EUROPEAN RAIL TIMETABLE

County Council

FOR REFERENCE ONLY

Published by
European Rail Timetable Limited
28 Monson Way
Oundle
Northamptonshire
PE8 4QG
United Kingdom

© European Rail Timetable Limited 2016

ISBN 978–0–9929073–7–2

Director and Editor-in-Chief : John Potter

Editor : Chris Woodcock

Editorial team : Peter Bass, David Turpie, Peter Weller

Additional compiling : Brendan Fox

Marketing and Advertising Manager: Keri Blunston

Commercial Manager : Gemma Donaldson

Social Media Manager: Reuben Turner

Subscriptions : Peter Weller

Telephone (Editorial & Sales) +44 (0)1832 270198

e-mail (Sales): sales@europeanrailtimetable.eu

e-mail (Editorial): editorial@europeanrailtimetable.eu

Website and on-line bookshop : www.europeanrailtimetable.eu

Cover created by Andrea Collins:
www.millstonecreative.co.uk
millstonecreative@btinternet.com

Front cover photograph:
Train *REX* 1870, the 0732 from Bolzano to Innsbruck, at Sankt Jodok,
between Brennero/Brenner and Innsbruck (Table 595) on March 9, 2016.
© Laurence Sly

Printed and bound by CPI Group (UK) Ltd, Croydon, CR0 4YY

INTRODUCTION

This **Winter 2016/2017** edition is a specially enlarged version of the regular European Rail Timetable, published by European Rail Timetable Limited and recognised throughout the world as the indispensable compendium of European rail schedules. Seasonal editions appear twice a year, in Summer and Winter versions, and they now replace the June and December monthly editions. Regular monthly printed editions also appear in February, April, August and October. Digital editions continue to be published every month (including digital versions of the seasonal Summer and Winter editions). These editions continue to be updated every month with the latest schedules from around Europe.

Previously published by Thomas Cook, the European Rail Timetable is still compiled by the same dedicated team and has been the travelling companion of the tourist and business traveller, Interrailer and Eurailer for many years.

The intention of this special seasonal edition is to make the timetable more widely available to the increasing numbers of holidaymakers who are touring Europe by train, whether using Interrail, Eurail or one of the other popular European rail passes, or simply travelling point to point. It includes additional information of use to rail travellers, especially those trying this kind of holiday for the first time.

Our feature on **Rail Passes** (pages v to xi) includes full details of the InterRail Global Pass and InterRail One Country Pass schemes (for European residents), as well as latest details of the various Eurail passes for those resident outside Europe. Many other passes are also featured, including a selection of citywide tickets and visitor cards for those visiting major European cities.

The **Country-by-Country** section (pages xii to xxiv) is packed with useful information about each country, and there is a chart of visa requirements on page xxiv. In the main body of the timetable, **Newslines** on page 3 has information about the latest changes and about the particular contents of this edition. Pages 8 and 9 help you make vital preparations for your journey, whilst a little time spent reading the notes on pages 4 to 7, explaining how to read the timetable, will be amply repaid when you get down to the task of planning your travels.

Whether you intend to travel only in one or two countries, or are attempting a spectacular grand tour of Europe, the timetables in this book will cover most of the routes you will need and will enable you to pre-plan your journey, which is often half the fun. Rail timetables are, however, always liable to change and you are recommended to consult the latest monthly edition of the European Rail Timetable or local information before travelling.

BEYOND EUROPE

Our Beyond Europe pages cover eight different areas of the world, with each section appearing at least twice a year in our regular monthly editions. As a special bonus we include the latest information from all eight areas in this special edition. Further details will be found on page 577.

www.hiddenEurope.co.uk

Enjoy the journey as much as the destination — *hidden europe* magazine invites you to look beyond the usual tourist trails. Rail journeys galore in Europe's premier magazine for devotees of Slow Travel.

ACCOMMODATION

Hotels:

Europe offers an excellent choice, from five-star hotels to room only. Your main problem may lie in finding something to suit your budget. Rooms in private houses are often a good, inexpensive and friendly option (local tourist offices often have lists), but you may be expected to stay for more than one night. The quality of cheaper hotels in Eastern Europe may still be less than inspiring and you may do better with a private room. Local tourist offices are almost always your best starting point if you haven't pre-booked. If they don't handle bookings themselves (there's usually a small charge), they will re-direct you to someone who does and/or supply you with the information to do it yourself – tell them your price horizons.

Hostels:

For those on a tight budget, the best bet is to join **HI** (Hostelling International); there's no age limit. Membership of a national association will entitle you to use over 5000 HI hostels in 60 different countries and, apart from camping, they often provide the cheapest accommodation. The norm is dormitory-style, but many hostels also have single and family rooms.

Many offer excellent-value dining and many have self-catering and/or laundry facilities. Some hostels are open 24 hours, but most have lock-out times and reception's hours are usually limited; advise them if you are arriving out of hours. Reservation is advisable – many hostels fill well in advance and even those with space are likely to limit your stay to three nights if you just turn up without booking. In winter (except around Christmas) you may be able to get special price deals.

Buy the HI's directory Europe, which lists hostel addresses, contact numbers, locations and facilities; the HI website is *www.hihostels.com.*

Camping:

This is obviously the cheapest accommodation if you're prepared to carry the equipment. There are campsites right across Europe, from basic (just toilets and showers) to luxury family-oriented sites with dining-rooms, swimming pools and complexes of permanent tents. The drawback is that sites are often miles from the city centres. There's no really good pan-European guide to campsites, but most tourist offices can provide a directory for their country.

WHAT TO TAKE WITH YOU

Luggage:

Backpack (not more than 50 litres for women or 60 litres for men) plus day sack; sort your luggage into see-through polythene bags (makes fishing out your socks from the backpack much easier), plus take plastic bags for dirty clothes etc, and elastic bands for sealing them. If flying to or from your holiday you will need to check your airlines baggage regulations.

Clothing:

Lightweight clothing, preferably of a type that doesn't need ironing; smart casual clothes for evening wear, swimsuit, sun hat, long-sleeved garment to cover shoulders (essential in some churches/temples; women may need headscarves); non-slip foot-wear – and don't forget underwear! All-purpose hiking boots (useful for big walks around cities) or rubber sandals with chunky soles are good when it's hot; flip flops for the shower etc.

First Aid/Medical:

Insect repellent and antihistamine cream, sun-screen cream, after-sun lotion, water-sterilising tablets, something for headaches and tummy troubles, antiseptic spray or cream, medicated wet-wipes, plasters for blisters, bandage, contraceptives and tampons (especially if visiting Eastern Europe, where they can be sometimes difficult to get – or try the luxury shop in the city's biggest hotel). Spare spectacles/contact lenses and a copy of your prescription.

Overnight Equipment:

Lightweight sleeping-bag (optional), sheet liner (for hostelling), inflatable travel pillow, earplugs, and eyemask.

Documents:

Passport, tickets, photocopies of passport/visas (helps if you lose the passport itself) and travel insurance, travellers' cheques counterfoil, passport photos, student card, numbers of credit cards and where to phone if you lose them.

Other items:

A couple of lightweight towels, small bar of soap, water-bottle, pocket knife, torch (flashlight), sewing kit, padlock and chain (for anchoring your luggage), safety matches, mug and basic cutlery, toothbrush, travel wash, string (for a washing-line), travel adapter, mobile (cell) phone charger, universal bath plug (often missing from wash-basins), sunglasses, alarm clock, notepad and pen, pocket calculator (to convert money), a money-belt and a good book/game (for long journeys).

EUROPEAN RAIL PASSES

Rail passes represent excellent value for train travellers who are touring around Europe (or parts of it) or making a number of journeys within a short period. They can offer substantial savings over point-to-point tickets, as well as greater flexibility. Passes may cover most of Europe (e.g. Interrail or Eurail), a specific group of countries, single countries, or just a certain area. Interrail passes are only available to European residents, whereas Eurail passes are only for non-European residents. Most passes cannot be used in your country of residence.

Passes either cover a specified number of consecutive days, or are of the *flexi* type where you get so many 'travel days' within a specified period (there are boxes on the pass where you write each date). Free travel requires the use of a travel day, whereas discounted travel does not.

With Interrail and Eurail *flexi* passes, direct night trains or ferries leaving after 1900 hrs can count as the next travel day (as long as it's not the first day of validity). Free overnight ferries count as either the day of departure or the next day. Passes generally cover the ordinary services of the national rail companies, but supplements often have to be paid for travel on high-speed services, night trains, and 'global price' trains. 'Independent' operators may not accept passes but may give discounts to passholders. Extra charges always apply for travel in sleeping cars or couchettes.

Passes can be purchased from appointed agents and their websites, and some may be available from principal railway stations. Your passport may be required for identification, also one or two passport-size photos.
In this feature USD = US dollars, € = euros, £ = pounds sterling.

Interrail

Europe-wide or single-country passes for European residents   website: www.interrail.eu

INTERRAIL GLOBAL PASS - valid in 30 European countries:
Austria, Belgium, Bosnia-Herzegovina, Bulgaria, Croatia, Czech Republic, Denmark, Finland, France, Germany, Great Britain, Greece, Hungary, Ireland (including Northern Ireland), Italy, Luxembourg, FYR Macedonia, Montenegro, Netherlands, Norway, Poland, Portugal, Romania, Serbia, Slovakia, Slovenia, Spain, Sweden, Switzerland and Turkey.
NOT VALID in the passholder's country of residence (but see below).

PRICES - GLOBAL PASS

	Youth 1st/2nd cl.	Adult 2nd class	Adult 1st class
Youth is 12-25 years			
5 days within 15 days (flexi)	€331/200	€264	€413
7 days within 1 month (flexi)	€393/246	€315	€491
10 days within 1 month (flexi)	€471/292	€374	€588
15 days within 1 month (flexi)	€579/361	€463	€723
15 days continuous	€520/338	€414	€650
22 days continuous	€608/374	€484	€760
1 month continuous	€787/479	€626	€983

Prices correct as at 14/01/16. Accompanied children aged 4-11 travel free with a Child Pass; two children can travel with each adult. Global Pass Senior (60+) gives 10% discount (not for One Country passes).

INTERRAIL ONE COUNTRY PASS (O.C.P.) - valid in one country

Covers any one of the participating countries above (except Bosnia-Herzegovina and Montenegro). NOT available for the passholder's country of residence. Note that Benelux (Belgium, Luxembourg and Netherlands) counts as one country. *Greece Plus* and *Italy Plus* passes includes Italy-Greece ferry services operated by Attica Group (Superfast Ferries - some routes are run jointly with Anek Lines). 1st class Youth passes are also available (except Norway). Prices correct as at 14/01/16.

PRICES - ONE COUNTRY PASS   *3, 4, 6 or 8 days within 1 month*

France, Germany or Great Britain:

	Youth	2nd	1st		Youth	2nd	1st
3 days	€154	€203	€317	6 days	€208	€283	€445
4 days	€164	€223	€349	8 days	€232	€313	€492

Austria, Italy Plus, Norway (2nd class only), Spain or Sweden:

	Youth	2nd	1st		Youth	2nd	1st
3 days	€131	€173	€272	6 days	€187	€256	€401
4 days	€145	€197	€308	8 days	€219	€297	€465

Benelux, Denmark, Finland, Greece Plus, Ireland, Italy or Switzerland:

	Youth	2nd	1st		Youth	2nd	1st
3 days	€87	€118	€185	6 days	€141	€199	€311
4 days	€108	€149	€233	8 days	€176	€239	€376

Bulgaria, Croatia, Czech Republic, Greece, Hungary, Poland, Portugal, Romania, Slovakia, Slovenia or Turkey:

	Youth	2nd	1st		Youth	2nd	1st
3 days	€57	€78	€121	6 days	€93	€125	€197
4 days	€69	€95	€148	8 days	€107	€148	€231

FYR Macedonia or Serbia:

	Youth	2nd	1st		Youth	2nd	1st
3 days	€42	€56	€89	6 days	€81	€106	€166
4 days	€57	€78	€121	8 days	€91	€126	€199

WHO CAN BUY INTERRAIL PASSES

Any national of a European country (including Russia) with a valid passport, or anyone who has lived in Europe for at least six months. Passes can be purchased up to three months before travel begins.

SUPPLEMENTS AND RESERVATION FEES

Required for certain types of high-speed or 'global price' train.

International day train examples, 2nd class (subject to change): France-Italy *TGV* €33-60 (€48-80 in 1st class); *Berlin-Warszawa Express* €4; *EC Switzerland-Italy* €11; *Eurostar* passholder fare (e.g. London-Paris from €89); *TGV/ICE* France-Germany €13; *TGV Lyria* (France-Switzerland) from €25; *Thalys* passholder fare from €15; *TGV* Brussels-France €9; *SJ Snabbtåg* Stockholm-København €7. *IC bus*

Klagenfurt-Venezia €9 (€13 1st class). Domestic examples: **Croatia** *IC/ICN* €1. **Czech Republic** *SC* €8. **Finland** *Pendolino* €3-7. **France** *TGV* €9 (peak €18), *Intercités* with compulsory reservation €6. **Germany** free on *ICE*. **Greece** *IC* €7-28. **Hungary** *IC* €3. **Italy** *FA*, *FB* and *FR* €10, *IC* €3. **Norway** long-distance trains €6.3. **Poland** *EIP* €10, *EIC/TLK* free. **Portugal** *AP/IC* €5. **Romania** *IC/IR* €1-1.2. **Slovakia** *IC* €5. **Slovenia** *ICS* €3.4 (€5.1 1st class). **Spain** *AVE* €10, most other long-distance trains €6.5, *MD* €4.5. **Sweden** *Snabbtåg* €7.

Night trains: Passes do not include sleeping accommodation, which is typically €15 to €75 for a couchette, and €35 to €155 for a berth in a sleeping car. Some trains also include reclining seats. Many night trains are globally priced and fares for passholders vary widely. *Thello* (France/Italy) gives 25% discount. Holders of a Global or Sweden One Country Pass can obtain a couchette berth on the *Berlin Night Express* (Berlin-Malmö and v.v.) for €29.

The number of seats allocated to Interrail holders may be limited (e.g. on *TGV* and *Thalys* trains). If sold out, you may have to buy an ordinary ticket. The fold-out Travel Report inside the ticket cover must be filled in. Direct night trains or ferries leaving after 1900 hrs can count as next day.

FREE TRAVEL TO THE BORDER, AIRPORT OR SEAPORT

Although it is not possible to purchase an Interrail pass for the holder's own country of residence, from 2016 a Global pass entitles the holder to two free journeys (one outbound, one inbound) between any station in their country of residence and its border, an airport or seaport. Each journey must be completed in one day (no overnight stops allowed), within the overall validity of the pass, or include a travel day if using a flexi pass. Details must be entered in the travel diary.

VALIDITY ON PRIVATE RAILWAYS

Interrail passes are valid on the national railway companies in each country, plus many privately run railways (some give discounts). For details see the Interrail Traveller's Guide or www.interrail.eu. Selected details are as follows (subject to change): **Austria**: free travel on WESTbahn and ROeEE. **Denmark**: free travel on Arriva and DSB-Øresund, 50% discount on Nordjyske Jernbaner (Hjørring-Hirtshals and Frederikshavn-Skagen). **France**: SNCF bus services included. **Germany**: free on most regional services. **Hungary**: GySEV services are included. **Italy**: not valid on NTV's *Italo* trains. **Netherlands**: privately run regional lines are included. **Norway**: Flåmsbana (Myrdal-Flåm) gives 30% discount. **Spain**: FGC gives 50% discount. **Sweden**: most private operators are included. **Switzerland**: free travel on BLS, FART/SSIF, MOB, RhB, SOB, THURBO and ZB. Many others offer 25-50% discount, including AB, ASM, CJ, FB, LEB, MBC, NStCM, RA, RB, RBS, SZU, TMR, TPC, TPF, TRN, WB, WSB. The MGB (Disentis-Brig-Zermatt) offers 50% to under-26s only. Discounted fare on William Tell Express (rail and boat tour). No discounts available on BRB or narrow gauge railways in Jungfrau area (BOB, JB, WAB).

VALIDITY ON FERRY AND BUS SERVICES

The pass includes free deck passage between Italy and Greece on SuperFast Ferries and Minoan Lines (you pay port taxes €7, high-season surcharge €10 June/Sept., €20 July/Aug., and possibly a fuel surcharge); free air-type seats for 1st class pass holders. Many other ferry companies offer discounts (not on cabins), for example: Balearia 20%, Finnlines 30%, Fjord Line 20% (10% high-season), Grimaldi 20%, Irish Ferries 30%, Stena Line 30%, Tallink Silja 20% (high-season), 40% (low-season), Viking Line 50%. Special fares apply on Destination Gotland.

Most Swiss lakes give 50% discount, as does Fjord1 on Norwegian Fjords. Certain bus services in Scandinavia (including Luleå-Haparanda-Tornio-Kemi) and some railway museums are free or discounted. A limited number of tourist attractions, hotels, hostels and cycle hire outlets also offer discounts.

Eurail

Eurail Global Pass *For non-European residents.*   website: www.eurail.com   www.eurailgroup.org

Area of validity

The *Eurail Global Pass* is valid for unlimited travel on the national railways of 28 European countries, namely Austria, Belgium, Bosnia-Herzegovina, Bulgaria, Croatia, Czech Republic, Denmark, Finland, France, Germany, Greece, Hungary, Ireland (including Northern Ireland), Italy, Luxembourg, Montenegro, the Netherlands, Norway, Poland, Portugal, Romania, Serbia, Slovakia, Slovenia, Spain, Sweden, Switzerland and Turkey.

Who can buy the pass?

The pass can be purchased by anyone resident outside Europe (but excluding residents of Russia and CIS or Turkey). Passes are sold through official Eurail Sales Agents (see www.eurailgroup.org) and can also be bought directly from Eurail through www.eurail.com.

The option exists to buy the passes after arrival in Europe but it is much cheaper to buy them beforehand, and since you can buy them up to eleven months in advance, there is no point in waiting until the last minute. Pass validity cannot be changed once in Europe, and passes must be validated before first use.

Periods of validity and prices

Adult *Eurail Global Passes* are only available as a first class pass (naturally you can also travel in second class). Prices (from eurail.com) in US dollars are as follows:

Youth is 12 - 25 years	Youth 1st class	Youth 2nd class	Adult 1st class
5 days within 1 month	424 USD	345 USD	528 USD
7 days within 1 month	516 USD	420 USD	643 USD
10 days within 2 months	636 USD	518 USD	793 USD
15 days within 2 months	833 USD	678 USD	1039 USD
15 days continuous	541 USD	441 USD	673 USD
22 days continuous	696 USD	566 USD	868 USD
1 month continuous	854 USD	695 USD	1065 USD
2 months continuous	1203 USD	979 USD	1501 USD
3 months continuous	1482 USD	1206 USD	1851 USD

Prices correct as at 14/01/16. Accompanied children aged 4 - 11 travel free with a Child Pass; two children can travel with each adult.

Supplements payable

Eurostar and *Thalys* charge a passholder rate, as do other 'global price' trains (see the Interrail page for further details). French *TGV* and certain *Intercités* require the reservation fee only. In Spain most long-distance trains have a supplement/reservation fee (sample 2nd class rates: regional trains €4.5, long-distance €6.5, *AVE* Turista class €10; where meal provided in 1st/Preferente class €23.5). Supplements are also payable on *Freccia* services in Italy (€10) and *SJ Snabbtåg* (€7). Further details are given in the Interrail section on the previous page.

As with all passes, sleeper/couchette supplements and seat reservations are extra.

Validity on other railways

Eurail passes are valid on the principal railway companies in each country, but may not be valid on 'private' or locally run railways (some give discounts). Selected details are as follows (some require reservations): **Austria**: free travel on WESTbahn and ROeEE. **Denmark**: free travel on Arriva and DSB-Øresund, 50% discount on Hjørring - Hirtshals and Frederikshavn - Skagen. **France**: SNCF buses included. **Hungary**: GySEV services are included. **Italy**: not valid on NTV's *Italo* trains. **Norway**: Flåmsbana (Myrdal - Flåm) gives 30% discount. **Spain**: FGC gives 50% discount. **Sweden**: most private operators are included. **Switzerland**: free travel on many railways including AB, ASM, BLS, BLT, CJ, FART/SSIF, FB, LEB, MBC, MOB, NStCM, RA, RhB, SOB, SZU, THURBO, TMR, TPC, TPF, TRN, WB, WSB, ZB. There is 50% discount on Arth-Goldau/Vitznau - Rigi, the Pilatus line (and cable car) offers 30%, and there is a 25% discount on railways in the Jungfrau region (BOB, BLM, JB, WAB) and the MGB (Disentis - Brig - Zermatt). There are reductions on some cable cars as well. A list of bonuses is included in the Traveler's Guide issued with your pass.

Ferry services

Free passage or fare reductions are available on various ferry services; the main ones are shown below. Ferry discounts usually exclude cabin accommodation, and other restrictions (such as compulsory reservation) may apply: free deck passage between Italy and Greece on SuperFast Ferries and Minoan Lines (you pay port taxes €7, high-season surcharge €10 June/Sept., €20 July/Aug., and possibly a fuel surcharge); free airline-type seats for 1st class pass holders. Many other ferry companies offer discounts (not on cabins), for example: Balearia 20%, Blue Star 30% (domestic routes), Finnlines 30%, Fjord Line 20% (10% high-season), Grimaldi 20%, Irish Ferries 30%, SNAV 20%, Stena Line 30%, Tallink Silja 40% (20% high-season), Viking Line 50%. Special fares apply on Destination Gotland. Most boat services on the Swiss lakes are included. Bodensee ferries operated by BSB, SBS, ÖBB give 50% discount. There are also reductions on some river cruises (e.g. certain DDSG sailings); KD Line gives a 20% discount on its scheduled Rhine and Mosel boats.

Other discounts

Certain bus services in Norway offer a 50% discount. Some railway museums offer free or discounted entry and a limited number of tourist attractions, hotels and hostels offer discounts. If in doubt, ask!

Note regarding flexi passes: free travel requires the use of a 'travel day', whereas discounted travel does not, provided it is within the overall validity of the pass. For free overnight travel by ferry you can enter either the day of departure or day of arrival. A direct overnight train leaving after 1900 hrs requires only the following day to be used as a 'travel day'.

Eurail Select Pass *For non-European residents*

Revamped for 2016 combining the Select with the former Regional pass, a *Eurail (Two/Three/Four Country) Select Pass* allows unlimited travel in 2, 3 or 4 bordering countries selected from the following (some countries are grouped together and count as one):

- Austria • Benelux (Belgium/Netherlands/Luxembourg) • Bulgaria
- Croatia/Slovenia • Czech Republic • Denmark • Finland • France
- Germany • Greece • Hungary • Ireland (including NIR) • Italy
- Norway • Poland • Portugal • Romania • Serbia/Montenegro
- Slovakia • Spain • Sweden • Switzerland • Turkey.

'Bordering' means linked by a direct train (not through another country) or shipping line included in the Eurail scheme; for example Italy's links include Spain and Greece.

The Two Country Select Pass is available for 4, 5, 6, 8 or 10 travel days within a two-month period, in both youth (12 - 25 years) and adult 1st and 2nd class versions. The Three and Four Country Select passes offer 5, 6, 8 and 10 days travel within a two-month period; there is no 2nd class adult version. Prices vary depending on countries chosen; some examples are shown below. Children aged 4 - 11 travel free with a Child Pass when accompanied by an adult; two children can travel with each adult.

International Ferries: *Select* and *One Country* passes must be valid in both the countries of departure and arrival to obtain free travel, but only need to be valid in one of the countries to obtain discounted travel.

Two Country Select Pass (examples):

Austria & Germany; France & Switzerland; Portugal & Spain.

(USD prices)	4 days	5 days	6 days	8 days	10 days
Youth 1st/2nd cl.	294/240	331/271	365/298	425/347	479/390
Adult 1st/2nd cl.	365/294	411/331	455/365	529/425	596/479

Three Country Select Pass (examples):

Czech Republic, Slovakia & Hungary; France, Spain & Portugal; Greece, Italy & Slovenia/Croatia.

(USD prices)	5 days	6 days	8 days	10 days
Youth 1st/2nd cl.	310/253	343/280	398/325	450/367
Adult 1st class	385	426	496	561

Four Country Select Pass (examples):

France, Italy, Portugal & Spain; Benelux, France, Germany & Italy.

(USD prices)	5 days	6 days	8 days	10 days
Youth 1st/2nd cl.	387/316	421/344	492/401	561/457
Adult 1st class	481	525	612	699

Denmark, Sweden, Norway & Finland; Austria, Czech Republic, Slovakia & Hungary; Bulgaria, Greece, Italy & Romania.

(USD prices)	5 days	6 days	8 days	10 days
Youth 1st/2nd cl	339/276	373/304	435/355	490/400
Adult 1st class	421	464	541	611

Eurail One Country Passes *For non-European residents*

A *Eurail One Country Pass* allows unlimited travel in a single European country as listed below (Benelux and Scandinavia each count as one). Each pass has its own characteristics regarding class of travel, number of travel days (usually 3, 4, 5 or 8 days within 1 month), and availability of adult, youth and family versions. For prices and further information see www.eurail.com.

- Austria • Benelux (Belgium, Luxembourg, the Netherlands)
- Bulgaria • Croatia • Czech Republic • Denmark • Finland
- Greece • Greek Islands • Hungary • Ireland • Italy • Norway
- Poland • Portugal • Romania • Scandinavia (Denmark, Finland, Norway, Sweden) • Slovakia • Slovenia • Spain • Sweden

BritRail

BritRail is a pass for overseas visitors to Great Britain, allowing unlimited travel on the national rail network in England, Scotland and Wales. It is not available to residents of Great Britain, Northern Ireland, the Isle of Man or the Channel Islands. It is best to buy the pass before arriving in Britain. Youth prices apply to ages 16 to 25, senior applies to 60+. Child prices (ages 5 to 15) are approx 50% of the adult fare. Prices correct as at 19/01/16. See www.britrail.net.

BRITRAIL CONSECUTIVE PASS

Travel for a certain number of consecutive days, First or Standard class.

(USD prices)	Adult 1st cl.	Youth 1st cl.	Senior 1st cl.	Adult Std cl.	Youth Std cl.	Senior Std cl.
3 days	339	271	288	224	179	224
4 days	421	337	358	278	222	278
8 days	600	480	510	403	323	403
15 days	886	709	754	600	480	600
22 days	1126	901	957	750	600	750
1 month	1334	1067	1134	886	709	886

BRITRAIL FLEXIPASS

Flexi version gives 3, 4, 8 or 15 days travel within a one-month period.

(USD prices)	Adult 1st cl.	Youth 1st cl.	Senior 1st cl.	Adult Std cl.	Youth Std cl.	Senior Std cl.
3 days	410	328	347	277	222	277
4 days	504	403	427	347	277	347
8 days	741	593	629	497	398	497
15 days	1106	885	939	747	598	747

BRITRAIL ENGLAND PASSES

The Britrail England Pass excludes Wales and Scotland. A Britrail South West pass is also available. Both passes are available in Consecutive and Flexi versions.

BRITRAIL LONDON PLUS PASS

This 'flexi' pass allows unlimited rail travel in London and the surrounding area for either 3, 4 or 8 days within a one-month period. You can visit such places as Canterbury, Salisbury, Bristol, Bath, Oxford, Cambridge, Stratford-Upon-Avon, Worcester, and anywhere on the coast between Harwich to Weymouth.

(USD prices)	Adult 1st cl.	Youth 1st cl.	Senior 1st cl.	Adult Std cl.	Youth Std cl.	Senior Std cl.
3 days	242	193	205	172	138	172
4 days	279	224	238	210	168	210
8 days	395	316	336	291	233	291

BRITRAIL SCOTLAND PASSES

Three different passes are available; Freedom of Scotland (available as 4 days within 8, and 8 days within 15 versions), Central Scotland (3 days within 7), and Highlands (4 days within 8; standard (2nd) class only).

DISCOUNTS

The following reductions are available on passes but only one type of discount can be used. Discounts cannot be applied to London Plus and any Scotland passes.

Saver Discount: small groups of 3 to 9 people receive a discount of up to 20%. Passes must be of the same type and duration and the party must travel together at all times.

Family Discount: if any adult or senior pass is purchased, one accompanying child (aged 5-15) may receive a free pass of the same type and duration. Any further children travelling receive a 50% discount. All children under 5 travel free.

Other International Passes

BALKAN FLEXIPASS

Unlimited travel (see note below) in Bosnia, Bulgaria, Greece, Macedonia, Montenegro, Romania, Serbia and Turkey for any 5/7/10/15 days in one month. 1st class €120/162/210/252, 2nd class €88/120/156/186. 40% discount for under 26s, 20% for over 60s, 50% for children (4-12). Supplements for IC trains. Allows travel on Attica Group (Superfast) ferries international routes and 30% discount on domestic routes. Prices correct as at 19/01/16 from Bosnian Railways (ŽRS). Only 1st class 5, 10 and 15 day passes are usually offered outside participating countries (with increased prices). Not available to residents of the above countries.

Note that if purchased from one of the above countries the pass allows only a return journey from place of issue to the border of a neighbouring participating country before unlimited travel is possible.

EUREGIO-BODENSEE TAGESKARTE

One day's unlimited travel by rail, bus and ferry in border region Austria/Germany/Switzerland surrounding Lake Constance. In Germany valid only on DB local trains. Adult 45 CHF/€31, small groups (1 or 2 adults and up to 4 children) 84 CHF/€58. Zonal versions also available for smaller areas.

EUREGIO TICKET MAAS-RHEIN

One days unlimited travel in border region Belgium/Netherlands/Germany by rail and bus (covers Liège, Hasselt, Maastricht, Roermond, Aachen, Düren). In Germany and Belgium covers only local trains and buses. Price €18.5. At weekends/public holidays valid as a family ticket (2 adults plus 3 children under 12).

EUROPEAN EAST PASS

Offers unlimited rail travel throughout Austria, Czech Republic, Hungary and Slovakia for any 5 to 10 days within a month. Valid also on direct services through Germany between Kufstein and Salzburg (the passholder cannot leave the train). Now available to European residents (except those from countries where the ticket is valid) as well as non-European residents. Price for 5 days: 1st class €236, 2nd class €162 (up to 5 extra days €25/21 per day 1st/2nd class). Children aged 4-11 half price. Discounts available on river cruises, Children's Railway etc.

ÖRESUND RUNDT

Two days unlimited travel on trains and buses in the København, Malmö and Helsingborg area (includes the metro in København), 249 SEK. Children 7-15 half price. The Öresund can only be crossed by rail in one direction; the Helsingborg - Helsingør ferry (operated by Scandlines, included) must be used in the other direction. Available in Denmark from København Tourist Office and in Sweden from Skånetrafiken.

PASS ALSACE-RHEIN-NECKAR

A day ticket valid on Saturdays, Sundays and public holidays covering local trains, buses and trams in the Rhein-Neckar area (VRN) of Germany, plus local trains in the Bas Rhin area of France. Therefore covers the Mannheim, Heidelberg and Strasbourg areas. Price €17.50 for one person or €28.50 for a group of 2-5 people.

PASSBASK

Covers the area between Bayonne in France and San Sebastian in Spain on SNCF trains (includes TGV but not night trains) and EuskoTren services. Valid for one day in July or August, or for Saturdays and Sundays (i.e. two days) rest of the year. A barrier pass for EuskoTren should be obtained at Hendaye station. Price €11, child aged 4-12 €7.

SAAR-LOR-LUX TICKET

One day's unlimited 2nd class travel on Saturday or Sunday throughout Saarland (i.e. Saarbrücken area of Germany, local trains only), Lorraine (i.e. Metz, Nancy, Épinal area of France) and all CFL trains in Luxembourg. Price €26; for groups of 2-5 people add €10 per extra person. Not valid on TGV or ICE trains.

OTHER PASSES

A range of day tickets is available covering areas of the Czech Republic and adjoining countries, i.e. **Euro-Neisse Tageskarte** (Liberec, Jelenia Góra, Zittau/Görlitz; www.zvon.de), the **EgroNet-Ticket** (Cheb, Karlovy Vary, Plauen, Zwickau; www.egronet.de), the **Bayern-Böhmen Ticket** (Bavaria/Bohemia), the **Sachsen-Böhmen Ticket** (Saxony/Bohemia) and the **Elbe-Labe Ticket**.

Railplus

Railplus cards are valid for one year and offer a discount of 25% on cross-border rail travel (excluding supplements) between the participating countries, which are Austria, Belgium, Bulgaria, Croatia, Czech Republic, Denmark, Finland, Germany, Great Britain, Greece, Hungary, Italy, Latvia, Lithuania, Luxembourg, Macedonia, Montenegro, Netherlands, Poland, Romania, Serbia, Slovakia, Slovenia, Switzerland and Ukraine.

France, Norway, Portugal, Spain and Sweden only grant discounts to youth (12-25) and seniors (60+). Cards are not available for sale in all participating countries, and you may be required to hold a national railcard for the country where you buy the pass, in addition to the Railplus card.

Passes for Domestic Travel

Every effort has been made to show latest prices, but some may have changed. Most cities offer day tickets valid on public transport (some include local trains), and larger cities often have Visitor Cards available from airports and tourist information offices (often also from hotels and online).

AUSTRIA

European residents : InterRail Global Pass and One Country Pass. Non-European residents : Eurail Global Pass, Eurail Select / One Country Passes.
Also European East Pass, Euregio-Bodensee Tageskarte.

Einfach-Raus-Ticket : one day's 2nd class travel on regional and local trains for groups of 2 to 5 people, €33 - 45. On Mon to Fri not valid before 0900 hrs.

Vorteilscard annual cards giving 45-50% discount; the *Classic* version (€99) is available to all but there are cheaper cards for families, seniors and those under 26.

ÖSTERREICHcard Classic gives unlimited travel for 1 year, €1,719 (1st class €2,414). Cheaper cards for families, seniors and youths.

Wien metro / tram / bus : 24 / 48 / 72 hours €7.6 / 13.3 / 16.5; any 8 days (not necessarily consecutive) €38.4; weekly ticket (only available from Monday 0000 to the following Monday 0900) €16.2. For journeys from / to the airport buy an additional zone ticket (€2.2). **Wien-Karte** : unlimited travel on local transport in Vienna plus discounted museum entry, 48 / 72 hours €18.9 / 21.9. One child up to age 15 free.

Other visitor cards giving local travel plus museum / sights discounts for 24 / 48 / 72 hours: **Salzburg Card** €27 / 36 / 42 (reduced by €3 - 5 low season Nov to Apr); **Innsbruck Card** €33 / 41 / 47. Children half price.

BELARUS

Minsk : 10-day public transport passes are available from metro stations.

BELGIUM

European residents : InterRail Global Pass and One Country Pass. Non-European residents : Eurail Global Pass, Eurail Select / One Country (Benelux) Passes. Also Euregio Ticket Maas-Rhein.

Nettreinkaart / Carte Train Réseau : unlimited travel on rail network; 1 month €292 / 450, 3 months €818 / 1260, 1 year €2923 / 4502. Add-ons for city transport also available.

Discounts on SNCB point to point tickets : **Rail Pass** (age 26 +) allows 10 single journeys between two specified stations (not frontier) for €76 2nd class, €117 1st class, valid 1 year. **Go Pass 10** is under 26 version, €51 2nd class. **Weekend Ticket** : 50% discount, from Friday 1900 hrs. **Senior Ticket** (65 +), flat fare of €6 2nd class, €13 1st class, from 0900 Mon-Fri, not Sat/Sun in peak summer.

Brussels : **Jump ticket** covers all transport in greater Brussels (De Lijn / SNCB / STIB / TEC) 1 / 2 / 3 days €7.5 / 14 / 18. Personal Mobib or Mobib Basic card required (€5).

De Lijn has 1 / 3 / 5 day system passes €6 / 12 / 17 (in advance). Day Pass may also be purchased from driver (€8). Includes coastal tram. Also West Flanders province 7 day pass valid by tram and bus €24 (€36 for 2 people).

BOSNIA-HERZEGOVINA

European residents : InterRail Global Pass. Also Balkan Flexipass. Non-European residents : Eurail Global Pass.

BULGARIA

European residents : InterRail Global Pass and One Country Pass. Non-European residents : Eurail Global Pass, Eurail Select / One Country Passes. Also Balkan Flexipass.

Sofia : all SKGT metro, tram and bus: 1 day 4 BGN, 10 trips 8 BGN.

CROATIA

European residents : InterRail Global Pass and One Country Pass. Non-European residents : Eurail Global Pass, Eurail Select / One Country passes.

Zagreb : day ticket (dnevna karta) all ZET tram / bus (zone 1): 30 HRK. Also multi-day tickets (višednevne karte): 3 / 7 / 15 / 30 days, 70 / 150 / 200 / 400 HRK. **Zagreb Card** adds museums, discounts, 24 hrs 60 HRK, 72 hrs 90 HRK.

CZECH REPUBLIC

European residents : InterRail Global Pass and One Country Pass. Non-European residents : Eurail Global Pass, Eurail Select / One Country Passes. Also European East Pass.

Day ticket (Celodenní Jízdenka): 2nd class travel on whole rail network 579 CZK (on *SC* trains 200 CZK reservation payable). 13 regional areas also available, 159 - 239 CZK. Certain regions also have day tickets including border areas of Germany or Poland, 250 - 300 CZK. Other day tickets cover specific cross-border areas: Vltava-Dunaj (486 CZK), EgroNet (200 CZK), Labe-Elbe (250 CZK), Euro-Nisa (160 CZK).

Group Weekend ticket (Skupinová víkendová jízdenka): 2nd class travel on whole network on Sat or Sun for 2 adults and up to 3 children, 679 CZK (829 CZK including local transport in Praha). Reservation fee payable on *SC* trains. Valid cross-border to first station on local trains (except Austria). Regional areas also available, 229 - 319 CZK. Versions for Czech Republic plus border areas of Germany or Poland, including regional areas, are also available.

Praha : all public transport (including most trains): 24 hrs 110 CZK, 3 days 310 CZK. Wider areas available. **Prague Card** : 2 / 3 / 4 day admission card, includes transport when booked online, €46 - 65 (student €33 - 47). Most cities have day tickets for city transport.

DENMARK

European residents : InterRail Global Pass and One Country Pass. Non-European residents : Eurail Global Pass, Eurail Select / One Country Passes (also Scandinavia). Also Öresund Rundt.

Fares based on national zonal system; 30-day **Pendlerkort** for commuters (photocard required) including all-zones version. 10-journey tickets also available. **Rejsekortet** is a new pre-pay travel card aimed at Danish residents, but a **Rejsekort Anonymt** may be purchased by anyone (card costs 80 DKK, plus an initial 600 DKK for travel purposes).

København : **City Pass** zones 1 - 4 (including from / to airport) on bus, metro and train 24 / 72 hrs 80 / 200 DKK (child half price). **24-Hour Ticket** adds greater København, 130 DKK (child 65 DKK). **FlexCard** : 7 days travel in choice of zones, 250 - 675 DKK.

Copenhagen Card : greater København public transport, free entry to 72 attractions, 24 / 48 / 72 / 120 hrs €48 / 65 / 78 / 110 (2 children under 10 free).

ESTONIA

Tallinn : tram / bus / trolley-bus **Ühiskaart** pre-pay travel card (deposit €2) available for 1 / 3 / 5 / 30 days: €3 / 5 / 6 / 23 (supplement on express buses). One hour ticket €1.10. **Tallinn Card** : adds museums etc., 24 hrs €32, 48 hrs €42, 72 hrs €52. Under 15s half price.

FINLAND

European residents : InterRail Global Pass and One Country Pass. Non-European residents : Eurail Global Pass, Eurail Select / One Country Passes (also Scandinavia).

Helsinki : single-charge electronic cards for all public transport including local trains: 1 / 2 / 3 days €8 / 12 / 16; 7 days €32 (1 - 7 days available). **Helsinki Card** : public transport plus free entry to main sights, 24 / 48 / 72 hrs €39 / 49 / 59, child 7-16 €22 / 27 / 32.

FRANCE

European residents : InterRail Global Pass and One Country Pass. Non-European residents : Eurail Global Pass and Eurail Select Pass. Also Pass Alsace - Rhein-Neckar, Passbask, Saar-Lor-Lux.

France Railpass : only available to non-European residents, valid for 1 - 9 days within one month. Adult 3 days 256 / 206 USD 1st / 2nd class plus approx 35 / 30 USD per extra day (9-day: 468 / 374 USD). Approx 30% discount for Youth (aged 12 - 25), 12% discount for Senior (60 +). Saver version for 2 - 5 people: 15% discount. Also, 15 days within two month pass 610 / 488 USD, 1st / 2nd class. Passes also available for 4, 5, 8 and 15 days continuous travel: 1st / 2nd class, 155 / 126 - 488 / 391 USD.

Reservations required for most trains. Special Passholder fare payable on *Eurostar*. Pass is available from RailEurope and other agents.

Annual railcards are available for children, young people (ages 12 - 27) and seniors (60 +) giving 25% - 50% discount off rail fares. A **Carte Week-End** is available for all ages giving discounts at weekends.

Regional Tickets : several regions offer day tickets on TER (local) trains at weekends and holidays. Conditions vary and some only valid in summer. Details generally available on TER website www.sncf.com/fr/trains/ter. The **Lille City Pass** 24 / 48 / 72 hrs, €25 / 35 / 45 includes local transport (photocard required) including all-zones version. 10-journey (3-day pass includes TER trains in Nord-Pas de Calais region on one day). **Alsa Plus 24h** : a zonal day pass for Alsace, €35.9 for the whole region; group ticket (2-5 people) available at weekends for €37.

Paris Visite : public transport within Paris, plus discounted entry to attractions: zones 1 - 3: €11.15 / 18.15 / 24.80 / 35.70 for 1 / 2 / 3 / 5 days. Zones 1 - 5 (includes suburbs and airports): €23.50 / 35.70 / 50.05 / 61.25. Children 4 - 11 half price. **Mobilis** : Paris one-day ticket (not available on airport services): €7 (zones 1 - 2) to €16.6 (zones 1 - 5).

Most cities have bus / tram day tickets, e.g. **Lyon** €5.5, **Lille** €4.8.

GERMANY

European residents : InterRail Global Pass and One Country Pass. Non-European residents : Eurail Global Pass and Eurail Select Pass. Also Euregio-Bodensee, Euregio Mass-Rhein, Sar-Lor-Lux.

For non-European residents, **German Rail Pass FLEXI** : 3, 4, 5, 7 and 10 days unlimited travel within one month. 3 days €258 / 191 1st / 2nd class; 4 days €277 / 205, 5 days €296 / 219, 7 days €367 / 272, 10 days €471 / 348. **German Rail Pass CONSECUTIVE** : 5 / 10 / 15 consecutive days 1st class €288 / 417 / 585 (€213 / 309 / 434 2nd class). A **Twin**

Pass offers a discount of approximately 50% for second adult. Youth passes also available. No supplements on *ICE, IC, EC.* 20% discount on Romantische Strasse bus.

Schönes-Wochenende-Ticket: one day's unlimited travel on Saturday or Sunday (to 0300 following day) on local trains (IRE/RE/RB/S-Bahn), 2nd class. Price €40 from machines, €42 from ticket offices. Valid for up to 5 people (+ €4 for each additional traveller), buy on the day. Also valid on trams/buses in certain areas, and on certain rail lines across the border into Poland.

Quer-durchs-Land-Ticket: one day's unlimited travel (not before 0900 Mon - Fri, but valid until 0300 following day) on local trains (IRE/RE/RB/S-Bahn), 2nd class. Valid for up to 5 people. €44 for one person, then add €8 for each additional person in the group (€76 for a group of five).

Regional tickets (Länder-Tickets): one day's unlimited 2nd class travel for up to 5 people on DB local trains (not before 0900 on Mon-Fri, valid to 0300 the following day). **Baden-Württemberg** €23 for one person (add €5 for each additional person). **Bayern** €23 for one person (add €5 for each additional person). **Brandenburg-Berlin** €29. **Hessen** (includes most buses) €33. **Mecklenburg-Vorpommern** €23 for one person (add €4 for each additional person). **Niedersachsen** €23 for one person (add €4 for each additional person). **Nordrhein-Westfalen** (SchönerTag Ticket) one person €29.5, 2-5 people €43. **Rheinland-Pfalz** plus **Saarland** €24 for one person (add €5 for each additional person). **Sachsen** including **Sachsen-Anhalt** and **Thüringen** €23 for one person (add €5 for each additional person). **Schleswig-Holstein** €28 for one person (add €3 for each additional person; includes public transport in Hamburg). All Länder tickets may be purchased on the day from ticket machines (most cost €2 more if purchased from travel centres).

Bahncard 25/50: valid for 1 year, giving discounts of 25% or 50% on all national DB trains for €62 or €255 in 2nd class (1st class €125/515). Both cards entitle the holder to a 25% discount for international journeys between Germany and 30 European countries (except where global fares are charged). Half price Bahncards available for young people and seniors. **Bahncard 100** (passport photo required) gives unlimited travel for 1 year, €4,090 in 2nd class, €6,890 in 1st class. All available from DB London.

Harz: HSB narrow gauge railway 3/5 days €78/117, child 6 - 11 50%.

Tageskarte (day ticket): most urban areas offer 24/48/72 hour tickets valid on most public transport; generally a zonal system operates.

Welcome Tickets: most public transport in selected cities, also includes free or reduced entry to many museums and visitor attractions. Buy from Tourist Information, main stations, some airports and hotels. Examples: **Berlin Welcome Card**: one adult and up to 3 children under 15; 48 hrs €21.5, 72 hrs €29.5, 4 days €34.5, 5 days €40.5, 6 days €45.5. Covers zones A, B and C and includes DB trains. **Dresden City Card**: 1 day €10; family card also available for 2 adults and up to 4 children under 15 €15. Includes ferry trips within the Dresden tariff zone. **Frankfurt Card**: 1 day €10.5, 2 days €15.5; group ticket (up to 5) €20.5 (1 day)/€30.5 (2 days). Includes travel from/to the airport. **Hamburg Card**: Day Ticket €9.9. Also 2-5 days €18.9 - 40.9. Group versions (up to 5) €17.9/32.9 - 72.9. **Hannover Card**: 1 day €9.5, 2 days €15, 3 days €18, group ticket (up to 5) €20/27/35. **Köln Welcome Card**: 24/48 hrs €9/18, group ticket (up to 5) €19/38. Wider areas also available. **Leipzig Card**: 1 day €11.5, 3 days €22.5, 3 day group (2 adults and up to 3 children under 14) €39.9. **Nürnberg Card**: 2 days €25 (accompanied children aged 6-11 €5).

GREAT BRITAIN

European (non-UK) residents: InterRail Global Pass and One Country Pass. Non-UK residents: Britrail.

Railcards: annual cards giving 34% discount on most rail fares; 16 - 25 Railcard, Two Together, Family & Friends, Senior: all £30; Disabled Persons £20. Network Railcard gives off-peak discount in South East England. £30.

All-Line Rail Rover: covers whole National Rail network. 1st/standard class £731/483 (7 days), £1117/731 (14 days), children 5 - 15 half price. 34% discount for holders of Senior/Disabled/Two Together railcard, and (standard class only) 16 - 25/Family & Friends railcard. Some restrictions before 1000 Mon - Fri. Not valid on Eurostar, Heathrow Express, London Underground. Valid on Ffestiniog Railway but not other private railways.

Spirit of Scotland Travelpass: all rail services in Scotland (includes Carlisle and Berwick) plus Caledonian MacBrayne ferry services and some buses. Standard class only. Valid 4 out of 8 days, £134; not before 0915 Mon to Fri (except on Glasgow - Oban/Mallaig/Stranraer services and north of Inverness). 34% discount with 16 - 25/Two Together/Senior/Disabled railcard; 50% discount for children (5 - 15). 20% discount on Northlink Ferries to Orkney and Shetland. Smaller areas also available: **Highland Rover**, 4 days out of 8 £81.50; **Central Scotland Rover** 3 in 7 days £36.30.

Explore Wales: standard class rail travel on any 4 days out of 8 (not valid before 0930 Mon - Fri), price £99, children half price. Tickets available online and at most staffed stations. Other areas available: South Wales (£69), North and Mid Wales (£69).

A range of **Rover** tickets is available covering various areas, typically for 7 days, 3 in 7 days, 4 in 8 days, or 8 in 15 days. Most not valid until after the morning peak on Mon to Fri. Examples: Anglia Plus, Coast and Peaks, East Midlands, Heart of England, Kent, North Country, North Wales, Severn & Solent, Thames.

Ranger day tickets also available: e.g. Cambian coast, Cheshire, Cornwall, Cotswolds, Cumbria, Devon, East Midlands, Isle of Wight, Lakes, Lancashire, Lincolnshire, North Downs, Oxfordshire, South Pennines, Thames branches, Tyne & Tees, West Midlands, West Wales, West Yorkshire, Yorkshire Coast. Details: nationalrail.co.uk.

All-day tickets (some off-peak) covering local rail and most buses are available in Derbyshire, Glasgow, Greater Manchester, Merseyside, South Yorkshire, West Yorkshire, Tyneside and West Midlands.

London: Day Travelcards cover almost all transport (Underground, bus and rail) in the London area; peak version from £12.10 (central London, zones 1 - 4) to £17.20 (zones 1 - 6), off-peak version (not before 0930 Mon - Fri) £12.10 (zones 1 - 6). 7-day tickets from £32.40 (zones 1 - 2) to £59.10 (zones 1 - 6), no off-peak version. Travelcard holders may take up to four children aged 1 - 15 for £2 each after 1000 (otherwise half fare). For single journeys contactless debit and credit cards, or stored-value Oyster cards offer the best value as prices are capped. Visitor Oyster cards are available preloaded from £10 to £50 (plus £3 fee, non-refundable). Children under 11 travel free on buses and trams (also on Tube, DLR and some rail services when accompanied by a fare paying adult; up to four children per adult).

Isle of Man Go Explore cards (£2 fee): most trains (not Groudle Glen) and buses: 1/3/5/7 days, £16/32/39/47, children 5 - 15 half price. Family card: 2 adults and up to 3 children £39/75/95/115.

GREECE

European residents: InterRail Global Pass and One Country Pass (also Greece Plus).

Non-European residents: Eurail Global Pass, Eurail Select/One Country Passes. Also Balkan Flexipass.

Athens: 24-hour ticket valid on metro, tram and bus €4.5, 5 days €9 (excludes airport, €9 single). 3-day tourist ticket including airport €22.

HUNGARY

European residents: InterRail Global Pass and One Country Pass. Non-European residents: Eurail Global Pass, Eurail Select/One Country Passes. Also European East Pass. Travel by rail and local transport is free for over-65s with an EU passport or ID card.

START Klub Card: gives 50% discount on 2nd class travel. Valid for either 6 months or one year: HUF 19900/34900 (HUF 14900/24900 under 26 years). Requires passport style photograph. Cardholders may obtain 50% discount for a second person on Saturday.

Balaton Mix: rail and shipping services around Lake Balaton, valid Mar. 26 - Oct. 23, 2016. 3-day ticket gives 1 day's unlimited travel HUF 3590, child 6 - 14 HUF 2190, family (2 adults + 2 children) HUF 9490. 7-day ticket gives any 2 days travel for HUF 5990/3590/16190. 50% discount on rail journey to/from the area within period of validity.

Budapest: BKV tram/metro/bus/rail, 24 hrs HUF 1650, 72 hrs HUF 4150, 7 days HUF 4950. Also 24 hr group ticket (2 - 5 people), HUF 3300. **Budapest Card** also includes museums, walking tour and discounts: 24 hrs HUF 4900, 48 hrs HUF 7900, 72 hrs HUF 9900.

IRELAND

European residents: InterRail Global Pass and One Country Pass. Non-European residents: Eurail Global/Select/One Country Passes. InterRail and Eurail passes valid in the Republic of Ireland are also valid in Northern Ireland.

REPUBLIC OF IRELAND ONLY:

Irish Explorer: any 5 days in 15 on IÉ rail services, €160 (child €80), standard class. **Trekker** gives 4 consecutive days on Irish Rail for €110.

Dublin area: **Short Hop Zone** tickets: Rail only 1 day €11.4, 3 days €26.5. **Leap Visitor Card**: 1 day €10, 3 days €19.5, 7days €40. Includes rail in short hop zone, Luas tram and bus (also Airlink); purchase at airport or tourist offices (not railway stations). Luas **Flexi** ticket (tram only): 1 day €6.8, 7 day €24.9 (child €2.8/8.9). **Rambler** (bus only, includes Airlink): 5 days €30.6.

NORTHERN IRELAND ONLY:

iLink integrated smartcard gives unlimited bus and rail travel on Translink services (Northern Ireland Railways, Ulsterbus and Belfast Citybus). Zone 4 covers the whole of Northern Ireland: 1 day £17.50, 7 days £61, 1 month £211. Zone 1 covers Belfast city (£6.50/23/78). Children half price. New North West zone: £14.50/52/181. Initial £1 fee for card. **Belfast Visitor Pass** includes visitor discounts: 1/2/3 days, adult £6.50/11/14.50, child £3.75/6/7.75. **Select**: 3 days travel within 7 on pre-selected dates and journeys gives 16% discount on normal fares.

ITALY

European residents: InterRail Global Pass and One Country Pass (also Italy Plus).

Non-European residents: Eurail Global Pass, Eurail Select/One Country Passes.

Mobilcard Südtirol: regional trains, buses, funiculars and cable cars in Bolzano, Malles, Brennero area: 1/3/7 days; €15/23/28 respectively.

Roma: Biglietto Integrato Giornaliero (BIG) covers rail/metro/bus in urban area for one day, €6 (excludes Fiumicino airport, restrictions on rail/metro). Biglietto Turistico Integrato (BTI) valid 3 days €16.5, weekly ticket (CIS) €24. **Roma Pass**: 2/3 day transport pass (€28/36) with museum discounts.

Milano: 24 hour ticket (abbonamento giornaliero): ATM city services plus local Trenitalia, Trenord rail services, €4.5. Also 48 hour ticket €8.25.

Napoli: 'Campania > artecard' is a transport + museum visitors card, with various options. The 3 day card (€32) allows free entry to two museums with 50% off others; the 7 day version (€34) allows 5 free then 50% off.

Venezia: Travel cards for ACTV buses and boats: 1/2/3/7 days €20/30/40/60. Each card is also available with airport transfer add-on (€8).

LATVIA

Riga Card: public transport, bus tour, plus free/discounted museum entry; €25/30/35 for 24/48/72 hours.

LITHUANIA

Vilnius: 1/3/10 day tickets available on local VVT buses/trolleybuses; €3.5/6/12. **Vilnius Card** includes public transport, museums and discounts; 24/72 hrs, €20/30.

LUXEMBOURG

European residents: InterRail Global Pass and One Country Pass (Benelux).

Non-European residents: Eurail Global Pass, Eurail Select/One Country Passes (Benelux). See also Sar-Lor-Lux Ticket.

Dagesbilljee/Billet longue durée: day ticket €4, unlimited 2nd class travel on all public transport throughout the country (until 0400 hrs following morning); not valid to border points. €5 if bought on board the train. Carnet of 5 day tickets €16. **Oeko Pass**: valid one month €50 2nd class, €75 1st class; from CFL offices.

Luxembourg Card: unlimited travel on trains and buses throughout the country, plus free entry to 70 attractions. 1 day €13, 2 days €20, 3 days €28. Family pass for 2-5 people (max 3 adults) for 1/2/3 days: €28/48/68.

MACEDONIA

European residents: InterRail Global Pass and One Country Pass. Also Balkan Flexipass.

MONTENEGRO

European residents: InterRail Global Pass and One Country Pass. Non-European residents: Eurail Global Pass, Eurail Select Pass. Also Balkan Flexipass.

NETHERLANDS

European residents: InterRail Global Pass and One Country Pass (Benelux).

Non-European residents: Eurail Global Pass, Eurail Select/One Country Passes (Benelux). Also Euregio Maas-Rhein.

A national stored-value OV-chipkaart is used for public transport, initial cost €7.50, which can be loaded with day tickets. A single-use chipcard or e-ticket may be used by less frequent travellers. **Day ticket**: unlimited travel on NS trains; 1st/2nd class €89.4/52.6. **Railrunner**: Children aged 4-11 travel for a flat rate of €2.50 each in 2nd class. Must be accompanied by an adult in 1st class; maximum 3 children per adult. Excludes Thalys.

Amsterdam Travel Ticket: GVB tram/bus/metro (also includes one return journey from/to airport on NS train): 24 hrs €15, 48 hrs €20, 72 hrs €25. **Amsterdam & Region Day Ticket**: a 1-day GVB ticket including Connexxion and EBS (not valid on trains), €13.5. **I amsterdam Card**: GVB tram/bus/metro, one free canal tour plus free/discounted entry to various attractions; 24/48/72/96 hrs, €55/65/75/85.

NORWAY

European residents: InterRail Global Pass and One Country Pass. Non-European residents: Eurail Global Pass, Eurail Select/One Country Passes (also Scandinavia).

Oslo: 24 hour ticket for all 'Ruter' public transport in zone 1 (wider areas available): 90 NOK, 7 days 240 NOK; children half price. **Oslo Pass**: all public transport including NSB local trains (zones 1-2, excludes airport), free entry to attractions, discounts on sightseeing buses/boats: 24/48/72 hours 335/490/620 NOK (children pay approximately 50%).

Bergen Card: local bus travel plus free or discounted entry to various attractions; 24/48/72 hrs, 240/310/380 NOK (children aged 3-15, 90/120/150 NOK).

POLAND

European residents: InterRail Global Pass and One Country Pass.

Non-European residents: Eurail Global Pass, Eurail Select/One Country Passes.

PKP Intercity operates *EIC, EIP, IC, TLK* trains and offers the following passes for its trains: **Bilet Weekendowy** (weekend ticket): valid 1900 Fri to 0600 Mon (extended if Thurs or Mon is a public holiday). Basic ticket valid only in *TLK* and *IC* trains (with seats); 79/109 PLN 2nd/1st class (this version was formerly called Bilet Podróżnika). **Weekendowy MAX**: valid in *EIC, EIP, IC* and *TLK*: 154 PLN 2nd class, 247 PLN 1st class (supplement of 10 PLN for each *EIP* journey). Seat reservations free (but not compulsory). Both the above also available from train conductor.

Bilety Sieciowe (network tickets): 3 months 2900/4050 PLN (2nd/1st class); 6 months 5400/7500 PLN; annual 9900/14600 PLN. Versions with unnamed holder are also available.

Przewozy Regionalne (PR) operates REGIO, IR and RE trains: **Bilety Sieciowe** (network tickets): weekly/monthly 159/369 PLN. **REGIOkarnet**: valid for any 3 days out of 2 months, 75 PLN; 65 PLN for REGIO trains only; validate at ticket office before travel. **Bilet Turystyczny** (tourist ticket): valid 1800 Friday to 0600 Monday, 45 PLN; 39 PLN for REGIO trains only. **Bilet Turystyczny + Czechy** adds border area of Czech Republic; 55 PLN. Passes valid on REGIO trains also valid on Arriva RP and Koleje Dolnośląskie.

Koleje Mazowieckie (KM) trains: wide area around Warsaw, 24 hr Bilet dobowy imienny 35 PLN.

Warsaw ZTM tram/bus/metro/rail (includes Chopin airport): 1 day zone 1 only, 15 PLN; zones 1 & 2, 26 PLN. Weekend ticket valid 1900 Fri - 0800 Mon valid zones 1 & 2, 24 PLN.

PORTUGAL

European residents: InterRail Global Pass and One Country Pass. Non-European residents: Eurail Global Pass, Eurail Select/One Country Passes.

Intra-Rail: for ages 12-30 with free nights at youth hostels; *Xcape* version valid 3 days €58 (€64 without youth card). *Xplore* version valid 7 days €127 (€146 without youth card). Not valid on *AP* trains. Buy at major stations. Card and ID must be presented to obtain a (free) travel ticket.

Lisboa: Carris tram/bus/metro - one-day ticket (bilhete 24h Rede) €6 in conjunction with reusable *7 Colinas* smartcard (€0.50). Includes the funiculars and lift. **Lisboa Card** includes free and discounted attractions: 24/48/72 hrs, €18.5/31.5/39 (ages 4-15: €11.5/17.5/20.5).

Coimbra: day ticket on SMTUC local buses €3.50.

Porto: *Andante Tour Card* gives metro + STCP bus + local rail, all zones, 24 hrs €7, 72 hrs €15. **Porto Card** also includes free/discounted entry to tourist attractions, 1 day €13, 2 days €20, 3 days €25.

ROMANIA

European residents: InterRail Global Pass and One Country Pass. Non-European residents: Eurail Global Pass, Eurail Select/One Country Passes. Also Balkan Flexipass.

Bucuresti: RATB tram, bus and trolleybus network (not express buses): 1/7/15 days, 8/17/25 RON. An 'Activ' or 'Multiplu' card may be required (1.6 RON). The **Bucharest City Card** is issued *free* and includes museum and other discounts, valid 3 days.

RUSSIA

Moskva: smart cards for unlimited number of journeys on metro; 1 day 210 RUB, 3 days 400 RUB, 7 days 800 RUB. Bus/tram tickets available from kiosks in strips of 10/20. Monthly *yediniy bilyet* covers bus/tram/metro (limited to 70 journeys) 2550 RUB. No tourist tickets.

St Peterburg: bus/tram tickets available in packs of 10; multi-journey cards can be bought for the metro. A **Guest Petersburg Card** is available for 2/3/5/7 days.

SERBIA

European residents: InterRail Global Pass and One Country Pass. Non-European residents: Eurail Global Pass, Eurail Select Pass. Also Balkan Flexipass.

SLOVAKIA

European residents: InterRail Global Pass and One Country Pass. Non-European residents: Eurail Global Pass, Eurail Select/One Country Passes. Also European East Pass.

Bratislava: urban tram/bus network, 24 hrs €6.9, 3 days €8, 7 days €11.4 **Bratislava City Card** includes many discounts, 1 day €10, 2 days €12, 3 days €15, available from tourist offices.

SLOVENIA

European residents: InterRail Global Pass and One Country Pass. Non-European residents: Eurail Global Pass, Eurail Select/One Country Passes.

Ljubljana City Card: city buses, castle funicular, tourist boat and museums, valid for 24, 48 or 72 hours, €23/30/35 (10% discount available online).

Passes for Domestic Travel

SPAIN

European residents: InterRail Global Pass and One Country Pass. Non-European residents: Eurail Global Pass, Eurail Select/One Country Passes. Also Passbask.

RENFE Spain Pass: for people resident outside Spain giving 4, 6, 8, 10 or 12 individual journeys. Tickets must be obtained in advance using the pass; reservations are compulsory but free. Valid 1 month from first journey. Can be purchased online (www.renfe.com).

Madrid: **Abono Turístico** (Tourist Ticket) gives all public transport in zone A, 1/2/3 days €8.4/14.2/18.4, also 5/7 days €26.8/35.4, children 50%. Available for wider area (zone T) at double the price. **Madrid Card** gives discounts at various attractions, 24/48/72/120 hrs €47/60/67/77 (cheaper online); combine with Tourist Ticket above for transport.

Barcelona T-Dia ticket: valid 1 day on metro/TMB bus/tram/local rail, from €8.4 (zone 1, includes airport) to €22.5 (all 6 zones, wide area around the city). **Hola BCN** zone 1 travelcards available for 2/3/4/5 days, €14/20.5/26.5/32 (cheaper online). **Barcelona Card**: adds free or discounted museums, 3 to 5 days €45/55/60 (children 4-12 years €21/27/32).

SWEDEN

European residents: InterRail Global Pass and One Country Pass. Non-European residents: Eurail Global Pass, Eurail Select/One Country Passes (also Scandinavia). Also Öresund Rundt.

Stockholm: all SL public transport in Greater Stockholm, 24/72 hours 115/230 SEK. 7 days 300 SEK, plus smartcard 20 SEK. Reduced 40% for under 20s/over 65s. **Stockholm Pass** includes museums, 710/1025/1225/1755 SEK for 24/48/72/120 hours (approximately half price for ages 6-17). A cheaper version excluding travel is also available.

SWITZERLAND

European residents: InterRail Global Pass and One Country Pass. Non-European residents: Eurail Global Pass, Eurail Select Pass. Also Euregio-Bodensee.

Swiss Travel Pass: available to all non-Swiss residents. Consecutive days on Swiss Railways, boats and most alpine postbuses and city buses. Valid for 3, 4, 8 or 15 days; 1st class 336/402/581/704 CHF, 2nd class 210/251/363/440 CHF. Youth Pass (16-25 years) gives approximately 20% reduction. All versions give 50% reduction on most funicular and mountain railways. Also includes the Swiss Museum Pass - free entrance to over 400 sites. Children aged 6-15 travel free with a Family Card if accompanied by a parent (not other relatives), otherwise half fare.

Swiss Travel Pass Flex: as above but for 3/4/8/15 non-consecutive days within 1 month. Prices 1st/2nd class: 382/239 CHF (3 days), 458/286 CHF (4 days), 651/407 CHF (8 days), 774/484 CHF (15 days). Youth discounts. Offers 50% reduction on most funicular and mountain railways on selected days only.

Swiss Transfer Ticket: return ticket from any airport/border station to any other Swiss station; use within 1 month. Each journey must be completed on day of validation and by the most direct route. 1st class 226 CHF, 2nd class 141 CHF. Family Card valid, see above. Cannot be obtained in Switzerland.

Swiss Transfer Ticket Combi: as Swiss Transfer Ticket but also offers unlimited half-fare tickets for 1 month on trains, buses, boats and most mountain railways and cable cars. 1st/2nd class 286/201 CHF. Family

card valid, see above under Swiss Travel Pass. No youth discount. Cannot be obtained in Switzerland.

Swiss Half Fare Card: discount card offering 50% off most public transport, valid for 1 month, 120 CHF.

Swiss Half Fare Card Combi: available to holders of the Swiss Travel Pass Flex or Swiss Transfer Ticket, 60 CHF. Offers the same benefits as the Swiss Half Fare Card.

The **9 o'clock Travelpass** is valid for travel within the GA area after 0900 hrs (not valid at weekends) to holders of Half Fare travelcards; 1st/2nd class 96/58 CHF. Packs of 6 can be bought for price of 5.

The above passes are available online (some may be printed at home), from Switzerland Travel Centre or from major Swiss stations. Not available to Swiss residents.

Bernese Oberland Regional Pass: valid May to October. Available for 4, 6, 8 or 10 days unlimited travel; 240/300/340/380 CHF 2nd class, 288/360/408/456 CHF 1st class.

Regional Passes: several other areas are available including Adventure Card Upper Valais - Uri - Grisons, Graubünden Pass, Lake Geneva - Alps and Tell-Pass.

Jungfrau Travel Pass: valid May to October for 3/4/5/6 days consecutive travel, 180/205/230/255 CHF. Covers most routes; 50% discount Eigergletscher - Jungfraujoch. 5 and 6 day passes also include boats on Lakes Brienz and Thun. **Summer Season Pass**: unlimited travel May to November, 550 CHF. Covers most routes; 50% discount Eigergletscher - Jungfraujoch. Discounts for holders of Half Fare Card, GA or Swiss Travel Pass on both the above. Not available in Switzerland.

Bern: day ticket for all transport in city 12.4 CHF. The **Bern Ticket** is issued to overnight guests offering free bus and tram travel within the inner city.

Genève: Day ticket (Carte 24 Heures) includes buses, trams, trains and boats: 10 CHF (valid for 2 people at weekends). **Carte 9 h** is valid from 0900 hrs, 8 CHF. Day ticket for wider regional area 18.5 CHF (13.2 CHF after 0900). The **Geneva Transport Card** is given to those staying at a hotel or youth hostel in the city and allows unrestricted travel on all public transport for the duration of the stay.

Zürich: ZVV Tageskarte gives 24 hours on all transport including SBB trains, 14.2/8.6 CHF 1st/2nd class (central zone only); all zones in Canton 55.6/33.6 CHF. Off-peak version is 9-UhrPass, all zones, not before 0900 Mon - Fri, 42.8/26 CHF. **Zürich Card** includes all museums: 24 hours 24 CHF, 72 hours 48 CHF (children 16/32 CHF), includes airport.

TURKEY

European residents: InterRail Global Pass and One Country Pass. Non-European residents: Eurail Global Pass, Eurail Select Pass. Also Balkan Flexipass.

Tren Tur Karti: 30 day network pass. *Ekspres* version covers day trains excluding high-speed (YTL 210), *Yatakli Karti* includes night trains (YTL 550). Various *YHT* cards cover high-speed lines. Buy from main stations.

UKRAINE

Kyïv: a unlimited use metro pass valid for 1 calendar month is available, 95 UAH (48 UAH if purchased after the 15th), but there are no tourist tickets.

Where to Buy your Pass

Sources of rail passes (and point to point tickets) include the following:

IN THE UNITED KINGDOM

ACP Rail - see www.acprail.com and www.britrail.net

Deutsche Bahn UK (German Railways)
UK Booking Centre, ✆ 08718 80 80 66 www.bahn.com

eRail Travel Ltd
17 Tileyard Studios, Tileyard Road, London, N7 9AH
✆ 0207 619 1083 www.etrains4u.com

Ffestiniog Travel
Unit 6, Snowdonia Business Park, Penrhyndeudraeth, Gwynedd LL48 6LD
✆ 01766 772030 www.ffestiniogtravel.com

International Rail
PO Box 153, Alresford, Hampshire SO24 4AQ
✆ 0871 231 0790 www.internationalrail.com

Rail Canterbury
39 Palace Street, Canterbury, Kent CT1 2DZ
✆ 01227 450088 www.rail-canterbury.co.uk

RailTourGuide
Suite 42, 7 - 15 Pink Lane, Newcastle upon Tyne, NE1 5DW
✆ 0191 246 0708 www.railtourguide.com

Real Russia
Unit 5, The Ivories, Northampton Street, Islington, London, N1 2HY
✆ 0207 100 7370 www.realrussia.co.uk

Switzerland Travel Centre
30 Bedford Street, 1st Floor, London, WC2E 9ED
0207 420 49 34 www.stc.co.uk

Trainseurope
4 Station Approach, March, Cambs PE15 8SJ
Also at St Pancras International station.
✆ 0871 700 7722 www.trainseurope.co.uk

Voyages sncf
www.voyages-sncf.com

IN THE USA AND CANADA

Rail Europe Inc.
44 South Broadway, White Plains, NY 10601, USA
✆ 1-800-622-8600 www.raileurope.com

Rail Europe, Canada
✆ 1-800-361 7245 (1-800-361-RAIL) www.raileurope.ca

See also **Rick Steve's** comprehensive website: www.ricksteves.com. For a list of **Eurail** agents worldwide see www.eurailgroup.org.

AUSTRIA

CAPITAL
Vienna (Wien).

CURRENCY
Euro (EUR / €). 1 euro = 100 cent. For exchange rates see page 9.

EMBASSIES IN VIENNA
Australia: Mattiellistraße 2-4, ✆ 1 506 740. **Canada**: Laurenzenberg 2, ✆ 1 531 383 000. **New Zealand** Mattiellistraße 2-4/3, ✆ 1 505 3021. **UK**: Jaurèsgasse 12, ✆ 1 716 130. **USA**: Boltzmanngasse 16, ✆ 1 313 390.

EMBASSIES OVERSEAS
Australia: 12 Talbot St, Forrest, Canberra, ACT 2603, ✆ 2 629 515 33. **Canada**: 445 Wilbrod St, Ottawa ON, KIN 6M7, ✆ 613 789 1444. **UK**: 18 Belgrave Mews West, London SW1X 8HU, ✆ 020 7344 3250. **USA**: 3524 International Court NW, Washington DC 20008, ✆ 202 895 6700.

LANGUAGE
German. English is widely spoken in tourist areas.

PUBLIC TRANSPORT
Most long-distance travel is by rail (see below). Inter-urban buses operated by ÖBB-Postbus (www.postbus.at); stops usually located by rail stations or post offices. City transport is efficient with integrated ticketing; buy tickets from machines or Tabak/Trafik booths. Wien has an extensive metro and tram system; for day tickets see Passes section. Other cities with tram networks include Graz, Innsbruck and Linz. Taxis are metered; extra charges for luggage (fixed charges in smaller towns).

RAIL TRAVEL
See Tables **950 - 999**. Operated by Österreichische Bundesbahnen (ÖBB) www.oebb.at. *RJ* (*Railjet*) / *EC* / *IC*) operate every 1 – 2 hrs on main domestic and international routes. *ICE* trains operate certain international services to / from Germany. Other train categories: *D* (ordinary fast trains); *REX* (semi-fast local trains); *R* (local stopping trains); *EN* (overnight trains, see below); S-Bahn services operate in major cities. Private operator *Westbahn* also operate fast trains between Wien and Salzburg. Most overnight trains, many of which are now branded *ÖBB nightjet*, convey sleeping-cars (up to three berths), couchettes (four or six berth) and 2nd class seats. Seat reservations available on long-distance services.

TELEPHONES
Dial in: ✆ +43 then number (omit initial 0). Outgoing: ✆ 00. Emergency: ✆ 112. Police: ✆ 133. Fire: ✆ 122. Ambulance: ✆ 144.

TOURIST INFORMATION
Austrian National Tourist Office (*Fremdenverkehrsbüro*) www.austria. info. Vienna: Albertinaplatz / Maysedergasse, ✆ 01 24 555.

TOURIST OFFICES OVERSEAS
Australia: 36 Carrington St, 1st floor, Sydney NSW 2000, ✆ 02 9299 3621, info@antosyd.org.au. **Canada**: 2 Bloor St West, Suite 400, Toronto ON, M4W 3E2, ✆ 416 967 3381, travel@austria. info. **UK**: 9-11 Richmond Buildings, off Dean St., London W1D 3HF, ✆ 0845 101 18 18, holiday@austria.info. **USA**: P.O. Box 1142, New York NY 10108-1142, ✆ 212 944 6880, travel@austria.info.

VISAS
See page xxiv for visa requirements.

BELGIUM

CAPITAL
Brussels (Bruxelles / Brussel).

CURRENCY
Euro (EUR / €). 1 euro = 100 cent. For exchange rates see page 9.

EMBASSIES IN BRUSSELS
Australia: Ave des Arts 56, ✆ 02 286 0500. **Canada**: Avenue de Tervueren 2, ✆ 02 741 0611. **New Zealand**: Avenue des Nerviens 9/31, ✆ 02 512 1040. **UK**: Avenue d'Auderghem 10, ✆ 02 287 6211. **USA**: Boulevard du Regentlaan 27, ✆ 02 811 4000.

EMBASSIES OVERSEAS
Australia: 19 Arkana St, Yarralumla, Canberra, ACT 2600, ✆ 2 627 325 01. **Canada**: 360 Albert St, Suite 820, Ottawa ON, K1R 7X7, ✆ 613 236 7267. **UK**: 17 Grosvenor Crescent, London SW1X 7EE, ✆ 020 7470 3700. **USA**: 3330 Garfield St NW, Washington DC 20008, ✆ 202 333 6900.

LANGUAGE
Dutch (north), French (south) and German (east). Many speak both French and Dutch, plus often English and/or German.

PUBLIC TRANSPORT
National bus companies: De Lijn (Flanders), TEC (Wallonia, i.e. the French-speaking areas); few long-distance buses. Brussels has extensive metro / tram / bus system operated by STIB with integrated ticketing; tickets can be purchased from tram / bus driver but it's cheaper to buy in advance from machines at metro stations or special kiosks (also offices labelled *Bootik*). For day tickets see Passes section. Some tram and bus stops are request stops – raise your hand. Taxis seldom pick up in the street, so find a rank or phone; double rates outside city limits.

RAIL TRAVEL
See Tables **400 - 448**. Operated by NMBS (in Dutch) / SNCB (in French) www.b-rail.be. Rail information offices: 'B' in an oval logo. Some platforms serve more than one train at a time; check carefully. Left luggage and cycle hire at many stations. Timetables usually in two sets: Mondays to Fridays and weekends/holidays.

TELEPHONES
Dial in: ✆ +32 then number (omit initial 0). Outgoing: ✆ 00. Emergency: ✆ 112. Police: ✆ 101. Fire, ambulance: ✆ 100.

TOURIST INFORMATION
Dutch: *Dienst voor Toerisme*. French: *Office de Tourisme*. Toerisme Vlaanderen www.toervl.be / www.visitflanders.co.uk. Office de Promotion du Tourisme de Wallonie et de Bruxelles www.belgium-tourism.net. Brussels: Hôtel de Ville, Grand Place or rue Royale 2, ✆ 025 138 940.

TOURIST OFFICES OVERSEAS
UK: Tourism Flanders-Brussels, 1a Cavendish Square, London W1G 0LD. ✆ 020 7307 7738, info@visitflanders.co.uk; Belgian Tourist Office Brussels-Wallonia, 217 Marsh Wall, London E14 9FJ. ✆ 020 7531 0390, ✆ 0800 954 5245, info@belgiumtheplaceto.be. **USA / Canada**: 220 East 42nd St, Suite 3402, New York NY 10017, ✆ 212 758 8130, info@visitbelgium.com.

VISAS
See page xxiv for visa requirements.

BULGARIA

CAPITAL
Sofia (Sofiya).

CURRENCY
Lev (BGN or Lv.); 1 lev = 100 stotinki (st). Tied to euro. For exchange rates see page 9.

EMBASSIES IN SOFIA
Australia *refer to Australian Embassy in Greece*. **Canada**: (Consulate) 7 Pozitano St, ✆ 02 969 9710. **New Zealand**: *refer to NZ Embassy in Belgium*. **UK**: ul. Moskovska 9, ✆ 02 933 9222. **USA**: ulitsa Kozyak 16, ✆ 02 937 5100.

EMBASSIES OVERSEAS
Australia: 29 Pindary Crescent str. O'Malley, Canberra, ACT 2606, ✆ 2 628 697 11. **Canada**: 325 Steward St, Ottawa ON, K1N 6K5, ✆ 613 789 3215. **UK**: 186 - 188 Queen's Gate, London SW7 5HL, ✆ 020 7584 9400. **USA**: 1621 22nd St NW, Washington DC 20008, ✆ 202 387 0174.

LANGUAGE
Bulgarian (written in the Cyrillic alphabet). English, German, Russian and French in tourist areas.

PUBLIC TRANSPORT
There is an extensive bus network but quality is variable. They are slightly more expensive than trains but both are very cheap for hard currency travellers. In Sofia buses and trams use the same ticket; punch it at the machine after boarding, get a new ticket if you change. For day tickets see Passes section.

RAIL TRAVEL

See Tables 1500 - 1560. Bulgarian State Railways (BDZ) www.bdz.bg run express, fast and stopping trains. Reservations are recommended (obligatory for express trains). Overnight trains convey 1st- and 2nd-class sleeping cars and seats. One platform may serve two tracks, platforms and tracks are both numbered. Station signs are in Cyrillic.

TELEPHONES

Dial in: ✆ +359 then number (omit initial 0). Outgoing: ✆ 00. Emergency: ✆ 112.

TOURIST INFORMATION

Bulgarian Tourism Authority www.bulgariatravel.org. Sofia: St Kliment Ohridski Sofia University, ✆ 02 491 83 44.

TOURIST OFFICES OVERSEAS

UK and **USA**: Tourist information available at the Bulgarian Embassies listed above.

VISAS

See page xxiv for visa requirements. Passports must have 3 months validity remaining. Visitors staying with friends or family (i.e. not in paid accommodation) need to register on arrival.

CROATIA

CAPITAL

Zagreb.

CURRENCY

Kuna (HRK or kn); 1 kuna = 100 lipa. For exchange rates see page 9.

EMBASSIES IN ZAGREB

Australia: Centar Kaptol, 3rd Floor, Nova Ves 11, ✆ 1 4891 200. **Canada**: Prilaz Gjure Dezelica 4, ✆ 1 4881 200. **New Zealand** (Consulate): Vlaska ulica 50A, ✆ 1 4612 060. **UK**: Ivana Lučiča 4, ✆ 1 6009 100. **USA**: Ulica Thomasa Jeffersona 2, ✆ 1 6612 200.

EMBASSIES OVERSEAS

Australia: 14 Jindalee Crescent, O'Malley, Canberra, ACT 2606, ✆ 2 6286 6988. **Canada**: 229 Chapel St, Ottawa ON, K1N 7Y6, ✆ 613 562 7820. **New Zealand** (Consulate): 131 Lincoln Rd, Henderson, PO Box 83-200, Edmonton, Auckland, ✆ 9 836 5581. **UK**: 21 Conway St, London, W1T 6BN, ✆ 020 7387 2022. **USA**: 2343 Massachusetts Ave. NW, Washington DC 20008-2803, ✆ 202 588 5899.

LANGUAGE

Croatian. English, German and Italian spoken in tourist areas.

PUBLIC TRANSPORT

Buses and trams are cheap, regular and efficient. Zagreb and Osijek have tram networks. Jadrolinija maintains most domestic ferry lines; main office in Rijeka, ✆ +385 51 666 111.

RAIL TRAVEL

See Tables 1300 - 1359. National railway company: Hrvatske željeznice (HŽ) www.hzpp.hr. Zagreb is a major hub for international trains. Efficient services but there is a limited network and services can be infrequent on some routes. Daytime trains on the Zagreb - Split line are operated by modern tilting diesel trains. Station amenities: generally left luggage, a bar and WCs.

TELEPHONES

Dial in: ✆ +385 then number (omit initial 0). Outgoing: ✆ 00. Police: ✆ 92. Fire: ✆ 93. Ambulance: ✆ 94.

TOURIST INFORMATION

Croatian National Tourist Board www.croatia.hr. Zagreb: Iblerov trg 10/IV, ✆ 014 699 333. Zagreb Tourist Board www.infozagreb.hr, Kaptol 5, ✆ 014 898 555.

TOURIST OFFICES OVERSEAS

UK: Elsinore House, 77 Fulham Palace Rd, London, W6 8JA, ✆ 020 8563 7979, info@croatia-london.co.uk. **Germany**: Rumfordstrasse 7, 80469 Munich ✆ 089 223 344, kroatien-tourismus@online.de. **USA**: 350 Fifth Ave., Suite 4003, New York NY 10118, ✆ 212 279 8672, cntony@earthlink.net or info@htz.hr.

VISAS

See page xxiv for visa requirements.

CZECH REPUBLIC

CAPITAL

Prague (Praha).

CURRENCY

Czech crown or koruna (CZK or Kč); 1 koruna = 100 haléřu. For exchange rates see page 9.

EMBASSIES IN PRAGUE

Australia (Consulate): 6th Floor, Solitaire Building, ulica Klimentska 10, ✆ 221 729 260. **Canada**: Ve Struhach 95/2, ✆ 272 101 800. **New Zealand** (Consulate): Václavské náměstí 11, ✆ 234 784 777. **UK**: Thunovská 14, ✆ 257 402 111. **USA**: Tržíště 15, ✆ 257 022 000.

EMBASSIES OVERSEAS

Australia: 8 Culgoa Circuit, O'Malley, Canberra, ACT 2606, ✆ 2 6290 1386. **Canada**: 251 Cooper St., Ottawa ON, K2P 0G2, ✆ 613 562 3875. **New Zealand** (Consulate): 110 Customs Street West, Auckland 1010, ✆ 9 306 5883. **UK**: 26–30 Kensington Palace Gardens, London W8 4QY, ✆ 020 7243 1115. **USA**: 3900 Spring of Freedom St NW, Washington DC 20008, ✆ 202 274 9100.

LANGUAGE

Czech. Czech and Slovak are closely related Slavic tongues. English, German and Russian are widely understood, but Russian is less popular.

PUBLIC TRANSPORT

Extensive long-distance bus network competing with the railways, run by private companies (many previously part of the nationalised ČSAD). In Prague the long-distance bus station is close to Florenc metro station. If boarding at a bus station with a ticket window, buy your ticket in advance, otherwise pay the driver. Good urban networks with integrated ticketing. Prague (Praha) has metro and tram system - see Passes feature for day tickets. Other cities with trams include Brno, Ostrava, Plzeň, Olomouc, Liberec.

RAIL TRAVEL

See Tables 1100 - 1169. National rail company is České Dráhy (ČD) www.cd.cz. An extensive network with many branch lines and cheap fares, but sometimes crowded trains. The best mainline trains are classified IC, EC or Ex. The fastest Praha - Ostrava trains are classified SC meaning SuperCity and are operated by Pendolino tilting trains - a compulsory reservation fee of CZK 250 or €9.00 applies on these. Other fast (R for rychlík) trains are shown in our tables with just the train number. Semi-fast trains are Sp or spešný, local trains (very slow) are Os or osobný. Some branch lines are now operated by private companies, and on the Praha - Ostrava route ČD compete with two private operators: RegioJet and Leo Express. Many long-distance trains have dining or buffet cars. Seats for express trains may be reserved at least one hour before departure at the counter marked R at stations.

TELEPHONES

Dial in: ✆ +420 then number. Outgoing: ✆ 00. Police: ✆ 158. Fire: ✆ 150. Ambulance: ✆ 155. Also 112.

TOURIST INFORMATION

Czech Tourism www.czechtourism.com. Prague: Vinohradská 46, 120 41 Praha 2, Vinohrady, ✆ 221 580 611. Prague Information Service, www.prague.eu, Information centre, Old Town Hall, Staroměstské náměstí 1, Praha 1.

TOURIST OFFICES OVERSEAS

Canada: See USA. **UK**: 13 Harley Street, London W1G 9QG, ✆ 020 7631 0427, info-uk@czechtourism.com. **USA**: 1109 Madison Ave., New York NY 10028, ✆ 212 288 0830, info-usa@czechtourism.com.

VISAS

See page xxiv for visa requirements.

DENMARK

CAPITAL

Copenhagen (København).

CURRENCY

Danish crown or krone, DKK or kr; 1 krone = 100 øre. For exchange rates see page 9.

EMBASSIES IN COPENHAGEN

Australia: Dampfaergevej 26, ✆ 70 26 36 76. **Canada**: Kristen Bernikowsgade 1, ✆ 33 48 32 00. **New Zealand** (Consulate): Store Strandstraede 21, ✆ 33 37 77 02. **UK**: Kastelsvej 36-40, ✆ 35 44 52 00. **USA**: Dag Hammarskjölds Allé 24, ✆ 33 41 71 00.

EMBASSIES OVERSEAS

Australia: 15 Hunter St, Yarralumla, Canberra, ACT 2600, ✆ 2 6270 5333. **Canada**: 47 Clarence St, Suite 450, Ottawa ON, K1N 9K1, ✆ 613 562 1811. **New Zealand** (Consulate): 273 Bleakhouse Rd, Howick, Auckland 2014, ✆ 9 537 3099. **UK**: 55 Sloane St, London SW1X 9SR, ✆ 020 7333 0200. **USA**: 3200 Whitehaven St NW, Washington DC 20008-3683, ✆ 202 234 4300.

LANGUAGE

Danish. English is almost universally spoken.

PUBLIC TRANSPORT

Long-distance travel is easiest by train (see below). Excellent regional and city bus services, many connecting with trains. Modern and efficient metro www.m.dk and suburban rail network in and around the capital; see Passes feature for day tickets. No trams in København; bus network can be tricky to fathom. Bridges or ferries link all the big islands. Taxis: green *Fri* sign when available; metered, and most accept major credit cards. Many cycle paths and bike hire shops; free use of City Bikes in Copenhagen central area (returnable coin required).

RAIL TRAVEL

See Tables **700 - 728**. Operator: Danske Statsbaner (DSB) www.dsb. dk. Some independent lines, and certain former DSB services are operated by private company ArrivaTog www.arriva.dk. *IC* trains reach up to 200 km/h. *Re* (regionaltog) trains are frequent, but slower. Reservations are recommended (not compulsory) on *IC* and *Lyn* trains - DKK 30 in standard class; reservation included in business class. Reservations close 15 minutes before a train leaves its originating station. Nationwide reservations ✆ 70 13 14 15. Baggage lockers at most stations, usually DKK 30 per 24 hrs. Usually free trolleys, but you may need a (returnable) coin.

TELEPHONES

Dial in: ✆ +45 then number. Outgoing: ✆ 00.
Emergency services: ✆ 112. Police ✆ 114.

TOURIST INFORMATION

Danish Tourist Board www.visitdenmark.com.

TOURIST OFFICES OVERSEAS

UK: 55 Sloane St, London SW1X 9SY, ✆ 020 7259 5958, london@visitdenmark.com. **USA / Canada**: P.O.Box 4649, Grand Central Station, New York NY 10163-4649, ✆ 212 885 9700, info@goscandinavia.com.

VISAS

See page xxiv for visa requirements.

ESTONIA

CAPITAL
Tallinn.

CURRENCY
Euro (EUR / €). 1 euro = 100 cent. For exchange rates see page 9.

EMBASSIES IN TALLINN

Australia (Consulate): c/- Standard Ltd Marja 9, ✆ 650 9308. **Canada** (Consulate): Toom Kooli 13, ✆ 627 3311. **New Zealand**: See Germany. **UK**: Wismari 6, ✆ 667 4700. **USA**: Kentmanni 20, ✆ 668 8100.

EMBASSIES OVERSEAS

Australia (Consulate): Suite 1, 144 Pacific Highway, Sydney, NSW 2060, ✆ 2 8014 8999. **Canada**: 260 Dalhousie St, Suite 210, Ottawa ON, K1N 7E4, ✆ 613 789 4222. **New Zealand** (Consulate): 3 Olliver Grove, Waikanae Beach, Wellington 5036, ✆ 4 293 1361. **UK**: 16 Hyde Park Gate, London SW7 5DG, ✆ 020 7838 5388. **USA**: 2131 Massachusetts Ave. NW, Washington DC 20008, ✆ 202 588 0101.

LANGUAGE

Estonian. Some English is spoken but some Finnish is also useful, plus Russian in Tallinn and the north-east.

PUBLIC TRANSPORT

Long-distance bus services are often quicker, cleaner, and more efficient than rail, but more expensive. The main domestic long-distance bus operator is Tpilet www.tpilet.ee; for international bus journeys book in advance with Luxespress www.luxexpress.eu or ecolines www. ecolines.net. Tallinn has a tram network.

RAIL TRAVEL

See Tables **1800 - 1890**. Local rail services are operated by Elron www. elron.ee. Comfortable overnight train to Moscow via St Peterburg. Very little English spoken at stations.

TELEPHONES

Dial in: ✆ +372 then number. Outgoing: ✆ 00.
Police: ✆ 110. Fire, ambulance: ✆ 112.

TOURIST INFORMATION

Estonian Tourist Board www.visitestonia.com, tourism@eas.ee. Tallinn: Niguliste 2 / Kullassepa 4, ✆ 645 7777, turismiinfo@tallinnlv.ee.

TOURIST OFFICES OVERSEAS

UK: Tourism brochures available from the Estonian Embassy (see above) Mon-Fri 0900 - 1700. **Germany**: Baltikum Tourismus Zentrale, Katharinenstraße 19-20, 10711 Berlin, ✆ 030 89 00 90 91, www. baltikuminfo.de, info@baltikuminfo.de.

VISAS

See page xxiv for visa requirements.

FINLAND

CAPITAL
Helsinki (Helsingfors).

CURRENCY
Euro (EUR / €). 1 euro = 100 cent. For exchange rates see page 9.

EMBASSIES IN HELSINKI

Australia (Consulate): c/- Tradimex Oy, Museokatu 25B, ✆ 04 204 492. **Canada**: Pohjoisesplanadi 25B, ✆ 09 228 530. **New Zealand** (Consulate): Erottajankatu 9, ✆ 50 342 9950. **UK**: Itäinen Puistotie 17, ✆ 09 2286 5100. **USA**: Itäinen Puistotie 14B, ✆ 09 616 250.

EMBASSIES OVERSEAS

Australia: 12 Darwin Ave., Yarralumla, Canberra, ACT 2600, ✆ 2 6273 3800. **Canada**: 55 Metcalfe St, Suite 850, Ottawa ON, K1P 6L5, ✆ 613 288 2233. **New Zealand** (Consulate): 1 Kimberley Rd, Epsom, Auckland 1023, ✆ 9 368 5711. **UK**: 38 Chesham Place, London SW1X 8HW, ✆ 020 7838 6200. **USA**: 3301 Massachusetts Ave. NW, Washington DC 20008, ✆ 202 298 5800.

LANGUAGE

Finnish, and, in the north, Lapp/Sami. Swedish, the second language, often appears on signs after the Finnish. English is widely spoken. German is also reasonably widespread.

PUBLIC TRANSPORT

There are more than 300 bus services daily from Helsinki to all parts of the country. The main long-distance bus operators are Matkahuolto www.matkahuolto.fi and the Expressbus consortium www.expressbus. com. Bus stations (*Linja-autoasema*) often have restaurants and shops. It is usually cheaper to buy tickets in advance. Bus stop signs show a black bus on a yellow background (local services) or a white bus on a blue background (long distance). Helsinki has metro / tram / bus network with integrated ticketing.

RAIL TRAVEL

See Tables **790 - 799**. National rail company: VR www.vr.fi. Long distance train types: *S* (Pendolino), *IC* (InterCity) and *P* (express). Travel classes are referred to as *Eco* (2nd class) and *Extra* (1st class). For all except purely local journeys, tickets are sold for travel by a specific train with seat reservations included. Standard *Eco* fares are referred to as 'Basic', whilst cheaper advance puchase 'Saver' fares are also available in limited numbers. In both cases tickets can be changed to a different date / departure time for a €5 fee (plus any price difference). Tickets can be upgraded to a seat in *Extra* class for a variable fee (dependent on the length of journey). Sleeping-cars: one, two or three berth compartments (variable supplement in addition to the appropriate *Eco* class fare). Rail station: *Rautatieasema*. some larger stations have luggage lockers. Only the largest stations have open ticket offices, although most have automatic ticket machines.

TELEPHONES

Dial in: ✆ +358 then number (omit initial 0). Outgoing: ✆ 00. Emergency services: ✆ 112.

TOURIST INFORMATION

Finnish Tourist Board www.visitfinland.com. Helsinki: PO Box 625, Töölönkatu 11, ✆ 029 50 58000, mek@visitfinland.com.

TOURIST OFFICES OVERSEAS

USA: 297 York Street, Jersey City, NJ 07302, ✆ 917 863 5484.

VISAS

See page xxiv for visa requirements.

FRANCE

CAPITAL

Paris, divided into *arrondissements* 1 to 20 (1er, 2e etc).

CURRENCY

Euro (EUR/€). 1 euro = 100 cent. For exchange rates see page 9.

EMBASSIES IN PARIS

Australia: 4 rue Jean Rey, ✆ 01 40 59 33 00. **Canada**: 35 avenue Montaigne, ✆ 01 44 43 29 00. **New Zealand**: 7 ter, rue Léonard de Vinci, ✆ 01 45 01 43 43. **UK**: 35 rue du Faubourg St Honoré, ✆ 01 44 51 31 00. **USA**: 2 avenue Gabriel, ✆ 01 43 12 22 22.

EMBASSIES OVERSEAS

Australia: 6 Perth Ave. Yarralumla, Canberra, ACT 2600, ✆ 2 6216 0100. **Canada**: 42 Sussex Drive, Ottawa ON, K1M 2C9, ✆ 613 789 1795. **New Zealand**: 34-42 Manners St, Wellington, ✆ 4 384 2555. **UK**: 58 Knightsbridge, London SW1X 7JT, ✆ 020 7073 1000. **USA**: 4101 Reservoir Rd, NW, Washington DC 20007, ✆ 202 944 6000.

LANGUAGE

French. Many people can speak a little English, particularly in Paris.

PUBLIC TRANSPORT

In Paris, use the Métro where possible: clean, fast, cheap and easy. For urban and suburban transport, *carnets* (sets of 10 tickets) are cheaper than individual tickets; for day tickets see Passes feature. Bus and train timetable leaflets (free) are available from tourist offices, bus and rail stations. Many cities have modern tram/light rail networks; Lyon, Marseille and Toulouse also have metro systems. Bus services are infrequent after 2030 and on Sundays. Sparse public transport in rural areas, and few long-distance bus services. Licensed taxis (avoid others) are metered; white roof-lights when free; surcharges for luggage, extra passengers, and journeys beyond the centre.

RAIL TRAVEL

See Tables 250 - 399. Société Nationale des Chemins de fer Français (SNCF) www.sncf.com, ✆ 3635 (premium rate, in French), followed by 1 for traffic status, 2 for timetables, 3 for reservations and tickets, 4 for other services. Excellent network from Paris to major cities with *TGV* trains using dedicated high-speed lines (up to 320 km/h on the *Est Européen* line to eastern France) as well as conventional track. However, some cross-country journeys can be slow and infrequent. Trains can get very full at peak times, so to avoid having to spend the journey standing, book a seat. Prior reservation is compulsory on *TGV* high-speed trains and the charge is included in the ticket price; rail pass holders will have to pay at least the reservation fee. Tickets can cost more at busy times (known as 'white' periods). Long distance trains on non-TGV routes are usually branded *Intercités* using refurbished rolling stock - some have compulsory reservation as shown in our tables. Reservation is also compulsory on all overnight trains: most convey couchettes and reclining seats only (sleeping cars are only conveyed on international trains). A certain number of couchette compartments are reserved for women only or those with small children; otherwise, couchette accommodation is mixed. There is a minimal bar/trolley service on some long-distance trains. Larger stations have 24-hour coin-operated left-luggage lockers, and sometimes pay-showers.

TELEPHONES

Dial in: ✆ +33 then number (omit initial 0). Outgoing: ✆ 00. Emergency: ✆ 112. Police: ✆ 17. Fire: ✆ 18. Ambulance: ✆ 15.

TOURIST INFORMATION

Maison de la France www.franceguide.com. Paris: 79/81 Rue de Clichy, ✆ 0 142 967 000. Local tourist offices: *Syndicat d'Initiative* or *Office de Tourisme*.

TOURIST OFFICES OVERSEAS

Australia: Level 13, 25 Bligh St, Sydney NSW 2000, ✆ 02 9231 6277, info.au@franceguide.com. **Canada**: 1800 avenue McGill College, Suite 1010, Montréal QC, H3A 3J6, ✆ 514 288 2026, canada@franceguide.com. **UK**: Lincoln House, 300 High Holborn, London WC1V 7JH, ✆ 0207 061 6600, info.uk@franceguide.com. **USA**: 825 Third Avenue, 29th floor, New York NY 10022, ✆ 212 838 7800, info.us@franceguide.com. Also in Los Angeles and Chicago.

VISAS

See page xxiv for visa requirements.

GERMANY

CAPITAL

Berlin.

CURRENCY

Euro (EUR/€). 1 euro = 100 cent. For exchange rates see page 9.

EMBASSIES IN BERLIN

Australia: Wallstraße 76-79, ✆ 030 88 00 880. **Canada**: Leipziger Platz 17, ✆ 030 203 12 470. **New Zealand**: Friedrichstraße 60, ✆ 030 206 210. **UK**: Wilhelmstraße 70/71, ✆ 030 204 570. **USA**: Clayallee 170, ✆ 030 830 50.

EMBASSIES OVERSEAS

Australia: 119 Empire Circuit, Yarralumla, Canberra, ACT 2600, ✆ 2 6270 1911. **Canada**: 1 Waverley St, Ottawa ON, K2P 0T8, ✆ 613 232 1101. **New Zealand**: 90-92 Hobson St, Thorndon, Wellington, ✆ 4 473 6063. **UK**: Embassy, 23 Belgrave Sq., London SW1X 8PZ, ✆ 020 7824 1300. **USA**: 2300 M Street, NW, Suite 300 Washington DC, 20037, ✆ 202 298 4000.

LANGUAGE

German. English and French widely spoken.

PUBLIC TRANSPORT

Most large cities have U-Bahn (U) underground railway and S-Bahn (S) urban rail service, many have trams. City travel passes cover these and other public transport, including local ferries in some cities (e.g. Hamburg). International passes usually cover S-Bahn. Single fares are expensive; a day card (*Tagesnetzkarte*) or multi-ride ticket (*Mehrfahrkarte*) pays for itself if you take more than three rides (see Passes feature for selected day tickets). Long-distance buses are not common.

RAIL TRAVEL

See Tables 800 - 949. Deutsche Bahn (DB) www.bahn.de. ✆ 01805 99 66 33 (20ct per call) for timetable and fares information, ticket purchase and reservations. Timetable freephone (automated): ✆ 0800 1507090. UK booking centre ✆ 08718 80 80 66 (calls are charged). *Sparpreis* are good value single fares valid for travel on a fixed day/train. Long-distance day trains: *ICE* (modern high-speed trains; up to 300km/h; higher fares but no extra charge for Interrail pass holders), *IC* and *EC*. Regional trains: *IRE*, *RE*, *RB* (modern, comfortable and connect with long-distance network). Frequent local S-Bahn services operate in major cities. Many local services are now run by private operators. Overnight services (*EN*) usually convey sleeping-cars (up to three berths) and couchettes (four or six berth), also 2nd class seats. Overnight trains between Germany and Austria/Switzerland are operated by Austrian Railways and are branded *ÖBB nightjet*. Reservation on overnight *EN* trains is usually compulsory. Most long-distance day trains convey a bistro or restaurant car (an at-seat service is offered in first class). Seat reservations possible on long-distance trains. Stations are well staffed, often with left luggage and bicycle hire. Main station is *Hauptbahnhof* (Hbf).

TELEPHONES

Dial in: ✆ +49 then number (omit initial 0). Outgoing: ✆ 00. Police: ✆ 110. Fire: ✆ 112. Ambulance: ✆ 112.

TOURIST INFORMATION

German National Tourist Office www.germany-tourism.de. Main office: Beethovenstraße 69, 60325 Frankfurt am Main, ✆ 069 974 640, info@germany.travel.

TOURIST OFFICES OVERSEAS

Australia: c/o Gate 7 Pty Ltd, Level 1, 97 Rose St. Chippendale, Sydney NSW 2008, ✆ 02 9331 6202, germanytourism@smink.com.au. **Canada**: Vox International Inc, 2 Bloor St West, Suite 2601, Toronto ON, M4W 3E2, ✆ 416 935 1896, info@-gnto.ca. **UK**: PO Box 2695, London W1A 3TN, ✆ 020 7317 0908, office-britain@germany.travel. **USA**: 122 East 42nd Street, New York NY 10168-0072, ✆ 212 661 7200, office-usa@germany.travel. Also in Chicago (✆ 773 539 6303) and Los Angeles (✆ 310 545 1350).

VISAS

See page xxiv for visa requirements.

GREECE

CAPITAL

Athens (Athina).

CURRENCY

Euro (EUR / €). 1 euro = 100 cent. For exchange rates see page 9.

EMBASSIES IN ATHENS

Australia: Level 6, Thon Building, Kifisias / Alexandras, Ambelokipi, ✆ 210 870 4000. **Canada**: Ioannou Ghennadiou 4, ✆ 210 727 3400. **New Zealand** (Consulate): Kifissias Avenue 76, Ambelokipi, ✆ 210 6924 136. **UK**: Ploutarchou 1, ✆ 210 727 2600. **USA**: Vasilissis Sophias 91, ✆ 210 721 2951.

EMBASSIES OVERSEAS

Australia: 9 Turrana St, Yarralumla, Canberra, ACT 2600, ✆ 2 6273 3011. **Canada**: 76-80 MacLaren St, Ottawa ON, K2P 0K6, ✆ 613 238 6271. **New Zealand**: 38 - 42 Waring Taylor St, Wellington 6142, ✆ 4 473 7775. **UK**: 1A Holland Park, London W11 3TP, ✆ 020 7229 3850. **USA**: 2217 Massachusetts Ave. NW, Washington DC 20008, ✆ 202 939 1300.

LANGUAGE

Greek. English widely spoken in Athens and tourist areas (also some German, French or Italian).

PUBLIC TRANSPORT

KTEL buses: fast, punctual, fairly comfortable long-distance services; well-organised stations in most towns (tickets available from bus terminals), www.ktelbus.com. Islands connected by ferries and hydrofoils. City transport: bus or (in Athens) trolleybus and metro. Outside Athens, taxis are plentiful and good value.

RAIL TRAVEL

See Tables 1400 - 1499. Operator: TrainOSE S.A. (OSE) www.trainose.gr. English language call centre for reservations and information (0600 - 2300): ✆ 14511. Limited rail network, especially away from the main Athens - Thessaloniki axis. Reservations are essential on most express trains. *ICity* trains are fast and fairly punctual, but supplements can be expensive. Stations: often no left luggage or English-speaking staff, but many have bars.

TELEPHONES

Dial in: ✆ + 30 then number. Outgoing: ✆ 00.
Emergency: ✆ 112. Police: ✆ 100. Fire: ✆ 199. Ambulance: ✆ 166. Tourist police (24 hrs, English-speaking): ✆ 171.

TOURIST INFORMATION

Greek National Tourist Organisation www.visitgreece.gr. Athens: Tsoha 7, ✆ 2 108 707 000. Athens information: Amalias 26, ✆ 2 103 310 392.

TOURIST OFFICES OVERSEAS

Australia: 37-49 Pitt St, Sydney NSW 2000, ✆ 02 9241 1663, hto@tpg.com.au. **UK**: 4 Great Portland St, London W1W 8QJ, ✆ 020 7495 9300, info@gnto.co.uk. **USA**: 305 East 47th Street, New York NY10017, ✆ 212 421 5777, info@greektourism.com.

VISAS

See page xxiv for visa requirements.

HUNGARY

CAPITAL

Budapest.

CURRENCY

Forint (HUF or Ft). For exchange rates see page 9.

EMBASSIES IN BUDAPEST

Australia: *refer to Australian Embassy in Austria*. **Canada**: Ganz utca 12–14, ✆ 1 392 3360. **New Zealand** (Consulate): Nagymazö utca 47, ✆ 1 302 2484. **UK**: Harmincad utca 6, ✆ 1 266 2888. **USA**: Szabadság tér 12, ✆ 1 475 4400.

EMBASSIES OVERSEAS

Australia: 17 Beale Crescent, Deakin, Canberra, ACT 2600, ✆ 2 6282 3226. **Canada**: 299 Waverley St, Ottawa ON, K2P 0V9, ✆ 613 230 2717. **New Zealand** (Consulate): 23 Fife St, Coxs Bay, Auckland 1144, ✆ 9 376 3609. **UK**: 35 Eaton Place, London SW1X 8BY, ✆ 020 7201 3440. **USA**: 3910 Shoemaker St NW, Washington DC 20008, ✆ 202 362 6730.

LANGUAGE

Hungarian. English and German are both widely understood.

PUBLIC TRANSPORT

Long-distance buses: *Volánbusz* www.volanbusz.hu, ✆ +36 1 382 0888. Extensive metro / tram / bus system in Budapest with integrated tickets; for day tickets see Passes section. Purchase tickets in advance and validate on board. Debrecen, Miskolc and Szeged also have trams. Ferry and hydrofoil services operate on the Danube.

RAIL TRAVEL

See Tables 1200 - 1299. A comprehensive network operated by Hungarian State Railways (MÁV) www.mav.hu connects most towns and cities. Express services link Budapest to major centres and Lake Balaton: *IC* trains require compulsory reservation, also a supplement which varies according to distance (passholders pay only the reservation fee). Most *EC* trains do not require reservation for international journeys; trains to Romania have compulsory reservation. Other trains include *gyorsvonat* (fast trains) and *sebesvonat* (semifast). Local trains (*személyvonat*) are very slow. Book sleepers well in advance.

TELEPHONES

Dial in: ✆ +36 then number (omit initial 06, which is only used when dialing from city to city within Hungary). Outgoing: ✆ 00.
Emergency: ✆ 112. Police: ✆ 107. Fire: ✆ 105. Ambulance: ✆ 104.

TOURIST INFORMATION

Hungarian National Tourist Office (*Tourinform*) www.gotohungary.com. Call Centre 0800 - 2000 Mon - Fri, ✆ 01 438 80 80, info@itthon.hu.

TOURIST OFFICES OVERSEAS

UK: 46 Eaton Place, London SW1X 8AL, ✆ 020 7823 0132, htlondon@hungarytourism.hu. **USA**: 470 7th Avenue, Suite 2601, New York NY 10123, ✆ 212 695 1221, info@gotohungary.com.

VISAS

See page xxiv for visa requirements.

IRELAND

CAPITAL

Dublin. For Northern Ireland see under United Kingdom.

CURRENCY

Euro (EUR / €). 1 euro = 100 cent. For exchange rates see page 9.

EMBASSIES IN DUBLIN

Australia: Fitzwilton House, Wilton Terrace, ✆ 01 664 5300. **Canada**: 7–8 Wilton Terrace, ✆ 01 234 4000. **New Zealand** (Consulate): P.O. Box 9999, Dublin, ✆ 01 660 4233. **UK**: 29 Merrion Road, ✆ 01 205 3700. **USA**: 42 Elgin Road, ✆ 01 668 8777.

EMBASSIES OVERSEAS

Australia: 20 Arkana St, Yarralumla, Canberra, ACT 2600, ✆ 2 6214 0000. **Canada**: Suite 1105, 130 Albert St, Ottawa ON, K1P 5G4, ✆ 613 233 6281. **New Zealand** (Consulate): 205 Queen Street, Auckland 1140, ✆ 9 977 2252. **UK**: 17 Grosvenor Place, London SW1X 7HR, ✆ 020 7235 2171. **USA**: 2234 Massachusetts Ave. NW, Washington DC 20008, ✆ 202 462 3939.

LANGUAGE

Most people speak English. The Irish language (Gaeilge) is spoken in several areas (known as the Gaeltacht) scattered over seven counties and four provinces, mostly along the western seaboard. Official documents use both languages.

PUBLIC TRANSPORT

A modern tramway system in Dublin called Luas www.luas.ie has two unconnected lines; the red line is the most useful for visitors as it connects Connolly and Heuston stations. Dublin Bus operates an extensive network throughout the capital. Almost all bus services outside Dublin are operated by Bus Éireann www.buseireann.ie, ✆ 01 836 6111 (daily 0830–1900). Long distance services leave from the Dublin bus station (Busáras) in Store St, near Connolly rail station.

RAIL TRAVEL

See Tables 230 - 249. Rail services are operated by Iarnród Éireann (IÉ) www.irishrail.ie. Timetable and fares enquiries: ✆ 01 850 366 222 (0900–1700 Mon-Fri). The Enterprise express service Dublin - Belfast is operated jointly with Northern Ireland Railways. Local IÉ north-south electric line in Dublin is called DART.

TELEPHONES

Dial in: ✆ +353 then number (omit initial 0). Outgoing: ✆ 00 (048 for Northern Ireland). Emergency services: ✆ 112 or 999.

TOURIST INFORMATION

Fáilte Ireland www.discoverireland.ie or www.ireland.com. Dublin: 14 Upper O'Connell Street, infooconnell@failteireland.ie.

TOURIST OFFICES OVERSEAS

Australia: Level 5, 36 Carrington St, Sydney NSW 2000, ✆ 02 9964 6900. **Canada**: 2 Bloor St West, Suite 3403, Toronto ON, M4W 3E2, ✆ 416 925 6368. **UK**: 103 Wigmore St, London W1U 1QS, ✆ 020 7518 0800. **USA**: 345 Park Avenue, 17th floor, New York NY 10154, ✆ 212 418 0800.

VISAS

See page xxiv for visa requirements.

ITALY

CAPITAL
Rome (Roma).

CURRENCY
Euro (EUR/€). 1 euro = 100 cent. For exchange rates see page 9.

EMBASSIES IN ROME

Australia: Via Antonio Bosio 5, ✆ 06 852 721. **Canada**: Via Zara 30, ✆ 06 85 44 42 911. **New Zealand**: Via Clitunno 44, ✆ 06 853 7501. **UK**: Via XX Settembre 80a, ✆ 06 4220 0001. **USA**: Via Vittorio Veneto 121, ✆ 06 46 741.

EMBASSIES OVERSEAS

Australia: 12 Grey St, Deakin, Canberra ACT 2600, ✆ 2 6273 3333. **Canada**: 275 Slater St, Ottawa ON, K1P 5H9, ✆ 613 232 2401. **New Zealand**: 34-38 Grant Rd, Thorndon, Wellington, ✆ 4 473 5339. **UK**: 14 Three Kings Yard, London W1K 4EH, ✆ 020 7312 2200. **USA**: 3000 Whitehaven St NW, Washington DC 20008, ✆ 202 612 4400.

LANGUAGE

Italian. Standard Italian is spoken across the country though there are marked regional pronunciation differences. Some dialects in more remote areas. Many speak English in cities and tourist areas. In the south and Sicily, French is often more useful than English.

PUBLIC TRANSPORT

Buses are often crowded, but regular, and serve many areas inaccessible by rail. Services may be reduced at weekends. Tickets are usually purchased from newsagents. Roma, Milano and Napoli have metro systems; most major cities have trams. Taxis (metered) can be expensive; steer clear of unofficial ones.

RAIL TRAVEL

See Tables 580 - 648. The national operator is Trenitalia, a division of Ferrovie dello Stato (FS) www.trenitalia.com. 24-hr national rail information ✆ 89 20 21 (from abroad +39 06 68 47 54 75; 0700 - 2400). The trunk high-speed line from Torino to Salerno via Milano, Roma and Napoli allows fast journey times between major cities. Core services are branded Frecciarossa, whilst tilting Frecciargento trains divert off the high-speed lines to serve other cities. Frecciabianca services are fast premium fare services which use traditional lines. Reservation is compulsory on all types of service except EC (EuroCity) trains to Austria operated in Italy by LeNord. Other services are classified Regionale Veloce (fast regional train) and Regionale (stops at most stations). Services are reasonably punctual. Some long-distance trains do not carry passengers short distances. Sleepers: single or double berths in 1st class, three (sometimes doubles) in 2nd. Couchettes: four berths in 1st class, six in 2nd, although there is a number of four-berth 2nd-class couchettes. Refreshments on most long-distance trains. There are often long queues at stations; buy tickets and make reservations at travel agencies (look for FS symbol).

TELEPHONES

Dial in: ✆ +39 then number. Outgoing: ✆ 00.
Carabinieri: ✆ 112. Police: ✆ 113. Fire: ✆ 115. Ambulance: ✆ 118.

TOURIST INFORMATION

Italian State Tourist Board www.enit.it. Roma: Via Marghera 2/6, ✆ 0 649 711, sedecentrale@enit.it. Most towns and resorts have an Azienda Autonoma di Soggiorno e Turismo (AAST), many with their own websites, or Pro Loco (local tourist board).

TOURIST OFFICES OVERSEAS

Australia: Ground Floor, 140 William St, East Sydney NSW 2011, ✆ 02 9357 2561, sydney@enit.it. **Canada**: 110 Yonge Street, Suite 503, Toronto ON, M5C 1T4, ✆ 416 925 4882, toronto@enit.it. **UK**: 1 Princes St, London W1B 2AY, ✆ 020 7408 1254, info. london@enit.it. **USA**: 630 Fifth Avenue, Suite 1965, New York NY 10111, ✆ 212 245 5618, newyork@enit.it. Also Chicago (✆ 312 644 0996) chicago@enit.it. and Los Angeles (✆ 310 820 1898) losangeles@enit.it.

VISAS
See page xxiv for visa requirements.

LATVIA

CAPITAL
Riga.

CURRENCY
Euro (EUR/€). 1 euro = 100 cent. For exchange rates see page 9.

EMBASSIES IN RIGA

Australia: (Consulate) c/- Airtour, 7 Vilandes ✆ 6732 0509. **Canada**: Baznicas iela 20/22, ✆ 6781 3945. **New Zealand**: refer to NZ Embassy in Germany. **UK**: J Alunana iela 5, ✆ 6777 4700. **USA**: Samnera Velsa St. 1, ✆ 6710 7000.

EMBASSIES OVERSEAS

Australia: (Consulate) 2 Mackennel Street, Melbourne, VIC 3079, ✆ 3 9499 6920. **Canada**: 350 Sparks St, Suite 1200, Ottawa ON, K1R 7S8, ✆ 613 238 6014. **New Zealand** (Consulate): 166 St Asaphs St., Te Whare Ta Wahi, Christchurch 8140, ✆ 3 365 3505. **UK**: 45 Nottingham Place, London W1U 5LY, ✆ 020 7312 0041. **USA**: 2306 Massachusetts Ave. NW, Washington DC 20008, ✆ 202 328 2840.

LANGUAGE

Latvian is the majority language. Russian is the first language of around 30% and is widely understood. English and German can often be of use, especially in the larger towns.

PUBLIC TRANSPORT

Very cheap for Westerners. Taxis generally affordable (agree fare first if not metered). Long-distance bus network preferred to slow domestic train service.

RAIL TRAVEL

See Tables 1800 - 1899. The national operator is Latvian Railways www. ldz.lv. Comfortable overnight train to Moscow and St Peterburg; best to take berth in 2nd-class coupé (4-berth compartment). Reservation is compulsory for all sleepers; Russia-bound sleepers may require proof of entry visa when booking. Very little English spoken at stations.

TELEPHONES

Dial in: ✆ +371 then number. Outgoing: ✆ 00.
Emergency: ✆ 112. Police: ✆ 02. Fire: ✆ 01. Ambulance: ✆ 03.

TOURIST INFORMATION

Latvian Tourism Development Agency www.latvia.travel/en.
Riga: Brivibas iela 55, ✆ 67 229 945, info@latvia.travel. Tourist Hotline:
✆ 1188.

TOURIST OFFICES OVERSEAS

Germany: Baltikum Tourismus Zentrale, Katharinenstraße 19-20,
10711 Berlin, ✆ 030 89 00 90 91, info@baltikuminfo.de.

VISAS

See page xxiv for visa requirements. Applications may take up to 30
days; confirmed hotel reservations are required. Visas may also be valid
for Estonia and Lithuania. Passports must be valid for at least 3 months
following the stay. Visas issued on arrival at the airport (not train border
crossings) are valid 10 days.

LITHUANIA

CAPITAL

Vilnius.

CURRENCY

Euro (EUR / €). 1 euro = 100 cent. For exchange rates see page 9.

EMBASSIES IN VILNIUS

Australia (Consulate): 23 Vilniaus St. ✆ 05 212 33 69.
Canada (Consulate): Jogailos St. 4, ✆ 05 249 09 50.
New Zealand: *refer to NZ Embassy in Germany*. **UK**: Antakalnio Str. 2,
✆ 05 246 29 00. **USA**: Akmenu gatve 6, ✆ 05 266 55 00.

EMBASSIES OVERSEAS

Australia (Consulate): 39 The Boulevarde. Doncaster, VIC 3108,
✆ 3 9840 0070. **Canada**: 150 Metcalfe St. Suite 1600, Ottawa ON,
K2P 1P1, ✆ 613 567 5458. **UK**: 2 Bessborough Gardens, London
SW1V 2JE, ✆ 020 7592 2840. **USA**: 2622 16 Street NW, Washington
DC 20009, ✆ 202 234 5860.

LANGUAGE

Lithuanian. Russian is the first language of around 10% of the
population. English and German can often be of use, especially in the
larger towns.

PUBLIC TRANSPORT

Similar to Latvia (see above).

RAIL TRAVEL

See Tables 1800 - 1899. The national operator is Lithuanian Railways
www.litrail.lt. Comfortable overnight train to Moscow via Minsk. Very
little English spoken at stations.

TELEPHONES

Dial in: ✆ +370 then number (omit initial 8). Outgoing: ✆ 00.
Emergency: ✆ 112. Police: ✆ 02. Fire: ✆ 01. Ambulance: ✆ 03.

TOURIST INFORMATION

Lithuania State Department of Tourism www.tourism.lt and www.travel.
lt. Vilnius: Vilniaus g. 22, ✆ 526 296 60, tic@vilnius.lt.

TOURIST OFFICES OVERSEAS

Germany: Lituanian Tourism, Jösephspitalstr 15, 80331 Muenchen,
✆ 089 55 25 33 406, info@baltikuminfo.de.
UK: Lithuanian National Tourism Office, 11 Blades Court, London
SW15 2NU, ✆ 0208 877 4546, lithuania@representationplus.co.uk.

VISAS

See page xxiv for visa requirements.

LUXEMBOURG

CAPITAL

Luxembourg City (Ville de Luxembourg).

CURRENCY

Euro (EUR / €). 1 euro = 100 cent. For exchange rates see page 9.

EMBASSIES IN LUXEMBOURG

Australia: *refer to Australian Embassy in Belgium.*
Canada (Consulate): 15, rue Guillaume Schneider, ✆ 26 270 570.
New Zealand: *refer to NZ Embassy in Belgium.* **UK**: 5 Boulevard
Joseph II, ✆ 22 98 64. **USA**: 22 Boulevard Emmanuel Servais,
✆ 46 01 23.

EMBASSIES OVERSEAS

Australia (Consulate): 6 Damour Ave, Sydney, NSW 2070,
✆ 2 9880 8002. **UK**: 27 Wilton Crescent, London SW1X 8SD,
✆ 020 7235 6961 (visa info. between 1000 and 1145).
USA / Canada: 2200 Massachusetts Ave. NW, Washington DC 20008,
✆ 202 265 4171.

LANGUAGE

Luxembourgish is the national tongue, but almost everyone also speaks
fluent French and/or German, plus often some English.

PUBLIC TRANSPORT

Good bus network between most towns. Taxis not allowed to pick up
passengers in the street; most stations have ranks.

RAIL TRAVEL

See Table 449 for local services. Operator: Société Nationale des
Chemins de fer Luxembourgeois (CFL) www.cfl.lu, ✆ +352 2489 2489.
Frequent rail services converge on Luxembourg City. Inexpensive multi-
ride passes (good for one hour or up to 24 hours) are valid on trains and
local buses. Most rail stations are small with few facilities.

TELEPHONES

Dial in: ✆ +352 then number. Outgoing: ✆ 00.
Police: ✆ 113. Fire and ambulance: ✆ 112.

TOURIST INFORMATION

Office National du Tourisme www.visitluxembourg.com. Luxembourg:
Gare Centrale, P.O. Box 1001, ✆ 42 82 82 10, info@visitluxembourg.
com. Luxembourg City Tourist Office www.lcto.lu, 30 Place Guillaume
II, ✆ 222 809, touristinfo@lcto.lu.

TOURIST OFFICES OVERSEAS

Germany: Klingelofer Straße 7 D 10785 Berlin, ✆ 03 2575 773,
info@visitluxembourg.de. **USA**: 17 Beekman Place, New York NY
10022, ✆ 212 935 8888, info@visitluxembourg.com.

VISAS

See page xxiv for visa requirements.

NETHERLANDS

CAPITAL

Amsterdam is the capital city. The Hague (Den Haag) is the seat of
government.

CURRENCY

Euro (EUR / €). 1 euro = 100 cent. For exchange rates see page 9.

EMBASSIES IN THE HAGUE

Australia: Carnegielaan 4, ✆ 0 70 310 8200. **Canada**: Sophialaan 7,
✆ 0 70 311 1600. **New Zealand**: Eisenhowerlaan 77N,
✆ 0 70 346 9324. **UK**: Lange Voorhout 10, ✆ 0 70 427 0427.
USA: Lange Voorhout 102, ✆ 0 70 310 2209.

EMBASSIES OVERSEAS

Australia: 120 Empire Circuit, Yarralumla, Canberra, ACT 2600,
✆ 2 6220 9400. **Canada**: Constitution Square Building, 350 Albert St,
Suite 2020, Ottawa ON, K1R 1A4, ✆ 1 877 388 2443.
New Zealand: Investment House, cnr Ballance & Featherston Streets,
Wellington, ✆ 4 471 6390. **UK**: 38 Hyde Park Gate, London SW7 5DP,
✆ 020 7590 3200. **USA**: 4200 Linnean Ave. NW, Washington DC
20008, ✆ 202 244 5300.

LANGUAGE

Dutch. English is very widely spoken.

PUBLIC TRANSPORT

Premium rate number for all rail and bus enquiries (computerised, fast
and accurate): ✆ 09 009 292 www.9292ov.nl. Taxis are best boarded at
ranks or ordered by phone as they seldom stop in the street. In many
cities (not Amsterdam) a *Zonetaxi* can be prebooked for an onward
journey at a fixed price (€6 for the first two kilometres, then an extra
€3 for every two kilometres thereafter; ✆ 0900 6798294 or purchase
on-line). A nationwide stored value contactless Smartcard system
called OV-Chipcard is used for all public transport. Personalised and
anonymous cards are available, together with disposable cards for
visitors. These can be purchased at ticket offices and also from
machines (payment by cash or credit card). OV-Chipcard readers are
located on railway platforms and on trams and buses etc. (remember to
swipe your card at the beginning and end of your journey).

RAIL TRAVEL

See Tables **450 - 499**. National rail company Nederlandse Spoorwegen (NS) www.ns.nl provides most services, though private operators run local train services in some parts of the north and east. Through tickets can be purchased between all stations in the Netherlands, regardless of operator. Cycle hire and cycle and baggage storage are usually available at larger stations. Smaller stations are usually unstaffed, but all stations have ticket vending machines. Most paper tickets have been replaced by the OV-Chipcard (see previous paragraph). Travellers found to have boarded a train without a valid ticket must pay a fine of €35 plus the cost of their fare. *Intercity direct* are fast services between Amsterdam, Schiphol, Rotterdam and Breda via the high-speed line (supplement payable, except for local journeys Amsterdam - Schiphol and Rotterdam - Breda). Other fast trains, calling only at principal stations, are classified *Intercity*. Local stopping trains are branded *Sprinter*. Seat reservations are not available except for international journeys and for travel on *Intercity direct* services.

TELEPHONES

Dial in: ℘ + 31 then number (omit initial 0). Outgoing: ℘ 00. Emergency services: ℘ 112.

TOURIST INFORMATION

Netherlands Board of Tourism *Vereniging voor Vreemdelingenverkeer* www.holland.com, Vlietweg 15, 2260 MG Leidschendam, ℘ 070 370 5705, info@holland.com.

TOURIST OFFICES OVERSEAS

See www.holland.com.

VISAS

See page xxiv for visa requirements.

NORWAY

CAPITAL

Oslo.

CURRENCY

Norwegian crown or krone (NOK or kr); 1 krone = 100 øre. For exchange rates see page 9.

EMBASSIES IN OSLO

Australia (Consulate): Wilh. Wilhelmsen ASA, Strandveien 20, Lysaker, ℘ 67 58 48 48. **Canada**: Wergelandsveien 7, ℘ 22 99 53 00. **New Zealand** (Consulate): c/o Halfdan Ditlev-Simonsen & Co AS, Strandveien 50, Lysaker, ℘ 67 11 00 30. **UK**: Thomas Heftyesgate 8, ℘ 23 13 27 00. **USA**: Henrik Ibsens gate 48, ℘ 21 30 85 40.

EMBASSIES OVERSEAS

Australia: 17 Hunter St, Yarralumla, Canberra, ACT 2600, ℘ 2 6270 5700. **Canada**: 150 Metcalfe St. Suite 1300, Ottawa ON, K2P 1P1, ℘ 613 238 6571. **New Zealand** (Consulate): 6b Wagener Place, Mt Albert, Auckland 1025, ℘ 21 780 726. **UK**: 25 Belgrave Sq., London SW1X 8QD, ℘ 020 7591 5500. **USA**: 2720 34th St NW, Washington D.C. 20008, ℘ 202 333 6000.

LANGUAGE

Norwegian, which has two official versions: *Nynorsk* and *Bokmål*. Norwegian has three additional vowels: æ, ø, á, which (in that order) follow z. Almost everyone speaks English; if not, try German.

PUBLIC TRANSPORT

Train, boat and bus schedules are linked to provide good connections. It is often worth using buses or boats to connect two dead-end rail lines (e.g. Bergen and Stavanger), rather than retracing your route. Rail passes sometimes offer good discounts, even free travel, on linking services. NorWay Bussekspress www.nor-way.no, Karl Johans gate 2, N-0154 Oslo, ℘ 82 021 300 (premium rate) has the largest bus network with routes going as far north as Kirkenes. Long-distance buses are comfortable, with reclining seats, ample leg room. Tickets: buy on board or reserve, ℘ 81 544 444 (premium-rate). Taxis: metered, can be picked up at ranks or by phoning; treat independent taxis with caution.

RAIL TRAVEL

See Tables **770 - 789**. Operated by: Norges Statsbaner (NSB) www.nsb. no. All trains convey 2nd-class seating. Most medium- and long-distance trains also convey *NSB Komfort* accommodation, a dedicated area with complimentary tea/coffee and newspapers (supplement payable). Sleeping cars have one- and two-berth compartments; a sleeper supplement is payable per compartment (for two people travelling together, or sole use for single travellers). Long-distance

trains convey a bistro car serving hot and cold meals, drinks and snacks. Reservation possible (and recommended) on all long-distance trains, ℘ (within Norway) 81 500 888, then dial 9 for an english speaking operator. Reserved seats not marked, but your confirmation specifies carriage and seat/berth numbers. Carriage numbers shown by the doors, berth numbers outside compartments, seat numbers on seat-backs or luggage racks. Most larger stations have luggage lockers. Narvesen chain (at most stations; open long hours) sells English-language publications and a good range of snacks.

TELEPHONES

Dial in: ℘ + 47 then number. Outgoing: ℘ 00.
Police: ℘ 112. Fire: ℘ 110. Ambulance: ℘ 113.

TOURIST INFORMATION

Innovation Norway www.visitnorway.com. Oslo: Akersgata 13, ℘ 2200 2500. Tourist offices (*Turistkontorer*) and bureaux (*Reiselivslag / Turistinformasjon*) exist in almost all towns.

TOURIST OFFICES OVERSEAS

UK: Charles House, 5 Lower Regent St, London SW1Y 4LR, ℘ 020 7389 8800, infouk@innovationnorway.no. **USA**: 655 Third Avenue, 18th floor, New York NY 10017, ℘ 212 885 9700, newyork@innovationnorway.no.

VISAS

See page xxiv for visa requirements.

POLAND

CAPITAL

Warsaw (Warszawa).

CURRENCY

Złoty (PLN or zł); 1 złoty = 100 groszy. For exchange rates see page 9.

EMBASSIES IN WARSAW

Australia: ul. Nowogrodzka 11, ℘ 22 521 34 44. **Canada**: ul. Jana Matejki 1/5, ℘ 22 584 31 00. **New Zealand**: Aleje Ujazdowskie 51, ℘ 22 521 05 00. **UK**: ul Kawalerii 12, ℘ 22 311 00 00. **USA**: Aleje Ujazdowskie 29/31, ℘ 22 504 20 00.

EMBASSIES OVERSEAS

Australia: 7 Turrana St, Yarralumla, Canberra, ACT 2600, ℘ 2 6272 1000. **Canada**: 443 Daly Ave., Ottawa ON, K1N 6H3, ℘ 613 789 0468. **New Zealand**: 142 - 4 Featherston St, Wellington, ℘ 4 475 9453. **UK**: 47 Portland Place, London W1B 1JH, ℘ 020 7291 3520. **USA**: 2640 16th St NW, Washington DC 20009, ℘ 202 499 1700.

LANGUAGE

Polish. Many older Poles speak German, younger Poles are likely to understand English. Russian is widely understood, but unpopular.

PUBLIC TRANSPORT

Buses are cheap and sometimes more practical than trains. Main long-distance bus station in Warszawa is adjacent to the Zachodnia (western) station. Some services (including PolskiBus) leave from suburban metro stations. Tickets normally include seat reservations (seat number on back), bookable from bus station. In rural areas, bus drivers will often halt between official stops if you flag them down. Extensive tram networks in Warszawa and most other cities; Warszawa also has a modern north-south metro line.

RAIL TRAVEL

See Tables **1000 - 1099**. Most long-distance trains are classified *EC*, *EIC*, *EIP* or *TLK* and are operated by PKP Intercity, www.intercity.pl. *TLK* are lower-cost daytime and overnight services. Reservation is compulsory on all trains operated by PKP Intercity. Purely local trains (*osobowy*) are classified *R* (REGIO) and are operated by a separate company, Przewozy Regionalne (www.przewozyregionalne.pl), which also operates longer distance *IR* (InterREGIO) and *RE* services, often in competition with PKP Intercity, but tickets are not interchangeable. In some areas local services are operated by different companies (e.g. Koleje Śląskie around Katowice). At stations, departures (*odjazdy*) are shown on yellow paper, arrivals (*przyjazdy*) on white. Note that long distance trains are shown in red print on timetables at stations. Fares are about 50% higher for 1st class, but still cheap by western standards and probably worth it. Overnight trains usually have 1st and 2nd-class sleepers, plus 2nd-class couchettes and seats. Left luggage and refreshments in major stations.

TELEPHONES

Dial in: ✆ +48 then number (omit initial 0). Outgoing: ✆ 0*0 *(wait for tone after first 0). Police: ✆ 997. Fire: ✆ 998. Ambulance: ✆ 999. Emergency (from mobile): ✆ 112.

TOURIST INFORMATION

Polish National Tourist Office www.poland.travel.

TOURIST OFFICES OVERSEAS

UK: Level 3, Westgate House, West Gate, London W5 1YY, ✆ 0300 303 1812, london@poland.travel. **USA**: 5 Marine View Plaza, Hoboken NJ 07030, ✆ 201 420 9910, info.na@poland.travel.

VISAS

See page xxiv for visa requirements.
For travellers in Germany, visas are obtainable from the Polish consulate in Berlin www.berlin.polemb.net.

PORTUGAL

CAPITAL

Lisbon (Lisboa).

CURRENCY

Euro (EUR / €). 1 euro = 100 cent. For exchange rates see page 9.

EMBASSIES IN LISBON

Australia: Avenida da Liberdade 200, ✆ 21 310 1500.
Canada: Avenida da Liberdade 198–200, ✆ 21 316 4600.
New Zealand: (Consulate) Rua da Sociedade Farmaceutica 68 ✆ 213 140 780. **UK**: Rua de São Bernardo 33, ✆ 21 392 4000.
USA: Avenida das Forças Armadas, ✆ 21 727 3300.

EMBASSIES OVERSEAS

Australia: 32 Thesiger Court, Deakin, ACT 2600, ✆ 2 6260 4970.
Canada: 645 Island Park Dr., Ottawa ON, K1Y OB8, ✆ 613 729 2922.
New Zealand: (Consulate) 21 Marion St, Wellington, ✆ 4 382 7655.
UK: 11 Belgrave Sq., London SW1X 8PP, ✆ 020 723 5533.
USA: 2012 Massachusetts Ave. NW, Washington DC 20036, ✆ 202 332 3007.

LANGUAGE

Portuguese. Older people often speak French as a second language, young people Spanish and/or English. English, French, and German in some tourist areas.

PUBLIC TRANSPORT

Usually buy long-distance bus tickets before boarding. Bus stops: *paragem;* extend your arm to stop a bus. Taxis: black with green roofs or beige; illuminated signs; cheap, metered in cities, elsewhere fares negotiable; drivers may ask you to pay for their return journey; surcharges for luggage over 30 kg and night travel; 10% tip. City transport: single tickets can be bought as you board, but day tickets or passes are cheaper.

RAIL TRAVEL

See Tables 690 - 699. Operator: Comboios de Portugal (CP) www.cp.pt. Cheap and generally punctual; 1st/2nd class on long-distance. Fastest trains are *IC* and *AP* (Alfa Pendular), modern, fast; supplement payable; seat reservations compulsory, buffet cars. CP information line, ✆ 808 208 208. Left-luggage lockers in most stations.

TELEPHONES

Dial in: ✆ +351 then number. Outgoing: ✆ 00.
Emergency services: ✆ 112.

TOURIST INFORMATION

Portuguese National Tourist Office www.visitportugal.com. info@visitportugal.com, ✆ 211 140 200.

TOURIST OFFICES OVERSEAS

UK: 11 Belgrave Square, London SW1X 8PP, ✆ 0207 201 6666, tourism.london@portugalglobal.pt. **USA**: 590 Fifth Avenue, 4th floor, New York NY 10036, ✆ 646 723 0200, tourism@iecp.pt.

VISAS

See page xxiv for visa requirements.

ROMANIA

CAPITAL

Bucharest (Bucuresti).

CURRENCY

Leu (plural: lei). 1 leu = 100 bani. For exchange rates see page 9.

EMBASSIES IN BUCHAREST

Australia (Consulate): The Group, Praga St 3 ✆ 21 206 22 00.
Canada: 1 - 3 Tuberozelor St, ✆ 21 307 50 00. **New Zealand**: *refer to NZ Embassy in Belgium*. **UK**: Jules Michelet 24, ✆ 21 201 72 00.
USA: Dr Liviu Librescu Blvd. 4–6, ✆ 21 200 33 00.

EMBASSIES OVERSEAS

Australia: 4 Dalman Crescent, O'Malley, Canberra ACT 2606, ✆ 2 6286 2343. **Canada**: 655 Rideau St, Ottawa ON, K1N 6A3, ✆ 613 789 3709. **New Zealand** (Consulate): 53 Homewood Ave, Karori, Wellington 6012, ✆ 4 476 6883. **UK**: Arundel House, 4 Palace Green, London W8 4QD, ✆ 020 7937 9666. **USA**: 1607 23rd St NW, Washington DC, 20008, ✆ 202 332 4846.

LANGUAGE

Romanian. English is understood by younger people, plus some French, German, and Hungarian throughout Transylvania.

PUBLIC TRANSPORT

Buy bus/tram/metro tickets in advance from kiosks (as a rule) and cancel on entry. Taxis are plentiful and inexpensive; if the meter is not in use agree price first and always pay in lei, not foreign currency. Avoid unlicensed vehicles. Trains are best for long-distance travel, although bus routes are expanding and connect important towns and cities.

RAIL TRAVEL

See Tables 1600 - 1699. Societatea Naţională de Transport Feroviar de Călători (CFR) operates an extensive network linking all major towns www.cfrcalatori.ro. Most main lines are electrified and quite fast, but branch line services are very slow. Trains are fairly punctual and very cheap. Except for local trains, reserve and pay a speed supplement in advance (tickets issued abroad include the supplement): cheapest are *regio* (very slow), then *Interregio* and finally *IC* trains (prices approaching Western levels). Food and drink is normally available only on *IC* and some *IR* trains. Couchette (*cuşetă*) or sleeper (*vagon de dormit*) accommodation is inexpensive. An increasing number of services are now operated by private operators, such as Regiotrans, Transferoviar Grup SA, and Softrans S.R.L.

TELEPHONES

Dial in: ✆ +40 then number (omit initial 0). Outgoing: ✆ 00.
Emergency: ✆ 112. Police: ✆ 955. Fire: ✆ 981. Ambulance: ✆ 961.

TOURIST INFORMATION

Romanian National Tourist Office www.romaniatourism.com.
Bucharest TIC www.tourism-bucharest.com: ✆ 021 305 55 00, turism@bucuresti-primaria.ro.

TOURIST OFFICES OVERSEAS

UK: 12 Harley St, London W1G 9PG, ✆ 020 7224 3692, romaniatravel@btconnect.com. **USA**: 355 Lexington Ave., 8th floor, New York NY 10017, ✆ 212 545 8484, info@romaniatourism.com.

VISAS

See page xxiv for visa requirements. Make sure you keep your visa papers when you enter – you'll pay a large fine if you don't have them when you leave Romania.

SLOVAKIA

CAPITAL

Bratislava.

CURRENCY

Euro (EUR / €). 1 euro = 100 cent. For exchange rates see page 9.

EMBASSIES IN BRATISLAVA

Australia: *refer to Australian Embassy in Austria*. **Canada**: Carlton Court Yard & Savoy Buildings, Mostova 2, ✆ 2 5920 4031.
New Zealand: *refer to NZ Embassy in Austria*. **UK**: Panská 16, ✆ 2 5998 2000. **USA**: Hviezdoslavovo námestie 4, ✆ 2 5443 0861.

EMBASSIES OVERSEAS

Australia: 47 Culgoa Circuit, O'Malley, Canberra, ACT 2606, ✆ 2 6290 1516. **Canada**: 50 Rideau Terrace, Ottawa ON, K1M 2A1, ✆ 613 749 4442. **New Zealand** (Consulate): 188 Quayt St, Auckland 1010, ✆ 9 366 5111. **UK**: 25 Kensington Palace Gardens, London W8 4QY, ✆ 020 7313 6470. **USA**: 3523 International Court NW, Washington DC 20008, ✆ 202 237 1054.

LANGUAGE

Slovak, a Slavic tongue closely related to Czech. Some Russian (unpopular), German, Hungarian (especially in the south), plus a little English and French.

PUBLIC TRANSPORT

There is a comprehensive long-distance bus network, often more direct than rail in upland areas. Buy tickets from the driver; priority is given to those with bookings.

RAIL TRAVEL

See Tables 1170 - 1199. The national rail operator is Železničná spoločnosť' (ŽSSK) www.slovakrail.sk, running on the network of ŽSR. Trains are cheap, but often crowded. Apart from a small number of *EC* trains (for which higher fares apply), the fastest trains are *expresný* (*Ex*) and *Rýchlik* (*R*). Cheaper are *zrýchlený* (semi-fast) and *osobný* (very slow). At stations, departures (*odjezdy*) are shown on yellow posters, arrivals (*prijezdy*) on white. Sleeping cars/couchettes (reserve at all main stations, well in advance in summer) are provided on most overnight trains. Seat reservations (at station counters marked R) are recommended for express trains. Private operators Regiojet and Leo Express also run on main route to Kosice.

TELEPHONES

Dial in: ✆ +421 then number (omit initial 0). Outgoing: ✆ 00. Emergency: ✆ 112. Police: ✆ 158. Fire: ✆ 150. Ambulance: ✆ 155.

TOURIST INFORMATION

Slovak Tourist Board www.slovakia.travel. Main office: Námestie L'. Štúra 1, P.O. Box 35, 974 05 Banská Bystrica, ✆ 0 484 136 146, sacr@sacr.sk. Bratislava Tourist Information Centre: Klobučnicka 2, www.bratislava.sk, ✆ 0 216 186, touristinfo@bratislava.sk.

TOURIST OFFICES OVERSEAS

Germany: Slowakische Zentrale für Tourismus, Zimmerstr. 27, D-10969, Berlin, ✆ +49 (0)30 2594 2640. **USA** Phorall LLC, 18 Florence St., Edison NY08817 nyoffice@slovakia.travel

VISAS

See page xxiv for visa requirements.

SLOVENIA

CAPITAL

Ljubljana.

CURRENCY

Euro (EUR/€). 1 euro = 100 cent. For exchange rates see page 9.

EMBASSIES IN LJUBLJANA

Australia (Consulate): *refer to Australian Embassy in Austria*. **Canada** (Consulate): Linhartova cesta 49a, ✆ 1 252 4444. **New Zealand**: (Consulate) Lek d.d., Verovskova 57, ✆ 1 580 3055. **UK**: Trg Republike 3, ✆ 1 200 3910. **USA**: Prešernova 31, ✆ 1 200 5500.

EMBASSIES OVERSEAS

Australia: 26 Akame Circuit, O'Malley, Canberra, ACT 2606, ✆ 2 6290 0000. **Canada**: 150 Metcalfe St. Suite 2200, Ottawa, ON, K2P 1P1, ✆ 613 565 5781. **UK**: 10 Little College St, London SW1P 3SH, ✆ 020 7222 5700. **USA**: 2410 California St., Washington DC 20008, ✆ 202 386 6610.

LANGUAGE

Slovenian. English, German and Italian are often spoken in tourist areas.

PUBLIC TRANSPORT

Long-distance bus services are frequent and inexpensive; normally, buy your ticket on boarding. Information: Trg Osvobodilne Fronte 5, next to Ljubljana station, ✆ 012 344 606. On city buses pay by dropping the exact flat fare or a cheaper token (available from news-stands and post offices) into the farebox next to the driver. Daily and weekly passes are available in the main cities.

RAIL TRAVEL

See Tables 1300 - 1359. Operator: Slovenske železnice (SŽ) www.slo-zeleznice.si. Information: ✆ 012 913 332 (+386 129 13 332 from abroad). Good, efficient network, but fewer services run on Saturdays. Reserve for *ICS* trains; supplements are payable on other express services.

TELEPHONES

Dial in: ✆ +386 then number (omit initial 0). Outgoing: ✆ 00. Police: ✆ 113. Fire and ambulance: ✆ 112.

TOURIST INFORMATION

Slovenian Tourist Board www.slovenia.info. Ljubljana: Krekov trg 10, ✆ 01 306 45 75, stic@visitljubljana.si.

TOURIST OFFICES OVERSEAS

UK: Slovenian Tourist Board, 10 Little College Street, London SW1P 3SH, ✆ 0870 225 53 05, london@slovenia.info. **USA**: 2929 East Commercial Boulevard, Suite 201, Fort Lauderdale, FL 33308, ✆ 954 491 0112, info@slovenia.info.

VISAS

See page xxiv for visa requirements.

SPAIN

CAPITAL

Madrid.

CURRENCY

Euro (EUR/€). 1 euro = 100 cent. For exchange rates see page 9.

EMBASSIES IN MADRID

Australia: Paseo de la Castellana, 259D, ✆ 913 536 600. **Canada**: Paseo de la Castellana, 259D, ✆ 913 828 400. **New Zealand**: Pinar 7, ✆ 915 230 226. **UK**: Paseo de la Castellana 259D, ✆ 917 146 300. **USA**: Serrano 75, ✆ 915 872 200.

EMBASSIES OVERSEAS

Australia: 15 Arkana St, Yarralumla, Canberra, ACT 2600, ✆ 2 6273 3555. **Canada**: 74 Stanley Avenue, Ottawa ON, K1M 1P4, ✆ 613 747 2252. **New Zealand**: 50 Manners St, Wellington 6142, ✆ 4 802 5665. **UK**: 39 Chesham Place, London SW1X 8SB, ✆ 020 7235 5555. **USA**: 2375 Pennsylvania Ave. NW, Washington DC 20037, ✆ 202 452 0100.

LANGUAGE

Castilian Spanish is the most widely spoken language. There are three other official languages: Catalan in the east; Galician (*Galego*) in the north-west, and Basque (*Euskera*) in the Basque country and parts of Navarre. English is fairly widely spoken in tourist areas. Note that in Spanish listings *Ch* often comes after the *C*'s, *Ll* after the *L*'s, and *Ñ* after the *N*'s.

PUBLIC TRANSPORT

Numerous regional bus companies provide a fairly comprehensive and cheap (if sometimes confusing) service. The largest bus operating groups are ALSA www.alsa.es and Avanzabus www.avanzabus.com. City buses are efficient and there are metro systems in Madrid, Barcelona, València and Bilbao.

RAIL TRAVEL

See Tables 650 - 689. National rail company: Red Nacional de los Ferrocarriles Españoles (RENFE) www.renfe.es. FEVE and a number of regionally-controlled railways operate lines in coastal regions. General information: RENFE ✆ 902 320 320; FEVE ✆ 902 100 818; AVE (high-speed): ✆ 915 066 329; Grandes Líneas (other long-distance): ✆ 902 105 205; international: ✆ 934 901 122. Spain's high-speed network has expanded considerably over the last few years and the Barcelona - Madrid service has some of the fastest trains in Europe. As well as *AVE* high-speed trains, other long-distance categories include *Altaria*, *Euromed*, *Talgo* (light articulated trains) and IC expresses (see page 321 for further train categories). *Trenhotel* (hotel train): night train offering sleeping compartments with their own shower and WC. Long-distance trains convey 1st and 2nd-class accommodation (known as *Preferente* and *Turista*) and require advance reservation. *Regionales*: local stopping service; *Cercanías*: suburban trains. In remoter parts of country, services may be very infrequent. Reservation is compulsory on all services for which a train category (*Talgo*, *IC* etc) is shown in the timing column of this timetable. RENFE offer money back if their AVE trains on the Sevilla line arrive more than 5 minutes late.

TELEPHONES

Dial in: ✆ +34 then number. Outgoing: ✆ 00.
Emergency (police / fire / ambulance): ✆ 112.

TOURIST INFORMATION

Spanish Tourist Office / Turespaña (*Oficinas de Turismo*) www.tourspain.es. Also in the USA: www.spain.info/en_US, and in the UK: www.spain.info/en_GB.

TOURIST OFFICES OVERSEAS

Canada: 2 Bloor Street West, Suite 3402, Toronto ON M4W 3E2, ✆ 416 961 3131, toronto@tourspain.es. **UK**: 64 North Row, 6th floor, London W1K 7DE, ✆ 0207 317 2011, londres@tourspain.es. **USA**: 60 East 42nd Street, Suite 5300 (53rd floor), New York NY 10165-0039, ✆ 212 265 8822, nuevayork@tourspain.es. Also in Chicago ✆ 312 642 1992, Los Angeles ✆ 323 658 7188, Miami ✆ 305 476 1966.

VISAS

See page xxiv for visa requirements.

SWEDEN

CAPITAL

Stockholm.

CURRENCY

Swedish crown or krona (SEK, kr, or Skr); 1 krona = 100 öre. For exchange rates see page 9.

EMBASSIES IN STOCKHOLM

Australia: Klarabergsviadukten 63, ✆ 08 613 2900. **Canada**: Klarabergsgatan 23, ✆ 08 453 3000. **New Zealand**: *refer to NZ Embassy in Belgium*. **UK**: Skarpögatan 6–8, ✆ 08 671 3000. **USA**: Dag Hammarskjölds Väg 31, ✆ 08 783 5300.

EMBASSIES OVERSEAS

Australia: 5 Turrana St, Yarralumla, Canberra, ACT 2600, ✆ 2 6270 2700. **Canada**: 377 Dalhousie St, Ottawa ON, K1N 9N8, ✆ 613 244 8200. **New Zealand** (Consulate): Molesworth House, 101 Molesworth Street, Wellington, ✆ 4 499 9895. **UK**: 11 Montagu Pl., London W1H 2AL, ✆ 020 7917 6400. **USA**: 2900 K Street NW, Washington DC 20007, ✆ 202 467 2600.

LANGUAGE

Swedish. English is widely spoken.

PUBLIC TRANSPORT

The transport system is highly efficient; ferries are covered (in whole or part) by rail passes and city transport cards. Swebus www.swebus.se, ✆ 0771 218 218 (+46 771 218 218 from abroad) is the biggest operator of long-distance buses. Advance booking is essential, tickets may be purchased at sales offices, by telephone or via the website. Bus terminals usually adjoin rail stations.

RAIL TRAVEL

See Tables **730 - 769**. National rail company: SJ AB, formerly part of Statens Järnvägar (SJ) www.sj.se or www.samtrafiken.se. Best services are operated by high-speed trains (*Snabbtåg*, shown as *Sn* in our tables) running at up to 200 km/h and using either SJ 2000 trains (formerly X2000) or new SJ 3000 units. Supplements are required on *Snabbtåg*. Some local lines are run by regional authorities or private companies such as Veolia Transport www.veolia.se; see page 349 for other operators. SJ information and sales line, ✆ (0) 771 75 75 75, Veolia ✆ (0) 771 260 000. Sleeping-cars: one or two berths in 2nd class; couchettes: six berths; female-only compartment available. 1st-class sleeping-cars (en-suite shower and WC) on many overnight services; 2nd-class have wash-basins, shower and WC at the end of the carriage. Long-distance trains have a refreshment service. Many trains have a family coach with a playroom, and facilities for the disabled. Seat reservations are compulsory on *Sn* and night trains. *Sn* services also operate between Sweden and Copenhagen via the Öresund bridge and tunnel but it is better to use the frequent local trains for short journeys. 'C' (for Central) in timetables etc. means the town's main station. *Biljetter* indicates the station ticket office, often with limited opening hours, but ticket machines are widely in use. *Pressbyrån* kiosks (at stations) sell snacks and English-language publications.

TELEPHONES

Dial in: ✆ +46 then number (omit initial 0). Outgoing: ✆ 00.
Emergency services (police / fire / ambulance): ✆ 112.

TOURIST INFORMATION

Swedish Travel & Tourism Council www.visitsweden.com, info@visitsweden.com. Stockholm Visitor Centre: Kulturhuset, Sergels Torg 3, ✆ 085 0828 508, touristinfo@stockholm.se.

TOURIST OFFICES OVERSEAS

UK: 5 Upper Montagu St, London W1H 2AG, ✆ 020 7108 6168, uk@visitsweden.com. **USA**: PO Box 4649, Grand Central Station, New York NY10163-4649, ✆ 212 885 9700, usa@visitsweden.com.

VISAS

See page xxiv for visa requirements.

SWITZERLAND

CAPITAL

Berne (Bern).

CURRENCY

Swiss franc (CHF or Sfr.); 1 franc = 100 centimes. For exchange rates see page 9.

EMBASSIES IN BERNE

Australia (Consulate in Geneva): Chemin des Fins 2, Geneva, ✆ 0 22 799 91 00. **Canada**: Kirchenfeldstrasse 88, ✆ 0 31 357 32 00. **New Zealand** (Consulate in Geneva): 2 Chemin des Fins, Geneva, ✆ 0 22 929 03 50. **UK**: Thunstrasse 50, ✆ 0 31 359 77 00. **USA**: Sulgeneckstrasse 19, ✆ 0 31 357 70 11.

EMBASSIES OVERSEAS

Australia: 7 Melbourne Avenue, Forrest, Canberra, ACT 2603, ✆ 2 6162 8400. **Canada**: 5 Marlborough Avenue, Ottawa ON, K1N 8E6, ✆ 613 235 1837. **New Zealand**: 10 Customhouse Quay, Wellington 6040, ✆ 4 472 1593. **UK**: 16-18 Montagu Place, London W1H 2BQ, ✆ 020 7616 6000. **USA**: 2900 Cathedral Ave. NW, Washington DC 20008, ✆ 202 745 7900.

LANGUAGE

German, French, Italian, and Romansch are all official languages. Most Swiss people are at least bilingual. English is widespread.

PUBLIC TRANSPORT

Swiss buses are famously punctual. Yellow postbuses call at rail stations; free timetables from post offices. Swiss Pass valid (see Passes feature), surcharge for some scenic routes. The best way to get around centres is often on foot. Most cities have efficient tram and bus networks with integrated ticketing.

RAIL TRAVEL

See Tables **500 - 579**. The principal rail carrier is Swiss Federal Railways (SBB / CFF / FFS) www.sbb.ch. Information: ✆ 0 900 300 300 (English-speaking operator). There are also many local lines with independent operators. Services are fast and punctual, trains spotlessly clean. Reservations are required on some sightseeing trains (e.g. Glacier Express, Bernina-Express). All main stations have information offices (and usually tourist offices), shopping and eating facilities. Bicycle hire at most stations.

TELEPHONES

Dial in: ✆ +41 then number (omit initial 0). Outgoing: ✆ 00.
Emergency: ✆ 112. Police: ✆ 117. Fire: ✆ 118. Ambulance: ✆ 114.

TOURIST INFORMATION

Switzerland Tourism www.myswitzerland.com. Zürich: Tödistrasse 7, (Not open to the public). International toll-free ✆ 00800 100 200 29.

TOURIST OFFICES OVERSEAS

Canada: 480 University Ave, Suite 1500, Toronto ON, M5G 1V2, ✆ 800 794 7795 (toll-free), info.caen@myswitzerland.com. **UK**: 30 Bedford Street, London WC2E 9ED, ✆ 00800 100 200 29 (free-phone), info.uk@myswitzerland.com. **USA**: 608 Fifth Ave., New York NY 10020, ✆ 01 800 794 7795 (toll-free), info.usa@myswitzerland.com.

VISAS

See page xxiv for visa requirements.

TURKEY

CAPITAL
Ankara.

CURRENCY
New Turkish lira (TRY or YTL). 1 lira = 100 kurus. For exchange rates see page 9.

CONSULATES IN ISTANBUL
Australia: Ritz Carlton residences, Asker Ocaği Caddesi No 15, Elmadağ 34367, ⌀ 393 8542. **Canada**: 209 Buyukdere Caddesi Tekfen Tower, ⌀ 385 9700. **New Zealand**: Inonu Caddesi No 48/3 Taksim, Istanbul 34437, ⌀ 244 0272. **UK**: Mesrutiyet Caddesi No 34, Tepebasi Beyoglu, ⌀ 334 6400. **USA**: İstinye Mahallesi, Kaplı calar Mekvii Sokak No 2, istinye 34460, ⌀ 335 9000.

EMBASSIES OVERSEAS
Australia: 6 Moonah Place, Yarralumla, Canberra, ACT 2600, ⌀ 2 6234 0000. **Canada**: 197 Wurtemburg St., Ottawa ON, K1N 8L9, ⌀ 613 244 2470. **New Zealand**: 17-17 Murphy St, Thorndon, Wellington 6011, ⌀ 4 472 1290. **UK**: (Consulate) Rutland Lodge Rutland Gardens, Knightsbridge, London SW1 1BW, ⌀ 020 7591 6900. **USA**: 2525 Massachusetts Ave, NW, Washington, DC 20008, ⌀ 202 612 6700.

LANGUAGE
Turkish, which is written using the Latin alphabet. English and German are often understood.

PUBLIC TRANSPORT
An excellent long-distance bus system, run by competing companies (amongst the best are Varan and Ulusoy), generally provides quicker journeys than rail. *Dolmus* minibuses that pick up passengers like a taxi, but at much cheaper rates and operating along set routes, can be used for shorter journeys. Istanbul has a modern metro line, as well as a light-rail and tram route. Passenger ferries link major ports.

RAIL TRAVEL
See Tables I570 - I590 (also I550 for European Turkey). Operator: TCDD (Turkish State Railways) www.tcdd.gov.tr. Traditional routes are tortuous and journeys slow, but the coaching stock is generally comfortable. Ankara and Istanbul are connected by a new high-speed route via Eskişehir with another high-speed section linking these cities with Konya. Further high speed lines are under construction. The Marmaray Tunnel under the Bosphorus opened in 2013, joining the Asian and European parts of Istanbul by rail for the first time. The historic terminal stations of Sirkeci and Haydarpasa are currently closed to all rail traffic. No domestic passenger rail services currently operate in European Turkey, other than in and around Istanbul itself.

TELEPHONES
Dial in: ⌀ +90 then number (omit initial 0). Outgoing: ⌀ 00. Emergency: ⌀ 112. Police: ⌀ 155. Fire: ⌀ 110. Ambulance: ⌀ 112.

TOURIST INFORMATION
Turkish National Tourist Office www.gototurkey.com. Ministry of Culture and Tourism www.kultur.gov.tr: Atatürk Bulvarı 29, 06050 Opera, Ankara, ⌀ 312 309 0850.

TOURIST OFFICES OVERSEAS
UK: 4th Floor, 29-30 St James's Street, London SW1A 1HB, ⌀ 020 7839 7778, info@gototurkey.co.uk. **USA**: 825 3rd Avenue 5 floor, New York NY 10022, ⌀ 212 687 2194, ny@tourismturkey.org. Also Los Angeles ⌀ 323 937 8066, Washington ⌀ 202 612 6800.

VISAS
See page xxiv for visa requirements.

UNITED KINGDOM

CAPITAL
London.

CURRENCY
Pounds Sterling (GBP or £). £1 = 100 pence (p). For exchange rates see page 09.

EMBASSIES IN LONDON
Australia (High Commission): Australia House, The Strand, ⌀ 020 7379 4334. **Canada** (High Commission) Macdonald House, 1 Grosvenor Square, ⌀ 020 7258 6600. **New Zealand** (High Commission): New Zealand House, 80 Haymarket, ⌀ 020 7930 8422. **USA**: 24 Grosvenor Square, ⌀ 020 7499 9000.

EMBASSIES OVERSEAS
Australia (High Commission): Commonwealth Ave, Yarralumla, Canberra, ACT 2600, ⌀ 2 6270 6666. **Canada** (High Commission): 80 Elgin St, Ottawa ON, K1P 5K7, ⌀ 613 237 1530. **New Zealand** (High Commission): 44 Hill St, Wellington, ⌀ 4 924 2888. **USA**: 3100 Massachusetts Ave. NW, Washington DC 20008, ⌀ 202 588 6500.

LANGUAGE
English, plus Welsh in Wales and Gaelic in parts of Scotland.

PUBLIC TRANSPORT
Intercity express bus services (coaches) are generally cheaper, but slower, than trains, and mostly require prebooking. The main long-distance coach operator in England and Wales is National Express www.nationalexpress.com, or Citylink www.citylink.co.uk in Scotland. Comprehensive local bus network; most companies belong to large groups such as Stagecoach, First or Arriva. Bus stations are rarely adjacent to railway stations. Traveline www.traveline.org.uk is an on-line and telephone service for all UK timetables: ⌀ 0871 200 22 23 (10p per minute). Extensive 'Underground' railway network in London operated by Transport for London www.tfl.gov.uk who also control the bus service using private companies. In Northern Ireland, Ulsterbus (part of Translink) is the principal bus operator www.translink.co.uk.

RAIL TRAVEL
See Tables I00 - 234. Passenger services in Great Britain are provided by a number of train operating companies, working together as National Rail www.nationalrail.co.uk. Through tickets are available to all stations in the country. If asked, booking-office staff will quote the cheapest through fare regardless of operator (time period restrictions apply to the very cheapest fares). National Rail enquiries: ⌀ 08457 48 49 50. Fast trains, comfortable and frequent, have first and standard class. Other long- and medium-distance regional services are often standard-class only. Refreshments are often available on board. Sleepers: cabins are two-berth or (higher charge) single. Advance reservation (essential for sleepers) is available for most long-distance services - a fee may be charged. Travel between Saturday evening and Sunday afternoon is sometimes interrupted by engineering works and buses may replace trains.
In Northern Ireland, trains are operated by Northern Ireland Railways (NIR), part of Translink. NIR enquiries: ⌀ 028 90 666 630.

TELEPHONES
Dial in: ⌀ +44 then number (omit initial 0). Outgoing: ⌀ 00. Emergency services: ⌀ 999 or 112.

TOURIST INFORMATION
VisitBritain www.visitbritain.com. London: 20 Great Smith Street, ⌀ 020 7578 1000. There are local tourist offices in most towns and cities.

TOURIST OFFICES OVERSEAS
Australia: The Gateway, 1 Macquarie Place Sidney, NSW 2000, ⌀ 2 8247 2275. **Canada**: 777 Bay Street Suite, 2800 Toronto ON M5G 2G2, ⌀ 664 666 77. **USA** 845 Third Avenue, 10th Floor New York NY 10022, ⌀ 212 850 0349. Also in Los Angeles, ⌀ 310 481 2989. Intending visitors should refer to the website www.visitbritain.com.

VISAS
See page xxiv for visa requirements.

Visa Requirements

The table below shows whether nationals from selected countries (shown in columns) need visas to visit countries in Europe (shown in rows) - the symbol ▲ indicates that a visa **is** required. This information applies to tourist trips for up to 30 days - different requirements may apply for longer trips or for visits for other purposes, also if you are resident in a country other than your own. To enter certain countries you may need up to three months remaining validity on your passport. Holders of biometric ordinary passports sometimes do not require a visa.

The first row and column, labelled **Schengen area**, apply to the 26 European countries which have signed the Schengen Agreement whereby border controls between the member countries have been abolished. It is possible to obtain a single Schengen visa to cover all these countries, which are:

Austria, Belgium, Czech Republic, Denmark, Estonia, Finland, France, Germany, Greece, Hungary, Iceland, Italy, Latvia, Liechtenstein, Lithuania, Luxembourg, Malta, Netherlands, Norway, Poland, Portugal, Slovakia, Slovenia, Spain, Sweden, Switzerland.

Note that the Schengen area and the European Union (EU) differ in the following respects: Iceland, Liechtenstein, Norway and Switzerland are not in the EU but have implemented the Schengen agreement, whereas the United Kingdom and the Republic of Ireland are in the EU but have opted out of Schengen. Andorra is not included in the Schengen area. Croatia, Cyprus, Romania and Bulgaria are in the EU and are legally obliged to join Schengen once certain requirements are met.

Visas should generally be applied for in advance from an Embassy or Consulate of the country you are visiting, although sometimes they are available on arrival. Transit visas may be available for those travelling through a country in order to reach another, but these may also need to be purchased in advance. **WARNING! The information show below is given as a guide only - entry requirements are subject to change and should be confirmed from official sources.**

NATIONALS OF →
▲ VISA REQUIRED
TRAVELLING TO ↓

	Schengen area	Albania	Belarus	Bosnia-Herzegovina	Bulgaria	Croatia	Cyprus	Macedonia	Moldova	Montenegro	Romania	Russia	Serbia	Switzerland	Turkey	UK / Ireland	Ukraine	Australia	Canada	Japan	New Zealand	USA
Schengen area	–		▲									▲			▲		▲					
Albania ◇		–	▲					▲				▲										
Belarus	▲	▲	–	▲	▲	▲	▲	▲		▲	▲			▲		▲		▲	▲	▲	▲	▲
Bosnia-Herzegovina			▲	–						▲												
Bulgaria		▲¹	▲	▲¹	–			▲¹	▲¹	▲¹		▲	▲¹		▲		▲					
Croatia			▲			–						▲			▲		▲					
Cyprus		▲¹	▲	▲¹			–	▲¹	▲¹	▲¹		▲	▲¹		▲		▲					
Macedonia		▲¹	▲					–	▲	▲¹		▲¹										
Moldova			▲						–			▲¹										
Montenegro			▲							–												
Romania		▲¹	▲	▲¹				▲¹	▲¹	▲¹	–	▲	▲¹		▲		▲					
Russia	▲	▲			▲	▲	▲	▲			▲	–		▲		▲		▲	▲	▲	▲	▲
Serbia								▲¹					–									
Switzerland		▲¹	▲	▲¹				▲¹	▲¹	▲¹		▲	▲¹	–	▲		▲					
Turkey	●²					●	●								–	●		●	●			●
UK / Ireland		▲	▲	▲				▲	▲	▲		▲	▲		▲	–	▲					
Ukraine	▲	▲															–	▲			▲	

NOTES

▲ – Visa required (see also general notes above table).

▲¹ – Visa not required by holders of 'biometric' passports.

● – Electronic visa required before entering the country (prices vary according to nationality). For further information and to make a visa application see www.evisa.gov.tr.

●² – ● applies to nationals of Austria, Belgium, Malta, Netherlands, Norway, Poland, Portugal and Spain.

◇ – Tax of 10 euro may be payable on entry to Albania.

EUROPEAN RAIL TIMETABLE

DECEMBER 2016

GENERAL INFORMATION

REGULAR FEATURES

TIMETABLES

CONTACT DETAILS

Director and Editor-in-chief	John Potter
Editor	Chris Woodcock
Editorial Team	Peter Bass
	David Turpie
	Peter Weller
Additional compiling	Brendan Fox
Marketing and Advertising Manager	Keri Blunston
Commercial Manager	Gemma Donaldson
Subscriptions Manager	Peter Weller
Social Media Manager	Reuben Turner
Regular Correspondents	Nicky Gardner
	Susanne Kries
General sales enquiries	Mon-Fri 0900 - 1700
	+44 (0)1832 270198
	sales@europeanrailtimetable.eu

Every care has been taken to render the timetable correct in accordance with the latest advices, but changes are constantly being made by the administrations concerned and the publishers cannot hold themselves responsible for the consequences of either changes or inaccuracies.

ISSN 1748-0817   Published monthly.
Printed and bound by CPI Group (UK) Ltd, Croydon, CR0 4YY

Cover created by Andrea Collins   website: www.millstonecreative.co.uk
e-mail: millstonecreative@btinternet.com

European Rail Timetable Limited
28 Monson Way
Oundle
Northamptonshire PE8 4QG, United Kingdom

website: www.europeanrailtimetable.eu
e-mail: editorial@europeanrailtimetable.eu
sales: sales@europeanrailtimetable.eu

© European Rail Timetable Limited, 2016

Company Number 8590554

2016

CALENDRIER   CALENDARIO   KALENDER   CALENDARIO

2016

JULY
M T W T F S S
① ② ③ ④ ⑤ ⑥ ⑦
– – – – 1 2 3
4 5 6 7 8 9 10
11 12 13 14 15 16 17
18 19 20 21 22 23 24
25 26 27 28 29 30 31

AUGUST
M T W T F S S
① ② ③ ④ ⑤ ⑥ ⑦
1 2 3 4 5 6 7
8 9 10 11 12 13 14
15 16 17 18 19 20 21
22 23 24 25 26 27 28
29 30 31 – – – –

SEPTEMBER
M T W T F S S
① ② ③ ④ ⑤ ⑥ ⑦
– – – 1 2 3 4
5 6 7 8 9 10 11
12 13 14 15 16 17 18
19 20 21 22 23 24 25
26 27 28 29 30 – –

OCTOBER
M T W T F S S
① ② ③ ④ ⑤ ⑥ ⑦
31 – – – – 1 2
3 4 5 6 7 8 9
10 11 12 13 14 15 16
17 18 19 20 21 22 23
24 25 26 27 28 29 30

NOVEMBER
M T W T F S S
① ② ③ ④ ⑤ ⑥ ⑦
– 1 2 3 4 5 6
7 8 9 10 11 12 13
14 15 16 17 18 19 20
21 22 23 24 25 26 27
28 29 30 – – – –

DECEMBER
M T W T F S S
① ② ③ ④ ⑤ ⑥ ⑦
– – – 1 2 3 4
5 6 7 8 9 10 11
12 13 14 15 16 17 18
19 20 21 22 23 24 25
26 27 28 29 30 31 –

2017

JANUARY
M T W T F S S
① ② ③ ④ ⑤ ⑥ ⑦
30 31 – – – – 1
2 3 4 5 6 7 8
9 10 11 12 13 14 15
16 17 18 19 20 21 22
23 24 25 26 27 28 29

FEBRUARY
M T W T F S S
① ② ③ ④ ⑤ ⑥ ⑦
– – 1 2 3 4 5
6 7 8 9 10 11 12
13 14 15 16 17 18 19
20 21 22 23 24 25 26
27 28 – – – – –

MARCH
M T W T F S S
① ② ③ ④ ⑤ ⑥ ⑦
– – 1 2 3 4 5
6 7 8 9 10 11 12
13 14 15 16 17 18 19
20 21 22 23 24 25 26
27 28 29 30 31 – –

APRIL
M T W T F S S
① ② ③ ④ ⑤ ⑥ ⑦
– – – – – 1 2
3 4 5 6 7 8 9
10 11 12 13 14 15 16
17 18 19 20 21 22 23
24 25 26 27 28 29 30

MAY
M T W T F S S
① ② ③ ④ ⑤ ⑥ ⑦
1 2 3 4 5 6 7
8 9 10 11 12 13 14
15 16 17 18 19 20 21
22 23 24 25 26 27 28
29 30 31 – – – –

JUNE
M T W T F S S
① ② ③ ④ ⑤ ⑥ ⑦
– – – 1 2 3 4
5 6 7 8 9 10 11
12 13 14 15 16 17 18
19 20 21 22 23 24 25
26 27 28 29 30 – –

JULY
M T W T F S S
① ② ③ ④ ⑤ ⑥ ⑦
31 – – – – 1 2
3 4 5 6 7 8 9
10 11 12 13 14 15 16
17 18 19 20 21 22 23
24 25 26 27 28 29 30

AUGUST
M T W T F S S
① ② ③ ④ ⑤ ⑥ ⑦
– 1 2 3 4 5 6
7 8 9 10 11 12 13
14 15 16 17 18 19 20
21 22 23 24 25 26 27
28 29 30 31 – – –

SEPTEMBER
M T W T F S S
① ② ③ ④ ⑤ ⑥ ⑦
– – – – 1 2 3
4 5 6 7 8 9 10
11 12 13 14 15 16 17
18 19 20 21 22 23 24
25 26 27 28 29 30 –

OCTOBER
M T W T F S S
① ② ③ ④ ⑤ ⑥ ⑦
30 31 – – – – 1
2 3 4 5 6 7 8
9 10 11 12 13 14 15
16 17 18 19 20 21 22
23 24 25 26 27 28 29

NOVEMBER
M T W T F S S
① ② ③ ④ ⑤ ⑥ ⑦
– – 1 2 3 4 5
6 7 8 9 10 11 12
13 14 15 16 17 18 19
20 21 22 23 24 25 26
27 28 29 30 – – –

DECEMBER
M T W T F S S
① ② ③ ④ ⑤ ⑥ ⑦
– – – – 1 2 3
4 5 6 7 8 9 10
11 12 13 14 15 16 17
18 19 20 21 22 23 24
25 26 27 28 29 30 31

2017

PUBLIC HOLIDAYS 2017

JOURS FÉRIÉS   GIORNI FESTIVI   FEIERTAGE   DÍAS FESTIVOS

The dates given below are those of national public holidays. They do not include regional, half-day or unofficial holidays. Passengers intending to travel on public holidays, or on days immediately preceding or following them, are strongly recommended to reserve seats and to confirm timings locally. Further information regarding special transport conditions applying on holiday dates may be found in the introduction to each country.

Austria: Jan. 1, 6, Apr. 17, May 1, 25, June 5, 15, Aug. 15, Oct. 26, Nov. 1, Dec. 8, 25, 26.

Belarus: Jan. 1, 7, Mar. 8, Apr. 25, May 1, 9, July 3, Nov. 7, Dec. 25.

Belgium: Jan. 1, Apr. 16, 17, May 1, 25, June 4, 5, July 21, Aug. 15, Nov. 1, 11, Dec. 25.

Bosnia-Herzegovina: Jan. 1, 2, Mar. 1, May 1, 2, 9, Nov. 25. *Other religious holidays are observed in certain areas.*

Bulgaria: Jan. 1, Mar. 3, Apr. 14 – 17, May 1, 6, 24, Sept. 6, 22, Dec. 24, 25, 26.

Croatia: Jan. 1, 6, Apr. 16, 17, May 1, June 15, 22, 25, Aug. 5, 15, Oct. 8, Nov. 1, Dec. 25, 26.

Czech Republic: Jan. 1, Apr. 14, 17, May 1, 8, July 5, 6, Sept. 28, Oct. 28, Nov. 17, Dec. 24, 25, 26.

Denmark: Jan. 1, Apr. 13, 14, 16, 17, May 12, 25, June 4, 5, Dec. 25, 26.

Estonia: Jan. 1, Feb. 24, Apr. 14, 16, May 1, June 4, 23, 24, Aug. 20, Dec. 24, 25, 26.

Finland: Jan. 1, 6, Apr. 14, 16, 17, May 1, 25, June 4, 24, Nov. 4, Dec. 6, 25, 26.

France: Jan. 1, Apr. 17, May 1, 8, 25, June 5, July 14, Aug. 15, Nov. 1, 11, Dec. 25.

Germany: Jan. 1, 6*, Apr. 14, 17, May 1, 25, June 5, 15*, Aug. 15*, Oct. 3, 31*, Nov. 1*, 22*, Dec. 25, 26. * Observed in certain regions: see also page 367.

Great Britain: *England & Wales*: Jan. 2, Apr. 14, 17, May 1, 29, Aug. 28, Dec. 25, 26.
Scotland: Jan. 2, 3, Apr. 14, May 1, 29, Aug. 7, Nov. 30, Dec. 25, 26.

Greece: Jan. 1, 6, Feb. 27, Mar. 25, Apr. 14, 16, 17, May 1, June 5, Aug. 15, Oct. 28, Dec. 25, 26.

Hungary: Jan. 1, Mar. 15, Apr. 16, 17, May 1, June 5, Aug. 20, Oct. 23, Nov. 1, Dec. 25, 26.

Iceland: Jan. 1, Apr. 13, 14, 16, 17, 20, May 1, 25, June 4, 5, 17, Aug. 7, Dec. 25, 26.

Ireland (Northern): Jan. 2, Mar. 17, Apr. 14, 17, May 1, 29, July 12, Aug. 28, Dec. 25, 26.

Ireland (Republic): Jan. 1, 2, Mar. 17, Apr. 17, May 1, June 5, Aug. 7, Oct. 30, Dec. 25, 26.

Italy: Jan. 1, 6, Apr. 16, 17, 25, May 1, June 2, Aug. 15, Nov. 1, Dec. 8, 25, 26.

Latvia: Jan. 1, Apr. 14, 16, 17, May 1, 4, June 23, 24, Nov. 18, Dec. 24, 25, 26, 31.

Lithuania: Jan. 1, Feb. 16, Mar. 11, Apr. 16, 17, May 1, June 24, July 6, Aug. 15, Nov. 1, Dec. 24, 25, 26.

Luxembourg: Jan. 1, Apr. 17, May 1, 25, June 5, 23, Aug. 15, Nov. 1, Dec. 25, 26.

Macedonia: Jan. 1, 2, 7, Apr. 17, May 1, 24, June 26, Aug. 2, Sept. 8, Oct. 11, 23, Dec. 8. *Other religious holidays are observed in certain areas.*

Moldova: Jan. 1, 2, 7, 8, Mar. 8, Apr. 16, 17, 24, May 1, 9, Aug. 27, 28, 31, Dec. 25.

Netherlands: Jan. 1, Apr. 16, 17, 27, May 25, June 4, 5, Dec. 25, 26.

Norway: Jan. 1, Apr. 13, 14, 16, 17, May 1, 17, 25, June 4, 5, Dec. 25, 26.

Poland: Jan. 1, 6, Apr. 16, 17, May 1, 3, June 4, 15, Aug. 15, Nov. 1, 11, Dec. 25, 26.

Portugal: Jan. 1, Apr. 14, 16, 25, May 1, June 10, 15, Aug. 15, Oct. 5, Nov. 1, Dec. 1, 8, 25.

Romania: Jan. 1, 2, 24, Apr. 16, 17, May 1, June 4, 5, Aug. 15, Nov. 30, Dec. 1, 25, 26.

Russia: Jan. 1 – 7, Feb. 23, Mar. 8, May 1, 8, 9, June 12, Nov. 4, 6.

Serbia: Jan. 1, 2, 7, Feb. 15, 16, Apr. 14 – 17, May 1, 2, Nov. 11.

Slovakia: Jan. 1, 6, Apr. 14, 17, May 1, 8, July 5, Aug. 29, Sept. 1, 15, Nov. 1, 17, Dec. 24, 25, 26.

Slovenia: Jan. 1, Feb. 8, Apr. 16, 17, 27, May 1, 2, June 4, 25, Aug. 15, Oct. 31, Nov. 1, Dec. 25, 26.

Spain: Jan. 1, 6, Mar. 19*, Apr. 13*, 14, 17*, May 1, July 25*, Aug. 15, Oct. 12, Nov. 1*, Dec. 6*, 8, 25. * Observed in certain regions.

Sweden: Jan. 1, 6, Apr. 14, 16, 17, May 1, 25, June 4, 6, 24, Nov. 4, Dec. 25, 26.

Switzerland: Jan. 1, 2*, 6*, Mar. 19*, Apr. 14*, 17*, May 1*, 25 June 5*, 15*, Aug. 1, 15*, Nov. 1*, Dec. 8*, 25, 26*. *Also some local holidays.* * Observed in certain regions.

Turkey: Jan. 1, Apr. 23, May 1, 19, Aug. 30, Oct. 29 (also 2017 festival periods June 25 – 27, Sept. 1 – 4).

Ukraine: Jan. 1, 2, 7, 8, 9, Mar. 8, Apr. 16, 17, May 1, 2, 9, June 4, 5, 28, Aug. 24.

MOVABLE HOLIDAYS

Fêtes mobiles   –   Feste mobile
Bewegliche Feste   –   Fiestas movibles

	2017	2018
Good Friday	Apr. 14	Mar. 30 ●
Easter Monday	Apr. 17	Apr. 2 ●
Ascension Day	May 25	May 10 ●
Whit Monday (Pentecost)	June 5	May 21 ●
Corpus Christi	June 15	May 31

● *One week later in the Orthodox calendar*

TIME COMPARISON

COMPARAISON DES HEURES   COMPARAZIONE DELLE ORE   ZEITVERGLEICH   COMPARACIÓN DE LAS HORAS

West European Time	WINTER: GMT SUMMER: GMT + 1	Ireland Portugal United Kingdom	Iceland *(GMT all year)*				
Central European Time	WINTER: GMT + 1 SUMMER: GMT + 2	Albania Austria Belgium	Bosnia Croatia Czech Rep.	Denmark France Germany	Hungary Italy Luxembourg	Macedonia Malta Montenegro	Netherlands Norway Poland	Serbia Slovakia Slovenia	Spain Sweden Switzerland
East European Time	WINTER: GMT + 2 SUMMER: GMT + 3	Bulgaria Estonia Finland	Greece Latvia Lithuania	Moldova Romania Turkey	Ukraine	Belarus *(GMT + 3 all year)* Kaliningrad *(GMT + 3 all year)* Western Russia *(GMT + 3 all year)*			

Daylight Saving Time ('Summer Time') applies between 0100 GMT on March 26 and 0100 GMT on October 29, 2017 *(GMT = Greenwich Mean Time = UTC)*.

What's new this month

WELCOME

Welcome to the Winter 2016/2017 edition of the European Rail Timetable which includes new schedules for most European countries valid from December 11. We have been able to include new timings for most trains but, as is often the case for the December edition, only partial information was available for certain countries as we went to press. Readers are therefore advised to check individual country headings for details of the current validity status. Please be aware that many tables have been compiled using advance data which is sometimes liable to change and readers may wish to confirm timings before travelling. All our tables will be checked over the coming weeks as schedules are confirmed.

Regretfully, we have had to increase the price of our printed timetables by one pound. This is the first price rise since we took over production of the European Rail Timetable from Thomas Cook nearly three years ago and is due to increased production and distribution costs. Our digital version is not directly affected by these costs and so will remain at its current price. A summary of the latest prices for individual copies and subscriptions will be found on page 10.

ROUTE OF THE MONTH

The European Rail Timetable gives a great overview of ferry and inshore shipping services around Europe's coasts. That inspired our regular correspondents, Nicky Gardner and Susanne Kries, to switch from trains to boats for the Route of the Month feature in our Winter 2016/17 timetable. Turn to page 34 and join them on a Hebridean adventure as they sample some of the Caledonian MacBrayne shipping routes in Table **219**.

TIP OF THE MONTH

Continuing with the island hopping theme of our *Route of the Month*, Nicky and Susanne offer some practical advice for readers who may be tempted to explore the Hebridean islands for themselves. Containing useful information on schedules, fares and accommodation, the article will be found on page 35.

CAR TRAINS

Austrian Railways has introduced two new services from Innsbruck; to Hamburg which operates daily, and Düsseldorf which runs three days per week.

Treinreiswinkel will introduce a second destination from its Düsseldorf base for the summer season. In addition to the established Verona service, it will be possible to travel to Livorno once a week between July 5 and August 31, outbound on Wednesday and returning on Thursday (Table **1**).

INTERNATIONAL

German Railways ceased running all its *City Night Line* services from December 11. However, Austrian Railways has now taken over the operation of certain trains and, together with its existing *EuroNight* services, will run them under a new *nightjet* brand. A summary of the various changes to overnight services are listed below.

Table 28: *CNL* **419/418** *Pollux* Amsterdam – München has been withdrawn. A new *nightjet* service **421/420** Düsseldorf – Frankfurt – Nürnberg – München – Innsbruck will run, together with a portion Düsseldorf – Nürnberg – Wien (numbered **40421/40420**).

Tables 20, 54 and 56: *EN* **447/446** *Jan Kiepura* Köln – Berlin – Warszawa and *CNL* **40447/40458** *Kopernikus* Köln – Berlin – Praha have been withdrawn.

Table 52: Former *CNL* **458/40470** *Canopus* Zürich – Praha (via Frankfurt) is diverted to run via Innsbruck, being conveyed with the Zürich – Budapest cars of *nightjet* service **40467/40462** between Zürich and Linz (Table **86**).

Tables 54 and 73: Former *CNL* services **479/478** *Komet* Hamburg – Basel – Zurich and **471/470** *Sirius* Berlin – Basel – Zürich are now combined, running as new *nightjet* service **471/470** Hamburg – Berlin – Basel – Zürich.

Table 64: *EN* **491/490** Hamburg – Nürnberg – Wien becomes a *nightjet* branded service which now also conveys a portion running Hamburg – Nürnberg – München – Innsbruck (numbered **40491/40490**).

Table 70: Former *CNL* trains **485/484** *Lupus* München – Innsbruck – Roma and **40485/40481** *Apus* München – Innsbruck – Milano are diverted to run via Villach and Tarvisio as *nightjet* service **295/294**. Trains **40463/40236** *Pictor* München – Villach – Tarvisio – Venezia are renumbered **463/236**.

Table 73: *CNL* **40419/40478** *Pegasus* Amsterdam – Köln – Zürich is withdrawn.

Other changes from the mid-December timetable changes are outlined below.

Tables 10, 11 and 17: Eurostar services London – Paris/Brussels are valid until May 27. In Table **17**, the London to Marne la Vallée-Chessy (station for Disneyland) service is valid until July 7 and London to Marseille until November 4, 2017. Owing to engineering work taking place on the high-speed line between Calais and Paris, Eurostar services will depart Paris up to 12 minutes earlier and arrive up to 12 minutes later from January 23 to February 4, 2017.

Table 11: A number of long-distance *TGV* services have been withdrawn as follows: **5102/5144** between Lille and Marseille; **9800** Brussels – Toulon; the Sundays only **5137** Lille – Montpellier; **6811/6859** between Lyon and Toulouse; also the train pair **5211/5214** and **5278/5280** betweeen Lille and Nantes / Rennes.

Table 15a: The line between Hoek van Holland Haven and Schiedam Centrum is to be integrated into the Rotterdam metro system later this year. Work to convert the line is due to commence on April 1, 2017 and therefore the service is subject to alteration from that date.

Table 17: Eurostar **9084/9087** will be running between London and Marseille on December 17, 2016, February 11, 18, 2017. This service has not previously run during the winter months.

Table 20: The 1155 Thalys service from Paris to Köln (**9437**) is extended to Düsseldorf on Saturdays, and to Essen on Mondays to Fridays and Sundays. In the reverse direction, train **9448**, the 1245 from Köln, starts back at Essen.

Tables 20 and 21: Three extra *ICE* services are now running between Brussels and Frankfurt: one daily, one daily except Saturdays, and the other on Fridays and Sundays only. However, the first *ICE* trains from both Brussels and Frankfurt no longer run on Sundays.

Table 24: Train **24/23** Paris – Moskva reduces in frequency from three times a week to weekly and no longer calls at Épernay.

Table 28: A new early morning *ICE* has been introduced between Frankfurt and Amsterdam. *ICE* **222** departs Frankfurt (Main) Hbf at 0456 on Mondays to Fridays (daily from Köln at 0628), arriving Amsterdam at 0928.

Table 44: The afternoon Milano to Paris trains **9248** and **9250** are combined to depart Milano at 1440 every day of the week.

Table 50: *Snälltåget* has announced that train **301** *Berlin Night Express* will run on April 12 and May 25 from Malmö to Berlin and, in the reverse direction, train **300**, will run on April 16 and May 28. During the summer months it will run three times a week in each direction.

Table 56: Russian Railways has introduced a new twice weekly sleeper service between Moskva and Berlin using Talgo stock.

Table 61: **293/292** *Nusic* Beograd – Sofia and **481/480** *Serdica* Budapest – Vidin – Sofia are both withdrawn. Train **491** *Balkan* Beograd – Sofia is retimed to run two hours later, departing Beograd at 0925, but the connection at Sofia with train **491** *Balkan Express* to istanbul is maintained as the latter train is also retimed. In the opposite direction, train **490** *Balkan* Sofia – Beograd runs almost two hours earlier, departing Sofia at 0940. However, as with the eastbound journey, the connection with retimed train **490** *Balkan Express* from istanbul continues to apply.

Table 62: **411/410** Ljubljana – Zagreb – Beograd, which was previously reported as withdrawn, has been reprieved but only runs over the Christmas / New Year period and during the Summer. In addition, it has been extended to run to and from Villach, conveying first and second class seats.

Table 68: *EC* **111/110** München – Klagenfurt is now formed of *Railjet* coaches.

CONTINUED ON PAGE 36

EXPLANATION OF SYMBOLS	EXPLICATION DES SIGNES	DELUCIDAZIONE DEI SEGNI	ZEICHENERKLÄRUNG	EXPLICACIÓN DE LOS SIGNOS
SERVICES	**SERVICES**	**SERVIZI**	**DIENSTE**	**SERVICIOS**
Through service (1st and 2nd class seats)	Relation directe (places assises 1re et 2e classe)	Relazione diretta (con posti di 1ª e 2ª classe)	Direkte Verbindung (Sitzplätze 1. und 2. Klasse)	Relación directa (con asientos de 1ª y 2ª clase)
Sleeping car	Voiture-lits	Carrozza letti	Schlafwagen	Coche-camas
Couchette car	Voiture-couchettes	Carrozza cuccette	Liegewagen	Coche-literas
Restaurant car	Voiture-restaurant	Carrozza ristorante	Speisewagen	Coche-restaurante
Snacks and drinks available (see page 8)	Voiture-bar ou vente ambulante (voir page 8)	Carrozza bar o servizio di buffet (vedere pagina 8)	Imbiss und Getränke im Zug (siehe Seite 8)	Servicio de cafetería o bar móvil (véase pág. 8)
2 Second class only	Uniquement deuxième classe	Sola seconda classe	Nur zweite Klasse	Sólo segunda clase
Bus or coach service	Service routier	Servizio automobilistico	Buslinie	Servicio de autobuses
Shipping service	Service maritime	Servizio marittimo	Schifffahrtslinie	Servicio marítimo
DAYS OF RUNNING	**JOURS DE CIRCULATION**	**GIORNI DI EFFETTUAZIONE**	**VERKEHRSTAGE**	**DÍAS DE CIRCULACIÓN**
Mondays to Saturdays except holidays*	Du lundi au samedi, sauf les fêtes*	Dal lunedì al sabato, salvo i giorni festivi*	Montag bis Samstag außer Feiertage*	De lunes a sábado, excepto festivos*
Ⓐ Mondays to Fridays except holidays*	Du lundi au vendredi, sauf les fêtes*	Dal lunedì al venerdì, salvo i giorni festivi*	Montag bis Freitag außer Feiertage*	De lunes a viernes, excepto festivos*
Ⓑ Daily except Saturdays	Tous les jours sauf les samedis	Giornalmente, salvo il sabato	Täglich außer Samstag	Diario excepto sábados
Ⓒ Saturdays, Sundays and holidays*	Les samedis, dimanches et fêtes*	Sabato, domenica e giorni festivi*	Samstage, Sonn- und Feiertage*	Sábados, domingos y festivos*
† Sundays and holidays*	Les dimanches et fêtes*	Domenica e giorni festivi*	Sonn- und Feiertage*	Domingos y festivos*
①② Mondays, Tuesdays	Les lundis, mardis	Lunedì, martedì	Montag, Dienstag	Lunes, martes
③④ Wednesdays, Thursdays	Les mercredis, jeudis	Mercoledì, giovedì	Mittwoch, Donnerstag	Miércoles, jueves
⑤⑥ Fridays, Saturdays	Les vendredis, samedis	Venerdì, sabato	Freitag, Samstag	Viernes, sábados
⑦ Sundays	Les dimanches	Domenica	Sonntag	Domingos
①–④ Mondays to Thursdays	Des lundis aux jeudis	Dal lunedì al giovedì	Montag bis Donnerstag	De lunes a jueves
OTHER SYMBOLS	**AUTRES SIGNES**	**ALTRI SIMBOLI**	**SONSTIGE SYMBOLE**	**OTROS SÍMBOLOS**
IC 29 Train number (**bold figures** above train times)	Numéro du train (en **caractères gras** au-dessus de l'horaire du train)	Numero del treno (in **neretto** sopra gli orari del treno)	Zugnummer (über den Fahrplanzeiten in **fetter Schrift** gesetzt)	Número del tren (figura en **negrita** encima del horario del tren)
♦ See footnotes (listed by train number)	Renvoi aux notes données en bas de page (dans l'ordre numérique des trains)	Vedi in calce alla pagina l'annotazione corrispondente al numero del treno	Siehe die nach Zugnummern geordneten Fußnoten	Véase al pie de la página la nota correspondiente al número del tren
Ⓡ Reservation compulsory	Réservation obligatoire	Prenotazione obbligatoria	Reservierung erforderlich	Reserva obligatoria
Frontier station	Gare frontalière	Stazione di frontiera	Grenzbahnhof	Estación fronteriza
✦ Airport	Aéroport	Aeroporto	Flughafen	Aeropuerto
| Train does not stop	Sans arrêt	Il treno non ferma qui	Zug hält nicht	El tren no para aquí
Separates two trains in the same column between which no connection is possible	Sépare deux trains de la même colonne qui ne sont pas en correspondance	Separa due treni della stessa colonna che non sono in coincidenza	Trennt zwei in derselben Spalte angegebene Züge, zwischen denen kein Anschluß besteht	Separa dos trenes de la misma columna entre los cuales no hay enlace
→ Continued in later column	Suite dans une colonne à droite	Continuazione più avanti a destra	Fortsetzung weiter rechts	Continuación a la derecha
← Continued from earlier column	Suite d'une colonne à gauche	Seguito di una colonna a sinistra	Fortsetzung von links	Continuación desde la izquierda
v.v. Vice versa	Vice versa	Viceversa	Umgekehrt	A la inversa
* Public holiday dates for each country are given on page 2. *Other, special symbols are explained in table footnotes or in the introduction to each country.*	* Les dates des fêtes légales nationales sont données en page 2. *D'autres signes particuliers sont expliqués dans les notes ou bien dans l'avant-propos relatif à chaque pays.*	* Per le date dei giorni festivi civili nei diversi paesi vedere pagina 2. *Altri segni particolari vengono spiegati nelle note in calce ai quadri o nella introduzione attinente a ogni paese.*	* Gesetzlichen Feiertage der jeweiligen Länder finden Sie auf Seite 2. *Besondere Symbole sind in den Fußnoten bzw. in der Einleitung zu den einzelnen Ländern erklärt.*	* Las fechas de los días festivos en cada país figuran en la página 2. *La explicación de otros signos particulares se da en las notas o en el preámbulo correspondiente a cada país.*

What is the European Rail Timetable?

The European Rail Timetable is a concise guide to rail and ferry schedules throughout Europe, and also includes selected areas of the world outside Europe. Needless to say, it cannot be comprehensive (it would run into thousands of pages), but through our knowledge and experience, together with valuable feedback from our readers, we can select those services which we believe will satisfy the needs of most travellers.

When do the services change?

There is a major annual timetable change in mid-December affecting almost all European countries, with many countries having a second change in mid-June. There are, of course, exceptions. For example, the British summer timetable starts in late May, Sweden changes again in mid-August, whilst Russia and the other CIS countries have their main change at the end of May. Many holiday areas also have separate timetables for the high-summer period, particularly areas of France and Italy. In fact, changes can happen at any time of year, and railways issue amendments either on set dates or as and when necessary. Engineering work also causes frequent changes, and shipping schedules can change at any time.

How are the trains selected for inclusion?

People travel for many reasons, whether for leisure, business, sightseeing, visiting friends or relations, or just for the fun of it, and there are no hard and fast rules for selecting the services that we show. Naturally, major towns and inter-city services are shown as a matter of course, but the level of smaller places and local trains shown will depend on the country and even the area. It's surprising just how many minor lines we manage to squeeze in! Generally we will show a greater number of local trains in areas which are popular tourist destinations or where other services are sparse.

It is not possible to show suburban trains within cities or conurbations, or most outer-suburban routes to places close to large cities. However, where there are places of particular interest or importance in this category we do try to show brief details of frequency and journey time.

When should I use the International section?

The rail tables are divided into two sections - International (Tables 9 to 99) and Country by Country (Tables 100 upwards). For some international services between adjacent countries (for example Stockholm - Oslo or Hamburg - Århus) it is necessary to use the relevant Country tables - the index or maps will guide you. Local trains which cross international frontiers will usually only be found in the Country sections.

Some international trains also carry passengers internally within each country and will therefore be found in the Country tables as well as the International section. Some services are primarily for international travel and will therefore only be found in the International section - this includes *Eurostar* trains (London - Paris/Brussels) and *Thalys* services (Paris - Brussels - Amsterdam/ Köln), as well as certain long-distance night trains.

What about places outside Europe?

The European Rail Timetable includes the whole of Turkey and Russia. Furthermore, our Beyond Europe section at the back of each edition features timetables from different areas of the world each month. Eight areas are featured, each appearing at least twice a year. The areas covered are **India**, **South East Asia**, **Australia**, **New Zealand**, **China**, **Japan**, **South America**, **North America**, **South Korea**, **Africa and the Middle East**. Details of when each region appears will be found in the introduction of the Beyond Europe section. Please note that we include **all** of the latest Beyond Europe sections in our expanded Winter and Summer editions.

What else does it contain?

A summary of international sleeper services will be found on page 33, listing types of accommodation, operators and facilities on board.

We also include a summary of European rail passes (see the list of contents on page 1 for its current location) with a more detailed version appearing in our expanded Summer and Winter editions.

Each month a different rail journey is described in our *Route of the Month* feature, written by Nicky Gardner and Susanne Kries, editors of Hidden Europe magazine. They also offer useful information in our *Tip of the Month*.

Our timetables and other products may be purchased from our website **www.europeanrailtimetable.eu**.

Using the index

INDEX
pages 11-26

Placenames ❶

Major city ❸

Selected places reached from city above ❹

Middelburg, 450
Middelfart, 700, 705, 710
Middelkerke, 406
Middlesbrough, 187, 209, 210, 211
Midzylesie, 1095
Miercurea Ciuc, 1640, 1645
Mikkeli, 798
Mikonos, 2800

MILANO
 city plan, page 32
▶ Amsterdam, 73
▶ Ancona, 630
▶ Arona, 590
▶ Athina, 74
▶ Avignon, 90
▶ Barcelona, 90

Table numbers ❷

Table numbers ❷

Look up the two places between which you are travelling. It can often be helpful to start your search from the smaller of the two locations. ❺

Using the maps

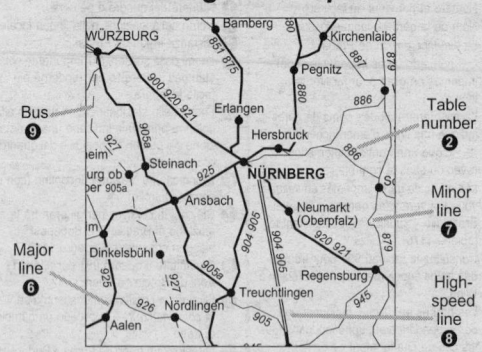

Bus ❾

Major line ❻

Table number ❷

Minor line ❼

High-speed line ❽

The maps can be the quickest way of finding the required table number, if you already know the geographical location of the places required. ❿

COMMENT TROUVER VOTRE TRAIN	COME TROVARE IL VOSTRO TRENO	WIE FINDE ICH MEINEN ZUG?	COMO BUSCAR SU TREN
❶ Localité.	❶ Località.	❶ Ortsname.	❶ Localidad.
❷ Numéros des tableaux.	❷ Numeri dei quadri-orario.	❷ Tabellennummer.	❷ Números de los cuadros horarios.
❸ Grande ville.	❸ Grandi città.	❸ Großstadt.	❸ Gran ciudad.
❹ Localités sélectionnées à gagner de la grande ville en haut.	❹ Principali destinazione raggiungibili dalla località in neretto sopra.	❹ Knotenpunkte erreichbar von der Großstadt oben.	❹ Principales destinos accesibles a través de esta localidad.
❺ Cherchez les deux bouts du parcours désiré sur la liste des villes. Commencer par la ville de moindre importance peut faciliter la recherche.	❺ Cercate le località' tra le quali dovrete viaggiare; spesso può essere di aiuto iniziare la ricerca dalla località più piccola.	❺ Suchen Sie Ihre Start- und Endbahnhof im Ortsverzeichnis. Dazu empfehlen wir, Ihre Suche aus der Richtung des kleineren Ortes aufzunehmen.	❺ Busque los dos lugares a través de los cuales viaja. Normalmente facilita la búsqueda empezar por la localidad más pequeña.
❻ Ligne principale.	❻ Principale linea ferroviaria.	❻ Hauptstrecke.	❻ Línea principal.
❼ Ligne secondaire.	❼ Linea ferroviaria secondaria.	❼ Nebenstrecke.	❼ Línea secundaria.
❽ Ligne à grande vitesse.	❽ Linea ad alta velocità.	❽ Hochgeschwindigkeitsstrecke.	❽ Línea de alta velocidad.
❾ Liaison en autocar.	❾ Autobus.	❾ Busverbindung.	❾ Línea de autobuses.
❿ La consultation des cartes – si vous savez déjà la location géographique de vos points de départ et d'arrivée – est le moyen le plus rapide de repérer les numéros des tableaux relatifs à votre parcours.	❿ Le mappe sono il metodo più rapido per trovare i numeri dei quadri-orario di cui avete bisogno, quando gia' siete a conoscenza della collocazione geografica delle località' di partenza e arrivo del vostro viaggio.	❿ Kennen Sie die geographische Lage der Ausgangs- und Bestimmungsorte Ihrer Reise, dann empfehlen wir einen Blick in die im Kursbuch enthaltene Übersichtskarte.	❿ Los mapas pueden ser la forma más rápida de encontrar los cuadros que debe consultar, si ya conoce el punto de inicio y conclusión de su viaje.

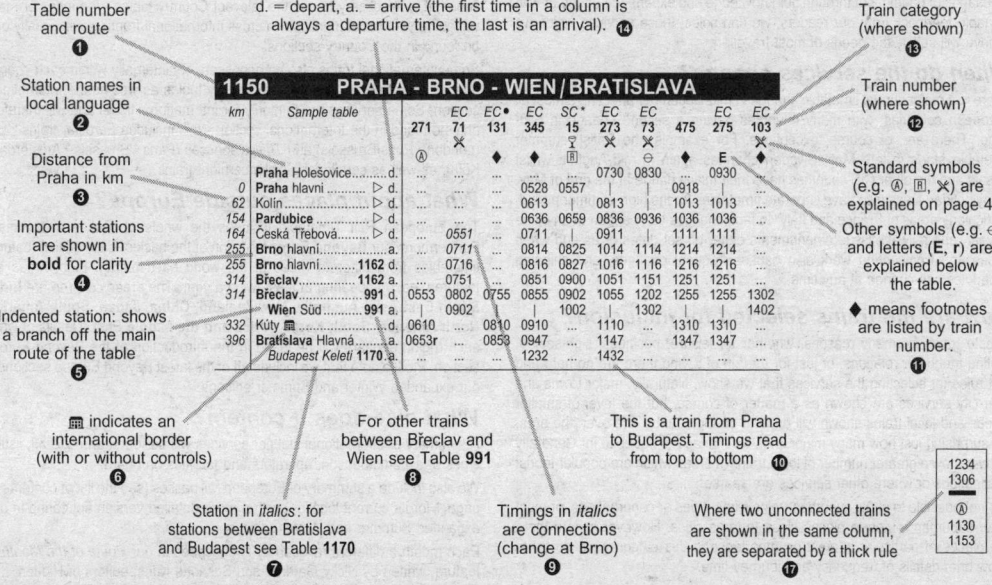

Numbers in circles refer to translations below

Reading the tables

Trains run daily unless otherwise shown by symbol or footnote ⑮

d. = depart, a. = arrive (the first time in a column is always a departure time, the last is an arrival). ⑭

Table number and route ❶

Train category (where shown) ⑬

Station names in local language ❷

Train number (where shown) ⑫

Distance from Praha in km ❸

Important stations are shown in **bold** for clarity ❹

Standard symbols (e.g. Ⓐ, ⓧ, ⓧ) are explained on page 4.

Other symbols (e.g. ⊖) and letters (**E, r**) are explained below the table.

Indented station: shows a branch off the main route of the table ❺

♦ means footnotes are listed by train number. ⑪

1150		PRAHA - BRNO - WIEN/BRATISLAVA									
km	Sample table	EC 271	EC• 71	EC 131	EC 345	SC* 15	EC 273	EC 73	475	EC 275	EC 103
		Ⓐ	ⓧ		♦	ⓧ ⊖ Ⓡ	♦	ⓧ	♦	E	♦
	Praha Holešovice ▷ d.	...	...	...	...	...	0730	0830	...	0930	...
0	**Praha** hlavní ▷ d.	...	...	...	0528	0557		0918		...	...
62	Kolín ▷ d.	...	...	...	0613		0813		1013	1013	...
154	**Pardubice** ▷ d.	...	...	...	0636	0659	0836	0936	1036	1036	...
164	Česká Třebová ▷ d.	...	0551	...	0711		0911		1111	1111	...
255	**Brno** hlavní a.	...	0711	...	0814	0825	1014	1114	1214	1214	...
255	**Brno** hlavní **1162** d.	...	0716	...	0816	0827	1016	1116	1216	1216	...
314	**Břeclav** **1162** a.	...	0751	...	0851	0900	1051	1151	1251	1251	...
314	**Břeclav** **991** d.	0553	0802	0755	0855	0902	1055	1202	1255	1255	1302
	Wien Süd **991** a.		0902			1002		1302			1402
332	Kúty ⌂ d.	0610		0810	0910		1110		1310	1310	...
396	**Bratislava** Hlavná a.	0653r		0853	0947		1147		1347	1347	...
	Budapest Keleti **1170** a.				1232		1432				...

⌂ indicates an international border (with or without controls) ❻

For other trains between Břeclav and Wien see Table **991** ❽

This is a train from Praha to Budapest. Timings read from top to bottom ❿

Station in *italics*: for stations between Bratislava and Budapest see Table **1170** ❼

Timings in *italics* are connections (change at Brno) ❾

Where two unconnected trains are shown in the same column, they are separated by a thick rule ⑰

| 1234 |
| 1306 |
| Ⓐ |
| 1130 |
| 1153 |

CLASSES OF TRAVEL:
Trains have 1st and 2nd class seats unless otherwise shown. However, local trains may only have 2nd class seats. ⑮

TIME ZONES:
Times are in local time (Russian times are in Moscow time). For time zones see page 2. Timings are given in 24 hour clock (see page 9). ⑯

COMMENT LIRE LES TABLEAUX

❶ Numéro et parcours du tableau.
❷ Nom de la gare en langue locale.
❸ La distance en km de Praha.
❹ Les noms des gares importantes sont imprimés en **gras** pour faciliter la lecture.
❺ La mise en retrait des noms de gares indique une ligne d'embranchement.
❻ ⌂ indique une frontière internationale (avec ou sans le contrôle).
❼ Les noms de gares imprimés en *italique*: vous trouverez des gares sur le trajet Bratislava - Budapest en consultant le tableau **1170**.
❽ Consultez le tableau **991** pour trouver des trains supplémentaires de Břeclav à Wien.
❾ Les heures en *italique* indiquent une *correspondance* et supposent dans tous les cas un changement de train.
❿ Ici un train de Praha à Budapest. Lire de haut en bas.
⑪ Les signes conventionnels sont expliqués à la page 4. Les autres signes et lettres sont expliqués en bas du tableau. Le symbole ♦ à l'en-tête d'une colonne signifie qu'il faut consulter la note qui porte le numéro du train concerné.
⑫ Le numéro du train (en cas échéant).
⑬ Indication de catégorie (en cas échéant).
⑭ d. = départ, a. = arrivée. Pour chaque train la *première* mention est toujours une heure de *départ*, la *dernière* toujours une heure d'*arrivée*.
⑮ Sauf indication contraire, les trains circulent *tous les jours* et y compris des places assises de 1ère et 2ème classe.
⑯ Toutes les indications horaires sont données en heures locales (voir page 2). En Russie c'est à l'heure Moskva.
⑰ Deux trains de la même colonne qui ne sont pas en correspondance sont séparés par une règle épaisse.

COME SI CONSULTA UN QUADRO ORARIO

❶ Numero del quadro e percorso.
❷ Nome della stazione nella lingua locale.
❸ Distanze in km da Praha.
❹ I nomi delle stazioni piu' importante sono stampati in *neretto* per renderne più facile la lettura.
❺ I nomi delle stazioni rientrati rispetto alla colonna principale indicano una diramazione del percorso principale del quadro-orario in questione.
❻ ⌂ indica una stazione di confine (con o senza il controllo).
❼ Stazioni in *corsivo*: per gli orari tra le stazione di Bratislava e Budapest bisogna consultare il quadro **1170**.
❽ Consultare il quadro **991** per ulteriori treni da Břeclav a Wien.
❾ Gli orari *in corsivo* si riferiscono a servizi in *coincidenza* che implicano un cambio di treno.
❿ Questo è un' treno da Praha a Budapest. La lettura viene fatta dall'alto verso il basso.
⑪ I simboli convenzionali sono spiegate a pagina 4. Altri simboli e lettere sono spiegati sotto il quadro-orario in questione. Il simbolo ♦ all'inizio di una colonna-orario significa che bisogna fare riferimento alla nota corrispondente al numero del treno in questione.
⑫ Numero del treno (quando indicato).
⑬ Classificazione del treno (quando indicato).
⑭ d. = partenza, a. = arrivo. Notare che l'orario che compare per *primo* nel quadro-orario è sempre un l'orario di *partenza*, mentre quello che compare per *ultimo* è sempre l'orario di *arrivo*.
⑮ Se non ci sono altre indicazioni i treni si intendono giornalieri, con prima e seconda classe di viaggio.
⑯ Gli orari sono sempre espressi in ora locale (in Russia e' utilizzati l'ora di Mosca). Per informazioni sui fusi orari vedere a pagina 2.
⑰ Quando nella colonna-orario ci sono due treni che non sono in coincidenza tra loro, questo e' indicato dalla linea in grassetto che li separa.

WIE LESE ICH DIE FAHRPLÄNE

❶ Tabellennummer und Strecke.
❷ Bahnhof in der Landessprache.
❸ Entfernungsangabe.
❹ Wichtige Bahnhöfe sind **fett** gedruckt um das Lesen zu vereinfachen.
❺ Eingerückte Bahnhöfe befinden sich auf einer abzweigenden Strecke.
❻ ⌂ Bezeichnet eine internationale Grenze (mit oder ohne Grenzkontrolle).
❼ *Kursiv* gedruckte Bahnhofsnamen: Bahnhöfe zwischen Bratislava und Budapest finden Sie in Tabelle **1170**.
❽ Zusätzliche Züge finden Sie in Tabelle **991**.
❾ *Kursiv* gedruckte Zeitangaben weisen immer auf das Umsteigen hin.
❿ Ein Zug von Praha nach Budapest. Sie lesen von oben nach unten.
⑪ Eine Erklärung der überall in dem Kursbuch verwendeten konventionellen Zeichen finden Sie auf Seite 4. Anderen Zeichen und Buchstaben finden Sie unter der Fahrplantabelle. Das Zeichen ♦ im Kopf der Zugspalte bedeutet: Sehen Sie bei der Fußnote des Zuges mit der betreffenden Zugnummer nach.
⑫ Zugnummer (wo zutreffend).
⑬ Zuggattung (wo zutreffend).
⑭ d. = Abfahrt, a. = Ankunft. Es handelt sich stets bei der ersten für einen Zug angegebenen Zeit um eine Abfahrtzeit, bei der letzten um eine Ankunftzeit.
⑮ Sofern nicht anders angemeldet, verkehren die Züge *täglich*. Im Allgemeinen führen die Züge die 1. und 2. Wagenklasse.
⑯ Fahrzeiten sind immer in der jeweiligen Landeszeit angegeben (Seite 2). Russische Fahrzeiten sind auf Moskauer Zeit.
⑰ Im Falle von zwei Zügen in der gleichen Spalte ohne Anschlussmöglichkeit, liegt das Zeichen ▬▬ zwischen den Zügen.

COMO LEER LOS CUADROS

❶ Número y línea del cuadro.
❷ Nombre de las estaciones en el idioma local.
❸ Distancia en km de Praga.
❹ Los nombres de las estaciones más importantes están impresas en **negrita** facilitar la lectura.
❺ La impresión sangrada de los nombres de estas estaciones significa un ramal de la línea principal.
❻ ⌂ significa una frontera internacional (con o sin control de aduanas).
❼ Estaciones impresas en *cursiva*: para las estaciones entre Bratislava y Budapest debe consultar el cuadro **1170**.
❽ Consultar el cuadro **991** para encontrar más trenes desde Břeclav hasta Viena.
❾ Los horarios en cursiva, hacen referencia a servicios de enlace, que requieren un cambio de tren.
❿ Esto un tren desde Praga hasta Budapest. Leer de arriba a abajo.
⑪ La explicación de los signos convencionales se da en la página 4. Ostros símbolos y letras se explican al pie del cuadro. El símbolo ♦ en el encabezamiento de la columna quiere decir: consulte la nota que lleva el número del tren interesado.
⑫ Número de tren (si se indica).
⑬ Tipo de tren (si se indica).
⑭ d. = salida, a. = llegada. Nótese que el primer horario indicado en las columnas es siempre un horario de salida, y el último un horario de llegada.
⑮ Salvo indicación contraria, los trenes circulan a diario y llevan plazas sentadas de primera y segunda clases.
⑯ Todas las indicaciones horarias son en horario local (Para Rusia se utiliza la hora local de Moscù). Para comprobar las franjas horarias mirar la página 2. Los horarios utilizan el sistema horario de 24h (ver página 9).
⑰ Cuando dos trenes que no tienen conexión aparecen en la misma columna, estos se encuentran separados por el símbolo ▬▬.

Reading the footnotes

These footnotes relate to the sample table on page 6
❶

In certain tables, footnotes are listed by train number, shown by ♦ on relevant trains
❷

♦ –	**NOTES** (LISTED BY TRAIN NUMBERS)
102/3 –	POLONIA – ⬜ ✗ Warszawa - Ostrava - Břeclav - Wien and v.v.
131 –	MORAVIA – ⬜ Bohumin - Ostrava - Břeclav - Bratislava.
345 –	AVALA – ⬜ ✗ Praha - Bratislava - Budapest - Beograd. Conveys on ⑤ June 12 - Sept. 18 ▬ 2 cl. Praha - Beograd (**335**) - Thessaloniki.
475 –	JADRAN – June 19 - Sept. 4. ▬ 1, 2 cl., ▬ 2 cl., ⬜ Praha - Bratislava - Zagreb - Split (Table **92**); ⬜ Praha - Bratislava.

E –	SLOVAN, not June 19 - Sept. 4.
r –	0659 on ©.
▷ –	See also Table **1160**.
⊖ –	Runs 10 mins later on Aug. 15.
● –	*Ex* in Slovakia.
* –	Pendolino tilting train. Classified *EC* in Austria.

OTHER TRAIN NAMES:

71 –	GUSTAV MAHLER
73 –	FRANZ SCHUBERT

Letters and symbols may be found above the timings (e.g. **E**) or against individual times (e.g. **r**).

Symbols may also appear in the station column (e.g. ▷).
❻

Train names are sometimes listed separately.
❺

Train 345 is named 'AVALA' and runs daily from Praha to Beograd with 1st and 2nd class seats and a restaurant car. On Fridays June 12 to September 18, a through couchette car runs from Praha to Thessaloniki, attached to train 335 between Beograd and Thessaloniki.
❸

Train 475 is named 'JADRAN' and runs only from June 19 to September 4. It has a sleeper, couchettes and second class seats from Praha to Split via Bratislava and Zagreb, as well as first and second class seats only going as far as Bratislava. Further details will be found in Table 92.
❹

Always read the footnotes; they may contain important information. Standard symbols are explained on page 4.
❼

Dates shown are where a train **starts** its journey (unless otherwise noted). Some notes show both directions of the train (e.g. **102/3**) with "and v.v."
❽

FURTHER HINTS ON READING THE TIMETABLE

- Refer to the introduction to each country for important information such as train types, supplements, compulsory reservation, and the dates of validity of the timings. Exceptions are noted in individual tables.
- For dates of public holidays see page 2.

- Please allow adequate time for changing trains, especially at large stations. Connections are not guaranteed, especially when late running occurs (connecting trains are sometimes held for late running trains).
- A Glossary of common terms appears on page 10.

LES NOTES EN BAS DU TABLEAU

❶ Ces notes se rapportent à l'exemple de tableau à la page 6.

❷ Dans certains tableaux, le symbole ♦ à l'en-tête d'une colonne signifie qu'il faut consulter la note qui porte le numéro du train concerné.

❸ Le train 345 s'appelle AVALA et circule tous les jours de Praha à Beograd avec des places assises de 1ère et 2ème classe et une voiture-restaurant. Tous les vendredis du 12 juin jusqu'au 18 sept il y a aussi une voiture-couchettes de Praha à Thessaloniki, qui se joint au train 335 entre Beograd et Thessaloniki.

❹ Le train 475 s'appelle JADRAN et circule seulement entre le 19 juin et le 4 septembre. Il comprend des voitures-lits, couchettes et places assises de 2ème classe à Split via Zagreb, et des places assises de 1ère et 2ème classe jusqu'à Bratislava. Voir le tableau **92**.

❺ Les noms des trains sont parfois indiqués séparément.

❻ Les lettres et signes sont situés à l'en-tête d'une colonne ou à côté d'une heure dans la colonne. Une signe peut sortir également à côté d'un nom de gare.

❼ Les notes peuvent vous donner des informations importantes. Les signes conventionnels sont expliqués à la page 4.

❽ Sauf indication contraire, les jours et dates de circulation mentionnés sont ceux applicables à la *gare d'origine* du train (mentionnée si elle ne figure pas sur le tableau même dans les notes). Les notes peuvent expliquer les deux sens d'un train (e.g. **102/3**) utilisant "and v.v." (et vice versa).

PLUS DE CONSEILS

- Il vous est fortement recommandé de consulter aussi l'introduction à chaque section nationale: vous y trouverez des précisions concernant la classification des trains, les prestations offertes à bord des trains, les suppléments, la réservation des places, etc.
- Jours fériés - voir page 2.
- Aucune correspondance n'est garantie pourtant. N'oubliez pas non plus que dans les grandes gares les changements peuvent entraîner une longue marche et l'emprunt d'escaliers.
- Lexique - voir page 10.

NOTE ALLA FINE DEL QUADRO-ORARIO

❶ Queste note si riferiscono all' esempio a pagina 6.

❷ In certi quadri-orario, il simbolo ♦ nelle note di testa significa che bisogna fare riferimento alla nota con il numero di treno corrispondente.

❸ Il treno 345 si chiama AVALA ed e' giornaliero tra Praha a Beograd con posti di 1ª e 2ª classe e carrozza ristorante. Il venerdì dal 12 giugno fino al 18 settembre e' aggiunta a Beograd una carrozza cuccette diretta a Thessaloniki, combinandosi con il treno 335 tra Beograd e Thessaloniki.

❹ Il treno 475 si chiama JADRAN ed e' operativo solo dal 19 giugno al 4 settembre. Il treno si compone di carrozze letti, carrozze cuccette, e posti di 2ª classe tra Praha e Split, via Bratislava e Zagrabria; inoltre ci sono anche posti di 1ª e 2ª classe fino a Bratislava. Consultare anche il quadro-orario **92** al riguardo.

❺ I nomi dei treni sono talvolta indicati separatamente.

❻ Lettere e simboli possono essere sia alla testa di una colonna-orario, che accanto all'orario del treno stesso. Un simbolo potrebbe anche essere accanto al nome di una stazione.

❼ E' importante leggere sempre le note a le informazioni a fine quadro. I segni convenzionali sono elencati e spiegati a pagina 4.

❽ Salvo casi in cui sia diversamente indicato, le date di circolazione dei treni si riferiscono sempre alla stazione dove il treno inizia il suo viaggio (come viene riportato nelle note a fine quadro, e Inoltre nel quadro stesso).

ALTRI CONSIGLI UTILI

- Vi consigliamo vivamente di consultare anche l'introduzione dedicata ad ogni nazione. Troverete importanti informazioni riguardanti i servizi di trasporto di ciascun paese, così come le categorie dei treni, la ristorazione, il pagamento di supplementi, la necessità di prenotazione, ecc.
- I giorni festivi suddivisi per paese sono elencati a pagina 2.
- Le coincidenze indicate non sono garantite. Tenete presente che che nelle grandi stazioni il trasferimento tra due binari potrebbe significare un lungo tratto da percorrere a piedi e con l'uso di scale.
- Il glossario si trova a pagina 10.

FUSSNOTEN

❶ Fußnoten beziehen sich auf die Beispieltabelle auf Seite 6.

❷ ♦ : Sehen Sie bei der Fußnote des Zuges mit der betreffenden Zugnummer nach.

❸ Zug 345 heißt AVALA und fährt täglich zwischen Praha und Beograd mit Sitzplätzen 1. und 2. Klasse. An Freitagen vom 12. Juni bis 18. September führt dieser Zug durchgehende Liegewagen von Praha nach Thessaloniki (mit Zug 335 vereinigt von Beograd nach Thessaloniki).

❹ Zug 475 heißt JADRAN und fährt nur von 19. Juni bis 4. September. Er führt Schlaf-, Liege und Sitzwagen 2. Klasse von Praha nach Split über Zagreb, auch Sitzwagen 1. und 2. Klasse, die nur bis Bratislava fahren. Auf Tabelle 92 finden Sie weitere Informationen.

❺ Zugnamen können besonders aufgeführt sein.

❻ Zeichen und Buchstaben finden sich im Kopf der Zugspalte oder neben einer bestimmten Zeitangabe. Zeichen sind auch in der Bahnhofsspalte möglich.

❼ In Fußnoten findet man wichtige Informationen. Standardzeichen sind auf Seite 4 erklärt.

❽ Die erwähnten Tage und Zeitabschnitte für Züge, die nicht täglich verkehren, gelten für den Ausgangsbahnhof des Zuges (wenn dieser nicht in der Tabelle steht, ist er in der Fußnote erwähnt). Fußnoten dürfen beide Richtungen erklären (z.B. **102/3**), mit "and v.v." (und abgekehrt).

WEITERE HINWEISE

- Es ist zu empfehlen, die Einleitungen zu jedem einzelnen Land zu lesen. Darin werden Sie wichtige Informationen über die Besonderheiten jedes Landes finden: Zugcharakterisierung, Services an Bord der Züge, Zuschlagpflicht, Reservierungsbedingungen usw.
- Feiertage - siehe Seite 2.
- Anschlussversäumnisse durch Verspätung oder Ausfall von Zügen sind immer möglich. Bitte beachten Sie, dass auf Großstadtbahnhöfen häufig längere Fußwege zurückgelegt bzw. Treppen benutzen werden müssen.
- Glossar - siehe Seite 10.

LAS NOTAS AL PIE DEL CUADRO

❶ Estas notas hacen referencia al ejemplo de la página 6.

❷ El símbolo ♦ ciertas tablas horarias significa: que hay que consultar la nota a pie de página con el número correspondiente.

❸ El Tren 345 se llama AVALA y circula a diario entre Praga y Belgrado con plazas sentadas de 1ra y 2da clase, además de con coche-restaurante. Los Viernes del 12 de junio al 18 de septiembre el tren lleva coches litera desde Praga hasta Tesalónica que se combinan con el tren 335 entre Belgrado y Tesalónica.

❹ El Tren 475 se llama JADRAN y circula solamente del 19 de junio al 4 de septiembre. El Tren 475 se llama JADRAN y circula del 19 de junio al 4 de sept. El tren dispone de lleva vagones de coches cama, litera, y plazas sentadas de 2da clase entre Praga y Split a través de Zagreb, también plazas sentadas de 1ra y 2da clase hasta Bratislava. Consulte el cuadro **92**.

❺ Los nombres de los Trenes a veces son enumerados por separado.

❻ Las letras y signos se encuentran en el encabezamiento de las distintas columnas horarias o adyacentes a horas de salida individuales. Los símbolos también pueden aparecer en la columna de la estación.

❼ Lea siempre las notas a pie de cuadro ya que pueden contener información importante. La explicación de los signos convencionales se da en la página 4.

❽ Salvo indicación contraria los días y fechas de circulación de los trenes son aquéllos mencionados en la estación de *origen* del tren. Algunas notas muestran ambas direcciones del tren mediante la nota "and v.v." (y viceversa).

INFORMACIÓN ADICIONAL

- Se recomienda vivamente que consulte también los preámbulos al comienzo de cada sección nacional: le proporcionarán datos importantes sobre las particularidades de cada país: tipos de trenes, restauración, pago de suplementos, y necesidades de reservación anticipada.
- Días festivos - consulte la página 2.
- Los trasbordos no se pueden garantizar, sobretodo en el caso de retrasos. Hay que ser consciente también que el trasbordo en las estaciones de grandes ciudades puede suponer un desplazamiento bastante largo a pie y el uso de escaleras.
- Glosario - consulte la página 10.

The following is designed to be an outline guide to travelling around Europe by train. For further details of types of accommodation available, catering, supplements etc., see the introduction to each country.

BUYING YOUR TICKET

Train tickets must be purchased before travelling, either from travel agents or at the station ticket office (or machine). Where a station has neither a ticket office nor a ticket machine, the ticket may usually be purchased on the train.

Tickets which are not dated when purchased (for example in France and Italy) must be validated before travel in one of the machines at the entrance to the platform.

In certain Eastern European countries foreign nationals may have to buy international rail tickets at the office of the state tourist board concerned and not at the railway station. The tickets can sometimes only be purchased in western currency and buying tickets can take a long time.

Most countries in Europe offer two classes of rail accommodation, usually 1st and 2nd class. 1st class is more comfortable and therefore more expensive than 2nd class. Local trains are often 2nd class only. In Southern and Eastern Europe, 1st class travel is advisable for visitors as fares are reasonable and 2nd class can be very overcrowded.

RESERVATIONS

Many express trains in Europe are restricted to passengers holding advance seat reservations, particularly in France, Italy, Sweden and Spain. This is indicated by the symbol ▣ in the tables, or by notes in the introduction to each country. All *TGV, Eurostar* and *Thalys* trains require advance reservation, as do all long-distance trains in Spain.

Reservations can usually be made up to two months in advance. A small fee is charged, but where a supplement is payable the reservation fee is often included. Reservations can often be made on other long-distance services and this is recommended at busy times.

SUPPLEMENTS

Many countries have faster train services for which an extra charge is made. This supplement is payable when the ticket is purchased and often includes the price of a seat reservation. The supplement can sometimes be paid on the train, but usually at extra cost. The introduction to each country gives further information. On certain high-speed services, the first class fare includes the provision of a meal.

RAIL PASSES

Passes are available which give unlimited travel on most trains in a given area. These range from Interrail and Eurail passes which cover most of Europe for up to one month, to local passes which cover limited areas for one day. Further details of Interrail and Eurail passes appear elsewhere in this edition, and a special feature on rail passes appears in the twice-yearly Independent Travellers Edition.

FINDING YOUR TRAIN

At most stations departures are listed on large paper sheets (often yellow), and/or on electronic departure indicators. These list trains by departure, giving principal stops, and indicate from which platform they leave.

On each platform of principal European stations, a display board can be found giving details of the main trains calling at that platform. This includes the location of individual coaches, together with their destinations and the type of accommodation provided.

A sign may be carried on the side of the carriage indicating the train name, principal stops and destination and a label or sign near the door will indicate the number allocated to the carriage, which is shown on reservation tickets. 1st class accommodation is usually indicated by a yellow band above the windows and doors and/or a figure '1' near the door or on the windows

A sign above the compartment door will indicate seat numbers and which seats are reserved. In non-compartment trains, reserved seats have labels on their headrests. In some countries reserved seats are not marked and occupants will be asked to move when the passenger who has reserved the seat boards the train.

LUGGAGE & BICYCLES

Luggage may be registered at many larger stations and sent separately by rail to your destination. In some countries, bicycles may also be registered in advance and certain local and some express trains will convey bicycles (there may be a charge). The relevant railways will advise exact details on request.

✕ CATERING ♀

Many high-quality and long-distance trains in Europe have restaurant cars serving full meals, usually with waiter service. An at-seat service may also be provided to passengers in first class accommodation. Such trains are identified with the symbol ✕ in the tables. Full meals may only be available at set times, sometimes with separate sittings, and may only be available to passengers holding first class tickets. However, the restaurant car is often supplemented by a counter or trolley service offering light snacks and drinks.

Other types of catering are shown with the symbol ♀. This varies from a self-service buffet car serving light meals (sometimes called bistro or café) to a trolley which is wheeled through the train, serving drinks and light refreshments. Where possible, the introduction to each country gives further information on the level of catering to be expected on particular types of train.

Please note that the catering shown may not be available throughout the journey and may be suspended or altered at weekends or on holidays.

SLEEPING CARS 🛏

Sleeping cars are indicated by the symobol 🛏 in the tables. Standard sleeping car types have bedroom style compartments with limited washing facilities and full bedding. Toilets are located at one or both ends of the coach. An attendant travels with each car or pair of cars and will serve drinks, snacks and breakfast at an extra charge. 1st class sleeping compartments have one or two berths (in Britain and Norway, and in older Swedish sleeping cars, two berth compartments require only 2nd class tickets) and 2nd class compartments have three berths. Some trains convey special T2 cabins, shown as 🛏 (T2) in the tables, with one berth in 1st class and two berths in 2nd class.

Compartments are allocated for occupation exclusively by men or by women except when married couples or families occupy all berths. Children travelling alone, or who cannot be accommodated in the same compartment as their family, are placed in women's compartments. In Russia and other countries of the CIS, however, berths are allocated in strict order of booking and men and women often share the same compartments.

Some trains have communicating doors between sleeping compartments which can be opened to create a larger room if both compartments are occupied by the same family group. Berths can be reserved up to 2 months (3 months on certain trains) before the date of travel and early reservation is recommended as space is limited, especially on French ski trains and in Eastern Europe. Berths must be claimed within 15 minutes of boarding the train or they may be resold.

HOTEL TRAINS

High quality overnight trains, often referred to as Hotel trains, run on a selection of national and international routes. The facilities are of a higher standard than those offered in conventional sleeping cars, and special fares are payable. The trains fall into the following categories:

ÖBB nightjet : Many night trains radiating from Germany and Austria, are operated by Austrian Railways and are branded *ÖBB nightjet*. They operate on 17 routes serving four countries and all convey sleeping-car, couchette and seating accommodation. Standard sleeping-car compartments can be configured with one, two or three berths and have a washbasin (with toiletries provided). *Deluxe* sleeping-car compartments can also be configured with one, two or three berths and have an en-suite washroom with WC, washbasin and shower (shower gel and towels are provided). The sleeping-car fare includes a welcome drink, a bottle of water, a newspaper and a full breakfast served in the morning (including free hot drink refills). Four and six berth couchettes are available, the price of which includes a bottle of water and a small breakfast. Women only, family and wheelchair couchette compartments are provided. 2nd class seating cars (with six seat compartments) are also conveyed. Reservation is compulsory in all categories of accommodation and special all-inclusive fares are available. Please note that Interrail and Eurail pass holders must pay a special pass holders fare.

Trenhotel (Spain). These *Talgo*-type trains run on the international routes from Madrid to Lisboa and from Irún/Hendaye to Lisboa. They also operate on internal routes within Spain, from Barcelona to A Coruña, Granada and Vigo, and from Madrid to A Coruña, Ferrol and Pontevedra. The highest class of accommodation is *Gran Clase*, which has shower and toilet facilities in each compartment and can be used for single or double occupancy.

Compartments with showers are also available on some domestic overnight services in Sweden and Italy, and on certain other international routes as indicated on our international overnight services summary on page 33.

COUCHETTES ▭

Couchettes (▭) are a more basic form of overnight accommodation consisting of simple bunk beds with a sheet, blanket and pillow. The couchettes are converted from ordinary seating cars for the night, and there are usually 4 berths per compartment in 1st class, 6 berths in 2nd class. On certain trains (e.g. in Austria and Italy), 4 berth compartments are available to 2nd class passengers, at a higher supplement. Washing and toilet facilities are provided at the ends of each coach. Men and women are booked into the same compartments and are expected to sleep in daytime clothes. A small number of trains in Germany, however, have women-only couchette compartments.

INTERNATIONAL OVERNIGHT SERVICES

A summary of international overnight services will be found on page 33 which specifies the various types of accommodation and catering provided on each individual service (including details of the operator).

CAR-SLEEPERS

Trains which convey motor cars operate throughout much of Europe and are shown in Table **1** for international services and Table **2** for other services. The motor cars are conveyed in special wagons while passengers travel in sleeping cars or couchettes, usually (but not always) in the same train.

WHEELCHAIR ACCESS ♿

Most main-line domestic and international trains, together with an increasing number of local trains, are specially equipped to accommodate passengers in wheelchairs. Access ramps are available at many stations and some trains are fitted with special lifts. These trains have at least one wheelchair space, and are equipped with accessible toilets.

Most railways publish guides to accessibility, and many countries provide dedicated staff to assist disabled travellers. Wheelchair users normally need to reserve in advance, stating their requirements.

HEALTH REQUIREMENTS

It is not mandatory for visitors to Europe to be vaccinated against infectious diseases unless they are travelling from areas where these are endemic. For travellers' peace of mind, however, protection against the following diseases should be considered:

HIV	Cholera
Hepatitis A	Hepatitis B
Polio	Rabies
Tetanus	Typhoid

Full information is available from the manual published by the World Health Organisation, and travellers should seek advice from their Travel Agent.

DRINKING WATER

Tap water is usually safe to drink in most parts of Europe. The water in washrooms or toilets on trains is, however, not suitable for drinking. Those who doubt the purity of the tap water are recommended to boil it, to use sterilisation tablets, or to drink bottled water.

CLIMATE

Most of Europe lies within the temperate zone but there can be considerable differences between North and South, East and West, as illustrated in the table below. Local temperatures are also affected by altitude and the difference between summer and winter temperatures tends to be less marked in coastal regions than in areas far removed from the sea.

	Bucuresti	Dublin	Madrid	Moskva
JANUARY				
Highest	2°	8°	10°	− 6°
Lowest	− 6°	3°	3°	− 12°
Rain days	6	13	9	11
APRIL				
Highest	18°	11°	18°	10°
Lowest	6°	4°	7°	2°
Rain days	7	10	11	9
JULY				
Highest	29°	19°	31°	23°
Lowest	16°	11°	18°	14°
Rain days	7	9	3	12
OCTOBER				
Highest	18°	14°	19°	8°
Lowest	6°	8°	10°	2°
Rain days	5	11	9	10

Highest = Average highest daily temperature in °C
Lowest = Average lowest daily temperature in °C
Rain days = Average number of days with recorded precipitation
Source: World Weather Information Service

FIND US ON FACEBOOK!

www.facebook.com/EuropeanRailTimetable

and on **Twitter** @EuropeanRailTT

METRIC CONVERSION TABLES

The Celsius system of temperature measurement, the metric system of distance measurement and the twenty-four hour clock are used throughout this book. The tables below give Fahrenheit, mile and twelve-hour clock equivalents.

CURRENCY CONVERSION

The information shown below is intended to be indicative only.
Rates fluctuate from day to day and commercial exchange rates normally include a commission element.

Country	unit	1 GBP =	1 USD =	1 EUR =	100 JPY =
Euro zone (‡)	**euro**	**1.18**	**0.93**	**1.00**	**0.82**
Albania	lek	160.96	126.63	135.92	111.13
Belarus	rubl	2.55	2.00	2.15	1.76
Bosnia	marka	2.32	1.82	1.96	1.60
Bulgaria	lev	2.32	1.82	1.96	1.60
Croatia	kuna	8.93	7.03	7.54	6.15
Czech Republic	koruna	32.02	25.19	27.03	22.10
Denmark	krone	8.81	6.93	7.44	6.08
Georgia	lari	3.25	2.56	2.75	2.24
Hungary	forint	371.11	291.96	313.37	256.21
Iceland	krona	140.40	110.45	118.56	96.93
Macedonia	denar	72.93	57.3	61.58	50.34
Moldova	leu	25.57	20.12	21.60	17.65
Norway	krone	10.65	8.34	8.99	7.35
Poland	złoty	5.29	4.16	4.46	3.65
Romania	leu nou	5.33	4.19	4.50	3.68
Russia	rubl	81.21	63.89	68.56	56.07
Serbia	dinar	145.98	114.84	123.26	100.78
Sweden	krona	11.60	9.13	9.80	8.01
Switzerland	franc	1.28	1.01	1.08	0.88
Turkey	yeni lira	4.37	3.44	3.69	3.02
Ukraine	hryvnya	33.17	26.10	28.01	22.90
United Kingdom	pound	1.00	0.78	0.84	0.69
United States	dollar	1.27	1.00	1.07	0.87

‡ – Austria, Belgium, Cyprus, Estonia, Finland, France, Germany, Greece, Ireland, Italy, Latvia, Lithuania, Luxembourg, Malta, the Netherlands, Portugal, Slovakia, Slovenia and Spain.

The euro is also legal tender in Andorra, Kosovo, Monaco, Montenegro, San Marino, and the Vatican City.

PASSPORTS AND VISAS

Nationals of one country intending to travel to or pass through another country normally require a valid passport and will also require a visa unless a special visa-abolition agreement has been made between the countries concerned. The limit of stay permitted in each country is usually 3 months.

Applications for visas should be made well in advance of the date of travel to the local consulate of the country concerned. Consuls usually make a charge for issuing a visa. Before issuing a transit visa, a consul normally requires to see the visa of the country of destination.

The possession of a valid passport or visa does not necessarily grant the holder automatic access to all areas of the country to be visited. Certain countries have zones which are restricted or prohibited to foreign nationals.

All border controls have been abolished, however, between those countries which have signed the **Schengen Agreement** (see list below), and a visa allowing entry to any of these countries is valid in all of them.

LIST OF SCHENGEN AREA COUNTRIES

Austria, Belgium, Czech Republic, Denmark, Estonia, Finland, France, Germany, Greece, Hungary, Iceland, Italy, Latvia, Lithuania, Luxembourg, Malta, Netherlands, Norway, Poland, Portugal, Slovakia, Slovenia, Spain, Sweden, Switzerland.

TEMPERATURE

°C	°F
−20	−4
−15	5
−10	14
−5	23
0	32
5	41
10	50
15	59
20	68
25	77
30	86
35	95
40	104

Conversion formulae :
°C = (°F – 32) x 5 / 9
°F = (°C x 9 / 5) + 32

DISTANCE

km	miles	km	miles	km	miles
1	0.62	45	27.96	300	186.41
2	1.24	50	31.07	400	248.55
3	1.86	55	34.18	500	310.69
4	2.49	60	37.28	600	372.82
5	3.11	65	40.39	700	434.96
6	3.73	70	43.50	800	497.10
7	4.35	75	46.60	900	559.23
8	4.97	80	49.71	1000	621.37
9	5.59	85	52.82	1100	683.51
10	6.21	90	55.92	1200	745.65
15	9.32	95	59.03	1300	807.78
20	12.43	100	62.14	1400	869.92
25	15.53	125	77.67	1500	932.06
30	18.64	150	93.21	2000	1242.74
35	21.75	175	108.74	3000	1864.11
40	24.85	200	124.27	4000	2485.48

TIME

24 hour clock

Midnight departure = 0000
1 am = 0100
5 am = 0500
5.30 am = 0530
11 am = 1100
12 noon = 1200
1 pm = 1300
3.45 pm = 1545
Midnight arrival = 2400

⚬━	FRANCAIS	ITALIANO	DEUTSCH	ESPAÑOL
additional trains	d'autres trains	ulteriori treni	weitere Züge	otros trenes
also	[circule] aussi	[si effettua] anche	[verkehrt] auch	[circula] también
alteration	modification	variazione	Änderung	modificación
approximately	environ	circa	ungefähr	aproximadamente
arrival, arrives (a.)	arrivée, arrive	arrivo, arriva	Ankunft, kommt an	llegada, llega
and at the same minutes past each hour until	puis toutes les heures aux mêmes minutes jusqu'à	poi ai stessi minuti di ogni ora fino a	und so weiter im Takt bis	luego a los mismos minutos de cada hora hasta
calls at	s'arrête à	ferma a	hält in	efectúa parada en
certain	déterminé	certo	bestimmt	determinado
change at	changer à	cambiare a	umsteigen in	cambiar en
composition	composition	composizione	Zugbildung	composición
confirmation	confirmation	conferma	Bestätigung	confirmación
connection	correspondance, relation	coincidenza, relazione	Anschluss, Verbindung	correspondencia, enlace
conveys	comporte, achemine	ha in composizione	befördert, führt	lleva
daily	tous les jours	giornalmente	täglich	diariamente
delay	retard	ritardo	Verspätung	retraso
departure, departs (d.)	départ, part	partenza, parte	Abfahrt, fährt ab	salida, sale
earlier	plus tôt	più presto	früher	más temprano
engineering work	travaux de voie	lavori sul binario	Bauarbeiten	obras de vía
even / uneven dates	jours pairs / impairs	giorni pari / dispari	gerade / ungerade Daten	fechas pares / impares
every 30 minutes	toutes les 30 minutes	ogni 30 minuti	alle 30 Minuten	cada 30 minutos
except	sauf	escluso	außer	excepto
fast(er)	(plus) rapide	(più) rapido	schnell(er)	(más) rápido
for	pour	per	für	para
from Rennes	(en provenance) de Rennes	(proviene) da Rennes	von Rennes	(procede) de Rennes
from Jan. 15	à partir du 15 janvier	dal 15 di gennaio	vom 15. Januar (an)	desde el 15 de enero
hourly	toutes les heures	ogni ora	stündlich	cada hora
hours (hrs)	heures	ore	Stunden	horas
journey	voyage, trajet	viaggio, percorso	Reise	viaje, trayecto
journey time	temps de parcours	tempo di tragitto	Reisezeit	duración del recorrido
later	plus tard	più tardi	später	más tarde
may	peut, peuvent	può, possono	kann, können	puede(n)
minutes (mins)	minutes	minuti	Minuten	minutos
not	ne [circule] pas	non [si effettua]	[verkehrt] nicht	no [circula]
not available	pas disponible	non disponibile	nicht erhältlich	no disponible
on the dates shown in Table 81	les jours indiqués dans le tableau 81	nei giorni indicati nel quadro 81	an den in der Tabelle 81 angegebene Daten	los días indicados en el cuadro 81
only	seulement	esclusivamente	nur	sólo
operator	entreprise de transports	azienda di trasporto	Verkehrsunternehmen	empresa de transportes
other	autre	altro	andere	otros
runs	circule	circola, si effettua	verkehrt	circula
sailing	traversée	traversata	Überfahrt	travesía
ship	bateau, navire	nave, battello	Schiff	barco
stopping trains	trains omnibus	treni regionali	Nahverkehrszüge	trenes regionales
stops	s'arrête	ferma	hält	efectúa parada
subject to	sous réserve de	soggetto a	vorbehaltlich	sujeto a
summer	été	estate	Sommer	verano
supplement payable	avec supplément	con pagamento di supplemento	zuschlagpflichtig	con pago de suplemento
then	puis	poi	dann	luego
through train	train direct	treno diretto	durchgehender Zug	tren directo
timings	horaires	orari	Zeitangaben	horarios
to York	vers, à destination de York	(diretto) a York	nach York	(continúa) a York
to / until July 23	jusqu'au 23 juillet	fino al 23 di luglio	bis zum 23. Juli	hasta el día 23 de julio
to pick up	pour laisser monter	per viaggiatori in partenza	zum Zusteigen	para recoger viajeros
to set down	pour laisser descendre	per viaggiatori in arrivo	zum Aussteigen	para dejar viajeros
unless otherwise shown	sauf indication contraire	salvo indicazione contraria	sofern nicht anders angezeigt	salvo indicación contraria
valid	valable	valido	gültig	válido
when train 44 runs	lors de la circulation du train 44	quando circola il treno 44	beim Verkehren des Zuges 44	cuando circula el tren 44
winter	hiver	inverno	Winter	invierno

INDEX OF PLACES by table number

The BEYOND EUROPE section is indexed separately - see the back of each edition

🚍 Connection by train from the nearest station shown in this timetable.
🚢 Connection by boat from the nearest station shown in this timetable.
🚌 Connection by bus from the nearest station shown in this timetable.
10 / 355 Consult both indicated tables to find the best connecting services.

CRUISE TRAINS

The services shown in the European Rail Timetable are the regular scheduled services of the railway companies concerned. However, a number of specialised operators also run luxurious cruise trains taking several days to complete their journey. Overnight accommodation is provided either on the train or in hotels. Cruise trains are bookable only through the operating company or its appointed agents and normal rail tickets are not valid on these trains. A selection of operators is shown below.

The Danube Express : Fully escorted holidays in central and eastern Europe by luxury private train based in Budapest. Operator: Danube Express, Offley Holes Farm, Charlton Road, Preston, Hitchin, SG4 7TD, UK; ✆ +44 (0)1462 441400. Website: www.danube-express.com

Belmond Royal Scotsman : Luxury tours of Scotland starting from Edinburgh. Operator: Belmond Royal Scotsman, Shackleton House, 4 Battle Bridge Lane, London, SE1 2HP, UK; ✆ 0845 217 0799 (UK only) or +44 (0) 20 3117 1300. Website: www.royalscotsman.com

El Transcantábrico and **El Expreso de La Robla** : Rail cruises along Spain's northern coast. Operator: Trenes Turísticos de Lujo, Plaza de los Ferroviarios s/n., 33012 Oviedo, Asturias, Spain; ✆ + 34 902 555 902, fax + 34 985 981 711. Website: www.trenesturisticosdelujo.com

Trans-Siberian Express : Tours by private hotel train along the Trans-Siberian Railway. Operator: Golden Eagle Luxury Trains, Denzell House, Denzell Gardens, Dunham Road, Altrincham, WA14 4QF, UK; ✆ +44 (0)16 1 928 9410, fax +44 (0)161 941 6101. Website: www.goldeneagleluxurytrains.com

Venice Simplon-Orient-Express : This well-known luxury train runs once or twice weekly from late March to early November, mostly on its established London - Paris - Venezia route. Operator: Belmond VSOE, Shackleton House, 4 Battle Bridge Lane, London, SE1 2HP, UK; ✆ 0845 217 0799 (UK only) or +44 (0) 20 3117 1300. Website: www.vsoe.com

LIST OF ADVERTISERS

CITY STATION LOCATION PLANS

———	Passenger railway	▬█▬	Main station
- - - -	Metro	▬■▬	Local station
·····🚌···🚃····	Bus / tram line	🚌	Bus station
·····⛴·····	Ferry	✈	Airport

Only those metro, bus, and tram lines which provide inter-station links or connect outlying main stations to the city centre are shown.

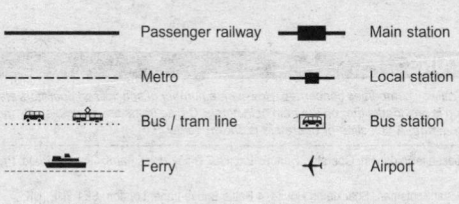

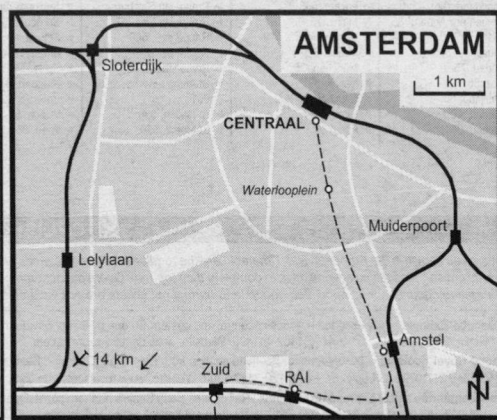

AMSTERDAM

1 km

Sloterdijk

CENTRAAL

Waterlooplein

Muiderpoort

Lelylaan

Amstel

✈ 14 km ↙

Zuid

RAI

N

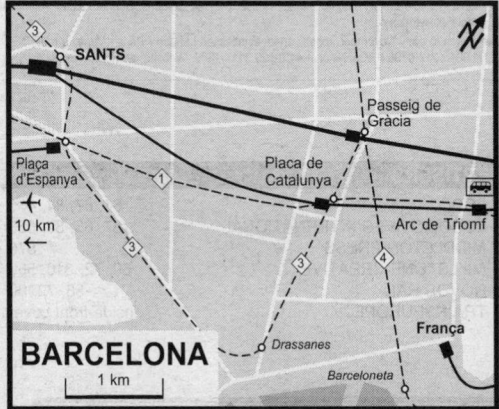

BARCELONA

1 km

SANTS

Passeig de Gràcia

Plaça d'Espanya

Plaça de Catalunya

10 km ←

Arc de Triomf

França

Drassanes

Barceloneta

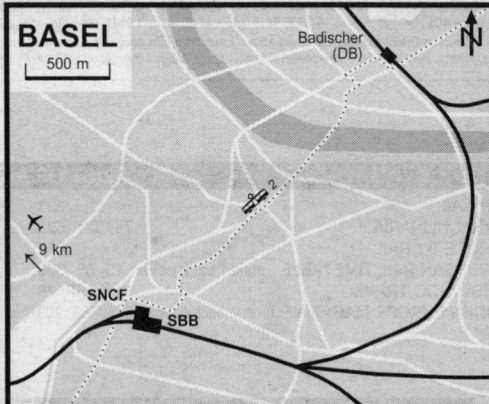

BASEL

500 m

Badischer (DB)

✈ 9 km ↙

SNCF

SBB

N

BELFAST

250 m

Ferry Terminal

✈ City ↗

Laganside

✈ International 26 km ←

City Hall

Europa

Great Victoria Street

CENTRAL

City Hospital

Botanic

N

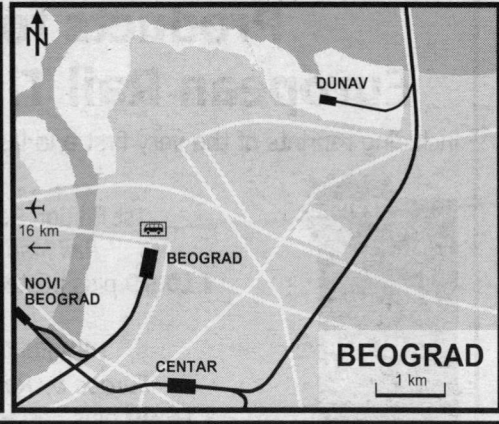

BEOGRAD

1 km

DUNAV

✈ 16 km ←

BEOGRAD

NOVI BEOGRAD

CENTAR

N

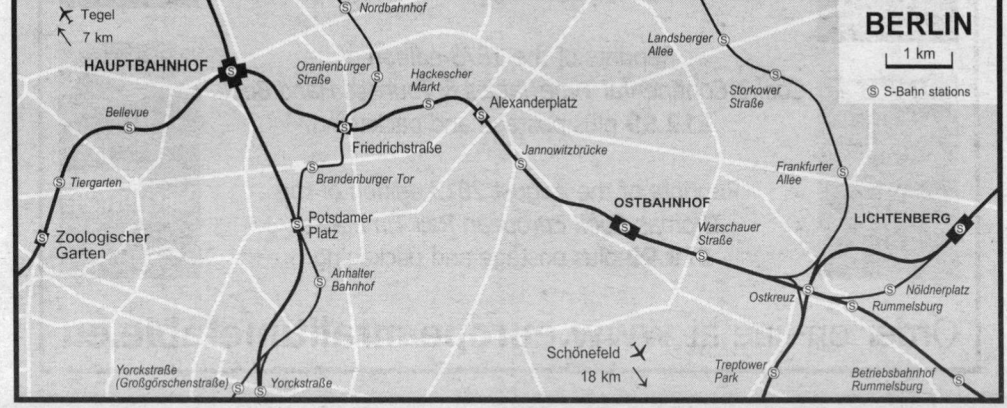

BERLIN

1 km

Ⓢ S-Bahn stations

✈ Tegel 7 km ↖

Nordbahnhof

HAUPTBAHNHOF

Oranienburger Straße

Hackescher Markt

Landsberger Allee

Alexanderplatz

Storkower Straße

Bellevue

Ⓢ Tiergarten

Friedrichstraße

Jannowitzbrücke

Brandenburger Tor

Frankfurter Allee

Potsdamer Platz

OSTBAHNHOF

LICHTENBERG

Zoologischer Garten

Warschauer Straße

Anhalter Bahnhof

Nöldnerplatz

Ostkreuz

Rummelsburg

Yorckstraße (Großgörschenstraße)

Yorckstraße

Schönefeld ✈ 18 km ↘

Treptower Park

Betriebsbahnhof Rummelsburg

BRUSSELS

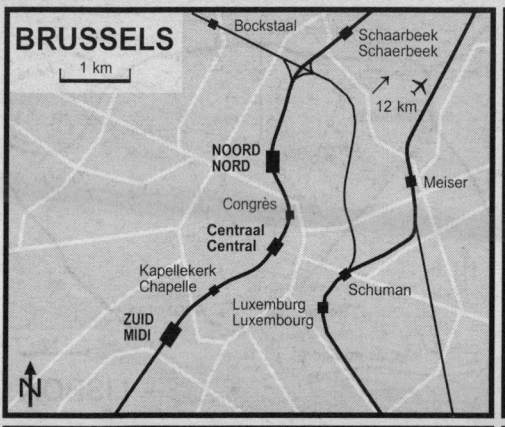

1 km

Bockstaal
Schaarbeek
Schaerbeek
✈ 12 km
NOORD
NORD
Meiser
Congrès
Centraal
Central
Kapellekerk
Chapelle
Luxemburg
Luxembourg
Schuman
ZUID
MIDI
N

BUDAPEST

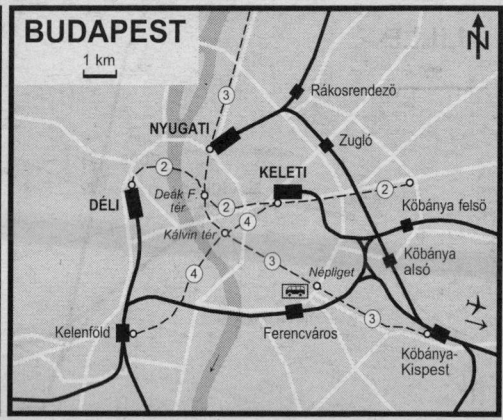

1 km

N
Rákosrendezö
③
NYUGATI
Zugló
KELETI
②
Deák F.
DÉLI ② tér
Köbánya felsö
②
Kálvin tér
④
Köbánya
alsó
④
Népliget
③
Kelenföld
Ferencváros
③
Köbánya-
Kispest

DUBLIN

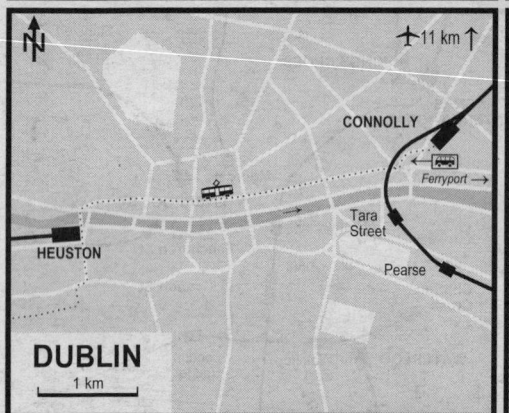

N
✈ 11 km ↑

CONNOLLY
Ferryport →
Tara
Street
HEUSTON
Pearse

1 km

FRANKFURT / MAIN

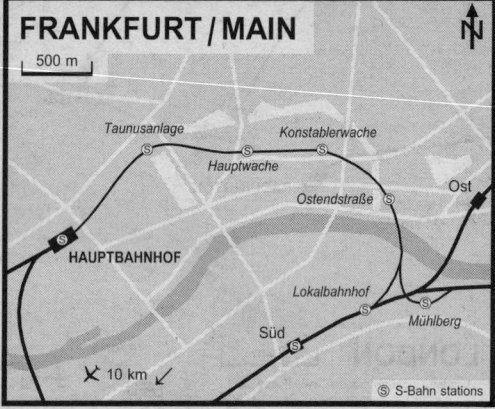

500 m
N

Taunusanlage
Konstablerwache
Ⓢ
Ⓢ
Hauptwache
Ostendstraße
Ⓢ
Ⓢ Ost
Ⓢ
HAUPTBAHNHOF
Lokalbahnhof
Ⓢ
Süd
Mühlberg
✈ 10 km ↙
Ⓢ S-Bahn stations

GENÈVE

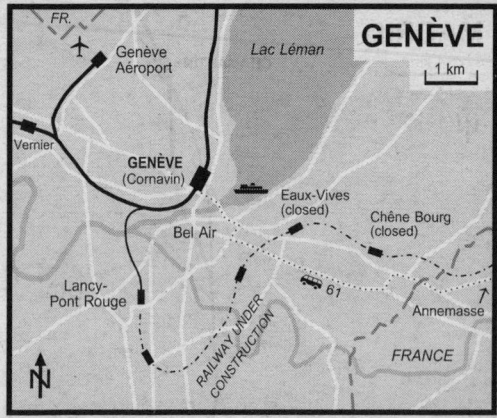

FR.
Genève
Aéroport
Lac Léman
1 km
Vernier
GENÈVE
(Cornavin)
Eaux-Vives
(closed)
Chêne Bourg
(closed)
Bel Air
Lancy-
Pont Rouge
61
Annemasse
RAILWAY UNDER
CONSTRUCTION
FRANCE
N

GLASGOW

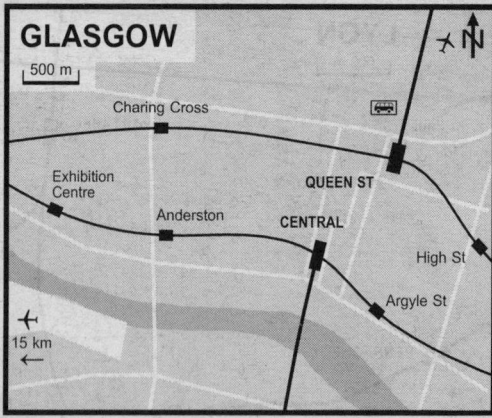

500 m
N ✈

Charing Cross
QUEEN ST
Exhibition
Centre
Anderston
CENTRAL
High St
✈
15 km
←
Argyle St

HAMBURG

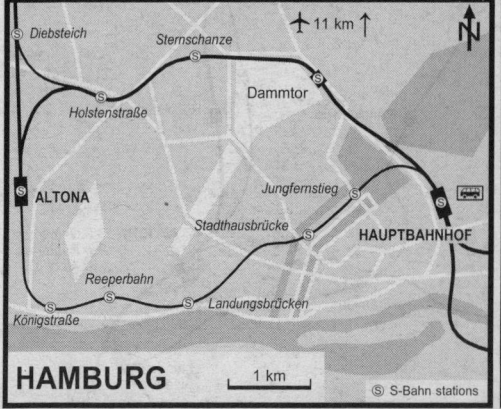

✈ 11 km ↑
N

Ⓢ Diebsteich
Sternschanze
Ⓢ
Dammtor
Holstenstraße
Ⓢ
Jungfernstieg
Ⓢ
ALTONA
Stadthausbrücke
Ⓢ
HAUPTBAHNHOF
Reeperbahn
Ⓢ
Landungsbrücken
Königstraße Ⓢ

1 km
Ⓢ S-Bahn stations

KØBENHAVN

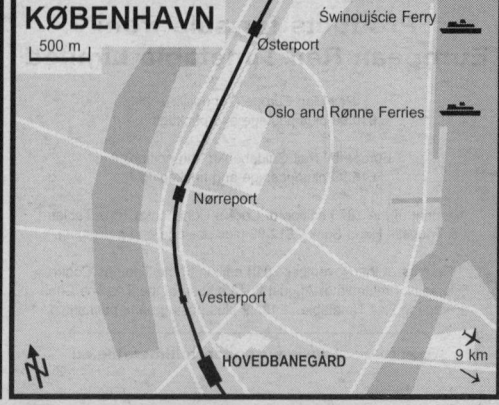

500 m

Świnoujście Ferry
Østerport
Oslo and Rønne Ferries
Nørreport
Vesterport
N ✈
9 km
↘
HOVEDBANEGÅRD

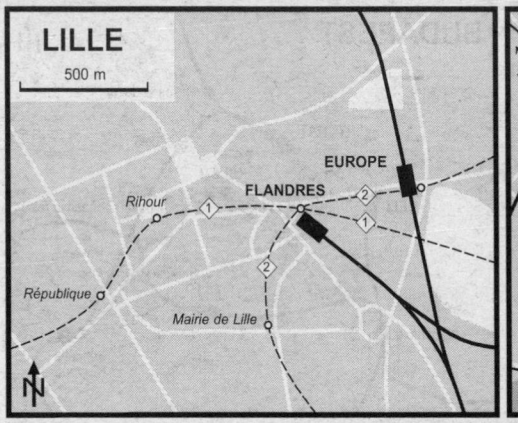

LILLE
500 m

Rihour · FLANDRES · EUROPE
République · Mairie de Lille

LISBOA

Sete Rios · Entrecampos · Roma · Roma-Areeiro
Sintra · Campolide · Areeiro · Oriente
São Sebastião · Alameda
Marquês de Pompal · Oriente
Rato · Restauradores · SANTA APOLÓNIA
Rossio · Baixa-Chiado · Rossio
Cais do Sodré · Terreiro do Paço
Cascais · Barreiro
1 km

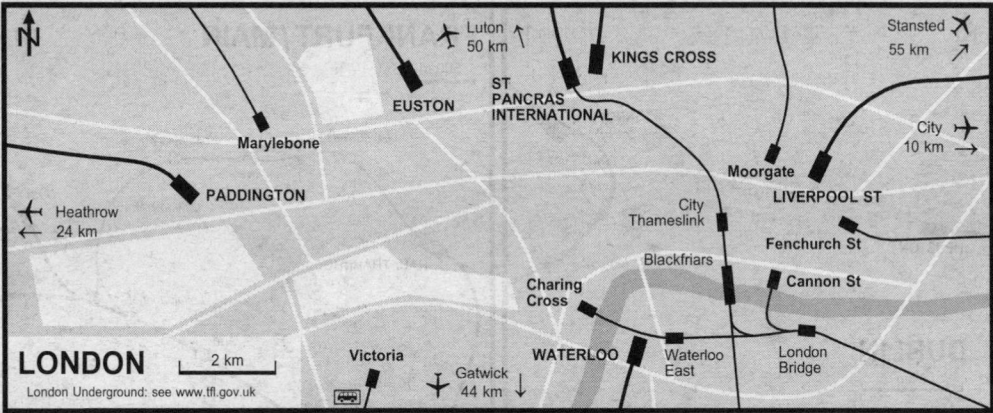

LONDON
2 km
London Underground: see www.tfl.gov.uk

Luton 50 km · KINGS CROSS · Stansted 55 km
ST PANCRAS INTERNATIONAL
EUSTON · City 10 km
Marylebone · Moorgate
Heathrow 24 km · PADDINGTON · LIVERPOOL ST
City Thameslink · Fenchurch St
Blackfriars · Cannon St
Charing Cross · London Bridge
Victoria · WATERLOO · Waterloo East
Gatwick 44 km

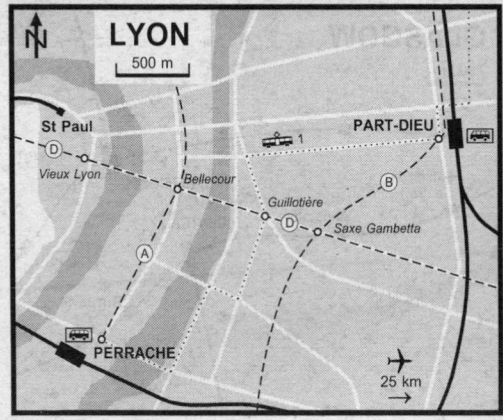
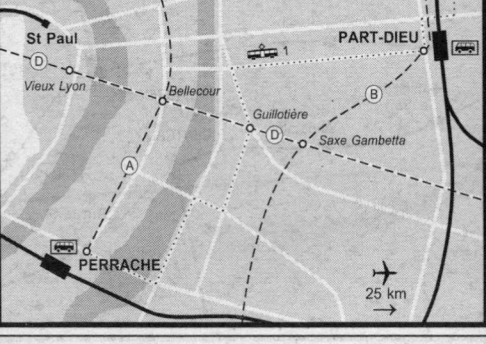

LYON
500 m

St Paul · PART-DIEU
Vieux Lyon · Bellecour
Guillotière · Saxe Gambetta
PERRACHE
25 km

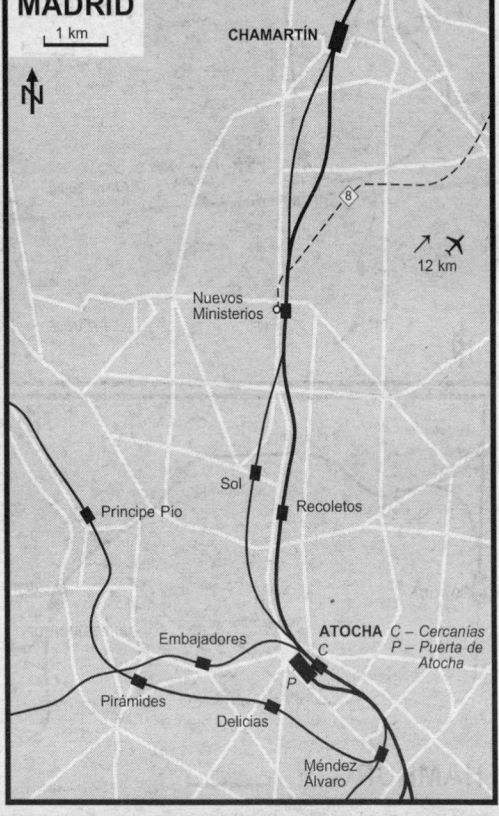

MADRID
1 km

CHAMARTÍN
12 km
Nuevos Ministerios
Príncipe Pío · Sol · Recoletos
Embajadores · ATOCHA · C – Cercanías · P – Puerta de Atocha
Pirámides · Delicias
Méndez Álvaro

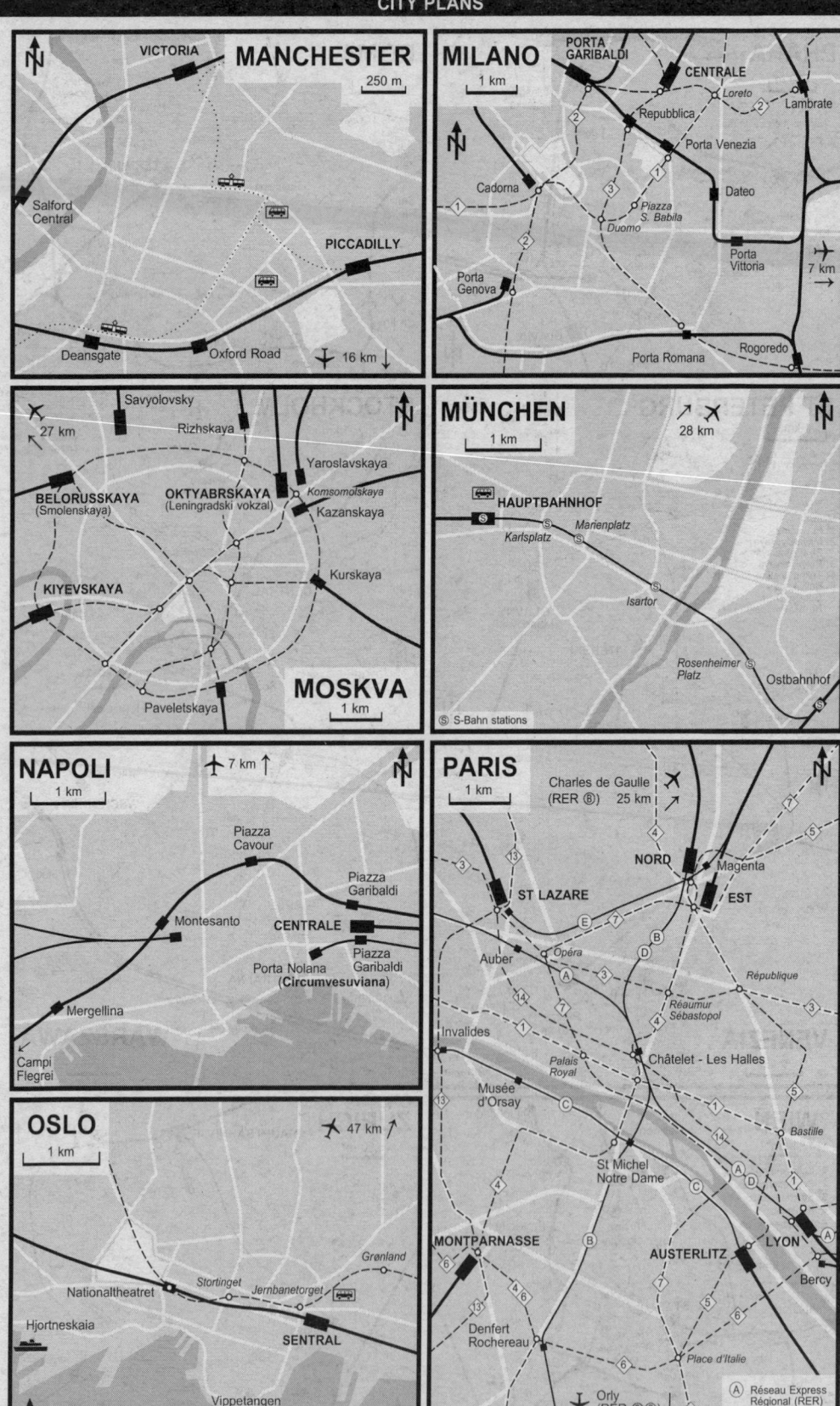

MANCHESTER
250 m

VICTORIA
Salford Central
PICCADILLY
Deansgate
Oxford Road
16 km ↓

MILANO
1 km

PORTA GARIBALDI
CENTRALE
Loreto
Lambrate
Repubblica
Porta Venezia
Cadorna
Piazza S. Babila
Dateo
Duomo
Porta Genova
Porta Vittoria
7 km →
Porta Romana
Rogoredo

MOSKVA
1 km

27 km
Savyolovsky
Rizhskaya
Yaroslavskaya
Komsomolskaya
BELORUSSKAYA (Smolenskaya)
OKTYABRSKAYA (Leningradski vokzal)
Kazanskaya
KIYEVSKAYA
Kurskaya
Paveletskaya

MÜNCHEN
1 km

28 km
HAUPTBAHNHOF
Marienplatz
Karlsplatz
Isartor
Rosenheimer Platz
Ostbahnhof
Ⓢ S-Bahn stations

NAPOLI
1 km
✈ 7 km ↑

Piazza Cavour
Piazza Garibaldi
Montesanto
CENTRALE
Porta Nolana
Piazza Garibaldi (Circumvesuviana)
Mergellina
Campi Flegrei

PARIS
1 km

Charles de Gaulle (RER Ⓑ) 25 km
NORD
Magenta
ST LAZARE
EST
Auber
Opéra
République
Réaumur Sébastopol
Invalides
Palais Royal
Châtelet - Les Halles
Musée d'Orsay
Bastille
St Michel Notre Dame
MONTPARNASSE
AUSTERLITZ
LYON
Bercy
Denfert Rochereau
Place d'Italie
Orly (RER Ⓑ Ⓒ) 15 km
Ⓐ Réseau Express Régional (RER)
① Métro urbain (selected lines)

OSLO
1 km
✈ 47 km ↗

Grønland
Nationaltheatret
Stortinget
Jernbanetorget
Hjortneskaia
SENTRAL
Vippetangen

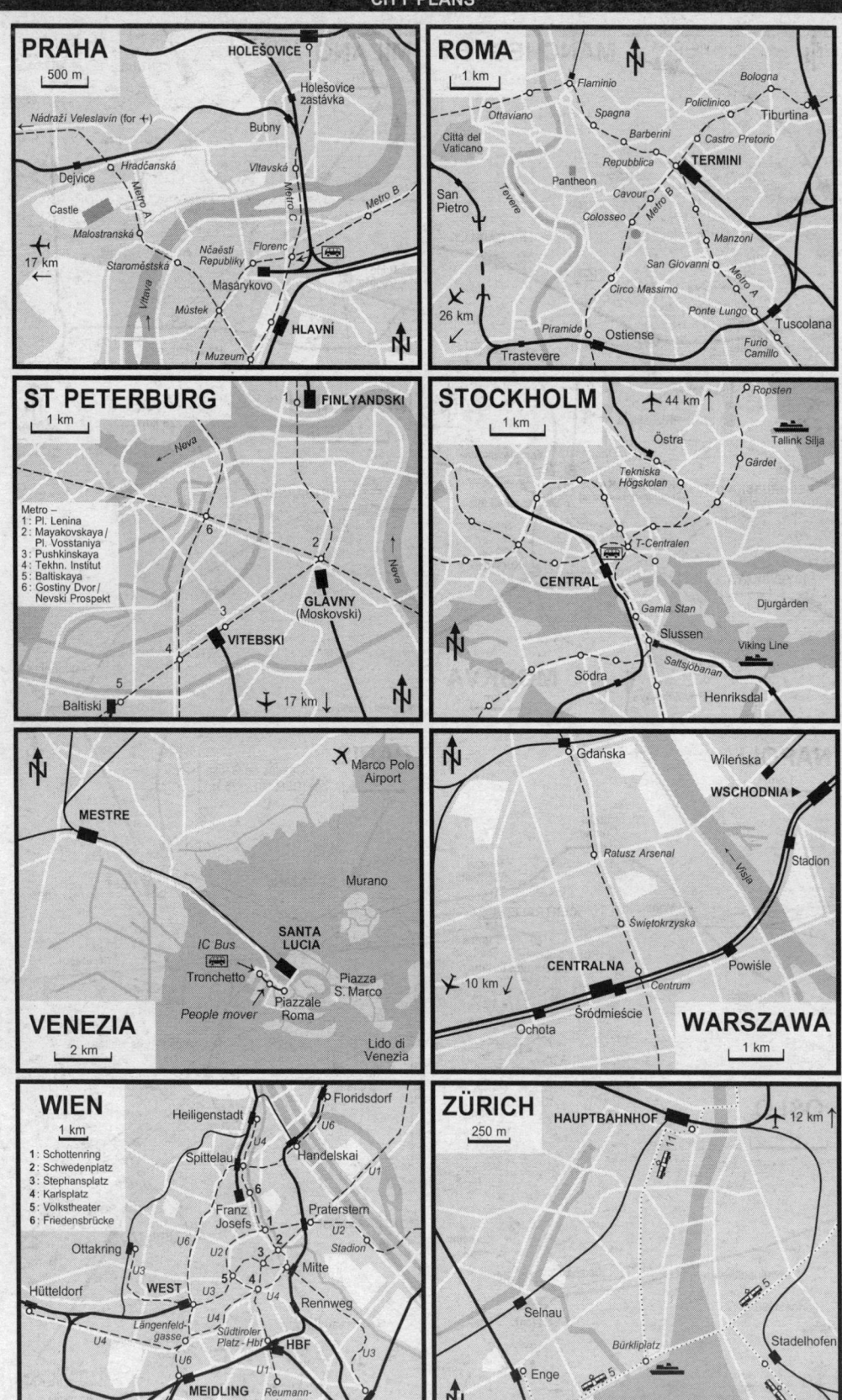

PRAHA

500 m

HOLEŠOVICE
Holešovice
zastávka
Nádraží Veleslavin (for ✈)
Bubny
Vltavská
Hrádčanská
Dejvice
Metro A
Metro C
Metro B
Castle
Malostranská
✈ 17 km
Staroměstská
Nčaěsti
Republiky
Florenc
Masarykovo
Můstek
Muzeum
Vltava
HLAVNÍ
N

ROMA

1 km
N
Flaminio
Bologna
Ottaviano
Policlinico
Spagna
Tiburtina
Città del
Vaticano
Barberini
Castro Pretorio
Repubblica
TERMINI
Pantheon
Cavour
Metro B
Colosseo
Manzoni
San
Pietro
Tevere
San Giovanni
Metro A
✈ 26 km
Circo Massimo
Piramide
Ponte Lungo
Tuscolana
Ostiense
Furio
Camillo
Trastevere

ST PETERBURG

1 km
FINLYANDSKI
Nova
Metro –
1 : Pl. Lenina
2 : Mayakovskaya /
Pl. Vosstaniya
3 : Pushkinskaya
4 : Tekhn. Institut
5 : Baltiskaya
6 : Gostiny Dvor /
Nevski Prospekt
6
2
3
GLAVNY
(Moskovski)
4
VITEBSKI
Neva
5
Baltiski
✈ 17 km
N

STOCKHOLM

1 km
✈ 44 km
Ropsten
Östra
Tallink Silja
Tekniska
Högskolan
Gärdet
T-Centralen
CENTRAL
Gamla Stan
Djurgården
Slussen
Viking Line
N
Södra
Saltsjöbanan
Henriksdal

VENEZIA

N
✈ Marco Polo
Airport
MESTRE
Murano
SANTA
LUCIA
IC Bus
Piazza
S. Marco
Tronchetto
Piazzale
Roma
People mover
2 km
Lido di
Venezia

WARSZAWA

N
Gdańska
Wileńska
WSCHODNIA ▶
Ratusz Arsenal
Wisła
Stadion
Świętokrzyska
CENTRALNA
Powiśle
✈ 10 km
Centrum
Ochota
Śródmieście
1 km

WIEN

1 km
Floridsdorf
Heiligenstadt
1 : Schottenring
2 : Schwedenplatz
3 : Stephansplatz
4 : Karlsplatz
5 : Volkstheater
6 : Friedensbrücke
U4
U6
Spittelau
Handelskai
U1
6
Franz
Josefs
Praterstern
1
U6
U2
Stadion
Ottakring
2
U2
3
Mitte
U3
5 4
Hütteldorf
WEST
Rennweg
U3
U4
Längenfeld
gasse
Südtiroler
Platz - Hbf
HBF
U4
U3
MEIDLING
U6
U1
Reumann-
platz
Simmering

ZÜRICH

250 m
HAUPTBAHNHOF
✈ 12 km
11
5
Selnau
Bürkliplatz
Stadelhofen
N
Enge
5
11

From	To	Train Number	Brand	Facilities and owner	Train Name	International table number
Düsseldorf	Wien	40421/40490	Nightjet	🛏 1, 2 cl.🚿(öbb), 🚃 2 cl.(öbb), ¶		28, 66
Düsseldorf	Innsbruck	421/420	Nightjet	🛏 1, 2 cl.🚿(öbb), 🚃 2 cl.(öbb), ¶		28
München	Budapest	463/462	Euro Night	🛏 1, 2 cl.(mav), 🚃 2 cl.(mav)	Kálmán Imre	32, 65
Wien	Bucuresti	347/346	Euro Night	🛏 1, 2 cl.(cfr), 🚃 2 cl.(cfr), 🍴(cfr)	Dacia	32, 61
Budapest	Bucuresti	473/472	Euro Night	🛏 1, 2 cl.(cfr), 🚃 1, 2 cl.(cfr)	Ister	32, 61
Paris	Venezia	221/220	Thello Euro Night	🛏 1, 2 cl.(ti), 🚃 2 cl.(ti), 🍴(ti)		44
Irún / Hendaye	Lisboa	312/310	Trenhotel talgo	🛏 1, 2 cl.🚿(renfe), 🍴(renfe)	Surex / Sud Expresso	45
Lisboa	Madrid	335/332	Trenhotel talgo	🛏 1, 2 cl.🚿(renfe), 🍴(renfe)	Lusitania	45
Berlin	Malmö	301/300	Euro Night	🚃 2 cl.(bne)	Berlin Night Express	50
Zürich	Praha	50467/50466	Euro Night	🛏 1, 2 cl.		52
Zürich	Hamburg	471/470	Nightjet	🛏 1, 2 cl.🚿(öbb), 🚃 2 cl.(öbb), ¶		54, 73
Zürich	Berlin	471/470	Nightjet	🛏 1, 2 cl.🚿(öbb), 🚃 2 cl.(öbb), ¶		54, 73
Warszawa	Kyïv	68/67		🛏 1, 2 cl.(uz)	Kyïv Ekspres	56
Warszawa	Moskva	10/9		🛏 1, 2 cl.(rzd)	Polonez	56
Berlin	Budapest	477/476	Euro Night	🛏 1, 2 cl.(cd), 🚃 2 cl.(mav)	Metropol	60
Berlin	Wien	40477/40406	Euro Night	🛏 1, 2 cl.(cd), 🚃 2 cl.(mav)	Metropol	60
Praha	Budapest	477/476	Euro Night	🛏 1, 2 cl.🚿(cd), 🚃 2 cl.(cd)	Metropol	60
Budapest	Beograd	341/340		🛏 1, 2 cl.(zs), 🚃 2 cl.(zs)	Beograd	61
Beograd	Thessaloníki	335/334		🚃 2 cl.(mz)	Hellas Express	61
Bucuresti	istanbul	461/492 ❖		🛏 1, 2 cl.(cfr), 🚃 2 cl.(tcdd)	Bosphor	61
Hamburg	Wien	491/490	Nightjet	🛏 1, 2 cl.🚿(öbb), 🚃 2 cl.(öbb), ¶		64
Hamburg	Innsbruck	40491/40420	Nightjet	🛏 1, 2 cl.🚿(öbb), 🚃 2 cl.(öbb), ¶		64
München	Roma	295/294	Nightjet	🛏 1, 2 cl.🚿(db), 🚃 2 cl.(db), ¶		70
München	Venezia	40463/40236	Nightjet	🛏 1, 2 cl.🚿(db), 🚃 2 cl.(db), ¶		70
München	Milano	40295/40235	Nightjet	🛏 1, 2 cl.🚿(db), 🚃 2 cl.(db), ¶		70
München	Zagreb	50463/498	Euro Night	🛏 1, 2 cl.(hz), 🚃 2 cl.(hz)		86
Zürich	Zagreb	40465/414	Euro Night	🛏 1, 2 cl.(hz), 🚃 2 cl.(hz)		86
Zürich	Budapest	40467/40462	Euro Night	🛏 1, 2 cl.(mav), 🚃 2 cl.(mav)		86
Zürich	Graz	465/464	Nightjet	🛏 1, 2 cl.🚿(öbb), 🚃 2 cl.(öbb)		86
Zürich	Wien	467/466	Nightjet	🛏 1, 2 cl.🚿(öbb), 🚃 2 cl.(öbb)		86
Wien	Roma	40233/40294	Nightjet	🛏 1, 2 cl.🚿(öbb), 🚃 2 cl.(öbb)		88
Wien	Venezia	237/236	Nightjet	🛏 1, 2 cl.🚿(öbb), 🚃 2 cl.(öbb)		88
Wien	Milano	233/235	Nightjet	🛏 1, 2 cl.(ti), 🚃 2 cl.(ti)		88
Praha	Moskva	22/21		🛏 1, 2 cl.(rzd)	Vltava	95
Wien	Moskva	22/21		🛏 1, 2 cl.(rzd)	Vltava	95
Krakow	Kyïv	36/35		🛏 1, 2 cl.🚿(pkp)		1075
Praha	Kyïv	443/771		🛏 1, 2 cl.(uz)		96
Bratislava	Kyïv	801/771		🛏 1, 2 cl.(uz)		96
Budapest	Kyïv	34/81		🛏 1, 2 cl.(uz)	Latorca	96
Warszawa	Lviv	35/36		🛏 1, 2 cl.(uz)		97
Warszawa	Budapest	407/476		🛏 1, 2 cl.(pkp), 🚃 2 cl.(pkp)		99
Warszawa	Wien	407/406		🛏 1, 2 cl.(pkp), 🚃 2 cl.(öbb)	Chopin	99
Warszawa	Praha	407/445		🛏 1, 2 cl.(pkp), 🚃 2 cl.(pkp)		99
Kraków	Budapest	402/476		🛏 1, 2 cl.(pkp), 🚃 2 cl.(pkp)		99
Kraków	Wien	402/50406		🛏 1, 2 cl.(pkp), 🚃 2 cl.(pkp)		99
Kraków	Praha	403/443		🛏 1, 2 cl.(cd), 🚃 2 cl.(cd)	Silesia	99
Wrocław	Kyïv	36/35		🛏 1, 2 cl.🚿(pkp)		1075
Helsinki	Moskva	31/32	Firménny	🛏 1, 2 cl.🚿(rzd), 🍴	Lev Tolstoi	1910

Non daily sleepers (other seasonal services operate):

Paris	Moskva	453/452	Euro Night	🛏 1, 2 cl.🚿(rzd), 🍴(pkp, rzd)	Trans European Express	24
Nice	Moskva	18/17		🛏 1, 2 cl.🚿(rzd), 🍴(pkp, rzd)		25

Key to ownership of sleeping cars:

bdz - Bulgarian, bc - Belarussian, bne - Berlin Night Express, cd - Czech, cfr - Romanian, cnl - City Night Line, db - German, hz - Croatian, mav - Hungarian, mz - Macedonain, öbb - Austrian, pkp - Polish, renfe - Spanish, rzd - Russian, sbb - Swiss, ti - Italian, uz - Ukrainian, zs - Serbian.

Note : This list excludes trains not shown in our International section (e.g. Czech Republic to Slovakia, Ukraine to Russia etc.).

¶ – Reported as not running most nights.
* No sleeping cars conveyed until further notice.
🚿 – Shower.
🍴 – Restaurant car.
❖ – The composition of this train is subject to confirmation.

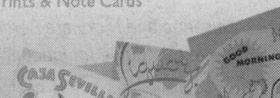

Homage to the Hebrides (Table 219)

Nicky Gardner and Susanne Kries find inspiration in Table 219. Join our regular roving correspondents on a Hebridean adventure.

Winter is in the offing, ushering in the season when we sit by the fire discussing quite which is our favourite table in each national section of the *European Rail Timetable*. In Britain, the choice is easy. You just can't beat Table 219. Oddly, there are no trains at all in this table which is devoted to ferry services in western Scotland, among them the Hebridean routes operated by Caledonian MacBrayne (CalMac). These services run from four mainland ports, namely (from north to south) Ullapool, Mallaig, Oban and Kennacraig. In addition, CalMac operate ferries to the islands of Harris and North Uist (both in the Outer Hebrides) from the small port of Uig on the Isle of Skye.

Our view is that Caledonian MacBrayne's comprehensive network of ferry services to, from and between the Hebridean islands offers some of the finest inshore shipping routes in Europe, with superb opportunities for island hopping by scheduled ferry services. Rail travellers often head for Mallaig, at the very end of the West Highland Line, whence there are year-round scheduled ferry services to six different Hebridean islands (five in the Inner Hebrides, plus South Uist in the Outer Isles). The destination list from Oban also runs to half-a-dozen islands ranging from serene Colonsay (in the Inner Hebrides) to beautiful Barra (at the southern end of the Outer Hebrides).

Direct trains from Glasgow run to both Oban and Mallaig (see Table 218). At each port it is just a short walk from train to ship. Once on board the boat, travellers will find every creature comfort with a great choice of Scottish fare on offer in the restaurants which are a popular feature of the larger boats. All ferries convey cars, but it's very easy to devise creative itineraries through the Hebrides relying entirely on public transport.

Trips to the Hebrides are always special, and the journey really can be as much fun as the destination. Table 219 gives the bare facts about key routes. But it hides one essential detail, namely that these are real, working boats providing lifeline links to some of Scotland's remotest communities. On a breezy Tuesday in November, for example, ferry operator Caledonian MacBrayne advised that gusting winds might cause disruption to the *MV Clansman* as she set off on her scheduled journey from Oban to Coll and Tiree. A footnote in that CalMac advisory, indicated that "the captain is fine with taking livestock" – it was a nice reminder that the company's vessels are part of the fabric of Hebridean life. During the late summer and autumn, the company laid on extra sailings to accommodate livestock sales in Tiree and the Uists. In October 2016, CalMac sponsored the Royal National Mòd festival of Gaelic literature, music and arts in the Isle of Lewis, providing extra sailings on the Ullapool to Stornoway route to get everyone to and from the island.

From time to time CalMac ferries deviate from their regular schedules to assist vessels in distress or to make extra port calls to ensure that travellers left stranded after storms can all be ferried without further delay to their destinations.

For a first taste of the Hebrides, and with a full week to spare, we recommend sailing out from Oban to Barra, then tracking north through the Outer Hebrides to Tarbert on Harris, from where it's just a short hop across to Uig on Skye. One might then enjoy a day or two on Skye before crossing the Sound of Sleat on the ferry from Armadale to Mallaig, where one can rejoin the mainland rail network. This itinerary requires five ferries in all, with an all-inclusive fare for those five boats of just £29.60 per person – using CalMac's Hopscotch ticket no. 23. The fare quoted is valid until 30 March 2017. For more advice on winter journeys to the Hebrides see our *Tip of the Month* opposite.

© 2016 Nicky Gardner and Susanne Kries

Susanne and Nicky are Berlin-based travel writers. They are the authors of 'Europe by Rail: The Definitive Guide for Independent Travellers'. The 14th edition was published in June 2016.

Island Hopping in Winter

by Nicky Gardner and Susanne Kries

Visitors to many offshore islands around Europe are deterred by high ferry fares. But the tariffs for journeys to the Hebrides are very reasonable. One-way fares from the mainland to the Outer Hebrides start at just £10.15. That's the fare (valid until 30 March 2017) for a foot passenger from Mallaig to the South Uist port of Lochboisdale.

The Caledonian MacBrayne (CalMac) vessel *MV Lord of the Isles* plies the route thrice weekly during the current winter season with a crossing time of just under four hours. As this issue of the *European Rail Timetable* goes to press, CalMac have not yet announced their summer 2017 schedules, which will come into effect in late March. Chances are that the summer season will see enhanced frequencies on the Mallaig-Lochboisdale route and on other CalMac routes to the Outer Hebrides.

Winter journeys to the Scottish islands need careful planning, but they can be immensely rewarding. There are some ferry routes *between* islands which don't run at all in winter. For example, the regular summer season weekly link from both Coll and Tiree to Barra is now on hold until the spring. The direct boat from Eigg to Canna (both in the Small Isles off the south coast of Skye) runs twice weekly in the summer but not at all from late October until the very end of March.

Off-season accommodation options may be limited. Many B&Bs in the Outer Hebrides close entirely for the winter months. But island hotels may offer cosy hospitality at greatly discounted prices. For example, the Coll Hotel (on the Isle of Coll, five sailings a week direct from Oban, crossing time three hours) stays open all year and regular off-season visitors claim that the seafood tastes even better during the winter months.

While the *Spirit of Scotland Travelpass* (launched last spring by VisitScotland) does include CalMac ferry routes, it's hardly worth investing in the pass merely for a journey to the Hebrides. Other than on Skye, there are very few island bus services on which the pass is valid. But it may be worth getting a *Spirit of Scotland Travelpass* if you include a side trip to the Hebrides as part of a wider Scottish itinerary. The pass covers rail travel throughout Scotland as well as many bus and ferry routes. Discounted prices apply during winter, with adult passes starting at £107 for travel on four days in any eight-day period. This price applies until 31 March 2017. Discounts are available for railcard holders.

The one essential prerequisite for winter island hopping in the Hebrides is a measure of flexibility. Winter storms can and do affect ferries. CalMac's advance warning system on likely delays is excellent, but don't plan too packed an itinerary. That way you'll not fret when a gale rolls in off the Atlantic and you find yourself unexpectedly stranded for a day or two. Indeed, some of our most memorable island-hopping trips have been the ones when everything did *not* go entirely to plan.

© Nicky Gardner and Susanne Kries

---◆---

The authors together produce and publish *hidden europe* magazine (www.hiddeneurope.co.uk). The current edition of *hidden europe* (issue 50, published in mid-November 2016) features the Outer Hebrides, Bessarabia, Albania, Slovakia, Dalmatia, Bohemia and much more.

INTERNATIONAL (continued)

Table 82: The Gotthard Base Tunnel is now open for regular passenger services and Swiss Railways has introduced a revised service along the route. The number of Zürich to Milano services has increased from seven to eight per day with a reduced journey time of 3 hours 36 minutes (37 minutes faster than previous timings). The new schedules also include a new Basel – Arth-Goldau – Milano service.

Table 95: The twice weekly Moskva – Cheb sleeping car, which is conveyed in train **22/21** *Vltava* Moskva – Terespol – Praha, has been withdrawn. Train **10/9** Moskva – Warszawa – Budapest – Sofia has been cut back to run only between Moskva and Warszawa; the provision of a direct Moskva – Warszawa – Kraków sleeping car on this train was unable to be verified at the time of going to press.

GREAT BRITAIN

The link from Oxford Parkway to Oxford has been completed meaning services from London Marylebone can now run through to Oxford's main station (Table **128**).

Virgin East Coast has enhanced its service provision at weekends. On Saturdays there are three additional services between London and Leeds, with four extra trains running in the opposite direction. On Sundays the London to Leeds route benefits from two additional trains northbound and one southbound whilst Edinburgh gains two additional trains to and from London Kings Cross (Table **180**).

A number of trains between York and Manchester Airport, operated by *TransPennine Express*, have been extended to run from and to Newcastle (Table **188**).

Cross Country is now making full use of the recently opened Norton Bridge flyover, located to the north of Stafford, by accelerating many of its Manchester services by up to 15 minutes (Table **122**).

Services on the Leeds to Carlisle route continue to be disrupted as work to repair the line between Armathwaite and Carlisle continues (Table **173**). The line is expected to fully to re-open by the spring of 2017.

IRELAND

Iarnród Éireann issued a new timetable from November 20, 2016 with minor retimings throughout the network and our Irish tables have been updated accordingly.

FRANCE

Engineering work on the route between Brest and Quimper commences on December 19 and will run throughout the year until December 8, 2017 (Table **286**).

Rail services on the branch line from Cannes to Grasse are suspended for approximately twelve months to allow upgrade work to be carried out. A very limited replacement bus service is provided on Mondays to Fridays (Table **361**).

The Paris Austerlitz to Cerbère service is the latest French overnight train to be withdrawn. The only remaining overnight services operating in France are Paris to Nice / Briançon, Paris to Latour de Carol / Rodez / Albi and Paris to Hendaye. The Hendaye service is also expected to be withdrawn when the new high-speed line between Tours and Bordeaux is opened in July.

BELGIUM

The recently introduced service linking Brussels Airport with the city's European quarter (Brussels Schumann and Luxembourg stations) now also runs at weekends, as shown in Table **401**.

NETHERLANDS

There has been a major revision of the Dutch timetable with a number of key route changes and many amended timings.

All services from Amsterdam Centraal heading towards Den Haag, Rotterdam and Vlissingen (Table **450**) now operate via Haarlem, no longer serving Schiphol Airport. *Intercity direct* services in Table **451** continue to run via Schiphol and, together with various local trains (summarised in Table **452**), a very frequent service is maintained between Amsterdam Centraal and the airport.

All long distance services between Groningen / Leeuwarden and Den Haag via Lelystad, together with a new half-hourly service between Lelystad and Dordrecht, operate via Amsterdam Zuid and Schiphol (Table **460**). The stopping service between Zwolle and Amsterdam continues to provide a through service to Amsterdam Centraal and there is also a fast shuttle service operating between the main stations of Almere and Amsterdam (Table **459**).

The Den Haag – Rotterdam – Eindhoven service now runs over the high-speed line between Rotterdam and Breda, saving nine minutes (Table **471**). A change of trains at Breda will be required for the time being, although through services are expected to recommence later in 2017. Please note that these services no longer run between Eindhoven and Venlo (see below) and, because of the diversion over the high-speed line, they no longer serve Dordrecht (although good connections are provided at Breda, as shown in Table **471**).

Services between Eindhoven and Venlo are now part of a new through route from Schiphol via Amsterdam Zuid and Utrecht, timings for which will be found in Table **470**. For most of the day they are formed as a portion of the existing Schiphol to Heerlen service.

Other services generally run on the same routes as before, although there are varying degrees of retiming across the network.

SWITZERLAND

Opening of the Gotthard Base Tunnel - the world's longest and deepest rail tunnel - to regular passenger traffic has enabled the schedules of principal services to be reduced by approximately 30 minutes. Consequently, a small restructuring of Table **550** has been made and services which continue to use the traditional mountain route are now shown in new Table **550a**.

ITALY

Only partial information for the new timetable was available as we went to press, although all trains shown with a train number within our tables have been checked. However, there has been much renumbering of trains this year so precise running days, exception dates, as well as timings for local services remain subject to confirmation. As always, it is advisable for travellers to recheck information locally.

Services between Milano and Brescia have been speeded up by ten minutes owing to the opening of a 40 kilometre section of new high-speed railway (Table **605**).

As part of the ongoing upgrade works on the Ligurian coast, Imperia Porto Maurizio and Imperia Oneglia stations have been replaced by a single station named Imperia (Table **580**).

SPAIN

Engineering work between Zaragoza and Barcelona (via both Caspe and Lleida) has resulted in many services being retimed (Table **652**).

AVE service **3944/3994** Barcelona – Sevilla / Málaga now runs on Saturdays only, with the return service *AVE* **3945/3995** operating only on Sundays (Table **660**).

Many *Euromed* services between Barcelona and València have been retimed with an additional stop at L'Aldea - Amposta inserted (Table **672**); most *Reginal Exprés* services have also been retimed.

A new weekend Intercity service has been introduced between Madrid and Vinaròs (Tables **668**, **672**). Departing Madrid Puerta de Atocha on Fridays at 1710, *IC* **5570** arrives Vinaròs at 2118. The return service, *IC* **5481**, returns on Sundays departing Vinaròs at 1543 and arriving back in the Spanish capital at 1943.

Eva Transportes has issued a new timetable for services between Lagos and Sevilla (Table **676**).

DENMARK

The new timetable reveals numerous, albeit fairly minor, schedule changes, and tables have been updated accordingly.

The practice of principal *IC* and *Lyn* trains serving København Lufthavn (Kastrup) has been discontinued (Table **700**).

NORWAY

Journeys on the Vestfold line between Oslo and Skien (Table **783**) are a few minutes quicker following the opening of the 12 kilometre Holmestrand Tunnel. Within the tunnel is a brand new station serving Holmestrand itself. On Mondays to Fridays, two faster trains are provided in each direction between Oslo and Skien omitting certain stops and completing the journey in approximately 2 hours and 30 minutes.

The early morning service on Mondays to Fridays from Göteborg to Oslo, together with the mid-afternoon return train, has been withdrawn between Göteborg and Halden (Table **770**).

CONTINUED ON PAGE 558

Car-carrying trains are composed of special wagons or vans for the conveyance of motorcars usually with sleeping cars and couchettes enabling the driver and passengers to travel overnight in comfort in the same train. Some services (particularly in France) convey vehicles separately allowing passengers a choice of trains for their own journey. Some shorter distance services run by day and convey seating coaches.

Cars are often loaded on the trains at separate stations from the passenger station and may be loaded some time before the passenger train departs. International car-carrying trains are shown in Table **1**, Domestic car-carrying trains in Table **2**. Some services also carry passengers without cars.

Details of Channel Tunnel shuttle services may be found on page 46. Austrian and Swiss alpine tunnel car-carrying trains are shown in the relevant country section - see pages 458 and 260 respectively for details.

Readers should be careful to check that dates refer to current schedules, as old dates may be left in the table until such time as current information is received. Loading and train times may vary on some dates, but will be confirmed by the agent when booking.

Some services shown in Table **1** are operated by organisations other than national railway companies. Contact details for these are:

Services from Germany (except Düsseldorf - Livorno and Verona services):
ÖBB AutoZug, (booking centre); ✆ +43 (0)5 1717.

Düsseldorf - Livorno and Verona services:
Treinreiswinkel, ANVR 2407, Oude Vest 7 - 9, 2312 XP Leiden; ✆ 071-513 70 08.

Certain Eastern European services (see table for details):
Optima Tours, Karlstrasse 56, 80333 D - München; ✆ +49 89 54880 - 111, fax +49 89 54880 - 155.

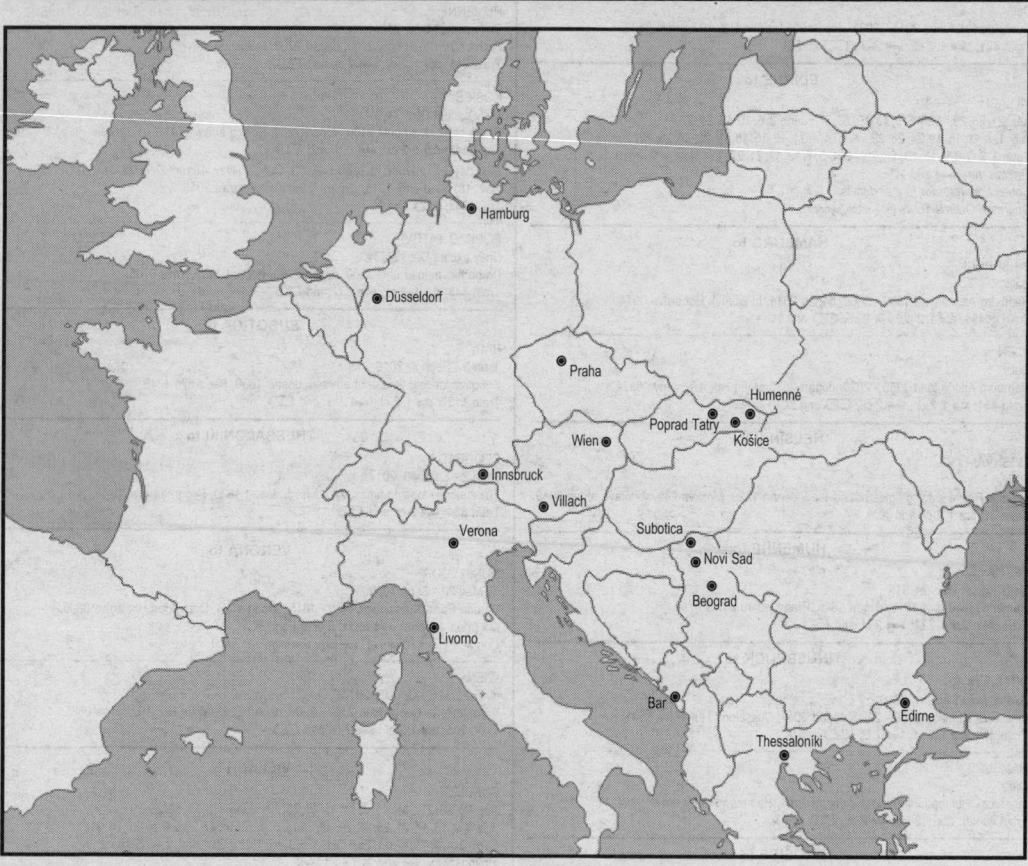

BAR to

BEOGRAD:
Daily.
Bar loading times not advised, depart 1900, Beograd arrive 0706.
Train **432**: 🛏 1, 2 cl., 🍴 2 cl. and �car.

NOVI SAD:
June 3 - Sept. 4, 2017.
Bar loading times not advised, depart 1650, Novi Sad arrive 0635.
Train **1136**: 🛏 1, 2 cl. 🍴 2 cl. and �car.

SUBOTICA:
June 4 - Sept. 5, 2016.
Bar loading times not advised, depart 1700, Subotica arrive 0909.
Train **1136**: 🛏 1, 2 cl., 🍴 2 cl. and �car.

BEOGRAD to

BAR:
Daily.
Beograd loading times not advised, depart 2110, Bar arrive 0902.
Train **433**: 🛏 1, 2 cl., 🍴 2 cl. and �car.

THESSALONÍKI:
June 1 - Sept. 9, 2017.
Beograd loading times not advised, depart 1835, Thessaloníki arrive 1005.
Train **335**: 🍴 2 cl. and �car.

DÜSSELDORF to

INNSBRUCK:
③⑤⑦ from Dec. 11, 2016.
Düsseldorf Hbf load 1945 - 2015, depart 2054, Innsbruck Hbf arrive 0914.
Train **421**: 🛏 1, 2 cl., 🚗 2 cl., 🚗 and ✕.

LIVORNO:
③ July 5 - Aug. 30, 2017.
Düsseldorf Hbf load 1530 - 1715, depart 1830, Livorno Centrale arrive 1000 (times subject to alteration).
🛏 (max. 3 berth), 🚗 (max. 5 berth) and ✕.
Contact: Treinreiswinkel (see table heading).

VERONA:
⑤ May 19 - Sept. 29, 2017.
Düsseldorf Hbf load 1530 - 1715, depart 1831, Verona Porta Nuova arrive 0840.
🛏 (max. 3 berth), 🚗 (max. 5 berth) and ✕.
Contact: Treinreiswinkel (see table heading).

WIEN:
Daily.
Düsseldorf Hbf load 2015 - 2035, depart 2054, Wien Hbf ARZ arrive 0828.
Train **421**: 🛏 1, 2 cl., 🚗 2 cl., 🚗 and ✕.

EDIRNE to

VILLACH:
Apr. 21, 25, 29, May 5, 9, 13, 19, 23, 27, June 2, 6, 10, 16, 21, 27,
July 1, 7, 11, 15, 19, 24, 28, 29, Aug. 1, 4, 11, 12, 15, 18, 19, 22, 25, 26, 29,
Sept. 1, 2, 5, 8, 9, 15, 19, 23, 29, Oct. 3, 7, 13, 17, 21, 27, 31, Nov. 4, 9, 2016.
Timings vary. 🚗 and ✕.
Contact operator for further details.
Operator: Optima Tours (see table heading).

HAMBURG to

INNSBRUCK:
Daily.
Hamburg Altona load 1930 - 2000, depart 2014, Innsbruck Hbf arrive 0914.
Train **40491**: 🛏 1, 2 cl., 🚗 2 cl., 🚗 and ✕.

WIEN:
Daily.
Hamburg Altona load 1950 - 2020, depart 2035, Wien Hbf ARZ arrive 0824.
Train **491**: 🛏 1, 2 cl., 🚗 2 cl., 🚗 and ✕.

HELSINKI to

MOSKVA:
Daily.
Helsinki Pasila loading times not advised, depart 1729, Moskva Oktyabrskaya arrive 0919.
Train **31**: 🛏 1, 2 cl. and ✕.

HUMENNÉ to

PRAHA:
Daily except Dec. 24, 31.
Humenné load until 1845, depart 1946, Praha hlavní arrive 0739.
Train **442**: 🛏 1, 2 cl., 🚗 2 cl. and 🚗.

INNSBRUCK to

DÜSSELDORF:
②④⑥ from Dec. 11, 2016.
Innsbruck Hbf load 2000 - 2030, depart 2044, Düsseldorf Hbf arrive 0841.
Train **420**: 🛏 1, 2 cl., 🚗 2 cl., 🚗 and ✕.

HAMBURG:
Daily.
Innsbruck Hbf load 2000 - 2030, depart 2044, Hamburg Altona arrive 0854.
Train **40420**: 🛏 1, 2 cl., 🚗 2 cl., 🚗 and ✕.

KOŠICE to

PRAHA:
Daily except Dec. 24, 31.
Košice load until 2035, depart 2208, Praha hlavní arrive 0739.
Train **442**: 🛏 1, 2 cl., 🚗 2 cl. and 🚗.
Also daytime train on ⑦ (also Mar. 28, July 6; not Dec. 27, Mar. 27, July 3): load until 1045, depart 1144, Praha hlavní arrive 1915.
Train **242**: 🚗 and ✕.

LIVORNO to

DÜSSELDORF:
④ July 6 - Aug. 31, 2017.
Livorno Centrale load 1430 - 1615, depart 1730, Düsseldorf Hbf arrive 1000 (times subject to alteration).
🛏 (max. 3 berth), 🚗 (max. 5 berth) and ✕.
Contact: Treinreiswinkel (see table heading).

WIEN:
④⑥ Apr. 6 - Oct. 28, 2017 (also Apr. 17, May 1, June 5, Aug. 15).
Livorno Centrale load 1630 - 1800, depart 1920, Wien Hbf arrive 0840 (0922 on ⑤, also Mar. 29, May 17, Aug. 16).
Train **1234**: 🛏 1, 2 cl. and 🚗.

MOSKVA to

HELSINKI:
Daily.
Moskva Oktyabrskaya loading times not advised, depart 2310, Helsinki Pasila arrive 1250.
Train **32**: 🛏 1, 2 cl. and ✕.

NOVI SAD to

BAR:
June 2 - Sept. 3, 2017.
Novi Sad loading times not advised, depart 2131, Bar arrive 1157.
Train **1137**: 🛏 1, 2 cl., 🚗 2 cl. and 🚗.

POPRAD TATRY to

PRAHA:
Daily except Dec. 24, 31.
Poprad Tatry load until 2040, depart 2153, Praha hlavni arrive 0639.
Train **444**: 🛏 1, 2 cl., 🚗 2 cl. and 🚗.

PRAHA to

HUMENNÉ:
Daily except Dec. 24, 31.
Praha hlavní load until 2100, depart 2200, Humenné arrive 1033.
Train **445**: 🛏 1, 2 cl., 🚗 2 cl. and 🚗.

KOŠICE:
Daily except Dec. 24, 31.
Praha hlavní load until 2100, depart 2200, Košice arrive 0741.
Train **445**: 🛏 1, 2 cl., 🚗 2 cl. and 🚗.
Also daytime train on ⑤ (also Dec. 23, Oct. 27, Nov. 16; not Dec. 25, Jan. 1, Oct. 28, Nov. 18): load until 1215, depart 1306, Košice arrive 2045.
Train **243**: 🚗 and ✕.

POPRAD TATRY:
Daily except Dec. 24, 31.
Praha hlavní load until 2200, depart 2309, Poprad Tatry arrive 0705.
Train **443**: 🛏 1, 2 cl., 🚗 2 cl. and 🚗.

SUBOTICA to

BAR:
June 3 - Sept. 4, 2016.
Subotica loading times not advised, depart 1830, Bar arrive 1049.
Train **1137**: 🛏 1, 2 cl., 🚗 2 cl. and 🚗.

THESSALONÍKI to

BEOGRAD:
June 2 - Sept. 10, 2017.
Thessaloníki loading times not advised, depart 1830, Beograd arrive 0746.
Train **334**: 🚗 2 cl. and 🚗.

VERONA to

DÜSSELDORF:
⑥ May 20 - Sept. 30, 2017.
Verona Porta Nuova load 1430 - 1615, depart 1734, Düsseldorf Hbf arrive 0805.
🛏 (max. 3 berth), 🚗 (max. 5 berth) and ✕.
Contact: Treinreiswinkel (see table heading).

WIEN:
⑤⑦ Apr. 28 - Oct. 15, 2017.
Verona Porta Nuova load 2100 - 2200, depart 2252, Wien Hbf ARZ arrive 0855.
Train **235**: 🛏 1, 2 cl., 🚗 2 cl. and 🚗.

VILLACH to

EDIRNE:
Apr. 18, 23, 27, May 1, 7, 11, 15, 21, 25, 29, June 4, 8, 12, 18, 25, 29,
July 3, 9, 13, 17, 21, 23, 27, 30, 31, Aug. 3, 6, 13, 14, 17, 20, 21, 24, 27, 28, 31,
Sept. 3, 4, 7, 11, 17, 21, 25, Oct. 1, 5, 9, 15, 19, 23, 29, Nov. 2, 6, 2016.
Timings vary. 🚗 and ✕.
Contact operator for further details.
Operator: Optima Tours (see table heading).

WIEN to

DÜSSELDORF:
Daily.
Wien Hbf ARZ load 2030 - 2050, depart 2127, Düsseldorf Hbf arrive 0841.
Train **420**: 🛏 1, 2 cl., 🚗 2 cl., 🚗 and ✕.

HAMBURG:
Daily.
Wien Hbf ARZ load 1930 - 2000, depart 2027, Hamburg Altona arrive 0806.
Train **490**: 🛏 1, 2 cl., 🚗 2 cl., 🚗 and ✕.

LIVORNO:
③⑤ Apr. 5 - Oct. 27, 2017 (also Apr. 16, 30, June 4, Aug. 14).
Wien Hbf ARZ load 1815 - 1945, depart 2010, Livorno Centrale arrive 0850.
Train **1237**: 🛏 1, 2 cl., 🚗 2 cl. and 🚗.

VERONA:
④⑥ Apr. 27 - Oct. 14, 2017.
Wien Hbf ARZ load 1810 - 1850, depart 1910, Verona Porta Nuova arrive 0635.
Train **233**: 🛏 1, 2 cl., 🚗 2 cl. and 🚗.

AUSTRIA
to 09/12/17

Feldkirch - Graz: daily.
Feldkirch - Villach: daily,
Feldkirch - Wien Hbf ARZ: daily.
Graz - Feldkirch: daily.
Villach - Feldkirch: daily.
Wien Hbf ARZ - Feldkirch: daily.

CROATIA
to 09/12/17

Split - Zagreb: daily in summer (dates to be confirmed).
Zagreb - Split: daily in summer (dates to be confirmed).

FINLAND
to 30/05/17

Helsinki - Kemijärvi: ⑤ Dec. 16 - May 5.
Helsinki - Kolari: daily Dec. 14 - Jan. 8; ③⑤⑥ Jan. 9-22; ②③④⑤⑥⑦ Jan. 23 - Feb. 5; daily Feb. 6 - Apr. 22; ③⑤⑥⑦ Apr. 24-30 (not Dec. 24). Additional train on ⑤ Feb. 10 - Apr. 21 (also Apr. 12,16).
Helsinki - Oulu: daily Dec. 11 - May 7 (not Dec. 24).
Helsinki - Rovaniemi: daily Dec. 11 - May 7 (not Dec. 24). Additional train on ⑤ Feb. 10 - Apr. 21 (also Apr. 12,16).
Kemijärvi - Helsinki: ⑥ Dec. 17 - May 6.
Kolari - Helsinki: daily Dec. 14 - Jan. 8; ④⑥⑦ Jan. 9-22; ①③④⑤⑥⑦ Jan. 24 - Feb. 5; daily Feb. 6 - Apr. 23; ①④⑥⑦ Apr. 24 - May 1 (not Dec. 24). Additional train on ⑥ Feb. 11 - Apr. 22 (also Apr. 13,17).
Kolari - Tampere: daily Dec. 14 - Jan. 8; ④⑥⑦ Jan. 9-22; ①③④ Jan. 24 - Feb. 5; ①②③④ Feb. 6 - Apr. 23; ①④⑥⑦ Apr. 24 - May 1 (also Mar. 4; not Dec. 24).
Oulu - Helsinki: daily Dec. 11 - May 7 (not Dec. 24).
Rovaniemi - Helsinki: daily Dec. 11 - May 7 (not Dec. 24). Additional train on ⑥ Feb. 11 - Apr. 22 (also Apr. 13,17).
Rovaniemi - Tampere: daily Dec. 11 - May 7 (not Dec. 24).
Rovaniemi - Turku: daily Dec. 11 - May 7 (not Dec. 24).
Tampere - Kolari: daily Dec. 14 - Jan. 8; ③⑤⑥ Jan. 9-22; ②③⑦ Jan. 23 - Feb. 5; ①③⑤⑦ Feb. 6 - Apr. 22; ③⑤⑥⑦ Apr. 24-30 (also Feb. 24; not Dec. 24).
Tampere - Rovaniemi: daily Dec. 11 - May 7 (not Dec. 24).
Turku - Rovaniemi: daily Dec. 11 - May 7 (not Dec. 24).

Note: Helsinki trains load and unload at Pasila station (3 km north of Helsinki station)

FRANCE
to 09/12/17

Avignon - Paris: ⑥ Dec. 17, 2016 - Mar. 25; ④⑥ Apr. 1 - June 24; daily June 27 - Sept. 11; ④⑥ Sept. 14 - Oct. 7; ⑥ Oct. 14 - Dec. 9, 2017.
Biarritz - Paris▲: ⑥ Apr. 1 - May 6; ④⑥ May 11 - June 17; ②④⑥ June 20 - July 1; ①②④⑤⑥ July 3-22; ①②③④⑤⑥ July 24 - Sept. 4; ④⑥ Sept. 7-30, 2017.
Bordeaux - Paris: ⑥ Dec. 17, 2016 - May 6; ④⑥ May 11 - June 17; ②④⑥ June 20 - July 1; ①②④⑤⑥ July 3-23; ①②③④⑤⑥ July 24 - Sept. 2; ④⑥ Sept. 7-30, 2017.
Briançon - Paris▲: ④⑥ June 15-24; ②④⑥ June 27 - Sept. 11, 2017.
Fréjus-St. Raphaël – see St. Raphaël.
Lyon - Paris: ⑥ Dec. 17, 2016 - June 24; ②⑥ June 27 - Sept. 11; ⑥ Sept. 14 - Dec. 9, 2017.
Marseille - Paris: ⑥ Dec. 17, 2016 - Mar. 25; ④⑥ Apr. 1 - June 24; daily June 27 - Sept. 11; ④⑥ Sept. 14 - Oct. 7; ⑥ Oct. 14 - Dec. 9, 2017.
Narbonne - Paris▲: ⑥ Dec. 17, 2016 - May 6; ④⑥ May 11 - June 17; ②④⑥ June 20 - July 1; ①②④⑤⑥ July 3-22; ①②③④⑤⑥ July 24 - Sept. 4; ④⑥ Sept. 7-30, 2017.
Nice - Paris▲: ⑥ Dec. 17, 2016 - Mar. 25; ④⑥ Apr. 7 - May 13; ②④⑥ May 6 - June 24; daily June 27 - Sept. 11; ②④⑥ Sept. 12 - Oct. 7; ④⑥ Oct. 12-28; ⑥ Nov. 4 - Dec. 9, 2017.
Paris - Avignon: ⑤ Dec. 16, 2016 - Mar. 24; ③⑤ May 31 - June 23; daily June 26 - Sept. 10; ③⑤ Sept. 13 - Oct. 6; ⑤ Oct. 13 - Dec. 8, 2017.
Paris - Biarritz▲: ⑤ Mar. 31 - May 5; ③⑤ May 10 - June 16; ①③⑤ June 19-30; ①③④⑤⑥ July 1-22; ①②③④⑤⑥ July 24 - Sept. 2; ③⑤ Sept. 6-29, 2017.
Paris - Bordeaux: ⑤ Dec. 16, 2016 - May 5; ③⑤ May 10 - June 16; ①③⑤ June 19-30; ①③④⑤⑥ July 1-22; ①②③④⑤⑥ July 24 - Sept. 2; ③⑤ Sept. 6-29, 2017.
Paris - Briançon▲: ③⑤ June 14-23; ①③⑤ June 26 - Sept. 10, 2017.
Paris - Lyon: ⑤ Dec. 16-31, 2016; ④ Jan. 1 - Apr. 30; ⑤ May 1 - June 23; ①⑤ June 26 - Sept. 8; ⑤ Sept. 15 - Dec. 8, 2017.
Paris - Marseille: ⑤ Dec. 16, 2016 - Mar. 24; ③⑤ May 31 - June 23; daily June 26 - Sept. 10; ③⑤ Sept. 13 - Oct. 11; ⑤ Oct. 13 - Dec. 8, 2017.
Paris - Narbonne▲: ⑤ Dec. 16, 2016 - May 5; ③⑤ May 10 - June 16; ①③⑤ June 19-30; ①③④⑤⑥ July 1-22; ①②③④⑤⑥ July 24 - Sept. 2; ③⑤ Sept. 6-29, 2017.
Paris - Nice▲: ⑤ Dec. 16, 2016 - Mar. 24; ③⑤ Apr. 4 - May 12; ①③⑤ May 15 - June 23; daily June 26 - Sept. 10; ①③⑤ Sept. 11 - Oct. 6; ③⑤ Oct. 11-27; ⑤ Nov. 3 - Dec. 8, 2017.

FRANCE (continued)
to 09/12/17

Paris - St. Raphaël▲: ⑤ Dec. 16, 2016 - Mar. 24; ③⑤ Mar. 31 - May 12; ①③⑤ May 15 - June 23; daily June 26 - Sept. 10; ①③⑤ Sept. 11 - Oct. 6; ③⑤ Oct. 11-27; ⑤ Nov. 3 - Dec. 8, 2017.
Paris - Toulon▲: ⑤ Dec. 16, 2016 - Mar. 24; ③⑤ Apr. 4 - May 12; ①③⑤ May 15 - June 23; daily June 26 - Sept. 10; ①③⑤ Sept. 11 - Oct. 6; ③⑤ Oct. 11-27; ⑤ Nov. 3 - Dec. 8, 2017.
Paris - Toulouse▲: ⑤ Dec. 16 - May 5; ③⑤ May 10 - June 16; ①③⑤ June 19-30; ①③④⑤⑥ July 1-22; ①②③④⑤⑥ July 24 - Sept. 2; ③⑤ Sept. 6-29, 2017.
St. Raphaël - Paris▲:
Toulon - Paris▲: ⑥ Dec. 17, 2016 - Mar. 25; ④⑥ Apr. 7 - May 13; ②④⑥ May 6 - June 24; daily June 27 - Sept. 11; ②④⑥ Sept. 12 - Oct. 7; ④⑥ Oct. 12-28; ⑥ Nov. 4 - Dec. 9, 2017.
Toulouse - Paris▲: ⑥ Dec. 17, 2016 - May 6; ④⑥ May 11 - June 17; ②④⑥ June 20 - July 1; ①②④⑤⑥ July 3-23; ①②③④⑤⑥ July 24 - Sept. 4; ④⑥ Sept. 7-30, 2017.

Passengers are offered a choice of departure times, mostly by day train but those noted ▲ also include night trains (Briançon night train only).

GERMANY
to 09/12/17

Basel (Lörrach) - Hamburg Altona ♦: ④⑥ Dec. 17, 2016 - Jan. 7; ⑥ Jan. 14 - Apr. 1; ①⑥ Apr. 3 - July 3; ①④⑥ July 6 - Sept. 2; ①⑥ Sept. 4-30; ⑥ Oct. 7-28, 2017 (also Dec. 26, Jan. 1, Apr. 13, May 25, June 22, Oct. 3; not Dec. 24, 31).
Hamburg Altona - Basel (Lörrach) ♦: ③⑤ Dec. 16, 2016 - Jan. 6; ⑤ Jan. 13 - Mar. 31; ⑤⑦ Apr. 2 - July 2; ③⑤⑦ July 5 - Sept. 3; ⑤⑦ Sept. 8 - Oct. 1; ⑤ Oct. 6-27, 2017 (also Apr. 12, May 24, June 21).
Niebüll - Westerland: Daily shuttle service; 18-28 per day in summer, 12-14 per day in winter.
Westerland - Niebüll: Daily shuttle service; 18-28 per day in summer, 12-14 per day in winter.

♦ – Operated by BahnTouristikExpress ✆ +49 (0)911 240 388.

GREECE
to 09/12/17

Athína - Thessaloníki: daily.
Thessaloníki - Athína: daily.

RUSSIA
to 09/12/17

Moskva - Astrakhan and v.v.
Moskva - Petrozavodsk and v.v.
Moskva - Pskov and v.v.
Moskva - St. Peterburg and v.v.
Moskva - Sochi - Adler and v.v.
St. Peterburg - Astrakhan and v.v.
St. Peterburg - Sochi - Adler and v.v.

Contact operator for days and dates of running.

SLOVAKIA
to 09/12/17

Bratislava - Humenné: daily (not Dec. 24, 31).
Humenné - Bratislava: daily (not Dec. 24, 31).

SLOVENIA
to 09/12/17

Bohinjska Bistrica - Podbrdo - Most na Soči: daily.
Most na Soči - Podbrdo - Bohinjska Bistrica: daily.

Note: service operates through the Julian Alps. Passengers remain in their vehicles. Also accepts passengers without vehicles.

Scenic Rail Routes of Europe

The following is a list of some of the most scenic rail routes of Europe, timings for most of which can be found within the timetable (the relevant table number has been specified in **bold**). Routes marked * are some of the editorial team's favourite journeys. Please note that this list does not include specialised mountain and tourist railways.

Types of scenery : **C**-Coastline, **F**-Forest, **G**-Gorge, **L**-Lake, **M**-Mountain, **R**-River.

ALBANIA

Route							Table
Elbasan - Pogradec	M	L	G		R		1390

AUSTRIA

Route							Table
Bruck an der Mur - Villach	M				R		980
Gmunden - Stainach Irdning*	M	L					961
Innsbruck - Brennero	M						595
Innsbruck - Garmisch*	M						895
Innsbruck - Schwarzach-St Veit	M		G				960
Krems - Emmersdorf					R		991
Landeck - Bludenz*	M						951
St Pölten - Mariazell*	M						994
Salzburg - Villach*	M		G				970
Selzthal - Kleinreifling - Steyr	M		G		R		976/977
Wiener Neustadt - Graz	M						980

BELGIUM and LUXEMBOURG

Route							Table
Liège - Luxembourg*					R		444
Liège - Marloie					R		
Namur - Dinant					R		440

BULGARIA

Route							Table
Septemvri - Dobriniste	M						1510
Sofia - Burgas	M						1500
Tulovo - Gorna Oryakhovitsa	M						1525

CROATIA and BOSNIA

Route							Table
Rijeka - Ogulin	M						1310
Ogulin - Split	M						1330
Sarajevo - Ploče	M		G		R		1355

CZECH REPUBLIC

Route							Table
Karlovy Vary - Mariánské Lázně					R	F	1123
Karlovy Vary - Chomutov					R		1110
Praha - Děčin					R		1100

DENMARK

Route							Table
Struer - Thisted		C					716

FINLAND

Route							Table
Kouvola - Joensuu				L		F	797

FRANCE

Route							Table
Aurillac - Neussargues	M		G				331
Bastia - Ajaccio	M						369
Bourg-en-Bresse - Bellegarde	M						341
Chambéry - Bourg St Maurice	M						366
Chambéry - Modane	M	L					367
Chamonix - Martigny*	M		G				572
Clermont Ferrand - Béziers	M		G				332
Clermont Ferrand - Nîmes*	M		G		R		333
Gap - Briançon	M	L					362
Genève - Aix les Bains	M				R		364
Grenoble - Veynes - Marseille	M						632
Marseille - Ventimiglia		C					360/361
Mouchard - Montbéliard					R		378
Nice - Digne	M						359
Nice - Cuneo*	M		G				581
Perpignan - Latour de Carol*	M		G				354
Portbou - Perpignan		C					355
Sarlat - Bergerac					R		318
Toulouse - Latour de Carol	M						312
Valence - Veynes	M						362

GERMANY

Route							Table
Arnstadt - Meiningen	M						870
Dresden - Děčin			G		R		1100
Freiburg - Donaueschingen			G			F	938
Garmisch - Reutte - Kempten	M						888
Heidelberg - Neckarelz					R		923/924
Koblenz - Mainz*			G		R		911/914
München - Lindau	M						935
Murnau - Oberammergau	M	L					897
Naumburg - Saalfeld					R		849/851
Niebüll - Westerland		C					821
Nürnberg - Pegnitz			G		R		880

GERMANY - continued

Route							Table
Offenburg - Konstanz	M					F	916
Pforzheim - Nagold / Wildbad						F	941
Plattling - Bayerisch Eisenstein						F	929
Rosenheim - Berchtesgaden	M	L					890/891
Rosenheim - Wörgl	M						951
Siegburg/Bonn - Siegen					R		807
Stuttgart - Singen						F	940
Titisee - Seebrugg				L		F	938
Trier - Koblenz - Giessen					R		906/915
Ulm - Göppingen	M						930
Ulm - Tuttlingen					R		938

GREAT BRITAIN and IRELAND

Route							Table
Alnmouth - Dunbar		C					180
Barrow in Furness - Maryport		C					159
Coleraine - Londonderry		C					231
Dun Laoghaire - Wicklow		C					237
Edinburgh - Aberdeen		C					224
Exeter - Newton Abbot		C					115/116
Glasgow - Oban / Mallaig*	M	L					218
Inverness - Kyle of Lochalsh*	M	C					226
Lancaster - Carlisle - Carstairs	M		G		R		151
Liskeard - Looe					R		118
Llanelli - Craven Arms	M						146
Machynlleth - Pwllheli	M	C					148
Perth - Inverness	M						221
Plymouth - Gunnislake					R		118
St Erth - St Ives		C					118
Sheffield - Chinley	M						193/206
Shrewsbury - Aberystwyth	M				R		147
Skipton - Settle - Carlisle	M				R		173

GREECE

Route							Table
Korinthos - Patras		C					1450
Diakoptó - Kalávrita	M		G				1455

HUNGARY

Route							Table
Budapest - Szob					R		1255
Eger - Szilvásvárad	M						1299
Székesfehérvár - Balatonszentgyörgy				L			1220
Székesfehérvár - Tapolca				L			1225

ITALY

Route							Table
Bologna - Pistoia	M						609
Bolzano - Merano	M						597
Brennero - Verona*	M						595
Brig - Arona	M	L					590
Domodossola - Locarno*	M		G				551
Firenze - Viareggio	M						614
Fortezza - San Candido	M						596
Genova - Pisa		C					610
Genova - Ventimiglia		C					580
Lecco - Tirano	M	L					593
Messina - Palermo		C					641
Napoli - Sorrento		C					639
Roma - Pescara	M						624
Salerno - Reggio Calabria		C					640
Taranto - Reggio Calabria		C					635
Torino - Aosta	M						586
Ventimiglia - Cuneo*	M		G				581

NORWAY

Route							Table
Bergen - Oslo*	M	L					780/781
Bodø - Trondheim	M	L					787
Dombås - Åndalsnes	M						785
Drammen - Larvik		C					783
Myrdal - Flåm*	M	C					781
Oslo - Kongsvinger					R		750
Oslo / Røros - Trondheim	M	L					784/785
Stavanger - Kristiansand		C					775

POLAND

Route							Table
Jelenia Góra - Walbrzych	M						1084
Kraków - Zakopane	M						1066
Olsztyn - Elk				L			1035
Olsztyn - Morag				L			1035
Tarnów - Krynica	M						1078

PORTUGAL

Route							Table
Covilhã - Entroncamento	M				R		691
Pampilhosa - Guarda	M						692
Porto - Coimbra		C			R		690
Porto - Pocinho*					R		694
Porto - Valenca	M	C					696

ROMANIA

Route							Table
Brasov - Ploesti	M						1600
Caransebes - Craiova	M		G		R		1620
Fetesti - Constanta					R		1680
Oradea - Cluj Napoca	M				R		1612

SERBIA and MONTENEGRO

Route							Table
Priboj - Bar	M	L					1370

SLOVAKIA

Route							Table
Banská Bystrica - Brezno - Košice	M						1192
Žilina - Poprad Tatry	M						1180

SLOVENIA

Route							Table
Jesenice - Sežana	M		G		R		1302
Maribor - Zidani Most	M						1315
Maribor - Bleiburg	M		G		R		1315
Villa Opicina - Ljubljana - Zagreb			G		R		1305

SPAIN

Route							Table
Algeciras - Ronda	M				R		673
Barcelona - Latour de Carol	M						656
Bilbao - San Sebastián	M						686
Bilbao - Santander	M						687
Ferrol - Gijón*		C					687
Granada - Almeria	M						673
Huesca - Canfranc	M		G		R		670
León - Monforte de Lemos	M						682
León - Oviedo	M						685
Lleida - La Pobla de Segur	M	L					655
Málaga - Bobadilla			G				673
Santander - Oviedo	M	C					687
Zaragoza - València	M				R		670

SWEDEN

Route							Table
Bollnäs - Ånge - Sundsvall	M	L					761
Borlänge - Mora	M	L				F	758
Borlänge - Ludvika - Frövi	M					F	755
Narvik - Kiruna	M					F	765
Östersund - Storlien				L		F	761

SWITZERLAND

Route							Table
Andermatt - Göschenen			G				576
Basel - Delémont - Moutier	M				R		505
Chur - Arosa	M		G				541
Chur - Brig - Zermatt*	M						575/576
Chur - St Moritz*	M		G				540
Davos - Filisur	M		G				545a
Davos - Landquart	M						545
Interlaken Ost - Jungfraujoch*	M	L					564
Interlaken Ost - Luzern	M	L					561
Interlaken West - Spiez				L			560
Lausanne - Brig	M				R		570
Lausanne - Neuchâtel - Biel	M	L					505
Montreux - Zweisimmen - Lenk	M	L	G				566
Rorschach - Kreuzlingen				L			532
St Moritz - Scuol Tarasp	M						546
St Moritz - Tirano*	M						547
Spiez - Zweisimmen			G				563
Thun - Kandersteg - Brig*	M	L					562
Zürich / Luzern - Chiasso	M	L					550
Zürich - Chur	M	L					520

Airport code and name	City	Distance	Journey	Transport ‡	City terminal	Table
AAR Aarhus	Aarhus	37 km	40 mins	🚍 flybus, connects with flights	Banegårdspladsen, Central rail station	
ABZ Aberdeen, Dyce	Aberdeen	11 km	33 mins	🚍 **727**, ①-⑤ every 30 mins; ⑥⑦ hourly	Union Square bus station. Also ①-⑤ 🚍 **80** to Dyce rail station	
ALC Alacant	Alacant	12 km	30 mins	🚍 **C6**, every 20 mins 0600 - 0000	Plaza Puerta del Mar	
AMS Amsterdam, Schiphol	Amsterdam	17 km	20 mins	Train, every 10 mins	Centraal rail station	451, 454
	Rotterdam	65 km	45 mins	Train, every 30 mins	Centraal rail station	450, 454
	Den Haag	43 km	35 mins	Train, every 30 mins	Centraal rail station	450, 454
AOI Ancona, Falconara	Ancona	16 km	30 mins	1) 🚍 Linea J, 2) Train hourly at peak times: 17 mins	Main rail station	
ATH Athína, Elefthérios Venizélos	Athína	27 km	39 mins	Metro (line **3**), 2 per hour	Syntagma	1440
	Pireás	41 km	90 mins	🚍 **X96**, 3 - 4 per hour	Platía Karaiskáki	
BCN Barcelona, Aeroport del Prat	Barcelona	14 km	19 mins	Train, 2 per hour	Sants. Also calls at Passeig de Gràcia rail station (26 mins)	659
BSL Basel - Mulhouse - Freiburg	Basel	9 km	20 mins	🚍 **50**, ①-⑤ 8 per hour; ⑥⑦ 6 per hour	SBB rail station / Kannenfeldplatz	
	Freiburg	60 km	55 mins	🚍 ①-⑤ every 1 - 2 hours; ⑥⑦ every 2 hours	Rail station	
BHD Belfast, City, George Best	Belfast	2 km	15 mins	🚍 Airlink **600**, ①-⑤ every 20 mins; ⑦ every 40 mins	Europa Buscentre. Also train from Sydenham rail station	
BFS Belfast, International	Belfast	26 km	40 mins	🚍 Airbus **300**, Ⓐ every 15 mins; ⑥ every 20; ⑦ every 30	Europa Buscentre (adjacent to Great Victoria St rail station)	
BEG Beograd, Nikola Tesla	Beograd	18 km	30 mins	🚍 **72**, every 32 minutes	Rail station	
SXF Berlin, Schönefeld	Berlin	24 km	28 mins	Train, AirportExpress **RE7/ RB14** 2 per hour 0631 - 2331	Hbf, also Ost, Alexanderplatz and Zoo rail stations	847
TXL Berlin, Tegel	Berlin	7 km	40 mins	🚍 JetExpressBus **TXL**, Ⓐ every 10 mins, Ⓒ every 20 mins	Hauptbahnhof rail station	
BIQ Biarritz - Anglet - Bayonne	Biarritz	3 km	12 mins	🚍 STAB **6**, every hour approx.	Town centre	
	Bayonne	7 km	28 mins	🚍 STAB **6**, every hour approx.	Rail station	
BIO Bilbao, Sondika	Bilbao	10 km	45 mins	🚍 Bizkaibus **A-3247**, every hour 0620 - 0000	Plaza Moyúa (Metro station Moyúa)	
BLL Billund	Vejle	25 km	34 mins	🚍 Sydtrafik **43**	Town centre	
BHX Birmingham, International	Birmingham	12 km	11 mins	Train, ①-⑥ + 9 per hour, ⑦ 6 per hour	New Street rail station from International	129, 142, 143
BLQ Bologna, Guglielmo Marconi	Bologna	8 km	25 mins	🚍 Aerobus **BLQ**, every 15 mins 0600 - 2315	Centrale rail station	
BOD Bordeaux, Mérignac	Bordeaux	12 km	45 mins	🚍 Jet 'Bus, every 45 mins 0745 - 2245	St Jean rail station	
BOH Bournemouth, Hurn	Bournemouth	10 km	15 mins	🚍 **A 1** Airport Shuttle, hourly 0730 - 1830	Rail station, Bus station (Travel Interchange)	
BTS Bratislava, Milan Rastislav Štefánika	Bratislava	10 km	25 mins	🚍 **61**, 3 - 4 per hour	Main rail station (Hlavná stanica)	
BRE Bremen	Bremen	3 km	20 mins	Tram **6**, ①-⑥ every 10 mins, ⑦ every 20 mins	Main rail station	
VBS Brescia, Montichiari, Verona	Verona	50 km	45 mins	🚍, connects with Ryanair flights	Main rail station	
	Brescia	18 km	20 mins	🚍, connects with Ryanair flights	Main rail station	
BRS Bristol, International	Bristol	13 km	30 mins	🚍 International Flyer, ①-⑥ 3 - 6 per hour; ⑦ 2 - 6 per hour	Temple Meads rail station, also bus station	
BRQ Brno	Brno	8 km	30 mins	🚍 **76**, 2 per hour	Main rail station, also bus station	
BRU Brussels, Nationaal / Zaventem	Brussels	12 km	25 mins	Train, 6 per hour	Midi / Zuid rail station (also calls at Central and Nord)	401
	Antwerpen	38 km	34 mins	Train, Ⓐ 2 per hour, Ⓒ hourly.	Centraal	420, 432
OTP Bucuresti, Henri Coanda, Otopeni	Bucuresti	16 km	45 mins	🚍 **783**, ①-⑤ every 15 - 30 mins; ⑥⑦ every 30 mins	Piata Victoriei (800m from Nord station or 1 stop on subway)	
BUD Budapest, Ferihegy	Budapest	16 km	40 mins	🚍 **200E**, every 10 - 20 mins	Köbánya-Kispest metro station (metro connection to city centre)	
	Budapest	18 km	25 mins	Train, 2 - 6 per hour	🚍 **200E**, to Ferihegy station then train to Nyugati rail station.	
BZG Bydgoszcz	Bydgoszcz	4 km	30 mins	🚍 **80**, 2 per hour	Main rail station	
CCF Carcassonne, Salvaza	Carcassonne	5 km	10 mins	🚍, connects with Ryanair flights	Place Davilla and Carcassonne rail station	
CWL Cardiff	Cardiff	19 km	40 mins	🚍 Airbus Xpress **T9**, ①-⑥ hourly, ⑦ every 2 hours	Central rail station, city centre	
	Cardiff	19 km	50 mins	🚍 to Rhoose then Train: ①-⑥ hourly, ⑦ every 2 hours	Central rail station	
CRL Charleroi, Brussels South	Brussels	55 km	60 mins	🚍 Brussels City Shuttle, every 30 mins	Brussels Midi (corner of Rue de France / Rue de l'Instruction)	
	Charleroi		18 mins	🚍 Line **A**, ①-⑤ 2 per hour, ⑥⑦ hourly	Main rail station	
ORK Cork	Cork	8 km	25 mins	🚍 **226**, ①-⑥ 2 per hour, ⑦ hourly	Rail station, also Parnell Place bus station	
LDY Derry (Londonderry)	Londonderry	11 km	30 mins	🚍 connects with flights	Foyle Street bus station	
DNR Dinard - Pleurtuit - St-Malo	St Malo	14 km	20 mins	Taxis only. Dinard 6 km 10 mins		
DSA Doncaster - Sheffield	Doncaster	10 km	25 mins	🚍 **91**, ①-⑥ 2 per hour; ⑦ hourly	Frenchgate Interchange (bus station)	
DOK Donetsk	Donetsk	13 km	40 mins	Fixed-run taxi **5**	Main rail station	
DTM Dortmund, Wickede	Dortmund	10 km	25 mins	🚍 every hour, AirportExpress	Main rail station (Hbf). Also 🚍 to Holzwickede rail station	
DRS Dresden	Dresden	15 km	21 mins	Train (S-Bahn **S2**) every 30 mins	Main rail stations (Hbf and Neustadt)	857a
DUB Dublin	Dublin	11 km	60 mins	🚍 Airlink **747**, every 10 mins (15 - 20 mins on ⑦)	Bus station (Busáras) in O'Connell St., Heuston rail station	
	Belfast	157 km	130 mins	🚍 **001 / 200**, hourly 0520 - 2120 also 2320, 0120, 0320	Europa Buscentre. Also 2220, 0020, 0220, 0420 June 3 - Sept. 22	
DBV Dubrovnik, Čilipi	Dubrovnik	24 km	30 mins	🚍 Atlas Bus, connects with flights	Bus station	
DUS Düsseldorf, International	Düsseldorf	7 km	12 mins	Train (S-Bahn **S1**) Ⓐ every 20 mins, Ⓒ every 30 mins	Main rail station (Hauptbahnhof)	800, 802
EMA East Midlands, Nottingham - - Leicester - Derby	East Midlands	10 km	10 mins	Taxi shuttle	East Midlands Parkway rail station	
	Nottingham	21 km	55 mins	🚍 Skylink, every 30 min. 0505 - 0105, also 0205, 0305, 0405	Broadmarsh bus station	
	Derby	19 km	40 mins	🚍 Skylink every 30 min. 0615 - 1855; (60 mins 1945 - 0545)	Bus station	
	Loughborough	8 km	25 mins	🚍 Skylink every 30 min. 0715 - 2017; (60 mins 2057 - 0657)	Swan Street	
	Leicester	23 km	55 mins	🚍 Skylink every 30 min. 0715 - 1948; (60 mins 2057 - 0657)	St Margaret's bus station	
EDI Edinburgh, Turnhouse	Edinburgh	11 km	25 mins	🚍 Airlink **100**, every 10 mins. **N 22** 2400 - 0600 every 30mins.	Haymarket rail station; Waverley Bridge (next to Waverley station)	
ERF Erfurt	Erfurt	6 km	22 mins	Tram, Line **4**, Ⓐ 3 - 6 per hour; Ⓒ 2 per hour	Main rail station (Hauptbahnhof)	
EBJ Esbjerg	Esbjerg	12 km	21 mins	🚍 **8**, hourly	Bybusterminal	
EXT Exeter	Exeter	8 km	25 mins	🚍 **56, 56A, 56B**, 1 per hour	St Davids rail station	
FAO Faro	Faro	6 km	20 mins	🚍 Proxima **16**, 1 per hour	Rail station, Bus station	
FLR Firenze, Amerigo Vespucci	Firenze	7 km	20 mins	🚍 Ataf Vola in bus **62**, every 30 mins	Santa Maria Novella rail station	
HHN Frankfurt, Hahn	Frankfurt	120 km	105 mins	🚍, connects with Ryanair flights	Mannheimer Straße, adjacent to main rail station (Hauptbahnhof)	
	Also 🚍 to Bingen, 60 mins; Heidelberg hbf, 140 mins; Koblenz, 70 mins; Köln hbf, 135 mins; Luxembourg, 105 mins; Mainz, 70 mins; Mannheim, 110 mins					
FRA Frankfurt	Frankfurt	10 km	15 mins	Train (S-Bahn **S8** or **S9**), 4 - 6 times hourly	Main rail station (Hauptbahnhof)	917a
FDH Friedrichshafen	Friedrichshafen	4 km	7 mins	1 - 2 trains per hour	Main rail station (Stadt) or Harbour (Hafen)	933
GDN Gdańsk, Lech Walesa	Gdańsk	10 km	22 mins	Train **PKM**, Port Lotniczy, 3 - 4 per hour	Wrzeszcz rail station, then 3 stops (every 15 mins) to Główny	
GVA Genève	Genève	6 km	6 mins	Train, 5 times hourly	Cornavin rail station	500, 570
GOA Genova, Cristoforo Colombo	Genova	7 km	20 mins	🚍 Volabus, 1 - 2 per hour	Principe rail station	
GRO Girona	Girona	12 km	25 mins	🚍, hourly	Rail / Bus station (Estación autobuses)	
	Barcelona	102 km	70 mins	🚍, connects with Ryanair flights	Estacio del Nord, corner of carrer Ali Bei 80 / Sicilia	

‡ –   The frequencies shown apply during daytime on weekdays and are from the airport to the city centre. There may be fewer journeys in the evenings, at weekends and during the winter
months. Extended 🚍 journey times could apply during peak hours.

Airport code and name	City	Distance	Journey	Transport ‡	City terminal	Table
GLA Glasgow, International	Glasgow	15 km	15 mins	🚌 *GlasgowFlyer*, ①–⑥ every 10 mins, ⑦ every 15 mins.	Central rail station	
PIK Glasgow, Prestwick	Glasgow	61 km	50 mins	Train, ①–⑥ 4 per hour, ⑦ 2 per hour	Central rail station	216
GSE Göteborg, City	Göteborg	17 km	30 mins	🚌, connects with Ryanair, Air Berlin and Wizz Air flights	Nils Ericson Terminalen (bus station) / Central rail station	
GOT Göteborg, Landvetter	Göteborg	25 km	30 mins	🚌, ①–⑤ 3 per hour, ⑥⑦ 2 - 3 per hour	Nils Ericson Terminalen (bus station) / Central rail station	
GRZ Graz	Graz	9 km	9 mins	Train ①–⑥ 1 - 2 per hour, ⑦ every 2 hours	Main rail station (Hauptbahnhof)	980
GNB Grenoble, St Geoirs	Grenoble	37 km	45 mins	🚌, connects with flights	Main rail station, also bus station	
HAM Hamburg, Fuhlsbüttel	Hamburg	11 km	24 mins	Train (S-Bahn **S1**), every 10 mins	Main rail station (Hauptbahnhof)	
HAJ Hannover, Langenhagen	Hannover	15 km	17 mins	Train (S-Bahn **S5**), every 30 mins	Main rail station (Hauptbahnhof)	809
HEL Helsinki, Vantaa	Helsinki	19 km	35 mins	Train ①–⑥ 4 - 6 per hour, ⑦ 3 - 4 per hour	Main rail station	
NOC Ireland West Airport Knock	Ballyhaunis	22 km	30 mins	🚌 **64**, 0855, 1250	Rail station	235
IOM Isle of Man, Ronaldsway	Douglas	16 km	30 mins	🚌 **1**, hourly (every 30 mins in peak periods)	Lord street	
IST İstanbul, Atatürk	İstanbul	28 km	40 mins	🚌, *Havas Airport Shuttle* hourly 0400 - 2400	Taksim	
	İstanbul	28 km	60 mins	Metro to Zeytinburnu, then over bridge for Tram **T1**	Sirkeci rail station	
SAW İstanbul, Sabiha Gökcen	İstanbul	32 km	60 mins	🚌, 1–2 per hour, 0540 - 2040	Bus station. Also Pendik rail station is 4km from airport	
XRY Jerez	Jerez	10 km	9 mins	Train, 11 trains per day	Jerez de la Frontera, then to Cadiz	671
FKB Karlsruhe - Baden-Baden	Baden-Baden	8 km	15 mins	🚌 **205**, connects with Ryanair flights	Rail station; also 🚌 **140** to Karlsruhe Hbf, 25 mins	
KTW Katowice, Pyrzowice	Katowice	34 km	50 mins	🚌 *Lotnisko, PKM*, 1 per hour approx	Katowice Dworzec (main rail station)	
KUN Kaunas	Kaunas	13 km	40 mins	🚌 **120, 29**	City centre	
	Vilnius	102 km	90 mins	🚌 connects with Ryanair flights	Hotel Panorama, close to bus and rail stations	
KLU Klagenfurt	Klagenfurt	5 km	25 mins	🚌 **45**, to Annabichl rail station, then train or 🚌 **40**	Main rail station and bus station	
CPH København, Kastrup	København	12 km	15 mins	Train, every 10 mins	Main rail station (Hovedbanegård)	703
	Malmö	36 km	22 mins	Train, every 20 mins	Central rail station	703
CGN Köln / Bonn, Konrad Adenauer	Bonn	25 km	32 mins	🚌 **SB60**, ①–⑤ 2 per hour; ⑥⑦ 1 - 2 per hour	Main rail station (Hauptbahnhof)	
	Köln	15 km	16 mins	Train **S13**, ①–⑤ every 20 mins, ⑥⑦ every 30 mins	Main rail station (Hbf). Also to Mönchengladbach, Koblenz	802
KRK Kraków John Paul II Airport (Balice)	Kraków	12 km	18 mins	Train, 2 per hour, from Lotnisko station	Kraków Główny	1099
KBP Kyïv, Boryspil	Kyïv	34 km	60 mins	🚌 **322** *Polit*, 2 - 3 per hour	Main rail station	
LBA Leeds - Bradford	Leeds	16 km	40 mins	🚌 **757**, 2 per hour	Main rail station and bus station	
	Bradford	11 km	40 mins	🚌 **737, 747**, 2 per hour	Interchange rail station	
AOC Leipzig, Altenburg - Nobitz	Leipzig	75 km	70 mins	🚌 **250** *ThüSac*, connects with Ryanair flights	Main rail station. Also stops at Altenburg rail station after 15 mins	
LEJ Leipzig - Halle	Leipzig	20 km	14 mins	Train, 2 - 3 per hour	Main rail station (Hauptbahnhof)	856
	Halle	18 km	12 mins	Train, 2 per hour	Main rail station (Hauptbahnhof)	856
LNZ Linz, Blue Danube	Linz	12 km	19 mins	🚌, connects with Ryanair flights	Main rail station. Also free 🚌 to Hörsching rail station, 3 mins	
LIS Lisboa, Portela	Lisboa	3 km	9 mins	Train, Red (Vermelho) line. Every 5 - 9 mins	Oriente rail station. For Santa Apolónia change at São Sebastião	
LPL Liverpool, John Lennon	Liverpool	11 km	37 mins	🚌 **500**, every 30 mins 0545 - 1945	Lime Street rail station, Liverpool One bus station	
LJU Ljubljana, Jože Pučnik, Brnik	Ljubljana	26 km	45 mins	🚌, Ⓐ hourly 0500 - 2000; Ⓒ 0700, every 2 hours 1000 - 2000	Bus station (Avtobusna postaja)	
LCJ Łódź, Lublinek	Łódź	6 km	20 mins	🚌 **65**	Kaliska rail station	
LCY London, City	London	12 km	20 mins	Train (Docklands Light Railway), every 8 - 10 mins	Bank underground (tube) station	140
LGW London, Gatwick	London	44 km	30 mins	Train *Gatwick Express*, every 15 minutes	Victoria rail station	103, 105, 140
LHR London, Heathrow	London	24 km	15 mins	Train *Heathrow Express*, every 15 minutes	Paddington rail station	140
	London	24 km	58 mins	Underground train (tube), every 5 mins	King's Cross St Pancras rail station	140
LTN London, Luton	London	50 km	35 mins	🚌 6 - 7 per hour / 🚌 between ✈ and Parkway rail station)	St Pancras International rail station	103, 140, 170
SEN London, Southend	London	64 km	55 mins	Train, 3 per hour	Liverpool Street rail station	
STN London, Stansted	London	55 km	46 mins	Train *Stansted Express*, every 15 minutes	Liverpool Street rail station	140
LBC Lübeck, Blankensee	Lübeck	8 km	30 mins	🚌 **6**, every 20 mins	Bus station (bus stop 5). Also train from Flughafen 300m walk	827
	Hamburg	59 km	75 mins	🚌 *VHHAG*, connects with Ryanair flights	Corner Adenaueralle / Brockesstrasse (ZOB) near main rail station	
LUZ Lublin	Lublin	10 km	15 mins	Train, ①–⑥ 5 per day, ⑦ 3 per day, connects with flights	Main rail station	
LUX Luxembourg, Findel	Luxembourg	7 km	25 mins	🚌 **16**, every 15 mins ①–⑥, every 30 mins ⑦	Central rail station	
LWO Lviv, Skniliv	Lvov	10 km		🚌, Taxi-bus *Marshrutka*	City Centre	
LYS Lyon, St Exupéry	Lyon	23 km	30 mins	Tram *RhôneExpress*, 4 per hour	Part Dieu rail station	
	Chambéry	87 km	60 mins	🚌 *Altibus*, 4 - 5 times daily	Bus station (gare routière)	
	Grenoble	91 km	65 mins	🚌 *Faure Vercors*, 0630 Ⓐ, hourly 0730 - 2330	Bus station (gare routière); Place de la Résistance	
MAD Madrid, Barajas T4	Madrid	12 km	11 mins	Train, *Cercanías*, from T4, every 30 mins 0558 - 2227	Chamartín, also Atocha 25 mins. 🚌 from T4 to T1, T2 and T3.	
AGP Málaga	Málaga	8 km	12 mins	Train, every 30 mins	María Zambrano (renfe) and Centro-Alameda rail stations	662
MMX Malmö, Sturup	Malmö	30 km	45 mins	🚌 *flygbussarna*, 1 - 2 per hour	Central rail station	
MAN Manchester	Manchester	16 km	14 mins	Train, up to 9 per hour (hourly through the night)	Piccadilly rail station	
MSE Manston	Ramsgate	3 km	9 mins	🚌 **38**, ①–⑥ hourly 0943 - 1343	Rail station	
MRS Marseille, Provence	Marseille	28 km	25 mins	🚌, every 20 mins. See also rail / bus on Table 351	St Charles rail station; also 🚌 to Aix TGV rail stn. every 30 mins	
FMM Memmingen	Memmingen	5 km	10 mins	🚌 **2, 810, 811**	Bus station and rail station; also 🚌 to München, 95 mins	
LIN Milano, Linate	Milano	9 km	20 mins	1) 🚌 **73** every 10 mins; 2) 🚌 *Starfly*, every 30 mins	1) Piazza S. Babila, Metro line 1; 2) Centrale rail station	
MXP Milano, Malpensa	Milano	45 km	40 mins	1) *Malpensa Express* train, every 30 mins; 2) 1 - 2 per hour	1) Cadorna and Bovisa rail stations; 2) Centrale rail station	583
			50 mins	🚌 *Bus Express*, 2 per hour / *Shuttle Air* 3 per hour	Centrale rail station. Also 🚌 to Gallarate (Table 590)	
BGY Milano, Orio al Serio, Bergamo	Milano	45 km	60 mins	🚌, 1 - 2 per hour	Centrale rail station (Air Terminal)	
	Bergamo	4 km	15 mins	🚌, 2 per hour	Rail station	
MSQ Minsk	Minsk	42 km	90 mins	🚌 **112, 300**,	Vostochniy and Moskovskiy bus stations	
DME Moskva, Domodedovo	Moskva	35 km	47 mins	Train, *Aeroexpress*, 1 - 2 per hour approx	Paveletskaya rail station	1901
SVO Moskva, Sheremetyevo	Moskva	35 km	35 mins	Train, *Aeroexpress*, 1 - 2 per hour approx	Belorusskaya rail station	1901
VKO Moskva, Vnukovo	Moskva	28 km	40 mins	Train, *Aeroexpress*, 1 per hour approx	Kiyevskaya rail station	1901
MUC München, International	München	37 km	40 mins	Train **S1, S8** for Hbf, every 10 mins; **S8** for Ost, every 20 mins	Main rail stations (Hauptbahnhof, Ostbahnhof)	892
	Freising	6 km	24 mins	🚌 *MVV* **635**, every 20 mins	Rail station for connections to Regensburg, Passau	878, 944
NTE Nantes, Atlantique	Nantes	9 km	30 mins	🚌 *Tan Air*, ± hourly; connects with flights	Main rail station	
NAP Napoli, Capodichino	Napoli	7 km	20 mins	🚌 *ANM* **3S** line, 2 per hour; *Alibus*, 2 per hour	Piazza Garibaldi (Centrale rail station)	
NCL Newcastle, International	Newcastle	9 km	25 mins	Metro train, every 12 mins	Main rail station	

‡ – The frequencies shown apply during daytime on weekdays and are from the airport to the city centre. There may be fewer journeys in the evenings, at weekends and during the winter months. Extended 🚌 journey times could apply during peak hours.

¶ – Graz Airport - Feldkirchen rail station is located about 300 metres away from the airport.

Airport code and name	City	Distance	Journey	Transport ‡	City terminal	Table
NCE Nice, Côte d'Azur	Nice	7 km	20 mins	🚌 99, 2 per hour	SNCF rail station ¶	
		7 km	20 mins	🚌 98, 3 per hour	City centre, Riquier	
FNI Nîmes - Arles - Camargue	Nîmes	12 km	20 mins	🚌, connects with Ryanair flights	Rail station	
NWI Norwich	Norwich	8 km	24 mins	🚌 603, ①–⑥ 4 per hour 0700 - 1800, 1835, 1905, 1935, 2002 Bus station		
NUE Nürnberg	Nürnberg	6 km	12 mins	Train, U-bahn U2, 4 - 6 per hour	Main rail station (Hauptbahnhof)	
ODS Odesa	Odesa	9 km	30mins	🚌 129	Rail station	
OSL Oslo, Gardermoen	Oslo	49 km	19 mins	Train Flytoget, 3 - 6 per hour	Central rail station	771
TRF Oslo, Sandefjord Torp	Oslo	123 km	116 mins	🚌 to Torp rail station (4 mins) for train to Oslo	Also 🚌 to Oslo Bus terminal	783
RYG Oslo, Rygge	Oslo	69 km	51 mins	🚌 connects with Ryanair flights, to Rygge rail station (4 km).	Sentral rail station (51 mins Rygge to Sentral)	770
PMO Palermo, Falcone-Borsellino	Palermo	24 km	45 mins	Train Trinacria express, ①–⑥ 2 per hour, ⑦ hourly	Centrale rail station	
PMI Palma, Mallorca	Palma	11 km	30 mins	🚌 1, every 15 mins	Paseo de Mallorca, Placa d'Espanya (for rail stations), the Port	
BVA Paris, Beauvais	Paris	80 km	75 mins	🚌, connects with Ryanair and WizzAir flights	Porte Maillot, Metro (Line 1) for Châtelet Les Halles, Gare de Lyon	
CDG Paris, Charles de Gaulle	Paris	25 km	35 mins	RER train, (Line B), every 7 - 15 mins	Nord, Châtelet Les Halles, and St Michel rail stations	398
	Disneyland	23 km	45 mins	🚌 VEA Navette / Shuttle, every 20 minutes	Disneyland Resort, Disneyland hotels	
ORY Paris, Orly	Paris	15 km	35 mins	🚌 to Pont de Rungis, then RER train, (Line C) 4 per hr.	Austerlitz, St Michel, Musée d'Orsay, and Invalides rail stns.	398
	Paris	15 km	33 mins	ORLYVAL shuttle to Antony then RER train, (Line B) 4 per hr.	Châlet-Les-Halles, Nord rail stations	398
PGF Perpignan, Rivesaltes	Perpignan	5 km	15 mins	🚌, connects with flights	Rail station, bus station (gare routière)	
PSA Pisa, Galileo Galilei	Pisa	2 km	8 mins	🚌 every 10 minutes	Centrale rail station	613
OPO Porto	Porto	17 km	35 mins	Metro Train, Line E, 3 per hour	Campanhã rail station	
POZ Poznań, Ławica	Poznań	6 km	20 mins	🚌 L MPK, 2 per hour	Rail station	
PRG Praha, Václav Havel	Praha	19 km	46 mins	🚌 AE Airport Express, every 20 - 30 mins	hlavní rail station	
	Praha	17 km	60 mins	🚌 119, every 10 mins	Nádraží Veleslavín metro station, then Metro line A to muzeum	
PUY Pula	Pula	6 km	15 mins	🚌, connects with Ryanair flights	Town centre	
REU Reus	Reus	6 km	20 mins	🚌 50, Hispano Igualadina, hourly	Rail station	652
	Barcelona	90 km	90 mins	🚌 Hispano Igualadina connects with Ryanair flights	Sants rail station	
KEF Reykjavík, Keflavík	Reykjavík	50 km	45 mins	🚌 flybus, connects with all flights	BSÍ bus terminal	
RIX Riga	Riga	13 km	30 mins	🚌 22, every 10 - 30 mins	Abrenes iela (street) next to rail station	
RJK Rijeka	Rijeka	30 km	45 mins	🚌 Autotrans, connects with flights	Bus station, Jelačić Square	
CIA Roma, Ciampino	Roma	15 km	40 mins	🚌 Terravision 1 - 3 per hour	Termini rail station	622
FCO Roma, Fiumicino	Roma	26 km	42 mins	Train, ①–⑥ 4 per hour, ⑦ 2 per hour	Ostiense and Tiburtina rail stations	622
(also known as Leonardo da Vinci)	Roma	26 km	31 mins	Leonardo Express rail service, every 30 mins	Termini rail station	622
RTM Rotterdam	Rotterdam	5 km	20 mins	Airport Shuttle 33, ①–⑤ every 10 mins, ⑥⑦ every 15 mins	Groot Handelsgebouw (adjacent to Centraal rail station)	
RZE Rzeszów, Jasionka	Rzeszów	15 km	20 mins	🚌 L, connects with flights	Main rail station and bus station	
LED St Peterburg, Pulkovo II	St Peterburg	17 km	60 mins	🚌 13	Moskovskaya Metro station, Line 2 for Nevski Pr. (see City Plans)	
SZG Salzburg, W. A. Mozart	Salzburg	5 km	22 mins	🚌 2, ①–⑥ every 10 - 20 mins, ⑦ every 20 mins	Main rail station	
SIP Simferopol	Simferopol	12 km	28 mins	🚌 9 (trolleybus), every 10–15 mins	Main rail station	
SKP Skopje, Alexander the Great	Skopje	14 km	25 mins	🚌 Vardar Ekspres, connects with flights	Bus station	
SOF Sofia, International	Sofia	10 km	26 mins	Train, Line 1 from Terminal 2, every 10 mins	City centre. Change at Serdika for Line 2, for Central rail station	
SOU Southampton	Southampton	8 km	8 mins	Train, 50 metres from terminal, 4 - 5 trains per hour	Central rail station	108, 129
SPU Split, Kaštela	Split	16 km	50 mins	🚌 connects with flights	Bus station. Departs 200m from Airport terminal	
SVG Stavanger, Sola	Stavanger	14 km	30 mins	🚌 ①–⑤ every 20 mins, ⑥ 2 per hour, ⑦ hourly	Atlantic Hotel / Fiskepiren	
ARN Stockholm, Arlanda	Stockholm	44 km	20 mins	Arlanda Express train, every 15 mins	Central rail station	747, 760
NYO Stockholm, Skavsta	Stockholm	103 km	80 mins	🚌, connects with Ryanair flights	Cityterminal (bus station), also 🚌 to Nyköping rail station	
VST Stockholm, Västerås	Stockholm	107 km	75 mins	🚌, connects with Ryanair flights	Cityterminal (bus station), also 🚌 941 to Västerås rail station	
SXB Strasbourg, Entzheim	Strasbourg	10 km	9 mins	Train from Entzheim Aéroport (300m walk) 1 - 4 per hour	Gare Centrale (Central rail station)	388
STR Stuttgart, Echterdingen	Stuttgart	20 km	27 mins	Train (S-Bahn S2, S3), 2 - 4 times hourly	Main rail station (Hauptbahnhof)	932
SZZ Szczecin, Goleniów	Szczecin	35 km	35 mins	Train, 14 - 20 per day.	Szczecin Główny.	
TLL Tallinn, Ülemiste	Tallinn	5 km	22 mins	🚌 90K, every 30 mins 0800 - 1800	Balti jaam (rail station)	
TMP Tampere, Pirkkala	Tampere	18 km	25 mins	🚌, connects with Ryanair flights	Main rail station	
TBS Tbilisi	Tbilisi	19 km	30 mins	Train, 2 per day: 0845, 1805	Rail station	
TIA Tirana (Tiranë), Nënë Tereza	Tirana	12 km	45 mins	🚌 Rinas Express, every hour 0600 - 1800	National Museum in city centre	
TRN Torino, Caselle	Torino	16 km	20 mins	SATTI train every 30 mins	Torino Dora rail station, Piazza Baldissera	
	Torino	16 km	40 mins	🚌, ①–⑥ 2 - 3 per hour; ⑦ 1 - 2 per hour	Torino Porta Nuova and Porta Susa rail stations	
TLS Toulouse, Blagnac	Toulouse	8 km	38 mins	Tram, T2 every 15 minutes for Arènes then Metro line A	for Marengo-SNCF, then 300m to Matabiau rail station	
	Toulouse	8 km	20 mins	🚌 Aero, every 20 minutes	Place Jeanne d'Arc / Matabiau rail / bus station (gare routière)	
TRS Trieste, Ronchi dei Legionari	Trieste	33 km	50 mins	🚌 51, ①–⑥ 1 - 2 per hour; ⑦ hourly	Bus station, next to rail station	
	Monfalcone	4 km	17 mins	🚌 10, ①–⑥ 1 - 2 per hour; ⑦ hourly	Rail station	
TRD Trondheim, Værnes	Trondheim	33 km	37 mins	🚌, ①–⑤ hourly, ⑥⑦ every two hours	Rail station. Værnes rail station is 220m from Airport terminal	787
VLC València	València	9 km	22 mins	Train, Lines 3, 5, Ⓐ every 6 - 9 mins; ⑥⑦ every 8 - 12 mins	Xàtiva for Nord rail station	
VCE Venezia, Marco Polo	Venezia	12 km	25 mins	🚌 5, 2 per hour	Piazzale Roma (see city plans p32)	
	Venezia		80 mins	Waterbus Alilaguna ± every 30 mins	Lido 53 - 63 mins / Piazza S. Marco, 72 - 80 mins	
TSF Venezia, Treviso	Venezia	30 km	70 mins	🚌, connects with flights	Mestre rail station, Piazzale Roma (see city plans p32)	
VRN Verona, Villafranca	Verona	12 km	20 mins	🚌, every 20 mins 0635 - 2335	Rail station	
VNO Vilnius	Vilnius	4 km	7 mins	Train, every ± 40 minutes	Rail station	1812
WAW Warszawa, Frederic Chopin, Okęcie,	Warszawa	13 km	23 mins	SKM / KM train, 3 - 5 per hour	Śródmieście (2 - 3 per hr) or Centralna (1 - 2 per hr) rail stations	
WMI Warszawa, Modlin	Warszawa	44 km	47 mins	🚌, to Modlin rail stn, then train, approx 1 - 2 per hour	Centralna or Gdánska rail stations	1030
NRN Weeze, Niederrhein	Düsseldorf	70 km	75 mins	🚌, connects with Ryanair flights	Main rail station (Hauptbahnhof) Worringer Street	
	Düsseldorf	74 km	82 mins	🚌 SW1, to Weeze rail station, then train, Table 802	Main rail station (Hauptbahnhof)	802
VIE Wien, Schwechat	Wien	21 km	16 mins	City Airport Train (CAT), every 30 mins; special fares	Mitte rail station	985
	Wien	21 km	25 mins	S-bahn, every 30 mins	Mitte rail station	985
	Bratislava	54 km	60 mins	🚌 ÖBB - Postbus / Slovak Lines, hourly	AS Mlynské nivy (bus station) / Einsteinnova/Petrzalka	985
WRO Wrocław, Copernicus	Wrocław	10 km	30 mins	🚌 406, ①–⑥ 2 - 3 per hour; ⑦ every 40 mins	Rail station, bus station	
ZAG Zagreb	Zagreb	17 km	25 mins	🚌, 1 - 2 per hour	Bus station (Autobusni kolodvor), Avenija Marina Drzica	
ZAZ Zaragoza	Zaragoza	10 km	30 mins	🚌, ①–⑥ 1 - 2 per hour 0615 - 2315; ⑦ hourly 0645 - 2245	Paseo Maria Agustin, 150m from Portillo rail station	
ZRH Zürich	Zürich	10 km	13 mins	Train, 7 - 8 per hour	Main rail station (HB)	529

‡ – The frequencies shown apply during daytime on weekdays and are from the airport to the city centre. There may be fewer journeys in the evenings, at weekends and during the winter months. Extended 🚌 journey times could apply during peak hours.

¶ – Also train, from Nice St Augustin, ± hourly; 800m from Terminal 1.

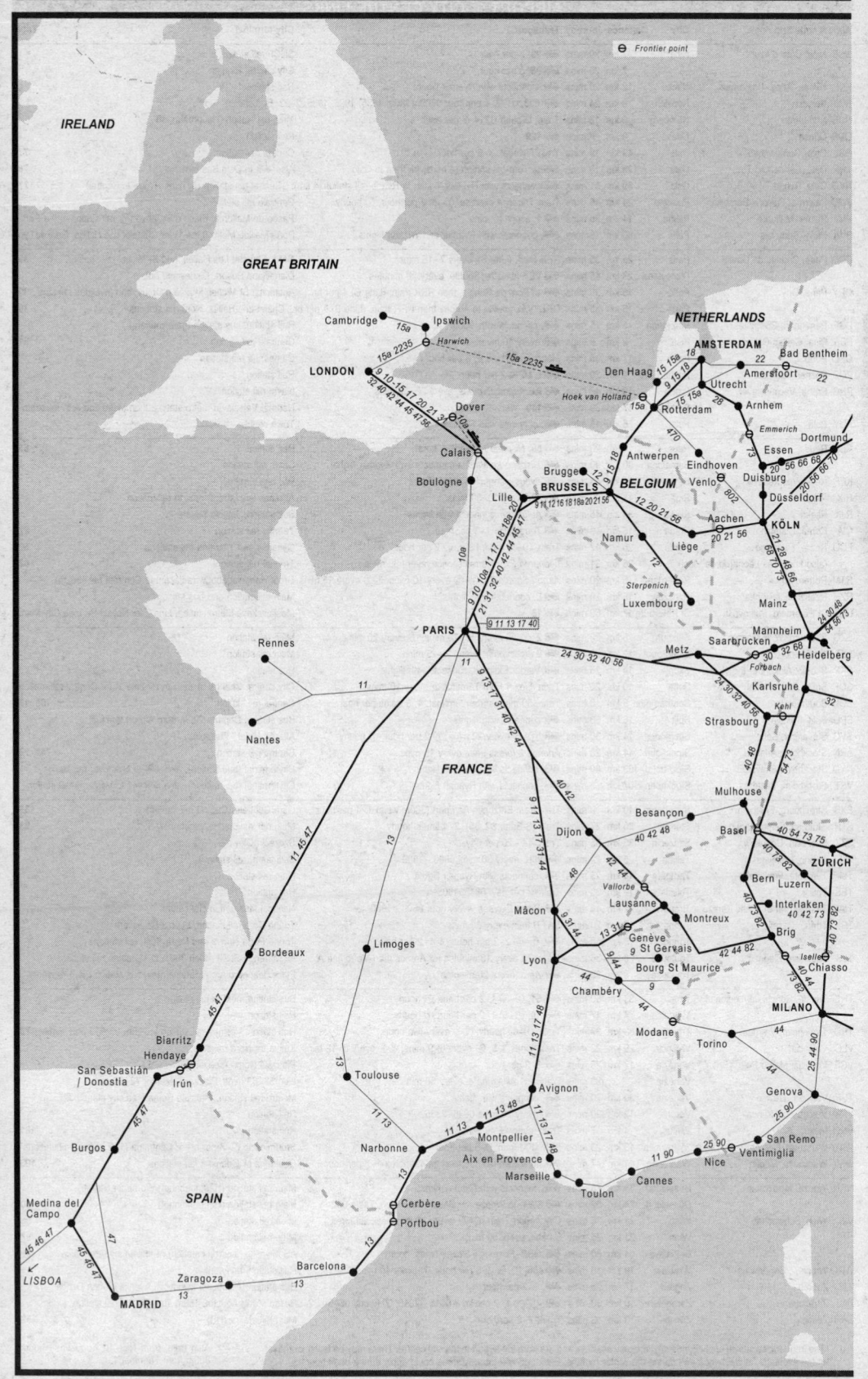

⊖ Frontier point

IRELAND

GREAT BRITAIN

NETHERLANDS

Cambridge 15a Ipswich
15a 2235 Harwich
LONDON 15a 2235
9 10 15 17 20 21 31
32 40 42 44 45 47 56

Dover

Calais

Boulogne

AMSTERDAM
Bad Bentheim
Den Haag 15 15a 18 Amersfoort 22
9 15 18 Utrecht 22
Hoek van Holland 15 15a Arnhem
15a Rotterdam Emmerich Dortmund
470 Essen 20 56 66 68
Antwerpen Eindhoven Duisburg 20 56 66 70
Brugge Venlo Düsseldorf
BRUSSELS BELGIUM 802
Lille 12 16 18 18a 20 21 56 KÖLN
9 11 12 16 18 18a 20 21 Aachen 21 28 48 66
Namur Liège 20 21 56 68 70 73
Sterpenich Mainz
Luxembourg 24 30 48
Metz Saarbrücken 32 68 Heidelberg
24 30 32 40 56 30 Forbach
Karlsruhe 32
Kehl
Strasbourg

PARIS
9 11 13 17 40

Rennes
11
Nantes

FRANCE

Bordeaux

Limoges

Biarritz
Hendaye
San Sebastián / Donostía
Irún

Burgos

Medina del Campo

LISBOA

Zaragoza
MADRID

SPAIN

Cerbère
Portbou

Barcelona

Narbonne
Toulouse

Montpellier
Aix en Provence
Marseille
Toulon
Cannes

Avignon

Lyon
Chambéry
Modane

Dijon
Besançon
Mâcon
Vallorbe
Lausanne
Genève
St Gervais
Bourg St Maurice

Mulhouse
Basel
Bern Luzern
Interlaken
Montreux Brig
Iselle
Torino

Nice
San Remo
Ventimiglia

Genova

MILANO

ZÜRICH
Chiasso

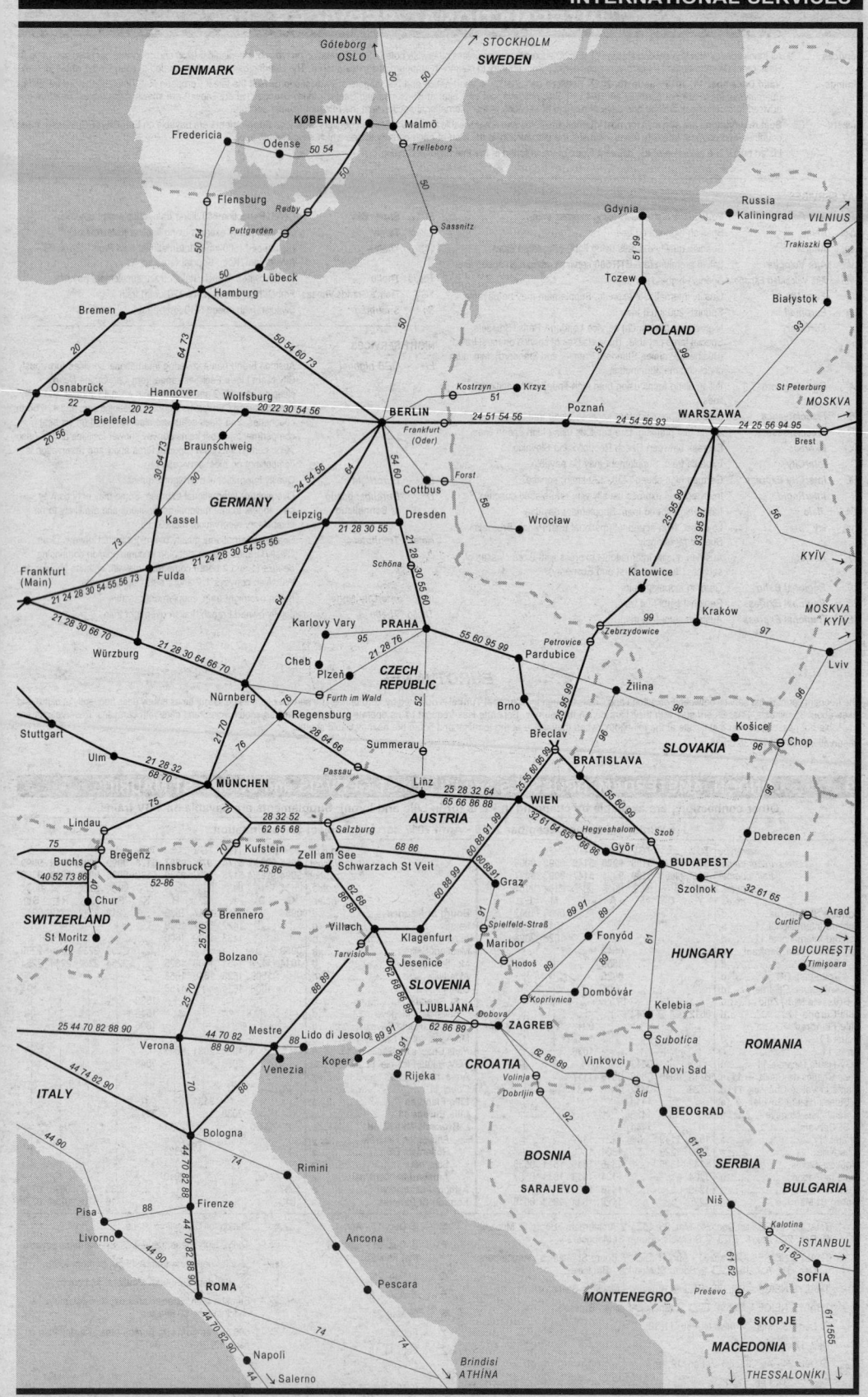

INTERNATIONAL SERVICES

Services	All trains convey first and second classes of seating accommodation unless otherwise noted. For information on types of sleeping car (🛏) and couchette car (⊨) see page 8. Restaurant (✕) and buffet (♀) cars vary considerably from country to country in standard of service offered. The catering car may not be carried or open for the whole journey.
Timings	**Valid December 11, 2016 - June 10, 2017.** Services can change at short notice and passengers are advised to consult the latest European Rail Timetable before travelling. International trains are not normally affected by public holidays, but may alter at Christmas and Easter - these changes (where known) are shown in the tables. Readers are advised to cross-check timings and days of running of services in the International section with the relevant country section.
Tickets	**Seat reservations** are available for most international trains and are advisable as some trains can get very crowded. **Supplements** are payable on **EuroCity** (EC) trains in most countries and on most InterCity trains – consult the introduction at the start of each country to see which supplements apply. Listed below is a selection of the different types of trains found in the International Section.

DAY SERVICES:

AP	*Alfa Pendular*	Portuguese high-quality tilting express train.
Alvia	*Alvia*	Spanish high-speed train.
Alta	*Altaria*	Spanish quality express using light, articulated stock.
AV	*Alta Velocità*	Italian premium fare **ETR 500** services using high-speed lines.
AVE	*Alta Velocidad Española*	Spanish high-speed train.
EC	*EuroCity*	Quality international express. Supplement may be payable.
Em	*Euromed*	Spanish 200 km/h train.
☆	*Eurostar*	High-speed (300 km/h) service London - Paris / Brussels. Special fares payable. Three classes of service on most trains: (Business Premier, Standard Premier and Standard). Minimum check-in time 30 minutes.
FA	*Frecciargento*	Italian tilting trains using both high-speed and traditional lines.
FB	*Frecciabianca*	Italian fast premium fare services using traditional lines.
FR	*Frecciarossa*	Italian fast premium fare services using high-speed lines.
Ex	*Express*	Express between Czech Republic and Slovakia.
IC	*InterCity*	Express train. Supplement may be payable.
ICE	*InterCity Express*	German high-speed (230 - 320 km/h) service.
IR	*InterRegio*	Inter-regional express usually with refurbished coaches.
ITA	*.italo*	Italian high-speed train. Supplement payable.
izy	*izy*	Low cost, high-speed international train Paris - Brussels. Special fares apply.
RJ	*Railjet*	Austrian quality international express with three classes of service: (Business, First and Economy).
RB	*Regional Bahn*	German stopping train.
RE	*Regional Express*	Regional semi-fast train.
REX	*Regional Express*	Austrian semi-fast train.

SC	*Super City*	Czech Pendolino **680** tilting train, supplement payable.
Talgo	*Talgo*	Spanish quality express using light, articulated stock.
⇌	*Thalys*	High-speed (300 km/h) international train Paris - Brussels - Amsterdam / Köln. Special fares apply.
Thello	*Thello*	Jointly owned French / Italian train, supplement payable.
TGV	*Train à Grande Vitesse*	French high-speed (270 - 320 km/h) train.
Sn	*Snabbtåg*	Swedish high-speed (210 km/h) train.

NIGHT SERVICES:

EN	*ÖBB nightjet*	Austrian brand name covering international services (previously City Night Line). Facilities range from *Comfortline Deluxe* sleeping cars (1, 2 and 3 berth) with en-suite shower and WC, to modernised *Comfortline Economy* sleeping cars and 4 / 6 berth couchettes. 2nd class seats are also conveyed (in six seat compartments). Most trains convey shower facilities and ♀ (also ✕ on certain services). Special fares apply and reservation is compulsory on most services.
EN	*EuroNight*	Quality international overnight express.
D	*Durchgangszug* or *Schnellzug*	Overnight or international express. Some may only convey passengers to international destinations and are likely to be compulsory reservation, marked Ⓡ.
Hotel	*Trenhotel*	Spanish international quality overnight train. Conveys Gran Clase / Grande Classe sleeping accommodation comprising *de luxe* (1 and 2 berth) compartments with en-suite shower and WC. Also conveys 1, 2 and 4 berth sleeping cars.
ICN	*InterCity Notte*	Italian overnight train, supplement payable.
Thello	*Thello*	Jointly owned French / Italian overnight train.

EUROTUNNEL

The frequent car-carrying service between Folkestone and Calais through the **Channel Tunnel** is operated by Eurotunnel. The service operates up to four times hourly (less frequently at night) and takes about 35 minutes. Passengers stay with their cars during the journey. Separate less-frequent trains operate for lorries, coaches, motorcycles, and cars with caravans. Reservations are advisable but passengers can buy tickets at the toll booths when they arrive at the terminal and board the next available shuttle.
Reservations: ✆ 08443 35 35 35.

9 LONDON, AMSTERDAM, BRUSSELS and LILLE - ST GERVAIS and BOURG ST MAURICE

Other connections are available by changing in Paris (or in Lille and Lyon). Supplements are payable on TGV trains.

Winter ski trains December 2016 - April 2017 service. Subject to confirmation.

train type	TGV	⇌	TGV	⇌	TGV	☆	☆
train number	964	9904/5	5108	9920	5146	9092	9096
train number	965	9906/7	5109	9921	5147	9093	9097
notes						Ⓡ	Ⓡ
notes	Y	C	F	A	F	M	E ❶
London St Pancras ....d.	...	...	...	...	...	0945	1942
Ashford International 11 ......a.	...	...	...	...	...	1015	2019
Ashford International 11 ......a.	...	...	...	...	...	1028	2028
Amsterdam Centraal .....d.	...	...	...	0542	...		...
Schiphol ....d.	...	...	...	0559	...		...
Rotterdam CS ....d.	...	...	...	0625	...		...
Antwerpen Centraal ....d.	...	...	...	0705	...		...
Brussels Midi / Zuid ....d.	...	0713	...	0753v	...		...
Lille Europe 11 ....d.	0612	...	0743	...	...		...
Lille Flandres ◇ ....d.		...	...	...	0943		...
Douai 11 ....d.		...	...	...	1012		...
Arras 11 ....d.		...	...	...	1030		...
TGV Haute Picardie 11 ....d.		...	0813	...			...
Paris Charles de Gaulle ✛ 11..d.	0713	0845	0853	0916	1117		...
Marne la Vallée Chessy § 11...d.	0728	...	0912	...	1131		...
Cluses (Haute Savoie).......a.			1418				...
Salanches Megève ......a.			1436				...
St Gervais ....a.			1444				...
Chambéry...................a.	1030	1149	...	1221	1427		...
Albertville.................a.	1109	1229	...	1304	1506		...
Moûtiers-Salins ....a.	1142	1305	...	1346	1545	1811	0533
Aime la Plagne ....a.	1204	...	...	1404	1613	1831	0557
Landry........................a.	1215	...	...	1416	1623		...
Bourg St Maurice ....a.	1225	...	...	1428	1634	1850	0616

train type	☆	⇌	TGV	TGV	⇌	TGV	☆	☆	☆	☆
train number	9095	9963/2	5174	970	9987	5178	9099	9099	9099	9099
train number	9094	9965/4	5175	971	9986	5179	9098	9098	9098	9098
notes	Ⓡ	Ⓡ	Ⓡ		Ⓡ	Ⓡ	Ⓡ	Ⓡ	Ⓡ	Ⓡ
notes	G	D	K	Z	B	K	P ❶	Q ❶	R ❶	S ❶
Bourg St Maurice ....d.	0934	...	1413	1517	1539	...	2212	2212	2212	2212
Landry........................d.		...	1422	1527	1549	...				
Aime la Plagne ....d.		...	1433	1539	1600	...				
Moûtiers-Salins ....d.	0959	...	...	...	...	...	2239	2239	2239	2239
Moûtiers-Salins ....d.	1014	1427	1451	1608	1625	...	2254	2254	2254	2254
Albertville.................d.		1509	1528	1646	1658	...				
Chambéry...................d.		1600	1614	...	1750	...				
St Gervais ....d.			...			1530				
Salanches Megève ......d.			...			1548				
Cluses (Haute Savoie)......d.			...			1606				
Marne la Vallée Chessy § 11 .....a.			1917	2017		...				
Paris Charles de Gaulle ✛ 11 ....a.		1908	1934	2031	2045	...				
TGV Haute Picardie 11 ....a.			2006	...		2048				
Arras 11 ....a.			...			...				
Douai 11 ....a.			...			...				
Lille Flandres ◇ ....a.			...	2131		...				
Lille Europe 11 ....a.			2038	...	2117	...				
Brussels Midi / Zuid..........a.		2036	...	2211	...	...				
Antwerpen Centraal.......a.			...	2256		...				
Rotterdam CS ....a.			...	2333		...				
Schiphol ....a.			...	2354		...				
Amsterdam Centraal ......a.			...	0010		...				
Ashford International 11 ......a.	1537	...	...	...	...	...	0633	...	0633	0707
London St Pancras ....a.	1613	...	...	...	...	...	0716	0705	0734	0750

A – THALYS NEIGE – ⑥ Dec. 24 - Mar. 25: 🛏 ♀ Amsterdam - Bourg St Maurice; ⑥ Dec. 24 - Apr. 8. 🛏 ♀ Brussels - Bourg St Maurice.

B – THALYS NEIGE – ⑥ Dec. 31 - Apr. 1. 🛏 ♀ Bourg St Maurice - Amsterdam; ⑥ Dec. 31 - Apr. 15: 🛏 ♀ Bourg St Maurice - Brussels.

C – THALYS NEIGE – Feb. 25: 🛏 ♀ Brussels - Moûtiers-Salins.

D – THALYS NEIGE – Mar. 4: 🛏 ♀ Moûtiers-Salins - Brussels.

E – ⑤ Dec. 23 - Mar. 31 (also ⑥ Feb. 11, 18).

G – ⑥ Dec. 24 - Apr. 8 (also ⑦ Feb. 12, 19).

K – Dec. 24, 31, Feb. 11, 18.

M – ⑥ Dec. 17 - Apr. 1.

P – ⑥ Dec. 31 - Mar. 18 (not Feb. 25).

Q – ⑥ Feb. 25.

R – ⑥ Apr. 1, 8.

S – ⑥ Mar. 25.

Y – Feb. 4, 11.

Z – Feb. 11, 18.

v – 0759 Dec. 24 - Jan. 21.

§ – Station for Disneyland, Paris.

⇌ – *Thalys* high-speed train Ⓡ ♀. Special fares payable.

❶ – ✕ after departure from Ashford. ✕ from 0500.

❶ – ✕ after departure from Moûtiers. ✕ from 0500.

☆ – Eurostar train. Special fares payable. Minimum check-in time 30 minutes.

◇ – 500 metres from Lille Europe (see Lille City Plan on page 30).

For explanation of standard symbols see page 4

LONDON - LILLE - PARIS and BRUSSELS *by Eurostar* 10

Minimum check-in time is 30 minutes, but passengers are advised to allow longer due to immigration procedures. Not available for London - Ebbsfleet - Ashford or v.v. Special fares payable that include three classes of service: business premier, standard premier and standard. All times shown are local times (France and Belgium are one hour ahead of Great Britain). All Eurostar services are Ⓡ, non-smoking and convey ✕ in Business Premier and Standard Premier, 🍸 in Standard.

Service December 11 - May 27. No service December 25.

Due to engineering work from January 23 until May 27 on the high speed line between Calais and Paris, services will depart Paris up to 12 minutes earlier and arrive up to 12 minutes later.

km	km	*train number*	9080	9108	9002	9110	9110	9004	9008	9008	9114	9010	9010	9116	9116	9014	9018	9126	9126	9020	9022	9060	9024
		notes	①–⑤		⑥		⑥	①–⑤	⑥	①–⑤		⑦					Ⓑ	①–⑥	⑦	⑥			
		notes	j	P		L		q		q	J	y	R	V	X			q	y		S	Z	
0	0	**London** St Pancras d.	0540	0613	0618	0650	0657	0701	0752	0755	0804	0819	0831	0855	0858	0924	1024¶	1058	1104	1101	1131	1201	1224
35	35	Ebbsfleet International d.	0558	0630	|	0707	|	|	0812	0812	|	0838	|	0915	0915	0941	1042¶	1115	|	|	|	|	1242
90	90	Ashford International d.	0624	0653	0655	0728	0728	|	|	|	|	|	|	|	|	|	|	|	|	|	|	|	|
166	166	Calais Fréthun a.	|	|	|	0859	|	|	|	|	|	|	|	|	1059	|	|	|	|	|	|	|	|
267	267	Lille Europe a.	|	|	|	0930	0926	|	|	|	1026	|	|	1126	1130	|	|	1326	1326	|	|	|	|
	373	**Brussels** Midi / Zuid a.	|	0922	|	1007	1005	|	|	|	1105	|	|	1205	1208	|	|	1405	1405	|	|	|	|
492		**Paris** Nord a.	0917	...	0947	...	...	1017	1117	1117	...	1147	1147	...	...	1248	1347	...	...	1417	1447	1529	1547

train number	9132	9028	9136	9032	9140	9036	9038	9144	9040	9148	9044	9152	9046	9152	9048	9050	9156	9158	9054	9162	9056		
notes					Ⓑ		⑤⑦	⑥				⑦	①–⑤		⑤⑦	Ⓑ	⑥⑦	①–⑤		⑦	⑦		
notes		Q	N				B			W	h	y	q	G	C		z	q	h	m	g		
London St Pancras d.	1258	1331	1404	1422	1504	1531	1601	1604	1631	1704	1731	1755	1801	1804	1831	1901	1904	1934	2001	2003	2031	...	...
Ebbsfleet International d.	1315	|	|	|	|	|	|	|	|	|	|	|	|	|	|	|	|	|	|	|	|	...	...
Ashford International d.	|	|	|	1455c	|	|	|	|	|	|	|	1828c	|	|	|	|	|	|	|	|	|	...	...
Calais Fréthun a.	1459	|	|	|	|	|	|	|	|	|	|	|	|	|	|	|	2059	2129	|	|	|	...	...
Lille Europe a.	1530	|	1626	|	1726	|	|	1826	|	1926	|	2026	|	2026	|	|	2130	2200	|	2226	|	...	...
Brussels Midi / Zuid a.	1608	|	1705	|	1805	|	|	1905	|	2005	|	2105	|	2105	|	|	2208	2238	|	2305	|	...	...
Paris Nord a.	...	1647	...	1747	...	1847	1917	...	1947	...	2047	...	2117	...	2147	2217	...	...	2317	...	2347	...	...

train number	9109	9005	9007	9113	9009	9011	9117	9013	9015	9019	9125	9023	9129	9027	9133	9029	9029	9031	9035	9037	9141	9141	9039
notes	①	①	①–⑥	①–⑥	①–⑤	⑥⑦							⑦		①–⑥		⑦	①–⑥	⑥⑦	⑤	⑦	①–⑥	
notes	k	p	w	f	q	y		D		T	E		r	F	q	M	y	q	r		y	q	x
Paris Nord d.	...	0643	0713	...	0743	0813	...	0843	0913	1013	...	1113	...	1213	...	1231	1243	1313	1413	1443	...	...	1513
Brussels Midi / Zuid d.	0656	|	|	0756	|	|	0852	|	|	|	1056	|	1156	|	1252	|	|	|	|	|	1452	1456	|
Lille Europe d.	0735	|	|	0835	|	|	0930	|	|	|	1135	|	1235	|	1330	|	|	|	|	|	1530	1535	|
Calais Fréthun d.	|	|	|	|	|	|	1001	|	|	|	|	|	|	|	1401	|	|	|	|	|	1601	|	|
Ashford International a.	|	|	|	|	|	|	|	|	|	|	|	1208c	|	|	|	|	|	|	|	|	|	|	|
Ebbsfleet International a.	|	|	|	|	|	|	|	|	1018	|	|	|	|	|	1345	|	1348	1418	|	|	1545	1545	1618
London St Pancras a.	0759	0802	0832	0857	0900	0930	0957	1000	1039	1130	1157	1239	1258	1330	1405	1400	1409	1439	1530	1602	1605	1605	1639

train number	9145	9043	9045	9149	9149	9047	9153	9153	9051	9157	9053	9055	9161	9059	9061	9063							
notes			⑦	⑦	①–⑥		①–⑤	⑦	Ⓑ						⑦	Ⓑ							
notes	K		y	y	q		q	y		H	A	h	h	h	y								
Paris Nord d.	...	1613	1643	...	...	1713	...	...	1813	...	1843	1913	...	2013	2043	2113	...	...	...	...	...	...	...
Brussels Midi / Zuid d.	1556	|	|	1656	1656	|	1756	1756	|	1856	|	|	1952	|	|	|	...	...	...	...	...	...	...
Lille Europe d.	1635	|	|	1734	1735	|	1835	1835	|	1935	|	|	2030	|	|	|	...	...	...	...	...	...	...
Calais Fréthun d.	|	|	|	|	|	|	|	|	|	|	|	|	2101	|	|	|	...	...	...	...	...	...	...
Ashford International a.	|	|	1737c	|	1734	|	|	1835c	|	|	|	2007c	|	|	|	|	...	...	...	...	...	...	...
Ebbsfleet International a.	|	1718	|	1745	|	|	1845	|	1918	|	|	|	2045	2118	|	2218	...	...	...	...	...	...	...
London St Pancras a.	1657	1739	1812	1805	1806	1832	1903	1910	1939	1957	2004	2039	2103	2139	2200	2239	...	...	...	...	...	...	...

A – ④⑤⑦ Dec. 11–31 (also Dec. 26, 27). ⑤⑦ Jan. 1 - May 27 (also Jan. 2, Apr. 13, 17, May 1, 25; not Apr. 30).
B – ⑤⑦ (also Dec. 26, 27, Jan. 2, Apr. 17, May 1).
C – ⑤⑦ (also Dec. 17, 26, 27, Jan. 2, Apr. 17, May 1).
D – ②–⑤ Jan. 1 - Feb. 4 (not Dec. 27). ①–⑤ Feb. 5 - May 27 (not Apr. 17, May 1).
E – ①–⑤ Dec. 11–31. ⑤ Jan. 1 - Mar. 25 (also Jan. 2). ①–⑥ Mar. 26 - May 27 (not Apr. 1, 15, 17, May 1).
F – ⑤⑦ Dec. 11–31 (also Dec. 26, 27). ⑦ Jan. 1 - Mar. 25 (also Jan. 2, Feb. 10). ①⑤⑦ Mar. 26 - May 27.
G – ①–⑤ Dec. 11–31 (not Dec. 26, 27). ⑤ Jan. 1 - Mar. 25. ①–⑤ Mar. 26 - May 27 (not Apr. 17, May 1).
H – Ⓑ Dec. 11–31. ⑦ Jan. 1 - Feb. 4 (also Jan. 2). ⑤⑦ Feb. 5 - Mar. 25. Ⓑ Mar. 26 - May 27.
J – ①–⑤ Dec. 11–31 (not Dec. 26, 27). ⑤ Feb. 5 - Mar. 25. ①–⑤ Mar. 26 - May 27 (not Apr. 17, May 1).
K – ⑤⑦ Dec. 11–31 (also Dec. 26, 27, Jan. 2). ⑤ Feb. 5 - May 27 (also Feb. 19, Mar 5, Apr. 13, 30, May 25).
L – ①–⑤ Dec. 11 - Mar. 25 (not Dec. 26, 27, Jan 2). ②–④ Mar. 26 - May 27 (not Apr. 17, May 1).
M – Feb. 10. ⑤ Mar. 26 - May 27.
N – ⑤⑦ Dec. 11–31 (also Dec. 26, 27). Jan. 2, Feb. 10, 17, 19, Mar. 5. ⑤ Mar. 26 - May 27 (also Apr. 13, May 1, 25).
P – ①⑤ Mar. 26 - May 27 (not Apr. 17, May 1).
Q – ④⑤⑥⑦ Dec. 11–31 (also Dec. 26, 27). ①⑤⑥ Jan. 1 - Feb. 4 (also Jan. 2). ①⑤⑥⑦ Feb. 5 - Mar. 25. Daily Mar. 26 - May 27.
R – ①④⑤⑥ Dec. 11–31 (not Dec. 26). ①⑤⑥ Jan. 1 - May 27 (also Apr. 13, May 25; not Jan. 2, Apr. 17, May 1).
S – ⑤⑥ Dec. 11–31. ⑥ Jan. 1 - Mar. 25 (also Feb. 10, 12). ①⑤⑥⑦ Mar. 26 - May 27 (also Apr. 13; not Apr. 30).
T – ①④⑤⑥⑦ Dec. 11–31 (also Dec. 27). ①⑤⑥ Jan. 1 - Feb. 4 (not Jan. 2). ①⑤⑥ Feb. 5 - Mar. 25. ①–⑥ Mar. 26 - May 27 (not Apr. 30).
V – ①–⑤ Dec. 11 - Mar. 25 (not Dec. 27). ②–④ Mar. 26 - May 27.
W – Ⓑ Dec. 11 - Mar. 25. Daily Mar. 26 - May 27 (not Apr. 1, 15).
X – ⑥⑦ Dec. 11 - Mar. 25 (also Dec. 27). ①⑤⑥⑦ Mar. 26 - May 27.
Z – Dec. 23, 30, Feb. 10. ⑤ Mar. 26 - May 27.

c – Not Feb. 26.
f – Also Dec. 26, 27, Jan. 2, Apr. 17, May 1, 25.
g – Also Dec. 27, Jan. 2, May 1.
h – Not Dec. 24, 31.
j – Not Dec. 26, 27, Jan 2, Apr. 17, May 1, 8, 25.
k – Not Dec. 26, Jan 2, Apr. 17, May 1.
m – Not Jan. 1.
p – Not Dec. 26, Jan. 2, Apr. 17, May 1, 8.
q – Not Dec. 26, 27, Jan 2, Apr. 17, May 1.
r – Also Apr. 17, May 1.
w – Not Dec. 26, 27, Jan 2, Apr. 17, May 1, 25,
x – Not Jan. 1, Apr. 16, 30.
y – Also Dec. 26, 27, Jan. 2, Apr. 17, May 1.
z – Also Dec. 26, 27, Jan. 2, Apr. 17, May 1; not Dec. 24, 31.
¶ – On Feb. 26 depart London 1014, Ebbsfleet 1032.

LONDON – PARIS *by rail – sea – rail* 10a

Other services are available by taking normal service trains between London and Dover (Tables **100**, **101**), sailings between Dover and Calais (Table **2110**) and normal service trains between Calais and Paris, by changing at Boulogne (Table **261**), passengers making their own way between stations and docks at Dover and Calais, allowing at least 1 hour for connections.

French train number	⚡	⚡	⛴	TGV⚡	2	2026				⚡	⚡	⛴	2	2030	2	2030	2034		⚡	⛴	2	2036	
sea crossing (see below)	⑥	①–⑤	①–⑥	7254	①–⑥	①–⑥	⑦	⑥	①–⑤	⑥	Ⓑ		⑦	⑦	①–⑤	①–⑤	⑥	⑦	⑦	⑦	⑦	⑦	
notes		p		Ⓡ A	f	f	q		p				h	h	f	f		q	q		h	h	
London St Pancras d.	0637	0722	...	...	...	...	...	...	...	0934	0937	...	...	...	...	...	...	...	1137	...	...	...	...
London Charing Cross d.	|	|	...	...	...	...	0840c	0840	0833	|	|	...	...	...	...	...	...	1040c	|	...	...	...	...
Dover Priory ❦ a.	0741	0828	...	...	...	...	1031	1031	1033	1041	1041	...	...	...	...	...	...	1231	1241	...	...	...	...
Dover Eastern Docks 🏛 ❦ d.	...	...	0955	...	...	...	...	...	...	...	...	1210	...	...	...	...	...	...	...	1425	...	...	...
Calais Port 🏛 ✣ a.	...	...	1225	...	...	...	...	...	...	...	...	1440	...	...	...	...	...	...	...	1655	...	...	...
Calais Ville ✣ d.	...	...	...	1327	1335	...	...	...	...	...	...	...	1548	...	1558	...	...	...	...	...	1807	...	...
Boulogne Ville d.	...	...	...	|	1410	1433	...	...	...	...	...	...	1623	1633	1633	1645	1733	...	...	...	1847	1933	...
Amiens a.	...	...	...	|	...	1609	...	...	...	...	...	...	...	1809	...	1809	1909	...	...	...	...	2109	...
Paris Nord a.	...	...	...	1514	...	1729	...	...	...	...	...	...	...	1929	...	1929	2029	...	...	...	...	2229	...

French train number	TGV⚡	⛴	⚡		2005	2	2009	2	⛴			2011	2	⛴			2017	2	2021	2	⛴	⚡	
sea crossing (see below)	7223	①–⑥	①–⑥	①–⑥	①–⑤	①–⑤	⑥	⑥	①–⑥	⑥	⑥	⑦	⑦	⑦	⑦	⑦	Ⓑ	①–⑤	⑥	⑥⑦			①–⑥
notes	Ⓡ A		p	p	f	f						h	h					f		h			
Paris Nord d.	0946	...	...	...	0731	...	0831	...	...	...	...	0931	...	...	...	...	1331	...	1431	...	...	...	...
Amiens d.	|	...	...	...	0853	...	0951	...	...	...	...	1051	...	...	...	...	1451	...	1551	...	...	...	...
Boulogne Ville d.	|	...	...	...	1016	1227	1126	1227	...	...	...	1226	1248	...	...	...	1614x	1711	1714	1723	...	...	...
Calais Ville ✣ a.	1132	...	...	...	...	1310	...	1310	...	...	...	...	1323	...	...	...	...	1750	...	1757	...	...	...
Calais Port 🏛 ✣ d.	...	1305	...	...	...	...	...	...	1410	...	...	...	...	1525	...	...	...	...	...	...	2000	...	...
Dover Eastern Docks 🏛 ❦ a.	...	1335	...	...	...	...	...	...	1440	...	...	...	...	1555	...	...	...	...	...	...	2030	...	...
Dover Priory ❦ d.	...	...	1449	1500	...	...	...	...	...	1549	1603	...	...	...	1725	1745	...	...	...	...	...	2145	2203
London Charing Cross a.	...	...	|	1655	...	...	...	...	...	|	1752	...	...	...	1922	|	...	...	...	...	...	|	2357
London St Pancras a.	...	...	1554	...	...	...	...	...	...	1654	...	...	...	...	...	1853	...	...	...	...	...	2254	...

A – ①–⑥ (not Apr. 17, May 1, 8, 25).
c – London **Cannon Street**.
f – Not Apr. 17, May 1, 8, 25.
h – Also Apr. 17, May 1, 8, 25.
p – Not Jan. 2, Apr. 17.
q – Also Jan. 2, Apr. 17.
x – 1626 on ⑦.
⚡ – Supplement payable.

⛴ – Ship service, operated by P & O Ferries. ✕ on ship. One class only on ship. For additional ferry services see Table **2110**.
❦ – Passengers make their own way between Dover Priory and Dover Eastern Docks.
✣ – 🚌 service (not a guaranteed connection):
From Calais Port to Calais Ville station 1120, 1220, 1305, 1405, 1500, 1640, 1740, 1835.
From Calais Ville station to Calais Port 1040, 1135, 1235, 1320, 1420, 1515, 1655, 1755.

11 LONDON / BRUSSELS - LILLE - CHARLES DE GAULLE ✈ - WESTERN / SOUTHERN FRANCE

DAY TRAINS (FOR NIGHT TRAINS SEE TABLE 13). Supplements are payable on *TGV* trains. Connections at Lille are not guaranteed. Other connections available via Paris.

km		TGV	TGV	TGV	TGV	TGV		TGV	TGV	TGV	☆	☆	☆	☆	EC	☆	TGV	TGV
	train number	5104	6813	5200	5110	9810		9870	9812	5202	9108	9110	9110	9084	147	9114	5164	9826
	train number	5105	6812	5201	9811	9811	17483	9871	9813					9085	148			9827
	notes	R	R	R	R	R		R	R	R	R✗	R✗	R✗	R✗	♣	R✗	R	R
											X	L		M		J		
	London St Pancras **12** ...d.										0613	0650	0657	0719x		0804		
	Ebbsfleet International **12** ...d.										0630	0707						
	Ashford International **12** ...d.										0653	0728	0728	0755				
	Brussels Midi / Zuid **12** ...d.				0710			0717	0817									1031
	Lille Europe **12** ...a.							0752	0852		0922	0930	0926			1026		
0	**Lille** Europe ...d.	0534		0717c		0654f		0802	0902	0918						1043y		
	Douai ...d.					0716												
	Arras ...d.	0558				0732												
99	TGV Haute Picardie ...d.	0617		0747												1115y		
203	Paris Charles de Gaulle ✈ ...a.	0653		0814	0821	0826		0854	0953	1012						1144	1149	
203	Paris Charles de Gaulle ✈ ...d.	0658		0819	0830	0830		0859	0958	1016						1157	1157	
227	Marne la Vallée § ...d.	0711		0833	0843	0843			1011	1033						1210	1210	
	Strasbourg ...a.								1049									
289	Massy TGV ...d.			0908						1108								
	Le Mans ...a.																	
	Rennes ...a.																	
	Angers St Laud ...a.																	
	Nantes ...a.																	
	St Pierre des Corps ...a.				1001					1159								
	Poitiers ...a.				1042					1242								
	Angoulême ...a.				1135					1335								
	Bordeaux ...a.				1234					1434								
	Le Creusot TGV ...a.																	
521	**Lyon** Part Dieu ...a.	0900	0936			1030	1030			1200					1300z		1400	1400
645	**Lyon** Perrache ...a.																	
	Valence TGV ...a.	0945	1011		1110	1110				1244					1408		1439	1439
	Avignon TGV ...a.				1143	1143												
	Nîmes ...a.	1033	1056							1332								
	Montpellier ...a.	1102	1127							1402								
	Béziers ...a.		1210															
	Narbonne ...a.		1225															
	Toulouse Matabiau ...a.		1341															
	Perpignan ...a.						17483											
	Aix en Provence TGV ...a.																1534	1534
	Marseille St Charles ...a.				1220	1220	1231								1445	1531	1549	1549
	Toulon ...a.						1314									1614		
	St Raphaël - Valescure ...a.						1409									1709		
	Cannes ...a.						1436									1735		
	Nice ...a.						1506									1803		

		☆	☆	TGV	☆	TGV	☆	☆	TGV	TGV	TGV	☆	TGV	TGV	TGV	TGV	TGV
	train number	9116	9116	9828	9074	5452	9126	9126	5232	5209	5222	9132	5134	6183	5119	6217	9874
	train number			5028		5453			5233		5223		5135			6824	9875
	notes	R✗	R✗	R	R✗	R	R✗	R✗	R	R	R	R✗	R	R	R	R	R
							①-⑥	⑦								⑤⑥⑦	
		B	C		A	Y	q	k			W		w				
	London St Pancras **12** ...d.	0855	0858		1014		1058	1104				1258					
	Ebbsfleet International **12** ...d.	0915	0915		1034		1115					1315					
	Ashford International **12** ...d.				1058												
	Brussels Midi / Zuid **12** ...d.			1217p													1517
	Lille Europe **12** ...a.	1126	1130	1253		1254s	1326	1326				1530					1552
	Lille Europe ...d.			1303					1352c	1352c	1445f		1554		1554		1603
	Douai ...d.										1508						
	Arras ...d.										1526						
	TGV Haute Picardie ...d.										1550		1622		1622		
	Paris Charles de Gaulle ✈ ...a.			1353					1444	1444	1617		1651		1651		1654
	Paris Charles de Gaulle ✈ ...d.			1358					1449	1449	1621		1656		1656		1659
	Marne la Vallée § ...d.			1411	1402	1433			1503	1503	1634		1711		1711		
	Strasbourg ...a.																1901e
	Massy TGV ...d.				1508				1538	1538	1708						
	Le Mans ...a.								1627	1627							
	Rennes ...a.								1747								
	Angers St Laud ...a.									1708							
	Nantes ...a.									1752							
	St Pierre des Corps ...a.				1600						1758						
	Poitiers ...a.				1642						1842						
	Angoulême ...a.				1732						1935						
	Bordeaux ...a.				1837						2036						
	Le Creusot TGV ...a.																
	Lyon Part Dieu ...a.			1600								1900	1900	1936			
	Lyon Perrache ...a.																
	Valence TGV ...a.												1945				
	Avignon TGV ...a.			1706										2006			
	Nîmes ...a.													2033	2103		
	Montpellier ...a.													2102	2130	2141	
	Béziers ...a.													2209	2226		
	Narbonne ...a.													2225	2242		
	Toulouse Matabiau ...a.														2341		
	Perpignan ...a.															2318	
	Aix en Provence TGV ...a.			1734									2034	2121			
	Marseille St Charles ...a.			1749									2049				
	Toulon ...a.			1843										2209			
	St Raphaël - Valescure ...a.			1939										2300			
	Cannes ...a.			2009										2331			
	Nice ...a.			2036										2359			

A – Daily Dec. 11 - Jan. 2 (not Dec. 17). ①③⑤⑦ Feb. 5 - July 7 (daily Feb. 10 – 20, daily Apr. 1 – 15, also Apr. 29, daily May 27 - June 3). On Feb. 26 depart London 1024, Ebbsfleet 1044, not calling at Ashford.

B – ①–⑤ Dec. 11 - Mar. 25 (not Dec. 27). ②–④ Mar. 26 - May 27.

C – ⑥⑦ Dec. 11 - Mar. 25 (also Dec. 27). ①⑤⑥⑦ Mar. 26 - May 27.

J – ①–⑤ Dec. 11–31 (not Dec. 26, 27). ①④⑤ Feb. 5 - Mar. 25. ①–⑤ Mar. 26 - May 27 (not Apr. 17, May 1).

L – ①–⑤ Dec. 11 - Mar. 25 (not Dec. 26, 27, Jan 2). ②–④ Mar. 26 - May 27 (not Apr. 17, May 1).

M – Dec. 17, 23, 30, Feb. 11, 18. ①③⑤ Mar. 31 - May 27. ①④⑤⑥⑦ May 28 - Sept. 28. ①⑤⑥ Sept. 29 - Nov. 4. See Table 17.

W – ①②③④⑦.

X – ①⑤ Mar. 26 - May 27 (not Apr. 17, May 1).

Y – July 3 - Aug. 28.

c – Depart 6 – 9 minutes earlier on certain dates.

e – 1852 on ⑦.

f – Lille **Flandres** (◇).

k – Also Dec. 26, 27, Jan. 2, Apr. 17, May 1.

p – 1205 Jan. 23 - Feb. 28.

q – Not Dec. 26, 27, Jan 2, Apr. 17, May 1.

s – Calls to set down only.

w – Also Apr. 17, May 1, 8, June 5; not Mar. 18, 19.

x – 0715 on ⑦.

y – Jan 23 - Apr. 23, May 29 - July 1 depart Lille 1034, TGV Haute Picardie 1106.

z – Not Sept. 23, 30.

♣ – EC Thello. To Milano, Table 90.

⊖ – To St Malo on dates in Table 261.

§ – Marne la Vallée - Chessy (station for Disneyland).

☆ – Eurostar train. Special fares payable. ✗ in Business Premier and Standard Premier, ♈ in Standard. Business Premier not available to Marne la Vallée - Chessy and Marseille. Minimum check-in time 30 minutes. Valid Dec. 11 - May 27, 2017.

◇ – 500 metres from Lille Europe (see Lille City Plan on page 30).

LONDON / BRUSSELS - LILLE - CHARLES DE GAULLE ✈ - WESTERN / SOUTHERN FRANCE 11

DAY TRAINS (FOR NIGHT TRAINS SEE TABLE 13). Supplements payable on all *TGV* services. Connections at Lille are not guaranteed. Other connections available via Paris.

train type	☆	*TGV*	*TGV*		☆	*TGV*	*TGV*	*TGV*		☆	*TGV*		☆	*TGV*	*TGV*								
train number	**9136**	**9836**	**5240**		**9140**	**5237**	**5230**	**5124**		**9144**	**5130**		**9148**	**5234**	**9846**								
train number		**9837**	**5241**				**5231**	**5125**			**5131**			**5235**	**9847**								
notes	R ✕	R 🍸	R 🍸		R ✕ Ⓑ	R 🍸	R 🍸	R 🍸		R ✕ ⑥	R 🍸		R ✕	R 🍸	R 🍸								
	F		**h**			△	▽				▷		**W**	**A**									
London St Pancras **12** d.	1404	...	...	...	1504	...	...	...	...	1604	...	...	1704	...	...	...	...	...	...	...	...	...	...
Ebbsfleet International **12** d.	|	...	...	...	|	...	...	...	...	|	...	...	|	...	...	...	...	...	...	...	...	...	...
Ashford International **12** d.	|	...	...	...	|	...	...	...	...	|	...	...	|	...	...	...	...	...	...	...	...	...	...
Brussels Midi / Zuid **12** d.	|	1617	...	...	|	...	...	...	...	|	...	...	|	...	1917	...	...	...	...	...	...	...	...
Lille Europe **12** a.	1626	1653	...	...	1726	...	...	...	...	1826	...	...	1926	...	1952	...	...	...	...	...	...	...	...
Lille Europe d.	...	1703	1709f	...	...	1752c	1752c	1826	...	...	1900f	...	...	1952	2002	...	...	...	...	...	...	...	...
Douai d.	...	|	|	...	...	|	|	|	...	...	|	...	...	|	|	...	...	...	...	...	...	...	...
Arras d.	...	|	|	...	...	|	|	|	...	...	|	...	...	|	2028	...	...	...	...	...	...	...	...
TGV Haute Picardie d.	...	|	|	...	...	|	|	1854	...	...	|	...	...	|	|	...	...	...	...	...	...	...	...
Paris Charles de Gaulle ✈ a.	...	1753	1804	...	...	1842	1842	1923	...	...	1954	...	...	2044	2112	...	...	...	...	...	...	...	...
Paris Charles de Gaulle ✈ d.	...	1758	1809	...	...	1847	1847	1928	...	...	1958	...	...	2049	2117	...	...	...	...	...	...	...	...
Marne la Vallée § d.	...	1811	1833	...	...	1900	1900	1941	...	...	2007	...	...	2103	2130	...	...	...	...	...	...	...	...
Strasbourg a.	...	|	|	...	...	|	|	|	...	...	...	...	...	|	|	...	...	...	...	...	...	...	...
Massy TGV d.	...	|	1908	...	...	1938	1938	|	...	...	...	...	...	2138	|	...	...	...	...	...	...	...	...
Le Mans a.	...	|	|	...	...	2028	2028	|	...	...	...	...	...	2228	|	...	...	...	...	...	...	...	...
Rennes a.	...	|	|	...	...	2158	|	|	...	...	...	...	...	|	|	...	...	...	...	...	...	...	...
Angers St Laud a.	...	|	|	...	...	...	2110	|	...	...	...	...	...	2309	|	...	...	...	...	...	...	...	...
Nantes a.	...	|	|	...	...	...	2154	|	...	...	...	...	...	2347	|	...	...	...	...	...	...	...	...
St Pierre des Corps a.	...	|	1959	...	...	...	...	|	...	...	...	...	...	...	|	...	...	...	...	...	...	...	...
Futuroscope a.	...	|	|	...	...	...	...	|	...	...	...	...	...	...	|	...	...	...	...	...	...	...	...
Poitiers a.	...	|	2041	...	...	...	...	|	...	...	...	...	...	...	|	...	...	...	...	...	...	...	...
Angoulême a.	...	|	2135	...	...	...	...	|	...	...	...	...	...	...	|	...	...	...	...	...	...	...	...
Bordeaux a.	...	|	2234	...	...	...	...	|	...	...	...	...	...	...	|	...	...	...	...	...	...	...	...
Le Creusot TGV a.	...	|	...	...	...	...	...	|	...	...	...	...	...	...	2239	...	...	...	...	...	...	...	...
Lyon Part Dieu a.	...	2000	...	...	...	...	...	2130	...	...	...	...	...	...	2324	...	...	...	...	...	...	...	...
Lyon Perrache a.	...	|	...	...	...	...	...	|	...	...	...	...	...	...	...	...	...	...	...	...	...	...	...
Lyon St Exupéry ✈ a.	...	|	...	...	...	...	...	|	...	...	...	...	...	...	...	...	...	...	...	...	...	...	...
Valence TGV a.	...	2045	...	...	...	...	...	|	...	...	...	...	...	...	...	...	...	...	...	...	...	...	...
Avignon TGV a.	...	|	...	...	...	...	...	2238	...	...	...	...	...	...	...	...	...	...	...	...	...	...	...
Nîmes a.	...	2133	...	...	...	...	...	|	...	...	...	...	...	...	...	...	...	...	...	...	...	...	...
Montpellier a.	...	2202	...	...	...	...	...	|	...	...	...	...	...	...	...	...	...	...	...	...	...	...	...
Béziers a.	...	2252t	...	...	...	...	...	|	...	...	...	...	...	...	...	...	...	...	...	...	...	...	...
Narbonne a.	...	2308t	...	...	...	...	...	|	...	...	...	...	...	...	...	...	...	...	...	...	...	...	...
Toulouse Matabiau a.	...	|	...	...	...	...	...	|	...	...	...	...	...	...	...	...	...	...	...	...	...	...	...
Perpignan a.	...	2347t	...	...	...	...	...	|	...	...	...	...	...	...	...	...	...	...	...	...	...	...	...
Aix en Provence TGV a.	...	...	...	...	...	...	...	2307	...	...	...	...	...	...	...	...	...	...	...	...	...	...	...
Marseille St Charles a.	...	...	...	...	...	...	...	2321	...	...	...	...	...	...	...	...	...	...	...	...	...	...	...
Toulon a.	...	...	...	...	...	...	...	...	...	...	...	...	...	...	...	...	...	...	...	...	...	...	...
St Raphaël - Valescure a.	...	...	...	...	...	...	...	...	...	...	...	...	...	...	...	...	...	...	...	...	...	...	...
Cannes a.	...	...	...	...	...	...	...	...	...	...	...	...	...	...	...	...	...	...	...	...	...	...	...
Nice a.	...	...	...	...	...	...	...	...	...	...	...	...	...	...	...	...	...	...	...	...	...	...	...

train type	*TGV*	*TGV*	*TGV*	☆	*TGV*	*TGV*	*TGV*	*TGV*	☆	☆	*TGV*	*TGV*	*TGV*	☆	*TGV*	*TGV*	*TGV*	*TGV*	*TGV*	*TGV*	*TGV*	☆	
train number	**9809**	**9852**	**9890**	**9117**	**5152**	**5254**	**5252**	**9854**	**9125**	**9129**	**5062**	**9862**	**5260**	**9133**	**6869**	**9860**	**5166**	**5270**	**5272**	**5264**	**5264**	**9141**	
train number		**9853**	**9891**		**5153**	**5255**		**5065**				**9863**	**5261**		**6868**	**9861**	**9860**	**5271**		**5265**	**5265**		
notes	R 🍸 Ⓐ	R 🍸	R 🍸	R ✕	R 🍸	R 🍸 ⚒	R 🍸 ⚒	R 🍸	R ✕	R ✕ ⑦	R 🍸 Ⓑ	R 🍸	R 🍸	R ✕ ①–⑥	R 🍸	R 🍸	R 🍸	R 🍸	R 🍸	R 🍸 Ⓐ	R 🍸 Ⓒ	R ✕	
					▷				**E**	**y**				**j**				▽	△				
Nice d.	...	...	...	...	...	...	...	...	...	...	...	...	...	...	...	...	...	...	...	...	...	...	...
Cannes d.	...	...	...	...	...	...	...	...	...	...	...	...	...	...	...	...	...	...	...	...	...	...	...
St Raphaël - Valescure d.	...	...	...	...	...	...	...	...	...	...	...	...	...	...	...	...	...	...	...	...	...	...	...
Toulon d.	...	...	...	...	...	...	...	...	...	...	...	...	...	...	...	...	...	...	...	...	...	...	...
Marseille St Charles d.	...	...	...	...	...	...	...	0611	...	...	...	...	...	...	...	0911	...	...	...	...	...	...	...
Aix en Provence TGV d.	...	...	...	...	...	...	...	0625	...	...	...	...	...	...	...	0925	...	...	...	...	...	...	...
Perpignan d.	...	...	...	...	...	...	...	|	...	...	...	0515z	...	...	...	|	...	...	...	...	...	...	...
Toulouse Matabiau d.	...	...	...	...	...	...	...	|	...	...	...	|	...	...	0545	|	...	...	...	...	...	...	...
Narbonne d.	...	...	...	...	...	...	...	|	...	...	...	0552z	...	...	0704	|	...	...	...	...	...	...	...
Béziers d.	...	...	...	...	...	...	...	|	...	...	...	0608z	...	...	0720	|	...	...	...	...	...	...	...
Montpellier d.	...	...	...	...	...	...	...	|	...	...	0658	0658	...	...	0803	|	0858	...	...	...	...	...	...
Nîmes d.	...	...	...	...	...	...	...	|	...	...	0727	0727	...	...	0831	|	0926	...	...	...	...	...	...
Avignon TGV d.	...	...	...	...	...	...	...	|	...	...	|	|	...	...	|	|	|	...	...	...	...	...	...
Valence TGV d.	...	...	...	...	...	...	...	0721	...	...	0819	0819	...	...	|	|	1015	...	...	...	...	...	...
Lyon St Exupéry ✈ d.	...	...	...	...	...	...	...	|	...	...	|	|	...	...	|	|	|	...	...	...	...	...	...
Lyon Perrache d.	...	...	...	...	...	...	...	|	...	...	|	|	...	...	|	|	|	...	...	...	...	...	...
Lyon Part Dieu d.	...	0550	...	...	...	...	...	0800	...	...	0900	0900	...	...	0950	1100	1100	...	...	...	...	...	...
Le Creusot TGV d.	...	0633	...	...	...	...	...	|	...	...	|	|	...	...	...	|	|	...	...	...	...	...	...
Bordeaux d.	...	|	...	...	...	...	...	|	...	...	|	|	0726	...	...	|	|	...	...	0926	0925	...	...
Angoulême d.	...	|	...	...	...	...	...	|	...	...	|	|	0826	...	...	|	|	...	...	1026	1026	...	...
Poitiers d.	...	|	...	...	...	...	...	|	...	...	|	|	0917	...	...	|	|	...	...	1117	1117	...	...
Futuroscope d.	...	|	...	...	...	...	...	|	...	...	|	|	|	...	...	|	|	...	...	|	|	...	...
St Pierre des Corps d.	...	|	...	...	...	...	...	|	...	...	|	|	1000	...	...	|	|	...	...	1200	1200	...	...
Nantes d.	...	|	...	...	...	...	0555	|	...	...	|	|	|	...	...	|	|	0957	...	|	|	...	...
Angers St Laud d.	...	|	...	...	...	...	0645	|	...	...	|	|	|	...	...	|	|	1043	...	|	|	...	...
Rennes d.	...	|	...	...	...	0610	|	|	...	...	|	|	|	...	...	|	|	|	1005	|	|	...	...
Le Mans d.	...	|	...	...	...	0733	0733	|	...	...	|	|	|	...	...	|	|	1133	1133	|	|	...	...
Massy TGV d.	...	|	...	...	...	0825	0825	|	...	...	|	|	1055	...	...	|	|	1225	1225	1255	1255	...	...
Strasbourg d.	...	|	0608	...	...	|	|	|	...	...	|	|	|	...	...	|	|	|	|	|	|	...	...
Marne la Vallée § d.	...	0749	|	...	0853	0901	0901	0952	...	...	1052	1052	1135	...	...	1252	1252	1301	1301	|	1331	...	...
Paris Charles de Gaulle ✈ a.	...	0800	0757	...	0903	0912	0912	1002	...	...	1102	1102	1145	...	...	1302	1302	1311	1312	1331	1341	...	...
Paris Charles de Gaulle ✈ d.	...	0808	0808	...	0907	0915	0915	1006	...	...	1107	1107	1157	...	...	1307	1307	1316	1316	1336	1346	...	...
TGV Haute Picardie d.	...	|	|	...	|	0950	0950	1037	...	...	|	|	1231	...	...	1336	1336	|	|	|	|	...	...
Arras a.	...	|	|	...	|	|	|	|	...	...	|	|	|	...	...	1356e	1356e	|	|	|	|	...	...
Douai a.	...	|	|	...	|	|	|	|	...	...	|	|	|	...	...	|	|	|	|	|	|	...	...
Lille Europe a.	...	0856	0856	...	0958	1017	1017	1103	...	...	1156	1156	1301f	...	...	1421e	1421e	1407	1407	1430	1437	...	...
Lille Europe **12** d.	0732	0908	0908	0930	...	...	...	1117	1135	1235	...	1208	...	1330	...	1435e	...	...	...	...	...	1535v	...
Brussels Midi / Zuid **12** a.	0807	0943	0943	|	...	...	...	1151	|	|	...	1243	...	|	...	1512e	...	...	...	...	...	|	...
Ashford International **12** a.	...	...	...	|	...	...	...	...	|	|	...	...	...	|	...	...	...	...	...	...	...	|	...
Ebbsfleet International **12** a.	...	...	...	|	...	...	...	...	|	|	...	...	...	1345	...	...	...	...	...	...	...	1545	...
London St Pancras **12** a.	...	...	...	0957	...	...	...	...	1157	1258	...	...	...	1405	...	...	...	...	...	...	...	1605	...

A – ⑤ Dec. 16 - 30, Apr. 14 - June 30 (also May 24).
E – ①–⑤ Dec. 11–31. ⑤ Jan. 1 - Feb. 4 (also Jan. 2).
①–⑤ Feb. 5 - Mar. 25.
①–⑥ Mar. 26 - May 27 (not Apr. 1, 15, 17, May 1).
F – ⑤⑦ Dec. 11–31 (also Dec. 26, 27).
⑦ Jan. 1 - Mar. 25 (also Jan. 2, Feb. 10, 17).
⑤ Mar. 26 - May 27 (also Apr. 13, May 1, 25).
W – Ⓑ Dec. 11 - Mar. 25. Daily Mar. 26 - May 27 (not Apr. 1, 15).

c – Depart 6 - 9 minutes earlier on certain dates.

e – On Ⓒ does not call at Arras, arrives Lille 1404, Brussels 1457.
f – Lille **Flandres** (◇).
h – Not Apr. 15, 16, 29, 30, May 20, 24, 25, June 4, 10, 17, 24.
j – Not Dec. 26, 27, Jan 2, Apr. 17, May 1.
t – ⑤⑦.
v – 1530 on ⑦ (also Dec. 26, 27, Jan 2, Apr. 17, May 1).
y – Also Also Apr. 17, May 1.
z – ①⑥.

▽ – To / from Le Croisic on dates in Table **288**.
△ – To / from Lorient or Quimper on dates in Table **285**.
▷ – To / from Dijon, Besancon and Mulhouse (Table **370**).
§ – Marne la Vallée - Chessy. Station for Disneyland Paris.
◇ – 500 metres from Lille Europe (see Lille City Plan on page 30).
☆ – Eurostar train. Special fares payable. ✕ in Business Premier and Standard Premier, 🍸 in Standard. Minimum check-in time 30 minutes. Valid Dec. 11 - May 27, 2017.

12 ⚒ – Daily except Sundays and holidays † – Sundays and holidays Ⓐ – Mondays to Fridays, except holidays Ⓑ – Daily except Saturdays 49

DAY TRAINS (FOR NIGHT TRAINS SEE TABLE 13). Supplements payable on all *TGV* services. Connections at Lille are not guaranteed. Other connections available via Paris.

	TGV	☆	TGV	☆	☆	☆	TGV	☆	☆	☆	TGV	TGV	☆
train number	5256	9145	9866	9149	9149	9057	9894	9153	9153	9057	5192	9868	9161
train number	5257		5066				9895				5193	9869	
notes	℞☿ ⑦	℞☿✕	℞☿	℞☿✕ ⑦	℞☿✕ ①–⑥	℞✕		℞✕ ①–⑤	℞✕ ⑦	℞✕	℞☿	℞☿	℞☿✕
	F			q	y	R		y	q	S			h
Nice ....d.			0919										
Cannes ....d.			0948										
St Raphaël - Valescure ....d.			1019										
Toulon ....d.			1117										
Marseille St Charles ....d.			1210								1408		
Aix en Provence TGV ....d.			1224								1423		
Perpignan ....d.													
Toulouse Matabiau ....d.													
Narbonne ....d.													
Béziers ....d.													
Montpellier ....d.												1458	
Nîmes ....d.												1526	
Avignon TGV ....d.			1253								1451		
Valence TGV ....d.												1615	
Lyon St Exupéry ✈ ....d.													
Lyon Perrache ....d.													
Lyon Part Dieu ....d.			1400								1600	1700	
Le Creusot TGV ....d.													
Bordeaux ....d.													
Angoulême ....d.													
Poitiers ....d.													
Futuroscope ....d.													
St Pierre des Corps ....d.													
Nantes ....d.													
Angers St Laud ....d.													
Rennes ....d.	1110												
Le Mans ....d.	1232												
Massy TGV ....d.	1325												
Strasbourg ....d.							1510						
Marne la Vallée § ....d.	1401		1552			1652					1752	1852	
Paris Charles de Gaulle ✈ .....a.	1412		1602			1704					1802	1902	
Paris Charles de Gaulle ✈ .....d.	1417		1607			1709					1807	1907	
TGV Haute Picardie ....d.											1841		
Arras ....a.											1859		
Douai ....a.											1917		
Lille Europe ....a.	1507		1657				1758				1944f	1956	
Lille Europe 12 ....d.		1635	1707	1734	1735		1810	1835	1835			2008	2030
Brussels Midi / Zuid 12 .....a.			1743				1843					2043	
Ashford International 12 ....a.				1734		1806			1835c	1904			
Ebbsfleet International 12 .....a.				1745		1827		1845		1926			2045
London St Pancras 12 ......a.		1657		1805	1806	1847		1903	1910	1946			2103

	☆	☆	TGV	TGV	TGV	TGV	TGV	TGV	TGV
train number	9087	9087	5266	6861	9882	5284	5284	5186	5180
train number	9086	9086	5267	6860	9883	5285	5285	5187	5186
notes	℞✕	℞✕	℞☿	℞☿	℞☿	℞☿	℞☿	℞☿	℞☿
	M	M				Ⓐ	Ⓒ		
Nice ....d.									
Cannes ....d.									
St Raphaël - Valescure ....d.									
Toulon ....d.									
Marseille St Charles ....d.	1522			1710					1810
Aix en Provence TGV ....d.				1724					1825
Perpignan ....d.									
Toulouse Matabiau ....d.					1445				
Narbonne ....d.					1604				
Béziers ....d.					1619				
Montpellier ....d.					1706			1758	
Nîmes ....d.					1733			1826	
Avignon TGV ....d.	1559				1752			1852	
Valence TGV ....d.								1916	
Lyon St Exupéry ✈ ....d.									
Lyon Perrache ....d.									
Lyon Part Dieu ....d.	1725z			1850	1900			2000	2000
Le Creusot TGV ....d.									
Bordeaux ....d.			1526			1723	1723		
Angoulême ....d.			1626			1825	1826		
Poitiers ....d.			1716				1913		
Futuroscope ....d.			1725				1921		
St Pierre des Corps ....d.			1802			2002	2000		
Nantes ....d.									
Angers St Laud ....d.									
Rennes ....d.									
Le Mans ....d.									
Massy TGV ....d.			1855			2055	2055		
Strasbourg ....d.									
Marne la Vallée § ....d.			1931		2052	2131	2131	2152	2152
Paris Charles de Gaulle ✈ .....a.			1941		2102	2141	2141	2202	2202
Paris Charles de Gaulle ✈ .....d.			1950		2107	2146	2146	2207	2207
TGV Haute Picardie ....d.			2033			2215	2215	2238	2238
Arras ....a.			2049						
Douai ....a.									
Lille Europe ....a.	2021		2111f		2156	2244	2244	2304	2304
Lille Europe 12 ....d.		2136			2222				
Brussels Midi / Zuid 12 .....a.					2256				
Ashford International 12 ....a.		2134							
Ebbsfleet International 12 .....a.									
London St Pancras 12 ......a.		2212							

F – ⑤⑦ Dec. 11–31 (also Dec. 26, 27). ⑦ Jan. 1 - Feb. 4 (also Jan. 2).
  ⑤⑦ Feb. 5 - Mar. 25. ⑤ Mar. 26 - May 27, (also Apr. 13, 30, May 25).

M – Dec. 17, 23, 30, Feb. 11, 18. ①⑤⑥ Mar. 31 - May 27. ①④⑤⑥⑦
  May 28 - Sept. 28. ①⑤⑥ Sept. 29 - Nov. 4. See Table 17.

R – ⑤⑦ Dec. 11 - Jan. 2 (also Dec. 24, 31). ⑤⑦ Feb. 5 - July 7,
  (also Feb. 11, 18, Apr. 1, 8, 15, May 27, June 3). See Table 17.

S – Dec. 12, 14, 19–22, 26, 29, Jan. 2, 3. ①③ Feb. 5 - July 7,
  (also Feb. 14, 16, Apr. 4, 6, 11, 13, May 30, June 1). See Table 17.

V – July 3 - Aug. 28.

c – Not Feb. 26.
f – Lille **Flandres** (◇).
h – Not Dec. 24, 31.
q – Also Dec. 26, 27, Jan. 2, Apr. 17, May 1.
y – Not Dec. 26, 27, Jan. 2, Apr. 17, May 1.
z – Not Sept. 23, 30.

⊖ – From St Malo on dates in Table **261**.

☆ – Eurostar train. Special fares payable. ✕ in Business Premier and Standard Premier, ☿ in Standard. Business Premier not available from Marne la Vallée - Chessy and Marseille. Minimum check-in time 30 minutes. Valid Dec. 11 - May 27, 2017.

◇ – 500 metres from Lille Europe (see Lille City Plan on page 30).

§ – Marne la Vallée - Chessy, station for Disneyland Paris.

All times shown are local times (France and Belgium are one hour ahead of Great Britain).
For the complete service London - Lille see Table 10. For other services Lille - Brussels (by TGV) see Table 16.
All Eurostar services are ℝ and convey ✕ in Business Premier and Standard Premier, ♟ in Standard.

Eurostar service Dec. 11 – May 27, 2017.

km	train type	☆	☆	ICE 15 ♟		☆	9110		☆ 9114			☆		☆ 9116	☆ 9116		☆		☆ 9126	☆ 9126	ICE 17 ♟	
	train number	9108	9110			9110			9114					9116	9116				9126	9126		
	notes				Ⓐ	⑥				Ⓐ		Ⓒ		B	C z	Ⓐ		Ⓒ	①–⑥	j	y	
	notes	Pz	Lz						J													
0	**London** St Pancras ...... d.	0613	0650	...	...	0657		...	0804		...		...	0855	0858		...		1058	1104		
35	Ebbsfleet International .... d.	0630	0707	...	...	...		...	...		...		...	0915	0915		...		1115	...		
90	Ashford International ...... d.	0652	0728	...	...	0728		...	...		...		...	...	...		...		...	...		
267	Lille Europe .... a.		0930	...	...	0926		...	1026		...		...	1126	1133		...		1326	...		
267	Lille Europe .... d.		0933	...	...	0930		...	1030		...		...	1130	1133		...		1330	1326		
373	**Brussels** Midi / Zuid ..... a.	0922	1007	1025	1026	1031	1005	1033	1058	1105	1105	1124	1131	1133	1158	1205	1208	1226	1231	1233	1258	1405	1405	1425	1431x	1433
	Brugge .... a.				1124					1201		1224							1324			1524		
	Leuven .... a.				1057				1125				1157		1225				1257	1325			1457x	
	Liège Guillemins .... a.		1112		1155				1200				1255		1300				1355	1400			1512	1555	
	Namur .... a.					1139								1239					1346					1539
	Luxembourg .... a.					1340								1445					1552					1740

	train type	☆			☆ 9136	⇌ 9461		☆		☆		☆	ICE 19 ♟		☆		☆ 9144	⇌ 9473	
	train number	9132			9136	9461								9140				9144	9473	
	notes		Ⓐ						Ⓐ		Ⓒ		B		Ⓐ		Ⓒ	⑥		Ⓒ
	notes	z			A															
London St Pancras ......d.	1258	...	...	1404			...	1504		...			1604		...				
Ebbsfleet International ....d.	1315	...	...	...			...	...		...			...		...				
Ashford International ......d.	...	...	...	...			...	...		...			...		...				
Lille Europe ....a.	1530	...	...	1626			...	1726		...			1826		...				
Lille Europe ....d.	1533	...	...	1630			...	1730		...			1830		...				
Brussels Midi / Zuid ......a.	1608	1626	1631	1633	1658		1705	1726	1728	1731	1733	1758	1805	1825	1826	1831	1833	1858	1905	1926	1928	1933	1958
Brugge ....a.		1724					1824						1924						2024	
Leuven ....a.			1657		1725			1757			1825			1857		1925				2025
Liège Guillemins ....a.			1755	1800				1811	1855	1900			1912	1955	2000			2011	2039	2100
Namur ....a.			1740					1840					1939				2039		2240
Luxembourg ....a.			1940					2040					2140				2240		

	train type	☆			☆ 9152	☆ 9152		☆		☆		☆ 9156		☆		☆ 9158		☆		☆	☆ 9162	
	train number	9148			9152	9152							9156				9158					9162	
	notes		Ⓐ		⑦	①–⑤		Ⓐ		Ⓒ		⑥⑦		Ⓒ		①–⑤	Ⓐ		Ⓒ		Ⓒ	⑦	
	notes	W			y	G						h z				jz						c	
London St Pancras ......d.	1704	...	...	1755	1804		...	1904		...			1934		...						2003	
Ebbsfleet International ....d.	...	...	...	...	...		...	...		...			...		...						...	
Ashford International ......d.	...	...	...	1828e	...		...	...		...			...		...						...	
Lille Europe ....a.	1926	...	...	2026	2026		...	2130		...			2200		...						2225	
Lille Europe ....d.	1930	...	...	2030	2030		...	2133		...			2203		...						2230	
Brussels Midi / Zuid ......a.	2005	2026	2031	2033	2058		2105	2105	2126	2131	2133	2158	2208	2226	2258	2233		2238	2257	2258	2305	2333	2304
Brugge ....a.		2124					2224						2324								0001	
Leuven ....a.			2057		2125			2157			2225			2327				2323	2327				
Liège Guillemins ....a.			2155	2200				2255		2302			0023				0023	0023				0046
Namur ....a.			2139					2241					2339								0046	
Luxembourg ....a.			2340																			

	train type	☆			☆ 9109			☆		☆ 9113			☆ 9117			☆		☆		☆ 9125			☆	☆ 9129	
	train number				9109					9113			9117							9125				9129	
	notes	Ⓐ		Ⓐ		Ⓐ		Ⓒ		①–⑥		Ⓐ							Ⓐ			Ⓐ		⑦	
	notes			k						f			z							X				r	
Luxembourg ....d.													0620	0650					0720					
Namur ....d.	0411						0551				0651		0820	0843		0851			0921		0951			
Liège Guillemins ......d.		0443						0600				0700				0900						1000		
Leuven ....d.		0537						0637				0734				0937						1037		
Brugge ....d.		0450			0557	0559			0658					0859						0959				
Brussels Midi / Zuid ....d.	0545	0555	0603	0656	0655	0655	0657	0703	0756		0755	0757	0803	0852	0907	0927	0955	1003	1056	1027	1055	1057	1103	1156
Lille Europe ....a.			0731						0830					0926					1130					1230
Lille Europe ....d.			0735						0835					0930					1135					1235
Ashford International ....a.																								
Ebbsfleet International ....a.																								
London St Pancras ....a.			0759						0857					0957					1157					1258

	train type				☆ 9133			☆ 9141	☆ 9141			☆ 9145				☆ 9149	☆ 9149		
	train number				9133			9141	9141			9145				9149	9149		
	notes				①–⑤			⑦	①–⑥							⑦	①–⑥		
	notes				j z			y z	j			K				y	j		
Luxembourg ....d.	0820			1020				1120			1220							
Namur ....d.	1021		1051	1221		1251	1321	1351		1421	1451						
Liège Guillemins ......d.			1100		1300			1400			1500					
Leuven ....d.			1137		1337			1437			1537					
Brugge ....d.		1059			1259		1359			1459					
Brussels Midi / Zuid ....d.	1127	1155	1157	1203	1252	1327	1355	1357	1403	1452	1456	1427	1455	1457	1503	1556	1527	1555	1557	1603	1656	1656
Lille Europe ....a.				1326			1526	1532			1630				1730	1732	
Lille Europe ....d.				1330			1530	1535			1635				1734	1735	
Ashford International ....a.														1734		
Ebbsfleet International ....a.				1345			1545	1545							1745		
London St Pancras ....a.				1405			1605	1605			1657				1805	1806	

	train type				☆ 9153	☆ 9153			☆ 9157			☆ 9161		
	train number				9153	9153			9157			9161		
	notes				①–⑤	⑦			H			h z		
	notes				j	y								
Luxembourg ....d.	1324			1420				1520					
Namur ....d.	1521		1551	1621		1651		1721	1751				
Liège Guillemins ......d.			1600		1700			1800				
Leuven ....d.			1637		1737			1837				
Brugge ....d.		1559			1659		1759				
Brussels Midi / Zuid ....d.	1627	1655	1657	1703	1756	1756	1727	1755	1757	1803	1856	1827	1855	1857	1903	1952
Lille Europe ....a.				1830	1830			1930			2026		
Lille Europe ....d.				1835	1835			1935			2030		
Ashford International ....a.					1835e								
Ebbsfleet International ....a.				1845							2045		
London St Pancras ....a.				1905				1957			2103		

A – ⑤⑦ Dec. 11–31 (also Dec. 26,27). ⑦ Jan. 1 - Mar. 25 (also Jan. 2, Feb. 10, 17). ⑤ Mar. 26 - May 27 (also Apr. 13, May 1,25).

B – ①–⑤ Dec. 11 - Mar. 25 (not Dec. 27). ②–④ Mar. 26 - May 27.

C – ⑥⑦ Dec. 11 - Mar. 25 (also Dec. 27). ①⑤⑥⑦ Mar. 26 - May 27.

G – ①–⑤ Dec. 11–31 (not Dec. 26,27). ⑤ Jan. 1 - Feb. 4. ①–⑤ Feb. 5 - May 27 (not Apr. 17, May 1).

H – ⑧ Dec. 11–31. ⑦ Jan. 1 - Feb. 4 (also Jan. 2). ①④⑤⑦ Feb. 5 - Mar. 25. ⑧ Mar. 26 - May 27.

J – ①–⑤ Dec. 11–31 (not Dec. 26,27). ①④⑤⑥ Feb. 5 - Mar. 25. ①–⑤ Mar. 26 - May 27 (not Apr. 17, May 1). ⑤⑦ Feb. 5 - Mar. 25. ⑤ Feb. 4 (also Jan. 2). ⑤⑦ Feb. 5 - Mar. 25. ⑤ Mar. 26 - May 27, (also Apr. 13,30, May 25).

K – ⑤⑦ Dec. 11–31 (also Dec. 26,27). ⑦ Jan. 1 - Feb. 4 (also Jan. 2). ①–⑤ Feb. 5 - Mar. 25. ①–⑥ Mar. 26 - May 27 (not Apr. 1, 15, 17, May 1).

L – ①–⑤ Dec. 11 - Mar. 25 (not Dec. 26, 27, Jan 2). ②–④ Mar. 26 - May 27 (not Apr. 17, May 1).

P – ①⑤ Mar. 26 - May 27 (not Apr. 17, May 1). ①–⑤ Mar. 26 - May 27 (not Apr. 1, 15).

W – ⑧ Dec. 11 - Mar. 25. Daily Mar. 26 - May 27 (not Apr. 17, May 1).

X – ①–⑤ Dec. 11–31. ⑤ Jan. 1 - Feb. 4 (also Jan. 2). ①–⑤ Feb. 5 - Mar. 25. ①–⑥ Mar. 26 - May 27 (not Apr. 1, 15, 17, May 1).

Notes continued on next page →

13   LONDON - PARIS - BARCELONA - MADRID

train type	AVE	AVE	AVE	TGV	AVE	TGV	AVE	☆		☆	TGV	AVE	AVE	TGV	☆	AVE	AVE		☆	
train number	9729	3122	9730 9731	9711	3142	9713	3172	9084 9085		9110	5164 9826	9743	3202	9756 9757	9014	3212	3412		9022	
notes	B			C				Q		K					⑤⑦	V			T	
London St Pancras 10 ....d.	...	...	...	...	...	...	...	0719r	...	0804	...	...	...	...	0924	...	...	...	1131	...
Lille Europe ....d.	...	...	...	...	...	...	...		...	1026	1043	...	...	...		...	...	...		...
Paris Nord 10 ....a.	...	...	...	...	...	...	...		...			...	...	1248		...	...	...	1447	...
															TGV				TGV	
															9715				9717	
																			A S	
Paris Gare de Lyon ....d.	...	...	...	0715	...	1007	...		...			...	...	1407		...	...	...	1607	...
Paris Austerlitz ....d.	...	...	...		...		...		...			...	...			...	...	...		...
Les Aubrais-Orléans ....d.	...	...	...		...		...		...			...	...			...	...	...		...
Genève 🚄 ....d.	...	...	...		...		...	1130	...			...	1242			...	1500	...		...
Lyon Part Dieu ....d.	...	...	...		...	1221	...	1300e	1324		1400	1423	1436			...		...		...
Valence TGV ....d.	...	...	0803		...	1221	...					1503		1510	1621	...	1804	1821		...
Marseille St Charles ....d.	...	...	0803		...		...									...				...
Aix en Provence TGV ....d.	...	...	0818		...		...									...				...
Avignon TGV ....d.	...	...	0845		...		...									...				...
Nimes ....d.	...	...	0904	1008	...	1308	...					1548		1708		...		1907		...
Montpellier ....d.	...	...	0933	1037	...	1338	...					1625		1738		...		1941		...
Béziers ....d.	...	...	1016		...	1418	...					1716				...		2029		...
Toulouse Matabiau ....d.	0806	...			...		...									...				...
Carcassonne ....d.	0857	...			...		...									...				...
Narbonne ....d.		...	1033	1135	...	1435	...					1733		1835		...		2048		...
Perpignan ....d.	1000	...	1117	1212	...	1513	...					1810		1913		...		2125		...
Cerbère 🚄 ....a.		...			...		...									...				...
Portbou 🚄 ....a.		...			...		...									...				...
Figueres Vilafant ◇ ....a.	1023	...	1140	1236	...	1536	...					1833		1936		...		2148		...
Girona ....a.	1040	...	1157	1253	...	1553	...					1850		1953		...		2205		...
Barcelona Sants ....a.	1121	...	1238	1334	...	1634	...					1931		2034		...		2246		...
Barcelona Sants ....d.	...	1200	1250		1400		1700					2000			2100	2115		...		...
Zaragoza Delicias ....d.	...	1340	1423		1540		1828					2140			2240	2240		...		...
Madrid Puerta de Atocha ....a.	...	1510	1545		1710		1950					2310			0002	0002		...		...

train type	TGV	☆	AVE		TGV	☆	AVE	AVE	TGV	AVE		AVE	TGV	TGV		AVE	TGV	AVE	AVE
train number	9700	9039	9734		9866 9867	9149	3053	3061	9702	9055		3093	9704	5380 5381		3123	9706	9724 9725	9732
notes	R D	h					①④⑤	①–④		k							C		E
Madrid Puerta de Atocha ....d.	...	...	...	...	...	...	0550	0610	...	...	...	0930	...	...	...	1230	...	1325	...
Zaragoza Delicias ....d.	...	...	...	...	...	...	0706		...	...	...	1046	...	...	...	1346	...	1451	...
Barcelona Sants ....a.	...	...	...	...	...	...	0855	0840	...	...	...	1234	...	...	...	1530	...	1624	...
Barcelona Sants ....d.	0610	...	0720	...	...	...			0925	...	...		1320	...	...	1620	1645	1830	
Girona ....d.	0651	...	0801	...	...	...			1006	...	...		1401	...	...	1701	1726	1911	
Figueres Vilafant ◇ ....d.	0708	...	0818	...	...	...			1023	...	...		1418	...	...	1718	1743	1928	
Portbou 🚄 ....a.		...		...	...	...				...	...			...	...				
Cerbère 🚄 ....a.		...		...	...	...				...	...			...	...				
Perpignan ....a.	0731	...	0843	...	...	...			1046	...	...	1443		...	...	1742	1806	1951	
Narbonne ....a.	0811	...	0922	...	...	...			1127	...	...	1524		...	...	1823	1854		
Carcassonne ....a.		...		...	...	...				...	...			...	...			2056	
Toulouse Matabiau ....a.		...		...	...	...				...	...			...	...			2142	
Béziers ....a.	0829	...	0938	...	...	...			1220	...	...		1618	1627	...	1839	1910		
Montpellier ....a.	0924	...	1024	...	...	...			1220	...	...		1618	1627	...	1920	1954		
Nimes ....a.	0952	...	1056	...	...	...			1252	...	...		1652	1655	...	1952	2022		
Avignon TGV ....a.		...		...	...	...				...	...			...	...			2042	
Aix en Provence TGV ....a.		...		...	...	...				...	...			...	...			2109	
Marseille St Charles ....a.		...		...	...	...				...	...			...	...			2125	
Valence TGV ....a.		...	1146	...	...	...			1338	...	1357		1738	1746	...				
Lyon Part Dieu ....a.		...	1226	1238	1400	...				...			1824	1836	...				
Genève 🚄 ....a.		...	...	1427		...				1700				2027	...				
Les Aubrais-Orléans ....a.		...	...			...				...				...	...				
Paris Austerlitz ....a.		...	...			...				...				...	...				
Paris Gare de Lyon ....a.	1245	...	...			...			1553	...			1953	...	...	2245			
		☆								☆									
		9037								9051									
		⑤								⑧									
Paris Nord 10 ....d.	1443	1513	...	...		...			1813	1913	...	...	...	...	...	...	...	...	...
Lille Europe ....a.			...	...	1657	1735					...	...	...	...	...	...	...	...	...
London St Pancras 10 ....a.	1602	1639	...	...	1806				1939	2039	...	...	...	...	...	...	...	...	...

A – July 3 - Aug. 28.
B – Apr. 2 - Sept. 26.
C – June 2 - Aug. 28.
D – Calls at Agde, a. 0843, Sète, a. 0858.
E – Apr. 3 - Sept. 27.
K – ①–⑤ Dec. 11–31 (not Dec. 26,27). ①④⑤ Feb. 5 - Mar. 25. ①–⑤ Mar. 26 - May 27 (not Apr. 17, May 1).
Q – ①⑤⑥ Mar. 31 - May 27. ①④⑤⑥⑦ May 28 - Sept. 28 (not Sept. 23,30). ①⑤⑥ Sept. 29 - Nov. 4. see Table **17**.
R – July 4 - Aug. 28.
S – Calls at Sète 1958, Agde 2014.
T – ⑤⑥ Dec. 11–31. ⑥ Jan. 1 - Mar. 25 (also Feb. 10,12,17,19). ①⑤⑥⑦ Mar. 26 - May 27 (also Apr. 13; not Apr. 30).

V – ①②③④⑥.
e – Not Sept. 23, 30.
h – Not Jan. 1, Apr. 16, 30.
k – Not Dec. 24, 31.
r – 0715 on ⑦.
z – Not Aug. 29, Nov. 11.

TGV – *Train à Grande Vitesse* 🅁 🍴 ✗.
AVE – *Alta Velocidad Española* 🅁 🍴 ✗.
✗ – Supplement payable.

◇ – 🚌 connections available to Figueres bus station (Table **657**).
☆ – Eurostar train. 🅁, ✗ in Business Premier and Standard Premier, 🍴 in Standard. Special fares payable. Minimum check-in time 30 minutes. Additional services are shown on Table **10**. Valid Dec. 11 - May 27, 2017.

←Table 12 notes continued from previous page.

c – Not Jan. 1.
e – Not Feb. 26.
f – Also Dec. 26, 27, Jan. 2, Apr. 17, May 1, 25.
h – Also Dec. 26, 27, Jan. 2, Apr. 17, May 1; not Dec. 24, 31.
j – Not Dec. 26, 27, Jan. 2, Apr. 17, May 1.
k – Not Dec. 26, Jan 2, Apr. 17, May 1.
r – Also Apr. 17, May 1.
x – 27–28 minutes later on Ⓒ.

y – Also Dec. 26, 27, Jan. 2, Apr. 17, May 1.
z – Calls at Calais Fréthun, see Table **10**.

⇌ – *Thalys* high-speed train. 🅁 🍴. Special fares payable. Valid Dec. 11 - Apr. 1, 2017.
☆ – Eurostar train. 🅁, ✗ in Business Premier and Standard Premier, 🍴 in Standard. Special fares payable. Minimum check-in time is 30 minutes. Not available for London - Ebbsfleet - Ashford or v.v. journeys. Valid Dec. 11 - May 27, 2017.

train type	☆	☆	☆	IC	☆	IC	⇌	☆	☆	IC	⇌	☆	☆	IC	⇌	⇌
train number	9108	9110	9110	9231	9114	9235	9327	9116	9116	9239	9993	9126	9126	9247	9397	9351
notes	P	A	⑥	❖	K	❖		Y	B	❖		E	J	❖	①-④	
London St Pancras **12** d.	0613	0650	0657	…	…	0804	…	…	0855	0858	…	…	1058	1104	…	
Ebbsfleet International 12 d.	0630	0707		…				0915	0915				1115			
Ashford International 12 d.	0653	0728	0728	…												
Lille Europe 12 d.	|	0933	0930	…	1030			1130	1133	…			1330	1330	…	
Brussels Midi/Zuid **12** a.	0922	1007	1005	…	1105			1205	1208	…			1405	1405	…	
Brussels Midi/Zuid **12** d.				1045		1145	1152			1245	1252			1445	1452	1552
Antwerpen Centraal a.				1143		1243	1227			1343	1327			1543	1527	1627
Roosendaal ▥ a.				1211		1311				1411				1611		
Rotterdam Centraal a.				1250		1350	1302			1450	1402			1650	1602	1702
Den Haag HS a.				1322		1422				1522				1722		
Schiphol ✈ a.				1350		1450	1324			1550	1424			1750	1624	1724
Amsterdam Centraal a.				1406		1506	1342			1606	1442			1806	1642	1742

train type	☆	IC	⇌	☆	IC	⇌	☆	IC	⇌	☆	IC	⇌
train number	9132	9255	9357	9136	9259	9363	9140	9263	9369	9144	9267	9375
notes	❖	⑧w		F	❖	①-④	⑥	❖	⑥	.⋄		⑧H
London St Pancras **12** d.	1258			1404			1504			1604		
Ebbsfleet International 12 d.	1315											
Ashford International 12 d.												
Lille Europe 12 d.	1533			1630			1730			1830		
Brussels Midi/Zuid **12** d.	1608			1705			1805			1905		
Brussels Midi/Zuid **12** d.		1645	1652		1745	1752		1845	1852		1945	1952
Antwerpen Centraal a.		1743	1727		1843	1827		1943	1927		2043	2027
Roosendaal ▥ a.		1811			1911			2011			2111	
Rotterdam Centraal a.		1850	1802		1950	1902		2050	2002		2150	2102
Den Haag HS a.		1922			2022			2122			2222	
Schiphol ✈ a.		1950	1824		2050	1924		2150	2024		2250	2124
Amsterdam Centraal a.		2006	1842		2106	1942		2206	2042		2306	2142

train type	☆	IC	⇌	☆	☆				☆	☆	☆	☆
train number	9148	9271	9381	9152	9152	9995						
notes	W	❖		⑦y	Q	⑤⑥⑦			①-⑥	⑦	⑥	⑧
London St Pancras **12** d.	1704			1755	1804	k			0804	1104	1601	1704
Ebbsfleet International 12 d.									|	|	|	|
Ashford International 12 d.				1828c								
Lille Europe 12 d.	1930			2030	2030				|	|	|	|
Brussels Midi/Zuid **12** d.	2005			2105	2105				1058	1358	1858	1958
Brussels Midi/Zuid d.		2045	2052			2152			1102	1402	1902	2002
Antwerpen Centraal a.		2143	2127			2227			1138	1438	1938	2038
Roosendaal ▥ a.		2211										
Rotterdam Centraal a.		2250	2202			2302			1212	1512	2012	2112
Den Haag HS a.		2322										
Schiphol ✈ a.		2350	2224			2324			1238	1538	2038	2138
Amsterdam Centraal a.		0006	2242			2342			1254	1554	2054	2154

> Eurostar has submitted the proposed timetable for its planned London – Amsterdam service to the Belgian rail regulator.
>
> Proposed timings for the service, due to start in Dec. 2017, are shown on the right.

train type	⇌	☆	IC	☆	☆	⇌	IC	☆	⇌	IC	☆
train number	9310	9117	9322	9216	9125	9328	9220	9129	9334	9224	9133
notes	①-⑤		■		X	Y	■	⑦r	⑥⑦	■	E
Amsterdam Centraal d.	0617			0817	0652	0917	0752		1017	0852	…
Schiphol ✈ d.	0634			0834	0707	0934	0807		1034	0907	…
Den Haag HS d.					0740		0840			0940	
Rotterdam Centraal d.	0658			0858	0808	0958	0908		1058	1008	…
Roosendaal ▥ d.					0847		0947			1047	
Antwerpen Centraal d.	0734			0933	0917	1033	1017		1133	1117	…
Brussels Midi/Zuid **12** d.	0808			1008	1015	1108	1115		1208	1215	…
Brussels Midi/Zuid **12** d.		0852			1056		1156		1252		
Lille Europe 12 a.		0926			1130		1230		1330		
Ashford International 12 a.											
Ebbsfleet International 12 a.											1345
London St Pancras **12** a.		0957			1157		1257				1405

train type	IC	⇌	☆	⇌	☆	⇌	IC	☆	⇌	IC	⇌	☆	⇌	IC	☆	⇌
train number	9232	9340	9346	9141	9141	9352	9236	9145	9358	9240	9149	9149	9364	9244	9153	9153
notes	■	①-⑤	⑦y		E		■	F	⑧w	■	⑦y	E	9996	■	C	⑦y
Amsterdam Centraal d.	1052	1117	1217			1317	1152		1417	1252			1517	1352		
Schiphol ✈ d.	1107	1134	1234			1334	1207		1434	1307			1534	1407		
Den Haag HS d.	1140						1240			1340				1440		
Rotterdam Centraal d.	1208	1158	1258			1358	1308		1458	1408			1558	1508		
Roosendaal ▥ d.	1247						1347			1447				1547		
Antwerpen Centraal d.	1317	1233	1333			1433	1417		1533	1517			1633	1617		
Brussels Midi/Zuid **12** d.	1415	1308	1408			1508	1515		1608	1615			1708	1715		
Brussels Midi/Zuid **12** d.				1452	1456			1556			1656	1656			1756	1756
Lille Europe 12 a.				1526	1530			1632			1732	1732			1832	1832
Ashford International 12 a.												1734			1835	
Ebbsfleet International 12 a.				1545	1545						1745				1845	
London St Pancras **12** a.				1605	1605			1657			1805	1806			1903	1910

train type	⇌	IC	☆	⇌	IC	☆		☆	☆	☆	☆	☆
train number	9370	9248	9157	9376	9252	9161						
notes	9998	■	R		⑧w	b		①-⑥	⑦	⑥	①-⑤	⑦
Amsterdam Centraal d.	1617	1452		1717	1552			0748	0925	1418	1648	1721
Schiphol ✈ d.	1634	1507		1734	1607			0804	0941	1435	1704	1737
Den Haag HS d.		1540			1640							
Rotterdam Centraal d.	1658	1608		1758	1708			0830	1006	1506	1730	1806
Roosendaal ▥ d.		1647			1747							
Antwerpen Centraal d.	1733	1717		1833	1817							
Brussels Midi/Zuid **12** d.	1808	1815		1908	1915			0937	1137	1638	1837	1938
Brussels Midi/Zuid **12** d.			1856			1952		1005	1205	1702	1902	2005
Lille Europe 12 a.			1930			2026						
Ashford International 12 a.						2045						
Ebbsfleet International 12 a.						2045						
London St Pancras **12** a.			1957			2103		1057	1257	1757	1957	2057

> Eurostar has submitted the proposed timetable for its planned London – Amsterdam service to the Belgian rail regulator.
>
> Proposed timings for the service, due to start in Dec. 2017, are shown on the right.

A – ①-⑤ Dec. 11 - Mar. 25 (not Dec. 26, 27, Jan 2). ②-④ Mar. 26 - May 27 (not Apr. 17, May 1).
B – ⑥⑦ (also Dec. 27).
C – ①-⑤ (not Dec. 26, 27, Jan. 2, Apr. 17, May 1).
E – ①-⑥ (not Dec. 26, 27, Jan. 2, Apr. 17, May 1).
F – ⑤⑦ Dec. 11-31 (also Dec. 26, 27). ⑦ Jan. 1 - Feb. 4 (also Jan. 2). ⑤⑦ Feb. 5 - Mar. 25. ⑤ Mar. 26 - May 27, (also Apr. 13, 30, May 25).
H – ⑧ (not Dec. 25). Train number 9975 on ①-④.
J – ①-⑤ Dec. 11-31 (not Dec. 26, 27).
K – ①-⑤ Dec. 11-31 (not Dec. 26, 27). ①④⑤ Feb. 5 - Mar. 25. ①-⑤ Mar. 26 - May 27 (not Apr. 17, May 1).

Q – ①-⑤ Dec. 11-31 (not Dec. 26, 27). ⑤ Jan. 1 - Feb. 4. ①-⑤ Feb. 5 - May 27 (not Apr. 17, May 1).
R – ⑧ Dec. 11-31. ⑦ Feb. 1 - Feb. 4 (also Jan. 2). ①④⑤⑦ Feb. 5 - Mar. 25. ⑧ Mar. 26 - May 27.
W – ⑧ Dec. 11 - Mar. 25. Daily Mar. 26 - May 27 (not Apr. 1, 15).
X – ①-⑤ Dec. 11-31. ⑤ Jan. 1 - Feb. 4 (also Jan. 2). ①-⑤ Feb. 5 - Mar. 25. ①-⑥ Mar. 26 - May 27 (not Apr. 1, 15, 17, May 1).
Y – ①-⑥ (also Dec. 25).

Z – ①-⑤ Dec. 11 - Mar. 25 (not Dec. 27). ②-④ Mar. 26 - May 27.
b – Not Dec. 24, 31.
c – Not Feb. 26.
k – Also Dec. 31.
r – Also Apr. 17, May 1.
w – Not Dec. 25.
y – Also Dec. 26, 27, Jan. 2, Apr. 17, May 1.
⇌ – *Thalys* high-speed train. ⑧ ⑨. Valid Dec. 11 - Apr. 1, 2017. Special fares payable.
■ – Service calls at Dordrecht 14-15 minutes after Rotterdam Centraal and at Mechelen 18 minutes after Antwerpen Centraal; see Table 18 for full timings.

☆ – Eurostar train. ⑧, ✗ in Business Premier and Standard Premier, ⑨ in Standard. Special fares payable. Minimum check-in time 30 minutes. Not available for London - Ebbsfleet - Ashford or v.v. journeys. Valid Dec. 11 - May 27, 2017.
❖ – Service calls at Mechelen 37 minutes after Brussels Midi/Zuid and 28 minutes after Roosendaal; see Table 18 for full timings.

15a LONDON - AMSTERDAM *by rail–sea–rail via Harwich - Hoek van Holland*

From April 1, 2017 the Hoek van Holland Haven - Schiedam Centrum - Rotterdam Centraal service is subject to alteration.

notes		①–⑥	⑥	①–⑤	①–⑥	①–⑥	①–⑥	①–⑥		⑦	⑦	⑦	⑦	⑦	⑦		①–⑤	⑥	①–⑥	①–⑥	②–⑦	②–⑦	②–⑦		
					⛴							⛴								⛴					
London Liverpool Street	d.	...	0638	0638	...	...	...	...	...	...	0755	...	...	...	...	...	1932	1932	...	...	...	...	...	...	...
Colchester	d.	...	0740	0743	...	...	...	...	...	...	0859	...	...	...	...	...	2025	2032	...	...	...	...	...	...	...
Manningtree	d.	...	0748	0751	...	...	...	...	...	...	0907	...	...	...	...	...	2034	2040	...	...	...	...	...	...	...
Cambridge	d.	...	|	|	...	...	...	...	...	...	|	...	...	...	...	...	|	|	1944	...	...	...	...	...	...
Ipswich	d.	0659	|	|	...	...	...	...	...	0751	|	...	...	...	...	...	|	|	2101	...	...	...	...	...	...
Harwich International 🏨	d.	0727	0809	0810	0900	...	...	...	...	0816	0925	1000	...	...	...	...	2054	2056	2129	2300	...	...	...	...	...
Hoek van Holland Haven 🏨	a.	...	...	...	1715	1756	...	...	...	...	...	1800	1856	...	...	...	...	...	...	0800	0826	...	...	...	...
Schiedam Centrum	a.	...	...	...	...	1821	1826	...	...	...	...	...	1921	1926	...	...	...	...	...	...	0851	...	0856	...	...
Rotterdam Centraal	a.	...	...	...	...	1827	|	1835	...	...	...	...	1927	|	1935	...	...	...	...	...	0857	0905	|	...	...
Utrecht Centraal	a.	...	...	...	...	...	|	1913	...	...	...	...	...	|	2013	...	...	...	...	...	...	0943	|	...	...
Amersfoort	a.	...	...	...	...	...	|	1934	...	...	...	...	...	|	2034	...	...	...	...	...	...	1004	|	...	...
Den Haag HS	a.	...	...	...	...	...	1843	...	...	...	...	...	...	1943	...	...	...	...	...	...	...	...	0913	...	...
Schiphol ✈	a.	...	...	...	...	...	1914	...	...	...	...	...	...	2014	...	...	...	...	...	...	...	...	0944	...	...
Amsterdam Centraal	a.	...	...	...	...	...	1931	...	...	...	...	...	...	2031	...	...	...	...	...	...	...	...	1001	...	...

notes		⑦•	⑦	⑦	①	①	①		
				⛴					
London Liverpool Street	d.	1932	...	...	...	...	...	...	...
Colchester	d.	2046	...	...	...	...	...	...	...
Manningtree	d.	2055	...	...	...	...	...	...	...
Cambridge	d.	|	1912	...	...	...	...	...	...
Ipswich	d.	|	2036	...	...	...	...	...	...
Harwich International 🏨	d.	2114	2105	2300	...	...	...	...	...
Hoek van Holland Haven 🏨	a.	...	...	0800	0826	...	...	...	...
Schiedam Centrum	a.	...	...	...	0851	...	0856	...	...
Rotterdam Centraal	a.	...	...	...	0857	0905	|	...	...
Utrecht Centraal	a.	...	...	...	...	0943	|	...	...
Amersfoort	a.	...	...	...	...	1004	|	...	...
Den Haag HS	a.	...	...	...	...	...	0913	...	...
Schiphol ✈	a.	...	...	...	...	...	0944	...	...
Amsterdam Centraal	a.	...	...	...	...	...	1001	...	...

notes		⑥⑦	⑥⑦	⑥⑦	⑥⑦	⑦	⑥	⑦	⑥		
					⛴						
Amsterdam Centraal	d.	1128	...	...	...	...	...	...	...	...	...
Schiphol ✈	d.	1146	...	...	...	...	...	...	...	...	...
Den Haag HS	d.	1219	...	...	...	...	...	...	...	...	...
Amersfoort	d.	|	1126	...	...	...	...	...	...	...	...
Utrecht	d.	|	1147	...	...	...	...	...	...	...	...
Rotterdam Centraal	d.	|	1225	1232	...	...	...	...	...	...	...
Schiedam Centrum	d.	1233	...	1237	...	...	...	...	...	...	...
Hoek van Holland Haven 🏨	d.	...	...	1302	1345	...	...	...	...	...	...
Harwich International 🏨	a.	...	...	...	1945	2035	2045	2110	2138	...	...
Ipswich	a.	...	...	...	...	|	|	2137	2203	...	...
Cambridge	a.	...	...	...	...	|	|	...	...	...	...
Manningtree	a.	...	...	...	...	2048	2058	...	...	...	...
Colchester	a.	...	...	...	...	2057	2107	...	...	...	...
London Liverpool Street	a.	...	...	...	...	2202	2214	...	...	...	...

notes		①–⑤	①–⑤	①–⑤	①–⑤	①–⑤	①–⑤						①–⑤	⑥	⑦	①–⑥	⑦								
					⛴							⛴													
Amsterdam Centraal	d.	1128	...	...	...	...	...	...	...	1928	...	...	...	...	...	...	...	...	...	...	...	...	...	...	...
Schiphol ✈	d.	1146	...	...	...	...	...	...	...	1946	...	...	...	...	...	...	...	...	...	...	...	...	...	...	...
Den Haag HS	d.	1219	...	...	...	...	...	...	...	2019	...	...	...	...	...	...	...	...	...	...	...	...	...	...	...
Amersfoort	d.	|	1126	...	...	...	...	...	1926	|	...	...	...	...	...	...	...	...	...	...	...	...	...	...	...
Utrecht	d.	|	1147	...	...	...	...	...	1947	|	...	...	...	...	...	...	...	...	...	...	...	...	...	...	...
Rotterdam Centraal	d.	|	1225	1232	...	...	...	...	2025	|	2032	...	...	...	...	...	...	...	...	...	...	...	...	...	...
Schiedam Centrum	d.	1233	...	1237	...	...	...	...	...	2033	2037	...	...	...	...	...	...	...	...	...	...	...	...	...	...
Hoek van Holland Haven 🏨	d.	...	...	1302	1415	...	...	...	...	...	2102	2200	...	...	...	...	...	...	...	...	...	...	...	...	...
Harwich International 🏨	a.	...	...	...	1945	2045	2138	...	...	...	...	0630	0715	0720	0720	0750	0830	...	...	...	...	...	...	...	...
Ipswich	a.	...	...	...	...	|	2204	...	...	...	...	...	|	|	|	0817	0856	...	...	...	...	...	...	...	...
Cambridge	a.	...	...	...	...	|	...	...	...	...	...	...	|	|	|	0939	1025	...	...	...	...	...	...	...	...
Manningtree	a.	...	...	...	...	2058	...	...	...	...	...	...	0731	0733	0733	...	...	...	...	...	...	...	...	...	...
Colchester	a.	...	...	...	...	2107	...	...	...	...	...	...	0741	0742	0742	...	...	...	...	...	...	...	...	...	...
London Liverpool Street	a.	...	...	...	...	2214	...	...	...	...	...	...	0854	0845	0859	...	...	...	...	...	...	...	...	...	...

SEA CROSSING (for rail / sea / rail journeys): ⛴ – Ship operated by Stena Line. Ⓡ. Stena Plus lounge (supplement payable) and ✗ on ship. A cabin must be booked on night sailings.

16 LILLE - BRUSSELS (Summary Table)

train type		TGV	TGV	☆	☆	☆	TGV	☆	☆	⇌	TGV	☆	TGV	TGV	☆	☆	TGV	☆	TGV	☆	⇌	☆	TGV	☆	⇌	☆	☆	☆
train number		**9809**	**9853**	**9110**	**9110**	**9114**	**9855**	**9116**	**9116**	**9993**	**9863**	**9126**	**9861**	**9861**	**9132**	**9136**	**9867**	**9140**	**9895**	**9144**	**9975**	**9148**	**9869**	**9152**	**9995**	**9156**	**9158**	**9162**
notes		Ⓐ		⑥									Ⓒ	Ⓐ				Ⓑ		⑥	①–④				⑤⑥⑦	⑥⑦	①–⑤	⑦
notes					**C**	**J**		**V**	**D**	**Z**						**F**					**Z**	**W**		**B**	**Z**	**z**	**j**	**x**
Lille Europe	d.	0732	0908	0930	0933	1030	1117	1130	1133	1159	1208	1330	1422	1435	1533	1630	1707	1730	1810	1830	1907	1930	2008	2030	2104	2133	2203	2230
Brussels Midi / Zuid	a.	0807	0943	1005	1007	1105	1151	1205	1208	1235	1243	1405	1457	1512	1608	1705	1743	1805	1843	1905	1943	2005	2043	2105	2141	2208	2238	2305

train type		☆	TGV	☆	TGV	☆	⇌	☆	☆	TGV	☆	☆	☆	TGV	☆	TGV	☆	⇌	☆	⇌	☆	TGV	☆					
train number		**9109**	**9870**	**9113**	**9812**	**9117**	**9994**	**9125**	**9129**	**9828**	**9133**	**9141**	**9141**	**9874**	**9145**	**9836**	**9149**	**9996**	**9153**	**9998**	**9157**	**9846**	**9161**					
notes		①		①–⑥					⑦		①–⑥	⑦	①–⑥					①–④	Ⓑ	⑤⑥⑦								
notes		**k**		**j**			**Z**	**X**	**r**		**q**	**y**	**q**		**K**			**Z**		**Z**	**H**		**h**					
Brussels Midi / Zuid	d.	0656	0717	0756	0817	0852	0917	1056	1156	1217**p**	1252	1452	1456	1517	1556	1617	1656	1717	1756	1817	1856	1917	1952	...	...	...	...	...
Lille Europe	a.	0730	0752	0830	0852	0926	0953	1130	1230	1253	1326	1526	1532	1552	1630	1653	1730	1753	1830	1853	1930	1952	2026	...	...	...	...	...

B – Ⓑ Dec. 11–31. ⑤⑦ Jan. 1 - Feb. 4 (also Jan. 2). Ⓑ Feb. 5 - May 27.
C – ①–⑤ Dec. 11 - Mar. 25 (not Dec. 26, 27, Jan 2). ②–④ Mar. 26 - May 27 (not Apr. 17, May 1).
D – ⑥⑦ Dec. 11 - Mar. 25 (also Dec. 27). ①⑤⑥⑦ Mar. 26 - May 27.
F – ⑤⑦ Dec. 11–31 (also Dec. 26, 27). ⑦ Jan. 1 - Mar. 25 (also Jan. 2, Feb. 10, 17). ⑤ Mar. 26 - May 27 (also Apr. 13, May 1, 25).
H – Ⓑ Dec. 11–31. ⑦ Jan. 1 - Feb. 4 (also Jan. 2). ①④⑤⑦ Feb. 5 - Mar. 25. Ⓑ Mar. 26 - May 27.
J – ①–⑤ Dec. 11–31 (not Dec. 26, 27). ①④⑤ Feb. 5 - Mar. 25. ①–⑤ Mar. 26 - May 27 (not Apr. 17, May 1).
K – ⑤⑦ Dec. 11–31 (also Dec. 26, 27). ⑦ Jan. 1 - Feb. 4 (also Jan. 2). ⑤⑦ Feb. 5 - Mar. 25. ⑤ Mar. 26 - May 27, (also Apr. 13, 30, May 25).
L – ①–⑤ (not Dec. 26, 27, Jan 2).
V – ①–⑤ Dec. 11 - Mar. 25 (not Dec. 27). ②–④ Mar. 26 - May 27.
W – Ⓑ Dec. 11 - Mar. 25. Daily Mar. 26 - May 27 (not Apr. 1, 15).
X – ①–⑤ Dec. 11–31. ⑤ Jan. 1 - Feb. 4 (also Jan. 2). ①–⑤ Feb. 5 - Mar. 25. ①–⑥ Mar. 26 - May 27 (not Apr. 1, 15, 17, May 1).
Z – To / from Amsterdam (Table **18**).

h – Not Dec. 24, 31.
j – Also Dec. 26, 27, Jan. 2, Apr. 17, May 1, 25.
k – Not Dec. 26, Jan 2, Apr. 17, May 1.
p – 1205 Jan. 23 - Feb. 28.
q – Not Dec. 26, 27, Jan 2, Apr. 17, May 1.
r – Also Apr. 17, May 1.
x – Not Jan. 1.
y – Also Dec. 26, 27, Jan. 2, Apr. 17, May 1.
z – Also Dec. 26, 27, Jan. 2, Apr. 17, May 1; not Dec. 24, 31.

⇌ – *Thalys* high-speed train. Valid Dec. 11 - Apr. 1. Ⓡ 🍷.
TGV – High-speed train. Ⓡ 🍷.
☆ – Eurostar train. Ⓡ, ✗ in Business Premier and Standard Premier, 🍷 in Standard. Special fares payable. Minimun check-in time 30 minutes departure from Brussels. Valid Dec. 11 - May 27, 2017.

17 LONDON - MARSEILLE and MARNE LA VALLÉE

train type		☆		☆	☆		
train number		**9084**		**9074**	**9074**		
train number		**9085**					
notes		**M**		**A**	**Y**		
London St Pancras	d.	0719**f**	...	1014	1024	...	...
Ebbsfleet International	d.	|	...	1034	1044	...	...
Ashford International	d.	0755	...	1058	|	...	...
Lille Europe	a.	|	...	1254**s**	1254**s**	...	...
Marne la Vallée §	a.	|	...	1403	1403	...	...
Lyon Part Dieu	a.	1300**x**	...	...	...	...	...
Avignon TGV	a.	1408	...	...	...	...	...
Marseille St Charles	a.	1445	...	...	...	...	...

train type		☆	☆	☆	☆	☆	
train number		**9057**	**9057**	**9057**	**9087**	**9087**	
train number					**9086**	**9086**	
notes		**Y**	**B**	**C**	**M**	**M**	
Marseille St Charles	d.	...	...	...	1522	...	...
Avignon TGV	d.	...	...	...	1559	...	...
Lyon Part Dieu	d.	...	...	...	1725**x**	...	...
Marne la Vallée §	d.	1652	1652	1802	|	...	...
Lille Europe	d.	|	|	|	2021	2136	...
Ashford International	a.	|	1806	1904	...	2134	...
Ebbsfleet International	a.	1827	1827	1926	...	|	...
London St Pancras	a.	1847	1847	1946	...	2212	...

A – Daily Dec. 11 - Jan. 2 (not Dec. 17). ①③⑤⑦ Feb. 5 - July 7 (daily Feb. 10–20, not Feb. 26, daily Apr. 1–15, also Apr. 29, daily May 27 - June 3).
B – ⑤⑦ Dec. 11 - Jan. 2 (also Dec. 24, 31). ⑤⑦ Feb. 5 - July 7 (also Feb. 11, 18, Apr. 1, 8, 15, May 27, June 3).
C – Dec. 12, 14, 19–22, 26, 29, Jan. 2, 3. ①③ Feb. 5 - July 7 (also Feb. 14, 16, Apr. 4, 6, 11, 13, May 30, June 1).
M – Dec. 17, 23, 30, Feb. 11, 18. ①⑤⑥ Mar. 31 - May 27. ①④⑤⑥⑦ May 28 - Sept. 28. ①⑤⑥ Sept. 29 - Nov. 4.

Y – Feb. 26.
f – 0715 on ⑦.
s – Calls to set down only.
☆ – Eurostar train. Ⓡ, ✗ in Standard Premier, 🍷 in Standard. Special fares payable. Minimum check-in time 30 minutes. Not available for London - Ashford or v.v. journeys. Valid Dec. 11 - Nov. 4, 2017.

x – Not Sept. 23, 30.
§ – Marne la Vallée - Chessy (station for Disneyland).

Brussels - Disneyland: see Table 11

AMSTERDAM - BRUSSELS - PARIS 18

For the full service London - Brussels and v.v. see Table **12**. Connections at Brussels are not guaranteed.

		train type	⇌	⇌	⇌	⇌	⇌	⇌	⇌	⇌	*IC*	⇌	*IC*	⇌	⇌	*IC*	⇌	*IC*	⇌	⇌	*IC*	⇌	*IC*	⇌
		train number	**9302**	**9304**	**9308**	**9920/1**	**9310**	**9412**	**9316**	**9994**	**9212**	**9322**	**9216**	**9424**	**9328**	**9220**	**9334**	**9224**	**9336**	**9340**	**9228**	**9346**	**9232**	**9448**
		notes	①-④	①-⑤	①-⑥	⊕	①-⑤		①-⑥						①-⑥		⑥⑦		①-⑤			①-⑤		
			S		**h**	**A**			**f**	**K**					**f**									
0	*0*	**Amsterdam** Centraal d.	...	...	...	0542	0617	...	...	0717	0552	0817	0652	...	0917	0752	1017	0852	...	1117	0952	1217	1052	...
17	*17*	Schiphol ✈ ⊕ d.	...	...	...	0559	0634	...	...	0734	0608	0834	0708	...	0934	0808	1034	0908	...	1134	1008	1234	1108	...
60		Den Haag HS d.	...	...	...	|	|	...	...	|	0640	|	0740	...	|	0840	|	0940	...	|	1040	|	1140	...
82	*70*	**Rotterdam** Centraal d.	...	...	...	0625	0658	...	...	0758	0705j	0858	0805j	...	0958	0908	1058	1005j	...	1158	1108	1258	1205j	...
		Dordrecht d.	...	...	...	|	|	...	...	|	0720	|	0820	...	|	0922	|	1020	...	|	1122	|	1220	...
140		Roosendaal 🏛 d.	...	...	...	|	|	...	...	|	0747	|	0847	...	|	0947	|	1047	...	|	1147	|	1247	...
181	*165*	**Antwerpen** Centraal d.	...	...	...	0705	0734	...	...	0833	0817	0933	0917	...	1033	1017	1133	1117	...	1233	1217	1333	1317	...
		Mechelen d.	...	...	...	|	|	...	...	|	0835	|	0935	...	|	1035	|	1135	...	|	1235	|	1335	...
		Brussels Nationaal ✈ d.	...	...	...	|	|	...	...	|	0849	|	0949	...	|	1049	|	1149	...	|	1249	|	1349	...
229	*212*	**Brussels** Midi/Zuid △ a.	...	...	...	|	0808	...	...	0908	0915	1008	1015	...	1108	1115	1208	1215	...	1308	1315	1408	1415	...
229	*212*	**Brussels** Midi/Zuid d.	0637	0713	0743	0753v	0813	0843	0913	0917	...	1013	...	1043	1113	...	1213	...	1237	1313	...	...	...	1443
		Lille Europe a.	|	|	|	...	|	|	|	0953	...	|	...	|	|	...	|	...	|	|	...	...	...	|
541	*524*	**Paris** Nord a.	0759	0835	0905	...	0935	1005	1035	...	...	1135	...	1205	1235	...	1335	...	1359	1435	...	...	...	1605

train type	⇌	*IC*	⇌	⇌	⇌	*IC*	⇌	⇌	⇌	⇌	*IC*	⇌	⇌	⇌	⇌	*IC*	⇌	⇌	⇌	*IC*	⇌	⇌	*IC*	⇌
train number	**9352**	**9236**	**9356**	**9358**	**9358**	**9240**	**9360**	**9364**	**9996**	**9364**	**9244**	**9368**	**9370**	**9998**	**9370**	**9248**	**9472**	**9376**	**9376**	**9252**	**9380**	**9382**	**9256**	**9484**
notes			⑤	Ⓑ	⑥			①-④	①-④	⑤⑥⑦		Ⓑ	⑦	⑤⑥⑦	①-⑤			⑥	Ⓑ		⑤			
				w	**f**		**G**					**b**	**w**					**f**	**w**					
Amsterdam Centraal d.	1317	1152	...	1417	...	1252	...	...	1517	1517	1352	...	...	1617	1617	1452	...	...	1717	1552	...	1817	1652	...
Schiphol ✈ ⊕ d.	1334	1208	...	1434	...	1308	...	...	1534	1534	1408	...	...	1634	1634	1508	...	...	1734	1608	...	1834	1708	...
Den Haag HS d.	|	1240	...	|	...	1340	...	...	|	|	1440	...	...	|	|	1540	...	...	|	1640	...	|	1740	...
Rotterdam Centraal d.	1358	1308	...	1458	...	1405j	...	...	1558	1558	1508	...	...	1658	1658	1608j	...	...	1758	1708	...	1858	1805j	...
Dordrecht d.	|	1322	...	|	...	1420	...	...	|	|	1522	...	...	|	|	1620	...	...	|	1722	...	|	1820	...
Roosendaal 🏛 d.	|	1347	...	|	...	1447	...	...	|	|	1547	...	...	|	|	1647	...	...	|	1747	...	|	1847	...
Antwerpen Centraal d.	1433	1417	...	1533	...	1517	...	...	1633	1633	1617	...	...	1733	1733	1717	...	...	1833	1817	...	1933	1917	...
Mechelen d.	|	1435	...	|	...	1535	...	...	|	|	1635	...	...	|	|	1735	...	...	|	1835	...	|	1935	...
Brussels Nationaal ✈ d.	|	1449	...	|	...	1549	...	...	|	|	1649	...	...	|	|	1749	...	...	|	1849	...	|	1949	...
Brussels Midi/Zuid △ a.	1508	1515	...	1608	...	1615	...	...	1708	1708	1715	...	...	1808	1808	1815	...	...	1908	1915	...	2008	2015	...
Brussels Midi/Zuid d.	1513	...	1543	1613	1613	...	1637	1713	1717	1713	...	1743	1813	1817	1813	...	1843	1913	1913	...	1943	2013	...	2043
Lille Europe a.	|	...	|	|	|	...	|	|	1753	|	...	|	|	1853	|	...	|	|	|	...	|	|	...	|
Paris Nord a.	1635	...	1705	1735	1735	...	1759	1835	...	1835	...	1905	1935	...	1935	...	2005	2035	2035	...	2105	2135	...	2205

train type	⇌	*IC*	⇌	⇌	⇌	*IC*	*IC*	*IC*
train number	**9388**	**9260**	**9390**	**9394**	**9394**	**9264**	**9268**	**9272**
notes	Ⓑ		⑤	①-⑤	⑦			
	w				**w**	**x**	**x**	**x**
Amsterdam Centraal d.	1917	1752	...	2017	2017	1852	1952	2052
Schiphol ✈ ⊕ d.	1934	1808	...	2034	2034	1908	2008	2108
Den Haag HS d.	|	1840	...	|	|	1940	2040	2140
Rotterdam Centraal d.	1958	1908	...	2058	2058	2005j	2108	2205j
Dordrecht d.	|	1922	...	|	|	2020	2122	2220
Roosendaal 🏛 d.	|	1947	...	|	|	2047	2147	2247
Antwerpen Centraal d.	2033	2017	...	2133	2133	2117	2217	2317
Mechelen d.	|	2035	...	|	|	2135	2235	2335
Brussels Nationaal ✈ d.	|	2049	...	|	|	2149	2249	2349
Brussels Midi/Zuid △ a.	2108	2115	...	2208	2208	2215	2315	0015
Brussels Midi/Zuid d.	2113	...	2137	...	2213	...	...	...
Lille Europe a.	|	...	|	...	|	...	...	...
Paris Nord a.	2235	...	2259	...	2335	...	...	...

train type	*IC*	⇌	*IC*	⇌	*IC*	⇌	⇌	*IC*	⇌
train number	**9211**	**9391**	**9215**	**9401**	**9219**	**9303**	**9305**	**9223**	**9309**
notes		①-⑤				①-⑤	①		①-⑥
							t		**f**
Paris Nord d.	...	...	...	0601	...	0625	0655	...	0725
Lille Europe d.	...	...	...	|	...	|	|	...	|
Brussels Midi/Zuid a.	...	...	...	0723	...	0747	0817	...	0847
Brussels Midi/Zuid ▽ d.	0545	0652	0645	...	0745	0752	...	0845	0852
Brussels Nationaal ✈ d.	0611	|	0711	...	0811	|	...	0911	|
Mechelen d.	0625	|	0725	...	0825	|	...	0925	|
Antwerpen Centraal a.	0643	0727	0743	...	0843	0827	...	0943	0927
Roosendaal 🏛 a.	0711	|	0811	...	0911	|	...	1011	|
Dordrecht a.	0736	|	0836	...	0936	|	...	1036	|
Rotterdam Centraal a.	0750	0803	0850	...	0950	0902	...	1050	1002
Den Haag HS a.	0822	|	0922	...	1022	|	...	1122	|
Schiphol ✈ ⊗ a.	0850	0824	0950	...	1050	0924	...	1150	1024
Amsterdam Centraal a.	0906	0842	1006	...	1106	0942	...	1206	1042

train type	⇌	*IC*	⇌	⇌	*IC*	⇌	⇌	*IC*	⇌	*IC*	⇌	⇌	⇌	*IC*	⇌	⇌	⇌	*IC*	*IC*	⇌	*IC*	⇌	⇌	*IC*
train number	**9413**	**9227**	**9315**	**9319**	**9231**	**9321**	**9325**	**9235**	**9327**	**9239**	**9993**	**9333**	**9437**	**9243**	**9339**	**9341**	**9397**	**9247**	**9251**	**9351**	**9255**	**9357**	**9461**	**9259**
notes				⑤			①-⑤					①				⑤⑦	①-④					Ⓑ		
						H	**y**									**d**						**w**		
Paris Nord d.	0755	...	0825	0901	...	0925	1001	...	1025	...	...	1125	1155	...	1225	1246	...	...	...	1425	...	1525	1555	...
Lille Europe d.	|	...	|	|	...	|	|	...	|	...	1159	|	|	...	|	|	...	...	...	|	...	|	|	...
Brussels Midi/Zuid a.	0917	...	0947	1023	...	1047	1123	...	1147	...	1235	1247	1317	...	1347	1412	...	...	...	1547	...	1647	1717	...
Brussels Midi/Zuid ▽ d.	...	0945	0952	...	1045	...	...	1145	1152	1245	1252	...	...	1345	1352	...	1452	1445	1545	1552	1645	1652	...	1745
Brussels Nationaal ✈ d.	...	1011	|	...	1111	...	...	1211	|	1311	|	...	...	1411	|	...	|	1511	1611	|	1711	|	...	1811
Mechelen d.	...	1025	|	...	1125	...	...	1225	|	1325	|	...	...	1425	|	...	|	1525	1625	|	1725	|	...	1825
Antwerpen Centraal a.	...	1043	1027	...	1143	...	...	1243	1227	1343	1327	...	...	1443	1427	...	1527	1543	1643	1627	1743	1727	...	1843
Roosendaal 🏛 a.	...	1111	|	...	1211	...	...	1311	|	1411	|	...	...	1511	|	...	|	1611	1711	|	1811	|	...	1911
Dordrecht a.	...	1136	|	...	1236	...	...	1336	|	1436	|	...	...	1536	|	...	|	1636	1736	|	1836	|	...	1936
Rotterdam Centraal a.	...	1150	1102	...	1250	...	...	1350	1302	1450	1402	...	...	1550	1502	...	1602	1650	1750	1702	1850	1802	...	1950
Den Haag HS a.	...	1222	|	...	1322	...	...	1422	|	1522	|	...	...	1622	|	...	|	1722	1822	|	1922	|	...	2022
Schiphol ✈ ⊗ a.	...	1250	1124	...	1350	...	...	1450	1324	1550	1424	...	...	1650	1524	...	1624	1750	1850	1724	1950	1824	...	2050
Amsterdam Centraal a.	...	1306	1142	...	1406	...	...	1506	1342	1606	1442	...	...	1706	1542	...	1642	1806	1906	1742	2006	1842	...	2106

train type	⇌	⇌	⇌	*IC*	⇌	⇌	*IC*	⇌	⇌	⇌	⇌	*IC*	⇌	⇌	⇌	⇌	⇌	⇌	⇌
train number	**9363**	**9363**	**9365**	**9263**	**9369**	**9473**	**9267**	**9975**	**9375**	**9375**	**9377**	**9271**	**9381**	**9995**	**9387**	**9987/6**	**9389**	**9393**	**9399**
notes	⑤⑦	①-④						①-④	⑤⑦					⑤⑥⑦	⑤⑦	⊗		⑤	⑦
	w		**L**	**x**			**x**		**w**	**D**	**V**	**x**		**X**	**w**	**B**	**T**		**w**
Paris Nord d.	1625	...	1655	...	1725	1755	...	...	1825	1825	1855	...	1925	...	2025	...	2055	2125	2225
Lille Europe d.	|	...	|	...	|	|	...	1907	|	|	|	...	|	2104	|	...	|	|	|
Brussels Midi/Zuid a.	1747	...	1817	...	1847	1917	...	1943	1947	1947	2017	...	2047	2141	2147	2211	2217	2247	2347
Brussels Midi/Zuid ▽ d.	1752	1752	...	1845	1852	...	1945	1952	1952	...	...	2045	2052	2152	...	|	...	...	...
Brussels Nationaal ✈ d.	|	|	...	1911	|	...	2011	|	|	...	...	2110	|	|	...	|	...	...	...
Mechelen d.	|	|	...	1925	|	...	2025	|	|	...	...	2125	|	|	...	|	...	...	...
Antwerpen Centraal a.	1827	1827	...	1943	1927	...	2043	2027	2027	...	...	2143	2127	2227	...	2256	...	...	...
Roosendaal 🏛 a.	|	|	...	2011	|	...	2111	|	|	...	...	2211	|	|	...	|	...	...	...
Dordrecht a.	|	|	...	2036	|	...	2136	|	|	...	...	2236	|	|	...	|	...	...	...
Rotterdam Centraal a.	1902	1902	...	2050	2002	...	2150	2102	2102	...	...	2250	2202	2302	...	2333	...	...	...
Den Haag HS a.	|	|	...	2122	|	...	2222	|	|	...	...	2322	|	|	...	|	...	...	...
Schiphol ✈ ⊗ a.	1924	1924	...	2150	2024	...	2250	2124	2124	...	...	2350	2224	2324	...	2354	...	...	...
Amsterdam Centraal a.	1942	1942	...	2206	2042	...	2306	2142	2142	...	...	0006	2242	2342	...	0010	...	...	...

b – Not Dec. 19, Dec. 25-30, Jan. 2.
d – Not Dec. 25, Jan. 1.
f – Also Dec. 25.
h – Also Dec. 25; not Dec. 30, Jan. 6.
j – 3 minutes later on ⑥⑦.
t – Not Dec. 19, 26, Jan. 2.
v – 0759 Dec. 24 - Jan. 21.
w – Not Dec. 25.
y – Not Dec. 30, Jan. 6.
x – Not Dec. 31.

⊗ – Calls to set down only.
⊕ – Calls to pick up only.

A – THALYS NEIGE – ⑥ Dec. 24 - Mar. 25: [12] 🍷 Amsterdam - Brussels - Bourg St Maurice; ⑥ Dec. 24 - Apr. 8: [12] 🍷 Brussels - Bourg St Maurice (Table **9**). +
B – THALYS NEIGE – ⑥ Dec. 31 - Apr. 1: [12] 🍷 Bourg St Maurice - Brussels - Amsterdam; ⑥ Dec. 31 - Apr. 15: [12] 🍷 Bourg St Maurice - Brussels (Table **9**).
D – ①②③④⑥ (also Dec. 25).
G – ②③④ (not Jan. 3, 4, 5).
H – ①②③④⑥⑦.
K – Not Amsterdam - Brussels on Jan. 1.
L – ②③④⑤⑦ (not Dec. 20-22, 25, 27-29, Jan. 1).
S – Not Dec. 26 - Jan. 5.
T – ①②③④⑥⑦.
V – ①-④ (not Jan. 3-5).
X – Not Brussels - Amsterdam on Dec. 31.

⇌ – *Thalys* high-speed train. 🅁 🍷. Special fares payable. Valid Dec. 11 - Apr. 1, 2017.
▽ – All services, except *Thalys*, call at Brussels Central 4 minutes, and Brussels Noord 10 minutes, after Brussels Midi/Zuid.
△ – All services, except *Thalys*, call at Brussels Noord 10 minutes, and Brussels Central 5 minutes, before Brussels Midi/Zuid.

izy

PARIS - BRUSSELS 18a (Winter)

train type/number	*izy*	*izy*	*izy*	*izy*	*izy*	*izy*	*izy*	*izy*	*izy*
train number									
notes	⑥	①⑤	A	⑦	⑥	①-⑤	⑦		
Brussels Midi/Zuid d.	0829	1028	1446	1629	1821	1859	2031	...	...
Paris Nord a.	1042	1250	1700	1844	2032	2129	2243	...	...

train type/number	*izy*	*izy*	*izy*	*izy*	*izy*	*izy*	*izy*	*izy*
train number								
notes	①	B	⑦	⑥	⑤	⑦	⑦	①-⑤
Paris Nord d.	0949	1134	1344	1506	1536	1728	1949	2001
Brussels Midi/Zuid a.	1208	1344	1552	1714	1755	1953	2211	2212

A – ②③④⑤⑦. B – ②③④⑤⑥. Low-cost *TGV* services branded **izy**, internet booking only through www.izy.com, special conditions apply.

For the full service London - Brussels and v.v. see Table **12**. For Paris - Brussels and v.v. see Table **18**. Connections at Brussels are not guaranteed.

train type	ICE	ICE	IC	⇌	ICE	IC	⇌	ICE	ICE	ICE	IC	⇌	ICE	IC	⇌	☆	☆	☆	ICE	ICE	IC
train number	11	545	2310	9401	847	1028	9303	13	13	557	2216	9413	859	2226	9315	9108	9110	9110	15	549	2218
notes	①–⑥						①–⑤	①–⑤		⑥⑦							P	L			⑥
										S											
London St Pancras....d.	...	...	...	...	...	...	...	...	...	...	...	...	...	...	...	0613	0650	0657	...	...	...
Ebbsfleet International ....d.	...	...	...	...	...	...	...	...	...	...	...	...	...	...	...	0630	0707		...	...	...
Ashford International....d.	...	...	...	...	...	...	...	...	...	...	...	...	...	...	...	0653	0728	0728	...	...	...
Lille Europe ....d.	...	...	...	...	...	...	...	...	...	...	...	...	...	...	...		0933	0930	...	...	...
Paris Nord ....d.	...	...	...	0601	...	0625	...	...	...	0755	...	...	...	0825					...	...	...
Brussels Midi/Zuid ....a.	...	...	...	0723	...	0747	...	...	...	0917	...	...	...	0947	0922	1007	1005	...	...	...	...
Brussels Midi/Zuid ....d.	0625	...	...	0728	...	...	...	0824	0825	...	0928	...	...	...				1025	...	...	...
Brussels Nord ....d.	0633	...	...	...	...	...	...	...	0834	...	...	...	...	...				1034	...	...	...
Liège Guillemins ....d.	0712	...	...	0814	...	...	...	0914	0914	...	1014	...	...	...				1114	...	...	...
Aachen 🚉....a.	0737	...	...	0836	...	...	...	0936	0936	...	1036	...	...	...				1136	...	...	...
Köln Hbf....a.	0815	...	...	0915	...	...	...	1015	1015	...	1115	...	...	...				1215	...	...	...
Köln Hbf....d.	...	0828	0909	0918	0928	1010	...	...	...	1048	1109	1119	1148	1210				...	1248	1309	
Wuppertal Hbf....a.	...					1041	...	...	...	1114			1214	1241				...	1314		
Hagen Hbf....a.	...					1100	...	...	...	1133			1233	1259				...	1333		
Düsseldorf Hbf....a.	...	0850	0931	0940	0950		...	...	...		1131	1140						...		1331	
Duisburg Hbf....a.	...	0908	0944	0954	1008		...	...	...		1144	1200						...		1344	
Essen Hbf....a.	...	0921	0957	1008	1021		...	...	...		1157	1214						...		1357	
Bochum Hbf....a.	...	0933	1008		1033		...	...	...		1208							...		1408	
Dortmund Hbf....a.	...	0946	1021	...	1046	1123	...	...	...		1221	1241		1321				...		1421	
Hamm (Westf)....a.	...	1006		...	1106		...	...	...	1202			1302					...	1402		
Bielefeld Hbf....a.	...	1036		...	1136		...	...	...	1236			1336					...	1436		
Münster....a.	...		1054	...		1155	...	...	...		1254			1354				...		1454	
Osnabrück Hbf....a.	...		1121	...		1222	...	...	...		1321			1421				...		1521	
Bremen Hbf....a.	...		1215	...		1315	...	...	...		1414			1515				...		1615	
Hannover Hbf....a.	...	1128		...	1228		...	...	...	1328			1428					...	1528		
Hamburg Hbf....a.	...		1313	...	1413		...	...	...		1511		1613					...		1713	
Berlin Hbf....a.	...	1307		...	1409		...	...	...	1506			1609					...	1706		...

train type	⇌	☆	☆	ICE	ICE	IC		⇌	⇌	ICE	ICE	⇌	☆	☆	⇌	ICE	ICE	EC	⇌	ICE	ICE	ICE	EC
train number	9327	9116	9116	211	651	2312		9437	9437	953	1026	9339	9126	9126	9341	17	653	8	9351	215	215	655	6
notes		⑤⑦						⑥	⑧	⑧			①–⑤	⑦	⑤⑦					①–⑤	⑦		⑧
		V	**X**										**j**	**y**	**k**								**p**
London St Pancras....d.	...	0855	0858	...	...	...		...	...	...	...	...	1058	1104		...	...	...	...	...	...	...	...
Ebbsfleet International ....d.	...	0915	0915	...	...	...		...	...	...	...	...	1115			...	...	...	...	...	...	...	...
Ashford International....d.	...			...	...	...		...	...	...	...	...				...	...	...	...	...	...	...	...
Lille Europe ....d.	...	1130	1134	...	...	...		...	...	...	...	...	1330	1330		...	...	...	...	...	...	...	...
Paris Nord ....d.	1025			...	...	...		1155	1155	...	1225	...		1245		...	...	...	1425	...	...	...	...
Brussels Midi/Zuid ....a.	1147	1205	1208	...	...	...		1317	1317	...	1347	1405	1405	1412		...	...	...	1547	...	...	...	...
Brussels Midi/Zuid ....d.	...			1225	...	...		1328	1328	...		...		1425		...	1616	1625	...	...	...	...	...
Brussels Nord ....d.	...			1234	...	...		...	...	...		...		1434		...	1625	1634	...	...	...	...	...
Liège Guillemins ....d.	...			1314	...	...		1414	1414	...		...		1514		...	1714	1714	...	...	...	...	...
Aachen 🚉....a.	...			1336	...	...		1436	1436	...		...		1536		...	1736	1736	...	...	...	...	...
Köln Hbf....a.	...			1415	...	...		1515	1515	...		...		1615		...	1815	1815	...	...	...	...	...
Köln Hbf....d.	...	...	...	...	1448	1509		1519	1526	1548	1610	...			...	1648	1710	...	...	1848	1910		
Wuppertal Hbf....a.	...	...	...	...	1514				1614	1641		...			...	1714		...	...	1914			
Hagen....a.	...	...	...	...	1533				1633	1700		...			...	1733		...	...	1933			
Düsseldorf Hbf....a.	...	...	...		1531	1553	1553				...	...			...		1731	...	...		1931		
Duisburg Hbf....a.	...	...	...		1544		1615				...	...			...		1744	...	...		1944		
Essen Hbf....a.	...	...	...		1557		1631				...	...			...		1757	...	...		1957		
Bochum Hbf....a.	...	...	...		1608						...	...			...		1808	...	...		2008		
Dortmund Hbf....a.	...	...	...		1621					1721	...	...			...		1821	...	...		2021		
Hamm (Westf)....a.	...	...	...	1606					1702		...	...			...	1802		...	...	2002			
Bielefeld....a.	...	...	...	1636					1736		...	...			...	1836		...	...	2036			
Münster....a.	...	...	...		1654					1755	...	...			...	1854		...	...	2054			
Osnabrück....a.	...	...	...		1721					1821	...	...			...	1921		...	...	2121			
Bremen Hbf....a.	...	...	...		1815					1914	...	...			...	2015		...	...	2216			
Hannover Hbf....a.	...	...	...	1728					1828		...	...			...	1928		...	...	2128			
Hamburg Hbf....a.	...	...	...		1913					2013	...	...			...	2113		...	...	2314			
Berlin Hbf....a.	...	...	...	1906					2009		...	...			...	2106		...	...	2306		...	

L – ①–⑤ Dec. 11 - Mar. 25 (not Dec. 26, 27, Jan 2).
②–④ Mar. 26 - May 27 (not Apr. 17, May 1).

P – ①⑤ Mar. 26 - May 27 (not Apr. 17, May 1).

S – Calls at Düsseldorf Flughafen ✈, arrives 1149.

V – ①–⑤ Dec. 11 - Mar. 25 (not Dec. 27).
②–④ Mar. 26 - May 27.

X – ⑥⑦ Dec. 11 - Mar. 25 (also Dec. 27).
①⑤⑥⑦ Mar. 26 - May 27.

k – Not Dec. 25, Jan. 1.

j – Not Dec. 26, 27, Jan 2,
Apr. 17, May 1.

m – Not Dec. 27.

p – Not Dec. 25.

w – Also Dec. 27.

y – Also Dec. 26, 27, Jan. 2,
Apr. 17, May 1.

⇌ – *Thalys* high-speed train. ℝ ☕. Special fares payable. Valid Dec. 11 - Apr. 1, 2017.

☉ – 🚉 between Hamburg and København is Rødby, see Table **720**.

☆ – Eurostar train. ℝ, ✗ in Business Premier and Standard Premier, ☕ in Standard. Special fares payable. Minimum check-in time 30 minutes. Not available for London - Ebbsfleet - Ashford or v.v. journeys. Valid Dec. 11 - May 27, 2017.

For the full service London - Brussels and v.v. see Table **12**. For Paris - Brussels and v.v. see Table **18**. Connections at Brussels are not guaranteed.

train type	☆	☆	⇌	ICE	ICE	☆	⇌	ICE	ICE	IC	ICE	ICE	☆	⇌	ICE	ICE	IC	IC
train number	9132	9136	9461	947	26	9140	9365	19	657	2318	1102	102	9144	9473	1522	512	2020	2241
notes		F			⑧	L	y		⑦	⑧	p	⑥	⑥		G	y		✗
London St Pancras ...d	1258	1404				1504							1604					
Ebbsfleet International ...d	1315																	
Ashford International ...d																		
Lille Europe ...d	1533	1630				1730							1830					
Paris Nord ...d			1555				1655							1755				
Brussels Midi/Zuid ...a	1608	1705	1717			1805	1817						1905	1917				
Brussels Midi/Zuid ...d			1728					1825						1928				
Brussels Nord ...d								1834										
Liège Guillemins ...d			1814					1914						2014				
Aachen ...a			1836					1936						2036				
Köln Hbf ...a			1915					2015						2115				
Köln Hbf ...a				1918	1927			2010	2048	2110	2111	2111			2118	2210	2211	0213
Wuppertal Hbf ...a								2041		2114		2141				2241		
Hagen Hbf ...a								2059		2133		2159				2300		
Düsseldorf Hbf ...a				1940	1950				2131	2131					2141		2231	0234
Duisburg Hbf ...a				1953	2008				2144	2144					2200		2244	0251
Essen Hbf ...a				2006	2021				2157	2157					2215		2257	0307
Bochum Hbf ...a					2033				2208	2208								0317
Dortmund Hbf ...a				2036	2046			2122	2221	2221	2221				2241	2321		0334
Hamm (Westf) ...a					2106				2202	2247	2247							
Bielefeld Hbf ...a					2136				2235	2319	2319							
Münster ...a								2154	2254j						2356	0415	0538	
Osnabrück Hbf ...a								2221								0446	0602	
Bremen Hbf ...a								2316								0552		
Hannover Hbf ...a					2228				2328		0018	0018					0718	
Hamburg Hbf ...a					0009			0014								0651		
Berlin Hbf ...a									0110								0922	

train type	IC	⇌	ICE	IC	ICE	⇌	☆	☆	ICE	EC	⇌	☆	ICE	EC	EC	ICE	ICE	⇌	⇌	☆
train number	2021	9412	101	2319	18	9322	9125	9129	1521	115	9424	9129	9133	7	119	656	214	9334	9336	9133
notes	H			✗	①-⑥		X	r	⍾			⑦	①-⑥	⍾	⍾	Ⓐ		⑥⑦	①-⑤	q
Berlin Hbf ...d																	0430			
Hamburg Hbf ...d	2246															0442f				
Hannover Hbf ...d																	0621			
Bremen Hbf ...d	2344															0540f				
Osnabrück Hbf ...d	0037															0637f				
Münster ...d	0105			0503c						0631						0703f	0727			
Bielefeld Hbf ...d																0721				
Hamm (Westf) ...d	0125															0754				
Dortmund Hbf ...d	0144	0520	0537	0537					0636					0737	0749					
Bochum Hbf ...d	0155		0549																	
Essen Hbf ...d	0206	0542	0600							0750				0800	0823					
Duisburg Hbf ...d	0219	0556	0613						0734	0803				0813	0838					
Düsseldorf Hbf ...d	0240	0617	0627						0751	0818				0827	0852					
Hagen Hbf ...d			0557						0657								0824			
Wuppertal Hbf ...a			0615						0714								0841			
Köln Hbf ...a	0302	0642	0646	0650					0747	0815	0842			0850		0915	0915			
Köln Hbf ...d		0645								0845							0943			
Aachen ...d		0724			0821					0924							1021			
Liège Guillemins ...a		0752			0846					0949							1046			
Brussels Nord ...a					0926												1126			
Brussels Midi/Zuid ...a		0832			0935					1032							1135			
Brussels Midi/Zuid ...d		0843				1013	1056	1156		1043		1156	1252					1213	1237	1252
Paris Nord ...a		1005				1135					1205							1335	1359	
Lille Europe ...a							1130	1230				1230	1326							1326
Ashford International ...a																				
Ebbsfleet International ...a													1345							1345
London St Pancras ...a							1157	1257				1257	1405							1405

F – ⑤⑦ Dec. 11–31 (also Dec. 26, 27). ⑦ Jan. 1 - Mar. 25 (also Jan. 2, Feb. 10, 17). ⑤ Mar. 26 - May 27 (also Apr. 13, May 1, 25).

G – Calls at Düsseldorf Flughafen ✈ arrives 2148.

H – Calls at Düsseldorf Flughafen ✈ departs 0607.

L – ②③④⑤⑦ (not Dec. 20-22, 25, 27-29, Jan. 1).

X – ①-⑤ Dec. 11–31. ⑤ Jan. 1 - Feb. 4 (also Jan. 2). ①-⑤ Feb. 5 - Mar. 25. ①-⑥ Mar. 26 - May 27 (not Apr. 1, 15, 17, May 1).

c – ① (also Dec. 27; not Dec. 26).

f – ①-⑥ (not Dec. 26).

j – ⑦ (also Dec. 26; not Dec. 25, Jan. 1).

p – Not Dec. 25, Jan. 1.

q – Not Dec. 26, 27, Jan 2, Apr. 17, May 1.

r – Also Apr. 17, May 1.

y – Not Dec. 24, 31.

☆ – Eurostar train. Ⓡ, ✗ in Business Premier and Standard Premier, ⍾ in Standard. Special fares payable. Minimum check-in time 30 minutes. Not available for London - Ebbsfleet - Ashford or v.v. journeys. Valid Dec. 11 - May 27, 2017.

⇌ – *Thalys* high-speed train. Ⓡ ⍾. Special fares payable. Valid Dec. 11 - Apr. 1, 2017.

LOCOMOTIVES
INTERNATIONAL

INTERNATIONAL

20 — BERLIN, HAMBURG and KÖLN - BRUSSELS, PARIS and LONDON

For the full service Brussels - London and v.v. see Table 12. For Brussels - Paris and v.v. see Table 18. Connections at Brussels are not guaranteed.

	EC 9	ICE 654	ICE 16	⇌ 9448	☆ 9141	☆ 9141	IC 2023	ICE 944	⇌ 9448	☆ 9145	☆ 9149	☆ 9149	IC 2313	ICE 652	ICE 210	⇌ 9358	☆ 9149	☆ 9149	IC 2217	ICE 650	ICE 14	⇌ 9370	☆ 9157
notes					y	q				①–⑤	①–⑥		F	y	q	⑤⑦	⑦	⑤			⑧	h	H
Berlin Hauptbahnhof . d.		0652						0749						0852						1052			
Hamburg Hbf .... d.	0646						0746						0845						1046				
Hannover Hbf .... d.		0831						0931						1031						1231			
Bremen Hbf .... d.	0744						0844						0943						1144				
Osnabrück Hbf .... d.	0837						0937						1035						1237				
Münster .... d.	0903						1003						1102						1303				
Bielefeld Hbf .... d.		0922						1022						1122						1322			
Hamm (Westf) .... d.		0954						1054						1154						1354			
Dortmund Hbf .... d.	0937						1036						1137						1337				
Bochum Hbf .... d.	0949												1148						1349				
Essen Hbf .... d.	1000												1159		1125				1400				
Duisburg Hbf .... d.	1013												1212		1138				1413				
Düsseldorf Hbf .... d.	1027												1226		1154				1427				
Hagen Hbf .... d.		1024					1057	1124						1224						1424			
Wuppertal Hbf .... d.		1041					1115	1141						1241						1441			
Köln Hbf .... a.	1050	1109					1147	1209					1250	1309	1229				1450	1509			
Köln Hbf .... d.			1143					1243						1343							1542		
Aachen .... d.			1221					1324						1421							1621		
Liège Guillemins ..... d.			1246					1349						1446							1646		
Brussels Nord .... a.			1326											1526							1726		
Brussels Midi/Zuid .... a.			1335					1432						1535							1735		
Brussels Midi/Zuid .... d.				1443	1452	1456			1443	1556	1656	1656				1613	1656	1656				1813	1856
Paris Nord .... a.				1605					1605							1735						1935	
Lille Europe .... a.					1526	1530				1630	1730	1730					1730	1730					1930
Ashford International .. a.												1734						1734					
Ebbsfleet International . a.					1545	1545					1745						1745						
London St Pancras ... a.					1605	1605				1657	1801	1806					1805	1806					1957

	IC 2327	ICE 950	⇌ 9472	☆ 9161	IC 2311	ICE 558	ICE 12	⇌ 9382	IC 2229	ICE 858	⇌ 9484	IC 2213	ICE 556	ICE 10	⇌ 9394
notes	2027		x				⑧						✕	⑦	h
Berlin Hauptbahnhof . d.		1149				1252				1349			1452		
Hamburg Hbf .... d.	1146				1246				1346			1446			
Hannover Hbf .... d.		1331				1431				1531			1631		
Bremen Hbf .... d.	1244				1344				1444			1544			
Osnabrück Hbf .... d.	1337				1437				1537			1637			
Münster .... d.	1403				1503				1603			1703			
Bielefeld Hbf .... d.		1422				1522				1622			1722		
Hamm (Westf) .... d.		1454				1554				1654			1754		
Dortmund Hbf .... d.	1436	1514			1537				1636			1737			
Bochum Hbf .... d.					1549							1749			
Essen Hbf .... d.			1550		1600						1750	1800			
Duisburg Hbf .... d.			1603		1612						1803	1813			
Düsseldorf Hbf .... d.			1618		1627						1818	1827			
Hagen Hbf .... d.	1457	1524				1624			1657	1724			1824		
Wuppertal Hbf .... d.	1515	1541				1641			1715	1741			1841		
Köln Hbf .... a.	1547	1609	1641		1650	1709			1747	1809	1841	1850	1909		
Köln Hbf .... d.			1644				1743				1844			1943	
Aachen .... d.			1724				1821				1924			2021	
Liège Guillemins ..... d.			1749				1846				1949			2046	
Brussels Nord .... a.							1926							2126	
Brussels Midi/Zuid .... a.			1832				1935				2032			2135	
Brussels Midi/Zuid .... d.			1843	1952				2013			2043				2213
Paris Nord .... a.			2005					2135			2205				2335
Lille Europe .... a.				2026											
Ashford International .. a.				2045											
Ebbsfleet International . a.															
London St Pancras ... a.				2103											

F – ⑤⑦ Dec. 11–31 (also Dec. 26,27). ⑦ Jan. 1 - Feb. 4 (also Jan. 2). ⑤⑦ Feb. 5 - Mar. 25. ⑤ Mar. 26 - May 27, (also Apr. 13,30, May 25).

H – ⑧ Dec. 11–31. ⑦ Jan. 1 - Feb. 4 (also Jan. 2). ①④⑤⑦ Feb. 5 - Mar. 25. ⑧ Mar. 26 - May 27.

h – Not Dec. 25.
q – Not Dec. 26, 27, Jan. 2, Apr. 17, May 1.
x – Not Dec. 24, 31.
y – Also Dec. 26,27, Jan. 2, Apr. 17, May 1.

☆ – Eurostar train. Ⓑ, ✕ in Business Premier and Standard Premier, Ⓨ in Standard. Special fares payable. Minimum check-in time 30 minutes. Not available for London - Ebbsfleet - Ashford or v.v. journeys. Valid Dec. 11 - May 27, 2017.

⇌ – Thalys high-speed train. Ⓑ Ⓨ. Special fares payable. Valid Dec. 11 - Apr. 1, 2017.

⊙ – 🚇 between Hamburg and København is Rødby (Table 720).

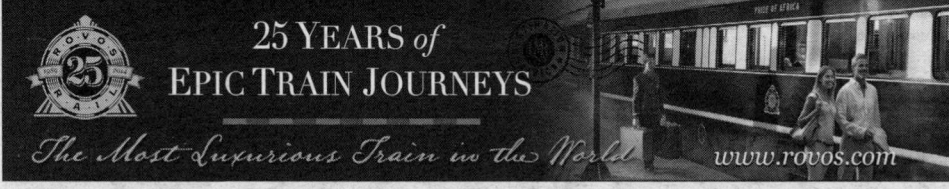

	ICE 11	ICE 593	ICE 529	⇌ 42012	ICE 9401	ICE 621	ICE 515	⇌ 27	⇌ 42014	ICE 13	ICE 13	ICE 595	ICE 623	⇌ 9413	ICE 625	ICE 517	IC 2023	⇌ 9315	☆ 9108	☆ 9110	☆ 9110	ICE 15	ICE 597	ICE 627	⇌ 42016
notes	①-⑥	1091		® ♀			♀	® ♀ S	♀	①-⑤	⑥⑦								P	L	⑥				® U
London St Pancras … d.																			0613	0650	0657				
Ebbsfleet International … d.																			0630	0707					
Ashford International … d.																			0653	0728	0728				
Lille Europe … d.																				0933	0932				
Paris Nord … d.					0601									0755				0825							
Brussels Midi/Zuid … a.					0723									0917				0947	0922	1007	1005				
Brussels Midi/Zuid … d.	0625				0728					0824	0825		0928											1025	
Brussels Nord … d.	0633										0834													1034	
Liège Guillemins … d.	0712				0814					0914	0914		1014											1114	
Aachen Hbf … a.	0737				0836					0936	0936		1036											1136	
Köln Hbf … a.	0815				0915					1015	1015		1115											1215	
Köln Hbf … d.	0827				0936x	0955	0953			1026	1026							1130x	1155	1153				1218	
Bonn Hbf … a.							1012																	1212	
Koblenz Hbf … a.	⊖					⊖	⊖					1046	⊖											1246	
Mainz Hbf … a.												1138												1338	
Frankfurt Flughafen + … a.	0916				1033	1049	1159			1116	1116		1233		1249		1359					1316			
Frankfurt (Main) Hbf … a.	0930	0950	0954		1048		1213			1130	1130	1150	1154		1248			1412				1330	1350	1354	
Würzburg Hbf … a.			1102			1202	1331					1301	1402											1502	
Nürnberg Hbf … a.			1159	1340		1259	1427	1540				1403	1459											1559	1740
Praha hlavni … ¶ a.				1718				1918																	2118
Mannheim Hbf … a.		1027			1123							1227			1323								1427		
Stuttgart Hbf … a.		1108			1208							1308			1408								1508		
Ulm Hbf … a.		1207			1308							1407			1508								1607		
Augsburg Hbf … a.		1253			1353							1453			1553								1653		
München Hbf … a.		1327	1304		1404	1427					1508	1528	1606		1627								1727	1704	

	⇌ 9327	☆ 9116	☆ 9116	ICE 599	ICE 721	ICE 9437	ICE 125	ICE 723	ICE 611	IC 2027	⇌ 9339	☆ 9126	☆ 9126	⇌ 9341	ICE 17	ICE 17	ICE 691	ICE 725	⇌ 9351	ICE 215	ICE 215	ICE 691	ICE 729
notes		⑤⑦ V	X			⑧	j	k			①-⑥	⑦	⑤⑦ g	①-⑤	⑥⑦				①-⑤	⑦			
London St Pancras … d.		0855	0858				1058	1104															
Ebbsfleet International … d.		0915	0915				1115																
Ashford International … d.																							
Lille Europe … d.		1130	1133								1330	1330											
Paris Nord … d.	1025						1155				1225			1245					1425				
Brussels Midi/Zuid … a.	1147	1205	1208				1317				1347	1405	1405	1412					1547				
Brussels Midi/Zuid … d.					1225		1328								1425	1425					1616	1625	
Brussels Nord … d.					1234										1434	1434				1625	1634		
Liège Guillemins … d.					1314		1414								1514	1514				1714	1714		
Aachen Hbf … a.					1336		1436								1536	1536				1736	1736		
Köln Hbf … a.					1415		1515								1615	1615				1815	1815		
Köln Hbf … d.			1426					1529	1555	1553					1620	1620				1819	1819		
Bonn Hbf … a.									1612														
Koblenz Hbf … a.			⊖					⊖	1646						⊖	⊖				⊖	⊖		
Mainz Hbf … a.									1738														
Frankfurt Flughafen + … a.			1516				1616	1649	1759						1709	1726				1909	1909		
Frankfurt (Main) Hbf … a.			1530	1550	1554		1630	1654	1813						1722	1741	1750	1754		1925	1925	1950	1954
Würzburg Hbf … a.				1702			1802	1931										1902					2102
Nürnberg Hbf … a.				1759			1859	2027										1959					2159
Praha hlavni … ¶ a.																							
Mannheim Hbf … a.				1627				1723										1827					2027
Stuttgart Hbf … a.				1708				1808										1908					2108
Ulm Hbf … a.				1807				1908										2007					2207f
Augsburg Hbf … a.				1853				1953										2053					2253f
München Hbf … a.				1927	1907			2004	2027						2127	2107				2329f	2307		

L – ①-⑤ Dec. 11 - Mar. 25 (not Dec. 26, 27, Jan 2). ②-④ Mar. 26 - May 27 (not Apr. 17, May 1).

P – ①⑤ Mar. 26 - May 27 (not Apr. 17, May 1).

S – 🚆 ✕ Hamburg - Dortmund - Köln - Wien (Table **66**).

U – ⑧ Mar. 29 - Oct. 4.

V – ①-⑤ Dec. 11 - Mar. 25 (not Dec. 27). ②-④ Mar. 26 - May 27.

X – ⑥⑦ Dec. 11 - Mar. 25 (also Dec. 27). ①⑤⑥⑦ Mar. 26 - May 27.

f – ⑧ (not Dec. 25).

g – Not Dec. 25, Jan. 1.

j – Not Dec. 26, 27, Jan 2, Apr. 1, May 1.

k – Also Dec. 26, 27, Jan. 2, Apr. 17, May 1.

x – Köln **Messe/Deutz** (Table **910**). Connections from Köln Hbf depart every 2-5 minutes, journey time 2-3 minutes.

z – 11 - 19 minutes later on ⑥⑦.

⊖ – Via Köln - Frankfurt high speed line.

⇌ – *Thalys* high-speed train. ® ♀. Special fares payable. Valid Dec. 11 - Apr. 1, 2017.

🚌 – **DB/ČD** *ExpressBus*. ® ♀. Rail tickets valid. 🏠 is Waidhaus (Germany). (Table **76**).

¶ – For connections to Praha by train, via Nürnberg and Regensburg, see Table **76**.

☆ – Eurostar train. ®, ✕ in Business Premier and Standard Premier, ♀ in Standard. Special fares payable. Minimum check-in time 30 minutes. Not available for London - Ebbsfleet - Ashford or v.v. journeys. Valid Dec. 11 - May 27, 2017.

	☆	☆	⇌	IC	ICE	☆	☆	ICE	ICE	IC	IC	EN	☆	⇌	ICE	ICE	IC	ICE
train type																		
train number	9132	9136	9461	1029	615	9140	9365	19	773	1029	2315 2215	421	9144	9473	221	1552	2221 2321	619
notes	⑧	⑧ F			g	⑧	G	g	g	g	g	A	⑥			⑥		g
London St Pancras d.	1258	1404				1504							1604					
Ebbsfleet International d.	1315																	
Ashford International d.																		
Lille Europe d.	1533	1630				1730							1830					
Paris Nord d.			1555				1655							1755				
Brussels Midi/Zuid a.	1608	1705	1717			1805	1817						1905	1917				
Brussels Midi/Zuid d.			1728											1928				
Brussels Nord d.								1834										
Liège Guillemins d.			1814					1914						2014				
Aachen Hbf a.			1836					1936						2036				
Köln Hbf a.			1915					2015						2115				
Köln Hbf d.				1953	1957			2028			2053	2121			2126		2153	2230
Bonn Hbf a.				2012							2112	2141					2212	
Koblenz Hbf a.				2046	⊖			⊖			2146	2215					2246	⊖
Mainz Hbf a.				2141							2238	2315					2338	
Frankfurt Flughafen + a.					2049			2116	2121		2202	2350			2216			2347
Frankfurt (Main) Hbf a.								2130			2213	0004f			2230	2308		2400
Würzburg Hbf a.											2344							
Nürnberg Hbf a.											0042	0237						
Praha hlavní ¶ a.																		
Mannheim Hbf a.					2123			2154										0104
Stuttgart Hbf a.					2208			2250								0050		0320
Ulm Hbf a.					2308													0440
Augsburg Hbf a.					2352							0625						0529
München Hbf a.					0027							0705						0602

	⇌	IC	ICE	ICE	⇌	☆	IC	EN	ICE	ICE	⇌	☆	ICE	ICE	ICE	⇌	☆	IC	ICE	ICE	ICE	ICE	⇌	☆	☆
train type																									
train number	9412	2212	618 1018	18	9322	9125	2220 2320	420	616	220	9424	9129	822	694	214	9334	9133	2216	728	692	16	16	9448	9141	9141
notes		q	①–⑥	①–⑥		X		A				⑦ r	①–⑥			⑥⑦	①–⑥		h		⑦	①–⑥		⑦ y	①–⑥ h
München Hbf d.			0001				2252	0324					0449							0652	0629c				
Augsburg Hbf d.			0032				2329	0357													0706c				
Ulm Hbf d.			0116					0440													0751c				
Stuttgart Hbf d.			0230					0551					0651						0737		0851				
Mannheim Hbf d.			0440					0636					0732						0839		0932				
Nürnberg Hbf d.									0246					0600				0800							
Würzburg Hbf d.														0655				0855							
Frankfurt (Main) Hbf d.			0544	0629				0527f		0727			0804	0808	0816					1004	1008	1016	1029		
Frankfurt Flughafen + d.			0601	0643				0538	0709	0743					0831							1031	1043		
Mainz Hbf d.									0617n	0604					0920										
Koblenz Hbf d.		0605	⊖	⊖					0713	0707			⊖		1013										
Bonn Hbf d.		0646							0746						1046										
Köln Hbf a.		0705	0705	0739				0805	0815	0805	0833		0939		1105						1133	1133			
Köln Hbf d.	0645		0705	0743							0845		0943								1143	1143			
Aachen Hbf a.	0724		0821								0924		1021								1221	1221			
Liège Guillemins d.	0752		0846								0949		1046								1246	1246			
Brussels Nord a.			0926										1126								1326	1326			
Brussels Midi/Zuid a.	0832		0935								1032		1135								1335	1335			
Brussels Midi/Zuid d.	0843				1013	1056					1043	1156				1213	1252						1443	1452	1456
Paris Nord a.	1005				1135						1205					1335							1605		
Lille Europe a.						1130						1230					1326							1526	1530
Ashford International a.																									
Ebbsfleet International a.																	1345							1545	1545
London St Pancras a.						1157						1257					1405							1605	1605

A – ÖBB *nightjet* ⇌ 1, 2 cl., ⇌ 2 cl. (4, 6 berth), 🚗 Düsseldorf - Köln - München - Innsbruck and v.v. Special fares apply.

F – ⑤⑦ Dec. 11–31 (also Dec. 26, 27). ⑦ Jan. 1 - Mar. 25 (also Jan. 2, Feb. 10, 17). ⑤ Mar. 26 - May 27 (also Apr. 13, May 1, 25).

G – ②③④⑤⑦ (not Dec. 20-22, 25, 27-29, Jan. 1).

X – ①–⑤ Dec. 11–31. ⑤ Jan. 1 - Feb. 4 (also Jan 2). ①–⑥ Feb. 5 - Mar. 25. ①–⑥ Mar. 26 - May 27 (not Apr. 1, 15, 17, May 1).

c – ①–⑤ (not Dec. 26, 27).

f – Frankfurt (Main) **Süd**.

g – Not Dec. 24, 31.

h – Not Dec. 26, 27, Jan 2, Apr. 17, May 1.

n – ①–⑥.

q – Not Dec. 25, Jan. 1.

r – Also Apr. 17, May 1.

y – Also Dec. 26, 27, Jan 2, Apr. 17, May 1.

¶ – For connections to / from Praha by train, via Nürnberg and Regensburg, see Table **76**.

⇌ – *Thalys* high-speed train. Ⓡ ✕. Special fares payable. Valid Dec. 11 - Apr. 1, 2017.

☆ – *Eurostar* train. Ⓡ, ✕ in Business Premier and Standard Premier, ✕ in Standard. Special fares payable. Minimum check-in time 30 minutes. Valid Dec. 11 - May 27, 2017.

⊖ – Via Köln - Frankfurt high speed line.

	IC 2226	ICE 612	ICE 726	⇌ 9448	☆ 9145	IC 2218	ICE 690	ICE 724	ICE 210	⇌ 9358	☆ 9149	☆ 9149	IC 2312	🚌 42005	ICE 228	ICE 598	ICE 720	ICE 14	⇌ 9370	☆ 9157	ICE 518	🚌 42007	ICE 628	⇌ 9472	☆ 9161
notes			796					794	794					Ⓡ							⑧	Ⓡ			
notes		①–⑥			A				⑤⑦		⑤	⑦		Ⓡ				y		B		Q			k
München Hbf d.		0727	0755			0828	0852								1028	1055					1128		1155		
Augsburg Hbf d.			0803				0903									1103					1203				
Ulm Hbf d.			0850													1151					1250				
Stuttgart Hbf d.			0951		0937	1051										1251					1351				
Mannheim Hbf d.		1036				1132										1332					1436				
Praha hlavní ¶ d.													0700								0812				
Nürnberg Hbf d.	0729c		0900			1000							1050	1129	1200						1150		1300		
Würzburg Hbf d.	0826c		0955			1055								1227	1257								1355		
Frankfurt (Main) Hbf d.	0942		1110			1208	1204	1229						1336	1408	1404	1429						1510		
Frankfurt Flughafen + d.	0958	1109	1122					1243									1443				1509		1525		
Mainz Hbf d.	1020				1120						1320														
Koblenz Hbf d.	1113	⊖			1213			⊖			1413					⊖									
Bonn Hbf d.	1146				1246						1446														
Köln Hbf a.	1205	1205	1225x		1305			1332					1505				1533				1605		1614x		
Köln Hbf d.				1245				1343									1542							1644	
Aachen Hbf 🚇 d.				1324				1421									1621							1724	
Liège Guillemins d.				1349				1446									1646							1749	
Brussels Nord a.								1526									1726								
Brussels Midi/Zuid a.				1432				1535									1735							1832	
Brussels Midi/Zuid d.				1443	1556					1613	1656	1656							1813	1856				1843	1952
Paris Nord a.				1605						1735									1935					2005	
Lille Europe a.					1630						1730	1730								1930					2026
Ashford International a.												1734													
Ebbsfleet International a.																									
London St Pancras a.					1657						1806	1803								1957					2103

	ICE 596	ICE 28	ICE 626	EC 8	ICE 12	⇌ 9382	ICE 516	ICE 624	⇌ 9484	🚌 42009	ICE 26	ICE 1090	ICE 622	ICE 572	EC 6	ICE 10	⇌ 9394
notes			826					754		Ⓡ		594	752				
notes			Ⓑ	Ⓑ				1124		Ⓡ		F		k		⑦	
München Hbf d.	1228		1255				1328	1355				1428	1455				
Augsburg Hbf d.	1303						1403					1503					
Ulm Hbf d.	1351						1450					1551					
Stuttgart Hbf d.	1451						1551					1651	1725				
Mannheim Hbf d.	1532						1636					1732	1806				
Praha hlavní ¶ d.									1042								
Nürnberg Hbf d.		1329	1400					1500			1420	1529	1600				
Würzburg Hbf d.		1427	1455					1555			1627		1655				
Frankfurt (Main) Hbf d.	1608	1536	1604			1627		1710			1736	1808	1804	1829			
Frankfurt Flughafen + d.						1643	1709	1725						1837	1843		
Mainz Hbf d.				1520											1720		
Koblenz Hbf d.				1613	⊖		⊖								1813		⊖
Bonn Hbf d.				1644											1846		
Köln Hbf a.			1705	1739			1805	1813x						1905	1939		
Köln Hbf d.				1743				1844						1943			
Aachen Hbf 🚇 d.				1821				1924						2021			
Liège Guillemins d.				1846				1949						2046			
Brussels Nord a.				1926										2126			
Brussels Midi/Zuid a.				1935				2032						2135			
Brussels Midi/Zuid d.						2013			2043								2213
Paris Nord a.						2135			2205								2335
Lille Europe a.																	
Ashford International a.																	
Ebbsfleet International a.																	
London St Pancras a.																	

A – ⑤⑦ Dec. 11–31 (also Dec. 26, 27). ⑦ Jan. 1 - Feb. 4 (also Jan. 2).
⑤⑦ Feb. 5 - Mar. 25. ⑤ Mar. 26 - May 27, (also Apr. 13, 30, May 25).

B – Ⓑ Dec. 11–31. ⑦ Jan. 1 - Feb. 4 (also Jan. 2). ①④⑤⑦ Feb. 5 - Mar. 25.
Ⓑ Mar. 26 - May 27.

F – 🛌🍴 Wien - Nürnberg - Frankfurt - Köln - Dortmund - Hamburg.

Q – Mar. 28 - Oct. 4.

c – ①–⑥ (also Dec. 25; not Dec. 26).

k – Not Dec. 24, 31.

x – Köln Messe/Deutz (Table 910). Connections to Köln Hbf depart every
2-5 minutes, journey time 2-3 minutes.

y – Not Dec. 25.

⊖ – Via Köln - Frankfurt high speed line.

¶ – For connections from Praha by train, via Regensburg and Nürnberg, see Table 76.

⇌ – *Thalys* high-speed train. Ⓡ 🍴. Special fares payable. Valid Dec. 11 - Apr. 1, 2017.

🚌 – DB/ČD *ExpressBus.* Ⓡ 🍴. Rail tickets valid. 1st and 2nd class. 🚇 is Waidhaus
(Germany). Timings subject to alteration (Table 57).

☆ – Eurostar train. Ⓡ 🍴 in Business Premier and Standard Premier, 🍴 in Standard. Special
fares payable. Minimum check-in time 30 minutes. Not available for London - Ebbsfleet -
Ashford or v.v. journeys. Valid Dec. 11 - May 27, 2017.

22 AMSTERDAM - BERLIN

train type		IC		IC		IC		IC		IC		IC		IC	IC	IC	ICE	RE	RE	IC			
train number		245		141		143		145		147		149		241	241	241	645			243			
notes		①–⑥												⑥	Ⓑ	⑦	655			⑦			
		C													A	q				w			
Amsterdam Centraal d.	...	0500	...	0700	...	0900	...	1100	...	1300	...	1500	...	1700	1700	1700	...	...	...	1900	...	...	...
Hilversum d.	...	0526	...	0722	...	0922	...	1122	...	1322	...	1522	...	1722	1722	1722	...	...	...	1922	...	...	...
Amersfoort d.	...	0536	...	0736	...	0936	...	1136	...	1336	...	1536	...	1736	1736	1736	...	...	...	1936	...	...	...
Apeldoorn d.	...	0603	...	0802	...	1002	...	1202	...	1402	...	1602	...	1802	1802	1802	...	...	...	2002	...	...	...
Deventer d.	...	0615	...	0819	...	1019	...	1219	...	1419	...	1619	...	1819	1819	1819	...	...	...	2019	...	...	...
Almelo d.	...	0640	...	0846	...	1046	...	1246	...	1446	...	1646	...	1846	1846	1846	...	...	...	2046	...	...	...
Hengelo d.	...	0654	...	0859	...	1059	...	1259	...	1459	...	1659	...	1859	1859	1859	...	...	...	2059	...	...	...
Bad Bentheim 🏛 a.	...	0711	...	0916	...	1116	...	1316	...	1516	...	1716	...	1916	1916	1916	...	1957	...	2116	...	...	...
Rheine a.	...	0733	...	0940	...	1140	...	1340	...	1540	...	1740	...	...	1940	1940	...	2012	...	2140	...	...	...
Osnabrück Hbf a.	...	0803	...	1006	...	1206	...	1406	...	1606	...	1806	...	...	2006	2006	...	2046	2116	2206	...	...	...
Minden a.	...	0847	...	1047	...	1247	...	1447	...	1647	...	1847	...	...	2047	2047	...	...	2207	2250	...	...	...
Hannover Hbf a.	...	0918	...	1118	...	1318	...	1518	...	1718	...	1918	...	...	2118	2118	2131	...	2251	2324	...	...	...
Wolfsburg a.	...	0953	...	1153	...	1353	...	1553	...	1753	...	1953	...	...	...	2153	|	...	...	...	...	...	...
Stendal a.	...	1025	...	1225	...	1425	...	1625	...	1825	...	2025	...	...	...	2225	|	...	...	...	...	...	...
Berlin Hauptbahnhof a.	...	1122	...	1322	...	1522	...	1722	...	1922	...	2122	...	...	...	2322	2306	...	...	...	...	...	...
Berlin Ostbahnhof a.	...	1134	...	1334	...	1534	...	1734	...	1934	...	2134	...	...	...	2334	...	...	...	...	...	...	...

train type		IC		ICE	IC		RE	RE	IC	IC	IC		IC		IC		IC		IC		IC		
train number		244		646	242				240	240	240		148		146		144		142		140		
notes		①		①–⑤	①–⑥				①–⑥	①–⑥	⑦												
		D			p				p	B													
Berlin Ostbahnhof d.	...	...	...	...	...	...	...	...	0623	...	...	...	0823	...	1023	...	1223	...	1423	...	1623	...	...
Berlin Hauptbahnhof d.	...	...	...	0430	...	...	...	...	0634	...	...	...	0834	...	1034	...	1234	...	1434	...	1634	...	...
Stendal d.	...	...	...	0516	...	...	...	...	0734	...	...	...	0934	...	1134	...	1334	...	1534	...	1734	...	...
Wolfsburg d.	...	...	...	0548	...	...	...	...	0804	...	...	...	1004	...	1204	...	1404	...	1604	...	1804	...	...
Hannover Hbf d.	...	...	...	0618	0640	...	0709	...	0840	0840	...	...	1040	...	1240	...	1440	...	1640	...	1840	...	...
Minden d.	...	...	...	...	0712	...	0752	...	0912	0912	...	...	1112	...	1312	...	1512	...	1712	...	1912	...	...
Osnabrück Hbf d.	...	...	...	...	0753	...	0841	0914	0953	0953	...	...	1153	...	1353	...	1553	...	1753	...	1953	...	...
Rheine d.	...	...	...	...	0821	...	...	0948	1021	1021	...	...	1221	...	1421	...	1621	...	1821	...	2021	...	...
Bad Bentheim 🏛 d.	...	0744	...	...	0844	...	...	1003	1044	1044	1044	...	1244	...	1444	...	1644	...	1844	...	2044	...	...
Hengelo a.	...	0801	...	...	0901	...	...	...	1101	1101	1101	...	1301	...	1501	...	1701	...	1901	...	2101	...	...
Almelo a.	...	0814	...	...	0914	...	...	...	1114	1114	1114	...	1314	...	1514	...	1714	...	1914	...	2114	...	...
Deventer a.	...	0843	...	...	0943	...	...	...	1143	1143	1143	...	1343	...	1543	...	1743	...	1943	...	2143	...	...
Apeldoorn a.	...	0858	...	...	0958	...	...	...	1158	1158	1158	...	1358	...	1558	...	1758	...	1958	...	2158	...	...
Amersfoort a.	...	0924	...	...	1024	...	...	...	1224	1224	1224	...	1424	...	1624	...	1824	...	2024	...	2224	...	...
Hilversum a.	...	0938	...	...	1038	...	...	...	1238	1238	1238	...	1438	...	1638	...	1838	...	2038	...	2238	...	...
Amsterdam Centraal a.	...	1000	...	...	1100	...	...	...	1300	1300	1300	...	1500	...	1700	...	1901	...	2101	...	2301	...	...

A – Ⓑ (daily Apr. 2 - Nov. 10).
B – ①–⑥ (daily Apr. 3 - Nov. 11).
C – ①–⑥ Apr. 8 - Nov. 4.
D – ① Apr. 10 - Oct. 30.
p – Not Dec. 26.
q – Also Dec. 26.
w – Also Dec. 26; not Dec. 25.

24 PARIS - MOSKVA

train number	JI	24JI
train number	453	453
notes	AP	AQ
	⑤	⑤
Paris Est d.	1858	1858
Épernay d.	|	|
Strasbourg d.	2325	2325
Karlsruhe Hbf d.	0044	0044
Frankfurt (Main) Süd d.	0156	0156
Erfurt Hbf d.	0443	0443
Berlin Hbf a.	0708	0708
Berlin Hbf d.	0713	0713
Berlin Lichtenberg a.	0729	0729
Berlin Lichtenberg d.	0750	0750
Frankfurt (Oder) 🏛 d.	0855	0855
Rzepin d.	1016	1016
Poznań Gł. d.	1135	1135
Warszawa Centralna d.	1430	1430
Warszawa Wschodnia a.	1436	1436
Warszawa Wschodnia d.	1525	1525
Terespol a.	1707	1707
Terespol 🏛 d.	1747	1747
Brest Tsentralny 🏛 a.	1933	2033
Brest Tsentralny d.	2143	2243
Baranavichy a.	2345	0045
Minsk a.	0126	0226
Orsha Tsentralnaya § a.	0357	0457
Smolensk Tsentralny § a.	0526	0626
Vyazma a.	0712	0812
Moskva Belorusskaya a.	1001	1101

train number	23JI	23JI
train number	452	452
notes	BP	BQ
	③	③
Moskva Belorusskaya d.	2115	2215
Vyazma d.	0008	0108
Smolensk Tsentralny § d.	0155	0255
Orsha Tsentralnaya § d.	0320	0420
Minsk d.	0559	0659
Baranavichy d.	0756	0856
Brest Tsentralny a.	0950	1050
Brest Tsentralny 🏛 d.	1203	1303
Terespol 🏛 a.	1121	1121
Terespol d.	1206	1206
Warszawa Wschodnia a.	1354	1354
Warszawa Wschodnia d.	1424	1424
Warszawa Centralna d.	1435	1435
Poznań Gł. d.	1722	1722
Rzepin d.	1903	1903
Frankfurt (Oder) 🏛 a.	1924	1924
Berlin Lichtenberg a.	2022	2022
Berlin Lichtenberg d.	2045	2045
Berlin Hbf a.	2104	2104
Berlin Hbf d.	2109	2109
Erfurt d.	2322	2322
Frankfurt (Main) Süd a.	0216	0216
Karlsruhe a.	0339	0339
Strasbourg a.	0450	0450
Épernay a.	|	|
Paris Nord a.	0933	0933

25 NICE - MOSKVA

train number	18BJ	18BJ	
notes	⑥	⑥	
notes	DP	DQ	
Nice d.	2229	2229	⑥
Monaco-Monte Carlo d.	2246	2246	:
Menton d.	2257	2257	:
Ventimiglia 🏛 d.	2350	2350	:
Bordighera d.	2359	2359	:
San Remo d.	0009	0009	:
Genova Piazza Principe d.	0222	0222	⑦
Milano Rogoredo d.	0437	0437	:
Verona d.	0627	0627	:
Bolzano / Bozen d.	0830	0830	:
Brennero / Brenner 🏛 d.	1037	1037	:
Innsbruck Hbf d.	1138	1138	:
Zell am See d.	1356	1356	:
Linz Hbf d.	1706	1706	:
Wien Hbf d.	1841	1841	:
Břeclav 🏛 d.	2006	2006	:
Bohumín 🏛 d.	2027	2027	:
Zebrzydowice 🏛 d.	2248	2248	:
Katowice d.	2345	2345	:
Warszawa Centralna a.	0252	0252	①
Warszawa Wschodnia a.	0303	0303	:
Warszawa Wschodnia d.	0328	0328	:
Terespol a.	0525	0525	:
Terespol 🏛 d.	0605	0605	:
Brest Tsentralny 🏛 a.	0751	0851	:
Brest Tsentralny d.	1001	1101	:
Baranavichy a.	1200	1300	:
Minsk a.	1346	1446	:
Orsha Tsentralnaya § a.	1617	1717	:
Smolensk Tsentralny § a.	1748	1848	:
Vyazma a.	1933	2033	:
Moskva Belorusskaya a.	2225	2325	:

train number	17BJ	17BJ	
notes	④	④	
notes	CP	CQ	
Moskva Belorusskaya d.	1018	1118	④
Vyazma d.	1346	1436	:
Smolensk Tsentralny § d.	1538	1638	:
Orsha Tsentralnaya § d.	1705	1805	:
Minsk d.	1938	2038	:
Baranavichy d.	|	|	:
Brest Tsentralny a.	2324	0024	:
Brest Tsentralny 🏛 d.	0150	0250	⑤
Terespol 🏛 a.	0108	0108	:
Terespol d.	0158	0158	:
Warszawa Wschodnia a.	0349	0349	:
Warszawa Wschodnia d.	0419	0419	:
Warszawa Centralna d.	0430	0430	:
Katowice d.	0717	0717	:
Zebrzydowice 🏛 d.	0823	0823	:
Bohumín 🏛 d.	0907	0907	:
Břeclav 🏛 d.	1118	1118	:
Wien Hbf d.	1241	1241	:
Linz Hbf d.	1426	1426	:
Zell am See d.	1840	1840	:
Innsbruck Hbf d.	2144	2144	:
Brennero / Brenner 🏛 d.	2243	2243	:
Bolzano / Bozen d.	2355	2355	:
Verona d.	0136	0136	⑥
Milano Rogoredo d.	0257	0257	:
Genova Piazza Principe d.	0454	0454	:
San Remo d.	0646	0646	:
Bordighera d.	0700	0700	:
Ventimiglia 🏛 d.	0803	0803	:
Menton a.	0814	0814	:
Monaco-Monte Carlo a.	0824	0824	:
Nice a.	0840	0840	:

Notes for tables 24 and 25

A – TRANSEUROPEAN EXPRESS ⑤: 🛏 1, 2 cl. Paris (**453**) - Berlin - Brest (**24** *JI*) - Moskva. ✕ (PKP) Paris - Warszawa. ✕ (RZD) Brest - Moskva.

B – TRANSEUROPEAN EXPRESS ③: 🛏 1, 2 cl. Moskva (**23** *JI*) - Brest (**452**) - Berlin - Paris. ✕ (RZD) Moskva - Brest. ✕ (PKP) Warszawa - Paris.

C – ④: 🛏 1 cl. (lux), 🛏 1, 2 cl. Moskva - Nice. ✕ (RZD) Moskva - Brest and ✕ (PKP) Warszawa - Nice (journey two nights).

D – ⑥: 🛏 1 cl. (lux), 🛏 1, 2 cl. Nice - Moskva. ✕ (PKP) Nice - Warszawa and ✕ (RZD) Brest - Moskva (journey two nights).

P – Mar. 26, 2017 - Oct. 28, 2017.

Q – Dec. 11, 2016 - Mar. 25, 2017.

✕ (PKP) – Polish railways restaurant car.

✕ (RZD) – Russian railways restaurant car.

§ – 🏛: Osinovka (BY) / Krasnoye (RU).

train type	ICE	ICE	ICE		ICE	ICE	ICE	🚌		ICE	ICE	ICE	ICE	ICE		ICE	ICE	ICE
train number	121	621	515		105	595	27	42014		123	629	519	229	42018		125	723	611
notes	①–⑤	①–⑥						Ⓡ 🍴						Ⓡ 🍴		Ⓑ		Ⓑ
		y			E			2						2			p	
Amsterdam Centraal...d.		0637			0802					1037						1237		
Rotterdam Centraal ...d.	0605			0735			1005						1205				1405	
Utrecht Centraal ...d.	0643	0704		0813	0830		1043	1104					1243	1304			1443	1504
Arnhem ◐...d.		0737			0908			1137						1337				1537
Oberhausen Hbf ◐...d.		0826			1000			1226						1426				1626
Duisburg Hbf ...d.		0834			1008			1234						1438				1638
Düsseldorf Hbf ...d.		0848			1022			1248						1454				1653
Köln Hbf ...a.		0912			1045			1315						1518				1718
Köln Hbf ...d.		0927			1055			1328						1529				1728
Bonn Hbf ...d.																		
Koblenz ...d.			⊖			⊖							⊖			⊖		
Mainz ...d.																		
Frankfurt Flughafen ✈...a.		1016	1052		1149	1202		1416		1452		1616		1652		1816	1852
Frankfurt (Main) Hbf ...a.		1030	1054		1213			1430	1454		1621		1630	1654		1830	1854
Würzburg ...a.			1202			1331			1602	1731		1802			2002	
Nürnberg ...a.			1259			1427	1540		1659	1827	1840	1859			2059	
Regensburg ...a.						1525				1925						
Praha hlavní ...a.							1918				2230					
Mannheim ...a.			1123		1223	1230			1523			1723			1923
Stuttgart ...a.			1208			1308			1608			1808			2008
Ulm ...a.			1308			1407			1707			1908			2108
Augsburg ...a.			1353			1453			1753			1953			2153
München Hbf ...a.			1404	1427		1528			1804	1827		2004	2027		2205	2226
Passau ▥ ...a.						1634					2034					
Linz ...a.						1743					2143					
Wien Hbf ...a.						1909					2309					

train type	ICE	ICE	ICE		ICE	EN	EN			train type	ICE		EN	EN	ICE	ICE		ICE	ICE	ICE
train number	129	821	615		221	40421	421			train number	222		420	40490	616	220		614	820	128
notes		Ⓑ								notes										①–⑥
			w			A	B				p		C	A					w	y
Amsterdam Centraal...d.		1632f			1837					**Wien** Hbf ...d.			2039							
Rotterdam Centraal ...d.	1605			1805						Linz ...d.			2215							
Utrecht Centraal ...d.	1643	1704		1843	1904					Passau ▥ ...d.			2325							
Arnhem ◐...d.		1737			1937					Innsbruck Hbf ...d.			2044							
Oberhausen Hbf ◐...d.		1826			2026					**München** Hbf ...d.		2252		0324		0524	0552			
Duisburg Hbf ...d.		1834			2034					Augsburg ...d.		2329		0357		0601				
Düsseldorf Hbf ...d.		1848			2048	2054	2054			Ulm ...d.				0440		0650				
Köln Hbf ...a.		1912			2112	2118	2118			**Stuttgart** ...d.				0551		0751				
Köln Hbf ...d.		1921			2126	2121	2121			Mannheim ...d.				0636		0836				
Bonn Hbf ...d.						2143	2143			**Praha** hlavní ...d.										
Koblenz ...d.			⊖			2217	2217			Regensburg ...d.				0027						
Mainz ...d.						2317	2317			**Nürnberg** ...d.		0240	0246							
Frankfurt Flughafen ✈...a.		2010	2035	2052		2216	2350	2350			Würzburg ...d.							0755			
Frankfurt (Main) Hbf ...a.		2025	2048		2230	0004k	0004k			**Frankfurt** (Main) Hbf ...a.	0456t		0527k	0527k		0727		0904	0909	
Würzburg ...a.			2203			0134				Frankfurt Flughafen ✈ ...a.	0512t		0536a	0536a	0706	0743		0906	0943	
Nürnberg ...a.			2259j			0237	0237			Mainz ...a.			0602	0602						
Regensburg ...a.						0410				Koblenz ...a.			0705	0705		⊖		⊖		
Praha hlavní ...a.										Bonn Hbf ...a.										
Mannheim ...a.			2123							**Köln** Hbf ...a.	0621t		0815	0815		0833				1032
Stuttgart ...a.			2208							**Köln** Hbf ...d.	0628		0817	0817		0844				1041
Ulm ...a.			2308							Düsseldorf Hbf ...a.	0652		0841	0841		0911				1105
Augsburg ...a.			2352				0625			Duisburg Hbf ...a.	0709					0925				1122
München Hbf ...a.		0007j	0027				0705			Oberhausen Hbf ◐ ...a.	0719					0932				1132
Innsbruck Hbf ...a.							0914			Arnhem ◐ ...a.	0828				1028					1228
Passau ▥ ...a.						0518				Utrecht Centraal ...a.	0900	0917			1100	1117		1300	1317
Linz ...a.						0633				Rotterdam Centraal ...a.		0955			1155				1355
Wien Hbf ...a.						0819				**Amsterdam** Centraal ...a.	0928				1128			1328	

train type	ICE	ICE	ICE		IC	ICE	ICE	ICE		EC	ICE	ICE	ICE	ICE		🚌	ICE	ICE	ICE		ICE	🚌	ICE	ICE
train number	612	726	126		2024	610	722	124		8	28	596	626	122		42009	26	1090	104		514	42011	620	120
notes		796					792									Ⓡ 🍴						Ⓡ 🍴		Ⓑ
		①–⑥					1122						756			2		594			E		2	p
													826											
Wien Hbf ...d.										0850						1050								
Linz ...d.										1017						1217								
Passau ▥ ...d.					0717					1124						1324								
München Hbf ...d.	0727	0755				0928	0955				1228	1255				1428		1528			1555	
Augsburg ...d.	0803					1003					1303					1503		1603			
Ulm ...d.	0850					1051					1351					1551		1650			
Stuttgart ...d.	0951					1151					1451					1651		1751			
Mannheim ...d.	1036					1236				1439	1532				1729	1736		1836			
Praha hlavní ...d.					0827					1229				1042				1242			
Regensburg ...d.					0929					1429											
Nürnberg ...d.		0900				1100					1329	1400			1420	1529			1620	1700	
Würzburg ...d.		0955			1026		1155				1427	1455			1627				1755	
Frankfurt (Main) Hbf ...d.		1104	1129		1142		1304	1329			1536	1608	1604	1629		1742			1904	1929
Frankfurt Flughafen ✈...d.	1106		1143		1158	1306		1343						1643		1755		1809		1906	1943
Mainz ...a.					1218					1518											
Koblenz ...a.			⊖		1311			⊖		1611			⊖						⊖		
Bonn Hbf ...a.					1344					1644											
Köln Hbf ...a.		1232	1405			1433			1705				1739			1905				2033
Köln Hbf ...d.		1241				1446							1746			1914				2042
Düsseldorf Hbf ...a.		1305				1511							1812			1936				2105
Duisburg Hbf ...a.		1322				1526							1825			1949				2121
Oberhausen Hbf ◐...a.		1332				1534							1833			1956				2132
Arnhem ◐...a.		1428				1628							1928			2058				2228
Utrecht Centraal ...a.		1500	1517			1700	1717					2000	2017			2130	2147			2300
Rotterdam Centraal ...a.			1555				1755						2055				2225			
Amsterdam Centraal ...a.		1528				1728						2026				2156				2326

A – ÖBB *nightjet* 🛏 1, 2 cl., ➞ 2 cl. (4, 6 berth), 🚗 Düsseldorf - Köln - Frankfurt - Nürnberg - Wien and v.v. Special fares apply.

B – ÖBB *nightjet* 🛏 1, 2 cl., ➞ 2 cl. (4, 6 berth), 🚗 Düsseldorf - Köln - Frankfurt - Nürnberg - München - Innsbruck. Conveys *EN* 40491 ÖBB *nightjet* 🛏 1, 2 cl., ➞ 2 cl. (4, 6 berth), 🚗 Hamburg (490) - Nürnberg (421) - München - Innsbruck. Special fares apply.

C – ÖBB *nightjet* 🛏 1, 2 cl., ➞ 2 cl. (4, 6 berth), 🚗 Innsbruck - München - Nürnberg - Frankfurt - Köln - Düsseldorf. Conveys *EN* 40420 ÖBB *nightjet* 🛏 1, 2 cl., ➞ 2 cl. (4, 6 berth), 🚗 Innsbruck (420) - München - Nürnberg (490) - Hamburg. Special fares apply.

E – 🚗 🍴 Amsterdam - Mannheim - Basel and v.v. (Table 73).

a – Arrival time.
f – 1637 on ⑥⑦.
j – ④⑤⑦ (not Dec. 25).

k – Frankfurt (Main) **Süd**.
p – Not Dec. 25.
t – ①–⑤ (not Dec. 26).
w – Not Dec. 24, 31.
y – Not Dec. 26.

🚌 – **DB** / **ČD** *ExpressBus*. Ⓡ 🍴. Rail tickets valid. 2nd class only. (Table 76).

RJ – ÖBB *Railjet* service. 🚗 (business class), 🚗 (first class), 🚗 (economy class) ✗.

◐ – ▥ between Arnhem and Oberhausen is Emmerich.
⊖ – Via Köln - Frankfurt high speed line.

30   PARIS - FRANKFURT - BERLIN, LEIPZIG, DRESDEN and PRAHA

Alternative services Paris - Frankfurt are available via Brussels (Table **21**).   Alternative services Paris - Berlin are available via Brussels (Table **20**).

train type	TGV	ICE	ICE	EC	ICE	TGV	ICE	ICE	EC	ICE		ICE	ICE	ICE	ICE	ICE	ICE	ICE	ICE	ICE	IC		ICE	EN	
train number	9561	372	1559	177	623	9551	370	1651	179	627		9553	276	1655	725	9563	274	1657	729	9555	1659	2029		9557	470	
notes	ℝ★	🍴	🍴	✕	🍴	ℝ★	🍴	🍴	✕	🍴		ℝ★	🍴	🍴	🍴	🍴	🍴	🍴	🍴	ℝ★	🍴	🍴		ℝ★		
notes	①–⑥																			⑧	⑧			9559 ℝ★		
	w	J		A					D											m				C		
Paris Est..............d.	0720				0906							1301				1520				1710				1906		
Strasbourg..............d.	0913												1713													
Forbach 🚻..............d.					1047															1859				2049		
Saarbrücken..............d.					1058				1459											1859				2059		
Kaiserlautern..............d.					1133				1537											1937				2137		
Karlsruhe Hbf..............d.	0955									1755																
Mannheim..............d.	1021				1219				1619							1821				2019				2219	2359	
Frankfurt (Main) Hbf..d.	1058	1113	1119		1154	1258	1313	1319		1354		1658	1713	1720	1754	1858	1913	1919	1958	2058	2119	2221		2258	0054f	
Würzburg..............a.			1301					1502						1902				2102				2344				
Nürnberg..............a.			1403					1559						1959				2159				0042				
Fulda..............a.		1209	1212				1409	1412				1809	1812			2009	2012			2212						
Erfurt..............a.			1337					1537						1937				2137				2341				
Leipzig Hbf..............a.			1422					1622						2022				2222				0026r				
Dresden Hbf..............a.			1535	1708				1735	1908					2135				2342t								
Děčín (🚻 = Schöna)..a.				1753					1953																	
Praha Holešovice..a.				1918					2118																	
Praha hlavní..............a.				1928					2128																	
Kassel Wilhelmshöhe..a.		1241					1441						1841				2041									
Göttingen..............a.		1301					1501						1901				2101									
Braunschweig..............a.		1357					1557						1957				2157									
Wolfsburg..............a.		1415					1615						2015				2215									
Berlin Hauptbahnhof..a.		1528					1728						2128				2330							0606		

train type	EN	ICE	ICE	ICE	ICE	ICE	ICE	ICE		ICE	ICE	ICE	ICE	ICE	TGV	TGV	ICE	EC	ICE	TGV	ICE	EC	ICE	ICE
train number	471	9558	9568	9586	822	1656	275	9584		277	9554	9554	724	1652	279	9552	9552	626	373	176	1558	9560	622	174	1556	375	9550
notes		ℝ★	ℝ★	ℝ★	🍴	🍴	🍴	ℝ★		ℝ★	🍴	🍴	🍴	🍴	🍴	ℝ★	ℝ★	🍴	🍴	🍴	🍴	ℝ★	🍴	🍴	🍴	ℝ★
notes		①–⑤	⑧		①–⑥	①–⑤	⑥	①–⑤		⑥	⑦			⑧	⑥					J	A				E		⑧
	C	w		h		g		Jg	p	w			q				h	p						J	A		E	h
Berlin Hauptbahnhof..d.	2302					0432			0630				0830				1230								1430	
Wolfsburg..............d.						0540			0740				0940				1340								1540	
Braunschweig..............d.						0558			0758				0958				1358								1558	
Göttingen..............d.						0655			0855				1055				1455								1655	
Kassel Wilhelmshöhe..d.						0716			0916				1116				1516								1716	
Praha hlavní..............d.																0822				1022					
Praha Holešovice..d.																0833				1033					
Děčín (🚻 = Schöna)..d.																1000				1200					
Dresden Hbf..............d.					0613j				0813							1043	1213				1243	1413				
Leipzig Hbf..............d.			0529				0729						0929				1329				1529					
Erfurt..............d.			0618				0818						1018				1418				1618					
Fulda..............d.			0744	0748			0944	0948					1144	1148			1548	1544			1744	1748				
Nürnberg..............d.				0600							1000					1400					1600					
Würzburg..............d.				0655							1055					1455					1655					
Frankfurt (Main) Hbf..d.	0402f	0558	0659	0658	0804	0837	0844	0856	0856	1037	1044	1058	1058	1204	1237	1244	1258	1604	1644		1637	1644	1804	1837	1844	1858
Mannheim..............a.	0440	0639	0739	0738		0940	0940			1142	1142			1340	1340			1740				1939
Karlsruhe Hbf..............a.			0807			1006												1807					
Kaiserlautern..............a.		0721		0822			1022			1224	1224			1422	1422							2022
Saarbrücken..............a.		0800		0902			1101			1305	1305			1501	1501							2101
Forbach 🚻..............a.		0809		0911					🚻	1315				1510				🚻				2110
Strasbourg..............a.		0847				1047												1847				
Paris Est..............a.		0951	1038	1054			1238	1250		1454	1457			1650	1701			2041				2258

A – JOHANNES BRAHMS – 🛏 ✕ Praha - Dresden - Berlin - Hamburg and v.v.
C – ÖBB *nightjet* 🛏 1, 2 cl., 🚃 2 cl. (4, 6 berth), 🛏 Zürich - Basel - Mannheim - Frankfurt - Berlin - Hamburg and v.v. Special fares apply.
D – ALOIS NEGRELLI – 🛏 ✕ Hamburg - Berlin - Dresden - Praha.
E – ROBERT SCHUMANN – 🛏 ✕ Praha - Dresden - Berlin - Hamburg.
J – 🛏 🍴 Interlaken Ost - Basel - Mannheim - Berlin and v.v.
T – Runs as *ICE* 9566 on certain dates.

f – Frankfurt (Main) **Süd**.
g – Not Dec. 26.
h – Not Apr. 16, 30, June 4.
j – ①–⑥ (not Dec. 26).
m – Not Apr. 16, 17, 30, June 4.
p – Also Apr. 16, 30, June 4.
q – Also Apr. 17, May 1, June 5.

r – ①⑥.
t – Not ⑥.
w – Not Apr. 17, May 1, June 5.

🚻 – 🚻 is at Kehl.
★ – *Alleo* ICE / TGV service.
A DB / SNCF joint enterprise.

---

31   LONDON - GENÈVE

For the full service Paris - Genève, see Table **341**. 90 minutes (including Eurostar check-in time of 30 minutes) has been allowed from Paris Gare de Lyon to Paris Nord. 60 minutes has been allowed from Paris Nord to Paris Gare de Lyon. Additional Eurostar services are available, see Table **10**.

train type	☆	☆	TGV			☆	TGV	TGV	☆	TGV	☆	TGV		☆	TGV	☆	TGV	☆	TGV
train number	9002	9004	9773		9110	9110	9114	5164	9750	9018	9775	9022	9777		9028	9781	9032	9785	9036	9789
notes	⑥	①–⑤			⑥			ℝ	ℝ	⑧		ℝ	⑧			R	♥		♥		⑤
notes			j		L		J	q			♥		S		R		♥		♥	
London St Pancras **10**..d.	0618	0701			0650	0657	0804			1024¶		1131			1331		1422		1531	
Lille Europe..............d.					0930	0926	1026	1043												
Paris Nord **10**..............a.	0947	1017							1347		1447				1647		1747		1847	
Paris Gare de Lyon..a.			1211						1511		1611				1811		1911		2011	
Lyon Part Dieu..............a.								1400	1534											
Bellegarde..............a.			1457					1645	1748		1858				2058		2151		2251	
Genève..............a.			1528					1717	1817		1928				2128		2221		2321	

train type	TGV	☆	TGV	TGV	☆		TGV	☆		TGV	☆	TGV	TGV		TGV	☆	TGV	☆		TGV	☆
train number	9760	9023	9764	9029	9031		9768	9039		9770	9047	9756	5192	9868	9161	9772	9055		9774	9059
notes	⚒	♥		⑦	①–⑥					①–⑤		ℝ				©️	h		A️	
notes			y	j			n			♥					h		h			h
Genève..............d.	0614		0741				0941			1141		1241			1341		1441			
Bellegarde..............d.	0643		0810				1010			1210		1311			1410		1510			
Lyon Part Dieu..............d.												1426	1600	1700						
Paris Gare de Lyon..d.	0927		1049				1452				1649		1749			
Paris Nord **10**..............d.		1113		1243	1313			1513		1713			1913		2013	
Lille Europe..............d.											1944f	1956	2030			
London St Pancras **10**..a.		1239		1409	1439		1630			1832			2103		2039		2139	

J – ①–⑤ Dec. 11–31 (not Dec. 26,27). ①④⑤ Feb. 5 - Mar. 25. ①–⑤ Mar. 26 - May 27 (not Apr. 17, May 1).
L – ①–⑤ Dec. 11 - Mar. 25 (not Dec. 26, 27, Jan 2). ②–④ Mar. 26 - May 27 (not Apr. 17, May 1).
R – ④⑤⑥⑦ Dec. 11–31 (also Dec. 26, 27). ①⑤⑥ Jan. 1 - Feb. 4 (also Jan. 2). ①⑤⑥⑦ Feb. 5 - May 27.
S – ⑤⑥ Dec. 11–31. ⑥ Jan. 1 - Mar. 25 (also Feb. 10, 12, 17, 19). ①⑤⑥⑦ Mar. 26 - May 27 (also Apr. 13; not Apr. 30).

f – Lille **Flandres** (◇).
h – Not Dec. 24, 31.
j – Not Dec. 26, 27, Jan 2, Apr. 17, May 1.
n – Not Jan. 1, Apr. 16, 30.
q – Jan 23 - Apr. 23, May 29 - July 1 depart Lille 1034, TGV Haute Picardie 1106.
y – Also Dec. 26, 27, Jan. 2, Apr. 17, May 1.

◇ – 500 metres from Lille Europe (see Lille City Plan on page 30).
¶ – On Feb. 26 depart London 1014, Ebbsfleet 1032.
♥ – *TGV Lyria* service. ℝ special fares payable. At-seat meal service in first class.
🚅 – *SNCF* service; see table 366a.
☆ – Eurostar train. ℝ, ✕ in Business Premier and Standard Premier, 🍴 in Standard. Special fares payable. Minimum check-in time 30 minutes. Additional services are shown in Table **10**. Connections across Paris between *TGV* and Eurostar services are not guaranteed. Valid Dec. 11 - May 27.

Alternative services London - München and London - Wien - Budapest are available via Brussels (Table **21**)

train type	RJ	EN	IC	RJ	ICE	EC	RJ	EC	EN		TGV	ICE	TGV	EC	RJ		ICE		RJ	☆	TGV	ICE	EC	RJ
train number	61	473	2261	65	9571	113	563	147	347		9551	595	9591	219	167		9573	517	261	9014	9575	599	391	361
train number/notes															567		9593							
notes	✕	¶	☕	✕	★	☕	✕	✕	M		★	☕		A	✕		☕		✕		★	☕		✕
			S											x										
London St Pancras 10 .... d.	...	...	...	...	...	...	...	...	...		...	...	...	...	...		...	...	...	0924	...	...	...	...
Paris Nord 10 .... a.	...	...	...	...	...	...	...	...	...		...	...	...	...	...		...	...	...	1248	...	...	...	...
Paris Est .... d.	...	...	...	0640		...	...	...	...		0906	...	0925	...	...		1055	...	...		1355	...	...	...
Strasbourg .... d.	☒			0831		...	...	...	...		...	...	1127	...	...		1246	...	...		1546	...	...	☒
Kehl 🚲 .... d.	☒					...	...	...	...		☒			☒	...		☒	...	...		☒	...	...	☒
Karlsruhe Hbf .... d.	...	0806		0910		...	...	...	...		1216	1230	1221	...	...		1328	...	...		1628	...	...	...
Mannheim Hbf .... d.	...					...	...	...	...					...	...			...	...			...	...	...
Stuttgart Hbf .... d.	...	0853		0948	0958	...	...	...	...		1313	1318	1358	...	...		1404	1414	...		1704	1712	1758	...
Ulm Hbf .... d.	...	0956			1057	...	...	...	...		1409	1420	1456	...	...		1510	...	...		1809	1856	...
Augsburg Hbf .... d.	...	1039			1142	...	...	...	...		1455	1507	1542	...	...		1555	...	...		1855	1942	...
München Pasing .... a.	...	1101				...	...	...	...		1518		1518	...	...		1618	...	...		1918		...
München Hbf .... a.	...	1111			1211	...	...	...	...		1528	1545	1611	...	...		1627	...	...		1927	2011	...
München Hbf .... d.	0725	...	1130	1217		...	...	...	...				1617	...	...		1730	...	...			2017f	...
Salzburg Hbf 🚲 .... a.	0858	...	1258	1359	1408	...	...	...	...			1759	1808	...	...		1858	...	...		2202f	2208	...
Linz Hbf .... a.	1012	...	1412		1512	...	...	...	...				1912	...	...		2012	...	...			2312	...
St Pölten Hbf .... a.	1100	...	1500		1600	...	...	...	...				2000	...	...		2100	...	...			2400	...
Wien Hbf .... a.	1130	...	1530		1630	1639	1939	...	...				2030	...	...		2130	...	...			0030	...
Hegyeshalom 🚲 .... a.	1225	...	1625			1725	2025	...	...					...	...			...	...				...
Györ .... a.	1253	...	1653			1753	2053	...	...					...	...			...	...				...
Budapest Keleti .... a.	1419	1910	1819			1919	2220	...	...					...	...			...	...				...
Bucuresti Nord .... a.		1210					1600																	

train type	☆	☆	TGV	EN	☆	TGV	TGV	ICE	☆	ICE	ICE		train type	RJ	ICE	ICE	☆	TGV	ICE	ICE	☆	☆
train number	9018	9020	9577	463	9024	9579	9579	693	9032	9557	1093		train number	66	616	9558	9023	9578	9586	9568	9027	9031
train number/notes										9559	695		train number/notes	1066								
notes	⑧	⑥	⑧h		K	⑥p	⑧	⑧f		★			notes	✕	①–⑤	★w		★w	⑥	⑧h	U	j
London St Pancras 10 ..... d.	1024c	1101		1224				1422					**Bucuresti** Nord .... d.									
Paris Nord 10 .... d.	1347	1417		1547				1747					**Budapest** Keleti .... d.	1340								
Paris Est .... d.	...	...	1555		...	1755	1755		...	1906			**Györ** .... d.	1502								
Strasbourg .... d.	...	...	1746		...	1946	1946		...				**Hegyeshalom** 🚲 .... d.	1532								
Kehl 🚲 .... d.	...	...			...				☒				**Wien** Hbf .... d.	1630								
Karlsruhe Hbf .... d.	...	...	1828		...	2028	2028		...				**St Pölten** Hbf .... d.	1700								
Mannheim Hbf .... d.	...	...			...			2217	...	2231			**Linz** Hbf .... d.	1748								
Stuttgart Hbf .... d.	...	...	1922e		...	2112	2104	2113	...		2308		**Salzburg** Hbf 🚲 .... d.	1856								
Ulm Hbf .... d.	...	...	2020		...	2210	2209		...				**München** Hbf .... a.	2032								
Augsburg Hbf .... d.	...	...	2103		...	2258	2255		...				**München** Hbf .... d.	2044n	0324							
München Pasing .... a.	...	...			...			2320	...				**München** Pasing .... d.		0333							
München Hbf .... a.	...	...	2136		...	2329	2329		...				**Augsburg** Hbf .... d.	2117n	0357							
München Hbf .... d.	...	...		2336	...				...				**Ulm** Hbf .... d.	2204n	0440							
Salzburg Hbf 🚲 .... a.	...	...		0118	...				...				**Stuttgart** Hbf .... d.	2305n	0551			0654				
Linz Hbf .... a.	...	...		0455	...				...				**Mannheim** Hbf .... d.	2345n	0628	0639			0738	0739		
St Pölten Hbf .... a.	...	...		0600	...				...				**Karlsruhe** Hbf .... d.				0732			0807		
Wien Hbf .... a.	...	...		0635	...				...				**Kehl** 🚲 .... d.			☒		☒		☒		
Hegyeshalom 🚲 .... a.	...	...		0725	...				...				**Strasbourg** .... a.			0811						
Györ .... a.	...	...		0753	...				...				**Paris** Est .... a.			0951		1005	1054	1038		
Budapest Keleti .... a.	...	...		0924	...				...				**Paris** Nord 10 .... d.				1113				1213	1313
Bucuresti Nord .... a.													**London** St Pancras 10 .... a.				1239				1330	1439

train type	IC	EN	TGV	TGV	☆	☆	IC	ICE	TGV	RJ	EC	ICE	ICE	☆	ICE	TGV	EN	RJ	RJ	EC	TGV	ICE	EN	RJ	IC
train number	72	462	9576	9576	9035	9039	1296	690	9574	160	218	596	9572	9059	1090	9560	346	60	564	112	9590	592	472	62	2262
train number/notes										560			9592			594									
notes	T	K	①–⑤	⑥⑦	⑥⑦	①–⑥		☕	★	✕	☕	★		g	☕		M	✕	✕	☕	★	☕	S	✕	
Bucuresti Nord .... d.	0545	...	...	...	...	...	...	...	...	...	...	...	...	...	...	...	1400	...	...	...	...	1745	...	...	...
Budapest Keleti .... d.	1850	2040	...	...	...	...	...	...	...	...	...	...	...	...	...	...	0540	0740	...	...	...	0850	0940	...	...
Györ .... d.	...	2202	...	...	...	...	...	...	...	...	...	...	...	...	...	...	0702	0902	...	...	...		1102	...	...
Hegyeshalom 🚲 .... d.	...	2232	...	...	...	...	...	...	...	...	...	...	...	...	...	...	0732	0932	...	...	...		1132	...	...
Wien Hbf .... d.	...	2325	...	...	...	...	...	...	...	0730	...	...	...	...	...	...	0821	1030	1130	...	...		1230	...	...
St Pölten Hbf .... d.	...	0000	...	...	...	...	...	...	...	0800	...	...	...	...	...	...		1100	1200	...	...		1300	...	...
Linz Hbf .... d.	...	0105	...	...	...	...	...	...	...	0848	...	...	...	...	...	...	1148	1248	...	...		1348	...	...
Salzburg Hbf 🚲 .... d.	...	0428	...	...	...	0545	...	0952	1000	...	...	...	...	...	...	1300	1352	1400	...	...		1500	...	...
München Hbf .... a.	...	0610	...	...	...	0731	...		1141	...	...	...	...	...	...	1430		1541	...	...		1631	...	...
München Hbf .... d.	...	...	0623	0628	...	0746	0828	...		1147	1228	...	1428	...	...		1547	1609	1628	...	...		1647
München Pasing .... d.	...	...			...		0837	...			1237	...	1437	...	...			1637	TGV	...	...		1656
Augsburg Hbf .... d.	...	...	0656	0705	...	0817	0903	...		1217	1303	...	1503	...	...		1617	1640	1703	9570	...		1721
Ulm Hbf .... d.	...	...	0742	0750	...	0904	0951	...		1304	1351	...	1551	...	...		1703	1725	1751	★	...		1804
Stuttgart Hbf .... d.	...	...	0854	0854	...	0959	1046	1054		1359	1446	1454	1651	...	...		1759	1832	1846	1854	...		1911
Mannheim Hbf .... d.	...	...			...								1729	1740	...				1807		...		1953
Karlsruhe Hbf .... d.	...	...	0932	0932	...		1132				1532			...	...		1918		1932		...		
Kehl 🚲 .... d.	...	...			...				☆				☒	...	...						...		
Strasbourg .... a.	...	...	1012	1012	...			1213	9043		1613			...	...		2019		2013		...		
Paris Est .... a.	...	...	1205	1205	...		1405				1805		2041	...	...		2205		2205		...		
Paris Nord 10 .... d.	...	...			1413	1513			1613				2013	...	...						...		
London St Pancras 10 .... a.	...	...			1530	1639			1739				2139	...	...						...		

A – Apr. 14, 17, May 25, 28, Sept. 22, 24, 29, Oct. 1.
K – KÁLMÁN IMRE – 🛏 1, 2 cl., 🛏 2 cl. (4, 6 berth), 🚌 München - Budapest and v.v.
M – DACIA – 🛏 1, 2 cl., 🛏 2 cl., 🚌 ✕ Wien - Budapest - Bucuresti and v.v.
S – EuroNight ISTER – 🛏 1, 2 cl., 🛏 1, 2 cl., 🚌 ✕ Budapest - Bucuresti and v.v.
T – TRAIANUS – 🚌 Bucuresti - Budapest.
U – ⑤⑦ Dec. 11–31 (also Dec. 26, 27). ⑦ Jan. 1 - Mar. 25 (also Jan. 2, Feb. 10, 17). ①⑤⑦ Mar. 26 - May 27.

b – Not Jan. 1, Apr. 16, 30.
c – 1014 on Feb. 26.
e – Arrive 18 minutes earlier.
f – ⑧ (not Dec. 25).
g – Not Dec. 24, 31.
h – Not Apr. 16, 30, June 4.
j – Not Dec. 26, 27, Jan 2, Apr. 17, May 1.

n – ⑤⑥.
p – Also Apr. 16, 30, June 4.
r – Also Apr. 17, May 1.
w – Not Apr. 17, May 1, June 5.
x – To Graz (arrive 2214; Table **68**).

☒ – 🚲 is at Forbach.
RJ – ÖBB *Railjet* service. ✕, 🚌 (business class), 🚌 (first class), 🚌 (economy class).
★ – *Alleo* ICE / TGV service. A DB / SNCF joint enterprise.
TGV – 🅁, supplement payable, ☕.
¶ – Compulsory reservation for international journeys between Hungary and Romania.
☆ – Eurostar train. 🅁, ✕ in Business Premier and Standard Premier, ☕ in Standard. Special fares payable. Minimum check-in time 30 minutes. Additional services are shown in Table **10**. Valid Dec. 11 - May 27.

40 — LONDON - PARIS - BASEL - ZÜRICH, INTERLAKEN, BRIG and MILANO

Southbound (London → Milano), part 1

train type	TGV	IC	IC	IC	IC	EC	EC	☆	TGV	IC	IC	IC	IR	EC	☆	☆	TGV	IC	IC	IC	IR	EC
train number	9203	567	1067	967	671	57	19	9080	9211	573	1073	820	2327	21	9002	9004	9213	577	1077	824	2331	23
notes	①–⑥					RℙℸⓍ	RℙℸⓍ	h	♥					Ⓧ	①–⑤	q	♥	ℸ				Ⓧ
London St Pancras d								0540							0618	0701						
Paris Nord a								0917							0947	1017						
Paris Gare de Lyon d	0723								1023								1223					
Dijon d									1201								1401					
Besançon TGV ⊝ d																						
Belfort TGV ⊡ d	0941																					
Mulhouse d	1006								1306								1506					
Basel SBB a	1026								1326								1526					
Basel SBB d	1033		1031	1059	1104	1231			1333		1331		1404				1533		1531			1604
Zürich HB a	1126	1137					1309		1426	1437				1509			1626	1637				1709
Landquart a		1241								1541								1741				
Chur a		1252								1552								1752				
Chur d		1258								1558								1758				
St Moritz a		1455								1755								1955				
Luzern a			1205								1505								1705			
Arth Goldau a			1246			1346x					1546			1546x					1746			1746x
Bellinzona a			1348			1448					1648								1848			
Locarno a			1427			1527					1727								1927			
Lugano a			1417			1517					1717								1917			
Chiasso ▨ a			1546			1546					1746								1946			
Bern a				1124	1156		1324					1424	1506							1624	1706	
Thun a				1152	1221		1352					1452	1524							1652	1724	
Spiez a				1202	1231		1402					1502	1534							1702	1734	
Interlaken West a					1251							1522								1722		
Interlaken Ost a					1257							1528								1728		
Brig a				1240			1440						1611								1811	
Como San Giovanni a							▥															
Milano Centrale a						1637	1635							1835								2035

Southbound, part 2

train type	☆	TGV	EC		IC	IR	EC	☆	☆	TGV	IC	IC	ICE	IR	ICN	ICN	☆	☆	TGV	RE	TGV	IR
train number	9014	9215	59		581	2335	25	9018	9022	9219	585	1085	373	2339	889	889	9024	9028	9223	5093	9225	2343
notes	♥ B	♥	RℙℸⓍ				Ⓧ	⑧	A	♥					①–⑤	⑥⑦		R	♥		♥	RℙℸⓍ
London St Pancras d	0924							1024f	1131								1224	1331				
Paris Nord a	1248							1347	1447								1547	1647				
Paris Gare de Lyon d		1423								1623									1823		1823	
Dijon d																			2001		2001	
Besançon TGV ⊝ d																						
Belfort TGV ⊡ d		1641								1842									2106		2106	
Mulhouse d		1706								1907									2106		2106	
Basel SBB a		1726								1926									2126		2126	
Basel SBB d			1731		1733		1804			1933	1931		1959	2004					2133		2136	2202
Zürich HB a					1826		1909			2026	2037				2109	2132			2226		2312	2312
Landquart a					1941						2141											0037
Chur a					1952						2152											0047
Chur d					1958																	
St Moritz a					2157																	
Luzern a												1905			2105	2215						2305
Arth Goldau a							1946x					1946			2146x	2215						
Bellinzona a												2048			2248	2323						
Locarno a												2127			2327	2357						
Lugano a												2117			2317	2352						
Chiasso ▨ a												2146			2344	0021						
Bern a			1824								2024		2056								2250	
Thun a			1852								2052		2124									
Spiez a			1902			1905					2102		2134									
Interlaken West a			1923										2151									
Interlaken Ost a			1928										2157									
Brig a			1940								2140			2156								
Como San Giovanni a			▥																			
Milano Centrale a			2137				2235															

Northbound (Milano → London)

train type	RE	IR	IC	IC	TGV	☆	☆	IC	IC	IR	IC	IC	TGV	TGV	☆	EC	EC	IR	IC	IC	TGV	☆
train number	2408	2308	1058	558	9206	9031	9035	858	1060	2312	562	1062	9214	9210	9039	12	50	2316	1066	566	9218	9047
notes					①–⑥ q	⑥⑦ r							♥	♥ B	t	Ⓧ	RℙℸⓍ				♥	ℸ
Milano Centrale d																0725	0723					
Como San Giovanni d																▥						
Brig d																0920						
Interlaken Ost d			0627											0830					1030			
Interlaken West d			0632											0835					1035			
Spiez d			0654						0754					0854			0954		1054			
Thun d			0704						0804					0904			1004		1104			
Bern d			0736						0836				0936	0910			1036		1136			
Chiasso ▨ d								0613								0815						
Lugano d								0641								0842						
Locarno d								0635								0835						
Bellinzona d								0711								0911						
Arth Goldau d	0611	0614						0813z			0814					1013z				1014		
Luzern d		0654									0854									1054		
St Moritz d																			0802			
Chur d																			1003			
Chur d				0609						0809									1009			
Landquart d				0619						0819									1019			
Zürich HB d	0651			0723	0734			0851			0923			0934			1051		1123	1134		
Basel SBB a		0755	0829		0827				0929		0955	1029	1023	1027				1129	1155	1229	1227	
Basel SBB d					0834								1034	1034						1234		
Mulhouse d													1053	1053						1254		
Belfort TGV ⊡ d					0918																1319	
Besançon TGV ⊝ d																						
Dijon d													1158	1158								
Paris Gare de Lyon a					1137								1337	1337							1537	
Paris Nord a						1313	1413															1713
London St Pancras a						1439	1530															1832

A – ⑤⑥ Dec. 11–31. ⑥ Jan. 1 - Mar. 25 (also Feb. 10, 12, 17, 19). ①⑤⑥⑦ Mar. 26 - May 27 (also Apr. 13; not Apr. 30).
B – Apr. 3 - July 1.
R – ④⑤⑥⑦ Dec. 11–31 (also Dec. 26, 27). ①⑤⑥ Jan. 1 - Feb. 4 (also Jan. 2). Daily Feb. 5 - May 27.
f – 1014 on Feb. 26.
h – Not Dec. 26, 27, Jan 2, Apr. 17, May 1, 8, 25.
q – Not Dec. 26, 27, Jan 2, Apr. 17, May 1.
r – Also Apr. 17, May 1.
t – Not Jan. 1, Apr. 16, 30.

x – Depart 4 minutes later.
z – Arrive 4 minutes earlier.
⊝ – Full name: Besancon Franche-Comté TGV.
⊡ – Full name: Belfort Montbéliard TGV.
♥ – TGV Lyria service. ℙ ℸ special fares payable. At-seat meal service in first class.
Ⓧ – Compulsory reservation for international journeys. Supplement payable for international journeys and for internal journeys within Italy.
☆ – Eurostar train. ℙ, ✗ in Business Premier and Standard Premier, ℸ in Standard. Special fares payable. Minimum check-in time 30 minutes. Valid Dec. 11 - May 27, 2017.
▥ – ▨ between Brig and Milano is Domodossola. Ticket point is Iselle.

MILANO, BRIG, INTERLAKEN and ZÜRICH - BASEL - PARIS - LONDON 40

train type	EC	IC	IR	IC	IC	TGV	☆		EC	EC	IR	IC	IC	TGV	☆		EC	IC	IR	IC	IC	TGV	
train number	14	1068	2320	1070	570	9222	9055		16	52/152	2324	1074	574	9226	9063		18	1076	2328	578	1078	9230	
notes	[R] 🍷 ⊗					♥	h		[R] 🍷 ⊗	[R] 🍷 ⊗				♥ Ⓑ	Ⓑ		[R] 🍷 ⊗					♥	
Milano Centrale d.	0925	...	...	...	...	...	...	...	1125	1123	...	...	...	...	...	...	1325	...	...	...	...	...	...
Como San Giovanni d.	1003	...	...	...	...	...	...	...	1203	◧	...	...	...	...	...	...	|	...	...	...	...	...	...
Brig d.	|	1120	...	...	...	...	...	...	|	1320	...	...	...	...	...	...	|	1520	...	...	...	...	...
Interlaken Ost d.	|	|	...	1230	...	...	...	...	|	|	...	1430	...	...	...	...	|	|	...	...	1630	...	...
Interlaken West d.	|	|	...	1235	...	...	...	...	|	|	...	1435	...	...	...	...	|	|	...	...	1635	...	...
Spiez d.	|	1154	...	1254	...	...	...	...	|	1354	...	1454	...	...	...	...	|	1554	...	...	1654	...	...
Thun d.	|	1204	...	1304	...	...	...	...	|	1404	...	1504	...	...	...	...	|	1604	...	...	1704	...	...
Bern d.	|	1236	...	1336	...	...	...	...	|	1436	...	1536	...	...	...	...	|	1636	...	...	1736	...	...
Chiasso 🏛 d.	1015	|	...	|	...	...	...	...	1215	|	...	|	...	...	...	...	1415	|	...	...	|	...	...
Lugano d.	1042	|	...	|	...	...	...	...	1242	|	...	|	...	...	...	...	1442	|	...	...	|	...	...
Locarno d.	*1035*	|	...	|	...	...	...	...	*1235*	|	...	|	...	...	...	...	*1435*	|	...	...	|	...	...
Bellinzona d.	1111	|	...	|	...	...	...	...	1311	|	...	|	...	...	...	...	1511	|	...	...	|	...	...
Arth Goldau d.	1213**x**	|	1214	|	...	...	...	...	1413**x**	|	1414	|	...	...	...	...	1613**x**	|	1614	...	|	...	...
Luzern d.	|	|	1254	|	...	...	...	...	|	|	1454	|	...	...	...	...	|	|	1654	...	|	...	...
St Moritz d.	|	|	|	|	*1002*	...	...	...	|	|	|	|	*1202*	...	...	...	|	|	|	*1302*	|	...	...
Chur d.	|	|	|	|	*1203*	...	...	...	|	|	|	|	*1403*	...	...	...	|	|	|	*1503*	|	...	...
Chur d.	|	|	|	|	1209	...	...	...	|	|	|	|	1409	...	...	...	|	|	|	1609	|	...	...
Landquart d.	|	|	|	|	1219	...	...	...	|	|	|	|	1419	...	...	...	|	|	|	1619	|	...	...
Zürich HB d.	1251	|	|	|	1323	1334	...	...	1451	|	|	|	1523	1534	...	...	1651	|	|	1734	|	...	...
Basel SBB a.	...	1329	1355	1429	...	1427	...	...	...	1529	1555	1629	...	1627	...	...	...	1729	1755	1827	1829	...	...
Basel SBB d.	...	...	...	...	...	1434	...	...	...	...	...	...	...	1634	...	...	...	...	...	...	...	1834	...
Mulhouse a.	...	...	...	...	...	1453	...	...	...	...	...	...	...	1653	...	...	...	...	...	...	...	1856	...
Belfort TGV ⊡ a.	...	...	...	...	...	|	...	...	...	...	...	...	...	|	...	...	...	...	...	...	...	1921	...
Besançon TGV ⊖ a.	...	...	...	...	...	|	...	...	...	...	...	...	...	|	...	...	...	...	...	...	...	|	...
Dijon a.	...	...	...	...	...	1558	...	...	...	...	...	...	...	1758	...	...	...	...	...	...	...	|	...
Paris Gare de Lyon a.	...	...	...	...	...	1737	...	...	...	...	...	...	...	1937	...	...	...	...	...	...	...	2137	...
Paris Nord d.	...	...	...	...	...	...	1913	...	...	...	...	...	...	...	2113	...	...	...	...	...	...	...	...
London St Pancras a.	...	...	...	...	...	...	2039	...	...	...	...	...	...	...	2239	...	...	...	...	...	...	...	...

h – Not Dec. 24, 31.
x – Arrive 4 minutes earlier.

⊖ – Full name: Besancon Franche-Comté TGV.
⊡ – Full name: Belfort Montbéliard TGV.

◧ – 🏛 between Brig and Milano is Domodossola. Ticket point is **Iselle**.
☆ – Eurostar train. [R], ✗ in Business Premier and Standard Premier, 🍷 in Standard. Special fares payable. Minimum check-in time 30 minutes. Valid Dec. 11 - May 27, 2017.
♥ – *TGV Lyria* service. [R] 🍷 special fares payable. At-seat meal service in first class.
⊗ – Compulsory reservation for international journeys. Supplement payable for international journeys and for internal journeys within Italy.

LONDON - PARIS - LAUSANNE - BRIG 42

train type	TGV	IR	TGV		☆	☆	TGV	IR		TGV	☆	TGV	IR		☆	TGV	IR			☆	TGV	IR	
train number	9261	1717	9263		9002	9004	9269	1725		9773	9014	9271	1731		9022	9273	1737			9028	9277	1741	
notes	♥ 🍷		♥ 🍷 A		⑥	①–⑤ g	♥ 🍷			♥ 🍷 ①–④	⑦	♥ 🍷 ⑦			Q	♥ 🍷				R	♥ 🍷		
London St Pancras **10** d.	...	...	...	...	0618	0701	...	...	...	...	0924	...	...	...	1131	...	...	...	...	1331	...	...	...
Paris Nord **10** a.	...	...	...	...	0947	1017	...	...	...	...	1248	...	...	...	1447	...	...	...	...	1647	...	...	...
Paris Gare de Lyon d.	0757	...	0757	...	...	...	1157	...	...	1211	...	1357	...	...	...	1557	...	...	...	...	1757	...	...
Dijon d.	0932	...	0932	...	...	...	1336	...	...	|	...	1531	...	...	...	1732	...	...	...	...	1932	...	...
Frasne a.	1042	...	1042	...	...	...	1442	...	...	◧	...	1639	...	...	...	1842	...	...	...	...	2042	...	...
Vallorbe 🏛 a.	1057	...	1057	...	...	...	1457	...	...	|	...	1657	...	...	...	1857	...	...	...	...	2057	...	...
Lausanne a.	1137	...	1137	...	...	...	1537	...	...	1615	...	1737	...	...	...	1937	...	...	...	...	2137	...	...
Lausanne d.	...	1220	|	...	...	...	...	1620	...	...	...	...	1818	...	...	...	2020	...	...	...	...	2220	...
Montreux a.	...	1240	1213	...	...	...	...	1640	...	...	...	...	1835	...	...	...	2040	...	...	...	...	2240	...
Aigle a.	...	1251	1227	...	...	...	...	1651	...	...	...	...	1846	...	...	...	2051	...	...	...	...	2251	...
Martigny a.	...	1311	1252	...	...	...	...	1711	...	...	...	...	1905	...	...	...	2111	...	...	...	...	2311	...
Sion a.	...	1325	1316	...	...	...	...	1725	...	...	...	...	1920	...	...	...	2125	...	...	...	...	2325	...
Sierre a.	...	1337	1330	...	...	...	...	1737	...	...	...	...	1932	...	...	...	2137	①–⑥	⑦	...	...	2337	...
Visp a.	...	1353	1404	1408	...	...	...	1753	1808	...	...	...	1953	2008	...	...	2153	2241	2323	...	...	2353	...
Zermatt a.	...	|	|	1513	...	...	...	|	1913	...	...	...	|	2113	...	...	|	2336	0018	...	...	|	...
Brig a.	...	1402	1418	...	...	...	...	1802	...	...	...	...	2002	...	...	...	2202	...	...	...	...	0002	...

train type	IR	TGV	☆	IR	IR	TGV	☆		IR	TGV	☆	☆		IR	EC	TGV	TGV		TGV	IR	TGV		
train number	1806	9260	9027	1712	1710	9264	9039		1720	9268	9051	9055		1728	34	9270	9778		9272	1732	9272		
notes		♥ 🍷 X	U	Ⓒ	Ⓐ	♥ 🍷	t			♥ 🍷	Ⓑ	h			[R] 🍷 ⊗	♥ 🍷 ⑤⑦	♥ 🍷 ①–④		♥ 🍷 W		♥ 🍷		
Brig d.	0428	...	...	0558	0601	...	...	...	0958	...	...	...	...	1358	1418			...	1551	1558	...	...	...
Zermatt d.	|	...	...	|	|	...	...	0837	|	...	...	...	1237	|	|	...	...	1437	|	|	...	...	...
Visp d.	0435	...	...	0606	0609	...	...	0945	1006	...	...	...	1345	1406	|	...	...	1545	1602	1606	...	...	...
Sierre d.	0453	...	...	0622	0628	...	...	...	1021	...	...	...	...	1421	|	...	...	...	1629	1622	...	...	...
Sion d.	0505	...	...	0634	0640	...	...	...	1033	...	...	...	...	1433	1446	...	...	...	1641	1634	...	...	...
Martigny d.	0518	...	...	0648	0654	...	...	...	1047	...	...	...	...	1447	|	...	...	...	1705	1648	...	...	...
Aigle d.	0542	...	...	0707	0714	...	...	...	1106	...	...	...	...	1506	|	...	...	...	1732	1707	...	...	...
Montreux d.	0553	...	...	0718	0725	...	...	...	1117	...	...	...	...	1517	1525	...	...	...	|	1718	...	...	...
Lausanne a.	0614	...	...	0740	0743	...	...	...	1139	...	...	...	...	1539	1542	...	...	...	|	1740	...	...	...
Lausanne d.	...	0623	...	...	...	0823	...	...	...	1223	...	...	...	...	...	1623	1638	...	1823	...	1823	...	...
Vallorbe 🏛 d.	...	0700	...	...	...	0900	...	...	...	1300	...	...	...	...	...	1700	|	...	1900	...	1900	...	...
Frasne a.	...	0713	...	...	...	0914	...	...	...	1314	...	...	...	...	...	1714	◧	...	1914	...	1914	...	...
Dijon a.	...	0823	...	...	...	1023	...	...	...	1424	...	...	...	...	...	1822	|	...	2022	...	2022	...	...
Paris Gare de Lyon a.	...	1003	...	...	...	1203	...	...	...	1603	...	...	...	...	...	2003	2049	...	2203	...	2203	...	...
Paris Nord **10** d.	...	...	1213	...	...	...	1513	...	...	...	1813	1913	...	...	...	...	...	...	...	...	...	...	...
London St Pancras **10** a.	...	...	1330	...	...	...	1639	...	...	...	1939	2039	...	...	...	...	...	...	...	...	...	...	...

Q – ⑤⑥ Dec. 11–31. ⑥ Jan. 1 - Mar. 25 (also Feb. 10, 12, 17, 19). ①⑤⑥⑦ Mar. 26 - May 27 (also Apr. 13; not Apr. 30).
R – ④⑤⑥⑦ Dec. 11–31 (also Dec. 26, 27). ①⑤⑥ Jan. 1 - Feb. 4 (also Jan. 2). Daily Feb. 5 - May 27.
U – ⑤⑦ Dec. 11–31 (also Dec. 26, 27). ⑦ Jan. 1 - Mar. 25 (also Jan. 2, Feb. 10, 17). ①⑤⑦ Mar. 26 - May 27.
W – ⑥ Dec. 17 - Apr. 1.
X – ①–⑤ Dec. 11 - Apr. 7. ①–⑥ Apr. 8 - July 1.

g – Not Dec. 26, 27, Jan 2, Apr. 17, May 1.
h – Not Dec. 24, 31.
t – Not Jan. 1, Apr. 16, 30.
◧ – Via Genève.

◇ – Stopping train. 2nd class only.
♥ – *TGV Lyria* service. [R]. Special fares payable. At-seat meal service in first class.
⊗ – Compulsory reservation for international journeys. Supplement payable for international journeys and for internal journeys within Italy.
☆ – Eurostar train. [R], ✗ in Business Premier and Standard Premier, 🍷 in Standard. Special fares payable. Minimum check-in time 30 minutes. Valid Dec. 11 - May 27, 2017. Additional Eurostar services are available, see Table **10**.

train type	TGV	FR✒	IC	FB	ITA		TGV	☆		TGV	FB	ITA		FR✒	FR✒
train number	9241	9569	597	9727	9925		9245	9080	17905	9245	9745	9977		9655	9557
notes	ℝ✕	9571	✒	ℝ☂	9927		ℝ✕			ℝ✕	ℝ☂	ℝ✕		ℝ✕	ℝ✕
notes	♣	ℝ✕		✒	ℝ✕		♣	b		♣	✒	✒		✒	✒
		⑧					P			Q					
London St Pancras **10 12**.........d.	...	...	...	...	...		...	0540	...	...	...	...		...	...
Paris Nord **10** ....a.	...	...	...	...	...		...	0917	...	...	...	...		...	...
Paris Gare de Lyon ....d.	0629	...	...	...	...		0941f	...	...	1041	...	...		...	...
Lyon Part Dieu ....d.	0831	...	...	...	...		...	...	1150	...	...	...		...	...
Lyon St Exupéry TGV ✚ ....d.	...	...	...	...	...		1138f	...	...	1236	...	...		...	...
Chambéry................................d.	0942	...	...	...	...		...	...	1316	1345	...	...		...	...
Modane ▥ ....a.	1055	...	...	...	...		1455	...	...	1455	...	...		...	...
Oulx ▲ ....a.	1123	...	...	...	...		1523	...	...	1523	...	...		...	...
Torino Porta Susa § ....a.	1224	1320	...	1319	1335		1615	...	...	1615	1710	1712		1800	1822
Torino Porta Nuova § ....a.			...			1330		...	...				1730		
Novara....................................a.			...	1411			1711	...	...	1711	1811				
Milano Porta Garibaldi.............a.	1350	1418d	...				1750	...	...	1750					
Milano Centrale.......................a.	...	...	...	1450	1425		...	...	...	...	1854	1800		1850	1910
Milano Centrale.......................d.	...	...	1450	1505	1435		...	...	...	1905	1815			1900	1920	1920
Alessandria ....a.	...	...			1429		...	...	...	...	...	1829			
Genova Piazza Principe ....a.	...	...			1530		...	...	...	...	...	1930			
La Spezia ....a.	...	...					...	...	...	...	...				
Viareggio.................................a.	...	...					...	...	...	...	...				
Pisa Centrale........................a.	...	...					...	...	...	...	...				
Livorno....................................a.	...	...					...	...	...	...	...				
Grosseto..................................a.	...	...					...	...	...	...	...				
Brescia.................................a.	...	...		1551			...	...	...	1951					
Verona Porta Nuova..............a.	...	...		1628			...	...	...	2028					
Vicenza....................................a.	...	...		1654			...	...	...	2054					
Padova.....................................a.	...	...		1712			...	...	...	2112					
Venezia Mestre.....................a.	...	...		1728			...	...	...	2128					
Venezia Santa Lucia..............a.	...	...		1740			...	...	...	2140					
Piacenza.................................a.	...	...	1543				...	...	...	...	...			2012	
Parma.....................................a.	...	...	1614				...	...	...	...	...			2054	
Reggio Emilia ....a.	...	1509	1631		1521		...	...	...	...	...			2112	
Modena....................................a.	...	...	1648				...	...	...	...	...			2132	
Bologna Centrale...................a.	...	1537	1714		1547		...	...	...	...	...			2022	2214
Firenze SMN.........................a.	...	1615	1817v		1625		...	...	...	...	...			2059	
Roma Tiburtina......................a.	...	1743	2118		1753		...	...	...	...	...			2228	
Roma Termini........................a.	...				1805		...	...	...	...	2110		2155	2240	
Napoli Centrale......................a.	...	1855	2330		1925		...	...	...	...	2230		2315		
Salerno....................................a.	...	1942			2016		...	...	...	...	...				

train type	☆		TGV		ICN	ICN		☆	EN	FR✒		ITA	IC	EC	IC	ITA	FR✒
train number	9014	17909	9249		797	799		9032	221	9503	2004	9901	583	141	505	9961	9509
notes		83237	ℝ✕		ℝ✕	ℝ✕				9505		ℝ✕	ℝ☂	✒	✒	9963	ℝ✕
notes			♣		H	E		V		ℝ☂		✒	✒			ℝ✕	✒
										✕							
												Ⓐ					
London St Pancras **10 12** .....d.	0924	...	...		...	...		1422	...	...	...	...	...	...	...	...	...
Paris Nord **10**.......................a.	1248	...	...		...	...		1747	...	...	...	...	...	...	...	...	...
Paris Gare de Lyon..................d.	...	...	1441		...	...		...	1911	...	...	...	...	...	...	...	...
Dijon......................................d.	...	...	...		...	...		...	2157	...	...	...	...	...	...	...	...
Lyon Part Dieu....................d.	...	1550	...		...	...		...	...	...	...	...	...	...	...	...	...
Lyon St Exupéry TGV ✚..........d.	...	...	1637		...	...		...	...	...	...	...	...	...	...	...	...
Chambéry................................d.	...	1716	1744		...	...		...	...	...	...	...	...	...	...	...	...
Modane ▥.................................d.	...	...	1855		...	...		...	⊙	...	...	...	...	...	...	...	...
Oulx ▲....................................a.	...	...	1923		...	...		...	...	...	...	...	...	...	...	...	...
Torino Porta Susa §................a.	...	...	2018		2140			...	...	...	...	...	...	...	...	...	...
Torino Porta Nuova §..............a.	...	...			2130	2155		...	...	...	...	...	...	...	...	...	...
Novara....................................a.	...	...			2238d			...	...	...	...	...	...	...	...	...	...
Milano Porta Garibaldi.............a.	...	...	2150		2317d			...	...	...	...	...	...	...	...	...	...
Milano Centrale.......................a.	...	...						...	0550	...	...	...	...	...	...	...	...
Milano Centrale.......................d.	...	...						...	...	0615	0618	0635	0650	0705		0715	0720
Novara....................................a.	...	...						...	...	0656							
Torino Porta Susa.....................a.	...	...						...	...	0758							
Alessandria ....a.	...	...	2229		2257			...	...	...	...	...	...	...	...	...	...
Genova Piazza Principe........a.	...	...	2330		2350			...	...	...	...	...	...	0840	0851	...	...
La Spezia ....a.	...	...			0124			...	...	...	...	...	...	...	1004	...	...
Viareggio.................................a.	...	...			0216			...	...	...	...	...	...	...	1039	...	...
Pisa Centrale........................a.	...	...			0216			...	...	...	...	...	...	...	1056	...	...
Livorno....................................a.	...	...			0237			...	...	...	...	...	...	...	1119	...	...
Grosseto..................................a.	...	...			0355			...	...	...	...	...	...	...	1228	...	...
Brescia.................................a.	...	...						...	0712	...	...	...	...	...	...	...	...
Verona Porta Nuova..............a.	...	...						...	0754	...	...	...	...	...	...	...	...
Vicenza....................................a.	...	...						...	0843	...	...	...	...	...	...	...	...
Padova.....................................a.	...	...						...	0906	...	...	...	...	...	...	...	...
Venezia Mestre.....................a.	...	...						...	0923	...	...	...	...	...	...	...	...
Venezia Santa Lucia..............a.	...	...						...	0935	...	...	...	...	...	...	...	...
Piacenza.................................a.	...	...			0008			...	...	...	...	...	...	0743	...	...	...
Parma.....................................a.	...	...			0059			...	...	...	...	...	...	0814	...	...	...
Reggio Emilia ....a.	...	...						...	...	0701		0721	0831				...
Modena....................................a.	...	...						...	...	...	...	...	0848				...
Bologna Centrale...................a.	...	...			0215			...	...	0722		0747	0914			0822	...
Firenze SMN.........................a.	...	...			0407t			...	...	0759		0825	1011v			0859	...
Roma Tiburtina......................a.	...	...			0717			...	...	0928		0953	1317		1420o	1028	...
Roma Termini........................a.	...	...				0554o		...	...	0940c	1005			1433		1010c	1040c
Napoli Centrale......................a.	...	...			0938	0817		...	...	1100			1529			1130	1200
Salerno....................................a.	...	...			1032	0912		...	...	1154						1232	...

E – 🛏 1, 2 cl., ▭ 2 cl., ▱ Torino - Roma - Napoli - Salerno.

H – 🛏 1, 2 cl., ▭ 2 cl. (4 berth), ▱ Torino - Milano - Salerno.

P – Apr. 3 - July 1.

Q – Dec. 11 - Apr. 2.

V – Thello - 🛏 1, 2 cl. (1, 2, 3 berth), ▭ 2 cl. (4, 6 berth), ✕ Paris - Milano - Venezia.
For use by passengers making international journeys only. Special fares payable.

b – Not Dec. 26, 27, Jan 2, Apr. 17, May 1, 8, 25.

c – Depart 10 - 19 minutes later.

d – Departure time.

f – On ⑥⑦ Apr. 8 - July 1 depart Paris Gare de Lyon 0945, Lyon St Exupéry TGV ✚ 1138.

o – Roma Ostiense.

t – Firenze Campo di Marte.

v – Firenze Rifredi.

✒ – Supplement payable.

♣ – TGV France-Italy service. ℝ ✕ Special fares payable.

▲ – Station for the resorts of Cesana, Claviere and Sestriere.

☆ – Eurostar train. ℝ, ✕ in Business Premier and Standard Premier, ☂ in Standard. Special fares payable. Minimum check-in time 30 minutes. Valid Dec. 11 - May 27, 2017. Additional Eurostar services are available, see Table **10**.

⊙ – Frontier / ticketing points ▥ are Vallorbe and Domodossola. Ticket point for Domodossola is **Iselle**.

§ – Local train services (Tables **585**, **586**) and metro services run between Torino **Porta Susa** and Torino **Porta Nuova**.

train type	TGV			☆	ICN	ICN	IC	TGV		☆	☆
train number	9240	83262	18550	9039	798	796	500	9244	18556	9051	9055
notes	R✗				R✗	R✗		R✗			R✗ 83472
notes	♣	©	Ⓐ	f	H	E	✗	♣ h	ⓑ		k
Salerno .... d					2038	2050					
Napoli Centrale .... d					2132	2142					
Roma Termini .... d							0003o				
Roma Tiburtina .... d					2343						
Firenze SMN .... d					0257t						
Bologna Centrale .... d					0418						
Modena .... d											
Reggio Emilia .... d											
Parma .... d					0521						
Piacenza .... d					0602						
Venezia Santa Lucia .... d											
Venezia Mestre .... d											
Padova .... d											
Vicenza .... d											
Verona Porta Nuova ..... d											
Brescia .... d											
Grosseto .... d						0153					
Livorno .... d						0309					
Pisa Centrale .... d						0326					
Viareggio .... d											
La Spezia .... d						0425					
Genova Piazza Principe . d						0606	0708				
Alessandria .... d						0657	0757				
Milano Centrale .... a											
Milano Centrale .... a											
Milano Porta Garibaldi .. d	0600				0711a			0845			
Novara .... d	0631					0805					
Torino Porta Nuova § .... d							0810	0855			
Torino Porta Susa § ..... d	0739					0910		1011			
Oulx ▲ .... d	0836							1113			
Modane 🚋 .... a	0905							1144			
Chambéry .... a	1015	1035	1207					1250	1344		
Lyon St Exupéry TGV ✈ ... a	1123										
Lyon Part Dieu .... a		1210	1326					1510			
Paris Gare de Lyon ...... a	1319							1611			
Paris Nord 10 .... a				1513						1813	1913
London St Pancras 10 12 . a				1630						1939	2039

train type	FB	FB	ITA	FR	TGV	FB	IC	FR	IC	ITA	FR	EN	☆	☆
train number	9714	9810	9908 9910	9622	9248	9826	728	9552	1534	9940	9654	220	9027	9031
notes	R♨	R♨	R✗	R✗	R✗	R✗	R♨	R✗	R	R✗	R✗		①–⑥	①–⑥
notes	✗	✗	✗	✗	♣	✗		✗	✗	✗	✗	V	U	p
Salerno .... d					0737		1536							
Napoli Centrale .... d			0825	0940			1615	1700			1725			
Roma Termini .... d			0945	1100				1820		1845	1900			
Roma Tiburtina .... d			0955					1829			1855			
Firenze SMN .... d			1125					2000		2025				
Bologna Centrale .... d		1118	1203			1918		2038		2103				
Modena .... d		1141				1941								
Reggio Emilia .... d		1154	1224			1954				2124	2118			
Parma .... d		1210				2010								
Piacenza .... d		1241				2041								
Venezia Santa Lucia .... d	1050											1920		
Venezia Mestre .... d	1102											1932		
Padova .... d	1118											1948		
Vicenza .... d	1135											2012		
Verona Porta Nuova ..... d	1202											2050		
Brescia .... d	1239											2133		
Grosseto .... d							1604							
Livorno .... d							1718							
Pisa Centrale .... d							1736							
Viareggio .... d							1753							
La Spezia .... d							1838							
Genova Piazza Principe . d			1330				2018							
Alessandria .... d			1431											
Torino Porta Susa ...... d									2002					
Novara .... d									2103					
Milano Centrale .... a	1325	1325	1315	1355		2125	2140	2145	2150	2215	2202	2240		
Milano Centrale .... a			1325	1405								2305		
Milano Porta Garibaldi .. d					1440									
Novara .... d														
Torino Porta Nuova § .... d		1530												
Torino Porta Susa § ..... d			1413	1452	1611									
Oulx ▲ .... a					1716								☉	
Modane 🚋 .... a					1746									
Chambéry .... a					1853									
Lyon St Exupéry TGV ✈ ... a														
Lyon Part Dieu .... a					2028									
Dijon .... a												0642		
Paris Gare de Lyon ...... a					2231y							0955		
Paris Nord 10 .... a													1213	1313
London St Pancras 10 12 . a													1330	1439

E – 🛏 1, 2 cl., 🛋 2 cl., 🚋 Salerno - Napoli - Roma - Torino.

H – 🛏 1, 2 cl., 🛋 2 cl. (4 berth), 🚋 Salerno - Torino.

U – ⑤⑦ Dec. 11–31 (also Dec. 26, 27). ⑦ Jan. 1 - Mar. 25 (also Jan. 2, Feb. 10, 17). ①⑤⑦ Mar. 26 - May 27.

V – *Thello* – 🛏 1, 2 cl. (1, 2, 3 berth), 🛋 2 cl. (4, 6 berth), ✗ Venezia - Milano - Paris. For use by passengers making international journeys only. Special fares payable.

a – Arrival time.

f – Not Jan. 1, Apr. 16, 30.

h – Calls at Aix les Bains at 1304, Bourg-en-Bresse 1410, Mâcon Loché TGV 1432.

k – Not Dec. 24, 31.

o – Roma **Ostiense**.

p – Not Dec. 26, 27, Jan 2, Apr. 17, May 1.

t – Firenze **Campo di Marte**.

y – 2237 on ⑥.

✗ – Supplement payable.

♣ – *TGV* France-Italy service. R ✗ Special fares payable.

▲ – Station for the resorts of Cesana, Claviere and Sestriere.

☆ – Eurostar train. R, ✗ in Business Premier and Standard Premier, 🍴 in Standard. Special fares payable. Minimum check-in time 30 minutes. Valid Dec. 11 - May 27, 2017. Additional Eurostar services are available, see Table 10.

☉ – Frontier / ticketing points 🚋 are Vallorbe and Domodossola. Ticket point for Domodossola is **Iselle**.

§ – Local train services (Tables 585, 586) and metro services run between Torino **Porta Susa** and Torino **Porta Nuova**.

45 — LONDON - PARIS/MADRID - LISBOA and PORTO

train type/number train number notes	☆ 9008 g	TGV 8537 ①-⑥ ⍟ A	Hotel 312 ⍟ ⍟ A	Hotel 332 ⍟ ⍟ L	IR 823 ⍟ ⍟
London St Pancras 10 .... d.	0755f	...	...	...	...
Paris Nord 10 .... a.	1117	...	...	...	...
Paris Montparnasse .... d.	...	1228	...	...	...
Bordeaux St Jean .... d.	...	1551	...	...	...
Biarritz .... d.	...	1747	...	...	...
Hendaye .... d.	...	1820	...	...	...
Irún 🚇 .... d.	...	1826	1850	...	...
San Sebastián / Donostia... a.	...	...	1908	...	...
Vitoria / Gasteiz .... a.	...	...	2045	...	...
Miranda de Ebro .... a.	...	...	2109	...	...
Burgos Rosa de Lima .... a.	...	...	2204	...	...
Valladolid Campo Grande ... a.	...	...	2320	...	...
Madrid Chamartín .... d.	...	...		2150	...
Ávila .... d.	...	...		2311	...
Medina del Campo .... a.	...	...	2351	2355	...
Salamanca .... a.	...	...	0057	0057	...
Ciudad Rodrigo .... a.	...	...	0206	0206	...
Fuentes d'Oñoro 🚇 ES d.	...	...	0230	0230	...
Vilar Formoso 🚇 PT d.	...	...	0150	0150	...
Guarda .... a.	...	...	0222	0222	...
Mangualde .... a.	...	...	0323	0323	...
Coimbra-B .... a.	...	...	0446	0446	0520
Pombal .... a.	...	...	0521	0521	...
Entroncamento .... a.	...	...	0605	0605	...
Lisboa Oriente .... a.	...	...	0720	0720	...
Lisboa Santa Apolónia ...... a.	...	...	0730	0730	...
Aveiro .... a.	...	...	...	...	0601
Porto Campanhã .... a.	...	...	...	...	0650

train type/number train number notes	IR 822	Hotel 335 ⍟ ⍟ L	Hotel 310 ⍟ ⍟ B	TGV 8544 ⍟ ⑧
Porto Campanhã .... d.	2155	...	...	...
Aveiro .... d.	2245	...	...	...
Lisboa Santa Apolónia ... d.	...	2125	2125	...
Lisboa Oriente .... d.	...	2134	2134	...
Entroncamento .... d.	...	2230	2230	...
Pombal .... d.	...	2306	2306	...
Coimbra-B .... d.	2325	2332	2332	...
Mangualde .... d.	...	0046	0046	...
Guarda .... d.	...	0145	0146	...
Vilar Formoso 🚇 PT d.	...	0235	0235	...
Fuentes d'Oñoro 🚇 ES d.	...	0340	0340	...
Ciudad Rodrigo .... d.	...	0359	0359	...
Salamanca .... d.	...	0456	0456	...
Medina del Campo .... d.	...	0618	0600	...
Ávila .... a.	...	0705		...
Madrid Chamartín .... a.	...	0840		...
Valladolid Campo Grande . d.	...		0629	...
Burgos Rosa de Lima .... d.	...		0748	...
Miranda de Ebro .... d.	...		0848	...
Vitoria / Gasteiz .... d.	...		0912	...
San Sebastián / Donostia... d.	...		1055	...
Irún 🚇 .... a.	...		1118	...
Hendaye .... a.	...		1128	1435
Biarritz .... a.	...			1501
Bordeaux St Jean .... a.	...			1711
Paris Montparnasse ..... a.	...			2033
Paris Nord 10 .... a.	...			...
London St Pancras 10 ... a.	...			...

46 — MADRID - LISBOA

For train services see Table 45	🚌 C ①	🚌 C ①-⑤	🚌 C
Madrid Estación Sur ✛ .. d.	1000	1430	2100
Cáceres .... d.	...	1915	...
Badajoz ⚐ .... 🚌 ES d.	1530	2030	0230
Elvas .... 🚌 PT d.	...	...	...
Lisboa Oriente .... a.	1700	2200	0400

For train services see Table 45	🚌 C ①-⑤	🚌 C	🚌 C
Lisboa Oriente .... d.	0915	1215	2015
Elvas .... 🚌 PT d.	...	...	...
Badajoz ⚐ .... 🚌 ES d.	1330	1630	0015
Cáceres .... a.	...	1800	...
Madrid Estación Sur ✛ .. a.	1840	2155	0530

NOTES FOR TABLES 45 AND 46

f – 0752 on ⑥.
g – Not Dec. 26, 27, Jan 2, Apr. 17, May 1.

✗ – Supplement payable.
ES – Spain (Central European Time).
PT – Portugal (West European Time).
✛ – Madrid south bus station close to Méndez Álvaro metro (see Madrid city plan on page 30).
⚐ – Badajoz railway station is 1 km north of Badajoz city centre and Badajoz bus station is 2.5 km south of Badajoz city centre.
☆ – Eurostar train. ⍟, ✗ in Business Premier and Standard Premier, ⍟ in Standard. Special fares payable. Minimum check-in time 30 minutes. Valid Dec. 11 - May 27, 2017. Additional Eurostar services are available, see Table 10.

NOTES FOR TABLES 45 AND 46

A – SUREX / SUD EXPRESSO *Trenhotel* - 🛏 *Gran Clase / Gran Classe* (1, 2 berths), 🛏 *Preferente* (1, 2 berths), 🛏 *Turista* (4 berths), 🚻 ⍟ Irún (312) - Vilar Formoso (313) - Lisboa.
B – SUD EXPRESSO / SUREX *Trenhotel* - 🛏 *Gran Clase / Gran Classe* (1, 2 berths), 🛏 *Preferente* (1, 2 berths), 🛏 *Turista* (4 berths), 🚻 ⍟ Lisboa (310) - Vilar Formoso (311) - Hendaye.
C – 🚌 operated by Avanza, additional buses operate, rail tickets not valid; www.avanzabus.com
L – LUSITANIA *Hotel Train* - 🛏 *Gran Clase / Gran Classe* (1, 2 berths), 🛏 *Preferente* (1, 2 berths), 🛏 *Turista* (4 berths), 🚻 ⍟ 🚻 Madrid (332/3) - Medina del Campo (312) - Lisboa and Lisboa (310) - Medina del Campo (330/5) - Madrid. Special fares apply.

47 — LONDON - PARIS - HENDAYE / IRÚN - MADRID

train type/number train number notes	TGV 8531 ⍟ ①-⑥	MD 18014 2	Alvia 4166	MD 18310 2	☆ 9044 h	4053 P✛	MD 18012 2	RE 18318 2
London St Pancras 10 .... d.	...	...	...	...	1731	...	...	...
Paris Nord 10 .... a.	...	...	...	...	2047	...	...	...
Paris Montparnasse ..... d.	0728	...	...	...	...	...	...	...
Paris Austerlitz .... d.	...	...	...	...	...	2152	...	...
Les Aubrais-Orléans .... d.	...	...	...	...	...	2252	...	...
Bordeaux St Jean .... d.	1051	...	...	...	...	...	...	...
Biarritz .... d.	1248	...	...	...	0848	...	...	...
Hendaye .... a.	1320	...	...	...	0914a	...	...	...
Irún 🚇 .... a.	1329	1350	1615	...	0925	1050	...	...
San Sebastián / Donostia... a.	...	1407	1631	...	...	1107	...	...
Vitoria / Gasteiz .... a.	...	1555	1807	...	...	1255	...	...
Miranda de Ebro .... a.	...	1616	1829	...	...	1316	...	...
Burgos Rosa de Lima .... a.	...	1713	1931	...	...	1413	...	...
Valladolid Campo Grande ... a.	...	1845	2048	2135	...	1543	1905	...
Medina del Campo .... a.	...	1911		2209	...	1609	1932	...
Salamanca .... a.	...			2252	...			2021
Ávila .... a.	...	1958			...	1658		...
Madrid Chamartín .... a.	...	2144	2206		...	1840		...

train type/number train number notes	RE 18302 2	Alvia 4087 ⍟	TGV 8544 ⑧	MD 18061 2	Av 8109	MD 18061 2	4052	☆ 9015 Q✛
Madrid Chamartín .... d.	...	0800	...	0905	1015	...	...	...
Ávila .... a.	...	...	...	1038		...	...	...
Salamanca .... d.	0712	...	...			...	...	...
Medina del Campo .... d.	0802	...	...	1125	←	...	...	...
Valladolid Campo Grande ... d.	0830	0918	...	1149	1120	1150	...	...
Burgos Rosa de Lima .... d.	...	1028	...	→		1320	...	...
Miranda de Ebro .... d.	...	1128	...			1417	...	...
Vitoria / Gasteiz .... d.	...	1151	...			1440	...	...
San Sebastián / Donostia... d.	...	1326	...			1629	...	...
Irún 🚇 .... d.	...	1348	...			1651	...	...
Hendaye 🚇 .... a.	...	1355	1435				...	1924
Biarritz .... a.	...	1501					...	1954
Bordeaux St Jean .... a.	...	1711					...	...
Les Aubrais-Orléans .... d.	...						0608	...
Paris Austerlitz .... a.	...						0720	...
Paris Montparnasse ..... d.	...		2033					...
Paris Nord 10 .... d.	...							0913
London St Pancras 10 ... a.	...							1039

P – INTERCITÉS – for dates of running see Table 305. 🛏 1, 2 cl. 🛋 (reclining) Paris - Irún ✛.
Q – INTERCITÉS – for dates of running see Table 305. 🛏 1, 2 cl. 🛋 (reclining) Hendaye - Paris ✛.

h – Not Dec. 24, 31.
a – Subject to confirmation.
✗ – Supplement payable.
Alvia – ⍟ ⍟ ✗.

☆ – Eurostar train. ⍟, ✗ in Business Premier and Standard Premier, ⍟ in Standard. Special fares payable. Minimum check-in time 30 minutes. Valid Dec. 11 - May 27, 2017. Additional Eurostar services are available, see Table 10.

48 — FRANKFURT - STRASBOURG - LYON - MARSEILLE

train type train number notes	ICE 9568 ①-⑤ ⑧ h	TGV 9877 9876 ⍟ ★	TGV 5340 5349	ICE 107	TGV 9580 ⍟ ★	TGV 9837 9581 ⍟ ★
Köln Hbf .... d.	...	...	...	1255	...	...
Frankfurt (Main) Hbf .... d.	...	0659	...		1358	...
Mannheim .... d.	...	0740	...	1423	1439	...
Karlsruhe .... d.	...	0808	...		1512	...
Baden-Baden .... d.	...		...		1534	...
Offenburg .... d.	0734	0804			1434	1504
Kehl 🚇 .... d.	0754	0822			1452	1522
Strasbourg .... a.	0805	0834	0847		1504	1534 1600
Strasbourg .... d.	...		0906			1615
Mulhouse .... d.	...		0952			1705
Belfort Montbéliard TGV..... d.	...		1026			1731
Besançon TGV ⊖ .... d.	...		1050			1755
Chalon sur Saône .... d.	...					1857
Lyon Part Dieu .... a.	...		1256	1336		1956 2010
Avignon TGV .... a.	...		1425			2105
Aix en Provence TGV .... a.	...		1453			2133
Marseille St Charles .... a.	...		1512			2148
Nîmes .... a.	...			1501		2133
Montpellier .... a.	...			1530		2202

train type train number notes	TGV 9862 9863 ⍟ ★	TGV 9582 9583 ①-⑤	ICE 106	TGV 6874 6875 ⍟ ★	TGV 9577 ⑧	ICE 100 698	ICE 590 992
Montpellier .... d.	0658	...	...	...	...	...	...
Nîmes .... d.	0727	...	...	...	...	...	...
Marseille St Charles .... d.		0810	...	1239	...	...	...
Aix en Provence TGV .... d.		0825	...	1253	...	...	...
Avignon TGV .... d.		0853	...	1322	...	...	...
Lyon Part Dieu .... d.	0854	1000	...	1433	...	...	...
Chalon sur Saône .... d.		1102	...		...	...	...
Besançon TGV ⊖ .... d.		1206	...	1657v	...	...	...
Belfort Montbéliard TGV..... d.		1230	...	1730	...	...	...
Mulhouse .... d.		1255	...	1804	...	...	...
Strasbourg .... a.		1344	...	1857	...	...	...
Strasbourg .... d.	1355	1422	1452		1922	1947	...
Kehl 🚇 .... a.		1433	1503		1933		...
Offenburg .... a.		1452	1522		1952		...
Baden-Baden .... a.	1422					2028	...
Karlsruhe .... a.	1446					2025 2059	...
Mannheim .... a.	1518		1536			2124 2132	...
Frankfurt (Main) Hbf..... a.	1558					2208	...
Köln Hbf .... a.			1705			2307	...

h – Not Apr. 16, 30, June 4.   v – Besançon Viotte.   ★ – *Alleo* ICE / TGV service. A DB / SNCF joint enterprise.   ⊖ – Full name: Besançon Franche-Comté TGV.

OSLO, STOCKHOLM and KØBENHAVN - HAMBURG - BERLIN — 50

train type	EC	ICE	EC	ICE	1/3		EC	ICE	Sn		EC	ICE	Sn	Sn		EC	ICE	IC
train number	238	1511	38	901	[R]		36	1515	519	1039	34	1517	521	523	1051	232	903	2073
notes	⚲	⚲	⚲	⚲	(B)		⚲	⚲	①-⑤	①-⑥	⚲	⚲	①-⑥	①-⑤		⚲	⚲	⚲
notes	P c			c	J		c		Q		c					P c		
Stockholm Central ...d.					2310				0521				0621	0721				
Göteborg ...d.									0655						0855			
Malmö C ...d.			0653		0648	0653	0833		0950	0953	1033		1050	1147	1153	1233		
København H ...d.	0537	0728	0737		0728	0908	0937		1024	1028	1108	1137	1124		1228	1308	1337	
Rødby Ferry ...d.	0736		0936				1136					1336				1536		
Puttgarden ...a.	0836		1036				1236					1436				1636		
Lübeck Hbf ...a.			1137				1337					1537				1737		
Hamburg Hbf ...a.	1021	1036	1220	1236			1421	1436				1622	1636			1821	1836	1851
Berlin Hbf ...a.		1219		1419				1619					1819				2019	2055

train type	Sn	391		EC	EC	ICE	ICE		Sn	Sn		EC	EC		EN	IC
train number	527	105	1063	32	1232	1701	905		529	531	1075	30	1230		301	230
notes		①-⑥		⚲	⚲	(B)			R			Tc	Wc		Gb	K / 1130
notes				Xc	Tc											
Oslo Sentral ...d.		0701														
Stockholm Central ...d.	0921								1021	1121						
Göteborg ...d.		1040	1055								1255					
København H ...d.															1552	
Malmö C ...d.	1347		1353	1433					1450	1547	1553	1633			1626	1700
København H ...d.			1428	1508	1537	1537			1524		1628	1708	1737	1737		2255
Rødby Ferry ...d.					1736	1736						1936	1936			
Puttgarden ...a.					1836	1836						2036	2036			
Lübeck Hbf ...a.					1937	1937						2137	2137			
Hamburg Hbf ...a.					2021	2021	2036	2151				2223	2223			0528
Berlin Hbf ...a.						2219		2354							0625	

train type	EN		394	Sn	EC		398	Sn	Sn		IC	EC		Sn	IC	EC		
train number	300	1020	124	528	31	1056	134	540	512	2070	33	1068	544	2072	233	1080		
notes	③⑤⑦			M	Vc			(B)	⑥		1233				P c			
notes	C b										⚲ c							
Berlin Hbf ...d.	1928										0706			0906				
Hamburg Hbf ...d.					0724						0911	0928		1111	1128			
Lübeck Hbf ...d.					0806							1006			1206			
Puttgarden ...d.					0908							1108			1308			
Rødby Ferry ...a.					1008							1208			1408			
København H ...d.					1222	1232	1332		1424			1422	1432	1532	1622	1632	1732	
Malmö C ...d.	0725	0733	0808		0811		1306	1406	1411	1459		1506	1606	1611		1706	1806	
København H ...d.		0808																
Göteborg ...a.			1105	1300			1705	1755					1905			2105		
Stockholm Central ...a.				1239				1839	1939				2039					
Oslo Sentral ...a.			1652				2149											

train type	ICE	EC		Sn	ICE		EC	2		ICE	EC		ICE	EC		IC	Sn
train number	1616	35	1092	550	1614	37		[R]	800	39	1610	239		231	516		
notes	①-⑥			(B)				(B)				1131			526		
notes		c			c		J		c		P c			K			
Berlin Hbf ...d.	1039				1239			1439			1639						
Hamburg Hbf ...d.	1221	1328		1422	1528			1621	1728		1823	1928		2342			
Lübeck Hbf ...d.		1406			1606			1806			2006						
Puttgarden ...d.		1508			1708			1908			2108						
Rødby Ferry ...d.		1608			1808			2008			2208						
København H ...a.		1819	1832	1932			2022	2032		2219	2232		0022	0112	0657	0612	
Malmö C ...a.			1906	2006	1911			2106	2237		2306		0146		0646	0711	
Göteborg ...a.			2305								2039						
Stockholm Central ...a.				2339				0616							1139		

C — BERLIN NIGHT EXPRESS – Apr. 16, May 28, ③⑤⑦ June 26 - Aug. 13: ⛴ 2 cl., ⚲ (X on board ferry) Berlin - Malmö. [R] Special fares apply.

G — BERLIN NIGHT EXPRESS – Apr.12, May 25, ①④⑥ June 26 - Aug. 13: ⛴ 2 cl., ⚲ (X on board ferry) Malmö - Berlin. [R] Special fares apply. EN 301 arrives Berlin Hbf 0625, passengers are allowed on until 0700.

J — (B): ⛴ 1,2 cl., 2 cl., ⚲ [R] Stockholm - Malmö and v.v.

K — (B) Dec. 16 - Jan. 1 (also Dec. 17), daily June 2 - Sept. 2. Via Flensburg ⛴ and Padborg ⛴.

L — (B) Dec. 16-30 (not Dec. 25), daily June 2 - Sept. 2. Via Padborg ⛴ and Flensburg ⛴.

M — ①-⑤ Apr. 4 - July 4. ①⑥ July 9 - Aug. 13. ①-⑤ Aug. 15 - Dec. 9.

P — June 23 - Aug. 13.

Q — Not June 24 - Aug. 28.

R — July 3 - Aug. 13.

T — June 23 - Aug. 13.

V — Dec. 17-31 (not Dec. 25), Apr. 1 - Oct. 1.

W — Dec. 11 - June 22, Aog. 14 - Oct. 1.

X — (B) Dec. 16 - Jan. 1 (also Dec. 17), Mar. 31 - June 22, Aug. 14 - Dec. 9.

b — Train is conveyed by train-ferry Trelleborg - Sassnitz Fährhafen ⛴ (Mukran) and v.v.

c — Passengers to / from Rødby or Puttgarden may be required to leave / board the train on board the ferry.

Sn – Snabbtåg high speed train. [R] (X).

(D) – Additional services Malmö - København and v.v. are available, see Table 703.

BERLIN - TORUN / GDYNIA — 51

train type	EC			train type		EC
train number	55	88100		train number	88033	54
notes	[R]			notes		[R]
notes	H	A		notes	A	H
Berlin Hbf ...d.	1437			Gdynia Gł. ...d.		0716
Berlin Ost ...d.	1450			Sopot ...d.		0724
Berlin Lichtenberg ...d.		1837		Gdańsk Gł. ...d.		0740
Frankfurt (Oder) ⛴ ...d.	1545			Tczew ...d.		0757
Rzepin ...a.	1605			Toruń Gł. ...d.		
Kostrzyn ⛴ ...a.		1948		Bydgoszcz Gł. ...d.		0903
Gorzów Wlkp. ...a.		2030		Piła ...d.		
Krzyż ...a.		2118		Inowrocław ...d.		0930
Poznań Gł. ...a.	1723			Gniezno ...d.		1001
Gniezno ...a.	1759			Poznań Gł. ...d.		1031
Inowrocław ...a.	1829			Krzyż ...d.	0732	
Piła ...a.				Gorzów Wlkp. ...d.	0828	
Bydgoszcz Gł. ...a.	1855			Kostrzyn ⛴ ...d.	0911	
Toruń Gł. ...a.	2002			Rzepin ...a.		1152
Tczew ...a.	2019			Frankfurt (Oder) ⛴ ...a.		1212
Gdańsk Gł. ...a.	2034			Berlin Lichtenberg ...a.	1028	
Sopot ...a.	2043			Berlin Ost ...a.		1318
Gdynia Gł. ...a.	2043			Berlin Hbf ...a.		1343

A — Operated by Arriva (Table 1000).

H — BERLIN GDANSK EXPRESS (X) [R] Berlin - Poznań - Gdynia and v.v. (Table 1020).

PRAHA - LINZ - ZÜRICH — 52

train type			1547		train type	RJ	EC	RJ	EC	RJ	50467
train number	1541	1543	1545	50466	train number	765	163	563	165	869	1540
notes				B	notes	(X)		(X)		(X)	(X) A
Praha Holešovice ...d.		0942	1342		Zürich HB ...d.		0840		1040		2140
Praha hlavni ...d.	0602	1002	1402	1802	Innsbruck Hbf ...d.	0817	1211	1217	1411	1514	0128
Tábor ...d.	0715	1115	1515	1915	Salzburg ...d.	1008		1408		1708	0350
Veseli nad Lužnici ...d.					Linz Hbf ...a.	1112		1512		1812	0455
České Budějovice ...d.	0804	1206	1606	2006							
Summerau ...d.	0909	1309	1709	2109							
Linz Hbf ...a.	1008	1408	1808	2207	Linz Hbf ...d.	1152		1552		1835	0635

train number	162	166	760		train number	RJ		RJ		RJ	
notes	(X)	(X)	(X)			1542		1544		1546	
Linz Hbf ...d.	1048	1448	1848	0105	Summerau ...a.	1250		1650		1950	0750
Salzburg ...a.	1152	1552	1952	0210	České Budějovice ...a.	1351		1751		2050	0851
Innsbruck Hbf ...a.	1344	1744	2144	0423	Veseli nad Lužnici ...a.					2124	
Zürich HB ...a.	1720	2120		0820	Tábor ...a.	1442		1842		2142	0941
					Praha hlavni ...a.	1557		1957		2257	1057
					Praha Holešovice ...a.	1619					

A — ⛴ 1, 2 cl. Zürich (EN 40467) - Linz (1540) - Praha. Linz - Praha.

B — ⛴ 1, 2 cl. Praha (1547) - Linz (EN 40462) - Zürich. Praha - Linz.

RJ – ÖBB Railjet service. (premium class), (first class), (economy class), (X).

TRAIN NAMES:
1540 / 1541 – F A GERSTNER
1542 / 1543 – ANTON BRUCKNER
1544 / 1545 – FERDINAND KINDERMANN
1546 / 1547 – VÁSA PŘÍHODA

54 — HAMBURG - BERLIN - BASEL - ZÜRICH

Station		EN 471 A
Hamburg Altona	d	2036
Hamburg Hbf	d	2052
Berlin Spandau	d	2241
Berlin Hbf	d	2302
Berlin Südkreuz	d	2311
Halle (Saale) Hbf	d	0020
Frankfurt (Main) Süd	d	0402
Mannheim Hbf	d	0442
Karlsruhe Hbf	d	0510
Offenburg	d	0545
Freiburg (Brsg) Hbf	d	0620
Basel Bad Bf ▣	a	0706
Basel SBB	a	0720
Zürich HB	a	0905

Station		EN 470 A
Zürich HB	d	2000
Basel SBB	d	2113
Basel Bad Bf ▣	d	2122
Freiburg (Brsg) Hbf	d	2158
Offenburg	d	2230
Karlsruhe Hbf	d	2304
Mannheim Hbf	d	2359
Frankfurt (Main) Süd	d	0054
Halle (Saale) Hbf	d	0450
Berlin Südkreuz	a	0559
Berlin Hbf	a	0606
Berlin Spandau	a	0618
Hamburg Hbf	a	0830
Hamburg Altona	a	0901

A – ÖBB nightjet 🛏 1, 2 cl., 🛏 2 cl. (4, 6 berth), 🍴 Zürich - Basel - Berlin - Hamburg and v.v. Special fares apply.

55 — FRANKFURT - LEIPZIG - DRESDEN - PRAHA

Station	EC 259	IC 2043	EC 171	ICE 1543	IC 2447	EC 173	ICE 1545	IC 2445	EC 379	ICE 1547	IC 2443	EC 175	ICE 1549	IC 2441	EC 177	ICE 1641	IC 2049	EC 179	ICE 1643	IC 2047	EN 477	EN 40477
notes	①–⑥ J	Ⓐ	✗ L	✗		✗ C	✗		✗	✗		✗	✗		✗ P	✗		✗ Q	✗	Ⓑ	M	B
Frankfurt Flughafen ✈ d							0811			1011			1211			1411			1610			
Frankfurt (Main) Hbf d				0618																		
Frankfurt (Main) Süd d							0822			1022			1222			1422			1622			
Fulda d				0714			0914			1114			1314			1514			1714			
Erfurt Hbf d				0839			1039			1239			1439			1639			1841			
Leipzig Hbf d	0557	0729		0923	0929		1123	1129		1323	1329		1523	1529		1723	1729		1925	1929		
Dresden Hbf d	0708	0837	0908		1037	1108		1237	1308		1437	1508		1637	1708		1837	1908		2037	2110	2110
Bad Schandau ▣ 🚪 d	0738		0938			1138			1338			1538			1738			1938				
Děčín ▣ 🚪 d	0758		0958			1158			1358			1558			1758			1958			2156	2156
Praha Holešovice a	0918		1118			1318			1518			1718			1918			2118			2318	2318
Praha hlavní a	0928		1128			1328			1528			1728			1928			2128			2327	2327
Wien Hbf 1150 a						1750																0655
Bratislava hlavná 1150 a						2035															0536	
Budapest Keleti 1175 a																					0837	

Station	EC 178	IC 2048	ICE 1640	EC 176	IC 2440	ICE 1548	EC 174	IC 2442	ICE 1546	EC 378	IC 2444	ICE 1544	EC 172	IC 2446	ICE 1542	EC 170	IC 2030	EC 258	EN 476	EN 40406	IC 2046	ICE 1642
notes	✗ D		✗	✗ P		✗	✗		✗	✗		✗	C		✗	L	Ⓑ	Ⓑ K	M	B		✗
Budapest Keleti 1175 d													0725						2005			
Bratislava hlavná 1150 d													1010						2301			
Wien Hbf 1150 d																				2250		
Praha hlavní d	0627			0827			1027			1227			1427			1627		1827	0406	0406		
Praha Holešovice d	0636			0836			1036			1236			1436			1636		1836	0415	0415		
Děčín ▣ 🚪 d	0800			1000			1200			1400			1600			1800		2000	0542	0542		
Bad Schandau ▣ 🚪 d	0815			1015			1215			1415			1615			1815		2015				
Dresden Hbf a	0844	0920		1044	1120		1244	1320		1444	1520		1644	1720		1844	1920	2045	0627	0627	0720	
Leipzig Hbf a		1028	1035		1228	1235		1428	1435		1628	1635		1828	1835		2028	2226			0828	0835
Erfurt Hbf a			1119			1319			1519			1719			1919							0919
Fulda a			1242			1442			1642			1842			2042							1042
Frankfurt (Main) Süd a			1337			1537			1737						2138							1137
Frankfurt (Main) Hbf a												1940										
Frankfurt Flughafen ✈ a			1349			1549			1749						2149							1149

B – METROPOL – 🛏 1, 2 cl., 🛏 2 cl. (4, 6 berth), 🍴 Berlin - Praha - Wien and v.v.
C – HUNGARIA – 🍴 ✗ Hamburg - Berlin - Dresden - Praha - Budapest and v.v.
D – ALOIS NEGRELLI – 🍴 ✗ Praha - Dresden - Berlin.
J – ①–⑥: KOPERNIKUS – 🍴 ✗ Leipzig - Dresden - Praha.
K – ⑦: KOPERNIKUS – 🍴 ✗ Praha - Dresden - Leipzig.
L – CARL MARIA VON WEBER – 🍴 ✗ Berlin - Dresden - Praha and v.v.
M – METROPOL – 🛏 1, 2 cl., 🛏 2 cl. (4, 6 berth), 🍴 Berlin - Dresden - Praha - Budapest and v.v.

P – JOHANNES BRAHMS – 🍴 ✗ Hamburg - Berlin - Dresden - Praha and v.v.
Q – ALOIS NEGRELLI – 🍴 ✗ Hamburg - Berlin - Dresden - Praha.

🚪 – Ticketing point is Schöna.

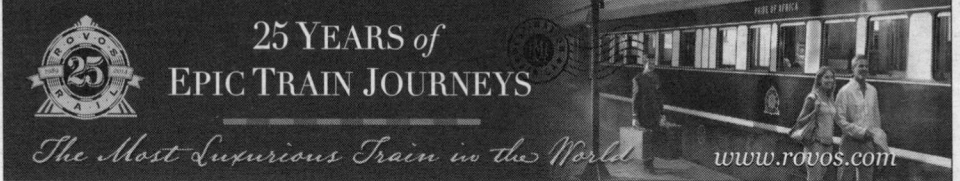

LONDON - KÖLN - BERLIN - WARSZAWA - MOSKVA 56

train type / number / notes / code	EC 41 ①-⑥ T	☆ 9032	24JI 453 ①-⑥ MY	24JI 453 MZ	ICE 541 b♉ T	EC 43 PY	10SZ PZ	10SZ C	68KJ	ICE 855 ♉ A	EC 45 T	⇄ 9401	ICE 857 A	EC 55 N	⇄ 9413	ICE 859 ♉ A	EC 47 ⑧	☆ 9110 ①-⑥	ICE 15 A	ICE 559 ♉ T	441 14MJ ⑰ JY	441 14MJ ⑰ JZ
London St Pancras ... d.		1422																0650				
Ashford International ... d.		1455c																0728				
Lille Europe ... d.																		0930				
Paris Nord ... d.		1747	1858e	1858e						0601		0755										
Brussels Midi/Zuid ... d.										0728		0928						1007	1025			
Liège Guillemins ... d.										0814		1014							1114			
Aachen 🚇 ... d.										0840		1040							1140			
Köln Hbf ... a.										0915		1115							1215			
Köln Hbf ... d.					0429					0748		0948				1148			1248			
Bielefeld Hbf ... d.					0640					0938		1138				1338			1438			
Hannover Hbf ... d.					0731					1031		1231				1431			1531			
Berlin Hbf ... a.			0708	0708	0906					1209		1409				1609			1706			
Berlin Hbf ... d.	0637		0713	0713		0937				1237		1437				1637						
Berlin Ostbahnhof ... d.	0650		0750k	0750k		0950				1250		1450				1650					1850	1850
Frankfurt (Oder) 🚇 ... d.	0745		0855	0855		1045				1345		1545				1745					1947	1947
Rzepin ... d.	0808		1016	1016		1108				1408		1608				1808					2015	2015
Poznań Gł. ... d.	0938		1135	1135		1240				1540		1724				1930					2134	2134
Warszawa Centralna ... a.	1215		1426	1426		1515	1840	1940	1850	1815						2205					0013	0013
Warszawa Wschodnia ... a.	1237		1525	1525		1532	1921	2021	1858	1832						2227					0033	0033
Terespol 🚇 ... a.			1707	1707			2137	2237													0213	0213
Brest Tsentralny 🚇 ... a.			1933	2033			0103	0203													0438	0538
Yahodyn 🚇 ... a.									0030													
Kyïv ... a.									1320													
Minsk ... a.			0126	0226			0702	0802													0812	0912
Orsha Tsentralnaya § ... a.			0357	0457			1000	1100													1043	1143
Smolensk Tsentralny § ... a.			0526	0626			1129	1229													1210	1310
Moskva Belorusskaya ‡ ... a.			1001	1101			1600	1700														
Moskva Kurskaya ... a.																					1625	1725

train type / number / notes / code	440 13MJ ⑥⑦ KY	440 13MJ ⑥⑦ KZ	ICE 954 ①-⑥ A	⇄ 9448	ICE 652 A	ICE 210 ⑤⑦	☆ 9149	EC 46 ①-⑥ T	ICE 950 A	☆ 9472	ICE 9161 h	EC 54 N	⇄ 858 ♉	ICE 9484	9SZ PY	9SZ PZ	67KJ C	EC 44 T	ICE 856 ♉	EC 42 ⑧ T	ICE 842 ♉	EC 40 ①-⑥ T	23JI 452 FY	23JI 452 FZ	☆ 9023
Moskva Kurskaya ... d.	1205	1305																							
Moskva Belorusskaya ‡ ... d.															1409	1509							2115	2215	
Smolensk Tsentralny § ... d.	1616	1716													1852	1952							0155	0255	
Orsha Tsentralnaya § ... d.	1747	1847													2017	2117							0320	0420	
Minsk ... d.	2009	2109													2301	0001							0559	0659	
Kyïv ... d.																	1615								
Yahodyn 🚇 ... d.																	0415								
Brest Tsentralny 🚇 ... d.	2332	0032													0520	0620							1203f	1303f	
Terespol 🚇 ... d.	2357	2357													0518	0518							1206	1206	
Warszawa Wschodnia ... d.	0138	0138						0548							0737	0737	0901	0948		1343		1743	1354	1354	
Warszawa Centralna ... d.	0158	0158						0600							0755	0755	0910	1000		1400		1800	1435	1435	
Poznań Gł. ... d.	0433	0433						0832				1032						1232		1632		2032	1722	1722	
Rzepin ... d.	0551	0551						0952				1152						1352		1752		2152	1903	1903	
Frankfurt (Oder) 🚇 ... d.	0612	0612						1012				1212						1412		1812		2207	1924	1924	
Berlin Ostbahnhof ... a.	0719	0719						1118				1306						1518		1918		2258	2022k	2022k	
Berlin Hbf ... a.								1143				1315						1543		1943		2321	2104	2104	
Berlin Hbf ... d.			0749		0852						1149		1349						1549		1949		2109	2109	
Hannover Hbf ... a.			0928		1031						1328		1528						1728		2128				
Bielefeld Hbf ... a.			1020		1122						1420		1620						1820		2220				
Köln Hbf ... a.			1209		1309						1609		1809						2009		0030				
Köln Hbf ... d.									1243	1343									1644		1844				
Aachen 🚇 ... d.									1320	1420									1720		1920				
Liège Guillemins ... d.									1346	1446									1746		1946				
Brussels Midi/Zuid ... a.				1432		1535	1656				1832		1952	2032							2205				
Paris Nord ... a.				1605									2005										0933e	0933e	1113
Lille Europe ... a.							1730			2026															
Ashford International ... a.																									1208c
London St Pancras ... a.							1806			2103															1239

A – 🚌 ✕ Köln - Wuppertal - Hamm - Berlin and Düsseldorf - Hamm - Berlin and v.v. Table **810**.

C – KYÏV EKSPRES / KIEV EXPRESS – 🛏 1,2 cl. Warszawa - Kyïv and v.v.

F – TRANSEUROPEAN EXPRESS ③: 🛏 1, 2 cl. Moskva (**23 JI**) - Brest (**452**) - Berlin - Paris. ✕ (RZD) Moskva - Brest. ✕ (PKP) Warszawa - Paris.

J – ①⑦: 🛏 1 cl. (lux), 🛏 1,2 cl., 🚌 ✕ 🍽 Berlin - Moskva, Talgo train.

K – ⑥⑦: 🛏 1 cl. (lux), 🛏 1,2 cl., 🚌 ✕ 🍽 Moskva - Berlin, Talgo train.

M – TRANSEUROPEAN EXPRESS ⑤: 🛏 1, 2 cl. Paris (**453**) - Berlin - Brest (**24 JI**) - Moskva. ✕ (PKP) Paris - Warszawa. ✕ (RZD) Brest - Moskva.

N – BERLIN GDANSK EXPRESS 🚌 ✕ 🍽 Berlin - Poznań - Gdynia and v.v.

P – POLONEZ – 🛏 1,2 cl., 🍽 Warszawa - Moskva and v.v. ✕ Brest - Moskva and v.v.

T – BERLIN WARSZAWA EXPRESS – 🚌 ✕ Berlin - Poznań - Warszawa and v.v. 🅁 Special fares apply. Supplement payable in Poland.

X – ①-⑤ Dec. 11-31. ⑤ Jan. 1 - Feb. 4 (also Jan. 2). ①-⑤ Feb. 5 - Mar. 25.

Y – Mar. 26 - Oct. 28.

Z – Dec. 11 - Mar. 25.

b – Not Oct. 3.

c – Not Feb. 26, 2017.

e – Paris **Est**.

f – Arrive 1050.

h – Not Dec. 24, 31.

k – Berlin **Lichtenberg**.

r – Depart 2107.

⇄ – *Thalys* high-speed train. 🅁 🍽. Special fares payable. Valid Dec. 11 - Apr. 1, 2017.

§ – 🚉: Osinovka (BY) / Krasnoye (RU).

‡ – Also known as Moskva **Smolenskaya** station.

☆ – *Eurostar* train. Special fares payable. ✕ in Business Premier and Standard Premier, 🍽 in Standard. Minimum check-in time 30 minutes. Valid Dec. 11 - May 27, 2017.

BERLIN - COTTBUS - FORST - WROCLAW 58

	RE 5825 ⑥⑦ K			RE 5826 ⑦ K	RE 5824 ⑥ K
Berlin Lichtenberg ... d.	0831		Wrocław Gł. ... d.	1629	1921
Berlin Ostkreuz ... d.	0836		Legnica ... d.	1713	2006
Cottbus ... a.	0953		Żagań ... d.	1846	2133
Forst 🚇 ... a.			Żáry ... d.	1858	2148
Forst 🚇 ... d.	1008		Tuplice ... d.		
Tuplice ... d.			Forst 🚇 ... a.	1930	2220
Żáry ... d.	1041		Forst 🚇 ... d.		
Żagań ... d.	1058		Cottbus ... a.	2005	2236
Legnica ... d.	1219		Berlin Ostkreuz ... a.	2126	2348
Wrocław Gł. ... a.	1305		Berlin Lichtenberg ... a.	2135	2354

K – KULTURZUG - 🚌 Berlin - Wrocław and v.v. For Intenational journeys only. Special fares apply.

Table 1 — Hamburg → Budapest / Wien / Graz

	271	273	71	275	73	259	277	75	171	279	77	131	173	79	379	281	371	175	283	373	177	179	477	477	40477
train type	EC	EC	RJ	EC	RJ	EC	EC	RJ	EC	EC	RJ	EC	EC	RJ	EC	EC	RJ	EC	EC	RJ	EC	EC	EN	EN	EN
notes	✕	✕	✕	✕	✕	①-⑥ Q	✕ S	✕	✕	✕	✕	✕ V	✕ J	✕	✕ H	✕	✕	✕	✕	✕	✕	✕	C	A	B
Hamburg Altona .... d.													0636								1239	1437			
Hamburg Hbf .... d.													0648	0851							1251	1451			
Berlin Hbf .... d.							0658						0903	1100			1300				1500	1700	1901		1901
Berlin Südkreuz .... d.							0704						0910	1107			1307				1507	1707	1907		1907
Leipzig Hbf .... a.					0557																				
Dresden Hbf .... d.						0708	0908						1108	1308				1508			1708	1908	2108		2108
Bad Schandau ✕⊖.. d.						0738	0938						1138	1338				1538			1738	1938			
Děčín .... d.						0756	0956						1156	1356				1556			1756	1956	2156		2156
Ústí nad Labem hlavní d.						0815	1015						1215	1415				1615			1815	2015	2215		2215
Praha Holešovice ... a.						0917	1117						1317	1517				1717			1917	2117	2317		2317
Praha hlavní .... a.						0927	1127						1327	1527				1727			1927	2127	2327		2327
Praha hlavní .... d.		0549	0650	0752	0852		0952	1052		1152	1252			1352	1452	1552	1652	1752	1852				2358	2358	2358
Pardubice .... d.		0647	0747	0849	0947		1049	1147		1249	1347			1449	1547	1649	1747	1849	1947				0108	0108	0108
Brno hlavní .... d.	0622	0823	0923	1023	1123		1223	1323		1423	1523	1624		1723	1823	1923	2028	2123					0315	0315	0315
Břeclav .... a.	0652	0852	0952	1052	1152		1252	1352		1452	1552	1653		1752	1852	1952	2057	2152					0347	0347	0347
Břeclav .... d.	0659	0859	0955	1059	1155		1259	1355	1459	1559	1559	1659		1755	1859	1955	2059	2155					0440	0440	0549
Wien Hbf .... a.			1049		1249			1449			1649			1849			2049			2249					0655
Wien Meidling ... a.			1102		1302			1502			1702			1902			2105								
Wiener Neustadt Hbf a.			1128		1328			1528			1730			1928			2128								
Graz Hbf .... a.			1333		1533			1733			1933			2133			2333								
Kúty .... d.	0713	0913		1113			1313			1513		1613	1713			1913		2113					0455	0455	
Bratislava hlavná ... d.	0753	0953		1153			1353			1553		1653	1753			1953		2150					0548	0548	
Štúrovo ✕△ .... d.	0911	1111		1311			1511			1711		1811	1911			2111							0710	0710	
Budapest Keleti ..... a.	1035	1235		1435			1635			1835		1935	2035			2235							0837	0837	

Table 2 — Budapest / Wien / Graz → Hamburg

	178	176	282	174	70	280	378	72	172	130	74	278	170	76	276	258	78	274	370	272	372	270	40406	476	476
train type/number	EC	EC	EC	EC	RJ	EC	EC	RJ	EC	EC	RJ	EC	EC	RJ	EC	EC	RJ	EC	RJ	EC	RJ	EC	EN	EN	EN 524
notes	✕	✕	✕	✕	✕	✕ G	✕	✕	✕ K	✕ V	✕	✕	✕	✕	✕ T	✕ P	®	✕	✕	✕	✕	✕	X	A	D
Budapest Keleti ..... d.				0525					0725	0822			0925		1125			1325		1525		1725		2005	2005
Štúrovo ✕△ .... d.				0649					0849	0949			1049		1249			1449		1649	1850			2124	2124
Bratislava hlavná ... d.			0610	0810					1010	1110			1210		1410			1610		1810		2010		2301	2301
Kúty .... d.			0649	0849					1049	1149			1249		1449			1649		1849	2049			2343	2343
Graz Hbf .... d.					0626			0826						1026			1226	1426		1626					
Wiener Neustadt Hbf d.					0832			1032			1032			1232			1432	1632		1832					
Wien Meidling ... d.					0858			1058			1058			1258			1458	1658		1858					
Wien Hbf .... d.				0709	0909			1109			1109			1309			1509	1709		1909	2250				
Břeclav .... a.		0701		0804	0901	1004		1101	1201	1301		1404	1501												
Břeclav .... d.		0707		0807	0907	1007		1107	1207	1307		1407	1507												
Brno hlavní .... a.		0738		0838	0938	1038	1138	1238	1338	1438	1538		1638	1738	1838	1938		2038	2136						
Pardubice .... d.		0910		1012	1110	1206	1212	1310	1412	1510		1612	1710	1812	1910	2012		2112	2218						0533
Praha hlavní .... a.		1006		1106	1206	1306	1406	1506	1606	1706	1806		1906	2006	2106	2209	2313						0345	0345	0639x
Praha hlavní .... d.	0628	0828		1028			1228	1428					1628		1828								0406	0406	
Praha Holešovice ... d.	0637	0837		1037			1237	1437					1637		1837								0415	0415	
Ústí nad Labem hlavní d.	0741	0941		1141			1341	1541					1741		1941								0522	0522	
Děčín .... d.	0800	1000		1200			1400	1600					1800		2000								0542	0542	
Bad Schandau ✕⊖.. a.	0815	1015		1215			1415	1615					1815		2015										
Dresden Hbf .... a.	0843	1044		1244			1444	1644					1844		2045								0626	0626	
Leipzig Hbf .... a.															2226										
Berlin Südkreuz ..... a.	1050	1250		1450			1650	1850					2050										0858	0858	
Berlin Hbf .... a.	1058	1258		1458			1658	1858					2058										0907	0907	
Hamburg Hbf .... a.		1511		1710			1911	2115																	
Hamburg Altona .... a.		1525		1724			2137																		

A – METROPOL – 🛏 1,2 cl., 🛋 2 cl., 🍴 Berlin - Praha - Budapest and v.v.

B – METROPOL – 🛏 1,2 cl., 🛏 2 cl. (4,6 berth), 🍴 Berlin (477) - Praha - Břeclav (407) - Wien.

C – 🛏 1,2 cl., 🛋 2 cl., 🍴 Praha - Pardubice - Břeclav - Budapest.

D – 🛏 1,2 cl., 🛋 2 cl., 🍴 Budapest (476) - Břeclav - Pardubice (524/898) - Praha.

G – PORTA BOHEMICA – 🍽 ✕ Praha - Berlin - Hamburg - Kiel (arrive 2018).

H – PORTA BOHEMICA – 🍽 ✕ Kiel (depart 0742) - Hamburg - Berlin - Praha.

J – HUNGARIA – 🍽 ✕ Hamburg - Berlin - Praha - Břeclav - Budapest. Conveys ②⑤ June 16 - Sept. 1: 🛏 1,2 cl., 🛋 2 cl. Praha (173) - Budapest (341) - Bar.

K – HUNGARIA – 🍽 ✕ Budapest - Břeclav - Praha - Berlin - Hamburg. Conveys ④⑦ June 18 - Sept. 3: 🛏 1,2 cl., 🛋 2 cl. Bar (340) - Budapest (172) - Praha.

P – ⑥ (not Dec. 25, Apr. 16): KOPERNIKUS – 🍽 ✕ Praha - Dresden - Leipzig.

Q – ①-⑥ (not Dec. 26, Apr. 17): KOPERNIKUS – 🍽 ✕ Leipzig - Dresden - Praha.

S – SLOVAN – 🍽 ✕ Praha - Břeclav - Budapest. Conveys on ②⑤ June 20 - Sept. 1: 🛏 1,2 cl. Praha - Budapest - Split.

T – SLOVAN – 🍽 ✕ Budapest - Břeclav - Praha. Conveys on ③⑥ June 21 - Sept. 2: 🛏 1,2 cl. Split - Budapest - Praha.

V – VARSOVIA – 🍽 ✕ Warszawa - Katowice - Břeclav - Budapest and v.v. (Table 99).

X – METROPOL – 🛏 1,2 cl., 🛏 2 cl. (4,6 berth), 🍴 Wien (406) - Břeclav (476) - Praha - Berlin.

x – 0703 on ⑥⑦ in train 898.

△ – Routeing point for international tickets: Szob.

⊖ – Routeing point for international tickets: Schöna.

RJ – ÖBB Railjet service. 🛋 (business class), 🛋 (first class), 🛋 (economy class), ✕.

OTHER TRAIN NAMES:

70/71 –	GUSTAV MAHLER
72/73 –	BEDŘICH SMETANA
74/75 –	FRANZ SCHUBERT
76/77 –	ANTONÍN DVOŘÁK
78/79 –	JOHANN STRAUSS
130/131 –	VARSOVIA
170/171 –	CARL MARIA VON WEBER
172/173 –	HUNGARIA
174/175 –	ROBERT SCHUMANN
176/177 –	JOHANNES BRAHMS
178/179 –	ALOIS NEGRELLI
270/271 –	PETROV
272/273 –	CSÁRDÁS
274/275 –	JAROSLAV HAŠEK
278/279 –	DANUBIUS
280/281 –	JÁN JESÉNIUS/JESZENSZKY JÁNOS
282/283 –	SLOVENSKÁ STRELA
370/371 –	JOSEPH HAYDN
372/373 –	W. A. MOZART

WIEN - BUDAPEST - BEOGRAD / BUCUREŞTI and İSTANBUL / THESSALONÍKI 61

Services to / from İstanbul are subject to alteration until further notice. Trains are replaced by 🚌 Çerkezköy - İstanbul and v.v.

train type	IC	IC		IC		EC				493		EN			463	461			EN		
train number	73	343	335	75		345	341	337	491	81031		473	1095	463	465	465	461		347		
notes	R	🍷		R		✕	R	≋	2			R		R	493	493	R		R		
	H	B	K	P		A	G	Y	D	C		R	J	XJ	R Z	R S	WT		E		
Wien Hbf d.	...	...	...	...	...	0839	...	...	...	...	...	...	...	...	...	...	...	...	1939	...	...
Budapest Kelenföld d.	...	...	...	...	...	1104	...	...	...	...	...	...	...	...	...	...	...	...	2204	...	...
Budapest Keleti d.	0710	0805	...	0910	...	1205	2225	...	...	...	...	1910	...	...	...	...	...	...	2250	...	...
Lökösháza a.	1010	|	...	1210	...	|	|	...	...	...	...	2210	...	...	...	...	...	...	0140	...	...
Curtici 🛃 a.	1200	|	...	1400	...	|	|	...	...	...	...	0001	...	...	...	...	...	...	0335	...	...
Arad a.	1244	|	...	1439	...	|	|	...	...	...	...	0039	...	...	...	...	...	...	0419	...	...
Timişoara a.	1333	|	...	|	...	|	|	...	...	...	...	|	...	...	...	...	...	...	|	...	...
Craiova a.	1940	|	...	|	...	|	|	...	...	...	...	|	...	...	...	...	...	...	|	...	...
Braşov a.	|	|	...	2310	...	|	|	...	...	...	...	0932	...	...	...	...	...	...	1316	...	...
Bucureşti Nord a.	2238	|	...	...	...	|	|	...	...	...	...	1210	...	...	...	...	...	...	1600	...	...
Bucureşti Nord d.	...	|	...	...	...	|	|	...	...	...	...	...	1245	...	...	1245	1245	...	...	...	...
Videle a.	...	|	...	...	...	|	|	...	...	...	...	...	1339	...	...	1339	1339	...	...	...	...
Giurgiu Nord 🛃 a.	...	|	...	...	...	|	|	...	...	...	...	...	1445	...	...	1445	1445	...	...	...	...
Giurgiu Nord 🛃 d.	...	|	...	...	...	|	|	...	...	...	...	...	1510	...	...	1510	1510	...	...	...	...
Ruse 🛃 a.	...	|	...	...	...	|	|	...	...	...	...	...	1535	...	...	1535	1535	...	...	...	...
Ruse 🛃 d.	...	|	...	...	...	|	|	...	...	...	...	...	...	1630	1630	1630	1630	...	...	...	...
Gorna Oryakhovitsa a.	...	|	...	...	...	|	|	...	...	...	...	...	...	1828	1828	1828	1828	...	...	...	...
Varna a.	...	|	...	...	...	|	|	...	...	...	...	...	...	|	|	|	|	...	...	...	...
Burgas a.	...	|	...	...	...	|	|	...	...	...	...	...	...	|	|	|	|	...	...	...	...
Subotica 🛃 a.	...	1155	...	...	...	1555	0154	...	...	...	...	...	...	...	|	|	|	|	...	...	...	...
Novi Sad a.	...	1454	...	...	...	1849	0445	...	...	...	...	...	...	...	|	|	|	|	...	...	...	...
Beograd a.	...	1622	1835	...	...	2015	0613	0735	0925	...	...	...	...	...	|	|	|	|	...	...	...	...
Niš a.	...	...	2302	...	...	...	...	1144	1342	...	...	...	...	...	|	|	|	|	...	...	...	...
Tabanovci 🛃 a.	...	...	0314	...	...	...	...	1602	|	...	...	...	...	...	|	|	|	|	...	...	...	...
Skopje a.	...	...	0420	...	...	...	...	1715	|	...	...	...	...	...	|	|	|	|	...	...	...	...
Idomeni 🛃 a.	...	..	0828	...	...	...	...	...	|	...	...	...	...	...	|	|	|	|	...	...	...	...
Dimitrovgrad (Serbia) 🛃 a.	...	...	|	...	...	...	...	...	1658	...	...	...	...	...	|	|	|	|	...	...	...	...
Kalotina Zapad 🛃 a.	...	...	|	...	...	...	...	...	1828	...	...	...	...	...	|	|	|	|	...	...	...	...
Pleven a.	...	...	|	...	...	...	...	...	|	...	...	...	...	...	1939	|	|	1939	...	...	...	...
Mezdra a.	...	...	|	...	...	...	...	...	|	...	...	...	...	...	2055	|	|	2055	...	...	...	...
Vidin 🛃 a.	...	...	|	...	...	...	...	...	|	...	...	...	...	...	|	|	|	|	...	...	...	...
Sofia a.	...	...	|	...	...	...	...	...	2010	...	...	...	...	...	2225	|	|	2225	...	...	...	...
Sofia d.	...	...	|	...	...	...	...	...	...	2040	...	...	...	...	...	|	|	...	...	...	...	...
Dimitrovgrad (Bulgaria) a.	...	...	|	...	...	...	...	...	...	2355	...	...	...	...	...	2315	2315	...	...	...	...	...
Svilengrad a.	...	...	|	...	...	...	...	...	...	0102	...	...	...	...	...	0102	0102	...	...	...	...	...
Kapikule 🛃 a.	...	...	|	...	...	...	...	...	...	0205	...	...	...	...	...	0205	0205	...	...	...	...	...
İstanbul Sirkeci a.	...	...	|	...	...	...	...	...	...	*0750**	...	...	...	...	...	*0750**	*0750**	...	...	...	...	...
Kulata 🛃 a.	...	...	|	...	...	...	...	...	...	...	...	...	...	...	...	...	...	...	...	...	...	...
Thessaloníki a.	...	...	1005	...	...	...	...	...	...	...	...	...	...	...	...	...	...	...	...	...	...	...

train type/number	EN			EN		492		492				81032				EC	IC		IC	IC	
train number	346		336	472		464	460	464	462	1094		492	490	340		344	74	334	342	72	
notes	R		≋	R		460	R	462	R				2	R		✕	R		🍷	R	
	E		Y	R		R F	WT	R V	XJ	J		C	D	G		A	P	L	B	H	
Thessaloníki d.	...	...	...	...	...	...	...	...	...	...	...	...	...	...	...	...	...	1830	...	...	...
Kulata 🛃 d.	...	...	...	...	...	...	...	...	...	...	...	...	...	...	...	...	...	|	...	...	...
İstanbul Sirkeci d.	...	...	...	...	...	*2200**	...	*2200**	...	...	...	*2200**	...	...	...	...	...	|	...	...	...
Kapikule 🛃 d.	...	...	...	...	...	0345	...	0345	...	...	...	0345	...	...	...	...	...	|	...	...	...
Svilengrad d.	...	...	...	...	...	0450	...	0450	...	...	...	0450	...	...	...	...	...	|	...	...	...
Dimitrovgrad (Bulgaria) d.	...	...	...	...	...	0650	...	0650	...	...	...	0550	...	...	...	...	...	|	...	...	...
Sofia a.	...	...	...	...	...	|	...	|	...	...	...	0910	...	...	...	...	...	|	...	...	...
Sofia d.	...	...	...	...	...	|	0900	|	0900	...	...	...	0940	...	...	...	...	|	...	...	...
Vidin 🛃 d.	...	...	...	...	...	|	|	|	|	...	...	...	|	...	...	...	...	|	...	...	...
Mezdra d.	...	...	...	...	...	|	1029	|	1029	...	...	...	|	...	...	...	...	|	...	...	...
Pleven d.	...	...	...	...	...	|	1148	|	1148	...	...	...	|	...	...	...	...	|	...	...	...
Kalotina Zapad 🛃 d.	...	...	...	...	...	|	|	|	|	...	...	...	1121	...	...	...	...	|	...	...	...
Dimitrovgrad (Serbia) 🛃 d.	...	...	...	...	...	|	|	|	|	...	...	...	1100	...	...	...	...	|	...	...	...
Idomeni 🛃 d.	...	...	...	...	...	|	|	|	|	...	...	...	|	...	...	...	...	2011	...	...	...
Skopje d.	...	...	0820	...	...	|	|	|	|	...	...	...	|	...	...	...	...	2219	...	...	...
Tabanovci 🛃 d.	...	...	0926	...	...	|	|	|	|	...	...	...	|	...	...	...	...	2329	...	...	...
Niš d.	...	...	1335	...	...	|	|	|	|	...	...	...	1408	...	...	...	...	0329	...	...	...
Beograd d.	...	...	1808	...	...	|	|	|	|	...	...	...	1814	2150	...	0736	...	0746	1135	...	...
Novi Sad d.	...	...	...	...	...	|	|	|	|	...	...	...	...	2318	...	0904	...	...	1301	...	...
Subotica 🛃 d.	...	...	...	...	...	|	|	|	|	...	...	...	...	0216	...	1202	...	...	1602	...	...
Burgas d.	...	...	...	...	...	|	|	|	|	...	...	...	...	|	...	|	...	...	|	...	...
Varna d.	...	...	...	...	...	|	|	|	|	...	...	...	...	|	...	|	...	...	|	...	...
Gorna Oryakhovitsa d.	...	...	...	...	...	1310	1310	1310	1310	...	...	...	...	|	...	|	...	...	|	...	...
Ruse 🛃 a.	...	...	...	...	...	1505	1505	1505	1505	...	...	...	...	|	...	|	...	...	|	...	...
Ruse 🛃 d.	...	...	...	...	...	1610	1610	...	...	1610	...	...	...	|	...	|	...	...	|	...	...
Giurgiu Nord 🛃 a.	...	...	...	...	...	1635	1635	...	...	1635	...	...	...	|	...	|	...	...	|	...	...
Giurgiu Nord 🛃 d.	...	...	...	...	...	1658	1658	...	...	1658	...	...	...	|	...	|	...	...	|	...	...
Videle d.	...	...	...	...	...	1806	1806	...	...	1806	...	...	...	|	...	|	...	...	|	...	...
Bucureşti Nord a.	...	...	...	...	...	1858	1858	...	...	1858	...	...	...	|	...	|	...	...	|	...	...
Bucureşti Nord d.	1400	...	...	1745	...	...	...	...	...	...	...	...	...	|	...	|	...	...	|	0545	...
Braşov d.	1637	...	...	2019	...	...	...	...	...	...	...	...	...	|	...	|	0545	...	|	|	...
Craiova d.	|	...	...	|	...	...	...	...	...	...	...	...	...	|	...	|	|	...	|	0855	...
Timişoara d.	|	...	...	|	...	...	...	...	...	...	...	...	...	|	...	|	|	...	|	1438	...
Arad d.	0116	...	...	0518	...	...	...	...	...	...	...	...	...	|	...	|	1415	...	|	1531	...
Curtici 🛃 d.	0200	...	...	0559	...	...	...	...	...	...	...	...	...	|	...	|	1459	...	|	1614	...
Lököshaza d.	0150	...	...	0549	...	...	...	...	...	...	...	...	...	|	...	|	1449	...	|	1549	...
Budapest Keleti a.	0450	...	...	0850	...	...	...	...	...	...	...	...	...	0546	...	1554	1750	...	1954	1850	...
Budapest Kelenföld a.	0554	...	...	...	...	...	...	...	...	...	...	...	...	...	...	1653	...	...	...	...	...
Wien Hbf a.	0821	...	...	...	...	...	...	...	...	...	...	...	...	...	...	1921	...	...	...	...	...

A – AVALA – (12) ✕ Wien - Budapest - Beograd and v.v.
B – IVO ANDRIC – (12) 🍷 Budapest - Beograd and v.v.
C – BALKAN EXPRESS – 🛏 2 cl. Sofia - İstanbul and v.v.
D – BALKAN – (2) Beograd - Sofia and v.v.
E – DACIA – 🛌 1, 2 cl., 🛏 2 cl., (2) ✕ Wien - Bucureşti and v.v.
F – June 2 - Oct. 2: BOSPHOR – 🛌 1, 2 cl., 🛏 2 cl. İstanbul (**492/82032**) - Dimitrovgrad (**464**) - Gorna Oryakhovitsa (**460**) - Ruse - Bucureşti. ✣.
G – BEOGRAD – 🛌 1, 2 cl., 🛏 2 cl., (12) Budapest - Beograd and v.v.
H – TRAIANUS – (12) Budapest - Bucureşti and v.v.
J – Dec. 11 - June 1, Oct. 3 - Dec. 9.
K – June 1 - Sept. 9 HELLAS EXPRESS – 🛌 1, 2 cl., 🛏 2 cl., (2) Beograd - Skopje - Thessaloníki.
L – June 2 - Sept. 10 HELLAS EXPRESS – 🛌 1, 2 cl., 🛏 2 cl., (2) Thessaloníki - Skopje - Beograd.
P – TRANSSYLVANIA / TRANSILVANIA – (12) Budapest - Braşov and v.v.
R – *EuroNight* ISTER – 🛌 1, 2 cl., 🛏 1, 2 cl., (2) ✕ Budapest - Bucureşti and v.v.
S – June 2 - Oct. 2: BOSPHOR – 🛌 1, 2 cl., 🛏 2 cl. Bucureşti (**461**) - Ruse - Gorna Oryakhovitsa (**465**) - Dimitrovgrad (**493/81031**) - İstanbul. ✣.
T – June 2 - Oct. 2.
V – Dec. 11 - June 1, Oct. 3 - Dec. 9: BOSPHOR – 🛌 1, 2 cl., 🛏 2 cl. İstanbul (**492/82032**) - Dimitrovgrad (**464**) - Gorna Oryakhovitsa (**462**) - Ruse. ✣.
W – (2) ROMANIA – Bucureşti - Ruse - Sofia and v.v.
X – (2) Ruse - Sofia and v.v.
Y – OLYMPUS – (2) Beograd - Skopje and v.v. ≋.
Z – Dec. 11 - June 1, Oct. 3 - Dec. 9: BOSPHOR – 🛌 1, 2 cl., 🛏 2 cl. Ruse (**463**) - Gorna Oryakhovitsa (**465**) - Dimitrovgrad (**493/81031**) - İstanbul. ✣.

≋ – Service suspended due to engineering work.
¶ – Train number for international bookings.
✗ – Supplement payable.
* – 🚌 Çerkezköy - İstanbul and v.v., see Table 1550.
✣ – The compostion of this train is subject to confirmation.

62   MÜNCHEN - LJUBLJANA - ZAGREB - BEOGRAD - THESSALONÍKI

train type / number	RJ	D	EC113	EC	D	D	D		EN	D	
train number	111	211	EC213	115	315	315	337	491	50463	415	335
notes	♀			♀			411 ☂				
		T	M	W			P	K	L	B	G
München Hbf.............d.	0818	...	...	1218	1417	...	...	...	...	2336	...	...
Salzburg Hbf ▥.........d.	1012	...	...	1412	1612	...	...	...	...	0134	...	...
Bischofshofen ....d.	1054	...	...	1454	1654	...	...	...	...		...	...
Schwarzach St Veit....d.	1111	...	...	1511	1711	...	...	...	...		0423	...
Bad Gastein..............d.	1142	...	...	1542	1742	...	...	...	...		0501	...
Villach Hbf...............d.	1243	1253	...	1653	1843	1853	1853	...	...	0415	0625	...
Jesenice ▥.............a.	...	1333	...	1733	...	1933	1933	...	...	0455	0705	...
Ljubljana ....a.	...	1431	...	1832	...	2040	2040	...	...	0559	0813	...
Dobova ▥...............a.	...	1621	...	2006	...	2242	2242	...	...	0806	0957	...
Zagreb ....a.	...	1713	...	2053	...	...	2336	...	...	0853	1043	...
Zagreb ....d.	...	1739	...	...	...	...	2352	...	...	...	1107	...
Vinkovci ....a.	...	2101	...	...	...	...	0313	...	...	...	1433	...
Šid ▥.....................a.	...	...	...	...	...	...	0345	...	...	...	1515	...
Beograd ....a.	...	...	...	...	...	...	0555	0735	0925	...	1737	1835
Niš ▥.....................a.	...	...	...	...	...	...	...	1144	1342	...	...	2302
Dimitrovgrad ▥........a.	...	...	...	...	...	...	...		1658	...	...	...
Kalotina Zapad ▥.....a.	...	...	...	...	...	...	...		1828	...	...	...
Sofia ....a.	...	...	...	...	...	...	...		2010	...	...	...
Tabanovci ▥............a.	...	...	...	...	...	...	...	1602	...	...	0314	...
Skopje ▥.................a.	...	...	...	...	...	...	...	1715	...	...	0420	...
Idoméni ▥...............a.	...	...	...	...	...	...	...	...	...	...	0828	...
Thessaloníki ....a.	...	...	...	...	...	...	...	...	...	...	1005	...

train type		D	EN			D	D	EC	EC212		D	RJ
train number	334	414	498	336	490	410	314	114	EC112	210	110
notes				☂		314		✕			
	H	C	L	K	A	Q		W	M	T	♀
Thessaloníki...............d.	...	1830	...	...	...	...	...	...	...	...	...
Idoméni ▥.................d.	...	2011	...	...	...	...	...	...	...	...	...
Skopje ▥...................d.	...	2219	...	0820	...	...	...	...	...	...	...
Tabanovci ▥..............d.	...	2329	...	0926	...	...	...	...	...	...	...
Sofia ....d.	...		...	...	0940	...	...	...	...	...	...
Kalotina Zapad ▥.......d.	...		...	...	1121	...	...	...	...	...	...
Dimitrovgrad ▥..........d.	...		...	...	1100	...	...	...	...	...	...
Niš ▥.......................d.	0329	...	...	1408	1408	...	...	...	...	...	...
Beograd ....d.	0746	1055	...	1814	1814	2120	...	...	...	...	...
Šid ▥.......................d.	...	1353	...	...	...	0025	...	...	...	...	...
Vinkovci ....d.	...	1442	...	...	...	0105	...	...	...	0901	...
Zagreb ....a.	...	1813	...	...	...	0425	...	...	...	1224	...
Zagreb ....d.	...	1837	2120	...	...	0437	...	...	0650	1235	...
Dobova ▥...................d.	...	1926	2207	...	...	0540	0540	...	0744	1338	...
Ljubljana ....d.	...	2110	2355	...	...	0728	0728	...	0923	1527	...
Jesenice ▥.................d.	...	2205	0050	...	...	0827	0827	...	1017	1627	...
Villach Hbf.................a.	...	2243	0131	...	...	0908	0908	0916	1058	1709	1716
Bad Gastein................a.	...	0024		...	...	...	...	1016	1216	...	1816
Schwarzach St Veit......a.	...	0057		...	...	...	...	1047	1247	...	1848
Bischofshofen ....a.	...	...		...	...	...	...	1103	1303	...	1903
Salzburg Hbf ▥...........a.	...	...	0409	...	...	...	...	1147	1347	...	1948
München Hbf..............a.	...	...	0610	...	...	...	...	1340	1541	...	2142

A –   BALKAN – ▭ Beograd - Sofia and v.v.
B –   ▭ Zürich (465) - Schwarzach St Veit (415) - Zagreb - Beograd. ▭ Villach - Beograd.
Conveys EN40465 ⊯ 1,2 cl., ▬ 2 cl. (4, 6 berth) Zürich - Zagreb. (Table 86).
C –   ▭ Beograd (414) - Zagreb - Schwarzach St Veit (464) - Zürich. ▭ Beograd - Villach.
Conveys EN414 ⊯ 1,2 cl., ▬ 2 cl. (4,6 berth) Zagreb - Zürich. (Table 86).
F –   ▭ Zürich (465) - Schwarzach St Veit (415) - Zagreb - Beograd and Beograd (414) -
Zagreb - Schwarzach St Veit (464) - Zürich. ▭ Villach - Beograd and v.v.
Conveys ⊯ 1,2 cl., ▬ 2 cl. Zürich - Zagreb and v.v. (Table 86).
G –   June 1 - Sept. 9 HELLAS EXPRESS – ⊯ 1,2 cl., ▬ 2 cl., ▭ Beograd - Skopje -
Thessaloníki.
H –   June 2 - Sept. 10 HELLAS EXPRESS – ⊯ 1,2 cl., ▬ 2 cl. ▭ Thessaloníki - Skopje -
Beograd.
K –   OLYMPUS – ▭ Beograd - Skopje and v.v. ☂.
L –   LISINSKI – ⊯ 1,2 cl., ▬ 2 cl. (4, 6 berth), ▭ München - Salzburg - Zagreb and v.v.

M –   ▭ Frankfurt - München - Zagreb and v.v. ✕ München - Villach and v.v.
P –   Dec. 22 - Jan. 14, June 24 - Sept. 10: ▭ Villach - Jesenice ▥ - Ljubljana -
Zagreb - Beograd.
Q –   Dec. 23 - Jan. 15, June 25 - Sept. 11: ▭ Beograd - Zagreb - Ljubljana -
Jesenice ▥ - Villach.
T –   SAVA – ▭ Villach - Jesenice ▥ - Ljubljana - Zagreb - Vinkovci and v.v.
W –   WÖRTHERSEE – ▭ ✕ Münster - Klagenfurt and Klagenfurt - Dortmund.

◫ –   Supplement payable: Jesenice ▥ - Zagreb - Beograd and v.v.
✗ –   Supplement payable.
☂ –   Service suspended due to engineering work.

64   HAMBURG and BERLIN - WIEN - BUDAPEST

For alternative services via Břeclav see Table **60**

train type	ICE	ICE	ICE	RJ	ICE	ICE	RJ	ICE	IC	ICE	EN	ICE	ICE	IC	ICE	ICE		EN	EC
train number	1003	783	23	65	1005	91	67	787	2355	27	347	1609	789	29	2301	881	229	491	345
	1583				1605														
notes	①–⑥	①–⑥	♀	♀	♀	♀	✕	♀	♀	♀	ℝ	♀	♀	♀	♀	♀	♀		♀
				C			C				D							A	J
Hamburg Hbf...............d.	...	0555	...	...	0803	...	1001	...	...	...	...	1201	...	...	1401	...	...	2029	...
Hannover Hbf................d.	...	0726	...	...	0926	...	1126	...	...	...	...	1326	...	...	1526	...	...	2157	...
Berlin Hbf....................d.	0432		...	0730		...		0930	...	1130	...	...	1330	...	...	...	...	...	...
Leipzig Hbf...................d.	0543		...	0848		...		1043	...	1248	...	...	1448	...	...	...	...	...	...
Nürnberg Hbf................d.	0928	1024	1029	1223	1230	...	1424	1425	1430	...	1623	1624	1629	1823	1824	1830	...	0307	...
Passau ▥.....................d.	...	...	1238	...	1438	...	...	...	1638	...	...	1838	...	...	2038	...	...	0524	...
Linz Hbf......................a.	...	...	1342	1414	1543	1614	...	...	1742	...	...	1942	...	...	2143	...	...	0633	...
Wien Hbf.....................a.	...	...	1508	1514	1708	1730	...	...	1908	1942	...	2108	...	...	2308	...	0819	0842	...
Budapest Keleti §...........a.	...	...	1819	...	2019	...	...	...	...	2220	...	...	...	...	...	...	...	1119	...

train type	ICE	ICE	ICE	EN	ICE	ICE	IC	RJ	ICE	ICE	ICE	RJ	ICE	ICE	RJ	ICE	ICE	EC	RJ	EN
train number	228	880	1610	346	28	788	2356	60	26	786	1006	62	90	1604	64	22	782	344	42	490
notes	♀	♀	♀	ℝ	♀	♀	♀	♀	♀	♀	704	♀	♀	♀	♀	♀	1182	⑤⑦	♀	
				D				C			C				C			J	J	B
Budapest Keleti §...........d.	...	...	...	0540	...	...	0740	...	...	...	0940	...	...	1140	...	...	...	1640	1740	...
Wien Hbf.....................d.	0652	...	...	0818	0852	...	1030	1052	...	...	1230	1252	...	1430	1452	...	...	1918	2018	2039
Linz Hbf......................d.	0816	...	...	1016	...	1146	1216	...	...	...	1346	1416	...	1546	1616	...	...	2146	2215	...
Passau ▥.....................a.	0917	...	...	1117	...	1317	...	...	...	...	1518	...	...	1717	...	...	...	...	2322	...
Nürnberg Hbf................a.	1125	1133	1134	...	1325	1333	1334	...	1525	1534	1534	...	1726	1736	...	1925	1934	1935	...	0127
Leipzig Hbf...................a.	...		1510	...	...	1710	...	...	...	1910	...	...	2110	...	...	...	2308	...	...	...
Berlin Hbf....................a.	...		1630	...	...	1830	...	...	...	2033	...	...	2230	...	...	...	0030	...	...	...
Hannover Hbf................a.	...	1432	...	...	1632	...	...	1832	...	...	2032	...	...	2240	...	...	...	...	0649	...
Hamburg Hbf................a.	...	1554	...	...	1753	...	...	1953	...	...	2153	...	...	...	...	...	2240	...	...	0836

A –   ÖBB nightjet ⊯ 1,2 cl., ▬ 2 cl. (4, 6 berth), ▭ Hamburg - Wien. Special fares apply. Conveys EN40491 ÖBB
nightjet ⊯ 1,2 cl., ▬ 2 cl. (4,6 berth), ▭ Hamburg (491) - Nürnberg (421) - München - Innsbruck.
B –   ÖBB nightjet ⊯ 1,2 cl., ▬ 2 cl. (4, 6 berth), ▭ Wien - Hamburg. Special fares apply. Conveys EN40420 ÖBB
nightjet ⊯ 1,2 cl., ▬ 2 cl. (4,6 berth), ▭ Innsbruck (420) - München - Nürnberg (490) - Hamburg.
C –   ÖBB Railjet service: München - Wien - Budapest and v.v.
D –   DACIA – ⊯ 1,2 cl., ▬ 2 cl., ✕ Wien - Bucuresti and v.v.
J –   AVALA – ▭ ♀ Wien - Budapest - Beograd and v.v.

§ –   ▥ is at Hegyeshalom.
RJ –   ÖBB Railjet service. ✕, ▭ (business class),
▭ (first class), ▭ (economy class).

For explanation of standard symbols see page 4

MÜNCHEN - SALZBURG - WIEN - BUDAPEST - BUCUREŞTI 65

train type	RJ	RJ	EC	RJ	RJ	RJ	RJ	RJ	RJ	EC	EC	RJ	EN	EC	EC	RJ	EC	RJ	EN	EC	RJ	EC	IC	EC	EN
train number	41	761	345	949	49	265	61	111	63	217	145	65	473	113	147	67	115	69	347	219	261	117 1217	1269	391	463
notes	✕	✕	🍷 K	✕ ⑦	✕	✕	✕	✕	✕ F	🍷	🍷	✕	🅁 Y	🍷	🍷 G	✕	🍷	✕	🅁 D	🍷	✕	🍷	Ⓑ	Ⓑ f	A
München Hbf d.	...	...	...	...	...	0624	0728	0818	0930	1018	...	1130	...	1218	...	1330	1418	1530	...	1617	1730	1818	1917	2017	2336
Salzburg Hbf 🛃 a.	...	...	...	...	...	0758	0858	0959	1058	1159	...	1258	...	1359	...	1458	1559	1658	...	1759	1858	1959	2100	2202	0118
						|	|	RJ	|	RJ		|		RJ		|	RJ	|		RJ	|	RJ	RJ	RJ	|
						|	|	765	|	161		|		563		|	165	|		167	|	169	663	361	|
						|	|	✕	|	✕		|		✕		|	✕	|		✕	|	✕	✕	✕	|
Salzburg Hbf 🛃 d.	...	0605	...	0708	0708r	0808	0908	1008	1108	1208	...	1308	...	1408	...	1508	1608	1708	...	1808	1908	2008	2108	2208	0350
Linz Hbf d.	...	0714	...	0814	0814r	0914	1014	1114	1214	1314	...	1414	...	1514	...	1614	1714	1814	...	1914	2014	2114	2214	2314	0510
St Pölten Hbf d.	...	0802	...	0902	0902r	1002	1102	1202	1302	1402	...	1502	...	1602	...	1702	1802	1902	...	2002	2102	2202	2302	0002	0602
Wien Meidling d.	...	0825	...	0925	0925r	1025	1125	1225	1325	1425	...	1525	...	1625	...	1725	1825	1925	...	2025	2125	2225	2325	0025	0630
Wien Hbf d.	0739	0830	0839	0930	0942	1030	1139	1230	1339	1430	1439	1542	...	1630	1639	1739	1842	1930	1939	2030	2130	2230	2330	0030	0639
Hegyeshalom 🛃 a.	0825	...	0925	...	1025	...	1225	...	1425	...	1525	1625	...	...	1725	1825	1925	...	2025	...	...	...	...	...	0725
Győr a.	0853	...	0953	...	1053	...	1253	...	1453	...	1553	1653	...	...	1753	1853	1953	...	2053	...	...	...	...	...	0753
Budapest Keleti a.	1019	...	1119	...	1219	...	1419	...	1619	...	1719	1819	1910	...	1919	2019	2119	...	2220	...	...	...	...	...	0924
Bucureşti Nord a.	...	...	...	...	...	...	...	...	...	...	...	...	1210	...	...	...	...	...	1600	...	...	...	...	...	...

train type	RJ	RJ	RJ	EN	RJ	RJ	RJ	EC	RJ	EN	RJ	RJ	RJ	RJ	RJ	RJ	RJ	EC	RJ	RJ	EC	EN	IC	EN	
train number	362	260	160	346	262	162	60	140	564	472	62	166	64	168	66 1066	760	68	344	762	42	148	466	72	462	
notes	✕ C	✕	✕	🅁 D	✕	✕	✕	🍷 J	✕	🅁 Y	✕	✕	✕	✕	✕ F	✕	✕	🍷 K	✕	✕	🍷	W	🅁 H	A	
Bucureşti Nord d.	...	...	...	1400	...	...	...	...	...	1745	...	...	...	...	...	...	...	...	...	...	...	...	0545	...	...
Budapest Keleti d.	...	...	...	0540	...	0640	0740	0840	...	0850	0940	...	1140	...	1340	...	1540	1640	...	1740	1840	...	1850	2040	...
Győr d.	...	...	...	0702	...	0802	0902	1002	...	...	1102	...	1302	...	1502	...	1702	1802	...	1902	2002	...	...	2202	...
Hegyeshalom 🛃 d.	...	...	...	0732	...	0832	0932	1032	...	...	1132	...	1332	...	1532	...	1732	1832	...	1932	2032	...	...	2232	...
Wien Hbf d.	0530	0630	0730	0821	0830	0930	1030	1121	1130	...	1230	1330	1430	1530	1630	1730	1830	1921	1930	2030	2121	2128	...	2325	...
Wien Meidling d.	0537	0637	0737	...	0837	0937	1037	...	1137	...	1237	1337	1437	1537	1637	1737	1837	...	1937	2037	...	2136	...	2333	...
St Pölten Hbf d.	0600	0700	0800	...	0900	1000	1100	...	1200	...	1300	1400	1500	1600	1700	1800	1900	...	2000	2100	...	2203	...	0000	...
Linz Hbf d.	0648	0748	0848	...	0948	1048	1148	...	1248	...	1348	1448	1548	1648	1748	1848	1948	...	2048	2148	...	2300	...	0105	...
Salzburg Hbf 🛃 a.	0752	0852	0952	...	1052	1152	1252	...	1352	...	1452	1552	1652	1752	1852	1952	2052	...	2152	2252	...	0022	...	0210	...
	EC	|	EC		|	EC	|		EC		|	EC	|	79042	|	RJ	|			79050				|	
	390	|	218		|	114	|		112		|	216	|	2	|	110	|			2				|	
Salzburg Hbf 🛃 d.	0800	0900	1000	...	1100	1200	1300	...	1400	...	1500	1600	1700	1815	1856	2000	2100	...	...	2300	...	...	...	0428	...
München Hbf a.	0941	1030	1141	...	1230	1341	1430	...	1541	...	1630	1741	1830	2006	2029	2142	2231	...	...	0057	...	...	...	0610	...

A – KÁLMÁN IMRE – 🛏 1, 2 cl., 🛌 2 cl. (4, 6 berth), [2] 🍷 München - Wien - Budapest and v.v.
C – ①–⑥ (not Dec. 26, Apr. 17, May 1, June 5).
D – DACIA – 🛏 1, 2 cl., 🛌 2 cl., [2] ✕ Wien - Budapest - Bucureşti and v.v.
F – From / to Frankfurt (Main) Hbf on dates shown in Table **930**.
G – [12] Wien - Budapest - Szolnok (arrive 2102) - Debrecen (2233).
H – TRAIANUS – [12] 🍷 Bucureşti - Budapest.
J – [12] Debrecen (depart 0527) - Szolnok (0657) - Budapest - Wien.
K – AVALA – [12] 🍷 Wien - Budapest - Beograd and v.v.

W – WIENER WALZER ÖBB *nightjet* 🛏 1, 2 cl., 🛌 2 cl. (4, 6 berth), [2] Zürich - Salzburg - Wien and v.v.
Y – *EuroNight* ISTER – 🛏 1, 2 cl., 🛌 1, 2 cl., [2] ✕ Budapest - Bucureşti and v.v.

f – Not Dec. 25.
r – ①–⑥ (not Dec. 26, Apr. 17, May 1, June 5, Aug. 14).

RJ – ÖBB *Railjet* service, ✕, [1] (business class), [1] (first class), [2] (economy class).

DORTMUND - KÖLN - FRANKFURT - WIEN - BUDAPEST 66

train type	ICE	RJ	ICE	ICE	ICE	RJ	ICE	EN	ICE	ICE	EN	EC
train number	21	63	23	1521	91	67	27	347	29	229	40421	345
notes	🍷	✕	🍷		🍷	✕	🍷	D 🅁	🍷	🍷	A	🍷
Dortmund Hbf d.	...	...	0437	0636	...	...	0838	...	...	...	...	...
Düsseldorf Hbf d.	...	...	0527	⊙	...	...	0927	...	...	...	2054	...
Köln Hbf d.	...	...	0553	0753	...	...	0953	...	...	...	2121	...
Bonn Hbf d.	...	...	0614	0814	...	...	1014	...	...	...	2143	...
Koblenz Hbf d.	...	...	0648	0848	...	...	1048	...	...	...	2217	...
Mainz Hbf d.	...	...	0739	0940	...	...	1140	...	...	...	2317	...
Frankfurt Flug. ✈ d.	...	...	0802	1002	...	...	1202	...	...	...	2353	...
Frankfurt (M) Hbf d.	0622	...	0819	1018	...	...	1221	...	1416	1621	0007f	...
Würzburg Hbf d.	0733	...	0933	1125	1135	...	1333	...	1533	1733	|	...
Nürnberg Hbf d.	0830	...	1030	▬	1230	...	1430	...	1630	1830	0307	...
Regensburg Hbf d.	0927	...	1127	RJ	1327	...	1527	...	1727	1927	0413	...
Passau Hbf 🛃 d.	1040	...	1240	**65**	1440	...	1640	...	1840	2040	0524	...
Linz a.	1143	...	1343	✕	1543	...	1743	...	1943	2143	0633	...
Wien Hbf a.	1309	1339	1509	1542	1709	1739	1909	1939	2109	2309	0820	0839
Hegyeshalom 🛃 a.	...	1425	...	1625	...	1825	...	2025	...	...	...	0925
Budapest Keleti a.	...	1619	...	1819	...	2019	...	2220	...	...	...	1119

train type	ICE	EN	ICE	RJ	ICE	RJ	ICE	RJ	ICE	RJ	ICE	EC	EN
train number	228	346	28	60	26	62	90	64	22	66	20	344	40490
notes	🍷	D 🅁	🍷	✕	🍷	✕	🍷	✕	🍷	✕	🍷	🍷	A
Budapest Keleti d.	...	0540	...	0740	...	0940	...	1140	...	1340	...	1640	...
Hegyeshalom 🛃 d.	...	0732	...	0932	...	1132	...	1332	...	1532	...	1832	...
Wien Hbf d.	0650	0821	0850	1021	1050	1221	1250	1421	1450	1618	1650	1921	2039
Linz d.	0817	...	1017	...	1217	...	1417	▬	1617	...	1817	...	2216
Passau Hbf 🛃 a.	0918	...	1118	...	1318	...	1518	ICE	1718	...	1918	...	2323
Regensburg Hbf a.	1027	...	1227	...	1427	...	1627	**1522**	1827	...	2027	...	0024
Nürnberg Hbf a.	1125	...	1325	...	1525	...	1725	🍷	1925	...	2125	...	0127
Würzburg Hbf a.	1224	...	1424	...	1624	...	1822	1829	2024	...	2224	...	|
Frankfurt (M) Hbf a.	1340	...	1536	...	1736	...	...	1936	2136	...	2339	...	0523f
Frankfurt Flug. ✈ a.	...	...	...	...	1757	...	...	1956	2157	...	...	...	0536
Mainz Hbf a.	...	...	...	...	1818	...	...	2018	2218	...	...	...	0602
Koblenz Hbf a.	...	...	...	...	1911	...	...	2111	2311	...	...	...	0705
Bonn Hbf a.	...	...	...	...	1942	...	...	2143	2342	...	...	...	|
Köln Hbf a.	...	...	...	...	2005	...	...	2205	0005	...	...	...	0815
Düsseldorf Hbf a.	...	...	...	...	⊙	...	...	⊙	0032	...	...	...	0841
Dortmund Hbf a.	...	...	...	...	2120	...	...	2322	0121	...	...	...	...

A – ÖBB *nightjet* 🛏 1, 2 cl., 🛌 2 cl. (4, 6 berth), [2] Düsseldorf - Köln - Frankfurt - Nürnberg - Wien and v.v. Special fares apply.
D – DACIA – 🛏 1, 2 cl., 🛌 2 cl., [2] ✕ Wien - Budapest - Bucureşti and v.v.

f – Frankfurt (Main) **Süd**.

⊙ – Via Hagen, Wuppertal (Table **800**).
RJ – ÖBB *RailJet* service. [1] (business class), [1] (first class), [2] (economy class), ✕.

DORTMUND - KÖLN - MÜNCHEN - GRAZ and KLAGENFURT 68

train type / number	RJ	EC	EC	IC	EC	EC	EC	D	EC	EC	EN
train number	111	211	217	690	113	113 213	115	315	219	117 1217	50463
notes	🍷	H	✕ Y	🍷	✕	A	✕ W		🍷	✕	L
Dortmund Hbf d.	...	...	...	...	...	...	...	...	...	...	...
Münster Hbf d.	...	...	...	...	...	...	0631	...	...	...	...
Köln Hbf d.	...	...	...	...	...	...	0818	...	...	...	...
Frankfurt (Main) Hbf d.	...	...	...	...	0822	0822	|	...	1220	1420t	...
Saarbrücken d.	...	...	0528	...	|	|	|	...	|	|	...
Mannheim d.	...	...	0712	...	|	|	1101	...	|	|	...
Heidelberg d.	...	...	|	...	0913	0913	|	...	1314	1514t	...
Stuttgart Hbf d.	...	...	0758	...	0958	0958	1157	...	1358	1557	...
Ulm d.	...	...	0856	...	1054	1054	1255	...	1456	1655	...
Augsburg d.	...	...	0942	...	1142	1142	1342	...	1542	1741	...
München Hbf d.	0818	...	1018	...	1218	1218	1417	...	1617	1818	2336
Salzburg 🛃 a.	0959	...	1159	1212	1359	1359	1558	...	1759	1958	0119
Bischofshofen a.	1052	...	1302	1252	1452	1452	1652	...	1902	2052	|
Selzthal a.	|	...	1439	|	|	|	|	...	2039	|	|
Graz a.	|	...	1614	|	|	|	|	...	2214	|	|
Schwarzach St Veit a.	1109	...	...	1309	1509	1509	1709	...	...	2109	|
Villach Hbf a.	1243	1253	...	1443	1643	1643	1843	1853	...	2243	0351
Klagenfurt a.	1316	|	...	...	1715	|	1915	|	...	2315	|
Ljubljana a.	...	1431	...	...	...	1831	...	2040	...	...	0559

train type / number	IC	EC	D	EC	EC	EC	EC	EC	RJ	EN	
train number	693	218	314	114	112	212 112	216	210	110	498	
notes	🍷	🍷		✕ W	🍷	A	✕ Y	H	🍷	L	
Ljubljana d.	...	...	0726	...	...	0922	...	1525	...	2355	...
Klagenfurt d.	0645	...	|	0842	1027	|	...	|	1642	|	...
Villach Hbf d.	0716	...	0907	0916	1116	1116	...	1707	1716	0146	...
Schwarzach St Veit d.	0850	...	...	1049	1249	1249	...	...	1850	|	...
Graz d.	|	0545	...	|	|	|	1145	...	|	|	...
Selzthal d.	|	0719	...	|	|	|	1319	...	|	|	...
Bischofshofen d.	0905	0857	...	1105	1305	1305	1457	...	1905	|	...
Salzburg 🛃 d.	0948	1000	...	1200	1400	1400	1600	...	2000	0427	...
München Hbf a.	...	1141	...	1340	1541	1541	1741	...	2142	0610	...
Augsburg a.	...	1214	...	1415	1615	1615	1815	...	...	...	...
Ulm a.	...	1302	...	1502	1701	1701	1901	...	...	...	...
Stuttgart Hbf a.	...	1401	...	1600	1800	1800	2000	...	...	...	...
Heidelberg a.	...	1444	...	|	1843	1843	|	...	...	...	...
Mannheim a.	...	|	...	1657	|	|	2047	...	...	...	...
Saarbrücken a.	...	|	...	|	|	|	2219	...	...	...	...
Frankfurt (Main) Hbf a.	...	1540	...	|	1940	1940	...	...	...	...	...
Köln Hbf a.	...	...	...	1942	...	...	...	...	...	...	...
Münster Hbf a.	...	...	...	|	...	...	...	...	...	...	...
Dortmund Hbf a.	...	...	...	2100	...	...	...	...	...	...	...

A – [12] 🍷 Frankfurt - Stuttgart - München - Villach - Ljubljana - Zagreb and v.v.
H – SAVA – [2] Villach - Jesenice 🛃 - Ljubljana - Zagreb - Vinkovci and v.v. ✕ Jesenice 🛃 - Zagreb and v.v.
L – LISINSKI – 🛏 1, 2 cl., 🛌 2 cl. (4, 6 berth), [2] München - Ljubljana - Zagreb and v.v.
W – WÖRTHERSEE – [12] ✕ Münster - Klagenfurt and Klagenfurt - Dortmund.

Y – [12] ✕ Saarbrücken - Mannheim - Graz and v.v.

t – Not ⑥.

Table 70 — Part 1

	ICE 823 ①–⑤	EC 1289 ✗♥ ⑥⑦	EC 81 ✗♥ ①–⑤	EC 37 ✗	FB 9732 Ⓡ	ICE 521	ICE 699 ⊗	EC 85 ♥ RJ 63 R	FB 8718 Ⓡ	FR 9439/9441 ✓ 2	IC 2021	ICE 1125 ⑦	ICE 525 ①–⑥	ICE 2265	EC 87 ✗	FA 42 Ⓡ✓	8525 Ⓡ	ICE 513	ICE 529	EC 89 ✗ ⊗	2107 2	FB 9758 Ⓡ♥
Dortmund Hbf d.											0144	0514	0524					0637	0724			
Bochum Hbf d.											0155	0526	0538					0649	0738			
Essen Hbf d.											0206	0538	0553					0700	0754			
Duisburg Hbf d.											0219	0550	0607					0712	0808			
Düsseldorf Hbf d.											0239	0605	0621					0727	0822			
Köln Messe/Deutz d.												0628	0644						0844			
Köln Hbf d.				0418							0353							0755				
Bonn Hbf d.											0416											
Koblenz Hbf d.				⊖							0531											
Mainz Hbf d.											0628											
Frankfurt Flughafen ✈ d.				0534							0648	0736	0735					0853	0935			
Frankfurt (Main) Hbf d.				0551							0702	0754	0754						0954			
Mannheim Hbf d.																		0931				
Heidelberg Hbf d.																						
Nürnberg Hbf d.	0558			0802							1002	1002							1202			
Stuttgart Hbf d.						0656								0853				1013				
Ulm Hbf d.						0756								0956				1109				
Augsburg Hbf d.						0842								1039				1155				
München Hbf d.	0703	0734	0734		0904	0913	0934					1104	1104	1111	1134			1227	1304			1334
München Ost ▲ d.		0744	0744												1144				1344			
Kufstein 🚃 a.		0834	0834				1034								1234							1436
Wörgl a.		0844	0844				1044								1244							1446
Jenbach a.		0859	0859				1059								1259							1459
Innsbruck Hbf a.		0918	0918				1118								1318							1518
Innsbruck Hbf d.		0924	0924				1124								1324							1524
Brennero/Brenner 🚃 a.		1000	1000				1200								1400							1600
Bolzano/Bozen a.		1115	1127				1327								1527							1727
Trento a.		1148	1202				1402								1602							1802
Verona a.		1237	1256	1402	1330		1458		1521	1532					1658	1732	1752			1858	1921	2002
Padova a.		1326		1412					1636						1742						2036	
Venezia Santa Lucia a.		1356		1440					1648						1810						2048	
Milano Centrale a.					1515					1655							1855					2115
Bologna Centrale a.			1407					1620		1653						1840				2020		
Firenze SMN a.										1730						1925¶						
Roma Termini a.										1910						2045						
Napoli Centrale a.										2035												

Table 70 — Part 2

	IC 119 K	EC 115 ✗ Q	ICE 515	ICE 623	IC 2261	EC 83 ✗	FB 9759 Ⓡ	ICE 517 ♥	ICE 627	EC 287 ✗	ICE 721 ♥	EC 289 ✗	ICE 599	EN 295 B	EN 40295 D	ICE 729	EN 40463 C	EN 421 A
Dortmund Hbf d.			0837					1037			1325							
Bochum Hbf d.								1049			1338							
Essen Hbf d.	0823		0941					1100		1153	1353					1754		
Duisburg Hbf d.	0838	0734	0955					1112		1207	1407					1808		
Düsseldorf Hbf d.	0852	0751	1012					1127		1221	1421					1822		2054
Köln Messe/Deutz d.				1033						1244	1444					1844		
Köln Hbf d.	0918	0818	0955					1155										2121
Bonn Hbf d.	0937	0837																2143
Koblenz Hbf d.	1017	0917								⊖								2217
Mainz Hbf d.	1112	1017																2317
Frankfurt Flughafen ✈ d.			1053	1135				1253	1332		1535					1935		2353
Frankfurt (Main) Hbf d.				1154					1354			1550				1954		0007k
Mannheim Hbf d.	1154	1102	1131					1331			1554	1630						
Heidelberg Hbf d.	1206																	
Nürnberg Hbf d.				1406						1602	1802					2202		0342
Stuttgart Hbf d.	1257	1158	1213		1253			1413					1712					
Ulm Hbf d.	1411	1256	1309		1356			1509					1809					
Augsburg Hbf d.		1342	1355		1440			1555					1855					
München Hbf d.		1411	1427	1508	1512	1534		1627	1704	1734	1907	1934	1927	2010	2010	2307	2336	0717
München Ost ▲ d.						1544				1744		1944		2020	2020		2346	
Kufstein 🚃 d.						1636				1836		2036						0825
Wörgl d.						1644				1846		2046						0836
Jenbach a.						1659				1859		2059						0853
Innsbruck Hbf a.	1901					1718				1918		2118						0914
Innsbruck Hbf d.						1724												
Brennero/Brenner 🚃 a.						1800								▯	▯		▯	
Bolzano/Bozen a.						1927												
Trento a.						2002												
Verona a.						2056	2130							0635x	0539x			
Padova a.						2212											0824	
Venezia Santa Lucia a.						2240									0910			
Milano Centrale a.																		
Bologna Centrale a.														0506				
Firenze SMN a.														0607				
Roma Termini a.														0922				
Napoli Centrale a.																		

A – ÖBB *nightjet* 🛏 1, 2 cl., ⇌ 2 cl. (4, 6 berth), 🚗 Düsseldorf - Köln - Frankfurt - München - Innsbruck and v.v. Special fares apply.

B – ÖBB *nightjet* 🛏 1, 2 cl., ⇌ 2 cl. (4, 6 berth), 🚗 München - Villach - Tarvisio 🚃 - Roma. Special fares apply.

C – ÖBB *nightjet* 🛏 1, 2 cl., ⇌ 2 cl. (4, 6 berth), 🚗 München (463) - Villach (237) - Tarvisio 🚃 - Venezia. Special fares apply.

D – ÖBB *nightjet* 🛏 1, 2 cl., ⇌ 2 cl. (4, 6 berth), 🚗 München (295) - Villach (235) - Tarvisio 🚃 - Verona - Milano. Special fares apply.

K – 🚗 ♈ Munster - Köln - Stuttgart - Lindau 🚃 - Innsbruck and v.v.

Q – WÖRTHERSEE – 🚗 ✗ Münster - München - Klagenfurt.

R – On ⑤⑥ June 2 - Sept. 9 to Rimini, arrive 1729.

k – Frankfurt (Main) Süd.

x – Calls at Padova before Verona.

▯ – 🚃 is Tarvisio (Table 88).

⊗ – Compulsory reservation for international journeys. Supplement payable for international journeys and for internal journeys within Italy.

⊖ – Via Köln - Frankfurt high speed line.

¶ – Firenze **Campo di Marte**.

✓ – Supplement payable.

▲ – Change here for München Airport (Table 892).

♥ – DB-ÖBB EuroCity service.

Table 70 — Part 1

	EC 288	ICE 610	ICE 722	IC 118	EC 286	ICE 626	ICE 516	FB 8706	FB 9705	EC 88	ICE 622	ICE 514	FR 8502	FB 9712	FB 8709	EC 80	ICE 528	ICE 512	FB 9715	FB 9717	FB 9724	FR 9518	EC 84	ICE 524	ICE 510
notes	×		1122	K	♥			R	R	♥			R	R	R	×♥			R	R⑥⑦	R	R	×♥ R		1010/1110
Napoli Centrale d.																									
Roma Termini d.													0645									0800	0920		
Firenze SMN d.													0803c										1100		
Bologna Centrale d.										0752			0845										1135	1152	
Milano Centrale d.						0715								0905							0945	1015			
Venezia Santa Lucia d.								0720					0820										1050		
Padova d.								0748					0848									1118			
Verona d.								0830	0828	0904			0947	0930	1028	1102				1058	1128	1200		1304	
Trento d.										0959			1041			1159								1359	
Bolzano / Bozen d.										1034			1114			1234								1434	
Brennero / Brenner d.										1200						1400								1602	
Innsbruck Hbf a.										1236						1436								1636	
Innsbruck Hbf d.	0717			0901	1040					1240						1440								1640	
Jenbach d.	0735				1101					1301						1501								1701	
Wörgl a.	0749				1116					1316						1516								1716	
Kufstein a.	0757				1124					1324						1524								1726	
München Ost ▲ a.	0849				1215					1415						1615								1816	
München Hbf a.	0901	0928	0955	1226	1255	1328				1426	1455	1528				1625	1652	1727					1827	1855	1928
Augsburg Hbf a.		1000				1400						1600					1800								2000
Ulm Hbf a.		1047	1345			1447						1647					1847								2047
Stuttgart Hbf a.		1145	1458			1546						1746					1946								2146
Nürnberg Hbf a.			1057	1357							1557							1757						1957	
Heidelberg Hbf a.			1553																						
Mannheim Hbf a.		1228	1606								1628	1828					2028								2229
Frankfurt (Main) Hbf a.		1304		1604												1804	2004							2204	
Frankfurt Flughafen ✈ a.		1306	1322							1622	1706	1906				1822	2022	2106						2222	2308
Mainz Hbf a.			1646																						
Koblenz Hbf a.		⊖	1741							⊖														⊖	
Bonn Hbf a.			1820																						
Köln Hbf a.		1405	1842							1805		2005												2205	
Köln Messe/Deutz a.	1414			1714												1914	2114							2339	
Düsseldorf Hbf a.	1431	1436	1907	1736						1831		2031				1944	2136	2231						2400	
Duisburg Hbf a.	1444	1449	1922	1749						1844		2044				1957	2149	2244						0013	
Essen Hbf a.	1457	1505	1934	1802						1857		2057				2015	2202	2257						0026	
Bochum Hbf a.	1508									1908		2108				2027	2214							0036	
Dortmund Hbf a.	1521									1921		2121				2042	2230							0049	

Table 70 — Part 2

	FA 8512	FB 8717	EC 86	ICE 990	ICE 520	FB 8721	FB 8720	EC 82	EC 1288	EC 420	EN 40236	ICE 728	ICE 612	EN 294	EN 40235	ICE 724	ICE 610
notes	R✂	R✂	×	1590	1620 / 922	R✂	R✂	×♥ ①-⑤	×♥ ⑥⑦	A	C			B	D		
Napoli Centrale d.																	
Roma Termini d.	1045													1904			
Firenze SMN d.	1203c													2214			
Bologna Centrale d.	1245				1410			1552						2310			
Milano Centrale d.		1305				1505									2040		
Padova d.															2344x		
Venezia Santa Lucia d.			1350				1520		1550		2057						
Verona d.	1337	1428	1502			1538	1628	1630	1702	1702					2252x		
Trento d.			1559						1759	1759							
Bolzano / Bozen d.			1634						1834	1834							
Brennero / Brenner d.			1800						2000	2000	▯			▯	▯		
Innsbruck Hbf a.			1836						2036	2036							
Innsbruck Hbf d.			1840						2040	2040	2044						
Jenbach d.			1901						2101	2101	2106						
Wörgl a.			1916						2116	2116	2123						
Kufstein a.			1924						2124	2124	2135d						
München Ost ▲ a.			2014						2216	2216							
München Hbf a.			2025	2044	2055			2227	2227	2238	0610	0652	0727	0819	0819	0852	0928
Augsburg Hbf a.			2115							2327		0800					1000
Ulm Hbf a.			2202									0847					1047
Stuttgart Hbf a.			2259									0945					1145
Nürnberg Hbf a.				2201							0116		0757			0957	
Heidelberg Hbf a.																	
Mannheim Hbf a.			2345										1028			1228	
Frankfurt (Main) Hbf a.			0042r	0004						0523k		1004				1204	
Frankfurt Flughafen ✈ a.			0023r							0536		1022	1106			1222	
Mainz Hbf a.										0602							
Koblenz Hbf a.										0705		⊖				⊖	
Bonn Hbf a.																	
Köln Hbf a.										0815						1205	
Köln Messe/Deutz a.											1114					1324	
Düsseldorf Hbf a.										0841	1136	1231				1346	
Duisburg Hbf a.											1149	1244				1400	
Essen Hbf a.											1202	1257				1414	
Bochum Hbf a.											1214					1427	
Dortmund Hbf a.											1230					1442	

A – ÖBB nightjet 1, 2 cl., 2 cl. (4, 6 berth), Innsbruck - München - Frankfurt - Köln - Düsseldorf. Special fares apply.

B – ÖBB nightjet 1, 2 cl., 2 cl. (4, 6 berth), Roma - Tarvisio ▯ - Villach - München. Special fares apply.

C – ÖBB nightjet 1, 2 cl., 2 cl. (4, 6 berth), Venezia (236) - Tarvisio ▯ - Villach (498) - München. Special fares apply.

D – ÖBB nightjet 1, 2 cl., 2 cl. (4, 6 berth), Milano (235) - Verona - Tarvisio ▯ - Villach (294) - München. Special fares apply.

K – ☕ Innsbruck - Lindau ▯ - Stuttgart - Köln - Munster.

R – On ⑥⑦ June 3 - Sept. 10 from Rimini, depart 1035.

c – Firenze **Campo di Marte.**

d – Departure time.

k – Frankfurt (Main) **Süd.**

r – Train stops at Frankfurt Flughafen before Frankfurt (Main).

x – Train stops at Verona before Padova.

▯ – ▯ is Tarvisio (Table 88).

⊖ – Via Köln - Frankfurt high speed line.

✂ – Supplement payable.

▲ – Change here for München Airport (Table 892).

♥ – DB-ÖBB EuroCity service.

73 — AMSTERDAM, BERLIN, DORTMUND and KÖLN - BASEL - ZÜRICH and MILANO

train type	ICE	EC	ICE	ICE	IR	EC	ICE	ICE	EC	ICE	EC	ICE	ICE	ICE	IR	EC	ICE	ICE	EC	ICE	EC	EC
train number	3	15	271	5	2319	17	101	275	57	71	7	121	515	277	2327	21	105	73	9	279	9	23
notes		⊗	①-⑥	M		⊗			⊗	B/1271	①-⑥	y				⊗		✕ D/1173	✕ D			[R] ⊗
Hamburg Hbf .... d.	...	...	0045e	...	...	...	...	...	...	0618	0442v	...	...	...	...	...	0824	0646	...	...	...	...
Bremen Hbf .... d.											0540v							0744				
Berlin Hbf .... d.								0432p												0830		
Hannover Hbf .... d.			0210e							0741							0941					
Dortmund Hbf .... d.							0537			0737	0837							0937				
Essen Hbf .... d.										0800								1000				
Amsterdam Centraal .... d.												0637					0802					
Utrecht Centraal .... d.												0704					0830					
Arnhem ⊙ .... d.												0737					0908					
Duisburg Hbf .... d.											0813	0834	h				1008	1013				
Düsseldorf Hbf .... d.											0827	0848					1022	1027				
Köln Hbf .... d.								0654			0853	0927	0955				1055	1053				
Bonn Hbf .... d.												0914					1114					
Koblenz Hbf .... d.												0948 ⊖					1148 ⊖					
Mainz Hbf .... d.												1040					1240					
Frankfurt Flughafen ✈ .... d.						0751						1018	1052				1151					
Frankfurt (Main) Hbf .... d.			0550	0650			0850			1005	1030	1050					1205		1250			
Mannheim Hbf .... d.			0633	0736			0836	0936		1045	1123		1123	1136			1236	1245	1323	1336		
Karlsruhe Hbf .... d.	0555p		0658	0800			0900	1000		1110	1149			1200			1300	1310	1349	1400		
Freiburg (Brsg) Hbf .... d.	0702p		0802	0901			1007	1101		1212	1251			1306			1401	1412	1455	1501		
Basel Bad Bf 🚻 .... a.	0735p		0834	0934			1038	1134		1245	1322			1338			1434	1445	1527	1534	←	
Basel SBB .... a.	0747p		0847	0947			1047	1147		1254	1330			1347			1447	1454	1535	1547	1535	
Basel SBB ★ .... d.	0807		0907	1004				1159	1241	1307	1359						1507	1607			1607	
Bern .... a.								1256		1324				1456					→			
Interlaken Ost .... a.								1357			1557											
Zürich HB .... a.	0900	0909	1000			1109				1400	1522					1509	1600		1700		1709	
Chur .... a.				1122																		
Arth-Goldau .... a.		0946			1144	1146x									1544	1546x						1746
Bellinzona .... a.		1048				1248									1648							1848
Lugano .... a.		1117				1317									1717							1917
Chiasso 🚻 .... a.		1146				1346			◫						1746							1946
Como San Giovanni .... a.						1356																
Milano Centrale .... a.		1235				1435			1637						1835							2035

train type	ICE	ICE	EC	EC	ICE	ICE	ICE	ICE	ICE	ICE	ICE	EN	IR	EC
train number	107	75	59	25	123	371	109	77	125	373	79	471	2315	15
notes		1175	[R]	[R]				1277			1279	A		[R] ⊗
Hamburg Hbf .... d.		1024					1224				1424	2052		
Bremen Hbf .... d.														
Berlin Hbf .... d.						1034			1230			2302		
Hannover Hbf .... d.		1141					1341			1541				
Dortmund Hbf .... d.						1337c								
Essen Hbf .... d.														
Amsterdam Centraal .... d.					1037				1237					
Utrecht Centraal .... d.					1104				1304					
Arnhem ⊙ .... d.					1137				1337					
Duisburg Hbf .... d.					1234		h		1438					
Düsseldorf Hbf .... d.					1248				1454					
Köln Hbf .... d.	1255				1328		1455		1529					
Bonn Hbf .... d.														
Koblenz Hbf .... d.	⊖			⊖		⊖		⊖						
Mainz Hbf .... d.	1351				1418		1551		1618					
Frankfurt (Main) Hbf .... d.		1405			1430	1450		1605	1630	1650	1805	0402z		
Mannheim Hbf .... d.	1434	1445			1536	1636	1645	1736	1845			0442		
Karlsruhe Hbf .... d.	1458	1510			1600	1700	1710	1800	1910			0510		
Freiburg (Brsg) Hbf .... a.	1601	1612			1701	1801	1812	1901	2012			0620		
Basel Bad Bf 🚻 .... a.	1634	1645			1734	1834	1845	1934	2045			0706		
Basel SBB .... a.	1647	1654			1747	1847	1854	1947	2054			0720		
Basel SBB ★ .... d.		1707	1731		1759			1907		1959	2107		0804	
Bern .... a.			1824		1856					2056				
Interlaken Ost .... a.					1957					2157				
Baden .... a.														
Zürich HB .... a.		1800	1909				2000				2200		0905	
Chur .... a.		1922												
Arth-Goldau .... a.			1946									0944	0950	
Bellinzona .... a.			2048										1048	
Lugano .... a.			2117										1117	
Chiasso 🚻 .... a.			◫ 2146										1146	
Como San Giovanni .... a.			2156											
Milano Centrale .... a.			2137	2235									1235	

A – ÖBB nightjet 🛏 1,2 cl., 🛏 2 cl. (4,6 berth), 🍴 Hamburg - Berlin - Frankfurt - Zürich. Special fares apply.

B – 🍴 ✕ (Hamburg ①–⑥, not Dec. 26) - Dortmund - Köln - Basel - Interlaken Ost.

D – 🍴 ✕ Hamburg - Dortmund - Köln - Basel - Zürich.

M – 🍴 🍽 (Hamburg ①, also Dec. 27; not Dec. 26) - (Frankfurt ①–⑥, not Dec. 26) - Basel - Chur.

c – Not ⑥.

e – ① (also Dec. 27; not Dec. 26).

h – Via Hagen and Wuppertal.

p – ①–⑤ (not Dec. 26).

v – ①–⑥ (not Dec. 26).

x – depart 4 minutes later.

y – Not Dec. 26.

z – Frankfurt (Main) Süd.

⊖ – 🚃 is at Emmerich.

◫ – Via Brig. 🚃 is at Domodossola; ticket point is Iselle.

⊖ – Via Köln - Frankfurt high speed line.

★ – Connections at Basel are not guaranteed.

⊗ – Compulsory reservation for international journeys. Supplement payable for international journeys and for internal journeys within Italy.

CONNECTING SERVICES

Basel - Luzern - Chiasso : Table 550,   Basel - Bern - Interlaken and Brig : Table 560.

Zürich - Landquart - Chur : Table 520,   Chur - St Moritz : Table 540,   Zürich - Bellinzona - Chiasso : Table 550.

	ICE 78	ICE 372	ICE 126	ICE 76	ICE 370	ICE 124	ICE 74	EC 12	EC 8	EC 50	ICE 278	EC 8	ICE 72	ICE 122	ICE 276	EC 6	EC 14	ICE 70	ICE 104
notes	1278			1276			1274		⊗	⊗		⊗	1272		G	⊗		1270	
Milano Centrale d.							0725		0723									0925	
Como San Giovanni d.																		1003	
Chiasso d.							0815		▢									1015	
Lugano d.							0842											1042	
Bellinzona d.							0911											1111	
Arth-Goldau d.							1013											1214	
Chur d.													1039						1239
Zürich HB d.	0600			0800				1000	1051	1100			1200					1251	1400
Interlaken Ost d.		0600									1000				1200				
Bern d.		0704								1036	1104	←			1304				
Basel SBB ★ a.	0653	0759		0853			1053	1153	1129	1159	1153		1253		1359			1453	
Basel SBB d.	0706	0813		0906	1013		1106			1220	1213	1220	1306		1413	1427		1506	1513
Basel Bad Bf d.	0715	0823		0915	1023		1115		→		1223	1230	1315		1423	1435		1515	1523
Freiburg (Brsg) Hbf d.	0749	0857		0949	1057		1149				1257	1304	1349		1455	1507		1549	1557
Karlsruhe Hbf d.	0851	1000		1051	1200		1251				1400	1412	1451		1601	1612		1651	1700
Mannheim Hbf a.	0914	1023		1114	1224		1314				1423	1437	1514		1624	1637		1714	1723
Frankfurt (Main) Hbf a.	0953	1108	1129	1153	1308	1329	1353				1508		1553	1629	1708			1753	
Frankfurt Flughafen ✈ a.			1140			1340								1640					1806
Mainz Hbf a.											1518				1718				
Koblenz Hbf a.			⊖			⊖					1611		⊖		1811				
Bonn Hbf a.											1644				1844				
Köln Hbf a.			1232			1433					1705			1739	1905				1905
Düsseldorf Hbf a.			1305			1511					1731			1812	1931				1936
Duisburg Hbf a.			1322			1526					1744			1825	1944				1949
Arnhem ⊙ a.			1428			1628								1928					2058
Utrecht Centraal a.			1500			1700								2000					2130
Amsterdam Centraal a.			1528			1728								2026					2156
Essen Hbf a.											1757				1957				
Dortmund Hbf a.											1821				2021				
Hannover Hbf a.	1217			1417			1617						1817					2017	
Berlin Hbf a.		1528			1728											1928	2128		
Bremen Hbf a.											2015				2216x				
Hamburg Hbf a.	1335			1535			1735				2113		1935		2314x			2138	

	EC 52/152	ICE 274	ICE 120	ICE 376 / 396	ICE 102 / 1102	EC 18 / 1172	ICE 272 / 292	ICE 100	EC 20	ICE 4	EN 470
notes	⊗		m			⊗	y		⊗		A
Milano Centrale d.	1123					1325			1525		
Como San Giovanni d.						1603					
Chiasso d.	▢					1415			1615		
Lugano d.						1442			1642		
Bellinzona d.						1511			1711		
Arth-Goldau d.						1613			1813		
Chur d.											
Zürich HB d.						1651	1700		1851	1900	2000
Baden d.											
Interlaken Ost d.				1500		1604					
Bern d.	1436			1604							
Basel SBB ★ a.	1529			1659		1753			1953		2053
Basel SBB d.	1613	1706		1713	1813	1913			2013	2113	
Basel Bad Bf d.	1623	1715		1723	1823	1923			2023	2122	
Freiburg (Brsg) Hbf d.	1655	1749		1756	1857	1956			2055	2158	
Karlsruhe Hbf d.	1801	1851		1900	2000	2101			2201	2304	
Mannheim Hbf a.	1824	1908	1914	1924	2024	2124			2233	2359	
Frankfurt (Main) Hbf a.	1929	1953				2108			2313		0051z
Frankfurt Flughafen ✈ a.			1940	2006		2206					
Mainz Hbf a.											
Koblenz Hbf a.			⊖	⊖		⊖					
Bonn Hbf a.											
Köln Hbf a.			2033	2105		2307					
Düsseldorf Hbf a.			2105			2338					
Duisburg Hbf a.			2121	h		2355					
Arnhem ⊙ a.			2228								
Utrecht Centraal a.			2300								
Amsterdam Centraal a.			2326								
Essen Hbf a.						0008					
Dortmund Hbf a.				2221		0031					
Hannover Hbf a.				2217j	0018		2341f				
Berlin Hbf a.		2330								0606	
Bremen Hbf a.											
Hamburg Hbf a.				2351j		0111f					0830

A – ÖBB *nightjet* 🛌 1, 2 cl., 🛏 2 cl. (4, 6 berth), 🚃 Zürich - Frankfurt - Berlin - Hamburg. Special fares apply.
G – 🚃 ✕ Interlaken Ost - Basel - Köln - Dortmund (- Hamburg) ⑧ not Dec. 25).
T – ⑤ (daily Mar. 18 - Oct. 30).

f – Not ⑥.
h – Via Wuppertal, Hagen.
j – ⑤⑦ (also Dec. 26; not Dec. 25).
m – Not Dec. 25.
x – ⑧ (not Dec. 25).
y – Not Dec. 24, 31.
z – Frankfurt (Main) **Süd**.

⊙ – 🚃 is at Emmerich.
▢ – Via Brig. 🚃 is at Domodossola; ticket point is **Iselle**.
★ – Connections at Basel are not guaranteed.
⊖ – Via Köln - Frankfurt high speed line.
⊗ – Compulsory reservation for international journeys. Supplement payable for international journeys and for internal journeys within Italy.

CONNECTING SERVICES

① – Mondays   ② – Tuesdays   ③ – Wednesdays   ④ – Thursdays   ⑤ – Fridays   ⑥ – Saturdays   ⑦ – Sundays   ⑧ – Not Saturdays

74 — MILANO and ROMA - PÁTRA - ATHÍNAI

		FB		IC	FB	FA
train type		FB	⛴	IC	FB	FA
train number	2320	9803		605	9809	9355
notes	R X		SF	R X	R X	SF
Milano Centrale.....d.	...	0735	...	...	1035	...
Bologna.....d.	...	0942	...	1000	1242	...
Roma Termini.....d.	0545		...			1450
Foligno.....d.	0742					
Ancona.....d.	0950	1129		1217	1431	
Ancona Marittima.....d.	...		1330			
Pescara Centrale.....d.	...			1352	1540	
Caserta.....d.	...					1603
Foggia.....d.	...			1538	1714	1750
Bari Centrale.....a.	...			1700	1820	1848
Bari Marittima.....a.	...					2000
Pátra.....a.	...		1430			1300
Athína Lárisa.....a.	...	❖		...		❖

		FB	IC			FB	IC	FA
train type		FB	IC		⛴	FB	IC	FA
train number	⛴	9818	2327	541		9822	612	9354
notes	SF	R X	R X		SF	R X	R X	R X
Athína Lárisa.....d.	...		1430	...	...			...
Pátra.....d.	1430			...		1800		
Bari Marittima.....a.						0930		
Bari Centrale.....a.						1138	1204	1317
Foggia.....a.						1237	1319	1413
Caserta.....a.								1602
Pescara Centrale.....a.						1412	1503	
Ancona Marittima.....a.	1030							
Ancona.....a.		1326	1344	1530		1523	1633	
Foligno.....a.		1543	1711					
Roma Termini.....a.		1746	1856					1720
Bologna.....a.	1514					1714	1900	
Milano Centrale.....a.	1725					1925		

ᵪ – Supplement payable.   ❖ – For ⛴/rail connections Pátra - Athína and v.v. see Table 1450.   SF – Superfast Ferries, for days of running see Tables 2715, 2755.

75 — MÜNCHEN - ZÜRICH

train type	EC	EC	EC	EC	
train number	196	194	192	190	
notes	X	X	X	X	
München Hbf.....d.	0717	1233	1633	1833	...
Buchloe.....d.	0758	1317	1717	1917	...
Memmingen.....d.		1346	1746	1946	...
Kempten Hbf.....d.	0841				
Lindau.....d.	0954	1455	1854	2054	...
Bregenz.....a.	1006	1506	1906	2106	...
St Margrethen.....a.	1018	1518	1918	2118	...
St Gallen.....a.	1041	1541	1941	2141	...
Winterthur.....a.	1126	1626	2026	2226	...
Zürich Flughafen +.....a.	1141	1641	2041	2241	...
Zürich HB.....a.	1153	1653	2053	2253	...
Basel SBB.....a.	...	...	2212	...	

train type	EC	EC	EC	EC	
train number	191	193	195	197	
notes	X	X	X	X	
Basel SBB.....d.	0547	0747	...	...	
Zürich HB.....d.	0709	0909	1309	1809	
Zürich Flughafen +.....d.	0721	0921	1321	1821u	
Winterthur.....d.	0737	0937	1337	1837u	
St Gallen.....d.	0821	1021	1420	1921u	
St Margrethen.....d.	0842	1042	1442	1942u	
Bregenz.....d.	0855	1055	1455	1955	
Lindau.....a.	0905	1105	1505	2005	
Kempten Hbf.....d.				2122	
Memmingen.....a.	1013	1213	1613		
Buchloe.....a.	1041	1241	1641	2203	
München Hbf.....a.	1128	1328	1728	2245	

u – Calls to pick up only.

76 — MÜNCHEN and NÜRNBERG - PRAHA

train type	RE	ALX	ALX	🚌	🚌	🚌	RE	ALX	🚌	🚌	🚌	🚌	RE	ALX	🚌	🚌	🚌	🚌	RE	ALX	🚌
train number		351	351	P	Q	P		353	Q	P	P	P		355	Q	P	P	Q		357	P
notes	①–⑥			R	R	R			R	R	R	B			R	R	R	⑦			R
notes	¶	¶						¶					𝟋					m	𝟋		
München Hbf.....d.	...	0455	...	0715	...	...	0901	1015	...	...	...	...	1244	1415	...	...	1700	1702			
Nürnberg Hbf.....d.	0536		0740		0940	0943			1130	1240	1340	1343	1419		1540	1740		1743		1840	
Regensburg.....d.		0623					1031											1835			
Schwandorf.....d.	0643	0705	0705			1048	1107				1448	1507				1848	1909				
Furth im Wald.....a.		0750	0750	◐		◐	1150		◐	◐	◐	1550		◐	◐	1952	◐				
Plzeň hlavní.....a.		0857	0857		1210		1257					1657			2059	2110					
Praha hlavní.....a.		1041	1041	1118	1153	1318		1441	1453	1508	1618	1718		1841	1853	1918	2118	2153	2241	2218	

train type	ALX	RE	🚌	🚌	🚌	ALX	RE	🚌	🚌	🚌	🚌	ALX	RE	🚌	🚌	🚌	🚌	ALX	RE	🚌
train number	356		P	Q	P	354		P	Q	P	P	352		P	P	P	Q	350		P
notes	𝟋		R	R	R	𝟋		R	R	R	⑦	𝟋		R	R	R	R	𝟋		R
notes			r		B															
Praha hlavní.....d.	0512	...	0712	0800	0830	0912	...	1042	1115	1130	1242	1312	...	1415	1530	1612	1715	1712	...	1842
Plzeň hlavní.....d.	0700	...	0820		1100			1500				1900								
Furth im Wald.....a.	0810	...	◐		1210			◐	1610			◐	2012					◐		
Schwandorf.....a.	0854	0906			1254	1306		1655	1705			2056	2106							
Regensburg.....a.	0929				1330			1736				2133								
Nürnberg Hbf.....a.		1014	1050	1208		1414	1420		1508	1620	1814		1853	1908	1950	2153	2205	2222	2220	
München Hbf.....a.	1118	...	1253	1505	1553	1915	2305													

B – ①④⑤⑥.

P – 🚌 DB/ČD IC Bus. Rail tickets valid. R ?. Supplement payable. 2nd class only. At Praha hlavní railway station the bus stop is located outside the old building on the upper level (access from platform one); street name is Wilsonova. At Nürnberg Hbf the bus stop is at Bahnhofvorplatz Hauptausgang (main entrance). At Plzeň the bus stop is located at Plzeň Autobusove nadrazi (Husova).

Q – 🚌 DB/Czech Student Agency IC Bus. Rail tickets valid. R ?. Supplement payable. 2nd class only. At Praha hlavní railway station the bus stop is located outside the old building on the upper level (access from platform one); street name is Wilsonova. The bus stop for München is at Hackerbrücke (approx. 700 metres from München Hbf).

m – Also calls at München Flughafen Terminal 2, Halt 22 (depart 1745).
r – Calls at München Flughafen Terminal 2, Halt 22 (arrive 1208).

¶ – Ex in the Czech Republic.
◐ – 🚌 is Waidhaus (Germany).
ALX – Arriva Länderbahn Express.

OTHER TRAIN NAMES: 351/352 – JAN HUS   350/353 – ALBERT EINSTEIN   354/357 – FRANZ KAFKA   355/356 – KAREL ČAPEK

CONNECTING SERVICES
Hamburg - Hannover - Nürnberg: Table 900
Köln - Frankfurt - Nürnberg: Table 920
Karlsruhe - Stuttgart - Nürnberg: Table 925

train type	IR	EC	IC	EC	IR	EC	IR	EC	FB	IC	EC	FR	IR	EC	FR	IR	EC	FR✓	IR	EC	IR	EC	FR✓	FB
train number	2309	11	802	35	2311	13	1807	51	9723	806	37	9529	2315	15	9533	2319	17	9541	2323	19	1819	57	9549	9749
notes		⊗	R🍴	⊗		R🍴	⊗	R🍴	✓	⊗	R🍴	✓	R🍴	⊗	✓	R🍴	⊗	R🍴✓	R🍴	⊗	R🍴	⊗	R🍴✓ 9551	✓
Genève Aéroport ✈ ....d.																					1151			
Genève ....d.			0539			0609					0739										1200			
Lausanne.......................d.			0618			0650					0818										1250			
Montreux........................d.			0636			0711					0836										1311			
Aigle..............................d.						0722															1322			
Martigny.........................d.						0743															1343			
Sion...............................d.				0712		0758					0912										1358			
Zürich HB...................d.		0609		0709									0909				1109			1309				
Basel SBB ....d.	0504			0604				0631			0804			1004			1204					1231		
Olten..............................d.	0530			0630				0657			0830			1030			1230					1257		
Bern............................d.			0606					0734		0806												1334		
Spiez..............................d.			0636					0805		0836												1405		
Luzern.........................d.	0618			0718									0918	1118						1318				
Arth-Goldau...................d.	0646	0650		0746	0750						0946	0950			1146	1150			1346	1350				
Bellinzona......................d.		0750			0850								1050			1250				1450				
Lugano...........................d.		0818			0918								1118			1318				1518				
Chiasso 🚋......................d.		0852			0952								1152			1352				1552				
Como San Giovanni ......a.					0956											1356								
Visp...............................d.		0703				0825	0832			0903											1425	1432		
Brig 🚋 ¶.........................d.		0711	0744			0832	0844			0911	0944										1432	1444		
Domodossola 🚋 ¶..........a.				0812			0912				1012											1512		
Stresa............................a.			0838				0938																	
Gallarate........................a.											1102											1602		
Milano Centrale.............a.		0935		0937		1035	1037				1137			1235			1435				1635	1637		

Connecting trains from Milano Centrale:

	FR✓	FB			FR			FB			FB			FB			FB
	9523	9717			9525			8717			8721			9747			
	9521																
	X🔁 ⑥⑦				R			R🍴			R🍴			R🍴			
Milano Centrale.............d.	1020	1015		1120	1145		1205	1220		1305	1320		1505	1520		1715	1720 1745
Verona Porta Nuova......a.		1128			1258	1328		1428			1628			1828	1858		
Venezia Mestre ....a.		1228			1358	1428		1528			1728			1928	1958		
Venezia Santa Lucia .....a.				1410	1440			1540			1740			2010			
Bologna Centrale ....a.	1122			1222			1322			1422			1622			1822	
Firenze SMN ....a.	1159			1259			1359			1459			1659			1859	
Roma Termini ....a.	1340			1440			1540			1640			1840			2040	
Napoli Centrale...............a.	1500			1602			1700			1800			2000			2200	

train type	IC	IC	EC	FB	FR	IR	EC	FB	FR	EC	FR✓	EC	IR	EC	IR	EC	IC	ICN	IC	EC	IR	EC
train number	971	818	39	8727	9553	2327	21	8731	9557	153	9759	9559	2331	23	1829	59	2117	797	828	41	2335	25
notes				R🍴✓	R🍴X		R🍴X	R🍴✓	R🍴X	R🍴X	R🍴✓	R🍴X		R🍴X	R🍴	R🍴	⊗	K	⊗	R🍴		R🍴X
Genève Aéroport ✈ ....d.																	1651					
Genève ....d.			1339														1700		1839			
Lausanne.......................d.			1418														1750		1918			
Montreux........................d.			1436														1811		1936			
Aigle..............................d.																	1822					
Martigny.........................d.																	1843					
Sion...............................d.			1512														1858		2012			
Zürich HB...................d.						1509								1709							1909	
Basel SBB ....d.	1259				1404		1504					1604			1731					1804		
Oltern.............................d.	1329				1430		1530					1630			1757					1830		
Bern............................d.	1356	1406													1834			1906				
Spiez..............................d.		1436														1905		1936				
Luzern.........................d.				1518			1618				1718								1918			
Arth-Goldau...................d.				1546		1550	1650				1746	1750							1946	1950		
Bellinzona......................d.							1650				1750				1850					2050		
Lugano...........................d.							1718				1818				1924					2118		
Chiasso 🚋......................d.							1752				1852				1952					2152		
Como San Giovanni ......a.											1856									2156		
Visp...............................d.		1503													1928	1932			2003			
Brig 🚋 ¶.........................d.		1511	1544												1932	1944			2011	2044		
Domodossola 🚋 ¶..........a.			1612												2012					2112		
Stresa............................a.			1638																2103	2138		
Gallarate........................a.																			2103			
Milano Centrale.............a.			1737			1835				•1945				2035		2137			2237	2235		

Connecting trains from Milano Centrale:

				FB	FR		IR		FR	EC		FR	EC						IC	EC		
Milano Centrale.............d.				1805	1820			1905	1920			2015	2020						2225	2317g		
Verona Porta Nuova......a.					1928			2028				2128							0020			
Venezia Mestre ....a.					2028			2128				2228										
Venezia Santa Lucia .....a.								2140				2240										
Bologna Centrale ....a.				1922				2022				2122							0215			
Firenze SMN ....a.				1959				2059				2159							0407y			
Roma Termini ....a.				2140				2240				2340							0717t			
Napoli Centrale...............a.				2300															0938			

K – 🛏 1,2 cl., 🛏 2 cl. (4 berth), 🚗 Milano - Napoli - Salerno.
g – Milano **Porta Garibaldi**.
t – Roma **Tiburtina**.
y – Firenze **Campo di Marte**.
✓ – Supplement payable.
¶ – Ticketing point is **Iselle**.
⊗ – Compulsory reservation for international journeys. Supplement payable for international journeys and for internal journeys within Italy.

82 — ROMA, VENEZIA and MILANO - ZÜRICH, BASEL and GENÈVE

train type	EC	IR	EC	ICN		EC	IC	IC	FB	FR	FR	FR	FR	FR	FR	IR	FR	FR	IR	EC	IR	FB	FR	IC	ICE
train number	12	2316	50	798	2122	32	817	968	9702	9600	9502	2320	9504	9606	8706	2420	9712	9508	2324	52/152	1822	9716	9514/9512	825	376/396
notes	⊗		⊗	A		⊗			✗	①–⑥	①–⑥		①–⑥	✗	✗		✗	✗		⊗		✗			
Napoli Centrale d.	…	…	…	2101	…	…	…	…	…	…	…	…	…	…	…	…	…	…	…	…	…	…	…	…	0700
Roma Termini d.	…	…	…	2315t	…	…	…	0600	…	…	0620	0700	…	…	…	…	…	0720	…	…	…	…	0820		
Firenze SMN d.	…	…	…	0315y	…	…	…	…	…	…	0730	0800	…	…	…	…	…	0900	…	…	…	…	1000		
Bologna Centrale d.	…	…	…	0427	0528	…	…	…	…	…	0808	…	…	0838	…	…	…	0938	…	…	…	…	1038		
Venezia Santa Lucia d.							0620								0720	0820									
Venezia Mestre d.							0632								0732	0832						0902			
Verona Porta Nuova d.							0732									0832	0932					1002			
Milano Centrale a.	…	…	…	0711g	0800	…	…	…	0845	0855	0910	0942	0959	0955	…	…	1045	…	…	1040	…	1115	1140		

Sub-trains from Milano Centrale:
EC 14 [R][Y] · EC 158 [R][Y] ⊗ · EC 16 [R][Y] · EC 34 [R][Y] ⊗

	EC	IR	EC	ICN		EC	IC	IC	FB	FR	FR	FR	FR	FR	FR	IR	FR	FR	IR	EC	IR	FB	FR	IC	ICE
	12	2316	50	798	2122	32	817	968	9702	9600	9502	2320	9504	9606	8706	2420	9712	9508	2324	52/152	1822	9716	9514	825	376
Milano Centrale d.	0725	…	0723	…	0823	…	…	…	…	…	0925	…	…	…	…	…	1015	…	…	…	1125	1123	…	1223	
Gallarate d.		0757 (IR)																				1221		1321	
Stresa d.		1814		0921																		1248		1348	
Domodossola d.		0848			0948																	1316	1328	1416 1449	
Brig a.		0916	0928		1016	1049																1326	1334	1455	
Visp a.		0926	0934			1055																			
Como San Giovanni d.											1003						1103			1203					
Chiasso d.	0808										1008						1108			1208					
Lugano a.	0841										1041						1141			1241					
Bellinzona a.	0910										1110						1210			1310					
Arth-Goldau a.	1009	1014									1209	1214					1309	1313		1409	1414				
Luzern a.		1041										1241					1341				1441				
Spiez a.			0953		1124															1353				1524	
Bern a.			1023		1154	1204														1423				1554	1604
Olten a.			1127	1102		1230						1327					1427			1527	1502				1630
Basel SBB a.			1155	1129		1259						1355					1455			1555	1529				1659
Zürich HB a.	1051										1251						1351			1451					
Sion a.	…	…	…	1001	…	1047	…	…	…	…	…	…	…	…	…	…	…	…	…	1401	…	1447			
Martigny a.	…	…	…	1015	…	…	…	…	…	…	…	…	…	…	…	…	…	…	…	1415					
Aigle a.	…	…	…	1036	…	…	…	…	…	…	…	…	…	…	…	…	…	…	…	1436					
Montreux a.	…	…	…	1047	1122	…	…	…	…	…	…	…	…	…	…	…	…	…	…	1447	1523				
Lausanne a.	…	…	…	1110	1142	…	…	…	…	…	…	…	…	…	…	…	…	…	…	1510	1542				
Genève a.	…	…	…	1200	1221	…	…	…	…	…	…	…	…	…	…	…	…	…	…	1600	1621				
Genève Aéroport ✈ a.	…	…	…	1209	…	…	…	…	…	…	…	…	…	…	…	…	…	…	…	1609					

---

train type/number	FB	FR	IR	FR	FR	IR	FR	FB	IC	EC	IR	FR	FB	FR	IR	EC	IR	FR	EC	IC	ICE	EC
train number	9720	9518	2328	9728	9526/9524	2332	9532	8718	1084	22	2336	9536	8720	9638	1836	10	2338	9540	42	1088	338	24
notes	©	✗		✗	✗		✗	✗		⊗	✗	✗	✗	⊗		⊗		✗	⊗			⊗
Napoli Centrale d.	…	0800	…	1000	…	1200	…	…	…	1300	…	…	…	…	…	…	…	1400	…	…	…	…
Roma Termini d.	…	0920	…	1120	…	1320	…	…	…	…	1420	…	1500	…	…	…	…	1520	…	…	…	…
Firenze SMN d.	…	1100	…	1300	…	1500	…	…	…	…	1600	…	…	…	…	…	…	1700	…	…	…	…
Bologna Centrale d.	…	1138	…	1338	…	1538	…	…	…	…	1638	…	…	…	…	…	…	1738	…	…	…	…
Venezia Santa Lucia d.					1150			1420				1520						1620				
Venezia Mestre d.	1002				1202			1432				1532						1632				
Verona Porta Nuova d.	1102				1302			1532				1632						1732				
Milano Centrale a.	1215	1240	…	1415	1440	…	…	1640	1655	…	1740	1755	1755	…	…	…	…	1842	1855	…	…	…

Sub-trains from Milano Centrale:
EC 18 [R][Y] ⊗ · EC 20 [R][Y] ⊗ · EC 36 [R][Y] ⊗ · EC 56 [R][Y] ⊗

	FB	FR	IR	FR	FR	IR	FR	FB	IC	EC	IR	FR	FB	FR	IR	EC	IR	FR	EC	IC	ICE	EC
	9720	9518	2328	9728	9526	2332	9532	8718	1084	22	2336	9536	8720	9638	1836	10	2338	9540	42	1088	338	24
Milano Centrale d.	…	1325	…	1525	…	…	1723	…	1725	…	…	1823	…	1825	…	…	…	1923	…	1925		
Gallarate d.																		1957				
Stresa d.							1821					1921						2048				
Domodossola d.							1848					1948										
Brig a.							1916	1920				2016	2023					2116	2120			
Visp a.							1926					2026	2029					2126			2003	
Como San Giovanni d.				1603																	2003	
Chiasso d.		1408		1608						1808				1908							2008	
Lugano a.		1441		1641						1841				1941							2041	
Bellinzona a.		1510		1710						1910				2010							2110	
Arth-Goldau a.		1609	1614	1809	1814					2009				2109	2114						2209	
Luzern a.		1641			1841					2041					2141							
Spiez a.							1953					2053						2153				
Bern a.							2023					2123						2223	2236			
Olten a.			1727		1927		2102		2127			2202				2227			2303			
Basel SBB a.		1755			1955		2129		2155			2229				2259			2330			
Zürich HB a.		1651			1851				2051						2151					2251		
Sion a.	…	…	…	…	1947	…	…	…	…	…	…	2059	…	…	…	2147	…	…	…	…		
Martigny a.	…	…	…	…	…	…	…	…	…	…	…	2113	…	…	…	…	…	…	…	…		
Aigle a.	…	…	…	…	…	…	…	…	…	…	…	2136	…	…	…	…	…	…	…	…		
Montreux a.	…	…	…	…	…	…	2022	…	…	…	…	2147	…	…	…	2222	…	…	…	…		
Lausanne a.	…	…	…	…	…	…	2042	…	…	…	…	2210	…	…	…	2242	…	…	…	…		
Genève a.	…	…	…	…	…	…	2121	…	…	…	…	2307	…	…	…	2321	…	…	…	…		
Genève Aéroport ✈ a.	…	…	…	…	…	…	…	…	…	…	…	2316	…	…	…	…	…	…	…	…		

A – 🛏 1, 2 cl., 🛏 2 cl. (4 berth),
🛌 Salerno - Napoli - Milano.
g – Milano **Porta Garibaldi**.
t – Roma **Tiburtina**.
y – Firenze **Campo di Marte**.
✗ – Supplement payable.
¶ – Ticketing point is **Iselle**.
⊗ – Compulsory reservation for international journeys. Supplement payable for international journeys and for internal journeys within Italy.

train type/number	RJ	RJ	IC	RJ	D	RJ	RJ	EC	EC	RJ	EC	EC	EC	RJ	EC	D	IC	RJ	EC	RJ	EC	RJ	RJ	EN	EN	EN	EN
train number	49	765	515	111	211	161	596	217	163	563	147	113	113	165	115	315	611	167	219	169	117	361	363	465	40465	40467	467
notes	✗	✗	⛲	✗	2	✗	✗	⛲	B	✗	D	⛲	213	✗	⛲	411 P		✗	⛲	✗	✗	1217	⛲	Z	A	C	W
Zürich HB .... d.				0640		0840				1040				1240		1440		1640	1840	2040	2040	2140	2140				
Sargans .... d.				0737		0937				1137				1337		1537		1737	1937	2137	2137	2237	2237				
Buchs .... d.		0548		0754		1000				1154				1354		1554		1759	1954	2205	2205	2303	2303				
Bregenz .... d.		0548																									
Feldkirch .... d.		0613		0817		1017				1217				1417		1617		1817	2017	2245	2245	2324	2324				
Bludenz .... d.		0626		0830		1030				1230				1430		1630		1830	2030	2301	2301	2340	2340				
Langen am Arlberg d.		0652																				2335	2335				
St Anton am Arlberg d.		0703		0903		1103				1303				1503		1703		1903	2103	2345	2345						
Landeck-Zams .... d.		0727		0927		1127				1327				1527		1727		1927	2127	0009	0009						
Ötztal .... d.		0751		0948		1148				1348				1548		1748		1951	2151								
Innsbruck Hbf ... d.	0510x	0817	0821	1017		1221e	1217			1417				1617		1817		2017	2214	0056	0056	0128	0128				
Jenbach .... d.	0527x	0844				1244														0119	0119						
Wörgl .... d.	0541x	0843	0900	1043		1300	1243			1443				1643		1843		2043		0138	0138						
Kitzbühel .... d.			0930			1330																					
St Johann in Tirol d.			0938			1338																					
Saalfelden ...... d.			1006			1406																					
Zell am See ..... d.			1017			1417																					
Schwarzach St Veit d.																				0324	0420						
Salzburg Hbf .... d.	0708x	1008		1012		1208	1212	1215		1408				1608	1612	1615	1808	1815	2008	2012	2208					0350	0438
Bischofshofen ... a.				1052		1252	1302							1652	1702		1902	2052							0336		
Schwarzach St Veit a.			1046	1109		1309		1446			1511	1511		1709					2109								
Selzthal .... a.			1239			1439	1639							1839		2039						0504					
Graz Hbf .... a.			1414			1614	1814							2014		2214						0700					
Villach Hbf ..... a.			1243	1253		1443				1643	1643			1843	1853				2243			0605					
Klagenfurt ...... a.			1316								1718			1916					2316								
Jesenice .... a.			1333								1733			1933								0705					
Ljubljana .... a.			1431								1831			2040								0813					
Zagreb .... a.			1713								2053			2336								1043					
Vinkovci .... a.			2101											0313								1433					
Beograd .... a.														0555								1737					
Linz Hbf .... a.	0812x	1112		1312				1512						1712			1912	2112	2312			0455	0601				
St Pölten .... a.	0900x	1200	RJ	1400	EC			1600						1800			2000	2200	2400			0600	0713				
Wien Meidling ... a.	0923x	1223	63	1423	145			1623						1823			2023	2223	0023			0627	0746				
Wien Hbf .... a.	0930x	1230	✗	1430	⛲			1630						1830			2030	2230	0030			0635	0755				
Wien Hbf .... d.	0942	1339		1439				1639						1842								0639					
Hegyeshalom .... d.	1025	1425		1525				1725						1925								0725					
Györ .... d.	1053	1453		1553				1753						1953								0753					
Budapest Keleti . a.	1219	1619		1719				1919						2119								0924					

train type/number	RJ	RJ	EC	RJ	RJ	IC	D	EC	RJ	RJ	EC	RJ	EC	EC	EC	EC	RJ	RJ	IC	EC	RJ	RJ	EN	EN	EN	EN
train number	360	362	218	691	160	512	410	114	162	60	860	212	112	164	216	62	166	64	168	610	210	66	760	466	40462	414	464
notes	✗	✗	⛲	✗	✗	⛲	314 Q	⛲	✗	✗	✗	112	⛲	✗	✗	✗ B	⛲	✗	2	⛲	✗	✗	✗	W	E	A	Z
Budapest Keleti ... d.							0640	0740							0940		1140				1340			2040			
Györ .... d.							0802	0902							1102		1302				1502			2202			
Hegyeshalom .... d.							0832	0932							1132		1332				1529			2232			
Wien Hbf .... a.							0918	1021							1221		1421				1618			2321			
Wien Hbf .... d.		0530x		0730			0930	1030	1030						1330		1530				1730	2128	2325				
Wien Meidling ... d.		0537x		0737			0937	1037	1037						1337		1537				1737	2136	2333				
St Pölten .... d.		0600x		0800			1000	1100	1100						1400		1600				1800	2203	0000				
Linz Hbf .... d.		0648x		0848			1048	1148	1148						1448		1648				1848	2300	0105				
Beograd .... d.						2120																1055					
Vinkovci .... d.						0105																1442					
Zagreb .... d.						0437				0650							1235	RJ				1837					
Ljubljana .... d.						0728				0922						RJ	1525	110				2110					
Jesenice .... d.						0827				1017						793	IC	1627 ✗				2205					
Klagenfurt ...... d.						0908	0842			1027					518	1245				1642							
Villach Hbf ..... d.			0716			0916				1116	1116				1316 ⛲			1709	1716			2316					
Graz Hbf .... d.			0545		0745					0945	1145				1345		1545					2224					
Selzthal .... d.			0719		0919					1119	1319				1519		1719					0029					
Schwarzach St Veit d.				0850		1050				1248	1248	1313			1450				1850								
Bischofshofen ... d.			0857	0905	1057	1105							1457	1505		1650		1857	1905			0158					
Salzburg Hbf .... d.		0756	0944	0948	0956	1144		1148	1156	1252	1256			1544	1548	1556		1756	1944	1948	1956	0230	0230				
Schwarzach St Veit d.																1713						0232	0232				
Zell am See ..... d.												1344				1744											
Saalfelden ...... d.												1354				1754											
St Johann in Tirol d.												1422				1822											
Kitzbühel .... d.												1430				1830											
Wörgl .... d.		0919		1119				1319		1415		1502				1719	1902	1919				2119					
Jenbach .... d.								1429				1502															
Innsbruck Hbf ... d.	0745	0948		1148				1348	1448			1548				1748	1939	1948				2148	0431	0431	0453	0453
Ötztal .... d.	0809	1012		1212				1412				1612				1812		2012				2212				
Landeck-Zams .... d.	0833	1033		1233				1433	1533			1633				1833		2036				2236	0545	0545		
St Anton am Arlberg d.	0857	1057		1257				1457				1657				1857		2100				2300	0610	0610		
Langen am Arlberg d.									1604													2310	0620	0620		
Bludenz .... d.	0931	1131		1331				1531	1631			1731				1931		2134				2337	0620	0706	0706	
Feldkirch .... d.	0944	1147		1348				1548	1648			1744				1948		2148				2350	0637	0637	0738	0738
Bregenz .... a.									1717													0013				
Buchs .... a.	0959	1206		1406				1606				1758				2006		2203					0656	0656	0753	0753
Sargans .... a.	1023	1223		1423				1623				1823				2023		2223					0723	0723	0823	0823
Zürich HB .... a.	1120	1320		1520				1720				1920				2120		2320					0820	0820	0920	0920

A – ALPINE PEARLS ÖBB *nightjet* 🛏 1,2 cl., 🛏 2 cl. (4, 6 berth). 🍽 Zürich - Zagreb and v.v. 🛏 Zürich - Beograd and v.v. 🛏 Villach - Beograd and v.v.

B – TRANSALPIN 🚃 (observation car), 🍽 ⛲ Zürich - Innsbruck - Graz and v.v.

C – 🛏 1,2 cl., 🛏 2 cl. 🚃 Zürich - Wien - Budapest. Conveys 🛏 1,2 cl. (50467) Zürich - Linz - Praha (Table 52). Special fares payable.

D – 🚃 ✗ Wien - Budapest - Szolnok (arrive 2102) - Debrecen (2233).

E – 🛏 1,2 cl., 🛏 2 cl., 🚃 Budapest - Wien - Zürich. Conveys 🛏 1,2 cl. (50466) Praha - Linz - Zürich (Table 52). Special fares payable.

P – Dec. 22 - Jan. 14, June 24 - Sept. 10: 🚃 Villach - Jesenice 🚋 - Ljubljana - Zagreb - Beograd.

Q – Dec. 23 - Jan. 15, June 25 - Sept. 11: 🚃 Beograd - Zagreb - Ljubljana - Jesenice 🚋 - Villach.

W – WIENER WALZER ÖBB *nightjet* 🛏 1,2 cl., 🛏 2 cl. (4, 6 berth). 🚃 Zürich - Wien and v.v. Special fares payable.

Z – ZÜRICHSEE ÖBB *nightjet* 🛏 1,2 cl., 🛏 2 cl. (4, 6 berth), 🚃 Zürich - Graz and v.v.

e – Arrive 1211.

x – ①–⑥ (not Dec. 26, Apr. 17, May 1, June 5).

RJ – ÖBB *Railjet* service. ✗, 🚃 (business class), 🚃 (first class), 🚃 (economy class).

☉ – 🚋 between Ljubljana and Zagreb is Dobova.

⊕ – 🚋 between Vinkovci and Beograd is Šid.

88 — WIEN - KLAGENFURT - VENEZIA, MILANO and ROMA

train type		REX	EC	RJ		RJ		RJ	REX	EN	EN	EN	EN
train number	831	1881	31	533	835	535	837	539	1883	40233	233	1237	237
notes	R		2		X / Y	X / Y	X / Y	X	2	R	M	C	V ♥
Wien Hbf ....d.	...	...	0625	...	0825	...	1025	...	1425	...	1923	1923	2023	2127
Wien Meidling ....d.	...	...	0632	...	0832	...	1032	...	1432	...	1931	1931	2031	2135
Bruck an der Mur .....d.	...	...	0815	...	1015	...	1215	...	1615	...	2127	2127	2222	...
Klagenfurt Hbf ....d.	0605	...	1022	...	1222	1210	1422	1410	1822	...	2337	2337	0021	...
Linz Hbf ....d.														2300
Salzburg Hbf ....d.														0140
Villach Hbf ....d.	0650	0945	1050	...	1246	1256	1446	1456	1846	1929	0055	0134	0045	0445
Tarvisio 🚍 ....a.	...	1012	1112							1956	0119		0108	0508
Udine ....a.	0825	1130	1216	...	1430	...	1630	...	2115				0217	0623
Venezia Mestre ....a.	1000	...	1353	...	1605	...	1805							0812
Venezia Tronchetto ★ ..a.	1020	...		...	1625	...	1825							
Venezia Santa Lucia ....a.	...	...	1405											0824
Padova ....a.											0409	0539	0415	
Verona Porta Nuova ..a.												0635		
Milano Centrale ....a.												0910		
Bologna Centrale .....a.											0520		0541	
Firenze SMN ....a.											0619		0653	
Pisa Centrale ....a.													0831	
Livorno Centrale ......a.													0850	
Roma Termini ....a.											0922			

> **OTHER CONNECTING SERVICES**
> Venezia - Roma : Table **600**
> Venezia - Milano : Table **605**

train type	REX	RJ		RJ		RJ	EC		EN	EN	EN	EN	EN
train number	1880	534	830	538	832	630	30	838	236	1234	235	40294	1234
notes	2	X	R	Y	R	X	X	Y	♥	V	D	M	R / E
Roma Termini ....d.												1904	
Livorno Centrale ......d.										1920			1920
Pisa Centrale ....d.										1946			1946
Firenze SMN ....d.										2105		2149	2105
Bologna Centrale .....d.										2223		2246	2223
Milano Centrale ....d.											2040		
Verona Porta Nuova ..d.											2252		
Padova ....d.										2349	2344	0003	2349
Venezia Santa Lucia ....d.							1555		2057				
Venezia Tronchetto ★ ..d.			0920		1120			1820	2109				
Venezia Mestre ....d.			0940		1140		1607	1840	2109				
Udine ....d.	0707		1115		1315		1746	2015	2247	0201			0201
Tarvisio 🚍 ....d.	0827						1849			0319		0305	0319
Villach Hbf ....a.	0854	0914	1250	1314	1450	1514	1911	2150	0042	0341	0307	0327	0341
Salzburg Hbf ....a.									0404				
Linz Hbf ....a.									0601				
Klagenfurt Hbf ....a.		0937	1335	1337	1535	1537	1937	2235		0407	0439	0439	0407
Bruck an der Mur .....a.		1144		1544		1744	2144			0621	0639	0639	0621
Wien Meidling ....a.		1328		1728		1928	2328		0746	0826	0839	0839	0905
Wien Hbf ....a.		1335		1735		1935	2335		0755	0832	0846	0846	0915

C – ③⑤ Apr. 5 - Oct. 27 (also Apr. 16, 30, June 4, Aug. 14): ÖBB *nightjet* 🛏 1, 2 cl., 🛏 2 cl. (4, 6 berth), 💺 Wien - Firenze - Pisa - Livorno.

D – ⑥ Apr. 6 - Oct. 28: ÖBB *nightjet* 🛏 1, 2 cl., 🛏 2 cl. (4, 6 berth), 💺 Livorno - Pisa - Firenze - Wien.

E – ④ Apr. 6 - Oct. 28 (also Apr. 17, May 1, June 5, Aug. 15): ÖBB *nightjet* 🛏 1, 2 cl., 🛏 2 cl. (4, 6 berth), 💺 Livorno - Pisa - Firenze - Wien.

M – ÖBB *nightjet* 🛏 1, 2 cl., 🛏 2 cl. (4, 6 berth), 💺 Wien - Milano and v.v.

R – ÖBB *nightjet* 🛏 1, 2 cl., 🛏 2 cl. (4, 6 berth), 💺 Wien - Roma and v.v.

V – ÖBB *nightjet* 🛏 1, 2 cl., 🛏 2 cl. (4, 6 berth), 💺 Wien - Venezia and v.v.

Y – Mar. 19 - Oct. 26.

✗ – Supplement payable.

★ – See Venezia City Plan on page 32.

RJ – ÖBB *Railjet* service. 💺 (business class), 💺 (first class), 💺 (economy class), X.

🚌 – ÖBB *IC Bus.* Rail tickets valid. R Supplement payable. 1st and 2nd class. Y in first class. Connections to / from Wien are made at Villach.

♥ – From June 1 to Sept. 15, an ÖBB *IC Bus* departs Venezia Mestre 0825 for Lido di Jesolo (arrives 0920). Also departs Lido di Jesolo 1945 for Venezia Mestre (arrives 2040). Rail tickets **not** valid.

89 — VENEZIA - LJUBLJANA - ZAGREB - BUDAPEST and BEOGRAD

train type	IC	D	EC	IC	🚌	EC	1604		480
train number	205	415	247	205	832	213	1247	1205	1247
notes	A	p	M	R			K	C	E
Venezia Santa Lucia ..d.									
Venezia Tronchetto ...d.					1120				
Venezia Mestre ....d.					1140				
Villach Hbf ....d.		0625			1450	1653			
Koper ....a.						2015			
Rijeka ....d.	0535								2050
Ljubljana ....a.		0825	0908		1835	0015			0015
Dobova 🚍 ....d.		1015			2021				
Split ....d.								1817	
Zagreb ....a.	0931	1043			2053		0213		
Zagreb ....d.	1003	1107	1537				0232		
Vinkovci ....d.		1433							
Šid 🚍 ....d.		1515							
Beograd ....d.		1737							
Koprivnica 🚍 ....d.	1121		1655		▣		0404		
Gyékényes ....a.	1134		1709				0418		
Nagykanizsa ....a.							0554		
Kaposvár ....a.	1319		1901						
Dombóvár ....a.	1348		1946						
Fonyód ....a.							0705		
Siófok ....a.							0755		
Székesfehérvár ....a.			1641				0741	0839	0741
Budapest Déli ....a.			1729				0829		0829
Budapest Keleti ....a.	1614		2214					0936	

train type	D	EC	EC	IC	D	EC	IC		1246		1246
train number	314	31	212	835	800	414	246	204	1204	481	1605
notes	Q		T	A			M	R	D	G	J
Budapest Keleti ....a.	...	...		0545			1445	1815			
Budapest Déli ....a.					0830				2030	2030	
Székesfehérvár ....d.					0916		1914	2116	2116		
Siófok ....d.							1954				
Fonyód ....d.							2052				
Dombóvár ....d.					0803		1700				
Kaposvár ....d.					0831		1731				
Nagykanizsa ....d.							2154				
Gyékényes ....d.					1011		1916	2253			
Koprivnica 🚍 ....a.					1030		▣	1930	2309	▣	
Beograd ....d.	2120						1055				
Šid 🚍 ....d.	0025						1353				
Vinkovci ....d.	0105						1442				
Zagreb ....a.	0425				1139	1813		2059	0022		
Zagreb ....d.	0437	0650			1200	1837			0035		
Split ....d.			0744				1926		0757		
Dobova 🚍 ....d.	0540						1926				
Ljubljana ....a.	0728	0923			2110	1630			0635	0612	
Rijeka ....a.			1541						0925		
Koper ....a.										0840	
Villach Hbf ....a.	0908	1050	1058	1256		2243					
Venezia Mestre ....a.		1353		1605							
Venezia Tronchetto ..a.				1625							
Venezia Santa Lucia ..a.		1405									

A – KVARNER 💺 Y Budapest - Zagreb - Rijeka and v.v.

C – ADRIA ①③⑥ June 19 - Sept. 2: 🛏 1, 2 cl., 🛏 2 cl., 💺 Split - Zagreb - Budapest. Conveys on ③⑥ June 21 - Sept. 2: 💺 Split (**1205**) - Budapest (**276**).

D – ADRIA ②⑤⑦ June 18 - Sept. 1: 🛏 1, 2 cl., 🛏 2 cl., 💺 Budapest - Zagreb - Split. Conveys on ②⑤ June 20 - Sept. 1: 🛏 1, 2 cl. Praha (**277**) - Budapest (**1204**) - Split.

E – ISTRA ②⑤ June 24 - Aug. 26: 🛏 2 cl., 💺 Rijeka - Hodoš - Budapest (Table **91**).

G – ISTRA ①④ June 23 - Aug. 25: 🛏 2 cl., 💺 Budapest - Hodoš - Rijeka (Table **91**).

J – ISTRA ①④ June 23 - Aug. 25: 🛏 2 cl., 💺 Budapest - Hodoš - Koper (Table **91**).

K – ISTRA ②⑤ June 30 - Aug. 29: 🛏 2 cl., 💺 Koper - Hodoš - Budapest (Table **91**).

M – CITADELLA – 💺 X Ljubljana - Hodoš - Budapest and v.v. (Table **91**).

Q – Dec. 23 - Jan. 15, June 25 - Sept. 11: 💺 Beograd - Zagreb - Ljubljana - Jesenice 🚍 - Villach. Daily 💺 Dobova - Villach.

P – Dec. 22 - Jan. 14, June 25 - Sept. 10: 💺 Villach - Jesenice 🚍 - Ljubljana - Zagreb - Beograd. Daily 💺 Villach - Dobova.

R – RIPPL-RÓNAI – 💺 X Zagreb - Budapest and v.v.

T – Mar. 19 - Oct. 26.

k – Budapest Kelenfold.

▣ – 🚍 is Hodoš.

🚌 – ÖBB *IC Bus.* R Rail tickets valid. Supplement payable. 1st and 2nd class. Y in first class.

MARSEILLE - NICE - MILANO, ROMA and VENEZIA 90

	train type	EC	FB	IC	FB	FR			IC	IC	FB	FR	FR		EC	EC	IC	FR	FB		EC	EC	ICN
	train number	139	9773	511	9723	9533		17473	745	665	9777	9727	9541		145	145	673	9557	9749		147	147	799
	notes	140							746						146	146					148	148	
	notes		✗	Ⓡ♀	✗	Ⓡ✗		Ⓐ	Ⓡ	Ⓡ✗	✗	Ⓡ♀	Ⓡ✗		♣	♣	Ⓡ♀	Ⓡ✗	✗		♣	♣	Ⓡ
	notes	♣					◇		Ⓡ				✗		①	②-⑦					①-⑤	⑥⑦	Ⓐ
Marseille St Charles	d.	...	...	...	...	0630		...	...	...	...	...	...		1131	...	...	...	1531		...	...	...
Toulon	d.	...	...	...	...	0713		...	...	...	...	...	...		1218	...	...	...	1617		...	...	...
Cannes	d.	...	...	...	...	0839		...	...	...	...	...	...		1335	...	...	...	1738		...	...	...
Nice	d.	0808	...	...	0906	0950		...	...	...	...	...	...		1406	1406	...	...	1807		1807	...	...
Monaco - Monte Carlo	d.	0825	...	...	...	1016		...	...	...	...	...	...		1423	1423	...	...	1825		1825	...	...
Ventimiglia 🚲	d.	0901	...	...	1040	1049		...	...	...	...	...	...		1502	1502	...	...	1902		1902	...	...
San Remo	d.	0913	...	...	...	1108		...	...	...	...	...	...		1513	1513	...	...	1913		1913	...	...
Genova Piazza Principe	a.	1107	1212	1238	...	1306		1347	1502	...	...	...	...		1707	1707	1747	...	2106		2106	2353	
Milano Centrale	a.	1250			1305	1320			1450			1505	1520		1850	1850		1920	2005		2250	2250	
Verona	a.	...			1428							1628			...				2128			
Venezia Santa Lucia	a.	...			1540							1740			...				2240			
La Spezia	a.	...	1312	1355							1521	1618			...			1921				0124
Pisa Centrale	a.	...	1355	1452								1710			...			2017				0216
Firenze SMN	a.	...				1459							1659					2059				
Roma Termini	a.	...	1632	1803		1640						2003	1840					2240				0555o
Napoli Centrale	a.	...			2029	1800							2000									0817

	train type	ICN	IC	EC	TGV	FB	FB	FR	FR	EC		IC	FB	FR	EC	EC		FR	FB	FB	IC
	train number	796	658	142	6864	9708	9764	9508	9610	9710		17490	674	9718	9526	160	159		9532	9726	9774	675
	notes	Ⓡ	Ⓡ		Ⓡ♀	✗	Ⓡ♀	Ⓡ✗	Ⓡ♀	Ⓡ		144	Ⓡ✗	✗	Ⓡ✗	160	160		Ⓡ✗	✗	Ⓡ	676
	notes	Ⓐ		♣		①-⑤		①-⑤		♣		♣			♣						Ⓡ	◇
	notes														①-④	⑤⑥⑦						Ⓡ
Napoli Centrale	d.	2142	...	...	...	...	0640					...	...	...	1000	...		1200	...	...	...
Roma Termini	d.	0003o	...	...	...	0657	0720	0800				...	...	...	1120	...		1320	...	1357	...
Firenze SMN	d.	...	...	...	...	...	0900					...	...	...	1300	...		1500	...	...	...
Pisa Centrale	d.	0326	0542	...	...	0947					1342				...			...	1629		
La Spezia	d.	0425	0638	...	...	1039					1438				...			...	1715		
Venezia Santa Lucia	d.			...	...	0750		0832q			1150				...		1320				
Verona	d.			...	...	0902		0932			1302				...		1432				
Milano Centrale	d.			0705	...	1025		1040	1055	1055	1110			1425	1440	1510	1510		1640	1555		1705
Genova Piazza Principe	d.	0601	0815	0856	...	1156					1258	1615		1658	1658				1816	1858	
San Remo	a.			1049	...						1447			1848	1848					2054	
Ventimiglia 🚲	a.			1101	...						1501			1901	1901				2115	2240	
Monaco - Monte Carlo	a.			1148	...						1543			1946	1946					2305	
Nice	a.			1204	1223				1600	1655				2005	2006					2330	
Cannes	a.			1253							1719			2038							
Toulon	a.			1412							1844			2156							
Marseille St Charles	a.			1459							1929			2242							

A – 🛏 1, 2 cl., 🛌 2 cl. (4 berth), 🚃 Torino - Genova - Napoli - Salerno and v.v.
j – Firenze Campo di Marte.
o – Roma Ostiense.
q – Venezia Mestre.
✗ – Supplement payable.
♣ – EC Thello.
◇ – Stopping train. Alternative services available, see Table 361.
★ – Service offering Executive, Business, Premium and Standard class.

WIEN - LJUBLJANA and ZAGREB 91

	train type	EC			EC	EC	IC	1246	1246			train type / number	IC	IC	EC	EC		EC	480	1604
	train number	151	483	2752	246	159	523	1605	481			train number	508	514	158	247	2751	482	150	1247	1247
	notes	✗		2		✗	✗					notes	Ⓡ			2		✗			
	notes														C	M			E	K	Q
	notes			E			M	C	P	J											
Wien Hbf	d.	0758	...	...	1558	...					Rijeka	d.	...	...	...	1200	...	2050	...		
Wien Meidling	d.	0805	...	...	1605	...					Koper	d.	0525	...	...	1003	...	...	2015		
Wiener Neustadt Hbf	d.	0832	...	...	1632	...					Ljubljana	d.	0748	0758	...	0908	1240	1450	1600	0015	015
Graz Hbf	d.	1038	...	...	1838	...					Zagreb	d.	...	0725	...						
Spielfeld-Straß 🚲	d.	1120	...	...	1920	...					Dobova 🚲	d.	...	0813	...						
Budapest Déli	d.			0830		...	2030	2030				Zidani Most	d.	...	0850	1004	...	1657	0108	0108		
Hodoš 🚲	d.			1305		...	0103	0103				Pragersko	d.	...	0942	1000	1114	...	1800	0225	0225	
Maribor	a.	1137	...	...	1938	1945	0231	0231				Maribor	d.	...	0956	1019	...	1819	...		
Pragersko	a.	1205	...	...	1424	2011	2001	0356				Hodoš 🚲	a.	...		1230	...		0338	0338		
Zidani Most	a.	1310	...	...	1531		2052	0506	0505			Budapest Déli	a.	...		1729	...		0829	0829		
Dobova 🚲	a.			2156								Spielfeld-Straß 🚲	a.	...	1036	...	1836	...			
Zagreb	a.			2242								Graz Hbf	a.	...	1120	...	1920	...			
Ljubljana	a.	1406	1510	1542	1630	...	2153	0605	0605			Wiener Neustadt Hbf	a.	...	1328	...	2128	...			
Koper	a.	...	1813	...	...			0840				Wien Meidling	a.	...	1355	...	2155	...			
Rijeka	a.	...	1755	...	...			0925				Wien Hbf	a.	...	1402	...	2202	...			

C – CROATIA 🚃 ✗ Wien - Zagreb and v.v.
E – EMONA 🚃 ✗ Wien - Ljubljana and v.v.
M – CITADELLA 🚃 ✗ Budapest - Hodoš - Ljubljana and v.v. (Table 89).
J – ISTRA ①④ June 23 - Aug. 25: 🛌 2 cl., 🚃 Budapest - Hodoš - Rijeka.
K – ISTRA ②⑤ June 24 - Aug. 26: 🛌 2 cl., 🚃 Rijeka - Hodoš - Budapest.
P – ISTRA ①④ June 23 - Aug. 25: 🛌 2 cl., 🚃 Budapest - Hodoš - Koper.
Q – ISTRA ②⑤ June 30 - Aug. 29: 🛌 2 cl., 🚃 Koper - Hodoš - Budapest.

✗ – Supplement payable.
◇ – Stopping train.

ZAGREB - SARAJEVO 92

train number	397		train number	396
notes	A		notes	A
Zagreb	d.	0859	Sarajevo	d.	1021
Sunja	d.	1015	Zenica	d.	1146
Volinja	d.	1112	Doboj	d.	1330
Dobrljin 🚲	d.	1145	Banja Luka	d.	1509
Novi Grad	d.	1201	Novi Grad	d.	1645
Banja Luka	d.	1337	Dobrljin 🚲	d.	1721
Doboj	d.	1523	Volinja	d.	1759
Zenica	d.	1700	Sunja	d.	1827
Sarajevo	a.	1823	Zagreb	a.	1942

A – 🚃 Zagreb - Sarajevo and v.v.

WARSZAWA - VILNIUS 93

	train number	10113		TLK		TLK	11083		TLK			train number	TLK		141	IC	TLK		145
		143		31011		41109	149		10109				10118		11140	14108	13010		10102
	notes	2	2	H			2		2			notes	W		2	2	H		2
	notes	⑥⑦					⑤⑥⑦		⑧				①-⑥		①⑥⑦				⑥⑦
Warszawa Centralna	d.	...	...	0736		1205	...		1505			Vilnius	d.	...	0730	...	...	1445		...
Warszawa Wschodnia	d.	...	...	0744		1214	...		1514			Kaunas	d.	...	0849	0900	...	1617		1655
Małkinia	d.	...	...	0905		1332	...		1641			Šeštokai	d.	...		...	...			...
Białystok	d.	0743	...	1016		1429	1519		1754			Mockava 🚲 Ⓞ	d.	...		...	...			...
Suwałki	d.	0940	...	1217		1740	...		1953			Suwałki	d.	0443	1112	...	1536		1903	
Mockava 🚲 Ⓞ	a.	...	...				...					Białystok	d.	0651	1310	1333	1744		2108	
Šeštokai	a.	...	...				...					Małkinia	d.	0750		1429	1844		...	
Kaunas	a.	1335	1352			2135	2145		...			Warszawa Wschodnia	a.	0911		1546	2009		...	
Vilnius	a.	...	...	1521			2301		...			Warszawa Centralna	a.	0922		1556	2020		...	

H – HAŃCZA – 🚃 Ⓡ Kraków - Warszawa - Białystok - Suwałki - Mockava and v.v.
W – WIGRY – 🚃 Ⓡ Warszawa - Białystok - Suwałki and v.v.

Ⓞ – 🚲 = Trakiszki (Poland) / Mockava (Lithuania); ticketing point is Mockava.

94 MOSKVA / St PETERBURG - WARSZAWA

train number	57*MJ*	57*MJ*	21*EJ*	21*EJ*	13*MJ*	13*MJ*	17*BJ*	17*BJ*	9*SZ*	9*SZ*	23*JI*	23*JI*
train number	**404**	**404**	**404**	**404**	⑥⑦	⑥⑦					**452**	**452**
notes	**SW**	**SX**	**PW**	**PX**	**KW**	**KX**	**HW**	**HX**	**RW**	**RX**	**BW**	**BX**
Moskva Belorusskaya ... d.	...	...	0533	0633	1205k	1305k	1018	1118	1409	1509	2115	2215
Smolensk Tsentralny 🛂 § d.	...	...	1009	1109	1616	1716	1538	1638	1852	1952	0155	0255
St Peterburg Vitebski .. d.	2146	2146	|	|	|	|	|	|	|	|	|	|
Orsha Tsentralnaya .... § d.	1138z	1238z	1138	1238	1747	1847	1705	1805	2017	2117	0320	0420
Minsk ... d.	1414	1514	1414	1514	2009	2109	1938	2038	2301	0001	0559	0659
Brest Tsentralny 🛂 ... d.	2032	2132	2032	2132	2332	0032	0150	0250	0520	0620	1203	1303
Terespol ... a.	1950	1950	1950	1950	2312	2312	0108	0108	0438	0438	1121	1121
Warszawa Wschodnia ... a.	2230	2230	2230	2230	0138	0138	0349	0349	0737	0737	1354	1354
Warszawa Centralna ... a.	2246	2246	2246	2246	0156	0156	0425	0425	0755	0755	1430	1430

train number	24*JI*	24*JI*	10*SZ*	10*SZ*	14*MJ*	14*MJ*	18*BJ*	18*BJ*	22*AJ*	22*AJ*	22*AJ*	22*AJ*
train number	**453**	**453**			①⑦	①⑦					**52***BJ*	**52***BJ*
notes	**AW**	**AX**	**RW**	**RX**	**JW**	**JX**	**GW**	**GX**	**QW**	**QX**	**TW**	**TX**
Warszawa Centralna ... d.	1430	1430	1940	1940	0015	0015	0257	0257	0258	0258	0258	0258
Warszawa Wschodnia ... d.	1525	1525	2021	2021	0033	0033	0328	0328	0328	0328	0328	0328
Terespol ... d.	1747	1747	2317	2317	0258	0258	0605	0605	0605	0605	0605	0605
Brest Tsentralny 🛂 ... a.	1933	2033	0103	0203	0438	0538	0751	0851	0751	0851	0751	0851
Minsk ... a.	0126	0226	0702	0802	0812	0912	1346	1446	1346	1446	1346	1446
Orsha Tsentralnaya ..... § a.	0357	0457	1000	1100	1043	1143	1617	1717	1617	1717	1617	1717
St Peterburg Vitebski .. a.	|	|	|	|	|	|	|	|	|	|	0723	0723
Smolensk Tsentralny 🛂 .§ a.	0526	0626	1129	1229	1210	1310	1748	1848	1748	1848	...	...
Moskva Belorusskaya ... a.	1001	1101	1600	1700	1625k	1725k	2225	2325	2225	2325	...	...

A – TRANSEUROPEAN EXPRESS ⑤: 🛏 1, 2 cl. Paris (**453**) - Berlin - Brest (**24** *JI*) - Moskva. ✕ (RZD) Brest - Moskva.

B – TRANSEUROPEAN EXPRESS ③: 🛏 1, 2 cl. Moskva (**23** *JI*) - Brest (**452**) - Berlin - Paris. ✕ (RZD) Moskva - Brest.

G – ⑥: 🛏 1 cl. (lux), 🛏 1, 2 cl. Nice - Warszawa - Moskva. ✕ (RZD) Brest - Moskva (journey two nights).

H – ④: 🛏 1 cl. (lux), 🛏 1, 2 cl. Moskva - Warszawa - Nice. ✕ (RZD) Moskva - Brest (journey two nights).

J – ①⑦: 🛏 1 cl. (lux), 🛏 1, 2 cl., 🚃 ✕ Ⓡ Berlin - Warszawa - Moskva, Talgo train.

K – ⑥⑦: 🛏 1 cl. (lux), 🛏 1, 2 cl., 🚃 ✕ Ⓡ Moskva - Warszawa - Berlin, Talgo train.

P – VLTAVA ⑤: 🛏 1, 2 cl. Moskva (**21***EJ*) - Terespol (**404**) - Praha (Table **95**). Conveys on ⑤: 🛏 1, 2 cl. Moskva - Wien.

Q – VLTAVA ⑥: 🛏 1, 2 cl. Praha (**405**) - Brest (**22***AJ*) - Moskva (Table **95**). Conveys on ⑥: 🛏 1, 2 cl. Wien - Moskva.

R – POLONEZ – 🛏 1, 2 cl. 🍸 Moskva - Warszawa and v.v. ✕ Moskva - Brest and v.v. Conveys, subject to confirmation, 🛏 1, 2 cl. Moskva - Warszawa - Kraków and v.v.

S – ④: 🛏 1, 2 cl. St Peterburg (**57***MJ*) - Orsha (**21***JA*) - Terespol (**404**) - Praha (journey 2 nights).
Conveys 🛏 1, 2 cl. St Peterburg (**57***MJ*) - Orsha (**21***JA*) - Terespol (**404**) - Bohumín (**101**) - Wien (journey 2 nights).

T – ⑥: 🛏 1, 2 cl. Praha (**405**) - Brest (**22***AJ*) - Orsha (**52***BJ*) - St Peterburg (journey 2 nights).
Conveys on ⑥: 🛏 1, 2 cl. Wien (**100**) - Bohumín (**405**) - Brest (**22***AJ*) - Orsha (**20***GJ*) - St Peterburg (journey 2 nights).

W – Mar. 26 - Oct. 28.

X – Dec. 11 - Mar. 25.

k – Moskva **Kurskaya**.

z – Arrive 0907.

§ – 🛂: Osinovka (BY) / Krasnoye (RU).

95 MOSKVA and St PETERBURG - PRAHA, WIEN and BUDAPEST

Times in Russia and Belarus subject to alteration from March 26, 2017

train number	57*MJ*	57*MJ*	21*EJ*	21*EJ*		17*BJ*		9*SZ*
notes	**B**	**Q**	**V**	**C**		**S**		**D**
Moskva Belorusskaya ... d.	...	...	0633	0633	...	1118	...	1509
Smolensk Tsentralny 🛂 ....§ d.	...	...	1109	1109	...	1638	...	1952
St Peterburg Vitebski ... d.	2146	2146	|	|	...	|	...	|
Orsha Tsentralnaya ... § d.	1238x	1238x	1238	1238	...	1805	...	2117
Minsk ... d.	1514	1514	1514	1514	...	2035	...	0001
Brest Tsentralny 🛂 ... a.	1856	1856	1856	1856	...	0024	...	0328
Brest Tsentralny 🛂 ... d.	2132	2132	2132	2132	...	0250	...	0620
Terespol ... a.	1950	1950	1950	1950	...	0108	...	0438
Warszawa Centralna ... a.	2246	2246	2246	2246	...	0425	...	0737
Kraków Gł. ... a.	|	|	|	|	...	|	...	1123z
Katowice ... a.	0158	0158	0158	0158	...	0713	...	...
Bohumín 🛂 ... a.	0310	0310r	0310	0310r	...	0843	...	...
Ostrava hlavní ... a.	0605	0658	0605	0658	...	|	...	...
Břeclav ... a.	|	0850	|	0850	...	1050	...	...
Wien Hbf ... a.	|	0949	|	0949	...	1232	...	...
Olomouc ... a.	0719	...	0719	...	...	...	...	...
Pardubice ... a.	0837	...	0837	...	...	...	...	...
Praha hlavní ... a.	0939	...	0939	...	...	...	...	...

train number	10*NJ*		22*IJ*	18*BJ*	22*AJ*	22*IJ*	22*AJ*	
notes	**E**		**H**	**T**	**W**	**P**	**A**	
Praha hlavní ... d.	...	...	...	...	1822	...	1822	...
Pardubice ... d.	...	...	...	...	1921	...	1921	...
Olomouc ... d.	...	...	...	...	2041	...	2041	...
Wien Hbf ... d.	...	...	1809	1841	|	1809	|	...
Břeclav ... d.	...	...	1911	2006	|	1911	|	...
Ostrava hlavní ... d.	...	...	2101	|	2151	2101	2151	...
Bohumín 🛂 ... d.	...	...	2227	2227	2227	2227	2227	...
Katowice ... d.	...	...	2345	2345	2345	2345	2345	...
Kraków Gł. ... d.	1438z	...	|	|	|	|	|	...
Warszawa Centralna ... d.	1710	...	0258	0257	0258	0258	0258	...
Terespol ... d.	2317	...	0605	0605	0605	0605	0605	...
Brest Tsentralny 🛂 ... a.	0203	...	0851	0851	0851	0851	0851	...
Brest Tsentralny 🛂 ... d.	0418	...	1100	1100	1100	1100	1100	...
Minsk ... a.	0802	...	1446	1446	1446	1446	1446	...
Orsha Tsentralnaya ... § a.	1100	...	1717	1717	1717	1717t	1717t	...
St Peterburg Vitebski ... a.	|	...	|	|	|	0723	0723	...
Smolensk Tsentralny 🛂 .§ a.	1229	...	1848	1848	1848	...	...	...
Moskva Belorusskaya ... a.	1700	...	2325	2325	2325	...	...	...

A – ⑥: 🛏 1, 2 cl. Praha (**405**) - Brest (**22***AJ*) - Orsha (**52***BJ*) - St Peterburg (journey 2 nights).

B – ④: 🛏 1, 2 cl. St Peterburg (**57***MJ*) - Orsha (**21***EJ*) - Terespol (**404**) - Praha (journey 2 nights).

C – ⑤: 🛏 1, 2 cl. Moskva (**21***EJ*) - Terespol (**404**) - Bohumín (**101**) - Wien.

D – 🛏 1, 2 cl. Moskva - Brest - Warszawa. 🛏 1, 2 cl. Moskva - Brest - Warszawa - Kraków ✣.

E – 🛏 1, 2 cl. Warszawa - Brest - Moskva. 🛏 1, 2 cl. Kraków - Warszawa - Brest - Moskva ✣.

H – ⑥: 🛏 1, 2 cl. Wien (**100**) - Bohumín (**405**) - Brest (**22***IJ*) - Moskva.

P – ⑥: 🛏 1, 2 cl. Wien (**100**) - Ostrava (**405**) - Brest (**22***IJ*) - Orsha (**52***BJ*) - St Peterburg, (journey 2 nights).

Q – ④: 🛏 1, 2 cl. St Peterburg (**57***MJ*) - Orsha (**21***EJ*) - Terespol (**404**) - Ostrava (**101**) - Wien, (journey 2 nights).

S – ④: 🛏 1 cl. (lux), 🛏 1, 2 cl. Moskva - Wien - Nice. ✕ (RZD) Moskva - Brest and ✕ (PKP) Warszawa - Nice (journey two nights).

T – ⑥: 🛏 1 cl. (lux), 🛏 1, 2 cl. Nice - Wien - Moskva. ✕ (PKP) Nice - Warszawa and ✕ (RZD) Brest - Moskva (journey two nights).

V – VLTAVA ⑤: 🛏 1, 2 cl. Moskva (**21***EJ*) - Terespol (**404**) - Praha.

W – VLTAVA ⑥: 🛏 1, 2 cl. Praha (**405**) - Brest (**22***AJ*) - Moskva.

r – Depart 0650.

t – Depart 2055.

x – Arrive 0907.

z – Subject to confirmation.

§ – 🛂: Osinovka (BY) / Krasnoye (RU).

✣ – Subject to confirmation.

96 BUDAPEST / PRAHA / BRATISLAVA - KYÏV

train number	801	443	*IC* 34
train number	**82**	**82**	**81***LJ*
notes	**A**	**C**	**L**
Budapest Nyugati ... d.	...	...	0723
Szolnok ... d.	...	...	0838
Debrecen ... d.	...	...	0954
Záhony 🛂 ... a.	...	...	1121
Praha hlavní ... d.	...	2309	|
Bratislava hlavná ... d.	2349	|	|
Žilina ... d.	|	0516	|
Zvolen ... d.	0316	|	|
Košice ... d.	1006	1006	|
Čierna nad Tisou 🛂 ... a.	1151	1151	|
Chop 🛂 ... a.	1410	1410	1340
Lviv ... a.	2224	2224	2224
Khmelnytsky ... a.	0228	0228	0228
Vinnytsya ... a.	0432	0432	0432
Kyïv ... a.	0743	0743	0743

train number	81*DJ*	771	771
train number	*IC* **33**	**800**	**107**
notes	**L**	**B**	**D**
Kyïv ... d.	2108	2324	2324
Vinnytsya ... d.	0015	0215	0215
Khmelnytsky ... d.	0215	0538	0538
Lviv ... d.	0646	1010	1010
Chop 🛂 ... d.	1420	1735	1735
Čierna nad Tisou 🛂 ... d.	|	1805	1805
Košice ... a.	|	1954	1954
Zvolen ... a.	|	0155	|
Žilina ... a.	|	|	0115
Bratislava hlavná ... a.	|	0525	|
Praha hlavní ... a.	|	...	0739
Záhony 🛂 ... a.	1337	...	...
Debrecen ... a.	1601	...	...
Szolnok ... a.	1720	...	...
Budapest Nyugati ... a.	1837	...	...

A – ①–⑤ (not Dec. 26, Jan. 6, Apr. 14, 17, May 1, 8): 🛏 1, 2 cl. Bratislava (**801**) - Košice (**8807**) - Čierna nad Tisou (**8862**) - Chop (**82**) - Lviv - Kyïv (journey two nights).

B – ①②③⑥⑦ (not Dec. 24, Jan. 4, Apr. 12, 15, 29, May 6): 🛏 1, 2 cl. Kyïv (**771**) - Khmelnytsky - Lviv (**107**) - Chop (**8863**) - Čierna nad Tisou (**8820**) - Košice (**800**) - Bratislava (journey two nights).

C – 🛏 1, 2 cl. Praha (**443**) - Košice (**8807**) - Čierna nad Tisou (**8862**) - Chop (**82**) - Lviv - Kyïv (journey two nights).

D – 🛏 1, 2 cl. Kyïv (**771**) - Khmelnytsky - Lviv (**107**) - Chop (**8863**) - Čierna nad Tisou (**8820**) - Košice (**442**) - Praha (journey two nights).

L – LATORCA – 🛏 1, 2 cl. Budapest - Lviv - Kyïv and v.v.

97 WARSZAWA - LVIV

train type/number	1326	1326
notes	**6307**	**6307**
notes	**35**	**51**
	AP	**AQ**
Warszawa Centralna . d.	1855	1855
Kraków Gł. ... d.	2214	2214
Przemyśl ... d.	0252	0356
Medyka 🛂 ... d.	|	|
Mostiska **II** 🛂 ... ‡ a.	0421	0530
Lviv ... ‡ a.	0603	0715

train type/number	36	52
notes	**3606**	**3606**
notes	**3124**	**3124**
	BQ	**BP**
Lviv ... ‡ d.	2259	2315
Mostiska **II** 🛂 ... ‡ d.	0045	0101
Medyka 🛂 ... d.	|	|
Przemyśl ... a.	0020	0036
Kraków Gł. ... a.	0538	0538
Warszawa Centralna d.	0905	0905

A – LVIV EXPRESS – 🛏 2 cl. Warszawa (**1326**) - Kraków (**6307**) - Przemyśl (**35/51**) - Lviv. Conveys 🛏 2 cl. Wrocław (**6307**) - Kraków - Przemyśl - Lviv.

B – LVIV EXPRESS – 🛏 2 cl. Lviv (**52/36**) - Przemyśl (**3606**) - Kraków (**3124**) - Warszawa. Conveys 🛏 2 cl. Lviv - Przemyśl (**3606**) - Kraków - Wrocław.

P – Runs on even dates in Jan., Apr., May, Aug., Nov., Dec. 2017; uneven dates in Dec. 2016, Feb., Mar., June, July, Sept., Oct.

Q – Runs on even dates in Dec. 2016, Feb., Mar., June, July, Sept., Oct.; uneven dates in Jan., Apr., May, Aug., Nov., Dec. 2017.

‡ – Ukrainian (East European) time.

88 Standard-Symbole sind auf Seite 4 erklärt 12

WARSZAWA and KRAKÓW - PRAHA, WIEN and BUDAPEST — 99

train type/train number	EC	EC	EC		EC	RJ	Ex	EC	EC	EC		EC				402	EN	402		Ex	EC
train number	116	103	277		131	77	114	105	281	112		110	407	407	407	407	402	402		101	273
notes/train number													477			444	477	407			
notes	⚊	⚊	⚊		⚊	⚊				⚊		⚊ Ⓡ									
notes	Y	X	Z		V		L	W	K	M		T	B	C	P	A	D	R		H	N
Gdynia Główny .... d.	...	...	...	...	...	...	0925	...	...	...		...	...	...	...	...	...	...		...	...
Gdańsk Główny .... d.	...	...	...	...	...	...	0950	...	...	...		...	...	...	...	...	...	...		...	...
Warszawa Wschodnia ..... d.	0539	0644	...	...	0924	...	1234	1339	...	1738		2112	2112	2112	...	...	...	2240			
Warszawa Centralna ...... d.	0550	0655	...	...	0955	...	1255	1355	...	1754		2125	2125	2125	...	...	...	2251			
Kraków Główny .... d.	...	...	...	...	...	1042e	...	...	...	...		...	...	...	2202	2202	2202	...			
Katowice .... d.	0828	0930	...	...	1231	...	1528	...	1631	2027		0008	0010	0008	...	...	0200	...			
Zebrzydowice 🚩 .... d.		1023	...	...	1323	...	1623	...	...	...		0103	0103	0103	0054	0054	0054	0251			
Bohumín 🚩 .... a.	0947	1040	...	...	1340	1331e	1640	...	1749	...		0121	0121	0121	0112	0112	0112	0410			
Bohumín 🚩 .... d.	1008	1050	...	...	1350	1410	1650	...	1808	...		0220	0220	0214	0220	0220	0329	0650			
Ostrava hlavní .... a.	1016	1058	...	...	1358	1416	1658	...	1816	2155		0228	0228	0222	0228	0228	0336	0658			
Přerov .... a.		1149	...	...	1449	...	1749	...	...	...		0318	0318	0311	0318	0318	...	0749			
Olomouc .... a.	1119		...	...		1519	...	1919	...	...		...	...	0356	...	...	0440	...			
Pardubice .... a.	1237		...	...		1637	...	2037	...	...		...	...	0523	...	...	0607	...			
Praha hlavní .... a.	1339		...	...		1739	...	2139	...	...		...	...	0633	...	...	0722	...			
Břeclav .... a.	...	1250	1259	...	1550	1555	...	1850	1859	...		0414	0414	...	0414	0414	...	0850	0859		
Wien Hbf .... a.	...	1349		...		1649	...	1949	...	...		0655	...	0655	...	0949	...			
Kúty 🚩 .... a.	...	...	1311	...	1611	...	...	...	1911	...		0453	...	0453	...	...	...	0911		
Bratislava hlavná .... a.	...	...	1350	...	1650	...	...	...	1950	...		0536	...	0536	...	...	...	0950		
Štúrovo 🚩 △ .... a.	...	...	1511	...	1811	...	...	...	2111	...		0710	...	0710	...	...	...	1111		
Budapest Keleti .... a.	...	...	1635	...	1935	...	...	...	2235	...		0837	...	0837	...	...	...	1235		

train type/train number	EC	EC	EC	EC		Ex	RJ	EC	EC	EC	EC		EC	Ex	EC		EN	EN	476		476			
train number	111	113	280	104		115	74	130	276	102	117		272	100			406	50406	476	406	445	443		
notes/train number	⚊ Ⓡ		⚊	⚊					⚊		⚊		⚊					403	406	403	406	403		
notes	①–⑥																							
notes	Tz	M	K	W		J		V	Z	X	Y		N	H			C	E	G	F	Q	S		
Budapest Keleti .... d.	...	...	0525	...		...	0822	1125	...	...	...		1525	...		...	...	2005	2005	...		
Štúrovo 🚩 △ .... d.	...	...	0649	...		...	0949	1249	...	...	...		1649	...		...	...	2124	2124	...		
Bratislava hlavná .... d.	...	...	0810	...		...	1110	1410	...	...	...		1810	...		...	...	2301	2301	...		
Kúty 🚩 .... d.	...	...	0849	...		...	1149	1449	...	...	...		1849	...		...	...	2343	2343	...		
Wien Hbf .... d.	...	...	...	0809		1109		1204	1409	...	...		...	1809		2250	2250	...	...	...		
Břeclav .... d.	...	...	0901	0911		...	1204	1211	1501	1511	...		1901	1911		0013	0013	0013	0013	...		
Praha hlavní .... d.	...	0622	...		1022	...	...	...	1422	...	...		...	...		...	...	...	...	2200	2309	
Pardubice .... d.	...	0721	...		1121	...	...	...	1521	...	...		...	...		...	...	...	...	2316	0023	
Olomouc .... d.	...	0841	...		1241	...	...	...	1641	...	...		...	...		...	...	...	...	0041	0155	
Přerov .... d.	...		1009			...	1309	...	1609	...	...		2009			0105	0105	0105	0105	0126		
Ostrava hlavní .... d.	0556	0944	1101		1344	...	1401	...	1701	1744	...		2101			0156	0156	0156	0156	0217	0302	
Bohumín 🚩 .... a.		0952	1108		1352	...	1408	...	1708	1752	...		2108			0203	0203	0203	0203	0226	0309	
Bohumín 🚩 .... d.		1007	1120		1429x	...	1420	...	1720	1809	...		2246			0300	0404	0300	0404	0300	0404	
Zebrzydowice 🚩 .... d.			1138			...	1438	...	1738	...	...		2306			0319	0423	0319	0423	0319	0423	
Katowice .... a.	0727	1129	1230			...	1526	...	1830	1933	...		2339			0416		0416		0416		
Kraków Główny .... a.	...	...	...		1721x	...	...	...	...	...	...		...	...		...	0705		0705		0705	
Warszawa Centralna ...... a.	1005	1405	1505			...	1800	...	2105	2205	...		0256			0700		0700		0700		
Warszawa Wschodnia ..... a.	1031	1416	1526			...	1836	...	2126	2226	...		0307			0712		0712		0712		
Gdańsk Główny .... a.	...	...	1808																			
Gdynia Główny .... a.	...	...	1833																			

A – 🛏 1, 2 cl., ⚊ 2 cl., 🍴 Kraków (402) - Bohumín (407) - Břeclav (477) - Budapest.

B – 🛏 1, 2 cl., ⚊ 2 cl., 🍴 Warszawa (407) - Břeclav (477) - Bratislava - Budapest.

C – CHOPIN – 🛏 1, 2 cl., ⚊ 2 cl. (4, 6 berth) 🍴 Warszawa - Wien and v.v.

D – 🛏 1, 2 cl., (also ⚊ 2 cl. (4, 6 berth) Dec. 13 - Jan. 11, not Dec. 25, Jan. 1, also Mar. 12 - Nov. 2), 🍴 Kraków (402) - Bohumín (407) - Wien.

E – 🛏 1, 2 cl., (also ⚊ 2 cl. (4, 6 berth) Dec. 13 - Jan. 11, not Dec. 25, Jan. 1, also Mar. 12 - Nov. 2), 🍴 Wien (406) - Bohumín (403) - Kraków.

F – 🛏 1, 2 cl., ⚊ 2 cl., 🍴 Budapest (476) - Břeclav (406) - Bohumín (403) - Kraków.

G – 🛏 1, 2 cl., ⚊ 2 cl., 🍴 Budapest (476) - Břeclav (406) - Warszawa.

H – MORAVIA – 🍴 Bohumín - Ostrava - Břeclav - Wien and v.v. Conveys on dates in Table 95 🛏 2 cl. Moskva / St Peterburg - Bohumín - Wien and v.v.

J – CRACOVIA – 🍴 Praha - Bohumín - (Apr. 13 - Sept. 30 Kraków).

K – JÁN JESENIUS / JESZENSZKY JÁNOS – 🍴 🍴 Praha - Břeclav - Budapest and v.v. (Table 60).

L – CRACOVIA – 🍴 (Apr. 14 - Oct. 1 Kraków) - Bohumín - Praha.

M – PORTA MORAVICA – 🍴 🍴 Warszawa - Katowice - Praha and v.v.

N – CSÁRDÁS – 🍴 🍴 Praha - Břeclav - Budapest and v.v. (Table 60).

P – 🛏 1, 2 cl., 🍴 (also ⚊ 2 cl. Dec. 10 - Jan. 8, not Dec. 24, 31, also Mar. 9 - Nov. 1) Warszawa (407) - Bohumín (444) - Praha.

Q – 🛏 1, 2 cl., 🍴 (also ⚊ 2 cl. Dec. 11 - Jan. 9, not Dec. 24, 31, Jan. 2, also Mar. 10 - Nov. 2) Praha (445) - Bohumín (406) - Warszawa.

R – SILESIA – 🛏 1, 2 cl., 🍴 (also ⚊ 2 cl. Dec. 16 - Jan. 9, not Dec. 24, 31, also Apr. 6 - Nov. 6) Kraków (402) - Bohumín (442) - Praha.

S – SILESIA – 🛏 1, 2 cl., ⚊ 2 cl. 🍴 (also ⚊ 2 cl. Dec. 15 - Jan. 8, not Dec. 24, 31, also April 5 - Nov. 5) Praha (443) - Bohumín (403) - Kraków.

T – COMENIUS – 🍴 🍴 Warszawa - Katowice - Ostrava and v.v.

V – VARSOVIA – 🍴 🍴 Warszawa - Katowice - Břeclav - Budapest and v.v.

W – SOBIESKI – 🍴 🍴 Gdynia - Warszawa - Katowice - Wien and v.v.

X – POLONIA – 🍴 🍴 Warszawa - Katowice - Wien and v.v.

Y – PRAHA – 🍴 🍴 Warszawa - Katowice - Praha and v.v.

Z – SLOVAN – 🍴 🍴 Praha - Břeclav - Budapest and v.v. (Table 60).

e – Apr. 14 - Oct. 1.

x – Apr. 13 - Sept. 30.

y – Not Dec. 25, Apr. 16.

z – Not Dec. 26, Apr. 17.

△ – Routeing point for international tickets : Szob.

⚊ – Supplement payable in Poland; Reservation compulsory in Poland.

SC – SUPERCITY PENDOLINO train, 🍴 Ⓡ ✗; operated by tilting trains.

✗ – Ⓡ with supplement payable.

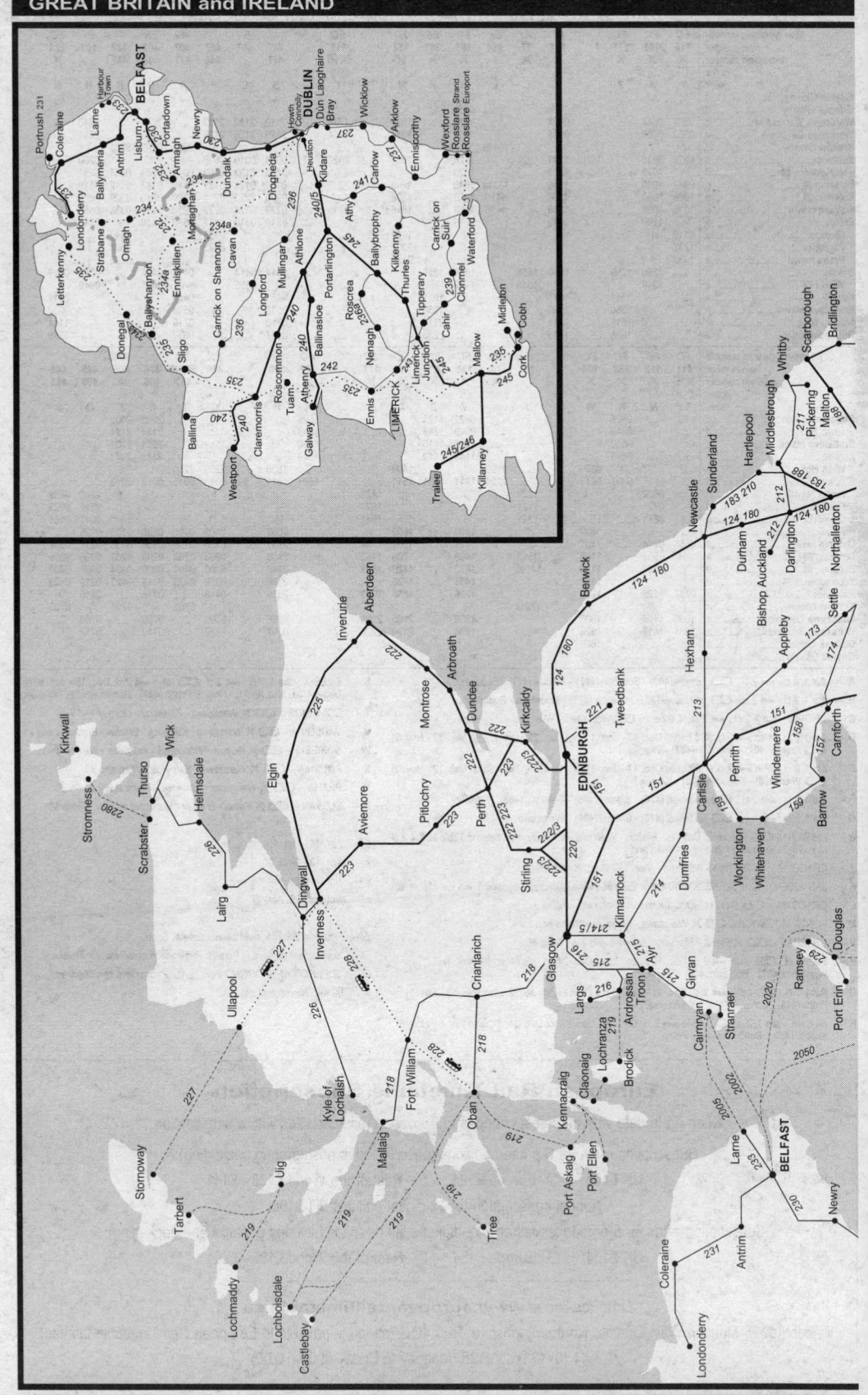

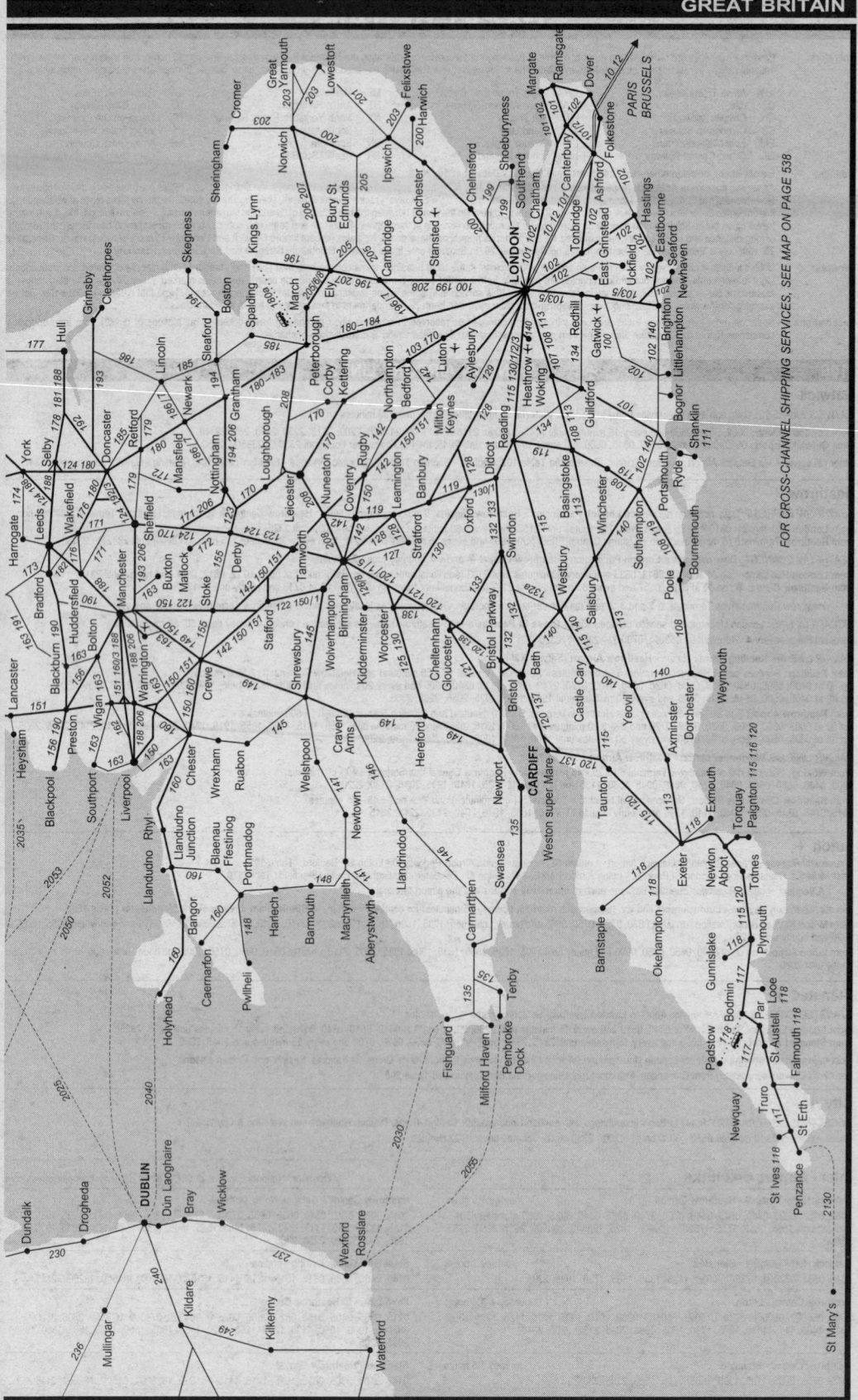

FOR CROSS-CHANNEL SHIPPING SERVICES, SEE MAP ON PAGE 538

GREAT BRITAIN

Operators: Passenger services are provided by a number of private passenger train companies operating the **National Rail** (www.nationalrail.co.uk) network on lines owned by the British national railway infrastructure company **Network Rail**. The following Network Rail codes are used in the table headings to indicate the operators of trains in each table:

AW	Arriva Trains Wales	GR	Virgin Trains East Coast	ME	Merseyrail	SW	South West Trains
CC	c2c	GW	Great Western Railway	NT	Arriva Rail North	TL	Thameslink Railway
CH	Chiltern Railways	HT	Hull Trains	NY	North Yorkshire Moors Railway	TP	TransPennine Express
CS	Caledonian Sleeper	IL	Island Line	SE	Southeastern	VT	Virgin Trains West Coast
EM	East Midlands Trains	LE	Greater Anglia	SN	Southern	XC	Arriva Cross Country
GC	Grand Central Railway	LM	London Midland	SR	Abellio ScotRail		

Timings: Except where indicated otherwise, timings are valid **May 15 - December 10, 2016.**

As service patterns at weekends (especially on ⑦) usually differ greatly from those applying on Mondays to Fridays, the timings in most tables are grouped by days of operation : Ⓐ = Mondays to Fridays ; ✕ = Mondays to Saturdays ; ⑥ = Saturdays ; ⑦ = Sundays. Track engineering work, affecting journey times, frequently takes place at weekends, so it is advisable to confirm your journey details locally if planning to travel in the period between the late evening of ⑥ and the late afternoon of ⑦. Confirm timings, too, if you intend travelling on public holidays (see page 2) as there may be alterations to services at these times. Suburban and commuter services are the most likely to be affected; the majority of long-distance and cross-country trains marked Ⓐ and ✕ run as normal on these dates. No trains (except limited Gatwick and Heathrow Express services) run on **December 25**, with only a limited service on certain routes on December 26. In Scotland only trains between Edinburgh / Glasgow and England run on **January 1**.

Services: Unless indicated otherwise (by '2' in the train column or '2nd class' in the table heading), trains convey both **first** (1st) and **standard** (2nd) classes of seated accommodation. Light refreshments (snacks, hot and cold drinks) are available from a **buffet car** or a **mobile trolley service** on board those trains marked ♈ and ✕ : the latter also convey a **restaurant car** or serve meals to passengers at their seats (this service is in some cases available to first-class ticket holders only). Note that catering facilities may not be available for the whole of a train's journey. **Sleeping-cars** (🛏) have one berth per compartment in first class and two in standard class.

Reservations: Seats on most long-distance trains and berths in sleeping-cars can be reserved in advance when purchasing travel tickets at rail stations or directly from train operating companies (quote the departure time of the train and your destination). Seat reservation is normally free of charge.

100   LONDON AIRPORT LINKS

Gatwick ✈

GATWICK EXPRESS : Daily non-stop rail service from/ to **London Victoria**. Journey time : 30 minutes (35 minutes on ⑦).

From **London** Victoria : 0002, 0030, 0500 and every 15 minutes until 2045, 2100⑥, 2115Ⓑ, 2130⑥, 2145Ⓑ, 2200, 2215, 2230, 2300, 2330, 2345.
From **Gatwick** Airport : 0020, 0035, 0050, 0135, 0545, 0600 and every 15 minutes until 2045, then 2-3 trains per hour until 2330⑥, 2335Ⓐ, 2350⑦.

Other rail services via Gatwick Airport : London Victoria - Eastbourne Table 102; Bedford - Brighton Table 103; London Victoria - Brighton Table 105; Reading - Gatwick Airport Table 134.

Heathrow ✈

HEATHROW EXPRESS : Daily non-stop rail service **London Paddington - Heathrow** Terminal 5 and v.v. Journey times : **Heathrow** Central ♣ 15 minutes, Heathrow Terminal 5 21 minutes.

From **London** Paddington : 0510✕/0625⑦ and every 15 minutes until 2155, then every 30 minutes (15 minutes on ⑤⑦) until 2325.
From **Heathrow** Terminal 5 (5 mins. later from Heathrow Central) : 0507✕/0618⑦ and every 15 minutes until 2212, then every 30 minutes (15 mins. on ⑤⑦) until 2342✕ / 2348⑦.

HEATHROW CONNECT : Daily rail service **London Paddington - Heathrow** Central ♣ and v.v. Journey time 32 minutes.

From **London** Paddington : on ✕ at 0442, 0513, 0533 and every 30 minutes until 2103 (additional later trains on ⑤⑥); on ⑦ at 0612, 0712, 0812, 0907 and hourly until 2312.
From **Heathrow** Central ♣ : on ✕ at 0529, 0557 and every 30 minutes until 2127 (additional later trains on ⑤⑥); on ⑦ at 0713 and hourly until 2313.

♣ –   Heathrow Central serves Terminals 1, 2 and 3. A free rail transfer service operates every 15 minutes Heathrow Central - Heathrow **Terminals 4 and 5 and v.v.**

PICCADILLY LINE : London Underground service between **Kings Cross St Pancras** and all Heathrow terminals via Central London. Journey time : 50 - 58 minutes.
Frequent trains (every 4 - 10 minutes) 0530✕ / 0730⑦ - 2300✕ / 2330⑦.

RAILAIR LINK 🚌 **Reading** railway station - **Heathrow Airport** (Service **X25**).
From **Reading** : Services call at Heathrow Terminal 5 (±40 minutes), Heathrow Terminal 1 (±50 minutes) and Heathrow Terminal 3 (±56 minutes) :
On Ⓐ at 0400, 0500, 0530, 0555, 0608, 0620, 0640, 0700, 0720, 0740, 0800, 0820, 0840, 0905 and every 20 minutes until 1805, 1835, 1905, 1935, 2005, 2035, 2105, 2205, 2305.
On ⑥ at 0400, 0500, 0545, 0615, 0645 and every 30 minutes until 1915, 1945, 2025, 2055, 2205, 2305.
From **Heathrow** Airport Bus Station : Services call at Heathrow Terminal 5 (± 10 minutes) and Reading Railway Station (± 50 minutes).
On Ⓐ at 0005, 0500, 0600, 0630, 0657, 0720 and every 20 minutes until 1000, 1015, and every 20 minutes until 1755, 1815, 1835, 1855, 1915, 1940, 2010, 2040, 2110, 2140, 2215, 2305.
On ⑥ at 0005, 0500, 0600, 0700, 0730 and every 30 minutes until 1900, 1920, 1950, 2020, 2050, 2130, 2200, 2305.

RAILAIR LINK 🚌 **Woking** rail station - **Heathrow Airport** (Service **701**).
From **Woking** : Services call at Heathrow Terminal 5 (± 25 - 45 minutes) and Heathrow Central Bus Station (± 40 - 60 minutes) :
0300, 0400, 0500, 0600, 0640, 0740, 0845, 0945, 1050, 1135 and hourly until 1735, 1845, 1945, 2045, 2130, 2220.
From **Heathrow** Central Bus Station : Services call at Heathrow Terminal 5 (± 15 minutes) and Woking (± 45 - 65 minutes).
0645, 0745, 0845, 0950, 1040, 1140, 1230 and hourly until 1630, 1735, 1835, 1940, 2040, 2130, 2215, 2315.

Luton ✈

Thameslink Railway services Brighton - Gatwick Airport - London St Pancras - Luton Airport Parkway 🔲 - Luton 🔲 - Bedford : Table 103.
East Midlands Trains services London St Pancras - Luton Airport Parkway 🔲 - Luton 🔲 - Leicester - Nottingham / Derby / Sheffield : Table 170.
🔲 –   A frequent shuttle 🚌 service operates between each of the railway stations and the airport terminal.

🚌 service Milton **Keynes - Luton** Airport and v.v. (Stagecoach route **99**. Journey 55 minutes) for connections from/ to **Birmingham**, **Liverpool** and **Manchester** (Table 150).
From **Milton Keynes** railway station : on Ⓐ at 0630, 0720, 0750, 0855 and hourly until 1655, 1735, 1805, 1835, 1905, 2010, 2110, 2210; on ⑥ at 0630, 0750, 0855 and hourly until 2055; on ⑦ at 0920 and hourly until 2120.
From **Luton** Airport : on Ⓐ at 0540, 0650, 0750, 0905 and hourly until 1705, 1735, 1805, 1835, 1905, 1935, 2005, 2110; on ⑥ at 0540, 0650, 0750, 0905 and hourly until 2005; on ⑦ at 0820 and hourly until 2020.

Stansted ✈

STANSTED EXPRESS : Daily rail service from/ to **London Liverpool St**. Journey time ± 45 minutes.
From **London** Liverpool St : on ✕ at 0440, 0510 and every 15 minutes until 2255, 2325; on ⑦ at 0440, 0510, 0540, 0610 and every 15 minutes until 2255, 2325.
From **Stansted** Airport : on ✕ at 0600 and every 15 minutes until 2345, 2359; on ⑦ at 0530, 0600, 0630, 0700 and every 15 minutes until 2345, 2359.

Most trains call at **Tottenham Hale** for London Underground (Victoria Line) connections to/from Kings Cross, St Pancras, Euston, and Victoria stations.
For *Cross Country* services to / from Cambridge, Peterborough, Leicester and Birmingham see Table **208**.

City ✈

DOCKLANDS LIGHT RAILWAY from/ to **Bank** (interchange with London Underground : Central, Circle, District, Northern, and Waterloo & City Lines).
Trains run every 7 - 10 minutes 0530 - 0030 on ✕, 0700 - 2330 on ⑦. Journey time: ± 22 minutes.

Inter - Airport 🚌 links

Operator : National Express ✆ 08717 81 81 81. www.nationalexpress.com

Gatwick North Terminal - **Heathrow** Central.   Journey 1½ hours
0055, 0155, 0320, 0440, 0540, 0640, 0700, 0740, 0825, 0840, 0925, 0955 and every 30 minutes until 1555, 1655, 1735, 1755Ⓒ, 1805Ⓐ, 1825, 1955Ⓒ, 2005Ⓐ, 2055, 2200, 2255, 2355.

Heathrow Central - **Gatwick** North Terminal.
0015, 0035, 0240, 0340, 0535, 0635, 0720Ⓐ, 0735Ⓒ, 0835, 0905, 0935, 1025, 1035, 1120, 1135, 1235, 1245, 1335, 1340, 1435, 1455, 1535, 1545, 1635, 1720, 1735, 1835, 1920, 1935, 1950, 2035, 2130, 2205, 2305.

Gatwick North Terminal - **Stansted**.   Journey 3 hours
0340, 0535, 0720Ⓐ, 0735Ⓒ, 0935, 1135, 1335, 1535, 1735, 1935, 2205.

Stansted - **Gatwick** North Terminal.
0140, 0405, 0605, 0815, 1015, 1215, 1415, 1615Ⓒ, 1625Ⓐ, 1815Ⓒ, 1825Ⓐ, 2115.

Heathrow Central - **Luton**.   Journey 1–1½ hours
0005, 0550Ⓒ, 0605Ⓒ, 0730, 0750Ⓐ, 0805Ⓒ, 0830, 0930, 1005, 1030, 1130, 1205, 1300, 1330, 1405, 1415, 1530, 1605, 1730, 1805, 1930, 2005, 2130, 2205, 2345.

From Luton to **Heathrow** Central.
0215, 0355, 0405, 0450, 0520, 0605, 0625Ⓒ, 0640Ⓒ, 0740Ⓐ, 0755Ⓒ, 0805, 0820Ⓐ, 0850Ⓒ, 1005, 1050, 1130, 1205, 1250, 1400, 1450, 1605, 1650, 1725, 1805, 1850, 1955, 2005, 2205.

Heathrow Central - **Stansted**.   Journey 1½ hours
0505, 0705, 0905, 1105, 1305, 1505, 1705, 1905, 2105, 2335.

Stansted - **Heathrow** Central.
0140, 0405, 0605, 0815, 1015, 1215, 1415, 1615Ⓒ, 1625Ⓐ, 1815Ⓒ, 1825Ⓐ, 2115.

SE 2nd class

LONDON - MARGATE via HS1 HIGH SPEED LINE 101

Special fares are payable for high-speed services. For slower services see Table **102**.

Via Faversham

km			Ⓐ	Ⓐ F	Ⓐ	Ⓐ F		Ⓐ F	Ⓐ	Ⓐ	Ⓐ	Ⓐ	Ⓐ	Ⓐ	Ⓐ		Ⓐ	Ⓐ	Ⓐ A	Ⓐ	Ⓐ	Ⓐ		⑥ F	⑥	⑥ F	⑥
0	**London** St Pancras d.	Ⓐ	0655	0722	0758	0825		1525	1555	1625	1658	1725	1755	1825	1855		2125	2155	2225	2255	2325	2355	⑥	0725	0755	0825	0852
9	Stratford Int'l d.		0702	0729	0805	0832	and at	1532	1602	1632	1705	1732	1802	1832	1902	and at	2132	2202	2232	2302	2332	0002		0732	0802	0832	0859
35	Ebbsfleet Int'l d.		0713	0740	0816	0843	the same	1543	1613	1643	1716	1743	1813	1844	1913	the same	2143	2213	2243	2313	2343	0013		0743	0813	0843	0913
52	Rochester d.		0731	0758	0834	0901	minutes	1601	1631	1701	1734	1758	1830	1902	1931	minutes	2201	2231	2301	2331	0001	0031		0801	0831	0901	0931
54	Chatham d.		0735	0801	0837	0904	past each	1604	1634	1704	1738	1802	1834	1906	1934	past each	2204	2234	2304	2334	0004	0034		0804	0834	0904	0934
70	Sittingbourne d.		0752	0818	0854	0921	hour until	1621	1651	1721	1755	1820	1852	1924	1953	hour until	2221	2251	2321	2351	0021	0051		0821	0851	0921	0951
83	Faversham a.		0801	0826	0903	0929	♣	1629	1700	1730	1803	1828	1900	1932	2006	♣	2229	2300	2329	0002	0030	0100		0829	0900	0929	1000
100	Herne Bay a.		...	0842	...	0944		1646	...	...	...	1843	1915	1948	...		2246	...	2346	...	...	...		0844	...	0944	...
118	**Margate** a.		...	0859	...	0959		1702	...	...	...	1857	1931	2004	...		2302	...	0002	...	...	...		0859	...	0959	...

	⑥ F	⑥	⑥ F		⑥ F	⑥	⑥	⑥	⑥	⑥	⑥	⑥		⑦ F	⑦ F	⑦ F	⑦ F	⑦ F	⑦		⑦ K	⑦	⑦	⑦	⑦	⑦	⑦
London St Pancras d.	0927	0955	1022		2025	2055	2125	2155	2225	2255	2325	2355	⑦	0825	0927	1027	1125	1225	1252		2025	2055	2125	2155	2225	2255	2325
Stratford Int'l d.	0934	1002	1032	and at	2032	2102	2132	2202	2232	2302	2332	0002		0832	0934	1034	1132	1232	1259	and at	2032	2102	2132	2202	2232	2302	2332
Ebbsfleet Int'l d.	0945	1013	1043	the same	2043	2113	2143	2213	2243	2313	2343	0013		0843	0945	1045	1143	1243	1313	the same	2043	2113	2143	2213	2243	2313	2343
Rochester d.	1002	1031	1101	minutes	2101	2131	2201	2231	2301	2331	0001	0031		0901	1002	1102	1201	1301	1331	minutes	2101	2131	2201	2231	2301	2334	0001
Chatham d.	1005	1034	1104	past each	2104	2134	2204	2234	2304	2334	0004	0034		0904	1005	1105	1204	1304	1334	past each	2104	2134	2204	2234	2304	2337	0004
Sittingbourne d.	1022	1051	1121	hour until	2121	2151	2221	2251	2321	2351	0021	0051		0921	1022	1122	1221	1321	1351	hour until	2121	2151	2221	2251	2321	2355	0021
Faversham a.	1030	1100	1129	♣	2129	2200	2229	2300	2329	0001	0030	0100		0929	1030	1130	1229	1329	1404	♣	2129	2204	2229	2304	2329	0004	0030
Herne Bay a.	1044	...	1144		2144	...	2244	...	2344	...	...	...		0944	1044	1144	1244	1344	...		2144	...	2244	...	2344	...	...
Margate a.	1059	...	1159		2159	...	2259	...	2359	...	...	...		0959	1059	1159	1259	1359	...		2159	...	2259	...	2359	...	...

		Ⓐ	Ⓐ	Ⓐ	Ⓐ	Ⓐ	Ⓐ	Ⓐ	Ⓐ	Ⓐ	Ⓐ	Ⓐ G	Ⓐ	Ⓐ G		Ⓐ G	Ⓐ	Ⓐ	Ⓐ G	Ⓐ	Ⓐ	Ⓐ	Ⓐ	Ⓐ G		⑥	⑥	⑥
Margate d.	Ⓐ	...	...	...	0605	0634	0703	...	...	0826	...	0926	...	1030		1730	...	1826	1838	1930	...	2030	...	2130	⑥	...	...	0630
Herne Bay d.		...	...	...	0619	0648	0717	...	...	0843	...	0943	...	1044	and at	1744	...	1843	1854	1944	...	2044	...	2144		...	...	0644
Faversham d.		0458	0528	0558	0634	0702	0731	0759	0828	0859	0926	0959	1026	1059	the same	1759	1829	1859	1928t	1959	2028	2059	2126	2159		0528	0628	0659
Sittingbourne d.		0507	0537	0607	0642	0710	0739	0807	0837	0907	0937	1007	1037	1107	minutes	1807	1837	1907	1937	2007	2037	2107	2137	2207		0537	0637	0707
Chatham d.		0524	0554	0624	0659	0727	0758	0824	0854	0924	0954	1024	1054	1124	past each	1824	1854	1924	1954	2024	2054	2124	2154	2224		0554	0654	0724
Rochester d.		0528	0558	0628	0703	0730	0802	0828	0858	0928	0958	1028	1058	1128	hour until	1828	1858	1928	1958	2028	2058	2128	2158	2228		0558	0658	0728
Ebbsfleet Int'l a.		0546	0616	0646	0717	0747	0817	0847	0916	0946	1016	1046	1116	1146	♣	1849	1916	1946	2016	2046	2116	2146	2216	2246		0616	0716	0746
Stratford Int'l a.		0558	0628	0658	0729	0800	0830	0859	0928	0959	1028	1058	1129	1159		1902	1928	1959	2028	2102	2128	2159	2228	2258		0628	0728	0758
London St Pancras a.		0606	0636	0707	0737	0807	0838	0907	0936	1006	1036	1106	1140	1206		1910	1936	2006	2036	2109	2136	2207	2236	2306		0636	0736	0806

	⑥	⑥ H	⑥	⑥ G		⑥	⑥ G	⑥	⑥ G	⑥	⑥ G	⑥	⑥ G		⑦	⑦		⑦	⑦ H	⑦ G	⑦	⑦ G		⑦	⑦ G	⑦	⑦ G
Margate d.	...	0730	...	0830		...	1830	...	1930	...	2030	...	2130	⑦	...	...	...	0830	0930	1030	...	1130		...	2030	...	2130
Herne Bay d.	...	0744	...	0844	and at	...	1844	...	1944	...	2044	...	2144		...	...	...	0844	0944	1044	...	1144	and at	...	2044	...	2144
Faversham d.	0728	0759	0828	0859	the same	1826	1859	1926	1959	2026	2059	2126	2159		0659	0759	...	0859	0959	1059	1129	1159	the same	2029	2059	2129	2159
Sittingbourne d.	0737	0807	0837	0907	minutes	1837	1907	1937	2007	2037	2107	2137	2207		0707	0807	...	0907	1007	1107	1137	1207	minutes	2037	2107	2137	2207
Chatham d.	0754	0824	0854	0924	past each	1854	1924	1954	2024	2054	2124	2154	2224		0724	0824	...	0924	1024	1124	1154	1224	past each	2054	2124	2154	2224
Rochester d.	0758	0828	0858	0928	hour until	1858	1928	1958	2028	2058	2128	2158	2228		0728	0828	...	0928	1028	1128	1158	1228	hour until	2058	2128	2158	2228
Ebbsfleet Int'l a.	0816	0846	0916	0946	♣	1916	1946	2016	2046	2116	2146	2216	2246		0746	0846	...	0946	1046	1146	1216	1246	♣	2116	2146	2216	2246
Stratford Int'l a.	0829	0858	0929	0958		1928	1958	2028	2102	2128	2158	2228	2258		0758	0858	...	0958	1058	1159	1228	1258		2128	2159	2228	2258
London St Pancras a.	0836	0906	0936	1006		1936	2006	2036	2109	2136	2206	2236	2306		0806	0906	...	1006	1106	1207	1236	1306		2136	2207	2236	2306

Via Ashford and Dover

km			②–⑤	Ⓐ	Ⓐ	Ⓐ D	Ⓐ	Ⓐ	Ⓐ D	Ⓐ	Ⓐ D		Ⓐ	Ⓐ D	Ⓐ	Ⓐ	Ⓐ	Ⓐ	Ⓐ	Ⓐ	Ⓐ	Ⓐ	Ⓐ	Ⓐ	Ⓐ	Ⓐ D
0	**London** St Pancras d.	Ⓐ	0012	0640	0704	0725	0737	0812	0837	0909	0937		1612	1637	1650	1707	1720	1737	1750	1807	1820	1837	1850	1907	1920	1937
9	Stratford International d.		0019	0647	0711	0732	0744	0819	0844	0916	0944	and at	1619	1644	1657	1714	1727	1744	1757	1814	1827	1845	1857	1914	1927	1944
35	Ebbsfleet International d.		0030	0659	0722	|	0755	0830	0855	0927	0955	the same	1630	1655	|	1726	|	1756	|	1826	|	1856	|	1926	|	1955
90	Ashford International d.		0050	0722	0742	0801	0817	0852	0915	0952	1015	minutes	1652	1718	1726	1747	1756	1817	1826	1847	1856	1917	1926	1947	1956	2015
112	**Folkestone** Central d.		...	|	|	0819	0837	|	0930	|	1030	past each	|	1733	|	1803	|	1833	|	1903	|	1934	|	2003	|	2030
124	**Dover** Priory a.		...	|	|	0830	0847	|	0941	|	1041	hour until	|	1744	|	1815	|	1844	|	1915	|	1945	|	2015	|	2041
112	Canterbury West d.		...	0740	0758	|	|	0909	|	1009	|	♠	1709	|	1742	...	1812	|	1842	...	1912	...	1942	...	2012	|
140	Ramsgate a.		...	0803	0818	0910	0924	0927	1018	1027	1118		1729	1823	1801	...	1831	1925	1901	...	1931	...	2001	...	2031	2118
149	**Margate** a.		...	...	0831	0926	...	0939	1030	1039	1130		1741	1837	1815	...	1845	...	1915	...	1945	...	2015	...	2045	2130

	Ⓐ	Ⓐ	Ⓐ	Ⓐ	Ⓐ B	Ⓐ	②–⑤	①	Ⓐ		⑥	⑥ D	⑥ D	⑥		⑥ D	⑥	⑥	⑥	⑥	⑥	⑥	⑥	⑥		⑦
London St Pancras d.	2012	2037	2112	2137	2212	2237	2312	2312	2337	⑥	0012	...	0637	0708		1937	2012	2037	2112	2137	2212	2237	2312	2337	⑦	0012
Stratford International d.	2019	2044	2119	2144	2219	2244	2319	2319	2344		0019	...	0644	0715	and at	1944	2019	2044	2119	2144	2219	2244	2319	2344		0019
Ebbsfleet International d.	2030	2055	2130	2155	2230	2255	2330	2330	2355		0030	...	0655	0726	the same	1955	2030	2055	2130	2155	2230	2255	2330	2355		0030
Ashford International d.	2052	2115	2152	2215	2252	2315	2352	2352	0015		0050	0615	0715	0752	minutes	2015	2052	2115	2152	2215	2252	2315	2352	0015		0050
Folkestone Central d.	|	2130	|	2230	|	2330	|	|	0030		...	0630	0730	|	past each	2030	|	2130	|	2230	|	2330	|	0030		...
Dover Priory a.	|	2141	|	2241	|	2341	|	|	0041		...	0641	0741	|	hour until	2041	|	2141	|	2241	|	2341	|	0041		...
Canterbury West d.	2109	|	2209	|	2309	|	0009	*0034*p	|		...	|	|	0809	♠	|	2109	|	2209	|	2309	|	0009	|		...
Ramsgate a.	2131	2219	2227	2319	2330	0019	0030	0043	0121		...	0718	0818	0827		2119	2127	2219	2227	2321	2327	0021	0027	0121		...
Margate a.	2142	...	2239	...	2339	...	0039r	0058	...		...	0730	0830	0839		2130	2139	...	2239	...	2339	...	0039	...		...

	⑦ D	⑦ D	⑦		⑦ D	⑦	⑦	⑦	⑦	⑦	⑦	⑦	⑦
London St Pancras d.	...	0837	0909		1937	2012	2037	2112	2137	2212	2237	2312	2337
Stratford International d.	...	0844	0916	and at	1944	2019	2044	2119	2144	2219	2244	2319	2344
Ebbsfleet International d.	...	0855	0927	the same	1955	2030	2055	2130	2155	2230	2255	2330	2355
Ashford International d.	0815	0915	0952	minutes	2015	2052	2115	2152	2215	2252	2315	2352	0015
Folkestone Central d.	0830	0930	|	past each	2030	|	2130	|	2230	|	2330	|	...
Dover Priory a.	0841	0941	|	hour until	2041	|	2141	|	2241	|	2342	|	...
Canterbury West d.	|	|	1009	♠	|	2109	|	2209	|	2309	|	0009	...
Ramsgate a.	0918	1018	1027		2118	2127	2218	2227	2318	2327	0018	0027	...
Margate a.	0930	1030	1039		2130	2139	...	2239	...	2339	...	0039	...

		Ⓐ	Ⓐ	Ⓐ	Ⓐ	Ⓐ	Ⓐ	Ⓐ	Ⓐ
Margate d.	Ⓐ	...	...	0546	...	0615	...	0646	...
Ramsgate d.		0455	...	0558	...	0628	0614	0658	...
Canterbury West d.		0518	...	0618	...	0648	|	0718	...
Dover Priory d.		|	0545	|	0618	|	0648	|	0716
Folkestone Cent. d.		|	0556	|	0629	|	0659	|	0727
Ashford Int'l d.		0543	0613	0636	0646	0706	0716	0736	0744
Ebbsfleet Int'l a.		0602	0632	0655	0705	|	0735	|	|
Stratford Int'l a.		0614	0644	0707	0717	0734	0747	0804	0812
London St Pancras a.		0621	0651	0714	0725	0742	0754	0813	0820

	Ⓐ	Ⓐ	Ⓐ	Ⓐ	Ⓐ	Ⓐ	Ⓐ E	Ⓐ		Ⓐ E	Ⓐ	Ⓐ	Ⓐ	Ⓐ	Ⓐ		Ⓐ	Ⓐ	Ⓐ	Ⓐ	Ⓐ	Ⓐ		⑥	⑥	⑥
Margate d.	0716	0656	0749	...	0851	...	0859	0953		1702	1753	...	1853	...	1953	...	...	2053	2100	2153	...	2253	⑥	...	...	0553
Ramsgate d.	0728	0712	0801	...	0903	0932	0912	1005	and at	1713	1805	...	1905	...	2005	...	...	2105	2112	2205	2212	2305		0505	...	0605
Canterbury West d.	0748	|	0825	...	0923	0952	|	1025	the same	|	1825	...	1925	...	2025	...	...	2125	|	2225	|	2325		0525	...	0625
Dover Priory d.	|	0748	|	0849	|	|	0949	|	minutes	1749	|	1849	|	1949	|	...	2049	|	2149	|	2249	|		|	0549	|
Folkestone Central d.	|	0759	|	0900	|	|	1000	|	past each	1800	|	1900	|	2000	|	...	2100	|	2200	|	2300	|		|	0600	|
Ashford International d.	0806	0816	0843	0916	0943	1010	1016	1043	hour until	1816	1843	1916	1943	2016	2043	...	2116	2143	2216	2243	2316	2341		0543	0616	0643
Ebbsfleet International a.	|	0835	0902	0935	1002	|	1035	1102	♠	1835	1902	1935	2002	2035	2102	...	2135	2202	2235	2302	2335	...		0602	0635	0702
Stratford International a.	0834	0847	0914	0947	1014	1038	1047	1114		1847	1914	1947	2014	2047	2114	...	2147	2214	2247	2314	2347	...		0614	0647	0714
London St Pancras a.	0842	0854	0921	0954	1021	1046	1055	1121		1854	1921	1954	2021	2054	2121	...	2154	2221	2254	2321	2354	...		0621	0654	0721

	⑥	⑥	⑥	⑥	⑥	⑥	⑥ E		⑥	⑥ E	⑥		⑦	⑦	⑦		⑦	⑦	⑦	⑦	⑦ E		⑦ E	⑦	⑦ E
Margate d.	...	0653	0657	0753	...	0853	0859		2153	2159	2253	⑦	...	...	0753	...	...	0853	...	0953	0959		2059	2153	2159
Ramsgate d.	0612	0705	0712	0805	0812	0905	0912	and at	2205	2212	2305		...	0712	0805	...	0812	0905	0912	1005	1012	and at	2112	2205	2212
Canterbury West d.	|	0725	|	0825	|	0925	|	the same	2225	|	2325		...	|	0825	...	|	0925	|	1025	|	the same	|	2225	|
Dover Priory d.	0649	|	0749	|	0849	|	0949	minutes	|	2249	|		...	0749	|	...	0849	|	0949	|	1049	minutes	2149	|	2249
Folkestone Central d.	0700	|	0800	|	0900	|	1000	past each	|	2300	|		...	0800	|	...	0900	|	1000	|	1100	past each	2200	|	2300
Ashford International d.	0716	0743	0816	0843	0916	0943	1016	hour until	2243	2316	2341		0743	0816	0843	...	0916	0943	1016	1043	1116	hour until	2216	2243	2315
Ebbsfleet International a.	0735	0802	0835	0902	0935	1002	1035	♠	2302	2335	...		0802	0835	0902	...	0935	1002	1035	1102	1135	♠	2235	2302	...
Stratford International a.	0747	0814	0847	0914	0947	1014	1047		2314	2347	...		0814	0847	0914	...	0947	1014	1047	1114	1147		2247	2314	...
London St Pancras a.	0754	0821	0855	0921	0954	1021	1055		2321	2354	...		0821	0854	0921	...	0954	1021	1054	1121	1154		2254	2321	...

A – ② departure from London St Pancras is operated by 🚌 after Faversham (Faversham d. 2336, Herne Bay d. 0012, Margate a. 0043).
B – ② departure from London St Pancras is operated by 🚌 after Ramsgate (Ramsgate d. 2335, Margate a. 2354).
D – To London St Pancras (see upper table).
E – From London St Pancras (see upper table).
F – To London St Pancras (see lower table).
G – From London St Pancras (see lower table).
H – From Ashford International (see lower table).
K – To Ashford International (see lower table).
p – Connection by 🚌 from Ashford; continues to Ramsgate (arr. 0112) and Margate (arr. 0131).
r – Not ②.
t – Arrives 1910.
♠ – Timings may vary by up to ± 4 minutes.
♣ – Timings may vary by up to ± 3 minutes.

Typical off-peak journey time in hours and minutes
READ DOWN   READ UP
↓   ↑

Journey times may be extended during peak hours on Ⓐ (0600 - 0900 and 1600 - 1900) and also at weekends.
The longest journey time by any train is noted in the table heading.

LONDON VICTORIA - RAMSGATE
Longest journey : 2 hours 10 minutes   SE

km					
0	0h00	↓	d.**London** Victoria.....a.	↑	1h57
18	0h17		d.Bromley South ....d.		1h40
53	0h47	↓	d.Rochester ....d.	↑	1h12
55	0h50		d.Chatham...............d.		1h10
72	1h09	↓	d.Sittingbourne.......d.	↑	0h50
84	1h21		d.Faversham..........d.		0h42
101	1h36	↓	d.Herne Bay ....d.	↑	0h26
119	1h49		d.Margate.............d.		0h10
128	1h59		a.**Ramsgate**.........d.		0h00

From London Victoria: on Ⓐ at 0007②–⑥ f, 0522, 0552, 0622 g, 0652 g, 0736, 0837 and hourly until 1537, 1637 g, 1636 c, 1657, 1727, 1730 c m, 1752 c m, 1757 m, 1812 c, 1827, 1844 c, 1857, 1937, 2037, 2137, 2207 f g, 2237 f, 2307 f; on ⑥ at 0707 g, 0737 and hourly until 2237, 2307; on ⑦ at 0007, 0745 and hourly until 2045, 2104h, 2145, 2204h, 2245, 2304 h, 2345 h.
From Ramsgate: on Ⓐ at 0432, 0506, 0539, 0608, 0629 m c, 0632, 0651 m c, 0703, 0708 m c, 0719 b, 0754 and hourly until 1354, 1450, 1545, 1648, 1748, 1848, 1954, 2050, 2154, 2310 h; on ⑥ at 0430, 0554 and hourly until 2154, 2310 h; on ⑦ at 0705, and hourly until 2105, 2120 g, 2235.

b – To London Blackfriars, not Victoria.
c – From/to London Cannon Street, not Victoria.
f – On Tuesday nights/Wednesday mornings does not call at Herne Bay or Margate.
h – To Faversham.
g – Change at Faversham.
m – To/from Margate.

LONDON VICTORIA - DOVER
Longest journey : 2 hours 10 minutes   SE

km					
0	0h00	↓	d.**London** Victoria.....a.	↑	2h02
18	0h17		d.Bromley South ....d.		1h43
53	0h47	↓	d.Rochester ....d.	↑	1h17
55	0h50		d.Chatham...............d.		1h15
72	1h09	↓	d.Sittingbourne.......d.	↑	0h58
84	1h21		d.Faversham..........d.		0h47
99	1h37	↓	d.Canterbury East..d.	↑	0h27
124	1h58		a.**Dover** Priory......d.		0h00

From London Victoria: on Ⓐ at 0522 g, 0552 g, 0622, 0652, 0734, 0807, 0834 and at the same minutes past each hour until 1407, 1437 g, 1507, 1537 g, 1607, 1636 c g, 1637, 1657 g, 1708 c, 1730 c g, 1757 g, 1827, 1857, 1927 b, 1937 g, 2007, 2034 e, 2107, 2134 e, 2207; on ⑥ at 0522, 0634, 0707, 0734 and at the same minutes past each hour until 1934, 2007, 2034 e, 2107, 2134 e, 2207; on ⑦ at 0745, 0804 e, 0845, 0904 e and at the same minutes past each hour until 2004 e, 2045, 2104 h, 2145.
From Dover Priory: on Ⓐ at 0430, 0500 g, 0545 b, 0605 g, 0628 g, 0702, 0735, 0820, 0852, 0920, 0952 and at the same minutes past each hour until 1520, 1551, 1620, 1651 g, 1720, 1751, 1820, 1851, 1920, 2005, 2105, 2205, 2305h; on ⑥ at 0520, 0620, 0652 and at the same minutes past each hour until 1920, 2005, 2105, 2205, 2305h; on ⑦ at 0705, 0805, 0903 e, 0905 and at the same minutes past each hour until 2005, 2103 e, 2105, 2203 e, 2235 g.

b – From/to London Blackfriars, not Victoria.   c – From London Cannon Street, not Victoria.   e – To/from Canterbury East.   g – Change at Faversham.   h – To Faversham.

LONDON CHARING CROSS - CANTERBURY WEST
Longest journey : 1 hour 55 minutes   SE

km					
0	0h00	↓	d.**London** C Cross ...a.	↑	1h46
1	0h03		d.**London** Waterloo ‡ a.		1h42
3	0h08	↓	d.**London** Bridge .....d.		1h36
36	0h32		d.Sevenoaks.........d.		1h13
48	0h40	↓	d.Tonbridge ....d.	↑	1h04
90	1h20		a.Ashford Int'l ....d.		0h27
113	1h38	↓	a.**Canterbury** West....d.	↑	0h00

From London Charing Cross: on Ⓐ at 0530 b, 0636 c, 0709, 0738, 0817 g, 0923, 0940 d, 1010 and at the same minutes past each hour until 1609, 1638, 1709, 1738, 1800d, 1808 c g, 1840, 1910, 1940 d, 2010, 2110, 2210 e, 2310 e, 2340 e h; on ⑥ at 0602, 0710, 0740 d, 0810 and at the same minutes past each hour until 1910, 2010, 2110, 2210, 2310, 2340 d; on ⑦ at 0810, 0840 d, 0910 and at the same minutes past each hour until 1710 then hourly until 2210.
From Canterbury West: on Ⓐ at 0518 d, 0600, 0634 c g, 0703, 0718 d, 0806 d, 0836, 0906 d, 0937, 1006 d, 1042 and at the same minutes past each hour until 1542 g, 1606 d, 1641, 1706 d, 1740, 1806 d, 1836, 1939, 2039, 2139; on ⑥ at 0539, 0637, 0737, 0806 d, 0840, 0906 d, 0938, 1006 d, 1042 at the same minutes past each hour until 1942, 2006 d, 2039, 2139; on ⑦ at 0740, 0840, 0906 d, 0943 and at the same minutes past each hour until 1843, 1906 d, 1940, 2040, 2140.

c – To/from London Cannon Street.   e – On ① change trains at Ashford for 🚌 connection to Canterbury.   ‡ – London Waterloo East.
d – Change trains at Ashford.   g – Does not call at London Bridge.   h – On ②–⑤ change trains at Ashford.

LONDON CHARING CROSS - DOVER
Longest journey : 2 hours 06 minutes   SE

km					
0	0h00	↓	d.**London** C Cross ...a.	↑	2h58
1	0h03		d.**London** Waterloo ‡ a.		1h53
3	0h08	↓	d.**London** Bridge .....d.		1h42
36	0h32		d.Sevenoaks.........d.		1h18
48	0h40	↓	d.Tonbridge ....d.		1h06
90	1h20		d.Ashford Int'l ....d.		0h29
113	1h40	↓	d.Folkestone Central...d.	↑	0h12
124	1h52		a.**Dover** Priory......d.		0h00

From London Charing Cross: on Ⓐ at 0530, 0709, 0738, 0836, 0940 and hourly until 1240, 1310, 1340, 1410, 1440, 1510, 1540, 1609, 1638, 1650f, 1724 b c, 1738 d, 1745 c f, 1800, 1832 b c, 1910, 1940, 2040, 2140, 2240, 2340; on ⑥ at 0740 and hourly until 2340; on ⑦ at 0840 and hourly until 2240.
From Dover Priory: on Ⓐ at 0429 c, 0529, 0559 c, 0628, 0711 b c f, 0724, 0758, 0825, 0858, 0925, 0958 and hourly until 1458 b, 1558 b, 1625, 1658, 1725, 1758, 1825, 1858, 1958, 2058, 2158 e; on ⑥ at 0458 and hourly until 2058, 2158 e; on ⑦ at 0759 and hourly until 2059.

b – Does not call at London Bridge   c – From/to London Cannon Street.   f – To/from Folkestone Central.
d – Change trains at Ashford.   e – Terminates at Tonbridge.   ‡ – London Waterloo East.

LONDON VICTORIA - ASHFORD INTERNATIONAL
Longest journey : 1 hours 40 minutes   SE

km					
0	0h00	↓	d.**London** Victoria.....a.	↑	1h29
18	0h17		d.Bromley South ....d.		1h14
28	0h28	↓	d.Swanley.............d.		1h03
56	0h52		d.West Malling ....d.		0h42
64	1h03	↓	d.Maidstone East ....d.	↑	0h30
68	1h09		d.Bearsted.............d.		0h25
95	1h31		a.**Ashford** Int'l ....d.		0h00

From London Victoria: on Ⓐ at 0022②–⑤, 0555, 0637, 0707, 0752, 0822, 0852 and every 30 minutes until 1622, 1652, 1712, 1742, 1747 b, 1818, 1842, 1904 b, 1922, 1952, 2022, 2052, 2122, 2152, 2222, 2252, 2322; on ⑥ at 0022, 0622, 0722, 0752 and every 30 minutes until 2322; on ⑦ at 0022, 0736 and hourly until 2336.
From Ashford International: on Ⓐ at 0514, 0532 b, 0547, 0601, 0617, 0624 b, 0656, 0711, 0748, 0830, 0910, 0930, 1010, 1038 and at the same minutes past each hour until 1538, 1602, 1638, 1702, 1738, 1802, 1838, 1900, 1938, 2002, 2038, 2102, 2132, 2232; on ⑥ at 0532, 0610, 0638 and at the same minutes past each hour until 2038, 2110, 2132, 2232; on ⑦ at 0646 and hourly until 2146.

b – From/to Blackfriars, not Victoria.

LONDON CHARING CROSS - HASTINGS
Longest journey : 1 hour 53 minutes   SE

km					
0	0h00	↓	d.**London** C Cross ...a.	↑	1h43
1	0h03		d.**London** Waterloo ‡ a.		1h39
3	0h08	↓	d.**London** Bridge .....d.		1h35
36	0h34		d.Sevenoaks.........d.		1h09
48	0h43	↓	d.Tonbridge ....d.	↑	1h00
55	0h55		d.Tunbridge Wells ...d.		0h49
89	1h33	↓	d.Battle.................d.	↑	0h16
100	1h45		a.**Hastings** ....d.		0h00

From London Charing Cross: on Ⓐ at 0628, 0715, 0745 c d, 0819 d, 0842 c d, 0914 c d, 0945 and every 30 minutes until 1545, 1612, 1622 c d *, 1642, 1702 c d, 1714 *, 1737 c d *, 1756 *, 1828 c d *, 1845, 1905 c d, 1915, 1945, 2015, 2045, 2145, 2245, 2345; on ⑥ at 0715, 0745, 0815, 0845 and every 30 minutes until 2015, 2045, 2145, 2245, 2345; on ⑦ at 0825, 0855, and every 30 minutes until 1925, 1955, 2025, 2125, 2225, 2325.
From Hastings: on Ⓐ at 0517, 0537 c d, 0548 c d, 0604 *, 0620 *, 0628 *, 0643 c d *, 0703 *, 0725 c d *, 0744, 0804 c d *, 0814, 0847, 0929, 0947, 1031, 1050 and at the same minutes past each hour until 1450 d, 1531 d, 1545 c d, 1619 d, 1645, 1719, 1750 *, 1819, 1846, 1950, 2050, 2150; on ⑥ at 0548, 0620, 0650, 0720, 0750, 0820, 0850, 0931, 0950 and at the same minutes past each hour until 1650, 1720, 1750, 1820, 1850, 1950, 2050, 2150; on ⑦ at 0720, 0750, 0831, 0850 and at the same minutes past each hour until 1831, 1850, 1950, 2050, 2150.

c – From/to London Cannon Street.   * – Does not call at Sevenoaks and Tonbridge. Frequent trains call at these stations.
d – Does not call at London Bridge.   ‡ – London Waterloo East.

LONDON VICTORIA - EASTBOURNE
Longest journey : 1 hour 44 minutes   SN

km					
0	0h00	↓	d.**London** Victoria.....a.	↑	1h26
17	0h16		d.East Croydon ....d.		1h09
43	0h33	↓	d.Gatwick Airport ......d.	↑	0h53
61	0h50		d.Haywards Heath ....d.		0h34
81	1h06	↓	d.Lewes................d.	↑	0h19
106	1h27		a.**Eastbourne**..........d.		0h00

From London Victoria: on Ⓐ at 0005②–⑤, 0532, 0647, 0747, 0817, 0847, 0917 and every 30 minutes until 1647, 1722 b, 1727, 1757, 1823 b, 1846, 1917, 1947, 2017, 2047, 2117, 2147, 2247; on ⑥ at 0005, 0747 and every 30 minutes until 2147, 2247; on ⑦ at 0005, 0847 and hourly until 2247.
From Eastbourne: on Ⓐ at 0508, 0543 b, 0621 b, 0654 g, 0712 g b, 0731 g, 0757, 0818, 0853, 0931, 0955, 1035, 1055 and at the same minutes past each hour until 1435, 1453, 1535, 1553, 1635, 1653, 1733, 1755, 1831, 1931, 1955 c, 2031, 2131, 2216; on ⑥ at 0503, 0628, 0655, 0735, 0755 and at the same minutes past each hour until 1935, 1955 d, 2035, 2135, 2218; on ⑦ at 0658, 0755, 0859 and hourly until 2059.

b – From/to London Bridge, not Victoria.   c – From Jan. 2.   d – From Jan. 7.   g – Does not call at Gatwick Airport.

ASHFORD - HASTINGS - EASTBOURNE - BRIGHTON
Longest journey : 2 hours 07 minutes   SN

km					
0	0h00	↓	d.**Ashford** Int'l ....a.	↑	1h46
25	0h23		d.Rye....................d.		1h24
42	0h47	↓	d.**Hastings** ....d.	↑	1h04
50	0h52		d.Bexhill................d.		0h52
67	1h07	↓	d.**Eastbourne**..........d.	↑	0h37
67	1h15		d.**Eastbourne**..........d.		0h32
93	1h35	↓	d.Lewes................d.	↑	0h12
106	1h48		a.**Brighton** ....d.		0h00

From Ashford International: on Ⓐ at 0614, 0715, 0833, 0853 h, 0933 and hourly until 1933, 1959 h, 2033, 2133, 2234 h; on ⑥ at 0615, 0733 and hourly until 2133, 2234 h; on ⑦ at 0811, 0916 and hourly until 2116, 2234 h.
From Brighton: on Ⓐ at 0512 e, 0521 h, 0546 h, 0619 h, 0615, 0732 and hourly until 1532, 1632, 1709 h, 1730, 1832, 1932, 2030; on ⑥ at 0510 e, 0520 h, 0618 h, 0632 and hourly until 2032; on ⑦ at 0722 h, 0814 h, 0812 and hourly until 2012.

e – Change at Eastbourne.   h – Ashford - Hastings and v.v.
🚌 Additional local services are available Brighton/Lewes - Eastbourne - Hastings v.v.

Typical off-peak journey time in hours and minutes
READ DOWN ↓   READ UP ↑

Journey times may be extended during peak hours on Ⓐ (0600 - 0900 and 1600 - 1900) and also at weekends.
The longest journey time by any train is noted in the table heading.

LONDON BRIDGE - UCKFIELD
Longest journey : 1 hour 19 minutes   SN

km						
0	0h00	↓	d.**London** Bridge ......a.	↑	1h15
16	0h16	↓	d.East Croydon.............d.	↑	0h59
32	0h29	↓	d.Oxted.........................d.	↑	0h44
57	0h55	↓	d.Eridge △..................d.	↑	0h17
70	1h01	↓	d.Crowborough ....d.	↑	0h12
74	1h15	↓	a.**Uckfield** ....d.	↑	0h00

From London Bridge : on Ⓐ at 0602, 0638, 0703, 0755, 0902, 1008 and hourly until 1508, 1538, 1608, 1638, 1708, 1806, 1908, 2004, 2104, 2204, 2304; on Ⓖ at 0608 and hourly until 2208, 2304.
From Uckfield : on Ⓐ at 0516, 0540, 0630, 0705, 0731, 0801, 0833, 0934 and hourly until 1534, 1633, 1732, 1832, 1900, 1933, 2004, 2034, 2134, 2234; on Ⓖ at 0634 and hourly until 2234.
On ⑦ services run Oxted - Uckfield and v.v. only. Connections available from / to London Victoria (see East Grinstead Table). From Oxted at 0937⑦ and hourly until 2237⑦. From Uckfield at 1034⑦ and hourly until 2234⑦.

△ – **Spa Valley Railway** (🚂 Eridge - Tunbridge Wells West: 8 km). ✆ 01892 537715. www.spavalleyrailway.co.uk

LONDON VICTORIA - EAST GRINSTEAD
Longest journey : 60 minutes   SN

km						
0	0h00	↓	d.**London** Victoria......a.	↑	0h56
17	0h17	↓	d.East Croydon.............d.	↑	0h37
33	0h37	↓	d.Oxted.........................d.	↑	0h16
42	0h43	↓	d.Lingfield....................d.	↑	0h12
48	0h54	↓	a.**East Grinstead** ▽..d.	↑	0h00

From London Victoria : on Ⓐ at 0526, 0547, 0624, 0654, 0710, 0718 b, 0732, 0750 b, 0824 b, 0853 and every 30 minutes until 1653, 1713 b, 1723, 1744 b, 1753, 1817 b, 1823, 1847 b, 1853 and every 30 minutes until 2323; on Ⓖ at 0523, 0623, 0653 and every 30 minutes until 2253, 2324; on ⑦ at 0747, 0853, 0923, 0953 and every 30 minutes until 1953, 2053, 2153, 2236.
From East Grinstead : on Ⓐ at 0545 b, 0555, 0613 b, 0632, 0640 b, 0702, 0716 b, 0733, 0749 b, 0807, 0817 b, 0837 and every 30 minutes until 1807, 1817 b, 1837 and every 30 minutes until 2237, 2254; on Ⓖ at 0637 and every 30 minutes until 2237, 2257; on ⑦ at 0820, 0912, and every 30 minutes until 2012, 2112, 2212, 2309.

b – From / to London Bridge (not Victoria).   ▽ – **Bluebell Railway** (🚂 East Grinstead - Sheffield Park: 18 km). ✆ 01825 720800. www.bluebell-railway.com

LONDON VICTORIA - LITTLEHAMPTON
Longest journey : 1 hour 47 minutes   SN

km						
0	0h00	↓	d.**London** Victoria......a.	↑	1h42
17	0h16	↓	d.East Croydon.............d.	↑	1h25
43	0h33	↓	d.Gatwick Airport ....a.	↑	1h09
61	0h50	↓	d.Haywards Heath ....a.	↑	0h54
82	1h06	↓	d.Hove ....d.	↑	0h35
96	1h21	↓	d.Worthing....................d.	↑	0h21
114	1h41	↓	a.**Littlehampton** ....d.	↑	0h00

From London Victoria : on Ⓐ at 0747, 0817, 0847 and every 30 minutes until 1617, 1657 b g, 1718, 1740 b g, 1746, 1810 b g, 1817 g, 1846, 1917, 1947, 2017, 2047, 2147; on Ⓖ at 0747, 0817, 0847 and every 30 minutes until 2017, 2047, 2147; on ⑦ at 0817 and hourly until 2117.
From Littlehampton : on Ⓐ at 0552 b, 0629 b g, 0640 g, 0700 g, 0729, 0814, 0851, 0914, 0947, 1014, 1051 and at the same minutes past each hour until 1514, 1549, 1614, 1651, 1714, 1751, 1814, 1914, 2014, 2114 Ⓖ; on Ⓖ at 0545, 0614, 0651 and at the same minutes past each hour until 1814, 1914, 2014, 2114; on ⑦ at 0715 and hourly until 2015.

b – From / to London Bridge (not Victoria).   g – Does not call at Gatwick Airport.

LONDON VICTORIA - BOGNOR REGIS
Longest journey : 1 hour 57 minutes   SN

km						
0	0h00	↓	d.**London** Victoria......a.	↑	1h50
17	0h16	↓	d.East Croydon.............d.	↑	1h30
43	0h37	↓	d.Gatwick Airport ....d.	↑	1h08
61	1h03	↓	d.Horsham ....d.	↑	0h50
94	1h30	↓	d.Arundel.....................d.	↑	0h16
110	1h40	↓	d.Barnham ....d.	↑	0h07
116	1h46	↓	a.**Bognor Regis** ....d.	↑	0h00

From London Victoria : on Ⓐ at 0602, 0803, 0832, 0902, 0932, 1006 and every 30 minutes until 1636, 1702 g, 1734 g, 1803 g, 1834 g, 1902, 1932, 2002, 2032, 2117 k, 2217 k; on Ⓖ at 0736, 0806, 0836 and every 30 minutes until 1836, 1902, 1932, 2002, 2032, 2117 k, 2217 k; on ⑦ at 0702 and hourly until 2202.
From Bognor Regis : on Ⓐ at 0605, 0640 g, 0717 g, 0755, 0826, 0856, 0930, 0956 and at the same minutes past each hour until 1456, 1527, 1556, 1630, 1656, 1730, 1756, 1833 k, 1940 k, 2040 k; on Ⓖ at 0630, 0656 and at the same minutes past each hour until 1756, 1833 k, 1930 k, 1940 k, 2040 k; on ⑦ at 0652, 0759 and hourly until 2159.

g – Does not call at Gatwick Airport.   k – Does not call at Arundel and Horsham.   n – From Jan. 7.

SEAFORD - BRIGHTON
Longest journey : 42 minutes   SN

km						
0	0h00	↓	d.**Seaford**...................a.	↑	0h36
4	0h05	↓	d.Newhaven Harbour..d.	↑	0h30
5	0h07	↓	d.Newhaven Town ......d.	↑	0h28
15	0h19	↓	d.Lewes.......................d.	↑	0h18
22	0h26	↓	d.Falmer......................d.	↑	0h09
28	0h35	↓	a.**Brighton**.................d.	↑	0h00

From Seaford : on Ⓐ at 0509, 0544, 0627, 0717, 0733, 0759, 0855, 0925, 0954 and at the same minutes past each hour until 1654, 1720, 1757, 1824, 1841, 1859, 1917, 1937, 1957, 2028, 2057, 2128, 2157, 2220, 2257, 2325; on ⑦ at 0505, 0628, 0657, 0725, 0757 and at the same minutes past each hour until 1957, 2028, 2057, 2128, 2157, 2220, 2257, 2325; on ⑦ at 0757. 0828, 0857, 0928, 0957 and every 30 minutes until 2127, 2153, 2227, 2253.
From Brighton : on Ⓐ at 0545, 0639, 0652, 0717, 0740, 0810, 0845, 0910 and every 30 minutes until 1710, 1745, 1802, 1822, 1838, 1908, 1940, 2010, 2040, 2104, 2140, 2204, 2234, 2336; on Ⓖ at 0552, 0610, 0640 and every 30 minutes until 2040, 2104, 2140, 2204, 2236, 2336; on ⑦ at 0715, 0749, 0817, 0849, 0917, 0947 and every 30 minutes until 2147, 2209, 2239.

BRIGHTON - PORTSMOUTH HARBOUR
Longest journey : 1 hour 49 minutes   SN

km	✕	⑦			✕	⑦
0	0h00	0h00	↓	d.**Brighton**................d.	↑	1h19	1h36
2	0h04	0h10	↓	d.Hove ....d.	↑	1h15	1h31
16	0h22	0h31	↓	d.Worthing...................d.	↑	1h01	1h17
35	0h39	0h54	↓	d.Barnham ....d.	↑	0h39	0h48
45	0h47	1h02	↓	d.Chichester................d.	↑	0h31	0h39
59	1h02	1h23	↓	d.Havant......................d.	↑	0h17	0h19
71	1h14	1h37	↓	a.**Portsmouth** S ▽.d.	↑	0h04	0h04
72	1h18	1h41	↓	a.**Portsmouth** H .....d.	↑	0h00	0h00

From Brighton : on Ⓐ at 0553, 0635, 0715, 0737, 0803, 0904, 1003 and hourly until 1503, 1603 p, 1705, 1800, 1900 p, 2003, 2033, 2133, 2203; on Ⓖ at 0601, 0703 and hourly until 1903, 1956, 2103, 2133, 2203; on ⑦ at 0715 r, 0719, 0820 r, 0830 and hourly until 2030, 2125, 2146 r.
From Portsmouth Harbour : on Ⓐ at 0528, 0604, 0701, 0720, 0829 and hourly until 1629, 1640, 1729, 1827, 1932 p, 2032 p, 2115 p t, 2215 t, 2240 t; on Ⓖ at 0629, 0648, 0729 and hourly until 1929, 2028, 2111 t, 2215 t, 2244 t; on ⑦ at 0714 and hourly until 1914, 2011, 2114, 2144.

p – To / from Portsmouth & Southsea only.   t – Runs in ⑦ (slower) timings.   ▽ – Portsmouth and Southsea.
r – Runs in ✕ (faster) timings.

BRIGHTON - SOUTHAMPTON CENTRAL
Longest journey : 2 hours 1 minute   SN

km	✕	⑦			✕	⑦
0	0h00	0h00	↓	d.**Brighton**................d.	↑	1h45	1h50
2	0h04	0h04	↓	d.Hove ....d.	↑	1h41	1h46
16	0h22	0h21	↓	d.Worthing...................d.	↑	1h23	1h25
35	0h44	0h48	↓	d.Barnham ....d.	↑	1h00	1h03
45	0h52	0h56	↓	d.Chichester................d.	↑	0h52	0h54
59	1h04	1h08	↓	d.Havant......................d.	↑	0h38	0h42
75	1h23	1h25	↓	d.Fareham ....d.	↑	0h23	0h24
98	1h46	1h56	↓	a.**Southampton** C ..d.	↑	0h00	0h00

From Brighton : on Ⓐ at 0512, 0530, 0627, 0705, 0730, 0833, 0859, 0933 and hourly until 1633, 1702, 1733, 1828, 1930, 2030; on Ⓖ at 0515, 0527, 0634, 0733, 0833, 0900, 0933 and hourly until 1633, 1700, 1733, 1833, 1929, 2030; on ⑦ at 0800 and hourly until 2100.
From Southampton Central : on Ⓐ at 0610, 0733, 0832 and hourly until 1332, 1426, 1434, 1532 and hourly until 2032, 2113; on Ⓖ at 0632 and hourly until 1332, 1426, 1434, 1532 and hourly until 2032, 2113; on ⑦ at 0730, 0827, 0930 and hourly until 1930, 2029, 2130.

LONDON WATERLOO - READING
Longest journey : 1 hour 35 minutes   SW

km						
0	0h00	↓	d.**London** Waterloo ..a.	↑	1h22
16	0h16	↓	d.Richmond ....d.	↑	1h03
18	0h20	↓	d.Twickenham............d.	↑	0h58
30	0h33	↓	d.Staines ....d.	↑	0h36
46	0h53	↓	d.Ascot ....d.	↑	0h28
70	1h20	↓	a.**Reading** ....d.	↑	0h00

From London Waterloo : on Ⓐ at 0505, 0550, 0620, 0650, 0720, 0750, 0807, 0820, 0837, 0850 and every 30 minutes until 1550, 1605, 1620, 1635, 1650, 1720, 1735, 1750, 0820, 1805, 1905, 2005, 2105 and every 30 minutes until 2350; on ⑦ at 0709, 0809 and every 30 minutes until 2339.
From Reading : on Ⓐ at 0542, 0612, 0623, 0642, 0712, 0723, 0742, 0812, 0842, 0912, 0925, 0942, 0956, 1012 and every 30 minutes until 1642, 1712, 1723, 1742, 1753, 1812, 1842, 1852, 1912 and every 30 minutes until 2242, 2312; on Ⓖ at 0542 and every 30 minutes until 2242, 2312; on ⑦ at 0754, 0824, 0854 and every 30 minutes until 2154, 2224, 2254.

LONDON WATERLOO - WINDSOR
Longest journey : 1 hour 09 minutes   SW

km						
0	0h00	↓	d.**London** Waterloo ..a.	↑	0h56
16	0h20	↓	d.Richmond ....d.	↑	0h34
18	0h24	↓	d.Twickenham............d.	↑	0h30
30	0h39	↓	d.Staines ....d.	↑	0h15
41	0h53	↓	a.**Windsor** ▷ ....d.	↑	0h00

From London Waterloo : on Ⓐ at 0558 and every 30 minutes until 2328; on Ⓖ at 0558 and every 30 minutes until 2328; on ⑦ at 0644, 0744, 0825, 0844 and at the same minutes past each hour until 2044, 2144, 2244.
From Windsor and Eton Riverside : on Ⓐ at 0553, 0623 and every 30 minutes until 2223, 2253; on Ⓖ at 0553, 0623 and every 30 minutes until 2223, 2253; on ⑦ at 0701, 0801, 0901, 0934 and at the same minutes past each hour until 2101, 2201, 2301.

▷ – Windsor and Eton Riverside.

103 BEDFORD - LUTON ✈ - LONDON - GATWICK ✈ - BRIGHTON

Additional trains are available London Bridge - Brighton and v.v.

Other services: Bedford - Luton Airport - London St Pancras see Table **170**; London Victoria - Gatwick Airport - Brighton see Table **105**; London Victoria - Gatwick Airport *Gatwick Express* see Table **100**.

km	Ⓐ	Ⓐ	Ⓐ	Ⓐ	Ⓐ	Ⓐ	Ⓐ	Ⓐ	Ⓐ	Ⓐ	Ⓐ	Ⓐ	Ⓐ	Ⓐ	Ⓐ	Ⓐ	Ⓐ	Ⓐ	Ⓐ	Ⓐ	Ⓐ	Ⓐ	Ⓐ		Ⓐ	Ⓐ	Ⓐ
0	**Bedford** d.	0040	0140	0220	0240	0320	0340	0416	0445	0518	0544	0600	0618	0654	0658	0730	0734	0748	0804	0824	0840	0854	0910	and at	1440	1454	1510
31	Luton d.	0104	0204	0244	0304	0344	0404	0440	0510	0542	0604	0624	0638	0714	0722	0750	0758	0812	0828	0848	0904	0918	0934	the same	1504	1518	1534
33	Luton Airport ✈ d.	0107	0207	0247	0307	0347	0407	0443	0513	0544	|	0627	0641	|	0725	|	0800	0815	0831	0851	0907	0921	0937	minutes	1507	1521	1537
48	St Albans City d.	0119	0219	0259	0319	0359	0419	0455	0525	0556	0616	0638	0652	0726	0738	0802	0812	0828	0843	0903	0918	0933	0948	past	1518	1533	1548
80	**London** St Pancras d.	0154	0254	0324	0354	0424	0454	0524	0552	0620	0634	0656	0714	0744	0756	0820	0832	0848	0904	0924	0940	0954	1010	each	1540	1554	1610
85	**London** Blackfriars d.	0205	0305	0335	0405	0435	0505	0535	0603	0633	0646	0708	0728	0756	0808	0832	0844	0900	0918	0938	0952	1008	1022	hour	1552	1608	1622
101	East Croydon d.	0236	0336	0406	0436	0506	0532	0602	0632	0702	0716	0736	0758	0826	0838	0858	0912	0931	0949	1004	1019	1034	1049	until	1619	1634	1651
127	Gatwick Airport ✈ d.	0255	0355	0425	0457	0527	0548	0618	0648	0717	0732	0754	0814	0842	0854	0914	0928	0958	1005	1034	1035	1102	1105		1635	1702	1707
145	Haywards Heath d.	...	...	...	0512	0542	0602	0634	0704	0731	0748	0808	0830	0858	...	0928	0945	...	1019	...	1049	...	1119	♣	1649	...	1721
166	**Brighton** a.	...	...	...	0534	0602	0622	0654	0726	0750	0808	0823	0850	0918	...	0948	1005	...	1039	...	1109	...	1139		1709	...	1743

	Ⓐ	Ⓐ	Ⓐ	Ⓐ	Ⓐ	Ⓐ	Ⓐ	Ⓐ	Ⓐ	Ⓐ	Ⓐ	Ⓐ	Ⓐ	Ⓐ	Ⓐ	Ⓐ	Ⓐ	Ⓐ	Ⓐ	Ⓐ	Ⓐ	Ⓐ	Ⓐ	Ⓐ	⑥	⑥	⑥	⑥
Bedford d.	1524	1550	1608	1626	1640	1708	1720	1734	1800	1810	1824	1840	1854	1908	1940	2010	2040	2110	2140	2152	2222	2240	2310	2340	0040	0140	0220	0240
Luton d.	1548	1610	1632	1650	1704	1732	1744	1758	1819	1834	1848	1904	1918	1932	2004	2034	2104	2134	2204	2216	2246	2306	2334	0004	0104	0204	0244	0304
Luton Airport ✈ d.	1551	1613	1635	1652	1707	1735	1747	1801	1822	1837	1851	1907	1921	1935	2007	2037	2107	2137	2207	2219	2249	2309	2337	0007	0107	0207	0247	0307
St Albans City d.	1603	1624	1647	1704	1718	1748	1758	1812	1834	1848	1903	1918	1933	1946	2018	2048	2118	2148	2218	2230	2300	2321	2349	0019	0119	0219	0259	0319
London St Pancras d.	1624	1646	1708	1728	1740	1808	1818	1834	1854	1910	1924	1940	1954	2010	2040	2110	2140	2210	2240	2254	2324	2354	0024	0054	0154	0254	0324	0354
London Blackfriars d.	1638	1658	1720	1740	1752	1820	1830	1846	1908	1922	1938	1952	2008	2022	2052	2122	2152	2222	2252	2308	2336	0005	0035	0105	0205	0305	0335	0405
East Croydon d.	1704	1726	1748	1809	1825	1850	1901	1918	1939	1951	2010	2021	2039	2051	2121	2151	2221	2251	2321	2339	0006	0032	0106	0136	0236	0336	0406	0436
Gatwick Airport ✈ d.	1729	1742	1814	1824	1852	1906	1927	1935	2003	2007	2026	2037	2054	2107	2137	2207	2237	2307	2340	2357	0026	0055	0126	0155	0255	0355	0425	0455
Haywards Heath d.	...	1758	1832	1840	...	1920	...	1949	...	2021	...	2051	2110	2121	2153	2221	2253	2321	2355	0011	0043	...	...	...	...	...	...	...
Brighton a.	...	1819	1852	1903	...	1942	...	2010	...	2041	...	2111	2124	2141	2213	2241	2313	2341	0015	0031	0103	...	...	...	...	...	...	...

	⑥	⑥	⑥	⑥	⑥	⑥	⑥	⑥	⑥	⑥		⑥	⑥	⑥	⑥	⑥	⑥	⑥	⑥		⑥	⑥	⑥	⑥	⑥	⑥	⑥	⑥
Bedford d.	0320	0340	0412	0450	0520	0540	0554	0610	0624	0640	and at	1754	1810	1824	1840	1854	1910	1940	2010	...	2040	2110	2140	2152	2222	2240	2310	2340
Luton d.	0344	0404	0436	0514	0544	0604	0618	0634	0648	0704	the same	1818	1834	1848	1904	1918	1934	2004	2034	...	2104	2134	2204	2216	2246	2306	2334	0004
Luton Airport ✈ d.	0347	0407	0439	0517	0547	0607	0621	0637	0651	0707	minutes	1821	1837	1851	1907	1921	1937	2007	2037	...	2107	2137	2207	2219	2249	2309	2337	0007
St Albans City d.	0359	0419	0451	0528	0558	0618	0633	0648	0703	0718	past	1833	1848	1903	1918	1933	1948	2018	2048	...	2118	2148	2218	2230	2300	2321	2349	0019
London St Pancras d.	0424	0454	0524	0554	0624	0640	0654	0710	0724	0740	each	1854	1910	1924	1940	1954	2010	2040	2110	...	2140	2210	2240	2254	2324	2354	0024	0054
London Blackfriars d.	0435	0505	0535	0608	0638	0652	0708	0722	0738	0752	hour	1908	1922	1938	1952	2008	2022	2052	2122	...	2152	2222	2252	2308	2336	0005	0035	0105
East Croydon d.	0506	0532	0602	0634	0704	0719	0734	0749	0804	0819	until	1934	1951	2004	2021	2034	2051	2121	2151	...	2221	2251	2321	2339	0004	0032	0106	0136
Gatwick Airport ✈ d.	0526	0548	0618	0650	0720	0735	0802	0805	0834	0835		2002	2007	2034	2037	2102	2107	2137	2207	...	2237	2307	2337	2357	0024	0054	0125	0155
Haywards Heath d.	0544	0603	0633	0703	0733	0751	...	0819	...	0849	♣	...	2021	...	2051	2116	2121	2153	2221	...	2253	2321	2353	0011	0041	0109	...	...
Brighton a.	0606	0624	0654	0724	0754	0811	...	0839	...	0909		...	2041	...	2111	2132	2141	2213	2241	...	2313	2341	0013	0031	0101	0129	...	...

	⑦	⑦	⑦	⑦	⑦	⑦	⑦	⑦	⑦		⑦	⑦	⑦	⑦	⑦	⑦	⑦	⑦	⑦	⑦	⑦	⑦	⑦	⑦	⑦	⑦	⑦
Bedford d.	...	0558	0628	0658	0728	0750	0806	0820	0836	and at	1636	1650	1706	1720	1736	1806	1836	1906	1936	2006	2028	2058	2128	2158	2228	2300	2340
Luton d.	...	0622	0652	0722	0752	0814	0830	0844	0900	the same	1700	1714	1730	1744	1800	1830	1900	1930	2000	2030	2052	2122	2152	2222	2252	2324	0004
Luton Airport ✈ d.	...	0625	0655	0725	0755	0817	0833	0847	0903	minutes	1703	1717	1733	1747	1803	1833	1903	1933	2003	2033	2055	2125	2155	2225	2255	2327	0007
St Albans City d.	...	0637	0707	0737	0807	0829	0845	0859	0915	past	1715	1729	1745	1759	1815	1845	1915	1945	2015	2045	2107	2137	2207	2237	2307	2339	0019
London St Pancras d.	...	0710	0740	0810	0840	0854	0910	0924	0940	each	1740	1754	1810	1824	1840	1910	1940	2010	2040	2110	2140	2210	2240	2310	2340	0014	0054
London Blackfriars d.	0652	0722	0752	0822	0852	0906	0922	0936	0952	hour	1752	1806	1822	1836	1852	1922	1952	2022	2052	2122	2152	2222	2252	2322	2352	0025	0105
East Croydon d.	0723	0753	0821	0856	0926	0939	0956	1009	1026	until	1826	1839	1856	1909	1926	1956	2026	2056	2126	2156	2226	2256	2326	2357	0029	0059	0136
Gatwick Airport ✈ d.	0744	0818	0842	0912	0942	0956	1012	1026	1042		1842	1856	1912	1926	1942	2012	2042	2112	2142	2212	2242	2312	2342	0020	0049	0119	0156
Haywards Heath d.	0758	0834	0856	0926	0956	...	1028	...	1056	♣	1856	...	1928	...	1956	2028	2056	2128	2158	2228	2256	2328	2356	0036	...	...	...
Brighton a.	0818	0854	0916	0948	1016	...	1048	...	1116		1916	...	1948	...	2016	2048	2116	2148	2216	2248	2316	2348	0016	0056	...	...	...

	②–⑤	Ⓐ	Ⓐ	Ⓐ	Ⓐ	Ⓐ	Ⓐ	Ⓐ	Ⓐ	Ⓐ	Ⓐ	Ⓐ	Ⓐ	Ⓐ	Ⓐ	Ⓐ	Ⓐ	Ⓐ	Ⓐ	Ⓐ	Ⓐ	Ⓐ	Ⓐ	Ⓐ	Ⓐ	Ⓐ	
Brighton d.	0010	...	...	...	...	...	...	...	0510	0530	0544	0606	0619	0657	0722	0748	0800	0818	0833	0905	0935	1005	1035	...	1105	...	and at
Haywards Heath d.	0025	...	...	...	...	...	...	...	0531	0551	0603	0629	0642	0720	0746	0809	0822	0839	0856	0926	0956	1026	1056	...	1126	...	the same
Gatwick Airport ✈ d.	0039	0121	0221	0321	0351	0421	0455	0525	0548	0608	0617	0643	0700	0738	0801	0823	0839	0853	0910	0940	1010	1040	1110	1108	1140	1138	minutes
East Croydon d.	0100	0140	0240	0340	0410	0440	0517	0547	0603	0623	0639	0658	0723	0754	0824	0839	0854	0910	0925	0955	1025	1055	1125	1138	1155	1208	past
London Blackfriars d.	0129	0209	0309	0409	0439	0509	0546	0612	0630	0652	0708	0726	0754	0822	0850	0910	0922	0938	0954	1024	1054	1124	1154	1208	1224	1238	each
London St Pancras d.	0140	0220	0320	0420	0450	0520	0556	0622	0640	0702	0718	0736	0804	0832	0900	0920	0932	0948	1004	1034	1104	1134	1204	1218	1234	1248	hour
St Albans City d.	0214	0254	0354	0454	0514	0554	0618	0644	0703	0723	0743	0757	0825	0852	0920	0940	0952	1009	1025	1055	1125	1155	1225	1239	1255	1309	until
Luton Airport ✈ d.	0226	0306	0406	0506	0526	0606	0630	0656	0714	0734	0754	0808	0837	0903	0929	0952	1003	1021	1037	1107	1137	1206	1237	1251	1307	1321	
Luton d.	0229	0309	0409	0509	0529	0609	0633	0659	0717	0737	0757	0811	0840	0906	0932	0955	1006	1024	1040	1110	1140	1210	1240	1254	1310	1324	♣
Bedford a.	0255	0337	0435	0535	0557	0637	0701	0725	0743	0803	0823	0837	0905	0926	0957	1020	1025	1053	1105	1135	1205	1235	1305	1319	1335	1349	

	Ⓐ	Ⓐ	Ⓐ	Ⓐ	Ⓐ	Ⓐ	Ⓐ	Ⓐ	Ⓐ	Ⓐ	Ⓐ	Ⓐ	Ⓐ	Ⓐ	Ⓐ	Ⓐ	Ⓐ	Ⓐ	Ⓐ	Ⓐ	Ⓐ	Ⓐ	Ⓐ	Ⓐ	Ⓐ	Ⓐ	Ⓐ	Ⓐ	Ⓐ
Brighton d.	...	1505	...	1535	...	1602	...	1635	...	1701	...	1735	...	1805	1835	...	1905	...	1933	...	2003	...	2033	2105	2133	2205	2233	2305	2337
Haywards Heath d.	...	1526	...	1556	...	1623	...	1656	...	1722	...	1756	...	1826	1856	...	1926	...	1954	...	2026	...	2054	2126	2154	2226	2254	2326	2358
Gatwick Airport ✈ d.	1508	1540	1538	1610	1608	1640	1638	1710	1710	1740	1745	1810	1815	1840	1910	1917	1940	1947	2010	2018	2040	2047	2110	2140	2210	2240	2310	2340	0015
East Croydon d.	1538	1555	1608	1625	1638	1656	1703	1725	1739	1755	1804	1825	1834	1855	1925	1934	1955	2008	2025	2038	2055	2108	2125	2155	2225	2255	2325	2356	0038
London Blackfriars d.	1608	1622	1638	1652	1708	1722	1736	1752	1810	1822	1836	1852	1906	1924	1954	2008	2024	2038	2054	2108	2124	2138	2154	2222	2252	2322	2352	0024	0104
London St Pancras d.	1618	1632	1648	1702	1718	1732	1746	1802	1820	1832	1846	1902	1916	1934	2004	2018	2034	2048	2104	2118	2134	2148	2204	2232	2302	2332	0002	0034	0114
St Albans City d.	1639	1650	1709	1720	1736	1750	1806	1820	1842	1850	1906	1920	1936	1955	2025	2039	2055	2109	2125	2139	2155	2209	2225	2257	2327	2357	0027	0108	0148
Luton Airport ✈ d.	1651	|	1721	|	1748	|	1818	|	1854	|	1919	|	1948	2007	2037	2051	2107	2121	2137	2151	2207	2221	2237	2309	2339	0009	0039	0120	0200
Luton d.	1654	1702	1724	1732	1751	1802	1821	1832	1857	1902	1922	1932	1951	2010	2040	2054	2110	2124	2140	2154	2210	2224	2240	2312	2342	0012	0042	0123	0203
Bedford a.	1719	1723	1749	1753	1813	1823	1846	1853	1926	1923	1948	1953	2013	2035	2105	2119	2135	2150	2205	2219	2235	2249	2305	2340	0008	0038	0108	0149	0229

	⑥	⑥	⑥	⑥	⑥	⑥	⑥	⑥	⑥	⑥	⑥	⑥	⑥	⑥	⑥	⑥	⑥	⑥	⑥		⑥	⑥	⑥	⑥	⑥	⑥	⑥
Brighton d.	0010	...	...	...	...	...	...	0533	0605	0602	0635	0632	0705	0737	0734	0805	...	0835	...	and at	2005	...	2033	...	2105	2133	2205
Haywards Heath d.	0025	...	...	...	...	...	...	0554	0626	0620	0656	0647	0726	0756	0751	0826	...	0856	...	the same	2026	...	2054	...	2126	2154	2226
Gatwick Airport ✈ d.	0039	0121	0221	0321	0421	0455	0525	0610	0640	0638	0710	0708	0740	0810	0808	0840	0838	0910	0908	minutes	2040	2038	2110	2108	2140	2210	2240
East Croydon d.	0100	0140	0240	0340	0440	0517	0547	0625	0655	0708	0725	0738	0755	0825	0838	0855	0908	0925	0938	past	2055	2108	2125	2138	2155	2225	2255
London Blackfriars d.	0129	0209	0309	0409	0509	0542	0614	0654	0724	0738	0754	0808	0824	0854	0908	0924	0938	0954	1008	each	2124	2138	2154	2208	2224	2252	2322
London St Pancras d.	0140	0220	0320	0420	0520	0552	0624	0704	0734	0748	0804	0818	0834	0904	0918	0934	0948	1004	1018	hour	2134	2148	2204	2218	2234	2302	2332
St Albans City d.	0148	0254	0354	0454	0554	0625	0645	0725	0755	0809	0825	0839	0855	0925	0939	0955	1009	1025	1039	until	2155	2209	2225	2239	2259	2327	2357
Luton Airport ✈ d.	0200	0306	0406	0506	0606	0637	0657	0737	0807	0821	0837	0851	0907	0937	0951	1007	1021	1037	1051		2207	2221	2237	2251	2311	2339	0009
Luton d.	0203	0309	0409	0509	0609	0640	0700	0740	0810	0824	0840	0854	0910	0940	0954	1010	1024	1040	1054	♣	2210	2224	2240	2254	2314	2342	0012
Bedford a.	0229	0335	0436	0537	0635	0708	0725	0805	0835	0849	0905	0919	0935	1005	1019	1035	1049	1105	1119		2235	2249	2305	2319	2340	0008	0038

	⑥	⑥	⑥	⑦	⑦	⑦	⑦	⑦	⑦	⑦	⑦	⑦	⑦		⑦	⑦	⑦	⑦	⑦	⑦	⑦	⑦	⑦	⑦	⑦	⑦	⑦
Brighton d.	2233	2305	2337	0010	0606	0636	0703	0736	0804	...	0844	...	0914	and at	...	1844	...	1914	1944	2014	2044	2114	2144	2214	2244	2312	2342
Haywards Heath d.	2254	2326	2358	0026	0624	0654	0724	0754	0824	...	0903	...	0933	the same	...	1903	...	1933	2003	2033	2103	2133	2203	2233	2303	2331	0002
Gatwick Airport ✈ d.	2310	2340	0015	0039	0638	0708	0738	0808	0838	0859	0917	0929	0947	minutes	1859	1917	1929	1947	2017	2047	2117	2147	2217	2247	2317	2345	0015
East Croydon d.	2325	2356	0038	0100	0657	0727	0757	0827	0856	0917	0933	0947	1003	past	1917	1933	1947	2003	2033	2103	2133	2203	2233	2303	2333	0002	0038
London Blackfriars d.	2352	0024	0104	0129	0724	0754	0824	0854	0924	0954	1008	1022	1038	each	1952	2008	2022	2038	2108	2138	2208	2238	2308	2338	0008	0032	0104
London St Pancras d.	0002	0034	0114	0140	0734	0804	0834	0904	0934	1004	1018	1032	1048	hour	2002	2018	2032	2048	2118	2148	2218	2248	2318	2348	0018	0044	0114
St Albans City d.	0027	0108	0148	0214	0808	0838	0908	0938	1008	1038	1043	1057	1113	until	2027	2043	2057	2113	2143	2213	2243	2322	2352	0022	0052	0118	0148
Luton Airport ✈ d.	0039	0120	0200	0226	0820	0850	0920	0950	1020	1050	1055	1109	1125		2039	2055	2109	2125	2155	2225	2255	2334	0004	0034	0104	0130	0200
Luton d.	0042	0123	0203	0229	0823	0853	0923	0953	1023	1053	1058	1112	1128	♣	2042	2058	2112	2128	2158	2228	2258	2337	0007	0037	0107	0133	0203
Bedford a.	0108	0149	0229	0255	0849	0919	0949	1019	1049	1119	1125	1138	1154		2108	2124	2138	2154	2225	2254	2324	0003	0033	0103	0133	0159	0229

♣ – Timings may vary by up to 5 minutes.

SN LONDON - GATWICK ✈ - BRIGHTON 105

km			②–⑤	Ⓐ	Ⓐ	Ⓐ	Ⓐ	Ⓐ	Ⓐ	Ⓐ	Ⓐ	Ⓐ	Ⓐ	Ⓐ	Ⓐ	Ⓐ	Ⓐ	Ⓐ	Ⓐ	Ⓐ	Ⓐ		Ⓐ	Ⓐ	Ⓐ	Ⓐ	Ⓐ
0	**London** Victoria.....d.	Ⓐ	0005	0100	0400	0452	0606	0615	0617	0630	0715	0736	0800	0807	0821	0830	0838	0900	0920	0930	0950	and at the same	1550	1600	1620	1630	1706
17	East Croydon.........d.		0027	0124	0427	0519	0623	|	0635	|	|	0752	|	0823	0841	|	0854	|	0936	|	1006	minutes past	1606	|	1636	|	1723
43	Gatwick Airport ✈..d.		0045	0150	0452	0548	|	0646	0706	0704	0750	0808	0833	|	0857	0902	0910	0932	0952	1002	|	each hour until	|	1632	1652	1702	|
82	**Brighton** ....a.		0118	0225	0523	0626	0705	0716	0741	0735	0820	0838	0857	0912	0938	0927	0942	0954	1017	1024	1046	❖	1646	1654	1720	1732	1812

	Ⓐ	Ⓐ	Ⓐ	Ⓐ	Ⓐ	Ⓐ	Ⓐ	Ⓐ	Ⓐ	Ⓐ	Ⓐ	Ⓐ	Ⓐ	Ⓐ	Ⓐ	Ⓐ	Ⓐ	Ⓐ	Ⓐ	Ⓐ	Ⓐ	Ⓐ	Ⓐ	Ⓐ		⑥	⑥	⑥	⑥
London Victoria .....d.	1730	1742	1800	1815	1830	1844	1900	1920	1930	1950	2000	2020	2030	2050	2100	2120	2130	2150	2200	2220	2230	2250	2307	2332	⑥	0005	0100	0400	0502
East Croydon..........d.	|	|	|	|	1847	|	|	1936	|	2007	|	2036	|	2106	|	2136	|	2206	|	2238	|	2306	2323	2350		0027	0124	0424	0524
Gatwick Airport ✈...d.	1807	1815	1837	1847	|	1917	1932	1952	2002	2023	2032	2051	2102	2122	2132	2152	2202	2222	2232	2254	2302	2322	|	0015		0045	0151	0449	0553
Brighton ....a.	1839	1848	1912	1921	1939	1953	2002	2019	2027	2049	2057	2119	2127	2148	2158	2216	2230	2246	2257	2319	2327	2346	0003	0053		0118	0226	0517	0630

	⑥	⑥	⑥	⑥	⑥	⑥	⑥	⑥	⑥	⑥	⑥		⑥	⑥	⑥	⑥	⑥	⑥	⑥	⑥		⑥	⑥	⑥	⑥	⑥	⑥
London Victoria .....d.	0532	0600	0630	0700	0720	0730	0750	0800	0820	0830	0850	and at the same	2000	2020	2030	2050	2100	2120	2130	2150	...	2200	2220	2230	2250	2307	2332
East Croydon..........d.	0548	|	|	|	0736	|	0806	|	0836	|	0906	minutes past	|	2036	|	2106	|	2136	|	2206	...	|	2236	|	2306	2324	2349
Gatwick Airport ✈...d.	0622	0632	0702	0732	0751	0802	|	0832	0852	0902	|	each hour until	2032	2052	2102	2122	2132	2152	2202	2222	...	2232	2252	2302	2322	|	0013
Brighton ....a.	0706	0702	0727	0757	0816	0824	0846	0854	0916	0924	0946	❖	2054	2118	2124	2148	2157	2221	2227	2247	...	2259	2318	2327	2346	0003	0050

		⑦	⑦	⑦	⑦	⑦	⑦	⑦	⑦	⑦	⑦	⑦	⑦	⑦	⑦		⑦	⑦	⑦	⑦	⑦	⑦	⑦	⑦	⑦	⑦	
London Victoria .....d.	⑦	0005	0100	0400	0502	0547	0632	0726	0832	0907	0927	0932	1006	1027	1032	and at the same	1906	1927	1932	2006	2027	2032	2106	2127	2227	2332	...
East Croydon..........d.		0027	0126	0426	0525	0610	0655	0748	0853	0923	0942	0949	1023	1042	1049	minutes past	1923	1942	1949	2023	2042	2049	2123	2142	2242	2353	...
Gatwick Airport ✈...d.		0046	0154	0453	0550	0633	0723	0813	0913	0939	1006	|	1039	1106	|	each hour until	1939	2006	|	2039	2106	|	2139	2207	2306	0015	...
Brighton ....a.		0117	0225	0522	0620	0709	0759	0851	0951	1003	1043	1024	1103	1143	1124	❖	2003	2043	2024	2103	2143	2124	2203	2243	2345	0052	...

		Ⓐ	Ⓐ	Ⓐ	Ⓐ	Ⓐ	Ⓐ	Ⓐ	Ⓐ	Ⓐ	Ⓐ	Ⓐ	Ⓐ	Ⓐ	Ⓐ	Ⓐ	Ⓐ		Ⓐ	Ⓐ	Ⓐ	Ⓐ	Ⓐ		Ⓐ	Ⓐ	Ⓐ
Brighton ....d.	Ⓐ	0350	0523	0614	0630	0640	0646	0712	0729	0744	0815	0830	0846	0918	0928	0948	0958	and at the same	1418	1428	1448	1458	1518	...	1526	1548	1618
Gatwick Airport ✈...d.		0505	0555	0652	0704	0719	|	0749	0802	0820	0849	0906	0914	0945	0953	1015	|	minutes past	1445	1453	1515	|	1545	...	1553	1615	1645
East Croydon..........d.		0532	0610	0716	|	|	0739	|	|	|	|	|	0929	|	1008	|	1038	each hour until	|	1508	|	1538	|	...	1608	|	|
London Victoria .....a.		0552	0628	0735	0741	0754	0758	0823	0839	0855	0923	0939	0949	1016	1026	1045	1056	❖	1515	1524	1546	1554	1615	...	1626	1647	1717

	Ⓐ	Ⓐ	Ⓐ	Ⓐ	Ⓐ	Ⓐ	Ⓐ	Ⓐ	Ⓐ	Ⓐ	Ⓐ	Ⓐ	Ⓐ	Ⓐ	Ⓐ	Ⓐ	Ⓐ	Ⓐ	Ⓐ	Ⓐ	Ⓐ	Ⓐ	Ⓐ	Ⓐ			⑥	⑥	⑥
Brighton ....d.	1648	1720	1728	1750	1758	1818	1828	1848	1859	1915	1928	1948	1958	2020	2028	2048	2058	2120	2128	2149	2158	2226	2255	2310	...	⑥	0350	0523	0550
Gatwick Airport ✈...d.	1716	1748	1753	1817	1823	1850	1853	1921	1940	1945	1953	2015	2023	2045	2053	2115	2123	2145	2153	2215	2223	2250	2320	2353	...		0503	0553	0626
East Croydon..........d.	|	|	1808	|	1838	|	1909	|	2003	|	2008	|	2038	|	2108	|	2138	|	2208	|	2238	|	|	0020	...		0529	0608	0641
London Victoria .....a.	1747	1822	1824	1852	1856	1926	1928	1951	2020	2015	2026	2044	2056	2117	2125	2144	2156	2214	2224	2243	2257	2321	2354	0042	...		0556	0624	0657

	⑥	⑥	⑥	⑥	⑥	⑥	⑥	⑥	⑥		⑥	⑥	⑥	⑥	⑥	⑥	⑥	⑥	⑥	⑥	⑥	⑥	⑥	⑥	⑥	⑥	⑥
Brighton ....d.	0556	0618	0628	0648	0658	0718	0728	0748	0758	and at the same	1818	1828	1848	1858	1918	1928	1948	1958	2018	2028	2048	2058	2118	2128	2148	2158	2218
Gatwick Airport ✈...d.	0633	0645	0653	0715	|	0745	0753	0815	|	minutes past	1845	1853	1915	1923	1945	1953	2015	2024	2045	2053	2115	2124	2145	2153	2215	2225	2245
East Croydon..........d.	0653	|	0708	|	0738	|	0808	|	0838	each hour until	|	1908	|	1938	|	2008	|	2039	|	2108	|	2139	|	2208	|	2240	|
London Victoria .....a.	0710	0715	0724	0746	0754	0815	0824	0845	0854	❖	1915	1924	1945	1954	2015	2024	2045	2055	2115	2125	2146	2155	2215	2224	2245	2256	2315

	⑥	⑥		⑦	⑦	⑦	⑦		⑦	⑦	⑦	⑦	⑦	⑦	⑦	⑦		⑦	⑦	⑦	⑦	⑦	⑦		⑦	⑦	⑦
Brighton ....d.	2255	2308	⑦	0350	0613	0706	0747	...	0825	0838	0910	0859	0935	1010	0959	1035	and at the same	1910	1859	1935	2010	1959	2035	...	2104	2204	2305
Gatwick Airport ✈...d.	2321	2354		0502	0648	0743	0830	...	|	0901	|	0941	0957	|	1041	1057	minutes past	|	1941	1957	|	2041	2057	...	2141	2241	2346
East Croydon..........d.	|	0020		0527	0706	0804	0858	...	0908	0916	0946	1001	1014	1046	1101	1114	each hour until	1946	2001	2014	2046	2101	2114	...	2201	2301	0018
London Victoria .....a.	2355	0041		0555	0727	0825	0914	...	0924	0932	1003	1018	1030	1103	1118	1130	❖	2003	2018	2031	2105	2118	2130	...	2218	2319	0040

❖ – Timings may vary by ± 3 minutes.

☛ For other services London - Gatwick Airport - Brighton and v.v. see Tables **100** and **103**.

SW 🍸 on most trains LONDON - GUILDFORD - PORTSMOUTH 107

km			①	Ⓐ	Ⓐ	Ⓐ	Ⓐ	Ⓐ	Ⓐ	Ⓐ	Ⓐ	Ⓐ	Ⓐ		Ⓐ	Ⓐ	Ⓐ	Ⓐ	Ⓐ	Ⓐ	Ⓐ	Ⓐ	Ⓐ	Ⓐ	Ⓐ
0	**London** Waterloo....... **113** d.	Ⓐ	0050	...	0500	0520	0615	0645	0730	0800	0830	0900	0930	and at	1600	1730	1700	1730	1800	1815	1830	1900	1930	2000	2030
39	Woking..................... **113** d.		0118	...	0553	0611	0643	0713	0755	0825	0855	0925	0955	the same	1625	1756	1725	1756	|	|	1858	1925	1955	2025	2055
49	Guildford ....d.		0126**s**	0516	0604	0630**a**	0655	0725	0804	0840	0907	0934	1004	minutes	1634	1808	1737	1808	1833	1851	1908	1937	2004	2034	2104
69	Haslemere........................d.		|	0530	0628	0655	0720	0753	0825	0856	0925	0949	1021	past each	1651	1826	1754	1826	1852	1906	1926	1953	2023	2055	2122
88	Petersfield ....d.		|	0547	0645	0711	0736	0811	0836	0907	0936	1000	1032	hour until	1702	1837	1805	1837	1903	1923	1937	2004	2034	2106	2133
107	Havant ....a.		0200**s**	0602	0659	0727	0751	0826	0849	0919	0949	1015	1049		1714	1850	1819	1850	1915	1940	1951	2016	2048	2118	2145
118	**Portsmouth** & Southsea ... a.		0214**s**	0618	0716	0746	0807	0843	0902	0932	1003	1028	1102	♥	1728	1903	1832	1903	1929	1959	2004	2029	2101	2132	2158
120	**Portsmouth** Harbour .... a.		0219	0622	0720	0751	0812	0848	0907	0937	1008	1033	1107		1738	1910	1839	1910	1936	...	2010	2034	2106	2137	2202

	Ⓐ	Ⓐ	Ⓐ	Ⓐ	Ⓐ	Ⓐ	Ⓐ		⑥	⑥	⑥	⑥	⑥	⑥		⑥	⑥	⑥	⑥	⑥		⑥	⑥	⑥	⑥
London Waterloo .... **113** d.	2100	2130	2200	2230	2245	2315	2345	⑥	...	0520	0645	0730	0800	0830	and at	1900	1930	2000	2030	2100	...	2130	2200	2230	2245
Woking .... **113** d.	2125	2155	2225	2256	2313	2343	0013		...	0613	0713	0755	0825	0855	the same	1925	1955	2025	2055	2125	...	2155	2225	2255	2313
Guildford............................d.	2134	2204	2234	2305	2325	2352	0025		0515	0625	0725	0804	0834	0904	minutes	1934	2004	2034	2104	2134	...	2204	2234	2304	2325
Haslemere ....d.	2155	2225	2255	2325	2350	0012	0050		0530	0645	0745	0821	0849	0921	past each	1949	2021	2049	2121	2155	...	2225	2255	2325	2350
Petersfield ....d.	2206	2236	2306	2336	0006	0023	0106		0546	0701	0801	0832	0900	0932	hour until	2000	2032	2100	2132	2206	...	2236	2306	2336	0006
Havant..................................a.	2218	2248	2318	2348	0020	0036	0121		0601	0719	0816	0849	0915	0949		2015	2049	2115	2144	2218	...	2248	2318	2348	0020
Portsmouth & Southsea ....a.	2232	2303	2331	0002	0038	0050	0138		0618	0735	0832	0902	0928	1002	♥	2028	2102	2128	2158	2232	...	2302	2331	0002	0037
Portsmouth Harbour..........a.	2237	2308	2336	0007	...	0055	...		0622	0740	0837	0907	0933	1007		2033	2107	2133	2203	2236	...	2308	2336	0007	...

	⑥	⑥		⑦	⑦	⑦	⑦		⑦	⑦	⑦		⑦	⑦	⑦	⑦		⑦	⑦	⑦	⑦	⑦	⑦	⑦	⑦
London Waterloo .... **113** d.	2315	2345	⑦	...	0800	0830	0900	...	0930	1000	1030	and at	1800	1830	1900	1930	...	2000	2030	2100	2130	2200	2230	2300	2330
Woking .... **113** d.	2343	0013		0732	0835	0904	0935	...	1004	1032	1102	the same	1832	1902	1932	2002	...	2032	2102	2132	2202	2232	2302	2332	0003
Guildford............................d.	2352	0025		0741	0845	0914	0945	...	1014	1042	1112	minutes	1842	1912	1942	2012	...	2042	2112	2142	2212	2242	2312	2342	0012
Haslemere ....d.	0012	0050		0807	0912	0929	1012	...	1029	1107	1127	past each	1907	1927	2007	2027	...	2107	2127	2207	2227	2307	2327	0007	0027
Petersfield ....d.	0023	0106		0823	0928	0940	1028	...	1040	1123	1138	hour until	1923	1938	2023	2038	...	2123	2138	2223	2238	2323	2338	0023	0038
Havant..................................a.	0036	0121		0838	0943	0952	1043	...	1052	1138	1150		1938	1950	2038	2050	...	2138	2150	2238	2250	2338	2350	0038	0050
Portsmouth & Southsea ....a.	0049	0137		0853	0958	1006	1058	...	1105	1153	1204	♥	1953	2004	2053	2104	...	2153	2204	2253	2304	2353	0004	0053	0104
Portsmouth Harbour..........a.	0054	...		0857	1003	1011	1103	...	1111	1158	1211		1958	2011	2058	2109	...	2158	2208	2258	2309	2358	0009	0058	0109

		Ⓐ	Ⓐ	Ⓐ	Ⓐ	Ⓐ	Ⓐ	Ⓐ	Ⓐ	Ⓐ	Ⓐ	Ⓐ	Ⓐ	Ⓐ		Ⓐ	Ⓐ	Ⓐ	Ⓐ	Ⓐ	Ⓐ	Ⓐ	Ⓐ	Ⓐ	Ⓐ
Portsmouth Harbour..........d.	Ⓐ	0430	0519	0550	0615	...	0642	...	0713	0745	0815	0845	0915	0945	and at	1445	1515	...	1545	1615	...	1645	1715	1745	1815
Portsmouth & Southsea ....d.		0435	0524	0555	0620	...	0647	...	0718	0750	0820	0850	0920	0950	the same	1450	1520	...	1550	1620	...	1650	1720	1750	1820
Havant..................................d.		0451	0540	0611	0634	0650	0700	0711	0732	0804	0834	0904	0934	1004	minutes	1504	1534	1554	1604	1634	1656	1704	1734	1804	1834
Petersfield ....d.		0508	0557	0629	0648	0707	0714	0725	0746	0818	0848	0918	0948	1018	past each	1518	1548	1610	1618	1648	1710	1718	1748	1818	1848
Haslemere ....d.		0526	0616	0647	0702	0726	0735	0740	0800	0832	0902	0932	1002	1032	hour until	1532	1602	1624	1637	1702	1732	1737	1802	1832	1902
Guildford ....d.		0550	0631	0707	0717	0745	0754	0803	0815	0854	0917	0947	1017	1047		1547	1617	1647	1700	1717	1747	1800	1817	1855	1921
Woking .... **113** a.		0600	0640	0715	0725	0755	|	0811	0826	|	0927	0959	1025	1057	♥	1557	1625	1657	1711	1725	1758	1811	|	1903	1929
London Waterloo .... **113** a.		0629	0712	0745	0754	0824	0832	0841	0855	0931	0955	1027	1051	1124		1624	1651	1727	1743	1754	1827	1843	1859	1929	1959

	Ⓐ	Ⓐ	Ⓐ	Ⓐ	Ⓐ	Ⓐ	Ⓐ	Ⓐ			⑥		⑥	⑥	⑥	⑥	⑥		⑥	⑥	⑥	⑥	⑥	⑥	⑥
Portsmouth Harbour..........d.	1845	1915	1945	2015	2045	2119	2219	2319	...	⑥	0443	...	0519	0619	0645	0715	0745	and at	1615	1645	...	1719	1745	1815	1845
Portsmouth & Southsea ....d.	1850	1920	1950	2020	2050	2124	2224	2324	...		0448	...	0524	0624	0650	0720	0750	the same	1620	1650	1710	1724	1750	1820	1850
Havant..................................d.	1904	1934	2004	2034	2104	2140	2240	2340	...		0504	...	0540	0640	0704	0734	0804	minutes	1634	1704	1726	1740	1804	1834	1904
Petersfield ....d.	1918	1948	2018	2048	2118	2157	2257	2357	...		0520	...	0557	0657	0718	0748	0818	past each	1648	1718	1743	1757	1818	1848	1918
Haslemere ....d.	1932	2002	2032	2102	2132	2215	2315	0015	...		0539	...	0615	0715	0732	0802	0832	hour until	1702	1732	1802	1815	1832	1902	1932
Guildford ....d.	1947	2017	2047	2117	2147	2239	2339	0037	...		0602	...	0634	0734	0747	0817	0847		1717	1747	1817	1834	1847	1917	1947
Woking .... **113** a.	1957	2025	2058	2125	2157	2249	2349	...	...		0611	...	0644	0744	0757	0826	0857	♣	1725	1757	1825	1844	1857	1925	1957
London Waterloo .... **113** a.	2024	2050	2129	2150	2227	2319	0033	...	...		0640	...	0713	0813	0823	0851	0923		1751	1823	1851	1913	1923	1951	2023

	⑥	⑥	⑥	⑥	⑥	⑥	⑥			⑦	⑦	⑦		⑦	⑦	⑦		⑦	⑦	⑦		⑦	⑦	⑦	⑦
Portsmouth Harbour..........d.	1915	1945	2015	2045	2119	2219	2319	...	⑦	0648	0732	0748	...	0832	0848	0932	...	0948	1032	1048	and at	2132	2148	2232	2248
Portsmouth & Southsea ....d.	1920	1950	2020	2050	2124	2224	2324	...		0653	0737	0753	...	0837	0853	0937	...	0953	1037	1053	the same	2137	2153	2237	2253
Havant..................................d.	1934	2004	2034	2104	2140	2240	2340	...		0707	0750	0807	...	0850	0907	0950	...	1007	1050	1107	minutes	2150	2207	2250	2307
Petersfield ....d.	1948	2018	2048	2118	2157	2257	2357	...		0724	0804	0824	...	0904	0924	1004	...	1024	1104	1124	past each	2204	2224	2304	2324
Haslemere ....d.	2002	2032	2102	2132	2215	2315	0015	...		0742	0817	0842	...	0917	0942	1017	...	1042	1117	1142	hour until	2217	2242	2317	2342
Guildford ....d.	2017	2047	2117	2149	2239	2339	0037	...		0805	0835	0905	...	0935	1005	1035	...	1106	1135	1206		2235	2305	2335	0005
Woking .... **113** a.	2025	2059	2125	2157	2249	2349	...	...		0813	0842	0915	...	0942	1015	1042	...	1113	1142	1213	♥	2242	2313	2342	0013
London Waterloo .... **113** a.	2050	2127	2150	2224	2318	0032	...	...		0850	0916	0948	...	1014	1046	1114	...	1149	1214	1244		2314	2344	0014	...

a – Arrives 0621.

♣ – Arrivals into London Waterloo may vary by ± 6 minutes.

♥ – Timings may vary by ± 3 minutes.

108 LONDON - SOUTHAMPTON - BOURNEMOUTH - WEYMOUTH

🍷 on most trains. SW

km	Ⓐ	②–⑤	Ⓐ	Ⓐ	Ⓐ	Ⓐ	Ⓐ	Ⓐ	Ⓐ	Ⓐ	Ⓐ	Ⓐ		Ⓐ	Ⓐ	Ⓐ	Ⓐ	Ⓐ	Ⓐ	Ⓐ	Ⓐ	Ⓐ	Ⓐ	Ⓐ
0	**London** Waterloo 113 d.	0005	...	...	...	0530	0630	0703	0735	0805	0835	0905		1635	1705	1735	1805	1835	1905	1935	2005	2035	2105	2135
39	Woking 113 d.	0037	...	...	...	0601	0657	0730	0800	|	0900	|	and	1700u	|	|	|	|	|	2000	|	2100	2132	2200
77	Basingstoke 119 d.	0056	...	...	0540	0621	0718	0750	0820	0849	|	0949	at	|	|	|	|	|	1949	|	2049	|	2152	|
107	Winchester 119 d.	0113	...	...	0559	0638	0734	0806	0837	0905	0933	1005	the	1733	1800	1830	1900	1930	2005	2033	2105	2133	2208	2233
120	**Southampton** Airport 119 d.	0126	...	...	0613	0653	0749	0815	0852	0914	0942	1014	same	1742	1809	1839	1909	1939	2014	2042	2115	2142	2222	2242
128	**Southampton** Central 119 d.	0137	...	...	0625	0701	0759	0827	0901	0924	0951	1024	minutes	1753	1821	1851	1919	1951	2024	2051	2125	2151	2231	2251
149	Brockenhurst 119 d.	0153s	...	0616	0644	0718	0820	0846	0918	0938	1005	1038	past	1808	|	|	1936	|	2038	2108	2144	2205	2250	2305
174	**Bournemouth** 119 d.	0215	0611	0644	0711	0746	0848	0913	0945	1004	1024	1104	each	1824	1850	1921	2007	2021	2104	2127	2212	2224	2317	2329
183	Poole d.	...	0624	0657	0724	0758	0900	0926	0958	1014	1037	1114	hour	1837	1903	1934	2019	2034	2115	2139	2223	2237	2329	2342
193	Wareham d.	...	0638	0711	0738	0812	0912	0940	1010	1028	1050	1128	until	1849	1917	1946	2033	2046	2127	2151	...	2249	...	2354
219	Dorchester South d.	...	0658	0731	0758	0833	0933	1000	1026	1054	1106	1149	♠	1908	1937	2003	2054	2102	2147	2212	...	2309	...	0014
230	**Weymouth** a.	...	0709	0742	0809	0844	0944	1011	1035	1106	1115	1202		1919	1950	2015	2107	2115	2200	2223	...	2320	...	0025

	Ⓐ	Ⓐ	Ⓐ	⑥	⑥	⑥	⑥	⑥	⑥	⑥	⑥	⑥	⑥		⑥	⑥	⑥	⑥	⑥	⑥	⑥	⑥	⑥	⑥	⑥
London Waterloo 113 d.	2205	2235	2305	⑥	0005	...	...	...	0530	0630	0735	0805	0835		1805	1835	1905	1935	2005	2035	2105	2135	2205	2235	2305
Woking 113 d.	2232	2300	2332		0037	...	...	...	0601	0657	0800	|	0900	and	|	1900	|	2000	|	2100	2132	2200	2232	2300	2332
Basingstoke 119 d.	2252	|	2353		0056	...	...	...	0621	0718	0821	0849	|	at	1849	|	1949	|	2049	|	2152	|	2252	|	2352
Winchester 119 d.	2308	2333	0012		0113	...	...	...	0641	0734	0838	0905	0933	the	1905	1933	2005	2033	2105	2133	2208	2233	2308	2333	0011
Southampton Airport 119 d.	2322	2342	0028		0126	...	...	...	0656	0748	0851	0914	0942	same	1914	1942	2014	2042	2114	2142	2222	2242	2322	2342	0025
Southampton Central 119 d.	2330	2351	0038		0137	...	...	0621	0705	0800	0900	0924	0951	minutes	1924	1951	2024	2051	2124	2151	2230	2251	2330	2351	0035
Brockenhurst 119 d.	2349	0005	0054s		0153s	...	0616	0640	0722	0817	0917	0938	1005	past	1938	2005	2038	2105	2143	2205	2249	2305	2349	0005	0051s
Bournemouth 119 d.	0016	0022	0118		0215	0611	0644	0711	0749	0844	0944	1004	1024	each	2004	2024	2104	2124	2210	2224	2317	2326	0016	0022	0115
Poole d.	0028	0035	0130		...	0624	0657	0724	0802	0857	0957	1014	1037	hour	2014	2037	2114	2137	2223	2237	2329	2339	0030	0035	0127
Wareham d.	...	...	...		...	0638	0711	0738	0814	0909	1009	1028	1049	until	2028	2049	2128	2149	...	2249	...	2350	...	...	...
Dorchester South d.	...	...	...		...	0658	0731	0758	0834	0929	1027	1049	1105	♠	2049	2105	2149	2209	...	2309	...	0011	...	...	...
Weymouth a.	...	...	...		...	0709	0742	0809	0845	0940	1035	1100	1113		2100	2113	2200	2220	...	2320	...	0022	...	...	...

⑦	⑦	⑦	⑦	⑦	⑦	⑦	⑦	⑦	⑦		⑦	⑦	⑦	⑦	⑦		⑦	⑦	⑦	⑦		⑦	⑦
London Waterloo 113 d.	0005	...	...	...	0754	0835	0854	0935	0954		1435	1454	1535	1605	1635		2005	2035	2105	2135	...	2205	2305
Woking 113 d.	0037	...	...	...	0828	0909	0928	1008	1028	and	1507	1528	1607	1637	1707	and	2037	2107	2137	2207	...	2237	2337
Basingstoke 119 d.	0056	...	0748	...	0848	0929	0948	1028	1048	at	1528	1548	1628	1657	1728	at	2057	2128	2157	2228	...	2257	2357
Winchester 119 d.	0113	...	0808	...	0908	0946	1008	1044	1108	the	1544	1608	1644	1714	1744	the	2114	2144	2214	2244	...	2314	0014
Southampton Airport 119 d.	0126	...	0827	...	0927	0955	1027	1053	1127	same	1553	1627	1653	1727	1753	same	2127	2153	2227	2253	...	2327	0028
Southampton Central 119 d.	0137	...	0835	0903	0935	1003	1035	1103	1135	minutes	1603	1635	1703	1736	1803	minutes	2136	2203	2236	2303	...	2336	0042
Brockenhurst 119 d.	0153s	...	0857	0917	0957	1018	1057	1117	1157	past	1617	1657	1717	1757	1817	past	2157	2217	2257	2317	...	2355	0058s
Bournemouth 119 d.	0215	0839	0927	0939	1024	1039	1124	1139	1224	each	1639	1724	1739	1825	1839	each	2225	2239	2325	2339	...	0022	0122
Poole d.	...	0851	0936	0951	1033	1051	1133	1151	1233	hour	1651	1733	1751	1834	1851	hour	2234	2251	2334	2351	...	0034	0134
Wareham d.	...	0903	...	1003	...	1103	...	1203	...	until	1703	...	1803	...	1903	until	...	2303	...	0003	...	...	...
Dorchester South d.	...	0924	...	1024	...	1124	...	1224	...	♠	1724	...	1824	...	1924	♠	...	2325	...	0025	...	...	...
Weymouth a.	...	0935	...	1035	...	1135	...	1235	...		1735	...	1835	...	1935		...	2336	...	0036	...	...	...

Ⓐ	Ⓐ	Ⓐ	Ⓐ	Ⓐ	Ⓐ	Ⓐ	Ⓐ	Ⓐ	Ⓐ	Ⓐ	Ⓐ	Ⓐ	Ⓐ		Ⓐ	Ⓐ	Ⓐ	Ⓐ	Ⓐ	Ⓐ	Ⓐ	Ⓐ	Ⓐ	Ⓐ
Weymouth d.	...	...	...	0555	...	0625	...	0655	...	0725	0755	0820	0903		1703	1720	1803	1820	1903	1920	2010	2110	2210	2310
Dorchester South d.	...	...	...	0607	...	0637	...	0707	...	0737	0807	0833	0913	and	1713	1733	1813	1833	1913	1937	2022	2122	2222	2322
Wareham d.	...	...	...	0627	...	0657	...	0727	...	0757	0827	0853	0928	at	1728	1753	1828	1853	1928	1957	2042	2142	2242	2342
Poole d.	0500	0545	*0611*	0641	...	0711	...	0741	0755	0811	0841	0907	0940	the	1740	1807	1840	1907	1940	2009	2054	2154	2254	2354
Bournemouth 119 d.	0515	0557	*0625*	0656	0634	0726	0704	0759	0810	0825	0859	0918	0955	same	1759	1822	1859	1922	1959	2022	2112	2212	2312	0003
Brockenhurst 119 d.	0538	0614	|	|	0703	|	0733	0815	0841	0852	0915	0941	1011	minutes	1815	1845	1915	1945	2015	2045	2140	2240	2340	...
Southampton Central 119 d.	0555	0630	0700	0725	0730	0755	0800	0830	0900	*0916*	0930	1000	1030	past	1830	1900	1930	2000	2030	2100	2200	2300	2359	...
Southampton Airport 119 d.	0603	0638	0708	...	0738	...	0808	0838	0908	*0923*	0938	1008	1038	each	1838	1908	1938	2008	2038	2108	2208	2308	0010	...
Winchester 119 d.	0618	0648	0718	...	0748	...	0818	0848	0918	*0932*	0948	1018	1048	hour	1848	1918	1948	2018	2048	2118	2218	2324	...	...
Basingstoke 119 a.	0634	|	|	...	|	...	0834	|	0935	*0946*	|	1034	|	until	|	1934	|	2034	|	2134	2234	2343	...	...
Woking 113 a.	0653	|	|	...	|	...	0853	0922	0954	...	1020	|	1119	♠	1925	|	2019	|	2119	|	2254	0018	...	...
London Waterloo 113 a.	0724	0747	0816	...	0850	...	0925	0953	1023	...	1049	1120	1149		1952	2020	2049	2124	2149	2222	2323	0104	...	...

⑥	⑥	⑥	⑥	⑥	⑥	⑥	⑥	⑥	⑥	⑥	⑥	⑥		⑥	⑥	⑥	⑥	⑥	⑥	⑥	⑥	⑥	⑥	⑥
Weymouth d.	...	...	...	0542	0620	0655	0720	0803	0820	0903	0920	1003		1703	1720	1803	1820	1903	1920	2010	...	2110	2210	2310
Dorchester South d.	...	...	...	0552	0633	0707	0733	0813	0833	0913	0933	1013	and	1713	1733	1813	1833	1913	1933	2022	...	2122	2222	2322
Wareham d.	...	...	...	0610	0653	0727	0753	0828	0853	0928	0953	1028	at	1728	1753	1828	1853	1928	1953	2042	...	2142	2242	2342
Poole d.	...	...	0528	0624	0707	0741	0807	0840	0907	0940	1007	1040	the	1740	1807	1840	1907	1940	2007	2054	...	2154	2254	2354
Bournemouth 119 d.	...	...	0542	0642	0722	0759	0822	0859	0922	0959	1022	1059	same	1759	1822	1859	1922	1959	2022	2112	...	2212	2312	0003
Brockenhurst 119 d.	...	...	0610	0710	0745	0815	0845	0915	0945	1015	1045	1115	minutes	1815	1845	1915	1945	2015	2045	2140	...	2240	2340	...
Southampton Central 119 d.	0512	0600	0630	0730	0800	0830	0900	0930	1000	1030	1100	1130	past	1830	1900	1930	2000	2030	2100	2200	2230	2300	2359	...
Southampton Airport 119 d.	0520	0608	0638	0738	0808	0838	0908	0938	1008	1038	1108	1138	each	1838	1908	1938	2008	2038	2108	2208	2238	2308	0010	...
Winchester 119 d.	0534	0623	0652	0748	0818	0848	0918	0948	1018	1048	1118	1148	hour	1848	1918	1948	2018	2048	2118	2218	2255	2324	...	...
Basingstoke 119 a.	0550	0639	0708	|	0834	|	0934	|	1034	|	1134	|	until	|	1934	|	2034	|	2134	2234	2311	2343	...	...
Woking 113 a.	0628	0658	0727	0821	|	0919	|	1019	|	1119	|	1219	♠	1919	|	2019	|	2119	|	2253	2332	0018	...	...
London Waterloo 113 a.	0705	0731	0753	0849	0920	0949	1020	1049	1120	1149	1221	1251		1949	2020	2049	2124	2149	2222	2322	0003	0104	...	...

⑦	⑦	⑦	⑦	⑦	⑦	⑦	⑦	⑦		⑦	⑦	⑦	⑦	⑦		⑦	⑦	⑦	⑦	⑦	⑦	⑦	⑦
Weymouth d.	...	...	...	0748	...	0848	...	0948		...	1248	...	1348	...		1748	...	1848	...	1958	2058	2158	2258
Dorchester South d.	...	...	...	0800	...	0900	...	1000	and	...	1300	...	1400	...	and	1800	...	1900	...	2010	2110	2210	2310
Wareham d.	...	...	...	0820	...	0920	...	1020	at	...	1320	...	1420	...	at	1820	...	1920	...	2030	2130	2230	2330
Poole d.	...	0650	0750	0832	0855	0932	0955	1032	the	1255	1332	1355	1432	1455	the	1832	1855	1932	1955	2050r	2150r	2250r	2350r
Bournemouth 119 d.	...	0706	0806	0850	0906	0950	1006	1050	same	1306	1350	1406	1450	1506	same	1850	1906	1950	2006	2106	2206	2306	0003
Brockenhurst 119 d.	...	0734	0834	0909	0934	1009	1034	1109	minutes	1334	1409	1434	1509	1534	minutes	1909	1934	2009	2034	2134	2234	2334	...
Southampton Central 119 d.	0655	0755	0855	0925	0955	1025	1055	1125	past	1355	1425	1455	1525	1555	past	1925	1955	2025	2055	2155	2255	2353	...
Southampton Airport 119 d.	0703	0803	0903	0933	1003	1033	1103	1133	each	1403	1433	1503	1533	1603	each	1933	2003	2033	2103	2203	2303	...	...
Winchester 119 d.	0723	0823	0923	0942	1023	1042	1123	1142	hour	1423	1442	1523	1542	1617	hour	1942	2017	2042	2117	2218	2323	...	...
Basingstoke 119 a.	0742	0842	0942	0958	1042	1058	1142	1158	until	1442	1458	1542	1558	1633	until	1958	2033	2058	2133	2235	2342	...	...
Woking 113 a.	0802	0902	1002	1019	1102	1118	1202	1218	♠	1502	1518	1602	1618	1653	♠	2018	2053	2118	2153	2254	0002	...	...
London Waterloo 113 a.	0846	0941	1039	1050	1139	1150	1237	1249		1537	1549	1637	1649	1724		2049	2124	2149	2224	2325	0033	...	...

Brockenhurst - Lymington Pier (for ⛴ to Isle of Wight).
Journey 11 minutes. Trains call at Lymington Town 6 minutes later:
Ⓐ: 0559 and every 30 minutes until 0929, 1012 and every 30 minutes until 1812, 1848 and every 30 minutes until 2218.
⑥: 0612, 0642 and every 30 minutes until 2112, 2148, 2218.
⑦: 0859, 0929 and every 30 minutes until 2059, 2129, 2159.

Lymington Pier - Brockenhurst.
Journey 11 minutes. Trains call at Lymington Town 2 minutes later:
Ⓐ: 0614 and every 30 minutes until 0944, 1027 and every 30 minutes until 1827, 1903 and every 30 minutes until 2203, 2236.
⑥: 0627, 0657 and every 30 minutes until 2127, 2203, 2236.
⑦: 0914, 0944 and every 30 minutes until 2114, 2144, 2214.

r – Arrives 8 minutes earlier.
s – Calls to set down only.
u – Calls to pick up only.
♠ – Timings may vary by ± 3 minutes.
☛ For ⛴ services Weymouth / Poole – Jersey / Guernsey / St Malo and v.v., see Table **2100**.

111 PORTSMOUTH - RYDE - SHANKLIN

2nd class IL

Through fares including ferry travel are available. Allow 10 minutes for connections between trains and ferries. Operator: Wightlink ✆ 0871 376 4342. www.wightlink.co.uk

Portsmouth Harbour - Ryde Pierhead: ⛴
0515Ⓐ, 0615⚒, 0715 and hourly until 1815, 1920, 2020, 2120, 2245.

Ryde Pierhead - Portsmouth Harbour — Journey time: ± 20 minutes
0547Ⓐ, 0647⚒, 0747 and hourly until 2147, 2310.

Service until December 18, 2016. Additional services operate on Ⓐ and on public holidays.

Ryde Pierhead - Shanklin: *14 km*
⚒: 0549, 0607, 0649, 0707, 0749, 0807, 0849, 0907, 0949, 1007, 1049*, 1107, 1149*, 1207*, 1249*, 1307*, 1349, 1407, 1449*, 1507*, 1549*, 1607*, 1649, 1707, 1749, 1807, 1849, 1907, 1949, 2007, 2049, 2149.
⑦: 0649, 0749, 0849, 0907 **a**, 0949, 1007 **a**, 1049*, 1107 **a**, 1149*, 1207***a**, 1249*, 1307*, 1349, 1407, 1449*, 1507*, 1549*, 1607*, 1649, 1707, 1749, 1807, 1849, 1907 **a**, 1949, 2049, 2149.

Shanklin - Ryde Pierhead — Journey time: ± 24 minutes
⚒: 0618, 0638, 0718, 0738, 0818, 0838, 0918, 0938, 1018, 1038*, 1118, 1138*, 1218*, 1238*, 1318*, 1338, 1418, 1438*, 1518*, 1538*, 1618*, 1638, 1718, 1738, 1818, 1838, 1918, 1938, 2018, 2118, 2238.
⑦: 0718, 0818, 0838 **a**, 0918, 0938 **a**, 1018, 1038***a**, 1118, 1138***a**, 1218*, 1238***a**, 1318*, 1338, 1418, 1438*, 1518*, 1538*, 1618*, 1638, 1718, 1738, 1818, 1838 **a**, 1918, 1938 **a**, 2018, 2118, 2238.

a – From Apr. 9.
* – Also calls at Smallbrook Junction (connection with **Isle of Wight Steam Railway**, see note △) 9 minutes from Ryde / 15 minutes from Shanklin, when Steam Railway is operating.
△ – **Isle of Wight Steam Railway** (🚂 Smallbrook Junction - Wootton: *9 km*). ✆ 01983 882204. www.iwsteamrailway.co.uk

SW 🍷 on most services London - Axminster and v.v. **LONDON - SALISBURY - EXETER** 113

km		Ⓐ	Ⓐ	Ⓐ	Ⓐ	Ⓐ	Ⓐ	Ⓐ	Ⓐ	ⒶB	Ⓐ	Ⓐ	ⒶB	Ⓐ	Ⓐ	Ⓐ	Ⓐ	Ⓐ	Ⓐ	Ⓐ	Ⓐ	Ⓐ	Ⓐ	Ⓐ	Ⓐ	ⒶB
0	**London** W'loo 108 d.	Ⓐ	...	...	...	...	*0630*	0710	0820	0920	1020	1120	1220	1250	1320	1350	1420	1520	1550	1620	1650	1720	1750	1820	1850	1920
39	Woking 108 d.		...	...	...	...	*0657*	0736	0846	0946	1046	1146	1246	1316	1346	1416	1446	1546	1616	1646	1716u	1746u	|	1846	1918	1946
77	Basingstoke 108 d.		...	...	...	...	0722	0757	0907	1007	1107	1207	1307	1338	1407	1438	1507	1607	1638	1707	1738	1807	1838	1907	1939	2007
107	Andover d.		...	...	...	...	0744	0819	0924	1024	1124	1224	1324	1400	1424	1500	1524	1624	1700	1729	1800	1829	1900	1929	2001	2029
134	**Salisbury** a.		...	...	...	...	0803	0839	0943	1042	1142	1242	1343	1419	1442	1520	1542	1642	1720	1748	1820	1850	1920	1948	2021	2049
134	**Salisbury** d.		...	...	0608	0740	0808	0847	0947	1047	1147	1247	1347	1424	1447	1523	1547	1647	1723	1753	1823	1854	1923	1953	2025	2053
169	Gillingham d.		...	0551	0642	0811	0837	0917	1017	1117	1217	1317	1417	|	1517	1552	1617	1717	1753	1819	1851	1919	1954	2022	2052	2119
190	Sherborne d.		...	0606	0657	0826	...	0932	1032	1132	1232	1332	1432	◧	1532	1607	1632	1732	1808	1834	1906	1934	2009	2037	2107	2134
197	**Yeovil** Junction a.		...	0611	0703	0832	...	0938	1038	1138	1238	1338	1438	|	1538	1613	1638	1738	1813	1840	1912	1939	2015	2043	2113	2140
197	**Yeovil** Junction d.		...	0615	0707	0839	...	0939	1039	1139	1239	1339	1439	|	1539	1620	1639	1739	...	1843	1917	1941	2020	2044	2117	2141
200	**Yeovil** Pen Mill 139 a.		...	|	|	|	...	|	|	|	|	|	|	1539	|	1627	|	|	...	|	1925	|	2025	|	2123	|
211	Crewkerne d.		...	0624	0716	0849	...	0949	1049	1149	1249	1349	1449	...	1549	...	1649	1749	...	1853	...	1950	...	2054	...	2151
233	Axminster d.		0552	0656c	0737	0903	...	1003	1103	1203	1303	1403	1503	...	1603	...	1703	1803	...	1907	...	2004	...	2108	...	2205
249	Honiton d.		0607	0712	0753	0916	...	1016	1116	1216	1316	1416	1516	...	1616	...	1716	1818	...	1919	...	2017	...	2120	...	2219
277	**Exeter** St Davids △ a.		0635	0742	0821	0944	...	1042	1143	1243	1343	1443	1544	...	1643	...	1742	1843	...	1946	...	2043	...	2147	...	2247

	Ⓐ	Ⓐ	Ⓐ	①–④	⑤a		⑥	⑥	⑥	⑥	⑥	⑥	⑥B	⑥		⑥		⑥B	⑥	⑥	⑥	⑥	⑥	⑥	⑥B	⑥
London Waterloo 108 d.	2020	2120	2220	2340	2340	⑥	...	...	...	...	0710	0820	0920	1020	...	1120	...	1220	1320	1420	1520	1620	1720	1820	1920	2020
Woking 108 d.	2046	2149	2249	0008	0008		...	...	...	...	0736	0846	0946	1046	...	1146	...	1246	1346	1446	1546	1646	1746	1846	1946	2046
Basingstoke 108 d.	2107	2214	2311	0028	0028		...	...	...	...	0759	0907	1007	1107	...	1207	...	1307	1407	1507	1607	1707	1807	1907	2007	2107
Andover d.	2129	2236	2333	0050	0050		...	...	...	...	0821	0924	1024	1124	...	1224	...	1324	1424	1524	1624	1724	1824	1924	2024	2129
Salisbury a.	2148	2255	2353	0110	0110s		...	...	...	...	0842	0942	1042	1142	...	1242	...	1342	1442	1542	1642	1742	1843	1943	2042	2148
Salisbury d.	2206	2303	...	...	|		...	...	0615	0745	0847	0947	1047	1147	...	1247	...	1347	1447	1547	1647	1747	1847	1947	2047	2153
Gillingham d.	2235	2327s	...	...	0136s		...	...	0642	0811	0917	1017	1117	1217	...	1317	...	1417	1517	1617	1717	1817	1919	2017	2117	2218
Sherborne d.	2250	2342s	...	...	0151s		...	...	0657	0826	0932	1032	1132	1232	...	1332	...	1432	1532	1632	1732	1832	1934	2032	2132	2233
Yeovil Junction a.	2255	2348	...	...	0157		...	...	0703	0832	0938	1038	1138	1238	...	1338	...	1438	1538	1638	1738	1838	1939	2038	2138	2241
Yeovil Junction d.	2257	...	...	...	...		...	0615	0707	0839	0939	1039	1139	1239	...	1339	...	1439	1539	1639	1739	1839	1941	2039	2139	2242
Yeovil Pen Mill 139 a.	|	...	...	...	...		...	|	|	|	|	|	|	|	...	|	...	|	|	|	|	|	|	|	|	|
Crewkerne d.	2306	...	...	...	...		...	0624	0716	0849	0949	1049	1149	1249	...	1349	...	1449	1549	1649	1749	1849	1950	2049	2149	2252
Axminster d.	2320	...	...	...	...		0552	0656c	0738	0903	1003	1103	1203	1303	...	1403	...	1503	1603	1703	1803	1903	2005	2103	2203	2305
Honiton d.	2332	...	...	...	...		0607	0712	0754	0916	1016	1116	1216	1316	...	1416	...	1516	1616	1716	1817	1916	2017	2117	2217	...
Exeter St Davids △ a.	0001	...	...	...	...		0635	0742	0822	0944	1042	1142	1242	1342	...	1442	...	1542	1642	1742	1842	1942	2044	2142	2245	...

	⑥	⑥	⑥		⑦	⑦	⑦	⑦	⑦	⑦	⑦B	⑦	⑦	⑦	⑦	⑦	⑦	⑦B	⑦	⑦	⑦	⑦	⑦	⑦e	⑦	⑦
London Waterloo 108 d.	2120	2220	2340	⑦	...	...	0815	0915	1015	1115	1215	1315	1415	1515	1615	1715	1745	1815	1845	1915	1945	2015	2045	2115	2215	2335
Woking 108 d.	2149	2249	0008		...	...	0847	0947	1046	1146	1246	1346	1446	1546	1646	1746	|	1846	|	1946	|	2046	|	2146	2246	0008
Basingstoke 108 d.	2214	2311	0028		...	0805	0908	1008	1107	1207	1307	1407	1507	1607	1707	1807	|	1907	|	2007	|	2107	|	2207	2307	0040
Andover d.	2236	2333	0050		...	0827	0930	1025	1129	1224	1329	1424	1529	1624	1729	1824	1849	1929	1949	2024	2049	2129	|	2226	2329	0102
Salisbury a.	2255	2353	0110		...	0846	0946	1045	1145	1245	1345	1445	1545	1645	1745	1845	1905	1945	2005	2045	2105	2145	2205	2245	2348	0122
Salisbury d.	2303	...	...		0706	0851	0951	1051	1151	1251	1351	1451	1551	1651	1751	1851	...	1951	...	2051	...	2151	...	2251	...	...
Gillingham d.	2327s	...	...		0731	0921	1021	1121	1221	1321	1421	1521	1621	1721	1821	1921	...	2021	...	2121	...	2221	...	2322	...	...
Sherborne d.	2342s	...	...		0746	0936	1036	1136	1236	1336	1436	1536	1636	1736	1836	1936	...	2036	...	2136	...	2236	...	2337	...	...
Yeovil Junction a.	2348	...	...		0751	0941	1041	1141	1241	1341	1441	1541	1641	1741	1841	1941	...	2041	...	2141	...	2242	...	2343	...	...
Yeovil Junction d.	...	...	...		0753	0943	1043	1143	1243	1343	1443	1543	1643	1743	1843	1943	...	2043	...	2143	...	...	...	2344	...	...
Yeovil Pen Mill 139 a.	...	...	...		|	|	|	|	|	|	|	|	|	|	|	|	...	|	...	|	...	...	...	|	...	...
Crewkerne d.	...	...	...		0802	0952	1052	1152	1252	1352	1452	1552	1652	1752	1852	1952	...	2052	...	2152	...	...	...	2354	...	...
Axminster d.	...	...	...		0816	1006	1106	1206	1306	1406	1506	1606	1706	1806	1906	2006	...	2106	...	2206	...	...	...	0008	...	...
Honiton d.	...	...	...		0831	1018	1118	1218	1318	1418	1518	1618	1718	1818	1918	2018	...	2118	...	2220	...	...	...	0020	...	...
Exeter St Davids △ a.	...	...	...		0859	1045	1145	1245	1345	1445	1545	1645	1745	1845	1945	2045	...	2146	...	2248	...	...	...	0046	...	...

		Ⓐ	Ⓐ	Ⓐ	Ⓐ	Ⓐ	Ⓐ	Ⓐ	Ⓐ	Ⓐ	ⒶB	Ⓐ	Ⓐ	Ⓐ	ⒶB	Ⓐ	Ⓐ	Ⓐ	ⒶB	Ⓐ	Ⓐ	Ⓐ	Ⓐ	Ⓐ	Ⓐ	Ⓐ
Exeter St Davids ▽ d.	Ⓐ	...	...	...	...	0510	...	0641	0725	...	0823	0925	1025	1125	1225	1325	1425	...	1525	...	...	1624	1725	1746	1825	...
Honiton d.		...	...	...	...	0541	0619	0712	0752	...	0855	0955	1055	1155	1255	1355	1455	...	1555	...	...	1656	1755	1819	1859	...
Axminster d.		...	...	...	...	0552	0630	0723	0803	...	0906	1006	1106	1206	1306	1406	1506	...	1606	...	...	1707	1806	1829	1910	...
Crewkerne d.		...	...	...	...	0605	0643	0736	0816	...	0919	1019	1119	1219	1319	1419	1519	...	1619	...	...	1720	1819	...	1923	...
Yeovil Pen Mill 139 d.		...	...	...	0541	|	|	|	|	...	|	|	|	|	|	|	|	1544	|	1631	1653	|	|	...	|	1927
Yeovil Junction a.		...	...	...	0546	0614	0652	0745	0825	...	0927	1027	1127	1227	1327	1427	1527	1549	1627	1636	|	1728	1827	...	1931	|
Yeovil Junction d.		...	...	0514	0550	0620	0653	0750	0829	...	0929	1029	1129	1229	1329	1429	1529	1553	1629	...	1646b	1730	1829	...	1933	1917b
Sherborne d.		...	...	0520	0556	0626	0700	0756	0835	...	0935	1035	1135	1235	1335	1435	1535	1559	1635	...	◧	1736	1835	...	1939	◧
Gillingham d.		...	...	0536	0612	0642	0715	0812	0851	0918	0951	1051	1151	1251	1351	1451	1551	1617	1651	...	|	1752	1851	...	1955	|
Salisbury a.		...	...	0601	0639	0707	0740	0837	0916	0942	1016	1116	1216	1316	1416	1516	1616	1643	1716	...	1817	1822	1923	...	2022	2042
Salisbury d.		0515	0543	0606	0645	0715	0745	0847	0921	0947	1021	1121	1221	1321	1421	1521	1621	1647	1721	...	1827	1827	1926	...	2026	...
Andover d.		0535	0603	0626	0705	0735	0805	0906	0938	1006	1038	1138	1238	1338	1438	1538	1638	1706	1738	...	1844	1844	1945	...	2045	...
Basingstoke 108 a.		0558	0626	0649	0728	0758	0828	0928	0955	1028	1055	1155	1255	1355	1455	1555	1655	1729	1755	...	1901	1901	2008	...	2108	...
Woking 108 a.		0618	0646	|	|	0818	0848	0949	1015	1049	1115	1215	1315	1415	1515	1615	1715	1749	1815	...	1921	1921	2029	...	2129	...
London Waterloo 108 a.		0649	0714	0739	0814	0846	0917	1019	1049	1119	1149	1249	1349	1449	1549	1649	1749	1821	1849	...	1950	1950	2100	...	2204	...

	Ⓐ	Ⓐ	Ⓐ	Ⓐ	Ⓐ		⑥	⑥	⑥	⑥	⑥	⑥	⑥	⑥	⑥B	⑥	⑥	⑥	⑥B	⑥	⑥	⑥B	⑥	⑥	⑥	⑥
Exeter St Davids ▽ d.	1925	...	2025	2125	2257	⑥	...	...	...	...	0510	...	0641	0725	0824	0925	1025	1125	1225	1325	1425	1525	1625	1725	1825	1925
Honiton d.	1955	...	2057	2159	2332		...	...	...	...	0541	0619	0713	0755	0855	0955	1055	1155	1255	1355	1455	1555	1655	1757	1855	1955
Axminster d.	2006	...	2108	2210	2343		...	...	...	...	0552	0630	0724	0806	0906	1006	1106	1206	1306	1406	1506	1606	1706	1808	1906	2006
Crewkerne d.	2019	...	2121	2223	2356		...	...	...	...	0605	0643	0737	0819	0919	1019	1119	1219	1319	1419	1519	1619	1719	1821	1919	2019
Yeovil Pen Mill 139 d.	|	2030	|	|	|		...	...	...	...	|	|	|	|	|	|	|	|	|	|	|	|	|	|	|	|
Yeovil Junction a.	2028	2035	2129	2231	0004		...	...	...	...	0614	0652	0745	0827	0927	1027	1127	1227	1327	1427	1527	1627	1727	1829	1927	2027
Yeovil Junction d.	2029	...	2131	2233	0006		...	...	...	...	0620	0653	0750	0829	0929	1029	1129	1229	1329	1429	1529	1629	1729	1831	1929	2029
Sherborne d.	2036	...	2137	2239	|		...	...	...	...	0626	0700	0756	0835	0935	1035	1135	1235	1335	1435	1535	1635	1735	1837	1935	2035
Gillingham d.	2051	...	2153	2255	|		...	...	...	...	0642	0715	0812	0851	0951	1051	1151	1251	1351	1451	1551	1651	1751	1853	1951	2051
Salisbury a.	2122	...	2218	2329	0043		...	...	...	...	0707	0740	0837	0916	1016	1116	1216	1316	1416	1516	1616	1716	1816	1918	2016	2116
Salisbury d.	2126	...	2226	...	...		0515	0547	0621	0647	0721	0747	0847	0921	1021	1121	1221	1321	1421	1521	1621	1721	1821	1926	2026	2126
Andover d.	2145	...	2245	...	...		0535	0606	0638	0706	0738	0806	0906	0938	1038	1138	1238	1338	1438	1538	1638	1738	1838	1945	2045	2145
Basingstoke 108 a.	2207	...	2307	...	...		0558	0628	0655	0728	0755	0828	0928	0955	1055	1155	1255	1355	1455	1555	1655	1755	1855	2008	2108	2207
Woking 108 a.	2228	...	*2331*	...	...		0618	0649	0715	0749	0817	0849	0949	1015	1115	1215	1315	1415	1515	1615	1715	1815	1915	2029	2129	2228
London Waterloo 108 a.	2258	...	*0008*	...	...		0649	0719	0749	0819	0849	0919	1019	1049	1149	1249	1349	1449	1549	1649	1749	1849	1949	2104	2204	2257

	⑥	⑥	⑥		⑦	⑦	⑦	⑦	⑦	⑦	⑦	⑦	⑦	⑦	⑦	⑦	⑦B	⑦	⑦	⑦	⑦	⑦	⑦	⑦	⑦	⑦
Exeter St Davids ▽ d.	2025	2125	2257	⑦	...	...	...	...	...	0925	1025	1125	1225	1325	1425	...	1525	...	1625	...	1725	1825	1925	2025	2125	2315
Honiton d.	2056	2157	2332		...	...	...	...	0858	0957	1057	1157	1257	1357	1457	...	1557	...	1657	...	1757	1857	1957	2057	2159	2340s
Axminster d.	2107	2208	2343		...	...	...	...	0909	1009	1109	1209	1309	1409	1509	...	1609	...	1709	...	1809	1909	2009	2109	2210	2351s
Crewkerne d.	2120	2221	2356		...	...	...	...	0922	1022	1122	1222	1322	1422	1522	...	1622	...	1722	...	1822	1922	2022	2122	2223	0012s
Yeovil Pen Mill 139 d.	|	|	|		...	...	...	...	|	|	|	|	|	|	|	...	|	...	|	...	|	|	|	|	|	|
Yeovil Junction a.	2129	2229	0004		...	...	...	...	0930	1030	1130	1230	1330	1430	1530	...	1630	...	1730	...	1830	1930	2030	2131	2232	0021s
Yeovil Junction d.	2130	2231	0006		...	...	0732	...	0932	1032	1132	1232	1332	1432	1532	...	1632	...	1732	...	1832	1932	2032	2132	2233	|
Sherborne d.	2137	2237	|		...	...	0738	...	0938	1038	1138	1238	1338	1438	1538	...	1638	...	1738	...	1838	1938	2038	2138	2240	|
Gillingham d.	2152	2253	|		...	...	0754	0854	0954	1054	1154	1254	1354	1454	1554	1621	1654	1721	1754	...	1854	1954	2054	2154	2256	|
Salisbury a.	2223	2329	0041		...	...	0820	0920	1020	1120	1220	1320	1420	1520	1620	1647	1720	1747	1820	...	1920	2020	2120	2220	2321	0057
Salisbury d.	2227	...	...		0645	0727	0827	0927	1027	1129	1227	1327	1427	1527	1627	1652	1727	1752	1827	1852	1927	2027	2127	2227	...	...
Andover d.	2247	...	...		0702	0746	0846	0946	1044	1146	1244	1346	1444	1546	1644	1709	1746	1809	1844	1909	1946	2044	2146	2246	...	...
Basingstoke 108 a.	2309	...	...		0719	0808	0908	1002	1106	1204	1306	1402	1506	1602	1706	1726	1802	1826	1906	1926	2002	2106	2203	2308	...	...
Woking 108 a.	2332	...	...		0739	0828	0928	1028	1128	1228	1328	1428	1528	1628	1728	1748	1828	1848	1928	1948	2028	2128	2228	*0002*	...	...
London Waterloo 108 a.	0003	...	...		0820	0912	1011	1104	1204	1304	1359	1459	1559	1659	1759	1819	1859	1919	1959	2019	2059	2159	2259	*0033*	...	...

☛ Full service **London** Waterloo - **Salisbury** and v.v. :

From **London** Waterloo on ✕ at 0710, 0750, 0820, 0850 and every 30 minutes until 1920, 1950, 2020, 2120, 2220, 2340; on ⑦ at 0815 and hourly until 2215, 2335 (also 1745, 1845, 1945, 2045. Please see timings above for calling points between London and Salisbury).

From **Salisbury** on Ⓐ at 0515, 0543, 0606, 0645, 0715, 0745, 0815, 0847, 0921, 0947 and at the same minutes past each hour until 1747, 1827, 1847, 1926, 2026, 2126; on ⑥ at 0515, 0547, 0621, 0647, 0721, 0747, 0821, 0847, 0947, 1021, 1047 and at the same minutes past each hour until 1847, 1926, 2026, 2126; on ⑦ at 0645, 0727, 0827, 0927, 1027, 1129, 1227 and hourly until 2127 (also 1652, 1752, 1852).

B – Conveys 12 London Waterloo - Bristol and v.v. (Table **140**).

a – Not Dec. 30.

b – Calls at Yeovil Junction before Yeovil Pen Mill.

c – Arrives 0643.

e – Does not call at Exeter Central.

s – Calls to set down only.

u – Calls to pick up only.

◧ – Via Westbury (Table **140**).

△ – Trains to Exeter St Davids also call at **Exeter Central** 5 – 6 minutes earlier.

▽ – Trains from Exeter St Davids also call at **Exeter Central** 4 – 5 minutes later.

115 LONDON - EXETER - PAIGNTON and PLYMOUTH GW

km			Ⓐ2 B★	Ⓐ2 ★	Ⓐ 2	Ⓐ 🍷	Ⓐ 🍷★	Ⓐ 2	Ⓐ2 C★	Ⓐ 🍷		Ⓐ C2	Ⓐ ✕	Ⓐ 🍷★	Ⓐ 🍷	Ⓐ 🍷	Ⓐ ✕	Ⓐ 2	Ⓐ ✕	Ⓐ C2	Ⓐ 2★	Ⓐ 🍷	⑤ 2
0	**London** Paddington 132 d.	Ⓐ	...	...	...	0706	0730	...	...	0906	...	...	1006	1000	1106	1133	1205	...	1305	...	...	1406	...
58	**Reading** 132 d.		...	...	...	0733	0759	...	...	0935u	...	...	1032	1027	1133	1201	1233	...	1333	...	...	1434	...
85	Newbury d.		...	...	...	0749	|	...	...	|	...	...	|	|	|	1223	|	...	|	...	...	|	...
154	Westbury 139 d.		...	...	...	0826	|	...	...	|	...	...	|	|	1217	1300	|	...	|	...	...	|	1520
186	Castle Cary 139 d.		...	...	...	|	|	...	...	1031	...	...	|	|	1235	|	|	...	|	...	...	|	1550
	Bristol Temple Meads 120a 120 d.		...	0524	0642	|	0913	...	0855	|	...	0955	|	1147	|	|	|	1319	|	1357	...	|	|
230	Taunton 120a 120 d.		...	0620	0739	0903	0945	...	1001	1053	...	1100	|	1229	1259	1340	|	1400	1448	1458	...	1549	1621
253	Tiverton Parkway 120 d.		...	0635	0755	0916	|	...	|	1106	...	1116	|	|	1312	|	|	1415	1501	1514	...	1602	1637
279	**Exeter** St Davids 120 a.		...	0652	0812	0930	1009	...	1031	1121	...	1132	1206	1254	1328	1404	1406	1433	1516	1533	...	1617	1658
279	**Exeter** St Davids 116 120 d.		0628	0655	0814	0933	1010	1018	1032	1125	...	1135	1208	1257	1329	...	1410	...	1519	...	1550	1620	...
311	Newton Abbot 116 120 d.		0655	0728	0835	0955	1038	1041	1101	1145	...	1157	1229	1323	1349	...	1429	...	1542	...	1621	1641	...
321	Torquay 116 120 d.		|	|	|	|	1050	|	1113	|	...	1209	|	1337	|	...	|	...	|	...	|	|	...
324	**Paignton** 116 120 a.		|	|	|	|	1057	|	1120	|	...	1242	|	1345	|	...	|	...	|	...	|	|	...
325	Totnes 120 d.		0709	0742	0849	1007	...	1053	...	1158	...	...	|	...	1403	...	|	...	1554	...	1633	1653	...
363	**Plymouth** 120 a.		0740	0811	0919	1033	...	1124	...	1227	...	...	1305	...	1433	...	1505	...	1623	...	1705	1721	...
	Newquay **117** a.		...	|	|	|	...	|	...	|	...	...	|	...	...	...	|	...	...	...	...	|	...
	Penzance **117** a.		...	1016	1123	1237	...	1325	...	*1439*	...	...	1511	...	...	...	1712	...	...	...	...	1933	...

	Ⓐ 🍷	Ⓐ 🍷	①–④ 🍷	⑤ 🍷	Ⓐ 🍷	Ⓐ 🍷★	Ⓐ ✕		Ⓐ 🍷	①–④ 🍷	⑤ 🍷	①–④ ✕	⑤ ✕	Ⓐ 🍷	Ⓐ 🍷	Ⓐ 2	Ⓐ 2	Ⓐ 🍷	Ⓐ A		⑥2 ★	⑥2 ★	⑥ 2
London Paddington 132 d.	1506	1606	1636	1636	1703	1733	1803	...	1805	1835	1835	1903	1903	1945	2035	...	...	2145	2345‡	⑥	...	...	...
Reading 132 d.	1533	1632	1704	1704	1730	1801	1831	...	1838	1903	1903	1933	1933u	2012	2102	...	...	2212	0046u		...	...	...
Newbury d.	|	|	1720	1720	1748	1819	|	...	1904	1919	1919	1950	1950	2028	2119	...	...	|	|		...	...	...
Westbury 139 d.	1623	|	1803	1803	|	1900	|	...	1955	2006	2006	|	|	2106	2156	...	...	|	|		...	...	...
Castle Cary 139 d.	1641	|	1822	1822	|	1919	|	...	...	2024	2024	|	|	2126	2215	...	...	|	|		...	...	...
Bristol Temple Meads 120a 120 d.	|	|	|	|	|	|	|	...	...	|	|	|	|	|	|	2156	2306	2336	|		0524	0636	...
Taunton 120a 120 d.	1705	1750	1844	1844	1852	1942	1948	...	...	2046	2047	2054	2054	2148	2237	2303	0014s	0037s	0235		0618	0725	...
Tiverton Parkway 120 d.	1718	1803	1857	1857	1905	1955	|	...	...	2059	2059	2107	2107	2202	2250	2319	0031s	0050s	|		0633	0741	...
Exeter St Davids 120 a.	1733	1818	1914	1913	1920	2009	2013	...	...	2116	2116	2122	2122	2217	2305	2337	0052	0108	0307		0652	0759	...
Exeter St Davids 116 120 d.	1737	1822	...	1916	1922	2020	2016	...	...	...	2117	2125	2125	2219	2308	...	...	...	0411		0653	0800	0928
Newton Abbot 116 120 d.	1758	1843	...	1936	1942	2058	2036	...	...	...	2137	2145	2145	2240	2328	...	...	...	0433		0727	0831	0949
Torquay 116 120 d.	|	|	...	|	|	2112	|	...	...	...	|	|	|	|	|	...	...	...	|		|	|	|
Paignton 116 120 a.	|	|	...	|	|	2122	|	...	...	...	|	|	|	|	|	...	...	...	|		|	|	|
Totnes 120 d.	1811	1856	...	|	1956	...	2050	...	...	...	|	2158	2158	2253	2342	...	...	...	|		0740	0845	1001
Plymouth 120 a.	1839	1926	...	2015	2024	...	2118	...	...	...	2215	2226	2226	2325	0011	...	...	...	0514		0813	0916	1032
Newquay **117** a.	|	|	...	...	|	...	|	...	...	...	...	|	|	...	...	...	...	...	|		|	|	|
Penzance **117** a.	2042	2131	...	...	2228	...	2313	...	...	...	...	*0046*	0040	...	...	...	...	...	0753		1018	1126	1236

	⑥ 🍷	⑥ 🍷	⑥ 🍷	⑥ 🍷	⑥ 2★	⑥ 🍷		⑥ 🍷	⑥ 🍷	⑥ 🍷	⑥ 🍷	⑥ 2★	⑥ 🍷	⑥ 🍷	⑥ 🍷	⑥ 🍷	⑥ 🍷	⑥ 🍷★	⑥ C2	⑥ 🍷		⑦ 2★	⑦ 2★
London Paddington 132 d.	0730	0806	0906	1006	...	1106	...	1206	1306	1406	1506	...	1606	1706	1630	1806	1906	2006	...	2030	⑦	...	...
Reading 132 d.	0759	0835	0933	1035	...	1133	...	1235	1333	1435	1534	...	1635	1733	1659	1835	1933	2035	...	2059		...	...
Newbury d.	|	0859	|	|	...	|	...	|	|	|	|	...	|	|	|	|	1949	2050	...	|		...	...
Westbury 139 d.	|	0943	|	|	...	1222	...	|	|	|	1624	...	|	1823	|	|	2027	2129	...	|		...	...
Castle Cary 139 d.	|	1002	|	|	...	1240	...	|	|	|	1642	...	|	1841	|	|	2045	2147	...	|		...	...
Bristol Temple Meads 120a 120 d.	0918	|	|	|	*1144*	|	...	|	|	|	|	*1644*	|	|	1818	|	|	|	2159	2217		0726	0828
Taunton 120a 120 d.	0952	1025	1049	|	*1216*	1303	...	|	1449	1550	1705	*1717*	1750	1904	1908	1950	2108	2209	2305	2318		0820	0932
Tiverton Parkway 120 d.	|	1038	1102	|	*1228*	1316	...	|	1502	1603	1718	*1730*	1803	1917	1923	|	2121	2222	2321	2331		0835	0947
Exeter St Davids 120 a.	1015	1053	1116	1208	*1241*	1330	...	1409	1516	1617	1731	*1743*	1817	1932	1938	2012	2135	2235	2339	2347		0853	1004
Exeter St Davids 116 120 d.	1019	...	1119	1212	1252	1333	...	1413	1518	1619	1738	1753	1819	1934	1940	2015	2139	2239	...	...		0905	1006
Newton Abbot 116 120 d.	1040	...	1140	1236	1321	1354	...	1434	1539	1640	1759	1822	1842	1955	2001	2037	2200	2304	...	...		0928	1032
Torquay 116 120 d.	|	...	|	|	|	|	...	|	|	|	|	|	|	|	2014	|	|	|	...	...		|	|
Paignton 116 120 a.	|	...	|	|	|	|	...	|	|	|	|	|	|	|	2022	|	|	|	...	...		|	|
Totnes 120 d.	1053	...	1153	|	1334	1407	...	|	1553	1653	1812	1835	1855	2008	...	2051	2213	2319	...	...		0941	1044
Plymouth 120 a.	1120	...	1224	1313	1405	1434	...	1510	1622	1724	1838	1905	1924	2034	...	2118	2240	2346	...	...		1012	1113
Newquay **117** a.	|	...	...	|	|	...	...	|	|	|	|	|	...	|	...	|	...	...	...	...		|	|
Penzance **117** a.	1320	...	...	1517	*1621*	...	...	1710	1824	1924	2041	2108	...	2242	...	2322	...	...	...	...		1224	1315

	⑦ 🍷★	⑦ 🍷	⑦ 2	⑦ 🍷	⑦ 🍷		⑦ 🍷★	⑦ 🍷	⑦ 🍷	⑦ 🍷	⑦ 2★	⑦ 🍷	⑦ 🍷	⑦ 🍷		⑦ 🍷	⑦ 2	⑦ 🍷	⑦ 🍷★	⑦ 🍷	⑦ 🍷	⑦ 🍷	⑦ A
London Paddington 132 d.	0800	0857	...	0957	1057	...	1133	1157	1257	1300	...	1357	1457	1557	...	1657	...	1757	1857	1903	1957	2057	2350‡
Reading 132 d.	0839	0932	...	1032	1132	...	1210	1232	1332	1338	...	1432	1532	1632	...	1732	...	1832	1932	1938	2032	2132	0038u
Newbury d.	|	0948	...	|	|	...	|	1248	|	|	...	1448	|	1648	...	|	...	1848	|	|	2048	|	|
Westbury 139 d.	|	1022	...	|	|	...	1305	|	1418	|	...	|	|	1724	...	|	...	1927	|	|	2127	|	|
Castle Cary 139 d.	|	|	...	1134	|	...	1324	|	|	|	...	1536	|	1743	...	|	...	|	2029	|	2144	|	|
Bristol Temple Meads 120a 120 d.	1000	|	...	|	|	...	|	|	|	1455	...	|	|	|	...	|	1830	|	|	2055	|	|	|
Taunton 120a 120 d.	1034	1058	...	1156	1246	...	1345	1354	1455	1529	...	1557	1651	1805	...	1850	1933	2001	2051	2150	2206	2246s	|
Tiverton Parkway 120 d.	1048	1112	...	|	|	...	1359	1407	|	|	...	|	1704	1818	...	1903	1949	2016	2105	2204	2219	2300s	|
Exeter St Davids 120 a.	1102	1126	...	1221	1312	...	1413	1421	1518	1553	...	1623	1718	1834	...	1918	2007	2029	2120	2220	2235	2319	0305
Exeter St Davids 116 120 d.	1105	1126	1215	1223	1313	...	1415	1424	1521	1555	1605	1625	1721	1836	...	1920	...	2030	2121	...	2236	...	0435
Newton Abbot 116 120 d.	1132	1147	1236	1244	1335	...	1442	1447	1542	1616	1637	1644	1740	1858	...	1939	...	2053	2148	...	2257	...	0456
Torquay 116 120 d.	|	|	|	|	|	...	1453	|	|	|	|	|	|	|	...	|	...	|	|	...	|	...	|
Paignton 116 120 a.	|	|	|	|	|	...	1502	|	|	|	|	|	|	|	...	|	...	|	|	...	|	...	|
Totnes 120 d.	1144	1201	1248	1257	|	...	...	1459	1554	|	1651	1700	1754	|	...	1953	...	2106	2202	...	2310	...	|
Plymouth 120 a.	1214	1230	1318	1325	1411	...	...	1527	1622	1653	1721	1729	1820	1934	...	2020	...	2133	2230	...	2340	...	0535
Newquay **117** a.	|	...	|	...	|	...	...	|	|	...	|	|	|	|	...	|	...	|	...	...	...	...	|
Penzance **117** a.	1416	...	1525	...	1612	...	...	1729	1824	...	1937	*1937*	2028	*2142*	...	2222	...	2334	...	...	...	...	0859

A – THE NIGHT RIVIERA – Conveys 🛏 1, 2. cl and 2 (reclining seats).
B – To Par (Table **117**).
C – To / from Cardiff (Table **120a**).

b – Also calls at Dawlish 0621.
c – Also calls at Teignmouth at 0554.
s – Stops to set down only.

u – Stops to pick up only.

NOTES CONTINUE ON NEXT PAGE →

116 EXETER - PAIGNTON 2nd class GW

km			Ⓐ	Ⓐ	Ⓐ	Ⓐ	Ⓐ	Ⓐ	Ⓐ	Ⓐ	Ⓐ	Ⓐ	Ⓐ	Ⓐ	Ⓐ	Ⓐ	Ⓐ	Ⓐ	Ⓐ	Ⓐ	Ⓐ	Ⓐ	Ⓐ
0	**Exeter** St Davids 115 120 d.	Ⓐ	0534	0611	0718	0750	0842	0858	0958	1032	1058	1158	1249	1303	1358	1503	1558	1628	1655	1728	1751	1836	1933
20	Dawlish 115 120 d.		0555	0631	0738	0810	0857	0925	1019	1048	1118	1228	|	1324	1428	1523	1619	1648	1715	1755	1812	1902	1959
24	Teignmouth 115 120 d.		0600	0636	0743	0815	0902	0930	1024	1053	1123	1233	|	1329	1433	1528	1624	1653	1720	1800	1817	1907	2004
32	Newton Abbot 115 120 d.		0609	0645	0752	0824	0911	0938	1032	1101	1132	1241	1313	1338	1442	1537	1632	1702	1729	1810	1826	1916	2013
42	Torquay 115 120 d.		0620	0656	0803	0836	0922	0950	1044	1113	1143	1253	1324	1349	1453	1548	1644	1713	1740	1821	1837	1927	2024
45	**Paignton** 🚂 115 120 a.		0628	0706	0812	0844	0929	0957	1053	1120	1152	1301	1333	1358	1500	1557	1654	1722	1750	1830	1846	1934	2032

	Ⓐ	Ⓐ	Ⓐ		⑥	⑥	⑥	⑥	⑥	⑥	⑥	⑥	⑥	⑥	⑥	⑥	⑥	⑥	⑥	⑥	⑥	⑥	⑥
Exeter St Davids 115 120 d.	2020	2129	2249	⑥	0518	0536	0611	0750	0837	0856	0956	1025	1035	1059	1157	1258	1359	1430	1458	1558	1655	1727	1827
Dawlish 115 120 d.	2043	2149	2309		0539	0557	0631	0810	0851	0925	1016	|	1051	1119	1217	1318	1429	1446	1518	1617	1715	1753	1846
Teignmouth 115 120 d.	2050	2154	2314		0544	0602	0636	0815	0856	0930	1021	|	1056	1124	1222	1323	1434	1451	1523	1622	1720	1758	1851
Newton Abbot 115 120 d.	2058	2203	2334a		0552	0611	0645	0824	0906	0939	1031	1048	1104	1136	1238a	1332	1444	1500	1532	1631	1729	1808	1901
Torquay 115 120 d.	2112	2214	2344		0603	0622	0656	0835	0916	0950	1042	1059	1114	1147	1248	1343	1456	1511	1543	1642	1740	1819	1912
Paignton 🚂 115 120 a.	2122	2223	2353		0611	0630	0706	0844	0925	0958	1050	1107	1123	1157	1256	1351	1504	1519	1553	1652	1750	1826	1921

	⑥	⑥	⑥	⑥			⑦	⑦	⑦	⑦	⑦	⑦	⑦	⑦	⑦	⑦	⑦	⑦	⑦	⑦	⑦	⑦	⑦
Exeter St Davids 115 120 d.	1856	1913	2019	2056	...	⑦	0849	0954	1053	1158	1302	1326	1359	1415	1505	1531	1600	1657	1757	1857	1957	2102	2202
Dawlish 115 120 d.	1909	1933	2039	2116	...		0909	1014	1113	1218	1317	1339	1419	1429	1517	1543	1615	1710	1817	1917	2017	2115	2222
Teignmouth 115 120 d.	1914	1938	2044	2121	...		0914	1019	1118	1223	1322	1344	1424	1435	1522	1548	1620	1715	1822	1922	2022	2120	2227
Newton Abbot 115 120 d.	1922	1947	2053	2132	...		0924	1037a	1127	1232	1330	1352	1435	1442	1530	1556	1629	1723	1831	1931	2031	2128	2236
Torquay 115 120 d.	1932	1958	2104	2143	...		0935	1048	1138	1243	1341	1404	1446	1453	1542	1607	1640	1735	1842	1942	2042	2140	2247
Paignton 🚂 115 120 a.	1940	2006	2111	2150	...		0942	1054	1145	1251	1348	1411	1452	1502	1550	1615	1647	1742	1849	1949	2049	2147	2255

a – Arrives 7 - 9 minutes earlier.

🚂 – Dartmouth Steam Railway (Paignton - Kingswear: *10 km*). ✆ 01803 555 872. www.dartmouthrailriver.co.uk

GW PLYMOUTH and PAIGNTON - EXETER - LONDON 115

km			Ⓐ 🍸w	Ⓐ 🍸	Ⓐ 🍸	Ⓐ 2	Ⓐ ✖	Ⓐ 🍸b	Ⓐ 🍸c	Ⓐ ✖	Ⓐ 🍸	Ⓐ 🍸☆	Ⓐ 2☆	Ⓐ 🍸	Ⓐ 🍸	Ⓐ 🍸	Ⓐ 🍸☆	Ⓐ ✖	Ⓐ 2☆	Ⓐ ✖	Ⓐ 🍸☆
	Penzance 117 d.	Ⓐ	...	...	...	...	...	...	...	0505	0541	...	0600	0645	0741	0844	...	1000	...	*1046*	...
	Newquay 117 d.		...	...	...	...	...	...	...	|	|	...	|	|	|	|	...	|	...	|	...
0	**Plymouth** 120 d.		...	...	...	...	0553	0530	0509	0655	0748	...	0809	0853	0948	1044	...	1201	...	1256	...
38	Totnes 120 d.		...	...	...	...	|	0558	|	|	0816	...	0839	0923	1019	|	...	1229	...	1324	...
	Paignton 116 120 d.		...	...	...	...	|	|	|	|	|	0740	|	|	|	|	1132	|	1248	|	1413
	Torquay 116 120 d.		...	...	...	...	|	|	|	|	|	0746	|	|	|	|	1138	|	1254	|	1419
52	Newton Abbot 116 120 d.		...	...	...	...	0631	0611	0547	0732	0829	0806	0852	0936	1032	|	1150	1242	1308	1337	1432
84	**Exeter** St Davids 116 120 a.		...	...	...	...	0651	0633	0610	0752	0849	0839	0918	0956	1054	1137	1215	1302	1332	1357	1458
84	**Exeter** St Davids 120 d.		...	...	0546	0600	0652	0635	0612	0753	0851	0841	0933	0958	1056	1139	1217	1304	1336	1359	1501
110	Tiverton Parkway 120 d.		...	...	0602	0617	|	0651	0627	|	0906	|	0950	1013	1111	|	1232	1319	1353	|	1516
133	Taunton 120a 120 d.		...	...	0617	0634	0718	0706	0654	0819	0921	0905	1007	1028	1125	|	1246	1334	1410	1424	1531
205	**Bristol** Temple Meads 120a 120 a.		0518	...	|	0741	|	|	0757	|	|	0957	1110	|	1158	|	|	|	1513	|	|
	Castle Cary d.		|	...	0639	...	|	0727	|	|	0942	|	|	|	|	|	1306	|	...	1446	1553
	Westbury d.		0603	0616	0701	...	|	0751	|	|	1002	|	|	1105	|	|	1327	|	...	1504	|
	Newbury a.		0648	0706	0745	...	|	0829	|	|	|	|	|	|	|	|	1403	|	...	|	|
337	**Reading** 132 a.		0716	0737	0806	...	0832	0847	0914	0932	1050	1108	...	1150	1308	1316	1420	1450	...	1549	1650
395	**London** Paddington 132 a.		0747	0809	0838	...	0900	0921	0944	1002	1124	1139	...	1224	1340	1344	1454	1521	...	1622	1724

	Ⓐ 🍸	Ⓐ 🍸	Ⓐ 🍸	Ⓐ 🍸	Ⓐ ✖	Ⓐ 2☆	①–④ 🍸	⑤ 🍸	⑤ ✖	①–④ ✖	Ⓐ 🍸	Ⓐ 2☆	Ⓐ 2☆	Ⓐ A		⑥ 2	⑥ 🍸	⑥ 🍸	⑥ 🍸	⑥ 🍸	⑥ 2☆
Penzance 117 d.	...	1303	*1345*	*1449*	1559	...	*1644*	*1644*	1742	1742	...	...	*1916*	2145‡	⑥	...	...	...	...	*0537*	...
Newquay 117 d.	...	|	|	|	|	...	|	|	|	|	...	...	|	|		...	|	|	...	|	...
Plymouth 120 d.	...	1503	1602	1657	1803	...	*1844*	*1844*	1944	1944	...	...	2125	2354		...	0540	0655	...	0747	0806
Totnes 120 d.	...	|	1629	1728	1831	...	*1913*	*1913*	2012	2012	...	...	2154	0022		...	0607	|	...	0814	0835
Paignton 116 120 d.	...	|	|	|	|	1852	|	|	|	|	*2014*	2035	|	|		...	|	|	...	|	|
Torquay 116 120 d.	...	|	|	|	|	1857	|	|	|	|	*2020*	2040	|	|		...	|	|	...	|	|
Newton Abbot 116 120 d.	...	1541	1642	1741	1844	1909	*1926*	*1926*	2025	2025	*2031*	*2053*	2206	0036		...	0620	0732	...	0827	0848
Exeter St Davids 116 120 a.	...	1601	1702	1801	1903	1939	*1948*	*1948*	2044	2044	*2050*	*2128*	2240	0058		...	0640	0752	...	0847	0914
Exeter St Davids 120 d.	1453	1603	1708	1803	1906	1939	1955	*1948*	2046	2046	*2052*	2149	...	0106		0600	0641	0754	0729	0849	...
Tiverton Parkway 120 d.	1508	1618	1723	1818	1921	|	2010	*2005*	2101	2101	*2105*	2206	...	|		0617	0656	0809	0744	0904	...
Taunton 120a 120 d.	1523	1633	1737	1833	1936	2010	2025	2027	2115	2115	2129	2223	...	0142		0634	0711	0824	0759	0919	...
Bristol Temple Meads 120a 120 a.	|	|	|	|	|	2054	|	|	2145	2145	2232	2313	...	|		0741	|	|	0857	|	...
Castle Cary d.	|	|	|	1854	|	...	2046	2046	|	|	|	...	...	|		|	0733	|	|	0940	...
Westbury d.	1608	|	|	1914	|	...	2105	2105	|	|	|	...	...	|		|	0756	|	|	1001	...
Newbury a.	1649	|	|	1951	|	...	2142	2142	|	|	|	...	...	|		|	0833	|	|	|	...
Reading 132 a.	1716	1749	1851	2008	2050	...	2159	2159	2308	2304	2355	...	...	0401s		...	0851	0942	1011	1050	...
London Paddington 132 a.	1745	1821	1924	2039	2124	...	2239	2230	2341	2344	0036	...	...	0523y		...	0922	1010	1039	1121	...

	⑥ 🍸	⑥ 🍸☆	⑥ 🍸	⑥ 🍸	⑥ 🍸	⑥ 🍸	⑥ 🍸	⑥ 🍸	⑥ 🍸	⑥ 🍸	⑥ 🍸	⑥ 🍸	⑥ 🍸	⑥ 2☆	⑥ 🍸	⑥ 2☆		⑦ 2	⑦ 🍸	⑦ 2	⑦ 🍸☆
Penzance 117 d.	0650	...	0759	0844	...	1000	1058	*1146*	...	*1300*	1401	*1452*	1552	1641	1740	1906	⑦	...	...	...	...
Newquay 117 d.	...	|	...	|	...	|	|	|	...	|	|	|	|	|	|	|		...	...	...	...
Plymouth 120 d.	0852	...	1001	1043	...	1159	1254	1400	...	1504	1600	1656	1754	1851	1942	2115		...	...	...	0840
Totnes 120 d.	0919	...	1031	|	...	1229	1321	|	...	1531	1628	1727	1821	1922	2009	2144		...	...	...	0907
Paignton 116 120 d.	|	0918	|	|	...	|	|	|	*1355*	|	|	|	|	|	|	|		...	...	...	|
Torquay 116 120 d.	|	0925	|	|	...	|	|	|	*1401*	|	|	|	|	|	|	|		...	...	...	|
Newton Abbot 116 120 d.	0932	0939	1044	|	...	1242	1335	1435	*1412*	1544	1641	1740	1834	1935	2022	2156		...	...	...	0921
Exeter St Davids 116 120 a.	0952	1013	1104	1136	...	1302	1355	1456	*1435*	1604	1701	1800	1854	2001	2042	2222		...	...	...	0947
Exeter St Davids 120 d.	0954	1015	1106	1138	1154	1304	1357	1459	*1437*	1606	1703	1802	1856	...	2044	...		0801	0839	0933	0949
Tiverton Parkway 120 d.	1009	1030	1121	|	1209	1319	|	1514	*1450*	1621	1717	1817	1911	...	2059	...		0818	0854	0951	|
Taunton 120a 120 d.	1024	1045	1136	|	1224	1334	1423	1529	1519	1636	1732	1832	1926	...	2114	...		0835	0908	1018	1013
Bristol Temple Meads 120a 120 a.	|	1127	|	|	|	|	|	|	|	|	|	|	|	...	2147	...		0938	|	1120	|
Castle Cary d.	|	|	|	|	1246	|	1444	1550	|	|	|	1853	1947	...	|	...		...	0930	...	|
Westbury d.	1102	|	|	|	1305	|	1502	|	1607	|	|	1913	2006	...	|	...		...	0950	...	1049
Newbury a.	|	|	|	|	1351	|	|	|	1653	|	|	1947	|	...	|	...		...	1027	...	1123
Reading 132 a.	1147	1245	1251	1315	1419	1449	1549	1648	1721	1751	1848	2004	2056	...	2304	...		...	1045	...	1144
London Paddington 132 a.	1221	1314	1321	1344	1450	1521	1621	1721	1751	1821	1921	2037	2132	...	2344	...		...	1122	...	1222

	⑦ 🍸	⑦ 🍸	⑦ 🍸	⑦ 🍸	⑦ 🍸	⑦ 2☆	⑦ 🍸	⑦ 🍸	⑦ 🍸	⑦ 🍸☆	⑦ 2	⑦ 🍸		⑦ 2☆	⑦ 🍸	⑦ 🍸	⑦ 🍸	⑦ 🍸	⑦ 🍸	⑦ 2☆	⑦ A
Penzance 117 d.	...	0830	0947	1100	...	1205	1256	...	...	...	1339	...		1437	1500	...	1613	1731	...	1900	2115‡
Newquay 117 d.	...	|	|	|	...	|	|	...	...	...	|	...		|	|	...	|	|	...	|	|
Plymouth 120 d.	1010	1035	1145	1300	1345	1407	1455	1510	1542	...	1551	1610	...	1638	1700	1749	1815	1930	2000	2115	2320
Totnes 120 d.	1040	1103	1214	1328	1413	1436	1525	|	1608	...	1620	1637	...	1707	1728	1816	1842	1957	|	2144	2348
Paignton 116 120 d.	|	|	|	|	|	|	|	|	|	1545	|	|	...	|	|	|	|	|	|	|	|
Torquay 116 120 d.	|	|	|	|	|	|	|	|	|	1550	|	|	...	|	|	|	|	|	|	|	|
Newton Abbot 116 120 d.	1054	1119	1228	1341	1426	1449	1538	1547	1623	1605	1633	1655	...	1720	1740	1829	1854	2010	2036	2157	0001
Exeter St Davids 116 120 a.	1114	1139	1248	1401	1448	1515	1558	1607	1643	1631	1654	1715	...	1746	1801	1850	1915	2030	2057	2222	0023
Exeter St Davids 120 d.	1118	1141	1249	1403	1450	...	1601	1609	1644	1633	...	1717	...	1747	1802	1852	1917	2031	2059	...	0059
Tiverton Parkway 120 d.	1133	1156	|	1417	|	...	1616	1624	1700	|	...	1732	...	|	1819	|	1932	2047	2114	...	|
Taunton 120a 120 d.	1148	1210	1315	1432	1513	...	1631	1639	1714	1658	...	1746	...	1818	1834	1916	1946	2100	2127	...	|
Bristol Temple Meads 120a 120 a.	1224	|	|	|	|	...	|	1720	|	1757	...	1822	...	1917	|	|	|	|	2159	...	|
Castle Cary d.	|	1231	|	|	1535	...	|	|	1736	|	...	|	...	...	|	|	2008	2124	|	...	|
Westbury d.	|	1251	1359	|	1553	...	|	|	1756	|	...	|	...	...	|	1955	2028	2144	|	...	|
Newbury a.	|	1328	|	|	1632	...	|	|	1833	|	...	|	...	...	|	2028	|	2219	|	...	|
Reading 132 a.	1344	1347	1445	1550	1650	...	1749	1843	1850	1919	...	1943	...	...	1950	2048	2114	2240	2326	...	0403s
London Paddington 132 a.	1422	1427	1527	1627	1727	...	1827	1922	1927	1957	...	2022	...	...	2028	2127	2157	2327	0004	...	0503

← **NOTES** (continued from previous page)

w – Via Trowbridge (Table **140**).

y – Arrives 0512 on ⑥.

★ – Also calls at Dawlish (10–15 minutes after Exeter) and Teignmouth (15–18 minutes after Exeter).

☆ – Also calls at Teignmouth (7–10 minutes after Newton Abbot) and Dawlish (12–15 minutes after Newton Abbot).

‡ – Passengers may occupy cabins at London Paddington from 2230 and at Penzance from 2045⑦/2115Ⓐ.

GW 2nd class PAIGNTON - EXETER 116

		Ⓐ	Ⓐ	Ⓐ	Ⓐ	Ⓐ	Ⓐ	Ⓐ	Ⓐ	Ⓐ	Ⓐ	Ⓐ	Ⓐ	Ⓐ	Ⓐ	Ⓐ	Ⓐ	Ⓐ	Ⓐ	Ⓐ	Ⓐ	Ⓐ	Ⓐ
Paignton 🚂 115 120 d.	Ⓐ	0603	0634	0711	0740	0820	0912	0934	1021	1033	1115	1213	1308	1421	1513	1612	1630	1657	1726	1752	1834	1937	2035
Torquay 115 120 d.		0608	0639	0716	0746	0825	0917	0939	1026	1038	1120	1218	1313	1426	1518	1617	1635	1702	1731	1757	1839	1942	2040
Newton Abbot 115 120 d.		0621	0652	0737b	0806b	0838	0939b	0950	1039	1051	1133	1231	1326	1439	1531	1631	1648	1715	1744	1810	1852	1954	2053
Teignmouth 115 120 d.		0628	0659	0745	0813	0845	0945	|	1046	1058	1140	1238	1333	1446	1538	1638	1655	1722	1751	1817	1859	2002	2100
Dawlish 115 120 d.		0633	0704	0750	0819	0850	0950	|	1051	1103	1145	1243	1338	1451	1543	1643	1701	1727	1756	1822	1904	2007	2105
Exeter St Davids 115 120 a.		0703	0733	0814	0839	0912	1014	*1020*	1113	1128	1208	1313	1408	1513	1612	1711	1718	1751	1819	1845	1932	2029	2128

	Ⓐ	Ⓐ	Ⓐ		⑥	⑥	⑥	⑥	⑥	⑥	⑥	⑥	⑥	⑥	⑥	⑥	⑥	⑥	⑥	⑥	⑥	⑥	⑥
Paignton 🚂 115 120 d.	2135	2245	2355	⑥	0613	0634	0711	0806	0904	0930	1015	1058	1120	1213	1243	1313	1412	1513	1543	1613	1711	1752	1856
Torquay 115 120 d.	2141	2250	2359		0618	0639	0716	0811	0909	0935	1020	1103	1125	1218	1248	1318	1417	1518	1548	1618	1716	1757	1901
Newton Abbot 115 120 d.	2200	2303	0013		0631	0652	0727	0834b	0935b	0949	1033	1122b	1138	1232	1307	1338b	1439b	1533	1606b	1631	1729	1810	1914
Teignmouth 115 120 d.	*2213*	2310	0020		0638	0659	...	0841	0942	0956	1040	1130	1145	1239	1314	1346	1447	1541	1613	1638	1736	1817	1921
Dawlish 115 120 d.	*2218*	2315	0025		0643	0704	...	0846	0947	1002	1045	1135	1150	1244	1319	1351	1452	1546	1618	1643	1741	1822	1926
Exeter St Davids 115 120 a.	*2240*	2337	0048		0706	0733	...	0909	1009	1018	1114	1148	1213	1313	1336	1413	1513	1613	1631	1714	1810	1844	1949

	⑥	⑥	⑥	⑥	⑥	⑥		⑦	⑦	⑦	⑦	⑦	⑦	⑦	⑦	⑦	⑦	⑦	⑦	⑦	⑦	⑦	⑦
Paignton 🚂 115 120 d.	1921	1951	2013	2047	2115	2153	⑦	0949	1058	1149	1257	1352	1419	1457	1555	1619	1654	1749	1855	1955	2055	2152	2300
Torquay 115 120 d.	1926	1956	2018	2053	2120	2158		0954	1103	1154	1302	1357	1424	1501	1600	1624	1659	1754	1900	2000	2100	2157	2305
Newton Abbot 115 120 d.	1940	2008	2031	2105	2133	2211		1007	1121b	1207	1315	1409	1437	1516	1613	1637	1712	1807	1913	2014	2113	2209	2318
Teignmouth 115 120 d.	1947	2015	2038	|	2140	2218		1014	1128	1214	1322	1416	1444	1523	1620	1644	1719	1814	1920	2021	2120	2216	2325
Dawlish 115 120 d.	1952	2020	2043	|	2145	2223		1019	1133	1219	1327	1421	1449	1528	1625	1649	1724	1819	1925	2026	2125	2221	2330
Exeter St Davids 115 120 a.	2025	2037	2105	2125	2207	2245		1040	1147	1242	1340	1442	1512	1541	1638	1711	1741	1840	1948	2049	2138	2242	2352

b – Arrives 8-10 minutes earlier.

🚂 – Dartmouth Steam Railway (Paignton - Kingswear). ✆ 01803 555 872. www.dartmouthrailriver.co.uk

117 PLYMOUTH - NEWQUAY and PENZANCE

GW, XC

km			②–⑤	①	②–⑤		①	Ⓐ	Ⓐ	Ⓐ	Ⓐ	Ⓐ	Ⓐ	Ⓐ	Ⓐ	Ⓐ	Ⓐ	Ⓐ	Ⓐ	Ⓐ	Ⓐ	Ⓐ	Ⓐ
			A				A	🍷	2B	2	2	2	🍷	2	2B	2	🍷	2	2	🍷	2	2	2
	London Paddington **115**	d.	2345p	...	...	...	2350p	...	...	...	...	...	0706	...	*0730*e	*0906*	1006	...	...	1205	...	...	*1305*
	Bristol Temple Meads **115 120**	d.	|	...	...	...	|	...	...	0524	...	0642	|	...	*0913*e	*0944*	*1045*	...	*1147*	*1245*	...	*1344*	*1445*
0	**Plymouth**	d.	0543	0600	0628	...	0628	0702	0753	0814	...	0921	1039	...	1125	1239	1311	...	1349	1512	...	1557	1701
7	Saltash	d.	|	|	|	...	|	0715	0802	0824	...	0931	|	...	1134	1248	|	...	1358	|	...	1612	1714
29	Liskeard	d.	0608	0623	0651	...	0709	0736	0820	0843	...	0950	1103	...	1153	1307	1335	...	1417	1537	...	1633	1738
43	Bodmin Parkway 🚂	d.	0622	0635	0703	...	0723	0749	0833	0855	...	1002	1116	...	1205	1319	1348	...	1429	1550	...	1645	...
49	Lostwithiel	d.	0628	0641	0708	...	0729	0755	0840	0900	...	1007	|	...	1211	1324	|	...	1434	|	...	1650	...
56	Par ♡	d.	0637	0648	0715	...	0738	0803	0854	0908	0917	1015	1128	1140	1218	1332	1400	1407	1442	1601	1610	1658	...
89	**Newquay** ♡	a.	|	|	|	...	|	|	...	|	1009	|	|	1231	|	|	|	1459	|	|	1702	|	...
63	St Austell	d.	0646	0655	0721	...	0746	0811	...	0916	...	1022	1136	...	1225	1339	1407	...	1449	1608	...	1706	...
86	Truro	d.	0706	0711	0738	...	0806	0829	...	0934	...	1040	1154	...	1242	1357	1425	...	1507	1626	...	1723	...
101	Redruth	d.	0718	0723	0749	...	0820	0841	...	0947	...	1053	1206	...	1256	1410	1437	...	1520	1638	...	1736	...
107	Camborne	d.	0726	0730	0755	...	0827	0848	...	0953	...	1059	1214	...	1302	1416	1445	...	1526	1646	...	1742	...
119	St Erth	d.	0742	0743	0807	...	0845	0902	...	1008	...	1110	1225	...	1314	1428	1459	...	1538	1700	...	1754	...
128	**Penzance**	a.	0753	0752	0816	...	0859	0912	...	1016	...	1123	1237	...	1325	1439	1511	...	1549	1712	...	1806	...

(Ⓐ)

		Ⓐ	Ⓐ	Ⓐ	Ⓐ	Ⓐ	Ⓐ	Ⓐ	Ⓐ	Ⓐ	Ⓐ	Ⓐ		Ⓐ	⑤	①–④		⑥	⑥	⑥	⑥	⑥	⑥	⑥
		🍷	2	2	2	🍷	C	🍷	2	D	🍷	C		🍷	🍷	2		2	A	2		2	2	2
London Padddington **115**	d.	1406	...	...	...	1506	...	1606	...	...	1703	...	...	1803	1903	*1903*	⑥	...	2345p	...	...	...	...	...
Bristol Temple Meads **115 120**	d.	*1513*e	...	*1544*	...	|	1645	|	...	1744	|	1844	...	|	*1945*	*1945*		...	|	...	...	0524	...	0636
Plymouth	d.	1723	...	1755	1817	1842	1901	1931	...	1949	2026	2050	...	2120	2229	2242		...	0543	...	0628	0818	...	0919
Saltash	d.	1734	...	1804	1831	|	|	1940	...	|	2037	|	...	|	2239	2251		...	|	...	|	0828	...	0928
Liskeard	d.	1754	...	1820	1854	1907	1924	1957	...	2012	2056	2113	...	2145	2259	2310		...	0608	...	0651	0847	...	0949
Bodmin Parkway 🚂	d.	1807	...	1832	...	1919	1936	2010	...	2024	2109	2125	...	2159	2313	2326		...	0622	...	0703	0859	...	1002
Lostwithiel	d.	1813	...	1837	...	|	|	|	...	|	|	2131	...	|	2319	2331		...	0628	...	0708	0904	...	|
Par ♡	d.	1822	1829	1845	...	1931	1946	2022	2028	2034	2121	2137	...	2211	2328	2339		0609	0637	0652	0714	0912	0918	1014
Newquay ♡	a.	|	1921	|	...	|	|	|	2120	|	|	|	...	|	|	|		|	|	0744	|	|	1010	|
St Austell	d.	1829	...	1853	...	1939	1952	2029	...	2041	2128	2144	...	2218	2335	2346		0616	0646	...	0721	0920	...	1022
Truro	d.	1847	...	1910	...	2000	2018	2047	...	2102	2146	2203	...	2237	2353	0005		0635	0706	...	0737	0937	...	1040
Redruth	d.	1859	...	1923	...	2010	2029	2059	...	2118	2158	2214	...	2248	0006	0018		0648	0718	...	0748	0950	...	1055
Camborne	d.	1907	...	1929	...	2018	2035	2107	...	2125	|	2220	...	|	0014	0024		0654	0726	...	0755	0956	...	1102
St Erth	d.	1921	...	1942	...	2028	2046	2120	...	2135	2214	2232	...	|	0028	0035		0704	0742	...	0807	1008	...	1117
Penzance	a.	1933	...	1954	...	2042	2054	2131	...	2143	2228	2241	...	2313	0040	0046		0716	0753	...	0815	1018	...	1126

		⑥	⑥		⑥	⑥	⑥	⑥	⑥	⑥	⑥	⑥	⑥	⑥	⑥	⑥	⑥	⑥	⑥	⑥	⑥	⑥	⑥	⑥
		2	2B	🍷	2	2	🍷	2	2	🍷	2	2	🍷	🍷	2	2	🍷	C	2B	2	D	🍷	C	🍷
London Padddington **115**	d.	...	...	0730	...	*0906*	1006	...	...	1206	...	...	1306	1406	...	...	1506	...	...	...	*1606*	1706	...	1806
Bristol Temple Meads **115 120**	d.	...	*0812*e	0918	...	*1044*	|	...	*1144*	*1244*	...	*1345*	|	*1512*e	...	*1544*	|	1644	...	...	1744	|	1844	|
Plymouth	d.	0951	1033	1123	...	1245	1316	...	1415	1513	...	1603	1626	1726	...	1752	1843	1855	1908	...	1948	2040	2058	2121
Saltash	d.	1001	1044	|	...	1254	|	...	1424	|	...	1612	|	|	...	1806	|	|	1917	...	|	2051	|	|
Liskeard	d.	1022	1103	1148	...	1313	1341	...	1445	1538	...	1633	1651	1751	...	1826	1908	1921	1936	...	2011	2111	2125	2146
Bodmin Parkway 🚂	d.	1034	1115	1201	...	1325	1354	...	1458	1551	...	1645	1704	1804	...	1838	1921	1933	1948	...	2023	2124	2137	2200
Lostwithiel	d.	1039	1120	|	...	1330	|	...	1504	|	...	1650	|	|	...	1844	|	|	1953	...	2028	|	|	|
Par ♡	d.	1046	1128	1212	1215	1337	1406	1410	1512	1603	1615	1657	|	1816	1821	1852	1932	1944	2001	2015	2035	2136	2147	2212
Newquay ♡	a.	|	|	|	1307	|	|	1457	|	|	1707	|	|	|	1913	|	|	|	|	2107	|	|	|	|
St Austell	d.	1054	1137	1220	...	1345	1414	...	1521	1610	...	1704	1721	1824	...	1859	1941	1952	2008	...	2041	2144	2201	2219
Truro	d.	1110	1155	1239	...	1402	1432	...	1539	1629	...	1723	1739	1842	...	1917	2000	2015	2026	...	2102	2203	2218	2238
Redruth	d.	1124	1208	1251	...	1415	1445	...	1553	1641	...	1736	1752	1855	...	1930	2012	2027	2043	...	2113	2215	2229	2250
Camborne	d.	1130	1214	1258	...	1421	1452	...	1600	1649	...	1742	1759	1902	...	1936	2020	2035	2049	...	2119	|	2235	2258
St Erth	d.	1142	1225	1310	...	1433	1507	...	1612	1700	...	1754	1814	1914	...	1948	2030	2046	2058	...	2131	2232	2245	2312
Penzance	a.	1155	1236	1320	...	1442	1517	...	1621	1710	...	1803	1824	1924	...	1957	2041	2056	2108	...	2140	2242	2254	2322

			⑦	⑦	⑦	⑦	⑦	⑦	⑦	⑦	⑦	⑦	⑦	⑦	⑦	⑦	⑦		⑦	⑦	⑦	⑦	⑦	⑦
			2a	2b	2	2	2	🍷	2	F	2B	🍷	2	🍷	2	🍷	2B		🍷	E	2	🍷	C	🍷
London Padddington **115**	d.	⑦	...	...	...	...	...	0800	...	*0857*	*0957*	1057	...	1157	...	1257	*1300*	...	1457	...	*1557*	1657	...	1757
Bristol Temple Meads **115 120**	d.		...	...	...	0726	0828	1000	...	1057	|	*1154*	...	*1254*	...	*1344*	*1455*	...	*1614*e	1644	|	*1744*	1844	|
Plymouth	d.		0911	0915	...	1020	1115	1215	...	1255	1331	1415	1450	1530	...	1625	1735	...	1825	1853	1943	2025	2050	2135
Saltash	d.		0921	0925	...	1030	1126	|	...	|	1339	|	1459	|	...	|	1745	...	|	|	1952	|	|	|
Liskeard	d.		0943	0943	...	1051	1145	1243	...	1318	1358	1440	1518	1554	...	1650	1806	...	1852	1916	2011	2049	2113	2200
Bodmin Parkway 🚂	d.		0955	0955	...	1103	1157	1256	...	1330	1410	1454	1530	1609	...	1703	1818	...	1906	1928	2023	2102	2125	2213
Lostwithiel	d.		1001	1001	...	1108	1202	|	...	|	|	|	1536	|	...	|	1823	...	|	|	2028	|	|	|
Par ♡	d.		1009	1009	1018	1116	1210	1308	1315	1340	1421	|	1544	1621	1634	1714	1831	...	1917	1938	2036	2113	2135	2226
Newquay ♡	a.		|	|	1110	|	|	|	1407	|	|	|	|	|	1726	|	|	...	|	|	|	|	|	|
St Austell	d.		1016	1016	...	1125	1218	1315	...	1351	1429	1510	1551	1629	...	1722	1838	...	1925	1945	2043	2120	2143	2234
Truro	d.		1035	1035	...	1144	1235	1334	...	1409	1445	1528	1610	1647	...	1740	1856	...	1941	2001	2100	2137	2200	2249
Redruth	d.		1048	1048	...	1157	1248	1346	...	1420	1459	1539	1623	1659	...	1753	1909	...	1954	2012	2114	2151	2211	2304
Camborne	d.		1054	1054	...	1203	1254	1354	...	1427	1505	1547	1629	1707	...	1801	1915	...	2004	2021	2120	2157	2220	2311
St Erth	d.		1106	1106	...	1214	1305	1406	...	1437	1516	1559	1641	1719	...	1813	1925	...	2016	2031	2132	2210	2230	2323
Penzance	a.		1115	1115	...	1224	1315	1416	...	1447	1525	1612	1651	1729	...	1824	1937	...	2028	2039	2142	2222	2242	2334

A – THE NIGHT RIVIERA – Conveys 🛏 1, 2. cl and (2). See also note ‡ on page 101.
B – From Exeter St Davids (Table **115**).
C – From Glasgow Central (Table **120**).
D – From Aberdeen (Tables **222** / **120**).
E – From Edinburgh (Table **120**).
F – From Birmingham New Street (Table **120**).

G – From Newquay.
H – From York (Table **120**).
J – From Dundee (Tables **222** / **120**).

a – From Apr. 2.
b – Until Mar 26.
e – Change at Exeter St Davids.

p – Previous night.
s – Stops to set down only.
u – Stops to pick up only.

♡ – Par - Newquay: *'The Atlantic Coast Line'*.
🚂 – Bodmin & Wenford Railway (Bodmin Parkway - Bodmin General - Boscarne Junction *10 km*). ✆ 01208 73555. www.bodminrailway.co.uk

118 BRANCH LINES and BUS CONNECTIONS IN DEVON and CORNWALL

2nd class GW

EXETER - EXMOUTH *'The Avocet Line'* *18 km*

From Exeter St Davids: on ⚒ at 0544, 0606Ⓐ, 0629, 0708, 0736, 0815, 0845, 0915, 0948 and at the same minutes past each hour until 1616, 1646, 1715, 1745⑥, 1753Ⓐ, 1816⑥, 1821Ⓐ, 1847⑥, 1850Ⓐ, 1931, 2031⑥, 2034Ⓐ, 2131Ⓐ, 2141⑥, 2231Ⓐ, 2241⑥, 2309⑥, 2328Ⓐ; on ⑦ at 0830, 0940, 1013, 1044, 1122**a**, 1151, 1226**a**, 1247, 1322**a**, 1348, 1446, 1518, 1546, 1622**a**, 1646, 1716, 1746, 1846, 1951, 2052, 2148, 2248, 2325.

From Exmouth: on ⚒ at 0001Ⓐ, 0004⑥, 0614, 0643Ⓐ, 0712, 0751, 0821, 0852, 0921, 0953 and at the same minutes past each hour until 1653, 1723, 1753⑥, 1801Ⓐ, 1825⑥, 1832Ⓐ, 1854⑥, 1859Ⓐ, 1939, 2007⑥, 2015Ⓐ, 2111Ⓐ, 2116⑥, 2207Ⓐ, 2219⑥, 2307Ⓐ, 2317⑥, 2345⑥; on ⑦ at 0910, 1019, 1054**b**, 1124, 1200**b**, 1228, 1255, 1324, 1358, 1427, 1523, 1555**b**, 1623, 1655, 1723, 1755, 1823, 1923, 2028, 2128, 2227, 2329.

Journey: 37–40 minutes. Trains call at Exeter Central 3–4 minutes from Exeter St Davids.

a – Starts from Exeter Central.   b – Terminates at Exeter Central.

EXETER - BARNSTAPLE *'The Tarka Line'* *63 km*

From Exeter St Davids: on ⚒ at 0550Ⓐ, 0554⑥, 0648Ⓐ, 0655⑥, 0831, 0927, 1027, 1127, 1227, 1327, 1427, 1527, 1657⑥, 1702Ⓐ, 1757, 1859, 2100, 2253⑤; on ⑦ at 0843, 0954, 1203, 1408, 1604, 1807, 2001.

From Barnstaple: on ⚒ at 0700Ⓐ, 0705⑥, 0843, 0943, 1043, 1143, 1243, 1343, 1443, 1543, 1708⑥, 1713Ⓐ, 1813, 1916, 2024, 2216Ⓐ, 2230⑥; on ⑦ at 1000, 1129, 1323, 1529, 1721, 1926, 2130.

Journey: 65 minutes. Trains call at ***Crediton*** *(11 minutes from Exeter / 54 minutes from Barnstaple) and* ***Eggesford*** *(40 minutes from Exeter / 25 minutes from Barnstaple).*

PLYMOUTH - GUNNISLAKE *'The Tamar Valley Line'* *24 km*

From Plymouth: on Ⓐ at 0506, 0641, 0840, 1054, 1254, 1454, 1637, 1823, 2131; on ⑥ at 0640, 0854, 1054, 1254, 1454, 1639, 1823, 2131; on ⑦ at 0920, 1106, 1306, 1511, 1741.

From Gunnislake: on Ⓐ at 0551, 0731, 0929, 1145, 1345, 1545, 1729, 1913, 2221; on ⑥ at 0731, 0945, 1145, 1345, 1545, 1729, 1913, 2221; on ⑦ at 1018, 1207, 1358, 1604, 1835.

Journey: 45–60 minutes.

LISKEARD - LOOE *'The Looe Valley Line'* *14 km*

From Liskeard: on Ⓐ at 0605, 0714, 0833, 0959, 1111, 1216, 1321, 1425, 1541, 1641, 1806, 1918; on ⑥ at 0601, 0713, 0835, 0958, 1108, 1212, 1324, 1428, 1543, 1656, 1801, 1928; on ⑦ from Apr. 2 at 1012, 1126, 1250, 1402, 1523, 1635, 1740, 2015.

From Looe: on Ⓐ at 0637, 0746, 0909, 1030, 1143, 1248, 1353, 1459, 1613, 1715, 1840, 1952; on ⑥ at 0633, 0747, 0909, 1032, 1137, 1244, 1356, 1456, 1615, 1728, 1833, 2000; on ⑦ from Apr. 2 at 1044, 1158, 1322, 1434, 1555, 1707, 1815, 2050.

Journey: 28–33 minutes.

EXETER - OKEHAMPTON *Service runs only summer ⑦.* 40 km

From Exeter St. Davids: on summer ⑦.
From Okehampton: on summer ⑦.
Journey: 40–42 minutes. Trains call at ***Crediton*** *(approx. 10 minutes from Exeter).*

GW, XC — PENZANCE and NEWQUAY - PLYMOUTH — 117

		Ⓐ 🍷	Ⓐ 2	Ⓐ 🍷	Ⓐ 2	Ⓐ D		Ⓐ 🍷	Ⓐ 🍷	Ⓐ D	Ⓐ 🍷	Ⓐ E	Ⓐ 2	Ⓐ 🍷	Ⓐ 2		Ⓐ 2	Ⓐ 2	Ⓐ 🍷	Ⓐ 2	Ⓐ 2	Ⓐ 2	Ⓐ 🍷
Penzance d.	Ⓐ	0505	0520	0541	0600	0628	...	0645	0741	0828	0844	0935	...	1000	1046	...	1141	...	1303	1345	...	1449	1559
St Erth d.		|	|	|	0609	0636	...	0655	0751	0836	0854	0943	...	1010	1055	...	1150	...	1313	1354	...	1458	1610
Camborne d.		|	0539	0559	0622	0646	...	0707	0806	0846	0907	0956	...	1023	1108	...	1203	...	1325	1407	...	1511	1621
Redruth d.		0526	|	0606	0628	0652	...	0714	0813	0852	0914	1003	...	1030	1114	...	1209	...	1332	1413	...	1517	1629
Truro d.		0538	0554	0619	0640	0704	...	0727	0826	0904	0927	1015	...	1043	1126	...	1220	...	1345	1424	...	1528	1642
St Austell d.		0556	...	0636	0657	0720	...	0745	0844	0920	0944	1031	...	1100	1143	...	1237	...	1402	1441	...	1545	1659
Newquay ♡ d.		|	...	|	|	|	...	|	|	|	|	|	1013	|	|	...	|	1303	|	|	1501	|	|
Par ♡ d.		|	...	0643	0703	0727	...	0752	0851	0927	0951	1038	1102	1108	1150	...	1244	1352	1410	1448	1547	1552	1707
Lostwithiel d.		|	...	0651	0710	|	...	0800	|	|	|	1045	...	|	1156	...	1250	...	|	1455	...	1558	1714
Bodmin Parkway 🚂 d.		0614	...	0657	0716	0737	...	0806	0903	0937	1003	1051	...	1119	1202	...	1256	...	1421	1501	...	1604	1721
Liskeard d.		0627	...	0711	0729	0753	...	0820	0916	0950	1016	1104	...	1133	1217	...	1309	...	1434	1514	...	1617	1734
Saltash d.		|	...	0730	0747	|	...	0839	0934	|	|	|	...	|	1234	...	1328	...	|	1532	...	1637	|
Plymouth a.		0651	...	0741	0804	0820	...	0849	0946	1018	1040	1127	...	1157	1244	...	1337	...	1459	1543	...	1651	1758
Bristol Temple Meads **115 120** a.		*0926*	...	|	1110	1025	...	*1124*	1158	1224	*1324*	1355	...	*1426*	*1523*	...	*1623*	...	*1724*	*1823*	...	*1925*	*2025*
London Padddington **115** a.		1002	...	1124	...	...	...	1224	1340	...	1344	...	...	1521	*1622*	...	...	...	1821	*1924*	...	*2039*	2124

	Ⓐ 2	①–④ 2 B	⑤ 2 C	Ⓐ 2	⑤ 🍷	①–④ 🍷	Ⓐ 2	Ⓐ 2		①–④ 2	⑤ 🍷	Ⓐ 2	Ⓐ A	Ⓐ		⑥ 2	⑥ 2	⑥ D		⑥ 🍷	⑥ 2	⑥ 2	⑥ 🍷
Penzance d.	...	1644	1644	...	1742	1742	...	1916	...	2018	2018	...	2145	2210	⑥	0520	0537	0630	...	0650	...	0735	0759
St Erth d.	...	1653	1653	...	1752	1752	...	1925	...	2027	2027	...	2155	2218		|	0545	0638	...	0700	...	0748	0809
Camborne d.	...	1706	1706	...	1807	1807	...	1938	...	2042	2042	...	2209	2231		0538	0559	0651	...	0712	...	0803	0924
Redruth d.	...	1712	1712	...	1815	1815	...	1944	...	2050	2050	...	2217	2238		0544	0605	0657	...	0719	...	0810	0831
Truro d.	...	1725	1725	...	1827	1827	...	1956	...	2103	2103	...	2230	2249		0556	0616	0709	...	0732	...	0821	0844
St Austell d.	...	1742	1742	...	1844	1844	...	2013	...	2120	2120	...	2248	2305		...	0633	0725	...	0749	...	0837	0902
Newquay ♡ d.	...	|	|	1722	|	|	1924	|	...	|	|	2126	|	|		...	|	|	...	|	0748	|	|
Par ♡ d.	...	1748	1748	1813	1852	1852	2013	2019	...	2127	2127	2216	2257	2312		...	0639	0732	...	0756	0839	0844	0909
Lostwithiel d.	...	1755	1755	...	|	|	...	2026	...	2134	2134	...	|	2319		...	0646	0739	...	0804	...	0851	|
Bodmin Parkway 🚂 d.	...	1801	1801	...	1904	1904	...	2032	...	2140	2140	...	2309	2325		...	0652	0746	...	0810	...	0857	0920
Liskeard d.	1749	1814	1814	...	1917	1917	...	2045	...	2153	2153	...	2325	2337		...	0707	0758	...	0823	...	0910	0933
Saltash d.	1806	1832	1832	...	|	|	...	2104	...	2211	2211	...	|	|		...	0726	|	...	|	...	0929	|
Plymouth a.	1818	1842	1842	...	1941	1941	...	2119	...	2224	2224	...	2348	0001		...	0742	0821	...	0848	...	0940	0958
Bristol Temple Meads **115 120** a.	*2025*	|	|	...	2145	2145	...	...	...	...	...	...	|	...		...	|	1025	...	*11234*	...	...	|
London Paddington **115** a.	...	*2239***e**	*2230***n**	...	2341	2344	...	...	...	...	...	...	0523**c**	...		...	*1121*	...	...	*1221*	...	...	1321

	⑥ D	⑥ 🍷	⑥ E	⑥ 2	⑥ 🍷	⑥ 2		⑥ 🍷	⑥ 2	⑥ 2	⑥ 2	⑥ 🍷	⑥ 2	⑥ 2		⑥ 🍷	⑥ 2 B	⑥ 2	⑥ 🍷	⑥ 2	⑥ 2 B	⑥ 2	⑥
Penzance d.	0828	0844	0943	...	1000	1037	...	1058	1146	...	1300	1401	...	1452	...	1552	1641	...	1740	...	1906	...	2129
St Erth d.	0836	0854	0951	...	1010	1045	...	1108	1155	...	1309	1411	...	1501	...	1602	1651	...	1750	...	1915	...	2138
Camborne d.	0846	0906	1001	...	1022	1059	...	1120	1209	...	1322	1423	...	1515	...	1614	1706	...	1805	...	1928	...	2149
Redruth d.	0852	0913	1007	...	1029	1105	...	1127	1215	...	1328	1430	...	1521	...	1621	1713	...	1812	...	1934	...	2156
Truro d.	0904	0926	1019	...	1042	1116	...	1140	1227	...	1339	1443	...	1532	...	1634	1726	...	1825	...	1945	...	2209
St Austell d.	0920	0944	1035	...	1059	1133	...	1157	1244	...	1356	1500	...	1549	...	1652	1744	...	1842	...	2002	...	2226
Newquay ♡ d.	|	|	|	1012	|	|	...	|	|	1309	|	|	1459	|	...	|	|	1721	|	1917	|	2118	|
Par ♡ d.	0927	0951	1041	1101	1107	1139	...	|	1253	1358	1403	1507	1548	1555	...	1659	1751	1810	1849	2003	2009	2209	2233
Lostwithiel d.	|	|	1048	...	|	1146	...	|	1300	...	1409	|	...	1602	...	1706	1758	...	|	...	2015	2218	|
Bodmin Parkway 🚂 d.	0937	1002	1055	...	1118	1152	...	1213	1306	...	1415	1519	...	1608	...	1713	1805	...	1901	...	2021	2224	2244
Liskeard d.	0950	1015	1107	...	1131	1207	...	1226	1319	...	1428	1533	...	1621	...	1726	1819	...	1914	...	2035	2237	2258
Saltash d.	|	|	|	...	|	1226	...	|	1339	...	1447	|	...	1640	...	|	1838	...	|	...	2054	2255	|
Plymouth a.	1017	1039	1130	...	1156	1237	...	1251	1350	...	1458	1557	...	1650	...	1750	1849	...	1938	...	2110	2312	2322
Bristol Temple Meads **115 120** a.	1225	|	1355	...	*1425*	...	...	*1525*	*1625*	...	*1725*	*1825*	...	*1924*	...	*2022*	...	...	2147	...	...	...	...
London Paddington **115** a.	...	1344	...	...	1521	...	...	1621	*1721*	...	*1821*	1921	...	*2037*	...	2132	...	...	2344	...	...	...	...

		⑦ 🍷	⑦ F	⑦ 🍷	⑦ 2	⑦ 🍷		⑦ 2 B	⑦ E	⑦ 🍷		⑦ 2 B	⑦ 2	⑦ 2	⑦ 🍷	⑦ G	⑦ 🍷	⑦ 2	⑦ 🍷	⑦ 2 B		⑦ 2	⑦ A
Penzance d.	⑦	0830	0930	0947	...	1100	...	1205	1230	1256	...	1339	1437	...	1500	1530	1613	...	1731	1900	...	2005	2115
St Erth d.		0839	0938	0956	...	1110	...	1213	1238	1306	...	1349	1447	...	1510	1538	1623	...	1740	1909	...	2014	2125
Camborne d.		0856	0948	1009	...	1124	...	1226	1251	1320	...	1402	1500	...	1523	1549	1636	...	1753	1921	...	2027	2139
Redruth d.		0902	0954	1015	...	1130	...	1232	1258	1326	...	1408	1506	...	1530	1555	1643	...	1800	1927	...	2033	2146
Truro d.		0916	1006	1028	...	1143	...	1244	1309	1339	...	1419	1517	...	1542	1607	1656	...	1812	1939	...	2045	2201
St Austell d.		0932	1022	1045	...	1200	...	1300	1326	1357	...	1436	1534	...	1600	1623	1713	...	1831	1956	...	2102	2219
Newquay ♡ d.		|	|	|	1112	|	...	|	|	|	...	|	|	1510	|	|	|	1738	|	|	...	|	|
Par ♡ d.		0940	1029	1053	1201	1207	...	1306	1332	1403	...	1443	1540	1559	1607	1630	1719	1827	1838	2003	...	2109	|
Lostwithiel d.		|	|	|	...	|	...	1313	1339	|	...	1449	1547	...	|	|	|	...	|	2009	...	2115	|
Bodmin Parkway 🚂 d.		0952	1039	1106	...	1219	...	1319	1346	1416	...	1455	1553	...	1618	1640	1731	...	1849	2015	...	2122	2235
Liskeard d.		1005	1052	1119	...	1233	...	1333	1358	1429	...	1508	1609	...	1631	1652	1745	...	1902	2028	...	2136	2250
Saltash d.		1021	|	|	...	|	...	1354	|	|	...	1526	1626	...	|	|	1801	...	|	2047	...	2154	|
Plymouth a.		1029	1115	1143	...	1257	...	1403	1423	1453	...	1534	1636	...	1656	1715	1810	...	1926	2100	...	2204	2314
Bristol Temple Meads **115 120** a.		|	1323	*1354*	...	*1526*	...	*1625*	1647	*1720*	...	*1822*	1917	...	|	1922	*2025*	...	*2159*	...	...	...	|
London Paddington **115** a.		1427	...	1527	...	1627	...	...	...	1827	...	*2022*	...	...	2028	*2127*	2157	...	2327	...	...	...	0503

A – THE NIGHT RIVIERA – Conveys 🛏 1, 2. cl and (2). See also note ‡ on page 101.
B – To Exeter St Davids (Table **115**).
C – To Taunton (Table **115**).
D – To Glasgow Central (Table **120**).
E – To Manchester Piccadilly (Table **120**).
F – To Edinburgh (Table **120**).
G – To Leeds (Table **120**).
H – To Dundee (Tables **120**/**222**).
J – To Penzance.
K – To Newton Abbot (Table **115**).
c – Arrives 0512 on ⑥ mornings.
e – Change at Exeter St Davids.
g – Arrives 1402.
n – Change at Taunton.
♡ – Par - Newquay: *'The Atlantic Coast Line'.*
🚂 – Bodmin & Wenford Railway (Bodmin Parkway - Bodmin General - Boscarne Junction *10 km*). ✆ 01208 73555. www.bodminrailway.co.uk

GW 2nd class — BRANCH LINES and BUS CONNECTIONS IN DEVON and CORNWALL — 118

Rail tickets are generally not valid on 🚌 services shown in this table.

BODMIN PARKWAY - PADSTOW — *Plymouth City Bus 🚌 service 11A*

From Bodmin Parkway station: on ⚒ at 0627, 0727, 0827, 0922, 1022, 1122, 1222, 1322, 1422, 1522, 1622, 1727, 1822; on ⑦ at 0751, 1001, 1201, 1401, 1601, 1756.

From Padstow Bus Terminus: on ⚒ at 0620, 0735, 0835, 0935, 1035, 1135, 1235, 1335, 1435, 1535, 1635, 1730, 1835, 1930; on ⑦ at 0855, 1105, 1305, 1505, 1705, 1905.

Journey: 60 minutes. Buses also make calls in Bodmin town centre and at Bodmin General station, and call at ***Wadebridge*** *(35 minutes after Bodmin / 25 minutes after Padstow).*

TRURO - FALMOUTH DOCKS — *'The Maritime Line'* — *20 km*

From Truro: on ⚒ at 0604, 0631, 0714, 0747, 0820, 0851 and at the same minutes past each hour until 1620, 1651, 1727, 1759, 1831, 1902, 2004, 2105, 2208Ⓐ, 2212⑥; on ⑦ at 0901, 1039, 1209, 1308, 1412, 1535, 1700, 1813, 1946, 2103, 2204.

From Falmouth Docks: on ⚒ at 0631, 0715, 0747, 0820, 0850 and at the same minutes past each hour until 1620, 1650, 1727, 1759, 1831, 1902, 1929, 2031, 2132, 2235Ⓐ, 2239⑥; on ⑦ at 0935, 1106, 1236, 1335, 1439, 1614, 1735, 1840, 2013, 2130, 2233.

Trains call at ***Falmouth Town*** *22 minutes after Truro and 3 minutes after Falmouth Docks.*

Journey: 25 minutes.

ST AUSTELL - EDEN PROJECT — *First Kernow 🚌 service 101*

From St Austell bus station: on Ⓐ at 0845, 0930, 1035, 1140, 1240, 1405, 1454, 1545, 1735; on ⑥ at 0845, 0930, 1035, 1135, 1235, 1410, 1504, 1553, 1642, 1735; on ⑦ at 0845, 0937, 1030, 1125, 1220, 1325, 1435, 1535, 1630, 1730.

From Eden Project: on Ⓐ at 0908, 1110, 1210, 1330, 1432, 1515, 1615, 1715, 1800; on ⑥ at 0908, 1105, 1205, 1330, 1436, 1525, 1620, 1705, 1800; on ⑦ at 0908, 0958, 1055, 1150, 1250, 1355, 1505, 1559, 1655, 1800.

Journey: 20 minutes.

ST ERTH - ST IVES — *'The St Ives Bay Line'* — *7 km*

From St Erth: on Ⓐ at 0706, 0759, 0905, 0938 and every 30 minutes until 1648, 1717, 1748 and every 30 minutes until 2048, 2123, 2158; on ⑥ at 0650, 0800, 0903, 0935, 1013, 1048, 1119, 1148 and every 30 minutes until 1648, 1717, 1759, 1859, 1953, 2033, 2106, 2147; on ⑦ at 1030**b**, 1118**b**, 1148**b**, 1156**a**, 1218**b**, 1230**a**, 1248**b**, 1318, 1348, 1418, 1448, 1518, 1548, 1618, 1648, 1726, 1755 1830, 1931.

From St Ives: on Ⓐ at 0725, 0815, 0922, 0953, 1033 and every 30 minutes until 1703, 1731, 1803, 1833, 1905, 1932, 2003, 2033, 2103, 2137, 2231; on ⑥ at 0712, 0815, 0920, 0950, 1027, 1103 and every 30 minutes until 1703, 1732, 1817, 1926, 2010, 2049, 2124, 2205; on ⑦ at 1053**b**, 1133**b**, 1203**b**, 1213**a**, 1233**b**, 1248**a**, 1303**b**, 1333, 1403, 1432, 1503, 1533, 1603, 1633, 1703, 1740, 1810, 1850, 1950.

Journey: 15 minutes.

a – Until Mar. 26.
b – From Apr. 2.

12 *La explicación de los signos convencionales se da en la página 4* 103

Table 1

km		⚒	⚒	⚒	⑥	Ⓐ	⚒ A		⚒	⚒		⚒	⚒		Ⓐ	⑥	Ⓐ	⑥ E		⚒	⚒		⚒	⚒
	Manchester Piccadilly 122 d.			0511				0727			0827			0927	0927		1027			1127				
	Newcastle 124 d.								0623		0725	0735		0835		0935							
	York 124 d.								0727		0826	0835		0935		1035							
	Leeds 124 d.					0616																	
	Sheffield 124 d.						0718		0821		0924	0924		1024		1124							
	Derby 124 d.				0648	0648	0706	0750		0853		0953	0953		1053		1153						
0	Birmingham New Street 150 d.	0604	0633	0704	0733	0733	0804	0833	0904	0933	1004	1033	1033	1104	1104	1133	1204	1233	1304				
13	Birmingham Intl ✈ 150 d.	0614		0714			0814		0914		1014			1114	1114		1214		1314				
-30	Coventry 150 d.	0625		0725			0825		0925		1025			1125	1125		1225		1325				
45	Leamington Spa 128 d.	0637	0700	0738	0800	0759	0838	0900	0938	1000	1038	1100	1100	1138	1138	1200	1238	1300	1338				
77	Banbury 128 d.	0654	0719	0755	0819	0816	0855	0919	0955	1019	1055	1119	1119	1155	1155	1219	1255	1319	1355				
114	Oxford a.	0714	0741	0814	0839	0839	0914	0941	1015	1041	1114	1141	1141	1214	1214	1241	1314	1341	1414				
	Oxford 131 d.	0716	0743	0816	0843	0843	0916	0943	1016	1043	1116	1143	1143	1216	1216	1243	1316	1343	1416				
158	Reading 131 a.	0741	0809	0841	0909	0908	0941	1010	1041	1111	1140	1209	1206	1241	1241	1309	1340	1409	1441				
	Reading d.	0746	0820	0846			0946	1020	1046		1146	1220	1250	1250	1246		1346	1418	1446				
183	Basingstoke 108 a.	0808	0841	0908			1008	1039	1108		1208	1239	1308	1308		1408	1440	1508					
213	Winchester 108 a.	0824	0856	0925			1024	1054	1124		1224	1254	1255	1324	1324		1424	1455	1524				
226	Southampton Airport ✈ 108 a.	0833	0908	0933			1032	1108	1133		1232	1308	1308	1332	1332		1434	1508	1532				
234	Southampton Central 108 a.	0844	0917	0943			1043	1117	1143		1241	1317	1317	1341	1341		1441	1517	1541				
255	Brockenhurst 108 a.	0859		0958			1058		1158		1257		1356	1357		1457		1557					
280	Bournemouth 108 a.	0914		1013			1113		1213		1312		1411	1412		1512		1612					

Table 2

	⚒	⚒	⚒	⚒ G	⚒	⚒	⚒	⚒	⚒	⚒	⑥	Ⓐ	⚒	⚒	Ⓐ
Manchester Piccadilly 122 d.		1227		1327		1427		1527		1627		1727		1827		1927
Newcastle 124 d.	1035		1135		1234	1335		1435	1505	1635	1635		1732			
York 124 d.	1135	*	1235		1335	1435		1535	1605	1735	1735		1835			
Leeds 124 d.									1640							
Sheffield 124 d.	1224		1324		1424	1524		1624	1724	1824	1824		1924			
Derby 124 d.	1253		1353		1453	1553		1653	1753	1853	1853		1954			
Birmingham New Street 150 d.	1333	1404	1433	1504	1533	1604	1633	1704	1733	1804	1833	1904	1933	1933	2004	2033	2104	2204
Birmingham Intl ✈ 150 d.		1414		1514		1614		1714		1814		1914			2014	2114	2214
Coventry 150 d.		1425		1525		1625		1725		1825		1925			2025	2125	2225
Leamington Spa 128 d.	1400	1438	1500	1538	1601	1638	1700	1738	1801	1838	1900	1938	2003	2004	2038	2100	2138	2238
Banbury 128 d.	1419	1455	1519	1555	1619	1655	1719	1755	1819	1855	1919	1955	2020	2022	2055	2119	2155	2255
Oxford a.	1440	1514	1541	1614	1640	1714	1740	1814	1841	1914	1941	2014	2040	2040	2114	2141	2214	2314
Oxford 131 d.	1443	1516	1543	1616	1643	1716	1743	1816	1843	1915	1943	2016	2043	2042	2116	2143	2216	2316
Reading 131 a.	1508	1541	1611	1641	1710	1740	1810	1842	1910	1941	2009	2041	2108	2107	2142	2216	2245	2347
Reading d.		1546	1620	1646		1750	1850		1946	2046		2150		2222	2248
Basingstoke 108 a.		1608	1640	1708		1808	1908		2009	2109		2209		2239	2307
Winchester 108 a.		1624	1658	1724		1824	1924		2024	2124		2224		2256	2324
Southampton Airport ✈ 108 a.		1632	1708	1732		1833	1932		2033	2133		2234		2312	2336
Southampton Central 108 a.		1641	1717	1741		1843	1941		2041	2140		2242		2320	2343
Brockenhurst 108 a.		1657		1757		1857	1957		2058	2156		2258			
Bournemouth 108 a.		1712		1815		1912	2012		2115	2215		2319			

Table 3

	⑦	⑦	⑦	⑦	⑦	⑦	⑦	⑦	⑦	⑦	⑦	⑦	⑦	⑦	⑦	⑦ E	⑦	⑦	⑦ G	⑦
Manchester Piccadilly 122 d.		0827	0927	1027		1127		1226		1326		1427		1527		1627		1727		1827		1927
Newcastle 124 d.													1335		1435		1524		1635		1735	
York 124 d.												1435		1535		1624		1735		1835	
Leeds 124 d.																					
Sheffield 124 d.											1422		1524		1624		1724		1824		1924	
Derby 124 d.									1355		1453		1553		1654		1754		1854		1956
Birmingham New Street 150 d.		0904	1004	1104	1204	1233	1304	1333	1404	1433	1504	1533	1604	1633	1704	1733	1804	1833	1904	1933	2004	2033	2104
Birmingham Intl ✈ 150 d.		0914	1014	1114	1204	1245	1314		1414	1445	1514		1614	1645	1714		1814	1845	1914	1945	2014		2114
Coventry 150 d.		0925	1025	1125	1225	1255	1325		1425	1455	1525		1625	1655	1725		1825	1855	1925	1955	2025		2124
Leamington Spa 128 d.		0938	1038	1138	1238	1308	1338	1359	1438	1508	1538	1559	1638	1708	1738	1759	1838	1908	1938	2008	2038	2100	2136
Banbury 128 d.		0955	1055	1155	1255	1325	1355	1416	1455	1526	1555	1616	1655	1725	1755	1817	1855	1925	1955	2025	2055	2119	2153
Oxford a.		1014	1114	1214	1314	1343	1414	1435	1514	1544	1614	1635	1714	1743	1814	1835	1914	1944	2014	2043	2114	2138	2211
Oxford 131 d.		1016	1116	1216	1316	1345	1416	1436	1516	1546	1616	1636	1716	1745	1816	1838	1916	1946	2016	2044	2116	2140	2212
Reading 131 a.		1042	1140	1240	1341	1409	1440	1504	1540	1611	1640	1701	1739	1809	1840	1904	1939	2008	2040	2114	2140	2206	2238
Reading d.	0952	1052	1152	1252	1352		1452		1552		1652		1752		1852		1952		2052		2152		
Basingstoke 108 a.	1011	1109	1208	1308	1408		1508		1608		1708		1808		1909		2009		2108		2209		
Winchester 108 a.	1026	1124	1224	1324	1424		1524		1624		1724		1824		1924		2024		2124		2223		
Southampton Airport ✈ 108 a.	1035	1133	1233	1333	1433		1533		1633		1733		1833		1933		2033		2133		2233		
Southampton Central 108 a.	1042	1142	1242	1342	1442		1542		1642		1740		1842		1940		2041		2142		2242		
Brockenhurst 108 a.	1106	1206	1306	1406	1506		1603		1706		1806		1903		2006		2106		2206				
Bournemouth 108 a.	1126	1226	1326	1426	1526		1626		1726		1826		1926		2026		2126		2226				

A – From Nottingham (Table 121).   E – From Edinburgh Waverley (Table 124).   G – To Guildford (Table 134).

XC Most services convey 🍷 BOURNEMOUTH - SOUTHAMPTON - READING - BIRMINGHAM 119

		⑥	Ⓐ	Ⓐ G	⑥ G	Ⓐ	⑥	Ⓐ	⑥	Ⓐ	⑥	Ⓐ	⑥	Ⓐ	⑥	⑥	Ⓐ	⚒	⚒	⚒	⑥	Ⓐ	⚒	Ⓐ	⑥	⚒
Bournemouth 108 d.	⚒	...	...	...	...	...	...	...	0625	0630	0637	...	...	0730	0747	...	...	0845	...	0945	...	...	1045	...	...	1145
Brockenhurst 108 d.		...	...	...	...	...	...	...	0639	0645	0655	...	...	0750	0802	...	...	0900	...	1000	...	...	1100	...	...	1200
Southampton Central 108 d.		0509	0515	...	...	0615	0620	...	0653	0715	0720	...	0747	0815	0820	...	...	0916	0946	1017	...	...	1117	1146	1147	1217
Southampton Airport ✈ 108 d.		0516	0522	...	...	0622	0627	...	0701	0722	0727	...	0754	0822	0827	...	...	0923	0955	1024	...	...	1124	1153	1154	1224
Winchester 108 d.		0525	0531	...	...	0631	0636	...	0709	0731	0736	0812	0803	0831	0836	...	...	0932	1003	1033	...	...	1133	1202	1203	1233
Basingstoke 108 d.		0541	0547	...	...	0647	0652	...	0725	0747	0752	0828	0819	0847	0852	...	...	0949	1019	1049	...	...	1149	1218	1219	1249
Reading a.		0600	0605	...	...	0704	0708	...	0742	0804	0808	0844	0835	0904	0908	...	...	1008	1037	1107	...	...	1208	1237	1235	1308
Reading 131 d.		0615	0615	0645	0645	0715	0715	0746	0747	0815	0815	0850	0845	0915	0912	0945	0945	1015	1045	1115	1145	1145	1215	1245	1245	1315
Oxford 131 a.		0637	0637	0706	0710	0736	0738	0810	0810	0838	0838	0913	0910	0937	0934	1010	1013	1038	1110	1138	1210	1210	1238	1311	1310	1338
Oxford d.		0639	0638	0708	0712	0739	0740	0812	0812	0839	0840	0915	0912	0939	0936	1012	1015	1039	1112	1139	1212	1212	1239	1312	1312	1356
Banbury 128 d.		0657	0657	0725	0729	0757	0757	0830	0829	0857	0857	0933	0929	0957	0953	1029	1032	1057	1129	1157	1229	1232	1257	1331	1329	1357
Leamington Spa 128 d.		0714	0714	0743	0747	0814	0814	0847	0847	0914	0914	0950	0947	1014	1011	1047	1050	1114	1147	1214	1247	1250	1314	1348	1347	1414
Coventry 150 d.		0727	0727	|	|	0827	0827	|	|	0927	0927	|	|	1027	1027	|	|	1127	|	1227	|	|	1327	|	|	1427
Birmingham Intl ✈ 150 d.		0738	0738	|	|	0838	0838	|	|	0938	0938	|	|	1038	1038	|	|	1138	|	1238	|	|	1338	|	|	1438
Birmingham New Street 150 a.		0748	0748	0812	0818	0848	0848	0918	0918	0948	0948	1018	1018	1048	1048	1118	1118	1148	1218	1248	1318	1318	1348	1418	1418	1448
Derby **124** a.		|	|	0905	0905	|	|	1005	1006	|	|	1105	1105	|	|	1205	1205	|	1305	|	1405	1405	|	1505	1505	|
Sheffield **124** a.		|	|	0944	0944	|	|	1044	1044	|	|	1144	1144	|	|	1244	1244	|	1344	|	1444	1444	|	1544	1544	|
Leeds **124** a.		|	|	|	|	|	|	|	|	|	|	|	|	|	|	|	|	|	|	|	|	|	|	|	|	|
York **124** a.		|	|	1039	1039	|	|	1139	1139	|	|	1240	1239	|	|	1339	1340	|	1439	|	1539	1539	|	1639	1639	|
Newcastle **124** a.		|	|	1145	1146	|	|	1245	1246	|	|	1345	1345	|	|	1446	1443	|	1545	|	1646	1645	|	1745	1745	|
Manchester Piccadilly **122** a.		0926	0939	...	...	1026	1026	...	...	1126	1126	...	...	1226	1226	...	...	1326	...	1426	...	...	1526	...	...	1626

	Ⓐ	⑥	⚒	Ⓐ E	⑥	⚒	⚒	⚒	Ⓐ	⑥	⚒	Ⓐ	⑥	⚒	⑥	Ⓐ	Ⓐ	⑥	⑥	Ⓐ	Ⓐ	⑥	Ⓐ	⑥	Ⓐ	⑥
Bournemouth 108 d.	...	...	1245	...	...	1345	...	1445	...	...	1545	...	...	1645	...	...	1745	1747	...	...	1845	1847	...	...	1945	1947
Brockenhurst 108 d.	...	...	1300	...	...	1400	...	1500	...	...	1600	...	...	1700	...	...	1800	1802	...	...	1900	1902	...	...	2000	2002
Southampton Central 108 d.	...	...	1316	1346	1347	1417	...	1516	1546	1547	1617	...	...	1717	1747	1746	1815	1820	...	...	1916	1920	...	...	2017	2019
Southampton Airport ✈ 108 d.	...	...	1323	1354	1354	1424	...	1523	1553	1554	1624	...	...	1724	1754	1753	1822	1827	...	...	1923	1927	...	...	2024	2026
Winchester 108 d.	...	...	1332	1403	1403	1433	...	1532	1602	1603	1633	...	...	1733	1803	1802	1831	1836	...	...	1932	1936	...	...	2033	2036
Basingstoke 108 d.	...	...	1349	1419	1419	1449	...	1548	1618	1618	1649	...	...	1749	1818	1818	1847	1852	...	...	1949	1952	...	...	2049	2052
Reading a.	...	...	1408	1436	1435	1507	...	1607	1634	1634	1708	...	...	1807	1835	1835	1904	1908	...	...	2005	2008	...	...	2106	2108
Reading 131 d.	1345	1345	1415	1445	1445	1515	1545	1615	1645	1645	1715	1745	1745	1815	1845	1845	1915	1915	1945	1945	2015	2015	2045	2045	2111	2115
Oxford 131 a.	1411	1410	1438	1509	1510	1538	1611	1638	1708	1710	1738	1808	1810	1838	1910	1911	1938	1938	2010	2009	2036	2038	2112	2110	2134	2138
Oxford d.	1413	1412	1439	1513	1512	1539	1612	1639	1713	1712	1739	1810	1812	1838	1912	1913	1939	1940	2012	2013	2039	2040	2114	2112	2136	2139
Banbury 128 d.	1431	1429	1457	1532	1529	1557	1629	1657	1732	1729	1757	1827	1829	1857	1929	1930	1957	1957	2030	2032	2057	2057	2133	2129	2154	2157
Leamington Spa 128 d.	1450	1447	1514	1550	1547	1614	1647	1714	1750	1747	1814	1845	1847	1914	1947	1948	2014	2015	2048	2050	2114	2115	2152	2147	2211	2214
Coventry 150 d.	|	|	1527	|	|	1627	|	1727	|	|	1827	|	|	1927	|	|	2027	2027	|	|	2127	2127	|	2159	2225	2226
Birmingham Intl ✈ 150 d.	|	|	1538	|	|	1638	|	1738	|	|	1838	|	|	1938	|	|	2038	2038	|	|	2138	2138	|	2211	2235	2237
Birmingham New Street 150 a.	1518	1518	1548	1618	1618	1648	1718	1748	1818	1818	1848	1918	1918	1948	2018	2018	2048	2048	2116	2123	2148	2148	2218	2221	2245	2247
Derby **124** a.	1605	1606	|	1705	1705	|	1805	|	1905	1905	|	2005	2005	|	2124	2109	|	|	...	...	|	|	...	...	...	...
Sheffield **124** a.	1644	1644	|	1742	1745	|	1844	|	1940	1947	|	2040	2049	|	2159	2150	|	|	...	...	|	|	...	...	...	...
Leeds **124** a.	|	|	|	1834	1829	|	|	|	|	|	|	|	|	|	|	|	|	|	...	...	|	|	...	...	...	...
York **124** a.	1740	1739	|	1901	1901	|	1939	|	2038	2040	|	2140	2144	|	2246	2252	|	|	...	...	|	|	...	...	...	...
Newcastle **124** a.	1847	1841	|	2001	2001	|	2042	|	2144	2144	|	2247	2247	|	...	...	|	|	...	...	|	|	...	...	...	...
Manchester Piccadilly **122** a.	...	...	1726	...	...	1826	...	1925	...	...	2026	...	...	2126	...	...	2227	2233	...	...	2339a	2329	...	...	...	...

	⑥	Ⓐ		⑦	⑦	⑦	⑦	⑦ G	⑦	⑦	⑦	⑦	⑦	⑦ E	⑦	⑦	⑦	⑦	⑦	⑦	⑦	⑦	⑦	⑦	⑦	⑦
Bournemouth 108 d.	...	...	⑦	...	...	0940	1040	...	1140	...	1240	...	1340	...	1440	...	1540	...	1640	...	1740	...	1840	...	1940	...
Brockenhurst 108 d.	...	...		...	...	0957	1057	...	1157	...	1257	...	1357	...	1457	...	1557	...	1657	...	1757	...	1857	...	1957	...
Southampton Central 108 d.	...	...		...	0915	1015	1115	...	1215	...	1315	...	1415	...	1515	...	1615	...	1715	...	1815	...	1915	...	2015	...
Southampton Airport ✈ 108 d.	...	...		...	0922	1022	1122	...	1222	...	1322	...	1422	...	1522	...	1622	...	1722	...	1822	...	1922	...	2022	...
Winchester 108 d.	...	...		...	0931	1031	1131	...	1231	...	1331	...	1431	...	1531	...	1631	...	1731	...	1831	...	1931	...	2031	...
Basingstoke 108 d.	...	...		...	0947	1047	1147	...	1247	...	1347	...	1447	...	1547	...	1647	...	1747	...	1847	...	1947	...	2047	...
Reading a.	...	...		...	1004	1103	1203	...	1304	...	1403	...	1505	...	1603	...	1703	...	1803	...	1903	...	2003	...	2103	...
Reading 131 d.	2145	2145		0912	1011	1111	1211	1254	1311	1341	1411	1441	1511	1541	1611	1641	1711	1741	1811	1841	1911	1941	2011	2041	2111	2141
Oxford 131 a.	2210	2223		0935	1035	1135	1235	1315	1335	1404	1435	1504	1535	1604	1635	1704	1735	1804	1835	1903	1935	2003	2035	2104	2135	2202
Oxford d.	2212	2230		0937	1037	1137	1237	1317	1337	1406	1437	1506	1537	1606	1637	1706	1737	1806	1837	1906	1937	2006	2037	2106	2137	2206
Banbury 128 d.	2229	2248		0955	1055	1155	1255	1335	1355	1424	1455	1524	1555	1624	1655	1724	1755	1824	1855	1924	1955	2024	2055	2124	2154	2224
Leamington Spa 128 d.	2247	2305		1012	1112	1212	1312	1352	1412	1442	1512	1540	1612	1640	1712	1740	1812	1842	1912	1941	2012	2041	2112	2141	2212	2242
Coventry 150 d.	|	2317		1029	1129	1228	1327	|	1427	1454	1527	1554	1627	1654	1727	1754	1827	1855	1927	1954	2027	2054	2127	2153	2224	2254
Birmingham Intl ✈ 150 d.	|	2327		1040	1141	1240	1338	|	1438	1504	1538	1604	1638	1704	1738	1804	1838	1905	1938	2004	2038	2104	2138	2203	2234	2304
Birmingham New Street 150 a.	2317	2356		1050	1151	1250	1348	1419	1448	1514	1548	1614	1648	1714	1748	1814	1848	1915	1948	2014	2048	2115	2148	2214	2243	2314
Derby **124** a.	...	...		|	|	|	|	1501	|	1601	|	1702	|	1802	|	1903	|	2001	|	...	|	...	|	...	...	...
Sheffield **124** a.	...	...		|	|	|	|	1547	|	1648	|	1749	|	1845	|	1940	|	2041	|	...	|	...	|	...	...	...
Leeds **124** a.	...	...		|	|	|	|	|	|	|	|	1851	|	|	|	|	|	|	|	...	|	...	|	...	...	...
York **124** a.	...	...		|	|	|	|	1638	|	1740	|	1921	|	1939	|	2039	|	2143	|	...	|	...	|	...	...	...
Newcastle **124** a.	...	...		|	|	|	|	1744	|	1841	|	2019	|	2041	|	2144	|	2312	|	...	|	...	|	...	...	...
Manchester Piccadilly **122** a.	...	...		1241	1329	1429	1524	...	1629	...	1730	...	1829	...	1928	...	2028	...	2129	...	2226	...	2324	...	...	...

E – To Edinburgh Waverley (Table **124**). G – From Guildford (Table **134**). a – Arrives 2326 until Feb. 10 and from Mar. 24 (also on ⑤ Feb.17 - Mar. 17).

GW 2nd class BRISTOL - TAUNTON 120a

km			Ⓐ B	Ⓐ B	Ⓐ A	Ⓐ	Ⓐ C	Ⓐ D	Ⓐ	Ⓐ	Ⓐ	Ⓐ E	Ⓐ	Ⓐ	Ⓐ	Ⓐ	Ⓐ	Ⓐ	Ⓐ	Ⓐ E	Ⓐ E	Ⓐ E		⑥ B	⑥	⑥ B	⑥ A
	Cardiff Central **136** d.	Ⓐ	...	...	...	...	0759	0900	0959	1059	1159	1300	1359	1500	1600	1700	1800	1900	2000	...	...	...	⑥	...	...	...	...
0	**Bristol** T Meads .. 120 132 d.		0524	0642	0718	0826	0855	0955	1053	1153	1253	1357	1453	1553	1653	1755	1856	1955	2055	2156	2306	2335		0524	0618	0636	0718
31	Weston-super-Mare 132 d.		0547	0706	0749	0901	0929	1024	1122	1221	1323	1425	1528	1627	1728	1830	1930	2029	2133	2231	2342	0006s		0545	0646	0656	0751
43	Highbridge and Burnham d.		0557	0717	0800	0911	0940	1035	1133	1232	1334	1436	1538	1638	1739	1841	1940	2039	2144	2242	2354	0017s		0555	0657	|	0802
53	Bridgwater d.		0605	0725	0808	0919	0948	1043	1141	1240	1342	1444	1546	1646	1747	1849	1948	2047	2152	2250	0002	0025s		0603	0705	|	0810
72	**Taunton** 120 132 a.		0618	0738	0824	0932	1001	1059	1155	1256	1358	1458	1601	1701	1801	1903	2004	2103	2207	2302	0014	0037		0616	0719	0724	0824

	⑥	⑥	⑥	⑥	⑥	⑥	⑥		⑥	⑥	⑥	⑥	⑥	⑥	⑥ E	⑥		⑦ B	⑦ B	⑦	⑦ A	⑦	⑦	⑦	⑦ E	⑦	⑦
Cardiff Central **136** d.	0800	0900	1000	1059	1200	1300	1400	...	1500	1600	1700	1800	1900	...	2100	...	⑦	...	...	...	...	...	...	...	...	...	...
Bristol T Meads .. 120 132 d.	0857	0953	1054	1153	1253	1355	1453	...	1553	1653	1753	1853	1953	2054	2159	2217		0726	0828	1023	1110	1305	1555	1655	1830	1905	2025
Weston-super-Mare 132 d.	0932	1022	1124	1222	1323	1423	1523	...	1623	1723	1823	1923	2024	2128	2233	2247s		0749	0858	1052	1137	1332	1629	1726	1900	1940	2059
Highbridge and Burnham d.	0944	1033	1135	1233	1334	1434	1535	...	1634	1734	1834	1934	2034	2139	2244	2258s		|	0909	1103	1147	1343	1639	1739	1911	1950	2109
Bridgwater d.	0952	1041	1143	1241	1342	1442	1543	...	1642	1742	1842	1942	2042	2147	2252	2305s		0805	0917	1111	1155	1351	1647	1744	1919	1958	2117
Taunton 120 132 a.	1006	1057	1156	1257	1359	1500	1600	...	1657	1759	1856	2000	2100	2159	2305	2317		0818	0930	1124	1209	1403	1702	1759	1933	2011	2132

		Ⓐ	Ⓐ	Ⓐ E	Ⓐ D	Ⓐ	Ⓐ C	Ⓐ	Ⓐ	Ⓐ B	Ⓐ	Ⓐ	Ⓐ	Ⓐ C	Ⓐ	Ⓐ	Ⓐ	Ⓐ	Ⓐ	Ⓐ	Ⓐ	Ⓐ		⑥	⑥ E	⑥	⑥
Taunton 120 132 d.	Ⓐ	0512	0602	0634	0654	0712	0812	0836	0938	1007	1104	1207	1307	1410	1457	1607	1706	1808	1917	2030	2129	2245	⑥	0539	0634	0654	0735
Bridgwater d.		0524	0614	0646	0705	0723	|	0848	0950	1019	1116	1219	1319	1422	1509	1619	1717	1819	1929	2042	2140	2257		0551	0646	0705	0747
Highbridge and Burnham d.		0532	0621	0654	0713	0731	|	0856	0957	1027	1124	1227	1327	1431	1516	1627	1725	1827	1936	2050	2147	2305		0559	0654	0712	0755
Weston-super-Mare 132 a.		0543	0632	0704	0724	0742	0832	0909	1008	1038	1134c	1238	1338	1441	1527b	1637	1737	1838	1947	2100	2159	2315		0609	0705	0724	0805
Bristol T Meads .. 120 132 a.		0620	0709	0741	0757	0825	0854	0943	1042	1110	1212	1309	1412	1513	1612	1711	1812	1913	2020	2136	2232	2351		0644	0741	0758	0839
Cardiff Central **136** a.		...	0824	...	...	...	...	...	...	1221	1323	1418	1525	1618	1727	1818	1922	2020	...	...	...	...		...	...	...	...

	⑥ E	⑥	⑥	⑥	⑥	⑥	⑥	⑥	⑥	⑥	⑥	⑥	⑥	⑥		⑦ E	⑦ E	⑦	⑦ C	⑦	⑦	⑦ C	⑦	⑦ B	⑦	⑦	⑦
Taunton 120 132 d.	0759	0910	1012	1104	1207	1307	1407	1507	1607	1707	1807	1907	2017	2135	⑦	0835	1018	1136	1200	1334	1519	1658	1719	1818	1856	2025	2136
Bridgwater d.	0810	0922	1024	1116	1219	1319	1419	1519	1619	1719	1819	1919	2029	2147		0847	1030	1148	|	1346	1531	1709	1730	1830	1906	2037	2148
Highbridge and Burnham d.	0817	0930	1032	1124	1227	1327	1427	1527	1627	1727	1827	1927	2037	2155		0855	1038	1155	|	1353	1538	1717	1737	1837	1914	2045	2155
Weston-super-Mare 132 a.	0827	0942	1042	1134	1237	1337	1437	1537	1637	1737	1839	1937	2048	2205		0906	1048	1205	1219	1404	1548	1727	1748	1848	1924	2057	2205
Bristol T Meads .. 120 132 a.	0857	1012	1112	1211	1309	1411	1510	1609	1711	1811	1910	2009	2124	2240		0938	1120	1243	1308	1436	1620	1757	1819	1917	1950	2131	2238
Cardiff Central **136** a.	...	1120	1217	1318	1419	1518	1618	1717	1815	1918	2015	...	2231	...		...	...	...	...	...	...	...	...	...	...	...	...

A – From Gloucester (Table **140**).
B – To / from Penzance (Table **115**).
C – To / from Paignton (Table **115**).
D – To / from Plymouth (Table **115**).
E – To / from Exeter St Davids (Table **115**).
b – Departs 1543.
c – Departs 1146.
s – Calls to set down only.

120 BIRMINGHAM - BRISTOL - PAIGNTON and PLYMOUTH

Most services convey ⅄ XC

km		Ⓐ	Ⓐ	Ⓐ	Ⓐ	Ⓐ	Ⓐ	Ⓐ	Ⓐ	Ⓐ	Ⓐ	Ⓐ	Ⓐ	Ⓐ	Ⓐ	Ⓐ	Ⓐ	Ⓐ	Ⓐ	Ⓐ	Ⓐ	Ⓐ
									★d							A					★	B
	Glasgow Central 124 d.	...	...	...	...	...	...	...	...	...	...	...	...	0601	...	...	...	0750	...	0900	...	...
	Edinburgh Waverley 124 d.	...	...	...	...	...	...	...	...	...	...	0606	...	0707	...	0810	...	0908	...	1010	...	1106
	Newcastle 124 d.	...	...	...	...	...	...	...	...	0645	...	0740	...	0843	...	0942	...	1042	...	1144	...	1241
	York 124 d.	...	...	...	...	...	...	0640	...	0743	...	0845	...	0945	...	1045	...	1145	...	1245	...	1345
	Leeds 124 d.	...	...	...	...	0600	...	0705	...	0811	...	0911	...	1011	...	1111	...	1211	...	1311	...	1411
	Sheffield 124 d.	...	...	...	...	0652	...	0753	...	0854	...	0954	...	1055	...	1154	...	1255	...	1355	...	1455
	Derby 124 d.	...	...	0610	...	0727	...	0828	...	0928	...	1030	...	1128	...	1230	...	1328	...	1428	...	1528
	Manchester Piccadilly 122 d.	...	...	|	0600	|	0707	|	0807	|	0907	|	1007	|	1107	|	1207	|	1307	|	1407	|
0	**Birmingham** New Street 121 d.	...	0642	0712	0742	0812	0842	0917	0942	1017	1042	1117	1142	1217	1242	1317	1342	1417	1442	1517	1542	1612
73	Cheltenham Spa 121 a.	...	0721	0751	0824	0850	0924	0958	1024	1059	1124	1157	1224	1259	1324	1357	1424	1458	1524	1558	1624	1649
135	**Bristol** Parkway a.	...	0754	0826	0854	0925	0954	1030	1054	1131	1154	1229	1254	1330	1354	1429	1454	1529	1554	1630	1654	1724
145	**Bristol** Temple Meads a.	...	0805	0839	0910	0939	1008	1042	1110	1141	1205	1242	1309	1341	1408	1442	1510	1541	1611	1643	1710	1739
145	**Bristol** Temple Meads 120a 115 d.	0634	0810	0844	...	0944	...	1045	1115	1144	...	1245	...	1344	...	1445	1513	1544	...	1645	1713	1744
217	Taunton 120a 115 a.	0707	0842	0914	...	1015	...	1116	1158	1214	...	1316	...	1414	...	1516	1544	1614	...	1716	1744	1815
240	Tiverton Parkway 115 a.	0719	0854	0926	...	1028	...	1129	1210	1226	...	1328	...	1426	...	1528	1556	1626	...	1728	1756	1827
266	**Exeter** St Davids 115 a.	0732	0907	0940	...	1042	...	1143	1224	1240	...	1343	...	1440	...	1543	1612	1640	...	1742	1811	1841
298	Newton Abbot 115 a.	0754	0927	0959	...	1104	...	1204	1248	1259	...	1403	...	1459	...	1603	...	1704	...	1811	1835	1905
308	Torquay 115 a.	|	0939	|	...	|	...	|	1300	|	...	|	...	|	...	|	...	|	...	|	1847	|
311	**Paignton** 115 a.	|	0947	|	...	|	...	|	1308	|	...	|	...	|	...	|	...	|	...	|	1855	|
312	Totnes 115 a.	0807	...	1014	...	1117	...	1218	...	1311	...	1416	...	1511	...	1619	...	1716	...	1823	...	1917
350	**Plymouth** 115 a.	0833	...	1042	...	1144	...	1247	...	1338	...	1443	...	1540	...	1648	...	1742	...	1849	...	1943
	Newquay 117 a.	...	...	...	...	...	...	...	...	...	...	...	...	...	...	...	...	...	...	|	...	|
	Penzance 117 a.	...	...	...	...	...	...	...	...	...	...	...	...	...	...	...	...	...	...	2054	...	2143

	Ⓐ	Ⓐ	Ⓐ	Ⓐ	Ⓐ	Ⓐ	Ⓐ	Ⓐ	Ⓐ	Ⓐ	Ⓐ	⑥	⑥	⑥	⑥	⑥	⑥	⑥	⑥	⑥	⑥	⑥
				b	D					c									★d			
Glasgow Central 124 d.	...	1100	...	...	...	1300	...	...	...	1500	...	...	...	...	...	...	...	...	...	...	...	...
Edinburgh Waverley 124 d.	...	1208	...	1307	...	1408	...	1508	...	1606	1707	...	...	...	...	...	...	...	...	...	...	0608
Newcastle 124 d.	...	1343	...	1442	...	1541	...	1641	...	1741	1843	...	...	...	...	...	...	...	...	0645	...	0741
York 124 d.	...	1445	...	1545	...	1645	...	1745	...	1845	1945	...	...	...	...	...	...	0620	...	0745	...	0845
Leeds 124 d.	...	1511	...	1611	...	1711	...	1811	...	1911	2011	...	...	...	...	0600	...	0711	...	0811	...	0911
Sheffield 124 d.	...	1555	...	1655	...	1758	...	1858	...	1958	2058	...	...	...	...	0650	...	0756	...	0855	...	0955
Derby 124 d.	...	1628	...	1729	...	1829	...	1930	...	2029	2129	...	...	0610	...	0726	...	0828	...	0930	...	1028
Manchester Piccadilly 122 d.	1507	|	1607	|	1705	|	1805	|	1907	|	|	...	...	|	0600	|	0707	|	0807	|	0907	|
Birmingham New Street 121 d.	1642	1712	1742	1812	1842	1912	1942	2012	2042	2112	2212	...	0642	0712	0742	0812	0842	0912	0942	1012	1042	1112
Cheltenham Spa 121 a.	1724	1751	1824	1850	1924	1950	2024	2052	2125	2151	2251	...	0724	0750	0824	0851	0924	0951	1024	1051	1124	1153
Bristol Parkway a.	1754	1828	1854	1932	1954	2030	2054	2125	2201	2233	2322	...	0753	0824	0853	0924	0953	1029	1054	1125	1153	1229
Bristol Temple Meads a.	1807	1841	1906	1942	2009	2041	2105	2136	2214	2243	2340	...	0805	0838	0906	0939	1004	1042	1109	1138	1204	1242
Bristol Temple Meads 120a 115 d.	...	1844	...	1945	...	2044	2113	2144	...	...	...	0608	0812	0845	...	0944	...	1044	1112	1144	...	1244
Taunton 120a 115 a.	...	1915	...	2016	...	2115	2143	2215	...	...	...	0715	0842	0915	...	1017	...	1115	1159	1215	...	1315
Tiverton Parkway 115 a.	...	1927	...	2029	...	2127	2155	2227	...	...	...	0727	0854	0927	...	1030	...	1127	1211	1227	...	1327
Exeter St Davids 115 a.	...	1942	...	2043	...	2144	2209	2241	...	...	...	0740	0907	0940	...	1044	...	1141	1225	1241	...	1341
Newton Abbot 115 a.	...	2002	...	2103	...	2205	2228	2301	...	...	...	0759	0928	1000	...	1109	...	1201	1250	1300	...	1401
Torquay 115 a.	...	|	...	|	...	|	|	|	...	...	...	|	0939	|	...	|	...	|	1302	|	...	|
Paignton 115 a.	...	|	...	|	...	|	|	|	...	...	...	|	0947	|	...	|	...	|	1310	|	...	|
Totnes 115 a.	...	2014	...	2116	...	2217	2241	2313	...	...	...	0812	...	1012	...	1122	...	1213	...	1312	...	1416
Plymouth 115 a.	...	2040	...	2146	...	2243	2313	2339	...	...	...	0838	...	1039	...	1151	...	1240	...	1339	...	1444
Newquay 117 a.	...	|	...	...	...	...	...	...	...	...	...	...	...	...	...	...	...	...	...	...	...	...
Penzance 117 a.	...	2241	...	...	...	...	...	...	...	...	...	...	...	...	...	...	...	...	...	...	...	...

	⑥	⑥	⑥	⑥	⑥	⑥	⑥	⑥	⑥	⑥	⑥	⑥	⑥	⑥	⑥	⑥	⑥	⑥	⑥	⑥	⑦	⑦
				A					★	B					D					c		
Glasgow Central 124 d.	...	0601	...	...	...	0750	...	0900	...	...	...	1100	...	...	...	1300	...	...	...	1500	...	...
Edinburgh Waverley 124 d.	...	0707	...	0805	...	0908	...	1005	...	1108	...	1204	...	1309	...	1405	...	1508	...	1605	...	...
Newcastle 124 d.	...	0843	...	0942	...	1044	...	1142	...	1244	...	1344	...	1444	...	1544	...	1644	...	1744	...	...
York 124 d.	...	0945	...	1045	...	1145	...	1245	...	1345	...	1445	...	1545	...	1645	...	1745	...	1845	...	...
Leeds 124 d.	...	1011	...	1111	...	1211	...	1311	...	1411	...	1511	...	1611	...	1711	...	1811	...	1911	...	...
Sheffield 124 d.	...	1055	...	1155	...	1255	...	1355	...	1455	...	1555	...	1655	...	1755	...	1858	...	1955	...	...
Derby 124 d.	...	1130	...	1230	...	1328	...	1430	...	1528	...	1628	...	1728	...	1829	...	1929	...	2028	...	...
Manchester Piccadilly 122 d.	1007	|	1107	|	1207	|	1307	|	1407	|	1507	|	1607	|	1706	|	1805	|	1907	|	...	...
Birmingham New Street 121 d.	1142	1212	1242	1312	1342	1412	1442	1512	1542	1612	1642	1712	1742	1812	1842	1912	1942	2012	2042	2112	...	0930
Cheltenham Spa 121 a.	1224	1251	1325	1350	1424	1451	1524	1550	1624	1650	1724	1750	1824	1850	1924	1950	2024	2051	2124	2150	...	1008
Bristol Parkway a.	1253	1324	1354	1426	1454	1524	1554	1629	1653	1725	1753	1829	1853	1925	1954	2029	2053	2122	2158	2231	...	1037
Bristol Temple Meads a.	1307	1338	1405	1440	1509	1538	1607	1642	1707	1738	1807	1842	1904	1938	2005	2042	2104	2135	2212	2241	...	1048
Bristol Temple Meads 120a 115 d.	...	1345	...	1444	1512	1544	...	1644	1710	1744	...	1844	...	1944	...	2044	2111	2144	...	...	0844	1057
Taunton 120a 115 a.	...	1415	...	1516	1542	1614	...	1716	1740	1815	...	1915	...	2015	...	2115	2142	2215	...	...	0915	1129
Tiverton Parkway 115 a.	...	1427	...	1528	1554	1626	...	1729	1752	1827	...	1927	...	2027	...	2127	2154	2229	...	...	0927	1141
Exeter St Davids 115 a.	...	1441	...	1543	1609	1640	...	1743	1805	1841	...	1944	...	2040	...	2143	2208	2244	...	...	0939	1154
Newton Abbot 115 a.	...	1502	...	1603	...	1700	...	1810	1830	1904	...	2005	...	2100	...	2204	2227	2311	...	...	0959	1214
Torquay 115 a.	...	|	...	|	...	|	...	|	1841	|	...	|	...	|	...	|	|	|	...	...	|	|
Paignton 115 a.	...	|	...	|	...	|	...	|	1849	|	...	|	...	|	...	|	|	|	...	...	|	|
Totnes 115 a.	...	1514	...	1616	...	1712	...	1823	...	1916	...	2017	...	2112	...	2220	2239	2327	...	...	1012	1226
Plymouth 115 a.	...	1541	...	1643	...	1739	...	1851	...	1942	...	2043	...	2138	...	2250	2306	2356	...	...	1037	1252
Newquay 117 a.	...	...	...	...	...	...	...	|	...	|	...	|	...	...	...	...	...	...	...	...	...	|
Penzance 117 a.	...	...	...	...	...	...	...	2056	...	2140	...	2254	...	...	...	...	...	...	...	...	...	1447

	⑦	⑦	⑦	⑦	⑦	⑦	⑦	⑦	⑦	⑦	⑦	⑦	⑦	⑦	⑦	⑦	⑦	⑦	⑦	⑦	⑦	⑦
							★								★a	B				c		
Glasgow Central 124 d.	...	...	...	...	...	...	...	...	...	...	...	1055	...	1200	...	...	...	1348	...	1455	...	...
Edinburgh Waverley 124 d.	...	...	...	...	...	0908	...	1008	...	1105	...	1208	...	1308	...	1408	...	1508	...	1608	...	1708
Newcastle 124 d.	...	...	...	0935	...	1039	...	1140	...	1240	...	1340	...	1440	...	1540	...	1640	...	1740	...	1840
York 124 d.	...	...	0933	1033	...	1141	...	1241	...	1341	...	1441	...	1541	...	1641	...	1741	...	1841	...	1941
Leeds 124 d.	0810	0900	1000	1100	...	1211	...	1311	...	1411	...	1511	...	1611	...	1711	...	1811	...	1911	...	2011
Sheffield 124 d.	0854	0957	1057	1157	...	1257	...	1357	...	1455	...	1555	...	1654	...	1754	...	1855	...	1955	...	2054
Derby 124 d.	0928	1033	1129	1229	...	1332	...	1429	...	1526	...	1627	...	1727	...	1826	...	1927	...	2027	...	2126
Manchester Piccadilly 122 d.	|	|	|	|	...	|	1307	|	1407	|	1507	|	1607	|	1707	|	1807	|	1907	|	2007	|
Birmingham New Street 121 d.	1030	1130	1212	1312	1342	1412	1442	1512	1542	1612	1642	1712	1742	1812	1842	1912	1942	2012	2042	2112	2142	2212
Cheltenham Spa 121 a.	1109	1208	1251	1351	1423	1450	1524	1550	1624	1650	1724	1751	1824	1851	1924	1951	2024	2051	2124	2151	2223	2252
Bristol Parkway a.	1139	1238	1320	1420	1453	1523	1559	1620	1654	1720	1803	1820	1854	1921	2003	2020	2056	2120	2159	2233	2252	2322
Bristol Temple Meads a.	1151	1249	1331	1431	1508	1534	1611	1631	1708	1733	1814	1835	1908	1932	2014	2031	2106	2130	2210	2244	2302	2333
Bristol Temple Meads 120a 115 d.	1154	1254	1344	1444	...	1544	1614	1644	...	1744	...	1844	...	1944	2019	2044	...	2144	...	...	...	...
Taunton 120a 115 a.	1225	1325	1414	1514	...	1614	1644	1714	...	1817	...	1916	...	2017	2058	2114	...	2214	...	...	...	...
Tiverton Parkway 115 a.	1235	1336	1426	1526	...	1626	1656	1726	...	1829	...	1928	...	2029	2111	2126	...	2227	...	...	...	...
Exeter St Davids 115 a.	1252	1352	1439	1539	...	1640	1709	1739	...	1845	...	1945	...	2043	2127	2139	...	2245	...	...	...	...
Newton Abbot 115 a.	1312	1412	1459	1600	...	1701	1736	1800	...	1905	...	2007	...	2101	2153	2159	...	2304	...	...	...	...
Torquay 115 a.	|	|	|	|	...	|	1748	|	...	|	...	|	...	|	|	|	...	|	...	...	...	...
Paignton 115 a.	|	|	|	|	...	|	1756	|	...	|	...	|	...	|	|	|	...	|	...	...	...	...
Totnes 115 a.	1325	1425	1511	1612	...	1714	...	1812	...	1917	...	2019	...	2113	|	2217	...	2317	...	...	...	...
Plymouth 115 a.	1352	1452	1537	1638	...	1742	...	1838	...	1943	...	2045	...	2141	2237	2245	...	2346	...	...	...	...
Newquay 117 a.	...	...	...	...	...	...	...	...	...	...	...	...	...	...	...	...	...	...	...	...	...	...
Penzance 117 a.	...	...	...	...	...	...	...	2039	...	...	...	2242	...	...	...	...	...	...	...	...	...	...

A – From Dundee (Table 222).
B – From Aberdeen (Table 222).
D – To Cardiff Central (Table 121).
a – Also calls at Weston-super-Mare (a. 2036).

b – Also calls at Gloucester (a. 1901).
c – Also calls at Gloucester (a. 2202 on Ⓐ and ⑦, 2200 on ⑥).
d – Also calls at Weston-super-Mare (a. 1132 on Ⓐ, 1129 on ⑥).
★ – Also calls at Dawlish (10 – 15 minutes after Exeter) and Teignmouth (15 – 18 minutes after Exeter).

XC Most services convey 🍸 PLYMOUTH and PAIGNTON - BRISTOL - BIRMINGHAM 120

	Ⓐ	Ⓐ	Ⓐ	Ⓐ	Ⓐ	Ⓐ	Ⓐ	Ⓐ	Ⓐ	Ⓐ	Ⓐ	Ⓐ	Ⓐ	Ⓐ	Ⓐ	Ⓐ	Ⓐ	Ⓐ	Ⓐ	Ⓐ	Ⓐ	Ⓐ
		E			D		☆e					B	☆			A					☆a	
Penzance 117 d.	Ⓐ	...	...	...	...	...	...	...	...	0628	...	...	...	0828	...	...	0935	...	...	...	...	...
Newquay 117 d.		...	...	...	...	...	...	...	...	|	...	...	...	|	...	...	|	...	...	...	...	...
Plymouth 115 d.		...	...	0520	...	0625	...	0725	...	0825	...	0925	...	1025	...	1125	1150	1225	...	1325	...	1425
Totnes 115 d.		...	...	0545	...	0650	...	0750	...	0850	...	0950	...	1050	...	1150	1215	1251	...	1351	...	1450
Paignton 115 d.		...	...	|	...	|	0702	|	...	|	...	|	1007	|	...	|	|	|	...	|	1404	|
Torquay 115 d.		...	...	|	...	|	0708	|	...	|	...	|	1013	|	...	|	|	|	...	|	1410	|
Newton Abbot 115 d.		...	...	0602	...	0703	0719	0803	...	0903	...	1003	1024	1103	...	1203	1228	1304	...	1404	1421	1503
Exeter St Davids 115 d.		...	...	0624	...	0724	0745	0824	...	0924	...	1024	1050	1124	...	1224	1250	1324	...	1424	1448	1524
Tiverton Parkway 115 d.		...	...	0637	...	0737	0758	0837	...	0938	...	1037	1103	1137	...	1238	1306	1338	...	1438	1502	1537
Taunton 120a 115 d.		...	...	0651	...	0751	0812	0851	...	0951	...	1051	1117	1151	...	1251	1322	1351	...	1451	1515	1551
Bristol Temple Meads 120a 115 a.		0620	...	0726	...	0827	0854	0926	...	1025	...	1124	1152	1224	...	1324	1355	1426	...	1523	1556	1623
Bristol Temple Meads d.		0627	0700	0730	0800	0830	0900	0930	1000	1030	1100	1130	1200	1230	1300	1330	1400	1430	1500	1530	1600	1630
Bristol Parkway d.		0638	0709	0739	0809	0839	0909	0939	1009	1039	1109	1139	1209	1239	1309	1339	1409	1440	1509	1540	1609	1639
Cheltenham Spa 121 d.		0710	0740	0811	0840	0912	0942	1010	1041	1111	1142	1211	1240	1311	1342	1410	1441	1511	1542	1611	1641	1711
Birmingham New Street 121 a.		0756	0826	0856	0926	0958	1023	1056	1126	1158	1226	1256	1326	1356	1423	1456	1523	1556	1623	1656	1723	1756
Manchester Piccadilly 122 a.		|	0959	|	1059	|	1159	|	1259	|	1359	|	1459	|	1559	|	1659	|	1800	|	1859	|
Derby 124 a.		0841	...	0939	...	1038	...	1138	...	1241	...	1339	...	1440	...	1540	...	1641	...	1739	...	1839
Sheffield 124 a.		0917	...	1017	...	1118	...	1217	...	1317	...	1418	...	1517	...	1618	...	1718	...	1818	...	1918
Leeds 124 a.		1001	...	1101	...	1201	...	1301	...	1401	...	1501	...	1601	...	1704	...	1802	...	1903	...	2005
York 124 a.		1030	...	1130	...	1230	...	1330	...	1430	...	1530	...	1630	...	1730	...	1831	...	1930	...	2030
Newcastle 124 a.		1129	...	1230	...	1329	...	1431	...	1529	...	1700	...	1730	...	1833	...	1932	...	2033	...	2128
Edinburgh Waverley 124 a.		1306	...	1410	...	1507	...	1606	...	1706	...	1807	...	1906	...	2009	...	2108	...	2214	...	2303
Glasgow Central 124 a.		1412	...	...	...	1612	...	...	...	1811	...	...	...	2015	...	...	...	2224	...	...	...	...

	Ⓐ	Ⓐ	Ⓐ	Ⓐ	Ⓐ	Ⓐ	Ⓐ	Ⓐ	Ⓐ		⑥	⑥	⑥	⑥	⑥	⑥	⑥	⑥	⑥	⑥	⑥	⑥
						b					c			D		☆					B	☆
Penzance 117 d.	...	...	...	...	...	...	...	...	...	⑥	...	...	...	...	...	...	...	...	0630	...	...	...
Newquay 117 d.	...	...	...	...	...	...	...	...	...		...	...	...	...	...	...	...	...	|	...	...	...
Plymouth 115 d.	...	1525	...	1625	...	1725	...	1825	...		...	...	0525	...	0625	...	0725	...	0825	...	0925	...
Totnes 115 d.	...	1551	...	1650	...	1751	...	1850	...		...	...	0550	...	0650	...	0750	...	0850	...	0950	...
Paignton 115 d.	...	|	...	|	...	|	...	|	2014		...	...	|	...	|	0702	|	...	|	...	|	1006
Torquay 115 d.	...	|	...	|	...	|	...	|	2020		...	...	|	...	|	0708	|	...	|	...	|	1012
Newton Abbot 115 d.	...	1604	...	1703	...	1804	...	1903	2031		...	...	0603	...	0703	0719	0803	...	0903	...	1003	1023
Exeter St Davids 115 d.	...	1624	1654	1724	...	1825	...	1924	2052		...	...	0623	...	0723	0745	0823	...	0923	...	1023	1049
Tiverton Parkway 115 d.	...	1638	1708	1737	...	1839	...	1937	2105		...	...	0637	...	0737	0758	0837	...	0937	...	1037	1102
Taunton 120a 115 d.	...	1651	1722	1751	...	1851	...	1951	2119		...	...	0650	...	0750	0811	0850	...	0950	...	1050	1117
Bristol Temple Meads 120a 115 a.	...	1724	1754	1823	...	1925	...	2025	2152		...	...	0722	...	0824	0849	0925	...	1025	...	1124	1154
Bristol Temple Meads d.	1700	1730	1800	1830	1900	1930	2000	2030	2200		0615	0700	0730	0800	0830	0900	0930	1000	1030	1100	1130	1200
Bristol Parkway d.	1709	1740	1809	1839	1909	1940	2009	2040	2210		0624	0709	0739	0809	0839	0909	0939	1009	1039	1109	1139	1209
Cheltenham Spa 121 d.	1742	1811	1841	1911	1940	2011	2056	2117	2242		0711	0741	0811	0841	0911	0941	1011	1041	1111	1141	1211	1241
Birmingham New Street 121 a.	1823	1856	1923	1956	2022	2051	2137	2202	2343		0756	0825	0856	0926	0956	1025	1056	1126	1156	1226	1256	1326
Manchester Piccadilly 122 a.	1959	|	2058	|	2200	|	...	...	...		|	0959	|	1059	|	1159	|	1259	|	1359	|	1459
Derby 124 a.	...	1940	...	2038	...	2143	...	...	...		0841	...	0939	...	1038	...	1138	...	1238	...	1338	...
Sheffield 124 a.	...	2018	...	2115	...	2224	...	...	...		0917	...	1017	...	1117	...	1217	...	1317	...	1418	...
Leeds 124 a.	...	2106	...	2204	...	2315	...	...	...		1001	...	1101	...	1200	...	1302	...	1401	...	1501	...
York 124 a.	...	...	...	...	...	...	...	...	...		1030	...	1130	...	1230	...	1330	...	1430	...	1530	...
Newcastle 124 a.	...	...	...	...	...	...	...	...	...		1129	...	1229	...	1329	...	1428	...	1529	...	1629	...
Edinburgh Waverley 124 a.	...	...	...	...	...	...	...	...	...		1302	...	1406	...	1504	...	1604	...	1707	...	1803	...
Glasgow Central 124 a.	...	...	...	...	...	...	...	...	...		1412	...	...	...	1612	...	...	...	1811	...	...	...

	⑥	⑥	⑥	⑥	⑥	⑥	⑥	⑥		⑥	⑥	⑥	⑥	⑥	⑥		⑥	⑥	⑥		⑦	⑦
			A					☆a													c	
Penzance 117 d.	0828	...	...	0943	...	...	...	...	...	...	...	...	...	...	...	...	...	...	...	⑦	...	...
Newquay 117 d.	|	...	...	|	...	...	...	...	...	...	...	...	...	...	...	...	...	...	...		...	...
Plymouth 115 d.	1025	...	1125	1148	1225	...	1325	...	...	1425	...	1525	...	1625	...	...	1725	...	1825		...	...
Totnes 115 d.	1050	...	1150	1213	1251	...	1350	...	...	1450	...	1550	...	1650	...	...	1751	...	1850		...	...
Paignton 115 d.	|	...	|	|	|	...	|	1355	...	|	...	|	...	|	...	...	|	...	|		...	...
Torquay 115 d.	|	...	|	|	|	...	|	1401	...	|	...	|	...	|	...	...	|	...	|		...	...
Newton Abbot 115 d.	1103	...	1203	1225	1304	...	1403	1412	...	1503	...	1603	...	1703	...	...	1804	...	1903		...	...
Exeter St Davids 115 d.	1123	...	1223	1248	1323	...	1425	1437	...	1523	...	1623	1653	1723	...	...	1824	...	1923		...	...
Tiverton Parkway 115 d.	1137	...	1237	1302	1337	...	1438	1450	...	1537	...	1637	1707	1737	...	...	1838	...	1937		...	...
Taunton 120a 115 d.	1150	...	1250	1315	1350	...	1451	1503	...	1550	...	1650	1721	1750	...	...	1851	...	1950		...	...
Bristol Temple Meads 120a 115 a.	1225	...	1323	1355	1425	...	1525	1549	...	1625	...	1725	1755	1825	...	...	1924	...	2022		...	...
Bristol Temple Meads d.	1230	1300	1330	1400	1430	1500	1530	1600	...	1630	1700	1730	1800	1830	1900	...	1930	2000	2030		0915	1030
Bristol Parkway d.	1239	1309	1339	1409	1440	1509	1539	1609	...	1639	1709	1739	1809	1839	1909	...	1940	2009	2039		0924	1039
Cheltenham Spa 121 d.	1311	1341	1411	1441	1511	1541	1611	1641	...	1711	1741	1813	1841	1911	1941	...	2011	2041	2111		1012	1110
Birmingham New Street 121 a.	1356	1426	1456	1526	1556	1626	1656	1726	...	1756	1826	1856	1926	1958	2026	...	2052	2138	2152		1049	1148
Manchester Piccadilly 122 a.	|	1559	|	1659	|	1759	|	1859	...	|	1959	|	2059	|	2202	...	|	...	...		|	|
Derby 124 a.	1438	...	1540	...	1640	...	1738	...	...	1840	...	1938	...	2040	...	...	2143	...	...		1137	1238
Sheffield 124 a.	1517	...	1618	...	1717	...	1817	...	...	1917	...	2022	...	2119	...	...	2223	...	...		1218	1318
Leeds 124 a.	1601	...	1701	...	1802	...	1901	...	...	2004	...	2104	...	2202	...	...	2325	...	...		1301	1401
York 124 a.	1630	...	1729	...	1830	...	1930	...	...	2030	...	2155	...	...	...	...	...	...	...		1327	1427
Newcastle 124 a.	1729	...	1831	...	1932	...	2028	...	...	2128	...	...	...	...	...	...	...	...	...		1426	1526
Edinburgh Waverley 124 a.	1906	...	2006	...	2108	...	2208	...	...	2257	...	...	...	...	...	...	...	...	...		1602	1656
Glasgow Central 124 a.	2012	...	...	...	2220	...	...	...	...	...	...	...	...	...	...	...	...	...	...		...	1812

	⑦	⑦	⑦	⑦	⑦	⑦		⑦	⑦	⑦	⑦	⑦		⑦	⑦	⑦	⑦	⑦	⑦	⑦		⑦
	B		☆a									d										
Penzance 117 d.	...	...	...	0930	...	...	...	...	...	...	...	1230	...	...	...	...	...	1530	...	...	...	...
Newquay 117 d.	...	...	...	|	...	...	...	...	...	...	...	|	...	...	...	...	...	|	...	...	...	...
Plymouth 115 d.	0925	1025	...	1125	1200	1225	...	1252	1325	...	1425	1435	...	1524	...	1625	...	1725	...	1825	...	...
Totnes 115 d.	0950	1050	...	1150	|	1250	...	|	1351	...	1451	1501	...	1550	...	1650	...	1750	...	1852	...	...
Paignton 115 d.	|	|	1050	|	|	|	...	|	|	...	|	|	...	|	...	|	...	|	1820	|	...	...
Torquay 115 d.	|	|	1056	|	|	|	...	|	|	...	|	|	...	|	...	|	...	|	1826	|	...	...
Newton Abbot 115 d.	1003	1103	1108	1203	1236	1303	...	1327	1404	...	1504	1513	...	1603	...	1703	...	1803	1837	1905	...	...
Exeter St Davids 115 d.	1023	1123	1133	1223	1256	1323	...	1347	1424	...	1524	1532	...	1624	...	1726	...	1823	1858	1925	...	...
Tiverton Parkway 115 d.	1037	1137	1147	1237	1310	1337	...	|	1438	...	1537	1546	...	1637	...	1739	...	1837	1911	1938	...	...
Taunton 120a 115 d.	1050	1152	1200	1250	1323	1350	...	|	1451	...	1551	1559	...	1651	...	1753	...	1850	1924	1952	...	...
Bristol Temple Meads 120a 115 a.	1124	1227	1244	1326	1354	1421	...	1442	1526	...	1626	1647	...	1726	...	1827	...	1922	1957	2025	...	...
Bristol Temple Meads d.	1130	1230	1300	1330	1400	1430	...	1500	1530	1600	1630	1700	...	1730	1800	1830	1900	1930	2000	2030	...	2210
Bristol Parkway d.	1139	1239	1309	1339	1409	1439	...	1509	1540	1609	1640	1709	...	1740	1809	1839	1909	1939	2009	2040	...	2220
Cheltenham Spa 121 d.	1210	1310	1341	1410	1441	1510	...	1540	1611	1640	1712	1741	...	1811	1840	1910	1941	2010	2040	2111	...	2249
Birmingham New Street 121 a.	1249	1348	1427	1448	1527	1548	...	1627	1649	1726	1749	1827	...	1848	1926	1948	2027	2049	2118	2148	...	2340
Manchester Piccadilly 122 a.	|	|	1559	|	1659	|	...	1759	|	1859	|	1959	...	|	2100	|	2200	|	|	|	...	...
Derby 124 a.	1337	1439	...	1537	...	1638	...	...	1740	...	1839	...	...	1940	...	2039	...	2141	...	2240	...	...
Sheffield 124 a.	1417	1517	...	1618	...	1717	...	...	1819	...	1920	...	...	2018	...	2116	...	2218	...	2318	...	...
Leeds 124 a.	1501	1602	...	1701	...	1801	...	...	1904	...	2005	...	...	2107	...	2204	...	2301	...	0008	...	...
York 124 a.	1527	1627	...	1727	...	1827	...	...	1929	...	2030	...	...	2132	...	...	...	...	...	...	...	...
Newcastle 124 a.	1625	1725	...	1825	...	1925	...	...	2031	...	2131	...	...	...	...	...	...	...	...	...	...	...
Edinburgh Waverley 124 a.	1757	1856	...	1957	...	2056	...	...	2212	...	2304	...	...	...	...	...	...	...	...	...	...	...
Glasgow Central 124 a.	...	2019	...	...	...	2213	...	...	...	...	...	...	...	...	...	...	...	...	...	...	...	...

A – To Dundee (Table 222).
B – To Aberdeen (Table 222).
D – From Cardiff Central (Table 121).
E – From Bath Spa (d. 0609).

a – Also calls at Weston-super-Mare (d. 1538 on Ⓐ, 1529 on ⑥, 1221 on ⑦).
b – Also calls at Gloucester (d. 2046).
c – Also calls at Gloucester (d. 0700 on ⑥, 1000 on ⑦).
d – Also calls at Weston-super-Mare (d. 1628).
e – Also calls at Weston-super-Mare (d. 0833).

☆ – Also calls at Teignmouth (7 – 10 minutes after Newton Abbot) and Dawlish (12 – 15 minutes after Newton Abbot).

121 BIRMINGHAM - CARDIFF

AW, XC

km	Station	(Ⓐ)	Ⓐ 2	Ⓐ	Ⓐ	Ⓐ 2	Ⓐ 🍷	Ⓐ 2	Ⓐ		Ⓐ 🍷	Ⓐ 2	Ⓐ 🍷	Ⓐ 2	Ⓐ 🍷	Ⓐ 🍷		Ⓐ 2	Ⓐ 🍷	Ⓐ 2 B	Ⓐ 🍷	Ⓐ 🍷
	Nottingham **123** d.		...	...	...	...	0600	...	0704	...	0812	...	0910	...	1010	1110	...	...	1210	...	1310	1410
	Derby **123** d.		...	...	...	...	0636	...	0736	...	0837	...	0936	...	1037	1137	...	...	1237	...	1337	1436
0	**Birmingham** New Street **120** d.		...	0500	0537	...	0730	...	0830	...	0930	...	1030	...	1130	1230	...	...	1330	...	1430	1530
73	Cheltenham **120** d.		0537	0602	0643	0746	0811	0846	0910	...	1010	1045	1110	1146	1210	1310	...	1345	1410	...	1510	1610
83	Gloucester d.		0550	0614	0701**d**	0758	0825**c**	0858	0925**c**	...	1025**c**	1058	1125**c**	1159	1225**c**	1325**c**	...	1358	1425	1448	1525**c**	1625**c**
115	Lydney 🚂 d.		0609	0633	0720	0817	|	0917	|	...	1044	1117	|	1218	|	1344	...	1417	|	1507	|	1644
127	Chepstow d.		0619	0642	0729	0827	0851	0927	0951	...	|	1127	1151	1228	1251	|	...	1427	1451	1517	1551	1653
138	Caldicot d.		0626	0651	0738	0835	|	0935	|	...	|	1135	|	1236	|	|	...	1435	|	1525	|	|
155	Newport **132 136 149** a.		0641	0705	0752	0850	0912	0951	1011	...	1111	1150	1210	1251	1309	1410	...	1450	1510	1540	1612	1711
174	**Cardiff** Central **132 136 149** a.		0700	0721	0808	0907	0929	1011	1028	...	1128	1212	1226	1308	1326	1426	...	1515	1530	1558	1630	1730

Station	Ⓐ 2	Ⓐ 🍷	Ⓐ 2	Ⓐ	Ⓐ 2	Ⓐ	Ⓐ A	Ⓐ 2	Ⓐ	Ⓐ	Ⓐ 2	⑤ 2	(⑥)	⑥ 2	⑥	⑥	⑥ 2	⑥ 🍷		⑥ 2	⑥	⑥ 🍷
Nottingham **123** d.	...	1510	...	1610	...	1710	...	...	1810	1910	...	...		...	...	...	...	0558	...	...	0658	0809
Derby **123** d.	...	1537	...	1637	...	1737	...	...	1837	1937	*2129*	...		...	...	...	...	0636	...	...	0736	0837
Birmingham New Street **120** d.	...	1630	...	1730	...	1830	1842	...	1930	2030	*2212*	2300		...	0500	0542	...	0730	...	...	0830	0930
Cheltenham **120** d.	1645	1714	1745	1817	1845	1913	1925	1945	2011	2110	2300	0008		...	0603	0642	0745	0810	...	0845	0910	1010
Gloucester d.	1658	1725	1758	1831	1900	1925	|	1958	2025**c**	2121	2313	0019		0550	0614	0657**c**	0758	0822	...	0858	0922	1022
Lydney 🚂 d.	1717	1744	1817	|	1920	|	|	2017	|	2140	2333	...		0609	0633	0716	0817	|	...	0917	|	1041
Chepstow d.	1727	|	1827	|	1929	|	|	2027	|	2149	2342	...		0619	0642	0726	0827	0848	...	0927	0948	|
Caldicot d.	1735	|	1835	|	1937	|	|	2035	|	2158	2351	...		0627	0651	0734	0835	|	...	0935	|	|
Newport **132 136 149** a.	1750	1811	1849	1914	1953	2011	2047	2050	2110	2212	0006	...		0642	0705	0748	0850	0906	...	0950	1005	1106
Cardiff Central **132 136 149** a.	1810	1828	1909	1933	2012	2028	2103	2110	2128	2235**a**	0025	...		0703	0721	0804	0910	0925	...	1009	1021	1124

Station	⑥ 2	⑥ 🍷	⑥ 2	⑥ 🍷	⑥ 🍷		⑥ 2	⑥ 🍷	⑥ B	⑥ 🍷		⑥ 🍷	⑥ 2	⑥ 🍷	⑥ 2	⑥	⑥ 2	⑥	⑥ A	⑥ 2	⑥	⑥
Nottingham **123** d.	...	0910	...	1010	1110	...	...	1210	...	1310	...	1410	...	1510	...	1610	...	1710	...	...	1810	1910
Derby **123** d.	...	0936	...	1037	1137	...	...	1237	...	1337	...	1437	...	1537	...	1637	...	1737	...	...	1837	1937
Birmingham New Street **120** d.	...	1030	...	1130	1230	...	...	1330	...	1430	...	1530	...	1630	...	1730	...	1830	1842	...	1930	2030
Cheltenham **120** d.	1045	1110	1146	1210	1310	...	1345	1410	...	1510	...	1610	1645	1710	1745	1816	1845	1910	1925	1945	2010	2110
Gloucester d.	1058	1122	1158	1222	1322	...	1358	1422	1442	1522	...	1622	1658	1722	1758	1827	1858	1922	|	1958	2022	2121
Lydney 🚂 d.	1117	|	1217	|	1341	...	1417	|	1501	|	...	1641	1717	1741	1817	|	1917	|	|	2017	|	2140
Chepstow d.	1127	1148	1227	1248	|	...	1427	1449	1511	1548	...	1651	1727	|	1827	|	1927	|	|	2027	|	2150
Caldicot d.	1135	|	1235	|	|	...	1435	|	1519	|	...	|	1735	|	1835	|	1934	|	|	2035	|	2158
Newport **132 136 149** a.	1150	1205	1250	1305	1406	...	1450	1509	1535	1606	...	1708	1750	1806	1850	1910	1950	2003	2044	2050	2109	2217
Cardiff Central **132 136 149** a.	1206	1223	1307	1321	1422	...	1509	1526	1553	1625	...	1724	1810	1824	1912	1930	2011	2020	2100	2109	2126	2242

Station	⑥ 🍷	⑥ 2	(⑦)	⑦ 2	⑦ 🍷	⑦ 🍷	⑦ 2	⑦ 🍷	⑦ 🍷	⑦ 2	⑦ 🍷		⑦ 🍷	⑦ 2	⑦	⑦ 🍷	⑦ 2	⑦ 🍷	⑦ 🍷	⑦ 2	⑦ 🍷	⑦ 2
Nottingham **123** d.	...	...		...	...	0954	...	1111	1210	...	1310	...	1410	...	1510	1610	...	1710	1810	...	...	...
Derby **123** d.	2028	...		...	...	1018	...	1136	1236	...	1338	...	1434	...	1534	1634	...	1735	1835	...	2027	...
Birmingham New Street **120** d.	2112	...		...	1012	1112	...	1230	1330	...	1430	...	1530	...	1630	1730	...	1830	1930	...	2112	...
Cheltenham **120** d.	2151	...		...	1052	1152	1219	1310	1410	1419	1510	...	1610	1619	1711	1810	1835	1912	2010	2019	2152	...
Gloucester d.	2200	2309		1048	1105	1205	1232	1323	1424**c**	1433	1523	...	1623	1637**c**	1723	1823	1848	1928	2022	2033	2202	2233
Lydney 🚂 d.	...	2328		1107	|	|	1251	|	|	1452	|	...	|	1656	|	|	1907	|	|	2052	...	2252
Chepstow d.	...	2338		1117	|	|	1301	|	|	1502	|	...	|	1707	|	|	1917	|	|	2102	...	2302
Caldicot d.	...	2346		1125	|	|	1309	|	|	1510	|	...	|	1713	|	|	1925	|	|	2110	...	2309
Newport **132 136 149** a.	...	0011		1139	1147	1244	1324	1406	1501	1525	1606	...	1704	1729	1806	1906	1950	2006	2106	2125	...	2330
Cardiff Central **132 136 149** a.	...	0035		1204	1209	1307	1348	1427	1528	1550	1629	...	1726	1752	1829	1927	2014	2030	2127	2148	...	2351

Station	(Ⓐ)	Ⓐ C	Ⓐ 2	Ⓐ	Ⓐ 2	Ⓐ A	Ⓐ		Ⓐ	Ⓐ 2	Ⓐ 🍷	Ⓐ 2	Ⓐ		Ⓐ 🍷	Ⓐ 2	Ⓐ 🍷	Ⓐ 2	Ⓐ 🍷	Ⓐ 🍷	Ⓐ 2	Ⓐ 🍷
Cardiff Central **132 136 149** d.		...	0612	0640	0705	0700	0745	...	0845	0912	0945	1009	1045	...	1145	1212	1245	1312	1345	1445	1512	1545
Newport **132 136 149** d.		...	0628	0655	0723	0715	0802	...	0900	0927	1000	1027	1100	...	1200	1228	1301	1326	1400	1500	1528	1600
Caldicot d.		...	0641	0708	0738	|	|	...	|	0939	|	1040	|	...	|	1242	|	1340	|	|	1541	|
Chepstow d.		...	0650	0716	0749	|	|	...	0918	0948	1018	1049	|	...	1218	1251	1318	1349	|	1518	1550	1618
Lydney 🚂 d.		...	0659	0725	0758	|	0825	...	|	0957	|	1058	1125	...	|	1300	|	1358	1425	|	1559	|
Gloucester d.		0710	0722	0746	0821	|	0849**c**	...	0950**c**	1020	1050**c**	1121	1150**c**	...	1248**c**	1322	1350**c**	1420	1450**c**	1550**c**	1622	1650**c**
Cheltenham **120** d.		0721	0733	0757	0832	0840	0900	...	1001	1031	1101	1132	1201	...	1258	1333	1401	...	1501	1601	1631	1701
Birmingham New Street **120** a.		0816	*0826*	0845	...	0926	0945	...	1045	...	1145	...	1245	...	1345	...	1445	...	1545	1645	...	1745
Derby **123** a.		...	...	0934	...	...	1034	...	1134	...	1234	...	1334	...	1434	...	1534	...	1634	1734	...	1834
Nottingham **123** a.		...	...	1003	...	...	1103	...	1203	...	1303	...	1403	...	1503	...	1603	...	1703	1803	...	1903

Station	Ⓐ 2	Ⓐ 🍷		Ⓐ 2	Ⓐ 🍷	Ⓐ 2	Ⓐ 🍷	Ⓐ	Ⓐ	Ⓐ 2	Ⓐ	Ⓐ 2	(⑥)	⑥	⑥ C	⑥ 2	⑥	⑥ 2	⑥ A	⑥	⑥	⑥ 2
Cardiff Central **132 136 149** d.	1610	1645	...	1712	1745	1808	1845	1950	2105	2112	2150	2320		...	...	0610	0640	0707	0700	0745	0845	0910
Newport **132 136 149** d.	1627	1700	...	1728	1800	1824	1900	2005	2121	2127	2205	2338		...	...	0626	0655	0723	0715	0800	0900	0925
Caldicot d.	1640	|	...	1741	|	1837	|	2018	|	2140	|	0001		...	...	0640	0708	0736	|	|	|	0937
Chepstow d.	1649	|	...	1750	1818	1846	1917	2026	|	2149	|	0010		...	...	0649	0716	0745	|	|	0918	0947
Lydney 🚂 d.	1658	1725	...	1759	|	1855	|	2035	|	2158	|	0019		...	...	0658	0725	0754	|	0825	|	0955
Gloucester d.	1723**c**	1750**c**	...	1821	1846	1921**c**	1945	2059**c**	2204	2223	2247	0039		0700	0707	0721	0746	0822	|	0850**c**	0950**c**	1021
Cheltenham **120** d.	1732	1801	...	1830	1857	1931	1957	2111	2215	2234	2258	...		0711	0718	0732	0757	0833	0841	0901	1001	1032
Birmingham New Street **120** a.	...	1845	...	...	1945	...	2040	2151	2305	...	2359	...		0756	0808	...	0845	...	0926	0945	1045	...
Derby **123** a.	...	1934	...	...	2034	...	2132	...	...	...	...	...		0841	...	...	0934	...	...	1034	1134	...
Nottingham **123** a.	...	2004	...	...	2103	...	2208	...	...	...	...	...		...	...	...	1003	...	...	1103	1203	...

Station	⑥ 🍷	⑥ 2	⑥		⑥ 🍷	⑥ 2	⑥ 🍷	⑥ 2 🍷	⑥ 🍷	⑥ 🍷	⑥ 2	⑥ 🍷	⑥ 2	⑥ 🍷	⑥ 2	⑥ 🍷	⑥ 2	⑥ 🍷	⑥	⑥	⑥ 2	⑥ 2
Cardiff Central **132 136 149** d.	0945	1010	1045	...	1145	1209	1245	1312	1345	1445	1508	1545	1608	1645	1709	1745	1807	1845	2000	2050	2111	2318
Newport **132 136 149** d.	1000	1027	1100	...	1200	1227	1300	1327	1400	1500	1527	1600	1623	1700	1725	1800	1827	1900	2015	2105	2127	2337
Caldicot d.	|	1040	|	...	|	1240	|	1341	|	|	1538	|	1637	|	1738	|	1840	|	2028	|	2140	2359
Chepstow d.	1018	1049	|	...	1218	1249	1318	1350	|	1518	1547	1618	1646	|	1747	1818	1849	1918	2036	|	2149	0008
Lydney 🚂 d.	|	1058	1125	...	|	1258	|	1359	1425	|	1556	|	1655	1725	1756	|	1858	|	2045	|	2158	0017
Gloucester d.	1050	1122	1150**c**	...	1248**c**	1322	1350**c**	1420	1450**c**	1550**c**	1621	1650**c**	1720	1750**c**	1824**c**	1846	1921	1946	2107	2149	2219	0037
Cheltenham **120** d.	1101	1132	1201	...	1259	1332	1401	...	1501	1601	1632	1701	1730	1801	1833	1857	1931	1957	2118	2200	...	...
Birmingham New Street **120** a.	1145	...	1245	...	1345	...	1445	...	1545	1645	...	1745	...	1845	...	1945	...	2042	2207	2242	...	...
Derby **123** a.	1235	...	1334	...	1434	...	1535	...	1634	1734	...	1835	...	1932	...	2034	...	2133	2253	...	...	...
Nottingham **123** a.	1303	...	1403	...	1503	...	1603	...	1703	1803	...	1903	...	2004	...	2103	...	2208	2327	...	...	...

Station	(⑦)	⑦ 2	⑦ 🍷	⑦ 🍷	⑦ 2	⑦ 🍷	⑦ 🍷		⑦ 2	⑦ 🍷	⑦ 🍷	⑦ 2	⑦ 🍷		⑦ 🍷	⑦ 2	⑦ 🍷		⑦ D	⑦ 2	⑦	⑦ 2
Cardiff Central **132 136 149** d.		1030	1045	1145	1225	1245	1345	...	1425	1445	1545	1623	1645	...	1745	1824	1845	...	1945	2024	2045	2226
Newport **132 136 149** d.		1048	1106	1205	1247	1305	1405	...	1445	1505	1605	1645	1703	...	1804	1846	1903	...	2003	2045	2105	2246
Caldicot d.		1102	|	|	1258	|	|	...	1500	|	|	1700	|	...	|	1859	|	...	|	2059	|	2259
Chepstow d.		1111	|	|	1307	|	|	...	1509	|	|	1709	|	...	|	1908	|	...	|	2108	|	2308
Lydney 🚂 d.		1120	|	|	1316	|	|	...	1518	|	|	1718	|	...	|	1917	|	...	|	2117	|	2317
Gloucester d.		1142	1150	1248	1340**c**	1348	1448	...	1540	1548	1648	1740	1748	...	1848	1942**c**	1950	...	2049	2142	2148	2339
Cheltenham **120** d.		1153	1201	1258	1349	1358	1458	...	1550	1558	1658	1750	1758	...	1858	1953	2000	...	2100	...	2159	...
Birmingham New Street **120** a.		...	1243	1341	...	1441	1541	...	...	1641	1741	...	1841	...	1941	...	2043	...	2144	...	2242	...
Derby **123** a.		...	1333	1434	...	1533	1634	...	...	1733	1833	...	1933	...	2034	...	2133	...	*2240*	...	...	...
Nottingham **123** a.		...	1400	1500	...	1600	1700	...	...	1800	1900	...	2000	...	2100	...	2200	...	...	...	...	...

A – 🚃12 Manchester Piccadilly - Bristol Temple Meads - Cardiff Central and v.v. (Tables **120** / **122**).
B – 🚃2 🍷 Gloucester - Fishguard Harbour (Table **135**).
C – 🚃12 Gloucester - Stansted Airport (Table **208**).
D – 🚃12 Cardiff - Leicester (Table **208**).

a – Arrives 2230 on ⑤.
c – Arrives 4 – 6 minutes earlier.
d – Arrives 8 minutes earlier.

🚂 – DEAN FOREST RAILWAY (Lydney Junction - Parkend. 7 *km*). ✆ 01594 845840. www.deanforestrailway.co.uk. Lydney Junction station is 10 minutes walk from the National Rail station.

XC — Most services convey 🍸 — BIRMINGHAM - MANCHESTER — 122

km			Ⓐ	Ⓐ	Ⓐ	Ⓐ	Ⓐ	Ⓐ	Ⓐ	Ⓐ	Ⓐ	Ⓐ	Ⓐ	Ⓐ	Ⓐ	Ⓐ	Ⓐ	Ⓐ	Ⓐ	Ⓐ	Ⓐ	Ⓐ	Ⓐ	Ⓐ
										A												H		
	Bournemouth **119** d.	Ⓐ	...	...	...	...	...	...	...	...	0630	...	0730	...	0845	...	0945	...	1045	...	1145	...	1245	...
	Southampton Central **119** d.		...	...	...	...	0515	...	0615	...	0715	...	0815	...	0916	...	1017	...	1117	...	1217	...	1316	...
	Reading **119** d.		...	...	...	...	0615	...	0715	...	0815	...	0915	...	1015	...	1115	...	1215	...	1315	...	1415	...
	Paignton **120** d.		...	...	...	...	|	...	|	...	|	0702	|	...	|	...	|	1007	|	...	|	...	|	...
	Exeter St Davids **120** d.		...	...	...	...	|	...	|	...	|	0745	|	...	|	...	|	1050	|	...	|	1250	|	...
	Bristol T Meads **120** d.		...	...	...	...	|	0700	|	0800	|	0900	|	1000	|	1100	|	1200	|	1300	|	1400	|	1500
0	**Birmingham** New Street **150** d.		0557	0622	0657	0731	0757	0831	0857	0931	0957	1031	1057	1131	1157	1231	1257	1331	1357	1431	1457	1531	1557	1631
20	Wolverhampton **150** d.		0616	0641	0715	0750	0815	0849	0915	0949	1015	1049	1115	1149	1215	1249	1315	1349	1415	1449	1515	1549	1615	1649
46	Stafford **150** d.		0632	0655	0731	0802	0833	0902	0928	1002	1028	1102	1128	1202	1228	1302	1328	1402	1428	1502	1528	1603	1628	1702
72	Stoke on Trent **150** d.		0651	0714	|	0820	0854	0920	0944	1020	1044	1120	1144	1220	1244	1320	1344	1420	1444	1520	1544	1620	1644	1720
104	Macclesfield **150** d.		0712	0731	|	0837	0911	|	1002	|	1102	|	1202	|	1302	|	1402	|	1502	|	1602	|	1702	|
123	Stockport **150** d.		0726	0750	0824	0850	0927	0950	1014	1050	1114	1150	1214	1250	1314	1350	1414	1450	1514	1550	1614	1650	1714	1751
132	**Manchester** Piccadilly **150** a.		0734	0800	0834	0859	0939	0959	1026	1059	1126	1159	1226	1259	1326	1359	1426	1459	1526	1559	1626	1659	1726	1800

	Ⓐ	Ⓐ	Ⓐ	Ⓐ	Ⓐ	Ⓐ	Ⓐ	Ⓐ	Ⓐ	Ⓐ	①–④	Ⓐ	①–④		⑥	⑥	⑥	⑥	⑥	⑥	⑥	⑥	⑥	⑥
										a	b	a	b									A		
Bournemouth **119** d.	1345	...	1445	...	1545	...	1645	...	1745	1845	1845	...	...	⑥	...	...	...	...	...	...	...	...	0637	...
Southampton Central **119** d.	1417	...	1516	...	1617	...	1717	...	1815	1916	1916	...	...		...	...	...	...	0509	...	0620	...	0720	...
Reading **119** d.	1515	...	1615	...	1715	...	1815	...	1915	2015	2015	...	...		...	...	...	...	0615	...	0715	...	0815	...
Paignton **120** d.	|	1404	|	...	|	...	|	...	|	|	|	...	...		...	...	...	...	|	...	|	...	|	0702
Exeter St Davids **120** d.	|	1448	|	...	|	1654	|	...	|	|	|	...	...		...	...	...	...	|	...	|	...	|	0745
Bristol T Meads **120** d.	|	1600	|	1700	|	1800	|	1900	|	|	|	...	...		...	...	...	...	|	0700	|	0800	|	0900
Birmingham New Street **150** d.	1657	1731	1757	1831	1857	1931	1957	2031	2057	2157	2157	2230	2230		0557	0631	0657	0731	0757	0831	0857	0931	0957	1031
Wolverhampton **150** d.	1715	1749	1815	1849	1915	1949	2015	2049	2116	2215	2226	2248	2259		0615	0649	0715	0749	0815	0849	0915	0949	1015	1049
Stafford **150** d.	1728	1802	1828	1902	1928	2002	2028	2102	2129	2228	2239	2301	2314		0628	0702	0731	0802	0828	0902	0928	1002	1028	1102
Stoke on Trent **150** d.	1744	1820	1844	1920	1944	2020	2044	2119	2146	2244	2256	2320	2332		0645	0720	|	0820	0844	0920	0944	1020	1044	1120
Macclesfield **150** d.	1802	|	1902	|	2002	|	2102	|	2203	2302	2313	|	|		0706	0737	|	0837	0902	|	1002	|	1102	|
Stockport **150** d.	1815	1850	1914	1951	2014	2049	2114	2149	2216	2316	2328	|	|		0719	0750	0816	0850	0914	0950	1014	1050	1114	1150
Manchester Piccadilly **150** a.	1825	1859	1924	1959	2026	2058	2126	2200	2227	2326	2339	0011	0026		0728	0759	0829	0859	0926	0959	1026	1059	1126	1159

	⑥	⑥	⑥	⑥	⑥	⑥	⑥	⑥	⑥	⑥	⑥	⑥	⑥	⑥	⑥	⑥	⑥	⑥	⑥	⑥		⑥	⑥	⑥
										H														
Bournemouth **119** d.	0747	...	0847	...	0947	...	1047	...	1147	...	1247	...	1347	...	1447	...	1547	...	1647	...	...	1747	1847	...
Southampton Central **119** d.	0820	...	0918	...	1017	...	1120	...	1220	...	1318	...	1420	...	1518	...	1620	...	1720	...	...	1820	1920	...
Reading **119** d.	0912	...	1015	...	1115	...	1215	...	1315	...	1415	...	1515	...	1615	...	1715	...	1815	...	...	1915	2015	...
Paignton **120** d.	|	...	|	...	|	1006	|	...	|	...	|	...	|	1355	|	...	|	...	|	...	...	|	|	...
Exeter St Davids **120** d.	|	...	|	...	|	1049	|	...	|	1248	|	...	|	1437	|	...	|	1653	|	...	...	|	|	...
Bristol T Meads **120** d.	|	1000	|	1100	|	1200	|	1300	|	1400	|	1500	|	1600	|	1700	|	1800	|	1900	...	|	|	...
Birmingham New Street **150** d.	1057	1131	1157	1231	1257	1331	1357	1431	1457	1531	1557	1631	1657	1731	1757	1831	1857	1931	1957	2031	...	2057	2157	2231
Wolverhampton **150** d.	1115	1149	1215	1249	1315	1349	1415	1449	1515	1549	1615	1649	1715	1749	1815	1849	1915	1949	2015	2049	...	2117	2215	2249
Stafford **150** d.	1128	1202	1228	1302	1328	1402	1428	1502	1528	1602	1628	1702	1728	1802	1828	1902	1928	2002	2028	2102	...	2130	2228	2302
Stoke on Trent **150** d.	1144	1220	1244	1320	1344	1420	1444	1520	1544	1620	1644	1720	1744	1820	1844	1920	1944	2020	2044	2120	...	2147	2244	2320
Macclesfield **150** d.	1202	|	1302	|	1402	|	1502	|	1602	|	1702	|	1802	|	1902	|	2002	2037	2102	2138	...	2205	2302	2339
Stockport **150** d.	1214	1250	1314	1350	1414	1450	1514	1550	1614	1650	1714	1750	1814	1850	1914	1950	2014	2050	2114	2153	...	2221	2314	2354
Manchester Piccadilly **150** a.	1226	1259	1326	1359	1426	1459	1526	1559	1626	1659	1726	1759	1826	1859	1925	1959	2026	2059	2126	2202	...	2233	2329	0010

		⑦	⑦	⑦	⑦	⑦	⑦	⑦	⑦	⑦	⑦		⑦	⑦	⑦	⑦	⑦	⑦	⑦	⑦	⑦	⑦	⑦	⑦
											F			F				H						
Bournemouth **119** d.	⑦	...	...	...	...	0940	...	1040	...	1140	...	...	1240	...	1340	...	1440	...	1540	...	1640	...	1740	1840
Southampton Central **119** d.		...	...	...	0915	1015	...	1115	...	1215	...	...	1315	...	1415	...	1515	...	1615	...	1715	...	1815	1915
Reading **119** d.		...	...	0912	1011	1111	...	1211	...	1311	...	...	1411	...	1511	...	1611	...	1711	...	1811	...	1911	2011
Paignton **120** d.		...	...	|	|	|	...	|	1050	|	...	...	|	...	|	...	|	...	|	...	|	...	|	|
Exeter St Davids **120** d.		...	...	|	|	|	...	|	1133	|	1256	...	|	1347	|	...	|	1532	|	...	|	...	|	|
Bristol T Meads **120** d.		...	...	|	|	|	...	|	1300	|	1400	...	|	1500	|	1600	|	1700	|	1800	|	1900	|	|
Birmingham New Street **150** d.		0901	1001	1101	1157	1257	1331	1357	1431	1457	1531	...	1557	1631	1657	1731	1757	1831	1857	1931	1957	2031	2057	2157
Wolverhampton **150** d.		0919	1019	1119	1216	1316	1349	1415	1449	1515	1549	...	1615	1649	1715	1749	1815	1849	1915	1949	2015	2053	2117	2215
Stafford **150** d.		0933	1033	1132	1229	1329	1402	1428	1502	1528	1602	...	1628	1702	1729	1802	1828	1902	1928	2002	2028	2106	2130	2228
Stoke on Trent **150** d.		|	1052	1152	1246	1345	1420	1445	1521	1545	1619	...	1645	1721	1746	1821	1847	1921	1947	2021	2045	2122	2146	2245
Macclesfield **150** d.		|	1109	1210	1305	1405	|	1502	|	1605	|	...	1705	|	1805	|	1905	|	2005	|	2103	|	2204	2302
Stockport **150** d.		1026	1123	1230	1317	1417	1451	1515	1550	1617	1650	...	1717	1750	1817	1850	1918	1950	2017	2050	2115	2151	2216	2315
Manchester Piccadilly **150** a.		1037	1133	1241	1329	1429	1500	1524	1559	1629	1659	...	1730	1759	1829	1859	1928	1959	2028	2100	2129	2200	2226	2324

		Ⓐ	Ⓐ	Ⓐ	Ⓐ	Ⓐ	Ⓐ	Ⓐ	Ⓐ	Ⓐ	Ⓐ	Ⓐ	Ⓐ	Ⓐ	Ⓐ	Ⓐ	Ⓐ	Ⓐ	Ⓐ	Ⓐ	Ⓐ	Ⓐ	Ⓐ	Ⓐ
Manchester Piccadilly **150** d.	Ⓐ	0511	0600	0627	0707	0727	0807	0827	0907	0927	1007	1027	1107	1127	1207	1227	1307	1327	1407	1427	1507	1527	1607	1627
Stockport **150** d.		|	0608	0635	0716	0736	0816	0836	0916	0935	1016	1036	1116	1136	1216	1236	1316	1336	1416	1436	1516	1536	1616	1636
Macclesfield **150** d.		|	|	0648	|	0749	|	0849	|	0949	|	1049	|	1149	|	1249	|	1349	|	1449	|	1549	|	1649
Stoke on Trent **150** d.		0607	|	0706	0744	0807	0844	0907	0944	1007	1045	1107	1144	1207	1244	1307	1344	1407	1444	1507	1544	1607	1644	1707
Stafford **150** d.		0625	0700	0724	0801	0825	0902	0925	1000	1025	1102	1125	1201	1225	1301	1325	1401	1425	1501	1525	1603	1625	1702	1725
Wolverhampton **150** d.		0641	0716	0745	0816	0841	0916	0942	1017	1041	1116	1141	1216	1241	1317	1341	1417	1441	1517	1541	1617	1641	1717	1741
Birmingham New Street **150** a.		0657	0733	0807	0833	0858	0933	0958	1033	1058	1133	1158	1233	1258	1333	1358	1433	1458	1533	1558	1633	1658	1733	1758
Bristol T Meads **120** a.		|	0910	...	1008	|	1110	|	1205	|	1307	|	1408	|	1510	|	1611	|	1710	|	1807	|	1906	|
Exeter St Davids **120** a.		|	...	...	...	|	1224	|	...	|	...	|	...	|	1612	|	...	|	1811	|	...	|	...	|
Paignton **120** a.		|	...	...	...	|	1308	|	...	|	...	|	...	|	...	|	...	|	1855	|	...	|	...	|
Reading **119** a.		0840	...	...	...	1041	...	1140	...	1241	...	1340	...	1440	...	1541	...	1640	...	1740	...	1842	...	1940
Southampton Central **119** a.		0943	...	...	...	1143	...	1241	...	1341	...	1441	...	1541	...	1641	...	1741	...	1843	...	1940	...	2041
Bournemouth **119** a.		1013	...	...	...	1213	...	1311	...	1411	...	1511	...	1611	...	1711	...	1815	...	1912	...	2011	...	2115

	Ⓐ	Ⓐ	Ⓐ	Ⓐ	Ⓐ	Ⓐ	Ⓐ	Ⓐ	Ⓐ	①–④	Ⓐ	①–④		⑥	⑥	⑥	⑥	⑥	⑥	⑥	⑥	⑥	⑥	⑥
	A		F						a	b	a	b												
Manchester Piccadilly **150** d.	1705	1727	1805	1827	1907	1927	2007	2027	2127	2127	2207	2207	⑥	0511	0600	0707	0727	0807	0827	0907	0927	1007	1027	1107
Stockport **150** d.	1714	1735	1813	1836	1916	1936	2017	2036	2136	2136	2216	2216		|	0608	0716	0736	0816	0836	0916	0937	1016	1036	1116
Macclesfield **150** d.	1728	|	1826	|	|	1949	|	2049	2149	2149	2229	2229		|	0621	|	0749	|	0849	|	0950	|	1049	|
Stoke on Trent **150** d.	1745	|	1844	1907	1944	2007	2045	2107	2206	2206	2246	2246		0608	0640	0744	0807	0844	0907	0944	1008	1044	1107	1144
Stafford **150** d.	1802	1825	1901	1925	2001	2025	2102	2125	2224	2224	2303	2303		0626	0700	0801	0825	0901	0925	1001	1025	1101	1125	1201
Wolverhampton **150** d.	1816	1841	1917	1941	2017	2044	2116	2141c	2241	2241	2316	2316		0641	0716	0817	0841	0917	0941	1017	1041	1117	1141	1217
Birmingham New Street **150** a.	1833	1858	1933	1958	2033	2100	2132	2200	2259	2312	2336	2343		0657	0733	0833	0858	0933	0958	1033	1058	1133	1159	1233
Bristol T Meads **120** a.	2009	|	2105	|	2214	|	...	...	...	...	...	...		|	0906	1004	|	1109	|	1204	|	1307	|	1405
Exeter St Davids **120** a.	...	|	2209	|	...	|	...	...	...	...	...	...		|	...	...	|	1225	|	...	|	...	|	...
Paignton **120** a.	...	|	...	|	...	|	...	...	...	...	...	...		|	...	...	|	1310	|	...	|	...	|	...
Reading **119** a.	...	2041	...	2142	...	2242	...	...	...	...	...	...		0841	...	...	1041	...	1138	...	1241	...	1340	...
Southampton Central **119** a.	...	2140	...	2242	...	2343	...	...	...	...	...	...		0940	...	...	1141	...	1241	...	1341	...	1441	...
Bournemouth **119** a.	...	2215	...	2319	...	...	...	...	...	...	...	...		1011	...	...	1212	...	1312	...	1412	...	1512	...

A – From / to Cardiff (Table **121**).
F – To / from Plymouth (Table **120**).
H – From Penzance (Tables **117** and **120**).

a – Until Feb. 10 and from Mar. 24 (also on ⑤ Feb. 17 - Mar. 17).
b – Feb. 13 - Mar. 23.
c – Not ①–④ Feb. 13 - Mar. 23.

122 — MANCHESTER - BIRMINGHAM

Most services convey 🍴   XC

	⑥	⑥	⑥	⑥	⑥	⑥	⑥	⑥	⑥	⑥	⑥ A	⑥	⑥ G	⑥	⑥	⑥	⑥	⑥	⑥	⑥	⑥	⑦	⑦	⑦
Manchester Piccadilly 150 d.	1127	1207	1227	1307	1327	1407	1427	1507	1527	1607	1627	1706	1727	1805	1827	1907	1927	2007	2027	2107	2127	⑦	0827	0927
Stockport 150 d.	1136	1216	1236	1316	1336	1416	1436	1516	1536	1616	1636	1715	1736	1813	1836	1916	1936	2016	2035	...	2135		0836	0936
Macclesfield 150 d.	1149	|	1249	|	1349	|	1449	|	1549	|	1649	1727	|	1826	|	1949	|	2049	|	2149				0949
Stoke on Trent 150 d.	1207	1244	1307	1344	1407	1444	1507	1544	1607	1644	1707	1745	1807	1844	1907	1944	2007	2045	2107	2144	2207			1007
Stafford 150 d.	1225	1301	1325	1401	1425	1501	1525	1601	1625	1701	1725	1801	1825	1901	1925	2001	2025	2102	2125	2202	2230		0926	1025
Wolverhampton 150 d.	1241	1317	1341	1417	1441	1517	1541	1617	1641	1717	1741	1817	1841	1917	1941	2017	2041	2115	2142	2217	2245		0941	1041
Birmingham New Street 150 a.	1258	1333	1358	1433	1458	1533	1558	1633	1658	1733	1758	1833	1858	1933	1959	2033	2058	2131	2159	2233	2301		0957	1057
Bristol T Meads 120 a.		1509		1607		1707		1807		1904		2005		2104		2212								
Exeter St Davids 120 a.		1609				1805								2208										
Paignton 120 a.						1849																		
Reading 119 a.	1441	...	1540	...	1641	...	1739	...	1841	...	1941	...	2041	...	2142	...	2245	...					1140	1240
Southampton Central 119 a.	1541	...	1641	...	1741	...	1841	...	1941	...	2041	...	2140	...	2242	...	2341	...					1242	1342
Bournemouth 119 a.	1612	...	1712	...	1812	...	1912	...	2012	...	2112	...	2215	...	2318	...							1326	1426

	⑦	⑦	⑦	⑦	⑦	⑦	⑦	⑦	⑦	⑦	⑦	⑦ G	⑦	⑦	⑦	⑦	⑦	⑦	⑦	⑦	⑦
Manchester Piccadilly 150 d.	1027	1127	1226	1307	...	1327	1407	1427	1507	...	1527	1607	1627	...	1727	1807	1827	1907	...	1927	2007	2107	2207
Stockport 150 d.	1036	1136	1235	1316	...	1336	1416	1436	1516	...	1536	1616	1636	...	1716	1736	1816	1836	1916	...	1936	2016	2116	2216
Macclesfield 150 d.	1049	1149	1249	|	...	1349	|	1449	|	...	1549	|	1649	...	1749	|	1849	|	...	1949	2029	2129	2229
Stoke on Trent 150 d.	1107	1207	1307	1344	...	1407	1444	1507	1544	...	1607	1644	1707	...	1744	1807	1844	1907	1944	...	2007	2047	2147	2247
Stafford 150 d.	1127	1225	1325	1401	...	1425	1501	1525	1601	...	1625	1701	1725	...	1801	1825	1901	1925	2001	...	2025	2104	2204	2304
Wolverhampton 150 d.	1142	1241	1341	1415	...	1441	1517	1541	1615	...	1641	1715	1741	...	1815	1841	1915	1941	2015	...	2041	2117	2222	2319
Birmingham New Street 150 a.	1158	1257	1357	1431	...	1457	1531	1557	1631	...	1657	1731	1757	...	1831	1857	1931	1957	2031	...	2057	2133	2240	2336
Bristol T Meads 120 a.		|	1611		1708		1814		1908		2014		2106		2210				2302	
Exeter St Davids 120 a.		|	1709										2127							
Paignton 120 a.		|	1756																	
Reading 119 a.	1341	1440	1540	...	1640	...	1739	...	1840	1939	...	2040	...	2140	...	2238
Southampton Central 119 a.	1442	1542	1642	...	1740	...	1842	...	1940	2041	...	2142	...	2242
Bournemouth 119 a.	1526	1626	1726	...	1826	...	1926	...	2026	2126	...	2226

A – To Cardiff (Table 121).   G – To Plymouth (Table 120).

123 — BIRMINGHAM - NOTTINGHAM

XC

km		Ⓐ	Ⓐ	Ⓐ	Ⓐ	Ⓐ	Ⓐ	Ⓐ	Ⓐ	Ⓐ		Ⓐ	Ⓐ	Ⓐ		⑥	⑥	⑥	⑥	⑥
	Cardiff Central 121 d.	Ⓐ	...	...	...	...	...	0640	...	0745	and at	1745	1845	1950		⑥	...	...	...	...	...
0	Birmingham New Street d.		0619	0649	0719	0749	0819	0849	0919	0949	the same	1919	1949	2049	2203	2309		0619	0649	0719	0749	0819
28	Tamworth d.		0639	0707	0739	0807	0836	0909	0936	1007	minutes	1936	2009	2109	2227	2328		0639	0707	0739	0807	0836
48	Burton-on-Trent d.		0651	0720	0750	0819	0848	0921	0948	1019	past each	1948	2021	2121	2239	2340		0651	0719	0750	0819	0848
67	Derby a.		0704	0735	0805	0836	0900	0934	1000	1034	hour until	2000	2034	2132	2251	2353		0703	0734	0805	0835	0900
67	Derby d.		0708	0743	0810	0840	0908	0940	1008	1040		2008	2040	2138	2259	2357		0709	0740	0809	0840	0908
93	Nottingham a.		0738	0809	0834	0906	0928	1003	1028	1103		2028	2103	2208	2327	0016		0738	0806	0834	0906	0928

	⑥	⑥	⑥	⑥		⑥	⑥	⑥	⑥	⑥	⑥		⑦	⑦	⑦	⑦	⑦	⑦	⑦	⑦	⑦	⑦	⑦
Cardiff Central 121 d.	0640	...	0745	...	and at	1645	...	1745	1845	2000	...	⑦	...	...	...	...	...	...	...	...	...	...	1945
Birmingham New Street d.	0849	0919	0949	1019	the same	1849	1919	1949	2049	2210	2249		1149	1249	1349	1449	1549	1649	1749	1849	1949	2049	2203
Tamworth d.	0909	0936	1007	1036	minutes	1909	1936	2009	2227	2308			1207	1307	1407	1509	1607	1707	1807	1909	2007	2106	2219
Burton-on-Trent d.	0921	0948	1019	1048	past each	1921	1948	2021	2121	2239	2320		1219	1319	1419	1521	1619	1719	1819	1921	2019	2119	
Derby a.	0934	1000	1034	1100	hour until	1932	2000	2034	2133	2253	2333		1234	1333	1434	1533	1634	1733	1833	1933	2034	2133	2240
Derby d.	0940	1008	1040	1108	▽	1940	2040	2140	2259				1240	1340	1440	1540	1640	1740	1840	1940	2040	2140	
Nottingham a.	1003	1028	1103	1128		2004	2028	2103	2208	2327			1300	1400	1500	1600	1700	1800	1900	2000	2100	2200	

	Ⓐ	Ⓐ A	Ⓐ	Ⓐ	Ⓐ	Ⓐ	Ⓐ	Ⓐ		Ⓐ	Ⓐ	Ⓐ	Ⓐ	Ⓐ		⑥	⑥ A	⑥	⑥	⑥	⑥	⑥
Nottingham d.	Ⓐ	0600	0637	0704	0737	0812	0841	0910	and at	1841	1910	1940	2040	2139		⑥	0558	0637	0658	0737	0809	0841	0910
Derby a.		0632	0659	0731	0802	0833	0907	0931	the same	1906	1931	2006	2104	2208		0630	0659	0729	0802	0829	0909	0931
Derby d.		0636	0706	0736	0806	0837	0911	0936	minutes	1910	1937	2010	2110	2212	2245	0636	0706	0736	0806	0837	0912	0936
Burton-on-Trent d.		0648	0717	0750	0818	0849	0922	0950	past each	1921	1949	2021	2124	2223	2256	0648	0717	0750	0818	0849	0924	0949
Tamworth d.		0701	0730	0803	0830	0902	0934	1002	hour until	1933	2003	2033	2134	2235	2307	0701	0730	0802	0830	0902	0935	1002
Birmingham New Street a.		0725	0753	0825	0855	0924	0955	1024		1955	2025	2055	2157	2301	2325	0724	0752	0824	0855	0924	0956	1024
Cardiff Central 121 a.		0929	...	1028	...	1128	...	1226		...	...	2235a				0925	...	1021	...	1124	...	1223

	⑥	⑥	⑥	⑥	⑥		⑥	⑥	⑥	⑥	⑥		⑦	⑦	⑦	⑦	⑦	⑦	⑦	⑦	⑦	⑦	⑦	⑦	⑦
Nottingham d.	and at	1841	1910	1941	2037	2139	⑦	0954	1111	1210	...	1310	1410	1510	...	1610	1710	1810	1910	2010	2110	...
Derby a.	the same	1906	1932	2007	2102	2208		1012	1131	1230	...	1330	1429	1530	...	1634	1729	1833	1935	2035	2130	...
Derby d.	minutes	1910	1937	2011	2110	2212	2226	1018	1136	1236	...	1338	1434	1534	...	1634	1735	1835	1935	2035	2137	2226
Burton-on-Trent d.	past each	1921	1949	2022	2124	2222	2237	1029	1147	1247	...	1349	1447	1547	...	1647	1747	1847	1947	2047	2148	2237
Tamworth d.	hour until	1933	2002	2034	2135	2235	2247	1042	1200	1300	...	1400	1500	1600	...	1700	1800	1900	1959	2059	2200	2247
Birmingham New Street a.	△	1955	2024	2055	2156	2302	2306	1102	1221	1321	...	1422	1520	1621	...	1719	1819	1921	2021	2118	2223	2305
Cardiff Central 121 a.		...	2242	...	...	...		1307	1427	1528	...	1629	1726	1829	...	1927	2030	2127

A – To Bournemouth (Table 119).

a – On ⑤ arrives 2230.

▲ – Arrivals in Cardiff may be up to 7 minutes later after 1500.
△ – Arrivals in Cardiff may vary ± 7 minutes.
▽ – Arrivals in Nottingham may be up to 3 minutes later after 1700.

XC BIRMINGHAM - SHEFFIELD - LEEDS - YORK - NEWCASTLE - EDINBURGH - GLASGOW 124

km			Ⓐ	Ⓐ	Ⓐ	Ⓐ	Ⓐ	Ⓐ	Ⓐ	Ⓐ	Ⓐ	Ⓐ	Ⓐ	Ⓐ	Ⓐ	Ⓐ	Ⓐ	Ⓐ	Ⓐ	Ⓐ	Ⓐ	Ⓐ	Ⓐ	Ⓐ	Ⓐ
									H	G				A			B		C		B		D		
	Plymouth **120** d.	Ⓐ	...	...	...	...	...	...	...	...	0520	...	0625	...	0725	...	0825	...	0925	...	1025	...	1125	...	1225
	Bristol T Meads **120** d.		...	...	...	...	...	...	0627	...	0730	...	0830	...	0930	...	1030	...	1130	...	1230	...	1330	...	1430
	Southampton Central **119** d.		...	...	...	...	...	...	|	...	|	...	|	...	|	...	|	0946	|	...	|	1146	|	...	|
	Reading **119** d.		...	...	...	...	...	...	|	0645	|	0746	|	0850	|	0945	|	1045	|	1145	|	1245	|	1345	|
0	**Birmingham** New Street **123** d.		...	...	0600	0630	0703	0730	0803	0830	0903	0930	1003	1030	1103	1130	1203	1230	1303	1330	1403	1430	1503	1530	1603
28	Tamworth **123** d.		...	...	|	|	0719	|	0819	|	|	|	1019	|	|	|	1219	|	|	|	1419	|	|	|	1620
48	Burton on Trent **123** d.		...	...	|	|	0731	|	0829	|	0927	|	|	|	1126	|	|	|	1328	|	|	|	1526	|	|
67	**Derby** **123 170** d.		...	0556	0635	0713	0744	0813	0844	0916**a**	0944**b**	1016**a**	1044**b**	1116**a**	1144**b**	1216**a**	1244	1316**a**	1344**b**	1416**a**	1444	1516**a**	1544	1616**a**	1643
105	Chesterfield **170** d.		...	0617	0654	0732	0803	0832	0903	|	1003	|	1103	|	1203	|	1303	|	1403	|	1503	|	1603	|	1704
125	**Sheffield** **170** d.		...	0633	0709	0754**d**	0822**b**	0847	0921	0947	1021	1047	1121	1147	1221	1247	1321	1347	1421	1447	1521	1547	1621	1647	1721
154	Doncaster **180** d.		...	0703**b**	|	0825	|	0919	|	1019	|	1119	|	1219	|	1319	|	1419	|	1519	|	1619	|	1720	|
171	Wakefield Westgate **180** d.		...	|	0737	|	0848	|	0947	|	1047	|	1147	|	1247	|	1347	|	1447	|	1547	|	1650	|	1749
187	**Leeds** **190 180** d.		...	|	0757**d**	|	0908**d**	|	1008**d**	|	1108**d**	|	1208**d**	|	1308**d**	|	1408**d**	|	1508**d**	|	1608**d**	|	1708	|	1808**b**
199	**York** **190 180** a.		...	0723	0822	0847	0930	0940	1030	1039	1130	1139	1230	1240	1330	1340	1430	1439	1530	1539	1630	1639	1730	1740	1831
	York **180** d.		...	0732	0829	0850	0932	0950	1032	1048	1132	1150	1232	1248	1332	1350	1432	1448	1532	1548	1632	1648	1732	1748	1833
270	Darlington **180** d.		...	0800	0858	0917	0958	1016	1100	1115	1159	1216	1300	1315	1400	1416	1500	1515	1600	1615	1700	1715	1800	1815	1901
305	Durham **180** d.		...	0818	0915	0934	1016	1033	1117	1132	1216	1233	1317	1332	1416	1433	1517	1532	1617	1632	1718	1732	1817	1833	1919
328	**Newcastle** **180** a.		...	0838	0927	0947	1029	1046	1129	1145	1230	1245	1329	1345	1431	1445	1529	1545	1629	1645	1730	1745	1833	1847	1932
	Newcastle **180** d.		0735	...	0935	...	1035	...	1140	...	1239	...	1338	...	1435	...	1537	...	1637	...	1737	...	1840	...	1935
384	Alnmouth **180** a.		|	...	0958	...	|	...	|	...	|	...	1401	...	|	...	1600	...	1700	...	1800	...	|	...	2000
436	Berwick upon Tweed **180** a.		0818	...	1019	...	|	...	1221	...	|	...	1422	...	|	...	1621	...	|	...	1821	...	1921	...	2023
528	**Edinburgh** Waverley **180 220** a.		0900	...	1106	...	1204	...	1306	..	1410	...	1507	...	1606	...	1706	...	1807	...	1906	...	2009	...	2108
599	Motherwell **220** a.		1002	...	1152	...	...	...	1353	...	...	...	1552	...	...	...	1752	...	...	...	1953	...	...	...	2207
620	**Glasgow** Central **220** a.		1025	...	1212	...	...	...	1412	...	...	...	1612	...	...	...	1811	...	...	...	2015	...	...	...	2224

	Ⓐ	Ⓐ	Ⓐ	Ⓐ	Ⓐ	Ⓐ	Ⓐ	Ⓐ	Ⓐ	Ⓐ		⑥	⑥	⑥	⑥	⑥	⑥	⑥	⑥	⑥	⑥	⑥	⑥	⑥	⑥
																			G		E				
Plymouth **120** d.	...	1325	...	1425	...	1525	...	1625	...	1725	⑥	...	...	...	...	...	...	...	...	0525	...	0625	...	0725	...
Bristol T Meads **120** d.	...	1530	...	1630	...	1730	...	1830	...	1930		...	...	...	...	...	...	0615	...	0730	...	0830	...	0930	...
Southampton Central **119** d.	1346	|	...	|	1546	|	...	|	1746	|		...	...	...	...	...	...	|	...	|	0653	|	0747	|	...
Reading **119** d.	1445	|	1545	|	1645	|	1745	|	1845	|		...	...	...	...	...	...	|	0645	|	0747	|	0845	|	0945
Birmingham New Street **123** d.	1630	1703	1730	1803	1830	1903	1930	2003	2030	2103		...	...	0557	0630	0703	0730	0803	0830	0903	0930	1003	1030	1103	1130
Tamworth **123** d.	|	|	|	1819	|	|	|	2019	|	2119		...	...	0613	0646	0719	0746	0819	|	|	|	1019	|	|	|
Burton on Trent **123** d.	|	1726	|	|	|	1929	|	|	|	2130		...	...	0624	0656	0731	0756	0829	|	0928	|	|	|	1128	|
Derby **123 170** d.	1711**b**	1742	1816**a**	1844**b**	1909	1943	2009	2044**b**	2119**a**	2144		...	0556	0638	0713	0744	0813**b**	0844	0916**a**	0944**b**	1016**a**	1044**b**	1116**a**	1144**b**	1216**a**
Chesterfield **170** d.	|	1803	|	1903	1928	2004	|	2103	2138	2207		...	0631	0657	0732	0803	0832	0903	|	1003	|	1103	|	1203	|
Sheffield **170** d.	1747**b**	1821	1847	1926**d**	1956**g**	2021	2053**a**	2121**b**	2154	2230**b**		...	0649**b**	0712	0754**d**	0822**b**	0847	0921	0947	1021	1047	1121	1147	1221	1247
Doncaster **180** d.	|	|	1918	|	2018	|	2120	|	2231	|		...	0719	|	0825	|	0919	|	1019	|	1119	|	1219	|	1319
Wakefield Westgate **180** d.	1819	1848	|	1951	|	2048	|	2148	|	2301		...	|	0740	|	0848	|	0947	|	1047	|	1147	|	1247	|
Leeds **190 180** d.	1838	1908**b**	|	2008	|	2106	|	2204	|	2315		...	|	0757	|	0908**d**	|	1008**d**	|	1108**d**	|	1208**d**	|	1308**b**	|
York **190 180** a.	1901	1930	1939	2030	2038	...	2140	...	2252	...		...	0743	0819	0847	0930	0940	1030	1039	1130	1139	1230	1239	1330	1339
York **180** d.	1904	1933	1945	2032	2048	...	2147	...	...	...		...	0748	0829	0850	0932	0948	1032	1048	1132	1150	1232	1248	1332	1350
Darlington **180** d.	1932	2002	2012	2059	2115	...	2213	...	...	...		...	0815	0858	0917	0959	1018	1100	1115	1158	1216	1300	1315	1359	1417
Durham **180** d.	1949	2020	2029	2116	2132	...	2230	...	...	...		...	0832	0915	0934	1016	1035	1117	1132	1215	1233	1317	1332	1416	1434
Newcastle **180** a.	2001	2033	2042	2128	2144	...	2247	...	...	...		...	0845	0927	0947	1029	1047	1129	1146	1229	1246	1329	1345	1428	1446
Newcastle **180** d.	2003	2036	...	2135	...	...	...	...	...	..		0738	...	0935	...	1035	...	1136	...	1236	...	1335	...	|	...
Alnmouth **180** a.	2026	|	...	2158	...	...	...	...	...	....		|	...	0958	...	|	...	|	...	|	...	1358	...	|	...
Berwick upon Tweed **180** a.	|	2124	...	|	...	...	...	...	....	...		0821	...	1019	...	|	...	1219	...	|	...	1419	...	|	...
Edinburgh Waverley **180 220** a.	2128	2214	...	2303	...	...	...	...	...	...		0907	...	1103	...	1205	...	1302	...	1406	...	1504	...	1604	...
Motherwell **220** a.	...	...	...	...	...	...	...	...	...	...		0954	...	1152	...	...	...	1353	...	...	...	1552	...	...	...
Glasgow Central **220** a.	...	...	...	...	...	...	...	...	...	...		1015	...	1212	...	...	...	1412	...	...	...	1612	...	...	...

	⑥	⑥	⑥	⑥	⑥	⑥	⑥	⑥		⑥	⑥	⑥	⑥	⑥	⑥	⑥	⑥	⑥	⑥		⑥			⑦	⑦
	B		C		B		D																		
Plymouth **120** d.	0825	...	0925	...	1025	...	1125	...	...	1225	...	1325	...	1425	...	1525	...	1625	...	...	1725	...	⑦	...	...
Bristol T Meads **120** d.	1030	...	1130	...	1230	...	1330	...	...	1430	...	1530	...	1630	...	1730	...	1830	...	...	1930	...		...	...
Southampton Central **119** d.	|	0947	|	...	|	1147	|	...	...	|	1347	|	...	|	1547	|	...	|	1747	...	|	...		...	...
Reading **119** d.	|	1045	|	1145	|	1245	|	1345	...	|	1445	|	1545	|	1645	|	1745	|	1845	...	|	...		...	...
Birmingham New Street **123** d.	1203	1230	1303	1330	1403	1430	1503	1530	...	1603	1630	1703	1730	1803	1830	1903	1930	2003	2030	...	2103	...		...	...
Tamworth **123** d.	1219	|	|	|	1419	|	|	|	...	1619	|	|	|	1819	|	|	|	2019	|	...	2119	...		...	...
Burton on Trent **123** d.	|	|	1327	|	|	|	1527	|	...	|	1654	1726	|	|	|	1927	|	|	|	...	2130	...		...	...
Derby **123 170** d.	1244**b**	1316**a**	1344**b**	1416**a**	1444**b**	1516**a**	1544	1616**a**	...	1643	1716**a**	1744**b**	1816**a**	1844	1916**a**	1944**b**	2016**a**	2044	2127	...	2146	...		...	...
Chesterfield **170** d.	1303	|	1403	|	1503	|	1603	|	...	1704	|	1803	|	1903	1935	2005	2035	2105	2147	...	2208	...		...	...
Sheffield **170** d.	1321	1347	1421	1447	1521	1547	1621	1647	...	1721	1747	1821	1847	1921	1956**d**	2024	2053	2121	2203	...	2230**d**	...		...	...
Doncaster **180** d.	|	1419	|	1519	|	1619	|	1719	...	|	|	|	1919	|	2019	|	2124	|	2226	...	2253	...		...	...
Wakefield Westgate **180** d.	1347	|	1447	|	1547	|	1647	|	...	1748	1815	1848	|	1951	|	2049	|	2148	|	...	2311	...		...	...
Leeds **190 180** d.	1408**d**	|	1508**d**	|	1608**d**	|	1708**d**	|	...	1808**b**	1838**d**	1908**d**	|	2008	|	2119**g**	|	2202	|	...	2325	...		...	0920
York **190 180** a.	1430	1439	1530	1539	1630	1639	1729	1739	...	1830	1901	1930	1939	2030	2040	2155	2144	...	2246	...	...	...		...	0942
York **180** d.	1432	1448	1532	1546	1632	1648	1731	1746	...	1832	1904	1932	1945	2032	2048	...	2148	...	...	...	...	...		...	0944
Darlington **180** d.	1500	1515	1600	1616	1700	1715	1757	1812	...	1901	1932	1959	2012	2059	2115	...	2215	...	...	...	...	...		...	1011
Durham **180** d.	1517	1532	1617	1633	1717	1732	1814	1829	...	1919	1949	2016	2029	2116	2132	...	2232	...	...	...	...	...		...	1028
Newcastle **180** a.	1529	1545	1629	1646	1729	1745	1831	1841	...	1932	2001	2028	2042	2128	2144	...	2247	...	...	...	...	...		...	1040
Newcastle **180** d.	1535	...	1634	...	1735	...	1837	...	...	1935	...	2035	...	2132	...	...	...	...	...	...	...	...		0945	1042
Alnmouth **180** a.	1558	...	1657	...	1759	...	|	...	...	2000	...	|	...	2155	...	...	...	...	...	...	...	...		1011	|
Berwick upon Tweed **180** a.	1619	...	|	...	1819	...	1918	...	...	2023	...	2118	...	|	...	...	...	...	...	...	...	...		|	1123
Edinburgh Waverley **180 220** a.	1707	...	1803	...	1906	...	2006	...	...	2108	...	2208	...	2257	...	...	...	...	...	...	...	...		1111	1207
Motherwell **220** a.	1752	...	...	...	1953	...	...	...	...	2159	...	...	...	...	...	...	...	...	...	...	...	...		...	1258
Glasgow Central **220** a.	1811	...	...	...	2012	...	...	...	...	2220	...	...	...	...	...	...	...	...	...	...	...	...		...	1318

	⑦	⑦	⑦	⑦	⑦	⑦		⑦	⑦	⑦	⑦	⑦	⑦		⑦	⑦	⑦	⑦	⑦	⑦	⑦	⑦	⑦	⑦	⑦
								C			G	B												B	
Plymouth **120** d.	...	...	...	...	...	...	...	0925	...	1025	...	1125	...	...	1225	...	1325	...	1425	...	1524	...	1625	1725	1825
Bristol T Meads **120** d.	...	...	...	0915	1030	...	...	1130	...	1230	...	1330	...	...	1430	...	1530	...	1630	...	1730	...	1830	1930	2030
Southampton Central **119** d.	...	...	...	|	|	...	...	|	...	|	...	|	...	...	|	...	|	...	|	...	|	...	|	|	|
Reading **119** d.	...	...	...	|	|	...	...	|	...	|	1254	|	1341	...	|	1441	|	1541	|	1641	|	1741	|	|	|
Birmingham New Street **123** d.	...	0903	1003	1103	1203	1230	...	1303	1330	1403	1430	1503	1530	...	1603	1630	1703	1730	1803	1830	1903	1930	2003	2103	2203
Tamworth **123** d.	...	0919	1018	|	1219	|	...	|	|	1419	|	|	|	...	1619	|	|	|	1819	|	|	|	2019	2119	2219
Burton on Trent **123** d.	...	0928	1029	1125	|	|	...	1326	|	|	|	1525	|	...	|	|	1728	|	|	|	1926	|	|	2129	|
Derby **123 170** d.	...	0944	1044	1144**d**	1244**b**	1311**a**	...	1344**d**	1411**a**	1444**b**	1511**a**	1544**d**	1611**a**	...	1644**b**	1712**a**	1743	1812**a**	1843	1906	1942	2009**d**	2044**b**	2144	2242
Chesterfield **170** d.	...	1003	1103	1203	1303	1330	...	1403	1430	1503	|	1603	|	...	1703	|	1804	|	1905	|	2003	|	2103	2203	2303
Sheffield **170** d.	0921	1021**b**	1121	1221	1321	1351**d**	...	1421	1451**b**	1521	1551	1621	1651	...	1721	1752	1821	1852**d**	1921	1952**a**	2021	2052**a**	2121**b**	2221	2319
Doncaster **180** d.	|	|	|	|	|	1417	...	|	1522**d**	|	1618	|	1719**b**	...	|	1817	|	1919	|	2018	|	2123	|	|	|
Wakefield Westgate **180** d.	0946	1046	1146	1246	1346	|	...	1446	|	1546	|	1646	|	...	1745	1835	1849	|	1950	|	2053	|	2148	2244	|
Leeds **190 180** d.	1008**b**	1105**b**	1205	1305	1405	|	...	1505	|	1605	|	1705	|	...	1805	1859**d**	1908	|	2008	|	2108	|	2204	2301	0008
York **190 180** a.	1029	1127	1227	1327	1427	1437	...	1527	1543	1627	1638	1727	1740	...	1827	1921	1929	1939	2030	2039	2132	2143	...	...	...
York **180** d.	1032	1129	1229	1329	1429	1448	...	1529	1545	1629	1647	1729	1745	...	1829	1923	1932	1945	2032	2048	...	2149	...	...	...
Darlington **180** d.	1059	1156	1256	1357	1457	1515	...	1556	1612	1656	1714	1756	1811	...	1856	1950	2000	2012	2100	2115	...	2226	...	...	...
Durham **180** d.	1116	1213	1313	1414	1514	1532	...	1613	1629	1713	1731	1813	1828	...	1913	2007	2018	2029	2118	2132	...	2243	...	...	...
Newcastle **180** a.	1128	1225	1325	1426	1526	1544	...	1625	1642	1725	1744	1825	1841	...	1925	2019	2031	2041	2131	2144	...	2312	...	...	...
Newcastle **180** d.	1134	1230	1328	1432	1528	...	...	1628	...	1728	...	1828	...	...	1928	...	2034	2056	2134	...	...	...	...	...	...
Alnmouth **180** a.	|	|	1351	|	1552	...	...	1651	...	1751	...	|	...	...	1951	...	|	|	2159	...	...	...	...	...	...
Berwick upon Tweed **180** a.	1217	|	1412	|	1612	...	...	|	...	1812	...	1909	...	...	2012	...	2121	|	|	...	...	...	...	...	...
Edinburgh Waverley **180 220** a.	1259	1400	1456	1602	1656	...	...	1757	...	1856	...	1957	...	...	2056	...	2212	2221	2304	...	...	...	...	...	...
Motherwell **220** a.	1353	...	1554	...	1755	...	...	...	...	1959	...	...	...	...	2156	...	...	...	...	...	...	...	...	...	...
Glasgow Central **220** a.	1412	...	1611	...	1812	...	...	...	...	2019	...	...	...	...	2213	...	...	...	...	...	...	...	...	...	...

A – From Winchester (Table **119**).
B – From Penzance (Tables **117** / **120**).
C – To Aberdeen (Table **222**).
D – To Dundee (Table **222**)
E – From Bournemouth (Table **119**).
G – From Guildford (Table **134**).
H – From Bath Spa (Table **120**).
J – From Paignton (Table **120**).
a – Arrives 10 – 12 minutes earlier.
b – Arrives 5 – 6 minutes earlier.
d – Arrives 7 – 9 minutes earlier.
g – Arrives 15 – 16 minutes earlier.

Block 1 — Ⓐ (column markers: D, B, CB, G, B)

Station	Times
Glasgow Central 220 d.	0601 … 0750 … 0900 … 1100
Motherwell 220 d.	0617 … 0805 0915 … 1116
Edinburgh Waverley 180 220 d.	0606 0700 0707 … 0810 0908 1010 1106 1208 … 1307
Berwick upon Tweed 180 d.	0647 0741 … 0851 0951 1049 1149 1248
Alnmouth 180 d.	0708 0801 … 1209 … 1411
Newcastle 180 d.	0738 0832 0836 … 0939 … 1038 1137 1238 1334 1439
Newcastle 180 d.	0625 0645 0725 0740 0835 0843 0935 0942 1035 1144 1234 1241 1335 1343 1436 1442 1505
Durham 180 d.	0638 0658 0738 0755 0848 0856 0949 0956 1048 1055 1149 1157 1248 1254 1349 1356 1449 1456 1518
Darlington 180 d.	0655 0715 0755 0812 0905 0913 1007 1013 1105 1113 1206 1214 1305 1313 1407 1413 1506 1513 1534
York 180 d.	0722 0741 0821 0840 0932 0941 1033 1041 1132 1140 1232 1240 1331 1340 1433 1440 1533 1541 1601
York 190 180 d.	0640 0727 0743 0826 0845 0935 0945 1035 1045 1135 1145 1235 1245 1335 1345 1435 1445 1535 1545 1605
Leeds 190 180 d.	0600 0616 0705 … 0811 … 0911 … 1011 … 1111 … 1211 … 1311 … 1411 … 1511 … 1611 1640c
Wakefield Westgate 180 d.	0612 0628 0719 … 0823 … 0923 … 1023 … 1124 … 1223 … 1323 … 1423 … 1523 … 1623 1652
Doncaster 180 d.	0646 … 0756b … 0851 … 0959 … 1059 … 1159 … 1259 … 1359 … 1459 … 1559
Sheffield 170 d.	0601 0652e 0718d 0753 0821 0854 0924d 0954 1024 1055 1124 1154 1224 1255 1324 1355 1424 1455 1524 1555 1624 1655 1724
Chesterfield 170 d.	0626 0706 0730 0806 0833 0907 … 1008 … 1107 … 1208 … 1307 … 1407 … 1507 … 1607 … 1708
Derby 123 170 d.	0610 0648b 0727 0750 0828 0853 0928 0953 1030 1053 1128 1153 1230 1253 1328 1353 1428 1453 1528 1553 1628 1653 1729 1753
Burton on Trent 123 d.	0620 0658 0738 0800 0838 … 0938 … 1338 … 1538 … 1740
Tamworth 123 d.	0631 0709 0750 0811 0850 … 1050 … 1249 … 1447 … 1647
Birmingham New Street 123 a.	0652 0727 0808 0827 0910 0927 1008 1027 1109 1127 1207 1227 1308 1327 1408 1427 1508 1527 1602 1628 1708 1728 1806 1827
Reading 119 a.	0908 … 1010 … 1109 … 1209 … 1307 … 1409 … 1508 … 1611 … 1708 … 1808 … 1910 … 2009
Southampton Central 119 a.	1117 … 1317 … 1517 … 1716
Bristol T Meads 120 a.	0839 … 0939 … 1042 … 1141 … 1242 … 1341 … 1442 … 1541 … 1643 … 1739 … 1841 … 1942
Plymouth 120 a.	1042 1144 1247 1338 1443 1540 1648 1742 1849 1943 2040 2146

Block 2 — Ⓐ then ⑥

Station	Times
Glasgow Central 220 d.	1300 … 1500 … 1700 1900 … 0601
Motherwell 220 d.	1316 … 1516 … 1716 1916 … 0617
Edinburgh Waverley 180 220 d.	1408 1508 1606 1707 1805 2002 … 0608 0700 0707
Berwick upon Tweed 180 d.	1450 … 1751 1852 2045 … 0647 0740
Alnmouth 180 d.	1702 … 1910 2105 … 0707 0800
Newcastle 180 d.	1534 1634 1734 1837 1939 2134 … 0736 0831 0836
Newcastle 180 d.	1541 1635 1641 1732 1741 1835 1843 1935 1942 … 0623 0645 0735 0741 0835 0843
Durham 180 d.	1554 1648 1653 1748 1754 1848 1856 1950 1955 … 0638 0658 0748 0754 0848 0856
Darlington 180 d.	1613 1706 1712 1805 1813 1907 1913 2007 2013 … 0655 0715 0805 0813 0905 0913
York 180 d.	1640 1731 1740 1832 1839 1933 1940 2032 2040 … 0721 0741 0831 0840 0932 0940
York 190 180 d.	1645 1735 1745 1835 1845 1936 1945 2035 2045 … 0620 0727 0745 0835 0845 0935 0945
Leeds 190 180 d.	1711 … 1811 … 1911 … 2011 … 2111 … 0600 0616 0711e … 0811 … 0911 … 1011
Wakefield Westgate 180 d.	1723 … 1823 … 1923 … 2024 … 2123 … 0612 0629 0723 … 0824 … 0924 … 1024
Doncaster 180 d.	1759 … 1859 … 2000 … 2102 … 0647 0756d … 0859 … 0959
Sheffield 170 d.	1758d 1824 1858d 1924 1958d 2024 2058b 2129 2200d … 0650c 0718d 0756b 0820 0855 … 0924 0955 1024 … 1055
Chesterfield 170 d.	1810 … 1911 … 2010 … 2121 2141 2225 … 0704 0730 0808 0832 0907 … 1007 … 1107
Derby 123 170 d.	1829 1853 1930 1954 2029 2054 2129 2202 2245 … 0610 0648 0726 … 0751 0828 0853 0930b … 0953 1028 1053 … 1130b
Burton on Trent 123 d.	1941 … 2140 … 2256 … 0620 0658 0737 … 0800 0838 … 0941 … 1141
Tamworth 123 d.	1848 … 2047 … 2150 … 2307 … 0631 0709 0748 … 0811 0849 … 1048
Birmingham New Street 123 a.	1908 1927 2007 2027 2107 2129 2209 2251 2325 … 0650 0728 0808 … 0827 0908 0927 1006 … 1027 1107 1127 … 1208
Reading 119 a.	2107 … 2216 … 0909 … 1008 … 1111 … 1206 1309
Southampton Central 119 a.	2320 … 1117 … 1317
Bristol T Meads 120 a.	2041 2136 2243 2340 … 0838 … 0939 … 1042 … 1138 … 1242 … 1338
Plymouth 120 a.	2243 2339 … 1039 … 1151 … 1240 … 1339 … 1444 … 1541

Block 3 — ⑥ (column markers: D, B, CB, G, B)

Station	Times
Glasgow Central 220 d.	0750 … 0900 … 1100 … 1300 … 1500 … 1700
Motherwell 220 d.	0805 0915 1116 1316 1516 1716
Edinburgh Waverley 180 220 d.	0805 0908 1005 1108 1204 1309 1405 1508 1605 1708 1808
Berwick upon Tweed 180 d.	0847 0951 1045 1151 1246 1447 1752 1851
Alnmouth 180 d.	0909 1211 1409 1703 1911
Newcastle 180 d.	0939 … 1038 … 1240 … 1334 … 1348 … 1532 … 1634 … 1734 … 1838 … 1911
Newcastle 180 d.	0935 0942 1035 1044 1135 1142 1235 1244 1335 1344 1435 1444 1505 1544 1635 1644 1732 1744 1835 1844 1935 1945
Durham 180 d.	0949 0956 1048 1056 1149 1155 1248 1256 1349 1356 1448 1456 1518 1556 1648 1656 1749 1756 1849 1857 1950
Darlington 180 d.	1006 1013 1105 1113 1206 1212 1305 1313 1406 1413 1513 1515 1613 1619 1713 1719 1806 1813 1906 1914 2007 2014
York 180 d.	1032 1041 1131 1140 1232 1240 1331 1341 1432 1440 1531 1540 1601 1640 1731 1740 1831 1841 1932 1941 2033 2041
York 190 180 d.	1035 1045 1135 1145 1235 1245 1335 1345 1435 1445 1535 1545 1606 1646 1735 1745 1835 1845 1936 1945 2035 2045
Leeds 190 180 d.	1111 1211 1311 1411 1511 1611 1640c 1711 1811 1911 2011 2111
Wakefield Westgate 180 d.	1123 1223 1323 1423 1523 1623 1652 1723 1823 1924 2023 2123
Doncaster 180 d.	1059 1159 1259 1359 1459 1559 1759 1859 2000 2059
Sheffield 170 d.	1124 1155 1224 1255 1324 1355 1424 1455 1524 1555 1624 1655 1724 1755 1824 1858d 1924 1955 2024 2055 2125 2155
Chesterfield 170 d.	1209 1307 1408 1507 1607 1707 1807 1907 2007 2107 2137 2207
Derby 123 170 d.	1153 1230 1253 1328 1353 1430 1453 1528 1553 1628 1653 1728 1753 1829b 1853 1929 1954 2028 2053 2128 2156 2226
Burton on Trent 123 d.	1338 1538 1738 1939 2138 2237
Tamworth 123 d.	1249 1449 1648 1845 2046 2149 2247
Birmingham New Street 123 a.	1227 1308 1327 1402 1426 1508 1527 1602 1627 1707 1727 1807 1827 1907 1927 2006 2027 2104 2125 2206 2244 2306
Reading 119 a.	1408 1508 1609 1710 1810 1910 2009 2108 2214
Southampton Central 119 a.	1517 1717 2320
Bristol T Meads 120 a.	1440 1538 1642 1738 1842 1938 2042 2135 2241
Plymouth 120 a.	1643 1739 1851 1942 2043 2138 2250 2356

Block 4 — ⑦ (column markers: B, B, C, G)

Station	Times
Glasgow Central 220 d.	0750 … 1055 1200 1348 1455 1655 1900
Motherwell 220 d.	0805 1113 1217 1404 1512 1712 1914
Edinburgh Waverley 180 220 d.	0908 1008 1105 1208 1308 1355 1408 1508 1608 1708 1808 2018
Berwick upon Tweed 180 d.	0949 1148 1248 1434 1447 1751 1851 2039
Alnmouth 180 d.	1105 1208 1408 1705 2103
Newcastle 180 d.	1036 1136 1237 1335 1437 1520 1535 1634 1736 1837 1937 2149
Newcastle 180 d.	0935 1039 1140 1240 1335 1340 1435 1440 1524 1540 1635 1640 1735 1740 1825 1840 1926 1940
Durham 180 d.	0948 1053 1153 1253 1348 1353 1449 1454 1537 1553 1648 1653 1748 1755 1837 1853 1939 1953
Darlington 180 d.	1005 1110 1210 1310 1406 1411 1506 1511 1554 1611 1710 1716 1805 1811 1854 1910 1956 2010
York 180 d.	1031 1138 1237 1337 1432 1437 1532 1537 1622 1636 1731 1737 1832 1838 1920 1937 2022 2037
York 190 180 d.	0933 1033 1141 1241 1341 1435 1441 1535 1541 1625 1641 1735 1741 1835 1841 1924 1944 2024 2041
Leeds 190 180 d.	0810 0900 1000 1100 1211b 1311d 1411d 1511d 1611d 1711b 1811b 1911d 2011b 2111d
Wakefield Westgate 180 d.	0823 0911 1012 1112 1224 1324 1423 1523 1623 1723 1823 1923 2023 2123
Doncaster 180 d.	0932 1030 1130 1459 1559 1651 1759 1859 1954b 2051
Sheffield 170 d.	0854 0957 1057 1157 1257 1357 1422 1455 1524 1555 1624 1654 1724 1754 1824 1855 1924 1955 2021 2054 2120 2154
Chesterfield 170 d.	0907 1009 1109 1209 1309 1409 1432 1507 1607 1707 1807 1907 2007 2106 2132 2206
Derby 123 170 d.	0928 1033 1133 1229 1332 1429 1453 1526 1553 1627 1654 1727 1754 1826 1854 1927 1956 2027 2054b 2126 2153 2226
Burton on Trent 123 d.	1140 1343 1537 1737 1938 2137 2203 2237
Tamworth 123 d.	1053 1248 1448 1648 1845 2046 2147 2214 2247
Birmingham New Street 123 a.	1018 1121 1205 1306 1409 1505 1526 1602 1626 1705 1726 1802 1826 1904 1928 2005 2027 2103 2126 2205 2231 2305
Reading 119 a.	1701 1809 1904 2008 2114 2206
Southampton Central 119 a.	
Bristol T Meads 120 a.	1151 1249 1331 1431 1534 1631 1733 1835 1932 2031 2130 2244 2333
Plymouth 120 a.	1352 1452 1537 1630 1742 1838 1943 2045 2245 2346

A – To Winchester (Table 119).
B – To Penzance (Tables 117/120).
C – From Aberdeen (Table 222).
D – From Dundee (Table 222).
E – To Bournemouth (Table 119).
G – To Guildford (Table 134).
H – To Paignton (Table 120).
b – Arrives 5–6 minutes earlier.
c – Arrives 9–10 minutes earlier.
d – Arrives 7–8 minutes earlier.
e – Arrives 12 minutes earlier.

LM 2nd class BIRMINGHAM - WORCESTER - HEREFORD 125

km		Ⓐ	Ⓐ	Ⓐ	Ⓐ		Ⓐ	Ⓐ	Ⓐ	Ⓐ	Ⓐ	Ⓐ	Ⓐ	Ⓐ	Ⓐ	Ⓐ	⑥	⑥		⑥	⑥	⑥	⑥	⑥
0	**Birmingham** New St. d.	0659	0719	0759	0849		1549	1649	1719	1749	1759	1819	1919	1959	2059	2300	0649	0749		1749	1849	1919	2059	2210
21	Bromsgrove d.	0721	0744	0821	0910		1610	1710	1740	1809	1820	1842	1942	2019	2120	2320	0710	0810		1810	1910	1940	2120	|
32	Droitwich Spa d.	0730	0754	0830	0920	and	1620	1720	1752	1819	1835	1857	1952	2029	2130	2330	0720	0820	and	1820	1920	1951	2130	2235
41	**Worcester** Foregate St d.	0742	0811	0840	0932	hourly	1630	1735	1807	1835	1857	1910h	2015	2036h	2141	2339h	0732	0832	hourly	1835	1938	2001	2150	2243h
54	Great Malvern 130 d.	0800	0822	0853	0945	until	1643	1747	1819	1849	1910	*1954*	2027	*2100*	2154	...	0745	0845	until	1848	1950	2025	2202	...
65	Ledbury 130 d.	0813	...	0907	0959		1659	1800	1831	1904	...	*2010*	2041	*2116*	2209	...	0759	0859		1901	...	2039	2215	...
87	**Hereford** 130 a.	0833	...	0927	1019		1719	1821	1851	1923	...	*2029*	2101	*2134*	2228	...	0819	0919		1919	...	2102	2235	...

	⑦	⑦	⑦	⑦	⑦	⑦	⑦	⑦	⑦
Birmingham New St. d.	1000	1200	1400	1558	1758	1900	2000	2100	2205
Bromsgrove d.	1020	1220	1420	1618	1818	1920	2020	2120	2225
Droitwich Spa d.	1030	1232	1430	1628	1828	1930	2030	2130	2236
Worcester Foregate St d.	1054	1250	1454	1642	1842	1944	2100	2144	2254
Great Malvern 130 d.	1106	1302	1506	1703	1859	*2033*	*2139*	2156	2307
Ledbury 130 d.	1118	1315	1518	1716	1912	*2048*	...	2209	...
Hereford 130 a.	1134	1332	1534	1734	1930	*2104*	...	2227	...

	Ⓐ	Ⓐ	Ⓐ	Ⓐ	Ⓐ	Ⓐ	Ⓐ	Ⓐ	Ⓐ		Ⓐ
Hereford 130 d.	*0450*	*0528*	...	...	0709	0732	...	0845	0939		1739
Ledbury 130 d.	|	*0545*	...	...	0725	0750	...	0906	0958		1758
Great Malvern 130 d.	0548	*0559*	0647	0702	0737	0807	0840	0917	1010	and	1810
Worcester F'gate St. d.	0602	0626h	0658	0716	0749	0824	0852	0930	1024	hourly	1824
Droitwich Spa d.	0611	0633	0713	0733	0805	0833	0901	0943	1033	until	1833
Bromsgrove d.	0621	0643	0723	|	|	0843	0911	0953	1043		1842
Birmingham N St... a.	0649	0710	0748	0810	0840	0907	0939	1019	1109		1909

	Ⓐ	Ⓐ	Ⓐ	Ⓐ	Ⓐ	⑥	⑥	⑥	⑥		⑥	⑥	⑥	⑥	⑥	⑥	⑦	⑦	⑦	⑦	⑦	⑦	⑦	⑦
Hereford 130 d.	1848	1950	2056	2129	2259	...	*0617*	0739	0839		1739	1911	1959	*2020*	*2135*	2249	1005	1202	1405	1609	*1634*	1809	*1830*	2005
Ledbury 130 d.	1904	2009	2114	2145	2315	...	*0634*	0758	0858		1758	1928	2015	*2040*	*2151*	2305	1022	1218	1422	1625	*1652*	1825	*1848*	2022
Great Malvern 130 d.	1915	2020	2125	2156	2327	0622	0717	0810	0910	and	1810	1939	2027	2130	*2203*	2317	1034	1230	1434	1637	*1705*	1837	*1911*	2037
Worcester Foregate St d.	1928	2031	2136	2210	2339	0634	0728	0824	0924	hourly	1824	1951	2040	2142	2247h	2328	1046	1242	1446	1649	1757h	1849	1949	2049
Droitwich Spa d.	1937	2045	...	2219	...	0643	0743	0833	0933	until	1833	2000	2049	2202	2255	...	1106	1303	1503	1703	1805	1903	2003	2103
Bromsgrove d.	1947	2055	...	2229	...	0653	0753	0843	0943		1843	|	2059	|	|	...	1115	1313	1513	1713	1815	1913	2013	2113
Birmingham New St. a.	2018	2120	...	2254	...	0718	0818	0909	1009		1909	2055n	2120	2255n	2336n	...	1138	1338	1538	1738	1838	1938	2038	2138

h – Worcester Shrub Hill. n – Birmingham Snow Hill.

LM 2nd class BIRMINGHAM - KIDDERMINSTER - WORCESTER 126

km		Ⓐ	Ⓐ	Ⓐ	Ⓐ	Ⓐ	Ⓐ	Ⓐ	Ⓐ	Ⓐ	Ⓐ	Ⓐ	Ⓐ	Ⓐ	Ⓐ	Ⓐ	Ⓐ	Ⓐ	Ⓐ		Ⓐ	Ⓐ	Ⓐ	Ⓐ	Ⓐ	Ⓐ
0	**Birmingham** Moor St. d.	0604	0649	0719	0749	0834	0909	0939	1009	1039	1109	1139	1209	1239	1309	1339	1409	1439	1509	...	1539	1609	1639	1709	1732	1749
1	**Birmingham** Snow Hill d.	0607	0653	0723	0753	0843	0913	0943	1013	1043	1113	1143	1213	1243	1313	1343	1413	1443	1513	...	1543	1613	1643	1713	1736	1753
31	Kidderminster △ d.	0648	0734	0804	0834	0920	0947	1018	1047	1118	1147	1218	1247	1318	1347	1418	1447	1518	1552	...	1620	1647	1722	1752	1814	1832
45	Droitwich Spa d.	0658	0747	0817	0847	0930	1000	1030	1100	1130	1200	1230	1300	1330	1400	1430	1500	1530	1606	...	1631	1700	1737	1804	1828	1845
54	**Worcester** Shrub Hill a.	|	|	0824	|	0940	|	|	|	1138	|	1238	|	|	1408	1440	1510	|	1614	...	|	|	|	1812	|	|
54	**Worcester** Foregate St a.	0709	0757	0833	0858	...	1009	1039	1109	...	1209	...	1309	1340	...	1446	...	1539	1625	...	1640	1709	1746	...	1839	1854

	Ⓐ	Ⓐ	Ⓐ	Ⓐ	Ⓐ	Ⓐ	⑥	⑥	⑥	⑥	⑥	⑥	⑥	⑥		⑥	⑥	⑥	⑥	⑥	⑥	⑥	⑥	⑥	⑥	⑥
Birmingham Moor St... d.	1839	1924	1954	2053	2154	2257	0633	0701	0749	0845	0909	0939	1009	1039	...	1109	1139	1209	1239	1309	1339	1409	1439	1509	1539	1609
Birmingham Snow Hill . d.	1843	1928	1958	2058	2158	2301	0637	0705	0753	0853	0913	0943	1013	1043	...	1113	1143	1213	1243	1313	1343	1413	1443	1513	1543	1613
Kidderminster △ d.	1920	2009	2039	2139	2239	2342	0717	0745	0831	0933	0947	1018	1047	1118	...	1147	1218	1247	1318	1347	1418	1447	1518	1547	1618	1647
Droitwich Spa d.	1932	2022	2050	2152	2252	2354	0731	0756	0842	0944	1000	1030	1100	1130	...	1200	1230	1300	1330	1400	1430	1500	1530	1600	1630	1700
Worcester Shrub Hill a.	|	|	2059	2159	2259	0005	0740	0805	|	0952	|	1038	|	1138	...	|	|	|	1338	|	1439	|	1538	|	|	|
Worcester Foregate St. a.	1943	2031	...	2208	2310	...	...	0813	0851	...	1009	...	1109	*1156*	...	1209	1239	1309	...	1409	1446	1509	...	1609	1639	1709

	⑥	⑥	⑥	⑥	⑥	⑥	⑥	⑥	⑥	⑥	⑦	⑦	⑦	⑦	⑦	⑦	⑦	⑦	⑦		⑦	⑦	⑦	⑦	⑦	⑦
Birmingham Moor St... d.	1639	1709	1739	1819	1849	1924	1953	2052	2152	2257	0924	1015	1115	1215	1315	1415	1515	1615	1702	...	1715	1815	1915	2015	2143	2252
Birmingham Snow Hill . d.	1643	1713	1743	1823	1853	1928	1956	2056	2156	2301	0928	1022	1122	1222	1322	1422	1522	1622	1706	...	1722	1822	1922	2022	2146	2255
Kidderminster △ d.	1718	1749	1822	1900	1934	2009	2036	2136	2236	2342	1003	1059	1159	1259	1357	1459	1557	1657	1733	...	1757	1859	1957	2057	2220	2329
Droitwich Spa d.	1730	1802	1837	1914	1946	2022	2048	2148	2250	2354	1015	1111	1211	1311	1408	1511	1608	1708	1745	...	1809	1911	2009	2109	2231	2341
Worcester Shrub Hill a.	|	1812	|	|	1954	2031	2056	2156	2257	0005	1022	1119	1219	|	|	|	|	|	1752	...	|	1919	2017	2117	2239	2349
Worcester Foregate St. a.	1739	*1822*	1846	1923	...	...	2101	...	2304	...	1032	1135	...	1320	1417	1520	1617	1717	...	...	1819	...	...	2124	...	...

	Ⓐ	Ⓐ	Ⓐ	Ⓐ	Ⓐ	Ⓐ	Ⓐ	Ⓐ	Ⓐ	Ⓐ	Ⓐ	Ⓐ	Ⓐ	Ⓐ	Ⓐ	Ⓐ	Ⓐ	Ⓐ	Ⓐ	Ⓐ	Ⓐ	Ⓐ	Ⓐ	Ⓐ	Ⓐ	Ⓐ
Worcester Foregate St. d.	...	...	...	...	0714	...	0802	0839	0903	...	1016	...	1116	1151	1216	...	...	1351	1416	...	...	1533	1613	1634	1647	1715
Worcester Shrub Hill d.	0530	0612	0635	0650	|	0735	|	0845	|	0952	|	1052	|	|	|	1252	1317	|	|	1452	1517	1547	|	1640	|	|
Droitwich Spa d.	0538	0620	0643	0703	0723	0743	0811	0853	0912	1000	1025	1100	1125	1200	1225	1300	1325	1400	1425	1500	1525	1555	1622	1648	1655	1725
Kidderminster △ d.	0548	0633	0656	0716	0736	0754	0824	0906	0925	1010	1038	1110	1138	1210	1238	1310	1338	1410	1438	1510	1538	1606	1635	1701	1706	1738
Birmingham Snow Hill . a.	0627	0722	0738	0759	0815	0835	0907	0945	1004	1045	1115	1145	1215	1245	1315	1345	1415	1445	1515	1545	1616	1645	1718	1739	1745	1817
Birmingham Moor St... a.	0638	0728	0743	0806	0820	0840	0911	0950	1010	1050	1120	1150	1220	1250	1320	1350	1420	1450	1520	1550	1620	1650	1725	1745	1750	1825

	Ⓐ	Ⓐ	Ⓐ	Ⓐ	Ⓐ	Ⓐ	Ⓐ	⑥	⑥	⑥	⑥	⑥	⑥	⑥	⑥	⑥	⑥	⑥	⑥	⑥	⑥	⑥	⑥	⑥	⑥	⑥
Worcester Foregate St. d.	1756	...	1846	1946	2051	...	2217	...	...	...	0747	...	0856	0916	...	1016	...	...	1151	1216	1251	...	1351	1416	...	1516
Worcester Shrub Hill d.	|	1837	|	|	|	2154	2227	0544	0625	0701	|	0815	|	|	0948	|	1052	1117	|	|	|	1317	|	|	1452	|
Droitwich Spa d.	1805	1845	1855	1955	2100	2202	2235	0552	0633	0709	0756	0823	0905	0925	0956	1025	1100	1125	1200	1225	1300	1325	1400	1425	1500	1525
Kidderminster △ d.	1815	1855	1910	2010	2113	2213	2248	0605	0646	0722	0806	0836	0916	0938	1006	1038	1110	1138	1210	1238	1310	1338	1410	1438	1510	1538
Birmingham Snow Hill . a.	1855	1934	1955	2055	2155	2255	2328	0647	0732	0805	0845	0915	0956	1015	1041	1115	1145	1215	1245	1315	1345	1415	1445	1515	1545	1615
Birmingham Moor St... a.	1900	...	2000	2100	2200	2300	2337	0653	0740	0810	0850	0920	1001	1020	1050	1120	1150	1220	1250	1320	1350	1420	1450	1520	1550	1620

	⑥	⑥	⑥	⑥	⑥	⑥	⑥	⑥	⑥	⑥	⑥	⑦	⑦	⑦	⑦	⑦	⑦	⑦	⑦	⑦	⑦	⑦	⑦	⑦	⑦	⑦
Worcester Foregate St. d.	1547	1614	1647	...	1747	1812	1851	1951	...	2142	...	0920	1026	1114	1220	1326	1426	1528	1545	1626	1727	1826	...	...	2118	2223
Worcester Shrub Hill d.	|	|	|	1715	|	1817	|	|	2052	2154	2247	0926	|	1126	1226	|	|	|	|	|	|	|	1938	2037	2125	2229
Droitwich Spa d.	1556	1623	1656	1723	1756	1825	1900	2000	2100	2202	2255	0935	1035	1135	1235	1335	1435	1537	1554	1635	1736	1835	1946	2046	2133	2237
Kidderminster △ d.	1610	1636	1706	1736	1806	1837	1913	2013	2113	2213	2305	0945	1045	1145	1245	1345	1445	1547	1604	1645	1746	1845	1956	2056	2143	2247
Birmingham Snow Hill . a.	1645	1715	1745	1815	1845	1916	1955	2055	2154	2255	2336	1022	1122	1222	1322	1422	1522	1623	1636	1722	1824	1921	2033	2133	2219	2325
Birmingham Moor St... a.	1650	1720	1750	1820	1858	1920	2000	2100	2200	2300	2340	1029	1130	1230	1330	1430	1530	1630	1645	1730	1830	1925	2037	2137	2223	...

△ – **Severn Valley Railway** (Kidderminster - Bridgnorth: *26 km*). ✆ 01299 403816. www.svr.co.uk.

LM 2nd class STRATFORD UPON AVON - BIRMINGHAM 127

km		Ⓐ	Ⓐ	Ⓐ	Ⓐ	Ⓐ	Ⓐ	Ⓐ		Ⓐ	Ⓐ	Ⓐ	Ⓐ	Ⓐ	Ⓐ	Ⓐ	Ⓐ	Ⓐ	Ⓐ	Ⓐ	Ⓐ	⑥	⑥
0	**Stratford upon Avon** d.	0626	0652	0719	0743	0826	0926	1003	and at	1603	1626	1727	1755	1827	1851	1903	1926	2026	2126	2233	2330	0700	0743
13	Henley in Arden d.	0641	0707	0735	0758	0841	0941	|	the same	|	1641	1743	1807	1843	1907	|	1941	2041	2139	2246	|	0715	0758
40	**Birmingham** Moor St. d.	0724	0749	0808	0839	0918	1018	1049	minutes past each	1649	1719	1818	1839	1919	1935	1954	2018	2118	2218	2319	0006	0755	0838
41	**Birmingham** Snow Hill a.	0726	0751	0810	0841	0920	1020	1052	hour until	1652	1721	1821	1841	1922	1937	1956	2020	2120	2220	2321	0008	0757	0840

	⑥	⑥		⑥	⑥	⑥	⑥	⑥	⑥	⑥	⑥	⑥	⑥	⑦	⑦	⑦	⑦	⑦	⑦	⑦	⑦	⑦	⑦	⑦
Stratford upon Avon d.	0826	0903	and at	1703	1726	1754	1813	1848	1926	2026	2126	2233	2330	0929	1029	1129	1229	1329	1429	1529	1629	1729	1829	1929
Henley in Arden d.	0841	|	the same minutes	|	1741	1808	1828	1903	1941	2041	2140	2247	|	0943	1043	1143	1243	1343	1443	1543	1643	1743	1843	1943
Birmingham Moor St d.	0918	0949	past each	1749	1819	1839	1909	1944	2018	2118	2218	2319	0008	1015	1115	1215	1315	1415	1515	1615	1715	1815	1915	2015
Birmingham Snow Hill a.	0920	0952	hour until	1752	1821	1843	1911	1946	2020	2120	2220	2322	0010	1017	1117	1217	1317	1417	1517	1617	1717	1817	1917	2017

	Ⓐ	Ⓐ	Ⓐ	Ⓐ	Ⓐ	Ⓐ	Ⓐ		Ⓐ	Ⓐ	Ⓐ	Ⓐ	Ⓐ	Ⓐ	Ⓐ	Ⓐ	Ⓐ	Ⓐ	Ⓐ	Ⓐ	⑥	⑥	⑥
Birmingham Snow Hill d.	0553	0630	0640	0725	0828	0858	0928	and at	1458	1528	1628	1703	1728	1747	1758	1828	1928	2028	2128	2228	0725	0828	0858
Birmingham Moor St d.	0556	0633	0643	0728	0831	0901	0931	the same minutes	1501	1531	1631	1706	1731	1750	1801	1831	1931	2031	2131	2231	0728	0831	0901
Henley in Arden d.	|	0705	0720	0806	0906	|	1006	past each	|	1606	1707	1736	1807	1828	|	1907	2007	2107	2207	2307	0806	0906	|
Stratford upon Avon a.	0648	0720	0736	0823	0923	0949	1023	hour until	1541	1623	1724	1749	1824	1843	1859	1923	2023	2123	2223	2323	0821	0923	0949

	⑥	⑥	⑥		⑥	⑥	⑥	⑥	⑥	⑥	⑥	⑥	⑥		⑦	⑦	⑦	⑦	⑦	⑦	⑦	⑦	⑦	⑦
Birmingham Snow Hill d.	0928	0958	1028	and at	1628	1658	1707	1747	1828	1928	2028	2128	2228	...	0927	1026	1127	1227	1327	1427	1527	1627	1727	1827
Birmingham Moor St d.	0931	1001	1031	the same minutes	1631	1701	1710	1750	1831	1931	2031	2131	2231	...	0930	1029	1130	1230	1330	1430	1530	1630	1730	1830
Henley in Arden d.	1006	|	1106	past each	1706	|	1748	1828	1906	2007	2107	2207	2307	...	1001	1101	1201	1301	1401	1501	1601	1701	1801	1901
Stratford upon Avon a.	1023	1041	1123	hour until	1723	1741	1803	1843	1923	2023	2123	2223	2323	...	1015	1115	1215	1315	1415	1515	1615	1715	1815	1915

– THE SHAKESPEARE EXPRESS – 12. ✕ (1st class only) and 🍸 Birmingham Snow Hill - Stratford upon Avon and v.v. Runs ⑦ July 17 - Sept. 4, 2016. National Rail tickets NOT valid. From Birmingham Snow Hill 1023 and 1356 (Birmingham Moor Street 5 minutes later). From Stratford upon Avon at 1023 and 1356. Journey time: 59 – 74 minutes. To book contact Vintage Trains Ltd. ✆ 0121 708 4960. www.shakespeareexpress.com.

12 Standard-Symbole sind auf Seite 4 erklärt 113

128 LONDON - OXFORD, STRATFORD UPON AVON and BIRMINGHAM

2nd class CH

LONDON - BIRMINGHAM

km			Ⓐ	Ⓐ	Ⓐ	Ⓐ	Ⓐ	Ⓐ	Ⓐ	Ⓐ	Ⓐ	Ⓐ	Ⓐ	Ⓐ	Ⓐ	Ⓐ	Ⓐ	Ⓐ	Ⓐ	Ⓐ	Ⓐ	Ⓐ	Ⓐ
0	**London** Marylebone ◇ d.	Ⓐ	...	0605	0711	0748	0814	0837	0910	0940	1010	1040	1110	1140	1210	1240	1310	1340	1410	1440	1510	1540	1615
45	High Wycombe ◇ d.		...	|	|	0814	|	|	0936	|	1036	|	1134	|	1234	|	1334	|	1434	|	1536	|	|
88	Bicester North ◇ d.		0546	0647	0754	0836	|	0926	|	1030	|	1131	|	1227	|	1327	|	1427	|	1527	|	1627	|
111	Banbury ◇ d.		0604	0703	0807	0850	0908	0940	1008	1043	1107	1145	1210	1240	1307	1340	1410	1440	1507	1540	1609	1640	1708
143	Leamington Spa d.		0624	0721	0825	0907	0926	0958	1025	1101	1125	1204	1227	1258	1325	1358	1427	1458	1525	1558	1626	1658	1726
146	Warwick d.		0629	0726	0829	0912	0930	1003	|	1105	|	1209	|	1302	|	1402	|	1502	|	1602	|	1702	|
147	Warwick Parkway d.		0632	0729	0833	0915	0934	1017	1032	1109	1132	1213	1233	1306	1332	1406	1433	1506	1530	1606	1632	1706	1732
169	Solihull a.		0648	0750	0844	0930	0945	1023	1044	1124	1144	1230	1244	1321	1344	1421	1444	1521	1544	1621	1643	1721	1744
180	**Birmingham** Moor Street 126 a.		0658	0802	0853	0942	0954	1035	1053	1133	1156	1241	1256	1333	1356	1433	1456	1533	1556	1633	1653	1736	1754
181	**Birmingham** Snow Hill 126 a.		0703	0807	0858	...	0959	...	1058	1139	...	1248	...	1338	...	1438	...	1538	...	1638	1658	1741	1757
198	Stourbridge Junction a.		...	...	...	...	...	...	...	...	...	...	...	...	...	...	...	...	...	...	...	...	1825
210	Kidderminster 126 a.		...	...	...	...	...	...	...	...	...	...	...	...	...	...	...	...	...	...	...	...	1841

	Ⓐ	Ⓐ	Ⓐ	Ⓐ	Ⓐ	Ⓐ	Ⓐ	Ⓐ	Ⓐ	Ⓐ	Ⓐ	Ⓐ	Ⓐ	Ⓐ	Ⓐ		⑥	⑥	⑥	⑥	⑥	⑥	⑥
London Marylebone ◇ d.	1621	1647	1715	1747	1815	1847	1915	1947	2010	2040	2110	2140	2210	2237	2307	⑥	...	0700	0810	0840	0910	0940	1010
High Wycombe ◇ d.	1648	|	|	|	|	|	|	|	2034	2105	2136	2204	2235	2302	|		0612	0724	0834	|	0934	|	1034
Bicester North ◇ d.	1711	1734	|	1835	|	1936	2003	2034	2058	2126	2201	2228	2259	2327	2350		0645	0751	0857	0926	|	1024	|
Banbury ◇ d.	1724	1747	1809	1848	1910	1951	2016	2047	2112	2139	2214	2241	2313	2341	0003		0703	0804	0910	0940	1007	1037	1107
Leamington Spa d.	1741	1804	1827	1905	1928	2009	2035	2104	2130	2157	2231	2259	2331	2359	0021		0721	0823	0928	0958	1025	1055	1125
Warwick d.	|	1808	|	1909	|	2013	|	2108	|	2201	|	2303	|	0003	0025		0725	|	0932	1002	|	1059	|
Warwick Parkway d.	1747	1812	1834	1913	1934	2017	2043	2112	2136	2205	2238	2307	2337	0007	0029		0729	0829	0935	1006	1031	1103	1132
Solihull a.	1802	1826	1849	1928	1950	2032	2058	2133	2148	2220	2250	2330	2348	0023	0040		0747	0846	0950	1021	1043	1120	1144
Birmingham Moor Street 126 a.	1811	1838	1859	1938	2000	2041	2110	2143	2158	2230	2300	2339	0001	0036	0052		0800	0859	1001	1033	1055	1133	1156
Birmingham Snow Hill 126 a.	1819	...	1902	1943	2004	2046	...	2148	2206	2235	2304	2344	...	...	...		...	0904	1006	1038	...	1138	...
Stourbridge Junction a.	...	...	1926	...	2033	...	...	...	2236	...	2349	...	...	...	...		...	...	...	...	...	...	...
Kidderminster 126 a.	...	...	1938	...	2045	...	...	...	2247	...	...	...	...	...	...		...	...	...	...	...	...	...

	⑥	⑥	⑥	⑥	⑥	⑥	⑥	⑥	⑥	⑥	⑥	⑥	⑥	⑥	⑥	⑥	⑥	⑥	⑥	⑥	⑥	⑥	⑥
London Marylebone ◇ d.	1040	1110	1140	1210	1240	1310	1340	1410	1440	1510	1540	1610	1640	1710	1740	1810	1840	1910	1940	2010	2040	2110	2210
High Wycombe ◇ d.	|	1134	|	1234	|	1334	|	1434	|	1534	|	1634	|	1734	|	1834	|	1934	|	2034	|	2134	2234
Bicester North ◇ d.	1127	|	1224	|	1324	|	1424	|	1524	|	1624	|	1724	|	1824	|	1924	|	2024	|	2124	2157	2257
Banbury ◇ d.	1143	1210	1237	1307	1337	1409	1437	1507	1537	1609	1637	1707	1737	1809	1837	1907	1937	2009	2037	2107	2137	2210	2310
Leamington Spa d.	1201	1227	1255	1325	1355	1426	1455	1525	1555	1626	1655	1725	1755	1826	1855	1926	1955	2027	2055	2125	2155	2228	2328
Warwick d.	1205	|	1259	|	1359	|	1459	|	1559	|	1659	|	1759	|	1859	|	1959	|	2059	|	2159	2232	2332
Warwick Parkway d.	1209	1234	1303	1332	1403	1433	1503	1532	1603	1633	1703	1732	1803	1833	1903	1933	2003	2033	2103	2132	2203	2236	2337
Solihull a.	1224	1245	1320	1344	1420	1444	1520	1544	1620	1644	1720	1744	1820	1847	1918	1946	2018	2045	2118	2144	2218	2256	2354
Birmingham Moor Street 126 a.	1233	1256	1333	1356	1433	1456	1533	1556	1633	1656	1733	1756	1833	1858	1927	1958	2027	2057	2127	2157	2227	2306	0006
Birmingham Snow Hill 126 a.	1238	...	1338	...	1438	...	1538	...	1638	...	1738	...	1838	1904	1932	2004	2032	...	2132	...	2232	2311	...
Stourbridge Junction a.	...	...	...	...	...	...	...	...	...	...	...	...	...	...	...	...	...	...	...	...	...	...	...
Kidderminster 126 a.	...	...	...	...	...	...	...	...	...	...	...	...	...	...	...	...	...	...	...	...	...	...	...

		⑦	⑦	⑦	⑦	⑦	⑦	⑦	⑦	⑦		⑦	⑦	⑦	⑦	⑦		⑦	⑦	⑦	⑦	⑦
London Marylebone ◇ d.	⑦	0815	0910	0940	1010	1040	1110	1140	1210	1240		1710	1740	1810	1840	1910	...	1940	2010	2040	2110	2208
High Wycombe ◇ d.		0845	0934	|	1034	|	1134	|	1234	|	and at	1734	|	1835	|	1934	...	|	2034	|	2134	2234
Bicester North ◇ d.		0910	|	1024	|	1124	|	1224	|	1326	the	|	1826	|	1926	|	...	2026	|	2126	|	2256
Banbury ◇ d.		0929	1007	1037	1107	1137	1207	1237	1307	1339	same	1807	1839	1907	1939	2007	...	2039	2107	2139	2207	2309
Leamington Spa d.		0947	1025	1055	1125	1155	1225	1255	1325	1357	minutes	1825	1857	1925	1957	2025	...	2057	2125	2157	2225	2327
Warwick d.		0951	|	1059	|	1159	|	1259	|	1401	past	|	1901	|	2001	|	...	2101	|	2201	2229	2331
Warwick Parkway d.		0955	1032	1103	1132	1203	1232	1303	1332	1405	each	1832	1905	1932	2005	2032	...	2105	2132	2205	2234	2334
Solihull a.		1016	1044	1118	1144	1218	1244	1320	1344	1420	hour	1844	1920	1943	2020	2044	...	2128	2144	2220	2257	2349
Birmingham Moor Street a.		1024	1053	1127	1156	1227	1256	1329	1356	1429	until	1856	1929	1956	2029	2056	...	2137	2156	2229	2306	2358
Birmingham Snow Hill a.		1029	1058	1132	...	1232	...	1334	...	1434		...	1934	...	2034	...	...	2142	...	2234	2311	0004

		Ⓐ	Ⓐ	Ⓐ	Ⓐ	Ⓐ	Ⓐ	Ⓐ	Ⓐ	Ⓐ	Ⓐ	Ⓐ	Ⓐ	Ⓐ	Ⓐ	Ⓐ	Ⓐ	Ⓐ	Ⓐ	Ⓐ	Ⓐ	Ⓐ	Ⓐ
Kidderminster 126 d.	Ⓐ	...	...	...	...	...	0609	...	0705	0730	...	0809	...	...	...	...	...	...	...	...	...	...	...
Stourbridge Junction d.		...	...	...	...	...	0618	0638	0714	0738	...	0823	...	...	...	...	...	...	...	...	...	...	...
Birmingham Snow Hill 126 d.		...	...	...	...	...	0650	0707	0750	0807	0822	0852	0912	...	1012	...	1112	...	1212	...	1312	...	1412
Birmingham Moor Street 126 d.		...	0515	0542	0610	0628	0655	0711	0755	0810	0825	0855	0915	0955	1015	1055	1115	1155	1215	1255	1315	1355	1415
Solihull d.		...	0524	0551	0619	0638	0704	0720	0804	0819	0837	0907	0924	1004	1024	1104	1124	1204	1224	1304	1324	1404	1424
Warwick Parkway d.		...	0536	0605	0634	0659	0718	0739	0816	0834	0902	0919	0939	1016	1039	1116	1139	1216	1239	1316	1339	1416	1439
Warwick d.		...	|	0608	|	0702	|	|	|	0837	0906	|	0942	|	1042	|	1142	|	1242	|	1342	|	1442
Leamington Spa d.		...	0541	0613	0641	0706	0724	0746	0822	0842	0912	0925	0946	1022	1046	1123	1146	1222	1246	1322	1346	1422	1446
Banbury ◇ d.		0517	0559	0631	0659	0724	|	0806	0840	0900	0930	0944	1004	1040	1104	1140	1204	1240	1304	1340	1404	1440	1504
Bicester North ◇ d.		0533	0611	0646	0711	0739	|	|	|	0913	0942	|	1016	|	1116	|	1216	|	1317	|	1416	|	1516
High Wycombe ◇ d.		0600	|	|	|	|	|	|	|	|	1008	|	|	1110	|	1210	|	1310	|	1410	|	1510	|
London Marylebone ◇ a.		0630	0703	0735	0802	0833	0834	0907	0938	0959	1036	1040	1108	1140	1208	1241	1308	1341	1408	1441	1508	1538	1608

	Ⓐ	Ⓐ	Ⓐ	Ⓐ	Ⓐ	Ⓐ	Ⓐ	Ⓐ	Ⓐ	Ⓐ	Ⓐ	Ⓐ		⑥	⑥	⑥	⑥	⑥	⑥	⑥	⑥	⑥	⑥
Kidderminster 126 d.	...	...	...	...	...	...	...	...	...	...	...	...	⑥	...	...	...	...	0637	0712	...	0813	...	0910
Stourbridge Junction d.	...	...	...	...	...	...	...	...	...	...	...	...		...	...	...	...	0645	0722	...	0824	...	0920
Birmingham Snow Hill 126 d.	...	1512	...	1612	1652	1707	1752	1812	1840	1917	2015	2115		...	...	0612	0646	0712	0751	...	0853	0912	0951
Birmingham Moor Street 126 d.	1455	1515	1555	1615	1655	1710	1755	1815	1843	1920	2018	2118		...	...	0615	0649	0715	0755	0815	0856	0915	0955
Solihull d.	1504	1524	1604	1624	1704	1719	1806	1824	1852	1929	2027	2127		...	...	0624	0702	0724	0805	0824	0905	0924	1004
Warwick Parkway d.	1516	1539	1616	1639	1716	1736	1822	1845	1907	1949	2042	2147		...	...	0644	0714	0739	0818	0839	0916	0939	1019
Warwick d.	|	1542	|	1642	1719	1739	|	1848	|	1952	2045	2150		...	...	0647	|	0742	|	0842	|	0942	|
Leamington Spa d.	1522	1546	1622	1646	1723	1743	1828	1853	1912	1957	2050	2155		...	...	0652	0720	0746	0824	0846	0922	0946	1025
Banbury ◇ d.	1540	1604	1640	1704	1741	1801	1846	1912	1930	2015	2113	2213		0604	0629	0710	0739	0804	0844	0904	0940	1004	1044
Bicester North ◇ d.	|	1616	|	1716	|	1814	1858	1928	1946	2027	2125	2225		0616	0646	0722	0751	0816	|	0916	|	1016	|
High Wycombe ◇ d.	1610	|	1710	|	1811	1838	|	|	2013	|	2145	2245		0645	0710	0746	0811	|	0914	|	1014	|	1118
London Marylebone ◇ a.	1641	1712	1742	1813	1839	1911	1944	2023	2043	2113	2212	2311		0723	0736	0813	0840	0910	0941	1010	1041	1110	1146

	⑥	⑥	⑥	⑥	⑥	⑥	⑥	⑥	⑥	⑥	⑥	⑥	⑥	⑥	⑥	⑥	⑥	⑥	⑥	⑥	⑥	⑥	⑥
Kidderminster 126 d.	...	...	...	...	...	...	...	...	...	...	...	...	...	...	...	...	...	...	...	...	...	...	...
Stourbridge Junction d.	...	...	...	...	...	...	...	...	...	...	...	...	...	...	...	...	...	...	...	...	...	...	...
Birmingham Snow Hill 126 d.	1012	...	1112	...	1212	...	1312	...	1412	...	1512	...	1612	...	1712	...	1812	...	1912	...	2012	...	2115
Birmingham Moor Street 126 d.	1015	1055	1115	1155	1215	1255	1315	1355	1415	1455	1515	1555	1615	1655	1715	1755	1815	1855	1915	1955	2015	2045	2118
Solihull d.	1024	1104	1124	1204	1224	1304	1324	1404	1424	1504	1524	1604	1624	1704	1724	1804	1824	1904	1924	2004	2024	2055	2127
Warwick Parkway d.	1039	1116	1139	1220	1239	1316	1339	1416	1439	1516	1539	1616	1639	1716	1739	1816	1839	1916	1939	2016	2039	2113	2149
Warwick d.	1042	|	1142	|	1242	|	1342	|	1442	|	1542	|	1642	|	1742	|	1842	|	1942	|	2042	2117	2152
Leamington Spa d.	1046	1121	1146	1226	1246	1322	1346	1422	1446	1522	1546	1622	1646	1722	1746	1822	1846	1922	1946	2022	2046	2122	2157
Banbury ◇ d.	1104	1139	1204	1244	1304	1340	1407	1440	1504	1540	1604	1640	1704	1740	1804	1840	1904	1940	2004	2040	2104	2140	2215
Bicester North ◇ d.	1116	|	1216	|	1316	|	1420	|	1516	|	1616	|	1716	|	1816	|	1916	|	2016	|	2116	2152	2230
High Wycombe ◇ d.	|	1214	|	1314	|	1414	|	1514	|	1614	|	1714	|	1814	|	1914	|	2014	|	2114	|	2214	2301
London Marylebone ◇ a.	1211	1241	1310	1341	1411	1441	1510	1541	1610	1646	1710	1741	1810	1841	1910	1941	2010	2041	2110	2141	2210	2241	2347

		⑦	⑦	⑦	⑦	⑦	⑦	⑦	⑦	⑦	⑦	⑦		⑦	⑦	⑦	⑦	⑦	⑦	⑦	⑦	⑦
Birmingham Snow Hill d.	⑦	...	...	...	0912	...	1012	...	1112	...	1212	...		...	1712	...	1812	...	1912	...	2012	2115
Birmingham Moor Street d.		...	0825	0855	0915	0955	1015	1055	1115	1155	1215	1255	and at	1655	1715	1755	1815	1855	1915	1939	2015	2118
Solihull d.		...	0834	0904	0924	1004	1024	1104	1124	1204	1224	1304	the	1704	1724	1804	1824	1904	1924	1948	2024	2127
Warwick Parkway d.		...	0849	0916	0939	1016	1039	1116	1139	1216	1239	1316	same	1716	1739	1816	1839	1916	1939	|	2039	2144
Warwick d.		...	0852	|	0942	|	1042	|	1142	|	1242	|	minutes	|	1742	|	1842	|	1942	2011	2042	2147
Leamington Spa d.		...	0858	0922	0946	1022	1046	1122	1146	1222	1246	1322	past	1722	1746	1822	1846	1922	1946	2017	2046	2152
Banbury ◇ d.		0849	0916	0940	1004	1040	1104	1140	1204	1240	1304	1340	each	1740	1804	1840	1904	1941	2004	2036	2104	2215
Bicester North ◇ d.		0903	0929	|	1016	|	1116	|	1216	|	1316	|	hour	|	1816	|	1916	1953	2016	2052	2116	2230
High Wycombe ◇ d.		0932	|	1013	|	1114	|	1213	|	1313	|	1413	until	1812	|	1913	|	2016	|	2116	|	2301
London Marylebone ◇ a.		1006	1018	1041	1108	1142	1210	1240	1308	1340	1410	1440		1840	1910	1940	2010	2043	2108	2153	2212	2342

◇ – Frequent additional services are available between these stations.

CH 2nd class LONDON - OXFORD, STRATFORD UPON AVON and BIRMINGHAM 128

LONDON - STRATFORD UPON AVON

km			Ⓐ	Ⓐ	Ⓐ	Ⓐ	Ⓐ		Ⓐ	Ⓐ	Ⓐ	Ⓐ
0	**London** Marylebone d.	Ⓐ	...	0617	0814	1010	1210	...	1410	1621	1824	2043
45	High Wycombe d.		...	0701	|	1036	1234	...	1434	1648	1900	2114
88	Bicester North d.		0546	0733	|	|	|	...	|	1711	1941	2143
111	Banbury d.		0604	0749	0908	1107	1307	...	1507	1724	2006	2201
143	Leamington Spa a.		0623	0808	0925	1124	1324	...	1524	1741	2025	2219
	Leamington Spa d.		0653	0808	0940	1132	1332	...	1532	1811	2026	2220
146	Warwick d.		0658	0813	0945	1137	1337	...	1537	1816	|	2224
165	**Stratford u. Avon** Pkwy. a.		0722	0837	1008	1157	1401	...	1601	1846	2050	2245
167	**Stratford upon Avon** a.		0728	0843	1014	1203	1407	...	1607	1851	2054	2252

		⑥	⑥	⑥	⑥	⑥	⑥	⑥		⑦	⑦	⑦		⑦	⑦
London Marylebone d.	⑥	0700	1010	1210	1410	1610	1810	2010	⑦	0943	1210	1410	...	1610	1810
High Wycombe d.		0724	1034	1234	1434	1634	1834	2034		1018	1234	1434	...	1634	1835
Bicester North d.		0751	|	|	|	|	|	|		1047	|	|	...	|	|
Banbury d.		0804	1107	1307	1507	1707	1907	2107		1111	1307	1507	...	1707	1907
Leamington Spa a.		0822	1124	1324	1524	1724	1924	2124		1130	1324	1524	...	1724	1924
Leamington Spa d.		0830	1132	1332	1532	1732	1932	2132		1132	1332	1532	...	1732	1932
Warwick d.		0834	1138	1337	1537	1737	1937	2137		1138	1337	1537	...	1737	1937
Stratford u. Avon Pkwy. a.		0901	1155	1400	1558	1805	2000	2200		1157	1356	1556	...	1756	1956
Stratford upon Avon a.		0909	1202	1406	1605	1812	2007	2207		1204	1403	1603	...	1803	2003

		Ⓐ	Ⓐ	Ⓐ	Ⓐ	Ⓐ	Ⓐ	Ⓐ	Ⓐ	Ⓐ	Ⓐ
Stratford upon Avon d.	Ⓐ	0606	0733	0900	1037	1240	1437	1736	1912h	2139	2315
Stratford u. Avon Pkwy. d.		0610	0737	0904	1041	1244	1441	1740	1916h	2143	|
Warwick d.		0640	0803	0927	1104	1304	1505	1803	1952	2206	2334
Leamington Spa a.		0645	0807	0934	1111	1311	1515	1807	1956	2210	2338
Leamington Spa d.		0706	0808	0946	1123	1322	1546	1808	1957	2210	2339
Banbury d.		0724	0827	1004	1140	1340	1604	1827	2015	2230	2357
Bicester North d.		0739	0841	1016	|	|	1616	1843	2027	2246	...
High Wycombe d.		|	0905	|	1210	1410	|	|	|	2317	...
London Marylebone a.		0833	0935	1108	1241	1441	1712	1941	2113	2358	...

		⑥	⑥	⑥	⑥	⑥	⑥	⑥	⑥		⑦	⑦	⑦	⑦	⑦	⑦
Stratford upon Avon d.	⑥	0756	1040	1242	1442	1641	1841	2042	2215	⑦	0938	1246	1446	1646	1846	2038
Stratford u. Avon Pkwy. d.		0800	1044	1246	1446	1645	1845	2046	|		0941	1250	1450	1650	1850	2042
Warwick d.		0824	1108	1309	1509	1709	1909	2109	2235		1001	1311	1511	1711	1911	2103
Leamington Spa a.		0828	1115	1316	1516	1716	1916	2115	2240		1005	1317	1517	1717	1917	2107
Leamington Spa d.		0829	1146	1346	1546	1746	1946	2157	2241		1006	1346	1546	1746	1946	2108
Banbury d.		0848	1204	1407	1604	1804	2004	2215	2302		1024	1404	1604	1804	2004	2128
Bicester North d.		0903	1216	1420	1616	1816	2016	2230	...		1036	1416	1616	1816	2016	2142
High Wycombe d.		0930	|	|	|	|	|	2301	...		1103	|	|	|	|	2213
London Marylebone a.		1005	1310	1510	1710	1910	2110	2347	...		1139	1510	1710	1910	2108	2253

LONDON - OXFORD via High Wycombe

km			Ⓐ	Ⓐ	Ⓐ	Ⓐ	Ⓐ	Ⓐ	Ⓐ	Ⓐ	Ⓐ	Ⓐ	Ⓐ	Ⓐ		Ⓐ	Ⓐ	Ⓐ	Ⓐ	Ⓐ	Ⓐ	Ⓐ	Ⓐ	Ⓐ
0	**London** Marylebone d.	Ⓐ	0609	0648	0714	0740	0811	0837	0900	0935	1006	1035	1107	1135	and at the same minutes past each hour until ♥	1435	1507	1535	1618	1650	1718	1750	1818	1850
45	High Wycombe d.		0642	0713	0738	0804	|	0903	|	1001	|	1100	|	1200		1502	|	1559	|	1715	|	1815	|	1916
90	Bicester Village d.		0713	0745	0802	0832	0855	0924	0952	1024	1053	1124	1154	1223		1525	1554	1621	1706	1740	1805	1840	1908	1941
103	**Oxford** Parkway a.		0723	0753	0811	0839	0902	0933	1001	1032	1101	1132	1201	1230		1532	1601	1630	1713	1748	1812	1848	1915	1949
	Oxford a.		0729	0802	0822	0854	0911	0940	1011	1038	1110	1138	1210	1238		1546	1610	1638	1722	1756	1821	1855	1925	1958

	Ⓐ	Ⓐ	Ⓐ	Ⓐ		Ⓐ	Ⓐ	Ⓐ	Ⓐ		⑥	⑥	⑥	⑥	⑥	⑥	⑥	⑥	⑥	⑥		⑥	⑥	⑥
London Marylebone d.	1950	2007	2037	2102	...	2132	2207	2240	2310	⑥	0557	0625	0705	0735	0805	0835	0905	0935	1005	1035	and at the same minutes past each hour until ♥	1835	1905	1935
High Wycombe d.	2014	|	|	|	...	2159	|	2307	2339		0627	0652	0729	0759	|	0859	|	0959	|	1059		1859	|	1959
Bicester Village d.	2038	2055	2124	2155	...	2226	2256	2333	0010		0656	0724	0757	0827	0854	0922	0954	1022	1054	1124		1922	1954	2022
Oxford Parkway a.	2047	2104	2131	2202	...	2236	2303	2341	0018		0704	0734	0804	0836	0901	0931	1001	1029	1101	1131		1929	2001	2029
Oxford a.	2055	2113	2145	2210	...	2242	2312	2349	0026		0711	0745	0812	0844	0910	0939	1009	1038	1109	1139		1936	2009	2036

		⑥	⑥	⑥		⑥	⑥	⑥	⑥			⑦		⑦	⑦	⑦		⑦	⑦	⑦	⑦		⑦	⑦
London Marylebone d.	...	2005	2035	2105	...	2135	2205	2235	2310	...	⑦	0735	...	0835	0905	0935	and at the same minutes past each hour until ♥	2005	2035	2105	2135	...	2215	2315
High Wycombe d.	...	|	2059	|	...	2159	|	2306	2336	...		0805	...	0859	|	0959		|	2059	|	2159	...	|	2347
Bicester Village d.	...	2054	2122	2154	...	2222	2254	2331	2359	...		0834	...	0922	0953	1022		2053	2122	2153	2222	...	2305	0018
Oxford Parkway a.	...	2101	2131	2201	...	2229	2301	2338	0009	...		0843	...	0929	1000	1031		2100	2129	2200	2231	...	2312	0026
Oxford a.	...	2110	2138	2210	...	2238	2309	2345	0017	...		0850	...	0936	1008	1038		2108	2136	2208	2238	...	2320	0034

		Ⓐ	Ⓐ	Ⓐ	Ⓐ	Ⓐ	Ⓐ		Ⓐ	Ⓐ	Ⓐ	Ⓐ	Ⓐ	Ⓐ	Ⓐ	Ⓐ	Ⓐ	Ⓐ	Ⓐ		Ⓐ	Ⓐ	Ⓐ	Ⓐ
Oxford d.	Ⓐ	0536	0602	0625	0643	0720	0744	...	0801	0821	0840	0910	0942	1010	1041	1110	1142	1211	1240	and at the same minutes past each hour until ♥	1611	1638	1723	1803
Oxford Parkway d.		0542	0607	0631	0648	0725	0750	...	0808	0827	0850	0916	0947	1017	1047	1115	1147	1217	1247		1617	1645	1729	1809
Bicester Village d.		0552	0617	0640	0657	0735	0759	...	0820	0836	0859	0925	0957	1026	1056	1124	1156	1226	1256		1626	1656	1738	1822
High Wycombe d.		0625	0646	|	0725	|	0827	...	0850	|	0927	0950	|	1051	|	1151	|	1251	|		1651	|	1806	|
London Marylebone a.		0700	0723	0730	0757	0820	0857	...	0927	0930	0956	1019	1043	1118	1146	1218	1246	1318	1346		1721	1744	1835	1912

	Ⓐ	①–④	⑤	Ⓐ	Ⓐ	Ⓐ	Ⓐ	Ⓐ	Ⓐ	Ⓐ	Ⓐ	Ⓐ		⑥	⑥	⑥	⑥	⑥	⑥	⑥	⑥		⑥	⑥
Oxford d.	1822	1903	1903	1920	2000	2026	2055	2115	2137	2215	2242	2315	⑥	0612	0635	0710	0738	0811	0840	0909	0943	and at the same minutes past each hour until ♥	1911	1943
Oxford Parkway d.	1829	1909	1909	1929	2007	2031	2101	2121	2146	2221	2247	2320		0618	0641	0715	0745	0817	0847	0915	0948		1917	1948
Bicester Village d.	1838	1918	1918	1939	2019	2040	2110	2130	2155	2230	2258	2330		0628	0650	0726	0755	0826	0857	0926	0957		1926	1957
High Wycombe d.	1906	|	|	2007	|	2110	2138	|	2221	2300	2326	0004		0656	|	0754	|	0851	|	0951	|		1951	|
London Marylebone a.	1933	2008	2015	2037	2109	2138	2205	2218	2253	2352	0011	...		0727	0740	0828	0854	0918	0946	1018	1047		2018	2048

	⑥	⑥	⑥		⑥	⑥		⑦	⑦		⑦	⑦	⑦	⑦	⑦		⑦	⑦	⑦	⑦	⑦	⑦	⑦	⑦
Oxford d.	2011	2042	2109	...	2142	2209	⑦	0743	0810	...	0838	0901	0942	1011	1042	and at the same minutes past each hour until ♥	1811	1841	1909	1941	2011	2109	2148	2211
Oxford Parkway d.	2017	2048	2115	...	2148	2214		0749	0816	...	0844	0907	0948	1017	1048		1817	1847	1915	1947	2017	2114	2154	2216
Bicester Village d.	2026	2057	2126	...	2157	2225		0758	0825	...	0853	0918	0957	1026	1057		1826	1856	1926	1956	2026	2125	2203	2224
High Wycombe d.	2051	|	2151	...	2222	2251		0823	0850	...	|	0944	|	1051	|		1851	|	1951	|	2051	2150	|	2251
London Marylebone a.	2118	2147	2218	...	2249	2327		0851	0925	...	0942	1011	1045	1118	1145		1918	1945	2017	2048	2118	2216	2256	2316

h – Change at **Hatton** (a. 1936/d. 1944).

♥ – Timings may vary by up to 2 minutes.

CH 2nd class LONDON - AYLESBURY 129

Until December 23 services from Aylesbury Vale Parkway, Aylesbury and Amersham depart 3 minutes earlier

km			Ⓐ	Ⓐ	Ⓐ	Ⓐ	Ⓐ	Ⓐ	Ⓐ	Ⓐ	Ⓐ	Ⓐ	Ⓐ	Ⓐ	Ⓐ	Ⓐ	Ⓐ	Ⓐ	Ⓐ	Ⓐ	Ⓐ	Ⓐ	Ⓐ	Ⓐ	Ⓐ
0	**London** Marylebone △ d.	Ⓐ	0633	0652	0757	0857	0957	1057	1157	1257	1357	1457	1527	1612	1642	1730	1759	1832	1859	1932	1956	2057	2157	2257	2357
38	Amersham △ d.		0708	0727	0832	0932	1032	1132	1232	1332	1432	1532	1602	1647	1717	|	1829	|	1934	2008	2031	2132	2232	2332	0032
60	**Aylesbury** △ d.		0730	0756	0854	0954	1054	1154	1254	1354	1454	1554	1626	1709	1739	1824	1855	1925	2003	2030	2053	2154	2254	2354	0054
65	**Aylesbury** Vale Parkway a.		0739	0804	0903	1003	1103	1203	1303	1403	1503	1603	1634	1718	1748	1832	1904	1933	2011	2039	2102	2203	2303	0003	0103

		⑥	⑥	⑥	⑥	⑥		⑥	⑥	⑥	⑥		⑦	⑦	⑦	⑦	⑦		⑦	⑦	⑦		⑦
London Marylebone △ d.	⑥	...	0727	0757	0857	0957	and at the same minutes past each hour until	2057	2157	2227	2257	⑦	0757	0857	0957	1057	1157	and at the same minutes past each hour until	1957	2057	2127	...	2227
Amersham △ d.		0702	0802	0832	0932	1032		2132	2232	2302	2332		0832	0932	1032	1132	1232		2032	2132	2202	...	2302
Aylesbury △ d.		0726	0824	0854	0954	1054		2154	2254	2324	2354		0854	0954	1054	1154	1254		2054	2154	2224	...	2324
Aylesbury Vale Parkway a.		...	0833	0903	1003	1103		2203	2303	2333	0003		0903	1003	1103	1203	1303		2103	2203	2233	...	2333

		Ⓐ	Ⓐ	Ⓐ	Ⓐ	Ⓐ	Ⓐ	Ⓐ	Ⓐ	Ⓐ	Ⓐ	Ⓐ	Ⓐ	Ⓐ	Ⓐ	Ⓐ	Ⓐ	Ⓐ	Ⓐ	Ⓐ	Ⓐ		Ⓐ	Ⓐ	Ⓐ
Aylesbury Vale Parkway d.	Ⓐ	0516	0544	0619	0653	0725	0751	0812	0839	0918	1013	1113	1213	1313	1413	1513	1613	1643	1734	1809	1842	...	1943	2048	2113
Aylesbury ▽ d.		0521	0549	0624	0658	0730	0802	0817	0844	0923	1018	1118	1218	1318	1418	1518	1618	1648	1750	1821	1847	...	1948	2053	2118
Amersham ▽ d.		0543	0611	0647	0721	0753	0825	0839	0905	0944	1039	1139	1239	1339	1439	1539	1639	1709	1811	1842	1908	...	2009	2114	2139
London Marylebone ▽ a.		0616	0649	0722	0753	0826	0900	0916	0944	1023	1120	1220	1320	1420	1520	1620	1720	1748	1850	1918	1948	...	2049	2152	2219

		⑥	⑥	⑥	⑥		⑥	⑥	⑥	⑥			⑦	⑦	⑦	⑦	⑦		⑦	⑦	⑦	⑦	⑦
Aylesbury Vale Parkway d.	⑥	0613	0713	0813	0913	and at the same minutes past each hour until	1913	2013	2113	2213	...	⑦	0713	0813	0913	1013	1113	and at the same minutes past each hour until	1813	1913	2013	2113	2243
Aylesbury ▽ d.		0618	0718	0818	0918		1918	2018	2118	2218	2318		0718	0818	0918	1018	1118		1818	1918	2018	2118	2248
Amersham ▽ d.		0639	0739	0839	0939		1939	2039	2139	2239	2342		0739	0839	0939	1039	1139		1839	1939	2039	2139	2309
London Marylebone ▽ a.		0718	0818	0920	1020		2020	2120	2220	2320	...		0820	0920	1020	1120	1220		1920	2020	2120	2220	2347

△ – Additional trains London Marylebone - Aylesbury on Ⓐ at 0727 and hourly until 1427, 1557, 1627, 1711, 1742, 1812, 1843, 1918, 2023, 2127, 2227, 2327; on ⑥ at 0827 and hourly until 2127, 2327, 2357; on ⑦ at 1527 and hourly until 2027, 2157, 2257, 2327.

▽ – Additional trains Aylesbury - London Marylebone on Ⓐ at 0607, 0638, 0712, 0741, 0902, 0948 and hourly until 1548, 1715, 1918, 2021, 2148, 2248; on ⑥ at 0648 and hourly until 2148; on ⑦ at 0848, 0948, 1448 and hourly until 2148.

130 LONDON - WORCESTER - HEREFORD

Most trains convey 🍸 GW

Other services: London Paddington - Oxford see Table **131**; Worcester - Hereford see Table **125**.

km			Ⓐ	Ⓐ	Ⓐ	Ⓐ	Ⓐ	Ⓐ	Ⓐ	Ⓐ	Ⓐ	Ⓐ	Ⓐ	Ⓐ	Ⓐ	Ⓐ	Ⓐ	Ⓐ	Ⓐ	Ⓐ	Ⓐ	Ⓐ	Ⓐ	⑤		⑥	⑥
0	**London** Padd. **131 132** d.	Ⓐ	...	0512	0545	0652	0750	0821	0921	1022	1120	1220	1322	1421	1522	1552	1622	1722	1749	1822	1922	2022	2148	2318	⑥	0517	0621
58	Reading **131 132** d.		...	0550	0619	0722	0822	0853	0953	1052	1152	1251	1352	1453	1552	1620	1652**u**	1750	1822	1851	1952	2053	2225	0005		0554	0654
103	**Oxford** **131** d.		0514	0621	0650	0801	0858	0924	1019	1119	1221	1321	1418	1520	1621	1646	1725	1817	1850	1922	2021	2121	2254	0036		0624	0723
148	Moreton in Marsh d.		0542	0648	0727	0839	0936	0959	1055	1156	1259	1357	1456	1555	1656	1725	1812	1855	1929	2001	2059	2157	2335	0115		0701	0757
172	Evesham a.		0559	...	0744	0856	...	1018	1109	1216	1317	1416	1511	1612	1715	...	1831	1915	1945	2020	2118	2217	2354	...		0720	0816
172	Evesham d.		0559	...	0751	0857	...	1025	1110	1224	1318	1428	1511	1621	1717	...	1838	1915	1946	2022	2122	2218	2355	...		0724	0821
194	**Worcester** Shrub Hill a.		0619	...	0810	0915	...	1044	1128	1243	1338	1449	1525	1640	1736	...	1857	1935	2005	2041	2147	2240	0015	...		0743	0840
195	**Worcester** Foregate St a.		0625	...	0816	0919	...	1050	1134	1248	1342	...	1540	1644	1744	...	1911	1939	...	2045	2151	2244	...	...		0748	0844
208	Great Malvern a.		...	...	...	0932	...	1107	...	1302	1357	...	...	...	1758	...	1926	1953	...	2059	2207	2259	...	...		0802	0901
219	Ledbury a.		...	...	...	...	...	1120	...	1323	...	...	...	...	...	...	...	2008	...	2114	2235	...	...	...		...	...
241	**Hereford** a.		...	...	...	...	...	1141	...	1347	...	...	...	...	...	...	...	2029	...	2134	2255	...	...	...		...	...

	⑥	⑥	⑥	⑥	⑥	⑥	⑥	⑥	⑥	⑥	⑥	⑥	⑥		⑦	⑦	⑦	⑦	⑦	⑦	⑦	⑦	⑦	⑦	⑦	⑦	⑦
London Padd. **131 132** d.	0721	0821	0921	1021	1121	1321	1421	1521	1621	1721	1821	1950	2148	⑦	0803	0842	0935	1042	1242	1342	1442	1542	1642	1742	1842	1942	2142
Reading **131 132** d.	0754	0853	0954	1055	1154	1354	1454	1554	1654	1755	1854	2022	2221		0845	0922	1016	1122	1322	1422	1522	1622	1725	1825	1925	2022	2222
Oxford **131** d.	0823	0924	1025	1123	1225	1425	1523	1623	1723	1823	1923	2049	2251		0917	0952	1052	1152	1352	1452	1556	1656	1756	1856	1956	2054	2254
Moreton in Marsh d.	0857	1001	1059	1200	1300	1503	1557	1657	1804	1900	1959	2126	2328		0952	1025	1125	1230	1430	1526	1630	1728	1833	1932	2032	2131	2331
Evesham a.	0916	1020	1118	1219	1318	1521	1616	1716	1823	1919	2019	2143	2345		1010	1041	1142	1249	1449	1544	1649	1744	1849	1954	2050	2150	2350
Evesham d.	0921	1024	1131	1227	1323	1522	1621	1721	1824	1920	2023	2143	2346		1014	1045	1148	1250	1450	1545	1649	1744	1850	1955	2051	2151	2351
Worcester Shrub Hill a.	0940	1043	1150	1246	1342	1541	1640	1740	1844	1939	2043	2202	0008		1033	1101	1207	1310	1510	1604	1708	1803	1908	2014	2111	2210	0013
Worcester Foregate St. a.	0944	1048	1156	1250	1344	1545	1644	1744	1856	1944	2049	2205	...		1036	1105	1210	1314	1514	1607	1711	1806	1913	2018	...	2214	...
Great Malvern a.	1000	1101	...	1305	1400	1600	1700	1801	1910	...	2102	2220	...		1054	1119	1222	1327	1528	...	1723	...	1925	2032	...	2227	...
Ledbury a.	...	1121	...	1321	...	...	...	...	1924	...	2116	...	...		...	1134	...	1342	1542	...	1736	...	...	2046	...	...	...
Hereford a.	..	1140	...	1339	...	...	...	...	1945	...	2135	...	...		...	1153	...	1407	1601	...	1753	...	...	2104	...	...	...

		Ⓐ	Ⓐ	Ⓐ	Ⓐ	Ⓐ	Ⓐ	Ⓐ	Ⓐ	Ⓐ	Ⓐ	Ⓐ	Ⓐ	Ⓐ	Ⓐ	Ⓐ	Ⓐ	Ⓐ	Ⓐ	Ⓐ	Ⓐ	Ⓐ	Ⓐ		⑥	⑥	⑥
Hereford d.	Ⓐ	...	0450	0528	...	...	0642	...	...	...	...	...	1209	...	...	...	1514	...	...	...	...	...	2151	⑥	...	0617	0710
Ledbury d.		...	|	0545	...	...	0659	...	...	...	...	...	1224	...	...	...	1531	...	...	...	...	...	2209		...	0634	0730
Great Malvern d.		...	0517	0559	...	...	0712	...	...	0954	...	...	1236	1425	...	...	1545	...	...	1835	1944	...	2222		0556	0649	0744
Worcester Foregate St. d.		...	0531	0614	...	0653	0728	0826	...	1007	...	1206	1256	1439	...	1550	1601	...	1728	1848	1956	2059	2234		0609	0704	0759
Worcester Shrub Hill d.		0511	0536	0619	...	0655	0732	0839	...	1010	1122	1208	1258	1443	1521	1554	1605	...	1731	1852	2004	2103	2243		0612	0708	0804
Evesham a.		0525	0553	0635	...	0712	0749	0854	...	1026	1136	1224	1316	1501	1535	1607	1622	...	1746	1908	2019	2120	2300		0629	0725	0821
Evesham d.		0527	0558	0637	...	0712	0750	0905	...	1030	1136	1232	1330	1502	1535	1608	1625	...	1747	1908	2019	2121	2301		0629	0726	0825
Moreton in Marsh d.		0547	0614	0656	0710	0727	0811	0923	0950	1048	1152	1250	1349	1522	1552	1624	1645	1732	1805	1926	2047	2141	2326		0648	0745	0845
Oxford **131** a.		0624	0652	0732	0751	0812	0849	0959	1028	1127	1227	1325	1423	1559	1628	1653	1728	1801	1901	2000	2124	2227	2358		0725	0826	0925
Reading **131 132** a.		0653	0725	0756	0822	...	0916	1024	1054	1153	1255	1354	1454	1625	1654	1724	1754	1825	1931	2024	2155	2253	0042**b**		0754	0852	0952
London Padd. **131 132** a.		0728	0757	0829	0851	...	0947	1057	1129	1227	1330	1428	1530	1659	1729	1759	1829	1859	2006	2059	2242**a**	2338	0122		0828	0927	1025

	⑥	⑥	⑥	⑥	⑥	⑥	⑥	⑥	⑥	⑥	⑥	⑥	⑥		⑦	⑦	⑦	⑦	⑦		⑦	⑦	⑦	⑦	⑦	⑦	⑦
Hereford d.	...	...	...	...	1213	...	1513	...	...	...	...	2020	...	⑦	...	...	...	...	1332	...	1432	...	1634	...	1830	...	...
Ledbury d.	...	...	...	...	1231	...	1531	...	...	...	...	2040	...		...	...	...	...	1351	...	1452	...	1652	...	1848	...	...
Great Malvern d.	0843	0951	1058	...	1246	1434	1544	1634	1749	1835	...	2053	2241		0922	...	1115	1320	1407	...	1509	...	1705	...	1911	2015	...
Worcester Foregate St. d.	0858	1004	1111	1206	1301	1457	1559	1655	1802	1849	2002	2111	2253		0934	1025	1128	1332	1422	...	1524	1628	1724	1826	1929	2028	...
Worcester Shrub Hill d.	0902	1008	1115	1210	1306	1501	1604	1702	1806	1902	2006	2115	2256		0940	1029	1131	1336	1429	...	1528	1632	1728	1830	1933	2031	2128
Evesham a.	0919	1024	1131	1226	1323	1518	1620	1718	1823	1918	2023	2132	2314		0956	1045	1147	1352	1446	...	1546	1646	1747	1848	1948	2048	2145
Evesham d.	0929	1030	1132	1230	1326	1526	1621	1726	1827	1927	2024	2133	...		0957	1055	1155	1355	1455	...	1555	1655	1755	1855	1955	2049	2149
Moreton in Marsh d.	0948	1049	1150	1249	1345	1545	1641	1744	1845	1945	2043	2152	...		1016	1113	1213	1413	1513	...	1613	1713	1813	1913	2013	2108	2208
Oxford **131** a.	1028	1124	1226	1324	1426	1623	1723	1823	1924	2023	2126	2235	...		1049	1149	1249	1449	1550	...	1653	1753	1850	1953	2053	2148	2243
Reading **131 132** a.	1054	1152	1255	1352	1452	1654	1754	1853	1953	2051	2156	2310	...		1127	1227	1327	1524	1627	...	1727	1823	1923	2023	2121	2220	2314
London Padd. **131 132** a.	1128	1227	1330	1427	1526	1728	1829	1927	2027	2125	2229	2352	...		1204	1303	1404	1603	1705	...	1805	1900	2002	2100	2202	2301	2359

a – 2236 on ⑤. b – 0037 on ⑦. u – Calls to pick up only.

131 LONDON - OXFORD via Reading

GW

km			②–⑤	Ⓐ	Ⓐ	Ⓐ	Ⓐ	Ⓐ	Ⓐ	Ⓐ	Ⓐ	Ⓐ	Ⓐ	Ⓐ	Ⓐ	Ⓐ	Ⓐ	Ⓐ	Ⓐ	Ⓐ	Ⓐ	Ⓐ	Ⓐ	Ⓐ	Ⓐ	Ⓐ
0	**London** P ◇ **130 132** d.	Ⓐ	0022	0512	0545	0620	0652	0721	0750	0821	0851	0921	0950	1022	1050	1120	1150	1220	1250	1322	1350	1421	1450	1522	1552	1622
58	Reading **130 132** d.		0101	0550	0619	0651	0722	0753	0822	0853	0922	0953	1022	1052	1122	1152	1222	1251	1320	1352	1420	1453	1522	1552	1620	1652**u**
85	Didcot Parkway **132** d.		0119	0607	|	0708	0744	|	|	|	0938	|	|	|	1138	|	|	|	1335	|	|	|	1538	|	|	|
102	**Oxford** **130** a.		0134	0619	0648	0723	0758	0819	0848	0918	0952	1017	1048	1117	1151	1219	1248	1316	1350	1416	1447	1517	1550	1616	1644	1723

	Ⓐ	Ⓐ	Ⓐ	Ⓐ	Ⓐ		Ⓐ	Ⓐ	Ⓐ	Ⓐ	Ⓐ	Ⓐ	⑤	①–④	⑤	①–④	Ⓐ	⑤	Ⓐ		⑥	⑥	⑥	⑥	⑥	⑥
London P ◇ **130 132** d.	1649	1722	1749	1822	1850	...	1922	1950	2022	2048	2118	2148	2218	2218	2248	2248	2318	2342	2333	⑥	0022	0517	0550	0621	0650	0721
Reading **130 132** d.	1721	1750	1822	1851	1923	...	1952	2022	2053	2122	2151	2225	2250	2300	2329	2334	0005	0027	0027		0104	0554	0622	0654	0722	0754
Didcot Parkway **132** d.	1738	|	|	|	|	...	|	|	|	|	|	|	|	|	|	|	|	0046	0056		0122	0608	0638	|	|	|
Oxford **130** a.	1753	1814	1848	1919	1952	...	2020	2052	2117	2151	2218	2248	2325	2330	2357	0001	0034	0102	0118		0137	0621	0652	0719	0748	0818

	⑥	⑥		⑥	⑥	⑥	⑥		⑥	⑥	⑥	⑥		⑦	⑦	⑦	⑦		⑦	⑦	⑦		⑦	⑦
London P ◇ **130 132** d.	0750	0821	and at the same	1950	2018	2050	2118	...	2148	2218	2250	2333	⑦	0803	0842	0935	1042	and	1942	2042	2142	...	2203	2242
Reading **130 132** d.	0822	0853	minutes past	2022	2051	2122	2154	...	2221	2255	2328	0017		0845	0922	1016	1122	hourly	2022	2120	2222	...	2246	2321
Didcot Parkway **132** d.	|	|	each hour until	|	|	2139	2210	...	2237	2312	2347	0033		0901	0938	1032	1138	until	2038	2137	2238	...	2302**a**	2339**a**
Oxford **130** a.	0847	0916	♥	2047	2116	2151	2223	...	2248	2326	0001	0054		0912	0949	1044	1149		2052	2150	2252	...	*2355**	*0015**

		②–⑤	②–⑤	Ⓐ	Ⓐ	Ⓐ	Ⓐ	Ⓐ	Ⓐ	Ⓐ	Ⓐ	Ⓐ	Ⓐ	Ⓐ	Ⓐ	Ⓐ	Ⓐ	Ⓐ	Ⓐ	Ⓐ	Ⓐ	Ⓐ	Ⓐ	Ⓐ	Ⓐ	Ⓐ
Oxford **130** d.	Ⓐ	0007	0027	0400**b**	0501	0542	0559	0630	0655	0734	0753	0808	0851	0901	0931	1001	1031	1101	1131	1201	1231	1301	1329	1401	1431	1501
Didcot Parkway **132** d.		0021	0046	0412	0516	0600	0613	|	0710	|	|	0821	|	0916	|	|	|	|	|	|	|	|	|	|	|	|
Reading **130 132** a.		0037	0113	0440	0541	0616	0626	0653	0725	0756	0822	0834	0916	0932	0954	1024	1054	1124	1153	1225	1255	1324	1354	1425	1454	1524
London P ◇ **130 132** a.		0122	0207	0547	0644	0654	0711	0728	0757	0829	0851	0907	0947	1013	1029	1057	1129	1159	1227	1313	1330	1358	1428	1500	1530	1601

	Ⓐ	Ⓐ	Ⓐ	Ⓐ	Ⓐ	Ⓐ	Ⓐ	Ⓐ	Ⓐ	Ⓐ	Ⓐ	Ⓐ	⑤	①–④	Ⓐ	Ⓐ	Ⓐ		⑥	⑥	⑥	⑥	⑥	⑥	⑥	⑥
Oxford **130** d.	1531	1601	1631	1701	1730	1801	1831	1905	1931	2001	2031	2101	2132	2132	2211	2230	2309	⑥	0007	0027	0359	0514	0549	0631	0659	0730
Didcot Parkway **132** d.	|	|	|	|	|	|	|	|	|	|	|	|	|	|	2226	|	2323		0021	0046	0410	0531	0601	|	|	|
Reading **130 132** a.	1554	1625	1654	1724	1754	1825	1855	1931	1955	2024	2053	2126	2155	2155	2243	2253	2341		0042	0113	0430	0557	0627	0657	0723	0754
London P ◇ **130 132** a.	1629	1659	1729	1759	1829	1859	1929	2006	2030	2059	2128	2201	2236	2242	2325	2338	0027		0122	0207	0531	0701	0731	0737	0758	0828

	⑥	⑥		⑥	⑥	⑥	⑥	⑥	⑥	⑥	⑥	⑥		⑦	⑦	⑦		⑦	⑦	⑦	⑦	⑦	⑦	⑦
Oxford **130** d.	0801	0829	and at the same	1929	2001	2027	2101	2128	2201	2235	2301	2310	⑦	*0715**	0852	1000	and	1755	1855	1955	2055	2150	2245	*2300**
Didcot Parkway **132** d.	|	|	minutes past	|	|	|	|	2142	2213	2251	2315	2342		0759	0903	1013	hourly	1808	1908	2008	2107	2204	2258	2350
Reading **130 132** a.	0825	0852	each hour until	1953	2025	2051	2125	2156	2228	2310	2332	0002		0818	0919	1027	until	1823	1923	2023	2121	2220	2314	0016
London P ◇ **130 132** a.	0859	0927	♥	2027	2059	2125	2159	2229	2302	2352	0017	0105		0900	0958	1105		1900	2002	2100	2202	2301	2359	0115

a – Arrival time.
b – ②–⑤ only.
u – Calls to pick up only.
* – Connection by 🚐.
◇ – London Paddington.
♥ – Timings may vary by up to 3 minutes.

GW 🍸 available on most services **LONDON - BRISTOL - CARDIFF - SWANSEA** 132

LONDON - BRISTOL TEMPLE MEADS - TAUNTON

Timings may vary ± 4 minutes until 31 December

km			Ⓐ	Ⓐ	Ⓐ	Ⓐ	Ⓐ	Ⓐ	Ⓐ	Ⓐ	Ⓐ	Ⓐ	Ⓐ	Ⓐ	Ⓐ	Ⓐ	Ⓐ	Ⓐ	Ⓐ	Ⓐ	Ⓐ	Ⓐ	Ⓐ	Ⓐ
			Q			A					A													
0	**London** Paddington. 130 131 d.	Ⓐ	0518	0630	0700	0730	0800	0830	0900	0930	1000	1030	1100	1130	1200	1230	1300	1330	1400	1430	1500	1530	1600	1630
58	Reading 130 131 d.		0555	0657	0730	0759	0828	0859	0928	0959	1027	1059	1127	1159	1227	1259	1328	1359	1428	1459	1527	1558	1628	1659
85	Didcot Parkway 131 d.		0610	0712	0744	|	0841	|	0942	|	1043	|	1142	|	1242	|	1342	1413	|	1514	|	1612	|	1712
124	Swindon d.		0628	0730	0801	0827	0900	0933	1000	1025	1059	1126	1200	1229	1300	1328	1400	1430	1456	1530	1556	1629	1657	1730
151	Chippenham d.		0642	0744	0817	0842	0915	0945	1014	1039	1114	1140	1214	1244	1313	1343	1414	1444	1510	1544	1609	1644	1711	1745
172	Bath a.		0655	0757	0829	0855	0927	0959	1028	1054	1129	1156	1228	1259	1327	1356	1428	1459	1524	1600	1623	1658	1724	1759
190	**Bristol** Temple Meads.. 120a a.		0710	0817	0845	0910	0943	1015	1043	1111	1144	1213	1243	1315	1345	1412	1443	1515	1540	1615	1638	1714	1739	1814
221	Weston-super-Mare 120a a.		...	...	...	|	...	...	...	...	1206	...	...	...	...	...	...	...	...	1652	...	1752	...	1851
262	**Taunton** 120a a.		...	...	...	0944	...	...	...	...	1229	...	...	...	...	...	...	...	...	...	...	...	...	1929

	Ⓐ	Ⓐ	Ⓐ	Ⓐ	Ⓐ	⑤	Ⓐ		Ⓐ	Ⓐ	Ⓐ	⑤	①–④	Ⓐ		⑥	⑥	⑥	⑥	⑥	⑥	⑥	⑥	⑥
											B			C				D						
London Paddington.. 130 131 d.	1700	1730	1800	1830	1900	1912	1930	...	2000	2045	2145	2215	2215	2330	⑥	0630	0700	0730	0800	0830	0900	0930	1000	1030
Reading 130 131 d.	1727	1757	1828	1858	1928	1938	1959	...	2029	2112	2212	2243	2255	0010		0700	0729	0759	0828	0858	0928	0959	1028	1059
Didcot Parkway 131 d.	1742	1811	1842	1913	1942	1954	2012	...	2042	2127	2232	2303	2314	0028		0714	|	0813	|	0913	|	1013	|	1114
Swindon d.	1800	1830	1900	1930	2001	2011	2030	...	2100	2144	2250	2322	2333	0048		0733	0757	0832	0857	0931	0955	1031	1056	1132
Chippenham d.	1815	1845	1914	1946	2016	|	2044	...	2116	2158	2304	2336	2346	0103		0747	0811	0846	0910	0946	1010	1046	1111	1146
Bath a.	1828	1858	1928	1959	2029	k	2059	...	2129	2212	2318	2349	2358	0115		0800	0824	0900	0924	1000	1024	1100	1124	1200
Bristol Temple Meads... 120a a.	1844	1913	1943	2014	2044	2059	2114	...	2144	2228	2332	0004	0014	0130		0815	0839	0915	0939	1015	1039	1115	1139	1215
Weston-super-Mare 120a a.	...	1948	...	2053	...	...	2150	...	...	...	0006s	...	...	...		...	...	|	...	...	...	...	...	...
Taunton 120a a.	...	2023	...	...	...	...	...	...	...	...	0037	...	...	...		...	...	0950	...	...	...	...	...	...

	⑥	⑥	⑥	⑥	⑥	⑥	⑥	⑥	⑥	⑥		⑥	⑥	⑥	⑥	⑥	⑥	⑥	⑥	⑥	⑥	⑥	⑥	⑥
													A								B			
London Paddington.. 130 131 d.	1100	1130	1200	1230	1300	1330	1400	1430	1500	1530	...	1600	1630	1700	1730	1800	1830	1900	1930	2000	2030	2130	2235	2330
Reading 130 131 d.	1128	1159	1228	1259	1328	1359	1428	1459	1528	1600	...	1628	1659	1728	1759	1828	1859	1928	1959	2028	2059	2159	2303	0006
Didcot Parkway 131 d.	|	1214	|	1314	|	1414	|	1513	|	1614	...	|	1713	|	1812	|	1913	|	2013	2042	2114	2214	2322	0023
Swindon d.	1156	1232	1255	1332	1357	1433	1456	1531	1556	1633	...	1656	1731	1756	1831	1856	1931	1956	2031	2101	2132	2232	2341	0042
Chippenham d.	1210	1245	1310	1346	1410	1446	1510	1546	1610	1647	...	1710	1746	1810	1845	1910	1946	2010	2046	2116	2146	2247	2355	0056
Bath a.	1224	1259	1324	1400	1424	1500	1524	1600	1624	1700	...	1724	1800	1824	1858	1924	2000	2024	2059	2129	2200	2300	0009	0110
Bristol Temple Meads... 120a a.	1239	1314	1342	1415	1439	1515	1541	1615	1639	1715	...	1739	1815	1840	1913	1938	2015	2040	2114	2145	2214	2315	0023	0124
Weston-super-Mare 120a a.	...	...	...	...	...	...	...	...	...	...	...	...	1836	...	1950	...	2036	2126	...	...	2247s	...	...	...
Taunton 120a a.	...	...	...	...	...	...	...	...	...	...	...	...	1907	...	...	...	2102	2159	...	...	2317	...	...	...

		⑦	⑦	⑦	⑦	⑦	⑦	⑦	⑦	⑦	⑦	⑦	⑦	⑦	⑦	⑦	⑦	⑦	⑦	⑦	⑦	⑦	⑦	⑦
		D					E										B							
London Paddington.. 130 131 d.	⑦	0800	0900	1000	1100	1200	1300	1400	1500	1527	1600	1627	1700	1730	1800	1827	1903	1927	2003	2103	2203	2237	2303	2337
Reading 130 131 d.		0839	0940	1040	1140	1240	1338	1438	1538	1603	1638	1700	1738	1806	1838	1903	1938	2003	2038	2143	2246	2317	2346	0020
Didcot Parkway 131 d.		0855	0958	1053	1153	1253	1353	1453	1553	|	1653	|	1753	|	1853	|	1953	|	2053	2200	2303	2332s	0002s	0035s
Swindon d.		0914	1015	1111	1211	1311	1411	1511	1611	1630	1711	1728	1811	1833	1911	1929	2011	2028	2110	2218	2322	2348s	0021s	0053s
Chippenham d.		0929	1029	1125	1225	1325	1425	1525	1625	1645	1725	1741	1825	1848	1925	1944	2025	2042	2125	2232	2337	|	0035s	0106s
Bath a.		0942	1044	1139	1239	1339	1439	1539	1639	1659	1739	1757	1839	1902	1939	1959	2039	2059	2141	2246	2351	p	0051s	0123s
Bristol Temple Meads... 120a a.		0956	1059	1155	1255	1355	1453	1555	1653	1713	1753	1813	1855	1920	1955	2014	2055	2113	2154	2302	0006	0030	0105	0139
Weston-super-Mare 120a a.		|	...	1231	...	1428	|	...	1724	...	...	...	...	1957	...	...	2125	...	2229	...	...	...	...	...
Taunton 120a a.		1033	...	...	...	...	1528	...	1759	...	...	...	...	...	...	...	2148	...	...	...	...	...	...	...

LONDON - BRISTOL PARKWAY - CARDIFF - SWANSEA

Timings beyond Bristol Parkway may vary ± 4 minutes until December 31

km			Ⓐ	Ⓐ	Ⓐ	Ⓐ	Ⓐ	Ⓐ	Ⓐ	Ⓐ	Ⓐ	Ⓐ	Ⓐ	Ⓐ	Ⓐ	Ⓐ	Ⓐ	Ⓐ	Ⓐ	Ⓐ	Ⓐ	Ⓐ	Ⓐ	Ⓐ
												✕												
0	**London** Paddington. 130 131 d.	Ⓐ	0518	0645	0715	0745	0815	0845	0915	0945	1015	1045	1115	1145	1215	1245	1315	1345	1415	1445	1515	1545	1615	1645
58	Reading 130 131 d.		0555	0711	0742	0811	0841	0911	0941	1011	1042	1111	1142	1211	1241	1310	1341	1411	1441	1511	1541	1611	1642	1711
85	Didcot Parkway 131 d.		0610	|	0757	|	0854	|	0956	|	1056	|	1156	|	1256	|	1356	|	1455	|	1556	|	1657	|
124	Swindon d.		0628	0739	0815	0841	0916	0940	1014	1042	1113	1140	1213	1242	1313	1338	1415	1442	1516	1539	1614	1641	1715	1739
180	**Bristol** Parkway d.		0716t	0808	0841	0908	0943	1008	1041	1108	1143	1208	1242	1309	1341	1408	1442	1508	1544	1608	1640	1708	1741	1808
215	Newport 136 149 a.		0748	0832	0907	0929	1005	1031	1106	1131	1204	1231	1304	1331	1402	1430	1505	1531	1607	1630	1706	1732	1803	1830
234	**Cardiff** Central . 135 136 149 a.		0803	0850	0922	0949	1022	1046	1123	1145	1221	1246	1322	1346	1422	1445	1523	1546	1622	1645	1723	1748	1821	1848
266	Bridgend 135 a.		0826	0914	...	1010	...	1109	...	1208	...	1309	...	1409	...	1508	...	1609	...	1708	...	1811	1849	1909
286	Port Talbot 135 a.		0839	0927	...	1023	...	1122	...	1221	...	1322	...	1423	...	1521	...	1622	...	1721	...	1824	1902	1922
295	Neath 135 a.		0847	0934	...	1031	...	1130	...	1229	...	1330	...	1432	...	1529	...	1629	...	1729	...	1830	1910	1930
307	**Swansea** 135 a.		0900	0948	...	1045	...	1143	...	1242	...	1343	...	1446	...	1542	...	1643	...	1742	...	1845	1923	1945

	Ⓐ	Ⓐ	Ⓐ	Ⓐ	①–④	⑤	⑤	①–④	Ⓐ	⑤	①–④	⑤	①–④		⑥	⑥	⑥	⑥	⑥	⑥		⑥	⑥	⑥
	G																							
London Paddington.. 130 131 d.	1715	1745	1815	1845	1915	1915	2015	2015	2115	2245	2245	2330	2330	⑥	...	0745	0845	0945	1045	1145	...	1245	1345	1445
Reading 130 131 d.	1742	1811	1840	1911	1942	1948u	2040	2040	2142	2311	2323	0010	0010		...	0812	0912	1012	1112	1212	...	1312	1412	1512
Didcot Parkway 131 d.	1758	|	1856	|	1957	|	2056	2056	2201	2332	2343	0028	0028		...	|	|	|	|	|	...	|	|	|
Swindon d.	1815	1845	1916	1941	2016	2017	2115	2115	2219	2350	0001	0048	0048		...	0840	0939	1040	1139	1240	...	1340	1441	1539
Bristol Parkway d.	1842	1910	1941	2008	2042	2043	2141	2141	2247	0016	0027	0137t	0137t		0711	0909	1009	1109	1209	1309	...	1409	1509	1609
Newport 136 149 a.	1910	1933	2005	2031	2104	2105	2203	2204	2319	0038	0055	0203s	0210s		0731	0930	1031	1131	1230	1331	...	1431	1531	1630
Cardiff Central .. 135 136 149 a.	1925	1948	2021	2051	2119	2118	2223	2225	2341	0054	0116	0220	0230		0747	0947	1047	1146	1246	1347	...	1446	1546	1646
Bridgend 135 a.	1949	2010	2044	2115	2145	2144	2246	2248	0003	0119	0141	...	...		0809	1009	1109	1209	1309	1409	...	1509	1609	1709
Port Talbot 135 a.	2002	2025	2057	2128	2158	2157	2300	2302	0017	0133	0155	...	...		0822	1022	1122	1222	1322	1422	...	1522	1622	1722
Neath 135 a.	2009	2033	2104	2135	2206	2205	2308	2310	0025	0141	0203	...	...		0830	1030	1130	1230	1334	1430	...	1530	1630	1730
Swansea 135 a.	2021	2046	2118	2150	2220	2219	2322	2324	0039	0155	0217	...	...		0844	1043	1143	1243	1343	1443	...	1543	1643	1743

	⑥	⑥	⑥	⑥	⑥	⑥	⑥	⑥		⑦	⑦	⑦	⑦	⑦	⑦	⑦	⑦	⑦	⑦	⑦	⑦	⑦	⑦	⑦
			G		a						G		G		G									
London Paddington.. 130 131 d.	1545	1645	1745	1845	1915	1945	2045	2200	⑦	0837	0930	1037	1137	1237	1337	1437	1537	1637	1737	1837	1900	1937	2037	2137
Reading 130 131 d.	1612	1712	1812	1912	1942	2012	2112	2230		0916	1007	1114	1214	1314	1414	1514	1613	1714	1814	1914	1936	2014	2114	2215
Didcot Parkway 131 d.	|	|	|	|	1956	|	|	2248		0933	|	1129	1229	1329	1429	1529	1627	1729	1829	1929	|	2029	2129	2230
Swindon d.	1639	1740	1839	1940	2014	2039	2139	2306		0951	1041	1148	1248	1348	1448	1548	1648	1748	1848	1948	2004	2048	2147	2250
Bristol Parkway d.	1709	1809	1909	2009	2043	2109	2212f	2333		1017	1106	1214	1314	1414	1514	1614	1714	1814	1914	2014	2032	2114	2214	2317
Newport 136 149 a.	1730	1832	1930	2030	2104	2131	2244	0002		1036	1125	1233	1333	1435	1535	1635	1737	1835	1935	2035	2051	2135	2240	2338
Cardiff Central .. 135 136 149 a.	1746	1847	1946	2046	2119	2148	2306	0023		1059	1149	1258	1358	1458	1558	1658	1803	1858	1958	2058	2116	2158	2301	0002
Bridgend 135 a.	1809	1909	2009	2109	2145	2210	2328	...		1122	1212	1318	1417	1518	1620	1720	1823	1920	2020	2120	2138	2220	2322	0024
Port Talbot 135 a.	1822	1922	2022	2122	2158	2224	2341	...		1135	1225	1330	1431	1531	1634	1731	1837	1931	2031	2133	2151	2233	2337	0036
Neath 135 a.	1830	1930	2030	2130	2206	2232	2349	...		1144	1232	1338	1438	1539	1642	1739	1845	1939	2039	2140	2200	2240	2345	0044
Swansea 135 a.	1846	1943	2043	2143	2220	2246	0003	...		1157	1246	1353	1453	1559	1656	1756	1859	1958	2056	2154	2214	2257	0002	0059

A – To Paignton (Table 115).
B – To Exeter St Davids (Table 115).
C – To Cardiff Central (See lower panel).
D – To Penzance (Tables 115/117).
E – To Plymouth (Table 115).
G – To Carmarthen (Table 135).
Q – To Swansea (See lower panel).

a – ⑥ until Dec. 31.
f – Arrives 9 minutes earlier.
k – Also calls Bristol Parkway a. 2036/d. 2038.
p – Also calls Bristol Parkway (to set down only) a. 0018.
s – Calls to set down only.
t – Bristol Temple Meads.
u – Calls to pick up only.

132 SWANSEA, CARDIFF and BRISTOL - LONDON

🍸 available on most services GW

TAUNTON - BRISTOL TEMPLE MEADS - LONDON

Timings may vary ± 4 minutes until December 31

		Ⓐ	Ⓐ	Ⓐ	Ⓐ	Ⓐ	Ⓐ	Ⓐ	Ⓐ	Ⓐ	Ⓐ	Ⓐ	Ⓐ	Ⓐ	Ⓐ	Ⓐ	Ⓐ	Ⓐ	Ⓐ	Ⓐ	Ⓐ	Ⓐ	Ⓐ
		R						E	T				A				D						
Taunton 120a d.	Ⓐ	...	...	...	...	...	...	0654	...	0712	...	...	0905	...	...	...	1125	...	...	...	...	...	...
Weston-super-Mare 120a d.		...	...	...	...	0620	0648	0725	...	0749	...	...	0929	...	...	...	|	...	...	...	...	...	...
Bristol Temple Meads 120a d.		0447	0529	0600	0633	0700	0730	0800	0812	0830	0900	0930	1000	1030	1100	1130	1200	1230	1300	1330	1400	1430	1500
Bath d.		|	0541	0613	0646	0713	0743	0813	0830	0843	0913	0943	1013	1043	1113	1143	1212	1243	1313	1343	1413	1443	1513
Chippenham d.		|	0554	0625	0658	0725	0755	0825	0845	0855	0925	0955	1025	1055	1125	1155	1225	1255	1325	1355	1425	1455	1525
Swindon d.		0523	0610	0641	0715	0741	0811	0841	0904	0911	0941	1011	1041	1111	1141	1211	1241	1311	1341	1411	1441	1511	1541
Didcot Parkway 131 a.		0541	0627	0658	|	0801	0828	0858	...	0928	|	1031	|	1128	|	1229	|	1328	|	1428	|	1528	|
Reading 130 131 a.		0556	0641	0713	0743	0816	0843	0914	...	0944	1008	1046	1108	1143	1208	1243	1308	1343	1408	1443	1509	1543	1608
London Paddington 130 131 a.		0624	0715	0744	0814	0845	0912	0942	...	1015	1037	1114	1139	1214	1238	1312	1340	1414	1438	1514	1542	1614	1640

	Ⓐ	Ⓐ	Ⓐ	Ⓐ	Ⓐ	Ⓐ	Ⓐ	Ⓐ	Ⓐ	Ⓐ	Ⓐ		⑥	⑥	⑥	⑥	⑥	⑥	⑥	⑥	⑥	⑥	⑥
										D				Q						B			
Taunton 120a d.	...	...	...	...	...	...	...	...	...	2115	2129	⑥	...	...	...	...	...	0654	...	0759	...	...	...
Weston-super-Mare 120a d.	...	...	...	...	1710	...	1809	...	...	|	2201		...	...	...	0624	...	0724	...	0830	...	...	...
Bristol Temple Meads 120a d.	1530	1600	1630	1700	1730	1800	1830	1930	2030	2150	2235		0530	0600	0630	0700	0730	0800	0830	0900	0930	1000	1030
Bath d.	1543	1613	1643	1713	1743	1813	1843	1943	2043	2202	2247		0543	0613	0643	0713	0743	0813	0843	0913	0943	1013	1043
Chippenham d.	1555	1625	1655	1725	1755	1825	1855	1955	2055	2215	2300		0555	0625	0655	0725	0755	0825	0855	0925	0955	1025	1055
Swindon d.	1611	1641	1711	1741	1811	1841	1911	2011	2111	2232	2316		0611	0641	0711	0742	0811	0842	0911	0941	1011	1042	1111
Didcot Parkway 131 a.	1628	|	1728	1759	1828	|	1928	2028	2128	2250	2333		0628	0659	0728	0759	0828	0859	0928	|	1028	|	1128
Reading 130 131 a.	1643	1708	1743	1813	1844	1909	1943	2043	2144	2308	2354		0642	0714	0743	0813	0843	0914	0943	1011	1044	1108	1143
London Paddington 130 131 a.	1714	1737	1814	1844	1914	1939	2014	2114	2213	2342	0034		0714	0744	0814	0844	0914	0944	1015	1039	1114	1138	1214

	⑥	⑥	⑥	⑥	⑥	⑥	⑥	⑥	⑥	⑥	⑥	⑥	⑥	⑥	⑥	⑥	⑥	⑥	⑥	⑥		⑦	⑦
		A																	D				
Taunton 120a d.	...	1045	...	...	...	...	...	...	...	...	...	...	...	...	...	...	...	...	2114	2130	⑦	...	...
Weston-super-Mare 120a d.	...	1107	...	...	...	...	...	...	...	...	...	...	...	...	...	...	...	2010	|	2153		...	...
Bristol Temple Meads 120a d.	1100	1130	1200	1230	1300	1330	1400	1430	1500	1530	1600	1630	1700	1730	1800	1830	1930	2033	2147	2228		0745	0815
Bath d.	1113	1143	1213	1243	1313	1343	1413	1443	1513	1543	1613	1643	1713	1743	1813	1843	1943	2046	2202	2246		0758	0828
Chippenham d.	1125	1155	1225	1255	1325	1355	1425	1455	1525	1555	1625	1655	1725	1755	1825	1855	1955	2058	2215	2258		0810	0840
Swindon d.	1141	1211	1242	1311	1341	1411	1443	1511	1541	1611	1641	1711	1742	1811	1841	1911	2011	2114	2231	2314		0826	0856
Didcot Parkway 131 a.	|	1228	|	1328	|	1428	|	1528	|	1628	|	1728	|	1828	|	1928	2027	2131	2248	2332		0844	|
Reading 130 131 a.	1209	1245	1309	1343	1411	1443	1509	1543	1610	1644	1708	1743	1808	1845	1908	1943	2043	2146	2304	2348		0900	0926
London Paddington 130 131 a.	1239	1314	1338	1414	1440	1514	1538	1614	1638	1714	1738	1814	1838	1914	1938	2014	2114	2214	2344	0033		0940	1004

	⑦	⑦	⑦	⑦	⑦	⑦	⑦	⑦	⑦	⑦	⑦	⑦	⑦	⑦	⑦	⑦	⑦	⑦	⑦	⑦	⑦	⑦	⑦
							E									E	A	E					E
Taunton 120a d.	...	...	...	...	...	...	1148	...	...	...	...	...	...	...	...	1639	1658	1746	...	...	1856	...	2127
Weston-super-Mare 120a d.	0811	...	0956	...	...	...	|	...	...	1320	...	1451	...	...	...	1701	1729	|	...	...	1925	2026	|
Bristol Temple Meads 120a d.	0845	0948	1030	1105	1130	1205	1230	1305	1330	1405	1505	1530	1600	1630	1705	1730	1805	1830	1905	1930	2000	2100	2210
Bath d.	0858	1001	1043	1118	1143	1218	1243	1318	1343	1418	1518	1543	1613	1643	1718	1743	1818	1843	1918	1943	2013	2113	2223
Chippenham d.	0910	1013	1055	1130	1155	1230	1255	1330	1355	1430	1530	1555	1625	1655	1730	1755	1830	1855	1930	1955	2025	2125	2235
Swindon d.	0926	1029	1111	1146	1211	1246	1311	1346	1411	1446	1546	1611	1641	1711	1746	1811	1846	1911	1946	2011	2041	2141	2252
Didcot Parkway 131 a.	0943	1045	1127	1203	1227	1303	1327	|	1427	|	1602	|	1657	|	1802	|	1902	|	2002	|	2058	2158	2310
Reading 130 131 a.	0959	1102	1144	1219	1244	1319	1344	1414	1444	1514	1619	1642	1714	1742	1819	1843	1919	1943	2019	2043	2114	2216	2326
London Paddington 130 131 a.	1041	1142	1227	1257	1322	1357	1422	1459	1522	1557	1659	1722	1757	1822	1857	1922	1957	2022	2057	2122	2152	2258	0004

SWANSEA - CARDIFF - BRISTOL PARKWAY - LONDON

Timings may vary ± 4 minutes until 31 December

		Ⓐ	Ⓐ	Ⓐ	Ⓐ	Ⓐ	Ⓐ	Ⓐ	Ⓐ	Ⓐ	Ⓐ	Ⓐ	Ⓐ	Ⓐ	Ⓐ	Ⓐ	Ⓐ	Ⓐ	Ⓐ	Ⓐ	Ⓐ	Ⓐ	Ⓐ
		S				✕					G												
Swansea 135 d.	Ⓐ	...	0352	0458	0527	0558	0628	0658	0728	0758	0829	...	0928	...	1029	...	1129	...	1229	...	1328	...	1428
Neath 135 d.		...	0404	0510	0539	0610	0640	0710	0740	0810	0841	...	0940	...	1041	...	1141	...	1241	...	1340	...	1440
Port Talbot 135 d.		...	0412	0518	0547	0618	0648	0718	0748	0818	0849	...	0948	...	1049	...	1149	...	1249	...	1348	...	1448
Bridgend 135 d.		...	0425	0531	0600	0631	0701	0731	0801	0831	0902	...	1001	...	1102	...	1202	...	1302	...	1401	...	1501
Cardiff Central 135 136 149 d.		...	0512	0554	0623	0654	0725	0755	0825	0855	0926	0955	1026	1055	1126	1155	1226	1255	1326	1355	1425	1456	1526
Newport 136 149 d.		...	0532	0609	0638	0709	0739	0809	0839	0909	0939	1009	1040	1109	1140	1209	1240	1309	1340	1409	1439	1509	1540
Bristol Parkway d.		0457	0601	0632	0702	0732	0802	0832	0902	0932	1003	1032	1103	1132	1203	1232	1302	1332	1402	1432	1502	1532	1602
Swindon d.		0523	0627	0658	0728	0758	0828	0859	0929	0959	1029	1059	1130	1159	1230	1259	1330	1359	1429	1459	1529	1559	1629
Didcot Parkway 131 a.		0541	0645	|	0745	|	|	|	|	1015	1045	1116	|	1215	1246	1315	|	1415	1445	1516	|	1616	1645
Reading 130 131 a.		0556	0659	0728	0800	|	0855	0925	0958	1030	1101	1130	1157	1230	1301	1331	1356	1430	1500	1530	1558	1630	1701
London Paddington 130 131 a.		0624	0730	0759	0833	0854	0924	0957	1032	1059	1132	1202	1229	1300	1332	1407	1432	1507	1533	1610	1633	1701	1730

	Ⓐ	Ⓐ	Ⓐ	Ⓐ	Ⓐ	Ⓐ	Ⓐ	Ⓐ	①–④	⑤		⑥	⑥	⑥	⑥	⑥	⑥	⑥	⑥	⑥	⑥	⑥	⑥
																						G	
Swansea 135 d.	...	1529	...	1629	...	1729	1829	1929	2029	2029	⑥	0359	0459	0529	0559	0629	0659	0729	0759	0829	0929	1029	1129
Neath 135 d.	...	1541	...	1641	...	1741	1841	1940	2041	2041		0411	0511	0541	0611	0641	0711	0741	0811	0841	0941	1041	1141
Port Talbot 135 d.	...	1549	...	1649	...	1749	1849	1948	2049	2049		0419	0519	0549	0619	0649	0719	0749	0819	0849	0949	1049	1149
Bridgend 135 d.	...	1602	...	1702	...	1802	1902	2001	2102	2102		0431	0532	0602	0632	0702	0732	0802	0832	0902	1003	1102	1202
Cardiff Central 135 136 149 d.	1556	1622	1656	1726	1756	1825	1926	2025	2125	2125		0456	0556	0626	0656	0726	0756	0826	0856	0926	1026	1126	1226
Newport 136 149 d.	1609	1640	1709	1740	1809	1840	1940	2039	2139	2139		0510	0610	0640	0710	0740	0810	0840	0910	0940	1040	1140	1240
Bristol Parkway d.	1632	1703	1733	1803	1832	1902	2003	2104	2202	2202		0600t	0634	0704	0733	0804	0833	0904	0933	1004	1104	1204	1304
Swindon d.	1659	1730	1800	1830	1859	1929	2030	2133	2228	2228		0641	0701	0731	0800	0831	0900	0931	0959	1031	1131	1231	1331
Didcot Parkway 131 a.	1716	|	1817	1847	|	1946	2047	2152	|	|		0659	|	|	0816	|	0917	|	1016	|	|	|	|
Reading 130 131 a.	1731	1759	1831	1901	1925	2001	2101	2211	2300	2302		0714	0727	0757	0832	0857	0932	0957	1031	1058	1157	1259	1357
London Paddington 130 131 a.	1809	1832	1902	1932	1954	2032	2132	2251a	2342	2338		0744	0800	0830	0902	0930	1002	1028	1102	1132	1230	1333	1430

	⑥	⑥	⑥	⑥	⑥	⑥	⑥	⑥		⑦	⑦	⑦	⑦	⑦	⑦	⑦	⑦	⑦	⑦	⑦	⑦	⑦	⑦
																			G		G		G
Swansea 135 d.	1229	1329	1429	1529	1629	1729	1829	1929	⑦	...	0810	0928	1028	1124	1224	1324	1424	1524	1551	1651	1751	1851	1959
Neath 135 d.	1241	1341	1441	1541	1641	1741	1841	1941		...	0822	0940	1040	1136	1236	1336	1436	1536	1603	1703	1803	1903	2011
Port Talbot 135 d.	1249	1349	1449	1549	1649	1749	1849	1949		...	0829	0947	1047	1143	1243	1343	1443	1543	1610	1710	1810	1910	2018
Bridgend 135 d.	1302	1402	1502	1602	1702	1802	1902	2002		...	0843	1000	1100	1156	1256	1356	1456	1556	1623	1723	1823	1923	2031
Cardiff Central 135 136 149 d.	1326	1426	1526	1626	1726	1826	1926	2026		0800	0905	1025	1125	1220	1320	1420	1520	1620	1650	1750	1850	1950	2055
Newport 136 149 d.	1340	1440	1540	1640	1740	1840	1940	2040		0821	0928	1044	1144	1239	1339	1439	1539	1639	1709	1809	1908	2009	2114
Bristol Parkway d.	1404	1504	1604	1704	1804	1903	2004	2103		0851	0950	1106	1206	1301	1401	1501	1601	1701	1731	1831	1931	2031	2138
Swindon d.	1431	1531	1631	1731	1831	1929	2031	2130		0919	1018	1133	1233	1329	1429	1529	1629	1729	1759	1859	1959	2059	2205
Didcot Parkway 131 a.	|	|	|	|	|	|	|	2147		|	|	|	|	1346	1446	1546	1646	1746	1816	1916	2016	|	|
Reading 130 131 a.	1457	1557	1657	1758	1857	1957	2057	2201		0952	1045	1201	1301	1400	1502	1601	1701	1801	1831	1931	2031	2128	2240
London Paddington 130 131 a.	1530	1631	1731	1832	1930	2030	2129	2238		1029	1128	1244	1342	1442	1542	1642	1742	1842	1906	2006	2106	2204	2322

A – From Paignton (Table **115**).
B – From Exeter St Davids (Table **115**).
D – From Penzance (Tables **115**/**117**).
E – From Plymouth (Table **115**).

G – From Carmarthen (Table **135**).
Q – From Swansea (See lower panel).
R – Via Bristol Parkway (See lower panel).
S – From Bristol Temple Meads (See upper panel).

T – From Gloucester (Table **138**).

a – Arrives 2244 on ⑤.
t – Bristol Temple Meads.

GW 2nd class — SWINDON - WESTBURY — 132a

km		Ⓐ	Ⓐ	Ⓐ	Ⓐ	Ⓐ	Ⓐ	Ⓐ	Ⓐ	Ⓐ	⑥	⑥	⑥	⑥	⑥	⑥	⑥	⑥	⑦	⑦	⑦	⑦	⑦
		A							AB									B					
	Gloucester 133 140 d.	0517	...	...	...	...	...	...	1754	...	...	...	...	...	...	...	...	2014	...	...	...	...	...
0	**Swindon** 133 132 d.	0612	0849	1047	1247	1319	1512	1736	1848	2006	0836	1036	1236	1436	1522	1736	1936	2108	1128	1328	1528	1718	1953
27	Chippenham 132 d.	0629	0906	1104	1304	1336	1529	1753	1905	2023	0853	1053	1253	1453	1539	1753	1953	2125	1145	1345	1545	1735	2010
37	Melksham d.	0638	0915	1113	1313	1347	1539	1803	1915	2032	0902	1102	1302	1503	1548	1802	2002	2134	1154	1354	1554	1744	2019
46	Trowbridge 140 d.	0648	0933	1124	1323	1359	1549	1813	1924	2042	0912	1112	1312	1512	1558	1812	2012	2144	1203	1403	1603	1754	2029
52	**Westbury** 140 a.	0655	0942	1133	1332	1407	1557	1821	1931	2049	0920	1120	1320	1520	1605	1818	2020	2152	1210	1410	1610	1801	2036

	Ⓐ	Ⓐ	Ⓐ	Ⓐ	Ⓐ	Ⓐ	Ⓐ	Ⓐ	Ⓐ	⑥	⑥	⑥	⑥	⑥	⑥	⑥	⑥	⑦	⑦	⑦	⑦	⑦	⑦
	B								B														B
Westbury 140 d.	0704	0733	0948	1147	1220	1414	1621	1832	1932	0732	0822	0930	1132	1332	1506	1633	1832	1030	1230	1435	1620	1839	1941
Trowbridge 140 d.	0710	0739	0954	1153	1226	1420	1627	1838	1938	0738	0828	0936	1138	1338	1512	1639	1838	1035	1235	1440	1625	1845	1946
Melksham d.	0720	0749	1004	1203	1236	1430	1637	1848	1947	0748	0837	0946	1148	1348	1521	1649	1848	1046	1246	1450	1635	1854	1957
Chippenham 132 d.	0730	0800	1014	1212	1245	1441	1646	1900	2000	0800	0847	1000	1200	1400	1531	1700	1900	1100	1300	1500	1645	1904	2007
Swindon 133 132 a.	0748	0819	1034	1236	1305	1503	1706	1923	2021	0820	0906	1022	1220	1420	1550	1722	1922	1120	1320	1519	1705	1922	2025
Gloucester 133 140 a.	0852	...	...	...	...	...	...	...	2123	...	...	...	...	...	...	...	...	...	...	...	...	...	2121

A – To Southampton Central (Table **140**).

B – From / to Cheltenham Spa (Table **133**).

GW Most London trains convey 🍸 — LONDON - CHELTENHAM — 133

km		Ⓐ	Ⓐ	Ⓐ	Ⓐ	Ⓐ	Ⓐ	Ⓐ	Ⓐ	Ⓐ	Ⓐ	Ⓐ	Ⓐ	Ⓐ	Ⓐ	Ⓐ	Ⓐ	Ⓐ	Ⓐ	⑥	⑥	⑥	⑥	⑥
			2A		2		2		2		2		2			2A		2	2	2		2		2
0	**London** Paddington 132 d.	...	...	0736	...	0936	...	1136	...	1336	...	1536	...	1742	1847	...	1948	...	...	...	0815	...	1015	...
58	Reading 132 d.	...	...	0802	...	1003	...	1203	...	1404	...	1602	...	|	1919	...	2018	...	...	...	0842	...	1042	...
85	Didcot Parkway 132 d.	...	...	0818	...	1018	...	1218	...	1419	...	1617	...	1821	1934	...	2034	...	...	...	0855	...	1056	...
124	**Swindon** 132 d.	0640	0750	0841	0936	1039	1136	1239	1336	1439	1536	1638	1754	1841	1955	2025	2055	2154	2336	0716	0914	1014	1114	1214
164	Stroud d.	0709	0820	0910	1005	1107	1205	1307	1405	1507	1605	1708	1822	1911	2025	2053	2124	2223	0005	0745	0945	1043	1145	1243
183	Gloucester a.	0731	0848	0930	1028	1130	1228	1330	1428	1530	1628	1729	1849	1931	2046	2115	2146	2246	0028	0806	1006	1105	1207	1303
194	**Cheltenham** Spa 138 a.	0749	0905	0953	1048	1152	1245	1352	1447	1552	1647	1752	1905	1947	2102	2133	2202	2304	0045t	0824	1022	1122	1222	1324
	Worcester Shrub Hill 138 a.	...	...	...	...	...	...	...	...	...	...	...	...	...	...	...	2224	...	...	...	...	...	...	...

	⑥	⑥	⑥		⑥	⑥	⑥	⑥	⑥	⑥	⑥	⑦	⑦		⑦	⑦		⑦	⑦	⑦	⑦	⑦	⑦	⑦	⑦
		2			2		2		2		2		2					2			2		2A		2
London Paddington 132 d.	1215	...	1415	...	...	1615	...	1815	...	2015	...	0827	...	...	1027	1227	...	...	1427	1630	...	1830	...	2027	...
Reading 132 d.	1242	...	1442	...	...	1642	...	1842	...	2042	...	0903	...	...	1103	1303	...	...	1503	1703	...	1906	...	2103	...
Didcot Parkway 132 d.	1256	...	1456	...	...	1656	...	1855	...	2055	...	|	...	...	|	|	...	...	|	|	...	|	...	|	...
Swindon 132 d.	1314	1414	1514	...	1614	1714	1814	1914	2000	2117	2241	0937	1044	...	1137	1337	...	1425	1537	1737	1843	1937	2029	2133	2257
Stroud d.	1345	1443	1545	...	1643	1745	1843	1945	2029	2145	2310	1004	1113	...	1204	1404	...	1455	1604	1804	1911	2004	2058	2201	2326
Gloucester a.	1406	1503	1605	...	1703	1806	1903	2006	2050	2206	2331	1026	1133	...	1226	1426	...	1516	1626	1826	1934	2026	2118	2222	2346
Cheltenham Spa 138 a.	1422	1525	1621	...	1725	1822	1925	2022	2102	2221	...	1043	1147	...	1243	1445	...	1533	1645	1845	...	2045	2130	2240	0007
Worcester Shrub Hill 138 a.	...	...	...	...	...	...	...	...	...	...	...	...	...	...	...	...	...	...	...	...	...	...	...	...	...

	Ⓐ	Ⓐ	Ⓐ	Ⓐ	Ⓐ	Ⓐ		Ⓐ	Ⓐ	Ⓐ	Ⓐ	Ⓐ	Ⓐ		Ⓐ	Ⓐ	Ⓐ	Ⓐ	Ⓐ	Ⓐ	Ⓐ	⑥	⑥	⑥
	2B			C				2		2		2			2		2B		2	2	2	2		
Worcester Shrub Hill 138 d.	...	0528	...	...	0708	...	...	...	...	...	...	...	...	...	...	...	...	...	...	...	...	...	...	0836
Cheltenham Spa 138 d.	...	0554	0630	...	0731	0831	...	0918	1036	1120	1236	1320	1436	...	1520	1620	1740	1834	2001	2100	2201	0530	0731	0859
Gloucester d.	0517	0610	0645	0705	0746	0848	...	0932	1051	1133	1252	1333	1452	...	1533	1643	1754	1850	2013	2121	2213	0543	0747	0915
Stroud d.	0535	0631	0705	|	0806	0908	...	0952	1113	1152	1314	1352	1514	...	1552	1704	1812	1911	2031	2138	2232	0601	0806	0935
Swindon 132 d.	0605	0701	0735	0904	0836	0945	...	1023	1145	1224	1345	1424	1545	...	1624	1735	1842	1941	2105	2209	2305	0632	0837	1005
Didcot Parkway 132 a.	...	0718	0755	...	0853	1002	...	...	1202	...	1402	...	1602	...	...	|	...	1958	...	...	...	...	0853	1022
Reading 132 a.	...	0733	0811	...	0908	1016	...	...	1217	...	1417	...	1617	...	...	1803	...	2014	...	...	...	...	0908	1036
London Paddington 132 a.	...	0807	0840	...	0938r	1045	...	...	1245	...	1446	...	1653	...	...	1839	...	2043r	...	...	...	...	0940	1109

	⑥	⑥		⑥	⑥	⑥	⑥	⑥	⑥	⑥	⑥	⑥	⑥	⑦	⑦		⑦	⑦		⑦	⑦	⑦	⑦	⑦	⑦
	2			2		2		2		2		2A	2	2			2				2		2		2
Worcester Shrub Hill 138 d.	...	...	...	...	...	...	...	...	...	...	...	...	...	...	...	...	...	...	...	...	...	...	...	...	...
Cheltenham Spa 138 d.	1001	1100	...	1201	1300	1401	1500	1601	1700	1801	1900	2001	2120	0924	1118	...	1232	1346	...	1546	1632	1746	...	2001	2147
Gloucester d.	1014	1115	...	1214	1316	1414	1515	1614	1715	1814	1917	2014	2135	0937	1134	...	1245	1402	...	1602	1645	1802	1944	2016	2159
Stroud d.	1032	1135	...	1232	1336	1432	1535	1632	1735	1832	1936	2032	2153	0955	1154	...	1303	1422	...	1622	1702	1822	2002	2036	2217
Swindon 132 a.	1104	1205	...	1304	1406	1504	1605	1704	1805	1904	2006	2103	2225	1024	1222	...	1332	1450	...	1652	1733	1852	2031	2105	2247
Didcot Parkway 132 a.	...	1222	...	...	1423	...	1622	...	1822	...	2023	...	...	...	|	...	...	1509	...	|	...	|	...	|	...
Reading 132 a.	...	1236	...	...	1437	...	1636	...	1836	...	2037	...	...	...	1251	...	...	1523	...	1722	...	1922	...	2136	...
London Paddington 132 a.	...	1307	...	...	1506	...	1707	...	1906	...	2107	...	...	...	1328	...	...	1559	...	1800	...	1959	...	2222	...

A – To / from Westbury (Table **132a**).

B – To Southampton Central (Tables **132a** and **140**).

C – Via Bristol and Bath (Tables **132** and **140**).

r – Arrives up to 3 minutes later until Dec. 30.

t – On ②–⑤ mornings arrives 0040.

GW — GATWICK AIRPORT ✈ - READING — 134

km		Ⓐ	Ⓐ	Ⓐ	Ⓐ	Ⓐ	Ⓐ	Ⓐ		Ⓐ	Ⓐ	Ⓐ	Ⓐ	Ⓐ	Ⓐ	Ⓐ	Ⓐ	Ⓐ	⑥	⑥	⑥	⑥		⑥
		A																	A					
0	**Gatwick** Airport ✈ d.	...	0531	0556	0658	0758	0910	1003	and	1503	1603	1703	1803	1913	2003	2103	2222	2318	...	0531	0603	0703	and	1903
10	Redhill △ d.	...	0543	0613	0710	0808	0923	1014	hourly	1514	1614	1713	1813	1927	2014	2114	2233	2334	...	0542	0613	0713	hourly	1914
43	Guildford △ d.	0602	0613	0643	0743	0838	0954	1044	until	1544	1644	1744	1847	1956	2044	2144	2314	0002	0609	0612	0644	0744	until	1944
84	**Reading** △ a.	0632	0700	0731	0830	0919	1025	1121		1626	1721	1826	1927	2034	2121	2221	0003	0042	0643	0701	0719	0819		2019

	⑥	⑥		⑥	⑥	⑦	⑦		⑦	⑦	⑦	⑦	⑦	⑦	⑦	⑦		⑦	⑦	⑦	⑦	⑦	⑦		⑦	⑦	⑦
													A														
Gatwick Airport ✈ d.	2003	2103	...	2219	2318	0611	0711	...	0811	0909	1009	1109	...	1209	1309	1409	...	1509	1609	1709	1809	1909	2009	...	2109	2209	2309
Redhill △ d.	2014	2114	...	2233	2329	0620	0720	...	0820	0920	1020	1120	...	1220	1320	1420	...	1520	1620	1720	1820	1920	2020	...	2120	2220	2320
Guildford △ d.	2044	2144	...	2314	0002	0651	0752	...	0900	0952	1100	1152	1214	1300	1352	1500	...	1552	1700	1752	1900	1952	2100	...	2152	2300	2352
Reading △ a.	2119	2219	...	0001	0037	0726	0835	...	0938	1035	1135	1235	1248	1335	1435	1535	...	1635	1735	1835	1935	2035	2136	...	2236	2336	0037

	Ⓐ	Ⓐ	Ⓐ	Ⓐ	Ⓐ	Ⓐ		Ⓐ	Ⓐ	Ⓐ	Ⓐ	Ⓐ	Ⓐ	Ⓐ		Ⓐ	Ⓐ	Ⓐ	Ⓐ	⑥	⑥		⑥	⑥
												A												A
Reading ▽ d.	0432	0522	0632	0732	0832	0932	and	1432	1526	1632	1732	1821	1832	1932	...	2032	2132	2232	2332	0434	0534	and	1734	1823
Guildford ▽ d.	0510	0600	0710	0818	0913	1010	hourly	1510	1610	1710	1818	1859	1910	2010	...	2110	2218	2318	0021	0510	0610	hourly	1810	1901
Redhill ▽ a.	0539	0629	0738	0846	0942	1038	until	1538	1640	1738	1847	...	1942	2038	...	2145	2248	2358	0049	0539	0639	until	1838	...
Gatwick Airport ✈ a.	0555	0642	0750	0859	0957	1050		1551	1659	1754	1900	...	1956	2050	...	2204	2304	0011	0103	0558	0650		1850	...

	⑥	⑥	⑥	⑥	⑥	⑥	⑦	⑦	⑦	⑦	⑦		⑦	⑦	⑦	⑦	⑦	⑦	⑦	⑦	⑦		⑦	⑦	⑦	⑦	⑦
																									A		
Reading ▽ d.	1834	1934	2034	2134	2234	2334	0603	0703	0820	0918	1020	...	1118	1220	1318	1420	1518	1620	1718	1820	1918	...	2020	2118	2214	2219	2315
Guildford ▽ d.	1910	2010	2110	2218	2318	0021	0639	0747	0856	1001	1056	...	1201	1256	1401	1456	1601	1656	1801	1856	2001	...	2056	2201	2242	2256	2359
Redhill ▽ a.	1938	2038	2146	2253	2358	0049	0708	0816	0935	1035	1135	...	1235	1335	1435	1535	1635	1735	1835	1935	2035	...	2135	2235	...	2335	0030
Gatwick Airport ✈ a.	1950	2050	2159	2305	0008	0100	0728	0828	0947	1047	1147	...	1247	1347	1447	1547	1647	1747	1847	1947	2047	...	2147	2247	...	2347	0041

A – To / from Newcastle (Table **124**).

△ – Additional trains Redhill - Reading on Ⓐ at 0624, 0728, 0833, 0934 and hourly until 1434, 1529, 1632, 1743, 1843, 2034, 2135; on ⑥ at 0634 and hourly until 2034, 2136. Journey time 80–92 minutes.

▽ – Additional trains Reading - Redhill on Ⓐ at 0552, 0702 and hourly until 1802, 2002; on ⑥ at 0604 and hourly until 2004. Journey time 85–90 minutes.

135 CARDIFF - SWANSEA - SOUTH WEST WALES

2nd class AW

km			Ⓐ	Ⓐ	Ⓐ	Ⓐ 🍷	Ⓐ	Ⓐ 🍷	Ⓐ 🍷	Ⓐ	Ⓐ	Ⓐ	Ⓐ 🍷	Ⓐ 🍷	Ⓐ 🍷	Ⓐ 🍷	Ⓐ 🍷	Ⓐ 🍷	Ⓐ 🍷	Ⓐ 🍷	Ⓐ 🍷	Ⓐ	Ⓐ	Ⓐ 🍷	Ⓐ 🍷	Ⓐ
	Manchester Picc. **149** d.	Ⓐ	...	...	...	...	...	...	...	...	...	...	...	...	...	0630	0730	...	...	0830	0930	...	...	1030	1130	...
0	**Cardiff** Central **149 132** d.		...	...	...	...	...	...	0535	0642	...	0714	0750	0903	...	1004	1042	1058	...	1138	1239	...	1313	1340	1443	...
32	Bridgend **132** d.		...	...	...	...	...	...	0607	0705	...	0739	0809	0923	...	1023	1101	1119	...	1159	1258	...	1334	1404	1502	...
52	Port Talbot **132** d.		...	...	...	...	...	...	0623	0722	...	0758	0825	0936	...	1036	1114	|	...	1211	1311	...	1350	1418	1515	...
61	Neath **132** d.		...	...	...	...	...	...	0634	0733	...	0809	0835	0943	...	1043	1121	|	...	1218	1318	...	1401	1425	1522	...
73	**Swansea** **132** a.		...	...	...	...	...	...	0651	0749	...	0825	0852	0955	...	1055	1134	|	...	1234	1333	...	1419	1434	1534	...
73	**Swansea** **146** d.		...	...	...	...	...	0545	0653	0752	0814	...	0901	1002	...	1100	1138	|	1200	1240	1337	1400	*1435*	1438	1537	1600
91	Llanelli **146** d.		...	...	...	...	...	0604	0711	0810	0831	...	0920	1021	...	1118	1154	1210a	1219	1259	1356	1416	*1451*	1457	1556	1618
124	**Carmarthen** a.		...	...	...	...	...	0638	0743	0841	|	...	0950	1053	...	1144	1226	|	1248	1322	1428	1445	...	1522	1629	1647
124	**Carmarthen** d.		0450	0530	0550	0558	...	0639	0746	0843	|	...	0959	...	1058	1148	...	|	1251	1330	...	1451	...	1528	...	1651
147	Whitland d.		0503	0547	0605	0613	...	0656	0800	0902	0910	...	1014	...	1113	1201	...	1245	1306	1345	...	1506	...	1543	...	1706
172	Tenby a.		|	0614	|	|	...	0724	|	0930	|	...	|	...	1141	|	...	|	1334	|	...	1534	...	|	...	1734
191	**Pembroke Dock** a.		|	0654	|	|	...	0803	|	1014	|	...	|	...	1220	|	...	|	1416	|	...	1616	...	|	...	1816
166	Clarbeston Road d.		0518x	...	0620x	0627x	0720	...	0814x	...	0925x	...	1028x	...	...	1215x	...	|	...	1359x	...	...	...	1557x	...	...
174	Haverfordwest d.		0529	...	|	0635	|	...	0823	...	|	...	1036	...	...	1223	...	|	...	1408	...	...	...	1606	...	...
189	**Milford Haven** a.		0550	...	|	0656	|	...	0843	...	|	...	1053	...	...	1244	...	|	...	1427	...	...	...	1625	...	...
191	**Fishguard** Harbour a.		...	...	0644	...	0744	...	...	...	0950	...	...	...	...	...	...	1323	...	...	...	...	...	...	...	...

	Ⓐ 🍷	Ⓐ 🍷 B	Ⓐ 🍷	Ⓐ 🍷	Ⓐ	Ⓐ	Ⓐ 🍷	Ⓐ	Ⓐ A	Ⓐ 🍷		①–④	⑤	Ⓐ	Ⓐ		⑥	⑥	⑥	⑥	⑥	⑥	⑥ 🍷		⑥	⑥
Manchester Picc. **149** d.	1230	...	1330	1430	...	...	1530	...	...	1630	...	1830	1832	...	1930	⑥	...	...	...	...	...	...	...	...	...	...
Cardiff Central **149 132** d.	1539	1604	1704	1739	...	1806	1904	...	1929	1946	2104	2215	2208	...	2315		...	...	...	...	...	...	0533	...	0642	...
Bridgend **132** d.	1601	1625	1727	1800	...	1830	1923	...	1950	2005	2127	2241	2235	...	2345		...	...	...	...	...	...	0604	...	0702	...
Port Talbot **132** d.	1614	1641	1742	1818	...	1847	1938	...	2003	2021	2145	2254	2247	...	0001		...	...	...	...	...	...	0620	...	0718	...
Neath **132** d.	1621	1649	1752	1826	...	1858	1948	...	2010	2028	2152	|	2254	...	0013		...	...	...	...	...	...	0631	...	0729	...
Swansea **132** a.	1635	1702	1807	1839	...	1914	2004	...	2021	2042	2205	|	2307	...	0028		...	...	...	...	...	...	0648	...	0745	...
Swansea **146** d.	1640	1705	1814	1841	...	*1934*	2011	...	2033	2048	2227	|	2311	2345	0045		...	...	...	...	...	0545	0653	...	0750	...
Llanelli **146** d.	1659	1724	1833	1900	...	*1954*	2030	...	2050	2111	2246	2324	2331	0002	0102s		...	...	...	...	...	0604	0711	...	0808	...
Carmarthen a.	1728	1755	1902	1928	...	*2029*	2055	...	2123	2139	2315	2359	0005	0033	0138		...	...	...	...	...	0637	0743	...	0840	...
Carmarthen d.	1731	1757	1905	1930	...	...	...	2110	...	2141	2320	...	...	0035	...		0450	0530	0550	0558	...	0638	0746	...	0843	...
Whitland d.	1746	1813	1921	1946	...	...	...	2125	...	2156	2335	...	...	0051	...		0503	0546	0606	0613	...	0656	0800	...	0902	0907
Tenby a.	|	|	1952	|	...	...	...	2152	...	|	|	...	...	|	...		|	0614	|	|	...	0724	|	...	0930	|
Pembroke Dock a.	|	|	*2031*	|	...	...	...	2224	...	|	|	...	...	|	...		|	0655	|	|	...	0803	|	...	1014	|
Clarbeston Road d.	1800x	1827x	...	2000x	2005	...	...	...	...	2210x	2350x	...	...	0104x	...		0518x	...	0621x	0627x	0720	...	0815x	...	...	0922x
Haverfordwest d.	1808	|	...	2009	|	...	...	...	...	2223	2358	...	...	|	...		0530	...	|	0635	|	...	0823	...	...	|
Milford Haven a.	1827	|	...	2028	|	...	...	...	...	2242	0017	...	...	|	...		0551	...	|	0656	|	...	0848	...	...	|
Fishguard Harbour a.	...	1852	...	...	2029	...	...	...	...	...	...	...	...	0131	...		...	...	0646	...	0744	...	...	...	...	0947

	⑥	⑥ 🍷	⑥ 🍷	⑥	⑥ 🍷	⑥ 🍷	⑥	⑥ 🍷	⑥	⑥ 🍷	⑥	⑥ 🍷	⑥	⑥ 🍷	⑥ 🍷	⑥	⑥	⑥ 🍷	⑥ 🍷 B	⑥ 🍷		⑥	⑥ 🍷	⑥	⑥ 🍷	⑥ A
Manchester Picc. **149** d.	...	...	...	...	0630	...	...	0730	...	0830	...	0930	...	1030	1130	...	...	1230	...	1330	...	...	1430	...	1530	...
Cardiff Central **132** d.	0714	0758	0904	0914	1000	1059	...	1105	1114	1204	...	1304	1310	1404	1504	...	1514	1540	1604	1704	...	1738	1804	...	1904	1950
Bridgend **132** d.	0738	0817	0923	0934	1019	1119	...	1124	1134	1223	...	1323	1332	1423	1523	...	1534	1559	1624	1725	...	1758	1825	...	1924	2010
Port Talbot **132** d.	0754	0830	0936	0952	1031	|	...	1138	1150	1236	...	1336	1348	1436	1536	...	1550	1617	1640	1740	...	1814	1841	...	1939	2023
Neath **132** d.	0805	0837	0943	1003	1038	|	...	1146	1201	1243	...	1343	1359	1443	1543	...	1601	1624	1648	1750	...	1825	1849	...	1949	2031
Swansea **132** a.	0822	0851	0955	1019	1051	|	...	1159	1218	1255	...	1357	1416	1455	1555	...	1617	1636	1701	1805	...	1842	1902	...	2005	2043
Swansea **146** d.	...	0900	1004	▬	1100	|	1150	1205	...	1302	1350	1405	...	1500	1600	1609	1623	1640	1706	1809	...	...	1905	1934	2013	2100
Llanelli **146** d.	...	0919	1022	⑥	1118	1202	1211	1224	...	1322	1406	1424	...	1520	1619	1628	1641	1659	1724	1828	...	...	1924	1954	2032	2117
Carmarthen a.	...	0948	1051		1145	|	1240	1253	...	1347	1440	1453	...	1545	1651	1659	...	1728	1755	1901	...	...	1951	2029	2057	2148
Carmarthen d.	...	0957	...	1056	1148	|	1258	...	...	1351	1458	...	...	1549	...	1701	...	1731	1757	1905	...	...	1955	▬	2100	...
Whitland d.	...	1014	...	1111	1203	1238	1312	...	...	1406	1512	...	...	1604	...	1716	...	1746	1813	1921	...	...	2010	...	2115	...
Tenby a.	...	|	...	1139	|	|	1340	...	...	|	1540	...	...	|	...	1743	...	|	|	1953	...	...	|	⑥	2142	...
Pembroke Dock a.	...	|	...	1216	|	|	1416	...	...	|	1616	...	...	|	...	1818	...	|	|	2024	...	...	|		2214	...
Clarbeston Road d.	...	1028x	...	...	1217x	|	...	...	...	1420x	...	...	...	1618x	...	...	...	1800x	1827x	...	...	...	2025x	2030	...	...
Haverfordwest d.	...	1036	...	...	1225	|	...	...	...	1429	...	...	...	1626	...	...	...	1808	|	...	...	...	2033	|	...	...
Milford Haven a.	...	1053	...	...	1244	|	...	...	...	1448	...	...	...	1645	...	...	...	1827	|	...	...	...	2052	|	...	...
Fishguard Harbour a.	...	...	...	...	...	1319	...	...	...	...	...	...	...	...	...	...	...	...	1851	...	...	...	...	2054	...	...

	⑥ 🍷	⑥		⑥ 🍷	⑥	⑥		⑦	⑦	⑦ 🍷	⑦	⑦ A	⑦ 🍷	⑦	⑦ A	⑦ 🍷 c	⑦ 🍷 b	⑦	⑦ A	⑦ 🍷	⑦	⑦ 🍷	⑦	⑦	⑦ 🍷	⑦
Manchester Picc. **149** d.	1630	...	...	1830	...	...	⑦	...	...	...	...	...	...	...	...	1031	1031	...	...	1233	...	1430	...	...	...	...
Cardiff Central **132** d.	2001	2104	...	2208	...	2235		...	...	0956	1119	1150	1205	...	1359	1405	1412	...	1601	1614	...	1810d	...	...	2013	2230
Bridgend **132** d.	2020	2123	...	2235	...	2302		...	...	1026	1139	1213	1235	...	1418	1434	1442	...	1621	1643	...	1839	...	...	2035	2251
Port Talbot **132** d.	2033	2139	...	2247	...	2319		...	...	1041	1153	1226	1251	...	1431	1451	1458	...	1634	1659	...	1855	...	...	2052	2305
Neath **132** d.	|	2146	...	2254	...	2331		...	...	1049	1201	1233	|	...	1439	1459	1506	...	1642	1707	...	1903	...	...	2100	2313
Swansea **132** a.	|	2157	...	2307	...	2347		...	...	1101	1214	1246	|	...	1453	1511	1519	...	1656	1723	...	1918	...	...	2112	2325
Swansea **146** d.	|	2225	...	2310	2347	0008		...	...	1104	1216	1252	|	1402	1502	1544	1536	1638	1708	1725	1837	1922	...	2050	2118	2338
Llanelli **146** d.	2103	2244	...	2329	0004	0027s		...	...	1124	1235	1310	1321	1422	1519	1603	1555	1658	1726	1744	1857	1941	...	2110	2137	2358
Carmarthen a.	2131	2316	...	0001	0035	0100		...	...	1156	1306	1339	1354	1455	1549	1633	1624	1730	1755	1814	1929	2009	...	2142	2206	0030
Carmarthen d.	2205	...	...	...	0037	...		0955	1019	1206	1308	...	1355	1457	...	1635	1627	1732	...	1820	1932	2010	...	...	2210	0034
Whitland d.	2220	...	...	...	0053	...		1011	1034	1222	1323	...	1411	1512	...	1653	1644	1748	...	1837	1948	2030	2037	...	2226	0050
Tenby a.	|	...	...	...	|	...		|	1101	|	|	...	|	1540	...	|	|	1816	...	|	|	|	2102	...	|	|
Pembroke Dock a.	|	...	...	...	|	...		|	1141	|	|	...	|	1615	...	|	|	1851	...	|	|	|	2136	...	|	|
Clarbeston Road d.	2234x	...	...	...	0106x	...		1027x	...	1238x	|	...	1427x	...	...	1708x	1652x	...	...	1853x	2004x	2046x	...	...	2242x	0103x
Haverfordwest d.	2242	...	...	...	|	...		1035	...	1246	|	...	1435	...	...	1717	1708	...	...	1901	2012	2054	...	...	2250	|
Milford Haven a.	2301	...	...	...	|	...		1055	...	1306	|	...	1455	...	...	1736	1728	...	...	1921	...	2116	...	...	2310	|
Fishguard Harbour a.	...	...	...	...	0131	...		...	...	...	1400	...	...	...	...	...	...	...	...	...	...	...	...	...	...	0128

		②–⑤	Ⓐ	Ⓐ 🍷	Ⓐ 🍷	Ⓐ 🍷	Ⓐ 🍷	Ⓐ	Ⓐ 🍷	Ⓐ 🍷	Ⓐ 🍷	Ⓐ 🍷	Ⓐ 🍷	Ⓐ	Ⓐ 🍷	Ⓐ 🍷	Ⓐ	Ⓐ	Ⓐ 🍷	Ⓐ 🍷	Ⓐ 🍷	Ⓐ 🍷	Ⓐ 🍷	Ⓐ 🍷	Ⓐ 🍷	Ⓐ
Fishguard Harbour d.	Ⓐ	...	0150	...	...	...	...	0650	...	...	0750	...	...	0954	...	...	...	...	...	...	1329	...	...	...	...	...
Milford Haven d.		0018	|	...	...	...	0555	|	0705	...	|	0908	...	|	...	1108	...	...	...	1308	|	...	...	1508	...	...
Haverfordwest d.		0033	|	...	...	...	0610	|	0720	...	|	0923	...	|	...	1123	...	...	...	1323	|	...	...	1523	...	...
Clarbeston Road d.		0041x	0212x	...	...	...	0618x	0713	0728x	...	0811x	0931x	...	1017x	...	1131x	...	...	...	1331x	|	...	...	1531x	...	...
Pembroke Dock d.		|	|	...	...	...	|	▬	|	0658	|	|	0909	|	...	|	...	1109	...	|	|	1309	...	|	...	1509
Tenby d.		|	|	...	...	...	|	...	|	0728	|	|	0938	|	...	|	...	1143	...	|	|	1341	...	|	...	1541
Whitland d.		0054	0224	...	...	...	0631	Ⓐ	0741	0755	0824	0944	1007	1032	...	1144	...	1211	...	1344	1404	1409	...	1544	...	1609
Carmarthen a.		0116	0241	...	...	...	0647	A	0755	0814	0843	1003	1024	1049	...	1200	...	1229	...	1400	1421	1430	...	1600	...	1627
Carmarthen d.		...	0303	0503	0547	0615	0650	0730	0801	0817	0900	1006	1031	...	1103	1205	...	1233	1302	1405	1426	1438	1503	1605	...	1631
Llanelli d.		...	0325	0528	0615	0644	0719	0805	0830	0846	0925	1032	1057	...	1131	1230	1245	1259	1330	1430	1448	1503	1532	1630	1645	1657
Swansea a.		...	0344	|	0635	0704	0738	0821	0849	0907	0951	1049	1120	...	1152	1249	1304	1318	1351	1449	|	1523	1551	1649	1702	1720
Swansea **132** d.		...	*0352*	|	0640	0706	0742	0828	0853	0910	0955	1055	...	...	1155	1254	1310	...	1355	1455	|	...	1555	1655	1712	...
Neath **132** d.		...	*0404*	|	0653	0717	0753	0840	0904	0925	1006	1106	...	...	1206	1305	1325	...	1406	1506	|	...	1606	1706	1727	...
Port Talbot **132** d.		...	*0412*	0601	0704	0724	0800	0848	0911	0936	1013	1113	...	...	1213	1312	1336	...	1413	1513	|	...	1613	1713	1738	...
Bridgend **132** d.		...	*0425*	0616	0720	0740	0815	0902	0924	0953	1026	1126	...	...	1226	1325	1353	...	1426	1526	1535	...	1626	1726	1755	...
Cardiff Central **132** a.		...	*0501*	0645	0747	0803	0838	0923	0945	1018	1048	1146	...	...	1248	1350	1415	...	1447	1547	1559	...	1647	1746	1815	...
Manchester Picc. **149** a		...	...	1011	...	1110	1210	...	1310	...	1410	1510	...	...	1610	1710	...	...	1810	1910	...	...	2014	2101	...	...

A – From/to London (operated by GW, see Table **132**). Conveys (12) and 🍷.
B – From Gloucester (Table **121**).

a – Arrives 10 minutes earlier.
b – Until Jan. 1.
c – From Jan. 8.

d – Departs 1758 until Jan. 1.
s – Calls to set down only.
x – Calls on request.

SOUTH WEST WALES - SWANSEA - CARDIFF — 135

AW — 2nd class

	⑥Ⓐ ⑥Ⓐ ⑥Ⓐ ⑥Ⓐ ⑥Ⓐ ⑥Ⓐ ⑥Ⓐ ⑥Ⓐ ⑥Ⓐ ⑥Ⓐ	⑥ ⑥Ⓨ ⑥Ⓨ ⑥Ⓨ ⑥ ⑥Ⓨ ⑥ ⑥Ⓨ ⑥Ⓐ
Fishguard Harbour d.	… … 1908 … … 2050 … … … …	… 0150 … … … 0650 … … 0750
Milford Haven d.	… 1708 … 1912 2036 … … … 2318	0018 … … 0555 0705 … … …
Haverfordwest d.	… 1723 … 1927 2051 … … … 2333	0033 … … 0610 0720 … … …
Clarbeston Road d.	… 1731x … 1929 1935x … 2059x 2112x … 2341x	0041x 0212x … 0618x 0713 0728x … 0811x
Pembroke Dock d.	… … 1709 — 1919 … … 2109 2228	… … … … 0659 …
Tenby d.	… … 1738 … 1957 … … 2153 2255	… … … 0729 …
Whitland d.	… 1745 1807 Ⓐ 1948 2027 2112 2126 … 2221 2325 2354	0054 0224 … 0631 … 0741 0756 … 0824
Carmarthen a.	1802 1824 … 2004 2045 2134 2149 … 2239 2344 0016	0116 0241 … 0647 … 0755 0815 … 0843
Carmarthen d.	1658 1806 1831 1850 2009 2047 … … 2244	0244 0504 0555 0620 … 0650 … 0801 0818 … 0900 0938
Llanelli d.	1726 1835 1857 1921 2033 2117 … … 2201 2314	0306 0529 0624 0648 … 0719 … 0830 0848 0855 0928 1006
Swansea a.	1746 1855 1920 1943 2055 2142 … … 2222 2339	0325 … 0643 0708 … 0738 … 0849 0907 0922 0950 1022
Swansea 132 d.	1749 1858 … 1951 2058 2145 … … 2232	0359 … 0647 0711 … 0744 … 0855 0910 0933 0954 1029
Neath 132 d.	1803 1913 … 2002 2109 2200 … … 2247	0411 … 0658 0726 … 0755 … 0906 0925 0945 1006 1041
Port Talbot 132 d.	1814 1924 … 2009 2116 2211 … … 2258	0419 0602 0705 0737 … 0802 … 0913 0936 0952 1013 1049
Bridgend 132 d.	1829 1940 … 2023 2131 2227 … … 2315	0431 0617 0720 0753 … 0817 … 0932 0953 1010 1028 1102
Cardiff Central 132 a.	1850 200 … 2046 2200 2255 … … 2338	0453 0644 0743 0831 … 0844 … 0953 1018 1033 1048 1123
Manchester Picc. 149 a.	2210	… 1011 1110 … 1210 … 1310 … 1410 …

	⑥Ⓨ ⑥ ⑥Ⓨ ⑥Ⓨ ⑥Ⓨ ⑥Ⓨ ⑥Ⓨ ⑥Ⓨ ⑥ ⑥ ⑥ ⑥ ⑥ ⑥ ⑥ ⑥ ⑥
Fishguard Harbour d.	… 0953 … … … 1328 … … … 1900 … 2100
Milford Haven d.	0908 … 1108 … 1308 … … 1508 … 1708 … 1908 … 2116
Haverfordwest d.	0923 … 1123 … 1323 … … 1523 … 1723 … 1923 … 2131
Clarbeston Road d.	0931x 1014x 1131x … 1331x … … 1531x … 1731x … 1921 1931x … 2122x 2139x
Pembroke Dock d.	… 0909 … … 1109 … 1309 … 1509 … 1712 … 1913 …
Tenby d.	… 0937 … … 1141 … 1342 … 1543 … 1746 … 1951 …
Whitland d.	0944 1005 1029 … 1144 1209 1344 1403 … 1411 … 1544 … 1612 … 1745 1815 … 1944 2021 … 2136 2152
Carmarthen a.	1002 1023 1046 … 1200 1227 1400 1419 … 1428 … 1600 … 1629 … 1803 1832 … 2004 2039 … 2159 2214
Carmarthen d.	1004 1027 … 1109 1205 … 1233 1302 1405 1424 … 1433 1503 1605 … 1632 1702 1807 1834 … 2007 2047 …
Llanelli d.	1031 1053 … 1137 1230 1242 1259 1330 1430 1447 … 1458 1532 1630 1647 1651 1730 1836 1902 1925 … 2031 2117 2138
Swansea a.	1048 1117 … 1156 1249 1301 1318 1349 1449 … 1520 1551 1649 1704 1720 1748 1856 1924 1947 … 2051 2142 2202
Swansea 132 d.	1055 … 1200 1253 1307 … 1400 1455 … 1510 … 1555 1658 1710 … 1754 1900 … 1952 … 2055 2143 2220
Neath 132 d.	1106 … 1211 1304 1322 … 1411 1506 … 1525 … 1606 1709 1725 … 1805 1911 … 2003 … 2106 2159 2235
Port Talbot 132 d.	1113 … 1218 1311 1333 … 1418 1513 … 1536 … 1613 1716 1736 … 1812 1919 … 2010 … 2113 2210 2246
Bridgend 132 d.	1128 … 1231 1326 1352 … 1431 1526 1531 1553 … 1628 1731 1752 … 1827 1933 … 2024 … 2126 2226 2302
Cardiff Central 132 a.	1148 … 1252 1348 1414 … 1452 1551 1553 1616 … 1649 1752 1815 … 1847 1954 … 2047 … 2147 2250 2323
Manchester Picc. 149 a.	1510 … 1610 1709 … 1810 1910 … 2011 2111 … 2209 2344 …

	⑥ ⑥ ⑦ ⑦ ⑦ ⑦ ⑦Ⓨ ⑦ ⑦Ⓨ ⑦ ⑦ABC ⑦ ⑦Ⓨ ⑦ABC ⑦ ⑦A ⑦ ⑦ ⑦ ⑦ ⑦ ⑦
Fishguard Harbour d.	0150 🚌 … … 1422 … … … … …
Milford Haven d.	… 2318 … … 1123 1318 … 1513 … 1740 … 1938 … 2135 2315
Haverfordwest d.	… 2333 … … 1138 1331 … 1528 … 1755 … 1953 … 2151 2330
Clarbeston Road d.	… 2341x … … 1147x 1340x … 1537x … 1803x … 2001x … 2159x 2339x
Pembroke Dock d.	2109 2218 … … 1155 … … 1625 … 1900 … 2145 …
Tenby d.	2142 2245 … … 1223 … … 1653 … 1928 … 2213 …
Whitland d.	2211 2315 2354 0224s … 1203 1254 1357 … 1457 1554 1724 1816 … 1959 2017 … 2214 2244 2353
Carmarthen a.	2228 2334 0016 0242 … 1221 1317 1415 … 1514 1611 1742 1835 … 2018 2036 … 2231 2305 0014
Carmarthen d.	2235 … 0245 0250 0940 1030 1053 1224 1320 1421 1458 1540 1626 1655 1747 … 1905 … 2021 … 2115 2234
Llanelli d.	2305 … 0308s … 1010 1056 1123 1250 1350 1451 1527 1609 1646 1722 1818 … 1932 1959 2053 … 2141 2304
Swansea a.	2328 … … 0350 1034 1118 1147 1313 1413 1513 1543 1624 1715 1739 1845 … 1949 2020 2115 … 2204 2327
Swansea 132 d.	… … 0810 … 1128 1221 1343 … 1531 1551 1651 1730 1751 1851 … 1959r 2040 … 2210 2331
Neath 132 d.	… … 0822 … 1139 1233 1354 … 1542 1603 1703 1741 1803 1903 … 2011r 2051 … 2221 2343
Port Talbot 132 d.	… … 0829 … 1146 1240 1401 … 1549 1610 1710 1748 1810 1910 … 2018r 2058 … 2228 2350
Bridgend 132 d.	… … 0843 … 1201 1253 1417 … 1604 1623 1723 1803 1823 1923 … 2031r 2112 … 2245 0006
Cardiff Central 132 a.	0408 0904 … 1233 1317 1448 … 1637 1647 1747 1832 1848 1948 … 2053 2135 … 2310 0030
Manchester Picc. 149 a.	… 1611 … 1813 … 2011 … 2214 …

A – To London (operated by GW, see Table 132). Conveys 🛏 and Ⓨ.
r – Departs 4 mins earlier until Jan. 1.
s – Calls to set down only.
x – Calls on request.

CARDIFF - BRISTOL — 136

GW — 2nd class

km		Ⓐ	Ⓐ A	Ⓐ B	Ⓐ C	Ⓐ A	Ⓐ G	Ⓐ					⑥	⑥ E	⑥ A	⑥ B	⑥	⑥ G
0	Cardiff Central d.	Ⓐ	0628 0700 0730 0759 0830 0900 0930	and at the same minutes past each hour until		Ⓐ 1930 Ⓐ A Ⓐ G Ⓐ D 2000 2030 2100 2129	… 2204 2236 2327		⑥	0456 0630 0700 0730 0800
19	Newport d.		0642 0715 0744 0815 0844 0915 0944			1944 2015 2044 2115 2143	… 2219 2352 2345			0510 0644 0715 0744 0815
61	Bristol T Meads a.		0719 0751 0818 0852 0919 0954 1019	▽ H		2017 2053 2117 2151 2225	… 2307 0033			0555 0719 0751 0819 0854

		⑥	⑥	⑥	⑥	⑥ F		⑦	⑦ A	⑦ A	⑦ A	⑦ A	⑦ A	⑦ A	⑦ A	⑦ A	⑦	⑦ J	⑦ A	⑦ A	⑦ K
Cardiff Central d.	and at the same minutes past each hour until	1900	1930	1954	2030	2100	2200	⑦	0808 0913 1008 1108 1208 1308 1408 1508 1608 1635 1708 1739 1808c 1908 2018 2118 K
Newport d.		1915	1944	2010	2044	2115	2215		0827 0934 1029 1129 1227 1327 1428 1529 1627 1653 1729 1759 1828 1929 2038 2137 2228
Bristol T Meads a.		1952	2019	2048	2117	2151	2301		0908 1013 1103 1203 1304 1403 1503 1604 1703 1728 1802 1837 1904 2005 2113 2220 2313

		②–⑤			Ⓐ	Ⓐ	Ⓐ					⑥	⑥
		Ⓐ E	D E G M	0716 0720 0754 0824	0854 0921	and at the same minutes past each hour until		Ⓐ G 1921 Ⓐ A Ⓐ B 1954 2015 2054 2119 2155 2254	⑥	⑥ E
Bristol T Meads d.		0137 0554 0619	0716 0720 0754 0824	0854 0921			1921 1954 2015 2054 2119 2155 2254	0137 0650 0721 0754 0823
Newport a.		0210s 0634 0659 0725	0748 0807 0827 0902	0924 0958			2001 2027 2047 2126 2158 2235b 2334	0203s 0726 0758 0828 0901
Cardiff Central a.		0231 0655 0718 0744	0803 0824 0846 0925	0943 1021	▽		2020 2047 2103 2145 2222b 2259a 2356	0220 0744 0817 0843 0923

		⑥				Ⓐ			⑦	⑦	⑦	⑦	⑦ M	⑦ A	⑦ A	⑦ A	⑦ J	⑦	⑦ A	nd	⑦ A	⑦ A
Bristol T Meads d.		A 0854 0921	and at the same minutes past each hour until			G 1921 Ⓐ A Ⓐ B 1954			⑦	0848 0948 1048 1147 1248 1348 1416 1448 1548 1612 1648 hourly 2148
Newport a.		0924 0958				1956 2023				0919 1019 1121 1221 1319 1420 1447 1520 1619 1643 1721 until 2223
Cardiff Central a.		0942 1018	▽			2015 2044				0938 1041 1143 1241 1341 1421 1509 1541 1643 1707 1743 ▲ 2246

A 0854 0921	G A	B A G A A		M A A A J A nd A A
0854 0921	1921 1954	2010 2054 2129 2157 2255		0848 0948 1048 1147 1248 1348 1416 1448 1548 1612 1648 2148
0924 0958	1956 2023	2044 2123 2210 2238 2335		0919 1019 1121 1221 1319 1420 1447 1520 1619 1643 1721 2223 2320
0942 1018	2015 2044	2100 2142 2231 2300 2356		0938 1041 1143 1241 1341 1421 1509 1541 1643 1707 1743 2246 2341

A – To/from Portsmouth Harbour (Table 140).
B – To/from Manchester Piccadilly (Tables 121/122).
C – To/from Paignton (Table 115).
D – To/from Westbury (Table 140).
E – To/from London Paddington (Table 132).
F – To Exeter St Davids (Table 115).
G – To/from Taunton (Table 120a).
H – 0900 from Cardiff extended to Plymouth; 1300 from Cardiff extended to Exeter St Davids (Table 115).
J – To/from Brighton (Table 140).
K – To Warminster (Table 140).
M – From Frome (Table 140).

a – Arrives 2251 on ⑤.
b – Arrives 6 minutes earlier on ⑤.
c – Departs 1812 from Jan. 8.
s – Calls to set down only.
▽ – Timings may vary by up to 6 minutes.
▲ – Timings may vary by up to 3 minutes.

138 WORCESTER - GLOUCESTER - BRISTOL

2nd class GW

km		Ⓐ	ⒶA	ⒶC	Ⓐ	ⒶB	ⒶB	ⒶC	ⒶB	Ⓐ	ⒶD	ⒶB	ⒶC	ⒶB	ⒶB	ⒶC	ⒶD	Ⓐ	Ⓐ	Ⓐ	Ⓐ	⑥A	⑥
	Great Malvern d.	...	...	...	...	...	...	0850	...	1050	...	1251	...	1450	...	1648	...	1850	...	...	...	...	...
0	**Worcester** Shrub Hill d.	0528	...	...	...	0649	*0708*	0906	...	1106	...	1306	...	1506	...	1706	...	1907	...	2146	2228	...	...
24	Ashchurch for Tewkesbury d.	0544	...	...	*0627*	0705	|	0924	...	1124	...	1324	...	1524	...	1724	...	1924	...	2202	2251	...	*0633*
36	Cheltenham Spa ◧ d.	0554	...	0624	*0643*	0716	*0731*	0933	...	1133	...	1333	...	1533	...	1733	...	1934	2048	2212	2305	...	0648
46	**Gloucester** ◧ a.	0603	...	0634	*0653*	0726	*0740*	0942	...	1145	...	1344	...	1544	...	1744	...	1943	2058	2223	2317	...	0658
46	**Gloucester** d.	...	0616	0642	0705	0741	0841	0944	1041	1147	1241	1346	1441	1546	1640	1746	1841	1945	2115	2228	...	0621	0702
97	**Bristol** Parkway d.	...	0657	0724	0749	0820	0919	1022	1120	1223	1319	1423	1520	1624	1720	1823	1922	2027	2152	2305	...	0701	0740
108	**Bristol** Temple Meads a.	...	0713	0740	0800	0836	0935	1039	1135	1235	1335	1439	1538	1639	1735	1839	1938	2038	2211	2319	...	0713	0755

	⑥B	⑥B	⑥C	⑥B	⑥	⑥D	⑥B	⑥C	⑥B	⑥B	⑥C	⑥D	⑥	⑥	⑥	⑥	⑦A	⑦	⑦	⑦	⑦	⑦	⑦
Great Malvern d.	...	...	...	...	1046	...	...	...	1450	...	1650	...	1850	...	2115	...	...	...	...	...	...	...	...
Worcester Shrub Hill d.	0647	...	0908	...	1106	...	1254	...	1506	...	1706	...	1906	...	2131	2225	...	1138	1436	1640	1840	2038	...
Ashchurch for Tewkesbury d.	0703	...	0927	...	1124	...	1310	...	1524	...	1724	...	1924	...	2151	2241	...	1153	1451	1656	1856	2054	...
Cheltenham Spa ◧ d.	0713	...	0936	...	1134	...	1320	...	1534	...	1734	...	1934	2102	2201	2251	1004	1203	1501	1706	1906	2103	2201
Gloucester ◧ a.	0725	...	0945	...	1145	...	1332	...	1544	...	1745	...	1945	2112	2211	2301	1014	1214	1511	1716	1916	2113	2211
Gloucester d.	0740	0842	0948	1041	1147	1242	1343	1442	1547	1642	1747	1842	1947	2114	...	...	1016	1218	1513	1719	1919	2115	...
Bristol Parkway d.	0820	0920	1025	1121	1225	1320	1422	1520	1624	1720	1825	1920	2025	2152	...	...	1055	1258	1555	1757	1958	2153	...
Bristol Temple Meads a.	0834	0936	1039	1135	1239	1334	1437	1534	1639	1734	1839	1935	2039	2204	...	...	1107	1309	1608	1809	2010	2207	...

	Ⓐ	Ⓐ	ⒶC	ⒶC	ⒶC	Ⓐ	Ⓐ	Ⓐ	Ⓐ	ⒶC	ⒶB	ⒶC	ⒶB	ⒶC	Ⓐ	Ⓐ	Ⓐ	Ⓐ		⑥	⑥	⑥C	⑥C
Bristol Temple Meads d.	...	...	0734	0841	0940	1041	1141	1241	1340	1441	1541	1641	1741	1834	1941	2041	...	2212	...	...	...	0741	0841
Bristol Parkway d.	...	...	0746	0852	0952	1055	1152	1252	1352	1452	1552	1652	1753	1846	1952	2052	...	2223	...	...	...	0752	0852
Gloucester a.	...	...	0832	0933	1032	1134	1233	1334	1432	1534	1633	1734	1833	1928	2032	2132	...	2303	...	...	...	0833	0933
Gloucester ◧ d.	0600	0714	...	0937	...	1136	...	1337	...	1536	...	1737	...	1948	2035	2133	2152	...	...	0550	0715	...	0938
Cheltenham Spa ◧ a.	0611	0724	...	0946	...	1146	...	1346	...	1546	...	1747	...	2001	2048	2144	2202	...	...	0559	0724	...	0947
Ashchurch for Tewkesbury a.	0619	0733	...	0955	...	1156	...	1355	...	1556	...	1756	...	2010	...	2153	|	...	...	0608	0733	...	0956
Worcester Shrub Hill a.	0641	0754	...	1014	...	1213	...	1414	...	1614	...	1816	...	2030	...	2214	2224	...	...	0633	0752	...	1014
Great Malvern a.	...	0812	...	1032	...	1233	...	1435	...	1632	...	1836	...	...	...	...	...	...	...	...	...	...	1032

	⑥C	⑥	⑥B	⑥	⑥B	⑥	⑥B	⑥C	⑥C	⑥B	⑥	⑥	⑥		⑦	⑦		⑦	⑦	⑦	⑦		⑦	⑦
Bristol Temple Meads d.	0941	1041	1141	1241	1341	1441	1541	1641	1741	1841	1941	2043	2206	...	0920	1211	...	1441	1641	1837	2041	...	2230	...
Bristol Parkway d.	0952	1052	1153	1252	1352	1452	1552	1652	1753	1852	1952	2054	2218	...	0929	1222	...	1451	1651	1846	2050	...	2239	...
Gloucester a.	1032	1132	1234	1335	1435	1533	1633	1733	1833	1933	2033	2134	2301	...	1010	1304	...	1533	1733	1930	2133	...	2321	...
Gloucester ◧ d.	...	1137	...	1338	...	1538	...	1738	...	1938	2038	2138	...	...	1012	1305	...	1551	1735	1937	2137	...	...	2356
Cheltenham Spa ◧ a.	...	1147	...	1347	...	1547	...	1747	...	1948	2049	2148	...	...	1021	1316	...	1602	1745	1946	2146	...	...	0007
Ashchurch for Tewkesbury a.	...	1157	...	1357	...	1556	...	1756	...	1956	...	2157	...	...	1030	1325	...	1612	1755	1956	...	...	...	...
Worcester Shrub Hill a.	...	1215	...	1415	...	1614	...	1815	...	2015	...	2218	...	...	1051	1344	...	1629	1815	2022	...	...	...	...
Great Malvern a.	...	...	...	1432	...	1632	...	1836	...	2040	...	...	...	...	...	...	...	...	...	...	...	...	...	...

A – To Taunton (Table **137**). B – To / from Weymouth (Table **139**). C – To / from Westbury (Table **139**). D – To Frome (Table **139**). ◧ – See also Tables **121** and **133**.

140 BRISTOL - WESTBURY - SOUTHAMPTON, PORTSMOUTH and WEYMOUTH

GW, SW

km		Ⓐ	⑥	Ⓐ	Ⓐ	⑥	Ⓐ	⑥	⚒C	⚒	⚒A	⚒	⑥A	ⒶA	⚒	⚒	⚒A	⚒	⚒A	⚒	⚒A	⚒	ⒶA	⑥A	⚒	⚒	⚒A
	Cardiff Central **136** d.	...	...	...	...	...	...	...	...	0628	...	0730	...	...	...	0830	...	0930	...	1030	...	1130	...	...	...	1230	...
0	**Bristol** Temple Meads d.	...	...	0518	0544	0549	...	...	...	0722	0747	0822	0839	0841	0851	0922	0949	1022	1049	1122	1149	1222	1239	1243	1249	1322	1349
19	Bath Spa d.	...	...	|	0603	0607	...	...	...	0735	0807	0836	0857	0859	0907	0936	1007	1035	1107	1135	1207	1235	1256	1301	1307	1335	1407
34	Bradford on Avon d.	...	...	0542	0619	0623	...	...	...	0747	0823	0847	0913	0915	0921	0948	1023	1047	1123	1147	1223	1247	1312	1313	1319	1347	1423
39	Trowbridge **132a** d.	...	...	0549	0626	0629	...	...	...	0753	0829	0853	0919	0921	0927	0954	1029	1053	1129	1153	1229	1253	1318	1320	1327	1353	1429
46	**Westbury** **132a** d.	0549	0602	0603	0640**c**	0643**c**	0646	0647	0701	0801	0836	0901	0927	0932**d**	0939	1001	1037	1101	1136	1201	1237	1301	1330**d**	1328	1339**d**	1401	1437
	Frome d.	|	|	|	|	|	0655	0656	|	|	...	|	0936	0941	|	|	1046	|	...	|	1247	|	|	|	|	|	1451
	Castle Cary d.	|	|	|	|	|	0714	0715	|	|	...	|	0953	1000	|	|	1103	|	...	|	1304	|	|	|	|	|	...
	Yeovil Pen Mill d.	|	|	|	|	|	0735	0729	|	|	...	|	1007	1014	|	|	1117	|	...	|	1317	|	|	|	|	|	...
	Dorchester West d.	|	|	|	|	|	0809	0803	|	|	...	|	1040	1048	|	|	1154	|	...	|	1354	|	|	|	|	|	...
	Weymouth a.	|	|	|	|	|	0824	0817	|	|	...	|	1057	1103	|	|	1209	|	...	|	1409	|	|	|	|	|	...
53	Warminster d.	0557	0610	|	0648	0651	...	...	0712	0809	...	0909	...	...	0946	1010	...	1109	...	1209	...	1309	1339	1337	1346	1409	...
85	**Salisbury** d.	0619	0632	|	0711	0724	...	...	0736	0832	...	0932	...	...	1009	1031	...	1132	...	1232	...	1332	1402	1400	1412	1432	...
	London W'loo **113** a.	|	|	0746**p**	|	|	...	...	|	|	...	|	...	...	1149	|	...	|	...	|	...	|	|	|	1549	|	...
112	Romsey d.	0638	0651	...	0730	0744	...	...	0755	0850	...	0950	...	...	...	1050	...	1150	...	1251	...	1350	1421	1420	...	1450	...
123	**Southampton** Central a.	0649	0702	...	0740	0802	...	...	0809	0904	...	1004	...	...	...	1104	...	1204	...	1304	...	1404	1432	1432	...	1504	...
147	Fareham a.	0715	0727	...	0805	0827	...	...	...	0927	...	1027	...	...	...	1127	...	1227	...	1327	...	1427	1458	1454	...	1527	...
164	**Portsmouth** & S a.	0738	0746	...	0824	0846	...	...	...	0946	...	1046	...	...	...	1146	...	1246	...	1346	...	1446	**B**	**B**	...	1546	...
165	**Portsmouth** Harbour a.	0745	0752	...	0830	0852	...	...	...	0952	...	1054	...	...	...	1154	...	1254	...	1354	...	1454	...	...	...	1554	...

	ⒶE	⚒	⚒A	⚒	⑥A	ⒶA	⚒	Ⓐ	⚒A	ⒶG	⑥	Ⓐ	⚒A	⚒	ⒶD	⚒A	⚒	ⒶG	⚒A	⑥	Ⓐ	⚒	⑥D	⚒	ⒶG	⚒	⑥	Ⓐ
Cardiff Central **136** d.	...	1330	...	1430	...	...	...	1530	...	...	1630	1629	...	1730	...	...	1830	...	...	1930	1930	...	...	2030	...	...	...	...
Bristol Temple Meads d.	...	1422	1448	1522	1538	1544	1551	1622	1649	...	1722	1723	1749	1822	...	1849	1922	...	1949	2022	2022	2049	...	2122	...	2223	2309	2320
Bath Spa d.	...	1435	1506	1535	1557	1602	1607	1635	1707	...	1736	1736	1807	1835	...	1907	1935	...	2007	2036	2036	2107	...	2136	...	2236	2327	2338
Bradford on Avon d.	...	1447	1522	1547	1613	1618	1624	1647	1723	...	1748	1748	1823	1847	...	1923	1947	...	2023	2048	2047	2123	...	2148	...	2247	2342	2354
Trowbridge **132a** d.	...	1453	1528	1554	1619	1624	1630	1653	1730	...	1754	1754	1829	1853	1924	1929	1953	...	2029	2054	2053	2129	2144	2154	...	2253	2349	2359
Westbury **132a** d.	1457	1501	1537	1602	1626	1633	1639	1701	1738	1745	1802	1805	1840**d**	1902	1940**c**	1939	2001	2011	2037	2102	2101	2139	2152	2201	2218	2305**d**	2356	0008
Frome d.	1507	|	1546	|	...	...	|	|	1747	|	|	|	1849	|	|	...	|	|	2048	|	|	2150	...	|	|	|	0007	0019
Castle Cary d.	1524	|	1609	|	...	...	|	|	1805	|	|	|	1906	|	|	...	|	|	...	|	|	2208	...	|	|	|	...	...
Yeovil Pen Mill d.	1539	|	1624	|	...	...	|	|	1821	|	|	|	1919	|	|	...	|	|	...	|	|	2223	...	|	|	|	...	...
Dorchester West d.	...	|	1658	|	...	...	|	|	1854**e**	|	|	|	1954	|	|	...	|	|	...	|	|	2258	...	|	|	|	...	...
Weymouth a.	...	|	1710	|	...	...	|	|	1912	|	|	|	2010	|	|	...	|	|	...	|	|	2313	...	|	|	|	...	...
Warminster d.	...	1509	...	1609	...	...	1647	1709	...	1752	1810	1813	...	1910	1950	...	2009	2019	...	2110	2109	...	...	2211	2226	2312	...	...
Salisbury d.	...	1532	...	1632	...	...	1709	1732	...	1817	1833	1835	...	1932	2011	...	2032	2042	...	2133	2132	...	...	2232	2246	2338	...	...
London W'loo **113** a.	...	|	...	|	...	...	1849	|	...	1950	|	|	...	|	|	...	|	...	...	|	|	...	...	|	...	...	...	...
Romsey d.	...	1550	...	1650	...	...	...	1750	...	...	1851	1854	...	1950	2030	...	2050	...	...	2151	2150	...	...	2253	...	...	...	...
Southampton Central a.	...	1604	...	1704	...	...	...	1803	...	...	1903	1904	...	2003	2044	...	2104	...	...	2203	2202	...	...	2304	...	...	...	...
Fareham a.	...	1627	...	1727	...	...	...	1827	...	...	1927	1927	...	2027	...	...	2127	...	...	2227	2242	...	...	2327	...	...	...	...
Portsmouth & S a.	...	1646	...	1746	...	...	...	1852**r**	...	...	1946	1946	...	2046	...	...	2146	...	...	2246	2258	...	...	2348	...	...	...	...
Portsmouth Harbour a.	...	1654	...	1754	...	...	...	1900**r**	...	...	1952	1954	...	2054	...	...	2153	...	...	2252	2303	...	...	2354	...	...	...	...

	⑦	⑦	⑦	⑦	⑦B		⑦	⑦B		⑦	⑦	⑦	⑦	⑦	⑦	⑦	⑦B	⑦	⑦	⑦	⑦	⑦	⑦	⑦	⑦	⑦	⑦
Cardiff Central **136** d.	...	0808	...	0913	1008	...	1108	1208	...	...	1308	1408	...	1508	1608	...	1635	...	1708	1739	1812	1908	...	2018	...	...	2208
Bristol Temple Meads d.	0823	0910	0925	1015	1110	...	1210	1310	...	...	1413	1510	1604	1615	1710	...	1740	1743	1810	1847	1910	2015	2048	2125	2135	2215	2315
Bath Spa d.	0841	0929	0944	1027	1126	...	1222	1327	...	...	1427	1527	1620	1627	1727	...	1752	1801	1827	1900	1926	2027	2106	2139	2149	2233	2329
Bradford on Avon d.	0857	0940	1000	1044	1139	...	1239	1340	...	...	1443	1540	1631	1644	1740	...	1805	1816	1839	1913	1938	2044	2123	2151	2200	2250	2341
Trowbridge **132a** d.	0903	0947	1007	1050	1147	...	1246	1347	...	...	1450	1547	1637	1650	1747	...	1812	1824	1847	1919	1946	2051	2130	2157	2206	2256	2347
Westbury **132a** d.	0912	1000**d**	1018**d**	1101	1201**c**	...	1301**c**	1401**d**	...	1425	1501**d**	1603**c**	1646	1701	1801**c**	1816	1821	1831	1901**c**	1931**d**	1959**d**	2101	2138	2205	2215	2303	2355
Frome d.	0922	|	1031	|	|	...	|	|	...	1434	|	|	|	|	|	1804**g**	|	1839	|	|	|	|	2148	|	|	...	0004
Castle Cary d.	0940	|	1048	|	|	...	|	|	...	1451	|	|	|	|	|	|	|	1858	|	|	|	|	2205	|	|	...	...
Yeovil Pen Mill d.	0956	|	1103	|	|	...	|	|	...	1505	|	|	|	|	|	|	|	1912	|	|	|	|	2219	|	|	...	...
Dorchester West d.	1030	|	1141	|	|	...	|	|	...	1540	|	|	|	|	|	|	|	1947	|	|	|	|	2253	|	|	...	...
Weymouth a.	1042	|	1154	|	|	...	|	|	...	1554	|	|	|	|	|	|	|	2001	|	|	|	|	2306	|	|	...	...
Warminster d.	...	1008	...	1108	1210	...	1308	1410	...	...	1508	1612	1653	1708	1808	1823	1830	...	1908	1938	2008	2108	...	2213	2222	...	...
Salisbury d.	...	1032	...	1132	1232	...	1332	1436	...	...	1532	1632	1716	1732	1832	1843	1856	...	1932	2001	2032	2132	...	2236	2246	...	...
London W'loo **113** a.	...	|	...	|	|	...	|	|	...	...	|	|	1859	|	|	2019	|	...	|	|	|	|	...	|	...	...	...
Romsey d.	...	1050	...	1150	1250	...	1350	1454	...	...	1550	1650	...	1750	1850	...	1914	...	1950	2020	2050	2150	...	2256	...	...	...
Southampton Central a.	...	1103	...	1203	1303	...	1403	1503	...	...	1603	1703	...	1803	1903	...	1925	...	2003	2030	2103	2203	...	2306	...	...	...
Fareham a.	...	1126	...	1226	1329	1344	1426	1527	1544	...	1626	1726	...	1826	1924	...	1949	...	2026	2055	2126	2226	...	2330	...	...	...
Portsmouth & S a.	...	1145	...	1244	**B**	1408	1444	**B**	1608	...	1644	1744	...	1844	1944	...	**B**	...	2045	2116	2145	2245	...	2348	...	...	...
Portsmouth Harbour a.	...	1152	...	1252	...	1413	1452	...	1613	...	1652	1752	...	1853	1952	...	...	...	2052	2126	2152	2252	...	2356	...	...	...

A – From Gloucester, Cheltenham Spa, Worcester or Great Malvern (see Table **138**).
B – To Brighton (journey time from Fareham: 1 hr 16 m - 1 hr 29 m), also calling at Havant, Chichester, Worthing and Hove.
C – From Gloucester on Ⓐ (Table **132a**).
D – From Cheltenham Spa (Table **132a**).
E – From London Waterloo (see other direction of table).
G – From Yeovil (see other direction of table).
c – Arrives 7 – 9 minutes earlier.
d – Arrives 4 – 5 minutes earlier.
e – 1858 on Ⓐ.
f – Arrives 12 minutes earlier.
g – Calls at Frome before Westbury.
p – London Paddington (Table **115**).
r – 4 minutes earlier on ⑥.

GW, SW — PORTSMOUTH, SOUTHAMPTON and WEYMOUTH - WESTBURY - BRISTOL — 140

km		⚒	Ⓐ	⚒	⚒A	Ⓐ	⚒	Ⓐ	⚒A	Ⓐ	⑥	⚒	⑥A	ⒶA	Ⓐ	⑥	⚒A	⚒	⑥A	Ⓐ	⚒	⚒	ⒶA	⑥A	⚒	⑥A	Ⓐ	⚒
	Portsmouth Harbour d.		...	...	...	...	...	...	...	0600	0600	...	...	...	0705	0723	...	0823	...	...	0923	...	...	...	1023	...	...	1123
	Portsmouth & S d.		...	...	...	...	...	...	...	0604	0604	...	...	...	0709	0727	...	0827	...	...	0927	...	B	B	1027	...	...	1127
	Fareham d.		...	...	...	...	...	...	...	0624	0628	...	...	...	0729	0747	...	0847	...	...	0947	...	1013	1016	1047	...	...	1147
	Southampton Central d.		...	...	...	...	...	...	...	0646	0653	...	...	...	0753	0810	0823	0910	...	...	1010	...	1042	1042	1110	...	...	1210
	Romsey d.		...	...	...	...	...	...	...	0700	0711	...	...	...	0811	0821	0835	0921	...	...	1021	...	1054	1053	1121	...	...	1221
	London W'loo **113** d.		...	...	...	...	...	...	...	|	|	...	...	...	|	|	|	|	...	...	|	0920	|	|	|	...	...	|
	Salisbury d.		...	0602	...	...	0640	...	...	0719	0730	...	...	...	0830	0840	0901	0940	...	...	1040	1052	1113	1113	1140	...	...	1240
	Warminster d.		...	0624	...	...	0700	...	0723	0739	0750	...	...	...	0852	0901	0923	1001	...	...	1101	1112	1132	1135	1201	...	...	1301
0	**Weymouth** d.		...	|	...	...	|	0533	|	|	|	0638	...	...	|	|	|	|	0846	0853	|	|	|	|	|	1110	1110	|
11	Dorchester West d.		...	|	...	...	|	0545	|	|	|	0651	...	...	|	|	|	|	0859	0906	|	|	|	|	|	1126	1123	|
44	Yeovil Pen Mill d.		...	|	...	...	|	0620	|	|	|	0730	...	...	|	|	|	|	0934	0941	|	|	|	|	|	1205	1205	|
63	Castle Cary d.		...	|	...	...	|	0644b	|	|	|	0744	...	...	|	|	|	|	0948	0955	|	|	|	|	|	1221	1223	|
86	Frome d.		...	|	...	0645	|	0703	|	|	|	0802	...	...	|	|	|	|	1007	1015	|	|	|	|	|	1239	1242	|
95	**Westbury** **132a** d.		0558	0633	0638	0655	0709	0717e	0738e	0753e	0802	0817e	0838	0845	0910d	0910	0935	1010	1038h	1038b	1110	1121	1141	1147	1210	1249	1252	1310
105	Trowbridge **132a** d.		0604	...	0644	0702	0715	0723	0744	0800	0808	0823	0844	0851	0916	0916	0941	1016	1044	1044	1116	1127	1148	1153	1216	1256	1258	1316
110	Bradford on Avon d.		0610	...	0650	0708	0721	0729	0750	0806	0814	0829	0850	0857	0922	0922	0947	1022	1050	1050	1122	1133	1154	1159	1222	1302	1304	1322
125	Bath Spa a.		0628	...	0708	0725	0735	0747	0808	0822	0831	0847	0905	0913	0936	0936	1005	1036	1108	1108	1136	1147	1211	1217	1236	1319	1322	1336
144	**Bristol** Temple Meads a.		0646	...	0727	0746	0752	0805	0829	0842	0844	0906	0927	0935	0951	0948	1028	1048	1127	1128	1148	1205	1228	1235	1248	1337	1343	1348
	Cardiff Central **136** a.		0744	...	...	0846	...	...	...	0943	0942	...	...	...	1044	1043	...	1146g	...	...	1242	...	...	...	1343	...	...	1443

	ⒶA	⑥A	⚒	⚒	⚒A	ⒶD	⚒	⚒A	⚒	⚒A	⚒	ⒶC	ⒶA	⑥A	⚒	⚒c	⚒	⑥	Ⓐ	⚒	Ⓐs	⚒	⚒	⚒	⚒	⚒	⚒	Ⓐs
Portsmouth Harbour d.	...	...	1223	...	...	...	1323	...	1423	...	1523	...	...	...	1623	...	1723	...	...	...	...	1823	...	1923	...	...	2023	...
Portsmouth & S d.	...	...	1227	...	...	...	1327	...	1427	...	1527	...	...	...	1627	...	1727	...	...	B	...	1827	...	1927	...	...	2027	...
Fareham d.	...	...	1247	...	...	...	1347	...	1447	...	1547	...	...	...	1647	...	1747	...	...	1814	...	1847	...	1947	...	...	2047	...
Southampton Central d.	1227	1227	1309	...	...	...	1410	...	1510	...	1610	...	...	...	1710	...	1810	...	...	1842	...	1910	...	2010	...	...	2110	...
Romsey d.	1239	1238	1320	...	...	...	1421	...	1521	...	1621	...	...	...	1721	...	1821	...	...	1853	...	1921	...	2021	...	...	2121	...
London W'loo **113** d.	|	|	|	1220	...	1250	|	...	|	...	|	...	...	...	|	...	|	...	...	|	1650	|	...	|	1920	...	|	1850
Salisbury d.	1306	1303	1339	1352	...	1424	1440	...	1540	...	1640	...	...	...	1740	...	1840	...	...	1915	1823	1940	...	2040	2057	...	2140	2025
Warminster d.	1334	1325	1400	1412	...	1444	1501	1528	1601	...	1701	...	1728	1728	1801	...	1901	...	...	1932n	|	2001	...	2101	2117	...	2201	|
Weymouth d.	|	|	|	|	1310	|	|	|	|	1508	|	...	|	|	|	...	|	1728	1730	|	|	|	...	|	|	2021	|	|
Dorchester West d.	|	|	|	|	1323	|	|	|	|	1521	|	...	|	|	|	...	|	1741	1743	|	|	|	...	|	|	2034	|	|
Yeovil Pen Mill d.	|	|	|	|	1406	|	|	|	|	1556	|	1653	|	|	|	...	|	1818	1823	|	1927	|	...	|	|	2106n	|	2127
Castle Cary d.	|	|	|	|	1420	|	|	|	|	1610	|	1707	|	|	|	...	|	1832	1837	|	1939	|	...	|	|	2118n	|	2141
Frome d.	|	|	|	|	1439	|	|	|	|	1629	|	1724	|	|	|	...	|	1857	1906	|	1957	|	...	|	|	2138n	|	2158
Westbury **132a** d.	1344	1338e	1410	1421	1448	1451	1510	1538	1610	1638	1710	1733	1738	1746d	1810	1838	1910	1917e	1921e	1941n	2006	2010	2038	2110	2125	2155	2210	2212
Trowbridge **132a** d.	1350	1344	1416	1427	1455	...	1516	1544	1616	1644	1716	...	1744	1752	1816	1844	1916	1923	1927	1948n	...	2016	2044	2116	2131	2202	2216	...
Bradford on Avon d.	1356	1350	1422	1433	1501	...	1522	1550	1622	1650	1722	...	1750	1758	1822	1850	1922	1929	1933	1954n	...	2022	2050	2122	2137	2208	2222	...
Bath Spa a.	1414	1408	1436	1447	1518	...	1536	1608	1636	1712g	1736	...	1808	1816	1836	1906	1936	1947	1951	2006n	...	2035	2106	2136	2151	2225	2236	...
Bristol Temple Meads a.	1435	1429	1448	1505	1537	...	1548	1629	1648	1731g	1748	...	1828	1836	1849	1929	1948	2005	2009	2029	...	2048	2129	2149	2206	2245	2250	...
Cardiff Central **136** a.	...	...	1545	...	...	...	1644	...	1743	...	1843	...	...	...	1946g	...	2047	...	...	...	...	2145	...	2300v	...	...	2356	...

	Ⓐ	⑥	Ⓐ	⑦	⑦	⑦	⑦	⑦	⑦	⑦	⑦	⑦	⑦	⑦	⑦	⑦	⑦	⑦	⑦	⑦	⑦	⑦	⑦	⑦	⑦	⑦	⑦	⑦
Portsmouth Harbour d.	...	...	2123		...	0908	...	...	1108	...	...	1308	...	1408	1508	...	...	1608	...	1708	...	1808	...	...	1908	...	2008	2205
Portsmouth & S d.	...	...	2127		...	0912	...	...	1112	B	...	1312	...	1412	1512	...	...	1612	B	1712	...	1812	...	B	1912	...	2012	2212
Fareham d.	...	...	2148		...	0932	...	...	1132	1232	...	1332	...	1432	1532	...	...	1632	1703	1732	...	1832	...	1905	1932	...	2032	2232
Southampton Central d.	2120	2127	2222		...	0954	...	...	1154	1254	...	1354	...	1454	1554	...	...	1654	1726	1754	...	1854	...	1928	1954	...	2054	2257
Romsey d.	2131	2138	2234		...	1006	...	...	1206	1306	...	1406	...	1506	1606	...	...	1706	1739	1806	...	1906	...	1940	2006	...	2106	2308
London W'loo **113** d.	|	|	|		...	|	...	...	|	|	1215	|	...	|	|	...	...	|	|	|	...	|	1815	|	|	...	|	|
Salisbury d.	2153	2204	2300		...	1025	...	...	1225	1325	1355	1425	...	1525	1625	1710	...	1725	1801	1825	...	1925	1955	2001	2025	...	2125	2328
Warminster d.	2215	2226	2320		...	1049	...	...	1244	1344	1415	1444	...	1544	1644	1736	...	1744	1821	1844	...	1944	2015	2021	2044	...	2144	2350
Weymouth d.	|	|	|		...	|	...	1105	|	|	|	|	1415	|	|	|	1610	|	|	|	1756	|	|	|	|	2009	|	|
Dorchester West d.	|	|	|		...	|	...	1119	|	|	|	|	1428	|	|	|	1623	|	|	|	1809	|	|	|	|	2022	|	|
Yeovil Pen Mill d.	|	|	|		...	|	...	1154	|	|	|	|	1504	|	|	|	1658	|	|	|	1844	|	|	|	|	2057	|	|
Castle Cary d.	|	|	|		...	|	...	1208	|	|	|	|	1518	|	|	|	1713	|	|	|	1859	|	|	|	|	2110	|	|
Frome d.	|	|	|		0935	|	1140	1227	|	|	|	|	1537	|	|	1757f	1731	|	|	|	1918	|	|	|	|	2129	|	|
Westbury **132a** d.	2226	2238	2331		0953d	1058	1150	1236	1256	1356	1424	1500	1547	1604d	1700	1748	1741	1800	1832	1900	1934e	2000	2023	2035e	2100	2147d	2200	2359
Trowbridge **132a** d.	*2238*	2244	...		0959	1105	1156	...	1302	1402	1430	1506	1553	1610	1706	...	1748	1806	1838	1906	1940	2006	2029	2041	2106	2155	2206	...
Bradford on Avon d.	*2244*	2250	...		1005	1111	1202	...	1308	1408	1436	1512	1559	1616	1712	...	1754	1812	1844	1912	1948	2012	2035	2047	2112	2201	2212	...
Bath Spa a.	*2302*	2309	...		1022	1124	1220	...	1323	1425	1451	1525	1617	1629	1725	...	1809	1830	1856	1925	2009	2025	2050	2105	2125	2219	2225	...
Bristol Temple Meads a.	*2323*	2328	...		1040	1144	1238	...	1341	1444	1506	1540	1635	1641	1744	...	1827	1844	1917	1939	2029	2039	2105	2123	2141	2237	2241	...
Cardiff Central **136** a.	...	...	...		1143	1243	...	...	1443	1541	...	1643	...	1743	1842	...	...	1942	...	2045	...	2140	...	...	2246	...	2341	...

A – To Gloucester, Cheltenham Spa, Worcester or Great Malvern (see Table **138**).
B – From Brighton (journey time to Fareham 1hr 14m - 1hr 22m), also calling at Hove, Worthing, Chichester and Havant.
C – From Yeovil Junction (dep.1648). To London (see other direction of table).
D – To Yeovil (see other direction of table).
b – Arrives 11–14 minutes earlier.
c – Note **A** applies on ⑥.
d – Arrives 8–10 minutes earlier.
e – Arrives 5–6 minutes earlier.
f – Arrival time. Calls after Westbury.
g – 4–5 minutes earlier on ⑥.
h – Arrives 1016.
n – 3–5 minutes later on ⑥.
s – To Salisbury (see other direction of table).
v – 2251 on ①–④.

SN — EAST CROYDON - MILTON KEYNES — 141

km		Ⓐ	Ⓐ	Ⓐ	Ⓐ	Ⓐ	Ⓐ	Ⓐ	Ⓐ	Ⓐ	Ⓐ	Ⓐ		Ⓐ	Ⓐ	Ⓐ	Ⓐ	Ⓐ	Ⓐ		⑥	⑥	⑥
0	**East Croydon** d.		...	...	...	...	...	...	0750	0808	0910	1010		1710	1811	1912	...	...	...	...		...	...
12	Clapham Junction ▶ d.		0503	0530	0555	0620	0638	0739	0819	0839	0939	1039	and at	1739	1839	1939	2039	2139	2239	...		0508	0538
18	Kensington Olympia ⊙ ▶ d.		0514	0544	0607	0630	0649	0750	0831	0850	0950	1050	the same	1750	1850	1950	2050	2150	2250	...		0519	0549
27	Wembley Central d.		|	0602	0624	0647	0707	0808	0847	0908	1008	1109	minutes	1809	1909	2009	2108	|	|	...		|	0607
40	Watford Junction **142** d.		0540	0614	0636	0657	0719	0820	0901	0920	1020	1121	past each	1821	1921	2021	2120	2223	2332	...		0547	0620
76	Leighton Buzzard **142** d.		...	0642	...	...	0751	0848	...	0948	1048	1148	hour until	1848	1948	2048	2150	...	...	...		...	0647
87	Bletchley **142** d.		...	0649	...	...	0758	0855	..	0955	1057	1155		1855	1955	2055	2158	...	...	...		...	0655
92	**Milton Keynes** **142** a.		...	0656	...	...	0803	0901	...	1001	1102	1200	❖	1900	2000	2100	2205	...	...	...		...	0700

	⑥	⑥	⑥		⑥	⑥	⑥	⑥	⑥	⑥	⑦	⑦	⑦	⑦	⑦	⑦	⑦		⑦	⑦	⑦	⑦
East Croydon d.	...	0610	0710		1710	1810	1910	...	...	...		...	...	...	...	...	...		...	...	...	...
Clapham Junction ▶ d.	0609	0636	0739	and at	1739	1839	1938	2025	2150	2241		0815	0915	1015	1115	1205	1305	and at	1905	2005	2115	2215
Kensington Olympia ⊙ ▶ d.	0620	0647	0750	the same	1750	1852	1948	2036	2201	2251		0826	0926	1026	1126	1216	1316	the same	1916	2016	2125	2226
Wembley Central d.	0638	0709	0809	minutes	1809	1909	|	|	|	|		|	|	|	|	|	|	minutes	|	|	|	|
Watford Junction **142** d.	0650	0721	0821	past each	1821	1921	2015	2109	2230	2319		0855	0957	1055	1154	1242	1342	past each	1942	2042	2153	2256
Leighton Buzzard **142** d.	...	0748	0848	hour until	1848	...	...	...	...	...		...	...	...	...	...	...	hour until	...	...	...	...
Bletchley **142** d.	...	0755	0855		1855	...	...	...	...	...		...	...	...	...	...	...		...	...	...	...
Milton Keynes **142** a.	...	0800	0900	❖	1900	...	...	...	...	...		...	...	...	...	...	...	❖	...	...	...	...

	Ⓐ	Ⓐ	Ⓐ	Ⓐ	Ⓐ	Ⓐ	Ⓐ	Ⓐ	Ⓐ		Ⓐ	Ⓐ	Ⓐ	Ⓐ	Ⓐ	Ⓐ	Ⓐ	Ⓐ		⑥	⑥	⑥	
Milton Keynes **142** d.		...	...	...	0701	0813	...	0913	1013		1713	1813	1915	2013	2113	...	2211	...	...		...	...	...
Bletchley **142** d.		...	...	...	0706	0817	...	0917	1017	and at	1717	1817	1920	2017	2117	...	2215	...	...		...	...	...
Leighton Buzzard **142** d.		...	...	...	0713	0824	...	0924	1024	the same	1724	1824	1927	2024	2124	...	2222	...	...		...	...	...
Watford Junction **142** d.		0554	0653	0725	0738	0852	0915	0952	1052	minutes	1752	1851	1954	2051	2151	2227	2253	2336	...		0552	0655	...
Wembley Central d.		0605	0705	0737	0750	0904	0927	1004	1104	past each	1804	1905	2006	2104	|	|	|	|	...		|	0706	...
Kensington Olympia ⊡ ▶ d.		0632	0722	0758	0807	0922	0947	1022	1122	hour until	1822	1920	2023	2122	2222	2251	2323	0007	...		0623	0724	...
Clapham Junction ▶ a.		...	0732	0809	0817	0932	0957	1032	1132		1832	1930	2033	2132	2233	2301	2333	0017	...		0633	0734	...
East Croydon a.		...	...	...	0904	1001	...	1101	1201	❖	1903	...	...	...	...	...	2359	...	...		0656	0801	...

	⑥		⑥	⑥	⑥	⑥	⑥	⑥	⑥	⑥		⑦	⑦	⑦	⑦	⑦		⑦	⑦	⑦	⑦	⑦
Milton Keynes **142** d.	0713		1713	1813	...	1914	...	...	...	...	...		...	...	...	...		...	...	...	...	...
Bletchley **142** d.	0717	and at	1717	1817	...	1918	...	...	...	...	...		...	...	...	...	and at	...	...	...	...	...
Leighton Buzzard **142** d.	0724	the same	1724	1824	...	1925	...	...	...	...	...		...	...	...	...	the same	...	...	...	...	...
Watford Junction **142** d.	0752	minutes	1752	1851	1931	1951	2043	2144	2248	2325	...		0917	1017	1122	1222	minutes	1922	2022	2117	2217	2317
Wembley Central d.	0804	past each	1804	1903	1942	|	|	|	|	|	...		|	|	|	|	past each	|	|	|	|	|
Kensington Olympia ⊡ ▶ d.	0822	hour until	1822	1921	2001	2022	2111	2212	2316	2353	...		0947	1047	1149	1250	hour until	1950	2049	2147	2247	2347
Clapham Junction ▶ a.	0832		1832	1931	2010	2032	2121	2221	2326	0002	...		0958	1058	1159	1259		1959	2059	2200	2257	2357
East Croydon a.	0901	❖	1901	2001	...	2101	...	...	...	...	...		...	...	...	...	❖	...	...	...	...	0023

⊙ – All trains call at Shepherd's Bush, 2–3 minutes after Kensington Olympia.
⊡ – All trains call at Shepherd's Bush, 2–3 minutes before Kensington Olympia.
❖ – Timings may vary by up to 2 minutes.
▶ – Additional local services run between Clapham Junction and Shepherd's Bush.

142 LONDON - NORTHAMPTON - BIRMINGHAM and CREWE LM

LONDON - NORTHAMPTON - BIRMINGHAM

km		Ⓐ	Ⓐ	Ⓐ	Ⓐ	Ⓐ	Ⓐ	Ⓐ	Ⓐ	Ⓐ	Ⓐ	Ⓐ	Ⓐ	Ⓐ	Ⓐ	Ⓐ		Ⓐ	Ⓐ	Ⓐ	Ⓐ	Ⓐ	Ⓐ	Ⓐ	Ⓐ
0	**London Euston** d.		...	...	...	0534	...	0624	0634	0713	0749	0754	0813	0849	0854	0913	and	1449	1454	1513	1549	1554	1613	1650	1713
28	Watford Junction d.		...	...	...	0555	...	0641	0654	|	0803	0811	|	0903	0911	|	at	1503	1511	|	1603	1611	|	|	|
64	Leighton Buzzard d.		...	...	...	0628	...	0709	0725	0742	|	0836	0842	|	0936	0942	the	|	1536	1542	|	1636	1642	1720	|
75	Bletchley d.		...	...	...	0635	...	0716	0732	0750	|	0843	0850	0924y	0943	0950	same	|	1543	1550	|	1643	1650	1727	|
80	Milton Keynes d.		...	0537	...	0640	...	0721	0737	0754	0825	0849	0854	0929y	0949	0954	minutes	1525	1549	1554	1625	1649	1654	1732	1748
106	**Northampton** a.		...	0553	...	0656	...	0739	0753	0810	0840	0906	0911	0944y	1006	1010	past	1544	1606	1610	1640	1706	1713	1748	1810
106	**Northampton** d.		0516	0555	0616	0658	0716	0745	0755	0813	0855	0916	*0925*	0955	...	1016	each	1555	...	1616	1655	1716	...	1755	1819
136	Rugby d.		0538	0617	0638	0720	0738	0804	0817	0835	0917	0938	*0947*	1017	...	1038	hour	1617	...	1638	1717	1738	...	1817	1841
154	Coventry d.		0550	0630	0650	0732	0750	...	0830	0850	0930	0950	*1011*	1030	...	1050	until	1630	...	1650	1730	1750	...	1830	1853
171	**Birmingham Int'l ✈** d.		0605	0646	0705	0748	0805	...	0846	0905	0946	1005	*1029*	1046	...	1105	△	1646	...	1705	1746	1805	...	1846	1908
185	**Birmingham New St.** a.		0617	0701	0717	0805	0817	...	0902	0917	1001	1017	*1042*	1101	...	1117		1702	...	1717	1801	1817	...	1901	1920

	Ⓐ	Ⓐ	Ⓐ	Ⓐ	Ⓐ	Ⓐ	Ⓐ	Ⓐ	Ⓐ	Ⓐ	Ⓐ	Ⓐ	Ⓐ	Ⓐ	Ⓐ	Ⓐ	Ⓐ	Ⓐ	Ⓐ	⑥	⑥	⑥	⑥	⑥	⑥	⑥
London Euston d.	1724	1749	1752	1813	1816	1849	1852	1913	1949	1954	2013	2049	2054	2113	2149	2154	2224	2304	2324		...	...	0534	...	...	0624
Watford Junction d.	1744	|	1811	|	|	|	|	|	|	2011	|	|	2111	|	|	2215	2241	2329	2341		...	...	0552	...	...	0641
Leighton Buzzard d.	1809	1820	|	|	1844	|	1920	1942	2018	2036	2042	2118	2136	2144	2218	2247	2307	0002	0007		...	...	0625	...	...	0709
Bletchley d.	1816	|	1841	|	|	|	1927	|	|	2043	2049	|	2143	2152	|	2254	2314	0009	0014		0531	...	0631	...	...	0719
Milton Keynes d.	1822	1831	1846	1846	1854	1923	1932	1956	2029	2049	2054	2129	2149	2157	2232	2302	2323	0018	0023		0537	...	0637	...	...	0724
Northampton a.	1838	1848	1908	1904	1915	1937	1953	2011	2045	2106	2111	2146	2209	2215	2250	2320	2340	0036	0040		0553	...	0653	...	...	0741
Northampton d.	1839	1857	...	1919	1931	1946	1955	2019	2055	...	2116	2155	...	2219	2255	...	...	...	...		0555	0616	0655	0716	0737	*0755*
Rugby d.	1901	1919	...	1941	1956	2005	2017	2041	2117	...	2138	2217	...	2241	2317	...	...	...	...		0617	0638	0717	0738	0759	*0817*
Coventry d.	1911	1932	...	1953	2011	...	2030	2053	2130	...	2150	2230	...	2253	2330	...	...	...	...		0630	0650	0730	0750	0811	*0830*
Birmingham Int'l ✈ d.	1929	1948	...	2008	2029	...	2046	2108	2146	...	2205	2246	...	2311	2348	...	...	...	...		0646	0705	0746	0805	0829	*0846*
Birmingham New St. a.	1942	2003	...	2020	2042	...	2102	2120	2202	...	2218	2302	...	2322	0004	...	...	...	...		0701	0717	0801	0817	0842	*0901*

	⑥	⑥	⑥	⑥	⑥	⑥	⑥	⑥	⑥		⑥	⑥	⑥	⑥	⑥	⑥	⑥	⑥	⑥	⑥	⑥	⑥	⑥	⑥	⑥
London Euston d.	...	0705	0749	0754	...	0849	0854	0913	0949	and	1754	1813	1849	1854	1913	...	1946	2034	2040	2107	2128	2154	2234	2304	2340
Watford Junction d.	...	0726	0803	0811	...	0903	0911	|	1003	at	1811	|	1903	1911	|	...	2002	2050	2101	2124	2144	2214	2250	2324	2359
Leighton Buzzard d.	...	0758	|	0836	...	|	0936	0942	|	the	1836	1844	|	1936	1942	...	2034	2118	|	2150	2208	2247	2316	2356	0032
Bletchley d.	...	0805	|	0843	...	0924	0943	0950	1024x	same	1843	1852	|	1943	1950	...	2041	2125	2131	2157	2215	2254	2323	0003	0039
Milton Keynes d.	...	0810	0825	0849	...	0929	0949	0954	1029x	minutes	1849	1856	1925	1949	1954	...	2049	2133	2140	2206	2224	2303	2331	0011	0047
Northampton a.	...	0826	0840	0905	...	0944	1006	1013	1045x	past	1906	1913	1944	2006	2011	...	2106	2150	2156	2223	2243	2320	2348	0028	0104
Northampton d.	0816	0837	0855	0916	0937	0955	...	1016	1055	each	...	1916	1955	...	2022	2055	2116	2159	2216	...	2255	...	...	...	...
Rugby d.	0838	0859	0917	0938	0959	1017	...	1038	1117	hour	...	1938	2017	...	2044	2117	2138	2221	2238	...	2317	...	...	...	...
Coventry d.	0850	0911	0930	0950	1011	1030	...	1050	1130	until	...	1950	2030	...	2056	2130	2150	2233	2250	...	2330	...	...	...	...
Birmingham Int'l ✈ d.	0905	0929	0946	1005	1029	1046	...	1105	1146	△	...	2005	2046	...	2114	2146	2205	2249	2305	...	2349	...	...	...	...
Birmingham New St. a.	0917	0942	1001	1017	1042	1101	...	1117	1201		...	2017	2102	...	2125	2201	2217	2304	2317	...	0004	...	...	...	...

	⑦	⑦	⑦	⑦	⑦	⑦	⑦	⑦	⑦	⑦	⑦	⑦	⑦	⑦	⑦	⑦		⑦	⑦	⑦	⑦	⑦	⑦	⑦	⑦
London Euston d.		0654	0724	0752	0824	0855	0924	0954	1001	1024	1028	1054	1124	1154	1234	1250	and	1950	2034	2106	2130	2200	2228	2258	2334
Watford Junction d.		0713	0745	0810	0845	0914	0945	1010	1019	1040	1046	1114	1142	1214	1250	1306	at	2006	2050	2123	2150	2219	2249	2317	2355
Leighton Buzzard d.		0741	0814	0839	0914	0941	1014	1035	1047	1105	1115	1143	1212	1243	1315	1327	the	2027	2115	2149	2219	2247	2318	2350	0028
Bletchley d.		0748	0821	0845	0921	0948	1021	1042	|	1112	|	1150	1219	1250	1322	|	same	|	2122	2156	2226	2254	2325	2357	0035
Milton Keynes d.		0758	0830	0851	0927	0957	1027	1050	1058	1120	1128	1158	1228	1258	1328	1337	minutes	2037	2128	2204	2234	2303	2333	0005	0043
Northampton a.		0815	0847	0909	0944	1014	1044	1106	1116	1138	1145	1215	1244	1315	1344	1351	past	2054	2146	2221	2250	2319	2350	0023	0100
Northampton d.		...	...	0926	1000	...	1100	1108	...	1140	1158	...	1255	...	1355	1402	each	2106	2155	...	2252	2332	...	...	...
Rugby d.		...	...	0948	1022	...	1122	1130	...	1202	1220	...	1317	...	1417	1424	hour	2128	2217	...	2314	2354	...	...	...
Coventry d.		...	...	1000	1034	...	1134	...	...	...	1232	...	1330	...	1430	...	until	...	2230	...	2338	0007	...	...	...
Birmingham Int'l ✈ d.		...	...	1009	1052	...	1152	...	...	...	1250	...	1348	...	1448	...	△	...	2248	...	2356	...	...	...	...
Birmingham New St. a.		...	...	1026	1103	...	1203	...	...	...	1301	...	1359	...	1459	...		...	2259	...	0007	...	...	...	...

	Ⓐ	Ⓐ	Ⓐ	Ⓐ	Ⓐ	Ⓐ	Ⓐ	Ⓐ	Ⓐ	Ⓐ	Ⓐ	Ⓐ	Ⓐ	Ⓐ	Ⓐ	Ⓐ	Ⓐ	Ⓐ	Ⓐ	Ⓐ	Ⓐ		Ⓐ	Ⓐ	Ⓐ
Birmingham New St. d.		...	...	...	...	...	...	...	0553	...	0614	0654	0714	0733	0754	*0814*	0833	0854	0914	0933	0954	and	1554	...	1633
Birmingham Int'l ✈ d.		...	...	...	...	...	...	...	0605	...	0630	0705	0730	0745	0805	*0830*	0845	0905	0930	0945	1005	at	1605	...	1645
Coventry d.		...	...	...	...	...	0557	...	0621	...	0648	0721	0742	0804	0821	*0848*	0900	0925	0948	1000	1021	the	1621	...	1700
Rugby d.		...	...	...	0516	...	0612	...	0632	*0647*	0659	0732	0753	0815	0839	*0859*	0912	0938	0959	1012	1032	same	1632	...	1716
Northampton a.		...	...	...	0537	...	0633	...	0654	*0709*	0724	0754	0816	0837	0900	*0920*	0933	0959	1020	1033	1054	minutes	1657	...	1738
Northampton d.		0415	0448	0505	0546	0618	0638	0700	0710	0732	0738	0805	0825	0847	0905	0925	0950	1005	1025	1050	1105	past	1705	1725	1750
Milton Keynes d.		0430	0504	0521	0603	0635	0655	0718	0731	0747	0755	0822	0841	0905	0922	0941	1007	1022	1041	1107	1122	each	1722	1741	1807
Bletchley d.		0435	0509	0526	0608	0640	0700	|	|	0752	0800	0827	0846	|	0927	0946	|	1027	1046	|	1127	hour	1727	1746	|
Leighton Buzzard d.		0442	0515	0533	0615	0647	0707	0727	0740	0759	0807	0833	0853	|	0933	0953	|	1033	1053	|	1133	until	1733	1753	|
Watford Junction d.		0511	0550	0602	0635	0705	|	|	|	0827	|	|	|	0928	0959	|	1031	1059	|	1131	1159	△	1759	|	1831
London Euston a.		0534	0611	0620	0651	0722	0739	0802	0812	0848	0839	0910	0927	0946	1018	1023	1046	1117	1127	1146	1217		1818	1827	1846

	Ⓐ	Ⓐ	Ⓐ	Ⓐ	Ⓐ	Ⓐ	Ⓐ	Ⓐ	Ⓐ	Ⓐ	Ⓐ	Ⓐ	Ⓐ	Ⓐ	Ⓐ	Ⓐ	⑥	⑥	⑥	⑥	⑥	⑥	⑥	⑥	⑥	⑥
Birmingham New St. d.	1654	1714	1733	1754	1814	1833	1854	1914	1933	1954	2033	2054	2134	2154	...	2254		...	...	...	0614	0654	0714	0733	0754	0814
Birmingham Int'l ✈ d.	1705	1726	1745	1805	1830	1845	1905	1930	1945	2005	2045	2105	2145	2205	...	2305		...	...	...	0630	0705	0730	0745	0805	0830
Coventry d.	1721	1742	1800	1821	1848	1900	1921	1948	2000	2021	2100	2121	2200	2221	...	2321		...	...	...	0648	0721	0748	0800	0821	0848
Rugby d.	1732	1756	1812	1832	1859	1918	1932	1959	2015	2032	2114	2132	2212	2232	...	2332		...	...	...	0659	0732	0759	0812	0832	0859
Northampton a.	1756	1817	1837	1853	1921	1941	1954	2023	2038	2053	2135	2154	2235	2253	...	2355		...	...	...	0720	0754	0820	0836	0857	0920
Northampton d.	1805	1825	1850	1905	1925	1950	2005	2025	...	2105	2137	2205	...	2255	2335	...		0515	0605	0705	0735	0805	0825	0850	0905	0925
Milton Keynes d.	1822	1841	1907	1922	1941	2007	2025	2041	...	2122	2153	2222	...	2313	2353	...		0531	0621	0721	0752	0822	0841	0907	0922	0941
Bletchley d.	1827	1846	|	1927	1946	|	2030	2046	...	2127	2158	2227	...	2318	2358	...		0536	0627	0727	0757	0827	0846	|	0927	0946
Leighton Buzzard d.	1833	1853	|	1933	1953	|	2037	2053	...	2133	2204	2233	...	2324	0004	...		0543	0633	0733	0803	0833	0853	|	0933	0953
Watford Junction d.	1859	|	1931	1959	|	2031	2101	|	...	2159	2233	2303	...	2359	0033	...		0616	0701	0759	0828	0859	|	0934	0959	|
London Euston a.	1918	1928	1947	2020	2027	2048	2120	2128	...	2222	2252	2321	...	0021	0055	...		0638	0720	0818	0846	0917	0927	0949	1017	1027

	⑥	⑥	⑥	⑥		⑥	⑥	⑥	⑥	⑥	⑥	⑥	⑥	⑥	⑥	⑥	⑥	⑥	⑥	⑥	⑥	⑥	⑥	⑥	⑥
Birmingham New St. d.	0833	0854	0914	0933	and	1554	1614	1633	1654	1714	1733	1754	1814	1833	1854	1914	1933	1954	...	2033	2054	2134	2154	2214	2254
Birmingham Int'l ✈ d.	0845	0905	0930	0945	at	1605	1630	1645	1705	1731	1745	1805	1830	1845	1905	1930	1945	2005	...	2045	2105	2145	2205	2230	2305
Coventry d.	0900	0921	0948	1000	the	1621	1648	1700	1721	1749	1800	1821	1848	1900	1921	1948	2000	2021	...	2100	2121	2200	2221	2248	2321
Rugby d.	0912	0932	0959	1012	same	1632	1659	1712	1732	1759	1812	1832	1859	1912	1932	1959	2012	2032	2047	2112	2132	2212	2232	2259	2332
Northampton a.	0934	0954	1020	1034	minutes	1654	1720	1734	1753	1821	1834	1854	1920	1934	1953	2020	2035	2053	2106	2135	2153	2233	2253	2321	2355
Northampton d.	0950	1005	1025	1050	past	1705	1725	1750	1805	1831	1850	1905	1931	...	2002	2032	...	2102	2120	...	2205	2243	...	2330	...
Milton Keynes d.	1007	1022	1041	1107	each	1722	1741	1807	1822	1847	1907	1922	1947	...	2018	2047	...	2118	2134	...	2221	2259	...	2346	...
Bletchley d.	|	1027	1046	|	hour	1727	1746	|	1827	1852	|	1927	1952	...	2023	|	...	|	2139	...	2226	2304	...	2351	...
Leighton Buzzard d.	|	1033	1053	|	until	1733	1753	|	1833	1859	|	1933	1959	...	2030	2056	...	|	2146	...	2232	2311	...	2358	...
Watford Junction d.	1031	1059	|	1131	△	1759	|	1831	1859	1927	1931	1959	2027	...	2052	2126	...	2152	2219	...	2307	2346	...	0020	...
London Euston a.	1046	1117	1127	1146		1817	1827	1846	1917	1946	1946	2018	2046	...	2112	2146	...	2212	2237	...	2327	0006	...	0040	...

	⑦	⑦	⑦	⑦	⑦	⑦	⑦	⑦	⑦	⑦	⑦	⑦	⑦	⑦	⑦		⑦	⑦	⑦	⑦	⑦	⑦	⑦	⑦	⑦
Birmingham New St. d.		...	...	...	...	...	...	...	0914	...	1014	...	1114	...	1214	and	...	1914	...	...	2014	...	2114	...	2214
Birmingham Int'l ✈ d.		...	...	...	...	...	...	...	0925	...	1025	...	1125	...	1225	at	...	1925	...	...	2025	...	2125	...	2225
Coventry d.		...	...	...	...	...	...	...	0944	...	1044	...	1144	...	1244	the	...	1944	...	...	2044	...	2144	...	2244
Rugby d.		...	...	...	...	...	...	...	0955	...	1055	1120	1155	1220	1255	same	1920	1955	2017	...	2055	2120	2155	...	2255
Northampton a.		...	...	...	...	...	...	...	1017	...	1117	1141	1217	1241	1317	minutes	1941	2017	2038	...	2117	2141	2217	...	2319
Northampton d.		...	0620*	0753	0823	0853	0930	1009	1037	1108	1126	1150	1226	1250	1326	past	1950	2025	2051	...	2129	2155	2226	2300	...
Milton Keynes d.		0642	0711	0809	0839	0909	0946	1026	1055	1124	1142	1207	1242	1307	1342	each	2007	2041	2107	2115	2145	2211	2242	2316	...
Bletchley d.		0647	0716	0814	0844	0914	0951	1031	1100	1129	1147	|	1247	|	1347	hour	|	2046	|	2120	2150	2216	2246	2321	...
Leighton Buzzard d.		0653	0723	0821	0851	0921	0958	1037	1106	1136	1153	1215	1253	1315	1353	until	2015	2052	2116	2126	2156	2222	2253	2327	...
Watford Junction d.		0725	0754	0853	0922	0952	1029	1105	1137	1206	1218	1240	1318	1335	1418	△	2035	2122	2138	2156	2226	2253	2323	2359	...
London Euston a.		0745	0814	0913	0945	1013	1051	1126	1159	1226	1238	1301	1338	1353	1438		2054	2142	2157	2219	2248	2315	2343	0021	...

x – Trains 11xx and hourly to 17xx do not call at Bletchley and then run 4 minutes earlier to Northampton.
y – Trains 11xx and hourly to 14xx do not call at Bletchley and then run 4 minutes earlier to Northampton.
* – Connection by 🚌.
△ – Timings may vary by up to 3 minutes.

LONDON - NORTHAMPTON - BIRMINGHAM - CREWE and LIVERPOOL 142

LONDON - CREWE

km		Ⓐ	Ⓐ	Ⓐ	Ⓐ	Ⓐ	Ⓐ	Ⓐ	Ⓐ	Ⓐ	Ⓐ	Ⓐ	Ⓐ	Ⓐ	Ⓐ	Ⓐ	Ⓐ	Ⓐ		⑥	⑥	⑥	⑥
0	**London** Euston 150 d.	...	...	0624	0746	0846	0946	1046	1146	1246	1346	1446	1546	1646	1746	1849	2046	2049	...	...	...	0624	0746
27	Watford Junction 150 d.	...	...	0641	|	|	|	|	|	|	|	|	|	|	|	|	|	|	...	...	...	0641	|
78	Milton Keynes 150 d.	...	...	0721	0819	0919	1019	1119	1219	1319	1419	1519	1619	1719	1819	1923	2119	2129	...	...	...	0724	0819
104	Northampton d.	0545	0635	0745	|	|	|	|	|	|	|	|	|	|	|	1946	|	2155	...	0541	0638	0745	|
135	Rugby 150 d.	0606	0659	0804	0842	0942	1042	1142	1242	1342	1442	1542	1642	1747	1847	2006	2145	2217	...	0602	0658	0804	0842
158	Nuneaton d.	0620	0712	0816	0854	0954	1054	1154	1254	1354	1454	1554	1654	1800	1900	2019	2200	|	...	0616	0712	0816	0854
178	Tamworth (Low Level) d.	0635	0729	0829	0909	1009	1109	1209	1309	1409	1509	1609	1709	1815	1915	2032	2215	|	...	0629	0729	0829	0909
188	Lichfield Trent Valley d.	0641	0735	0835	0917	1017	1117	1217	1317	1417	1517	1617	1717	1822	1922	2038	2222	|	...	0635	0735	0835	0917
217	Stafford 150 d.	0700	0755	0855	0942	1042	1142	1242	1342	1442	1542	1642	1742	1842	1942	2055	|	2353	...	0658	0755	0855	0942
231	Stone d.	0709	0804	0904	0951	1050	1151	1251	1351	1451	1551	1651	1750	|	|	2104	|	|	...	0707	0804	0904	0951
243	Stoke on Trent 150 d.	0721	0812	0912	1002	1102	1202	1302	1402	1502	1602	1702	1802	1907	2002	2112	2251	|	...	0715	0815	0915	1002
268	**Crewe** 150 a.	0743	0834	0934	1024	1124	1224	1324	1424	1524	1624	1724	1824	1926	2025	2134	2310	0022	...	0737	0837	0937	1024

	⑥	⑥	⑥	⑥	⑥	⑥	⑥	⑥	⑥	⑥	⑥		⑦	⑦	⑦	⑦	⑦	⑦	⑦	⑦	⑦	⑦	⑦	⑦
London Euston 150 d.	0846	0946	1046	1146	1246	1346	1446	1546	1646	1746	1846	...	*0752*	0954	1024	1124	1250	1350	1450	1550	1650	1750	1850	1950
Watford Junction 150 d.	|	|	|	|	|	|	|	|	|	|	|	...	*0810*	1010	1040	1142	1306	1406	1506	1606	1706	1806	1906	2006
Milton Keynes 150 d.	0919	1019	1119	1219	1319	1419	1519	1619	1719	1819	1919	...	*0851*	1050	1120	1228	1337	1437	1537	1637	1737	1837	1937	2037
Northampton d.	|	|	|	|	|	|	|	|	|	|	|	...	0940	1108	1140	1302	1402	1502	1602	1702	1802	1902	2002	2106
Rugby 150 d.	0942	1042	1142	1242	1342	1442	1542	1642	1742	1842	1942	...	1003	1130	1203	1326	1426	1526	1626	1726	1826	1926	2026	2130
Nuneaton d.	0954	1054	1154	1254	1354	1454	1554	1654	1754	1854	1958	...	1016	1143	1216	1340	1440	1540	1640	1740	1840	1940	2040	2143
Tamworth (Low Level) d.	1009	1109	1209	1309	1409	1509	1609	1709	1809	1909	2014	...	1030	1157	1230	1355	1455	1555	1655	1755	1855	1955	2055	2158
Lichfield Trent Valley d.	1017	1117	1217	1317	1417	1517	1617	1717	1817	1917	2021	...	1037	1204	1237	1401	1501	1601	1701	1801	1901	2001	2101	2204
Stafford 150 d.	1042	1142	1242	1342	1442	1538	1642	1742	1844	1942	2044	...	1100	1221	1300	1421	1521	1621	1721	1821	1921	2021	2121	2223
Stone d.	1051	1151	1251	1351	1451	1551	1651	1751	1853	1951	|	...	1109	1230	1309	1430	1530	1630	1730	1830	1930	2030	2130	2232
Stoke on Trent 150 d.	1102	1202	1302	1402	1502	1602	1702	1802	1902	2002	2102	...	1117	1241	1317	1440	1541	1638	1741	1841	1941	2041	2141	2241
Crewe 150 a.	1124	1224	1324	1424	1524	1624	1724	1824	1927	2024	2122	...	1141	1302	1341	1502	1602	1703	1803	1906	2003	2106	2203	2302

	Ⓐ	Ⓐ	Ⓐ	Ⓐ	Ⓐ	Ⓐ	Ⓐ		Ⓐ	Ⓐ	Ⓐ	Ⓐ	Ⓐ	Ⓐ	Ⓐ	Ⓐ		⑥	⑥	⑥	⑥	⑥	⑥
Crewe 150 d.	0521	0652	0755	0902	1002	1102	1202	...	1302	1402	1502	1602	1702	1802	1902	2010	...	0601	0700	0718	0802	0902	1002
Stoke on Trent 150 d.	|	0717	0817	0928	1028	1128	1228	...	1328	1428	1528	1628	1728	1828	1928	2033	...	0624	0722	0738	0828	0928	1028
Stone d.	|	|	0825	0936	1036	1136	1236	...	1336	1436	1536	1636	1736	1836	1936	2041	...	|	0731	|	0836	0936	1036
Stafford 150 d.	|	0739	0837	0955	1055	1155	1255	...	1355	1455	1555	1655	1755	1855	1950	2100	...	0648	0748	0808	0855	0955	1055
Lichfield Trent Valley d.	0608	0757	0854	1013	1113	1213	1313	...	1413	1513	1613	1713	1813	1913	2008	2118	...	0705	0805	0825	0913	1013	1113
Tamworth (Low Level) d.	0615	0803	0901	1020	1120	1220	1320	...	1420	1520	1620	1720	1820	1920	2015	2125	...	0711	0811	0831	0920	1020	1120
Nuneaton d.	0631	0819	0916	1036	1136	1236	1336	...	1436	1536	1636	1736	1836	1936	2030	2140	...	0727	0827	0847	0936	1036	1136
Rugby 150 d.	0646	0834	0932	1053	1153	1253	1353	...	1453	1553	1653	1753	1853	1953	2047	2158	...	0743	0843	0903	0953	1053	1153
Northampton d.	0716	|	|	|	|	|	|	...	|	|	|	|	|	|	2107	2217	...	|	|	|	|	|	|
Milton Keynes 150 d.	|	0900	0954	1115	1215	1315	1415	...	1515	1615	1715	1815	1915	2015	...	...	...	0805	0915	0925	1015	1115	1215
Watford Junction 150 d.	|	|	|	|	|	|	|	...	|	|	|	|	|	|	...	...	...	|	|	|	|	|	|
London Euston 150 a.	0805	0937	1029	1150	1250	1350	1450	...	1550	1650	1750	1852	1950	2051	...	...	...	0840	0952	1000	1050	1150	1250

	⑥	⑥	⑥	⑥	⑥	⑥	⑥	⑥	⑥		⑦	⑦	⑦	⑦		⑦	⑦	⑦	⑦		⑦	⑦	⑦	⑦
Crewe 150 d.	1102	1202	1302	1402	1502	1602	1702	1802	1902	...	0932	1037	1137	1237	...	1337	1432	1537	1637	...	1737	1837	1937	2042
Stoke on Trent 150 d.	1128	1228	1328	1428	1528	1628	1728	1828	1928	...	0953	1059	1159	1259	...	1359	1453	1559	1659	...	1759	1859	1959	2107
Stone d.	1136	1236	1336	1436	1536	1636	1736	1836	1936	...	1001	1107	1207	1307	...	1407	1501	1607	1707	...	1807	1907	2007	2115
Stafford 150 d.	1155	1255	1355	1455	1555	1655	1755	1855	1951	...	1019	1119	1219	1319	...	1419	1519	1619	1719	...	1819	1922	2019	2127
Lichfield Trent Valley d.	1213	1313	1413	1513	1613	1713	1813	1913	2008	...	1036	1136	1236	1336	...	1436	1536	1636	1736	...	1836	1939	2036	2144
Tamworth (Low Level) d.	1220	1320	1420	1520	1620	1720	1820	1920	2015	...	1043	1143	1243	1343	...	1443	1543	1643	1743	...	1843	1946	2043	2151
Nuneaton d.	1236	1336	1436	1536	1636	1736	1836	1936	2031	...	1058	1158	1258	1358	...	1458	1558	1658	1758	...	1858	2001	2058	2206
Rugby 150 d.	1253	1353	1453	1553	1653	1753	1853	1952	2047	...	1120	1220	1320	1420	...	1520	1620	1720	1820	...	1920	2017	2120	2222
Northampton d.	|	|	|	|	|	|	|	2012	2120	...	1150	1250	1350	1450	...	1550	1650	1750	1850	...	1950	2051	2155	2244
Milton Keynes 150 d.	1315	1415	1515	1615	1715	1815	1915	...	2134	...	1207	1307	1407	1507	...	1607	1707	1807	1907	...	2007	2107	2211	...
Watford Junction 150 d.	|	|	|	|	|	|	|	...	2219	...	1240	1335	1435	1535	...	1635	1735	1835	1935	...	2035	2138	2253	...
London Euston 150 a.	1350	1450	1550	1650	1750	1850	1950	...	2237	...	1301	1353	1453	1553	...	1653	1753	1853	1953	...	2054	2157	2315	...

BIRMINGHAM - CREWE - LIVERPOOL

km		Ⓐ	Ⓐ	Ⓐ	Ⓐ	Ⓐ	Ⓐ	Ⓐ		Ⓐ	Ⓐ	Ⓐ	Ⓐ	Ⓐ	Ⓐ	Ⓐ	Ⓐ	Ⓐ	Ⓐ	⑥	⑥	⑥	⑥
0	**Birmingham** New St. d.	...	...	...	0601	0636	0701	0736	and at	1701	1736	1801	1836	1901	1936	2036	2134	2239	2309	...	...	...	0601
19	Wolverhampton d.	...	...	...	0621	0654	0720	0754	the same	1720	1754	1820	1854	1920	1954	2054	2154a	2305	2336	...	...	...	0620
43	Stafford d.	...	...	...	0637	0710	0736	0810	minutes	1736	1810	1836	1910	1945	2010	2110	2210a	2321	2353	...	...	...	0636
82	**Crewe** d.	0540	0603	0633	0659	0733	0757	0832	past each	1757	1832	1859	1933	2032	2033	2132	2242	2358	0022	0548	0614	0633	0659
118	Runcorn d.	0600	0630	0700	0725	0800	0825	0852	hour until	1825	1857	1922	1956	...	2056	2155	2307	...	...	0608	0633	0700	0725
131	**Liverpool** SP ‡ d.	0609	0639	0709	0733	0809	0833	0901	★	1833	1906	1931	2005	...	2105	2204	2316	...	...	0617	0642	0709	0733
140	**Liverpool** Lime St a.	0621	0651	0721	0746	0821	0844	0911		1844	1917	1942	2017	...	2118	2215	2331	...	...	0627	0654	0721	0744

	⑥	⑥	⑥	⑥	⑥		⑥	⑥	⑥	⑥	⑥	⑥	⑥	⑥	⑥	⑦	⑦	⑦	⑦		⑦	⑦	⑦
Birmingham New St. d.	0636	0701	0736	0801	0836	and at	1701	1736	1801	1836	1901	2001	2036	2136	2239	0942	1042	1142	1235	and at	1835	1935	2142
Wolverhampton d.	0654	0720	0754	0820	0854	the same	1720	1754	1820	1854	1920	2022	2054	2159	2306	1000	1100	1200	1253	the same	1853	1953	2200
Stafford d.	0710	0736	0810	0836	0910	minutes	1736	1810	1836	1910	1936	2038	2110	2216	2322	1017	1117	1217	1309	minutes	1909	2009	2217
Crewe d.	0733	0759	0832	0857	0932	past each	1757	1832	1857	1930	1957	2059	2149	2236	2342	1038	1138	1238	1331	past each	1931	2031	2238
Runcorn d.	0800	0825	0852	0922	0952	hour until	1825	1852	1922	...	2025	2121	*2224*	...	...	1101	1201	1301	1354	hour until	1954	2054	2300
Liverpool SP ‡ d.	0809	0833	0901	0931	1001	★	1833	1901	1931	...	2033	2130	|	...	...	1110	1210	1310	1403		2003	2103	2310
Liverpool Lime St a.	0821	0844	0911	0942	1011		1844	1911	1942	...	2044	2140	*2246*	...	...	1121	1221	1321	1414		2014	2114	2324

	Ⓐ	Ⓐ	Ⓐ	Ⓐ	Ⓐ	Ⓐ	Ⓐ		Ⓐ	Ⓐ	Ⓐ	Ⓐ	Ⓐ	Ⓐ	Ⓐ	Ⓐ	Ⓐ	Ⓐ	Ⓐ	⑥	⑥	⑥	⑥
Liverpool Lime St d.	...	...	0630	0704	0734	0804	0834	and at	1704	1734	1804	1834	1912	1934	2004	2034	2134	2234	2334	...	...	0632	0704
Liverpool SP ‡ d.	...	...	0640	0715	0744	0815	0844	the same	1716	1744	1815	1844	1922	1944	2015	2044	2144	2246	2346	...	...	0642	0715
Runcorn d.	...	...	0648	0723	0752	0823	0852	minutes	1725	1752	1825	1852	1930	1952	2025	2052	2152	2255	2355	...	...	0650	0723
Crewe d.	0619	0649	0716	0749	0817	0849	0919	past each	1749	1819	1849	1919	1955	2019	2047	2119	2219	2324	0026	0611	0649	0719	0749
Stafford d.	0641	0710	0740	0810	0840	0910	0940	hour until	1810	1843	1910	1939	2016	2039	2110	2139	2240	...	...	0631	0710	0740	0810
Wolverhampton a.	0658	0726	0758	0827	0858	0927	0957	★	1827	1859	1928	1957	2032	2056	2127	2157	2259	...	...	0647	0727	0756	0827
Birmingham New St. a.	0720	0750	0818	0848	0918	0948	1018		1848	1918	1948	2018	2050	2118	2148b	2218b	2328	...	...	0715	0750	0818	0848

	⑥	⑥	⑥		⑥	⑥	⑥	⑥		⑥	⑥	⑥	⑥		⑥	⑦	⑦	⑦		⑦	⑦	⑦	⑦
Liverpool Lime St d.	0734	0804	0834	and at	1704	1734	1804	1834	...	1904	1934	2034	2134	...	2204	...	1134	1234	and at	1934	2034	2134	2330
Liverpool SP ‡ d.	0744	0815	0844	the same	1716	1744	1815	1844	...	1915	1944	2044	2144	...	2215	...	1144	1244	the same	1944	2044	2144	2342
Runcorn d.	0752	0825	0852	minutes	1725	1752	1824	1852	...	1925	1952	2052	2152	...	2223	...	1152	1252	minutes	1952	2052	2152	2352
Crewe d.	0819	0849	0919	past each	1749	1822	1849	1919	...	1951	2019	2119	2224	...	2247	1021	1219	1319	past each	2019	2119	2222	0020
Stafford d.	0840	0910	0940	hour until	1810	1843	1910	1940	...	2012	2040	2140	2245	...	...	1042	1240	1340	hour until	2040	2140	2242	...
Wolverhampton a.	0858	0927	0958	★	1828	1859	1928	1957	...	2028	2057	2158	2302	...	...	1101	1256	1357		2057	2157	2259	...
Birmingham New St. a.	0918	0948	1018		1848	1918	1948	2018	...	2048	2118	2218	2320	...	...	1119	1315	1415		2115	2215	2317	...

NUNEATON - COVENTRY

From Nuneaton: 2nd class only Journey ± 20 minutes *16 km*

Ⓐ: 0633, 0737, 0833, 1014 and hourly until 2014, 2114, 2214.

⑥: 0644, 0814, 0914, 1014 and hourly until 1814, 1944, 2114, 2214.

⑦: 1236, 1411, 1511, 1611, 1711, 1811, 2011, 2200.

From Coventry:

Ⓐ: 0604, 0704, 0804, 0904, 1042 and hourly until 1842, 1942, 2042, 2142.

⑥: 0615, 0715, 0842, 0942, 1042 and hourly until 1742, 1842, 2015, 2142.

⑦: 1146, 1339, 1439, 1539, 1639, 1739, 1939, 2132.

BEDFORD - BLETCHLEY

From Bedford: 2nd class only Journey ± 44 minutes *26 km*

Trains call at **Woburn Sands** 30 minutes later:

0625Ⓐ, 0631⑥, 0731⚒, 0831⑥, 0834Ⓐ, 0934⚒, 1055⚒, 1155⚒, 1255⚒, 1355⚒, 1455⚒, 1555⚒, 1640⚒, 1740⚒, 1823⑥, 1826Ⓐ, 1923⚒, 2055⚒, 2200⚒.

From Bletchley:

Trains call at **Woburn Sands** 11 minutes later:

0531Ⓐ, 0541⑥, 0634⑥, 0642Ⓐ, 0731⚒, 0822Ⓐ, 0839⑥, 1005⚒, 1105⚒, 1201⚒, 1301⚒, 1401⚒, 1501⚒, 1551⚒, 1651⚒, 1731⑥, 1736Ⓐ, 1831⚒, 2001⚒, 2101⚒.

a – Departs 7 minutes later on ①-④ Feb. 13 - Mar. 23.

b – Arrives 9 minutes later on ①-④ Feb. 13 - Mar. 23.

‡ – Liverpool South Parkway. 🚌 connections available to/from Liverpool John Lennon Airport.

★ – Timings may vary by ± 3 minutes.

145 BIRMINGHAM - SHREWSBURY - CHESTER

2nd class AW

km			⑥	Ⓐ	⚒A	⑥🍷	ⒶB	⑥🍷	Ⓐ🍷	⚒	Ⓐ🍷	⑥🍷	⑥🍷	Ⓐ🍷	⚒	⑥🍷	Ⓐ🍷	⚒	⚒🍷	⚒🍷	ⒶC	⚒	⚒🍷	⑥C	Ⓐ🍷
	London Euston **150** d.	⚒	...	...	...	M	...	...	L	...	L	...	...	...	...	...	...	...	...	...	1023	...	...	1123	...
0	**Birmingham** International ✈ d.		...	...	...	...	...	...	...	...	0709	0709	...	...	0809	0910	0910	1009	...	1110	1133	1209	...	1233	1308
13	**Birmingham** New Street d.		...	...	0530	...	...	...	...	0625	0723	0724	...	...	0825	0925	0925	1025	...	1125	1153	1225	...	1253	1325
34	Wolverhampton d.		...	...	0548	...	...	...	...	0643	0742	0742	...	...	0843	0943	0943	1043	...	1142	1211	1243	...	1311	1343
59	Telford Central d.		...	...	|	...	...	...	...	0659	0759	0759	...	...	0900	1000	0959	1059	...	1159	1228	1259	...	1328	1400
65	Wellington d.		...	...	|	...	...	...	...	0706	0805	0805	...	...	0907	1006	1005	1106	...	1205	1235	1306	...	1335	1406
81	**Shrewsbury** a.		...	...	|	...	...	...	...	0722	0819	0820	...	...	0920	1018	1021	1119	...	1221	1251	1320	...	1354	1420
	Aberystwyth **147** a.		...	...	|	...	...	...	...	0919	|	|	...	...	1120	|	|	1319	...	|	...	1518	...	...	|
	Cardiff Central **149** d.		...	...	|	...	...	0520	0508	...	|	|	0721	0721	...	|	|	...	0921	|	...	...	1121	...	|
81	**Shrewsbury** d.		0520	0520	|	0610	*0610*	0722	0724	...	0821	0822	0925	0924	...	1022	1023	...	1124	1222	...	...	1324	...	1425
110	Gobowen d.		0539	0539	|	0630	*0630*	0743	0743	...	0840	0841	0944	0943	...	1042	1044	...	1143	1242	...	...	1343	...	1445
122	Ruabon d.		0551	0551	|	0642	*0642*	0754	0754	...	0852	0853	0955	0954	...	1054	1056	...	1155	1254	...	...	1354	...	1457
129	Wrexham General d.		0558	0604	|	0650	0700	0801	0802	...	0900	0901	1002	1002	...	1101	1102	...	1201	1300	...	...	1402	...	1503
149	**Chester** **160** a.		0617	0625	0643	0710	0716	0819	0821	...	0919	0918	1020	1020	...	1120	1121	...	1220	1322	...	...	1420	...	1521
	Holyhead **160** a.		...	...	0823	...	...	1011	...	...	...	1104	1209	1219	...	1312	1315	...	1414	1508	...	...	1614	...	1716

	⑥🍷	⚒	⚒🍷	⚒🍷	⚒	⚒🍷	Ⓐ	Ⓐ🍷	⑥🍷	Ⓐ✕	⚒	⑥	Ⓐ	Ⓐ🍷	⚒🍷	⚒C	⑥	Ⓐ	Ⓐ	⑥J	Ⓐ	①-④	⑥	⑥	⑥
London Euston **150** d.	...	...	...	...	...	...	...	L	...	...	...	...	...	...	...	1823	...	...	...	...	Ma	Mb	...	...	...
Birmingham International ✈ d.	1310	1409	...	1509	1609	...	...	1709	1709	...	1809	...	...	...	1904e	1933	2009	2004	...	...	2104	2104	2109	...	...
Birmingham New Street d.	1325	1425	...	1525	1625	...	...	1725	1725	...	1825	...	...	...	1925	1950	2025	2025	...	...	2125	2125	2125	...	2235
Wolverhampton d.	1342	1443	...	1542	1643	...	...	1742	1743	...	1843	...	...	...	1943	2019	2043	2043	...	...	2142	2154	2143	...	2253
Telford Central d.	1359	1459	...	1558	1659	...	...	1801	1800	...	1859	...	...	...	2000	2036	2059	2059	...	...	2158	2208	2200	...	2309
Wellington d.	1406	1506	...	1605	1706	...	...	1806	1807	...	1906	...	...	...	2006	2043	2106	2105	...	...	2206	2215	2206	...	2316
Shrewsbury a.	1419	1520	...	1620	1720	...	...	1820	1820	...	1919	...	...	...	2020	2055	2120	2118	...	...	2218	2228	2223	...	0011
Aberystwyth **147** a.	|	1719	...	|	1919	...	...	|	|	...	2123	...	...	...	|	...	2330	2336	...	...	|	|	|	...	...
Cardiff Central **149** d.	|	...	1321	|	...	1521	1621	|	|	1716	...	1721	...	1821	|	...	...	...	1934	1934	|	|	|	2055	...
Shrewsbury d.	1422	...	1526	1624	...	1724	1810	1825	1822	1909	...	1924	1924	2013	2024	...	...	...	2139	2137	2224	2233	2225	2306	...
Gobowen d.	1442	...	1545	1644	...	1743	|	1844	1842	|	...	1943	1943	|	2043	...	...	...	2158	2156	2243	2253	2244	|	...
Ruabon d.	1454	...	1556	1656	...	1754	|	1856	1854	|	...	1954	1955	|	2055	...	...	...	2209	2207	2255	2304	2256	|	...
Wrexham General d.	1500	...	1604	1703	...	1803	|	1905	1902	1943	...	2002	2002	|	2102	...	...	...	2214	2213	2303	2311	2303	|	...
Chester **160** a.	1521	...	1624	1721	...	1822	1905	1924	1921	2002	...	2022	2024	2108	2121	...	...	...	2234	2232	2320	2333	2322	0020	...
Holyhead **160** a.	1714	...	1821	1917c	...	2020d	...	...	2128	2141	...	2225	...	...	...	...	...	...	0048	...	...	...	...	...	...

	Ⓐ	Ⓐ	⑥	Ⓐ		⑦🍷	⑦	⑦	⑦🍷	⑦🍷	⑦🍷	⑦🍷	⑦🍷	⑦🍷	⑦	⑦🍷	⑦🍷	⑦🍷	⑦	⑦C	⑦	⑦	⑦	⑦	⑦
London Euston **150** d.	...	...	...	...	⑦	...	...	...	...	...	...	...	...	...	...	...	...	...	...	1900	...	...	...	...	...
Birmingham International ✈ d.	...	...	...	...		...	0951	1048	1207	1307	...	1407	1507	1607	...	1707	1807	1907	2008	2013	2108	...	2211	2240	2308
Birmingham New Street d.	...	2332	2335	2252		...	1004	1105	1224	1324	...	1424	1524	1624	...	1724	1824	1924	2024	2027	2124	...	2224	2255	2324
Wolverhampton d.	...	0002	2354	2327		...	1022	1127	1242	1342	...	1443	1543	1643	...	1743	1843	1943	2043	2056	2143	...	2242	2316	2346
Telford Central d.	...	0029	0022	|		...	1049	1154	1259	1358	...	1459	1559	1659	...	1759	1859	1959	2059	2113	2210	...	2309	|	0013
Wellington d.	...	0036	0030	|		...	1057	1201	1305	1404	...	1506	1606	1706	...	1805	1906	2006	2106	2120	2217	...	2316	|	0020
Shrewsbury a.	...	0052	0043	|		...	1110	1215	1324	1418	...	1519	1622	1719	...	1819	1919	2019	2119	2135	2230	...	2331	|	0035
Aberystwyth **147** a.	...	▬	▬	|		...	1316	|	1520	|	...	1717	|	1919	...	|	2120	|	2314	...	|	...	...	|	...
Cardiff Central **149** d.	2117	⑥	Ⓐ	|		...	...	|	...	|	1313	...	|	...	1513	|	...	|	▬	...	|	2101	...	|	...
Shrewsbury d.	2318	2333	2337	|		1016	...	1217	...	1420	1524	...	1624	...	1730	1820	...	2024	...	...	2232	2319	...	|	...
Gobowen d.	|	2352	2357	|		1035	...	1237	...	1439	1544	...	1643	...	1749	1840	...	2044	⑦	...	|	|	...	|	...
Ruabon d.	|	0004	0009	|		1047	...	1249	...	1451	1556	...	1655	...	1801	1851	...	2056		...	|	|	...	|	...
Wrexham General d.	|	0014	0015	|		1054	...	1256	...	1458	1602	...	1706	...	1808	1858	...	2103	2235	...	|	|	...	|	...
Chester **160** a.	0026	0033	0035	0037		1114	...	1317	...	1518	1622	...	1727	...	1825	1922	...	2120	2255	...	2331	0033	...	0022	...
Holyhead **160** a.	...	...	...	0215		...	...	...	...	...	1834	...	...	...	2018	2125	...	...	...	...	...	...	...	0215	...

		⑥	Ⓐ	Ⓐ	⑥	Ⓐ	⑥	Ⓐ	⑥🍷	Ⓐ🍷	⚒	⑥C	⑥🍷	Ⓐ✕	Ⓐ	Ⓐ🍷	⑥🍷	⚒	⑥🍷	Ⓐ🍷	Ⓐ🍷	Ⓐ🍷	⑥🍷	⚒	⚒🍷
Holyhead **160** d.	⚒	...	...	...	...	...	...	...	0425	0425	...	...	0522	0533	...	0628	0635	...	0715	L	...	0805	0820	...	0923
Chester **160** d.		0422	0422	...	...	0530	0537	0545	0620	0618	...	...	0721	0714	...	0819	0819	...	0930	0926	...	1020	1019	...	1130
Wrexham General d.		|	|	...	...	0546	0555	0603	0638	0637	...	...	0737	0732	0747	0834	0834	...	0946	0942	...	1036	1035	...	1145
Ruabon d.		|	|	...	...	0553	▬	▬	0645	0643	...	...	0744	|	0755	0841	0841	...	0953	0949	...	1042	1042	...	1153
Gobowen d.		|	|	...	...	0605	...	...	0657	0655	...	...	0756	|	0807	0852	0853	...	1005	1001	...	1053	1054	...	1205
Shrewsbury a.		|	|	...	...	0627	...	...	0717	0716	...	...	0820	0807	0828	0913	0913	...	1029	1022	...	1114	1114	...	1229
Cardiff Central **149** a.		|	|	...	...	|	...	...	0917	0916	...	...	|	0958	▬	1115	1115	...	|	1211	...	1318	1313	...	|
Aberystwyth **147** d.		|	|	...	...	|	⑥	ⒶC	...	...	0530	...	|	...	Ⓐ🍷	...	...	0730	|	...	...	...	...	0930	|
Shrewsbury d.		|	|	0518	0522	0633	0633	0639	...	...	0733	0818	0833	...	0832	...	...	0933	1033	...	1032	...	...	1133	1233
Wellington d.		|	|	0531	0535	0646	0646	0653	...	...	0746	0832	0846	...	0845	...	...	0946	1046	...	1046	...	...	1146	1246
Telford Central d.		|	|	0538	0542	0653	0653	0700	...	...	0753	0839	0853	...	0852	...	...	0953	1053	...	1052	...	...	1153	1253
Wolverhampton a.		0539	0539	0558	0601	0711	0711	0717	...	...	0811	0900	0911	...	0910	...	...	1010	1111	...	1109	...	...	1212	1310
Birmingham New Street a.		0558	0610	0615	0619	0730	0730	0747	...	...	0829	0921	0927	...	0929	...	...	1030	1128	...	1130	...	...	1232	1329
Birmingham International ✈ a.		...	...	0649	0649	0749	0749	0759	...	...	0849	0939	0950	...	0949	...	...	1049	1149	...	1149	...	...	1250	1350
London Euston a.		...	...	...	...	...	...	0915	...	...	...	1056	...	...	...	...	...	...	...	...	...	...	...	...	...

	⑥🍷	Ⓐ🍷	⚒	⑥🍷	Ⓐ🍷	Ⓐ🍷	⑥🍷	⚒C	⚒	Ⓐ🍷	⑥🍷	⑥🍷	Ⓐ🍷	⚒	⑥🍷	Ⓐ🍷	⚒🍷	⚒	Ⓐ🍷	⑥🍷	ⒶB	⑥	⑥	Ⓐ	ⒶD
Holyhead **160** d.	1033	1040	...	1123	1127	1232	1238	...	...	1324	1328	1425	1434	...	1523	1544	1650	...	1730	1730	...	...	...	...	...
Chester **160** d.	1219	1219	...	1330	1330	1419	1419	...	...	1530	1530	1619	1619	...	1728	1730	1828	...	1917	1928	2022	2026	...	...	2135
Wrexham General d.	1234	1234	...	1346	1346	1434	1434	...	...	1546	1546	1635	1635	...	1744	1748	1845	...	1933	1944	2038	2042	...	...	|
Ruabon d.	1241	1241	...	1353	1353	1441	1441	...	...	1553	1553	1642	1642	...	1751	1754	1851	...	1940	1951	*2056*	2050	...	...	|
Gobowen d.	1253	1253	...	1405	1405	1452	1453	...	...	1605	1605	1654	1653	...	1803	1806	1903	...	1952	2003	*2107*	2101	...	...	|
Shrewsbury a.	1313	1314	...	1428	1427	1513	1513	...	...	1629	1629	1714	1714	...	1824	1827	1924	...	2014	2025	*2128*	2121	...	...	|
Cardiff Central **149** a.	1521	1510	...	|	|	1716	1708	...	...	|	|	1912	1917	...	|	|	2135h	...	...	...	...	...	...	...	|
Aberystwyth **147** d.	...	...	1130	|	|	...	...	...	1330	|	|	...	...	1530	|	|	...	1730	...	...	...	...	1930	1930	|
Shrewsbury d.	...	...	1334	1433	1433	...	...	1524	1533	1633	1633	...	...	1733	1833	1833	...	1932	...	...	...	...	2133	2133	|
Wellington d.	...	...	1348	1446	1446	...	...	1538	1546	1647	1647	...	...	1746	1846	1846	...	1946	...	...	...	...	2146	2147	|
Telford Central d.	...	...	1354	1453	1453	...	...	1544	1553	1654	1653	...	...	1753	1853	1853	...	1953	...	...	...	...	2153	2153	|
Wolverhampton a.	...	...	1412	1511	1511	...	...	1601	1610	1709	1708	...	...	1811	1911	1911	...	2011	...	...	...	...	2209	2211	2227
Birmingham New Street a.	...	...	1432	1528	1530	...	...	1622	1630	1730	1728	...	...	1830	1928	1930	...	2029	...	...	...	...	2228	2231g	2250f
Birmingham International ✈ a.	...	...	1449	1550	1549	...	...	1639	1649	1749	1750	...	...	1849	1949	1949	...	2049	...	...	...	...	...	...	...
London Euston a.	...	...	...	...	...	...	...	1756	...	...	...	...	...	...	...	...	...	...	...	...	...	...	...	...	...

	Ⓐ	⑥	⚒		⑦	⑦	⑦	⑦	⑦🍷	⑦	⑦🍷	⑦	⑦C	⑦🍷	⑦🍷	⑦🍷	⑦	⑦	⑦🍷	⑦	⑦🍷	⑦	⑦	⑦	⑦
Holyhead **160** d.	1921	1921	...	⑦	...	...	...	...	...	1020	...	...	...	...	...	...	...	1625	...	...	1825	...	...	...	...
Chester **160** d.	2121	2120	2228		0808	...	0922	...	1131	1221	...	1331	...	...	1531	...	1731	1824	...	1926	2027	...	2126	2204	2300
Wrexham General d.	2137	2137	2244		0827	...	0938	...	1148	1238	...	1348	...	...	1548	...	1748	1841	...	1942	|	...	2144	2223	|
Ruabon d.	2144	2144	2251		▬	...	0945	...	1155	1245	...	1355	...	...	1555	...	1755	1847	...	1949	|	...	2151	...	|
Gobowen d.	2155	2157	2303		...	...	0957	...	1207	1257	...	1407	...	...	1607	...	1807	1859	...	2001	|	...	2202	...	|
Shrewsbury a.	2216	2217	2323		...	...	1018	...	1227	1318	...	1427	...	...	1627	...	1827	1920	...	2021	|	...	2222	...	0014
Cardiff Central **149** a.	|	|	|		...	...	|	...	|	1533	...	|	...	...	|	...	|	2131	...	|	|	...	|	...	...
Aberystwyth **147** d.	|	|	|		⑦	...	|	0930	|	...	1130	|	...	1330	|	1530	|	...	1730	|	|	1930	|	...	...
Shrewsbury d.	2218	2231	2326		0810	0909	1020	1140	1231	...	1331	1431	1524	1533	1640	1733	1831	...	1931	2023	|	2131	2223	...	...
Wellington d.	2232	2245	2340		0824	0923	1034	1154	1245	...	1345	1445	1538	1547	1654	1747	1845	...	1945	2037	|	2145	2237	...	...
Telford Central d.	2238	2251	2347		0831	0930	1040	1200	1251	...	1351	1451	1544	1553	1700	1753	1851	...	1951	2044	|	2151	2245	...	...
Wolverhampton a.	2255	2307	0017		0859	0958	1056	1216	1307	...	1407	1507	1601	1609	1715	1809	1907	...	2007	2112	2129	2207	2314	...	...
Birmingham New Street a.	2328	2328	...		0915	1014	1113	1232	1323	...	1423	1524	1620	1625	1737	1827	1926	...	2025	2129	2153	2227	...	...	...
Birmingham International ✈ a.	...	...	...		0932	1032	1131	1258	1357	...	1457	1557	1639	1657	1757	1857	1957	...	2057	2157	2208	2257	...	...	...
London Euston a.	...	...	...		...	...	...	...	...	...	...	...	1757	...	...	...	...	...	...	...	...	...	...	...	...

A – [12] and 🍷 Birmingham New Street - Crewe - Holyhead (Table **150**).
B – [12] and 🍷 Wrexham - London Euston and v.v. (Table **150**).
C – [12] and 🍷 Shrewsbury - London Euston and v.v. (Table **150**).
D – [12] and 🍷 Bangor - Crewe - Birmingham New Street (Table **150**).
J – To / from Llandudno Junction (Table **165**).
L – To / from Llandudno (Table **165**).
M – To / from Manchester Piccadilly (Table **160**).

a – Until Feb. 10 and from Mar. 24 (also ⑤ Feb. 17 - Mar. 17).
b – Feb. 13 - Mar. 23.
c – Arrives 1913 on ⑥.
d – Arrives 2013 on ⑥.
e – Departs 1909 on ⑥.
f – Arrives 2258 on ①-④ Feb. 17 - Mar. 24.
g – Arrives 2250 on ①-④ Feb. 17 - Mar. 24.
h – Arrives 2131 on ⑥.

146 — SHREWSBURY - SWANSEA

AW 2nd class

km		ⓐ	⑥	ⓐ	⑥	ⓐ	⑦	⑥	ⓐ	⑥	⑥	ⓐ		⑥	ⓐ	0603	⑥	0933	1112	1312	1435	1526	1819	1821
0	Shrewsbury .... 149 d.	0445	0516	0556	0900	1009	1204	1356	1405	1618	1758	1824	Swansea .... 135 d.	0431		0603	0915	0933	1112	1312	1435	1526	1819	1821
20	Church Stretton 149 d.	0503	0533	0614	0919	1027	1222	1414	1423	1636	1814	1842	Llanelli .... 135 d.	0450	0520	0625	0934	0954	1132	1332	1453	1548	1841	1842
32	Craven Arms .. 149 d.	0514	0547	0624	0930	1037	1233	1424	1434	1647	1824	1854	Pantyffynnon ......d.	0510	0539	0644	0955	1013	1153	1353	1512	1608	1900	1901
52	Knighton ....d.	0536	0612	0656	0954	1101	1257	1448	1458	1711	1848	1918	Llandeilo ....d.	0529	0555	0706	1015	1033	1213	1413	1532	1632	1920	1921
84	Llandrindod ......a.	0610	0646	0734	1032	1139	1335	1526	1536	1749	1926	1956	Llandovery ....d.	0551	0621	0728	1037	1055	1235	1435	1554	1654	1942	1943
84	Llandrindod ......d.	—	0654	0735	1035	1200	1341	1540	1541	1758	1949	1956	Llanwrtyd ....d.	0616	—	0808	1105	1120	1300	1501	1624	1730	2008	2031
110	Llanwrtyd ....d.		0723	0809	1107	1231	1412	1611	1623	1829	2008	2030	Llandrindod ......a.	0644		0838	1136	1151	1331	1531	1654	1750	2037	2102
128	Llandovery ....d.	0642	0747	0834	1132	1256	1437	1636	1648	1855	2034	2059	Llandrindod ......d.	0655	0618	0845	1140	1201	1343	1542	1659	1801	2043	2102
146	Llandeilo ....d.	0703	0808	0855	1154	1318	1459	1658	1710	1916	2055	2117	Knighton ....d.	0732	0703	0923	1218	1240	1422	1621	1737	1840	2118	2158
159	Pantyffynnon ......d.	0721	0825	0913	1211	1335	1516	1715	1727	1934	2113	2135	Craven Arms ... 149 a.	0753	0727	0946	1240	1302	1444	1642	1759	1902	2139	2220
178	Llanelli .... 135 a.	0741	0845	0933	1235	1358	1537	1735	1747	1954	2133	2155	Church Stretton 149 a.	0806	0742	0958	1253	1317	1457	1655	1812	1917	2152	2235
196	Swansea .... 135 a.	0808	0922	1002	1301	1425	1603	1804	1814	2020	2202	2222	Shrewsbury .... 149 a.	0822	0757	1014	1309	1332	1512	1711	1828	1933	2209	2252

147 — SHREWSBURY - ABERYSTWYTH

AW 2nd class

km		⚒	⚒		0625	0825		1025	1225	1425	1625	...		1825		ⓐ	⑥	⑥	⑥	2025	2025	⑦		⑦	1004	⑦	1224	⑦	1424		⑦	1624	...	⑦	1824	⑦	2024
	B'mingham N S 145..d.				0625	0825		1025	1225	1425	1625				1825						2025	2025	⑦	0830	1128	1327	1527	1629	1727	1828	1927	2127
0	Shrewsbury..........d.		0625	0727	0930	1029	1127	1329	1530	1727	1831	1827	1930	2030	2039	2143	2150		0905	1150	1349	1551	1651	1749	1850	1949	2149
32	Welshpool ....d.		0647	0749	0952	1051	1149	1351	1552	1749	1853	1849	1952	2052	2105	2205	2212		0930	1204	1403	1605	1705	1803	1904	2003	2203
54	Newtown............d.		0702	0803	1006	1106	1203	1405	1606	1803	1907	1903	2006	2110	2116	2220	2227		0945	1211	1411	1612	1712	1811	1911	2010	2210
63	Caersws.............d.		0709	0810	1013	1113	1210	1412	1613	1810	1914	1910	2013	2123	2123	2227	2234		1025	1242	1443	1643	1741	1842	1940	2044	2239
98	Machynlleth........d.		0740	0844	1045	1141	1243	1443	1644	1841	1945	1942	2047	2145	2151	2255	2302		1025	1247	1450	1648	1747	1848	1945	2048	2245
98	Machynlleth........d.		0746	0848	1050	1141	1247	1449	1650	1849	1948	1945	2049	2146	2151	2302	2307		1255	1458	1655	1755	1856	1954	2057	2252
104	Dovey Junction ‡..d.		0756	0855	1056	1153	1254	1456	1656	1857	1957	2100	2057	2154	2159	2308	2313		1050	1305	1508	1705	1805	1906	2004	2107	2302
118	Borth ....d.		0806	0905	1106	1203	1304	1505	1706	1907	2007	2110	2107	2204	2209	2318	2323		1055	1313	1516	1713	1813	1916	2014	2117	2312
131	Aberystwyth..........a.		0819	0919	1118	1216	1319	1518	1719	1919	2019	2123	2123	2217	2222	2330	2336		1110	1316	1520	1717	1817	1917	2017	2122	2314

		⚒	⚒	ⓐ	⑥																					⑦	⑦	⑦	⑦	⑦	⑦	⑦	⑦	⑦
Aberystwyth........d.		0530	0730	0730	0830	0930	1130	1130	1230	1330	1530	1730	1732	1833	1833	1930	1930		0930	1030	1130	1330	1433	1530	1730	1930
Borth ....d.		0541	0641	0741	0741	0841	0941	1141	1141	1241	1341	1541	1741	1741	1843	1843	1941	1941		0943	1043	1141	1341	1444	1543	1743	1941
Dovey Junction ‡..d.	⚒	0552	0653	0753	0754	0858	0952	1153	1155	1257	1352	1552	1751	1751	1854	1854	1959	1959	⑦	0953	1056	1151	1356	1457	1553	1753	1951
Machynlleth........a.		0600	0700	0800	0803	0905	1001	1201	1202	1305	1401	1601	1758	1759	1901	1901	2006	2006		1000	1103	1158	1403	1504	1600	1800	1958
Machynlleth........d.		0600	0703	0805	0808	0906	1008	1204	1207	1306	1407	1608	1805	1805	1909	1909	2011	2011		1008	1105	1206	1406	1508	1605	1805	2005
Caersws.............d.		0627	0730	0828	0931	0933	1035	1232	1234	1333	1434	1631	1828	1830	1932	1932	2034	2034		1031	1128	1229	1429	1531	1630	1829	2028
Newtown............d.		0634	0737	0839	0842	0940	1042	1239	1241	1340	1441	1642	1839	1841	1943	1943	2044	2044		1041	1138	1240	1440	1541	1641	1840	2039
Welshpool ....d.		0649	0752	0854	0856	0955	1056	1253	1255	1354	1455	1656	1853	1856	1957	2000	2102	2059		1056	1154	1254	1455	1556	1656	1854	2053
Shrewsbury..........a.		0713	0814	0916	0918	1018	1118	1316	1317	1418	1519	1720	1915	1918	2022	2022	2124	2121		1118	1216	1316	1517	1620	1717	1916	2115
B'mingham N S 145..a.					1030		1232	1430	1432			1630	1830	2029	2029			2228	2231a		1232		1423	1625			1827	2025	2227

▷ — Additional journeys Machynlleth - Aberystwyth and v.v.:
From Machynlleth at 0453⚒, 0545⚒, 0647⚒, 0850⑦, 0947⑦, 1049⑦, 1349⑦, 1800⚒.
From Aberystwyth at 1830⑦, 2030⑧, 2036⑥, 2130⑧, 2136⑥, 2230⚒, 2320⑦, 2335⑥, 2340ⓐ.

a — Arrives 2250 on ①–④ Feb. 17 - Mar. 24.

‡ — Trains call on request.

148 — MACHYNLLETH - PWLLHELI

AW 2nd class

km			ⓐ	ⓐ		0625	0825	...	1025	1225	1425	1625	1825		⑥	⑥		0625	0825	...	1025	1225	1425	1625		1825	⑦
	Birmingham N S 145..d.					0625	0825		1025	1225	1425	1625	1825					0625	0825		1025	1225	1425	1625		1825	1624
	Shrewsbury 147....d.	ⓐ		0727	0930		1127	1329	1530	1729	1930						0729	0931		1129	1329	1530	1727		1930	1727
0	Machynlleth..........d.		0507	0643	0852	1055		1251	1456	1655	1903	2143	⑥	0507	0643	0853	1056		1252	1455	1655	1903	2143	⑦	1755
	Dovey Junction ‡....d.		0513	0649	0858	1101		1257	1502	1701	1909	2149		0513	0649	0859	1101		1258	1501	1701	1909	2149		1901
16	Aberdovey ....d.		0526	0702	0911	1114		1310	1515	1714	1922	2202		0526	0702	0912	1114		1311	1514	1714	1922	2202		1914
22	Tywyn ....d.		0533	0711	0920	1123		1319	1524	1724	1931	2211		0533	0711	0921	1123		1319	1523	1724	1931	2211		1920
22	Tywyn ....d.		0533	0716	0929	1130		1325	1526	1729	1932	2216		0533	0714	0929	1132		1326	1525	1729	1932	2216		1920
37	Fairbourne..........d.		0552	0734	0948	1149		1344	1545	1747	1950	2234		0552	0732	0948	1150		1344	1544	1747	1950	2234		1939
41	Barmouth ....a.		0604	0745	0959	1159		1355	1556	1758	2002	2245		0604	0745	0959	1201		1355	1555	1758	2001	2245		1947
41	Barmouth ....d.			0747	1001	1201		1357	1558	1800	2003	2247			0747	1001	1202		1357	1557	1800	2003	2247		1949
58	Harlech ....a.			0811	1025	1225		1421	1622	1824	2029	2311			0811	1025	1226		1421	1621	1824	2029	2311		2015
58	Harlech ....d.			0825	1027	1227		1431	1629	1833	2029	2314			0825	1027	1229		1431	1629	1833	2029	2314		2017
67	Penrhyndeudraeth..d.			0838	1040	1240		1444	1642	1846	2042	2327			0838	1040	1242		1444	1642	1846	2042	2327		2031
69	Minffordd ....160 d.			0842	1044	1244		1448	1645	1849	2046	2330			0842	1044	1245		1448	1645	1849	2046	2330		2034
72	Porthmadog......160 d.			0850	1052	1252		1456	1653	1857	2054	2338			0850	1052	1253		1456	1653	1857	2054	2338		2040
80	Criccieth............d.			0857	1059	1259		1503	1700	1904	2102	2346			0857	1059	1301		1503	1700	1904	2102	2345		2048
93	Pwllheli.............a.			0912	1114	1315		1520	1717	1920	2117	0001			0913	1114	1316		1519	1716	1920	2117	0001		2105

			ⓐ	ⓐ	ⓐ		ⓐ	ⓐ	ⓐ		ⓐ	ⓐ		⑥	⑥	⑥		⑥	⑥	⑥	⑥	⑥		⑦
Pwllheli..............d.			0629	0724	0934		1137	1338	1537		1742	2026		0629	0724	0934		1137	1338	1537	1742	2026		1348
Criccieth............d.	ⓐ		0643	0738	0948		1151	1352	1551		1756	2040		0643	0738	0948		1151	1352	1551	1756	2040	⑦	1402
Porthmadog......160 d.			0653	0747	0957		1201	1402	1601		1806	2055b		0653	0747	0958		1201	1402	1601	1806	2055b		1412
Minffordd ....160 d.			0657	0752	1001		1205	1406	1605		1810	2059		0657	0752	1002		1205	1406	1605	1810	2059		1416
Penrhyndeudraeth..d.			0701	0756	1005		1209	1410	1609		1814	2103		0701	0756	1006		1209	1410	1609	1814	2103		1420
Harlech ....a.			0715	0809	1020		1224	1425	1624		1827	2117		0715	0809	1021		1224	1425	1624	1827	2117		1432
Harlech ....d.			0717	0821	1029		1228	1428	1629		1830	2119		0717	0821	1029		1228	1428	1629	1830	2119		1434
Barmouth ....a.			0742	0845	1054		1253	1453	1654		1855	2144		0742	0845	1053		1253	1452	1654	1855	2144		1459
Barmouth ....d.			0645	0746	0852	1059		1255	1455	1656		1857	2146	⑥	0643	0746	0852	1101		1255	1455	1656	1857	2146	1501
Fairbourne..........d.			0653	0754	0900	1107		1303	1503	1704		1905	2154		0651	0754	0900	1109		1303	1502	1704	1905	2154		1509
Tywyn ....d.			0713	0812	0920	1127		1323	1524	1724		1925	2214		0711	0812	0920	1129		1323	1523	1724	1925	2214		1527
Tywyn ....d.			0714	0816	0927	1130		1325	1526	1727		1934	2217		0713	0816	0927	1130		1325	1526	1727	1935	2217		1528
Aberdovey ....d.			0720	0822	0933	1136		1331	1532	1733		1940	2223		0719	0822	0933	1136		1331	1531	1733	1941	2223		1535
Dovey Junction ‡....a.			0735	0838	0947	1149		1345	1546	1747		1956	2238		0734	0838	0947	1151		1345	1545	1747	1956	2238		1549
Machynlleth..........a.			0743	0845	0954	1157		1352	1554	1755		2004	2245		0742	0845	0954	1158		1353	1554	1755	2003	2245		1558
Shrewsbury 147....a.			0916	1017	1118	1316		1519	1720	1918		2118			0918	1018	1118	1317		1519	1719	1915	2124			1717
Birmingham New Str. 145..a.			1030	...	1230	1430		1630	1830	2029		2231a			1030	...	1232	1432		1630	1830	2029	2228			1827

a — Arrives 2250 on ①–④ Feb. 17 - Mar. 24.   b — Arrives 2048.   ‡ — Trains call on request.

149 — CARDIFF - HEREFORD - CREWE - MANCHESTER

AW 2nd class   Most trains convey ⓧ

Most Manchester trains continue to/from destinations on Table 135

km		ⓐ	ⓐ	ⓐ	ⓐ	ⓐ	ⓐ	ⓐ	ⓐ	ⓐ	ⓐ	ⓐ	ⓐ	ⓐ	ⓐ	ⓐ	ⓐ	ⓐ	ⓐ	ⓐ	ⓐ	ⓐ	ⓧ	ⓐ
			J																					
0	Cardiff Central.... 132 d.	ⓐ	0435	0508	0538	0650	0721	0805	0850	0921	1005	1050	1121	1205	1250	1321	1405	1450	1521	1550	1621	1650	1716	1750	1821	1853
19	Newport .... 132 d.		0453	0527	0557	0704	0738	0905	0935	1019	1114	1136	1219	1304	1339	1419	1504	1536	1604	1635	1704	1731	1804	1835	1905
30	Cwmbrân ....d.		0505	0539	0608	0714	0746	0829	0915	0946	1029	1114	1146	1229	1314	1346	1429	1514	1546	1614	1644	1714	1742	1815	1845	1919
35	Pontypool & New Inn d.		0511	0545	0614		0752		0951			1152		1351			1552	1619		1749	1820		2113
52	Abergavenny ....d.		0522	0554	0623	0727	0801	0842	0928	1001	1042	1127	1201	1242	1326	1401	1443	1527	1601	1629	1657	1727	1800	1829	1859	1934
89	Hereford ....d.		0547	0625	0649	0753	0827	0908	0959	1027	1108	1153	1227	1308	1355	1425	1508	1553	1627	1654	1724	1753	1855	1924	1949
109	Leominster ....d.		0600	0638	0702	0806		0921		1040		1121	1206		1321	1408		1521	1606	1640	1707		1806		1908		2012
127	Ludlow ....d.		0611	0649	0713	0817	0848	0932	1018	1048	1132	1217	1248	1332	1419	1446	1532	1617	1651	1718		1819	1919	1945	2023
138	Craven Arms ....146 d.		0620	0657	0721	0825	0856		1026	1057		1225	1256		1427	1455		1627		1727		1825	1927		2032
150	Church Stretton ..146 d.		0629	0708	0730	0834	0905		1039	1106		1238	1305		1436	1504		1708	1736		1841		1936		2041
170	Shrewsbury ......146 a.		0643	0722	0744	0848	0919	0958	1052	1121	1158	1252	1321	1359	1450	1528	1558	1648	1724	1750	1809	1855	1906	1950	2011	2055
170	Shrewsbury ......¶ d.		0644	0724	0746	0851	0924	1000	1053	1124	1201	1325	1325	1359	1452	1526	1559	1650	1751	1751	1810	1856	1909	1952	2013	2056
200	Whitchurch ....¶ d.		0704		0806	0908		1112		1310		1509		1710		1809		1913		2113
223	Crewe ....¶ a.		0724		0824	0927		1028	1128		1228	1328		1428	1528		1628	1727		1827	1843	1933		2022	2043	2133
	Chester 145, 160 ... a.			0821			1020			1220			1420			1624			1821	1905		2002	2108		
	Holyhead 145, 160 ... a.					1219			1414			1614			1821			2020			2141			
263	Stockport ....a.		0753		0859	0957		1058	1158		1258	1358		1458	1558		1659	1758		1858		2003		2050	2201
273	Manchester Piccadilly a.		0803		0910	1011		1110	1210		1310	1410		1510	1610		1710	1810		1910		2014		2101	2210

J — To/from Llandudno (Tables 145/160).   L — To Llandudno Junction (Tables 145/160).   For continuation of Table and additional footnotes see next page ▶ ▶ ▶

149 CARDIFF - HEREFORD - CREWE - MANCHESTER

Most trains convey 🍷 2nd class AW

Most Manchester trains continue to / from destinations on Table **135**

	Ⓐ	Ⓐ	Ⓐ	Ⓐ		⑥	⑥	⑥		⑥	⑥	⑥	⑥	⑥		⑥	⑥	⑥	⑥	⑥	⑥	⑥	⑥	⑥	⑥	⑥	⑥
Cardiff Central ... **132** d.	1934	2017	2117	2155	⑥	0435	0520	0537	...	0650	0721	0750	0850	0921	...	0955	1055	1121	1155	1255	1321	1355	1455	1521	1555	1618	1655
Newport ... **132** d.	1948	2031	2132	2212		0452	0535	0556	...	0704	0736	0804	0904	0935	...	1009	1109	1135	1209	1309	1335	1409	1509	1536	1609	1634	1709
Cwmbrân ... d.	1958	2041	2143	2224		0503	0545	0608	...	0714	0746	0814	0914	0946	...	1019	1119	1146	1219	1319	1346	1419	1519	1546	1619	1644	1719
Pontypool & New Inn . d.	2003	2047	|	2230		0509	0551	0613	...	|	0751	|	|	0952	...	|	|	1150	|	|	1350	|	|	1552	1625	1650	|
Abergavenny ... d.	2012	2056	2156	2240		0522	0600	0623	...	0727	0801	0827	0927	1001	...	1032	1132	1200	1232	1332	1401	1432	1532	1601	1634	1702	1732
Hereford ... d.	2039	2122	2221	2308		0547	0625	0648	...	0753	0827	0853	0953	1026	...	1058	1158	1228	1258	1358	1427	1458	1558	1629**d**	1700	...	1758
Leominster ... d.	2052	2135	2234	2321		0601	0638	0702	...	0806	|	0906	1006	|	...	1111	1211	|	1311	1411	|	1511	1611	1643	1713	...	1811
Ludlow ... d.	2103	2146	2245	2332		0612	0649	0713	...	0817	0848	0917	1017	1048	...	1122	1222	1249	1322	1422	1448	1522	1622	1654	1724	...	1822
Craven Arms ... **146** d.	2112	2154	2254	2342		0620	0657	0721	...	0826	0856	|	1026	1057	...	|	1231	1257	|	1431	1456	|	1631	|	|	...	1831
Church Stretton .. **146** d.	2121	2204	2303	2351		0629	0706	0730	...	0835	0905	|	1035	1107	...	|	1240	1306	|	1441	1505	|	1640	1708	|	...	1840
Shrewsbury ... **146** a.	2137	2218	2317	0007		0643	0722	0744	...	0851	0923	0943	1049	1123	...	1148	1253	1322	1348	1454	1523	1548	1654	1722	1750	...	1854
Shrewsbury ... **145**¶ d.	2139	2220	2318	0012		0647	0722	0746	...	0852	0925	0947	1050	1125	...	1150	1254	1324	1350	1455	1528	1550	1655	1724	1752	...	1856
Whitchurch ... ¶ d.	|	2243	2344	0038		0707	|	0806	...	0909	|	1004	1107	|	...	1206	|	|	1406	|	|	1606	|	|	1808	...	|
Crewe ... ¶ a.	|	2304	0005	0103		0725	|	0824	...	0927	|	1023	1125	|	...	1225	1326	|	1425	1525	|	1625	1726	|	1827	...	1926
Chester **145, 160** ... a.	2234	|	0026	...		|	0819	|	...	|	1020	|	|	1219	...	|	|	1419	|	|	1624	|	|	1822	|	...	|
Holyhead **145, 160** .. a.	0048	|	...	...		|	1011	|	...	|	1209	|	|	1413	...	|	|	1613	|	|	1819	|	|	2013	|	...	|
Stockport ... a.	...	2332	...	...		0754	...	0858	...	0958	...	1058	1158	...	...	1258	1358	...	1458	1558	...	1659	1758	...	1858	...	1958
Manchester P'dilly ... a.	...	2348	...	...		0805	...	0910	...	1011	...	1110	1210	...	...	1310	1410	...	1510	1610	...	1709	1810	...	1910	...	2011

	⑥	⑥	⑥	⑥	⑥	⑥	⑥		⑦	⑦	⑦	⑦	⑦	⑦	⑦	⑦	⑦	⑦	⑦	⑦		⑦	⑦	⑦	⑦	⑦	⑦
				L										a	b												
Cardiff Central ... **132** d.	1721	1755	1850	1934	2010	2055	2154	⑦	...	0830	0917	1034	1135	1235	1236	1313	1340	1456	1513	1556	...	1640	1735	1836	1940	2101	2315
Newport ... **132** d.	1735	1809	1904	1948	2026	2110	2212		...	0849	0941	1053	1154	1253	1254	1335	1358	1514	1533	1614	...	1658	1753	1858	1959	2119	2336
Cwmbrân ... d.	1746	1820	1915	1958	2037	2121	2224		...	0859	0951	1104	1205	1304	1309	1347	1409	1524	1543	1624	...	1709	1804	1909	2010	2130	2347
Pontypool & New Inn . d.	1752	1825	1920	2003	2042	|	2229		...	0905	0957	1110	1211	1311	1315	|	|	|	1549	|	...	1715	1810	|	2016	2136	2353
Abergavenny ... d.	1801	1835	1930	2012	2052	2134	2239		...	0914	1008	1120	1222	1320	1325	1400	1422	1538	1558	1637	...	1725	1820	1922	2026	2146	0003
Hereford ... d.	1827	1900	1955	2039	2120	2200	2303		...	0941	1036	1150	1254**d**	1355**n**	1355**d**	1426	1448	1604	1628**d**	1704	...	1753**d**	1849**d**	1949	2054	2214	0035
Leominster ... d.	|	1914	2009	2052	2133	2214	—		...	0955	1050	1203	1308	1408	1408	|	1501	|	1641	|	...	1807	1903	2003	2108	2227	...
Ludlow ... d.	1848	1925	2020	2103	2144	2225	...		...	1006	1101	1214	1319	1419	1419	1448	1512	1625	1652	1726	...	1818	1914	2014	2119	2238	...
Craven Arms ... **146** d.	1856	|	2028	2112	2154	2233	...		...	1014	|	1224	|	1428	1428	|	|	|	1700	|	...	1826	|	2022	2129	2248	...
Church Stretton .. **146** d.	1905	|	2037	2121	2204	2242	⑥		...	1023	|	1233	|	1437	1437	|	|	|	1709	|	...	1835	|	2031	2138	2257	...
Shrewsbury ... **146** a.	1919	1951	2053	2135	2217	2257			...	1037	1130	1248	1348	1451	1451	1521	1538	1651	1723	1752	...	1849	1941	2045	2156	2314	...
Shrewsbury ... **145**¶ d.	1924	1952	2057	2137	2219	2306	2330		0955	1039	1131	1251	1350	1453	1453	1524	1540	1653	1730	1754	...	1854	1942	2048	*2232*	2319	...
Whitchurch ... ¶ d.	|	2009	|	|	2244	2331	2355		|	1100	1158	|	|	|	|	|	1606	|	|	|	...	|	2007	|	|	2346	...
Crewe ... ¶ a.	|	2027	2128	|	2304	2353	0016		1025	1119	1222	1326	1425	1525	1525	|	1627	1725	|	1825	...	1924	2028	2121	*2303*	0009	...
Chester **145, 160** ... a.	2022	|	|	2232	|	0020	...		|	|	*1317*t	|	*1518*t	|	|	1622	|	|	1825	*1922*t	...	|	*2120*t	|	*2331*	0033	...
Holyhead **145, 160** .. a.	2225	|	|	...	|	...	...		|	|	|	|	|	|	|	1834	|	|	2018	*2125*t	...	|	|	|	...	...	...
Stockport ... a.	...	2059	2159	...	2332	...	...		1058	|	1258	1359	1458	1558	1558	...	1658	1758	...	1858	...	1958	2057	2158	...	...	...
Manchester P'dilly ... a.	...	2111	2209	...	2344	...	...		1113	1157	1311	1412	1512	1611	1611	...	1711	1813	...	1911	...	2011	2111	2214	...	...	...

		Ⓐ	Ⓐ	Ⓐ	Ⓐ	Ⓐ	Ⓐ	Ⓐ	Ⓐ	Ⓐ	Ⓐ	Ⓐ	Ⓐ	Ⓐ	Ⓐ	Ⓐ	Ⓐ	Ⓐ	Ⓐ	Ⓐ	Ⓐ	Ⓐ	Ⓐ	Ⓐ	Ⓐ	Ⓐ	Ⓐ
								✕				J															
Manchester P'dilly ... d.	Ⓐ	...	...	...	...	...	0630	...	0730	...	0830	...	0930	...	1030	1130	...	1230	1330	...	1430	1530	...	1630	1730	...	1830
Stockport ... d.		...	...	...	...	...	0639	...	0739	...	0839	...	0939	...	1040	1140	...	1240	1340	...	1440	1540	...	1640	1740	...	1839
Holyhead **145, 160** .. d.		...	...	...	...	0425	|	0533	|	0628	|	...	|	0805	|	|	1040	|	|	1232	|	|	1434	|	|	1650	|
Chester **145, 160** ... d.		...	...	...	...	0618	|	0714	|	0819	|	0926	|	1020	|	|	1219	|	|	1419	|	|	1619	|	|	1828	|
Crewe ... ¶ d.		...	0449	...	0558	|	0708	|	0808	|	0908	|	1008	|	1108	1208	|	1308	1408	|	1508	1608	|	1708	1809	|	1908
Whitchurch ... ¶ d.		...	0508	...	0619	|	|	|	|	|	|	|	|	|	|	|	|	|	1428	|	|	1628	|	|	1829	|	1929
Shrewsbury ... **145**¶ a.		...	0528	...	0645	0716	0742	0807	0837	0913	0937	1022	1037	1114	1137	1237	1314	1337	1445	1513	1537	1647	1714	1737	1848	1924	1955
Shrewsbury ... **146** d.		...	0530	0610	0647	0718	0744	0810	0840	0914	0940	1024	1039	1116	1139	1239	1315	1340	1450	1515	1540	1650	1716	1740	1850	1925	1956
Church Stretton .. **146** d.		...	0545	0626	0702	|	0759	|	|	0930	|	|	1054	|	1154	|	1330	|	1505	1530	|	1706	1731	|	1905	1940	2011
Craven Arms ... **146** d.		...	0553	0634	0710	|	0807	|	|	0938	|	|	|	1137	|	|	1338	|	1513	1538	|	1714	1739	|	1913	1948	2019
Ludlow ... d.		...	0601	0643	0717	0744	0815	|	0906	0945	1006	|	1108	1144	1208	1305	1345	1406	1520	1546	1606	1721	1746	1806	1920	1956	2027
Leominster ... d.		...	0611	0654	0728	0754	0826	|	0916	|	1016	|	1118	|	1218	1315	|	1416	1531	|	1616	1732	1757	1816	1931	|	2037
Hereford ... d.		0526	0641**e**	0710	0745	0811	0842	0858	0933	1010	1033	|	1135	1208	1235	1332	1411	1433	1551	1611	1633	1751	1814	1833	1948	2022	2054
Abergavenny ... d.		0551	0704	0734	0808	0834	0905	|	0958	1033	1056	|	1158	1231	1258	1355	1433	1456	1614	1634	1656	1814	1837	1856	2011	2045	2122
Pontypool & New Inn . d.		0602	0714	0745	0818	0844	|	|	|	1043	|	|	|	1242	|	1405	|	|	1623	1644	|	1824	|	|	2021	|	2132
Cwmbrân ... d.		0607	0719	0750	0823	0849	0917	|	1011	1048	1109	|	1211	1247	1311	1410	|	1509	1628	1649	1709	1829	1849	1909	2026	2057	2137
Newport ... **132** a.		0619	0729	0800	0837	0900	0934	0940	1022	1101	1120	1153	1222	1256	1322	1420	1454	1521	1639	1659	1721	1839	1900	1922	2037	2115	2150
Cardiff Central ... **132** a.		0643	0749	0818	0855	0916	0959	0958	1039	1115	1138	1211	1237	1318	1340	1437	1510	1539	1657	1716	1739	1855	1917	1943	2058	2135	2211**f**

	Ⓐ	Ⓐ	Ⓐ	Ⓐ	Ⓐ		⑥	⑥	⑥	⑥	⑥	⑥	⑥	⑥	⑥		⑥	⑥	⑥	⑥	⑥	⑥	⑥	⑥	⑥	⑥	⑥
Manchester P'dilly ... d.	1930	2030	2136	...	2236	⑥	...	...	...	...	...	0630	0730	...	0830	...	0930	...	1030	1130	...	1230	1330	...	1430	1530	...
Stockport ... d.	1939	2040	2145	...	2244		...	...	...	...	...	0639	0739	...	0839	...	0940	...	1040	1140	...	1240	1340	...	1440	1540	...
Holyhead **145, 160** .. d.	|	|	|	...	|		...	...	...	...	0425	|	|	0635	|	...	|	0820	|	|	1033	|	|	1238	|	|	1425
Chester **145, 160** ... d.	|	|	|	...	|		...	...	...	...	0620	|	|	0819	|	...	|	1019	|	|	1219	|	|	1419	|	|	1619
Crewe ... ¶ d.	2010	2121	2212	...	2314		...	0454	...	0555	|	0708	0808	|	0908	...	1008	|	1108	1208	|	1308	1408	|	1509	1608	|
Whitchurch ... ¶ d.	2029	2142	2233	...	2334		...	0513	...	0616	|	0728	0827	|	|	...	|	|	|	1227	|	|	1427	|	|	1627	|
Shrewsbury ... **145**¶ a.	2048	2208	2301	...	0003		...	0533	...	0642	0717	0747	0845	0913	0937	...	1036	1114	1137	1245	1313	1337	1445	1513	1538	1643	1714
Shrewsbury ... **146** d.	2050	2209	...	2308	...		...	0540	0613	0644	0719	0750	0850	0915	0940	...	1038	1115	1140	1250	1315	1340	1446	1515	1540	1645	1716
Church Stretton .. **146** d.	2105	2224	...	2324	...		...	0555	0628	0659	|	0805	0905	|	0955	...	1054	|	1155	1305	1330	|	1501	|	1555	1700	|
Craven Arms ... **146** d.	2113	2232	...	2332	...		...	0603	0636	0707	|	0813	0913	|	1003	...	1102	|	1203	1313	1338	|	1509	|	1603	1708	|
Ludlow ... d.	2120	2240	...	2341	...		...	0610	0644	0714	0745	0820	0920	0944	1010	...	1109	1141	1210	1320	1344	1406	1517	1541	1610	1715	1742
Leominster ... d.	2131	2250	...	2352	...		...	0621	0655	0725	0755	0831	0931	|	1021	...	1120	|	1221	1331	|	1416	1527	|	1621	1726	|
Hereford ... d.	2150**d**	2311	...	0009	...		0542	0642**d**	0711	0744**d**	0812	0851	0950	1009	1038	...	1147**h**	1206	1238	1351	1410	1433	1546	1606	1638	1746**d**	1807
Abergavenny ... d.	2216	2334	...	0033	...		0607	0705	0734	0807	0835	0914	1013	1032	1101	...	1210	1229	1301	1414	1432	1456	1609	1629	1701	1809	1830
Pontypool & New Inn . d.	|	2343	...	|	...		0618	0715	0744	0817	0845	|	|	1042	|	...	|	1239	|	|	1443	|	|	1639	|	|	1840
Cwmbrân ... d.	2228	2348	...	0046	...		0623	0720	0749	0822	0850	0926	1025	1047	1113	...	1222	1244	1313	1426	1448	1509	1621	1644	1713	1821	1845
Newport ... **132** a.	2241	2359	...	0059	...		0634	0737	0800	0831	0901	0937	1036	1057	1127	...	1240	1254	1328	1436	1504	1521	1635	1654	1733	1836	1855
Cardiff Central ... **132** a.	2304	0023	...	0122	...		0654	0754	0820	0850	0917	0959	1102	1115	1157	...	1257	1313	1353	1453	1521	1537	1654	1708	1753	1855	1912

	⑥	⑥	⑥	⑥	⑥	⑥	⑥	⑥	⑥		⑦	⑦	⑦	⑦	⑦	⑦	⑦	⑦	⑦	⑦	⑦	⑦	⑦	⑦	⑦	⑦	⑦
	k	m									🚌																
Manchester P'dilly ... d.	1630	1630	1730	...	1830	1930	2030	2133	2235	⑦	...	...	0930	1031	1124	...	1233	1330	1430	1530	1630	1730	...	1830	1930	2030	...
Stockport ... d.	1640	1640	1740	...	1840	1940	2039	2143	2244		...	...	0940	1040	1140	...	1243	1340	1440	1539	1639	1739	...	1839	1939	2039	...
Holyhead **145, 160** .. d.	|	|	|	1650	|	|	|	|	|		...	...	|	|	|	1020	|	|	|	|	|	|	1625	|	|	|	...
Chester **145, 160** ... d.	|	|	|	1829	|	|	|	|	|		...	...	|	|	*1131*t	1221	|	*1331*t	|	*1531*t	|	*1731*t	1824	|	*1926*t	|	2300
Crewe ... ¶ d.	1708	1708	1809	|	1910	2009	2109	2212	2314		...	...	1013	1111	1213	|	1313	1413	1510	1613	1713	1813	|	1913	2010	2113	2323
Whitchurch ... ¶ d.	1727	1727	1828	|	1931	2028	2130	2233	2334		...	...	1035	|	|	|	1334	|	|	|	1734	|	|	1934	|	2135	2345
Shrewsbury ... **145**¶ a.	1743	1744	1846	1924	1956	2047	2153	2301	0004		...	...	1101	1141	1243	1318	1359	1443	1544	1643	1800	1843	1920	2000	2044	2203	0014
Shrewsbury ... **146** d.	1745	1746	1850	1926	1958	2048	2155	...	—		0750	...	1103	1145	1244	1319	1401	1444	1547	1644	1801	1844	1921	2001	2045	2204	...
Church Stretton .. **146** d.	1800	1801	1905	1941	2013	2103	2210	...	...		0815	...	1119	|	|	1335	|	1500	|	1700	|	|	1937	|	2101	2220	...
Craven Arms ... **146** d.	1808	1809	1913	1949	2021	2111	2218	...	...		0835	...	1127	|	|	1343	|	1508	|	1708	|	|	1945	|	2110	2229	...
Ludlow ... d.	1815	1816	1920	1955	2028	2119	2226	...	⑥		0855	...	1136	1213	1313	1351	1428	1516	1617	1716	1829	1912	1953	2029	2118	2237	...
Leominster ... d.	1826	1827	1931	|	2039	2129	2237	...			0920	...	1147	1223	1324	1402	1439	1526	1628	1726	1839	|	2004	2039	2130	2249	...
Hereford ... d.	1843	1846**d**	1951	2021	2056	2146	2253	...	2315		0950	1007	1203	1239	1340	1419	1456	1543	1644	1743	1857	1936	2021	2055	2146	2305	...
Abergavenny ... d.	1906	1909	2014	2044	2119	2209	2316	...	2338		...	1031	1227	1302	1403	1442	1519	1606	1708	1806	1920	1959	2046	2118	2210	2329	...
Pontypool & New Inn . d.	|	|	2023	|	2128	|	2325	...	|		...	1041	|	1312	|	1452	|	1616	|	1816	|	|	2056	|	2221	2339	...
Cwmbrân ... d.	1918	1921	2028	2057	2133	2222	2330	...	2350		...	1046	1240	1317	1416	1457	1531	1621	1721	1821	1933	2011	2101	2131	2226	2344	...
Newport ... **132** a.	1934	1934	2040	2114	2144	2233	2344	...	0002		...	1057	1253	1329	1426	1510	1546	1632	1735	1834	1943	2027	2110	2144	2235	2354	...
Cardiff Central ... **132** a.	1958	1958	2055	2131	2205	2255	0005	...	0029		...	1118	1316	1356	1447	1534	1611	1653	1807	1854	2007	2047	2132	2205	2258	0015	...

◄◄◄ For additional notes see previous page.

a – Until Jan. 1.
b – From Jan. 8.
d – Arrives 4 – 6 minutes earlier.
e – Arrives 0630.
f – Arrives 2205 on ⑤.
g – Arrives 0618.
h – Arrives 1135.
k – Until Dec. 31.
m – From Jan. 7.
n – Arrives 1344.
t – Change at Shrewsbury.

¶ – Additional journeys Shrewsbury - Whitchurch - Crewe and v.v.:
From Shrewsbury at 0531Ⓐ, 0544⑥, 0757⑥, 0800Ⓐ, 1018⚒, 1224⚒, 1424⚒, 1624⚒, 1825⑥, 1830Ⓐ, 2032⚒, 2330⑥.
From Crewe at 0640Ⓐ, 0720⑥, 0734Ⓐ, 0914Ⓐ, 0920⑥, 1120⚒, 1320⚒, 1520⑥, 1522Ⓐ, 1720⚒.

VT LONDON - BIRMINGHAM, CHESTER, HOLYHEAD, MANCHESTER and LIVERPOOL 150

LONDON - BIRMINGHAM - WOLVERHAMPTON

Certain services continue to / from destinations on Table 151. For trains via Northampton see Table 142.

km			Ⓐ	Ⓐ	Ⓐ	Ⓐ	Ⓐ	C	Ⓐ	Ⓐ	Ⓐ	Ⓐ	ⒶD	Ⓐ	Ⓐ	Ⓐ	Ⓐ	Ⓐ	Ⓐa	①-④b	Ⓐa	①-④b	Ⓐa	①-④b	Ⓐa
0	**London** Euston ... d.	Ⓐ	0620	0643	0703	0723	0743	and	1703	1723	1743	1803	1823	1843	1903	1923	1943	2003	2023	2023	2043	2043	2103	2103	2143
28	Watford Junction ... △ d.		0634	|	|	0737	|	at the	|	1737	|	|	1837	|	|	1937	|	|	2037	2037	|	|	|	|	2158
80	Milton Keynes ... d.		|	0713	|	|	0813	same	|	|	1813u	|	|	1913	|	|	2013	|	|	|	2113	2113	2135	2135	2217
133	Rugby ... a.		0712	|	0751	|	|	minutes	1751	|	|	1851	|	|	1951	|	|	2051	|	|	|	|	2156	2156	|
151	Coventry ... a.		0722	0742	0802	0822	0842	past	1802	1822	1842	1902	1922	1942	2002	2022	2042	2102	2124	2124	2142	2142	2207	2207	2246
168	Birmingham Int'l ✈ ... a.		0733	0753	0813	0833	0853	each	1813	1833	1853	1913	1933	1953	2013	2033	2053	2113	2134	2134	2153	2153	2218	2218	2300
182	**Birmingham** New St. a.		0745	0808	0827	0845	0908	hour	1827	1845	1908	1927	1945	2008	2027	2045	2108	2127	2146	2146	2205	2205	2230	2230	2316
190	Sandwell & Dudley ... a.		...	0824	...	...	0924	until	...	...	1924	|	1958	2024	...	2058	2124	|	2159	|	2216	|	2241	|	2333
202	**Wolverhampton** ... a.		...	0837	...	...	0937		...	...	1937	2000	2011	2037	...	2112	2137	2158	2212	2216	2230	2237	2256	2303	2347

	①-④b	Ⓐ	①-④	⑤		⑥	⑥	⑥	⑥	⑥	⑥	⑥	E	⑥	⑥	⑥	⑥	⑥D	⑥	⑥	⑥	⑥	⑥	⑥	⑥
London Euston ... d.	2143	2230	2330	2330	⑥	0623	0703	0723	0743	0803	0823	0843	and	1703	1723	1743	1803	1823	1843	1903	1923	1943	2025	2103	2143
Watford Junction ... △ d.	2158	2245	|	|		0637	|	0737	|	|	0837	|	at the	|	1737	|	|	1837	|	|	1937	|	2040	2118	2158
Milton Keynes ... d.	2217	2329	0029	0028		|	|	|	0813	|	|	0913	same	|	|	1813	|	|	1913	|	|	2020	|	2150	2230
Rugby ... a.	|	2358	0100	0105		|	0751	|	|	0851	|	|	minutes	1751	|	|	1851	|	|	1951	|	|	|	2211	2252
Coventry ... a.	2246	0010	0113	0118		0722	0802	0822	0842	0902	0922	0942	past	1802	1822	1842	1902	1922	1942	2002	2022	2050	2136	2222	2302
Birmingham Int'l ✈ ... a.	2300	0021	0124	0129		0733	0813	0833	0853	0913	0933	0953	each	1813	1833	1853	1913	1933	1953	2013	2033	2101	2150	2233	2313
Birmingham New St . a.	2316	0032	0136	0141		0745	0827	0845	0908	0927	0945	1008	hour	1827	1845	1908	1927	1945	2008	2027	2045	2113	2204	2245	2325
Sandwell & Dudley ... a.	|	|	|	|		...	...	...	0924	...	...	1024	until	...	1858	1924	1943	1958	2024	2053	2058	|	2224	2256	2336
Wolverhampton ... a.	2348	0103	0207	0210		...	...	...	0937	...	...	1037		...	1911	1937	1956	2011	2037	2109	2112	2138	2238	2310	2350

		⑦	⑦	⑦	⑦	⑦	⑦	⑦	⑦		⑦	⑦	⑦	⑦	⑦D	⑦	⑦	⑦		⑦	⑦	⑦	⑦	⑦	⑦
London Euston ... d.	⑦	0850	0950	1050	1150	1220	1240	1300	1320	and	1740	1800	1820	1840	1900	1920	1940	2000	...	2018	2038	2054	2155	2225	2325
Watford Junction ... △ d.		0907	1005	1105	1205	1234	|	|	1334	at the	|	|	1834	|	|	1934	|	|	...	2032	|	2110	2209	2239	2339
Milton Keynes ... d.		0939	1038	1138	1230	|	1313	|	|	same	1813	|	|	1913	|	|	2013	|	...	|	2116	2143	2245	2312	0012
Rugby ... a.		1013	1113	1213	1249	|	|	1351	|	minutes	|	1851	|	|	1952	|	|	2051	...	|	|	2205	2322	2346	0046s
Coventry ... a.		1024	1123	1223	1259	1322	1342	1402	1422	past	1844	1902	1922	1942	2003	2022	2042	2103	...	2120	2146	2216	2333	2357	0058s
Birmingham Int'l ✈ ... a.		1035	1134	1234	1310	1333	1353	1413	1433	each	1854	1913	1933	1953	2013	2033	2053	2113	...	2131	2157	2227	2344	0008	0109s
Birmingham New St . a.		1047	1147	1247	1325	1346	1408	1425	1445	hour	1908	1925	1945	2008	2025	2045	2108	2125	...	2145	2209	2239	2356	0021	0122s
Sandwell & Dudley ... a.		1058	1158	1258	...	1356	1425	...	...	until	1925	1948	...	2024	2035	2056	2124	...	...	2156	2224	2251	|	|	|
Wolverhampton ... a.		1111	1211	1310	...	1408	1437	...	...	☆	1937	2000	...	2037	2047	2111	2137	...	...	2208	2236	2303	0015	0041	0142

		Ⓐ	Ⓐ	Ⓐ	Ⓐ	Ⓐ	Ⓐ		Ⓐ	Ⓐ	ⒶD	ⒶK	Ⓐ	Ⓐ	Ⓐ	Ⓐ	F	Ⓐ	Ⓐ	Ⓐ	Ⓐ	Ⓐ	Ⓐ	Ⓐ	Ⓐ
Wolverhampton ... d.	Ⓐ	0500	0524	0545	0604	0627	0645	...	0705	...	0724	0745	...	...	0845	...	and	...	1845	...	1945	...	2047	2143	2242
Sandwell & Dudley ... d.		|	0534	0555	0615	0638	0656	...	0715	...	|	0757	...	...	0855	...	at the	...	1855	...	1955	...	2057	2155c	2255c
Birmingham New St . d.		0529	0550	0610	0630	0650	0710	...	0730	...	0750	0810	0830	0850	0910	0930	same	1850	1910	1930	2010	2050	2110	2210	2310
Birmingham Intl ✈ ... d.		0540	0600	0620	0640	0700	0720	...	|	0741	0800	0821	0840	0900	0920	0940	minutes	1900	1920	1940	2020	2100	2120	2220	2320
Coventry ... d.		0551	0611	0631	0651	0711	0731	...	|	0752	0811	0831	0851	0911	0931	0951	past	1911	1931	1951	2031	2111	2131	2231	2331
Rugby ... d.		0603	|	|	|	|	|	...	|	|	0823	|	|	0923	|	|	each	1923	|	2003	|	2123	|	2245	2344
Milton Keynes ... d.		0626	0638	0659	|	0740s	|	...	|	|	|	|	0920	|	1000	|	hour	|	2000	|	2100	|	2159	2308	0024
Watford Junction ... ▽ a.		0647	|	|	0737	|	|	...	|	|	|	0916	|	|	|	1039	until	|	|	2041	2119	|	2220	2339	0052
London Euston ... a.		0705	0713	0734	0753	0815	0831	...	0843	0850	0915	0934	0955	1015	1032	1056	☆	2015	2034	2058	2139	2213	2243	0006	0115

		⑥	⑥	⑥	⑥		⑥	⑥	⑥	⑥		⑥	⑥	⑥	⑥D	⑥	⑥	⑥	F	⑥	⑥	⑥	⑥	⑥	⑥
Wolverhampton ... d.	⑥	...	0545	0606	0627	...	0645	0705	0725	0745	...	...	...	...	0905	...	0945	...	and	...	...	1845	1945	2045	2109
Sandwell & Dudley ... d.		...	0555	0617	0637	...	0656	0715	|	0755	...	...	...	...	|	...	0955	...	at the	...	...	1855	1955	2055	2119
Birmingham New St . d.		0550	0610	0630	0650	...	0710	0730	0750	0810	...	0830	0850	0910	0930	0950	1010	1030	same	1830	1850	1910	2010	2110	2130
Birmingham Intl ✈ ... d.		0600	0620	0640	0700	...	0720	0740	0800	0820	...	0840	0900	0920	0940	1000	1020	1040	minutes	1840	1900	1920	2020	2120	2140
Coventry ... d.		0611	0631	0651	0711	...	0731	0751	0811	0831	...	0851	0911	0931	0951	1011	1031	1051	past	1851	1911	1931	2031	2131	2151
Rugby ... d.		0624	|	|	0723	...	|	|	0823	|	...	|	0923	|	|	1023	|	|	each	|	1923	1943	2043	2143	2203
Milton Keynes ... d.		|	0659	|	|	...	0759	|	|	0859	...	|	|	0959	|	|	1059	|	hour	|	|	2007	2105	2205	2226
Watford Junction ... ▽ a.		|	0719	0736	|	...	|	0837	|	|	...	0939	|	|	1039	|	|	1139	until	1939	|	2034	2135	2234	2312
London Euston ... a.		0717	0738	0755	0817	...	0835	0856	0915	0935	...	0959	1015	1034	1056	1115	1133	1155	☆	1956	2023	2055	2157	2255	2331

		⑦	⑦	⑦	⑦	⑦	⑦	⑦		⑦	⑦D	⑦	⑦	⑦	⑦	⑦	⑦	⑦	⑦	⑦	⑦	⑦	⑦	⑦	⑦
Wolverhampton ... d.	⑦	0805	0905	1005	1105	...	1145	...	and	1545	1604	...	1645	...	...	1745	...	...	1845	...	1945	...	2105	2205	2237
Sandwell & Dudley ... d.		0815	0915	1015	1115	...	1155	...	at the	1555	|	...	1655	...	...	1755	...	...	1855	...	1955	...	2117	2216	2248
Birmingham New St . d.		0830	0930	1030	1130	1150	1210	1230	same	1610	1630	1650	1710	1730	1750	1810	1830	1850	1910	1930	2010	2030	2130	2230	2300
Birmingham Intl ✈ ... d.		0840	0940	1040	1140	1200	1220	1240	minutes	1619	1640	1700	1720	1740	1800	1820	1840	1900	1920	1940	2020	2040	2140	2240	2310
Coventry ... d.		0851	0951	1051	1151	1211	1231	1251	past	1631	1651	1711	1730	1751	1811	1831	1851	1911	1931	1951	2031	2051	2151	2251	2321
Rugby ... d.		0904	1004	1104	1205	1225	|	|	each	|	|	1725	|	|	1825	|	|	1926	|	|	|	2105	2204	2304	2335
Milton Keynes ... d.		0939	1039	1139	1227	|	1301	|	hour	1659	|	|	1759	|	|	1859	|	|	2000	|	2101	2128	2237	2337	0013s
Watford Junction ... ▽ a.		1007	1111	1208	|	|	|	1338	until	|	1738	|	|	1838	|	|	1938	|	|	2039	|	2202	2305	0006	0043
London Euston ... a.		1027	1131	1227	1306	1320	1338	1357	☆	1738	1757	1818	1838	1857	1917	1939	1957	2018	2039	2057	2148	2223	2325	0027	0105

LONDON - CHESTER (- HOLYHEAD)

km			ⒶA	Ⓐ	Ⓐ	Ⓐ		Ⓐ	Ⓐ	Ⓐ	Ⓐ	Ⓐ	Ⓐ	Ⓐ		Ⓐ	ⒶG	Ⓐ	Ⓐ			⑥A	⑥
0	**London** Euston ... d.	Ⓐ	...	0710	0810	0910	...	1010	1110	1210	1310	1410	1510	1610	...	1710	1810	1910	2010	...	⑥	...	0810
80	Milton Keynes ... d.		...	0741	0843	0941	...	1041	1141	1241	1341	1441	1541	1641u	...	1741u	1841u	1941	2041	...		...	0841
254	Crewe ... d.		0623	0849	0953	1049	...	1149	1249	1352	1449	1549	1649	1749	...	1857	1956	2055	2149	...		0623	0949
288	**Chester** ... a.		0643	0913	1013	1113	...	1213	1313	1413	1513	1613	1713	1808	...	1916	2015	2120	2213	...		0643	1013
	Bangor **160** ... a.		0749	*1051*	1124	1216	...	*1331*	*1435*	*1530*	*1642*	*1738*	*1846*	1921	...	2028	2125	2229	*0013*	...		0749	*1135*
	Holyhead **160** ... a.		0823	*1122*	1158	1250	...	*1414*	*1508*	*1614*	*1716*	*1821*	*1917*	*2020*	...	2059	2159	2303	*0048*	...		0823	*1209*

	⑥	⑥	⑥	⑥	⑥	⑥	⑥	⑥	⑥	⑥			⑦	⑦	⑦	⑦	⑦	⑦	⑦	⑦	⑦		⑦
London Euston ... d.	0910	1010	1110	1210	1310	1410	1510	1610	1710	1810	...	⑦	*0815*	*0945*	*1115*	*1337*	*1437*	1508	1608	1708	1808	...	1908
Milton Keynes ... d.	0941	1041	1141	1241	1341	1441	1541	1641	1741	1841	...		|	*1033*	*1204*	|	|	1542	1642	1742	1842	...	1942
Crewe ... d.	1049	1156	1249	1352	1449	1549	1649	1749	1852	1949	...		1042	1227	1327	1527	1627	1652	1752	1901	1952	...	2055
Chester ... a.	1113	1217	1313	1416	1513	1610	1713	1810	1911	2013	...		1102	1252	1351	1549	1649	1713	1813	1919	2013	...	2113
Bangor **160** ... a.	1216	*1332*	*1438*	*1532*	*1636*	1717	*1841*	1921	2023	*2124*	...		1209	1417	1512	1712	1817	*1914*	*1947*	2034	2123	...	2222
Holyhead **160** ... a.	1250	*1413*	*1508*	*1613*	*1714*	1751	*1913*	1955	2058	*2225*	...		1240	1448	1552	1752	1849	*1949*	*2018*	2103	2154	...	2253

		ⒶH	Ⓐ	ⒶG	Ⓐ	Ⓐ		Ⓐ	Ⓐ	Ⓐ	Ⓐ	Ⓐ	Ⓐ	Ⓐ	Ⓐ	Ⓐ	ⒶB		⑥H	⑥	⑥	⑥	⑥
Holyhead **160** ... d.	Ⓐ	...	0448	0551	0655	*0715*	...	0855	*0923*	*1040*	*1127*	1252	1358	*1434*	*1544*	*1730*	*1921*	⑥	...	*0425*	0652	0755	0855
Bangor **160** ... d.		...	0514	0618	0722	*0802*	...	0922	*1002*	*1107*	*1200*	1320	1425	*1504*	*1623*	*1809*	2020		...	*0456*	0720	0822	0922
Chester ... d.		0422	0626	0735	0835	0935	...	1035	1135	1235	1335	1435	1535	1635	1735	1935	2135		0422	0717	0835	0935	1035
Crewe ... a.		0444	0647	0754	0854	0954	...	1054	1154	1254	1354	1454	1554	1654	1754	1954	2154		0443	0736	0854	0954	1054
Milton Keynes ... a.		*0651*	|	|	1002	1102	...	1202	1302	1402	1502	1602	1702	1802	1901	2104	...		*0711*	0852	1002	1102	1202
London Euston ... a.		*0729*	0834	0941	1039	1139	...	1239	1339	1439	1539	1639	1739	1839	1939	2143	...		*0753*	0930	1039	1138	1239

	⑥	⑥	⑥		⑥	⑥	⑥		⑥	⑥			⑦	⑦	⑦	⑦	⑦	⑦		⑦	⑦	⑦	⑦
Holyhead **160** ... d.	*0923*	*1033*	*1123*	...	*1238*	1358	*1425*	...	*1523*	*1823*	...	⑦	0845	*0845*	1055	1150	1250	1355	...	*1530*	*1625*	*1730*	*1825*
Bangor **160** ... d.	*1002*	*1105*	*1202*	...	*1307*	1425	*1453*	...	*1602*	*1902*	...		0912	*0912*	1122	1217	1318	1422	...	*1558*	*1704*	*1759*	*1904*
Chester ... d.	1135	1235	1335	...	1435	1535	1635	...	1735	2035	...		1039	1128	1233	1330	1433	1533	...	1735	1835	1935	2037
Crewe ... a.	1154	1254	1354	...	1454	1554	1654	...	1754	2054	...		1103	1147	1253	1350	1454	1552	...	1753	1853	1956	2056
Milton Keynes ... a.	1302	1402	1502	...	1602	1702	1802	...	|	...	...		|	1304	1403	1503	1603	1703	...	1904	2003	*2136*	*2304*
London Euston ... a.	1339	1439	1539	...	1639	1739	1839	...	*2005*	...	...		*1313*	1346	1444	1545	1644	1744	...	1944	2046	*2228*	*2354*

A – From Birmingham New Street (d. 0530), Wolverhampton (d. 0548) and Stafford (d. 0601).
B – To Wolverhampton (a. 2227) and Birmingham New Street (a. 2250 **a**, 2258 **b**).
C – The 1023 from London continues to Shrewsbury (Table **145**) calling at Wolverhampton (a. 1210).
D – To / from Shrewsbury (Table **145**).
E – The 1123 from London continues to Shrewsbury (Table **145**) calling at Wolverhampton (a. 1310).
F – The 1630 from Birmingham New Street starts from Shrewsbury (Table **145**) calling at Wolverhampton (d. 1604).
G – Conveys 🛏 London Euston - Wrexham and v.v. (Table **145**).
H – To Stafford (a. 0524), Wolverhampton (a. 0539), and Birmingham New Street (a. 0558 ⑥, 0610 Ⓐ).
K – From Manchester Piccadilly.

a – To Feb. 10 and from Mar. 24 (also ⑤ Feb. 17 - Mar. 17).
b – Feb. 13 - Mar. 23.
c – Not ①–④ Feb. 13 - Mar. 23.
s – Calls to set down only.
u – Calls to pick up only.
☆ – Timings may vary by up to 3 minutes.
△ – Trains call here to pick up only.
▽ – Trains call here to set down only.

150 LONDON - BIRMINGHAM, CHESTER, HOLYHEAD, MANCHESTER and LIVERPOOL VT

LONDON - MANCHESTER

km		Ⓐ	Ⓐ	Ⓐ	Ⓐ	Ⓐ	Ⓐ	Ⓐ	Ⓐ	Ⓐ	Ⓐ	Ⓐ	Ⓐ		Ⓐ	Ⓐ	Ⓐ	④-⑤2	Ⓐ		Ⓐ	Ⓐ	Ⓐ	Ⓐ
0	**London** Euston d.		0616	0636	0655	0720	0735	0800	0820	0840	0900	0920	0940	and at	1800	1820	1840	1857	1900	...	1920	1940	2000	2040
80	Milton Keynes d.		0646		0727	0750	0806		0850			0950		the same		1850u				...	1950			
235	Stoke on Trent d.		0745		0825	0848		0925	0948		1025	1048		minutes	1925	1948			2025	...	2050		2126	
267	Macclesfield d.		0802		0841			0941			1041			past each	1941					...	2107		2142	
	Crewe d.			0811			0911			1011			1111	hour until			2018	2033s		...		2123		2213
	Wilmslow d.			0827			0927			1027			1127				2033			...		2138		2229
287	Stockport d.		0817	0837	0856	0917	0937	0955	1017	1037	1056	1117	1137	a ♡	1956	2017	2043		2053	...	2120		2155	2239
296	**Manchester** Piccadilly a.		0828	0849	0907	0928	0949	1007	1028	1049	1107	1128	1149		2007	2028	2053	2110	2108	...	2131	2157	2207	2248

	Ⓐ	Ⓐ		Ⓐ	Ⓐ	⑥	⑥	⑥	⑥	⑥	⑥		⑥	⑥	⑥	⑥	⑥		⑥	⑥	⑥	⑥	⑥b	⑥
London Euston d.	2100	2140	...	2200	2300		0636	0655	0720	0735	0800	...	0820	0840	0900	0920	0940	and at	1900	1920	1940	2020	2031	2100
Milton Keynes d.	2131		...	2240				0727	0750	0806		...	0850			0950		the same		1950		2105		2145
Stoke on Trent d.	2228	2305	...		0118s			0825	0848		0925	...	0948		1025	1048		minutes	2025	2048		2205		
Macclesfield d.	2244	2321	...		0134s			0841			0941	...			1041			past each	2041			2221		
Crewe d.			...	0017			0811			0911		...		1011			1111	hour until			2119		2230	2259
Wilmslow d.			...	...			0827			0927		...		1027			1127				2134			2315
Stockport d.	2259	2339	...	...	0148s		0837	0856	0917	0937	0955	...	1017	1037	1055	1117	1137		2056	2120	2145	2236		2327
Manchester Piccadilly a.	2311	2350	...	...	0159		0849	0907	0928	0949	1007	...	1028	1049	1107	1128	1149		2107	2130	2153	2251	2035	2339

	⑦	⑦	⑦	⑦	⑦		⑦	⑦	⑦	⑦	⑦	⑦	⑦		⑦	⑦	⑦	⑦	⑦	⑦	⑦	⑦	⑦	⑦
London Euston d.		0810	0820	0920	1020	...	1120	1217	1237	1257	1317	1337	1357	and at	1817	1837	1857	1917	1937	1957	2015	2035	2125	2151
Milton Keynes d.		0856	0906	1007	1107	...	1208	1250			1350			the same	1850			1950			2048		2214	2239
Stoke on Trent d.			1021	1123	1225	...	1311	1350		1426	1450		1526	minutes	1950		2026	2050		2126	2150		2329	
Macclesfield d.			1038	1139	1242	...	1328			1442			1542	past each			2042			2142			2346	
Crewe d.		1019				...			1413			1513		until		2013			2113			2221		0016s
Wilmslow d.		1034				...			1429			1529				2029			2129			2236		
Stockport d.		1044	1052	1153	1256	...	1342	1421	1439	1456	1520	1539	1556	☆	2021	2039	2057	2121	2139	2159	2220	2246	0001	0038s
Manchester Piccadilly a.		1054	1102	1204	1305	...	1350	1432	1448	1506	1531	1548	1605		2030	2048	2106	2131	2149	2209	2229	2254	0009	0048

km		Ⓐ	Ⓐ	Ⓐ	Ⓐ	Ⓐ	Ⓐ	Ⓐ	Ⓐ	Ⓐ	Ⓐ	Ⓐ	Ⓐ	Ⓐ	Ⓐ	Ⓐ	Ⓐ	Ⓐ		Ⓐ	Ⓐ	Ⓐ	Ⓐ	Ⓐ
0	**Manchester** Piccadilly d.		0505	0555	0610	0635	0643	0700	0715	0627	0735	0755	0815	0835	0855	0915	0935	0955	and at	1655	1715	1735	1755	1815
9	Stockport d.		0513	0603	0618	0643	0651	0707u	0723	0635	0743	0804	0823	0843	0904	0923	0943	1004	the same	1704	1723	1743	1804	1823
30	Wilmslow d.			0611			0659					0811			0911			1011	minutes	1711			1811	
50	Crewe d.		0536	0628			0717					0829			0929			1029	past each	1729			1829	
	Macclesfield d.				0631	0656				0648	0756			0856			0956		until			1756		
	Stoke on Trent d.				0648	0712			0750	0706	0812		0850	0912		0950	1012				1750	1812		1850
	Milton Keynes a.		0651						0846	c			0949			1046			d		1848		1933	1946
304	**London** Euston a.		0729	0808	0823	0846	0854	0900	0924	0934	0952	1019	1026	1053	1108	1124	1143	1205		1909	1924	1943	2008	2024

	Ⓐ	Ⓐ	Ⓐ	Ⓐ	Ⓐ	Ⓐ	⑥	⑥	⑥	⑥	⑥	⑥	⑥	⑥	⑥	⑥	⑥	⑥	⑥	⑥	⑥		⑥	⑥
Manchester Piccadilly d.	1835	1855	1915	1955	2015	2115		0525	0555	0610	0635	0655	0715	0735	0755	0815	0835	0855	0915	0935	0955	and at	1715	1735
Stockport d.	1843	1903	1923	2004	2023	2123		0534	0603	0618	0643	0704	0723	0743	0804	0823	0843	0904	0923	0943	1004	the same	1723	1743
Wilmslow d.		1911		2011				0541	0611			0711			0811			0911			1011	minutes		
Crewe d.		1929		2029				0600	0629			0729			0829			0929			1029	past each		
Macclesfield d.	1856		1936		2036	2136				0631	0656			0756			0856			0956		until		1756
Stoke on Trent d.	1912		1952		2052	2153				0648	0712		0750	0812		0850	0912		0950	1012			1750	1812
Milton Keynes a.		2031	2048	2135	2151	2300		0711	0731				0846			0946			1046			d	1848	
London Euston a.	2042	2106	2126	2213	2228	2351		0753	0810	0828	0846	0905	0924	0943	1011	1024	1043	1108	1124	1143	1205		1925	1943

	⑥	⑥	⑥	⑥	⑥	⑥	⑦	⑦	⑦	⑦	⑦	⑦	⑦	⑦	⑦	⑦		⑦	⑦	⑦	⑦	⑦	⑦	⑦
Manchester Piccadilly d.	1755	1815	1835	1855	1935	2035		0805	0820	0920	1020	1035	1115	1135	1155	1215	and at	1815	1835	1855	1915	1935	2021	2055
Stockport d.	1804	1823	1843	1904	1943	2043		0814	0828	0928	1029	1046	1124	1142	1203	1223	the same	1822	1842	1904	1922	1941	2027	2103
Wilmslow d.	1811			1911				0822			1037				1211		minutes			1911				
Crewe d.	1829			1929				0843			1055				1230		past each			1929				
Macclesfield d.			1856		1956	2056			0841	0940		1057		1155			until		1855			1954	2040	2116
Stoke on Trent d.		1849	1912		2012	2112			0857	1000		1115	1152	1212		1251		1850	1912		1950	2011	2057	2133
Milton Keynes a.		1945			2110	2210				1116		1221	1250			1347	☆	1948			2046		2203	2246
London Euston a.	2005	2034	2059	2120	2201	2302		1058	1102	1209	1257	1300	1328	1348	1410	1428		2027	2048	2110	2131	2201	2257	2349

LONDON - LIVERPOOL

km		⚒	Ⓐ	⚒	⑥	Ⓐ	Ⓐ	⑥	⚒	⚒		⚒	⚒	⚒	⚒	⚒	⑥	Ⓐ	⑥	Ⓐ	⚒	⑥	Ⓐ
0	**London** Euston d.		0527	0707	0807	0807	0907	0907	1007	1107	...	1207	1307	1407	1507	1607	1633	1707	1707	1733	1807	1833	1833
80	Milton Keynes d.		0615			0838					...												
135	Rugby d.										...									1823			1923
155	Nuneaton d.		0645								...								1803				
215	Stafford d.		0708	0823	0924	0927	1024	1026	1124	1224	...	1324	1424	1524	1624	1724	1759	1824	1827	1856	1923	1959	1954
254	Crewe d.		0728	0843	0943		1043	1046	1143	1243	...	1343	1443	1543	1643	1743		1844	1847	1916	1943		2016
290	Runcorn d.		0745	0900	1000	1000	1100	1103	1200	1300	...	1400	1500	1600	1700	1800	1832	1900	1904	1933	2000	2032	2033
312	**Liverpool** Lime Street a.		0805	0921	1021	1021	1121	1121	1221	1321	...	1421	1521	1621	1721	1821	1852	1921	1925	1952	2021	2053	2053

	Ⓐ	⑥	Ⓐ	⑥	Ⓐ	⑦	⑦	⑦	⑦	⑦		⑦	⑦	⑦	⑦	⑦	⑦		⑦	⑦	⑦	⑦	⑦
London Euston d.	1907	1907	2007	2011	2107		0815	0914	1015	1115	...	1205	1305	1405	1505	1605	1705	...	1805	1905	2005	2008	2121
Milton Keynes d.					2139					1204	...							...				2041	
Rugby d.				2115							...							...					
Nuneaton d.		2003	2103		2208		0944	1045	1147		...						1804	...		2004	2104		2253
Stafford d.		2027	2127	2146			1008	1114	1214	1253	...	1325	1425	1525	1625	1726		...	1925	2029		2133	2318
Crewe d.		2047	2148	2206	2251		1030	1135	1234	1315	...	1345	1445	1545	1645	1746	1846	...	1945	2049	2146	2155	2344
Runcorn d.	2050	2105	2205	2224	2309		1047	1152	1251	1332	...	1402	1502	1602	1702	1802	1902	...	2002	2106	2203	2212	0004
Liverpool Lime Street a.	2108	2125	2225	2246	2334		1105	1210	1308	1351	...	1420	1520	1623	1721	1821	1921	...	2020	2123	2220	2229	0027

	⚒	Ⓐ	⑥	Ⓐ	⑥	Ⓐ	⑥	Ⓐ	⑥	Ⓐ		⑥	⚒	⚒	⚒	⚒	⚒	⚒	⚒	Ⓐ	⑥	⑥	Ⓐ
Liverpool Lime Street d.		0526	0547	0605	0645	0700	0720	0747	0747	0847	...	0847	0947	1047	1147	1247	1347	1447	1547	1647	1647	1747	1747
Runcorn d.		0543	0603	0621	0701	0715u	0737	0803	0803	0903	...	0903	1003	1103	1203	1303	1403	1503	1603	1703	1703	1803	1803
Crewe d.		0602			0720		0757	0823	0822	0925	...	0924	1022	1122	1222	1324	1422	1522	1622		1723		1824
Stafford d.		0622	0636	0654	0739		0816	0843	0842	0944	...	0943	1042	1142	1242	1343	1442	1542	1642	1736	1743	1836	1843
Nuneaton d.			0659						0905		...												
Rugby d.		0654									...												
Milton Keynes d.		0714									...									1824			
London Euston a.		0751	0805	0823	0900	0904	0947	1001	1006	1105	...	1105	1159	1259	1400	1505	1559	1659	1759	1903	1907	1959	2007

	Ⓐ	⑥	Ⓐ	⑥	Ⓐ	⑦	⑦	⑦	⑦		⑦	⑦	⑦	⑦	⑦	⑦	⑦		⑦	⑦	⑦	⑦	⑦
Liverpool Lime Street d.	1847	1847	1947	1948	2048		0818	0838	0938	...	1038	1147	1247	1347	1447	1547	1618	...	1647	1747	1847	1947	2047
Runcorn d.	1903	1903	2003	2004	2104		0835	0854	0954	...	1054	1203	1303	1403	1503	1603	1634	...	1703	1803	1903	2003	2103
Crewe d.	1922	1923	2024	2023	2124		0853	0913	1014	...	1114	1223	1323	1423	1523	1623	1654	...	1723	1823	1923	2024	2124
Stafford d.	1942	1942		2043	2144			0933	1034	...	1136	1244	1344	1444	1544	1644		...	1744	1844	1944	2043	2144
Nuneaton d.			2102		2218			0956	1057	...	1159							...					2219
Rugby d.					2232					...								...					2233
Milton Keynes d.					2255		1021		1147	...							1805	...				2137	2306
London Euston a.	2104	2117	2209	2215	2346		1108	1137	1232	...	1313	1404	1504	1604	1705	1803	1844	...	1904	2005	2103	2228	2354

a – The 1520 Ⓐ from London Euston arrives Manchester Piccadilly at 1734.
b – Jan. 7 - Feb. 11.
c – Via Birmingham New Street.
d – The 1255 from Manchester Piccadilly arrives London Euston 1509; the 1315 from Manchester Piccadilly arrives London Euston 1530.

s – Calls to set down only.
u – Calls to pick up only.

☆ – Timings may vary by up to 3 minutes.
♡ – The 1720 Ⓐ from London calls at Milton Keynes to pick up only.

TP, VT LONDON, BIRMINGHAM and MANCHESTER - PRESTON - EDINBURGH and GLASGOW 151

km			Ⓐ	⚒	⚒	⚒	Ⓐ	⑥	Ⓐ	⚒	⑥	Ⓐ	⑥	⑥ W	⚒	Ⓐ ◐	⑥	⚒	⚒	Ⓐ W	⚒ ◐	⚒	⚒	⑥ ◐
0	**London Euston** 150 d.	⚒	...	...	...	...	...	...	0531	...	0605	...	...	...	0730	0643	...	...	0830	...	0743	...	0930	0843
80	Milton Keynes 150 d.		...	...	...	...	...	...	0623	...	0641	...	...	...	|	0713	...	...	|	...	0813	...	|	0913
	Birmingham New Street 150 d.		...	...	...	0615	...	...	|	...	|	0715	0715	...	|	0815	0815	...	|	...	0915	...	|	1015
	Wolverhampton 150 d.		...	...	...	0637	...	...	|	...	|	0737	0737	...	|	0837	0837	...	|	...	0937	...	|	1037
253	Crewe 150 d.		...	0557	...	0709	...	...	0732	...	0755	0809	0809	...	|	0909	0909	...	|	...	1009	...	|	1109
291	Warrington Bank Quay d.		...	0615	...	0727	...	...	0749	...	0812	0827	0827	...	0914	0927	0927	...	1014	...	1027	...	1114	1127
	Manchester Airport ✈ d.		...	|	0558	|	0700	0700	|	0729	|	|	|	0829	|	|	|	0900	|	...	|	1000	|	|
	Manchester Piccadilly d.		0457	|	0615	|	0715	0715	|	0744	|	|	|	0846	|	|	|	0915	|	...	|	1015	|	|
310	Wigan North Western d.		|	0625	0643	0738	0743	0743	0800	0810	0823	0838	0838	|	0925	0938	0938	0943	1025	...	1038	1043	1125	1138
334	**Preston** d.		0542f	0640	0658	0753	0758	0758	0815	0825	0837	0853	0853	0932	0941	0954	0953	0958	1041	1029	1053	1058	1141	1153
368	Lancaster d.		0558	0654	0714	0808	0814	0814	0830	0841	0852	0908	0913	0948	0955	1008	1008	1014	1055	1100	1108	1114	1155	1208
398	Oxenholme d.		0612	0709	0729	0822	|	0829	0843	0855	0906	|	|	1004	|	1022	1022	1029	1108	1120	|	|	|	1221
450	Penrith d.		|	0734	0754	|	0852	0854	|	0920	0932	0944	0948	...	1031	|	|	1054	|	...	1145	|	1230	|
478	Carlisle d.		0652	0751	0811	0901	0910	0911	0922	0937	0948	1001	1003	...	1047	1101	1101	1111	1147	...	1202	1206	1247	1301
519	Lockerbie d.		0711	0810	0830	|	0929	0930	|	0956	|	|	|	...	|	|	|	1130	|	...	|	|	|	|
	Haymarket a.		|	|	0930s	1013	|	|	|	1057s	|	|	|	...	|	1216	1217	|	|	...	|	1320s	|	1411
641	**Edinburgh** Waverley a.		|	|	0937	1022	|	|	|	1103	|	|	|	...	|	1222	1222	|	|	...	|	1326	|	1417
643	**Glasgow** Central a.		0818	0913	...	...	1029	1029	1036	...	1059	1116	1116	...	1201	...	...	1229	1301	...	1317	...	1401	...

	Ⓐ ◐	⚒	Ⓐ	⑥	Ⓐ ◐	⑥ ◐	⚒	⚒	⚒ ◐	Ⓐ	⑥	⚒	⚒ ◐	⚒	Ⓐ	⑥	⚒ ◐	Ⓐ	⑥	⑥	Ⓐ	⑥ ◐	Ⓐ ◐	⚒
London Euston 150 d.	0843	...	1030	1030	0943	0943	...	1130	1043	...	...	1230	1143	...	1330	1330	1243	...	...	1430	1430	1343	1343	...
Milton Keynes 150 d.	0913	...	|	|	1013	1013	...	|	1113	...	...	|	1213	...	|	|	1313	...	...	|	|	1413	1413	...
Birmingham New Street 150 d.	1015	...	|	|	1115	1115	...	|	1215	...	...	|	1315	...	|	|	1415	...	...	|	|	1515	1515	...
Wolverhampton 150 d.	1037	...	|	|	1137	1137	...	|	1237	...	...	|	1337	...	|	|	1437	...	...	|	|	1537	1537	...
Crewe 150 d.	1109	...	|	|	1209	1209	...	|	1309	...	...	|	1409	...	|	|	1509	...	...	|	|	1609	1609	...
Warrington Bank Quay d.	1127	...	1214	1214	1227	1227	...	1314	1327	...	...	1414	1427	...	1514	1514	1527	...	...	1614	1614	1627	1627	...
Manchester Airport ✈ d.	|	1100	|	|	|	|	1200	|	|	1300	1300	|	|	1400	|	|	|	1500	1500	|	|	|	|	1600
Manchester Piccadilly d.	|	1115	|	|	|	|	1215	|	|	1315	1315	|	|	1415	|	|	|	1515	1515	|	|	|	|	1615
Wigan North Western d.	1138	1143	1225	1225	1238	1238	1242	1325	1338	1343	1343	1425	1438	1443	1525	1525	1538	1543	1543	1625	1625	1638	1638	1643
Preston d.	1153	1158	1241	1241	1253	1255	1258	1341	1353	1358	1402	1441	1453	1458	1541	1541	1553	1558	1558	1641	1641	1653	1653	1658
Lancaster d.	1208	1214	|	1255	1308	1310	1314	1355	1408	1414	|	1455	1508	1514	|	1555	1608	1614	1614	1655	1655	1708	1708	1714
Oxenholme d.	1221	1229	|	1308	1322	1325	1329	1408	|	|	|	|	1522	1529	1606	1610	|	1629	1629	|	1709	1722	1722	1729
Penrith d.	|	|	1328	|	|	|	1354	|	1443	1451	|	1530	|	1554	1631	|	1644	|	1654	1730	1735	|	1747	1754
Carlisle d.	1301	1308	1345	1347	1401	1403	1411	1447	1459	1508	1508	1546	1602	1611	1647	1648	1701	1711	1711	1747	1751	1802	1806	1811
Lockerbie d.	|	1327	|	|	|	|	1430	|	|	1527	1527	|	|	1630	|	|	|	1730	1730	|	|	|	|	1830
Haymarket a.	1412	|	|	|	|	|	1534s	|	1616	|	|	|	|	1729s	|	|	1814	|	|	|	|	|	|	1931s
Edinburgh Waverley a.	1422	|	|	|	|	|	1540	|	1622	|	|	|	|	1736	|	|	1822	|	|	|	|	|	|	1940
Glasgow Central a.	...	1429	1501	1501	1517	1517	...	1601	...	1627	1627	1701	1717	...	1801	1801	...	1830	1830	1901	1915	1916	1923	...

	⚒	⚒ ◐	Ⓐ	⑥	Ⓐ	⑥	⚒ ◐	⚒	Ⓐ A	Ⓐ	Ⓐ	⑥	Ⓐ ◐	⑥ ◐	Ⓐ	⚒	Ⓐ ◐	⑥ ◐	⑥	Ⓐ	⑤	Ⓐ	⑥	⚒ ◐
London Euston 150 d.	1530	1443	...	...	1630	1630	1543	...	1633	1657	1730	1730	1643	1643	1757	1830	1743	1743	...	...	1846	1930	1930	1843
Milton Keynes 150 d.	|	1513	...	...	|	|	1613	...	|	|	|	|	1713	1713	|	|	1813u	1813	...	...	1919	|	|	1913
Birmingham New Street 150 d.	|	1615	...	...	|	|	1715	...	|	|	|	|	1815	1815	|	|	1915	1915	...	...	|	|	|	2015
Wolverhampton 150 d.	|	1637	...	...	|	|	1737	...	|	|	|	|	1837	1837	|	|	1937	1937	...	...	|	|	|	2037
Crewe 150 d.	|	1709	...	...	|	|	1809	...	1820	|	|	|	1909	1909	|	|	2009	2009	...	...	2042s	|	2105	2116
Warrington Bank Quay d.	1714	1727	...	...	1815	1814	1827	...	1837	1850	1914	1914	1927	1927	1950	2014	2027	2027	...	...	2101s	2116	2123	...
Manchester Airport ✈ d.	|	|	1700	1700	|	|	|	1800	|	|	|	|	|	|	|	|	|	|	2000	2000	|	|	|	...
Manchester Piccadilly d.	|	|	1715	1715	|	|	|	1815	|	|	|	|	|	|	|	|	|	|	2016	2015	|	|	|	...
Wigan North Western d.	1725	1738	|	1743	1826	1825	1838	1843	1848	1901	1925	1925	1938	1938	2001	2025	2038	2038	|	2043	2112s	2127	2133	...
Preston d.	1741	1753	1758	1758	1843	1841	1853	1858	1902	1915	1941	1941	1953	1954	2015	2041	2053	2057	2058	2058	2131	2142	2149	...
Lancaster d.	1755	1808	1814	1814	1858	1855	1908	1914	...	1930	1955	1955	2008	...	2031	2055	2108	...	2113	2114	...	2157	...	...
Oxenholme d.	1808	1823	1829	1829	|	1908	1921	1929	...	1945	2008	2008	|	...	...	2110	2123	...	...	2129	...	2210	...	...
Penrith d.	|	1848	1854	1854	1932	1934	|	1954	...	2010	|	2034	2045	...	...	2135	|	...	...	2154	...	2235	...	...
Carlisle d.	1847	1904	1911	1911	1948	1951	2001	2011	...	2025	2047	2051	2102	...	...	2150	2202	...	...	2211	...	2251	...	...
Lockerbie d.	|	|	1930	1930	|	|	|	|	...	2044	|	|	|	...	...	2209	|	...	...	2230	...	|	...	...
Haymarket a.	|	2013	|	|	|	|	|	2130s	...	|	|	|	2213	...	...	|	|	...	...	2328s	...	|	...	...
Edinburgh Waverley a.	|	2023	|	|	|	|	|	2138	...	|	|	|	2222	...	...	|	|	...	...	2337	...	|	...	...
Glasgow Central a.	2001	...	2034	2034	2101	2101	2117	...	...	2148	2202	2201	...	...	...	2311	2317	...	...	...	...	0005	...	...

	Ⓐ	⑥ c	Ⓐ ◐	Ⓐ	Ⓐ		⑦	⑦	⑦		⑦	⑦	⑦	⑦	⑦	⑦	⑦	⑦	⑦	⑦	⑦	⑦	⑦	⑦
London Euston 150 d.	2030	2031	1943	...	2110	⑦	...	...	...	...	...	0845	...	...	0945	...	...	1045	...	...	1228	...	...	1328
Milton Keynes 150 d.	|	|	2013	...	|		...	...	...	...	...	0933	...	...	1033	...	...	1133	...	...	|	...	...	|
Birmingham New Street 150 d.	|	|	2115	...	|		0845	0920	...	...	...	|	1020	...	|	1120	...	|	1220	...	|	1320	...	|
Wolverhampton 150 d.	|	|	2137	...	|		0904	0937	...	...	...	|	1037	...	|	1137	...	|	1237	...	|	1337	...	|
Crewe 150 d.	|	2231	2218	...	2259		0937	1009	...	...	1027	1057	1109	...	1157	1209	...	1258	1309	...	|	1409	...	|
Warrington Bank Quay d.	2223	2248	2235	...	2321		0954	1027	...	...	1043	1113	1127	...	1214	1227	...	1315	1327	...	1416	1427	...	1516
Manchester Airport ✈ d.	|	|	|	2200	|		|	|	1000	...	|	|	|	1100	|	|	1200	|	|	1300	|	|	1400	|
Manchester Piccadilly d.	|	|	|	2216	|		|	|	1015	...	|	|	|	1115	|	|	1215	|	|	1315	|	|	1415	|
Wigan North Western d.	2234	2302	2246	2255	2332		1006	1038	1042	...	1054	1124	1138	1143	1225	1238	1243	1326	1338	1343	1427	1438	1443	1527
Preston d.	2253	2317	2300	2313	2350		1019	1102e	1106e	...	1119f	1139	1153	1158	1240	1253	1258	1342	1353	1358	1442	1453	1457	1542
Lancaster d.	...	...	...	2328	...		...	1118	1123	...	1136	1154	1208	1214	1255	1308	1314	1357	1408	1414	1458	1509	1514	1558
Oxenholme d.	...	...	...	...	...		...	1133	1138	...	...	1208	1224	1229	1308	1322	1329	1410	|	1429	|	1524	1528	1611
Penrith d.	...	...	...	...	...		...	|	1202	...	...	1234	|	|	1334	|	1354	1436	1445	1454	1532	|	1553	|
Carlisle d.	...	...	...	...	...		...	1212	1223	...	...	1249	1303	1309	1350	1402	1411	1452	1503	1511	1548	1603	1611	1649
Lockerbie d.	...	...	...	...	...		...	|	1242	...	...	|	|	1327	|	|	1430	|	|	|	|	|	1629	|
Haymarket a.	...	...	...	...	...		...	|	1343s	...	...	|	1414	|	|	|	1528s	|	1614	|	|	|	1728s	|
Edinburgh Waverley a.	...	...	...	...	...		...	|	1348	...	...	|	1419	|	|	|	1535	|	1620	|	|	|	1735	|
Glasgow Central a.	...	...	...	...	...		...	1327	...	...	...	1402	...	1430	1502	1515	...	1604	...	1628	1701	1714	...	1801

	⑦ ◐	⑦	⑦	⑦ ◐	⑦	⑦	⑦ ◐	⑦	⑦	⑦ ◐	⑦	⑦	⑦ ◐	⑦ h	⑦ k	⑦ ◐h	⑦ ◐k	⑦ a	⑦ k	⑦ b	⑦ ◐	⑦	⑦ ◐	⑦
London Euston 150 d.	1240	...	1428	1340	...	1528	1440	...	1628	1540	...	1728	1640	1828	1828	1740	1740	1928	1928	1928	1840	2025	1940	2050
Milton Keynes 150 d.	1313	...	|	1413	...	|	1513	...	|	1613	...	|	1713	|	|	1813	1813	|	|	|	1913	|	2013	2137
Birmingham New Street 150 d.	1415	...	|	1515	...	|	1615	...	|	1715	...	|	1815	|	|	1915	1915	|	|	|	2015	|	2115	|
Wolverhampton 150 d.	1437	...	|	1537	...	|	1637	...	|	1737	...	|	1837	|	|	1937	1937	|	|	|	2037	|	2137	|
Crewe 150 d.	1509	...	|	1609	...	|	1709	...	|	1809	...	|	1909	|	|	2009	2009	|	|	|	2110	2213	2217	2251
Warrington Bank Quay d.	1527	...	1616	1627	...	1716	1727	...	1816	1827	...	1917	1927	2016	2016	2027	2027	2116	2116	2116	...	2230	2236	2308
Manchester Airport ✈ d.	|	1500	|	|	1600	|	|	1700	|	|	1800	|	|	|	|	|	|	|	|	|	...	|	|	|
Manchester Piccadilly d.	|	1515	|	|	1616	|	|	1715	|	|	1815	|	|	|	|	|	|	|	|	|	...	|	|	|
Wigan North Western d.	1538	1543	1627	1638	1643	1727	1738	1743	1827	1838	1843	1928	1938	2027	2027	2038	2038	2127	2127	2127	...	2241	2247	2319
Preston d.	1553	1558	1642	1653	1658	1742	1753	1758	1842	1853	1858	1942	1953	2042	2042	2053	2053	2142	2142	2142	...	2255	2301	2339
Lancaster d.	1608	1614	1657	1708	1714	1757	1809	1814	1857	1908	1914	1957	2008	2057	2057	2108	2108	2157	2157	2157	...	...	...	...
Oxenholme d.	|	1628	|	1723	1729	1811	1823	1829	1911	1922	1929	2012	|	2111	2111	2123	2123	2211	2211	2211	...	...	...	...
Penrith d.	1645	|	1732	|	1754	|	1848	1854	1936	|	1954	2037	2045	2136	2136	|	|	2236	2236	2236	...	...	...	...
Carlisle d.	1702	1708	1748	1803	1811	1849	1904	1917	1953	2001	2011	2051	2102	2152	2152	2202	2202	2252	2252	2252	...	...	...	...
Lockerbie d.	|	1727	|	|	1830	|	|	1936	|	|	2030	|	|	|	|	2221	2221	|	|	|	...	...	...	...
Haymarket a.	1811	|	|	|	1929s	|	2014	|	|	|	2128s	|	2214	|	|	|	|	|	|	|	...	...	...	...
Edinburgh Waverley a.	1818	|	|	|	1937	|	2022	|	|	|	2134	|	2220	|	|	|	|	|	|	|	...	...	...	...
Glasgow Central a.	...	1828	1900	1912	...	1959	...	2038	2103	2111	...	2201	...	2305	2313	2320	2329	0001	0016	0026	...	...	...	...

A – To Blackpool North (a. 1931).
W – To Windermere (Table **158**).

a – To Jan. 1 and from Apr. 2.
b – Jan. 8 - Feb. 12.

c – To Dec. 31 and from Feb. 18.
e – Arrives 10 - 11 minutes earlier.
f – Arrives 7 minutes earlier.
h – To Feb. 12 and from Apr. 2.
k – Feb. 19 - Mar. 26.

s – Calls to set down only.

◐ – Via Table **150**.

151 GLASGOW and EDINBURGH - PRESTON - MANCHESTER, BIRMINGHAM and LONDON

TP, VT

km		⚒	Ⓐ	⑥	Ⓐ B	Ⓐ	Ⓐ	⑥	⑥ ◐	Ⓐ	⑥	⚒	Ⓐ ◐	⑥	⚒ ◐	⚒	⚒	⚒ ◐	⚒	⚒	⑤2	⚒ ◐	⚒
	Glasgow Central d.		...	...	...	...	0428	0426	...	0422	...	0540	...	...	0550	...	0630	...	0709	0735	...	0800	...
	Edinburgh Waverley d.		...	...	...	...	|	|	...	|	...	|	...	...	|	0615	|	0652	|	|	...	|	0812
	Haymarket d.		...	...	...	...	|	|	...	|	...	|	...	...	|	0619u	|	0656	|	|	..	|	0816u
	Lockerbie d.		...	...	...	...	|	|	...	0550	...	|	...	...	|	|	0725	|	0808	|	...	|	0911
	Carlisle d.		...	...	...	...	0544	0544	...	0622	...	0649	...	...	0702	0733	0746	0807	0833	0849	...	0910	0933
	Penrith d.		...	...	...	...	0558	0558	...	0642	...	|	...	...	0717	0748	0800	0822	0848	|	...	|	0948
	Oxenholme d.		...	...	...	...	0621	0621	...	0709	...	0724	...	...	0741	0812	0823	|	0912	0923	...	|	1012
	Lancaster d.		0513	0538	...	...	0636	0636	...	0724	0724	0738	0658	0658	0756	0827	0838	0857	0927	0938	...	0956	1027
0	**Preston** d.		0533	0558	0600	0617	0657	0657	0617	0744	0744	0758	0717	0717	0817	0847	0858	0917	0947	0958	0952	1017	1047
24	Wigan North Western d.		0545	0609	0611	0628	0709	0709	0628	0756	0756	0809	0728	0728	0828	0858	0909	0928	0959	1009	1004	1028	1059
57	**Manchester** Piccadilly a.		|	|	|	|	|	|	|	0827	0827	|	|	|	|	0928	|	|	1028	|	|	|	1128
73	**Manchester** Airport ✈ a.		|	|	|	|	|	|	|	0847	0848	|	|	|	|	0947	|	|	1047	|	|	|	1147
—	Warrington Bank Quay d.		0556	0620	0622	0639	0719	0719	0639	...	...	0820	0739	0739	0839	...	0920	0939	...	1020	1016	1039	...
0	Crewe 150 a.		|	|	0642	0659	|	|	0657	...	...	|	0757	0757	0857	...	|	0958	...	|	1038	1057	...
63	Wolverhampton 150 a.		|	|	|	0735	|	|	0732	...	...	|	0833	0833	0933	...	|	1033	...	|	|	1133	...
82	**Birmingham** New St 150 a.		|	|	|	0801	|	|	0805	...	...	|	0905	0905	1005	...	|	1105	...	|	|	1205	...
	Milton Keynes 150 a.		|	0738	|	...	|	|	0858	...	...	|	0958	...	1058	...	|	1159	...	|	|	1258	...
	London Euston 150 a.		0758	0817	0834	...	0907	0913	0935	...	...	1013	1032	...	1134	...	1116	1234	...	1213	1231	1334	...

	⚒	Ⓐ ◐	⑥ ◐	⑥ W	⑥	Ⓐ	Ⓐ W	⚒	⚒ ◐	Ⓐ	⑥	⚒	⚒ ◐	Ⓐ	⑥	⚒	⚒ ◐	Ⓐ	⑥	⚒	⚒ ◐	⚒	⚒
Glasgow Central d.	0840	...	...	...	0906	0906	...	0940	1000	...	...	1040	...	1109	1109	1140	1200	...	...	1240	...	1309	1340
Edinburgh Waverley d.	|	0851	0852	...	|	|	...	|	|	1011	1012	|	1052	|	|	|	|	1212	1212	|	1252	|	|
Haymarket d.	|	0857	0857	...	|	|	...	|	|	1016u	1016u	|	1057	|	|	|	|	1216u	1216u	|	1257	|	|
Lockerbie d.	|	|	|	...	1007	1012	...	|	|	1110	1111	|	|	1207	1207	|	|	1311	1311	|	|	1408	|
Carlisle d.	0949	1008	1009	...	1030	1033	...	1049	1111	1133	1133	1149	1208	1231	1231	1249	1311	1333	1333	1349	1408	1430	1449
Penrith d.	1003	|	|	...	1045	1048	...	|	1125	1148	1148	|	|	1247	1247	1303	|	|	1348	|	1422	1445	|
Oxenholme d.	|	1042	1043	1101	1109	|	1113	1123	|	1212	1212	1223	1243	1312	|	|	|	1410	1412	1424	|	1509	1523
Lancaster d.	1038	1057	1057	1117	1124	1124	1132	1138	|	1227	1227	1238	1257	1327	1327	1338	1356	1425	1427	1439	1456	1525	1538
Preston d.	1058	1117	1117	1137	1147	1147	1151	1158	1217	1247	1247	1258	1317	1347	1347	1358	1417	1447	1447	1458	1517	1547	1558
Wigan North Western d.	1109	1128	1128	...	|	1159	...	1209	1228	1258	1259	1309	1328	1359	1359	1409	1428	1459	1459	1509	1528	1559	1609
Manchester Piccadilly a.	|	|	|	...	1228	1228	...	|	|	1328	1328	|	|	1428	1428	|	|	1528	1528	|	|	1628	|
Manchester Airport ✈ a.	|	|	|	...	1247	1247	...	|	|	1347	1347	|	|	1447	1447	|	|	1547	1547	|	|	1647	|
Warrington Bank Quay d.	1120	1139	1139	...	...	...	...	1220	1239	...	...	1320	1339	...	...	1420	1439	...	...	1520	1539	...	1620
Crewe 150 a.	|	1157	1157	...	...	...	...	|	1257	...	...	|	1357	...	...	|	1457	...	...	|	1557	...	|
Wolverhampton 150 a.	|	1232	1233	...	...	...	...	|	1333	...	...	|	1433	...	...	|	1533	...	...	|	1633	...	|
Birmingham New St 150 a.	|	1305	1305	...	...	...	...	|	1405	...	...	|	1505	...	...	|	1605	...	...	|	1705	...	|
Milton Keynes 150 a.	|	1358	1358	...	...	...	...	|	1458	...	...	|	1558	...	...	|	1658	...	...	|	1758	...	|
London Euston 150 a.	1313	1433	1433	...	...	...	...	1413	1534	...	...	1514	1634	...	...	1613	1733	...	...	1713	1834	...	1813

	⚒ ◐	⚒	⚒	Ⓐ ◐	⑥ ◐	Ⓐ	⑥	Ⓐ	⑥	Ⓐ ◐	⑥ ◐	⚒	Ⓐ	⑥	⑥ W	Ⓐ W	Ⓐ ◐	⑥ ◐	⚒	Ⓐ	⑥	Ⓐ	⑥
Glasgow Central d.	1400	...	1440	...	...	1509	1509	1540	1540	1600	1600	...	1640	1640	...	...	...	...	1709	1730	1740	1740	1800
Edinburgh Waverley d.	|	1418	|	1451	1452	|	|	|	|	|	|	1612	|	|	...	...	1652	1652	|	|	|	|	|
Haymarket d.	|	1422u	|	1458	1457	|	|	|	|	|	|	1616u	|	|	...	...	1657	1657	|	|	|	|	|
Lockerbie d.	|	1517	|	|	|	1608	1608	|	|	|	|	1710	|	|	...	...	|	|	1808	|	1832	1835	|
Carlisle d.	1510	1540	1549	1608	1608	1630	1630	1648	1649	1710	1710	1733	1753	1752	...	...	1808	1807	1830	1846	1852	1857	1910
Penrith d.	|	|	|	1621	1622	1645	1645	1703	1703	|	|	1748	1807	|	...	...	|	|	1845	1900	1906	|	|
Oxenholme d.	1544	1616	1624	|	|	1714	1709	|	|	1744	1744	1812	1831	1826	1831	1834	1842	1843	1909	1923	1929	1932	|
Lancaster d.	|	1630	1638	1657	1657	1729	1725	1737	1738	|	|	1827	1845	1841	1847	1903a	1859	1858	1925	1937	1944	1947	1957
Preston d.	1617	1650	1658	1717	1717	1747	1746	1758	1758	1817	1819	1847	1905	1901	1906	1926	1917	1918	1947	1958	2004	2007	2017
Wigan North Western d.	1628	|	1709	1728	1728	1759	1759	1809	1809	1828	1830	1859	1916	1912	...	...	1931	1929	1959	2009	2015	2019	2028
Manchester Piccadilly a.	|	1730	|	|	|	1828	1828	|	|	|	|	1929	|	|	...	...	|	|	2029	|	|	|	|
Manchester Airport ✈ a.	|	1748	|	|	|	1847	1847	|	|	|	|	1947	|	|	...	...	|	|	2047	|	|	|	|
Warrington Bank Quay d.	1639	...	1720	1739	1739	...	...	1820	1820	1839	1841	...	1927	1923	...	...	1941	1940	...	2020	2026	2032	2039
Crewe 150 a.	1657	...	|	1757	1757	...	...	|	|	1857	1900	...	|	|	...	...	2000	1959	...	2039	2045	2051	2059
Wolverhampton 150 a.	1733	...	|	1833	1832	...	...	|	|	1933	1934	...	|	|	...	...	2038	2032	...	|	|	2130	2132
Birmingham New St 150 a.	1805	...	|	1905	1905	...	...	|	|	2005	2005	...	|	|	...	...	2105	2105	...	|	|	2158b	2155
Milton Keynes 150 a.	1858	...	|	1958	2005	...	...	|	|	2058	2104	...	2045	2042	...	...	2158	2204	...	2148	2151	...	...
London Euston 150 a.	1933	...	1915	2034	2055	...	...	2012	2019	2139	2157	...	2125	2138	...	...	2243	2255	...	2225	2245	...	...

	⚒	Ⓐ	⑥	Ⓐ	⑥	Ⓐ	Ⓐ	⑦	⑦	⑦	⑦	⑦	⑦	⑦	⑦	⑦ ◐	⑦	⑦	⑦ ◐	⑦	⑦	⑦ ◐	⑦
Glasgow Central d.	...	1840	1840	...	...	2010	...		...	...	...	...	...	...	0938	...	...	1038	...	1116	1138	1155	...
Edinburgh Waverley d.	1813	|	|	1852	1852	|	2014		...	...	...	...	...	...	|	...	1012	|	1051	|	|	|	1212
Haymarket d.	1817u	|	|	1856	1856	|	2018u		...	...	...	...	...	...	|	...	1016u	|	1055	|	|	|	1216u
Lockerbie d.	1912	|	|	|	|	2105	2112		...	...	...	...	...	...	|	...	1110	|	|	|	|	|	1310
Carlisle d.	1934	1949	1948	2007	2009	2126	2135		...	...	...	...	...	...	1050	...	1133	1151	1207	1233	1249	1307	1333
Penrith d.	1949	|	2002	|	2024	2139	|		...	...	...	...	...	...	1104	...	1148	1205	|	1248	|	|	1348
Oxenholme d.	2013	2024	2025	2042	2047	2203	2212		...	...	...	...	...	...	1127	...	1212	1229	1243	1312	1323	|	1412
Lancaster d.	2028	2038	2040	2056	2102	2218	2227		...	...	...	...	...	1124	1142	1158	1227	1243	1257	1327	1338	1353	1427
Preston d.	2048	2058	2100	2117	2122	2240	2247	⑦	0900	1000	1017	1058	1117	1147	1202	1217	1247	1304	1317	1347	1358	1417	1447
Wigan North Western d.	2101	2109	2111	2128	2133	2252	2259		0911	1012	1028	1109	1128	|	1213	1228	1259	1315	1328	1359	1409	1428	1459
Manchester Piccadilly a.	2130	|	|	|	|	|	2328		|	|	|	|	|	1227	|	|	1328	|	|	1429	|	|	1528
Manchester Airport ✈ a.	2147	|	|	|	|	|	2347		|	|	|	|	|	1247	|	|	1347	|	|	1447	|	|	1547
Warrington Bank Quay d.	...	2120	2122	2139	2144	2303	...		0922	1022	1039	1120	1139	...	1224	1239	...	1326	1339	...	1420	1439	...
Crewe 150 a.	...	|	2141	2159	2204	2326	...		0941	1041	1059	|	1159	...	|	1259	...	|	1359	...	|	1458	...
Wolverhampton 150 a.	...	|	2222	2232	2239	...	...		|	|	1131	|	1232	...	|	1332	...	|	1432	...	|	1534	...
Birmingham New St 150 a.	...	|	2248	2302b	2259	...	...		|	|	1150	|	1250	...	|	1406	...	|	1506	...	|	1606	...
Milton Keynes 150 a.	...	2240	...	...	...	...	...		1107	1207	...	|	...	...	|	1458	...	|	1558	...	|	1658	...
London Euston 150 a.	...	2339	...	...	...	...	...		1206	1247	...	1322	...	...	1416	1539	...	1521	1639	...	1613	1738	...

	⑦	⑦ ◐	⑦	⑦	⑦ ◐	⑦	⑦	⑦ ◐	⑦	⑦	⑦ ◐		⑦	⑦	⑦	⑦	⑦	⑦	⑦	⑦	⑦ W	⑦	⑦
Glasgow Central d.	1238	...	1316	1338	1355	...	1438	...	1516	1538	1557	...	...	1638	...	1716	1738	...	1838	...	...	...	2008
Edinburgh Waverley d.	|	1251	|	|	|	1412	|	1451	|	|	|	...	1612	|	1651	|	|	1812	|	1851	...	1957	|
Haymarket d.	|	1255	|	|	|	1416u	|	1455	|	|	|	...	1616u	|	1655	|	|	1816u	|	1856	...	2001u	|
Lockerbie d.	|	|	|	|	|	1510	|	|	1615	|	|	...	1710	|	|	|	1832	1910	|	|	...	2055	2103
Carlisle d.	1349	1407	1436	1449	1511	1533	1549	1607	1636	1649	1709	...	1733	1751	1807	1833	1852	1933	1946	2007	...	2117	2124
Penrith d.	|	1422	|	|	|	1548	|	1622	|	1703	|	...	1748	1805	|	1848	1906	1948	|	2022	...	|	2139
Oxenholme d.	1423	|	1512	1523	1545	1612	1623	|	1712	|	1744	...	1812	1828	1842	1912	1929	2012	2022	|	2101	2153	2203
Lancaster d.	1438	1457	1527	1538	|	1627	1638	1657	1727	1738	|	...	1827	1843	1857	1927	1944	2027	2036	2057	2121	2208	2218
Preston d.	1458	1517	1547	1558	1617	1647	1658	1717	1747	1758	1817	...	1847	1903	1917	1947	2004	2047	2056	2117	2142	2228	2238
Wigan North Western d.	1509	1528	1559	1609	1629	1659	1709	1729	1759	1809	1828	...	1859	1914	1928	2001	2015	2059	2108	2129	...	2240	2252
Manchester Piccadilly a.	|	|	1629	|	|	1728	|	|	1830	|	|	...	1928	|	|	2030	|	2128	|	|	...	2309	|
Manchester Airport ✈ a.	|	|	1647	|	|	1747	|	|	1847	|	|	...	1947	|	|	2047	|	2147	|	|	...	2326	|
Warrington Bank Quay d.	1520	1539	...	1620	1640	...	1720	1740	...	1820	1839	...	...	1925	1939	...	2026	...	2120	2139	...	...	2303
Crewe 150 a.	|	1559	...	|	1659	...	|	1759	...	|	1858	...	...	|	1959	...	2045	...	2139	2159	...	...	2321
Wolverhampton 150 a.	|	1632	...	|	1732	...	|	1833	...	|	1934	...	...	|	2033	...	|	...	2214	2232	...	...	...
Birmingham New St 150 a.	|	1706	...	|	1805	...	|	1906	...	|	2006	...	...	|	2051	...	|	...	2232	2255	...	...	...
Milton Keynes 150 a.	|	1758	...	|	1858	...	|	1958	...	|	2059	...	...	|	...	...	2152	...	...	...	...	...	...
London Euston 150 a.	1711	1838	...	1814	1939	...	1911	2039	...	2013	2148	...	...	2122	...	...	2255	...	...	...	...	...	...

B – From Blackpool North (d. 0525).
W – From Windermere (Table **158**).

a – Arrives 9 minutes earlier.

b – Arrives 4 – 5 mintes earlier on Ⓐ to Feb. 10 and from Mar. 17 (also ⑤ Feb. 17 - Mar. 17).
u – Calls to pick up only.

◐ – Via Table **150**.

EM 2nd class CREWE - STOKE - DERBY 155

For other trains Crewe - Stoke on Trent and v.v. see Table **142**

km		Ⓐ	Ⓐ	Ⓐ	Ⓐ		Ⓐ	Ⓐ		⑥	⑥	⑥	⑥		⑥	⑥		⑦	⑦	⑦	⑦	⑦	⑦	⑦	⑦	⑦
0	**Crewe** d.		0607	0658	0807	and at	1907	2045	...		0607	0707	0807	and at	1907	2045	...		1404	1505	1608	1708	1808	1908	2015	2116
24	**Stoke on Trent** d.		0633	0724	0833	the same	1933	2118	...		0633	0733	0833	the same	1933	2119			1429	1532	1635	1735	1835	1935	2040	2142
33	Blythe Bridge d.		0646	0736	0845	minutes	1945	2130	...		0645	0745	0845	minutes	1945	2131			1441	1544	1647	1747	1847	1947	2052	2154
51	Uttoxeter d.		0658	0749	0858	past each	1958	2142	...		0658	0758	0858	past each	1958	2144			1454	1557	1659	1759	1859	1959	2105	2206
82	**Derby** a.		0725	0816	0926	hour until	2025	2208	...		0724	0826	0926	hour until	2022	2210			1519	1624	1727	1828	1928	2028	2134	2236

	Ⓐ	Ⓐ	Ⓐ	Ⓐ		Ⓐ	Ⓐ		⑥	⑥	⑥	⑥		⑥	⑥		⑦	⑦	⑦	⑦	⑦	⑦	⑦	⑦
Derby d.		0640	0740	0842	and at	1942	2042	...		0640	0740	0842	and at	1942	2042	...		1438	1538	1638	1741	1842	1941	2040
Uttoxeter d.		0705	0807	0907	the same	2007	2107	...		0707	0807	0907	the same	2007	2107	...		1503	1603	1703	1806	1906	2006	2105
Blythe Bridge d.		0719	0821	0921	minutes	2021	2121	...		0721	0821	0921	minutes	2021	2121	...		1517	1617	1717	1820	1920	2020	2119
Stoke on Trent a.		0732	0832	0933	past each	2033	2133	...		0734	0832	0933	past each	2033	2133	...		1530	1631	1730	1833	1934	2034	2133
Crewe a.		0759	0859	1001	hour until	2101	2159	...		0759	0859	1001	hour until	2101	2201	...		1600	1700	1802	1901	2003	2100	2200

NT 2nd Class only MANCHESTER - PRESTON - BLACKPOOL 156

For other trains Manchester - Preston and v.v. see Tables **151** and **157**

km		Ⓐ	Ⓐ	Ⓐ	Ⓐ	Ⓐ	Ⓐ	Ⓐ	Ⓐ		Ⓐ	Ⓐ	Ⓐ	Ⓐ	Ⓐ	⑤	①–④	⑤	①–④	①–④	⑤	①-④	⑥	⑥	⑥	⑥	⑥
0	**Manchester** Airport d.		0527	0618	0757	0825	0929	1029	1129	and at	1629	1729	1829	1929	2029	2129	2129	2229	2229	2330	2330	🚌		0527	0629	0757	0929
16	**Manchester** Piccadilly d.		0544	0633	0816	0846	0946	1046	1146	the same	1646	1746	1846	1946	2046	2146	2146	2246	2246	2346	2346	2355		0544	0646	0816	0946
34	Bolton d.		0603	0653	0833	0907	1007	1107	1207	minutes	1706	1808	1907	2007	2107	2207	2207	2307	2307**d**	|	2359**s**	0020**s**		0603	0707	0833	1007
66	**Preston** a.		0632	0722	0903	0937	1036	1136	1237	past each	1733	1838	1939	2036	2136	2233	2238	2337	2337	0031	0036	0055**s**		0633	0739	0902	1035
66	**Preston** d.		0635	0725	0905	0939	1038	1138	1238	hour until	1735	1842	1941	2038	2138	2238	...	2339	...	...	0038	|		0635	0741	0904	1038
94	**Blackpool** North a.		0703	0754	0934	1004	1104	1204	1304	♧	1803	1911	2004	2104	2204	2303	...	0004	...	...	0104	0135		0704	0809	0933	1103

	⑥	⑥	⑥	⑥	⑥	⑥	⑥	⑥	⑥	⑥	⑥	⑥	⑥	⑦	⑦🚌	⑦🚌	⑦	⑦	⑦	⑦	⑦		⑦	⑦	⑦	⑦	⑦🚌
Manchester Airport d.	1029	1129	1229	1329	1429	1529	1629	1729	1829	1929	2029	2129	2229		0005	0530	0848	0929	1029	1129	1229	and at	1929	2029	2129	2229	2330
Manchester Piccadilly d.	1046	1146	1246	1346	1446	1546	1646	1746	1846	1946	2046	2147	2246		0030	0555	0904	0947	1046	1146	1246	the same	1946	2046	2146	2246	2346
Bolton d.	1107	1207	1307	1407	1507	1607	1707	1807	1907	2007	2107	2207	2307		0055**s**	0620**s**	0924	1007	1106	1207	1307	minutes	2007	2107	2208	2308	|
Preston a.	1136	1235	1336	1436	1536	1636	1733	1839	1937	2036	2133	2236	2338		0130**s**	0655**s**	0957	1037	1136	1237	1336	past each	2037	2134	2243	2346	0036
Preston d.	1138	1238	1340	1438	1538	1637	1738	1842	1939	2038	2138	2238	2339**c**		|	|	...	1039	1138	1239	1338	hour until	2039	*2220*	...	2348	...
Blackpool North a.	1204	1303	1404	1504	1604	1706	1806	1912	2004	2104	2203	2304	0004**c**		0210	0735	...	1102	1204	1304	1403	♧	2104	*2247*	...	0017	...

	Ⓐ	Ⓐ	Ⓐ	Ⓐ	Ⓐ	Ⓐ	Ⓐ		Ⓐ	Ⓐ	Ⓐ	Ⓐ	Ⓐ	Ⓐ	Ⓐ	Ⓐ	Ⓐ	Ⓐ	⑥	⑥	⑥	⑥	⑥	⑥	⑥	⑥	⑥
Blackpool North d.		...	...	...	0635	0753	0840	and at	1440	1540	1635	1712	1753	1840	1940	2040	2140	2245		0337	0446	0638	0740	0835	0940	1040	1140
Preston a.		...	...	...	0703	0818	0904	the same	1504	1604	1704	1742	1819	1904	2005	2103	2204	2309		|	0509	0705	0807	0859	1004	1104	1204
Preston d.		0402	0512	0641	0705	0820	0905	minutes	1505	1609	1705	1743	1821	1909	2010	2105	2205	2310		0402**u**	0512	0707	0809	0905	1012	1105	1205
Bolton d.		|	|	0708	0734	0857	0934	past each	1534	1635	1734	1813	1855	1934	2036	2134	2234**b**	2339**b**		0435**u**	0540	0734	0834	0934	1035	1134	1234
Manchester Piccadilly a.		0444	0600	0727	0757	0918	0957	hour until	1557	1656	1757	1837	1920	1957	2058	2157	2259	2358		0452	0601	0756	0857	0957	1056	1157	1257
Manchester Airport a.		0502	0617	0747	0818	*0947*	1023	♧	1617	1717	1817	1855	*1947*	2022	2117	2215	2316	0024		0508	0618	0817	0923	1022	1123	1223	1322

	⑥	⑥	⑥	⑥	⑥	⑥	⑥	⑥	⑥	⑥	⑥	⑦	⑦🚌	⑦🚌	⑦	⑦	⑦	⑦	⑦	⑦	⑦	⑦		⑦	⑦	⑦	⑦
Blackpool North d.	1239	1340	1440	1540	1635	1735	1840	1940	2040	2140	2245		0320	0520	...	...	1044	1140	1240	1340	1435	1540	and at	1940	2040	2140	...
Preston a.	1303	1404	1504	1604	1704	1804	1904	2003	2104	2204	2309		|	|	...	...	1108	1204	1304	1404	1459	1604	the same	2004	2104	2204	...
Preston d.	1305	1412	1509	1605	1705	1805	1912	2005	2105	2205	2310		0400**u**	0600**u**	0905	1005	1109	1205	1305	1405	1509	1605	minutes	2008	2105	2205	2335
Bolton d.	1334	1435	1535	1634	1734	1834	1935	2034	2134	2234	2339		0435**u**	0635**u**	0934	1034	1135	1234	1334	1434	1535	1634	past each	2037	2134	|	|
Manchester Piccadilly a.	1357	1458	1556	1657	1757	1859	1957	2057	2157	2257	2358		0500**u**	0700**u**	0957	1057	1156	1257	1357	1457	1556	1657	hour until	2100	2157	2257	0026
Manchester Airport a.	1423	1523	1623	1723	1823	1917	2018	2116	2215	2316	0024		0525	0725	1016	1115	1215	1317	1415	1515	1615	1715	♧	2117	2215	2315	0044

b – ⑤ only.
c – Jan. 7 - Feb. 11.
d – To Dec. 29 and from Mar. 27.
s – Calls to set down only.
u – Calls to pick up only.
♧ – Timings may vary by up to 3 minutes.

NT MANCHESTER - PRESTON - BARROW IN FURNESS 157

For other trains Manchester - Preston / Lancaster and v.v. see Tables **151** and **156**.

km		Ⓐ	Ⓐ2	Ⓐ2	Ⓐ2D	Ⓐ2	Ⓐ2	Ⓐ	Ⓐ2A	Ⓐ	Ⓐ2	Ⓐ2A	Ⓐ	Ⓐ2	Ⓐ2	Ⓐ2	Ⓐ2	Ⓐ	Ⓐ2E	Ⓐ2	Ⓐ	Ⓐ	⑥	⑥	⑥2A	⑥
0	**Manchester** Airport ✈ d.		...	*0558*	...	*0802*	...	0929	...	...	...	...	...	...	...	*1603*	*1700*	1729	...	...	...	2200		*0558*	...	...
16	**Manchester** Piccadilly d.		...	*0615*	...	0831**f**	...	0946	...	...	...	...	...	...	...	1627	1714**f**	1746	...	...	...	2216		*0614*	...	...
34	Bolton d.		...	|	...	0852	...	1007	...	...	...	...	...	...	...	1649	1731	1808	...	...	...	|		|	...	...
66	**Preston** d.		0519	*0658*	...	0927	1004	1048	...	...	...	...	1546	...	...	1728	1805	1847	2006	2109	2147	2313		*0658*	0842	0945
100	Lancaster d.		0542	0733	0848	0947	1025	1105	1219	1320	1437	1533	1602	1648	1720	1748	1826	1903	2026	2129	2203	2329		0733	0902	1001
110	Carnforth d.		0552	0742	0857	0957	1035	1113	1229	1328	1447	1543	1610	1658	1730	1758	1838	1911	2038	2139	2211	2337		0742	0912	1009
119	Arnside d.		0602	0752	0908	1008	1047	1123	1239	1338	1457	1554	1620	1709	1741	1809	1848	1921	2048	2150	2221	2347		0752	0922	1019
124	Grange over Sands d.		0608	0758	0914	1014	1053	1129	1245	1344	1503	1600	1626	1715	1747	1815	1854	1927	2054	2156	2227	2352		0758	0928	1025
140	Ulverston d.		0625	0815	0931	1030	1112	1143	1302	1400	1520	1615	1642	1732	1803	1831	1911	1943	2111	2212	2243	0008		0815	0944	1041
156	**Barrow in Furness** a.		0646	0838	0950	1054	1133	1205	1323	1423	1542	1637	1705	1756	1825	1856	1934	2006	2132	2236	2306	0030		0838	1006	1104

	⑥2A	⑥	⑥2A	⑥	⑥2	⑥	⑥2E	⑥2	⑥	⑥	⑥2E	⑥		⑥	⑦	⑦2		⑦	⑦2	⑦2	⑦2		⑦	⑦2	⑦2	⑦
Manchester Airport ✈ d.	...	...	...	...	...	...	...	...	1629	...	...	2000	...	...		...	...	...	...	...	...	...	1629	...	...	2029
Manchester Piccadilly d.	...	...	...	...	...	...	...	...	1646	...	...	2016	...	...		...	...	...	...	...	...	...	1646	...	...	2046
Bolton d.	...	...	...	...	...	...	...	...	1707	...	...	2034	...	...		...	...	...	...	...	...	...	1707	...	...	2107
Preston d.	...	...	...	1407	...	1546	...	...	1745	1908	2003	2058	...	...		1117	...	1204	1402	1604	...	...	1747	2004	...	2147
Lancaster d.	1119	1223	1332	1423	1520	1602	1700	1731	1801	1929	2023	2114	...	2314		1133	...	1220	1422	1625	1720	...	1803	2024	2103	2203
Carnforth d.	1128	1231	1341	1431	1530	1610	1710	1740	1810	1939	2033	2122	...	2322		1141	...	1228	1432	1635	1730	...	1811	2034	2128	2211
Arnside d.	1139	1241	1352	1440	1540	1620	1721	1752	1820	1949	2044	2132	...	2334		1151	...	1238	1443	1645	1741	...	1821	2044	2138	2226
Grange over Sands d.	1145	1247	1358	1445	1546	1626	1727	1758	1825	1955	2050	2138	...	2339		1157	...	1244	1449	1651	1747	...	1827	2050	2144	2231
Ulverston d.	1201	1303	1414	1458	1603	1642	1744	1816	1842	2012	2106	2154	...	2355		1213	...	1300	1505	1708	1802	...	1843	2107	2200	2247
Barrow in Furness a.	1223	1326	1436	1518	1624	1705	1806	1840	1905	2035	2128	2217	...	0017		1236	...	1323	1529	1731	1826	...	1906	2130	2224	2311

	Ⓐ	Ⓐ	Ⓐ2	Ⓐ2	Ⓐ🍸		Ⓐ2	Ⓐ2A	Ⓐ2	Ⓐ2	Ⓐ2	Ⓐ2	Ⓐ2A	Ⓐ2	Ⓐ2A		Ⓐ2	Ⓐ🍸B	Ⓐ2	Ⓐ	Ⓐ2		⑥	⑥2	⑥	⑥
Barrow in Furness d.		0435	0523	0615	0648	...	0713	0806	0850	1009	1113	1213	1332	1441	1524	...	1610	1720	1803	2015	2143	...		0435	0532	0615
Ulverston d.		0451	0539	0634	0707	...	0731	0827	0908	1028	1132	1232	1350	1457	1543	...	1628	1737	1821	2034	2201	...		0451	0547	0634
Grange over Sands d.		0503	0551	0650	0723	...	0745	0845	0924	1044	1148	1247	1406	1509	1559	...	1644	1752	1837	2050	2217	...		0503	0600	0650
Arnside d.		0509	0557	0656	0729	...	0751	0851	0930	1050	1154	1253	1412	1515	1605	...	1650	1758	1843	2056	2223	...		0509	0606	0656
Carnforth d.		0519	0608	0707	0740	...	0803	0905	0942	1108	1206	1305	1424	1525	1617	...	1702	1809	1856	2107	2236	...		0519	0616	0707
Lancaster a.		0531	0616	0718	0748	...	0813	0913	0952	1118	1215	1314	1434	1533	1628	...	1714	1818	1904	2115	2245	...		0531	0623	0718
Preston a.		...	0639	...	0807	...	...	0937	1024	...	1240	...	...	1553	...	...	...	...	1932	2135	2311	...		...	0642	...
Bolton a.		...	0708	...	0834	...	...	...	...	...	...	...	...	1634	...	...	...	...	...	...	...	...		...	0708	...
Manchester Piccadilly a.		...	0727	...	0856	...	...	...	...	...	...	...	...	1656	...	...	...	...	...	...	...	...		...	0727	...
Manchester Airport ✈ a.		...	0747	...	0916	...	...	...	...	...	...	...	...	1717	...	...	...	...	...	...	...	...		...	0747	...

	⑥2	⑥2	⑥	⑥2C	⑥	⑥2A	⑥		⑥2A	⑥	⑥2	⑥🍸B	⑥2A	⑥	⑥2		⑦	⑦		⑦	⑦2	⑦2	⑦	⑦2	⑦2	⑦2D
Barrow in Furness d.	0707	0808	0850	1009	1120	1211	1333	...	1455	1525	1629	1720	1803	1917	2135	...		0922	...	1023	1210	1310	1348	1612	1815	1911
Ulverston d.	0726	0826	0907	1028	1137	1229	1352	...	1515	1541	1647	1737	1821	1936	2153	...		0941	...	1042	1229	1329	1405	1631	1834	1929
Grange over Sands d.	0742	0842	0922	1044	1152	1245	1408	...	1532	1553	1703	1752	1837	1952	2209	...		0957	...	1058	1245	1345	1419	1647	1850	1945
Arnside d.	0748	0848	0928	1050	1158	1251	1414	...	1539	1559	1709	1758	1843	1958	2215	...		1003	...	1104	1251	1351	1425	1653	1856	1951
Carnforth d.	0800	0900	0939	1102	1209	1303	1425	...	1556	1609	1721	1809	1856	2009	2228	...		1014	...	1115	1304	1404	1437	1706	1909	2004
Lancaster a.	0808	0909	0947	1111	1219	1315	1433	...	1608	1617	1736	1818	1905	2017	2240	...		1024	...	1123	1312	1415	1444	1715	1917	2014
Preston a.	0841	...	1007	...	...	...	1452	...	...	1637	...	...	1931	2037	...	...		...	...	1143	1337	...	1504	1740	1942	...
Bolton a.	...	...	1034	...	...	...	...	...	...	...	...	...	...	...	...	...		...	...	1208	...	...	1534	...	...	...
Manchester Piccadilly a.	...	...	1056	...	...	...	...	...	...	...	...	...	...	...	...	...		...	...	1227	...	...	1556	...	...	...
Manchester Airport ✈ a.	...	...	1121	...	...	...	...	...	...	...	...	...	...	...	...	...		...	...	1247	...	...	1613	...	...	...

A – From / to Carlisle (Table **159**).
B – To Windermere (Table **158**).
C – From Sellafield (Table **159**).
D – To / from Morcambe (Table **174**).
E – To Millom (Table **159**).
f – Manchester **Oxford Road**.

158 PRESTON - OXENHOLME - WINDERMERE

2nd Class NT

km			Ⓐ	Ⓐ	Ⓐ	Ⓐ	Ⓐ	Ⓐ	Ⓐ	Ⓐ	Ⓐ	Ⓐ	Ⓐ	Ⓐ	Ⓐ	Ⓐ	Ⓐ	Ⓐ	Ⓐ		⑥	⑥	⑥	⑥	⑥
															B										M
	Preston 151 d.	Ⓐ	...	...	...	...	...	1029	...	...	...	...	...	...	...	...	...	...	...	⑥	...	...	...	...	0932
	Lancaster 151 d.		0546	...	...	...	...	1100	...	...	...	...	...	...	1821	...	...	...	...		0602	...	...	...	0948
0	**Oxenholme** 151 d.		0623	0733	0826	0911	1033	1120	1226	1333	1422	1534	1622	1734	1838	1934	2022	2115	2218		0622	0721	0826	0911	1004
4	Kendal d.		0628	0737	0830	0915	1037	1125	1230	1337	1426	1538	1626	1738	1843	1938	2026	2119	2222		0627	0725	0830	0915	1009
16	**Windermere** a.		0641	0752	0846	0931	1050	1142	1243	1354	1443	1555	1643	1755	1858	1953	2041	2132	2237		0641	0742	0846	0931	1026

	⑥	⑥	⑥	⑥	⑥	⑥	⑥	⑥	⑥	⑥	⑥				⑦	⑦	⑦	⑦	⑦	⑦	⑦	⑦	⑦	⑦	⑦
								B			🚌				🚌										
Preston 151 d.	1044	...	1248	...	1430	...	1704	...	...	...	...	...	⑦	...	0905	...	...	...	...	...	...	...	...	...	...
Lancaster 151 d.	|	...	1304	...	...	...	1720	1825	...	...	...	...		...	0955	1129	...	...	...	...	...	...	...	...	...
Oxenholme 151 d.	1120	1226	1321	1417	1519	1634	1737	1842	1934	2022	2120	...		...	1040	1145	1227	1335	1421	1535	1621	1733	1841	1927	2016
Kendal d.	1125	1230	1325	1421	1524	1638	1741	1846	1938	2026	2130	...		...	1050	1149	1231	1339	1425	1539	1625	1737	1845	1931	2020
Windermere a.	1142	1243	1341	1436	1541	1655	1756	1901	1953	2041	2205	...		...	1125	1202	1246	1354	1440	1554	1640	1752	1901	1944	2036

		Ⓐ	Ⓐ	Ⓐ	Ⓐ	Ⓐ	Ⓐ	Ⓐ	Ⓐ	Ⓐ	Ⓐ	Ⓐ	Ⓐ	Ⓐ	Ⓐ	Ⓐ	Ⓐ	Ⓐ		⑥	⑥	⑥	⑥	⑥	⑥
Windermere d.	Ⓐ	0645	0756	0850	0947	1056	1147	1247	1358	1458	1600	1649	1803	1906	1958	2050	2140	2245	⑥	0657	0747	0850	0937	1040	1147
Kendal d.		0659	0811	0902	1001	1108	1202	1302	1413	1513	1613	1704	1818	1918	2012	2104	2154	2259		0712	0802	0902	0952	1054	1202
Oxenholme 151 a.		0704	0816	0907	1006	1113	1207	1307	1418	1518	1618	1709	1823	1923	2017	2109	2159	2304		0717	0807	0907	0957	1059	1207
Lancaster 151 a.		...	...	...	...	1131	...	...	...	...	...	...	1854	...	...	...	...	2322		...	...	...	|	1117	...
Preston 151 a.		...	...	...	...	1151	...	...	...	...	...	...	1926	...	...	...	...	2342		...	...	...	1039	1137	...

	⑥	⑥	⑥	⑥	⑥	⑥	⑥	⑥	⑥	⑥				⑦	⑦		⑦	⑦	⑦	⑦	⑦	⑦	⑦	⑦	⑦
										🚌				🚌											
Windermere d.	1251	1345	1441	1550	1707	1803	1906	1958	2045	2140	...	⑦	...	1043	1206	...	1250	1358	1447	1558	1648	1802	1905	1948	2040
Kendal d.	1306	1359	1455	1605	1722	1817	1918	2012	2056	2215	...		...	1108	1220	...	1302	1412	1501	1612	1702	1816	1918	2002	2055
Oxenholme 151 a.	1311	1404	1500	1610	1727	1822	1923	2017	2101	2225	...		...	1118	1225	...	1307	1417	1506	1617	1707	1821	1923	2007	2100
Lancaster 151 a.	1333	...	1517	...	1748	1846	...	...	2118	|	...		...	...	...	...	...	...	...	...	...	1838	...	...	2120
Preston 151 a.	1406	...	1537	...	1811	1906	...	...	...	2350	...		...	...	...	...	...	...	...	...	...	1858	...	...	2144

B – From Barrow in Furness (Table **157**). M – From Manchester Airport (Table **151**).

159 BARROW - WHITEHAVEN - CARLISLE

2nd class NT

km			Ⓐ	Ⓐ	Ⓐ	Ⓐ	Ⓐ	Ⓐ	Ⓐ	Ⓐ	Ⓐ	Ⓐ	Ⓐ	Ⓐ	Ⓐ	Ⓐ	Ⓐ	Ⓐ	Ⓐ	Ⓐ			⑥	⑥
	Lancaster 151 157 d.	Ⓐ	...	...	...	...	...	...	...	...	...	1219	...	1533	...	...	...	...	2026	...	...	⑥	...	...
0	**Barrow in Furness** 157 d.		...	0546	0651	0744	...	0920	1010	1140	1236	1331	1437	1643	1731	1830	1940	...	2134	...	...		...	0546
26	Millom d.		...	0621	0719	0812	...	0948	1038	1214	1304	1359	1512	1711	1805	1858	2010	...	2204	...	...		...	0621
47	Ravenglass for Eskdale … 🚂 d.		...	0642	0737	0829	...	1005	1055	1235	1321	1416	1533	1728	1826	1915	...	...	...	...	...		...	0642
56	Sellafield d.		...	0656	0751	0840	...	1019	1108	1248	1336	1428	1547	1740	1840	1925	...	...	...	...	...		...	0656
74	**Whitehaven** d.		0624	0718	0812	...	0904	1037	1128	1310	1356	1454	1612	1800	1915	1946	...	2030	...	2151	...		0622	0718
85	Workington d.		0642	0739	0831	...	0922	1055	1146	1332	1414	1513	1634	1818	1936	2004	...	2048	...	2211	...		0640	0739
92	Maryport d.		0650	0749	0839	...	0930	1104	1154	1342	1422	1522	1644	1826	1946	2013	...	2056	...	...	...		0648	0749
119	Wigton d.		0711	0812	0900	...	0951	1126	1216	1405	1443	1544	1707	1847	2010	2034	...	2117	...	...	...		0709	0812
138	**Carlisle** a.		0733	0833	0925	...	1013	1149	1238	1426	1506	1604	1728	1910	2031	2055	...	2139	...	...	...		0731	0833

	⑥	⑥	⑥	⑥		⑥	⑥	⑥	⑥		⑥	⑥	⑥	⑥	⑥	⑥	⑥	⑥			⑦	⑦	⑦	⑦
Lancaster 151 157 d.	...	...	...	...	...	0902	...	1119	...	...	1332	...	...	1700	...	...	...	2023	...	⑦	...	...	...	...
Barrow in Furness 157 d.	0655	0741	...	0845	...	1010	1138	1239	1350	...	1452	1533	1732	1810	...	1940	...	2130	...		...	...	...	...
Millom d.	0724	0809	...	0919	...	1038	1212	1307	1418	...	1520	1601	1806	1840	...	2010	...	2200	...		...	...	...	...
Ravenglass for Eskdale … 🚂 d.	0742	0826	...	0940	...	1055	1233	1324	1435	...	1537	1618	1827	...	...	...	...	...	...		...	...	...	...
Sellafield d.	0756	0839	...	0954	...	1108	1246	1336	1447	...	1550	1630	1841	...	...	...	...	...	...		...	...	...	...
Whitehaven d.	0816	...	0906	1019	...	1128	1308	1355	1507	...	1611	1656	1913	...	1943	...	2030	...	...		1233	1433	1633	1933
Workington d.	0834	...	0924	1040	...	1146	1329	1413	1525	...	1629	1714	1934	...	2001	...	2048	...	...		1251	1451	1651	1951
Maryport d.	0842	...	0932	1051	...	1154	1340	1421	1533	...	1637	1722	1944	...	2009	...	2056	...	...		1259	1459	1659	1959
Wigton d.	0904	...	0953	1114	...	1216	1403	1442	1555	...	1659	1744	2008	...	2030	...	2117	...	...		1318	1518	1718	2018
Carlisle a.	0926	...	1015	1137	...	1238	1426	1505	1617	...	1719	1806	2029	...	2053	...	2139	...	...		1341	1541	1741	2041

		Ⓐ	Ⓐ	Ⓐ	Ⓐ	Ⓐ	Ⓐ	Ⓐ	Ⓐ	Ⓐ	Ⓐ	Ⓐ	Ⓐ	Ⓐ	Ⓐ	Ⓐ	Ⓐ	Ⓐ	Ⓐ	Ⓐ	Ⓐ			⑥
																A								
Carlisle d.	Ⓐ	...	0515	...	0737	...	0842	0938	1054	1208	1252	1435	1513	1631	1737	1814	...	1915	2037	...	2200	...	⑥	...
Wigton d.		...	0534	...	0755	...	0901	0956	1112	1226	1310	1454	1531	1649	1756	1832	...	1933	2055	...	2218	...		...
Maryport d.		...	0558	0646	0816	...	0925	1017	1133	1247	1331	1517	1552	1710	1820	1853	...	1954	2116	...	2239	...		...
Workington d.		...	0609	0704	0827	...	0935	1028	1144	1258	1342	1528	1604	1721	1831	1904	...	2005	2127	...	2250	...		...
Whitehaven d.		...	0631	0724	0847	...	0956	1048	1205	1318	1403	1549	1623	1741	1852	1925	...	2025	2147	...	2310	...		...
Sellafield d.		...	0652	0742	...	0900	1018	1108	1225	1335	1421	1611	1644	1804	1917	...	...	...	...	...	...	...		...
Ravenglass for Eskdale … 🚂 d.		...	0706	0753	...	0910	1031	1118	1235	1345	1431	1624	1655	1814	1930	...	...	...	...	...	...	...		...
Millom d.		0609	0727	0812	...	0929	1052	1136	1254	1404	1450	1645	1715	1835	1951	...	2016	...	...	2209	...	...		0609
Barrow in Furness 157 a.		0642	0803	0845	...	1000	1130	1208	1326	1436	1522	1723	1749	1910	2031	...	2049	...	...	2242	...	...		0641
Lancaster 151 157 a.		...	0913	...	...	...	...	...	1433	...	1628	...	...	...	...	...	...	...	...	...	...	...		...

	⑥	⑥	⑥	⑥	⑥	⑥	⑥	⑥	⑥	⑥	⑥	⑥	⑥	⑥	⑥	⑥	⑥	⑥			⑦	⑦	⑦	⑦
													A											
Carlisle d.	0515	0735	...	0842	0938	1054	1156	1252	1433	1525	1636	1740	1814	1900	...	2015	...	2145	...	⑦	1410	1710	1910	2110
Wigton d.	0534	0753	...	0901	0956	1112	1215	1310	1452	1543	1654	1758	1832	1918	...	2032	...	2203	...		1427	1727	1927	2127
Maryport d.	0557	0814	...	0925	1017	1133	1239	1331	1515	1604	1715	1819	1853	1939	...	2052	...	2224	...		1447	1747	1947	2147
Workington d.	0608	0825	...	0935	1028	1144	1251	1342	1526	1616	1726	1830	1904	1950	...	2104	...	2235	...		1459	1759	1959	2159
Whitehaven d.	0630	0845	...	0956	1048	1204	1315	1402	1547	1636	1748	1850	1925	2010	...	2125	...	2255	...		1520	1820	2020	2220
Sellafield d.	0651	...	0905	1018	1108	1222	1336	1419	1612	1656	1808	1911	...	...	...	...	...	...	...		...	...	...	...
Ravenglass for Eskdale … 🚂 d.	0705	...	0915	1031	1118	1232	1350	1429	1625	1706	1818	1921	...	...	...	...	...	...	...		...	...	...	...
Millom d.	0725	...	0934	1052	1136	1251	1411	1448	1646	1725	1837	1939	...	...	2016	...	2208	...	...		...	...	...	...
Barrow in Furness 157 a.	0803	...	1005	1130	1208	1325	1449	1520	1723	1757	1911	2013	...	...	2049	...	2241	...	...		...	...	...	...
Lancaster 151 157 a.	...	...	1111	...	1315	...	1608	...	...	1905	...	...	...	...	...	...	...	...	...		...	...	...	...

A – From Newcastle (Table **213**).

🚂 – Ravenglass and Eskdale Railway. ✆ 01229 717171. www.ravenglass-railway.co.uk

191 BLACKPOOL - PRESTON - CLITHEROE - HELLIFIELD

2nd class NT

TABLE TEMPORARILY RELOCATED FROM PAGE 151

km			⑦				⑦	
0	**Blackpool North** 156 190 d.	...		...	...	...	*1240*	...
29	**Preston** 156 190 d.	...	0839	...	...	...	1319	...
48	Blackburn 163 190 d.	...	0904	...	...	...	1339	...
63	Clitheroe 163 d.	...	0927	...	...	...	1402	...
85	Hellifield a.	...	0952	...	...	...	1427	...
	Appleby 173 a.	...	*1110*	...	...	...	*1556*	...

		⑦		⑦			
Appleby 173 d.	...		...	*1339*	...	...	...
Hellifield d.	...	1030	...	1455	...	...	...
Clitheroe 163 d.	...	1055	...	1518	...	...	...
Blackburn 163 190 d.	...	1125	...	1545	...	...	...
Preston 156 190 a.	...	1147	...	1605	...	...	...
Blackpool North 156 190 a.	...	...	...	1633	...	...	...

AW, VT 2nd class HOLYHEAD - CHESTER - MANCHESTER 160

km		(Ⓐ)	Ⓐ	Ⓐ	Ⓐ	Ⓐ	Ⓐ	Ⓐ	Ⓐ	Ⓐ	Ⓐ	Ⓐ	Ⓐ	Ⓐ	Ⓐ	Ⓐ	Ⓐ	Ⓐ	Ⓐ	Ⓐ	Ⓐ	Ⓐ	Ⓐ	Ⓐ	Ⓐ	Ⓐ	Ⓐ
						🍷C	🍷A		🍷	🍴C	🍴A			🍷C	🍴A	🍷	🍷	🍷C	🍷	🍷C	🍴A	🍷	🍷B	🍷	🍷C	🍷	🍷B
0	**Holyhead** d.		...	...	...	0425	0448	...	0514	0533	0551	...	...	0628	0655	...	0715	...	...	0805	0855	...	0923	...	1040	...	1127
40	Bangor d.		...	...	...	0457	0514	...	0543	0601	0618	...	...	0706	0722	...	0802d	...	...	0902c	0922	...	1002	...	1107	...	1200
	Llandudno ‡ d.		...	...	...	|	|	...	|	|	|	...	0646	|	|	0745	|	0830	...	|	|	0945	|	1044	|	1144	|
64	Llandudno Junction ‡ d.		...	0438	...	0515	0532	0546	0607	0619	0636	...	0656	0725	0740	0754	0825	0839	0854	0925	0940	0954	1025	1053	1125	1153	1223
71	Colwyn Bay d.		...	0444	...	0521	0538	0552	0613	0627	0642	...	0702	0731	0747	0800	0831	0845	0900	0931	0947	1000	1031	1059	1131	1159	1229
88	Rhyl d.		...	0457	...	0531	0549	0602	0626	0638	0653	...	0715	0741	0758	0813	0841	0856	0913	0941	0958	1013	1041	1112	1141	1212	1240
94	Prestatyn d.		...	0502	...	0537	|	0608	0631	|	0658	...	0721	0747	0804	0819	0847	|	0919	0947	1004	1019	1047	1118	1147	1218	1245
116	Flint d.		...	0516	...	0550	|	0621	0645	0655	0712	...	0735	0800	0817	0832	0900	|	0932	1000	1017	1032	1100	1131	1200	1231	1259
136	**Chester** a.		...	0534	...	0605	0617	0638	0702	0709	0726	...	0753	0815	0831	0850	0914	0923	0950	1015	1031	1050	1115	1149	1214	1249	1313
136	**Chester 150** ♥ d.		0334	0537	0538	...	0626	0640	0712	...	0735	0738	0755	...	0835	0852	0916	...	0952	...	1035	1052	...	1152	...	1252	...
170	**Crewe 150** ♥ a.		|	0558	|	...	0647	|	|	...	0754	|	0818	...	0854	|	0937	...	|	...	1054	|	...	|	...	|	...
165	Warrington Bank Quay a.		|	...	0605	...	...	0709	0739	...	...	0808	...	...	...	0918	...	...	1018	...	...	1118	...	1220	...	1318	...
201	**Manchester** Piccadilly a.		0442	...	0639	...	...	0746	0813	...	...	0851	...	...	...	0952	...	...	1052	...	...	1152	...	1252	...	1352	...
217	**Manchester** Airport a.		0459	...	...	...	...	...	...	...	...	...	...	...	...	1015	...	...	1115	...	...	1215	...	1315	...	1415	...

	Ⓐ	Ⓐ	Ⓐ	Ⓐ	Ⓐ	Ⓐ	Ⓐ	Ⓐ	Ⓐ	Ⓐ	Ⓐ	Ⓐ	Ⓐ	Ⓐ	Ⓐ	Ⓐ	Ⓐ	Ⓐ	Ⓐ	Ⓐ	Ⓐ	Ⓐ	Ⓐ	Ⓐ	Ⓐ	Ⓐ	Ⓐ
	🍷	🍷C	🍷A	🍷	🍷B	🍷A	🍷	🍷	🍷C		🍷	🍷B	🍷	🍷C		🍷D						B	🍷B				Ka
Holyhead d.	...	1232	1252	1305	1324	1358	...	...	1434	...	...	1544	...	1650	...	1730	...	...	1823	...	...	1921	...	...	2032	...	...
Bangor d.	...	1307	1320	1332	1404	1425	...	...	1504	...	...	1623	...	1718	...	1809	...	...	1902	...	...	2000	2020	...	2101	...	...
Llandudno ‡ d.	...	|	|	|	|	|	1440	1508	|	...	1607	|	1705	|	...	|	...	1844	|	1934	...	|	|	2043	|	2145	...
Llandudno Junction ‡ d.	1253	1325	1339	1350	1429	1443	1449	1517	1527	1618	1625	1646	1715	1737	...	1832	1839	1853	1926	1946	...	2023	2038	2052	2128	2155	...
Colwyn Bay d.	1259	1331	1345	1358	1435	1450	1455	1523	1533	1624	1631	|	1721	1743	...	|	1845	1859	1932	1954	...	2029	2044	2058	2134	2201	...
Rhyl d.	1312	1341	1356	1412	1445	1500	1508	1536	1544	1634	1644	|	1733	1753	...	|	1855	1912	1942	2009	...	2039	2055	2111	2147	2216	...
Prestatyn d.	1318	1347	1401	1418	1451	|	1514	1542	1549	1640	1649	|	1739	1759	...	|	1901	1918	1948	2016	...	2045	2101	2117	2152	2222	...
Flint d.	1331	1400	1415	1431	1504	|	1527	1555	1603	1653	1703	|	1752	1812	...	|	1914	1931	2001	2030	...	2058	2114	2130	2206	2237	...
Chester a.	1349	1415	1428	1445	1525	1528	1544	1613	1617	1707	1720	1726	1811	1826	...	1911	1930	1949	2016	2044	...	2116	2128	2147	2222	2255	...
Chester 150 ♥ d.	1350	...	1435	1447	...	1535	1548	1622	...	...	1722	...	1816	...	1849	...	...	1952	2018	2046	2050	...	2135	2151	2224	2301	2322
Crewe 150 ♥ a.	|	...	1454	|	...	1554	|	|	...	...	|	...	|	...	|	...	...	|	2041	2106	|	...	2154	|	2249	2326	|
Warrington Bank Quay a.	1418	...	...	1517	...	...	1618	1651	...	...	1749	...	1845	...	1918	...	...	2018	...	...	2119	...	...	2217	...	...	2351
Manchester Piccadilly a.	1452	...	...	1551	...	...	1651	1726	...	...	1825	...	1925	...	1952	...	...	2052	...	...	2152	...	...	2253	...	...	0023
Manchester Airport a.	1515	...	...	...	...	...	...	...	...	...	...	...	...	...	2015	...	...	2114	...	...	...	...	...	...	...	...	...

	①–④	(⑥)	⑥	⑥	⑥		⑥	⑥	⑥	⑥	⑥	⑥	⑥	⑥	⑥	⑥	⑥	⑥	⑥	⑥	⑥	⑥	⑥	⑥	⑥	⑥	⑥
	Ke						🍷C			🍷C	🍷B	🍷	🍷C	🍷A	🍷	🍷B	🍷A	🍷	C🍷	🍷A	🍷	🍷B	🍷	🍷C	🍷	🍷B	🍷
Holyhead d.	...		...	...	...	...	0425	...	...	...	0522	...	0635	0652	...	0715	0755	...	0820	0855	...	0923	...	1033	...	1123	...
Bangor d.	...		...	...	...	...	0457	...	...	...	0601	...	0707	0720	...	0802	0822	...	0902	0922	...	1002	...	1105	...	1202	...
Llandudno ‡ d.	...		...	...	...	...	|	...	...	...	|	0634	|	|	0745	|	|	0845	|	|	0945	|	1044	|	1144	|	1236
Llandudno Junction ‡ d.	...		...	0438	...	...	0515	...	0537	...	0624	0644	0725	0738	0754	0825	0840	0854	0925	0940	0954	1025	1053	1125	1153	1225	1253
Colwyn Bay d.	...		...	0444	...	...	0521	...	0543	...	0630	0650	0731	0744	0800	0831	0847	0900	0931	0947	1000	1031	1059	1131	1159	1231	1259
Rhyl d.	...		...	0457	...	...	0531	...	0556	...	0640	0703	0741	0755	0813	0841	0858	0913	0941	0958	1013	1041	1112	1141	1212	1241	1312
Prestatyn d.	...		...	0502	...	...	0537	...	0601	...	0646	0708	0747	0801	0819	0847	0904	0919	0947	1003	1019	1047	1118	1147	1218	1247	1318
Flint d.	...		...	0516	...	...	0550	...	0615	...	0659	0721	0800	0815	0832	0900	0917	0932	1000	|	1032	1100	1131	1200	1231	1300	1331
Chester a.	...		...	0533	...	...	0606	...	0633	...	0715	0738	0815	0828	0850	0915	0931	0950	1014	1028	1050	1116	1149	1216	1249	1315	1349
Chester 150 ♥ d.	2339		0336	0537	0538	...	...	0613	0635	0712	...	0740	...	0835	0852	...	0935	0952	...	1035	1052	...	1150	...	1251	...	1352
Crewe 150 ♥ a.	|		|	0558	|	...	...	|	0659	|	...	|	...	0854	|	...	0954	|	...	1054	|	...	|	...	|	...	|
Warrington Bank Quay a.	0010		|	...	0605	...	...	0639	...	0738	...	0806	...	...	0918	...	...	1018	...	...	1118	...	1217	...	1320	...	1420
Manchester Piccadilly a.	0044		0441	...	0638	...	...	0714	...	0813	...	0852	...	...	0952	...	...	1052	...	...	1152	...	1252	...	1353	...	1452
Manchester Airport a.	...		0459	...	...	...	...	...	...	...	...	0915	...	...	1015	...	...	1115	...	...	1215	...	1315	...	1417	...	1515

	⑥	⑥	⑥	⑥	⑥	⑥	⑥	⑥	⑥	⑥	⑥	⑥	⑥	⑥	⑥	⑥	⑥	⑥	⑥	⑥	⑥	(⑦)	⑦	⑦	⑦	⑦	⑦
	🍷C	🍷	🍷B	🍷A	🍷	🍷C	🍷	🍷B	🍷	🍷C	🍷	🍷D				B										🍷	🍷A
Holyhead d.	1238	...	1328	1358	...	1425	...	1523	...	1650	...	1730	...	1823	...	1921	...	...	2037	...	...		...	...	0845	...	...
Bangor d.	1307	1333	1407	1425	...	1453	...	1602	...	1718	...	1809	...	1902	...	2000	...	...	2106	...	...		...	...	0912	...	...
Llandudno ‡ d.	|	|	|	|	1442	|	1544	|	1644	|	1744	|	1844	|	1942	|	2043	...	|	2145	...		...	...	|	...	...
Llandudno Junction ‡ d.	1325	1356	1425	1443	1451	1516	1553	1625	1653	1736	1753	1832	1853	1926	1951	2023	2052	...	2129	2155	...		...	...	0936	...	...
Colwyn Bay d.	1331	1402	1431	1450	1457	1522	1559	1631	1659	1742	1759	1838	1859	1932	1957	2029	2058	...	2135	2201	...		...	...	0942	...	...
Rhyl d.	1341	1415	1441	1500	1510	1533	1612	1641	1712	1752	1812	1848	1912	1942	2010	2039	2111	...	2148	2216	...		...	...	0955	...	...
Prestatyn d.	1347	1421	1447	|	1516	1538	1618	1647	1718	1758	1818	1854	1918	1948	2016	2045	2117	...	2154	2222	...		...	...	1000	...	...
Flint d.	1400	1434	1500	|	1529	1552	1631	1700	1731	1811	1831	1907	1931	2001	2029	2058	2130	...	2207	2237	...		...	...	1014	...	...
Chester a.	1414	1452	1517	1527	1546	1605	1649	1715	1749	1825	1849	1924	1949	2016	2047	2113	2148	...	2223	2255	...		...	...	1031	...	...
Chester 150 ♥ d.	...	1453	...	1535	1548	...	1650	...	1750	...	1850	...	1950	2018	2050	...	...	2153	2226	2301	2322		0839	0942	1039	1036	1128
Crewe 150 ♥ a.	...	|	...	1554	|	...	|	...	|	...	|	...	|	2041	|	...	...	|	2249	2326	|		|	|	1103	|	1147
Warrington Bank Quay a.	...	1520	...	...	1617	...	1719	...	1818	...	1920	...	2018	...	2119	...	...	2220	...	...	2350		0907	1009	...	1103	...
Manchester Piccadilly a.	...	1552	...	...	1652	...	1752	...	1851	...	1952	...	2052	...	2151	...	...	2252	...	...	0022		0940	1044	...	1136	...
Manchester Airport a.	...	1615	...	...	1715	...	1816	...	...	...	2013	...	...	...	...	...	...	...	...	...	...		...	...	...	...	...

	⑦	⑦	⑦	⑦	⑦	⑦	⑦	⑦	⑦	⑦	⑦	⑦	⑦	⑦	⑦	⑦	⑦	⑦	⑦	⑦	⑦	⑦	⑦	⑦	⑦	⑦	⑦
		🍷C	🍷A	🍷	🍷A	🍷	🍷A	🍷	🍷A		🍷			🍷A		🍷C	🍷A				🍷K						
Holyhead d.	...	1020	1055	...	1150	...	1250	...	1355	...	1430	...	1530	...	...	1625	...	...	1730	...	1825	...	1940	...	...	2035	2140
Bangor d.	...	1059	1122	...	1217	...	1318	...	1422	...	1508	...	1558	...	...	1704	...	...	1759	...	1904	...	2009	...	...	2114	2209
Llandudno ‡ d.	...	|	|	...	|	...	|	...	|	...	|	...	|	...	...	|	...	...	|	...	|	...	|	...	...	|	|
Llandudno Junction ‡ d.	...	1122	1140	...	1235	...	1336	...	1440	...	1526	...	1625	...	...	1725	...	...	1824	...	1924	...	2037	...	...	2137	2227
Colwyn Bay d.	...	1128	1146	...	1242	...	1342	...	1446	...	1532	...	1631	...	...	1731	...	...	1830	...	1930	...	2043	...	...	2143	2233
Rhyl d.	...	1141	1157	...	1253	...	1353	...	1457	...	1545	...	1644	...	...	1744	...	...	1843	...	1943	...	2056	...	...	2156	2243
Prestatyn d.	...	1146	1203	...	1259	...	1359	...	1503	...	1551	...	1649	...	...	1749	...	...	1848	...	1948	...	2102	...	...	2201	2249
Flint d.	...	1200	1216	...	|	...	1413	...	|	...	1604	...	1703	...	...	1803	...	...	1902	...	2002	...	2116	...	...	2215	2302
Chester a.	...	1218	1230	...	1324	...	1426	...	1531	...	1624	...	1720	...	...	1821	...	...	1921	...	2019	...	2134	...	...	2232	2316
Chester 150 ♥ d.	1136	...	1233	1236	1330	1336	1433	1436	1533	1536	1636	1627	1722	1735	1736	...	1835	1836	1924	1936	2027	2036	2136	2143	2206	2235	...
Crewe 150 ♥ a.	|	...	1253	|	1350	|	1454	|	1552	|	|	1651	1744	1753	|	...	1853	|	1945	|	2048	|	2200	|	|	2300	...
Warrington Bank Quay a.	1203	...	...	1303	...	1403	...	1503	...	1603	1703	...	...	...	1803	...	...	1903	...	2003	...	2103	...	2210	2233	...	...
Manchester Piccadilly a.	1235	...	...	1335	...	1436	...	1535	...	1635	1735	...	...	...	1835	...	...	1935	...	2035	...	2135	..	2244	2305	...	...
Manchester Airport a.	...	...	...	...	...	...	...	...	...	...	...	...	...	...	...	...	...	...	...	...	...	...	...	...	...	...	...

LLANDUDNO - BLAENAU FFESTINIOG

km		⚒	⚒	Ⓐ	⑥	⚒	⚒		⑥	Ⓐ	
0	**Llandudno** d.	...	*0708*	1008	1022	1308	1620	...	1903	1905	...
5	**Llandudno** Junction d.	0530	0726	1028	1034	1330	1633	...	1918	1920	...
18	Llanrwst d.	0548	0749	1050	1056	1352	1655	...	1940	1942	...
24	Betws y Coed d.	0554	0755	1056	1102	1358	1701	...	1946	1948	...
44	**Blaenau Ffestiniog** d.	0621	0826	1127	1133	1429	1732	...	2015	2017	...

	⚒	Ⓐ	⑥	⚒	Ⓐ	⑥	Ⓐ	⑥	⚒	
Blaenau Ffestiniog d.	0624	0835	0846	1135	1457	1457	1736	1737	2023	...
Betws y Coed d.	0650	0902	0913	1202	1524	1524	1803	1804	2050	...
Llanrwst d.	0656	0908	0919	1208	1530	1530	1809	1810	2056	...
Llandudno Junction a.	0720	0933	0944	1233	1555	1555	1834	1835	2121	...
Llandudno a.	*0739*	0956	1011	1243	1611	1607	1849	1849	2141	...

A – Conveys 🛏12 to/from London Euston (Table **150**).
B – To/ from Birmingham New Street (Table **145** or **150**).
C – To/ from Cardiff Central (Tables **145** and **149**).
D – To/ from Shrewsbury (Table **145**).
E – (FR Pink service) Dec. 26, 2016 - Jan. 1, 2017, Mar. 25–31, Apr. 1, 2, 3, 7, 8, 24, 28, May 5–8, 12–15, 19, 22, 26, June 5, 9, 12, 16, 19, 23, 26, Sep. 18, 22, 25, 29, Oct. 1, 2, 6–9, 13–16, 20, Nov. 3, 4, 5.
F – (FR Blue service) Apr. 4, 5, 6, 9–23, 25–27, 29, 30, May, 1–4, 9–11, 16–18, 20, 21, 23–25, 27–31, June 1–4, 6–8, 10, 11, 13–15, 17, 18, 20–22, 24, 25, 27–30, July 1 - Sept. 17, Sept. 19–21, 23, 24, 26–28, 30, Oct. 3–5, 10–12, 17–19, 21–31, Nov. 1, 2.
G – (WHR Yellow service) Mar. 25, 26, 28–30, Apr. 1–13, 19–27, May 2–4, 6, 7, 9–11, 14, 16–18, 21–27, June 3–8, 10–15, 17–22, 24–26, 30, July 1–3, 7–9, 14–17; 21–23, 28, Sept. 2–4, 8–30, Oct. 1, 3–5, 7, 8, 10–12, 14, 15, 17–19, 21–31, Nov. 1–4.
H – (WHR Red service) Apr. 14–18, 29, 30, May 1, 19, 20, 28–31, June 1, 2, 27–29, July 4–6, 11–13, 18–20, 24–27, 29–31, Aug. 1–31, Sept. 1, 5–7.

K – To/from Birmingham International (Table **145**).

a – Until Feb. 10 and from Mar. 24; also ⑤ Feb. 17 - Mar. 24.
b – Runs 15 minutes later on certain dates.
c – Arrives 20 minutes earlier.
d – Arrives 10 minutes earlier.
e – Feb. 13 - Mar. 23.

* – Connection by 🚐.
‡ – For full service Llandudno - Llandudno Junction and v.v. see next page.
♥ – For full service Chester - Crewe and v.v. see next page.
§ – Additional trains operate ②–④, Jun. 27 - Sep.14 and ①, July 24 - Aug. 28 from Blaenau Ffestiniog - Porthmadog and v.v. - check with operator for details.
△ – Operators: Ffestiniog Railway and Welsh Highland Railways. www.festrail.co.uk Ffestiniog Railway ✆ 01766 516024. Welsh Highland Railway ✆ 01286 677018.

160 MANCHESTER - CHESTER - HOLYHEAD

2nd class AW, VT

		① K	②–⑤ B	Ⓐ 🍷B	Ⓐ 🍷	Ⓐ 🍷	Ⓐ 🍷	Ⓐ 🍷C	Ⓐ 🍷	Ⓐ 🍷B	Ⓐ 🍷	Ⓐ 🍷	Ⓐ 🍷A	Ⓐ 🍷C	Ⓐ 🍷	Ⓐ 🍷A	Ⓐ 🍷B	Ⓐ 🍷	Ⓐ 🍷C	Ⓐ 🍷	Ⓐ 🍷B	Ⓐ 🍷	Ⓐ 🍷C	Ⓐ 🍷	Ⓐ 🍷B	Ⓐ 🍷
Manchester Airport d.	Ⓐ	...	...	...	0533	...	...	...	...	...	...	...	...	...	...	...	...	1036	...	1136	...	1236	...	1336	...	1436
Manchester Piccadilly d.		...	...	...	0548	...	0650	...	0750	...	0850	...	...	...	0950	...	...	1052	...	1152	...	1252	...	1352	...	1452
Warrington Bank Quay d.		...	...	...	0621	...	0725	...	0824	...	0926	...	...	...	1027	...	...	1126	...	1227	...	1326	...	1426	...	1526
Crewe 150 ♥ d.		0001	0015	0623	|	0654	|	...	|	...	|	...	0953	...	|	1049	...	|	...	|	...	|	...	|	...	|
Chester 150 ♥ a.		0022	0037	0643	0649	0717	0752	...	0853	...	0953	...	1013	...	1058	1113	...	1153	...	1255	...	1353	...	1454	...	1553
Chester d.		0038	0040	0644	0655	0719	0755	0822	0855	0923	0958	1002	1016	1024	1100	1116	1125	1155	1224	1256	1324	1355	1424	1455	1525	1555
Flint d.		0051	0053	0657	0708	0734	0810	0838	0908	0938	|	1018	1029	1039	|	|	1138	1210	1237	1311	1337	1410	1437	1510	1538	1610
Prestatyn d.		0104	0106	0710	0721	0747	0823	0852	0921	0951	|	1031	1042	1053	1124	|	1151	1223	1250	1325	1350	1423	1450	1524	1552	1623
Rhyl d.		0110	0112	0716	0727	0753	0829	0858	0927	0957	|	1037	1048	1059	1131	1143	1157	1229	1256	1331	1356	1429	1456	1530	1558	1629
Colwyn Bay d.		0121	0123	0727	0738	0807	0843	0912	0938	1011	|	1051	1059	1109	|	1154	1211	1243	1307	1345	1407	1443	1507	1544	1608	1643
Llandudno Junction ‡ d.		0128	0129	0733	0744	0816	0851	0918	0944	1018	1036	1058	1106	1116	1146	1201	1218	1250	1313	1351	1413	1450	1513	1550	1620	1650
Llandudno ‡ a.		|	|	|	0756	|	...	0927	|	1027	|	1109	|	|	|	|	|	...	|	1402	|	1501	|	1601	|	1701
Bangor d.		0144	0146	0750	...	0838	...	...	1008	...	1053	...	1125	1139	1202	1217	1236	...	1331	...	1437	...	1531	...	1644	...
Holyhead ▽ a.		0215	0215	0823	...	0918	...	...	1036	...	1122	...	1158	1219	1236	1250	1315	...	1414	...	1508	...	1614	...	1716	...

	Ⓐ 🍷C	Ⓐ 🍷	Ⓐ 🍷B	Ⓐ 🍷	Ⓐ 🍷A	Ⓐ 🍷C	Ⓐ 🍷	Ⓐ 🍷	Ⓐ 🍷A	Ⓐ 🍷B	Ⓐ	Ⓐ C🍴	Ⓐ 🍷A	Ⓐ	Ⓐ	Ⓐ 🍷A	Ⓐ	Ⓐ	Ⓐ	Ⓐ C	Ⓐ	Ⓐ		⑥ B	⑥ 🍷B	⑥ 🍷
Manchester Airport d.	...	1536	...	...	...	...	...	...	...	...	...	...	...	...	...	...	2032	...	2132	...	...	...		...	...	0533
Manchester Piccadilly d.	...	1552	...	1650	...	...	1719	1750	...	...	1850	...	...	...	1950	...	2050	...	2150	...	2212	2314	⑥	...	...	0548
Warrington Bank Quay d.	...	1626	...	1728	...	...	1752	1824	...	...	1922	...	...	...	2026	...	2126	...	2224	...	2257	2348		...	...	0621
Crewe 150 ♥ d.	...	|	...	|	1749	...	|	|	1857	...	|	...	1956	...	|	2055	|	2136	|	...	|	|		0015	0623	|
Chester 150 ♥ a.	...	1654	...	1801	1808	...	1822	1853	1916	...	1950	...	2015	...	2053	2120	2155	2159	2251	...	2325	0015		0037	0643	0649
Chester d.	1627	1655	1725	1803	1810	1824	...	1855	1923	1932	...	2006	2026	2034	...	2124	...	2204	...	2256	...	...		0040	0644	0655
Flint d.	1640	1710	1740	|	1823	1839	...	1910	1936	1947	...	2018	|	2049	...	2137	...	2219	...	2311	...	...		0053	0657	0710
Prestatyn d.	1654	1723	1753	1826	1836	1853	...	1923	1949	2000	...	|	|	2102	...	2150	...	2232	...	2324	...	...		0106	0710	0723
Rhyl d.	1700	1729	1759	1833	1842	1859	...	1929	1955	2006	...	2035	2053	2108	...	2157	...	2238	...	2330	...	...		0112	0716	0729
Colwyn Bay d.	1710	1743	1813	1845	1853	1913	...	1940	2006	2020	...	2047	2104	2122	...	2208	...	2252	...	2344	...	...		0123	0727	0743
Llandudno Junction ‡ d.	1716	1750	1825	1852	1900	1919	...	1950	2013	2030	...	2054	2110	2129	...	2214	...	2259	...	2352	...	...		0129	0733	0750
Llandudno ‡ a.	|	1801	|	1903	|	|	...	|	|	2038	...	|	|	|	...	|	...	|	...	|	...	...		|	|	0801
Bangor d.	1739	...	1847	...	1921	1935	...	2015	2029	...	...	2111	2127	2152	...	2231	...	2322	...	0014	...	...		0146	0750	...
Holyhead ▽ a.	1821	...	1917	...	...	2020	...	2042	2059	...	...	2141	2159	2230	...	2303	...	0002	...	0048	...	...		0215	0823	...

	⑥ 🍷	⑥ 🍷	⑥ 🍷C	⑥ 🍷	⑥ 🍷B	⑥ 🍷	⑥ 🍷C	⑥ 🍷	⑥ 🍷A	⑥ 🍷B	⑥ 🍷	⑥	⑥ 🍷C	⑥ 🍷	⑥ 🍷B	⑥ 🍷	⑥ 🍷C	⑥ 🍷	⑥ 🍷B	⑥ 🍷	⑥ 🍷A	⑥ 🍷C	⑥ 🍷	⑥ 🍷B	⑥ 🍷	⑥ 🍷A
Manchester Airport d.	...	...	...	...	...	...	...	0936	...	...	1036	...	...	1136	...	1236	...	1336	...	1436	...	...	1536	...	1636	...
Manchester Piccadilly d.	...	0650	...	0750	...	0850	...	0952	...	...	1052	...	...	1152	...	1252	...	1352	...	1452	...	...	1552	...	1652	...
Warrington Bank Quay d.	...	0723	...	0825	...	0926	...	1026	...	...	1126	...	...	1227	...	1326	...	1426	...	1527	...	...	1626	...	1726	...
Crewe 150 ♥ d.	0703	|	...	|	...	|	...	|	1049	...	|	...	...	|	...	|	...	|	...	|	1549	...	|	...	|	1749
Chester 150 ♥ a.	0723	0750	...	0854	...	0953	...	1053	1113	...	1153	...	...	1255	...	1353	...	1453	...	1554	1610	...	1654	...	1753	1810
Chester d.	0725	0755	0822	0856	0924	0955	1023	1055	1116	1124	1155	...	1223	1256	1326	1355	1423	1455	1522	1556	1612	1627	1655	1724	1755	1816
Flint d.	0739	0810	0836	0911	0937	1010	1036	1110	|	1139	1210	...	1236	1311	1339	1410	1436	1510	1537	1611	1625	1642	1710	1739	1810	1829
Prestatyn d.	0752	0823	0849	0924	0950	1023	1050	1123	|	1152	1223	...	1250	1325	1352	1423	1450	1523	1550	1624	1638	1655	1724	1752	1823	1842
Rhyl d.	0758	0829	0855	0930	0956	1029	1056	1129	1143	1158	1229	...	1257	1331	1358	1429	1457	1529	1556	1630	1645	1701	1730	1758	1829	1849
Colwyn Bay d.	0809	0843	0906	0944	1007	1043	1106	1143	1154	1209	1243	...	1309	1345	1409	1443	1509	1543	1607	1644	1656	1712	1744	1812	1843	1900
Llandudno Junction ‡ d.	0815	0850	0912	0951	1013	1050	1113	1150	1201	1215	1250	1257	1315	1351	1415	1450	1515	1550	1614	1651	1702	1717	1750	1819	1850	1906
Llandudno ‡ a.	|	0901	|	1002	|	1101	|	1201	|	|	|	1307	|	1402	|	1501	|	1601	|	1702	|	|	1802	|	1901	|
Bangor d.	0838	...	0936	...	1031	...	1136	...	1217	1233	1312	...	1333	...	1440	...	1532	...	1637	...	1719	1741	...	1843	...	1923
Holyhead ▽ a.	0918	...	1011	...	1104	...	1209	...	1250	1312	...	...	1413	...	1508	...	1613	...	1714	...	1751	1819	...	1913	...	1955

	⑥ 🍷C	⑥ 🍷	⑥ 🍷A	⑥ 🍷B	⑥	⑥ C	⑥	⑥	⑥	⑥ C	⑥ 🚌	⑥	⑥	⑥			⑦ 🚌	⑦	⑦	⑦ 🍷A	⑦	⑦	⑦ 🍷	⑦ 🍷	⑦ 🍷	⑦ 🍷
Manchester Airport d.	...	1736	...	...	1836	...	...	...	2032	...	...	...	...	...		...	...	...	...	...	...	...	...	...	...	...
Manchester Piccadilly d.	...	1752	...	...	1852	...	1951	...	2050	...	...	2151	2226	2314	⑦	...	0718	...	0956	...	1052	...	1156	...	1256	...
Warrington Bank Quay d.	...	1826	...	...	1926	...	2030	...	|	...	...	2224	2256	2348		...	0838	...	1028	...	1126	...	1227	...	1329	...
Crewe 150 ♥ d.	...	|	1852	...	|	...	|	2100	2128	...	...	|	|	|		...	|	0924	|	1042	|	1127	|	1227	|	1327
Chester 150 ♥ a.	...	1853	1911	...	1954	...	2057	2121	2157	...	...	2254	2325	0015		...	0938	0946	1059	1102	1154	1150	1255	1252	1358	1351
Chester d.	1824	1855	1918	1932	...	2032	...	2126	...	2236	...	...	...	...		...	...	0948	...	1107	...	1203	...	1302	...	1402
Flint d.	1839	1910	1931	1947	...	2047	...	2141	...	2251	...	...	...	...		...	...	1003	...	|	...	1218	...	1317	...	1417
Prestatyn d.	1852	1923	1944	2000	...	2100	...	2154	...	2305	...	...	...	...		...	...	1016	...	1130	...	1231	...	1330	...	1430
Rhyl d.	1858	1929	1951	2006	...	2106	...	2200	...	2311	...	...	...	...		...	...	1022	...	1137	...	1237	...	1336	...	1436
Colwyn Bay d.	1909	1943	2002	2020	...	2119	...	2214	...	2325	...	...	...	...		...	...	1036	...	1148	...	1248	...	1350	...	1450
Llandudno Junction ‡ d.	1916	1950	2008	2027	...	2126	...	2221	...	2335	2348	...	...	...		...	...	1043	...	1154	...	1254	...	1357	...	1457
Llandudno ‡ a.	|	2001	|	|	...	|	...	|	...	...	|	...	...	...		...	...	|	...	|	...	|	...	|	...	|
Bangor d.	1933	...	2025	2048	...	2143	...	2245	...	...	0013	...	...	...		...	...	1105	...	1211	...	1311	...	1419	...	1514
Holyhead ▽ a.	2013	...	2058	2128	...	2225	...	2315	...	...	0048	...	...	...		...	...	1144	...	1240	...	1341	...	1448	...	1552

	⑦ 🍷	⑦ 🍷	⑦ 🍷	⑦	⑦ 🍷C	⑦ 🍷	⑦	⑦ 🍷A	⑦	⑦	⑦ 🍷A	⑦ 🍷C	⑦	⑦ 🍷	⑦ 🍷A	⑦ 🍷B	⑦	⑦ 🍷A	⑦	⑦ 🍷A	⑦	⑦	⑦	⑦	⑦	⑦
Manchester Airport d.	...	...	...	...	...	...	...	...	...	...		...	...	...	...	...	...	...	...	...	...	...	...	...	...	...
Manchester Piccadilly d.	1356	...	1456	...	...	1556	...	...	1656	...	...	...	...	1756	...	...	1856	...	1956	...	2056	...	2156	...	2256	2325
Warrington Bank Quay d.	1427	...	1528	...	...	1627	...	...	1727	...	...	...	...	1827	...	...	1930	...	2031	...	2128	...	2226	...	2330	2354
Crewe 150 ♥ d.	|	1427	|	1527	...	|	1627	1652	|	1727	1752	...	1827	|	1901	...	|	1952	|	2055	|	2128	|	2229	|	|
Chester 150 ♥ a.	1455	1451	1556	1549	...	1655	1649	1713	1755	1749	1813	...	1849	1855	1919	...	1958	2013	2059	2113	2156	2151	2254	2252	2357	0024
Chester d.	...	1502	...	1602	1636	...	1702	...	...	1802	...	1829	1852	...	1929	1938	...	2018	...	2117	...	2200	...	2300	...	...
Flint d.	...	1517	...	1617	1651	...	1717	...	...	1817	...	1844	1907	...	1942	1953	...	2031	...	2130	...	2215	...	2315	...	...
Prestatyn d.	...	1530	...	1630	1704	...	1730	...	...	1830	...	1857	1921	...	1955	2006	...	2044	...	2143	...	2228	...	2328	...	...
Rhyl d.	...	1536	...	1636	1710	...	1736	...	...	1836	...	1903	1927	...	2002	2012	...	2051	...	2150	...	2234	...	2334	...	...
Colwyn Bay d.	...	1550	...	1650	1724	...	1750	...	...	1850	...	1917	1941	...	2013	2026	...	2102	...	2201	...	2248	...	2345	...	...
Llandudno Junction ‡ d.	...	1557	...	1657	1731	...	1757	...	...	1857	...	1924	1947	...	2019	2033	...	2108	...	2207	...	2255	...	2351	...	...
Llandudno ‡ a.	...	|	...	|	|	...	|	...	...	|	...	|	|	...	|	|	...	|	...	|	...	|	...	|	...	...
Bangor d.	...	1619	...	1714	1754	...	1819	...	...	1914	...	1948	2009	...	2036	2055	...	2125	...	2224	...	2312	...	0014	...	...
Holyhead ▽ a.	...	1648	...	1752	1834	...	1849	...	...	1949	...	2018	2039	...	2103	2125	...	2154	...	2253	...	2350	...	0044	...	...

CAERNARFON - PORTHMADOG - BLAENAU FFESTINIOG △ §

km		🚂 H	🚂 G	🚂 EF	🚂 H		🚂 G	🚂 F	🚂 H	🚂 EF	🚂 F
0	**Blaenau Ffestiniog** d.	...	...	1135	...	...	...	1340	...	1505**b**	1720
19	Minffordd d.	...	...	1230	...	...	...	1435	...	1555**b**	1815
22	**Porthmadog** Harbour d.	0940	1045	1245	1255	...	1410	1450	1540	1610**b**	1830
35	Beddgelert d.	1025	1125	...	1335	...	1450	...	1620	...	...
42	Rhyd Ddu d.	1100	1155	...	1400	...	1515	...	1645	...	...
50	Waunfawr d.	1125	1220	...	1430	...	1545	...	1715	...	...
61	**Caernarfon** a.	1205	1300	...	1510	...	1615	...	1750	...	...

	🚂 EF	🚂 F	🚂 GH	🚂 EF		🚂 H	🚂 F	🚂 G	🚂 H	
Caernarfon d.	...	...	1000	...	...	1300	...	1415	1545	...
Waunfawr d.	...	...	1030	...	...	1330	...	1445	1615	...
Rhyd Ddu d.	...	...	1055	...	...	1400	...	1515	1645	...
Beddgelert d.	...	...	1125	...	...	1430	...	1540	1710	...
Porthmadog Harbour d.	1005	1125	1210	1335	...	1510	1545	1625	1755	...
Minffordd d.	1015	1135	...	1345	...	...	1555	...	...	...
Blaenau Ffestiniog d.	1120	1240	...	1445	...	...	1700	...	...	...

♥ – All trains **Chester** - **Crewe**. Journey time ± 23 minutes:
On ⚒: 0422, 0455, 0537, 0551, 0626Ⓐ, 0635⑥, 0645Ⓐ, 0717⑥, 0735Ⓐ, 0755, 0835, 0855, 0916, 0935, 0955, 1035, 1055 and at the same minutes past each hour until 1535, 1555, 1635, 1655, 1735, 1755, 1855, 1935Ⓐ, 1955, 2018, 2035⑥, 2046Ⓐ, 2055, 2135Ⓐ, 2224Ⓐ, 2226⑥, 2301.
On ⑦: 0840, 0939, 1039, 1128, 1221, 1233, 1320, 1330, 1423, 1433, 1533, 1627, 1722, 1735, 1835, 1859, 1924, 1935, 1950, 2027, 2037, 2050, 2136, 2150, 2235, 2300.

‡ – All trains **Llandudno Junction** - **Llandudno**. Journey time ± 10 minutes:
On ⚒: 0540Ⓐ, 0613, 0651, 0731, 0744Ⓐ, 0750⑥, 0817Ⓐ, 0828⑥, 0850⑥, 0918Ⓐ, 0928⑥, 0948Ⓐ, 0951⑥, 1003⑥, 1018Ⓐ, 1028⑥, 1050⑥, 1058Ⓐ, 1126⑥, 1128Ⓐ, 1150⑥, 1228⑥, 1235, 1257, 1351, 1428, 1450, 1530⑥, 1550, 1559⑥, 1603Ⓐ, 1626⑥, 1650, 1728⑥, 1750, 1826, 1841, 1852, 1928⑥, 1950⑥, 1955Ⓐ, 2030, 2058Ⓐ, 2132.
On ⑦ from Apr. 16: 1100, 1200, 1258, 1400, 1504, 1600, 1700.

♥ – All trains **Crewe** - **Chester**. Journey time ± 23 minutes:
On ⚒: 0001①, 0007②–⑥, 0010① 0015②–⑥, 0623, 0654Ⓐ, 0703⑥, 0711Ⓐ, 0723⑥, 0823, 0849Ⓐ, 0923, 0940Ⓐ, 0949⑥, 0953Ⓐ, 1023, 1049, 1123, 1149Ⓐ,1156⑥, 1223, 1249 and at the same minutes past each hour until 1823, 1845Ⓐ, 1852⑥, 1857Ⓐ, 1923, 1949⑥, 1956Ⓐ, 2023, 2048Ⓐ, 2055Ⓐ, 2100⑥, 2136, 2149Ⓐ, 2223, 2321⑥, 2330Ⓐ, 2357⑥.
On ⑦: 0924, 1007, 1042, 1105, 1127, 1155, 1227, 1254, 1327, 1357, 1427, 1457, 1527, 1627, 1652, 1727, 1752, 1827, 1901, 1924, 1952, 2027, 2055, 2128, 2203, 2229, 2306, 2338.

‡ – All trains **Llandudno** - **Llandudno Junction**. Journey time ± 10 minutes:
On ⚒: 0554Ⓐ, 0634⑥, 0646Ⓐ, 0708, 0745, 0802Ⓐ, 0808⑥, 0830Ⓐ, 0845⑥, 0908⑥, 0945, 1008, 1022⑥, 1044, 1108⑥, 1112Ⓐ, 1144, 1208⑥, 1236⑥, 1246, 1308, 1408, 1440Ⓐ, 1442⑥, 1508, 1544⑥, 1607, 1620, 1644⑥, 1705Ⓐ, 1708⑥, 1744⑥, 1808, 1844, 1903⑥, 1905Ⓐ, 1913⑥, 1934Ⓐ, 1942⑥, 2008, 2043, 2111Ⓐ, 2145.
On ⑦ from Apr. 16: 1119, 1218, 1319, 1419, 1515, 1612, 1712.

← FOR OTHER NOTES SEE PREVIOUS PAGE

136 La explicación de los signos convencionales se da en la página 4 12

📭 Sleeper trains LONDON - SCOTLAND 📭 161

CS

All trains in this table convey 📭 1, 2 cl., 🛏 (reservation compulsory) ✕ and ☕.

km			⑦	Ⓐ		⑦	Ⓐ					①–④	⑤			Ⓐ	⑦	
0	**London** Euston 150 ....d.		2057	2115	...	2328	2350		Fort William 218 ....d.			...	...	...	...	1950	1900	
28	Watford Junction 150 ....d.		2117u	2133u	...	2349u	0010u		Inverness 223 ....d.			...	...	...	...	2044	2026	
254	Crewe 150 151 ....d.		2336u	2356u	...				Perth 223 ....d.			...	...	...	...	2356u	2306u	
336	Preston 151 ....d.		0035u	0100u	...				Aberdeen 222 ....d.			...	...	...	...	2143	2143	
481	Carlisle 151 ....a.				...	0441s	0516s		Dundee 222 ....d.			...	...	...	...	2306u	2306u	
625	Motherwell.....................a.				...	0652s	0655s		**Edinburgh** Waverley 151 ..d.			2315	2340	2340			
646	**Glasgow** Central 151 .... 🚉 a.				...	0720	0720		**Glasgow** Central 151 ....d.			2315	2340	2340			
646	**Edinburgh** Waverley 151 . 🚉 a.				...	0721	0721		Motherwell.....................d.			2330u	0001u	0001u			
	Dundee 222 ....a.		0611s	0611s	...				Carlisle 151 ....d.			0144u	0146u	0147u			
	Aberdeen 222 .... 🚉 a.		0739	0739	...				Preston 151 ....a.			...	...	...	...	0436s	0444s	
	Perth 223 ....a.		0539s	0539s	...				Crewe 150 151 ....a.			...	...	...	...	0538s	0538s	
	Inverness 223 ....a.		0838	0838	...				Watford Junction 150 ....a.			0643s	0643s	0639s			
	Fort William 218 ....a.		0955	0955	...				**London** Euston 150 ...... 🚉 a.			0707	0707	0702		0747	0747

s – Calls to set down only.
u – Calls to pick up only.

🚉 – Sleeping-car passengers may occupy their cabins until 0800 following arrival at these stations.

PRESTON - LIVERPOOL 162

NT 2nd class

km			✕☕	✕☕	⑥	Ⓐ	✕☕			✕☕	✕☕	✕☕	✕☕			⑦	⑦	⑦		⑦	⑦	⑦
0	**Preston**................d.	⛏	0730	0830	0930	0930	1030	and	1630	1730	1830	1930	...	2030	2140	2242	⑦	0925	1025	and	2125	2225	2310
24	Wigan North Western. d.		0750	0851	0950	0950	1050	hourly	1650	1750	1850	1950	...	2050	2202	2304		0847	0946	1046	hourly	2146	2247	2331
38	St Helens Central........ d.		0807	0907	1006	1006	1106	until	1706	1806	1906	2006	...	2106	2220	2323		0903	1003	1103	until	2203	2304	2348
57	**Liverpool** Lime Street a.		0836	0929	1027	1031	1128	★	1731	1828	1929	2028	...	2128	2254	2354		0934	1035	1135	★	2235	2336	0020

			✕☕	✕☕	✕☕	✕☕			✕☕	✕☕	✕☕	✕☕	⑥	✕☕	✕☕		⑦	⑦	⑦		⑦	⑦	⑦
Liverpool Lime Street ....d.		⛏	0657	0757	0828	0928	and	1628	1716	1732	1800	1930	2030	2147	2147	2302	⑦	0847	0947	1047	and	2047	2147	2247
St Helens Central ....d.			0717	0815	0849	0949	hourly	1649	1744	1801	1821	1949	2049	2216	2215	2331		0914	1014	1114	hourly	2114	2214	2314
Wigan North Western...........d.			0731	0831	0903	1003	until	1703	1804	1820	1851	2003	2103	2234	2238	2348		0930	1030	1130	until	2131	2230	2330
Preston...........................a.			0755	0858	0927	1027	★	1727	1830	1851a	1917	2027	2132	2258	2302	0013		0953	1053	1153	★	2155	2253	2353

a – 1845 on ⑥.

★ – Timings may vary by up to 3 minutes.

MANCHESTER and LIVERPOOL local services 163

ME, NT 2nd class

MANCHESTER - CLITHEROE
Journey time: ± 77 – 85 minutes 57 km NT

From Manchester Victoria:

Ⓐ : Trains call at Bolton ± 25 and Blackburn ± 55 minutes later: 0555, 0700, 0752p, 0903, 1003, 1103, 1203, 1303, 1403, 1503, 1603, 1635, 1703, 1803, 1903, 2003, 2103, 2203.

⑥ : Trains call at Bolton ± 20 and Blackburn ± 52 minutes later: 0555, 0700, 0752p, 0903, 1003, 1103, 1203, 1303, 1403, 1503, 1603, 1635, 1703, 1803, 1903, 2003, 2103, 2203.

⑦ : Trains call at Bolton ± 18 and Blackburn ± 50 minutes later: 0802, 0903 and hourly until 2103.

From Clitheroe:

Ⓐ : Trains call at Blackburn ± 23 and Bolton ± 54 minutes later: 0645, 0705, 0745, 0825, 0946, 1046, 1146, 1246, 1346, 1446, 1528, 1646, 1745, 1810, 1846, 1946, 2046, 2144, 2244⑤.

⑥ : Trains call at Blackburn ± 24 and Bolton ± 51 minutes later: 0705, 0745, 0825, 0946, 1046, 1146, 1246, 1346, 1446, 1528, 1645, 1745, 1803, 1845, 1946, 2045, 2144, 2248.

⑦ : Trains call at Blackburn ± 24 and Bolton ± 53 minutes later: 0946, 1044 and hourly until 2244.

MANCHESTER - BUXTON
Journey time: ± 60 – 70 minutes 41 km NT

From Manchester Piccadilly:

Trains call at Stockport ± 11, Hazel Grove ± 22 and New Mills Newtown ± 31 minutes later.

Ⓐ : 0649, 0749, 0849, 0949, 1049, 1149, 1249, 1349, 1449, 1549, 1621, 1649, 1722, 1749, 1821, 1849, 1949, 2049, 2149, 2310.

⑥ : 0649, 0749, 0849, and hourly until 1649, 1721, 1749, 1849, 1949, 2049, 2154, 2310.

⑦ : 0856, 0950, 1051, 1149 and hourly until 1949, 2049, 2149, 2249.

From Buxton:

Trains call at New Mills Newtown ± 21, Hazel Grove ± 34 and at Stockport ± 46 minutes later.

Ⓐ : 0602, 0623, 0653, 0724, 0748, 0826, 0927, 1029, 1129, 1229, 1329, 1429 1529, 1629, 1702, 1728, 1802, 1829, 1929, 2029, 2126, 2257.

⑥ : 0602, 0627, 0725, 0803, 0827, 0927, 1028 and hourly until 1929, 2029, 2129, 2257.

⑦ : 0823, 0920, 1027, 1127 and hourly until 1927, 2027, 2129, 2227.

MANCHESTER - NORTHWICH - CHESTER
Journey time: ± 90 – 95 minutes 73 km NT

From Manchester Piccadilly:

Trains call at Stockport ± 13, Altrincham ± 28 and Northwich ± 55 minutes later.

✕ : 0618, 0717, 0817, 0917, 1017, 1117, 1217, 1317, 1417, 1517, 1617, 1709Ⓐ,1717⑥, 1817, 1917, 2017, 2117⑥, 2122Ⓐ, 2217, 2317.

⑦ : 0923, 1122, 1322, 1522, 1722, 1922, 2122.

From Chester:

Trains call at Northwich ± 30, Altrincham ± 55 and Stockport ± 74 minutes later.

✕ : 0602, 0659, 0804, 0859, 0959, 1059, 1159, 1259, 1359, 1459, 1559, 1659, 1804, 1904, 2004, 2133, 2248.

⑦ : 0902, 1104, 1304, 1504, 1704, 1904, 2104.

MANCHESTER - ST HELENS - LIVERPOOL
Journey time: ± 63 minutes 51 km NT

From Manchester Victoria:

Trains call at St Helens Junction ± 30 minutes later.

✕ : 0539, 0602, 0702, 0738, 0802, 0838, 0902 and hourly until 1702, 1738, 1802, 1902, 2002, 2109, 2209, 2309.

⑦ : 0859p, 1001p, 1101p, and hourly (note p applies to all trains) until 2301p.

From Liverpool Lime Street:

Trains call at St Helens Junction ± 28 minutes later.

✕ : 0520, 0620, 0720, 0742, 0820 and hourly until 1620, 1642, 1721, 1739, 1820, 1920, 2020, 2120, 2220, 2319.

⑦ : 0812p 0915p, and hourly (note p applies to all trains) until 2315p.

MANCHESTER - WIGAN - SOUTHPORT
Journey time: ± 75 minutes 62 km NT

From Manchester Piccadilly:

Trains call at Wigan Wallgate ± 35 minutes later.

Ⓐ : 0641v, 0703v, 0738v, 0810v, 0822 and hourly until 1822, 1923, 2020, 2122, 2238.

⑥ : 0641v, 0703v, 0822 and hourly until 1822, 1924, 2020, 2122, 2236.

⑦ : 0835, 0935, 1031, 1133, 1231, 1335 and hourly until 2035.

From Southport:

Trains call at Wigan Wallgate ± 30 minutes later.

Ⓐ : 0621, 0652v, 0719, 0757v, 0823 and hourly until 1623, 1732, 1815, 1920, 2020, 2218.

⑥ : 0621, 0719, 0822, 0923 and hourly until 1623, 1732, 1815, 1920, 2122v, 2218.

⑦ : 0910, 1005 and hourly until 2205.

MANCHESTER AIRPORT - CREWE
Journey time: ± 33 minutes 37 km NT

From Manchester Airport:

✕ : 0634, 0730⑥, 0831, 0934, 1034, 1134 and hourly until 1533, 1634, 1733, 1834.
Additional later services (and all day on ⑦) available by changing at Wilmslow.

From Crewe:

✕ : 0547, 0711, 0811, 0911 and hourly until 1611, 1711⑥, 1713Ⓐ, 1811.
Additional later services (and all day on ⑦) available by changing at Wilmslow.

LIVERPOOL - BIRKENHEAD - CHESTER
Journey time: ± 42 minutes 29 km ME

From Liverpool Lime Street:

Trains call at Liverpool Central ± 2 minutes and Birkenhead Central ± 9 minutes later.

✕ : 0538, 0608, 0643, 0713, 0743, 0755Ⓐ, 0813, 0820Ⓐ, 0843, 0858⑥, 0913, 0928, 0943, 0958 and every 15 minutes until 1858, 1913 and every 30 minutes until 2343.

⑦ : 0813, 0843 and every 30 minutes until 2313, 2343.

From Chester:

Trains call at Birkenhead Central ± 33 minutes and Liverpool Central ± 44* minutes later.

✕ : 0555, 0630, 0700, 0722Ⓐ, 0730⑥, 0737Ⓐ, 0752Ⓐ, 0800⑥, 0807Ⓐ, 0815⑥, 0831, 0845 and every 15 minutes until 1830, 1900 and every 30 minutes until 2300.

⑦ : 0800, 0830 and every 30 minutes until 2300.

LIVERPOOL - SOUTHPORT
Journey time: ± 44 minutes 30 km ME

From Liverpool Central:

✕ : 0608, 0623, 0638, 0653, 0708 and every 15 minutes until 2308, 2323, 2338.

⑦ : 0808, 0823, 0853, 0923, 0953 and every 30 minutes until 2253, 2323, 2338.

From Southport:

✕ : 0538, 0553, 0608, 0623, 0643, 0658, 0713, 0728, 0738Ⓐ, 0743⑥, 0748Ⓐ, 0758, 0803Ⓐ, 0813 and every 15 minutes until 2258, 2316.

⑦ : 0758, 0828, 0858, 0928, 0958 and every 30 minutes until 2258, 2316.

p – Starts / terminates at Manchester **Piccadilly**, not Victoria.
v – Starts / terminates at Manchester **Victoria**, not Piccadilly.

* – Trains FROM Chester call at Liverpool Lime Street, then Liverpool Central.

170 LONDON - LEICESTER - NOTTINGHAM, DERBY and SHEFFIELD

Most trains convey 🍷 EM

km			②–⑥	⚒	Ⓐ	⑥	Ⓐ	⑥S	⚒	Ⓐ	⑥	Ⓐ	⑥	⑥	Ⓐ	⚒	Ⓐ	Ⓐ	⑥	⚒	⚒	⚒	⚒	⚒	ⒶF	⚒
0	**London** St Pancras ... d.	⚒	0015	...	0545	0545	0632	0637	...	0652	0652	0655	0701	...	0724	0729	...	0758	0757	0801	0815	0826	0829	0856	...	0900
47	Luton ✈ Parkway ... d.		0043	...	|	|	|	|	...	0713	0713	|	|	...	|	0749	...	|	|	|	|	|	0849	|	...	|
49	Luton ... d.		0047	...	0612	0612	0654	0659	...	|	|	0718	0722	...	|	|	...	|	|	0822	|	|	|	|	...	0922
80	Bedford ... d.		0111	...	0627	0627	0709	|	...	|	|	0733	0736	...	|	0804	...	|	|	0837	|	|	0904	|	...	0937
105	Wellingborough ... d.		0131	...	0639	0639	0721	|	...	|	|	0746	0748	...	|	0817	...	|	|	0849	|	|	0917	|	...	0949
116	Kettering ... d.		0141	...	0647	0647	0729	0727	0738	|	|	0756	0758	...	|	0823	0832	|	|	0900	|	|	0923	|	...	1000
128	**Corby** ... a.		|	...	|	|	|	|	0747	|	|	|	|	...	|	|	0841	|	|	0911	|	|	|	|	0926	1011
133	Market Harborough ... d.		0153	...	0657	0657	0739	0737	...	|	|	0807	0808	...	0816	0834	...	|	|	...	0910	|	0934	|	|	...
159	**Leicester** ... d.		0210	...	0712	0712	0752	0753	...	0758	0800	0823	0823	0830	0830	0848	...	0901	0901	...	0925	0930	0948	1001	|	...
180	Loughborough ... d.		▬	...	0722	0723	0802	0803	...	0808	0809	0834	0833	0840	0840	0858	...	|	|	...	|	0940	0958	|	|	...
191	E. Midlands Parkway . d.		...	...	0729	|	|	0811	...	0816	|	0842	0841	0848	0848	|	...	|	|	...	0942	0948	|	|	1031	...
204	**Nottingham** ... a.		⚒	...	|	|	|	|	...	0832	0831	0854	0854	|	|	0918	...	|	|	...	0955	|	1018	|	|	...
207	**Derby** ... a.		0627	0721	0745	0743	0817	0823	...	...	...	...	...	0903	0903	...	...	0923	0923	...	...	1003	...	1023	1045	...
246	Chesterfield ... d.		0646	0743	0810	0810	0838	0844	...	...	...	...	...	0927	0927	...	...	0943	0943	...	...	1027	...	1043	...	...
265	**Sheffield** ... a.		0713	0800	0827	0826	0855	0858	...	...	...	...	...	0940	0941	...	...	0958	0958	...	...	1041	...	1100	...	...

	⚒	⚒	⚒	⚒	⚒	⚒	⚒	⚒	⚒	⚒	⚒	⚒	⚒	⚒	⚒	⚒	⚒	⚒	⚒	⚒	⚒	⚒	⚒	⚒	⚒	⚒
London St Pancras ... d.	0915	0926	0929	0958	1001	1015	1026	1029	1058	1101	1115	1126	1129	1158	1201	1215	1226	1229	1258	1301	1315	1326	1329	1358	1401	1415
Luton ✈ Parkway ... d.	|	|	0949	|	|	|	|	1049	|	|	|	|	1149	|	|	|	|	1249	|	|	|	|	1349	|	|	|
Luton ... d.	|	|	|	|	1022	|	|	|	|	1122	|	|	|	|	1222	|	|	|	|	1322	|	|	|	|	1422	|
Bedford ... d.	|	|	1004	|	1037	|	|	1104	|	1137	|	|	1204	|	1237	|	|	1304	|	1337	|	|	1404	|	1437	|
Wellingborough ... d.	|	|	1017	|	1049	|	|	1117	|	1149	|	|	1217	|	1249	|	|	1317	|	1349	|	|	1417	|	1449	|
Kettering ... d.	|	|	1023	|	1100	|	|	1123	|	1200	|	|	1223	|	1300	|	|	1323	|	1400	|	|	1423	|	1500	|
Corby ... a.	|	|	|	|	1111	|	|	|	|	1212	|	|	|	|	1311	|	|	|	|	1412	|	|	|	|	1512	|
Market Harborough ... d.	1010	|	1034	|	...	1110	|	1134	|	...	1210	|	1234	|	...	1310	|	1334	|	...	1410	|	1434	|	...	1510
Leicester ... d.	1025	1030	1048	1101	...	1125	1130	1148	1201	...	1225	1230	1248	1301	...	1325	1330	1348	1401	...	1425	1430	1448	1501	...	1525
Loughborough ... d.	|	1040	1058	|	...	|	1140	1158	|	...	|	1240	1258	|	...	|	1340	1358	|	...	|	1440	1458	|	...	|
E. Midlands Parkway . d.	1042	1048	|	|	...	1142	1148	|	|	...	1242	1248	|	|	...	1342	1348	|	|	...	1442	1448	|	|	...	1542
Nottingham ... a.	1055	|	1118	|	...	1155	|	1218	|	...	1255	|	1318	|	...	1355	|	1418	|	...	1455	|	1518	|	...	1555
Derby ... a.	...	1103	...	1123	...	...	1203	...	1223	...	...	1303	...	1323	...	...	1403	...	1423	...	...	1503	...	1523	...	...
Chesterfield ... d.	...	1127	...	1143	...	...	1227	...	1243	...	...	1327	...	1343	...	...	1427	...	1443	...	...	1527	...	1543	...	...
Sheffield ... a.	...	1141	...	1159	...	...	1241	...	1259	...	...	1341	...	1402	...	...	1441	...	1500	...	...	1541	...	1558	...	...

	⚒	⚒	⚒	⚒	⚒	⑥	Ⓐ	⚒	⚒	⚒	⚒	⚒	⑥	Ⓐ	⚒	⑥	Ⓐ	Ⓐ	⑥	Ⓐ	⑥	⑥B	Ⓐ	⚒	Ⓐ	⑥
London St Pancras ... d.	1426	1429	1458	1501	1515	1526	1526	1529	1558	1601	1615	1626	1629	1629	1657	1701	1700	1700	1715	1715	1726	1729	1730	1757	1745	1801
Luton ✈ Parkway ... d.	|	1449	|	|	|	|	|	1549	|	|	|	|	1649	1649	|	|	|	|	|	|	|	1749	|	|	1808	|
Luton ... d.	|	|	|	1522	|	|	|	|	|	1622	|	|	|	1653	|	1722	|	|	|	1740	|	|	|	|	|	1822
Bedford ... d.	|	1504	|	1537	|	|	|	1604	|	1637	|	|	1704	1707	|	1737	1737	1737	|	|	|	1804	1804	|	|	1837
Wellingborough ... d.	|	1517	|	1549	|	|	|	1617	|	1649	|	|	1717	1719	|	1749	1749	1749	|	|	|	1817	1817	|	1832	1849
Kettering ... d.	|	1523	|	1600	|	|	|	1623	|	1700	|	|	1723	1726	|	1800	1806g	1814g	|	|	|	1823	1823	|	1844	1900
Corby ... a.	|	|	|	1611	|	|	|	|	|	1711	|	|	|	|	|	1811	1815	|	|	|	|	|	|	|	|	1911
Market Harborough ... d.	|	1534	|	...	1610	|	|	1634	|	...	1710	|	1734	1736	|	...	...	|	1810	1816	|	1834	1834	|	1856	...
Leicester ... d.	1530	1548	1601	...	1625	1630	1630	1648	1701	...	1725	1730	1748	1751	1801	...	...	1837	1825	1832	1830	1848	1848	1901	1914	...
Loughborough ... d.	1540	1558	|	...	|	1640	1640	1658	|	...	|	1740	1758	1801	|	...	...	1847	|	|	1840	1858	1858	|	1926	...
E. Midlands Parkway . d.	1548	|	|	...	1642	1648	1648	|	|	...	1742	1748	|	|	|	...	...	1856	1842	1850	1848	|	1905	|	1934	...
Nottingham ... a.	|	1618	|	...	1655	|	|	1718	|	...	1755	|	1818	1821	|	...	...	|	1855	1909	|	1918	1920	|	1947	...
Derby ... a.	1603	...	1623	...	...	1703	1703	...	1723	...	...	1803	...	...	1823	...	...	1913	...	...	1903	...	...	1923	2031	...
Chesterfield ... d.	1627	...	1643	...	...	1727	1734	...	1743	...	...	1827	...	...	1843	...	...	1934	...	...	1927	...	...	1943	...	...
Sheffield ... a.	1641	...	1659	...	...	1742	1748	...	1800	...	...	1841	...	...	1900	...	...	1950	...	...	1941	...	...	1959	...	...

	ⒶC	⑥	Ⓐ	⑥L	ⒶL	⑥	ⒶB	⑥	Ⓐ	⑥	Ⓐ	Ⓐ	⑥	⑥	Ⓐ	⑥	ⒶL	⑥L	ⒶL	Ⓐ	⑥	⚒	⚒	Ⓐ	⑥	⑥
London St Pancras ... d.	1800	1826	1825	1815	1815	1829	1830	1858	1857	1901	1900	1915	1915	1926	1928	1929	1955	1958	1932	2000	2001	2015	2026	2030	2030	2056
Luton ✈ Parkway ... d.	|	|	|	|	|	1849	1850	|	|	|	|	|	|	|	|	1949	|	|	1953	|	|	|	|	2049	2050	|
Luton ... d.	1822	|	1850	|	|	|	|	|	|	1922	1924	|	|	|	|	|	|	|	|	2022	2025	|	|	|	|	|
Bedford ... d.	1837	|	|	|	|	1904	1907	|	|	1937	1940	|	|	|	|	2004	|	|	2009	2037	2039	|	|	2104	2104	|
Wellingborough ... d.	1849	|	|	|	1903	1917	1920	|	|	1949	1954	|	|	|	|	2017	|	|	2022	2049	2051	|	|	2118	2117	|
Kettering ... d.	1906	|	|	|	1911	1923	1926	|	|	2000	2006	|	|	|	2019	2023	|	|	|	2101	2100	|	|	2123	2124	|
Corby ... a.	1916	|	|	|	|	|	|	|	|	2011	2017	|	|	|	|	|	|	|	|	2112	2111	|	|	|	|	|
Market Harborough ... d.	...	|	1927	1910	|	1934	|	|	1949	...	...	2010	2010	|	2029	2034	|	|	2038	...	...	2109	|	2134	2134	|
Leicester ... d.	...	1930	1942	1925	1934	1948	1952	2001	2002	...	...	2025	2025	2030	2045	2048	2102	2105	2053	...	...	2122	2130	2148	2148	2201
Loughborough ... d.	...	1940	1953	|	1945	1958	|	|	2013	...	...	|	|	2040	2055	2058	|	|	2103	...	...	|	2140	2158	2158	|
E. Midlands Parkway . d.	...	1948	|	1942	1954	|	2009	|	2021	...	...	2038	2042	2051	2102	|	|	|	|	...	...	2136	2148	|	2207	|
Nottingham ... a.	...	|	|	1955	2008	2018	2023	|	|	...	...	2051	2055	|	|	2118	|	|	2128	...	...	2150	|	2218	2221	|
Derby ... a.	...	2003	2015	|	|	...	...	2023	2034	...	...	...	...	2108	2119	...	2129	2131	|	...	...	...	2205	...	...	2223
Chesterfield ... d.	...	2027	2039	2052	2109	...	...	2043	2054	...	...	...	...	...	...	...	2153	2203	2222	...	...	...	...	...	...	2247
Sheffield ... a.	...	2041	2055	2105	2123	...	...	2059	2109	...	...	...	...	...	...	...	2208	2217	2236	...	...	...	...	...	...	2300

	Ⓐ	Ⓐ	⑥	⑥	Ⓐ	⚒	⚒	⚒	⑥	Ⓐ	⑥	Ⓐ	Ⓐ		⑦Y	⑦	⑦	⑦	⑦	⑦	⑦	⑦	⑦	⑦	⑦	⑦
London St Pancras ... d.	2055	2100	2101	...	...	2125	2130	2200	...	...	2226	2225	2315	⑦	...	0900	0930	1000	1030	1100	1130	1210	1230	1310	1340	1410
Luton ✈ Parkway ... d.	|	|	|	...	...	|	2151	|	...	...	2247	2248	|		...	0928	|	1029	|	1129	1159	1231	1253	1331	1402	1431
Luton ... d.	|	2123	2124	...	...	|	|	2224	...	...	|	|	2346		...	|	0959	|	1102	1133	1203	1234	1257	1334	1407	|
Bedford ... d.	|	2138	2139	...	...	|	2205	2239	...	...	2303	2303	0012	❖	...	0950	1019	1054	1125	1154	1223	1249	1312	1349	1422	1446
Wellingborough ... d.	|	2150	2152	...	...	|	2218	2252	...	...	2315	2317	0024		...	1003	1031	1108	1136	1207	1235	1302	1326	1402	1436	1459
Kettering ... d.	|	2157	2202	2206	2211	|	2225	2300	2305	2311	2322	2326	0042		...	1010	1038	1116	1143	1215	1242	1309	1334	1409	1443	1506
Corby ... a.	|	|	|	2221	2226	|	|	|	2319	2326	|	|	|		...	|	|	|	|	|	|	|	|	|	|	|
Market Harborough ... d.	|	2207	2213	...	...	2218	2235	2311	...	...	2332	2337	0052		...	1020	1049	1127	1153	1225	1252	1319	1345	1419	1455	1516
Leicester ... d.	2203	2222	2229	...	...	2233	2249	2327	...	...	2346	2353	0107		1020	1036	1105	1145	1210	1241	1309	1336	1403	1436	1513	1533
Loughborough ... d.	|	2232	2245	...	...	2243	2259	2338	...	...	2356	0004	0119		1030	1046	1115	1156	1220	1251	1319	1346	1414	1446	1524	1543
E. Midlands Parkway . d.	|	2239	|	...	...	2250	2307	2347	...	...	0004	0012	0130		1037	1053	1123	1205	1227	1259	1326	1353	1423	1453	1533	1550
Nottingham ... a.	|	|	|	...	...	2304	|	0006	...	...	|	|	0145		|	1108	|	1216	|	1312	|	1407	|	1507	|	1605
Derby ... a.	2225	2254	2259	...	...	...	2325	...	...	...	0019	0026	0210		1054	...	1143	...	1243	...	1342	...	1443	...	1549	...
Chesterfield ... d.	2245	...	...	...	...	...	...	...	...	...	...	0048	...		1114	...	1210	...	1312	...	1411	...	1514	...	1612	...
Sheffield ... a.	2301	...	...	...	...	...	...	...	...	...	...	0104	...		1128	...	1228	...	1328	...	1425	...	1529	...	1629	...

	⑦L	⑦	⑦	⑦	⑦	⑦	⑦	⑦	⑦	⑦	⑦	⑦	⑦	⑦	⑦	⑦	⑦	⑦	⑦	⑦	⑦	⑦L	⑦	⑦	⑦	⑦
London St Pancras ... d.	1440	1510	1540	1610	1635	1640	1705	1710	1735	1740	1805	1810	1835	1840	1905	1910	1935	1940	2000	2010	2035	2040	2110	2130	2230	2300
Luton ✈ Parkway ... d.	|	1533	|	1631	|	|	|	1731	|	|	|	1831	|	|	|	1931	|	|	|	2031	|	|	2131	|	2251	2327
Luton ... d.	1504	|	1604	|	|	1702	|	|	|	1802	|	|	|	1902	|	|	|	2002	|	|	|	2104	|	2152	|	|
Bedford ... d.	1519	1548	1619	1646	|	1716	|	1746	|	1816	|	1846	|	1916	|	1946	|	2016	|	2047	|	2120	2146	2206	2313	2351
Wellingborough ... d.	1533	1602	1633	1659	|	1729	|	1758	|	1829	|	1858	|	1929	|	1958	|	2029	|	2058	|	2133	2159	2219	2326	0004
Kettering ... d.	1541	1611	1641	1706	|	1737	|	1806	|	1837	|	1905	|	1937	|	2005	|	2037	|	2106	|	2141	2206	2227	2333	0012
Corby ... a.	|	|	|	|	|	|	|	|	|	|	|	|	|	|	|	|	|	|	|	|	|	|	|	|	|	|
Market Harborough ... d.	1552	1622	1652	1716	|	1747	|	1815	|	1847	|	1915	|	1947	|	2015	|	2047	|	2116	|	2152	2216	2237	2343	0022
Leicester ... d.	1610	1638	1710	1733	1744	1803	1811	1833	1841	1903	1910	1932	1945	2003	2022	2033	2041	2103	2110	2133	2141	2210	2233	2254	0004	0042
Loughborough ... d.	1621	1651	1721	1743	|	1813	|	1843	|	1913	|	1942	|	2013	|	2043	|	2113	2121	2143	2151	|	2247	2304	0014	0052
E. Midlands Parkway . d.	1630	1659	1730	1750	1800	1821	1825	1850	1855	1921	1925	1949	2001	2021	2039	2050	2055	2121	2129	2150	2159	2226	2258	2316	0026	0104
Nottingham ... a.	|	1711	|	1805	|	|	1836	1905	|	|	1936	2005	|	|	2051	2105	|	|	2145	2205	|	|	2311	|	0042	|
Derby ... a.	1647	...	1747	...	1814	1836	...	...	1908	1937	...	...	2013	2037	...	...	2107	2136	...	...	2211	2240	...	2335	...	0119
Chesterfield ... d.	1713	...	1811	...	1837	...	...	...	1934	...	...	...	2037	...	...	...	2129	...	...	...	...	2309	...	2355	...	...
Sheffield ... a.	1728	...	1825	...	1851	...	...	...	1950	...	...	...	2051	...	...	...	2143	...	...	...	...	2323	...	0008	...	...

B – To/from Lincoln (Table **187**).
C – To/from Melton Mowbray (see panel on page 139).
D – To/from London St. Pancras (Table **170**).
E – 12-car Derby - Corby - London St Pancras.
F – Via Melton Mowbray (see panel on page 139).
L – To/from Leeds (Table **171**).
R – From York (d. 1750) and Doncaster (d. 1813).

S – To Doncaster (a. 0953) and York (a. 1017).
V – From York (d. 1750) and Doncaster (d. 1813⑦, 1818⑥).
Y – To Doncaster (a. 1152) and York (a. 1215).

e – Arrives 1121.
f – Arrives Kettering 9 minutes after Corby.
g – Arrives 1800.

h – Also calls at Doncaster (d. 0557).
k – Arrives 7–9 minutes earlier.
n – Arrives 0919.
p – On Ⓐ Chesterfield d.0002, Nottingham a. 0040.

❖ – For Kettering - Corby service on ⑦, see next page.

EM Most trains 🍷 SHEFFIELD, DERBY and NOTTINGHAM - LEICESTER - LONDON 170

	✖	Ⓐ	Ⓐ	⑥	⑥	Ⓐ	Ⓐ C	⑥	Ⓐ	⑥	✖	⑥	Ⓐ	Ⓐ	⑥	Ⓐ	Ⓐ L h	⑥	⑥	Ⓐ	Ⓐ	Ⓐ	⑥	Ⓐ	⑥
Sheffield d.	...	...	...	...	0529	...	...	...	0530	...	...	...	...	0600	0629	...	0629	...	...	...	...	0649	...	...	...
Chesterfield d.	...	...	...	...	0541	...	...	...	0542	...	...	...	...	0613	0641	...	0640	...	...	...	...	0701	...	...	...
Derby d.	...	0500	0519	0521	0601	...	...	...	0604	...	...	0621	...	0633	0701	...	0705	...	0721	...	...	0722	...	...	...
Nottingham d.	...	|	|	|	|	0532	...	0605	|	0632	...	|	0630	|	|	0652	|	0705	|	0710	...	|	0730	0755	...
E. Midlands Parkway d.	...	0511	|	0535	|	0543	...	|	0617	0643	...	0635	0642	|	|	0704	|	|	0735	0725	...	0733	0743	0804	...
Loughborough d.	...	0518	|	0542	|	0552	...	0621	0626	|	...	0642	|	0653	|	|	0722	0721	0742	|	...	0741	|	|	...
Leicester d.	0445	0529	0543	0553	0624	0604	...	0632	0639	0700	...	0653	0659	0706	0724	0719	0736	0732	0753	0742	...	0756	0801	0819	...
Market Harborough d.	|	0543	0558	0607	|	0620	...	0646	0654	0714	...	|	0713	|	|	0733	|	0746	|	0757	...	|	0815	|	...
Corby d.	|	|	|	|	|	|	0635	|	|	|	0706	|	|	|	|	|	|	|	|	|	0802	|	|	|	0816
Kettering d.	0505	0554	0608	0617	|	0631	0645	0656	0706	|	0717	0726	0724	0730	|	0743	0759	0756	|	0809	0811	0817	|	|	0826
Wellingborough d.	0517	0602	0616	0624	|	0640	0654	0703	0714	|	...	0734	0732	0738	|	0751	0807	0803	|	|	...	0825	|	|	0834
Bedford d.	0538	|	0630	0638	|	|	0709	0717	|	|	...	0747	|	0755	|	|	|	0817	|	0829	...	|	|	|	0847
Luton d.	|	0625	|	0653	|	|	0724	|	|	|	...	0803	0757	|	|	0815	|	|	|	|	...	|	|	|	0903
Luton ✈ Parkway d.	0556	|	|	|	|	0705	|	0732	0740	|	...	|	|	0811	|	|	|	0832	|	|	...	|	|	|	|
London St Pancras a.	0620	0649	0708	0718	0729	0731	0748	0756	0807	0814	...	0827	0823	0839	0831	0842	0856	0856	0900	0906	...	0910	0914	0926	0926

	✖	Ⓐ	✖ B	⑥	Ⓐ	Ⓐ L	⑥ L	✖	✖	✖	✖	Ⓐ	⑥ L	✖	✖	✖	✖	✖	✖	✖	✖	✖	✖	✖	✖	✖
Sheffield d.	0729	...	...	...	0746	0724	0737	...	0829	...	0849	...	0834	...	0929	...	0949	...	...	1029	...	1049	...	...	1129	...
Chesterfield d.	0741	...	...	...	0759	0737	0750	...	0841	...	0901	...	0847	...	0941	...	1001	...	...	1041	...	1101	...	...	1141	...
Derby d.	0801	0736	...	0821	0819	|	|	...	0901	...	0921	...	|	...	1001	...	1021	...	...	1101	...	1121	...	...	1201	...
Nottingham d.	|	|	0805	|	|	0832k	0832k	...	|	0905	|	0932	0932n	...	|	1005	|	1032	...	|	1105	|	1132	...	|	1205
E. Midlands Parkway d.	|	|	|	0835	0835	0843	0843	...	|	|	0935	0943	0943	...	|	|	1035	1043	...	|	|	1135	1143	...	|	|
Loughborough d.	|	0754	0821	0842	0842	|	|	...	|	0921	0942	|	|	...	|	1021	1042	|	...	|	1121	1142	|	...	|	1221
Leicester d.	0824	0805	0832	0853	0856	0900	0900	...	0924	0932	0953	1000	1000	...	1024	1032	1053	1100	...	1124	1132	1153	1200	...	1224	1232
Market Harborough d.	|	0819	0846	|	|	0914	0914	...	|	0946	|	1014	1014	...	|	1046	|	1114	...	|	1146	|	1214	...	|	1246
Corby d.	|	|	|	|	|	|	|	0916	|	|	|	|	|	1016	|	|	|	|	1116	|	|	|	|	1216	|	|
Kettering d.	|	0829	0856	|	|	|	|	0926	|	0956	|	|	|	1026	|	1056	|	|	1126	|	1156	|	|	1226	|	1256
Wellingborough d.	|	0842	0903	|	|	|	|	0934	|	1003	|	|	|	1034	|	1103	|	|	1134	|	1203	|	|	1234	|	1303
Bedford d.	|	0905	0917	|	|	|	|	0947	|	1017	|	|	|	1047	|	1117	|	|	1147	|	1217	|	|	1247	|	1317
Luton d.	|	0919	|	|	|	|	|	1003	|	|	|	|	|	1103	|	|	|	|	1203	|	|	|	|	1303	|	|
Luton ✈ Parkway d.	|	|	0932	|	|	|	|	|	|	1032	|	|	|	|	|	1132	|	|	|	|	1232	|	|	|	|	1332
London St Pancras a.	0933	0945	0956	0959	1006	1017	1014	1026	1030	1056	1100	1114	1114	1126	1130	1156	1201	1214	1226	1231	1256	1300	1314	1326	1331	1357

	✖	✖	✖	✖	✖	✖	✖	✖	✖	✖	✖	✖	✖	✖	✖	✖	✖	✖	✖	✖	⑥	Ⓐ	⑥	Ⓐ	✖	⑥
Sheffield d.	1149	...	...	1229	...	1249	...	...	1329	...	1349	...	...	1429	...	1449	...	...	1529	...	1549	1549	...	...	...	1629
Chesterfield d.	1201	...	...	1241	...	1301	...	...	1341	...	1401	...	...	1441	...	1501	...	...	1541	...	1601	1601	...	...	...	1641
Derby d.	1221	...	...	1301	...	1321	...	...	1401	...	1421	...	...	1501	...	1521	...	...	1601	...	1621	1621	...	...	...	1701
Nottingham d.	|	1232	...	|	1305	|	1332	...	|	1405	|	1432	...	|	1505	|	1532	...	|	1605	|	|	1632	1630	...	|
E. Midlands Parkway d.	1235	1243	...	|	|	1335	1343	...	|	|	1435	1443	...	|	|	1535	1543	...	|	|	1635	1635	1643	1641	...	|
Loughborough d.	1242	|	...	|	1321	1342	|	...	|	1421	1442	|	...	|	1521	1542	|	...	|	1621	1642	1642	|	|	...	|
Leicester d.	1253	1300	...	1324	1332	1353	1400	...	1424	1432	1453	1500	...	1524	1532	1553	1600	...	1624	1632	1653	1653	1700	1658	...	1726
Market Harborough d.	|	1314	...	|	1346	|	1414	...	|	1446	|	1514	...	|	1546	|	1614	...	|	1646	|	|	1714	1712	...	|
Corby d.	|	|	1316	|	|	|	|	1416	|	|	|	|	1516	|	|	|	|	1616	|	|	|	|	|	|	1716	|
Kettering d.	|	|	1326	|	1356	|	|	1426	|	1456	|	|	1526	|	1556	|	|	1626	|	1656	|	1714	|	|	1726	|
Wellingborough d.	|	|	1334	|	1403	|	|	1434	|	1503	|	|	1534	|	1603	|	|	1634	|	1703	|	|	|	|	1734	|
Bedford d.	|	|	1347	|	1417	|	|	1447	|	1517	|	|	1547	|	1617	|	|	1647	|	1717	|	|	|	|	1747	|
Luton d.	|	|	1403	|	|	|	|	1503	|	|	|	|	1603	|	|	|	|	1703	|	|	|	|	|	1749	1803	|
Luton ✈ Parkway d.	|	|	|	|	1431	|	|	|	|	1532	|	|	|	|	1632	|	|	|	|	1732	|	|	|	|	|	|
London St Pancras a.	1400	1414	1427	1430	1456	1459	1514	1527	1531	1556	1559	1614	1627	1632	1656	1700	1715	1726	1730	1756	1800	1807	1814	1815	1826	1829

	Ⓐ	✖	⑥	Ⓐ	✖	Ⓐ E	⑥	✖	✖	Ⓐ	⑥	✖	Ⓐ	⑥	✖	✖	Ⓐ	⑥	⑥ V	✖	Ⓐ	✖	⑥	⑥	Ⓐ	Ⓐ
Sheffield d.	1629	...	1649	1649	...	...	...	1729	...	1738	1749	...	...	...	1829	...	1849	...	1849	...	...	1929	...	...	...	...
Chesterfield d.	1641	...	1701	1701	...	...	...	1741	...	1754	1801	...	...	...	1841	...	1901	...	1901	...	...	1941	...	...	...	...
Derby d.	1701	...	1721	1721	...	1636	...	1801	...	1821	1821	...	...	...	1901	...	1921	...	1921	...	...	2001	...	...	...	...
Nottingham d.	|	1705	|	|	1732	|	...	|	1805	|	|	1832	...	...	|	1905	|	...	|	1932	...	|	...	2005	2002	...
E. Midlands Parkway d.	|	|	1735	1735	1743	1648	...	|	|	1835	1835	1843	...	...	|	|	1935	...	1935	1943	...	|	...	2017	2015	...
Loughborough d.	|	1721	1742	1742	|	|	...	|	1821	1842	1842	|	...	...	|	1921	1942	...	1942	|	...	|	...	2025	2022	...
Leicester d.	1724	1732	1753	1753	1800	|	...	1824	1832	1853	1853	1900	...	...	1924	1932	1953	...	1953	2000	...	2024	...	2036	2033	...
Market Harborough d.	|	1746	|	|	1814	|	...	|	1846	|	|	1914	...	...	|	1946	|	...	|	2014	...	|	...	2049	2047	...
Corby d.	|	|	|	|	|	1751	1816	|	|	|	|	|	1856	1916	|	|	|	1950	|	|	1953	|	2043	|	|	2051
Kettering d.	|	1756	|	1814	|	1823f	1826	|	1856	|	|	|	1926f	1926	|	1956	|	2026f	2014	|	2026f	|	2126f	2058	2057	2118f
Wellingborough d.	|	1803	|	|	|	1834	1834	|	1903	|	|	|	1934	1934	|	2003	|	2034	|	|	2034	|	2134	2107	2104	2127
Bedford d.	|	1817	|	|	|	1847	1847	|	1917	|	|	|	1947	1947	|	2017	|	2047	|	|	2047	|	2147	2121	2118	2142
Luton d.	1811	|	|	|	|	1903	1903	|	|	|	|	|	2003	2003	|	|	|	2103	|	|	2103	|	2203	|	|	2159
Luton ✈ Parkway d.	|	1832	|	|	|	|	|	|	1932	|	|	|	|	|	|	2032	|	|	|	|	|	|	|	2136	2132	|
London St Pancras a.	1836	1856	1900	1903	1915	1926	1926	1933	1958	2002	2000	2016	2027	2027	2033	2056	2101	2126	2103	2116	2126	2134	2226	2159	2157	2224

	Ⓐ	⑥	⑥	Ⓐ	⑥	⑥	Ⓐ	✖	Ⓐ	⑥	⑥	Ⓐ	✖		⑦	⑦	⑦	⑦	⑦	⑦	⑦	⑦	⑦	⑦ L	⑦ L	⑦
Sheffield d.	...	2029	...	2049	...	...	...	2137	2201	2242	2320	2321	2337	⑦	...	...	...	...	0818	...	0925	...	1025	1035	1143	...
Chesterfield d.	...	2040	...	2101	...	...	...	2155	2213	2256	2332	2345	2353p		...	...	...	...	0831	...	0938	...	1037	1048	1155	...
Derby d.	...	2100	...	2121	...	...	...	|	2234	|	0006	0005	|		0650	...	0751	...	0851	...	0959	...	1057	|	1217	...
Nottingham d.	2102	|	...	|	2105	2132	2132	2235	...	2328	...	...	0030p	✣	|	0729	|	0822	|	0920	|	1030	|	1139e	|	1249
E. Midlands Parkway d.	2114	2113	...	2135	2117	|	|	▬	...	...	...	...	...		0702	0739	0805	0835	0905	0931	1013	1045	1111	1150	1234	1303
Loughborough d.	2122	2120	...	2142	2125	2147	2147	...	...	...	...	...	...		|	|	0813	0843	0912	0940	1020	1053	1119	1159	1242	1312
Leicester d.	2133	2131	...	2153	2137	2158	2158	...	...	...	...	...	...		0720	0755	0825	0855	0924	0954	1032	1108	1130	1213	1256	1326
Market Harborough d.	2147	...	...	|	2150	2212	2212	✖	...	...	...	...	...		0738	0811	0841	0911	0940	1011	1045	1122	1143	1227	1310	1340
Corby d.	|	...	2143	|	|	|	|	2243	...	...	...	...	...		|	|	|	|	|	|	|	|	|	|	|	|
Kettering d.	2157	...	2152	|	2158	2223	2223	2252	...	...	...	...	...		0749	0821	0851	0921	0950	1022	1055	1133	1153	1238	1321	1351
Wellingborough d.	2204	...	...	|	2207	2230	2230	...	...	...	...	...	...		0801	0832	0902	0932	1002	1030	1102	1141	1201	1246	1329	1359
Bedford d.	2218	...	...	|	2221	2243	2245	...	...	...	...	...	...		0815	0845	0915	0945	1015	1045	1116	1157	1215	1302	1344	1415
Luton d.	2235	...	...	|	2236	2301	2302	...	...	...	...	...	...		0834	|	0935	|	1035	|	1136	|	1230	|	1401	|
Luton ✈ Parkway d.	2239	...	...	|	2240	|	|	...	...	...	...	...	...		|	0907	|	1007	|	1106	|	1213	|	1318	|	1431
London St Pancras a.	2305	...	...	2301	2315	2340	2338	...	...	...	...	...	...		0915	0945	1015	1048	1117	1148	1214	1239	1254	1344	1427	1457

	⑦	⑦	⑦	⑦	⑦	⑦	⑦	⑦ L	⑦	⑦	⑦	⑦	⑦	⑦	⑦	⑦	⑦	⑦	⑦	⑦ V	⑦	⑦	⑦	⑦	⑦	⑦
Sheffield d.	1249	...	1343	...	1449	...	...	1529	1550	...	...	...	1649	...	...	...	1750	...	...	1847	...	1928	2026	...	2236	2330
Chesterfield d.	1301	...	1356	...	1501	...	...	1542	1602	...	...	...	1700	...	...	...	1802	...	...	1900	...	1941	2039	...	2248	2344
Derby d.	1322	...	1417	...	1522	...	...	1602	1626	...	...	1657	1723	...	...	1804	1826	...	...	1919	...	2003	2101	...	2323	|
Nottingham d.	|	1349	|	1452	|	1543	1552	|	|	1645	1650	|	|	1745	1752	|	|	1845	1852	|	1951	|	|	2121	...	0023
E. Midlands Parkway d.	1336	1403	1431	1504	1536	1553	1605	1616	1637	1655	1703	1711	1736	1755	1804	1820	1837	1855	1905	1934	2004	2018	2113	2131	...	...
Loughborough d.	1344	1412	1439	1512	1543	|	1612	1625	|	|	1711	1719	|	|	1812	1828	|	1902	1912	1942	2011	2027	|	2139	...	...
Leicester d.	1355	1426	1455	1524	1555	1612	1624	1639	1655	1710	1723	1731	1754	1814	1825	1840	1854	1914	1925	1955	2023	2041	2132	2154	...	...
Market Harborough d.	1408	1440	1508	1537	|	|	1637	1653	|	|	1736	1744	|	|	1838	1853	|	1927	1938	2008	2036	2055	2146	2208	...	...
Corby d.	|	|	|	|	|	|	|	|	|	|	|	|	|	|	|	|	|	|	|	|	|	|	|	|	...	...
Kettering d.	1418	1451	1518	1547	|	|	1647	1703	|	|	1746	1755	|	|	1848	1905	|	1937	1948	2015	2046	2106	2157	2218	...	...
Wellingborough d.	1426	1459	1525	1554	|	|	1655	1712	|	|	1754	1802	|	|	1855	1912	|	1945	1955	2025	2053	2114	2205	2225	...	...
Bedford d.	1439	1515	1540	1609	|	|	1709	1728	|	|	1808	1817	|	|	1909	1928	|	1959	2009	2040	2109	2131	2221	2239	...	...
Luton d.	1454	|	1555	|	1642	|	|	1745	|	|	|	1831	|	|	|	1944	|	2015	|	2054	2123	2146	2237	2254	...	...
Luton ✈ Parkway d.	|	1531	|	1624	|	|	1725	|	|	|	1824	|	|	|	1924	|	|	|	2024	2058	|	|	|	|	...	...
London St Pancras a.	1518	1557	1619	1648	1709	1723	1748	1810	1802	1817	1847	1855	1909	1925	1948	2007	2000	2039	2049	2121	2148	2213	2303	2324	...	...

✣ – **Kettering - Corby** and v.v. trains on ⑦. Journey time: 10 minutes.
From Kettering at 0955, 1055, 1155, 1255, 1355, 1455, 1555, 1650, 1750, 1855, 1950, 2050, 2155.
From Corby at 0930, 1025, 1125, 1220, 1330, 1425, 1525, 1625, 1720, 1820, 1920, 2020, 2125.

← FOR OTHER NOTES SEE PREVIOUS PAGE

CORBY - MELTON MOWBRAY - DERBY

km		Ⓐ	Ⓐ D			Ⓐ D	Ⓐ E	
0	**Corby** d.	0926	1916	...	**Derby** d.	...	1636	...
23	Oakham d.	0947	1936	...	East Mids Parkway d.	...	1648	...
43	**Melton Mowbray** d.	1000	1948	...	**Melton Mowbray** d.	0600	1714	...
81	East Mids Parkway d.	1031	...	...	Oakham d.	0612	1727	...
97	**Derby** a.	1045	...	...	**Corby** a.	0635	1751	...

171 NOTTINGHAM - SHEFFIELD - HUDDERSFIELD and LEEDS 2nd class NT

NOTTINGHAM - SHEFFIELD - LEEDS

km		⚒	Ⓐ	⚒	⚒	Ⓐ	⚒	Ⓐ	⚒	Ⓐ	⑥	⚒	⚒	⚒	⚒		⚒	⚒	⑥	Ⓐ	⚒	⚒	⚒	⚒	⑥A
0	**Nottingham** ..170 206 d.		...	...	0520	...	...	0621	0639	0712	0711	0746	0817	0847	0917	and	1644	1717	1744	1747	1817	1847	1917	...	2016
18	Langley Mill d.		...	...	|	...	...	0640	|	0731	0730	|	0836	|	0936	at	|	1736	1800	1803	1836	|	1936	...	2033
29	Alfreton 206 d.		...	...	|	...	...	0648	0700	0739	0738	0809	0844	0908	0944	the	1705	1744	1808	1811	1844	1908	1944	...	2041
45	Chesterfield...170 206 d.		...	...	0549	0626	...	0658	0710	0749	0748	0820	0855	0920	0955	same	1715	1755	1818	1820	1855	1920	1955	...	2052
64	**Sheffield** ......170 206 a.		...	...	0615	0646	...	0716	0728	0804	0811	0837	0914	0937	1014	minutes	1737	1814	1834	1838	1914	1937	2014	...	2105
64	**Sheffield** ......192 193 d.		0550	0606	...	0649	0706	0718	0751	0818	0818	0850	0918	0950	1018	past	1750	1818	1850	1850	1916f	1952	2018	2106	2126
70	Meadowhall...192 193 d.		0556	0612	...	0655	0712	0724	0757	0825	0825	0856	0924	0956	1024	each	1756	1824	1856	1856	1922f	1958	2024	2112	|
90	Barnsley d.		0610	0633	...	0712	0733	0741	0812	0842	0842	0912	0942	1012	1042	hour	1813	1842	1915	1915	1943	2013	2043	2134	|
107	Wakefield Kirkgate d.		0628	0650	...	0728	0751	0758	0828	0858	0858	0928	0958	1027	1058	until	1828	1858	1932	1931	1959	2028	2059	2152	2202e
130	**Leeds** a.		0649	0728	...	0751	0826	0819	0849	0919	0919	0949	1017	1049	1118	◇	1851	1926	1951	1952	2018	2049	2120	2228	2217

	ⒶA	⚒A	①–④	⑥	⑥	Ⓐ	ⒶA	⑦	⑦	⑦B	⑦	⑦	⑦	⑦	⑦	⑦	⑦	⑦	⑦A	⑦	⑦	⑦	⑦	⑦	⑦	⑦A
Nottingham ..170 206 d.	2033	...	...	2117	...	2114	2146		...	...	...	1008	1117	1217	1317	1417	1512	1617	...	1717	1817	1917	1943	2015	2133	...
Langley Mill d.	2050	...	...	2136	...	2141	2203		...	...	...	1032	1136	1236	1336	1436	1536	1636	...	1736	1836	1936	|	2034	2157	...
Alfreton 206 d.	2058	...	...	2144	...	2149	2211		...	...	...	1040	1144	1244	1344	1444	1544	1644	...	1744	1844	1944	2004	2042	2205	...
Chesterfield ..170 206 d.	2109	...	...	2155	...	2201	2222		...	...	...	1051	1154	1254	1354	1454	1556	1654	...	1754	1854	1954	2014	2052	2216	...
Sheffield ......170 206 a.	2123	...	...	2214	...	2220	2236		...	...	...	1110	1215	1315	1415	1515	1615	1715	...	1815	1915	2015	2031	2117	2236	...
Sheffield ......192 193 d.	2126	2217	2206	...	2224	...	2253		0839	1017	1039	1117	1217	1317	1417	1517	1617	1717	1734	1817	1917	2017	2039	2136	2239	2326
Meadowhall ..192 193 d.	|	|	2212	...	2231	...	|		0845	1023	1045	1123	1223	1323	1423	1523	1623	1723	|	1823	1923	2023	2045	2142	2245	|
Barnsley d.	|	|	2233	...	|	...	|		0910	1037	1110	1137	1237	1337	1437	1537	1637	1737	|	1837	1937	2037	2110	|	2310	|
Wakefield Kirkgate d.	2201e	2247e	2255	...	2320e	...	2323e		0930	1056	1130	1156	1259	1356	1456	1556	1656	1756	1806e	1856	1956	2056	2130	2228e	2330	2352e
Leeds a.	2218	2305	2330	...	2340	...	2342		1005	1116	1205	1216	1318	1416	1516	1616	1716	1816	1823	1916	2016	2116	2205	2250	0005	0007

	⚒	Ⓐ	⑥	Ⓐ	ⒶA	Ⓐ	⑥	Ⓐ	ⒶA	⑥A	⚒	⚒	⑥A	⚒	⚒	⚒		⚒	⚒	⚒	⑥	Ⓐ	⚒	⚒	⚒
Leeds d.		...	...	...	0525	...	...	0605	0634	0634	0638	0705	0738	0740	0805	0840	and	1706	1740	1806	1840	1840	1906	1945	2030
Wakefield Kirkgate d.		...	...	...	0538e	0604	...	0622	0647e	0646e	0709	0725	0751e	0758	0825	0858	at	1725	1758	1825	1858	1858	1925	2002	2049
Barnsley d.		...	...	0523	|	0622	0622	0638	|	|	0727	0742	|	0814	0840	0914	the	1740	1814	1840	1914	1918	1940	2019	2105
Meadowhall ..192 193 d.		...	...	0545	|	0642	0643	0652	|	|	0749	0755	|	0830	0854	0930	same	1754	1829	1854	1932	1935	1954	2036	2122
Sheffield ......192 193 a.		...	...	0554	0620	0653	0652	0700	0722	0722	0758	0805	0822	0840	0902	0937	minutes	1803	1838	1903	1939	1942	2002	2044	2130
Sheffield ......170 206 d.		0505	0554	0603	...	...	0703	0703	0724	0737	...	0808	0834	...	0905	...	past	1805	...	1905	...	...	2005	...	2137
Chesterfield ..170 206 d.		0520	0619	0619	...	...	0719	0720	0737	0750	...	0824	0847	...	0922	...	each	1822	...	1922	...	...	2022	...	2154
Alfreton 206 d.		|	0629	0630	...	...	0729	0731	0748	0801	...	0834	0857	...	0932	...	hour	1832	...	1932	...	...	2032	...	2205
Langley Mill d.		|	0637	0637	...	...	0737	0739	0757	0809	...	0842	|	...	0940	...	until	1840	...	1940	...	...	2040	...	2213
Nottingham ..170 206 a.		0607	0702	0701	...	...	0755	0757	0823	0825	...	0902	0919	...	1000	...	◇	1900	...	2000	...	...	2100	...	2235

	⚒	⚒	Ⓐ	⑥	Ⓐ	⑥	⑦	⑦	⑦	⑦	⑦A	⑦	⑦A	⑦	⑦	⑦	⑦	⑦	⑦A	⑦	⑦	⑦	⑦B	⑦	⑦	⑦	⑦
Leeds d.	2037	2137	...	...	2237	2244		...	0832	0905	0950	1002	1050	1105	1205	1305	1405	1434	1505	1605	1705	1803	1905	2022	2145	2217
Wakefield Kirkgate d.	2108	2208	...	...	2310	2300e		...	0903	0922	1003e	1019	1103e	1121	1222	1322	1422	1447e	1521	1622	1722	1822	1921	2052	2200e	2248
Barnsley d.	2126	2229	...	...	2331	|		...	0924	0941	|	1038	|	1141	1241	1341	1441	|	1541	1641	1741	1841	1941	2113	|	2312
Meadowhall ..192 193 d.	2148	2250	...	...	2351	2345		...	0945	0957	|	1053	|	1156	1254	1356	1457	|	1557	1657	1758	1857	1954	2136	2246	2336
Sheffield ......192 193 a.	2157	2301	...	...	0002	2358		...	0955	1004	1030	1102	1131	1203	1304	1405	1506	1517	1605	1705	1805	1904	2004	2143	2256	2343
Sheffield ......170 206 d.	...	...	2337	2338	...	...		0905	...	1007	1035	1103	...	1207	1306	1407	1507	...	1607	1707	1807	1907	2007	...	2330	...
Chesterfield ..170 206 d.	...	...	0002	2353	...	...		0921	...	1023	1048	1120	...	1223	1323	1423	1523	...	1623	1723	1823	1923	2023	...	2344	...
Alfreton 206 d.	...	...	|	|	...	...		0932	...	1033	|	1130	...	1233	1333	1433	1533	...	1633	1733	1833	1933	2033	...	2355	...
Langley Mill d.	...	...	|	|	...	...		0940	...	1041	|	1138	...	1241	1341	1441	1541	...	1641	1741	1841	1941	2041	...	0002	...
Nottingham ..170 206 a.	...	...	0040	0030	...	...		1000	...	1101	1121	1158	...	1301	1401	1501	1601	...	1701	1801	1901	1959	2101	...	0023	...

SHEFFIELD - HUDDERSFIELD *'The Penistone Line'*

km		⚒	Ⓐ	⚒	⚒		⚒	Ⓐ	⑥	⑥	Ⓐ	⚒	⚒	⚒	⚒	⚒	⑦	⑦	⑦	⑦	⑦	⑦	⑦	⑦	⑦
0	**Sheffield** d.		0536	0636	0736	and at the same	1536	1633	1636	1737	1737	1836	1937	2042	2140	2241		0939	1149	1236	1339	1539	1654	1740	1939
6	Meadowhall d.		0542	0642	0842	minutes	1542	1639	1642	1743	1743	1842	1943	2048	2146	2247		0945	1155	1242	1345	1545	1700	1747	1945
26	Barnsley d.		0601	0701	0801	past each	1601	1700	1703	1804	1804	1903	2008	2108	2208	2308		1006	1216	1306	1406	1606	1715	1810	2006
38	Penistone d.		0618	0718	0818	hour until	1618	1717	1720	1821	1824	1920	2025	2125	2225	2325		1023	1233	1323	1423	1623	1732	1827	2023
59	**Huddersfield** a.		0650	0749	0849	◇	1649	1747	1750	1851	1855	1953	2057	2157	2257	2359		1054	1303	1353	1453	1654	1803	1858	2053

	⚒	⚒	⚒	⚒	⚒		⚒	Ⓐ	⑥	Ⓐ	⚒	⚒	⚒	⚒		⑦	⑦	⑦	⑦	⑦	⑦	⑦	⑦	⑦
Huddersfield d.		0610	0710	0808	0913	and at	1713	1751	1813	1818	1918	2018	2118	2218	...		0919	1015	1119	1319	1415	1519	1723	1919
Penistone d.		0642	0742	0842	0944	the same	1744	1831	1844	1849	1950	2052	2149	2249	...		0950	1046	1150	1350	1446	1550	1755	1950
Barnsley d.		0658	0758	0858	1001	minutes	1801	1848	1901	1906	2007	2112	2206	2306	...		1012	1103	1207	1412	1503	1612	1812	2012
Meadowhall 192 193 d.		0722	0822	0921	1021	past each	1822	1906	1920	1925	2028	2131	2226	2327	...		1035	1121	1230	1435	1521	1636	1836	2035
Sheffield 192 193 a.		0729	0829	0928	1030	hour until ◇	1831	1914	1930	1933	2036	2140	2236	2336	...		1044	1128	1238	1443	1528	1644	1844	2043

A – From/to London St. Pancras (Table **170**).
B – To/from Armathwaite (Table **173**).
e – Wakefield Westgate.
f – Departs 6 minutes later on Ⓐ.
◇ – Timings may vary by up to 2 minutes.

172 NOTTINGHAM - WORKSOP and MATLOCK 2nd class EM

NOTTINGHAM - WORKSOP *'The Robin Hood Line'*

km		⚒	⚒	⑥	Ⓐ	⑥	Ⓐ	⚒	⚒		⚒	⚒	⚒	⚒	⚒	⚒	⑥	⑦	⑦	⑦	⑦	⑦	⑦	⑦	⑦	⑦
0	**Nottingham** d.		0540	0605	0605	0703	0701	0826	0926	and	1726	1755	1855	1955	2055	2205	2305		0807	0942	1128	1328	1525	1653	1829	2025
28	Mansfield d.		0613	0638	0638	0740	0740	0900	0957	hourly	1803	1836	1929	2036	2136	2242	2343		0840	1016	1202	1401	1558	1726	1902	2058
50	**Worksop** a.		0649	0719	0723	0814	0818	0933	1033	until	1837	1908	2005	2109	2208	2314	...		...	...	...	...	...	...	...	...

	⚒	⚒	⚒	⚒	⚒	⚒		⚒	⚒	⚒	⚒	⚒	⚒	⚒	⚒		⑦	⑦	⑦	⑦	⑦	⑦	⑦	⑦	⑦
Worksop d.		0550	0656	0738	0838	0938	and	1538	1642	1746	1841	1922	2022	2122	2222	...		...	...	...	...	...	...	...	...
Mansfield d.		0621	0729	0810	0910	1010	hourly	1610	1714	1818	1913	1953	2053	2153	2253	...		0855	1033	1217	1415	1612	1739	1921	2110
Nottingham a.		0656	0805	0845	0943	1043	until	1643	1746	1852	1948	2030	2125	2226	2326	...		0931	1107	1251	1450	1646	1813	1955	2144

NOTTINGHAM - DERBY - MATLOCK

km		⚒	⚒	Ⓐ	⑥	⚒	⚒	⚒		⚒	⚒	Ⓐ	⑥		⑦	⑦	⑦	⑦	⑦	⑦		⑦	⑦
0	**Nottingham** 123 d.		...	0617	0620	0720	0820	0920		1920	2020	2139	2139	...		0926	1127	1323	1528	1722	...	1922	2124
26	**Derby** 123 a.		...	0650	0650	0750	0850	0950	and	1950	2050	2208	2208	...		0954	1155	1351	1556	1751	...	1950	2152
26	**Derby** d.		0542	0651	0652	0752	0852	0952	hourly	1952	2052	2215	2216	...		0956	1156	1356	1558	1756	...	1952	2155
34	Duffield ◧ d.		0549	0658	0659	0759	0859	0959	until	1959	2059	2222	2223	...		1003	1204	1403	1605	1803	...	1959	2202
46	Whatstandwell ◧ d.		0604	0713	0714	0814	0914	1014		2014	2114	2237	2239	...		1018	1219	1418	1620	1818	...	2014	2217
50	Cromford d.		0610	0719	0720	0820	0920	1020	★	2020	2120	2243	2245	...		1024	1224	1424	1626	1824	...	2020	2223
52	Matlock Bath ◧ d.		0612	0721	0722	0822	0922	1022		2022	2122	2245	2247	...		1026	1227	1426	1628	1826	...	2022	2225
53	**Matlock** ◧ a.		0615	0725	0726	0826	0926	1026		2026	2126	2249	2250	...		1030	1230	1430	1632	1830	...	2026	2229

	⚒	⚒		⚒	⚒	⚒	⚒		⚒	⚒	⚒	⚒		⑦	⑦	⑦		⑦	⑦	⑦		⑦	⑦
Matlock ◧ d.		0620	...	0737	0837	0937	1037		1937	2037	2141	2255	...		1038	1238	...	1441	1638	1838	...	2038	2244
Matlock Bath ◧ d.		0622	...	0739	0839	0939	1039	and	1939	2039	2143	2257	...		1040	1240	...	1443	1640	1840	...	2040	2246
Cromford d.		0625	...	0742	0842	0942	1042	hourly	1942	2042	2146	2300	...		1043	1243	...	1446	1643	1843	...	2043	2249
Whatstandwell ◧ d.		0630	...	0747	0847	0947	1047	until	1947	2047	2151	2305	...		1048	1248	...	1451	1648	1848	...	2048	2254
Duffield ◧ d.		0646	...	0803	0903	1003	1103		2003	2103	2203	2321	...		1105	1305	...	1507	1705	1905	...	2105	2311
Derby d.		0654	...	0811	0911	1011	1111	★	2011	2111	2216	2328	...		1112	1312	...	1515	1712	1912	...	2112	2318
Derby 123 d.		0700	...	0813	0913	1013	1113		2013	2113	2259	2330	...		1114	1314	...	1516	1714	1914	...	2114	...
Nottingham 123 a.		0720	...	0846	0942	1041	1141		2043	2141	2327	0002	...		1141	1341	...	1543	1744	1944	...	2141	...

★ – Timings may vary by up to 2 minutes.

◧ – Visitor attractions near these stations:
Duffield: Ecclesbourne Valley Railway (shares National Rail station). ✆ 01629 823076.
Whatstandwell: National Tramway Museum (1.6 km walk). ✆ 01773 854321.
Matlock Bath: Heights of Abraham (short walk to cable car). ✆ 01629 582365.
Matlock: Peak Rail (shares National Rail station). ✆ 01629 580381.

NT 2nd class — LEEDS - SETTLE - CARLISLE — 173

A replacement 🚌 service is currently operating Appleby/Armathwaite - Carlisle and v.v. due to emergency engineering works. Timings shown are valid until further notice.

km		Ⓐ	Ⓐ	🚌	⑥	⚒	⑦	⚒	Ⓐ	⑥	⑦C		⚒	⑦	⑥	Ⓐ	⑦	⑥	Ⓐ	⚒		ⒶA	⑥A	⑦A
	London Kings Cross **180** d.	🚌	...	...	...	...	...	...	...	...	...	...	...	...	...	...	...	...	...	...	...	1803	1835	1835
0	**Leeds** **176** d.	...	0529	...	0619	0849	0900	0947	1049	1049	1120	...	1249	1357	1449	1449	1741	1750	1806	1919	...	2039	2055	2101
27	Keighley **176** d.	...	0556	...	0642	0912	0929	1012	1112	1112	1142	...	1312	1421	1512	1512	1802	1813	1829	1942	...	2057**s**	2113**s**	2121**s**
42	Skipton **176** d.	...	0615	...	0656	0926	0948	1026	1126	1126	1155	...	1326	1435	1526	1526	1815	1835	1846	2000	...	2113	2127	2139
58	Hellifield d.	...	0627	...	0708	0940	1002	|	1137	1137	|	...	1340	1449	1537	1537	1828	1849	1900	2015	...	...	...	...
66	**Settle** d.	...	0636	...	0715	0950	1011	1044	1146	1146	1214	...	1348	1458	1545	1545	1835	1857	1908	2024	...	...	...	...
76	Horton in Ribblesdale d.	...	|	...	0724	0958	1020	|	1154	1154	|	...	1357	1507	1553	1553	1844	1906	1917	2032	...	...	...	...
84	Ribblehead d.	...	0651	...	0732	1006	1028	|	1202	1202	|	...	1405	1515	1601	1601	1851	1914	1925	2042	...	...	...	...
99	Garsdale d.	...	0706	...	0747	1021	1043	|	1217	1217	|	...	1420	1530	1616	1616	1907	1929	1940	...	...	...	...	...
115	Kirkby Stephen d.	...	0718	...	0759	1034	1056	1122	1230	1230	1251	...	1432	1543	1628	1629	1919	1941	1952	...	...	...	...	...
132	Appleby a.	...	0730	...	0813	1046	1108	1137	1242	1242	1303	...	1444	1555	1641	1641	1934	1956	2007	...	...	...	...	...
132	Appleby d.	0657	0732	0740	0823	1047	1110	*1147*	1243	1243	1304	...	1445	1556	1641	1642	*1944*b	*2006*b	*2017*b	...	...	...	...	...
166	Armathwaite a.	0747	0808	|	0857	1124	1147	|	1319	1320	1340	...	1521	1632	1718	1719	*2034*	*2056*	*2107*	...	...	...	...	...
166	Armathwaite d.	0747	*0818*	|	*0907*	*1133*	*1156*	|	*1328*	*1329*	*1350*	...	*1531*	*1642*	*1727*	*1728*	*2034*	*2056*	*2107*	...	...	...	...	...
182	**Carlisle** a.	0817	*0848*	0840	*0937*	*1203*	*1226*	1247	*1358*	*1359*	*1420*	...	*1601*	*1712*	*1757*	*1758*	*2104*b	*2126*b	*2137*b	...	...	...	...	...

	⑥A	ⒶA	⑥	Ⓐ	⑥	Ⓐ	⑦	⑥	⑥	Ⓐ	⑦	Ⓐ		⑥	Ⓐ	⑦D	⑥	⚒	⑦	⑥	Ⓐ	Ⓐ	⑥	Ⓐ🚌
Carlisle d.	...	...	...	*0458*c	*0704*c	*0733*c	*0837*c	*0822*c	*1048*c	*1048*c	*1111*c	*1243*c	...	*1244*c	*1433*	*1305*c	*1446*c	*1446*c	*1557*c	*1642*c	*1643*c	...	...	1814
Armathwaite a.	...	...	...	*0528*	*0734*	*0803*	*0907*	*0852*	*1118*	*1118*	*1141*	*1313*	...	*1314*	|	*1335*	*1516*	*1516*	*1627*	*1712*	*1713*	...	...	1839
Armathwaite d.	...	...	...	*0528*	*0734*	0813	*0907*	0902	1128	1128	1151	1323	...	1324	|	1345	1526	1526	1637	1722	1723	...	...	1839
Appleby a.	...	...	...	*0618*	*0824*	0847	*0957*	0938	1204	1203	1227	1359	...	1400	*1533*	1420	1602	1602	1713	1758	1759	...	...	1929
Appleby d.	...	...	...	0630c	0834c	0935c	1007c	1006c	1233c	1236c	1339c	1447c	...	1504c	1543	1557c	1626c	1701c	1743c	1849c	1856c	...	...	1929
Kirkby Stephen d.	...	...	...	0643	0847	0948	1021	1019	1246	1249	1353	1500	...	1517	1556	1610	1639	1714	1757	1902	1909	...	...	1954s
Garsdale d.	...	...	...	0656	0900	1002	1034	1033	1259	1302	1406	1513	...	1530	|	|	|	1727	1810	1915	1922	...	...	2029s
Ribblehead d.	...	...	0714	0711	0915	1017	1049	1047	1314	1317	1421	1529	...	1545	|	|	|	1742	1825	1930	1937	2100	2100	2112s
Horton in Ribblesdale d.	...	...	0720	0717	0921	1024	1056	1054	1320	1324	1428	1536	...	1551	|	|	|	1748	1832	1936	1943	2106	2106	2127s
Settle d.	...	...	0728	0725	0929	1032	1104	1102	1328	1332	1436	1545	...	1559	1634	1646	1717	1757	1841	1944	1951	2114	2114	2142s
Hellifield d.	...	...	0737	0734	0937	1039	1113	1109	1337	1339	1445	1553	...	1607	|	|	|	1806	1851	1952	1959	2123	2123	2154s
Skipton **176** a.	0655	0655	0753	0749	0952	1054	1129	1124	1355	1356	1502	1610	...	1623	1654	1707	1738	1823	1907	2007	2014	2138	2140	2214s
Keighley **176** a.	0708u	0707u	0808	0807	1008	1107	1140	1137	1407	1407	1516	1622	...	1637	1707	1720	1751	1837	1918	2018	2025	2202	*2203*	2234s
Leeds **176** a.	0734	0731	0837	0837	1035	1136	1205	1207	1436	1437	1545	1653	...	1707	1738	1746	1817	1907	1948	2045	2050	2234	*2234*	2333
London Kings Cross **180** a.	0951	0957	...	...	...	...	...	...	...	...	...	...	...	...	...	...	...	...	...	...	...	...	...	...

A – (12) and 🍷 London Kings Cross - Skipton and v.v. (Table **180**).
C – From Sheffield (Table **171**).
D – To Nottingham (Table **171**).
b – An additional fast 🚌, not calling at Armathwaite, taking 60 minutes, operates Appleby - Carlisle departing at the same time.
c – An additional fast 🚌, not calling at Armathwaite, departs Carlisle 72 minutes prior to departure of the train from Appleby.
s – Calls to set down only.
u – Calls to pick up only.

NT 2nd class — LEEDS - LANCASTER - HEYSHAM — 174

km	km		Ⓐ	⑥		⑥	Ⓐ		⑦	Ⓐ		⑥	⑦		Ⓐ	⑥		⑦	⑥		Ⓐ	⑦		
0	0	**Leeds** 173 176 d.	...	0554	...	0819	0818	...	0840	1017	...	1019	1100	...	1316	1350	...	1459	1646	...	1645	1720	...	...
27	27	Keighley 173 176 d.	...	0621	...	0843	0841	...	0907	1043	...	1042	1123	...	1340	1413	...	1522	1710	...	1709	1747	...	...
42	42	Skipton 173 176 d.	0541	0638	...	0900	0855	...	0926	1100	...	1100	1140	...	1401	1433	...	1538	1725	...	1725	1803	...	...
58	58	Hellifield 173 d.	0556	0652	...	0914	0910	...	0940	1114	...	1114	1154	...	1415	1448	...	1552	1740	...	1739	1818	...	...
66	66	Giggleswick 173 d.	0607	0703	...	0925	0920	...	0952	1124	...	1125	1204	...	1425	1459	...	1602	1750	...	1750	1828	...	...
103	103	Carnforth a.	0642	0738	...	1000	0956	...	1028	1200	...	1200	1239	...	1501	1534	...	1638	1826	...	1825	1903	...	...
113		**Lancaster** a.	0652	0750	...	1013	1008	...	1038	1211	...	1211	1251	...	1516	1545	...	1647	1838	...	1838	1912	...	...
120	112	Morecambe a.	*0736*	*0838*	...	1031	1032	...	1055	1243	...	1236	1316	...	1535	1602	...	1714	1858	...	1901	1935	...	...
127	119	**Heysham Port** a.	...	...	...	...	...	...	...	1301	...	1254	...	...	...	...	...	...	...	...	...	...	...	...

		Ⓐ	⑥		⑥	Ⓐ		⑦	⑥		Ⓐ	⑦		Ⓐ	⑥		⑦	Ⓐ		⑥	⑦		
Heysham Port d.	...	...	...	...	...	...	...	...	1315	...	1317	...	...	...	...	...	...	...	...	...	...	...	...
Morecambe d.	...	*0610*	*0736*	...	1034	1034	...	1222	1331	...	1333	1446d	...	1619d	1616	...	1723	1908	...	1909	1946	...	...
Lancaster d.	...	0707	0823	...	1049	1049	...	1248	1348	...	1349	1429d	...	1605d	1640	...	1737	1924	...	1925	2002	...	...
Carnforth d.	...	0718	0833	...	1107	1107	...	1258	1358	...	1359	1500	...	1632	1650	...	1754	1934	...	1935	2012	...	...
Giggleswick 173 d.	...	0752	0907	...	1142	1142	...	1332	1433	...	1434	1535	...	1708	1725	...	1829	2009	...	2010	2047	...	...
Hellifield 173 d.	...	0803	0919	...	1153	1153	...	1344	1446	...	1444	1546	...	1720	1736	...	1840	2020	...	2020	2058	...	...
Skipton 173 176 a.	...	0821	0936	...	1210	1210	...	1401	1503	...	1503	1603	...	1737	1753	...	1857	2038	...	2037	2115	...	...
Keighley 173 176 a.	...	0837	0951	...	1222	1223	...	1416	1520	...	1520	1617	...	1750	1807	...	1910	2050	...	2048	2126	...	...
Leeds 173 176 a.	...	0905	1020	...	1250	1253	...	1444	1548	...	1547	1646	...	1815	1836	...	1944	2115	...	2116	2154	...	...

d – Calls at Lancaster, then Morecambe.

NT 2nd class — LEEDS - HARROGATE - YORK — 175

km		⚒	Ⓐ	⑥	Ⓐ	⑥	⑥	Ⓐ	⑥	Ⓐ	⑥	Ⓐ	⚒	⚒	and at	⚒	⚒	Ⓐ	⑥	⚒	⚒	⚒	Ⓐ
0	**Leeds** 124 188 d.		0609	0610	0631	0636	0713	0714	0741	0743	0755	0801	0829	0859	the same	1529	1559	1629	1629	1659	1713	1729	1743
29	**Harrogate** d.		0646	0647	0708	0713	0749	0751	0818	0820	0832	0838	0906	0936	minutes	1606	1636	1707	1706	1736	1750	1806	1820
36	Knaresborough d.		0654	0657	0718	0723	0759	0759	0826	0829	0843	0849	0915	0947	past each	1615	1647	1715	1714	1747	1801	1815	1837
62	**York** 124 188 a.		0725	0726	0747	0750	0827	0832	0859	0858	...	...	0946	...	hour until	1645	...	1745	1744	...	...	1846	1904

	⚒	⚒	Ⓐ	⚒	⚒	⑥	Ⓐ		⑦	⑦	⑦	⑦		⑦	⑦	⑦		⑦	⑦	⑦		⑦	⑦	⑦
Leeds 124 188 d.	1759	1829	1859	1930	2029	2120	2129	...		0954	1054	1154	...	1254	1354	1454	...	1554	1654	1754	...	1855	1954	2119
Harrogate d.	1836	1906	1936	2007	2106	2157	2206	...		1048	1130	1233	...	1333	1430	1533	...	1633	1733	1833	...	1933	2033	2156
Knaresborough d.	1847	1916	1947	2016	2115	2208	2216	...		1057	1141	1245	...	1347	1445	1544	...	1644	1745	1844	...	1945	2044	2205
York 124 188 a.	...	1945	...	2045	2144	...	...	...		1125	1204	1310	...	1413	1509	1609	...	1707	1810	1908	...	2008	2107	...

	⚒	⑥	Ⓐ	⑥	Ⓐ	Ⓐ	⑥	Ⓐ	⚒	⑥	Ⓐ	⑥	Ⓐ	⚒	⚒	⚒	and at	⚒	⚒	⚒	⚒	⚒	⑥
York 124 188 d.		...	...	0652	0649	...	...	...	0754	...	...	0843	0847	0911	...	1011	the same	...	1611	...	1704	1728	...
Knaresborough d.		0647	0657	0720	0719	0742	0750	0757	0819	0850	0855	0908	0911	0936	1006	1036	minutes	1605	1636	1706	1735	1755	1808
Harrogate d.		0656	0707	0729	0740	0751	0759	0806	0829	0859	0904	0918	0921	0945	1015	1045	past each	1614	1645	1715	1745	1805	1817
Leeds 124 188 a.		0733	0746	0806	0816	0830	0836	0840	0908	0936	0937	0955	0957	1022	1052	1122	hour until	1652	1722	1752	1822	1842	1854

	Ⓐ	Ⓐ	⑥	Ⓐ	⚒	⚒	⚒	⑥	Ⓐ		⑦	⑦	⑦	⑦		⑦	⑦	⑦	⑦	⑦		⑦	⑦	⑦
York 124 188 d.	...	1805	1812	...	1913	2011	2111	2157	2211	...		1114	1217	1320	...	1418	1517	1617	1718	1817	...	1918	2017	2127
Knaresborough d.	1810	1834	1837	1906	1938	2036	2136	2222	2237	...		1142	1242	1344	...	1442	1542	1641	1743	1842	...	1942	2042	2151
Harrogate d.	1824	1843	1846	1915	1947	2045	2146	2236	2248	...		1153	1253	1354	...	1452	1553	1652	1753	1853	...	1952	2053	2202
Leeds 124 188 a.	1901	1924	1923	1952	2024	2123	2223	2313	2326	...		1228	1330	1430	...	1529	1630	1730	1830	1930	...	2029	2130	2239

Additional trains	⚒A	⑦A	⑦	Ⓐ	⑥	⑥	⑦	Ⓐ	
Leeds d.	1959	2034	2230	2238	2233	2322	2323	2332	...
Harrogate a.	2025	2100	2307	2317	2311	0001	2359	0012	...

Additional trains	⚒	Ⓐ	ⒶA	⑥A	Ⓐ	⑦	⑦	⑦A	⑦
Harrogate d.	0605	0625	0734	0813	0815	0953	1053	1707	2312
Leeds a.	0644	0701	0806	0845	0852	1031	1129	1733	2349

A – (12) and 🍷 Harrogate - Leeds - London Kings Cross and v.v. (Table **180**).

NT 2nd class — WEST YORKSHIRE LOCAL SERVICES — 176

BRADFORD FORSTER SQUARE - SKIPTON

Journey: ± 38 minutes *30 km*

From Bradford Forster Square: Trains call at **Keighley** ± 22 minutes later.

Ⓐ: 0603, 0638, 0715, 0741, 0811, 0841, 0911 and every 30 minutes until 1541, 1612, 1638, 1711, 1738, 1816, 1841, 1908, 1936, 2009, 2109, 2209, 2309.

⑥: 0609, 0709, 0811, 0842, 0911 and every 30 minutes until 1541, 1612, 1638, 1711, 1738, 1811, 1841, 1908, 1936, 2009, 2112, 2202, 2309.

⑦: 1055, 1255, 1455, 1655, 1855, 2055, 2255.

From Skipton: Trains call at **Keighley** ± 14 minutes later.

Ⓐ: 0556, 0626, 0700, 0724, 0800, 0831, 0900 and every 30 minutes until 1430, 1458, 1530, 1558, 1630, 1700, 1724, 1800, 1830, 1900, 1931, 1954, 2054, 2154.

⑥: 0600, 0704, 0730, 0800, 0831, 0900 and every 30 minutes until 1430, 1458, 1530, 1600, 1630, 1700, 1728, 1800, 1830, 1900, 1930, 1954, 2057, 2155.

⑦: 0932, 1142, 1342, 1542, 1742, 1942, 2124.

Table continues on next page ▶ ▶ ▶

176 WEST YORKSHIRE local services

2nd class NT

LEEDS - DONCASTER

Stopping trains. For faster trains see Table 180.

Journey: ± 50 minutes *48 km*

From Leeds:

Ⓐ: 0620, 0721, 0821 and hourly until 1621, 1657, 1721, 1821, 1921, 2022, 2121, 2240.

⑥: 0621, 0721, 0821 and hourly until 1921, 2022, 2121, 2219.

⑦: 1021, 1221, 1421, 1621, 1821, 2021, 2121.

From Doncaster:

Ⓐ: 0626, 0708, 0726, 0756, 0826 and hourly until 1826, 1922, 2026, 2127, 2227.

⑥: 0626, 0726, 0827, 0926, 1027, 1126, 1227, 1326 and hourly until 1826, 1922, 2026, 2122, 2226.

⑦: 0912, 1112, 1312, 1512, 1712, 1927, 2152.

LEEDS - SKIPTON

See also Tables 173/174

Journey: ± 45 minutes *42 km*

From Leeds: Trains call at **Keighley** ± 24 minutes later.

Ⓐ: 0529, 0616, 0657, 0725, 0749, 0825, 0856, 0926, 0956 and every 30 minutes until 1726, 1740, 1756, 1826, 1856, 1926, 1956, 2022, 2055, 2126, 2156, 2226, 2256, 2319.

⑥: 0554, 0650, 0750, 0825, 0856, 0926, 0956 and every 30 minutes until 1956, 2026, 2100, 2126, 2204, 2226, 2256, 2319.

⑦: 0840, 0900, 1009, 1109, 1216 and hourly until 2116, 2220, 2320.

From Skipton: Trains call at **Keighley** ± 13 minutes later.

Ⓐ: 0545, 0614, 0640, 0706, 0718, 0730, 0745, 0813, 0837, 0917, 0947 and every 30 minutes until 1617, 1647, 1715, 1747, 1817, 1847, 1915, 1947, 2022, 2045, 2117, 2217.

⑥: 0545, 0644, 0745, 0816, 0847, 0917, 0947, and every 30 minutes until 1917, 1947, 2022, 2050, 2117, 2149, 2217.

⑦: 0832, 0912, 1012 and hourly until 1612, 1714, 1812, 1922, 2012, 2122, 2212, 2312.

LEEDS - BRADFORD FORSTER SQUARE

For Leeds - Bradford Interchange see Table 190

Journey: ± 21 minutes *22 km*

From Leeds:

Ⓐ: 0645, 0739, 0810, 0832, 0841, 0910, 0942, 1012, 1040, and every 30 minutes until 1540, 1607, 1638, 1709, 1736, 1810, 1837, 1908, 2101.

⑥: 0710, 0810, 0841, 0910, 0939, 1010, 1040, and every 30 minutes until 1540, 1607, 1638, 1708, 1736, 1810, 1837, 1910, 2158.

⑦: 0831, 0941 and hourly until 1641, 1745, 1841, 1942, 2041, 2141, 2241.

From Bradford Forster Square:

Ⓐ: 0558, 0630, 0654, 0757, 0826, 0902, 0930, 1000 and every 30 minutes until 1600, 1630, 1701, 1730, 1800, 1830, 1900, 1930.

⑥: 0600, 0658, 0733, 0758, 0826, 0901, 0930, 1000 and every 30 minutes until 1600, 1630, 1701, 1730, 1800, 1831, 1900, 1930.

⑦: 0901, 1003, 1113 and hourly until 1713, 1815, 1913, 2013, 2113, 2213, 2313.

LEEDS - ILKLEY

Journey: ± 30 minutes *26 km*

From Leeds:

Ⓐ: 0600, 0634, 0704, 0729, 0733, 0758, 0835, 0902 and every 30 minutes until 1602, 1632, 1702, 1716, 1732, 1746, 1802, 1832, 1902, 1933, 2007, 2107, 2207, 2315.

⑥: 0602, 0702, 0758, 0832, 0902, 0932, 1004, 1032 and every 30 minutes until 1832, 1903, 1933, 2007, 2107, 2208, 2315.

⑦: 0905 and hourly until 2005, 2108, 2215, 2310.

From Ilkley:

Ⓐ: 0602, 0633, 0710, 0737, 0756, 0805, 0816, 0838 and every 30 minutes until 1438, 1510, 1536, 1612, 1638, 1712, 1743, 1804, 1812, 1842, 1910, 1938, 2028, 2118, 2218, 2318.

⑥: 0610, 0710, 0810, 0838, 0910, 0940, 1010, 1038 and every 30 minutes until 1538, 1612, 1638, 1712, 1738, 1812, 1842, 1910, 1938, 2028, 2118, 2224, 2318.

⑦: 0905 and hourly until 2105, 2215, 2315.

HUDDERSFIELD - WAKEFIELD WESTGATE

Journey: ± 33 minutes *25 km*

From Huddersfield:

Ⓐ: 0531, 0631, 0735, 0831, 0931 and hourly until 1931, 2031, 2135.

⑥: 0640, 0735, 0831, 0931, and hourly until 1931, 2031, 2135.

From Wakefield Westgate:

Ⓐ: 0643, 0744, 0844, and hourly until 1844, 1946, 2050, 2142, 2248.

⑥: 0730, 0844, 0944, and hourly until 1844, 1944, 2050, 2144, 2248.

BRADFORD FORSTER SQUARE - ILKLEY

Journey: ± 31 minutes *22 km*

From Bradford Forster Square:

Ⓐ: 0615, 0642 0711, 0745, 0816, 0846 and every 30 minutes until 1315, 1346, 1416, 1446, 1516, 1546, 1616, 1643, 1716, 1748, 1811, 1846, 1941 2038, 2140, 2240, 2326.

⑥: 0615, 0716, 0816, 0846 and every 30 minutes until 1716, 1743, 1816, 1846, 1946, 2038, 2140, 2240, 2320.

⑦: 1027, 1227, 1426, 1627, 1827, 2027, 2237.

From Ilkley:

Ⓐ: 0617, 0652, 0720, 0748, 0824, 0852, 0921, 0951 and every 30 minutes until 1651, 1720, 1751, 1821, 1851, 1921, 2009, 2043, 2143, 2243.

⑥: 0621, 0721, 0821, 0852, 0921, 0951 and every 30 minutes until 1851, 1921, 2009, 2048, 2143, 2243.

⑦: 0925, 1125, 1325, 1525, 1725, 1925, 2130.

177 HULL - BRIDLINGTON - SCARBOROUGH

2nd class NT

km		⚒	⚒	⚒	⚒		⚒	⚒	⑥		Ⓐ	⚒	Ⓐ	⑥		⑦	⑦	⑦	⑦		⑦	⑦	⑦
0	**Hull** △ d.	0653	0814	0947	1114	...	1314	1444	1614	...	1618	1738	1915	1922	...	0925	1025	1205	1405	...	1605	1800	1859
13	Beverley △ d.	0707	0828	1001	1128	...	1328	1458	1628	...	1632	1752	1929	1936	...	0939	1039	1219	1419	...	1619	1814	1913
31	Driffield △ d.	0724	0842	1015	1140	...	1340	1512	1643	...	1647	1809	1943	1951	...	0956	1054	1234	1434	...	1634	1826	1928
50	**Bridlington** △ a.	0739	0857	1030	1156	...	1354	1527	1658	...	1702	1825	1958	2006	...	1011	1109	1249	1449	...	1649	1839	1946
50	**Bridlington** d.	0741	0900	1038	1206	...	1406	1535	1704	...	1704	1835	2003	2019	...	1014	1111	1255	1455	...	1655	1844	...
71	Filey d.	0802	0922	1100	1228	...	1428	1557	1726	...	1726	1857	2025	2041	...	1036	1133	1317	1517	...	1717	1906	...
87	**Scarborough** a.	0821	0940	1118	1246	...	1446	1615	1744	...	1744	1915	2043	2059	...	1054	1151	1335	1535	...	1735	1924	...

		⚒	⚒	⚒	⚒		⚒	⚒	⚒		⚒		⑥	Ⓐ		⑦	⑦	⑦		⑦	⑦	⑦	⑦
Scarborough d.	...	0650	0902	1000	1128	...	1328	1457	1625	...	1757	...	1940	2004	...	...	1111	1206	...	1406	1606	1806	1937
Filey d.	...	0705	0917	1015	1143	...	1343	1512	1640	...	1812	...	1955	2019	...	...	1126	1221	...	1421	1621	1821	1952
Bridlington a.	...	0727	0939	1037	1205	...	1405	1534	1702	...	1834	...	2017	2041	...	...	1148	1243	...	1443	1643	1843	2014
Bridlington △ d.	...	0730	0941	1041	1211	...	1411	1536	1705	...	1841	...	2023	2044	...	0951	1150	1246	...	1446	1646	1856	2016
Driffield △ d.	...	0747	0957	1057	1224	...	1424	1552	1719	...	1857	...	2039	2100	...	1007	1206	1259	...	1459	1659	1912	2029
Beverley △ d.	...	0806	1012	1112	1237	...	1437	1607	1731	...	1912	...	2054	2115	...	1022	1221	1312	...	1512	1712	1929	2042
Hull △ a.	...	0822	1028	1128	1253	...	1454	1623	1748	...	1930	...	2110	2131	...	1038	1237	1328	...	1528	1728	1946	2058

△ – All trains Hull - Bridlington and v.v.:

From Hull on ⚒ at 0556, 0620, 0653, 0714, 0752, 0814, 0916, 0947, 1014, and every 30 minutes until 1544, 1614⑥, 1618Ⓐ, 1644, 1714, 1738, 1814, 1915Ⓐ, 1922⑥, 2015, 2148; on ⑦ at 0900, 0925, 1025, 1125, 1205, 1255, 1405, 1500, 1605, 1655, 1715, 1800, 1859.

From Bridlington on ⚒ at 0644, 0712, 0730, 0808, 0905, 0941 and every 30 minutes until 1511, 1536, 1611, 1641, 1705⑥, 1706Ⓐ, 1736, 1815, 1841, 1908Ⓐ, 1911⑥, 2023⑥, 2044Ⓐ, 2128, 2242; on ⑦ at 0951, 1150, 1246, 1346, 1446, 1545, 1646, 1720, 1746, 1816, 1856, 1956, 2016.

178 HULL - YORK

2nd class NT

km		⚒	⑦	Ⓐ	⑥	⚒	⑥	⑦	⚒	⑥	Ⓐ	⑦	⑥	⑦	Ⓐ	⑥	Ⓐ	⑦	Ⓐ	⑥	⑥	Ⓐ	⑦	⚒	⑦	⑦	⑥
0	**Hull** .... 181 189 d.	0707	0854	0902	0903	1012	1107	1146	1204	1308	1315	1317	1415	1420	1422	1503	1503	1606	1610	1610	1711	1717	1725	1918	1925	2030	2102
50	Selby .. 181 189 d.	0748	0928	0942	0939	1049	1141	1220	1239	1349	1358	1351	1449	1454	1458	1537	1541	1640	1649	1649	1800	1804	1759	1954	2000	2104	2137
84	**York** a.	0822	0952	1016	1011	1120	1205	1252	1304	1422	1427	1417	1522	1526	1528	1602	1606	1706	1713	1715	1823	1828	1825	2025	2025	2128	2159

	Ⓐ	⑥	⚒	⑥	Ⓐ	⑦	⑥	⚒	⑦	⚒	⚒	⑦	⑥	⑦	Ⓐ	⑦	⑥	Ⓐ	⑦	⚒	⑥	Ⓐ	⑦	⑥	⑦	⑥	Ⓐ
York d.	0730	0740	0843	0951	1019	1040	1047	1145	1205	1247	1344	1354	1447	1452	1502	1606	1606	1611	1714	1725	1809	1844	1916	1950	2150	2212	2229
Selby .. **181 189** d.	0750	0759	0906	1009	1039	1058	1106	1204	1224	1306	1408	1423	1506	1511	1521	1635	1632	1637	1733	1750	1838	1913	1935	2008	2210	2230	2247
Hull .... **181 189** a.	0846	0856	0948	1053	1123	1136	1153	1251	1306	1351	1451	1504	1551	1552	1602	1716	1722	1728	1814	1834	1927	2002	2016	2048	2250	2316	2335

179 LINCOLN - SHEFFIELD

2nd class NT

km		⚒	⚒	⚒	⚒		⚒	⑥	⚒		⚒	⑥	⚒	⚒	⚒	⚒	⑥	⚒	⚒	⚒	⚒	⑦	⑦	⑦	⑦	⑦	⑦
0	**Lincoln** d.	...	...	0700	0825		1125	...	1227		1523	...	1625	1722	...	1825	...	1943	2027	2127	...	...	1515	1715	1915	2108	...
26	Gainsborough ‡ d.	...	...	0721	0845	and	1144	1211a	1246	and	1543	1617a	1646	1741	...	1844	1932a	2004	2048	2148	...	...	1536	1736	1936	2129	...
40	Retford d.	...	0701	0739	0901	hourly	1200	1231	1302	hourly	1559	1636	1701	1757	1814	1900	1954	2019	2103	2203	2245	1450	1551	1751	1951	2144	2224
52	Worksop ▽ d.	0630	0713	0751	0913	until	1211	1243	1314	until	1611	1648	1713	1809	1825	1912	2005	2031	2115	2215	2258	1502	1603	1803	2003	2156	2236
78	**Sheffield** ▽ a.	0703	0749	0825	0948	▲	1248	1317	1348	▲	1648	1723	1748	1834	1858	1953b	2040	2105	2146	2250	2332	1535	1635	1835	2035	2228	2308

	⚒	⚒	⚒	⚒	⑥	⚒		⚒	⑥	⚒		⚒	⑥	⚒	⚒	⚒		⚒	⚒	⚒	⑦	⑦	⑦	⑦	⑦	⑦
Sheffield ▽ d.	0539	0546	0644	0730	0803	0844		1144	1203	1244		1544	1601	1644	1723	1744	...	1844	1949	2142	1342	1355	1543	1743	1932	2106
Worksop ▽ d.	0603	0623	0715	0801	0834	0915	and	1215	1237	1315	and	1615	1637	1716	1754	1815	...	1916	2020	2214	1403	1426	1614	1814	2003	2137
Retford d.	0613	0637	0725	0811	0845	0925	hourly	1225	1247	1325	hourly	1625	1646	1727	1808	1825	...	1926	2030	2229	1413	1438	1624	1824	2013	2148
Gainsborough ‡ d.	0628	...	0740	0825	0902a	0943	until	1240	1304a	1340	until	1640	1702a	1742	...	1840	...	1941	2045	...	1428	...	1639	1839	2028	...
Lincoln a.	0656	...	0807	0853	...	1007	▲	1306	...	1406	▲	1707	...	1806	...	1906	...	2007	2110	...	1454	...	1703	1903	2053	...

a – Gainsborough Central.
b – Arrives 1748 on ⑥.
‡ – Gainsborough Lea Road.
▲ – Timings may vary ± 2 minutes.
▽ – Additional journeys Worksop - Sheffield and v.v: **From Worksop** at 0813Ⓐ, 2126⑥, 2130Ⓐ and 2328⚒. **From Sheffield** at 2045⚒ and 2244⚒.

GR Most services convey 🍸 LONDON - LEEDS, YORK, NEWCASTLE and EDINBURGH 180

For additional services see Tables **124**, **181**, **182**, **183**, **184** and **188**.

km			Ⓐ	Ⓐ	Ⓐ	Ⓐ	Ⓐ	Ⓐ	Ⓐ	Ⓐ	Ⓐ	Ⓐ	Ⓐ	Ⓐ	Ⓐ	Ⓐ	Ⓐ	Ⓐ	Ⓐ	Ⓐ	Ⓐ	Ⓐ	Ⓐ	Ⓐ	Ⓐ	Ⓐ
					A																	A			
0	**London** Kings Cross . d.	Ⓐ	...	...	...	0550	0615	0630	0700	0705	0708	0730	0735	0800	0806	0830	0835	0900	0903	0908	0930	0935	1000	1003	1008	1030
44	Stevenage d.		...	...	...	0611	0635	0650	|	|	0728	|	0755	|	|	|	0855	|	|	0929	|	0955	|	|	1029	|
123	Peterborough d.		...	...	...	0642	0706	0721	0746	0752	0759	0816	|	|	0853	0916	|	0946	0952	1000	1016	|	|	1051	1101	1116
170	Grantham d.		...	...	...	0702	0726	0740	|	|	0819	|	0840	|	|	|	0940	|	|	1021	|	1040	|	|	1121	|
193	Newark North Gate d.		...	...	...	0714	0738	|	|	|	0831	0844	|	|	|	0944	|	|	|	1033	1044	|	|	|	1135	1144
223	Retford d.		...	...	...	0729	0754	|	|	|	0846	|	|	|	|	|	|	|	|	1049	|	|	|	|	...	|
251	Doncaster d.		...	0615	...	0745	0811	0813	|	0842	0901	0910	0914	|	0942	1010	1014	|	1043	1105	1111	1114	|	1142	...	1210
283	Wakefield Westgate a.		...	|	...	0802	|	0832	|	0900	|	|	0931	|	1000	|	1031	|	1100	|	|	1131	|	1200	...	|
299	**Leeds** a.		...	|	0710	0818	|	0848	|	0917	|	|	0946	|	1015	|	1048	|	1116	|	|	1147	|	1216	...	|
303	**York** d.		...	0639	0737	...	0835	...	0855	...	0925	0935	...	0953	...	1035	...	1055	...	1130	1136	...	1154	...	...	1235
351	Northallerton d.		...	|	|	...	0853	...	|	...	...	|	...	|	...	1054	...	|	...	...	|	...	|	...	...	1254
374	Darlington d.		...	0707	0806	...	0908	...	0923	...	...	1004	...	1022	...	1108	...	1123	...	...	1205	...	1222	...	...	1308
409	Durham a.		...	0723	0822	...	0924	...	|	...	...	1020	...	|	...	1124	...	|	...	...	1221	...	|	...	...	1324
432	**Newcastle** a.		0622	0739	0838	...	0940	...	0951	...	...	1037	...	1050	...	1142	...	1151	...	...	1239	...	1250	...	...	1342
488	Alnmouth a.		0653	0808	|	...	|	...	|	...	...	1107	...	|	...	...	...	|	...	...	1310	...	|	...	...	|
540	Berwick upon Tweed a.		0717	0832	0929	...	|	...	1038	...	...	|	...	1136	...	...	...	1238	...	...	|	...	1337	...	...	1429
632	**Edinburgh** Waverley a.		0807	0921	1020	...	1112	...	1120	...	...	1209	...	1219	...	...	...	1320	...	...	1413	...	1420	...	...	1514

	Ⓐ	Ⓐ	Ⓐ	Ⓐ	Ⓐ	Ⓐ	Ⓐ	Ⓐ	Ⓐ	Ⓐ	Ⓐ	Ⓐ	Ⓐ		Ⓐ	Ⓐ	Ⓐ	Ⓐ	Ⓐ	Ⓐ	Ⓐ	Ⓐ	Ⓐ	Ⓐ	Ⓐ	Ⓐ
							B											A					K			C
London Kings Cross . d.	1035	1100	1105	1108	1130	1135	1200	1203	1208	1230	1235	1300	1305	...	1308	1330	1335	1400	1405	1408	1430	1435	1500	1505	1508	1530
Stevenage d.	1055	|	|	1129	|	1156	|	|	1229	|	1255	|	|	...	1329	|	1355	|	|	1428	|	1455	|	|	1529	|
Peterborough d.	|	|	1152	1159	1216	|	|	1251	1300	1316	|	1346	1352	...	1400	1416	|	|	1451	1500	1516	|	|	1551	1600	1616
Grantham d.	1140	|	|	1219	|	1241	|	|	1322	|	1340	|	|	...	1421	|	1440	|	|	1520	|	1540	|	|	1621	|
Newark North Gate d.	|	|	|	1231	1244	|	|	|	1334	1344	|	|	|	...	1434	1444	|	|	|	1534	1544	|	|	|	1633	1644
Retford d.	|	|	|	1246	|	|	|	|	...	|	|	|	|	...	1449	|	|	|	|	...	|	|	|	|	1649	|
Doncaster d.	1214	|	1242	1305	1310	1314	|	1342	...	1410	1414	|	1442	...	1504	1511	1514	|	1542	...	1610	1614	|	1641	1705	1710
Wakefield Westgate a.	1231	|	1300	|	|	1332	|	1400	...	|	1431	|	1459	...	|	|	1531	|	1559	...	|	1631	|	1659	|	|
Leeds a.	1248	|	1316	|	|	1348	|	1416	...	|	1448	|	1516	...	|	|	1548	|	1616	...	|	1648	|	1716	|	|
York d.	...	1253	...	1329	1336	...	1355	...	...	1435	...	1454	...	...	1530	1535	...	1555	...	...	1635	...	1654	...	1729	1736
Northallerton d.	...	|	...	...	|	...	|	...	...	1454	...	|	...	...	...	1554	...	|	...	...	1654	...	|	...	...	1754
Darlington d.	...	1321	...	...	1406	...	1423	...	...	1508	...	1522	...	...	...	1608	...	1623	...	...	1708	...	1722	...	...	1809
Durham a.	...	|	...	...	1422	...	|	...	...	1524	...	|	...	...	...	1624	...	|	...	...	1724	...	|	...	...	1825
Newcastle a.	...	1349	...	...	1439	...	1452	...	...	1540	...	1550	...	...	...	1640	...	1651	...	...	1740	...	1750	...	...	1841
Alnmouth a.	...	|	...	...	1509	...	|	...	...	...	...	|	...	...	...	1710	...	|	...	...	...	...	|	...	...	1909
Berwick upon Tweed a.	...	|	...	...	|	...	1539	...	...	...	...	1638	...	...	...	|	...	1739	...	...	...	...	1837	...	...	|
Edinburgh Waverley a.	...	1517	...	...	1613	...	1622	...	...	...	...	1721	...	...	...	1813	...	1823	...	...	...	...	1920	...	...	2013

	Ⓐ	Ⓐ	Ⓐ	Ⓐ	Ⓐ	Ⓐ	Ⓐ	Ⓐ	Ⓐ	Ⓐ	Ⓐ	Ⓐ	Ⓐ	Ⓐ	Ⓐ		Ⓐ	Ⓐ	Ⓐ	Ⓐ	Ⓐ	Ⓐ	Ⓐ	Ⓐ	Ⓐ	Ⓐ
		A							D		E			F				G			H			J		
London Kings Cross . d.	1535	1600	1606	1609	1630	1633	1700	1703	1719	1730	1733	1749	1800	1803	1819	...	1830	1833	1900	1903	1906	1930	1933	2000	2005	2035
Stevenage d.	1555	|	|	1630	|	1653	|	|	|	|	1755	|	|	|	|	...	|	1853	|	|	1928	|	1953	|	|	2055
Peterborough d.	|	|	1654	1701	1716	|	|	1750	1808	1817	|	1837	|	1851	1907	...	1918	|	|	1953	2000	2016	|	|	2051	2126
Grantham d.	1641	|	|	1722	|	1740	|	|	1829	|	1842	1906	|	|	1927	...	|	1942	|	|	2021	|	2040	|	|	2146
Newark North Gate d.	|	|	|	1736	1744	|	|	|	1841	1846	|	|	|	1922	|	...	1946	|	|	|	2036	2044	|	|	2120	2159
Retford d.	|	|	|	...	|	1802	|	|	|	|	|	1928	|	|	|	...	|	2005	|	|	...	|	|	|	|	|
Doncaster d.	1714	|	1745	...	1810	1818	|	1841	1910	|	1915	1944	|	1950	|	...	2012	2021	|	2041	...	2110	2114	|	2145	2223
Wakefield Westgate a.	1731	|	1805	...	|	1835	|	1859	...	|	1933	2002	|	2007	|	...	|	2038	|	2100	...	|	2131	|	2207	2240
Leeds a.	1748	|	1820	...	|	1851	|	1917	...	|	1948	2020	|	2021	|	...	|	2053	|	2117	...	|	2149	|	2223	2257
York d.	...	1754	...	...	1836	...	1853	...	...	1929	...	...	1951	...	2020	...	2036	...	2053	...	...	2134	...	2153	...	...
Northallerton d.	...	|	...	...	1856	...	|	...	...	|	...	...	|	...	2038	...	|	...	|	...	...	2152	...	|	...	...
Darlington d.	...	1823	...	...	1910	...	1922	...	...	1957	...	...	2019	...	2053	...	2105	...	2121	...	...	2207	...	2221	...	...
Durham a.	...	|	...	...	1926	...	|	...	...	2013	...	...	|	...	2109	...	2121	...	|	...	...	2223	...	2237	...	...
Newcastle a.	...	1851	...	...	1942	...	1950	...	...	2029	...	...	2047	...	2125	...	2137	...	2149	...	...	2239	...	2254	...	...
Alnmouth a.	...	|	...	...	|	...	|	...	...	2058	...	...	|	...	...	...	2209	...	|	...	...	2311f	...	...	...	...
Berwick upon Tweed a.	...	1939	...	...	|	...	2037	...	...	|	...	...	2135	...	...	...	|	...	2238	...	...	2336f	...	...	...	...
Edinburgh Waverley a.	...	2022	...	...	2112	...	2122	...	...	2208	...	...	2220	...	...	...	2315	...	2328	...	...	0026f	...	...	...	...

	Ⓐ	Ⓐ	Ⓐ	Ⓐ		⑥	⑥	⑥	⑥	⑥	⑥	⑥	⑥	⑥	⑥	⑥	⑥	⑥	⑥	⑥	⑥	⑥	⑥	⑥	⑥	⑥
								A												A						
London Kings Cross . d.	2100	2135	2200	2330	⑥	...	...	...	0615	0700	0703	0730	0800	0803	0830	0833	0900	0903	0930	1000	1003	1030	1100	1103	1130	1135
Stevenage d.	2121	2157	|	|		...	...	...	0635	0720	0725	|	|	|	|	|	|	0923	|	|	|	|	|	1123	|	|
Peterborough d.	2152	2228	2247	0017s		...	...	...	0706	|	0755	0816	|	0849	0916	|	|	0954	1016	|	1051	1116	|	1154	1216	1223
Grantham d.	|	2249	2309	0045s		...	...	...	0726	|	0814	|	|	0909	|	0940	|	1015	|	|	1110	|	|	1214	|	|
Newark North Gate d.	2220	2302	2321	0057s		...	...	...	0738	|	0826	|	|	0921	0944	|	|	1027	|	|	1123	1144	|	1226	|	|
Retford d.	|	2319	|	|		...	...	...	0754	|	|	0855	|	|	|	1004	|	|	1054	|	|	|	|	|	1254	|
Doncaster d.	2246	2335	2352	0124s		...	0610	...	0810	|	0851	0912	|	0951	1012	1021	|	1051	1110	|	1151	1211	|	1251	1311	1314
Wakefield Westgate a.	|	2352	|	|		...	|	...	|	|	0907	|	|	1008	|	1037	|	1107	|	|	1207	|	|	1307	|	1331
Leeds a.	|	0008	|	0234		...	|	0710	|	|	0926	|	|	1024	|	1054	|	1125	|	|	1224	|	|	1325	|	1348
York d.	2312	...	0042	...		...	0634	0737	0835	0855	...	0935	0953	...	1036	...	1053	...	1135	1154	...	1235	1253	...	1336	...
Northallerton d.	2342	...	0110s	...		...	0652	|	0853	|	...	|	|	...	1054	...	|	...	|	|	...	1254	|	...	|	...
Darlington d.	2357	...	0124s	...		...	0707	0806	0908	0923	...	1005	1024	...	1108	...	1121	...	1204	1222	...	1308	1321	...	1404	...
Durham a.	0013	...	0143s	...		...	0723	0822	0924	|	...	1021	|	...	1125	...	|	...	1221	|	...	1324	|	...	1421	...
Newcastle a.	0041	...	0214	...		0630	0739	0837	0940	0952	...	1037	1052	...	1141	...	1149	...	1237	1251	...	1340	1349	...	1437	...
Alnmouth a.	...	...	...	...		0657	0808	|	|	|	...	1105	|	...	|	...	|	...	1306	|	...	|	|	...	1505	...
Berwick upon Tweed a.	...	...	...	...		0721	0832	0931	|	1039	...	|	1139	...	|	...	1239	...	|	1339	...	|	1439	...	|	...
Edinburgh Waverley a.	...	...	...	...		0815	0920	1024	1110	1127	...	1212	1227	...	1310	...	1326	...	1413	1425	...	1510	1527	...	1610	...

	⑥	⑥	⑥	⑥	⑥	⑥	⑥	⑥	⑥	⑥		⑥	⑥	⑥	⑥	⑥	⑥	⑥	⑥	⑥	⑥	⑥	⑥	⑥	⑥	⑥
	B							A													D		E			H
London Kings Cross . d.	1200	1203	1230	1233	1300	1303	1330	1400	1403	1430	...	1500	1503	1530	1533	1600	1603	1630	1700	1703	1710	1730	1735	1800	1803	1808
Stevenage d.	|	|	|	|	|	1324	|	|	|	|	...	|	1524	|	1553	|	|	|	|	1724	|	|	|	|	|	1829
Peterborough d.	|	1252	1316	1321	|	1354	1416	|	1450	1516	...	|	1554	1616	1624	|	1651	1716	|	1754	1800	1817	1823	|	1850	1900
Grantham d.	|	1315	|	|	1403	1414	|	|	1511	|	...	|	1614	|	|	|	1712	|	|	1814	1821	|	|	|	|	1921
Newark North Gate d.	|	1327	1344	|	|	1426	|	|	1524	1544	...	|	1626	|	1652	|	1725	1744	|	1826	|	1846	|	|	1918	1935
Retford d.	|	|	|	1404	|	|	1455	|	|	|	...	|	|	1654	|	|	|	|	|	|	|	|	|	|	1933	...
Doncaster d.	|	1354	1410	1421	|	1452	1512	|	1550	1611	...	|	1651	1710	|	|	1751	1810	|	1851	1856	1911	1915	|	1949	...
Wakefield Westgate a.	|	1411	|	1438	|	1508	|	|	1607	|	...	|	1707	|	1732	|	1808	|	|	1908	...	|	1932	|	2006	...
Leeds a.	|	1429	|	1456	|	1525	|	|	1624	|	...	|	1725	|	1748	|	1825	|	|	1924	...	|	1948	|	2022	...
York d.	1354	...	1435	...	1456	...	1536	1553	...	1635	...	1654	...	1735	...	1752	...	1837	1853	...	...	1936	...	1954	...	...
Northallerton d.	|	...	1454	...	|	...	|	|	...	1654	...	|	...	|	...	|	...	1856	|	...	...	|	...	|	...	...
Darlington d.	1423	...	1508	...	1524	...	1605	1622	...	1708	...	1722	...	1803	...	1821	...	1910	1922	...	...	2005	...	2022	...	...
Durham a.	|	...	1524	...	|	...	1621	|	...	1724	...	|	...	1819	...	|	...	1926	|	...	...	2021	...	|	...	...
Newcastle a.	1451	...	1540	...	1552	...	1637	1650	...	1740	...	1750	...	1835	...	1849	...	1942	1950	...	...	2040	...	2050	...	...
Alnmouth a.	|	...	|	...	|	...	1705	|	...	|	...	|	...	1906	...	|	...	|	|	...	...	...	...	2124	...	...
Berwick upon Tweed a.	1539	...	|	...	1641	...	|	1739	...	|	...	1843	...	|	...	1939	...	|	2037	...	...	...	...	2149	...	...
Edinburgh Waverley a.	1624	...	1712	...	1728	...	1810	1825	...	1911	...	1928	...	2012	...	2024	...	2114	2122	...	...	...	...	2237	...	...

A – To/from Aberdeen (Table **222**).
B – To/from Inverness (Table **223**).
C – To/from Glasgow Central (Table **220**).
D – To/from Hull (Table **181**).
E – To/from Harrogate (Table **175**).

F – To/from Skipton (Table **173**).
G – To/from Bradford Forster Square (Table **182**).
H – To/from Lincoln (Table **186**).
J – To/from Sunderland (Table **210**).
K – To/from Stirling (Table **222**).

f – ⑤ only.
s – Calls to set down only.
u – Calls to pick up only.

180 LONDON - LEEDS, YORK, NEWCASTLE and EDINBURGH

Most services convey 🍸 GR

For additional services see Tables **124, 181, 182, 183, 184** and **188**.

	⑥	⑥ F	⑥	⑥	⑥ G	⑥	⑥	⑥	⑥
London Kings Cross d.	1830	1835	1900	1904	1930	2000	2030	2100	2200
Stevenage d.	|	|	|	|	1950	|	|	|	|
Peterborough d.	1916	1924	|	1957	2021	2048	2116	2148	2247
Grantham d.	|	|	|	|	2041	|	2136	|	2307
Newark North Gate d.	1944	|	|	|	2053	2116	2148	|	2319
Retford d.	|	|	|	|	|	|	2203	|	2334
Doncaster d.	2012	2015	|	2047	2118	2141	2219	|	2349
Wakefield Westgate a.	|	2032	|	2104	2134	|	2236	|	0005
Leeds a.	|	2047	|	2121	2150	|	2252	|	0023
York d.	2035	...	2053	...	...	2206	...	2258	...
Northallerton d.	2054	...	|	...	...	|	...	2316	...
Darlington d.	2108	...	2121	...	...	2235	...	2331	...
Durham a.	2124	...	|	...	...	2251	...	2347	...
Newcastle a.	2142	...	2151	...	...	2309	...	0005	...
Alnmouth a.	...	...	...	...	...	...	...	...	...
Berwick upon Tweed a.	...	...	...	...	...	...	...	...	...
Edinburgh Waverley a.	...	...	...	...	...	...	...	...	...

⑦

	⑦	⑦	⑦	⑦	⑦	⑦	⑦	⑦ A	⑦	⑦	⑦	⑦	⑦	⑦	⑦	⑦ B	⑦
London Kings Cross d.	...	...	...	0845	0900	0903	0930	1000	1003	1010	1030	1100	1103	1120	1130	1200	1203
Stevenage d.	...	...	...	|	|	0923	|	|	|	|	|	|	1123	|	|	|	|
Peterborough d.	...	...	...	|	|	0954	1016	|	1050	1056	1116	|	1154	|	1216	|	1250
Grantham d.	...	...	...	|	|	1014	|	|	|	1117	|	|	1214	1225	|	|	1310
Newark North Gate d.	...	...	...	|	|	1026	|	|	|	1129	1144	|	1226	|	|	|	1322
Retford d.	...	...	...	|	|	|	1055	|	|	|	|	|	|	|	1255	|	|
Doncaster d.	...	...	0937	|	|	1051	1111	|	1140	1155	1211	|	1251	|	1311	|	1347
Wakefield Westgate a.	...	...	|	|	|	1108	|	|	|	1212	|	|	1308	|	|	|	1404
Leeds a.	...	0830	|	|	|	1126	|	|	|	1229	|	|	1325	|	|	|	1421
York d.	...	0900	1001	1037	1049	...	1135	1152	1208	...	1235	1251	...	1317	1335	1352	...
Northallerton d.	...	0918	|	|	|	...	|	|	|	...	1253	|	...	1335	|	|	...
Darlington d.	...	0935	1029	1105	1117	...	1203	1221	1238	...	1308	1319	...	1350	1403	1421	...
Durham a.	...	0951	1045	1121	|	...	1219	|	1255	...	1324	|	...	1406	1419	|	...
Newcastle a.	0915	1006	1101	1138	1145	...	1235	1249	1311	...	1340	1347	...	1422	1435	1449	...
Alnmouth a.	|	1042	|	|	|	...	1309	|	|	...	|	|	...	|	1508	|	...
Berwick upon Tweed a.	0959	1107	1148	|	1233	...	|	1337	|	...	|	1434	...	|	|	1537	...
Edinburgh Waverley a.	1045	1158	1232	1310	1318	...	1419	1420	1446	...	1508	1518	...	1558	1618	1620	...

	⑦	⑦	⑦	⑦	⑦	⑦	⑦ A	⑦	⑦	⑦	⑦	⑦	⑦	⑦	⑦ C	⑦	⑦	⑦	⑦ D	⑦	⑦	⑦	⑦ E	⑦	⑦	⑦ F	⑦
London Kings Cross d.	1220	1230	1233	1300	1303	1330	1400	1403	1430	1500	1503	1530	1600	1605	1630	1635	1700	1705	1720	1730	1735	1800	1803	1827	1830	1835	1900
Stevenage d.	|	|	1255	|	1323	|	|	|	|	|	1523	|	|	|	|	1655	|	|	|	|	1755	|	|	|	|	1855	|
Peterborough d.	1309	1316	|	|	1354	1416	|	1452	1516	|	1554	1617	|	1653	1716	|	|	1751	|	1817	|	1846	1851	|	|	|	|
Grantham d.	|	|	1342	|	1414	|	|	1512	|	|	1614	1638	|	1713	|	1740	|	|	1826	1838	1843	|	|	|	|	1941	|
Newark North Gate d.	|	1344	|	|	1426	|	|	1524	1544	|	1626	|	|	1725	1744	|	|	1819	1838	|	|	|	1920	|	1945	|	|
Retford d.	|	|	|	|	|	1455	|	|	|	|	1642	|	|	|	|	1803	|	|	|	|	|	|	|	|	|	2004	|
Doncaster d.	1358	1411	1420	|	1451	1511	|	1550	1611	|	1658	1712	|	1751	1810	1820	|	1844	1905	1912	1916	|	1948	|	2010	2020	|
Wakefield Westgate a.	|	|	1437	|	1508	|	|	1607	|	|	1715	|	|	1810	|	1839	|	1901	...	|	1933	|	2005	|	|	2037	|
Leeds a.	|	|	1454	|	1525	|	|	1625	|	|	1731	|	|	1828	|	1856	|	1918	...	|	1951	|	2023	|	|	2052	|
York d.	1423	1435	...	1453	...	1535	1552	...	1635	1652	...	1736	1749	...	1835	...	1851	...	...	1938	...	1959	...	2026	2036	...	2053
Northallerton d.	|	1453	...	|	...	|	|	...	1653	|	...	|	|	...	1853	...	|	...	...	|	...	|	...	|	2055	...	|
Darlington d.	1451	1508	...	1521	...	1603	1621	...	1708	1720	...	1805	1817	...	1908	...	1919	...	...	2006	...	2027	...	2054	2109	...	2122
Durham a.	1507	1524	...	|	...	1619	|	...	1724	|	...	1821	|	...	1924	...	|	...	...	2022	...	|	...	2111	2125	...	|
Newcastle a.	1525	1540	...	1549	...	1635	1649	...	1740	1748	...	1838	1845	...	1940	...	1947	...	...	2038	...	2055	...	2129	2141	...	2150
Alnmouth a.	...	|	...	|	...	1703	|	...	|	|	...	1906	|	...	|	...	|	...	...	2110	...	|	...	...	|	...	2223
Berwick upon Tweed a.	...	|	...	1636	...	|	1737	...	|	1835	...	|	1936	...	|	...	2035	...	...	|	...	2143	...	...	2228	...	2248
Edinburgh Waverley a.	...	1709	...	1720	...	1809	1820	...	1908	1920	...	2013	2020	...	2114	...	2120	...	...	2218	...	2228	...	...	2313	...	2340

	⑦	⑦ H	⑦	⑦	⑦	⑦	⑦	⑦	⑦	⑦	⑦	⑦
London Kings Cross d.	1903	1908	1930	1935	2000	2005	2035	2100	2135	2200	2204	2235
Stevenage d.	|	1929	|	1955	|	|	2055	|	2156	|	|	|
Peterborough d.	1950	2001	2018	2026	2046	2052	2126	2146	2227	2247	2251	2323s
Grantham d.	|	2022	|	2046	|	|	2146	|	2248	|	2315	2344s
Newark North Gate d.	2018	2036	2047	|	|	|	2158	|	2300	|	2327	2355s
Retford d.	|	...	|	|	|	2132	|	|	2316	|	|	|
Doncaster d.	2043	...	2115	2119	|	2148	2223	|	2340	2343	0001	0024s
Wakefield Westgate a.	2100	...	|	2136	|	2206	2239	|	2357	|	...	|
Leeds a.	2118	...	|	2152	|	2222	2257	|	0014	|	...	0130
York d.	...	...	2140	...	2157	...	...	2302	...	0035	...	...
Northallerton d.	...	...	|	...	|	...	...	2336	...	0106s	...	...
Darlington d.	...	...	2219	...	2239	...	...	2351	...	0120s	...	...
Durham a.	...	...	2235	...	2255	...	...	0007	...	0138s	...	...
Newcastle a.	...	...	2308	...	2327	...	...	0039	...	0210	...	...
Alnmouth a.	...	...	...	...	...	...	...	...	...	...	...	...
Berwick upon Tweed a.	...	...	...	...	...	...	...	...	...	...	...	...
Edinburgh Waverley a.	...	...	...	...	...	...	...	...	...	...	...	...

Ⓐ

	Ⓐ	Ⓐ	Ⓐ	Ⓐ		Ⓐ	Ⓐ	Ⓐ	Ⓐ G
Edinburgh Waverley d.	...	...	...	...	...	...	...	...	...
Berwick upon Tweed d.	...	...	...	...	...	...	...	...	...
Alnmouth d.	...	...	...	...	...	...	...	...	...
Newcastle d.	...	...	...	0445	...	...	0525	...	...
Durham d.	...	...	...	0500	...	...	0539	...	...
Darlington d.	...	...	...	0518	...	...	0558	...	...
Northallerton d.	...	...	...	0529	...	...	0609	...	...
York d.	...	...	...	0600	...	...	0631	...	...
Leeds d.	...	0505	0530	|	...	0605	|	0640	0700
Wakefield Westgate d.	...	0518	0544	|	...	0618	|	0653	0713
Doncaster d.	0507	0536	0603	0624	...	0636	0654	0712	|
Retford d.	|	0551	|	|	...	0651	|	|	|
Newark North Gate d.	0536	0606	0629	0647	...	0707	|	0737	|
Grantham d.	0548	0618	0641	0700	...	0720	0726	|	|
Peterborough d.	0610	0639	0701	0721	...	0741	0750	|	|
Stevenage a.	|	|	|	|	...	|	|	|	|
London Kings Cross a.	0700	0729	0752	0812	...	0834	0843	0850	0859

	Ⓐ J	Ⓐ H	Ⓐ	Ⓐ	Ⓐ	Ⓐ	Ⓐ D	Ⓐ F	Ⓐ	Ⓐ E	Ⓐ	Ⓐ K	Ⓐ	Ⓐ	Ⓐ	Ⓐ	Ⓐ	Ⓐ	Ⓐ	Ⓐ C	Ⓐ	Ⓐ	Ⓐ	Ⓐ	Ⓐ	Ⓐ	Ⓐ
Edinburgh Waverley d.	...	...	...	...	...	0540	...	...	...	...	0548	0626	...	...	0655	0730	...	...	...	0800	0830	...	...	...	0900	0930	...
Berwick upon Tweed d.	...	...	...	...	0600	|	...	...	...	...	0634	0710	...	...	|	0812	...	...	...	|	0912	...	...	...	|	1012	...
Alnmouth d.	...	...	...	...	0621	|	...	...	...	...	0655	|	...	...	|	|	...	...	...	0900	|	...	...	...	|	|	...
Newcastle d.	0559	...	...	0630	0655	0704	...	...	...	...	0729	0757	...	...	0825	0859	...	...	...	0930	1000	...	...	...	1026	1059	...
Durham d.	0612	...	...	0644	0708	|	...	...	←	...	0742	|	...	...	0838	|	...	...	...	0943	|	...	...	...	1039	|	...
Darlington d.	0632	...	...	0703	0731	|	...	...	0731	...	0801	0828	...	...	0857	0928	...	...	...	1001	1029	...	...	...	1058	1128	...
Northallerton d.	|	...	...	0715	→	|	...	...	|	...	|	|	...	...	0908	|	...	...	...	|	|	...	...	...	1109	|	...
York d.	0701	...	...	0737	...	|	...	...	0802	...	0831	0857	...	...	0931	0958	...	1003	...	1031	1059	...	...	...	1131	1157	...
Leeds d.	|	...	0715	|	...	|	...	0740	|	0817	|	|	0845	0916	|	|	0945	|	1015	|	|	1045	...	1115	|	|	1145
Wakefield Westgate d.	|	...	0728	|	...	|	...	0753	|	0830	|	|	0858	0929	|	|	0958	|	1028	|	|	1058	...	1128	|	|	1158
Doncaster d.	|	...	0746	|	...	|	0757	0813	|	0848	0855	|	0917	0947	0955	|	1017	1025	1046	1058	|	1117	...	1146	1155	|	1217
Retford d.	|	...	|	|	...	|	|	|	0836	|	|	|	|	|	|	|	|	1039	|	|	|	|	...	|	|	|	|
Newark North Gate d.	|	0757	|	|	...	|	0822	0838	|	|	0919	|	|	|	1019	|	|	1054	|	1121	|	|	1154	|	1219	|	|
Grantham d.	|	|	0818	|	...	|	0835	|	|	0921	|	|	|	1018	|	|	|	1106	1118	|	|	|	1207	1218	|	|	|
Peterborough d.	0812	0827	|	0843	...	|	0902	0907	|	|	0950	|	1009	|	1051	|	1108	1128	|	1152	|	1209	1228	|	1250	|	1307
Stevenage a.	|	0856	0902	|	...	|	|	|	|	1008	|	|	|	1101	|	|	|	1156	1201	|	|	|	1256	1302	|	|	|
London Kings Cross a.	0906	0924	0929	0937	...	0940	0955	0957	1002	1035	1042	1051	1100	1128	1142	1151	1159	1223	1228	1242	1250	1300	1324	1328	1341	1349	1358

	Ⓐ	Ⓐ	Ⓐ	Ⓐ A	Ⓐ	Ⓐ	Ⓐ	Ⓐ	Ⓐ B	Ⓐ	Ⓐ	Ⓐ	Ⓐ	Ⓐ A	Ⓐ	Ⓐ	Ⓐ	Ⓐ	Ⓐ	Ⓐ	Ⓐ	Ⓐ	Ⓐ	Ⓐ	Ⓐ	Ⓐ	Ⓐ
Edinburgh Waverley d.	...	...	1000	1030	...	...	...	...	1130	...	...	...	1200	1230	...	...	...	1300	1330	...	...	...	1400	1430	...	...	...
Berwick upon Tweed d.	...	...	|	1112	...	...	...	...	|	...	...	...	|	1312	...	...	...	|	1412	...	...	...	|	1512	...	...	...
Alnmouth d.	...	...	1100	|	...	...	...	...	|	...	...	...	1300	|	...	...	...	|	|	...	...	...	1500	|	...	...	...
Newcastle d.	...	...	1130	1200	...	...	...	1225	1257	...	...	...	1330	1400	...	...	...	1426	1500	...	...	...	1533	1559	...	...	...
Durham d.	...	...	1143	|	...	...	...	1238	|	...	...	...	1343	|	...	...	...	1439	|	...	...	...	1546	|	...	...	...
Darlington d.	...	...	1201	1229	...	...	...	1257	1328	...	...	...	1401	1429	...	...	...	1458	1527	...	...	...	1605	1628	...	...	...
Northallerton d.	...	...	|	|	...	...	...	1308	|	...	...	...	|	|	...	...	...	1509	|	...	...	...	|	|	...	...	...
York d.	1203	...	1231	1259	...	...	...	1331	1357	...	1402	...	1431	1459	...	...	...	1531	1557	...	1602	...	1635	1657	...	...	...
Leeds d.	|	1215	|	|	1245	...	1315	|	|	1345	|	1415	|	|	1445	...	1515	|	|	1545	|	1615	|	|	1645	...	1715
Wakefield Westgate d.	|	1228	|	|	1258	...	1328	|	|	1358	|	1428	|	|	1458	...	1528	|	|	1558	|	1628	|	|	1658	...	1728
Doncaster d.	1225	1246	1255	|	1317	...	1346	1354	|	1417	1425	1446	1455	|	1517	...	1546	1554	|	1617	1625	1646	1658	|	1717	...	1746
Retford d.	1240	|	|	|	|	...	|	|	|	|	1441	|	|	|	|	...	|	|	|	|	1641	|	|	|	|	...	1800
Newark North Gate d.	1255	|	1319	|	|	1354	|	1417	|	|	1456	|	1519	|	|	1552	|	1620	|	|	1656	|	1721	|	|	1754	|
Grantham d.	1307	1318	|	|	|	1406	1418	|	|	|	1508	1517	|	|	|	1604	1619	|	|	|	1708	1718	|	|	|	1806	1824
Peterborough d.	1328	|	1351	|	1409	1427	|	1452	|	1509	1529	|	1552	|	1608	1625	|	1650	|	1709	1730	|	1751	|	1809	1828	|
Stevenage a.	1357	1402	|	|	|	1456	1501	|	|	|	1557	1601	|	|	|	1655	1702	|	|	|	1759	1804	|	|	|	1857	1907
London Kings Cross a.	1425	1428	1442	1451	1459	1524	1527	1544	1551	1600	1625	1628	1642	1651	1659	1721	1729	1742	1753	1800	1827	1831	1844	1850	1901	1925	1935

← FOR NOTES SEE PREVIOUS PAGE

180a PETERBOROUGH - KINGS LYNN

First Excel service **X1**

From **Peterborough** railway station: Journey 75 minutes. Buses call at **Wisbech** bus station ± 39 minutes later.

Ⓐ: 0704, 0734, 0809 and every 30 minutes until 1109, 1149, 1219 and every 30 minutes until 1449, 1520, 1550, 1620, 1650, 1720, 1755, 1833, 1903, 1933, 2033, 2233.

⑥: 0739, 0809 and every 30 minutes until 1109, 1149, 1219 and every 30 minutes until 1719, 1754, 1833, 1903, 1933, 2033, 2233.

⑦: 0909, 1009 and hourly until 2009.

Table **180a** continues on the next page.

GR Most services convey 🍸 EDINBURGH - NEWCASTLE - YORK and LEEDS - LONDON 180

For additional services see Tables **124**, **181**, **182**, **183**, **184** and **188**.

	Ⓐ	Ⓐ	Ⓐ	Ⓐ	Ⓐ	Ⓐ		Ⓐ	Ⓐ	Ⓐ	Ⓐ	Ⓐ	Ⓐ	Ⓐ	Ⓐ	Ⓐ	Ⓐ	⑥	⑥	⑥	⑥	⑥	⑥	⑥	⑥	⑥
													A				A								D	
Edinburgh Waverley . d.	...	1530	...	...	...	1600	...	1630	...	...	1700	...	1731	...	1830	1935	2100		...	...	...	...	...	...	...	...
Berwick upon Tweed.. d.	...	1612	...	...	...	|	...	1712	...	...	|	...	1818	...	1916	2017	2148		...	...	...	...	...	...	...	...
Alnmouth .... d.	...	|	...	...	...	|	...	|	...	...	1800	...	|	...	1939	2040	2211		...	...	...	...	...	...	...	...
Newcastle .... d.	1625	1659	...	...	...	1726	...	1759	...	...	1830	...	1906	...	2016	2115	2246		...	...	0445	...	0559	...	...	0630
Durham .... d.	1638	|	...	...	...	1739	...	|	...	...	1843	...	|	...	2029	2128	2300		...	...	0500	...	0612	...	...	0643
Darlington .... d.	1657	1727	...	...	...	1758	...	1828	...	...	1901	...	1935	...	2048	2147	2322		...	...	0518	...	0632	...	...	0702
Northallerton .... d.	1709	|	...	...	...	1809	...	|	...	...	|	...	|	...	|	2158	2348s		...	...	0529	...	|	...	...	0713
York .... d.	1731	1757	...	1802	...	1831	...	1857	...	...	1931	...	2005	...	2117	2220	0018		...	...	0600	...	0701	...	...	0735
Leeds .... d.	|	|	1745	|	1815	|	...	|	1845	1916	|	1945	|	2045	|	|	0045		0505	0530	|	0605	|	0705	...	|
Wakefield Westgate d.	|	|	1758	|	1828	|	...	|	1858	1929	|	1958	|	2058	|	|	...		0518	0543	|	0618	|	0718	...	|
Doncaster .... d.	1755	|	1817	1826	1846	1855	...	|	1917	1947	1955	2017	2028	2116	2140	2243	...		0536	0601	0624	0636	0725	0736	0745	0758
Retford .... d.	|	|	|	1840	|	|	...	|	|	|	|	|	|	2131	|	|	...		0550	|	|	0650	|	|	|	|
Newark North Gate .... d.	1819	|	|	1855	|	1919	...	|	|	|	2019	|	|	|	2204	2307	...		0605	0625	|	0705	|	0800	|	0822
Grantham .... d.	|	|	|	1907	1918	|	...	|	|	2018	|	|	|	2154	2216	2319	...		0617	0639	|	0717	|	0812	0818	|
Peterborough .... d.	1849	|	1908	1929	|	1951	...	|	2008	|	2049	2105	2117	2215	2237	2347	...		0639	0701	0713	0738	0815	0833	0840	0851
Stevenage .... a.	|	|	|	1958	2003	2019	...	2025	|	2102	2117	|	2148	2245	2307	0028s	...		0707	|	|	0806	|	0901	|	|
London Kings Cross . a.	1943	1950	2000	2025	2028	2046	...	2052	2059	2128	2142	2156	2213	2311	2335	0103	...		0734	0753	0804	0835	0908	0928	0935	0942

	⑥	⑥	⑥	⑥	⑥	⑥	⑥	⑥	⑥	⑥	⑥	⑥	⑥		⑥	⑥	⑥	⑥	⑥	⑥	⑥	⑥	⑥	⑥	⑥	⑥
	F		G				H	E					C									A			B	
Edinburgh Waverley . d.	...	...	...	...	...	0620	...	...	0655	...	0730	...	0800	...	0830	...	0900	...	0930	...	1000	1030	...	1100	1130	...
Berwick upon Tweed.. d.	...	...	...	...	...	0706	...	...	|	...	0813	...	|	...	0913	...	|	...	1013	...	|	1113	...	|	1213	...
Alnmouth .... d.	...	...	...	...	...	0727	...	...	|	...	|	...	0900	...	|	...	|	...	|	...	1100	|	...	|	|	...
Newcastle .... d.	...	0655	...	0722	...	0801	...	...	0825	...	0900	...	0930	...	1000	...	1026	...	1100	...	1130	1200	...	1226	1301	...
Durham .... d.	...	0708	...	0736	...	|	...	...	0838	...	|	...	0943	...	|	...	1039	...	|	...	1143	|	...	1239	|	...
Darlington .... d.	...	0727	...	0754	...	0829	...	...	0857	...	0929	...	1001	...	1029	...	1057	...	1129	...	1201	1229	...	1257	1329	...
Northallerton .... d.	...	|	...	0808	...	|	...	...	0908	...	|	...	|	...	|	...	1109	...	|	...	|	|	...	1309	|	...
York .... d.	...	0757	...	0830	...	0859	...	...	0930	...	0959	...	1031	...	1059	...	1131	...	1159	...	1231	1259	...	1331	1400	...
Leeds .... d.	0738	|	0805	|	0840	|	...	0905	|	0940	|	1005	|	...	|	1105	|	1140	|	1205	|	|	1305	|	|	1405
Wakefield Westgate d.	|	|	0818	|	0854	|	...	0918	|	0953	|	1018	|	...	|	1118	|	1153	|	1218	|	|	1318	|	|	1418
Doncaster .... d.	0811	0820	0838	0855	0912	|	...	0936	0953	|	|	1037	1055	...	|	1136	1156	1212	|	1236	1255	|	1336	1355	|	1436
Retford .... d.	|	|	0854	|	|	|	...	|	1007	|	|	|	|	...	|	|	1210	|	|	|	|	|	|	1409	|	|
Newark North Gate .... d.	|	|	0909	0919	|	|	0954	1000	|	|	|	1101	1119	...	|	1159	|	|	|	1302	1319	|	1400	|	|	1504
Grantham .... d.	0843	|	|	0931	|	|	1006	1014	1030	|	|	1115	|	...	|	1212	|	|	|	1314	|	|	1412	|	|	1516
Peterborough .... d.	|	|	0938	0953	1002	1006	1029	1036	1052	1058	|	1136	1151	...	|	1234	1251	|	|	1335	1351	|	1433	1451	|	1537
Stevenage .... a.	|	|	|	|	|	|	1100	1107	|	|	|	|	|	...	|	1302	|	|	|	|	|	|	1501	|	|	|
London Kings Cross . a.	0951	0954	1030	1045	1053	1058	1126	1136	1143	1151	1155	1228	1242	...	1253	1329	1342	1353	1356	1427	1442	1452	1529	1542	1555	1629

	⑥	⑥	⑥	⑥	⑥	⑥	⑥	⑥	⑥	⑥	⑥	⑥	⑥	⑥	⑥	⑥	⑥	⑥	⑥	⑥	⑥	⑥	⑥	⑦	⑦	⑦
			A																	A						
Edinburgh Waverley . d.	1200	...	1230	...	1300	1330	...	...	1400	1430	...	1500	1530	...	1600	1630	...	1700	...	1730	...	1830	1900		...	...
Berwick upon Tweed.. d.	|	...	1313	...	|	1412	...	...	|	1512	...	|	1612	...	|	1712	...	|	...	1816	...	1912	1945		...	...
Alnmouth .... d.	1300	...	|	...	|	|	...	...	1500	|	...	|	|	...	|	|	...	1800	...	|	...	|	2008		...	...
Newcastle .... d.	1330	...	1400	...	1426	1500	...	...	1530	1559	...	1626	1659	...	1726	1759	...	1830	...	1904	...	1959	2043		...	...
Durham .... d.	1343	...	|	...	1439	|	...	...	1544	|	...	1639	|	...	1739	|	...	1843	...	|	...	...	2056		...	...
Darlington .... d.	1401	...	1429	...	1457	1529	...	...	1603	1628	...	1657	1728	...	1757	1828	...	1902	...	1933	...	...	2115		...	...
Northallerton .... d.	|	...	|	...	1509	|	...	...	|	|	...	1709	|	...	1809	|	...	|	...	|	...	...	2128		...	...
York .... d.	1431	...	1459	...	1531	1558	...	...	1633	1657	...	1731	1758	...	1831	1857	...	1931	...	2003	...	...	2150		0800	...
Leeds .... d.	|	1440	|	1505	|	|	1540	1605	|	|	1705	|	|	1805	|	|	1905	|	1940	|	2005	...	|		|	0805
Wakefield Westgate d.	|	1453	|	1518	|	|	1553	1618	|	|	1718	|	|	1818	|	|	1919	|	1953	|	2018	...	|		|	0818
Doncaster .... d.	1455	1512	|	1536	1555	|	1612	1636	1656	|	1736	1755	|	1839	1855	|	1937	1955	2014	2026	2036	...	2215		0823	0836
Retford .... d.	|	|	|	|	1609	|	|	|	|	|	|	1809	|	|	|	|	|	|	|	|	2050	...	...		|	0850
Newark North Gate .... d.	1519	|	|	1600	|	|	1644	1659	1720	|	1800	|	|	1903	1919	|	2001	|	2038	|	2105	...	...		|	0905
Grantham .... d.	|	|	|	1612	|	|	|	1711	|	|	1812	|	|	1915	|	|	2013	2027	|	2058	|	...	...		|	0917
Peterborough .... d.	1551	1601	|	1634	1651	|	|	1733	1751	|	1833	1851	|	1936	1951	|	2034	2051	2107	2121	2134	...	...		0911	0941
Stevenage .... a.	|	|	|	1703	|	|	|	|	|	|	1901	|	|	|	2019	|	2102	|	|	2150	|	...	...		0939	|
London Kings Cross . a.	1643	1653	1656	1731	1744	1752	1800	1825	1842	1852	1929	1942	1952	2028	2046	2051	2129	2142	2158	2218	2225	...	...		1007	1033

	⑦	⑦	⑦	⑦	⑦	⑦	⑦	⑦	⑦	⑦	⑦	⑦	⑦	⑦	⑦	⑦	⑦	⑦	⑦	⑦	⑦	⑦	⑦	⑦	⑦	⑦
																						A				
Edinburgh Waverley . d.	...	...	...	...	...	...	...	...	0900	0930	...	1000	1030	...	1100	1120	1130	...	...	1200	1220	1230	...	...	1300	1319
Berwick upon Tweed.. d.	...	...	...	...	...	...	...	...	|	1013	...	|	1112	...	|	|	1213	...	...	|	|	1313	...	...	1343	|
Alnmouth .... d.	...	...	...	...	...	...	...	...	|	|	...	1100	|	...	|	|	|	...	...	1300	|	|	...	...	|	|
Newcastle .... d.	0755	...	...	0855	...	0925	1000	...	1029	1100	...	1130	1200	...	1226	1251	1301	...	1315	1330	1352	1400	...	1420	1431	1445
Durham .... d.	0809	...	...	0908	...	0938	|	...	1042	|	...	1143	|	...	1239	1304	|	...	1328	1343	1405	|	...	1433	|	1459
Darlington .... d.	0827	...	...	0928	...	0957	1028	...	1101	1130	...	1202	1229	...	1258	1323	1329	...	1348	1401	|	1430	...	1453	1500	1517
Northallerton .... d.	|	...	...	|	...	1008	|	...	1112	|	...	|	|	...	1310	|	|	...	1401	|	|	|	...	|	|	1532
York .... d.	0858	...	...	0958	...	1031	1058	...	1134	1159	...	1232	1258	...	1332	1356	1400	...	1424	1431	1449	1459	...	1523	1530	1557
Leeds .... d.	|	0843	0905	|	1005	|	|	1105	|	|	1205	|	|	1305	|	|	|	1405	|	|	|	|	1505	|	|	|
Wakefield Westgate d.	|	0856	0918	|	1018	|	|	1118	|	|	1218	|	|	1318	|	|	|	1418	|	|	|	|	1518	|	|	|
Doncaster .... d.	|	0920	0937	|	1036	1055	|	1136	1157	|	1236	1255	|	1336	1355	|	|	1436	1448	1455	|	|	1537	1546	1553	|
Retford .... d.	|	|	|	|	1051	|	|	|	1211	|	|	|	|	|	1409	|	|	|	|	|	|	|	|	|	1608	|
Newark North Gate .... d.	|	|	1000	|	1106	1119	|	1200	|	|	1259	1319	|	1400	|	|	|	1459	|	1519	|	|	1600	1609	|	|
Grantham .... d.	|	|	1012	|	1119	|	|	1212	|	|	1311	|	|	1412	|	|	|	1511	|	|	1540	|	1612	|	|	|
Peterborough .... d.	1005	1011	1034	1104	1141	1151	1204	1234	1251	|	1333	1351	|	1434	1451	|	|	1533	1540	1551	|	|	1634	1642	1651	|
Stevenage .... a.	|	|	1104	|	|	|	|	1306	|	|	|	|	|	1503	|	|	|	|	|	|	|	|	1704	|	|	|
London Kings Cross . a.	1057	1108	1132	1156	1233	1242	1255	1333	1342	1352	1424	1442	1450	1532	1542	1550	1556	1624	1632	1642	1646	1652	1732	1735	1743	1750

	⑦	⑦	⑦	⑦	⑦	⑦	⑦	⑦	⑦	⑦	⑦	⑦	⑦	⑦	⑦	⑦	⑦	⑦	⑦	⑦	⑦	⑦	⑦	⑦	⑦	⑦
	B			A							E				A											
Edinburgh Waverley . d.	1330	...	1400	1430	...	...	1447	...	1500	1530	...	...	1600	1620	1630	...	...	1700	1730	...	1800	...	1830	1900	2000	2100
Berwick upon Tweed.. d.	1413	...	|	|	...	...	1532	...	|	1612	...	...	|	|	1713	...	...	|	1816	...	|	...	1912	1946	2047	2147
Alnmouth .... d.	|	...	1501	|	...	...	|	...	|	|	...	...	1700	|	|	...	...	|	|	...	1900	...	|	|	2110	2210
Newcastle .... d.	1500	...	1531	1558	...	1552	1621	...	1627	1701	...	...	1730	1750	1800	...	...	1829	1903	...	1930	...	2001	2033	2145	2239
Durham .... d.	|	...	1544	|	...	|	1634	...	1640	|	...	...	1743	|	|	...	...	1842	|	...	1944	...	|	2046	2159	...
Darlington .... d.	1531	...	1603	|	...	1630	1653	...	1659	1729	...	...	1801	1817	1830	...	...	1901	1932	...	2003	...	2029	2105	2219	...
Northallerton .... d.	|	...	|	|	...	1641	|	...	|	|	...	...	|	1829	|	...	...	1912	|	...	|	...	|	|	2232	...
York .... d.	1601	...	1633	1659	...	1707	1722	...	1731	1759	...	...	1831	1853	1859	...	...	1933	2001	...	2032	...	2059	2135	2306	...
Leeds .... d.	|	1616	|	|	1645	|	|	1716	|	|	1745	1815	|	|	|	1845	1916	|	|	1945	|	2045	|	|	2336	...
Wakefield Westgate d.	|	1629	|	|	1659	|	|	1729	|	|	1759	1828	|	|	|	1859	1929	|	|	1959	|	2058	|	|	...	...
Doncaster .... d.	|	1647	1656	|	1720	1736	|	1747	1757	|	1819	1846	1855	|	|	1920	1947	1957	|	2020	2055	2116	2125	2158	...	...
Retford .... d.	|	|	|	|	|	|	|	1801	|	|	|	|	|	|	|	|	2001	|	|	|	|	2130	|	|	...	...
Newark North Gate .... d.	|	|	1719	|	1745	|	1803	|	|	|	1844	|	1919	|	|	1945	|	2021	|	2046	2119	|	2149	2221	...	...
Grantham .... d.	|	1718	|	|	|	1808	|	1824	1830	|	|	1917	|	1943	|	|	2024	|	2050	|	|	2153	2201	2233	...	...
Peterborough .... d.	|	|	1751	|	1814	|	1834	|	1852	|	1914	|	1950	|	|	2014	|	2051	2110	2115	2151	2214	2223	2255	...	...
Stevenage .... a.	|	1801	|	|	|	|	|	1908	|	|	|	2001	|	|	|	|	2108	|	|	|	|	2244	2253	2333s	...	...
London Kings Cross . a.	1755	1830	1842	1852	1906	1919	1925	1935	1944	1949	2007	2027	2042	2048	2055	2107	2134	2142	2202	2207	2243	2310	2318	2359	...	...

FOR NOTES SEE PAGE 143

First Excel service **X1** 🚌 KINGS LYNN - PETERBOROUGH 🚌 180a

From **Kings Lynn** bus station: Journey 80 minutes. Buses call at **Wisbech** bus station ± 32 minutes later.

Ⓐ: 0534, 0604, 0634, 0704, 0734, 0805, 0835, 0905, 0935, 1015 and every 30 minutes until 1615, 1655, 1725, 1755, 1900, 2110.

⑥: 0604, 0634, 0704, 0734, 0805, 0835, 0905, 0935, 1015 and every 30 minutes until 1615, 1655, 1725, 1755, 1900, 2110.

⑦: 0740 and hourly until 1840.

181 — LONDON - HULL

All trains ☕ HT

km		Ⓐ	Ⓐ	Ⓐ	Ⓐ	Ⓐ	Ⓐ△	Ⓐ	Ⓐ	Ⓐ		⑥	⑥	⑥	⑥	⑥	⑥△	⑥	⑥		⑦	⑦	⑦	⑦	⑦	⑦
0	London Kings Cross .... 180 d.	Ⓐ	0722	0948	1148	1348	1548	1719	1850	2030		⑥	0713	0948	1148	1448	1710	1748	1948	⑦	1048	1248	1448	1720	1744	1950
170	Grantham .... 180 d.		0825	1049	1249	1449	1649	1829	1952	2132			0820	1049	1249	1549	1821	1849	2052		1147	1347	1547	1826	1848	2051
223	Retford .... 180 d.		0851	1110	1310	1511	1711		2013	2153			0843	1110	1310	1609		1911	2113		1208	1408	1608		1908	2112
251	Doncaster .... 180 a.		0905	1123	1324	1525	1724	1906	2026	2206			0857	1123	1324	1623	1854	1924	2126		1222	1422	1625	1903	1923	2126
280	Selby .... a.		0922	1139	1339	1540	1740	1925	2047	2222			0914	1139	1340	1640	1911	1940	2142		1243	1444	1645	1921	1945	2142
330	Hull .... a.		1001	1214	1414	1615	1818	2005	2123	2300			1001	1218	1414	1725	1953	2015	2217		1320	1521	1722	2002	2020	2217
330	Hull .... d.		...	...	...	...	...	...	...	2135			...	...	...	...	...	2025	...		...	...	...	...	2030	...
343	Beverley .... a.		...	...	...	...	...	...	...	2145			...	...	...	...	...	2036	...		...	...	...	...	2041	...

		Ⓐ	Ⓐ	Ⓐ	Ⓐ	Ⓐ	Ⓐ△	Ⓐ	Ⓐ		⑥	⑥	⑥	⑥	⑥	⑥	⑥		⑦	⑦	⑦	⑦	⑦
Beverley .... d.	Ⓐ	0602	...	...	...	...	...	...	...	⑥	...	...	0955	...	...	...	...	⑦	...	1053	...	...	...
Hull .... a.		0613	...	...	...	...	...	...	...		...	...	1006	...	...	...	...		...	1104	...	...	...
Hull .... d.		0626	0700	0823	1030	...	1233	1513	1710	1911	0620	0650	0823	1031	1331	1530	1836	0906	1112	1436	...	1632	1848
Selby .... d.		0700	0737	0901	1106	...	1306	1547	1745	1945	0658	0725	0903	1106	1405	1605	1910	0940	1146	1510	...	1706	1922
Doncaster .... 180 d.		0721	0757	0925	1125	...	1325	1605	1803	2003	0715	0745	0925	1126	1426	1624	1929	1000	1204	1528	...	1727	1940
Retford .... 180 d.		0740		0939	1139	...	1339	1619	1817	2017		0759	0939	1140	1440	1638	1943	1014	1218	1542	...	1741	1954
Grantham .... 180 d.		0803	0835	1001	1201	...	1401	1640	1839	2040	0746	0818	0959	1201	1502	1700	2006	1035	1239	1605	...	1802	2016
London Kings Cross .... 180 a.		0913	0955	1110	1307	...	1510	1745	1945	2146	0852	0935	1108	1308	1608	1806	2110	1140	1344	1714	...	1915	2119

△ – Operated by GR (Table 180).

182 — LONDON - BRADFORD

All trains ☕ GC

km		Ⓐ	Ⓐ	Ⓐ	Ⓐ	Ⓐ		⑥	⑥	⑥	⑥△	⑥		⑦	⑦	⑦	⑦	⑦
0	London Kings Cross .... 180 d.	Ⓐ	1048	1448	1603	1833	1952	⑥	1048	1548	1636	1923	1930	...	⑦	1150	1550	1845	1922	...
251	Doncaster .... 180 a.		1222	1622	1735	2020	2119		1216	1718	1816	2051	2116	...		1319	1717	2024	2057	...
278	Pontefract Monkhill .... a.		1247	1647																
292	Wakefield Kirkgate .... a.		1304	1704	1804	2038e	2145		1243	1742	1844	2131	2134e			1347	1746	2054	2120	...
	Mirfield .... a.		1316	1716	1820		2159		1255	1755	1856	2142				1359	1759	2112	2135	
313	Brighouse .... a.		1324	1724	1828		2207		1308	1809	1910	2151				1408	1808	2123	2143	
322	Halifax .... 190 a.		1339	1739	1840		2223		1320	1821	1922	2203				1420	1820	2136	2155	
335	Bradford Interchange .... 190 a.		1354	1754	1855	2123f	2238		1337	1838	1938	2219	2220f			1436	1835	2152	2210	

		Ⓐ	Ⓐ	Ⓐ	Ⓐ	Ⓐ		⑥	⑥△	⑥	⑥	⑥		⑦a	⑦b	⑦	⑦	⑦
Bradford Interchange .... 190 d.	Ⓐ	0630f	0655	0752	1021	1433	⑥	0655	0733f	0851	1021	1521	⑦	0755	0810	1205	1505	1559
Halifax .... 190 d.			0708	0805	1034	1447		0709		0905	1035	1535		0810		1219	1520	1613
Brighouse .... d.			0719	0816	1048	1503		0720		0915	1048	1549		0821		1230	1535	1623
Mirfield .... d.			0727	0824	1057	1513		0728		0924	1057	1557		0830		1238	1543	1631
Wakefield Kirkgate .... d.		0713e	0744	0855	1113	1535		0743	0818e	0940	1114	1614		0846	0846	1255	1602	1648
Pontefract Monkhill .... d.			0801		1136	1554		0800		0957	1133	1634						
Doncaster .... 180 d.			0831	0931	1207	1621		0832	0838	1025	1206	1711		0911	0911	1321	1627	1713
London Kings Cross .... 180 a.		0859	1010	1113	1343	1810		1006	1030	1156	1343	1844		1040	1040	1452	1757	1845

a – Until Feb. 12 and from Apr. 2.   e – Wakefield Westgate.   △ – Operated by GR (Table 180).
b – Feb. 19 - Mar. 26.   f – Bradford Forster Square.

183 — LONDON - YORK - SUNDERLAND

All trains ☕ GC

km		Ⓐ	Ⓐ	Ⓐ	Ⓐ	Ⓐ		⑥	⑥	⑥	⑥	⑥		⑦	⑦	⑦	⑦
0	London Kings Cross ..... 180 d.	Ⓐ	0803	1121	1253	1650	1918	⑥	0811	1120	1320	1647	1911	⑦	0948	1348	1647	1822	...
303	York .... 180 d.		0958	1321	1451	1841	2119		1019	1319	1519	1842	2101		1139	1539	1842	2014	...
339	Thirsk .... d.		1015	1337	1514	1858	2136		1036	1336	1536	1858	2118		1155	1556	1901	2030	...
351	Northallerton .... 180 d.		1024	1346	1524	1907	2146		1045	1345	1546	1907	2128		1204	1606	1912	2040	...
375	Eaglescliffe .... a.		1042	1403	1541	1924	2203		1104	1403	1604	1925	2146		1222	1623	1929	2057	...
399	Hartlepool .... a.		1108	1423	1607	1944	2223		1123	1423	1623	1944	2206		1241	1652	1952	2117	...
428	Sunderland .... a.		1138	1451	1638	2021	2251		1150	1450	1650	2021	2236		1308	1721	2020	2151	...

		Ⓐ	Ⓐ	Ⓐ	Ⓐ	Ⓐ		⑥	⑥	⑥	⑥	⑥		⑦	⑦	⑦	⑦
Sunderland .... d.	Ⓐ	0645	0842	1228	1518	1731	⑥	0643	0830	1218	1529	1729	⑦	0920	1212	1412	1812	...
Hartlepool .... d.		0710	0908	1252	1550	1757		0710	0855	1242	1553	1754		0945	1236	1440	1840	...
Eaglescliffe .... d.		0732	0928	1312	1611	1822		0731	0917	1302	1612	1814		1005	1304	1504	1904	...
Northallerton .... 180 d.		0753	0947	1331	1631	1842		0752	0943	1320	1631	1832		1024	1324	1524	1924	...
Thirsk .... d.		0801	0959	1344	1643	1851		0801	0952	1330	1643	1843		1033	1333	1533	1933	...
York .... 180 d.		0821	1027	1406	1702	1911		0820	1012	1356	1702	1902		1052	1352	1552	1953	...
London Kings Cross ..... 180 a.		1020	1230	1610	1906	2105		1014	1208	1546	1853	2057		1243	1544	1744	2144	...

184 — LONDON - PETERBOROUGH

TL

km		Ⓐ	Ⓐ	Ⓐ	Ⓐ	Ⓐ	Ⓐ	Ⓐ	Ⓐ	Ⓐ	Ⓐ	Ⓐ	and at	Ⓐ	Ⓐ	Ⓐ	Ⓐ	Ⓐ	Ⓐ	Ⓐ	Ⓐ	Ⓐ
0	London Kings Cross ...... 180 d.	Ⓐ	0034	0134	0522	0622	0634	0722	0734	0811	0821	0834	the same	1522	1534	1622	1640	1650	1707	1713	1737	1743	1807
4	Finsbury Park .... d.		0040	0140	0528	0628	0640	0728	0740		0828	0840	minutes	1528	1540	1628		1656		1719		1749	
44	Stevenage .... 180 d.		0112	0221	0559	0647	0713	0747	0813		0847	0913	past each	1547	1613	1649		1717		1740		1809	
95	Huntingdon .... d.		0150s	0259s	0638	0723	0749	0823	0849	0854	0922	0949	hour until	1623	1649	1732	1727	1755	1800	1818	1830	1846	1858
123	Peterborough .... 180 a.		0212	0318	0655	0739	0806	0839	0907	0912	0938	1006	▽	1639	1706	...	1743	1812	1819	1838	1853	1903	1921

		Ⓐ	Ⓐ	Ⓐ	Ⓐ	Ⓐ	Ⓐ	Ⓐ	Ⓐ	Ⓐ	Ⓐ	Ⓐ	Ⓐ	Ⓐ		⑥	⑥	⑥		⑥	⑥	⑥	⑥	⑥	⑥
London Kings Cross ...... 180 d.	Ⓐ	1813	1837	1843	1910	1922	1952	2010	2022	2107	2122	2207	2222	2301	2322	⑥	0001	0034	0134	...	0522	0622	0634	0722	0734
Finsbury Park .... d.		1819		1849		1928	1958		2028		2128		2228		2328			0040	0140	...	0528	0628	0640	0728	0740
Stevenage .... 180 d.		1839		1910		1948	2019		2047		2147		2247		2347		0022	0112	0221	...	0559	0647	0713	0747	0813
Huntingdon .... d.		1916	1927	1947	2000	2024	2057	2053	2123	2154	2223	2254	2323	2348	0023		0057s	0150s	0256s	...	0638	0723	0749	0823	0849
Peterborough .... 180 a.		1932	1943	2003	2019	2041	2114	2111	2139	2210	2240	2310	2343	0014	0042		0113	0212	0318	...	0655	0739	0806	0839	0906

		⑥	⑥	and at	⑥	⑥	⑥	⑥	⑥	⑥	⑥	⑥	⑥	⑥	⑥	⑥		⑥	⑥	⑥	⑥	⑥	⑥	⑥a
London Kings Cross ...... 180 d.		0822	0834	the same	1622	1634	1640	1722	1734	1740	1822	1834	1840	1922	1934	2022	2034	...	2122	2134	2222	2252	2322	2352
Finsbury Park .... d.		0828	0840	minutes	1628	1640		1728	1740		1828	1840		1928	1940	2028	2040	...	2128	2140	2228	2258	2328	2358
Stevenage .... 180 d.		0847	0913	past each	1647	1713		1747	1813		1847	1913		1947	2013	2047	2113	...	2147	2213	2247	2317	2347	0026
Huntingdon .... d.		0923	0949	hour until	1723	1749	1727	1823	1849	1827	1923	1949	1927	2023	2049	2123	2149	...	2222	2249	2323	2353	0023	0104s
Peterborough .... 180 a.		0939	1008	▽	1739	1806	1743	1839	1906	1844	1939	2006	1943	2039	2106	2139	2206	...	2238	2307	2341	0014	0044	0125

		⑦b	⑦b	⑦b	⑦	⑦	⑦	⑦	⑦	⑦	⑦	⑦	⑦	⑦	⑦	⑦	⑦	⑦	⑦	⑦	⑦	⑦	⑦	⑦	⑦
London Kings Cross ...... 180 d.	⑦	0022	0054	0704	0822	0922	1022	1122	1222	1322	1422	1522	1622	1710	1722	1810	1822	1840	1922	2022	2122	2222	2233	2322
Finsbury Park .... d.		0028	0100	0710	0828	0928	1028	1128	1228	1328	1428	1528	1628		1728		1828		1928	2028	2128	2228	2239	2328
Stevenage .... 180 d.		0057	0133	0746	0847	0947	1047	1147	1247	1347	1447	1547	1647		1747		1847		1947	2047	2147	2247	2313	2347
Huntingdon .... d.		0134s	0211s	0828	0923	1023	1123	1223	1323	1423	1522	1623	1723	1757	1823	1855	1923	1932	2023	2123	2223	2323	2349	0023
Peterborough .... 180 a.		0156	0233	0844	0939	1039	1139	1240	1339	1439	1539	1640	1739	1819	1839	1913	1939	1951	2040	2139	2239	2343	0007	0043

For return service and footnotes see next page ▷ ▷ ▷

TL — PETERBOROUGH - LONDON — 184

		Ⓐ	Ⓐ	Ⓐ	Ⓐ	Ⓐ	Ⓐ	Ⓐ	Ⓐ	Ⓐ	Ⓐ	Ⓐ	Ⓐ	Ⓐ	Ⓐ	Ⓐ	Ⓐ	Ⓐ	Ⓐ	Ⓐ	Ⓐ	and at	Ⓐ
Peterborough 180 d.	Ⓐ	0325	0410	0510	0540	0547	0615	0632	0655	0715	0706	0726	0733	0746	0816	0846	0919	0930	0946	1016	1046	the same	1616
Huntingdon d.		0340	0425	0525	0555	0601	0630	0646	0710	0733	0722	0740	0748	0801	0830	0900	0934	0944	1000	1033	1100	minutes	1633
Stevenage 180 d.		0416	0504	0604	|	0639	0658	0724	0736	0758	0801	|	0827	0832	0907	0937	1003	1021	1036	1111	1136	past each	1712
Finsbury Park d.		0453s	0538	0624	|	0706	|	0744	|	|	0821	|	0848	|	0928	1000	|	|	1056	1143	1156	hour until	1743
London Kings Cross 180 a.		0502	0547	0629	0642	0712	0721	0750	0800	0822	0829	0828	0855	0856	0934	1006	1027	1047	1103	1149	1202	▽	1749

	Ⓐ	Ⓐ	Ⓐ	Ⓐ	Ⓐ	Ⓐ	Ⓐ	Ⓐ	Ⓐ	Ⓐ	Ⓐ	Ⓐ	Ⓐ			⑥	⑥	⑥	⑥	⑥	⑥	⑥	⑥	⑥
Peterborough 180 d.	1646	1721	1754	1821	1846	1916	1946	2016	2044	2121	2146	2222	2244	...	⑥	0325	0416	0516	0546	0616	0646	0716	0746	0810
Huntingdon d.	1700	1740	1810	1839	1901	1934	2000	2033	2058	2136	2200	2236	2258	...		0340	0433	0533	0600	0633	0700	0733	0800	0825
Stevenage 180 d.	1736	1819	1848	1917	1936	2012	2036	2110	2136	2213	2236	2317	2336	...		0416	0511	0611	0636	0711	0736	0811	0836	|
Finsbury Park d.	1756	1851	1909	1950	1956	2043	2056	2143	2156	2244	2256	2347	2356	...		0453s	0543	0643	0656	0743	0756	0843	0856	|
London Kings Cross 180 a.	1802	1857	1915	1956	2002	2050	2103	2148	2202	2250	2302	2353	0001	...		0459	0549	0649	0702	0749	0802	0849	0902	0912

	⑥	⑥	⑥	⑥	⑥	⑥	⑥	⑥	and at	⑥	⑥	⑥	⑥	⑥		⑥	⑥	⑥	⑥		⑥	⑥	⑥
Peterborough 180 d.	0818	0846	0909	...	0946	1012	1016	1046	the same	1716	1746	1816	1846	1916	...	1946	2016	2046	2116	...	2146	2216	2246
Huntingdon d.	0833	0900	0924	0933	1000	1027	1033	1100	minutes	1733	1800	1833	1900	1933	...	2000	2033	2100	2133	...	2200	2233	2300
Stevenage 180 d.	0911	0936	|	1011	1036	|	1111	1136	past each	1811	1836	1911	1936	2011	...	2036	2111	2136	2211	...	2236	2311	2336
Finsbury Park d.	0945	0956	|	1043	1056	|	1143	1156	hour until	1843	1856	1943	1956	2043	...	2056	2143	2156	2243	...	2256	2343	2359s
London Kings Cross 180 a.	0951	1002	1011	1049	1102	1115	1149	1202	▽	1849	1902	1949	2002	2049	...	2102	2149	2202	2249	...	2302	2349	0009

		⑦b	⑦b	⑦b	⑦	⑦	⑦	⑦	⑦	⑦	⑦	⑦	⑦		⑦	⑦	⑦	⑦		⑦	⑦	⑦	⑦	⑦
Peterborough 180 d.	⑦	0546	0646	0746	0846	0915	0946	1015	1046	1115	1146	1246	1346	...	1446	1546	1646	1746	...	1846	1946	2046	2146	2301
Huntingdon d.		0601	0700	0800	0900	0930	1000	1030	1100	1130	1200	1300	1400	...	1500	1600	1700	1800	...	1900	2000	2100	2200	2315
Stevenage 180 d.		0640	0739	0836	0936	|	1036	|	1136	|	1236	1336	1436	...	1536	1635	1736	1836	...	1936	2036	2136	2236	2352
Finsbury Park d.		0714	0802	0859	0956	|	1056	|	1156	|	1256	1356	1456	...	1556	1655	1756	1856	...	1956	2056	2157	2256	0017s
London Kings Cross 180 a.		0723	0810	0905	1002	1017	1102	1116	1202	1216	1302	1402	1502	...	1602	1701	1802	1902	...	2002	2102	2203	2302	0026

a – From Feb. 18. b – From Feb. 19. s – Calls to set down only. ▽ – Timings may vary by up to 2 minutes.

EM 2nd class — PETERBOROUGH - LINCOLN - DONCASTER — 185

km		⑥	Ⓐ	⚒T	⚒	⚒	ⒶD	⚒	⑥	Ⓐ	Ⓐ		⚒E	⚒	Ⓐ	⚒	⚒	⑥	ⒶD	⚒	⚒D	⚒	Ⓐ	⑥	⚒
0	**Peterborough** d.	...	...	0630	...	0730	...	0833	0932	0935	1040	...	1150	1241	1341	1511	1625	...	...	1732	...	1836	...	...	2030
27	Spalding d.	...	...	0653	...	0753	...	0854	0953	0956	1101	...	1213	1302	1404	1532	1646	...	...	1755	...	1859	...	...	2053
57	Sleaford d.	0650	0653	...	0743	...	0840	0918	1020	1021	1125	...	1241	1326	1429	1614	1718	1754	1756	...	1900	...	2005	2010	...
91	**Lincoln** a.	0722	0726	...	0815	...	0913	0956	1053	1053	1201	...	1314	1403	1503	1647	1751	1827	1829	...	1932	...	2039	2044	...

	Ⓐ	⚒	Ⓐ	⑥	⚒	⚒N	Ⓐ	Ⓐ	⑥	⚒	Ⓐ	ⒶR	⑥R	⚒	Ⓐ	ⒶR	⑥R	⚒	⑥	Ⓐ	⚒	⚒	⑥	Ⓐ	⚒L	⑥T	ⒶT
Lincoln d.	0617	...	...	...	0705	0800	0910	1018	1018	1110	1210	1330	1330	1441	1512	1600	1601	...	1715	1718	1810	...	1905	1915	2048	...	...
Sleaford d.	0645	...	...	...	0737	0834	0942	1051	1051	1142	1242	1403	1403	1516	1544	1634	1634	...	1747	1753	1842	...	1937	1947	2120	...	...
Spalding d.	...	0700	0800	0805	...	0900	1006	1113	1119	1204	1307	1425	1427	1538	...	1656	1657	1808	...	...	...	1959	...	...	...	2103	2105
Peterborough a.	...	0722	0822	0827	...	0924	1030	1134	1143	1228	1330	1446	1451	1602	...	1718	1723	1831	...	...	...	2022	...	...	...	2125	2127

km		Ⓐ	ⒶS	⑥	⚒	ⒶP	⑥	⑥	ⒶS	⚒S
0	**Lincoln** d.	0700	0915	0915	1154	1315	1410	1510	1831	1932
26	Gainsborough Lea Road d.	0721	0935	0935	1215	1335	1430	1530	1855	1952
60	**Doncaster** a.	0907	1002	1005	1245	1407	1458	1600	1925	2023

	⑥	Ⓐ	Ⓐ	⑥	Ⓐ	⑥	⑥	Ⓐ	⚒
Doncaster d.	1024	1024	1301	1305	1427	1507	1627	1936	2033
Gainsborough Lea Road d.	1048	1053	1329	1329	1452	1531	1652	2001	2056
Lincoln a.	1110	1116	1354	1354	1515	1557	1719	2023	2125

D – To/from Doncaster (lower panel).
E – To/from Doncaster on Ⓐ (lower panel).
L – To Boston (Table **194**).
N – From Nottingham (Table **186**).
P – To/from Peterborough (upper panel).
R – From Newark North Gate (Table **186**).
S – To/from Sleaford (upper panel).
T – To/from Nottingham (Table **206**).

EM 2nd class — GRIMSBY - LINCOLN - NOTTINGHAM — 186

km			Ⓐ	Ⓐ	Ⓐ	ⒶA	ⒶB	Ⓐ	Ⓐ	Ⓐ	Ⓐ	Ⓐ	Ⓐ	Ⓐ	Ⓐ	Ⓐ	Ⓐ	Ⓐ	Ⓐ	Ⓐ	Ⓐ	Ⓐ	Ⓐ	Ⓐ	Ⓐ	Ⓐ
0	**Grimsby Town** d.	Ⓐ	...	...	0556	...	...	...	0703	...	...	...	0920	...	...	...	1128	...	...	...	1349	...	...	...	1545	...
47	Market Rasen d.		...	...	0632	...	...	...	0739	...	...	...	0955	...	...	...	1203	...	...	...	1425	...	...	...	1621	...
71	**Lincoln** a.		...	...	0651	...	...	...	0757	...	...	...	1014	...	...	...	1222	...	...	...	1444	...	...	...	1640	...
71	**Lincoln** d.		0526	0646	0654	0704	0730	0736	0759	0836	0907	0937	1016	1036	1135	1140	1223	1234	1337	1436	1446	1536	1542	1634	1643	1726
97	Newark North Gate a.		0556	|	0722	|	0755	|	0824	|	0932	|	1040	|	1200	|	1250	|	|	|	1511	|	1611	|	1711	|
98	Newark Castle ♧ d.		0609	0714	...	0729	...	0806	...	0907	...	1007	...	1107	...	1207	...	1305	1407	1506	...	1608	...	1705	...	1756
126	**Nottingham** ♧ a.		0647	0740	...	0756	...	0833	...	0930	...	1030	...	1130	...	1230	...	1330	1430	1530	...	1630	...	1730	..	1830

	Ⓐ	Ⓐ	Ⓐ	Ⓐ	Ⓐ	Ⓐ	Ⓐ		⑥	⑥A	⑥	⑥	⑥	⑥	⑥B	⑥	⑥	⑥	⑥	⑥	⑥	⑥	⑥	⑥	⑥
Grimsby Town d.	...	...	1828	...	...	2124	...	⑥	...	...	...	0650	...	...	...	...	0920	...	...	...	1128	...	...	...	1349
Market Rasen d.	...	...	1904	...	...	2200	...		...	...	...	0726	...	...	...	...	0955	...	...	...	1203	...	...	...	1425
Lincoln a.	...	...	1923	...	...	2219	...		...	...	...	0744	...	...	...	...	1014	...	...	...	1222	...	...	...	1444
Lincoln d.	1818	1835	1925	2031	2140	...	2226		0526	0704	0726	0746	0835	0901	0930	0936	1015	1036	1130	1140	1223	1236	1337	1432	1446
Newark North Gate a.	1846	|	1953	|	|	...	|		0556	|	|	0812	|	0925	0953	|	1044	|	1152	|	1252	|	|	|	1511
Newark Castle ♧ d.	...	1903	...	2058	2207	...	2255		0610	0729	0755	...	0904	...	...	1007	...	1104	...	1204	...	1306	1405	1501	...
Nottingham ♧ a.	...	1930	...	2127	2239	...	2328		0647	0757	0823	...	0931	...	...	1030	...	1131	...	1227	...	1329	1429	1525	...

	⑥	⑥	⑥	⑥	⑥	⑥	⑥	⑥	⑥		⑦	⑦		⑦			⑦	⑦	⑦		⑦	⑦		⑦	⑦
Grimsby Town d.	...	...	1600	...	...	1828	...	1945	...	⑦	...	...	...	...	...	...	...	...	...	...	...	...	...	...	...
Market Rasen d.	...	...	1635	...	...	1902	...	2020	...		...	...	...	...	...	...	...	...	...	...	...	...	...	...	...
Lincoln a.	...	...	1653	...	...	1921	...	2039	...		...	...	...	...	...	...	...	...	...	...	...	...	...	...	...
Lincoln d.	1526	1635	1655	1725	1830	1924	1939	...	2045		1105	1245	...	1508	...	...	1709	1805	1903	...	2005	2100	...	2126	2210
Newark North Gate d.	|	|	1722	|	|	1953	|	...	|		1130	1310	...	1536	...	...	1734	|	|	...	|	2127	...	2155	|
Newark Castle ♧ d.	1557	1705	...	1754	1859	...	2004	...	2110		...	...	...	1550	...	...	...	1834	1933	...	2035	2140	...	...	2239
Nottingham ♧ a.	1627	1730	...	1829	1924	...	2031	...	2137		...	...	...	1620	...	...	...	1911	2005	...	2103	2209	...	...	2316

		Ⓐ	Ⓐ	ⒶP	Ⓐ	Ⓐ	Ⓐ	Ⓐ	Ⓐ	Ⓐ	Ⓐ	Ⓐ	Ⓐ	Ⓐ	ⒶP	Ⓐ	Ⓐ	Ⓐ	ⒶP	Ⓐ	Ⓐ	Ⓐ	Ⓐ	Ⓐ	Ⓐ
Nottingham ♧ d.	Ⓐ	...	0554	0653	...	...	0812	0925	...	...	1029	1129	...	1229	...	1329	...	1429	...	1529	...	1627	...	1721	1750
Newark Castle ♧ d.		...	0630	0727	...	...	0840	0952	...	...	1051	1153	...	1253	...	1352	...	1453	...	1553	...	1653	...	1752	1818
Newark North Gate d.		...	|	|	0742	0831	|	|	0957	1050	|	|	1206	|	1302	|	...	|	1528	|	1646	|	1728	|	|
Lincoln a.		...	0702	0756	0812	0902	0908	1017	1023	1114	1126	1221	1236	1323	1330	1423	...	1522	1555	1623	1713	1717	1800	1824	1849
Lincoln d.		0557	...	...	0815	...	...	...	1025	...	...	...	1237	...	...	...	1437	...	...	...	1722	...	...	...	...
Market Rasen d.		0613	...	...	0832	...	...	...	1042	...	...	...	1254	...	...	...	1454	...	...	...	1739	...	...	...	...
Grimsby Town a.		0655	...	...	0912	...	...	...	1122	...	...	...	1335	...	...	...	1534	...	...	...	1818	...	...	...	...

	Ⓐ	Ⓐ	Ⓐ	Ⓐ	ⒶB	ⒶA	Ⓐ	Ⓐ		⑥	⑥	⑥P	⑥	⑥	⑥	⑥	⑥	⑥	⑥	⑥	⑥	⑥	⑥P	⑥	⑥
Nottingham ♧ d.	1817	...	1919	...	...	2030	2120	2226	⑥	...	0555	0653	...	...	0811	...	0922	...	1029	1129	...	1229	...	1329	1419
Newark Castle ♧ d.	1853	...	1954	...	...	2054	2155	2257		...	0630	0726	...	...	0842	...	0950	...	1051	1155	...	1250	...	1350	1442
Newark North Gate d.	|	1935	|	2003	2036	|	|	2310		...	|	|	...	0820	|	0935	|	1049	|	|	1205	|	1302	|	|
Lincoln a.	1922	2001	2021	2027	2102	2122	2222	2340		...	0703	0758	...	0855	0909	0959	1018	1117	1124	1226	1236	1319	1330	1422	1510
Lincoln d.	...	2002	...	...	...	...	...	...		0538	...	...	0808	...	...	1006	...	...	...	...	1236	...	...	*1453*	...
Market Rasen d.	...	2019	...	...	...	...	...	...		0554	...	...	0825	...	...	1023	...	...	...	...	1254	...	...	*1510*	...
Grimsby Town a.	...	2056	...	...	...	...	...	...		0636	...	...	0912	...	...	1102	...	...	...	...	1334	...	...	*1550*	...

	⑥P	⑥	⑥	⑥	⑥	⑥	⑥B	⑥A	⑥	⑥	⑥		⑦		⑦		⑦	⑦	⑦	⑦	⑦	⑦B	⑦	⑦	⑦
Nottingham ♧ d.	...	1528	1621	1729	...	1823	...	1929	...	2030	2124	⑦	...	...	...	...	1633	...	1726	1836	1935	...	2039	...	2228
Newark Castle ♧ d.	...	1550	1652	1750	...	1850	...	1953	...	2104	2157		...	...	...	...	1659	...	1801	1859	1958	...	2103	...	2303
Newark North Gate d.	1529	|	|	|	1807	|	1935	|	2032	|	2206		1135	...	1335	...	|	1755	|	1928a	|	2036	|	2210	2317
Lincoln a.	1556	1622	1708	1823	1834	1923	2001	2026	2056	2132	2240		1202	...	1402	...	1731	1820	1833	1957	2030	2102	2135	2237	2348
Lincoln d.	...	...	*1722*	...	1835	...	...	...	2057	...	...		...	...	...	...	...	...	...	...	...	...	...	...	...
Market Rasen d.	...	...	*1738*	...	1852	...	...	...	2115	...	...		...	...	...	...	...	...	...	...	...	...	...	...	...
Grimsby Town a.	...	...	*1818*	...	1934	...	...	...	...	...	...		...	...	...	...	...	...	...	...	...	...	...	...	...

A – To/from London St Pancras (Table **170**).
B – To/from London Kings Cross (Table **180**).
P – To Peterborough (Table **185**).
a – Arrives 1909.

♧ – Additional journeys Newark Castle - Nottingham and v.v. Journey time: 28–36 minutes.
From Newark Castle at 0642Ⓐ, 0739Ⓐ, 0741⑥, 0841Ⓐ, 0843⑥, 0938⚒, 1047⚒, 1139⚒, 1247⚒, 1347Ⓐ, 1349⑥, 1439⚒, 1547⚒, 1638⑥, 1639Ⓐ, 1739⚒, 1847⑥, 1947⚒.
From Nottingham at 0756Ⓐ, 0758⑥, 0854⚒, 0949Ⓐ, 0951⑥, 1049Ⓐ, 1052⑥, 1153⑥, 1154Ⓐ, 1249⚒, 1349⚒, 1452⑥, 1453Ⓐ, 1549⚒, 1649⚒, 1852Ⓐ, 1857⑥.

Block 1

km		②-⑤	①	⑥	②-⑤	①	⑥	②-⑤	①	⑥	Ⓐ	✗	✗	✗	✗	✗	✗	✗	✗	✗	✗	Ⓐ
0	Newcastle d.											0533		0602			0706					
23	Durham d.											0546		0620			0719					
34	Middlesbrough d.												0554			0631	0715					
58	Darlington d.											0603		0637			0736					
81	Northallerton d.											0622		0649	0659		0743					
93	Thirsk d.											0630			0710		0755					
▯	Scarborough d.													0630	0700		0738					
▯	Malton d.													0653	0723		0801					
129	York a.										0636 0648		0712 0718	0728	0747		0738 0801					
129	York d.	0138	0138	0138	0252	0252	0252	0400	0420	0521 0555	0616 0640 0645 0651	0714	0723 0737	0750	0810 0813	0826	0840					
▯	Hull d.										0548		0637		0735							
▯	Selby d.										0623		0709		0808							
170	Leeds a.	0220	0204	0219	0333	0318	0333	0411	0446	0547 0618	0640 0647 0705 0708	0717 0733	0740 0750	0804 0820	0832 0840	0851	0904					
170	Leeds d.	0220	0205	0220	0335	0320	0335	0449	0449	0550 0620	0635 0644 0652 0711	0710 0720	0735 0744	0753 0809	0820 0836	0844 0854	0909					
185	Dewsbury d.									0601 0631	0646	0722 0721	0746	0820	0847		0920					
198	Huddersfield d.	0243	0243	0256	0358	0358	0411	0526	0526	0611 0640	0655 0702 0710 0731	0731 0739	0746 0802	0811 0830	0842 0856	0902 0912	0932					
227	Stalybridge d.									0630 0659	0714 0728 0750 0750	0759 0817		0850	0915		0950					
239	Manchester Victoria a.		0330h		0445h						0735		0835		0935							
255	Manchester Piccadilly a.	0343	0343e	0329	0458	0458g	0443	0557	0557	0607 0645	0707 0714 0730 0743	0806 0805	0816 0833	0845 0905	0913 0932	0945	1005					
255	Manchester Airport + a.	0400	0400e	0349	0515	0515g	0505	0619	0619	0710	0740	0810	0840	0910	0939	1010						
265	Warrington Central a.									0628 0728		0831 0830		0930			1030					
286	Liverpool South Parkway a.											0847 0847		0947			1046					
295	Liverpool Lime Street a.									0656 0753	0809	0859 0859	0909	0959		1009	1059					

Block 2

	⑥	✗	✗	✗	✗	✗	✗	✗	✗	✗	✗	✗	✗	✗	✗	✗	✗	✗
Newcastle d.		0748d	0806			0910			1003		1048k 1106a			1206		1248k	1310
Durham d.		0801d	0822			0923			1020		1101d 1119a			1222		1301d	1323
Middlesbrough d.			0827			0927		1027		1127			1227				
Darlington d.		0818d	0839			0940			1037		1118 1136a			1239		1318	1340
Northallerton d.			0850 0856		0951 0956			1049 1056		1147a 1156			1250 1256			1351
Thirsk d.			0904		1004			1104		1204			1304			
Scarborough d.	0750		0850			0950			1050		1150			1250
Malton d.	0813		0913			1013			1113		1213			1313
York a.	0838 0850d		0915 0922 0938		1014 1022 1038			1113 1122 1138 1151		1210a 1222 1238		1313 1322 1338 1351		1415
York d.	0840 0853		0915 0923 0940 0953		1015 1023 1040 1053			1115 1123 1140 1153		1215 1223 1240 1253		1315 1323 1340 1353		1415
Hull d.		0838		0938			1038		1138			1238		1338
Selby d.		0910		1010			1110		1210			1310		1410
Leeds a.	0904 0916	0934 0940 0949 1004	1017 1034 1040 1049	1104 1116 1134 1139	1150 1204 1216 1234	1239 1249 1304 1316	1334 1349 1404 1416	1434 1444
Leeds d.	0909 0920	0936 0944 0953 1009	1020 1044 1053 1109	1110 1120 1136 1144	1153 1209 1220 1236	1244 1253 1309 1320	1336 1351 1409 1421	1436 1444
Dewsbury d.	0920	0947	1020	1047	1120	1147	1220	1247	1320	1347	1420	1447
Huddersfield d.	0930 0940	0956 1002 1011 1030	1040 1056 1102 1111	1130 1140 1156 1202	1211 1230 1240 1256	1302 1311 1330 1340	1356 1402 1409 1430	1440 1456 1502
Stalybridge d.	0950	1015		1100 1115		1150 1215		1250 1315		1350 1415		1450 1515
Manchester Victoria d.		1035			1135			1235			1335			1435			1535
Manchester Piccadilly a.	1005 1013 1032	1044 1105 1113 1132	1144 1205 1213 1232	1244 1305 1313 1332	1342 1405 1413 1432	1444 1505 1513 1532
Manchester Airport + a.	1039	1110 1139	1210 1239	1310 1339	1410 1439	1510 1541
Warrington Central a.	1030		1130		1230		1330		1430		1530
Liverpool South Parkway a.	1046		1147		1247		1347		1447		1547
Liverpool Lime Street a.	1059	1109	1159	1209	1259	1309	1359	1409	1459	1509	1559	1609

Block 3

	✗	✗	✗	Ⓐ	⑥	✗	Ⓐ	⑥	✗	✗	✗	✗	✗	⑥	Ⓐ	✗	Ⓐ	⑥	✗	✗	✗	✗
Newcastle d.			1403 1406		1447 1452	1508			1606		1651		1703 1706		1804
Durham d.			1420 1422		1501	1523			1622		1719 1722			1726		1822
Middlesbrough d.	1327		1427			1527			1626			1726			
Darlington d.			1437 1439		1518 1519	1540			1639		1718		1736 1739		1839
Northallerton d.	1356		1448 1450 1456			1551 1556			1650 1654			1747 1750 1754		1850
Thirsk d.	1404		1504			1604			1702			1802		
Scarborough d.		1350			1450			1550			1650			1750
Malton d.		1413			1513			1613			1713			1813
York a.	1422 1438		1511 1513 1522 1538	1550 1551		1615 1622 1638		1713 1720 1738 1751		1810 1815 1820 1838		1913
York d.	1423 1440 1453		1515 1515 1523 1540	1553 1553		1615 1622 1640 1653		1715 1722 1740 1753 1753		1815 1815 1822 1840 1853 1915		1415
Hull d.			1438		1538			1638		1738			1849
Selby d.			1510		1610			1710		1810			1910
Leeds a.	1449 1504	1510 1524 1540 1539	1549 1606 1616 1616	1634 1639 1649 1706	1716 1735 1740 1749	1804 1816 1834 1840	1840 1849 1904 1915	1928 1943
Leeds d.	1453 1509	1517 1536 1544 1544	1553 1609 1620 1620	1636 1644 1653 1709	1720 1737 1744 1753	1809 1820 1820 1836	1844 1844 1853 1909	1941 1941
Dewsbury d.	1520	1547		1620	1647		1720 1731	1748		1820	1847		1920
Huddersfield d.	1511 1530	1535 1556 1602 1602	1611 1630 1640 1640	1656 1702 1711 1730	1740 1757 1802 1811	1830 1840 1840 1856	1902 1902 1911 1930	1940 2002
Stalybridge d.	1550	1615		1650	1715		1750 1816		1850	1915		1950
Manchester Victoria d.		1635 1635			1735			1835			1935 1935			2035
Manchester Piccadilly a.	1542 1605 1613 1634	1644 1705 1716 1716	1717 1732 1746 1805	1817 1833 1842 1905	1916 1932 1942 2005	2013
Manchester Airport + a.	1610	1639	1712	1739	1810 1839	1916 1940	2010
Warrington Central a.	1630		1730		1830		1930		2030
Liverpool South Parkway a.	1647		1747		1847		1947		2047
Liverpool Lime Street a.	1659	1711 1709	1759	1809	1859	1910	1959	2012 2010	2059	2114n

Block 4

	✗	✗	✗	✗	✗	Ⓐ	⑥	Ⓐ	⑥	✗	✗	✗	✗	✗	p	Ⓐ	⑥	q	⑦ r 🚌 v	⑦ r 🚌 v	⑦ r 🚌 v	⑦ r 🚌 v	⑦ r 🚌 v
Newcastle d.		1910			2027			2155 2155 2155		⑦													
Durham d.		1923			2045			2210 2210 2210															
Middlesbrough d.	1827		1930			2052 2052		2150															
Darlington d.		1940			2102			2219 2227 2227 2227															
Northallerton d.	1856	1951	1958		2113	2120 2120		2230 2238 2238 2238															
Thirsk d.	1904		2006			2128 2128		2238															
Scarborough d.		1850		1950	2045	2050		2207															
Malton d.		1913		2013	2109	2113		2230															
York a.	1922 1938 2014		2025 2038	2133 2136 2138 2146 2152		2255 2257 2302 2302 2302		0130 0218t 0330 0348t 0500t 0455 0600t 0555 0700t										
York d.	1923 1940 2016		2040 2116		2140 2140 2148	2228		2305 2305 2305															
Hull d.		1959			2138																		
Selby d.		2030			2212																		
Leeds a.	1951 2004 2039 2059		2104 2139		2205 2205 2213	2240 2305		2332 2332 2332		0220 0256 0420 0426 0538 0545 0638 0645 0738							
Leeds d.	1953 2009 2041		2109 2141		2140 2140 2209	2241 2309		2335 2335 2335		0220 0300 0420 0430 0540 0540 0545 0640 0640 0738							
Dewsbury d.		2020 2052		2120 2152		2220 2220		2346 2346 2346		0610 0651 0710 0751									
Huddersfield d.	2011 2030 2102		2130 2202		2230 2230	2302 2330		2355 2355 0001		0255 0318 0455 0448 0558 0605 0651 0735 0801						
Stalybridge d.		2050		2150		2250 2250				0720 0719 0820 0819									
Manchester Victoria d.																							
Manchester Piccadilly a.	2042 2105 2133		2205 2233		2305 2305	2337 0004		0027 0028 0032		0355 0349 0555 0519 0630 0745 0734 0845s 0838					
Manchester Airport + a.	2110	2154		2256				0046 0050 0110*		0420 0408 0620 0538 0650 0810 0754 0910 0854					
Warrington Central a.		2130			2230		2330 2330																
Liverpool South Parkway a.		2147			2245		2345 2345																
Liverpool Lime Street a.		2159			2256		2356 2356																

a – Runs 4 minutes later on ⑥.
c – Runs 8 minutes later on ⑥.
d – ⑥ only.
e – From Jan. 23. until Jan 16 change at Manchester Victoria for a connecting 🚌 (Manchester Piccadilly a. 0350, Manchester Airport a. 0415).
g – From Jan. 23. until Jan 16 change at Manchester Victoria for a connecting 🚌 (Manchester Piccadilly a. 0505, Manchester Airport a. 0530).

h – Until Jan. 16.
k – Runs 3 minutes later on Ⓐ.
n – On ⑥ arrives 2109.
p – To Feb. 11 and from Apr. 1.
q – Feb. 18 - Mar. 25.
r – Feb. 19 - Mar. 26.
s – Calls to set down only.

t – From Apr. 2 departs 12 minutes later.
v – To Feb. 12 and from Apr. 2.
* – Connection by 🚌.
▯ – Distances : York (0 km) - Malton (33 km) - Scarborough (67 km). Hull (0 km) - Selby (34 km) - Leeds (83 km).

TP THE NORTH EAST and YORKSHIRE - MANCHESTER and LIVERPOOL 188

	⑦	⑦ r	⑦r 🚌	⑦	⑦	⑦	⑦	⑦	⑦	⑦	⑦	⑦	⑦	⑦	⑦	⑦	⑦	⑦	⑦	⑦	⑦	⑦	⑦	⑦	⑦	⑦	⑦	⑦	⑦
Newcastle d.	...	...	...	...	...	0800	...	...	...	...	0906	...	...	1004	...	...	...	1110	1120	...	...	1206	...	...	...	1306	1310	...	...
Durham d.	...	...	...	...	...	0813	...	...	...	...	0919	...	...	1020	...	...	...	1123	1133	...	...	1222	...	...	...	1319	|	...	...
Middlesbrough d.	...	...	...	...	...	|	...	...	...	...	|	...	...	|	1027	...	...	|	|	...	...	|	1227	...	...	|	|	...	...
Darlington d.	...	...	...	...	...	0831	...	...	...	...	0936	...	...	1039	|	...	...	1140	1150	...	...	1240	|	...	...	1336	1341	...	...
Northallerton d.	...	...	...	...	...	0842	...	...	...	...	0947	...	...	1050	1056	...	...	1151	|	...	...	1251	1256	...	...	|	1353	...	...
Thirsk d.	...	...	...	...	...	0850	...	...	...	...	|	...	...	|	1104	...	...	|	|	...	...	|	1304	...	...	|	|	...	...
Scarborough d.	...	...	...	...	...	|	...	...	0853	...	|	...	...	|	|	1053	...	|	|	1153	...	|	|	1253	...	|	|	1353	...
Malton d.	...	...	...	...	...	|	...	...	0916	...	|	...	...	|	|	1116	...	|	|	1216	...	|	|	1316	...	|	|	1416	...
York a.	...	...	...	...	...	0909	...	...	0941	...	1010	...	...	1113	1122	1141	...	1214	1222	1241	...	1314	1322	1341	...	1408	1416	1441	...
York d.	...	...	0655	0809	0850	0911	...	0928	0944	...	1012	1028	1045	1115	1123	1145	...	1215	1223	1245	...	1315	1323	1345	...	1415	1423	1445	...
Hull d.	...	...	|	|	|	|	0835	|	|	0934	|	|	|	|	|	|	1137	|	|	|	1237	|	|	|	1339	|	|	|	1429
Selby d.	...	...	|	|	|	|	0910	|	|	1006	|	|	|	|	|	|	1208	|	|	|	1308	|	|	|	1410	|	|	|	1500
Leeds a.	...	...	0745	0835	0913	0934	0938	0953	1008	1032	1036	1051	1108	1138	1147	1208	1234	1240	1247	1308	1334	1339	1347	1408	1434	1439	1447	1508	1527
Leeds d.	...	...	0745	0840f	0916	0944	...	0953	1010	1036	1044	1053	1110	1144	1153	1210	1236	1244	1253	1310	1336	1344	1353	1410	1436	1444	1453	1510	1536
Dewsbury d.	...	...	0810	0851f	0927	|	...	|	1021	1047	|	|	1121	|	|	1221	1247	|	|	1321	1347	|	|	1421	1447	|	|	1521	1547
Huddersfield d.	...	...	0835	0901f	0936	1002	...	1011	1030	1056	1102	1111	1130	1202	1211	1230	1256	1302	1311	1330	1356	1402	1411	1430	1456	1502	1511	1530	1556
Stalybridge d.	...	0919	0920s	0919f	0955	|	...	|	1050	|	|	|	1150	|	|	1250	|	|	|	1350	|	|	|	1450	|	|	|	1550	|
Manchester Victoria d.	...	|	|	|	|	1035	...	|	|	|	1135	|	|	1235	|	|	|	1335	|	|	|	1435	|	|	|	1535	|	|	|
Manchester Piccadilly a.	0912	0934	0945	0934f	1010	|	...	1047	1106	1131	|	1142	1206	|	1242	1306	1331	|	1344	1406	1431	|	1442	1506	1531	|	1542	1606	1631
Manchester Airport ✈ a.	|	0954	...	0954f	|	|	...	1118	|	...	|	1209	|	|	1311	|	...	|	1405	|	...	|	1508	|	...	|	1605	|	...
Warrington Central d.	0933	...	...	...	1033	|	...	...	1130	...	|	...	1230	|	...	1330	...	|	...	1430	...	|	...	1530	...	|	...	1630	...
Liverpool South Parkway a.	0949	...	...	...	1049	|	...	...	1147	...	|	...	1247	|	...	1347	...	|	...	1447	...	|	...	1547	...	|	...	1647	...
Liverpool Lime Street a.	1001	...	...	...	1101	1109t	...	...	1159	...	1209t	...	1258	1309t	...	1359	...	1409t	...	1458	...	1509t	...	1559	...	1609t	...	1658	...

	⑦	⑦	⑦	⑦	⑦	⑦	⑦	⑦	⑦	⑦	⑦ p	⑦ q	⑦ q	⑦	⑦	⑦	⑦	⑦	⑦	⑦	⑦	⑦	⑦	⑦	⑦	⑦	⑦	⑦	⑦
Newcastle d.	1405	...	...	...	1510	1517	...	...	1604	...	...	1643	...	...	1710	1719	...	1804	...	...	...	1910	...	2010	...	...	...	...	2200
Durham d.	1421	...	...	...	1523	1530	...	...	1620	...	...	1657	...	...	1723	|	...	1822	...	...	...	1923	...	2023	...	...	...	...	2214
Middlesbrough d.	|	1423	...	...	|	|	...	...	|	1623	...	|	...	...	|	|	...	|	...	1819	...	|	...	|	...	2041	...	2208	|
Darlington d.	1438	|	...	...	1540	1547	...	...	1638	|	...	|	...	...	1741	1746	...	1840	...	|	...	1940	...	2040	...	|	...	|	2231
Northallerton d.	|	1451	...	...	1551	|	...	...	|	1652	...	|	...	...	1753	1758	...	|	...	1847	...	1951	...	2051	...	2109	...	2237	2243
Thirsk d.	|	1459	...	...	|	|	...	...	|	1700	...	|	...	...	|	|	...	|	...	1859	...	|	...	|	...	2117	...	2245	|
Scarborough d.	|	|	1453	...	|	|	1553	...	|	|	1653	|	1703	...	|	|	1753	|	...	|	1853	|	1953	|	...	|	2138	|	|
Malton d.	|	|	1516	...	|	|	1616	...	|	|	1716	|	1727	...	|	|	1816	|	...	|	1916	|	2016	|	...	|	2201	|	|
York a.	1512	1522	1541	...	1614	1619	1641	...	1711	1722	1741	1744	1751	...	1815	1821	1841	1913	...	1917	1941	2014	2041	2114	...	2143	2226	2309	2315
York d.	1515	1523	1545	...	1615	1623	1645	...	1715	1723	1745	1746	1753	...	1815	1823	1845	1915	...	1923	1945	2015	2045	2115	...	2145	2228	...	2317
Hull d.	|	|	|	1539	|	|	|	1643	|	|	|	|	|	1739	|	|	|	|	1842	|	|	|	|	|	2049	|	|	...	|
Selby d.	|	|	|	1610	|	|	|	1714	|	|	|	|	|	1810	|	|	|	|	1914	|	|	|	|	|	2120	|	|	...	|
Leeds a.	1539	1548	1608	1634	1640	1647	1708	1738	1742	1748	1808	1808	1818	1834	1839	1848	1908	1938	1942	1947	2008	2039	2108	2139	2147	2208	2251	...	2343
Leeds d.	1544	1553	1610	1636	1644	1653	1710	1738	1744	1753	1810	1810	...	1836	1844	1853	1910	1941	...	1953	2010	2041	2110	2141	...	2210	2253	...	2345
Dewsbury d.	|	|	1621	1647	|	|	1721	|	|	|	1821	1821	...	1847	|	|	1921	1952	...	|	2021	2052	2121	2152	...	2221	2304	...	2356
Huddersfield d.	1602	1611	1630	1656	1702	1711	1730	1756	1802	1811	1830	1830	...	1856	1902	1911	1930	2002	...	2011	2030	2102	2130	2202	...	2230	2313	...	0005
Stalybridge d.	|	|	1650	|	|	|	1750	|	|	|	1850	1850	...	|	|	|	1950	|	...	|	2050	|	2150	|	...	2250	2332	...	|
Manchester Victoria d.	1635	|	|	|	1735	|	|	|	1835	|	|	|	...	|	1935	|	|	2033	...	|	|	|	|	|	...	|	|	...	|
Manchester Piccadilly a.	|	1643	1706	1731	|	1746	1806	1831	|	1842	1906	1906	...	1931	|	1944	2006	|	...	2045	2106	2135	2206	2233	...	2305	2349	...	0037
Manchester Airport ✈ a.	|	1708	|	...	|	1805	|	...	|	1908	|	|	...	...	|	2006	|	|	...	2108	|	...	|	2254	...	|	...	...	0058
Warrington Central d.	|	...	1730	...	|	...	1830	...	|	...	1930	1930	...	...	|	...	2030	|	...	...	2130	...	2230	...	...	2330	...	...	...
Liverpool South Parkway a.	|	...	1747	...	|	...	1847	...	|	...	1947	1947	...	...	|	...	2047	|	...	...	2147	...	2246	...	...	2346	...	...	...
Liverpool Lime Street a.	1709t	...	1759	...	1809t	...	1859	...	1909t	...	1959	1959	...	...	2009t	...	2059	2107t	...	...	2159	...	2259	...	...	2359	...	...	...

		②–⑤	⑥	① m	① n	⚒	① m	Ⓐ k	⑥	⚒	⚒	⚒	⚒		⚒	⚒	⚒	⚒	⚒	⚒	⚒	⚒	⚒	Ⓐ	⑥	⚒	⚒	⚒	⚒
Liverpool Lime Street d.	⚒	...	...	...	...	...	...	...	...	...	...	...	...	...	...	0612	...	0622	...	...	0712	...	0715	...	...	...	0812	...	0822
Liverpool South Parkway d.		...	...	...	...	...	...	...	...	...	...	...	...	...	...	|	...	0632	...	...	|	...	0725	...	...	...	|	...	0832
Warrington Central d.		...	...	...	...	...	...	...	...	...	...	...	...	...	...	|	...	0645	...	...	|	...	0741	...	...	...	|	...	0845
Manchester Airport d.		0038	0038	0025*	0045	...	0405*	0422	0425	...	0530	...	...	...	...	|	0634	|	0706	...	|	0732	|	0806	0806	...	|	0834	|
Manchester Piccadilly d.		0053	0055	0050*	0100	...	0430*	0437	0440	...	0547	...	0615	...	0626	|	0657	0712	0726	0740	|	0757	0811	0826	0826	0841	|	0857	0911
Manchester Victoria d.		|	|	0112	|	...	0450	|	|	...	|	...	|	...	|	0646	|	|	|	|	0751	|	|	|	|	|	0851	|	|
Stalybridge d.		|	|	|	|	...	|	|	|	...	0600	...	0627	...	|	0658	|	0725	|	0752	|	|	0825	|	|	0854	|	|	0925
Huddersfield d.		|	0125	|	|	...	0540	0540	0540	...	0618	...	0646	...	0655	0717	0727	0746	0755	0812	0821	0827	0846	0855	0855	0913	0921	0927	0946
Dewsbury d.		|	|	|	|	...	|	|	|	...	0627	...	0655	...	0705	0726	|	0755	0804	0823	|	|	0855	|	|	0923	|	|	0955
Leeds a.		0159	0202	0209	0209	...	0559	0559	0559	...	0642	...	0708	...	0718	0739	0747	0810	0817	0836	0840	0846	0909	0915	0915	0936	0940	0946	1008
Leeds d.		0205	0205	0215	0215	...	0601	0601	0601	...	0643	...	0714	...	0722	0743	0749	0812	0820	0838	0843	0848	0912	0917	0917	0938	0943	0948	1012
Selby d.		|	|	|	|	...	|	|	|	...	|	...	|	...	0742	|	|	|	|	0858	|	|	|	|	|	0958	|	|	|
Hull a.		|	|	|	|	...	|	|	|	...	|	...	|	...	0820	|	|	|	|	0933	|	|	|	|	|	1034	|	|	|
York a.		0245	0244	0244	0244	...	0624	0624	0624	...	0706	...	0737	...	...	0806	0812	0838	0843	...	0906	0914	0936	0940	0940	...	1006	1013	1036
York d.		...	...	...	...	0600	0626	0626	0626	0640	0708	0718	0740	...	...	0808	0815	0840	...	...	0908	0915	0940	0942	0942	...	1008	1015	1040
Malton d.		...	...	...	...	|	|	|	|	0704	|	|	0804	...	...	|	|	0904	...	...	|	|	1004	|	|	...	|	|	1104
Scarborough a.		...	...	...	...	|	|	|	|	0729	|	|	0829	...	...	|	|	0930	...	...	|	|	1029	|	|	...	|	|	1129
Thirsk d.		...	...	...	...	0616	|	|	|	...	0725	0734	...	...	...	|	0831	...	...	...	|	0931	...	|	|	...	|	1031	...
Northallerton d.		...	...	...	...	0624	0647	0647	0647	...	0733	0742	...	...	...	0829	0840	...	...	...	0929	0940	...	|	|	...	1029	1040	...
Darlington d.		...	...	...	...	0640	0700	0700	0700	...	0745	|	...	...	...	0841	|	...	...	...	0941	|	...	|	1012	...	1041	|	...
Middlesbrough a.		...	...	...	...	0707	|	|	|	...	|	0817	...	...	...	|	0912	...	...	...	|	1012	...	|	|	...	|	1112	...
Durham d.		...	...	...	...	...	0717	0717	0717	...	0801	...	...	...	...	0857	...	...	...	...	0957	...	...	1027	1029	...	1057	...	...
Newcastle a.		...	...	...	...	...	0735	0735	0735	...	0819	...	...	...	...	0914	...	...	...	...	1015	...	...	1042	1044	...	1112	...	...

	⚒	⚒	⚒	⚒	⚒	⚒	⚒	⚒	⚒	⚒	⚒	⚒	⚒	⚒	⚒	⚒		⚒	⚒	⚒	⚒	⚒	⚒	⚒	⚒	⚒	Ⓐ	⑥	⚒
Liverpool Lime Street d.	...	...	0912	...	0922	...	...	1012	...	1022	...	...	1111	...	1122	...	...	...	1212	...	1222	...	...	1312	...	1322	...	...	...
Liverpool South Parkway d.	...	...	|	...	0932	...	...	|	...	1032	...	...	|	...	1132	...	...	...	|	...	1232	...	...	|	...	1332	...	...	...
Warrington Central d.	...	...	|	...	0945	...	...	|	...	1045	...	...	|	...	1145	...	...	...	|	...	1245	...	...	|	...	1345	...	...	...
Manchester Airport d.	0906	...	|	0933	|	1006	...	|	1033	|	1106	...	|	1133	|	1206	...	...	|	1233	|	1306	...	|	1333	|	1406	1406	...
Manchester Piccadilly d.	0926	0941	|	0957	1011	1026	1041	|	1057	1111	1126	1141	|	1157	1211	1226	...	1241	|	1257	1311	1326	1341	|	1357	1411	1426	1426	1441
Manchester Victoria d.	|	|	0951	|	|	|	|	1051	|	|	|	|	1151	|	|	|	...	|	1251	|	|	|	|	1351	|	|	|	|	|
Stalybridge d.	|	0954	|	|	1025	|	1054	|	|	1125	|	1154	|	|	1225	|	...	1254	|	|	1325	|	1354	|	|	1425	|	|	1454
Huddersfield d.	0955	1013	1021	1027	1046	1055	1113	1121	1127	1146	1155	1213	1221	1227	1246	1255	...	1313	1321	1327	1346	1355	1413	1421	1427	1446	1455	1455	1513
Dewsbury d.	|	1023	|	|	1055	|	1123	|	|	1155	|	1223	|	|	1255	|	...	1323	|	|	1355	|	1423	|	|	1455	|	|	1523
Leeds a.	1015	1036	1040	1046	1108	1114	1136	1140	1146	1208	1215	1236	1240	1246	1308	1315	...	1336	1340	1346	1408	1415	1436	1440	1446	1508	1515	1515	1536
Leeds d.	1017	1038	1043	1048	1112	1117	1138	1143	1148	1212	1217	1238	1243	1248	1312	1317	...	1338	1343	1348	1412	1417	1438	1443	1448	1512	1517	1517	1538
Selby d.	|	1058	|	|	|	|	1158	|	|	|	|	1258	|	|	|	|	...	1358	|	|	|	|	1458	|	|	|	|	|	1558
Hull a.	|	1135	|	|	|	|	1235	|	|	|	|	1335	|	|	|	|	...	1435	|	|	|	|	1535	|	|	|	|	|	1635
York a.	1040	...	1106	1113	1136	1140	...	1206	1212	1236	1240	...	1306	1313	1336	1340	...	...	1406	1413	1436	1440	...	1506	1513	1536	1540	1540	...
York d.	...	...	1108	1115	1140	1142	...	1208	1215	1240	...	...	1308	1315	1340	1342	...	...	1408	1415	1440	...	...	1508	1515	1540	...	1542	...
Malton d.	...	...	|	|	1204	|	...	|	|	1304	...	...	|	|	1404	|	...	...	|	|	1504	...	...	|	|	1604	...	|	...
Scarborough a.	...	...	|	|	1229	|	...	|	|	1329	...	...	|	|	1429	|	...	...	|	|	1529	...	...	|	|	1629	...	|	...
Thirsk a.	...	...	|	1131	...	|	...	|	1231	...	...	...	|	1331	...	|	...	...	|	1431	...	...	...	|	1531	...	...	|	...
Northallerton a.	...	...	1129	1140	...	|	...	1229	1240	...	...	...	1329	1340	...	|	...	...	1429	1440	...	...	...	1529	1540	...	...	|	...
Darlington a.	...	...	1141	|	...	|	...	1241	|	...	...	...	1341	|	...	|	...	...	1441	|	...	...	...	1541	|	...	...	|	...
Middlesbrough a.	...	...	|	1212	...	|	...	|	1312	...	...	...	|	1412	...	|	...	...	|	1512	...	...	...	|	1612	...	...	|	...
Durham a.	...	...	1157	...	...	1227	...	1257	...	...	...	...	1357	...	...	1427	...	...	1457	...	...	...	...	1557	...	...	...	1627	...
Newcastle a.	...	...	1215	...	...	1242	...	1316	...	...	...	...	1415	...	...	1443	...	...	1512	...	...	...	...	1615	...	...	...	1642	...

f – To Feb. 12 and from Apr. 2.
k – Runs ②–⑤ (also ① from Jan. 23).
m – Until Jan. 16.
n – From Jan . 23.
p – Until Jan. 1.
q – From Jan. 8.
r – Feb. 19 - Mar. 26.
s – Stop to set down only.
t – From Feb. 19.
* – Connection by 🚌.

Table 1

Station	Times
Liverpool Lime Street …..d.	1412 1422 … … 1511 … 1522 … … 1612 … … 1622 … … … 1710 … 1722 … … 1812 … 1822 … … 1912
Liverpool South Parkway d.	1432 … 1532 … 1632 … 1732 … 1832
Warrington Central………..d.	1445 … 1545 … 1645 … 1745 … 1845
Manchester Airport ………d.	1433 1506 … 1533 1606 … 1633 1703t 1706 … 1733 1806t … 1833 1924
Manchester Piccadilly ……d.	1457 1511 1526 1541 1557 1611 1626 1641 1656 1711 1725 1725 1741 1754 1811 1826 1841 1857 1911 1926 1942
Manchester Victoria ……..d.	1451 … 1551 … 1651 … 1751 … 1851 … 1951
Stalybridge ……………….d.	1525 1554 1625 1654 1725 1738 1738 1756 1825 1854 1925
Huddersfield ……………..d.	1521 1527 1546 1555 1613 1621 1627 1646 1655 1713 1721 1727 1746 1757 1757 1816 1821 1827 1846 1855 1914 1921 1927 1946 1956 2012 2021
Dewsbury ………………..d.	1555 1623 1655 1723 1755 1825 1855 1924 1956
Leeds ……………………..a.	1540 1546 1608 1615 1636 1640 1646 1708 1715 1736 1742 1746 1808 1816 1816 1838 1842 1846 1909 1916 1937 1942 1946 2009 2017 2031 2042
Leeds ……………………..d.	1543 1548 1612 1617 1638 1643 1648 1712 1717 1740 1744 1749 1812 1818 1818 1841 1845 1849 1912 1917 1939 1943 1949 2012 2020 2033 2043 2105
Selby ……………………..d.	1658 1801 1904 2001 2055 2128
Hull ………………………..a.	1735 1838 1939 2041 2135 2207
York ……………………….a.	1606 1613 1636 1640 1706 1713 1736 1743 1807 1814 1836 1844 1844 1908 1913 1936 1940 2006 2012 2035 2058 2107
York ……………………….d.	1608 1615 1640 1708 1715 1740 1809 1816 1840 1857 1857 1910 1916 1940 2008 2016 2040 2109
Malton …………………….d.	1704 1804 1904 2004 2104
Scarborough ……………..a.	1729 1829 1929 2029 2129
Thirsk …………………….a.	1631 1731 1832 1933 2035 2126
Northallerton ……………a.	1629 1640 1729 1740 1830 1840 1931 1941 2029 2043 2134
Darlington ………………..a.	1641 1741 1842 1927 1943 2041 2146
Middlesbrough …………..a.	1712 1812 1914 2014 2115
Durham …………………..a.	1657 1757 1858 1943 1944 2001 2057 2202
Newcastle ………………..a.	1712 1815 1914 1957 1958 2019 2113 2219

Table 2

Station	Times
Liverpool Lime Street …..d.	1922 … 2022 … 2022 … 2130 2230 2230 2230 (p) (q) … ⑦ 0100 0100 0425 0330 0530 0630 … 0605
Liverpool South Parkway d.	1932 2032 2032 2140 2240 2240 2240
Warrington Central………..d.	1945 2045 2045 2153 2253 2253 2253
Manchester Airport ………d.	2024 2024 2124 2224 (v) (w) 2320 2320 2320 2325 0100 0100 0425 0330 0530 0630 0605
Manchester Piccadilly ……d.	2011 2042 2042 2111 2111 2142 2219 2242 2321 2321 2321 2335 2335 2334 2350 0117 0125 0442 0355 0555 0647 0630
Manchester Victoria ……..d.	2351 2351 2351 2351
Stalybridge ……………….d.	2025 2125 2125 2231 2254 2334 2334 2334 0700 0655
Huddersfield ……………..d.	2046 2112 2112 2146 2146 2211 2250 2313 2352 2351 2352 0021 0021 0021 0052 0050 0147 0225 0512 0455 0655 0718 0740
Dewsbury ………………..d.	2055 2155 2155 2229 2322 0030* 0030 0030 030s 0102s 0115 0720 0727 0805
Leeds ……………………..a.	2108 2131 2131 2208 2208 2230 2312 2335 0011 0055* 0031 0043 0043 0044 0115 0140 0206 0300 0531 0530 0745 0740 0830
Leeds ……………………..d.	2112 2121 2133 2133 2211 2211 2221 2233 2316 2337 0015 0055* 0034 0045 0048 0047 0123 0140 0208 0300 0533 0530 0745 0743 0843
Selby ……………………..d.	2145 2243
Hull ………………………..a.	2223 2319
York ……………………….a.	2137 2157 2158 2234 2236 2258 2342 0003 0043 0145* 0113 0113 0129 0129 0207 0230 0252b 0350 0617b 0620 0835 0827b 0906
York ……………………….d.	2200 2212 2235 2242 0847 0908
Malton …………………….d.	2224 2236 2306
Scarborough ……………..a.	2249 2301 2331
Thirsk …………………….a.	2258 0903
Northallerton ……………a.	2306 0911 0929
Darlington ………………..a.	2318 0925 0941
Middlesbrough …………..a.	0952
Durham …………………..a.	2334 0957
Newcastle ………………..a.	0008 1015

Table 3

Station	Times
Liverpool Lime Street …..d.	… … … … … … 0822 … 0912f … 0922 1010f … 1022 … 1112f … 1122 1210f … 1222 … 1312f … 1322 1405f
Liverpool South Parkway d.	0832 0932 1032 1132 1132 1232 1332 1345
Warrington Central………..d.	0844 0944 1044 1145 1145 1245 1345
Manchester Airport ………d.	0729 0802 0810* 0824 0935 1033 1133 1233 1333
Manchester Piccadilly ……d.	0747 0820 0847 0847 0911 0928 1003 1011 1057 1111 1143 1157 1211 1211 1257 1311 1343 1357 1411 1443
Manchester Victoria ……..d.	0951 1045 1151 1245 1351 1425
Stalybridge ……………….d.	0800 0833 0900 0900 0924 1025 1125 1225 1225 1325 1425
Huddersfield ……………..d.	0818 0852 0918 0918 0946 1005 1021 1032 1046 1114 1127 1146 1213 1221 1227 1246 1246 1314 1327 1346 1413 1421 1427 1446 1509 1515
Dewsbury ………………..d.	0827 0901 0927 0927 0955 1015 1055 1155 1255 1355 1455 1525
Leeds ……………………..a.	0840 0914 0940 0940 1008 1030 1040 1051 1109 1134 1146 1209 1236 1240 1309 1309 1334 1409 1436 1440 1509 1528 1538
Leeds ……………………..d.	0843 0915 0915 0943 0943 0943 1012 1030 1040 1053 1112 1148 1148 1212 1238 1243 1248 1312 1338 1349 1412 1438 1443 1449 1512 1536 1540 1603
Selby ……………………..d.	0952 1104 1301 1458 1603
Hull ………………………..a.	1014 1140 1336 1532 1637
York ……………………….a.	0906 0938 0938 1006 1006 1006 1049 1038 1106 1116 1139 1201 1211 1235 1306 1311 1336 1336 1402 1411 1439 1506 1511 1540 1601
York ……………………….d.	0908 0942 0942 1008 1008 1008 1042 1108 1117 1142 1203 1212 1242 1308 1314 1342 1340 1404 1413 1442 1508 1514 1542 1606
Malton …………………….d.	1006 1005 1106 1206 1306 1406 1506 1606
Scarborough ……………..a.	1031 1031 1131 1231 1331 1432 1531 1631
Thirsk …………………….a.	1134 1331 1531
Northallerton ……………a.	0929 1029 1029 1029 1129 1142 1233 1329 1340 1425 1529 1540
Darlington ………………..a.	0941 1041 1041 1041 1141 1245 1341 1411 1437 1443 1541 1636
Middlesbrough …………..a.	1214 1412 1612
Durham …………………..a.	0957 1057 1057 1057 1302 1357 1428 1500 1557 1653
Newcastle ………………..a.	1015 1114 1114 1114 1215 1300 1317 1416 1444 1506 1515 1615 1708

Table 4

Station	Times
Liverpool Lime Street …..d.	… 1422 1512f 1522 1612f … 1622 1712f … 1722 1812f … 1822 … 1912f 1922 … 2012f 2022 … 2152
Liverpool South Parkway d.	1432 1532 1632 1732 1832 1932 2032 2202
Warrington Central………..d.	1445 1545 1645 1745 1845 1945 2045 2215
Manchester Airport ………d.	1433 1533 1633 1733 1833 1920 2020 2120 2120
Manchester Piccadilly ……d.	1457 1511 1543 1557 1611 1643 1657 1711 1743 1757 1811 1857 1911 1942 2012 2042 2112 2142 2242 2346
Manchester Victoria ……..d.	1551 1651 1751 1851 1951 2051
Stalybridge ……………….d.	1525 1625 1725 1825 1925 2025 2125 2255
Huddersfield ……………..d.	1527 1546 1613 1621 1630 1646 1713 1721 1727 1746 1813 1821 1846 1846 1921 1927 1946 2011 2021 2046 2111 2121 2146 2211 2313 0021
Dewsbury ………………..d.	1555 1623 1655 1723 1755 1823 1855 1955 2055 2155 2220 2322 0030
Leeds ……………………..a.	1546 1609 1636 1640 1649 1709 1736 1740 1746 1808 1836 1840 1846 1909 1940 1946 2008 2030 2040 2108 2133 2140 2208 2233 2335 0043
Leeds ……………………..d.	1548 1612 1637 1643 1650 1712 1738 1743 1749 1812 1838 1843 1849 1912 1943 1949 2012 2018 2043 2112 2138 2143 2211 2221 2236 2341 0045
Selby ……………………..d.	1657 1800 1901 2051 2201 2243
Hull ………………………..a.	1732 1835 1936 2127 2237 2319
York ……………………….a.	1611 1635 1706 1713 1737 1806 1811 1842 1906 1912 1936 2006 2014 2035 2056 2106 2137 2206 2234 2304 0022 0113
York ……………………….d.	1613 1642 1708 1715 1742 1808 1813 1842 1908 1915 1942 2008 2042 2100 2108 2208 2235
Malton …………………….d.	1706 1806 1906 2006 2106 2232
Scarborough ……………..a.	1731 1831 1931 2031 2131 2257
Thirsk …………………….a.	1731 1933 2116 2258
Northallerton ……………a.	1634 1729 1740 1834 1929 1944 2029 2124 2129 2306
Darlington ………………..a.	1646 1741 1839 1846 1941 2041 2141 2318
Middlesbrough …………..a.	1812 2016 2158
Durham …………………..a.	1702 1757 1856 1902 1957 2057 2157 2334
Newcastle ………………..a.	1717 1815 1913 1917 2014 2114 2214 0007

a – To Feb. 12 and from Apr. 2.
b – From Apr. 2 arrives 16 minutes earlier.
c – Feb. 19 - Mar. 26.
d – Until Mar. 26.
e – From Apr. 2.
f – From Feb. 19.
h – From Jan. 8.
k – Until Feb. 12.
p – To Feb. 11 and from Apr. 1.
q – Feb. 18 - Mar. 25.
r – ①–④ only.
s – Calls to set down only.
t – ⑥ only.
v – From Apr. 1.
w – Until Feb. 11.
* – Connection by 🚌.

NT 2nd class — YORK - LEEDS - HALIFAX - BLACKPOOL and MANCHESTER — 190

km		⚒	Ⓐ	⑥	⚒	Ⓐ	⑥	Ⓐ	⚒	⚒	⚒	⚒	⚒	⚒	⚒	⚒	⚒		⚒	⚒	⚒	⚒	⚒	⚒	⚒
0	**York** 124 188 d.		...	...	...	...	...	0535	...	0620	...	...	...	0718a	...	...	...		1718	...	...	...	1827	...	...
41	**Leeds** 124 188 d.		0508	0535	0557	0608	0618	0623	0651	0708	0718	0723	0751	0805	0818	0826	0851		1805	1818	1823	1851	1905	1919	1951
56	Bradford Interchange d.		0531	0558	0617	0631	0641	|	0714	0728	0741	|	0814	0826	0841	|	0914	and	1826	1841	|	1914	1926	1942	2014
69	**Halifax** d.		0544	0611	0629	0644	0654	|	0727	0740	0754	|	0827	0839	0854	|	0927	at	1838	1854	|	1927	1939	1955	2027
	Dewsbury d.		|	|	|	|	|	0639	|	|	|	0739	|	|	|	0842	|	the	|	|	1841	|	|	|	|
	Brighouse d.		|	|	|	|	|	0659	|	|	|	0758	|	|	|	0859	|	same	|	|	1859	|	|	|	|
83	Hebden Bridge d.		0559	0627	0646	0659	0710	0717	0742	0752	0805	0817	0842	0852	0906	0918	0942	minutes	1852	1906	1917	1942	1952	2011	2042
90	Todmorden d.		0607	0634	|	0707	0717	0724	0750	|	0813	0824	0850	|	0913	0925	0950	past	|	1913	1925	1950	|	2018	2050
104	Rochdale d.		0623	0651	|	0720	0734	0741	0804	|	0825	0841	0900	|	0924	0942	1000	each	|	1924	1941	2000	|	2035	2100
120	**Manchester** Victoria a.		0647	0717	|	0737	0758	0803	0824	|	0847	0904	0917	|	0942	1004	1017	hour	|	1942	2006	2018	|	2100	2117
103	Burnley Manchester Road d.		...	...	0705	...	...	...	...	0812	...	...	...	0912	...	...	...	until	1912	...	...	...	2012	...	...
113	Accrington d.		...	...	0714	...	...	...	...	0821	...	...	...	0921	...	...	...		1921	...	...	...	2021	...	...
123	Blackburn 191 d.		...	...	0723	...	...	...	...	0829	...	...	...	0930	...	...	...	❖	1930	...	...	...	2030	...	...
142	Preston 156 191 a.		...	...	0746	...	...	...	...	0852	...	...	...	0947	...	...	...		1947	...	...	...	2047	...	...
171	**Blackpool** North 156 191 a.		...	...	0814	...	...	...	...	0923	...	...	...	1015	...	...	...		2017	...	...	...	2115	...	...

	⚒	⚒	⚒	⚒	⚒	⑦	⑦	⑦	⑦	⑦	⑦	⑦	⑦	⑦	⑦	⑦		⑦	⑦	⑦	⑦	⑦	⑦	⑦	⑦
York 124 188 d.	1918	...	...	...	...		...	0812	...	0905	...	1015	...	...	1118a	...		1827	...	1918	...	2027	...	...	...
Leeds 124 188 d.	2005	2035	2108	2135	2235		0818	0853	0908	0953	1008	1053	1108	1151	1208	1251		1908	1951	2008	2052	2108	2135	2208	2235
Bradford Interchange d.	2026	2058	2128	2158	2258		0841	0913	0933	1014	1033	1113	1133	1215	1228	1314	and	1928	2014	2028	2115	2128	2158	2231	2259
Halifax d.	2039	2111	2140	2211	2311		0854	0926	0945	1026	1045	1126	1145	1228	1240	1327	at	1940	2027	2040	2128	2140	2211	2246	2314
Dewsbury d.	|	|	|	|	|		|	|	|	|	|	|	|	|	|	|	the	|	|	|	|	|	|	|	|
Brighouse d.	|	|	|	|	|		|	|	|	|	|	|	|	|	|	|	same	|	|	|	|	|	|	2257	2325
Hebden Bridge d.	2052	2126	2154	2226	2326		0909	0940	1001	1041	1101	1140	1201	1244	1252	1342	minutes	1952	2042	2052	2144	2152	2226	...	...
Todmorden d.	|	2134	|	2234	2334		0917	|	1009	|	1109	|	1209	1251	|	1350	past	|	2050	|	2152	|	2234	...	...
Rochdale d.	|	2150	|	2250	2350		0929	|	1021	|	1121	|	1221	1304	|	1403	each	|	2103	|	...	|	2250	...	...
Manchester Victoria a.	|	2215	|	2315	0008		0946	|	1039	|	1139	|	1239	1320	|	1420	hour	|	2120	|	...	|	2313	...	...
Burnley Manchester Road d.	2113	...	2214	...	...		...	1001	...	1103	...	1201	...	...	1312	...	until	2012	...	2112	...	2212	...	...	...
Accrington d.	2121	...	2223	...	...		...	1009	...	1111	...	1209	...	...	1320	...		2020	...	2120	...	2220	...	...	...
Blackburn 191 d.	2130	...	2232	...	...		...	1018	...	1120	...	1218	...	...	1329	...	❖	2029	...	2129	...	2229	...	...	...
Preston 156 191 a.	2148	...	2251	...	...		...	1041	...	1140	...	1240	...	...	1348	...		2048	...	2147	...	2252	...	...	...
Blackpool North 156 191 a.	...	...	2321c	...	...		...	1108	...	1210	...	1310	...	...	1414	...		2113	...	2216	...	...	...	...	...

	⚒	⚒	⚒	⑥	Ⓐ	⚒	⚒	⚒	⚒	⚒	⚒	⚒	⚒	⚒	⚒	⚒		⚒	⚒	⚒	⚒	⚒	⚒	⚒	⚒
Blackpool North 156 191 d.		...	0511b	...	...	...	0611b	...	...	...	...	0711	...	...	...	0811		...	...	...	1656	...	...	...	1811
Preston 156 191 d.		...	0537	...	...	...	0638	...	...	...	...	0737	...	...	...	0836		...	...	...	1725	...	...	...	1837
Blackburn 191 d.		...	0555	...	...	...	0655	...	...	...	...	0755	...	...	...	0855	and	...	...	...	1753	...	...	...	1856
Accrington d.		...	0603	...	...	...	0703	...	...	...	...	0803	...	...	...	0903	at	...	...	...	1801	...	...	...	1904
Burnley Manchester Road d.		...	0612	...	...	...	0712	...	...	...	...	0812	...	...	...	0912	the	...	...	...	1812	...	...	...	1913
Manchester Victoria d.		0547	|	0608	0612	0636	|	...	0712	0726	0748	|	0816	0826	0848	|	same	1708	1725	1745	|	1810	1826	1848	|
Rochdale d.		0602	|	0627	0626	0653	|	...	0726	0747	0802	|	0830	0847	0902	|	minutes	1727	1747	1803	|	1827	1847	1902	|
Todmorden d.		0612	|	0644	0643	0710	|	...	0743	0804	0813	|	0841	0904	0913	|	past	1743	1804	1816	|	1841	1904	1913	|
Hebden Bridge d.		0619	0634	0651	0650	0717	0734	0739	0750	0811	0820	0834	0848	0911	0920	0934	each	1750	1811	1822	1834	1848	1911	1920	1935
Brighouse d.		|	|	|	|	|	|	0756	|	0829	|	|	|	0929	|	|	hour	|	1829	|	|	|	1929	|	|
Dewsbury d.		|	|	|	|	|	|	0811	|	0842	|	|	|	0941	|	|	until	|	1841	|	|	|	1941	|	|
Halifax d.		0637	0648	0709	0707	0734	0749	|	0807	|	0833	0848	0906	|	0933	0947		1807	|	1835	1847	1906	|	1934	1949
Bradford Interchange d.		0652	0704	0724	0723	0750	0804	|	0823	|	0849	0904	0921	|	0949	1002	❖	1824	|	1852	1903	1922	|	1949	2004
Leeds 124 188 a.		0714	0722	0746	0746	0811	0822	0834	0845	0904	0910	0923	0944	1003	1012	1021		1844	1903	1915	1923	1944	2003	2011	2026
York 124 188 a.		...	0803	...	...	...	0904	...	...	...	...	1000	...	...	...	1103		...	...	...	2004	...	...	...	...

	⚒	⚒	⚒	⚒	⚒	⚒	Ⓐ	⑥	Ⓐ	⑦	⑦	⑦	⑦	⑦	⑦	⑦		⑦	⑦	⑦	⑦	⑦	⑦	⑦	⑦
Blackpool North 156 191 d.	...	...	1911	...	2029	...	...	...	...		...	...	...	...	...	1111		1811	...	1911	...	2011	...	2111	...
Preston 156 191 d.	...	...	1937	...	2056	...	...	...	...		...	0937	...	1038	...	1137		1837	...	1937	...	2037	...	2137	...
Blackburn 191 d.	...	...	1955	...	2124	...	...	...	...		...	0955	...	1055	...	1155	and	1855	...	1955	...	2055	...	2155	...
Accrington d.	...	...	2003	...	2132	...	...	...	...		...	1003	...	1103	...	1203	at	1903	...	2003	...	2103	...	2203	...
Burnley Manchester Road d.	...	...	2012	...	2141	...	...	...	...		...	1012	...	1112	...	1212	the	1912	...	2012	...	2112	...	2212	...
Manchester Victoria d.	1916	1926	|	2026	|	2126	2226	2254	2321		0915	|	1015	|	1115	|	same	|	1915	|	2015	|	2115	|	2210
Rochdale d.	1931	1947	|	2047	|	2147	2247	2308	2342		0929	|	1029	|	1129	|	minutes	|	1929	|	2029	|	2129	|	2231
Todmorden d.	1942	2004	|	2104	|	2204	2304	2325	2359		0942	|	1042	|	1142	|	past	|	1942	|	2042	|	2142	|	2248
Hebden Bridge d.	1949	2011	2034	2111	2203	2211	2311	2331	0006		0949	1034	1049	1134	1149	1234	each	1934	1949	2034	2049	2134	2149	2234	2255
Brighouse d.	|	2029	|	|	|	|	|	|	|		|	|	|	|	|	|	hour	|	|	|	|	|	|	|	|
Dewsbury d.	|	2041	|	|	|	|	|	|	|		|	|	|	|	|	|	until	|	|	|	|	|	|	|	|
Halifax d.	2007	|	2049	2129	2218	2229	2329	2349	0023		1007	1047	1107	1147	1207	1247		1947	2007	2049	2107	2149	2207	2249	2313
Bradford Interchange d.	2022	|	2104	2144	2233	2244	2345	0004	0039		1023	1103	1123	1203	1223	1303	❖	2003	2024	2105	2123	2205	2223	2305	2328
Leeds 124 188 a.	2044	2103	2126	2206	2253	2309	0006	0026	0057		1044	1122	1144	1224	1244	1322		2022	2044	2122	2144	2226	2246	2324	2351
York 124 188 a.	2130b	...	2230d	...	2340	...	...	...	...		...	1158	...	1303	...	1400		...	...	2203	...	...	...	...	...

a – Departs xx27 on the even hours except on ⑥ when departs 0818, 0918, 1027.
b – ⑥ only.
c – Ⓐ only.
d – 2218 on ⑥.
❖ – Timings may vary by ± 5 minutes.

NT 2nd class — BLACKPOOL PRESTON - CLITHEROE - HELLIFIELD — 191

THIS TABLE HAS TEMPORARILY MOVED TO PAGE 134

NT 2nd classs — HULL - DONCASTER - SHEFFIELD — 192

km		Ⓐ	Ⓐ	Ⓐ	Ⓐ	Ⓐ	Ⓐ	Ⓐ	Ⓐ	Ⓐ	Ⓐ	Ⓐ	Ⓐ	Ⓐ	Ⓐ	Ⓐ	Ⓐ	Ⓐ	Ⓐ	Ⓐ	⑥	⑥	⑥	⑥	⑥	⑥
0	**Hull** 181 d.		0520	0641	0803	0857	0957	1057	1156	1257	1357	1457	1557	1657	1743	1757	1857	2003	2057	2220		0520	0640	0803	0857	0957
38	Goole d.		0547	0717	0830	0924	1024	1124	1223	1324	1424	1524	1624	1725	1821	|	1924	2036	2124	2254		0547	0716	0830	0924	1024
66	**Doncaster** 181 a.		0617	0747	0854	0949	1047	1148	1247	1347	1447	1548	1648	1747	1851	1848	1949	2106	2147	2324		0617	0746	0857	0948	1047
66	**Doncaster** 193 d.		0628	0748	0856	0950	1049	1148	1249	1348	1449	1549	1649	1749	1902	1850	1950	2107	2149	2325		0629	0748	0902	0949	1049
90	Meadowhall 193 d.		0657	0825	0916	1010	1110	1210	1309	1410	1510	1610	1710	1810	1929	1910	2010	2134	2212	2354		0658	0825	0924	1010	1110
96	**Sheffield** 193 a.		0706	0833	0926	1019	1120	1219	1319	1420	1519	1620	1720	1820	1939	1917	2017	2142	2221	0004		0707	0832	0931	1019	1120

	⑥	⑥	⑥	⑥	⑥	⑥	⑥	⑥	⑥	⑥	⑥	⑥	⑥	⑦	⑦	⑦	⑦	⑦	⑦	⑦	⑦	⑦	⑦	⑦	⑦	⑦
Hull 181 d.	1058	1157	1257	1357	1457	1557	1657	1743	1755	1857	2003	2057	2216		0840	0943	1050	1241	1330	1441	1532	1637	1732	1835	2001	2140
Goole d.	1124	1224	1324	1426	1524	1624	1725	1821	|	1924	2036	2124	2250		0908	1017	1118	1314	1402	1509	1602	1708	1802	1903	2034	2208
Doncaster 181 a.	1147	1247	1347	1447	1547	1648	1748	1851	1847	1947	2106	2147	2320		0930	1047	1146	1337	1426	1532	1627	1731	1831	1934	2059	2235
Doncaster 193 d.	1149	1249	1348	1449	1549	1649	1749	1901	1849	1950	2107	2149	2321		0939	*1130*	1148	1339	1429	1533	1629	1732	1834	1936	2101	2240
Meadowhall 193 d.	1210	1310	1410	1510	1610	1710	1810	1929	1910	2010	2134	2212	2350		1000	|	1208	1359	1452	1554	1654	1754	1853	1957	2128	2307
Sheffield 193 a.	1220	1320	1420	1520	1617	1720	1817	1939	1919	2017	2142	2222	2359		1008	*1153*	1218	1408	1503	1601	1701	1801	1904	2006	2138	2315

	Ⓐ	Ⓐ	Ⓐ	Ⓐ	Ⓐ	Ⓐ	Ⓐ	Ⓐ	Ⓐ	Ⓐ	Ⓐ	Ⓐ	Ⓐ	Ⓐ	Ⓐ	Ⓐ	Ⓐ	Ⓐ	Ⓐ	⑥	⑥	⑥	⑥	⑥	⑥	⑥
Sheffield 193 d.		0529	0741	0841	0941	1041	1141	1241	1341	1441	1541	1641	1741	1753	1841	1944	2000	2115	2234		0529	0741	0841	0941	1041	1141
Meadowhall 193 d.		0535	0747	0847	0947	1047	1147	1247	1347	1447	1547	1647	1747	1759	1847	1950	2006	2121	2240		0535	0747	0847	0947	1047	1147
Doncaster 193 a.		0606	0819	0915	1015	1115	1215	1314	1415	1517	1615	1715	1812	1835	1911	2013	2037	2154	2312		0606	0820	0914	1015	1112	1218
Doncaster 181 d.		0610	0824	0919	1019	1119	1219	1319	1419	1519	1619	1719	1819	1839	1917	2017	2044	2156	2315		0612	0824	0919	1019	1118	1219
Goole d.		0636	0844	0938	1038	1138	1238	1338	1438	1537	1638	1742	1838	1912	1937	2036	|	2222	2343		0638	0843	0938	1038	1137	1238
Hull 181 a.		0718	0913	1010	1110	1209	1308	1410	1511	1607	1709	1811	1908	1950	2010	2106	2144	2257	...		0720	0915	1010	1110	1209	1310

	⑥	⑥	⑥	⑥	⑥	⑥	⑥	⑥	⑥	⑥	⑥	⑥	⑦	⑦	⑦	⑦	⑦	⑦	⑦	⑦	⑦	⑦	⑦	⑦	⑦	⑦
Sheffield 193 d.	1241	1341	1441	1541	1641	1741	1753	1841	1944	2000	2115	2233		0845	...	1026	1228	1324	1428	1529	1628	1728	1828	2002	2128	2215
Meadowhall 193 d.	1247	1347	1447	1547	1647	1747	1759	1847	1950	2006	2121	2239		0851	...	1032	1235	1332	1434	1535	1635	1735	1835	2009	2134	2221
Doncaster 193 a.	1316	1416	1516	1616	1712	1813	1837	1912	2016	2036	2154	2309		0922	...	1051	1256	1403	1456	1556	1656	1755	1855	2030	2204	2240
Doncaster 181 d.	1319	1419	1519	1619	1719	1819	1841	1917	2017	2043	2156	2310		0926	1019	1057	1258	1405	1500	1558	1656	1758	1856	2030	2206	2245
Goole d.	1338	1438	1537	1638	1742	1838	1911	1937	2036	|	2222	2338		0948	1040	1116	1317	1425	1519	1619	1716	1817	1922	2050	2225	2306
Hull 181 a.	1410	1509	1609	1709	1811	1910	1951	2009	2107	2146	2259	...		1021	1118	1150	1354	1455	1557	1652	1748	1851	1956	2122	2257	2340

193 CLEETHORPES - DONCASTER - SHEFFIELD - MANCHESTER TP

km		⚒	①	②–⑥	⚒	⚒	⑥	Ⓐ	⚒	⚒	⚒	⚒		⚒	⚒	⚒	⚒	⚒	⚒	⚒		⚒	⚒
0	**Cleethorpes** d.		...	...	...	...	0505	0507	0620	0726	0826	0926	...	1026	1126	1226	1326	1426	1526	1626	...	1726	1826
5	Grimsby Town d.		...	...	...	...	0513	0515	0628	0734	0834	0934	...	1034	1134	1234	1334	1434	1534	1634	...	1734	1834
48	Scunthorpe d.		...	...	...	...	0546	0546	0703	0809	0908	1008	...	1108	1208	1308	1408	1508	1608	1708	...	1808	1908
85	**Doncaster** a.		...	...	...	...	0623	0623	0733	0838	0938	1038	...	1138	1238	1338	1438	1538	1638	1738	...	1838	1938
85	**Doncaster** 192 d.		...	...	...	0540	0625	0625	0735	0842	0942	1042	...	1142	1242	1342	1442	1542	1642	1742	...	1840	1942
109	Meadowhall 192 d.		...	...	...	0601	0646	0646	0752	0901	1001	1101	...	1201	1301	1401	1501	1601	1701	1801	...	1901	2001
115	**Sheffield** 192 a.		...	...	...	0608	0655	0655	0801	0908	1008	1108	...	1208	1308	1408	1508	1608	1708	1808	...	1908	2008
115	**Sheffield** 206 d.		0325	0325	0511	0611	*0708*	0708	0804	0911	1011	1111	...	1211	1311	1411	1511	1611	1711	1811	...	1911	2011
175	Stockport 206 a.		|	|	|	0653	*0752*	0753	0852	0952	1052	1152	...	1252	1352	1452	1552	1652	1752	1852	...	1952	2052
184	**Manchester** Piccadilly 206 a.		0417	0451	0603	0703	*0802*	0802	0903	1002	1103	1203	...	1303	1403	1503	1603	1703	1803	1903	...	2003	2103
200	**Manchester** Airport a.		0442	0512	0628	0727	*0825*	0826	0927	1027	1133a	1227	...	1327	1429	1527	1633a	1729	1827	1925	...	2039	2132

	⚒	Ⓐ	⑥		⑦	⑦	⑦	⑦		⑦		⑦	⑦		⑦	⑦	⑦	⑦	⑦	⑦	⑦	⑦	⑦
Cleethorpes d.	1926	2026	2026	...		...	...	...	...	0926	...	1026	1126	...	...	1326	1426	1526	1626	1726	1826	1926	2026
Grimsby Town d.	1934	2034	2034	...		...	...	...	...	0934	...	1034	1134	...	...	1334	1434	1534	1634	1734	1834	1934	2034
Scunthorpe d.	2008	2108	2108	...		...	...	...	...	1010	...	1108	1211	...	...	1408	1508	1608	1708	1810	1908	2010	2111
Doncaster a.	2040	2140	2140	...		...	...	...	...	1040	...	1140	1240	...	...	1438	1535	1634	1738	1839	1939	2040	2141
Doncaster 192 d.	2042	2142	2142	...		...	...	...	...	1042	...	1142	1242	...	1342	1442	1542	1642	1742	1842	1942	2042	2142
Meadowhall 192 d.	2109	2159	2159	...		...	...	...	...	1101	...	1201	1301	...	1401	1501	1601	1701	1801	1901	2001	2101	2206
Sheffield 192 a.	2119	2208	2207	...		...	...	...	...	1108	...	1208	1308	...	1409	1508	1607	1708	1808	1908	2008	2108	2214
Sheffield 206 d.	...	2211	*2224*	...		0751	0911	1011	...	1110	...	1210	1310	...	1411	1511	1611	1711	1811	1911	2011	2111	...
Stockport 206 a.	...	2252	*2322*	...		0832	0953	|	...	1153	...	1251	1352	...	1453	1552	1652	1752	1852	1952	2052	2153	...
Manchester Piccadilly 206 a.	...	2302	*2337*	...		0841	1003	1103	...	1206	...	1303	1403	...	1503	1602	1702	1802	1903	2002	2103	2203	...
Manchester Airport a.	...	2323	...	...		0909	1029	1127	...	1229	...	1328	1429	...	1529	1628	1727	1829	1929	2029	2129	2229	...

	⚒	⑥	⑥	Ⓐ	⚒	⚒	⚒	⚒	⚒	⚒	⚒	⚒	⚒	⑥	Ⓐ		⚒	⚒	Ⓐ	⑥		⚒	Ⓐ
Manchester Airport d.		0550	...	0550	0655	0753	0855	0955	1055	1155	1255	1355	1455	1555	1555	...	1655	1755	1855	1855	...	1955	...
Manchester Piccadilly 206 d.		0613	...	0613	0720	0820	0920	1020	1120	1220	1320	1420	1520	1620	1620	...	1718	1820	1918	1918	...	2020	...
Stockport 206 d.		0621	...	0621	0728	0828	0928	1028	1128	1228	1328	1428	1528	1628	1628	...	1726	1828	1926	1926	...	2028	...
Sheffield 206 a.		0702	...	0702	0810	0908	1008	1109	1208	1308	1408	1508	1608	1709	1709	...	1810	1910	2009	2009	...	2112	...
Sheffield 192 d.		▬	0709	0712	0812	0910	1010	1110	1210	1310	1410	1510	1610	1710	1710	...	1812	1912	2011	2027	...	...	2134
Meadowhall 192 d.		...	0715	0718	0818	0916	1016	1116	1216	1316	1416	1516	1616	1716	1716	...	1818	1918	2017	2033	...	...	2140
Doncaster 192 a.		Ⓐ	0739	0738	0837	0935	1035	1135	1235	1335	1435	1535	1635	1737	1737	...	1845	1941	2045	2101	...	...	2202
Doncaster d.		0530	0743	0739	0839	0937	1037	1137	1237	1337	1437	1537	1637	1739	1747	...	1847	1948	2046	2107	...	...	2205
Scunthorpe d.		0600	0809	0805	0905	1003	1103	1203	1303	1403	1503	1603	1703	1805	1813	...	1915	2015	2112	2133	...	...	2231
Grimsby Town a.		0643	0847	0846	0940	1039	1137	1240	1337	1439	1537	1639	1737	1843	1849	...	1948	2048	2148	2209	...	...	2309
Cleethorpes a.		0654	0856	0855	0951	1051	1149	1251	1349	1451	1549	1651	1750	1856	1859	...	2000	2101	2200	2221	...	...	2320

	⚒	⑥	Ⓐ	⑥	⚒	Ⓐ		⑦	⑦	⑦	⑦	⑦	⑦	⑦	⑦	⑦	⑦	⑦	⑦	⑦	⑦	⑦	⑦
Manchester Airport d.	...	...	2047	2047	2147	2327	...		0838	1054	1155	1255	1355	1455	1555	1655	1755	1855	1955	2055	...	2155	2255
Manchester Piccadilly 206 d.	2043	...	2120	2120	2222	2353	...		0858	1118	1218	1320	1420	1520	1620	1720	1820	1920	2018	2120	...	2216	2316
Stockport 206 d.	2054	...	2128	2128	|	|	...		0906	1127	1228	1328	1428	1529	1627	1727	1828	1928	2027	2127	...	2224	2324
Sheffield 206 a.	2135	...	2209	2211	2315	0121	...		0947	1207	1308	1408	1509	1609	1708	1808	1908	2008	2108	2211	...	2306	0006
Sheffield 192 d.	...	2152	2210	...	...	...	...		0951	1210	1310	1410	1510	1610	1710	1810	1910	2010	2110	...	2231	...	...
Meadowhall 192 d.	...	2158	2216	...	...	...	...		0958	1216	1316	1416	1516	1616	1716	1816	1916	2016	2116	...	2237	...	...
Doncaster 192 a.	...	2220	2243	...	...	...	...		1028	1235	1335	1435	1535	1635	1735	1835	1935	2035	2135	...	2256	...	...
Doncaster d.	...	2225	2245	...	...	...	...		1029	1237	...	1437	1537	1637	1737	1837	1937	2037	2137	...	2258	...	...
Scunthorpe d.	...	2259	2319	...	...	...	...		1055	1303	...	1503	1603	1703	1803	1903	2003	2103	2203	...	2324	...	...
Grimsby Town a.	...	2335	2355	...	...	...	...		1132	1337	...	1538	1639	1737	1839	1937	2037	2139	2239	...	2358	...	...
Cleethorpes a.	...	2347	0009	...	...	...	...		1142	1349	...	1549	1651	1749	1851	1949	2049	2151	2251	...	0010	...	...

km	NT 2nd class only	⚒	⚒	⚒	⑥	⚒	⚒	⑥	⚒	⑥	⚒	⑥	⚒	Ⓐ	⑥	⚒	⚒	⚒	⑥	Ⓐ	⑦	⑦	⑦	⑦	⑦	⑦	⑦	⑦
0	**Sheffield** ⊙ d.		0618	0712	0814	0914	1014	1114	1214	1314	1414	1514	1614	1714	1714	1814	1914	2035	2224	2248		0914	1114	1314	1514	1714	1914	2214
16	Grindleford d.		0634	0730	0828	0928	1028	1129	1228	1328	1429	1528	1628	1729	1728	1829	1928	2051	2238	2302		0929	1129	1329	1529	1729	1930	2229
18	Hathersage d.		0639	0733	0832	0932	1032	1132	1232	1332	1433	1532	1632	1732	1732	1832	1932	2054	2242	2306		0933	1133	1333	1533	1733	1934	2233
24	Hope d.		0647	0741	0839	0939	1039	1140	1239	1339	1440	1539	1639	1740	1739	1840	1939	2101	2249	2313		0940	1140	1340	1540	1740	1941	2240
32	Edale d.		0655	0749	0847	0947	1047	1148	1247	1347	1448	1547	1647	1748	1747	1848	1947	2109	2256	2322		0948	1148	1348	1548	1748	1949	2248
41	Chinley d.		0703	0757	0855	0955	1055	1156	1255	1355	1456	1555	1655	1756	1755	1856	1955	2117	2304	2330		0956	1156	1356	1556	1756	1957	2256
67	**Manchester** P'dilly ⊙ a.		0734	0835	0934	1034	1134	1234	1334	1434	1534	1634	1734	1831	1836	1935	2035	2205	2337	2359		1034	1233	1434	1634	1833	2034	2329

NT 2nd class only	⚒	⚒	⑥	Ⓐ	⑥	⚒	⑥	⚒	⑥	⚒	⑥	⚒	⚒	⚒	⚒	⚒	Ⓐ	⑥	⚒	⑦	⑦	⑦	⑦	⑦	⑦	⑦	⑦	⑦
Manchester P'dilly ⊙ d.		0546	0635	0708	0749	0849	0949	1049	1149	1249	1349	1449	1549	1649	1749	1849	2045	2049	2228		0744	0922	1140	1340	1540	1740	1940	2211
Chinley d.		0614	0714	0748	0823	0923	1025	1123	1225	1323	1425	1523	1623	1723	1823	1923	2120	2123	2253		0823	0959	1217	1417	1617	1817	2017	2243
Edale d.		0623	0723	0758	0833	0933	1034	1133	1234	1333	1434	1533	1633	1733	1833	1933	2129	2133	2301		0833	1008	1227	1427	1627	1827	2027	2251
Hope d.		0629	0729	0804	0839	0939	1040	1139	1240	1339	1440	1539	1639	1739	1839	1939	2135	2139	2307		0839	1014	1233	1433	1633	1833	2033	2257
Hathersage d.		0636	0736	0811	0845	0946	1046	1145	1246	1346	1446	1546	1646	1746	1846	1946	2142	2146	2315		0845	1021	1240	1440	1640	1840	2040	2303
Grindleford d.		0640	0740	0815	0849	0949	1050	1149	1250	1350	1450	1550	1650	1750	1850	1949	2146	2150	2319		0849	1024	1244	1444	1644	1844	2044	2312
Sheffield ⊙ a.		0657	0757	0832	0906	1006	1106	1206	1305	1406	1506	1606	1706	1808	1908	2007	2201	2207	2335		0906	1043	1300	1459	1700	1900	2100	2326

a – On Ⓐ arrives 7 minutes earlier.

⊙ – Additional journeys on ⑦ from Apr. 2:
From **Sheffield** at 1020, 1215, 1415, 1614, 1815.
From **Manchester Piccadilly** at 0823, 1040, 1240, 1440, 1645.

194 SKEGNESS - NOTTINGHAM 2nd class EM

km		Ⓐ	Ⓐ	Ⓐ	Ⓐ	Ⓐ	Ⓐ	Ⓐ		Ⓐ	Ⓐ	Ⓐ	Ⓐ	Ⓐ	Ⓐ	Ⓐ	Ⓐ	Ⓐ	Ⓐ	Ⓐ	⑥	⑥	⑥	⑥
0	**Skegness** d.		...	...	0709	0810	0906	1015	...	1115	1215	1315	1415	1509	1611	1730	1814	1914	2015	2102		...	...	0709
38	Boston d.		...	0613	0746	0845	0941	1050	...	1150	1250	1350	1450	1544	1648	1805	1848	1949	2050	2137		...	0613	0746
66	Sleaford d.		...	0635	0811	0907	1003	1112	...	1212	1313	1413	1512	1610	1713	1827	1913	2013	2118	2200		...	0635	0811
89	Grantham a.		...	0704	0842	0939	1031	1141	...	1241	1342	1442	1541	1641	1742	|	1941	2040	2145	|		...	0707	0842
89	Grantham 206 d.		0610	0710	0845	0945	1036	1145	...	1245	1348	1445	1545	1645	1745	|	1945	2044	2149	|		0610	0710	0845
126	**Nottingham** 206 a.		0654	0753	0920	1021	1114	1222	...	1323	1422	1523	1622	1720	1822	1922	2025	2120	2226	2253		0654	0752	0920

	⑥	⑥	⑥	⑥	⑥		⑥	⑥	⑥	⑥	⑥	⑥	⑥	⑥	⑥	⑦	⑦	⑦	⑦	⑦	⑦	⑦	⑦	⑦
Skegness d.	0815	0915	1015	1115	1215	...	1315	1415	1509	1611	1724	1814	1919	2015	2102		...	...	...	1410	1610	1807	1915	...
Boston d.	0850	0950	1050	1150	1250	...	1350	1450	1544	1648	1759	1849	1954	2050	2137		...	1213	...	1445	1650	1842	1950	...
Sleaford d.	0912	1014	1112	1212	1312	...	1413	1512	1610	1713	1821	1913	2018	2112	2200		...	1235	...	1507	1712	1904	2012	2142
Grantham a.	0941	1043	1141	1241	1341	...	1442	1541	1641	1742	|	1941	2045	2143	|		...	1304	...	1535	1741	1933	2041	2210
Grantham 206 d.	0945	1046	1145	1245	1346	...	1445	1545	1645	1745	|	1945	2048	2147	|		1252	...	1509	1540	1745	1937	2045	2213
Nottingham 206 a.	1021	1123	1222	1323	1423	...	1523	1622	1720	1822	1921	2024	2125	2225	2254		1330	...	1539	1617	1820	2012	2120	2249

	Ⓐ	Ⓐ	Ⓐ	Ⓐ	Ⓐ	Ⓐ	Ⓐ	Ⓐ	Ⓐ	Ⓐ	Ⓐ		Ⓐ	Ⓐ	Ⓐ	Ⓐ	Ⓐ	Ⓐ A	Ⓐ	⑥	⑥	⑥	⑥	⑥
Nottingham 206 d.		0507	0550	0641	0735	0845	0955	1045	1145	1245	1345	...	1445	1545	1645	1744	1844	...	2051		0507	...	0550	0641
Grantham 206 a.		0546	0627	0719	0812	0926	|	1123	1219	1323	1423	...	1522	1625	1728	1825	1923	...	2132		0546	...	0627	0718
Grantham d.		▬	0631	0723	0816	0932	|	1127	1225	1327	1427	...	1526	1629	1732	1829	1926	...	2138		...	...	0631	0724
Sleaford d.		Ⓐ	0657	0751	0845	1003	1044	1153	1250	1355	1452	...	1552	1655	1801	1855	1955	2120	2203		...	...	0657	0751
Boston d.		0625	0725	0818	0912	1026	1111	1219	1315	1421	1517	...	1620	1721	1826	1921	2019	2153	2229		...	0625	0725	0818
Skegness a.		0703	0805	0856	0949	1100	1150	1258	1354	1500	1556	...	1659	1800	1905	1959	2057	...	...		...	0703	0805	0856

	⑥		⑥	⑥	⑥	⑥	⑥	⑥		⑥	⑥	⑥	⑥	⑥	⑥ A	⑥	⑦	⑦	⑦	⑦	⑦	⑦	⑦	⑦ B
Nottingham 206 d.	0731	...	0840	0955	1045	1145	1245	1345	...	1445	1545	1645	1744	1845	...	2051		1157	1240	...	1456	1623	1831	1948
Grantham 206 a.	0809	...	0923	|	1123	1219	1325	1423	...	1522	1625	1728	1825	1923	...	2131		1229	1313	...	1531	1703	1908	2022
Grantham d.	0817	...	0930	|	1127	1225	1329	1427	...	1526	1629	1732	1829	1926	...	2136		1233	...	1350	1536	1707	1913	2027
Sleaford d.	0846	...	0956	1044	1153	1250	1355	1452	...	1552	1655	1801	1855	1955	2121	2201		1259	...	1416	1602	1736	1941	2055
Boston d.	0912	...	1022	1111	1219	1315	1421	1517	...	1620	1721	1826	1921	2019	2153	2229		1324	...	1445	1629	1802	2010	...
Skegness a.	0948	...	1100	1150	1258	1354	1500	1556	...	1659	1800	1905	1959	2057	...	...		1400	...	1524	1708	1838	...	...

A – From Lincoln (Table **185**). B – From Liverpool (Table **206**).

TL LONDON - KINGS LYNN 196

km		Ⓐ	Ⓐ	Ⓐ	Ⓐ	Ⓐ	Ⓐ	Ⓐ	Ⓐ	Ⓐ	Ⓐ	Ⓐ	Ⓐ	Ⓐ	Ⓐ	Ⓐ	Ⓐ	Ⓐ	Ⓐ	Ⓐ	Ⓐ	Ⓐ	Ⓐ	Ⓐ
0	London Kings Cross ...... 197 d.		...	0542	0644	0714	0744	0844	0944	1044	1144	1244	1344	1444	1544	1558p	1644	1707p	1714	1744	1814	1807p	1844	1907p
93	Cambridge ...... 197 d.		0617	0652	0733	0806	0838	0935	1035	1135	1235	1335	1435	1535	1635	1722	1740	1817	1806	1839	1909	1919	1939	2014
117	Ely ...... d.		0633	0708	0751	0822	0854	0951	1051	1151	1251	1351	1451	1551	1652	1739	1757	1833	1821	1856	1924	1935	1956	2030
142	Downham Market ...... d.		0653	0725	0807	0838	0910	1007	1107	1207	1307	1407	1507	1607	1710	...	1813	1850	...	1912	1939	1952	2012	2047
160	Kings Lynn ...... a.		0707	0740	0821	0852	0925	1021	1121	1221	1321	1421	1521	1621	1724	...	1827	1908	...	1927	1954	2010	2026	2105

	Ⓐ	Ⓐ	Ⓐ	Ⓐ	Ⓐ	Ⓐ	Ⓐ	Ⓐ	⑥	⑥	⑥	⑥	⑥	⑥	⑥	⑥	⑥	⑥	⑥	⑥	⑥	⑥	⑥	⑥
London Kings Cross ...... 197 d.	1944	2014	2044	2114	2144	2214	2244	2314		...	0644	0744	0844	0944	1044	1144	1244	1344	1444	1544	1644	1744	1814	1844
Cambridge ...... 197 d.	2040	2110	2140	2210	2240	2310	2340	0010		0635	0735	0835	0935	1035	1135	1235	1335	1435	1535	1635	1735	1835	1905	1935
Ely ...... d.	2056	2126	2156	2226	2257	2326	2357	0026		0651	0751	0851	0951	1051	1151	1251	1351	1451	1551	1651	1751	1851	1919	1951
Downham Market ...... d.	2112	2142	2212	2242	...	2342	...	0042		0707	0807	0907	1007	1107	1207	1307	1407	1507	1607	1707	1807	1907	1935	2007
Kings Lynn ...... a.	2126	2156	2226	2256	...	2356	...	0056		0721	0821	0921	1021	1121	1221	1321	1421	1521	1621	1721	1821	1921	1951	2021

	⑥	⑥	⑥	⑥	⑥	⑥	⑥	⑦	⑦	⑦	⑦	⑦	⑦	⑦	⑦	⑦	⑦	⑦	⑦	⑦	⑦	⑦	⑦	⑦
London Kings Cross ...... 197 d.	1914	1944	2014	2044	2114	2214	2314		0752	0915	1015	1115	1215	1315	1415	1515	1615	1715	1815	1915	2015	2115	2215	2315
Cambridge ...... 197 d.	2006	2035	2106	2140	2207	2310	0010		0906	1006	1106	1206	1306	1406	1506	1606	1706	1806	1906	2006	2106	2206	2306	0007
Ely ...... d.	2022	2051	2122	2157	2223	2326	0026		0922	1022	1122	1222	1322	1422	1522	1622	1722	1822	1922	2022	2122	2222	2322	0023
Downham Market ...... d.	2038	2108	2138	...	2239	2342	0042		0938	1038	1138	1238	1338	1438	1538	1638	1738	1838	1938	2038	2138	2238	2338	0039
Kings Lynn ...... a.	2053	2121	2153	...	2253	2356	0056		0953	1053	1153	1253	1353	1453	1553	1653	1753	1853	1953	2052	2153	2253	2353	0054

	Ⓐ	Ⓐ	Ⓐ	Ⓐ	Ⓐ	Ⓐ	Ⓐ	Ⓐ	Ⓐ	Ⓐ	Ⓐ	Ⓐ	Ⓐ	Ⓐ	Ⓐ	Ⓐ	Ⓐ	Ⓐ	Ⓐ	Ⓐ	Ⓐ	Ⓐ	Ⓐ	Ⓐ
Kings Lynn ...... d.		0455	0519	0551	0610	0617	0651	...	0714	0725	...	0754	0827	0857	...	0954	1054	1154	1254	1354	1454	1554	1636	...
Downham Market ...... d.		0509	0533	0605	0622	0631	0705	...	0728	0737	...	0808	0841	0911	...	1008	1108	1208	1308	1408	1508	1608	1651	1710
Ely ...... d.		0526	0552	0622	0647r	0650	0722	0730	0748	0756	0802	0826	0858	0928	1008	1025	1125	1225	1326	1425	1525	1625	1709	1726
Cambridge ...... 197 a.		0542	0610	0639	0703	0708	0739	0747	0804	0810	0820	0843	0915	0945	1024	1041	1141	1241	1342	1441	1541	1641	1725	1740
London Kings Cross ...... 197 a.		0636	0725p	0737	0807	0825p	0837	0920p	0910	0910	0950p	0945	1013	1043	1132	1135	1238	1335	1435	1535	1636	1738	1833	1836

	Ⓐ	Ⓐ	Ⓐ	Ⓐ	Ⓐ	Ⓐ	Ⓐ	Ⓐ	⑥	⑥	⑥	⑥	⑥	⑥	⑥	⑥	⑥	⑥	⑥	⑥	⑥	⑥	⑥	⑥
Kings Lynn ...... d.	1736	...	1836	1937	...	2037	2137	2229		...	0554	0654	0754	...	0854	0930	0954	1054	1154	1254	1354	1454	1554	1654
Downham Market ...... d.	1750	...	1850	1953	...	2051	2151	2243		...	0608	0708	0808	...	0908	0942	1008	1108	1208	1308	1408	1508	1608	1708
Ely ...... d.	1808	1829	1908	2010	2029	2108	2208	2300		0525	0625	0725	0825	0859	0925	0959	1025	1125	1225	1325	1425	1525	1625	1725
Cambridge ...... 197 a.	1824	1843	1924	2026	2043	2124	2224	2318		0541	0641	0741	0841	0913	0941	1014	1041	1141	1241	1341	1441	1541	1641	1741
London Kings Cross ...... 197 a.	1936	1939	2035	2132	2133	2232	2332	0050		0639	0735	0836	0937	1002	1035	1105	1137	1235	1335	1435	1534	1634	1736	1835

	⑥	⑥	⑥	⑥	⑥	⑥	⑥	⑦	⑦	⑦	⑦	⑦	⑦	⑦	⑦	⑦	⑦	⑦	⑦	⑦	⑦	⑦	⑦	⑦
Kings Lynn ...... d.	1754	1835	1935	2035	2135	2226	2310		0827	0927	1027	1127	1227	1327	1427	1527	1627	1727	1757	1827	1927	2027	2127	2227
Downham Market ...... d.	1808	1849	1949	2049	2149	2240	2324		0841	0941	1041	1141	1241	1341	1441	1541	1641	1741	1809	1841	1941	2041	2141	2241
Ely ...... d.	1825	1906	2006	2106	2206	2257	2342		0858	0958	1058	1158	1258	1358	1458	1558	1658	1758	1826	1858	1958	2058	2158	2258
Cambridge ...... 197 a.	1841	1922	2022	2122	2222	2313	2359		0915	1015	1115	1215	1315	1415	1515	1615	1715	1815	1840	1915	2015	2115	2215	2314
London Kings Cross ...... 197 a.	1935	2032	2132	2232	2332	0040	...		1009	1108	1209	1308	1408	1508	1609	1709	1808	1909	1936	2009	2109	2210	2311	0042

p – London **Liverpool Street**.

r – Arrives 5 minutes earlier.

TL LONDON KINGS CROSS - CAMBRIDGE 197

km		Ⓐ	Ⓐ	Ⓐ	Ⓐ	Ⓐ	Ⓐ	Ⓐ	Ⓐ		Ⓐ	Ⓐ	Ⓐ	Ⓐ	Ⓐ	Ⓐ	Ⓐ	Ⓐ	Ⓐ	Ⓐ	Ⓐ	Ⓐ	Ⓐ	Ⓐ
0	London Kings Cross . d.		0004	0542	0644	0714	0744	0814	0844	and at the same minutes past each hour until ☆	1514	1544	1552	1614	1644	1714	1744	1814	1844	1914	1944	2014	2044	2114
93	Cambridge ...... a.		0130	0650	0731	0804	0833	0904	0930		1601	1630	1655	1702	1735	1804	1834	1908	1934	2005	2035	2105	2135	2205

	Ⓐ	Ⓐ	Ⓐ	Ⓐ	Ⓐ	⑥	⑥	⑥	⑥	⑥	⑥	⑥		⑥	⑥	⑥	⑥	⑥	⑥	⑥	⑥	⑥	⑥	⑥
London Kings Cross . d.	2144	2214	2244	2314	2344		0004	0031	0544	0644	0744	0814	and at the same minutes past each hour until ☆	1744	1814	1844	1914	1944	2014	2044	2114	2144	2214	2244
Cambridge ...... a.	2235	2305	2335	0005	0040		0124	0128	0655	0730	0830	0903		1830	1901	1930	2001	2030	2101	2135	2202	2237	2305	2337

	⑥	⑦	⑦	⑦	⑦	⑦	⑦	⑦	⑦	⑦	⑦	⑦		⑦	⑦	⑦	⑦	⑦	⑦	⑦	⑦	⑦	⑦	⑦
London Kings Cross . d.	2314		0014	0635	0752	0852	0915	0952	1015	1052	1115	1152	and at the same minutes past each hour until ☆	1815	1852	1915	1952	2015	2052	2115	2152	2215	2252	2315
Cambridge ...... a.	0005		0122	0745	0855	0955	1001	1055	1101	1155	1201	1255		1901	1955	2001	2055	2101	2155	2201	2255	2301	2355	0006

	Ⓐ	Ⓐ	Ⓐ	Ⓐ	Ⓐ	Ⓐ	Ⓐ	Ⓐ	Ⓐ	Ⓐ	Ⓐ	Ⓐ	Ⓐ	Ⓐ	Ⓐ	Ⓐ		Ⓐ	Ⓐ	Ⓐ	Ⓐ	Ⓐ	Ⓐ	Ⓐ
Cambridge ...... d.		0514	0545	0615	0645	0715	0745	0815	0850	0920	0927	0950	1015	1047	1115	1147	and at the same minutes past each hour until ☆	1815	1845	1915	1945	2015	2045	2115
London Kings Cross . a.		0610	0636	0716	0737	0807	0837	0910	0945	1013	1032	1043	1105	1135	1205	1238		1911	1939	2005	2036	2106	2133	2205

	Ⓐ	Ⓐ	Ⓐ	Ⓐ	⑥	⑥	⑥	⑥	⑥	⑥	⑥	⑥	⑥		⑥	⑥	⑥	⑥	⑥	⑥	⑥	⑥	⑥	⑥
Cambridge ...... d.	2145	2215	2230	2322		0545	0647	0715	0747	0815	0847	0915	0947	and at the same minutes past each hour until ☆	1815	1847	1915	1945	2015	2045	2115	2145	2215	2230
London Kings Cross . a.	2237	2305	2332	0050		0639	0735	0805	0836	0904	0937	1004	1035		1905	1935	2005	2035	2105	2134	2204	2234	2302	2332

	⑥	⑦	⑦	⑦	⑦	⑦	⑦	⑦	⑦	⑦	⑦		⑦	⑦	⑦	⑦	⑦	⑦	⑦	⑦	⑦	⑦	⑦	⑦
Cambridge ...... d.	2315		0628	0728	0828	0920	0928	1020	1028	1120	1128	and at the same minutes past each hour until ☆	1820	1828	1845	1920	1928	2020	2028	2120	2128	2220	2228	2316
London Kings Cross . a.	0040		0739	0835	0935	1009	1029	1108	1130	1209	1230		1909	1930	1936	2009	2030	2109	2130	2210	2230	2311	2330	0042

☆ – Timings may vary by up to 3 minutes.

CC, LE LONDON - SOUTHEND and CAMBRIDGE 199

Typical off-peak journey time in hours and minutes
READ DOWN ↓ READ UP ↑

Journey times may be extended during peak hours on Ⓐ (0600 - 0900 and 1600 - 1900) and also at weekends.
The longest journey time by any train is noted in the table heading.

LONDON FENCHURCH STREET - SOUTHEND CENTRAL — Longest journey: 1 hour 08 minutes — CC

km	A				A
0	0h00	↓	d.London F Street ....a.	↑	1h04
8	0h09	↓	d.West Ham ....d.	↑	0h56
12	0h14	↓	d.Barking ....d.	↑	0h50
39	0h34	↓	d.Basildon ....d.	↑	0h29
56	0h53	↓	a.Southend Central ..d.	↑	0h10
63	1h03		a.Shoeburyness ....d.		0h00

From London Fenchurch Street: 0500⚒/0634⑦ and at least every 30 minutes (every 10 - 20 minutes 0840Ⓐ - 2010Ⓐ) until 2341.

From Southend Central*: 0424⚒/0544⑦ and at least every 30 minutes (every 15 minutes 0424Ⓐ - 2020Ⓐ) until 2249⑦, 2335⚒.

A – During peak hours on Ⓐ (0600 - 0900 and 1600 - 1900) trains may not make all stops.

* – Trains depart Shoeburyness 10 minutes before Southend Central.

☛ On ⑦ passengers for Basildon and Shoeburyness should change at Barking.

LONDON LIVERPOOL STREET - SOUTHEND VICTORIA — Longest journey: 1 hour 14 minutes — LE

km					
0	0h00	↓	d.London L Street ....a.	↑	0h58
6	0h07	↓	d.Stratford ....d.	↑	0h49
32	0h25	↓	d.Shenfield ....d.	↑	0h35
53	0h43	↓	d.Rayleigh ....d.	↑	0h16
64	0h54	↓	a.Southend Airport ...d.	↑	0h05
66	1h01		a.Southend Victoria .d.		0h00

From London Liverpool Street: 0535⚒/0714⑦ and at least every 30 minutes (every 20 minutes 0635⚒ - 2213⚒) until 2344.

From Southend Victoria: 0400⚒/0615⑦ and at least every 30 minutes (every 20 minutes 0626⚒ - 2130⚒) until 2249⑦/2300⚒.

LONDON LIVERPOOL STREET - CAMBRIDGE — Longest journey: 1 hour 39 minutes — LE

km					
0	0h00	↓	d.London L Street ....a.	↑	1h23
10	0h12	↓	d.Tottenham Hale .....d.	↑	0h57
36	0h29	↓	d.Harlow Town ....d.	↑	0h38
48	0h42	↓	d.Bishops Stortford ...d.	↑	0h28
67	0h54	↓	d.Audley End ....d.	↑	0h15
89	1h23		a.Cambridge ....d.		0h00

From London Liverpool Street: on Ⓐ at 0528, 0558 and every 30 minutes until 1528, 1558, 1628, 1643, 1707, 1713, 1737, 1743, 1807, 1813, 1837, 1843, 1907, 1911, 1928, 1958, 2028 and every 30 minutes until 2258, 2328, 2358⑤; on ⑥ at 0520, 0558, 0628, 0658 and every 30 minutes until 2328, 2358; on ⑦ at 0742, 0828, 0857 and at the same minutes past each hour until 2228, 2257.

From Cambridge: on Ⓐ at 0448, 0520, 0548, 0551, 0618, 0621, 0647, 0651, 0717, 0721, 0747, 0751, 0818, 0821, 0848, 0918, 1004, 1021 and at the same minutes past each hour until 1521, 1551 and every 30 minutes until 1921, 2004, 2021, 2104, 2121, 2204, 2221, 2251; on ⑥ at 0438, 0521, 0604, 0621 and at the same minutes past each hour until 2221, 2251; on ⑦ at 0732, 0751 and at the same minutes past each hour until 2132, 2232.

12 Les signes conventionnels sont expliqués à la page 4 153

200 LONDON - HARWICH, IPSWICH and NORWICH

Most Norwich trains convey 🍸 LE

For Rail - Sea - Rail services London - Amsterdam and v.v. via Harwich and Hoek van Holland see Table **15a**.

km			Ⓐ	Ⓐ	Ⓐ	Ⓐ	Ⓐ	Ⓐ	Ⓐ	Ⓐ	Ⓐ	Ⓐ	Ⓐ	Ⓐ	Ⓐ	Ⓐ		Ⓐ	Ⓐ	Ⓐ	Ⓐ	Ⓐ	Ⓐ	Ⓐ	Ⓐ	Ⓐ
			P					C																		
0	**London** Liverpool Street d.	Ⓐ	...	...	0600	...	0625	...	0638	0700	0730	0755	...	0830	0900	...	and	1530	1600	...	*1602*	1630	1644	1700	1702	1730
48	Chelmsford d.		...	...	0630	...	0658	...	0710	|	0803	|	...	0903	|	...	at	1600	|	...	*1634*	|	1715	|	1736	|
84	Colchester d.		0540	0610	0650	...	0723	...	0743	0751	0823	0847	...	0923	0947	...	the	1621	1647	...	*1704*	1717	1747t	|	1801	|
97	Manningtree d.		0549	0618	0658	0724	0731	...	0751	0759	0831	0855	0900	0931	0955	1000	same	1629	1655	1700	1724	|	1757	|	1809	1827
112	**Harwich** International d.		|	0636	|	0741	|	0750	0810	|	|	|	0917	|	|	1017	minutes	|	|	1717	1741	|	1815	|	|	|
115	**Harwich** Town a.		|	0641	|	0746	|	|	0815	|	|	|	0922	|	|	1022	past	|	|	1722	1746	|	1822	|	|	|
111	**Ipswich** **205** d.		0600	...	0711	...	0744	0820	...	0812	0844	0908	...	0944	1008	...	each	1641	1708	...	...	1736	...	1800	1825	1839
130	Stowmarket **205** d.		0611	...	0722	...	0755	0834	...	0823	0855	|	...	0955	|	...	hour	1652	1719	...	...	1747	...	|	1836	1850
153	Diss d.		...	...	0735	...	0808	...	...	0836	0908	0929	...	1008	1029	...	until	1705	1732	...	...	1800	...	1821	1848	1903
185	**Norwich** a.		...	...	0754	...	0827	...	...	0855	0927	0948	...	1027	1050	...		1724	1753	...	...	1822	...	1842	1909	1925

	Ⓐ	Ⓐ	Ⓐ	Ⓐ	Ⓐ	Ⓐ	Ⓐ	Ⓐ	Ⓐ	Ⓐ	Ⓐ	Ⓐ	Ⓐ	Ⓐ	Ⓐ	Ⓐ	Ⓐ	Ⓐ	Ⓐ	Ⓐ	Ⓐ	Ⓐ	Ⓐ	Ⓐ	Ⓐ		⑥	⑥
																L											P	
London Liverpool St. d.	...	1750	...	1810	1830	...	1820	1900	...	1930	1932	...	2000	...	2030	...	2100	...	2102	2130	2200	...	2230	...	2330	⑥	...	...
Chelmsford d.	...	|	...	|	|	...	1857	|	...	|	2002	...	|	...	2103r	...	|	...	2134	2203	2228	...	2303	...	0003		...	...
Colchester d.	...	1843	...	1902	1923	...	1930	1947	...	2020	2025	...	2047	...	2119	...	2147	...	2204	2223	2247	...	2323	...	0023		0540	0552
Manningtree d.	1835	1852	1902	1911	1932	1938	1940	1955	2000	2028	2034	2038	2055	2100	2128	...	2156	2200	2212	2232	2255	2300	2332	2336	0033		0549	0600
Harwich Int'l d.	1852	|	1919	|	|	1955	2002	|	2017	|	2054	2055	|	2117	|	2138	|	2217	2228	|	|	2317	|	2353	|		|	0617
Harwich Town a.	1857	|	1924	|	|	2000	...	|	2022	|	...	2100	|	2122	|	|	|	2222	...	|	|	2322	|	2358	|		|	0622
Ipswich **205** d.	...	1904	...	1923	1944	...	...	2008	...	2041	...	...	2108	...	2141	2204	2209	...	...	2245	2308	...	2345	...	0045		0600	...
Stowmarket **205** d.	...	1916	...	1934	1955	...	...	2019	...	2052	...	...	2119	...	2153	...	2220	...	...	2256	...	...	2356	...	0056		0611	...
Diss d.	...	1929	...	1947	2008	...	...	2032	...	2105	...	...	2132	...	2206	...	2233	...	...	2309	...	...	0009	...	0109		...	...
Norwich a.	...	1950	...	2009	2030	...	...	2051	...	2124	...	...	2151	...	2229	...	2253	...	...	2329	...	...	0029	...	0135		...	...

	⑥	⑥	⑥	⑥	⑥	⑥	⑥	⑥	⑥	⑥		⑥	⑥	⑥	⑥	⑥	⑥	⑥	⑥	⑥	⑥	⑥	⑥	⑥	⑥	⑥	⑥
				C															L								
London Liverpool St. d.	0534	...	0630	...	0638	0700	...	0730	0800	...	and	1900	...	1930	1932	2000	...	2030	...	2100	...	2102	2130	2200	...	2230	...
Chelmsford d.	0610	...	0703	...	0712	|	...	0803	|	...	at	|	...	2003	2007	|	...	2103	...	|	...	2134	2203	2228	...	2303	...
Colchester d.	0640	...	0723	...	0740	0747	...	0823	0847	...	the	1947	...	2023	2032	2047	...	2123	...	2147	..	2204	2223	2248	...	2323	...
Manningtree d.	0648	0700	0731	...	0748	0755	0800	0831	0855	0900	same	1955	2000	2031	2040	2055	2100	2132	...	2155	2200	2212	2232	2256	2300	2332	2336
Harwich Int'l d.	|	0717	|	0750	0809	|	0817	|	|	0917	minutes	|	2017	|	2056	|	2117	|	2138	|	2217	2228	|	|	2317	|	2353
Harwich Town a.	|	0722	|	|	...	|	0822	|	|	0922	past	|	2022	|	...	|	2122	|	|	|	2222	...	|	|	2322	|	2358
Ipswich **205** d.	0700	...	0744	0820	...	0808	...	0844	0908	...	each	2008	...	2044	...	2108	...	2145	2203	2208	...	...	2245	2308	...	2345	...
Stowmarket **205** d.	*0721*	...	0755	0834	...	|	...	0855	|	...	hour	|	...	2055	...	|	...	2156	...	...	...	...	2256	...	...	2356	...
Diss d.	*0734*	...	0808	...	...	0829	...	0908	0929	...	until	2029	...	2108	...	2129	...	2209	...	...	...	...	2309	...	...	0009	...
Norwich a.	*0753*	...	0827	...	...	0850	...	0927	0950	...		2050	...	2127	...	2150	...	2229	...	...	...	...	2329	...	...	0035	...

	⑥		⑦	⑦	⑦	⑦	⑦	⑦	⑦	⑦	⑦		⑦	⑦	⑦	⑦	⑦	⑦	⑦	⑦	⑦	⑦	⑦	⑦	⑦	⑦	⑦
			C					P																			
London Liverpool St. d.	2330	⑦	...	...	0755	0802	0830	...	0902	...	0930	and	1902	...	1930	1932	2002	...	...	2030	2102	...	2130	2202	2230	2302	2330
Chelmsford d.	|		...	...	0836	0843	|	...	0943	...	|	at	1943	...	|	2011	2043	...	...	|	2143	...	|	2243	|	2343	|
Colchester d.	0026		...	0818	0859	0913	0925	0932	1013	...	1025	the	2013	...	2025	2046	2113	...	...	2125	2213	...	2225	2313	2325	0013	0025
Manningtree d.	0035		...	0826	0907	0921	0933	0940	1021	1026	1033	same	2021	2026	2033	2055	2121	...	2126	2134	2221	2226	2234	2321	2334	0021	0034
Harwich Int'l d.	|		0830	0843	0925	|	|	|	|	1043	|	minutes	|	2043	|	2114	|	2110	2143	|	|	2243	|	|	|	|	|
Harwich Town a.	|		|	0848	*0948*	|	|	|	|	1048	|	past	|	2048	|	...	|	|	2148	|	|	2248	|	|	|	|	|
Ipswich **205** d.	0048		0902	...	...	0935	0946	0955	1033	...	1046	each	2033	...	2046	...	2133	2137	...	2147	2233	...	2247	2333	2347	0039	0047
Stowmarket **205** d.	0100		0917	...	...	...	0957	1006	...	...	1057	hour	...	...	2057	...	...	...	...	2158	...	...	2258	...	2358	...	0058
Diss d.	0113		...	...	...	...	1010	...	...	...	1110	until	...	...	2110	...	...	...	...	2211	...	...	2311	...	0011	...	0111
Norwich a.	0138		...	...	...	...	1031	...	...	...	1131		...	...	2131	...	...	...	...	2231	...	...	2331	...	0031	...	0136

		Ⓐ	Ⓐ	Ⓐ	Ⓐ	Ⓐ	Ⓐ	Ⓐ	Ⓐ	Ⓐ	Ⓐ	Ⓐ	Ⓐ	Ⓐ	Ⓐ	Ⓐ	Ⓐ	Ⓐ	Ⓐ	Ⓐ	Ⓐ	Ⓐ		Ⓐ	Ⓐ	Ⓐ	Ⓐ
									L																		
Norwich d.	Ⓐ	...	...	0500	0530	...	0600	...	...	0624	0648	...	...	0705	0740	...	...	...	0800	0830	...	0900	and	1530	...	1600	...
Diss d.		...	...	0518	0548	...	0618	...	...	0642	0706	...	...	0723	0758	...	...	...	0817	0847	...	0917	at	1547	...	1617	...
Stowmarket **205** d.		...	...	0530	0600	...	0630	...	...	0654	0718	...	...	0735	|	...	0810	...	0829	|	...	0929	the	|	...	1629	...
Ipswich **205** d.		0514	...	0544	0614	...	0644	...	0659	0708	0732	...	...	0749	0820	...	0826	...	0843	0909	...	0943	same	1609	...	1643	...
Harwich Town d.		|	0524	|	|	0624	|	0652	|	|	|	...	0716	|	|	0758	|	0828	|	|	0928	|	minutes	|	1628	|	1653
Harwich Int'l d.		|	0529	|	|	0629	|	0657	0727	|	|	0715	0721	|	|	0803	|	0833	|	|	0933	|	past	|	1633	|	1658
Manningtree d.		0525	0546	0554	0624	0646	0654	0714	...	0718	0743	0731	0738	0759	|	0820	0836	0850	0853	0919	0950	0953	each	1619	1650	1653	1715
Colchester d.		0535	...	0605	0635	...	0705	...	...	0730	|	0742	0754t	0810	|	0837t	0845	...	0903	0930	...	1003	hour	1630	...	1703	...
Chelmsford d.		0558	...	|	|	...	|	...	...	|	|	0814	0819	|	|	0859	0904	...	0921	|	...	1021	until	|	...	1721	...
London Liverpool St. a.		0634	...	0654	0727	...	0758	...	...	0824	0842	0854	0858	0904	0924	0936	0939	...	0958	1019	...	1055		1719	...	1758	...

	Ⓐ	Ⓐ	Ⓐ	Ⓐ	Ⓐ	Ⓐ	Ⓐ	Ⓐ	Ⓐ	Ⓐ	Ⓐ	Ⓐ	Ⓐ	Ⓐ	Ⓐ	Ⓐ	Ⓐ	Ⓐ	Ⓐ	Ⓐ	Ⓐ	Ⓐ	Ⓐ	Ⓐ	Ⓐ		⑥	⑥
																C		P					P					
Norwich d.	1630	...	1700	1730	...	...	1800	1830	...	1900	1930	...	...	2000	...	...	2030	...	...	2100	...	2200	...	...	2305	⑥	0500	0530
Diss d.	1647	...	1717	1747	...	...	1817	1847	...	1917	1947	...	...	2017	...	...	2047	...	...	2117	...	2217	...	...	2322		0517	0547
Stowmarket **205** d.	|	...	1729	1759	...	...	1829	|	...	1929	|	...	...	2029	...	2045	|	2114	...	2129	...	2229	2308	...	2334		0529	|
Ipswich **205** d.	1709	...	1743	1813	...	...	1843	1909	...	1943	2009	...	...	2043	...	2101	2109	2128	...	2143	...	2243	2322	...	|		0543	0609
Harwich Town d.	|	1728	|	|	1800	1826	|	|	1928	|	|	2005	2028	|	...	|	|	|	2128	|	2228	|	|	2328	2348		|	|
Harwich Int'l d.	|	1733	|	|	1805	1831	|	|	1933	|	|	2010	2033	|	2045	2129	|	|	2133	|	2233	|	|	2333	...		|	|
Manningtree d.	1719	1750	1753	|	1822	1848	1853	1919	1950	1953	2019	2027	2050	2053	2058	...	2119	2138	2150	2153	2250	2253	2332	2350	...		0553	0619
Colchester d.	1730	...	1803	1830	*1843*	...	1903	1930	...	2003	2030	*2045*	...	2103	2112	...	2130	2151	...	2203	...	2303	2343	2359	...		0603	0630
Chelmsford d.	|	...	1821	|	*1909*	...	1921	|	...	2021	|	...	...	2121	2140	...	|	...	...	2221	...	2325	...	...	...		0621	|
London Liverpool St. a.	1819	...	1855	1918	*1946*	...	1955	2020	...	2055	2119	...	...	2155	2214	...	2219	...	...	2255	...	0003	...	...	...		0655	0719

	⑥	⑥	⑥	⑥	⑥	⑥	⑥	⑥		⑥	⑥	⑥	⑥	⑥	⑥	⑥	⑥	⑥	⑥	⑥	⑥	⑥	⑥	⑥	⑥	⑥	⑥
																			C		P					P	
Norwich d.	...	0600	...	0630	...	...	0700	0730	and	1730	...	1800	1830	...	1900	...	2000	...	...	...	...	...	2100	...	2200	...	...
Diss d.	...	0617	...	0647	...	...	0717	0747	at	1747	...	1817	1847	...	1917	...	2017	...	...	...	...	...	2117	...	2217	...	...
Stowmarket **205** d.	...	0629	...	|	...	...	0729	|	the	1759	...	1829	|	...	1929	...	2029	...	2045	...	2114	...	2129	...	2229	2308	...
Ipswich **205** d.	...	0643	0659	0709	...	...	0743	0809	same	1813	...	1843	1909	...	1943	...	2043	...	2101	2109	2128	...	2143	...	2243	2322	...
Harwich Town d.	0628	|	|	|	...	0728	|	|	minutes	|	1828	|	|	1928	|	2028	|	...	|	|	|	2128	|	2228	|	|	2328
Harwich Int'l d.	0633	|	0727	|	0720	0733	|	|	past	|	1833	|	|	1933	|	2033	|	2045	2129	|	|	2133	|	2233	|	|	2333
Manningtree d.	0650	0653	...	0719	0733	0750	0753	0819	each	|	1850	1853	1919	1950	1953	2050	2053	2058	...	2119	2138	2150	2153	2250	2253	2332	2350
Colchester d.	...	0703	...	0730	0743	...	0803	0830	hour	1830	...	1903	1930	...	2003	...	2103	2112	...	2130	2149	...	2203	...	2303	2343	2359
Chelmsford d.	...	0721	...	|	0809	...	0821	|	until	|	...	1921	|	...	2021	...	2121	2140	...	|	...	...	2221	...	2325	...	...
London Liverpool St. a.	...	0755	...	0819	0846	...	0855	0919		1919	...	1955	2019	...	2055	...	2155	2214	...	2217	...	...	2255	...	0010	...	...

		⑦	⑦	⑦	⑦	⑦	⑦	⑦	⑦	⑦	⑦		⑦	⑦	⑦	⑦	⑦	⑦	⑦	⑦	⑦	⑦	⑦	⑦	⑦	⑦	⑦
																	C				P						
Norwich d.	⑦	...	0700	...	...	0800	...	...	0900	...	...	and	1900	...	...	...	...	2000	...	...	...	2100	...	...	2200	...	2305
Diss d.		...	0717	...	...	0817	...	...	0917	...	...	at	1917	...	...	...	...	2017	...	...	...	2117	...	...	2217	...	2322
Stowmarket **205** d.		...	0729	...	...	0829	...	...	0929	...	...	the	1929	...	...	...	2018	2029	...	...	2111	2129	...	...	2229	...	2334
Ipswich **205** d.		...	0743	0751	0809	0843	...	0909	0943	...	1009	same	1943	...	2009	...	2036	2043	...	2109	2125	2143	...	2209	2243	...	|
Harwich Town d.		...	|	|	|	|	0853	|	|	0953	|	minutes	1953	1953	|	...	|	|	2053	|	|	|	2153	|	|	2253	2350
Harwich Int'l d.		0720	|	0816	|	|	0858	|	|	0958	|	past	|	1958	|	2035	2105	|	2058	|	|	|	2158	|	|	2258	...
Manningtree d.		0734	0753	...	0819	0853	0915	0919	0953	1015	1019	each	|	2015	2019	2048	...	2053	2115	2119	2135	2153	2215	2219	2253	2315	...
Colchester d.		0748	0803	...	0830	0903	...	0930	1003	...	1030	hour	2003	...	2030	2057	...	2103	...	2130	2146	2203	...	2230	2303	2324	...
Chelmsford d.		0810	|	...	0858	|	...	0958	|	...	1058	until	|	...	2058	2115	...	|	...	2158	...	|	...	2258	2325	...	...
London Liverpool St. a.		0859	0904	...	0944	1003	...	1044	1103	...	1144		2103	...	2144	2202	...	2204	...	2240	...	2303	...	2340	0007	...	...

C – To/from Cambridge (Table **205**).
P – To/from Peterborough (Table **205**).
L – To/from Lowestoft (Table **201**).

r – Calls at Chelmsford on ④⑤ only.
t – Arrives 7 – 8 minutes earlier.

201 IPSWICH - LOWESTOFT

km			Ⓐ 2	Ⓐ 2	⑥ 2	Ⓐ 2	⑥ 2	✕		Ⓐ 2	⑥ 2	Ⓐ 2	✕ 2	Ⓐ 2	✕ 2	Ⓐ 2	✕ 2	✕ 2	✕H		⑦		⑦ 2	⑦ 2	⑦ 2
0	Ipswich ...... d.		0620	...	0717	0735	0817	0917	and at	1517	1617	1717	1813	1817	1917	2017	2117	2217		⑦	1002	and every	1802	1907	2002	2202
17	Woodbridge .... d.	⚒	0637	...	0732	0753	0832	0932	the same	1532	1618	1632	1730	1830	1832	1932	2032	2132	2232		1019	two hours	1819	1924	2019	2219
36	Saxmundham . d.		0658	0744	0754	0815	0854	0954	minutes	1554	1640	1654	1754	1851	1854	1954	2054	2154	2254		1040	until	1840	1945	2040	2240
65	Beccles ...... d.		...	0816	0825	0846	0925	1025	past each	1625	1719	1725	1825	1925	1925	2025	2125	2225	2325		1112	☆	1912	2021	2312	2312
79	Lowestoft ...... a.		...	0833	0843	0906	0943	1043	hour until ☆	1643	1736	1751	1843	1943	1943	2043	2143	2243	2343		1130		1930	2039	2130	2330

		Ⓐ H	⑥	Ⓐ	⑥ 2	Ⓐ	⑥ 2	⑥ 2	✕		⑥	Ⓐ	✕ 2	✕ 2	✕ 2	✕ 2	✕ 2	✕ 2		⑦		⑦ 2	⑦ 2	⑦ 2	⑦
Lowestoft .... d.	⚒	0525	0607	0614	0641	0707	0727	0807	0907	and at	1507	1607	1607	1702	1707	1807	1907	2007	2107	⑦	0805	and every	1605	1705	1805	2005
Beccles .... d.		0541	0625	0630	0657	0725	0743	0825	0925	the same	1525	1625	1725	1725	1825	1925	2025	2125		0821	two hours	1621	1721	1821	2021
Saxmundham.... d.		0613	0657	0703	0729	0757	0817	0857	0957	minutes	1557	1657	1707t	1757	1757	1857	1957	2057	2157		0853	until	1653	1753	1853	2053
Woodbridge.... d.		0635	0718	0725	0751	0818	0839	0918	1018	past each	1618	1718	1728	1818	1818	1918	2018	2118	2218		0914	☆	1714	1814	1914	2114
Ipswich .... a.		0653	0736	0744	0809	0836	0857	0936	1036	hour until ☆	1636	1736	1746	1836	1836	1936	2037	2136	2236		0932		1732	1832	1932	2132

H – To / from Harwich International (Table 200). t – Arrives 6 minutes earlier.

☆ – All trains are 2nd class only except the following which also convey 1st class:
From Ipswich at 0917⑥, 1002⑦, 1117Ⓐ, 1317⑥, 1517Ⓐ, 1602⑦, 1717⑥, 1917Ⓐ, 2117⑥, 2202⑦, 2217✕.
From Lowestoft at 0525Ⓐ, 0607⑥, 0614Ⓐ, 0707⑥, 0805⑦, 0907Ⓐ, 1107⑥, 1307Ⓐ, 1405⑦, 1507⑥, 1702Ⓐ, 1907⑥, 2005⑦.

203 LE 2nd class — NORWICH and IPSWICH local services

NORWICH - GREAT YARMOUTH
Journey time ± 32 minutes 30 km (33 km via Reedham)

From Norwich: Trains noted 'r' call at **Reedham** 18–21 minutes later.
Ⓐ: 0506, 0613, 0652, 0736r, 0809, 0836, 0936, 1036, 1136r, 1236, 1336, 1440, 1536, 1638, 1706, 1736, 1804, 1840, 1933, 2038, 2140, 2300.
⑥: 0530r, 0636, 0706, 0736r, 0809, 0836, 0936, 1036, 1136r, 1236, 1336, 1436, 1536, 1640, 1706, 1736, 1806, 1840, 1933, 2040, 2140, 2300.
⑦: 0736r, 0845, 0936r, 1045, 1136r, 1245, 1336r, 1445, 1536r, 1645, 1736r, 1845, 1936r, 2045, 2136r, 2236.

From Great Yarmouth: Trains noted 'r' call at **Reedham** 12–14 minutes later.
Ⓐ: 0545, 0624, 0658, 0730, 0817, 0846, 0917, 1017, 1117, 1217, 1317, 1417, 1517r, 1617, 1717, 1747r, 1817, 1847r, 1917, 2017, 2117, 2217, 2334r.
⑥: 0615, 0717, 0745, 0817, 0847, 0917, 1017, 1117, 1217, 1317, 1417, 1512r, 1617, 1717, 1747r, 1817, 1847r, 1917, 2017, 2117, 2217, 2334r.
⑦: 0817r, 0922, 1017r, 1122, 1217r, 1322, 1417r, 1522, 1617r, 1722, 1817r, 1922, 2017r, 2122, 2217r, 2317r.

NORWICH - LOWESTOFT
Journey time ± 43 minutes 38 km

From Norwich: Trains noted 'r' call at **Reedham** 18–21 minutes later.
Ⓐ: 0536r, 0627r, 0645r, 0755r, 0855, 1005r, 1058, 1205r, 1258, 1405r, 1455r, 1550r, 1658r, 1750r, 1902r, 2005r, 2105r, 2205r, 2240r.
⑥: 0540r, 0650r, 0755r, 0855, 1005r, 1058, 1205r, 1258, 1405r, 1458r, 1550r, 1658r, 1750r, 1905r, 2005r, 2105r, 2205r, 2240r.
⑦: 0725, 0858r, 1058r, 1258r, 1458r, 1658r, 1858r, 2058r.

From Lowestoft: Trains noted 'r' call at **Reedham** 20–23 minutes later.
Ⓐ: 0542r, 0635r, 0735r, 0747r, 0850r, 0948r, 1057, 1148r, 1257, 1348r, 1457, 1548r, 1648r, 1748r, 1848r, 1955r, 2057, 2148r, 2248r, 2330r.
⑥: 0638r, 0740r, 0848r, 0948r, 1057, 1148r, 1257, 1348r, 1457, 1548r, 1648r, 1748r, 1848r, 1955r, 2057, 2148r, 2248r, 2330r.
⑦: 0946r, 1146r, 1346r, 1546r, 1746r, 1946r, 2146r, 2335r.

NORWICH - SHERINGHAM (🚂)
Journey time ± 57 minutes 49 km

From Norwich:
Trains call at **Hoveton and Wroxham** 🚂 ± 15 minutes, and **Cromer** ± 45 minutes later.
✕: 0510Ⓐ, 0520⑥, 0540Ⓐ, 0545⑥, 0715, 0821, 0945, 1045, 1145, 1245, 1345, 1445, 1545, 1645, 1745, 1855, 1955, 2115, 2245①–④, 2305⑤⑥.
⑦: 0836, 0945, 1036, 1145, 1236, 1345, 1436, 1546, 1636, 1745, 1836, 1945, 2036.

From Sheringham:
Trains call at **Cromer** ± 11 minutes, and **Hoveton and Wroxham** 🚂 ± 39 minutes later.
✕: 0007⑥, 0621⑥, 0631Ⓐ, 0716, 0822, 0944, 1047, 1144, 1247, 1344, 1447, 1546, 1649, 1749, 1852, 1956, 2110, 2217, 2347①–④, also 0553Ⓐ from Cromer).
⑦: 0007, 0942, 1041, 1142, 1241, 1342, 1441, 1542, 1641, 1742, 1841, 1942, 2041, 2142.

IPSWICH - FELIXSTOWE
Journey time ± 25 minutes 25 km

From Ipswich:
Ⓐ: 0504, 0604, 0714, 0825, 0857, 0958 and hourly until 2058, 2228.
⑥: 0558, 0658, 0758, 0858, 0958, 1058 and hourly until 2058, 2228.
⑦: 1055 and hourly until 1955.

From Felixstowe:
Ⓐ: 0534, 0636, 0747, 0854, 0928 and hourly until 2128, 2301.
⑥: 0628, 0728, 0828, 0928, 1028 and hourly until 2128, 2258.
⑦: 1125 and hourly until 2025.

r – Via Reedham.

🚂 – Heritage and Tourist railways :
NORTH NORFOLK RAILWAY : Sheringham - Holt and v.v. 8 km. ✆ 01263 820800. www.nnrailway.co.uk
BURE VALLEY STEAM RAILWAY : Wroxham - Aylsham and v.v. ✆ 01253 833858. www.bvrw.co.uk

205 LE — IPSWICH - CAMBRIDGE and PETERBOROUGH

km		✕ 2	✕ C	✕	Ⓐ	⑥	Ⓐ	✕ H	Ⓐ	✕	✕	✕	✕	✕	✕	✕	✕	✕	✕	✕	✕	✕	✕
0	Ipswich .... 200 d.	0510	0600	0616	0654	0720	0800	0803	0820	0920	0958	1020	1120	1158	1220	1320	1358	1420	1520	1558	1620	1720	1749
19	Stowmarket .... 200 d.	0526	0612	0631	0709	0735	0812	0816	0835	0935	1011	1035	1135	1211	1235	1335	1411	1435	1535	1611	1635	1735	1804
42	Bury St Edmunds.............d.	0549	0629	0654	0733	0757	0829	0832	0857	0957	1029	1057	1157	1229	1257	1357	1429	1457	1557	1629	1657	1757	1825
65	Newmarket ....d.	0609		0714	0752	0817			0916	1017		1116	1217		1316	1417		1516	1617		1717	1817	
88	Cambridge ....208 a.	0633		0739	0819	0839			0939	1039		1139	1239		1339	1439		1539	1639		1739	1839	
82	Ely .... 208 d.		0656				0858	0858			1058			1258			1458			1658			1858
108	March .... 208 d.		0714				0916	0916			1116			1316			1516			1716			1916
132	Peterborough .... 208 a.		0737				0939	0939			1139			1339			1539			1739			1939

		⑥	Ⓐ	⑥	Ⓐ	⑥	Ⓐ	✕	✕ 2	✕ 2		⑦ 2	⑦ H	⑦ C	⑦	⑦	⑦	⑦	⑦	⑦	⑦	⑦	⑦
Ipswich .... 200 d.		1758	1817	1820	1913	1920	1958	2000	2018	2117	2219	⑦	0732	0902	0955	1102	1155	1302	1355	1502	1555	1702	1755	1902	2102
Stowmarket .... 200 d.		1811	1832	1835	1928	1935	2011	2012	2035	2133	2235		0748	0918	1007	1118	1207	1318	1407	1518	1607	1718	1807	1918	2118
Bury St Edmunds............. d.		1829	1857b	1857	1957c	1957	2029	2029	2056	2156	2257		0811	0941	1024	1141	1241	1341	1424	1541	1624	1741	1824	1941	2141
Newmarket.....................d.		1916	1916	2017	2017				2217	2217			0831	1001		1201		1401		1601		1801		2001	2201
Cambridge .... 208 a.		1939	1939	2039	2039				2140	2240			0857	1025		1225		1425		1625		1825		2024	2224
Ely .... 208 d.	1858					2058	2059						1052		1252		1452		1652		1852		
March .... 208 d.	1916					2116	2117						1108		1308		1508		1708		1908		
Peterborough .... 208 d.	1939					2139	2139						1131		1331		1531		1731		1939		

		Ⓐ	Ⓐ 2	⑥ 2	✕	✕			⑦					
Peterborough .... 208 d.					0750				0950		1150		1350		1550
March .... 208 d.	⚒				0809				1009		1209		1409		1609
Ely .... 208 d.					0832				1032		1232		1432		1632
Cambridge .... 208 d.				0642	0744		0844	0944	1044	1144	1244	1344	1444	1544	1644	1744
Newmarket.....................d.				0702	0805		0904	1005	1104	1205	1304	1405	1504	1605	1705	1805
Bury St Edmunds.............d.		0531	0621	0623	0723	0824	0858	0924	1024	1058	1124	1224	1258	1324	1424	1458	1524	1624	1658	1725	1825
Stowmarket .... 200 a.		0552	0642	0644	0745	0843	0914	0945	1045	1114	1145	1245	1314	1345	1445	1514	1545	1645	1714	1745	1845
Ipswich .... 200 a.		0607	0700	0702	0802	0902	0928	1002	1102	1128	1202	1302	1328	1402	1502	1528	1602	1702	1728	1804	1902

		✕	✕ H	✕	✕ C	✕ C	✕ 2			⑦ 2					
Peterborough .... 208 d.		1750		1950		2145			⑦		1150		1350		1547		1745		1947	
March .... 208 d.		1809		2009		2204					1209		1409		1606		1804		2006	
Ely .... 208 d.		1832		2032		2226					1232		1432		1629b		1829b		2029b	
Cambridge .... 208 d.			1844	1944		2044	2144	2244		0912	1112	1312	512	1712	1912	2112	2250
Newmarket.....................d.			1904	2005		2104	2205	2306		0934	1134	1334	1534	1734	1934	2134	2312
Bury St Edmunds.............d.		1858	1924	2024	2058	2124	2224	2322	2327		0955	1155	1258	1355	1458	1555	1655	1755	1855	1955	2055	2155	2303
Stowmarket .... 200 a.		1914	1945	2045	2124	2145	2245	2308	2348		1018	1218	1314	1418	1514	1618	1711	1818	1911	2018	2111	2218	2355
Ipswich .... 200 a.		1928	2004	2100	2128	2202	2302	2322	0005		1036	1236	1328	1436	1528	1636	1725	1836	1925	2036	2125	2236	0011

C – To / from Colchester (Table 200).
H – To / from Harwich International (Table 200).
b – Arrives 4 – 5 minutes earlier.
c – Arrives 9 minutes earlier.

206 NORWICH - NOTTINGHAM - SHEFFIELD - MANCHESTER - LIVERPOOL

2nd class EM

km		Ⓐ	Ⓐ	Ⓐ	Ⓐ	Ⓐ	Ⓐ	Ⓐ		Ⓐ	Ⓐ	Ⓐ	Ⓐ	Ⓐ	Ⓐ AD	⑥	⑥	⑥	⑥	⑥	⑥
0	**Norwich** 207 d.	...	...	...	0550	0651	0757	0857	B	1457	1548	1657	1754	1857	...	...	...	...	0550	0653	0757
49	Thetford 207 d.	...	...	...	0623	0719	0824	0924		1524	1623	1727	1827	1924	...	...	...	...	0623	0722	0824
86	Ely 205 207 208 d.	...	...	...	0651	0744	0848	0946	and	1547	1647	1752	1852	1952	...	...	...	...	0648	0748	0848
111	March 205 208 d.	...	...	...	0707	0800	0907	|	at	|	|	|	1908	|	...	...	...	...	0707	0804	0905
135	**Peterborough** 180 205 208 d.	...	...	...	0727	0824	0927	1028	the	1627	1724	1826	1926	2027	2131	...	...	...	0727	0828	0925
181	Grantham 180 194 d.	...	...	...	0758	0855	0958	1100	same	1658	1757	1857	1959	2059	|	...	...	...	0758	0859	0953
218	**Nottingham** 194 a.	...	...	...	0840	0926	1035	1134	minutes	1735	1835	1935	2031	2133	2254	...	...	...	0839	0935	1035
218	**Nottingham** 171 d.	0521	0639	0746	0847	0947	1047	1147	past	1747	1847	1941	*2047*	*2146*	...	0520	0640	0746	0847	0947	1047
247	Alfreton 171 d.	|	0659	0810	0908	1008	1108	1208	each	1810	1908	2002	|	*2211*	...	|	0700	0809	0908	1008	1108
264	Chesterfield 171 d.	0549	0710	0820	0920	1020	1120	1220	hour	1820	1920	2012	*2131*	*2222*	...	0549	0711	0819	0920	1020	1120
283	**Sheffield** 171 193 d.	0618	0732	0840	0940	1040	1140	1240	until	1840	1940	2031	*2158*	*2236*	...	0620	0732	0840	0940	1040	1140
343	Stockport 193 a.	0722	0824	0924	1025	1125	1224	1325	♤	1924	2025	2124	...	...	...	0722	0824	0925	1025	1125	1224
352	**Manchester** Piccadilly 193 a.	0734	0836	0937	1036	1136	1236	1336		1936	2036	2136	...	...	...	0734	0836	0936	1036	1136	1236
378	Warrington Central 188 a.	0753	0857	0957	1057	1157	1257	1357		1957	2057	...	...	...	...	0753	0857	0957	1057	1157	1257
399	**Liverpool SP** ▷ 188 a.	0818	0915	1015	1115	1215	1315	1415		2018	2118	...	...	...	...	0818	0915	1015	1115	1215	1315
408	**Liverpool** Lime Street 188 a.	0832	0932	1031	1131	1231	1331	1431		2035	2136	...	...	...	...	0831	0931	1031	1131	1231	1331

	⑥		⑥	⑥	⑥	⑥	⑥	⑥ D	⑦	⑦	⑦	⑦	⑦	⑦	⑦	⑦	⑦	⑦	⑦	⑦	⑦	⑦
Norwich 207 d.	0857	B	1457	1552	1654	1750	1857	...	...	...	...	...	1047	...	...	1347	1453	1554	1654	1754	1856	2052
Thetford 207 d.	0924		1524	1623	1724	1823	1924	...	...	...	...	...	1114	...	...	1414	1520	1621	1721	1821	1923	2119
Ely 205 207 208 d.	0946	and	1547	1647	1747	1848	1948	...	...	...	...	...	1139	...	...	1440	1546	|	1748	1848	1948	2144
March 205 208 d.	|	at	|	|	|	1905	|	...	...	...	...	...	|	...	...	|	1603	|	|	|	|	|
Peterborough 180 205 208 d.	1022	the	1627	1725	1826	1930c	2026	2127	...	...	...	...	1216	...	1431	1523d	1624	1723a	1826c	1926	2030	2223b
Grantham 180 194 d.	1055	same	1656	1759	1858	2003c	2058	2202	...	...	...	...	1252c	...	1509	1555	1656	1755	1858	1957	2102	2255
Nottingham 194 a.	1136	minutes	1735	1834	1933	2036	2132	2232	...	...	...	...	1330	...	1539	1624	1731	1827	1933	2031	2134	2328
Nottingham 171 d.	1147	past	1744	1847	1939	*2117*	...	...	0947	1048	1144	1240	1342	1447	1547	1642	1739	1840	1943	*2133*	...	...
Alfreton 171 d.	1208	each	1808	1908	2000	*2144*	...	...	1004	1108	1207	1304	1405	1510	1607	1711	1804	1903	2003	*2205*	...	...
Chesterfield 171 d.	1220	hour	1818	1920	2010	*2155*	...	...	1018	1119	1218	1317	1416	1521	1618	1721	1815	1914	2013	*2216*	...	...
Sheffield 193 d.	1240	until	1837	1940	2032	*2214*	...	...	1041	1139	1239	1338	1437	1543	1639	1744	1836	1935	2035	*2236*	...	...
Stockport 193 a.	1325	♤	1924	2025	2117	...	...	...	1126	1225	1325	1425	1525	1625	1728	1825	1925	2025	2124	...	...	...
Manchester Piccadilly 193 a.	1336		1936	2036	2128	...	...	...	1137	1237	1337	1437	1537	1637	1738	1837	1937	2038	2137	...	...	...
Warrington Central 188 a.	1357		1957	2057	...	...	...	...	1158	1258	1358	1458	1558	1658	1758	1858	1958	...	...	...	...	...
Liverpool SP ▷ 188 a.	1415		2015	2120	...	...	...	...	1216	1316	1416	1516	1616	1716	1816	1916	2016	...	...	...	...	...
Liverpool Lime Street 188 a.	1431		2031	2133	...	...	...	...	1230	1330	1430	1530	1630	1730	1830	1930	2030	...	...	...	...	...

	Ⓐ A	Ⓐ D	Ⓐ A	Ⓐ	Ⓐ	Ⓐ	Ⓐ	Ⓐ		Ⓐ	Ⓐ	Ⓐ	Ⓐ	Ⓐ	Ⓐ	Ⓐ	⑥ A	⑥ D	⑥ A	⑥	⑥	⑥
Liverpool Lime Street 187 d.	...	...	...	...	...	0647	0742	0852		1452	1552	1652	1752	1852	1952	2137	...	...	...	...	...	0649
Liverpool SP ▷ 188 d.	...	...	...	...	...	0657	0753	0903		1503	1603	1703	1803	1903	2003	2147	...	...	...	...	...	0659
Warrington Central 188 d.	...	...	...	...	...	0715	0813	0919	and	1519	1619	1719	1819	1919	2019	2203	...	...	...	...	...	0715
Manchester Piccadilly 193 d.	...	...	...	...	...	0742	0843	0943	at	1543	1643	1743	1843	1943	2043	2228	...	...	...	...	...	0742
Stockport 193 d.	...	...	...	...	...	0754	0854	0954	the	1554	1654	1754	1854	1954	2054	2238	...	...	...	...	...	0754
Sheffield 171 d.	...	...	...	*0603*	*0724*	0837	0937	1037	same	1637	1741	1840	1937	2039	2138	2338	...	...	...	*0554*	*0737*	0837
Chesterfield 171 d.	...	...	...	*0619*	*0737*	0852	0952	1052	minutes	1653	1757	1857	1952	2054	2154	2353	...	...	...	*0619*	*0750*	0852
Alfreton 171 d.	...	...	...	*0630*	*0748*	0903	1003	1103	past	1704	1808	1908	2003	2105	2205	|	...	...	...	*0629*	*0801*	0903
Nottingham 171 a.	...	...	...	*0701*	*0823*	0927	1027	1127	each	1727	1829	1930	2027	2133	2234	0030	...	...	...	*0702*	*0825*	0927
Nottingham 194 d.	0456	0507	0610	0752	0835	0934	1034	1134	hour	1734	1837	...	2034	...	...	...	0505	0507	0610	0745	0834	0934
Grantham 180 194 d.	|	0551c	|	0828c	0912c	1011c	1110	1211	until	1811	1909	...	2107	...	...	...	|	0551c	|	0820c	0910	1009
Peterborough 180 205 208 d.	0627	0623	0736	0859	0940	1045c	1141	1242	♤	1845c	1941	...	2140	...	...	...	0627	0625	0735	0858	0943	1040
March 205 208 a.	0642	...	0752	|	|	|	|	|		1859	|	...	|	...	...	...	0642	...	0750	|	|	|
Ely 205 207 208 a.	0701	...	0811	0942	1013	1118	1213	1314		1919	2014	...	2213	...	...	...	0701	...	0811	0931	1016	1113
Thetford 207 a.	0728	...	0836	1006	1037	1143	1238	1339		1950	2038	...	2237	...	...	...	0730	...	0836	1006	1043	1137
Norwich 207 a.	0813	...	0913	1044	1112	1215	1313	1413		2022	2113	...	2319	...	...	...	0813	...	0915	1043	1115	1213

	⑥	⑥		⑥	⑥	⑥	⑥	⑥	⑥	⑥	⑥	⑦	⑦	⑦	⑦	⑦	⑦	⑦	⑦ C	⑦	⑦	⑦	⑦
Liverpool Lime Street 187 d.	0742	0852		1452	1552	1652	1752	1852	1952	2052	2137	...	...	...	1252	1352	1452	1552	1654	1752	1852	1952	2121
Liverpool SP ▷ 188 d.	0752	0903		1503	1603	1703	1803	1903	2003	2103	2147	...	...	...	1303	1403	1503	1603	1705	1803	1903	2003	2131
Warrington Central 188 d.	0813	0919	and	1519	1619	1719	1819	1919	2019	2119	2203	...	...	...	1319	1419	1519	1619	1721	1819	1919	2019	2147
Manchester Piccadilly 193 d.	0843	0943	at	1543	1643	1743	1843	1943	2043	2143	2228	...	...	1243	1344	1444	1544	1644	1746	1844	1944	2044	2211
Stockport 193 d.	0854	0954	the	1554	1654	1754	1854	1954	2054	2152	2238	...	...	1255	1354	1454	1554	1654	1755	1854	1954	2054	2228
Sheffield 171 d.	0937	1037	same	1637	1741	1840	1937	2039	2138	2242	2338	*1103*	1243	1348	1441	1539	1643c	1740c	1839c	1940c	2040c	2140c	2330
Chesterfield 171 d.	0952	1052	minutes	1653	1757	1857	1952	2054	2154	2256	2353	*1120*	1257	1402	1455	1553	1657	1754	1854	1954	2054	2156	2344
Alfreton 171 d.	1003	1103	past	1704	1808	1908	2003	2105	2205	2307	|	*1130*	1308	1412	1508	1603	1707	1805	1905	2005	2105	2206	2355
Nottingham 171 a.	1027	1127	each	1727	1829	1930	2027	2133	2234	2328	0030	*1158*	1334	1435	1532	1628	1730	1834	1933	2030	2133	2236	0023
Nottingham 194 d.	1034	1134	hour	1734	1837	...	2034	...	...	...	...	1240	1347	1445	1550	1645	1736	1846	1948	2045	...	...	...
Grantham 180 194 d.	1109	1207	until	1815	1909	...	2107	...	...	...	...	1315	1422	1520	1622	1721c	1817	1926c	2022	2120	...	...	...
Peterborough 180 205 208 d.	1141	1240	♤	1844	1941	...	2140	...	...	...	...	1343	1458c	1558c	1659c	1757c	1849	1959	...	2153	...	...	...
March 205 208 a.	|	|		1900	|	...	|	...	...	...	...	|	|	|	|	1812	|	|	...	|	...	...	...
Ely 205 207 208 a.	1213	1313		1919	2014	...	2213	...	...	...	...	1416	1531	1631	1732	1832	1922	2032	...	2226	...	...	...
Thetford 207 a.	1238	1337		1943	2038	...	2237	...	...	...	...	1443	1555	1655	1756	1856	1949	2056	...	2250	...	...	...
Norwich 207 a.	1313	1413		2016	2113	...	2319	...	...	...	...	1524	1635	1726	1830	1929	2026	2137	...	2324	...	...	...

A – Via Melton Mowbray (Table **208**).
B – The 1057 from Norwich also calls at March (d.1205⑥ / 1208Ⓐ).
C – To Sleaford (Table **194**).
D – From / to Spalding (Table **185**).

a – Arrives 1712.
b – Arrives 2216.
c – Arrives 5 – 6 minutes earlier.
d – Arrives 1513.

♤ – Timings may vary by up to 6 minutes.
▷ – Liverpool South Parkway.

207 CAMBRIDGE - NORWICH

LE

km		Ⓐ	⑥	⑥	Ⓐ	⚒	⚒		⚒	⚒	⑥	Ⓐ	⑥	Ⓐ	⑥	Ⓐ	⚒ 2	⚒	⑦	⑦	⑦	⑦
0	**Cambridge** d.	0605	0607	0700	0704	0812	0912	and at	1712	1812	1912	1925	2012	2020	2112	2113	*2140*	2255	0852	1052	1152	1252
24	Ely 206 d.	0620	0622	0716	0719	0828	0927	the same	1728	1828	1928	1940	2028	2037	2128	2130	2216	2310	0907	1107	1207	1307
63	Thetford 206 d.	0644	0647	0743	0747	0853	0951	minutes	1753	1853	1853	2004	2053	2101	2153	2156	2237	2334	0934	1134	1231	1334
84	Attleborough d.	0704	0706	0803	0806	0908	1006	past each	1808	1908	2008	2019	2108	2116	2208	2211	2251	2349	0949	1149	1246	1349
94	Wymondham d.	0711	0714	0813	0816	0915	1015	hour until	1815	1915	2015	2027	2115	2124	2215	2218	2258	2357	0956	1156	1254	1356
110	**Norwich** 206 a.	0727	0728	0830	0830	0930	1030	△	1830	1930	2030	2041	2130	2138	2232	2232	2319	0011	1013	1213	1312	1413

	⑦	⑦	⑦	⑦	⑦	⑦	⑦	⑦ 2	⑦	⑦ 2
Cambridge d.	1352	1452	1552	1652	1752	1852	1952	*2006*	2152	*2206*
Ely 206 d.	1407	1507	1607	1707	1807	1907	2007	2036	2207	2229
Thetford 206 d.	1431	1531	1634	1731	1831	1931	2031	2057	2231	2250
Attleborough d.	1446	1546	1649	1746	1846	1946	2046	2111	2246	2304
Wymondham d.	1454	1554	1656	1754	1854	1954	2054	2118	2254	2311
Norwich 206 a.	1513	1613	1713	1813	1910	2013	2110	2137	2323	2324

	Ⓐ	⑥	Ⓐ	⑥	Ⓐ	⑥	⚒	
Norwich 206 d.	0533	0537	0633	0640	0737	0740	0840	and at the
Wymondham d.	0545	0549	0645	0652	0749	0752	0852	same
Attleborough d.	0552	0556	0652	0659	0756	0759	0859	minutes
Thetford 206 d.	0606	0610	0706	0713	0810	0813	0913	past each
Ely 206 a.	0631	0635	0731	0738	0837	0838	0938	hour until
Cambridge a.	0652	0656	0753	0759	0859	0859	0959	△

	⚒	⑥	Ⓐ	⚒	⚒	⚒	⚒	⑥	Ⓐ	⚒	⑦	⑦	⑦	⑦	⑦	⑦	⑦	⑦	⑦	⑦	⑦ 2	⑦	⑦ 2	⑦
Norwich 206 d.	1440	1535	1540	1638	1735	1838	1938	2110	2115	2240	0903	1003	1103	1203	1303	1403	1503	1603	1703	1803	1856	2003	2052	2203
Wymondham d.	1452	1547	1552	1650	1747	1852	1950	2122	2127	2252	0915	1015	1115	1215	1315	1415	1515	1615	1715	1815	|	2015	|	2215
Attleborough d.	1459	1554	1559	1659	1754	1857	1958	2129	2134	2259	0922	1022	1122	1222	1322	1422	1522	1622	1722	1822	|	2022	|	2222
Thetford 206 d.	1513	1613	1613	1713	1813	1911	2012	2143	2148	2313	0936	1036	1136	1236	1336	1436	1536	1636	1736	1836	1923	2036	2119	2236
Ely 206 a.	1538	1638	1638	1738	1839	1938	2039	2210	2216	2338	1003	1101	1203	1301	1401	1501	1603	1701	1801	1901	1944	2101	2140	2301
Cambridge a.	1559	1659	1659	1759	1859	1959	2059	2229	2235	2359	1022	1123	1222	1322	1422	1522	1622	1722	1822	1922	*2007*	2122	*2207*	2322

△ – Timings may vary by up to 2 minutes.

XC STANSTED AIRPORT - CAMBRIDGE - PETERBOROUGH - LEICESTER - BIRMINGHAM 208

km			Ⓐ	⑥	⑥	Ⓐ	Ⓐ	⑥	⚒	⚒	⚒	⚒	⚒	⚒	⚒	⚒	⚒	⚒	⚒	⚒	⚒	ⒶB	Ⓐ		⑦	⑦
0	**Stansted Airport** ▽ d.	⚒	...	...	0525	0516	0612	0627	0721a	0821a	0921a	1027	1127	1227	1327	1427	1527	1627	1727	1821a	1921a	...	2021	⑦	1025	1125
40	**Cambridge** ▽ d.		0515	0515	0555	0555	0656	0657	0801	0901	1001	1101	1201	1301	1401	1501	1601	1701	1801	1901	2001	...	2101		1100	1200
64	Ely **205** d.		0530	0530	0610	0610	0712	0712	0815	0915	1015	1115	1215	1315	1415	1515	1615	1715	1815	1915	2015	...	2115		1115	1215
89	March **205** d.		0546	0546	0628	0628	0729	0729	0832	0932	1032	1132	1232	1332	1432	1532	1632	1732	1834	1932	2032	...	2132		1132	1232
113	**Peterborough** **205** d.		0610	0610	0652	0652	0752	0752	0852	0952	1052	1152	1252	1352	1452	1552	1652	1752	1852	1952	2052	2131	2159		1153	1253
131	Stamford d.		0623	0623	0705	0705	0805	0805	0905	1005	1105	1205	1305	1405	1505	1605	1705	1805	1905	2005	2105	2145	2212		1206	1306
154	Oakham d.		0637	0635	0719	0719	0819	0819	0919	1019	1119	1219	1319	1419	1519	1619	1719	1819	1919	2019	2119	2201	2226		1220	1320
174	Melton Mowbray d.		0648	0646	0730	0730	0830	0830	0930	1030	1130	1230	1330	1430	1530	1630	1730	1830	1930	2030	2130	2212	2237		1231	1331
197	**Leicester** d.		0710	0710	0748	0751	0848	0848	0948	1048	1148	1248	1348	1448	1548	1648	1748	1848	1948	2048	2148	...	2255		1250	1350
227	Nuneaton d.		0729	0729	0810	0817	0910	0910	1010	1110	1210	1310	1410	1510	1610	1710	1815	1910	2010	2110	2210	...	2314		1310	1409
244	Coleshill Parkway d.		0745	0747	0825	0832	0925	0925	1025	1125	1225	1325	1425	1525	1625	1725	1830	1925	2025	2125	2225	...	2329		1325	1425
259	**Birmingham** New St. a.		0758	0803	0838	0845	0938	0938	1038	1138	1238	1338	1438	1538	1638	1738	1844	1938	2038	2138	2238	...	2342		1338	1438

	⑦	⑦	⑦	⑦		⑦	⑦	⑦	⑦
Stansted Airport ▽ d.	1225	1325	1425	1525	...	1625	1725	1825	1925
Cambridge ▽ d.	1300	1400	1500	1600	...	1700	1800	1900	2000
Ely **205** d.	1315	1415	1515	1615	...	1715	1815	1915	2015
March **205** d.	1332	1432	1532	1632	...	1732	1832	1932	2032
Peterborough **205** d.	1353	1453	1553	1653	...	1753	1853	1953	2053
Stamford d.	1406	1506	1606	1706	...	1806	1906	2006	2106
Oakham d.	1420	1520	1620	1720	...	1820	1920	2020	2120
Melton Mowbray d.	1431	1531	1631	1731	...	1831	1931	2031	2131
Leicester d.	1450	1550	1650	1750	...	1850	1950	2050	2150
Nuneaton d.	1509	1609	1709	1809	...	1909	2010	2110	2210
Coleshill Parkway d.	1525	1625	1725	1825	...	1925	2025	2125	2225
Birmingham New St. a.	1538	1638	1738	1838	...	1938	2038	2138	2238

		ⒶA	⑥A	Ⓐ	⑥	⚒A	⚒	⚒	⚒C	⚒	⚒	⚒
Birmingham New St d.	⚒	...	...	0519	0522	...	0622	0722	0822	0922	1022	1122
Coleshill Parkway △ d.		...	...	0534	0536	...	0636	0735	0836	0936	1036	1136
Nuneaton d.		...	...	0549	0552	...	0652	0751	0852	0952	1052	1152
Leicester d.		...	...	0615	0615	...	0718	0818	0918	1018	1118	1218
Melton Mowbray d.		0536	0540	0632	0632	0653	0735	0835	0935	1035	1135	1235
Oakham d.		0549	0552	0643	0643	0705	0746	0846	0946	1046	1146	1246
Stamford d.		0605	0608	0657	0657	0719	0800	0900	1000	1100	1200	1300
Peterborough **205** d.		0627	0627	0712	0712	0735	0818	0918	1018	1118	1218	1318
March **205** d.		0643	0643	0731	0731	0751	0834	0934	1034	1134	1234	1334
Ely **205** d.		0701	0701	0752	0752	0811	0852	0952	1052	1152	1252	1352
Cambridge ▽ d.		...	...	0810	0810	...	0910	1010	1110	1210	1310	1410
Stansted Airport ▽ a.		...	...	0839	0839	...	0940	1040	1140	1240	1340	1440

	⚒	⚒	⚒	⚒	⚒	Ⓐ	⚒	⚒	⑥	Ⓐ	⑥	Ⓐ			⑦	⑦	⑦	⑦	⑦	⑦	⑦	⑦	⑦	⑦		⑦D
Birmingham New St d.	1222	1322	1422	1522	1622	1652	1722	1822	1922	1922	2022	2025	...	⑦	1122	1222	1322	1422	1522	1622	1722	1822	1922	2022	...	2152
Coleshill Parkway △ d.	1236	1336	1436	1536	1636	1706	1736	1836	1936	1936	2036	2038	...		1136	1236	1336	1436	1536	1636	1736	1836	1936	2036	...	2205
Nuneaton d.	1252	1352	1452	1552	1652	1722	1752	1852	1952	1952	2052	2054	...		1152	1252	1352	1452	1552	1652	1752	1852	1952	2052	...	2222
Leicester d.	1318	1418	1518	1618	1718	1755b	1818	1918	2018	2018	2118	2118	...		1219	1319	1419	1519	1619	1716	1819	1919	2019	2116	...	2248
Melton Mowbray d.	1335	1435	1535	1635	1735	1813	1835	1935	2035	2035	2135	2135	...		1236	1336	1436	1536	1636	1736	1836	1936	2036	2136	...	...
Oakham d.	1346	1446	1546	1646	1746	1825	1846	1946	2046	2046	2146	2146	...		1247	1347	1447	1547	1647	1748	1848	1948	2048	2147	...	...
Stamford d.	1400	1500	1600	1700	1800	1840	1900	2000	2100	2100	2200	2200	...		1301	1401	1501	1601	1701	1801	1902	2001	2101	2201	...	...
Peterborough **205** d.	1418	1518	1618	1718	1818	1859	1918	2018	2118	2118	2214	2218	...		1318	1418	1518	1618	1718	1818	1918	2018	2118	2216	...	...
March **205** d.	1434	1534	1634	1737	1834	1915	1934	2034	2134	2134	2229	2236	...		1334	1434	1534	1634	1734	1834	1934	2034	2134	2232	...	...
Ely **205** d.	1452	1552	1652	1759	1852	1934	1952	2052	2152	2152	2248	2254	...		1352	1452	1552	1652	1752	1852	1952	2052	2152	2251	...	...
Cambridge ▽ d.	1510	1610	1710	1818	1910	1952	2010	2110	2210	2210	2303	2310	...		1410	1510	1610	1710	1810	1910	2010	2110	2210	2306	...	...
Stansted Airport ▽ a.	1540	1640	1740	1854	1940	...	2040	2140	2240	2252	...	...	...		1445	1545	1645	1745	1845	1945	2045	2145	2245	...	...	...

A – [2] Nottingham - Norwich (Table **206**).
B – [2] Spalding - Nottingham (Tables **185** and **206**).
C – [12] Gloucester - Stansted Airport (Table **121**); 🍸 Birmingham - Peterborough.
D – [12] Cardiff Central - Leicester (Table **121**).

a – Departs 6 minutes later on ⑥.
b – Arrives 9 minutes earlier.

△ – 🚌 connections available to the National Exhibition Centre (NEC) and Birmingham International Airport.

☛ **Full service Leicester - Birmingham New Street and v.v.**

From Leicester: On ⚒ at 0549⑥, 0617Ⓐ, 0643Ⓐ, 0649⑥, 0710, 0722Ⓐ, 0748⑥, 0751Ⓐ, 0816, 0848, 0918, 0948 and every 30 minutes until 2018, 2048, 2116Ⓐ, 2118⑥, 2148, 2216⑥, 2227Ⓐ, 2255Ⓐ.
On ⑦ at 1022, 1119, 1219, 1250 and then at 19 and 50 minutes past each hour until 2019, 2050, 2150, 2219.

From Birmingham New Street: On ⚒ at 0519Ⓐ, 0522⑥, 0550Ⓐ, 0552⑥, 0622, 0652, 0722, 0752, 0822, 0852 and every 30 minutes until 1522, 1552, 1609Ⓐ, 1622, 1652, 1709Ⓐ, 1722, 1752, 1822, 1852, 1922, 1952, 2022⑥, 2025Ⓐ, 2052, 2222.
On ⑦ at 0952, 1052, 1122, 1152 and every 30 minutes until 2022, 2052, 2152.

▽ – **Full service Cambridge - Stansted Airport and v.v.**

From Cambridge: On ⚒ at 0444Ⓐ, 0456⑥, 0517Ⓐ, 0542⑥, 0610⑥, 0632Ⓐ, 0640⑥, 0710⑥, 0740, 0810, 0826⑥, 0910, 0926⑥, 0931Ⓐ, 1010, 1026, 1110, 1126, 1210, 1226, 1310, 1326, 1410, 1426, 1510, 1526, 1610, 1626⑥, 1710, 1726⑥, 1817⑥, 1818Ⓐ, 1826⑥, 1910, 1926⑥, 2010, 2026⑥, 2110, 2126, 2210.
On ⑦ at 0739, 0824, 0915, 0924, 1015, 1024, 1115, 1124, 1215, 1224, 1315, 1324, 1410, 1424, 1510, 1524, 1610, 1624, 1710, 1724, 1810, 1824, 1910, 1924, 2010, 2024, 2110, 2124, 2210.

From Stansted Airport: On ⚒ at 0516Ⓐ, 0525⑥, 0612Ⓐ, 0627⑥, 0648⑥, 0721Ⓐ, 0727⑥, 0748⑥, 0821Ⓐ, 0827⑥, 0905⑥, 0921Ⓐ, 0927⑥, 1005, 1027, 1105, 1127, 1205, 1227, 1305, 1327, 1405, 1427, 1505, 1527, 1605, 1627, 1705⑥, 1727, 1805⑥, 1821Ⓐ, 1827⑥, 1905⑥, 1921Ⓐ, 1927⑥, 2005⑥, 2021Ⓐ, 2027⑥, 2105⑥, 2127, 2205, 2227, 2257Ⓐ, 2327⑥.
On ⑦ at 0840, 0909, 1009, 1025, 1109, 1125, 1209, 1225, 1309, 1325, 1409, 1425, 1509, 1525, 1609, 1625, 1709, 1725, 1809, 1825, 1909, 1925, 2009, 2025, 2104, 2118, 2209, 2225, 2304.

NT 2nd class MIDDLESBROUGH - NEWCASTLE 210

km			ⒶA	⚒	⚒	⚒	⚒	⚒	and at	⚒	⚒	⚒	⚒	⚒	⑥X	Ⓐ		⑦	⑦	and at	⑦	⑦	⑦	⑦Y
0	**Middlesbrough** d.	⚒	...	...	0655	0732	0832	0932	the same	1532	1632	1743	1832	1942	2047	2110	⑦	0931	1031	the same	1632	1742	1831	1933
9	Stockton d.		...	...	0706	0743	0843	0943	minutes	1543	1643	1754	1843	1954	2058	2121		0942	1043	minutes	1643	1753	1842	1944
28	Hartlepool d.		...	0703	0725	0802	0902	1002	past each	1602	1702	1813	1902	2013	2117	2140		1001	1102	past each	1703	1815	1901	2003
57	Sunderland d.		0540	0730	0755	0830	0930	1030	hour until	1630	1730	1843	1929	2039	2142	2211a		1028	1128	hour until	1730	1843	1928	2029
77	**Newcastle** a.		0556	0751	0816	0853	0952	1053	❖	1653	1752	1907	1955b	2104	2204	2232		1048	1148	❖	1748	1908	1952	2050

		Ⓐ	⑥	⚒	⚒	and at	⚒	⚒	⚒	⚒	⚒	Ⓐ	⑥	Ⓐ	⑥	ⒶA		⑦W	and at	⑦	⑦	⑦	⑦	⑦
Newcastle d.	⚒	0600	0600	0700	0730	the same	1630	1653	1730	1830	1930	2030	2033	2118	2130	2300	⑦	1000	the same	1600	1700	1800	1900	2000
Sunderland d.		0620	0628a	0720	0750	minutes	1650	1715	1752	1851	1951	2051	2055	2138	2151	2320		1021	minutes	1621	1720	1821	1922	2021
Hartlepool d.		0646	0653	0745	0815	past each	1715	1739	1818	1915	2017	2115	2122	2203	2215	...		1046	past each	1646	1746	1845	1946	2045
Stockton d.		...	...	0804	0833	hour until	1733	1758	1837	1933	2036	2133	2140	2221	2234	...		1104	hour until	1705	1805	1904	2005	2104
Middlesbrough a.		...	...	0825	0848	❖	1748	1816	1852	1948	2049	2148	2155	2236	2248	...		1120	❖	1717	1825	1916	2021	2120

A – To/from London Kings Cross (Table **180**).
W – From Apr. 2 the 1000 departure continues to Whitby (Table **211**).
X – From Whitby (Table **211**).
Y – From Apr. 2 starts from Whitby (Table **211**).

a – Arrives 6 minutes earlier.
b – Arrives 1951 on Ⓐ.

❖ – Timings may vary by ± 3 minutes.

NT 2nd class MIDDLESBROUGH and PICKERING - WHITBY 211

km		⚒	⑦C	⚒	⑦B	⑦A	⚒	⑦D	⚒	
0	**Middlesbrough** d.	0704	0905	1028	1121	1356	1403	1616	1740	...
18	Battersby d.	0734	0935	1058	1151	1433	1435	1655	1810	...
41	Glaisdale d.	0808	1009	1131	1225	1507	1509	1728	1843	...
46	Grosmont d.	0817	1017	1139	1233	1515	1517	1736	1851	...
56	**Whitby** a.	0837	1038	1159	1252	1534	1536	1756	1911	...

	⚒	⑦A	⚒	⑦D	⑦B	⚒	⑦C	⚒	
Whitby d.	0845	1044	1215	1301	1547	1600	1804	1918	...
Grosmont d.	0902	1101	1232	1318	1604	1618	1821	1935	...
Glaisdale d.	0913	1112	1243	1329	1615	1628	1832	1946	...
Battersby d.	0947	1156	1318	1404	1650	1703	1906	2020	...
Middlesbrough a.	1015	1223	1346	1433	1718	1730	1933	2047	...

km		🚂	🚂		🚂	🚂	🚂		🚂	🚂
0	**Pickering** d.	...	0925	...	1100	1200	1300	...	1500	1610
29	Grosmont a.	...	1025	...	1205	1305	1405	...	1615	1710
29	Grosmont d.	0915	1040	...	...	1315	1430	...	...	1715
39	**Whitby** a.	0945	1110	...	...	1345	1500	...	...	1745

	🚂	🚂		🚂	🚂	🚂	🚂	🚂	
Whitby d.	1000	...	...	1245	1400	...	1640	1800	...
Grosmont a.	1025	...	...	1315	1425	...	1705	1825	...
Grosmont d.	1030	1130	...	1330	1430	1540	1715	...	...
Pickering a.	1140	1240	...	1440	1540	1650	1820	...	...

A – From Apr. 2.
B – From Apr. 2. To/from Newcastle (Table **210**).
C – From Apr. 2. To/from Bishop Auckland (Table **212**).
D – From Apr. 2. To/from Darlington (Table **212**).

🚂 – Apr. 2 - Oct. 29, 2017. National rail tickets **not** valid. An amended service operates on most ⑦ and on certain other dates. - please confirm with operator. The North Yorkshire Moors Railway (✆ 01751 472508. www.nymr.co.uk).

212 BISHOP AUCKLAND - DARLINGTON - MIDDLESBROUGH - SALTBURN
2nd class NT

km		⚒	⚒	Ⓐ	⑥	⚒	⚒	⚒	⚒	⚒	Ⓐ	⑥	⚒	⑦A	⑦		⑦	⑦	⑦A	⑦	⑦B	⑦
0	**Bishop Auckland** d.	0717	0821	0926	0926	1125	1325	1525	1623	1805	1902	1920	2110	0812	1007	...	1207	1507	...	1708	1838	1907
4	Shildon d.	0722	0826	0931	0931	1130	1330	1530	1628	1810	1907	1925	2115	0817	1012	...	1212	1512	...	1713	1843	1912
8	Newton Aycliffe d.	0727	0831	0936	0936	1135	1335	1535	1633	1815	1912	1930	2120	0822	1017	...	1217	1517	...	1718	1848	1917
19	**Darlington** a.	0743	0847	0953	0953	1151	1351	1551	1650	1831	1928	1947	2136	0838	1033	...	1233	1533	...	1734	1904	1933
19	**Darlington** ▶ d.	0744	0900	0955	0955	1153	1353	1553	1653	1833	1930	1955	2138	0840	1035	...	1235	1535	1550	1736	...	1935
43	**Middlesbrough** ▶ d.	0811	0927	1022	1024	1221	1421	1621	1720	1900	1957	2023	2206	0905	1103	...	1303	1603	1617	1803	...	2003
55	Redcar Central ▶ d.	*0909*	0938	1034	1036	1233	1433	1633	1732	1910	2009	*2110*	2218	*1013*	1115	...	1315	1615	...	1815	...	2015
63	**Saltburn** ▶ a.	*0926*	0955	1051	1053	1250	1450	1650	1750	1926	2026	*2126*	2235	*1028*	1130	...	1330	1630	...	1830	...	2030

	⚒	⚒	⑥	Ⓐ	⚒	⚒	⚒	⚒	⚒	⚒	⚒	⚒	⚒		⑦B	⑦	⑦	⑦	⑦A	⑦	⑦A	⑦
Saltburn ▷ d.	...	...	0621	0624	...	0754	0958	1157	1357	1457	1630	1730	1930	...	...	...	1036	1336	...	1536	*1636*	1736
Redcar Central ▷ d.	...	...	0634	0637	...	0807	1011	1210	1410	1510	1643	1743	1943	...	...	...	1049	1349	...	1549	*1649*	1749
Middlesbrough ▷ d.	0544	...	0647	0650	...	0820	1023	1221	1421	1521	1657	1755	1955	...	...	0850	1102	1402	1434	1602	1719	1802
Darlington ▷ a.	0613	...	0719	0720	...	0851	1053	1252	1452	1552	1726	1825	2026	...	...	0920	1130	1431	1459	1631	1747	1831
Darlington d.	...	0648	...	...	0749	0851	1054	1254	1454	1554	1728	1832	2032	...	0743	0929	1132	1431	...	1631	1749	1834
Newton Aycliffe d.	...	0702	...	...	0804	0906	1108	1308	1508	1608	1742	1846	2046	...	0757	0943	1146	1445	...	1645	1803	1848
Shildon d.	...	0707	...	...	0808	0910	1113	1313	1513	1613	1747	1851	2051	...	0802	0948	1151	1450	...	1650	1808	1853
Bishop Auckland a.	...	0715	...	...	0816	0918	1120	1320	1520	1620	1754	1858	2058	...	0810	0955	1158	1457	...	1657	1815	1900

A – From Apr. 2. To/from Whitby (Table **211**).
B – From Apr. 2.

▶ – All trains Darlington - Middlesbrough - Redcar - Saltburn:
⚒: 0629, 0658, 0725Ⓐ, 0730⑥, 0823⑥, 0831Ⓐ, 0900, 0931, 0955, 1032, 1053, 1131, 1153, 1232, 1253, 1332, 1353, 1432, 1453, 1531, 1553, 1631, 1653, 1730, 1754Ⓐ, 1800⑥, 1833, 1930, 2030⑥, 2032Ⓐ, 2138.
⑦: 0835, 0933, 1035, 1135, 1235, 1333, 1434, 1535, 1635, 1736, 1836, 1935, 2035, 2145.

▷ – All trains Saltburn - Redcar - Middlesbrough - Darlington:
⚒: 0621⑥, 0624Ⓐ, 0710, 0725Ⓐ, 0728⑥, 0754, 0830, 0930, 0958, 1030, 1057, 1130, 1157, 1230, 1257, 1330, 1357, 1430, 1457, 1530, 1555, 1630, 1655, 1730, 1757, 1829, 1857, 1930, 2030Ⓐ, 2034⑥, 2130, 2239.
⑦: 0936, 1036, 1136, 1236, 1336, 1436, 1536, 1636, 1736, 1836, 1936, 2042, 2136, 2243.

213 NEWCASTLE - CARLISLE
2nd class NT

km		⑥	Ⓐ	⚒	⚒	⚒	⚒	⚒	⚒	⚒	⚒	⚒	⚒	⚒	⚒	⚒	⚒	⚒	Ⓐ	⑦	⑦	⑦	⑦
0	**Newcastle** ▶ d.	0630	0646	0824	0924	1022	1122	1222	1323	1424	1524	1622	1716	1754	1824	1925	2016	2118	2235	0910	1010	1110	1210
6	MetroCentre ▶ d.	0638	0654	0832	0932	1033	1132	1232	1333	1432	1532	1632	1724	1802	1833	1934	2024	2126	2243	0918	1018	1118	1218
19	Prudhoe ▶ d.	0650	0704	0844	0944	1043	1142	1242	1344	1442	1542	1644	1737	1814	1848	1947	2039	2138	2258	0930	1032	1130	1232
36	Hexham ▶ d.	0709	0717	0858	0955	1055	1155	1255	1357	1455	1556	1703	1750	1833	1906	2005	2100	2157	2319	0949	1051	1149	1251
62	Haltwhistle d.	0732	0740	0921	1014	1118	1214	1318	1416	1518	1616	1726	1813	1855	1925	2028	...	2220	...	1011	1114	1208	1314
99	**Carlisle** a.	0807	0815	0957	1046	1200	1247	1356	1451	1557	1651	1800	1852	1932	1958	2103	...	2256	...	1047	1150	1240	1349
	Glasgow Central **214** a.	1037	1037	...	...	...	...	...	1737	...	...	...	2140	...	...	...	...	...	...	...	...	...	...

	⑦	⑦	⑦	⑦	⑦		⑦	⑦
Newcastle ▶ d.	1310	1410	1510	1610	1710	...	1810	2015
MetroCentre ▶ d.	1318	1418	1518	1618	1718	...	1818	2024
Prudhoe ▶ d.	1330	1432	1530	1632	1730	...	1832	2038
Hexham ▶ d.	1349	1451	1549	1651	1749	...	1851	2057
Haltwhistle d.	1408	1510	1611	1710	1808	...	1914	2120
Carlisle a.	1440	1542	1647	1742	1840	...	1949	2155
Glasgow Central **214** a.	...	...	...	...	...	...	...	...

	⚒	⑥	Ⓐ	⚒	⚒	⚒	Ⓐ	⑥	⚒
Glasgow Central **214** d.	...	...	...	...	...	0707	...	...	...
Carlisle d.	...	0625	0628	0718	0828	0943	1025	1028	1135
Haltwhistle d.	...	0657	0700	0750	0900	1011	1058	1100	1203
Hexham ▷ d.	0612	0719	0722	0812	0922	1029	1120	1122	1222
Prudhoe ▷ d.	0630	0737	0740	0829	0934	1041	1132	1134	1234
MetroCentre ▷ d.	0645	0750	0753	0846	0946	1053	1144	1146	1246
Newcastle ▷ a.	0655	0807	0807	0901	0959	1106	1157	1159	1259

	⚒	⚒	⚒	⚒	⚒	⚒	Ⓐ	⑥	⚒	⚒	⚒	Ⓐ	⑦	⑦	⑦	⑦	⑦	⑦	⑦	⑦	⑦	⑦	⑦
Glasgow Central **214** d.	...	...	1213	...	...	...	1613	1613	...	...	...	...	...	...	...	...	...	...	...	...	...	...	...
Carlisle d.	1228	1332	1436	1528	1628	1728	1838	1841	1941	...	2128	...	0901	1004	1108	1204	1308	1410	1508	1604	1708	1804	2015
Haltwhistle d.	1300	1404	1505	1556	1700	1800	1910	1913	2010	...	2200	...	0933	1036	1136	1236	1336	1438	1536	1636	1736	1836	2043
Hexham ▷ d.	1322	1426	1523	1615	1722	1822	1932	1935	2028	2112	2222	2322	0956	1058	1156	1258	1356	1458	1556	1658	1756	1858	2102
Prudhoe ▷ d.	1334	1438	1535	1626	1734	1840	1949	1952	2045	2130	2240	2340	1013	1115	1213	1315	1413	1515	1613	1715	1813	1915	2119
MetroCentre ▷ d.	1346	1450	1547	1638	1746	1853	2003	2006	2059	2145	2253	2353	1029	1129	1229	1329	1429	1529	1629	1729	1829	1929	2135
Newcastle ▷ a.	1400	1503	1558	1650	1759	1907	2017	2017	2113	2158	2306	0004	1039	1139	1241	1341	1441	1541	1641	1741	1841	1941	2148

▶ – Additional Trains Newcastle - Hexham. Journey time 43–45 minutes: 0625Ⓐ, 0753⚒, 0854⚒ and houly until 1454⚒, 1554⚒, 1654Ⓐ, 1656⑥ 1724⚒.

▷ – Additional Trains Hexham - Newcastle. Journey time 42–47 minutes: 0742⚒, 0845⚒, 0943⚒, 1045⚒, 1143⚒, 1245⚒, 1342⚒, 1445⚒, 1543⚒, 1645⚒, 1743⚒, 1843⚒.

214 CARLISLE - DUMFRIES - GLASGOW
2nd class SR

km		⚒	⑥	Ⓐ	⚒	⑥	Ⓐ	⑥	⚒	⑥	⚒	⑦	⑥	⚒	⑦	⚒	⑦	⑥	⚒	⑦	⚒		⑥	⚒	⑦	⚒
	Newcastle **213** d.	...	...	...	...	0630	0646	...	...	...	...	...	...	1323	...	...	...	...	...	...	1716	...	...	...	...	...
0	**Carlisle** d.	...	0525	0531	0608	0815	0815	0955	1115	1220	1312	1313	1422	1512	1515	1617	1712	1716	1757	1912	1917	...	2022	2112	2126	2310
16	Gretna Green d.	...	0536	0543	0619	0826	0826	1006	1126	1232	1323	1324	1433	1523	1526	1628	1723	1727	1808	1923	1928	...	2033	2123	2137	2321
28	Annan d.	...	0545	0553	0627	0834	0834	1014	1134	1240	1331	1332	1441	1531	1534	1636	1731	1735	1816	1931	1937	...	2041	2131	2145	2329
53	**Dumfries** d.	0546	0602	0610	0646	0853	0853	1032	1153	1258	1350	1351	1459	1550	1552	1654	1749	1753	1835	1950	1955	...	2059	2150	2203	2347
124	Auchinleck d.	0634	...	...	0735	0941	0941	...	1241	...	1438	1439	...	1638	...	...	...	...	1923	2038	2044	...	...	2238	...	...
146	**Kilmarnock** ▽ d.	0652	...	...	0755	0959	0959	...	1259	...	1458	1457	...	1657	...	...	...	...	1957a	2057	2101	...	...	2257	...	...
185	**Glasgow** Central ▽ a.	0732	...	...	0837	1037	1037	...	1335	...	1538	1536	...	1737	...	...	...	...	2037	2135	2140	...	...	2336	...	...

	⚒	⚒	Ⓐ	⑥	⚒	⚒	⑥	⚒	⑦	⑥	⚒	⚒	⑦	⑥	⑦	⚒	⚒	⑥	⑦	⚒	⚒	⑥	Ⓐ	⑦	⑥	Ⓐ
Glasgow Central ▽ d.	...	...	...	...	0707	0837	...	1013	...	...	1213	1313	...	...	1512	...	1613	...	...	1742	1913	...	2113	2212	2213	2313
Kilmarnock ▽ d.	...	...	...	...	0754	0918	...	1051	...	...	1250	1350	...	...	1553	...	1652	...	...	1825	1952	...	2153	2249	2253	0002
Auchinleck d.	...	...	...	...	0811	0935	...	1108	...	...	1307	1407	...	...	1610	...	1709	...	...	1842	2009	...	2210	2306	2309	0020
Dumfries d.	0458	0618	0743	0743	0901	1025	1102	1158	1300	1314	1357	1457	1501	1602	1700	1707	1759	1841	1901	1933	2100	2213	2300	2356	2359	0115
Annan d.	0513	0633	0758	0758	0916	1040	1117	1213	1315	1329	1413	1512	1516	1617	1715	1722	1814	1856	1916	1948	2115	2228	2315	0011	0014	...
Gretna Green d.	0522	0642	0807	0807	0925	1049	1126	1222	1324	1338	1421	1521	1525	1626	1724	1731	1823	1905	1925	1957	2124	2237	2324	0020	0023	...
Carlisle a.	0535	0655	0820	0820	0941	1104	1139	1235	1337	1354	1435	1534	1542	1639	1737	1744	1836	1918	1938	2011	2143	2250	2337	0033	0036	...
Newcastle **213** a.	...	0901	0958	...	1106	...	...	...	...	...	1558	...	...	...	...	...	2017	...	...	...	...	...	...	...	...	...

a – Arrive 1940.

▽ – Frequent additional services are available (half-hourly on ⚒, hourly on ⑦).

215 GLASGOW and KILMARNOCK - STRANRAER
2nd class SR

For ⛴ Cairnryan - Belfast and v.v. see Table 2002.

km		⚒	⚒	⚒	⚒	⚒	⚒	⑦	⚒	⚒	⑦	⚒	⚒	⑦	⚒	⚒	⚒	⑦	⚒	Ⓐ	⑥	⑦	⚒	B	⚒	A
0	**Glasgow** Central **216** d.	...	...	...	...	0807	...	...	...	...	...	...	...	...	1413	...	...	...	1713	1813	...	...	...	2013	...	2213
39	**Kilmarnock 214** a.	...	...	...	...	0849	...	...	...	...	...	...	...	...	1450	...	...	...	1752	1852	...	...	...	2052	...	2252
	Kilmarnock d.	...	...	...	0801	0900	...	...	1104	...	...	1303	...	...	1458	...	1700	...	1804	1904	1904	...	...	2104	...	2305
56	Troon **216** d.	...	...	...	0814	0912	...	...	1116	...	...	1315	...	...	1510	...	1712	...	1818	1916	1916	...	...	2116	...	2317
64	**Ayr** 🚐 **216** a.	...	...	...	0827	0923	...	...	1130	...	...	1328	...	...	1524	...	1723	...	1828	1927	1927	...	...	2127	...	2330
	Ayr d.	0525	0621	0716	0828	0923	1026	1106	1131	1226	1227	1329	1424	1505	1525	1625	1724	1805	1829	1927	1927	1927	2032	2128	2230	2331
97	Girvan d.	0552	0648	0756	0855	0954	1055	1136	1201	1253	1253	1359	1453	1535	1555	1652	1754	1835	1856	1958	1958	1953	2059	2153	2257	0001
121	Barrhill d.	...	...	0816	...	1013	...	1155	1220	...	1318	1418	...	1554	1614	...	1813	1854	...	2017	2017	2017	...	...	...	0020
162	**Stranraer** a.	...	...	0852	...	1049	...	1231	1256	...	1354	1454	...	1630	1650	...	1849	1930	...	2053	2053	2053	...	...	...	0056

	⚒	⚒	⚒	⚒	⚒	⚒	⚒	⑦	⚒	⑦	⚒		⚒	⑦	⚒	⚒	⚒	⑦	⚒	⚒	⚒	⑦	⑥	Ⓐ	⚒	⚒
Stranraer d.	...	...	0702	...	0858	...	1106	1041	...	1241	1304	...	...	1440	1500	...	1659	1740	...	1903	...	1940	2103	2103	...	...
Barrhill d.	...	...	0736	...	0932	...	1140	1116	...	1316	1338	...	...	1514	1534	...	1733	1814	...	1937	...	2015	2137	2137	...	...
Girvan d.	0557	0653	0754	0900	0952	1100	1159	1134	1300	1334	1357	...	1500	1533	1553	1658	1751	1833	1901	1956	2104	2033	2157	2157	2230	2302
Ayr a.	0627	0721	0823	0928	1020	1128	1229	1202	1328	1402	1429	...	1528	1601	1626	1727	1820	1901	1929	2026	2132	2101	2225	2225	2309	2330
Ayr 🚐 **216** d.	...	0722	0824	...	1021	...	1229	...	...	...	1430	...	...	...	1627	1728	1821	...	...	2027	...	...	2226	2226	...	...
Troon **216** d.	...	0733	0833	...	1029	...	1238	...	...	...	1441	...	...	...	1638	1739	1829	...	...	2038	...	...	2239	2239	...	...
Kilmarnock a.	...	0749	0852	...	1044	...	1254	...	...	...	1456	...	...	...	1653	1756	1844	...	...	2055	...	...	2256	2303	...	...
Kilmarnock 214 d.	...	...	0857	...	...	...	...	...	...	...	...	...	...	...	...	...	1857	...	...	...	...	...	...	...	...	...
Glasgow Central **216** a.	...	...	0937	...	...	...	...	...	...	...	...	...	...	...	...	...	1937	...	...	...	...	...	...	...	...	...

A – Runs Ⓐ from Glasgow, ⚒ from Kilmarnock.
B – Runs ⑥ from Glasgow, ⚒ from Kilmarnock.

☛ 🚐 connections to/from Cairnryan are available from Ayr for pre-booked Rail & Sail ticket holders - www.stenaline.co.uk/rail

158 Les signes conventionnels sont expliqués à la page 4 12

SR GLASGOW - AYR, ARDROSSAN and LARGS 216

Typical off-peak journey time in hours and minutes
READ DOWN ↓ READ UP ↑

Journey times may be extended during peak hours on Ⓐ (0600 - 0900 and 1600 - 1900) and also at weekends.
The longest journey time by any train is noted in the table heading.

GLASGOW CENTRAL - AYR — Longest journey: 1 hour 04 minutes SR

km	△				△
0	0h00	↓	**Glasgow** Central ......d.		0h49
43	0h25		Kilwinning ....d.	↑	0h22
48	0h29	↓	Irvine ....d.		0h18
56	0h37		Troon.......................d.	↑	0h11
61	0h41	↓	Prestwick Airport ✈ ..d.		0h07
67	0h52		**Ayr**..........................a.	↑	0h00

From Glasgow Central: On ⚒ at 0015②–⑥, 0600, 0630, 0700, 0730, 0746, 0800, 0830, 0838, 0900, 0930, 1000, 1030 and every 30 minutes until 1500, 1530, 1600, 1628, 1640, 1701, 1716Ⓐ, 1728Ⓐ, 1730⑥, 1800, and every 30 minutes until 2330. On ⑦ at 0900 and every 30 minutes until 1900, 2000, 2100, 2200, 2300.

From Ayr: On ⚒ at 0513, 0540, 0602, 0620Ⓐ, 0633, 0650, 0705, 0717, 0732Ⓐ, 0740, 0805, 0829, 0851, 0923, 0948 and at the same minutes past each hour until 1525, 1548, 1623, 1654, 1706, 1723, 1753, 1805, 1825, 1850, 1915 and every 30 minutes until 2215, 2300. On ⑦ at 0845 and every 30 minutes until 1945, 2045, 2145, 2300.

△ – Trains at 0015⚒ - 0838⚒ and 1900⚒ - 2330⚒ and all day on ⑦ call additionally at Paisley Gilmour Street.

GLASGOW CENTRAL - ARDROSSAN - LARGS — Longest journey: 1 hour 10 minutes SR

km					
0	0h00	↓	**Glasgow** Central ......d.	↑	0h59
12	0h10		Paisley Gilmour St ....d.		0h46
43	0h19	↓	Kilwinning ....d.	↑	0h25
50	0h28		**Ardrossan** Sth Beach ..d.		0h17
54	0h49	↓	Fairlie ....d.	↑	0h05
69	0h56		**Largs** ....a.		0h00

From Glasgow Central: On ⚒ at 0615, 0715, 0848 and hourly until 1448, 1548, 1631, 1714⑥, 1723Ⓐ, 1749, 1850, 1945, 2045, 2145, 2245, 2315①②③④⑥, 2345⑤. On ⑦ at 0940 and hourly until 2140, 2242.

From Largs: On ⚒ at 0642, 0722Ⓐ, 0742, 0833Ⓐ, 0853⑥, 0953 and hourly until 1553, 1648, 1733, 1852, 1952, 2052, 2152, 2252. On ⑦ at 0854 and hourly until 2154, 2300.

SR 2nd class GLASGOW - OBAN, FORT WILLIAM and MALLAIG 218

km		⚒	⚒	⚒ A	Ⓐ Ba	⚒ 🍷	⚒ 🍷	⑦ c	⑦ 🍷		⚒ 🍷	Ⓐ Ba	⑦ 🍷	⑦ 🍷 c	⚒ 🍷	⚒ 🍷		Ⓐ	⚒ 🍷	⑦ 🍷	⑦ 🍷	⚒ 🍷	①–④ 🍷	⑤ 🍷	⑥ 🍷
	Edinburgh **220** ....d.	...	...	0450	...	*0715*	*0715*	...	*0830*	...	*0930*	...	*1100*	*1100*	*1114*	*1114*	...	...	*1530*	*1700*	*1700*	*1715*	*1715*	*1715*	*1715*
0	**Glasgow** Queen St .....d.	...	0520	0548‡	...	0821	0821	...	0956	...	1037	...	1220	1220	1221	1221	...	...	1637	1820	1820	1821	1821	1821	1821
16	Dalmuir........................d.	...	0538	0604	...	0842	0842	...	1016	...	1056	...	1234	1234	1242	1242	...	...	1657	1834	1834	1841	1841	1841	1841
26	Dumbarton Central.......d.	...	0547	0615	...	0851	0851	...	1025	...	1105	...	1247	1247	1251	1251	...	...	1706	1847	1847	1850	1850	1850	1850
40	Helensburgh Upper .....d.	...	0603	0632	...	0906	0906	...	1040	...	1127	...	1306	1306	1306	1306	...	...	1722	1905	1905	1904	1904	1904	1904
51	Garelochhead ....d.	...	0614	0645	...	0917	0917	...	1051	...	1140	...	1318	1318	1318	1318	...	...	1733	1916	1916	1917	1917	1917	1917
68	Arrochar & Tarbet........d.	...	0634	0709	...	0937	0937	...	1111	...	1201	...	1338	1338	1338	1338	...	...	1757	1936	1936	1937	1937	1937	1937
81	Ardlui..........................d.	...	0652	0724x	...	0950	0950	...	1127	...	1214	...	1356	1356	1356	1356	...	...	1810	1951	1951	1951	1951	1951	1951
95	**Crianlarich**.................a.	...	0708	0745	...	1006	1006	...	1144	...	1230	...	1412	1412	1412	1412	...	...	1826	2007	2007	2007	2007	2007	2007
95	**Crianlarich**.................d.	...	0718	0747	...	1015	1021	...	1146	...	1233	...	1418	1424	1418	1424	...	...	1829	2014	2020	2014	2020	2020	2020
	Dalmally ....d.	...	0751	|	...	1042	|	...	1214	...	1259	...	1444	|	1444	|	...	1705	1855	2040	|	2040	|	|	|
	Taynuilt ....d.	...	0811	|	...	1103	|	...	1240	...	1320	...	1504	|	1505	|	...	1724	1920	2100	|	2100	|	|	|
162	**Oban** ....a.	...	0835	|	...	1127	|	...	1304	...	1343	...	1527	|	1528	|	...	1747	1943	2124	|	2124	|	|	|
115	Bridge of Orchy ....d.	...	...	0818	...	...	1048	...	...	...	...	...	...	1449	...	1449	...	...	...	...	2047	...	2045	2045	2045
140	Rannoch.......................d.	...	...	0846	...	...	1109	...	...	...	...	...	...	1512	...	1512	...	...	...	...	2108	...	2108	2108	2108
177	Roy Bridge ....d.	...	...	0931x	...	...	1148	...	...	...	...	...	...	1550	...	1550	...	...	...	...	2146	...	2146	2146	2146
183	Spean Bridge...............d.	...	...	0939	...	...	1155	...	...	...	...	...	...	1556	...	1556	...	...	...	...	2153	...	2153	2156	2153
197	**Fort William**...............a.	...	...	0955	...	...	1208	...	...	...	...	...	...	1609	...	1609	...	...	...	...	2206	...	2206	2209	2206
197	**Fort William**...............d.	0830	...	...	1015	...	1212	1212	...	...	...	1430	...	1619	...	1619	...	...	...	...	2214	...	2214	2217	2214
223	Glenfinnan...................d.	0905	...	...	1122	...	1246	1246	...	...	...	1545	...	1655	...	1655	...	...	...	...	2247	...	2247	2250	2247
251	Arisaig.........................d.	0938	...	...	|	...	1319	1319	...	...	...	|	...	1727	...	1727	...	...	...	...	2320	...	2320	2323	2320
259	Morar...........................d.	0946	...	...	|	...	1327	1327	...	...	...	|	...	1736	...	1736	...	...	...	...	2328	...	2328	2331	2328
264	**Mallaig**.......................a.	0953	...	...	1226	...	1334	1334	...	...	...	1629	...	1743	...	1743	...	...	...	...	2335	...	2335	2338	2335

	⚒ 🍷	⚒ 🍷	⚒	⚒	⚒	⑦	⑦ c	Ⓐ	Ⓐ Ba	⑦	⑥		Ⓐ		⚒	⚒	⑦	⑦	⑦ A			⚒	Ⓐ A	Ⓐ Ba
Mallaig..........................d.	...	0603	...	...	1010	...	1010	...	1409	...	...	...	...	...	1605	...	1605	...	...	...	...	...	...	1838
Morar.............................d.	...	0609	...	...	1017	...	1017	...	|	...	...	...	...	...	1612	...	1612	...	...	...	...	...	...	|
Arisaig...........................d.	...	0619	...	...	1027	...	1026	...	|	...	...	...	...	...	1621	...	1621	...	...	...	...	...	...	|
Glenfinnan......................d.	...	0651	...	...	1059	...	1059	...	1518	...	...	...	...	...	1654	...	1654	...	...	...	...	...	...	1947
Fort William..................a.	...	0725	...	...	1132	...	1132	...	1603	...	...	...	...	...	1728	...	1728	...	...	...	...	...	...	2031
Fort William..................d.	...	0744	...	...	1140	...	1140	...	...	...	...	...	...	...	1737	...	1737	...	1900	...	...	...	1950	...
Spean Bridge....................d.	...	0757	...	...	1156	...	1156	...	...	...	...	...	...	...	1751	...	1751	...	1920	...	...	...	2010	...
Roy Bridge ....d.	...	0804	...	...	1202	...	1202	...	...	...	...	...	...	...	1757	...	1757	...	1927x	...	...	...	2017x	...
Rannoch...........................d.	...	0847	...	...	1242	...	1242	...	...	...	...	...	...	...	1838	...	1838	...	2015	...	...	...	2107	...
Bridge of Orchy ....d.	...	0907	...	...	1303	...	1303	...	...	...	...	...	...	...	1858	...	1858	...	2048	...	...	...	2135	...
Oban ....d.	0521	|	0857	1211	|	1211	|	1441	...	1611	1611	...	1611	...	|	1811	|	1811	|	...	...	2036	|	...
Taynuilt...........................d.	0544	|	0920	1235	|	1238	|	1506	...	1638	1634	...	1634	...	|	1833	|	1833	|	...	...	2101	|	...
Dalmally ....d.	0603	|	0940	1300	|	1259	|	1526	...	1658	1654	...	1654	...	|	1856	|	1856	|	...	...	2120	|	...
Crianlarich.....................a.	0631	0931	1008	1332	1327	1326	1332	1554	...	1726	1722	...	...	...	1922	1927	1922	1927	2118	...	...	2147	2205	...
Crianlarich.....................d.	0633	0933	1014	1337	1337	1337	1337	1556	...	1727	1724	...	...	...	1932	1932	1932	1932	2119	...	...	2148	2206	...
Ardlui..............................d.	0651	0951	1029	1355	1355	1355	1355	1611	...	1743	1742	...	...	...	1952	1952	1952	1952	2140x	...	...	2204	2227x	...
Arrochar & Tarbet..............d.	0710	1005	1043	1409	1409	1409	1409	1627	...	1757	1756	...	...	...	2006	2006	2006	2006	2158	...	...	2218	2245	...
Garelochhead ....d.	0730	1032	1104	1431	1431	1429	1429	1649	...	1819	1819	...	...	...	2026	2026	2026	2026	2224	...	...	2238	2311	...
Helensburgh Upper............d.	0742	1044	1116	1443	1443	1440	1440	1700	...	1831	1831	...	...	...	2037	2037	2040	2040	2238	...	...	2249	2325	...
Dumbarton Central............a.	0756	1059	1129	1459	1459	1457	1457	1713	...	1847	1844	...	...	...	2050	2050	2053	2053	2252	...	...	2302	2339	...
Dalmuir.............................a.	|	1109	1138	1509	1509	1506	1506	1723	...	1856	1854	...	...	...	2104	2104	2104	2104	2304	...	...	2311	2351	...
Glasgow Queen St...........a.	0837	1130	1156	1529	1530	1528	1528	1748	...	1917	1919	...	...	...	2122	2122	2119	2119	2329¶	...	...	2333	0014¶	...
Edinburgh **220**.................a.	*0951*	*1239*	*1307*	*1639*	*1639*	*1655*	*1655*	*1851*	...	*2024*	*2021*	...	...	...	*2256*	*2256*	*2221*	*2221*	0024	...	...	...	0110	...

A – Ⓡ. 🛏12 (limited accommodation), 🛏 1, 2 cl. and ✕ London Euston - Fort William and v.v. (Table **161**).
B – THE JACOBITE – 🚂. Ⓡ. National Rail tickets **not** valid. To book ✆ 0845 128 4681 or visit www.westcoastrailways.co.uk.

a – 2017 dates and times to be advised.
c – From 26 March.
x – Calls on request.

‡ – Low-level platforms. Calls to pick up only.
¶ – Low-level platforms. Calls to set down only.

SCOTTISH ISLAND FERRIES 219

Caledonian MacBrayne Ltd operates numerous ferry services linking the Western Isles of Scotland to the mainland and to each other. Principal routes – some of which are seasonal – are listed below (see also the map on page **90**). Service frequencies, sailing-times and reservations: ✆ +44 (0)800 066 5000; fax +44 (0)1475 635 235; www.calmac.co.uk

Ardrossan – Brodick (Arran)
Ardrossan – Campbeltown (Kintyre)
Barra – Eriskay
Claonaig – Lochranza (Arran)
Colintraive – Rhubodach (Bute)
Fionnphort – Iona (Iona)
Kennacraig – Port Askaig (Islay)
Kennacraig – Port Ellen (Islay)
Kilchoan – Tobermory (Mull)
Largs – Cumbrae (Cumbrae)
Leverburgh (Harris) – Berneray (North Uist)
Lochaline – Fishnish (Mull)
Mallaig – Armadale (Skye)
Mallaig – Eigg, Muck, Rum and Canna
Mallaig/Oban – Lochboisdale (South Uist)
Oban – Castlebay (Barra)
Oban – Coll and Tiree
Oban – Colonsay, Port Askaig (Islay) and Kennacraig
Oban – Craignure (Mull)
Oban – Lismore
Portavadie (Cowal & Kintyre) – Tarbert Loch Fyne
Sconser (Skye) – Raasay
Tayinloan – Gigha
Tobermory (Mull) – Kilchoan
Uig (Skye) – Lochmaddy (North Uist)
Uig (Skye) – Tarbert (Harris)
Ullapool – Stornoway (Lewis)
Wemyss Bay – Rothesay (Bute)

220 EDINBURGH - GLASGOW

GR, SR, XC

EDINBURGH - FALKIRK - GLASGOW QUEEN STREET

km			⚒	⚒	Ⓐ	⚒	⚒	⚒	⚒	⚒	⚒	⚒	⚒	⚒	and at	⚒	⚒	⚒	⚒	⚒	⚒	⚒	⚒
0	**Edinburgh** Waverley d.	⚒	0555	0630	0645	0700	0715	0730	0745	0800	0815	0830	0845	0900	the same	1800	1815	1830	1845	1900	1915	1930	2000
2	Haymarket d.		0600	0634	0649	0704	0719	0735	0749	0805	0820	0834	0849	0905	minutes	1806	1820	1834	1849	1905	1920	1935	2005
28	Linlithgow d.		0615	0649	0705	│	0734	0750	0806	│	0835	│	0905	│	past each	│	1836	│	1905	│	1935	1950	2020
41	Falkirk High d.		0626	0701	0714	0727	0743	0801	0815	0830	0847	0855	0917	0925	hour until	1826	1848	1855	1916	1925	1946	1959	2031
76	**Glasgow** Queen Street a.		0649	0725	0737	0751	0808	0825	0840	0855	0907	0919	0937	0952	☆	1850	1909	1922	1936	1951	2009	2024	2051

	⚒	⚒	⚒	⚒	⚒	⚒	⚒		⑦	⑦	⑦	⑦	⑦	⑦	⑦	and at	⑦	⑦	⑦	⑦	⑦	⑦
Edinburgh Waverley d.	2030	2100	2130	2200	2230	2300	2330	⑦	0800	0830	0900	0930	1000	1030	1100	the same	2100	2130	2200	2230	2300	2330
Haymarket d.	2034	2105	2134	2204	2234	2304	2334		0804	0834	0904	0934	1004	1034	1104	minutes	2104	2134	2204	2234	2304	2334
Linlithgow d.	2049	2120	2150	2219	2250	2319	2349		0824	0854	0924	0954	1023	1049	1119	past each	2119	2152	2219	2251	2319	2350
Falkirk High d.	2058	2131	2159	2230	2259	2330	0001		0835	0903	0935	1003	1034	1058	1130	hour until	2130	2203	2230	2302	2330	0002
Glasgow Queen Street a.	2126	2151	2225	2251	2326	0001	0027		0859	0926	0955	1028	1055	1121	1151	☆	2151	2227	2251	2326	2354	0025

		⚒	Ⓐ	⑥	Ⓐ	⚒	⚒	⚒	⚒	⚒	⚒	⚒	⚒	and at	⚒	⚒	⚒	⚒	⚒	⚒	⚒	⚒
Glasgow Queen Street d.	⚒	0600	0630	0630	0645	0700	0715	0730	0745	0800	0815	0830	0845	the same	1800	1814	1830	1845	1900	1915	1930	2000
Falkirk High d.		0618	0651	0654	0707	0721	0734	0753	0804	0822	0834	0853	0904	minutes	1824	1834	1853	1905	1922	1934	1948	2022
Linlithgow d.		0629	0702	0705	0715	0732	0745	0800	0815	│	0843	│	0915	past each	│	1845	│	1916	│	1945	1959	2029
Haymarket ▽ a.		0645	0718	0720	0732	0750	0801	0818	0832	0846	0905	0915	0933	hour until	1844	1902	1914	1933	1946	2001	2018	2047
Edinburgh Waverley a.		0650	0723	0727	0737	0755	0806	0824	0837	0852	0911	0921	0939	☆a	1851	1907	1922	1940	1951	2007	2024	2052

	⚒	⑤⑥	①–④	⚒	⑤⑥	①–④	⚒	⚒	⚒		⑦	⑦	⑦	⑦	⑦	⑦	⑦	and at	⑦	⑦	⑦	⑦
Glasgow Queen Street d.	2030	2100	2100	2129	2200	2200	2230	2300	2330	⑦	0748	0830	0900	0930	1000	1030	1100	the same	2200	2230	2300	2330
Falkirk High d.	2049	2122	2122	2149	2222	2222	2249	2322	2352		0810	0848	0922	0949	1022	1048	1122	minutes	2222	2248	2322	2353
Linlithgow d.	2100	2129	2132	2200	2229	2232	2300	2333	0003		0820	0859	0929	1000	1029	1059	1129	past each	2232	2259	2329	0004
Haymarket ▽ a.	2115	2145	2151	2217	2246	2251	2315	2352	0020		0842	0920	0949	1020	1045	1115	1145	hour until	2251	2315	2345	0025
Edinburgh Waverley a.	2123	2150	2156	2222	2252	2256	2320	2357	0026		0847	0925	0954	1025	1050	1120	1150	☆	2257	2320	2350	0030

EDINBURGH - MOTHERWELL - GLASGOW CENTRAL

km			⚒	⚒	Ⓐ2	⑥2	⑥A	ⒶA	⚒2	⚒A	⚒2	⚒A	⚒2	⚒A	Ⓐ2	⑥2	⚒A	⚒2	⚒2	⚒A	ⒶB	⑥A	ⒶA	⚒2
0	**Edinburgh** Waverley d.	⚒	0624	0727	0740	0754	0914	0918	1019	1111	1153	1312	1352	1511	1549	1548	1711	1740	1826	1911	2017	2113	2114	2313
2	Haymarket d.		│	0731	0746	0758	0920	0924	1024	1116	1158	1316	1357	1516	1554	1553	1716	1746	1831	1916	2022	2118	2119	2317
71	Motherwell a.		0704	0812	0833	0900	0954	1002	1133	1152	1309	1353	1504	1552	1635	1704	1752	1834	1933	1953	2103	2159	2207	0021
92	**Glasgow** Central a.		0722	0829	0855	0923	1015	1025	1154	1212	1325	1412	1525	1612	1701	1723	1811	1854	1954	2015	2125	2220	2224	...

		⑦	⑦A	⑦A	⑦A	⑦A	⑦A	⑦A	⑦B
Edinburgh Waverley d.	⑦	1023	1217	1313	1510	1711	1918	2112	2122
Haymarket d.		│	1221	1318	1514	1715	1923	2117	2126
Motherwell a.		1103	1258	1353	1554	1755	1959	2156	2203
Glasgow Central a.		1128	1318	1412	1611	1812	2019	2213	2226

		⚒A	⚒B	⑥2	Ⓐ2	⚒A	⚒A	Ⓐ2	⑥2
Glasgow Central d.	⚒	0601	0650	0703	0705	0750	0900	0933	0948
Motherwell d.		0617	0706	0721	0721	0805	0915	0959	1004
Haymarket d.		0657	0748	0822	0829	0851	0957	1050	1113
Edinburgh Waverley a.		0701	0752	0829	0834	0858	1002	1054	1121

	⚒A	⚒2	⚒A	⚒2		⚒A	⚒2	⚒A	⚒A	⚒2	⑥	Ⓐ			⑦A	⑦A	⑦A	⑦A		⑦A	⑦A	⑦	
Glasgow Central d.	1100	1146	1300	1405	...	1500	1546	1700	1900	1948	2105	2105	...	⑦	1055	1200	1348	1455	...	1655	1900	2058	...
Motherwell d.	1116	1202	1316	1427	...	1516	1602	1716	1916	2006	│	2122	...		1113	1217	1404	1512	...	1712	1915	2118	...
Haymarket d.	1154	1249	1354	1519	...	1556	1705	1754	1954	2053	2154	│	...		1151	1256	1442	1552	...	1751	1959	2204	...
Edinburgh Waverley a.	1159	1258	1359	1524	...	1600	1711	1800	1958	2100	2159	2221	...		1156	1300	1447	1556	...	1755	2005	2208	...

OTHER SERVICES EDINBURGH - GLASGOW

EDINBURGH WAVERLEY – SHOTTS – GLASGOW CENTRAL

76 km Journey time: ±75 minutes (trains marked * ±90 minutes)

From Edinburgh Waverley:

⚒: 0552*, 0637 Ⓐ, 0641 ⑥, 0655*, 0757, 0825*, 0857, 0926*, 0956 and at the same minutes past each hour (⊡) until 1555, 1626*, 1656, 1720*, 1749, 1756*, 1856, 1926*, 2126* ⑤⑥ and 2256* ⑤⑥.

All trains call at **Haymarket** 4 minutes later and **Shotts** 38 minutes later (trains marked * 53 minutes later).

⑦: 1026, 1226, 1426, 1626, 1826 and 2026.

On ⑦ trains run **Edinburgh** to **West Calder** where a 🚌 connection is made serving **Shotts** and **Glasgow Central**. Journey time to **Haymarket** 4 mins; **Shotts** 78 mins; **Glasgow** 149 mins.

From Glasgow Central:

⚒: 0006* ⑥, 0616*, 0700, 0713*, 0803, 0817*, 0903, 0917*, 1005, 1017*, 1103, 1117* and at the same minutes past each hour until 1703, 1717*, 1802, 1816 ⑥, 1818 Ⓐ*, 1903 Ⓐ, 1907 ⑥, 1917*, 2117 ⑤⑥* and 2303 ⑤⑥*.

Trains call at **Shotts** 27 minutes later (trains marked * 36 minutes later) and **Haymarket** 59 minutes later (trains marked * 83 minutes later).

⑦: 0904, 1104, 1304, 1504, 1704 and 1904.

On ⑦ trains run **West Calder** to **Edinburgh**. A 🚌 connection runs from **Glasgow Central** calling at **Shotts** then **West Calder**. Journey time to **Shotts** 85 mins; **Haymarket** 160 mins and **Edinburgh** 164 mins.

EDINBURGH WAVERLEY – AIRDRIE – GLASGOW QUEEN STREET LOW LEVEL

71 km Journey time: ±74 minutes.

From Edinburgh Waverley:

⚒: 0607, 0621, 0638, 0648, 0707, 0720, 0737, 0749 ⑥, 0751 Ⓐ, 0808, 0821, 0839, 0849Ⓐ, 0852 ⑥, 0910, 0920, 0937, 0948, 1008, 1022, 1038, 1048, 1107, 1121, 1137, 1148, 1208, 1221, 1236, 1250 ⑥, 1255 Ⓐ, 1309, 1318 Ⓐ, 1321⑥, 1337, 1349, 1407, 1423, 1437, 1448, 1508, 1522, 1539, 1552, 1608, 1621, 1638, 1648, 1707, 1718 Ⓐ, 1723 ⑥, 1737, 1753, 1807, 1823, 1839, 1848, 1919 ⑥, 1922 Ⓐ, 1951, 2022, 2051 ⑥, 2054 Ⓐ, 2120 ⑥, 2123 Ⓐ, 2150, 2221 and 2250.

⑦: 0838, 0906, 0938, 1006, 1040, 1110, 1140, 1210, 1240, 1308 and every 30 minutes until 1809, 1840, 1940, 2040, 2140 and 2240.

All trains call at **Haymarket** 4 minutes later, **Bathgate** 25 minutes later and **Airdrie** 44–49 minutes later.

From Glasgow Queen Street Low Level:

⚒: 0545, 0601, 0616, 0638, 0647, 0707, 0717, 0738, 0747, 0808, 0816, 0838, 0848, 0909, 0918, 0938, 0946, 1007, 1016, 1038, 1047, 1109, 1117, 1138, 1147, 1208, 1216, 1238, 1247 and at the same minutes past each hour until 1808, 1817, 1838, 1847, 1908, 1938, 2008, 2039, 2109, 2138, 2208, 2238, 2308 **b** and 2338 **b**.

⑦: 0811, 0845, 0915, 0945, 1015, 1045 and every 30 minutes until 1815, 1845, 1945, 2045, 2145 and 2245 **b**.

All trains call at **Airdrie** 23 minutes later, **Bathgate** 40–45 minutes later and **Haymarket** 63–67 minutes later.

A – To/from destinations on Tables **120** and **124**.
B – To/from London Kings Cross (Table **180**).
a – 1730 from Glasgow also calls at Linlithgow (d. 1803).
b – Terminates at Bathgate.
☆ – Timings may vary by ± 5 minutes.
▽ – Trains call to set down only.
⊡ – Timings may vary by ± 2 minutes.

221 EDINBURGH - TWEEDBANK

2nd class SR

km			Ⓐ	⑥	Ⓐ	⑥	⚒	⚒	⚒	⚒	⚒	⚒		⚒	⚒	⚒	Ⓐ	⑥	⚒	⚒	Ⓐ	⑥	⚒	⚒	⚒
0	**Edinburgh** Waverley d.	⚒	0543	0555	0622	0625	0651	0723	0753	0824	0855	0924	and at	1524	1552	1624	1652	1654	1722	1755	1823	1826	1854	1924	1954
13	Eskbank d.		0608	0614	0641	0644	0711	0743	0812	0843	0914	0943	the same	1543	1613	1643	1713	1715	1743	1814	1842	1845	1914	1943	2014
15	Newtongrange d.		0612	0617	0644	0647	0714	0746	0815	0846	0917	0946	minutes	1546	1616	1646	1716	1718	1746	1817	1845	1848	1917	1946	2017
43	Stow d.		│	│	0706	0709	0736	0808	0837	0908	│	1008	past each	1608	│	1708	1738	1741	1808	1839	1907	1910	1939a	2008	2039
53	Galashiels d.		0644	0646	0715	0718	0745	0817	0846	0917	0946	1017	hour until	1617	1646	1717	1747	1749	1817	1848	1916	1919	1948	2017	2048
57	**Tweedbank** a.		0648	0650	0719	0722	0750	0823	0853	0922	0950	1021	♤	1623	1650	1722	1751	1754	1821	1853	1921	1923	1952	2024	2053

	⚒	⚒	⚒	⚒		⑦	⑦		⑦	⑦
Edinburgh Waverley d.	2053	2153	2254	2354	⑦	0911	1011	and at	2212	2311
Eskbank d.	2113	2213	2314	0013		0930	1030	the same	2232	2330
Newtongrange d.	2116	2216	2317	0016		0933	1033	minutes	2235	2333
Stow d.	2138	2238	2339	0038		0955	1055	past each	2257	2355
Galashiels d.	2147	2247	2348	0047		1004	1104	hour until	2306	0004
Tweedbank a.	2153	2253	2354	0052		1008	1108	♡	2310	0008

		Ⓐ	⑥	⚒	Ⓐ	⑥	Ⓐ	⑥	⚒	⚒	Ⓐ
Tweedbank d.	⚒	0520	0530	0558	0628	0629	0658	0700	0728	0758	0828
Galashiels d.		0524	0534	0602	0632	0633	0702	0704	0732	0802	0832
Stow d.		0533	0543	0611	0641	0642	0711	0713	0741	0811a	0841
Newtongrange d.		0553	0603	0631	0701	0702	0731	0733	0801	0831	0901
Eskbank d.		0556	0606	0634	0704	0705	0734	0736	0804	0834	0904
Edinburgh Waverley a.		0615	0625	0656	0728	0724	0759	0755	0824	0854	0923

	⑥	⚒	⚒	⚒	⚒		⚒	⚒	Ⓐ	⑥	Ⓐ	⑥	⚒	Ⓐ	⑥	⚒	⚒	⚒		⑦	⑦		⑦	⑦
Tweedbank d.	0831	0859	0930	0959	1029	and at	1730	1759	1828	1832	1859	1903	1931	2029	2032	2129	2229	2328	⑦	0845	0945	and at	2145	2246
Galashiels d.	0835	0903	0934	1003	1033	the same	1734	1803	1832	1836	1903	1907	1935	2033	2036	2133	2233	2332		0849	0949	the same	2149	2250
Stow d.	0844	│	0943	│	1042	minutes	1743	│	1841	1845	│	│	1944	2042	2045	2142	2242	2341		0858	0958	minutes	2158	2259
Newtongrange d.	0904	0931	1003	1031	1102	past each	1803	1831	1901	1905	1931	1935	2004	2102	2105	2202	2302	0001		0918	1018	past each	2218	2319
Eskbank d.	0907	0934	1006	1034	1105	hour until	1806	1834	1904	1908	1934	1938	2007	2105	2108	2205	2305	0004		0921	1021	hour until	2221	2322
Edinburgh Waverley a.	0926	0956	1028	1056	1128b	♤c	1829	1856	1925	1931	1954	1959	2027	2124	2127	2228	2326	0026		0940	1040	♡	2240	2341

a – Not ⑥.
b – Arrives 1124 on Ⓐ.
c – The 1557 and 1658 departures also call at Stow on Ⓐ.
♤ – Timings may vary by ± 4 minutes.
♡ – Timings may vary by ± 2 minutes.

GR, SR, XC ⊤ on most trains EDINBURGH and GLASGOW - DUNDEE - ABERDEEN

km		✕✕ B	✕✕ A			2			2		2			⑦		E			Ⓐ	⑥	⑦		⑥	Ⓐ	⑦
0	Edinburgh Waverley d.	...	...	...	0530	...	0630	0700	0728	...	0733	0800	0804	0828	...	0832	0900	0910	0930	0915	...	...			
2	Haymarket d.	...	...	...	0534	...	0634	0704	0733	...	0738	0804	0808	0833	...	0836	0904	0915	0934	0920	...	...			
42	Kirkcaldy d.	...	0520	...	0603	...	0706	0736	0802	...	0812	0836	0840	...	...	0907	0930	0950	...	...	1006	...			
54	Markinch d.	...	...	...	0612	...	0715	0745	...	...	0822	0845	...	...	...	0916	0945	...	...	...	1016	...			
82	Leuchars △ d.	...	0548	...	0633	...	...	0806	0825	...	...	0909	0906	0925	...	...	1005	1014	...	1023	1037	...			
	Glasgow Queen Street d.	...	...	...	...	0556	...	...	0742	...	...	...	0841	...	...	...	...	...	...	0941	0941	0937			
	Stirling d.	...	...	...	...	0625	...	...	0809u	...	...	...	0908	...	...	...	...	...	...	1008	1008	1010			
	Perth d.	...	...	0600	...	0700	0746	...	0842	0857	...	...	0942	0949	...	...	...	...	1040	1040	1047				
95	Dundee d.	0539a	0611	0625	0642	0652	0723	0812	0822	0843	0904	...	0927	0920	0940	1005	...	1022	1029	1034	1037	1052	1102	1102	1111
112	Carnoustie d.	0559a	0625	0640	...	0704	0735	...	...	0916	...	...	...	...	...	...	...	...	...				1117	1117	1126
123	Arbroath d.	0606a	0634	0647	0700	0712	0742	...	0859	0923	...	0936	0959	1021	...	1046	1051	1054	1109	1124	1124	1132
145	Montrose d.	0626	0650	0704	0715	0726	0757	...	0914	0938	...	0950	...	1040	...	1102	1105	1108	1124	1138	1144	1148
184	Stonehaven d.	0651	0715	0726	0737	0751	0821	...	0935	...	...	1010	1036	1102	...	1125	1126	1129	1146	1203	1212	1213
210	Aberdeen a.	0714	0739	0749	0757	0813	0847	...	0955	1017	...	1029	1055	1124	...	1147	1146	1149	1210	1223	1235	1237

	⑦ E	2		C	E	⑦		2	2			⑦		2			⑦	2		⑦	2		⑦	⑦
Edinburgh Waverley d.	0933	0935	1000	1028	...	1036	...	1050	1100	1131	1132	...	1136	...	1200	1230	...	1236	1203	...	1300	1327	1306	...	...
Haymarket d.	0937	0939	1004	1033	...	1041u	...	1054	1104	1135	1136	...	1141	...	1204	1234	...	1241	1245	...	1304	1334	1338	...	...
Kirkcaldy d.	1012	1013	1036	1105	...	1113u	...	1123	1136	...	1208	...	1213	...	1236	...	...	1313	1313	...	1336	...	1410	...	...
Markinch d.	1022	1022	1045	...	...	1122	...	...	1145	...	1217	...	1222	...	1245	...	...	1322	...	...	1345	...	1419	...	...
Leuchars △ d.			1105	1130	...	...	...	1147	1205	1224	1239	...	...	1305	1323	...	...	1337	...	1405	1423	1441	...
Glasgow Queen Street d.				1041	1045	...	...	...	...	1141	...	1145	...	...	1241	...	...	1245	...	...	1341	1345
Stirling d.				1109	1111	...	...	...	...	1207	...	1211	...	...	1307	...	...	1311	...	...	1408	1413
Perth d.	1054	1056	...	1139	1154	1142	...	1205	1210	1221	1240	1255	1237	1256	1246	...	1339	1355	...	1342	...	1438	1450
Dundee d.	...	...	1122	1144	1202	...	1205	1210	1221	1240	1255	1300	...	1310	1321	1339	1402	...	1351	1407	1421	1437	1457	1502	1513
Carnoustie d.	...	...	...	...	...	...	...	...	...	...	1312	...	...	...	...	...	...	...	...	...	...	1517	1525
Arbroath d.	...	...	1202	1218	...	1227	...	1256	...	1319	...	1326	...	1355	1418	...	1407	1423	...	1454	...	1524	1532
Montrose d.	...	...	1218	1233	...	1241	...	...	1333	...	1341	...	1410	1433	...	1421	1439	...	...	1541	1548
Stonehaven d.	...	...	1241	...	...	1303	...	1330	...	...	1402	...	1431	1454	...	1445	1500	...	1527	...	1610
Aberdeen a.	...	...	1303	1313	...	1323	...	1351	...	1415	...	1422	...	1450	1514	...	1505	1520	...	1549	...	1626	1633

	✕✕ E	⑦ E	✕✕ C	2	✕✕ C	⑦ F	2	2	✕✕ 2	2	⑦	✕✕ 2	2	✕✕ E	2		2	Ⓐ	⑥	⑦	✕✕ CE	✕✕ 2
Edinburgh Waverley d.	1334	1356	1400	1428	1433	...	1435	1500	1528	1534	...	...	1535	1550	1600	1605	1629	...	1632	1633
Haymarket d.	1340u	1400	1404	1433	1439	...	1441	1504	1534	1538	...	1540	1554	1604	1609	1633u	...	1637	1638
Kirkcaldy d.	1411u	1432	1436	1506	1511	...	1513	1536	...	1610	...	1613	1626	1636	1639	...	...	1713
Markinch d.	1420	...	1445	...	...	...	1522	1545	...	1621	...	1622	1635	1645	1649	...	1722
Leuchars △ d.		...	1505	1531	1536	...	1605	1623	1642	...	1706	1709	1724	...
Glasgow Queen Street d.				...	1441	1449	...	...	1541	...	1545	...	...	1611	1641	1641	1645
Stirling d.				...	1507	1518	...	...	1612	...	...	1639	...	1711	1711	1722
Perth d.	1450	1509	...	1540	1552	1555	...	1636	...	1647	1655	1707	...	1719	1741	1741	1741	1758	1754
Dundee d.	...	...	1521	1548	1550	1602	1615	...	1622	1639	1658	1658	...	1710	...	1724	1723	1740	1747	1804	1804	1802	...
Carnoustie d.	...	...	...	...	1614	...	...	...	1710	...	...	1737	1804	1816	1816
Arbroath d.	...	...	1605	1608	1621	1631	...	1655	...	1726	...	1744	1756	1812	1823	1823	1819
Montrose d.	...	...	1621	1636	1645	...	1709	1732	1741	...	1759	1812	...	1837	...
Stonehaven d.	...	...	1644	1647	...	1707	...	1733	1753	1805	...	1822	1837	...	1856	1856	1858
Aberdeen a.	...	...	1707	1708	1715	1726	...	1753	...	1813	1825	...	1842	1901	...	1916	1916	1918

	✕✕ 2	⑦ 2	✕✕	⑦ 2			2	2	✕✕ E	D	D	C	C	✕✕	2	✕✕ E	2	2	2	Ⓐ	⑥	⑦	✕✕ C	✕✕ B
Edinburgh Waverley d.	1700	1704	1734	1736	...	...	1741	1750	1804	1806	1811	1810	1813	1833	1836	...	1837c	1855	1900	...	1915	1925	1931	...
Haymarket d.	1705	1709	1738	1741	...	...	1745u	1754	1808	1811	1815	1815	1816	1838	1841	...	1844	1859	1904	...	1919	1932	1935	...
Kirkcaldy d.	1737	1739	1810	...	...	...	1816	1826	1840	1844	1847	1845	1913	1913	...	1919	...	1936	...	2002	...
Markinch d.	1746	...	1819	...	...	...	1826	1836	1850	1853	1857	1854	...	1929	2003	1945	...	2011	...
Leuchars △ d.	1809	1804	1841	1834	...	...	1910	...	1914	1923	1915	1938	1937	...	2006	...	1909	...	2032	...	2029	...
Glasgow Queen Street d.				1703b	1741	1745	...	...	1841	...	1909	...	...	1941
Stirling d.				1745	1816	1813	...	1900	...	1907	...	1936	2015	...	2008
Perth d.				1825	1855	1845	1858	1906	...	1936	...	1943	2001	2035	...	2013	...	2038
Dundee d.	1825	1818	1857	1848	1856	1918	1909	...	1926	...	1930	1936	1931	1955	1952	2005	...	2022	2038	2048	...	2043	2100
Carnoustie d.	...	...	...	1919	1929	1921	...	...	2019	...
Arbroath d.	...	1835	...	1905	...	1936	1928	...	1949	1952	1947	2012	2009	2026	...	2059	2117
Montrose d.	...	1850	...	1922	...	1951	1944	...	2003	2006	2001	2028	2025	2041	...	2114	2131
Stonehaven d.	...	1912	...	1944	2015	2009	...	2024	2027	2023	2051	2048	...	2135	2155
Aberdeen a.	...	1935	...	2007	2035	2029	...	2042	2048	2042	2113	2110	2122	...	2156	2215

	⑦ E	✕✕ 2	Ⓐ D	⑥ D	⑦ C	✕✕ 2		⑦	✕✕ 2	✕✕ 2	⑦	⑤–⑥	✕✕ 2	⑦ 2	Ⓐ 2	⑦ 2	Ⓐ 2	⑥ 2	⑦ 2	✕✕ 2	✕✕ 2
Edinburgh Waverley d.	1941	2000	2015	2014	2032	...	2037	2100	2105	2143	...	...	2134	2150	2208	2225	2237	2237	...	2309	2319
Haymarket d.	1945	2004	2018	2018	2037	...	2041	2105	2109	2147	...	2139	2155	2212	2229	2241u	2241	...	2313	2323
Kirkcaldy d.	2017	2047	...	2054	2111	...	2135	2135	2151	2215	...	...	2255	2312	2324	...	2356	...
Markinch d.	2026	2056	2103	2104	...	2124	2144	2200	...	2256	2306	2321	2333	...	0005	0024
Leuchars △ d.	...	2116	2127	2128	2139	...	2205	2222	2239	...	2328	2342	...	0025	
Glasgow Queen Street d.	1945	...	...	2041	...	2142	2145	...	2248	2248	2337	2345	...
Stirling d.	2012	...	2108	...	2208	2212	2225	...	2333	2333	0005	0020	...
Perth d.	2047	2100	...	2143	2157	...	2241	2247	2304	2333	...	2357	0005	0013	0009	0044	0057	...	0057
Dundee d.	2110	...	2132	2142	2143	2153	2209	...	2221	2238	2253	2310	...	2344	2358	...	0036	...	0041	...
Carnoustie d.	...	...	...	2220	...	2320	2322	...
Arbroath d.	2126	...	2211	2227	...	2240	...	2309	2327	2329	...
Montrose d.	2141	...	2227	2241	...	2255	...	2324	2341	2344	...
Stonehaven d.	2205	...	2250	2302	...	2316	...	2345	0005	0005	...
Aberdeen a.	2225	...	2310	2322	...	2339	...	0007	0015	0025	...

A – Ⓡ. 🛏 1, 2 class and �car London Euston - Aberdeen.
  Departs London previous day. Train stops to set down only. See Table **161**.
B – To Inverness (Table **225**).
C – From destinations on Table **180**.
D – From destinations on Table **124**.
E – To Inverness (Table **223**).
F – On Ⓐ to Inverness (Table **225**):

a – Ⓐ only.
b – Departs 1711 on Ⓐ.
c – Departs 1842 on Ⓐ.
s – Stops to set down only.
u – Stops to pick up only.

△ – Frequent 🚌 connections available to / from **St Andrews**. Journey 10 minutes.
  Operator : Stagecoach (routes 94, 96, 99).

222 ABERDEEN - DUNDEE - EDINBURGH and GLASGOW ☂ on most trains   GR, SR, XC

km		Ⓐ C	Ⓐ 2	⑥ 2	Ⓐ 2	☆ 2		D	☆ 2	☆ 2						⑦ 2	2F		G	⑦ 2	F	⑦ 2	
0	Aberdeen d	...	...	...	...	...	...	...	0526	0546	...	...	0633	...	0703	...	...	...	0740
26	Stonehaven d								0545	0602			0651		0720				0756
65	Montrose d								0610	0624			0714		0744				0817
87	Arbroath d								0625	0638			0727		0758				0831
97	Carnoustie d						0603		0645				0734		0805				0838
115	Dundee d		0553	0604	0632			0650	0658	0709	0738	0724	0752	0817	0820	0828		0845	0854
149	Perth d	0513	0518	0536	0614	0619		0656	0715			0801	0813	0841	0850	0850	0906	0915
202	Stirling d	0526	0554			0655		0717	0753				0844	0915		0939	0943
249	Glasgow Queen Street a		0634			0734			0834				0914	0948		1014	1018
	Leuchars △d					0617	0644		0712	0723	0751	0737				0841
	Markinch d	0544	0607	0646	0640	0711		0737	0747	0812	0759	0830	0903	0919
	Kirkcaldy d	0553	0616	0649	0721		0746	0741	0757	0821	0809	0840	0913	0925	0929
	Haymarket a	0611	0640	0703	0754	0735	0758	0814	0825	0817	0839	0858	0858	0920	0925	0956	1003	1018
	Edinburgh Waverley a	0617	0647	0708	0800	0740	0804	0819	0830	0823	0846	0906	0903	0926	0931	1002	1011	1023

		⑦ 2	☆ C	⑦ D	⑦ 2	☆ 2	☆ 2	CF	⑦ 2	☆	☆	☆	⑦ 2		H	☆ C	⑦ C	☆ 2		CF	F		
Aberdeen d		...	0752	0820				0842	0907				0924	0936	0947	0952			1030	1038		1103
Stonehaven d		0810	0838								0941	0954	1005	1010		1047	1120
Montrose d		0833	0859			0918	0946				1005	1016	1028	1033		1108	1114	1144
Arbroath d		0849	0915			0932	1000				1020	1030	1044	1049		1123	1128	1158
Carnoustie d						0939					1027	1036			1135
Dundee d		0907	0932	0924	0943		0954	1017		1032	1046	1054	1103	1107	1120	1128		1144	1150	1213	1217
Perth d	0916				0936	0957	1003	1016		1010	1102	1108	1116			1159	1202	1209	1212	1238
Stirling d	0951					1032		1044	1046			1143	1144		1235		1243	1243	1313
Glasgow Queen Street a						1115					1214	1216			1314	1315	1348
Leuchars △d		0921	0946	0937	0956			1030		1045		1117	1123	1133	1141			1230
Markinch d		1009	0959	1019	1005		1032		1106	1132		1155	1202	1231
Kirkcaldy d	0945	1017	1009	1028		1042		1116	1141		1141	1147	1205	1212	1241
Haymarket a	1040	1019	1049	1055	1109	1111	1112	1123		1126	1135	1158b	1217	1216	1220	1240	1249	1313	1319		1323
Edinburgh Waverley a	1045	1055	1100	1115	1116	1118	1130		1132	1141	1203b	1222	1222	1226	1245	1255	1321	1324		1333

		⑦ D	⑥ 2	☆ 2	⑦ F	⑦ F				☆ 2	☆ 2	☆ 2			⑦ 2	F		☆ 2	⑦ C	⑦ 2		⑦ F	⑦
Aberdeen d	1110			1129	1142	1147	1206				1229	1240	1247	1309		1331	1338	1347		1404	
Stonehaven d	1127		1145		1205	1224			1246	1256	1306	1325		1348	1356	1405		1420
Montrose d	1148		1208	1218	1228			1307	1320	1331	1347		1409	1418	1428
Arbroath d	1204		1222	1232	1244	1258			1322	1334	1345	1401		1424	1432	1444		1457
Carnoustie d			1239					1352		1439
Dundee d	1224	1234	1236		1243	1254	1302	1317	1320	1332		1343	1354	1407	1417	1434		1445	1454	1502	1513	1517	1515
Perth d				1255	1302	1305	1316				1402	1406	1415		1504	1508	1516		1537		1532
Stirling d					1338	1344			1438	1444		1542	1544	1614
Glasgow Queen Street a				1409	1416			1509	1516		1614	1618	1648
Leuchars △d	1237	1247	1249			1317	1330	1333	1345		1420	1430	1447		1516		1530	1528
Markinch d	1258	1308	1310	1323	1331		1355	1408		1446		1508	1531		1550	1600
Kirkcaldy d	1307	1318	1320	1332	1341		1342	1405	1416	1441		1518	1541		1541		1600	1610
Haymarket a	1337	1353	1357	1407	1417		1420	1423	1440	1453	1516		1518	1523	1555	1620		1618		1625	1635	1645
Edinburgh Waverley a	1343	1358	1404	1412	1422		1426	1428	1445	1458	1525		1523	1531	1600	1625		1625		1630	1640	1650

		☆ 2	☆	⑦ C	☆	⑦	⑦	⑦		☆ 2		☆	F	☆ 2	☆ 2		F	☆	⑦	Ⓐ	⑥	☆ 2		G	⑦
Aberdeen d		...	1431	1439	1452	1511	1528	1533			1602			1628		1627	1637	1709	1710		1736	1747	1818
Stonehaven d		1448		1510	1530	1544	1549		1619		1645	1645u	1655	1726		1752	1804	1836
Montrose d		1509	1515	1533	1551	1609	1610			1706		1710	1717	1751	1748		1817	1828	1859
Arbroath d		1524	1529	1549	1605	1623	1624		1655		1721		1726	1731	1805	1801	1821		1831	1843	1915
Carnoustie d			1536		1611			1702			1727	1838
Dundee d	1534		1545	1551	1607	1624	1643	1646	1649		1718		1721	1733	1742		1748	1750	1822	1818	1845		1854	1903	1932
Perth d		1600	1608	1613		1705	1711		1703		1722		1805	1806	1814	1814		1911	1926
Stirling d			1640	1641s		1738	1743			1837		1844	1843		1945	1958
Glasgow Queen Street a		1713	1718		1812	1817			1908		1916	1915		2017	2029
Leuchars △d	1547			1622	1637			1702		1731		1734	1746		1835	1831	1858		1946
Markinch d	1608	1629				1723	1732		1750	1756	1809		1835		1919	1940
Kirkcaldy d	1618	1638		1646	1702		1733	1742		1800	1806	1819		1845		1856	1929	1950		2011
Haymarket a	1653	1714		1720	1734		1817	1822	1827	1835	1841	1855		1920		1930	1928	2008	2027		2043
Edinburgh Waverley a	1659	1722		1726	1740		1823	1828	1832	1842	1846	1900		1926		1935	1933	2032	2032		2048

		Ⓐ C	☆ 2	☆ 2		Ⓐ	⑦ F	⑦ F				⑦ 2	☆ 2	☆	⑥ 2	☆ 2		F	⑥	☆	Ⓑ B	⑦	①–④	⑥	⑤
Aberdeen d	1818			1828	1912	1907				1936	1947	2007	2009	2042	2105		2129	2131		2143	2227	2227	2227	2323
Stonehaven d	1836		1849	1928	1924				1952	2005	2026	2025	2058	2121		2146	2149		2201u	2246	2246	2246	2342
Montrose d	1859		1912	1950	1945				2014	2027	2050	2046	2120	2145		2207	2210		2226u	2310	2310	2310	0006
Arbroath d	1915		1926	2006	1959				2028	2041	2104	2100	2134	2159		2223	2226		2244u	2324	2324	2324	0020
Carnoustie d			1933		2006				2107			2253u	2331	2331	2317	0037
Dundee d	1933	1916		1949	2023	2022	2042			2050	2101	2121	2119	2156	2216		2241	2245		2306u	2349	2349	2348	0045
Perth d			2002	2011			2106	2106		2111	2122		2217	2238		2243		0012	0012		0109
Stirling d				2042					2144	2150		2248	2310		2310
Glasgow Queen Street a				2115					2218	2221		2318	2343
Leuchars △d	1947	1929			2036	2035	2055			2134	2132		2229		2254	2258		2325u
Markinch d		1951	2032			2116	2133	2133		2157	2154		2251		2316	2319	2312
Kirkcaldy d	2011	2001	2041		2101	2126	2143	2143		2206	2203		2300		2324	2328		2354u
Haymarket a	2044	2047	2117		2129	2133	2211	2216	2221		2238	2248		2346		2357	2358	0022
Edinburgh Waverley a	2050	2052	2124		2136	2139	2216	2221	2228		2243	2253		2352		0002	0007	0027

OTHER SERVICES EDINBURGH and GLASGOW - STIRLING

From Edinburgh Waverley to Stirling: 75 km   Journey time: 54 minutes

☆: 0518, 0633 and every 30 minutes (☐) until 1933, 2033⑥, 2034⑤, 2134⑤⑥, 2135⑤, 2233⑤⑥, 2303⑥, 2304⑤, 2333⑤⑥.

⑦: 0934, 1035 and hourly until 1935 (also 1106 and hourly until 1806).

All trains call at **Haymarket** 4 minutes later, **Linlithgow** 22 minutes later and **Falkirk Grahamston** 35 minutes later.

From Glasgow Queen Street to Stirling: 47 km   Journey time: 45 minutes

☆: 0556, 0614, 0648, 0718, 0749, 0818, 0849, 0920, 0949 and every 30 minutes (☐) until 2248, 2319, 2348.

⑦: 1015 and hourly until 2215, 2345.

From Stirling to Edinburgh Waverley:

☆: 0530, 0637, 0717, 0749Ⓐ, 0807 and every 30 minutes (☐) until 1837, 1937, 2007, 2037, 2107⑤⑥, 2207⑤⑥, 2317⑤⑥.

⑦: 0905, 0951, 1110 and hourly until 1810, 1919, 2010 (also 1046 and hourly until 1646).

Trains call at **Falkirk Grahamston** 17 minutes later, **Linlithgow** 30 minutes later and **Haymarket** 50 minutes later.

From Stirling to Glasgow Queen Street:

☆: 0554, 0623, 0655, 0723, 0739, 0753, 0811, 0823 and every 30 minutes (☐) until 1723, 1751, 1819, 1853, 1923, 1953, 2021, 2053, 2123, 2153⑥, 2155Ⓐ, 2223, 2253.

⑦: 0926, 1026, 1125 and hourly until 2125, 2144.

B – ℞, ⇋ 1, 2 class and ⌫ Aberdeen - London Euston. Train stops to pick up only. See Table 161.
C – To destinations on Table 180.
D – To destinations on Table 124.
F – From Inverness (Table 223).
G – From Inverness (Table 225).
H – From Dyce (Table 225).

a – Arrives Haymarket 0916, Edinburgh 0921 on Ⓐ.
b – Arrives Haymarket 1151, Edinburgh 1156 on Ⓐ.
s – Stops to set down only.

☐ – Timings may vary by up to ± 5 minutes.

△ – Frequent 🚌 connections available to/from **St Andrews**. Journey 10 minutes. Operator: Stagecoach (routes 94, 96, 99).

SR EDINBURGH and GLASGOW - PERTH - INVERNESS 223

Most Inverness trains convey 🍷.

km		⚒	⚒ A	⚒ 2	⚒	⚒	⚒	⑦	⑦	⚒ 2	⚒	⚒	⚒	⑦ 2	⑦	⚒ 2	⚒	⚒	⚒	⑦	⑦	⑦ P	⚒ 2	⚒	⑦	⑦	⚒
0	**Edinburgh** Waverley d.	...	...	0630	...	...	0832	...	0933	0935	...	...	1036	1035	...	1136	...	...	1334	...	1356	...	1435	...	...	1550	...
2	Haymarket d.	...	...	0634	...	...	0836	...	0937	0939	...	...	1041u	1039	...	1141	...	...	1340u	...	1400	...	1441	...	...	1554	...
42	Kirkcaldy d.	...	...	0706	...	...	0907	...	1012	1013	...	...	1113u	|	...	1213	...	...	1411u	...	1432	...	1513	...	...	1626	...
54	Markinch d.	...	...	0715	...	...	0916	...	1022	1022	...	...	1122	|	...	1222	...	...	1420	...	|	...	1522	...	...	1635	...
	Glasgow Queen St. d.	...	...	|	0710	0841	|	0937	|	|	1010	1041	|	|	1111	|	1209	1341	|	1345	|	1438	|	1507	1545	|	1641
	Stirling d.	...	0455	|	0736	0908	|	1010	|	|	1037	1109	|	1126	1141	|	1237	1408	|	1413	|	1507	|	1537	1612	|	1711a
91	**Perth** d.	0508	0539	0745	0810	0941	0950	1046	1055	1056	1116	1138	1155	...	1217	1256	1313	1437	1451	1449	1513	1546	1555	1617	1646	1708	1740
116	Dunkeld & Birnam d.	0525	0600	...	0830	...	|	...	1111	...	1137	...	|	...	1235	...	1329	...	1508	...	1529	|	...	1634	...	1725	...
137	Pitlochry d.	0538	0616	...	0843	...	1022	...	1124	...	1150	...	1224	...	1248	...	1342	...	1521	...	1542	1613	...	1647	...	1738	...
148	Blair Atholl d.	0547	0628	...	0852	...	1031	...	1134	...	|	...	1233	...	|	...	1352	...	1530	...	1552	|	...	1656	...	|	...
186	Dalwhinnie d.	0613	0659	...	0917	...	1056	...	1158	...	|	...	1259	...	|	...	|	...	1555	...	1622	|	...	|	...	|	...
202	Newtonmore d.	|	0711	...	0927	...	|	...	1208	...	|	...	1309	...	|	...	|	...	|	...	1633	|	...	1728	...	|	...
207	Kingussie d.	0643	0719	...	0936	...	1109	...	1213	...	1235	...	1315	...	1334	...	1428	...	1608	...	1638	1657	...	1733	...	1822	...
226	Aviemore d.	0704	0743	...	0950	...	1123	...	1225	...	1247	...	1333	...	1346	...	1439	...	1619	...	1649	1710	...	1744	...	1833	...
237	Carrbridge d.	0719	0756	...	0959	...	|	...	1232	...	|	...	1341	...	1359	...	|	...	|	...	1659	|	...	1752	...	|	...
282	**Inverness** a.	0802	0838	...	1027	...	1158	...	1301	...	1329	...	1415	...	1427	...	1523	...	1654	...	1727	1745	...	1821	...	1908	...

	⚒ K	⑦	⑦ K	⚒	⚒	⑦	⑦	⚒ P	⚒	⑥	Ⓐ
Edinburgh Waverley d.	1632	...	1632	...	1741	1750	...	...	...	1941	1942
Haymarket d.	1637	...	1637	...	1745u	1754	...	...	...	1945	1946
Kirkcaldy d.	|	...	|	...	1816	1826	...	...	...	2017	2019
Markinch d.	|	...	|	...	1826	1836	...	...	...	2026	2028
Glasgow Queen St. d.	|	1645	|	1741	|	|	1811	1811	1941	|	|
Stirling d.	1723	1711	1722	1816	|	|	1840	1842	2008	|	|
Perth d.	1802	1738	1801	1852	1859	1906	1917	1921	2037	2101	2101
Dunkeld & Birnam d.	|	...	|	...	1918	...	1933	1938	...	2118	2118
Pitlochry d.	1831	...	1832	...	1931	...	1946	1951	...	2133	2133
Blair Atholl d.	|	...	|	...	|	...	1956	2001	...	2142	2142
Dalwhinnie d.	|	...	|	...	|	...	2019	2025	...	2207	2212
Newtonmore d.	|	...	|	...	|	...	2030	2035	...	2217	2223
Kingussie d.	1916	...	1917	...	2014	...	2035	2040	...	2222	2228
Aviemore d.	1929	...	1931	...	2026	...	2046	2052	...	2234	2239
Carrbridge d.	|	...	|	...	|	...	2054	|	...	2242	2247
Inverness a.	2004	...	2008	...	2101	...	2124	2126	...	2310	2316

	⚒ 2	⚒	⚒	⚒	⚒ L	⚒	⚒	⚒ 2	⑦ L	⑦	⚒	⚒
Inverness d.	0536	...	0650	...	0755	...	0845	...	0940	...	0941	...
Carrbridge d.	|	...	|	...	|	...	0916	...	1011	...	|	...
Aviemore d.	0612	...	0725	...	0830	...	0924	...	1019	...	1027	...
Kingussie d.	0627	...	0738	...	0843	...	0936	...	1032	...	1039	...
Newtonmore d.	|	...	|	...	|	...	0940	...	1037	...	|	...
Dalwhinnie d.	0640	...	|	...	|	...	|	...	|	...	1053	...
Blair Atholl d.	0712	...	|	...	|	...	|	...	1109	...	1114	...
Pitlochry d.	0726	...	0818	...	0924	...	1023	...	1123	...	1124	...
Dunkeld & Birnam d.	0739	...	0830	...	|	...	1034	...	1137	...	1137	...
Perth d.	0801	0813	0850	0915	0957	1016	1056	1102	1159	1209	1202	1212
Stirling d.	|	0844	|	0943	1032	1044	1129	|	1235	1243	|	1243
Glasgow Q St a.	|	0914	|	1018	|	1115	1213	|	|	1314	|	1315
Markinch d.	0830	...	|	...	|	...	...	1132	|	...	1231	...
Kirkcaldy d.	0840	...	0925	...	|	...	...	1141	|	...	1241	...
Haymarket a.	0920	...	1003	...	1112	...	...	1217	1313	...	1319	...
Edinburgh W. a.	0926	...	1011	...	1118	...	...	1222	1321	...	1324	...

	⚒	⚒	⑦	⑦	⑦	⚒	⚒	⑦	⑦	⚒	⚒ 2	⑦	⑦	⚒	⚒	⑦	⑦ 2	⚒	⚒ 2	⚒	⚒	⑦	⑦	⚒	⚒	⑦ B	Ⓐ B
Inverness d.	1045	...	1050	...	1243	1253	...	1330	...	1447	...	1522	...	1551	...	1624	...	1730	...	1846	...	1850	...	2015	...	2026	2044
Carrbridge d.	|	...	|	...	1315	1325	...	|	...	|	...	|	...	1627	...	1658	...	1807	...	1916	...	1922	...	2059	...	|	|
Aviemore d.	1123	...	1125	...	1323	1333	...	1406	...	1522	...	1557	...	1635	...	1710	...	1814	...	1928	...	1931	...	2107	...	2115	2134
Kingussie d.	1136	...	1137	...	1335	1345	...	1418	...	1534	...	1609	...	1647	...	1722	...	1826	...	1940	...	1943	...	2119	...	2129	2151
Newtonmore d.	|	...	|	...	1340	1349	...	|	...	|	...	|	...	1651	...	|	...	|	...	1945	...	1947	...	2123	...	2135	2157
Dalwhinnie d.	|	...	1151	...	|	|	...	|	...	1548	...	|	...	|	...	|	...	|	...	1957	...	1959	...	2135	...	2150	2211
Blair Atholl d.	|	...	|	...	1411	1420	...	|	...	|	...	|	...	1723	...	1755	...	|	...	2019	...	2021	...	2156	...	2215	2238
Pitlochry d.	1224	...	1220	...	1421	1431	...	1459	...	1617	...	1650	...	1733	...	1805	...	1906	...	2029	...	2031	...	2206	...	2229	2250
Dunkeld & Birnam d.	1237	...	1235	...	1434	1443	...	|	...	1634	...	1702	...	1745	...	1818	...	1918	...	2042	...	2042	...	2219	...	2243	2304
Perth d.	1302	1316	1255	1305	1454	1504	1516	1532	1608	1654	1703	1722	1805	1806	1814	1839	...	1938	2002	2106	2122	2106	2111	2238	2243	2306	2356
Stirling d.	|	1344	|	1338	1524	|	1544	|	1640	1729	|	|	1837	|	1844	1909	1919	2015	|	|	2150	|	2144	2310	|	...	...
Glasgow Queen St. a.	|	1416	|	1409	1558	|	1618	|	1713	1810	|	|	1908	|	1916	1941	|	2045	|	|	2221	|	2218	2343	|	...	...
Markinch d.	1331	...	1323	...	...	1531	...	1600	...	...	1732	1750	...	1835	...	...	|	...	2032	2133	...	2133	...	...	2312	...	...
Kirkcaldy d.	1341	...	1332	...	...	1541	...	1610	...	...	1742	1800	...	1845	...	...	|	...	2041	2143	...	2143	...	...	|	...	...
Haymarket a.	1417	...	1407	...	...	1620	...	1645	...	...	1822	1835	...	1920	...	...	2011	...	2117	2221b	...	2221	...	...	0022	...	...
Edinburgh Waverley a.	1422	...	1412	...	...	1625	...	1650	...	...	1828	1842	...	1926	...	...	2018	...	2124	2228b	...	2226	...	...	0027	...	...

A – Ⓡ. 🛏 1, 2 class and (2) London Euston - Inverness. Departs London previous day. Train stops to set down only. See Table **161**.
B – Ⓡ. 🛏 1, 2 class and (2) Inverness - London Euston. Train stops to pick up only. See Table **161**.
K – From London (Table **180**). Via Falkirk Grahamston (d. 1704).
L – To London (Table **180**). Via Falkirk Grahamston (d. 1046⚒/1249⑦).
P – To Elgin (Table **225**).

a – ⑥ only.
b – Arrives Haymarket 2216, Edinburgh 2221 on ⑥.
u – Calls to pick up only.

SR INVERNESS - ELGIN - ABERDEEN 225

km		⚒ A	⚒ 🍷	Ⓐ	⚒ C	⚒	⚒ 🍷	⚒ 🍷	⚒ 🍷	⚒ 🍷	Ⓐ	⑥	⚒ 🍷	⚒ 🍷	⚒	⚒	⚒	⑦ 🍷	⑦ 🍷	⑦ C	⑦ 🍷	⑦ B	⑦ 🍷	⑦ B
0	**Inverness** d.	0453	0554	...	...	0709	0900	1057	1246	1427	...	...	1529	1714	1813	2004	2133	0959	1233	1529	1713	1800	2103	2142
24	Nairn d.	0508	0609	...	...	0725	0916	1114	1301	1442	...	...	1546	1730	1828	2020	2148	1014	1248	1544	1729	1815	2118	2157
40	Forres d.	0519	0620	...	...	0737	0927	1125	1312	1453	...	...	1557	1741	1839	2031	2158	1025	1259	1555	1740	1826	2129	2208
59	**Elgin** d.	0533	0634	...	...	0752	0952	1141	1330	1509	...	...	1611	1759	1857	2047	2213	1039	1313	1609	1754	1841	2143	2223
89	Keith d.	0554	0655	...	...	0813	1011	1202	1349	1530	...	...	1635	1820	1919	...	2234	1100	1334	1631	1815	...	2205	...
109	Huntly d.	0609	0711	0746	...	0839	1026	1216	1403	1545	...	...	1650	1847	1942	...	2251	1120	1352	1646	1830	...	2221	...
130	Insch d.	0624	0729	0802	...	0857	1048	1235	1419	1603	...	...	1706	1902	1958	...	2306	1136	1408	1702	1851	...	2237	...
147	**Inverurie** d.	0637	0743	0816	...	0909	1100	1247	1431	1616	...	...	1719	1915	2010	...	2319	1148	1420	1714	1903	...	2249	...
164	Dyce ✈ d.	0651	0759	0829	0907	0921	1113	1302	1443	1630	1639	1705	1735	1929	2024	...	2332	1201	1435	1728	1917	...	2301	...
174	**Aberdeen** a.	0702	0811	0844	0918	0933	1125	1313	1455	1641	1650	1716	1746	1940	2035	...	2343	1212	1446	1739	1928	...	2313	...

	⚒	⚒	⚒	⚒ D	⚒ 🍷	⚒	⚒ 🍷	⚒ 🍷	⚒ 🍷	⚒ 🍷	Ⓐ	⑥	⑥ 🍷	Ⓐ 🍷 C	⚒ 🍷	⚒ 🍷		⑥ A	Ⓐ A	⑦ 🍷	⑦ 🍷	⑦ 🍷	⑦ 🍷	⑦ 🍷
Aberdeen d.	...	...	0614	0715	0819	0849	1013	1200	1338	1527	1619	1644	1721	1726	1822	2014	...	2156	2201	1000	1300	1522	1801	2127
Dyce ✈ d.	...	...	0623	0727	0830	0857	1022	1209	1347	1537	1629	1652	1732	1735	1831	2024	...	2205	2210	1009	1309	1531	1810	2136
Inverurie d.	...	...	0639	0743	0843	...	1034	1221	1359	1549	...	...	1750	1751	1844	2037	...	2217	2222	1021	1321	1543	1822	2148
Insch d.	...	...	0651	0755	0858	...	1047	1234	1412	1602	...	...	1803	1803	1857	2049	...	2229	2234	1034	1334	1556	1835	2201
Huntly d.	...	...	0713	0812	0914	...	1103	1250	1428	1618	...	...	1820	1820	1913	2107	...	2250	2255	1050	1351	1612	1858	2222
Keith d.	...	...	0727	0826	0928	...	1118	1305	1443	1640	...	...	1834	1834	1928	2121	...	2304	2309	1108	1406	1635	1913	2236
Elgin d.	0658	0723	0753	0847	0950	...	1140	1329	1508	1702	...	...	1857	1857	1950	2142	...	2325	2330	1129	1427	1656	1935	2257
Forres d.	0711	0743	0806	0902	1004	...	1153	1342	1522	1716	...	...	1913	1911	2003	2205	...	2339	2344	1142	1440	1710	1949	2311
Nairn d.	0727	0754	0817	0918	1015	...	1204	1353	1545	1731	...	...	1924	1922	2021	2216	...	2350	2355	1153	1451	1730	2000	2322
Inverness a.	0745	0812	0835	0936	1033	...	1222	1411	1603	1749	...	...	1942	1940	2039	2234	...	0008	0013	1211	1509	1748	2018	2340

Other trains **Inverurie - Dyce - Aberdeen**: On ⚒ at 0713, 0817⑥, 0846Ⓐ, 1038, 1133, 1333, 1524, 1638⑥, 1647Ⓐ, 1751, 1845, 1946, 2124; On ⑦ at 1102, 1255, 1458, 1620, 1730, 2122.
Other trains **Aberdeen - Dyce - Inverurie**: On ⚒ at 0750, 0958, 1103, 1250, 1457, 1552, 1652Ⓐ, 1754, 1912, 2055, 2250; On ⑦ at 1035, 1225, 1426, 1550, 1648, 2035.

A – To/from Edinburgh (Table **222**). B – From Glasgow (Table **223**). C – To/from Glasgow (Table **222**). D – From Dundee (Table **222**).

226 — INVERNESS - THURSO, WICK and KYLE OF LOCHALSH — 2nd class — SR

km																	⑦	⑦	⑦	⑦	⑦		⑦	⑦
			a	a		a	a					a					⑦							
0	Inverness........d.	0702	0855	1038	1100	1142	...	1335	1410	1450	1712	...	1754	1828	2106	2333		0940	1059	1253	1533	...	1754	2108
16	Beauly........d.	0717	0910	1053	1115	1157	...	1350	1415	1505	1727	...	1809	1843	2121	2348		0955	1115	1308	1548	...	1809	2123
21	Muir of Ord........d.	0725	0916	1059	1121	1206	...	1356	1423	1511	1733	...	1815	1849	2127	2354		1001	1121	1314	1556	...	1815	2129
30	Dingwall........d.	0740	0929	1112	1132	1218	...	1411	1437	1524	1747	...	1829	1905	2140	0007		1014	1134	1327	1609	...	1831	2142
49	Garve........d.		0952		1155		...	1433				...	1853					1158				...		
75	Achnasheen........d.		1018		1221		...	1500				...	1920					1225				...		
104	Strathcarron........d.		1048		1253		...	1530				...	1949					1255				...		
116	Stromeferry........d.		1105		1310		...	1547				...	2006					1312				...		
124	Plockton........d.		1117		1322		...	1559				...	2018					1324				...		
133	Kyle of Lochalsh........a.		1130		1335		...	1612				...	2031					1337				...		
51	Invergordon........d.	0758		1130			...		1454	1541	1804	...		1926	2157	0024		1032		1345	1626	...	1848	2200
71	Tain........d.	0817		1149			...		1513		1824	...		1945	2216	0043		1050		1403		...	1901	2218
93	Ardgay........d.	0833		1205			...		1529		1839	...		2001				...				...	1923	
108	Lairg........d.	0853		1221			...		1545			...		2017				...				...	1942	
136	Golspie........d.	0918		1246			...		1610			...		2042				...				...	2007	
146	Brora........d.	0929		1257			...		1621			...		2053				...				...	2018	
163	Helmsdale........d.	0947		1312			...		1636			...		2108				...				...	2033	
201	Forsinard........d.	1021		1346			...		1712			...		2142				...				...	2107	
237	Georgemas Jcn........a.	1045		1410			...		1736			...		2206				...				...	2131	
248	Thurso........a.	1059		1424			...		1750			...		2220				...				...	2145	
248	Thurso........d.	1102		1427			...		1753			...		2223				...				...	2148	
237	Georgemas Jcn........a.	1114		1439			...		1805			...		2235				...				...	2200	
260	Wick........a.	1131		1456			...		1822			...		2252				...				...	2217	

															⑦		⑦	⑦	⑦	⑦	⑦
						a					a	a			⑦						
Wick........d.			0618	0802			...	1234	1600		...			⑦		1158			...	
Georgemas Jcn........a.			0636	0820			...	1252	1618		...					1216			...	
Thurso........a.			0646	0830			...	1302	1628		...					1226			...	
Thurso........d.			0650	0834			...	1306	1632		...					1230			...	
Georgemas Jcn........d.			0703	0847			...	1319	1645		...					1243			...	
Forsinard........d.			0727	0913			...	1347	1711		...					1309			...	
Helmsdale........d.			0800	0946			...	1421	1744		...					1342			...	
Brora........d.			0816	1002			...	1436	1800		...					1358			...	
Golspie........d.			0825	1012			...	1447	1810		...					1408			...	
Lairg........d.		0628	0852	1038			...	1512	1836		...					1433			...	
Ardgay........d.	0616	0645	0907	1054			...	1530	1852	1928	...					1449			...	
Tain........d.	0632	0701	0923	1110			...	1546	1908	1946	2221	...	1055	1408	1505	...	2223
Invergordon........d.	0651	0720	0942	1131			...	1550 1606	1925	2005	2240	...	1114	1427	1524	1631	...	2242
Kyle of Lochalsh........d.			0612			1208	1346		1713			...				1512		
Plockton........d.			0628			1221	1359		1726			...				1525		
Stromeferry........d.			0640			1233	1411		1738			...				1537		
Strathcarron........d.			0659			1252	1430		1757			...				1556		
Achnasheen........d.			0727			1320	1501		1825			...				1624		
Garve........d.			0754			1347	1527		1852			...				1651		
Dingwall........d.	0710	0739	0817	1001	1153	1245	1410	1550	1610	1626	1919 1941	2024	2258	1135	1445	1543	1649	1714	2300
Muir of Ord........d.	0724	0752	0830	1014	1205	1258	1422	1603	1624	1638	1931 1952	2037	2311	1148	1457	1555	1702	1726	2313
Beauly........d.	0729	0758	0835	1019	1210	1303	1427	1608	1629	1644	1936	2042	2316	1153	1502	1601	1707	1732	2318
Inverness........a.	0744	0813	0850	1034	1225	1318	1442	1623	1646	1701	2000 2010	2057	2331	1208	1517	1616	1722	1747	2333

a — Conveys � on ①–⑤.

227 — 🚌 INVERNESS - ULLAPOOL - STORNOWAY — Valid until March 30, 2017

	①–⑥	①–⑥	①–⑤	①–⑤	⑥–⑦	⑥–⑦				①–⑥	①–⑥	①–⑤	①–⑤	⑥–⑦	⑥–⑦
Inverness........d.	0810		1500		1540	...		Stornoway........d.		0700		1400		1430	...
Garve........d.	0844		1534		1614	...		Ullapool........a.	0930		1630		1700	...	
Ullapool........a.	0930		1620		1700	...		Ullapool........d.		0950		1650		1720	...
Ullapool........d.		1030		1730		1830	...	Garve........d.		1032		1737		1802	...
Stornoway........a.		1300		2000		2100	...	Inverness........a.		1110		1810		1840	...

🚢 Latest passenger check-in for 🚢 is 30 minutes before departure.

Operators : 🚌 Scottish Citylink (service 961). www.citylink.co.uk. ✆ (0) 871 266 3333.
🚢 Caledonian MacBrayne. www.calmac.co.uk. ✆ (0)800 066 5000.

228 — 🚌 INVERNESS - FORT WILLIAM - OBAN — Valid until May 21, 2017.

Service number	19	19	19C	915	19	19	919	919	919	919	19	19
	①–⑥	①–⑤	①–⑥	⑦	①–⑥	①–⑥	①–⑥			①–⑥	19	19
Inverness bus station........d.	0520	0625	...	1045	1115	1245	1445	1645	1830	2015		
Fort Augustus bus stance..d.	0621	0726	0732	...	1143	1343	1543	1743	1931	2116		
Invergarry Jct..bus bay A82..d.	0633	...	0744	0948j	1153	1233	1353	1553	1753	1943	2128	
Fort William bus station......a.	0710	...	0847	1030	1235	1315	1435	1635	1835	2020	2205	

Service number			918				918					
Fort William bus station......d.	...	...	1100	...		...	1900	...				
Ballachulish Tourist Office......a.	...	...	1127	...		...	1927	...				
Oban Station Road........a.	...	...	1227	...		...	2027	...				

Service number	19	19	918	919	919	919	19B	19	918
	①–⑤	⑥	①–⑥		①–⑥	q	⑥		①–⑥
Oban Station Road........d.			0840					1640	
Ballachulish Tourist Office......d.			0939					1739	
Fort William bus station..a.			1008					1808	

Service number					919				915
					①–⑥				
Fort William bus station..d.	0720	0730	0900	1030	1215	1415	1520	1543	1840	2040
Invergarry Jct. bus bay A82..d.	0757	0807	0937	1108	1253	1453	1618	1620	1919r	2117
Fort Augustus........d.	0809	0819	0949	1118	1303	1503	1630	1632	...	2129
Inverness bus station........a.	0920	0920	1050	1216	1401	1601	1731	1733	...	2230

j – Picks up on A87 at Invergarry Hotel.
q – Operates ①–⑤ on school days (check locally for dates of running).
r – On A87 opposite Invergarry Hotel.

Operator : Scottish Citylink. www.citylink.co.uk. ✆ (0) 871 266 3333.

229 — ISLE OF MAN RAILWAYS — 2016 service — ✆ +44 (0)1624 663366

Please confirm all journeys locally as the exact service available may vary from that shown below

km	Manx Electric Railway	A	A	A	A	A	A			A	A	A	A	A	A
0	Douglas Derby Castle ‡.....d.	0940	1040	1140	1240	1410	1510		Ramsey........d.	1110	1210	1340	1440	1540	1640
4	Groudle........d.	0952	1052	1152	1252	1422	1522		Laxey........d.	1155	1255	1425	1525	1625	1725
11	Laxey........d.	1010	1110	1210	1310	1440	1540		Groudle........d.	1213	1313	1443	1543	1643	1743
29	Ramsey........a.	1055	1155	1255	1355	1525	1625		Douglas Derby Castle ‡.....a.	1225	1325	1455	1555	1655	1755

km	Snaefell Mountain Railway	B	B	B	B	B	B	B			B	B	B	B	B	B	B
0	Laxey........d.	1015	1115	1215	1315	1400	1455	1545		Summit........d.	1120	1225	1325	1425	1510	1605	1655
5	Summit........a.	1045	1145	1245	1345	1430	1525	1615		Laxey........a.	1150	1255	1355	1455	1540	1635	1725

km	Isle of Man Steam Railway	C	C	C	D			D			C	C	C	D
0	Douglas Railway Station ‡..d.	0950	...	1350	1550	...	1900		Port Erin........d.	...	1130	...	2115
9	Santon........d.	1011	...	1411	1611	...	...		Castletown........d.	...	1157	1427	1627	...	2142
16	Castletown........d.	1027	...	1427	1627	...	1947		Santon........d.	...	1217	1447	1647	...	...
25	Port Erin........a.	1050	...	...	...	...	2015		Douglas Railway Station ‡...a.	...	1235	1505	1705	...	2230

A — Mar. 18 - Sept. 30 (also ⑥⑦ in Oct.). Minimum service shown. Additional services operate on most dates. A reduced service operates on ②③④ in Oct.
B — Mar. 24 - Oct. 30 (not Oct. 3, 7, 10, 14, 17, 21). Minimum service shown. Additional services operate on most dates June - September.
C — Mar. 5 - Nov. 6. **Does not run every day.** Enhanced services with different timetables operate on most ④⑥⑦ in July and ④⑤⑥⑦ in August and on certain other dates.
D — ④ until Nov. 3.
‡ — 🚌 services 1, 1H, 2A, 12, 12A, connect Derby Castle and Lord Street Bus Station which is near the Steam Railway Station.

IRELAND

SEE MAP PAGE 90

Operators: Iarnród Éireann (**IÉ**), www.irishrail.ie Northern Ireland Railways (**NIR**), www.translink.co.uk Bus Éireann, www.buseireann.ie Ulsterbus, www.translink.co.uk and Dublin Area Rapid Transit (**DART**), www.irishrail.ie Most cross-border services are jointly operated.

Timings: **Rail**: **NIR** services are valid until further notice. **IÉ** services are valid from Nov. 20, 2016 until further notice. **DART** services are valid until further notice.
Bus: **Ulsterbus** services are valid until further notice. **Bus Éireann** services are valid until further notice.

Rail services: Except for *Enterprise* cross-border expresses (for details, see Table 230 below), **all trains** convey *Standard* (2nd) class seating. Most express trains in the Republic of Ireland, as noted in the tables, also have first class accommodation.
On public holiday dates in the **Republic of Ireland**, DART trains run as on Sundays; outer-suburban services to or from Drogheda and Dundalk do not run. Other services may be amended, though most main-line trains run normally. All services are subject to alteration during the Christmas, New Year and Easter holiday periods.

Bus services: **Bus Éireann** and **Ulsterbus**: services are shown in detail where there is no comparable rail service; only basic information is given for other routes. Buses do not always call at the rail station, but usually stop nearby. Where possible the stop details are given in the station bank or as a footnote. On longer routes, a change of bus may be required – please check with the driver. At holiday times bus travellers should consult detailed leaflets or seek further information from the operator. **Bus Éireann**: ✆ +353 1 836 6111 (Dublin) or + 353 21 450 8188 (Cork); **Ulsterbus**: ✆ + 028 9033 3000 (Translink, Belfast). **Dublin Busáras** (bus station) is a 5 minute walk from Dublin Connolly station.
The Dublin Tram service (Luas) connects Dublin Connolly and Heuston stations at frequent intervals. Journey time is 14 minutes, depending on traffic conditions. See Dublin City Plan on page 29.

BELFAST - DUNDALK - DUBLIN 230

NIR, IÉ

Enterprise express trains (*E*) convey Standard (2nd) class and Premium (1st) class seating, 🍸 (Café Bar and trolley service) and 🍴 (at-seat meal service in Premium)

km		Ⓐ	Ⓐ	Ⓐ 2	⑥	Ⓐ	🍴 *E*	⑥	🍴	🍴 *E*	🍴	🍴	🍴	🍴 *E*	🍴	🍴	🍴 *E*	🍴	🍴	🍴 *E*	🍴	⑤ 2	⑥	Ⓐ	🍴 *E*	🍴	Ⓐ
0	**Belfast** Central § d.	...	...	...	...	0625t	0645	...	0735x	0800	...	...	1010z	1035	...	1210z	1235	...	1340z	1405	...	...	1600t	1601t	1605	...	1709
13	Lisburn § d.	...	...	...	...	0648	|	...	0758	|	...	...	1032	|	...	1232	|	...	1402	|	...	...	1610	1612	|	...	1732
42	Portadown § d.	...	...	...	...	0714	0721	...	0825	0836	...	...	1058	1109	...	1258	1309	...	1428	1441	...	...	1636	1638	1641	...	1802
71	Newry d.	...	...	0630	...	▬	0742	...	▬	0857	...	...	...	1130	...	...	1330	...	...	1502	...	...	▬	▬	1702	...	1825
95	**Dundalk** d.	0540	0630	0659	0705	🍴	0800	0815	Ⓐ	0915	1010	1100	...	1147	1250	...	1347	...	...	1520	...	1605	🍴	🍴	1720	...	...
131	Drogheda d.	0604	0655	0720	0729	0800	0822	0839	0835	|	1034	1124	...	1208	1314	...	1408	1417	...	1541	1605	1630	1700	1730	1741	1800	...
148	Balbriggan d.	0619	0712	|	0746	0815	|	0854	0851	|	1049	1138	...	|	1329	...	|	1433	...	|	1621	|	1716	|	|	1815	...
154	Skerries d.	0626	0719	|	0752	0821	|	0900	0857	|	1055	1144	...	|	1335	...	|	1439	...	|	1627	|	1722	|	|	1821	...
168	Malahide d.	|	0736	|	0809	0837	|	0915	0912	|	1111	1159	...	|	1350	...	|	1454	...	|	1642	|	1737	|	|	1838	...
183	**Dublin** Connolly a.	0658	0759	0818	0830	0858	0900	0931	0930	1005	1130	1215	...	1240	1413	...	1440	1515	...	1620	1702	1714	1758	1813	1815	1857	...

	Ⓐ	🍴 *E*	🍴	🍴 w🍸	🍴	⑦	⑦ *E*	⑦ *E*	⑦ *E*	⑦ *E*	⑦ *E*
Belfast Central § d.	1801t	1805	1940t	2005	...	...	0900	1105	1305	1605	1905
Lisburn § d.	1812	|	2002	|	...	...	0913	|	|	|	|
Portadown § d.	1838	1841	2028	2041	...	...	0940	1136	1336	1636	1936
Newry d.	▬	1902	▬	2102	...	...	1001	1158	1358	1658	1958
Dundalk d.	🍴	1920	🍴	2120	...	0920	1019	1217	1417	1717	2017
Drogheda d.	1850	1941	2005	2141	2205	0945	1040	1240	1440	1740	2040
Balbriggan d.	1905	|	2021	|	2220	1000	|	|	|	|	|
Skerries d.	1911	|	2027	|	2226	1006	|	|	|	|	|
Malahide d.	1926	|	2042	|	2241	1021	|	|	|	|	|
Dublin Connolly a.	1945	2015	2100	2215	2301	1041	1120	1315	1515	1815	2115

	⑥	Ⓐ	Ⓐ	🍴 *E*	🍴	🍴 *E*	🍴	🍴	🍴 *E*	🍴	🍴	🍴 *E*
Dublin Connolly d.	...	...	0715	0735	0847	0930	1006	1035	1120	1117	1236	1320
Malahide d.	...	...	0730	|	0907	|	1025	1053	|	1142	1252	|
Skerries d.	...	...	0744	|	0922	|	1040	1108	|	1156	1307	|
Balbriggan d.	...	...	0750	|	0927	|	1045	1113	|	1202	1312	|
Drogheda d.	...	...	0804	0809	0945	1006	1103	1130	1156	1219	1329	1356
Dundalk d.	...	...	...	0831	1010	1028	▬	...	1218	1243	▬	1418
Newry d.	...	*0715*	...	0848	...	1046	🍴	...	1236	...	🍴	1436
Portadown § d.	0645	0740	...	0909	...	1108	1115	...	1258	...	1315	1458
Lisburn § a.	0708	0805	...	|	...	|	1138	...	|	...	1338	|
Belfast Central § a.	0740	0826	...	0945	...	1145	1159t	...	1335	...	1359t	1535

	🍴	🍴	🍴 *E*	🍴	🍴	🍴 *E*	🍴	Ⓐ	Ⓐ	⑥	🍴	🍴	🍴 *E*	🍴	🍴	🍴 *E*	🍴	Ⓐ	⑥	Ⓐ	🍴	⑦ *E*	⑦ *E*	⑦ *E*	⑦ *E*	⑦ *E*	⑦
Dublin Connolly d.	1336	1451	1520	1550	1621	1650	1653	...	1721	1721	1802	1840	1850	1920	2020	2050	...	2137	2207	2237	2337	1000	1200	1400	1600	1900	2122
Malahide d.	1354	1509	|	1609	1639	|	1712	...	|	1742	1827	|	|	1939	2038	|	...	2155	2225	2255	2356	|	|	|	|	|	2140
Skerries d.	1408	1524	|	1623	1654	|	1726	...	1751	1757	1841	1906	|	1953	2053	|	...	2209	2239	2309	0010	|	|	|	|	|	2155
Balbriggan d.	1414	1529	|	1629	1659	|	1732	...	1756	1802	1847	1912	|	1959	2058	|	...	2215	2245	2315	0016	|	|	|	|	|	2200
Drogheda d.	1431	1547	1554	1648	1716	|	1749	...	1813	1819	1904	1927	1928	2016	2115	2128	...	2232	2302	2332	0032	1032	1232	1432	1632	1933	2220
Dundalk d.	...	...	1616	▬	▬	1748	▬	...	1837	1845	1928f	...	1950	▬	...	2150	...	2256e	...	2356	*0059*	1054	1254	1454	1654	1955	2243
Newry d.	...	...	1633	Ⓐ	⑥	1806	🍴	1850	...	...	...	...	2008	🍴	...	2207	...	...	...	...	...	1112	1312	1512	1712	2013	...
Portadown § d.	...	...	1654	1705	1715	1828	1845	1915	...	...	...	...	2029	2045	...	2229	2235	...	...	...	...	1133	1333	1533	1733	2033	...
Lisburn § a.	...	...	|	1730	1738	|	1908	1938	...	...	...	...	|	2108	...	|	2258	...	...	...	...	|	|	|	|	|	...
Belfast Central § a.	...	...	1729	1739t	1748t	1905	1929t	2010	...	...	...	...	2105	2129t	...	2303	2319t	...	...	...	...	1208	1408	1608	1808	2108	...

e – ⑤ only.
f – Not ⑥.
t – Belfast **Great Victoria Street**.
w – Conveys 1st and 2nd class.
x – Belfast **Great Victoria Street**. On ⑥ depart 0740.
z – Belfast **Great Victoria Street**. On ⑥ depart 20 mins. later.
§ – Other local trains run Belfast - Lisburn - Portadown and v.v.

BELFAST - LONDONDERRY and PORTRUSH 231

NIR

km			Ⓐ	🍴	🍴		🍴	🍴	🍴	🍴			Ⓐ	Ⓐ			⑦	⑦	⑦	⑦	⑦	⑦	⑦		
	Belfast GVSt. ★ d.	...	0605	0710	0810	and at the	1910	2010	2110	2240	...		...	...	...	...	0920	1120	1320	1520	1720	1920	2120	...	...
0	**Belfast** Central d.	...	0615	0720	0820	same	1920	2020	2120	2250	...		1646	1746	...	...	0930	1130	1330	1530	1730	1930	2130	...	...
33	Antrim d.	...	0643	0747	0847	minutes	1947	2047	2147	2317	...	addi-	1714	1814	...	...	0957	1157	1357	1557	1757	1957	2157	...	...
52	Ballymena d.	...	0657	0803	0903	past each	2003	2103	2203	2330	...	tional	1728	1828	...	...	1011	1211	1411	1611	1811	2011	2211	...	...
97	**Coleraine** d.	...	0743	0843	0943	hour	2043	2143	2243	0005	...	trains	1810	1910	...	...	1052	1252	1452	1652	1852	2052	2247	...	...
107	Portrush a.	...	|	|	0955	until	|	2155	|	...	...	→	...	...	...	...	|	|	|	|	|	|	...	...	...
151	**Londonderry** a.	...	0825	0925	...		2125	...	2325	...	...		...	...	...	...	1134	1334	1534	1734	1934	2134	...	...	...

	Ⓐ	Ⓐ	⑥	Ⓐ	⑥	Ⓐ	Ⓐ	⑥	🍴	🍴		🍴	🍴	🍴	Ⓐ			⑦	⑦	⑦	⑦	⑦	⑦	⑦	
Londonderry d.	...	...	...	0605	0635	...	0713	0733	...	0933	and at the	...	1933	...	2133	...	...	...	0942	1142	1342	1542	1742	1942	...
Portrush d.	...	0605	0610	|	|	0705	|	|	0905	|	same	1905	|	2105	|	...	...	...	|	|	|	|	|	|	...
Coleraine d.	0550	0620	0623	0652	0721	0719	0819	0819	0919	1019	minutes	1919	2019	2119	2219	...	...	0828	1028	1228	1428	1628	1828	2028	...
Ballymena d.	0626	0700	0700	0730	0800	0800	0900	0900	1000	1100	past each	2000	2100	2200	2300	...	...	0904	1104	1304	1504	1704	1904	2104	...
Antrim d.	0644	0714	0714	0747	0814	0814	0914	0914	1014	1114	hour	2014	2114	2214	2316	...	...	0918	1118	1318	1518	1718	1918	2118	...
Belfast Central a.	0712	0739	0739	0816	0839	0839	0939	0939	1039	1139	until	2039	2139	2239	2341	...	...	0943	1143	1343	1543	1743	1943	2143	...
Belfast GVSt. ★ a.	0722	0750	0750	0825	0850	0851	0950	0950	1050	1150		2050	2150	2250	...	...	...	0953	1153	1353	1553	1753	1953	2153	...

km		Ⓐ	⑥	🍴	🍴	🍴	🍴	and at the same	🍴	🍴			⑦	⑦	⑦	⑦	⑦	⑦	⑦					
0	Coleraine d.	0550	0555	0645	0745	0845	0943	minutes past	2143	2245	...	...	0950	1055	1255	1455	1655	1855	2055	...	...	...	...	...
10	Portrush a.	0600	0605	0657	0757	0857	0955	each hour	2155	2257	...	...	1002	1107	1307	1507	1707	1907	2107	...	...	...	...	...

	Ⓐ	⑥	⑥	Ⓐ	🍴	🍴	and at the same	🍴	🍴	Ⓐ	⑥	Ⓐ	⑥			⑦	⑦	⑦	⑦	⑦	⑦	⑦		
Portrush d.	0605	0610	0703	0705	0803	0905	minutes past	2003	2105	2203	2223	2303	2305	...	...	1010	1210	1410	1610	1810	2010	2110	...	...
Coleraine a.	0616	0621	0715	0716	0815	0916	each hour	2015	2116	2214	2235	2315	2317	...	...	1022	1222	1422	1622	1822	2022	2122	...	...

★ – Belfast GVSt. (Belfast Great Victoria St.) is the nearest station to Belfast City Centre and the Europa Buscentre is adjacent.

Ulsterbus 212 express 🚌 service, Belfast - Londonderry. Journey time: 1 hour 40 minutes.
Ⓐ: 0630, 0745, 0830, 0900 and every 30 minutes until 1430, 1500 then 1520, 1540, 1600, 1620, 1640, 1700, 1720, 1740, 1800, 1830, 1900, 1930, 2030, 2130, 2300.
⑥: 0645, 0930, 1030, 1130, 1230, 1330, 1400 and every 30 minutes to 1800, 1830 then 1930, 2030, 2130, 2300.
⑦: 0830, 1000, 1130, 1330, 1430, 1600, 1730, 1930, 2030, 2130, 2215.

Ulsterbus 212 express 🚌 service, Londonderry - Belfast. Journey time: 1 hour 45 minutes.
Ⓐ: 0520, 0540, 0600, 0620, 0640, 0700, 0720, 0740, 0800, 0830 and every 30 minutes until 1630, 1700 then 1800, 1930, 2100.
⑥: 0700, 0800 and every 30 minutes to 1230, 1300 then 1400, 1500, 1600, 1700, 1800, 1930, 2100.
⑦: 0800, 0900, 1030, 1200, 1330, 1500, 1600, 1700, 1800, 1900.

232 🚌 BELFAST - ENNISKILLEN and ARMAGH — Ulsterbus **251**, **261**

From Belfast ★ to Enniskillen (Bus Stn) (journey time 2 hours 15 mins)
Ⓐ: 0805, 0905 and hourly until 1905, 2005.
⑥: 1005, 1205, 1405, 1505, 1605, 1805, 2005.
⑦: 1605, 2005.

From Enniskillen (Bus Stn) to Belfast ★
Ⓐ: 0725, 0825, and hourly until 1625, 1725, 1825 ◧.
⑥: 0725, 0925, 1125, 1225, 1325, 1525, 1725.
⑦: 1225, 1525, 1725.

From Belfast ★ to Armagh (Bus Stn) (journey time 1 hour 25 mins)
Ⓐ: 0800, 0945, 1045, 1145, 1245, 1345, 1445, 1645, 1715, 1745, 1845, 1945, 2115.
⑥: 1045, 1245, 1445, 1745, 1845, 2005.
⑦: 1335, 1735, 2015, 2200.

From Armagh (Bus Stn) to Belfast ★
Ⓐ: 0630, 0715, 0805, 0905, 1005, 1105, 1205, 1305, 1505, 1605, 1705, 1805.
⑥: 0730, 0905, 1105, 1305, 1605, 1705.
⑦: 1210, 1410, 1610, 1830, 2015.

Buses call at Portadown (Market Street) 40-75 minutes from Belfast and Portadown (Northern Bank) 20–30 minutes from Armagh (Bus Stn).

◧ – Change at Dungannon; arrive Europa Buscentre 2140.
★ – Europa Buscentre / Great Victoria St. Rail Station.

233 BELFAST - LARNE and BANGOR — NIR

From Belfast Central – Ⓐ: 0550, 0655, 0745 **H**, 0855 **H**, and hourly until 1355 **H**, 1455, 1523 **H**, 1555 **H**, 1644, 1714 **H**, 1744, 1825, 1925 **H**, 2025 **H**, 2125 **H**, 2225 **H**, 2325 **H**.
⑥: 0725 **H**, 0825 **H**, and hourly until 2225 **H**, 2325 **H**. ⑦: 0955 **H**, 1155 **H**, 1355 **H**, 1555 **H**, 1755 **H**, 1955 **H**, 2155 **H**.

From Larne Town – Ⓐ: 0558 **S**, 0628 **S**, 0653, 0735 **S**, 0800, 0858 **S**, 0958 **S** and hourly until 1458 **S**, 1553, 1625 **S**, 1706 **S**, 1736, 1828, 1928 **S**, 2028 **S**, 2128 **S**, 2228 **S**.
⑥: 0600 **S**, 0628 **S**, 0728 **S**, 0828 **S** and hourly until 2028 **S**, 2128 **S**, 2228 **S**. ⑦: 0858 **S**, 1058 **S**, 1258 **S**, 1458 **S**, 1658 **S**, 1858 **S**, 2058 **S**.

Trains call at: Carrickfergus 27-29 minutes from Belfast and 28-31 minutes from Larne and Whitehead 38-40 minutes from Belfast, 18-21 minutes from Larne.
Trains marked **H** arrive Larne **Harbour** 4 minutes after Larne **Town**. Trains marked **S** depart Larne **Harbour** 3 minutes before Larne **Town**. Journey time Belfast Central - Larne Harbour 57-65 mins.

A frequent train service operates between Belfast Central and Bangor. Journey time 30–31 minutes. 20 km. Approximate timings from Belfast ①–⑥: 2 per hour at xx12 and xx42 minutes past each hour, ⑦: xx42. Approximate timings from Bangor ①–⑥: 2 per hour at xx27 and xx57 minutes past each hour, ⑦: xx57.

234 🚌 DUBLIN - LONDONDERRY — Bus Éireann **33** / Ulsterbus **U274**

		A				A				
Dublin Busáras d.	0600	0800	1000	...	1230	1630	1815	...	2200	...
Dublin Airport ✈ △ d.	0620	0820	1020	...	1250	1650	1835	...	2220	...
Monaghan d.	0805	1005	1205	...	1435	1835	2020	...	2340	...
Omagh ▽ a.	0900	1100	1300	...	1530	1930	2115	...	0030	...
Strabane ▽ a.	0930	1130	1330	...	1600	2000	2145	...	0055	...
Londonderry a.	1000	1200	1400	...	1630	2030	2215	...	0120	...

									A	
Londonderry d.	0415	...	0700	...	1130	1330	...	1630	2200	0000
Strabane △ d.	0440	...	0730	...	1200	1400	...	1700	2230	0025
Omagh △ d.	0505	...	0800	...	1230	1430	...	1730	2255	0050
Monaghan d.	0600	...	0905	...	1335	1535	...	1835	0000	0155
Dublin Airport ✈ ▽ a.	0745	...	1040	...	1510	1710	...	2010	0130	0325
Dublin Busáras a.	0805	...	1100	...	1530	1730	...	2030	0150	0345

A – May 31 - Sept. 19. △ – Buses call here to pick up only. ▽ – Buses call here to set down only. ☛ The calling point in each town is the bus station unless otherwise indicated.

234a 🚌 DUBLIN - DONEGAL — Bus Éireann **30**

								⑦				
Dublin Busáras d.	0730	0930	1130	1330	1530	1730	1930	2100	2200	0000	...	...
Dublin Airport ✈ . △ d.	0750	0950	1150	1350	1550	1750	1950	|	2220	0020	...	...
Virginia d.	0855	1055	1255	1455	1655	1855	2055	|	2325	0125	...	...
Cavan d.	0925	1125	1325	1525	1725	1925	2125	2250	2350	0150	...	...
Enniskillen d.	1015	1215	1415	1615	1815	2015	2215	2335	0040	0240	...	...
Ballyshannon d.	1100	1300	1500	1700	1900	2100	2300	|	0125	0325	...	...
Donegal ⊡ a.	1120	1320	1520	1720	1920	2120	2320	0035	0145	0345	...	...

Donegal ⊡ d.	...	0100	...	0500	0700	0900	1100	1300	1500	1700	1900	...
Ballyshannon d.	...	0120	...	0520	0720	0920	1120	1320	1520	1720	1920	...
Enniskillen d.	...	0205	...	0605	0805	1005	1205	1405	1605	1805	2005	...
Cavan d.	...	0255	...	0655	0900	1100	1300	1500	1705	1900	2055	...
Virginia d.	...	0320	...	0725	0925	1125	1325	1525	1730	1925	2125	...
Dublin Airport ✈ ▽ a.	...	0445	...	0830	1030	1230	1430	1630	1835	2030	2230	...
Dublin Busáras a.	...	0505	...	0850	1050	1250	1450	1650	1855	2050	2250	...

● – Dublin **Busáras**. △ – Buses call here to pick up only. ▽ – Buses call here to set down only. ⊡ – Donegal **Abbey Hotel**.

235 🚌 LONDONDERRY - GALWAY and GALWAY - CORK — Bus Éireann **51**, **64**, **480**

	⚒									⑤⑦
Londonderry d.	...	...	...	0715	0915	1110	...	1530	1830	...
Letterkenny d.	...	...	...	0755	0957	1150	...	1610	1910	...
Donegal (Abbey Hotel) d.	...	0635	...	0840	1040	1240	...	1655	1955	...
Ballyshannon d.	...	0655	...	0900	1100	1300	...	1715	2015	...
Sligo d.	0600	0740	0800	1000	1200	1400	1600	1815	2105	2115
Ireland West Airport Knock d.	|	...	0905	1105	1305	1500	1705	|	...	|
Knock d.	0724	...	0924	1125	1324	1520	1725	1920	...	2230
Claremorris (Dalton St.) d.	|	...	|	1135	|	1530	1735	|	...	2240
Galway (Bus Station) ✣ a.	0900	...	1045	1240	1445	1635	1840	2040	...	2345

Galway (Bus Station) ✣ d.	...	...	0705	0805		1705	1805	1905	2005
Ennis d.	...	...	0820	0920		1820	1920	2020	2120
Shannon Airport ✈ d.	...	...	0850	0950	and	1850	1950	2050	2150
Limerick (Colbert Rail Station). a.	...	...	0920	1020	hourly	1920	2020	2120	2220
Limerick (Colbert Rail Station). d.	0725	0835	0935	1035	until	1935	2035	...	...
Mallow (Town Park) d.	0830	0940	1040	1140		2040	2140	...	...
Cork a.	0915	1025	1125	1225		2125	2225	...	...

Cork d.	...	...	0725	0825		1725	1825	1925	2055
Mallow (Town Park) d.	...	...	0800	0900		1800	1900	2000	2130
Limerick (Colbert Rail Station) a.	...	...	0910	1010	and	1910	2010	2110	2240
Limerick (Colbert Rail Station) d.	0725	0825	0925	1025	hourly	1925	2025	...	...
Shannon Airport ✈ d.	0755	0855	0955	1055	until	1955	2055	...	...
Ennis d.	0825	0925	1025	1125		2025	2125	...	...
Galway (Bus Station) ✣ a.	0945	1045	1145	1245		2145	2245	...	...

	⚒	⚒		⚒						⑤
Galway (Bus Station) ✣ d.	0600	...	0845	1030	...	1200	*1410*	1600	1810	...
Claremorris (Dalton St.) d.	0700	...	|	1135	...	1305	|	|	1911	...
Knock d.	0710	...	1005	1145	...	1315	*1530*	1725	1921	...
Ireland West Airport Knock d.	0730	...	1025	1205	...	1335	*1550*	1745	|	...
Sligo d.	0845	0855	1145	1310	1330	1500	1710	1905	2040	2100
Ballyshannon d.	...	0945	1232	...	1417	1547	1757	1952	...	2147
Donegal (Abbey Hotel) d.	...	1015	1252	...	1437	1607	1817	2012	...	2207
Letterkenny d.	...	1110	1340	...	1525	1655	1905	2100	...	2250
Londonderry a.	...	1145	1420	...	1605	1735	1945	2140	...	2330

✣ – Change buses at Galway. Minimum connection time 45 minutes.
☛ The calling point in each town is the bus station unless otherwise indicated.

236 DUBLIN - SLIGO — IÉ

km		⚒ 🍷		⚒ 🍷	⚒ 🍷	⚒ 🍷	⚒ 🍷	⚒ 🍷	Ⓐ	Ⓐ	⚒ 🍷		⑦ 🍷		⑦ 🍷		⑦ 🍷	⑦ 🍷	⑦ 🍷		⑦ 🍷		
0	**Dublin** Connolly d.	0800	...	1105	1305	1505	1600	1705	1715	1805	1905	...	0905	...	1305	...	1505	1600	1705	...	1905	...	...
26	Maynooth d.	0830	...	1136	1335	1535	1629	1734	1758	1835	1937	...	0932	...	1333	...	1534	1629	1733	...	1933	...	...
83	Mullingar d.	0910	...	1216	1416	1615	1715	1815	1844	1919	2023	...	1013	...	1413	...	1614	1714	1819	...	2016	...	...
125	**Longford** d.	0942	...	1247	1445	1646	1745	1846	1916	1950	2052	...	1043	...	1443	...	1644	1750	1849	...	2045	...	...
143	Dromod d.	1000	...	1259	1457	1658	1759	1901	...	...	2104	...	1056	...	1456	...	1656	1802	1904	...	2057	...	...
159	Carrick on Shannon d.	1016	...	1314	1513	1713	1815	1918	...	...	2121	...	1113	...	1512	...	1712	1817	1920	...	2114	...	...
173	Boyle d.	1028	...	1334	1534	1727	1834	1931	...	...	2133	...	1134	...	1534	...	1729	1836	1933	...	2127	...	...
219	**Sligo** a.	1109	...	1410	1610	1806	1909	2006	...	...	2209	...	1210	...	1610	...	1808	1910	2008	...	2204	...	...

	Ⓐ	Ⓐ	Ⓐ 🍷	⚒ 🍷	⚒ 🍷	⚒ 🍷	⚒ 🍷	⚒ 🍷		⚒ 🍷			⑦ 🍷		⑦ 🍷		⑦ 🍷		⑦ 🍷		⑦ 🍷		⑦ 🍷
Sligo d.	...	...	0545	0700	0900	1100	1300	1500	...	1800	...	...	0900	...	1100	...	1300	...	1500	...	1630	...	1800
Boyle d.	...	...	0617	0733	0933	1136	1333	1533	...	1834	...	...	0933	...	1133	...	1333	...	1533	...	1704	...	1835
Carrick on Shannon d.	...	...	0628	0745	0945	1148	1346	1546	...	1846	...	...	0945	...	1145	...	1345	...	1545	...	1717	...	1846
Dromod d.	...	...	0643	0800	1001	1202	1401	1601	...	1900	...	...	1000	...	1200	...	1400	...	1600	...	1732	...	1902
Longford d.	0540	0615	0657	0815	1016	1217	1416	1616	...	1919	...	...	1015	...	1215	...	1415	...	1615	...	1748	...	1917
Mullingar d.	0614	0649	0726	0845	1047	1253	1453	1652	...	1959	...	...	1051	...	1246	...	1452	...	1652	...	1819	...	1950
Maynooth d.	0657	0730	0810	0933	1128	1334	1534	1733	...	2040	...	...	1131	...	1327	...	1533	...	1733	...	1900	...	2038
Dublin Connolly a.	0736	0818	0847	1000	1158	1404	1604	1803	...	2108	...	...	1203	...	1355	...	1606	...	1800	...	1932	...	2109

236a BALLYBROPHY - ROSCREA - LIMERICK — IÉ

km		Ⓐ	⚒ 🍷	⚒		⚒h ◇🍴	⚒	⑦ ◇🍷	⑦		
0	**Dublin** Heuston d.	...	0900	...	...	1800	...	1825	...	...	...
107	Ballybrophy d.	...	0958	1005	...	1859	1905	1933	1940	...	...
123	Roscrea d.	...	...	1027	...	...	1927	|	2002	...	...
154	Nenagh d.	0745	...	1107	...	...	2007	|	2042	...	...
199	**Limerick** Colbert a.	0845	...	1205	...	...	2105	2042	2140	...	...

	⚒	⚒ 🍷		⚒	⚒ ◇🍷	⑦	⑦ 🍷			
Limerick Colbert d.	0630	0740	...	1655	...	1725	1820	...	...	...
Nenagh d.	0738	|	...	1750	...	1820	|	...	...	...
Roscrea d.	0818	|	...	1830	...	1900	|	...	...	...
Ballybrophy d.	0842	0845	...	1852	1855	1924	1927	...	...	...
Dublin Heuston a.	...	0955	...	...	2000	...	2042	...	...	...

h – 🍴 on Ⓐ, 🍷 on ⑥.
◇ – Also conveys 1st class.

IÉ DUBLIN - ROSSLARE 237

km		⚒		⚒ 🍷	Ⓐ	Ⓐ	⚒ § 🍷		⑦	⑦ 🍷	⑦ § 🍷	
0	**Dublin Connolly** ▲ d.	0940	...	1336	1637	1736	1838	...	1025	1345	1830	...
11	Dún Laoghaire ▲ d.	0958	...	1355	1658	1758	1857	...	1041	1402	1847	...
21	Bray ▲ d.	1017	...	1417	1717	1817	1917	...	1101	1423	1904	...
47	Wicklow d.	1040	...	1441	1742	1844	1942	...	1126	1446	1929	...
80	Arklow d.	1108	...	1510	1811	1916	2010	...	1154	1514	1957	...
97	Gorey d.	1121	...	1522	1824	1930	2023	...	1206	1527	2010	...
126	Enniscorthy d.	1142	...	1541	1844	1951	2042	...	1225	1546	2029	...
150	**Wexford** d.	1202	...	1604	1905	2012	2104	...	1248	1608	2051	...
160	Rosslare Strand d.	1219	...	1621	1919	...	2121	...	1304	1625	2108	...
166	**Rosslare** Europort a.	1226	...	1626	1925	...	2128	...	1310	1632	2115	...

	Ⓐ	Ⓐ y	⑥ y	⚒ 🍷		⚒ 🍷		⚒		⑦ 🍷	⑦ 🍷	⑦	
Rosslare Europort d.	...	0535	...	0720	...	1255	...	1755	...	0940	1420	1740	...
Rosslare Strand d.	...	0540	...	0724	...	1301	...	1801	...	0944	1426	1745	...
Wexford d.	...	0559	...	0743	...	1320	...	1820	...	1003	1445	1805	...
Enniscorthy d.	...	0623	...	0804	...	1341	...	1844	...	1024	1506	1827	...
Gorey d.	0555	0645	0645	0824	...	1401	...	1903	...	1044	1528	1847	...
Arklow d.	0608	0700	0700	0837	...	1413	...	1915	...	1057	1540	1900	...
Wicklow d.	0638	0733	0733	0904	...	1441	...	1942	...	1124	1608	1928	...
Bray ▲ d.	0704	0802	0802	0932	...	1503	...	2004	...	1147	1631	1953	...
Dún Laoghaire ▲ d.	0722	0820	0820	0950	...	1521	...	2022	...	1206	1648	2011	...
Dublin Connolly ▲ a.	0746	0846	0847	1015	...	1545	...	2044	...	1230	1710	2035	...

y – To Dundalk; see table **230**. § – Does not connect with Ferry: Rosslare - Fishguard. ▲ – Additional surburban trains (*DART*) run Howth - Dublin Connolly - Dún Laoghaire - Bray. Trains run every 10 - 15 minutes on ⚒, every 20 - 30 minutes on ⑦.

IÉ LIMERICK - WATERFORD 239

km			⚒ 🍷	⚒			⚒	⚒		
0	**Limerick Colbert** d.	...	0855	...	...	...	1745	...	...	...
35	**Limerick Junction** d.	...	0921	0945	...	...	1811	1840	...	...
40	Tipperary d.	...	...	0957	...	...	...	1852	...	...
62	Cahir d.	...	...	1020	...	...	...	1915	...	...
79	Clonmel d.	...	...	1037	...	...	...	1932	...	...
101	Carrick on Suir d.	...	...	1101	...	...	...	1956	...	...
124	**Waterford** a.	...	...	1126	...	...	...	2020	...	...

		⚒	⚒			⚒	⚒		
Waterford d.	...	0720	...	...	...	1625	...	...	...
Carrick on Suir d.	...	0745	...	...	...	1650	...	...	...
Clonmel d.	...	0808	...	...	...	1713	...	...	...
Cahir d.	...	0825	...	...	...	1730	...	...	...
Tipperary d.	...	0847	...	...	...	1751	...	...	...
Limerick Junction a.	...	0900	0940	...	...	1805	1834	...	...
Limerick Colbert a.	...	...	1014	...	...	...	1859	...	...

IÉ DUBLIN - GALWAY, BALLINA and WESTPORT 240

km		⚒	⚒ 🍷	⚒ 🍷	⚒ 🍷	⚒ 🍷	⚒ 🍷	⚒ 🍷	⚒ 🍷	⚒ 🍷	⚒ 🍷	⚒	⚒ 🍷	⚒ 🍷	⚒ 🍷	⚒ 🍷	⑦ 🍷	⑦	⑦ 🍷	⑦ 🍷	⑦ 🍷	⑦ 🍷	⑦ 🍷	⑦ 🍷	⑦ 🍷	⑦
0	**Dublin Heuston 245** d.	...	0735	0735f	0925	1125	1245	1325	1445	1535	1630	1710	1730	1815	1830	1935	0800	...	1135	1335	1435	1535	1635	1830	1845	2030
48	Kildare **245** d.	...	0801	0801f	|	|	|	|	|	|	1659	1739	|	|	|	|	0827	...	1203	1405	|	|	|	1902	1916	|
67	Portarlington **245** d.	...	0814	0814f	1002	1201	1322	1402	1522	1611	|	1756	1811	|	1913	2011	0840	...	1216	1419	1513	|	1714	1915	1929	2109
93	Tullamore d.	...	0830	0830f	1018	1218	1338	1418	1540	1631	1726	1813	1829	1906	|	2031	0856	...	1240	1443	1535	1632	1732	1933	1953	2125
129	**Athlone** d.	0730	0905	0908	1050	1242	1403	1444	1604	1659	1750	1848	1857	1927	1951	2100	0920	0940	1305	1509	1602	1658	1803	2000	2021	2151
152	Ballinasloe d.	0743	0921k	|	1105	1259	|	1459	|	1714	1807	|	1914	|	2008	2117	0937	|	1321	|	1619	|	1819	|	2037	2207
187	Athenry **242** d.	0816	0948k	|	1126	1323	|	1523	|	1737	1828	|	1935	|	2029	2140	1001	|	1346	|	1640	|	1848	|	2058	2227
208	**Galway 242** a.	0835	1010k	|	1150	1344	|	1543	|	1759	1848	|	1957	|	2050	2158	1022	|	1403	|	1707	|	1907	|	2118	2246
160	Roscommon d.	▬	...	0931	▬	...	1429	▬	1628	▬	...	1935f	...	1952	▬	...	...	1002	▬	1532	▬	1729	▬	2023	▬	...
186	Castlerea d.	...	...	0950	...	...	1448	...	1647	...	...	1954f	...	2011	...	...	...	1021	...	1552	...	1748	...	2043	...	...
204	Ballyhaunis d.	...	...	1003	...	...	1502	...	1701	...	...	2008f	...	2025	...	...	...	1034	...	1606	...	1802	...	2057	...	...
222	Claremorris d.	⚒	...	1017	⚒	...	1516	⚒	1715	⚒	...	2021f	...	2039	⚒	...	...	1048	⑦	1622	⑦	1822	⑦	2111	⑦	...
240	Manulla Junction § d.	0737	...	1031	1033	...	1529	1532	1728	1730	...	|	...	2052	2055	...	...	1102	1105	1635	1637	1835	1837	2124	2128	...
273	**Ballina** a.	0805	...	|	1101	...	|	1600	|	1758	...	|	...	|	2123		...	|	1133	|	1705	|	1905	|	2156	...
246	Castlebar d.	...	...	1037	...	...	1536	...	1735	...	...	2039f	...	2059	...	...	...	1109	...	1643	...	1843	...	2132	...	...
264	**Westport** a.	...	...	1055	...	...	1555	...	1755	...	...	2054f	...	2117	...	...	...	1130	...	1702	...	1900	...	2150	...	...

	Ⓐ	Ⓐ	Ⓐ 🍷	⚒ 🍷	⚒	⚒ 🍷	⚒	⚒ 🍷	⚒ 🍷	⚒	⚒ 🍷	⚒ 🍷	⚒	⚒ 🍷	⚒ 🍷	⚒	⑦	⑦ 🍷	⑦ 🍷	⑦	⑦ 🍷	⑦	⑦ 🍷	⑦ 🍷	⑦	⑦ 🍷
Westport d.	...	...	0520	...	...	0715	...	0945	...	...	1310	...	...	1815	...	...	...	0750	...	...	1315	...	1545	...	...	1745
Castlebar d.	...	...	0532	...	...	0728	...	0957	...	...	1323	...	...	1827	...	...	...	0803	...	...	1328	...	1558	...	...	1758
Ballina d.	...	...	|	...	0705	|	0935	|	...	1300	|	...	1805	|	...	2022	0740	|	...	1305	|	1535	|	...	1735	|
Manulla Junction § d.	...	...	|	...	0733	0736	1003	1005	...	1328	1330	...	1833	1835	...	2050	0808	0811	...	1333	1336	1603	1606	...	1803	1806
Claremorris d.	...	...	0550	...	▬4	0750	▬	1020	...	▬	1344	...	▬	1849	...	▬	▬	0825	...	▬	1350	▬	1620	...	▬	1820
Ballyhaunis d.	...	...	0603	...	...	0804	...	1033	...	...	1357	...	...	1902	...	...	...	0839	...	...	1404	...	1634	...	...	1834
Castlerea d.	...	...	0616	...	⚒	0818	⚒	1046	...	⚒	1410	...	⚒	1915	...	...	⑦	0853	...	⑦	1418	⑦	1648	...	⑦	1848
Roscommon d.	...	...	0634	...	🍷	0838	🍷	1105	...	🍷	1432	...	🍷	1934	...	Ⓐ	🍷	0913	...	🍷	1438	🍷	1708	...	🍷	1908
Galway **242** d.	...	0530	|	0630	0730	|	0930	|	1105	1305	|	1505	1720	|	1920	2215	0805	|	1100	1300	|	1505	|	1700	1800	|
Athenry **242** d.	...	0547	|	0646	0747	|	0945	|	1125	1322	|	1522	1738	|	1936	2231	0820	|	1118	1315	|	1522	|	1716	1817	|
Ballinasloe d.	...	0609	|	|	0807	|	1007	|	1147	1345	|	1547	1807	|	2009	2254	0843	|	1140	1342	|	1544	|	1740	1842	|
Athlone d.	0520	0627	0700j	0722	0825	0903	1024	1132	1205	1404	1458	1605	1824	2003	2026	2310	0901	0938	1158	1359	1506	1602	1740	1802	1902	1934
Tullamore d.	0543	0651	0722j	0744	0848	0929	1059	1159	1236	1438	1523	1636	1848	2031	2052	...	0931	1002	1221	1425	1534	1633	1807	1827	1932	2010
Portarlington **245** d.	0601	0709	0741j	|	0906	0947	1121	1222	1255	1505	1547	1651	1909	2050	2109	...	0949	1020	1239	1443	1552	1655	1826	1845	1951	2028
Kildare **245** d.	0615	0723	0756j	|	|	|	|	|	|	|	|	|	|	|	|	...	1002	|	1254	|	|	1709	1839	1859	|	|
Dublin Heuston **245** a.	0700	0759	0830j	0841	0947	1030	1200	1305	1340	1543	1630	1742	1954	2132	2147	...	1034	1105	1325	1527	1633	1740	1910	1935	2030	2110

✣ – An additional journey runs on ⑦: Galway depart 1925, Athenry 1942, Ballinasloe 2002, arrive Athlone 2020.
f – ⑤ only.
j – Also runs on ⑥.
k – Change at Athlone on ⑤.
§ – Passenger transfer point only.

IÉ DUBLIN - KILKENNY - WATERFORD 241

km		⚒ 🍷	⚒ 🍷	⚒ 🍷	⚒ 🍷	⑤ 🍷	⚒ 🍷	⚒ 🍷	⚒ 🍷	Ⓐ	⑦ 🍷	⑦ 🍷	⑦ 🍷	⑦ 🍷
0	**Dublin H** ◧ .. △ d.	0725	1015	1315	1510	1615	1640	1735	1835	2015	0910	1410	1745	1840
48	Kildare △ d.	0753	1042	|	1539	|	1717	1806	1905	2101	0940	1439	1814	1908
72	Athy d.	0813	1059	1358	1556	1702	1735	1825	1923	2116	0957	1458	1832	1927
90	Carlow d.	0827	1111	1412	1607	1714	1747	1837	1938	2128	1011	1510	1844	1939
106	Muine Bheag d.	0843	1122	1424	1619	|	1758	1848	1949	...	1025	1521	1858	1951
130	**Kilkenny** a.	0901	1140	1441	1636	|	1817	1906	2008	...	1043	1541	1917	2009
130	**Kilkenny** d.	0905	1145	1446	1640	|	1821	1910	2013	...	1047	1546	1921	2013
147	Thomastown d.	0916	1155	1456	1651	|	1831	1921	2023	...	1058	1556	1932	2024
179	**Waterford** a.	0940	1220	1525	1715	1810	1900	1946	2048	...	1120	1620	1956	2050

	Ⓐ	⚒ 🍷	⚒ 🍷	⚒ 🍷	⚒ 🍷	⚒ 🍷	⚒ 🍷	⑤⑥	⚒ 🍷	Ⓐ	⑦ 🍷	⑦ 🍷	⑦ 🍷	⑦ 🍷
Waterford d.	...	0600	0710	0750	1100	1305	1450	1600	1825	...	0905	1240	1510	1805
Thomastown d.	...	0619	|	0809	1119	1324	1511	|	1846	...	0924	1259	1529	1824
Kilkenny a.	...	0633	|	0824	1134	1339	1525	|	1900	...	0939	1314	1545	1839
Kilkenny d.	...	0637	|	0828	1141	1343	1530	|	1902	...	0943	1318	1549	1843
Muine Bheag d.	...	0651	|	0846	1155	1357	1545	|	1921	...	0957	1331	1603	1857
Carlow d.	0630	0703	0759	0858	1207	1411	1609	1652	1935	2135	1010	1343	1614	1908
Athy d.	0641	0715	0812	0910	1219	1423	1621	1704	1949	2145	1024	1355	1626	1926
Kildare △ d.	0658	0734	|	0928	1237	1441	1635	1721	2009	2200	1042	1416	1644	1945
Dublin H ◧ .. △ a.	0743	0808	0901	1000	1310	1515	1706	1750	2040	2245	1116	1450	1720	2020

◧ – Full name is **Dublin Heuston**. △ – For additional trains Dublin - Kildare and v.v, see Tables **240**, **245**.

IÉ LIMERICK JUNCTION - LIMERICK - GALWAY 242

km		⚒	⚒		⚒	⚒	⚒		⑦	⑦	⑦	⑦
0	**Limerick Jct** . **243** d.	...	0838	...	1340	...	...	...	...	1140	...	...
35	**Limerick** ¶ **245** d.	0555	0920	...	1420	1800	1945	...	0900	1220	1555	1815
74	Ennis **245** d.	0649x	0958	...	1458	1905	2025	...	0941	1304	1635	1857
103	Gort d.	0712	1020	...	1520	1932	2047	...	1003	1326	1701	1924
132	Athenry **240** d.	0743	1053	...	1553	2004	2118	...	1034	1357	1732	1955
152	**Galway** **240** a.	0810	1114	...	1612	2025	2140	...	1055	1417	1752	2015

	⚒	⚒		⚒	⚒	⚒	⚒	⑦	⑦	⑦	⑦
Galway **240** d.	0620	1030	...	1345	1750	1840	...	0830	1155	1610	1830
Athenry **240** d.	0641	1055	...	1406	1815	1906	...	0852	1215	1633	1853
Gort d.	0716	1121	...	1432	1840	1931	...	0918	1241	1701	1923
Ennis **245** d.	0745	1143	...	1500	1902	1953	2110	0940	1303	1723	1945
Limerick ¶ **245** a.	0825	1222	...	1539	1943	...	2149	1020	1342	1803	2023
Limerick Jct .. **243** a.	...	...	...	1611	2019	...	...	...	1415	...	...

x – Arrive 0634. ¶ – Limerick Colbert.

IÉ LIMERICK JUNCTION - LIMERICK 243

Shuttle service connecting with main-line trains. *35 km*. Journey time : 25 - 40 minutes. For through services to or from Dublin Heuston see Table **245**.

From Limerick Junction ⚒: 0807, 0838, 0940, 1040, 1140, 1240, 1340, 1440, 1540, 1622, 1740, 1813, 1834, 1940, 2047, 2238.
⑦: 1013, 1140, 1335, 1419, 1540, 1618, 1742, 1818, 1942, 2050.

From Limerick Colbert ⚒: 0530, 0615, 0725, 0855, 0945, 1045, 1145, 1245, 1345, 1445, 1545, 1645, 1745, 1850, 1950, 2045.
⑦: 0940, 1045, 1245, 1350, 1445, 1545, 1645, 1745, 1845, 1945.

245 DUBLIN - LIMERICK, TRALEE and CORK   IÉ

km			✠h ◇✕	✠	✠ ◇⚲	✠	✠ ◇⚲	✠	✠ ◇⚲	✠	✠ ◇⚲	✠	✠ ◇⚲	✠	✠ ◇⚲	✠	✠	✠ ◇⚲	✠	✠h ◇✕
0	Dublin Heuston.. 240 d.		0700	...	0800	...	0900	...	1000	...	1100	...	1200	...	1300	...	1400	...	1500	1525	...	1600	...	1625	1700
48	Kildare .... 240 d.			...																1552					
67	Portarlington .... 240 d.																		1605			1703	
82	Portlaoise ....d.		0742	...	0943	1042	1142	1242	1342	1442	1615	1713	
107	Ballybrophy..............d.			0958				1458		1631	1729	
127	Templemore..............d.			0902			1206		1643	1740	
139	Thurles..................d.		0813	0912	1015	1113	1215	1313	1413	1516	1609	1653	1709	1749	
172	Limerick Junction .. § d.		0834x	0838	0933x	0940	1036x	1040	1134x	1140	1236x	1240	1334x	1340	1434x	1440	1537x	1540	1730x	1740	1813	1827	1834
208	Limerick C ¶.§ 242 a.			0907	1014	1113	1216	1313	1414	1513	1613	1740	1800	1813	1840	1859
**	Ennis............. 242 a.			0957		1309		1457		1709	1837	
208	Charleville..............d.				1057		1257		1645	
232	Mallow .... 246 d.		0907	1007	1113	1207	1313	1407	1507	1611	1700	1803	1900	
	Tralee 246 ....a.												
266	Cork................ 246 a.		0935	1035	1145	1235	1345	1435	1535	1640	1730	1830	1930	

		✠h ◇✕	✠ ⚲	✠h ◇✕	✠ ◇⚲	✠ ◇		⑦	⑦ ◇⚲	⑦	⑦ ◇⚲	⑦ ⚲	⑦	⑦	⑦ ◇⚲	⑦	⑦	⑦ ◇⚲	⑦	⑦
Dublin Heuston .. 240 d.		1705	1725	1800	1900	2100		0830	...	1000	...	1125	1200	...	1300	1325	1400	1500	1525	1600	1700	1800
Kildare .... 240 d.			1754						1151		1351	1551	
Portarlington .... 240 d.			1806					1204		1404	1604	
Portlaoise ....d.		1800	1816	1948	2142		0912	1042	1214	1414	1614	
Ballybrophy..............d.		1832	1859	2003		1230	1430	1630	
Templemore..............d.		1812	1845	2014		1244	1443	1643	
Thurles..................d.		1821	1855	1916	2022	2213	0944	1112	1254	1308	1408	1453	1508	1608	1653	1708	1808	1908
Limerick Junction .. § d.			1936x	1940	2044x	2047	2234x	2238	1008x	1013	1137x	1140	1333x	1335	1531x	1731x	1931x
Limerick C ¶.§ 242 a.			1940	2005	2115	2303	1038	1205	1340	1400	1540	1613	1741	1813	2013
Ennis............. 242 a.			2023	2104		1129	1257	1449	1635	1857z	
Charleville..............d.		1857	2104		1028	1445	1751	
Mallow .... 246 d.		1914	1930	2010	2119	2307	1044	1050	1210	1406	1502	1605	1702	1808	1902	2005
Tralee 246 ....a.		2057					1220			
Cork................ 246 a.			1955	2035	2147	2335	1116	1235	1430	1530	1630	1730	1835	1930	2030

		⑦ ◇⚲	⑦ ⚲	⑦ ◇⚲		⑦	⑦	⑦					✠	✠	Ⓐ	✠	✠	✠h ◇✕	✠	✠ ◇⚲	✠
Dublin Heuston .. 240 d.		1825	1900	1905	1925	2100	2110		Cork................ 246 d.		0550	0615	...	0700	...	0800	
Kildare .... 240 d.		1854			1958	2139		Tralee 246 ....d.							0705	
Portarlington .... 240 d.		1907	1942	2011	2135	2152		Mallow .... 246 d.		0611		0721	0825	0837	
Portlaoise ....d.		1918	2022	2203		Charleville..............d.		0624			0852	
Ballybrophy..............d.		1933	2037		Ennis............. 242 d.			0650	0745	
Templemore..............d.		1946	2051		Limerick Colbert.. § 242 d.		0530	0615	0640	0725	0730	0740	0825	0855
Thurles..................d.		1955	2008	2021	2101	2212	2235		Limerick Junction .... § d.		0557	0646	0753	0756	0915	0923
Limerick Junction .. § d.			2047x	2050	2235x		Thurles..................d.		0619	0725	0816	0826	0943
Limerick C ¶.§ 242 a.		2042	2050	2115	2147	2320		Templemore..............d.		0628	0733	0834	
Ennis............. 242 a.			2129		Ballybrophy..............d.		0640	0744	0845	
Charleville..............d.			2104		Portlaoise ....d.		0654	0759	0900	
Mallow .... 246 d.		2102	2121	2130	2308		Portarlington .... 240 d.		0811	
Tralee 246 ....a.			2255		Kildare .... 240 d.		0717	0823	
Cork................ 246 a.		2130	2155	2335		Dublin Heuston .... 240 a.		0753	0820	0830	0857	0930	0955	1047	1059

		✠ ◇⚲	✠	✠ ◇⚲	✠	✠ ◇⚲	✠	✠ ◇⚲	✠	✠ ◇⚲	✠	✠ ◇⚲	✠	✠	✠ ◇⚲	✠	✠ ◇⚲	Ⓐ	✠
Cork................ 246 d.		...	0920	...	1020	...	1120	...	1220	...	1320	...	1420	...	1520	...	1620	...	1720	...	1820	...	1920	2020
Tralee 246 ....d.											
Mallow .... 246 d.		0941	1041	1141	1241	1341	1441	1541	1641	1741	1841	1941	2041
Charleville..............d.		1058	1458	1658	1858	
Ennis............. 242 d.		1000	1143	1500	1720	1902	
Limerick C ¶.§ 242 d.		0945	1045	1145	1245	1345	1404	1445	1545	1645	1745	1759	1850	1950	2045
Limerick Junction .... § d.		1012	1016	1111	1119	1216	1311	1316	1411	1416	1511	1519	1611	1616	1711	1719	1811	1817	1916	1919	2019	2021	2120
Thurles..................d.		1036	1236	1436	1539	1636	1739	1836	1939	2039	2138
Templemore..............d.		1144	1341	1748	1949	
Ballybrophy..............d.		1255	1855	
Portlaoise ....d.		1105	1308	1405	1505	1705	1811	1908	2012	2109	2207
Portarlington .... 240 d.					
Kildare .... 240 d.					
Dublin Heuston ... 240 a.		1155	1255	1400	1455	1555	1655	1755	1905	2000	2105	2200	2255

		⑦ ⚲	⑦	⑦ ◇⚲	⑦ ⚲	⑦ ◇⚲	⑦	⑦ ◇⚲		⑦ ◇⚲	⑦	⑦ ◇⚲	⑦	⑦ ◇⚲	⑦ ⚲	⑦	⑦ ◇⚲	⑦	Ⓐ	⑦
Cork................ 246 d.		...	0820	...	1020	...	1220	1320	...	1420	...	1520	...	1620	...	1720	...	1820	...	1920
Tralee 246 ....d.					1150		1340		1750	
Mallow .... 246 d.		0842	1041	1242	1316	1342	1441	1541	1641	1741	1842	1922	1941
Charleville..............d.		0858	1057	1258	1331	1457	1530	1657	1858	
Ennis............. 242 d.		0740	0940	1303	1515	1723	1900	
Limerick C ¶.§ 242 d.		0825	1020	1025	1045	1225	1245	1350	1420	1545	1620	1745	1820	1845	1945
Limerick Junction .... § d.		0917	1116	1317	1352	1415	1611	1614	1811	1814	1912	1917	1957	2011	2014
Thurles..................d.		0909	1110	1136	1309	1337	1413	1435	1506	1533	1609	1634	1704	1733	1834	1904	1937	2018	2034
Templemore..............d.		0918	1120	1318	1515	1713	1913	
Ballybrophy..............d.		0930	1132	1330	1529	1727	1927	
Portlaoise ....d.		0944	1146	1344	1547	1742	1942	
Portarlington .... 240 d.		0955	1157	1355	1559	1648	1753	1955	
Kildare .... 240 d.		1009	1211	1609	1612	1807	2009	
Dublin Heuston ... 240 a.		1040	1050	1243	1255	1441	1455	1535	1550	1642	1650	1730	1750	1840	1850	1950	2042	2055	2138	2150

h – ✕ on Ⓐ, ⚲ on ⑥.   z – Change at Limerick Colbert.   ◇ – Also conveys 🛏.   ** – Limerick - Ennis : 39 km.
x – Arrives 1 – 2 minutes earlier.   § – Also Table 243.   ¶ – Limerick Colbert.

246 (DUBLIN -) CORK - MALLOW - TRALEE   IÉ

km		✠	✠	✠	✠	✠	✠	✠h ◇✕	✠		⑦	⑦	⑦	⑦	⑦	⑦
0	Cork..........245 d.	0620	0855	1020	1220	1420	1655	1845	2055		0855	1020	1210	1435	1620	1845	2050
	Dublin 245 ... d.		0700	0900	1100	1300	1500	1700	1900	...		0830	1000	1300	1500	1700	1900	...
34	Mallow ....245 d.	0648	0923	1120	1310	1518	1725	1914	2124		0925	1044	1244	1517	1725	1925	2121
66	Millstreet...........d.	0712	0946	1144	1344	1542	1749	1943	2148		0947	1110	1310	1542	1748	1948	2145
100	Killarney.............d.	0743	1017	1218	1418	1618	1820	2019	2218		1014	1140	1340	1622	1825	2026	2218
134	Tralee ....a.	0821	1055	1255	1455	1655	1857	2057	2255		1049	1220	1415	1700	1859	2102	2255

		①	②–⑤	✠	✠	✠	✠	✠	✠h ◇✕	✠		⑦	⑦	⑦	⑦	⑦	⑦
Tralee ....d.		0445	0555	0705	0905	1105	1305	1505	1705	1905		0710	1150	1340	1510	1710	1750	1915
Killarney...........d.		0517	0627	0741	0937	1138	1337	1538	1737	1938		0741	1222	1421	1541	1744	1826	1946
Millstreet..........d.		0541	0651	0809	1007	1206	1406	1606	1810	2006		0807	1249	1448	1607	1810	1854	2012
Mallow ....245 d.		0607	0729z	0837	1036	1236	1436	1636	1845	2044		0843	1316	1514	1635	1844	1922	2045
Dublin 245 ....a.		0820	0930	1047	1255	1455	1655	1905	2105	2253		1050	1535	1730	1850	2055	2138	...
Cork..........245 a.		0720	0750	0915	1145	1345	1535	1730	1907	2105		0905	1348	1630	1730	1909	2030	2107

h – ✕ on Ⓐ, ⚲ on ⑥.   z – Arrive 0718.   ◇ – Also conveys 🛏 on ①–⑤.

CORK - MIDLETON   Journey time: 24 minutes   19 km.
✠ 0545, 0615, 0645 Ⓐ, 0715, 0745 Ⓐ, 0815, 0845 Ⓐ, 0915, 1015, then hourly until 1715, 1745,Ⓐ, 1815, 1915, 2015, 2115, 2215.
† 0815, 0915, 1115, 1215, 1415, 1615, 1715, 1815, 2015.

MIDLETON - CORK
✠ 0615, 0645, 0715 Ⓐ, 0745, 0815 Ⓐ, 0845, 0915 Ⓐ, 0945, 1045, then hourly until 1745, 1815 Ⓐ, 1845, 1945, 2045, 2145, 2245.
† 0845, 0945, 1145, 1245, 1445, 1645, 1745, 1845, 2045.

CORK - COBH   Journey time: 24 minutes   19 km.
✠ 0530 Ⓐ, 0600 ⑥, 0630 Ⓐ, 0700, 0730 Ⓐ, 0800, 0830 Ⓐ, 0900, 1000, then hourly until 1600, 1630, 1700, 1730, 1800, 1830, 1900 Ⓐ, 2000, 2100, 2230.
† 0800, 0900, 1100, 1200, 1300, 1430, 1600, 1700, 1800, 1940, 2100, 2200.

COBH - CORK
✠ 0600 Ⓐ, 0630 ⑥, 0700 Ⓐ, 0730, 0800 Ⓐ, 0830, 0900 Ⓐ, 0930, 1030, then hourly until 1630, 1700, 1730, 1800, 1830, 1900, 1930 Ⓐ, 2030, 2130, 2300.
† 0830, 0930, 1130, 1230, 1330, 1500, 1630, 1730, 1830, 2030, 2130, 2230.

FRANCE

SEE MAP PAGES 170/1

Operator: Société Nationale des Chemins de Fer Français (SNCF), unless otherwise shown.

Services: Most trains convey first and second classes of accommodation; many purely local services are second class only (it is not possible to show classes in the tables). *TGV* (*train à grande vitesse*) trains have a bar car in the centre of the train selling drinks and light refreshments. Selected *TGV* trains have an at-seat meal service in first class. On some *Intercité* services refreshments are available from a trolley wheeled through the train. Certain other long-distance trains also have refreshments available (sometimes seasonal or on certain days of the week), but it is not possible to identify these in the tables as this information is no longer supplied. Regional and local trains (outside Paris) are classified *TER* (*Train Express Regional*). Domestic night trains have sleeping accommodation which consists of modern four-berth couchettes (first class) or six-berth couchettes (second class). Women-only compartments are available on request. There are no sleeping cars on domestic trains in France. Note that all luggage placed on luggage racks must be labelled.

Timings: Valid from **December 11, 2016**, except where shown. Amended services operate on and around public holidays; whilst we try to show holiday variations, passengers are advised to confirm train times locally before travelling during these periods. Public holidays in 2017 are Jan. 1, Easter Monday (Apr. 17), May 1, May 8, Ascension Day (May 25), Whit Monday (June 5), July 14, Aug. 15, Nov. 1, 11, Dec. 25.
Engineering work can often affect schedules; major changes are shown in the tables where possible but other changes may occur at short notice.

Tickets: **Seat reservations are compulsory** for travel by all *TGV* and night trains (also *Intercité* shown with Ⓡ), and are also available for a small fee on many other long distance trains. Advance reservations are recommended for travel to ski resorts during the winter sports season. **Supplements** (which include the cost of seat reservation) are payable for travel in *TGV*, certain *Intercité* and night trains. All rail tickets (except passes) must be date-stamped before boarding the train using the self-service validating machines (composteurs) at the platform entrances. Note that where two *TGV* units are coupled together, they will often carry different train numbers for reservation purposes.

Note: The *TGV* services **Lille Europe - Charles de Gaulle ✈ - Marne-la-Vallée - Lyon / Bordeaux / Rennes / Nantes** are shown in the International section (Table **11**).

PARIS - LILLE - TOURCOING — 250

TGV Nord high-speed trains

For slower trains via Douai see Table **256**. For **Charles de Gaulle ✈ - Lille** see Table **11**. Certain trains continue to Dunkerque, Calais or Boulogne - see Table **265**.

km		*TGV* 7205	*TGV* 7007	*TGV* 7511*	*TGV* 7015	*TGV* 7021	*TGV* 7519	*TGV* 7223	*TGV* 7029	*TGV* 7033	*TGV* 7535*	*TGV* 7043	*TGV* 7045	*TGV* 7049	*TGV* 7053	*TGV* 7559*	*TGV* 7061	*TGV* 7265	*TGV* 7565	*TGV* 7065	*TGV* 7067	*TGV* 7269*	*TGV* 7271	*TGV* 7277
		Ⓐ	Ⓐ	①–⑥ b	Ⓐ	①–⑥ b	⑦ e	①–⑥ b	⑦ e				Ⓐ		⑤ f		Ⓐ	Ⓐ	⑥ t	⑦ e	Ⓐ		Ⓐ	
0	**Paris** Nord d.	0646	0716	0746	0816	0846	0846	0946	0946	1046	1146	1231	1316	1446	1516	1546	1616	1646	1646	1646	1716	1746	1816	1846
227	**Lille** Europe a.	0745	|	0845	|	|	0945	1045	|	|	1245	|	|	|	|	1645	|	1745	1745	|	|	1845	|	1945
227	**Lille** Flandres 415 a.	...	0818	...	0918	0948	...	...	1048	1148	...	1332	1418	1548	1618	...	1718	...	...	1748	1818	...	1918	...
237	Roubaix ◇ 415 a.	...	...	...	...	...	...	...	...	...	...	...	...	...	...	...	...	...	...	...	...	...	1951	...
240	**Tourcoing** 415 a.	...	...	...	...	...	...	...	...	...	...	...	...	...	...	...	...	...	...	...	...	...	1956	...

	TGV 7281	*TGV* 7083	*TGV* 7089	*TGV* 7091	*TGV* 7093	*TGV* 7093	*TGV* 7097	*TGV* 7097		
	Ⓐ	①–⑥ b	⑤ f	①–⑥ b	⑦ e§	⑤ f§	①–⑥ b⊗	⑦ e§		
Paris Nord d.	1916	1946	2016	2052	2143	2146	2221	2243	...	...
Lille Europe a.	|	|	|	⊡	|	|	⊡	|	...	...
Lille Flandres 415 a.	2018	2048	2118	2207	2251	2248	2339	2348	...	...
Roubaix ◇ 415 a.	2042	...	...	...	...	...	...	...	...	...
Tourcoing 415 a.	2048	...	...	...	...	...	...	...	...	...

	TGV 7000	*TGV* 7206*	*TGV* 7214	*TGV* 7208	*TGV* 7020	*TGV* 7228*	*TGV* 7530	*TGV* 7536*	
	Ⓐ	Ⓐ	Ⓐ	⑥ u	Ⓐ	①–⑥ b	Ⓐ		
Tourcoing 415 d.	...	0610	...	0640	...	...	...	...	...
Roubaix ◇ 415 d.	...	0615	...	0645	...	...	...	...	...
Lille Flandres 415 d.	0551	0641	...	0711	0741	...	...	...	...
Lille Europe d.	⊡	|	0713	|	|	0813	0842	0913	...
Paris Nord a.	0717	0744	0814r	0817	0844	0914	0944	1017	...

	TGV 7040	*TGV* 7046	*TGV* 7546	*TGV* 7248	*TGV* 7550	*TGV* 7254	*TGV* 7058	*TGV* 7066	*TGV* 7070	*TGV* 7572*	*TGV* 7074		*TGV* 7076	*TGV* 7082	*TGV* 7288*	*TGV* 7290		*TGV* 7292	*TGV* 7592	*TGV* 7094	*TGV* 7098	*TGV* 7096	*TGV* 7298	
		Ⓒ	Ⓐ	Ⓐ		①–⑥ b			⑤ f		Ⓐ			Ⓐ		Ⓐ		⑦ e	⑥ ⊡	⑤ f	⑦ e	①–⑥ b§	⑦ e	
Tourcoing 415 d.	...	...	...	1110	...	...	...	...	...	...	...	...	...	...	...	...	...	...	...	...	...	...	...	...
Roubaix ◇ 415 d.	...	...	...	1115	...	...	...	...	...	...	...	...	...	...	...	...	...	...	...	...	...	...	...	...
Lille Flandres 415 d.	1011	1111	...	1141	...	...	...	1611	1640	...	1740	...	1811	1840	...	...	...	...	...	2041	2111	2120	...	...
Lille Europe d.	|	|	1113	|	1313	1413	1513	|	|	1713	|	...	|	|	1913	1940	...	2013	2011	|	|	⊡	2213	...
Paris Nord a.	1124	1214	1220	1244	1423	1514	1617	1714	1744	1814	1844	...	1914	1944	2014	2041	...	2114	2132	2144	2220	2238	2314	...

b – Not Apr. 17, May 1, 8, June 5.
e – Also Apr. 17, May 1, 8, June 5.
f – Also May 24.
r – 0829 Jan. 23 - Mar. 31.
t – Also May 25.
u – On ⑥ Dec. 17 - Jan. 21 starts from Lille.

TGV –Ⓡ, supplement payable.
⊡ – Via Arras (Table **256**).
⊗ – Subject to alteration. On Ⓐ Jan. 23 - Mar. 3, Mar 20 - Apr. 21 and from May 29 Paris d. 2149, Lille a. 2313. Depart Paris 2218 on ⑥ Jan. 28 - July 1.
◇ – Also calls at Croix Wasquehal.

§ – Subject to alteration.
* – A different train number applies on certain days or for certain destinations.

Timings may vary due to engineering work.
Subject to alteration Dec. 18 - 31.

PARIS - SOISSONS - LAON — 251

km		Ⓐ	⑥	⚒	Ⓒ	Ⓐ	Ⓒ	Ⓐ	Ⓐ		⚒	Ⓐ	Ⓒ	Ⓐ	Ⓒ	Ⓐ	⑥	Ⓐ	Ⓐ		Ⓐ			
0	**Paris** Nord d.	0634	0731	0734	0831	0834	0931	1131	1231	1331	1431	1531	1631	1634	1731	1734	1831	1834	1934	2031	2131	...	...	...
61	Crépy-en-Valois d.	0710	0810	0811	0910	0910	1010	1211	1311	1411	1511	1611	1710	1711	1810	1811	1910	1911	2011	2110	2211	...	...	...
105	Soissons d.	0737	0839	0839	0939	0937	1039	1237	1337	1439	1537	1637	1736	1737	1839	1839	1939	1937	2037	2139	2239	...	...	...
140	**Laon** a.	0804	0905	0905	1006	1004	1105	1305	1405	1505	1605	1705	1805	1805	1905	1905	2005	2005	2105	2205	2305	...	...	...

	Ⓐ	Ⓐ	Ⓐ	⑥	Ⓐ	Ⓒ	†	⚒			Ⓐ		Ⓐ	Ⓒ	Ⓐ	Ⓒ	Ⓐ	Ⓐ	Ⓐ					
Laon d.	0506	0536	0636	0636	0736	0736	0836	0936	1136	1237	1336	...	1536	1536	1636	1733	1736	1837	1936	2037	...	...	...	...
Soissons d.	0530	0600	0701	0701	0801	0801	0901	1001	1201	1301	1401	...	1601	1601	1701	1759	1801	1904	2001	2101	...	...	...	...
Crépy-en-Valois d.	0605	0635	0735	0735	0835	0835	0935	1035	1235	1335	1435	...	1635	1635	1735	1835	1835	1935	2035	2135	...	...	...	...
Paris Nord a.	0640	0710	0810	0813	0910	0913	1013	1113	1313	1413	1513	...	1710	1713	1810	1913	1911	2013	2113	2213	...	...	...	...

Subject to alteration Dec. 24 - Jan. 1.

AMIENS - TERGNIER - LAON - REIMS — 252

km		①d	⑥	Ⓐ	Ⓐ	ⒶG	🚌 ⒶF	Ⓒ	Ⓐ	🚌 Ⓐ	†	⑥	🚌 Ⓐ	Ⓐ	†	ⒶG	⑥	Ⓐ	Ⓐ	⑥	Ⓑ	Ⓐ	⑥	Ⓐ	⑤	†
0	**Amiens** d.	0558	0626	0626	0718	0827	0827	0857	...	1227	1227	1327	1333	...	1557	1627	1627	1727	1757	1758	1827	1857	1857	1927	1927	1957
59	Ham (Somme) d.	0652	0720	0720	0815	0920	1011	0951	...	1411	1322	1422	1517	...	1651	1721	1720	1823	1853	1852	1922	1949	1951	2021	2021	2050
80	Tergnier d.	0709	0741	0742	0834	0942	1047	1007	1233	1447	1345	1443	1553	1612	1707	1742	1740	1845	1909	1908	1943	2005	2008	2044	2043	2106
108	**Laon** a.	0735	0807	0808	0900	1007	1132	1028	1302	1532	1411	1511	...	1634	1728	1808	1805	1910	1931	1929	2008	...	2029	...	2109	2127

	⚒	Ⓐ	⚒	⑥	ⒶG	ⒶF	🚌 ⒶF	†	Ⓐ	Ⓐ	🚌 Ⓐ	†	⑥	Ⓐ	🚌 Ⓐ	ⒶG	ⒶF	🚌 ⒶF	⚒	†	Ⓐ	Ⓐ	Ⓐ	Ⓐ	Ⓒ	⑤§
Laon d.	0550	0626	0650	0726	0726	0726	...	0829	0851	1150	...	1226	1326	1326	...	1602	1602	...	1650	1700	1726	1750	1834	1850r	1930	1950
Tergnier d.	0620	0655	0719	0758	0758	0748	0758	0852	0917	1220	1230	1259	1359	1349	1359	1631	1630	1640	1720	1728	1757	1819	1857	1919	1955	2020
Ham (Somme) d.	0642	0710	0742	0813	0812	...	0834	0909	...	...	1311	1314	1414	...	1435	1654	...	1721	1742	1750	1811	1840	1912	1941	2011	2042
Amiens a.	0733	0803	0833	0903	0903	...	1018	1000	...	...	1501	1403	1503	...	1619	1748	...	1911	1833	1843	1903	1933	2003	2033	2103	2133

LAON - REIMS

km		⚒	Ⓐ	Ⓐ	①d	⑥	Ⓒ	Ⓐ	Ⓐ	Ⓐ		
0	Laon d.	0633	0714	0733	0815	1046	1233	1333	1712	1740	1833	2046
52	Reims a.	0725	0750	0820	0850	1120	1320	1420	1750	1820	1920	2121

	①g	⚒	Ⓐ	†	⚒	⚒	Ⓑ	Ⓐ		Ⓐ	
Reims d.	0550	0640	0710	1110	1240	1510	1710	1740	1840	1940	...
Laon a.	0625	0728	0750	1157	1327	1546	1758	1827	1928	2028	...

F – Dec. 12 - Feb. 17.
G – From Feb. 20.
d – Not Apr. 17, May 1, 8, June 5.

g – Also Apr. 18, May 2, 9, June 6; not Apr. 17, May 1, 8, June 5.
r – From Feb. 20.

§ – Runs Ⓐ Laon - Tergnier.

Subject to alteration Dec. 25 - Jan. 1.

🚌 AMIENS - TGV HAUTE-PICARDIE — 253

SNCF 🚌 service

All *TGV* departures and arrivals at TGV Haute-Picardie (Table **11**) have 🚌 connections from / to Amiens and St Quentin. Departs 50 - 60 mins before the train; journey 40 minutes, Ⓡ.

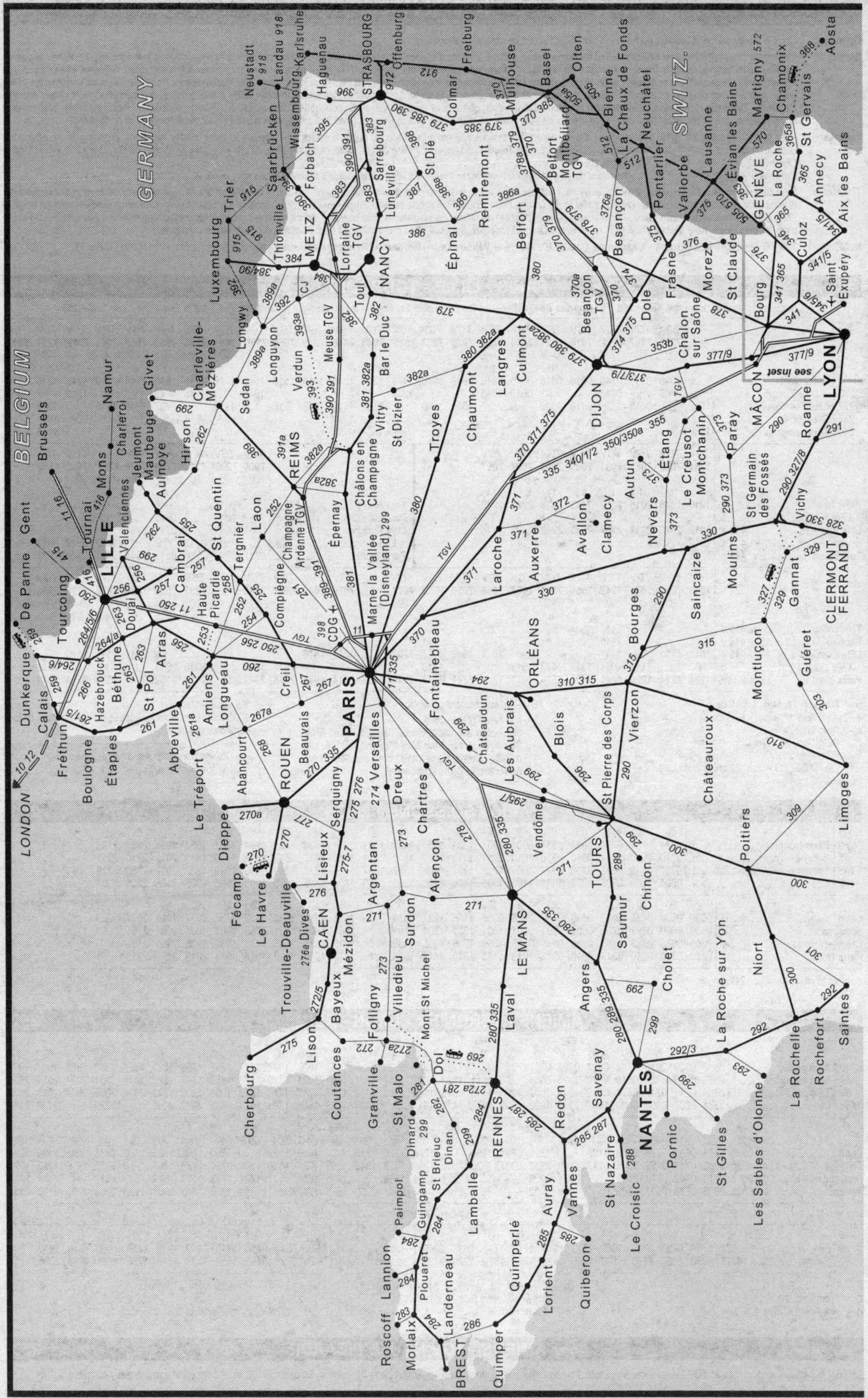
GERMANY
BELGIUM
SWITZ.
LONDON
PARIS
LILLE
ROUEN
CAEN
LE MANS
RENNES
NANTES
TOURS
ORLÉANS
DIJON
LYON
REIMS
METZ
NANCY
STRASBOURG
BREST
CLERMONT FERRAND
Brussels
Namur
Charleroi
Mons
Tournai
Gent
De Panne
Dunkerque
Calais
Fréthun
Boulogne
Étaples
Tourcoing
Hazebrouck
Béthune
St Pol
Arras
Douai
Valenciennes
Cambrai
Jeumont
Maubeuge
Aulnoye
Givet
Charleville-Mézières
Hirson
St Quentin
Tergnier
Laon
Haute Picardie
Amiens
Longueau
Abbeville
Le Tréport
Abancourt
Beauvais
Creil
Compiègne
Champagne Ardenne TGV
Épernay
Châlons en Champagne
Marne la Vallée (Disneyland)
CDG
Vitry
St Dizier
Bar le Duc
Meuse TGV
Verdun
Sedan
Longuyon
Longwy
Luxembourg
Trier
Thionville
Saarbrücken
Forbach
Wissembourg
Neustadt
Landau
Karlsruhe
Haguenau
Offenburg
Freiburg
Colmar
Mulhouse
Basel
Olten
Sarrebourg
Lunéville
St Dié
Lorraine TGV
Toul
Épinal
Remiremont
Belfort
Belfort Montbéliard TGV
Besançon
Besançon TGV
La Chaux de Fonds
Bienne
Neuchâtel
Pontarlier
Vallorbe
Frasne
Lausanne
Évian les Bains
Martigny
Chamonix
St Gervais
Aosta
La Roche
Annecy
Aix les Bains
Culoz
GENÈVE
St Claude
Morez
Dole
Bourg
Saint Exupéry
Chalon sur Saône
MÂCON
see inset
Paray
Le Creusot Montchanin
Étang
Autun
Roanne
Vichy
St Germain des Fossés
Moulins
Gannat
Montluçon
Guéret
Limoges
Culmont
Langres
Chaumont
Troyes
Laroche
Auxerre
Avallon
Clamecy
Nevers
Saincaize
Bourges
Vierzon
Châteauroux
Poitiers
Fontainebleau
Les Aubrais
Châteaudun
Blois
St Pierre des Corps
Vendôme
Chinon
Saumur
Angers
Cholet
Savenay
St Nazaire
Le Croisic
Pornic
St Gilles
Les Sables d'Olonne
La Roche sur Yon
Niort
La Rochelle
Rochefort
Saintes
Versailles
Chartres
Dreux
Serquigny
Lisieux
Trouville-Deauville
Dives
Le Havre
Fécamp
Dieppe
Argentan
Surdon
Alençon
Mézidon
Bayeux
Lison
Cherbourg
Coutances
Folligny
Villedieu
Granville
Mont St Michel
Dol
St Malo
Dinard
Dinan
St Brieuc
Lamballe
Guingamp
Paimpol
Plouaret
Lannion
Morlaix
Roscoff
Landerneau
Quimper
Quimperlé
Lorient
Auray
Vannes
Quiberon
Redon
Laval
TGV

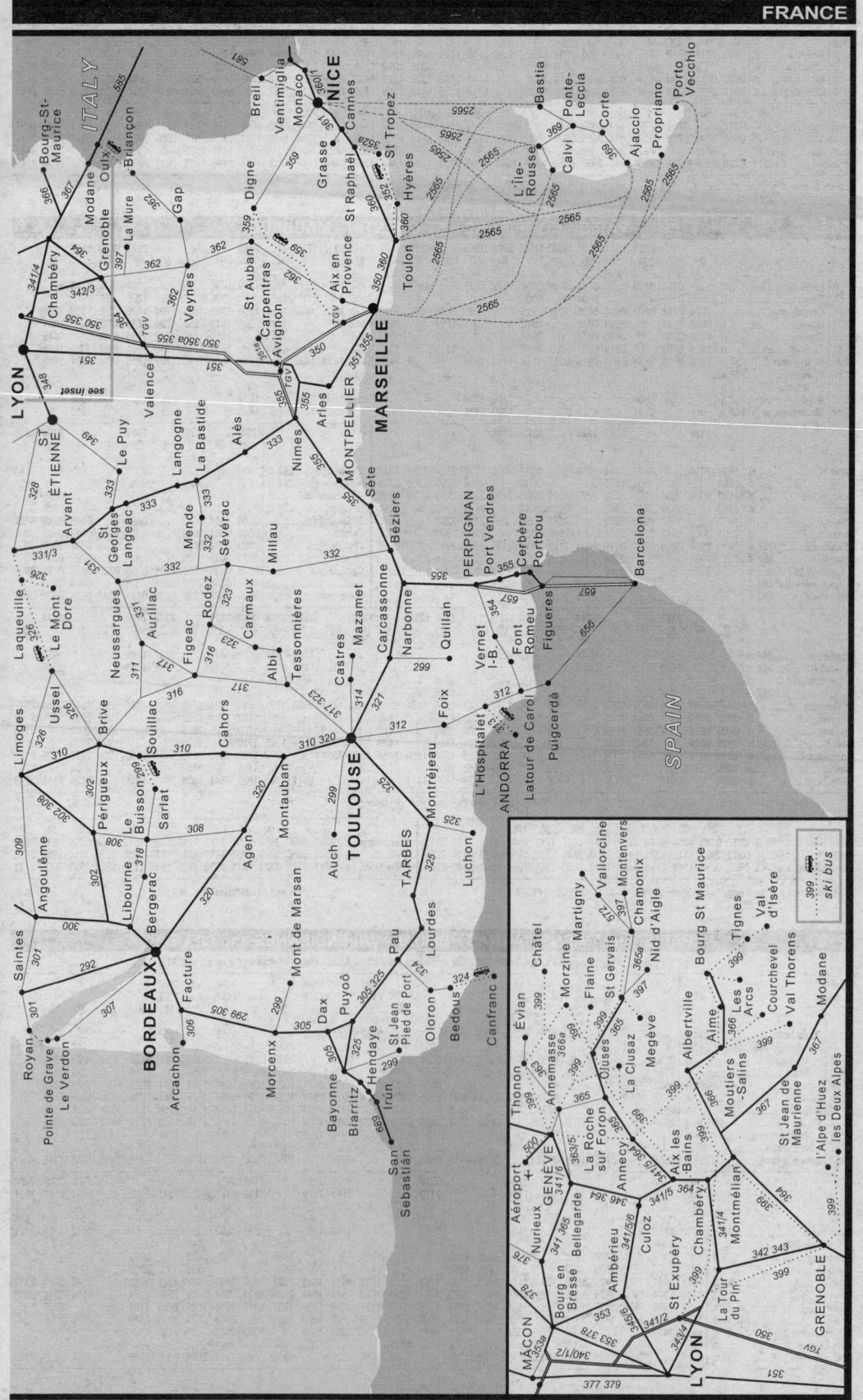

254 AMIENS - COMPIÈGNE

km		Ⓐ	Ⓐ	⑥	Ⓐ	†	Ⓐ	⑥	†	Ⓐ	†	⑥	Ⓐ	⑥	†	Ⓐ	Ⓒ	Ⓐ	Ⓐ	Ⓒ	Ⓐ	Ⓐ	†	⑥	Ⓐ	†	⑥
0	**Amiens** d.	0550	0618	0659	0735	0735	0855	0914	0932	1054	1118	1126	1229	1246	1330	1443	1619	1640	1703	1733	1752	1818	1835	1926	1931	2020	2032
5	Longueau d.	|	|	|	0741	|	|	0920	0938	|	|	|	1235	1252	1336	|	|	|	1709	1739	|	1825	1843	|	|	2026	2038
36	Montdidier d.	0620	0653	0730	0814	0806	0928	0951	1008	1124	1148	1156	1308	1323	1406	1513	1649	1710	1743	1810	1828	1903	1907	1956	2001	2056	2110
76	**Compiègne** a.	0647	0728	0759	0848	0835	0955	1030	1042	1151	1217	1225	1342	1359	1440	1540	1718	1737	1820	1845	1904	1937	1937	2025	2028	2130	2143

	Ⓐ	Ⓐ	Ⓐ	⑥	†	Ⓐ	Ⓐ	Ⓐ	⑥	†	Ⓐ	⑥	†	Ⓐ	⑥	†	Ⓐ	Ⓒ	Ⓐ	Ⓒ	Ⓐ	Ⓐ	⑥	Ⓐ	†	†	⑥
Compiègne d.	0547	0622	0659	0700	0738	0744	0823	0903	0918	0936	1059	1104	1119	1232	1248	1333	1447	1620	1644	1737	1751	1831	1904	1910	1913	2022	2037
Montdidier d.	0621	0654	0741	0729	0807	0814	0855	0929	0952	1009	1125	1131	1147	1307	1322	1407	1514	1648	1711	1811	1827	1904	1931	1937	1941	2057	2111
Longueau d.	0655	|	0819	|	0832	|	|	|	1023	1040	|	|	|	1338	1352	1438	|	|	|	1841	1859	|	|	|	|	2128	2142
Amiens a.	0701	0726	0826	0759	0839	0845	0930	0959	1028	1046	1156	1203	1218	1343	1357	1444	1544	1719	1744	1848	1905	1933	2003	2007	2012	2134	2147

Subject to alteration Dec. 25 - Jan. 1.

255 PARIS - COMPIÈGNE - ST QUENTIN - MAUBEUGE

km				2301			12303	12305	2307	2309		12311		12313	2317	12315		2319				2321	12321	2323		
		⚒	Ⓐ	Ⓐ	⚒	Ⓑ	Ⓐ		Ⓒ	Ⓐ	Ⓑ	⑥	⑥	Ⓑ	Ⓐ	†	⑥	⑥	Ⓐ	Ⓐ	Ⓐ	⑥	Ⓑ		⚒	
0	**Paris** Nord d.	...	0634	0719	...	0734	0819	0834	1019	1119	...	1219	...	1234	1319	1319	*1249*	1419	1434	...	...	1634	1634	1719	...	...
51	Creil d.	...	0705	|	...	0804	|	0905	|	|	...	|	...	1305	|	|	*1321*	|	1506	...	...	1705	1705	|	...	...
84	**Compiègne** d.	0625	0728	0800	0804	0828	0900	0928	1100	1200	1235	1300	1304	1328	1405	1400	1411	1500	1529	1635	1704	1728	1728	1800	1804	...
108	Noyon d.	0647	0742	|	0829	0842	|	0942	|	|	1259	|	1329	1342	|	|	1435	|	1543	1659	1729	1742	1742	|	1824	...
124	Chauny d.	0701	0754	|	0840	0853	|	0954	|	|	1313	|	1343	1354	|	|	1448	|	1554	1712	1742	1753	1754	|	1846	...
131	Tergnier d.	0709	0802	|	0849	0901	|	1002	|	|	1319	|	1349	1402	|	|	1454	|	1601	1718	1749	1801	1802	|	1853	...
154	**St Quentin** 257 d.	0728	0814	0834	0909	0914	0935	1014	1134	1234	1337	1332	1409	1414	1438	1432	1512	1534	1614	1740	1807	1815	1814	1834	1909	...
181	Busigny 257 d.	...	...	|	...	...	...	...	|	|	...	...	...	...	|	...	...	|	...	...	...	1834	...	|	...	...
207	*Cambrai* 257 a.	...	...	|	...	...	...	...	|	|	...	...	...	...	|	...	...	|	...	...	...	1856	...	|	...	...
217	Aulnoye Aymeries 262 a.	...	...	0904	...	...	...	...	1209	1304	...	...	...	...	1508	...	...	1604	...	...	...	...	...	1904	...	...
229	**Maubeuge** 262 a.	...	...	0915	...	...	...	...	1220	1315	...	...	...	...	1520	...	...	1615	...	...	...	...	...	1915	...	...

		2325			2327	2329		12331	2333				
	Ⓐ	Ⓐ		Ⓐ	†			Ⓐ	†	Ⓐ	Ⓑ	Ⓐ	Ⓒ
Paris Nord d.	1734	1819	...	1834	1834	1919	...	1934	2019	2034	2134	2234	2234
Creil d.	1804	|	...	1904	1905	|	...	2005	|	2104	2207	2308	2308
Compiègne d.	1828	1900	1904	1929	1928	2000	2004	2028	2100	2128	2229	2328	2330
Noyon d.	1842	|	1929	1942	1942	|	2029	2042	|	2142	2243	...	2344
Chauny d.	1853	|	1943	1953	1953	|	2042	2054	|	2153	2253	...	2355
Tergnier d.	1901	|	1949	2001	2001	|	2049	2102	|	2201	2301	...	0002
St Quentin 257 d.	1914	1934	2009	2014	2015	2034	2109	2114	2134	2214	2315	...	0015
Busigny 257 d.	...	1951	...	...	2034	|	...	...	|	...	...	...	...
Cambrai 257 a.	...	2015	...	...	2056	|	...	...	|	...	...	...	...
Aulnoye Aymeries 262 d.	...	...	...	...	...	2104	...	...	2204	...	...	...	...
Maubeuge 262 a.	...	...	...	...	...	2115	...	...	2215	...	...	...	...

	12300		12302		2304			2306	2308
	Ⓐ	⑥	Ⓐ	†	Ⓐ	Ⓐ	Ⓑ	⑥	Ⓐ
Maubeuge 262 d.	...	...	...	...	...	...	...	...	0642
Aulnoye Aymeries 262 d.	...	...	...	...	...	...	...	...	0653
Cambrai 257 d.	...	...	...	...	0536	...	...	0606	|
Busigny 257 d.	...	...	...	...	0608	...	...	0630	|
St Quentin d.	0446	0547	0546	...	0624	...	0646	0646	0724
Tergnier d.	0502	0601	0602	...	|	...	0702	0702	|
Chauny d.	0509	0609	0609	...	|	...	0709	0709	|
Noyon d.	0520	0621	0620	...	|	...	0720	0720	|
Compiègne d.	0535	0635	0635	0635	0700	0720	0735	0735	0800
Creil d.	0559	0658	|	0658	|	|	0759	0759	|
Paris Nord a.	0626	0726	0726	0726	0741	0817	0826	0826	0841

			2312			2314		2316	12318		2318	12320		12322		2324	2326	12328	2330		2332	2332			2334	
	Ⓑ	⑥	⚒	Ⓐ	⑥	†	Ⓐ	⚒	Ⓐ	⑥	†	Ⓐ	⑥	⑥	†	†	Ⓐ		†	Ⓐ	Ⓒ	Ⓐ		⚒	†	†
Maubeuge 262 d.	...	...	0742	...	...	0942	...	1042	...	...	...	...	...	...	...	1442	1538	...	1637	...	1737	1742	...	...	1952	...
Aulnoye Aymeries 262 d.	...	...	0753	...	...	0953	...	1053	...	...	...	...	...	...	...	1453	1550	...	1649	...	1748	1753	...	...	2004	...
Cambrai 257 d.	...	...	|	...	...	|	...	|	...	...	1206	...	...	...	...	|	|	...	|	...	|	|	...	...	|	...
Busigny 257 d.	...	...	|	...	...	|	...	|	...	...	1230	...	...	...	...	|	|	...	|	...	|	|	...	...	|	...
St Quentin d.	0746	0751	0824	0927	0950	1024	1046	1124	1246	1247	1246	1324	1351	1424	1451	1524	1621	1646	1724	1746	1824	1824	1851	1946	2034	2047
Tergnier d.	0802	0810	|	0944	1005	|	1102	|	1302	1302	1302	|	1410	|	1510	|	|	1702	|	1802	|	|	1910	2002	|	2102
Chauny d.	0809	0816	|	0950	1013	|	1109	|	1309	1309	1309	|	1416	|	1516	|	|	1709	|	1809	|	|	1918	2009	|	2110
Noyon d.	0820	0829	|	1000	1024	|	1120	|	1320	1321	1320	|	1429	|	1529	|	1645	1720	|	1820	|	|	1931	2020	|	2122
Compiègne d.	0835	0854	0900	1014	1038	1100	1135	1200	1335	1335	1335	1400	1454	1500	1554	1600	1700	1735	1800	1835	1900	1900	1954	2035	2109	2138
Creil d.	0859	...	|	...	1102	|	1159	|	1359	1358	1359	|	...	|	...	|	|	1759	|	1859	|	|	...	2059	|	2200
Paris Nord a.	0926	...	0941	...	1126	1141	1226	1241	1426	1423	1426	1441	...	1541	...	1641	1741	1826	1841	1926	1941	1941	...	2126	2153	2226

LOCAL TRAINS PARIS - COMPIÈGNE

	⑥	†	⚒	Ⓐ	⑥	Ⓐ	⚒	†	⚒	⚒		†	⑥
Paris Nord d.	0637	0837	0849	1037	1249	1337	1637	1737	1749	1840	1940	2037	2152
Creil d.	0710	0912	0922	1110	1321	1410	1710	1811	1822	1913	2013	2114	2225
Compiègne a.	0749	0950	0951	1147	1356	1450	1749	1850	1851	1954	2055	2150	2254

▽	Ⓐ		Ⓐ	†	⑥		⑥	Ⓑ		Ⓑ	⚒	Ⓐ
Compiègne d.	0505	0809	1019	1107	1112	1210	1509	1612	1709	1809	1910	2008
Creil d.	0545	0850	1048	1137	1151	1250	1538	1650	1750	1850	1950	2038
Paris Nord a.	0617	0923	1121	1211	1223	1323	1611	1723	1823	1923	2025	2111

▽ – Additional journeys from Compiègne: 0609⚒, 0638Ⓐ, 0703Ⓐ, 0710⑥.

Subject to alteration Dec. 25 - Jan. 1.

256 PARIS and AMIENS - ARRAS - DOUAI - VALENCIENNES and LILLE

For *TGV* trains Paris - Lille and v.v. see Table **250**. For additional *TGV* trains Arras - Douai - Lille and v.v. see Table **11**.

km ★			◇				◇					*TGV* 7151		*TGV* 7155			*TGV* 7157		*TGV* 7159					
		Ⓐ	Ⓐ	⑥	Ⓐ	⚒	Ⓐ	Ⓐ	†	Ⓐ	⑥	Ⓐ	Ⓐ	⑥ t	⑥	†	⑦ e	⑥	⚒	Ⓑ	⑥	Ⓐ	Ⓒ	
0	**Paris** Nord 264 d.	...	...	...	...	...	...	...	...	...	...	0752	...	0852	...	...	0952	...	1052	...	...	...	...	...
	Rouen 268 d.	...	...	...	...	...	...	...	...	0617	...	|	...	|	0818	...	|	...	|	...	...	1117	...	...
131	**Amiens** d.	0538	...	...	...	0638	...	...	...	0738	0738	|	0838	|	0938	0938	|	1038	|	1138	...	1238	1238	...
162	Albert d.	0558	...	...	...	0659	...	...	...	0759	0759	|	0859	|	0959	0959	|	1059	|	1159	...	1259	1259	...
199	Arras 264 a.	0623	...	...	...	0721	...	...	...	0823	0823	0841	0923	0941	1023	1023	1041	1123	1141	1223	...	1323	1323	...
199	Arras d.	0625	0647	...	...	0723	0747	...	*0757*	0825	0824	0844	0925	0944	1024	1024	1044	1124	1144	1225	1239	1325	1324	...
224	Douai a.	0637	|	...	...	0737	|	...	*0826*	0837	0837	0859	0937	0959	1037	1037	1059	1137	1158	1237	1303	1337	1337	...
224	Douai 257 ▶ d.	0639	|	0644	0708	0738	|	0809	0834	0839	0839	0909	0939	1009	1039	1039	1109	1139	1208	1239	1305	1339	1339	...
260	Valenciennes ▶ a.	|	|	|	|	|	|	|	|	|	|	0935	|	1035	|	|	1135	|	1234	|	|	|	|	...
257	**Lille** Europe a.	|	0708	|	|	|	0808	|	|	|	|	...	|	...	|	|	...	|	...	|	|	|	|	...
257	**Lille** Flandres 257 a.	0658	...	0725	0729	0758	...	0829	0913	0858	0858	...	0958	...	1058	1058	...	1158	...	1258	1330	1358	1358	...

	TGV 7165	*TGV* 7165					*TGV* 7169			*TGV* 7173	◇		*TGV* 7181	*TGV* 7179		*TGV* 7185	*TGV* 7187		*TGV* 7191			*TGV* 7091	*TGV* 7197	*TGV* 7097
	⑤ f	⑥ t	†	⑥	Ⓐ	Ⓒ		Ⓐ		Ⓐ	Ⓐ	Ⓑ	Ⓐ	⑦ e	Ⓐ	Ⓐ	⑦ e			Ⓐ		①–⑥ b	⑦ e	①–⑥ b§
Paris Nord 264 d.	1252	1252	...	...	...	...	1452	...	...	1652	...	...	1752	1752	...	1837	1852	...	1952	...	...	2052	2149	2221
Rouen 268 d.	|	|	...	...	...	...	|	...	...	|	...	...	|	|	...	|	|	1817	|	...	...	|	|	|
Amiens d.	|	|	...	1338	1438	...	|	1538	1638	|	...	1738	|	|	1838	|	|	1938	|	2038	...	|	|	|
Albert d.	|	|	...	1359	1459	...	|	1559	1659	|	...	1759	|	|	1859	|	|	1959	|	2059	...	|	|	|
Arras 264 a.	1341	1341	...	1423	1523	...	1541	1623	1723	1741	...	1823	1841	1841	1922	1926	1941	2023	2041	2123	...	2141	2241	2312
Arras d.	1344	1344	1408	1424	1525	1523	1544	1625	1725	1744	1800	1825	1844	1844	1924	1929	1944	2025	2044	2124	...	2144	2244	2318
Douai a.	1359	1359	1426	1437	1537	1537	1558	1637	1737	1758	|	1837	1858	1859	1937	1943	1958	2037	2059	2137	...	|	2259	|
Douai 257 ▶ d.	1409	1409	1428	1439	1539	1539	1608	1639	1739	1808	|	1839	1908	1909	1939	1954	2008	2039	2109	2139	...	|	2309	|
Valenciennes ▶ a.	1435	1435	|	|	|	|	1634	|	|	1835	|	|	1935	1935	|	2020	2037	|	2135	|	...	|	2335	|
Lille Europe a.	...	...	|	|	|	|	...	|	|	...	1821	|	...	...	|	...	...	|	...	|	...	|	...	|
Lille Flandres 257 a.	...	...	1458	1458	1558	1559	...	1700	1758	...	...	1858	...	...	1958	...	...	2058	...	2158	...	2207	...	2339

172 *For explanation of standard symbols see page 4* 12

LILLE and VALENCIENNES - DOUAI - ARRAS - AMIENS and PARIS — 256

Lille - Paris: see **250**

	TGV 7000 Ⓐ	⑥	TGV 7100 Ⓐ	TGV 7102 Ⓐ ‡	✕	TGV 7104 Ⓐ	TGV 7106 ⑥	⑥	Ⓐ	Ⓐ	TGV 7110 Ⓐ e	Ⓒ	Ⓐ	Ⓐ	Ⓐ	TGV 7118 Ⓐ	Ⓐ	✕	†	TGV 7120 ①-⑥ b	Ⓐ	Ⓐ	TGV 7126 ⑤	TGV 7126 Ⓒ
Lille Flandres 257 d.	0551	0602	0602	...	...	0702	...	...	0731	0802	0802	...	0902	0902	1002	1002	...	...	1102	1202	1202	...	1302	...
Lille Europe d.																								
Valenciennes ▶ d.				0555	0615		0650	0714			0815			1014			1214					1415	1415	
Douai 257 ▶ a.		0621	0621	0621	0640	0721	0716	0739	0753	0821	0821	0840	0921	0921	1021	1021	1039	1121	1221	1221	1239	1321	1440	1440
Douai d.		0623	0623	0632	0651	0723	0729	0751		0823	0823	0851	0923	0923	1023	1023	1051	1123	1223	1223	1251	1323	1451	1451
Arras a.	0614	0636	0636	0650	0705	0735	0744	0805		0835	0835	0905	0936	0937	1042	1036	1105	1136	1223	1236	1305	1335	1505	1505
Arras 264 d.	0617	0637	0637	0656	0716	0737	0758	0817		0837	0837	0917			1038	1117	1137	1237		1317	1337	1517	1517	
Albert d.		0657	0701		0801				0901	0901					1101	1159	1301		1401					
Amiens a.		0717	0721		0820				0921	0921					1121		1221	1321		1421				
Rouen 268 a.		0832	...						1044								1342							
Paris Nord 264 a.	0717			0759	0814		0859	0908			1014				1214					1414			1614	1614

	TGV 7130 Ⓑ h	Ⓐ	Ⓐ	⑥	Ⓐ	TGV 7136 Ⓑ h	Ⓐ	Ⓒ	Ⓐ	Ⓐ	TGV 7142 ⑥	†	Ⓐ	Ⓐ	TGV 7096 Ⓑ ①-⑥ b §	⑦	TGV 7160 Ⓒ e	Ⓐ
Lille Flandres 257 d.	1602	...	1630	1702	1702	...	1731	1802	1802	...	1902	...	1935	1935	2002	2102	2106	2208
Lille Europe d.					1721				1838								2115	...
Valenciennes ▶ d.		1615				1715				1915								
Douai 257 ▶ a.	1621	1640	1650	1721	1721		1740	1750	1821	1821	1921	1940	2017	2018	2021	2121	2136	2140 2241
Douai d.	1623	1651	1659	1723	1723		1751		1823	1823	1923	1951	2023	2023	2123		2138	2151 2243
Arras a.	1636	1705	1713	1736	1736	1743		1805	1837	1835	1859	1935	2006	2037	2035	2138	2143	2152 2205 2259
Arras 264 d.	1637	1717		1737			1817		1838	1837		1937	2017		2037		2147	2217
Albert d.	1701	...	1801					1901	1859	2001				2101				
Amiens a.	1720	...	1821					1922	1920	2021				2120				
Rouen 268 a.		...	1942						2042									
Paris Nord 264 a.		1817				1908					2108					2238	2314	

b – Not Apr. 17, May 1, 8, June 5.
e – Also Apr. 17, May 1, 8, June 5.
f – Also May 24.
h – Not May 25.
t – Also May 25.

TGV – Ⓡ, supplement payable.
◇ – TER à Grande Vitesse (via high-speed line). Supplement *Grande Vitesse* payable (€3 per day).
★ – Paris - Arras via high-speed line is 179 km.

▶ – Additional trains run Douai - Valenciennes (journey 30 - 40 mins).
§ – Subject to alteration (see Table **250**).
‡ – Timings may vary.

LILLE - DOUAI - CAMBRAI - ST QUENTIN — 257

km		Ⓐ P	⑥ P	Ⓐ	⑥	Ⓐ	⑥	✕	Ⓐ	†	⑥	†	† Ⓐ P	...	Ⓐ	⑥	✕	Ⓐ	†	⑥	⑥	Ⓐ	⑥	✕
0	Lille Flandres 256 d.	...	...	0602	0606	0706	0736	0806	0902	0906	1006		1110	1136	...	1206	1236	1302	1302	1406	...	1506	1536	1606
34	Douai 256 a.	...	...	0621	0638	0738	0808	0838	0921	0938	1038		1142	1208	...	1238	1308	1321	1321	1438	...	1538	1608	1638
34	Douai d.	...	...	0635	0640	0740	0811	0840	0940	0940	1040		1144	1211	...	1240	1311	1331	1340	1440	...	1540	1611	1640
66	Cambrai Ville a.	...	...	0713	0713	0813	0844	0913	1013	1013	1113		1213	1244	...	1313	1344	1401	1413	1513	...	1613	1643	1713
66	Cambrai Ville d.	0536	0606	0632	0715	0715	0815		0915		1015	1115	1206		1255		1315		1403		1513	1532			1715
82	Caudry d.	0554	0620	0646	0727	0727	0827		0927		1027	1127	1220		1310		1327		1416		1527	1544			1727
92	Busigny 255 d.	0608	0630	0658	0736	0736	0837		0937		1036	1137	1230		1320		1336		1425		1536	1553			1737
119	St Quentin 255 d.	0622	0644	0718	0757	0757	0857		0957		1057	1157	1246		1400				1557	1614					1757
	Paris Nord 255 a.	0741	0826										1426												

		Ⓐ	⑥	Ⓐ	†	Ⓐ	Ⓑ	⑥	Ⓐ	Ⓐ			Ⓐ	Ⓐ	✕	Ⓐ	Ⓐ	Ⓐ	Ⓐ	✕	†
Lille Flandres 256 d.		1636	1706	1706	1736	1806	1802	1836	1906	1935	2006		Paris Nord 255 d.	...	...	...	...	...	...	...	...
Douai 256 a.		1709	1738	1738	1808	1838	1821	1908	1938	2017	2038		St Quentin 255 d.	...	0505		0605		0703		...	0805
Douai d.		1711	1740	1740	1811	1840	1911	1940	2019	2040			Busigny 255 d.	...	0526		0626		0726	0725	...	0826
Cambrai Ville a.		1743	1813	1813	1843	1913	1913	1943	2013	2053	2113		Caudry d.	...	0535		0635		0735	0735	...	0835
Cambrai Ville d.			1815	1815		1915	1915		2015	2055	2115		Cambrai Ville a.	...	0546		0646		0746	0747	...	0846
Caudry d.			1827	1828		1928	1928		2028	2109	2128		Cambrai Ville d.	0506	0547	0617	0648	0717	0748	0749	0817 0848	0848
Busigny 255 d.			1838	1837		1937	1937		2037	2119	2137		Douai a.	0535	0617	0649	0720	0749	0820	0850	0850	0920 0920
St Quentin 255 d.			1857	1857		1958	1957		2057		2157		Douai 256 d.	0541	0652	0652	0722	0752	0822	0822		0922 0922
Paris Nord 255 a.		...	...	...	...	...	...	...	...	...	...		Lille Flandres 256 a.	0621	0655	0725	0755	0825	0855	0855		0955 0955

		Ⓐ	⑥	Ⓐ	†	Ⓐ n	⑥	Ⓐ	†	Ⓐ	⑥	⑥	Ⓒ	Ⓐ	†	⑥ P	Ⓐ	⑥	† P	⑥ P
Paris Nord 255 d.		...	...	...	...	...	...	...	...	...	...	...	1634		...	1819	1834			
St Quentin 255 d.		0842	1005		1205	1205	1205		1405		1442		1605	1605		1703	1805	1815	1842	1905	...	1905	1934	2015	2042
Busigny 255 d.		0903	1025		1226	1226	1225	1338	1426	1435	1503		1626	1626		1724	1826	1834	1903	1926	...	1926	1951	2034	2101
Caudry d.		0912	1035		1235	1235	1235	1351	1435	1444	1512		1635	1635		1735	1834	1844	1912	1935	...	1935	2004	2044	2112
Cambrai Ville a.		0924	1046		1246	1246	1246	1407	1447	1455	1524		1646	1646		1746	1846	1856	1924	1946	...	1946	2015	2056	2125
Cambrai Ville d.			1048	1147	1248	1248	1248	1417	1448	1456		1547		1648	1748	1848			1948	1948	1948			
Douai a.			1120	1220	1320	1319	1320	1450	1521	1529		1619		1720	1720	1749	1820	1820		2020	2020	2020		
Douai 256 d.			1122	1222	1322	1322	1339		1522	1539		1639		1722	1739	1752	1822	1822	1922	2022	2022	2039		
Lille Flandres 256 a.			1155	1255	1355	1355	1358		1556	1559		1700		1755	1758	1831	1855	1855	1955	2055	2055	2058		

P – For train numbers see Table **255**.
n – Not Dec. 19 - 30.

AMIENS - ST QUENTIN — 258

km		Ⓐ	Ⓐ	⑥	†	⑥	🚌	ⒶF	ⒶG	Ⓐ	n	⑥	🚌			Ⓐ	✕	ⒶD	ⒺE	†	⑥	🚌	Ⓐu	Ⓐz	⑥	†
0	Amiens d.	0649	0742	0744	1049	1249	1249	1649	1649	1749	1849	1949		St Quentin d.		0610	0710	0739	0803	0908	1210	1206	1710	1810	1816	2016
59	Ham (Somme) d.	0732	0824	0827	1134	1339	1352	1734	1752	1835	1933	2033		Ham (Somme) d.		0633	0733	0800	0827	0934	1233	1236	1733	1832	1839	2038
76	St Quentin a.	0756	0848	0851	1156	1359	1422	1756	1822	1858	1954	2100		Amiens a.		0712	0812	0912	0912	1012	1312	1339	1812	1912	1918	2114

D – Dec. 12 - Feb. 17.
E – From Feb. 20.
F – Dec. 26 - 30 and from Feb. 20.
G – Dec. 12 - 23, Jan. 2 - Feb. 17.
n – Not Dec. 19 - 30.
u – By 🚌 (a. 1843) Dec. 19 - 30.
z – By 🚌 (d. 1816, a. 1949) Dec. 12 - Feb. 17.
Subject to alteration on Dec. 25, 31, Jan. 1.

CALAIS - DUNKERQUE - DE PANNE — 259

km		Ⓐ	Ⓐ	⑥	Ⓐ	⑥	Ⓐ	⑥	Ⓐ	⑥			✕	Ⓐ	Ⓐ	⑥	⑥	Ⓐ	⑥	Ⓐ	⑥
0	Calais Ville d.	0541	0643	0712	0741	0812	1241	1300	1612	1741	1841		Dunkerque d.	0635	0710	0810	1219	1236	1336	1709	1736	1836	1936
23	Gravelines d.	0601	0700	0732	0801	0831	1301	1321	1631	1801	1901		Gravelines d.	0659	0731	0831	1244	1300	1400	1729	1800	1902	1959
46	Dunkerque a.	0624	0719	0753	0824	0850	1324	1343	1650	1824	1924		Calais Ville a.	0719	0747	0847	1305	1319	1419	1746	1819	1921	2019

Subject to alteration Dec. 26 - 30.

🚌 **DUNKERQUE - ADINKERKE (DE PANNE STATION)**

Operator: DK'BUS Marine (route 2B). Journey 40 - 50 minutes. Connects at De Panne station with coastal tram service (Table **406**).

From Dunkerque Gare: Ⓐ: 0605, 0701, 0759, 0903, 1003, 1103, 1159, 1256, 1359, 1501, 1557, 1655, 1758, 1903, 2007.
⑥ (also school holidays): 0602, 0701, 0755, 0858, 0959, 1059, 1159, 1302, 1402, 1502, 1558, 1656, 1759, 1903, 2008.
†: 0803, 0903, 1002, 1103, 1203, 1304, 1403, 1503, 1603, 1703, 1803, 1902, 2002.

From Adinkerke (De Panne station): Ⓐ: 0712, 0815, 0915, 1015, 1119, 1214, 1315, 1415, 1515, 1616, 1719, 1819, 1915, 2019, 2111.
⑥ (also school holidays): 0715, 0815, 0915, 1015, 1115, 1215, 1315, 1414, 1515, 1615, 1715, 1815, 1915, 2019, 2111.
†: 0915 and hourly to 2015, 2113.

260 PARIS - AMIENS

Trains numbered **2xxx** continue to/from Boulogne (Table **261**).

km		12001	12003	2005	12007		2009	12009				2011	2013			12015			2017	12019	2021	12023		2025		
		Ⓐ	⚒	Ⓐ	†	⑥	⑥	Ⓐ	†	Ⓐ	⑥	†	⚒	†	⚒	⚒	†	⑥	Ⓑ	Ⓐ	⑥	Ⓐ	⑥	Ⓐ	Ⓐ	Ⓒ
0	**Paris** Nord d.	0604	0704	0731	0804	0807	0831	0831	0907	0907	0907	0931	1031	1101	1107	1150	1204	1307	1331	1404	1431	1604	1604	1631	1704	1707
51	Creil d.	0630	0730	0758	0830	0841	|	|	0940	0940	0941	|	|	1135	1139	1219	1231	1340	|	1430	|	|	1631	1657	1731	1738
66	Clermont-de-l'Oise d.	0642	0742	|	0842	0856	|	|	0954	0956	0955	|	|	1152	1157	|	1242	1355	|	1442	|	1642	1642	|	1741	1752
81	St Just en Chaussée d.	0653	0753	|	0853	0914	|	|	1003	1007	1012	|	|	1205	1207	|	1253	1408	|	1453	|	1653	1653	|	1752	1812
126	Longueau d.	0716	0816	0835	0916	0945	0933	0933	1037	1040	1041	1033	1133	1238	...	1257	1316	1438	1433	1516	1533	1716	1716	1735	1816	1846
131	**Amiens** a.	0722	0822	0840	0922	0950	0938	0938	1043	1045	1046	1038	1138	1243	...	1302	1322	1443	1438	1522	1538	1723	1722	1740	1822	1851

	2027	12027			12029	12031			2035	12037	12039		
	Ⓒ	Ⓐ	Ⓐ	⑥	†	Ⓐ	Ⓐ			⚒	†		
Paris Nord d.	1731	1731	1801	1804	1804	1831	1904	1907	1931	2004	2031	2107	2228
Creil d.	|	|	1828	1831	1830	|	1931	1939	|	2030	|	2139	2303
Clermont-de-l'Oise d.	|	|	1840	1842	1842	|	1941	1955	|	2042	|	2155	2313
St Just en Chaussée d.	|	|	1851	1853	1853	|	1952	2013	|	2053	|	2206	2322
Longueau d.	1833	1833	1916	1916	1916	1932	2016	2046	2033	2116	2133	2238	2345
Amiens a.	1838	1839	1922	1922	1922	1938	2022	2051	2038	2123	2138	2243	2351

			12000			12002			12006
	Ⓐ	⑥	Ⓐ	Ⓐ	Ⓒ	Ⓐ	⚒	Ⓐ	Ⓐ
Amiens d.	0414	0517	0538	0606	0613	0621	0638	0706	0721
Longueau d.	0421	0523	0545	0612	0618	0628	0645	0712	0728
St Just en Chaussée d.	0454	0553	0610	0641	0645	|	0710	0742	|
Clermont-de-l'Oise d.	0506	0603	0620	0659	0702	|	0720	0801	|
Creil d.	0521	0620	0631	0720	0717	|	0731	0821	|
Paris Nord a.	0553	0653	0656	0753	0753	0729	0756	0853	0835

		2008	12010			12012	2014	12016	12018	12020	2022			12024		2026	12028	2030		12032	2034			2036		
		⚒	Ⓑ	⑥	†	⑥		Ⓐ	Ⓐ	⑥	Ⓐ	†	†	Ⓐ	Ⓒ			Ⓑ	†	Ⓐ	Ⓒ	Ⓒ	Ⓑ	†	Ⓐ	
Amiens d.	0738	0823	0838	0910	0917	1038	1123	1221	1238	1321	1423	...	1538	1538	1606	1623	1738	1823	...	1835	1923	1938	2038	2123	2156	...
Longueau d.	0745	0830	0845	0917	0923	1045	1130	1228	1245	1328	1430	...	1545	1545	1612	1630	1745	1830	...	1845	1930	1945	2044	2130	2203	...
St Just en Chaussée d.	0810	|	0910	0949	0953	1110	|	|	1310	|	|	1453	1608	1610	1641	|	1810	|	1853	1910	|	2008	2110	|	2228	...
Clermont-de-l'Oise d.	0820	|	0920	0959	1003	1120	|	|	1320	|	|	1504	1619	1620	1701	|	1820	|	1903	1920	|	2019	2120	|	2238	...
Creil d.	0831	|	0931	1019	1020	1131	|	|	1331	|	|	1521	1631	1631	1720	|	1831	|	1920	1931	|	2031	2131	|	2249	...
Paris Nord a.	0856	0929	0956	1053	1053	1156	1229	1329	1356	1429	1529	1553	1656	1656	1756	1729	1856	1929	1953	1956	2029	2056	2156	2229	2314	...

261 AMIENS - BOULOGNE - CALAIS

For *TGV* service Paris - Étaples / Boulogne / Calais see Table **265**. Faster services Paris - Calais are available by changing at Lille (Tables **250** / **266**) or Hazebrouck (Tables **264** / **266**).

km													2005			2009				2011				2013		
		Ⓐ	Ⓐ	⑥	Ⓐ	⚒	Ⓐ	†	⚒	⚒	Ⓐ	⑥	Ⓐ	†	†	⑥	Ⓐ	⑥	Ⓐ	†	†	Ⓐ	⑥	⚒	†	⑥
	Paris Nord **260** d.	...	...	...	...	...	...	...	...	...	...	...	0731	...	...	0831	...	...	...	0931	...	...	...	1031	...	...
0	**Amiens** d.	...	...	...	...	...	0624	...	0713	...	...	0847	0853	...	0947	0951	...	...	...	1051	...	...	...	1151	...	...
45	Abbeville d.	...	...	...	...	...	0657	...	0757	...	...	0918	0921	...	1019	1018	...	...	...	1118	...	...	...	1218	...	...
58	Noyelles sur Mer d.	...	...	...	...	...	0706	...	0806	...	...	0927	|	...	1028	1030	...	...	...	1131	...	...	...	1231	...	...
85	Rang du Fliers ⊙ d.	...	0604	...	...	...	0725	...	0823	...	...	0947	0946	...	1047	1055	⊖	⊖	...	1155	...	...	...	1255	...	*1402*
96	Étaples-Le Touquet § d.	...	0615	...	...	0700	0733	...	0832	...	...	0955	0957	...	1055	1106	1140	1148	...	1206	...	1251	...	1309	...	1433
123	**Boulogne** Ville § a.	...	0642	...	...	0726	0758	...	0848	...	...	1012	1016	...	1109	1126	1205	1214	...	1226	...	1311	...	1327	...	1453
123	**Boulogne** Ville d.	0546	0643	0627	0711	0727	0805	0811	0849	0911	0947	1013	...	1048	1111	...	1207	1217	1227	...	1248	1313	1311	...	1448	...
130	Wimille-Wimereux d.	0554	0652	0635	0720	0735	0812	0819	0857	0920	0955	1021	...	1056	1119	...	1216	1224	1235	...	1256	1321	1320	...	1457	...
140	Marquise-Rinxent d.	0602	0700	0642	0729	0742	0820	0828	0904	0928	1003	1029	...	1104	1128	...	1224	1232	1243	...	1303	1329	1329	...	1506	...
157	Calais Fréthun **265** d.	0613	0713	0701	0743	0800	0831	0841	0916	0941	1014	1041	...	1115	1140	...	1235	1250	1301	...	1314	1341	1341	...	1518	...
165	**Calais** Ville **265** a.	0622	0722	0710	0752	0810	0840	0850	0924	0950	1022	1050	...	1124	1150	...	1244	1259	1310	...	1323	1350	1350	...	1527	...

							2017	2017				2021								2025		2027				2035
	⑥	Ⓐ	†	⑥	Ⓐ	⑥	Ⓐ	†	†	⑥	Ⓐ	⑥	Ⓒ	Ⓐ	Ⓐ	E	†	⑥	Ⓐ	Ⓐ	Ⓐ	Ⓒ	⑥	Ⓑ	Ⓑ	
Paris Nord **260** d.	...	...	...	...	...	...	1331	1331	...	...	...	1431	...	...	...	...	...	...	...	1631	...	1731	...	...	...	1931
Amiens d.	...	1347	...	...	...	1447	1451	1451	...	...	...	1551	...	...	...	1647	...	1747	...	1753	1847	1851	...	1947	...	2051
Abbeville d.	...	1419	...	...	...	1519	1518	1518	...	...	...	1618	...	...	...	1719	...	1819	...	1819	1919	1918	...	2019	...	2118
Noyelles sur Mer d.	...	1429	...	...	...	1528	|	1531	...	...	...	|	...	...	...	1728	...	1828	...	1831	1928	1930	...	2028	...	2131
Rang du Fliers ⊙ d.	...	1446	⊖	...	...	1547	1544	1555	...	...	...	1644	...	...	1718	1747	...	1847	⊖	1855	1947	1955	...	2047	⊖	2155
Étaples-Le Touquet § d.	...	1454	1458	1521	...	1555	1555	1606	...	1630	...	1655	...	1700	1727	1755	...	1856	1835	1906	1955	2006	...	2055	2100	2206
Boulogne Ville § a.	...	...	1518	1541	...	...	1614	1626	...	1649	...	1714	...	1726	1744	1809	...	1911	1901	1926	2010	2026	...	2111	2118	2226
Boulogne Ville d.	1456	...	1520	1543	1611	...	...	...	1648	1651	1711	...	1723	1727	1746	1811	1848	1912	1922	...	2012	...	2036	...	2120	...
Wimille-Wimereux d.	1504	...	|	1551	1620	...	...	...	1656	1659	1720	...	1731	1735	1754	1819	1855	1920	1932	...	2020	...	2044	...	2129	...
Marquise-Rinxent d.	1511	...	1540	1559	1628	...	...	...	1703	1706	1728	...	1738	1743	1802	1828	1902	1929	1939	...	2029	...	2051	...	2138	...
Calais Fréthun **265** d.	1522	...	1552	1610	1641	...	...	...	1714	1717	1741	...	1749	1801	1813	1840	1913	1941	1957	...	2041	...	2102	...	2150	...
Calais Ville **265** a.	1531	...	1559	1618	1650	...	...	...	1723	1724	1750	...	1758	1810	1823	1850	1921	1950	2005	...	2050	...	2111	...	2159	...

			2008							2014			2014							2022						
	Ⓐ	Ⓐ	⚒	⚒	⑥	Ⓐ	Ⓐ	Ⓐ	Ⓒ	†		⑥	⚒	Ⓐ	Ⓐ	Ⓐ	Ⓒ	⑥	⚒	Ⓐ		⑥	Ⓐ	⑥	†	
Calais Ville **265** d.	...	0509	...	0609	0648	0709	0729	0809	0809	...	...	0901	...	0929	...	1009	1109	...	1148	...	...	1209	1216	1309	1309	...
Calais Fréthun **265** d.	...	0519	...	0621	0658	0723	0738	0820	0819	...	...	0910	...	0940	...	1022	1122	...	1157	...	...	1223	1225	1318	1322	...
Marquise-Rinxent d.	...	0531	...	0632	0716	0734	0756	0831	0831	...	...	0921	...	0954	...	1033	1133	...	1216	...	...	1234	1244	1331	1333	...
Wimille-Wimereux d.	...	0540	...	0640	0724	0741	0804	0839	0840	...	...	0929	...	1002	...	1040	1141	...	1224	...	...	1241	1251	1340	1341	...
Boulogne Ville a.	...	0548	...	0648	0732	0748	0811	0845	0848	...	...	0936	...	1009	...	1048	1148	...	1231	...	...	1248	1258	1348	1348	...
Boulogne Ville § d.	0449	0550	0627	...	...	0750	0812	...	0850	0933	...	...	0945	...	1040	...	...	1220	1232	1245	...	1250	1300	...	...	...
Étaples-Le Touquet § d.	0505	0606	0650	...	...	0806	0838	...	0905	0953	...	...	1008	...	1056	...	...	1239	1259	1306	...	1305	1316	...	...	...
Rang du Fliers ⊙ d.	0514	0615	0700	...	...	0815	⊖	...	0915	1004	...	...	1019	...	1111	...	...	1247	⊖	1317	...	1314	1324	...	...	...
Noyelles sur Mer d.	0531	0632	0723	...	...	0832	...	...	0932	1028	...	...	|	...	1130	...	...	...	...	|	...	1332	...	...	...	...
Abbeville d.	0541	0642	0735	...	...	0842	...	...	0942	1041	...	...	1043	...	1140	...	...	...	...	1343	...	1342	...	...	...	...
Amiens a.	0614	0713	0809	...	...	0913	...	...	1013	1109	...	...	1109	...	1213	...	...	...	...	1409	...	1413	...	...	...	...
Paris Nord **260** a.	...	...	0929	...	...	...	...	...	...	1229	...	...	1229	...	...	...	...	...	...	1529	...	...	...	...	...	...

		2026	2026				2030			2030		2034							2036							
	⚒	Ⓐ	Ⓒ	Ⓐ	†	⚒	†	Ⓐ	⑥	Ⓐ	Ⓐ	Ⓒ	Ⓐ	†	Ⓐ	†	⑥	Ⓐ	†		Ⓐ	†	⑥	Ⓐ	Ⓒ	
Calais Ville **265** d.	1335	...	...	1438	1440	1509	...	1558	1558	...	1648	...	1709	1712	1736	1807	1809	1830	...	...	1928	2009	2009	2038	2209	...
Calais Fréthun **265** d.	1344	...	...	1448	1450	1522	...	1607	1608	...	1657	...	1720	1720	1745	1817	1819	1841	...	...	1940	2018	2019	2048	2219	...
Marquise-Rinxent d.	1355	...	...	1458	1504	1533	...	1618	1619	...	1716	...	1734	1731	1804	1832	1831	1853	...	...	1953	2031	2032	2059	2231	...
Wimille-Wimereux d.	1402	...	...	1506	1514	1541	...	1626	1626	...	1724	...	1741	1739	1811	1840	1840	1900	...	...	2000	2040	2041	2106	2241	...
Boulogne Ville a.	1410	...	...	1513	1522	1548	...	1633	1633	...	1731	...	1748	1746	1818	1847	1848	1907	...	...	2007	2048	2048	2113	2248	...
Boulogne Ville § d.	...	1433	1445	...	1523	1550	1633	1635	...	1645	1732	1733	1750	1747	1819	...	1903	1908	1933	...	...	...	...	2115	...	...
Étaples-Le Touquet § d.	...	1453	1506	...	1545	1606	1653	1656	...	1706	1758	1754	1806	1802	1845	...	1919	1926	1953	...	...	...	...	2133	...	...
Rang du Fliers ⊙ d.	...	1504	1517	...	⊖	1615	1704	1703	...	1717	⊖	1805	1815	⊖	1852	...	1928	...	2004	...	...	...	...	2140	...	...
Noyelles sur Mer d.	...	1528	|	...	...	1633	1728	...	...	|	...	1828	1832	...	...	...	1946	...	2028	...	...	...	...	...	...	...
Abbeville d.	...	1541	1543	...	...	1642	1741	...	...	1743	...	1841	1842	...	...	...	1955	...	2041	...	...	...	...	...	...	...
Amiens a.	...	1609	1609	...	...	1713	1809	...	...	1809	...	1909	1913	...	...	...	2026	...	2109	...	...	...	...	...	...	...
Paris Nord **260** a.	...	1729	1729	...	...	...	1929	...	...	1929	...	2029	...	...	...	...	...	...	2229	...	...	...	...	...	...	...

ADDITIONAL JOURNEYS AMIENS - ABBEVILLE

ALSO:	Ⓐ	Ⓐ	Ⓐ	†	Ⓐ	⑥	Ⓐ		⚒	Ⓐ	Ⓑ	⚒	Ⓐ
Amiens d.	0646	0747	0812	0850	0947	1112	1247	1312	1612	1722	1812	1912	2012
Abbeville a.	0730	0820	0856	0922	1020	1156	1320	1356	1656	1807	1856	1956	2056

	⑥	Ⓐ	⚒	⚒	⚒	⑥	Ⓑ	⚒	Ⓐ	Ⓑ	Ⓐ
Abbeville d.	0546	0604	0647	0726	0804	1221	1304	1604	1704	1749	1947
Amiens a.	0620	0649	0729	0800	0849	1306	1349	1649	1749	1831	2029

E – Ⓐ from Amiens, ⚒ Boulogne - Calais.
⊖ – To / from Arras (Table 263).
⊙ – Rang du Fliers-Verton-Berck.
§ – See also Table 263.

Subject to alteration Dec. 26 - 30 and from Mar. 20

ABBEVILLE - LE TRÉPORT 261a

km																									
		🚌	🚌						🚌	🚌	🚌	🚌		🚌	🚌								🚌	🚌	
			⚒	⑦L	†J		⑦L	⑥N	†	Ⓐ	⑥	†		⚒	⚒	⑥		Ⓐu	⑦L	†J	Ⓐ	⑥	⑥	⑤	
	Laon 252 d.	...	...	...	...	...	0821	0826	...	...	...	...	...	...	...	...	...	...	...	...	...	...	...	...	...
	Amiens 261 d.	...	...	0847	...	...	|	0939	...	...	...	...	...	...	...	...	...	...	...	...	...	...	...	...	...
0	Abbeville d.	0641	0830	0917	0926	...	1001	1012	1129	1225	1225	1306	...	1406	1529	1627	...	1730	1750	1806	1924	1927	2006	2029	...
37	Le Tréport a.	0738	0924	0950	1006	...	1036	1046	1235	1319	1319	1400	...	1500	1623	1713	...	1821	1836	1852	2012	2013	2100	2123	...

	🚌							🚌	🚌		🚌		🚌	🚌			🚌				🚌			
	①g		⚒		Ⓐn		⑥	⚒	†		⚒		Ⓐ	†		†			⑥N	⑦L	⑥		⑦L	
Le Tréport d.	0447	...	0638	...	0745	...	0855	0937	0936	...	1237	...	1634	1638	...	1706	1738	...	1838	1841	1851	...	1927	...
Abbeville a.	0531	...	0724	...	0826	...	0936	1031	1030	...	1331	...	1731	1732	...	1745	1832	...	1912	1914	1945	...	2000	...
Amiens 261 a.	...	...	...	...	...	...	...	...	...	...	...	...	...	...	...	...	...	...	1940	|	...	...	2029	...
Laon 252 a.	...	...	...	...	...	...	...	...	...	...	...	...	...	...	...	...	...	...	2100	2100	...	...	...	...

J – To June 25/from Sept. 3.
L – ⑦ July 2 - Aug. 27 (also July 14, Aug. 15).
N – ⑥ July 1 - Aug. 26.
g – Also Apr. 18, May 2, 9, June 6.
n – Not Dec. 19-30.
u – By 🚌 (arrive 1855) on Dec. 19-30.

LILLE - VALENCIENNES - MAUBEUGE and CHARLEVILLE MÉZIÈRES 262

km		⑥	⚒	Ⓐ	Ⓐ	Ⓐ	⑥	Ⓐ	Ⓐ	⑥	Ⓐ	Ⓐ	⑥	Ⓐ	Ⓐ	Ⓒ	†	⑥	†	†	Ⓐ	⑥	Ⓐ	Ⓐ	⑥	⑥	⑥
0	Lille Flandres ▷ d.	0535	0535	...	0535	0635	0635	0705	0735	0735	0805	0835	0835	0905	0935	0935	...	...	1135	...	1201	1201	1235	...	1235	...	1305
48	Valenciennes ▷ d.	0621	0620	...	0620	0720	0722	0750	0820	0821	0843	0920	0921	0943	1020	1021	...	...	1221	...	1231	1232	1320	...	1321	...	1349
82	Aulnoye Aymeries a.	0649	0649	...	0649	0749	0750	0816	0849	0849	0909	0949	0949	1009	1049	1051	...	...	1249	...	1253	1253	1349	...	1348	...	1415
82	Aulnoye Aymeries d.	0652	0701	...	0711	0801	0801	0818	0901	0852	0911	1001	0952	1011	1101	1054	1101	1101	1301	1258	1255	1255	1355	1401	1400	...	1417
94	**Maubeuge** d.	0703	|	...	0725	|	|	0832	|	0904	0923	|	1004	1024	|	1105	|	|	|	1313	1304	1305	1406	|	|	...	1433
104	Jeumont a.	0710	|	...	0735	|	|	0839	|	0912	0930	|	1012	1031	|	1112	|	|	|	1320	|	1312	1413	|	|	...	1442
94	Avesnes d.	...	0717	...	...	0817	0817	...	0918	0917*	...	1013	...	...	1113	...	1112	1117	1312	...	1312*	1317*	...	1412	1411	...	...
123	Hirson a.	...	0746	0753	...	0846	0844	...	0946	0945*	...	1038	...	...	1138	...	1134	1145	1336	...	1338*	1344*	...	1438	1434	1442	...
184	**Charleville-Mézières** a.	...	...	0833	...	...	0925	...	...	...	...	...	...	...	...	...	1215	...	...	...	...	...	...	...	...	1522	...

	Ⓐ	†	†	⚒	⚒	Ⓐ	Ⓐ	Ⓒ	Ⓐ	Ⓐ	†	⑥	Ⓐ	Ⓐ	Ⓐ	Ⓐ		Ⓒ	†	Ⓐ	⑥	Ⓐ	Ⓐ			Ⓐ	Ⓐ
Lille Flandres ▷ d.	1335	1335	...	1435	...	1535	1605	1635	1701	1635	...	...	1731	1801	1831	...	1835	...	...	1901	...	1935	...	2035	...	2135	...
Valenciennes ▷ d.	1420	1418	...	1520	...	1620	1643	1720	1732	1720	...	...	1802	1832	1902	...	1920	...	...	1931	...	2020	...	2120	...	2220	...
Aulnoye Aymeries a.	1449	1445	...	1549	...	1649	1709	1749	1753	1749	...	...	|	1853	|	...	1949	...	...	1953	...	2049	...	2149	...	2249	...
Aulnoye Aymeries d.	1455	1454	1452	1555	1601	1701	1711	1752	1755	1801	1801	1801	|	1855	|	...	2001	...	1958	1955	2017	2055	2101	2155	2201	2255	2301
Maubeuge d.	1506	1505	|	1606	|	|	1725	1804	1805	|	|	|	|	1905	|	...	|	...	2013	2005	2033	2106	|	2206	|	2306	|
Jeumont a.	1513	1512	|	1613	|	|	1735	1812	1812	|	|	|	|	1912	|	...	|	...	2024	2012	2042	2113	|	2213	|	2313	|
Avesnes d.	1512*	...	1503	...	1612	1713	...	...	...	1813	1811	1817	1827	...	1928	...	2013	...	...	...	...	...	2112	...	2212	...	2312
Hirson a.	1538*	...	1527	...	1638	1738	...	...	...	1838	1834	1845	1846	...	1950	1955	2038	2041	...	...	...	...	2138	...	2238	...	2338
Charleville-Mézières a.	...	...	...	...	...	...	...	...	...	...	1915	...	1924	...	...	2033	...	2119	...	...	...	...	...	...	...	...	...

	Ⓐ	Ⓐ	Ⓐ	⑥	Ⓐ	Ⓐ	⚒	Ⓐ	†	⚒	Ⓐ	⚒	⚒	Ⓐ	Ⓒ	Ⓑ	⑥	Ⓐ	Ⓐ	Ⓐ	⑥	†	Ⓒ	Ⓐ	Ⓐ	⑥	⑥
Charleville-Mézières d.	...	...	...	...	...	...	...	0624	...	...	...	...	...	...	...	...	...	...	...	...	0939	...	...	1041	...	...	...
Hirson d.	...	...	0613	...	...	...	0616	0713	...	...	...	0716	...	0816	0822	...	...	0925	...	1025*	1027	1050	...	1125	...	1200	...
Avesnes d.	...	...	0634	...	...	...	0643	0734	...	...	...	0744	...	0844	0848	...	...	0950	...	1050*	1051	1115	...	1150	...	1226	...
Jeumont d.	0527	0549	|	0618	0623	0648	|	|	0718	0723	0749	|	0827	|	|	0849	0922	|	0949	1049	|	|	1122	|	1149	|	1218
Maubeuge d.	0536	0558	|	0630	0637	0656	|	|	0730	0737	0758	|	0836	|	|	0857	0931	|	0957	1057	|	|	1130	|	1157	|	1231
Aulnoye Aymeries a.	0548	0606	|	0642	0648	0704	0659	|	0742	0748	0806	0758	0848	0900	0857	0907	0942	1000	1009	1107	1100	1125	1142	1200	1207	1235	1242
Aulnoye Aymeries d.	0550	0608	|	0644	0650	0706	0709	|	0744	0750	0808	0811	0850	...	...	0911	0944	...	1011	1111	1114	...	1144	...	1211	...	1244
Valenciennes ▷ d.	0618	0631	0700	0711	0718	0728	0740	0800	0812	0818	0831	0841	0918	...	...	0941	1011	...	1041	1141	1143	...	1211	...	1241	...	1313
Lille Flandres ▷ a.	0655	0659	0731	0755	0755	0759	0825	0829	0855	0855	0859	0925	0955	...	...	1025	1055	...	1125	1225	1225	...	1255	...	1325	...	1355

	Ⓐ	⑥	†	†	†	Ⓐ	⚒	†		Ⓐ	Ⓐ	Ⓐ	†	⑥	Ⓒ	Ⓐ	Ⓐ	Ⓐ	†	Ⓐ	Ⓐ	†	†	⑥	⑥	Ⓐ	Ⓐ
Charleville-Mézières d.	...	1140	...	1320	...	...	...	...	...	...	...	...	1627	...	...	...	...	...	...	1841	...	...	1940	...	...	2053	...
Hirson d.	1216	1227	1227	1358	...	1425	1525	1535	...	...	1616	...	1718	1725	...	1716	1816	...	1901*	1925	...	...	2027	...	2127	2131	...
Avesnes d.	1243	1250	1251	1424	...	1450	1550	1559	...	...	1644	...	1744	1751	...	1745	1845	...	1926*	1950	...	...	2050	...	2151	2154	...
Jeumont d.	|	|	|	|	1418	|	|	|	1549	1627	|	1723	|	|	1748	|	|	1849	1915	|	1949	2048	|	2140	|	|	2149
Maubeuge d.	|	|	|	|	1426	|	|	|	1557	1636	|	1737	|	|	1756	|	|	1857	1928	|	1957	2056	|	2148	|	|	2157
Aulnoye Aymeries a.	1300	1259	1300	1435	1442	1500	1600	1608	1607	1648	1700	1748	1759	1800	1807	1800	1900	1907	1942	2000	2007	2107	2059	2159	2200	2203	2207
Aulnoye Aymeries d.	1311	1313	1314	...	1444	1511	...	...	1611	1650	1710	1750	...	...	1809	1811	...	1911	1944	...	2011	...	2113	...	2214	...	2211
Valenciennes ▷ d.	1341	1342	1343	...	1513	1541	...	...	1641	1718	1741	1818	...	...	1843	1841	...	1941	2010	...	2041	...	2142	...	2243	...	2241
Lille Flandres ▷ a.	1425	1425	1425	...	1555	1625	...	...	1725	1755	1825	1855	...	...	1925	1925	...	2025	2055	...	2125	...	2225	...	2325	...	2325

LOCAL TRAINS LILLE - VALENCIENNES

	Ⓐ	Ⓐ	Ⓐ	Ⓐ	Ⓒ	Ⓐ	Ⓐ	Ⓐ	†	Ⓐ	⑥	Ⓐ		Ⓐ	Ⓐ	†	⑥	Ⓐ		Ⓐ	Ⓒ	Ⓐ	Ⓒ	Ⓐ	
Lille Flandres d.	0512	0812	0912	1012	1035	1112	1205	1212	1235	1312	1335	1412	...	1612	1712	1735	1740	1812	...	1912	1935	2012	2135	2230	...
Valenciennes a.	0558	0855	0955	1055	1125	1201	1241	1255	1325	1355	1418	1455	...	1655	1755	1819	1830	1855	...	1955	2025	2055	2225	2323	...

	⑥	Ⓐ	Ⓐ	Ⓐ	Ⓐ	Ⓐ		Ⓐ	†	Ⓐ	⑥	Ⓐ		⑥	Ⓐ	†	Ⓐ	Ⓒ	Ⓐ		Ⓐ	Ⓐ	⑥		
Valenciennes d.	0434	0440	0605	0703	0804	0905	...	1105	1137	1203	1230	1303	...	1530	1603	1606	1703	1728	1802	...	1902	2004	2005	...	...
Lille Flandres a.	0526	0527	0648	0749	0848	0948	...	1148	1227	1248	1321	1348	...	1621	1648	1656	1748	1821	1848	...	1948	2048	2057	...	...

▷ – For additional trains see panel below main table.
* – Change at Aulnoye Aymeries.

Subject to alteration Dec. 26-30.

BOULOGNE - ST POL - ARRAS / BÉTHUNE 263

km		⚒	⚒	Ⓐ	⑥	⑥	Ⓐ	†	Ⓐ	†	⑥	Ⓐ	⚒	Ⓐ	†	†	†	⑥	Ⓐ	Ⓒ	⑥	⑥	Ⓐ	†	†
									🚌			🚌							b						
	Calais Ville 261 d.	...	...	...	...	...	0729	...	...	...	...	...	1148	...	...	...	1440	...	...	...	...	...	1648	1712	...
0	**Boulogne** Ville 261 d.	0454	...	0605	0618	...	0812	0841	...	...	...	1025	1232	...	1303	1439	1523	1528	1523	...	1716	...	1732	1747	...
27	Étaples Le Touquet 261 d.	0521	...	0639	0649	...	0840	0912	...	...	...	1058	1301	...	1323	1459	1547	1556	1556	...	1743	...	1800	1804	...
39	Montreuil d.	0537	...	0655	0705	...	0856	0927	...	...	...	1120	1316	...	1338	1514	1602	1612	1618	...	1800	...	1817	1820	...
60	Hesdin d.	0607	...	0729	0739	...	0927	0957	...	...	...	1150	1346	...	1415	1544	1632	1642	1705	...	1838	...	1850	1854	...
88	St Pol sur Ternoise a.	0646	...	0807	0817	...	1006	1032	...	...	...	1220	1425	...	1450	1625	1710	1721	1757	...	1917	...	1927	1929	...
88	St Pol sur Ternoise d.	0702	0656	0809	0819	0826	1012	1034	1040	1049	1056	1220	1426	1456	1504	1627	1712	1723	1812	1830	1918	1923	1934	1930	1936
127	**Arras** a.	0742	|	0846	0856	|	1043	1108	|	|	|	1300	1504	|	1530	1658	|	|	1848	1908	1951	|	2005	1959	|
120	Béthune ▷ d.	...	0750	...	...	0918	...	...	1141	1142	1150	...	...	1550	...	...	1805	1825	...	...	...	2012	...	...	2030
162	**Lille** Flandres ▷ a.	...	0825	...	...	0953	...	...	...	1221	1225	...	...	1625	...	...	1841	1902	...	...	...	2047	...	...	2109

	Ⓐ	Ⓐ	Ⓐ	Ⓒ	⑥	†	⑥	†	Ⓐ	⑥	Ⓐ	Ⓐ	Ⓐ	⑥	Ⓐ	Ⓐ	†		⑥	Ⓐ	†	Ⓐ	Ⓐ	⑥	⑥
		🚌																d					b		b
Lille Flandres ▷ d.	...	...	...	0842	...	...	...	1135	1210	1235	...	1526	...	...	1636	...	...	1736	...	...	...	1836	...	1920	...
Béthune ▷ d.	...	...	...	0923	...	...	...	1214	1252	1312	...	1602	...	...	1712	...	...	1812	...	...	...	1912	...	2013	...
Arras d.	0605	0739	0928	|	0946	0955	1221	1158	|	1328	1328	|	1621	1723	|	1728	1748	|	1828	1850	1828	|	1942	|	2008
St Pol sur Ternoise a.	0645	0822	1007	1015	1021	1030	1300	1304	1344	1403	1410	1654	1702	1755	1804	1808	1814	1904	1905	1930	1910	2004	2021	2104	2040
St Pol sur Ternoise d.	0650	0822	1014	...	1023	1036	1302	1333	...	1429	1429	...	1704	1757	...	1810	1816	...	1921	1932	1934	...	2036	...	2115
Hesdin d.	0728	0850	1054	...	1102	1115	1348	1411	...	1508	1507	...	1745	1836	...	1852	1853	...	2002	2014	2014	...	2104	...	2143
Montreuil d.	0758	0918	1124	...	1132	1146	1417	1441	...	1537	1535	...	1818	1907	...	1923	1923	...	2032	2045	2044	...	2132	...	2211
Étaples Le Touquet 261 d.	0812	0941	1140	...	1148	1215	1433	1458	...	1553	1550	...	1835	1923	...	1939	1939	...	2048	2101	2100	...	2155	...	2234
Boulogne Ville 261 a.	0842	1016r	1205	...	1214	1240	1453	1518	...	1615	1614	...	1901	1948	...	2004	2008	...	2105	2118	2118	...	2227	...	2306
Calais Ville 261 a.	...	...	1244	...	1259	...	...	1559	...	...	...	...	2005	...	...	...	...	...	...	2159	2159	...	...	...	...

b – By 🚌 Boulogne - St Pol and v.v.
d – On Ⓒ Lille 1741, Béthune 1822, St Pol 1913.
r – By train.
▷ – Additional trains run Béthune - Lille and v.v.

Subject to alteration Dec. 24-31.

264 — PARIS and LILLE - DUNKERQUE — High-speed trains

VIA LILLE — For local trains Lille Flandres - Dunkerque see Table 266

km		◇	TGV 7205 Ⓐ	TGV 7511 Ⓐ		◇	TGV 7567 Ⓐ	TGV 7269 Ⓐ	TGV 7571 ⑥			TGV 7214 Ⓐ	TGV 7530 Ⓐ	TGV 7552 ①-⑥ b	◇	TGV 7288 Ⓑ	TGV 7588 ⑥	TGV 7298 ⑥ e
					†	✗					Dunkerque....d.	0632	0724	0759 1031 1234	...	1631	1834	1834 2314...
	Paris Nord 250..d.	...	0646	0746	...	...	1646	1746	1746		Lille Europe...d.	0703	0754	0832 1105 1305	...	1707	1905	1905 2205
0	Lille Europe...d.	0712	0750	0850	1150	1250	1650	1750	1851 1850		Paris Nord 250.a.	0814	...	0944 1414	...	2014	2014	2314
76	Dunkerque.....a.	0744	0823	0923	1223	1323	1723	1823	1923 1923									

VIA BÉTHUNE — For local trains Arras - Béthune - Hazebrouck see Table 264a

km		TGV 7351 Ⓐ	TGV 7355 ⑥	TGV 7357 ⑦ t	TGV 7359 ⑥ e	TGV 7363 Ⓐ	TGV 7369 ①-⑥ b	TGV 7371 Ⓐ f	TGV 7373 Ⓐ	TGV 7385 Ⓑ z	TGV 7393 ⑤-⑦	TGV 7395 ⑤		TGV 7302 Ⓐ	TGV 7304 Ⓐ	TGV 7308 ⑥ t	TGV 7314 Ⓐ	TGV 7324 Ⓐ	TGV 7332 Ⓐ	TGV 7336 Ⓐ e	TGV 7354 ⑦	TGV 7346 ⑤⑦
0	Paris Nord....256 d.	0752	0852	0952	1052	1252	1352	1452	1552	1652	1837	1952 2052	Dunkerque....d.	0556	...	0756	0956	1356	1556	1656	...	1956 ...
199	Arras.....256 d.	0905	0950	1050	1150	1350	1550	1646	1750	1936	2050	2150	Hazebrouck....d.	0619	0646	0820	1019	1419	1619	1720	1918	2020 ...
219	Lens.....d.	0905	1005	1105	1205	1405	1605	1701	1805	1951	2105	2205	Béthune....d.	0642	0716	0843	1042	1442	1642	1743	1942	2043 ...
238	Béthune.....d.	0918	1018	1118	1218	1418	1618	1716	1818	2005	2118	2218	Lens....d.	0655	0733	0857	1056	1456	1655	1756	1955	2057 ...
272	Hazebrouck....d.	0939	1039	1139	1239	1439	1639	1738	1839	2029	2139	2239	Arras.....256 d.	0717	0756	0917	1117	1517	1717	1817	2017	2117 ...
312	Dunkerque.....a.	1004	1104	1204	1304	1504	1704	1802	1904	2055	2204	2304	Paris Nord..256 a.	0808	0847	1008	1208	1608	1808	1908	2108	2208 ...

A – Daily except ⑤ (not May 24).
b – Not Apr. 17, May 1, 8, June 5.
e – Also Apr. 17, May 1, 8, June 5.
f – Also May 24.
t – Also May 25.

z – On ⑦ depart 1852 and runs 10 - 15 mins later (train 7387).
TGV – Ⓡ, supplement payable.
◇ – TER à Grande Vitesse (TER GV) via high-speed line
(1, 2 class). Supplement *Grande Vitesse* €3 (valid all day).

> Departures from Dunkerque via Lille are up to
> 7 minutes earlier from Feb. 20

264a — ARRAS - BÉTHUNE - HAZEBROUCK — For TGV trains see Table 264

km		Ⓐ	⑥	Ⓐ	Ⓐ	Ⓐ	Ⓐ	Ⓐ	Ⓐ	†	✗	Ⓐ	⑥	Ⓐ	Ⓐ	⑥	Ⓐ	†	✗	Ⓐ	Ⓐ	Ⓐ d
0	Arras.......d.	0604	0623	0622	0657	0723	0804	0822	0856	0904	0923	1056	1204	1222	1225	1256	1257	1323	1356	1456	1556	1604 1617 1651 1714
20	Lens.......d.	0618	0642	0647	0713	0742	0818	0840	0913	0918	0942	1113	1218	1246	1244	1313	1313	1342	1413	1513	1613	1618 1636 1706 1728
39	Béthune.......d.	0635	0703	0706	0732	0801	0835	0859	0931	0935	1001	1130	1236	1303	1303	1331	1335	1401	1431	1531	1631	1655 1728 1743
51	Lillers.......d.	0644	0716	0716	0746	0810	0844	0940	0940	0943	1009	1139	1244	1316	1313	1340	1347	1410	1439	1540	1639	1643 1704 1740
73	Hazebrouck.......a.	0700	0736	0740	0806	0826	0900	0925	0956	1000	1026	1156	1300	1336	1334	1356	1406	1426	1456	1556	1656	1700 1719 1759 1803

		Ⓒ	Ⓒ	Ⓐ	Ⓐ	Ⓐ	Ⓐ	†	Ⓒ	Ⓒ	Ⓒ			Ⓐ	Ⓐ	Ⓐ	Ⓐ	Ⓐ	Ⓐ d	Ⓐ d	Ⓐ	
	Arras.......d.	1722	1756	1757	1822	1915	2000	1955	1956	2056	2104	2156	...	Hazebrouck.......d.	0506	0553	0604	0623	0634	0700	0704	0734 ...
	Lens.......d.	1746	1813	1813	1846	1933	2015	2013	2013	2113	2118	2213	...	Lillers.......d.	0522	0615	0620	0644	0651	0719	0721	0750 ...
	Béthune.......d.	1805	1831	1831	1917	1953	2031	2031	2031	2131	2135	2231	...	Béthune.......d.	0531	0629	0631	0658	0700	0731	0731	0801 ...
	Lillers.......d.	1816	1840	1840	1918	2001	2040	2040	2039	2140	2144	2240	...	Lens.......d.	0549	0649	0649	0716	0722	0750	0749	0821 ...
	Hazebrouck.......a.	1836	1856	1859	1937	2018	2057	2056	2056	2156	2200	2256	...	Arras.......a.	0607	0703	0703	0739	0739	0805	0803	0838 ...

		✗	Ⓐ	⑥ d	†					Ⓐ	Ⓐ	Ⓐ										
	Hazebrouck.......d.	0834	0934	0934	1004	1034	1134	1201	1234	1253	1434	1434	1501	1604	1634	1634	1653	1723	1734	1800	1823	1834 1901 1934 2001 2105
	Lillers.......d.	0850	0950	0950	1021	1050	1150	1218	1253	1314	1440	1451	1518	1621	1651	1651	1713	1744	1751	1817	1846	1851 1918 1951 2018 2121
	Béthune.......d.	0901	1001	1000	1031	1101	1200	1228	1304	1328	1501	1500	1528	1631	1701	1701	1728	1758	1801	1827	1858	1901 1928 2002 2027 2130
	Lens.......d.	0921	1021	1022	1049	1121	1222	1245	1324	1348	1521	1521	1545	1649	1717	1722	1749	1816	1822	1844	1921	1922 1945 2022 2044 2148
	Arras.......a.	0938	1038	1039	1103	1139	1239	1300	1339	1403	1539	1539	1600	1703	1738	1739	1803	1839	1839	1857	1939	1939 1957 2039 2058 2203

d – To / from Dunkerque (Table 266).   Subject to alteration Dec. 26 - 30

265 — (PARIS) - LILLE - CALAIS / BOULOGNE — High-speed trains

For Paris - Boulogne via Amiens see Table 260. For local trains Lille - Calais see Table 266. For local trains Calais - Boulogne - Rang du Fliers see Table 261.

km		TGV 7505 Ⓐ	TGV 7513 Ⓐ	TGV 7515 ⑥ t				TGV 7519 †	TGV 7223 ©	TGV 7535 ✗				TGV 7559 ⑥	TGV 7559 †		TGV 7265 Ⓐ	TGV 7565 ⑥		TGV 7569 Ⓐ	TGV 7569 †
	Paris Nord 250......d.	0646		0746	0746				0846	0946	1146				1546	1546		1646	1646		1746	1746
0	Lille Europe......d.	0755		0855	0855				0955	1054	1255				1655	1655		1756	1755		1856	1915
99	Calais Fréthun......d.	0823		0923	0923				1023	1122	1323				1723	1723		1824	1823		1924	1943
99	Calais Fréthun...261 d.	0832	0831	0932	0932	0941	0938	1012	1032	1124	1332	1341	1341	1612	1732	1735	1741	1833	1832	1840	1933	1957 1953
107	Calais Ville...261 a.		0840			0950	0954	1027		1132		1350	1427	1627		1750	1758		1850		2005	...
133	Boulogne Ville......a.	0855		0955	0953			1053		1354					1755	1755		1853	1853		1952	2014
160	Étaples-Le Touquet......a.			1012				1112		1413								1912			2011	...
171	Rang du Fliers ☉......a.			1023				1123		1424								1923			2023	...

		TGV 7277 † ⊕	TGV 7277 †					TGV 7279 † E §			TGV 7216 Ⓐ		TGV 7229 ①-⑥ b		TGV 7537 Ⓐ	TGV 7537 ⑥ t
	Paris Nord 250......d.	1846	1846					1916			Rang du Fliers ☉....d.		0630		0714	
	Lille Europe......d.	1955	1955					2038f 2054			Étaples-Le Touquet....d.		0642		0725	
	Calais Fréthun......a.	2023	2023					2115 2123			Boulogne Ville....d.		0703		0745 0744	
	Calais Fréthun...261 d.	1958	2035	2035	2039	2041	2112	2112 2125	2132 2132		Calais Ville...261 d.	0617	0702 0709		0745	
	Calais Ville...261 a.	2013			2054	2050	2110	2127 2146		2147	Calais Fréthun...261 a.	0626	0717 0722 0723		0800 0807 0807	
	Boulogne Ville......a.		2056	2056				2153			Calais Fréthun......d.	0629	0732		0815 0845	
	Étaples-Le Touquet......a.		2115								Lille Europe......a.	0658	0801		0845 0845	
	Rang du Fliers ☉......a.		2126								Paris Nord 250..a.	0814	0914		1014 1014	

		TGV 7546 Ⓐ		TGV 7551 Ⓐ	TGV 7551 ⑥		TGV 7555 †	TGV 7254 ①-⑥ b		TGV 7573 ✗ b			TGV 7586 ⑦ e		TGV 7290 Ⓐ	TGV 7292 ⑦ e	TGV 7592 ⑥ u
	Rang du Fliers ☉....d.			1130	1230				1527				1833				
	Étaples-Le Touquet....d.			1142	1242				1539				1844				
	Boulogne Ville....d.	1001		1203 1203	1303				1559		1801	1827	1904 1902				2035
	Calais Ville...261 d.	1009	1216		1302	1324	1432 1558		1807	1902		1807	1902			2032 2032	
	Calais Fréthun...261 d.	1021 1023 1047		1224 1223 1317	1323 1335	1447 1606	1620		1816 1823	1840 1848	1917	1924 1923	2047 2047 2058				
	Calais Fréthun......d.	1032		1232 1232	1332 1337		1632		1832	1900	1935	1932	2106				
	Lille Europe......a.	1101		1301 1301	1401 1405		1701		1901	1930	2004	2001	2134				
	Paris Nord 250..a.	1214		1414 1414	1514		1814		2014	2041	2114	2114	...				

E – Dec. 19 - 30.
f – Lille Flandres.
t – Also May 25.
u – Also May 25; not Dec. 24, 31.
TGV – Ⓡ, supplement payable.

◇ – TER à Grande Vitesse (TER GV) via high-speed line
(1, 2 class). Supplement *Grande Vitesse*
(€3, valid all day). Reservation not necessary.
⊕ – Not on Ⓐ Dec. 19 - 30.

§ – Full name: Rang du Fliers - Verton - Berck.
§ – Connects with *Eurostar* trains to / from Brussels
(Table 10).
🚌 – TER bus service. Rail tickets valid.

> From Jan. 23 arrivals at Paris may be
> up to 9 minutes later

> ALTERNATIVE ROUTES PARIS - CALAIS
> Via Lille (Tables 250 and 266)
> Via Hazebrouck (Tables 264 and 266)
> Via Amiens, Boulogne (Tables 260 and 261)

LILLE - DUNKERQUE and CALAIS — 266

Local trains

For trains via high-speed line see Table **264** Lille - Dunkerque and Table **265** Lille - Calais

km		Ⓐ	Ⓐ	Ⓐ b	⑥	⑥	Ⓐ	Ⓐ	Ⓐ	⑥	Ⓐ	⑥	Ⓐ	⚒	Ⓐ	Ⓐ	Ⓒ	Ⓐ	†	Ⓐ	Ⓐ	Ⓒ	Ⓒ	Ⓐ	Ⓐ	Ⓒ	Ⓒ
0	**Lille** Flandres d.	...	...	...	...	...	0615	0635	0645	0645	0700	...	0715	0735	...	0800	0815	0835	...	0845	0900	0935	...	1000	1015	1015	1135
22	Armentières d.	...	...	...	...	...	|	0649	0701	0659	0714	...	|	0750	...	0814	0829	0849	...	0902	0914	0950	...	1014	|	1029	1150
47	Hazebrouck d.	0543	0618	0633	0635	0647	0648	0713	0722	0718	0735	0746	0748	0813	0818	0835	0848	0913	0915	0918	0935	1013	1019	1037	1048	1048	1213
87	**Dunkerque** a.	|	0652	|	|	0720	0720	|	0756	0752	|	0820	0820	|	0852	|	0920	|	|	0952	|	|	1055	|	1120	1120	|
68	St Omer d.	0557	...	0650	0653	...	...	0726	...	...	0753	...	...	0827	...	0853	...	0926	0929	...	0953	1025	...	1055	...	...	1226
109	**Calais** Ville a.	0626	...	0727	0726	...	...	0756	...	...	0826	...	...	0856	...	0927	...	0956	0958	...	1026	1056	...	1126	...	...	1256

	Ⓒ	Ⓐ	Ⓐ	⑥	Ⓐ	Ⓐ	Ⓐ	⑥	⚒	Ⓐ	⑥	†	⑥	Ⓐ	⑥	Ⓐ	Ⓐ	Ⓒ	†		Ⓐ	Ⓐ	Ⓐ		†	Ⓐ	⑥
Lille Flandres d.	...	1200	1215	1215	1219	1235	1245	1245	...	1315	...	1315	1335	1345	...	1400	...	1435	...	1545	1600	1615	1619	1635	...	1645	...
Armentières d.	...	1214	|	1229	1234	1249	1302	1259	...	|	...	1329	1350	1401	...	1414	...	1450	...	1559	1614	|	1634	1649	...	1701	...
Hazebrouck d.	1217	1235	1248	1248	1253	1313	1318	1321	1333	1348	1348	1348	1413	1418	1419	1435	1447	1513	1519	1618	1635	1648	1653	1713	1719	1718	1719
Dunkerque a.	1253	|	1320	1319	|	|	1352	1355	|	1420	1420	1420	|	1452	1455	|	1520	|	1545	1652	|	1720	|	|	1743	1752	1753
St Omer d.	...	1253	...	...	1305	1326	...	...	1352	...	...	...	1426	...	...	1453	...	1526	...	...	1652	...	1705	1725	...	...	...
Calais Ville a.	...	1326	...	...	...	1356	...	...	1426	...	...	...	1456	...	...	1526	...	1556	...	...	1723	...	...	1756	...	...	...

	Ⓐ	Ⓐ	Ⓒ	Ⓐ	Ⓐ u	Ⓐ	Ⓐ	Ⓐ	Ⓐ	Ⓐ		Ⓐ	Ⓐ	Ⓐ	Ⓒ	Ⓐ	Ⓐ	Ⓐ		†	⑥	†	⚒	Ⓐ	† ⊖	Ⓐ	
Lille Flandres d.	1700	1715	1715	1719	...	1735	1745	1800	1815	1819	1835	1845	1900	...	1915	1919	1935	2015	2035	...	...	2115	2115	2215	2300	2312	...
Armentières d.	1714	|	1731	1734	...	1749	1802	1813	|	1834	1849	1902	1914	...	1931	1934	1949	|	2049	...	...	2129	2129	2229	2314	2326	...
Hazebrouck d.	1735	1748	1748	1753	1806	1812	1817	1835	1848	1853	1913	1918	1935	1947	1950	1953	2018	2048	2113	2119	2118	2148	2148	2247	2335	2349	...
Dunkerque a.	|	1820	1820	|	1828	|	1852	|	1920	|	|	1952	|	2020	2021	|	2052	2120	|	2145	2152	2211	2220	2320	|	...	...
St Omer d.	1753	...	...	1805	...	1825	...	1853	...	1905	1926	...	1953	...	...	2005	...	...	2126	...	...	...	...	...	2347	...	...
Calais Ville a.	1826	...	...	...	...	1856	...	1926	...	...	1956	...	2026	...	...	...	...	...	2156	...	...	...	...	...	0014	...	...

	Ⓐ	Ⓐ	Ⓐ	Ⓐ	Ⓐ	⑥	Ⓐ	Ⓐ	⑥	Ⓐ	⑥ u	Ⓐ u	Ⓐ	Ⓐ	Ⓐ	⑥	Ⓐ	⑥	Ⓐ	Ⓐ	⑥	Ⓐ	Ⓐ	⑥	Ⓐ	Ⓒ	Ⓐ
Calais Ville d.	...	0453	...	...	...	...	0534	...	...	0605	...	...	...	...	0634	0635	...	...	0706	...	...	...	0734	0735	...	...	0833
St Omer d.	...	0523	...	0554	...	...	0607	...	...	0635	...	...	0654	...	0708	0705	...	...	0735	0754	...	...	0808	0807	...	...	0909
Dunkerque d.	...	|	0507	|	0540	0540	|	0608	0608	|	0630	0636	|	0640	|	|	0708	0708	|	|	0739	0740	|	|	0808	0839	|
Hazebrouck d.	0448	0538	0543	0608	0613	0613	0626	0642	0642	0649	0702	0658	0708	0713	0726	0726	0743	0743	0749	0808	0811	0813	0826	0826	0843	0913	0926
Armentières d.	0511	...	0600	0626	|	0630	0645	0657	0659	0711	...	...	0726	|	0745	0745	0757	0800	0811	0826	...	|	0845	0844	0857	0930	0945
Lille Flandres a.	0525	...	0614	0640	0644	0644	0659	0714	0714	0725	...	...	0740	0744	0759	0759	0814	0814	0825	0840	...	0844	0859	0859	0914	0944	0959

	⑥ u	Ⓐ	†	Ⓐ	Ⓒ	Ⓐ	Ⓒ	Ⓐ	Ⓐ	Ⓐ	Ⓒ	⑥	Ⓐ	Ⓐ	Ⓐ	Ⓐ	Ⓐ	⑥	Ⓐ	Ⓒ		†	⑥	⑥	Ⓐ	Ⓐ	
Calais Ville d.	...	...	...	0906	0906	...	...	1034	...	1106	1135	...	...	1206	...	...	1234	1235	...	...	...	1335	1338	...	1434	...	...
St Omer d.	...	...	...	0935	0935	...	...	1108	...	1135	1209	...	...	1235	1254	...	1308	1307	...	...	...	1410	1411	...	1508	...	...
Dunkerque d.	0856	0908	0908	|	|	1040	1039	|	1108	|	|	1208	1213	...	|	1240	|	|	1308	1308	1339	|	|	1439	|	1508	...
Hazebrouck d.	0932	0943	0942	0949	0949	1113	1111	1126	1143	1149	1225	1244	1248	...	1308	1313	1325	1326	1343	1342	1411	1426	1426	1513	1526	1543	...
Armentières d.	...	0957	...	1011	1011	|	1128	1145	1157	1211	1245	1306	1302	...	1326	|	...	1345	1357	1400	...	1445	1445	1530	1545	1557	...
Lille Flandres a.	...	1014	...	1025	1025	1144	1144	1159	1214	1225	1259	1325	1320	...	1340	1344	...	1359	1414	1414	...	1459	1459	1544	1559	1614	...

		Ⓐ	Ⓒ	Ⓐ	Ⓐ	Ⓒ	Ⓐ	Ⓐ	Ⓐ	Ⓐ	⑥	†	Ⓐ	Ⓒ	Ⓐ	Ⓒ	Ⓒ	Ⓐ	Ⓒ	Ⓒ	Ⓐ	Ⓐ	Ⓒ	Ⓐ	Ⓐ	Ⓒ	
Calais Ville d.	...	1534	1539	...	...	...	1634	...	1706	...	...	...	1733	1735	...	...	...	1834	1835	...	...	1906	1935	...	2034	...	...
St Omer d.	...	1608	1611	...	...	...	1707	...	1735	...	...	...	1807	1810	...	...	...	1911	1908	...	...	1935	2010	...	2111	...	...
Dunkerque d.	1539	|	|	1608	1640	1639	|	1708	|	1740	1740	1744	|	|	1808	1808	1849	|	|	1908	1908	|	|	2008	|	2108	...
Hazebrouck d.	1611	1626	1626	1643	1713	1709	1726	1743	1749	1813	1811	1817	1826	1826	1843	1842	1921	1926	1925	1937	1942	1949	2026	2043	2126	2142	...
Armentières d.	...	1645	1645	1657	|	1727	1745	1757	1811	|	...	...	1845	1845	1857	1859	...	1945	1945	1956	...	2011	2045	2100	2145	2159	...
Lille Flandres a.	...	1659	1659	1714	1744	1744	1759	1814	1825	1844	...	...	1859	1859	1914	1914	...	1959	1959	2014	...	2025	2059	2114	2159	2214	...

b – From Bethune, depart 0602.
u – To/from Arras (Table **264a**).
⊖ – By 🚌 (Calais a. 0138) on Dec. 11, Jan. 8, 22.
Subject to alteration Dec. 24 - 31

PARIS - BEAUVAIS — 267

km		Ⓐ	⑥	Ⓐ	Ⓐ	⑥	† z	Ⓐ	Ⓒ	Ⓐ			⚒		⑥	Ⓐ	Ⓐ	Ⓒ	Ⓐ	Ⓐ	⑥	Ⓐ	Ⓐ	†	
0	**Paris** Nord d.	0607	0631	0637	0737	0801	0801	0850	0901	1001	1101	1201	1301	1401	1601	1607	1637	1701	1707	1737	1801	1807	1837	1844	...
80	**Beauvais** a.	0720	0750	0751	0851	0918	0918	1005	1018	1118	1218	1318	1418	1519	1720	1720	1747	1820	1820	1847	1920	1920	1947	2009	...

	⑥	Ⓐ	Ⓐ	⚒	Ⓑ	Ⓒ
Paris Nord d.	1901	1907	1937	2001	2101	2201
Beauvais a.	2019	2020	2048	2118	2218	2318

	Ⓐ	Ⓐ	⑥	Ⓐ	Ⓒ	Ⓐ	Ⓐ	Ⓒ	Ⓐ	⚒	†		⚒		⚒
Beauvais d.	0513	0540	0540	0613	0627	0640	0713	0737	0740	0840	0937	1037	1137	1237	1337
Paris Nord a.	0625	0655	0657	0725	0743	0755	0823	0857	0855	0957	1057	1157	1257	1357	1457

		Ⓐ	⑥	Ⓐ	Ⓐ	Ⓒ	Ⓐ	Ⓐ	Ⓒ	⑥	† z	Ⓐ	Ⓒ	†	† M	
Beauvais d.	1437	1640	1640	1710	1740	1741	1811	1840	1840	1937	1950	2010	2037	2137	2159	...
Paris Nord a.	1557	1755	1757	1823	1855	1857	1925	1955	1957	2057	2105	2127	2157	2257	2301	...

Most trains call at Persan-Beaumont (30 mins from Paris).
CREIL - BEAUVAIS: 14 journeys on Ⓐ, 7 on ⑥, 4 on †.

M – † July 9 - Aug. 27. From Le Tréport (Table **267a**).
z – To/from Le Tréport (Table **267a**).
Subject to alteration Dec. 19 - Jan. 1.

BEAUVAIS - LE TRÉPORT — 267a

km		Ⓐ	† L	† M	⑥	⚒	† M	⚒	Ⓐ	† L	⑥	⑤–⑦ v
	Paris Nord **267** d.	...	0801	0801	...	...	...	...	...	...	...	...
0	**Beauvais** d.	0740	0926	0926	0924	1234	1752	1759	...	1823	1853	2025
	Rouen ⊖ **268** d.	|	*0915*	*0915*	*0917*r	|	|	|	...	|	|	|
49	Abancourt **268** d.	0836	1021	1020	1021	1334	1851	1855	1905	1922	1949	2123
103	Eu d.	0928	1112	|	1112	1425	1943	...	1956	2013	2041	2214
106	**Le Tréport** a.	0932	1116	1109	1116	1430	1947	...	2000	2017	2045	2218

	Ⓐ	⑥	†	⑥	⚒	† u	⚒	† M	† L	† M
Le Tréport d.	0529	0643	0731	0847	1205	1238	1720	1800	1758	2001
Eu d.	0534	|	|	0852	1210	1243	1725	|	1803	2006
Abancourt **268** d.	0634	0735	0822	0944	1302	1334	1824	1849	1851	2052
Rouen ⊖ **268** a.	|	|	|	|	|	|	|	*1942*	|	|
Beauvais a.	0730	0830	0919	1049	1358	1430	1925	1945	1948	2150
Paris Nord **267** a.	...	...	...	...	...	...	...	2059	2105	2301

L – † to July 2/from Sept. 3.
M – † July 9 - Aug. 27.
r – ⑥ July 8 - Aug. 26.
u – By 🚌 on Dec. 25, Jan. 1.
v – Also holidays. By 🚌 on Dec. 25, Jan. 1.
⊖ – Rouen Rive-Droite. See Table **268** for other connections.

AMIENS - ROUEN — 268

km		① g	Ⓐ		⑥	†		Ⓐ	Ⓐ	⑥		†		①–④ n	⑤		Ⓑ	⑥	Ⓐ		Ⓐ	Ⓒ		
	Lille Flandres **256** d.	...	0602	...	0802	...	...	...	1102	...	...	...	...	...	...	...	...	...	1702	...	...	1802	...	...
0	**Amiens** d.	0555	0719	...	0927	0927	...	1027	1227	1244	...	1421	...	1655	1655	...	1727	1733	1827	...	1906	1926	...	...
31	Poix de Picardie d.	0614	0737	...	0946	0944	...	1045	1245	1305	...	1439	...	1717	1717	...	1745	1755	1845	...	1927	1944	...	...
52	Abancourt d.	0626	0749	...	0958	0956	...	1057	1258	1320	...	1451	...	1732	1732	...	1758	1810	1857	...	1942	1957	...	...
73	Serqueux d.	0642	0803	...	1011	1012	...	1110	1311	1336	...	1510	...	1749	1750	...	1813	1826	1913	...	1957	2010	...	...
121	**Rouen** Rive-Droite a.	0724	0832	...	1044	1044	...	1142	1342	1423	...	1542	...	...	1822	...	1842	1907	1942	...	...	2042	...	...

	Ⓐ	Ⓐ		Ⓐ		⑥		†	⑥ R		Ⓐ	⚒		Ⓐ			Ⓐ		⑤	†				
Rouen Rive-Droite d.	...	0617	...	0717	...	0818	...	0915	0917	...	1117	1217	...	1617	...	1817	1834	...	1917	1917	...	...	...	...
Serqueux d.	0614	0647	...	0747	...	0848	...	0948	0948	...	1149	1249	...	1651	...	1849	1915	...	1949	1949	...	...	...	...
Abancourt d.	0629	0703	...	0802	...	0902	...	1002	1004	...	1202	1302	...	1703	...	1902	1932	...	2002	2002	...	...	...	...
Poix de Picardie d.	0644	0715	...	0814	...	0915	...	1014	...	...	1215	1314	...	1715	...	1915	...	...	2014	2014	...	...	...	...
Amiens a.	0706	0732	...	0832	...	0932	...	1032	...	...	1232	1332	...	1732	...	1932	...	...	2032	2032	...	...	...	...
Lille Flandres **256** a.	...	0858	...	...	...	1058	...	...	...	...	1358	...	...	...	...	2058	...	...	...	...	...	...	...	...

R – ⑥ July 8 - Aug. 26.
g – Also Apr. 18, May 2.
n – Not holidays.

12 *French public holidays are on Dec. 25, Jan. 1, Apr. 17, May 1, 8, 25, June 5* 177

269 🚌 RENNES / DOL - MONT ST MICHEL

By 🚌 Keolis Emeraude

km	🚌		Ⓐ	Ⓒb		S	ⒸW			
0	**Rennes** Gare Routière ⊡ d.	0940	...	...	1135	...	...	1235	1640	...
	Dol (Gare SNCF) d.	|	1040	1115	|	1315	1315	|	|	...
68	**Mont St Michel** a.	1050	1110	1145	1245	1345	1345	1345	1750	...

🚌	Ⓐ	Ⓒ			S	W		⑦S	
Mont St Michel d.	0905	0935	1105	1435	1605	1610	1730	1840	...
Dol (Gare SNCF) a.	|	|	|	|	1640	1640	|	1910	...
Rennes Gare Routière ⊡ a.	1015	1045	1215	1545	...	...	1845	...	...

b – Runs 5 minutes later July 2 - Aug. 27. S – July 2 - Aug. 28. W – Aug. 29 - July 1. ⊡ – Adjacent to rail station. *Service to July 1, 2017*

Operator: Keolis Emeraude, St Malo. ✆ 02 99 19 70 70. www.keolis-emeraude.com Connections (not guaranteed) at Rennes or Dol with *TGV* services to / from Paris. Combined rail / bus tickets available from rail stations. Rail passes not valid. At Mont St Michel the coach terminates close to the tourist information office. A free *Passeur* shuttle service operates along the causeway to Mont St Michel itself, allow 25 mins (or 45 mins walk, *2.4 km*). Horse-drawn shuttles (*Maringotes*) are also available, fee payable.

270 PARIS - ROUEN - LE HAVRE

km								3101		13101		3103	3103	13103	3105	3105		13105	13191	3107	13193			13107	
		⚒	⑥	Ⓐ	Ⓐ	Ⓐ	⚒	Ⓐ	⑥	Ⓐ	⑦	⑥	Ⓐ		Ⓒ	Ⓐ		①–⑥	⑦	Ⓐ	⑥	Ⓒ	⚒		
											k	t		△				n	e		t				
0	**Paris** St Lazare § d.	...	...	...	...	...	0611	0653	...	0720	...	0750	0753	0820	0850	0853	...	1020	1036	1050	1050	...	...	1220	...
57	Mantes la Jolie § d.	...	...	...	0627	...	0644	|	0737	0752	...	|	|	0853	|	|	...	1052	1108	|	|	...	...	1252	...
79	Vernon-Giverny d.	...	...	...	0645	...	0706	|	0750	0807	...	|	|	0907	|	|	...	1107	1123	|	|	...	...	1307	...
111	Val de Reuil d.	...	...	...	0705	...	0727	|	0810	0828	...	|	|	0928	|	|	...	1128	1145	|	|	...	...	1328	...
126	Oissel d.	...	...	...	0717	...	0736	|	0822	0837	...	|	|	0937	|	|	...	1137	1156	|	|	...	...	1337	...
140	**Rouen** Rive-Droite a.	...	...	...	0730	...	0750	0802	0837	0848	...	0900	0902	0948	1000	1000	...	1148	1207	1200	1200	...	...	1348	...
140	**Rouen** Rive-Droite d.	0629	0700	0700	...	0740	...	0805	...	...	0904	0903	0905	...	1003	1003	...	...	...	1203	...	1217	1250	...	...
178	Yvetot d.	0659	0735	0735	...	0807	...	0833	...	...	0931	0931	0933	...	1032	1032	...	...	...	1232	...	1243	1328	...	...
203	Bréauté-Beuzeville ▲ d.	0712	0755	0755	...	0822	...	0848	...	...	0944	0946	0948	...	1047	1047	...	...	...	1247	...	1257	1348	...	...
228	**Le Havre** a.	0732	0809	0824	...	0837	...	0903	...	...	0959	1001	1002	...	1102	1102	...	...	...	1302	...	1311	1403	...	...

	3109	3113	3111	13109	3115	3117		3119	13111		3121		3123	13113	13115	3125		3127	3129	13117	13119		3131		
	①–⑥	⑥	⑤			Ⓐ	⑥	⑥	Ⓑ	⑦	Ⓐ	Ⓐ	Ⓐ	Ⓒ	Ⓐ		Ⓐ	①–④	⑤	Ⓒ	Ⓐ	Ⓒ	Ⓐ	Ⓐ	
	n	▷	F				b	t	h	e								m	f			b			
Paris St Lazare § d.	1250	1350	1350	1420	1450	1550	...	1620	1620	...	1650	1653	1725	1720	1730	1750	1753	1825	1825	1820	1830	...	1850	1853	...
Mantes la Jolie § d.	|	|	|	1452	|	|	...	1652	1652	...	|	1725	|	1752	|	|	1825	|	|	1852	|	...	|	1925	...
Vernon-Giverny d.	|	|	|	1507	|	|	...	1707	1707	...	|	1747	|	1807	1813	|	1847	|	|	1907	1913	...	1936	1946	...
Val de Reuil d.	|	|	|	1528	|	|	...	1728	1728	...	|	1810	|	1828	1832	|	1910	|	|	1928	1932	...	|	2006	...
Oissel d.	|	|	|	1537	|	|	...	1737	1737	...	|	1819	|	1837	1840	|	1919	|	|	1937	1940	...	|	2015	...
Rouen Rive-Droite a.	1400	1500	1500	1548	1600	1700	...	1748	1748	...	1800	...	1833	1848	1849	1900	...	1933	1933	1948	1949	...	2004	2025	...
Rouen Rive-Droite d.	1403	1503	...	...	1603	1703	1704	1751	...	1804	1803	...	1836	...	...	1903	...	...	1936	...	...	2004	2007	...	...
Yvetot d.	1432	1531	...	...	1632	1732	1731	1819	...	1831	1830	...	1902	...	...	1930	...	...	2002	...	...	2031	2035	...	...
Bréauté-Beuzeville ▲ d.	1447	1546	...	...	1647	1747	1744	1834	...	1845	1848	...	1919	...	...	1946	...	...	2019	...	...	2045	2051	...	...
Le Havre a.	1502	1601	...	...	1702	1802	1759	1848	...	1859	1902	...	1934	...	...	2001	...	...	2033	...	...	2100	2105	...	...

	13121	13123	3133	5376	13125	3135	3137	3137	13127	3139	3141	13129	3141	13131
	⑦	Ⓐ		TGV	Ⓐ	⑥	①–④	⑦	⑤	⑤	⑤	①–④	⑦	⑥
	e			♥y		t	w	u	f	f	f	D	v	E
Paris St Lazare § d.	1920	1930	1950	...	2020	2020	2050	2120	2120	2150	2205	2309	2350	2350
Mantes la Jolie § d.	1952	|	|	2033	2052	2052	|	2152	2152	|	2237	2352	0022	0022
Vernon-Giverny d.	2007	2013	|	|	2107	2107	2132	2207	2207	|	2252	0007	0036	0037
Val de Reuil d.	2028	2032	|	|	2128	2128	|	2228	2228	|	2312	0028	0056	0058
Oissel d.	2037	2040	|	|	2137	2137	|	2237	2237	|	2322	0037	0106	0107
Rouen Rive-Droite a.	2048	2049	2100	2114	2148	2148	2201	2248	2248	2300	2333	0048	0114	0118
Rouen Rive-Droite d.	...	...	2103	2118	...	2151	2204	2251	...	2303	2336	...	0117	...
Yvetot d.	...	...	2131	|	...	2218	2231	2319	...	2331	0004	...	0144	...
Bréauté-Beuzeville ▲ d.	...	...	2146	|	...	2234	2247	2334	...	2346	0019	...	0158	...
Le Havre a.	...	...	2201	2208	...	2248	2302	2348	...	0001	0033	...	0212	...

		13100	13102	3100		13104
	Ⓐ	Ⓐ	⑥	Ⓐ	Ⓐ	Ⓐ
			t			
Le Havre d.	...	...	...	0529	...	...
Bréauté-Beuzeville ▲ d.	...	...	...	0545	...	...
Yvetot d.	...	...	...	0601	...	...
Rouen Rive-Droite a.	...	...	...	0623	...	...
Rouen Rive-Droite d.	0526	0558	0612	0626	...	0648
Oissel d.	0540	0608	0623	|	0639	|
Val de Reuil d.	0550	0617	0632	|	0650	0703
Vernon-Giverny d.	0611	0639	0653	|	0711	0724
Mantes la Jolie § a.	0631	0656	0705	|	0731	|
Paris St Lazare § a.	0708	0735	0740	0738	0808	0815

	13106	3104	13108	3102			3106	13110		5316	3108	13112		13114	3110	3112	13116		3114	13118	3116		3118	13120	3120
	Ⓐ	⑥	⑦	Ⓐ	Ⓐ	⑥	Ⓐ	⚒	Ⓐ	TGV		⚒	Ⓐ	Ⓑ	⑥	⚒	⑥		⑦		⚒	⑥	Ⓐ		
		t	e					g		♥z				h	t		t		e						
Le Havre d.	...	0612	...	0629	...	0636	0702	...	0721	0749	0802	...	0902	...	0915	1002	...	...	1102	...	1155	1251	1256	...	1402
Bréauté-Beuzeville ▲ d.	...	0628	...	0646	...	0701	0718	...	0736	|	0818	...	0916	...	0931	1018	...	...	1118	...	1211	1309	1312	...	1418
Yvetot d.	...	0644	...	0702	...	0720	0734	...	0753	|	0834	...	0929	...	0947	1034	...	...	1134	...	1227	1328	1328	...	1434
Rouen Rive-Droite a.	...	0709	...	0725	...	0756	0756	...	0824	0840	0856	...	0957	...	1009	1056	...	...	1156	...	1256	1403	1356	...	1456
Rouen Rive-Droite d.	0658	0712	0712	0728	0712	...	0759	0812	...	0845	0859	0912	...	1012	1012	1059	1112	...	1159	1212	1259	...	1359	1413	1459
Oissel d.	0708	0723	0723	|	0740	...	|	0823	...	|	|	0923	...	1023	1023	|	1123	...	|	1223	|	...	|	1423	|
Val de Reuil d.	0717	0732	0732	|	0749	...	|	0832	...	|	|	0932	...	1032	1032	|	1132	...	|	1232	|	...	|	1432	|
Vernon-Giverny d.	0739	0753	0753	|	0811	...	|	0853	...	|	|	0953	...	1053	1053	|	1153	...	|	1253	|	...	|	1453	|
Mantes la Jolie § a.	0756	0805	0806	|	0831	...	|	0906	...	0930	|	1006	...	1106	1106	|	1206	...	|	1306	|	...	|	1506	|
Paris St Lazare § a.	0835	0840	0840	0839	0908	...	0915	0940	...	...	1010	1040	...	1140	1140	1210	1240	...	1310	1340	1410	...	1510	1540	1610

	3122	3138		13122	3124	13190	13124	13192	3126	3128		13126		3130		13128		13194	3132	3134		13130		3136	
	⑤		Ⓐ	⑦	Ⓐ	⑦	Ⓐ	⑥	⑦		Ⓐ	⑦	⑥	Ⓑ	⑥	Ⓐ		⑦		Ⓑ	⑥	⑦		⑦	
	f	Y		e		e		t	e			e		h	b			e		h	b	e		e	
Le Havre d.	...	1502	...	...	1555	...	...	...	1615	1655	...	...	...	1755	1803	...	...	...	1915	2002	2000	...	...	2115	...
Bréauté-Beuzeville ▲ d.	...	1518	...	...	1611	...	...	...	1631	1711	...	...	...	1811	1817	...	...	...	1931	2018	2015	...	...	2131	...
Yvetot d.	...	1534	...	...	1627	...	...	...	1647	1727	...	...	...	1827	1833	...	...	...	1947	2034	2031	...	...	2147	...
Rouen Rive-Droite a.	...	1556	...	...	1656	...	...	...	1709	1756	...	...	...	1856	1859	...	...	...	2009	2056	2055	...	...	2209	...
Rouen Rive-Droite d.	1555	1559	1612	1612	1659	1659	1712	1712	1712	1759	1812	1812	1823	1859	...	1912	...	1959	2012	2059	...	2110	...	2212	...
Oissel d.	|	|	1623	1623	|	|	1723	1723	1723	|	1823	1823	1838	|	...	|	...	|	2023	|	...	2122	...	2223	...
Val de Reuil d.	|	|	1632	1632	|	|	1732	1732	1732	|	1832	1832	1850	|	...	1932	...	|	2032	|	...	2131	...	2232	...
Vernon-Giverny d.	|	|	1653	1653	|	|	1753	1753	1753	|	1853	1853	1912	|	...	1953	...	|	2053	|	...	2153	...	2253	...
Mantes la Jolie § a.	|	|	1706	1706	|	|	1806	1805	1806	|	1906	1906	1925	|	...	2006	...	|	2106	|	...	2206	...	2306	...
Paris St Lazare § a.	1710	1711	1740	1740	1810	1810	1840	1840	1840	1910	1940	1940	...	2010	...	2040	...	2110	2140	2210	...	2240	...	2340	...

D – ①–④ Dec. 19 - 29, Mar. 20 - Apr. 20 (not Apr. 17), from May 22 (not May 24, 25). Dep. Paris 2320 from Mar. 20.
E – ⑥ Dec. 17 - Apr. 22.
F – Also May 24; not Apr. 14, 28, May 5, 26.
Y – Apr. 17, May 1, 8, June 5 only.

b – Not May 6, 7.
e – Also Apr. 17, May 1, 8, June 5.
f – Also May 24.
g – Not Feb. 4, 11.
h – Not May 25.
k – Also Apr. 17, May 1, June 5.

m – Not public holidays; not May 24.
n – Not Apr. 17, May 1, 8, June 5.
t – Also May 25.
u – Also Dec. 19 - 22, 26 - 29; ①–④ Mar. 20 - Apr. 21; also May 1, 8, 22, 23, ①–④ May 29 - June 29.
v – Also June 5; not May 21.
w – Not Dec. 19 - 29, Mar. 19 - Apr. 23.
y – Not Feb. 25, Mar. 24, 25.
z – Not Feb. 26, Mar. 20, 25, 26, Apr. 9, 15, 16, 23, 29, 30, May 7, 13, 14, 21, 28, June 4, 10, 11.

TGV – Ⓡ, supplement payable, 🍸.

♥ – To/from Lyon and Marseille (Table **335**).
▲ – 🚌 runs 2 - 8 times per day to Fécamp.
▷ – Also Apr. 14, 28, May 5, 25, 26.
△ – Not Jan. 15, 22, Feb. 4, 11, Mar. 5.
§ – Frequent suburban trains run Paris - Mantes-la-Jolie.

Timings Rouen to Le Havre may vary by a few minutes from Mar. 18. Departures from Paris may be 1 - 2 minutes earlier from Apr. 24.

270a ROUEN - DIEPPE

km		⑥	Ⓐ	Ⓐ	Ⓐ	⑦d	⚒		⚒	⑦d	⑥	Ⓐ	⑦S	⑥	⑥	Ⓐ	Ⓐ	Ⓐ		Ⓐr	Ⓐ		Ⓐ	⚒	†	
0	**Rouen** Rive-Droite d.	0640	0635	0711	0726	0841	0911	1011	1211	1225	1242	1339	1341	1412	1511	1611	1640	1710	1738	1812	1841	1911	2012	2124	2130	...
63	**Dieppe** a.	0740	0743	0758	0844	0940	0958	1058	1301	1310	1344	1443	1441	1458	1558	1657	1743	1758	1843	1858	1943	1958	2100	2209	2216	...

	Ⓐ	⚒	Ⓐ	Ⓐ	Ⓒ	Ⓐ	⚒		⚒		Ⓐ		†	Ⓐ	⑥	⑦S	Ⓐ	†	⚒	⑦K	Ⓐ	⚒	†	⑦S		
Dieppe d.	0530	0616	0700	0713	0751	0800	0813	1000	1200	1313	1359	...	1556	1600	1609	1700	1713	1800	1813	1844	1900	1959	2013	2101	...	...
Rouen Rive-Droite a.	0616	0718	0747	0818	0835	0848	0919	1048	1248	1419	1448	...	1642	1647	1655	1746	1819	1847	1919	1929	1953	2048	2113	2146	...	...

K – ⑦ July 2 - Aug. 27 (also July 14, Aug. 15).
S – ⑦ June 11 - Sept. 10 (also July 14, Aug. 15).

d – Also Apr. 17, May 1, 25, June 5; not May 7.
r – Also ⑥ June 10 - Sept. 9.

Timings may vary by a few minutes from Mar. 18.

CAEN - ALENÇON - LE MANS - TOURS 271

km		⚒	Ⓐ	Ⓐ	Ⓐ	⚒	†		⑥	Ⓐ					Ⓑ	†	⚒	⑥ 🚌	Ⓐ	†	Ⓐ	⑥	Ⓐ	Ⓐ	†	◇
0	**Caen** ... **275/7** d.	...	0535x	...	0559	0726	...	0900	1029	1039	...	1246	...	...	1647	...	...	...	1745	1745	1811	1825	...	2000	2029	...
23	Mézidon ... **275/7** d.	...	0550x	...	0614	0741	...	0915	1044	1053	...	1302	...	...	1702	...	...	...	1800	1801	1830	1840	...	2014	2044	...
67	Argentan ... **273** d.	...	0614	...	0643	0809	...	0941	1108	1116	...	1326	...	...	1730	...	...	...	1832	1835	1858	1908	...	2040	2108	...
82	Surdon ... **273** d.	...	|	...	0653	0818	...	|	1119	1126	...	1336	...	...	|	...	...	...	1842	1848	1908	1918	...	2049	|	2147
91	Sées ... d.	...	0628	...	0701	0826	...	|	1127	1133	...	1343	...	...	1744	...	...	...	1850	1855	1915	1925	...	2056	2123	2154
111	Alençon ... d.	...	0642	...	0715	0839	0838	1008	1140	1146	...	1357	...	1622r	1758	...	...	...	1902	1909	1928	1938	...	2113	2136	2206
166	**Le Mans** ... a.	...	0729	...	0805	0909	0909	1041	1219	1224	...	1429	...	1712	1831	...	...	...	...	1944	2003	2008	...	...	2207	...
166	**Le Mans** ... d.	0625	...	0739	...	...	...	1043	...	...	1240	1440	1638	...	1837	1903	1907	...	...	1947	...	...	2017	...	...	...
215	Château du Loir ... d.	0655	...	0809	...	...	...	1111	...	...	1310	1507	1708	...	1908	1948	1953	2000	...	2017	...	...	2102	...	...	...
262	St Pierre des Corps .. d.	|	...	|	...	...	...	1148	...	...	|	1541	|	...	|	|	...	|	...	|	...	...	|	...	...	...
265	**Tours** ... a.	0738	...	0838	...	...	...	1153	...	...	1339	1547	1739	...	1938	2031	...	2050	...	2048	...	...	2138	...	...	...

	Ⓐ	Ⓐ	†	⑥	Ⓐ	⚒	†	⚒	†	Ⓐ	⑥	⚒	⑥	Ⓐ	①–④ m	⑤ f		N	⑤ f	Ⓐ	Ⓑ	†	⑤ f	†	①–④ m	⑤⑦ w
Tours ... d.	...	*0527*x	...	...	0635	0749	0907	0908	1022	...	...	1159	1225	1422	...	1519	1654	...	...	1729	1822	...	...	1905	...	2121
St Pierre des Corps ... d.	...	|	...	...	|	|	0922	0922	|	...	...	|	|	|	...	|	|	...	...	|	|	...	...	1922	...	|
Château du Loir ... d.	...	*0557*x	...	...	0709	0821	0951	0952	1052	...	...	1229	1307	1453	...	1550	1724	...	...	1812	1852	...	...	1953	...	2151
Le Mans ... a.	...	*0643*x	...	...	0758	0853	1022	1023	1121	...	...	1259	1357	1523	...	1618	1752	...	...	1857	1921	...	...	2022	...	2221
Le Mans ... d.	0626x	0659	...	0735	*0859*	...	1034	1033	*1240*	1240	1240	...	...	1531	...	1623	1755	1858	1900	*1931*	...	1958	2002	2026	2029	...
Alençon ... d.	0657	0751	0757	0827	*0947*	...	1105	1104	*1333*	1332	1332	...	...	1609	1722	1722	1829	1929	1936	*2020*	...	2029	2034	2057	2107	...
Sées ... d.	0709	0803	0809	0839	...	...	1118	1118	...	1345	1345	...	...	1622	1735	1734	1843	1941	1949	...	...	2042	2045	2109	2120	...
Surdon ... **273** d.	0716	0811	0816	0847	...	...	1126	1126	...	1352	1353	...	...	|	1742	1741	1850	1948	1957	...	...	2049	2052	|	2128	...
Argentan ... **273** d.	0726	0821	...	0857	...	...	1136	1135	...	1403	1403	...	...	1636	1752	1751	1900	1958	2014	...	...	2059	2101	2123	2137	...
Mézidon ... **275/7** d.	0752	0850	...	0924	...	...	1202	1158	...	1430	1432	...	...	1700	1821	1821	1924	2025	2048	...	...	2126	2127	|	...	...
Caen ... **275/7** a.	0806	0904	...	0939	...	...	1214	1212	...	1445	1448	...	...	1715	1836	1836	1939	2043	2104	...	...	2141	2141	2158	...	...

N – ①②③④⑥ (not holidays).
f – Also May 24.
m – Not holidays.
r – 1624 on Ⓐ, 1641 on ⑥.
w – Also holidays.
x – ① (also Apr. 18, May 2, 9, June 6; not Apr. 17, May 1, 8, June 5).
◇ – 5 minutes later on Ⓒ.

CAEN - COUTANCES - GRANVILLE / RENNES 272

km	NOTES: SEE BELOW	① g	⚒	Ⓐ	⑥	Ⓐ	Ⓐ	⑥		Ⓐ		Ⓐ		⑥	Ⓐ	⑤ f	A	①–④ H	⑤ f	①–④ H	⑥	⑤ f	Ⓐ	N	†	⑤ f
0	**Caen** ... **275** d.	0547	0619	0711	0711	0830	0911	0911	1111	1211	1241	1343	1411	1601	1601	1710	1729	1735	1735	1807	1809	1814	1845	1911	1919	1929
30	Bayeux ... **275** d.	0604	0642	0728	0729	0852	0929	0929	1129	1229	1303	1404	1429	1623	1623	1727	1746	1756	1757	1830	1832	1837	1907	1934	1941	1952
57	Lison ... **275** d.	0618	0701	0744	0745	0910	0945	0945	1145	1245	1321	1421	1445	1641	1641	1743	1802	1815	1815	1849	1851	1856	1925	1953	2000	2010
75	St Lô ... d.	0633	0714	0758	0758	0923	0958	0958	1158	1259	1338	1436	1459	1654	1654	1757	1815	1828	1828	1902	1904	1909	1940	2006	2014	2024
105	**Coutances** ... a.	0653	0734	0818	0818	...	1020	1019	1218	1324	*1419*c	...	1519	*1737**	*1802**	1817	1836	*1908**	*1911**	1925	1926	1932	...	2027	2035	2044
143	Granville ... a.	*0740*r	*0814*a	|	*0859**	...	...	|	*1257*c	*1401**	*1452*c	...	*1558**	...	...	*1857**	*1916**	...	*1944**	...	...	...	...	...	*2114**	*2124**
252	*Rennes* **272a** ... a.	0850	...	1001	...	...	...	1202	...	...	...	...	1705	...	...	2003	2025	...	...	...	...	...	...	...	2220	2228

	⚒	Ⓐ 🚌	⚒	Ⓐ	Ⓐ	Ⓒ	⑥	Ⓐ	Ⓐ ‡	⚒	Ⓐ	Ⓐ	†		⑤ f	Ⓐ	A	⑤ f	①–④ H	⑤ f	†	⑥	①–④ H	⑤ f	†	†
Rennes **272a** ... d.	...	...	...	0550	...	...	0836	0900	...	...	...	...	1300	...	1456	...	...	...	...	1630	1648	1648	1654	1824	1859	2043
Granville ... d.	...	0547	*0601*z	*0645*n	...	*0749**	*0937**	*0955**	...	*1151**	*1251*v	...	*1346*n	...	*1552**	...	*1636*s	*1651**	*1710**	|	*1754**	*1754**	*1755**	*1920**	*1954**	*2132*n
Coutances ... d.	0609	0620	*0633**	0736	0825	0832	1020	1038	...	1234	1334	...	1437	*1526*a	1635	*1630*x	1717	1731	*1744**	1818	1837	1837	1838	2003	2037	2223
St Lô ... d.	0632	0657	0720	0758	0848	0855	1040	1059	1211	1258	1357	1511	1458	1613	1657	1715	1742	1756	1831	1838	1858	1904	1904	2025	2057	2243
Lison ... **275** d.	0649	0717	0736	0812	0905	0912	1054	1112	1227	1311	1411	1525	1512	1627	1712	1730	1756	1810	1844	1851	1912	1918	1918	2041	2111	2257
Bayeux ... **275** d.	0707	...	0753	0827	0920	0927	1108	1127	1244	1327	1426	1539	1527	1644	1727	1748	1811	1825	1901	1906	1927	1933	1932	2055	2125	2311
Caen ... **275** a.	0730	...	0815	0844	0938	0945	1125	1144	1306	1344	1444	1554	1544	1708	1744	1810	1829	1843	1922	1923	1944	1950	1949	2112	2142	2328

🚌 Lison - Coutances: 0634Ⓐ, 0722Ⓐ, 0807Ⓐ, 1540⑥, 1840†, 2038Ⓐ, 2140⑤–⑦, 2326Ⓑ. 🚌 Coutances - Lison: 0521Ⓐ, 0712Ⓒ, 1312Ⓒ, 1619†, 1630 **H**, 1949†. Journey 57 mins.

COUTANCES / GRANVILLE - DOL - ST MALO / RENNES 272a

km		① g	Ⓐ	⑥		⑤ f	A	†	⑤ f
0	*Caen* **272** ... d.	0547	0711	0911	1411	1710	1729	1919	1929
105	**Coutances** ... d.	0654	0819	1019	1521	1819	1839	2038	2045
•	Granville ... **273** d.	*0645**	*0809**	*1008**	*1510**	*1809**	*1845*t	*2028**	*2035**
132	Folligny ... **273** d.	0717	0839	1039	1540	1839	1900	2058	2105
151	Avranches ... d.	0733	0852	1053	1554	1853	1914	2111	2118
173	Pontorson ⊡ ... d.	0753	0909	1111	1612	1910	1931	2129	2135
194	Dol ... **281** d.	0815	0929	1130	1631	1930	1951	2148	2154
252	**Rennes** ... **281** a.	0850	1001	1202	1705	2003	2025	2220	2228

	Ⓐ	⑥	Ⓐ	†	⑤ f	⑤ f	†	⑥	H	⑤ f	†	†
Rennes ... **281** d.	0550	0836	0900	1300	1456	1630	1648	1648	1654	1824	1859	2043
Dol ... **281** d.	0622	0907	0933	1331	1527	1705	1719	1719	1728	1855	1930	2116
Pontorson ⊡ ... d.	0638	0923	0949	1347	1543	1720	1736	1736	1744	1911	1946	2132
Avranches ... d.	0657	0942	1005	1403	1600	1737	1754	1754	1801	1928	2003	2149
Folligny ... **273** d.	0715	0956	1018	1416	1613	1750	1809	1809	1815	1941	2016	2202
Granville ... **273** a.	*0740**	*1021**	*1043**	*1441**	*1638**	*1815**	*1834**	*1834**	*1840**	*2006**	*2041**	*2227**
Coutances ... a.	0734	1017	1037	1436	1633	1810	1830	1830	1835	2001	2036	2222
Caen **272** ... a.	0844	1125	1144	1544	1744	1923	1944	1950	1949	2112	2142	2328

NOTES FOR TABLES 272 / 272a

A – Daily except ⑤ (not May 24).
H – ①–④ (not holidays or May 24).
N – ①②③④⑥ (not holidays or May 24).
a – Ⓐ only. By 🚌.
c – Ⓒ only. By 🚌.
f – Also May 24.
g – Also Apr. 18, May 2, 9, June 6; not Apr. 17, May 1, 8, June 5.
n – By 🚌 from Granville (change to train at Folligny, Table **272a**).
r – By 🚌 Folligny (Table **272a**) - Granville.
s – ①②③④⑦ (not May 24). By 🚌.
t – By train (not on Ⓒ Jan. 7 - 29).
v – ⑤ (also May 24). By 🚌.
x – ①–④ **H**. By 🚌.
z – ⑥ only. By 🚌.
‡ – 12 - 13 minutes earlier on ⑤**f**.
⊡ – Pontorson-Mont St Michel (10 km from Mont St Michel).
• – Granville - Folligny is *15 km*.
* – Connection by 🚌.

Departures from Caen may be approx. 5 minutes earlier from Jan. 31

PARIS - DREUX - GRANVILLE 273

km			3411	3413	16511	16513		3421	3431	3435	16547		3441	3443	3445	16515	3451	3453	
		① g	Ⓐ	Ⓒ	† u	Ⓐ				⑤ f	⑥ u		Ⓐ	Ⓒ	⑤ f	Ⓐ	Ⓐ	Ⓒ	
0	**Paris Montparnasse** ⊖ d.	...	0738	0850	0927	0927	...	1055	1355	1528	1527	...	1643	1655	1713	1813	1943	1955	...
17	Versailles Chantiers . ▲ d.	...	|	0902	|	|	...	|	|	|	|	...	|	|	|	1827	|	2007	...
82	**Dreux** ... ▶ d.	0527	0825	0938	1014	1014	...	|	1443	|	1614	...	|	|	|	1914	2044	2044	...
118	Verneuil sur Avre ... d.	0550	0845	0957	1036	1036	...	1158	1503	|	1636	...	1801	1800	|	1936	2104	2103	...
142	L'Aigle ... d.	0603	0858	1011	1049	1049	...	1211	1516	1640	1650	...	1814	1814	1840	1950	2117	2117	...
183	Surdon ... **271** d.	0631	0919	1032	1118	1118	...	|	1537	|	1715	...	1835	1836	1901	2016	2138	2138	...
198	Argentan ... **271** d.	0641	0931	1043	1127	1130	...	1242	1548	1711	1725	...	1847	1848	1913	2026	2149	2148	...
226	Briouze ... d.	0657	0947	1100	1143	...	...	|	1605	|	...	...	|	|	1929	...	2205	2205	...
243	Flers ... d.	0708	0958	1110	1154	...	...	1305	1616	1734	...	...	1910	1913	1942	...	2216	2215	...
272	Vire ... d.	0724	1015	1127	1210	...	...	1322	1632	1751	...	...	1927	1930	1958	...	2232	2232	...
298	Villedieu les Poêles ... d.	0739	1030	1142	1224	...	...	1337	1647	1806	...	...	1942	1946	2014	...	2247	2247	...
313	Folligny ... **272** d.	0749	1040	1152	1235	...	...	|	|	|	...	...	|	|	2024	...	|	|	...
328	**Granville** ... **272** a.	0800	1051	1203	1246	...	...	1355	1704	1824	...	...	1959	2004	2034	...	2305	2304	...

	16510				3410	3410	3412	3420	16546	3430	16516	3432	3440	3444		13272	3450	3454	
	① g	Ⓐ	⑥ u	† u	⑥	Ⓐ	†		⑥ u	⚒	Ⓐ	†		†	⑤ f	†		†	
Granville ... **272** d.	0448	...	...	...	0555	0555	0655	0900	...	1154	...	1356	1504	1705	1712	...	1845	1954	...
Folligny ... **272** d.	|	...	...	...	|	|	|	|	...	|	...	|	|	|	1723	...	1856	2005	...
Villedieu les Poêles ... d.	0506	...	...	...	0613	0613	0714	0918	...	1212	...	1414	1523	1724	1733	...	1906	2015	...
Vire ... d.	0522	...	...	...	0629	0629	0730	0934	...	1228	...	1430	1539	1740	1749	...	1922	2031	...
Flers ... d.	0538	...	...	...	0646	0646	0746	0951	...	1245	...	1447	1555	1757	1806	...	1939	2048	...
Briouze ... d.	0549	...	...	...	0657	0657	0758	|	...	1256	...	1458	|	1808	1818	...	1950	2059	...
Argentan ... **271** d.	0606	0606	0609	0635	0715	0715	0816	1017	1209	1315	1405	1516	1621	1825	1835	1926	2009	2117	...
Surdon ... **271** d.	0616	0616	0619	0645	0725	0725	0826	1027	1219	1325	1415	1527	|	|	...	1936	2019	|	...
L'Aigle ... d.	0642	0642	0642	0713	0746	0746	0847	1048	1243	1346	1442	1548	1649	1853	...	2004	2041	2145	...
Verneuil sur Avre ... d.	0656	0656	0656	0726	0759	0759	0900	1101	1256	1359	1456	1601	1702	|	...	2019	2055	2158	...
Dreux ... ▶ d.	0720	0720	0720	0750	0820	0820	0921	|	1320	1420	1520	|	|	|	...	2043	2116	2219	...
Versailles Chantiers .. ▲ a.	0803	0803	|	|	|	|	|	|	|	|	|	|	|	|	...	2120	|	2255	...
Paris Montparnasse ⊖ a.	0816	0816	0805	0835	0905	0916	1006	1205	1405	1505	1605	1705	1805	2006	...	2131	2205	2307	...

f – Also May 24.
g – Also Apr. 18, May 2, 9, June 6; not Apr. 17, May 1, 8, June 5.
u – Will not run Paris - Dreux or v.v. on Jan. 7 - 29.
▲ – Paris - Versailles: see Table **274**.
▶ – Suburban trains run Paris - Versailles - Dreux approx hourly.
⊖ – Most trains use **Vaugirard** platforms (5 - 10 mins walk from Montparnasse main concourse).

274 PARIS - VERSAILLES

RER (express Métro) Line C: **Paris Austerlitz** - St Michel Notre Dame - **Versailles Rive Gauche** (for Château). Every 15 - 30 minutes. Journey 40 minutes.
Alternative service: RER Line C: Paris Austerlitz - St Michel Notre Dame - Versailles Chantiers. Journey 39 minutes.
SNCF suburban services: Paris St Lazare - Versailles Rive Droite (journey 28 - 35 minutes); Paris Montparnasse - Versailles Chantiers (journey 12 - 28 minutes). See also Table **278**.

275 PARIS - CAEN - CHERBOURG

For other trains Paris - Lisieux (- Trouville-Deauville) see Table **276**

km		3325								3331	3301			3333		3327		3335		3303	3337		3305		3341	
		①	⚒	Ⓐ	Ⓐ	⚒	Ⓐ	⚒	⚒	Ⓐ	Ⓐ	⚒		⑥	⑥		Ⓐ	Ⓐ	Ⓐ	Ⓒ	Ⓒ	Ⓒ	Ⓐ	Ⓐ	Ⓒ	Ⓒ
		g														T										
0	**Paris** St Lazare ▷ d.	0026	...	...	...	...	...	...	...	0645	0706	...	...	0745	...	0811	...	0844	...	0910	0944	...	1010	...	1143	...
57	Mantes la Jolie ▷ d.	|	...	...	...	...	...	...	...	|	|	...	...	|	...	|	...	|	...	|	|	...	|	...	|	...
108	Evreux ▷ d.	0133	...	...	...	...	0609	...	...	0743	|	...	...	0843	...	|	...	0943	...	|	1043	...	|	...	1243	...
160	Bernay d.	0211	...	...	...	...	0647	...	...	0810	|	...	...	0910	...	|	...	1010	...	|	1110	...	|	...	1310	...
191	Lisieux **277** d.	0243	...	0610	...	0651	0703	...	0751	0828	|	...	0851	0928	...	|	0951	1028	...	|	1128	...	|	...	1328	...
216	Mézidon **271 277** d.	|	...	0624	...	0705	0716	...	0805	|	|	...	0905	|	...	|	1005	|	...	|	|	...	|	...	|	...
239	**Caen** **271 277** a.	0320	...	0644	...	0725	0735	...	0825	0853	0858	...	0925	0953	...	1008	1025	1053	...	1101	1153	...	1200	...	1353	...
239	**Caen** **272** d.	0323	0558	...	0658	...	...	0803	...	...	0901	0911	...	...	1003	1011	...	...	1103	1104	...	1203	1203	1303	...	1403
269	Bayeux **272** d.	0350	0614	...	0714	...	...	0819	...	...	|	0928	...	...	1019	1028	...	...	1119	1122	...	1219	1221	1319	...	1419
296	Lison **272** d.	0411	0629	...	0729	...	...	0834	...	...	|	0944	...	...	1034	1044	...	...	1134	1137	...	1234	1236	1334	...	1434
314	Carentan d.	0425	0639	...	0739	...	...	0844	...	...	0937	...	...	...	1044	1056	...	...	1144	1149	...	1244	1248	1344	...	1444
343	Valognes d.	0445	0655	...	0755	...	...	0900	...	...	0953	...	...	...	1100	1113	...	...	1200	1204	...	1300	1303	1400	...	1500
371	**Cherbourg** a.	0501	0710	...	0810	...	...	0915	...	...	1008	...	...	...	1115	1129	...	...	1215	1220	...	1315	1319	1415	...	1515

	3307	3309		3343		3345	3347	3311			3313		3349	3315		3351	3317		3353	3319	3321	3355	3323	3357	3359	
	Ⓐ	⑥	Ⓐ	Ⓐ	Ⓐ	⑤	Ⓒ	Ⓐ	Ⓐ	Ⓐ	Ⓒ		Ⓐ	Ⓐ	Ⓐ		Ⓐ	Ⓒ	Ⓐ	⑤	Ⓒ		Ⓑ	⑥	⑤	
						f						u								f			h	t	f	
Paris St Lazare ▷ d.	1210	1310	...	1344	...	1410	1444	1509	...	...	1610	...	1642	1708	...	1744	1809	...	1843	1904	1910	1959	2044	2044	2145	...
Mantes la Jolie ▷ d.	|	|	...	|	...	|	|	|	...	...	|	...	|	|	...	|	|	...	|	|	|	2038	|	|	|	...
Evreux ▷ d.	|	|	...	1443	...	1509	1543	|	...	...	|	...	1743	|	...	1843	|	...	1943	|	|	2106	2140	2143	2243	...
Bernay d.	|	|	...	1510	...	1536	1610	|	...	...	|	...	1810	|	...	1910	|	...	2010	|	|	2133	2207	2210	2310	...
Lisieux **277** d.	|	|	1453	1528	...	1554	1628	|	1651	1721	|	1751	1828	|	1851	1928	|	...	2028	|	|	2152	2224	2228	2328	...
Mézidon **271 277** d.	|	|	1507	|	...	|	|	|	1705	1735	|	1805	|	|	1905	|	|	...	|	|	|	|	|	|	|	...
Caen **271 277** a.	1400	1500	1527	1553	...	1620	1653	1659	1725	1753	1800	1824	1853	1900	1925	1953	1958	...	2053	2058	2100	2216	2246	2253	2353	...
Caen **272** d.	1403	1503	...	...	1618	...	...	1702	...	1755	1803	1827	...	1903	...	...	2001	2003	...	2101	2103	...	2249	...	...	...
Bayeux **272** d.	1421	1521	...	...	1634	...	...	1720	...	1812	1821	1843	...	1921	...	...	2019	2019	...	2118	2121	...	2307	...	...	...
Lison **272** d.	1436	1536	...	...	1649	...	...	1735	...	1826	1836	1858	...	1936	...	...	2034	2034	...	2134	2136	...	2322	...	...	...
Carentan d.	1448	1548	...	...	1659	...	...	1747	...	1837	1848	1908	...	1948	...	...	2046	2044	...	2146	2148	...	2334	...	...	...
Valognes d.	1503	1603	...	...	1715	...	...	1802	...	1851	1903	1924	...	2003	...	...	2101	2100	...	2201	2203	...	2350	...	...	...
Cherbourg a.	1519	1619	...	...	1730	...	...	1818	...	1907	1919	1939	...	2019	...	...	2117	2115	...	2216	2219	...	0005	...	...	...

	3330	3332		3300	3334					3302			3338				3340	3304	3304			3306	3342			3344
	Ⓐ	⚒	Ⓐ	Ⓐ		Ⓐ	⑥	Ⓐ	Ⓒ		Ⓐ	Ⓒ		⚒			⑤	①–④	⑥	Ⓒ	†	⑤	Ⓒ	Ⓐ	⚒	Ⓐ
																	f	m				f		q		
Cherbourg d.	...	...	...	0543	...	0625	0630	0720	...	0735	...	...	...	0943	...	...	...	1035	1035	...	1143	1151	...	...	1243	...
Valognes d.	...	...	...	0601	...	0645	0645	0735	...	0752	...	...	...	0958	...	...	...	1052	1052	...	1158	1209	...	...	1258	...
Carentan d.	...	...	...	0616	...	0701	0701	0751	...	0808	...	...	...	1014	...	...	...	1108	1108	...	1214	1224	...	...	1314	...
Lison **272** d.	...	...	...	0628	...	0712	0712	0802	...	0819	0905	0912	...	1025	...	...	...	1119	1119	...	1225	|	...	...	1325	...
Bayeux **272** d.	...	...	...	0643	...	0729	0729	0816	...	0835	0920	0927	...	1039	...	...	...	1135	1135	...	1239	|	...	...	1339	...
Caen **272** a.	...	...	...	0659	...	0750	0750	0832	...	0851	0938	0945	...	1055	...	...	...	1151	1151	...	1255	1259	...	...	1355	...
Caen **271 277** d.	0505	0607	0635	0702	0742	0752	0752	0835	0835	0854	...	...	1007	...	1107	...	1150	1154	1154	1216	...	1302	1307	1307	...	1407
Mézidon **271 277** d.	|	|	0655	|	|	0811	0811	0854	0855	|	...	...	|	...	1127	...	|	|	|	1230	...	|	|	1327	...	|
Lisieux **277** d.	0532	0634	0709	|	0810	0825	0825	0908	0909	|	...	...	1034	...	1141	...	|	|	|	1243	...	1334	1334	1341	...	1434
Bernay d.	0551	0653	...	|	0828	...	...	...	...	|	...	...	1053	...	...	...	|	|	|	1258	...	1353	1353	...	...	1453
Evreux ▷ d.	0618	0720	...	|	0855	...	...	...	...	|	...	...	1120	...	...	...	|	|	|	...	...	1419	1420	...	...	1520
Mantes la Jolie ▷ a.	|	|	...	|	0922	...	...	...	...	|	...	...	|	...	...	...	|	|	|	...	...	|	|	...	...	|
Paris St Lazare ▷ a.	0718	0821	...	0859	0958	...	...	...	...	1047	...	...	1217	...	...	...	1347	1347	1347	...	...	1517	1517	...	...	1616

	3324	3308		3346			3348			3312	3310			3314		3350	3316			3318		3352	3320		3322	
			Ⓐ	Ⓒ	Ⓐ			Ⓐ	⚒	†	Ⓐ	Ⓐ	Ⓐ	Ⓐ	†	†	⑥	Ⓐ	⑥	†		†	Ⓐ	Ⓐ	†	
	R																									
Cherbourg d.	1253	1335	...	...	...	1520	...	...	1620	1635	1652	...	...	1735	1743	...	1752	1820	1820	1835	...	...	1909	1947	2005	...
Valognes d.	1311	1352	...	...	...	1535	...	...	1635	1652	|	...	...	1752	1759	...	1810	1835	1835	1852	...	...	1927	2002	2022	...
Carentan d.	1327	1408	...	...	...	1551	...	...	1651	1708	|	...	...	1808	1814	...	1825	1851	1851	1908	...	...	1942	2018	2038	...
Lison **272** d.	1339	1419	1525	...	...	1602	...	...	1702	1719	|	...	...	1819	1825	...	1837	1902	1902	1919	...	...	1954	2029	2049	...
Bayeux **272** d.	1355	1435	1539	...	...	1616	...	...	1716	1735	|	...	...	1835	1839	...	1852	1916	1916	1935	...	...	2009	2043	2105	...
Caen **272** a.	1411	1451	1554	...	...	1632	...	...	1732	1751	1751	...	...	1851	1855	...	1908	1932	1932	1951	...	...	2025	2059	2121	...
Caen **271 277** d.	1414	1454	1556	1607	1635	...	1707	1725	1735	1754	1754	1800	1835	1854	...	1907	1911	1935	...	1954	...	2007	2028	...	2124	...
Mézidon **271 277** d.	|	|	1610	|	1654	...	|	1745	1754	|	|	1819	1855	|	...	|	|	1954	...	|	...	|	|	...	|	...
Lisieux **277** d.	1441	|	1624	1634	1708	...	1734	1759	1808	|	|	1836	1909	|	...	1934	1936	2008	...	|	...	2034	2052	...	|	...
Bernay d.	1459	|	...	1653	...	...	1753	...	...	|	|	1854	...	|	...	1953	1953	...	...	|	...	2053	|	...	|	...
Evreux ▷ d.	1526	|	...	1720	...	...	1820	...	...	|	|	1933	...	|	...	2020	2020	...	...	|	...	2120	|	...	|	...
Mantes la Jolie ▷ a.	|	|	...	|	...	...	|	...	...	|	|	...	...	|	...	|	|	...	...	|	...	|	|	...	|	...
Paris St Lazare ▷ a.	1626	1650	...	1816	...	...	1917	...	...	1946	1946	...	...	2046	...	2117	2117	...	...	2146	...	2217	2226	...	2316	...

LOCAL TRAINS PARIS - EVREUX - SERQUIGNY △

	Ⓐ	Ⓐ	Ⓐ	Ⓐ	Ⓐ	Ⓐ	Ⓐ	Ⓐ	
Paris St Lazare d.	0907	1105	1310	1610	1711	1812	1913	2012	...
Mantes la Jolie d.	0941	1144	1344	1644	1746	1847	1947	2047	...
Evreux d.	1017	1222	1420	1721	1822	1922	2020	2120	...
Serquigny a.	...	1253	...	1754	1856	1956	...	...	...

	Ⓐ	Ⓐ	Ⓐ	Ⓐ	Ⓐ	Ⓐ		Ⓐ	Ⓐ
Serquigny d.	...	0604	0704	...	...	1304	...	...	1804
Evreux d.	0534	0639	0739	0844	1139	1339	...	1739	1839
Mantes la Jolie d.	0618	0715	0814	0918	1215	1415	...	1815	1911
Paris St Lazare a.	0652	0759	0855	0954	1249	1448	...	1849	...

R – Apr. 17, May 1, 8, June 5 only.
T – Apr. 15 only.

f – Also May 24.
g – Also Apr. 18, May 2, 9, June 6; not Apr. 17, May 1, 8, June 5.
h – Not May 25.
m – Not holidays.

q – On ③ runs 28 minutes later (Caen d. 1335).
t – Also May 25.
u – Runs 4 - 6 minutes later on ⑤.

▷ – For additional trains see panel below main table (also Table **276**).
△ – Frequent suburban trains run Paris - Mantes-la-Jolie. Additional local trains run Mantes la Jolie - Evreux.

180 De verklaring van de conventionele tekens vindt u op bladzijde 4 12

PARIS - LISIEUX - TROUVILLE DEAUVILLE 276

km				3371		3373	3375		3377		3379		3395	3381			3383		3385			3387	3389	3391	3393
		⚒	Ⓑ	Ⓐ	⑥	Ⓒ	Ⓐ	Ⓐ		Ⓐ	Ⓐ	Ⓒ			Ⓐ		⑤	①–④	⑤			⑤	⑦	⑥	Ⓐ
			h		t		S		F				Y	T			f	m	G	B	b	G	Q	P	
0	**Paris** St Lazare ..... ▷ d.	...	...	0741	...	0844	0943	...	1010	....	1143	...	1212	1345	...	...	1544	...	1627	...	...	1804	1815	1843	1910
108	Evreux ▷ d.	...	...	0843	...	0943	|	...	1109	...	1243	...	|	1443	...	...	1643	...	|	...	...	|	1919	1943	2012
160	Bernay ▷ d.	...	...	0910	...	1010	|	...	1136	...	1310	...	|	1510	...	...	1710	...	|	...	...	|	1946	2010	2042
191	**Lisieux** ▷ d.	0735	0837	0928	0935	1028	|	1035	1154	1235	1328	1335	|	1528	1535	1635	1728	1735	1823	1835	1935	1950	2006	2028	2102
209	Pont l'Évêque d.	0748	0850	0940	0948	1040	|	1048	1206	1248	1340	1348	|	1540	1548	1648	1740	1748	1835	1848	1946	2001	2018	2040	2113
221	**Trouville-Deauville** a.	0757	0859	0948	0957	1048	1132	1057	1216	1257	1348	1357	1408	1548	1557	1657	1748	1757	1844	1857	1955	2010	2027	2048	2122

		3370				3372	3372					3374	3376		3378			3380	3382	3384				3386	3388
	⚒	Ⓐ	†			Ⓐ	Ⓐ	⑥	Ⓐ	Ⓒ	Ⓐ		Ⓐ		⑦		Ⓐ	Ⓒ	⑦	Ⓐ	⑦	⑤	①–④	⑦	⑦
				B	z	J	K	t		⊡		E	S	▽	d		b		V		d	f	m	H	R
Trouville-Deauville d.	0700	0711	0738	0808	0959	1111	1110	1154	1204	1259	1404	1411	1415	1604	1638	1704	1807	1811	1853	1911	2004	2012	2020	2029	2057
Pont l'Évêque d.	0709	0722	0747	0817	1008	1122	1126	1207	1213	1308	1413	1422	1425	1613	1650	1713	1816	1822	|	1922	2013	2021	2029	|	2108
Lisieux ▷ d.	0722	0734	0800	0830	1021	1134	1139	1221	1226	1321	1426	1434	1440	1626	1704	1726	1829	1834	|	1934	2026	2034	2042	|	2120
Bernay ▷ d.	...	0753	...	...	...	1153	1156	...	...	...	...	1453	1459	...	1722	...	...	1853	|	1953	...	...	...	|	2139
Evreux ▷ d.	...	0820	...	...	...	1220	1223	...	...	...	...	1520	1526	...	1750	...	...	1920	|	2020	...	...	...	|	2206
Paris St Lazare ...... ▷ a.	...	0921	...	...	...	1317	1325	...	...	...	...	1616	1628	...	1846	...	...	2017	2046	2117	...	...	...	2226	2304

B – Ⓐ (also ⑥ July 8 - Aug. 26).
E – ⑦ June 25 - Aug. 27 (also Dec. 25, Jan. 1, June 5, 24).
F – ⑥ from Apr. 15 (also May 25, June 25).
G – ⑤ June 30 - Aug. 25.
H – ⑦ July 2 - Aug. 27 (also Apr. 17).
J – Ⓐ to June 23, also June 24.
K – Ⓐ June 26 - Aug. 25.
P – ⑥ June 24 - Aug. 26.
Q – ⑦ July 2 - Aug. 27 (also Aug. 15).

R – ⑦ May 28 - Sept. 24 (also May 25).
S – June 26 - Aug. 25 (also Jan. 2).
T – ⑥ from Mar. 25 (also May 25).
V – ⑦ June 4 - Sept. 24.
Y – Apr. 15, 22, May 25 only.

b – Not on ⑤ July 7 - Aug. 25.
d – Also Apr. 17, May 1, 8, June 5.
f – Also May 24.

h – Not May 25.
m – Not holidays or May 24.
t – Also May 25.
z – Runs 3 - 5 minutes later on Ⓒ.

⊡ – Also runs on ⑤ f (depart 1303, arrive 1325).
▽ – Not May 1, 8. Runs 5 mins earlier on Ⓒ.
▷ – For other trains see Table **275**.

TROUVILLE DEAUVILLE - DIVES CABOURG 276a

24 km Journey 30 minutes

December 11 - June 23

From Trouville Deauville: 1100⑥**u**, 1106⑦**x**, 1225⑥**E**, 1407⑥**v**, 1419⑦, 1604⑥**D**, 1645⑦**x**, 1900**T**, 2133④⑤**z**.
From Dives Cabourg: 0620①, 1140⑥**E**, 1144⑦**x**, 1217⑥**R**, 1322⑥**F**, 1522⑥**D**, 1558⑦**k**, 1731Ⓒ, 1949**T**.

June 24 - August 27

From Trouville Deauville: 0833Ⓐ, 0955Ⓐ, 1100Ⓒ, 1143Ⓐ, 1225Ⓒ, 1359Ⓐ**b**, 1407⑥⑦**n**, 1604⑥**t**, 1609Ⓐ, 1645⑦**e**, 1750Ⓐ**c**, 1900⑦**e**, 2005Ⓐ**d**, 2005⑥**t**, 2038⑦**e**, 2111⑥**t**, 2133Ⓐ.
From Dives Cabourg: 0620Ⓐ, 0913Ⓐ, 1023Ⓒ, 1032Ⓐ, 1140Ⓒ, 1322, 1522Ⓐ, 1523⑥**t**, 1558⑦**e**, 1710Ⓐ, 1731Ⓒ, 1833Ⓐ, 1949⑦**e**, 2042Ⓐ**d**. *Subject to alteration*

D – ⑥ Mar. 25 - June 17 (also May 25); ⑥ Sept. 2 - 23.
E – ⑥ Apr. 15 - June 17 (also May 25); ⑥ Sept. 2 - Oct. 21.
F – ⑥ Apr. 22 - June 17 (also Dec. 25, Jan. 1, May 1, 8, 25, June 5).
R – ⑥ Dec. 17 - Apr. 8.
T – Apr. 17, June 25 only.

b – Runs 20 minutes later on ⑤ **f**.
c – Runs 6 minutes later on ⑤ **f**.
d – Runs 15 minutes later on ⑤ **f**.
e – Also Aug. 15.
f – Also July 13.
k – Also Apr. 17.

n – Also Aug. 15.
t – Also July 14.
u – Also May 25.
v – 12 minutes later Apr. 15 - May 13.
x – Not May 25.
z – Also May 24.

ROUEN - LISIEUX - CAEN 277

km		Ⓐ	⑥	Ⓐ	Ⓐ	Ⓐ	†	⑥	Ⓐ	†	Ⓐ	⑥	Ⓐ	⑤	⑤	①–④	†	Ⓐ	⑥	⚒	†	Ⓐ	†	
									🚌				🚌	f	f	m								
0	**Rouen** Rive Droite d.	0604	0704	0707	0808	1004	1004	1004	1104	1204	1204	1304	1404	1504	1604	1608	1604	1704	1704	1804	1804	1904	1904	...
23	Elbeuf-St Aubin d.	0620	0720	0726	|	1020	1019	1019	|	1220	1219	1319	|	1520	1620	|	1619	1719	1720	1819	1820	1920	1919	...
73	Serquigny d.	0650	|	|	|	|	|	1050	|	1249	1249	1350	|	|	1648	|	1650	1747	1746	1854	1854	|	|	...
83	Bernay ▷ d.	0657	0752	0759	|	1052	1053	1058	|	1257	1257	1358	|	1552	1656	|	1658	1755	1754	1902	1902	1951	1953	...
114	Lisieux ▷ d.	0713	0809	0816	|	1109	1109	1114	|	1313	1314	1414	|	1609	1713	|	1714	1811	1811	1919	1919	2009	2009	...
139	Mézidon **271** ▷ d.	0728	0823	0830	|	1123	1123	1128	|	1328	1328	1427	|	1623	1728	|	1728	1826	1825	1933	1933	2023	2023	...
162	**Caen 271** ▷ a.	0742	0837	0843	0932	1137	1137	1141	1244*	1342	1343	1441	1544*	1637	1742	1731	1742	1841	1839	1947	1947	2037	2036	...

	Ⓐ	⑥	Ⓐ	Ⓐ		Ⓒ	Ⓐ	Ⓐ	Ⓐ	Ⓒ	Ⓐ		Ⓐ	Ⓐ	Ⓒ	⑥	†	Ⓐ	Ⓐ		⑤	⑥	†	
								🚌			🚌										f	S		
Caen 271 ▷ d.	0554	0715	0717	0805	...	1019	1021	1115*	1215	1216	1415*	...	1617	1719	1721	1815	1816	1818	1923	...	2016	2019	2024	...
Mézidon **271** ▷ d.	0608	0729	0731	|	...	1033	1035	|	1229	1230	|	...	|	1733	1735	1829	1830	1832	1937	...	2030	2033	2038	...
Lisieux ▷ d.	0622	0743	0745	|	...	1047	1048	|	1243	1243	|	...	|	1747	1748	1843	1843	1846	1950	...	2044	2047	2052	...
Bernay ▷ d.	0638	0800	0802	|	...	1104	1104	|	1300	1259	|	...	|	1804	1804	1900	1859	1903	2006	...	2100	2104	2109	...
Serquigny d.	0645	0808	0810	|	...	|	|	|	1308	1307	|	...	|	|	|	1908	1907	1911	|	...	|	|	|	...
Elbeuf-St Aubin d.	0721	0837	0837	|	...	1137	1137	|	1337	1337	|	...	|	1837	1837	1937	1937	1940	2039	...	2135	2137	2142	...
Rouen Rive Droite a.	0738	0853	0853	0929	...	1153	1153	1255	1353	1353	1555	...	1740	1855	1853	1953	1953	1956	2055	...	2153	2153	2158	...

S – ⑥ Apr. 1 - Sept. 2.
f – Also May 24.

m – Not holidays or May 24.
▷ – See also Table **275**.

* – Gare Routière (bus station).
🚌 – TER bus service, rail tickets valid.

PARIS - CHARTRES - LE MANS 278

For *TGV* trains Paris - Le Mans via the high-speed line see Table **280**

km		Ⓐ	⚒	⚒	Ⓐ	Ⓐ										Ⓒ	Ⓐ	Ⓐ	Ⓐ	†	⑥	Ⓑh	Ⓐ	Ⓐ	Ⓑh
0	**Paris** Montparnasse .. **274** d.	0533	0609	0639	0709	0740	0809	0906	1009	1106	1209	1306	1409	1506	1609	...	1622	1639	1705v	1706	1706	1709	1724	1754	1805
17	Versailles Chantiers .. **274** d.	0547	0625	0655	0725	0754	0825	0922	1025	1122	1225	1322	1425	1522	1625	...	1640	1655	1723*	1722	1722	1726	1739	1809	1822*
48	Rambouillet d.	0604	0645	0713	0745	0813	0845	0943	1045	1143	1245	1343	1445	1542	1645	...	1700	1715	|	|	1742	1746	1800	1830	|
88	**Chartres** d.	0641	0725	0742	0825	0851	0925	1009	1125	1209	1325	1411	1525	1609	1725	1731	1731	1755	1808	1809	1809	1826	1831	1859	1909
149	Nogent le Rotrou d.	*0736*	...	0819	...	...	...	1047	...	1247	...	1447	...	1647	...	1831	1831	...	1848	1847	1847	...	1925	...	1947
211	**Le Mans** a.	*0824*	...	0856	...	...	...	1124	...	1324	...	1524r	...	1724	...	1913	1913	...	1924	1924	1924	...	...	...	2024

		Ⓐ	Ⓐ		Ⓐ		Ⓑh		Ⓐ	①⑦
Paris Montparnasse .... **274** d.	1809	1824	1854	1905	1939	2009	2106	2209	2302	0002
Versailles Chantiers .... **274** d.	1825	1840	1910	1922	1954	2025	2122	2225	2321	0017
Rambouillet d.	1845	1900	1930	1943	2014	2045	2142	2245	2344	0045
Chartres d.	1925	1931	1959	2010	2055	2125	2210	2325	0022	0122
Nogent le Rotrou d.	...	2024	...	2046	...	...	2247	...	...	...
Le Mans a.	...	...	...	2128	...	...	2324	...	...	...

	Ⓐ	Ⓐ	⑥	Ⓐ	⚒	Ⓐ		Ⓐ	⚒
Le Mans d.	...	0336	...	...	...	...	...	0534	...
Nogent le Rotrou d.	...	0414	...	...	...	0530	...	0614	...
Chartres d.	0404	0452	0452	0534	0604	0627	0632	0652	0702
Rambouillet d.	0446	0519	0518	0616	0646	0701	0714	|	0744
Versailles Chantiers .... **274** d.	0508	0541	0540	0638	0708	0723	0738	0741*	0808
Paris Montparnasse.... **274** a.	0520	0553	0553	0650	0720	0736	0750	0753	0820

	Ⓐ	Ⓐ	⑥		Ⓐ	⚒	Ⓐ	⚒	⑦e										Ⓐ				Ⓑh	⑦e
Le Mans d.	0552	...	...	...	0632	...	...	0736	...	...	0936	...	1136	...	1336r	...	1536	...	...	1736	...	1936	...	2136
Nogent le Rotrou d.	0624	0630	0630	...	0710	...	0733	0814	0811	*0832*	1014	...	1214	...	1416	...	1613	...	...	1814	...	2014	...	2214
Chartres d.	0722	0730	0725	0734	0757	0802	0827	0852	0850	0934	1052	1134	1252	1334	1453	1534	1651	1734	1802	1851	1934	2051	2134	2252
Rambouillet d.	|	0801	...	0816	0831	0846	0901	0919	0919	1016	1119	1216	1319	1416	1519	1616	1720	1816	1847	1919	2016	2119	2216	2319
Versailles Chantiers .... **274** d.	0812*	0823	...	0838	0853	0908	0924	0941	0940	1038	1141	1238	1341	1438	1541	1638	1742	1838	1908	1941	2038	2141	2238	2341
Paris Montparnasse .... **274** a.	0824	0835	...	0850	0905	0920	0936	0953	0953	1050	1153	1250	1353	1450	1553	1650	1753	1850	1920	1953	2050	2153	2250	2353

e – Also Apr. 17, May 1, 8, June 5.
h – Not May 25.

r – ⚒ only.

v – Departs from Montparnasse Vaugirard platforms. On ⑤ departs 1652.
* – Will not convey passengers travelling Paris - Versailles or v.v.

Trains may be retimed a few minutes earlier owing to engineering work

TGV trains convey ♈. Many trains continue to destinations in Tables **281, 284, 285** and **293**.
For other trains Massy - Nantes/Rennes and v.v. see Table **11** (Lille services), Table **335** (services via St Pierre des Corps) and Table **391** (Strasbourg services).

Block 1

km	Station							8801	8903		8603	8603	8807	8081	8809	8053	8091	8911	8911	8013	8611	8813	8715
		Ⓐ	⑥	Ⓐ	Ⓐ	Ⓐ	Ⓐ	Ⓐ	Ⓐ	Ⓐ	Ⓐ	②–⑥	Ⓐ②–⑥	Ⓒ	①–⑥	⑥	①–⑥	⑥	②–⑤	①–⑥	Ⓐ	
0	Paris Montparnasse d.	…	…	…	…	…	…	0558	0653	0704	0705		0721	0736	0754	0808	0808	0852	0854	0908	0908	0954	1008
14	Massy TGV d.	…	…	…	…	…	…	…	0705	…	…		0738	0748	…	…	…	…	…	…	…	…	…
202	Le Mans d.	0612	0612	0620	0630	0650	0703	0704		0731		0824	0830		0906	0906					1052		1105
292	Laval d.				0731		0753				0840				0951	0951							
327	Vitré d.				0754		0822																
365	Rennes a.				0815		0848				0916	0916		0952		1025	1025			1113	1113		1213	
251	Sablé d.	0633	0639	0649		0713				0818			0846	0853									1126
299	Angers St Laud 289 a.	0655	0701	0730		0734		0748		0853			0909	0914		0924		1022	1027		1128		1147
387	Nantes 289 a.	0751	0751			0821		0832	0914				0955	1002		1009		1106	1114		1213		1234

Block 2

Station	8815*	8617	8817			8717	8819*	8621	8057	8821*	8623	8059	8629	8823			8825*	8827	8089	8729	8061	8829	8063	8633
	⑦	①–⑥	②–④	Ⓐ			⑤	①–④	⑤	①–④	⑤		⑤	⑤		v		⑦	Ⓒ	⑥–④	⑤	⑮①–④	⑦	
Paris Montparnasse d.	…	1054	1108	1154			1208	1221	1307	1341	1354d	1408	1408	1408	1421			1454	1454	1508	1508	1508	1554	1608	1608
Massy TGV d.																								
Le Mans d.	1138		1206		1223	1301	1306		1406	1440	1445			1515	1535	1536		1552						1515
Laval d.	1225		1249						1523			1544	1544		1624									
Vitré d.	1250		1308												1643									
Rennes a.	1323		1328			1419		1520	1558		1613	1620	1619		1702				1713	1713	1714		1812	1812
Sablé d.					1310	1324		1338						1557										
Angers St Laud 289 a.				1328	1344	1342		1359			1528			1619			1625	1628				1726		
Nantes 289 a.	1303c		1412		1435			1443			1612			1718			1710	1712				1813		

Block 3

Station	8831				8737*				8833	8747	8743*	8937	8935	8645			8649	8953	8841	8655	8657	8943		8095
	①–⑥	⑤	⑦	Ⓐ	⑥	①–⑤	⑦	Ⓐ	①–⑤	⑥⑦	⑤	⑤	①–③①–④	⑤	⑤	②–④①–④	⑤	⑤	①–④	⑤	⑤⑥	⑦	Ⓐ	
					p													j		u				
Paris Montparnasse d.	…	1623			1641				1654	1708	1708	1721	1721	1741			1741	1749	1754	1808	1808	1823		1841
Massy TGV d.																								
Le Mans d.	1702		1719	1722	1734	1738	1742	1742	1752		1806			1821	1823	1839		1851			1905	1905		2017
Laval d.						1822		1831			1850		1916		1923									2036
Vitré d.						1858		1848																2054
Rennes a.								1910		1914	1925		1953		1957				2014	2014				
Sablé d.	1726		1747	1755	1807		1805				1828		1830	1844	1846						1934	1941		
Angers St Laud 289 a.	1748	1757	1816	1826	1837			1828						1908	1909		1930				2005	2006		
Nantes 289 a.	1838	1845					1915		1919		1927	1933		1955	1958		2005	2014		2037				

Block 4

Station	8067	8945	8845	8977*	8663	8665			8761	8849	8949	8851	8071	8097		8853	8953	8077	8679	8075	8855	8857	8957	8779
	Ⓒ	①–④	⑤	⑤	⑥	⑤	⑥–④①–④	⑤	⑦	①–④①–⑤	⑤①–④⑤–⑦	⑤	⑤	①–③①–④	⑤	⑥⑦	⑤	①–④	⑤	⑦	①–④	⑤	⑤	
																			z					
Paris Montparnasse d.	1841	1850	1850	1854	1908	1908			1941	1954	1954	1954	2008	2024		2054	2054	2108	2108	2108	2123	2154	2154	2208
Massy TGV d.																								
Le Mans d.			1952	2006	2006	2013	2016				2052	2106	2120				2244		2206	2221	2252	2251		2349
Laval d.	2017											2149						2259	2311					
Vitré d.	2038																	2311						
Rennes a.	2057				2119	2120		2145				2225	2234				2319	2319	2330				0024	
Sablé d.			2014				2036	2039												2257	2329	2329		
Angers St Laud 289 a.			2036				2059	2101	2125	2125	2129				2224	2224				2257	2329	2329		
Nantes 289 a.		2100	2105	2123			2147	2150		2209	2209	2213			2307	2307				2341	0013	0013		

Block 5

Station	8800	8802	8052	8690	8804	8906	8908	8810	8704	8706	8812		8970	8080	8816		8712			8818	8082	8060		8062	8820
	①	Ⓐ	Ⓐ		①–⑤	②–⑤		①		Ⓐ	Ⓐ	①–⑤①–⑥②–⑥	Ⓐ	①–⑤	⑥		Ⓐ	②–⑤	①		Ⓐ	⑦	②–⑤	
	A		H			h	B		J			q							K						
Nantes 289 d.	0450	0515			0548	0616	0617	0622			0623	0649		0720			0727	0752			0843			0852	
Angers St Laud 289 d.	0541	0602			0640			0709		0714	0718	0740		0811			0818	0823	0839		0843			0940	
Sablé d.		0626															0846	0848			0908				
Rennes d.			0532	0605			0635	0635				0705	0713	0735					0805	0805		0905		
Vitré d.			0553										0732											
Laval d.			0615					0710	0712				0751											
Le Mans d.		0622	0650	0702				0750		0801	0804		0821		0838	0852	0913	0913			0926	0926	0932		
Massy TGV a.																								
Paris Montparnasse a.	0718	0745	0759	0812	0819	0837	0837	0845	0853	0856	0857		0910	0917	0945		0948			1014	1023			1113	1120

Block 6

Station	8618	8822	8618	8064	8824	8640		8928		8830	8974			8084		8084	8084	8832	8932	8730	8834	8836		8938
	⑥	⑥⑦	⑥	⑤	⑥		①–⑤①–⑥⑥⑦	⑥⑦		①–⑤		⑥		Ⓐ	①–⑤①–⑤⑥	Ⓐ	①–⑤		⑤	
	k				C			D				F		E				R		Q		
Nantes 289 d.		0852			0950		1058		1121	1135	1143	1154	1156	1200		1253	1253		1351			1435	1455
Angers St Laud 289 d.		0940			1035		1145		1209	1225	1240	1242	1246	1250		1340	1340		1439			1523	
Sablé d.											1247		1308	1312		1332							
Rennes d.	0905		0905	0935			1035		1105					1235		1235	1305		1405				
Vitré d.																							
Laval d.							1111		1141					1312		1311	1341						
Le Mans d.		1022	1022		1157f		1227		1310		1321	1333	1333	1357	1402	1406		1420r	1420		1520	1541	1607
Massy TGV a.																							
Paris Montparnasse a.	1117	1121	1121	1144	1215	1253f	1323	1323	1340		1420e	1418		1457		1506	1522	1518r	1518	1611a	1616	1638	1703	1710

Block 7

Station	8068		8842*	8646			8752	8844	8944	8976		8984	8088	8088			8660	8880	8980		8848	8762
	①–④	⑥	⑤		⑤	Ⓐ	⑤⑥①–④	⑤	Ⓐ	⑦	⑤⑤①–⑥	Ⓒ	Ⓐ	Ⓐ		⑤⑦④–⑥	⑤	⑥	Ⓒ	
									w			R										
Nantes 289 d.		1513	1530	1552				1640	1643	1653	1709	1719				1727		1748	1752		1826	
Angers St Laud 289 d.		1603	1620	1637		1648		1740	1740	1740	1801					1744	1809	1827		1840	1840	1844
Sablé d.		1625	1645			1718		1743				1822				1826	1838	1850		1904	1904	1928
Rennes d.	1505				1605		1637			1705			1735	1735				1805				1833
Vitré d.					1700																	1857
Laval d.					1642		1720						1813	1813								
Le Mans d.	1622	1648	1714		1726	1747	1806	1811		1823	1823	1823		1856	1858	1909	1913			2004		1957
Massy TGV a.																						
Paris Montparnasse a.	1718			1817	1822			1911	1920	1923	1920		1940	1945	1956			2011	2022	2019		2040	2056

FOR NOTES SEE NEXT PAGE →

NANTES and RENNES - LE MANS - PARIS   280

Trains may be retimed a few minutes earlier owing to engineering work

TGV trains convey ⚑. Many trains continue to destinations in Tables 281, 284, 285, 288 and 293.
For other trains Nantes/Rennes - Massy see Table 11 (Lille services), Table 335 (services via St Pierre des Corps) and Table 391 (Strasbourg services).

	TGV 8762	TGV 8670*	TGV 8668		TGV 8850	TGV 8950	TGV 8950		TGV 8676	TGV 8982	TGV 8852	TGV 8852	TGV 8092	TGV 8780	TGV 8854		TGV 8688	TGV 8794	TGV 8682	TGV 8682	TGV 8856	TGV 8958	TGV 8686	TGV 8960	TGV 8796
	Ⓐ	⑥⑦	Ⓐ	⑤	⑥	⑦	①–⑤	⑤	⑦	⑦	⑥⑦	⑤	⑦	①–④	⑤	⑦	⑦	①–④	⑤⑦	⑤⑦	⑦	⑦	⑦	⑦
											D			**x**						**x**	**s**				
Nantes 289 ....d.	...	...	1834	1852	1855	1900	1905	1920	...	1952	1953	...	...	2022	2023	...	...	...	2051	2154	...	2225	...
Angers St Laud 289 ..d.	...	...	1927	1940	1946	1948	1956	...	2041	2042	...	...	2109	2126	...	...	2139	...	...	2312	...
Sablé ....d.	...	...	1950	...	...	...	2018	...	...	...	...	2147	...	...	...	...	...	...	...	...	...
Rennes..............d.	1835	1905	1905	...	...	...	1935	...	2005	2005	...	...	2035	2105	2105	2105	...	...	2205	...	2235
Vitré ....d.	1857										2056			2144				2312
Laval ....d.									2043	2043					
Le Mans..............d.	...	...	2012	2022	2029	2029	2038	...	2051	...	...	...	2206	...	...	2220	...	...	...
Massy TGV ....a.																							
Paris Montparnasse ....a.	2054	2111	2111	...	2119	2125	2128	...	2139	2150	2214	2214	2219	2219	2244	...	2241	2310	2310	2323	2322	0005	0011	0043	0053

A – ①–⑤ Dec. 12-30; ① Jan. 2 - Feb. 27; ①–⑤ Mar. 6-31.
B – ⑥ Dec. 17-31, Mar. 11 - Apr. 1.
C – Not Jan. 31 - Feb. 24.
D – Not Feb. 4, 11, 18, 25.
E – Mar. 6-31.
F – Not Mar. 6-31.
H – Daily Dec. 12-15; ②–④ Jan. 31 - Feb. 23 (also Mar. 27).
J – Dec. 13-15.
K – Daily Dec. 13-15; ⑦ Dec. 18 - Mar. 26 (also Feb. 11, 18, 25; not Feb. 19, 26).
Q – Mar. 6-17.
R – Not ①–⑤ Mar. 6-17.

a – Arrive 1623 on ①–⑤ Mar. 6-17.
c – Arrive 1310 on ①–⑤ Mar. 20-31.
d – Departure time varies: 1338 - 1354.
e – Departure time varies: 1420 - 1430.

f – 9 – 11 minutes later from Mar. 6.
h – Also Feb. 10, 17.
j – Also Feb. 11, 18.
k – Not Feb. 5.
m – Not Feb. 4.
n – Also Feb. 19.
p – Not Feb. 10.
q – Not Feb. 18.
r – 20 - 22 minutes later Mar. 6-31.
s – Not Feb. 17.
t – Not Jan. 28.
u – Not Feb. 10, 17.
v – Not Mar. 24, 31.
w – Not Jan. 28, 29.
x – Not Jan. 27.
z – Dec. 16-30, Mar. 10-31.

* – Train number variations:
8622 runs as 8624 on ⑦;
8670 runs as 8672 on ⑥;
8737 runs as 8739 on ⑤;
8743 runs as 8745 on ⑦;
8815 runs as 8915 on ⑥;
8819 runs as 8919 on ⑤;
8821 runs as 8921 on ⑦–④;
8825 runs as 8925 on ⑥;
8842 runs as 8942 on ⑤⑥⑦;
8977 runs as 8979 on ⑥–④.

RENNES - ST MALO   281

km	TGV trains, Ⓡ	TGV 8081	TGV 8091	TGV 8083	TGV 8085		TGV 8089	TGV 8095	TGV 8099	TGV 8097	TGV trains, Ⓡ	TGV 8080	TGV 8082	TGV 8084	TGV 8084	TGV 8084		TGV 8088	TGV 8088	TGV 8092
		Ⓐ	Ⓒ	Ⓐ	Ⓒ		Ⓒ	Ⓐ	⑦	⑤		①–⑥	Ⓐ	①–⑤	①–⑤	⑥⑦		Ⓐ	Ⓒ	Ⓐ
														F	**E**				
	Paris Montparnasse 280..d.	0736	0808	1008	1008		1508	1841	1908	2024	St Malo ....d.	0606	0707	1144	1144	1215		1637	1637	1911
	Lille Flandres 11 ....d.										Dol 272 ....d.	0621	0722					1653	1653	1926
0	Rennes 272..........d.	0957	1032	1220	1220		1720	2058	2128	2241	Rennes 272 ....d.	0655	0759	1229	1229	1259		1729	1729	1959
58	Dol 272.............d.	1033	1107		1255			2130		2312	Lille Flandres 11.........a.								
81	St Malo ....a.	1046	1120	1302	1308		1804	2145	2210	2328	Paris Montparnasse 280..a.	0917	1023	1457	1506	1522		1956	1945	2219

Local services

	⑥	⑥	⑥	⑥	†	⑥	⑥	⑥	⑥·③	Ⓒ	Ⓐ	✕	⑤	Ⓒ		Ⓐ	Ⓐ	⑥	†	Ⓐ	⑥	†	Ⓐ
Rennes 272..........d.	0630	0630	0730	0730	0930	0940	1130	1245	1300	1315	1343	1343		1440	1535	1635	1637		1700	1730	1733	1800	1830	1831	1835
Dol 272..............d.	0709	0711	0808	0812	1008	1018	1208	1325	1343	1357	1417	1420		1516	1611	1710	1717		1738	1808	1811	1844	1911	1906	1910
St Malo ....a.	0728	0730	0825	0828	1022	1032	1222	1343	1401	1415	1431	1433		1530	1625	1724	1734		1752	1828	1825	1903	1930	1921	1925

	Ⓐ	⑤	⑥	†		①–④	⑤	†	✕		St Malo ....d.	Ⓐ	⑤	⑥	Ⓐ		Ⓐ	⑥		⑥	Ⓐ
Rennes 272..........d.	1908	1930	1940	1945	...	2005	2028	2030	2208		St Malo ....d.	0550	0620	0650	0650	...	0720	0750	...	0850	0930
Dol 272..............d.	1945	2008	2016	2023	...	2042	2106	2106	2246		Dol 272 ....d.	0604	0638	0703	0706	...	0738	0805	...	0904	0944
St Malo ....a.	2000	2022	2030	2037	...	2056	2120	2119	2300		Rennes 272 ....a.	0641	0719	0740	0744	...	0819	0844	...	0941	1019

	⑥	†	⑥		③	†	✕		Ⓐ	†	⑤	Ⓒ	Ⓐ	Ⓐ	†		⑥	Ⓐ	†	Ⓐ		†
St Malo ....d.	0950	0950	1050	...	1220	1250	1250	...	1450	1550	1550	1650	1720	1720	1750	1750	...	1815	1820	1830	1850	...	1955	2050
Dol 272 ....d.	1004	1005	1109	...	1239	1305	1309	...	1505	1604	1604	1704	1734	1738	1809	1808	...	1834	1835	1844	1906	...	2009	2104
Rennes 272 ....a.	1039	1043	1148	...	1320	1341	1349	...	1537	1636	1642	1736	1808	1819	1849	1850	...	1913	1915	1916	1945	...	2043	2137

E – From Mar. 6.   F – Until Mar. 3.

DOL - DINAN   282

km		Ⓐ	⑥		Ⓐ	Ⓒ		⑥	Ⓐ	†	⑥		Ⓒ	Ⓐ		Ⓐ	†		†	Ⓐ		⑤⑥
0	Dol.................d.	0702	0820	...	1035	1110	...	1305	1423	...	1428	1523	...	1725	1730	...	1850	1920	...	2111	2136	...	2251
28	Dinan..............a.	0725	0843	...	1058	1133	...	1328	1446	...	1451	1554	...	1756	1759	...	1920	1943	...	2134	2159	...	2314

		🚌	Ⓐ	✕		⑥			⑤		Ⓐ	†		⑥		Ⓐ				
Dinan ....d.		0540		0629	0732	...	0925	1230	...	1435	1622	...	1805	1838	...	1855	...	1936	...	2033	...
Dol ....a.		0610		0657	0800	...	0955	1258	...	1458	1645	...	1828	1901	...	1918	...	1959	...	2056	...

MORLAIX - ROSCOFF   283

km		Ⓐ 🚌	Ⓐ 🚌	✕ w		⑥ 🚌	†	✕	†		⑥ 🚌		⑤ 🚌	①–④ 🚌	Ⓒ 🚌		⑤ 🚌	† 🚌
0	Morlaix 284........d.	0810	0900	...	1025	...	1110	...	1151	...	1309	...	1526	...	1530	...	1715	...	1810	1815	...	2005	2010
21	St Pol de Léon......a.	0827	0915	...	1059	...	1125	...	1226	...	1343	...	1601	...	1545	...	1730	...	1825	1830	...	2020	2025
28	Roscoff............a.	0849	0935	...	1112	...	1140	...	1238	...	1356	...	1613	...	1600	...	1745	...	1845	1845	...	2037	2040

		Ⓐ 🚌	⑥ 🚌	⑥	✕ w	†		†	✕		⑥ 🚌	Ⓐ 🚌		⑥ 🚌	†		①–④ 🚌	Ⓐ 🚌	†		⑤ 🚌
Roscoff.............d.		0640	0800	0825		1120	...	1130	...	1320	1330	...	1416	1511	...	1630	...	1649	...	1715	1835	1935	...	2025
St Pol de Léon.......a.		0650	0815	0840		1131	...	1140	...	1331	1340	...	1427	1522	...	1640	...	1700	...	1730	1845	1940	...	2040
Morlaix 284.........a.		0710	0839	0905		1207	...	1205	...	1407	1405	...	1503	1558	...	1705	...	1736	...	1754	1910	2005	...	2100

w – Not Ⓐ Mar. 6-17.   🚌 journeys serve Roscoff port at sailing times.

Trains may be retimed a few minutes earlier owing to engineering work

TGV trains convey 🍴

Block 1 — TGV 8603 8603 / 8611 / 8617 8617

km	Station											TGV 8603	TGV 8603							TGV 8611				TGV 8617	TGV 8617	
	Paris Mont. 280 d.											0704	0708							0908				1106	1108	
0	Rennes d.			0612		0620	0640	0700	0720	0830	0920	0920		0957		1042	1040		1117			1238	1332	1332	
80	Lamballe 299 d.			0652		0723	0745		0813	0907	0959	0959		1035		1121	1120					1315		1412	
101	St Brieuc 299 d.			0705		0737	0800	0746	0828	0919	1012	1012		1048		1133	1131		1207	1223		1327	1422	1427	
132	Guingamp d.			0721						0939	1030	1030		1107		1151			1225	1243		1347	1440	1444	
158	Plouaret-Trégor d.		0619	0736	0742					0953			1121	1134	1205			1216	1301			1401	1457	1500	1508 1512
175	Lannion a.				0759								1151					1233	1318					1525	1529
189	Morlaix 283 d.	0614	0637	0725	0800				0830		1012	1101	1101	1112	1139			1223		1254		1305	1420	1516	1519
215	Landivisiau d.	0628	0657	0741	0815						1027			1127	1155		1239				1329	1435			
230	Landerneau 286 d.	0638	0709	0751	0828						1037			1138	1205		1248				1341	1445	1541	1543	
248	Brest 286 a.	0653	0724	0809	0840			0902			1049	1132	1132	1150	1217		1301		1326		1359	1457	1552	1554	

Block 2 — TGV 8627 / 8621 / 8623 8629

Station	TGV 8627						TGV 8621				TGV 8623	TGV 8629											
Paris Mont. 280 d.	1206						1307				1408	1408											
Rennes d.	1349	1428	1435	1436			1524	1600		1617	1623	1623		1650	1655	1710	1720	1729		1737	1744
Lamballe 299 d.	1447		1513	1515			1604	1638		1706	1703		1728	1757	1806	1807	1807		1838	1823
St Brieuc 299 d.	1502	1516	1526	1527			1617	1651	1709	1719	1716		1730	1741	1812	1820	1819	1820	1852	1835
Guingamp d.		1534	1543	1544			1636		1708		1727	1734		1752	1758				1835	1852
Plouaret-Trégor d.		1557	1558	1603	1617				1722	1729		1749		1754	1811	1813	1835		1850	1856	1906
Lannion a.				1620	1634			1746				1811	1828	1852				1913	
Morlaix 283 d.		1604	1615	1616	1630		1707	1720	1741		1757		1808	1807	1817	1831			1907		1925
Landivisiau d.			1630		1646			1744	1757				1826	1838	1847				1922	1941
Landerneau 286 d.			1640	1639	1656			1756	1807				1837	1847	1857				1932	1950
Brest 286 a.	1638	1654	1651	1708			1738	1814	1819		1828		1840	1852	1905	1910			1946	2002

Block 3 — TGV 8633 / 8647 / 8643 / 8645 8649 8691 8655 8657 8655 / 8663 8665 8667 8679 8689

Station	TGV 8633						TGV 8647	TGV 8643			8645	8649	8691	8655	8657	8655		8663	8665	8667	8679	8689
Paris Mont. 280 d.	1608						1712	1708														
Rennes d.	1817	1826	1838	1845	1849		1922	1927			1935	1940	1956	2001	2007	2018	2018	2018	2033	2123	2124 2128	2109 2359 / 2323
Lamballe 299 d.		1902	1937	1923	1942			2006			2027	2016	2036		2048			2124		2204	2212	
St Brieuc 299 d.		1908	1914	1947	1936		1953	2008			2012	2019	2038	2029	2049		2101	2108	2108	2135	2213 2219	2223 0013 0423
Guingamp d.		1927	1932		1952			2030	2037			2046			2117		2126	2125		2231	2236	0030 0440
Plouaret-Trégor d.	1924			2006	2013				2051	2057			2100			2133			2141	2247	2251	
Lannion a.	1941				2030					2114				2150								
Morlaix 283 d.		1956	2001		2024			2059	2111			2119		2129		2156	2159		2305	2309	0059 0516
Landivisiau d.					2041					2135				2135								0540
Landerneau 286 d.		2020			2051				2133			2145				2223			2329	2334		0540
Brest 286 a.		2031	2034		2103		2119		2130	2145		2157		2200		2217	2227	2234	2340	2345	0130 0552

Block 4 — TGV 8690 8612 8610 / 8618 8618 / 8620 / 8622 8624

Station	TGV 8690	TGV 8612	TGV 8610								TGV 8618	8618						TGV 8620			TGV 8622	8624	
Brest 286 d.		0444	0448			0540		0635			0638	0642	0702		0752		0817	0809			0842	0847 1022 1034
Landerneau 286 d.								0647			0654	0656	0719	0804			0826					1034 1045
Landivisiau d.								0657					0732	0814			0838					1055
Morlaix 283 d.		0517	0521			0611		0713			0717	0721	0755	0830		0849	0901			0916	0919 1057 1110
Lannion d.					0558		0613 0628		0656	0714					0836				0906	0908		0922 0925 0934 1127
Plouaret-Trégor d.							0642	0701	0711	0730			0747	0751			0852				0949 0948 1125 1141
Guingamp d.		0546	0550				0642	0701	0725	0730			0747	0751			0908		0918	0938	0949 0948 1125 1141
St Brieuc 299 d.	0506	0604	0608	0614	0631		0659	0724	0741	0751		0805	0809		0858		0933 0937			1007	1006 1143 1158 1236
Lamballe 299 d.	0518	0618		0626	0642		0711	0738	0753				0913		0948						1155 1210 1227
Rennes a.	0559	0659	0659	0725	0745		0753	0840	0850		0859	0859	1013		1048	1025			1055	1055	1236 1250 1340
Paris Mont. 280 a.	0815	0917	0917						1117	1121			1253a						1323	1323	

Block 5 — TGV 8634 / 8646 / 8660

Station		TGV 8634							TGV 8646				TGV 8660									
Brest 286 d.	1132			1135	1145	1201	1230	1308		1345		1432	1433	1525		1541		1558				1630
Landerneau 286 d.	1143			1146		1212	1247	1325				1443	1444	1536				1609				1641
Landivisiau d.	1154			1156		1222	1300	1338				1453	1454	1546				1619				1651
Morlaix 283 d.	1212			1212	1217	1238	1323	1401		1418		1509	1509	1603		1614		1635				1706
Lannion d.		1153	1204 1213					1401	1432			1554	1605		1627				1658 1658	
Plouaret-Trégor d.		1210	1221	1229	1236	1256		1418	1448		1527	1526	1611	1622	1632	1644	1653		1714 1715 1724
Guingamp d.		1244	1252	1310		1434		1447		1541	1540		1648		1707			1730		1740
St Brieuc 299 d.	1236			1301	1310	1327		1453		1506		1557	1556	1606		1707		1724 1723 1731		1759
Lamballe 299 d.	1250			1313		1339				1519		1609	1608	1620		1719		1736 1737 1743		1813
Rennes a.	1345			1353	1400	1421		1559		1650	1653	1720				1817	1837	1823		1854
Paris Mont. 280 a.				1614f					1825				2014								

Block 6 — TGV 8672 8670 8668 / 8676 / 8688 / 8696 8682 / 8686

Station	TGV 8672	TGV 8670	TGV 8668			TGV 8676							TGV 8688					TGV 8696	TGV 8682			TGV 8686	
Brest 286 d.		1647	1652	1658		1704		1711	1717	1726	1736	1800	1800	1815			1833		1849	1902	1933	1948 2102
Landerneau 286 d.						1718		1732	1747	1811	1817	1817		1844				1913	1951		2001 2113
Landivisiau d.		1719				1728		1745	1747	1757	1829	1830		1854				1923	2003			
Morlaix 283 d.		1719				1742		1743	1800	1803	1812	1852	1853	1848			1909	1921	1939	2018	2024 2135
Lannion d.	1703													1900			1918				2028 2036
Plouaret-Trégor d.	1720					1805		1821	1830	1912		1917	1917					2045	2053		2152
Guingamp d.	1735	1748	1751			1813		1835	1844		1917		1941	1947	1950	2011				2207
St Brieuc 299 d.	1755	1807	1810	1812	1824		1838	1852	1901		1940	1944	1957	2004	2028	2028		2106 2224
Lamballe 299 d.		1820		1838			1843	1904	1913		1958		2009	2017	2040			2236
Rennes a.	1900	1859	1900	1942		1925		1945	1953		2029	2053		2050	2059	2059	2121		2155 2316
Paris Mont. 280 a.	2111	2111	2114			2150					2241				2310	2313c			0011

Footnotes:

A – Not Feb. 17 - Mar. 3.
B – ①-④ Dec. 12 - Feb. 23; ① Feb. 27 - Mar. 27.
C – Until Dec. 29.
D – From Jan. 2.
E – ①②③④⑤⑥⑦ Dec. 11-29; ⑥⑦ Dec. 31 - Apr. 1.
F – ①-⑤ Dec. 12 - Feb. 10; ① Feb. 13-27; ①-⑤ Mar. 6-24 (also Mar. 27).
G – Dec. 12, Mar. 28-31.
L – Lannion - Brest and v.v.

a – Arrive 1304 from Mar. 6.
c – Arrive 2323 on ⑤.
f – Arrive 1623 on ①-⑤ Mar. 6-17.
p – Not Feb. 26.
q – Not Dec. 12, 19, Jan.30.
r – Not Mar. 25.
t – Not Feb. 10, 17.

Trains may be retimed a few minutes earlier owing to engineering work

km												TGV 8705	TGV 8705						TGV 8711						TGV 8715			
		Ⓐ	①-⑤	Ⓐ		⑥	①-⑤	①	②-⑤		①-⑤	①-⑤	⑥	⑥	⑦	⑥		⑥⑦	①-⑤	①-⑤	①-⑤	⑥		⑥	①-⑤		
					j							B	A	j				p		D	E	j		p			
0	Paris Mont 280 ....d.	...	...	...	...	...	...	...	...	...	0704	0704						0808					1008			
365	Rennes 287 ....d.	...	0622	...	0636	0654	0725				0924	0924	0926	0930k			0918	1029	1036			1127		1217		
	Nantes ....d.	...		0612				0730	0738	...							0918			1027	1029			1227	1251
	Nantes ....d.	...		0636				0752	0802	...										1051	1051			1249	1315
437	Redon 287 ....d.	...	0707	0712	0735	0738	0807	0830	0836	...			1008	1012	1013		1113	1122	1127	1127	1209		1259	1316	1343
492	Vannes ....d.	0634	0741	0807	0808	0832				1024	1036		1037	1038		1139		1156	1156t	1239		1325	1344	
511	Auray ....d.	0648	0753	0818	0820				1038	1049		1049	1050		1153		1209	1209t	1251		1338	1357	
545	Lorient ....d.	0718	0814	0843	0838	0858			1056	1108		1107	1110		1212		1230	1230t	1313		1356	1418	
565	Quimperlé ....d.	0733	0826		0850							1119	1122				1242	1242t	1325		1410	1430	
612	Quimper ....a.	0802	0853		0917	0931			1130	1141		1145	1148		1247		1309	1309t	1352		1438	1457	

	TGV 8717	TGV 8723												TGV 8729						
	⑥	①-⑤	⑤	①-⑤	⑤	①-④		⑦	①-④	①-⑤	⑥⑦	⑤	①-④	⑥-④	⑤		①-⑤	①-⑤	⑧
	p													j	J				
Paris Mont 280 ....d.	...	1206		1343			...				1508								
Rennes 287 ....d.	...	1340	1423			1610			1629	1636			1653		1717	1727			1750
Nantes ....d.	1312		1520			1620	1620				1618	1659				1702	1723	1724	
Savenay ....d.	1336					1642	1642				1642					1736	1745	1747	
Redon 287 ....d.	1405	1421	1604			1654	1708	1712		1715	1717	1720	1742	1738		1811	1805	1812	1822	1836
Vannes ....d.	1448	1526	1633	1656	1708	1723			1744		1742	1745	1809	1804	1802		1822	1837		1905
Auray ....d.	1500	1539	1646	1709	1719	1736			1758			1758		1817	1816		1835			1918
Lorient ....d.	1516	1558	1707v	1728	1750	1757			1817		1837	1840	1841		1854			1940
Quimperlé ....d.			1719v			1805	1809		1840			1852	1852					1952
Quimper ....a.	...	1631	1747v	1802		1834	1836		1907			1852	1911	1919	1922		1932			2019

	TGV 8739	TGV 8737		TGV 8747	TGV 8745	TGV 8743					TGV 8759		TGV 8757			TGV 8761		TGV 5237		TGV 8777
	⑥	⑥	⑤	①-⑤	⑤	①-④		①-⑤	⑦		⑦	⑤	①-④	①-④	①-④	⑦		⑦	⑤⑦		⑤
	j			q				j							r		n		♥h		h
Paris Mont 280 ....d.				1641	1641		1708	1708	1708			1808		1858			1941			2024
Rennes 287 ....d.	1752			1901	1901		1918	1929	1929			2022	2029	2031		2149		2203		2238
Nantes ....d.		1739	1805	1819						1940	1943	2000			2041				
Savenay ....d.		1803		1843						2002	2012	2026			2105				
Redon 287 ....d.	1837	1842	1853	1912	1944	1945			2015	2031	2041	2055		2119	2113		2131	2232		2245	2320
Vannes ....d.		1912	1922		2010	2009		2022	2035	2040			2126	2147	2140	2207		2258	2311		2346
Auray ....d.		1925	1934		2024			2035	2048	2053				2153	2221		2312	2324		2359
Lorient ....d.		1946	1954		2043			2055	2106	2111			2152		2212	2239		2333	2343		0018
Quimperlé ....d.		1958	2006					2108		2123					2224		2346	2355		0024
Quimper ....a.		2025	2033		2117			2136	2139	2150			2226		2252	2312		0014	0024		0051

	TGV 8704	TGV 8706	TGV 8712											TGV 8718					TGV 5272		TGV 8720	TGV 8722	TGV 8724	
	①	②-⑥	①-⑤	①-⑤	①-⑤	①	①-⑤			⑥	①-⑤	①-⑤	①-⑥	Ⓐ		⑥	①-⑤	①-⑤	①⑥	Ⓐ	①-⑤	⑦		①-⑤
		j										j						x		♥j	H	s		F G
Quimper ....d.	0414		0521		0528				0612		0630	0650	0704		0715			0736	0754	0806	0836	0836	0927	0920	0928
Quimperlé ....d.			0556				0701	0718	0733	0742		0806	0823	0836	0907	0907		0946	0955
Lorient ....d.	0451	0455	0557		0608		0645		0715	0733	0746	0755		0821	0838	0851	0922	0922	1002	1000	1008
Auray ....d.	0510		0629			0702		0734	0805	0805	0815		0840	0905	0912	0942	0942		1021	1029
Vannes ....d.	0523	0522	0623		0641		0653		0715		0748	0816	0818		0834		0854	0915	0926	0956	0956	1030	1033	1041
Redon 287 ....d.	0548	0549		0646	0711	0720	0724		0740	0743	0748	0813		0844	0851	0903		0919			1056	1104	1112
Savenay ....d.			0720		0747		0808		0819			0920					1131	1139x
Nantes ....a.			0745		0812		0832		0843			0945					1141	1155	1203x
Rennes 287 ....a.	0629	0629	0730		0754		0823		0827		0855		0923j	0942		0959		1029	1059	1059			
Paris Mont 280 ....a.	0853	0856	0951						1124							1253f	1323	1323			

	TGV 8730												TGV 8752								TGV 8762	TGV 8762	
	⑥	⑥⑦		⑦①-④	⑤	①-⑤	Ⓐ	⑤	⑥	⑥				⑦	⑤	⑥		⑦	⑦	⑤	⑦	①-⑤	Ⓐ
			C										p									j	
Quimper ....d.	0949	1032	1137	1219	1232	1238		1248	1317	1327	1330		1431		1512			1543	1546		1614	1614	1627
Quimperlé ....d.		1101		1246	1259	1305		1317	1344	1354	1357		1501		1539			1613					1656
Lorient ....d.	1023	1114	1214	1258	1312	1318		1332	1357	1408	1410		1517		1552			1630	1626		1653	1653	1711
Auray ....d.		1132	1235	1318	1331	1337		1358	1414	1429	1432		1537		1614			1651	1648		1713	1713	1737
Vannes ....d.	1050	1145	1249	1331	1344	1349		1411	1428	1442	1445		1552		1626		1646	1704	1700		1727	1727	1749
Redon 287 ....d.	1118	1211	1315	1400	1416	1415	1423		1506	1513	1514	1523	1524	1618		1657	1654	1716	1732	1732	1738	1743	
Savenay ....d.				1449		1530			1546	1547				1722	1727		1804	1810	
Nantes ....a.	1202		1445		1513			1553		1610	1611			1745	1750		1828	1836	
Rennes 287 ....a.		1250p	1355		1455	1455			1553j	1553k		1658		1755	1812	1811		1829	1829	
Paris Mont 280 ....a.		1614a									1914				2054	2056	

	TGV 8774							TGV 8776	TGV 8780				TGV 8794					TGV 8790		TGV 8798		TGV 8796	
	⑦	①-⑤①-④	⑦	Ⓐ	⑥			⑤①-⑤		⑤	①-④	⑥	①-④ ①-④	⑤		⑦	⑤	⑦	⑦		⑦
					j		h						h								
Quimper ....d.	1627		1715	1712		1722	1732		1743	1745	1757	1758	1807	1831	1832			1840	1916		1944	2003		2035	
Quimperlé ....d.	1654			1750	1800			1825	1825	1836	1902	1858			1943		2029		2102
Lorient ....d.	1707		1751	1748		1804	1813		1820	1822	1839	1837	1851	1916	1912			1917	1956		2022	2042	2056	2115
Auray ....d.	1729			1808		1832	1832		1840	1842	1858	1858	1913	1935	1929			1937	2018		2042	2103	2116	2134
Vannes ....d.	1741		1818	1821		1845	1844		1854	1856	1911	1909	1930	1949	1941			1952	2030		2056	2114	2129	2146
Redon 287 ....d.	1811	1841	1845	1848			1914			1938	1935		2015	2014	2020	2036		2059		2145		2212	
Savenay ....d.		1909										2046	2102				2211		
Nantes ....a.		1933										2110	2126				2235		
Rennes 287 ....a.	1853		1924	1929		1953			1959	2023	2015		2055	2053		2055	2139		2159		2230	2251	
Paris Mont 280 ....a.			2153					2208	2222			2310			2323		0011		0053	

A – Not Jan. 16 - 27.
B – Jan. 16 - 27.
C – Not Jan. 28 - Feb. 3, Feb. 6 - 10, Mar. 6 - 10, 13 - 17.
D – Jan. 31 - Feb. 24.
E – Dec. 12 - Jan. 30, Mar. 13 - 31.
F – Dec. 19, Jan. 9, 23, Feb. 20, Feb. 6, 20.
G – Not Dec. 19, Jan. 9, 23, Jan. 30 - Feb. 10, Feb. 20, Mar. 6, 20.
H – Not Jan. 30 - Feb. 10.
J – Not Feb. 3 - 24.

a – Arrive 1623 on ①-⑤ Mar. 6 - 17.
f – Arrive 1304 Mar. 6 - 31.
h – Not Jan. 27.
j – Not Jan. 28.
k – Not Jan. 29.
n – Not Jan. 27, 28.
p – Not Jan. 28, 29.
q – Not Feb. 10, 17.
r – Not Jan. 27, Feb. 10, 17.
s – Not Jan. 29, Feb. 26.
t – Not Jan. 16 - 27.
v – Not Jan. 31 - Feb. 25.
x – Not Mar. 6 - 10.

⊖ – To / from Brest (Table **286**).
◧ – See also **287** Nantes - Redon, **287/8** Nantes - Savenay.
♥ – From / to Lille Europe / Le Mans (Table **11**).

AURAY - QUIBERON : runs in Summer only

286   BREST - QUIMPER

Currently operated by 🚌 owing to engineering work

km		Ⓐ												Ⓒ										
0	Brest 284 ....d.	Ⓐ	0540		0744	...	1245	...	1725	...	1845	1900		Ⓒ	0700	0805	0830	0930	1130	1555	...	1800	2015	2030
18	Landerneau 284 ....d.			0700		0735	0855		1255		1740		1930					1005	1205	1630	1750			2105
72	Châteaulin ....d.			0625	0755		0828	0948		1348		1834		2010		0745			1046	1246	1711	1831		2100	2146
102	Quimper ....a.			0700	0830	0850	0901	1021	1351	1421	1831	1907	1950	2045		0820	0911	0936	1119	1319	1744	1904	1906	2135	2219

		Ⓐ	Ⓐ	Ⓐ	Ⓐ	Ⓐ	Ⓐ	Ⓐ	Ⓐ	Ⓐ	Ⓐ	Ⓐ		⑥	†	⑥		Ⓒ	Ⓒ		⑥	†		†	
	Quimper ....d.	0600	0640	0735	0740	1030	1050	1500	1500	1715	1810	1810	1900	Ⓒ	0700	0830	0945	...	1445	1755	1920	1920	...	2030	...
	Châteaulin ....d.	0633		0810			1123		1533	1750		1843	1935		0733	0903	1020	...	1518	1828		1953		2103	...
	Landerneau 284 ....d.	0727		0850		1216		1626		1937						0944		1559	1909			2144	...
	Brest 284 ....a.	...	0746	...	0845	1136	...	1606	...	1850	1916		2020		0817	1019	1105	...	1634	1944	2026	2037	...	2219	...

CAT 🚌 *31, journey approx 90 minutes.*   x – Not Dec. 25, Jan. 1.
From **Brest** : 0700Ⓐ, 0930†x, 1000⚹, 1415†x, 1445⚹, 1600⑤, 1805Ⓐ.
From **Quimper** : 0710Ⓐ, 1135⑤, 1245†x, 1255⚹, 1640⚹, 1730Ⓐ, 1740†x.

287   RENNES - REDON - NANTES

km		Ⓐ	①	Ⓐ	⑥	Ⓐ	Ⓐ	Ⓐ		Ⓐ	Ⓐ	⑥	①–④	⑥	⑤	⑤	⑦	①–④	⑤	⑥	†	Ⓐ	†	Ⓐ	Ⓐ
							a	d			c														
0	Rennes ...... § d.	...	...	0703	...	...	0850	0955	...	1203	1229	...	1406	...	...	1530	...	...	1636	1643	1656	...	...	1725	1742	...
72	Redon.......... § a.	...	...	...	...	...	...	...	...	...	...	...	...	...	...	...	...	...	...	...	...	...	...	...	...	...
72	Redon.......... § d.	0646	0720		0740	0748	0851		...	1423		1523	1524		1654		...	1738	1743		1841	
106	Savenay...... ◇ d.	0720	0747		0808	0818	0920	1012	1120		1449		1546	1547		1727		1804	1810		1909	
145	Nantes ...... ◇ a.	0745	0812	0826	0832	0843	0945	1012	1120	1325	1400	1513	1527	1610	1611	1652	1750	...	1806	1805	1818	1828	1836	1853	1903	1933

		⑥	Ⓐ	†		⑥	①–④	†	①–④	⑤		⑦				Ⓐ	Ⓐ	①–④	⑤	⑥		Ⓐ	Ⓐ	Ⓐ	Ⓐ
		c						c				n						c		b		c	e	c	
	Rennes .... § d.	1810	1829	1854	...	1920	1928	1946	...	...	2044	...		Nantes .... ◇ d.	0649	0724	0730	0730	0754	...	0913	1006	1007	1224	1253
	Redon............ § a.	1855	1918	1937				...			...			Savenay .... ◇ d.	0713		0752	0756		0937	1004	1029		
	Redon............ § d.	1859	1926	1945					2020	2036			Redon .... ◇ a.	0741		0830	0830		1005	1055	1055		
	Savenay.......... ◇ d.	1926	1954	2013					2046	2102			Redon .... § d.	0751				1011	1101	1101		
	Nantes .... ◇ a.	1950	2017	2037	...	2041	2054	2107	2110	2126	2209		Rennes .... § a.	0838	0846			0915	...	1053	1153	1154	1345	1415

		⑥	Ⓐ	⑥	①–④	⑤	⑤	①–④	⑤		⑤	†	①–④	⑤	⑤	⑦	⑥		⑦	⑤	⑥	Ⓐ	
				c																c		c	f
	Nantes .... ◇ d.	1251	1312	1438	1457	1555	1557	1618	1620	1646	...	1700	1723	1724	1725	1755	1757	1801	...	1819	1922	1940	1943	2000	2025	2041
	Savenay .... ◇ d.	1315	1336			1642	1642				...	1736	1745	1747	1747				1843		2002	2012	2026	2047	2105	
	Redon .... ◇ a.	1343	1405			1708	1710				...	1805	1812	1822	1822				1912		2031	2041	2055	2112	2131	
	Redon .... § d.																				2119		
	Rennes .... § a.			1559	1622	1717	1718	...	1807	...				1915	1917	1922	...		2044		2158	

a – Not Feb. 27 - Mar. 10.
b – Not Feb. 27 - Mar. 3.
c – Not Jan. 28.
d – Not Jan. 28, 29.

e – Not Jan. 29.
f – Not Jan. 27.
n – Dec. 11.

◇ – For other trains Redon - Nantes see Table 285, for Savenay - Nantes see Tables 285 and 288.
§ – For other trains see Table 285.

288   NANTES - ST NAZAIRE - LE CROISIC

km	TGV trains convey ▯											TGV 8903			TGV 8911	TGV 8911			TGV 8915		TGV 8919			TGV 8921			TGV 8925
		Ⓐ	Ⓐ	Ⓐ	Ⓐ	②–⑤	①	⑥	Ⓐ	⑥⑦	Ⓐ		⑦	①–⑥	⑤		⑥	⑥	⑤	⑤	⑦–④	Ⓐ	①–④	⑥
0	Nantes 285/7.......d.	0616	0640	0654	0753	0757	0757	0805	0919	0949	1006	1110	1117	1158	1218	1234	1306	1312	1446	1529	1604	1611	1640	1701	1714
	Paris Mont 280........d.								0653	...	0852	0854	...	...	1054	...	1221	...	1343	...	...	1454
39	Savenay 285/7.......d.	0648	0706	0720	0820	0835	0835	0845		1016	1029		1232	1242	1309		1347		1606	1636		1704	1735	
64	St Nazaire ....d.	0712	0726	0739	0835	0900	0913	0916	0955	1042	1045	1148	1154	1247	1301	1332	1343	1403	1524	1625	1650	1648	1728	1750	1752
79	Pornichet ....d.			0753		0910	0924	0927		1053	1058	1201		1312	1343	1356		1636	1700		1741	
83	La Baule Escoublac....d.			0800		0916	0929	0932		1058	1104	1209	1210		1321	1355	1405		1643	1706	1706	1748		1808
90	Le Croisic ....a.			0815		0927	0940	0943		1110	1117	1218	1222		1333	1406	1420		1550	1659	1717	1715	1802		1817

												TGV 8937	TGV 8937	TGV 8935			TGV 8943		TGV 8945		TGV 5230	TGV 8949		TGV 8953			TGV 8957
		Ⓐ	⑥	Ⓐ	①–④	⑤	Ⓐ	⑥	⑦	①–④	⑤		⑥	⑤	⑤⑥	⑤	①–④	⑥	①–④	⑥	⑤†		⑥	⑤	⑦	⑤⑥	⑥
	Paris Mont 280........d.									1721	1721	1721	...	...	1823	...	1850	...	1954	...	2054	...	2154
	Nantes 285/7.......d.	1717	1727	1734	1837	1841	1841	1900	1903	1931	1937	1939	1950	2001	2006	2041	2031	2104	2131	2200	2213	2222	2311	2325	2325	0017
	Savenay 285/7.......d.	1741	1753	1809	1913	1916	1917	1923	1940		2015	2030	2031		2100	2158		2249		2346	2354	
	St Nazaire ....d.	1757	1808	1832	1928	1930	1932	1939	2019	2007	2012	2039	2032	2047	2119	2121	2142	2212	2228	2330	2350	0007	0008	0053
	Pornichet ....d.	1809	1819		1939		1943	1950	2040		2031	2047	2100		2133		2223	2251	2302	2314		0013	0019	
	La Baule Escoublac....d.	1817	1826		1949		1951	1957	2040		2038	2055	2107		2135	2141	2158	2227	2258	2310	2321	0006	0020	0026	0109
	Le Croisic ....a.	1832	1839		2002		2005	2011	2052		2051	2110	2121		2144	2153	2207	2240	2312	2323	2323	0015	0035	0038	0118

		TGV 8906	TGV 8906	TGV 8908												TGV 5270	TGV 8926	TGV 8928			TGV 8932			TGV 8938
		①	⑥	②–⑤	Ⓐ	⑥	Ⓐ	Ⓐ	⑥	Ⓐ	Ⓐ	Ⓐ	Ⓒ	Ⓐ	⑥	①⑥	①–⑤	⑥⑦	Ⓐ	⑥	Ⓐ	⑦	Ⓐ	⑥	⑥
			A	B	h													♥	C	D					
	Le Croisic.......d.	0441	...	...		0545	0607		0632	0708		0730	0756	0828	0840	0951	1016	1036		1139	1229		...	1424
	La Baule Escoublac....d.	0453	...	...		0555	0621		0645	0720		0744	0810	0841	0854	1002	1027	1049		1153	1240		...	1434
	Pornichet.......d.	0501	...	...		0600	0629		0652	0728		0751	0815	0846	0902		1057		1200	1247		...	1441
	St Nazaire.......d.	0511	0529	0533	0533	0555	0611	0641	0645	0649	0703	0739	0742	0807	0827	0858	0915	1019	1042	1107	1210	1213	1258	1352	1414	1452
	Savenay 285/7.......d.	0525	0546	0550		0614	0624	0656	0704	0709	0726	0754	0757	0824	0841	0912		1121	1224		1320	1408		1503
	Nantes 285/7.......a.	0550	0610	0611	0611	0649	0648	0720	0720	0738	0743	0750	0820	0820	0851	0906	0936	0953	1052	1115	1140	1248	1247	1356	1440	1450	1541
	Paris Mont 280.......a.	...	0837	0840	0840												1323	1340		1518	...	1710

		TGV 8942	TGV 8944								TGV 8950	TGV 8950			TGV 8952	TGV 8952			TGV 8958		TGV 8960
		①–④	⑤–⑦	①–④	Ⓐ	⑥	Ⓐ	⑥	Ⓐ	⑥		⑤	①–⑤	①–④	⑥		⑤	⑥	Ⓐ	⑦	①–④	⑥	Ⓐ	⑦	⑥	⑥
											E										
	Le Croisic.......d.	...	1443	1534		1628		1651		1740	1746		1815	1841	1845	...	1853	1855	1933	1939	2000	2047		2112
	La Baule Escoublac....d.	...	1454	1545		1644		1705		1755	1801		1827	1852	1856		1908	1914	1947	1951	2032	2058		2126
	Pornichet.......d.	...				1651		1712		1802	1808		1834	1900			1914	1919	1952	1956	2038		2133
	St Nazaire.......d.	1456	1512	1601	1631	1701	1709	1724	1734	1800	1815	1821	1829	1846	1913	1912	1923	1932	2002	2008	2050	2115	2146	2213
	Savenay 285/7.......d.	1511				1648	1714	1728	1740	1756	1815		1848	1914		1938		2022	2110		2133		2229
	Nantes 285/7.......a.	1545	1546	1637	1716	1744	1757	1813	1830	1850	1849	1854	1917	1946	1947	1946	2005	2007	2012	2036	2046	2139	2148	2201	2219	2252
	Paris Mont 280.......a.	1817	1923								2125	2128			2214	2214			0005	...	0043

A – ① Feb. 6-20.
B – ① (not Feb. 6-20).
C – Not Jan. 31 - Feb. 24.
D – Not Feb. 4, 11, 18, 25.
E – Not Feb. 5, 12, 19.

h – Also Dec. 13, 15; not Dec. 14.
z – Dec. 16-30, Mar. 10-31.

TGV –🅁, supplement payable, ▯.
♥ – To/from Lille Europe (Table 11).

NANTES - ANGERS - TOURS 289

For other *TGV* trains Nantes - Angers - Lyon (via Massy) see Table **335**

km		TGV 5300 ① C	TGV 5302 ② 4	4402 ④	4402 ⑥ E	⑥ F	Ⓐ	Ⓐ	Ⓐ		TGV 5334 ♠	4406 ⑦ G	4406 Ⓐ H	5328 Ⓐ		⑤	①-④	⑤⑦	Ⓐ	14408 Ⓐ	Ⓐ	†	⑥	⑦
0	Nantes 280 ....d.	0444	0448		0611	0622	0701	0909	1110	...	1244	1336	1347	1444	...	1601	1601j		1631	1800	1838	2010	2015
88	Angers St Laud 280 ..d.	0534	0536	0634	0704	0704	0800	1001	1201	1254	1333	1429	1429	1534	...	1551	1700	1700	1735	1750	1901	1932	2101	2102
132	Saumur....d.	0558		0707	0727	0727	0822	1023	1222	1327	...	1452	1452	1558	...	1624	1722	1724	1808	1815	1924	1955	2123	2124
196	St Pierre des Corps ..a.	0629	0629				0851	1054	1256		1428			1628	...	1754	1755		1755		1955		2154	2156
199	Tours ....a.			0746	0800	0800				1419	...	1524	1524		1717	1805	1807	1849	1854		2038		
202	St Pierre des Corps ...d.			0824	0824						...	1547	1547										
	Orléans 296 .....a.	Ⓞ	Ⓞ				1005	1157	1411						...					2057		2257	2258
	Lyon Part Dieu 290 .a.	0930	0930		1340	1340					1730	2052	2106	1944									

				TGV 5352 Ⓐ A	Ⓐ	Ⓐ	①-⑤	✗		†		TGV 5368 ♠ ⑥⑦	TGV 5368 ①-⑤	①-⑥		†	†	Ⓐ	⑥		TGV 5380 ♠ B	4506 4507 ⑤-⑦ K	4506 4507 J
	Lyon Part Dieu 290 ..d.	...	...	0630	...	...	...	...		...		1428	1428		...			...			1830	...	1533	1533
	Orléans 296 .....d.	...	0657	0706	Ⓞ	1127			...	...	...			1702	...	...	1805	Ⓞ			...	2110	2114
	St Pierre des Corps ..d.																					2140	2116
	Tours ....d.	0714				1246		1512	1612	1612					1740	1842		1842	1842		2140	2116
	St Pierre des Corps ..d.		0801	0806	0934	1240					1733	1733	1806			1905				2133	2140	2116
	Saumur ....d.	0753	0837	0837		1317	1338	1552	1653	1653			1837		1842	1923	1938	1939	1945		2208	2216	2216
280	Angers St Laud 280 ..d.	0819	0900	0900	1035	1338	1411		1615	1717	1718	1825	1825	1901		1915	1948	2001	2016	2020	2233	2239	2239
280	Nantes 280 ....a.	0908	0946	0943	1107	1423		1700	1804	1806		1906	1912	1947				2046			2315	2320	2325

FOR NOTES SEE BELOW. Additional services operate Saumur - Tours and v.v. Frequent connecting services are available St Pierre des Corps - Tours and v.v. (journey time 5 minutes).

TOURS - BOURGES - NEVERS - MOULINS - LYON 290

Local service liable to alteration around public holidays. For faster *TGV* trains Nantes / Tours - Massy - Lyon and v.v. see Table **335**

km		Ⓐ Q	Ⓐ R	✗	4412 ①-⑤	4402 ⑥ E	4402 ⑥ F		16842 ①-⑤ P	16840 ⑥ N		4406 ⑦ G	4406 Ⓐ H	4416 ①-⑥ L	4416 Ⓐ M		Ⓑ T	Ⓐ	⑥	Ⓑ	Ⓑ
	Nantes 289 ....d.	...	...	...	0611	0622		...	...	...	1336	1347		...	...	...	...	...	...
0	Tours ....d.	...	...	0657	0819	0819	0819		1143	1157	1358	1542	1542	1542	1542		1659	1659	1758	1858
3	St Pierre des Corps ....d.	...	...	0704	0825	0827	0827		1150	1204	1405	1549	1549	1548	1549		1705	1705	1805	1905
	Orléans 315....d.	...	0607														1614	1715		
113	Vierzon 315 d.	...	0657		0828	0929	0929	0929		1328	1328	1528	1652	1652	1652	1652		1707	1807	1828	1928	2028
145	Bourges 315.d.	...	0730		0847	0948	0948	0948		1347	1347	1547	1715	1715	1715	1715		1730	1830	1847	1847	1951	2047
203	Saincaize ....a.																			
214	Nevers ....a.	...	0821		0925	1026	1024	1024		1424	1424	1625	1751	1751	1751	1751		1821a	1921	1925	1925	2038	2128
214	Nevers ....d.	0525		0825	0926	1037	1037	1037		1431	1431		1809	1809	1809	1809		1926			2128
	Dijon 373....a.				1154													2158		
203	Saincaize ....d.	0533	0834			1047	1047	1047					1818	1818	1818	1818				
252	Moulins-sur-Allier ....d.	0608	0901			1116	1116	1116		1502	1502		1845	1843	1843	1843				
	Digoin ....d.	0650	0942							1545	1545									
	Paray le Monial ....d.	0702	0954							1557	1557									
293	St Germain des Fossés 328 d.					1141	1141	1141					1908	1909	1906	1909				
359	Roanne ....328 d.					1229	1229	1229					1948	1954	1948	1954				
452	Lyon Part Dieu ..328 a.			1152		1334	1340	1340		1752	1752		2052	2106	2052	2106				
457	Lyon Perrache....328 a.	0902		1205		1347	1358	1352		1805	1805		2105	2118	2105	2118				

		Ⓐ	Ⓐ	Ⓐ	Ⓐ T	Ⓐ	Ⓐ	⑦ S	①-⑥		4504 ⑥	4504 Ⓐ	16848 16850 ⑥ D		Ⓐ	Ⓐ	Ⓑ		4506 ⑤-⑦ K	4506 J	4516 ①-④		†	Ⓒ	Ⓐ Q
	Lyon Perrache ....328 d.	...	...	...	...	...	...	...	...		0842	0900	1142		...	...	...		1521	1521	1521		...	1743	1810
	Lyon Part Dieu ....328 d.	...	...	...	...	...	...	...	...		0854	0912	1155		...	...	...		1533	1533	1533		...	1755	
	Roanne ....328 d.										1012	1024							1647	1647	1647				
	St Germain des Fossés 328 d.										1059	1117							1735	1735	1735				
	Paray le Monial ....d.												1350										2000	2026
	Digoin ....d.												1359										2010	2035
	Moulins-sur-Allier ....d.										1137	1142	1449						1802	1802	1802			2059	2123
	Saincaize ....a.										1204	1209							1833	1833	1833			2129	2148
	Dijon 373....d.								0706								1601							
	Nevers ....a.								0932		1215	1220	1521				1831		1845	1845	1845			2137	2155
	Nevers ....d.		0535	0635	0640	0735	0740	0935	0932		1230	1230	1528	1635	1639	1739	1832	1840	1859	1859	1859		1935	
	Saincaize ....a.																							
315	Bourges ....315 d.	0509e	0615	0713	0733	0814	0833	1013	1011		1310	1311	1605	1714	1733	1833	1917	1933	1945	1945	1945		2014	
315	Vierzon ....315 d.	0534	0634	0733	0755	0834	0855	1034	1034		1331	1336	1626	1734	1755	1855	1938	1955	2007	2006	2006		2034	
	Orléans 315 ....a.				0845		0945										1845	1946		2045a			
	St Pierre des Corps ..a.	0658	0751	0858		0955		1154	1155		1436	1438	1754	1855		2100		2108	2112	2112		2155	
	Tours ....a.	0706	0802	0905		1002		1201	1202		1443	1447	1801	1904		2107		2115	2119	2119		2202	
	Nantes 289....a.																		2320	2325			

NOTES FOR TABLES 289 AND 290

A – Dec. 19-23, Jan. 30 - Mar. 31.
B – Daily until Dec. 31; ⑤⑥⑦ from Jan. 1 (not Feb. 4, 11, 18, 25).
C – Dec. 13-29.
D – Not Ⓐ Jan. 30 - Feb. 10, Mar. 6-17.
E – Dec. 17-31.
F – From Feb. 4.
G – Dec. 11 - Jan. 29.
H – From Feb. 5.
J – ⑤⑥⑦ Dec. 11-31; ⑥⑦ Jan. 1-29.
K – From Feb. 3.
L – Dec. 12-28.
M – From Jan. 30.
N – Dec. 11 - Jan. 8, Jan. 14, 15, 21-29, Feb. 4-27, Mar. 1-5, 11, 12, 18-26, 28, 29, Apr. 1.

P – Jan. 9-20.
Q – Until Jan. 27.
R – Not Ⓐ Feb. 27 - Mar. 10.
S – Not Jan. 2-6, 9-13, Feb. 1, 2, 6-24, Mar. 3, 16, 17, 23, 28-31.
T – Not Dec. 19-30.
a – Ⓐ only.
j – Nantes d. 1610 on ⑦ Dec. 11 - Jan. 29; Nantes d. 1618 from Feb. 3.

♠ – To / from Marseille (Table 335 / 350).
♣ – From Montpellier, d. 1630 (Table 355).
Ⓞ – Via Massy.

Frequent connecting services are available St Pierre des Corps - Tours and v.v. (journey time 5 minutes).

ROANNE - ST ÉTIENNE 291

km		Ⓐ	Ⓐy	Ⓐz	Ⓐ	Ⓐy	Ⓐ		Ⓐy	w			Ⓐ	Ⓐy	Ⓑ	q	Ⓐ		v	⑦x
0	Roanne....d.	0524	0554	0624	0631	0654	0722	...	0824	0854	0954	1054	...	1219	1354	1454	...	1554	1654	1724	...	1824	1924	2024
80	St Étienne Châteaucreux ....a.	0637	0707	0737	0744	0807	0835	...	0937	1007	1107	1207	...	1332	1507	1607	...	1707	1807	1837	...	1937	2037	2137

		Ⓐy	✗		Ⓐ	x	Ⓐy	✗			t	Ⓐ		Ⓐy	✗r	q		x
	St Étienne Châteaucreux ....d.	0550	0623	...	0723	0823	0853	0953	...	1153	1223	...	1453	1553	1653	...	1719	1653	1753	...	1819	1853	1953	2053
	Roanne....a.	0703	0736	...	0836	0936	1006	1106	...	1306	1336	...	1606	1706	1806	...	1832	1806	1906	...	1932	2006	2106	2206

q – Not Dec. 25-30, Jan. 1.
r – Not Dec. 31.
t – Not Dec. 25, Jan. 1.
v – Not Dec. 26-31.
w – Not Dec. 25, 31, Jan. 1.
x – Not Dec. 25 - Jan. 1.
y – Not Dec. 26-30.
z – Not Dec. 31.

292 — NANTES - LA ROCHELLE - BORDEAUX

km			13899				3831			3835	3835						3837			
		Ⓐ	①–⑥	Ⓐ		Ⓐ		①–⑥	⑥	Ⓑ		Ⓐ	Ⓐ		m			①–④		
		t		◇		n		D					◇	v						
0	Nantes ▷ d.	...	...	...	...	...	0810	...	1210	1219	...	...	...	...	...	...	1705	...	...	...
77	La Roche sur Yon ▷ d.	...	...	...	...	...	0905	...	1304	1304	...	...	...	...	...	...	1749	...	...	...
113	Luçon d.	...	...	...	...	...	0946	...	1346	1346	...	...	...	...	...	...	1833	...	...	...
	La Rochelle Porte Dauphine d.	...	...	...	...	...		...			...	...	...	...	1802	...		...	2039	...
180	La Rochelle d.	...	0556	0633	...	0812	0945	...	1059	1151	...	1500	1500	1638	...	1743	1809	...	1950	2046
209	Rochefort d.	...	0622	0655	...	0834	1007	...	1121	1212	...	1522	1522	1700	...	1805	1839	...	2011	2117
253	Saintes d.	0610	0701	0731	...	0906	1039	...	1152	1244	...	1554	1554	1736	1744	1848	1917	...	2043	2145
376	Bordeaux St Jean a.	0741	0838	...	...	1034	...	...	1311	1410	...	1711	1711	...	1919	...	2015	...	2159	...

								3842			3854			3856			13898	3888			
		Ⓐ	⑥	Ⓐ	Ⓐ	Ⓐ	Ⓐ	⑥⑦	①–⑥	①–⑤		Ⓐ			Ⓐ		⑤⑦	①–④	⑦–④	⑤	
					◇		n		D	D		◇			m						
Bordeaux St Jean d.		...	...	...	...	...	0755	0823	1000	1255	...	1451	...	...	1655	1712	1745	1847	1851	2055	2055
Saintes d.		0532	0603	0620	0704	0742	0919	0948	1122	1422	1515	1608	1744	...	1816	1852	1922	2024	2035	2221	2222
Rochefort d.		0600	0641	0658	0740	0817	0951	1020	1154	1453	1547	1639	1819	...	1848	...	...	2056	2105	...	2257
La Rochelle d.		0632	0712	0729	0803	0843	1014	1043	1219	1516	1610	1704	1841	...	1912	...	...	2122	2125	...	2319
La Rochelle Porte Dauphine a.		0638	0718	0735	...	...															
Luçon d.		...	...	...	...	...	...	...	1329	...	...	1813	...	...	2022	...	...	...	...	...	...
La Roche sur Yon ▷ d.		...	...	...	...	...	...	...	1410	...	...	1902	...	...	2105	...	...	...	...	...	...
Nantes ▷ a.		...	...	...	...	...	...	...	1458	...	...	1947	...	...	2147	...	...	...	...	...	...

ADDITIONAL TRAINS LA ROCHELLE - ROCHEFORT

	Ⓐ	①–⑥			Ⓐ		Ⓐ	⑤⑥			Ⓐ	♻	♻		Ⓐ		Ⓐ
				D	D										D		D
La Rochelle Pte Dauphine d.	0650	0850	...	1230	1406	1605	1706	1829	2020	Rochefort d.	0755	0851	1051	...	1319	1610	1710	1749	1930
La Rochelle d.	0657	0857	...	1237	1413	1612	1713	1836	2027	La Rochelle d.	0827	0923	1121	...	1349	1640	1740	1818	2000
Rochefort d.	0727	0927	...	1306	1443	1642	1743	1906	2056	La Rochelle Pte D'phine a.	0833	0929	1127	...	1355	1646	1746	1825	2006

D – Not Feb. 13 - Mar. 10.

m – Not Feb. 18.
n – Not Feb. 19.
t – Not Dec. 23, 30, Mar. 27.
v – Not Dec. 23, 26, 30, Jan. 2, Mar. 27.

◇ – To / from Angoulême (Table **301**).
▷ – See also Table **293**.

293 — NANTES - LES SABLES D'OLONNE

km						TGV 8971												TGV 8979	TGV 8977	
		Ⓐ	Ⓐ	Ⓐ	Ⓒ			①–⑥	Ⓐ		Ⓐ	①–⑥	Ⓐ		Ⓐ	①–④⑤–⑦①–④		⑥–④	⑤	
	Paris Mont. **280** d.	...	...	...	...	0852	...	...	...	...	...	...	...	...	...	...	...	1854	1854	...
0	Nantes ▷ d.	0625	0725	0743	0825	1025	...	1125	...	1225	1425	1625	1725	...	1743	1825	1843	...	1925	1943	2025	2043	...	2133	2136	...
77	La Roche sur Yon ▷ a.	0715	0815	0836	0915	1115	...	1204	...	1315	1515	1715	1815	...	1836	1915	1936	...	2015	2036	2115	2136	...	2213	2217	...
77	La Roche sur Yon ▷ d.	0717	0817	...	0917	1117	...	1207	...	1317j	1517j	1717	1817	...	1917	...	2017	...	2117	...	2216	2220	...
114	Les Sables d'Olonne a.	0749	0849	...	0949	1149	...	1233	...	1349j	1549j	1749	1849	...	1949	...	2049	...	2149	...	2241	2245	...

		TGV 8970									TGV 8974				TGV 8976	TGV 8984	TGV 8980			TGV 8982	
		①–⑤	Ⓐ	⑥	Ⓐ	Ⓐ		Ⓐ	①–⑥	Ⓐ		①–⑥	⑥–⑥	Ⓑ	①–⑤	⑥	Ⓐ	Ⓐ	⑥	⑦	Ⓐ	
Les Sables d'Olonne d.	...	0532	...	0617	...	0717	...	0817	0917	1017	1037	1117	...	1317j	1517j	1535	1556	1624	1634	...	1717	...	1803	1817	1917
La Roche sur Yon a.	...	0555	...	0648	...	0748	...	0848	0948	1048	1102	1148	...	1348j	1548j	1600	1619	1649	1659	...	1748	...	1826	1848	1948
La Roche sur Yon ▷ d.	0526	0557	0626	0650	0650	0726	0750	0826	0850	0950	1050	1105	1150	1226	1350	1550	1603	1622	1651	1702	1726	1750	1826	1829	1850	1950
Nantes ▷ a.	0616	0640	0716	0743	0743	0816	0843	0916	0943	1043	1143	1145	1243	1316	1443	1643	1644	1704	1743	1743	1816	1843	1916	1911	1943	2043
Paris Mont. **280** a.	0910	...	...	...	...	...	...	...	...	...	1418	...	...	...	1920	1940	...	2019	...	...	2139	...	...

j – Not Ⓐ Mar. 6 - 17.

TGV – ℝ, supplement payable, ☂.
▷ – For additional trains see Table **292**.

294 — PARIS - LES AUBRAIS - ORLÉANS

km		Ⓐ	Ⓑ	Ⓐ	⑥⑦	①–⑥			⑥			Ⓐ	Ⓐ	Ⓐ	Ⓐ	Ⓐ	Ⓐ	①–⑥	⑤	Ⓑ	Ⓐ		Ⓐ	Ⓐ	Ⓐ	Ⓐ
							A	B				A	B	A												
0	Paris Austerlitz ▷ d.	0626	0738	0826	0837	0927	1055	1127	...	1238	1251	1310	1326	1405	1526	1626	1656	1726	1738	1757	...	1827	1837	1926	2027
119	Les Aubrais-Orléans ▷ a.	0725	0835	0925	0934	1025	1227	1225	...	1333	1357	1442	1425	1526	1625	1725	1755	1825	1834	1855	...	1925	1932	2025	2126
121	Orléans a.	0732	...	0932	...	1032	1234	1232	...	...	...	1432	1533	1632	1732	1802	1832	...	1902	...	1932	...	2032	2133

		①–⑥	Ⓐ	Ⓐ	Ⓐ	♻	♻	Ⓐ		Ⓐ	♻		Ⓒ	♻		Ⓒ	Ⓐ	♻	Ⓐ	⑤†		†	♻	⑤†	†
					y									z											
Orléans d.		0458	0558	0628	0658	...	0728	0828	0928	...	1132	...	...	1328	1528	...	1628	...	...	1728	...	1828	1928	2034
Les Aubrais-Orléans ▷ d.		0505	0605	0635	0705	0727	0735	0835	0935	1027	1138	...	1227	1240	1335	1535	1626	1635	...	1726	1735	1827	1835	1935	2040
Paris Austerlitz ▷ a.		0604	0704	0734	0807	0822	0834	0934	1034	1122	1237	...	1322	1350	1435	1634	1723	1734	...	1823	1834	1923	1934	2034	2140

LOCAL TRAINS

km		Ⓐ	♻	†	Ⓒ		Ⓐ				Ⓐ				Ⓐ	⑥	Ⓐ	⑦	⑥	Ⓐ	Ⓐ	Ⓐ
0	Paris Austerlitz § d.	0551	0652	1022	1223	...	1622	1722	1822	1935	Orléans d.	0624	0739	0755	1014	1235	1247	1724	1825	1938
56	Étampes § d.	0625	0726	1056	1257	...	1655	1758	1857	2011	Les Aubrais-Orléans d.	0630	0747	0801	1020	1241	1253	1730	1831	1944
88	Toury d.	0653	0754	1124	1325	...	1718	1825	1926	2035	Toury d.	0702	0817	0829	1048	1310	1310	1758	1859	2017
119	Les Aubrais-Orléans a.	0721	0822	1154	1354	...	1748	1850	1954	2058	Étampes d.	0731	0844	0850	1117	1336	1336	1831	1931	2045
121	Orléans a.	0727	0832	1200	1400	...	1754	1856	2000	2104	Paris Austerlitz § a.	0804	0915	0920	1149	1407	1407	1903	2003	2117

A – Dec. 12, 13, Feb. 6 - 9, Mar. 6 - 9.
B – Not Dec. 12, 13, Feb. 6 - 9, Mar. 6 - 9.
C – ①–⑥ (not Dec. 12, 13, 19 - 30, Feb. 6 - 9, Mar. 6 - 9).

y – Not Dec. 23, 30, Mar. 27.
z – Not Jan. 30 - Mar. 3.

◇ – For days of running see Table **315**.
▷ – For *Intercités* trains (ℝ) Paris - Les Aubrais-Orléans and v.v. see Table **310**; for other trains see Table **296** and **315**.
§ – Suburban trains run Paris Austerlitz - Étampes and v.v. approx every 30 mins (journey 55 min).

PARIS - TOURS 295

Direct *TGV* trains only via high-speed line – for additional *TGV* services requiring a change at St Pierre des Corps see Table 300. For other trains see Table 296. For Lille - Tours see Table 297

Trains may be retimed a few minutes owing to engineering work

km	*TGV* trains convey 🍸	*TGV* 8301 ①–⑥		*TGV* 8303		*TGV* 8321 ⑤		*TGV* 8323 Ⓐ		*TGV* 8325 Ⓐ		*TGV* 8327 Ⓒ	*TGV* 8327 Ⓐ		*TGV* 8331 Ⓐ		*TGV* 8333 ①–⑥		*TGV* 8335 ⑦		*TGV* 8337 ⑤			
0	**Paris** Montparnasse d.	0716	...	1216	...	1516	...	1616	...	1732	...	1816	1819	...	1837	...	1916	...	2016	...	2116	...	...	...
14	Massy-TGV d.	|	...	|	...	|	...	|	...	1744	...	|	|	...	|	...	|	...	|	...	|	...	...	...
162	Vendôme-Villiers TGV d.	0802	...	1302	...	1602	...	1702	...	1823	...	1902	|	...	1925	...	2002	...	2102	...	2202	...	...	...
221	St Pierre des Corps a.	0822	...	1322	...	1620	...	1722	...	1845	...	1921	1921	...	1944	...	2020	...	2122	...	2222	...	...	...
221	St Pierre des Corps d.	0825	...	1325	...	1623	...	1725	...	1852	...	1924	1924	...	1951	...	2023	...	2125	...	2225	...	...	...
224	**Tours** a.	0830	...	1330	...	1628	...	1730	...	1857	...	1929	1929	...	1956	...	2028	...	2130	...	2230	...	...	...

	TGV 8300 Ⓐ		*TGV* 8302 ①–④	*TGV* 8302 ⑤⑥		*TGV* 8306 Ⓐ		*TGV* 8308 ①–⑥		*TGV* 8310 Ⓒ	*TGV* 8310 Ⓐ		*TGV* 8320 ⑤⑦		*TGV* 8322		*TGV* 8324 Ⓐ		*TGV* 8326 ⑤⑦		*TGV* 8328 ⑤		*TGV* 8330 ⑦
Tours d.	0611	...	0649	0649	...	0735	...	0800	...	1131	1201	...	1631	...	1731	...	1831	...	1931	...	2031	...	2130
St Pierre des Corps a.	0616	...	0654	0654	...	0740	...	0805	...	1136	1206	...	1636	...	1736	...	1836	...	1936	...	2036	...	2135
St Pierre des Corps d.	0619	...	0657	0657	...	0743	...	0817	...	1139	1209	...	1639	...	1739	...	1839	...	1939	...	2039	...	2139
Vendôme-Villiers TGV d.	0641	...	0719	0719	...	|	...	0839	...	1201	1231	...	1701	...	1801	...	1901	...	2001	...	2101	...	2202
Massy-TGV a.	|	...	|	0755	...	|	...	|	...	|	|	...	|	...	|	...	|	...	|	...	|	...	|
Paris Montparnasse a.	0725	...	0804	0808	...	0841	...	0923	...	1245	1315	...	1745	...	1845	...	1945	...	2045	...	2145	...	2245

TGV –Ⓡ, supplement payable, 🍸.

Frequent connecting services are available St Pierre des Corps - Tours and v.v. (journey time 5 minutes).

ORLÉANS - BLOIS - TOURS 296

For fast *TGV* services Paris - Tours and v.v. see Table 295. Certain trains continue to / from Le Croisic (Table 288)

km		Ⓐ	Ⓒ		Ⓐ	Ⓐ	⚒		Ⓐ	Ⓑ			Ⓒ	Ⓒ		Ⓐ	Ⓐ		⑥	⚒		⑥	Ⓐ a	†
	Paris Austerlitz **294** d.	...	...	...	...	...	...	...	...	0738	...	...	0837	...	...	...	...	...	...	...	...	1238	1251	...
0	**Orléans** d.	...	0657	...	0706	0710	0742	...	0800	|	0842	...	|	1042	...	1127	1135	...	1222	...	...	|	|	1439
2	Les Aubrais-Orléans d.	...	|	...	|	|	|	...	|	0838	|	...	0937	|	...	|	|	...	|	...	...	1336	1400	|
30	Beaugency d.	...	0713	...	0721	0732	0800	...	0829	|	0900	...	|	1100	...	1142	1154	...	1252	...	...	|	|	1459
61	Blois d.	0636	0729	...	0738	0752	0819	...	0856	0904	0918	...	1002	1119	...	1204	1214	...	1314	1332	...	1403	1427	1519
93	Amboise d.	0658	0745	...	0753	0813	0837	...	...	0922	0936	...	1019	1137	...	1224	1235	...	...	1356	...	1419	1443	1538
115	St Pierre des Corps a.	0714	0759	...	0804	0827	0850	...	...	0935	0948	...	1031	1148	...	1238	1248	...	...	1415	...	1431	1454	1550
118	**Tours** a.	0721	|	...	|	0834	0857	...	...	0942	0955	...	1038	1156	...	|	1255	...	...	1422	...	1438	1503	1557
	Nantes **289** a.	...	0946	...	0943	...	...	...	...	...	...	...	...	...	...	1423	...	...	...	...	...	...	...	...

	⚒	Ⓐ b		Ⓐ			⚒	Ⓐ	†	Ⓐ		†	Ⓑ	⚒				Ⓐ c	Ⓐ				Ⓑ	
Paris Austerlitz **294** d.	...	1310	...	...	...	...	...	...	...	...	...	...	...	...	1738	...	...	...	1837	...	...	...	...	...
Orléans ▷ d.	1442	|	...	1542	1642	...	1702	1709	1736	1742	...	1805	...	1809	|	...	1844	1909	|	...	1942	2042	2142	...
Les Aubrais-Orléans ▷ d.	|	1451	...	|	|	...	|	|	|	|	...	|	...	|	1837	...	|	|	1935	...	|	|	|	...
Beaugency d.	1500	|	...	1600	1700	...	1718	1739	1804	1801	...	1820	...	1839	|	...	1902	1939	|	...	2000	2100	2200	...
Blois d.	1519	1524	...	1619	1719	...	1734	1757	1823	1821	...	1837	1844	1857	1903	...	1921	1957	2002	...	2019	2119	2219	...
Amboise d.	1537	1542	...	1637	1738	...	1750	...	...	1839	...	1852	1909	...	1918	...	1940	...	2019	...	2037	2137	2239	...
St Pierre des Corps a.	1550	1555	...	1650	1750	...	1804	...	...	1851	...	1903	1926	...	1933	...	1954	...	2031	...	2050	2150	2250	...
Tours a.	1557	1602	...	1657	1757	...	|	...	...	1900	...	|	1933	...	1938	...	2001	...	2038	...	2057	2157	2257	...
Nantes **289** a.	...	...	...	...	...	...	1947	...	...	...	...	2046	...	...	...	...	...	...	...	...	...	...	...	...

	Ⓐ	Ⓐ	⚒	⚒	Ⓐ	Ⓐ	Ⓐ		⚒	Ⓐ	Ⓒ	Ⓐ		Ⓒ	Ⓒ	Ⓐ	Ⓒ k	Ⓒ	Ⓐ	⑥	⑥		Ⓐ	Ⓐ
Nantes **289** d.	...	...	...	...	...	...	...	...	...	...	...	0701	...	...	...	...	0909	...	...	...	...	...	1110	...
Tours d.	0503	...	0603	0620	...	0629	0701	...	...	0750	0803	|	...	0922	1003	1003	|	1120	1119	1203	...	...	|	1239
St Pierre des Corps d.	0510	...	0610	0628	...	0636	0708	...	...	0757	0810	0857	...	0928	1010	1010	1056	1127	1126	1210	...	...	1258	1246
Amboise d.	0521	...	0621	0641	...	0650	0722	...	...	0808	0822	0908	...	0940	1022	1022	1109	1138	1140	1221	...	...	1309	1257
Blois d.	0542	0603	0642	0658	0703	0715	0741	...	0803	0828	0842	0926	...	0958	1042	1044	1126	1157	1213	1242	1255	...	1328	1336
Beaugency d.	0600	0621	0700	|	0722	...	0800	...	0822	0847	0900	0945	...	|	1100	1105	1142	|	|	1300	1322	...	1346	1358
Les Aubrais-Orléans a.	|	|	|	0724	|	...	|	...	|	|	|	|	...	1024	|	|	|	1224	1237	|	|	...	|	|
Orléans a.	0618	0651	0718	|	0751	...	0818	...	0851	0905	0919	1005	...	|	1118	1124	1157	|	|	1318	1351	...	1411	1420
Paris Austerlitz **294** a.	...	...	...	0822	...	...	...	...	...	...	...	...	...	1122	...	...	...	1322	1350	...	...	...	...	...

		⑤†	Ⓐ	⚒		†	Ⓐ	Ⓐ c	Ⓑ			⚒ c	⚒			Ⓐ		Ⓐ	Ⓑ		⑥	⑦ m	Ⓐ	
Nantes **289** d.	...	...	...	...	...	...	...	...	...	...	...	...	...	...	...	...	...	1800	...	...	2010	2015	...	...
Tours d.	1403	1503	1520	1603	...	1619	...	1627	1703	...	1719	...	1727	1803	...	1827	1910	|	2103	...	|	|	2213	...
St Pierre des Corps d.	1410	1510	1527	1610	...	1626	...	1635	1710	...	1728	...	1734	1810	...	1834	1917	1957	2110	...	2156	2158	2220	...
Amboise d.	1421	1521	1538	1621	...	1638	...	1652	1722	...	1741	...	1752	1821	...	1851	1929	2009	2121	...	2208	2209	2231	...
Blois d.	1441	1541	1557	1641	...	1657	1703	1715	1741	...	1758	1803	1813	1841	...	1914	1949	2027	2141	...	2225	2227	2251	...
Beaugency d.	1459	1559	|	1659	...	|	1730	...	1759	...	|	1830	...	1859	...	...	2007	2042	2159	...	2242	2242	2309	...
Les Aubrais-Orléans a.	|	|	1623	|	...	1723	|	...	|	...	1824	|	...	|	...	...	|	|	|	...	|	|	|	...
Orléans a.	1518	1618	|	1718	...	|	1759	...	1818	...	|	1858	...	1918	...	...	2025	2057	2218	...	2257	2258	2328	...
Paris Austerlitz **294** a.	...	...	1723j	...	...	1823	...	...	...	...	1923	...	...	...	...	...	...	...	...	...	...	...	...	...

a – Not Dec. 12, 13, Feb. 6 - 9, Mar. 6 - 9.
b – Dec. 12, 13, Feb. 6 - 9, Mar. 6 - 9.
c – Not Dec. 26 - 30.
j – Arrive 1731 Jan. 30 - Feb. 3.
k – Not Feb. 4 - 25.
m – Not Feb. 5 - 19.

Frequent connecting services are available St Pierre des Corps - Tours and v.v. (journey time 5 minutes).

LILLE - CHARLES DE GAULLE ✈ - TOURS 297

Trains continue to / from Bordeaux (Table **300**). Connections St Pierre des Corps - Tours are by local train.

TGV trains convey 🍸	*TGV* 5200		*TGV* 5202			*TGV* 5222		*TGV* 5240		
Lille Europe **11** d.	0708	...	0918	...	...	1445f	...	1709f	...	...
Charles de Gaulle ✈ d.	0819	...	1016	...	...	1621	...	1809	...	...
Marne la Vallée - Chessy d.	0833	...	1033	...	...	1634	...	1833	...	...
Massy-TGV d.	0908	...	1108	...	...	1708	...	1908	...	...
St Pierre des Corps a.	1001	...	1159	...	...	1758	...	1959	...	...
St Pierre des Corps d.	...	1004	...	1207	...	...	1819	...	2005	...
Tours a.	...	1009	...	1212	...	...	1824	...	2010	...

		TGV 5260		*TGV* 5264 Ⓐ	*TGV* 5264 Ⓒ		*TGV* 5266		*TGV* 5284 Ⓒ	*TGV* 5284 Ⓐ
Tours d.	0950	...	1147	...	...	1739	...	1947	...	...
St Pierre des Corps a.	0955	...	1152	...	...	1744	...	1952	...	...
St Pierre des Corps d.	...	1000	...	1200	1200	...	1802	...	2000	2002
Massy-TGV d.	...	1055	...	1255	1255	...	1855	...	2055	2055
Marne la Vallée - Chessy a.	...	1127	...	|	1327	...	1927	...	2127	2127
Charles de Gaulle ✈ a.	...	1145	...	1331	1341	...	1941	...	2141	2141
Lille Europe **11** a.	...	1301f	...	1430	1437	...	2111f	...	2244	2245

f – Lille **Flandres**.

Frequent connecting services are available St Pierre des Corps - Tours and v.v. (journey time 5 minutes).

ANGERS - CHOLET
Journey 45 - 50 minutes   60 km

Angers depart: 0645Ⓐ, 0721Ⓐ, 0745✗, 0938✗q, 1155✗q, 1202⑦, 1250Ⓐ, 1303⑥, 1548, 1638⑥, 1721Ⓐ, 1741Ⓐ, 1843Ⓐ, 1845⑥, 1938⑥, 2043⑦, 2047✗, 2147✗, 2248⑤⑦, 2308①–Ⓐ.
Cholet depart: 0615Ⓐ, 0638✗, 0656Ⓐ, 0717⑥, 0738Ⓐ, 0832⑦, 0843✗q, 0945Ⓐ q, 1103⑥, 1243⑥, 1245Ⓐ q, 1352, 1646⑥, 1733Ⓐ, 1737Ⓐ, 1838Ⓐ, 1843⑦, 1939⑥, 1953Ⓐ, 2146⑦.

BAYONNE - ST JEAN PIED DE PORT
50 km

		p		✗p				✗		⑤†
Bayonne .... d.	0745	...	1110	...	1455	...	1806	...	2110
Cambo les Bains .... a.	0807	...	1132	...	1518	...	1833	...	2132
St Jean Pied de Port .... a.	0843	...	1208	...	1554	...	1912	...	2208

	✗		p		p				†
St Jean Pied de Port .... d.	0610	...	0920	...	1341	...	1651	...	1917
Cambo les Bains .... d.	0649	...	0956	...	1417	...	1727	...	1953
Bayonne .... a.	0715	...	1017	...	1438	...	1748	...	2014

BORDEAUX - MONT DE MARSAN
147 km

	✗	Ⓐ		F		G			Ⓑ
Bordeaux.. **305** d.	0623	0858	1058	...	1258	1558	1730	...	2158
Morcenx .....**305** d.	0655	0736	1003	1203	...	1403	1703	1834	...	1959	2303
Mont de Marsan.a.	0724	0759	1026	1227	...	1427	1726	1859	...	2028	2327

	✗	✗			G	F		Ⓐ	†	Ⓐ
Mont de Marsan. d.	0533	0602	0733	1033	1233	1433	1633	1801	1832	1933	2033
Morcenx .....**305** d.	0558	0631	0759	1058	1258	1458	1658	1831	1902	1957	2105
Bordeaux...**305** a.	0702	...	0902	1202	1402	1602	1802	...	2005	2102	...

CARCASSONNE - LIMOUX - QUILLAN

	🚌		🚌	🚌			🚌	🚌	🚌	🚌
		✗	†	J	H			H	J	⑤
0	Carcassonne .... d.	0709	0940	1225	1236	...	1337	1847	1908	1916	2008
26	Limoux .... a.	0738	1018	1302	1308	...	1410	1925	1940	1953	2041
54	Quillan .... a.	0818	1058	1346	1346	...	1450	2005	2016	2037	2121

	🚌				🚌			🚌	🚌	🚌
	J	K	†	†		H	⑤	†	†	⑤
Quillan .... d.	0545	0603	0804	1103	...	1358	1400	1615	1624	1817	2005
Limoux .... d.	0627	0638	0844	1145	...	1432	1442		1708	1900	2045
Carcassonne .....a.	0707	0712	0917	1223	...	1507	1522	1705	1745	1937	2117

CHARLEVILLE MÉZIÈRES - GIVET
Journey 60 - 80 minutes   64 km

Charleville Mézières depart: 0557✗, 0643✗, 0751Ⓐ, 0851⑥, 0954✗n, 1051†, 1246✗n, 1346 n, 1500Ⓑ n, 1635, 1737✗, 1821Ⓐ, 1855Ⓐ, 1939, 2025Ⓐ, 2055.
Givet depart: 0445Ⓐ, 0531Ⓐ, 0546✗, 0614Ⓐ, 0639, 0717✗, 0922Ⓐ, 1046 n, 1219✗n, 1409✗n, 1436Ⓑ n, 1539Ⓑ n, 1651, 1758Ⓐ, 1913.

DINARD - ST MALO
Subject to alteration

🚌 : 7 - 10 times per day (fewer on †), journey 24 minutes. Operator: TIV. 11 km
⛴ : *Le Bus de Mer* passenger ferry operates 12 - 17 times daily from April to September. Journey time 10 minutes. Operator: Compagnie Corsaire.

LILLE - LENS
Journey 40 - 47 minutes   39 km

Lille Flandres depart: 0615Ⓐ, 0626Ⓐ, 0642Ⓐ, 0645⑥, 0715Ⓐ, 0719Ⓐ x, 0726Ⓐ, 0742⑥, 0819Ⓐ, 0826Ⓐ x, 0919✗, 1019 x, 1026†, 1118Ⓒ, 1126Ⓐ x, 1219✗, 1226, 1242Ⓐ x, 1318, 1326, 1518⑥, 1519†, 1542Ⓐ, 1619, 1626Ⓐ x, 1642Ⓐ, 1655Ⓐ x, 1715Ⓐ, 1719, 1726✗, 1742Ⓐ, 1815, 1819, 1826Ⓐ x, 1842Ⓐ, 1915 x, 1919, 1926✗x, 2018Ⓒ z, 2119Ⓐ.
Lens depart: 0454✗, 0544Ⓐ, 0554✗, 0639Ⓐ, 0644✗, 0655✗x, 0709Ⓐ, 0736Ⓐ x, 0740✗, 0744Ⓐ, 0754✗, 0810Ⓐ x, 0836Ⓐ x, 0838†, 0839⑥, 0854Ⓐ, 0944Ⓐ x, 0954Ⓒ, 1044†, 1054Ⓒ, 1110Ⓐ, 1134Ⓐ, 1154⑥, 1210Ⓐ x, 1244Ⓑ x, 1254, 1344✗x, 1354Ⓒ, 1444Ⓐ, 1454Ⓒ, 1546Ⓐ, 1554⑥, 1639Ⓐ, 1644Ⓐ, 1654Ⓒ, 1709Ⓐ, 1736Ⓐ, 1744Ⓐ, 1754, 1844, 1854, 1944Ⓐ x, 1954Ⓒ, 2010Ⓐ.

NANTES - CHOLET
Journey 45 - 68 minutes   65 km

Nantes depart: 0635Ⓐ🚌, 0816Ⓐ, 0835Ⓐ🚌, 0925Ⓒ🚌, 1030⑥🚌, 1216⑥, 1316⑥, 1355⑤†y🚌, 1405⑥🚌, 1425⑤🚌, 1620Ⓐ🚌, 1716Ⓐ, 1730🚌, 1815Ⓐ🚌, 1816†, 1916✗, 1945†🚌.
Cholet depart: 0633Ⓐ, 0645Ⓐ🚌, 0730⑥🚌, 0733Ⓐ, 0833⑥, 1025🚌, 1233†, 1245⑤🚌, 1545⑤🚌, 1558⑤†y🚌, 1633Ⓐ, 1745Ⓐ🚌, 1800†🚌, 1833Ⓐ, 1933†, 2030🚌.

NANTES - PORNIC

km			†	†		⑥	Ⓐ	⑥	Ⓐ		Ⓐ		Ⓐ
0	Nantes .... d.	1000	1125	...	1228	1628	1719	1740	...	1826	...	1942
	Ste Pazanne ... a.	1028	1154	...	1256	1658	1748	1812	...	1857	...	2011
60	Pornic .... a.	1057	1223	...	1325	1731	1821	1843	...	1926	...	2040

	Ⓐ	†	Ⓐ	†	Ⓐ		Ⓐ	Ⓐ	†	Ⓐ	Ⓐ	Ⓐ
Pornic.............. d.	0617	0708	0846	1016	1121	...	1413	1422	1446	1745	1746	1846
Ste Pazanne... d.	0647	0738	0915	1046	1150	...	1452	1451	1515	1814	1814	1915
Nantes.......... a.	0720	0808	0945	1117	1220	...	1522	1521	1545	1845	1845	1945

NANTES - ST GILLES CROIX DE VIE

km			Ⓐ	⑥	†		Ⓐ	†	⑥	Ⓐ		Ⓐ	Ⓐ	†
0	Nantes.......... d.	0702	1016	1019	...	1230	1233	1244	1421	...	1720	1806	1826
	Ste Pazanne .. d.	0732	1044	1048	...	1259	1302	1312	1450	...	1750	1837	1856
87	St Gilles Croix . a.	0814	1128	1130	...	1344	1342	1353	1532	...	1831	1918	1940

	Ⓐ	†	Ⓐ					①	①	Ⓐ	⑥
Nantes.................. d.	1923	2030	2034	...	St Gilles Croix... d.	0511	0535	0629	0725
Ste Pazanne...... d.	1952	2058	2102	...	Ste Pazanne....... d.	0551	0614	0709	0814
St Gilles Croix........ a.	2033	2140	2142	...	Nantes.................. a.	0615	0645	0743	0845

	Ⓐ	⑥	Ⓐ	Ⓐ	Ⓐ		Ⓐ	Ⓐ	Ⓐ	Ⓐ	Ⓐ	Ⓐ	Ⓐ	Ⓐ
St Gilles Croix d.	0739	0836	0940	1011	1220	1234	1536	1557	1644	1705	1710	1811	1843
Ste Pazanne.. d.	0818	0915	1016	1050	1301	1314	1615	1635	1727	1745	1751	1900	1927
Nantes............ a.	0848	0945	1050	1115	1332	1345	1645	1707	1759	1815	1822	1930	2001

Services call at Challans approx 1 hour after leaving Nantes.

PARIS - CHÂTEAUDUN - VENDÔME - TOURS

		Ⓐ	Ⓐ	h		Ⓐ	✗m	h	†	Ⓐ	g	†
0	Paris Austerlitz.. d.	...	0810	1010	...	1357	1610	...	1810	1910	2110
134	Châteaudun.. d.	...	0643	0717	0946	1149	1426	1523	1750	1800	1947	2053	2234
178	Vendôme ...... d.	0624	0724	0757	...	1248	1602	...	1843	...	2131	...
248	Tours........... a.	0724	0824	0857	...	1348	...	1943	...	...	...

	Ⓐ	✗g	†w	h	✗v	Ⓐ	h	⑤†	Ⓐ	†	Ⓐ	†
Tours............ d.	...	0906	...	1242	...	...	1536	...	1736	...	1836	2036
Vendôme ...... d.	0533	...	1006	...	1345	...	1622	1705	...	1838	1915	1939	2141
Châteaudun .. d.	0613	0715	1046	1211	1421	1604	1702	1743	1802	1917†	1957	2017	...
Paris Austerlitz. a.	0750	0850	...	1335	...	1745	1838	...	1931	...	2131	...

PARIS - DISNEYLAND (Marne la Vallée - Chessy)
32 km

Trains run approximately every 15 minutes 0500 - 2400 on RER Line A :
Paris Châtelet les Halles - Paris Gare de Lyon - Marne la Vallée Chessy (for Disneyland).
Operator: RATP. For *TGV* services serving Marne la Vallée see Tables **11** and **391**.
Journey 39 minutes.

ROYAN - POINTE DE GRAVE ⛴
Subject to alteration

Oct. - Feb. ⛴:
From Royan: 0745Ⓐ, 0830Ⓒ, 1000Ⓐ, 1015Ⓒ, 1200, 1500, 1715, 1915.
From Pointe de Grave: 0715Ⓐ, 0800Ⓒ, 0930Ⓐ, 0945Ⓒ, 1130, 1430, 1645, 1845.
Apr. - June and **Sept.**:
From Royan: 0750, 0930, 1100, 1230, 1400, 1545, 1715, 1900, 2030.
From Pointe de Grave (Le Verdon): 0715, 0855, 1025, 1155, 1325, 1510, 1640, 1825, 1955.
July - Aug.: approx every 40 - 50 minutes 0715 - 2115 (0630 - 2030 from Pointe de Grave).

⛴ – Oct. 16 - Nov. 1 the 1715 sailing from Royan is replaced by sailings at 1615 and 1745; the 1645 sailing from Pointe de Grave is replaced by sailings at 1545 and 1715:
Sailing time approx 20 minutes. ✆ 05 56 73 37 73. www.transgironde.fr

ST BRIEUC - DINAN

km		Ⓐ	⑥		†	✗		✗	†		Ⓐ
0	St Brieuc ..**284** d.	0651	0717	...	1248	1318	...	1718	1732	...	1908
21	Lamballe ..**284** d.	0714	0735	...	1305	1334	...	1734	1748	...	1924
62	Dinan........... a.	0804	0823	...	1354	1354	...	1823	1837	...	2012

	Ⓐ	Ⓐ	Ⓐ	Ⓒ	Ⓐ		Ⓐ	Ⓐ	⑥	†
Dinan.............. d.	0620	0643	...	1059	1134	...	1556	...	1830	1837	1903
Lamballe ..**284** d.	0710	0731	...	1144	1221	...	1646	...	1920	1927	1953
St Brieuc ..**284** a.	0726	0747	...	1159	1240	...	1701	...	1936	1943	2009

SOUILLAC - SARLAT 🚌
Subject to alteration   30 km

Souillac (rail station) depart: 0645Ⓐ, 0910⑥, 1500, 1836†, 2235⑤.
Sarlat depart: 1142, 1310③, 1638①②④⑤, 1712③⑥, 1720†, 1815①②④⑤.
Service by 🚌 (Trans Périgord Ligne 06). Journey 41 minutes.
Subject to alteration during school holidays.

TOULOUSE - AUCH
88 km

Toulouse Matabiau depart: 0624Ⓐ, 0724, 1224 p, 1424Ⓐ p, 1430Ⓒ, 1624Ⓐ, 1724, 1824, 2024.
Auch depart: 0606Ⓐ, 0706, 0806Ⓐ, 0906 p, 1106 p, 1406 p, 1706, 1806, 1906.
Journey 90 minutes.

TOURS - CHINON
49 km

Tours depart: 0743Ⓐ t, 0915 E, 1236 E, 1515 t, 1642Ⓐ, 1732Ⓐ, 1851 k, 2014Ⓑ.
Chinon depart: 0625✗ t, 0652✗t, 0749Ⓐ, 0839Ⓐ t, 1138 E, 1355 D, 1739✗, 1829Ⓑ, 2019†.
Journey 45 - 50 minutes.

VALENCIENNES - CAMBRAI
40 km

Valenciennes depart: 0604Ⓐ, 0626⑥, 0630Ⓐ x, 0733Ⓐ x, 0803⑥, 1006Ⓐ j, 1206Ⓐ j, 1230⑥, 1300⑥, 1306Ⓐ j, 1703Ⓐ x, 1730Ⓒ x, 1730Ⓒ, 1804Ⓐ, 2025†.
Cambrai depart: 0612Ⓐ, 0642⑥, 0650Ⓐ x, 0712Ⓐ, 0749⑥, 0750Ⓐ x, 0950⑥, 1112Ⓐ j, 1212Ⓐ j, 1215⑥, 1312Ⓐ j, 1351⑥, 1712Ⓐ x, 1745†, 1751Ⓒ, 1812Ⓐ, 1912Ⓐ x, 1922†.
Journey 40 - 50 minutes.

D – Daily Dec. 11 - Jan. 29; Ⓒ Feb. 4 - 26; daily Feb. 27 - Apr. 1.
E – ✗ Dec. 12 - Jan. 28; ⑥ Feb. 4 - 25; ✗ Feb. 27 - Apr. 1.
F – Daily Dec. 11 - Jan. 8; ⑥⑦ Jan. 14 - Feb. 5; daily Feb. 6 - Apr. 1.
G – ✗ Dec. 12 - Jan. 7; ⑥ Jan. 14 - Feb. 4; ✗ Feb. 6 - Apr. 1.
H – ✗ Dec. 12 - 31, Mar. 11 - Apr. 1.
J – ✗ Jan. 2 - Mar. 10.
K – ✗ Dec. 12 - 31, Mar. 13 - Apr. 1.

f – ⑤ only.
g – Not Jan. 28, Feb. 4, Mar. 25.
h – Not Jan. 28, 29, Feb. 4, Mar. 25, 26.
j – Not Dec. 26 - 30, Feb. 13 - 17, 20 - 24.
k – Not Mar. 26.
m – Not Jan. 23 - 27, Feb. 6, 20, 21.
n – Not Feb. 13 - 17, 20 - 24.
p – Not Mar. 6 - 10, 13 - 17.

q – Not Feb. 6 - 10, Mar. 13 - 17, 20 - 24.
t – Not Dec. 19 - 30.
v – Not Jan. 23 - 27, Feb. 10, 20, 21.
w – Not Dec. 11.
x – Not Dec. 26 - 30.
y – Not Dec. 25, Jan. 1.
z – Not Dec. 24, 31.

PARIS - POITIERS - LA ROCHELLE and BORDEAUX — 300

La Rochelle services subject to retiming on April 1

Certain *TGV* services continue to Toulouse (Table 320), Hendaye, Irún or Tarbes (Table 305) or Arcachon (Table 306).
Trains may be retimed a few minutes owing to engineering work

km	TGV trains convey ⓨ	TGV 8401	TGV 8501	TGV 8403	8371	8531	TGV 8341 8573	8461 8471	TGV 8407	5200	TGV 8503	TGV 8373	TGV 8473 8533	8411	TGV 5202	5450	5202	5450
		①–⑤	①–⑤	①–⑥	①–⑥	①–⑥	①–⑥	①–⑤		①–⑥	⑦		⑥⑦		①–⑤	①–⑤	⑥⑦	⑥⑦
	Lille Europe 11 ...d.									0708					0918		0918	
	Strasbourg 391 ...d.															0832		0832
	Charles de Gaulle ✈ ...d.									0819					1016		1016	
	Marne la Vallee-Chessy .d.									0833					1033	1033	1033	1033
0	Paris Montparnasse 295...d.		0604	0628		0641	0712	0728	0746		0828	0846	0928	1012	1028		1046	
14	Massy TGV 295 ...d.					0653				0908					1108	1108	1108	1108
162	Vendôme-Villiers TGV ...d.																	
221	St Pierre des Corps 295 ...a.					0745			0843	0945	1001				1145	1159	1159	1159 1159
	Tours ...d.		0615															
221	St Pierre des Corps 295 ...d.					0749			0847	0949	1005				1149	1203	1203	1203 1203
289	Châtellerault ...d.			0709			0756	0819		0916								
311	Futuroscope ⊖ ...d.			0722			0817			0928						1241	1241	
321	**Poitiers** ...a.			0729	0740		0825	0834	0852	0941	1031	1042		1152	1231	1242	1242	
321	**Poitiers** ...▷d.	0603	0656	0743	0755		0837	0855	0954		1034	1045	1048	1155	1234	1245	1245	
401	Niort ...d.	0709	0759		0849			0955	1049		1146	1250						
468	**La Rochelle** ...a.	0754	0848		0938			1047	1135		1235	1335						
434	Angoulême ...▷d.			0837			0926				1128	1138		1328	1338	1338	1338	1338
533	Libourne 302 ...▷d.						1008				1208			1410				
570	**Bordeaux** St Jean 302 ...▷a.			0933	0939		1029	1039		1141	1228	1234	1240	1339	1429	1434	1434	1435 1435

	TGV 8507	8375	8505 8537	8413	8381	8415	8417	8591	8433	8383	8511	8435	8385	8437	5222
	⑤	①–⑥	⑥	⑤ z	⑦ y	①–④⑤–⑦		①–⑤⑦–④		⑥⑦ ①–⑤ m	①–⑤		①–⑤ ⑦ h	①–⑤	
Lille Europe 11 ...d.															1445f
Strasbourg 391 ...d.															1621
Charles de Gaulle ✈ ...d.															1633
Marne la Vallee-Chessy ..d.															
Paris Montparnasse 295 ...d.	1128		1212	1228		1246	1312	1404	1404	1428	1446	1512	1528	1604 1612	1646
Massy TGV 295 ...d.															1708
Vendôme-Villiers TGV ...d.															
St Pierre des Corps 295 ...a.						1345	1507			1545				1723	1745 1758
Tours ...d.		1228				1349	1511			1549		1628			1749 1802
Châtellerault ...d.		1311		1353						1620	1653	1716		1809	
Futuroscope ⊖ ...d.		1332		1407							1715	1728		1821	
Poitiers ...a.		1340	1352	1414	1431	1452		1540		1652	1724	1736	1740	1752 1829	1831 1842
Poitiers ...▷d.	1254		1355		1434	1455		1543	1622	1655	1730		1743	1755 1826	1835 1845
Niort ...d.	1354		1446			1549			1721	1746	1835		1851	1931	
La Rochelle ...a.	1442		1529			1629			1811	1830	1925		1935	2018	
Angoulême ...▷d.				1528		1640	1637		1728			1837		1929	1938
Libourne 302 ...▷d.				1610					1810					2010	
Bordeaux St Jean 302 ...▷a.	1439		1541	1631		1733	1733	1739	1829		1839	1936		2032	2036

	TGV 8387	8593	8351	8441 8479	8391	8513	8445	8445	5240	5454	8393	8395	8449 8515	8481	8453	8397	8455	8353	8457	8355
	⑦–④		①–⑤	①–⑤		①–⑤	①–⑤	⑥⑦	⑤⑦	①–⑤	⑦	①–⑤	①–④		⑤	⑦–④	⑤	⑤⑦	①–⑤⑦	x
Lille Europe 11 ...d.								1709f												
Strasbourg 391 ...d.									1631											
Charles de Gaulle ✈ ...d.								1809												
Marne la Vallee-Chessy ..d.								1833	1833											
Paris Montparnasse 295 ...d.	1712	1728		1732	1804	1812	1828			1837	1846	1912	1912	1928	1946	2004	2012	2028 2036	2046	2201
Massy TGV 295 ...d.			1744					1908	1908										2122	
Vendôme-Villiers TGV ...d.				1823		1858				1925										
St Pierre des Corps 295 ...a.			1845					1944	1945	1959	1959			2045				2140 2145		2300
Tours ...d.			1828											2028						
St Pierre des Corps 295 ...d.			1849					1948	1949	2003	2003			2049				2143 2149		2304
Châtellerault ...d.			1912	1919				1953	2021	2021			2120	2116				2221		
Futuroscope ⊖ ...d.			1924		1941				2014					2128						
Poitiers ...a.	1852		1932	1942		1952		2023		2041	2041	2052	2052		2134	2135	2140	2152	2229	2346
Poitiers ...▷d.	1855		1935			1955			2044	2044	2055	2055		2137		2143	2155	2155	2207	
Niort ...d.	1946					2054				2146	2152			2253		2251	2306			
La Rochelle ...a.	2030					2138				2230	2237			2340		2336	2350			
Angoulême ...▷d.				2037				2128	2128	2138	2138				2225		2237		2328	
Libourne 302 ...▷d.								2210	2210										0010	
Bordeaux St Jean 302 ...▷a.		2040			2136		2140	2229	2229	2234	2234			2239		2333		2339		0029

LOCAL TRAINS ANGOULÊME - BORDEAUX and v.v.

	Ⓐ	✕	†	✕	†	✕	Ⓐ				Ⓐ	Ⓐ	†	†	✕	Ⓐ	Ⓒ
Angoulême ...d.	0605	...	0709	1009	...	...	1809	2005	2008	**Bordeaux** St Jean 302 d.	0628	0640	0828	0930	1140	1337	1440 1728 1840 2040
Coutras 302 d.	0656	0736	0757	1057	...	1237	1435	1856	2055 2055	Libourne 302 d.	0651	0713	0850	1003	1214	1417	1514 1750 1914 2114
Libourne 302 d.	0709	0750	0809	1109	...	1249	1447	1908	2107 2106	Coutras 302 d.	0704	0726	0903	1016	1227	1429	1527 1803 1927 2127
Bordeaux St Jean 302 a.	0735	0823	0832	1132	...	1323	1521	1932	2132 2128	Angoulême ...a.	0755	...	0953	...	1517	...	1854 ...

f – Lille **Flandres**.
h – Also Feb. 10, 17; not Dec. 25.
m – Also Dec. 23, Feb. 10, 17.
x – Not Jan. 8, 15, 22, Feb. 3, 5, 12, 19.
y – Not Feb. 5.
z – Not Feb. 10, 17.

TGV –Ⓡ, supplement payable, ⓨ.
⊖ – Not for journeys to/from Poitiers or Châtellerault.
▷ – For local trains Angoulême - Bordeaux see below main table. For local trains Poitiers - Angoulême see panel on next page.

La Rochelle services subject to retiming on April 1

Certain *TGV* services start from Toulouse (Table **320**), Hendaye or Tarbes (Table **305**) or Arcachon (Table **306**).
Trains may be retimed a few minutes owing to engineering work

TGV trains convey ☕	*TGV* 8340	*TGV* 8342	*TGV* 8342	*TGV* 8400		*TGV* 8370		*TGV* 8402	*TGV* 8402		*TGV* 8404 8470			*TGV* 8406		*TGV* 8372		*TGV* 5441	*TGV* 5260			*TGV* 8410	*TGV* 8410		*TGV* 8500
	①	⑥⑦	①–⑤	①–⑤		①–⑤		⑦	①–⑥	①–⑤	①–⑤		⑥	①–⑥		⑦		⑧				①–⑤	①–⑥	⑦	①	①–⑥ t
Bordeaux St Jean 302 ....▷ d.	...	...	...	0516	...	...		0531	0531	...	0618		...	0623		...		...	0726	0726		...	0731	0731	...	0821
Libourne 302 ....▷ d.	...	...	...	...	...	...		0553	0553	...			...	...		...		...	0753	0753		...	0753	0753	...	...
Angoulême ....▷ d.	...	...	...	0615	...	...		0635	0635	...			...	0725		...		...	0826	0826		...	0835	0835	...	...
La Rochelle .... d.	...	...	...	...	...	0527				...			0629	...		0734		...			0742	...			...	...
Niort .... d.	...	...	...	...	...	0613				...			0715	...		0819		...			0832	...			...	...
Poitiers ....▷ a.	...	...	...	...	...	0704				...			0810	0814		0904		...	0914	0914	0921	...			...	...
Poitiers .... d.	0515	0624	0624	0633	0707				0728		0800		0817	0854	0907			0917	0917			...			0929	...
Futuroscope ⊖ .... d.				0643					0736		0810			0902								...			0937	...
Châtellerault .... d.		0642	0642	0707				0742	0741	0747	0828			0915								...	0942	0947	0950	...
St Pierre-des-Corps 295 ... a.	0556	0710	0710					0810	0810									0956	0956			...	1010	1015		...
Tours .... a.										0832												...				...
St Pierre des Corps 295 ... d.	0600	0717	0714					0814	0817									1000	1000			...	1014	1019		...
Vendôme-Villiers TGV...... d.			0737						0839													...				...
Massy TGV **295** .... a.																		1052	1052			...				...
Paris Montparnasse **295**... a.	0658	0822	0822	0836		0852		0913	0926		0936			1000		1052						...	1116	1117		1139
Marne la Vallee - Chessy .. a.	...	...	...	...	...	...		...	...	...	...		...	...		...		1127	1127			...	...	...	...	...
Charles de Gaulle ✈ .... a.	...	...	...	...	...	...		...	...	...	...		...	...		...			1145			...	...	...	...	...
Strasbourg **391** .... a.	...	...	...	...	...	...		...	...	...	...		...	...		...		1328				...	...	...	...	...
Lille Europe **11** .... a.	...	...	...	...	...	...		...	...	...	...		...	...		...			1301f			...	...	...	...	...

	TGV 8412	*TGV* 8530	*TGV* 8374	*TGV* 5264	*TGV* 5264		*TGV* 8510	*TGV* 8380		*TGV* 8430		*TGV* 8540		*TGV* 8580	*TGV* 8432		*TGV* 8382	*TGV* 8434	*TGV* 8514		*TGV* 5266	*TGV* 5445	*TGV* 8436
	①–⑤			①–⑤	⑥⑦	⑥			t		①–⑥				①–⑤		①–⑤			q			⑤⑦
Bordeaux St Jean 302 ....▷ d.	...	0826	0921	...	0926	0925	...	1121	...	1131		1218	...	1319	1331	...	...	1427	1521	...	1526	1526	1531
Libourne 302 ....▷ d.	...	...	...	...	...	...			...	1153			...		1353	...	...			...			1553
Angoulême ....▷ d.	...	0925	...	...	1026	1026			...	1235			...		1435	...	...	1525		...	1626	1626	1635
La Rochelle .... d.	0821		0929	...				1137	...			1224	...			...	1430			...			...
Niort .... d.	0911		1015	...				1222	...			1314	...			...	1516			...			...
Poitiers ....▷ a.	1000	1014	1104	1114	1114			1307	...			1410	...		1524		1604			...	1713	1713	1723
Poitiers .... d.		1017	1107	1117	1117	1233		1310	...	1334			...	1527	1533	1607			...	1638	1716	1716	1726
Futuroscope ⊖ .... d.						1243				1333	1342		...		1543				...	1648	1725	1725	...
Châtellerault .... d.						1303				1354			...		1603		1629		...	1709			1742
St Pierre-des-Corps 295 ... a.				1156	1156					1410			...	1610					...	1758	1758	1811
Tours .... a.											1455		...						...			...
St Pierre des Corps 295 ... d.				1200	1200					1414			...	1614					...	1802	1802	1815
Vendôme-Villiers TGV...... d.													...						...			...
Massy TGV **295** .... a.				1252	1252								...						...	1852	1852	...
Paris Montparnasse **295**... a.		1200	1236	1249			1442	1452		1516		1536		1636	1716		1752	1800	1836		1852	1852	1918
Marne la Vallee - Chessy .. a.	...	...	...	...	1327		...	...		...		...		...	...		1927	1927	...		...	...	...
Charles de Gaulle ✈ .... a.	...	...	...	1331	1341		...	...		...		...		...	...		1941		...		...	...	...
Strasbourg **391** .... a.	...	...	...				...	...		...		...		...	...			2145	...		...	...	...
Lille Europe **11** .... a.	...	...	...	1430	1437		...	...		...		...		...	...		2111f		...		...	...	...

	TGV 8384	*TGV* 8440 8476		*TGV* 8582	*TGV* 8386	*TGV* 5284	*TGV* 5284	*TGV* 8350		*TGV* 8516		*TGV* 8442 8478	*TGV* 8584	*TGV* 8390		*TGV* 8444 8472	*TGV* 8392	*TGV* 8518	*TGV* 8392	*TGV* 8448	*TGV* 8394	*TGV* 8586
	⑧ n		⑧	①–⑤		⑤	①–⑤	⑥⑦	p		①–⑤			⑤		z n		⑤	⑦	⑤⑦	⑦	⑦
Bordeaux St Jean 302 ....▷ d.	...	1623		...	1719	...	1723	1723		1821		1825	1921			1931	...	2021	...	2031	...	2118	...
Libourne 302 ....▷ d.	...	...		...	...	...	...	...		...		1952				1952	...		...	2053	...		...
Angoulême ....▷ d.	...	1726		...	...	...	1825	1826		...		1926				2035	...		...	2135	...		...
La Rochelle .... d.	...	1629		1643	...	1723				1738		1826		1938	1942		2011		2033		2100		...
Niort .... d.	...	1715		1732	...	1804				1828		1915		2020	2032		2052		2115		2145		...
Poitiers ....▷ a.	...	1804		1814	1832		1904	1910		1928		2010	2014		2104	2121	2124	2149		2204	2224	2232	...
Poitiers .... d.	1734	1807		1817		1836		1907	1913		1917	1932		2017		2107		2127	2152		2207	2227	2235
Futuroscope ⊖ .... d.	1742					1846		1921	1927	1943								2210			2310		
Châtellerault .... d.	1753					1909			1941	2012													
St Pierre-des-Corps 295 ... a.								1958	1956	2008								2210			2310		
Tours .... a.	1846									2045b													
St Pierre des Corps 295 ... d.								2002	2000	2011								2214			2314		
Vendôme-Villiers TGV...... d.																							
Massy TGV **295** .... a.								2052	2052														
Paris Montparnasse **295**... a.		1952	2000			2036	2049			2118		2136		2200	2236	2249		2317	2329	2336	2344	0015	0019	0033
Marne la Vallee - Chessy .. a.	...	...	...			2127	2127			...		...		...	...		...	...	...	...	...	...	...
Charles de Gaulle ✈ .... a.	...	...	...			2141	2141			...		...		...	...		...	...	...	...	...	...	...
Strasbourg **391** .... a.	...	...	...							...		...		...	...		...	...	...	...	...	...	...
Lille Europe **11** .... a.	...	...	...			2245	2244			...		...		...	...		...	...	...	...	...	...	...

LOCAL TRAINS ANGOULÊME - POITIERS and v.v.

	Ⓐ	✾	Ⓐ	†		✾	Ⓑ	Ⓐ			Ⓐ		✾	Ⓐ		Ⓑ	Ⓐ
Angoulême .... d.	0624	0731	0840	0943	...	1240	1643	1743	1843	**Poitiers** .... d.	0620	0750	...	1306	1610	...	1718	1808	1923
Ruffec .... d.	0658	0757	0906	1010	...	1306	1710	1810	1909	Ruffec .... d.	0700	0836	...	1354	1654	...	1804	1857	2002
Poitiers .... a.	0745	0839	0950	1048	...	1351	1748	1848	1947	Angoulême .... a.	0727	0905	...	1420	1722	...	1830	1922	2028

b – ⑧ only.
f – Lille **Flandres**.
n – Not Dec. 25.
p – Not Dec. 24.
t – Not Jan. 28.
z – Not Feb. 10, 17.

TGV –🅁, supplement payable. ☕.
▷ – For local trains Bordeaux - Angoulême see panel on previous page. For local trains Angoulême - Poitiers see below main table.
⊖ – Not for journeys to/from Poitiers or Châtellerault.

ANGOULÊME - SAINTES - ROYAN — 301

km			① Ⓐ ◇	Ⓐ	Ⓐ	Ⓐ K	M	L	◇	✕	✕	Ⓑ	Ⓐ	†		⑥	⑤	Ⓑ D	⑤†	⑤	⑤
	Paris Austerlitz ❶ ....d.	...	...	...	...	...	...	...	...	...	...	...	...	...	...	...	...	...	...	...	...
0	**Angoulême** ....d.	...	0638	...	0731	...	0937	1231	...	1400	...	1643	...	1738	...	1843	1844	...	1949	2002	2050	2140	2141	...	2241
49	Cognac ....d.	...	0720	...	0815	...	1016	1314	...	1439	...	1722	...	1821	...	1923	1922	...	2029	2049	2131	2220	2220	...	2321
●77	Niort ....d.	0543		0631		0734			1507		1728		1820						2200				2321
75	**Saintes** ....a.	0645	0740	0747	0834	0834	1036	1334	...	1459	1604	1742	1832	1840	1925	1942	1941	...	2049	2108	2150	2240	2240	2255	2341
75	**Saintes** ....d.	...	...	0758	...	...	1101	...	...	1505	1617	...	...	1846	...	1949	2016	...	2056	2114	2158	2246	...	2310	2348
111	**Royan** ....a.	...	...	0831	...	...	1133	...	...	1537	1649	...	...	1920	...	2021	2048	...	2128	2146	2230	2319	...	2343	0020

		Ⓐ	Ⓐ	Ⓐ	⑥	Ⓐ	⑥	Ⓐ ◇	Ⓒ	Ⓐ	✕ K	M E	①-④ N	⑤†	†	Ⓐ		Ⓐ	⑦	⑤	†	⑤
Royan ....d.		...	...	0559	0621	0625	...	0830	0842	1026	...	1540	...	1655	...	1804	1902	1918	...	1941	...
Saintes ....a.		...	...	0631	0654	0658	...	0901	0914	1058	...	1613	...	1728	...	1836	1935	1950	...	2013	...
Saintes ....d.		0606	0616	0637	0706	0706	0712	0732	0913	0916	1105	1252	1619	1619	1619	1736	1739	1841	1842	1941	2010	2015	2023	2028
Niort ....a.		0715		0812	0812				1008	1010							1956		2104	2109		
Cognac ....d.		...	0635	0655	...	0731	0750	...	1124	...	1313	1638	1638	1638	1755	1758	1859	...	2000	...	2044	2048
Angoulême ....a.		...	0718	0738	...	0811	0829	...	1205	...	1350	1719	1719	1719	1835	1838	1943	...	2037	...	2128	2129
Paris Austerlitz ❶ ....a.		...	...	...	...	...	...	...	...	...	...	...	...	...	...	...	...	...	...	...	...	...

D – ①②③④⑥ only.
E – ①②③④⑥ (not Dec. 24, 31).
K – Not Ⓐ Feb. 6 - 24.
L – Not Ⓐ Feb. 6 - Mar. 3.
M – Not Ⓐ Feb. 13 - Mar. 3.
N – Feb. 6 - 23.
◇ – To / from La Rochelle (Table **292**).
❶ – See Table **300** for *TGV* connections at Niort or Angoulême.
● – Distance from Saintes.

BORDEAUX - PÉRIGUEUX - BRIVE and LIMOGES — 302

km		①-⑤⑥	4490 B	Ⓐ	4492 D	⑥	①-④	①-⑤⑤	4480 E	Ⓒ	①-⑥①-⑤			①-⑤		Ⓑ	①-⑤①-⑤	⑦	①-⑤⑤
0	**Bordeaux** St Jean ...... **300** d.	0558	0700	0735	0737	0831	0845	...	1039	1100	1234	1402	1602	...	1634	1700	1735	1800	1835	1835	...	1935	2035
37	Libourne ....**300** d.	0622	0723	0800	0800		0908	...	1100	1123	1257	1427	1626	...	1659	1724	1759	1826	1857	1901	...	1959	2059
53	Coutras ....**300** d.	0634	0733	0812	0810		0919	...	1110	1135	1308	1437	1635	...	1711	1736	1811	1835	1907	1910	...	2011	2111
93	Mussidan ....d.	0705	0803	0837	0838		0945	...	1137	1156	1336	1507	1704	...	1737	1807	1840	1904	1934	1936	...	2040	2139
129	Périgueux ....a.	0730	0833	0900	0859	0939	1006	...	1159	1215	1357	1532	1728	...	1758	1832	1902	1928	1955	1957	...	2101	2201
129	Périgueux ....▷ d.	0737		0902	0902j	0942		1055		1221	1402			1735		1840				2004	2005	...	
203	**Brive la Gaillarde** ......▷ a.	...		0956	0957j	1027																	
	Ussel **326** ....a.	...		1200																			
166	Thiviers ....d.	0802					1116	...	1243		1422			1801		1913				2025	2028	...	
228	**Limoges** ....▷ a.	0843					1155	...	1321		1459			1858		1958				2110	2118	...	

		①-⑤①-⑥①-⑤①-⑤				①-⑥		⑦①-⑥	t	F		①-⑤		①-⑤	Ⓑ ①-⑤		Ⓑ	4581	4591 ⑤⑦	①-⑤①-⑤	⑦	①-⑤
																				x			
Limoges ....▷ d.		...	...	0603	...	...	1103	1103r	...	...	1520	...	...	...	1711	...	1803	...	...	1842	2011	2014
Thiviers ....d.		...	...	0649	...	...	1147	1150r	...	...	1611	...	...	...	1800	...	1846	...	...	1935	2102	2108
Ussel **326** ....d.		...																1619				
Brive la Gaillarde ....▷ d.		...				0907			1304								1813				
Périgueux ....▷ a.		...		0717		1000	1210	1212r	1359		1639				1822		1908	1909	...	2002	2121	2128
Périgueux ....d.		0556	0633	0702	0733	0833	1002	1002	...	1235	1405	1405	1604	...	1702	1803	1828	1828	...	1921	1911	2008	...
Mussidan ....d.		0617	0657	0723	0757	0857	1023	1023	...	1258	1426	1426	1625	...	1723	1824	1857	1857	...	1944	1932	2029	...
Coutras ....**300** d.		0647	0726	0750	0826	0926	1050	1050	...	1326	1452	1452	1652	...	1750	1850	1926	1926	...	2021		2055	...
Libourne ....**300** d.		0659	0736	0800	0837	0936	1100	1100	...	1339	1502	1502	1702	...	1800	1901	1936	1936	...	2036	2004	2106	...
Bordeaux St Jean ....a.		0723	0758	0827	0902	0958	1121	1121	...	1402	1528	1528	1727	...	1826	1926	1958	1958	...	2100	2028	2128	...

ADDITIONAL TRAINS PÉRIGUEUX - BRIVE

		Ⓐ	Ⓐ	⑥	Ⓒ A	H	†	⑥	⑤†	✕	Ⓑ			Ⓐ	⑥	Ⓐ	H †		Ⓐ	G ⑤
Périgueux ....d.		0623	0740	0750	0902	1050	1306	1354	1454	1639	1811	2005	Brive la Gaillarde ... d.	0613	0708	0732	...	1116	1505	...	1705	1808	2012
Brive la Gaillarde ..... a.		0722	0834	0844	0957	1148	1405	1449	1549	1736	1919	2100	Périgueux .... a.	0718	0801	0828	...	1212	1559	...	1759	1907	2113

ADDITIONAL TRAINS PÉRIGUEUX - LIMOGES

		Ⓐ	Ⓐ	Ⓒ	✕	Ⓒ	Ⓐ	†	Ⓑ	†	Ⓐ	⑤†			⑥	Ⓐ	J	Ⓒ	Ⓐ	✕	Ⓐ	†	Ⓑ	⑥	K
Périgueux ....d.		0448	0623	0737	0840	...	1115	1310	1402	1550	1840	2005	2212	Limoges ....d.	0603	0722	0853	1431	1520	1734	1842	2011	2014	2103	2203	2308
Thiviers ....d.		0509	0648	0802	0901	...	1151	1345	1422	1610	1913	2028	2233	Thiviers ....d.	0649	0801	0935	1520	1611	1824	1935	2102	2108	2147	2247	2353
Limoges ....a.		0553	0736	0843	0946	...	1240	1434	1459	1655	1958	2118	2314	Périgueux ......a.	0717	0821	0955	1547	1639	1856	2002	2121	2128	2207	2307	0012

A – ①②③④ Jan. 3 - 26, Mar. 6 - 30.
B – ①-⑤ Dec. 16 - Jan. 2; ⑤ Jan. 6 - Mar. 31.
C – Not ①②③④ Feb. 13 - Mar. 9.
D – From Jan. 3.
E – Not Feb. 13 - Mar. 10.
F – Jan. 30 - Mar. 3.
G – ①②③④⑥ (not Dec. 19 - 31).
H – ①-⑤ Dec. 12 - Jan. 27, Mar. 6 - 31.
J – ①-⑤ Dec. 12 - Feb. 10, Mar. 13 - 31.
K – ⑧ Dec. 16 - Mar. 19; ⑤⑦ Mar. 24 - 31.

j – Jan. 3 - 26.
r – Not ①-⑤ Feb. 13 - Mar. 10.
t – Not ①-⑤ Jan. 30 - Mar. 3.
x – Not Dec. 25, Jan. 1.

▷ – See below main table for additional trains Périgueux - Brive and Périgueux - Limoges.

LIMOGES - MONTLUÇON — 303

🚌 service subject to alteration

km		Ⓐ F	Ⓒ	B	Ⓐ	🚌 C	Ⓐ	🚌			Ⓐ	B F	Ⓒ	Ⓐ	Ⓐ	Ⓒ
0	**Limoges** ....d.	0811	0957	1011	1211	...	1340	...	1611	...	**Montluçon** ....d.	0715	1134	1455	1534	...	1540	1634	...	1834
78	Guéret ....d.	0918	1103	1117	1318	...	1445	...	1718	1730	Guéret ....d.	0826	1236	1557	1636	...	1635	1736	...	1936
156	**Montluçon** ....a.	1020	1204	1216	1420	...	1545	...	1820	1839	**Limoges** ....a.	...	1342	1707	1742	...	1745	1842	...	2042

B – ①-④ Dec. 12 - Feb. 2.
F – ⑤ Dec. 16 - Feb. 3; daily Feb. 6 - Mar. 17.

For night train Paris - Tarbes - Hendaye - Irún see top of next page.

km	All TGV convey 🍴											TGV 8571			TGV 8531				TGV 8573			TGV 8533	TGV 8578
		Ⓐ	Ⓐ	Ⓐ	Ⓐ	✕		Ⓐ	Ⓐ			①–⑥	†	†				Ⓐ		Ⓐ	Ⓐ	①–⑤	
										M	✕	N			C	M	L		C	S		P
	Paris M'parnasse **300** ......d.	...	...	...	...	...	...	...	...	...	...	0628	...	...	0728	...	0828	...	...	...	1028	1028
0	**Bordeaux** St Jean ....d.	...	...	...	...	...	0645	0747	...	...	...	0951	0947	...	1051	...	1151	...	1251	...	1351	1351
109	Morcenx ....d.	...	...	...	...	...	0746	0842	...	...	...		1043	...		...		...	1347	...		
148	Dax ....a.	...	...	...	...	...	0809	0905	...	...	...	1101	1106	...	1202	...	1301	...	1410	...	1500	1500
148	Dax ....d.	0602	0642	0650	0712	0742	0814	0818	0910	0914	1012	1104	1111	1115	1205	1209	1304	1312	1415	1419	1505	1509
179	Puyoô **325** ....d.		0708					0832		0932				1133		1227			1437			
193	Orthez **325** ....d.		0719					0842		0942				1143		1237	1333		1447			1539
233	Pau **325** ....d.		0745					0906		1006		1154	1209		1302		1357		1511			1604
272	Lourdes **325** ....d.											1228	1237				1432					1641
293	**Tarbes 325** ....a.											1244	1251				1448					1656
199	**Bayonne 325** ....d.	0647	0727		0801	0826		0850	0942		1057		1159		1236			1357	1447		1536	
209	Biarritz **325** ....d.	0657	0737		0813			0900	0951		1107		1208		1248			1407	1456		1548	
222	St Jean de Luz **325** ....d.	0711	0751		0827			0914	1006		1121		1223		1304			1421	1511		1604	
235	Hendaye **325** ....a.	0725	0805		0842			0927	1020		1138		1237		1320			1435	1525		1619	
237	**Irún 325** ....a.							0934	1027						1329							

		TGV 8577				TGV 8537						TGV 8541	TGV 8591				TGV 8543	TGV 8593			TGV 7911
		Ⓐ		Ⓐ	Ⓐ		Ⓐ	Ⓐ			Ⓐ		⑤⑦		⑥			Ⓑ			⑤
																		t			
																		A	D		
	Paris M'parnasse **300** ......d.	...	1128	...	...	...	1228	...	...	...	...	...	1428	1428	...	...	...	1728	1728	...	1928
	Bordeaux St Jean ....d.	1445	1451	...	...	...	1551	...	...	1645	...	...	1751	1751	...	1847	...	2047	2047	...	2251
	Morcenx ....d.	1539		...	...	...		...	...	1746	...	...			...	1948	...			...	
	Dax ....a.	1601	1606	...	...	...	1700	...	...	1810	...	...	1903	1903	...	2012	...	2159	2159	...	0003
	Dax ....d.	1603	1609	1616	1642		1703	1712	1742	...	1815	1819	1842	1907	1911	1915	2015	2019	2203	2207	2211	0006
	Puyoô **325** ....d.			1634							1832						2037					
	Orthez **325** ....d.			1644							1843				1939			2047		2236		
	Pau **325** ....d.		1659	1708							1907				2003			2116		2303		
	Lourdes **325** ....d.		1730												2039			2143		2337		
	Tarbes 325 ....a.		1746												2055			2158		2353		
	Bayonne 325 ....d.	1633		1728			1735	1758	1826		1853	1927		1938		2000		2049		2235	2258	0036
	Biarritz **325** ....d.	1643		1738			1747	1807			1904	1936		1950		2010		2100		2247		0048
	St Jean de Luz **325** ....d.	1657		1752			1803	1821			1919	1950		2006		2024		2117		2300		0103
	Hendaye **325** ....a.	1711		1806			1817	1834			1933	2004		2021		2038		2133		2318		0118
	Irún 325 ....a.						1826															

						TGV 8561	TGV 8530												TGV 8540	TGV 8581		
		✕	✕	Ⓐ	Ⓐ	①–⑥		Ⓐ	Ⓐ	Ⓐ	Ⓐ	Ⓐ	Ⓐ	Ⓐ	Ⓒ	Ⓐ		Ⓐ	Ⓐ	Ⓐ		Ⓐ
		q	k				t													L		Q
	Irún 325 ....d.																0833					
	Hendaye **325** ....d.		0456	0506		0552			0635		0645	0721			0751		0839	0918		0937		1221	...
	St Jean de Luz **325** ....d.		0511	0521		0606			0650		0658	0735			0805		0853	0931		0953		1235	...
	Biarritz **325** ....d.		0525	0535		0620			0704		0712	0749			0819		0907	0945		1008		1248	...
	Bayonne 325 ....d.		0539	0549		0634		0701	0722		0729	0801			0831		0920	0958		1024		1301	...
	Tarbes 325 ....d.	0430					0610			0708		0807								1014			
	Lourdes **325** ....d.	0445					0626			0725		0822								1038			
	Pau **325** ....d.	0514		0625			0658			0754	0852	0852					0955			1105		1354	
	Orthez **325** ....d.	0538		0649			0722			0818	0916	0916					1019			1132		1419	
	Puyoô **325** ....d.	0549		0659						0829	0927	0927					1029					1430	
	Dax ....a.	0608	0612	0622	0717	0721	0744	0748	0752	0816	0847	0852	0946	0948		0950	1041	1048	1053	1157	1345	1448
	Dax ....d.		0617	0627		0726		0758	0758			0857		0955		1058		1200					
	Morcenx ....d.		0640	0651		0749						0918		1017		1017							
	Bordeaux St Jean ....a.		0745	0801		0845		0909	0909			1015		1115		1115		1209		1309			
	Paris M'parnasse **300** ......a.	...	...	...	...	...	1236	1236	...	...	...	...	...	...	...	...	...	1536	...	1636	...	...

		TGV 8544	TGV 8583				TGV 8585								TGV 8546			TGV 8548	TGV 8587			
		Ⓐ	⑤†	Ⓐ	⑤†	Ⓑ	Ⓐ	Ⓐ	Ⓑ	Ⓐ	Ⓑ	①–④	⑤†		Ⓐ	Ⓐ	✕	⑦	⑦	✕	†	†
		S	w	B																		
	Irún 325 ....d.	1334																					
	Hendaye **325** ....d.	1340		1435			1543	1619				1717	1717		1744			1839		1845		1940	
	St Jean de Luz **325** ....d.	1354		1449			1556	1633				1731	1731		1759			1854		1859		1954	
	Biarritz **325** ....d.	1408		1504			1610	1647				1746	1746		1813			1909		1913		2008	
	Bayonne 325 ....d.	1421	1457	1519			1621	1701		1732		1756	1758		1829	1837		1924		1926		2021	
	Tarbes 325 ....d.			1416		1542		1614										1820					
	Lourdes **325** ....d.			1438		1600		1638										1839					
	Pau **325** ....d.			1505	1631	1631		1705		1726					1859			1908		1952			
	Orthez **325** ....d.				1659	1659		1730		1750					1923					2019			
	Puyoô **325** ....d.				1710	1710				1800					1933					2030			
	Dax ....a.	1452	1543	1547	1551		1728	1728		1732	1755	1818	1822		1830		1855	1920	1951	1952	1956	1955	2049	2053
	Dax ....d.	1457		1557	1557			1737	1758			1835		1900				2002	2002	2002		2058	
	Morcenx ....d.	1520						1800				1858						2023				2121	
	Bordeaux St Jean ....a.	1615		1711	1711			1900	1909			2000		2009				2113	2113	2122		2216	
	Paris M'parnasse **300** ......a.	...	...	2036	2036	...	...	...	2236	...	...	...	...	2336	...	...	...	0033	0033	...	...	...

A – Daily Dec. 11 - Jan. 22; ⑤⑥⑦ Jan. 27 - Feb. 19; daily Feb. 20 - Mar. 5; ⑤⑥⑦ Mar. 10 - Apr. 1.
B – Not Feb. 6 - 10.
C – ①–⑥ Dec. 12 - Jan. 7; ⑥ Jan. 14 - Feb. 4; ①–⑥ Feb. 6 - Apr. 1.
D – Ⓑ Dec. 11 - Feb. 3; ①–⑤ Feb. 6 - 24; Ⓑ Feb. 27 - Mar. 31.
L – Daily Dec. 11 - Jan. 8; ⑥⑦ Jan. 14 - Feb. 5; daily Feb. 6 - Apr. 1.
M – Not ①–⑤ Feb. 20 - Mar. 3.
N – Not Feb. 6 - 10, 20 - 24, Feb. 27 - Mar. 3.
P – Jan. 9 - Feb. 3.
Q – Not ①–⑤ Feb. 6 - 17.
S – Dec. 12 - Jan. 6, Feb. 6 - Mar. 31.

k – Feb. 6, 13 only.
q – Not Feb. 6, 13.
t – Not Feb. 5, 12.
w – Not Jan. 29.

TGV – Ⓡ, supplement payable, 🍴.

PARIS - HENDAYE - IRÚN NIGHT TRAIN   305 (contd)

NIGHT TRAIN **PARIS - IRÚN** and **HENDAYE - PARIS**

🛏 1, 2 cl. and 🛋 (reclining).

See below for dates	4053 ℝ	4055 ℝ	See below for dates	4052 ℝ	4054 ℝ
	G	H		J	K
Paris Austerlitz ....d.	2152	2152	Irún ....d.	1921	1921
Les Aubrais-Orléans ....a.	2255	2252	Hendaye ....d.	1921	1921
Tarbes ....a.	0551	0551	St Jean de Luz ....d.	1934	1934
Lourdes ....a.	0607	0608	Biarritz ....d.	1949	1949
Pau ....a.	0635	0635	Bayonne ....d.	2005	2005
Orthez ....a.	0700	0700	Dax ....d.	2059	2059
Dax ....a.	0728	0728	Orthez ....d.	2128	2128
Bayonne ....a.	0833	0831	Pau ....d.	2152	2152
Biarritz ....a.	0845	0848	Lourdes ....d.	2220	2227
St Jean de Luz ....a.	0902	0905	Tarbes ....d.	2243	2245
Hendaye ....a.	0917	0920	Les Aubrais-Orléans......a.	0608	0608
Irún ....a.	0928	0930	Paris Austerlitz ....a.	0720	0720

G – ①②③④⑦ Dec. 18 - 29; ①⑦ Jan. 1 - 30; ①②③④⑦ Feb. 5 - Mar. 2; ①⑦ Mar. 5 - 27.
H – ⑤ Dec. 16 - Jan. 27; ⑤⑥ Feb. 3 - Mar. 4; ⑤ Mar.10 - 24 (also Dec. 17).
J – ①②③④⑤ Dec. 19 - 30; ①⑤ Jan. 2 - Feb. 3; ①②③④⑤ Feb. 6 - Mar. 3; ①⑤ Mar. 6 - 31.
K – ⑦ Dec. 18 - Jan. 29; ⑥⑦ Feb. 4 - Mar. 5; ⑦ Mar. 12 - 26 (also Dec. 17).

BORDEAUX - ARCACHON   306

TGV Trains

km	TGV services, ℝ		TGV 8471 ⑤–⑦ B		TGV 8473 ⑥⑦ n		TGV 8479 ⑤		TGV services, ℝ		TGV 8476 ⑥⑦ n		TGV 8478 Ⓒ		TGV 8472 ⑦
	Paris Montparnasse **300**....d.		0846	...	1028	...	1804	...	Arcachon...................d.	...	1533	...	1719	...	1839
0	Bordeaux St Jean..............d.	...	1238	...	1355	...	2141	...	La Teste ....d.		|	...	|	...	1845
40	Facture Biganos..............d.	...	1300	...	1419	...	2203	...	Facture Biganos...........d.	...	1551	...	1743	...	1900
56	La Teste ....a.		|	...	|	...	2219	...	Bordeaux St Jean ....a.	...	1613	...	1807	...	1923
59	Arcachon......................a.	...	1316	...	1443	...	2224	...	Paris Montparnasse **300**.a.	...	1957	...	2157	...	2314

Local services

		Ⓐ	✕	Ⓐ		Ⓐk	✕k	C	Ⓐj	C	Ⓐj					Ⓐ		Ⓐ		Ⓐ		Ⓐ			⑤†	⑤
Bordeaux St Jean ....d.	0635	0705	0735	0805	0835	0905	1105	1242	1305	1335	1405	1505	1605	1635	1705	1717	1735	1805	1835	1905	1935	2005	2105	2205	2305	2355
Facture Biganos........ a.	0704	0734	0804	0834	0904	0934	1134	1311	1335	1404	1434	1534	1634	1704	1734	1748	1804	1834	1904	1934	2004	2034	2134	2234	2334	0024
Arcachon............Ⓔ a.	0730	0800	0830	0900	0930	1000	1200	1337	1404	1430	1500	1600	1700	1730	1800	1814	1830	1900	1930	2000	2030	2100	2200	2300	0001	0050

	Ⓐ	✕n	Ⓐ	✕n	Ⓐ	Ⓐ	Ⓐ	Ⓐ	Ⓐ	Ⓐ		k		k	Ⓐj	C	C	Ⓐ	C	C	Ⓐ	Ⓐ	Ⓐ	Ⓐ	Ⓐ	†
Arcachon............Ⓔ d.	0510	0546	0618	0631	0645	0701	0731	0801	0901	1001	1101	...	1201	1231	1301	1401	1501	1601	1631	1701	1731	1801	1831	1901	2001	2101
Facture Biganos........ d.	0534	0610	0641	0655	0709	0725	0755	0825	0925	1025	1125	...	1225	1255	1325	1425	1525	1625	1655	1725	1755	1825	1855	1925	2025	2125
Bordeaux St Jean ....a.	0605	0641	0713	0725	0740	0755	0825	0855	0955	1055	1155	...	1255	1325	1355	1455	1555	1655	1725	1755	1825	1855	1925	1955	2055	2155

B – Not ⑤ Jan. 13 - Feb. 3.
C – Daily Dec. 11 - Jan. 8; Ⓒ Jan. 14 - 29; daily Feb. 4 - Mar. 31.

j – Not Ⓐ Jan. 9 - Feb. 3.
k – Not Ⓐ Jan. 9 - 27.
n – Not Mar. 11.

TGV – ℝ, supplement, ⚍.

Ⓔ – Trains also call at La Teste, 4 - 5 mins from Arcachon.

BORDEAUX - LE VERDON - POINTE DE GRAVE   307

km		Ⓐ	✕		Ⓐ	Ⓒ		Ⓐ j		⑥		Ⓐ j			P		Ⓐ			Ⓐ			Ⓐ	⑤†
0	Bordeaux St Jean .....d.	0611	0711	...	0814	0925	...	1019	...	1111	...	1219	...	1313	...	1611	...	1711	...	1811	...	1911	1944
19	Blanquefort ....d.	0639	0740	...	0847	0947	...	1047	...	1147	...	1246	...	1347	...	1648	...	1748	...	1848	...	1946	2015
35	Margaux ....d.	0703	0804	...	0908	1007	...	1108	...	1209	...	1307	...	1409	...	1710	...	1810	...	1910	...	2006	2035
57	Pauillac.....................d.	0728	0832	...	0928	1030	...	1130	...	1230	...	1330	...	1430	...	1731	...	1831	...	1931	...	2026	2055
76	Lesparre ....d.	0742	0847	...	0944j	1045	...	1144	...	1244	...	1344	...	1445	...	1746	...	1846	...	1946	...	2040	2110
102	Soulac sur Mer ....d.	...	0907	...	...	1104	...	...	...	...	...	...	...	1505	...	...	...	1906	...	2006	...	...	
109	Le Verdon ....d.	...	0914	...	...	1112	...	...	...	...	...	...	...	1512	...	...	...	1913	...	2013	...	...	
112	Pointe de Grave ....▷a.																							

	Ⓐ	⑥		Ⓐ	Ⓐ	Ⓒ		Ⓐ			Ⓐ			P		Ⓐ		Ⓐ	Ⓒ		Ⓐ		Ⓐ	Ⓐ
						h		j			j					j		j						
Pointe de Grave.................▷d.																								
Le Verdon ....d.	0547	...	...	0647	...	...	0747	...	0947	...	...	1147	...	...	...	1552	...	1647	...	...	1747			
Soulac sur Mer ....d.	0554	...	...	0653	...	...	0754	...	0954	...	...	1154	...	...	...	1600	...	1654	...	...	1754			
Lesparre ....d.	0614	0614	...	0712	...	0814	0814	...	1014	...	1114	1214	...	1414	...	1620	1620	1714	...	1814	1814			
Pauillac........................d.	0629	0629	...	0727	...	0831	0831	...	1029	...	1129	1229	...	1429	...	1635	1635	1730	...	1830	1830			
Margaux ....d.	0647	0647	...	0749	...	0853	0853	...	1053	...	1153	1253	...	1483	...	1655	1655	1754	...	1854	1854			
Blanquefort ....d.	0707	0707	...	0809	...	0914	0914	...	1115	...	1214	1313	...	1515	...	1715	1715	1815	...	1915	1915			
Bordeaux St Jean ....a.	0749	0749	...	0849	...	0949	0949	...	1138	...	1249	1338	...	1538	...	1739	1739	1849	...	1949	1949			

P – Daily Dec. 11 - Feb. 26; Ⓒ Mar. 4 - 19; daily Mar. 20 - Apr. 1.

h – Not Feb. 27 - Mar. 10.
j – Not Feb. 27 - Mar. 17.

▷ – For ferry schedule Pointe de Grave - Royan see Table 299.

PÉRIGUEUX - LE BUISSON - AGEN   308

km		①	Ⓐ	Ⓒ	F	✕	Ⓐ	⑤†		Ⓐ Ⓔ	✕	†	Ⓐ	F	†	⑥
0	Périgueux....................d.	0503	0757	0931	1230	1451	1715	1827 1908	1908	Agen ....d.	...	0728	1118	1406	...	1647	1836
40	Les Eyzies...................d.	0533	0827	1007	1302	1521	1752	1904 1945	1945	Monsempron Libos......d.	...	0803	1153	1447	...	1723	1915
57	Le Buisson ....d.	0551	0847	1029	1320	1539	1810	1920 2001	2002	Le Buisson ....d.	0637	0718	0839	0853 1243	1546 1724	1824	2010
108	Monsempron Libos ....d.	0640	0936	1121	1411	1629	1914	...	2052	Les Eyzies.................d.	0655	0735	0856	0911 1301	1604 1741	1844	2027
152	Agen ....a.	0720	1010	1158	1448	1709	1948	...	2127	Périgueux..................a.	0731	0811	0932	0947 1330	1633 1817	1919	2056

E – ①②③④⑥ (not Mar. 27).
F – Ⓒ (daily Dec. 11 - Jan. 29, Mar. 6 - 19).
G – Ⓐ Dec. 12 - Jan. 27, Mar. 6 - 17.
H – Ⓑ Dec. 11 - Jan. 29; † Feb. 5 - Mar. 5; daily Mar. 6 - 19 (also Mar. 26).

Ⓔ – Runs 9 minutes later throughout on ⑥.

309   LIMOGES - ANGOULÊME and POITIERS

km			J	Ⓐ	⑥		†	L	⑧	⑤	†			Ⓐ	D		A	③y		†	⑧	Ⓐ	Ⓒ		⑤
0	Limoges	d.	0503	0623	...	0808	...	1215	1221	...	1717	1814	1911	Angoulême	d.	0601	0730	...	1202	1225	...	1447	1712	...	1818	1909	...	2000
122	Angoulême	a.	0708	0840	...	1015	...	1425	1431	...	1931	2023	2120	Limoges	a.	0809	0936	...	1405	1432	...	1651	1929	...	2023	2121	...	2213

			Ⓐ	Ⓐ		Ⓐz	Ⓐz	Ⓐz					⑤				Ⓐ	⑥	Ⓐz	Ⓐz	⑥		Ⓐ	†	⑤
0	Limoges	d.	0604	0807	1206	1208	1302	1406	1607	1805	2007	2029	2229	Poitiers	d.	0559	0804	1005	1205	1205	1251	1405	1605	1651	1804	2005	2148	2225
139	Poitiers	a.	0755	0956	1356	1356	1507	1556	1756	1954	2156	2213	0012	Limoges	a.	0756	0955	1157	1355	1357	1457	1555	1757	1858	1957	2155	2341	0014

A – ①②④⑤⑥ (not Ⓐ Mar. 6 - 24).
D – ✗ (not ②③④⑤ Dec. 20 - 30).
J – ①⑤ Jan. 2 - Mar. 31 (also Dec. 12, 16).
L – ✗ (not Ⓐ Mar. 6 - 24).

y – Not Mar. 8, 15, 22.
z – Not Mar. 27 - 31.

310   PARIS - LIMOGES - TOULOUSE

For faster TGV services Paris - Agen - Toulouse and v.v. see Table 320

km				★ 3601				★ 3611	★ 3613	★ 3621				★ 3701	★ 3631	★ 3701		★ 3703	★ 3635		★ 3637
			①–⑥①–⑤	①–⑥①–⑤①–⑤①–⑥	⑦	①–⑥	⑦		①–⑤		①–⑥ ⑮	⑮	⑥⑦	Ⓒ	⑤⑦	⑤	⑤–⑦
			E			n		a		C		☆❅		☆❅ D		☆❅	
0	Lille Europe	d.															
	Paris Austerlitz 294 315	d.		0641		0752	0752	0841			0929	0941		1029	1152	1241
	Orléans 315	d.	0650	0750						1048				
119	Les Aubrais-Orléans 294 315	d.				0848	0848			1030	1039		1131		
200	Vierzon 315	d.	0649 0749 0810 0849				1010		1014		1133	1145	1318	
236	Issoudun	d.	0714 0814 0829 0912				1034			1154	1208		1427
263	Châteauroux	d.	0732 0832 0845 0932	0949	0949	1041		1049	1137	1208	1227	1248	1349	1444
294	Argenton sur Creuse	d.	0748 0849	0949		1058		1105		1223	1244		
341	La Souterraine	d.	0818	0923		1124		1134		1251			1523
400	Limoges	a.	0854	0954	1054	1054	1154		1219	1245	1254	1337	1409	1454	1554
400	Limoges	d.	0540	0957	1007	1057	1057	1157		1228	1249	1257		1413	1456
459	Uzerche	d.	0617		1056	1134	1134	1234		1317			1534
499	Brive la Gaillarde	a.	0644	1057	1056	1159	1159	1300		1345	1350	1356		1512	1600
499	Brive la Gaillarde	d.	0557	0702		1202	1202	1306		→	1359	1407	1515	1702
536	Souillac	d.	0628	0731		1231	1332		1429			1728
559	Gourdon	d.	0643	0747 ①–⑥		1248	1349		1447			1745
600	Cahors	d.	0612 0712	0812 0900	1309	1318	1416		1518	1525	1625	1813
639	Caussade	d.	0638 0738	0839 0926	1344	1441		1542			1840
662	Montauban 320	d.	0657 0757	0857 0945	1348	1400	1456		1557	1606	1704	1900
713	Toulouse Matabiau 320	a.	0735 0835	0935 1023	1415	1426	1538		1625	1632	1731	1935
	Portbou 355	a.											

			★ 3643				3651			★ 3655	★ 3661	★ 3669		★ 3665		★ 3667	★ 3663	★ 3681	TGV 5248		3751	3753
			⑦–④	①–⑤①–⑤①–⑤①–⑤①–⑤	⑦	①–⑤		⑥⑦①–⑤①–⑤	⑤⑦	①–④①–⑤	⑥⑦①–⑤		⑤			④–⑦ ❅	◆ ⓇP	◆ ⓇR
														1802		
	Lille Europe	d.													
	Paris Austerlitz 294 315	d.	1352	1552		1652	1752	1752	1811	1841	1913	1941	2212	2212
	Orléans 315	d.			1650			1850			2042	2327	2357
	Les Aubrais-Orléans 294 315	d.	1448						2012		2056	2107	2116
	Vierzon 315	d.	1649 1718	1733	1747	1821	1918	1933	1937	1949	2010	
	Issoudun	d.	1713	1754	1808	1842	1954	2013	2029	
	Châteauroux	d.	1549 1639	1732 1749	1809	1827	1846	1908	1950	1950	2008	2008	2030	2045	2126	2138	2148
	Argenton sur Creuse	d.	1655	1757	1825	1851	1926		2024	2029	2145	2155
	La Souterraine	d.	1722		1853	1924	1955	2053	2053	2124	2210	2221	2229
	Limoges	a.	1654	1755	†	1854	1938	1954	2054	2054	2137	2124	2154	2240	2252	2300
	Limoges	d.	1657 1707	1807 1837 1857	1907		2057	2057	2127		2243	2255	2303
	Uzerche	d.	1756	1856	1926	1933	1959	2134	2134	2204	2320	2332
	Brive la Gaillarde	a.	1755	1824	1924	1954	1959	2027	2159	2159	2229	2345	2358	0006
	Brive la Gaillarde	d.	1733 1758	2004	2202	2202	2232	2348	
	Souillac	d.	1759 1826	2031	2229	2229	2259	0018	0403
	Gourdon	d.	1816 1845	2049	2247	2247	2318	0034	0429
	Cahors	d.	1844 1916	2115	2315	2315	2348	0102	0510	0510
	Caussade	d.	1910 1942	2143		0543
	Montauban 320	d.	1927 1958	2203		0050	0203	0602	0602
	Toulouse Matabiau 320	a.	2005 2024	2235				0629	0629
	Portbou 355	a.						

			★ 3600	★ 3604	★ 3602	★ 3606	TGV 5296		★ 3612	★ 3610		★ 3620		★ 3700	★ 3630	★ 3634	★ 3632		★ 3640
			①–⑤①–⑤	①–⑤①–⑥	⑥⑦	①–⑤①–⑤①–⑥①–⑥	❅		①–⑥	①–⑥		⑦		①–⑥①–⑤	⑥⑦	⑤–①	⑤⑥	⑦	⑧
										F		☆❅	
	Cerbère 355	d.												
	Toulouse Matabiau 320	d.							0619	0640	0725		1038	1044
	Montauban 320	d.							0658	0708	0804		1106	1112
	Caussade	d.							0715		0820		1128
	Cahors	d.						0644	0742	0749	0848		1148	1155
	Gourdon	d.						0711	0811		0918e		1222
	Souillac	d.						0728	0827		0936e		1239
	Brive la Gaillarde	a.						0757	0853	0900	1001e		1300	1308
	Brive la Gaillarde	d.		0457	0457		0704		0732	0800	0800		0903		1318	1311	1357	1459
	Uzerche	d.		0523	0522			0801	0826	0826			1424	1525
	Limoges	a.		0600	0600		0749	0849	0902	0903		1002		1419	1411	1503	1603
	Limoges	d.	0503	0603	0603	0706	0723	0807	0823		0905	0906		1005	1223	1422	1414	1506	1506	1606
	La Souterraine	d.	0535		0607	0636		0738	0808	0837	0908		1037	1308		1537	1537	
	Argenton sur Creuse	d.		0636	←	0836	0910	0936		1101	⑥	1336		1610
	Châteauroux	d.	0613 0629	0710	0700	0715	0718	0817	0853	0920	0928	0951		1012	1011	1107		1119	1229	1351	1527		1616	1616	1635	1713
	Issoudun	d.	0630 0649	→	0730	0736		0907	0945		1124		1249		1631	1631	1651
	Vierzon 315	d.	0651 0716	0742	0751	0800	0849	0927	0953	1015		1209		1316		1651	1651	1717
	Les Aubrais-Orléans 294 315	a.					1027		1111	1111		1220		1637	1621	
	Orléans 315	a.	0810		0854		1109		1257		1410		1812
	Paris Austerlitz 294 315	a.	0819	0907	0920	1018		1209	1208		1318		1738	1718	1818	1818		1907
	Lille Europe	a.				1308								

FOR NOTES SEE NEXT PAGE

TOULOUSE - LIMOGES - PARIS   310

For faster TGV services Toulouse - Agen - Paris and v.v. see Table 320

		★ 3652 z	★ 3660 a	★ 3664	★ 3672		★ 3680 T			★ 3690 A	★ 3690 B					3752 ◆ ℝ R	3750 ◆ ℝ P
		⑥	⑤	①-⑥	①-⑥	①-⑤	⑦	①-⑤	①-⑥	⑧	⑤	⑧ ①-⑤	⑧	①-⑤ ⑥⑦	①-⑤		
Cerbère 355 ....d.		...	...	...	...	...	...	...	...	...	...	...	...	...	...	...	...
Toulouse Matabiau 320 ...d.		1325	1334	...	...	1434	1444	...	1544	1634	1634	1725	...	1825	1925	1927	...	2250	2250
Montauban 320 ....d.		1356	1402	...	...	1502	1530	...	1631	1702	1702	1804	...	1904	2004	2004	...	2319	2319
Caussade ....d.		1412	1418	...	...	1518	1544	...	1646	1718	1718	1821	...	1922	2019	2021	...	2337	
Cahors ....d.		1437	1445	...	...	1545	1608	...	1712	1745	1745	1848	...	1947	2047	2049	...	0007	0007
Gourdon ....d.		1509	1513	...	...	1613	1635	...	1742	1815	1815	1918	...	2016	2116	...	...	0038	
Souillac ....d.		1527	1531	...	...	1631	1651	...	1759	1834	1834	1935	...	2032	2132	...	...	0057	
Brive la Gaillarde ....a.		1555	1600	...	...	1700	1718	...	1825	1900	1903	2001	...	2057	2157	...	...		
Brive la Gaillarde ....d.		▬	1603	1603	...	1650	1703	...	▬	1736	1800	...	1836	1903	1906	...	2009		
Uzerche ....d.		...	...	...	...	1718	...	...	1805	1825	...	1905		...	...	...	2038		
Limoges ....a.		...	⑧	1703	1703	...	1755	1803	...	1854	1903	...	1954	2003	2005	...	2126		
Limoges ....d.		1623	1623	1706	1723	1736	...	1806	...	1823	1906	...	2006	2008	...	...		
La Souterraine ....d.		1708	1708	...	1737	1808	1808	...	...	1908	1937	...	...	...	...	...		
Argenton sur Creuse........d.		1736	1736	...	1801	1836	1832	...	...	1910	1936	...	...	...	...	...		
Châteauroux ....d.		1729	1751	1753	1811	1819	1853	1850	...	1911	1935	1951	...	2015	...	2112	2117		
Issoudun ....d.		1747	...	1807	...	1907	1906	...	1951	...	2031	...	...	...	...	...		
Vierzon 315 ....d.		1814	...	1827	...	1851	1927	1927	...	2017	...	2051	...	2144	2149	...	...		
Les Aubrais-Orléans 294 315 a.		...	1911	...	...	...	2011	...	...	...	2220	2222	...	...	0535	0535		
Orléans 315 ....a.		1910	...	...	...	...	2112	...	...	...	...	...	...	...	...	...		
Paris Austerlitz 294 315 ....a.		...	2007	2019	...	2053	2107	...	...	2218	...	2318	2318	...	...	0652	0652		
Lille Europe ....a.		...	...	...	...	...	...	...	...	...	...	...	...	...	...	...	...

◆ – NOTES (LISTED BY TRAIN NUMBER):

3750 - 3 – ▬ 1, 2 cl. and 🛏 (reclining) Paris – Toulouse and v.v.; ▬ 1, 2 cl. and 🛏 (reclining) Paris – Toulouse (**3980/1/3**) - Latour de Carol and v.v. Also conveys (to / from Brive) Paris – Rodez / Albi and v.v. on dates in Table **316**.

A – Jan. 23 - Mar. 3.
B – Daily Dec. 11 - Jan. 22; ⑥⑦ Jan. 28 - Feb. 5; daily Mar. 6 - Apr. 1.
C – ⑤ Dec. 16 - Jan. 6; ①-⑤ Jan. 9 - Mar. 31.
D – ①②③④⑥ Dec. 12 - Jan. 5; ⑥ Jan. 7 - Apr. 1.
E – Daily Dec. 11 - Mar. 12; ①-⑤ Mar. 13-31.
F – ①-⑤ Dec. 12 - Jan. 13; ⑤ Jan. 20 - Feb. 10; ①-⑤ Feb. 13 - Mar. 20; ⑤ Mar. 24 - 31.
N – ①②③④⑦ (also Dec. 25, Jan. 1; not Dec. 24, 31, Mar. 27).
P – ①②③④ only.
R – ⑤⑥⑦ (not Dec. 24, 31).
T – ①②③④⑥ only.

a – Not Dec. 26 - 30.
e – ① only.
n – Not Mar. 20 - 23, 27 - 30.
z – Not Dec. 23, 30.

TGV – ℝ, supplement payable, 🍴.
★ – *Intercités* service, ℝ.
☆ – Also conveys couchettes and reclining seats for daytime use (also vending machines).
🍴 – Subject to confirmation.

BRIVE - AURILLAC   311

km		Ⓐ P	Ⓐ K	⑥ Q	🍴 L	† T	⑥ Q	† M	Ⓐ Q			Ⓐ N	🍴 N	Ⓒ R	Ⓐ K		† T	⑤ Y	M
0	**Brive** la Gaillarde 316 ......d.	0715	1130	1211	1403	1422	1801	1803	2216	2239	**Aurillac** ....d.	0515	0700	1049	1112	...	1456	1557	1710
27	St Denis-près-Martel 316 ....d.	0741	1156	1242	1430	1454	1834	1834	2242	2306	St Denis-près-Martel 316 ...d.	0637	0824	1213	1237	...	1627	1721	1835
102	**Aurillac** ....a.	0910	1321	1406	1553	1619	2001	1957	0005	0029	**Brive** la Gaillarde 316......a.	0705	0850	1242	1303	...	1652	1746	1900

K – Jan. 9 - Mar. 10.   **M** – Jan. 9 - Mar. 12.   **P** – Jan. 9 - Mar. 19.   **R** – Jan. 14 - Mar. 12.   **Y** – Jan. 13 - Mar. 10.
L – Jan. 9 - Mar. 11.   **N** – Jan. 9 - Mar. 13.   **Q** – Jan. 14 - Mar. 11.   **T** – Jan. 15 - Mar. 12.

TOULOUSE - LATOUR DE CAROL   312

km		3981 ℝ P	3983 ℝ R										Ⓐ					Ⓐ	3980 ℝ L
	Paris Austerlitz 310 d.	2212	2212									**Latour de Carol** ....d.	0525	...	0721	0921c	...	1321	...	1721	1921
0	**Toulouse** Matabiau ...d.	0648	0755	0848v	1048v	1348	1448	1648	1748	1848	1948	**L'Hospitalet** ⊖.........d.	0552	...	0752	0951c	...	1351	...	1751	1952
65	Pamiers ....d.	0750	0850	0950	1150	1444	1550	1750	1851	1952	2050	Ax les Thermes ....d.	0620	0723	0820	1020	1123	1420	1523	1723	1820	2023
83	Foix ....a.	0803	0903	1003	1202	1504	1602	1802	1905	2004	2104	Foix ....d.	0704	0802	0904	1104	1203	1504	1603	1803	1906	2108
83	Foix ....d.	0805	0906	1005	1205	1506	1605	1805	1908	2005	2106	Foix ....a.	0705	0804	0905	1105	1204	1505	1604	1804	1907	2110
123	Ax les Thermes ....d.	0849	0952	1049	1249	1543	1649	1849	1944	2049	2143	Pamiers ....d.	0721	0821	0921	1121	1221	1521	1621	1823	1924	2124
144	L'Hospitalet ⊖ ....d.	0921	1023	1115	1321	...	1721	1921	...	2118	...	**Toulouse** Matabiau ....a.	0815	0915r	1015r	1215r	1315	1615	1715	1916	2015	2214
163	**Latour de Carol** .....a.	0950	1048	1136	1347	...	1747	1947	...	2139	...	*Paris* Austerlitz 310 .a.	...	...	...	...	...	...	...	...	...	0652

L – Not Dec. 24, 31: ▬ 1, 2 cl. and 🛏 (reclining) Latour de Carol - Toulouse (**3750/2**) - Paris.
P – ①②③④⑦ (also Mar. 31, Apr. 1): ▬ 1, 2 cl. and 🛏 (reclining) Paris (**3751/3**) - Toulouse - Latour de Carol.
R – ⑤⑥⑦ (not Dec. 24, 31, Mar. 31, Apr. 1): ▬ 1, 2 cl. and 🛏 (reclining) Paris (**3751/3**) - Toulouse - Latour de Carol.

c – ⑥⑦ only.
r – Not Feb. 13 - 17, 20 - 24.
v – Not Feb. 13 - 17.

⊖ – Full name: Andorre-L'Hospitalet. For 🚌 connections to / from Andorra see Table **313**.

ANDORRA 🚌   313

				⊖							⊖		
Andorre-L'Hospitalet (Gare) ..d.	0745	...	1945	...	and	...	...	**Andorra la Vella** ....d.	0545	...	1700	...	0745	and	1945	...
Pas de la Casa ....d.	0810	...	2000	...	hourly	2045	...	Soldeu ⊙ ....d.	0610	...	1735	...	0825	hourly	2025	...
Soldeu ⊙ ....d.	0825	...	2025	0855	until	2055	...	Pas de la Casa ....d.	0640	...	1815	...	0840	until	2040	...
Andorra la Vella ....a.	0910	...	2105	0940		2140	...	**Andorre-L'Hospitalet** (Gare)....a.	0710	...	1930	...				...

⊙ – Also calls at Canillo, Encamp and Escaldes.
⊖ – Additional journeys operated by Cooperativa Interurbana (service L4) run from Andorra at 0630, 0720 then hourly until 2020; from Pas de la Casa at 0715, 0820 then hourly until 2120.

Operator: La Hispano Andorrana, Av. Santa Coloma, entre 85 - 87, Andorra la Vella, ☎ + 376 821 372. www.andorrabus.com. Subject to cancellation when mountain passes are closed by snow.
Additional service: approx hourly (5 per day on ⑦) Escaldes - Andorra la Vella - Sant Julià de Lòria - Seu d'Urgell (Spain).

TOULOUSE - CASTRES - MAZAMET   314

km		Ⓐ	Ⓐ	🍴	†	y	y	Ⓐ	Ⓐ			Ⓐ	Ⓐ	Ⓐ		Ⓐy	⑧y	🍴y	y		Ⓐ
0	**Toulouse** ◇ ....d.	0543	0643	0750	0837	1144	1344	1544	1644	1722	1741	1847	2042	**Mazamet** ....d.	0531	0554	0636	0739	0842	1032	1232	1433	1731	1820	1938
86	Castres ....a.	0655	0758	0901	0952	1251	1452	1653	1750	1833	1853	1957	2154	Castres ....d.	0553	0616	0659	0802	0905	1054	1255	1456	1754	1857	2001
105	**Mazamet** ....a.	0721	0824	0927	1014	1317	1518	1715	1817	1859	1919	2023	2216	**Toulouse** ◇ ....d.	0701	0730	0805	0909	1011	1201	1401	1602	1905	2005	2112

y – Not Mar. 27 - 31.

◇ – Toulouse Matabiau.

315 PARIS - VIERZON - BOURGES - MONTLUÇON

km				3903			3909	3909							3915	3913						3917	3917	3921	
		Ⓐ ⊖	⚒	⚒	⑥	F	A	B	Ⓐ	Ⓑ ⊖H	Ⓐ		Ⓐ ⊖	⚒	⑤	G		①–④	†	Ⓐ	Ⓑ	D	C	⑤†	⑤†
0	**Paris** Austerlitz ...... 310 d.	...	...	0707	...	...	1151	1228	...	...	...	...	...	...	1707	1707	...	...	...	...	...	1907	1907	2107	...
	Orléans ...... 310 d.	0607	0715	|	...	0913	|	|	1450	1614	...	1650	1715	1748	|	|	1815	...	...	1915	1950	|	|	|	...
119	Les Aubrais-Orléans .... 310 d.	|	|	0805	...	|	1325	1325	|	|	...	|	|	|	1805	1805	|	...	...	|	|	2008	2008	2205	...
178	Salbris ...... d.	0644	0751	0835	...	0950	|	|	1529	1653	...	1729	1753	1827	1832	1832	1853	...	...	1952	2029	2035	2035	2232	...
200	Vierzon ...... 310 ▷ d.	0657	0805	0852	0902	1004	1403	1403	1545	1707	...	1744	1807	1842	1849	1849	1907	1924	...	2006	2044	2052	2052	2249	2300
232	**Bourges** ...... ▷ a.	0726	0826	0911	|	1025t	1421	1421	1613	1726	...	1811	1826	...	1907	1908	1927	|	...	2026	...	2111	2111	2308	|
	Bourges ...... d.	...	...	...	|	...	1438j	1438r	...	...	1729	...	...	...	1929	...	...	|	1930	...	...	...	2128	...	|
•291	St Amand-Montrond-Orval .. d.	...	...	...	0957	...	1525j	1525r	...	...	1823	...	...	...	2018	...	...	2020	2020	...	...	...	2215	...	2352
•341	**Montluçon** ...... a.	...	...	...	1031	...	1600j	1600r	...	...	1904	...	...	...	2053	...	...	2055	2103	...	...	...	2250	...	0027

						3904					3910		3916		3914			3918	3922					3924	
	Ⓐ H	⑥	Ⓐ	⚒	Ⓐ	⚒	⑥	Ⓐ	⚒ ⊖H	Ⓐ ⊖		J	†	K	⚒	Ⓐ	Ⓐ ⊖	E	†	Ⓒ	Ⓐ ⊖	Ⓐ	Ⓐ ⊖H	†	
Montluçon ...... d.	...	...	...	0535	...	...	0613	...	...	...	0844	1035	...	...	...	...	...	1641	...	...	...	1735	...	...	...
St Amand-Montrond-Orval ...... d.	...	...	...	0610	...	...	0650	0627	...	...	0920	1110	...	1326	...	...	...	1718	...	...	...	1829	...	...	...
Bourges ...... a.	...	...	...	|	...	...	|	0712	...	...	1011	|	...	1412	...	...	...	1812	...	...	...	1915	...	...	...
Bourges ...... ▷ d.	...	...	0633	|	...	0649	|	...	0733	0833	1030	|	1352	...	1549	1633	1733	1838	1838	1833	1833	...	1933	2049	...
Vierzon ...... 310 ▷ d.	0616	0650	0656	0702	0716	0709	0742	...	0755	0855	1049	1159	1412	...	1609	1655	1755	1901	1901	1855	1855	...	1955	2112	...
Salbris ...... d.	0631	0704	0709	...	0731	0725	...	...	0808	0909	|	...	1428	...	1625	1709	1809	1917	1917	1908	1909	...	2009	2126	...
Les Aubrais-Orléans ...... 310 a.	|	|	|	...	|	0752	...	...	|	|	1121	...	1455	...	1650	|	|	1950	1950	|	|	...	|	2154	...
Orléans ...... 310 a.	0710	0740	0745	...	0810	|	...	...	0845	0945	|	...	|	...	|	1745	1845	|	|	1945	1946	...	2045	|	...
Paris Austerlitz ...... 310 a.	...	...	...	...	...	0853	...	...	...	...	1219	...	1553	...	1753	...	...	2053	2049	...	...	...	...	2253	...

LOCAL TRAINS VIERZON - BOURGES (see also Table **290**)

	Ⓐ	⑥	Ⓐ	⚒	L	⚒M	H			Ⓐ	
Vierzon ...... d.	0618	0657	0740	0840	1040	1240	1440	1640	1836	1940	...
Bourges ...... a.	0646	0726	0808	0908	1108	1308	1508	1709	1903	2008	...

	Ⓐ		Ⓐ	Ⓐ N		⚒P	Ⓐ	Ⓐ		Ⓐ	
Bourges ...... d.	0653	0752	0852	1052	...	1252	1452	1553	1652	1750	1853
Vierzon ...... a.	0720	0820	0920	1120	...	1320	1520	1621	1720	1820	1920

A – Dec. 12, 13, Feb. 6 - 9, Mar. 6 - 9.
B – Daily Dec. 11 - Feb. 5; ⑤⑥⑦ Feb. 10 - 19; daily Feb. 22 - Mar. 5, Mar. 10 - Apr. 1 (not Dec. 12, 13).
C – Daily Dec. 11 - 31; ④⑤⑥ Jan. 5 - Feb. 18; daily Feb. 23 - Apr. 1.
D – ①②③⑦ Jan. 1 - Feb. 22.
E – Ⓐ Dec. 12 - 30; ⑤ Jan. 6 - Feb. 24; Ⓐ Feb. 27 - Mar. 31.
F – Not Jan. 2 - 4, 13, Feb. 20 - 24, Mar. 1, 21 - 23, 28, 29.
G – ①②③④⑦ only.
H – Not Ⓐ Dec. 19 - 30.

J – ⚒ Dec. 12 - 31; ⑥ Jan. 7 - Feb. 25; daily Feb. 27 - Mar. 18; ①⑤⑥ Mar. 20 - Apr. 1 (also Mar. 30; not Mar. 1).
K – Dec. 12 - 30, Feb. 27 - Mar. 31 (not Mar. 28, 29).
L – Dec. 11 - 18, 24, 25, 31, Jan. 1 - Feb. 19, Feb. 25, 26, 28, Mar. 1 - 12, 15 - 20, 25 - 27, 31, Apr. 1 (not Jan. 13).
M – Not Jan. 2 - 4, 10, 13, Feb. 20 - 24, 27, Mar. 21 - 24, 28 - 30.
N – Not Jan. 10, 13, Feb. 20 - 28, Mar. 1 - 3, 21 - 24.
P – Not Dec. 19 - 30, Jan. 2 - 4, 13, Feb. 20 - 27, Mar. 13, 14, 21 - 24, 28 - 30.

a – Ⓐ only.
j – Not Feb. 6 - 9.
r – Not ①②③④ Jan. 2 - Feb. 2, Feb. 22, 23.
t – Not Jan. 10.
⊖ – To/from Nevers (Table **290**).
▷ – For additional trains see below main table.
• – Via Bourges (Montluçon is *327* km direct).

316 BRIVE - FIGEAC - RODEZ

km		3755 Aa [R]	3755 Ab [R]	⚒	Ⓑ	Ⓐ		Ⓐ		Ⓑ
	Paris Austerlitz 310 ...... d.	2212	2212	...	...	...	...	...	...	...
0	**Brive la Gaillarde** ...... 311 d.	0345	0345	0608	0732j	1124j	1326j	1616	1825	2225
27	St Denis-près-Martel ...... 311 d.	0410	0411	0634	0758j	1150j	1352j	1646	1859	2249
45	Rocamadour-Padirac ...... d.	0426	0428	0649	0814j	1205j	1408j	1701	1914	2304
53	Gramat ...... d.	0435	0436	0656	0821j	1212j	1416j	1708	1921	2311
88	Figeac ...... 317 d.	0506	0510	0724	0849j	1240j	1444j	1735	1950	2339
94	Capdenac ...... 317 d.	0514	0519	0733	0856	1249	1452	1742	1959	2346
109	Viviez-Decazeville ...... d.	0530	0535	0747	0911	1304	1506	1757	2014	0001
161	**Rodez** ...... 323 a.	0617	0627	0832	0954	1349	1550	1841	2059	0045
227	Carmaux ...... 323 a.	0737f	0749f	...	...	...	...	...	...	...
244	**Albi** ...... 323 a.	0758f	0810f	...	...	...	...	...	...	...

	⚒	†	Ⓐ						3754 B [R]
Albi ...... 323 d.	...	...	...	...	...	...	...	...	2053e
Carmaux ...... 323 d.	...	...	...	...	...	...	...	...	2112e
Rodez ...... 323 d.	0631	0824	1021	1218	1420	1624	1752	...	2241
Viviez-Decazeville ...... d.	0717	0912	1106	1305	1507	1710	1841	...	2329
Capdenac ...... 317 d.	0732	0926	1122	1321	1524	1727	1901	...	2347
Figeac ...... 317 d.	0738	0933	1129j	1329j	1531	1736	1912	...	2355
Gramat ...... d.	0806	1001	1157j	1359j	1559	1805	1945	...	0027
Rocamadour-Padirac ...... d.	0815	1008	1206j	1409j	1606	1813	1952	...	0035
St Denis-près-Martel ...... 311 d.	0830	1023	1222j	1429j	1621	1829	2008	...	0051
Brive la Gaillarde ...... 311 a.	0856	1048	1245j	1453j	1645	1854	2032	...	0115
Paris Austerlitz 310 ...... a.	...	...	...	...	...	...	...	...	0652

A – Daily; not Dec. 25, Jan. 1 (from Paris): 🛏 1, 2 cl. and [2] (reclining) Paris (**3751/3**) - Brive - Rodez. Runs Paris - Brive - Rodez (**3757**) - Albi on ⑤.
B – Daily; also Mar. 27; not Dec. 24, 31, Mar. 28 (from Albi and Rodez): 🛏 1, 2 cl. and [2] (reclining) Rodez - Brive (**3750/2**) - Paris. Runs Albi (**3756**) - Rodez - Brive - Paris on ⑦.

a – Until Feb. 24.
b – From Mar. 3.
e – ⑦ only.
f – ⑥ only.
j – Not Mar. 27 - 31.

317 AURILLAC - FIGEAC - TOULOUSE

km		Ⓐ		†	⚒ q	Ⓐ	D		k	f
	Clermont Ferrand 331 ...... d.	...	...	...	...	...	...	...	...	...
0	**Aurillac** ...... d.	...	0646q	...	0847	...	1255	1652t	1831	2117
65	Figeac ...... 316 d.	0605	0805	1004	1004	1204t	1404	1805	1946	2230
71	Capdenac ...... 316 d.	0614	0814	1014	1014	1212j	1413	1815	...	...
100	Villefranche de Rouergue ...... d.	0641	0844	1044	1044	1239j	1442	1844	...	...
117	Najac ...... d.	0656	0859	1058	1058	1254j	1457	1859	...	...
170	Gaillac ...... 323 d.	0742	0949	1143	1143	1340	1543	1947	...	...
224	**Toulouse** Matabiau ...... 323 a.	0831	1031	1221	1221	1421	1623	2029	...	...

	⚒ n	①	②–⑤	†	⚒ A	n		Ⓐ	
Toulouse Matabiau .... 323 d.	...	0533	0654	0857	0857	1303	1704	1811	1909
Gaillac ...... 323 d.	...	0611	0742	0937	0937	1340	1742	1853	1947
Najac ...... d.	...	0657	0828j	1028	1028	1426	1828	1939	2034
Villefranche de Rouergue ... d.	...	0713	0843j	1043	1043	1443	1843	1954	2049
Capdenac ...... 316 d.	0547	0740	0914j	1112	1112	1513	1912	2022	2118
Figeac ...... 316 d.	0559	0747	0921r	1119	1120	1521	1918	2031	2125
Aurillac ...... a.	0724	...	...	...	1228	1633	2029f	2140t	2233c
Clermont Ferrand 331 ..... a.	...	...	...	...	...	1905	...	...	...

A – Gaillac - Capdenac: not Mar. 14 - 17, 20 - 24; Capdenac - Figeac: not Ⓐ Mar. 13 - 31; Figeac - Aurillac: runs ⚒ until Mar. 12 only.
D – Aurillac - Figeac: not Mar. 13 - 31; Figeac - Capdenac: not Ⓐ Mar. 13 - 31; Capdenac - Toulouse: not Ⓐ Mar. 17 - 24.

c – Ⓒ (not Mar. 18 - 26).
f – ⑤ (not Mar. 17 - 31).
j – Not Mar. 13 - 24.
k – Daily **except** ⑤.
n – Until Mar. 12.
q – ⚒ (not Ⓐ Mar. 13 - 24).
r – Not Mar. 14 - 31.
t – Not Mar. 13 - 31.

318 BORDEAUX - LIBOURNE - BERGERAC - SARLAT

km		①	Ⓐ	⚒			Ⓐ k	Ⓒ		⚒ k	Ⓐ k	k			Ⓐ	Ⓐ			Ⓐ		⑥–④	⑤		Ⓑ
0	**Bordeaux** St Jean ...... ▷ d.	...	0605	0705	0805	...	...	1005	...	1205	1305	1405	...	1605	1705	...	...	1805	1905	...	2005	2005	...	2205
37	Libourne ...... ▷ d.	...	0630	0732	0832	...	1031	1031	...	1235	1334	1431	...	1631	1734	1756	...	1834	1932	...	2031	2031	...	2233
77	Ste Foy la Grande ...... d.	...	0709	0812	0911	...	1110	1110	...	1309	1413	1512	...	1708	1810	1837	...	1911	2009	...	2109	2109	...	2308
99	**Bergerac** ...... a.	...	0730	0832	0930	...	1128	1128	...	1329	1433	1531	...	1727	1829	1858	...	1929	2029	...	2129	2129	...	2326
99	**Bergerac** ...... d.	0550	0735	...	0933j	...	1132	1132	...	...	...	1534r	...	1732	...	...	...	1934	...	...	...	2132	...	...
135	Le Buisson ...... d.	0627	0820	...	1018j	...	1217	1218	...	...	...	1618r	...	1820	...	...	...	2018	...	...	...	2205	...	...
168	**Sarlat** ...... a.	0658	0850	...	1046j	...	1246	1246	...	...	...	1646r	...	1850	...	...	...	2046	...	...	...	2235	...	...

	Ⓐ	Ⓐ	⚒	Ⓐ		Ⓐ	†	⚒		k	Ⓐ k		m	Ⓒ	Ⓐ k		j	Ⓑ			Ⓐ		⑤†	
Sarlat ...... d.	...	...	...	...	...	0607	...	0707	...	0909	...	...	1105	1325	...	...	1504	...	...	1705	...	...	1909	...
Le Buisson ...... d.	...	...	...	...	...	0641	...	0737	...	0939	...	...	1136	1356	...	...	1534	...	...	1736	...	...	1939	...
Bergerac ...... a.	...	...	...	...	...	0728	...	0829	...	1029	...	...	1225	1429	...	...	1628	...	...	1828	...	...	2028	...
Bergerac ...... d.	0530	0609	0627	0702	...	0733	0834	0835	...	1032	1134	...	1228	1432	1436	...	1631	1730	...	1832	1932	...	2032	...
Ste Foy la Grande ...... d.	0550	0628	0647	0725	...	0752	0853	0854	...	1052	1152	...	1249	1454	1455	...	1650	1751	...	1853	1951	...	2051	...
Libourne ...... ▷ d.	0624	0705	0729	0804	...	0827	0929	0929	...	1129	1227	...	1328	1528	1528	...	1728	1831	...	1927	2027	...	2128	...
Bordeaux St Jean ...... ▷ a.	0650	0729	0755	...	...	0853	0953	0953	...	1153	1253	...	1353	1553	...	...	1753	1855	...	1953	2053	...	2153	...

j – Not Ⓐ Mar. 6 - 24.
k – Not Ⓐ Mar. 6 - 31.
m – Not Mar. 4 - Apr. 1.
r – Not Mar. 18 - 26.
▷ – See also Tables **300** and **302**.

BORDEAUX - TOULOUSE   320

For Paris - Toulouse via Limoges see Table 310

km			4655 4654 ✕	4657 4656 ★	TGV 8501 ★	4659 4658 ①–⑥	TGV 8503 ★	4663 4662 ★		4665 4664 ★ ⑤	4665 4664 ★ ①–④	4665 4664 ★ ⑥⑦		TGV 8507 ⑤	TGV 8505 ⑥–④		4673 4672 ★ A	4667 4666 ★ ⑤⑦		4669 4668 ★	TGV 8511		TGV 8513 ⑤	TGV 8515 ⑤
	Paris M'parnasse 300 .... d.	...	...	...	0628	...	0928	...	...	...	...	...	...	1128	1228	...	...	...	...	...	1528	...	1828	1928
	Nantes 292 .... d.	...	...	...	...	...	...	...	...	...	...	...	...	...	...	...	...	...	...	...	...	...	...	...
0	**Bordeaux** St Jean .... d.	...	0731	0931	0947	1047	1247	1331	...	1437	1440t	1444f	...	1447	1547	...	1637	1645e	...	1729	1847	...	2147	2247
79	Marmande .... d.	...	...	...	...	...	1409		...				...			...		1809	...					
136	Agen .... d.	0825	0840	1040	1051	...	1353	1441	...	1553	1651	1714	...		1825	1841	1953	2025	2254	2351
206	Montauban .... d.	0914	0918	1118	1129	...	1432		...	1631	1729	1811	1819		1913	1918	2032	2114	2332	0029
257	**Toulouse** Matabiau .... a.	0941	0944	1144	1155	1252	1457	1544	...	1649	1649	1645	...	1657	1755	1840	1846	1846	1940	1944	2057	2140	2359	0055
	Narbonne 321 .... a.	...	1101	1301	...	...	...	1701	...				...			2002			2101			
	Montpellier 355 .... a.	...	1200	1401	...	1459	...	1801	...	1857	1857	1857	...	2104	2101		2159			
	Marseille 355 .... a.	...	1344j	1543	...	1641	...	1942	...	2040	2040	2040	...	2301	2237		2347			
	Nice 360 .... a.	...	...	...	1941r	...	...	...	2337	...	2337		...					

		TGV 8500 ①–⑥ z		TGV 8510		TGV 8512 ⑦	4754 4755 ★	TGV 8514		4756 4757 ★	TGV 8516	4760 4761 ★		TGV 8518	4762 4763 ★	4764 4765 ★		4768 4769 ★ B
		Ⓐ										y				Ⓐ		
Nice 360 .... d.	...	...	...	...	...	...	...	...	...	1022	...	...	...	...	1415
Marseille 355 .... d.	...	...	...	...	0815	...	...	1017	...	1318	...	1415	1518	...	1718
Montpellier 355 .... d.	...	...	...	...	0958	...	...	1158	...	1458	...	1558	1658	...	1858
Narbonne 321 .... d.	...	...	...	...	1059	...	...	1259	...	...	...	1659	...	...	...
Toulouse Matabiau .... d.	0604	0611	0655	0904	...	1104	1221	1304	1322	...	1418	1604	1710	1720	...	1804	1818	1822	1912	1920	...	2112
Montauban .... d.	0632	0640	0726	0932	...	1132		1332	1351	...	1444	1632		1749	...	1832	1844	1851	1949	...	
Agen .... d.	0710	0735	0817	1010	...	1210	1321	1410	1439	...	1522	1710		1837	...	1910	1921	1938	2037	...	
Marmande .... d.	...	...	...	...	...	...	1351		...	1552			...	1951	...		
Bordeaux St Jean .... a.	0812	...	...	1113	...	1312	1429	1512	...	1629	1813	1914	...	2012	2030	...	2113	...	2313
Nantes 292 .... a.	...	...	...	...	...	...	...	...	...	...	...	...	...	...	...	...	...	...	...
Paris M'parnasse 300 .... a.	1136	...	...	1439	...	1633		1833	...	2133	...	...	2333	...	...	...

FOR NOTES SEE TABLE 321 BELOW

Local trains Bordeaux - Agen (journey approx 90 mins):   *Subject to minor retiming*
From Bordeaux: 0552①, 0638✕, 0710Ⓐ, 1052, 1252✕, 1452, 1650Ⓑ, 1752, 1852, 2052Ⓑ.
From Agen: 0441✕, 0535Ⓐ, 0610⑥, 0626Ⓐ, 0739Ⓐ, 0841†, 1039, 1226⑥, 1240Ⓐ, 1444, 1640Ⓑ, 1732Ⓑ, 1840, 1947†.

TOULOUSE - CARCASSONNE - NARBONNE   321

km		TGV 6869 ♦	4655 4654 Ⓐ	✕	4657 4656 ★ Ⓐ	4659 4658 ★	Ⓒ	TGV 6861 Ⓐ	4663 4662 ★		4665 4664 ★ ⑤	4665 4664 ★ ①–④	4665 4664 ★ ⑥⑦		TGV 6857 Ⓐ	4673 4672 ★ A	4667 4666 ★ ⑤⑦	Ⓐ	4669 4668 ★
	Paris Austerlitz 310 .... d.	...	...	...	0731	...	0931	...	1047	...	...	1331	...	1437	1440t	1444f	...	...	1637	1645e	...	1729
	Bordeaux 320 .... d.	...	...	...	0731	...	0931	...	1047	...	1331	...	1437	1440t	1444f	...	...	1637	1645e	...	1729
0	**Toulouse** Matabiau .... d.	0545	0613	0713	0812	0948	1012	1149	1210	1257	1311	1445	1549	1553	1651	1650	1650	1655	...	1750	1753	1849	1851	1854	1948
55	Castelnaudary .... d.	...	0702	0749	0902		1101		1300		1400		1632		1732		1832		1932	
91	**Carcassonne** .... d.	0634	0729	0816	0927	1033	1128	1233	1327		1427	1533	1633	1659		1759		1837	1858	1935		1959	2033
128	Lézignan .... d.	...	0746	0835	0945		1145		1345		1445		1716		1816		1915		2016	
150	Narbonne .... a.	0701	0758	0849	0957	1101	1157	1301	1357		1457	1601	1701	1728		1828	1902	1928	2002		2028	2101
	Montpellier 355 .... a.	0758	...	...	...	1200	...	1401	...	1459	...	1701	1801	...	1857	1857	1857	1932	...	2001	...	2104	2101	...	2159
	Marseille 355 .... a.		...	...	1344j		1543		1641		1942		2040	2040	2040		...		2301	2237	...	2347
	Nice 360 .... a.		...	...			1941r						2337	...	2337					
	Lyon Part Dieu 350 .... a.	0950	...	...					1850							2150				
	Perpignan 355 .... a.	...	...	...	...	...	...	...	...	...	...	...	...	...	...	...	...	...	...	...
	Cerbère 355 .... a.	...	...	...	...	...	...	...	...	...	...	...	...	...	...	...	...	...	...	...
	Portbou 355 .... a.	...	...	...	...	...	...	...	...	...	...	...	...	...	...	...	...	...	...	...

		TGV 6809 Ⓐ	4754 4755 Ⓐ	✕	TGV 6813 Ⓐ	4756 4757 ★		4760 4761 Ⓐ		4762 4763 ★	4764 4765 ★		4768 4769 ★ B	4766 4767 ⑤⑦	TGV 6824 ♦
Cerbère 355 .... d.	...	...	...	...	...	...	...	...	...	...	...	...	...	...	...
Perpignan 355 .... d.	...	...	...	...	...	...	...	...	...	...	...	...	...	...	...
Lyon Part Dieu 350 .... d.	...	...	0706	...	0936	...	...	...	...	...	...	...	...	1936
Nice 360 .... d.	...	...	...	...	...	...	1022	...	...	...	1415	...	...	...
Marseille 355 .... d.	...	...	...	...	0815	...	1017	...	1318	...	1415	1518	...	1718	1918
Montpellier 355 .... d.	...	0617	0859	0958	...	1131	1158	...	1458	...	1558	1620	1658	...	1858	2058	...	2130
Narbonne .... d.	0632	0703	0732	0958	1059	...	1228	1259	1503		1603	1632		1659	1732	...	1803	1917	...	2159	2228
Lézignan .... d.	0645	0716	0745		...				1516		1616	1645			1745	...	1816	1930	...	
Carcassonne .... d.	0704	0735	0804	1029	1129		1256	1327	1535		1635	1709		1728	1804	...	1835	1949	...	2230	2259
Castelnaudary .... d.	0725	0756	0825						1556		1656	1727			1825	...	1856	2010	...	
Toulouse Matabiau ...... a.	0808	0845	0905	1111	1216		1341	1413	1645		1707	1745	1809		1813	1904	1907	...	1945	2059	2107	2313	...	2343
Bordeaux 320 .... a.	...	...	...	1429	...	1629	...	1914	...	2030	...	2113	...	2313
Paris Austerlitz 310 ...... a.	...	...	...	...	...	...	...	...	...	...	...	...	...	...

ADDITIONAL LOCAL TRAINS

	Ⓐ	Ⓐ		Ⓐ	Ⓒ	Ⓐ	Ⓐ	Ⓐ				Ⓐ	Ⓐ	Ⓒ			Ⓒ	Ⓐ	Ⓐ
Toulouse Mat. .... d.	...	...	0650	...	...	...	...	1715	1753	1955	**Narbonne** .... d.	...	0808	0908	1008	...	...	1713	1845
Castelnaudary .... d.	0552	...	0730	...	...	...	...	1805	1832	2045	Lézignan .... d.	...	0821	0921	1021	...	...	1727	1845
Carcassonne .... d.	0617	0645	0756	1011	1113	1727	1819	1827	1858	2109	**Carcassonne** ...... d.	0602	0636	0838	0941	1040	1202	...	1535	1744	1902
Lézignan .... d.	0634	0705		1032	1132	1745	1837		1915	...	Castelnaudary .... d.	0624	0656				1224	...	1556	...	
Narbonne .... a.	0647	0716		1045	1145	1758	1850		1928	...	**Toulouse** Mat. ..... a.	0704	0745				1304	...	1645	...	

♦ – NOTES FOR TABLES 320/1 (LISTED BY TRAIN NUMBER):

6824 – 🛏 🍴 Nancy - Dijon - Lyon - Montpellier - Toulouse.
6869 – 🛏 🍴 Toulouse - Montpellier - Lyon - Dijon - Nancy.

A – ①–④ from Jan. 23.
B – ①⑥⑦ only.

e – Depart 1640 Feb. 24 - Mar. 5.
f – Depart 1439 Feb. 25 - Mar. 5.
j – 9 minutes later Mar. 1 - 5.

r – 5 minutes later Jan. 14, 21.
t – 7 minutes later from Mar. 6.
v – 5 – 7 minutes later Feb. 20 - Mar. 5.
y – Not Jan. 28, 29, Feb. 4.
z – Not Jan. 28.

TGV – 🅁, supplement payable, 🍴.

★ – *Intercités* service, 🅁.

323 — TOULOUSE - ALBI - RODEZ - MILLAU

km		Ⓐ			①⑤			Ⓐ				Ⓐ	Ⓐ	Ⓐ	Ⓐ	†	✕	P Ⓡ		
0	Toulouse Matabiau ...... 317 d.	0607	0727	0915	1006	...	1117	1231	...	1307	1412	...	1637	1713	1737	1752	...	1814	1837	1914	1914	1928	...	2115
54	Gaillac .... 317 d.	0647	0812	1003	1052	...	1158	1318	...	1358	1500	...	1725	1757	1823	1841	...	1905	1922	2003	2019	...	2159
75	Albi Ville .... d.	0704	0826	1024	1108	...	1216	1338	...	1418	1514	...	1745	1818	1837	1902	...	1924	1935	2024	2025	2035	2053	2221
92	Carmaux .... d.	0722	0843	1039	1124	...	1233	1353	...	1433	1533	...	1801	...	1854	1918	...	...	1952	...	2041	2051	2112	2236
158	Rodez .... a.	0823	0946	...	1221	...	1332	...	...	1632	...	...	1952	...	...	2049	...	...	2138	2150	2209	...

		Ⓐ	✕	Ⓐ		Ⓐ	Pa Ⓡ	Pb Ⓡ	0739d	0836		1026		1224		Ⓐ		1435		1636	1730		1845	2055	† ✕
	Rodez .... d.					0622	0644	0653																	2057	
	Carmaux	0522	0558	0618	0646	0723	0739	0751	0844	0933	...	1125	1143	1321	...	1456	1532	1650	1735	1827	...	1953	2203	2204
	Albi Ville	0538	0614	0634	0705	0741	0758	0810	0901	0949	...	1141	1200	1340	...	1515	1548	1707	1753	1845	...	2009	2220	2222
	Gaillac .... 317 d.	0556	0633	0657	0725	0756	...	...	0919	1003	...	1158	1221	1358	...	1534	1602	1725	1808	1905	...	2031	2233	2233
	Toulouse Matabiau ..... 317 a.	0646	0719	0743	0820	0836	...	...	1000	1043	...	1237	1310	1437	...	1619	1641	1818	1850	1954	...	2118	2313	2313

km		②–⑤	⑥	①		Ⓑ	⑥	Ⓐ		†			①	Ⓑ		Ⓒ	⑤	①–④	①–④ z	⑤
0	Rodez .... d.	0624	0635	0705		1351	1715	1916		2038		Millau 332 .... d.	0455	0907		1522	1629	1753	2046	2107
44	Sévérac-le-Château 332 ..d.	0707	0718	0748		1435	1758	1959		2130		Sévérac-le-Château 332 .... d.	0527	0939		1552	1706	1823	2117	2138
74	Millau 332 .... a.	0739	0750	0820		1507	1830	2031		2202		Rodez .... d.	0608	1020		1635	1748	1906	2200	2220

P – ▬ 1, 2 cl. and ⊏⊐ (reclining) Paris - Brive - Rodez - Albi
and v.v. For days of running see Table **316**.

a – Until Feb. 24.
b – From Mar. 3.

d – ✕ only.
z – Not Jan. 2.

324 — PAU - OLORON - CANFRANC

km		🚌 ©P		🚌 Ⓐ	Ⓐ				©				Ⓐ				🚌 G	⑤†		
0	Pau .... d.			0730	...	0922	...	1225	...	1408	...	...	1532	...	1711	...	1834	1855	...	2025
36	Oloron-Ste-Marie .... d.	0700		0806	0815	...	0958	...	1300	1310	1444	...	1607	...	1747	...	1910	1931	...	2100
61	Bedous (Gare) .... d.	0733		...	0848	...	1027	1040	1343	1513	1525	...	...	1816	1830	...	1945	2000	...
77	Urdos (Douane) 🚋 .... d.	0755		...	0910	...	1102	1405	...	1547	...	...	1852	...	...	...	
96	Canfranc (Gare) .... 670 a.	0813		...	0928	...	1120	1423	...	1605	...	...	1910	...	...	...	

		①	②–⑤	⑥		🚌 Ⓐ	†	Ⓐ	©P	©			🚌 Ⓐ				🚌 G	🚌 G	⑤†	⑤†	🚌
	Canfranc (Gare) .... 670 d.	...	...	...		0835	...	1146		...	1446	...	...	1747		1807		...	1945
	Urdos (Douane) 🚋 .... d.	...	...	...		0852	...	1203		...	1503	...	...	1804		1823		...	2002
	Bedous (Gare) .... d.	...	...	0737		0915	0929	1226	1239	...	1526	1539	...	1827	1841	1847	1902	...	2025
	Oloron-Ste-Marie .... d.	0639	0646	0722	0810	0810	1002	...	1002	...	1308	1447	...	1612	1751	...	1914	1935	2101
	Pau .... a.	0714	0721	0757	0845	0845	1037	...	1037	...	1343	1522	...	1647	1826	...	1949	2010	...

G – ①②③④⑥ only.
P – Until Mar. 12.

325 — TOULOUSE - TARBES - PAU - BAYONNE - HENDAYE

km		Ⓐ	Ⓐ	⑥	Ⓐ			14143 N	14343 K	J		14145 K	14245 J	N	✕ Q		14151 14451 Q	†	Ⓐ Q		14155 14555 Q
0	Toulouse Matabiau ....d.	...	...	...	0600	...	0731	0931	1031	1031	...	1233	1232	1241	1441	...	1555	1631	...	1736	1806	...	1831	1941	2041
91	St Gaudens .... d.	...	...	...	0718	...	0829	1027	1119	1118	...			1352	1552	...	1650	1719	...	1833	1902	...		2051	2151
104	Montréjeau .... d.	...	...	...	0728	...	0838	1037			...	1328	1328	1401	1602	...	1700		...	1842	1912	...		2101	2200
121	Lannemezan .... d.	...	...	...	0740	...	0850	1049			...			1413	1618	...	1713		...	1854	1925	...	1940	2113	2213
158	Tarbes .... 305 d.	...	0628	0635	0809	...	0923	1122	1204	1206	...	1403	1407	1446	1644	...	1742	1804	...	1925	1954	...	2008	2144	2246
179	Lourdes .... 305 d.	...		0651	0825	...			1220	1221	...	1418	1422	1503f	1702	...		1820	...	1943		...	2023	2202	2302
218	Pau .... 305 d.	0614	0721	0730	0856	0936	...		1250	1250	...	1447	1450	1533f	1730	1736	...	1849	1936	2015	...		2051	2233	...
258	Orthez .... 305 d.	0638	0745	0800		1000	...		1313	1313	...	1511	1514		1802	...		1913	2000	...	2115	...	
272	Puyoô .... 305 d.	0649	0756	0813		1011	...				...				1813	...			2011	...		
323	Bayonne § .... 305 d.	0737	0837	0858		1058	...		1359	1359	...	1556	1556		1856	...		1955	2059	...	2157	...	
323	Bayonne § .... 305 d.	...	...	...			...				...					...				...		
333	Biarritz § .... 305 d.	...	...	...			...				...					...				...		
346	St Jean de Luz ...... 305 d.	...	...	...			...				...					...				...		
359	Hendaye .... 305 d.	...	...	...			...				...					...				...		
361	Irún .... 305 a.	...	...	...			...				...					...				...		

		Ⓐ R	©	⑥	Ⓑ R	Ⓐ	✕	Ⓐ PR	⑥	† w	Ⓐ PR	PR			14140 J	14240 K	14340 R		14244 M	14144 R		14148 Q		⑤ Q	⑦–④	Ⓑ		14150	†
	Hendaye .... 305 d.	...	...	...	...	...	...		...	...																		
	St Jean de Luz ...... 305 d.																											
	Biarritz § .... 305 d.																											
	Bayonne § .... 305 d.																											
	Bayonne § .... 305 d.				0608	0704	0805	0805	0805					1203	1203		1411		1603			1724	1803	2002	
	Puyoô .... 305 d.				0646	0745											1448					1806		2046	
	Orthez .... 305 d.				0657	0756											1459		1654			1817	1854	2058	
	Pau .... 305 d.	...	0549	0555	0727	0823	0914	0914	0914	0950	1212		1312	1314		1525	1548f	1717	1750	1750	1844	1919	2132	
	Lourdes .... 305 d.	0527	0520	0618	0624	0803	...	0944	0944	1019	1241		1342	1345		1617f	1742	1819	1819	1920	1945	2206	
	Tarbes .... 305 d.	0543	0535	0636	0640	0821	...	1000	1000	1000	1035	1300		1358	1402	1520		1633	1758	1838	1838	1938	2003	2222
	Lannemezan .... d.	0612		0603	0707	0709	...			1105	1330		1425	1428	1549		1701		1909	1909	2029	
	Montréjeau .... d.	0625	0615	0720	0722	...			1120	1344				1602		1716		1922	1923	...	
	St Gaudens .... d.	0633	0625	0729	0732	...	1045	1045	1045	1130	1354			1611		1726	1843	1932	1933	...	
	Toulouse Matabiau ....a.	0730	0735	0832	0830	...	1132	1132	1132	1232	1459		1532	1532	1722		1828	1932	2030	2030	...	2139	

TOULOUSE - LUCHON
For connections Toulouse - Montréjeau see also main table. 🚌 subject to confirmation

		©	🚌 ©	🚌 Ⓐ	🚌 A	🚌 ✕		🚌 Ⓐ	🚌
	Paris Aust. **310** ....d.	...	...	...	...	...	...	...	...
	Toulouse Mat. ....d.	0700		0741		...	1639	1700	...	1741	1900	...
	St Gaudens	0809		0856		...	1744	1816	...	1851	2020	...
	Montréjeau .... ♣ d.	0817	0836	0904	0932	1126	1608	1752	1826	1846	1859	2028	2108
	Luchon .... ♣ a.	...	0931	...	1022	1214	1656	...	1934	...	2156

		Ⓐ	Ⓐ	🚌 Ⓐ	🚌 P	Ⓐ	🚌	🚌 ©	©	🚌
	Luchon .... ♣ d.	...	...	0933	1054	...	1454	1605	...	1703	...	1800
	Montréjeau .... ♣ d.	0520	0557	0638	1023	1145	1155	1544	1655	1804	1754	1845	1851
	St Gaudens .... d.	0529	0606	0647		1204			1814		1854	
	Toulouse Mat. ...... a.	0645	0723	0757		1322			1922		1959	
	Paris Aust. **310** ..a.										

A – Ⓐ until Mar. 26; daily from Mar. 27.
J – Dec. 16 - Jan. 20.
K – Daily Jan. 21 - Feb. 5; ⓒ Feb. 11 - Mar. 5; daily Mar. 6 - Apr. 1.
M – Not Ⓐ Feb. 6 - Mar. 3.
N – Not Ⓐ Feb. 6 - 17.
P – Not Ⓐ Feb. 20 - Mar. 3.
Q – From Dec. 15.
R – From Dec. 16.

f – ⑤ only.
w – Not Dec. 11.

♣ – Additional 🚌 services **Montréjeau - Luchon and v.v.**:
From Montréjeau: 0726⑥, 0732Ⓐ, 0800✕, 1337†, 1420✕.
From Luchon: 0612⑥, 0617Ⓐ, 0846✕, 1223†, 1740⑥, 2000†.

§ – 🚌 services available to/from Biarritz town.

BRIVE LA GAILLARD and LIMOGES - USSEL - CLERMONT FERRAND 326

BRIVE - USSEL

km			4490		🚌	4492					
		Ⓐ		Ⓒ	Ⓐ	⑥p		Ⓑ		⑦	
			F				◇	h		e	
	Bordeaux **302** d.	...	0735	...	...	0910	...	...	...	...	...
0	**Brive la Gaillarde** ▷ d.	0620	0957	1019	1107	1115	1346	1710	1832	1920	...
26	Tulle ▷ d.	0652	1042z	1050	1147	1155z	1417	1751r	1910	1951	...
79	Meymac d.	0747	1146	1146	1255	1257	1511	1845	2008	2045	...
92	**Ussel** a.	0758	1200	1158	1317	1310	1523	1858	2019	2057	...

							4591			
	Ⓐ	⑥				⑤⑦	⑤†	①–④	⑥	Ⓑ
		k		⊖		d	E	w	k	h
Ussel d.	0545	0935	...	1204	...	1545	1619	1631	1716	1954
Meymac d.	0558	0948	...	1217	...	1559	1634	1644	1729	2007
Tulle ▷ d.	0656	1046	...	1314	...	1703r	1749r	1745r	1827	2107
Brive la Gaillarde ▷ a.	0725	1111	...	1339	...	1729	1811	1812	1853	2133
Bordeaux **302** a.	...	...	...	...	...	...	2028	...	...	...

LIMOGES - USSEL

km		①							Ⓐ		
		g				⊗				L	
0	**Limoges** d.	0557	...	1001	...	1319	...	1802	1937	2109	...
98	Meymac d.	0732	...	1132	...	1454	...	1938	2109	2237	...
111	**Ussel** a.	0744	...	1143	...	1506	...	1950	2121	2250	...

	Ⓐ	⑥	①						⑤⑦	
		k	g	⊕	⊙		B		d	
Ussel d.	0632	0702	0813	1031	1219	...	1353	...	1603	1754
Meymac d.	0645	0715	0826	1045	1232	...	1406	...	1616	1807
Limoges a.	0819	0849	0959	1223	1402	...	1536	...	1747	1947

🚌 USSEL and LE MONT DORE - CLERMONT FERRAND 🚌

	🚌	🚌	🚌	🚌	🚌	🚌	🚌	🚌	🚌	🚌	🚌	🚌	🚌	🚌	🚌
	①–⑥	①–⑥	①–⑥	⑦			⑥	Ⓒ		⑤†		⑤	⑤	⑦	Ⓑ
	b	b	b	s			p	t		v	H	f	f	s	
Ussel d.	...	0818	...	1008	...	1207	1319	1511	...	...	...	...	1915	...	2033
Le Mont Dore d.	0541	|	0841	|	1043	|	|	|	1533	1728	1743	1928	|	2046	|
Laqueuille d.	0603	0858	0903	1048	1105	1247	1359	1550	1556	1750	1805	1950	1955	2108	2113
Clermont Ferrand a.	0727y	...	1003	...	1229	1347	1459	...	1722	*1909*	1910	...	2055	...	2213

	🚌	🚌	🚌	🚌	🚌	🚌	🚌	🚌	🚌	🚌	🚌	🚌	🚌	🚌	🚌
			⑦	⑥		Ⓐ	⑤†	⚒	①–⑥			Ⓐ	⑤	⑤	⑦
			s	k			E		b	D			f	f	s
Clermont Ferrand d.	1010	...	*1246*	*1304*	1305	...	1424	1600	...	*1738*c	1804	1948	...	*2126*	*2145*
Laqueuille d.	1110	1115	1351	1423	1424	1436	1524	1700	1705	1859	1904	2048	2053	2221	2240
Le Mont Dore a.	|	1136	|	|	1448	|	|	|	1729	1922	|	2111	|	2244	2303
Ussel a.	1150	...	1431	1503	...	1516	1604	1740	...	...	1944	...	2131	...	...

B – ①②③④⑥ (not Apr. 17, May 1, 8, 24, June 5). Subject to alteration ①–④ Apr. 18 - May 18.
D – 🚌 runs 7 minutes later on †.
E – ⑤† (also Dec. 19–22, 24, 26–29, 31, Jan. 2, May 24; not Dec. 25, Jan. 1, Apr. 16, 30, May 7, 26, June 4).
F – ①–⑤ Dec. 16 - Jan. 2; ⑤ from Jan. 6 (also May 24; not May 26).
H – ①②③④⑥ (not Jan. 2, Apr. 17, May 1, 8, 24, June 5).
L – Ⓑ to May 21; ⑤⑦ from May 26 (also May 24).

b – Not Apr. 17, May 1, 8, June 5.
c – *1726* on ⑥**k**; *1745* on ⑦**e**. By train to Volvic, then 🚌 (d. 1809 **D**).
d – Also Apr. 17, May 1, 8, 24, June 5.
e – Also Apr. 17, May 1, 8, June 5.
f – Also May 24.
g – Also Apr. 18, May 2, 9, June 6; not Apr. 17, May 1, 8, June 5.
h – Not May 25.
k – Also May 25.
p – Also May 25; not May 27.
r – Arrives 10–15 minutes earlier.
s – Also Jan. 2, Apr. 17, May 1, 8, June 5; not Apr. 16, 30, May 7, June 4.
t – Not Apr. 16, 30, May 7, June 4.
v – Also Jan. 2, May 24; not Apr. 16, 30, May 7, 25, June 4.
w – Not Dec. 19 - Jan. 2, Apr. 17, May 1–18, 24, 25, June 5.
y – On Ⓐ operated by train Volvic (d. 0659) - Clermont Ferrand.
z – Arrives 18–21 minutes earlier.

◇ – Subject to alteration Mar. 6–9, 13–16, May 2–5, 9–12, 15–18.
⊖ – Subject to alteration Mar. 6–9, 13–16, Apr. 3–6, 10–13.
⊗ – Subject to alteration Apr. 18–21, 24–28, May 2–4, 9–11, 15–18.
⊕ – Subject to alteration Apr. 18–21, 24–28, May 5, 12, 19.
⊙ – Subject to alteration Apr. 18–21, 24–28.
▷ – Additional local trains run Brive - Tulle and v.v.

MONTLUÇON - LYON 327

For other rail journeys via Riom-Châtel-Guyon see Tables **328** and **329**. Services Vichy - Lyon and v.v. are subject to alteration May 25–28.

km		🚌		🚌		🚌		🚌		🚌	
		①g	⚒	⚒	⊡	Ⓐ	Ⓐ			†	⑦e
0	**Montluçon** 329 d.	0503	...	0729	...	0947	...	1600	...	1834	...
67	Gannat 329 d.	0621	...	0849	...	|	...	|	...	|	...
90	**St Germain des Fossés** d.	|	...	|	...	1112	1141	|	...	|	...
	Vichy 330 d.	0646	0657	0918	0928	...	|	|	...	2009	2028
156	Roanne 328 d.	...	0749	...	1016	...	1229	1810	1845	...	2116
249	**Lyon** Part Dieu 328 a.	...	0856	...	1120	...	1334	...	|	...	2219
254	**Lyon** Perrache 328 a.	...	0917	...	1131	...	1347	...	2020	...	2228

		🚌		🚌		🚌		🚌		🚌
	Ⓐ	Ⓐ				⑤†j		◧		⑤†j
Lyon Perrache 328 d.	0900	...	1000	...	1629	...	1729	...	2029	...
Lyon Part Dieu 328 d.	0912	...	1012	...	1640	...	1740	...	2040	...
Roanne 328 d.	1024	...	1130	1230	1746	...	1847	...	2145	...
Vichy 330 d.	|	...	...	|	1832	1845	1934	2004	2231	2245
St Germain des Fossés d.	1107	1136	...	|	...	|	...	|	...	|
Gannat 329 d.	...	|	...	|	...	|	...	2034	...	2315
Montluçon 329 a.	...	1302	...	1435	...	2012	...	2152	...	0034

e – Also Apr. 17, May 1, 8, June 5.
g – Also Jan. 3, Apr. 18, May 2, 9, June 6; not Apr. 17, May 1, 8, June 5.
j – Also May 24; not Apr. 16, 30, May 7, June 4.
⊡ – Subject to alteration ①–⑤ Feb. 20 - Apr. 14 (also on Mar. 19).
◧ – Runs 9 minutes **earlier** on †

CLERMONT FERRAND - LYON 328

Services Clermont Ferrand - Lyon and v.v. are subject to alteration May 25–28.

km		①–⑥	Ⓐ				Ⓑ		Ⓑ	⑦	
		b		⊡	⊕	⊗	h		h	e	
0	**Clermont Ferrand** ▷ d.	0624	0705	0857	1157	1357	1457	1657	1757	1957	...
14	Riom-Châtel-Guyon ▷ d.	0634	|	0906	1207	1406	1506	1706	1806	2006	...
55	Vichy 330 d.	0657	|	0928	1228	1428	1528	1728	1828	2028	...
129	Roanne 290 ▶ d.	0749	|	1016	1316	1516	1616	1816	1916	2116	...
222	**Lyon** Part Dieu 290 ▶ a.	0856	0918	1120	1420	1620	1720	1920	2020	2219	...
227	**Lyon** Perrache 290 a.	0917	0929	1131	1435	1631	1731	1931	2032	2228	...

	①–⑥							Ⓐ	
	b		⊖						
Lyon Perrache 290 d.	0629	...	1129	1429	1629	1729	1829	1926	2029
Lyon Part Dieu 290 ▶ d.	0640	...	1140	1440	1640	1740	1840	1940	2040
Roanne 290 ▶ d.	0745	...	1245	1545	1746	1847	1944	|	2145
Vichy 330 d.	0832	...	1334	1632	1832	1935	2032	|	2232
Riom-Châtel-Guyon ▷ d.	0855	...	1356	1656	1855	1957	2054	|	2255
Clermont Ferrand ▷ a.	0904	...	1405	1706	1905	2007	2102	2154	2304

CLERMONT FERRAND - ST ÉTIENNE

km		🚌		🚌	🚌		🚌	🚌		🚌	
		⚒	Ⓐ		Ⓐ	⚒⊙	Ⓒ	⑦e	⚒		Ⓐ
0	**Clermont Ferrand** ■ d.	0700	0757	0925	1050	1216	1305	1654	1719	1920	1937
46	Thiers ■ d.	0741	0842	|	1154	1258	1409	1757	1803	|	2024
112	Montbrison d.	|	...	|	1330	...	1545	1922	...	|	...
145	**St Étienne** Châteaucreux a.	0920	...	1110	1419	...	1634	2008	...	2105	...

		🚌		🚌		🚌	🚌		🚌
	⚒		⚒⊙		⑥	Ⓐ		Ⓐ	Ⓒ
St Étienne Châteaucreux d.	...	0720	...	1216	...	1632	1720	...	1800
Montbrison d.	...	|	...	1302	...	1727	|	...	1855
Thiers ■ d.	0708	|	1324	1427	1816	1854	|	1929	2022
Clermont Ferrand ■ a.	0752	0905	1411	1530	1900	1935	1905	2014	2132

b – Not Apr. 17, May 1, 8, June 5.
e – Also Apr. 17, May 1, 8, June 5.
h – Not May 25.
k – Also May 25.
p – To Lyon Perrache (not serving Lyon Part-Dieu). Terminates at Lyon Vaise Jan. 30 - Apr. 8.

⊡ – Subject to alteration ①–⑤ Feb. 20 - Apr. 14 (also on Mar. 19).
⊗ – Subject to alteration Feb. 6–10, Mar. 6–9, 13–17.
⊕ – Subject to alteration Feb. 6–10, Mar. 13–17.
⊖ – Subject to alteration Jan. 30 - Feb. 3, Mar. 6–10 and ①–⑤ Mar. 20 - Apr. 14.
⊙ – Subject to alteration ①–⑤ Apr. 24 - May 12.
▷ – See also Tables **329** and **330**.

▶ – Other trains Roanne - Lyon Part Dieu (journey 73–95 minutes):
From Roanne at 0503 Ⓐ, 0603, 0625 Ⓐ, 0706 ①–⑥ **b**, 0718 ⑦ **e**, 0728 ①–⑥ **b**, 0831 ①–⑥ **b**, 0931, 1131, 1245 **p**, 1445 Ⓐ **p**, 1645 ①–⑥ **b p**, 1745 Ⓑ **h p**, 1845 **p**.
From Lyon Part Dieu at 0612 ①–⑥ **b**, 0712, 0812 ①–⑥ **b**, 1012, 1212, 1412 Ⓐ, 1512 ①–⑥ **b**, 1612, 1712 ①–⑥ **b**, 1812, 1912 Ⓐ, 2012 Ⓑ **h**, 2112.
■ – Other trains Clermont Ferrand - Thiers and v.v.:
From Clermont Ferrand at 1645 Ⓐ, 1739 Ⓐ, 1814 Ⓐ and 1906 Ⓐ.
From Thiers at 0606 Ⓐ, 0638 Ⓐ, 0729 Ⓐ, 0807 ⑥ **k**, 0858 Ⓐ and 1740 Ⓐ.

MONTLUÇON - CLERMONT FERRAND 329

Subject to alteration April 3–28 and May 25–28

km		⑥	Ⓐ	Ⓐ		Ⓐ			Ⓑ		†
					E		⊙	◇			
0	**Montluçon** 327 d.	...	0601	0700	0828	1047	1221	...	1703	1843	1938
13	Commentry d.	...	0612	0711	0840	1059	1235	...	1716	1856	1949
67	Gannat 327 d.	0705	0706	0803	0926	1144	1327	1622	1804	1949	2043
94	Riom-Châtel-Guyon ▷ d.	0729	0730	0823	0943	1201	1346	1646	1830	2008	2102
108	**Clermont Ferrand** ▷ a.	0741	0742	0833	0952	1211	1356	1659	1840	2018	2111

	Ⓐ	①		⚒		Ⓑ	⚒	Ⓑ	⑤	†
		g		⊖	⊖				f	
Clermont Ferrand ▷ d.	0604	0635	0748	1218	1401	1648	1746	1910	2004	2012
Riom-Châtel-Guyon ▷ d.	0614	0645	0800	1231	1414	1702	1758	1923	2014	2022
Gannat 327 d.	0631	0707	0821	1249	1437	1727	1825	1950	2034	2042
Commentry d.	0721	0811	0909	1344	...	1818	1917	2040	2123	2132
Montluçon 327 a.	0734	0823	0920	1355	...	1829	1927	2051	2134	2143

E – ①⑥⑦ (also Jan. 3, Apr. 18, May 2, 9, 25, June 6).

f – Also May 24.
g – Also Jan. 3, Apr. 18, May 2, 9, June 6; not Apr. 17, May 1, 8, June 5.

⊙ – Subject to alteration Jan. 30 - Feb. 3, Mar. 6–10.
◇ – Runs 3–4 minutes later on Ⓐ (not Dec. 19–30).
⊖ – Subject to alteration Feb. 6–10, Mar. 13–17.
▷ – See also Tables **328** and **330**.

330   PARIS - NEVERS - CLERMONT FERRAND

Warning! Subject to alteration May 25–28, June 3, 4. Services from/to Paris are subject to alteration on May 20, 21, June 10.

km		5951 Ⓡ★		5955 Ⓡ★			5959 Ⓡ★	5963 Ⓡ★		5967 Ⓡ★			5971 Ⓡ★	5973 Ⓡ★		5977 Ⓡ★	5979 Ⓡ★	5983 Ⓡ★
		⚹	⚹r	Ⓐ	⚹	Ⓑ	①-⑥	⚹	⚹	Ⓐ	⑤	Ⓐ	Ⓑ	⑦	Ⓐ	⑦	⑦	Ⓐ
						b	b♠			⊙	D⊙	⊙		f	h		e	e
0	Paris Bercy ▶ d.	...	...	...	0700	...	0900	...	...	1300	1400	...	1500	...	1600	1700	1800	1800 1900
254	Nevers ▶ d.	...	...	0700	0904	...	1104	...	...	1504	1604	...	1704	...	1804	1904	...	2004 2104
314	Moulins sur Allier d.	0604	0641	0710	0741	0812	0932	...	1132	1211 1307	1411	1532	1632	1642	1712 1732	1750	1810	1832 1932 1937	...	2032 2132
355	St Germain des Fossés ▷ d.	0626	0707	0738	0808	0836		1137		1235 1337	1436			1708	1738		1807 1837	...	2001	...
365	Vichy d.	0638	0718	0749	0818	0846	1001	1149	1201	1247 1347	1447	1601	1701	1719	1749	1801	1817	1847 1901 2001 2011	...	2101 2201
406	Riom-Châtel-Guyon ▷ d.	0700	0740	0810	0839	0908	1024	1211	1224	1310 1408	1510	1624	1724	1741	1811	1824	1837	1909 1924 2024 2034	...	2124 2224
420	Clermont Ferrand ▷ a.	0709	0748	0818	0848	0917	1033	1223	1233	1318 1420	1518	1633	1733	1752	1821	1833	1847	1918 1933 2033 2044	2109	2133 2233

	5950 Ⓡ★	5954 Ⓡ★	5958 Ⓡ★			5962 Ⓡ★	5966 Ⓡ★		5970 Ⓡ★	5974 Ⓡ★		5978 Ⓡ★		5982 Ⓡ★		5986 Ⓡ★	5990 Ⓡ★
	Ⓐ	Ⓐ	Ⓐ	Ⓐ	Ⓐ	⚹	Ⓐ	⑥ ①-⑥	⚹	Ⓐ	Ⓐ	Ⓐ	Ⓐ	Ⓑ	⑦ D ⑥	Ⓐ	⑦
								k	b	⊗		e			h	e	e
Clermont Ferrand ▷ d.	0526	0555	0612	0628	0640	0716	0743	0828 0842	1028	1042	1242	1328	1428	1542	1628 1641 1710 1728 1742	1827	1828 1842 1928 2028
Riom-Châtel-Guyon ▷ d.	0537		0621	0639	0650	0725	0752	0839 0851	1039	1051	1339 1439 1551	1639 1651 1719 1739 1751	1836	1839 1851 1939 2038
Vichy ▷ d.	0559		0643	0701	0712	0745	0813	0900 0914	1100	1112	1312	1401	1501	1612	1701 1713 1742 1801 1814	1858	1902 1913 2001 2100
St Germain des Fossés ▷ d.		0653		0722	0754	0822		0923		1122	1322		1622		1723 1752		1823 1909		1923		2101
Moulins sur Allier d.	0628		0721	0730	0749	0821	0847	0929 0948	1129	1148	1348	1429	1530	1650	1730 1751 1815 1830 1849	1933	1931 1950 2030 2134
Nevers ▶ d.	0657		0756	0758	...	...	0918	0958	...	1158	...	1458	1559	...	1800	1859	...	1959	2059	...
Paris Bercy ▶ a.	0857	0901	...	0957	...	...	1157	...	1357	...	1657	1757	...	1957	...	2057	...	2157	2257	...

STOPPING TRAINS PARIS - NEVERS

km		5901 Ⓐ	5905 ①-⑥	5909		5911 Ⓐ	5915 Ⓒ	5917 Ⓐ	5919	5921			5900 Ⓐ	5904 ⑥	5906 Ⓐ	5908 ⑥		5910 Ⓐ	5912 Ⓐ	5914 ⚹	5916
			⊖	⊙	b					e			⊖	k	⊙			⊖	e		◇
0	Paris Bercy d.	...	0714	0915	...	1414	...	1705	1805	1805	1905	2004	Nevers d.	0452	0552	0622	0722	0834	0935	1021	1414	1622	1634	1822	2134
119	Montargis... d.	...	0814	1016	...	1518	...	1812	1909	1909	2011	2109	La Charité d.	0514	0613	0643	0742	0858	0955	1042	1434	1640	1658	1843	2158
155	Gien d.	...	0836	1037	...	1541	...	1835	1931	1931	2032	2131	Cosne d.	0530	0630	0702	0802	0922	1017	1101	1454	1701	1722	1902	2223
196	Cosne d.	0727	0900	1100	1232	1606	1739t	1859	1955	1955	2055	2155	Gien d.	0553	0654	0724	0825	...	...	1124	1519	1724	...	1925	...
228	La Charité... d.	0752	0919	1120	1257	1626	1804t	1915	2013	2013	2115	2212	Montargis d.	0621	0721	0750	0851	...	...	1150	1548	1751	...	1951	...
254	Nevers a.	0825	0943	1144	1325	1652	1836	1939	2038	2038	2138	2238	Paris Bercy a.	0732	0832	0849	0949	...	...	1249	1649	1849	...	2049	...

D – From/to Dijon (Table 373).
b – Not Apr. 17, May 1, 8, June 5.
e – Also Apr. 17, May 1, 8, June 5.
f – Also May 24; not May 26.
h – Not May 25.
k – Also May 25.
r – Not Dec. 19–31.
t – 3 minutes later on Ⓐ.

★ – *INTERCITÉS*. Ⓡ.
▶ – For additional trains see below main table.
▷ – See also Tables **328** and **329**.
♠ – Runs 8–12 minutes **earlier** on ⑥ (also May 25).
⊙ – Subject to alteration Jan. 30 - Feb. 3, Mar. 6–10.
⊗ – Subject to alteration Feb. 6–10, Mar. 13–17.
⊖ – Subject to alteration ①–⑤ Jan. 30 - Feb. 10, ①–⑤ Mar. 6–17.
◇ – Runs 1–2 minutes later Feb. 6 - June 9.

---

331   CLERMONT FERRAND - NEUSSARGUES - AURILLAC

km		Ⓐ	⑥	T ⊡		B				e		e		f △			Ⓐ				R	n		T			Ⓐ	Ⓐ	⑦ e
0	Clermont Ferrand ‡ d.	0545t	0732t	1030	1303	...	1648	1748	1757	1842	1957	2004	2123	Aurillac d.	0550	0733	0913	1022	1330n	1633	1741	1917	1951
36	Issoire ‡ d.	0613t	0800t	1058	1329	...	1718	1816	1815	1910	2025	2032	2151	Le Lioran d.	0624	0800	0946	1056	1403n	1711	1814	1950	2024
61	Arvant ‡ d.	0636	0824	1118	1349	...	1737	1838	1844	1929	2045	2054	2211	Murat (Cantal) d.	0635	0812	1000	1108	1415n	1723	1829	2001	2035
85	Massiac-Blesle d.	0652	0840	1138	1409	...	1757	1901	1905	1950	2106	2114	2232	Neussargues a.	0643	0827	1008	1116	1424n	1732	1838	2010	2043
111	Neussargues a.	0723	0911	1158	1430	...	1817	1922	1924	2009	2125	2134	2251	Neussargues d.	0644		1117	1437	1733	1839	2012	2044
111	Neussargues d.	0723	0911	1159	1438n	1610	1818	1926	1925	2014	2126	2135	2252	Massiac-Blesle d.	0706	0858		1140	1458	1758	1900	2033	2107
120	Murat (Cantal) d.	0738	0926	1208	1447n	1619	1827	1935	1934	2023	2135	2144	2301	Arvant ‡ d.	0726	0914		1201	1518	1818	1921	2052	2128
131	Le Lioran d.	0750	0938	1219	1458n	1631	1839	1951	1945	2034	2147	2155	2312	Issoire ‡ d.	0745	0945t		1219	1537	1836	1940	2111	2146
168	Aurillac a.	0837	1025	1252	1531n	1707	1912	2023	2020	2107	2220	2228	2345	Clermont Ferrand ‡ a.	0818	1015t		1248	1602	1905	2008	2139	2214

B – Daily to Mar. 19; ⑤ from Mar. 24 (also May 24). To Brive (Table 311).
R – Daily to Mar. 19. From Brive (Table 911).
T – To/from Toulouse (Table 317).
e – Also Apr. 17, May 1, 8, June 5.
f – Also Apr. 17, May 1, 8, 24, June 5.
n – Does not run on Ⓐ Apr. 3–21.
t – By train Clermont Ferrand - Arvant and v.v.
△ – Runs 14–15 minutes later on ⑦ (also Apr. 17, May 1, 8, June 5).
⊡ – Subject to alteration ①–⑤ Feb. 27 - Mar. 17.
‡ – See also Table **333**.

---

332   (CLERMONT FERRAND) - NEUSSARGUES - MILLAU - BÉZIERS

km		②-⑤ ⊗	⚹	⚹	⚹		⑤ d	⑤ d⊗	†	⑦ v⊗			⚹ ⊡	⚹		⑤ d	⑤ d⊗		A v⊗	⑦ v∇	⑦ d
		b⊗					d	d⊗		v⊗			⊡			d	d⊗		A	v∇	d
0	Clermont Ferrand 331 d.	...	...	...	...	1303	...	...	...	...	Béziers △ d.	0642	0800	0937	...	1644	1818	...	1857	1856
111	Neussargues 331 d.	...	...	...	...	1436	...	...	...	...	Bédarieux △ d.	0718	0834	1010	...	1719	1855	...	1940	1943
130	St Flour ⊖ d.	...	...	...	...	1459	...	...	...	...	Millau d.	0837	...	1127	1345	2013	...	2053	2100
168	St Chély d'Apcher d.	...	...	1134	...	1540	1631	...	...	...	Sévérac le Château d.	0905	...	1159	1413	D⊗	...	2128	...
201	Marvejols d.	0700	...	1209	...	1616	1707	1720	...	2228	Mende d.	...	...	1615	1730	2125	...	...
236	Mende d.	0747	...	...	...	...	1807	...	2311	Marvejols d.	0952	...	1248	1459	1702	1817	...	2207	2219	...
243	Sévérac le Château d.	...	...	1301	1703	1757	...	St Chély d'Apcher d.	1026	...	1325	1535	...	...	2253	...
273	Millau d.	0600	...	1331	1738	1827	2102	St Flour ⊖ d.	...	...	1405	...	...	...	...
352	Bédarieux △ d.	0717	0844	1446	1734	1854	1941	2220	Neussargues 331 a.	...	...	1425	...	...	...	...
394	Béziers △ a.	0750	0918	1520	1808	1928	2015	2255	Clermont Ferrand 331 a.	...	...	1602	...	...	...	...

		🚌 ⚹	🚌		⑤ f	Ⓑ j	Ⓐ †				🚌 ⚹	🚌		†		⑤ f	Ⓐ †
	Clermont Ferrand 331 d.	1050	1645	...	...	1945	2000	2125	2145	Mende d.	0635	...	0940	1440	...	1545	1730
	Massiac-Blesle 331 d.	1146		1804	1804	1910				Marvejols d.	0725	...	1035	1535	...	1635	1820
	St Flour d.	1210		1829	1829	1935		2240	2300	St Chély d'Apcher d.	0801	...	1122	1618	...	1653 1710	1858
	St Chély d'Apcher d.	1220	1820		1856		2120	2135	2310	2330	St Flour ⊖ d.	0631	0830	1104	...	1645 1718	1718 1745	1825 1930
	Marvejols d.	1300	1900		1934		2200	2215	2300	0010	Massiac-Blesle 331 a.	0656		1128	...	1742 1742		1850	...
	Mende a.	1340	1945		...		2245	2255	0035	0055	Clermont Ferrand 331 a.	...	0955	...	1300 1805	...	1910	...	2050

A – ①②③④⑥⑦ (also Dec. 23, 30, Feb. 10, 17, Apr. 7, 14, May 26; not May 24).
D – ①–④ (also Dec. 23, 30, Feb. 10, 17, Apr. 7, 14, May 26; not Apr. 17, May 1, 8, 24, 25, June 5).
b – Not Apr. 18, May 2, 9, 25, 26, June 6.
d – Also May 24; not Dec. 23, 30, Feb. 10, 17, Apr. 7, 14, May 26.
f – Also May 24.
j – Also May 24; not May 26.
v – Also Jan. 2, Apr. 17, May 1, 8, June 5; not Dec. 18, 25, Jan. 1, Feb. 5, 12, Apr. 2, 9, 16, 30, May 7, June 4.

⊖ – St Flour - Chaudes Aigues.
⊗ – Subject to alteration May 2 - June 30.
⊡ – Does not run St Chély d'Apcher - Millau and v.v. on ①–④ Apr. 10 - May 4.
∇ – From Montpellier (Table 355).
△ – Additional 🚌 journeys Bédarieux - Béziers and v.v.:
    From Bédarieux at 0619⚹, 0715†, 1221†, 1315⚹, 1609† and 1625⚹.
    From Béziers at 1049†, 1215⚹, 1445†, 1530⚹, 1730⚹ and 2045⑤f.

🚌 *Bus services in this table are operated on behalf of SNCF. Rail tickets valid.*

CLERMONT FERRAND - LE PUY EN VELAY and NÎMES 333

WARNING! Rail services Langogne/Mende - La Bastide - Alès and v.v. are subject to alteration from May 2. Other services are subject to alteration from June 6.

km																										
		Ⓐ	Ⓐ	🚌 Ⓐ	⑦	Ⓐ ⊡	🚌 Ⓐ	⑥	🚌 ⑥	🚌		⊗	🚌		🚌	Ⓒ s	Ⓐ		🚌	⚒	⑤ f	🚌 ①–④ c	⑥	🚌 ⑤f	†	Ⓐ
0	**Clermont Ferrand** ▷ d.	...	0545	...	...	0647	...	0732	...	...	...	0949	...	1250	...	1430	1448	1640	...	1757	1854	1900	1950	*2004*t	2118	2127
36	Issoire ▷ d.	...	0613	...	...	0715	...	0800	...	...	...	1017	...	1319	...	1509	1520	1709	...	1825	1922	1935	2030	*2032*t	2146	2205
61	Arvant ▷ d.	...	0632	...	...	0736	...	0820	...	...	...	1037	...	1341	...	1531	1541	1727	...	1845	1942	2008	2050	2056	2205	2226
71	Brioude d.	...	0643	...	...	0746	...	0829	...	...	...	1048	...	1352	1355	1540	1550	1737	...	1854	1951	2020	2058	2111	2215	2235
95	St Georges d'Aurac d.	...	0709	...	...	0805	...	0847	...	...	...	1112	...	|	|	▬	▬	1759	1802	1917	2015	|	...	|	2238	...
103	Langeac d.	...	|	...	...	0813	0819	0855	0859	...	...	|	...	1420	|	...	...	1808	|	|	|	|	...	2149	|	...
147	**Le Puy en Velay** a.	...	0756	...	...	|	0905	|	0945	...	...	1200	...	|	1503	⑤⑦	...	|	1854	2005	2101	2127	...	2235	2326	...
170	Langogne d.	...	▬	...	...	0936	...	1021	...	1230	...	...	...	1545	...	z	◧	1940	...	...	...	...	...	...	...	...
47•	**Mende** d.	0450	⑥p	0838	*0840*	|	...	|	...	|	1146	...	1445	|	...	1650	1832	|	...	...	...	...	...	...	...	...
188	La Bastide-St Laurent d.	0605	0706	0948	0959	0959	...	1040	...	1255	1305	...	1553	1606	...	1805	1942	2009	...	...	...	...	...	...	...	...
241	Grand Combe la Pise d.	0709	0808	...	1057	1057	...	1138	...	...	1407	...	...	1708	...	1909	...	2107	...	...	...	...	...	...	...	...
254	Alès a.	0724	0824	...	1112	1112	...	1152	...	...	1424	...	...	1724	...	1924	...	2122	...	...	...	...	...	...	...	...
254	Alès ▶ d.	0726	0826	...	1114	1122k	...	1159	...	...	1426	...	...	1726	...	1926	...	2126	...	...	...	...	...	...	...	...
303	**Nîmes 355** ▶ a.	0758	0858	...	1146	1154k	...	1231	...	...	1458	...	...	1758	...	1958	...	2158	...	...	...	...	...	...	...	...

	Ⓐ	⑥	① g	②–⑤ d	⚒ ⊗	⚒	① m	🚌 † w	⊙	🚌	⑥	🚌 Ⓐ		🚌		🚌		🚌	🚌 Ⓑ	Ⓐ	†	Ⓑ	🚌 ⑤f	◇	🚌	⑤ v
Nîmes 355 ▶ d.	...	...	...	...	...	...	0715	...	0812	...	...	...	1221	...	...	...	1413	...	...	...	...	1658	...	1811r	...	2118
Alès ▶ a.	...	...	...	...	...	...	0750	...	0843	...	...	...	1252	...	...	...	1443	...	...	...	...	1735	...	1845r	...	2150
Alès d.	...	...	...	...	...	...	0752	...	0845	...	...	...	1254	...	...	...	1445	...	...	...	...	1745	...	1852	...	2155
Grand Combe la Pise d.	...	...	...	...	...	...	0809	...	0900	...	...	...	1309	...	...	...	1501	...	...	...	...	1806	...	1907	...	2210
La Bastide-St Laurent d.	...	...	...	...	...	...	0913	...	0958	1001	...	...	1416	1417	...	...	1605	1612	...	...	...	1912	...	2013j	2013	2313
Mende a.	...	...	...	...	...	...	|	...	|	1111	...	...	1524	|	...	...	|	1720	...	...	...	|	...	2121	|	|
Langogne d.	...	...	...	...	...	...	0932	...	1023	...	...	...	...	1441	...	...	1624	...	...	...	...	1937	...	...	2038	*2346**
Le Puy en Velay d.	...	...	0526	0617	0808	...	...	1101	|	...	1210	1218	...	...	1606	1654	|	...	1910	...	1954	|	2026	...	...	...
Langeac d.	...	...	|	|	|	...	...	|	1148	...	|	|	...	...	|	|	1747	...	|	...	|	2103	2112	...	...	...
St Georges d'Aurac d.	...	...	0616	0705	0856	...	...	|	1155	...	1259	|	...	...	1655	1747	1757	...	|	...	2043	2111	|	...	...	...
Brioude d.	0557	0630	0641	0726	0916	1104	...	1204	1214	...	1319	1324	...	...	1716	...	1821	...	2018	...	2103	2129	2150	...	...	...
Arvant ▷ d.	0606	0638	0649	0738	0924	1112	...	...	1222	...	1331	1339	...	...	1725	...	1830	...	2035	2052	2113	2139	2201	...	...	...
Issoire ▷ d.	0626	0659	0710	0758	0944	1133	...	...	1242	...	1351	1421	...	...	1746	...	1849	...	...	2111	2133	2158	...	...	...	...
Clermont Ferrand ▷ a.	0657	0738	0742	0827	1015	1211	...	...	1310	...	1419	1501	...	...	1815	...	1916	...	...	2139	2200	2226	...	...	...	...

c – Not May 24, 25.
d – Not Jan. 3, Apr. 18, May 2, 9, 25, June 6.
f – Also May 24.
g – Also Jan. 3, Apr. 18, May 2, 9, June 6; not Apr. 17, May 1, 8, June 5.
j – Arrives 2008.
k – Not Feb. 13 - Mar. 3.
m – Also Jan. 3, Apr. 18, May 2, 9, June 6; not Dec. 19, 26, Jan. 2, Feb. 6, 13, Apr. 3, 10, 17, May 1, 8, June 5.
p – Also May 25; not Dec. 24, 31, Feb. 11, 18, Apr. 8, 15, May 27.
r – 5 minutes later on Dec. 11, Jan. 2, 8, 15, 22, 29, Feb. 19, 26, Mar. 5, 12, 19, 26, Apr. 17, 23, May 1, 8, 14, 21, 28, June 5, 11, 18, 25.

s – Not Apr. 16, 30, May 7, June 4.
t – By train Clermont Ferrand - Arvant.
v – Also May 24; not Dec. 23, 30, Feb. 10, 17, Apr. 7, 14, May 26.
w – Not Apr. 16, 30, May 7, June 4.
z – Also Apr. 17, May 1, 8, 24, 25, June 5; not Dec. 23, 30, Feb. 10, 17, Apr. 7, 14, May 26.

⊡ – Subject to alteration La Bastide - Nîmes from Apr. 24.
⊙ – Subject to alteration Nîmes - La Bastide Apr. 25–28.
⊗ – Subject to alteration on ①–⑤ Feb. 27 - Mar. 17.
¶ – Subject to alteration Feb. 13 - Mar. 3.
◧ – By train on ⑤ (not Dec. 23, 30, Feb. 10, 17, Apr. 7, 14); by 🚌 on other dates.

* – By 🚌 from La Bastide.
◇ – From Narbonne and Montpellier on Ⓐ (Table **355**).
• – Distance from La Bastide.
▷ – See also Table **331**.
▶ – Other trains Alès - Nîmes (journey time 32–40 minutes): Subject to alteration on June 4.
From Alès at 0600 Ⓐ, 0628 Ⓐ, 0656, 0800 ⚒, 0826, 0926 Ⓐ ¶, 1226 Ⓐ, 1256, 1526, 1641 Ⓐ, 1821 Ⓐ and 1926.
From Nîmes at 0618 Ⓐ, 0654 Ⓐ, 0715 ⚒, 0746 Ⓐ, 0918 Ⓐ ¶, 1018 ¶, 1123 Ⓐ ¶, 1318 Ⓐ, 1518 Ⓐ, 1618, 1733 ⚒, 1918 Ⓐ and 2118.

TGV services LYON - MASSY - LE MANS - RENNES and NANTES 335

For slower services via Bourges see Table **290**. For Lille - Massy - Rennes/Nantes see Table **11**. For Strasbourg - Massy - Rennes/Nantes see Table **391**.

	TGV **5352** Ⓐ t		*TGV* **5366** ①–⑤ h	*TGV* **5366** ⑥ d⊗	*TGV* **5366** ⑦ ⊖		*TGV* **5368** △	*TGV* **5394** ⑥ B	*TGV* **5393** ⑥ B	*TGV* **5378** ⊙	*TGV* **5371** p⊙	*TGV* **5380** ▽	*TGV* **5387** ▽	
Marseille St Charles **350** d.	...	...	0833	0837	0840	...	1239	...	...	1439	1439	...	...	...
Avignon TGV **350** d.	...	...	0919	0913	0916	...	1322	...	...	1522	1522	...	...	...
Montpellier **355** d.	...	...	|	|	|	...	|	...	...	|	|	1630	1630	...
Valence TGV **355** d.	...	...	0952	0951	0951	...	|	...	...	|	|	1748	1748	...
Bourg St Maurice **366** d.	...	...	|	|	|	...	|	1130	1130	|	|	|	|	...
Lyon Perrache d.	0616r	...	|	|	|	...	|	|	|	|	|	|	|	...
Lyon Part Dieu d.	0630	...	1032	1030	1030	...	1428	|	|	1630	1630	1830	1830	...
Massy TGV d.	0839	...	1238	1238	1238	...	1638	1805	1805	1838	1838	2039	2049	...
St Pierre des Corps a.	0930b	...	|	|	|	...	1729	|	|	|	|	2130	|	...
Le Mans **280** a.	|	...	1327	1328	1327	...	|	1852	1852	1928	1928	|	2136	...
Rennes 280 a.	|	...	1444	1444	1444	...	|	|	2020	|	2100	|	2252	...
Saumur a.	|	...	...	...	...	...	|	|	...	|	...	2205	...	...
Angers St Laud **280** a.	1022	...	...	...	...	...	1822	1935	...	2010	...	2230	...	...
Nantes 280 a.	1107y	...	...	...	...	...	1912v	2021	...	2053y	...	2309x	...	...

	TGV **5300** ① g	*TGV* **5300** ②–④ m	*TGV* **5338** ⊡	*TGV* **5336** n⊡	*TGV* **5308** ⑥ A	*TGV* **5310** ⑥ A	*TGV* **5326** ◇	*TGV* **5318** ◇	*TGV* **5334** ⊕	*TGV* **5328** Ⓐ	*TGV* **5346** ☆	*TGV* **5342** ⑤⑦ z	*TGV* **5344** ⑤⑦ z	
Nantes 280 d.	0444j	0448j	0656j	...	0704	...	0900j	...	1244j	1444j	...	1848f	...	...
Angers St Laud **280** d.	0534	0536	0743	...	0758	...	0946	...	1333	1534	...	1941f	...	...
Saumur d.	0558	|	|	...	|	...	|	...	|	1558	...	|	...	...
Rennes 280 d.	|	|	|	0710	|	0727	|	0910	|	|	1610	|	1910	...
Le Mans **280** d.	|	|	0832	0832	0909	0909	1032	1032	|	|	1732	2033	2033	...
St Pierre des Corps d.	0632	0632	|	|	|	|	|	|	1432	1631	|	|	|	...
Massy TGV d.	0725	0725	0925	0925	1004	1004	1125	1125	1525	1725	1825	2124	2124	...
Lyon Part Dieu a.	0930	0930	1130	1130	|	|	1330	1330	1730	1930	2030	2330	2330	...
Lyon Perrache a.	0943c	0943c	|	|	|	|	|	|	|	1944	|	2343	2343	...
Bourg St Maurice **366** a.	...	...	|	|	1632	1632	|	|	|	...	|	...	...	...
Valence TGV **355** a.	...	...	|	|	...	...	1412	1412	1810	...	2110	...	...	...
Montpellier **355** a.	...	...	|	|	...	...	1530	1530	|	...	|	...	...	...
Avignon TGV **350** a.	...	...	1240	1240	...	...	...	...	1843	...	2144	...	...	...
Marseille St Charles **350** a.	...	...	1325	1325	...	...	...	...	1921	...	2222	...	...	...

LYON - LE HAVRE	*TGV* **5376** ♥	
Marseille **350** d.	1539	...
Avignon TGV **350** d.	1616	...
Valence TGV **355** d.	1650	...
Lyon Part Dieu d.	1730	...
Massy-Palaiseau a.	1937	...
Versailles Chantiers a.	1955	...
Mantes la Jolie a.	2030	...
Rouen Rive Droite a.	2114	...
Le Havre a.	2208	...

LE HAVRE - LYON	*TGV* **5316** ♠	
Le Havre d.	0749	...
Rouen Rive Droite d.	0845	...
Mantes la Jolie d.	0933	...
Versailles Chantiers d.	1006	...
Massy-Palaiseau d.	1024	...
Lyon Part Dieu a.	1226	...
Valence TGV **355** a.	1308	...
Avignon TGV **350** a.	1341	...
Marseille **350** a.	1423	...

A – ⑥ Dec. 31 - Mar. 18 (not Feb. 4, 11, 18).
B – ⑥ Dec. 31 - Mar. 25 (not Feb. 11, 18, 25).

b – Not Dec. 19–23, Mar. 6–31.
c – Not Jan. 30 - Apr. 3.
d – Also May 25.
f – On ⑤ to Mar. 31 departs Nantes 1853, Angers 1943. From Apr. 7 departs Nantes 1905, Angers 1945.
g – Also Apr. 18, May 2, 9, June 6; not Apr. 17, May 1, 8, June 5.
h – Not May 25.
j – 8–10 minutes later from Apr. 3.
m – Not Apr. 18, May 2, 9, 24, 25, June 6. Service starts from Angers Jan. 3 - Apr. 6.
n – Not May 20, 21, 27, 28.
p – Not May 27.
r – Not Jan. 30 - Mar. 3, Apr. 3–7.
t – Not Dec. 26, Jan. 2, May 26.
v – 1906 on ⑥⑦ to Apr. 2; 1903 from Apr. 3.
x – Not ①–④ Jan. 2 - Apr. 6. Arrives 2315 until Apr. 2.
y – 5–6 minutes earlier from Apr. 3.
z – Also Apr. 17, May 1, 8, 24, June 5; not Apr. 16, 30.

TGV – 🅁, supplement payable, 🍷.

⊡ – Subject to alteration on Apr. 30, May 1, June 10, 11.
⊙ – Subject to alteration on May 20, June 10.
⊗ – Subject to alteration on May 20, 27, June 10.
⊖ – Subject to alteration on Apr. 16, 30, May 21, June 11.
△ – Subject to alteration on Apr. 15, 16, 29, 30, May 20, 25, 26, 27, June 10, 11, 17, 24.
▽ – Subject to alteration on Apr. 30, May 20, 26, 27, June 10.
◇ – Subject to alteration on Apr. 17, 30, May 1, 20, 21, 26, 27, 28, June 10, 11.
⊕ – Subject to alteration on May 20, June 10, 11.
☆ – Subject to alteration on Apr. 30, May 20, 27, June 10.
♥ – Subject to alteration from Apr. 3. Terminates at Mants la Jolie on Feb. 25.
♠ – Subject to alteration on ⑦ from Apr. 9 (also on Apr. 15, 29, May 13, June 10, 17, 24). Does not run Le Havre - Versailles on Feb. 26, Mar. 18, 19, 20, 25, 26. Departs Le Havre 0753 from Mar. 21 (also on Mar. 4, 11).

Subject to alteration March 17 – 19 and from April 3. Certain trains may not run during the Christmas/New Year period. Timings may vary on certain dates (please check your reservation). For Charles de Gaulle ✈ - Marne la Vallée - Lyon see Table 11. For Paris - Lyon St Exupéry ✈ see Table 342. Most trains not serving Lyon Perrache continue to / start from other stations.

km		TGV 6601 Ⓐ	TGV 6641 Ⓐ	TGV 6603 ①-⑥ b	TGV 6681 Ⓐ b	TGV 6643 Ⓐ	TGV 6605 ⑥	TGV 6605		TGV 6607	TGV 6609	TGV 6611	TGV 6613	TGV 6615	TGV 6685 ⑤	TGV 6617	TGV 6657	TGV 6619	TGV 6621	TGV 6659 Ⓐ	TGV 6623	TGV 6687	TGV 6663 Ⓐ	TGV 6627	TGV 6665 Ⓑ
0	**Paris** Gare de Lyon ... 341 d.	0550	0629	0659	0659	0729	0753	0753	...	0859	0959	1059	1153	1259	1259	1353	1429	1459	1553	1619	1657	1657	1729	1753	1841
303	Le Creusot TGV ... d.		0713				0913	0914	...				1314			1514				1714			1914		
363	Mâcon Loché TGV ... 341 d.						0933		...																
427	**Lyon** Part-Dieu ... a.	0756	0824	0826	0856	0856	0926	1000	...	1056	1156	1256	1356	1456	1456	1556	1624	1656	1756	1817	1856	1856	1926	1956	2044
432	**Lyon** Perrache ... a.	0809	0843	0909		0939	1013	1009	...	1109	1209n	1309n	1409	1509	...	1609	1637	1709	1809	...	1909	...	1939	2009	2057

	TGV 6689 ⑤⑥	TGV 6669 Ⓑ	TGV 6631 ①-④	TGV 6633 ⑤⑦	TGV 6635 h		TGV 6640 ①	TGV 6602 Ⓐ	TGV 6604 Ⓐ	TGV 6644 ①-④①-⑥-⑥ b	TGV 6604 ①-⑥ b	TGV 6648	TGV 6608	TGV 6610	TGV 6612 P	TGV 6614 ①-⑤ Q
Paris Gare de Lyon ... 341 d.	1857	1857	1929	1958	2059	2156	**Lyon** Perrache ⊠ ... d.	0521j	0551k	0621	0638	0646		0721	0751	0851	0951	0951	1046r
Le Creusot TGV ... d.				2118			**Lyon** Part-Dieu ... d.	0534	0604	0634	0651	0704	0704	0734	0804	0904	1004	1004	1104
Mâcon Loché TGV ... 341 a.				2137			Mâcon Loché TGV ... 341 a.		0601	0631					0832			1033	
Lyon Part-Dieu ... a.	2056	2056	2137	2203	2256	2356	Le Creusot TGV ... d.	0622	0652						0854		1046	1057	
Lyon Perrache ⊠ ... a.		2109	2139j	2218j			**Paris** Gare de Lyon ... 341 a.	0743	0813	0831	0849	0901	0901	0933	1015	1101	1207	1219	1301

	TGV 6692 Ⓐ	TGV 6616 Ⓐ	TGV 6616 ⑤	TGV 6618 Ⓑ	TGV 6694 ②-⑤ L	TGV 6620 s	TGV 6622 h	TGV 6624	TGV 6664 Ⓐ	TGV 6626 ⑤⑦	TGV 6696	TGV 6628	TGV 6638	TGV 6696	TGV 6630	TGV 6632 ⑤ e	TGV 6674 Ⓐ	TGV 6634 ⑤	TGV 6634		TGV 6672 e	TGV 6676 ⑦ e	TGV 6678 ⑦ e
Lyon Perrache ⊠ ... d.		1121r	1151	1246t		1351v	1451x	1551		1621	1651	1716c		1751			1847z	1951	2016d	2051	2055	...	2151k	2151	2221y
Lyon Part-Dieu ... d.	1104	1134	1204	1304	1304	1404	1504	1604	1604	1634	1704	1734	1734	1804	1834	1904	1904	2004	2104	2108	...	2204	2204	2234
Mâcon Loché TGV ... 341 d.								1630												2231			
Le Creusot TGV ... d.					1445		1646	1651						1846					2146	2150	...	2246	2252	
Paris Gare de Lyon ... 341 a.	1301	1331	1401	1501	1501	1607	1701	1808	1812	1831	1901	1932	1932	2007	2031	2101	2101	2207	2237	2307	2311	...	0007	0013	0031

L – ①⑥⑦ (also Apr. 18, May 2, 9, 25, June 6).
P – Daily to Mar. 17; ⑤⑦ Mar. 25 - Apr. 9; daily from Apr. 15.
Q – ①-⑤ Mar. 20 - Apr. 14.

b – Not Apr. 17, May 1, 8, June 5.
c – 1721 on ⑦.
d – Not Jan. 30 - Apr. 1.
e – Also Apr. 17, May 1, 8, June 5.
h – Not May 25.
j – Not Jan. 30 - Apr. 2.
k – Not ⑤ Feb. 3 - Mar. 31.

n – Not ①⑤ Jan. 30 - Mar. 31.
r – Not ①-④ Jan. 30 - Mar. 30.
s – Not Apr. 18, May 2, 9, 25, June 6.
t – Not Jan. 28 - Apr. 2.
v – Not ⑤-⑦ Feb. 3 - Apr. 2.
x – Not ① Jan. 30 - Mar. 27.
y – 2204 Feb. 5 - Apr. 2.
z – 1851 on Ⓐ.

TGV – Ⓡ, supplement payable, ⓘ.

Subject to alteration Mar. 17 – 19, May 25 – 27.

km		TGV 9241 ⑥⑦ c M	TGV 9241 ①-⑤ a M	TGV 6501 ⑥ B	TGV 6467 E	TGV 9761 ①-⑤ a	TGV 6933 Ⓐ	TGV 9765 ⑥	TGV 9765 e	TGV 9765 ①-⑤ a	TGV 6937	TGV 6503 D	TGV 6473 G	TGV 6939	TGV 9245 M	TGV 9773 Q	TGV 6941		TGV 9249 M	TGV 9775 ⑧ h	TGV 9777 h	TGV 6947	TGV 6949 k
0	**Paris** Gare de Lyon ... 340 366 d.	0629	0629	0711	0711	0711	0749	0811	0911	0917	0949	1011	1041	1041	1211	1245	...	1441	1511	1611	1645	1749
363	Mâcon Loché TGV ... 340 d.						0927				1127					1423	...			1823	1927	
406	Bourg-en-Bresse ... 365 d.					0903	0949	1004	1102		1149	1205	1205				...			1804		1949
439	Lyon St Exupéry TGV ✈ ... 342 a.	◨	◨											1236	1236		...	1637				
470	Bellegarde ... 346 d.			0948	0948	0950		1058	1148			1318	1318			1457	...		1748	1858		
503	Genève ... 346 a.					1018		1128	1217	1215						1528	...		1817	1928		
532*	Chambéry ... 366 a.	0940	0939									1338	1338		1538		...	1738			1938	
532*	Chambéry ... 345 364 d.	h										1349			1549		...	1948			1948	
546*	Aix les Bains ... 345 364 a.					1051					1251	1359			1559		...				1958	2051
585*	**Annecy** ... 345 364 a.					1129					1329	1429			1629		...				2029	2129

	TGV 9781 f	TGV 6511 ⑤ H	TGV 7951	TGV 6951 h	TGV 9785 v	TGV 9789 v	TGV 6953 ⑤			TGV 6960 ①-⑥ b	TGV 9760 ①-⑥ b	TGV 9764 ①-⑥	TGV 9764 e	TGV 6962 b	TGV 9768 b	TGV 6964	TGV 9240 M
Paris Gare de Lyon ... 340 366 d.	1811	1815	1815	1845	1911	2011	2019		**Annecy** ... 345 364 d.	0531		...	...	0730		0931	...
Mâcon Loché TGV ... 340 d.				2023			2157		Aix les Bains ... 345 364 d.	0601		...	...	0801		1001	...
Bourg-en-Bresse ... 365 d.					2104	2204	2221		Chambéry ... 345 364 d.	0613		...	...	0812		1012	...
Lyon St Exupéry TGV ✈ ... 342 d.									Chambéry ... 366 d.	0624		...	...	0824		1024	1024
Nurieux Brion ... a.	2030								Genève ... 346 d.		0614	0741	0741		0941		
Bellegarde ... 346 a.	2058	2111	2111		2151	2251			Bellegarde ... 346 d.		0643	0810	0810		1010		
Genève ... 346 a.	2128	⊖	⊖		2221	2321			Nurieux Brion ... d.		0709		0835				
Chambéry ... 366 a.				2138			2338		Lyon St Exupéry TGV ✈ ... 342 a.							1123	1123
Chambéry ... 345 364 a.				2148					Bourg-en-Bresse ... 365 d.		0737		0859	0902			
Aix les Bains ... 345 364 a.				2158			2324z		Mâcon Loché TGV ... 340 d.								
Annecy ... 345 364 a.				2229					**Paris** Gare de Lyon ... 340 366 a.	0915	0927		1049	1051	1115	1249	1319	1319

	TGV 6480 ⑥ B	TGV 9770 ①-⑤ a	TGV 9244 M	TGV 6972 c	TGV 9772 ⑥⑦	TGV 6482 ⓒ W	TGV 6508 T	TGV 9774 ①-⑤ a			TGV 6976 ⑤-⑦ r	TGV 7954 m R	TGV 9778 L	TGV 6980 ⑦ e	TGV 9780 ⑥ Y	TGV 6504 ⑥ U	TGV 6486 ⑧	TGV 6984 B k	TGV 9248 M	TGV 9240 M*
Annecy ... 345 364 d.					1231					Genève ... 346 d.	1531		1731			1831				
Aix les Bains ... 345 364 d.				1310y	1310					Bellegarde ... 346 d.	1601		1801			1909				
Chambéry ... 345 364 d.										Nurieux Brion ... d.	1613		1813							
Chambéry ... 366 d.			1253							Genève ... 346 d.	1624		1824					1856	1856	
Genève ... 346 d.		1141		1341	⊙	1441				Bellegarde ... 346 d.	1629	1741		⊙	1829	⊙				1941
Bellegarde ... 346 d.	1208	1210		1410	1503	1503	1510			Nurieux Brion ... d.	1659	1809		1818	1818	1900	1900	1900		2010
Nurieux Brion ... d.								1723		Lyon St Exupéry TGV ✈ ... 342 a.								◨	◨	
Lyon St Exupéry TGV ✈ ... 342 d.			1413	1413		1556	1556	1559		Bourg-en-Bresse ... 365 d.	1751	1858		1934	1934	1956	1956	2013		
Bourg-en-Bresse ... 365 d.			1435	1435						Mâcon Loché TGV ... 340 d.				1956	1956			2034		
Mâcon Loché TGV ... 340 d.						1749	1749	1749		**Paris** Gare de Lyon ... 340 366 a.	1919	1949	2049	2115	2133	2133	2149	2249	2211	2231	2237	2249
Paris Gare de Lyon ... 340 366 a.	1449	1452	1611	1611	1649	1749	1749	1749												

A – ①-⑤ to Mar. 31 (also Feb. 12, 19); Ⓑ from Apr. 3 (not May 25).
B – ⑥ to Apr. 29.
D – ⑥⑦ to Apr. 30; ⑥ from May 6 (also May 25).
E – ⑥⑦ to Apr. 2 (also Apr. 8, 15, 22, 29).
G – ⑥⑦ to Apr. 30.
H – ⑤ to Apr. 28.
L – Daily to Apr. 7; Ⓑ from Apr. 9 (not May 25).
M – ☐ Paris - Modane - Torino - Milano and v.v. (Table 44). Special 'global' fares payable.
Q – To Lausanne (a. 1615) on ①-④ (not Apr. 17, May 1, 8, 24, 25, June 5).
From Lausanne (d. 1638).
T – ⑥ to Apr. 29; ⑦ from May 7 (also May 8, June 5).

U – ⑥ to Apr. 1.
W – ⓒ to Apr. 30.
Y – ⑦ to Apr. 30.

a – Not Apr. 17, May 1, 8, 25, June 5.
b – Not Apr. 17, May 1, 8, 25, June 5.
c – Also Apr. 17, May 1, 8, 25, June 5.
e – Also Apr. 17, May 1, 8, June 5.
f – Also May 24.
h – Not May 25.
k – Not May 25, 26.
m – Not Apr. 17, May 1, 8, 24, 25, June 5.

r – Also Apr. 17, May 1, 8, 24, 25, June 5.
v – Not May 26.
y – Calls after Chambéry.
z – Calls before Chambéry.

TGV – Ⓡ, supplement payable, ⓘ.

¶ – Also calls at Le Creusot TGV (a. 2113, d. 2116).
⊖ – To / from Évian les Bains (Table 363).
⊙ – To / from St Gervais (Table 365).
◨ – Via Lyon Part Dieu.
* – Via St Exupéry TGV (Paris to Aix via Bourg is 511 km).

PARIS - LYON ST EXUPÉRY ✈ - GRENOBLE — 342

Shows complete service Paris - Lyon St Exupéry ✈ and v.v. Journeys not serving Grenoble continue to destinations in other tables. Subject to alteration March 17 – 19.

km	All trains convey 🍸	TGV 6901 ①–④ m	TGV 6905 D	TGV 6191 ①–⑥ b	TGV 6105	TGV 6199 ⑥ L	TGV 6911 ⊙	TGV 9245 ⊙	TGV 6917	TGV 6193 B		TGV 9249	TGV 6919		TGV 6921		TGV 6923 Ⓑ h	TGV 6195 Ⓑ h	TGV 6195 ⑥ k		TGV 6925 Ⓐ	TGV 6927		TGV 6929 ⑤⑦ w
0	**Paris** Gare de Lyon d.	0641	0741	0741	0837	0927	0945	1041	1141	1141	...	1441	1441	...	1641	...	1741	1741	1745	...	1849	1941	...	2045
441	Lyon St Exupéry ✈ a.	0834	0934	0934	1029	1122	1140	1233	1334	1334	...	1633	1633	...	1834	...	1934	1934	1940	...	2048	2134	...	2240
441	Lyon St Exupéry ✈ d.	0837	0938	...	...	...	1143	...	1338	...	...	...	1641	...	1838	...	1938	...	...	...	2052	2138	...	2243
553	**Grenoble** a.	0942	1042	...	...	...	1246	...	1442	...	...	...	1745	...	1942	...	2042	...	...	...	2154	2242	...	2346

	TGV 6900 ①–④ m	TGV 6902 Ⓐ		TGV 6904 ①–⑥ b		TGV 6906 ①–⑥ b		TGV 6908	TGV 9240		TGV 6910		TGV 6120 P	TGV 6920 ① g	TGV 6920 E		TGV 6976	TGV 6922 C	TGV 6922 Ⓐ	TGV 6198 Ⓒ		TGV 6924		TGV 6928 ⑦
Grenoble d.	0516	0616	...	0716	...	0816	...	1016	...	...	1316	...	...	1505	1516	...	...	1716	1716	...	...	1916	...	2116
Lyon St Exupéry ✈ a.	0621	0721	...	0821	...	0921	...	|	...	...	1423	...	...	1608	1621	...	...	|	1822	...	...	2021	...	2221
Lyon St Exupéry ✈ d.	0626	0726	...	0826	...	0926	...	|	1126	...	1426	...	1537	1613	1626	...	1726	|	1826	1924	...	2026	...	2226
Paris Gare de Lyon a.	0819	0919	...	1019	...	1119	...	1315	1319	...	1619	...	1730	1811	1819	...	1919	2015	2019	2119	...	2219	...	0019

B – Ⓑ to Mar. 17 (also Mar. 26, Apr. 8, 9); daily from Apr. 15.
C – ⑦ to Apr. 2; Ⓒ from Apr. 8. Also calls at Mâcon Loché TGV (d. 1838).
D – Daily to Apr. 8; ①–⑥ from Apr. 10 (not Apr. 17, May 1, 8, June 5).
E – ②–⑦ to Apr. 2; ②③④⑤⑦ from Apr. 4 (not Apr. 18, May 2, 9, 25, June 6).
L – Until Apr. 1.
P – Ⓑ (daily from Apr. 2).

b – Not Apr. 17, May 1, 8, June 5.
g – Also Apr. 18, May 2, 9, June 6; not Apr. 17, May 1, 8, June 5.
h – Not May 25.
k – Also May 25.
m – Not Apr. 17, May 1, 8, 24, 25, June 5.

w – Also Apr. 17, May 1, 8, 24, June 5.

TGV – Ⓡ, supplement payable, 🍸.

⊙ – Subject to alteration from Apr. 3.

LYON - GRENOBLE — 343

km		①–⑥ b	Ⓐ		Ⓐ		Ⓐ		Ⓐ ⊗	⊗					Ⓐ		Ⓐ		Ⓐ		Ⓐ		Ⓐ		Ⓐ
0	**Lyon** Part-Dieu 344 d.	0614	0644	0714	0744	0814	0844	0914	0944	1014	...	1114	1214	1314	1344	1414	1444	1514	1544	1614	1644	1714	1744	1814	1844
41	Bourgoin-Jallieu 344 d.	0641	0710	0741	0810	0841	0910	0941	1010	1041	...	1141	1241	1341	1410	1441	1510	1541	1610	1641	1710	1741	1810	1841	1910
56	La Tour du Pin 344 d.	0651	0721	0751	0821	0851	0921	0951	1021	1051	...	1151	1251	1351	1421	1451	1521	1551	1621	1650	1721	1751	1821	1850	1921
104	Voiron d.	0721	0752	0821	0852	0921	0952	1021	1052	1121	...	1221	1321	1421	1452	1521	1552	1621	1652	1721	1752	1821	1852	1921	1952
129	**Grenoble** a.	0738	0808	0838	0908	0938	1008	1038	1108	1138	...	1238	1338	1438	1508	1538	1608	1638	1708	1738	1808	1838	1908	1938	2008

		Ⓐ					Ⓑ h⊖	⑥k 🚌		🚌	
Lyon Part-Dieu 344 d.	1914	1944	2014	...	2114	...	2214	2206	...	2314	...
Bourgoin-Jallieu 344 d.	1941	2010	2041	...	2141	...	2244	2257	...	0005	...
La Tour du Pin 344 d.	1951	2021	2050	...	2151	...	2254	|	...	|	...
Voiron d.	2021	2052	2121	...	2221	...	2322	|	...	|	...
Grenoble a.	2038	2108	2138	...	2238	...	2338	0005	...	0110	...

	①–⑥ b	Ⓐ		Ⓐ		Ⓐ		Ⓐ	
Grenoble d.	0521	0552	0621	0652	0721	0750	0821	0852	0921
Voiron d.	0538	0608	0638	0708	0738	0808	0838	0908	0938
La Tour du Pin 344 d.	0608	0638	0708	0738	0808	0838	0908	0938	1008
Bourgoin-Jallieu 344 d.	0618	0648	0718	0748	0818	0848	0918	0948	1018
Lyon Part-Dieu 344 a.	0644	0716	0744	0814	0844	0914	0944	1014	1044

	Ⓐ			⊗			Ⓐ				Ⓐ		Ⓐ		Ⓐ		Ⓐ		Ⓐ		🚌			Ⓑ h△	⑥k 🚌
Grenoble d.	0952	1021	...	1121	...	1221	1252	1321	...	1421	1452	1521	1552	1621	1652	1721	1752	1821	1852	1921	1947	2021	...	2121	2123
Voiron d.	1008	1038	...	1138	...	1238	1308	1338	...	1438	1508	1538	1608	1638	1708	1738	1808	1838	1908	1938	|	2038	...	2138	2153
La Tour du Pin 344 d.	1038	1108	...	1208	...	1308	1338	1408	...	1508	1538	1608	1638	1708	1738	1808	1838	1908	1938	2008	|	2108	...	2208	2233
Bourgoin-Jallieu 344 d.	1048	1118	...	1218	...	1318	1348	1418	...	1518	1548	1618	1648	1718	1748	1818	1848	1918	1948	2018	|	2118	...	2218	2248
Lyon Part-Dieu 344 a.	1114	1144	...	1244	...	1344	1414	1444	...	1544	1614	1644	1718	1744	1814	1844	1914	1944	2014	2044	2116	2146	...	2244	2335

b – Not Apr. 17, May 1, 8, June 5.
h – Not May 25.
k – Also May 25.

⊗ – Subject to alteration on ①–⑤ Feb. 20 - Mar. 3.
⊖ – Subject to alteration on ①–④ Feb. 6 – 16 and ①–④ Mar. 27 - Apr. 13.
△ – Subject to alteration on Jan. 8, 29, Feb. 12, Mar. 12, Apr. 9.

LYON - CHAMBÉRY — 344

SERVICE UNTIL APRIL 29. Certain journeys continue to / from Bourg St Maurice (Table **366**) or Modane (Table **367**).

km		Ⓐ	⑥	Ⓐ	⑥	9241 ★			Ⓐ	Ⓒ				Ⓐ	Ⓒ	⑥	Ⓑ	⑥	Ⓐ	Ⓒ		Ⓐ	Ⓒ		Ⓐ	
0	**Lyon** Part Dieu 343 d.	0650	0650	0750	0750	0831	0850	0950	1032	1050	1150	1250	1350	1450	1450	1500	1550	1550	1650	1650	1750	1850	1850	1950	2050	2150
41	Bourgoin-Jallieu 343 d.	0718	0718	0817	0815	|	0917	1017	|	1117	1217	1317	1417	1518	1517	|	1617	1617	1718	1715	1817	1918	1917	2018	2118	2218
56	La Tour du Pin 343 d.	0730	0730	0828	0826	|	0929	|	a	1129	|	1329	|	1530	1529	|	|	|	1730	1726	|	1930	1929	|	2130	|
106	**Chambéry** a.	0816	0821	0916	0918	0940	1016	1118	1158	1217	1317	1417	1517	1616	1623	1622	1717	1722	1816	1821	1918	2016	2022	2116	2216	2310

	⚒	⚒	Ⓑ	⑥		Ⓐ	⑥	Ⓐ	Ⓒ	Ⓒ	⑥	Ⓐ				Ⓒ	Ⓐ		†	Ⓐ		9248 ★	Ⓐ	Ⓒ	Ⓒ △	Ⓐ
Chambéry d.	0544	0644	0743	0745	0838	0844	0848	0944	1035	1052b	1142	1207	1244	1344	1444	1538	1544	1641c	1739	1740	1844	1856	1944	1944	2034	2044
La Tour du Pin 343 d.	0629	|	0829	0829	|	|	|	1029	|	|	1230	|	|	1429	|	1631	1629	|	1831	1829	|	|	2027	2032	|	|
Bourgoin-Jallieu 343 d.	0641	0743	0841	0843	0943	0943	|	1041	|	1204	1242	|	1343	1441	1543	1643	1641	1743	1843	1841	1943	|	2040	2043	2143	2143
Lyon Part Dieu 343 a.	0710	0810	0910	0910	1010	1010	1010	1110	1210	1230	1310	1326	1410	1510	1610	1710	1710	1810	1910	1910	2010	2028	2110	2110	2210	2208

a – Via Aix les Bains (Table **345**).
b – 1049 on Feb. 4, 11, 12, 18, 19.
c – 1644 on Ⓐ.

★ – *TGV* service. Ⓡ and supplement payable. (12) and 🍸 Paris - Lyon - Modane - Milano and v.v.
△ – Subject to alteration on Jan. 8, 29, Feb. 12, Mar. 12, Apr. 9.

LYON - AIX LES BAINS - ANNECY — 345

Subject to alteration May 25 – 27

km		Ⓐ	🚌 Ⓐ	⚒h	⚒	🚌 †	⚒	Ⓐ	🚌 Ⓐ	Ⓒ	Ⓐ	Ⓐh		🚌 Ⓐ		🚌 Ⓐ	Ⓐ		Ⓐh		Ⓐ	h		
0	**Lyon** Part Dieu 344 346 d.	...	0608	...	0708	0708	0808	0908	1008	1008	1032	...	1208	1308	1408	1508	...	1608	...	1708	1808	...	1908	2108
46	Ambérieu 346 d.	0611	|	0713	0734	|	0834	0934	|	1034	|	1213	1234	|	1434	|	1611	1634	...	1734	1834	1913	1934	2134
96	Culoz 346 d.	0649	|	0751	0805	|	|	|	|	|	|	1251	|	|	|	|	1649	|	1751	|	|	1951	|	2205
118	Aix les Bains a.	0708	|	0810	0821	0835	0918	1018	|	1118	1145	1310	1318	|	1518	|	1708	1718	1810	1818	1918	2010	2018	2221
118	Aix les Bains 364 d.	0710	|	0812	0832	0835	0925	1025	|	1125	1147	1312	1325	|	1525	|	1710	1728	1812	1825	1925	2012	2025	2228
132	**Chambéry** 344 364 a.	0722	|	0825	|	|	|	|	|	|	1158	1325	|	|	|	|	1722	|	1824	|	|	2024	|	|
157	**Annecy** 364 a.	...	0759	...	0902	0910	1007	1107	1159	1207	...	...	1407	1459	1607	1659	...	1807	...	1907	2001	...	2107	2300

	Ⓐh	Ⓐ	⚒	Ⓐ		🚌 Ⓐ	⑥	🚌 †	Ⓐ	Ⓐ	Ⓒ	🚌 Ⓐ	⚒h	🚌 Ⓐ			Ⓐh			Ⓐ	Ⓐh		🚌 Ⓐ	⑦e
Annecy 364 d.	...	0600	0653	...	0753	0900	0953	1000	1053	...	1153	1200	...	1300	1353	1553	...	1653	...	1753	...	1853	2000	2053
Chambéry 344 364 d.	0533	|	|	0733	|	|	|	|	|	1123	|	|	1233	|	|	|	1633	|	1733	|	1833	|	|	|
Aix les Bains 364 a.	0547	0635	0735	0747	0831	|	1035	1030	1130	1135	1235	|	1247	|	1435	1635	1647	1726	1747	1835	1846	1935	|	2135
Aix les Bains d.	0549	0642	0742	0749	0838	|	1042	1030	1143	1143	1242	|	1249	|	1442	1642	1649	1740	1749	1842	1848	1942	|	2142
Culoz 346 d.	0609	|	|	0808	|	|	|	|	|	|	|	|	1309	|	|	|	1708	1757	1808	|	1909	|	|	|
Ambérieu 346 d.	0646	0728	0828	0846	0928	|	1128	|	1228	1228	1328	|	1346	|	1528	1728	...	1827	1846	1928	1946	2028	|	2228
Lyon Part Dieu 344 346 a.	...	0752	0852	...	0952	1052	1152	1210	1252	1252	1352	1352	...	1452	1552	1752	...	1852	...	1952	...	2052	2152	2252

e – Also Apr. 17, May 1, 8, June 5.
h – Not Dec. 26 – 30.

⚒ – Daily except Sundays and holidays
† – Sundays and holidays

346 — LYON - BELLEGARDE - GENÈVE

SERVICE UNTIL APRIL 29

km																	TGV 9750												
		①–⑤	⑥	✕		⑥	①–⑤	⑥		⑥					N			a							a		R	
			a			ⓐ	0823c	1023	1023			1223	1223		1423	1423												
0	Lyon Perrache ......d.	...	...	0625	0823c	1023	1023	△		△		1223	1223	△	1423	1423	N	△	△	a					a	△		
4	Lyon Part Dieu 345 d.	...	...	0636	0834	1036	1036	...	1136	1234	1236	1336	1436	1436	1534	1636	1636	1736	...	...	...	1834	...	2036	2036			
54	Ambérieu 345 d.	...	...	0701	0859	1101	1103	...	1203	1259	1303	1403	1501	1503		1701	1703	1804	...	...	2101	2101						
106	Culoz 345 d.	...	...	0735	0933	1135	1136	...	1233	1335	1335	1435	1535	1536		1736	1736	1839	...	1936	...	2137	2138						
139	Bellegarde 364 ⓞ d.	0623	0653	0800	1000	1200	1157	1253	1258	1400	1357	1456	1602	1557	1648	1800	1757	1904	1923	1934	2000	2127	2200	2204				
172	Genève 364 ⓞ a.	0657	0727	0828	1028	1228	1258	1327	1400	1428	1442	...	1628	1642	1717	1828	1858	...	1957	2000	2028	2201	2230					

														TGV 9756											
		①–⑤	✕	①–⑥	✕		ⓑ	⑥	⑥	⑥	①–⑤		⑥		⑥		①–⑤			✝	①–⑤		①–⑤	ⓑ	
		a		a			△	0928	△	a			△		△		a		△		a		a	b	
Genève 364 ⓞ d.		0503	...	0558	...	0729	0929	0928	1000	1129	1128	1203	1241	1329	1328	1529	1528	...	1603	1729	...	1903	1929	2018	2101
Bellegarde 364 ⓞ d.		0535	0552	0631	0655	0758	0958	1001	1055	1158	1201	1235	1311	1358	1401	1558	1601	1655	1635	1758	1855	1935	1958	2052	2126
Culoz 345 d.		0616	...	0718	...	0820	1023	1024	1119	1220	1224	...	1422	1424	1623	1624	1720	...	1823	1917	...	2023			
Ambérieu 345 d.		0653	...	0754	...	0858	1058	1058	1154	1258	1258	...	1458	1458	1658	1658	1754	...	1858	1958	...	2058			
Lyon Part-Dieu 345 a.		0724	...	0822	...	0922	1122	1122	1222	1322	1322	1426	1522	1522	1722	1722	1822	...	1922	2022	...	2122			
Lyon Perrache a.		...	...	...	...	0934	1135	1135	...	1333	1333	...	...	...	...	...	...	...	...	...	...	2135			

N – 🚆 Genève - Lyon - Marseille - Nice and v.v. (Table 350).
R – Not ⑤.

a – Not Dec. 26, Jan. 2, Apr. 14, 17.
b – Not Apr. 16.
c – ⓒ only.

ⓞ – Additional journeys: **From Bellegarde** at 0553 ①–⑤ a, 0723 ①–⑤ a, 1723 ①–⑤ a, 1823 ①–⑤ a and 2027 ①–⑤ a. **From Genève** at 1703 ①–⑤ a and 1803 ①–⑤ a.
△ – To / from Évian les Bains (Table 363) and / or St Gervais (Table 365).

TGV – ℝ, supplement payable, ☂.

348 — LYON - ST ÉTIENNE

TGV trains (Paris) - Lyon - St Étienne

	TGV 6681 ①–⑥ b		TGV 6685		TGV 6687		TGV 6689				TGV 6691 ①–⑥ b		TGV 6693		TGV 6695		TGV 6697 ⓐ	TGV 6697 ⓒ
Paris Gare de Lyon 340 ...d.	0659	...	1259	...	1657	...	1857	...	St Étienne Châteaucreux...d.	0613	...	1013	...	1213	...	1642	1813
Lyon Part-Dieu	0905	...	1505	...	1905	...	2105	...	Lyon Part-Dieu	0658	...	1058	...	1258	...	1728	1859
St Étienne Châteaucreux ...a.	0947	...	1547	...	1947	...	2147	...	Paris Gare de Lyon 340.....a.	0901	...	1301	...	1501	...	1932	2101

Local Trains Lyon - St Étienne SEE NOTE ✕

km		①–⑥ b	①–⑥ b	⑥ k	ⓐ	△		ⓐ			ⓐ			ⓐ			ⓐ	b	ⓐ		ⓐ		ⓐ
0	Lyon Part-Dieu..........d.	...	0624	...	0654	0705	...	0724	...	0754	...	0824	...	0854	0924	...	0954	1024	...	1054	1124	...	1154
	Lyon Perrache ....d.	0540		0640		...	0710		0732	0740		0810		0832			0932		1032			1132		
22	Givors Ville ....d.	0558	0641	0659	0658	0711	...	0728	0741	0758	0758	0828	0828	0841	0858	0911	0942	0958	1012	1042	1058	1112	1142	1158	1211
47	St Chamond ....d.	0617	0700	0717	0717	0730		0747	0800	0817	0817	0831	0847	0900	0917	0930	1000	1017	1031	1100	1117	1130	1200	1217	1230
59	St Étienne ⊙ ....a.	0626	0710	0726	0726	0740	0747	0756	0809	0826	0826	0840	0856	0909	0926	0940	1010	1026	1040	1110	1126	1140	1210	1226	1239

		①–⑥ b			ⓐ		ⓐ			ⓐ	b		ⓐ		⑥	ⓐ		①–⑤ b	ⓐ		ⓐ		ⓒ	ⓐ △		ⓐ
Lyon Part-Dieu......... d.	1206	1224		1254	1324	...	1354	1424		1454	1524	...	1554	...	1624	...	1654	1706	...	1724	...	...	1754	...	1824
Lyon Perrache .... d.			1232			1332			1432			1532		1602		1632	1640			1710z		1732	1740		1810	
Givors Ville .... d.	1242	1258	1312	1342	1358	1411	1442	1458	1512	1542	1558	1612	1642	1658	1712		1728	1742	1758	1758	1811	1828	1842
St Chamond .... d.	1300	1317	1330	1400	1417	1430	1500	1517	1530	1600	1617	1630	1647	1700	1717	1725	1731		1747	1801	1817	1817	1830	1847	1901
St Étienne ⊙ ....a.	1247	1310	1326	1340	1410	1426	1440	1510	1526	1539	1610	1626	1640	1656	1710	1726	1738	1741	1746	1756	1810	1826	1826	1839	1856	1910

		⑥ k	ⓐ		ⓐ b		ⓐ		ⓐ b	ⓐ h		ⓐ h		ⓐ		ⓐ c	ⓐ d	
Lyon Part-Dieu......... d.	...	...	1854	...	1924	...	1954	2024	...	2124	2224	2324	St Étienne ⊙ .... d.	0520	0534	0550	0604	0620	0634	0650	0704	0704	0711
Lyon Perrache .... d.	1832	1840		1902		1932			2032				St Chamond............ d.	0529	0543	0559	0613	0629	0643	0659	0713	0713	
Givors Ville .... d.	1858	1858	1911	1928	1942	1958	2011	2042	2058	2142	2242	2343	Givors Ville............ d.	0548	0602	0618	0632	0648	0702	0718	0732	0732	
St Chamond .... d.	1917	1917	1930	1947	2000	2017	2030	2100	2117	2200	2301	0002	Lyon Perrache ...... a.		0628		0658		0720		0750	0758	
St Étienne ⊙ ....a.	1926	1926	1939	1956	2010	2026	2039	2110	2126	2210	2310	0012	Lyon Part-Dieu ...... a.	0606		0636		0706		0736			0754

		ⓐ		ⓐ		ⓐ		ⓐ	b		ⓐ		①–⑥ b		ⓐ		ⓐ		ⓐ b		ⓐ		ⓐ
St Étienne ⊙ .... d.	0720	0734	0750	0804	0813	0820	0834	0850	0904	0920	0920	0934	0950	1004	1020	1050	1104	1120	1150	1204	1220	1250	1304	1330	1350	1404	1413	1420
St Chamond .... d.	0729	0743	0759	0813		0829	0843	0859	0913	0929	0959	1013	1029	1059	1113	1129	1159	1213	1229	1259	1313	1329	1359	1413		1429
Givors Ville .... d.	0748	0802	0818	0832		0848	0902	0918	0932	0948	1018	1031	1048	1118	1132	1148	1218	1232	1248	1318	1332	1348	1418	1432		1448
Lyon Perrache .... a.		0820		0850r		0928		0958		1058		1158		1258		1358		1458			
Lyon Part-Dieu.........a.	0806		0836		0854	0906		0936		1006	1036		1106	1136		1206	1236		1306	1336		1406	1436		1454	1506

		①–⑥ b		ⓐ	ⓐ △		ⓐ	⑥	ⓐ k	ⓐ		ⓐ		ⓒ	ⓐ		ⓐ		ⓐ	ⓐ k	h		ⓑ	h
St Étienne ⊙ .... d.	1450	1504	1520	1550	1604	1620	1634	1650	1704	1704	1720	1734	1750	1804	1804	1820	1834	1850	1904	1904	1913	1920	2004	2020	2118	2253
St Chamond .... d.	1459	1513	1529	1559	1613	1629	1643	1659	1713	1713	1729	1743	1813	1813	1829	1843	1913	1913		1929	2013	2029	2127	2302
Givors Ville .... d.	1518	1532	1548	1618	1632	1648	1702	1718	1732	1732	1748	1802	1818	1832	1832	1848	1902	1918	1932	1932		1948	2032	2048	2146	2322
Lyon Perrache .... a.		1558		1658		1720		1750	1758		1820		1850	1858		1920q		1950	1958		2058	
Lyon Part-Dieu.........a.	1536		1606	1636		1706		1736		1806		1836			1906		1936			1954	2006		2106	2204	2340

b – Not Apr. 17, May 1,8, June 5.
c – Not Dec. 19–30.
d – Also ①–⑤ Dec. 19–30.
h – Not May 25.
k – Also May 25.
q – 1928 Dec. 19–30.

r – 0858 on ⓒ (daily Dec. 17 - Jan. 1).
z – 1702 Dec. 19–30.

TGV – ℝ, supplement payable, ☂.

⊙ – St Étienne Châteaucreux.

△ – Timings may vary by up to 3 minutes Dec. 19–30.
✕ – Services from / to Lyon Perrache are subject to alteration Jan. 30 - Apr. 9.

TGV services are subject to alteration from Apr. 3

349 — ST ÉTIENNE - LE PUY

SERVICE UNTIL APRIL 2

km		ⓐ	✕		✕		ⓐ			ⓐ	✕	ⓐ			
	Lyon Part Dieu 348 ....d.	...	...	...	...	1206	...	1454	...	...	1706	...	...	...	...
0	St Étienne Châteaucreux ....d.	0531	0648	...	0846	1010	...	1251	1542	1553	...	1711	1748	1748	1845	...	2010	...	2157	...
15	Firminy ....d.	0548	0710	...	0903	1026	...	1310	...	1604	1610	...	1728	1806	1806	1902	...	2033	...	2220
88	Le Puy en Velay ....a.	0721	0827	...	1022	1138	...	1428	...	1720	...	1844	1917	1917	2017	...	2144	...	2328

		ⓐ	ⓐ	ⓐ			ⓐ						ⓑ			✝	
Le Puy en Velay ....d.	0430	...	0556	0639	0740	0834	...	1032	...	1232	...	1615	1728	...	1935	2040	...
Firminy ....d.	0541	...	0644	0708	0755	0858	0948	...	1148	...	1354	...	1726	1854	...	2053	2150
St Étienne Châteaucreux ......a.	0603	...	0706	0731	0810	0913	1005	...	1205	...	1410	...	1742	1910	...	2109	2207
Lyon Part Dieu 348 ....a.	...	0754	0820p	0854	...	...	...	1454	...	...	1954	...	...	...

p – Lyon **Perrache**. 0824 from Jan. 30.

TGV Méditerranée — PARIS / LYON - AVIGNON - MARSEILLE - TOULON - NICE — 350

For *TGV* trains Paris - Valence Ville - Avignon Centre see Table **351**. Certain Paris - Toulon trains continue to Hyères (Table **360**).

Services from Paris are subject to alteration on Mar. 18, 19. Timings may vary by a few minutes on certain dates – please check your TGV reservation for confirmed timings.

km	All *TGV* trains are 🄁	*TGV* 6805 Ⓐ	*TGV* 6805 Ⓒ ⊖	*TGV* 6101 Ⓐ a	*TGV* 6171	*TGV* 6103 ①–⑥ b	*TGV* 6890 C A	*TGV* 6105	*TGV* 9810	*TGV* 5110	*TGV* 6173	*TGV* 6820 ⊕	*TGV* 6886 B ⊕	*TGV* 6107 K	*TGV* 5338 N ⊗	*TGV* 6175	*TGV* 6109
	Brussels Midi **11** d.	...	...	...	...	...	...	...	0710	...	...	...	...	...	...	...	...
	Lille Europe **11** d.	...	...	...	...	...	...	...	|	0654f	...	...	...	...	...	...	...
	Charles de Gaulle ✈ **11** d.	...	...	...	...	...	...	...	0830	0830	...	...	...	...	...	...	...
	Marne la Vallée-Chessy § **11** d.	...	...	...	...	...	...	...	0843	0843	...	...	...	...	...	...	...
0	**Paris** Gare de Lyon ▶ d.	...	...	0607	0719	0737	...	0837	|	|	0921	...	...	0937	...	1019	1037
	Metz **379** d.	...	...	|	|	|	...	|	|	|	|	0544	...	|	...	|	|
	Strasbourg **379** d.	...	...	|	|	|	...	|	|	|	|	|	...	|	...	|	|
	Dijon **379** d.	...	...	|	|	|	...	|	|	|	|	0921	0921	|	...	|	|
	Genève **346** d.	...	...	|	|	|	...	|	|	|	|	|	|	|	...	|	|
◧	**Lyon** Part Dieu ▶ d.	0628	0702	|	|	|	...	|	1036	1036	|	1107	1107	|	1136	|	|
	Lyon St Exupéry ✈ ▶ d.	|	|	|	|	|	...	1032	|	|	|	|	|	|	|	|	|
527	Valence TGV ▶ d.	0704	|	0827	|	|	1006	|	1113	1113	|	|	|	|	|	|	|
657	**Avignon** TGV d.	0739	0806	0901	1000	1019	1040	1123	1146	1146	|	1210	1210	1218	1243	1258	1320
731	Aix en Provence TGV d.	0807	0834	0930	|	1047	1109	|	|	|	1220	1238	1238	1247	1312	|	1348
750	**Marseille** St Charles a.	0820	0848	0943	|	1059	1121	1200	1220	1220	|	1250	1250	1259	1325	|	1400
750	**Marseille** St Charles **360** d.	0831	0900	...	|	...	...	...	...	...	|	1302	...	...	...	|	...
817	**Toulon** **360** a.	0912	0941	...	1111	...	...	...	...	...	1308	1342	...	...	...	1408	...
885	Les Arcs-Draguignan **360** a.	0949	1019	...	1149	...	...	...	...	...	|	1420	...	...	...	1445	...
911	St Raphaël-Valescure **360** a.	1007	1037	...	|	...	...	...	...	...	1404	1438	...	...	...	1503	...
944	**Cannes** **360** a.	1037	1107	...	1233	...	...	...	...	...	1433	1508	...	...	...	1534	...
955	Antibes **360** a.	1049	1118	...	1245	...	...	...	...	...	1445	1520	...	...	...	1545	...
975	**Nice** **360** a.	1105	1134	...	1301	...	...	...	...	...	1505	1546	...	...	...	1601	...

	TGV 5316 H	*TGV* 6111	*TGV* 9877 X	*TGV* 9826	*TGV* 5164	*TGV* 6113	*TGV* 9756	*TGV* 6837 ◇	*TGV* 6177 V	*TGV* 9828	*TGV* 6145	*TGV* 6179 L	*TGV* 6117	*TGV* 5334 N ⊙	*TGV* 6169 ①–④ m	*TGV* 6119 ⑤⑦ d	*TGV* 6815	*TGV* 6121 Ⓑ h
Brussels Midi **11** d.	...	...	...	1031	...	...	...	...	...	1217	...	...	...	...	...	...	...	...
Lille Europe **11** d.	...	...	...	|	1034t	...	...	...	...	1252t	...	...	...	...	...	...	...	...
Charles de Gaulle ✈ **11** d.	...	...	...	1157	1157	...	...	...	...	1358	...	...	...	...	...	...	...	...
Marne la Vallée-Chessy § **11** d.	...	...	...	1210	1210	...	...	...	...	1411	...	...	...	...	...	...	...	...
Paris Gare de Lyon ▶ d.	...	1137	...	|	|	1237	...	...	1419	|	1437	1519	1537	...	1615	1615	...	1637
Metz **379** d.	...	|	0811	|	|	|	...	...	|	|	|	|	|	...	|	|	...	|
Strasbourg **379** d.	...	|	0906	|	|	|	...	1113	|	|	|	|	|	...	|	|	...	|
Dijon **379** d.	...	|	|	|	|	|	...	|	|	|	|	|	|	...	|	|	1606	|
Genève **346** d.	...	|	|	|	|	|	1241	|	|	|	|	|	|	...	|	|	|	|
Lyon Part Dieu ▶ d.	1236	|	1310	1406	1406	|	1436	1536	|	1606	|	|	|	1736	|	|	1806	|
Lyon St Exupéry ✈ ▶ d.	|	|	|	|	|	|	|	|	|	|	|	|	|	|	|	|	|	|
Valence TGV ▶ d.	1311	|	1350	1442	1442	|	1513	1613	|	|	|	|	|	1813	|	|	1841	|
Avignon TGV d.	1344	1420	1428	|	|	1519	1546	1646	|	1709	1716	1759	1819	1846	|	|	|	1920
Aix en Provence TGV d.	|	1448	1456	1537	1537	1548	|	|	1722	1737	1745	|	1847	|	|	|	1936	1948
Marseille St Charles a.	1423	1500	1512	1549	1549	1603	1620	1722	|	1749	1757	|	1859	1921	1925	1925	1948	2000
Marseille St Charles **360** d.	...	...	...	...	...	...	1632	...	|	1800	...	|	...	...	1936	1936	1958	...
Toulon **360** a.	...	...	...	...	...	...	1714	...	1810	1843	...	1909	...	...	2018	2018	2042	...
Les Arcs-Draguignan **360** a.	...	...	...	...	...	...	|	...	|	1920	...	|	...	...	|	...	2121	...
St Raphaël-Valescure **360** a.	...	...	...	...	...	...	1806	...	1902	1939	...	2000	...	...	2108	...	2140	...
Cannes **360** a.	...	...	...	...	...	...	1835	...	1932	2009	...	2030	...	...	2139	...	2211	...
Antibes **360** a.	...	...	...	...	...	...	1847	...	1943	2020	...	2043	...	...	2151	...	2223	...
Nice **360** a.	...	...	...	...	...	...	1903	...	2000	2036	...	2103	...	...	2207	...	2239	...

	TGV 6181	*TGV* 5134	*TGV* 6123	*TGV* 6183 ⑤–⑦ r	*TGV* 6153 ①–④ m	*TGV* 9580 ♣	*TGV* 6127 J	*TGV* 5347 R ⊖	*TGV* 6187 ⑤ Y	*TGV* 6129	*TGV* 6892 D A	*TGV* 5124 z	*TGV* 5124 E	*TGV* 6131 ②–④ ♥	*TGV* 6131 ②–④ M	*TGV* 6827 Ⓒ	*TGV* 6827 Ⓐ z ✣	*TGV* 6827 E	*TGV* 6131 S	*TGV* 6131 T	*TGV* 6137 ⑤⑦ Y
Brussels Midi **11** d.	...	...	...	...	...	...	...	...	...	...	...	...	...	...	...	...	...	...	...	...	...
Lille Europe **11** d.	...	1543t	...	...	...	...	...	...	...	...	...	1822t	1822t	...	...	...	...	...	...	...	...
Charles de Gaulle ✈ **11** d.	...	1656	...	...	...	...	...	...	...	...	...	1928	1928	...	...	...	...	...	...	...	...
Marne la Vallée-Chessy § **11** d.	...	1711	...	...	...	...	...	...	...	...	...	1941	1941	...	...	...	...	...	...	...	...
Paris Gare de Lyon ▶ d.	1719	|	1737	1819	1819	...	1837	...	1919	1937	...	|	|	2019	2019	...	...	...	2037	2037	2137
Metz **379** d.	|	|	|	|	|	...	|	...	|	|	...	|	|	|	|	...	...	...	|	|	|
Strasbourg **379** d.	|	|	|	|	|	1615	|	...	|	|	...	|	|	|	|	1803	1836	1836	|	|	|
Dijon **379** d.	|	|	|	|	|	|	|	...	|	|	...	|	|	|	|	2030	|	|	|	|	|
Genève **346** d.	|	|	|	|	|	|	|	...	|	|	...	|	|	|	|	|	|	|	|	|	|
Lyon Part Dieu ▶ d.	|	1906	|	|	|	2006	|	2036	|	|	...	2136	2136	|	|	2206	2206	2206	|	|	|
Lyon St Exupéry ✈ ▶ d.	|	|	|	|	|	|	|	|	|	|	...	|	|	|	|	|	|	|	|	|	|
Valence TGV ▶ d.	1932	|	|	|	|	|	|	2113	|	|	2157	|	|	|	|	|	|	|	|	|	|
Avignon TGV d.	|	2009	2019	|	|	2108	2121	2147	2159	2216	2231	2241	2252‡	2302	2313‡	2311	2311	2323‡	2320	2333‡	0021
Aix en Provence TGV d.	|	2037	2047	2121	2122	2136	2149	|	|	2245	2300	2310	|	2331	|	2342	2342	|	2350	|	0051
Marseille St Charles a.	|	2049	2100	|	|	2148	2203	2222	|	2257	2312	2321	2351	2343	0008	2354	2354	0018	0002	0028	0103
Marseille St Charles **360** d.	|	...	...	|	|	...	...	...	|	2309	...	...	...	...	...	...	...	...	...	...	...
Toulon **360** a.	2108	...	...	2209	2212	...	...	...	2309	2350	...	...	...	...	...	...	...	...	...	...	...
Les Arcs-Draguignan **360** a.	2145	...	...	|	...	...	...	...	|	...	...	...	...	...	...	...	...	...	...	...	...
St Raphaël-Valescure **360** a.	|	...	...	2300	...	...	...	...	0001	...	...	...	...	...	...	...	...	...	...	...	...
Cannes **360** a.	2228	...	...	2331	...	...	...	...	0030	...	...	...	...	...	...	...	...	...	...	...	...
Antibes **360** a.	2240	...	...	2343	...	...	...	...	0041	...	...	...	...	...	...	...	...	...	...	...	...
Nice **360** a.	2303	...	...	2359	...	...	...	...	0057	...	...	...	...	...	...	...	...	...	...	...	...

A – From Annecy (see panel).
B – From Basel (Table **379**).
C – Dec. 17, 31, Feb. 11, 18, 25, Apr. 8, 15, 22, 29, May 6, 25, June 3.
D – Dec. 18, Jan. 1, Feb. 19, 26, Mar. 5, Apr. 17, 23, May 1, 8, 28, June 5.
E – Jan. 16–19, 24–26, Feb. 27, 28, Mar. 1, 2, 7–9, Apr. 3–6, 11–13.
H – (12) Le Havre - Rouen - Massy - Lyon - Marseille (Table **335**). Subject to alteration on ⑦ from Apr. 9 (also on Apr. 15, 29, May 13, June 10, 17, 24).
J – Ⓑ (daily from Apr. 2).
K – ①–⑥ (daily from Apr. 3).
L – ⑤⑥ (daily from Apr. 3).
M – ②–④ Feb. 28 - Apr. 13 (not Mar. 14–30).
N – From Nantes via Massy TGV (Table **335**).
R – From Rennes via Massy TGV (Table **335**). Subject to alteration on Apr. 30, May 20, 27, June 10.
S – ①⑤⑥⑦ (also Apr. 18, May 24, June 6; not Feb. 27, Apr. 3). Subject to alteration on Jan. 16.
T – Runs on Feb. 27, Apr. 3 only.
V – To Ventimiglia (Table **360**).
X – From Luxembourg (Table **379**).
Y – From Apr. 7.

a – Not May 2, 9.
b – Not Apr. 17, May 1, 8, June 5.
d – Also Apr. 17, May 1, 8, 24, June 5.
f – Lille **Flandres**. Departs 0708 May 6–8.
h – Not May 25.
m – Not Apr. 17, May 1, 8, 24, 25, June 5.
r – Also Apr. 17, May 1, 8, June 5.
t – 4–11 minutes later to Jan. 22 and Apr. 24 - May 28.
z – Not Jan. 16–19, 24–26, Feb. 27, 28, Mar. 1, 2, 7–9, Apr. 3–6, 11–13.

TGV – 🄁, supplement payable, 🍸.

▶ – For Paris to Lyon see Table **340** (for Paris to St Exupéry ✈ see Table **342**). For additional trains from Paris and Lyon to Valence TGV see Table **355**. For Lyon to Valence Ville see Table **351**.
♥ – Not Feb. 28 - Mar. 9, Apr. 4–13, 18, May 2, 9, 24, 25, June 6. Subject to alteration Jan. 17–26.
◇ – Subject to alteration May 2–5, 15–19, 25–31, June 1, 2, 12–16, 26–30.
⊗ – Subject to alteration on Apr. 30, May 1, June 10, 11.
⊕ – Subject to alteration on Feb. 26, May 7, 21.
⊙ – Subject to alteration on May 20, June 10, 11.

ANNECY - MARSEILLE

	TGV 6890 C	*TGV* 6892 D
Annecy d.	0726	1931
Aix les Bains d.	0757	2001
Chambéry d.	0811	2016
Grenoble d.	0905	2056
Valence TGV a.	1001	2154
Marseille (see above) a.	1121	2312

⊖ – Subject to alteration on Jan. 15, 22.
‡ – Avignon **Centre**.
✣ – Subject to alteration.
♣ – From Frankfurt (Main), Table **47**.
◧ – Lyon Part Dieu to Valence TGV is 104 km.
§ – Station for Disneyland Paris.

Additional low-cost 'Ouigo' TGV trains run from Marne la Vallée-Chessy – see Table **350a**

For *TGV* trains Avignon Centre - Valence Ville - Paris see Table **351**. Certain Toulon - Paris trains start from Hyères (Table **360**).

Services to Paris are subject to alteration on Mar. 18, 19. Timings may vary by a few minutes on certain dates – please check your TGV reservation for confirmed timings.

All *TGV* trains are ℝ	TGV 6102 Ⓐ ①-④ m	TGV 6136	TGV 9854	TGV 6150 Ⓐ a	TGV 6898 Ⓐ	TGV 6898 Ⓒ	TGV 6106	TGV 6894 C A	TGV 9582 ♣	TGV 6108 Ⓐ	TGV 6108 Ⓑk	TGV 5366 ①-⑤ hR	TGV 5366 ⑥d R⊗	TGV 5366 ⑦ R⊖	TGV 6112	TGV 9860 Ⓒ	TGV 9860 Ⓐ	TGV 6172	TGV 6114	TGV 6814	TGV 6116
Nice .... 360 d.	...	...	...	...	...	...	...	...	...	...	...	...	...	...	...	...	...	0701	...	0723	...
Antibes .... 360 d.	...	...	...	...	...	...	...	...	...	...	...	...	...	...	...	...	...	0717	...	0743	...
Cannes .... 360 d.	...	...	...	...	...	...	...	...	...	...	...	...	...	...	...	...	...	0728	...	0755	...
St Raphaël-Valescure .. 360 d.	...	...	...	...	...	...	...	...	...	...	...	...	...	...	...	...	...	...	...	0823	...
Les Arcs-Draguignan .... 360 d.	...	...	...	...	...	...	...	...	...	...	...	...	...	...	...	...	...	0812	...	0842	...
Toulon .... 360 d.	...	...	...	0545	...	...	...	...	...	0745	0755	...	...	...	...	...	...	0851	...	0921	...
Marseille St Charles .. 360 a.	...	...	...	...	...	...	...	...	...	0826	0836	...	...	...	...	...	...	...	...	1002	...
Marseille St Charles ...d.	0520	0601	0611	...	0640	0640	0702	0750	0810	0838	0848	0833	0837	0840	0901	0911	0911	1001	1014	...	1202
Aix en Provence TGV ...... d.	0534	0616	0625	0637		0716	...	0804	0825						0915	0925	0925	1015	1029	...	1216
Avignon TGV .... d.	0603	0644		0705	0716	0716	0745	...	0832	0853		0919	0913	0916	0944	0953	0953	1004	1044	...	1245
Valence TGV ....▶ d.			0721		0750	0750		0904				0952	0951	0951					1125		
Lyon St Exupéry ✈ ....▶ d.																					
Lyon Part Dieu ....▶ a.			0754		0823	0823			0954			1026	1024	1024		1054	1054		1158		
Genève 346 .... a.																					
Dijon 379 .... a.					1000														1359		
Strasbourg 379 .... a.					1152	1219					1344										
Metz 379 .... a.																					
Paris Gare de Lyon ....▶ a.	0841	0923		0942			1023			1145	1159				1223			1241	1323		1523
Marne la Vallée-Chessy § 11 .. a.			0949													1248	1248				
Charles de Gaulle ✈ 11 ...... a.			1002													1302	1302				
Lille Europe 11 .... a.			1103													1404	1421				
Brussels Midi 11 .... a.			1151													1457	1512				

	TGV 9866 V	TGV 6174	TGV 5368 N△	TGV 6874 ¶	TGV 6118		TGV 9750	TGV 6176	TGV 9750		TGV 6120 J	TGV 5192	TGV 6122 N⊡	TGV 6864 ⊕	TGV 6885 B		TGV 5376 H	TGV 6124	TGV 9898 ⑤ X	TGV 9898 ②-④ X	TGV 9898 ① X	TGV 9898 ⑥⑦ X
Nice .... 360 d.	0919	1002	...	...	...	...	1055	1102	...	...	...	...	1222	...	...	...	...	...	...	...	...	...
Antibes .... 360 d.	0936	1019	...	...	...	...	1110	1118	...	...	...	...	1238	...	...	...	...	...	...	...	...	...
Cannes .... 360 d.	0948	1030	...	...	...	...	1121	1129	...	...	...	...	1250	...	...	...	...	...	...	...	...	...
St Raphaël-Valescure .. 360 d.	1019	1058	...	...	...	...	1148	1157	...	...	...	...	1317	...	...	...	...	...	...	...	...	...
Les Arcs-Draguignan .... 360 d.	1039		...	...	...	...			...	...	...	...	1336	...	...	...	...	...	...	...	...	...
Toulon .... 360 d.	1117	1151	...	...	...	...	1245	1250	←	...	...	...	1414	...	...	...	1450	...	...	...	...	...
Marseille St Charles .. 360 a.	1158		...	...	...	...	1329		1329	...	...	...	1456	...	...	...	1534	...	...	...	...	...
Marseille St Charles ...d.	1210		1239	1239	1303	...		1347		1400	1408	1439	1456	1508	1508	...	1539	1548	1602	1604	1604	1609
Aix en Provence TGV ...... d.	1224		1253	1253	1317	...		1401		1415	1423	1515	1523	1523		...		1604	1617	1618	1621	1625
Avignon TGV .... d.	1253	1303	1322	1322	1346	...		1404	1429	1443	1451	1522	1543	1551	1551	...	1616		1647	1646	1652	1653
Valence TGV ....▶ d.						...										...	1650	1658				
Lyon St Exupéry ✈ ....▶ d.						...				1537						...						
Lyon Part Dieu ....▶ a.	1354		1423	1423		...		1528			1554	1624		1654	1654	...	1724		1750	1750	1754	1754
Genève 346 .... a.						...		1717								...						
Dijon 379 .... a.						...								1847	1847	...						
Strasbourg 379 .... a.				1857		...										...			2155	2155	2155	2155
Metz 379 .... a.						...								2219		...			2256	2256	2256	2256
Paris Gare de Lyon ....▶ a.		1541			1623	...		1641		1730		1823			1915	...						
Marne la Vallée-Chessy § 11 .. a.	1548					...				1748						...						
Charles de Gaulle ✈ 11 ...... a.	1602					...				1802						...						
Lille Europe 11 .... a.	1657					...				1944f						...						
Brussels Midi 11 .... a.	1743					...										...						

	TGV 6178 L	TGV 6128 J	TGV 9882	TGV 6184		TGV 6130 W	TGV 5180*		TGV 6168 J	TGV 6896 D A	TGV 6132	TGV 6180		TGV 6806		TGV 6186 ⑦ U		TGV 6144 ⑦ U
Nice .... 360 d.	1352	...	...	1500r	...	...	...	...	1547	...	...	1654	...	1725	...	1802	...	...
Antibes .... 360 d.	1410	...	...	1515r	...	...	...	...	1604	...	...	1710	...	1742	...	1818	...	...
Cannes .... 360 d.	1422	...	...	1528	...	...	...	...	1616	...	...	1721	...	1753	...	1830	...	...
St Raphaël-Valescure .. 360 d.	1450	...	...	1555	...	...	...	...	1645	...	...		...	1820	...	1857	...	...
Les Arcs-Draguignan .... 360 d.	1510	...	...		...	...	...	...	1704	...	1805		...	1839	...		...	...
Toulon .... 360 d.	1549	...	...	1650	...	...	...	...	1742	...	1847		...	1918	...	1951	...	...
Marseille St Charles .. 360 a.		...	...		...	...	...	...	1823	...			...	2002	...		...	...
Marseille St Charles ...d.		1700	1710		...	1801	1810	...	1834	1846	1902		...	2013	...		2102	...
Aix en Provence TGV ...... d.		1714	1724		...	1815	1825	...		1900	1916		...	2027	...		2116	...
Avignon TGV .... d.	1702	1743	1752	1803	...	1844	1852	...	1928	1945	2003		...	2055	...	2104	2145	...
Valence TGV ....▶ d.					...			...	2000				...	2128	...			...
Lyon St Exupéry ✈ ....▶ d.					...			...					...		...			...
Lyon Part Dieu ....▶ a.			1854		...		1954	...					...	2203	...			...
Genève 346 .... a.					...			...					...		...			...
Dijon 379 .... a.					...			...					...		...			...
Strasbourg 379 .... a.					...			...					...		...			...
Metz 379 .... a.					...			...					...		...			...
Paris Gare de Lyon ....▶ a.	1941	2023		2041	...	2123		...	2145		2223	2241	...		...	2344	0023	...
Marne la Vallée-Chessy § 11 .. a.			2048		...		2148	...					...		...			...
Charles de Gaulle ✈ 11 ...... a.			2102		...		2202	...					...		...			...
Lille Europe 11 .... a.			2156		...		2305z	...					...		...			...
Brussels Midi 11 .... a.			2256		...			...					...		...			...

A – To Annecy (see panel).
B – To Basel (Table **379**).
C – Dec. 17, 31, Feb. 11, 18, 25, Apr. 8, 15, 22, 29, May 6, 25, June 3.
D – Dec. 18, Jan. 1, Feb. 19, 26, Mar. 5, Apr. 17, 23, May 1, 8, 28, June 5.
H – 🚏 Marseille - Lyon - Massy - Rouen - Le Havre (Table **335**). Subject to alteration from Apr. 3.
J – Ⓑ (daily from Apr. 2).
L – ⑥⑦ (daily from Apr. 1).
N – To Nantes via Massy TGV (Table **335**).
R – To Rennes via Massy TGV (Table **335**).
U – From Apr. 9.
V – From Ventimiglia (Table **360**).
W – Daily to Apr. 1; Ⓑ from Apr. 3 (not May 25).
X – To Luxembourg (Table **379**).

a – Not Apr. 18, May 2, 9, June 6.
d – Also May 25.
f – Lille **Flandres**. Arrives 1922 on May 6, 7, 8.
h – Not May 25.
k – Also May 25.
m – Not Apr. 17, May 1, 8, 24, 25, June 5.

r – On ⑤ departs Nice 1458, Antibes 1514.
z – Arrives Lille **Flandres** (not Lille Europe) Jan. 16–20.

TGV – ℝ, supplement payable, ⏛.

⊕ – Subject to alteration on Jan. 22, May 6, 7, 20, 21.
⊗ – Subject to alteration on May 20, 27, June 10.
⊖ – Subject to alteration on Apr. 16, 30, May 21, June 11.
¶ – Subject to alteration on May 25, 26, 27.
△ – Subject to alteration on Apr. 15, 16, 29, 30, May 20, 25, 26, 27, June 10, 11, 17, 24.
⊡ – Subject to alteration on May 20, June 10.
◇ – Subject to alteration on May 26, 27.
* – **5180** is combined with **5186** Lyon - Lille.
♣ – To Frankfurt (Main) Hbf, Table **47**.
▶ – For Lyon - Paris see Table **340** (for St Exupéry ✈ - Paris see Table **342**). For additional trains Valence TGV - Lyon and Paris see Table **355**. For Valence Ville - Lyon - Paris see Table **351**.
§ – Station for Disneyland Paris.

Additional low-cost 'Ouigo' TGV trains run to Marne la Vallée-Chessy – see Table **350a**

MARSEILLE - ANNECY

	TGV 6894 C	TGV 6896 D
Marseille (see above)..d.	0750	1846
Valence TGV ....d.	0907	2003
Grenoble ....a.	1000	2053
Chambéry ....a.	1042	2134
Aix les Bains ....a.	1055	2147
Annecy ....a.	1130	2225

Low-cost *TGV* services branded **Ouigo**, internet booking only through www.ouigo.com, special conditions apply. For regular *TGV* services see Tables **350** and **355**.

Timings and days of running are given as a guide only and may vary – please confirm when booking. Short-distance journeys may not be available for booking.

	TGV 6299 ①⑦	TGV 6299 ⑥	TGV 6299 ⑤		TGV 6258 ⑤	TGV 6250 ⑥⑦	TGV 6258 ①	TGV 6254 ②-④		TGV 6252 ①-⑤	TGV 6258 ⑥⑦		TGV 6260 ⑥	TGV 6262 ⑤⑦		TGV 6264 ①	TGV 6266 ②-④	TGV 6268 ⑤	TGV 6272 ⑤	TGV 6270 ①	TGV 6272 ⑦	
Marne la Vallée § ....d.	...	...	...	...	0913	0948	1020	1114	...	1222	1222	...	1748	1752	...	1909	1926	2018	2035	2042	2048	...
Lyon Part Dieu ....a.															...	...	2100	...	2208			
Lyon Perrache..............a.	0605	0605	0605									...										
Lyon St Exupéry + ...d.				...	1115	1135	1211	1302	...	1409	1411	...	1932	1948	...	2111s	...	...	2225s	2226s	2232s	...
Valence TGV..............a.														2011	...	2136	...	2258	2255	2258		
Avignon TGV..............a.	0705	0709	0712	...	1225				...	1458												
Aix en Provence TGV..........a.	0733	0738	0744	...					...			...	2052		...	2230	...	2357	2355	2358		
Marseille St Charles..........a.	0750	0754	0800	...		1304			...	1536		...	2107		...	2249	...	0012	0011	0013		
Nîmes ....a.	...	...	...	...	1220	...	1313	1405	...	...	1515	...	...	2056	...	...	...	...	...	...	...	...
Montpellier..............a.					1254	...	1349	1434		...	1549	...	...	2124								

	TGV 6276 ⑤	TGV 6278 ⑦	TGV 6276 ⑥	TGV 6280 ①	TGV 6282 ②-④	TGV 6284 ①-⑥	TGV 6296 ⑦		TGV 6286 ⑥⑦	TGV 6294 ⑤	TGV 6294 ①	TGV 6290 ②-④	TGV 6288 ①	TGV 6292 ⑤	TGV 6294 ②-④	TGV 3294 ⑥	TGV 3294 ⑦		TGV 6298 ⑥
Montpellier..............d.	...	...	...	...	...	...	...	...	1336	1433	1508	...	...	...	1638	1640	...	...	...
Nîmes ....d.	...	...	...	...	...	...	...	...	1405	1503	1540	...	...	...	1710	1710	...	...	...
Marseille St Charles..........d.	0516	...	0602	0618	...	0822	0831	...	1338			...	1608	1611	1617			...	2143
Aix en Provence TGV..........d.	...	...	...	...	...	0836	...	...	1353			...		1626				...	...
Avignon TGV..............d.	0553	...	0639	0657	...	...	0908	...				...	1644		1654			...	...
Valence TGV..............d.								...	1450	1553	1631	...				1757	1757	...	...
Lyon St Exupéry + ...d.	0647s	...	0731	0754	...	0949	1000	...	1512	1517	1622	1659	1752	1752	1747s	1823s	1826	...	...
Lyon Perrache..............d.			0713		0834			...										...	2318
Marne la Vallée § ....a.	0840	0911	0916	0940	1034	1134	1145	...	1701	1701	1809	1844	1938	1938	1938	2013	2013	...	...

TOURCOING - NANTES, RENNES and LYON

	TGV 7632 ①-⑥	TGV 7608 ⑦	TGV 7612	TGV 7602
Tourcoing..............d.	0829	...	1129	1947
TGV Haute-Picardie.....d.	0909	...	1214		
Charles de Gaulle + ...d.	0949	...	1248	2103
Marne la Vallée §.......d.	1003	...	1304		
Lyon Part Dieu ....a.				2308
Lyon Perrache..........d.		0807		
Massy TGV..............d.	1038	1038	1338	
Le Mans ....a.	1127	1127	1428	
Rennes..............a.			1544	
Angers St Laud..........a.	1208	1212	...	...
Nantes..............a.	1252	1259	...	...

	TGV 7600 ⑧	TGV 7630	TGV 7610 ⑧	TGV 7604 ⑥
Nantes ....d.		1400	...	...
Angers St Laud........d.		1448	...	...
Rennes..............d.			1810	1810
Le Mans ....d.		1533	1929	1929
Massy TGV..............d.		1625	2025	2026
Lyon Part Dieu.....a.	...			2225
Lyon Perrache......d.	0734			
Marne la Vallée § ...d.		1701	2100	
Charles de Gaulle + d.	0952	1716	2116	
TGV Haute-Picardie..a.			2144	
Tourcoing..............a.	1051	1827	2226	

s –   Calls to set down only.

§ –   Marne la Vallée - Chessy (station for Disneyland Paris). Journey from central Paris is approximately 40 minutes on RER Line A.

hidden europe

Discover Europe's rich diversity with *hidden europe* magazine.

Well penned prose about journeys and places — from the Ural Mountains to the Azores, from the Arctic to the Mediterranean.

Join us as we venture by train and ferry to the nerve ends of Europe. 'Slow Travel' at its best.

e-mail: info@hiddeneurope.co.uk
phone: +49 30 755 16 128

www.hiddeneurope.co.uk

351 LYON - VALENCE - AVIGNON - MARSEILLE

All *TGV* trains are Ⓡ. See Table **350** for *TGV* services Paris - Valence TGV - Avignon TGV - Marseille and v.v., Table **355** for *TGV* services Paris - Valence TGV - Montpellier and v.v.

km									*TGV*	*TGV*				*TGV*				*TGV*							
						17705			**6191**	**6191**	**17709**			**6199**	**17713**			**6193**	**17717**	**17717**		**17721**			
		⚒	⚒	①–⑥					①–⑥	①–⑤		①–⑤	⚒	⑥			①–⑤			①–⑤			Ⓐ		⚒
				b					**b**	**H**		**H**	**q**	**G**	**q**	**q**	**H**	**E**	**q**	**H**					
	Paris Gare de Lyon § d.	...	...	...	...	...	...	...	0741	0741	...	...	...	0927	...	...	...	1141	...	...	...	...	...	...	...
	Lyon St Exupéry TGV ✈ § d.	...	...	...	...	...	...	...	0942	0942	...	...	...	1128	...	...	...	1342	...	...	...	...	...	...	...
	Lyon Perrache ▷ d.	...	...	0540	...	...	...	...	|	|	...	...	...	|	...	...	...	|	...	...	...	...	1540	...	...
0	**Lyon** Part-Dieu ▷ d.	...	...	|	...	0720	...	0820	|	|	0920	1010	1020	|	1120	1220	1220	|	1320	1328	1420	1520	|	...	1620
32	Vienne ▷ d.	...	...	0603	...	0741	...	0840	|	|	0941	1030	1040	|	1141	1240	1240	|	1341	1351	1440	1541	1603	...	1640
87	Tain-l'Hermitage-Tournon ▷ d.	...	...	0641	...	0815	...	0920	|	|	1015	|	1118	|	1215	1318	|	|	1415	|	1520	1615	1641	...	1718
105	**Valence** Ville ▷ a.	...	...	0652	...	0826	...	0931	1011	1011	1026	|	1128	1158	1226	1328	|	1411	1426	|	1531	1626	1652	...	1728
105	**Valence** Ville d.	0612	0632	...	0702	0829	0932	...	1014	1014	1029	|	1132	1201	1229	1332	|	1414	1429	|	...	1629	1702	1702	1732
150	Montélimar d.	0635	0700	...	0730	0851	1000	...	1038	1038	1051	1215	1201	1225	1251	1401	1412	1437	1451	1516	...	1651	1730	1730	1801
202	Orange d.	0706	0735	...	0805	0924	1035	...	1103	1103	1124	1249	1235	1251	1324	1435	1447	1502	1524	1552	...	1724	1805	1805	1835
230	**Avignon** Centre a.	0729	0759	...	0828	0938	1059	...	1118	1118	1138	1311	1258	1304	1338	1458	1510	1516	1538	1608	...	1738	1828	1828	1858
230	**Avignon** Centre ▷ d.	0731	0804**a**	...	...	0941	...	...	...	1121	1141	...	...	1307	1341	...	...	1520	1541	1611	...	1741	...	...	...
265	Arles **355** ▷ d.	0749	0823**a**	...	...	1001	...	...	...	1143	1201	...	...	1325	1401	...	...	1542	1601	1631	...	1801	...	...	...
299	Miramas **355** ▷ d.	0809	0845**a**	...	...	1018	...	...	...	1203	1218	...	...	1345	1418	...	...	1601	1618	1651	...	1818	...	...	...
328	Vitrolles (for ✈) ⊖ **355** ▷ d.	0826	0901**a**	...	...	1036	...	...	...	...	1236	...	...	...	1436	...	...	...	1636	1711	...	1835	...	...	...
351	**Marseille** St Charles **355** ▷ a.	0842	0916**a**	...	...	1050	...	...	...	...	1254	...	...	...	1452	...	...	...	1650	1727	...	1849	...	...	...

						TGV	*TGV*			
	17725	**17725**				**6195**	**6195**	**17729**		
		⑤†	⑤			Ⓑ	⑥			
			f A			**h**	**k**			**n**
Paris Gare de Lyon § d.	...	...	...	...	...	1741	1745	...	...	...
Lyon St Exupéry TGV ✈ § d.	...	...	...	...	...	1941	1943	...	...	...
Lyon Perrache ▷ d.	...	...	...	1740	...	|	|	...	...	...
Lyon Part-Dieu ▷ d.	1720	1720	...	|	1820	|	|	1920	2020	2120
Vienne ▷ d.	1741	1741	...	1803	1840	|	|	1941	2040	2140
Tain-l'Hermitage-Tournon ▷ d.	1814	1814	...	1841	1918	|	|	2015	2120	2220
Valence Ville ▷ a.	1825	1825	...	1853	1928	2011	2012	2026	2131	2231
Valence Ville d.	1828	1828	1852	1902	1932	2014	2016	2029	...	...
Montélimar d.	1851	1851	1918	1931	2001	2037	2042	2051	...	...
Orange d.	1925	1925	1951	2005	2035	2102	2111	2124	...	...
Avignon Centre a.	1942	1942	2005	2028	2058	2118	2126	2138	...	...
Avignon Centre ▷ d.	...	1945	...	...	...	2121	2129	2141	...	...
Arles **355** ▷ d.	...	2006	...	...	...	2140	2148	2201	...	...
Miramas **355** ▷ d.	...	2025	...	...	...	2159	2207	2218	...	...
Vitrolles (for ✈) ⊖ **355** ▷ d.	...	|	...	...	...	...	...	2236	...	...
Marseille St Charles **355** ▷ a.	...	2053	...	...	...	...	...	2253	...	...

									TGV
			17702	**17702**					**6194**
	Ⓐ	⚒	①⑥	⚒		Ⓐ	⚒		①–⑤
			p△	△					**H**
Marseille St Charles **355** ▷ d.	...	...	0510	...	...	...	...	...	...
Vitrolles (for ✈) ⊖ **355** ▷ d.	...	...	|	...	...	...	...	...	...
Miramas **355** ▷ d.	...	...	0539	...	...	...	...	...	0714
Arles **355** ▷ d.	...	...	0558	...	...	...	...	...	0735
Avignon Centre ▷ a.	...	...	0619	...	...	...	...	...	0755
Avignon Centre d.	...	0538	0621	0621	0633	0633	0703	0733	0758
Orange d.	...	0601	0637	0637	0655	0655	0725	0756	0813
Montélimar d.	0533	0637	0713	0713	0731	0731	0801	0832	0840
Valence Ville a.	0601	0705	0733	0733	0758	0758	0828	0858	0901
Valence Ville ▷ d.	0608	0708	0735	0735	...	0808	0831	...	0904
Tain-l'Hermitage-Tournon ▷ d.	0619	0719	0746	0746	...	0819	0841	...	|
Vienne ▷ d.	0658	0758	0820	0820	...	0858	0920	...	|
Lyon Part-Dieu ▷ a.	|	|	0840	0840	...	|	0940	...	|
Lyon Perrache ▷ a.	0720	0820	...	...	...	0920	...	...	|
Lyon St Exupéry TGV ✈ § a.	...	...	...	...	...	...	...	...	|
Paris Gare de Lyon § a.	...	...	...	...	...	...	...	...	1123

			TGV					*TGV*									*TGV*	*TGV*							
	17706	**17706**	**6194**	**17704**	**17704**	**17714**	**17714**	**6196**			**17716**	**17718**					**6198**	**6198**	**17724**						
		①–⑤			①–⑤		①–⑤		①–⑥						Ⓐ	Ⓑ	Ⓐ	Ⓒ		⑦			⚒	Ⓑ	⑦
	q	**H**	**q**◇	**q**	**H**	**q**	**H**	**q**	**b**							**h**	¶			**z A**					**e**‡
Marseille St Charles **355** ▷ d.	0710	0708	...	0905	0906	1110	1110	...	...	...	1309	1502	...	...	...	...	...	...	1706	...	...	...	...	1858	...
Vitrolles (for ✈) ⊖ **355** ▷ d.	0726	0724	...	0924	0921	1126	1125	...	...	...	1325	1524	...	...	...	...	...	...	1723	...	...	...	...	1919	...
Miramas **355** ▷ d.	0743	0741	0759**v**	0940	0941	1143	1143	...	...	...	1342	1543	...	...	...	...	1658	1658	1741	...	...	...	...	1939	...
Arles **355** ▷ d.	0800	0758	0819**v**	0956	0958	1200	1200	...	...	...	1359	1600	...	...	...	...	1717	1717	1758	...	...	...	...	1958	...
Avignon Centre ▷ a.	0819	0816	0839	1018	1020	1219	1219	...	...	...	1418	1618	...	...	...	...	1738	1738	1818	...	...	...	...	2014	...
Avignon Centre d.	0821	0819	0842	1021	1023	1221	1222	1242	...	1302	1421	1621	...	1703	1726	...	1741	1741	1821	1843	1900	1933	1933	2016	...
Orange d.	0837	0837	0858	1041	1039	1237	1238	1300	...	1325	1437	1637	...	1725	1749	...	1758	1758	1837	1858	1923	1955	1955	2031	...
Montélimar d.	0910	0910	0925	1113	1115	1310	1311	1325	...	1400	1510	1710	...	1801	1830	...	1824	1824	1910	1931	1958	2031	2031	2102	...
Valence Ville a.	0932	|	0947	1135	|	1332	|	1347	...	1428	1531	1731	...	1828	1858	...	1845	1845	1931	1953	2025	2058	2058	2124	...
Valence Ville ▷ d.	0934	|	0950	1138	|	1334	|	1350	1429	...	1534	1734	1808	1831	...	1908	1848	1848	1934	...	2033	...	2101	...	2138
Tain-l'Hermitage-Tournon ▷ d.	0945	|	|	1149	|	1345	|	|	1439	...	1545	1745	1819	1841	...	1919	|	|	1945	...	2044	...	2112	...	2149
Vienne ▷ d.	1019	1035	|	1219	1240	1419	|	|	1519	...	1619	1819	1858	1920	...	1958	|	|	2019	...	2122	...	2152	...	2227
Lyon Part-Dieu ▷ a.	1040	1102	|	1240	1302	1440	1449	|	1540	...	1640	1840	|	1940	...	|	|	|	2040	...	2142	...	|	...	2250
Lyon Perrache ▷ a.	...	...	|	...	...	...	...	|	...	...	...	...	1920	...	...	2020	|	|	...	...	...	...	2212	...	...
Lyon St Exupéry TGV ✈ § a.	...	...	|	...	...	...	...	|	...	...	...	...	...	...	...	...	|	1919	...	...	...	...	...	...	...
Paris Gare de Lyon § a.	...	...	1215	...	...	...	...	1615	...	...	...	...	...	...	...	...	2111	2119	...	...	...	...	...	...	...

ADDITIONAL TRAINS LYON - VALENCE

	⚒	Ⓐ	Ⓐ	⚒⊗		Ⓐ	Ⓐ	Ⓑ**h**	Ⓐ	
Lyon Perrache d.	...	0640	0740	1340	1640	1710	1810	1840	1910	1940
Lyon Part Dieu d.	0620	|	|	|	|	|	|	|	|	|
Vienne d.	0640	0703	0803	1403	1703	1732	1832	1903	1932	2003
Tain-l'Hermitage-Tournon d.	0720	0741	0841	1441	1741	1810	1911	1941	2011	2041
Valence Ville a.	0731	0752	0852	1452	1752	1822	1922	1952	2022	2052

	Ⓐ	⚒	⑦**e**	⚒	Ⓐ⊗	⊗	Ⓑ**h**	⚒	Ⓑ**h**	⑦**w**
Valence Ville d.	0538	0629	0708	0738	1029	1229	1508	1608	1708	1921
Tain-l'Hermitage d.	0549	0639	0719	0750	1039	1239	1519	1619	1719	1934
Vienne d.	0628	0719	0758	0828	1119	1319	1558	1658	1758	2009
Lyon Part Dieu a.	|	0740	|	|	1140	1340	|	|	|	2030
Lyon Perrache a.	0650	...	0820	0850	...	...	1620	1720	1820	...

ADDITIONAL TRAINS AVIGNON - MARSEILLE

	Ⓐ	Ⓐ	Ⓐ	Ⓐ	⑥		Ⓐ		Ⓒ	⊙		**c**	Ⓐ	⊡	Ⓐ	⊡	⊡	Ⓐ				♥	Ⓐ	Ⓐ	
Avignon Centre d.	0542	0535**t**	0641	0617**t**	0617	0647	0717	0747	0834	0947	1217	1217	1417	1417	1517	1517	1617	1717	1747	1817	1817	1847	1905	1917	2035
Arles **355** d.	0601	|	0700	|	|	|	|	|	|	|	1234	|	1435	|	1536	|	|	|	|	1836	|	|	1924	|	2054
Cavaillon d.	|	0608	|	0651	0653	0722	0752	0822	0907	1022**c**	|	1251	|	1451	|	1551	1651	1751	1823	|	1851	1923	|	1951	|
Salon de Provence d.	|	0629	|	0713	0715	0744	0815	0844	0928	1044**c**	|	1312	|	1512	|	1613	1712	1813	1845	|	1913	1938	|	2013	|
Miramas **355** d.	0622	0640	0721	0725	0726	0756	0826	0856	0938	1056	1256	1323	1454	1522	1556	1624	1724	1824	1854	1858	1924	1946	1945	2022	2115
Vitrolles (for ✈) ⊖ **355** d.	0642	0701	|	0743	0747	0818	0850	0918	|	1118	1318	1346	...	...	1618	1646	1746	1846	...	1919	1946	*2009*	*2009*	...	2136
Marseille St Charles **355** a.	0658	0720	0755	0759	0813	0843	0916	0943	1106	1143	1343	1404	...	...	1643	1705	1805	1906	...	1944	2005	*2024*	*2024*	...	2152

	Ⓐ	Ⓐ		Ⓐ	Ⓐ	♥			⊕		**c**		⊡	Ⓐ**r**	**T**	⊡	Ⓐ	Ⓐ	Ⓐ	Ⓐ		Ⓐ		Ⓐ	
Marseille St Charles **355** d.	...	...	...	0630	0653	...	0755	0819	0855	1017	...	1217	1255	1417	1422	1517	1617	...	1655	1717	1755	1806	1854	1922	2032
Vitrolles (for ✈) ⊖ **355** d.	...	...	...	0647	0714	...	0814	0844	0914	1043	...	1243	1314	1443	1447	1543	1643	...	1714	1743	1814	1823	1914	1947	2058
Miramas **355** d.	0630	0638	0706	0709	0737	0806	0835	0906	0937	1106	1137	1306	1337	1506	1511	1606	1706	1721	1737	1806	1837	1841	1937	2010	2120
Salon de Provence d.	0639	|	0715	|	0746	0815	...	|	0946	|	1146	|	1346	1515	|	1615	1715	|	1747	1816	1846	|	1946	2019	|
Cavaillon d.	0700	|	0737	|	0808	0837	...	|	1008	|	1208	|	1408	1537	|	1637	1737	|	1808	1832	1906	|	2008	2041	|
Arles **355** d.	|	0700	|	0729	|	|	...	0927	|	1125	|	1327	|	|	|	|	|	1745	|	|	|	1901	|	|	2140
Avignon Centre a.	0733	0728**j**	0811	0750	0841	0911	...	0948	1041**c**	1148	1241	1348	1441	1612	1554	1711	1811	1805	1841	1901	1939	1919	2041	2114	2159

A – From / to Annecy (Table **364**).
E – Ⓑ to Mar. 17 (also Mar. 26, Apr. 8, 9); daily from Apr. 15.
G – ⑥ to Apr. 1.
H – ①–⑤ Mar. 20 - Apr. 14.
T – Dec. 12–16 and ①–⑤ Jan. 2 - Mar. 24.

a – Ⓐ only.
b – Not Apr. 17, May 1, 8, June 5.
c – ⑥⑦ (daily Dec. 17 - Jan. 1).
e – Also Apr. 17, May 1, 8, June 5.
f – Also May 24.
h – Not May 25.
j – 0718 from Apr. 24.
k – Also May 25.
n – Not Jan. 23–27, 30, 31, Feb. 1–3, Mar. 13–17, 20–24.
p – Not Apr. 17, May 1, 8, June 5.
q – Not ①–⑤ Mar. 20 - Apr. 14.
r – Not Dec. 12–16, Jan. 2 - Mar. 24.
t – 1–2 minutes earlier Jan. 30 - Feb. 24.
v – From Apr. 24 Miramas d. 0803, d. Arles 0822.
w – Also Apr. 17, May 1, 8, June 5; not Apr. 16, 30, May 7, June 4.
z – Also Apr. 17, May 1, 8, June 5; not Apr. 30, May 7.

TGV – Ⓡ, supplement payable, 🍸.

◇ – Also calls at Mâcon-Loché TGV (d. 1037).
¶ – Also calls at Mâcon-Loché TGV (d. 1934).
△ – Timings Avignon - Lyon may vary by up to 21 minutes Mar. 13 - Apr. 14. Timings may vary by up to 5 minutes from Apr. 24.

♥ – Does not run on ①–⑤ during school holiday periods.
⊗ – Subject to alteration on ①–⑤ Mar. 20 - Apr. 14.
⊕ – Subject to alteration Miramas - Cavaillon Feb. 13–17 and on Ⓐ Apr. 10 - May 12.
⊙ – Subject to alteration on ①–⑤ Jan. 2–20 and ①–⑤ Apr. 24 - May 12. Departs Avignon 0951 on ①–⑤ (not Dec. 19–30).
⊡ – Subject to alteration Dec. 12–16 and ①–⑤ Jan. 2 - Mar. 24.
‡ – Subject to alteration on Jan. 8, 29, Feb. 12, Mar. 12, Apr. 9.
§ – See Table 342 for full service Paris - Lyon St Exupéry and v.v.
▷ – For additional trains Lyon - Valence Ville and Avignon - Marseille see panels below main table.
⊖ – Vitrolles Aéroport Marseille-Provence ✈. A shuttle bus runs to the airport terminal (journey 5 minutes) connecting with trains.

Paris services are subject to alteration on Mar. 18, 19

AVIGNON TGV - AVIGNON CENTRE - CARPENTRAS   351a

km		Ⓐ	Ⓐn													Ⓐn	Ⓒ	Ⓐ				Ⓐn		Ⓐ		Ⓐn	†
0	Avignon TGV........ ◇ d.	...	0627	0657	0727	0757	0827	0857	0957	1157	1257	1327	1357	1427	1457	1557	1627	1657	1727	1757	1827	1857	1927	2027	2227
4	Avignon Centre .... ◇ d.	0602	0636	0707	0736	0807	0836	0907	1007	1207	1307	1337	1409	1437	1505	1607	1636	1707	1736	1807	1836	1907	1936	2037	2236
31	Carpentras ....a.	0638	0706	0736	0806	0836	0906	0936	1036	1236	1336	1407	1438	1506	1536	1636	1706	1736	1806	1836	1906	1936	2006	2107	2306

		Ⓐn	Ⓐ		Ⓐn	Ⓐ						Ⓐn	Ⓒ	Ⓐ△	Ⓒ	△		Ⓐn	Ⓐ		Ⓐn	Ⓐ	
Carpentras ....d.	0520	0624	0652	0722	0752	0822	0852	...	0954	...	1156	1222	1252	1322	1355	1452	1554	1622	1652	1722	1752	1822	1852	1922	1952
Avignon Centre .... ◇ d.	0545	0657	0727	0757	0827	0857	0927	...	1027	...	1227	1257	1327	1358	1428	1527	1627	1657	1727	1757	1827	1857	1927	1957	2027
Avignon TGV........ ◇ a.	0551	0703	0733	0803	0833	0903	0933	...	1033	...	1233	1303	1333	1404	1434	1533	1633	1703	1733	1803	1833	1903	1933	2003	2033

c – Ⓒ only.
n – Not Dec. 17 - Jan. 2.
t – Does not run on ①–⑤ Dec. 19 - Jan. 2.
△ – Subject to alteration during periods of engineering work. Please check.

◇ – Full service Avignon TGV - Avignon Centre and v.v. (journey 5–6 minutes):
From Avignon TGV at 0627 Ⓐ n, 0657, 0727, 0757, 0827 t, 0857, 0913, 0957, 1010, 1040, 1123, 1157, 1210, 1226, 1257, 1310 Ⓐ, 1327 t, 1357, 1410, 1427 Ⓐ, 1457, 1527, 1557, 1627, 1657, 1710, 1727 Ⓐ n, 1740, 1757, 1810, 1827 Ⓐ, 1839, 1857, 1910, 1927 t, 1956, 2027, 2057, 2127, 2157, 2227, 2257 and 2330. **From Avignon Centre** at 0545 Ⓐ n, 0627, 0657, 0727, 0757 t, 0827, 0857, 0914, 0927, 0957, 1027, 1057, 1127, 1157, 1227, 1242, 1257 Ⓐ n, 1311, 1327, 1358 Ⓐ, 1428, 1444, 1527△, 1557, 1615 Ⓐ, 1627, 1657 t, 1714, 1727, 1744, 1757, 1814 Ⓐ, 1827, 1844, 1857 t, 1927, 1942, 1957, 2027, 2057, 2147, 2227 and 2257.

🚌 routes 7801/2   ## 🚌 TOULON - ST TROPEZ   352

🚌 **Toulon** Gare Routière (adjacent to railway station) → Hyères → Le Lavandou → **St Tropez** Gare Routière.   *84 km.*

Service until March 31 (journey 2 hrs 5 mins - 2 hrs 15 mins).
From Toulon : 0550 ⋈, 0620 ⋈ d, 0650 ⋈, 0720 ⋈ d, 0810, 0900 ⋈ d, 1030 ⋈, 1210 d, 1300, 1415, 1530 ⋈ d, 1630, 1730 and 1815 d.
From St Tropez at 0600 ⋈ d, 0640 ⋈, 0845, 1040, 1110 ⋈ d, 1230, 1230 ⋈ d, 1440, 1630 d, 1700 ⋈, 1730 ⋈ d, 1830 Ⓐ d and 1930.

d – Direct (not via Le Lavandou), journey 1 hr 40 mins - 1 hr 45 mins.
Operator : Groupement SUMA, 13340 Rognac   ✆ (in France) 0 810 006 177   www.varlib.fr

---

🚌 route 7601   ## 🚌 ST RAPHAEL - ST TROPEZ   352a

🚌 **St Raphael** Gare Routière (adjacent to railway station) → St Aygulf → Ste Maxime → Grimaud → Port Grimaud (certain journeys) → **St Tropez** Gare Routière.   *35 km.*

Service until March 31 (journey 1 hr 10 mins - 1 hr 35 mins).
From St Raphael : 0600, 0750, 0915, 1100, 1300, 1340, 1500, 1615, 1745, 1915 and 2040.
From St Tropez : 0600, 0730, 0925, 1100, 1230, 1330, 1515, 1630, 1730, 1900 and 2100.

Operator : Groupement SUMA, 13340 Rognac   ✆ (in France) 0 810 006 177   www.varlib.fr

---

See also Table 378   ## LYON - BOURG EN BRESSE   353

km		Ⓐt		①–⑥	Ⓐt	Ⓐ	①–⑥	Ⓐ	Ⓐt		Ⓐ	①–⑥	Ⓐ	Ⓐt		Ⓐ	Ⓐt	①–⑥	Ⓐ	Ⓐt		Ⓐ	①–⑥	⑦	①–⑥
		⊖		b			b			⊖			b		⊖			b e		⊖			b e		b
0	Lyon Perrache.......... d.	...	0608	0708c		0808c	1008	1108		1215	1308	1408	1508		1608	1655		1708	1755		1808	1855	1908c	1955	2008c	2108z
5	Lyon Part Dieu.......... d.	...	0620	0720		0820	1020	1120		1227	1320	1420	1520		1620	1708		1720	1808		1820	1908	1920	2008	2020	2120z
△	Ambérieu ....d.	0652		0805			1305			1705			1805		1905			2044				
65	Bourg en Bresse..... a.	0716	0729	0829	0828	0929	1129	1228	1328	1329	1429	1529	1629	1728	1729	1757	1828	1829	1857	1928	1929	1957	2029	2102	2129	2229

		①–⑥	Ⓐ	①–⑥	Ⓐ	Ⓐt	①–⑥	Ⓐ	①–⑥	Ⓐ		Ⓐ		Ⓐ		Ⓐ	Ⓐt	①–⑥	Ⓐ	Ⓐt	Ⓐ	Ⓐt		Ⓐt	Ⓑ
										b			b		c		⊖				⊖				h
Bourg en Bresse...... d.	0531	0601	0631	0703	0734	0742	0731	0803	0831	0844	0844	1031	1131	1224	1231	1331	1431	1624	1631	1731	1734	1831	1834	1931	1934	2031
Ambérieu ....a.					0757	0842				0900	0900			1250				1650			1757		1857		1958	
Lyon Part Dieu.......... a.	0639	0708	0739	0752		0830	0839	0852	0939	0926	0926	1139	1239		1339	1439	1539		1739	1839		1939		2039		2139
Lyon Perrache ....a.	0651	0720c	0751	0803		0847	0851	0903	0951		0947	1152	1251		1351	1451	1551		1751c	1851c		1951		2052		2151c

b – Not Apr. 17, May 1, 8, June 5.
c – Not Jan. 30 - Apr. 8.
e – Also Apr. 17, May 1, 8, June 5.
h – Not May 25.
n – Not Dec. 26–30.
t – Not Dec. 19–30, Feb. 20 - Mar. 3, Apr. 18–28.
z – 5 minutes later on ⑤† (also May 24).
⊖ – To / from Mâcon Ville (Table **353a**).
△ – Ambérieu - Bourg en Bresse : *31 km.*

MÂCON - BOURG EN BRESSE   353a

km		Ⓐt	Ⓒd	Ⓐt	🚌	🚌	Ⓐ	Ⓐt	Ⓐt	🚌						🚌	Ⓐ	Ⓐt		Ⓐt	Ⓒd	Ⓐt	Ⓐt	Ⓒd
0	Mâcon Ville................d.	0704	0727	0757	0927	1304	1457	1704	1804	1904	2057			Ambérieu **353**........d.	0652		Ⓐt		Ⓐt	Ⓒd		1705	1805	1905	
37	Bourg en Bresse.........a.	0732	0829	0827	1029	1334	1559	1732	1832	1932	2130			Bourg en Bresse.........d.	0717	0938	1228	1338	1629	1638	1729	1829	1929	1938
	Ambérieu **353**........a.	0757						1757	1857	1958				Mâcon Ville................a.	0741	1041	1258	1441	1658	1741	1757	1857	1958	2041

Additional journeys by 🚌 : from Mâcon Ville at 1057 Ⓐ, 1657 Ⓒ d, 1757 Ⓒ d and 1957 Ⓒ d; from Bourg en Bresse at 0638 Ⓐ, 0738 and 1038 Ⓐ.

d – Runs daily Dec. 17 - Jan. 1, Feb. 18 - Mar. 5 and Apr. 15 - May 1.
t – Not Dec. 19–30, Feb. 20 - Mar. 3, Apr. 18–28.

DIJON - BOURG EN BRESSE   353b

km		Ⓐ		Ⓒ		C		Ⓐ				Ⓐ	Ⓐ		D		†	
0	Dijon......................d.	0633		0833	...	1245	...	1736	1847	...	Bourg en Bresse..........d.	0530	0632	...	1142	...	1737	...	1840	....
30	St Jean de Losne........d.	0705		0904	...	1315	...	1806	1916	...	Louhans...................d.	0602	0705	...	1215	...	1813	...	1912	....
86	Louhans...................d.	0744		0944	...	1354	...	1845	1953	...	St Jean de Losne........d.	0637	0740	...	1254	...	1847	...	1949	....
140	Bourg en Bresse..........a.	0816		1016	...	1426	...	1917	2025	...	Dijon......................a.	0703	0815	...	1326	...	1914	...	2014	....

C – Daily to Apr. 16; Ⓒ Apr. 22 - May 28; daily from June 3.
D – ⋈ to Apr. 8 (also Apr. 13, 14); ⑥ Apr. 15 - June 3; ⋈ from June 6.

PERPIGNAN - VILLEFRANCHE - LATOUR DE CAROL   354

km		⋈				Ⓐ		Ⓑ			⋈		Ⓐ			Ⓑ	
			z	z	z									z	z	z	
0	Perpignan.....................d.	0726	0826	1226	1426	1646	1746	1846	1946		Villefranche-Vernet les Bains ....d.	0625	0725	0825	1125	1325	1525	1745	1845
40	Prades-Molitg les Bains.........d.	0811	0911	1309	1509	1731	1831	1931	2031		Prades-Molitg les Bains..........d.	0633	0733	0833	1133	1333	1533	1753	1853
46	Villefranche-Vernet les Bains ......a.	0819	0919	1317	1517	1739	1839	1939	2039		Perpignan......................a.	0713	0813	0913	1213	1413	1613	1833	1933

VILLEFRANCHE - LATOUR DE CAROL *Petit Train Jaune* Narrow gauge, 2nd class. In summer most trains include open sightseeing carriages.
SERVICE UNTIL JUNE 2 (rail service is suspended Mar. 20–31)

km			†	A									B			†	
0	Villefranche-Vernet les Bains ...d.	0937	...	1357	1552	1552	...	1748		Latour de Carol ....d.	0814r	0905	...	...	1535n	...	...
28	Mont Louis la Cabanasse.......d.	1050	...	1506	1715	1715	...	1857		Bourg Madame.................d.	0832r	0923	...	...	1553n	...	...
35	Font Romeu-Odeillo-Via.......d.	1116	...	1525	1734	1737	...	1918		Font Romeu-Odeillo-Via..........d.	0934	1027	...	1556	1651	...	1749	...
56	Bourg Madame...............d.	1213n	...			1832	...	2013p		Mont Louis la Cabanasse.........d.	0959	1052	...	1617	1713	...	1813	...
63	Latour de Carol ....a.	1231n	...		1848	...	2029p		Villefranche-Vernet les Bains.....a.	1107	1156	...	1731	1827	...	1924	...

A – Villefranche - Font Romeu on ⑤⑥ Feb. 3 - Apr. 29 (not Mar. 10–31); Font Romeu - Latour de Carol on ⑤⑥ Feb. 3 - Mar. 4.
B – Latour de Carol - Villefranche on ⑥⑦ Feb. 4 - Mar. 5; Font Romeu - Villefranche on ⑥⑦ Feb. 4 - Apr. 30 (not Mar. 11–26).
n – Does not run Font Romeu - Latour de Carol and v.v. Mar. 20 - May 12.
p – Does not run Font Romeu - Latour de Carol Mar. 19 - May 12.
r – Does not run Latour de Carol - Font Romeu Mar. 20 - May 13.
z – Not ①–⑤ Apr. 18–28.

355 PARIS - MONTPELLIER - PERPIGNAN - PORTBOU

TGV timings may vary by a few minutes on certain dates – please check your reservation for confirmed timings.
Subject to alteration May 25–28, June 3, 4. Services from Paris are subject to alteration on Mar. 18, 19 and from April 3.

Table 1 (includes TGV 6809 ☆, TGV 9730 ■, TGV 6201)

km	Station	Times (in reading order)
	Brussels Midi 11 d.	
	Lille Europe 11 d.	
	Charles de Gaulle + 11 d.	
	Marne la Vallée § 11 d.	
0	Paris Gare de Lyon ► d.	0607
	Dijon 379 d.	
	Lyon Part Dieu ► d.	0706
527	Valence TGV ► d.	0743 · 0823
	Nice 360 d.	
∆128	Marseille St Charles 351 d.	0558 · 0718 · 0718 · 0803
∆105	Vitrolles Aéroport Marseille ‡ d.	0614 · 0733 · 0733
∆76	Miramas 351 d.	0634 · 0750 · 0750
∆42	Arles 351 d.	0654 · 0809 · 0809
∆49	Avignon Centre d.	0611r · 0638 · 0711 · 0738 · 0821 · 0821 · 0845v · 0838
∆28	Tarascon-sur-Rhône d.	0625r · 0652 · 0710h · 0725 · 0752 · 0852
686	Nîmes d.	0507 · 0543 · 0612 · 0643 · 0646 · 0712 · 0712 · 0731h · 0743 · 0747 · 0812 · 0829 · 0843 · 0843 · 0904 · 0908 · 0912
712	Lunel d.	0524 · 0600 · 0630 · 0659 · 0705 · 0730 · 0730 · 0800 · 0806 · 0829 · 0900 · 0900 · 0930
736	Montpellier a.	0539 · 0613 · 0645 · 0712 · 0729 · 0745 · 0745 · 0815 · 0830 · 0844 · 0855 · 0915 · 0915 · 0929 · 0934 · 0949
736	Montpellier d.	0549 · 0617 · 0649 · 0715 · 0749 · 0749 · 0749 · 0820 · 0848 · 0859 · 0920 · 0933 · 0938 · 0949
756	Frontignan d.	0603 · 0636 · 0703 · 0732 · 0803 · 0803 · 0803 · 0832 · 0902 · 0933 · 1003
763	Sète d.	0610 · 0642 · 0710 · 0738 · 0810 · 0810 · 0810 · 0841 · 0909 · 0916 · 0941 · 1010
786	Agde d.	0623 · 0658 · 0724 · 0754 · 0824 · 0824 · 0824 · 0857 · 0923 · 0957 · 1024
807	Béziers d.	0635 · 0713 · 0736 · 0809 · 0836 · 0836 · 0836 · 0911 · 0936 · 0941 · 1011 · 1016 · 1036
833	Narbonne a.	0650 · 0729 · 0750 · 0826 · 0850 · 0850 · 0850 · 0927 · 0950 · 0955 · 1025 · 1030 · 1039 · 1050
833	Narbonne d.	0657 · 0657 · 0732 · 0734 · 0757 · 0857 · 0857 · 0857 · 0957 · 0958 · 1033 · 1042 · 1057
	Carcassonne 321 a.	0802 · 1026
	Toulouse 321 a.	0905 · 1111
	Bordeaux 320 △ a.	
854	Port la Nouvelle d.	0710 · 0710 · 0747 · 0810 · 0910 · 0910 · 0910 · 1010 · 1110
896	Perpignan a.	0740 · 0740 · 0816 · 0840 · 0940 · 0940 · 0940 · 1040 · 1106 · 1114 · 1140
896	Perpignan d.	0620 · 0745 · 0745 · 0845 · 0945 · 0945 · 0945 · 1045
918	Argelès sur Mer d.	0635 · 0801 · 0801 · 0901 · 1001 · 1001 · 1101
923	Collioure d.	0640 · 0807 · 0807 · 0907 · 1007 · 1007 · 1107
926	Port Vendres d.	0644 · 0811 · 0811 · 0911 · 1011 · 1011 · 1111
931	Banyuls sur Mer d.	0649 · 0816 · 0816 · 0916 · 1016 · 1016 · 1111
938	Cerbère 657 a.	0654 · 0822 · 0822 · 0922 · 1022 · 1022 · 1122
940	Portbou 657 a.	1128

Table 2

Trains: 4754/4755 ★ · TGV 5104 · TGV 6813 ①–⑥ ⊡ · TGV 6205 Ⓐ b · 4756/4757 ★ S · TGV 6839 · TGV 6207 ⑥ H · TGV 6207 † G · ✕ · TGV 6207 Ⓐ · Ⓐ · TGV 9713 ♠ · TGV 9812 Ⓐ · 4760/4761 ★ ⑤f · TGV 5318/5326 N ★

Station	Times (in reading order)
Brussels Midi 11 d.	0817
Lille Europe 11 d.	0534t · 0900t
Charles de Gaulle + 11 d.	0658 · 0958
Marne la Vallée § 11 d.	0711 · 1011
Paris Gare de Lyon ► d.	0807 · 0915 · 0925 · 1007
Dijon 379 d.	0825 · 1005
Lyon Part Dieu ► d.	0910 · 0936 · 1005 · 1210 · 1336
Valence TGV ► d.	0950 · 1014 · 1022 · 1221 · 1249 · 1415
Nice 360 d.	1022
Marseille St Charles 351 d.	0818z · 1018z · 1150 · 1318
Vitrolles Aéroport Marseille ‡ d.	1205
Miramas 351 d.	1222
Arles 351 d.	0902z · 1242
Avignon Centre d.	0938 · 1138 · 1138 · 1211 · 1338 · 1338
Tarascon-sur-Rhône d.	0952 · 1157 · 1157 · 1225 · 1352 · 1352
Nîmes d.	0928 · 1012 · 1036 · 1059 · 1108 · 1120 · 1124 · 1208 · 1213 · 1213 · 1218 · 1247 · 1308 · 1312 · 1336 · 1412 · 1412 · 1504
Lunel d.	1031 · 1231 · 1231 · 1306 · 1331 · 1430 · 1430
Montpellier a.	0953 · 1046 · 1102 · 1127 · 1134 · 1144 · 1153 · 1234 · 1246 · 1246 · 1250 · 1329 · 1334 · 1346 · 1402 · 1445 · 1445 · 1453 · 1530
Montpellier d.	0958 · 1050 · 1131 · 1139 · 1149 · 1158 · 1249 · 1249 · 1305 · 1338 · 1350 · 1449 · 1449 · 1458
Frontignan d.	1104 · 1203 · 1303 · 1303 · 1323 · 1503 · 1503
Sète d.	1015 · 1111 · 1147 · 1158 · 1210 · 1215 · 1310 · 1310 · 1332 · 1409 · 1510 · 1510
Agde d.	1124 · 1214 · 1224 · 1324 · 1324 · 1345 · 1524 · 1524
Béziers d.	1041 · 1136 · 1212 · 1226 · 1236 · 1241 · 1336 · 1336 · 1400 · 1418 · 1436 · 1536 · 1536
Narbonne a.	1056 · 1150 · 1225 · 1250 · 1256 · 1350 · 1350 · 1416 · 1432 · 1450 · 1550 · 1550
Narbonne d.	1059 · 1157 · 1228 · 1257 · 1257 · 1259 · 1357 · 1357 · 1435 · 1457 · 1557 · 1557
Carcassonne 321 a.	1127 · 1255 · 1328
Toulouse 321 a.	1216 · 1341 · 1413 · 1707
Bordeaux 320 △ a.	1429 · 1629 · 1913
Port la Nouvelle d.	1210 · 1310 · 1310 · 1410 · 1410 · 1510 · 1609 · 1609
Perpignan a.	1240 · 1340 · 1340 · 1440 · 1440 · 1508 · 1540 · 1640 · 1640
Perpignan d.	1245j · 1445 · 1445 · 1545 · 1645 · 1711
Argelès sur Mer d.	1301j · 1501 · 1501 · 1601 · 1701 · 1728
Collioure d.	1307j · 1507 · 1507 · 1607 · 1707 · 1733
Port Vendres d.	1310j · 1511 · 1511 · 1611 · 1711 · 1736
Banyuls sur Mer d.	1316j · 1516 · 1516 · 1616 · 1716 · 1742
Cerbère 657 a.	1322j · 1522 · 1522 · 1622 · 1722 · 1748
Portbou 657 a.	1328j · 1528 · 1528 · 1754

Notes

G – Daily from Apr. 3 (not Apr. 8, 15).
H – ⑥ to Apr. 15.
N – From Nantes and Rennes (Table 335). Subject to alteration on Apr. 17, 30, May 1, 20, 21, June 10, 11.
S – From Strasbourg (Table 379).

b – Not Apr. 17, May 1, 8, June 5.
f – Also May 24; not May 26.
h – From Apr. 24 Tarascon d. 0705, Nîmes a. 0722.
j – 9–12 minutes later on Ⓐ Apr. 3–21.
r – Ⓐ only.
t – 2–3 minutes later to Jan. 22 and Apr. 24 – May 28.
v – Avignon TGV. Also calls at Aix en Provence (d. 0818).
z – 1–4 minutes earlier until Jan. 15.

TGV –ℝ, supplement payable, ⚹.

☆ – Also runs on ⑥ Nîmes - Montpellier.
⊡ – Subject to alteration on ①–⑤ Mar. 20 - Apr. 7.
⊗ – Subject to alteration Perpignan - Portbou on Ⓐ Apr. 3–21.
△ – Bordeaux timings are subject to alteration on May 6–8, June 4, 5.
♠ – To Barcelona (Table 13). Subject to confirmation from Apr. 3.
■ – 🚆 Marseille - Barcelona - Madrid. Subject to confirmation from Apr. 3.
★ – INTERCITÉS. ℝ.
∆ – Distance from Nîmes. Marseille to Nîmes via Avignon TGV is 135 km.
§ – Marne la Vallée - Chessy (station for Disneyland Paris).
‡ – Vitrolles Aéroport Marseille-Provence. A shuttle bus runs to the airport terminal (journey time 5 minutes). For additional trains see Table 351.
► – For additional trains from Paris and Lyon to Valence TGV see Table 350. For Lyon to Valence Ville see Table 351.

> Additional low-cost 'Ouigo' TGV trains run from Marne la Vallée-Chessy in the eastern suburbs of Paris. See Table 350a.

TGV timings may vary by a few minutes on certain dates – please check your reservation for confirmed timings.
Subject to alteration May 25–28, June 3, 4. Services from Paris are subject to alteration on Mar. 18, 19 and from April 3.

	TGV 6211	4762 4763	TGV 9743	4764 4765	TGV 9715							TGV 6235	4768 4769	TGV 9879
	Ⓐ	★	Ⓐ	Ⓐ ♠	★	Ⓐ ♠	Ⓑ	⑦	Ⓐ①–④	⑤	Ⓒ	⑤F	★	♣ Ⓐ Ⓐ
								e		m				
Brussels Midi 11 .... d.	…	…	…	…	…	…	…	…	…	…	…	…	…	…
Lille Europe 11 .... d.	…	…	…	…	…	…	…	…	…	…	…	…	…	…
Charles de Gaulle + 11 ...... d.	…	…	…	…	…	…	…	…	…	…	…	…	…	…
Marne la Vallée § 11 .... d.	…	…	…	…	…	…	…	…	…	…	…	…	…	…
Paris Gare de Lyon ▶ d.	1207					1407						1515		1525
Dijon 379 .... d.														
Lyon Part Dieu ▶ d.				1423										1710
Valence TGV ▶ d.	1422			1503		1621								1750
Nice 360 .... d.												1415y		
Marseille St Charles .... 351 d.		1418z			1518		1613	1616	1618			1718		1736
Vitrolles Aéroport Marseille ‡ . d.							1629	1631	1634					1751
Miramas .... 351 d.							1646	1648	1651					1809
Arles .... 351 d.		1502z			1538		1706	1709	1711					1829
Avignon Centre .... d.						1638r					1711		1811	
Tarascon-sur-Rhône .... d.					1552	1652r		1722	1724	1721	1725	1752		1825 1839
Nîmes .... d.	1508	1512	1528	1543 1548	1612	1643 1708 1712		1743	1743	1743 1747	1808 1812		1835	1847 1854
Lunel .... d.		1530		1600	1630	1700	1730		1800	1800	1800 1812	1830		1913
Montpellier .... a.	1534	1545 1553		1615 1621	1645 1653	1715 1734 1745		1815	1815	1815 1824	1834 1845	1853	1902	1924
Montpellier .... d.	1541	1549 1558		1620 1625	1649 1658	1705 1720 1738 1749	1755	1805	1820	1820 1818	1841 1849	1858		1927
Frontignan .... d.		1603		1633		1703 1723 1733		1809	1809	1823 1833	1836	1903		1946
Sète .... d.	1559	1610 1615		1641	1710	1730 1741		1810	1817	1830 1841	1841 1844	1901 1910		1952
Agde .... d.	1615	1624		1657	1724	1745 1757		1824	1831	1845 1857	1900	1916 1924		2007
Béziers .... d.	1627	1636 1641		1711 1716	1736	1800 1811		1836	1844	1906 1911	1911 1916	1931 1936		2023
Narbonne .... a.		1650 1656		1727 1730	1750	1816 1827	1832	1850		1916 1927	1927 1932	1944 1950		2039
Narbonne .... d.		1657 1659	1719	1732 1733	1757	1819	1835	1857				1947 1957		
Carcassonne 321 .... a.		1728		1802										
Toulouse 321 .... a.		1813	1904b		1907									
Bordeaux 320 .... △ a.		2029			2113									
Port la Nouvelle .... d.		1710	1731		1810	1831	1910					2010		
Perpignan .... a.		1740	1800	1805	1840	1900	1908	1940				2020 2040		
Perpignan .... d.		1745			1845		1945							
Argelès sur Mer .... d.		1801			1901		2001							
Collioure .... d.		1807			1907		2007							
Port Vendres .... d.		1811			1911		2011							
Banyuls sur Mer .... d.		1816			1916		2016							
Cerbère .... 657 a.		1822			1922		2022							
Portbou .... 657 a.		1928												

	TGV 6231		TGV 6215			4766 4767	TGV 5119	TGV 6824	TGV 6824	TGV 6217	TGV 6217	TGV 9836	TGV 9836	TGV 6219	TGV 6219		TGV 6221	TGV 6225
	Ⓐ		Ⓐ		Ⓑ	⑤⑦ p★	⊙	A ⑤⑦ ⊗⊙	⑤⑦	B ⑤⑦	⑤⑦	⑤⑦	⑤⑦	G	⑤ d	Ⓐ	⑤⑦	⑤⑦
												v				⊖		
Brussels Midi 11 .... d.	…	…	…	…	…	…	…	…	…	1617	1617					…	…
Lille Europe 11 .... d.	…	…	…	…	…	…	…	1543t		1703	1703					…	…
Charles de Gaulle + 11 ...... d.	…	…	…	…	…	…	…	1656		1758	1758					…	…
Marne la Vallée § 11 .... d.	…	…	…	…	…	…	…	1711		1811	1811					…	…
Paris Gare de Lyon ▶ d.	1607		1707						1807	1807				1904	1904		2015	2107
Dijon 379 .... d.							1729	1729									
Lyon Part Dieu ▶ d.							1910	1936	1936			2010	2010				
Valence TGV ▶ d.	1820		1922				1950	2014		2022	2029	2050	2050	2122	2122		2229	2322
Nice 360 .... d.																	
Marseille St Charles .... 351 d.			1818			1918j											
Vitrolles Aéroport Marseille ‡ . d.			1833														
Miramas .... 351 d.			1851														
Arles .... 351 d.			1911			2002											
Avignon Centre .... d.		1838 1838			1938 1938										2138		
Tarascon-sur-Rhône .... d.		1852 1852	1921		1952 1952												
Nîmes .... d.	1908	1912 1912	1943	2008 2009	2012		2028	2036	2100	2106	2108 2114	2136	2136	2208	2208 2212 2212		2314	0009
Lunel .... d.		1930		2000	2030									2230	2230			
Montpellier .... a.	1934	1945 1945	2015	2034	2045		2053	2102	2126	2130	2134 2139	2202	2202	2234	2234 2245 2245		2340	0048
Montpellier .... d.	1941	1949 1949	2020		2049		2058		2130	2134	2141 2146		2206	2241	2238 2249 2249			
Frontignan .... d.		2003 2003	2033		2103									2303	2303			
Sète .... d.	1959	2010 2010	2041		2110	2115				2200	2205	2225		2300	2257 2310 2310			
Agde .... d.	2015	2024 2024	2057		2124				2214	2220		2241		2315	2313 2324 2324			
Béziers .... d.	2029	2036 2036	2111		2136		2141	2212	2212	2228	2235	2254		2327	2327 2336 2336			
Narbonne .... a.	2043	2050 2050	2127		2150		2156	2225	2225	2242	2249	2308		2340	2351 2351			
Narbonne .... d.	2046	2057			2157	2157	2159	2228	2245	2245	2252	2311		2343				
Carcassonne 321 .... a.							2228	2256	2256									
Toulouse 321 .... a.							2313	2343	2341									
Bordeaux 320 .... △ a.																		
Port la Nouvelle .... d.		2110			2210	2210												
Perpignan .... a.	2118	2140			2240	2240					2318	2325		2347				0021
Perpignan .... d.		2145																
Argelès sur Mer .... d.		2202																
Collioure .... d.		2207																
Port Vendres .... d.		2211																
Banyuls sur Mer .... d.		2215																
Cerbère .... 657 a.		2222																
Portbou .... 657 a.																		

A – ①②③④⑥ (not Apr. 17, May 1, 8, 25, June 5). From Nancy (Table 379). Subject to alteration on June 3, 10, 17. Starts from Dijon on ①–④ from May 2.
B – ①②③④⑥.
F – ⑤ from Apr. 7 (also May 24; not May 26).
G – ①②③④⑦ (not May 24–28).
b – 1859 on ⑤ (also May 24).
d – Also May 24; not May 26.
e – ⑦ (also Jan. 2, Apr. 17, May 1, 8, June 5; not Dec. 18, 25, Jan. 1, Feb. 5, 12, Apr. 2, 9, 16, 30, May 7, June 4). To St Chély d'Apcher (Table 332).
h – Not May 25.
j – 1914 on Apr. 17, May 8, June 5.
k – 1725 until Apr. 23.
m – Not Apr. 17, May 1, 8, 25, June 5.
p – Also Apr. 17, May 1, 8, 24, June 5; not Apr. 16, 30, May 7, June 4.
r – Ⓐ only.
t – 11 minutes later to Jan. 22 and Apr. 24 - May 28.
v – Also Apr. 17, May 1, 8, 24, June 5; not Apr. 16, 30, May 7, 26, 28, June 4.
y – ①⑥⑦ (also Apr. 18, May 2, 9, 25, 26, June 6).
z – 3 minutes earlier until Jan. 15.

TGV – Ⓡ, supplement payable, ⏧.
⊖ – Not ⑤ Dec. 16 - Mar. 31. On ②–④ runs 3–4 minutes later Valence - Montpellier.
⊗ – Subject to alteration on Feb. 26, May 14, 21. Does not run Nancy - Dijon on ⑤ from May 5.
△ – Bordeaux timings are subject to alteration May 6–8, June 4, 5.
♠ – To Barcelona (Table 13). Subject to confirmation from Apr. 3.
♣ – ⏛ Luxembourg - Metz - Strasbourg - Montpellier (Table 379). Subject to alteration on Jan. 16, Feb. 6, 13, 20, June 10, 17.
⊙ – From Nancy (Table 379).
★ – INTERCITÉS. Ⓡ.
§ – Marne la Vallée - Chessy (station for Disneyland Paris).
‡ – Vitrolles Aéroport Marseille-Provence. A shuttle bus runs to the airport terminal (journey time 5 minutes). For additional trains see Table 351.
▶ – For Paris to Lyon see Table 340. For additional trains from Paris and Lyon to Valence TGV see Table 350. For Lyon to Valence Ville see Table 351.

Additional low-cost 'Ouigo' TGV trains run from Marne la Vallée-Chessy in the eastern suburbs of Paris. See Table 350a.

CERBÈRE - PERPIGNAN - MONTPELLIER - PARIS

TGV timings may vary by a few minutes on certain dates – please check your reservation for confirmed timings.
Subject to alteration May 25–28, June 3, 4. Services to Paris are subject to alteration on Mar. 18, 19 and from April 3.

		TGV 6202				TGV 6230							TGV 9862	TGV 9862	TGV 9862		TGV 6204						TGV 6869		
		Ⓐ	Ⓐ	Ⓐ	Ⓐ	①–⑥		Ⓐ				Ⓐ	①		⑥		Ⓐ	☆	☆	Ⓐ	Ⓒ		Ⓒ		Ⓐ
		A	B			b	A	D	E				g		p							☉			
Cerbère	d.																								0534
Banyuls sur Mer	d.																								0544
Port Vendres	d.																								0549
Collioure	d.																								0553
Argelès sur Mer	d.																								0558
Perpignan	a.																								0614
Perpignan	d.											0515	0515		0540		0545				0608				0619
Port la Nouvelle	d.															0615					0639				0650
Bordeaux 320 △	d.																					0545			
Toulouse 321	d.																					0634			
Carcassonne 321	d.																								
Narbonne	a.											0548	0549		0615	0627				0651	0701		0703		
Narbonne	d.					0529	0530	0532				0549	0552	0603	0618	0632	0632			0644	0654	0704	0709		
Béziers	d.	0430	0441	0445		0544	0545	0547				0605	0608	0617	0634	0648	0648			0701	0712	0720	←	0725	
Agde	d.	0445	0454	0458		0556	0557	0559				0620	0621	0632	0648	0659	0659			0715	0726		0732	0738	
Sète	d.	0502	0508	0512		0609	0611	0613				0635	0637	0647	0703	0713	0713			0731	→	0744	0749	0751	
Frontignan	d.			0514	0518		0615	0616	0618						0653		0718	0718			0736		0754	0757	
Montpellier	a.	0516j	0525	0529		0625	0629	0631				0654	0655	0710	0719	0730	0730			0755		0758	0811	0810	
Montpellier	d.	0523j	0527	0532		0626	0628	0632	0635	0638		0656n	0656	0659	0714	0726	0733	0733	0738		0802	0814	0814	
Lunel	d.		0542	0546			0642	0645	0648	0653					0731		0747	0753				0830	0823	
Nîmes	d.	0555	0601	0604	0649		0655	0703	0703	0706	0722		0727	0727	0727	0751	0755	0803	0803	0822		0831	0851	0851	
Tarascon-sur-Rhône	d.		0617	0619	0709			0719	0719	0722	0747f			0812t				0842				0909	0909	
Avignon Centre	a.				0723						0758f			0824t				0855				0922	0922	
Arles 351	d.		0632	0632			0732	0732	0732															
Miramas 351	d.		0652	0652			0752	0752	0752															
Vitrolles Aéroport Marseille ‡	d.		0709	0709			0809	0809	0809															
Marseille St Charles 351	a.		0725	0725			0829	0829	0829															
Nice 360	a.																							
Valence TGV	d.	0642				0742						0819	0819	0819									0916		
Lyon Part Dieu	a.											0854	0854	0854									0950		
Dijon 379	a.																						1133		
Paris Gare de Lyon	a.	0853				0953											1045								
Marne la Vallée § 11	a.											1048	1048	1048											
Charles de Gaulle ✈ 11	a.											1102	1102	1102											
Lille Europe 11	a.											1156	1156	1156											
Brussels Midi 11	a.											1252v	1252	1243											

		TGV 5166				TGV 6206	TGV 6878			TGV 6208	TGV 9734	4655 4654		TGV 9702				4657 4656	TGV 6882	
		Ⓐ		Ⓐ		Ⓐ	♣⊕			♠		☆ ⊗	◇	♠	◇	Ⓐ	Ⓐ	☆ ⊗	S⊕	
Cerbère	d.				0634		0704		0734			0934		1034						
Banyuls sur Mer	d.				0644		0714		0744			0944		1044						
Port Vendres	d.				0649		0719		0749			0949		1049						
Collioure	d.				0653		0722		0753			0953		1053						
Argelès sur Mer	d.				0658		0728		0758			0958		1058						
Perpignan	a.				0714		0743		0814			1014		1114						
Perpignan	d.			0641	0719	0740	0745		0819	0819	0847	1019	1053			1119			1219	
Port la Nouvelle	d.			0711	0750		0815		0849	0849		1050			1150				1250	
Bordeaux 320 △	d.											0731				0931				
Toulouse 321	d.											0948				1149				
Carcassonne 321	d.	0645										1033				1233				
Narbonne	a.	0716		0724	0803	0815	0827		0903	0903	0922	1101	1103	1127		1203		1301	1303	
Narbonne	d.	0719			0809	0818	0832		0909	0909	0925	1104	1109	1130		1209	1244	1304		
Béziers	d.	0737			0825	0835	0847		0925	0925	0941	1120	1125			1225	1301	1320		
Agde	d.	0751			0838	0849	0859		0938	0938		1138				1238	1315			
Sète	d.	0807			0852	0905	0912		0951	0951		1144	1151			1251	1331	1344		
Frontignan	d.	0813			0857		0918		0957	0957			1157			1257	1336			
Montpellier	a.	0831			0910	0921	0931		1010	1010	1024	1200	1210	1220		1310	1355	1401		
Montpellier	d.	0835	0856		0914	0927		1000	1014	1014	1031	1205	1214	1227	1242	1314		1405	1411	
Lunel	d.	0850			0931k			1031	1031			1231		1305		1331				
Nîmes	d.	0903	0926		0951k	0955		1027	1051	1051	1055	1059	1234	1251	1255	1327		1351		1433	1443
Tarascon-sur-Rhône	d.				1009k				1109	1109			1309		1346		1410			
Avignon Centre	a.								1122	1122			1322		1358		1423			
Arles 351	d.				1020							1259				1459				
Miramas 351	d.				1041															
Vitrolles Aéroport Marseille ‡	d.				1057															
Marseille St Charles 351	a.				1111							1344				1543				
Nice 360	a.																			
Valence TGV	d.	1015					1115			1141	1149		1341				1529			
Lyon Part Dieu	a.	1050					1150			1226							1604			
Dijon 379	a.						1337										1744			
Paris Gare de Lyon	a.				1245				1353c			1553								
Marne la Vallée § 11	a.	1248																		
Charles de Gaulle ✈ 11	a.	1302																		
Lille Europe 11	a.	1421z																		
Brussels Midi 11	a.																			

A – Jan. 16 - June 3.
B – To Jan. 13 and from June 6.
D – To Jan. 15.
E – From June 5.
S – To Strasbourg (Table 379).

b – Not Apr. 17, May 1, 8, June 5.
c – 1402 on Feb. 21, 22, June 13, 14.
f – 4–5 minutes earlier to Jan. 13 / from Apr. 24.
g – ① (also Apr. 18, May 2, 9, June 6; not Apr. 17, May 1, 8, June 5).
   Timings Narbonne - Montpellier may vary by 1–2 minutes to Jan. 9 / from June 6.
j – 3 minutes later to Jan. 13 / from June 6.
k – 1–3 minutes earlier to Jan. 15.
n – 0658 on ⑦ (also ①–⑤ to Jan. 13 / from June 5); 0659 on ⑥ (also May 25).
p – Also May 25; not May 27.
t – 2–3 minutes earlier from Apr. 24.
v – 1243 on ⑥⑦ (also May 25).
z – 1404 on Ⓒ.

TGV –Ⓡ, supplement payable.

◇ – Subject to alteration Cerbère - Perpignan on Ⓐ Apr. 3–21.
⊕ – Subject to alteration on June 10, 17.
△ – Bordeaux timings are subject to alteration May 6–8, June 4, 5.
⊗ – Timings Montpellier - Marseille may vary by a few minutes Mar. 1–5 (please check your reservation).
☉ – To Nancy (Table 379). Terminates at Dijon on Ⓐ from May 2.
♠ – From Barcelona (Table 13). Subject to confirmation from Apr. 3.
♣ – 🚈 Montpellier - Strasbourg - Metz - Luxembourg (Table 379).
★ – INTERCITÉS. Ⓡ.
‡ – Vitrolles Aéroport Marseille-Provence. A shuttle bus runs to the airport terminal (journey time 5 minutes). For additional trains see Table 351.
§ – Marne la Vallée - Chessy (station for Disneyland Paris).

Additional low-cost 'Ouigo' TGV trains run to Marne la Vallée-Chessy in the eastern suburbs of Paris. See Table 350a.

De verklaring van de conventionele tekens vindt u op bladzijde 4

TGV timings may vary by a few minutes on certain dates – please check your reservation for confirmed timings.
Subject to alteration May 25–28, June 3, 4. Services to Paris are subject to alteration on Mar. 18, 19 and from April 3.

	TGV 6212	TGV 9868	4659 4658 ★		TGV 9704 ♠	TGV 5380 5387 N ☉	Ⓐ ☉	Ⓐ ☉		TGV 6861	TGV 6218 Ⓑ h		Ⓐ ✈		TGV 5186	4663 4662 ★	Ⓒ		TGV 6220
Cerbère........................ d.	...	...	1234	...	...	...	...	...	...	1434	...	...	...	...	...	1534	...	...	...
Banyuls sur Mer.............. d.	...	...	1244	...	...	...	...	...	...	1444	...	...	...	...	...	1544	...	...	...
Port Vendres................. d.	...	...	1249	...	...	...	...	...	...	1449	...	...	...	...	...	1549	...	...	...
Collioure.................... d.	...	...	1253	...	...	...	...	...	...	1453	...	...	...	...	...	1553	...	...	...
Argelès sur Mer.............. d.	...	...	1258	...	...	...	...	...	...	1458	...	...	...	...	...	1558	...	...	...
Perpignan.................... a.	...	...	1314	...	...	...	...	...	...	1514	...	...	...	...	...	1614	...	...	...
Perpignan.................... d.	...	...	1319	1419	1450	...	...	...	...	1519	...	...	...	...	...	1619	1619	...	...
Port la Nouvelle............. d.	...	...	1350	1450	...	...	...	...	...	1550	...	...	...	...	...	1650	1650	...	...
Bordeaux 320........△ d.	...	1047	...	...	...	...	...	...	...	...	...	...	...	...	1331	...	...	...	...
Toulouse 321............. d.	...	1257	...	...	...	...	...	...	1445	...	...	...	...	...	1549	...	...	...	...
Carcassonne 321......... d.	...	...	...	...	...	...	...	...	1533	...	...	...	...	...	1633	...	...	...	...
Narbonne..................... a.	...	1403	...	1503	1524	...	...	...	1601	1603	...	...	...	...	1701	1703	1703	...	...
Narbonne..................... d.	...	1409	...	1509	1527	1532	...	...	1604	1609	...	1632	...	...	1704	1709	1709	...	...
Béziers...................... d.	1334	1425	...	1525	...	1547	...	...	1619	1625	...	1647	...	...	1719	1725	1725	1735	
Agde......................... d.	1348	1438	...	1538	...	1559	...	...	...	1637	...	1659	...	...	1738	1738	1749		
Sète......................... d.	1402	1451	...	1551	...	1613	...	...	1644	1651	...	1713	...	...	1743	1751	1751	1804	
Frontignan................... d.		1457	...	1557	...	1618	...	...	...	1657	...	1719	...	...	...	1757	1757		
Montpellier.................. a.	1419	...	1459	1510	1610	1618	...	1632	1701	1710	...	1731	...	...	1801j	1810	1810	1821	
Montpellier.................. d.	1426	1458	1504	1514	1614	1625	1630	1635	1635	1638	1706	1714	1726	...	1735	1738	1758	...	1805j	1814	1814	1827
Lunel....................... d.		1531		1631		1650	1650	1703		1731		1750	1801	...	1831	1831			
Nîmes....................... d.	1455	1526	1551	1551	1651	1655	1659	1706	1706	1722	1733	1751	1755	...	1803	1822	1826	1835j	1851	1851	1855
Tarascon-sur-Rhône..... d.		1609	1709		1721	1721	1742		1809		1842	...	1909	1909			
Avignon Centre......... a.	...	1622	1722			1754		1822		1854	...	1922	1922			
Arles.................351 d.				1732	1732						1859	...					
Miramas...............351 d.				1752	1752												
Vitrolles Aéroport Marseille ‡ d.				1810	1810												
Marseille St Charles....351 a.		1641		1829	1829						1942	...					
Nice 360.................... a.		1941															
Valence TGV.................. d.	1541	1615		1741	1748				1841		1916	...			1941		
Lyon Part Dieu............... a.		1650			1824			1850			1950	...					
Dijon 379................... a.																	
Paris Gare de Lyon........... a.	1753			1953					2053		2148	...			2153		
Marne la Vallée § 11........ a.		1848									2148	...					
Charles de Gaulle ✈ 11..... a.		1902									2202	...					
Lille Europe 11............. a.		1956									2305t						
Brussels Midi 11............ a.		2043															

	4665 4664 ★ ⬚	TGV 6222		Ⓒ	Ⓐ		TGV 9724 ■	TGV 6857	Ⓑ f	⑤ e	TGV 6224	TGV 6224	4667 4666 ⑤⑦ w★		Ⓐ ①–④	TGV 6228 ⑦ m	4669 4668 ★ R		
Cerbère........................ d.	...	...	1634	...	...	...	...	1734	...	...	...	...	...	1834	1834	...	...	1934	
Banyuls sur Mer.............. d.	...	...	1644	...	...	...	...	1744	...	...	...	...	...	1844	1844	...	...	1944	
Port Vendres................. d.	...	...	1649	...	...	...	...	1749	...	...	...	...	...	1849	1849	...	...	1949	
Collioure.................... d.	...	...	1653	...	...	...	...	1753	...	...	...	...	...	1853	1853	...	...	1953	
Argelès sur Mer.............. d.	...	...	1658	...	...	...	...	1758	...	...	...	...	...	1858	1858	...	...	1958	
Perpignan.................... a.	...	...	1714	...	...	...	...	1814	...	...	...	...	...	1914	1914	...	...	2014	
Perpignan.................... d.	...	...	1719	1748	...	...	...	1815	...	1819	...	1840	...	1919	1919	...	...	2019	
Port la Nouvelle............. d.	...	...	1750	...	...	...	...	...	...	1850	...	...	...	1950	1950	...	...	2050	
Bordeaux 320........△ d.	...	1447n	...	...	...	...	...	1750	...	...	...	1645	...	...	...	...	1731	...	
Toulouse 321............. d.	...	1654n	...	...	1655	1655	...	...	...	...	...	1851	...	...	...	...	1948	...	
Carcassonne 321......... d.	...	...	...	...	1758	1758	...	1837k	...	...	...	...	...	...	...	...	2033	...	
Narbonne..................... a.	...	...	1803	1823	1828	1828	1854	1902k	1903	...	1915	...	...	2003	2003	...	2101	2107	
Narbonne..................... d.	1720	...	1809	1826	1832	1832	1857	1905k	1909	...	1918	...	...	2009	2009	...	2104	2112	
Béziers...................... d.	1738	...	1825	1843	1848	1848	1913	1920	1925	...	1934	...	...	2025	2025	...	2120	2126	
Agde......................... d.	1753	...	1838	...	1859	1859	...	...	1938	...	1948	...	...	2038	2038	...	...	2138	
Sète......................... d.	1810	...	1851	...	1913	1913	...	1945	1951	2004	...	...	...	2051	2051	...	2144	2152	
Frontignan................... d.	1815	...	1857	...	1918	1918	...	...	1957	...	...	...	...	2057	2057	...	...	2159	
Montpellier.................. a.	1831	1857	1910	1922	1932	1931	1954	2001	2010	...	2020	...	2101	2110	2110	...	2159	2211	
Montpellier.................. d.	1835	1902	1914	1926	1938	1938	1958	2006	2014	2026	2027	...	2106	2114	2114	2126	...	2204	2215
Lunel....................... d.	1850	...	1931	...	1954	2001	...	...	2031	...	...	...	...	2131	2131	...	...	2231	
Nîmes....................... d.	1906	...	1951	1955	2009	2022	...	2025	2033	2048	2055	2055	...	2148	2148	2155	...	2233	2248
Tarascon-sur-Rhône..... d.	1922	...	2009	...	...	2042	...	...	...	...	...	...	...	...	...	...	...	...	
Avignon Centre......... a.	...	...	2022	...	...	2054	2042v	...	...	...	...	...	...	...	...	...	...	...	
Arles.................351 d.	1932	...	...	...	...	...	...	...	...	...	...	...	...	...	...	...	2259	...	
Miramas...............351 d.	1952	...	...	...	...	...	...	...	...	...	...	...	...	...	...	...	...	...	
Vitrolles Aéroport Marseille ‡ d.	2009	...	...	...	...	...	...	...	...	...	...	...	...	...	...	...	...	...	
Marseille St Charles....351 a.	2024	2040	...	...	...	...	2125	...	...	...	...	...	2237	...	...	...	2347	...	
Nice 360.................... a.	...	2337z	...	...	...	...	...	...	...	...	...	...	...	...	...	...	...	...	
Valence TGV.................. d.	...	...	...	...	...	...	...	...	...	...	2142	2143	...	...	2241	...	...	...	
Lyon Part Dieu............... a.	...	...	...	...	...	...	...	...	2150	...	...	...	...	...	...	...	...	...	
Dijon 379................... a.	...	...	...	...	...	...	...	...	...	...	...	...	...	...	...	...	...	...	
Paris Gare de Lyon........... a.	...	...	...	2245	...	...	...	...	...	2353	2353	...	...	...	0053	...	...	...	
Marne la Vallée § 11........ a.																			
Charles de Gaulle ✈ 11..... a.																			
Lille Europe 11............. a.																			
Brussels Midi 11............ a.																			

N – To Nantes and Rennes (Table **335**). Subject to alteration on Apr. 30, May 20, June 10.
R – From Apr. 9.

e – Also Apr. 17, May 1, 8, June 5.
f – Also May 24; not May 26.
h – Not May 25.
j – 2–3 minutes earlier until Jan. 15.
k – From June 5 Carcassonne d. 1834, Narbonne a. 1901, d. 1904.
m – Also May 26; not Apr. 17, May 1, 8, 24, 25, June 5.
n – May depart up to 10 minutes earlier until Mar. 5.
t – Jan. 16–20 arrives Lille **Flandres** 2308 (not Lille Europe).
v – Avignon **TGV** station. Also calls at Aix en Provence TGV (a. 2109).
z – ⑤–⑦ (also Apr. 17, May 1, 8, 25, June 5).

TGV –Ⓡ, supplement payable.

☉ – Runs up to 3 minutes earlier Béziers - Montpellier - Tarascon until Jan. 15.
⬚ – Until Jan. 15 departs Sète 1809, Montpellier 1833, Lunel 1847, Nîmes 1902, Tarascon 1919 (other timings as shown).
△ – Bordeaux timings are subject to alteration May 6–8, June 4, 5.
♠ – From Barcelona (Table **13**). Subject to confirmation from Apr. 3.
■ – 🚄 Madrid - Barcelona - Marseille. Subject to confirmation from Apr. 3.
★ – INTERCITÉS. Ⓡ.
☆ – To Mende (Table **333**).
‡ – Vitrolles Aéroport Marseille-Provence. A shuttle bus runs to the airport terminal (journey time 5 minutes). For additional trains see Table **351**.
§ – Marne la Vallée - Chessy (station for Disneyland Paris).

Additional low-cost 'Ouigo' TGV trains run to Marne la Vallée-Chessy
in the eastern suburbs of Paris. See Table **350a**.

359 NICE - ANNOT - DIGNE

SUBJECT TO CONFIRMATION 2nd class only

km	CP ▲						
0	**Nice** (Gare CP)	d.	0655	0925	1305	1715	1813
	Plan du Var	d.	0741	0957	1341	1757	1854
41	Villars sur Var	d.	0801	1017	1401	1818	1915
58	Puget Théniers	d.	0821	1038	1421	1839	1937
64	Entrevaux	d.	0830	1046	1429	1847	1945
78	Annot	d.	0851	1106	1449	1908	2001
96	Thorame Haute	d.	0915	1130	1512	1932	...
106	St André les Alpes	d.	0927	1144	1523	1945	...
150	**Digne**	a.	1020	1239	1620	2041	...

CP ▲		⚒	†				
Digne	d.	...	...	0715	1045	1425	1735
St. André les Alpes	d.	...	...	0812	1143	1524	1830
Thorame Haute	d.	...	...	0824	1156	1536	1842
Annot	d.	0540	0750	0850	1219	1600	1910
Entrevaux	d.	0558	0810	0908	1238	1619	1929
Puget Théniers	d.	0606	0822	0916	1246	1627	1938
Villars sur Var	d.	0627	0842	0937	1306	1648	1957
Plan du Var	d.	0649	0903	0958	1328	1710	2018
Nice (Gare CP)	a.	0731	0940	1030	1400	1745	2057

TRAIN DES PIGNES steam train, 2016

⑦ May 8 - Oct. 30 ⊠

Puget Théniers 1055 → Annot 1205
Annot 1500 → Puget Théniers 1540

Also calls at Entrevaux

www.traindespignes.fr

🚌 ★		🚌	🚌	🚌	🚌
		v			
Digne △	d.	0735	1100	1330	1640
Digne (Gare)	d.	0745	1110	1340	1650
Manosque-Gréoux	d.	0850	1215	1445	1800
Aix en Provence TGV	a.	0950	1315	1545	1900
Aéroport Marseille ✈	a.	1005	1330	1600	1915

🚌 ★		🚌	🚌	🚌	🚌
		⚒			z
Aéroport Marseille ✈	d.	0920	1255	1530	1820
Aix en Provence TGV	d.	0950	1325	1600	1850
Manosque-Gréoux	a.	1055	1430	1705	1955
Digne (Gare)	a.	1155	1530	1805	2050
Digne △	a.	1205	1540	1815	2055

🚌 ☆		🚌	🚌		🚌
		⚒			⑥
Digne △	d.	0700	1430	...	2000
Digne (Gare)	d.	|	1435	...	2003
Château Arnoux	a.	0725	1503	...	2029
Sisteron (Gare)	a.	0742	1520	...	2045
Veynes (Gare)	a.	...	1620	...	2140

🚌 ☆		🚌		🚌	🚌
				n	⚒
Veynes (Gare)	d.	0645	...	1245	...
Sisteron (Gare)	d.	0745	...	1345	1913
Château Arnoux	d.	0800	...	1400	1930
Digne (Gare)	a.	0828	...	1428	1956
Digne △	a.	0830	...	1430	2000

n – Not May 1.
v – Additional journey: 0500 ⚒.
z – Additional journey: 2035 (2100 from Aix TGV).

△ – Gare Routière (bus station).
▲ – Narrow gauge railway, operated by Chemins de Fer de Provence (CP).
☆ – LER route 33, operated by Autocars Payan or SCAL. SNCF rail tickets valid. For rail connections see **362**.

★ – LER (Lignes Express Régionales) Route 26, operated by Autocars Payan. Combined tickets 🚌 + TGV available.
⊠ – Also July 15, 22, 29, Aug. 12, 19, 26. An amended service runs on June 19.

360 MARSEILLE - TOULON - NICE - VENTIMIGLIA

Subject to alteration Jan. 14, 15, 21, 22. Services from Paris are subject to alteration on Mar. 18, 19. TGV timings may vary by a few minutes on certain dates – please check your reservation.

km	All *TGV* trains are 🄡		139		5773				17471	*TGV* 6805	*TGV* 6805	17473		*TGV* 6171	145	145		17475	*TGV* 6173	*TGV* 6155	*TGV* 6820	*TGV* 6175		
				Ⓐ		Ⓐ			Ⓐ	Ⓐ	Ⓒ				①									
			🄡♥		🄡B										🄡♥	🄡♥					⊕			
	Brussels Midi **11**	d.	...	...	...	...	...	...	...	...	...	...	...	...	...	...	...	...	...	...	...	...	...	...
	Lille Europe **11**	d.	...	...	...	...	...	...	...	...	...	...	...	...	...	...	...	...	...	...	...	...	...	...
	Paris Gare de Lyon **350**	▶ d.	...	...	2122a	...	...	...	...	...	...	...	...	0719	...	...	...	...	0921	0921	...	1019	...	...
	Strasbourg **379**	d.	...	...	|	...	...	...	...	...	...	...	...	|	...	...	...	...	|	|	...	|	...	...
	Metz **379**	d.	...	...	|	...	...	...	...	...	...	...	...	|	...	...	...	...	|	|	0544	|	...	...
	Dijon **379**	d.	...	...	|	...	...	...	...	...	...	...	...	|	...	...	...	...	|	|	0921	|	...	...
	Genève **346**	d.	...	...	|	...	...	...	...	...	...	...	...	|	...	...	...	...	|	|	|	|	...	...
	Lyon Part-Dieu **350**	d.	...	...	|	...	...	...	...	0628	0702	...	...	|	...	...	...	...	|	|	1107	|	...	...
	Bordeaux **320**	d.	...	...	|	...	...	...	...	|	|	...	...	|	...	...	...	...	|	|	|	|	...	...
	Toulouse **321**	d.	...	...	|	...	...	...	...	|	|	...	...	|	...	...	...	...	|	|	|	|	...	...
	Montpellier **355**	d.	...	...	|	...	...	...	...	|	|	...	...	|	...	...	...	...	|	|	|	|	...	...
0	**Marseille** St Charles	▶ d.	...	0529	|	0533	...	0628	0729	0831	0900	0931	...	|	1131	...	...	1214	|	|	1302	|	...	1429
67	**Toulon**	▶ a.	...	0610	0641	0632	...	0710	0812	0912	0941	1014	...	1111	1216	...	...	1258	1308	1308	1342	1408	...	1511
67	**Toulon**	▶ d.	...	0613	0644	0648	0648	0714	0816	0916	0945	1017	...	1115	1218	...	1221	1301	1316	1321	1346	1411	...	1514
	Hyères	▶ a.	...	|	|	|	|	|	|	|	|	|	...	|	|	...	|	|	|	1334	|	|	...	|
100	Carnoules	d.	...	0631	|	0719	0719	0732	|	|	|	1034	...	|	|	...	1251	1320	|	...	|	|	...	1532
135	Les Arcs-Draguignan	▷ d.	...	0651	0722	0746	0746	0752	0853	0952	1022	1056	...	1152	|	...	1320	1341	|	...	1423	1448	...	1553
162	St Raphaël-Valescure	▷ d.	...	0711	0740	...	...	0812	0914	1010	1040	1115	...	|	1311	...	...	1400	1407	...	1441	1506	...	1611
195	**Cannes**	▷ d.	...	0744	0811	...	...	0846	0944	1040	1110	1145	...	1237	1335	...	...	1430	1437	...	1512	1538	...	1643
206	Antibes	▷ d.	...	0755	0822	...	...	0858	0956	1052	1121	1156	...	1248	1347	...	...	1441	1448	...	1523	1548	...	1655
229	**Nice** Ville	▷ a.	...	0815	0836	...	...	0918	1009	1105	1134	1209	...	1301	1402	...	...	1459	1505	...	1546	1601	...	1714
229	**Nice** Ville	▷ d.	0808	0818	...	...	...	0921	...	...	...	...	...	...	1408	1408	...	...	...	...	...	...	...	1717
245	Monaco-Monte Carlo	▷ a.	0823	0837	...	...	...	0940	...	...	...	...	...	...	1424	1424	...	...	...	...	...	...	...	1736
252	Menton	▷ a.	|	0849	...	...	...	0952	...	...	...	...	...	...	|	|	...	...	...	...	...	...	...	1749
262	**Ventimiglia**	▷ a.	0845	0901	...	...	...	1004	...	...	...	...	...	...	1442	1442	...	...	...	...	...	...	...	...

		147	147		*TGV* 9756		4659 4658		*TGV* 6177	17479		*TGV* 9828	*TGV* 6179	17481		*TGV* 6169	*TGV* 6815	*TGV* 6181	*TGV* 6159	17483	4665 4664	*TGV* 6183		*TGV* 6187
		⑥⑦				Ⓐ	★	Ⓐ							Ⓐ	①–④			⑤⑦		⑤–⑦	⑤–⑦		⑤
		🄡♥	🄡♥										S			m			r		w★	z		Y
Brussels Midi **11**	d.	...	...	...	...	...	...	...	...	...	...	1217	...	...	...	...	...	...	...	...	...	...	...	...
Lille Europe **11**	d.	...	...	...	...	...	...	...	...	...	...	1252t	...	...	...	...	...	...	...	...	...	...	...	...
Paris Gare de Lyon **350**	▶ d.	...	...	...	...	...	...	...	1419	...	...	|	1519	...	...	1615	...	1719	1719	...	...	1819	...	1919
Strasbourg **379**	d.	...	...	...	...	...	...	...	|	...	...	|	|	...	...	|	...	|	|	...	...	|	...	|
Metz **379**	d.	...	...	...	...	...	...	...	|	...	...	|	|	...	...	|	...	|	|	...	...	|	...	|
Dijon **379**	d.	...	...	...	...	...	...	...	|	...	...	|	|	...	...	|	1606	|	|	...	...	|	...	|
Genève **346**	d.	...	...	...	1241	...	...	...	|	...	...	|	|	...	...	|	|	|	|	...	...	|	...	|
Lyon Part-Dieu **350**	d.	...	...	...	1436	...	...	...	|	...	...	1606	|	...	...	|	1806	|	|	...	...	|	...	|
Bordeaux **320**	d.	...	...	...	|	...	1047	...	|	...	...	|	|	...	...	|	|	|	|	...	1447v	|	...	|
Toulouse **321**	d.	...	...	...	|	...	1257	...	|	...	...	|	|	...	...	|	|	|	|	...	1654v	|	...	|
Montpellier **355**	d.	...	...	...	|	...	1504	...	|	...	...	|	|	...	...	|	|	|	|	...	1902	|	...	|
Marseille St Charles	▶ d.	1531	...	...	1632	1616	1658	...	|	1732	...	1800	|	1829	...	1936	1958	|	|	2022	2058	|	...	|
Toulon	▶ a.	1614	...	...	1714	1705	1741	...	1810	1814	...	1843	1909	1914	...	2018	2042	2108	2108	2105	2141	2209	...	2309
Toulon	▶ d.	1617	...	1647	1717	1721	1744	1750	1814	1820	1824	1846	1912	1917	1921	2021	2046	2111	2120	2114	2144	2212	...	2312
Hyères	▶ a.	|	...	|	|	|	|	|	|	|	|	|	|	|	|	|	|	|	2134	|	|	|	...	|
Carnoules	d.	|	...	1718	|	1751	|	1815	|	|	1854	|	|	|	1952	|	|	|	...	|	|	|	...	|
Les Arcs-Draguignan	▷ d.	|	...	1747	|	1811	1822f	1844	|	1856	1916	1923	|	1954	2020	|	2124	2148	...	2150	2221f	|	...	|
St Raphaël-Valescure	▷ d.	1712	...	...	1809	...	1841	...	1905	1916	...	1942	2003	2014	...	2111	2143	|	...	2208	2240	2303	...	0003
Cannes	▷ d.	1738	...	...	1839	...	1912	...	1935	1946	...	2013	2034	2046	...	2143	2215	2232	...	2241	2311	2335	...	0034
Antibes	▷ d.	1748	...	...	1850	...	1925	...	1946	1958	...	2023	2046	2057	...	2154	2226	2243	...	2252	2323	2346	...	0044
Nice Ville	▷ a.	1803	...	...	1903	...	1941	...	2000	2014	...	2036	2103	2113	...	2207	2239	2303	...	2307	2337	2359	...	0057
Nice Ville	▷ d.	1807	1807	...	...	...	...	...	2010j	...	...	...	...	...	...	...	...	...	...	...	...	...	...	...
Monaco-Monte Carlo	▷ a.	1824	1824	...	...	...	...	...	2023j	...	...	...	...	...	...	...	...	...	...	...	...	...	...	...
Menton	▷ a.	|	|	...	...	...	...	...	2034j	...	...	...	...	...	...	...	...	...	...	...	...	...	...	...
Ventimiglia	▷ a.	1842	1842	...	...	...	...	...	2048j	...	...	...	...	...	...	...	...	...	...	...	...	...	...	...

B – Not Dec. 24, 31. TRAIN BLEU – 🛏 1, 2 cl., (2) (reclining) Paris Austerlitz - Nice. Subject to alteration on Mar. 11, 18, 25.
S – ⑤⑥ (daily from Apr. 3).
Y – From Apr. 7.

a – Paris **Austerlitz**. Departs 2056 on May 20, 28, June 10.
f – From Mar. 3.
j – Not Jan. 29.
m – Not Apr. 17, May 1, 8, 24, 25, June 5.
r – Also Apr. 17, May 1, 8, 24, June 5.
t – 1303 to Jan. 22 and Apr. 24 - May 28.
v – May depart up to 10 minutes earlier until Mar. 5.
w – ⑤–⑦ (also Apr. 17, May 1, 8, 25, June 5).
z – Also Also Apr. 17, May 1, 8, June 5.

TGV – 🄡, supplement payable, 🍷.

⊕ – Subject to alteration on Feb. 26, May 7, 21.
▷ – For local trains Les Arcs - Cannes - Nice - Ventimiglia see Table **361**.
▶ – For complete *TGV* service Paris - Marseille - Toulon see Table **350**. For local trains Marseille - Toulon - Hyères see separate panel on next page.
★ – *INTERCITÉS*. 🄡.
♥ – International service to Italy. Operated by *Thello*. See Table **90**. **Subject to confirmation.**

VENTIMIGLIA - NICE - TOULON - MARSEILLE 360

Subject to alteration Jan. 14, 15, 21, 22. Services to Paris are subject to alteration on Mar. 18, 19. TGV timings may vary by a few minutes on certain dates – please check your reservation.

All *TGV* trains are [R]	⚒	Ⓐ		Ⓐ	*TGV* 6108 ⑥ p	Ⓐ		17470	*TGV* 6172	*TGV* 6814		Ⓑ		*TGV* 9866		*TGV* 6174	4760 4761 ★	*TGV* 9750	*TGV* 6176			142 [R]♥	*TGV* 6864	*TGV* 6124 ⊕
Ventimiglia ▷ d.	...	...	...	...	...	...	...	...	...	...	...	...	...	...	...	0910j	...	...	...	...	...	1114	...	...
Menton ▷ d.	...	...	...	0508	...	...	...	...	...	...	...	0808	...	...	...	0927j	...	...	...	...	...	|	...	...
Monaco-Monte Carlo ▷ d.	...	...	...	0526	...	...	...	...	...	...	...	0821	...	...	...	0938j	...	...	...	...	...	1139	...	...
Nice Ville ▷ a.	...	...	...	0545	...	...	...	...	...	...	...	0841	...	...	...	0952j	...	...	...	...	...	1152	...	...
Nice Ville ▷ d.	...	...	...	0547	...	...	...	0650	0701	0723	...	0844	0844	0919	...	1002	1022	1055	1102	...	...	...	1222	...
Antibes ▷ d.	...	...	...	0607	...	...	...	0707	0717	0743	...	0906	0906	0936	...	1019	1038	1110	1118	...	...	...	1238	...
Cannes ▷ d.	...	...	...	0618	...	...	...	0720	0728	0755	...	0919	0919	0948	...	1030	1049	1121	1129	...	...	...	1250	...
St Raphaël-Valescure ▷ d.	...	...	...	0646	...	...	...	0748	|	0823	...	0949	0949	1019	...	1058	1117	1148	1157	...	...	...	1317	...
Les Arcs-Draguignan ▷ d.	0546	0612	0643	0707	...	0713	0741	0808	0812	0842	...	1010	1010	1039	...	|	1135	|	|	...	1218	...	1336	...
Carnoules d.	0614	0640	0711	0726	...	0741	0809	|	|	|	...	1030	1030	|	...	|	|	|	|	...	1246	...	|	...
Hyères ▶ d.	|	|	|	|	0729	|	|	|	|	|	...	|	|	|	...	|	|	|	|	...	|	...	|	1434
Toulon ▶ a.	0644	0709	0741	0745	0748	0811	0839	0843	0848	0917	...	1048	1048	1114	...	1148	1213	1242	1247	...	1316	...	1411	1447
Toulon ▶ d.	0647	0712	...	0748	0755	...	...	0846	0851	0921	...	1051	1051	1117	...	1151	1216	1245	1250	...	...	...	1414	1450
Marseille St Charles ▶ a.	0737	0805	...	0833	0836	...	...	0929	|	1002	...	1133	1133	1158	...	|	1302	1329	|	...	...	...	1456	1534
Montpellier **355** a.	...	...	...	...	|	...	...	...	|	|	...	...	...	|	...	|	1453	|	|	...	...	...	|	|
Toulouse **321** a.	...	...	...	...	|	...	...	...	|	|	...	...	...	|	...	|	1707	|	|	...	...	...	|	|
Bordeaux **320** a.	...	...	...	...	|	...	...	...	|	|	...	...	...	|	...	|	1913	|	|	...	...	...	|	|
Lyon Part-Dieu **350** a.	...	...	...	...	|	...	...	...	|	1158	...	...	...	1354	...	|	...	1528	|	...	...	...	1654	|
Genève **346** a.	...	...	...	...	|	...	...	...	|	|	...	...	...	|	...	|	...	1717	|	...	...	...	|	|
Dijon **379** a.	...	...	...	...	|	...	...	...	|	1359	...	...	...	|	...	|	...	...	|	...	...	...	1847	|
Metz **379** a.	...	...	...	...	|	...	...	...	|	...	...	...	...	|	...	|	...	...	|	...	...	...	2219	|
Strasbourg **379** a.	...	...	...	...	|	...	...	...	|	...	...	...	...	|	...	|	...	...	|	...	...	...	...	|
Paris Gare de Lyon **350** ▶ a.	...	...	...	...	1159	...	...	...	1241	...	...	...	...	|	...	1541	...	...	1641	...	...	...	...	1915
Lille Europe **11** a.	...	...	...	...	...	...	...	...	...	...	...	...	...	1657	...	...	...	...	...	...	...	...	...	...
Brussels Midi **11** a.	...	...	...	...	...	...	...	...	...	...	...	...	...	1743	...	...	...	...	...	...	...	...	...	...

	TGV 6178 L	17474	4768 4769 ★ H		*TGV* 6184	17476	*TGV* 6168 J			144 [R]♥		*TGV* 6180	*TGV* 6806	Ⓐ	*TGV* 6186 ⑦ Y				160 ⑤–⑦ [R]♥	5774 [R] B				
Ventimiglia ▷ d.	...	...	...	...	...	...	...	...	...	1515	1546	...	...	...	...	...	...	...	1914	...	...	...	...	...
Menton ▷ d.	...	...	...	...	...	...	...	...	...	|	1606	...	...	1708	...	...	1805	...	|	...	...	...	...	...
Monaco-Monte Carlo ▷ d.	...	...	...	...	...	...	...	...	...	1540	1619	...	...	1721	...	...	1818	...	1939	...	...	...	...	...
Nice Ville ▷ a.	...	...	...	...	...	...	...	...	...	1600	1638	...	...	1741	...	...	1839	...	1952	...	...	...	...	...
Nice Ville ▷ d.	1352	1358	1415	...	1500r	1515	1547	...	...	...	1641	1654	1725	1744	1802	...	1842	...	1955	2005	...	...	...	...
Antibes ▷ d.	1410	1414	1431	...	1515r	1536	1604	...	...	...	1703	1710	1742	1807	1818	...	1904	...	2014	2022	...	...	...	...
Cannes ▷ d.	1422	1428	1444	...	1528	1546	1616	...	...	...	1714	1721	1753	1819	1830	...	1915	...	2025	2034	...	...	...	...
St Raphaël-Valescure ▷ d.	1450	1458	1516	...	1555	1613	1645	...	...	...	1749	|	1820	1849	1857	...	1945	...	2052	2100	...	...	...	...
Les Arcs-Draguignan ▷ d.	1510	1517	1535	...	|	1634	1704	1710	...	...	1811	1805	1839	1911	|	...	2007	...	|	2121	...	...	...	...
Carnoules d.	|	1539	|	...	|	|	|	1740	...	...	1833	|	|	1931	|	...	2027	...	|	|	...	...	...	...
Hyères ▶ d.	|	|	|	...	|	|	|	|	...	...	|	|	|	|	|	...	|	...	|	|	...	...	...	...
Toulon ▶ a.	1546	1557	1613	...	1647	1710	1739	1811	...	...	1850	1844	1914	1948	1947	...	2045	...	2142	2155	...	...	...	...
Toulon ▶ d.	1549	1600	1616	...	1650	1714	1742	...	...	...	1853	1847	1918	1951	1951	...	2049	...	2145	2158	...	...	...	...
Marseille St Charles ▶ a.	|	1645	1659	...	|	1804	1823	...	...	...	1935	|	2002	2033	|	...	2131	...	2231	|	...	...	...	...
Montpellier **355** a.	|	...	1853	...	|	...	|	...	...	...	...	|	|	...	|	...	...	...	...	|	...	...	...	...
Toulouse **321** a.	|	...	2107	...	|	...	|	...	...	...	...	|	|	...	|	...	...	...	...	|	...	...	...	...
Bordeaux **320** a.	|	...	2313	...	|	...	|	...	...	...	...	|	|	...	|	...	...	...	...	|	...	...	...	...
Lyon Part-Dieu **350** a.	|	...	...	...	|	...	|	...	...	...	...	|	2203	...	|	...	...	...	...	|	...	...	...	...
Genève **346** a.	|	...	...	...	|	...	|	...	...	...	...	|	...	...	|	...	...	...	...	|	...	...	...	...
Dijon **379** a.	|	...	...	...	|	...	|	...	...	...	...	|	...	...	|	...	...	...	...	|	...	...	...	...
Metz **379** a.	|	...	...	...	|	...	|	...	...	...	...	|	...	...	|	...	...	...	...	|	...	...	...	...
Strasbourg **379** a.	|	...	...	...	|	...	|	...	...	...	...	|	...	...	|	...	...	...	...	|	...	...	...	...
Paris Gare de Lyon **350** ▶ a.	1941	...	...	...	2041	...	2145	...	...	...	...	2241	...	...	2344	...	...	...	...	0738a	...	...	...	...
Lille Europe **11** a.	...	...	...	...	...	...	...	...	...	...	...	...	...	...	...	...	...	...	...	...	...	...	...	...
Brussels Midi **11** a.	...	...	...	...	...	...	...	...	...	...	...	...	...	...	...	...	...	...	...	...	...	...	...	...

LOCAL TRAINS MARSEILLE - TOULON - HYÈRES

km			Ⓐ	⚒		⚒		Ⓐ			Ⓐ	Ⓒ		Ⓐ		Ⓐ			Ⓐ		Ⓐ	Ⓐ		Ⓐ	Ⓒ
0	**Marseille** St Charles d.	...	0533	0601	0633	0702	0733	0802	0835	0935	1002	1033	1133	1154	1233	1306	1333	1433	1502	1522	1602	1616	1641	1652	1702
27	Cassis • d.	...	0556	0625	0655	0725	0755	0824	0857	0958	1025	1056	1156	1217	1257	1328	1356	1456	1525	1555	1624	|	1703	1725	1725
37	La Ciotat d.	...	0603	0632	0703	0733	0803	0831	0905	1005	1032	1103	1203	1224	1304	1335	1403	1503	1532	1602	1632	1642	|	1732	1732
51	Bandol d.	...	0615	0643	0715	0745	0815	0843	0916	1017	1045	1115	1215	1236	1316	1347	1415	1515	1545	1615	1644	|	1720	1744	1745
67	**Toulon** a.	...	0632	0701	0732	0802	0832	0901	0933	1034	1102	1132	1232	1254	1332	1405	1433	1532	1602	1632	1701	1705	1735	1802	1802
67	**Toulon** d.	0604	...	0706	0735	0805	0838t	...	0936	1037	...	1135	1235	...	1335	...	...	1535	1605	1635	1704	...	1738	1805	1805
87	**Hyères** a.	0625	...	0726	0757	0827	0901t	...	0957	1057	...	1157	1257	...	1357	...	...	1557	1625	1657	1725	...	1758	1826	1826

		Ⓐ	Ⓒ		Ⓐ						
Marseille St Charles d.	1738	1752	1804	1835	1902	1940	2002	2033	2102	2145	2233
Cassis • d.	1803	1826	1827	1858	1925	2002	2025	2056	2125	2208	2255
La Ciotat d.	1810	1833	1834	1905	1932	2009	2032	2103	2132	2215	2302
Bandol d.	1822	1846	1846	1917	1945	2021	2044	2116	2143	2228	2314
Toulon a.	1838	1903	1903	1933	2002	2038	2101	2133	2201	2245	2332
Toulon d.	1841	...	...	1936	2005	2039	...	2136	...	...	...
Hyères a.	1858	...	...	1957	2026	2058	...	2157	...	...	...

	Ⓐ n		Ⓐ	Ⓐ		Ⓐ	Ⓐ	Ⓐ		Ⓐ
Hyères ⊡ d.	...	...	0534	...	0602	...	0634	...	0702	0733
Toulon a.	...	...	0555	...	0623	...	0655	...	0720	0752
Toulon d.	0500	0522	0558	0614	0626	0647	0658	0712	0722	0755
Bandol d.	|	0539	0614	0629	0643	|	0715	|	0738	0812
La Ciotat d.	0522	0551	0626	0641	0655	0707	0727	0736	0750	0823
Cassis • d.	|	0558	0634	0649	0703	|	0735	|	0758	0831
Marseille St Charles a.	0550	0623	0658	0711	0727	0737	0759	0805	0822	0855

		Ⓐ					Ⓐ		Ⓐ								Ⓐ		Ⓐ						✣
Hyères ⊡ d.	0803	...	0906	...	...	1102	...	1202	...	1302	...	1402	...	...	...	1602	1634	1658	1731	1802	...	1902	2002	...	2103
Toulon a.	0823	...	0925	...	...	1122	...	1222	...	1323	...	1423	...	...	...	1623	1655	1717	1750	1822	...	1923	2023	...	2123
Toulon d.	0825	0857	0928	...	1055	1125	1158	1225	1258	1326	...	1426	...	1524	1604	1626	1658	1723	1753	1825	1858	1926	2026	...	2126
Bandol d.	0841	0912	0944	...	1110	1140	1214	1241	1314	1343	...	1443	...	1540	|	1643	1714	1738	1810	1842	1914	1943	2043	...	2142
La Ciotat d.	0853	0924	0956	...	1122	1152	1226	1252	1326	1355	...	1455	...	1552	1624	1655	1726	1751	1822	1854	1926	1955	2055	...	2155
Cassis • d.	0900	0932	1003	...	1129	1159	1233	1300	1334	1403	...	1502	...	1559	|	1703	1733	|	1834	1901	1933	2003	2102	...	2202
Marseille St Charles a.	0925	0956	1027	...	1154	1225	1258	1324	1358	1427	...	1527	...	1624	1654	1727	1758	1820	1858	1929	1958	2027	2127	...	2227

B – Not Dec. 24, 31. TRAIN BLEU – 🛏 1, 2 cl., (2) (reclining) Nice - Paris Austerlitz. Subject to alteration on Mar. 11, 18, 25. Departures are 43 – 68 minutes **earlier** on Mar. 17, 31.
H – ①⑥⑦ (also Apr. 18, May 2, 9, 25, 26, June 6).
J – Ⓑ (daily from Apr. 2).
L – ⑥⑦ (daily from Apr. 1).
Y – From Apr. 9.

a – Paris **Austerlitz**. Arrives 0838 Jan. 24 – 28, 31, Feb. 1 – 4, Mar. 14 – 17, 21 – 25. Arrives 0924 or 0947 Jan. 30, Feb. 13, Mar. 13, Apr. 3 – 8, 11 – 30, May 1 – 6, 8.
j – Not Jan. 29.
n – Not May 3 – 5, 10 – 12, 16 – 19, 23 – 25.
p – Also May 25.
r – On ⑤ departs Nice 1458, Antibes 1514.
t – 3 – 4 minutes earlier on ⑦ (also Mar. 18; not Jan. 15, 22, 29).

TGV – [R], supplement payable, 🍷.

⊕ – Subject to alteration on May 6, 7, 20, 21.
✣ – Subject to alteration Mar. 13 - May 26.
▷ – For local trains Ventimiglia - Nice - Cannes - Les Arcs see Table **361**.
▶ – For complete *TGV* service Toulon - Marseille - Paris see Table **350**. For local trains Hyères - Toulon - Marseille see separate panel below main table.
★ – *INTERCITÉS*. [R].
♥ – International service from Italy. Operated by *Thello*. See Table **90**. **Subject to confirmation**.
• – Cassis station is located 4 km from Cassis town.

361 LES ARCS - ST RAPHAEL - CANNES - NICE - MONACO - VENTIMIGLIA *Local trains*

Rail services Grasse - Cannes and v.v. are suspended during the currency of this timetable. A limited replacement 🚌 service operates on ①–⑤ (as shown).
Other local 🚌 services (numbers 600/610) operate daily between Grasse and Cannes bus stations. For long-distance trains see Table **360**. Subject to alteration on Jan. 14, 15, 21, 22, 29.

km		①–⑤	Ⓑ		①–⑤	①–⑤		①–⑤				①–⑤	①–⑤		①–⑥	①–⑤	Ⓐ		①–⑤	①–⑤		⑤–⑦		
		h										🚌				🚌	◇		🚌				◇	
0	**Les Arcs-Draguignan** d.	...	...	...	...	...	...	...	...	0554	...	...	...	...	0621	...	0651	...	...	0712	...	...	0752	...
23	Fréjus d.	...	...	...	...	...	...	...	...	0608	...	...	...	...	0636	...	0706	...	...	0726	...	...	0807	...
27	St Raphaël-Valescure d.	...	...	...	...	...	...	...	...	0613	...	...	...	...	0641	...	0711	...	...	0730	...	...	0812	...
31	Boulouris sur Mer d.	...	...	...	...	...	...	...	...	|	...	...	...	...	0645	...	|	...	...	|	...	...	|	...
	Grasse d.	...	...	...	...	...	...	...	...	|	...	0620	...	...	|	0650	|	...	0715	|	...	...	|	...
60	**Cannes** d.	...	0518	...	...	0544	...	0607	0614	0643	0646	0700	0705	0710	0723	0730	0744	0751	0755	0803	0816	0816	0846	0850
69	Juan les Pins d.	...	0528	...	...	0554	...	0615	0624	0651	0657	...	0713	0720	...	...	0751	0801	...	0811	0827	0827	0853	0900
71	Antibes d.	...	0531	...	...	0557	...	0619	0627	0655	0700	...	0716	0723	...	...	0755	0805	...	0814	0830	0830	0858	0903
80	Cagnes sur Mer d.	...	0543	...	...	0608	...	0626	0638	0702	0711	...	0723	0735	...	...	0802	0816	...	0831	0841	0841	0905	0914
94	**Nice** Ville a.	...	0559	...	...	0624	...	0640	0654	0715	0727	...	0737	0750	...	...	0815	0831	...	0845	0856	0856	0918	0929
94	**Nice** Ville d.	0530	0602	0602	0617	0627	0627	0643	0657	0718	0730	...	0743	0753	...	...	0818	0834	...	0848	0859	0859	0921	...
99	Villefranche sur Mer d.	0538	0610	0610	0625	0636	0636	0652	0706	0726	0739	...	0752	0801	...	...	0826	0842	...	0856	0908	0908	0929	...
101	Beaulieu sur Mer d.	0541	0613	0613	0628	0639	0639	0655	0709	0729	0742	...	0755	0805	...	...	0829	0845	...	0859	0911	0911	0932	...
104	Eze d.	0545	0617	0617	|	0643	0643	|	0713	|	0747	...	|	0809	...	...	|	0849	...	|	0915	0915	|	...
110	**Monaco-Monte Carlo** d.	0555	0628	0628	0639	0654	0654	0705	0723	0741	0758	...	0806	0829j	...	...	0840	0900	...	0910	0925	0925	0943	...
114	Cap Martin-Roquebrune d.	0601	0633	0633	|	0659	0659	|	0729	|	0804	...	|	0835	...	...	|	0905	...	|	0931	0931	|	...
117	Menton d.	0608	0640	0640	0649	0706	0706	0715	0735	0750	0811	...	0816	0841	...	...	0850	0912	...	0920	0937	0938	0953	...
127	**Ventimiglia** a.	0620	0653	0653	...	0719	0719	...	0748	...	0824	...	...	...	...	...	0901	0925	...	...	...	0950	1004	...

			Ⓐ				⑥⑦		①–⑤					⑥⑦						①–⑤				
			◇					◇								◇							◇	
Les Arcs-Draguignan d.	...	...	0853	...	...	0958	...	1056	...	...	...	...	...	...	...	1341	...	...	1429	...	...	...	1553	...
Fréjus d.	...	...	0908	...	...	1011	...	1110	...	...	...	...	...	...	...	|	...	...	1443	...	...	...	1606	...
St Raphaël-Valescure d.	...	0846	0914	...	...	1015	...	1115	...	...	...	...	...	...	...	1400	...	...	1448	...	...	...	1611	...
Boulouris sur Mer d.	...	0851	|	...	...	1020	...	|	...	...	...	...	...	...	...	|	...	...	|	...	...	...	|	...
Grasse d.	...	|	|	...	...	|	...	|	...	...	...	...	...	...	...	|	...	...	|	...	...	...	|	...
Cannes d.	0920	0925	0944	0951	1022	1051	1117	1145	...	1156	1213	1247	1304	1351	1414	1430	1451	1458	1521	...	1548	1617	1643	1646
Juan les Pins d.	0930	...	|	1001	1032	1100	1127	|	...	1206	1223	1257	1315	1401	1424	|	1501	1509	|	...	1558	1628	1651	1657
Antibes d.	0933	...	0956	1004	1035	1103	1130	1156	...	1209	1226	1300	1318	1404	1427	1441	1504	1512	1530	...	1601	1631	1655	1700
Cagnes sur Mer d.	0949	...	|	1016	1046	1114	1141	|	...	1221	1237	1311	1331	1415	1438	|	1516	1526	1538	...	1612	1642	1702	1711
Nice Ville a.	1005	...	1009	1031	1101	1130	1156	1209	...	1236	1253	1327	1348	1431	1454	1459	1531	1542	1552	...	1628	1657	1714	1726
Nice Ville d.	1008	...	...	1034	1104	1133	1159	...	1232	1239	1256	1330	1354	1434	1457	...	1534	1545	1555	1618	1631	1700	1717	1729
Villefranche sur Mer d.	1017	...	...	1042	1113	1142	1208	...	1241	1247	1304	1339	1402	1443	1505	...	1542	1553	1604	1626	1640	1708	1725	1738
Beaulieu sur Mer d.	1020	...	...	1045	1116	1145	1211	...	1244	1250	1307	1342	1405	1446	1508	...	1545	1556	1608	1629	1643	1712	1728	1741
Eze d.	1024	...	...	1049	1120	1149	1215	...	1248	1254	1311	1346	1409	1450	1512	...	1549	1600	|	|	1647	1716	|	1745
Monaco-Monte Carlo d.	1034	...	...	1100	1130	1200	1225	...	1259	1305	1322	1356	1430j	1500	1523	...	1600	1611	1619	1640	1658	1726	1739	1755
Cap Martin-Roquebrune d.	1040	...	...	1105	1136	1205	1231	...	1304	1311	1327	1402	1436	1506	1528	...	1605	1616	|	|	1704	1731	|	1801
Menton d.	1046	...	...	1112	1143	1212	1238	...	1310	1318	1334	1409	1442	1513	1535	...	1612	1623	1629	1650	1711	1738	1749	1808
Ventimiglia a.	1100	...	...	1125	1155	1225	1250	...	...	1331	1347	1421	...	1525	1550	...	1625	1636	...	...	1724	1751	...	1820

	①–⑤	①–⑤					①–⑤		①–⑤	①–⑤													⑤–⑦	⑥⑦
	🚌						🚌		🚌					◇			◇					◇	k	k
Les Arcs-Draguignan d.	...	...	...	1623	...	...	...	...	...	1755	...	...	...	1856	...	...	1954	...	...	...	...	2150	...	...
Fréjus d.	...	...	...	1638	...	...	...	...	...	1810	...	...	...	1910	...	...	2008	...	...	...	...	|	...	...
St Raphaël-Valescure d.	...	...	...	1643	...	...	...	...	...	1815	...	...	1846	1916	...	...	2014	...	...	...	...	2208	...	...
Boulouris sur Mer d.	...	...	...	1647	...	...	...	...	...	|	...	...	1850	|	...	...	|	...	...	...	...	|	...	...
Grasse d.	1620	...	...	|	...	...	1720	...	1750	|	...	...	|	|	...	...	|	...	...	...	...	|	...	...
Cannes d.	1700	1706	1717	1721	1742	1748	1800	1812	1830	1848	1854	1923	1924	1946	1952	2019	2046	2052	2100	2149	2219	2241	2248	2347
Juan les Pins d.	...	1713	1727	...	1749	1758	...	1822	...	1855	1905	1934	...	|	2002	2029	|	2102	2111	2159	2229	|	2258	2358
Antibes d.	...	1717	1730	...	1753	1801	...	1825	...	1859	1908	1937	...	1958	2005	2033	2057	2105	2120	2202	2233	2252	2301	0001
Cagnes sur Mer d.	...	1724	1742	...	1800	1812	...	1836	...	1906	1922	1955	...	|	2016	2044	|	2117	2138	2215	2244	|	2313	0012
Nice Ville a.	...	1739	1757	...	1813	1827	...	1852	...	1918	1937	2010	...	2014	2031	2059	2113	2132	2155	2231	2259	2307	2328	0027
Nice Ville d.	...	1742	1811	...	1817	1830	...	1855	...	1921	1940	2013	...	...	2034	2102	...	2135	2158	2234	2302	...	2331	...
Villefranche sur Mer d.	...	1750	1819	...	1827	1839	...	1904	...	1930	1948	2021	...	...	2043	2110	...	2143	2206	2242	2310	...	2339	...
Beaulieu sur Mer d.	...	1753	1822	...	1830	1842	...	1907	...	1933	1951	2024	...	...	2046	2113	...	2146	2209	2245	2313	...	2342	...
Eze d.	...	|	1826	...	|	1847	...	1911	...	|	1955	2028	...	...	2050	2117	...	2150	2213	2249	2317	...	2346	...
Monaco-Monte Carlo d.	...	1804	1837	...	1843	1858	...	1921	...	1944	2006	2039	...	...	2101	2128	...	2201	2224	2300	2328	...	2357	...
Cap Martin-Roquebrune d.	...	|	1843	...	|	1904	...	1927	...	|	2011	2045	...	...	2106	2133	...	2206	2229	2305	2333	...	0002	...
Menton d.	...	1815	1850	...	1855	1911	...	1934	...	1954	2018	2051	...	...	2112	2140	...	2213	2236	2311	2340	...	0009	...
Ventimiglia a.	...	...	1903	...	...	1924	...	1946	...	...	2031p	2104	...	...	...	2153	...	2226	2249	...	2353	...	0022	...

	Ⓑ	Ⓐ	①–⑤		Ⓑ	⑥		①–⑤		①–⑤		①–⑤		①–⑤		Ⓑ							⑥⑦	
		◇	🚌				◇	🚌		🚌						◇	◇							
Ventimiglia d.	...	...	...	...	0529	0532	...	...	0609	...	0633	...	0710	...	0731	...	...	...	0811	0833	0851	0933	1011	...
Menton d.	...	0508	...	...	0545	0548	...	...	0625	...	0649	0710	0726	0744	0748	0808	...	...	0827	0850	0907	0949	1027	...
Cap Martin-Roquebrune d.	...	|	...	...	0552	0554	...	...	0632	...	0656	|	0733	|	0755	|	...	...	0834	0857	0914	0956	1034	...
Monaco-Monte Carlo d.	...	0526	...	...	0559	0601	...	...	0639	...	0703	0722	0740	0757	0803	0821	...	...	0841	0904	0922	1003	1041	...
Eze d.	...	|	...	...	0608	0609	...	...	0648	...	0712	|	0749	|	0812	|	...	...	0850	0913	0931	1012	1050	...
Beaulieu sur Mer d.	...	0535	...	...	0611	0613	...	...	0652	...	0716	0731	0753	0806	0816	0830	...	...	0854	0917	0935	1016	1054	...
Villefranche sur Mer d.	...	0538	...	...	0615	0616	...	...	0655	...	0719	0734	0756	0809	0819	0834	...	...	0857	0920	0938	1019	1057	...
Nice Ville a.	...	0545	...	...	0622	0623	...	...	0703	...	0727	0741	0804	0816	0826	0841	...	...	0905	0928	0947	1027	1105	...
Nice Ville d.	0526	0547	...	0612	0625	0625	0650	...	0706	...	0730	0744	0807	0819	0829	0844	0844	...	0908	0931	0951	1030	1108	1108
Cagnes sur Mer d.	0541	0601	...	0627	0641	0641	|	...	0722	...	0746	0758	0822	0833	0845	0858	0858	...	0924	0947	1007	1046	1124	1124
Antibes d.	0555	0607	...	0641	0655	0655	0707	...	0733	...	0757	0807	0834	0841	0856	0906	0906	...	0941	1001	1023	1057	1136	1136
Juan les Pins d.	0559	0611	...	0645	0659	0659	|	...	0736	...	0800	0810	0837	0844	0900	0909	0909	...	0945	1005	1027	1100	1139	1139
Cannes d.	0607	0618	0630	0654	0707	0707	0720	0730	0745	0800	0811	0820	0845	0851	0908	0919	0919	0934	0955	1014	1035	1109	1148	1148
Grasse a.	...	|	0710	...	...	...	|	0810	...	0840	...	|	...	...	...	|	|	...	...	...	...	...	...	...
Boulouris sur Mer d.	...	|	...	...	...	...	|	...	...	...	...	|	...	...	...	|	|	1008	...	...	...	...	...	...
St Raphaël-Valescure d.	...	0646	...	...	...	...	0748	...	...	...	...	0849	...	...	...	0949	0949	1012	...	...	...	...	...	...
Fréjus d.	...	0650	...	...	...	...	|	...	...	...	...	0853	...	...	...	0953	0953	...	...	...	...	...	...	...
Les Arcs-Draguignan a.	...	0705	...	...	...	...	0805	...	...	...	...	0907	...	...	...	1008	1008	...	...	...	...	...	...	...

					①–⑤		⑥⑦												①–⑤				Ⓐ	①–⑤
									◇				◇					◇	🚌				◇	🚌
Ventimiglia d.	1033	...	1106	...	...	...	1210	1235	...	1306	1336t	1411	...	...	1438	1507	...	1546	...	1605	...	1632	...	...
Menton d.	1049	1111	1122	...	1146	1226	1226	1252	...	1323	1352	1427	...	...	1454	1523	1545	1606	...	1621	1641	1649	1708	...
Cap Martin-Roquebrune d.	1056	|	1129	...	1153	1233	1233	1258	...	1329	1359	1434	...	...	1501	1530	1552	|	...	1628	|	1656	|	...
Monaco-Monte Carlo d.	1103	1123	1143f	...	1200	1240	1240	1306	...	1337	1406	1441	...	...	1508	1544f	1559	1619	...	1635	1653	1704	1721	...
Eze d.	1112	|	1153	...	1209	1249	1249	1314	...	1345	1415	1450	...	...	1517	1554	1608	|	...	1644	|	1713	|	...
Beaulieu sur Mer d.	1116	1132	1157	...	1213	1253	1253	1319	...	1350	1419	1454	...	...	1521	1558	1612	1628	...	1648	1701	1717	1730	...
Villefranche sur Mer d.	1119	1135	1200	...	1216	1256	1256	1322	...	1353	1422	1457	...	...	1524	1601	1615	1631	...	1651	1705	1720	1734	...
Nice Ville a.	1127	1143	1207	...	1224	1304	1304	1329	...	1400	1430	1505	...	...	1532	1608	1623	1638	...	1659	1712	1727	1741	...
Nice Ville d.	1130	1146	1210	...	1227	...	1307	1332	1358	1403	1433	1508	1515	←	1535	1611	1626	1641	...	1702	1715	1730	1744	...
Cagnes sur Mer d.	1146	1200	1227	...	1243	...	1323	1348	|	1419	1449	1523	|	1524	1551	1627	1641	1655	...	1717	1730	1746	1758	...
Antibes d.	1157	1207	1242	...	1255	...	1335	1359	1414	1436	1501	→	1536	1539	1608	1638	1653	1703	...	1729	1747	1757	1807	...
Juan les Pins d.	1200	1210	1246	...	1258	...	1338	1402	|	1440	1504	...	|	1543	1612	1642	1656	1706	...	1732	1751	1801	1810	...
Cannes d.	1209	1219	1254	1304	1307	...	1347	1411	1428	1449	1513	...	1546	1552	1621	1650	1704	1714	1730	1740	1758	1809	1819	1830
Grasse a.	...	|	...	|	...	...	...	...	|	...	...	...	|	...	...	...	...	|	1810	...	...	...	|	1910
Boulouris sur Mer d.	...	|	...	1339	...	...	...	...	|	...	...	...	|	...	...	...	...	|	...	...	...	...	|	...
St Raphaël-Valescure d.	...	1249	...	1343	...	...	...	...	1458	...	...	...	1613	...	...	...	...	1749	...	...	...	...	1849	...
Fréjus d.	...	1253	...	1347	...	...	...	...	|	...	...	...	|	...	...	...	...	1753	...	...	...	...	1854	...
Les Arcs-Draguignan a.	...	1311	...	1403	...	...	...	...	1515	...	...	...	1632	...	...	...	...	1808	...	...	...	...	1909	...

FOR NOTES SEE NEXT PAGE

218 Ⓐ – Mondays to Fridays, except holidays Ⓑ – Daily except Saturdays Ⓒ – Saturdays, Sundays and holidays 12

Local trains

VENTIMIGLIA - MONACO - NICE - CANNES - ST RAPHAEL - LES ARCS — 361

Rail services Grasse - Cannes and v.v. are suspended during the currency of this timetable. A limited replacement 🚌 service operates on ①-⑤ (as shown).
Other local 🚌 services (numbers 600/610) operate daily between Cannes and Grasse bus stations. For long-distance trains see Table **360**. Subject to alteration on Jan. 14, 15, 21, 22, 29.

		①-⑤	①-⑤ 🚌		◇			①-⑤					①-⑤	△		⑥	z		⑤-⑦ w		⑤-⑦ w		⑥⑦ k	⑤-⑦
Ventimiglia d.	1709	...	...	1728	...	...	1807	...	1830	...	1905	1932	...	2014	2033	2112	...	...	2142r	...	2212r	2242	2242	2312
Menton d.	1726	1741	...	1746	1805	...	1823	1842	1848	1907	1921	1949	2010	2030	2049	2128	...	...	2158r	2228	2228	2258	2258	2328
Cap Martin-Roquebrune d.	1732	|	...	1753	|	...	1830	|	1854	|	1928	1956	|	2037	2056	2135	...	...	2205r	2235	2235	2305	2305	2335
Monaco-Monte Carlo d.	1740	1754	...	1800	1818	...	1837	1855	1902	1919	1943f	2003	2030	2044	2103	2142	...	2212	2212	2242	2242	2312	2312	2342
Eze d.	1748	|	...	1809	|	...	1846	|	1910	|	1952	2012	|	2053	2112	2151	...	2221	2221	2251	2251	2321	2321	2351
Beaulieu sur Mer d.	1753	1803	...	1813	1828	...	1850	1904	1915	1928	1956	2016	2039	2057	2116	2155	...	2225	2225	2255	2255	2325	2325	2355
Villefranche sur Mer d.	1756	1807	...	1816	1832	...	1853	1907	1918	1931	1959	2020	2042	2100	2119	2158	...	2228	2228	2258	2258	2328	2328	2358
Nice Ville a.	1803	1814	...	1824	1839	...	1901	1914	1925	1938	2007	2027	2050	2108	2127	2206	...	2236	2236	2306	2306	2336	2336	0006
Nice Ville d.	1806	1817	...	1827	1842	...	1904	1917	1928	1941	2010	2030z	2053	2111	2130z	2209	2209	...	2239	...	2309	...	2339	...
Cagnes sur Mer d.	1822	1831	...	1842	1856	...	1920	1931	1944	1955	2026	2046z	2107	2127	2146z	2225	2225	...	2255	...	2325	...	2355	...
Antibes d.	1834	1840	...	1854	1904	...	1932	1940	1955	2003	2038	2100z	2114	2138	2158z	2237	2237	...	2307	...	2339	...	0007	...
Juan les Pins d.	1837	1844	...	1857	1907	...	1935	1943	1958	2006	2041	2104z	2117	2141	2201z	2240	2240	...	2310	...	2343	...	0010	...
Cannes d.	1846	1852	1900	1905	1915	1933	1943	1949	2009	2012	2050	2112z	2126	2150	2209z	2248	2248	...	2318	...	2351	...	0019	...
Grasse a.	...	...	1940	...	|	|	...	...	|	...	...	...	|	...	...	...	...	...	...	...	...	...	...	...
Boulouris sur Mer d.	...	...	...	...	|	2007	...	...	2036	...	...	...	|	...	...	...	...	...	...	...	...	...	...	...
St Raphaël-Valescure d.	...	...	...	...	1945	2012	...	...	2041	...	...	...	2156	...	...	...	...	...	...	...	...	...	...	...
Fréjus d.	...	...	...	...	1949	2016	...	...	2045	...	...	...	2200	...	...	...	...	...	...	...	...	...	...	...
Les Arcs-Draguignan a.	...	...	...	...	2005	2030	...	...	2101	...	...	...	2217	...	...	...	...	...	...	...	...	...	...	...

f – Arrives 9–10 minutes earlier.
h – Not May 25.
j – Arrives 12 minutes earlier.
k – Also Apr. 17, May 1, 8, June 5.
p – Not ⑤.
r – ⑥ only.
t – ⑤-⑦ only.
w – Not Dec. 16, 23.
z – Not ①-④ Dec. 12–22.
△ – Runs 8 minutes earlier on ①-④ Dec. 12–22.
◇ – To/from Marseille (Table **360**).

BRIANÇON - GRENOBLE, LYON and MARSEILLE — 362

km		⚒ r	J	②-⑤ n	① w	②-⑤ p	① g	x	h	H	Ⓐ		Ⓐ	⊗	🚌 ⚒	⑥G	🚌 ⚒			⑤	†	①-④ d		🚌 Ⓐ	5790 🅁 D‡
0	**Briançon** d.	...	...	...	0435	...	...	0520	0600	0600	0652	0757	...	0940y	1015	1112	1115	1339	1456	1536	1550	1607	1722	1810	2029
13	L'Argentière les Écrins d.	...	...	...	0450	...	...	0533	0613	0613	0708	0813	...	0956y	1035	1126	1135	1355	1509	1550	1604	1622	1737	1830	2046
28	Montdauphin-Guillestre d.	...	...	...	0501	...	...	0545	0625	0625	0719	0826	...	1008y	1050	1138	1150	1406	1521	1601	1615	1634	1751	1845	2059
45	Embrun d.	...	...	...	0516	...	...	0559	0640	0640	0733	0842	...	1023	1125	1155	1225	1421	1538	1628	1630	1648	1807	1920	2116
82	**Gap** a.	...	...	...	0550	...	...	0635	0713	0717	0805	0919	...	1053	1210	1238	1310	1454	1611	1702	1702	1721	1838	1957	2151
82	**Gap** d.	0515	0531	...	0553	...	...	0641	0715	0753	...	0922	...	1055	...	1241	...	1456	1614	1705	1705	...	1841	...	2154
109	Veynes-Dévoluy a.	0535	0550	...	0611	...	...	0701	0734	0821	...	0951	...	1115	...	1310	...	1519	1637	1726	1726	...	1902	...	2218
109	Veynes-Dévoluy d.	0538	0553	0612	0614	...	0637	0719j	0758	0836	...	0954	...	1118	...	1323	...	1522	1640	1729	1729	...	1907	...	2221
172	Die d.	|	|	0718	0718	...	|	0823	|	|	...	|	...	1225	...	1430	...	|	1751	|	|	...	|	...	2329
209	Crest d.	|	|	0752	0752	...	|	0858	|	|	...	|	...	1301	...	1511	...	|	1826	|	|	...	|	...	0004
244	**Valence** Ville **364** a.	|	|	0816	0816	...	|	0922	|	|	...	|	...	1325	...	1535	...	|	1850	|	|	...	|	...	|
	Valence TGV a.	|	|	0828	0828	...	|	0933	|	|	...	|	...	1338	...	1546	...	|	1901	|	|	...	|	...	|
	Paris Austerlitz a.	|	|	...	...	...	|	...	|	|	...	|	...	...	...	...	...	|	...	|	|	...	|	...	0738b
159	Sisteron d.	0618	0634	...	...	0718	0719	...	0841	0919	...	1041	1238	...	...	...	...	1601	...	1812	1812	...	1949	...	...
176	Château Arnoux - St Auban d.	0631	0648	...	...	0733	0734	...	0854	0934	...	1054	1251	...	...	...	...	1614	...	1829	1829	...	2004	...	...
209	Manosque-Gréoux d.	0656	0714	...	...	0800	0800	...	0918	1006	...	1121	1315	...	...	...	...	1639	...	1904t	1908t	...	2030	...	...
278	Aix en Provence ▷ d.	0740	0759	...	...	0843	0843	...	1002	1059	...	1205	1401	...	...	...	...	1723	...	2000	2000	...	2121	...	...
315	**Marseille** St Charles ▷ a.	0824	0841	...	...	0915	0915	...	1033	1127	...	1239	1433	...	...	...	...	1753	...	2041	2041	...	2150	...	...

	Ⓐ	5789 🅁 D§	🚌 Ⓐ		①-④ d		Ⓐ	⚒ ⊗	⑥G	Ⓐ	Ⓒ	Ⓒ ▲	Ⓐ			①-④ m	⑤	†	①-⑤	⑤ f	Ⓑ	⑤ f	⑤† f	Ⓑ	🚌 ①-④ z
Marseille St Charles ▷ d.	...	...	...	...	...	0844	0949	...	...	1245	1245	...	...	...	1645	1735	1735	1744	...	...	1845	1845	...	...	...
Aix en Provence ▷ d.	...	...	...	...	...	0920	1039	...	...	1319	1319	...	...	...	1722	1821	1821	1821	...	...	1919	1919	...	...	...
Manosque-Gréoux d.	...	...	...	...	...	1002	1124	...	...	1401	1400	...	...	...	1804	1902	1905	1905	...	...	2005	2005	...	...	...
Château Arnoux - St Auban d.	...	...	...	...	...	1026	1148	...	...	1425	1424	...	...	...	1828	1926	1930	1931	...	...	2031	2031	...	...	...
Sisteron d.	...	...	...	...	...	1040	1201	...	...	1438	1438	...	...	...	1843	1939	1948	1948	...	...	2045	2045	...	...	...
Paris Austerlitz d.	...	2122c	...	...	...	|	...	...	...	|	|	...	...	...	|	...	|	|	...	...	|	|	...	...	...
Valence TGV d.	...	|	...	...	...	|	...	1021	1223	|	|	1421	...	1636	|	...	|	|	1825	1825	|	|	2011	2011	...
Valence Ville **364** d.	...	0405	...	...	...	|	...	1032	1234	|	|	1432	...	1647	|	...	|	|	1836	1836	|	|	2021	2021	...
Crest d.	...	0432	...	...	...	|	...	1058	1303	|	|	1458	...	1714	|	...	|	|	1903	1903	|	|	2050	2050	...
Die d.	...	0506	...	...	...	|	...	1134	1339	|	|	1532	...	1753	|	...	|	|	1938	1938	|	|	2126	2126	...
Veynes-Dévoluy a.	...	0615	...	...	...	1122	...	1242	1446	1518	1518	1636	...	1856	1935	...	2029	2029	2042	2042	2126	2126	2229	2229	...
Veynes-Dévoluy d.	...	0618	...	...	...	1123	...	1245	1449	1520	1521	1639	...	1903	1948	...	2032	2032	...	2047	2129	2129	2240	2240	...
Gap a.	...	0640	...	...	...	1144	...	1304	1516	1539	1540	1701	...	1923	2006	...	2053	2053	...	2108	2150	2150	2301	2301	...
Gap d.	0607	0643	0810	...	1057	1147	...	1307	1518	1542	1545	1704	1733	1935	2008	...	...	...	...	2111	...	2153	2304	...	2311
Embrun d.	0641	0734	0900	...	1130	1224	...	1340	1600	1618	1631	1735	1808	2020	2042	...	...	...	...	2157	...	2230	2338	...	2345
Montdauphin-Guillestre d.	0657	0753	0930	...	1144	1239	...	1410k	1615	1635	1648	1752	1823	2035	2058	...	...	...	...	2212	...	2245	2353	...	0000
L'Argentière les Écrins d.	0709	0812	0945	...	1156	1249	...	1422	1626	1646	1702	1804	1834	2048	2110	...	...	...	...	2222	...	2256	0004	...	0015
Briançon a.	0724	0830	1005	...	1211	1303	...	1436	1640	1701	1716	1817	1849	2102	2124	...	...	...	...	2236	...	2309	0017	...	0035

GAP - GRENOBLE *Subject to alteration May 29 - June 30*

km		⚒				L				
0	**Gap** d.	0515r	...	0729	...	1120	1330	1726	1926	...
27	Veynes-Dévoluy d.	0546	...	0750	...	1148	1351	1749	1952	...
117	St Georges de Commiers d.	0723	...	0922	...	1322	1527	1922	2125	...
136	**Grenoble** a.	0745	...	0945	...	1345	1547	1945	2145	...

	L					Ⓐ	Ⓒ			⑥
Grenoble d.	0810	1008	1210	1410	...	1608	1608	...	1810	1810
St Georges de Commiers d.	0833	1029	1231	1433	...	1628	1628	...	1831	1831
Veynes-Dévoluy d.	1006	1201	1406	1611	...	1803	1803	...	2004	2007
Gap a.	1027	1222	1427	1636	...	1824	1835	...	...	2028

LOCAL TRAINS MARSEILLE - AIX EN PROVENCE Journey time: 33–45 minutes

From Marseille at 0536, 0636, 0655⚒, 0719Ⓐ, 0734, 0805Ⓐ, 0815, 0855Ⓐ, 0924, 1116, 1215, 1255Ⓐ, 1335, 1406Ⓐ, 1415, 1456Ⓐ, 1526, 1534, 1603Ⓐ, 1614, 1654Ⓐ, 1720, 1803⚒, 1816, 1855, 1936, 2036, 2136, 2215 and 2256.

From Aix en Provence at 0540Ⓐ, 0620⚒r, 0639Ⓐ, 0700, 0720⚒, 0740†, 0802Ⓐ, 0820, 0900, 0922Ⓐ, 0940, 1140, 1220, 1300, 1321, 1340, 1420, 1500Ⓐ, 1540, 1620, 1639Ⓐ, 1700, 1740, 1801Ⓐ, 1820, 1841Ⓐ, 1920, 2021⚒, 2100, 2140Ⓐ and 2240s.

D – Conveys 🛏 1, 2 cl. and 💺 (reclining).
G – Until Apr. 1.
H – Dec. 17, 18, 24, Feb. 4, 5, 11, 12, 18 only.
J – Jan. 7, 14, 21, 28, Mar. 11, 18, 25 only.
L – ⚒ (daily from Apr. 24).

b – 0838 Jan. 24–28, 31, Feb. 1–4, Mar. 14–17, 21–25. Arrives 0924 or 0947 Jan. 30, Feb. 13, Mar. 13, Apr. 3–8, 11–30, May 1–6, 8.
c – Departs 2056 on May 20, 28, June 10.
d – Not Apr. 17, May 1, 8, 25, June 5.
f – Also May 24.
g – Also Apr. 18, May 2, 9, 26, June 6; not Apr. 17, May 1, 8, June 5.
h – Not Dec. 17, 18, 24, Feb. 4, 5, 11, 12, 18.
j – 0711 on Dec. 24, Feb. 4, 5, 11, 12.
k – Arrives 1354.
m – Not Apr. 17, May 1, 8, 24, 25, June 5.
n – Not Mar. 21 - Apr. 18, May 2, 9, June 6.
p – Not Apr. 18, May 2, 9, 25, 26, June 6.
r – Not Jan. 7, 14, 21, 28, Mar. 11, 18, 25.
s – Not Apr. 18–21, 24–28.
t – Arrives 1855.
u – Also May 25.
w – Also Mar. 21–24, 28–31, Apr. 4–7, 11–14, Apr. 18, May 2, 9, June 6; not Apr. 17, May 1, 8, June 5.
x – Not ①-⑤ Mar. 20 - Apr. 14.
y – 5–6 minutes earlier on Feb. 4, 11.
z – Not May 1.

⊗ – Subject to alteration on ①-⑤ Mar. 20 - Apr. 14.
▲ – Subject to alteration. May run later on certain dates.
§ – Not Dec. 24, 31. Train number **5793** on †. Subject to alteration on Dec. 16, 17, 23, Jan. 14, 21, Feb. 3, 4, 10, 11, 17, Mar. 11, 18, 25.
‡ – Not Dec. 24, 31. Train number **5792** on †. Subject to alteration on Dec. 23, 30, Jan. 14, 21, Feb. 10, 11, 17, 18, Mar. 11, 18, 25.
▷ – For other local trains see panel below main table.
◇ – Gare SNCF (rail station).

🚌 BRIANÇON - OULX

	🅁				
Briançon ◇ d.	0700	0925	...	1515	1755
Oulx ◇ a.	0805	1030	...	1620	1900

	🅁				
Oulx ◇ d.	0855	1145	...	1545	1945
Briançon ◇ a.	0955	1245	...	1645	2045

Operator: 05 voyageurs ✆ +33 (0)4 92 502 505
www.05voyageurs.com

363 BELLEGARDE - ANNEMASSE - ÉVIAN LES BAINS

Trains from Lyon / Bellegarde may divide at Belllegarde and / or Annemasse - take care to travel in the correct portion. For connections Paris - Bellegarde and v.v. see Table **341**.

SERVICE UNTIL APRIL 29

km							TGV 6501							TGV 6503										
		Ⓐ	Ⓐ		⚒		⑥	⊗		Ⓐ ⊗	Ⓑ ⊗	⑥	⑥	⑥⑦	Ⓑ ⊙	⑥	⑥	Ⓑ ⊙	⑥	Ⓐ	Ⓐ	Ⓐ	Ⓑ	⑥
	Paris Gare de Lyon **341** d.	...	...	...	...	...	0711	...	...	...	...	...	...	1011	...	...	...	...	...	...	...	...	...	...
	Lyon Part-Dieu **346** d.	...	...	...	*0636*	...	|	*0834*	...	...	*1036*	1036	1136	|	*1234*	1236	1336	*1436*	1436	...	...	...	*1636*	1636
0	**Bellegarde** **365** d.	...	0709	...	0809	...	0951	1009	...	...	1209	1209	1309	1324	1409	1409	1509	1609	1609	...	...	...	1809	1809
38	Annemasse **365** a.	...	0744	...	0843	...	1031	1043	...	...	1243	1243	1344	1404	1443	1443	1543	1643	1643	...	...	...	1843	1843
38	Annemasse d.	0715	0748	...	0853	...	1041	1053	...	1220	1253	1253	1353	1416	1453	1453	1553	1653	1653	1716	1753	1820	1853	1853
68	Thonon les Bains d.	0744	0825	...	0930	...	1111	1130	...	1249	1330	1330	1430	1454	1530	1530	1630	1727	1730	1749	1831	1851	1930	1930
77	**Évian les Bains** a.	0752	...	...	0938	...	1119	1138	...	1256	1338	1338	1438	1502	1538	1538	1638	1735	1738	1757	1838	1859	1938	1938

					TGV 6511				
	Ⓐ	Ⓑ		⑤ V	⑤		⑤	D	
Paris Gare de Lyon **341** d.	...	...	...	...	1815	...	...	...	...
Lyon Part-Dieu **346** d.	...	1736	*1834*	...	|	...	2036	*2036*	...
Bellegarde **365** d.	...	1909	2009	...	2116	...	2209	2209	...
Annemasse **365** a.	...	1944	2043	...	2200	...	2244	2244	...
Annemasse d.	1920	1953	2053	2128	2210	...	2253	2253	...
Thonon les Bains d.	1950	2030	2130	2152	2235	...	2330	2330	...
Évian les Bains a.	1959	2038	2138	2202	2242	...	2338	2338	...

	⚒	⚒		Ⓐ	Ⓐ	Ⓐ	†	Ⓑ	⑥
Évian-les-Bains d.	0502	0522	0622	0654	0715	0800	0821	...	0822
Thonon-les-Bains d.	0510	0531	0631	0703	0724	0808	0832	0832	0831
Annemasse a.	0542	0606	0706	0733	0804	0836	0907	0907	0907
Annemasse **365** d.	0547	0617	0717	...	...	...	0917	0917	0917
Bellegarde **365** a.	0620	0650	0750	...	...	...	0950	0950	0949
Lyon Part-Dieu **346** a.	...	0822	*0922*	...	...	...	*1122*	*1122*	1122
Paris Gare de Lyon **341** a.	...	...	...	...	...	...	...	...	...

									TGV 6508								TGV 6506		TGV 6504					
	⑥		Ⓑ ⊖	⑥		Ⓑ ⊗	⑥	Ⓐ ⊗	⑥		Ⓑ ⊗	⑥	⑥		⊙	Ⓐ ⊙	⑦ e	†	⑥ R	⑦ G	Ⓐ			Ⓑ
Évian-les-Bains d.	0922	...	1022	1022	...	1222	1222	1302	1314	...	1421	1422	1522	...	1622	1658	1656	1715	1720	1740	1802	1822	...	2044
Thonon-les-Bains d.	0931	...	1031	1031	...	1231	1231	1310	1328	...	1431	1431	1531	...	1631	1707	1706	1726	1731	1749	1810	1831	...	2054
Annemasse a.	1006	...	1107	1107	...	1307	1307	1339	1352	...	1507	1507	1607	...	1707	1737	1734	1806	1759	1812	1839	1907	...	2123
Annemasse **365** d.	1017	...	1117	1117	...	1317	1317	...	1413	...	1517	1517	1617	...	1717	...	1746	1817	1814	...	...	1917	...	2130
Bellegarde **365** a.	1050	...	1150	1149	...	1350	1349	...	1458	...	1550	1549	1650	...	1750	...	1815	1850	1856	...	...	1950	...	2203
Lyon Part-Dieu **346** a.	1222	...	*1322*	1322	...	*1522*	1522	...	|	...	*1722*	1722	1822	...	*1922*	...	|	2022	|	...	...	*2122*	...	...
Paris Gare de Lyon **341** a.	...	...	...	...	...	...	...	...	1749	...	...	...	...	...	...	...	2133	...	2149	...	...	...	...	...

D – Not ⑤.
G – ⑦ (also Apr. 17, May 1, 8, June 5; not Apr. 30, May 7). To Grenoble (Tables **365** and **364**).
R – ⑥ to Apr. 1.
V – ⑤ (also May 24). From Valence via Grenoble (Tables **364** and **365**).

e – Also Apr. 17.

TGV –[R], supplement payable, 🍷.

⊗ – Subject to alteration on ①–⑤ Dec. 12 – 23, ①–⑤ Mar. 13 - Apr. 7.
⊖ – Subject to alteration on ①–⑤ Dec. 12 – 23.
⊙ – Subject to alteration on ①–⑤ Mar. 13 - Apr. 7.

364 GENÈVE and ANNECY - CHAMBÉRY - GRENOBLE - VALENCE

Certain services are subject to alteration on some of the following dates: Mar. 20 – 24, 27 – 31, Apr. 29, 30, May 1, 6, 7, 8, 26, 27, June 3, 4, 5.

km		Ⓐ	①–⑥ b	Ⓐ t	Ⓐ	①–⑥ b		①–⑥ b	①–⑥ b			Ⓒ	Ⓐ t	⑥ c				Ⓒ					Ⓐ	A	Ⓑ h	t
0	**Genève** **341 346** d.	...	...	...	...	...	...	...	0658	...	...	...	...	...	1000	...	...	...	1200	...	...	...	1500	...	...	...
33	Bellegarde **341 346** d.	...	...	...	...	...	...	...	0728	...	...	...	...	...	1028	...	...	...	1228	...	...	...	1528	...	...	...
66	Culoz **346** d.	...	...	...	...	...	...	...	|	...	...	...	...	...	|	...	...	...	|	...	...	...	|	...	...	...
	Annecy **341 345** d.	...	...	...	...	0539	...	0639	|	0746	0839	0839	0939	0953	|	1039	...	1139	|	1245	1339	1439	|	1539	1639	...
88	Aix les Bains **341 345** d.	...	...	...	...	0625	...	0725	0805	0825	0925	0925	1025	1035	1105	1125	...	1225	1305	1325	1426	1525	1608	1625	1725	...
102	**Chambéry** **341 345** a.	...	...	...	...	0637	...	0737	0816	0837	0937	0937	1037	...	1117	1137	...	1237	1316	1337	1437	1537	1618	1637	1737	...
102	**Chambéry** d.	...	0540	0602	...	0640	...	0740	0818	0840	...	0940	...	...	1120	1140	1240	1240	1319	1340	1440	1540	1620	1640	1740	1802
116	Montmélian d.	...	0551	0612	...	0651	...	0751	|	0851	...	0951	...	...	|	1151	1251	1251	|	1351	1451	1551	|	1651	1750	1812
165	**Grenoble** a.	...	0627	0658	...	0727	...	0827	0904	0927	...	1027	...	...	1204	1227	1327	1327	1404	1427	1527	1627	1704	1727	1827	1858
165	**Grenoble** d.	0602	0630	...	0707	0730	0730	0830	...	0930	...	1030	...	...	1207	1230	1330	1330	...	1430	1530	1630	1707	1730	1830	...
242	Romans-Bourg de Péage d.	0701	0727	...	0758	0827	0827	0927	...	1027	...	1127	...	...	1258	1327	1427	1427	...	1527	1630	1727	1758	1827	1927	...
249	Valence TGV ⊙ a.	0708	0734	...	0805	0834	0834	0934	...	1034	...	1134	...	...	1305	1334	1434	1434	...	1534	1639	1734	1805	1834	1934	...
259	**Valence** Ville ⊙ a.	0718	0744	...	0815	0844	0844	0944	...	1044	...	1144	...	...	1315	1344	1444	1444	...	1544	1648	1744	1815	1844	1944	...

	①–④ m	⑤–⑦ f	①–⑥ b	⑦ e	①–⑥ b			E	
Genève **341 346** d.	1641	1641	...	...	...	...	1841	...	...
Bellegarde **341 346** d.	1709	1709	...	...	...	...	1910	...	...
Culoz **346** d.	1746	1746	...	...	...	...	1946	...	...
Annecy **341 345** d.	|	|	1739	1739	...	1839	|	1939	...
Aix les Bains **341 345** d.	1806	1805	1825	1825	...	1925	2005	2025	...
Chambéry **341 345** a.	1816	1816	1837	1837	...	1937	2016	2037	...
Chambéry d.	1818	1818	1840	1840	...	1940	2019	2040	...
Montmélian d.	|	|	1851	1851	...	1951	|	2051	...
Grenoble a.	1904	1904	1927	1927	...	2027	2104	2127	...
Grenoble d.	...	1907	1930	1930	1941	2030	...	...	...
Romans-Bourg de Péage d.	...	1955	2027	2031	2059	2127	...	...	...
Valence TGV ⊙ a.	...	2005	2034	2038	2105	2134	...	...	...
Valence Ville ⊙ a.	...	2016	2044	2048	2115	2144	...	...	...

	Ⓐ	①–⑥ b	①–⑥ d	Ⓐ t	Ⓐ	①–⑥ b	①–⑥ b	①–⑥ b	Ⓐ			①–⑥ b
Valence Ville ⊙ d.	...	...	...	...	...	...	0524	...	0615	...	0645	...
Valence TGV ⊙ d.	...	...	...	...	...	...	0534	...	0625	...	0657	...
Romans-Bourg de Péage d.	...	...	...	...	...	...	0543	...	0633	...	0705	...
Grenoble a.	...	...	...	...	...	...	0648	...	0729	...	0751	...
Grenoble d.	0507	...	0537	...	0632	0637	...	0654	0732	0732	0754	...
Montmélian d.	0544	...	0625	...	0710	0725	...	|	0810	0810	|	...
Chambéry a.	0554	...	0633	...	0719	0734	...	0740	0819	0819	0839	...
Chambéry **341 345** d.	0557	0622	...	0645	0723	...	...	0742	0822	0822	0842	...
Aix les Bains **341 345** d.	0610	0636	...	0657	0736	...	...	0756	0836	0836	0856	0925
Annecy **341 345** a.	|	0716	...	0745	0816	...	...	|	0916	0916	|	1007
Culoz **346** d.	0632	...	...	...	...	...	...	|	...	...	|	...
Bellegarde **341 346** d.	0701	...	...	...	...	...	...	0834	...	...	0934	...
Genève **341 346** a.	0728	...	...	...	...	...	...	0900	...	...	1000	...

	Ⓐ	Ⓑ v	†	Ⓐ		Ⓐ											E			Ⓐ	Ⓒ		Ⓑ h A		⑥ k	Ⓑ h ⊖
Valence Ville ⊙ d.	...	...	...	0715	0815	0915	1015	...	...	1215	1316	1346	1415	1515	1615	1645	1715	1745	...	1815	1815	1915	2015	2115	2115	2215
Valence TGV ⊙ d.	...	...	...	0725	0825	0925	1025	...	...	1225	1325	1357	1425	1525	1625	1657	1725	1757	...	1825	1825	1925	2025	2125	2125	2225
Romans-Bourg de Péage d.	...	...	...	0733	0833	0933	1033	...	...	1233	1333	1405	1433	1533	1633	1705	1733	1805	...	1833	1833	1933	2033	2133	2133	2232
Grenoble a.	...	...	...	0829	0929	1029	1129	...	...	1329	1429	1451	1529	1629	1729	1751	1829	1851	...	1929	1929	2029	2129	2229	2229	2329
Grenoble d.	0803	...	0837	...	0932	...	1132	1154	1232	1332	1432	1454	1532	1632	1732	1754	1832	...	1903	1932	1932	2032	2132	...	2232	...
Montmélian d.	0851	...	0925	...	1010	...	1210	|	1310	1410	1510	|	1610	1710	1810	|	1910	...	1951	2010	2010	2110	2210	...	2311	...
Chambéry a.	0859	...	0933	...	1019	...	1219	1240	1319	1419	1519	1539	1619	1719	1819	1839	1919	...	1959	2019	2019	2119	2219	...	2319	...
Chambéry **341 345** d.	...	0922	...	...	1022	...	1222	1243	1322	1422	1522	1542	1622	1723	1822	1842	1922	...	...	2022	2023	2122	2222	...	...	...
Aix les Bains **341 345** d.	...	0936	...	...	1036	...	1236	1256	1336	1436	1536	1556	1637	1736	1836	1856	1936	...	...	2036	2036	2136	2236	...	...	...
Annecy **341 345** a.	...	1016	...	...	1116	...	1316	|	1416	1516	1616	|	1716	1816	1916	|	2016	...	...	2116	2123	2216	2316	...	...	...
Culoz **346** d.	...	...	...	...	...	...	...	|	...	...	...	|	...	...	...	|	...	...	...	...	...	...	...	...	...	...
Bellegarde **341 346** d.	...	...	...	...	...	...	...	1334	...	...	...	1634	...	...	...	1934	...	...	...	...	...	...	...	...	...	...
Genève **341 346** a.	...	...	...	...	...	...	...	1400	...	...	...	1700	...	...	...	2000	...	...	...	...	...	...	...	...	...	...

A – To / from Avignon on dates in Table **351**.
E – To / from Évian les Bains on dates in Table **363**.

b – Not Apr. 17, May 1, 8, June 5.
c – Also May 25; not May 27.
d – Not Dec. 26 – 31, Apr. 17, May 1, 8, June 5.
e – Also Apr. 17, May 1, 8, June 5.
f – Also Apr. 17, May 25, June 5.
h – Not May 25.
k – Also Dec. 11, 25, Jan. 1, Feb. 5, Apr. 16, May 8, June 4; not Apr. 29, May 6.

m – Not Apr. 17, May 25, June 5.
t – Not Dec. 26 – 30.
v – Not Dec. 25 - Jan. 1, May 25.

⊖ – Subject to alteration on ①–④ Feb. 6 – 16, ①–④ Mar. 27 - Apr. 13.
⊙ – 🚌 runs 2 – 3 times per hour.

*See Table **350** for TGV services Annecy - Valence - Marseille*

🚌 GENÈVE AÉROPORT ✦ - CHAMBÉRY - GRENOBLE — 364a

Daily 🚌 service operated by Aerocar, www.aerocar.fr.　Journey 1 hr to Chambéry (Gare routière), 2 hrs 15 m to Grenoble (Gare routière). Rail tickets not valid. Reduced service on May 1.

Genève Aéroport (Level 0 - Arrivals) : depart 1030, 1300, 1530, 1800 and 2030.

Grenoble : depart 0600, 0830, 1100, 1330 and 1530 (from Chambéry 60 minutes later).

PARIS / ANNECY - LA ROCHE SUR FORON - ST GERVAIS — 365

Trains from Lyon / Bellegarde may convey portions for Évian les Bains.　For connections Genève Eaux-Vives - Annemasse / La Roche sur Foron see Table **366a**.

SERVICE UNTIL APRIL 29

km	TGV trains convey 🍴				TGV 6467	TGV 6467	TGV 9761			TGV 9765				TGV 6473			TGV 9773				
				ⓒ	⑦ Ⓐ	⑥ Ⓐ	Ⓐ		Ⓐ ⊗	⑥ ⊗	Ⓑ ⊗	⑥	☆ e	⑥⑦ ⊙	⑥	Ⓑ		⑥ ⊗	Ⓐ	⑥	Ⓑ ⊙
					T							e								
0	**Paris** Gare de Lyon ..... **341** d.	...	...	...	0711	0711	0711	...	...	0911	...	...	1011	...	...	1211	...	...	...	...
406	Bourg en Bresse .... **341** d.	...	...	...			0903	...	...	1102	...	...	1205	...	...	1404	...	...	...	...
	Lyon Perrache 346 .....d.	...	0625	...				0823c	...	1023	...	1023	...	...	1223	1223	...	...	1423	1423
	Lyon Part-Dieu 346 .....d.	...	0636	...				0834	...	1036	...	1036	1136	...	1236	1234	1336	...	1436	1436
470	Bellegarde .... **341** a.	...	0758	0948	0948	0950	0957	...	1157	1148	1158	1258	...	1318	1357	1357	1457	1456	1557	1559
470	Bellegarde .... **363** a.	...	0809	0951	0951	...	1009	...	1209	...	1209	1309	...	1324	1409	1409	...	1509	1609	1609
508	Annemasse .... **363** a.	...	0843	1022	1031	...	1043	...	1243	...	1243	1344	...	1404	1443	1443	...	1543	1643	1643
508	Annemasse ....▷ d.	0650	0850	1032	1032	...	1050	...	1250	...	1250	1351	...	1405	1450	1450	...	1550	1650	1650
•	**Annecy** ....▷ d.	...	0732	0932		...	1132		...	1332		...	...	...	1532		...	1732
525	La Roche sur Foron ...▷ a.	0707	0807	0907	1007	...	1107	1207	1307	...	1307	1407	1407	...	1507	1507	...	1607	1607	1707	1707	1807
525	La Roche sur Foron .....d.	0712	0812	0912	1012	...	1112	1212	1312	...	1312	1412	1412	...	1512	1512	...	1612	1612	1712	1712	1812
547	Cluses (Haute-Savoie) ....d.	0737	0837	0937	1037	1108	1108	1137	1237	1337	...	1337	1437	1437	1454	1537	1537	...	1637	1637	1737	1737	1837
566	Sallanches Megève ....d.	0750	0850	0950	1050	1128	1128	1150	1250	1350	...	1350	1450	1450	1511	1550	1550	...	1650	1650	1750	1750	1850
572	**St Gervais** ....a.	0756	0856	0956	1056	1133	1133	1156	1256	1356	...	1356	1456	1456	1518	1556	1556	...	1656	1656	1756	1756	1856

		TGV 9775			TGV 9777			TGV 9951	TGV 9785				TGV 9764					TGV 9768				
			⑥	Ⓑ	Ⓑ	⑥	Ⓑ h		⑤	⑤			✂			Ⓑ			Ⓑ	Ⓐ	⑥	Ⓑ ⑥
Paris Gare de Lyon ..... **341** d.	1511	...	1611	...	1815	1911	...		**St Gervais** .... d.	0504	0604	...	0704	0804	0804	...	0904	0904	1004	1004
Bourg en Bresse .... **341** d.		...	1804			2104			Sallanches Megève......... d.	0509	0609	...	0709	0809	0810	...	0909	0910	1009	1010
Lyon Perrache 346 ...... d.		1636	1636		1736	1834			Cluses (Haute-Savoie) ..... d.	0523	0623	...	0723	0823	0823	...	0923	0923	1023	1023
Lyon Part-Dieu 346 .... d.		1636			1736	1834		2036	La Roche sur Foron ...... a.	0547	0647	...	0747	0847	0847	...	0947	0947	1047	1047
Bellegarde .... **341** d.	1748	1757	1758	1858	1904	1957	2111	2151	2200	La Roche sur Foron ...▷ d.	0553	0653	...	0752	0853	0853	...	0952	0953	1053	1053
Bellegarde .... **363** d.		1809	1809		1909	2009	2116		2209	**Annecy** ....▷ d.	...	...	0829		...	1029		...	1029		...	...
Annemasse................ **363** d.		1843	1843		1944	2043	2200		2244	Annemasse ....▷ d.	0610	0710	...	...	0910	0910	...	...	1010	1110	1110
Annemasse.................▷ d.		1850	1850		1951	2050	2210		2251	Annemasse............... **363** d.	0617	0717	...	...	0917	0917	...	...	1017	1117	1117
Annecy ....▷ a.		...	...							Bellegarde .... **363** d.	0650	0750	...	...	0950	0949	...	...	1050	1150	1149
La Roche sur Foron ...▷ a.		1907	1907		2007	2107			2307	Bellegarde .... **341** d.	0655	0758	0810	...	0958	1001	1010	...	1055	1158	1201
La Roche sur Foron ..... d.		1912	1912		2012	2112			2312	Lyon Part-Dieu 346 .... a.	0822	0922		...	1122	1122		...	1222	1322	1322
Cluses (Haute-Savoie) ....d.		1937	1937		2037	2137	2242		2337	Lyon Perrache 346 .... a.	...	0934		...	1135	1135		...	1333	1333
Sallanches Megève .... d.		1951	1950		2051	2151	2256		2351	Bourg en Bresse........ **341** d.	...	0859r		...		...		...		...	...
St Gervais ....a.		1956	1956		2056	2156	2302		2356	**Paris** Gare de Lyon ... **341** a.	...	1049r		...	1249		...		...	...	...

		TGV 6480	TGV 9770			TGV 9772	TGV 6482					TGV 9776		TGV 9778	TGV 7954	TGV 6486		TGV 9780		TGV 9784		
		⑥	Ⓐ	ⓒ	Ⓑ	⑥	Ⓒ ⊗	Ⓐ	Ⓑ	⑥	⑥	⑤-⑦ e	⑤-⑦	①-④ m	⑥	Ⓐ	†	Ⓑ			Ⓑ	Ⓑ
St Gervais .... d.	1014	...	1104	1204	1204	...	1248	1304	1404	1404	1504	1504	...	1604	...	1631	1658	1704	1704	...	1804	...	...	1904	2004
Sallanches Megève ....d.	1022	...	1109	1209	1210	...	1256	1309	1409	1410	1510	1509	...	1609	...	1639	1706	1709	1710	...	1809	...	...	1909	2009
Cluses (Haute-Savoie) ...... d.	1038	...	1123	1223	1223	...	1311	1323	1423	1423	1523	1523	...	1623	...	1653	1720	1723	1723	...	1823	...	...	1923	2023
La Roche sur Foron ...... a.		...	1147	1247	1247	...		1347	1447	1447	1547	1547	...	1647	...		1747	1747	...	1847	...	...	1947	2047
La Roche sur Foron ...▷ d.		...	1152	1253	1253	...		1352	1453	1453	1553	1552	...	1653	...		1752	1753	...	1853	...	...	1952	2053
Annecy ....▷ a.		1229				...	1429					1629	...		...		1829		...		...	2029	...	...
Annemasse ....▷ a.	1123	...	1310	1310	...	1349		1510	1510	1610	...	1710	...	1728	1757		1810	...	1910	...	...	2110
Annemasse............... **363** d.	1133	...	1317	1317	...	1413		1517	1517	1617	...	1717	...	1746	1814		1817	...	1917	...	...	2130
Bellegarde .... **363** a.	1205	...	1350	1349	...	1458		1550	1549	1655	...	1750	...	1815	1856		1850	...	1950	...	...	2203
Bellegarde .... **341** d.	1208	1210	...	1358	1401	1410	1503		1558	1601	1655		1659	1758	1809	1818	1900	...	1855	1900	1958	2010	...	...
Lyon Part-Dieu 346 .... a.			...	1522	1522				1722	1722	1822		1922			...	2022		2122		...	...
Lyon Perrache 346 .... a.			...							...					...			2135		...	...
Bourg en Bresse........ **341** d.			...				1556			...	1756		1858	1934	1956			...		...	...
Paris Gare de Lyon ..... **341** d.	1449	1452	...			1649	1749			...	1949		2049	2133	2149		2149	...	2249	...	...

ANNECY - ANNEMASSE direct services

		✂ ⊗	Ⓐ ⊗	⑥		✂ ⊗	Ⓐ ⊗	Ⓐ	⑤f A				✂ ⊗	Ⓐ ⊗	Ⓐ	✂ A		Ⓑ ⊗	⑦w A		Ⓑ
Annecy ....d.	0632	0932	1032	1032	...	1432	1632	1832	1932	2032		**Annemasse**...............d.	0633	0833	...	1233	...	1633	1827	...	2033
La Roche sur Foron ......a.	0707	1007	1107	1107	...	1507	1707	1907	2007	2107		La Roche sur Foron ......a.	0649	0849	...	1249	...	1649	1843	...	2049
La Roche sur Foron ....d.	0710	...	1110	1119	...	1510	1710	1910	2010	2110		La Roche sur Foron ....d.	0652	0852	1208	1252	...	1652	1852	...	2052
Annemasse...............a.	0726	...	1126	1135	...	1526	1726	1926	2026	2126		**Annecy** ....a.	0729	0929	1240	1329	...	1729	1930	...	2129

A – 🚌 Grenoble - Chambéry - Annecy - Évian les Bains and v.v. See Tables **363** and **364**.

T – ⑦ to Apr. 2.

c – ⓒ only.

e – Also Apr. 17.

f – Also May 24.

h – Not May 25.

m – Not Apr. 17.

r – On ⑦ (also Apr. 17, May 1, 8, June 5) Bourg en Bresse d. 0902, Paris a. 1051.

w – Also Apr. 17, May 1, 8, June 5; not Apr. 30, May 7.

TGV – Ⓡ, supplement payable, 🍴.

▷ – For other trains Annemasse - La Roche sur Foron - Annecy see panel below main table.

☆ – Does not run La Roche - St Gervais and v.v. on ⑥ (see previous column for connecting train).

⊗ – Subject to alteration on ①–⑤ Mar. 20 - Apr. 14.

⊙ – Subject to alteration on ①–⑤ Mar. 13 - Apr. 7.

⊖ – Subject to alteration on ①–⑤ Mar. 13 - Apr. 14.

• – Annecy to La Roche sur Foron is 39 km.

ST GERVAIS - CHAMONIX — 365a

Many journeys continue to / from Le Châtelard or Martigny (Table **572**). Subject to alteration Apr. 18 - May 5.

km										A											A		
0	**St Gervais** ..... d.	0705	0805	0905	1005	1205	1305	1405	1505	1605	and	2005	**Chamonix** .. d.	0714	0814	0914	1014	1214	1314	1414	1514	1614	and	2014
9	Les Houches .. d.	0733	0833	0933	1033	1233	1333	1433	1533	1633	hourly	2033	Les Houches d.	0732	0832	0932	1032	1232	1332	1432	1532	1632	hourly	2032
20	**Chamonix** ..... a.	0748	0848	0948	1048	1248	1348	1448	1548	1648	until	2048	**St Gervais** .. a.	0757	0857	0957	1057	1257	1357	1457	1557	1657	until	2057

A – Until Apr. 2.

366 (PARIS) - CHAMBÉRY - ALBERTVILLE - BOURG ST MAURICE

SERVICE UNTIL APRIL 29. For Paris - Chambéry see Table **341**. For ski trains from/to Lille, Brussels, Amsterdam and London see Table **9**.

TGV services are subject to alteration Mar. 17 – 19. Local journeys between Chambéry and Bourg St Maurice are not usually permitted on *TGV* services.

km	*TGV* trains convey 🍷	🚌 Ⓐ		Ⓐ	🚌 Ⓐ	🚌 Ⓐ		Ⓐ ⊗	Ⓒ	*TGV* 6417 ⑥ B	🚌 Ⓐ	*TGV* 6419 ⑥	*TGV* 6419 ⑦ J	Ⓐ ⊗	⑥	*TGV* 6429 V	*TGV* 6429 ⑥	🚌 Ⓐ	*TGV* 6435 ⑥⑦ K	Ⓐ ⊕	Ⓒ	*TGV* 6437 ⑥	*TGV* 5308 ⑥ A ⊖	*TGV* 6439 ⑥⑦
0	**Paris Gare de Lyon** ...... **341** d.	...	...	...	...	...	...	...	...	0649	...	0749	0749	...	...	0845	0907	...	0949	...	...	1045	...	1145
	Lyon Part Dieu **344** .... d.	...	...	...	...	...	...	...	0750**k**	|	...	|	|	...	0950	|	|	...	|	1150	1150	|	...	|
	Aix les Bains .... d.	...	...	...	...	...	...	...	|	|	...	|	1055	...	|	|	|	...	1255	|	|	|	...	|
532	**Chambéry** .... **367** d.	0601	...	0706	...	0805	...	0931	0931	0953	0950	|	|	1131	1131	1200	|	1230	1310	1331	1331	1400	1414	|
545	Montmélian .... **367** d.	0621	...	0716	...	0825	...	0941	0941	|	|	|	|	1141	1141	|	|	|	|	1341	1341	|	|	|
557	St Pierre d'Albigny .... **367** d.	0639	...	0724	...	0840	...	0949	0950	|	|	|	|	1149	1150	|	|	|	|	1349	1350	|	|	|
580	Albertville .... a.	0717	...	0744	...	0905	...	1014	1014	1028	1040	1144	1144	1214	1217	1234	1243	1320	1342	1414	1416	1442	1507	1527
580	Albertville .... d.	0717	...	0754	...	0905	...	1021	1021	1041	1040	1154	1154	1221	1227	1248	1253	1320	1354	1421	1425	1454	1528	1543
608	**Moûtiers-Salins** .... d.	0745	...	0817	0855	0935	...	1050	1050	1114	1110	1216	1216	1250	1250	1314	1316	1350	1416	1450	1452	1519	1556	1616
623	Aime la Plagne .... d.	0800	...	...	0910	0950	...	1107	1108	1131	|	1232	1232	1307	1311	1331	1333	|	1431	1507	1510	1537	1615	1634
630	Landry .... d.	0810	...	...	0920	1000	...	1114	1118	1141	|	1243	1243	1315	1321	1341	1344	|	1441	1514	1524	1549	1625	1646
637	**Bourg St Maurice** .... a.	0822	...	...	0932	1012	...	1122	1126	1148	1140	1251	1251	1322	1329	1348	1351	1420	1448	1522	1532	1557	1632	1654

	Ⓒ	Ⓐ	🚌 Ⓐ	*TGV* 6443 ⑥ B	Ⓐ	⑥	Ⓐ	†	⑥	Ⓒ R	Ⓐ	*TGV* 6447 ⑤	Ⓐ	⑥ S	🚌 Ⓐ	Ⓐ	Ⓒ D	🚌 ⚒	*TGV* 6453 ④⑤ F	*TGV* 6451 ⑤ L		🚌 ⑤† f		*TGV* 6455 ⑤ L
Paris Gare de Lyon .... **341** d.	...	...	...	1245	...	...	...	...	...	...	...	1549	...	...	...	...	...	...	1827	1845	...	...	...	2234
Lyon Part Dieu **344** .... d.	1350	...	...	|	...	1500	1550	1550	1550	...	...	△	1750	1750	...	...	1850	...	|	|	...	...	...	|
Aix les Bains .... d.	|	...	...	|	...	|	|	|	|	...	...	|	|	|	...	...	|	...	|	|	...	...	...	|
Chambéry .... **367** d.	1531	1531	...	|	1631	1630	1729	1731	1731	1815	1829	1910	1931	1931	1950	2031	2030	2130	2147	2153	...	2245	...	|
Montmélian .... **367** d.	1541	1541	...	|	1641	1641	1741	1741	1741	1826	1840	|	1941	1941	|	2041	2040	2150	|	|	...	|	...	|
St Pierre d'Albigny .... **367** d.	1550	1549	...	|	1649	1650	1749	1750	1750	1843	1849	|	1949	1950	|	2049	2049	2205	|	|	...	|	...	|
Albertville .... a.	1613	1614	...	1629	1714	1712	1814	1816	1816	1902	1914	1944	2014	2013	2040	2114	2114	2230	2218	2228	...	2335	...	0530
Albertville .... d.	1621	...	1620	1645	1721	1721	1821	1823	1823	1909	1921	1956	2021	2023	2040	2121	2121	2230	2228	2238	...	2335	...	0544
Moûtiers-Salins .... d.	1651	...	1655	1711	1750	1749	1850	1844	1849	1944	1950	2019	2050	2050	2110	2150	2150	2305	2251	2300	...	0010	...	0614
Aime la Plagne .... d.	1709	...	1715	1730	1807	1808	1907	1908	1909	2001	2007	2035	2107	2109	|	2207	2208	|	2307	2317	...	0025	...	0632
Landry .... d.	1721	...	1725	1741	1815	1818	1915	1918	1919	2011	2014	2045	2115	2119	|	2215	2220	|	2316	2327	...	0035	...	0644
Bourg St Maurice .... a.	1729	...	1735	1748	1822	1826	1922	1926	1926	2019	2022	2052	2122	2126	2145	2222	2229	2345	2323	2335	...	0050	...	0651

	🚌 Ⓐ	🚌 Ⓐ		Ⓐ	⑥	🚌 Ⓐ	⑥	† T	Ⓐ	🚌 †	🚌 Ⓐ	Ⓐ	Ⓒ	🚌 Ⓐ	*TGV* 6420 ⑥⑦		*TGV* 6422 ⑥⑦ K	Ⓒ	Ⓐ ⊗		*TGV* 5394 ⑥ W ⊖	Ⓒ	Ⓐ ⊗	*TGV* 6426 ⑥
Bourg St Maurice .... d.	...	0426	...	0538	0538	0620	0632	0633	0638	0717	0805	...	0838	0904	0917	...	1011	1032	1038	...	1130	1234	1238	1313
Landry .... d.	...	|	...	0546	0548	|	0643	0643	0646	0724	0817	...	0848	0911	0927	...	1020	1042	1046	...	1140	1245	1246	1323
Aime la Plagne .... d.	...	|	...	0554	0559	|	0653	0654	0654	0733	0826	...	0859	0920	0937	...	1030	1052	1054	...	1152	1256	1254	1333
Moûtiers-Salins .... d.	0442	0456	...	0611	0615	0650	0710	0711	0711	0802	0845	0855	0919	0944	0954	...	1050	1113	1113	...	1214	1313	1313	1352
Albertville .... a.	0517	0531	...	0636	0637	0720	0734	0738	0738	0847	...	0916	0938	1019	1016	...	1109	1137	1138	...	1245	1341	1338	1413
Albertville .... d.	0517	0531	...	0645	0649	0720	0745	0745	0745	0847	...	0925	0945	1019	1029	...	1121	1145	1145	...	1305	1349	1345	1427
St Pierre d'Albigny .... **367** d.	0537	|	...	0712	0713	|	0811	0812	0812	0915	...	0949	1011	1049	|	...	|	1213	1212	...	|	1412	1412	|
Montmélian .... **367** d.	0542	0614	...	0720	0721	|	0819	0821	0820	0930	...	1000	1020	1104	|	...	|	1221	1220	...	|	1421	1420	|
Chambéry .... **367** a.	0612	0634	...	0730	0730	0812	0835	0831	0830	0950	...	1009	1029	1124	1058	...	1152	1230	1230	...	1348	1431	1430	1501
Aix les Bains .... a.	0631	...	...	|	|	...	|	...	|	...	...	...	|	...	|	...	|	|	...	...	...	|	...	|
Lyon Part Dieu **344** .... a.	...	...	...	0910	0910	...	1010	...	1010	...	...	...	1210	...	|	...	|	1410	...	...	...	1610	...	|
Paris Gare de Lyon .... **341** a.	...	...	...	...	...	...	...	...	...	...	...	...	...	...	1410	...	1515	...	...	...	...	...	...	1811

	Ⓒ	Ⓐ ⊕	*TGV* 6434 G		🚌 Ⓐ	Ⓐ		*TGV* 6436 E	Ⓒ D	Ⓐ	*TGV* 6438 ⑥ B		🚌 Ⓐ	*TGV* 6446 ⑦ J	Ⓒ D	Ⓐ	*TGV* 6442 ⑥⑦ R ¶		🚌 ⑤† f					
Bourg St Maurice .... d.	1431	1438	1449	...	1520	...	...	1615	1633	1638	1711	...	1746	1822	1830	1838	1907	...	1940	...	...	...	...	...
Landry .... d.	1441	1446	1501	...	1527	...	...	1625	1643	1646	1721	...	1753	1832	1841	1846	1917	...	1947	...	...	...	...	...
Aime la Plagne .... d.	1452	1454	1512	...	1536	...	...	1636	1653	1654	1731	...	1802	1843	1851	1854	1927	...	1956	...	...	...	...	...
Moûtiers-Salins .... d.	1517	1514	1537	...	1600	...	...	1654	1712	1713	1748	...	1826	1902	1914	1913	1945	...	2020	...	...	...	...	...
Albertville .... a.	1542	1538	1558	...	1635	...	...	1720	1738	1738	1806	...	1901	1926	1935	1938	2004	...	2055	...	...	...	...	...
Albertville .... d.	1549	1545	1615	...	...	1645	...	1733	1753	1745	1817	...	1901	1936	1947	1945	2017	...	2055	...	...	...	...	...
St Pierre d'Albigny .... **367** d.	1612	1612	|	...	...	1712	...	|	1812	1812	|	...	1931	|	2011	2012	|	...	2115	...	...	...	...	...
Montmélian .... **367** d.	1621	1620	|	...	...	1720	...	|	1820	1820	|	...	1946	|	2021	2020	|	...	2130	...	...	...	...	...
Chambéry .... **367** a.	1630	1630	1655	...	...	1730	...	1814	1829	1830	1848	...	2006	2010	2029	2028	2048	...	2150	...	...	...	...	...
Aix les Bains .... a.	|	...	|	...	...	|	...	|	|	...	|	...	...	|	|	...	|	...	...	...	...	...	...	...
Lyon Part Dieu **344** .... a.	1810	...	|	...	...	1910	...	|	2010	...	⊡	...	...	|	2210**n**	...	|	...	...	...	...	...	...	...
Paris Gare de Lyon .... **341** a.	...	...	2011	...	...	...	...	2115	...	...	2211	...	...	2315	...	...	2357	...	...	...	...	...	...	...

A – ⑥ Dec. 31 - Mar. 18 (not Feb. 4, 11, 18).
B – ⑥ to Apr. 1.
D – Ⓒ to Apr. 23.
E – ①⑤⑥⑦ to Apr. 2; ⑥ Apr. 8 – 29.
F – ④⑤ to Mar. 31.
G – ⑥⑦ to Apr. 2; ⑥ Apr. 8 – 29.
J – ⑦ to Apr. 2.
K – ⑥⑦ to Apr. 2.
L – ⑤ to Mar. 31.
R – ⑥⑦ to Apr. 23.
S – ⑥ to Apr. 22.
T – † to Apr. 23.
V – ①⑤⑦ to Apr. 2 (also Apr. 9, 16, 23).
W – ⑥ Dec. 31 - Mar. 25 (not Feb. 11, 18, 25).

f – Also May 24; not Apr. 16, 30, May 7, June 4.
k – ⑥ only.
n – Subject to alteration on Jan. 8, 29, Feb. 12, Mar. 12, Apr. 9.

TGV – 🅁, supplement payable, 🍷.

⊖ – To/from Nantes and Rennes (Table 335).
⊗ – Subject to alteration Apr. 3 – 21.
⊕ – Subject to alteration on ①–④ Apr. 3 – 20.
⊡ – Also calls at Bourg en Bresse (d. 2014) and Mâcon Loché TGV (d. 2036).
△ – Also calls at Mâcon Loché TGV (d. 1727) and Bourg en Bresse (d. 1748).
¶ – Also calls at Bourg en Bresse (d. 2206).

366a 🚌 GENÈVE - ANNEMASSE

🚌 TPG route 61 Genève Cornavin railway station - Annemasse rail station Journey time: 40 – 44 minutes *TER tickets valid between Genève Rieu and Annemasse*

From Genève Cornavin Ⓐ: 0645 and every 15 minutes until 1200, 1214, 1228, 1242, 1257 and every 15 minutes until 1857; then 1913, 1932, 1951, 2010, 2033, 2103, 2143, 2223.
⑥: 0633 and every 30 minutes until 2103; then 2143. ⑦ and holidays: 0833 and every 30 minutes until 2103; then 2143.

From Annemasse Ⓐ: 0551, 0615, 0631 and approximately every 15 minutes until 1754; then 1811, 1831, 1851, 1911, 1931, 1951, 2021, 2052, 2131.
⑥: 0551 and every 30 minutes until 2051. ⑦ and holidays: 0750, 0820, 0850, 0920, 0951, 1021 and every 30 minutes until 2051.

🚌 GENÈVE EAUX VIVES - ANNEMASSE - ANNECY

SNCF 🚌 service	🚌	🚌 ⚒	🚌	🚌	🚌	🚌	🚌 Ⓒ	🚌	🚌 ⊡	🚌	🚌
Genève Eaux-Vives .... d.	0648	0848	1045	1048	1248	1448	1648	1725	1800	1925	2115
Annemasse .... ▷ a.	0708	0908	|	1108	1308	1508	1708	|	|	|	2135
La Roche sur Foron ▷ a.	0741	0941	1120	1141	1341	1541	1741	1800	1845	2000	2200
Annecy .... ▷ a.	...	...	1155	...	...	...	...	1835	...	...	2235

	🚌 ⊖	🚌	🚌 Ⓐ	🚌 Ⓒ	🚌	🚌	🚌	🚌	🚌 ⚒⊠	🚌	🚌
Annecy .... ▷ d.	0615	0700	...	...	...	...	...	...	1640	...	...
La Roche sur Foron ▷ d.	0652	0735	0812	0812	1012	1212	1412	1612	1715	1812	2012
Annemasse .... ▷ d.	|	|	|	0847	1042	1242	1442	1647	|	1847	2042
Genève Eaux-Vives .... a.	0742	0825	0858	0912	1102	1302	1502	1702	1805	1912	2112

⊖ – ①–⑥ (not Apr. 17, May 25, June 5).
⊡ – ①–⑤ (not Apr. 17, May 25, June 5).

⊠ – Runs 15 minutes **earlier** on ⑥.
▷ – See also Table **365**.

CHAMBÉRY - MODANE 367

SERVICE UNTIL APRIL 29

km						🚌	TGV 9241	TGV 9241			TGV 6401			TGV 9245			TGV 6407					TGV 9249		
		Ⓐ	⑥	Ⓐ	⑥	Ⓐ	Ⓐ M	Ⓒ M	⑥⑦	Ⓐ	⑥	Ⓐ	Ⓒ	M ⊠	Ⓒ	Ⓐ	⑥⑦ B	Ⓐ	Ⓒ		Ⓐ	M	Ⓐ	⑥
	Paris Gare de Lyon **341** d.	...	...	...	...	...	0629	0629	...	...	0827	...	...	1041	...	...	1149	...	...	...	...	1441	...	...
	Lyon St Exupéry ✈ **342** d.	...	...	...	...	...	|	|	...	...	|	...	...	1236	...	...	|	...	...	...	...	1637	...	...
	Lyon Part Dieu **344** d.	...	...	...	0650	...	0831	0831	0850	...	|	...	1050	|	1250	...	|	1450	1450	...	...	|	...	...
0	**Chambéry** **366** d.	0635	0635	0735	0825	0830	0942	0944	1020	1110	1146	1236	1236	1345	1435	1445	1507	1635	1633	...	1735	1744	...	1750
14	Montmélian **366** d.	0645	0645	0745	0836	|	|	|	1030	1120	|	1246	1246	|	1445	1454	|	1646	1645	...	1745	|	←	1800
26	St Pierre d'Albigny **366** d.	0653	0654	0753	0844	|	|	|	1039	1127	|	1254	1258	|	1454	1503	|	1654	1654	...	1752	|	1801	1811
61	St Avre la Chambre d.	0721	0720	0821	0907	0943	|	|	1113	1155	1223	1324	1320	|	1519	1531	1545	1721	1718	...	→	|	1829	1836
71	St Jean de Maurienne d.	0729	0730	0829	0918	0958	|	|	1123	1209	1233	1332	1330	|	1529	1539	1558	1729	1729	...	...	1824	1837	1846
83	St Michel-Valloire d.	0738	0742	0838	0932	1014	|	|	1136	1221	1247	1344	1344	|	1543	1550	1612	1739	1743	...	...	|	1846	1859
99	**Modane** a.	0755	0759	0855	0946	1034	1045	1048	1153	1238	1307	1358	1359	1450	1559	1604	1632	1755	1759	...	...	1847	1903	1915

								🚌		🚌	
	Ⓒ	Ⓐ	Ⓐ	⑥	†	⑤†	Ⓐ	⑥	†	⑤	
Paris Gare de Lyon **341** d.	...	...	...	...	...	...	...	...	...	...	...
Lyon St Exupéry ✈ **342** d.	...	...	...	...	...	...	...	...	...	...	...
Lyon Part Dieu **344** d.	1650	...	...	...	1750	...	...	...	1950	...	...
Chambéry **366** d.	1829	1835	1935	1935	1935	2035	2135	2130	2136	2226	...
Montmélian **366** d.	1840	1845	1945	1946	1946	2045	2145	2150	2146	2246	...
St Pierre d'Albigny **366** d.	1850	1853	1953	1954	1954	2053	2153	2206	2154	2302	...
St Avre la Chambre d.	1913	1921	2021	2019	2024	2121	2221	2241	2220	2337	...
St Jean de Maurienne d.	1923	1929	2029	2029	2034	2129	2229	2256	2230	2352	...
St Michel-Valloire d.	1937	1938	2038	2042	2048	2138	2238	2312	2242	0008	...
Modane a.	1953	1955	2055	2059	2102	2155	2255	2332	2259	0028	...

					🚌		TGV 9240	
	⑥	Ⓐ	Ⓒ	Ⓐ	Ⓐ	Ⓒ	M	Ⓒ
Modane d.	0600	0605	0700	0706	0804	0848	0910	...
St Michel-Valloire d.	0616	0621	0717	0722	0824	0908	|	...
St Jean de Maurienne d.	0631	0632	0733	0733	0840	0922	0936	...
St Avre la Chambre d.	0640	0640	0743	0741	0855	0932	|	←
St Pierre d'Albigny **366** d.	0707	0707	0805	0808	|	0955	|	1005
Montmélian **366** d.	0716	0716	0815	0816	|	→	|	1014
Chambéry **366** a.	0724	0724	0824	0826	1008	...	1015	1025
Lyon Part Dieu **344** a.	...	...	1010	...	...	...	|	1230
Lyon St Exupéry ✈ **342** a.	...	...	...	...	...	...	1123	...
Paris Gare de Lyon **341** a.	...	...	...	...	...	...	1319	...

					TGV 9244			🚌				TGV 6406					TGV 6414	TGV 6414	TGV 9248	TGV 9248				
	Ⓐ	Ⓒ	⑥	Ⓐ	M	Ⓐ	Ⓒ	Ⓐ		Ⓐ	Ⓒ	⑥	Ⓐ	Ⓒ	†	Ⓐ	⑥ D	⑦ E	Ⓑ M	⑥ M	Ⓐ	Ⓒ n	Ⓐ	†
Modane d.	0953	1002	1002	1139	1149	...	1210	1216	...	1359	1411	1459	1605	1613	1613	1705	1729	1734	1752	1752	1805	1810	1926	2004
St Michel-Valloire d.	1007	1019	1019	1153	|	...	1227	1236	...	1412	1428	1515	1621	1630	1630	1721	1745	1750	|	|	1821	1828	1942	2021
St Jean de Maurienne d.	1023	1035	1035	1207	|	←	1243	1252	...	1428	1444	1532	1633	1646	1646	1732	1800	1805	|	|	1832	1844	1953	2037
St Avre la Chambre d.	1030	1045	1045	1214	|	1215	1253	1307	...	1436	1454	1542	1640	1656	1656	1740	1810	1815	|	|	1840	1855	2001	2047
St Pierre d'Albigny **366** d.	1100	1109	1109	→	|	1251	1317	1358	...	1505	1516	|	1707	1718	1718	1807	|	|	|	|	1907	1917	2028	2109
Montmélian **366** d.	1110	1118	1118	...	|	1300	1326	1414	...	1514	1525	|	1715	1726	1726	1816	|	|	|	|	1916	1925	2037	2117
Chambéry **366** a.	1119	1127	1127	...	1250	1309	1340	1434	...	1523	1534	1615	1724	1735	1735	1824	1844	1846	1853	1853	1925	1935	2046	2127
Lyon Part Dieu **344** a.	...	...	1310	...	|	...	1510	...	...	...	1710	|	...	...	1910	...	|	|	2028	2028	2110	2110	...	...
Lyon St Exupéry ✈ **342** a.	...	...	...	...	|	...	...	...	...	...	...	1723	...	...	...	...	|	|	|	|	...	...	...	...
Paris Gare de Lyon **341** a.	...	...	...	...	1611	...	...	...	...	...	...	1919	...	...	...	...	2211	2211	2231	2237	...	...	...	...

B – ⑥⑦ to Apr. 2. Also calls at Mâcon Loché TGV (d. 1327).
D – ⑥ to Apr. 1. Also calls at Bourg-en-Bresse (a. 2011), Mâcon Loché TGV (a. 2033).
E – ⑦ to Apr. 2. Also calls at Aix les Bains (a. 1901), Bourg-en-Bresse (a. 2010) and Mâcon Loché TGV (a. 2031).
M – 🚆12 and 🍷 Paris - Milano and v.v. (Table **44**). Ⓡ, special fares payable.

TGV – Ⓡ, supplement payable, 🍷.
n – Not Apr. 29.
⊠ – Subject to alteration from Apr. 3.

SAT/SAVDA 🚌 CHAMONIX - MONT BLANC TUNNEL - COURMAYEUR 368

SUBJECT TO CONFIRMATION

By 🚌, journey 45 minutes. Reservation compulsory by 1700 on previous day through SAT, Chamonix station ✆ +33 (0) 450 530 115 or SAVDA, Aosta bus station ✆ +39 0165 367 032.

Dec. 17 - Apr. 10: From Chamonix (Avenue de Courmayeur) at 0830, 0930, 1100, 1500, 1615, 1730. From Courmayeur (Piazzale Monte Bianco) at 0815, 0945, 1200, 1400, 1615, 1730.
Apr. 11 - July 1: From Chamonix (Avenue de Courmayeur) at 0830, 1145, 1530, 1715. From Courmayeur (Piazzale Monte Bianco) at 0945, 1045, 1545, 1700.
July 2 - Sept. 4: From Chamonix (Avenue de Courmayeur) at 0830, 1030, 1230, 1430, 1600, 1800. From Courmayeur (Piazzale Monte Bianco) at 0900, 1100, 1200, 1400, 1600, 1800.

SAVDA 🚌 COURMAYEUR - PRÉ ST DIDER - AOSTA

Courmayeur △ d.	0645	0735	0835	0935	and	1935	2035	2135	...	...
Pré St Didier d.	0653	0743	0843	0943	hourly	1943	2043	2143	...	...
Aosta ⊡ a.	0745	0835	0935	1035	until	2035	2135	2235	...	...

Aosta ⊡ d.	0645	0745	0845	0945	1045	1145	1245	1335	1445	and	2145
Pré St Didier d.	0737	0837	0937	1037	1137	1237	1337	1427	1537	hourly	2237
Courmayeur △ a.	0745	0845	0945	1045	1145	1245	1345	1436	1545	until	2245

△ – P. le Monte Bianco.

⊡ – Autostazione (bus station).

CORSICAN RAILWAYS 369

Narrow gauge. 2nd class. *Service until June 25*

km		Ⓐ	Ⓐ	⑥	Ⓐ	†	⑥	⑥	Ⓐ	†	⑥	Ⓐ	Ⓐ	⑥	†	Ⓐ	†	⑥	⑥	Ⓐ	Ⓐ	⑥	†c	Ⓐ	Ⓐ
0	**Bastia** ▷ d.	0603	0617	0619	0754	0855	0914	...	0944	1010	1056	1129	1510	1525	1535	1639	1650	1651	...	1657	...	1753	1817	1832	1927
10	Biguglia ▷ d.	0618	|	0632	0808	0909	0928	...	1002	1023	1111	1143	1523	1538	1548	1656	1703	1703	...	|	...	1808	1832	1850	1942
22	Casamozza ▷ d.	0632	0642	0645	0823	0923	0942	...	1016	1041	1125	1157	1538	1553	1602	1710	1720	1715	...	1722	...	1822	1849	1906	1956
47	Ponte Leccia a.	...	0718	0718	0900	0955	1016	...	1051	1115	1158	1230	1611	1626	1634	...	1754	1749	...	1757	...	▬	1921	1942	...
47	Ponte Leccia d.	...	0720	0723	0905	1001	1021	1030	1059	1120	1200	1232	1613	1628	1641	...	1800	1758	1805	1801	1805	...	1923	1944	...
98	Ile Rousse ▶ d.	...	|	|	|	|	|	1145	1215	1236	|	|	|	|	|	...	1916	|	1920	|	1920	...	|	|	...
120	**Calvi** ▶ a.	...	|	|	|	|	|	1220	1250	1311	|	|	|	|	|	...	1951	|	1955	|	2010	†b	|	|	...
74	Corté d.	...	0803	0802	0941	1040	1057	...	...	...	1240	1310	1649	1708	1722	...	...	1844	...	1841	...	1903	1956	2018	...
90	Vivario d.	...	0835	0834	1019	1110	1129	...	...	...	1312	1342	1726	1738	1752	...	...	1914	...	1913	...	1933	...	...	...
107	Vizzavona d.	...	0853	0855	1037	1128	1150	...	...	...	1330	1400	1748	1758	1813	...	...	1932	...	1931	...	1951	...	...	...
145	Mezzana △ d.	...	0943	0942	1127	1214	1237	...	...	...	1417	1447	1837	1844	1859	...	...	2018	...	2018	...	2037	...	...	...
158	**Ajaccio** △ a.	...	1001	1000	1145	1232	1255	...	...	...	1435	1505	1855	1902	1917	...	...	2036	...	2036	...	2055	...	...	...

	Ⓐ	⑥	Ⓐ	⑥	†	Ⓐ	⑥	Ⓐ	Ⓐ	†	⑥	⑥	Ⓐ	†	⑥	Ⓐ	†	⑥	⑥	Ⓐ	Ⓐ	†	Ⓐ	⑥	†b
Ajaccio △ d.	...	...	...	...	...	0602	0602	...	...	...	...	0743	0812	0843	1036	1106	...	...	1512	...	1523	1523	1635	1646	1700
Mezzana △ d.	...	...	...	...	...	0621	0621	...	...	...	...	0802	0831	0902	1055	1128	...	...	1531	...	1542	1542	1654	1705	1719
Vizzavona d.	...	...	...	...	...	0712	0713	...	...	...	...	0856	0925	0951	1149	1219	...	...	1621	...	1633	1632	1749	1757	1812
Vivario d.	...	...	...	...	...	0728	0729	...	...	...	...	0912	0941	1007	1205	1235	...	...	1636	...	1649	1647	1805	1812	1827
Corté d.	...	...	0621	0644	...	0802	0803	...	...	...	...	0943	1018	1041	1239	1311	...	...	1710	...	1724	1721	1842	1845	1855
Calvi ▶ d.	...	...	|	|	...	|	|	...	0700	0800	0815	|	|	|	|	|	1440	1550	|	1550	|	|	|	|	▬
Ile Rousse ▶ d.	...	...	|	|	...	|	|	...	0737	0837	0851	|	|	|	|	|	1517	1626	|	1627	|	|	|	|	...
Ponte Leccia a.	...	...	0655	0718	...	0836	0837	...	0854	0954	1008	1017	1052	1114	1313	1345	1634	1743	1744	1744	1758	1754	1916	1919	...
Ponte Leccia d.	...	...	0656	0722	...	0837	0839	...	0909	1002	...	1022	1055	1119	1314	1346	1640	...	1752	...	1802	1759	1918	1921	Ⓐ
Casamozza ▷ d.	0641	0714	0736	0757	0854	0917	0915	0933	0946	1040	...	1058	1130	1154	1350	1421	1719	...	1827	...	1837	1834	1958	1958	2003
Biguglia ▷ d.	0657	0728	0752	0811	0909	|	0928	0947	1002	1052	...	1111	1143	1206	1403	1433	1731	...	1839	...	1850	1847	|	2008	2017
Bastia ▷ a.	0712	0744	0812	0826	0924	0939	0941	1003	1015	1105	...	1124	1156	1219	1416	1446	1744	...	1852	...	1903	1903	2020	2020	2032

b – Not Dec. 18, 25, Jan. 1, Feb. 19, 26, Apr. 16, 23, 30, May 7, June 4.
c – Not Apr. 16, 30, May 7, June 4.
z – From Apr. 1.

△ – **Additional journeys** Ajaccio - Mezzana and v.v.: **From Ajaccio** at 0635 Ⓐ, 0654 ⑥, 0721 Ⓐ, 1215 ⚒, 1715 ⑥, 1725 Ⓐ, 1815 ⚒ and 1925 Ⓐ. **From Mezzana** at 0658 Ⓐ, 0717 ⑥, 0744 Ⓐ, 1330 Ⓐ, 1335 ⑥, 1740 ⑥, 1748 Ⓐ, 1900 Ⓐ, 1912 ⑥ and 1948 Ⓐ.

▶ – **Additional journeys** Ile Rousse - Calvi and v.v.: **From Ile Rousse** at 0900 Ⓐ, 0900 ⑥ **z**, 1020 † **z**, 1100 ⚒, 1320 † **z**, 1400 ⚒, 1620 † **z**, 1630 ⚒, 1820 † **z**, 1830 Ⓐ and 1830 ⑥ **z**. **From Calvi** at 0730 ⑥ **z**, 0800 Ⓐ, 0920 † **z**, 1000 ⚒, 1120 † **z**, 1305 ⚒, 1500 ⚒, 1520 † **z**, 1720 † **z**, 1730 Ⓐ and 1730 ⑥ **z**.

▷ – **Additional journeys** Bastia - Casamozza and v.v.: **From Bastia** at 0624 Ⓐ, 0640 ⑥, 0717 Ⓐ, 0723 ⑥, 0815 †, 0819 Ⓐ, 0835 ⑥, 0855 Ⓐ, 1010 ⑥, 1020 Ⓐ, 1210 ⑥, 1213 Ⓐ, 1225 †, 1325 Ⓐ, 1347 ⑥, 1450 Ⓐ, 1500 ⑥, 1605 Ⓐ, 1635 ⑥, 1719 Ⓐ, 1755 Ⓐ and 1922 ⑥. **From Casamozza** at 0719 Ⓐ, 0809 Ⓐ, 0826 ⑥, 0856 Ⓐ, 0928 ⑥, 1045 ⑥, 1054 Ⓐ, 1301 †, 1306 ⑥, 1316 Ⓐ, 1405 Ⓐ, 1422 ⑥, 1524 Ⓐ, 1555 ⑥, 1640 Ⓐ, 1718 ⑥, 1720 Ⓐ, 1756 Ⓐ, 1837 ⑥, 1852 Ⓐ and 2004 ⑥.

12 ⚒ – Daily except Sundays and holidays † – Sundays and holidays 223

370 PARIS - DIJON - BESANÇON - MULHOUSE - BASEL *TGV Rhin-Rhône*

Certain services are subject to alteration Mar. 11 - Apr. 3 (also on Apr. 8, 9 and ⑥⑦ June 10 – 25). For *TGV* trains Lyon - Dijon - Mulhouse - Strasbourg see Table **379**.
For *TGV* trains Paris - Dijon - Dole - Lausanne see Table **375**. Local services: Tables **371** Paris - Dijon, **374** Dijon - Besançon, **378** Besançon - Belfort, **370b** Belfort - Mulhouse.

km		*TGV* 6701	*TGV* 9203		*TGV* 6747	*TGV* 9211	*TGV* 6703	*TGV* 9213		*TGV* 9215	*TGV* 6755	*TGV* 6755	*TGV* 6741	*TGV* 9219	*TGV* 6759	*TGV* 9589	*TGV* 9223	*TGV* 9225	*TGV* 6757	*TGV* 6707	*TGV* 5130	*TGV* 5130	*TGV* 6709	*TGV* 6753
		Ⓐ	①–⑥ b		Ⓒ	⊗	⊕			A	Ⓐ n	Ⓑ r	⑤ d			Ⓑ h		N	Ⓑ h		⑥ ♥	Ⓑ h♥	Ⓑ h	⑤⑦ w
	Lille Europe **11** d.	...	...	...	...	...	...	...	...	...	...	...	...	...	...	...	...	...	...	...	1854f	1900f	...	...
0	**Paris** Gare de Lyon **375** d.	0653	0723	...	0953	1023	1123	1223	...	1423	1453	1453	1523	1623	1653	1723	1823	1823	1853	1923	|	|	2023	2053
212	Montbard d.	0800	|	...	1100	|	|	|	...	|	1600	1600	|	|	1800	|	|	|	2000	|	2109	2112	|	2200
287	**Dijon** **375** a.	0833	|	...	1134	1158	1258	1358	...	|	1634	1634	1657	|	1833	1857	1958	1958	2034	2057	2143	2200	2156	2234
287	**Dijon** **375** d.	0837	|	...	1140	1201	1302	1401	...	|	1637	...	...	|	1837	1901	2001	2001	2037	2101	2153	2204	2204	2237
333	Dole **375** a.	|	|	...	|	|	|	|	...	|	|	...	...	|	|	|	|	|	2102	|	|	|	|	2300k
364	**Besançon TGV** ⊖ d.	0908	|	...	1211	|	1331	|	...	|	1708	...	...	|	1908	1931	|	|	|	2131	2224	2234	2234	|
377	Besançon Viotte a.	|	|	...	1222	|	|	|	...	|	1720	...	...	|	1920	|	|	|	2129	|	|	|	|	2328k
446	Belfort Montbéliard TGV d.	0933	0941	...	...	|	1355	|	...	1641	...	...	...	1842	...	1955	|	|	...	2155	2248	2258	2258	...
491	Mulhouse **385** d.	0957	1006	...	...	1306	1417	1506	...	1706	...	...	...	1907	...	2023	2106	2106	...	2217	2310	2320	2320	...
	Freiburg (Brsg) Hbf a.	...	|	...	...	|	...	|	...	|	...	...	...	|	...	2111q	|	|	...	...	...	...	...	...
525	**Basel** **385** a.	...	1026	...	...	1326	...	1526	...	1726	...	...	...	1926	...	...	2126	2126	...	...	...	...	...	...
	Zürich HB **510** a.	...	1126	...	...	1426	...	1626	...	...	...	...	...	2026	...	...	2226		...	...	...	...	...	...

	TGV 6750	*TGV* 6700	*TGV* 5152	*TGV* 5152	*TGV* 6745	*TGV* 9588	*TGV* 9206		*TGV* 9210	*TGV* 9214	*TGV* 6704	*TGV* 6704	*TGV* 9218		*TGV* 9222	*TGV* 6706	*TGV* 6706	*TGV* 6784	*TGV* 9226	*TGV* 6710	*TGV* 6765	*TGV* 6765	*TGV* 9230	*TGV* 6767
	Ⓐ	①–⑥ b	①–⑥ b	⑦ e♠		①–⑥ m			A	B⊕	Ⓐ ⊙	Ⓒ	⊡		⊡	Ⓐ	⑦ e	⑦ s	Ⓑ h		⑦ e	Ⓐ		⑦ e
Zürich HB **510** d.	...	...	...	...	...	...	0734	...	0934	...	...	...	1134	...	1334	...	...	...	1534	...	...	...	...	...
Basel **385** d.	...	...	...	...	...	...	0834	...	1034	1034	...	...	1234	...	1434	...	...	...	1634	...	...	...	1834	...
Freiburg (Brsg) Hbf d.	...	...	...	...	...	0652	|	...	|	|	...	...	|	...	|	...	...	...	|	...	...	...	|	...
Mulhouse **385** d.	...	0542	0542	0557	...	0742	0856	...	1056	1056	1158	1158	1257	...	1456	1537	1542	...	1656	1742	...	...	1859	...
Belfort Montbéliard TGV d.	...	0607	0607	0622	...	0808	0921	...	|	|	1223	1223	1322	...	|	1602	1607	...	|	1807	...	...	1924	...
Besançon Viotte d.	0533y	|	|	|	0639	|	|	...	|	|	|	|	|	...	|	|	|	...	|	|	1835	1837	|	2047
Besançon TGV ⊖ d.	|	0630	0630	0645	0653	0832	|	...	|	|	1248	1249	|	...	|	1626	1630	...	|	1831	1849	1851	|	2101
Dole **375** d.	0559y	|	|	|	|	|	|	...	|	|	|	|	|	...	|	|	|	...	|	|	|	|	|	|
Dijon **375** a.	0623	0658	0658	0716	0720	0858	|	...	1158	1158	1315	1318	|	...	1558	1655	1658	...	1758	1858	1918	1922	|	2129
Dijon **375** d.	0625	0702	0702	0719	0724	0902	|	...	1201	1201	1318	1325	|	...	1601	1658	1701	1725	1801	1902	1925	1925	|	2132
Montbard d.	0703	|	0754	0754	0802	|	|	...	|	|	1404	1403	|	...	|	1736	|	1803	|	|	2003	|	|	|
Paris Gare de Lyon **375** a.	0807	0837	|	|	0905	1037	1137	...	1337	1337	1507	1507	1537	...	1737	1837	1837	1907	1937	2037	2107	2107	2137	2307
Lille Europe **11** a.	...	...	0958	0958	...	...	...	...	...	...	...	...	...	...	...	...	...	...	...	...	...	...	...	...

LOCAL TRAINS MULHOUSE - FREIBURG

km		①–⑤ a	⑥⑦ c	①–⑤ t		①–⑤ a	①–⑤ u	⑥⑦ v		
0	**Mulhouse** d.	0632	0831	0831	1023	1251	1434	1534	1751	1923
19	Neuenburg 🏛 d.	0658	0851	0851	1043	1311	1504	1604	1812	1944
22	Müllheim (Baden) a.	0702	0856	0856	1047	1316	1509	1609	1817	1949
22	Müllheim (Baden) **912** d.	*0707*	0857	*0906*	*1055*	*1323*j	1510	1610	*1823*	*1955*
51	**Freiburg** (Brsg) Hbf **912** a.	*0736*	0916	*0934*	*1122*	*1344*j	1529	1629	*1844*	*2021*

	①–⑤ a		⑥⑦ z			①–⑤ a			
Freiburg (Brsg) Hbf **912** d.	*0628*	0915	0926	...	*1115*	*1315*	1645	*1815*	*1936*
Müllheim (Baden) **912** a.	*0654*	0934	0944	...	*1134*	*1336*	1704	*1834*	*2004*
Müllheim (Baden) d.	0707	...	0945	0945	1140	1340	1705	1839	2009
Neuenburg 🏛 d.	0711	...	0950	0950	1145	1345	1710	1844	2014
Mulhouse a.	0730	...	1011	1011	1205	1406	1730	1904	2040p

A – From Apr. 3.
B – 🚂12 Bern - Basel - Paris.
N – 🚂12 Paris - Basel - Bern - Interlaken.

a – Not Dec. 26, Apr. 14, 17, May 1, 25, June 5.
b – Not Apr. 17, May 1, 8, June 5.
c – Also Dec. 26, Jan. 6, Apr. 14, 17, May 1, 25, June 5.
d – Also May 24; not May 26.
e – Also Apr. 17, May 1, 8, June 5.
f – Lille **Flandres**.
h – Not May 25.
j – Not Jan. 6.
k – 3 minutes later from May 19.

m – Not Apr. 17, May 1, 8, 26, June 5.
n – Not Apr. 18, May 2, 9, June 6.
p – 2033 on ⑥.
q – Not Apr. 16, 30, May 7, June 4.
r – Not Apr. 18, May 2, 9, 25, June 6.
s – Also Apr. 17, May 1, 8, June 5; not Apr. 16, 30, May 7, June 4.
t – Not Dec. 26, Jan. 6, Apr. 14, 17, May 1, 25, June 5.
u – Not Dec. 26, Jan. 6.
v – Also Dec. 26, Jan. 6.
w – Also Apr. 17, May 1, 8, 24, June 5.
y – From May 15 departs Besançon 0531, Dole 0556.
z – Also Dec. 26, Jan. 6, Apr. 14, 17, May 1, 25, June 5.

TGV – Ⓡ, supplement payable, 🍷.

⊗ – Subject to alteration Feb. 6 – 9 and ①–⑤ from June 6.
⊕ – Subject to alteration Feb. 6 – 9.
⊙ – Subject to alteration on Feb. 15, Apr. 17, 18, May 2 – 9, 15 – 19, 29 – 31, June 1, 2, 12 – 16, 26 – 30.
⊡ – Subject to alteration on June 6 – 30.
♥ – Also calls at Charles de Gaulle ✈ (d. 1958) and Marne la Vallée-Chessy (d. 2011). Subject to alteration Apr. 3 – 21 and from June 1.
♠ – Also calls at Marne la Vallée-Chessy (a. 0849) and Charles de Gaulle ✈ (a. 0903).
⊖ – Full name: Besançon Franche-Comté TGV.

370a BESANÇON VIOTTE - BESANÇON FRANCHE-COMTÉ TGV *Local connecting services*

km		⚒	†		⚒						Ⓐ				Ⓑ			Ⓒ			Ⓐ		
0	Besançon Viotte d.	0605	0620	0726	0806	...	0955	...	1143	1225	1305	1338	1415	...	1603	...	1735	1807	1848	1928	2006	2106	2159
13	Besançon Franche-Comté TGV a.	0620	0635	0741	0822	...	1010	...	1156	1238	1318	1353	1432	...	1616	...	1748	1822	1905	1941	2020	2121	2214

	⚒	†	†	⚒	⑥	Ⓐ		Ⓒ	Ⓐ		Ⓐ				Ⓑ					Ⓐ		⑥	Ⓑ
Besançon Franche-Comté TGV d.	0638	0652	0823	0839	0851	0915	...	1100	1104	1220	1301	1339	1422	1454	1638	1808	1849	1946	2022	2039	2138	2231	2241
Besançon Viotte a.	0658	0706	0837	0854	0906	0930	...	1115	1119	1237	1318	1354	1435	1509	1652	1822	1904	2001	2037	2054	2152	2244	2256

371 PARIS - SENS - AUXERRE and DIJON *Local Services*

For *TGV* services Paris - Dijon see Table **370**. Certain Paris - Auxerre trains continue to / from destinations in Table **372**.
WARNING! Certain services may be subject to alteration during the following periods: ①–⑥ Jan. 9 – 27, daily Mar. 11 - Apr. 2 (also Apr. 8, 9) and ⑥⑦ May 20 - June 10.
Please note that many trains are subject to complex timing variations during certain periods (the earliest known departure times are shown in the table).
Readers intending to use services in this table are strongly advised to check timings locally.

km		Ⓐ	⚒	Ⓐ	Ⓐ		⚒ △	⊗	◇	Ⓒ		Ⓑ ⊡	⚒	Ⓐ	Ⓑ		Ⓐ	Ⓒ	Ⓑ		Ⓐ	Ⓒ	†	Ⓐ		
0	**Paris** Bercy d.	...	...	0613	...	0739	0839	0926	1039	...	1238	...	1339	1438	...	1539	1631	1639	...	1731v	1831	1839	...	...	1931v	2039
113	Sens d.	...	0613	0719	...	0834	0934	1034	1134	...	1334	...	1434	1534	...	1634	1734	1734	...	1834	1934	1934	...	...	2034	2134
147	Joigny d.	...	0639	0748	...	0851	0950	1050	1150	...	1350	...	1450	1550	...	1650	1750	1750	...	1850	1950	1950	...	...	2051	2150
	Auxerre d.	0533	|	|	*0733*	|	|	|	|	*1139*	|	*1337*	|	|	1534a	|	|	|	1728	|	|	|	*1940*	*1945*	|	|
156	Laroche Migennes a.	0550	0646	0755	*0748*	0858	0956	1058	1156	*1152*	1356	*1352*	1458	1556	1553a	1658	1756	1756	1744	1858	1958	1956	*1954*	*2001*	2058	2156
156	Laroche Migennes d.	0552	0651	0759	0803	0900	1003e	1100	1158	1203	1406	1401	1500	1606	1601	1700	1806	1757	1801	1900	*2003*	1959h	2001	2006	2100	2159
175	**Auxerre** a.	|	|	0813	|	|	1017e	|	1213	|	1419	|	|	1620	|	|	1819	1814	|	|	*2018*	2014h	|	|	|	2214
197	Tonnerre d.	0624	0720	...	0826	0924	...	1124	...	1226	...	1428	1524	...	1628	1724	...	...	1828	1924	...	...	2028	2033	2124	...
243	Montbard d.	0648	0745	...	0851	0951	...	1151	...	1251	...	1453	1551	...	1653	1751	...	...	1852	1951	...	...	2053	2059	2151	...
315	**Dijon** a.	0730	0829	...	0932	1029	...	1235	...	1329	...	1530	1629	...	1733	1829	...	...	1933	2029	...	...	2130	2135	2229	...
	Lyon Part Dieu **377** a.	...	1044	...	...	1244	...	1444	...	...	...	...	1844	...	...	2048	...	...	...	2244t	...	...	...	...	...	...

	Ⓐ n	Ⓐ n	⑥	⚒	Ⓑ	k	⚒	⚒	⚒ ⊕	⊗		Ⓐ ⊙	Ⓒ		Ⓒ ⌛	Ⓐ ⌛			Ⓑ				Ⓐ	†		Ⓑ
Lyon Part Dieu **377** d.	...	...	...	...	...	...	0516g	...	...	0716	...	...	...	...	1116	1116	...	1316	...	...	1516	...	...	...	1716	...
Dijon d.	...	...	...	0522	0629	...	0727	0830	...	0927	...	1207	1229	...	1330	1330	...	1527	1629	...	1730	1829	...	...	1930	2029
Montbard d.	...	...	...	0559	0706	...	0806	0907	...	1003	...	1305	1306	...	1408	1417	...	1604	1706	...	1808	1906	...	...	2008	2123
Tonnerre d.	...	...	...	0626	0731	...	0832	0932	...	1030	...	1331	1331	...	1434	1442	...	1631	1731	...	1834	1931	...	...	2034	2148
Auxerre d.	0441	*0533*	0540	|	|	0733	|	|	0946	|	1139	|	|	1337	|	|	1536c	|	|	1738	|	|	1945	1940	|	|
Laroche Migennes a.	0455	*0550*	0554	0652	0757	0748	0855	0958	1001	1053	1152	1357	1357	1352	1458	1503	1553c	1653	1757	1752	1857	1957	2001	1954	2057	2213
Laroche Migennes d.	0457	0555	0556	0654	0807	0757	0856	1015r	1003	1056	1157	*1406*	*1406*	1357	1502	1505	1556	1655	*1806*a	1757	1858	2009r	2004	2004	2058	2220
Auxerre a.	|	|	|	|	0823	|	|	1031r	|	|	|	*1419*	*1419*	|	|	|	|	|	*1819*a	|	|	2026r	|	|	|	2236
Joigny d.	0505	0603	0604	0702	...	0805	0904	...	1010	1104	1205	...	...	1404	1509	1512	1605	1703	...	1805	1905	...	2012	2012	2105	...
Sens d.	0522	0621	0621	0719	...	0822	0920	...	1027	1120	1221	...	...	1421	1526	1528	1622	1720	...	1822	1921	...	2040	2039	2121	...
Paris Bercy a.	0628	0728	0722	0828	...	0922	1022	...	1135	1222	1322	...	...	1522	1622	1629	1722	1822	...	1922	2022	...	2148	2148	2222	...

CONTINUED ON NEXT PAGE (including other stopping services Paris Gare de Lyon - Laroche Migennes - Auxerre).

PARIS - SENS - AUXERRE and DIJON 371 (contd.)

LOCAL TRAINS PARIS - LAROCHE MIGENNES For faster trains see the main part of Table **371** on the previous page. See **WARNING** note on previous page for important information.

km							†	⚒				Ⓐ	Ⓒ	Ⓐ	Ⓐ	Ⓒ	Ⓐ	Ⓐ	Ⓒ	Ⓐ	Ⓐ		Ⓒ		❖	
0	**Paris** Gare de Lyon .. d.	0649	0749	0849	1049	1149	1249	1249	1349	1449	1549	1619	1649	1655	1719	1749	1755	1819	1849	1855	1919	1949	2049	2149	2239b	2249
45	Melun .... d.	0715	0815	0916	1116	1215	1316	1316	1415	1516	1615	1646	1715	|	1747	1815	|	1847	1915	|	1945	2016	2116	2215	|	2315
60	Fontainebleau-Avon .. d.	0727	0827	0928	1128	1227	1328	1328	1427	1528	1627	1658	1727	|	1758	1827	|	1858	1927	|	1957	2028	2128	2229	|	2327
79	Montereau .... d.	0750	0845	0950	1150	1245	1350	1350	1445	1550	1645	1720	1750	1748	1820	1850	1848	1920	1950	1948	2015	2050	2150	2245	|	2345
113	Sens .... d.	0838f	...	1038f	1220	...	1420	1438f	...	1638f	...	1749	1838f	1818	1849	1938f	1919	1949	2038f	2019	...	2138f	2219	...	2349	...
147	Joigny .... d.	0905	...	1105	1248	...	1448	1505	...	1705	...	1817	1905	1846	1917	2005	1947	2017	2105	2047	...	2205	2248	...	0018	...
156	**Laroche Migennes** ... a.	0913	...	1113	1255	...	1455	1513	...	1713	...	1825	1913	1854	1925	2013	1955	2025	2113	2055	...	2213	2300	...	0030	...

		Ⓐ	⑥	Ⓐ	Ⓐ	Ⓒ	Ⓐ	⑥	†	Ⓐ	Ⓐ							†	⚒		†	⚒	Ⓐ	Ⓒ		
Laroche Migennes ... d.	0401	0504	0504	0534	0559	0604	0634	0645	...	0704	...	0747	1007	...	1203	...	1405	1447	...	1547	1645	...	1745	1801	...	...
Joigny .... d.	0408	0511	0511	0541	0607	0611	0641	0652	...	0711	...	0754	1014	...	1211	...	1412	1454	...	1554	1652	...	1752	1809	...	...
Sens .... d.	0436	0539	0539	0610	0635	0639	0710	0737f	...	0740	...	0838f	1040	...	1237	...	1437	1537f	...	1636f	1737f	...	1837f	1837	...	...
Montereau .... d.	0511	0609	0612	0642	0710	0712	0742	0812	0812	0810	0819	0912	1112	1212	1312	1412	1512	1612	1612	1712	1812	1812	1912	1912	2012	2112
Fontainebleau-Avon ... d.	0529	|	0630	0701	|	0730	0801	0831	0830	|	0836	0931	1131	1229	1331	1430	1531	1631	1631	1732	1831	1830	1931	1931	2030	2130
Melun .... d.	0542	|	0643	0713	|	0743	0813	0844	0843	|	0849	0944	1144	1242	1344	1443	1544	1644	1644	1744	1844	1843	1944	1944	2043	2143
Paris Gare de Lyon ... a.	0611	0701	0711	0741	0800	0811	0841	0911	0911	0909	0917	1011	1211	1311	1411	1511	1611	1711	1715	1814	1911	1915	2011	2013	2111	2211

ADDITIONAL LOCAL TRAINS LAROCHE MIGENNES - AUXERRE

	⑥¶	⚒	†	⚒				⚒	†	D	E
Laroche Migennes ..... d.	0031	0706	0903	0908	1106	1510	1704	1908	1914	2106	2108
Auxerre .... a.	0044	0723	0916	0921	1123	1527	1721	1921	1932	2123	2121

	⑥‡	Ⓐ	◧	⊖			Ⓐ	†	⚒	⚒	†
Auxerre .... d.	0636	0637	0836	1037	1436	1636	1826	1830	1837	2036	2037
Laroche Migennes.. a.	0654	0653	0854	1051	1454	1654	1844	1844	1851	2054	2051

D – ①–④ (not Apr. 17, May 1, 8, 24, 25, June 5).
E – ⑤–⑦ (also Apr. 17, May 1, 8, 24, 25, June 5).
a – Ⓐ only.
b – Paris **Bercy**. Departs 2206 from May 14.
c – Ⓒ only.
e – 3 minutes later on ⑥.
f – Arrives 14–20 minutes earlier.
g – ① (also Apr. 18, May 9, June 6; not Apr. 17, May 1, 8, June 5).
h – 4–5 minutes later on †.

k – Runs up to 21 minutes later on †.
n – Not Feb. 27 - Mar. 24.
r – ⑥ only.
t – Ⓑ only. Change trains at Dijon on ⑤ (also May 24).
v – 8 minutes later on Ⓒ.
◧ – On ⑥ Auxerre d. 0837, Laroche a. 0851.
⊖ – On ⑥ Auxerre d. 1036, Laroche a. 1054.
△ – Subject to alteration on Ⓐ Mar. 13 - May 5.
⊗ – Subject to alteration on ①–⑤ Jan. 9 - Feb. 24, May 15–19, 29–31, June 1, 2, 19–23.

◇ – Subject to alteration on ①–⑤ Feb. 6 - Mar. 3. On Ⓒ runs 6–8 minutes later Laroche - Auxerre.
⊡ – Subject to alteration Feb. 6–9, May 2–5, 9–12. On †: Laroche d. 1403, Tonnerre d. 1426, Montbard d. 1451, Dijon a. 1532.
⊕ – Subject to alteration Mar. 6–10.
⊙ – Subject to alteration Feb. 6–9, 20–24, 27, 28, Mar. 1, 2, 3.
⊠ – Paris arrival may be up to 27 minutes later.
¶ – Runs 30 minutes earlier from May 20.
‡ – Runs 6 minutes earlier Jan. 7 - Feb. 25 and from June 17.
❖ – From May 14 departs Paris 2206, running up to 35 minutes earlier.

AUXERRE - CLAMECY / AVALLON 372

km		Ⓐ ⊖	†	⚒ ⊙	⑥	†	⑥	◇	Ⓐ	†	⑥	Ⓐ	†	Ⓐ	⑤–⑦ d
	Paris Bercy **371** .... ▲ d.	0613	...	...	0839	1039	1039	1238	1438	1639	...	...	...	...	...
	Laroche Migennes **371** ...... d.	0759	0903	0908	1006	1206	1206	1406	1606	1757	1908	1908	1914	2003	2108
0	**Auxerre** .... d.	0815	0918	0923	1022	1221	1222	1421	1622	1831	1923	1923	1941	2025	2123
17	Cravant-Bazarnes .... d.	0832	0934	0939	1039	1238	1239	1437	1638	1846	1939	1940	1956	2042	2139
53	Clamecy .... a.	|	1011	1014	|	1313	1315	|	1713	|	2014	|	2030	2118	|
86	Corbigny .... a.	|	1049	...	|	...	1353	|	...	|	...	|	2109	2156	|
41	Sermizelles-Vézelay .... d.	0856	...	...	1103	...	...	1502	...	1911	...	2002	...	...	2203
55	**Avallon** .... a.	0909	...	...	1115	...	...	1514	...	1924	...	2014	...	...	2215

	Ⓐ	⚒ ❖	⑥		Ⓑ ⊖	⊙		⑥			†	⑥	Ⓐ	†	†
Avallon .... d.	0545	...	0744	...	0944	...	...	1243	...	1643	...	...	...	...	1944
Sermizelles-Vézelay .... d.	0558	...	0756	...	0956	...	...	1256	...	1657	...	...	...	...	1956
Corbigny .... d.	|	0558	|	...	|	...	...	|	...	|	1657	1705	...	...	|
Clamecy .... d.	|	0638	|	...	|	1046	...	|	...	|	1737	1744	1745	1847	|
Cravant-Bazarnes .... d.	0620	0716	0820	...	1020	1122	...	1320	...	1721	1813	1821	1821	1923	2020
Auxerre .... a.	0635	0731	0835	...	1035	1137	...	1335	...	1736	1828	1835	1836	1938	2035
Laroche Migennes **371** ...... a.	0653	0748	0851	...	1051	1152	...	1352	...	1752	1844	1851	1851	1954	2051
Paris Bercy **371** .... ▲ a.	...	0922	...	...	...	1322	...	1522	...	1922	...	...	...	2148	...

d – Also Apr. 17, May 1, 8, 24, 25, June 5.
⊖ – Subject to alteration on ①–⑤ Feb. 27 - Mar. 10 and ①–⑤ Apr. 24 - May 5.
⊙ – Subject to alteration on ①–⑤ Feb. 27 - Mar. 10, Apr. 3–7, May 9–12.
◇ – Runs up to 15 minutes later Mar. 20–24.
❖ – Timings are up to 8 minutes later to Dec. 31 and Feb. 27 - May 13.
▲ – See **WARNING** note for Table **371** on page 224 for important information regarding services from / to Paris.

DIJON - ÉTANG - AUTUN and NEVERS 373

km		Ⓐ ♥	Ⓐ	①–⑥ b	Ⓑ	⚒ ⊖	¶	⚒	Ⓑ h	⚒	†	Ⓐ	
0	**Dijon** .... **377** d.	...	0607	0706	0806	1006	1204	1406	1601	1706	1806	1806	1906
37	Beaune .... **377** d.	...	0626	0725	0825	1025	1223	1425	1621t	1725	1825	1824	1925
81	**Montchanin** .... d.	...	0659	0757	0857	1100	1255	1459	1655	1758	1859	1901	1959
89	Le Creusot .... d.	...	0705	0804	0903	1107	1301	1505	1702	1805	1906	1908	2005
111	Étang .... d.	0605	0720	0819	0919	1123	1316	1520	1718	1820	1922	1928	2020
126	**Autun** .... a.	|	|	|	|	|	|	|	|	|	|	1946	|
179	Decize .... d.	0652	0805	0904	1006	1207	1401	1605	1804	1905	2008	...	2105
216	**Nevers** .... a.	0730	0830	0933	1031	1232	1426	1631	1831	1930	2033	...	2131
	Bourges **290** .... a.	...	...	1009‡	...	...	...	...	1915	...	...	...	...
	Vierzon **290** .... a.	...	...	1032‡	...	...	...	...	1936	...	...	...	...
	Tours **290** .... a.	...	...	1202‡	...	...	...	...	2107	...	...	...	...

	① g	②–⑤ v	⚒	Ⓑ	①–⑥ b	⑦ e	§	Ⓐ		Ⓑ	⑥	Ⓐ ♥	Ⓑ h⊖
Tours **290** .... d.	...	...	...	...	0657	...	...	...	...	...	...	...	1659
Vierzon **290** .... d.	...	...	...	...	0828	...	...	...	...	...	...	...	1828
Bourges **290** .... d.	...	...	...	...	0847	...	...	...	...	...	...	...	1847
Nevers .... d.	0525	...	0630	0729	0926	0930	1132	1330	1530	1731	1832	1846	1926
Decize .... d.	0551	...	0656	0755	0951	0956	1158	1356	1556	1757	1858	1918	1951
Autun .... d.	*0611*	0612	|	|	|	|	|	|	|	|	|	|	|
Étang .... d.	0635	0640	0740	0839	1034	1040	1242	1440	1640	1841	1942	2000	2035
Le Creusot .... d.	0655	0655	0755	0854	1050	1055	1257	1455	1655	1856	1957	...	2051
Montchanin .... d.	0702	0702	0803	0902	1100	1103	1305	1503	1703	1903	2004	...	2102
Beaune .... **377** d.	0730	0730	0829	0928	1128	1130	1330	1531	1730	1930	2031	...	2131
Dijon .... **377** a.	0754	0754	0854	0951	1154	1154	1355	1554	1754	1954	2054	...	2158

CONNECTIONS CHALON - MONTCHANIN

km		Ⓐ	⚒	⚒⊗	Ⓑ	⚒	Ⓑ	
0	**Chalon sur Saône** .... d.	...	0711	1412	1608	1712	1812	1912
15	Chagny .... d.	0625	0724	1425	1621	1725	1825	1925
44	**Montchanin** .... a.	0651	0751	1451	1647	1751	1851	1951

	Ⓐ	⚒	Ⓐ	§	Ⓐ	Ⓑ	Ⓑ	⑥
Montchanin .... ★ d.	0710	0810	0910	1110	1510	1710	1910	2010
Chagny .... ★ d.	0737	0837	0937	1138	1537	1737	1937	2038
Chalon sur Saône ★ a.	0750	0850	0950	1150	1550	1750	1950	2050

CONNECTIONS ÉTANG - AUTUN ⊡

	Ⓐ	⚒	⚒	🚌 ⚒	⑥	Ⓑ	🚌 ⚒	Ⓑ	Ⓐ♥	🚌 ⚒	†
Étang..... d.	0727	0827	1327	1525	1646	1727	1825	1846	2003	2041	2045
Autun..... a.	0745	0845	1345	1546	1704	1745	1846	1904	2021	2102	2103

	Ⓐ♥	⚒	🚌 ⚒	⚒	⚒	🚌 ⚒		Ⓑ	🚌 ⑥	🚌 Ⓐ	†
Autun..... d.	0545	0633	0709	0757	1214	1247	1614	1814	1911	1949	1954
Étang..... a.	0603	0651	0730	0816	1233	1308	1633	1833	1932	2010	2013

CONNECTIONS MONTCHANIN - PARAY LE MONIAL - MOULINS SUR ALLIER

km		Ⓐ	⑥	⚒◧		⚒	Ⓑ	⚒	Ⓑ	
	Dijon (see above) .... d.	...	...	1006	...	...	...	...	...	...
0	**Montchanin** .... d.	0708	0808	1106	1308	1508	1708	1808	1908	2008
15	Montceau les Mines .... d.	0721	0821	1121	1321	1520	1721	1821	1922	2021
50	Paray le Monial .... **290** d.	0751	0851	1158	1351	1545	1751	1851	1951	2051
61	Digoin .... **290** d.	...	...	1210	...	...	...	...	...	...
117	**Moulins sur Allier** .... **290** a.	...	...	1256	...	...	...	...	...	...
	Clermont Ferrand **330** .... a.	...	...	1420	...	...	...	...	...	...

	Ⓐ	⚒			⚒		Ⓑ	⑥	Ⓑ◇
Clermont Ferrand **330** ..... d.	...	...	...	...	...	...	...	...	1742
Moulins sur Allier ...... **290** d.	...	...	...	...	...	...	...	...	1903
Digoin .... **290** d.	...	...	...	...	...	...	...	...	1948
Paray le Monial .... **290** d.	0608	0708	1008	...	1408	1608	1808	1908	1959
Montceau les Mines .... d.	0638	0738	1038	...	1438	1638	1838	1938	2039
Montchanin .... d.	0651	0751	1051	...	1451	1651	1851	1951	2052
Dijon (see above) .... a.	...	...	...	...	...	...	...	...	2158

b – Not Apr. 17, May 1, 8, June 5.
e – Also Apr. 17, May 1, 8, June 5.
g – Also Apr. 18, May 2, 9, June 6; not Apr. 17, May 1, 8, June 5.
h – Not May 25.
t – ①②③④⑦ (not May 24).
v – Not Apr. 18, May 2, 9, 25, June 6.
♥ – (2) Autun - Étang - Nevers and v.v.

⊗ – Subject to alteration on ①–⑤ Mar. 27 - Apr. 7.
◧ – Subject to alteration Jan. 30 - Feb. 3, Mar. 6–10, May 26, 27, June 3.
¶ – Subject to alteration on ①–⑤ Mar. 13 - Apr. 7.
§ – Subject to alteration on ①–⑤ Mar. 13–24.
‡ – Subject to alteration Jan. 2–6, 9–13, Feb. 1, 2, 6–24, Mar. 3, 16, 17, 23, 28–31, Apr. 3, 4, 5, 7, 12, 18–29, May 6–19, 25–27, June 10.
◇ – Subject to alteration on May 25, 26, June 4.
⊖ – Conveys (12) Dijon - Montchanin - Clermont Ferrand and v.v.

★ – Additional journeys Montchanin - Chagny - Chalon: Montchanin d. 0656 ⑥ and 1810 ⑥.
⊡ – Additional 🚌 journeys: **From Étang** at 0745 ⚒, 1325 †, 1445 Ⓐ and 1925 †. **From Autun** at 1209 †, 1506 Ⓐ, 1749 ⚒ and 1849 †.

Timings Dijon - Nevers may vary by up to 5 minutes to Feb. 5 and from June 10 (earlier departures possible)

374 — DIJON - DOLE - BESANÇON
Local Services

Subject to alteration from May 15. For *TGV* services see Table 370 (Paris - Dijon - Besançon - Basel) and Table 379 (Strasbourg - Besançon - Dijon).

km			Ⓐ		Ⓑ	Ⓐ	✕				Ⓐ	Ⓐ	Ⓐ	G									
0	Dijon................375 d.	0509	0613	0641	0709	0713	0741	0809	1012	1109	1213	1241	1351	1509	1609	1613	1646	1711	1741	1813	1843	1913	2009	2109	2209
32	Auxonne..............d.	0529	0640	0701	0729	0740	0805	0829	1032	1129	1240	1301	1411	1529	1631	1640	1706	1740	1800	1840	1903	1941	2029	2129	2229
46	Dole................375 d.	0540	0650	0710	0739	0750	0811	0839	1042	1140	1250	1312	1420	1540	1641	1650	1717	1750	1809	1850	1913	1951	2039	2139	2239
91	Besançon Viotte ......a.	0605	0726	0737	0805	0826	0837	0905	1108	1205	1327	1337	1445	1605	1713	1726	1742	1826	1839	1927	1939	2026	2105	2205	2305
	Belfort 378 ....a.	0726	0856	...	...	...	...	...	...	...	...	...	...	...	1856	...	1956	...	...	...	...	...	...	...	...

			✕		Ⓐ		Ⓐ		Ⓐ		Ⓑ		Ⓐ	Ⓒ	Ⓐ	✕	†			
	Belfort 378 ....d.	...	...	...	...	0604	...	...	...	...	...	...	...	...	...	...	1704	...	...	
	Besançon Viotte ......d.	0514	0556	0607	0625	0656	0709	0733	0756h	0856	0956	1233	1356	1456	1556	1633	1656	1723	1733	1756	1823	1826	1833	1933	2023	2123k
45	Dole................375 d.	0522	0622	0633	0701	0722	0742	0810	0822	0922	1022	1311	1422	1522	1622	1711	1722	1749	1811	1822	1849	1853	1911	2011	2049	2149
59	Auxonne..............d.	0551	0631	0641	0710	0731	0751	0820	0831	0931	1031	1320	1431	1531	1631	1719	1731	1758	1820	1831	1858	1903	1920	2020	2059	2159
91	Dijon................375 a.	0610	0651	0707	0742	0751	0811	0847	0851	0953	1051	1347	1451	1551	1651	1747	1751	1818	1847	1851	1918	1922	1947	2047	2118	2218

G – ⑤–⑦ (also Apr. 17, May 1, 8, 24, 25, June 5).   h – 0754 on ① (also Apr. 18, May 2, 9; not Jan. 2, Apr. 17, May 1, 8).   k – 2121 on †.

375 — PARIS - DIJON - LAUSANNE and NEUCHÂTEL

Subject to alteration from May 15. Paris services are subject to alteration Mar. 17–19. See Table 970 for other *TGV* services Paris - Dijon and v.v.

km			①–⑤	✕	Ⓐ		TGV 9261				✕	†	TGV 9269	TGV 9773	TGV 9271	①–④	⑦	Ⓐ		TGV 9273				TGV 9277	TGV 9277		⑤†
			d⊖				‡						⊗	⊕	m	e¶	⊙⊖			⊗			b§	e¶		
0	Paris Gare de Lyon ......370 d.	...	...	...	0757	...	...	...	...	1157	...	1211	1357	...	...	...	1557	...	...	1757	1757	...
287	Dijon ....370 d.	...	...	...	0929	...	...	...	...	1333	...	...	1528	...	...	...	1729	...	...	1929	1929	...
287	Dijon ....374 d.	...	0509a	0641	0932	...	1012	...	...	1336	...	1531	...	1711	1723	...	1913	1932	1932	...
333	Dole ....374 376 d.	...	0614	0715	0959	...	1040	1118	1118	1401	...	1556	...	1748	1758	1814	1949	1958	1959	2014
365	Mouchard ....376 d.	...	0645	0740		...		1143	1143		...		...		1844			2016		2037
389	Andelot..............376 d.	...	0704			...		1204	1204		...		❶		1905					
410	Frasne................d.	0529	0719	0817		1044	1053	1218	1220	1444	1453		1641	1715	1802		1843	1920		2044	2044	2053
426	Pontarlier 🚲........a.		0735	0833			1104	1234	1236	1504			1725	1818		1936			2104	
490	Neuchâtel 511.......a.					1154				1554								2154	
434	Vallorbe 🚲...........a.	0549			1057			1457			1657			1857			2057	2057	
480	Lausanne............a.	1137						1537		1615	1737v			1937			2137	2137	

km			TGV 9260		TGV 9264		✕				TGV 9268	TGV 9270	TGV 9778	①–⑤	⑤⑦	Ⓐ				TGV 9272	TGV 9272		⑤†
			d⊖		Ⓐ		◇							⊖⊖	e	m					b§	e		
	Lausanne............d.	...	0623		0823		...		1223	1623	1638				1823	1823	...
	Vallorbe 🚲...........d.	...	0700		0900		...		1300	1652	1700				1901	1900	...
	Neuchâtel 511.......d.	...			0806		...	1206						1806		
	Pontarlier 🚲........d.	0515	0555		0742	0855	1128		1255			1742	1828	1855		
	Frasne................d.	0525	0612		0715	0758	0906	0916	1145		1306	1316	1710	1716		1758	1845	1906	1916	1916	
	Andelot..............376 d.	0625				1204	1204					1901			
	Mouchard ....376 d.	0647		0743		1221	1221				❶		1918		2121
	Dole ....374 376 d.	0710	0722	0801		1000	1245	1245	1311	1402	1759		1941	2011		1958	1959		2145	2149
	Dijon ....374 a.	0751	0823		1023		1347	1424	1822		2047		2022	2022		2218
	Dijon ....370 d.	0826		1026		1427	1825				2025	2025		
	Paris Gare de Lyon ......370 a.	1003		1203		1603	2003	2049			2223	2203		

A – ①–⑤ to Mar. 31; ①–⑥ from Apr. 3 (not Apr. 17, May 1, 8, June 5).
a – Ⓐ only.
b – Not Apr. 17, May 1, 8, June 5.
d – Not Dec. 26, Jan. 2, Apr. 14, 17, May 25, June 5.
e – Also Apr. 17, May 1, 8, June 5.
m – Not Apr. 17, May 1, 8, 24, 25, June 5.
v – 1803 on May 1, 8.

‡ – Subject to alteration on ⑦ Mar. 12 - Apr. 9.
§ – Subject to alteration on ⑥ Mar. 11 - Apr. 8.
¶ – Subject to alteration on Apr. 9.
◇ – Subject to alteration on ⑦ Mar. 12–24, 26–31, Apr. 2, 8, 9.
⊗ – Subject to alteration Mar. 11, 13–25, 27–31, Apr. 1, 8, 9.
⊙ – ①–⑤ (not Dec. 26, Jan. 2, Apr. 14, 17, May 1, 8, 25, June 5). Subject to alteration Feb. 20–23 and ①–④ Apr. 3–27.
⊕ – Subject to alteration on ①–⑤ Apr. 18–28.

❶ – Via Genève (Table 341).
⊖ – 🚌 Pontarlier - Frasne - Vallorbe and v.v.

TGV – TGV Lyria, 🅁, supplement payable, 🍴. Special 'global' fares including the reservation fee are payable for international journeys.

376 — DOLE / BESANÇON - MOREZ - ST CLAUDE

km			Ⓐ		⑤	Ⓐ	⑤⑦	🚌	⑤†			Ⓐ	①	✕	Ⓐ		⑤	①–④	🚌	⑤†	①–④
						u f		⊖ z					g n			f p			m
0	Dole.................375 d.	...	0614r	...	1014	1118	...	1814	...	2014t	St Claude.............d.	0442	0620	...	0954	...	1510	1551	...	1727	1727	...
	Besançon ....378 d.	0601	1004		1640	1751			Morez...............d.	0516	0652	1029	1545	1626	1800	1800	
32	Mouchard ...375 378 d.	0640	0645r	1034	1039	1143	1712	1820	1844	2044	Champagnole..........d.	0603	0738	1147j	1631	1712	1740	1846	1846	
56	Andelot............375 d.	0709	1101	1209	1736	1902	1910	1910	Andelot........ 375 d.	0618	0759	1158	1647	1800	1857	1909	
70	Champagnole..........d.	0740	1118	1221	1747	1923	1930	2126	Mouchard 375 378 d.	0636	0817	0841	1220	1225	1705	1830	1917	1925	1926
105	Morez................d.	0832	1212	1313	1843	2015	2017	2208	Besançon ....378 a.		0909	1255	1738	2002	2000
128	St Claude.............a.	0859	1240	1340	1910	2040	2057	2248	Dole................375 a.	0710	0845	1245	1804b	1917	1941

ST CLAUDE - OYONNAX - BOURG EN BRESSE

km			✕‡ ✕	🚌	⑦e	⊡	⊡	Ⓐu	🚌 Ⓒ	Ⓐ	⑦e			Ⓐ	🚌	Ⓒ	Ⓐ	⑦e	⊡	Ⓑh
0	St Claude ....d.	0552	0645	0807	0810	1025	1245	1345	1610	1710	1743	1825	Lyon P. Dieu 353 d.	...	...	...	...	...	...	...
32	Oyonnax ....d.	0631	0725	0852	0855	1110	1335	1430	1655	1755	1823	1910	Bourg en Bresse .....d.	0610	0740	1030	1038	1240	1335	1340	1605	1719	1821	1945
45	Brion Montréal § ......d.	0641	0740	0910	0920	1135	1340	1455	1720	1818	1838	1935	Nurieux Brion ....d.	0701	1120	1336	1800	1900	2038
48	Nurieux Brion ... ❶ d.	0649	0744	0917	0927	1344	1727	1827	1842	Brion Montréal § ......d.	0708	0825	1113	1124	1343	1420	1425	1650	1804	1904	2043
81	Bourg en Bresse .....a.	0726	0822	1010	1020	1220	1422	1540	1820	1920	1922	2020	Oyonnax ....d.	0733	0850	1138	1140	1408	1440	1450	1715	1824	1921	2103
	Lyon P. Dieu 353 a.	0830								St Claude ....a.	0809	0926	1214	1218	1444	1516	1526	1751	1903	1959	2139

b – Connection by 🚌 from Mouchard.
e – Also Apr. 17, May 1, 8, June 5.
f – Also May 24.
g – Also Apr. 18, May 2, 9, 26, June 6; not Apr. 17, May 1, 8, June 5.
h – Not May 25.
j – Arrives 1115.

m – Not Apr. 17, May 1, 8, 25, June 5.
n – Not Dec. 19–23, 26–30, Jan. 2, Feb. 20–24, 27, 28, Mar. 1–3, Apr. 18–21, 24–28.
p – Not Dec. 19 - Jan. 2, Feb. 20 - Mar. 2, Apr. 17 - May 11, May 24, 25, June 5.
r – ✕ only.
t – By train Dole - Mouchard.

u – Not May 2, 3, 4, 9, 10, 11.
z – Also Apr. 17, May 1, 8, 24, 25, June 5; not May 26.
⊡ – ①–⑥ (not Apr. 17, May 1, 8, June 5).
⊖ – ①②③④⑥ (not Apr. 17, May 1, 8, 24, 25, June 5).
‡ – Subject to alteration on May 26, 27.
❶ – For *TGV* connection Paris - Nurieux Brion and v.v. see Table 341.
§ – Brion Montréal la Cluse.

376a — BESANÇON - LE LOCLE - LA CHAUX DE FONDS

km			①–⑤ ①–⑤		Ⓐ ⑥	Ⓒ	Ⓐ		①–⑤		✕		Ⓐ
			b b		⊡		⊗			b b		⊗		
0	Besançon Viotte.......d.	...	...	0700	0728	0934	0935	1401	1725	1932	La Chaux de Fonds ..512 d.	0543	...	0656	0810	...	1608	1701	...	2145
67	Morteau...............d.	0510	0618	0729	0828	1000	1105	1105	1528	1857	2102	Le Locle............512 d.	0551	0818	1618	1711	
80	Le Locle ....512 d.	0529	0638	0750	1140	1140	1551	2121	Morteau...............d.	0610	0633	0721	0836	1234	1636	1733	1936	2208
88	La Chaux de Fonds 512 a.	0537	0648	0759	1147	1147	1558	2128	Besançon Viotte ......a.	0801	1008	1402	1802	1903	2105	

b – Not Dec. 26, Jan. 2, Apr. 14, 17, May 25, June 5.

⊡ – Includes a long stop at Le Valdahon (a. 0817, d. 0920).
⊗ – Subject to alteration Apr. 3–7, 10–14.

De verklaring van de conventionele tekens vindt u op bladzijde 4   12

Local Services — DIJON - CHALON SUR SAÔNE - LYON — 377

For *TGV* services Dijon - Lyon, see Table **379**. Paris Bercy timings are subject to alteration (see Table **371**).

km		Ⓐ		⚒	Ⓐ	s	Ⓐ		Ⓐ		Ⓐ		Ⓐ	⑦ e	⚒	†	Ⓐ		Ⓐ	⑥	†	Ⓐ	†	⚒	⊠
	Paris Bercy 371 d.	...	...	...	...	...	...	0739	...	0926	...	...	...	...	1339	...	...	1539	...	...	...	1731z	1739	...	...
0	**Dijon** 373 d.	0537	0637	0721	0737	0837	0937	1037	1137	1239	1337	1437	1537	...	1637	1637	1737	1837	1937	1944	2010	2037	2037	2044	2207
37	Beaune 373 d.	0558	0658	0747	0758	0858	0958	1057	1159	1258	1359	1458	1558	...	1657f	1658	1758	1859t	1958	2014	2049	2058	2058	2113	2235
52	Chagny d.	0613	0713	0801	0813	0913	1013	1113	1214	1313	1414	1513	1613	...	1713f	1713	1813	1914	2013	2030	2107	2113	2113	2130	2252
67	**Chalon sur Saône** d.	0626	0726	0818	0826	0926	1026	1126	1226	1326	1426	1526	1626	...	1726	1726	1826	1926	2026	2041	2121	2126	2126	2141	2307
125	Mâcon Ville d.	0657	0757	...	0857	0957	1057	1157	1257	1357	1457	1557	1657	1658	1757	1757	1857	1957	2057	...	...	2157	2157	...	...
163	Villefranche sur Saône ⊖ d.	0721	0821	...	0921	1021	1121	1221	1321	1421	1521	1621	1721	1721	1821	1821	1921	2021	2121	...	...	2221	2221	...	...
197	**Lyon** Part Dieu a.	0744	0844	...	0944	1044	1144	1244	1344	1444	1544	1644	1744	1744	1844	1844	1944	2048	2144	...	...	2244	2244	...	...

	Ⓐ	†	① g	②–⑥ d	Ⓐ	Ⓐ			Ⓐ			Ⓐ		Ⓐ		Ⓐ			Ⓐ			Ⓐ		Ⓐ	
Lyon Part Dieu d.	...	...	0516	...	0616	...	0716	...	0816	0916	...	1016	1116	1216	1316	1416	1516	...	1616	1716	...	1816	1916	2016	2116
Villefranche sur Saône ⊖ d.	...	...	0541	...	0641	...	0741	...	0841	0941	...	1041	1141	1241	1341	1441	1541	...	1641	1741	...	1841	1941	2041	2140
Mâcon Ville d.	...	...	0605	0605	0705	0735	0805	...	0905	1005	...	1105	1205	1305	1405	1505	1605	...	1705	1805	1820	1905	2005	2105	2202
Chalon sur Saône d.	0552	0607	0637	0637	0737	0819	0837	0911	0937	1037	1119	1137	1237	1337	1437	1537	1637	1720	1737	1837	1916j	1937	2037	2137	...
Chagny d.	0602	0617	0647	0647	0747	0830	0848	0922	0947	1047	1129	1147	1247	1347	1448	1547	1648	1729	1747	1848	1930	1947	2047	2148	...
Beaune 373 d.	0611	0628	0657	0658	0757	0842	0859	0942	0958	1058	1140	1158	1258	1358	1459	1558	1659	1743	1758	1900	1942	1958	2058	2202	...
Dijon 373 a.	0639	0702	0722	0722	0822	0915	0922	1017	1022	1122	1215	1222	1322	1422	1522	1622	1722	1816	1822	1926	2015	2022	2122	2227	...
Paris Bercy 371 a.	...	...	1022	1022	...	...	1222	...	...	...	...	...	1629v	...	1822	...	2022	...	...	2222	...	...	...	...	...

Additional local trains DIJON - CHALON SUR SAÔNE and MÂCON - LYON ◇

	⚒		Ⓐ		Ⓐ		Ⓐ			Ⓐ
Dijon d.	0643	0810	1044	1221	1444	1621r	1716	1744	1826	1921
Beaune d.	0711	0852	1114	1250	1513	1649r	1752	1815	1852	1948
Chagny d.	0727	0902	1130	1306	1530	1701	1807	1831	1905	2001
Chalon sur Saône a.	0742	0918	1141	1322	1541	1718	1821	1841	1921	2018

	Ⓐ	Ⓐ	⚒	Ⓐ		⚒	Ⓐ		Ⓐ	Ⓑ
Chalon sur Saône d.	0619	0643	0719	0743	1241	1421	1619	1643	1743	1817
Chagny d.	0630	0659	0729	0759	1255	1430	1629	1659	1759	1832
Beaune d.	0641	0707	0741	0808	1303	1442	1642	1709	1808	1845
Dijon a.	0715	0738	0815	0838	1333	1516	1715	1738	1838	1918

	Ⓐ	⚒	Ⓐ	Ⓐ	⑥	Ⓐ	Ⓐ		Ⓐ	
Mâcon Ville d.	0602	0635	0725	0735	0735	0825	0835	1235	1735	1835
Villefranche sur Saône ⊖ d.	0635	0706	0750	0806	0806	0850	0906	1306	1806	1906
Lyon Part Dieu a.	0700	|	0814	|	|	0914	|	|	|	|
Lyon Perrache ▷ a.	...	0735	0826	0835	0840	0926	0935	1335	1835	1935

	Ⓐ		Ⓐ	Ⓐ	Ⓐ	⚒	Ⓐ	Ⓐ		Ⓐ
Lyon Perrache ▷ d.	0725	0825	1324	1625	1633	1724	1733	1825	1925	2204n
Lyon Part Dieu d.	|	|	|	|	1646	|	1746	|	|	2216
Villefranche sur Saône ⊖ d.	0755	0855	1355	1655	1710	1756	1810	1855	2000	2240
Mâcon Ville a.	0825	0925	1425	1725	1733	1825	1833	1925	2030	2302

d – Not Apr. 18, May 2, 9, 26, June 6.
e – Also Apr. 17, May 1, 8, June 5.
f – 2–4 minutes later on ⑤ (also May 24).
g – Also Apr. 18, May 9, June 6; not Apr. 17, May 1, 8, June 5.
j – Arrives 1900.
n – Not Jan. 30 - Apr. 7.
r – 2 minutes earlier on ⑤ (also May 24).
s – From Sens on ⚒ (Table **371**).
t – Until May 14.
v – 1622 on ©.
z – Change trains at Dijon on ⑤ (also May 24).
⊠ – Runs 5–11 minutes later Jan. 16 - Apr. 16 and from June 5.
◇ – Certain trains continue beyond Lyon to / from Valence.
▷ – Lyon Perrache timings may vary by up to 3 minutes (earlier departures possible).
⊖ – Villefranche is also served by 🚌 service to Mâcon Loché TGV station, connecting with *TGV* trains to / from Paris (Tables **340/1**).

Local Services — LYON - LONS-LE-SAUNIER - BESANÇON - BELFORT — 378

For *TGV* services Lyon - Besançon Franche-Comté TGV - Belfort Montbéliard TGV (- Strasbourg) via high-speed line see Table **379**. Lyon services are subject to alteration May 25–28.

km		†	⚒	⚒	Ⓐ	Ⓐ	Ⓐ		Ⓐ	Ⓒ				⚒	*TGV* 6874 S	Ⓒ	Ⓐ	Ⓐ		Ⓒ	Ⓐ	Ⓑ	Ⓐ	Ⓒ	⑤† f
0	**Lyon** Perrache 353 d.	...	...	...	...	...	...	0717	...	...	...	...	...	...	...	...	...	...	...	1617	1617	1712	1817	1817	2113
5	**Lyon** Part-Dieu 353 d.	...	...	...	...	...	...	0734	0941	0941	...	...	...	...	1433	...	...	...	...	1630	1630	1730	1830	1830	2125
	Ambérieu 353 d.	...	...	...	...	...	...	|	|	|	...	...	...	...	|	...	...	...	...	|	|	1758	1859	1859	|
65	Bourg-en-Bresse 353 d.	...	...	...	...	...	0717	0817	1021	1020	...	...	...	...	1519	...	...	...	...	1719	1719	1817	1919	1919	2232
129	**Lons-le-Saunier** d.	...	0544	0613	0643	...	0759	0859	1101	1101	...	...	1218	1501	1600	1605	1605	1701	1713	1801	1801	1857	2001	2002	2312
178	Mouchard d.	...	0627	0702	0722	0802	0841	0937	1139	1139	...	1225	1302	1539	|	1641	1642	1737	1802	1841	1842	...	2041	2042	...
218	**Besançon** Viotte a.	...	0710	0742	0755	0844	0909	1009	1209	1209	...	1255	1342	1609	1654	1709	1709	1809	1844	1909	1909	...	2109	2109	...
218	**Besançon** Viotte ▷ d.	0711	0712	...	0811	...	...	1011	1211j	...	1232	...	...	...	1657	...	1711	1811	...	...	1911	...	...	2115	...
297	Montbéliard ▷ d.	0808	0808	...	0908	...	...	1109	1309j	...	1341	...	...	...	|	...	1809	1908	...	...	2010	...	...	2213	...
315	**Belfort** ▷ a.	0824	0824	...	0924	...	...	1125	1324j	...	1356	...	...	...	1727z	...	1825	1924	...	...	2025	...	...	2229	...

	⚒	Ⓐ	Ⓐ		Ⓐ	⚒	†		⚒		*TGV* 6837 S◇				⑥	Ⓐ	†	Ⓑ	Ⓐ		⑥	Ⓐ	Ⓐ		
Belfort ▷ d.	...	...	0504	...	0636	0736	...	...	0936	...	1232z	1204	...	1336	1536	1536	1536	...	1636	...	...	1732	...	1838	1937
Montbéliard ▷ d.	...	...	0518	...	0653	0751	...	...	0953	...	|	1218	...	1352	1553	1553	1552	...	1653	...	...	1748	...	1853	1953
Besançon Viotte ▷ a.	...	...	0620	...	0749	0849	...	...	1048	...	1259	1330	...	1449	1649	1649	1649	...	1749	...	...	1849	...	1951	2050
Besançon Viotte d.	...	0601	...	0651	0751	0851	0851	1004	1051	1218	1302	...	1351	1452	1651	1651	1651	1726	1751	1817	1850	1851	1925	1953	...
Mouchard d.	...	0641	...	0722	0822	0919	0920	1034	1121	1300	|	...	1423	1520	1721	1720	1722	1806	1822	1900	1922	1922	2004	2023	...
Lons-le-Saunier d.	0600	0730	...	0759	0857	1001	1001	...	1200	1344	1401	...	1500	1603	1800	1802	1802	...	1900	1944	2001	2000	...	2102	...
Bourg-en-Bresse 353 d.	0642	...	...	0844	...	1045	1045	...	...	...	1437	...	...	1646	...	1843	1846	...	...	...	...	...	...	2146	...
Ambérieu 353 d.	|	...	...	0902	...	|	|	...	...	...	|	...	...	|	...	...	|	...	...	...	...	...	...	|	...
Lyon Part-Dieu 353 a.	0731	...	...	0926	...	1126	1126	...	...	...	1526	...	...	1726	...	...	1926v	...	...	...	...	...	...	2230	...
Lyon Perrache 353 a.	0743	...	...	0947a	...	1139	1139	...	...	...	...	...	...	1738	...	...	1938v	...	...	...	...	...	...	2243b	...

ADDITIONAL LOCAL TRAINS BESANÇON - BELFORT

	Ⓐ	Ⓐ	Ⓑ		Ⓐ					Ⓐ
Dijon 374 d.	...	0509‡	...	0613	...	...	...	1613	1711	...
Besançon Viotte d.	0530	0608	0632	0732	1311	1511	1632	1732	1832	2011
Montbéliard d.	0640	0711	0741	0842	1408	1608k	1741	1842	1942	2108
Belfort a.	0655	0726	0756	0856	1424	1624k	1756	1856	1956	2124

	Ⓐ	Ⓐ	Ⓐ	†	Ⓐ						⚒
Belfort d.	0604	0704	0804	0836	0936	1136	1304	1704	1819	2034	2136
Montbéliard d.	0618	0718	0818	0853	0953	1153	1318	1718	1833	2050	2151
Besançon Viotte a.	0728	0828	...	0950	1049	1251	1428	1828	1944	2149	...
Dijon 374 a.	0847	...	...	...	...	...	...	1947‡	...	...	...

S – [12] Strasbourg - Lyon - Marseille and v.v. See also Table **379**.

a – Ⓐ (not Jan. 30 - Apr. 7).
b – Not Jan. 30 - Apr. 8.
f – Also May 24.
j – 4 minutes later on ① (also Apr. 18, May 2, 9, 26, June 6).
k – On ⑥ Montbéliard d. 1611, Belfort a. 1626.
v – On Apr. 17, May 1, 8, June 5 terminates at Lyon Part Dieu (a. 1934).
z – Belfort Montbéliard TGV station (see Table **379**).

TGV – [R], supplement payable, 🍷.

◇ – Subject to alteration May 2–5, 15–19, 25–31, June 1, 2, 12–16, 26–30.
‡ – Subject to alteration from May 15.
▷ – For additional trains Besançon - Belfort and v.v. see panel below main table.

Local trains BELFORT - MULHOUSE — 378a

	Ⓐ		Ⓐn	⚒	Ⓐ	Ⓒ	Ⓐn	Ⓐn	Ⓒ	Ⓐn	Ⓐ‡	Ⓐ	Ⓒ	Ⓐ	n	Ⓐn	Ⓐ	n	Ⓐ	†	Ⓐ	⚒n	†	Ⓐ	Ⓐn	⑥	†
Belfort d.	0529	0558	0631	0700	0732	0736	0806	0906	1004	1006	1106	1206	1211	1303	1404r	1506	1606	1706	1736	1754	1806	1843	1855	1905	2005	2015	2042
Altkirch d.	0550	0618	0652	0721	0752	0756	0827	0927	1026	1027	1127	1227	1235	1327	1426	1526	1627	1727	1758	1820	1828	1909	1921	1927	2026	2035	2106
Mulhouse a.	0609	0636	0710	0740	0810	0815	0839	0939	1039	1040	1139	1239	1246	1339	1439	1539	1639	1739	1809	1839	1840	1921	1939	1939	2039	2049	2119

km		Ⓐ		Ⓐn	Ⓐ		Ⓐn	Ⓐn‡	Ⓒ	Ⓐ			Ⓐn	Ⓐ	†	⚒n	Ⓐn	Ⓐ	n	Ⓐ	Ⓐ	⑥	†	Ⓐn	Ⓐ	n	Ⓐb
0	**Mulhouse** d.	0620	0646	0723	0801	0823	0923	1023	1123	1220	1315	...	1423	1522	1559	1619	1650	1719	1750	1823	1851	1928	1928	1931	2020	2056	2204
16	Altkirch d.	0632	0658	0735	0815	0835	0935	1035	1135	1235	1334	...	1435	1537	1618	1638	1708	1739	1808	1838	1910	1945	1947	1954	2038	2110	2229
19	**Belfort** a.	0653	0722	0757	0838	0856	0956	1056	1156	1256	1355	...	1456	1557	1639	1659	1729	1800	1829	1858	1932	2005	2011	2017	2059	2130	2321

b – Not Dec. 26, Apr. 14. By 🚌.
n – Not Dec. 26.
r – 1406 on Ⓐ.
‡ – Not May 9–12, 22–26, June 6–9, 19–23.

379 LUXEMBOURG - METZ - STRASBOURG - DIJON - LYON *TGV services*

Subject to alteration on June 10, 17. Timings may vary by a few minutes on certain dates – please check your TGV reservation for confirmed timings.

km		TGV 6839	TGV 6820	TGV 6886		TGV 9877		TGV 6837		TGV 9879	TGV 6815	TGV 6783		TGV 6825	TGV 6825		TGV 9580		TGV 6785		TGV 6827	TGV 6827	TGV 6827
												⑤		W	⑤⑦				⑥		Ⓒ	Ⓐ	E
			⊕	⊕				◇		⊠				T	ZT		F					✣	
	Luxembourg 384 d.	...	...	...	...	0723	...	...	...	1124	...	...	...	...	...	...	...	...	...	...	...	...	...
	Thionville 384 d.	...	...	...	...	0747	...	...	...	1146	...	...	...	...	...	...	...	...	...	...	...	...	...
	Metz 384 d.	...	0544	...	...	0811	...	...	...	1207	...	...	...	...	...	...	...	...	...	...	...	...	...
	Strasbourg 383 a.	...	|	...	...	0901	...	...	...	1255	...	...	...	...	...	...	...	...	...	...	...	...	...
0	**Strasbourg** 383 385 d.	0623	|	...	...	0906	...	1112	...	1304	...	...	...	...	...	...	1615	...	...	...	1803	1836	1836
65	Colmar 385 d.	|	|	...	...	0934	...	|	...	1332	...	...	...	...	...	...	|	...	...	...	1831	|	|
	Basel 385 d.	|	|	0732	...	|	...	|	...	|	...	...	...	...	...	...	|	...	...	...	|	|	|
106	**Mulhouse** 370 d.	|	|	0756	...	1004**b**	...	1207	...	1400**b**	...	...	...	...	...	...	1708	...	...	...	|	|	|
151	Belfort Montbéliard TGV 370 d.	0728	|	0820	...	1029	...	1232	...	1425	...	...	...	...	...	...	1734	...	...	...	1928	1943	1943
233	**Besançon TGV** ⊖ 370 d.	0751	|	0844	...	1053	...	1302**v**	...	1448	...	...	...	...	...	...	1758	...	...	...	1950	2006	2006
	Nancy d.	|	0624	|	...	|	...	|	...	|	...	...	...	1507	1507	...	|	...	...	...	|	|	|
	Toul d.	|	0647	|	...	|	...	|	...	|	...	...	...	|	|	...	|	...	...	...	|	|	|
	Neufchâteau d.	|	0717	|	...	|	...	|	...	|	...	...	...	|	|	...	|	...	...	...	|	|	|
	Culmont Chalindrey d.	|	0814	|	...	|	...	|	...	|	...	...	...	|	|	...	|	...	...	...	|	|	|
	Paris Gare de Lyon **370** d.	|	|	|	...	|	...	⊙	...	|	...	1453	...	|	|	...	|	...	1653	...	|	|	|
310	**Dijon** 370 a.	0818	0906	0911	...	|	...	|	...	1515	...	1634	...	1719	1719	...	|	...	1834	...	2018	|	|
310	**Dijon** 377 d.	0825	0921	0921	...	|	...	|	...	1525	1606	1644	...	1729	1729	1744	|	...	1846	...	2030	|	|
347	Beaune 377 d.	|	|	|	...	|	...	|	...	|	1632	1710	...	|	|	1815	|	...	1912	...	|	|	|
377	**Chalon sur Saône** 377 d.	|	1002	1002	...	|	...	|	...	|	1652	1730	...	|	|	1841	1859	...	1931	...	|	|	|
435	Mâcon Ville 377 d.	|	|	|	...	1221	...	|	...	|	1722	...	...	1844	1844	...	|	...	...	...	|	|	|
507	**Lyon** Part Dieu 377 a.	1001	1102	1102	...	1256	...	1526	...	1702	1756	...	...	1930	1930	...	1956	...	...	...	2156	2156	2156
	Lyon Perrache a.	|	|	|	...	|	...	|	...	|	|	...	...	|	|	...	|	...	...	...	|	|	|
	Valence TGV **350** a.	|	|	|	...	1344	...	1610	...	1745	1838	...	...	2011	|	...	|	...	...	...	|	|	|
	Avignon TGV **350** a.	|	1207	1207	...	1425	...	1643	...	|	|	...	...	|	|	...	2105	...	...	...	2308	2308	2320**c**
	Aix en Provence TGV **350** a.	|	1235	1235	...	1453	...	|	...	|	1933	...	...	|	|	...	2133	...	...	...	2339	2339	|
	Marseille **350** a.	|	1250	1250	...	1512	...	1722	...	|	1948	...	...	|	|	...	2148	...	...	...	2354	2354	0018
	Toulon **350** a.	|	1342	...	...	...	...	...	...	|	2042	...	...	|	|	...	...	...	...	...	...	...	...
	Nice **360** a.	|	1546	...	...	...	...	...	...	|	2239	...	...	|	|	...	...	...	...	...	...	...	...
	Nîmes **355** a.	1117	...	...	...	...	...	...	...	1832	...	...	...	2057	2103	...	...	...	...	...	...	...	...
	Montpellier **355** a.	1144	...	...	...	...	...	...	...	1902	...	...	...	2126	2130	...	...	...	...	...	...	...	...

km		TGV 6898	TGV 6898		TGV 6869	TGV 9582			TGV 9896	TGV 6814		TGV 6874		TGV 6784	TGV 6882		TGV 6885	TGV 6864		TGV 9898	TGV 9898	TGV 9898	TGV 9898
		Ⓐ	Ⓒ											⑦									
					T	F			⊗			¶		e	⊡			△		⑤	②–④	①	⑥⑦
	Montpellier **355** d.	...	...	...	0802	...	...	...	1000	...	...	...	...	...	1411	...	...	...	...	...	...	...	...
	Nîmes **355** d.	...	...	...	0831	...	...	...	1027	...	...	...	...	...	1443	...	...	...	...	...	...	...	...
	Nice **360** d.	...	...	...	|	...	...	...	|	0723	...	...	...	...	|	...	...	1222	...	...	...	...	...
	Toulon **350** d.	...	...	...	|	...	...	...	|	0921	...	...	...	...	|	...	...	1414	...	...	...	...	...
	Marseille **350** d.	0640	0640	...	|	0810	...	...	|	1014	...	1239	...	...	|	...	1508	1508	...	1602	1604	1604	1609
	Aix en Provence TGV **350** d.	|	|	...	|	0825	...	...	|	1029	...	1253	...	...	|	...	1523	1523	...	1617	1618	1621	1625
	Avignon TGV **350** d.	0716	0716	...	|	0853	...	...	|	|	...	1322	...	...	|	...	1551	1551	...	1647	1646	1652	1653
	Valence TGV **350** d.	0750	0750	...	0916	|	...	...	1115	1125	...	|	...	...	1529	...	|	|	...	|	|	|	|
	Lyon Perrache d.	|	|	...	|	|	...	...	|	|	...	|	...	...	|	...	|	|	...	|	|	|	|
0	**Lyon** Part Dieu 377 d.	0833	0833	...	0954	1000	...	...	1204	1208	...	1433	...	...	1608	...	1704	1704	...	1804	1804	1804	1804
72	Mâcon Ville 377 d.	|	|	...	1031	|	...	...	|	1245	...	|	...	...	|	...	|	|	...	1841	1841	1841	1841
130	**Chalon sur Saône** 377 d.	|	|	...	|	1102	1119	...	|	1314	...	|	...	1629	|	...	1808	1808	...	|	|	|	|
160	Beaune 377 d.	|	|	...	|	|	1140	...	|	1338	...	|	...	1649	|	...	|	|	...	|	|	|	|
197	**Dijon** 377 a.	|	1000	...	1133	|	1215	...	1337	1359	...	|	...	1715	1744	...	1847	1847	...	|	|	|	|
197	**Dijon** 370 d.	|	1008**n**	...	1143**t**	|	...	...	1346	...	...	|	...	1725	1759	...	1909	1905	...	|	|	|	|
	Paris Gare de Lyon **370** a.	|	|	...	|	|	...	...	|	...	...	⊙	...	1907	|	...	|	|	...	|	|	|	|
274	Culmont Chalindrey d.	|	|	...	|	|	...	...	|	...	...	|	...	...	|	...	|	1957	...	|	|	|	|
348	Neufchâteau d.	|	|	...	|	|	...	...	|	...	...	|	...	...	|	...	|	2045	...	|	|	|	|
392	Toul a.	|	|	...	|	|	...	...	|	...	...	|	...	...	|	...	|	2109	...	|	|	|	|
425	**Nancy** a.	|	|	...	1356**t**	|	...	...	|	...	...	|	...	...	|	...	|	2136	...	|	|	|	|
	Besançon TGV ⊖ 370 d.	1029	1037	...	...	1206	...	...	1415	...	...	1657**v**	...	...	1829	...	1939	|	...	2012	2012	2012	2012
	Belfort Montbéliard TGV 370 d.	1052	1100	...	...	1230	...	...	1438	...	...	1730	...	...	1853	...	2003	|	...	2036	2036	2036	2036
	Mulhouse 370 d.	|	1126	...	...	1255	...	...	1502	...	...	1804	...	...	|	...	2034**b**	|	...	2109**b**	2109**b**	2109**b**	2109**b**
	Basel 385 a.	|	|	...	...	|	...	...	|	...	...	|	...	...	|	...	2055	|	...	|	|	|	|
	Colmar 385 d.	|	1154	...	...	|	...	...	1531	...	...	|	...	...	|	...	...	|	...	2129	2129	2129	2129
	Strasbourg 385 a.	1152	1219	...	...	1344	...	...	1556	...	...	1857	...	...	1955	...	...	|	...	2155	2155	2155	2155
	Strasbourg 383 d.	...	...	...	...	...	...	...	1600	...	...	...	...	...	...	...	...	|	...	2208	2208	2208	2208
	Metz 383 384 a.	...	...	...	...	...	...	...	1648	...	...	...	...	...	...	...	...	2219	...	2256	2256	2256	2256
	Thionville 384 a.	...	...	...	...	...	...	...	1709	...	...	...	...	...	...	...	...	...	...	2316	2316	2316	2316
	Luxembourg 384 a.	...	...	...	...	...	...	...	1735	...	...	...	...	...	...	...	...	...	...	2351	2351	2351	2351

E – Jan. 16–19, 24–26, Feb. 27, 28, Mar. 1, 2, 7–9, Apr. 3–6, 11–13.
F – 12 Frankfurt - Strasbourg - Marseille and v.v. (Table **47**).
T – To / from Toulouse (Table **321**).
W – ①②③④⑥ (not Apr. 17, May 1, 8, 25, June 5). Subject to alteration on May 26, 27, June 3. Does not run Nancy - Dijon on ①–④ from May 2.
Z – Subject to alteration on Feb. 26, May 14, 21, 26, 28. Does not run Nancy -Dijon on ⑤ from May 5.

b – Arrives 9–12 minutes earlier.
c – Avignon **Centre**.
e – Also Apr. 17, May 1, 8, June 5.
n – 1005 from May 20.
t – Daily to Apr. 30; Ⓒ from May 6.
v – Besançon **Viotte**.

TGV –Ⓡ, supplement payable, 🍸.

✣ – Not Jan. 16–19, 24–26, Feb. 27, 28, Mar. 1, 2, 7–9, Apr. 3–6, 11–13. Subject to alteration.

⊡ – Subject to alteration on May 26, 27.
⊕ – Subject to alteration on Feb. 26, May 7, 21.
¶ – Subject to alteration on May 25, 26, 27.
△ – Subject to alteration on Jan. 22, May 6, 7, 20, 21.
⊗ – Subject to alteration on May 27, 28, June 4.
◇ – Subject to alteration May 2–5, 15–19, 25–31, June 1, 2, 12–16, 26–30.
⊠ – Subject to alteration on Jan. 16, Feb. 6, 13, 20, May 26, 27, 28.
⊙ – Via Lons le Saunier and Bourg en Bresse (Table **378**).
⊖ – Full name: Besançon Franche-Comté TGV.

380 PARIS - TROYES - BELFORT

km							11641	1541	1541	11643	1641		11645	1543	11647	1545		11649	1547	11741	11743	1549	1549	11745	11747
		⚒	⚒	Ⓐ	Ⓒ	Ⓐ	⚒		ⒶB	Ⓑ	⑥					Ⓑ	Ⓐ	Ⓐ	Ⓒ	Ⓐ			⑤E	Ⓑ	
					⊗			n														D			
0	**Paris** Est d.	...	...	...	...	...	0642	0742	0742	0842	0842	...	1212	1312	1412	1512	...	1642	1642	1712	1812	1842	1842	1942	2042
110	Nogent sur Seine d.	...	...	...	...	0651	0741	|	|	0941	0941	...	1311	|	1511	|	...	1741	1741	1817	1911	|	|	2041	2141
129	Romilly sur Seine d.	...	...	...	...	0703	0755	|	|	0955	0955	...	1325	|	1525	|	...	1755	1755	1831	1925	|	|	2055	2155
166	**Troyes** d.	...	...	0521	0650	0724	0816	0909	0909	1017	1019	...	1346	1439	1546	1639	...	1816	1816	1852	1949	2009	2017**f**	2117	2216
221	Bar sur Aube d.	...	...	0553	0722	0757	0852	|	|	...	|	...	1418	|	1619	|	...	1853	1853	...	2024	|	|	...	2248
262	Chaumont 382 d.	...	...	0616	0745	0818	0917	1001	1001	...	1109	...	1440	1530	1642	1731	...	1918	1918	...	2050	2103	2103	...	2311
296	Langres 382 d.	...	...	0637	0805	...	0938	|	|	...	|	...	1500	|	1703	|	...	1940	1940	...	2111	|	|	...	2331
307	Culmont Chalindrey 382 d.	...	...	0647	0825**f**	...	0946	|	1027	...	|	...	1508	|	1710	1757	...	1949	1951	...	2119	|	|	...	2338
	Dijon 382 a.	...	...	0736	0915	...	...	|	...	...	|	...	...	|	...	|	...	...	|	...	...	|	|	...	...
380	Vesoul d.	0731	0839	...	...	...	...	1104	...	...	1211	1239	...	1633**j**	...	1837	1912	...	2029**k**	...	...	2206	2203	...	...
410	Lure 386a d.	0751	0856	...	...	...	...	1124	...	...	...	1256	...	1654**j**	...	1857	1929	...	2050**k**	...	...	2225	2222	...	...
442	**Belfort** 386a a.	0820	0925	...	...	...	...	1144	...	...	...	1325	...	1714**j**	...	1917	1958	...	2112**k**	...	...	2246	2240	...	...

FOR BELFORT - TROYES - PARIS SEE NEXT PAGE

B – May 29 - June 23 only.
D – Daily to Feb. 9; ①②③④⑥⑦ from Feb. 11.
E – From Feb. 10.

f – Arrives 10 minutes earlier.
j – 8–11 minutes later Dec. 12–16.
k – 2–5 minutes later on Dec. 17, 24, 31.
n – Not ①–⑤ May 29 - June 23.
r – 8–9 minutes later on ⑥ to Feb. 25.
t – From Feb. 5.

⊗ – Subject to alteration on Feb. 26, June 11, 18, 25.
△ – Subject to alteration on ①–⑤ Feb. 6 - Mar. 17, ①–⑤ Apr. 17–28 (also on Feb. 26, June 11, 18, 25).
▽ – Subject to alteration on ①–⑤ Feb. 6 - Mar. 10, ①–⑤ Apr. 24 - May 12 (also on Feb. 26, June 10, 17).
◇ – On Mar. 10, Apr. 21, 28, May 5, 12, 19 does not run Belfort - Troyes.
⊠ – Until Jan. 29 departs Troyes 1547 and calls additionally at Romilly (d. 1608) and Nogent (d. 1622).

Subject to alteration Apr. 15–17, May 6–8, June 5

BELFORT - TROYES - PARIS — 380

	11640	11642	11644		1646	1540	11646	11648	1542	11740		1544		1642	1546	11746	11748	1548	11842	1644	1640
	Ⓐ	�ख	Ⓐ		Ⓐ		⑥	Ⓐ	†			†⊠		⑥	†			†	✕	Ⓐ	†
Belfort .... 386a d.	...	...	...	...	0459	0512	...	...	0820	...		1235	1320	...	1443	...	...	1648	...	1756	1808	...	1838	2035
Lure .... 386a d.	...	...	...	...	0519	0534	...	...	0842	...		1303	1342	...	1504	...	...	1709	...	1816	1828	...	1906	2103
Vesoul .... d.	...	...	...	...	0539	0554	...	...	0902	...		1321	1400	...	1520	1523	...	1729	...	1834	1847	...	1924	2121
Dijon .... 382 d.	...	...	...	...						1134			1405	...		1551	...		1858				
Culmont Chalindrey .. 382 d.	...	...	0525	0610	0619		0644	0817		1047	1223		1453			1644	...		1817	1915	1927	2000	
Langres .... 382 d.	...	...	0536	0619	0628		0654	0826		1056	1233		1503			1653	...		1826	1924		2011	
Chaumont .... 382 d.	...	...	0558	0640	0649	0657	0716	0847	1005	1116	1257	11742	1513	1524	1625	1626	...	1715	1833	1947	1945	1955	2053
Bar sur Aube .... d.	...	...	0620	0702	0711		0738	0909		1138	1319		1545			1738	...		1909	2007		2056	
Troyes .... d.	0512	0602r	0655	0732	0744	0742	0814	0945	1051	1212	1349	1412	1550	1616	1712	1712	1712	1812	1920	1942	2041	2042	2130
Romilly sur Seine ...... d.	0535	0625r	0718		0804	0804	0834	1005		1233		1435			1735	1735	1735	1833		2003		2056	
Nogent sur Seine .... d.	0548	0638r	0732		0818	0817	0848	1017		1246		1448			1748	1748	1748	1847		2017	2117t		
Paris Est .... a.	0646	0746	0831		0916	0916	0946	1116	1216	1346		1546	1716		1846	1846	1846	1946	2046	2116	2216	2216	

← FOR NOTES SEE FOOT OF PREVIOUS PAGE

PARIS - CHÂLONS EN CHAMPAGNE - BAR LE DUC — 381

km		Ⓐ	Ⓐ		Ⓐ	Ⓐ	⑥	Ⓐ	†		2777	Ⓐ	Ⓐ	†			2785 ①–④	⑤	2787 ©①–④	⑤	†
						◇		▽			♥ ♥꣸ ▥						♥ m	f	e♥	m	f h
0	Paris Est .... d.	0636	0736	...	0836	0836	1036	1036	1236	1426	1436	1636	1736	...	1836	1928	1936	1936	2028	2036	2136	2236
95	Château Thierry .... d.	0724	0824	...	0924	0924	1124	1124	1324		1524	1724	1831	...	1932		2031	2032		2124	2224	2224	2324
142	Épernay .... d.	0752	0852	...	0948	0952	1152	1152	1352		1552	1752	1858	...	1959		2058	2059		2152	2250	2252	2352
	Champagne-Ardenne TGV . d.							1511							2010			2112			
*172	Châlons en Champagne 382a d.	0810	0910	0915	1008	1010	1210	1210	1410	1535	1636	1810	1914	1928	2016	2037	2114	2121	2136	2208	2308	2310	0008
205	Vitry le François .... 382a d.	0828	0928	0934		1028	1228	1228		1428	1554	1628	1810		1949	2034	2056		2141	2156		2328	
234	St Dizier .... 382a a.	0846		0954		1054	1246	1252		1446		1646	1922z		2007	2052		2159			2357	
255	Bar le Duc .... 382a a.		0952			1052		1252		1618		1852			2120		2221			2352	

		Ⓐ	✕	Ⓐ	①–⑥	Ⓐ	②–⑤	A	†	⑥	Ⓐ	†	⑥				♥⊗	Ⓐ	Ⓑ	
					b♥		c				©	⊕	▱	◇						2784
											☉	⊕	▱	◇						
Bar le Duc .... 382a d.	...	...	0611	...	...	...	...	0937	...	1137	...	1337	...	...	1712	...	...	...	1937
St Dizier .... 382a d.	...	0558	...	0636	...	0737	0930	0933	0937	...	1122	...	1330	...	1537	...	1658	...	1737	1837	1937	...
Vitry le François ...... 382a d.	...	0617	0637	0658	...	0758	0950	0952	0958	...	1003	1143	1201	1351	1405	1558	...	1716	1738	1758	1858	1957	2002
Châlons en Champagne . 382a d.	0516	0613	0637	0655	0716	0815	0816	1008	...	1016	1016	1021	1204	1218	1410	1422	1616	1716	1733	1756	1816	1916	2015	2021
	Champagne-Ardenne TGV .. d.				0718															1820		
Épernay .... 382a d.	0535	0631	...	0732	0832	0832	...	1032	1037	1037	...	1233	...	1438	1632	1733	...	1832	1932	...	2037
Château Thierry .... d.	0601	0701	...	0801	0901	0901	...	1101	1101	1101	...	1301	...	1501	1701	1801	...	1901	2001	...	2117
Paris Est .... a.	0653	0753	...	0853	0953	0953	...	1153	1153	1153	...	1353	...	1553	1753	1853	...	1953	2053	...	2153

A – ①⑥⑦ (also Apr. 18, May 2, 9, 25, 26, June 6).
b – Not Apr. 17, May 1, 8, June 5.
c – Not Apr. 18, May 2, 9, 25, 26, June 6.
e – Also Apr. 17, May 1, 8, June 5.
f – Also May 24.
h – Not June 5.
m – Not Apr. 17, May 1, 8, 24, 25, June 5.
r – On † Reims 1036, Châlons 1116.
z – 1854 on †; 1858 on ⑥.

♥ – TGV train, ▥, supplement payable. ॰.
◇ – Subject to alteration from Feb. 13.
▽ – Subject to alteration on Feb. 28 and ①–⑤ Mar. 20 - Apr. 7.
▥ – Subject to alteration on Mar. 27–31, Apr. 3–7.
⊕ – Subject to alteration on Mar. 23, 27–31, Apr. 3–7. On ①–⑤ Feb. 13 - Mar. 24 (not Mar. 24; not Mar. 24) and on Ⓐ from May 29 does not run Bar le Duc – Châlons (departs Châlons 1215).
⊗ – Does not run Bar le Duc - Vitry Mar. 27–31, May 2-19.
† – Subject to alteration Mar. 13 - Apr. 28, May 15–26.

▱ – Subject to alteration Feb. 20 - Apr. 28, May 15–24.
꣸ – Subject to alteration Feb. 6–10, Mar. 31, Apr. 3–7. Terminates at Châlons Mar. 20–24. Terminates at Vitry Mar. 27–30, May 2–5, 8–19.
‡ – Subject to alteration on dates in Table 382a.
* – 188 km via high-speed line.

Certain services are subject to alteration on May 6, 7

BAR LE DUC - METZ / NANCY — 382

km		Ⓐ	✕	Ⓐ	Ⓐ	⑥	ⒶR	©R	⑥			Ⓐ			†	Ⓐ◇	✕⊗	Ⓑ◇	⑥			ⒶR		†	⑥R	†R
0	Bar le Duc ..♥ d.	0513	0554	0613	0726	0731	0754	0920	0926	1003	1113	1126	1213	1226	1305	1426	1506	1626	1713	1736	1821	1826	1905	1913	1929	2021	2126
40	Commercy .... d.	0539	0614	0639	0746	0750	0814	0944	0946	1024	1138	1146	1238	1246	1326	1446	1546	1646	1738	1746	1841	1846	1929	1938	1949	2044	2146
66	Toul .... d.	0559	0629	0658	0801	0804	0829	0957	1001	1037	1157	1201	1257	1301	1339	1501	1601	1701	1757	1801	1856	1901	1939	1957	2004	2059	2201
99	Nancy .... a.	0625	0653	0725	0825	0830	0854	1021	1025	1101	1224	1225	1325	1325	1404	1525	1625	1725	1826	1825	2005	2004	2025	2123	2225

		Ⓐ		ⒶR	⑥	✕	Ⓐ		©	Ⓐ◇	⑥		Ⓐ◇	⑥	©R	Ⓐ		⑥	ⒶR	Ⓑ R		✕	Ⓐ	Ⓑ	⑥E
Nancy .... d.	0507		0632	0640	0734	0834	0934		1032	1134	1234	1234	1334	1434	1434	1534	1607	1607	1634	1707	1734	1734	1834	1934	...	2034	2034
Toul .... d.	0531		0651	0704	0758	0858	0958		1051	1158	1258	1259	1359	1458	1458	1558	1630	1634	1657	1733	1758	1758	1858	1959	...	2058	2058
Commercy .... d.	0545		0704	0718	0812	0912	1012		1106	1212	1312	1314	1414	1512	1512	1612	1645	1653	1712	1812	1812	1912	2018	...	2112	2112
Bar le Duc ..♥ a.	0605		0723	0738	0832	0932	1032		1125	1232	1332	1342	1444	1532	1532	1632	1705	1718	1832	1832	1933	2043	...	2132	2132

E – From/to Épernay (Table 382a).
R – From/to Reims (Table 382a).
t – Not Dec. 26–30.

◇ – Subject to alteration on Ⓐ Feb. 20 - Apr. 21 and Ⓐ from May 29.
⊗ – Subject to alteration on Ⓐ Feb. 13 - Apr. 21 and Ⓐ from May 29.
† – Subject to alteration on ①–⑤ Feb. 6 - Mar. 10 and Apr. 24–28.

♥ – BAR LE DUC - METZ and v.v. (journey 55–61 minutes):
From Bar le Duc at 0716 ✕, 1308 Ⓐ t ◇, 1716 ⑥E and 1901 †.
From Metz at 0826 Ⓐ, 1235 ⑥, 1410 Ⓐ E ⊗, 1727 † and 1826 ✕.

Subject to alteration May 6–8

REIMS - CHÂLONS EN CHAMPAGNE - DIJON / BAR LE DUC — 382a

km		✕	✕	Ⓐ	Ⓐ	⑥	Ⓐ	②	Ⓐ	†	†	⑥	Ⓐ		Ⓐ	Ⓐ	†	Ⓐ	Ⓐ	†	⑥
							⊗	r‡	‡	▱	★								f△	
0	Reims .... ♠ d.	0552		0636	0725	0742	0836	1006	1136	1255	1506‡		1652	1656	1736	1736	1740	1806	1836	1835	1936a	2034	2236
	Épernay .... ♠ 381 d.	0644			0819						1614	1726			1826			1921			
58	Châlons en Champagne 381 d.	0704	0708	0726	0800	0841	0915	0919	1041	1211	1332	1546	1632	1742	1746	1813	1818	1820	1844	1928	1940	2021	2116j	2314
91	Vitry le François ... 381 d.	0723	0728		0819	0834	0934			1351	1608	1650	1759	1807	1813		1839	1901	1904	1949	1955	2041	2334
	Bar le Duc ...... 381 d.	0753			0923				1714	1825			1927			2020				
	Nancy 382 ...... a.	0854			1021				1925				2028			2123				
120	St Dizier .... 381 d.		0749		0841		0954		1410	1630		1831	1856		1858			1922	2007		2102	2353
193	Chaumont .... 380 d.		0835		0925				1454	1721		1925	1943						2149	
227	Langres .... 380 d.		0855		0946				1514	1741		1945	2003						2212	
238	Culmont Chalindrey .. 380 d.		0903		0956				1524	1751		1953	2013						2221	
315	Dijon .... 380 a.				1047				1626j	1855j			2101							

		✕	✕	Ⓐ	Ⓐ	⑥	Ⓐ	②	Ⓐ	⑥	Ⓐ	Ⓐ	Ⓐ	Ⓑ	⑤†	①–④	⑥	⑥	⑤
							¶		✔		¶					m			
Dijon .... 380 d.	...	...	...	...	...	...	1215	...	...	...	...	...	...	1809	1809	...	...	...
Culmont Chalindrey ...... 380 d.	...	0554	0649	...	...	1215	...	...	...	...	...	...	1859	1857	...	...	...
Langres .... 380 d.	...	0603	0658	...	...	1225	...	...	...	...	...	...	1909	1907	...	...	...
Chaumont .... 380 d.	...	0624	0718	...	1140	1246	...	...	...	...	...	1740	1750	1929	1928	...	...	...
St Dizier .... 381 d.	0558	0712	0807	...	1122	1248	1333	...	...	1658	...	...	1846	1859	...	2011	2012	...
Nancy 382 .... d.	...	0632	...	...	...	...	1434	...	1734	1734	...	...	...	...	...	...	2034
Bar le Duc ...... 381 d.	...	0724	...	...	...	1506	...	...	1833	1833	...	...	...	...	...	2133
Vitry le François ... 381 d.	0617	0733	0750	0828	...	1143	1250	1351	1531	1602	1716	...	1901	1902	1907	1920	2031	2039	2203
Châlons en Champagne 381 d.	0639	0752	0807	0854	0939t	1054	1204	1319	1410	1448b	1550	1586	1621	1654	1735	1849	1918	1920	1924	1938	1939c	2055	2101	2220
Épernay .... ♠ 381 d.	...	0838z	...	...	1605	1644	...	1940	2002v	...	...	2235
Reims .... ♠ a.	0730	0829	0906	0929	1029	1135	1259‡		1359	1529	...	1629	1715	1729	1825	1931	2007	2038	...	2029	2130	2140

a – Ⓐ only.
b – 1454 on Ⓐ.
c – 1954 on Ⓐ.
f – Also May 24.
j – 5–9 minutes earlier on ⑤.
m – Not Apr. 17, May 1, 8, 25, June 5.
r – On † Reims 1036, Châlons 1116.
¶ – 0954 on ⑤.
★ – Arrives 1935.
☀ – Arrives 0824.

★ – To Metz (a. 1817). Subject to alteration from Feb. 20.
● – From Metz (d. 1410). Subject to alteration Feb. 13 - Apr. 21 and from May 29.
⊗ – Subject to alteration Mar. 13 - Apr. 28 and May 15–26.
▱ – Subject to alteration on Ⓐ Jan. 30 - Apr. 12 and Apr. 24 - May 5.
‡ – Subject to alteration on ⑤ Jan. 30 - Feb. 17, Apr. 3–7, 24–28, May 2–5.
△ – Runs 2–4 minutes later Châlons - St Dizier on ⑤ (also May 24).
☙ – Subject to alteration Feb. 6–10 and Apr. 3–7.
☐ – Subject to alteration on ①–⑤ Feb. 20 - Mar. 17, Ⓐ Apr. 10–21.

♠ – Other local trains Épernay - Reims and v.v. (31 km; journey time 26–41 minutes):
From Épernay at 0533 Ⓐ, 0555 Ⓐ, 0618 Ⓐ, 0647 ✕, 0739 ✕, 0803 Ⓐ, 0933 Ⓐ, 0959 †, 1109 Ⓐ, 1203 †, 1206 Ⓐ, 1229 ✕Ⓐ, 1309 Ⓐ, 1403, 1533 ⑥, 1607 Ⓐ, 1637 Ⓐ, 1707 Ⓐ, 1730 Ⓐ, 1804, 1830 Ⓐ, 1903 Ⓐ, 2103 Ⓐ, 2203 Ⓐ and 2355 †.
From Reims at 0452 Ⓐ, 0652 ✕, 0722 Ⓐ, 0752 Ⓐ, 0822 Ⓐ, 0952, 1022 Ⓐ, 1052 Ⓐ, 1152 ⊡, 1222 ⑥, 1252 Ⓐ, 1322 Ⓐ, 1352 Ⓐ, 1422 ✕, 1552, 1652 †, 1722 Ⓐ, 1752 Ⓐ, 1822 Ⓐ, 1922 Ⓐ, 1952 ⑥, 2022 Ⓐ, 2052 Ⓐ, 2152 Ⓐ and 2222 ⑥.

383 METZ and NANCY - STRASBOURG

Subject to alteration Dec. 11 – 16. On Dec. 26, Apr. 14 most local services to / from Strasbourg run as on ⑦.

km		Ⓐ t	Ⓐ	⑥	Ⓐ	⚒	⚒	⚒	TGV 9877	Ⓐ	†		Ⓐ	Ⓒ	⚒	1001 ⑤⑥† w★	†	†	TGV 9879	TGV 2507 ⑦ e	Ⓐ	⚒	⑥	Ⓐ	Ⓐ
0	**Metz** ♥ d.	...	...	...	...	0634	...	0747	0811	...	...	...	0934	0942	...	...	1046	...	1207	...	...	1247	...	1343	...
	Paris Est d.	...	...	...	...	|	...	|	|	...	...	...	|	|	...	0821	|	...	|	1013	...	|	...	|	...
∆	**Nancy** 387 d.	...	...	...	0616	|	0716	|	|	0816	0816	...	|	|	1018	1109	|	1116	|	1151	1216	|	1316	|	1416
	Lunéville 387 d.	...	...	...	0634	|	0733	|	|	0834	0834	...	|	|	1036	1129	|	1134	|	|	1234	|	1332	|	1434
88	Sarrebourg ♥ d.	0535	0617	0633	0657	|	0800	0849	|	0857	0857	...	|	|	1059	1200	1149	1157	|	1232	1300	1349	1355	|	1457
91	Réding d.	0539	0622	0637	0701	0722	|	...	|	0901	|	...	1022	1030	|	|	...	|	|	|	|	...	1359	1430	1501
114	Saverne d.	0555	0638	0653	0716	0739	0816	...	|	0915	0915	...	1039	1046	1117	1220	...	1214	|	1250	1316	...	1414	1445	1515
159	**Strasbourg** a.	0634	0711	0734	0741	0811	0841	...	0901	0941	0941	...	1111	1111	1142	1246	...	1241	1255	1312	1341	...	1441	1511	1541

	†	Ⓐ	⑥	Ⓐ t	Ⓐ	†	†	Ⓑ	⑥	⑥	Ⓐ	Ⓐ	Ⓐ	Ⓐ	†	Ⓐ	Ⓑ	⚒	⑥	Ⓑ	Ⓐ	†	†	TGV 2583 Ⓐ y	TGV 2583 ⑦ z
Metz ♥ d.	...	...	...	...	...	1547	...	1643	1647	...	...	1717	...	1747	...	...	1843	...	1934	1947	...	...	2043	...	...
Paris Est d.	...	...	...	...	...	|	...	|	|	...	...	|	...	|	...	...	|	...	|	|	...	...	|	1913	1913
Nancy 387 d.	1416	...	1516	...	1616	|	1616	|	|	1716	1716	|	...	|	1816	1816	|	1916	|	|	...	2016	|	2048	2048
Lunéville 387 d.	1434	...	1533	...	1634	|	1634	|	|	1733	1734	|	...	|	1834	1834	|	1934	|	|	...	2033	|	2110	2110
Sarrebourg ♥ d.	1457	1551	1559	1618	1657	1649	1658	|	1749	1759	1800	1813	1818	1849	1856	1900	|	1957	2035	2049	2055	2057	|	2136	2139
Réding d.	|	1555	|	1623	1701	...	|	1730	...	|	|	...	1823	...	|	|	1931	|	|	...	|	|	2135	|	|
Saverne d.	1515	1611	1615	1639	1715	...	1715	1745	...	1815	1816	...	1840	...	1915	1915	1946	2016	2052	...	2111	2115	2151	2154	2157
Strasbourg a.	1541	1641	1641	1711	1741	...	1741	1811	...	1841	1841	...	1911	...	1941	1941	2011	2041	2117	...	2141	2141	2217	2217	2222

	TGV 2584 ①–⑥ b	⚒	Ⓐ	Ⓐ	Ⓐ	Ⓐ	⚒		†	Ⓐ	Ⓒ	⑥	Ⓐ	⚒		†	Ⓐ	Ⓐ	Ⓐ	⑥	Ⓐ t	1002 † ★[R]	TGV 2545 ⑦ e	TGV 9896 [R]	Ⓐ
Strasbourg d.	0541	...	0619	...	0649	0719	0749	0819	0949	1019	1019	...	...	1149	1219	1249	1249	1319	1419	1519	1519	1525	1551k	1600	...
Saverne d.	0606	...	0644	...	0715	0744	0814	0844	1015	1045	1044	...	...	1215	1245	1314	1315	1346	1445	1544	1549	1552	1615	|	...
Réding d.	|	...	|	...	0729	|	0828	|	1029	1100	|	...	...	1229	|	1329	1329	1359	|	|	1605	|	|	|	...
Sarrebourg ♥ d.	0624	0636	0700	0703	|	0800	|	0901	|	1104	1100	1111	1136	|	1303	|	|	1404	1503	1600	1609	1611	1632	|	1636
Lunéville 387 d.	0649	|	0725	|	|	0826	|	0925	|	1127	1126	|	|	|	1326	|	|	...	1526	1626	...	1635	|	|	|
Nancy 387 a.	0709	|	0744	|	|	0844	|	0944	|	1144	1145	|	|	|	1344	|	|	...	1544	1644	...	1655	1710	|	|
Paris Est a.	0846c	|	...	|	|	...	|	...	|	...	...	|	|	|	...	|	|	...	...	...	...	1954	1849	|	|
Metz ♥ a.	...	0736	...	0752	0815	...	0915	...	1116	...	...	1211	1236	1315	...	1415	1415	...	...	...	...	...	...	1648	1736

	Ⓐ	†	†	1002 ⑤ ★[R]	1002 ⑥ ★[R]	Ⓐ	Ⓐ	⑥	Ⓐ	⑥	†	Ⓐ	Ⓐ	†	†	Ⓐ	Ⓐ	⑥	†	Ⓐ	Ⓐ	⑥	†	Ⓐ	TGV 9898 [R]
Strasbourg d.	1619	1619	...	1613	1624	...	1649	1719	1719	...	1749	1749	...	1755	1819	1819	1849	1849	1849	1919	...	1949	1949	1949	2208
Saverne d.	1645	1645	...	1641	1651	...	1720	1745	1744	...	1822	1821	...	1837	1845	1844	1921	1915	1919	1945	...	2015	2015	2019	|
Réding d.	|	|	...	|	|	...	1727	1759	|	...	1839	1837	...	1851	|	1859	1937	1929	|	2000	...	|	|	2035	|
Sarrebourg ♥ d.	1703	1703	1711	1708	1711	1736	1740	1804	1802	1811	|	|	1842	1855	1903	1904	1940	|	1942	2004	2008	2033	2030	2038	|
Lunéville 387 d.	1726	1725	|	1738	1738	|	...	1826	1829	|	|	|	|	...	1926	1926	...	|	|	2026	|	2056	2056	...	|
Nancy 387 a.	1744	1745	|	1758	1758	|	...	1844	1846	|	|	|	|	...	1944	1944	...	|	|	2044	|	2114	2114	...	|
Paris Est a.	...	...	|	2053	2053	|	...	...	...	|	|	|	|	...	...	...	...	|	|	...	|	...	...	...	|
Metz ♥ a.	...	...	1811	...	...	1836	...	...	...	1911	1924	1926	1942	...	...	...	...	2015	2031	...	2057	...	...	...	2256

b – Not Apr. 17, May 1, 8, June 5.
c – 0848 on ⑥.
e – Also Apr. 17, May 1, 8, June 5.
k – 1543 on Dec. 11.
t – Not Dec. 26 – 30.

w – Not May 7, 8.
y – Not Dec. 26, Apr. 14.
z – Also Dec. 26, Apr. 14, 17, May 1, 8, June 5.

TGV – [R], supplement payable, 🍷.

★ – *INTERCITÉS 100% ÉCO.* Low-cost service via the classic route. [R].
♥ – Additional trains Metz to Sarrebourg and v.v.: From Metz at 0617 Ⓐ, 1617 Ⓐ and 1817 Ⓐ. From Sarrebourg at 0736 Ⓐ, 1211 †, 1411 ⑥ and 1849 †.
∆ – Nancy - Sarrebourg : *80* km.

384 LUXEMBOURG - METZ - NANCY

For *TGV* trains Luxembourg - Metz - Paris see Table **390**. For long distance trains to Lyon and southern France see Table **379**.

km		Ⓐ	Ⓐ	⚒	Ⓐ		Ⓐ	Ⓐ		⚒	Ⓐ		Ⓐ	⑥	Ⓐ		✣	Ⓐ			⚒⊗	Ⓐ⇊	Ⓒ🚌
0	**Nancy** d.	0528	0620	0650	0720	0750	0806	0820	0828	0850	0920	0950	1020	1050	1120	1150	and at the same	2020	2050	2150	2250	2328	2328
28	Pont-à-Mousson d.	0553	0637	0707	0737	0807	0824	0837	0853	0906	0937	1006	1037	1107	1137	1207	minutes past	2037	2106	2208	2307	2354	0019
37	Pagny sur Moselle d.	0602	0644	0714	0744	0815	0830	0844	0902	0913	0844	1013	1044	1114	1144	1214	each hour until	2044	2113	2216	2314	0002	|
57	**Metz** a.	0621	0657	0727	0757	0828	0844	0858	0921	0928	0958	1028	1058	1127	1158	1227		2058	2128	2228	2332	0021	0113

	Ⓐ	⚒	Ⓐ		Ⓐ		Ⓐ	⚒	Ⓐ	¶	Ⓐ	⚒	Ⓐ		Ⓐ	⊠		Ⓐ	w	Ⓑ		Ⓐ⇊	Ⓒ🚌
Metz d.	0602	0632	0702	0732	0802	0832	0902	0932	1002	1032	1102	1132	1202	1232	1302	and at the same	1932	2002	2032	2132	2232	2339	2339
Pagny sur Moselle d.	0617	0646	0716	0746	0816	0846	0916	0946	1016	1047	1116	1147	1216	1247	1316	minutes past	1947	2016	2046	2146	2246	2358	0009
Pont-à-Mousson d.	0624	0653	0723	0754	0823	0853	0923	0953	1023	1054	1123	1154	1223	1254	1323	each hour until	1954	2023	2053	2153	2253	0005	0024
Nancy a.	0641	0711	0740	0811	0839	0911	0940	1011	1040	1111	1140	1211	1240	1311	1340		2011	2040	2111h	2211	2311	0031	0116

(NANCY -) METZ - LUXEMBOURG

km		Ⓐ	Ⓐ t	⚒	Ⓐ	⚒	Ⓐ		Ⓐ t	⚒	†	Ⓐ	†	⑥	⚒⊙	✣	✣	✣	Ⓐ	Ⓐ		D	⑤ f		Ⓐ	
	Nancy ★ d.	...	...	...	0620	0650	0720	0750z	...	0850k	...	...	0950	...	1050k	1150	1250	1350	1450	...	1550	...	...	1650	1720	1750z
0	**Metz** d.	0533	0603	0633	0703	0733	0803	0833	0903	0933	0946	1030	1033	1042	1133	1233	1333	1433	1533	1603	1633	1703	1703	1732	1803	1833
18	Hagondange d.	0545	0615	0645	0715	0745	0815	0845	0918	0945	1002	1043	1045	1102	1145	1245	1345	1445	1545	1615	1645	1715	1719	1745	1815	1845
30	Thionville d.	0557	0627	0658	0727	0757	0827	0857	0934	0957	1017	1057	1057	1117	1157	1257	1357	1457	1557	1634	1657	1727	1734	1757	1827	1857
64	**Luxembourg** a.	0622	0652	0723	0753	0823	0852	0922	1001	1022	1046	1122	1122	1146	1222	1322	1422	1522	1622	1702	1722	1753	1802	1823	1852	1922

	Ⓐ			⑥	Ⓐ t	Ⓑ	t	Ⓐ	⑤⑥ p	
Nancy ★ d.	1820	1850z	1950z	2050	...	...	2150z	...	...	...
Metz d.	1903	1933	2033	2132	2133	2146	2233	2246	2316	...
Hagondange d.	1915	1945	2045	2145	2145	2202	2245	2302	2332	...
Thionville d.	1934	1957	2057	2157	2157	2217	2257	2317	2347	...
Luxembourg a.	2001	2022	2122	2222	2222	2246	2322	2346	0016	...

	Ⓐ	⚒	Ⓐ	Ⓐ	Ⓐ	⑥	Ⓐ	Ⓒ	Ⓐ	① g	E	⚒	Ⓐ
Luxembourg d.	0513	0538k	0543	...	0629	0629	0708	0738	0738	0759	0808	0838	...
Thionville d.	0546	0604	0616	0624	0704	0702	0734	0804	0807	0830	0834	0904	0924
Hagondange d.	0557	0616	0627	0640	0714	0713	0746	0816	0818	0844	0846	0916	0936
Metz a.	0614	0627	0643	0654	0727	0731	0757	0827	0830	0857	0857	0927	0952
Nancy ★ a.	...	0711	...	0740	0811	0810	0839	0911	...	...	...	1011k	1040

	¶	Ⓒ	Ⓐ		Ⓐ t		Ⓐ t	G	Ⓐ t	⚒		Ⓐ		Ⓐ		⑤	Ⓐ		Ⓐ t		Ⓐ	Ⓐ	Ⓐ		Ⓐ t	H
Luxembourg d.	0938	1013	1038	1138	1208	1238	1257	1338	1408	1438	1538	1608	1638	1657	1738	1757	1813	1838	1908	1938	2008	2038t	2113	2138t	2238	2313
Thionville d.	1004	1044	1104	1204	1234	1304	1336	1404	1434	1504	1604	1634	1704	1734j	1804	1834j	1846	1904	1937	2004	2034	2104	2145	2204	2304	2346
Hagondange d.	1016	1055	1116	1216	1246	1316	1347	1416	1446	1515	1616	1646	1716	1746	1816	1846	1857	1916	1949	2016	2046	2116	2156	2216	2316	2357
Metz a.	1029	1114	1129	1229	1259	1329	1401	1429	1459	1529	1627	1658	1727	1759	1827	1902	1914	1927	2000	2028	2057	2127	2214	2227	2327	0014
Nancy ★ a.	1111	...	1211	1311	...	1411	...	1511z	...	1611k	1711z	...	1811	...	1911	...	...	2011	...	2109z	...	2211	...	2311z	...	...

D – ①–④ (not Dec. 26 – 29, Apr. 17, May 1, 24, 25, June 5).
E – ②–⑤ (not May 25).
G – ②–⑦ (also Dec. 26, Jan. 16, Feb. 6, 13, 20, Apr. 17, May 1, 8, June 5).
H – ①–⑥ to Mar. 24 (also Dec. 25, Jan. 1, 22, 29, Feb. 5, Mar. 19); ⑦ Mar. 26 - Apr. 30 (also Apr. 14); ⚒ from May 2 (also May 7).

f – Also May 24.
g – Not Apr. 17, May 1, 8, June 5.
h – 2109 on Ⓒ.
j – Arrives 9 minutes earlier.

k – ⑥ only.
p – Not Feb. 10, 17, Mar. 10, 17, Apr. 21.
t – Not Dec. 26 – 30.
w – Runs 3 – 6 minutes earlier on Dec. 25, Jan. 1, Apr. 17, May 1, 8, 25, June 5.
z – Ⓒ only.

⊗ – Subject to alteration Mar. 27 – 31.
⊙ – Subject to alteration on ①–⑤ Feb. 27 - Mar. 24.
⇊ – Subject to alteration Feb. 27 - Mar. 10, Mar. 27 - Apr. 28.
¶ – Subject to alteration on ① Jan. 16 - Apr. 3.

⊠ – The 1432 from Metz runs on Ⓒ only.
✣ – The 1150, 1250 and 1350 from Nancy are subject to alteration on ①–⑤ Feb. 27 - Mar. 24.
★ – See panel above for full service Nancy - Metz and v.v.

On May 8 (a French public holiday) certain services to / from Luxembourg operate as on weekdays. On Dec. 26, June 23 (public holidays in Luxembourg) services to / from Luxembourg may operate as on ⑦. Please check if travelling on these dates.

STRASBOURG - MULHOUSE - BASEL — 385

For *TGV* trains Paris - Strasbourg - Colmar see Table **390**. For *TGV* trains Luxembourg - Metz - Strasbourg - Mulhouse - Lyon - Marseille/Montpellier see Table **379**.
On Dec. 26, Apr. 14 services run as on ⑦.

km			Ⓐ	Ⓐ	Ⓐ	⑥	Ⓐ	Ⓐ	† z	Ⓐ	Ⓐ	Ⓐ	Ⓐ	Ⓐ	Ⓐ	Ⓐ	Ⓒ	Ⓐ	Ⓐ	Ⓐ	Ⓒ	Ⓐ	Ⓐ	⅀	†	Ⓐ	Ⓐ	Ⓐ
0	Strasbourg	d.	...	0518	0551	0547	0618	0651	0650	0651	0721	0751	0751	0821	0851	0921	0951	0951	1021	1051	1121	1151	1151	1221	1251	1321	1351
43	Sélestat	d.	...	0538	0610	0614	0642	0710	0711	0740	0810	0816	0840	0910	0943	1010	1016	1040	1110	1142	1216	1241	1310	1340	1410
65	Colmar	d.	...	0550	0623	0626	0654	0723	0723	0723	0753	0823	0828	0853	0923	0956	1023	1028	1053	1123	1154	1223	1228	1253	1323	1353	1423
106	Mulhouse ★ ▷	d.	0546	0616	0646	0654	0716	0746	0746	0746	0816	0846	0855	0916	0946	1017	1046	1055	1114	1146	1215	1245	1255	1316	1346	1414	1446
140	Basel ▷	a.	0609	0639	0709	0750	0739	0809	0820	0820	0839	0909	...	0939	1009	...	1109	...	...	1209	...	1309	...	...	1409	...	1509

			Ⓒ		Ⓐ	Ⓐ	†	Ⓐ	Ⓐ	Ⓐ	Ⓐ	†	Ⓐ	Ⓐ	Ⓐ	Ⓐ	⑥	Ⓐ	Ⓐ	†	Ⓐ	⅀	†	Ⓐ			Ⓐ	Ⓐ r
Strasbourg		d.	1351	...	1451	1521	1551	1551	1551	1621	1651	1721	1745	1751	1821	1851	1851	1921	1921	1951	2021	2051	2121	2121	...	...	2221	2251	2320
Sélestat		d.	1416	...	1510	1540	1610	1610	1616	1640	1710	1740	1810	1810	1840	1910	1916	1940	1940	2011	2040	2118	2141	2146	...	...	2246	2310	2346
Colmar		d.	1428	...	1523	1553	1621	1623	1627	1653	1723	1753	1822	1823	1853	1923	1927	1953	1953	2023	2053	2131	2153	2159	...	...	2259	2323	2359
Mulhouse ★		d.	1455	...	1546	1616	1646	1646	1654	1716	1746	1816	1849	1846	1916	1946	1955	2014	2016	2046	2116	2154	2216	2220	...	...	2320	2344	0021
Basel ▷		a.	...	...	1609	1639	1709	1709	...	1739	1809	1839	...	1909	1939	2009	...	2039	2109	2139	...	2239	...	...	...	...	...	...	...

			Ⓐ	Ⓐ	Ⓐ	⑥	Ⓐ	Ⓒ	Ⓐ	Ⓐ	Ⓐ	Ⓒ	Ⓐ	Ⓐ	Ⓐ	Ⓒ	Ⓐ	Ⓐ	Ⓒ	Ⓐ	Ⓐ	Ⓐ	†	⑥
Basel ▷		d.	...	...	0521	0537t	...	0621	0651	...	0721	0751	0821	0851	...	...	0921	1021	...	...	1121	...	1221	...	1321	...
Mulhouse ▷		d.	0458	0533	0546	0600	0616	0646	0716	0735	0746	0816	0846	0916	0923	0935	0946	1046	1114	1135	1146	1213	1246	1314	1346	1414	1434	1435
Colmar		d.	0519	0559	0605	0629	0644	0707	0737	0802	0807	0837	0907	0937	0958	1002	1017	1036	1107	1136	1202	1207	1236	1307	1335	1407	1435	1501	1502
Sélestat		d.	0532	0611	0619	0642	0657	0719	0749	0813	0819	0849	0919	0949		1013	1019	1119	1148	1214	1219	1248	1319	1347	1419	1447	1513	1514
Strasbourg		a.	0558	0637	0639	0709	0724	0739	0809	0840	0839	0909	0939	1009		1034	1039	1039	1139	1209	1239	1239	1309	1339	1409	1439	1509	1539	1539

			Ⓐ	Ⓐ	†	⅀	Ⓐ	†	Ⓐ	⑥	Ⓐ	Ⓐ	⑥	Ⓑ	⑤† r	†	⅀	Ⓐ	†	⑥ ①–⑤ d	Ⓐ	†
Basel ▷		d.	1421	...	1521	1551	1621	1639	1651	1639	1721	1751	1821	1851	1839	1921	1951	1951	...	2021	2021	2039	2121	...	2239
Mulhouse ▷		d.	1446	1516	1532	1546	1616	1646	1704	1716	1735	1746	1816	1846	1916	1931	1946	2016	2014	2016	2035	2044	2046	2116	2146	2235	2310	2330	2338
Colmar		d.	1507	1537	1558	1607	1637	1707	1731	1737	1802	1807	1837	1907	1937	2002	2007	...	2037	2102	...	2107	2136	2207	2301	...	2358	0006
Sélestat		d.	1519	1549	1610	1619	1649	1719	1743	1749	1814	1819	1849	1919	1949	2014	2019	...	2049	2113	...	2119	2148	2219	2313	...	0013	0021
Strasbourg		a.	1539	1609	1636	1639	1709	1739	1809	1809	1839	1839	1909	1939	2009	2039	2039	...	2109	2139	...	2139	2214	2239	2339	...	0040	0048

a – Not Dec. 26 – 30, Apr. 14, 17, May 25, June 5.
c – Also Dec. 26, Apr. 14, 17, May 25, June 5.
d – Not Dec. 26, Apr. 14, 17, May 25, June 5.
h – Not Dec. 27 – 30.
r – Not Jan. 21.
t – 0531 from Apr. 10.
z – Not May 1, 8.

★ – Certain Mulhouse departures are 1 minute earlier Feb. 6 - Apr. 9.
◇ – From Apr. 10 Mulhouse d. 0550, Colmar d. 0609, Sélestat d. 0621, Strasbourg a. 0641.

▷ – **Other local trains** Mulhouse - Basel and v.v. (journey 31 minutes):
From Mulhouse at 0449 ①–⑤ a, 0549 ①–⑤ d, 0619 ①–⑥ d, 0649 ①–⑤ a, 0719 ⅀,
0749 ①–⑤ d, 0819 ①–⑤ a, 0919, 1056 ①–⑤ a, 1119, 1219 ①–⑤ a, 1319, 1419 ①–⑤ a,
1519 ⑥⑦ c, 1549 ①–⑤ d, 1619 ①–⑥ d, 1649 ①–⑤ a, 1719 ①–⑥ d, 1749 ①–⑤ d,
1819 h, 1849 ①–⑤ d, 1919 ①–⑥ d, 1949 ⑧ h and 2019 ①–⑤ d.
From Basel at 0609 ①–⑤ a, 0639 ①–⑤ d, 0709 ①–⑥ d, 0739 ①–⑤ a, 0809 ①–⑥ d,
0839, 0903 ①–⑤ a, 1039, 1139 ①–⑤ a, 1239, 1339 ①–⑤ a, 1439 ⑥⑦ c, 1539 ①–⑥ d,
1609 ①–⑤ a, 1639 ①–⑥ d, 1709 ①–⑤ d, 1739 h, 1809 ①–⑤ d, 1839 ①–⑥ d, 1909 ⑧ h,
1939 ①–⑤ d, 2039 and 2139 ①–⑤ a.

NANCY - ÉPINAL - REMIREMONT — 386

km			Ⓐ	Ⓐ	Ⓐ	⅀ v	⅀ ⊗	Ⓐ ⊗	† ⊗	Ⓐ	Ⓑ ⊗	⅀ ⊗	† ⊗	Ⓐ	Ⓐ	⅀ ⊗	⅀ ⊗	**2571** ♥ 1228	Ⓐ	Ⓐ	Ⓐ	⅀	Ⓐ	Ⓐ	Ⓐ	Ⓐ
0	Nancy	d.	0520	0555	0620	0655	0720	0755	0820	0855	0920	1020	1022	1055	1120	1220	1255	1320	1320	1403	1420	1520	1555	1620	1655	1720	1755
74	Épinal	a.	0613	0648	0718	0749	0813	0848	0913	0948	1013	1111	1117	1148	1213	1313t	1348	1413	1413	1444	1513	1613	1648	1713	1748	1813	1848
74	Épinal	d.	0620	...	0720	...	0820	...	0920	...	1020a	1120	...	...	1220	1320	...	1420	1447	1520a	1620	...	1720a	...	1820	...
100	Remiremont	a.	0652	...	0752	...	0850	...	0952	...	1052a	1150	...	...	1252	1352	...	1452	1508	1552a	1652	...	1752a	...	1852	...

Paris Est **390** ... d.

			⅀ v	Ⓐ	**2573** ♥ 1809	Ⓑ	⑥ h	Ⓐ	† k		Ⓐ	⅀	Ⓐ	⅀	**2574** ♥	⅀	⅀	Ⓐ		**2576** ⊗ Ⓒ
Paris Est **390**		d.								Remiremont		d.	0511a	...	0600	0615	...	0711a	...	0811	...	0906
Nancy		d.	1820	1855	1920	1955	2020	2120	2205	2220	2255	...	Épinal	a.	0540a	...	0620	0641	...	0740a	...	0840	...	0926
Épinal		a.	1913	1948	2013	2036	2113	2213	2304	2313	2354	...	Épinal	d.	0500	0546	0554	0623	0646	0646	0708	0746	0808	0846	0908	0929
Épinal		d.	1920	...	2020	2039	...	2220	...		...	Nancy	a.	0559	0640	0648	0705	0740	0740	0802	0841	0902	0940	1002	1012
Remiremont		a.	1952	...	2052	2103	...	2252	...		...	*Paris Est* **390**	a.	...	...	...	0846	...	...	...	...	...	...	1146

			Ⓐ	⅀ ⊗	Ⓐ	Ⓒ ⊗	Ⓐ ⊗	⑥ ⊗	Ⓐ ⊗	Ⓐ		**2578** ①–⑥ b♥	Ⓐ		**2580** ⑦ e♥	⅀	Ⓐ	Ⓑ		Ⓐ	⅀ ⊗	† k	Ⓐ
Remiremont		d.	0911	...	1011	1033	...	...	...	1211	1311	1411	1511a	1600	1615	...	1656	1711	...	1811	...	1911	...	2011	...
Épinal		a.	0940	...	1040	1102	...	...	1240	1340	1440	1540a	1622	1642	...	1716	1740	...	1840	...	1940	...	2039	...
Épinal		d.	0946	0946	1046	1106	1108	1142	1146	1208	1246r	1346	1446	1546	1623	1646	1708	1719	1746	1808	1846	1908	1946	2008	2046	2046	2146	2208
Nancy		a.	1040	1040	1140	1200	1202	1240	1240	1302	1340r	1440	1540	1640	1706	1740	1802	1802	1840	1902	1940	2002	2040	2102	2140	2140	2240	2302
Paris Est **390**		a.	...	...	...	...	...	...	...	...	...	...	...	1847	...	1949	...	...	...	...	...	...	...	...	...

a – Ⓐ only.
b – Not Apr. 17, May 1, 8, June 5.
e – Also Apr. 17, May 1, 8, June 5.
h – Not Apr. 15, 22.
k – Not Apr. 16, 23.
r – On † Épinal d. 1242, Nancy a. 1341.

t – 1316 on ⑥.
v – Not Dec. 26 – 30.

⊗ – Subject to alteration Feb. 13 – 17, 20 – 24, Apr. 10 – 14, 18 – 21.
♥ – *TGV* train, ℝ, ℤ, supplement payable.

ÉPINAL - BELFORT — 386a

km			⅀	Ⓑ	△	†	⅀				Ⓐ		▢		Ⓑ		†	⅀
0	Épinal	d.	0627	...	0957	...	1455	...	1849	1857	...	Belfort	**380** d.	0601	...	1101	...	1704	...	2001	2035
58	Luxeuil les Bains	d.	0712	...	1043	...	1539	...	1939	1943	...	Lure	**380** d.	0632	...	1132	...	1735	...	2032	2103
76	Lure	**380** d.	0726	...	1056	...	1552	...	1953	1956	...	Luxeuil les Bains	d.	0646	...	1146	...	1748	...	2045	2117
108	Belfort	**380** a.	0758	...	1128	...	1618	...	2025	2028	...	Épinal	a.	0733	...	1233	...	1836	...	2133	2202

△ – Subject to alteration on ①–⑤ Feb. 13 - Mar. 10.
▢ – Subject to alteration Feb. 20 – 24 and Apr. 10 – 14.

387 NANCY - LUNÉVILLE - ST DIÉ

km																2591											2593		2595	
		Ⓐ	Ⓐ	⑥	Ⓐ	Ⓒ	Ⓐ					Ⓐ	Ⓐ	⑥	†	Ⓐ	⑦e ♥	†	Ⓐ	✕	†	✕	Ⓐ	Ⓐ	Ⓒ	Ⓐ	⑦e ♥	Ⓐ
							⊗										⊗										⊗	
	Paris Est **390**........ d.																1413										1809		2009	
0	Nancy ....**383** d.	0545	0650	0750	0855	0900	0955	1027	1250	1411	1450	1550	1553	1650	1652	1711	1750	1758	1850	1941	1951	1951	1931	2151	2159
33	Lunéville ....**383** d.	0605	0710	0810	0914	0921	1014	1048	1310	1429	1510	1610	1614	1614	1710	1711	1730	1810j	1818	1910	1930		2011	2030	2213	2220
84	St Dié .... a.	0703	0753	0853	0953	1003	1103	1145	1354	1529	1553	1653	1656	1643	1753	1806	1829	1853	1858	1953k	2029	2045	2053	2129	2242	2258

					2596	2596														2598					
		Ⓐ	⑥	†	Ⓐ	♥	♥	Ⓐ	⑥	Ⓐ	Ⓐ	⑥	†	Ⓐ	Ⓐ	⑥	✕	✕	⑦e ♥	†	†	Ⓐ
										⊗									⊗			
St Dié........ d.	0507	0557	0607	0631	0657	0715	0715	0731	0805	0807	0907	1031	1107	1114	1207	1257	1431	1557	1610	1631	1707	1714	1807	1911	1931	2007
Lunéville ....**383** d.	0545	0638	0652	0728	0745			0830	0853	0849	0949	1130	1149	1156	1249	1346	1530	1639	1652	1729	1749	1745	1849v	2007	2029	2048t
Nancy ....**383** d.	0603	0658	0714	0749	0803			0811	0806	0913	0910	1010	1149	1210	1218	1310	1409	1549	1659	1712	1749	1808	1806	1908v	2029	2107t
Paris Est **390** .... a.						0946	0950															1949		

e – Also Apr. 17, May 1, 8, June 5.
j – 1813 on ⑥.
k – 2000 on ⑥.

n – Not May 25.
t – On Ⓒ Lunéville d.2049, Nancy a.2110.
v – On ⑥ Lunéville d.1900, Nancy a.1918.

♥ – TGV train, ⊞, ⏄, supplement payable.
⊗ – Subject to alteration on ①–⑤ Feb. 13–24.

388 STRASBOURG - ST DIÉ

km		⑥	†d	Ⓐ¶	⑥	†d		†h	⑤f	⑥		St Dié........ d.	Ⓐ	†d	⑥	⑥	Ⓐ¶		⑥	†d	†h	⑥	†h
0	Strasbourg........ ▷d.	0825	0950	0955	1225	1350	...	1750	1755	1805		St Dié........ d.	0850	0853	1143	1155	...	...	1615	1649	1737	1805	2051
9	Entzheim Aéroport ✈...▷d.	0833	0958	1004	1233	1358	...	1801	1806	1833		Molsheim........ d.	1024	1026	1319	1338	...	...	1747	1824	1915	1943	2124
19	Molsheim........ ▷d.	0841	1006	1012	1241	1406	...	1814	1815	1841		Entzheim Aéroport ✈...d.	1031	1033	1326	1345	...	...	1800	1831	1927	1956	2131
87	St Dié........ a.	1017	1138	1148	1419	1546	...	1947	1948	2013		Strasbourg........ a.	1039	1041	1335	1353	...	...	1811	1839	1939	2008	2139

d – Also Dec. 26.
f – Not Apr. 14.
h – Also Dec. 26, Apr. 14.

¶ – Not Dec. 26. Subject to alteration Apr. 3 – 21 and May 2 – 5.
▷ – Regular trains run Strasbourg - Entzheim Aéroport (300 metres from terminal) - Molsheim and v.v.: 2 – 3 per hour on ✕, 1 per hour on †.

388a ST DIÉ - ÉPINAL

km		Ⓐt	⑥	⑥	Ⓐt¶	Ⓒ	Ⓐ	Ⓒz	Ⓐt	⑤f	⑥n	†r			Ⓐ	Ⓐt	⑥	Ⓐt‡	⑥	Ⓒ	†	Ⓐt	✕	†r	⑤v
0	St Dié........d.	0615	0635	0733	1010	1215	1410	1644	1723	1832	1944	2010	2020		Épinal........d.	0613	0732	0800	1210	1235	1523	1558	1648	1833	1858	1945
60	Épinal........a.	0715	0735	0834	1110	1315	1511	1746	1825	1935	2046	2110	2121		St Dié........a.	0714	0834	0900	1315	1335	1623	1658	1745	1935	1958	2045

f – Also Dec. 24, 31, May 24; not Dec. 30.
n – Not Dec. 24, 31.
r – Also Apr. 16, 30, May 7, June 4.

t – Not Dec. 26 – 30.
v – Also May 16, 30, May 7, 24, June 4; not Dec. 30.
z – On † St Dié d.1730, Épinal a.1830.

¶ – By 🚌 Feb. 13 – 24, Apr. 10 – 21 (also ①②③④⑤ Mar. 6 – 31), Épinal a. 1351.
‡ – By 🚌 Feb. 13 – 24, Apr. 10 – 21 (also ①②③④⑤ Mar. 6 – 31), Épinal d. 1200, St Dié a. 1336.

389 PARIS - REIMS - CHARLEVILLE MÉZIÈRES - SEDAN

Warning! Subject to alteration from May 1

km				TGV 2709	TGV 2713	TGV 2715		TGV 2733		TGV 2743				TGV 2747		TGV 2753	TGV 2751		TGV 2785
		Ⓐ	✕	Ⓐ	①-⑥	①-⑥		Ⓐ		Ⓐ			Ⓐ	Ⓒ	⑥	Ⓐ			Ⓐ
				b		b	e	A	△		⊖			h	d	f	N		
0	Paris Est .... d.				0758		0928	0928	...	1306	...	1528			1728	...	1828	1828	...	1928
136	Champ. Ardenne TGV.§ d.												1639	1705					...	2007	2020
147	Reims ....§ a.					0844		1014	1014	1353		1616	1649	1712		1816		1914	1916		2032
147	Reims .... d.	0621	0651	0751	0848	0951		1018	1151	1232		1405	1451	1621	1651	1721	1721	1751		1821	1919	1921	1951
186	Rethel .... d.	0644	0713	0814	0911	1014		1041	1216	1254		1429	1514	1645	1715	1744	1745	1815		1843	1942	1944	2013
235	Charleville-Mézières ... a.	0716	0746	0847	0938	1046		1109	1241	1327		1500	1541	1718	1746	1816	1816	1850		1915	2010	2011	2046
255	Sedan .... a.	0739	...	0908	1004	1109x			1351c	1534				1815	1846	1846				1939g	2038	2112

		TGV 2757	TGV 2787	TGV 2759	TGV 2765				TGV 2706		TGV 2778		TGV 2712	TGV 2714	TGV 2716			TGV 2720
		⑤	①-④	⑤⑦	⑤⑦	⑦	†			Ⓐ		Ⓐ	✕	①-⑥	✕	Ⓐ	Ⓒ		Ⓐ	Ⓒ	Ⓐ
		v	m	r	p	e						b				k			
Paris Est .... d.		1958		2028		2058		2128		Sedan .... d.	...	0526		0617		0652	...	...	0744z	0747	0753
Champ. Ardenne TGV.§ d.			2109	2115			†			Charleville-Mézières ...... d.	0536	0558		0639		0718	...	0739	0808	0809	0819
Reims ....§ a.			2044		2127	2144		2214		Rethel .... d.	0611	0629		0712		0748	...	0812	0841	0841	0850
Reims .... d.	2037	2051		2129		2151	2218		Reims .... d.	0634	0653		0734		0808	0834	0904	0904	0909
Rethel .... d.	2059	2102		2113		2151	2213	2242		Reims ....§ d.		0645	0655		0745	0813	0815	...	0906	0906	0913
Charleville-Mézières ... a.	2132	2136		2146		2225	2246	2308		Champ. Ardenne TGV ....§ d.		0707	0718					...	0917	0921	
Sedan .... a.	2154			2209		2246	2308	2335		Paris Est .... a.		0731		0802		0831	0901	0901	...		1001

		TGV 2722	TGV 2724	TGV 2726		TGV 2738		TGV 2750			TGV 2754	TGV 2752		TGV 2784		TGV 2756	TGV 2760	TGV 2762		TGV 2766
		✕	Ⓐ	⑥		Ⓐ	⑥	⑥	†	⑥	⑦	Ⓐ	✕		Ⓐ	⑥	⑤⑦			⑥
				e	k		e	h		k		e				r		S	r		D
Sedan .... d.	0806	1017	1022		1052	1117x	1209		1440		1517	1543	1547		1632		1717	1746			2054
Charleville-Mézières ... d.	0838	1039	1048		1118	1139	1239		1500		1539	1605	1609	1618		1658		1739	1814		1939	2109	2120
Rethel .... d.	0911	1109	1118		1148	1211	1311		1536		1609	1638	1642	1649		1731		1811	1844		2011	2137	2150
Reims .... a.	0934	1134	1140		1210	1234	1334		1604		1634	1703	1705	1709		1755		1834	1910		2034	2204	2210
Reims ....§ d.		1145	1145	1215			1415		1615		1705		1714	1715		1803		1845	1916	1913	1945		2215
Champ. Ardenne TGV.§ d.								1717			1717			1817	1820		1928			
Paris Est .... a.		1232	1231	1303			1501		1704		1801	1801		1901		1934		1931	2001	2031		2303

A – ①⑤⑥ (also Apr. 18, 16, 30, May 2, 7, 9, 24, June 4; not Feb. 13, 17, Mar. 13, 17, 27, 31, Apr. 17, May 1, 8, June 5).
D – ⑥⑦ to Apr. 23 (daily Dec. 17 - Jan. 1, Jan. 21 - Mar. 19 and Mar. 25 - Apr. 2).
N – ①②③④⑥⑦ (not May 24).
R – ①②③④⑥ (not Apr. 17, May 1, 8, 24, June 5).
S – ①②③④⑥ (not Apr. 17, May 1, 8, 24, 25, June 5).
T – ①②③④⑥ (not Dec. 24, 31, Apr. 17, May 1, 8, 24, 25, June 5).

b – Not Apr. 17, May 1, 8, June 5.
c – Ⓒ only.

d – Also Dec. 24, 31; not Apr. 17.
e – Also Apr. 17, May 1, 8, June 5.
f – Also May 24.
g – ①②③④⑦ (not Apr. 16, 17, May 7, 8, 24, 25, June 4, 5).
h – Not May 24.
k – Also May 24.
m – Not May 24.
p – Also Dec. 24, 31, Apr. 17, May 1, 8, 24, June 5.
r – Also Apr. 17, May 1, 8, 24, June 5.
v – Also Dec. 24, 31, Apr. 16, 30, May 7, 24, June 4.
x – Not ①–⑤ Jan. 30 - Feb. 17, Apr. 24–28.

z – 0710 on ⑥.

TGV–⊞, supplement payable, ⏄.

⊖ – Subject to alteration on Mar. 23.
☐ – Subject to alteration Mar. 13–17, 23, 27–31.
△ – Subject to alteration Feb. 13–17, Mar. 13–17, 23, 27–31.
⊗ – Subject to alteration on ①–⑤ Jan. 30 - Feb. 17, Mar. 13–17, 23, 27–31, Apr. 24–28.
§ – For full service see Table 391a.

389a CHARLEVILLE MÉZIÈRES - THIONVILLE and METZ   *SERVICE UNTIL APRIL 23*

km		Ⓐ	✕	†	†	Ⓐ	⑥	⑤f				Ⓐ	⑥		Ⓐ ◇	⑥			
	Reims 389 .... d.				...	1405	1405				Metz .... **384** d.				...	...		...	...
0	Charleville-Mézières 389 d.	0540	0751	1122	...	1510	1510	1546	1723	1921		Thionville .... **384** d.	0517	0622		0847	0917		1743	1908
20	Sedan .... **389** a.	0557	0808	1140	...	1534	1535	1606	1741	1940		Hayange .... d.	0524	0629		0854	0925		1751	1916
20	Sedan .... **389** d.	0558	0809	1141	...	1535	1537	1607	1742	1941		Longuyon .... d.	0555	0704		0925	0955		1821	1946
69	Montmédy .... d.	0636	0841	1216	...	1607	1607	1640	1815	2012		Montmédy .... d.	0610	0717		0940	1009		1835	2000
91	Longuyon .... d.	0653	0855	1232	...	1622	1622	1655	1830	2026		Sedan .... **389** a.	0645	0747		1009	1039		1904	2031
	Hayange .... d.	0726	0931	1311	...	1653	1653	1726	1900	2107		Sedan .... **389** d.	0709				1905	2032
	Thionville .... **384** a.	0734	0938	1319	...	1700	1700	1733	1907	2115		Charleville-Mézières .. **389** a.	0734				1930	2049
170	Metz .... **384** a.	...	...	...	...	...	...	...	...	...		Reims **389** .... a.	...	...		...	...		...	...

f – Not Apr. 14.

◇ – Subject to alteration Jan. 30 - Feb. 17.

PARIS - STRASBOURG - COLMAR

For other connecting trains Strasbourg - Colmar and v.v., see Table 385

km	TGV trains: [R], 🍸 / ICE trains: [R], ✕	ICE 9571	TGV 9561	TGV 2363	TGV 2407		TGV 2365	ICE 9573	TGV 9593		TGV 2421	TGV 9575	TGV 2371	ICE 9563	TGV 9577	TGV 2443	TGV 2457	TGV 9579	TGV 2377		TGV 2465		TGV 2471
			①–⑥	①–⑥				Ⓑ	⑥				Ⓑ		Ⓑ		Ⓑ						⑤⑦
			r	b	♠			q	p				h		q ⊙		h	⊡					w
0	Paris Est d.	0640	0720	0720	0744	...	0925	1055	1055	...	1255	1355	1455	1520	1555	1655	1725	1755	1855	...	2025	...	2155
439	Strasbourg a.	0826	0904	0904	0943	...	1111	1241	1241	...	1446	1541	1641	1708	1741	1841	1913	1941	2041	...	2213	...	2341
439	Strasbourg 385 d.	0831	0909	0912	...	...	1117	1246	1246	...	...	1546	1646	1713	1746	...	...	1946	2046	...	...	...	...
	Stuttgart Hbf 931 a.	0948	|	|	...	...	|	1404	1404	...	...	1704	|	|	1904	...	...	2104	|	...	...	...	...
	Frankfurt Hbf 912 a.	...	1058	|	...	...	|	...	...	...	...	...	|	1858	...	...	...	...	|	...	...	...	...
482	Sélestat 385 a.	...	...	|	...	...	|	...	...	...	...	...	|	...	...	...	...	...	2104	...	...	...	...
504	Colmar 385 a.	...	...	0936⁝	...	...	1146◊	...	...	...	...	...	1711‡	...	...	...	...	...	2119‡	...	...	...	...

	TGV 2400	TGV 2404	TGV 2350	TGV 2410	TGV 2352	TGV 9578	ICE 9568	TGV 9576	TGV 2356	ICE 9566	ICE 9574	TGV 2358	TGV 2358	TGV 2430	TGV 2440	ICE 9572	TGV 9592	TGV 2450	TGV 2364	TGV 9560	TGV 9570	TGV 2470	TGV 2474
	①	Ⓐ	①–⑥	Ⓐ	⑦	①–⑥	Ⓑ		①–⑥	⑥		①–⑥	⑦		Ⓑ	Ⓑ	⑥		Ⓑ			⑤	⑦
	g		b		e	r	q	⊙	n	p		b	e		h	q	p		h♥			f	e
Colmar 385 d.	...	...	0640	...	0710	...	...	...	0951	...	...	1245	1300	...	...	...	...	...	1746	...	...	...	...
Sélestat 385 d.	...	...	0653	...	0724	...	...	...	|	...	...	|	|	...	...	...	...	...	|	...	...	...	...
Frankfurt Hbf 912 d.	...	...	|	...	|	...	0658	...	|	0856	...	|	|	...	...	...	...	...	|	1658	..	...	...
Stuttgart Hbf 931 d.	...	...	|	...	|	0654	|	0854	|	|	1054	|	|	...	...	1454	1454	...	|	|	1854	...	...
Strasbourg 385 a.	...	...	0713	...	0743	0811	0847	1012	1016	1047	1213	1313	1326	...	...	1613	1613	...	1812	1847	2013	...	...
Strasbourg d.	0615	0647	0719	0747	0747	0816	0851	1020	1020	1051	1219	1319	1331	1447	1547	1617	1617	1717	1817	1855	2019	2047	2147
Paris Est a.	0805	0835	0905	0935	0935	1005	1038	1205	1205	1238	1405	1505	1516	1635	1735	1805	1805	1905	2012	2041	2205	2235	2335

PARIS - METZ - LUXEMBOURG

For other connecting trains Metz - Luxembourg and v.v., see Table 384

km	TGV trains: [R], 🍸	TGV 2601	TGV 2803	TGV 2809	TGV 2809		TGV 2815	TGV 2815		TGV 2817	TGV 2617	TGV 2827	TGV 2831	TGV 2621	TGV 2833	TGV 2635	TGV 2839	TGV 2643	TGV 2843	TGV 2647			
		①	①–⑥	⑦	①–⑥		⑦	①–⑥		⑤⑦		①–④	⑤–⑦	Ⓑ		Ⓑ		①–⑥	⑦	⑤⑦			
		g	b	e △	b ⊕		e △	v ⊕		w △	Y	m	t △	h	▽	h	▽	b ▽	e	w			
0	Paris Est d.	0655	0740	0840	0840	...	1029	1040	...	1340	1340	1440	1540	1640	1740	1840	1940	2040	2040	2140	...	...	...
136	Champagne-Ardenne TGV d.	|	|	|	0924	...	1114	|	...	|	|	|	|	|	|	|	|	|	|	|	...	...	...
236	Meuse TGV a.	|	|	|	|	...	|	|	...	|	|	|	|	|	|	|	|	|	|	|	...	...	...
315	Metz a.	0820	0904	1004	1013	...	1204	1204	...	1504	1504	1604	1704	1804	1904	2004	2105	2205	2205	2304	...	...	...
315	Metz 384 d.	...	0909	1009	1018	...	1209	1209	...	1509	...	1609	1709	...	1909	...	2110	...	2209	...	...	...	...
345	Thionville 384 a.	...	0927	1029	1037	...	1227	1227	...	1527	...	1627	1727	...	1926	...	2127	...	2227	...	...	...	...
379	Luxembourg 384 a.	...	0952	1053	1101	...	1252	1252	...	1552	...	1652	1752	...	1951	...	2152	...	2253	...	...	...	...

	TGV 2650	TGV 2853	TGV 2654	TGV 2855		TGV 2861	TGV 2660		TGV 2865		TGV 2869		TGV 2672	TGV 2676	TGV 2881	TGV 2682	TGV 2877	TGV 2891	TGV 2684	TGV 2893			
	Ⓐ	Ⓐ	⑦	①–⑥		T	②–⑤							⑤–⑦	Ⓑ	①–④	⑤–⑦	Ⓐ	⑦	⑦			
			e △	b		△	u		⊠		✣		△	y △	h	m	c		e	e			
Luxembourg 384 d.	...	0604	...	0640	...	0810	...	...	1010	...	1309	...	...	...	1710	...	1809	1859	...	2003	...	...	...
Thionville 384 d.	...	0627	...	0703	...	0833	...	...	1033	...	1333	...	...	...	1733	...	1833	1924	...	2026	...	...	...
Metz 384 a.	...	0646	...	0721	...	0851	...	...	1054	...	1351	...	...	...	1751	...	1851	1946	...	2044	...	...	...
Metz d.	0623	0650	0726	0726	...	0856	0856	...	1057	...	1356	...	1556	1656	1756	1850	1856	1950	1956	2050	...	...	...
Meuse TGV d.	|	0720	|	|	...	|	|	...	|	...	|	...	|	|	|	|	|	|	|	|	...	...	...
Champagne-Ardenne TGV a.	|	|	|	|	...	|	|	...	|	...	|	...	|	|	|	1937	|	2037	|	2136	...	...	...
Paris Est a.	0750	0820	0850	0850	...	1020	1020	...	1220	...	1520	...	1720	1820	1920	2020	2020	2120	2120	2220	...	...	...

PARIS - NANCY

Certain trains continue beyond Nancy to Épinal and Remiremont (Table 386) or to Lunéville and St Dié (Table 387).

km	TGV trains: [R], 🍸	TGV 2501	TGV 2407	TGV 2503	TGV 2809	TGV 2507	TGV 2505	TGV 2815		TGV 2571	TGV 2509	TGV 2591	TGV 2777	TGV 2513	TGV 2515	TGV 2517	TGV 2573	TGV 2583	TGV 2785	TGV 2519	TGV 2595	TGV 2787	TGV 2521
		①–⑥			①–⑥	⑦	①–⑥	⑦			Ⓐ	⑦		⑥	Ⓑ	Ⓐ		Ⓑ	Ⓐ	①–⑥	⑦	⑦	⑤⑦
		b			b ⊕	e S	b	e △				e	B ❦	k	h			h S	B	b	e	e B	w
0	Paris Est d.	0709	0744	0809	0840	1013	1013	1029	...	1228	1409	1413	1426	1513	1609	1713	1809	1913	1928	2009	2009	2028	2113
136	Champagne-Ardenne TGV d.	0752	0826	|	0921	|	|	1110	...	|	|	|	1508	|	1652	|	|	|	2007	|	|	2109	|
236	Meuse TGV d.	|	0850	0913	...	|	|	...	...	|	1512	1515	...	|	|	|	1912	|	...	2112	2113	...	|
330	Nancy a.	0847	...	0947	...	1143	1145	...	...	1359	1547	1549	...	1644	1747	1845	1947	2044	...	2147	2147	...	2244

	TGV 2531	TGV 2778	TGV 2584	TGV 2533	TGV 2596	TGV 2597	TGV 2535	TGV 2577	TGV 2537	TGV 2541	TGV 2543	TGV 2579	TGV 2545	TGV 2784	TGV 2581	TGV 2547	TGV 2364	TGV 2682	TGV 2549	TGV 2890	TGV 2551	TGV 2892	TGV 2553
	Ⓐ	①–⑥	①–⑥	⑦	⑥	Ⓐ	Ⓐ	Ⓒ			Ⓐ	①–⑥	⑦		⑦	①–⑥	Ⓑ	①–④	⑤⑥	Ⓐ	Ⓑ	⑦	⑦
		b B	b S	e	k							b	e S	B ⊗	e	b	h	m	◧		h	e	
Nancy d.	0611	...	0716	0811	0811	0816	1011	1017	1224	1430	1611z	1716	1716	...	1811	1811	...	...	1916	...	2016	...	2116
Meuse TGV d.	|	...	|	0847	0847	|	|	|	1302	|	|	|	|	...	1847	1847	...	...	|	...	|	...	|
Champagne-Ardenne TGV d.	|	0718	|	|	|	|	1107	|	|	|	1706	|	|	1820	|	|	1929	1940	|	2040	|	2139	|
Paris Est a.	0746	0802	0846j	0949	0950	0946	1148	1146	1401	1605	1748	1847	1849	1901	1949	1950	2012	2020	2046	2120	2146x	2220	2246x

PARIS - SAARBRÜCKEN (- FRANKFURT)

km	TGV trains: [R], 🍸 / ICE trains: [R], ✕	TGV 9551		ICE 9553		ICE 9555		ICE 9557	TGV 9559	
						Ⓑ		Ⓑ	⑥	
						q		q	p	
0	Paris Est d.	0906	...	1301	...	1710	...	1906	1906	...
304	Lorraine TGV d.	|	...	1419	...	|	...	|	|	...
372	Forbach 🏛 a.	1045	...	|	...	|	...	2047	2046	...
383	Saarbrücken Hbf a.	1056	...	1457	...	1857	...	2057	2057	...
	Frankfurt (Main) Hbf 919 ▶ a.	1258	...	1658	...	2058	...	2258	2258	...

	ICE 9558	ICE 9586	ICE 9556	ICE 9554	ICE 9554	TGV 9552	TGV 9552		ICE 9550
	①–⑤	⑥	①–⑤	⑥	⑦	Ⓑ	⑥		Ⓑ
	r		r		d	q	p		q
Frankfurt (Main) Hbf 919 ▶ d.	0558	0658	0856	1058	1058	1258	1258	...	1858
Saarbrücken Hbf d.	0800	0902	1101	1305	1305	1501	1501	...	2101
Forbach 🏛 d.	0811	0913	|	|	1318	|	1512	...	2112
Lorraine TGV d.	|	|	|	|	|	|	1544	...	2145
Paris Est a.	0951	1054	1250	1454	1457	1650	1701	...	2258

B – To / from Bar le Duc (Table 381).
S – To / from Strasbourg via Sarrebourg (Table 383).
T – ①⑥⑦ (also May 25).
Y – ①②③④⑥ (not Apr. 17, May 1, 8, 24, June 5).

b – Not Apr. 17, May 1, 8, June 5.
c – Also Apr. 17, May 1, 8, 24, 25, June 5.
d – Also Apr. 17, May 1, June 5.
e – Also Apr. 17, May 1, 8, June 5.
f – Also May 24.
g – Also Apr. 18, May 2, 9, June 6; not Apr. 17, May 1, 8, June 5.
h – Not May 25.
j – 0848 on ⑥.
k – Also May 25.
m – Not Apr. 17, May 1, 8, 24, 25, June 5.
n – Not Dec. 26, Jan. 6, Apr. 17, May 1, 8, June 5.
p – Also Apr. 16, 30, June 4.
q – Not Apr. 16, 30, June 4.
r – Not Apr. 17, May 1, June 5.
t – Also Apr. 17, May 1, 8, 25, June 5.
u – Not Apr. 18, May 2, 9, 25, June 6.
v – Not Apr. 14, 17, May 1, 8, June 5.
w – Also Apr. 17, May 1, 8, 24, June 5.
x – 2–3 minutes later on ⑦ Jan. 8 - May 21.
y – Also Apr. 17, May 1, 8, 24, 25.
z – 1610 on ⑤ (also May 24).

◧ – Also May 24, 25. Arrives Paris 2049 on ⑥.
⁝ – 0939 Jan. 6 - Mar. 8.
◊ – 1149 Jan. 16 - Mar. 8 (also Jan. 13).
‡ – 3 minutes later Jan. 16 - Mar. 8.
♠ – Also calls at Champagne-Ardenne TGV (d. 0826) and Meuse TGV (d. 0853).
♥ – Also calls at Champagne-Ardenne TGV (a. 1926).
⊙ – To / from München (Table 32).
⊡ – To München (Table 32) on ⑥ (also Apr. 16, 30, June 4).
△ – Subject to alteration on May 7, 21.
▽ – Subject to alteration on May 6, 20.
⊕ – Subject to alteration on Feb. 6, 13.
⊠ – Subject to alteration on Jan. 16, Feb. 6, 13, 20, May 7, 21.
✣ – Subject to alteration on Jan. 16, Feb. 6 – 10, 13 – 17, 20, Apr. 11 – 13, 18 – 21, May 6, 7, June 13 – 16, 20 – 23.
❦ – Subject to alteration Feb. 6 – 10, Mar. 20 – 24, 27 – 31, Apr. 3 – 7, May 2 – 19.
⊗ – Subject to alteration Mar. 27 – 31, May 2 – 19.

391   STRASBOURG - NORTHERN and WESTERN FRANCE

		TGV 9890	TGV 5487	TGV 5470	TGV 5450	TGV 5450	TGV 5422		TGV 5424	TGV 5424		TGV 9894	TGV 5488	TGV 5454	
					Ⓐ	Ⓒ			⑥	Ⓑ					
		d	A	s⊗		☉			k	h		m	w		
Strasbourg	d.	0608	0731	0731	0832	0832	0959	...	1244	1247	...	1510	1510	1631	...
Lorraine TGV	d.	0645	0812	0812	0910	0910	1037	...	1321	1324	...	1552	1552	1710	...
Meuse TGV	d.						1059	...			...			1731	...
Champagne-Ardenne TGV	a.	0724	0853	0853	0948	0948	1122	...	1358	1402	...	1630	1630	1754	...
Champagne-Ardenne TGV	d.	0726f	0900	0900	0951	0951	1124	...	1401	1405	...	1633	1633	1757	...
Paris Charles de Gaulle ✈ +	a.	0800f					1201	...	1432	1436	...	1704	1704		...
Lille Europe	a.	0856						...	1526g	1537	...	1758			...
Brussels Midi/Zuid	a.	0943						...	...	...	...	1843			...
Marne la Vallée - Chessy §	a.		0929	0929	1023	1023		...	...	...	...		1728	1829	...
Massy TGV	a.		1005	1005	1105	1105		...	...	...	...		1803	1905	...
Le Mans	a.		1057	1057				...	...	...	...		1857		...
Angers	a.		1139					...	...	...	...		1941		...
Nantes	a.		1223v					...	...	...	...		2024t		...
Laval	a.				1149			...	...	...	...				...
Rennes	a.				1228			...	...	...	...				...
St Pierre des Corps	a.					1159	1159	...	...	...	...			1959	...
Futuroscope	a.						1238	...	...	...	...				...
Poitiers	a.						1242	...	...	...	...			2041	...
Angoulême	a.					1335	1335	...	...	...	...			2135	...
Bordeaux St Jean	a.					1434	1434	...	...	...	...			2234	...

		TGV 9870		TGV 5478	TGV 5441	TGV 5406		TGV 9874	TGV 9874	TGV 5480	TGV 5460		TGV 5416	TGV 5445	
				⚒ ⊖				⑦	①–⑥		Ⓐ				
								e	d						
Bordeaux St Jean	d.			⚒	0726c		...					...	1526c	...	
Angoulême	d.			⚒	0826		...					...	1626	...	
Poitiers	d.			⚒	0917		...					...	1716	...	
Futuroscope	d.						...					...	1725	...	
St Pierre des Corps	d.				1000		...					...	1801	...	
Rennes	d.						...			1433		...		...	
Laval	d.						...			1511		...		...	
Nantes	d.			0714b			...			1424b		...		...	
Angers	d.			0814			...			1513		...		...	
Le Mans	d.			0857			...			1602	1602	...		...	
Massy TGV	d.			0955	1055		...			1656	1656	...	1855	...	
Marne la Vallée - Chessy §	d.			1031	1131		...			1729	1729	...	1946n	...	
Brussels Midi/Zuid	d.	0717					...	1514q	1514q			...		...	
Lille Europe	d.	0759z					...	1558q	1558q			...	1754y	...	
Paris Charles de Gaulle ✈ +	d.	0859		1108p		1245	...	1659	1659			...	1858	...	
Champagne-Ardenne TGV	a.	0929		1137	1202r	1314	...	1729	1729	1759	1759	...	1929	2017	...
Champagne-Ardenne TGV	d.	0932		1140	1205r	1317	...	1735	1735	1805	1805	...	1935	2021	...
Meuse TGV	a.					1341	...					...		2044	...
Lorraine TGV	a.	1009		1218	1244r	1402	...	1813	1813	1846	1846	...	2014	2105	...
Strasbourg	a.	1049		1300	1328r	1441	...	1852	1901	1928	1928	...	2058	2145	...

CONNECTING 🚌 SERVICES (📞 03 87 78 67 09 for further details).   Nancy - Lorraine TGV (journey 35 minutes);   Verdun - Meuse TGV (journey 25 minutes).
Bus services connect with the trains in Table **391** on the following routes :   Metz - Lorraine TGV (journey 25 minutes);

A – ⑤–⑦ to Mar. 26; daily from Mar. 31.

b – 9 – 12 minutes later from Apr. 3.
c – 3 minutes earlier from Apr. 3.
d – Not Dec. 26, Apr. 14, 17, 18, May 1, 2, 8, 9, 25, June 5.
e – Also Dec. 26, Apr. 14, 17, May 1, 8, 25, June 5.
f – 2 – 4 minutes later on ① (also Apr. 18, May 2, 9, June 6; not Apr. 17, May 1, 8, June 5).
g – Jan. 28 - Apr. 8 diverted to Lille Flandres (a. 1530).
h – Not May 25.
k – Also May 25.
m – Not Apr. 16, 30, May 25.
n – Arrives 1927.
p – Arrives 1042.
q – Dec. 11 - Jan. 28 departs Brussels 1517, Lille 1603.
r – On ①⑥ from Apr. 3 Champagne-Ardenne a. 1159, d. 1202, Lorraine 1240, Strasbourg 1321.
s – Not Mar. 18, 19.
t – 2019 from Apr. 3.
v – Not Mar. 18, 19. Arrives 1218 from Apr. 3.
w – Not Apr. 30, May 7.
y – 1800 Dec. 11 - Jan. 22 and Apr. 24 - May 28.
z – 0802 Dec. 11 - Jan. 22 and Apr. 24 - May 28.

TGV – 🅁, supplement payable, ⑬.

⊗ – Subject to alteration on Apr. 29, 30, May 1, 20, 21, 27, June 10, 11.
☉ – Subject to alteration on May 20, 21, June 10, 11.
⊖ – Subject to alteration on May 20, June 10.
⊕ – Subject to alteration on Mar. 19.
⬚ – Subject to alteration on Apr. 15, 16, 29, 30, May 20, 27, June 10, 11, 17, 24.
§ – Station for Disneyland Paris.

391a   REIMS - CHAMPAGNE ARDENNE TGV

Certain trains continue to / from destinations in Table **389**

		⚒	⑥	⑥		⚒				Ⓐ				Ⓑ	†	⚒				Ⓐ	†	†
Reims	d.	0655	0731	0732	0800	0833	0906	1044	1100	1137	1304	1342	1453	1610	1625	1638	1705	1717	1803	1827	1904	1916	1956	2017	2039	2116
Champagne-Ardenne TGV	a.	0707	0743	0745	0812	0848	0921b	1056	1112	1149	1312	1354	1505	1622	1638	1650	1717	1729	1817	1839	1916	1928	2008	2029	2051	2128

		⚒	⑥	⑥		⚒				Ⓐ			†		Ⓐ			Ⓐ	Ⓒ	Ⓑ			Ⓐ	†	†
Champagne-Ardenne TGV	d.	0731	0755	0801	0840	0905	0957	1116	1149	1219	1322	1419	1516	1639	1655	1705	1818	1828	1849	1852	1936	1948	2020	2047	2115	2145
Reims	a.	0742	0808	0808	0852	0917	1009	1128	1200	1231	1334	1431	1528	1649	1707	1712	1832	1843	1902	1904	1950	2001	2032	2059	2127	2157

b – 1917 on Ⓒ.

392   LONGWY - NANCY / LUXEMBOURG

Longwy - Nancy

km		Ⓐ	⚒	Ⓐ	Ⓖ ✧	Ⓐ	Ⓒ	†	Ⓐ	⑦				Ⓐ	⚒		Ⓒ	Ⓖ ✧	†	Ⓐ	◇	⑤
							c v														f v	
0	Longwy 389a d.	0547	0647	0847	1047	1247r	1647	...	1859	1947	...	Nancy 384 d.	0554		0839		1239	1439	1639	1739	1839	1945
16	Longuyon 389a d.	0601	0700	0900	1100	1300	1700	...	1912	2000	...	Pont-à-Mousson 384 d.	0613		0859		1258	1458	1658	1758	1858	2002
57	Conflans-Jarny d.	0630	0730	0930	1130	1330	1730	...	1928	2030	...	Conflans-Jarny d.	0649		0931		1331	1531	1731	1831	1931	2030
100	Pont-à-Mousson 384 d.	0700	0800	1000	1200	1400	1800	...	1958	2016	...	Longuyon 389a d.	0721		1000		1400	1600	1800	1900	2000	...
128	Nancy 384 a.	0720	0820	1020	1220	1420	1820	...	2014	2036	...	Longwy 389a a.	0735		1012		1412	1612	1812	1912	2012	...

Longwy - Luxembourg

km		①–⑤	⑤	⑥	⑥	①–⑤	⑥	①–⑤	①–⑤	①–⑤	⑥			①–⑥	⑥	①–⑤	⑤	①–⑤	①–⑤	①–⑤	①–⑤	①–⑥	①–⑤	⑤
		n	n			n		A	n	A				n		n	A	n		n	n		n	n
0	Longwy d.	0617	0647	0728	0747	0817	0847	1317	1843	1907	...	Luxembourg d.	0615	0715	0741	1215	1615	1645	1715	1745	1812	1845	1915
8	Rodange 🚉 d.	0626	0655	0736	0756	0826	0856	1326	1852	1915	...	Rodange 🚉 d.	0639	0739	0809	1239	1639	1709	1739	1809	1839	1909	1939
27	Luxembourg a.	0648	0718	0827	0818	0848	0918	1348	1911	2012	...	Longwy a.	0646	0746	0816	1246	1646	1716	1746	1816	1846	1916	1946

A – ①–⑤ to Apr. 14 (not Dec. 26, Feb. 6 - Mar. 17).
G – Dec. 12 - Jan. 13, Feb. 6 – 24 and from Apr. 24.

c – Not Dec. 18, 25, Feb. 12, 19, Apr. 9, 16.
f – Not Dec. 23, 30, Feb. 17, 24, Apr. 14, 21.
n – Not Dec. 26, Apr. 17, May 1, 25, June 5, 23.

r – Until Jan. 13.
v – From / to Verdun (Table **393a**).

✧ – Subject to alteration on Mar. 5.
◇ – Subject to alteration on Mar. 4.

LONGWY - METZ 🚌 service (journey 55 minutes):
Subject to confirmation.
From Longwy at 0450 Ⓐ, 0645 Ⓐ, 0745, 0945 ⚒, 1245 ⚒, 1445 ⑤, 1645 Ⓐ, 1827 Ⓐ and 1930.
From Metz at 0631 Ⓐ, 0820 Ⓐ, 0920 ⚒, 1025 †, 1220 ⚒, 1520 ⑤, 1620 Ⓐ, 1820 ⚒, 2020 Ⓐ, 2120 † and 2220 ⚒.

393   🚌 CHÂLONS EN CHAMPAGNE - VERDUN

km		Ⓐ	Ⓒ	Ⓐ		Ⓐ	†	Ⓒ	Ⓐ				Ⓐ	Ⓒ		Ⓐ		Ⓐ		
0	Châlons en Champagne d.	0820	1020	1220	1420	1820	1930	2030	2040	...		Verdun d.	0542	0612	...	1017	1212	...	1517	...	1817
62	Ste Menehould Médiathèque d.	0923	1123	1323	1523	1923	2033	2133	2143	...		Ste Menehould Médiathèque d.	0627	0657	...	1102	1257	...	1602	...	1902
107	Verdun a.	1008	1208	1408	1608	2008	2118	2218	2228	...		Châlons en Champagne a.	0730	0800	...	1205	1400	...	1705	...	2005

VERDUN - METZ — 393a

km		⑥	Ⓐ	Ⓐ	▲	Ⓐs	Ⓐs	Ⓐt	⑥	Ⓐ	†jN	†
0	**Verdun** d.	...	0639	0739	1039	1239	1439	1639	1639	1815	1851	1939
40	Conflans-Jarny d.	0625	0722	0815	1115	1315	1515	1715	1715	1851	1927	2015
66	Hagondange . 384 d.	0705	|	0848	1148	1348	1548	1742	1748	|	...	|
84	**Metz** 384 a.	0716	0800	0901	1201h	1414	1601	1759	1801	1924	...	2059

	Ⓐ	Ⓐ⊙	⑥	Ⓐs	Ⓐs	Ⓒ◇	Ⓐ	†	Ⓐ	⑥	⑤fN
Metz 384 d.	0605	0846	0855	1038	1238	1255	1638z	1637	1821	1855	...
Hagondange 384 d.	|	0910	0910	1051	1251	1310	1651	1650‡	|	1910	...
Conflans-Jarny d.	0642	0943	0943	1123	1323	1343	1723	1728‡	1853	1943	2036
Verdun a.	0721	1019	1019	1159	1359	1419	1759	1819	1927	2019	2110

N – To/from Nancy (Table **392**).
f – Not Dec. 23, 30, Feb. 17, 24, Apr. 14, 21.
h – 1207 on ⑥⑦ from Apr. 1 (also Apr. 17, May 25).
j – Not Dec. 18, 25, Feb. 12, 19, Apr. 9, 16.
s – Not Dec. 26–30. Subject to alteration Feb. 13 - Apr. 21.
t – Not Dec. 26–30.
z – 1636 on certain dates.
‡ – 2–3 minutes later from Apr. 2.
▲ – Subject to alteration on Ⓐ (also on Apr. 2, 9).
⊙ – Subject to alteration Feb. 13–24, Apr. 10–21.
◇ – Subject to alteration on Apr. 2, 9.

METZ - FORBACH - SAARBRÜCKEN — 394

On Dec. 26, Apr. 14 the service between Forbach and Saarbrücken operates as on ⑦.

km		Ⓐ	⑥	Ⓐ	Ⓐ	⑥		†w	⑥	Ⓐ	Ⓐ⊙	Ⓒ	Ⓐ⊙	Ⓒ	Ⓐ⊙	⚒⊙	Ⓐ	Ⓐ	Ⓒ⊖	⚒				Ⓐ	Ⓒ	†	Ⓐ
0	**Metz** ▶ d.	0538	0608	0638	0738	0738	0838	...	0934	0938	1038	1038	1138	1238	1238	1338	1438	1538	1538	1638	1738	1838	1938	2038	2138	2238	2238
50	St Avold ▶ d.	0610	0639	0710	0810	0813	0911	...	1006	1010	1110	1113	1210	1313	1312	1410	1510	1610	1613	1710	1810	1910	2010	2110	2210	2310	2310
70	Forbach ▶ a.	0626	0656	0726	0826	0828	0926	...	1022	1026	1126	1126	1226	1326	1326	1426	1526	1626	1627	1726	1826	1926	2026	2126	2226	2326	2326
70	Forbach d.	0632	0659	0732	0832	...	0930r	0932	...	1032	1130	1132	1232	1330	1332	1432	1532	1632	1632	1732	1832	1932b	2032	2132	...	2330	2345
81	**Saarbrücken** a.	0642	0709	0742	0842	...	0940r	0942	...	1042	1140	1142	1242	1340	1342	1442	1542	1642	1642	1742	1842	1942b	2042	2142	...	2340	2355

	Ⓐz	⑥z	⚒	Ⓑ	⑥	⚒	Ⓐ		Ⓐ⊙	⊙	Ⓐ⊙	⑥	⑥	Ⓐ⊙	†	Ⓐ	⑥	Ⓐ	†		Ⓐ	Ⓐ	Ⓒ		Ⓑ	⑥	Ⓐ
Saarbrücken d.	0425	0450	0616a	0716	0721	0816a	0921	1016	1116	1221a	1316	1321	1416	1416	1421	1516	1521	1616	1616	1716	...	1816	1816	1916	2016	2016	2116
Forbach a.	0435	0500	0626a	0726	0731	0826a	0931	1026	1126	1231a	1326	1331	1426	1426	1431	1526	1531	1626	1626	1726	...	1826	1826	1926	2026	2026	2126
Forbach ▶ d.	0503	0503	0633	0733	0733	0833	0933	1033	1133	1233	1333	1333	1433	1433	1433	1533	1533	1633	1633	1733	1807	1833	1833	1933	2033	2033	2133
St Avold ▶ d.	0518	0518	0646	0748	0749	0848	0948	1047	1148	1247	1348	1348	1446	1448	1449	1549	1547	1648	1646	1748	1820	1848	1846	1948	2048	2046	2148
Metz ▶ a.	0550	0550	0722	0820	0820	0920	1020	1120	1220	1320	1420	1420	1520	1520	1522	1620	1620	1720	1720	1820	1856	1920	1921	2020	2120	2121	2220

a – Ⓐ only.
b – Not ⑥.
r – ⚒ only.
z – Not ②–⑥ Feb. 14–25, ②–⑥ Mar. 14–25, ②–⑥ May 2 - June 23.
⊖ – Change trains at Forbach on †.
⊗ – Subject to alteration on ①–⑤ Mar. 6–24 and Ⓐ from May 2.
⊙ – Subject to alteration on ①–⑤ Mar. 20 - Apr. 7 and Apr. 24–28.
▶ – Additional journeys Metz - Forbach and v.v.:
From Metz at 0704 Ⓐ, 1713 Ⓐ, 1813 Ⓐ and 1910 Ⓐ.
From Forbach at 0607 Ⓐ, 0707 Ⓐ and 0801 Ⓐ.

METZ - SARREGUEMINES Journey: 59–66 minutes.
From Metz at 0734 Ⓐ, 0834 Ⓐ, 1234 ⚒⊗, 1634 Ⓐ, 1734 ⑥, 1834 Ⓐ and 2034 Ⓑ.
From Sarreguemines at 0605 ⑥, 0611 Ⓐ, 0726 Ⓐ, 1126 Ⓐ ⊗, 1526 Ⓐ ⊗, 1621 ⑥, 1721 †, 1726 Ⓐ and 1926 Ⓐ.

STRASBOURG - SAARBRÜCKEN — 395

On Dec. 26, Apr. 14 services run as on ⑦.

km		Ⓐ¶	Ⓐ	⑥	Ⓐ	†	⑥	Ⓐ⊡	Ⓐ¶⊡	⚒⊡	†	Ⓐ¶⊡	†	Ⓐ	⑥	Ⓐ	†	Ⓐ¶	⑥	Ⓐ	†	Ⓐ	⑥	Ⓐ	†
0	**Strasbourg** d.	0544	0638	0740	0745	0845	0945	0945	1145	1245	1255	1444	1445	1545	1545	1645	1652	1715	1745	1759	1815	1845	1942	1955	2000
71	Diemeringen d.	0643	0737	0840	0848	0944	1044	1044	1244	1344	1354	1544	1544	1644	1644	1743	1751	1816	1844	1903	1914	1944	2041	2055	2102
97	Sarreguemines 🚋 ▲ d.	0704	0759	0902	0911	1011	1106	1105	1311	1406	1416	1606	1606	1705	1711	1806	1813	1837	1906	1925	1936	2006	2102	2117	2123
115	**Saarbrücken** Hbf ▲ a.	...	...	0922	0927	1027	...	...	1327	...	...	...	...	...	1727	...	...	...	...	...	...	...	2122§	...	...

	Ⓐ	Ⓐ¶	⚒	Ⓐ¶	Ⓐ	†	⑥	⚒⊡		†	⚒⊡		†	Ⓐ⊡	⑥		⑥	Ⓐ¶	Ⓐ	†	Ⓐ¶	Ⓑ	⑥	Ⓑ
Saarbrücken Hbf ▲ d.	...	...	...	...	...	0654‡	...	...	...	...	0954	...	1154	...	...	...	...	1354	...	...	...	...	1754	...
Sarreguemines 🚋 ▲ d.	0502	0544	0614	0644	0711	0715	0721	0814	...	1014	1015	...	1215	1221	1226	...	1414	1421	1507	1614	1620	1714	1815	1822
Diemeringen d.	0523	0605	0635	0705	0732	0737	0742	0835	...	1035	1035	...	1236	1242	1247	...	1435	1442	1528	1635	1641	1735	1835	1843
Strasbourg a.	0627	0707	0737	0807	0837	0838	0846	0937	...	1137	1137	...	1338	1345	1349	...	1537	1549	1637	1737	1745	1837	1937	1949

SAARBAHN LIGHT RAIL SERVICE **S1** **SARREGUEMINES - SAARBRÜCKEN** ⊖

	⚒	Ⓐ	⚒	Ⓐ				
Sarreguimes (Bahnhof) d.	0516	0546	0616	0646	0716	hourly ◐	2316	0016
Saarbrücken Hbf a.	0545	0615	0645	0715	0745	until	2345	0045

	⚒	Ⓐ	⚒	Ⓐ	⚒	Ⓐ			
Saarbrücken Hbf d.	0440	0510	0540	0610	0640	0710	0740	hourly ◧	2340
Sarreguimes (Bahnhof) a.	0510	0540	0610	0640	0710	0740	0810	until	0010

¶ – Not Dec. 26–30.
§ – Not Dec. 24.
‡ – Not Dec. 25.
◐ – Every 30 minutes 0716 - 0916 and 1216 - 2116 on Ⓐ, 0816 - 1816 on ⑥, 1216 - 1816 on †.
◧ – Every 30 minutes 0740 - 0840 and 1140 - 2040 on Ⓐ, 0740 - 1740 on ⑥, 1140 - 1740 on †.
⊡ – Subject to alteration on ①–⑤ Apr. 3–28.
▲ – For additional light rail service Sarreguemines - Sarrbrücken see below main table.
⊖ – Operated by Saarbahn (www.saarbahn.de). In Saarbrücken also serves city centre.

STRASBOURG - WISSEMBOURG — 396

Additional trains run Strasbourg - Haguenau and v.v.

km		⚒	Ⓐ	⑥	⑥	†	Ⓐ	⑥	Ⓐ	⑥	Ⓐ	†	⑥	Ⓐ	†	⑥	Ⓐ	†	⚒	†	Ⓐ	Ⓐ	†	Ⓐ	Ⓑ	⑥	Ⓑ
0	**Strasbourg** d.	0619	0735	0751	0851	0921	0935	1055	1121	1205	1251	1251	1351	1405	1451	1551	1621	1651	1721	1721	1751	1821	1851	1851	1921	1951	2035
34	Haguenau d.	0641	0811	0827	0913	0944	0959	1118	1150	1231	1314	1315	1415	1429	1515	1615	1644	1716	1743	1757	1817	1848	1916	1916	1946	2014	2109
66	**Wissembourg** a.	0717	0841	0853	0941	1010	1025b	1144	1217e	1309	1346b	1341	1441	1456b	1541	1641	1710	1742	1815	1823	1854	1914	1942	1953	2020	2046	2151*

	Ⓐ	Ⓐ	⑥	Ⓐ	⑥	†	Ⓐ	⑥	⑥	Ⓐ	†	†	Ⓐ	⑥	Ⓒ	Ⓐ	⑥	Ⓐ	†	Ⓐ	⑥	Ⓐ	⑥	†	Ⓐ	†
Wissembourg d.	0607	0641	0641	0730	0737	0844	0848	0948	1037	1040c	1045	1147	1230f	1237	1348	1402c	1548	1551c	1647	1741	1744	1821	1837	1838	1920	2049
Haguenau d.	0644	0714	0715	0804	0808	0915	0917	1015	1104	1106	1115	1214	1301	1303	1415	1429	1615	1618	1714	1818	1813	1847	1902	1913	1947	2115
Strasbourg a.	0711	0741	0738	0830	0830	0938	0939	1038	1138	1141	1138	1237	1324	1338	1437	1453	1637	1645	1737	1845	1837	1909	1937	1937	2009n	2138

b – By 🚌 from Haguenau Mar. 20 - Apr. 7 (arrives 18–41 minutes later).
c – By 🚌 to Haguenau Mar. 20 - Apr. 7 (departs 23–24 minutes **earlier**).
e – By 🚌 from Haguenau on ①②④⑤ Mar. 20 - Apr. 7 (a. 1228).
f – By 🚌 (d. 1142) to Haguenau on ①②④⑤ Mar. 20 - Apr. 7.
n – Not Dec. 27–30.
* – By 🚌.

PRIVATE TOURIST RAILWAYS — 397

MER DE GLACE - TRAIN DE MONTENVERS

✆ 04.50.53.22.75. www.compagniedumontblanc.fr

From Chamonix (200 metres from SNCF station) to Montenvers 'Mer de Glace' (altitude 1913 metres). Journey 20 minutes. **Service confirmed until April 30, 2017.**

A cable car takes visitors to the ice grotto inside the glacier

Dec. 17 - Mar. 17: from Chamonix 1000 - 1600, returning until 1630. Runs every 20–30 mins.
Mar. 18 - Apr. 30: from Chamonix 1000 - 1630, returning until 1700. Runs every 20–30 mins.
May 1 - July 8: from Chamonix 0830 - 1630‡, returning until 1700. Runs every 20–30 mins.
July 9 - Aug. 28: from Chamonix 0800 - 1800, returning until 1830. Runs every 20–30 mins.
Aug. 29 - Sept. 11: from Chamonix 0830 - 1700‡, returning until 1730. Runs every 20–30 mins.
Sept. 12 – 25: from Chamonix 0830 - 1630‡, returning until 1700. Runs every 20–30 mins.
Oct. 15 – 31: from Chamonix 1000 - 1600, returning until 1630. Runs every 30–60 mins.
Nov. 1 - Dec. 17: 1000, 1200, 1400, 1500, 1600, returning 1130, 1330, 1430, 1530, 1630.

‡ – Departure from Chamonix at 0900 (also 0930 return service) runs if sufficient demand.

PANORAMIQUE DES DÔMES *2016 service*

Electric rack railway from the foot to the summit of Le puy de Dôme. Journey: 15 minutes. No service on ①② until Mar. 15, Mar. 16–18, Oct. 10–14. www.panoramiquedesdomes.fr

Until Mar. 13 and Nov. 16 - Dec. 16: Hourly departures 1000 - 1700, returning 1030 - 1730.
Mar. 19 - July 1 and Sept. 5 - Oct. 2: Departures every 40 minutes 0900 - 1900, returning 0920 - 1920. **July 2 - Sept. 4**: Departures every 20 minutes 0900 - 2040, returning 0920 - 2100.
Oct. 3 - Nov. 13 and Dec. 17 – 31: Departures every 40 minutes 1000 - 1800, returning 1020 - 1820.

TRAMWAY DU MONT BLANC

The highest rack railway in France. www.compagniedumontblanc.fr
✆ 04.50.53.22.75.

Winter season : December 17, 2016 - March 26, 2017
Runs from St Gervais Le Fayet (opposite SNCF station) to Bellevue (altitude 1794 metres). Journey 60 minutes.

Mondays to Fridays (not school holidays):
Depart St Gervais : 0900, 1100, 1310, 1430.
Depart Bellevue : 1000, 1200, 1430, 1620 (to Feb. 3), 1650 (from Feb. 4).

Saturdays and Sundays (also during school holidays):
Depart St Gervais : 0900, 1000, 1100, 1310, 1410, 1510.
Depart Bellevue : 1000, 1100, 1200, 1410, 1510, 1620 (to Feb. 3), 1650 (from Feb. 4).

Summer season : June 11 - September 11, 2016
From St Gervais Le Fayet (opposite SNCF station) to Nid d'Aigle (altitude 2372 metres). Journey 70–80 minutes.

June 11 - July 8 and August 29 - September 11:
Depart St Gervais : 0820, 0930, 1030, 1100, 1220, 1330, 1430, 1510.
Depart Nid d'Aigle : 0935, 1040, 1155, 1225, 1335, 1445, 1600, 1700.

July 9 - August 28:
Depart St Gervais : 0720, 0830, 0930, 1000, 1110, 1220, 1330, 1400, 1520, 1630, 1740.
Depart Nid d'Aigle : 0835, 0940, 1050, 1125, 1230, 1340, 1455, 1610, 1640, 1750, 1900.

398 PARIS - PARIS AÉROPORTS

See page 31 for plan of central Paris

CHARLES DE GAULLE - PARIS

VAL shuttle train : air terminals - RER / TGV station.

Roissyrail (RER line B) : Aéroport Charles de Gaulle 2 TGV - Paris Châtelet les Halles. Frequent service 0450 - 2400.

Journey time from Charles de Gaulle :

Gare du Nord	35 minutes
Châtelet les Halles ★	38 minutes
St Michel Notre Dame	40 minutes
Antony (for Orly , see middle panel)	58 minutes

★ Cross - platform interchange with *RER* for Gare de Lyon.

ORLY - PARIS (*VAL + RER B*)

VAL light rail : Orly Sud - Orly Ouest - Antony (7 minutes). Frequent service ① - ⑤: 0600 - 2230; ⑦: 0700 - 2300. Cross platform interchange with RER line B (below).

RER line B : Antony - Paris. Frequent service 0510 - 0010.

Journey time from Antony :

St Michel Notre Dame	20 minutes
Châtelet les Halles ☆	25 minutes
Gare du Nord	29 minutes

☆ Interchange with *RER* for Gare de Lyon.

ORLY - PARIS (*Orlyrail*)

🚌 : Orly (Ouest and Sud) - Pont de Rungis Aéroport d'Orly station. Frequent shuttle service.

RER line C : Pont de Rungis Aéroport d'Orly - Paris. Every 15 minutes approx. 0500 - 2330 (0530 - 2400 from Paris).

Journey time from Pont de Rungis Aéroport d'Orly :

Paris Austerlitz	24 minutes
St Michel Notre Dame	27 minutes
Musée d'Orsay	31 minutes
Champ de Mars Tour Eiffel	39 minutes

399 SAVOIE SKI BUSES

Winter 2016 / 2017

🚌 *Ski buses* — GENÈVE AÉROPORT - ST GERVAIS - CHAMONIX

€★	Dec. 17, 2016 - Mar. 30, 2017		①⑤⑥⑦						⑥⑦	
–	**Genève** Gare Routière	d.	0730	1030	1230	1530	1730	2030	2230	...
–	**Genève** Arrivals terminal	d.	0800	1100	1300	1600	1800	2100	2300	...
–	Dormancy	a.	0900	1200	1400	1700	1900	2200	|	...
25	Megève ⊡	a.	*0925*	*1225r*	*1425r*	*1725*	*1925*	*2225*	|	...
25	St Gervais ⊡	a.	*0920*	*1220*	*1420*	*1720*	*1920*	*2220*	|	...
25	Les Contamines ⊡	a.	*0940*	*1240*	*1440*	*1740*	*1940*	*2240*	|	...
19	Les Houches	a.	0925	1225	1425	1725	1925	2225	0025	...
19	**Chamonix** Sud (Av. Courmayeur)	a.	0940	1240	1440	1740	1940	2240	0040	...

Dec. 17, 2016 - Mar. 30, 2017		①⑤⑥⑦						⑥⑦	
Chamonix Sud (Av. Courmayeur)	d.	0450	0750	0950	1250	1450	1750	1950	...
Les Houches	d.	0500	0800	1000	1300	1500	1800	2000	...
Les Contamines ⊡	d.	*0450*	*0750*	*0950*	*1250*	*1450*	*1750*	*1950*	...
St Gervais ⊡	d.	*0505*	*0805*	*1005*	*1305*	*1505*	*1805*	*2005*	...
Megève ⊡	d.	*0500*	*0800*	*1000*	*1300*	*1500*	*1800*	*2000*	...
Dormancy	d.	0530	0830	1030	1330	1530	1830	2030	...
Genève Arrivals terminal	a.	0640	0940	1140	1440	1640	1940	2140	...
Genève Gare Routière	a.	0700	1000	1200	1500	1700	2000	2200	...

r – Enquire for days of running.
⊡ – Connection from / to Dormancy.

★ – Best one-way fare in euros.

Reservations: www.ouibus.com. Reservation recommended.

🚌 *Ski buses* — GENÈVE AÉROPORT - ST GERVAIS - MEGÈVE

No service Dec. 25

€★	Dec. 17, 2016 - Apr. 1, 2017		⑥	⑥	
–	**Genève** Secteur International	d.	1330	1705	...
–	**Genève** Gare Routière	d.	1350	1725	...
–	Thonon, Place des Arts ▽	a.	1440	1825	...
35	Morzine, Gare Routière	a.	1535	1925	...
40	**Avoriaz 1800**	a.	1610	1955	...

Dec. 17, 2016 - Apr. 1, 2017		⑥	⑥	
Avoriaz 1800	d.	0930	1330	...
Morzine, Gare Routière	d.	1010	1400	...
Thonon, Place des Arts ▽	d.	1100	1500	...
Genève Gare Routière	a.	1150	1550	...
Genève Secteur International	a.	1215	1610	...

Geneve - Grand Bornand - St Jean de Sixt - **La Clusaz**: Dec. 17, 2016 - Apr. 2, 2017. Journey: Approx 2 hours.
From **Genève** 0810 ⑤–⑦, 1400 ⑥⑦, 1900 ⑤–⑦.
From **La Clusaz** at 0640 ⑤–⑦, 1130 ⑥⑦, 1700 ⑤–⑦.
www.gare-routiere.ch. Journeys to airport must be reserved in advance at the resort. Fare 41 CHF (68 CHF return).

★ – One-way fare in euros (return fare is €60 / 65, discount for groups).

Connections are available at Thonon to / from Abondance and Châtel.

Operator: SAT. Book on-line at www.sat-annemasse.com or ✆ +41 22 732 0230 (Gare Routière, Genève).

🚌 *Ski buses* — GENÈVE AÉROPORT - MORZINE - AVORIAZ

No service Dec. 25

€★	Dec. 17, 2016 - Apr. 9, 2017		⑥⑦ h	①⑤ E	⑥⑦ b	①⑤ E	①⑤ E	⑥⑦	⑥⑦	⑥⑦ b	①⑤ E
–	**Genève** Sect. Internat.	d.	0930	1030	1145	1300	1645	1730	1745	1800	1830
–	**Genève** Gare Routière	d.	0915	1015	1130	1245	1630	1700	1730	1745	1840
–	Annemasse, Gare Routière	d.	1015	1110	|	1345	1725	1815	|	|	1915
40	Les Carroz §	a.	|	|	1310	|	|	|	1910	|	|
45	Flaine §	a.	|	|	1330	|	|	|	1930	|	|
35	Morillon Télécabine	a.	1109	1209	|	1440	1835	1916	...	|	2016
35	Samoëns §	a.	1115	1215	|	1445	1840	1925	...	|	2025
35	Sixt-Fer à Cheval §	a.	1130	1230	|	1500	1855	1935	...	|	2035
25	Taninges, Café Central	a.	...	...	1300	...	...	...	...	1915	...
30	Les Gets, Gare Routière	a.	...	...	1315	...	...	...	...	1930	...
30	**Morzine**, Gare Routière	a.	...	...	1335	...	...	...	...	1950	...
35	Avoriaz-Prodains ⊡	a.	...	...	1345	...	...	...	...	2000	...

Dec. 17, 2016 - Apr. 9, 2017		⑥⑦ b	⑥⑦	①⑤ E	⑥⑦	①⑤ E	⑥⑦ b	⑥⑦	⑥⑦ b	⑥⑦
Avoriaz-Prodains ⊡	d.	...	...	0830	...	...	...	1430	...	1730
Morzine, Gare Routière	d.	...	...	0840	...	...	...	1440	...	1740
Les Gets, Gare Routière	d.	...	...	0900	...	...	...	1500	...	1800
Taninges, Café Central	d.	...	...	0915	...	...	...	1515	...	1815
Sixt-Fer à Cheval §	d.	0615	...	|	1200	1230	...	|	1630	|
Samoëns §	d.	0620	...	|	1215	1245	...	|	1645	|
Morillon Télécabine	d.	0625	...	|	1220	1250	...	|	1650	|
Flaine §	d.	|	0830	|	|	|	1400	|	|	|
Les Carroz §	d.	|	0850	|	|	|	1420	|	|	|
Annemasse, Gare Routière	a.	0738	|	|	1315	1345	|	|	1745	1900
Genève Gare Routière	a.	0820	1030	1045	1400	1415	1600	1645	1830	1945
Genève Sect. Internat.	a.	0805	1015	1030	1415	1430	1545	1630	1840	1930

E – ①⑤ Dec. 17 - Jan. 1, Jan. 29 - Mar. 12.
b – Also ①⑤ Dec. 17 - Jan. 1, Jan. 29 - Mar. 12.
h – Also at 0730⑥⑦.

⊡ – Avoriaz-Prodains, Téléphérique (for cable car to Avoriaz village).
§ – Office du Tourisme.
★ – One-way fare in euros.

Operators: Altibus (SAT Leman and Transdev).
Reservations: recommended. Book online at www.altibus.com or ✆ +41 22 732 0230 (Gare Routière, Genève). Reservation compulsory for return to airport at least 24 hours in advance at local tourist or bus office.

🚌 *Ski buses* — GENÈVE AÉROPORT - TARENTAISE SKI RESORTS

Not Dec. 25 (except **D** / **E**)

€★	Dec. 2, 2016 - Apr. 18, 2017		⑥⑦	C ⑥		⑥	⑥	D	C ⑥	F
–	**Genève** Gare Routière	d.	...	...	...	...	...	...	...	...
–	**Genève** , Secteur International	d.	1000	1100	1215	1330	1430	1530	1645	1915
70	**Moûtiers-Salins** Gare SNCF	a.	1200	1300	1415	1540	1630	1730	1845	2115
88	Courchevel-Valmorel / Pralognan ♥	a.	*1355*	*1440*	*1610*	*1700*	*1825*	*1910*	*2010*	*2240*
88	Méribel / St Martin de Belleville ⊡ ♥	a.	*1315*	*1400*	*1530*	*1700*	*1745*	*1830*	*1935*	*2200*
88	Les Menuires ⊡ / Brides les Bains ♥	a.	*1330*	*1415*	*1545*	*1715*	*1800*	*1845*	*1945*	*2215*
88	Val Thorens ⊡ ♥	a.	*1400*	*1445*	*1615*	*1745*	*1830*	*1915*	*2015*	*2245*
70	**Aime** Gare SNCF	a.	1220	1320	1435	1600	1650	1750	1905	2135
88	La Plagne ♥	a.	*1330*	*1430*	*1540*	*1720*	*1800*	*1900*	*2025*	*2250*
70	**Bourg St Maurice** Gare SNCF ☆	a.	1240	1340	1500	1620	1710	1810	1925	2155
88	Les Arcs / La Rosière ♥	a.	*1335*	*1435*	*1635*	*1710*	*1820*	*1910*	*2025*	*2250*
70	Tignes le Lac, Gare Routière	a.	1315	1415	1535	1655	1745	1845	2000	2230
70	Tignes Val Claret, Gare Routière	a.	1325	1425	1545	1705	1755	1855	2010	2240
70	**Val d'Isère** Gare Routière	a.	1400	1500	1620	1740	1830	1930	2045	2310

Dec. 3, 2016 - Apr. 19, 2017		B	E	⑥	F ⑧	F	⑥⑦
Val d'Isère Gare Routière	d.	0310	0600	0745	1000	1300	1515
Tignes Val Claret, Gare Routière	d.	0335	0625	0730	1030	1335	1540
Tignes le Lac, Gare Routière	d.	0350	0640	0745	1045	1350	1555
Les Arcs / La Rosière ♥	d.	|	⊙	⊙	⊙	⊙	⊙
Bourg St Maurice Gare SNCF ☆	d.	0430	0740	0845	1125	1445	1645
La Plagne ♥	d.	|	⊙	⊙	⊙	⊙	⊙
Aime Gare SNCF	d.	0450	0800	0915	1145	1515	1705
Val Thorens ⊡ ♥	d.	|	⊙	⊙	⊙	⊙	⊙
Les Menuires ⊡ / Brides les Bains ♥	d.	|	⊙	⊙	⊙	⊙	⊙
Méribel / St Martin de Belleville ⊡ ♥	d.	|	⊙	⊙	⊙	⊙	⊙
Courchevel-Valmorel / Pralognan ♥	d.	|	⊙	⊙	⊙	⊙	⊙
Moûtiers-Salins Gare SNCF	d.	0515	0845	1000	1225	1600	1750
Genève , Secteur International	a.	0700	1040	1210	1425	1800	1950
Genève Gare Routière	a.	...	...	...	...	...	...

B – ⑥ Dec. 31 - Mar. 25.
C – ⑥ Dec. 24 - Mar. 25.
D – Dec. 3 - Apr. 15 (including Dec. 25).
E – Dec. 3 - Apr. 19 (including Dec. 25).
F – Dec. 3 - Apr. 15 (not Dec. 25).
★ – One-way fare in euros. Return = single x 1.7. Discounts for groups (4 +).

♥ – Connecting 🚌 service. Approximate times.
⊙ – Times given at time of booking. Reservation compulsory.
⊡ – Through journeys also available on ⑤–⑦ through Voyages Loyet. www.loyet.com ✆ +33 479 55 64 76.
☆ – A funicular railway links Bourg St Maurice with Les Arcs 1600 every 20 mins during the winter sports period (free 🚌 connects to Les Arcs 1800 and 2000).

Reservations: recommended – book on-line at www.transdevsavoie.com or ✆ +41 22 732 0230 (Gare Routière, Genève). Reservations for the journey returning to the airport are compulsory at the local bus or tourist office 48 hours in advance, when departure times will be confirmed.
Operators : Transdev Martin, Transdev Savoie, Touriscar.
Journeys are not guaranteed during bad weather.

🚌 *Ski buses* — GENÈVE AÉROPORT ✈ - GRENOBLE - L'ALPE D'HUEZ / LES DEUX ALPES

See Table **364a** for daily services Genève Aéroport - Grenoble. Connections are available to l'Alpe d'Huez, Stations de l'Isère, Briancon and Serre Chevalier. Reservations: www.aerocar.fr

🚌 *Ski buses* — LYON ✈ - SAVOIE SKI RESORTS

Coach services operate from Lyon St Exupéry airport to most Savoie ski resorts from late December to mid April. Book on-line at www.altibus.com or ✆ +33 479 68 32 96 (or within France ✆ 0 820 320 368). e-mail : info@altibus.com. Reservations are compulsory, at least seven days in advance.

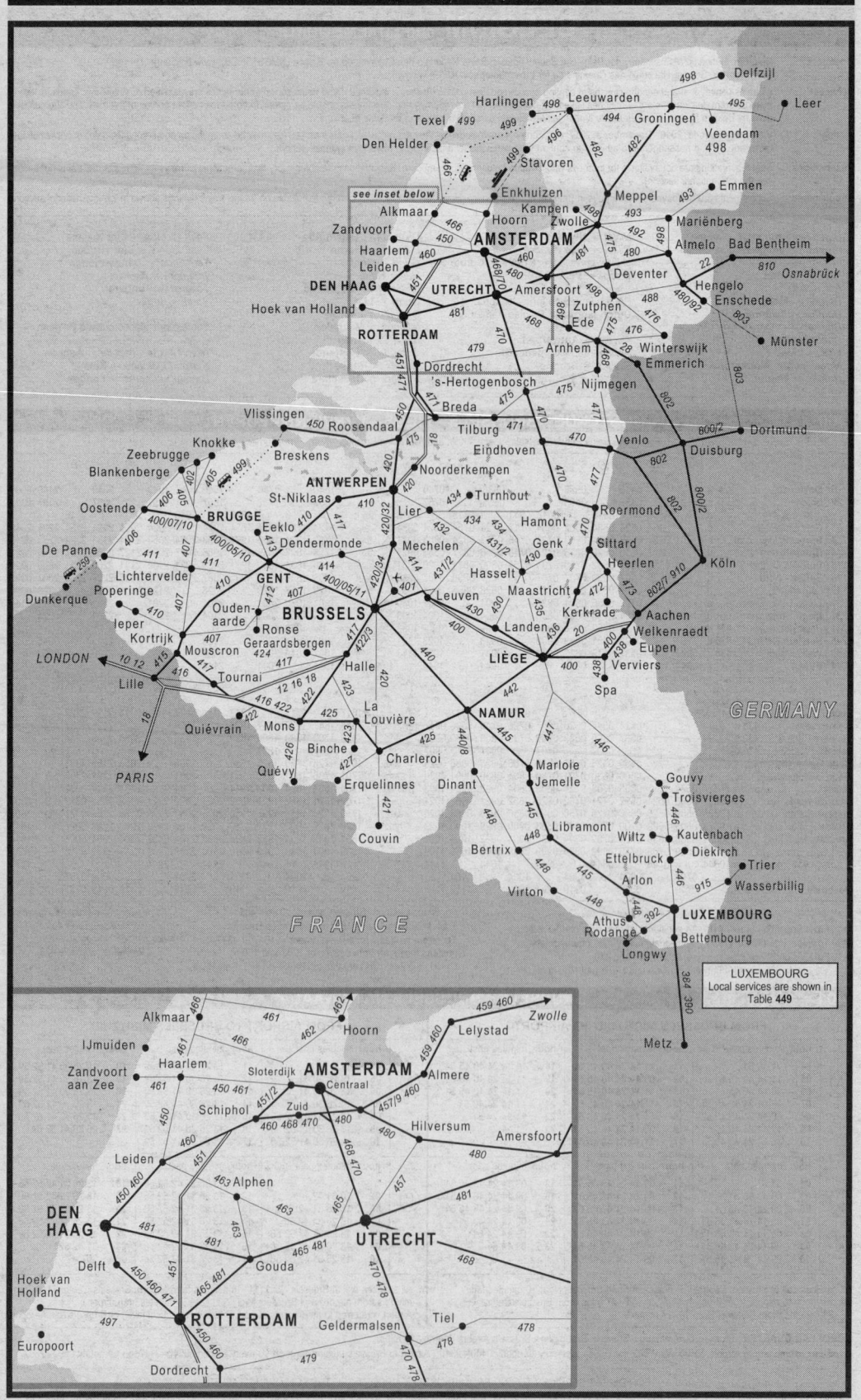

Delfzijl

Leer

Harlingen · 498 · Leeuwarden · 498 · 495

Texel · 499 · 499 · 494 · Groningen

Den Helder · 499 · Stavoren · 496 · 482 · 482 · Veendam · 498

466 · Enkhuizen · Meppel · 493 · Emmen

Alkmaar · 466 · Hoorn · Kampen · 498 · 493 · Mariënberg

Zandvoort · 450 · Zwolle · 492 · 498 · Almelo · Bad Bentheim

Haarlem · 460 · **AMSTERDAM** · 460 · 475 · 480 · Hengelo · 22 · 810 · Osnabrück

Leiden · **DEN HAAG** · **UTRECHT** · Amersfoort · Deventer · 481 · 488 · 480/91 · Enschede

Hoek van Holland · 481 · Zutphen · 803

ROTTERDAM · 470 · 468 · Ede · 475 · 476 · 28 · Winterswijk · Münster

Dordrecht · 479 · Arnhem · 468 · Emmerich

's-Hertogenbosch · 475 · Nijmegen · 802 · 803

Vlissingen · 450 · Roosendaal · Breda · 475 · 477

Zeebrugge · Knokke · Breskens · Tilburg · 471 · Venlo · 800/2 · Dortmund

Blankenberge · 405 · 499 · **ANTWERPEN** · Eindhoven · 470 · 802 · Duisburg

Oostende · 406 · 405 · St-Niklaas · 410 · Lier · 434 · Turnhout · Roermond · 802 · 800/2

De Panne · 411 · 407 · Eeklo · 410 · Mechelen · 434 · Hamont · 470 · Sittard · 802/7 910 · Köln

Dunkerque · Lichtervelde · 410 · **GENT** · 414 · Hasselt · 430 · Genk · 472 · Heerlen · 473

Poperinge · 407 · Ouden-aarde · 407 · Leuven · 430 · Landen · Maastricht · 435 · Kerkrade · Aachen

Ieper · Kortrijk · Ronse · Geraardsbergen · Halle · **LIÈGE** · 438 · Eupen

LONDON · 415 · Mouscron · 424 · 417 · 420 · 400 · 438 · Verviers

Lille · 416 · Tournai · La Louvière · 442 · Spa

Quiévrain · Mons · 425 · **NAMUR** · 445 · 447 · 446 · Gouvy · Troisvierges

PARIS · Quévy · Binche · Charleroi · 425 · Marloie · Jemelle · 446 · Wiltz · Kautenbach

Erquelinnes · Dinant · 448 · 445 · Libramont · Diekirch · Trier

Couvin · Bertrix · 448 · Ettelbruck · 446 · Wasserbillig

Virton · 445 · Arlon · 915

Athus · 448 · 392 · **LUXEMBOURG** · Bettembourg

Rodange · Longwy · 364 · 390

Metz

GERMANY

FRANCE

LUXEMBOURG
Local services are shown in
Table **449**

Inset

Alkmaar · 466 · 462 · Hoorn

IJmuiden · 461 · 466 · 462 · Lelystad · 459 460 · Zwolle

Zandvoort aan Zee · Haarlem · Sloterdijk · **AMSTERDAM** · Almere · 459 460

461 · 450 461 · 451/2 · Centraal · 457/9 460

Schiphol · Zuid · 460 468 470 · 480 · Hilversum · Amersfoort

Leiden · 460 · 451 · 468 470 · 480 · 480

450 460 · 463 · Alphen · 465 · 457 · 481

DEN HAAG · 481 · 463 · 465 481 · **UTRECHT**

Delft · 481 · Gouda · 470 478 · 468

Hoek van Holland · 450 460 471 · 465 481

Europoort · 497 · **ROTTERDAM** · Geldermalsen · Tiel · 478

Dordrecht · 479 · 470 478 · 478

BELGIUM and LUXEMBOURG

Operators: **Belgium**: Nationale Maatschappij der Belgische Spoorwegen / Société Nationale des Chemins de fer Belges (NMBS / SNCB). www.belgianrail.be
Luxembourg: Société Nationale des Chemins de fer Luxembourgeois (CFL). www.cfl.lu

Services: All trains convey first and second classes of seating accommodation unless otherwise indicated. Most trains shown in our tables are classified *IC* (InterCity). Trains for two or more different destinations are sometimes linked together for part of their journey and passengers should be careful to board the correct portion of the train. The line numbers used by Belgian Railways in their public timetables are shown as small numbers in the table headings.

Timings: Valid **December 11, 2016 - December 9, 2017.** Amendments are included as they are received. Local train services may be amended on and around the dates of public holidays (see page 2), and passengers are advised to confirm train times locally if planning to travel during these periods.

Reservations: Seat reservations are not available for journeys wholly within Belgium or Luxembourg. Reservations are compulsory for international journeys on *Thalys* or *ICE* trains (for timings see the International section).

Supplements: Supplements are not payable for journeys in Belgium or Luxembourg. However, a higher level of fares is payable on *Thalys* trains (timings shown in the International section).

Dutch-language forms of some **French-language** Belgian names

Aarlen = **Arlon**
Aat = **Ath**
Bergen = **Mons**
Doornik = **Tournai**
Duinkerke = **Dunkerque** (France)
Hoei = **Huy**
Luik = **Liège**
Moeskroen = **Mouscron**
Namen = **Namur**
Nijvel = **Nivelles**
Rijsel = **Lille** (France)
's Gravenbrakel = **Braine le Comte**
Wezet = **Visé**

French-language forms of some **Dutch-language** Belgian names

Anvers = **Antwerpen**
Audenarde = **Oudenaarde**
Bruges = **Brugge**
Courtrai = **Kortrijk**
Dixmude = **Diksmuide**
Furnes = **Veurne**
Gand = **Gent**
Hal = **Halle**
La Panne = **De Panne**
Lierre = **Lier**
Louvain = **Leuven**
Malines = **Mechelen**
Menin = **Menen**
Ostende = **Oostende**
Renaix = **Ronse**
Roulers = **Roeselare**
Saint Nicolas = **Sint Niklaas**
Saint Trond = **Sint Truiden**
Termonde = **Dendermonde**
Tirlemont = **Tienen**
Tongres = **Tongeren**
Ypres = **Ieper**

Some other places outside Belgium

Aken / Aix la Chapelle = **Aachen**
Keulen / Cologne = **Köln**
Londen / Londres = **London**

400 OOSTENDE - BRUSSELS - LIÈGE - VERVIERS - EUPEN

Lines 50a, 36, 37

For *Thalys* trains Paris - Brussels - Liège - Köln and *ICE* trains Brussels - Köln - Frankfurt see Table **21**

km			Ⓐ		Ⓐ		Ⓐ	Ⓐ ♠		Ⓐ		Ⓐ ⊡	
0	**Oostende** ▶ d.	...	...	0440	...	0538	...	...	0638r	...	0740	...	
22	Brugge ▷ d.	...	...	0457	...	0555	...	...	0655r	...	0757	...	
	Kortrijk **410** d.	...	0416	|	0516	|	0616	0641	|	0716	|	0816	and
62	Gent Sint-Pieters ▷ d.	...	0454	0524	0554	0622	0654	0717	0724	0754	0824	0854	at
114	**Brussels** Midi / Zuid ▷ a.	...	0524	0553	0624	0652	0724	0746	0753	0824	0853	0924	the
114	**Brussels** Midi / Zuid d.	...	0527	0556	0628	0656	0727	0748	0756	0827	0856	0927	same
116	Brussels Central d.	...	0531	0600	0632	0700	0731	0752	0800	0831	0900	0931	minutes
118	Brussels Nord d.	...	0535	0607	0639	0707	0737	0756	0807	0838	0907	0938	past
148	Leuven d.	...	...	0626	0658	0728	0758	...	0828	0855	0928	0957	each
221	**Liège** Guillemins a.	...	...	0702	0730	0801	0830	...	0901	...	1001	1030	hour
221	**Liège** Guillemins d.	...	...	0704	0733	0804	0836	...	0904	...	1004	1033	until
241	Pepinster **438** d.	...	...	|	0753	|	0854	...	|	...	|	1053	
245	**Verviers** Central **438** d.	...	...	0723	0801	0823	0902	...	0923	...	1023	1101	
258	Welkenraedt **438** d.	0637	...	0737	0815	0837	0914	...	0937	...	1037	1113	
264	**Eupen** a.	0644	...	0744	...	0844	...	...	0944	...	1044	...	

km			Ⓐ		Ⓐ		Ⓐ		Ⓐ		Ⓐ	△	△
0	**Oostende** ▶ d.	1640	...	1740	...	1840	...	1940	...	2040	...	2140	2305
22	Brugge ▷ d.	1657	...	1757	...	1857	...	1957	...	2057	...	2157	2322
	Kortrijk **410** d.	|	1716	|	1816	|	1916	|	2016	|	2116	|	|
62	Gent Sint-Pieters ▷ d.	1724	1754	1824	1854	1924	1954	2024	2054	2124	2154	2224	2349
114	**Brussels** Midi / Zuid ▷ a.	1753	1824	1853	1924	1953	2024	2053	2124	2153	2224	2253	0018
114	**Brussels** Midi / Zuid d.	1756	1827	1856	1927	1956	2027	2056	2127	2156	2227	2256	0021
116	Brussels Central d.	1800	1831	1900	1931	2000	2031	2100	2131	2200	2231	2300	0025
118	Brussels Nord d.	1808	1838	1907	1935	2007	2035	2107	2135	2207	2235	2307	0032
148	Leuven d.	1829	1857	1928	...	2028	...	2128	...	2228	...	2328	0050
221	**Liège** Guillemins a.	1901	1930	2001	...	2101	...	2201	...	2301	...	0022	0144
221	**Liège** Guillemins d.	1904	1933	2004	...	2104	...	2204	...	2304	...	0024	...
241	Pepinster **438** d.	|	1953	|	...	|	...	|	...	|	...	|	...
245	**Verviers** Central **438** d.	1923	2001	2023	...	2123	...	2223	...	2323	...	0045	...
258	Welkenraedt **438** d.	1937	2013	2037	...	2137	...	2235	...	2335	...	0057	...
264	**Eupen** a.	1944	...	2044	...	2144	...	...	...	...	...	...	...

	Ⓐ	△	Ⓐ	•	Ⓐ	•	Ⓐ	•	Ⓐ	•	Ⓐ ⊙	
Eupen d.	...	...	...	...	...	0617a	...	0717	...	0817	...	
Welkenraedt **438** d.	...	...	...	0524	0547	0626	0647	0726	0745	0826	0847	
Verviers Central **438** d.	...	...	...	0537	0600	0639	0700	0739	0800	0839	0900	and
Pepinster **438** d.	...	...	...	|	0607	|	0707	|	0807	|	0907	at
Liège Guillemins a.	...	...	...	0555	0625	0656	0725	0756	0825	0856	0925	the
Liège Guillemins d.	...	0440	...	0600	0630	0701	0730	0801	0830	0901	0930	same
Leuven d.	...	0534	...	0635	0703	0734	0803	0834	0903	0934	1003	minutes
Brussels Nord d.	0521	0555	0621	0652	0721	0752	0825	0852	0921	0952	1021	past
Brussels Central d.	0525	0559	0625	0656	0725	0756	0829	0856	0925	0956	1025	each
Brussels Midi / Zuid a.	0529	0603	0629	0700	0729	0800	0833	0900	0929	1000	1029	hour
Brussels Midi / Zuid ▷ d.	0532	0606	0636	0704	0732	0804	0836	0904	0932	1004	1032	until
Gent Sint-Pieters ▷ d.	0609	0639	0709	0739	0809	0839	0909	0939	1009	1039	1109	
Kortrijk **410** a.	0644	|	0744	|	0844	|	0944	|	1044	|	1144	
Brugge ▷ d.	...	0704	...	0804	...	0904	...	1004	...	1104	...	
Oostende ▶ a.	...	0719	...	0819	...	0919	...	1019	...	1119	...	

	•	Ⓐ	•	Ⓐ	•	Ⓐ	•	Ⓐ	•	•	△		Ⓐ ♥
Eupen d.	1617	...	1717	...	1817	...	1917	...	2017	2117	2222		...
Welkenraedt **438** d.	1626	1647	1726	1747	1826	...	1926	...	2026	2126	2231		...
Verviers Central **438** d.	1639	1700	1739	1800	1839	...	1939	...	2039	2139	2244		...
Pepinster **438** d.	|	1707	|	1807	|	...	|	...	|	|	|		...
Liège Guillemins a.	1656	1725	1756	1825	1856	...	1956	...	2056	2156	2303		...
Liège Guillemins d.	1701	1730	1801	1830	1901	...	2001	...	2101	2201	2308	A	...
Leuven d.	1734	1803	1834	1903	1934	...	2034	...	2134	2234	0001	L	...
Brussels Nord d.	1752	1821	1852	1921	1952	2021	2052	2121	2152	2252	0019	S	1604
Brussels Central d.	1756	1825	1856	1925	1956	2025	2056	2125	2156	2256	0023	O	1608
Brussels Midi / Zuid a.	1800	1829	1900	1929	2000	2029	2100	2129	2200	2300	0027		1612
Brussels Midi / Zuid ▷ d.	1804	1832	1904	1932	2004	2032	2104	2132	2204	2304	0029		1614
Gent Sint-Pieters ▷ d.	1839	1909	1939	2009	2039	2109	2139	2209	2239	2339	0112		1652
Kortrijk **410** a.	|	1944	|	2044	|	2144	|	2244	|	|	|		1721
Brugge ▷ d.	1904	...	2004	...	2104	...	2204	...	2304	0004	0137		...
Oostende ▶ a.	1919	...	2019	...	2119	...	2219	...	2319	0019	0151		...

a – Ⓐ only.
r – Runs 2 minutes later on Ⓒ.
♠ – From Poperinge (Table **410**). An additional journey runs one hour later.
♥ – To Poperinge (Table **410**). An additional journey runs one hour later.
▶ – For Oostende - Brugge see also Tables **407** and **410**.
△ – Via Landen (Table **430**) between Leuven and Liège (not high-speed line).
▷ – For Brugge - Gent - Brussels see also Table **405**.
⊡ – Train from Kortrijk at 1016 terminates at Leuven.
⊙ – There are no trains from Welkenraedt at 1047 or 1347 (instead they start from Leuven at 1203 and 1503).
• – On Ⓐ runs 2 - 4 mins later through Brussels Nord / Cent / Midi.

For slower trains Brussels - Liège via Landen see Table **430.**
For Aachen change at Verviers or Welkenraedt (Table **438***).*

401 BRUSSELS - BRUSSELS NATIONAAL ✈

Line 36c

FROM BRUSSELS MIDI / ZUID TO AIRPORT

	hour	minutes past	hour	minutes past	hour	minutes past
Ⓐ	**04**	11 40 51	**11**	11 14 24 40 45 51	**18**	11 14 24 40 45 51
	05	11 14 40 45 51	**12**	09 14 24 40 45 51	**19**	11 14 24 40 45 51
	06	06 14 40 45 51	**13**	11 14 24 40 45 51	**20**	11 14 24 40 45 51
	07	06 14 24 40 45 51	**14**	11 14 24 40 45 51	**21**	11 14 24 40 51
	08	06 14 24 40 45 52	**15**	11 14 24 40 45 51	**22**	11 14 24 51
	09	11 14 24 40 45 51	**16**	06 14 24 40 45 51	**23**	11 14 24
	10	06 14 24 40 45 51	**17**	11 14 24 40 45 51		
	hour	minutes past	hour	minutes past	hour	minutes past
Ⓒ	**04**	51	**11**	09 14 24 43 45 51	**18**	09 14 24 43 45 51
	05	09 43 45 51	**12**	09 14 24 43 45 51	**19**	09 14 24 43 45 51
	06	09 24 43 45 51	**13**	09 14 24 43 45 51	**20**	09 14 24 43 45 51
	07	09 14 24 43 45 51	**14**	09 14 24 43 45 51	**21**	09 14 24 43 51
	08	09 14 24 43 45 51	**15**	09 14 24 43 45 51	**22**	09 14 24 51
	09	09 14 24 43 45 51	**16**	09 14 24 43 45 51	**23**	09 14 51
	10	09 14 24 43 45 51	**17**	09 14 24 43 45 51		

All services call at Brussels Central 4 minutes later and Brussels Nord 10 minutes later. Journey time to airport: from Brussels Midi / Zuid 20 - 27 mins, from Brussels Centraal 16 - 23 minutes, from Brussels Nord 10 - 17 minutes.

FROM AIRPORT TO BRUSSELS MIDI / ZUID

	hour	minutes past	hour	minutes past	hour	minutes past
Ⓐ	**04**	41	**11**	13 26 30 41 52 59	**18**	13 26 30 41 52 59
	05	13 26 30 41	**12**	13 26 30 41 52 59	**19**	13 26 30 41 52 59
	06	13 26 30 41	**13**	13 26 30 41 52 59	**20**	13 26 30 41 52 59
	07	13 26 30 41 59	**14**	13 26 30 41 52 59	**21**	13 26 30 41 52 59
	08	13 26 31 41 52 59	**15**	13 26 30 41 52 59	**22**	13 26 30 41 52 59
	09	13 26 30 41 52 59	**16**	13 26 30 41 52 59	**23**	26 30 41 52 59
	10	13 26 30 41 52 59	**17**	13 26 30 41 52 59		
	hour	minutes past	hour	minutes past	hour	minutes past
Ⓒ			**11**	13 26 31 42 52 56	**18**	13 26 31 42 52 56
	05	26 31 42	**12**	13 26 31 42 52 56	**19**	13 26 31 42 52 56
	06	13 26 31 42 56	**13**	13 26 31 42 52 56	**20**	13 26 31 42 52 56
	07	13 26 31 42 56	**14**	13 26 31 42 52 56	**21**	13 26 31 42 52 56
	08	13 26 31 42 52 58	**15**	13 26 31 42 52 56	**22**	13 26 31 42 52 56
	09	13 26 31 42 52 56	**16**	13 26 31 42 52 56	**23**	31 42 52
	10	13 26 31 42 52 56	**17**	13 26 31 42 52 56	**00**	30

All services call at Brussels Nord (11 - 18 minutes from airport), Brussels Centraal (16 - 23 minutes from airport) and Brussels Midi / Zuid (21 - 28 minutes from airport).
Airport is referred to as Brussels Airport, Brussels Nat. Luchthaven or Brussels Nat. Aéroport.

EUROPEAN QUARTER: Brussels Luxembourg - Brussels Schumann - Brussels Airport. Journey 19 mins.
Brussels Luxembourg to Airport: on Ⓐ every 30 mins 0654 – 2254, on Ⓒ hourly 0440 – 2340. Airport to Brussels Luxembourg: on Ⓐ every 30 mins 0547 – 2147, on Ⓒ hourly 0602 – 2302.

FOR DIRECT SERVICES TO AND FROM BRUSSELS AIRPORT SEE THE FOLLOWING TABLES:
Aalst **411**, Antwerpen **420** / **432**, Brugge **405**, De Panne **411**, Denderleeuw **411**, Gent **405**, Hasselt **432**, Kortrijk **407**, Leuven **430** / **432**, Mechelen **432**, Mons **422**, Namur **440**, Tournai **417**.

ZEEBRUGGE - BRUGGE — 402

Line 50a

km			Ⓐ	ⒶN	Ⓐ	Ⓐ		Ⓐ	Ⓐ	ⒶN	Ⓐ	Ⓐ	Ⓐ	Ⓐ			Ⓒ	Ⓒ	Ⓒ	Ⓒ	Ⓒ	Ⓒ	Ⓒ	
0	Zeebrugge Strand ❦ d.	Ⓐ	...	...	...	...	and	...	...	...	...	...	...	...	...	Ⓒ	0806	1006	1206	1406	1606	1806	2006	...
0	Zeebrugge Dorp ❦ d.		0706	0732	0806	0906	hourly	1506	1606	1632	1706	1806	1906	2006	...		|	|	|	|	|	|	|	...
15	Brugge a.		0726	0752	0826	0926	until	1526	1626	1652	1726	1826	1926	2026	...		0826	1026	1226	1426	1626	1826	2026	...

		Ⓐ	ⒶN	Ⓐ	Ⓐ		Ⓐ	Ⓐ	ⒶN	Ⓐ	Ⓐ	Ⓐ				Ⓒ	Ⓒ	Ⓒ	Ⓒ	Ⓒ	Ⓒ	Ⓒ		
Brugge d.	Ⓐ	0634	0708	0734	0834	and	1534	1634	1716	1734	1834	1934	...	...	Ⓒ	0734	0934	1134	1334	1534	1734	1934	...	...
Zeebrugge Dorp ❦ a.		0654	0724	0754	0854	hourly	1554	1654	1736	1754	1854	1954	...	...		|	|	|	|	|	|	|	...	...
Zeebrugge Strand ❦ a.		...	...	...	...	until	...	...	...	...	...	...	...	...		0754	0954	1154	1354	1554	1754	1954	...	...

N – Not Dec. 26 - Jan. 6, Apr. 3 - 17, July 3 - Sept. 1.
❦ – On Ⓐ June 26 - Aug. 25 trains serve Zeebrugge Strand not Zeebrugge Dorp.

Most trains continue beyond Brugge as stopping services to Gent (not shown).
Change at Brugge for Brussels and faster service to Gent (Tables ***400*** */* ***405****).*

KNOKKE and BLANKENBERGE - BRUGGE - GENT - BRUSSELS — 405

Line 50a

On certain journeys passengers for Knokke should change at Brugge. For additional trains Brugge - Gent - Brussels see Table **400**. For Brugge - Gent (- Antwerpen) see Table **410**.

km		Ⓐ	Ⓐ		Ⓐ	E	Ⓐ	Ⓒ	E	Ⓐ ⊡	Ⓐ	Ⓒ		Ⓐ ◇	Ⓒ			Ⓐ	Ⓒ		Ⓐ			
0	**Knokke** d.	...	...	...	...	0536	...	...	0636	0657	...	...	0736	...	...	and	1836	...	...	1936	...	2036	2151	2249
•	Blankenberge d.	...	...	...	...	0542r	...	...	0642r	|	0714	...	0742r	...	...	at	1842r	...	...	1942r	...	2042r	2156t	2256t
22	Brugge a.	...	...	...	...	0559	...	...	0659	0719	0729	...	0759	...	...	the	1859	...	...	1959	...	2059	2214	2312
22	Brugge d.	0408	0432	0508	0532	0608	0632	...	0708	...	0732	...	0808	0832	...	same	1908	1932	...	2008	2032	2108	*2226*	*2322*
62	**Gent** Sint-Pieters d.	0438	0509	0540	0609	0640	0707	0710	0740	...	0808	0810	0840	0909	0910	minutes	1940	2009	2010	2040	2109	2140	*2250*	*2345*
119	**Brussels** Midi / Zuid a.	0509	0538	0609	0638	0709	0736	0739	0809	...	0837	0839	0909	0938	0939	past	2009	2038	2039	2109	2138	2209	...	*0018*
121	Brussels Central a.	0515	0543	0615	0643	0715	0743	0746	0814	...	0843	0846	0915	0943	0946	each	2015	2043	2046	2115	2143	2215	...	*0024*
123	Brussels Nord a.	0520	0548	0620	0648	0720	0748	0751	0819	...	0848	0851	0920	0948	0951	hour	2020	2048	2051	2120	2148	2220	...	*0029*
135	**Brussels Nationaal** ✈ a.	▽	0601	▽	0701	▽	0801	0803	▽	...	0901	0903	▽	1001	1003	until	▽	2101	2103	▽	2201	▽	...	...

	Ⓐ ⊡	G	G	Ⓒ		Ⓒ	Ⓐ		Ⓒ	Ⓐ			Ⓒ	Ⓐ		Ⓐ	F	Ⓐ		Ⓐ	Ⓒ		Ⓐ	Ⓐ ⊡
Brussels Nationaal ✈ d.	...	▽	▽	0656	▽	0756	0759	▽	0856	0859	▽	and	1956	1959	▽	2059	▽	2159	▽	2259	▽		1459	...
Brussels Nord d.	...	0540	0640	0709	0739	0809	0812	0839	0909	0912	0939	at	2009	2012	2040	2112	2140	2212	2240	2312	2340		1512	...
Brussels Central d.	...	0544	0644	0713	0743	0813	0816	0843	0913	0916	0943	the	2013	2016	2044	2116	2144	2216	2244	2316	2344	A	1516	...
Brussels Midi / Zuid d.	...	0551	0651	0721	0751	0821	0822	0851	0921	0922	0951	same	2021	2022	2051	2122	2151	2222	2251	2324	2351	L	1522	...
Gent Sint-Pieters d.	...	0624	0725	0750	0824	0850	0900	0924	0950	1000	1024	minutes	2050	2100	2124	2200	2224	2300	2324	0000	0024	S	1600	...
Brugge a.	...	0651	0752	...	0851	...	0929	0951	...	1029	1051	past	...	2129	2151	2229	2251	2329	2351	0029	0051	O	1629	...
Brugge d.	0502	0702	0802	...	0902	...	...	1002	...	...	1102	each	...	...	2202	...	2302	...	...	...	...		1631	1639
Blankenberge a.	0518s	0718s	0818s	...	0918s	...	...	1018s	...	...	1118s	hour	...	...	2218s	...	2318s	...	...	...	...		1646	|
Knokke a.	0523	0723	0823	...	0923	...	...	1023	...	...	1123	until	...	...	2223	...	2323	...	...	...	...		...	1701

E – Ⓐ from Knokke and Blankenberge, daily from Brugge.
F – Daily to Brugge, Ⓒ to Blankenberge and Knokke.
G – Ⓐ (daily Brugge to Blankenberge and Knokke).
r – Portion from Blankenberge attaches to main train at Brugge.
s – Portion for Blankenberge detaches from main train at Brugge (depart Brugge xx05).
t – Arrives Brugge 13 minutes later.
• – Blankenburg - Brugge: *15 km*.
◇ – 1732 journey starts from Blankenberge (d. 1714).
▽ – To / from Leuven, Hasselt / Genk (Table **430**).
⊡ – An additional journey runs one hour later.

KNOKKE - OOSTENDE - DE PANNE (Coastal Tramway) — 406

De Lijn 'Kusttram'

KNOKKE railway station - **OOSTENDE** railway station *Journey 63 mins*

Nov. 7 - Apr. 14: 0500⚒, 0600, 0700⚒, 0730, 0745Ⓐ, 0800⚒, 0825, 0900⚒, 0925 and every 20 minutes until 1905, 1929, 2031, 2131, 2231, 2331.

Apr. 15 - June 30: 0500⚒, 0600, 0700, 0730, 0745Ⓐ, 0800⚒, 0825, 0840⚒, 0855, 0910 and every 15 minutes until 1940, 2005, 2029, 2129, 2229, 2329.

Calls at Heist (+6 mins), Zeebrugge (+13 mins), Blankenberge (+25 mins).

DE PANNE railway station - **OOSTENDE** railway station *Journey 79 mins*

Nov. 7 - Apr. 14: 0419⚒, 0519⚒, 0619, 0712, 0737⚒, 0809, 0829⚒, 0849, 0909 and every 20 minutes until 1729, 1752, 1811, 1824, 1844, 1917, 1942, 2017, 2117, 2217, 2317.

Apr. 15 - June 30: 0419⚒, 0519⚒, 0619, 0712, 0737⚒, 0809, 0824, 0839⚒, 0854, 0909 and every 15 minutes until 1754, 1811, 1824, 1839, 1854, 1917, 1942, 2017, 2117, 2217, 2317.

Calls at Koksijde (+19 mins), Nieuwpoort (+38 mins), Middelkerke (+56 mins).

OOSTENDE railway station - **DE PANNE** railway station *Journey 79 mins*

Nov. 7 - Apr. 14: 0505⚒, 0605⚒, 0700⚒, 0710, 0735, 0805⚒, 0820, 0835, 0850, 0910 and every 20 minutes until 1830, 1900, 1930, 2032, 2132, 2232, 2332.

Apr. 15 - June 30: 0505⚒, 0605⚒, 0700⚒, 0710, 0735, 0750⚒, 0805, 0820, 0835, 0850, 0910, 0930 and every 15 minutes until 1830, 1900, 1930, 2000, 2030, 2130, 2230, 2330.

Calls at Middelkerke (+23 mins), Nieuwpoort (+41 mins), Koksijde (+60 mins).

OOSTENDE railway station - **KNOKKE** railway station *Journey 65 mins*

Nov. 7 - Apr. 14: 0455⚒, 0545⚒, 0645⚒, 0715⚒, 0725Ⓐ, 0745, 0827, 0855, 0910, 0930, 0950 and every 20 minutes until 1830, 1900, 1930, 2030, 2130, 2230, 2330.

Apr. 15 - June 30: 0455⚒, 0545⚒, 0645⚒, 0715, 0725Ⓐ, 0745, 0810, 0827, 0840, 0855, 0915 and every 15 minutes until 1900, 1930, 2000, 2030, 2130, 2230, 2330.

Calls at Blankenberge (+37 mins), Zeebrugge (+47 mins), Heist (+58 mins).

Note: daytime journeys are through journeys Knokke - Oostende - De Panne and v.v. Timings may vary at Christmas and New Year. *Subject to alteration from Apr. 15.*
Connections with rail services are available at Knokke (Table **405**), Zeebrugge (Table **402**), Blankenberge (Table **405**), Oostende (Tables **400/07/10**) and De Panne (Table **411**).

OOSTENDE - BRUGGE - KORTRIJK - BRUSSELS — 407

Lines 66, 89

For direct trains Oostende - Brugge - Brussels via Gent (also Kortrijk - Gent - Brussels) see Table **400**. For direct trains Brugge - Brussels - Brussels Nationaal ✈ see Table **405**.

km			Ⓐ	Ⓐ	Ⓐ	Ⓐ	Ⓐ	Ⓐ N	Ⓐ	Ⓐ	Ⓐ	Ⓐ		Ⓐ	Ⓐ	Ⓐ		Ⓒ	Ⓒ	Ⓒ	Ⓒ		Ⓒ	Ⓒ
0	**Oostende** ▷ d.	Ⓐ	...	...	...	...	0546	0634	0646	...	0746	0846		1946	2046	2146	Ⓒ	...	...	...	0646		1946	2046
22	Brugge ▷ d.		...	...	...	...	0605	0658	0705	...	0805	0905		2005	2105	2205		...	...	...	0706		2006	2106
39	Torhout d.		...	...	...	...	0621	0712	0721	...	0821	0921		2021	2121	2221		...	...	...	0721		2021	2121
44	Lichtervelde a.		...	...	...	...	0625	|	0725	...	0825	0925		2025	2125	2225		...	...	...	0725		2025	2125
44	Lichtervelde d.		...	...	...	...	0635	|	0735	...	0835	0935		2035	2135	2235		...	...	...	0735		2035	2135
52	Roeselare d.		...	...	...	...	0643	0723	0743	...	0843	0943	and	2043	2143	2243		...	...	...	0742	and	2042	2142
73	**Kortrijk** a.		...	...	...	...	0704	0741	0804	...	0904	1004		2104	2204	2304		...	...	...	0802		2102	2202
73	**Kortrijk** d.		0511	0544	0611	0645	0711	0745	0816	0811	0911	1011	hourly	2111	2211	...		0506	0606	0706	0806	hourly	2106	...
98	Oudenaarde d.		0531	0605	0632	0705	0732	0805	|	0832	0932	1032		2132	2232	...		0525	0625	0725	0825		2125	...
115	Zottegem d.		0547	0619	0647	0719	0747	0819	◇	0847	0947	1047	until	2147	2247	...		0542	0642	0742	0842	until	2142	...
136	Denderleeuw d.		0605	0638	0706	0741	0806	0845	|	0906	1006	1106		2206	2306	...		0606	0706	0806	0906		2206	...
158	**Brussels** Midi / Zuid a.		0621	0656	0721	0757	0821	0901	0924	0921	1021	1121		2221	2321	...		0621	0721	0821	0921		2221	...
160	Brussels Central a.		0627	0705	0727	0803	0827	0906	0930	0927	1027	1127		2227	2327	...		0627	0727	0827	0927		2227	...
162	Brussels Nord a.		0632	0710	0732	0808	0832	0911	0935	0932	1032	1132		2232	2332	...		0632	0732	0832	0932		2232	...
174	**Brussels Nationaal** ✈ a.		...	...	0747	...	0847	...	...	0947	1047	1147		2247	2347	...		0647	0747	0847	0947		2247	...

		Ⓐ ♡	Ⓐ	Ⓐ		Ⓐ	Ⓐ	Ⓐ	Ⓐ	Ⓐ	Ⓐ	Ⓐ	Ⓐ	Ⓐ	Ⓐ	Ⓐ		Ⓒ	Ⓒ		Ⓒ	Ⓒ	Ⓒ	Ⓒ
Brussels Nationaal ✈ d.	Ⓐ	...	0513	0613		1613	...	1713	...	1813	...	1913	2013	2113	2213	...	Ⓒ	...	0613		1913	2013	2113	2213
Brussels Nord d.		...	0528	0628		1628	1649	1728	1749	1828	1921	1928	2028	2128	2228	2315		...	0628		1928	2028	2128	2228
Brussels Central d.		...	0532	0632		1632	1653	1732	1753	1832	1925	1932	2032	2132	2232	2319		...	0632		1932	2032	2132	2232
Brussels Midi / Zuid d.		...	0539	0639		1638	1702	1738	1800	1839	1932	1939	2039	2139	2239	2327		...	0639		1939	2039	2139	2239
Denderleeuw d.		...	0558	0658		1658	1722	1758	1822	1858	|	1958	2058	2158	2258	2345		...	0658		1958	2058	2158	2258
Zottegem d.		...	0616	0716	and	1716	1743	1816	1843	1916	◇	2016	2116	2216	2316	0013		...	0722	and	2022	2122	2222	2322
Oudenaarde d.		...	0631	0731		1731	1757	1831	1857	1931	|	2031	2131	2231	2331	0029		...	0737		2037	2137	2237	2337
Kortrijk a.		...	0648	0748	hourly	1748	1816	1848	1914	1948	2044	2048	2148	2248	2348	...		...	0754	hourly	2054	2154	2254	2354
Kortrijk d.		0556	0656	0756		1756	...	1856	...	1956	2056	...	2156	...	...	...		0658	0758		2058	...	...	...
Roeselare d.		0618	0718	0818	until	1818	...	1918	...	2018	2118	...	2218	...	...	...		0718	0818	until	2118	...	...	...
Lichtervelde a.		0625	0725	0825		1825	...	1925	...	2025	2125	...	2225	...	...	...		0725	0825		2125	...	...	...
Lichtervelde d.		0635	0735	0835		1835	...	1935	...	2035	2135	...	2235	...	...	...		0735	0835		2135	...	...	...
Torhout d.		0640	0740	0840		1840	...	1940	...	2040	2140	...	2240	...	...	...		0740	0840		2140	...	...	...
Brugge ▷ a.		0655	0755	0855		1855	...	1954	...	2055	2155	...	2255	...	...	...		0754	0854		2154	...	...	...
Oostende ▷ a.		0713	0813	0913		1913	...	2013	...	2113	2213	...	2313	...	...	...		0813	0913		2213	...	...	...

N – Will not run Kortrijk - Brussels Dec. 26 - Jan. 6, Apr. 3 - 17, July 3 - Sept. 1.
◇ – Via Gent (Table **400**). To / from Welkenraedt.
▷ – See also Tables **400** and **410**.
♡ – Also at 0456.

Additional trains Brugge - Kortrijk: on Ⓐ hourly 0538 - 2238, on Ⓒ every 2 hours 0738 - 2138. **Kortrijk - Brugge** on Ⓐ 0534, 0634, hourly 0735 - 2135, on Ⓒ every 2 hours 0635 - 2035. Journey 47 mins.

410 — POPERINGE - KORTRIJK - GENT - ANTWERPEN — Lines 69, 75, 59

km		Ⓐ	Ⓐ			N			N			N♠									Ⓐ	Ⓐ	Ⓐ
0	Poperinge......d.	...	0410	0510	...	0553	0610	...	0653	0710	...	0810		...	2110	2210					...	0734	1654
10	Ieper.........d.	...	0418	0518	...	0601	0618	...	0701	0718	...	0818	and	...	2118	2218					...	0742	1702
32	Menen........d.	...	0437	0537	...	0621	0637	...	0721	0737	...	0837	at	...	2137	2237					...	0801	1721
43	**Kortrijk**......a.	...	0451	0551	...	0635	0651	...	0735	0751	...	0851	the	...	2151	2251					...	0815	1734
43	**Kortrijk**......d.	...	0457	0557	...	0641	0657	...	0741	0757	...	0857	same	2157	...	2257				A			
	Oostende....▷d.			0608			0708			0808		minutes	2108	...	2208				L			
	Brugge.......▷d.			0626			0726			0826		past	2126	...	2226				S			
85	**Gent Sint-Pieters**▷a.	...	0523	...	0623	0650	...	0711	0723	0750	...	0811	0823	0850	each	2150	2223	2250	2323	O	
85	**Gent Sint-Pieters**....d.	0426	0526	0553	0626	0653	0707	0717	0726	0753	0807	0817	0826	0853	0907	0926	hour	2153	2226	2253	2326
112	Lokeren......d.	0451	0551	0617	0651	0717	0734	▽	0751	0817	0834	▽	0851	0917	0934	0951	until	2217	2251	2317	2351
125	Sint-Niklaas...d.	0501	0601	0627	0701	0727	0744	...	0801	0827	0844	...	0901	0927	0944	1001	2227	2301	2327	0001
148	Antwerpen Berchem a.	0517	0617	0648	0717	0748	0802	...	0817	0848	0902	...	0917	0948	1002	1017	2248	2317	2348	0017
151	**Antwerpen** Centraal a.	0523	0623	0654	0723	0754	0809	...	0823	0854	0909	...	0923		1023	2254	2323	2354	0023

		Ⓐ	Ⓐ		N		Ⓐ		N		Ⓐ		N♥					Ⓐ	Ⓒ		Ⓐ	Ⓐ	Ⓐ
	Antwerpen Centraal...d.	0437	0506	0537	...	0606	0637	0651	0706	0737	0751	...	0806	0837	0851	...	2106	2137	2237	2337	2337	...
	Antwerpen Berchem...d.	0443	0512	0543	...	0612	0643	0656	0712	0743	0758	...	0812	0843	0858	...	2112	2143	2243	2343	2343	...
	Sint-Niklaas.....d.	0501	0535	0600	...	0635	0701	0714	0735	0801	0818	...	0835	0901	0918	and	2135	2201	2300	0001	0001	...
	Lokeren........d.	0511	0545	0609	...	0645	0711	0723	0745	0811	0828	...	0845	0911	0928	at	2145	2211	2309	0011	0011	...
	Gent Sint-Pieters...a.	0533	0607	0633	...	0707	0733	0749	0807	0833	0852	...	0907	0933	0952	the	2207	2233	2333	0033	0033	...	1645	1745
	Gent Sint-Pieters...▷d.	0536	0610	0635	...	0710	0736	...	0810	0836	...	0910	0936	same	2210	2236	2336		0036	...	1652	1752
	Brugge.........▷a.	0634	...	0734	...	0834	...	0934	minutes	2234						A
	Oostende.......▷a.	0652	...	0752	...	0852	...	0952	past	2252						L
	Kortrijk.......a.	0602	...	0702	...	0802	...	0902	...	1002	each	2302	0010	0110		S	...	1721	1821
	Kortrijk.......d.	0609	...	0709	0728	...	0809	...	0909	...	1009	hour	2309		O	1629	1726	1826
	Menen.........d.	0623	...	0723	0742	...	0823	...	0923	...	1023	until	2323		1643	1740	1840
	Ieper..........d.	0642	...	0742	0802	...	0842	...	0942	...	1042	2344		1702	1801	1901
	Poperinge......a.	0649	...	0749	0809	...	0849	...	0949	...	1049	2351		1709	1808	1908

ADDITIONAL TRAINS KORTRIJK - GENT

Kortrijk......d.	Ⓐ	0416	hourly	2216	Ⓒ	0521	hourly	2221	Gent Sint-Pieters......d.	Ⓐ	0609	hourly	2309	Ⓒ	0606	hourly	2306
Gent Sint-Pieters......a.		0451	until	2251		0554	until	2254	Kortrijk......a.		0644	until	2344		0639	until	2339

N – Not Dec. 26 - Jan. 6, Apr. 3 - 17, July 3 - Sept. 1.
♠ – Last journey is at 1707Ⓐ N (also 1810Ⓐ N).
♥ – Last journey is at 1851Ⓐ N.
▽ – To / from Brussels (Table 400).
▷ – See also Table 400.
§ – Most journeys continue to / from Brussels (Table 400).
Between Kortrijk and Antwerpen most trains are attached to Lille - Kortrijk - Antwerpen trains (Table 415).

411 — DE PANNE - GENT - AALST - DENDERLEEUW - BRUSSELS — Lines 73, 50

For direct trains Gent - Brussels see Tables 400 and 405 (faster journeys De Panne - Brussels may be available by changing at Gent)

km		Ⓐ	△	△				▯ N				Ⓐ		▽	▯	Ⓐ	Ⓐ	N		Ⓐ	Ⓐ	Ⓐ
0	De Panne §.....d.	...	0452	0552	0652		2052	0525	0725	**Brussels Nationaal** +.d.	...	0526	...	2026	2126	...			
5	Veurne.........d.	...	0501	0601	0701		2101	0533	0733	**Brussels** Nord....d.	...	0538	...	2038	2138	...	1635	1735
20	Diksmuide......d.	...	0513	0613	0713	and	2113	0544	0745	**Brussels** Central...d.	...	0542	...	2042	2142	...	1639	1739
39	Lichtervelde....d.	...	0530	0630	0730		2130	0603	0802	**Brussels** Midi/Zuid...d.	...	0548	and	2048	2148	...	1645	1745
56	Tielt...........d.	...	0542	0642	0742	hourly	2142	A	0615	0814	Denderleeuw.....d.	...	0609	...	2109	2209	A		
86	**Gent Sint-Pieters**...a.	0513	0607	0707	0806	until	2206	L	0642	0840	Aalst...........d.	...	0619	hourly	2119	2219	L		
86	**Gent Sint-Pieters**...d.	0513	0613	0713	0813		2213	S	0645	...	**Gent Sint-Pieters**...a.	...	0648		2148	2248	S	...	1715	1815
114	Aalst..........d.	0544	0644	0745	0844	until	2244	O		**Gent Sint-Pieters**...d.	0555	0655	until	2155	...	O	1620	1719	1819
121	Denderleeuw....d.	0554	0654	0754	0854		2254		Tielt..........d.	0619	0719	...	2219	...		1647	1746	1846
144	**Brussels** Midi/Zuid...a.	0612	0712	0812	0912		2312		0716	Lichtervelde....d.	0632	0732	...	2232	...		1700	1800	1900
146	Brussels Central....a.	0617	0717	0817	0917		2317		0721	Diksmuide......d.	0648	0749	...	2249	...		1715	1816	1916
148	Brussels Nord....a.	0622	0722	0822	0922		2322		0726	Veurne.........d.	0701	0801	...	2301	...		1726	1827	1927
160	Brussels Nationaal + a.	0635	0735	0835	0935		2335			De Panne §.....a.	0708	0808	...	2308	...		1734	1834	1934

N – Not Dec. 26 - Jan. 6, Apr. 3 - 17, July 3 - Sept. 1.
△ – On Ⓒ starts from Gent.
▽ – 2026 journey terminates at Gent on Ⓒ.
▯ – An additional journey runs one hour later.
§ – De Panne railway station is situated in Adinkerke. Connection available with the coastal tramway (Table 406).
Trains continue beyond Brussels to / from Leuven and Landen (Table 430).

ADDITIONAL TRAINS
Gent - Aalst - Denderleeuw - Brussels Midi - Brussels Nord: From Gent hourly 0540 - 2140 (also 0440Ⓐ). From Brussels Nord hourly 0607 - 2207 (also 2307Ⓐ to Gent, 2307Ⓒ to Aalst); from Brussels Midi 11 minutes later. On Ⓐ most trains continue beyond Brussels to / from Hasselt and Tongeren (Table 431).

412 — GENT - OUDENAARDE - RONSE — Line 86

km		Ⓐ			Ⓒ			Ⓒ		Ⓐ			Ⓒ			Ⓒ
0	Gent St-Pieters......d.	Ⓐ	0600	and	2100	Ⓒ	0800	every	2000	**Ronse**......d.	Ⓐ	0511	and	2211	Ⓒ	0709	every	2109
25	Oudenaarde......a.		0629	hourly	2129		0829	two	2029	Oudenaarde......a.		0522	hourly	2222		0720	two	2120
25	Oudenaarde......d.		0637	until	2137		0840	hours	2040	Oudenaarde......d.		0531	until	2231		0731	hours	2131
39	**Ronse**......a.		0648	△	2148		0851	until	2051	Gent St-Pieters......a.		0559	▽	2259		0759	until	2159

N – Not Dec. 26 - Jan. 6, Apr. 3 - 17, July 3 - Sept. 1.
△ – Also at 1628Ⓐ, 1728Ⓐ, 1828Ⓐ N.
▽ – Also at 0548Ⓐ N, 0649Ⓐ, 0749Ⓐ.
Most trains continue beyond Gent to / from Eeklo (Table 413).

413 — GENT - EEKLO — Line 58

km		Ⓐ			Ⓒ			Ⓒ		Ⓐ			Ⓒ			Ⓒ
0	Gent St-Pieters......d.	Ⓐ	0612	hourly	2112	Ⓒ	0812	every	2012	**Eeklo**......d.	Ⓐ	0511	hourly	2211	Ⓒ	0711	every	2111
7	Gent Dampoort......d.		0623	until	2123		0823	two	2023	Gent Dampoort......d.		0537	until	2237		0737	two	2137
27	**Eeklo**......a.		0646	△	2146		0846	hours	2046	Gent St-Pieters......a.		0547	▽	2247		0747	hours	2147

N – Not Dec. 26 - Jan. 6, Apr. 3 - 17, July 3 - Sept. 1.
△ – Also at 1732Ⓐ N.
▽ – Additional journey runs at 1649Ⓐ N.
Most trains continue beyond Gent to / from Ronse (Table 412).

414 — GENT - MECHELEN - LEUVEN — Line 53

For Mechelen - Leuven via Brussels Nationaal + see Table 432

		Ⓐ	Ⓐ	Ⓐ	Ⓐ	Ⓐ	Ⓐ			Ⓐ	Ⓐ	Ⓐ	Ⓒ	Ⓒ	Ⓒ	Ⓒ			Ⓒ	Ⓒ	Ⓒ
0	Gent St-Pieters...d.	Ⓐ	0420	...	0520	0601	...	0620	and at the same	2101	...	2120	2201	Ⓒ		0700	...	0800	and at the same	...	2200	...
30	Dendermonde.....d.		0501	0525	...	0601	0627	...	0701	minutes	2127	...	2127			0728	...	0828	minutes	...	2228	...
57	Mechelen........d.		0528	0548	0621	0628	0648	0721	0728	past each	2148	2221	2228	2248		0736	0754	0836	0854	past each	2236	2254	2336
82	**Leuven**.......a.		0618	0647	...	0718	0747	hour until	2218	2247	...	2318		0805	...	0905	hour until	2305	...	0005

		Ⓐ	Ⓐ	Ⓐ	Ⓐ	Ⓐ					Ⓒ	Ⓒ	Ⓒ	Ⓒ	Ⓒ			Ⓒ	Ⓒ	Ⓒ
	Leuven.......d.	Ⓐ	0512	0542	...	0613	0642	...	0713	and at the same	2142	...	2213	2242	Ⓒ	...	0655	...	0755	and at the same	2055	2155	2255
	Mechelen........d.		0538	0614	0632	0639	0714	0732	0739	minutes	2214	2232	2239	2314	0606	0706	0724	0806	0824	minutes	2106	2124	2224	2324
	Dendermonde.....d.		...	0637	0703	...	0738	0803	...	past each	2238	2303	...	2335	0634	0734	...	0834	past each	2134
	Gent St-Pieters....a.		...	0700	0739	...	0803	0839	...	hour until	2303	2339	...		0700	0800	...	0900	hour until	2200

Line 75 LILLE - MOUSCRON - KORTRIJK - (GENT - ANTWERPEN) 415

Lille - Mouscron is subject to alteration on French and Belgian public holidays

km		Ⓐ u	⚒	⚒	Ⓐ u					Ⓐ u		Ⓒ	Ⓐ	Ⓒ	⑥	Ⓑ		Ⓐ u	†	⚒	Ⓐ u				
0	**Lille** Flandres ▷ d.	0628	0708	0808	0828	0908	1008	1108	1208	1228	1308	1403	1408	1508	1603	1608	1708	1728	1803	1808	1828	1908	2008	2108	2208
10	Roubaix ▷ d.	0642	0718	0818	0842	0918	1018	1118	1218	1242	1318	1417	1418	1518	1618	1618	1718	1742	1818	1818	1842	1918	2018	2118	2218
12	Tourcoing 🚉 ▷ d.	0646	0722	0822	0846	0923	1022	1122	1222	1246	1322	1422	1422	1522	1622	1622	1722	1746	1822	1822	1846	1922	2022	2122	2222
18	Mouscron a.	...	0728	0828	...	0928	1032	1128	1228	...	1328	1428	1428	1528	1628	1628	1728	...	1828	1828	...	1928	2028	2128	2228
18	Mouscron d.	...	0738	0838	...	0938	1038	1138	1238	...	1338	1439	1438	1538	1638	1638	1738	...	1838	1838	...	1938	2038	2138	2238
30	**Kortrijk** a.	...	0746	0846	...	0946	1046	1146	1246	...	1346	1446	1446	1546	1646	1646	1746	...	1846	1846	...	1946	2046	2146	2246
	Gent Sint-P. **410** a.	...	0823	0923	...	1023	1123	1223	1323	...	1423	1523	1523	1623	1723	1723	1823	...	1923	1923	...	2023	2123	2223	2323
	Antwerpen **410** a.	...	0923	1023	...	1123	1223	1323	1423	...	1523	1623	1623	1723	1823	1823	1923	...	2023	2023	...	2123	2223	2323	0023

	⚒	Ⓐ u	Ⓐ	⑥	Ⓐ u		Ⓐ u		Ⓒ			Ⓐ u	Ⓐ	Ⓒ			Ⓐ	Ⓒ	Ⓐ u		Ⓐ u				
Antwerpen **410** d.	...	...	0537	0537	...	0637	...	0737	0837	0937	1037	...	...	1137	1237	1337	1437	1437	...	1537	...	1637	1737	1837	1937
Gent Sint-P. **410** d.	...	...	0635	0636	...	0736	...	0836	0936	1036	1136	...	...	1236	1336	1436	1536	1536	...	1636	...	1736	1836	1936	2036
Kortrijk d.	0613	...	0713	0713	...	0813	...	0913	1013	1113	1213	...	1313	1313	1413	1513	1613	1613	...	1713	...	1813	1913	2013	2113
Mouscron a.	0621	...	0721	0721	...	0821	...	0921	1021	1121	1221	...	1321	1321	1421	1521	1621	1621	...	1721	...	1821	1921	2021	2121
Mouscron d.	0629	...	0730	0729	...	0830	...	0930	1030	1131	1230	...	1331	1330	1430	1530	1630	1630	...	1730	...	1830	1930	2030	2130
Tourcoing 🚉 ▷ d.	0635	0715	0736	0736	0815	0836	0915	0936	1036	1137	1236	1313	1337	1336	1436	1536	1636	1636	1715	1736	1815	1836	1936	2036	2136
Roubaix ▷ d.	0639	0719	0741	0740	0819	0841	0919	0941	1040	1140	1241	1319	1341	1340	1440	1541	1640	1640	1719	1740	1819	1841	1940	2040	2140
Lille Flandres ▷ a.	0650	0733	0750	0754	0833	0850	0933	0950	1050	1150	1250	1333	1350	1350	1450	1550	1650	1653	1733	1750	1833	1850	1950	2050	2150

u – Not Dec. 26 - 30.

▷ – Frequent services Lille Flandres - Lille Europe - Roubaix and Tourcoing are operated by the Lille *VAL* métro (Line 2) or by tram. For *TGV* trains see Table **250**.

Between Kortrijk and Antwerpen these trains are attached to Poperinge - Kortrijk - Gent - Antwerpen trains (Table **410***).*

Lines 78, 118 LILLE - TOURNAI - MONS 416

km			Ⓐ	Ⓐ	Ⓐ	Ⓐ	Ⓐ	Ⓐ	Ⓐ	Ⓐ	Ⓐ	Ⓐ	Ⓐ	Ⓐ	Ⓐ	Ⓐ	Ⓐ	Ⓐ	Ⓐ	Ⓐ	Ⓐ ◇	Ⓐ	Ⓐ	Ⓐ	Ⓐ
0	**Lille** Flandres § d.	Ⓐ	...	0608	...	0708	...	0731	0808	0908	1006	...	1208	1306	...	1508	1608	1708	1736	1808	1908	2006	...	...	2206
	Mouscron **417** d.		0524	│	0624	│	0718	│	│	│	│	...	│	│	...	│	│	│	│	│	│	│	...	...	│
25	**Tournai** **417** a.		0541	0638	0641	0739	0735	0758	0838	0938	1033	...	1238	1333	...	1533	1638	1738	1810	1839	1933	2033	...	...	2233
25	**Tournai** d.		0544	...	0644	0744	0744	...	0844	0944	1044	1144	1244	1344	1444	1544	1644	1744	...	1844	1944	2044	2144	2224	...
64	Saint-Ghislain d.		0606	...	0706	0806	0806	...	0906	1006	1106	1206	1306	1406	1506	1606	1706	1806	...	1906	2006	2108	2208	2256	...
73	**Mons** a.		0614	...	0714	0814	0814	...	0914	1014	1114	1214	1314	1414	1514	1614	1714	1814	...	1914	2014	2116	2216	2308	...
	Charleroi Sud **425** a.		0649	...	0749	0849	0849	...	0949	1049	1149	1249	1349	1449	1549	1649	1749	1849	...	1949	2049	2149	2249	...	...
	Namur **425** a.		0722	...	0822	0922	0922	...	1022	1122	1222	1322	1422	1522	1622	1722	1822	1922	...	2022	2122	2222	2322	...	...

		Ⓐ	Ⓐ	Ⓐ ◇	Ⓐ	Ⓐ	Ⓐ ◇	Ⓐ	Ⓐ ◇	Ⓐ	Ⓐ ◇	Ⓐ	Ⓐ	Ⓐ	Ⓐ	Ⓐ	Ⓐ	Ⓐ	Ⓐ	Ⓐ	Ⓐ	Ⓐ ◇	Ⓐ ◇	Ⓐ	Ⓐ
Namur **425** d.	Ⓐ	...	...	...	0538	...	0638	0738	0838	0938	1038	1138	1238	1338	1438	...	1538	1538	1638	...	1738	1838	1938	2038	2138
Charleroi Sud **425** d.		...	...	...	0611	...	0711	0811	0911	1011	1111	1211	1311	1411	1511	...	1611	1611	1711	...	1811	1911	2011	2111	2211
Mons d.		0452	...	0552	0645	...	0745	0845	0945	1045	1145	1245	1345	1445	1545	...	1645	1645	1745	...	1845	1945	2045	2145	2245
Saint-Ghislain d.		0505	...	0605	0654	...	0754	0854	0954	1054	1154	1254	1354	1454	1554	...	1654	1654	1754	...	1854	1954	2054	2154	2256
Tournai a.		0536	...	0636	0715	...	0815	0915	1015	1115	1215	1315	1415	1515	1615	...	1715	1715	1815	...	1915	2015	2115	2215	2323
Tournai **417** d.		...	0622	0647	0722	0809	0822	0922	1022	1122	1222	1322	...	1522	1622	1649	1720	1724	1819	1822	1922	2022	2122	...	...
Mouscron **417** a.		...	│	│	│	│	│	│	│	│	│	│	...	│	│	│	1738	│	1837	│	│	│	│	...	...
Lille Flandres § a.		...	0651	0721	0751	0835	0851	0951	1051	1151	1251	1351	...	1551	1651	1723	...	1751	...	1851	1951	2051	2151	...	...

		Ⓒ	Ⓒ	Ⓒ		Ⓒ	Ⓒ	Ⓒ	
Mouscron **417** d.	Ⓒ	0613	0713	0813		2013	2113	2213	...
Tournai **417** d.		0630	0730	0830	and	2030	2130	2230	...
Saint-Ghislain d.		0701	0801	0901	hourly	2101	2202	2301	...
Mons a.		0712	0812	0912	until	2112	2213	2314	...
Charleroi Sud **425** a.		0749	0849	0949		2149	2249	...	
Namur **425** a.		0827	0927	1027		2227	2327	...	
Liège Guillemins **442** a.		0918	1018	1118		2318	...	...	

		Ⓒ	Ⓒ	Ⓒ	Ⓒ		Ⓒ	Ⓒ	
Liège Guillemins **442** d.	Ⓒ	...	...	0642	0742		1942	2042	...
Namur **425** d.		...	0633	0733	0833	and	2033	2133	...
Charleroi Sud **425** d.		0611	0711	0811	0911	hourly	2111	2211	...
Mons d.		0648	0748	0848	0948	until	2148	2248	...
Saint-Ghislain d.		0701	0801	0901	1001	△	2201	2301	...
Tournai **417** a.		0730	0830	0930	1030		2230	2331	...
Mouscron **417** a.		0747	0847	0947	1047		2247	2349	...

		⑥	⑥	Ⓒ	▽	Ⓒ	Ⓒ	Ⓒ	
Lille Flandres § d.	Ⓒ	0649	0749	0849	and hourly	1949	2049	2149	...
Tournai a.		0721	0821	0921	until	2021	2121	2221	...

		⑥	⑥	Ⓒ		Ⓒ	Ⓒ	Ⓒ	
Tournai d.	Ⓒ	0636	0736	0836	and hourly	1936	2036	2144	...
Lille Flandres § a.		0708	0809	0908	until	2008	2108	2208	...

△ – Mouscron arrivals at 0847, 1247, 1347, 1447, 1647, 1747, 2047, 2147 are 9 minutes later on ⑦.

▽ – 1249 departs 1256 on ⑦.

◇ – Change trains at Tournai.

§ – 🚉 between Lille and Tournai = Blandain.

Lines 94, 60 KORTRIJK - MOUSCRON - TOURNAI - BRUSSELS - SINT NIKLAAS 417

For direct trains Kortrijk - Brussels see Table **400** (via Gent) and Table **407** (via Oudenaarde)

km			Ⓐ	Ⓐ	Ⓐ	Ⓐ	Ⓐ	Ⓐ	Ⓐ	Ⓐ	Ⓐ	Ⓐ	Ⓐ	Ⓐ	Ⓐ		Ⓐ	Ⓐ	Ⓐ		Ⓒ		Ⓒ
0	**Kortrijk** d.	Ⓐ	...	...	...	...	...	...	...	...	0639	...	...	0739	...		2039	...	2139	Ⓒ	...		...
13	Mouscron **416** d.		...	...	...	...	0548	0607	...	...	0649	0707	...	0748	...		2048	...	2148		...		...
32	**Tournai** **416** d.		0444	0508	0544	0600	0609	0628	0644	0657	0710	0728	0744	0809	0844	and	2109	2144	2209		0544		2244
50	Leuze d.		0456	0521	0556	0612	0621	0640	0656	0709	0722	0740	0756	0821	0856	at	2121	2156	2221		0556		2256
62	Ath d.		0508	0534	0608	0624	0634	0652	0708	0721	0734	0752	0808	0834	0908	the	2134	2208	2234		0608	and	2308
100	Halle d.		0537	0603	0637	│	0703	│	0737	│	0803	│	0837	0903	0937	same	2203	2237	2303		0638		2338
116	**Brussels** Midi / Zuid a.		0548	0614	0648	0700	0715	0727	0748	0800	0815	0828	0848	0915	0948	minutes	2215	2248	2315		0648	hourly	2348
116	**Brussels** Midi / Zuid d.		0551	0617	0651	0703	0718	0730	0751	0803	0818	0830	0852	0918	0951	past	2218	2251	2318		0651		2351
118	Brussels Central d.		0555	0621	0655	0707	0722	0734	0755	0807	0822	0834	0856	0922	0955	each	2222	2255	2322		0655	until	2355
120	Brussels Nord d.		0602	0628	0702	0711	0728	0738	0801	0811	0828	0838	0902	0928	1002	hour	2228	2302	2328		0701		0001
132	**Brussels Nationaal** ✈ a.		0620	│	0720	...	│	...	0820	...	│	...	0920	│	1020	until	│	2320	│		0718		0018
154	Dendermonde a.		...	0655	...	...	0755	...	...	...	0855	...	...	0955	...		2255	...	0015		...		...
168	Lokeren **410** a.		...	0721	...	...	0821	...	...	...	0921	...	...	1021	...		2321	...	...		...		...
181	**Sint-Niklaas** **410** a.		...	0736	...	...	0836	...	...	...	0936	...	...	1036	...		2336	...	...		...		...

		Ⓐ	Ⓐ	Ⓐ	Ⓐ	Ⓐ		Ⓐ	Ⓐ	Ⓐ	Ⓐ	Ⓐ	Ⓐ		Ⓐ	Ⓐ	Ⓐ	Ⓐ			Ⓒ		Ⓒ
Sint-Niklaas **410** d.	Ⓐ	...	...	0524	...	0624		...	1924	...	2024	...	2124		...	...	...	...	...	Ⓒ	...		...
Lokeren **410** d.		...	...	0539	...	0639		...	1939	...	2039	...	2139		...	...	...	...	...		...		...
Dendermonde d.		...	...	0604	...	0704	and	...	2004	...	2104	...	2204		...	...	...	...	...		...		...
Brussels Nationaal ✈ d.		0441	0541	│	0641	│	at	1941	│	2041	│	2141	│		...	...	...	...	...		0542		2242
Brussels Nord d.		0501	0601	0634	0701	0734	the	2001	2034	2101	2134	2201	2234	A	1550	1617	1649	1717	...		0601	and	2301
Brussels Central d.		0505	0605	0638	0705	0738	same	2005	2038	2105	2138	2205	2238	L	1554	1621	1653	1721	...		0605		2305
Brussels Midi / Zuid a.		0509	0609	0642	0709	0742	minutes	2009	2042	2109	2142	2209	2242	S	1558	1625	1657	1725	...		0609	hourly	2309
Brussels Midi / Zuid d.		0512	0612	0645	0712	0745	past	2012	2045	2112	2145	2212	2245	O	1600	1627	1659	1727	...		0613		2313
Halle d.		0523	0623	0658	0723	0758	each	2023	2058	2123	2158	2223	2258		│	│	│	│	...		0623	until	2323
Ath d.		0554	0654	0729	0754	0829	hour	2054	2129	2154	2226	2254	2329		1639	1704	1739	1804	...		0654		2354
Leuze d.		0605	0705	0738	0805	0838	until	2105	2138	2205	...	2305	2338		1648	1713	1748	1813	...		0705		0005
Tournai **416** d.		0616	0716	0753	0816	0853		2116	2153	2216	...	2316	2351		1702	1728	1802	1827	...		0716		0016
Mouscron **416** d.		...	...	0812	...	0912		...	2212	...	...	...	...		...	1747	...	1846	...		...		...
Kortrijk a.		...	...	0821	...	0921		...	2221	...	...	...	...		...	...	...	...	...		...		...

420 ROOSENDAAL - ANTWERPEN - BRUSSELS - CHARLEROI

Lines 12, 25, 124

For *Thalys* services Paris - Brussels - Antwerpen - Amsterdam see Table **18**. For additional trains Antwerpen - Brussels Nationaal ✈ see Table **432**.

km				Ⓐ	Ⓐ	Ⓐ	Ⓐ	Ⓐ	Ⓐ	Ⓐ	Ⓐ	Ⓐ	Ⓐ	Ⓐ	Ⓐ	Ⓐ	Ⓐ	Ⓐ	Ⓐ	Ⓐ		Ⓐ	Ⓐ	Ⓐ	Ⓐ
																♥	◇					◇			
0	**Roosendaal**	d.	Ⓐ	...	...	...	...	...	...	...	...	...	...	...	...	...	0748	...	...	...		2048	...	...	...
8	Essen 🏛	d.		...	...	0507	...	...	...	0607	...	...	...	0707	...	...	|	...	0807	...		|	...	2107	...
26	Kapellen	d.		...	...	0525	...	...	...	0625	...	...	...	0725	...	...	|	...	0825	...	and	|	...	2125	...
41	**Antwerpen** Centraal	a.		...	...	0537	...	...	...	0637	...	...	...	0737	...	...	0815	...	0837	...	at	2115	...	2137	...
41	**Antwerpen** Centraal	d.		0454	...	0539	0554	0609	0625	0639	0654	0709	0725	0739	0754	0809	0817	0825	0839	0854	the	2117	2125	2139	2154
43	Antwerpen Berchem	d.		0500	...	0544	0600	0614	0631	0644	0700	0714	0731	0744	0800	0814	0823	0831	0844	0900	same	2123	2131	2144	2200
65	Mechelen	d.		0515	...	0604	0615	0634	0645	0704	0715	0734	0745	0804	0815	0834	0838	0845	0904	0915	minutes	2138	2145	2204	2215
	Brussels Nationaal ✈	a.		|	...	|	|	|	|	|	|	|	|	|	|	|	0849	|	|	|	past	2149	|	|	|
85	Brussels Nord	d.		0532	0602	0624	0632	0654	0702	0724	0732	0756	0802	0825	0832	0854	0907	0902	0924	0932	each	2207	2202	2224	2232
87	Brussels Central	d.		0536	0606	0628	0636	0658	0706	0728	0736	0800	0806	0829	0836	0858	0911	0906	0928	0936	hour	2211	2206	2228	2236
89	**Brussels** Midi / Zuid	a.		0540	0610	0632	0640	0702	0710	0732	0740	0804	0810	0833	0840	0902	0915	0910	0932	0940	until	2215	2210	2232	2240
89	**Brussels** Midi / Zuid	d.		0543	0613	...	0643	...	0713	...	0743	...	0813	...	0843	...	...	0913	...	0943		...	2213	...	2243
118	Nivelles	d.		0611	0641	...	0711	...	0741	...	0811	...	0841	...	0911	...	...	0941	...	1011		...	2241	...	2311
144	**Charleroi** Sud	a.		0636	0706	...	0736	...	0806	...	0836	...	0906	...	0936	...	...	1006	...	1036		...	2306	...	2336

		Ⓐ	Ⓐ	Ⓐ	Ⓐ	Ⓐ	Ⓐ	Ⓐ		Ⓒ	Ⓒ	Ⓒ	Ⓒ	Ⓒ	Ⓒ	Ⓒ	Ⓒ	Ⓒ		Ⓒ	Ⓒ	Ⓒ	Ⓒ	Ⓒ	Ⓒ
		◇			◇	⊡		⊡									◇				◇			◇	⊡
Roosendaal	d.	2148	...	...	2248	...	...	...	Ⓒ	...	...	...	...	...	...	...	0748	...		...	2148	...	...	2248	...
Essen 🏛	d.	|	...	2207	|	...	...	...		...	...	...	...	...	...	...	|	...		...	|	...	...	|	...
Kapellen	d.	|	...	2225	|	...	...	...		...	...	...	...	...	...	...	|	...	and	...	|	...	...	|	...
Antwerpen Centraal	a.	2215	...	2237	2315	...	...	...		...	...	...	...	...	...	...	0815	...	at	...	2215	...	...	2315	...
Antwerpen Centraal	d.	2217	2225	2239	2317	2305	2325	0010		...	0540	0609	0640	0709	0740	0809	0817	0840	the	2209	2217	2240	2309	2317	2348
Antwerpen Berchem	d.	2223	2231	2244	2323	2310	2331	0015		...	0545	0614	0645	0714	0745	0814	0823	0845	same	2214	2223	2245	2314	2323	2353
Mechelen	d.	2238	2245	2304	2338	2348	2345	0048		...	0604	0634	0704	0734	0804	0834	0838	0904	minutes	2234	2238	2304	2334	2338	0021
Brussels Nationaal ✈	a.	2249	|	|	2349	|	|	|		...	|	|	|	|	|	|	0849	|	past	|	2249	|	|	2349	|
Brussels Nord	d.	2307	2302	2324	0007	0014	0002	0119		0555	0624	0655	0724	0755	0824	0855	0907	0924	each	2255	2307	2324	2355	0007	0045
Brussels Central	d.	2311	2306	2328	0011	0018	0006	|		0559	0628	0659	0728	0759	0828	0859	0911	0928	hour	2259	2311	2328	2359	0011	0049
Brussels Midi / Zuid	a.	2315	2310	2332	0015	0022	0010	0130		0603	0632	0703	0732	0803	0832	0903	0915	0932	until	2303	2315	2332	0003	0015	0053
Brussels Midi / Zuid	d.	...	...	...	...	0025	...	...		0606	△	0706	△	0806	△	0906	...	△		2306	...	...	...	...	...
Nivelles	d.	...	...	...	...	0105	...	...		0634	...	0734	...	0834	...	0934	...	...		2334	...	...	...	...	...
Charleroi Sud	a.	...	...	...	...	0132	...	...		0657	...	0757	...	0857	...	0957	...	...		2357	...	...	...	...	...

			Ⓐ	Ⓐ	Ⓐ	Ⓐ	Ⓐ	Ⓐ	Ⓐ	Ⓐ	Ⓐ	Ⓐ	Ⓐ	Ⓐ	Ⓐ	Ⓐ	Ⓐ		Ⓐ	Ⓐ	Ⓐ	Ⓐ	Ⓐ	Ⓐ	Ⓐ
					⊡	◇					◇					◇						◇			
Charleroi Sud	d.	Ⓐ	...	...	0428	...	...	...	0524	...	...	0554	...	0624	...	...	0654		...	1924	...	...	1954	2024	...
Nivelles	d.		...	...	0456	...	...	...	0550	...	...	0620	...	0650	...	...	0720		...	1950	...	...	2020	2050	...
Brussels Midi / Zuid	a.		...	...	0535	...	...	...	0617	...	...	0647	...	0717	...	...	0746	and	...	2017	...	...	2047	2117	...
Brussels Midi / Zuid	d.		0450	0527	0539	0545	0550	0557	0620	0627	0645	0650	0657	0720	0727	0745	0748	at	1957	2020	2027	2045	2050	2120	2127
Brussels Central	d.		0454	0531	0543	0549	0554	0601	0624	0631	0649	0654	0701	0724	0731	0749	0752	the	2001	2024	2031	2049	2054	2124	2131
Brussels Nord	d.		0500	0537	0550	0555	0600	0607	0630	0637	0655	0700	0707	0730	0737	0755	0759	same	2007	2030	2037	2055	2100	2130	2137
Brussels Nationaal ✈	d.		|	|	|	0611	|	|	|	|	0711	|	|	|	|	0811	|	minutes	|	|	|	2111	|	|	|
Mechelen	d.		0517	0559	0621	0625	0617	0629	0648	0659	0725	0717	0729	0748	0759	0825	0817	past	2029	2048	2059	2125	2117	2148	2159
Antwerpen Berchem	d.		0531	0617	0651	0639	0631	0647	0702	0717	0739	0731	0747	0802	0817	0839	0831	each	2047	2102	2117	2139	2131	2202	2217
Antwerpen Centraal	a.		0535	0621	0655	0643	0635	0651	0706	0721	0743	0735	0751	0806	0821	0843	0835	hour	2051	2106	2121	2143	2135	2206	2221
Antwerpen Centraal	d.		...	0623	...	0645	...	...	...	0723	0745	...	...	...	0823	0845	...	until	...	...	2123	2145	...	...	2223
Kapellen	d.		...	0636	...	|	...	...	...	0736	|	...	...	...	0836	|	...		...	...	2136	|	...	...	2236
Essen 🏛	a.		...	0653	...	|	...	...	...	0753	|	...	...	...	0853	|	...		...	...	2153	|	...	...	2253
Roosendaal	a.		...	...	...	0711	...	...	...	...	0811	...	...	...	...	0911	...		...	...	...	2211	...	...	...

		Ⓐ	Ⓐ	Ⓐ	Ⓐ	Ⓐ	Ⓐ	Ⓐ			Ⓒ	Ⓒ	Ⓒ	Ⓒ	Ⓒ	Ⓒ		Ⓒ	Ⓒ	Ⓒ	Ⓒ	Ⓒ	Ⓒ	Ⓒ	Ⓒ
								⊡			◇			◇				◇							⊙
Charleroi Sud	d.	2054	2124	...	2154	2224	...	...	...	Ⓒ	...	0503	...	...	0603	...		...	2003	...	2103	...	2203	...	...
Nivelles	d.	2120	2150	...	2220	2250	...	2256	...		...	0528	...	...	0628	...		...	2028	...	2128	...	2228	...	...
Brussels Midi / Zuid	a.	2147	2217	...	2247	2318	...	2335	...		...	0554	△	...	0654	△	and	...	2054	△	2154	△	2255	△	...
Brussels Midi / Zuid	d.	2150	2220	2227	2250	2320	2327	2339	...		0545	0557	0628	0645	0657	0728	at	2045	2057	2128	2157	2228	2257	2328	0007
Brussels Central	d.	2154	2224	2231	2254	2324	2331	2343	...		0549	0601	0632	0649	0701	0732	the	2049	2101	2132	2201	2232	2301	2332	0011
Brussels Nord	d.	2200	2230	2237	2300	2328	2337	2349	...		0555	0608	0638	0655	0708	0738	same	2055	2108	2138	2208	2238	2308	2338	0017
Brussels Nationaal ✈	d.	|	|	|	|	...	|	|	...		0611	|	|	0711	|	|	minutes	2111	|	|	|	|	|	|	|
Mechelen	d.	2217	2248	2259	2317	...	2359	0021	...		0625	0629	0658	0725	0729	0758	past	2125	2129	2158	2229	2258	2329	2358	0041
Antwerpen Berchem	d.	2231	2302	2317	2331	...	0017	0051	...		0639	0647	0716	0739	0747	0816	each	2139	2147	2216	2247	2316	2347	0016	0108
Antwerpen Centraal	a.	2235	2306	2321	2335	...	0021	0055	...		0643	0651	0720	0743	0751	0820	hour	2143	2151	2220	2251	2320	2351	0020	0112
Antwerpen Centraal	d.	...	...	2323	...	...	...	...	...		0645	...	...	0745	...	...	until	2145	...	...	...	...	...	...	...
Kapellen	d.	...	...	2336	...	...	...	...	...		|	...	...	|	...	...		|	...	...	...	...	...	...	...
Essen 🏛	a.	...	...	2353	...	...	...	...	...		|	...	...	|	...	...		|	...	...	...	...	...	...	...
Roosendaal	a.	...	...	...	...	...	...	...	...		0711	...	...	0811	...	...		2211	...	...	...	...	...	...	...

LOCAL TRAINS ROOSENDAAL - ANTWERPEN

		Ⓐ			
Roosendaal	d.	0653	0723	and	2223
Essen 🏛	d.	0710	0733	hourly	2233
Kapellen	d.	0731	0754	until	2254
Antwerpen Cent.	a.	0749	0810		2310

					Ⓒ
Antwerpen Cent.	d.	0550	and	2050	2150
Kapellen	d.	0608	hourly	2108	2208
Essen 🏛	d.	0630	until	2130	2230
Roosendaal	a.	0637		2137	2237

ANTWERPEN - NOORDERKEMPEN

		◧	◧	
Antwerpen Centraal	d.	0640	hourly	2140
Noorderkempen	a.	0655	until	2155

		◐	◐	
Noorderkempen	d.	0605	hourly	2105
Antwerpen Centraal	a.	0620	until	2120

Noorderkempen station is situated on the high-speed line, 2 km from Brecht

♥ – No journey at 2109.
◧ – 0640 and 0740 run on Ⓐ only. No journeys at 1140 or 1340.
◐ – 0605 and 0705 run on Ⓐ only. No journeys at 1105 or 1305.
⊡ – Local train.
⊙ – Local train. Runs night of ⑥/⑦ and night of ⑦/①.
△ – To/from Binche via La Louvière (Table **423**).
◇ – *Benelux* train from/to Amsterdam via Schiphol ✈, Rotterdam, Den Haag (Table **18**).

421 CHARLEROI - MARIEMBOURG - COUVIN

Line 132

km				Ⓐ	Ⓐ	Ⓐ	Ⓐ		Ⓐ	Ⓐ	Ⓐ	Ⓐ	Ⓐ	Ⓐ	Ⓐ	Ⓐ		Ⓒ	Ⓒ	Ⓒ	Ⓒ	Ⓒ	Ⓒ	Ⓒ	Ⓒ	
0	**Charleroi** Sud	d.	Ⓐ	0555	0706	0814	0914		1614	1650	1720	1735	1814	1914	2014	2140	Ⓒ	0815	1015	1215	1415	1615	1815	2015	2215	...
18	Berzée	d.		0619	0729	0832	0932	and	1632	1713	1739	1758	1832	1932	2032	2203		0838	1038	1238	1438	1638	1838	2038	2238	...
22	Walcourt	d.		0625	0736	0837	0937	hourly	1637	1719	1744	1804	1837	1937	2037	2209		0846	1046	1246	1446	1646	1846	2046	2246	...
35	Philippeville	d.		0639	0750	0850	0950	until	1650	1734	1757	1819	1850	1950	2050	2223		0900	1100	1300	1500	1700	1900	2100	2300	...
48	Mariembourg ▲	d.		0650	0801	0901	1001		1701	1745	1809	1829	1901	2001	2101	2234		0911	1111	1311	1511	1711	1911	2111	2311	...
53	**Couvin**	a.		0658	0809	0909	1009		1709	1753	1817	1837	1909	2009	2109	2242		0919	1119	1319	1519	1719	1919	2119	2319	...

			Ⓐ	Ⓐ	Ⓐ	Ⓐ	Ⓐ	Ⓐ		Ⓐ	Ⓐ	Ⓐ	Ⓐ	Ⓐ	Ⓐ	Ⓐ		Ⓒ	Ⓒ	Ⓒ	Ⓒ	Ⓒ	Ⓒ	Ⓒ	Ⓒ	
				N																						
Couvin	d.	Ⓐ	0434	0459	0544	0618	0642	0750		1450	1550	1629	1757	1850	1950	2051	Ⓒ	0639	0839	1039	1239	1439	1639	1839	2039	...
Mariembourg ▲	d.		0444	0509	0554	0628	0653	0800	and	1500	1600	1639	1807	1900	2000	2101		0649	0849	1049	1249	1449	1649	1849	2049	...
Philippeville	d.		0455	0520	0605	0640	0704	0811	hourly	1511	1611	1651	1820	1911	2011	2112		0703	0903	1103	1303	1503	1703	1903	2103	...
Walcourt	d.		0509	0534	0618	0654	0719	0823	until	1523	1626	1705	1832	1923	2023	2126		0718	0918	1118	1318	1518	1718	1918	2118	...
Berzée	d.		0516	0539	0622	0658	0724	0828		1528	1631	1711	1836	1928	2028	2131		0724	0924	1124	1324	1524	1724	1924	2124	...
Charleroi Sud	a.		0540	0603	0640	0717	0748	0846		1546	1655	1735	1854	1946	2046	2155		0745	0945	1145	1345	1545	1745	1945	2145	...

N – Not Dec. 26 - Jan. 6, Apr. 3 - 17, July 3 - Sept. 1.
▲ – Service available on certain dates Mariembourg - Treignes and v.v. Some trains operated by steam locomotive.
Operator: Chemin de Fer à Vapeur des 3 Vallées (CFV3V), Chaussée de Givet 49-51, 5660 Mariembourg. www.cfv3v.com

BRUSSELS - MONS - QUIÉVRAIN — 422
Lines 96, 97

For additional trains Brussels - Halle - Braine-le-Comte see Table **423**

km		Ⓐ	Ⓐ	Ⓐ	Ⓐ◇	Ⓐ		Ⓐ	Ⓐ◇	Ⓐ	Ⓐ	Ⓐ	Ⓐ	Ⓐ		Ⓒ	Ⓒ
0	Brussels Nationaal + d.	0530		0630		0730		1930		2030	2130	2230	2330		0531	2231
12	Brussels Nord d.	0543	0613	0643	0713	0743	and	1913 1943	2013	2043 2113	2143	2213 2243	2313 2343		0543	2243
14	Brussels Central d.	0547	0617	0647	0717	0747	at	1917 1947	2017	2047 2117	2147	2217 2247	2317 2347		0547	2247
16	Brussels Midi / Zuid d.	0553	0624	0653	0724	0753	the	1924 1953	2024	2053 2124	2153	2224 2253	2324 2353		0554 and	2254
32	Halle d.		0634		0734		same	1934	2034	2134	2234	2334			hourly	
45	Braine-le-Comte d.	0616	0647	0716	0747	0816	minutes	1947 2016	2047	2116 2147	2216	2247 2316	2347 0016		0616 until	2316
51	Soignies d.	0622	0653	0722	0753	0822	past	1953 2022	2053	2122 2153	2222	2253 2322	2353 0022		0622	2322
76	Mons a.	0640	0711	0740	0811	0840	each	2011 2040	2111	2140 2211	2240	2311 2340	0011 0040		0640	2340
76	Mons d.		0714		0814		hour	2014	2114	2214	2314					□	□
86	Saint-Ghislain a.		0728		0828		until	2028	2128	2228	2328						
96	Quiévrain a.		0747		0847			2047									

		Ⓐ	Ⓐ	Ⓐ	Ⓐ◇	Ⓐ		Ⓐ◇	Ⓐ		Ⓒ	Ⓒ
	Quiévrain d.			0513	0613	0713	and	1913	2013			
	Saint-Ghislain d.			0532	0632	0732	at	1932	2032		□	□
	Mons a.			0546	0646	0746	the	1946	2046			
	Mons d.	0422 0449	0520 0549	0620 0649	0720 0749	0820	same	1949 2020	2049 2122 2122		0520	2220
	Soignies d.	0441 0507	0538 0607	0638 0707	0738 0807	0838	minutes	2007 2038	2107 2141 2241		0538	2238
	Braine-le-Comte d.	0449 0514	0546 0614	0646 0714	0746 0814	0845	past	2014 2045	2114 2149 2249		0546 and	2246
	Halle d.	0527	0627	0727	0827		each	2027	2127		hourly	
	Brussels Midi / Zuid a.	0509 0536	0604 0636	0704 0736	0804 0837	0907	hour	2036 2109	2136 2209 2309		0606 until	2306
	Brussels Central a.	0514 0542	0609 0642	0709 0742	0809 0842	0912	until	2042 2114	2142 2214 2314		0612	2312
	Brussels Nord a.	0519 0547	0614 0647	0714 0747	0814 0847	0917		2047 2119	2147 2219 2319		0617	2317
	Brussels Nationaal + a.	0532	0628	0729	0830	0930		2132	2232 2332		0629	2329

◇ – From / to Liège via Landen (Table **430**).   □ – MONS - QUIÉVRAIN LOCAL TRAINS ON Ⓒ: from Mons hourly 0654Ⓒ - 2054Ⓒ, from Quiévrain hourly 0737Ⓒ - 2137Ⓒ.

BRUSSELS - LA LOUVIÈRE - BINCHE — 423
Lines 96, 108

For additional trains Brussels - Halle - Braine-le-Comte see Table **422**

km		Ⓐ				Ⓒ						Ⓐ			Ⓒ			
0	Brussels Nord d.	0619		2019 2119	2219	0624		2224	Binche d.	0520		2120	0521 0614		2214
2	Brussels Central d.	0623		2023 2123	2223	0628		2228	La Louvière Sud d.	0534		2134	0534 0634		2234
4	Brussels Midi / Zuid d.	0630	and	2030 2130	2230	0635	and	2235	La Louvière Centre d.	0540	and	2140	0539 0639	and	2239
20	Halle d.	0641	hourly	2041 2141	2241	0644	hourly	2244	Braine-le-Comte d.	0603	hourly	2203	0602 0702	hourly	2302
33	Braine-le-Comte d.	0658	until	2058 2158	2258	0700	until	2300	Halle d.	0621	until	2221	0617 0717	until	2317
52	La Louvière Centre a.	0720		2120 2220	2320	0721		2321	Brussels Midi / Zuid a.	0630		2230	0625 0725		2325
55	La Louvière Sud a.	0726		2126 2226	2326	0726		2326	Brussels Central a.	0636		2236	0631 0731		2331
64	Binche a.	0740		2140		0746		2346	Brussels Nord a.	0641		2241	0636 0736		2336

On Ⓐ trains run beyond Brussels to / from Turnhout (Table **434**). On Ⓒ trains run beyond Brussels to / from Antwerpen (Table **420**).

BRUSSELS - GERAARDSBERGEN — 424
Lines 94, 123

km		Ⓐ		Ⓐ	Ⓒ		Ⓒ			Ⓐ		Ⓐ	Ⓒ		Ⓒ
0	Brussels Nord d.	0442		2042	0742		2042	Geraardsbergen d.	0425		2025	0725		2025
2	Brussels Centraal d.	0446	and	2046	0746	and	2046	Edingen d.	0446	and	2046	0746	and	2046
4	Brussels Midi / Zuid d.	0453	hourly	2053	0753	hourly	2053	Halle d.	0458	hourly	2058	0758	hourly	2058
18	Halle d.	0504	until	2104	0804	until	2104	Brussels Midi / Zuid a.	0507	until	2107	0807	until	2107
33	Edingen d.	0515		2115	0815		2115	Brussels Centraal a.	0513		2113	0813		2113
49	Geraardsbergen a.	0534		2134	0834		2134	Brussels Nord a.	0518		2118	0818		2118

MONS - CHARLEROI - NAMUR — 425
Lines 118, 130

km		Ⓐ		Ⓐ	Ⓐ	Ⓐ◇	Ⓐ	Ⓐ		Ⓐ	Ⓐ	Ⓐ		Ⓒ	Ⓒ	Ⓒ		Ⓒ♡	Ⓒ♡
	Tournai **416** d.			0544		0644		and at	1944		2044		2144			0630 0730			2030	2130
0	Mons d.	0437		0537 0617	0638	0717 0737	the	2017 2037	2118 2137	2218 2237	0615 0715 0815		2115 2215
20	La Louvière Sud d.	0454		0554 0633	0654	0733 0754	same	2052 2133	2154	2233 2254	0631 0731 0831	and	2131 2231
41	Charleroi Sud d.	0514 0552	0614 0652	0714 0752	0814	minutes	2052 2114	2152 2214	2252 2312	0651 0751 0851	hourly	2151 2251
56	Tamines d.	0527 0603	0627 0703	0727 0803	0827	past	2103 2127	2203 2227	2303	0704 0804 0904	until	2204 2304
61	Jemeppe-sur-Sambre d.	0535	0635	0735	0835	each	2135	2235	0712 0812 0912		2212 2312
78	Namur a.	0550 0622	0650 0722	0750 0822	0850	hour	2122 2150	2222 2250	2322	0727 0827 0927		2227 2327
	Liège Guillemins **442** a.	0642	0742	0842	0942	until	2242		0818 0918 1018		2318

		Ⓐ		Ⓐ		Ⓐ◇	Ⓐ	Ⓐ		Ⓐ	Ⓐ		Ⓒ	Ⓒ		Ⓒ♡	Ⓒ♡
	Liège Guillemins **442** d.			0518		0618		and at	1918		2018	2118	2218		0642		2042	2142
	Namur d.	0510 0538	0610 0638	0710 0738	the	2010 2038	2110 2138	2210 2238 2310	0633 0733		2133 2233
	Jemeppe-sur-Sambre d.	0525	0625	0725	same	2025	2125	2325	0648 0748	and	2148 2248
	Tamines d.	0534 0558	0634 0658	0734 0758	minutes	2034 2058	2134 2158	2234 2258 2334	0657 0757	hourly	2157 2257
	Charleroi Sud d.	0448 0548	0611 0648	0711 0748	past	2048 2111	2148 2211	2248 2309 2346	0611 0711 0811	until	2211 2310
	La Louvière Sud d.	0508 0608	0628 0708	0728 0808	0828	each	2108 2128	2208 2228	2308	0631 0731 0831		2231
	Mons a.	0522 0622	0642 0722	0742 0822	0842	hour	2122 2142	2222 2242	2322	0645 0745 0845		2245
	Tournai **416** a.		0715		0815		0915	until		2215	2323	0730 0830 0930		2330

◇ – Most journeys run from / to Lille (Table **416**).   ♡ – From / to Mouscron (Table **416**).

MONS - QUEVY — 426
Line 96

km		Ⓐ	Ⓐ	Ⓐ		Ⓐ	Ⓐ	Ⓐ§	Ⓐ§	Ⓐ	Ⓐ		Ⓐ‡	Ⓐ‡	Ⓐ	Ⓐ	Ⓐ	Ⓐ		Ⓐ	Ⓐ	Ⓐ	Ⓐ
0	Mons d.	0721	0821	0931	hourly	1631	1650	1728	1809	1918	2021	Quévy d.	0600	0615	0723	0755	0823	0913	hourly	1613	1723	1823	1923
18	Quévy d.	0737	0837	0947	until	1647	1704	1744	1827	1834	1937 2037	Mons a.	0617	0632	0739	0811	0839	0929	until	1629	1739	1839	1939

§ – From Brussels (depart Brussels Midi 1636 and 1715).
‡ – To Brussels (arrive Brussels Midi 0704 and 0719).

ADDITIONAL JOURNEYS: from Mons 1850Ⓐ; from Quévy 0524Ⓐ, 0655Ⓐ.   No service on Ⓒ.

CHARLEROI - ERQUELINNES — 427
Line 130a

km		Ⓐ		Ⓐ	Ⓒ		Ⓒ			Ⓐ		Ⓐ	Ⓒ		Ⓒ
0	Charleroi Sud d.	0655	and	1955	0614	every	2014	Erquelinnes d.	0504	and	2004	0704	every	2104
14	Lobbes d.	0712	hourly	2012	0629	two	2029	Lobbes d.	0521	hourly	2021	0724	two	2124
16	Thuin d.	0718	until	2018	0635	hours	2035	Thuin d.	0523	until	2023	0727	hours	2127
29	Erquelinnes a.	0734		2034	0653	until	2053	Charleroi Sud a.	0543		2043	0745	until	2145

Jeumont (France) is approximately 2 km from Erquelinnes station (for Jeumont - Lille see Table **262**).

BELGIUM and LUXEMBOURG *Timings may vary by 1 or 2 minutes*

430 BRUSSELS - LANDEN - HASSELT, GENK and LIÈGE

Lines 36, 21

For direct services Brussels - Liège via high-speed line see Table **400**. For other services Brussels - Hasselt on Ⓐ (via Aarshot) see Table **431**.

km			Ⓐ	Ⓐ	Ⓐ	Ⓐ	Ⓐ	Ⓐ		Ⓐ	Ⓐ	Ⓐ	Ⓐ	Ⓐ	Ⓐ	Ⓐ	Ⓐ		Ⓐ	Ⓐ	Ⓐ	Ⓐ	Ⓐ	Ⓐ
			♡		•	♡	△	•		♡	△	•	♡	△	b	△	b		N					
0	**Brussels** Midi / Zuid d.	Ⓐ	0512	0514	0539	0612	0614	0639		2112	2114	2139	2212	2214	2256	2314	0021		1548	1603	1634	1706	1734	1758
2	Brussels Central d.		0516	0518	0543	0616	0618	0643	and	2116	2118	2143	2216	2218	2300	2318	0025		1552	1607	1638	1710	1738	1802
4	Brussels Nord d.		0522	0525	0549	0622	0625	0649	at	2122	2125	2149	2222	2225	2307	2325	0032		1602	1614	1644	1716	1744	1808
33	**Brussels Nationaal ✈** d.		|	0538	|	|	0638	|	the	|	2138	|	|	2238	|	2338	|	A	|	|	|	|	|	|
33	Leuven d.		0543	0553	0610	0643	0653	0710	same	2143	2153	2210	2243	2253	2328	2353	0050	L	1621	1634	1703	1737	1803	1826
64	Tienen d.		0555	0607	0623	0655	0707	0723	minutes	2155	2207	2223	2255	2307	2340	0009	0102	S	1638	1647	1716	1750	1816	1840
64	Landen d.		0607	0621	0634	0707	0721	0734	past	2207	2221	2234	2307	2321	2351	0024	0113	O	1653	1659	1729	1801	1829	1851
75	Sint-Truiden d.		0616	...	|	0716	...	|	each	2216	...	|	2316	...	|	...	|		1704	|	1745	|	1845	...
92	**Hasselt** a.		0630	...	|	0730	...	|	hour	2230	...	|	2330	...	|	...	|		1721	|	1803	|	1903	...
108	Genk a.		0652	...	|	0752s	...	|	until	2252	...	|	...	...	|	...	|		...	|	...	|	1924	...
103	**Liège** Guillemins a.		...	...	0706	...	...	0807		...	...	2306	...	...	0022	...	0144		...	1734	...	1835	...	...

		Ⓒ	Ⓒ	Ⓒ	Ⓒ	Ⓒ	Ⓒ	Ⓒ	Ⓒ		Ⓒ	Ⓒ	Ⓒ	Ⓒ	Ⓒ	Ⓒ	Ⓒ	Ⓒ	Ⓒ	Ⓒ	Ⓒ	Ⓒ	Ⓒ	Ⓒ
		♡		♡		△	♡		△		♡		△	♡		△	♡		△	♡	△	b	△	b
Brussels Midi / Zuid d.	Ⓒ	0612	...	0712	...	0714	0812	...	0814		1912	...	1914	2012	...	2014	2112	...	2114	2212	2214	2256	2314	0021
Brussels Central d.		0616	...	0716	...	0718	0816	...	0818	and	1916	...	1918	2016	...	2018	2116	...	2118	2216	2218	2300	2318	0025
Brussels Nord d.		0622	...	0722	...	0724	0822	...	0824	at	1922	...	1924	2022	...	2024	2122	...	2124	2222	2224	2307	2324	0032
Brussels Nationaal ✈ d.		|	...	|	...	0738	|	...	0838	the	|	...	1938	|	...	2038	|	...	2138	|	2238	|	2338	|
Leuven d.		0643	...	0743	...	0751	0843	...	0853	same	1943	...	1951	2043	...	2053	2143	...	2151	2243	2253	2328	2351	0050
Tienen d.		0655	...	0755	...	...	0855	...	0907x	minutes	1955	...	...	2055	...	2107	2155	...	...	2255	2307	2340	...	0102
Landen d.		0707	0712	0807	0812	...	0907	0912	0921x	past	2007	2012	...	2107	2112	2121	2207	2212	...	2307	2321	2351	...	0113
Sint-Truiden d.		0716	|	0816	|	...	0916	|	...	each	2016	|	...	2116	|	...	2216	|	...	2316	...	|	...	|
Hasselt a.		0730	|	0830	|	...	0930	|	...	hour	2030	|	...	2130	|	...	2230	|	...	2330	...	|	...	|
Genk a.		0752	|	0852	|	...	0952	|	...	until	2052	|	...	2152	|	...	2252	|	...	2352	...	|	...	|
Liège Guillemins a.		...	0752	...	0852	...	...	0952	...		...	2052	...	...	2152	...	...	2252	...	...	...	0022	...	0144

		Ⓐ	Ⓐ	Ⓐ	Ⓐ	Ⓐ	Ⓐ	Ⓐ	Ⓐ		Ⓐ	Ⓐ	Ⓐ	Ⓐ			Ⓐ	Ⓐ	Ⓐ	Ⓐ	Ⓐ		Ⓐ	
		△	♡	b	•	△	♡	•	△		♡	•		b			N						N	
Liège Guillemins d.	Ⓐ	...	...	0440	0454	...	...	0554	...		...	2154	...	2308	...		...	...	0624	...	0724	...	...	...
Genk d.		...	...	|	|	...	0508r	|	...	and	2108	|	...	|	...		...	0533	|	0624	|	...	1537	...
Hasselt d.		...	0429	|	|	...	0529	|	...	at	2129	|	...	|	...		...	0557	|	0657	|	...	1558	...
Sint-Truiden d.		...	0445	|	|	...	0545	|	...	the	2145	|	...	|	...	A	...	0616	|	0716	|	...	1616	...
Landen d.		0439	0454	0510	0527	0539	0554	0627	0639	same	2154	2227	2239	2338	...	L	0604	0630	0659	0730	0759	...	1630	...
Tienen d.		0453	0505	0521	0538	0553	0605	0638	0653	minutes	2205	2238	2253	2349	...	S	0616	0643	0710	0742	0809	...	1643	...
Leuven d.		0509	0519	0534	0552	0609	0619	0652	0709	past	2219	2252	2309	0001	...	O	0630	0659	0724	0759	0824	...	1655	...
Brussels Nationaal ✈ a.		0523	|	|	|	0623	|	|	0723	each	|	|	2323	|	...		|	|	|	|	|	...	...	...
Brussels Nord a.		0536	0538	0552	0611	0636	0638	0711	0736	hour	2238	2311	2336	0017	...		0646	0716	0744	0816	0843	...	...	...
Brussels Central a.		0541	0543	0558	0616	0641	0643	0716	0741	until	2243	2316	2341	0022	...		0652	0721	0750	0821	0848	...	...	...
Brussels Midi / Zuid a.		0546	0548	0603	0621	0646	0648	0721	0746		2248	2321	2346	0027	...		0657	0726	0755	0826	0853	...	...	...

		Ⓒ	Ⓒ	Ⓒ	Ⓒ	Ⓒ	Ⓒ	Ⓒ	Ⓒ	Ⓒ	Ⓒ	Ⓒ	Ⓒ		Ⓒ	Ⓒ	Ⓒ	Ⓒ	Ⓒ	Ⓒ	Ⓒ	Ⓒ		
		△	b	△	△	♡	△		♡	△		♡	△			♡	△		♡		♡	b		
Liège Guillemins d.	Ⓒ	...	0440	...	...	...	...	0708	...	...	0808	...	...		2008	...	...	2108	...	2208	...	2308	...	...
Genk d.		...	|	...	...	...	...	|	0708	...	|	0808	...	and	|	2008	...	|	2108	|	2204	|	...	...
Hasselt d.		...	|	...	...	0629	...	|	0729	...	|	0829	...	at	|	2029	...	|	2129	|	2229	|	...	...
Sint-Truiden d.		...	|	...	...	0645	...	|	0745	...	|	0845	...	the	|	2045	...	|	2145	|	2245	|	...	...
Landen d.		...	0510	0539	...	0654	0739	0748	0754	...	0848	0854	0939z	same	2048	2054	...	2148	2154	2248	2254	2338	...	...
Tienen d.		...	0521	0553	...	0705	0753	...	0805	...	...	0905	0953z	minutes	...	2105	...	...	2205	...	2305	2349	...	...
Leuven d.		0509	0534	0609	0709	0719	0809	...	0819	0909	...	0919	1009	past	...	2119	2209	...	2219	...	2319	0001	...	...
Brussels Nationaal ✈ a.		0522	|	0622	0722	|	0822	...	|	0922	...	|	1022	each	...	|	2222	...	|	...	|	|	...	...
Brussels Nord a.		0536	0552	0636	0736	0738	0836	...	0838	0936	...	0938	1036	hour	...	2138	2236	...	2238	...	2338	0017	...	...
Brussels Central a.		0541	0558	0641	0741	0743	0841	...	0843	0941	...	0943	1041	until	...	2143	2241	...	2243	...	2343	0022	...	...
Brussels Midi / Zuid a.		0546	0603	0646	0746	0748	0846	...	0848	0946	...	0948	1046		...	2148	2246	...	2248	...	2348	0027	...	...

N – Not Dec. 26 - Jan. 6, Apr. 3 - 17, July 3 - Sept. 1.
b – From / to Brugge and Oostende (Table **400**).
r – 1308 departs at 1301.
s – 1312 from Brussels requires change at Hasselt.
x – Extends beyond Leuven to Landen every **two** hours (even hours from Brussels).
z – Every **two** hours from Landen 0939 - 1939.
♡ – From / to Brugge and Gent, Table **405** (most trains also from / to Knokke and Blankenberge).
△ – From / to Gent via Aalst, Table **411** (most trains also from / to De Panne).
• – From / to Mons (Table **422**).

431 BRUSSELS - AARSCHOT - HASSELT - TONGEREN

Line 35

No service on Ⓒ via this route. For other trains Brussels - Hasselt (via Landen) see Table **430**.

km			Ⓐ	Ⓐ		Ⓐ	Ⓐ	Ⓐ	
	Gent **411** ▷ d.	Ⓐ	0440	0540		1940	2040	2140	...
0	**Brussels** Midi / Zuid d.		0545	0645		2045	2145	2245	...
2	Brussels Central d.		0549	0649	and	2049	2149	2249	...
4	Brussels Nord d.		0555	0655	hourly	2055	2155	2255	...
46	Aarschot **432** d.		0621	0721	until	2121	2221	2321	...
63	Diest **432** d.		0634	0734		2134	2234	2334	...
84	**Hasselt** **432** a.		0649	0749		2149	2249	2349	...
110	Tongeren **435** a.		0722	0822		2222	...	...	...

		Ⓐ	Ⓐ	Ⓐ		Ⓐ	Ⓐ	
Tongeren **435** d.	Ⓐ	...	0538	0638r		2038	2138	...
Hasselt **432** d.		0511	0611	0711		2111	2211	...
Diest **432** d.		0527	0627	0727	and	2127	2227	...
Aarschot **432** d.		0541	0641	0741	hourly	2141	2241	...
Brussels Nord a.		0605	0705	0805	until	2205	2305	...
Brussels Central a.		0610	0710	0810		2210	2310	...
Brussels Midi / Zuid a.		0615	0715	0815		2215	2315	...
Gent **411** ▷ a.		0720	0820	0920		2320	0020	...

r – Journeys from Tongeren at 0938Ⓐ and 1938Ⓐ require a change at Hasselt.
▷ – Gent to Brussels is via Aalst and Denderleeuw (shown in footnote on Table **411**).

432 ANTWERPEN - BRUSSELS NATIONAAL ✈ - AARSCHOT - HASSELT

Lines 35, 36c, 16

For Antwerpen - Hasselt via Mol see Table **434**. For additional trains Brussels Nationaal ✈ - Leuven see Table **430**.

km	*Via Airport*		Ⓐ		Ⓐ		Ⓒ		Ⓒ	Ⓒ
							♠	♠	♠	♠
0	**Antwerpen** Centraal ▷ d.	Ⓐ	0445		2245	Ⓒ	0536		1936	2236
24	Mechelen ▷ d.		0507		2307		0556	and	1956	2256
40	**Brussels Nationaal ✈** ▷ d.		0521	and	2321		0610	every	2010	2310
59	Leuven d.		0543	hourly	2343		0634	**two**	2034	2334
75	Aarschot d.		0555	until	2355		0647	hours	2047	2347
92	Diest d.		0608		0008		0706	until	2106	0006
113	**Hasselt** a.		0622		0022		0723		2123	0023

		Ⓐ		Ⓐ		Ⓒ	Ⓒ		Ⓒ
						♥	♥	♥	♥
Hasselt d.	Ⓐ	0438		2238	Ⓒ	...	0637		2237
Diest d.		0453		2253		...	0654	and	2254
Aarschot d.		0507	and	2307		...	0715	every	2315
Leuven d.		0526	hourly	2326		0536	0736	**two**	2336
Brussels Nationaal ✈ ▷ a.		0539	until	2339		0550	0750	hours	2350
Mechelen ▷ a.		0553		2353		0604	0804	until	0004
Antwerpen Centraal ▷ a.		0615		0015		0624	0824		0024

km	*Via Lier*		Ⓐ		Ⓐ		Ⓒ		Ⓒ	Ⓒ
										◇
0	**Antwerpen** Centraal d.	Ⓐ	0631		2231	Ⓒ	0631		1931	2031
14	Lier d.		0649	and	2249		0649		1949	2049
41	Aarschot d.		0712	hourly	2312		0717	and	2017	2117
57	**Leuven** a.		0724	until	2324		◧	hourly	◧	◧
59	Diest d.		...		...		0730	until	2030	2130
80	**Hasselt** a.		...		...		0744		2044	2144
	Tongeren **435** a.		...		...		0813		2113	2213
	Liège Guillemins **435** a.		...		...		0851		2151	...

		Ⓐ		Ⓐ		Ⓒ	Ⓒ		Ⓒ
Liège Guillemins **435** d.	Ⓐ	...		...	Ⓒ	...	0609		2109
Tongeren **435** d.		...		...		...	0647		2147
Hasselt d.		...		...		0616	0716	and	2216
Diest d.		...		...		0631	0731	hourly	2231
Leuven d.		0636	and	2036		◧	◧	until	◧
Aarschot d.		0650	hourly	2050		0650	0750		2250
Lier d.		0713	until	2113		0713	0813		2312
Antwerpen Centraal a.		0729		2129		0729	0829		2329

♠ – Antwerpen - Leuven runs **hourly** 0436 - 2236.
♥ – Leuven - Antwerpen runs **hourly** 0536 - 2336.
◧ – On Ⓒ local trains run hourly Antwerpen - Aarschot - Leuven (journey 63 mins): from Antwerpen 0646 - 2246, from Leuven 0611 - 2211.
◇ – Also at 2131 to Tongeren, 2231 to Hasselt.
▷ – For additional trains see Table **420**.

Line 15 — BRUSSELS and ANTWERPEN - LIER - TURNHOUT / HASSELT / HAMONT — 434

km		Ⓐ	Ⓐ	Ⓐ	Ⓐ	Ⓐ	Ⓐ	Ⓐ	Ⓐ		Ⓐ	Ⓐ	Ⓐ	Ⓐ	Ⓐ	Ⓐ	Ⓐ
	Brussels Midi/Zuid ▷ d.	Ⓐ	...	...	0633	...	0733	...		...	1933	...	2033	...	2133	2233	...
	Brussels Centraal ▷ d.		...	...	0637	...	0737	...		...	1937	...	2037	...	2137	2237	...
	Brussels Nord ▷ d.		...	...	0643	...	0743	...	and	...	1943	...	2043	...	2143	2243	...
	Mechelen ▷ d.		...	...	0704	...	0804	...	at	...	2004	...	2104	...	2204	2304	...
0	Antwerpen Centraal d.		0609	0648	...	0709	0748	...	0809	the	1948	...	2009	2048	...	2109	2148	...	2225	...	2325
2	Antwerpen Berchem d.		0615	0653	...	0715	0753	...	0815	same	1953	...	2015	2053	...	2115	2153	...	2230	...	2330
15	Lier d.		0627	0704	0722	0727	0804	0822	0827	minutes	2004	2022	2027	2104	2122	2127	2204	2222	2246	2322	2346
34	Herentals d.		0643	0722	0738	0743	0822	0838	0843	past	2022	2038	2043	2122	2138	2143	2222	2238	2309	2338	0009
	Turnhout a.		...	0738	0754	...	0838	0854	...	each	2038	2054	...	2138	2154	...	2238	2254	...	2354	...
46	Geel d.		0655	...	...	0755	...	...	0855	hour	...	2055	...	...	2155	...	...	2321	...	0021
56	Mol a.		0607	0702	...	0802	...	...	0902	until	...	2102	...	...	2202	...	...	2328	...	0028
99	Hasselt a.		0652	0752r	...	0852r	...	...	0952r		...	2152r	...	...	2252r	...	...	...	...	...
77	Overpelt a.		...	0726	...	0826	...	...	0926		...	2126	...	...	2226	...	...	2345	...	...
79	Neerpelt a.		...	0728	...	0828	...	...	0928		...	2128	...	...	2228	...	...	2347	...	...
87	Hamont a.		...	0737	...	0837	...	...	0937		...	2137	...	...	2237	...	...	...	...	...

km		Ⓐ	Ⓐ	Ⓐ	Ⓐ	Ⓐ	Ⓐ	Ⓐ	Ⓐ		Ⓐ	Ⓐ	Ⓐ	Ⓐ	Ⓐ	Ⓐ	Ⓐ
	Hamont d.	Ⓐ	...	0528	...	0621	...	0721		...	1921	...	2021	...	2121		
	Neerpelt d.		...	0537	...	0630	...	0730		...	1930	...	2030	...	2130		
	Overpelt d.		...	0540	...	0633	...	0733	and	...	1933	...	2033	...	2133		
	Hasselt d.		...	...	...	0608s	...	0708s	at	...	1908s	...	2008s	...	2108s	2208	
	Mol d.		0458	...	0558	...	0658	...	0758	the	...	1958	...	2058	...	2158	2253
	Geel d.		0506	...	0606	...	0706	...	0806	same	...	2006	...	2106	...	2206	...
0	Turnhout d.		0459	0522	...	0606	0622	...	0706	0722	...	0806	minutes	1922	...	2006	2022	...	2106	...
18	Herentals d.		0519	0524	0542	0619	0624	0642	0719	0724	0742	0819	0824	past	1942	2019	2024	2042	2119	2124	2219
38	Lier d.		0535	0540	0557	0635	0640	0657	0735	0740	0757	0835	0840	each	1957	2035	2040	2057	2135	2140	2235
	Antwerpen Berchem d.		0545	...	0607	0645	...	0707	0745	...	0807	0845	hour	2007	2045	...	2107	2145	...	2245
	Antwerpen Centraal a.		0551	...	0612	0651	...	0712	0751	...	0812	0851	until	2012	2051	...	2112	2151	...	2251
55	Mechelen ▷ a.		...	0559	...	0659	...	0759		...	0859	...		...	2059	...	2159	...	
75	Brussels Nord ▷ a.		...	0617	...	0717	...	0817		...	0917	...		...	2117	...	2217	...	
77	Brussels Central ▷ a.		...	0622	...	0722	...	0822		...	0922	...		...	2122	...	2222	...	
79	Brussels Midi/Zuid ▷ a.		...	0627	...	0727	...	0827		...	0927	...		...	2127	...	2227	...	

		Ⓒ	Ⓒ	Ⓒ	Ⓒ			Ⓒ	Ⓒ	Ⓒ	△ ▽	Ⓒ
Antwerpen C. d.	Ⓒ	0609	0709	0752	0809			1952	2009	2052	2109
Ant. Berchem d.		0615	0715	0758	0815	and		1958	2015	2058	2115
Lier d.		0627	0727	0810	0827	at		2010	2027	2110	2127
Herentals d.		0643	0743	0832	0843	the		2032	2043	2132	2143
Turnhout a.		...	...	0847	...	same		2047	...	2147	...
Geel d.		0655	0755	...	0855	minutes		...	2055	...	2155
Mol a.		0702	0802	...	0902	past		...	2102	...	2202
Hasselt a.		0752r	...	...	0952x	each		...	2152x	...	...
Overpelt a.		0726	0826	...	0926	hour		...	2126	...	2226
Neerpelt a.		0728	0828	...	0928	until		...	2128	...	2228
Hamont a.		0737	0837	...	0937			...	2137	...	2237

		Ⓒ	Ⓒ	Ⓒ	Ⓒ			Ⓒ	Ⓒ	Ⓒ	Ⓒ	Ⓒ
Hamont d.	Ⓒ	...	...	...	0821			...	2021	...	2121	
Neerpelt d.		0630	...	0730	...	0830	and		...	2030	...	2130
Overpelt d.		0633	...	0733	...	0833	at		...	2033	...	2133
Hasselt d.		...	...	...	0808z	the		...	2008z	...	...
Mol d.		0658	...	0758	...	0858	same		...	2058	...	2158
Geel d.		0706	...	0806	...	0906	minutes		...	2106	...	2206
Turnhout d.		...	0713	...	...	...	past		2013	...	2113	...	2213
Herentals d.		0719	0730	0819	0830	0919	each		2030	2119	2130	2219	2230
Lier d.		0735	0752	0835	0850	0935	hour		2052	2135	2152	2235	2252
Ant. Berchem d.		0745	0802	0845	0902	0945	until		2102	2145	2202	2245	2302
Antwerpen C. a.		0751	0808	0851	0908	0951			2108	2151	2208	2251	2308

r – Portion for Hasselt is detached from main train at Mol (departs Mol xx07; Hamont portion departs xx10).
s – Portion from Hasselt attaches to main train at Mol (arrives Mol xx53; Hamont portion arrives xx49).
x – Portion for Hasselt runs every **two** hours (from Antwerpen 0809, 1009, 1209, 1409, 1609, 1809, 2009).
z – Portion from Hasselt runs every **two** hours (from Hasselt 0808, 1008, 1208, 1408, 1608, 1808, 2008).
▷ – See also Table **420**.

△ – Also at 2152, 2252, 2352.
▽ – Also at 2209, 2309.
▫ – Also at 0613.
⊙ – Also at 0458 from Mol and 0530 from Neerpelt.

*On Ⓐ Turnhout trains run beyond Brussels to/from Binche (Table **423**).*

Line 34 — LIÈGE - HASSELT — 435

km		Ⓐ		Ⓒ	Ⓒ				Ⓐ		Ⓒ	Ⓒ	Ⓒ
0	Liège Guillemins d.	Ⓐ 0722	and	2122	Ⓒ 0609	and	2109	Hasselt **431** d.	Ⓐ 0638	and	2038	Ⓒ 0550	and	2050 2150 2250
27	Tongeren **431** d.	0758	hourly	2158	0647	hourly	2147	Tongeren **431** d.	0703	hourly	2103	0615	hourly	2115 2213 2313
53	Hasselt **431** a.	0822	until	2222	0710	until	2210	Liège Guillemins a.	0738	until	2138	0651	until	2151 ... ...

◇ – From/to Maastricht (Table **436**).
▽ – Most journeys on Ⓒ run beyond Hasselt to/from Antwerpen (Table **432**).

Line 40 — LIÈGE - MAASTRICHT — 436

km		Ⓐ	Ⓐ	Ⓐ	Ⓐ					Ⓒ	Ⓒ	Ⓒ	Ⓒ		
0	Liège Guillemins d.	Ⓐ 0609	0640	0740	0840	and	2040 2140 2240		Ⓒ 0610	0709	0810	0910	and	2110 2210
19	Visé d.	0627	0658	0758	0858	hourly	2058 2158 2258		0628	0728	0828	0928	hourly	2128 2228
32	Maastricht a.	0642	0713	0813	0913	until	2113 2213 2313		0643	0743	0843	0943	until	2143 2243

		Ⓐ	Ⓐ	Ⓐ					Ⓒ	Ⓒ	Ⓒ	Ⓒ		
Maastricht d.	Ⓐ	...	0648	0748	0848	and	2048 2148 2248		Ⓒ 0718	0818	0918	1018	and	2218 2318
Visé d.		0615	0703	0803	0903	hourly	2103 2203 2303		0733	0833	0933	1033	hourly	2233 2333
Liège Guillemins a.		0633	0720	0820	0920	until	2120 2220 2320		0750	0850	0950	1050	until	2250 2350

◇ – To/from Hasselt (Table **435**).

Lines 37, 44 — SPA - VERVIERS - AACHEN — 438

For international trains Brussels - Aachen and beyond see Tables 20/21.

km		Ⓐ	Ⓐ	Ⓐ						Ⓐ	Ⓒ				Ⓐ	Ⓒ	Ⓒ
0	Spa Géronstère d.	...	0605	0646	0746		1946 2046 2046 2146	Aachen Hbf d.	...	0704a	0804			2004 2104 2104 2204
1	Spa d.	...	0608	0650	0750	and	1950 2050 2050 2150	Welkenraedt **400** d.	0620	0720	0820	and	2020 2118 2120 2218
13	Pepinster d.	...	0627	0712	0812	hourly	2012 2112 2112 2212	Verviers Central **400** a.	0634	0734	0834	hourly	2034 ... 2134 ...
17	Verviers Central a.	...	0634	0718	0818	until	2018 2118 2118 2218	Verviers central d.	0642	0742	0842	until	2042 ... 2142 ...
17	Verviers Central d.	...	0726	0826		2026 2126 2126 2218	Pepinster d.	0651	0751	0851		2051 ... 2151 ...
31	Welkenraedt **400** d.	0642	...	0742	0842		2042 2140 2142 2240	Spa a.	0710	0810	0910		2110 ... 2210 ...
50	Aachen Hbf a.	0656	...	0756	0856		2056 ... 2156 ...	Spa Géronstère a.	0714	0814	0914		2114 ... 2214 ...

a – Ⓐ only.

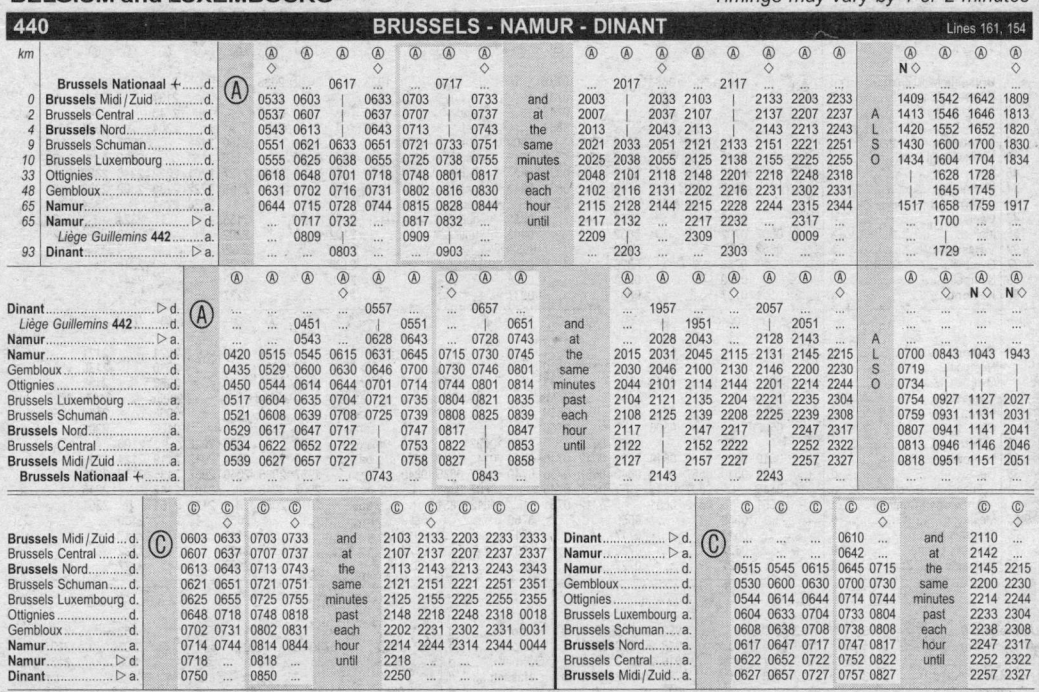

440 BRUSSELS - NAMUR - DINANT

Lines 161, 154

km			Ⓐ ◇	Ⓐ	Ⓐ	Ⓐ ◇	Ⓐ	Ⓐ	Ⓐ ◇		Ⓐ	Ⓐ	Ⓐ ◇	Ⓐ	Ⓐ	Ⓐ ◇	Ⓐ	Ⓐ		Ⓐ N ◇	Ⓐ	Ⓐ	Ⓐ ◇
	Brussels Nationaal ✈ d.	Ⓐ	...	...	0617	...	...	0717	...		...	2017	...	...	2117	...	...	...		...	...	...	...
0	**Brussels** Midi / Zuid d.		0533	0603	|	0633	0703	|	0733	and	2003	|	2033	2103	|	2133	2203	2233		1409	1542	1642	1809
2	Brussels Central d.		0537	0607	|	0637	0707	|	0737	at	2007	|	2037	2107	|	2137	2207	2237	A	1413	1546	1646	1813
4	**Brussels** Nord d.		0543	0613	|	0643	0713	|	0743	the	2013	|	2043	2113	|	2143	2213	2243	L	1420	1552	1652	1820
9	Brussels Schuman d.		0551	0621	0633	0651	0721	0733	0751	same	2021	2033	2051	2121	2133	2151	2221	2251	S	1430	1600	1700	1830
10	Brussels Luxembourg d.		0555	0625	0638	0655	0725	0738	0755	minutes	2025	2038	2055	2125	2138	2155	2225	2255	O	1434	1604	1704	1834
33	Ottignies d.		0618	0648	0701	0718	0748	0801	0817	past	2048	2101	2118	2148	2201	2218	2248	2318		|	1628	1728	|
48	Gembloux d.		0631	0702	0716	0731	0802	0816	0830	each	2102	2116	2131	2202	2216	2231	2302	2331		|	1645	1745	|
65	**Namur** a.		0644	0715	0728	0744	0815	0828	0844	hour	2115	2128	2144	2215	2228	2244	2315	2344		1517	1658	1759	1917
65	**Namur** ▷ d.		...	0717	0732	...	0817	0832	...	until	2117	2132	...	2217	2232	...	2317	...		...	1700	...	...
	Liège Guillemins **442** a.		...	0809	|	...	0909	|	...		2209	|	...	2309	|	...	0009	...		...	|	...	...
93	**Dinant** ▷ a.		...	...	0803	...	...	0903	...		...	2203	...	...	2303	...	...	...		...	1729	...	...

		Ⓐ	Ⓐ	Ⓐ	Ⓐ ◇	Ⓐ	Ⓐ	Ⓐ ◇	Ⓐ	Ⓐ		Ⓐ ◇	Ⓐ	Ⓐ	Ⓐ ◇	Ⓐ	Ⓐ	Ⓐ ◇		Ⓐ	Ⓐ ◇	Ⓐ N ◇	Ⓐ N ◇
Dinant ▷ d.	Ⓐ	...	...	...	...	0557	...	...	0657	...		...	1957	...	...	2057	...	...		...	...	...	...
Liège Guillemins **442** d.		...	...	0451	...	|	0551	...	|	0651	and	...	|	1951	...	|	2051	...		...	...	...	...
Namur ▷ a.		...	...	0543	...	0628	0643	...	0728	0743	at	...	2028	2043	...	2128	2143	...	A	...	...	...	...
Namur d.		0420	0515	0545	0615	0631	0645	0715	0730	0745	the	2015	2031	2045	2115	2131	2145	2215	L	0700	0843	1043	1943
Gembloux d.		0435	0529	0600	0630	0646	0700	0730	0746	0801	same	2030	2046	2100	2130	2146	2200	2230	S	0719	|	|	|
Ottignies d.		0450	0544	0614	0644	0701	0714	0744	0801	0814	minutes	2044	2101	2114	2144	2201	2214	2244	O	0734	|	|	|
Brussels Luxembourg a.		0517	0604	0635	0704	0721	0735	0804	0821	0835	past	2104	2121	2135	2204	2221	2235	2304		0754	0927	1127	2027
Brussels Schuman a.		0521	0608	0639	0708	0725	0739	0808	0825	0839	each	2108	2125	2139	2208	2225	2239	2308		0759	0931	1131	2031
Brussels Nord a.		0529	0617	0647	0717	|	0747	0817	|	0847	hour	2117	|	2147	2217	|	2247	2317		0807	0941	1141	2041
Brussels Central a.		0534	0622	0652	0722	|	0753	0822	|	0853	until	2122	|	2152	2222	|	2252	2322		0813	0946	1146	2046
Brussels Midi / Zuid a.		0539	0627	0657	0727	|	0758	0827	|	0858		2127	|	2157	2227	|	2257	2327		0818	0951	1151	2051
Brussels Nationaal ✈ a.		...	...	...	...	0743	...	...	0843	...		...	2143	...	...	2243	...	...		...	...	...	...

		Ⓒ	Ⓒ ◇	Ⓒ	Ⓒ ◇		Ⓒ	Ⓒ ◇	Ⓒ	Ⓒ	Ⓒ
Brussels Midi / Zuid d.	Ⓒ	0603	0633	0703	0733	and	2103	2133	2203	2233	2333
Brussels Central d.		0607	0637	0707	0737	at	2107	2137	2207	2237	2337
Brussels Nord d.		0613	0643	0713	0743	the	2113	2143	2213	2243	2343
Brussels Schuman d.		0621	0651	0721	0751	same	2121	2151	2221	2251	2351
Brussels Luxembourg d.		0625	0655	0725	0755	minutes	2125	2155	2225	2255	2355
Ottignies d.		0648	0718	0748	0818	past	2148	2218	2248	2318	0018
Gembloux d.		0702	0731	0802	0831	each	2202	2231	2302	2331	0031
Namur a.		0714	0744	0814	0844	hour	2214	2244	2314	2344	0044
Namur ▷ d.		0718	...	0818	...	until	2218	...	...	...	...
Dinant ▷ a.		0750	...	0850	...		2250	...	...	...	...

		Ⓒ	Ⓒ	Ⓒ	Ⓒ	Ⓒ ◇		Ⓒ	Ⓒ ◇
Dinant ▷ d.	Ⓒ	...	...	...	0610	...	and	2110	...
Namur ▷ a.		...	...	...	0642	...	at	2142	...
Namur d.		0515	0545	0615	0645	0715	the	2145	2215
Gembloux d.		0530	0600	0630	0700	0730	same	2200	2230
Ottignies d.		0544	0614	0644	0714	0744	minutes	2214	2244
Brussels Luxembourg a.		0604	0633	0704	0733	0804	past	2233	2304
Brussels Schuman a.		0608	0638	0708	0738	0808	each	2238	2308
Brussels Nord a.		0617	0647	0717	0747	0817	hour	2247	2317
Brussels Central a.		0622	0652	0722	0752	0822	until	2252	2322
Brussels Midi / Zuid a.		0627	0657	0727	0757	0827		2257	2327

N – Not Dec. 26 - Jan. 6, Apr. 3 - 17, July 3 - Sept. 1.
◇ – To / from Luxembourg or other destinations in Table **445**.
▷ – See also Table **448**.

442 NAMUR - LIÈGE

Line 125

km			Ⓐ	Ⓐ	Ⓐ	Ⓐ ◇	Ⓐ	Ⓐ ◇		Ⓐ	Ⓐ ◇	Ⓐ	Ⓐ ◇	Ⓐ ◇			Ⓒ	Ⓒ	Ⓒ ▽	Ⓒ ▽		Ⓒ ▽	Ⓒ ▽	Ⓒ ▽
	Mons **425** d.	Ⓐ	0437	...	0537	...	0637	...	and at	1937	...	2037	...	...	...	Ⓒ	...	0615	0715	0815		1915	2015	2115
	Charleroi Sud **425** d.		0514	...	0614	...	0714	...	the same	2014	...	2114	...	...	...		...	0651	0751	0851	and	1951	2051	2151
0	**Namur** d.		0553	0617	0653	0717	0753	0817	minutes	2053	2117	2153	2217	2317	...		0629	0729	0829	0929	hourly	2029	2129	2229
20	Andenne d.		0607	0631	0707	0731	0807	0831	past	2107	2131	2207	2231	2331	...		0643	0743	0843	0943	until	2043	2143	2243
31	Huy d.		0619	0645	0719	0745	0819	0845	each	2119	2145	2219	2245	2345	...		0655	0755	0855	0955		2055	2155	2255
60	**Liège** Guillemins a.		0642	0709	0742	0809	0842	0909	hour	2142	2209	2242	2309	0009	...		0718	0818	0918	1018		2118	2218	2318
63	Liège Palais a.		0651	0718	0751	0818	0851	0918	until	2151	2218	2251	2318	0018	...		0727	0827	0927	1027		2127	2227	2327

		Ⓐ ◇	Ⓐ	Ⓐ ◇	Ⓐ	Ⓐ ◇	Ⓐ	Ⓐ ◇		Ⓐ	Ⓐ ◇	Ⓐ	Ⓐ	Ⓐ			Ⓒ ▽	Ⓒ ▽	Ⓒ ▽	Ⓒ ▽		Ⓒ ▽	Ⓒ	Ⓒ
Liége Palais d.	Ⓐ	0442	0509	0542	0609	0642	0709	0742	and at	2009	2042	2109	2142	2209	...	Ⓒ	0633	0733	0833	0933		2033	2133	2233
Liège Guillemins d.		0451	0518	0551	0618	0651	0718	0751	the same	2018	2051	2118	2151	2218	...		0642	0742	0842	0942	and	2042	2142	2242
Huy d.		0516	0542	0616	0642	0716	0742	0816	minutes	2042	2116	2142	2216	2242	...		0705	0805	0905	1005	hourly	2105	2205	2305
Andenne d.		0527	0551	0627	0651	0727	0751	0827	past	2051	2127	2151	2227	2251	...		0716	0816	0916	1016	until	2116	2216	2316
Namur a.		0543	0607	0643	0707	0743	0807	0843	each	2107	2143	2207	2243	2307	...		0731	0831	0931	1031		2131	2231	2331
Charleroi Sud **425** a.		...	0646	...	0746	...	0846	...	hour	2146	...	2246	...	2346	...		0809	0909	1009	1109		2209	2310	...
Mons **425** a.		...	0722	...	0822	...	0922	...	until	2222	...	2322	...	...	...		0845	0945	1045	1145		2245	...	...

◇ – From / to Brussels (Table **440**).
▽ – From / to Mouscron via Tournai (Table **416**).

On Ⓐ June 26 - Aug. 25 the 0642 train from Liège extends to Oostende (a. 1016) and the 2118 arrival at Liège starts from Oostende (d. 1735).

On Ⓒ trains continue beyond Liège to / from Liers.

445 (BRUSSELS) - NAMUR - LUXEMBOURG

Line 162

km		Ⓐ	Ⓐ	Ⓐ									Ⓐ N		Ⓐ		Ⓐ			Ⓐ	s	s			Ⓐ
	Brussels Midi / Zuid **440** d.	...	0533	...	0633	0733	0833	0933	1033	1133	1233	1333	1409	1433	...	1533	...	1633	1733	1809	1833	1933	2033	2133	2233
	Brussels Central **440** d.	...	0537	...	0637	0737	0837	0937	1037	1137	1237	1337	1413	1437	...	1537	...	1637	1737	1813	1837	1937	2037	2137	2237
	Brussels Nord **440** d.	...	0543	...	0643	0743	0843	0943	1043	1143	1243	1343	1420	1443	...	1543	...	1643	1743	1820	1843	1943	2043	2143	2243
	Brussels Luxembourg **440** d.	...	0555	...	0655	0755	0855	0955	1055	1155	1255	1355	1434	1455	...	1555	...	1655	1755	1834	1855	1955	2055	2155	2255
0	**Namur** d.	0550	0651	0720	0751	0851	0951	1051	1151	1251	1351	1451	1520	1551	1622	1651	1726	1751	1851	1920	1951	2051	2151	2251	2351
29	Ciney d.	0613	0714	|	0814	0914	1014	1114	1214	1314	1414	1514	|	1614	1646	1714	1748	1814	1914	|	2014	2114	2214	2314	0014
52	Marloie d.	0629	0729	|	0829	0929	1029	1129	1229	1329	1429	1528	|	1629	1701	1729	1803	1829	1929	|	2029	2129	2229	2329	0029
58	Jemelle d.	0635	0735	|	0835	0935	1035	1135	1235	1335	1435	1535	|	1635	1707	1735	1810	1835	1935	|	2035	2135	2235	2335	0034
90	Libramont d.	0656	0757	0817	0856	0957	1057	1157	1257	1357	1457	1556	1617	1657	1729	1757	1833	1857	1957	2017	2057	2157	2257	2357	...
137	Arlon ▷ d.	0733	0833	0855	0933	1033	1133	1233	1333	1433	1533	1633	1655	1733	...	1833	1905	1933	2033	2055	2133	2233	2333	0028	...
165	**Luxembourg** ▷ a.	0751	0851	0913	0951	1051	1151	1251	1351	1451	1551	1651	1713	1751	...	1851	...	1951	2051	2113	2151	2251	2351	...	...

	Ⓐ	Ⓐ	Ⓐ	Ⓒ u	Ⓐ	u	Ⓐ			Ⓐ N										⑦ R	Ⓐ N				J
Luxembourg ▷ d.	...	...	0509	...	...	0609	0650	0709	0809	0848	0909	1009	1109	1209	1309	1409	1509	1609	1709	...	1747	1809	1909	2009	2109
Arlon ▷ d.	...	0432	0532	...	0557	0632	0713	0732	0832	0913	0932	1032	1132	1232	1332	1432	1532	1632	1732	1755	1813	1832	1932	2032	2132
Libramont d.	...	0504	0604	...	0629	0704	0742	0804	0904	0942	1004	1104	1204	1304	1404	1504	1604	1704	1804	1829	1842	1904	2004	2104	2204
Jemelle d.	0426	0526	0626	0626	0653	0726	|	0826	0926	|	1026	1126	1226	1326	1426	1526	1626	1726	1826	1852	|	1926	2026	2126	2226
Marloie d.	0433	0533	0633	0633	0659	0733	|	0833	0933	|	1033	1133	1233	1333	1433	1533	1633	1733	1833	1859	|	1933	2033	2133	2233
Ciney d.	0447	0547	0647	0647	0714	0747	|	0847	0947	|	1047	1147	1247	1347	1447	1547	1647	1747	1847	1915	|	1947	2047	2147	2248
Namur a.	0509	0609	0709	0709	0736	0809	0840	0909	1009	1040	1109	1209	1309	1409	1509	1609	1709	1809	1909	1937	1940	2009	2109	2209	2309
Brussels Luxembourg **440** a.	0604	0704	0804	0804	...	0904	0927	1004	1104	1127	1204	1304	1404	1504	1604	1704	1804	1904	2004	2028	2027	2104	2204	2304	...
Brussels Nord **440** a.	0617	0717	0817	0817	...	0917	0941	1017	1117	1141	1217	1317	1417	1517	1617	1717	1817	1917	2017	2041	2041	2117	2217	2317	...
Brussels Central **440** a.	0622	0722	0822	0822	...	0922	0946	1022	1122	1146	1222	1322	1422	1522	1622	1722	1822	1922	2022	2049	2046	2122	2222	2322	...
Brussels Midi / Zuid **440** a.	0627	0727	0827	0827	...	0927	0951	1027	1127	1151	1227	1327	1427	1527	1627	1727	1827	1927	2027	2054	2051	2127	2227	2327	...

J – Daily to Jemelle, Ⓐ to Namur.
N – Not Dec. 26 - Jan. 6, Apr. 3 - 17, July 3 - Sept. 1.
R – Also Apr. 17, May 1, 25, June 5, Nov. 1; not Dec. 25, Apr. 2, 9, July 2 - Sept. 3.
s – From Oostende on Ⓒ June 24 - Aug. 27 (d. 1712 and 1806).
u – To Oostende on Ⓒ June 24 - Aug. 27 (a. 0945 and 1045).

▷ – LOCAL TRAINS ARLON - LUXEMBOURG (journey 20 - 30 minutes):
From Arlon: 0437Ⓐ, 0537Ⓐ, 0607Ⓐ, 0627Ⓐ, 0633Ⓒ, 0652Ⓐ, 0707Ⓐ, 0737Ⓐ, 0755Ⓐ, 0807Ⓐ, 0837Ⓐ, 0855Ⓐ, 0907Ⓐ, 0937Ⓐ, 1107Ⓐ, 1237Ⓐ, 1307Ⓐ, 1413Ⓐ, 1507Ⓐ, 1637Ⓐ, 1655Ⓐ, 1707Ⓐ, 1737Ⓐ, 1807Ⓐ, 1837Ⓐ, 1911Ⓐ, 1937Ⓐ, 2107Ⓐ.
From Luxembourg: 0521Ⓐ, 0555Ⓐ, 0625Ⓐ, 0655Ⓐ, 0725Ⓐ, 0755Ⓐ, 0825Ⓐ, 0855Ⓐ, 1025Ⓐ, 1155Ⓐ, 1225Ⓐ, 1325Ⓐ, 1425Ⓐ, 1625Ⓐ, 1643Ⓐ, 1655Ⓐ, 1725Ⓐ, 1736Ⓐ, 1755Ⓐ, 1825Ⓐ, 1845Ⓐ, 1855Ⓐ, 2025Ⓐ, 2055Ⓐ, 2209Ⓐ, 2309Ⓐ, 2358.

Line 43/L10 — LIÈGE - GOUVY - CLERVAUX - LUXEMBOURG — 446

km		Ⓐ	Ⓐ	Ⓒ			Ⓐ N										Ⓐ N		Ⓐ			Ⓐ			
0	**Liège** Guillemins .. **447** d.	...	...	...	0608	...	0728	0808	...	1008	...	1208	...	1408	...	1608	1629	...	1708	1808	...	1908	2008	...	2208
23	Rivage .... **447** d.	...	...	...	0630	...	0751	0830	...	1030	...	1230	...	1430	...	1630	1653	...	1731	1830	...	1931	2030	...	2230
31	Aywaille .... d.	...	...	...	0639	...	0759	0839	...	1039	...	1239	...	1439	...	1639	1701	...	1739	1839	...	1939	2039	...	2239
58	Trois-Ponts .... d.	...	...	...	0701	...	0822	0901	...	1101	...	1301	...	1501	...	1701	1729	...	1802	1901	...	2002	2101	...	2301
70	Vielsalm .... d.	...	...	...	0713	...	0834	0913	...	1113	...	1313	...	1513	...	1713	1741	...	1814	1913	...	2014	2113	...	2313
81	Gouvy 🏛 .... d.	0525	0625	...	0726	...	0844	0926	...	1126	...	1326	...	1526	...	1726	1751	...	1824	1926	...	2024	2126	...	2324
91	Troisvierges .... d.	0536	0636	0636	0736	0836	...	0936	1036	1136	1236	1336	1436	1536	1636	1736	...	1836	...	1936	2036	...	2136	2236	...
99	**Clervaux** .... d.	0545	0645	0645	0745	0845	...	0945	1045	1145	1245	1345	1445	1545	1645	1745	...	1845	...	1945	2045	...	2145	2245	...
114	Kautenbach .... d.	0602	0702	0702	0802	0902	...	1002	1102	1202	1302	1402	1502	1602	1702	1802	...	1902	...	2002	2102	...	2202	2302	...
129	Ettelbruck .... d.	0617	0717	0717	0817	0917	...	1017	1117	1217	1317	1417	1517	1617	1717	1817	...	1917	...	2017	2117	...	2217	2317	...
141	Mersch .... d.	0628	0728	0728	0828	0928	...	1028	1128	1228	1328	1428	1528	1628	1728	1828	...	1928	...	2028	2128	...	2228	2328	...
160	**Luxembourg** .... a.	0642	0742	0742	0842	0942	...	1042	1142	1242	1342	1442	1542	1642	1742	1842	...	1942	...	2042	2142	...	2242	2342	...

	Ⓐ	Ⓐ		Ⓐ N												Ⓐ		Ⓐ							⑦
Luxembourg .... d.	...	...	...	...	0618	0718	0818	0918	1018	1118	1218	1318	1418	1518	1618	1645	1718	1745	1818	1918	2018	2118	2218	2318	0018
Mersch .... d.	...	...	...	...	0633	0733	0833	0933	1033	1133	1233	1333	1433	1533	1633	1703	1733	1803	1833	1933	2033	2133	2233	2333	0033
Ettelbruck .... d.	...	...	...	...	0644	0744	0844	0944	1044	1144	1244	1344	1444	1544	1644	1714	1744	1814	1844	1944	2044	2145	2244	2344	0044
Kautenbach .... d.	...	...	...	...	0700	0800	0900	1000	1100	1200	1300	1400	1500	1600	1700	1730	1800	1830	1900	2000	2100	2200	2300	0000	0100
Clervaux .... d.	...	...	...	...	0717	0817	0917	1017	1117	1217	1317	1417	1517	1617	1717	1747	1817	1847	1917	2017	2117	2217	2317	0017	0117
Troisvierges .... d.	...	...	...	...	0724	0826	0924	1026	1124	1226	1324	1426	1524	1626	1724	1756	1826	1856	1924	2026	2124	2226	2324	0024	0124
Gouvy 🏛 .... d.	0507	0547	0639	0707	...	0839	...	1039	...	1239	...	1439	...	1639	...	1805	1839	1905	...	2039	...	2239	...	...	...
Vielsalm .... d.	0518	0558	0649	0718	...	0849	...	1049	...	1249	...	1449	...	1649	...	...	1849	...	...	2049	...	2249	...	...	...
Trois-Ponts .... d.	0529	0609	0701	0729	...	0901	...	1101	...	1301	...	1501	...	1701	...	...	1901	...	...	2101	...	2301	...	...	...
Aywaille .... d.	0551	0631	0723	0751	...	0923	...	1123	...	1323	...	1523	...	1723	...	...	1923	...	...	2123	...	2323	...	...	...
Rivage .... **447** d.	0600	0640	0732	0800	...	0932	...	1132	...	1332	...	1532	...	1732	...	...	1932	...	...	2132	...	2332	...	...	...
Liège Guillemins ... **447** a.	0623	0701	0754	0823	...	0954	...	1154	...	1354	...	1554	...	1754	...	...	1954	...	...	2154	...	2354	...	...	...

N – Not Dec. 26 - Jan. 6, Apr. 3 - 17, July 3 - Sept. 1.

ADDITIONAL TRAINS TROISVIERGES - CLERVAUX - LUXEMBOURG:
From Troisvierges hourly 0406Ⓐ - 2206Ⓐ. From Luxembourg hourly 0645Ⓐ - 2245Ⓐ.

CONNECTIONS KAUTENBACH - WILTZ (journey 12 minutes):
From Kautenbach: on Ⓐ every 30 minutes 0602 - 2302; on Ⓒ 0602, 0702, hourly 0804 - 2304.
From Wiltz: on Ⓐ every 30 minutes 0416 - 2246; on Ⓒ 0546, 0646, 0746, hourly 0842 - 2242.

Line 43 — LIÈGE - MARLOIE — 447

km		Ⓐ	Ⓐ		Ⓐ	Ⓒ S		Ⓐ		Ⓐ		Ⓐ		Ⓐ k	Ⓐ		Ⓐ		Ⓐ					
0	**Liège** Guillemins .... **446** d.	0614	0714	0814	0914	0914	1014	1114	1214	1314	1414	1514	1614	1649	1714	1814	1914	2014	2114	2214	...	...	...	...
23	Rivage .... **446** d.	0641	0741	0841	0941	0941	1041	1141	1241	1341	1441	1541	1641	1718	1741	1841	1941	2041	2141	2241	...	...	...	...
43	Barvaux .... d.	0704	0804	0904	1004	1004	1104	1204	1304	1404	1504	1604	1704	1740	1804	1904	2004	2104	2204	2304	...	...	...	...
65	**Marloie** .... a.	0722	0822	0922	1022	1022	1122	1222	1322	1422	1522	1622	1722	1800	1822	1922	2022	2122	2222	2322	...	...	...	...

	Ⓐ	Ⓐ	Ⓐ n	Ⓐ		Ⓐ		Ⓐ		Ⓐ		Ⓐ		Ⓐ		Ⓐ		Ⓐ	Ⓒ					
Marloie .... d.	0438	0538	0613	0638	0738	0838	0938	1038	1138	1238	1338	1438	1538	1638	1738	1838	1938	2038	2138	...	...	...	...	...
Barvaux .... d.	0456	0556	0631	0656	0756	0856	0956	1056	1156	1256	1356	1456	1556	1656	1756	1856	1956	2056	2156	...	...	...	...	...
Rivage .... **446** d.	0519	0619	0654	0719	0819	0919	1019	1119	1219	1319	1419	1519	1619	1719	1819	1919	2019	2119	2219	...	...	...	...	...
Liège Guillemins .... **446** a.	0546	0646	0723	0746	0846	0946	1046	1146	1246	1346	1446	1546	1646	1746	1846	1946	2046	2146	2246	...	...	...	...	...

S – July 1 - Sept. 3.   k – To Jemelle, arrive 1811.   n – From Jemelle, depart 0606.

Lines 154, 166, 165 — ARDENNES LOCAL SERVICES — 448

km			Ⓒ	Ⓐ							Ⓐ	
0	**Namur** .... **440** d.	0552	0618	0632	0752	0952	1152	1352	1551	1752	1857	1951
28	Dinant .... **440** d.	0621	0650	0703	0821	1021	1221	1421	1619	1821	1929	2019
43	Houyet .... d.	0639	...	...	0839	1039	1239	1439	1637	1839	1947	2037
52	Beauraing .... d.	0647	...	...	0847	1047	1247	1447	1645	1847	1955	2045
100	Bertrix .... a.	0726	...	...	0926	1126	1326	1527	1724	1926	2034	2124
100	Bertrix .... d.	0733	...	...	0933	1133	1333	1534	1731	1933	...	2131
108	**Libramont** .... a.	0741	...	...	0941	1141	1341	1542	1739	1941	...	2139

		Ⓐ						Ⓐ			Ⓐ
Libramont .... d.	...	...	0719	0919	1119	1319	1516	...	1719	1916	2210
Bertrix .... a.	...	...	0728	0928	1128	1328	1525	...	1728	1925	2219
Bertrix .... d.	0535	0626	0735	0935	1135	1335	1532	1605	1735	1932	—
Beauraing .... d.	0613	0705	0813	1013	1213	1413	1609	1642	1813	2009	...
Houyet .... d.	0621	0713	0821	1021	1221	1421	1617	1650	1821	2017	d
Dinant .... **440** d.	0640	0732	0840	1040	1240	1440	1636	1708	1840	2036	2140
Namur .... **440** a.	0708	0801	0908	1108	1308	1508	1704	...	1908	2104	2209

km		Ⓐ					◇	Ⓐ			Ⓒ
0	**Libramont** .... d.	...	0809	1009	1209	1409	1609	1715	1809	2009	2209
8	Bertrix .... a.	...	0818	1018	1218	1418	1618	1724	1818	2018	2218
8	Bertrix .... d.	...	0821	1021	1221	1421	1621	1738	1824	2021	2221
33	Florenville ..... d.	...	0834	1034	1234	1434	1634	1751	1837	2034	2234
57	Virton .... a.	...	0852	1052	1252	1452	1652	1808	1855	2052	2252
57	Virton .... d.	0709	0909a	1109a	1309a	1509a	1654a	1809	1909a	2109a	...
85	Athus .... ▷ d.	0730	0932a	1132a	1332a	1532a	1732a	1832	1932a	2132a	...
98	**Arlon** .... a.	0744	0946a	1146a	1346a	1546a	1746a	1846	1946a	2146a	...

		Ⓐ	Ⓐ N							Ⓐ		Ⓐ
Arlon .... d.	...	...	0645	0711a	0914a	1114a	1314a	1514a	1714a	1814	1914a	2114
Athus .... ▷ d.	...	...	0701	0737a	0931a	1131a	1331a	1531a	1731a	1831	1931a	2137
Virton .... a.	...	...	0721	0757a	0952a	1152a	1352a	1552a	1752a	1852	1952a	2157
Virton .... d.	0608	0700	0722	0808	1008	1208	1408	1608	1808	...	2008	2208
Florenville .... d.	0625	0717	0739	0825	1025	1225	1425	1625	1825	...	2025	2225
Bertrix .... a.	0639	0731	0752	0839	1039	1239	1439	1639	1839	...	2039	2239
Bertrix .... d.	0642	0737	0753	0842	1042	1242	1442	1642	1842	...	2042	2242
Libramont .... a.	0651	0746	0802	0851	1051	1251	1451	1651	1851	...	2051	2251

N – Not Dec. 26 - Jan. 6, Apr. 3 - 17, July 3 - Sept. 1.
a – Ⓐ only.
d – On Ⓒ Dinant d. 2210, Namur a. 2242.
▷ – For connections Athus - Luxembourg see Table **449**.
◇ – Arrives Athus at 1714.

Operator: CFL — LUXEMBOURG – local services — 449

		⚒				
Luxembourg .... d.	0454	0524	0554	every 30 mins on ⚒	2354	...
Ettelbruck .... d.	0534	0604	0634	hourly on ⑦	0034	...
Diekirch .... a.	0539	0609	0639	(every 30 mins from 1154)	0039	...

	⚒	⚒	⚒			
Diekirch .... d.	0421	0451	0521	0551	every 30 mins on ⚒	2251
Ettelbruck .... d.	0427	0457	0527	0557	hourly on ⑦	2257
Luxembourg .... a.	0506	0536	0606	0636	(every 30 mins from 1251)	2336

		⚒				
Luxembourg .... d.	...	0522	0552	every 30 mins on ⚒	2352	...
Pétange .... d.	...	0545	0615	hourly on ⑦	0015	...
Rodange .... d.	...	0550	0620	(every 30 mins from 1152)	0020	...
Athus (Belgium) .... ▷ a.	...	0554	0624		0026	...

	⚒	⚒	⚒			
Athus (Belgium) .... ▷ d.	0504	0534	0604	0634	every 30 mins on ⚒	2334
Rodange .... d.	0510	0540	0610	0640	hourly on ⑦	2340
Pétange .... d.	0517	0547	0617	0647	(every 30 mins from 1134)	2347
Luxembourg .... a.	0538	0608	0638	0708		0008

Luxembourg → Bettembourg → Esch-sur-Alzette → Pétange → **Rodange** (journey 12 mins to Bettembourg, 20 mins to Esch, 45 - 50 mins to Pétange, 50 - 55 mins to Rodange):
⚒: 0503, 0533Ⓐ, 0600⚒, 0633 and every 15 minutes to 1948 then every 30 minutes to 2348.
†: 0618 and hourly to 1218 then every 30 minutes to 2348 then 0048, 0118.

Luxembourg → **Wasserbillig** (journey 35 - 42 minutes):
0518Ⓐt, 0610t, 0631Ⓐ, 0651Ⓐt, 0710Ⓒ, 0731t, 0751Ⓐ, 0810, 0831t, 0910, 0931t and at the same minutes past each hour until 1610, 1631t, 1659Ⓐt, 1710, 1731t, 1759Ⓐt, 1810, 1831t, 1859Ⓐt, 1910, 1931t, 2010, 2031t, 2110, 2131t, 2210, 2231t, 2310, 2331t.

Luxembourg → **Kleinbettingen** (journey 18 - 19 minutes):
Ⓐ: 0555, 0625, every 30 mins to 2055 (not 0925, 1125, 1525, 1925) also 2115, 2215, 2315.
Ⓒ: 0545, 0655 and hourly to 2255, 2358.

Bettembourg → Dudelange → **Volmerange-les-Mines** (journey 14 minutes):
0606Ⓐ, 0634⚒, 0706⚒, 0736⚒ and approx every 30 mins to 2336⚒
(on † runs only to Dudelange Usines, hourly 0634 - 1234, every 30 mins 1234 - 2334).

Rodange → Pétange → Esch-sur-Alzette → Bettembourg → **Luxembourg** (5 - 7 mins to Pétange, 26 - 32 mins to Esch, 39 - 45 mins to Bettembourg, 50 - 55 mins to Luxembourg):
⚒: at 06, 15, 36, 45 minutes past most hours 0536 - 1915, then every 30 mins to 2345.
†: 0545 and hourly to 1145 then every 30 minutes to 2345, also 0045.

Wasserbillig → **Luxembourg** (journey 35 - 42 minutes):
0434Ⓐ, 0508, 0554Ⓐt, 0608, 0627Ⓐt, 0639Ⓐ, 0654t, 0708, 0735Ⓐt, 0754, 0808Ⓐt, 0808Ⓒ, 0854t, 0908, 0954t, 1008, 1054t and at the same minutes past each hour until 2208, 2254t, 2308, 2354t.

Kleinbettingen → **Luxembourg** (journey 18 - 19 minutes):
Ⓐ: 0446 and approx every 30 mins to 2346 (not 1016, 1216, 2016, 2216, 2316).
Ⓒ: 0616, 0725 and hourly to 2325.

Volmerange-les-Mines → Dudelange → **Bettembourg** (journey 14 minutes):
0610⚒, 0639⚒, 0710, 0740 and approx every 30 mins to 2340⚒.
(on † runs only from Dudelange Usines, hourly 0617 - 1217, every 30 mins 1217 - 2347).

t – To/from Trier (Table **915**).
▷ – For connections to/from Arlon see Table **448**.

NETHERLANDS

SEE MAP PAGE 237

Operator: **NS** – Nederlandse Spoorwegen (unless otherwise indicated) www.ns.nl

Services: Trains convey first- and second-class seated accommodation, unless otherwise indicated in the tables. Some trains consist of portions for two or more destinations, and passengers should be careful to join the correct part of the train. The destination of each train portion is normally indicated beside the entrance doors.

Timings: Valid **December 11**, 2016 - **December 9**, 2017.

Holidays: Unless otherwise indicated, services marked ⚒ do not run on ⑦ or on Dec. 26, Apr. 17;
those marked Ⓐ do not run on ⑥⑦ or on Dec. 26, Apr. 17, 27, May 25, June 5;
those marked † run on ⑦ and on Dec. 26, Apr. 17;
those marked © run on ⑥⑦ and on Dec. 26, Apr. 17, 27, May 25, June 5.
No trains, other than international services, will run between ± 2000 hours on Dec. 31 and ± 0200 on Jan. 1.

Tickets: A nationwide smartcard system called *OV-chipkaart* is used for all public transport in the Netherlands. Personalised and anonymous cards are available (€7.50) which can be loaded and topped up with travel credit. Disposable single use cards can also be purchased from ticket machines and ticket offices for full fare single / return journeys and day tickets (a €1 supplement is payable for single use cards). You must always check-in and check-out your OV-chipkaart for each journey. Alternatively, e-tickets for full fare single and return journeys may be purchased on-line and printed yourself.

Supplements: A supplement is payable for journeys on *Intercity direct* services (except for local journeys Amsterdam - Schiphol and Rotterdam - Breda), also for internal journeys on *ICE* trains between Amsterdam and Arnhem. In both cases the single journey supplement is €2.30. Supplements may be purchased from special Supplement Pillars (using your OV-chipkaart) or from ticket machines.

450 AMSTERDAM - DEN HAAG - ROTTERDAM - ROOSENDAAL - VLISSINGEN

For *Intercity direct* services via the high-speed line, see Table **451**. For services via Amsterdam Zuid and Schiphol ✈, see Table **460**.
For Night Network services Amsterdam - Rotterdam and v.v., see Table **454**. For International services to / from Brussels, see Table **18**.

km		④⑤n	⊖	⑥⑦p	◇	⑥⑦p	⚒	Ⓐ	Ⓐ	⚒	⚒	Ⓐ		Ⓐ		Ⓐ		Ⓐ		⚒		⚒		⚒
0	**Amsterdam** Centraal ...... **461** d.	0004	0004	0034	0034	0104	...	...	...	0534	0604	0619	0634	0649	0704	0719	0734	0749	0804	0819	0834	0849	0904	0919
5	Amsterdam Sloterdijk .... d.	0009	0009	0039	0039	0109	...	...	...	0539	0609	0624	0639	0654	0709	0724	0739	0754	0809	0824	0839	0854	0909	0924
19	**Haarlem** .... **461** d.	0020	0020	0050	0050	0120	...	...	...	0550	0620	0636	0650	0706	0720	0736	0750	0806	0820	0836	0850	0906	0920	0936
47	Leiden Centraal .... a.	0040	0040	0110	0110	0140	...	...	...	0610	0640	0655	0710	0725	0740	0755	0810	0825	0840	0855	0910	0925	0940	0955
47	Leiden Centraal .... **460** d.	0043	0045	0115	0116	0145	...	...	...	0615	0645	0700	0715	0730	0745	0800	0815	0830	0845	0900	0915	0930	0945	1000
	Den Haag Centraal **460 471** a.	|	|	|	|	|	...	...	...	|	|	0711	|	0741	|	0811	|	0841	|	0911	|	0941	|	1011
63	**Den Haag** HS.......... **460 471** d.	0056	0058	0128	0131	0157	...	...	...	0628	0658	...	0728	...	0758	...	0828	...	0858	...	0928	...	0958	...
71	Delft .... **460 471** d.	0102	0104	0134	0137	...	...	...	...	0634	0704	...	0734	...	0804	...	0834	...	0904	...	0934	...	1004	...
81	Schiedam Centrum .... **460** d.	0110	0113	0143	0146	...	...	...	...	0643	0713	...	0743	...	0813	...	0843	...	0913	...	0943	...	1013	...
85	**Rotterdam** Centraal **460 471** a.	0115	0118	0148	0152	...	...	...	...	0648	0718	...	0748	...	0818	...	0848	...	0918	...	0948	...	1018	...
85	**Rotterdam** Centraal **460 471** d.	...	...	...	...	...	...	...	0621	0651	0721	...	0751	...	0821	...	0851	...	0921	...	0951	...	1021	...
105	Dordrecht .... **460 471** d.	...	...	...	...	...	0552	...	0637	0707	0737	...	0807	...	0837	...	0907	...	0937	...	1007	...	1037	...
143	**Roosendaal** .... a.	...	...	...	...	...	0625	...	0702	0729	0802	...	0829	...	0902	...	0929	...	1002	...	1029	...	1102	...
143	**Roosendaal** .... d.	...	...	...	...	...	...	0636	0706	0736	0806	...	0836	...	0906	...	0936	...	1006	...	1036	...	1106	...
156	Bergen op Zoom.................. d.	...	...	...	...	...	...	0645	0715	0745	0815	...	0845	...	0915	...	0945	...	1015	...	1045	...	1115	...
193	Goes .... d.	...	...	...	...	...	...	0716	0746	0816	0846	...	0916	...	0946	...	1016	...	1046	...	1116	...	1146	...
212	Middelburg........................... d.	...	...	...	...	...	...	0730	0800	0830	0900	...	0930	...	1000	...	1030	...	1100	...	1130	...	1200	...
218	**Vlissingen** .... a.	...	...	...	...	...	...	0739	0809	0839	0909	...	0939	...	1009	...	1039	...	1109	...	1139	...	1209	...

		⚒		⚒		⚒																
Amsterdam Centraal ...... **461** d.	0934	0949	1004	1019	1034	1049	1104	1119	1134	1149	and at the same minutes past each hour until	2004	2019	2034	2049	2104	2119	2134	2149	2204	2234	2304	2334
Amsterdam Sloterdijk .... d.	0939	0954	1009	1024	1039	1054	1109	1124	1139	1154		2009	2024	2039	2054	2109	2124	2139	2154	2209	2239	2309	2339
Haarlem .... **461** d.	0950	1006	1020	1036	1050	1106	1120	1136	1150	1206		2020	2036	2050	2106	2120	2136	2150	2206	2220	2250	2320	2350
Leiden Centraal .... a.	1010	1025	1040	1055	1110	1125	1140	1155	1210	1225		2040	2055	2110	2125	2140	2155	2210	2225	2240	2310	2340	0010
Leiden Centraal .... **460** d.	1015	1030	1045	1100	1115	1130	1145	1200	1215	1230		2045	2100	2115	2130	2145	2200	2215	2230	2245	2315	2345	0015
Den Haag Centraal **460 471** a.	|	1041	|	1111	|	1141	|	1211	|	1241		|	2111	|	2141	|	2211	|	2241	|	|	|	|
Den Haag HS.......... **460 471** d.	1028	...	1058	...	1128	...	1158	...	1228	...		2058	...	2128	...	2158	...	2228	...	2258	2328	2358	0028
Delft .... **460 471** d.	1034	...	1104	...	1134	...	1204	...	1234	...		2104	...	2134	...	2204	...	2234	...	2304	2334	0004	0034
Schiedam Centrum .... **460** d.	1043	...	1113	...	1143	...	1213	...	1243	...		2113	...	2143	...	2213	...	2243	...	2313	2343	0013	0043
Rotterdam Centraal **460 471** a.	1048	...	1118	...	1148	...	1218	...	1248	...		2118	...	2148	...	2218	...	2248	...	2318	2348	0018	0048
Rotterdam Centraal **460 471** d.	1051	...	1121	...	1151	...	1221	...	1251	...		2121	...	2151	...	2221	...	2251	...	2321	2351	0021	0051
Dordrecht............... **460 471** d.	1107	...	1137	...	1207	...	1237	...	1307	...		2137	...	2207	...	2237	...	2307	...	2337	0007	0037	0107
Roosendaal .... a.	1129	...	1202	...	1229	...	1302	...	1329	...		2202	...	2229	...	2302	...	2329	...	0002	0030	0109**j**	0139**k**
Roosendaal .... d.	1136	...	1206	...	1236	...	1306	...	1336	...		2206	...	2236	...	2306	...	2336	...	0006	...	...	...
Bergen op Zoom.................. d.	1145	...	1215	...	1245	...	1315	...	1345	...		2215	...	2245	...	2315	...	2345	...	0015	...	...	...
Goes .... d.	1216	...	1246	...	1316	...	1346	...	1416	...		2246	...	2316	...	2346	...	0016	...	0046	...	...	...
Middelburg........................... d.	1230	...	1300	...	1330	...	1400	...	1430	...		2300	...	2330	...	0000	...	0030	...	0100	...	...	...
Vlissingen .... a.	1239	...	1309	...	1339	...	1409	...	1439	...		2309	...	2339	...	0009	...	0039	...	0109	...	...	...

km		Ⓐ	⚒	Ⓐ	⚒	Ⓐ	Ⓐ		Ⓐ	⚒	Ⓐ		Ⓐ	⚒	⚒		⚒	⚒		⚒		⚒		⚒
	Vlissingen .... d.	...	...	...	...	...	...	...	...	...	0522	...	...	...	0552	...	...	0622	...	...	0652	...	0722	...
	Middelburg........................... d.	...	...	...	...	...	...	...	...	...	0529	...	...	...	0559	...	...	0629	...	...	0659	...	0729	...
	Goes .... d.	...	...	...	...	...	...	...	...	...	0543	...	...	...	0613	...	...	0643	...	...	0713	...	0743	...
	Bergen op Zoom.................. d.	...	...	...	...	...	0544	...	...	...	0612	...	...	...	0642	...	...	0712	...	...	0742	...	0812	...
	Roosendaal .... a.	...	...	...	...	...	0556	...	...	...	0624	...	...	...	0654	...	...	0724	...	...	0754	...	0824	...
	Roosendaal .... d.	...	...	...	0531**t**	...	0601	...	...	...	0631	0631**r**	...	...	0701	...	...	0731	...	...	0801	...	0831	...
	Dordrecht .... **460 471** d.	...	...	...	0554	...	0624	0624	...	...	0654	0654	...	...	0724	0724	...	0754	0754	...	0824	...	0854	...
	Rotterdam Centraal **460 471** a.	...	...	...	0609	...	0639	0639	...	...	0709	0709	...	...	0739	0739	...	0809	0809	...	0839	...	0909	...
	Rotterdam Centraal **460 471** d.	0512‡	0542	...	0612	...	0642	0642	...	...	0712	0712	...	...	0742	0742	...	0812	0812	...	0842	...	0912	...
	Schiedam Centrum .... **460** d.	0517‡	0547	...	0617	...	0647	0647	...	...	0717	0717	...	...	0747	0747	...	0817	0817	...	0847	...	0917	...
	Delft .... **460 471** d.	0524‡	0554	...	0624	...	0654	0654	...	...	0724	0724	...	...	0754	0754	...	0824	0824	...	0854	...	0924	...
	Den Haag HS.......... **460 471** d.	0533‡	0603	...	0633	...	0703	0703	...	...	0733	0733	...	...	0803	0803	...	0833	0833	...	0903	...	0933	...
0	**Den Haag** Centraal **460 471** d.	|	|	0618	|	0648	|	|	0718	...	|	|	0748	...	|	|	0818	|	|	0848	|	0918	|	0948
15	Leiden Centraal .... **460** a.	0545‡	0615	0630	0645	0700	0715	0715	0730	...	0745	0745	0800	...	0815	0815	0830	0845	0845	0900	0915	0930	0945	1000
15	Leiden Centraal .... d.	0550	0620	0635	0650	0705	0720	0720	0735	...	0750	0750	0805	...	0820	0820	0835	0850	0850	0905	0920	0935	0950	1005
43	**Haarlem** .... **461** d.	0610	0640	0655	0710	0725	0740	0740	0755	0755	0810	0810	0825	0825	0840	0840	0855	0910	0910	0925	0940	0955	1010	1025
57	Amsterdam Sloterdijk .... d.	0619	0649	0704	0719	0734	0749	0749	0804	0804	0819	0819	0834	0834	0849	0849	0904	0919	0919	0934	0949	1004	1019	1034
62	**Amsterdam** Centraal ...... **461** a.	0625	0655	0710	0725	0740	0755	0755	0810	0810	0825	0825	0840	0840	0855	0855	0910	0925	0925	0940	0955	1010	1025	1040

																				⊕				
Vlissingen .... d.	0752	...	0822	...	...	0852	...	0922	...	and at the same minutes past each hour until	1852	...	1922	...	1952	...	2022	2052	2122	2152	2222	2252	2322
Middelburg........................... d.	0759	...	0829	...	...	0859	...	0929	...		1859	...	1929	...	1959	...	2029	2059	2129	2159	2229	2259	2329
Goes .... d.	0813	...	0843	...	...	0913	...	0943	...		1913	...	1943	...	2013	...	2043	2113	2143	2213	2243	2313	2343
Bergen op Zoom.................. d.	0842	...	0912	...	...	0942	...	1012	...		1942	...	2012	...	2042	...	2112	2142	2212	2242	2312	2342	0012
Roosendaal .... a.	0854	...	0924	...	...	0954	...	1024	...		1954	...	2024	...	2054	...	2124	2154	2224	2254	2324	2354	0024
Roosendaal .... d.	0901	...	0931	...	...	1001	...	1031	...		2001	...	2031	...	2101	...	2131	2201	2231	2301	2331	0001	...
Dordrecht............... **460 471** d.	0924	...	0954	...	...	1024	...	1054	...		2024	...	2054	...	2124	...	2154	2224	2254	2324	2354	0024	...
Rotterdam Centraal **460 471** a.	0939	...	1009	...	...	1039	...	1109	...		2039	...	2109	...	2139	...	2210	2239	2309	2339	0009	0039	...
Rotterdam Centraal **460 471** d.	0942	...	1012	...	...	1042	...	1112	...		2042	...	2112	...	2142	...	2212	2242	2312	2342	0012	...	...
Schiedam Centrum .... **460** d.	0947	...	1017	...	...	1047	...	1117	...		2047	...	2117	...	2147	...	2217	2247	2317	2347	0017	...	...
Delft .... **460 471** d.	0954	...	1024	...	...	1054	...	1124	...		2054	...	2124	...	2154	...	2224	2254	2324	2354	0024	...	...
Den Haag HS.......... **460 471** d.	1003	...	1033	...	...	1103	...	1133	...		2103	...	2133	...	2203	...	2233	2303	2333	0003	0033	...	...
Den Haag Centraal **460 471** d.	|	1018**r**	|	1048**r**	...	|	1118	|	1148		|	2118	|	2148	|	2218	|	|	|	|	|	...	...
Leiden Centraal .... **460** a.	1015	1030**r**	1045	1100**r**	...	1115	1130	1145	1200		2115	2130	2145	2200	2215	2230	2245	2315	2345	0015	0045	...	...
Leiden Centraal .... d.	1020	1035**r**	1050	1105**r**	...	1120	1135	1150	1205		2120	2135	2150	2205	2220	2235	2250	2320	2350	0020	0050	...	...
Haarlem .... **461** d.	1040	1055	1110	1125	...	1140	1155	1210	1225		2140	2155	2210	2225	2240	2255	2310	2340	0010	0040	0110	...	...
Amsterdam Sloterdijk .... d.	1049	1104	1119	1134	...	1149	1204	1219	1234		2149	2204	2219	2234	2249	2304	2319	2349	0019	0049	0119	...	...
Amsterdam Centraal ...... **461** a.	1055	1110	1125	1140	...	1155	1210	1225	1240		2155	2210	2225	2240	2255	2310	2325	2355	0025	0055	0125	...	...

j – Mornings of ①–③ (not June 6).
k – Mornings of ④–⑦ (also June 6).
n – Not Apr. 28, May 26.
p – Also Apr. 28, May 26, June 6.
r – ⚒ only.
t – Ⓐ only.
⊖ – ①②③⑥⑦ (also Apr. 28, May 26).
◇ – Amsterdam - Den Haag on ①–⑤ (not Apr. 28, May 26, June 6). Den Haag - Rotterdam on ①–③ (not June 6).
‡ – 2–4 minutes on ④⑤.
⊕ – Change trains at Leiden on ①② (not Dec. 26, Apr. 17, June 5).

AMSTERDAM - ROTTERDAM - BREDA 451

Intercity direct services via the high-speed line. Supplement payable (except for local journeys Amsterdam - Schiphol and Rotterdam - Breda).

km		910 ⚒	1012 ⚒	912 ⚒	1014 ⚒	914	1016 ⚒◇	916	1018 ⚒⊖	918	1020 ⚒	920	1022 ⚒	922	1024 ⚒	924	1026 ⚒	926	1028 ⚒	928	1030 ⚒	930	1032	932	1034
0	**Amsterdam** Centraal..d.	0607	0622	0637	0649	0707	0722	0737	0749	0807	0822	0837	0849	0907	0922	0937	0949	1007	1022	1037	1049	1107	1122	1137	1149
17	**Schiphol** ✈ ....d.	0623	0638	0653	0705	0723	0738	0753	0805	0823	0838	0853	0905	0923	0938	0953	1006	1023	1038	1053	1105	1123	1138	1153	1205
70	**Rotterdam** Centraal ...a.	0649	0704	0719	0731	0749	0804	0819	0831	0849	0904	0919	0931	0949	1004	1019	1031	1049	1104	1119	1131	1149	1204	1219	1231
70	**Rotterdam** Centraal ...d.	0651	...	0721	...	0751	...	0821	...	0851	...	0921	...	0951	...	1021	...	1051	...	1121	...	1151	...	1221	...
117	**Breda**.........................a.	0715	...	0745	...	0815	...	0845	...	0915	...	0945	...	1015	...	1045	...	1115	...	1145	...	1215	...	1245	...

	★	968	1070	970	1072	972	974	976	978
Amsterdam Centraal...d.	and at the same minutes past each hour until	2037	2049	2107	2122	2137	2207	2237	2307
Schiphol ✈.................d.		2053	2105	2123	2138	2153	2223	2253	2323
Rotterdam Centraal ....a.		2119	2131	2149	2204	2219	2249	2319	2349
Rotterdam Centraal ....d.		2121	...	2151	...	2221	2251	...	2351
Breda..........................a.		2145	...	2215	...	2245	2315	...	0014

	903 ⚒	905 ⚒	1007 ⚒	907 ⚒	907	1009 ⚒	909	1011 ⚒	911	1013 ⚒
Breda ....d.	...	0644	...	0714	...	...	0744	...	0814	...
Rotterdam Centraal...........a.	...	0708	...	0738	...	...	0808	...	0838	...
Rotterdam Centraal...........d.	0640	0710	0728	0740	0740	0756	0810	0828	0840	0856
Schiphol ✈........................d.	0707	0737	0755	0807	0807	0823	0837	0855	0907	0923
Amsterdam Centraal...........a.	0721	0751	0809	0821	0821	0837	0851	0909	0921	0937

	913	1015 ⚒	915	1017 ⚒	917	1019 ⚒	919	1021 ⚒	921	1023 ⚒	923	1025 ⚒	925	1027	927	1029		963	1065	965	1067	967	969	971
Breda.........................d.	0844	...	0914	...	0944	...	1014	...	1044	...	1114	...	1144	...	1214	...	and at the same minutes past each hour until	2114	...	2144	...	2214	2244	2314
Rotterdam Centraal ....a.	0908	...	0938	...	1008	...	1038	...	1108	...	1138	...	1208	...	1238	...		2138	...	2208	...	2238	2308	2338
Rotterdam Centraal ....d.	0910	0928	0940	0956	1010	1028	1040	1056	1110	1128	1140	1156	1210	1228	1240	1256		2140	2156	2210	2228	2240	2310	2340
Schiphol ✈.................d.	0937	0955	1007	1023	1037	1055	1107	1123	1137	1155	1207	1223	1237	1255	1307	1323		2207	2223	2237	2255	2307	2337	0007
Amsterdam Centraal...a.	0951	1009	1021	1037	1051	1109	1121	1137	1151	1209	1221	1237	1251	1309	1321	1338		2221	2237	2251	2309	2321	2351	0021

◇ – 2 minutes later on ⑥ (also Apr. 27, May 25, June 5). ⊖ – 1–2 minutes later on Ⓐ. ★ – The 1649 and 1949 from Amsterdam Centraal run 1–2 minutes later on Ⓐ.

Local trains AMSTERDAM CENTRAAL - SCHIPHOL 452

See Table **451** for *Intercity direct* trains (which can be used without payment of a supplement between Amsterdam Centraal and Schiphol)

From Amsterdam Centraal

0001, 0011, 0031, 0042, 0515⚒, 0531⚒, 0542⚒, 0545⑥**k**, 0601⚒, 0611, 0631, 0642, 0701, 0711, 0731, 0742 and at 01, 11, 31 and 42 minutes past each hour until 2342.

k – Also Apr. 27, May 25, June 5.

From Schiphol Journey time: 17 – 18 minutes

0000, 0011, 0041, 0530Ⓐ, 0541, 0600Ⓐ, 0611, 0630⚒, 0641, 0700, 0711, 0730, 0741 and at 00, 11, 30 and 41 minutes past each hour until 2341.

UTRECHT - AMSTERDAM - ROTTERDAM - EINDHOVEN Night Network 454

	⑥⑦	⑥⑦		H	④⑤	④⑤	③	③		H	④⑤	④⑤	③	③		H	④⑤	④⑤	③	③		L	③	③	†	†
Utrecht Centraal........ d.	...	...	...	0101	0101	...	*0101*b	0101	...	0211	0211	...	*0217*b	0217	...	0317	0311	...	*0317*b	0317	...	0411	*0417*b	0417	0506	0605
Amsterdam Centraal. d.	...	...	...	0145	0145	...	|	0145	...	0246	0247	...	|	0246	...	0346	0347	...	|	0346	...	0446	|	0446	0542	0629
Schiphol ✈ .... d.	...	...	...	0205	0205	...	0203	|	...	0305	0305	...	0303	|	...	0405	0405	...	0403	|	...	0505	0503	|	0557	...
Leiden Centraal .... d.	...	...	...	0223	0223	🚌	0218	0223j	...	0323	0323	🚌	0318	0323j	...	0423	0423	🚌	0418	0423j	...	0530j	0518	0524j	0614	...
Den Haag HS........... d.	...	...	...	0238	0244j	0242	...	0238	...	0338	0344j	0342	...	0338	...	0438	0444j	0442	...	0438	...	0544	...	0539	0627	...
Delft .... d.	...	...	...	0245	|	0302	...	0245	...	0345	|	0402	...	0345	...	0445	|	0502	...	0445	...	0550	...	0546	0633	...
Rotterdam Centraal .. d.	0002	0102	...	0255	0325	...	...	0256	...	0356	0426	...	...	0356	...	0455	0526	...	...	0456	...	0601	...	0557	0644	...
Dordrecht.................. d.	0017	0117	...	...	...	...	...	...	...	...	...	...	...	...	...	...	...	...	...	...	...	...	...	...	...	...
Breda .... d.	0035	0135	...	...	...	...	...	...	...	...	...	...	...	...	...	...	...	...	...	...	...	...	...	...	...	...
Tilburg .... d.	0054	0154	...	...	...	...	...	...	...	...	...	...	...	...	...	...	...	...	...	...	...	...	...	...	...	...
Eindhoven .... a.	0117	0217	...	...	...	...	...	...	...	...	...	...	...	...	...	...	...	...	...	...	...	...	...	...	...	...

		④⑤	H	③	③	④⑤	④⑤	⑥⑦	H	③	③		④⑤	④⑤	⑥⑦	H	③	③		④⑤	④⑤	H	③	③	Ⓒ	†
Eindhoven .... d.	...	...	...	...	...	...	...	0030	...	...	...	...	...	...	0130	...	...	...	...	...	...	...	...	...	...	...
Tilburg .... d.	...	...	...	...	...	...	...	0102	...	...	...	...	...	...	0202	...	...	...	...	...	...	...	...	...	...	...
Breda .... d.	...	...	...	...	...	...	...	0119	...	...	...	...	...	...	0219	...	...	...	...	...	...	...	...	...	...	...
Dordrecht.................. d.	...	...	...	...	...	...	...	0141	...	...	...	...	...	...	0241	...	...	...	...	...	...	...	...	...	...	...
Rotterdam Centraal .. d.	...	0056	0100	0100	...	🚌	0132	0155	0200	0200	...	...	🚌	0232	0255	0300	0300	...	...	🚌	0332	0400	0400	...	0501	0600
Delft .... d.	...	0107	0112	0112	...	0158	|	...	0212	0212	...	...	0258	|	...	0312	0312	...	...	0358	|	0412	0412	...	0512	0612
Den Haag HS........... d.	...	0132t	0130j	0130j	...	0218	0223j	...	0221	0221	...	...	0318	0323j	...	0321	0321	...	...	0418	0423j	0421	0421	...	0528j	0628j
Leiden Centraal .... d.	...	0145	0145	0145	0146	...	0245j	...	0245j	0245j	0240	...	...	0345j	...	0345j	0345j	0340	...	...	0445j	0445	0445j	0440	0545	0646
Schiphol ✈ .... a.	...	0200	0200	|	0202	...	0300	...	0300	|	0257	...	...	0400	...	0400	|	0357	...	...	0500	0500	|	0457	0600	0701
Amsterdam Centraal. a.	0118	0216	0216	0217	|	...	0316	...	0316	0317	|	...	...	0416	...	0416	0417	|	...	...	0516	0516	0517	|	0617	0721
Utrecht Centraal....... a.	0145	0258	0244	0248	*0248*b	...	0358	...	0354	0349	*0349*b	...	...	0459	...	0454	0448	*0448*b	...	...	0600	0554	0548	*0548*b	0654	...

H – ①②⑥⑦. **L** – Not ③. **b** – Change trains at AmsterdamBijlmer Arena. **j** – Arrives 7 – 11 minutes earlier. **t** – Arrives 0113.

ALMERE - UTRECHT 457

km		Ⓐ	Ⓐ	Ⓐ	⚒	†	Ⓐ			Ⓐ				Ⓐ									
0	**Almere** Centrum.........d.	0549	0622	0652	0722	0722	0752	...	0822	0852	...	and at the same minutes past each hour until	1922	1952	...	...	2022	2122	2222	2322	...	...	...
20	Naarden-Bussum........d.	0608	0641	0711	0741	0741	0811	...	0841	0911	...		1941	2011	...	...	2041	2141	2241	2341	...	...	...
26	Hilversum ....d.	0615	0649	0719	0749	0748	0819	0819	0849	0919	0919		1949	2019	2019	...	2048	2148	2248	2348	...	...	...
43	**Utrecht** Centraal.........a.	0635	0705	0735	0805	0808	0835	0835	0905	0935	0935		2005	2035	2035	...	2108	2208	2308	0008	...	...	...

	⑥⑦c		⚒	Ⓐ		Ⓐ		⚒		Ⓐ			Ⓐ				Ⓐ						
Utrecht Centraal..........d.	0044	...	0622	0622	0652	0652	0722	0722	0752	0752	0822	0852	0852	and at the same minutes past each hour until	1922	1952	1952	...	2014	2114	2214	2314	2344
Hilversum ....d.	0112	...	0637	0642	0707	0712	0737	0742	0807	0812	0842	0907	0912		1942	2007	2012	...	2042	2142	2242	2342	0012
Naarden-Bussum.........d.	0119	...	...	0649	...	0719	...	0749	...	0819	0849	...	0919		1949	...	2019	...	2049	2149	2249	2349	0019
Almere Centrum.........d.	0138	...	...	0708	...	0738	...	0808	...	0838	0908	...	0938		2008	...	2038	...	2108	2208	2308	0008	0038

c – Also Apr. 28, May 26, June 6.

AMSTERDAM CENTRAAL - ALMERE - ZWOLLE 459

For fast services via Amsterdam Zuid, see Table **460**

km		Ⓐ	Ⓐ	⑥k	Ⓐ	Ⓐ	Ⓐ	⚒	†	⚒	⚒														
	Schiphol ✈.............d.	...	...	...	0530	...	0600	...	...	0630	...	0700	...	0730	...	and at the same minutes past each hour until	2200	...	2230	...	2300	...	2330	...	0000
0	**Amsterdam** Centraal d.	...	...	...	0553	0608	0623	0638	...	0653	0708	0723	0738	0753	0808		2223	2238	2253	2308	2323	2338	2353	0008	0023
14	Weesp ....d.	...	...	...	0610	|	0640	|	...	0710	|	0740	|	0810	|		2240	|	2310	|	2340	|	0010	|	0040
30	**Almere** Centrum.......d.	...	...	...	0625	0628	0655	0658	...	0725	0728	0755	0758	0825	0828		2255	2258	2325	2328	2355	2358	0025	0028	0055c
36	Almere Buiten ....d.	...	...	...	0631	...	0701	...	...	0731	...	0801	...	0831	...		2301	...	2331	...	0001	...	0031	...	0101c
54	**Lelystad** Centrum.....d.	0542	0611	0642	0654	...	0724	...	0742	0754	...	0824	...	0854	...		2324	...	2354	...	0019	...	0045	...	0115c
75	Dronten.....................d.	0554	0623	0654	0705	...	0735	...	0754	0805	...	0835	...	0905	...		2335	...	0005	...	...	...	...	...	...
88	Kampen Zuid ....d.	0602	0632	0702	0713	...	0743	...	0802	0813	...	0843	...	0913	...		2343	...	0013	...	...	...	...	...	...
104	**Zwolle**......................a.	0613	0643	0713	0724	...	0754	...	0813	0824	...	0854	...	0924	...		2355	...	0024	...	...	...	...	...	...

	Ⓐ	Ⓐ		Ⓐ		Ⓐ		⚒		⚒														
Zwolle......................d.	...	...	...	...	0537a	...	0607a	...	0637a	...	0707r	...	0737r	...	0807	...	0837	and at the same minutes past each hour until	...	2237	...	2307	...	2337	0007
Kampen Zuid ....d.	...	...	...	...	0547a	...	0617a	...	0647a	...	0717r	...	0747r	...	0817	...	0847		...	2247	...	2317	...	2347	0017
Dronten ....d.	...	...	...	...	0556a	...	0626a	...	0656a	...	0726r	...	0756r	...	0826	...	0856		...	2256	...	2326	...	2356	0026
Lelystad Centrum .....d.	0510	...	0540	...	0610	...	0640	...	0710	...	0740	...	0810	...	0840	...	0910		...	2310	...	2340	...	0010	0037
Almere Buiten............d.	0528	...	0558	...	0628	...	0658	...	0728	...	0758	...	0828	...	0858	...	0928		...	2328	...	2358	...	0028	...
Almere Centrum........d.	0536	0602	0606	0632	0636	0702	0706	0732	0736	0802	0806	0832	0836	0902	0906	0932	0936		2332	2336	0002	0006	0032	0036	...
Weesp.......................d.	0551	|	0621	|	0651	|	0721	|	0751	|	0821	|	0851	|	0921	|	0951		|	2351	|	0021	|	0051	...
Amsterdam Centraal. a.	0607	0623	0637	0653	0707	0723	0737	0753	0807	0823	0837	0853	0907	0923	0937	0953	1007		2353	0007	0023	0037	0053	0107	...
Schiphol ✈..............a.	0628	...	0659	...	0728	...	0759	...	0828	...	0859	...	0928	...	0959	...	1028		...	0028	...	0059	...	...	...

a – Ⓐ only. **c** – Weesp - Lelystad on the mornings of ①②③⑥⑦ (also Apr. 28, May 26). **k** – Also Apr. 27, May 25, June 5. **r** – ⚒ only.

460 — DEN HAAG - SCHIPHOL - AMSTERDAM ZUID - ALMERE - ZWOLLE

For services Amsterdam Centraal - Almere - Zwolle and v.v., see Table **459**. For services via Amersfoort and Utrecht, see Table **481**.

km				⑥k	Ⓐ	✶	✶		✶		✶		✶		✶
	Dordrecht	450 d.					0605	0639	0709	0739		0805	0839	0905	0939
	Rotterdam Centraal	450 d.			0556	0626	0656	0726	0756		0826	0856	0926	0956
	Schiedam Centrum	450 d.			0602	0632	0702	0732	0802		0832	0902	0932	1002
	Delft	450 d.			0609	0639	0709	0739	0809		0839	0909	0939	1009
	Den Haag HS	450 d.			0618	0648	0718	0748	0818		0848	0918	0948	1018
0	Den Haag Centraal	450 d.	0003 0033	0533 0603	0633	0703	0733	0803	0833	0903	0933	1003	1033
15	Leiden Centraal	450 d.	0017 0047	0547 0617 0632 0647 0702 0717	0732 0747 0802 0817 0832 0847 0902	0932 0947 1002	1017 1032 1047
42	Schiphol ✈	d.	0031 0101	0603 0633 0648 0703 0718 0733 0748 0803 0818 0833 0848 0903 0918 0933 0948 1003	1018 1033 1048 1103
51	Amsterdam Zuid	d.		0612 0642 0656 0712 0726 0742 0756 0812 0826 0842 0856 0912 0926 0942 0956 1012	1042 1056 1112
56	Duivendrecht	d.		0701 0731 0801 0831 0901 0931 1001 1031	1101
80	Almere Centrum	459 d.		0633 0703 0719 0733 0749 0803 0819 0833 0849 0903 0919 0933 0949 1003 1019 1033 1049 1103 1119 1133
86	Almere Buiten	459 d.		0723 0753 0823 0853 0923 0953 1023 1053	1123
104	Lelystad Centrum	459 d.	0542 0611 0642 0647 0717 0733 0747 0805 0817 0835 0847 0905 0917 0935 0947 1005 1017 1035 1047 1105 1117 1135 1147
154	Zwolle	459 a.	0613 0643 0713 0713 0743 0813 0843 0913 1013 1043 1113 1143 1213
	Leeuwarden 482	a.	0751	0855v	0951	1051	1151	1251
	Groningen 482	a.	0722	0829 0813	0913	1013	1113	1213	1313

					♥	♥														
Dordrecht	450 d.	1009t		1039	1105		1839	1905	1939	2005	2039	2105	2139
Rotterdam Centraal	450 d.	1026		1056	1126		1856	1926	1956	2026	2056	2126	2156
Schiedam Centrum	450 d.	1032		1102	1132		1902	1932	2002	2032	2102	2132	2202
Delft	450 d.	1039		1109	1139	and at	1909	1939	2009	2039	2109	2139	2209
Den Haag HS	450 d.	1048		1118	1148	the same	1918	1948	2018	2048	2118	2148	2218
Den Haag Centraal	450 d.		1103	1133		minutes	1903	1933	2003	2033	2103	2133	2203	2233 2303 2333
Leiden Centraal	450 d.	1102	1117 1132 1147 1202	past each	1917 1932 1947 2002 2017 2032 2047 2102 2117 2132 2147 2202 2217 2232 2247 2317 2347
Schiphol ✈	d.	1118	1133 1148 1203 1218	hour until	1933 1948 2003 2018 2033 2048 2103 2118 2133 2148 2203 2218 2233 2248 2303 2333 0001
Amsterdam Zuid	d.	1126	1142 1156 1212 1226		1942 1956 2012 2026 2042 2056 2112 2126 2142 2156 2212 2226 2242 2256 2312 2342
Duivendrecht	d.	1131	1201	1231	2001 2031 2100 2130 2200 2230 2300
Almere Centrum	459 d.	1149	1203 1219r 1233 1249r	2003 2019r 2033 2049r 2103 2133 2203 2233 2303 2333 0003
Almere Buiten	459 d.	1153	1223r	1253r	2023r 2053r
Lelystad Centrum	459 d.	1205	1217 1235r 1247 1305r	2017 2035r 2047 2105r 2117 2147 2217 2247 2317 2347 0017
Zwolle	459 a.		1243	1313	2043 2113 2143 2213 2243 2313 2343 0013 0043
Leeuwarden 482	a.		1351	2151	2351	0051	0151c
Groningen 482	a.		1413	2213	2313	0023	0123z

			✶	Ⓐ	Ⓐ		Ⓐ	✶d	✶		✶		✶		⑥⑤k
Groningen 482	d.					0532b		0648h		0748j		0848		0948
Leeuwarden 482	d.			0507a	0607a		0707	0808	0908
Zwolle	459 d.		0547a	0617a	0647	0717r	0747	0817	0847	0917	0947	1017	1047
Lelystad Centrum	459 d.	0613a 0625 0643a 0655 0713 0725a 0743r 0755a 0813 0825 0843 0855 0913 0925 0943 0955 1013 1025r 1043 1055r 1113
Almere Buiten	459 d.	0636	0706	0736a	0806a	0836	0906	0936	1006	1036r
Almere Centrum	459 d.	0629a 0643 0659 0713 0729 0743a 0759 0813a 0829 0843 0859 0913 0929 0943 0959 1013 1029 1043r 1059 1113r 1129
Duivendrecht	d.	0659	0729	0759a	0829a	0859	0959	1029	1059	1129
Amsterdam Zuid	d.	0650a 0706 0719 0735 0750 0803a 0819 0835a 0850 0859 0913 0929 0943 0959 1019 1035 1050 1105 1119 1135 1150
Schiphol ✈	d.	0558 0627 0643 0658 0713 0727 0743 0758 0813 0827 0843 0858 0913 0927 0943 0958 1013 1027 1043 1058 1113 1127 1143 1158
Leiden Centraal	450 d.	0615 0645 0700 0715 0730 0745 0800 0815 0830 0845 0900 0915 0930 0945 1000 1015 1030 1045 1100 1115 1130 1145 1200 1215
Den Haag Centraal	450 d.	0626 0656	0726	0756	0826	0856	0926	0956	1026	1056	1126	1156	1226
Den Haag HS	450 d.	0713	0743	0813	0843	0913	0943	1013	1043	1113	1143	1213
Delft	450 d.	0719	0749	0819	0849	0919	0949	1019	1049	1119	1149	1219
Schiedam Centrum	450 d.												
Rotterdam Centraal	450 d.	0735	0805	0835	0905	0935	1005	1035	1105	1135	1205	1235
Dordrecht	450 d.	0752	0822	0852	0923	0952	1023	1052	1123	1152	1223	1252

														⑤⑥k
Groningen 482	d.		1648		1748		1848		1948		2048	2148	2248 2326
Leeuwarden 482	d.		1708	1807	1908	2008	2108	2208
Zwolle	459 d.		1747	1817	1847	1917	1947	2017	2047	2117 2147 2217 2247 2317 2347 0036
Lelystad Centrum	459 d.	1125r and at 1813 1825r 1843 1855r 1913	1943	2013	2043	2113	2143 2213 2243 2313 2343 0013 0107
Almere Buiten	459 d.	1136r	1836r	1906r
Almere Centrum	459 d.	1143r the same 1829 1843r 1859 1913r 1929	1959	2029	2059	2129	2159 2229 2259 2329 2359 0029 0122
Duivendrecht	d.	1159	1859	1929	1959	2029	2129	2159
Amsterdam Zuid	d.	1205 minutes 1850 1905 1919 1935 1950 2005 2019 2035 2050 2105 2119 2135 2150 2205 2219 2250 2319 2350 0019 0050
Schiphol ✈	d.	1213	1858 1913 1927 1943 1958 2013 2027 2043 2058 2113 2127 2143 2158 2213 2227 2258 2327 2358 0026 0058
Leiden Centraal	450 d.	1230 past each 1915 1930 1945 2000 2015 2030 2045 2100 2115 2130 2145 2200 2215 2230 2315 2345 0015 0045 0115
Den Haag Centraal	450 d.	1926	1956	2026	2056	2126	2156	2226	2256 2326 2356 0026 0056 0126c
Den Haag HS	450 d.	1243 hour until 1943	2013	2043	2113	2143	2213	2243
Delft	450 d.	1249	1949	2019	2049	2119	2149	2219	2249
Schiedam Centrum	450 d.									
Rotterdam Centraal	450 d.	1305	2005	2035	2105	2135	2205	2235	2305
Dordrecht	450 d.	1323	2023	2052	2123	2152	2223	2252	2323

a – Ⓐ only.
b – 0536 on ①④⑤ (not Apr. 27, May 25, June 5). 0548 on ⑥ (also Apr. 27, May 25, June 5).
c – Mornings of ⑥⑦ (also Apr. 28, May 26, June 6).
d – Runs daily Schiphol - Den Haag.
h – 0636 on ⑥ (also Apr. 27, May 25, June 5).
j – 0732 on †.
k – Also Apr. 27, May 25, June 5.
r – ✶ only.
t – 1005 on ⑥ (also Apr. 27, May 25, June 5).
v – 0851 on ⑥ (also Apr. 27, May 25, June 5).
z – 0129 on the mornings of ④⑤ (not Apr. 28, May 26).
♥ – Certain trains depart Dordrecht at xx09 (not xx05); other timings follow the same pattern.

461 — AMSTERDAM - HAARLEM - HOORN and ZANDVOORT AAN SEE

km			Ⓐ	Ⓐ	Ⓐ	✶	✶	✶		✶											
0	Amsterdam C ⊙	450 d.		0611		0641 0711	0741 0741 0811 0841	and every	1811 1841 1911 1941 2011 2041 2111 2141 2211 2241 2311 2341
	Haarlem	450 d.		0631	0701 0731	0801 0801 0831 0901	30 minutes	1831 1901 1931 2001 2031 2101 2131 2201 2231 2301 2331 0001
11	Beverwijk	d.		0647	0717 0747	0817 0817 0847 0917	until	1847 1917 1947 2017 2047 2117 2147 2217 2247 2317 2347 0017
22	Castricum	466 d.		0700	0730 0800	0830 0830 0900 0930	1900 1930 2000 2030 2100 2130 2200 2230 2300 2330 0000 0030
34	Alkmaar	466 a.		0711	0741 0811	0841 0841 0911 0941	1911 1941 2011 2041 2111 2141 2211 2241 2311 2341 0011 0041
34	Alkmaar	466 d.	0615 0645 0715 0715 0745 0815 0815	0915 0945	1915 1945 2015 2115 2215 2315 0015
40	Heerhugowaard	466 d.	0623 0653 0723 0723 0753 0823 0823	0853 0923 0953	1923 1953 2023 2123 2223 2323 0023
57	Hoorn	a.	0639 0709 0739 0739 0809 0839 0839	0909 0939 1009	1939 2009 2039 2139 2239 2339 0039

			Ⓐ	Ⓐ	✶	✶															
Hoorn	d.		0550	0620	0650 0720 0750 0820 0850	0920 0950	1920 1950	2050	2150	2250	2350
Heerhugowaard	466 d.		0607	0637	0707 0737 0807 0837 0907	0937 1007	1937 2007	2107	2207	2307	0007
Alkmaar	466 d.		0615	0645	0715 0745 0815 0845 0915	0945 1015	1945 2015	2115	2215	2315	0015
Alkmaar	466 d.	0502 0521 0551 0621 0651 0651 0721 0751 0821 0851 0921	0951 1021	1951 2021 2051 2121 2151 2221 2251 2321 2351 0021
Castricum	466 d.	0513 0532 0602 0632 0632 0702 0702 0732 0802 0832 0902 0932	1002 1032	2002 2032 2102 2132 2202 2232 2302 2332 0002 0032
Beverwijk	d.	0525 0544 0614 0644 0644 0714 0714 0744 0814 0844 0914 0944	1014 1044	2014 2044 2114 2144 2214 2244 2314 2344 0014 0044
Haarlem	450 d.	0543 0602 0632 0702 0702 0732 0732 0802 0832 0902 0932	1032 1102	2032 2102 2132 2202 2232 2302 2332 0002 0032 0102
Amsterdam C ⊙	450 d.	0601 0620 0650 0720 0720 0750 0750 0820 0850 0920 0950	1050 1120	2050 2120 2150 2220 2250 2320 2350 0020 0050 0120

AMSTERDAM - HAARLEM - ZANDVOORT AAN SEE ⊠

Amsterdam C ⊙	450 d.	0026	0656a 0726r 0756r	0826 0856	and every	2326 2356		Zandvoort aan See	d.	0606 0636 0706 0736	0806 0836	and every	2306 2336
Haarlem	450 d.	0045	0715 0745 0815	0845 0915	30 minutes	2345 0015		Haarlem	450 d.	0617 0647 0717 0747	0817 0847	30 minutes	2317 2347
Zandvoort aan See	a.	0055	0725 0755 0825	0855 0925	until	2355 0025		Amsterdam C ⊙	450 a.	0635 0705 0735 0805	0835 0905	until	2335 0005

a – Ⓐ only.
r – ✶ only.
⊙ – Amsterdam Centraal. All trains also call at Amsterdam Sloterdijk (5 minutes from Centraal).
⊠ – Haarlem - Zandvoort is 8 km. Additional trains Haarlem - Zandvoort and v.v.: From Haarlem at 0545 Ⓐ, 0615 ✶, 0645 ✶. From Zandvoort at 0006, 0036 and 0106.

SCHIPHOL and AMSTERDAM - ENKHUIZEN 462

km			⑥⑦c	⑥⑦c		Ⓐ	Ⓐ	Ⓐ	Ⓐ	⑥k	Ⓐ	Ⓐ	⑥k	Ⓐ										
0	**Amsterdam Centraal** 466 d.	0001	0001	0031	...	0601	...	0636	...	0701	0706	...	0731	0736	...	0806	...	0836	and at	...	2306	...	2336	...
	Schiphol ✈ d.	|	|	|	...	|	0615	|	0645	|	|	0715	|	|	0745	|	0815	|	the same	2245	|	2315	|	2345
5	Amsterdam Sloterdijk 466 d.	0006	0006	0036	...	0606	0626	0644	0656	0706	0714	0726	0736	0744	0756	0814	0826	0844	minutes	2256	2314	2326	2344	2356
12	Zaandam 466 d.	0012	0012	0042	...	0612	0633	|	0703	0712	|	0733	0742	|	0803	|	0833	|	past each	2303	|	2333	|	0003
44	**Hoorn** d.	0041	0044	0114	...	0644	0659	0714	0729	0744	0744	0759	0814	0814	0829	0844	0859	0914	hour until	2329	2344	2359	0013	0029
62	**Enkhuizen** a.	...	0107	0137	...	0707	...	0737	...	0807	0807	...	0837	0837	...	0907	...	0937		...	0007	...	0036	...

	Ⓐ	⚒		Ⓐ	Ⓐ	Ⓐ	⚒	⚒	⚒	⚒		⚒	⚒											
Enkhuizen d.	0440	...	...	...	0522	...	0552	...	0622	...	0652	...	0722	...	0752	...	0822	and at	...	2252	...	2322	...	2352
Hoorn d.	0506	0506	...	0531	0550	0601	0620	0631	0650	0701	0720	0731	0750	0801	0820	0831	0850	the same	2301	2320	2331	2350	...	0020
Zaandam 466 d.	0535	0535	...	0557	|	0627	|	0657	|	0727	|	0757	|	0827	|	0857	|	minutes	2327	|	2357	|	...	|
Amsterdam Sloterdijk 466 a.	0541	0541	...	0602	0615	0632	0645	0702	0715	0732	0745	0802	0815	0832	0845	0902	0915	past each	2332	2345	0002	0015	...	0045
Schiphol ✈ a.	0554	0554	...	0616	|	0646	|	0716	|	0746	|	0816	|	0846	|	0916	|	hour until	2346	|	0016	|	...	|
Amsterdam Centraal 466 a.	...	...	...	...	0623	...	0653	...	0723	...	0753	...	0823	...	0853	...	0923		...	2353	...	0023	...	0053

c – Also Apr. 28, May 26, June 6. k – Also Apr. 27, May 25, June 5.

LEIDEN - ALPHEN - UTRECHT and GOUDA 463

km		Ⓐ	⚒	⚒																				
0	**Leiden** Centraal d.	0552	0622	0652	0722	0752	0822	0852	0922	0952	1022	1052	and every	1922	1952	2022	2052	2122	2152	2222	2252	2322	2352	0022
15	Alphen a/d Rijn d.	0607	0637	0707	0737	0807	0837	0907	0937	1007	1037	1107	30 minutes	1937	2007	2037	2107	2137	2207	2237	2307	2337	0007	0037
34	Woerden d.	0626	0656	0726	0756t	0826t	0856t	0926t	0956t	1026t	1056	1126	until	1956	2026	2056	2123	2153	2223	2253	2323	2353	0023	0053
50	**Utrecht** Centraal a.	0638	0708	0738	0808t	0838t	0908t	0938t	1008t	1038t	1108	1138		2008	2038	2108	2135	2205	2235	2305	2335	0005	0035	0105

	Ⓐ	⚒	⚒						
Utrecht Centraal d.	0554	0624	0654	0724	0754	and every	2324	2354	0024
Woerden d.	0606	0636	0706	0736	0806	30 minutes	2336	0006	0036
Alphen a/d Rijn d.	0623	0653	0723	0753	0823	until	2353	0023	0053
Leiden Centraal a.	0637	0707	0737	0807	0837		0007	0037	0107

t – 3 minutes earlier on †.

ALPHEN A/D RIJN - GOUDA and v.v. *17 km.* Journey time: 18–20 minutes.
From Alphen a/d Rijn at 0608 Ⓐ, 0638 Ⓐ, 0708 ⚒, 0738 ⚒, 0808, 0838 and every 30 minutes until 2308, 2338, 0008, 0038 and 0108.
From Gouda at 0532 Ⓐ, 0601 Ⓐ, 0632 ⚒, 0702 ⚒, 0732, 0802, 0833, 0902, 0932, 1002, 1033, 1102, 1132, 1202, 1233, 1302, 1332, 1402, 1433, 1502, 1532, 1602, 1633, 1702, 1732, 1802, 1833, 1902, 1932, 2002, 2033, 2102, 2132, 2202, 2233, 2302, 2332, 0002 and 0032.

AMSTERDAM - GOUDA - ROTTERDAM 465

For fast trains **Amsterdam - Rotterdam**, see Tables **450** and **451**. For other trains **Gouda - Rotterdam**, see Table **481**.

km		Ⓐ	⚒	⚒	⚒					
0	**Amsterdam Centraal** d.	0549	0619	0649	0719	0749	0819	and every	2319	2349
6	Amsterdam Amstel d.	0557	0627	0657	0727	0757	0827	30 minutes	2327	2357
9	Duivendrecht d.	0601	0631	0701	0731	0801	0831	until	2331	0001
27	Breukelen d.	0619	0649	0719	0749	0819	0849		2349	0019
40	Woerden d.	0629	0659	0729	0759	0829	0859		2359	0029
56	**Gouda** d.	0642	0712	0742	0812	0842	0912		0012	0042
70	Rotterdam Alexander d.	0654	0724	0754	0824	0854	0924		0024	0054
80	**Rotterdam Centraal** a.	0704	0734	0804	0834	0904	0934		0034	0104

	Ⓐ	Ⓐ	⚒	⚒					
Rotterdam Centraal d.	0525	0555	0625	0655	0725	0755	and every	2255	2325
Rotterdam Alexander d.	0535	0605	0635	0705	0735	0805	30 minutes	2305	2335
Gouda d.	0549	0619	0649	0719	0749	0819	until	2319	2349
Woerden d.	0602	0632	0702	0732	0802	0832		2332	0002
Breukelen d.	0611	0641	0711	0741	0811	0841		2341	0011
Duivendrecht d.	0628	0658	0728	0758	0828	0858		2358	0028
Amsterdam Amstel d.	0632	0702	0732	0802	0832	0902		0002	0032
Amsterdam Centraal a.	0641	0711	0741	0811	0841	0911		0011	0041

AMSTERDAM - ALKMAAR - DEN HELDER 466

Additional trains run Amsterdam - Alkmaar and v.v. on ⚒

km			⑥⑦c		Ⓐf	Ⓐ	Ⓐ	⚒	Ⓐ					†	⚒								
	Nijmegen 468 d.	...	2343p	...	...	...	...	...	...	0537a	0613r	0643r	0713	0737	0743	0813	0843	0913		2043	2113	2143	2213
	Arnhem 468 d.	...	0001	...	...	...	...	...	...	0601a	0631r	0701r	0731	0801	0801	0832	0901	0931		2102	2131	2201	2232
0	**Amsterdam Centraal** 459 d.	0013	0109	...	0517	...	0609	...	0639	0709	0739	0809	0839	0909	0909	0939	1009	1039	and every	2209	2239	2309	2339
5	Amsterdam Sloterdijk 459 d.	0018	0115	...	0522	...	0615	...	0645	0715	0745	0815	0845	0915	0915	0945	1015	1045	30 minutes	2215	2245	2315	2345
12	Zaandam 459 d.	0025	0122	...	0529	...	0622	...	0652	0722	0752	0822	0852	0922	0922	0952	1022	1052	until	2222	2252	2322	2352
29	Castricum 461 d.	0047	0134	...	0551	...	0634	...	0704	0734	0804	0834	0904	0934	0934	1004	1034	1104		2234	2304	2334	0004
41	**Alkmaar** 461 a.	0058	0146	...	0602	...	0646	...	0716	0746	0816	0846	0916	0946	0946	1016	1046	1116		2246	2316	2346	0016
41	**Alkmaar** 461 d.	0059	...	...	...	0620	0650	0650	0720	0750	0820	0850	0920	0950	0950	1020	1050	1120		2250	2320	2350	0020
48	Heerhugowaard 461 d.	0107	...	...	...	0628	0658	0658	0728	0758	0828	0858	0928	0958	0958	1028	1058	1128		2258	2328	2358	0028
83	**Den Helder** a.	0132z	...	...	...	0656	0726	0726	0756	0826	0856	0926	0956	1026	1026	1056	1126	1156		2326	2356	0033	0056

	⑥k	Ⓐ	†	Ⓐ	Ⓐ	†	⚒																
Den Helder d.	...	0504	...	0534	0604	...	0634	0704	0734		1804	1834	1904	1934	2004	2034	2104	2134	2204	...	2304	...	2357
Heerhugowaard 461 d.	...	0531	...	0601	0631	...	0701	0731	0801		1831	1901	1931	2001	2031	2101	2131	2201	2231	...	2331	...	0023
Alkmaar 461	...	0539	...	0609	0639	...	0709	0739	0809	and every	1839	1909	1939	2009	2039	2109	2139	2209	2239	...	2339	...	0031
Alkmaar 461 d.	0501	0544	0602	0614	0644	0702	0714	0744	0814	30 minutes	1844	1914	1944	2014	2044	2114	2144	2214	2244	...	2344	...	0032
Castricum 461 d.	0512	0555	0613	0625	0655	0713	0725	0755	0825	until	1855	1925	1955	2025	2055	2125	2155	2225	2255	...	2355	...	0043
Zaandam 459 d.	0535	0608	0635	0638	0708	0735	0738	0808	0838		1908	1938	2008	2038	2108	2138	2208	2238	2308	...	0008	...	0104
Amsterdam Sloterdijk 459 d.	0541	0614	0641	0644	0714	0741	0744	0814	0844		1914	1944	2014	2044	2114	2144	2214	2244	2314	...	0014	...	0110
Amsterdam Centraal 459 a.	0547	0620	0647	0650	0720	0747	0750	0820	0850		1920	1950	2020	2050	2120	2150	2220	2250	2320	...	0020	...	0115
Arnhem 468 a.	...	0729	...	0759	0829	...	0859	0929	0959		2029	2059	2129	2159	2230	2300	2330	2400	0030	...	0130	...	...
Nijmegen 468 a.	...	0747	...	0817	0847	...	0917	0947	1017		2047	2117	2147	2217	2247	2318	2347	0019t	0049	...	0149n	...	...

a – Ⓐ only.
c – Also Apr. 28, May 26, June 6.
f – Runs 4 minutes later on ①.
k – Also Apr. 27, May 25, June 5.
n – Arrival time varies (see Table **468**).
p – Previous day.
r – ⚒ only.
t – 0022 on the mornings of ⑦ (also Apr. 28, May 26, June 6).
z – *0218* on the mornings of ②③ (not Dec. 27, Apr. 18, June 6; by 🚌 from Heerhugowaard).

AMSTERDAM and SCHIPHOL ✈ - ARNHEM - NIJMEGEN 468

Certain Ede-Wageningen departures and Arnhem arrivals are 1 minute later on †.

km		A	①m	④⑤j			Ⓐ	Ⓐ	Ⓐ	Ⓐ	Ⓐ	⚒		Ⓐ	⚒		Ⓐ		⚒		⚒		⚒		⚒
0	**Amsterdam Centraal** 470 d.	0025	0025	...	...	...	...	...	0535	...	...	...	0625	...	...	0655	...	0725	...	0755	...	0825	...	0855	...
6	Amsterdam Amstel 470 d.	0033	0033	...	...	...	...	...	0543	...	...	...	0633	...	...	0703	...	0733	...	0803	...	0833	...	0903	...
	Schiphol ✈ 470 d.	|	|	...	...	...	...	...	|	...	...	...	|	...	...	|	0700	|	0730	|	0800	|	0830	|	0900
	Amsterdam Zuid 470 d.	|	|	...	...	...	...	...	|	...	...	...	|	...	...	|	0709	|	0739	|	0809	|	0839	|	0909
39	**Utrecht Centraal** 470 a.	0052	0052	...	...	...	...	...	0618	...	...	...	0652	...	...	0722	0734	0752	0804	0822	0834	0852	0904	0922	0934
39	**Utrecht Centraal** d.	0054	0054	...	...	...	0554	0609	...	0624	0639	0654	0654	0709	0709	0724	0739	0754	0809	0824	0839	0854	0909	0924	0939
79	Ede-Wageningen d.	0119	0119	...	...	...	0618	0632	...	0648	0702	0718	0718	0732	0732	0748	0802	0818	0832	0848	0902	0918	0932	0948	1002
96	**Arnhem** a.	0130	0133	🚌	...	...	0629	0644	...	0659	0714	0729	0729	0744	0744	0759	0814	0829	0844	0859	0914	0929	0944	0959	1014
96	**Arnhem** 475 d.	0135t	0138	0140	...	...	0635	0650	...	0705	0720	0735	0735	0750	...	0805	0820	0835	0850	0905	0920	0935	0950	1005	1020
114	**Nijmegen** 475 a.	0149t	0153	0211	...	...	0655	0702	...	0717	0732	0747	0747	0802	...	0817	0832	0847	0902	0917	0932	0947	1002	1017	1032

		⚒		⚒		⚒		⚒													Ⓑb	⑥k		
Amsterdam Centraal 470 d.	0925	...	0955	...	1025	...	1055	...	1125	...	1155	...	1225	and at	...	2055	...	2125	2155	2225	2255	2255	2325	2355
Amsterdam Amstel 470 d.	0933	...	1003	...	1033	...	1103	...	1133	...	1203	...	1233	the same	...	2103	...	2133	2203	2233	2303	2303	2333	0003
Schiphol ✈ 470 d.	|	0930	|	1000	|	1030	|	1100	|	1130	|	1200	|		2030	|	2100	|	|	|	|	|	|	|
Amsterdam Zuid 470 d.	|	0939	|	1009	|	1039	|	1109	|	1139	|	1209	|	minutes	2039	|	2109	|	|	|	|	|	|	|
Utrecht Centraal 470 a.	0952	1004	1022	1034	1052	1104	1122	1134	1152	1204	1222	1234	1252		2104	2122	2134	2152	2222	2252	2322	2322	2352	0022
Utrecht Centraal d.	0954	1009	1024	1039	1054	1109	1124	1139	1154	1209	1224	1239	1254	past each	2109	2124	2139	2154	2224	2254	2324	2324	2354	...
Ede-Wageningen d.	1018	1032	1048	1102	1118	1132	1148	1202	1218	1232	1248	1302	1318		2132	2148	2202	2219	2249	2319	2349	2349	0019	...
Arnhem a.	1029	1044	1059	1114	1129	1144	1159	1214	1229	1244	1259	1314	1329	hour until	2144	2159	2214	2230	2300	2330	2400	2400	0030	...
Arnhem 475 d.	1035	1050	1105	1120	1135	1150	1205	1220	1235	1250	1305	1320	1335		2150	2205	2220	2235	2305	2335	0005	0007	0035	...
Nijmegen 475 a.	1047	1102	1117	1132	1147	1202	1217	1232	1247	1302	1317	1332	1347		2202	2217	2232	2247	2318	2347	0019	0022	0049	...

FOR RETURN DIRECTION AND NOTES SEE NEXT PAGE →

468 NIJMEGEN - ARNHEM - SCHIPHOL ✈ and AMSTERDAM

Timings may vary by 1 – 2 minutes

km		Ⓐ	Ⓐ	⚒	Ⓐ	Ⓐ	⚒	†	⚒	⚒	†	⚒		⚒	†	⚒	⚒		⚒		⚒		⚒		⚒
	Nijmegen 475 d.	...	...	...	0537	...	0613	...	0628a	0643	...	0658a	0713	0728a	0737	0743	0758a	0813	0828a	0843	0858a	0913	0928	0943	0958
	Arnhem 475 a.	...	...	...	0556	...	0626	...	0640a	0656	...	0710a	0726	0740a	0756	0756	0810a	0826	0840a	0856	0910a	0926	0940	0956	1010
	Arnhem d.	...	0546	...	0601	0616	0631	...	0646	0701	...	0716	0731	0746	0801	0801	0816	0832	0846	0901	0916	0931	0946	1001	1016
	Ede-Wageningen d.	...	0557	...	0612	0627	0642	...	0657	0712	...	0727	0741	0757	0811	0812	0827	0843	0857	0911	0927	0941	0957	1011	1027
	Utrecht Centraal a.	...	0621	...	0636	0651	0706	...	0721	0736	...	0751	0807	0821	0837	0836	0851	0906	0921	0937	0951	1007	1021	1037	1051
0	**Utrecht** Centraal 470 d.	0556	0626	0638	0638	0656	0708	0708	0726	0738	0738	0756	0808	0826	0838	0838	0856	0908	0926	0938	0956	1008	1026	1038	1056
36	**Amsterdam** Zuid 470 d.	0623	0653	|	|	0723	|	|	0753	|	|	0823	|	0853	|	|	0923	|	0953	|	1023	|	1053	|	1123
45	**Schiphol** ✈ 470 a.	0629	0659	|	|	0729	|	|	0759	|	|	0829	|	0859	|	|	0929	|	0959	|	1029	|	1059	|	1129
	Amsterdam Amstel 470 d.	...	...	0656	0656	...	0726	0727	...	0756	0757	...	0826	...	0856	0856	...	0926	...	0956	...	1026	...	1056	...
	Amsterdam Centraal 470 a.	...	...	0705	0705	...	0735	0736	...	0805	0806	...	0835	...	0905	0905	...	0935	...	1005	...	1035	...	1105	...

		⚒																				⑤⑥k	
Nijmegen 475 d.	1013	1028	1043	1058	1113	1128	1143	and at the same minutes past each hour until	1858	1913	1928	1943	1958	2013	2028	2043	2113	2143	2213	2243	2313	2343	2343	...
Arnhem 475 a.	1026	1040	1056	1110	1126	1140	1156		1910	1926	1940	1956	2010	2026	2040	2056	2126	2156	2226	2256	2326	2356	2356	...
Arnhem d.	1032	1046	1101	1116	1131	1146	1201		1916	1932	1946	2001	2016	2031	2046	2102	2131	2201	2232	2301	2331	0001	0001	...
Ede-Wageningen d.	1043	1057	1111	1127	1142	1157	1212		1927	1943	1957	2012	2027	2042	2057	2113	2141	2211	2243	2311	2341	0011	0011	...
Utrecht Centraal a.	1106	1121	1137	1151	1206	1221	1236		1951	2006	2021	2036	2051	2106	2121	2138	2207	2237	2308	2337	0007	0037	0037	...
Utrecht Centraal 470 d.	1108	1126	1138	1156	1208	1226	1238		1956	2008	2026	2038	...	2108	...	2139	2208	2238	2309	2338	*0023*	...	0038	0042
Amsterdam Zuid 470 d.	|	1153	|	1223	|	1253	|		2023	|	2053	|	...	|	...	|	|	|	|	|	|	...	|	|
Schiphol ✈ 470 a.	|	1159	|	1229	|	1259	|		2029	|	2059	|	...	|	...	|	|	|	|	|	|	...	|	|
Amsterdam Amstel 470 d.	1126	...	1156	...	1226	...	1256		...	2026	...	2056	...	2126	...	2157	2226	2256	2327	2356	*0042*	...	0057	0116
Amsterdam Centraal 470 a.	1135	...	1205	...	1235	...	1305		...	2035	...	2105	...	2135	...	2206	2235	2305	2336	0005	*0051*	...	0106	0125

A – ②–⑦ (not Dec. 27, Apr. 18).
a – Ⓐ only.
b – Not Apr. 27, May 25, June 5.
j – Not Apr. 28, May 26.
k – Also Apr. 27, May 25, June 5.
m – Also Dec. 27, Apr. 18.
t – ②③⑥⑦ (also Apr. 28, May 26).

☛ Many trains from / to Amsterdam Centraal start from / continue to Den Helder (Table **466**). For INTERNATIONAL TRAINS **Amsterdam** – **Arnhem** – **Köln**, see Table **28**.

470 AMSTERDAM and SCHIPHOL ✈ - EINDHOVEN - MAASTRICHT, VENLO and HEERLEN

AMSTERDAM CENTRAAL - EINDHOVEN - MAASTRICHT

km		⚒	Ⓐ		Ⓐ		Ⓐ	⚒	Ⓐ		⚒		⚒													
0	**Amsterdam** Centraal 468 d.	...	...	...	...	...	0610	...	0640	...	0710	...	0740	...	0810	0840	0910	0940	1010	1040	and at the same minutes past each hour until	2210	2240	2308	2338
6	Amsterdam Amstel 468 d.	...	...	...	...	...	0618	...	0648	...	0718	...	0748	...	0818	0848	0918	0948	1018	1048		2218	2248	2316	2346
39	**Utrecht** Centraal 468 a.	...	...	...	...	...	0637	...	0707	...	0737	...	0807	...	0837	0907	0937	1007	1037	1107		2237	2307	2337	0007
39	**Utrecht** Centraal d.	...	...	...	...	...	0639	...	0709	...	0739	...	0809	0809	0839	0909	0939	1009	1039	1109		2239	2309	2339	0009
87	's-Hertogenbosch d.	...	*0549*	...	*0619*	...	0709	...	0739	...	0809	...	0839	0839	0909	0939	1009	1039	1109	1139		2309	2339	0009	0039
119	**Eindhoven** a.	...	*0623*	...	*0653*	...	0728	...	0758	...	0828	...	0858	0858	0928	0958	1028	1058	1128	1158		2328	2358	0028	0058
119	**Eindhoven** d.	...	0631	...	0701	...	0731	0731	0801	0801	0831	0831	0901	0901	0931	1001	1031	1101	1131	1201		2331	0001	...	...
148	Weert d.	...	0647	...	0717	...	0747	0747	0817	0817	0847	0847	0917	0917	0947	1017	1047	1117	1147	1217		2347	0017	...	...
172	Roermond d.	...	0703	0707r	0733	0737	0803	0803	0833	0833	0903	0903	0933	0933	1003	1033	1103	1133	1203	1233		0004	0033	...	...
196	Sittard d.	0625	0720	0725	0750	0755	0820	0820	0850	0850	0920	0920	0950	0950	1020	1050	1120	1150	1220	1250		0020	0050	...	...
218	**Maastricht** a.	0644	0734	0744	0804	0814	0834	0834	0904	0904	0934	0934	1004	1004	1035	1105	1134	1204	1235	1304		0034	0104	...	...

	Ⓐ	Ⓐ	Ⓐ	⚒	Ⓐ	⚒	⚒		⚒																
Maastricht d.	...	...	0525	...	0555	...	0625	...	0655	...	0725	0755	and at the same minutes past each hour until	1925	1955	2025	2055	2125	2155	2225	2255	...	2316	2355	0016
Sittard d.	...	...	0541	...	0611	...	0641	...	0711	...	0741	0811		1941	2011	2041	2111	2141	2211	2241	2311	...	2335	0011	0035
Roermond d.	...	...	0557	...	0627	...	0657	...	0727	...	0757	0827		1957	2027	2057	2127	2157	2227	2257	2327	...	2352	0027	...
Weert d.	...	...	0611	...	0641	...	0711	...	0741	...	0811	0841		2011	2041	2111	2141	2211	2241	2311	2341	...	...	0041	...
Eindhoven a.	...	...	0628	...	0658	...	0728	...	0758	...	0828	0858		2028	2058	2128	2158	2228	2258	2328	2358	...	...	0102	...
Eindhoven d.	0532	0602	0632	...	0702	0702	0732	0732	0802	0802	0832	0902		2032	2102	2132	2202	2232	2302	2332	...	0005	...	...	...
's-Hertogenbosch d.	0553	0623	0653	...	0723	0723	0753	0753	0823	0823	0853	0923		2053	2123	2153	2223	2253	2323	2353	...	0040	...	...	...
Utrecht Centraal a.	0621	0651	0721	...	0751	0751	0821	0821	0851	0851	0921	0951		2121	2151	2221	2251	2321	2351	0021	...	...	...	...	...
Utrecht Centraal 468 d.	0623	0653	0723	0723	0753	0753	0823	0823	0853	0853	0923	0953		2123	2153	2223	2253	2323	2353	0023	...	...	...	...	...
Amsterdam Amstel 468 d.	0641	0711	0741	0741	0811	0811	0841	0841	0911	0911	0941	1011		2141	2211	2241	2312	2342	0012	0042	...	...	...	...	...
Amsterdam Centraal 468 a.	0650	0720	0750	0750	0820	0820	0850	0850	0920	0920	0950	1020		2150	2220	2250	2321	2351	0021	0051	...	...	...	...	...

SCHIPHOL - AMSTERDAM ZUID - EINDHOVEN - HEERLEN and VENLO

km		Ⓐ	Ⓐ	Ⓐ	⚒	Ⓐ	A	A	B	B															
0	**Schiphol** ✈ 468 d.	...	...	...	...	...	0618	0618	0648	0648	0718	0718	0748r	0748	0818	0818	0848	0848	and at the same minutes past each hour until	1718	1718	1748	1748	1818	1848
9	**Amsterdam** Zuid 468 d.	...	...	...	...	...	0627	0627	0657	0657	0727	0727	0757r	0757	0827	0827	0857	0857		1727	1727	1757	1757	1827	1857
45	**Utrecht** Centraal 468 a.	...	...	...	...	...	0649	0649	0719	0719	0749	0749	0819r	0819	0849	0849	0919	0919		1749	1749	1819	1819	1849	1919
45	**Utrecht** Centraal ¶ d.	...	...	...	...	...	0654	0654	0724	0724	0754	0754	0824r	0824	0854	0854	0924	0924		1754	1754	1824	1824	1854	1924
93	's-Hertogenbosch ¶ d.	...	...	...	...	...	0726	0726	0756	0756	0826	0826	0856r	0856	0926	0926	0956	0856		1826	1826	1856	1856	1926	1956
	Eindhoven ¶ a.	...	...	...	...	...	0746	0746	0816	0816	0846	0846	0916r	0916	0946	0946	1016	1016		1846	1846	1916	1916	1946	2016
125	**Eindhoven** ¶ d.	...	0619	0649	0719	0721	0749	0751	0819	0821	0849	0851	0919	0921	0949	0951	1019	1021		1849	1851	1919	1921	1949	2019
	Helmond d.	...	0628	0658	0728	|	0758	|	0828	|	0858	|	0928	|	0958	|	1028	|		1858	|	1928	|	1958	2028
	Venlo a.	...	0658	0728	0758	|	0828	|	0858	|	0928	|	0958	|	1028	|	1058	|		1928	|	1958	|	2028	2058
154	Weert ¶ d.	...	━	━	━	0737	━	0807	━	0837	...	0907	...	0937	...	1007	...	1037		...	1907	...	1937	━	━
178	Roermond ¶ d.	...	⚒	⚒	...	0753	...	0823	...	0853	...	0923	...	0953	...	1023	...	1053		...	1923	...	1953	...	...
202	Sittard ¶ d.	0622	0652	0722	0752	0811	0822	0841	0852	0911	...	0941	...	1011	...	1041	...	1111		...	1941	...	2011	2052	2122
221	**Heerlen** a.	0643	0713	0743	0813	0826	0843	0856	0913	0926	...	0956	...	1026	...	1056	...	1126		...	1956	...	2026	2113	2143

Schiphol ✈ 468 d.	1918	1948	2018	2048	2118	2148	2218	2248	2318	2348	...
Amsterdam Zuid 468 d.	1927	1957	2027	2057	2127	2157	2227	2257	2327	2357	...
Utrecht Centraal 468 a.	1949	2019	2049	2119	2149	2219	2249	2319	2349	0019	...
Utrecht Centraal ¶ d.	1954	2024	2054	2124	━	━	━	━	━	...	...
's-Hertogenbosch ¶ d.	2026	2056	2126	2156	...	...	...	...	...	...	...
Eindhoven ¶ a.	2046	2116	2146	2216	...	...	...	...	...	...	...
Eindhoven ¶ d.	2049	2119	2149	2219	2249	2319	0019	...	...	...	...
Helmond d.	2058	2128	2158	2228	2258	2328	0028	...	...	...	...
Venlo a.	2128	2158	2228	2258	2328	2358	0058	...	...	...	...
Weert ¶ d.	━	━	━	━	...	...	...	...	...	...	...
Roermond ¶ d.	...	...	...	...	...	...	...	...	...	...	...
Sittard ¶ d.	2152	2222	2252	2322	...	...	...	2352	0022	...	...
Heerlen a.	2213	2243	2313	2343	...	...	...	0013	0043	...	...

	Ⓐ	Ⓐ	Ⓐ	Ⓐ	Ⓐ	⚒	⚒		⚒	
Heerlen d.	...	...	0535	...	0605	...	0635	...	0705	...
Sittard ¶ d.	...	...	0551	...	0621	...	0651	...	0721	...
Roermond ¶ d.	...	...	0608	...	0638	...	0708	...	0738	...
Weert ¶ d.	...	...	0622	...	0652	...	0722	...	0752	...
Venlo d.	...	0534	|	0604	|	0634	|	0704	|	0734
Helmond d.	...	0602	|	0632	|	0702	|	0732	|	0802
Eindhoven ¶ a.	...	0612	0639	0642	0709	0712	0739	0742	0809	0812
Eindhoven ¶ d.	...	0617	0647	0647	0717	0717	0747	0747	0817	0817
's-Hertogenbosch ¶ d.	0607	0637	0707	0707	0737	0737	0807	0807	0837	0837
Utrecht Centraal ¶ a.	0636	0706	0736	0736	0806	0806	0836	0836	0906	0906
Utrecht Centraal 468 d.	0641	0711	0741	0741	0811	0811	0841	0841	0911	0911
Amsterdam Zuid 468 d.	0705	0735	0805	0805	0835	0835	0905	0905	0935	0935
Schiphol ✈ 468 a.	0711	0741	0811	0811	0841	0841	0911	0911	0941	0941

Heerlen d.	0735	...	0805	...	and at the same minutes past each hour until	1735	...	1805	...	1835	...	...	...	...	...	...	1916	1946	2016	2046	2116	2146	2216	2246	2346
Sittard ¶ d.	0751	...	0821	...		1751	...	1821	...	1851	...	...	...	...	...	...	1937	2007	2037	2107	2137	2207	2237	2307	0008
Roermond ¶ d.	0808	...	0838	...		1808	...	1838	...	1908	...	...	...	...	...	...	━	━	━	...	...	...	...	...	...
Weert ¶ d.	0822	...	0852	...		1822	...	1852	...	1922	...	...	...	...	...	...	...	...	...	...	...	...	...	...	...
Venlo d.	|	0804	|	0834		|	1804	|	1834	|	1904	1934	2004	2034	2104	2134	2204	2234	2304	...	...	...	...	...	...
Helmond d.	|	0832	|	0902		|	1832	|	1902	|	1932	2002	2032	2102	2132	2202	2232	2302	2332	...	...	...	...	...	...
Eindhoven ¶ a.	0839	0842	0909	0912		1839	1842	1909	1912	1939	1942	2012	2042	2112	2142	2212	2242	2312	2342	...	...	...	...	...	...
Eindhoven ¶ d.	0847	0847	0917	0917		1847	1847	1917	1917	1947	1947	2017	2047	━	━	━	━	...	...	...	...	...	...	...	...
's-Hertogenbosch ¶ d.	0907	0907	0937	0937		1907	1907	1937	1937	2007	2007	2037	2107	...	...	...	...	...	...	...	...	...	...	...	...
Utrecht Centraal ¶ a.	0936	0936	1006	1006		1936	1936	2006	2006	2036	2036	2106	2136	...	...	...	...	...	...	...	...	...	...	...	...
Utrecht Centraal 468 d.	0941	0941	1011	1011		1941	1941	2011	2011	2041	2041	2111	2142	2211	2241	2312	2341	...	...	...	...	...	...	...	...
Amsterdam Zuid 468 d.	1005	1005	1035	1035		2005	2005	2035	2035	2105	2105	2135	2205	2235	2305	2335	0005	...	...	...	...	...	...	...	...
Schiphol ✈ 468 a.	1011	1011	1041	1041		2011	2011	2041	2041	2111	2111	2141	2211	2241	2311	2341	0011	...	...	...	...	...	...	...	...

A – Runs on Ⓐ Amsterdam to Eindhoven, ⚒ Eindhoven to Venlo / Heerlen.
B – Runs on ⚒ Schiphol to Utrecht, Ⓐ Utrecht to Eindhoven, daily Eindhoven to Venlo / Heerlen.
r – ⚒ only.
¶ – See also Amsterdam - Maastricht panel above.

DEN HAAG - EINDHOVEN 471

The Den Haag to Eindhoven service is expected to run with through trains later in 2017. Until then, a change of trains at Breda is required.

km																							
		Ⓐ	⚒	⚒	⚒	⚒																	
0	**Den Haag** Centraal d.	...	...	0545a	...	0615a	...	0645r	...	0715r	...	0745	...	0815	and at the same minutes past each hour until	...	2215	...	2245	...	...	...
2	**Den Haag** HS 450 460 d.	...	...	0551a	...	0621a	...	0651r	...	0721r	...	0751	...	0821		...	2221	...	2251	...	...	...
10	Delft 450 460 d.	...	...	0558a	...	0628a	...	0658r	...	0728r	...	0758	...	0828		...	2228	...	2258	...	...	...
24	**Rotterdam** Centraal 450 451 460 d.	0541	...	0611	...	0641	...	0711	...	0741	...	0811	...	0841		...	2241	...	2311	...	...	...
	Dordrecht 450 460 ★ d.	│	0557	│	0626	│	0657	│	0726	│	0757	│	0826	│		2226	│	2257	│	2326	...	2357
71	Breda 451 ★ a.	0604	0622	0634	0651	0704	0722	0734	0751	0804	0822	0834	0851	0904		2251	2304	2322	2334	2351	...	0022
71	Breda 475 d.	0607	0623a	0637	0653	0707	0723r	0737	0753	0807	0823	0837	0853	0907		2253	2307	2323	2337	2353	...	0023
92	Tilburg 475 d.	0621	0642a	0651	0712	0721	0742r	0751	0812	0821	0842	0851	0912	0921		2312	2321	2342	2351	0012	0037	0042
129	**Eindhoven** a.	0643	...	0713	...	0743	...	0813	...	0843	...	0913	...	0943		...	2343	...	0013	...	0109	...

km																						
		Ⓐ	⚒	Ⓐ	⚒	Ⓐ	⚒	⚒	⚒	⚒												
	Eindhoven d.	...	...	0544	...	0614	...	0644	...	0714	...	0744	...	0814	...	and at the same minutes past each hour until	2244	...	2314	...	2344	...
	Tilburg 475 d.	...	0549a	0608	0619a	0638	0649a	0708	0719	0738	0749r	0808	0819	0838	0849		2308	2319	2338	2349	0008	...
	Breda 475 a.	...	0608a	0621	0638a	0651	0708a	0721	0738	0751	0808r	0821	0838	0851	0908		2321	2338	2351	0008	0021	...
0	Breda 451 ★ d.	0601	0609	0623	0639	0653	0709	0723	0739	0753	0809	0823	0839	0853	0909		2323	2339	2353	0009	0024	0039
30	Dordrecht 450 460 ★ a.	0619	0633	│	0703	│	0733	│	0803	│	0833	│	0903	│	0933		│	0003	│	0033	│	0103
	Rotterdam Centraal 450 451 460 d.	...	...	0648	...	0718	...	0748	...	0818	...	0848	...	0918	...		2348	...	0018	...	0049	...
	Delft 450 460 d.	...	...	0659	...	0729	...	0759	...	0829	...	0859	...	0929	...		2359	...	0029	...	...	...
	Den Haag HS 450 460 a.	...	...	0707	...	0737	...	0807	...	0837	...	0907	...	0937	...		0007	...	0037	...	...	...
	Den Haag Centraal a.	...	...	0712	...	0742	...	0812	...	0842	...	0912	...	0942	...		0012	...	0042	...	...	...

a – Ⓐ only.
r – ⚒ only.

★ – Other fast shuttle services Dordrecht - Breda and v.v. (journey 18–20 minutes): **From Dordrecht** at 0634 Ⓐ, 0734 ⚒, 0834 ⚒, 0934 ⚒, 1034 ⚒, 1134 ⚒, 1234 and hourly until 1934. **From Breda** at 0701 ⚒, 0801 ⚒, 0901 ⚒, 1001 ⚒, 1101 ⚒, 1201 and hourly until 2001.

MAASTRICHT - HEERLEN - KERKRADE 472

Operated by **Arriva** (NS tickets valid)

km																							
				Ⓐ	⚒	⚒								A	Ⓐ	Ⓐ	Ⓐ	Ⓐ	⚒		⚒			
0	**Maastricht** d.	0029	...	0529	0559	0629	0659	0729	0759	and every	2329	2359	...	L	0649	0719	0749	0819	0849	and every	1119	1149	and every	2219
11	Valkenburg d.	0042	...	0542	0612	0642	0712	0742	0812	30 minutes	2342	0012	...	S	0659	0729	0759	0829	0859	30 minutes	1129	1159	30 minutes	2229
24	**Heerlen** d.	0058	...	0558	0628	0658	0728	0758	0828	until	2358	0028	...	O	0710	0740	0810	0840	0910	until	1140	1210	until	2240

				Ⓐ	⚒	⚒							A	Ⓐ	Ⓐ	Ⓐ	Ⓐ	⚒		⚒			
Heerlen d.	0002	0032	...	0532	0602	0632	0702	0732	and every	2302	2332	...	L	0646	0716	0746	0816	0846	and every	1116	1146	and every	2216
Valkenburg d.	0018	0048	...	0548	0618	0648	0718	0748	30 minutes	2318	2348	...	S	0656	0726	0756	0826	0856	30 minutes	1126	1156	30 minutes	2226
Maastricht a.	0031	0101	...	0601	0631	0701	0731	0801	until	2331	0001	...	O	0707	0737	0807	0837	0907	until	1137	1207	until	2237

HEERLEN - KERKRADE and v.v. *9 km*. Journey time: 13–14 minutes. **From Heerlen** at 0014, 0544 Ⓐ, 0614 ⚒, 0644 ⚒, 0714, 0744 and every 30 minutes until 2344.
From Kerkrade Centrum at 0000, 0030, 0600 Ⓐ, 0630 ⚒, 0700 ⚒, 0730, 0800, 0830 and every 30 minutes until 2330

HEERLEN - AACHEN 473

km		A	E							
0	**Heerlen** d.	0556	0656	0756	0856	and	2156	2256	...	...
10	Herzogenrath 🚌 802 a.	0610	0710	0810	0910	hourly	2210	2310	...	...
24	**Aachen** Hbf 802 a.	0631r	0731t	0831j	0931	until	2231	2345	...	...

	A	E						
Aachen Hbf 802 d.	0602r	0702	...	0802	and	2302	...	...
Herzogenrath 🚌 802 d.	0622	0722	...	0822	hourly	2322	...	...
Heerlen a.	0635	0735	...	0835	until	2335	...	...

A – ①–⑤ (not Dec. 26, Apr. 17, 27, May 25, June 5).
E – ①–⑥ (not Dec. 26, Apr. 17).
j – *0845* on ⑦ (also Dec. 26, Apr. 14, 17, May 1, 25, June 5, 15, Oct. 3, 31, Nov. 1).
r – Not Apr. 14, May 1, June 15, Oct. 3, 31, Nov. 1.
t – Not Apr. 14, May 1, 25, June 5, 15, Oct. 3, 31, Nov. 1. *0745* on ⑥.

ROOSENDAAL - 's-HERTOGENBOSCH - NIJMEGEN - ARNHEM - ZWOLLE 475

km																									
		Ⓐ	Ⓐ	Ⓐ	⚒	Ⓐ	⚒	†	⑥k	Ⓐ	†	⚒	†	⚒											
0	**Roosendaal** d.	...	...	...	...	0527	...	...	...	0557	...	0627	0654	0657	0727	0757	0827	0857	and every 30 minutes until	2127	2157	2227	...	2257	2327
23	Breda 471 d.	...	...	...	...	0550	...	...	...	0620	...	0650	0713	0720	0750	0820	0850	0920		2150	2220	2250	...	2320	2350
44	Tilburg 471 d.	...	...	...	...	0603	...	...	...	0633	...	0703	0733	0733	0803	0833	0903	0933		2203	2233	2303	...	2333	0003
67	**'s-Hertogenbosch** a.	...	...	...	...	0618	...	...	...	0648	...	0718	0748	0748	0818	0848	0918	0948		2218	2248	2318	...	2348	0018
67	**'s-Hertogenbosch** d.	...	...	0532	...	0623	...	...	...	0653	...	0723	0753	0753	0823	0853	0923	0953		2223	2253	2323	...	2353	...
86	Oss d.	...	...	0550	...	0635	...	...	...	0705	...	0735	0805	0805	0835	0905	0935	1005		2235	2305	2335	...	0005	...
110	**Nijmegen** a.	...	...	0614	...	0651	...	...	...	0721	...	0751	0821	0821	0851	0921	0951	1021		2251	2321	2351	...	0021	...
110	**Nijmegen** 468 d.	...	...	0624	...	0654	0654	0713	0716	0724	0746	0754	0824	0824	0854	0924	0954	1024		2254	2324	2354	0001	0024	...
129	**Arnhem** 468 a.	...	...	0637	...	0707	0707	0725	0734	0737	0804	0807	0837	0837	0907	0937	1007	1037		2307	2337	0007	0019	0037	...
129	**Arnhem** d.	...	0558	0641	...	0711	0711	0730	0741	0741	0811	0811	0841	0841	0911	0941	1011	1041		2311	2341	...	0025	...	...
145	Dieren d.	...	0620	0652	...	0722	0722	0750	0752	0752	0822	0822	0852	0852	0922	0952	1022	1052		2322	2352	...	0043	...	...
159	Zutphen d.	0604	0634	0704	0704	0734	0734	0804	0804	0804	0834	0834	0904	0904	0934	1004	1034	1104		2334	0004	...	0055	...	...
174	Deventer d.	0617	0647	0717	0717	0747	0747	0817	0817	0817	0847	0847	0917	0917	0947	1017	1047	1117		2347	0017	...	...	...	...
204	**Zwolle** a.	0641	0711	0741	0741	0811	0811	0841	0841	0841	0911	0911	0941	0941	1011	1041	1111	1141		0011	0041	...	...	...	...

	Ⓐ	Ⓐ	Ⓐ	Ⓐ	Ⓐ	⚒		Ⓐ	⚒		Ⓐ	⚒												
Zwolle d.	...	...	...	...	...	...	...	0620	...	...	0650	...	...	0720r	0750	0820	0850	⊠	2120	2150	2220	2250	...	2320	2350
Deventer d.	...	...	...	...	...	...	...	0645	...	...	0715	...	...	0745r	0815	0845	0915		2144	2215	2245	2315	...	2345	0015
Zutphen d.	...	...	...	0550	0609	...	...	0658	0658	...	0728	0728	...	0758	0828	0858	0928		2158	2228	2258	2328	...	2358	0028
Dieren d.	...	...	...	0601	0620	...	...	0708	0708	...	0738	0738	...	0808	0838	0908	0938		2208	2238	2308	2338	...	0008	0038
Arnhem a.	...	...	...	0621	0639	...	...	0721	0721	...	0751	0751	...	0821	0851	0921	0951	and every 30 minutes until	2221	2251	2321	2351	...	0021	0051
Arnhem 468 d.	...	...	0553	0623	0641	0653	...	0723	0723	...	0753	0753	0753	0823	0853	0923	0953		2223	2253	2323	2353	...	0035	...
Nijmegen 468 a.	...	...	0606	0636	0659	0706	...	0736	0736	...	0806	0806	0806	0836	0906	0936	1006		2236	2306	2336	0006	...	0049	...
Nijmegen d.	...	...	0609	0639	▬	0709	...	0739	0739	...	0809	0809	0809	0839	0909	0939	1009		2239	2309	2339	...	0016	...	...
Oss d.	...	...	0624	0654	...	0724	...	0754	0754	...	0824	0824	0824	0854	0924	0954	1024		2254	2324	2354	...	0045	...	...
's-Hertogenbosch a.	...	...	0637	0707	...	0737	...	0807	0807	...	0837	0837	0837	0907	0937	1007	1037		2307	2337	0007	...	0103	...	...
's-Hertogenbosch d.	...	0612	0642	0712	0712r	0742	0742	0812	0812	0812	0842	0842	0842	0912	0942	1012	1042		2312	2342	0012	...	...	...	...
Tilburg 471 d.	0549	0628	0658	0728	0728r	0758	0758	0828	0828	0828	0858	0858	0858	0928	0958	1028	1058		2328	2358	0028	...	...	...	...
Breda 471 d.	0615	0645	0715	0745	0745	0815	0815	0845	0845	0845	0915	0915	0915	0945	1015	1045	1115		2345	0015	0049	...	...	...	...
Roosendaal a.	0633	0703	0733	0803	0803	0833	0833	0903	0903	0903	0933	0933	0933	1003	1033	1103	1133		0003	0033	0107	...	...	...	...

k – Also Apr. 27, May 25, June 5.
r – ⚒ only.
⊠ – Certain services depart Deventer at xx44 (not xx45).

ARNHEM and ZUTPHEN - WINTERSWIJK 476

Operated by **Arriva** (NS tickets valid) 2nd class only

Arnhem - Winterswijk

km		H		Ⓐ	Ⓐ	Ⓐ	Ⓐ	⑥k	†	Ⓐ		Ⓐ															
0	**Arnhem** d.	0004	...	0602	0632	0702	0731	0731	0734	0802	0832t	0901	0932t	1032t	1131	1232t	1331	1432t	1531	1632t	1731	1832t	1931	2034	2134	2234	2334
14	Zevenaar d.	0018	...	0616	0646	0716	0746	0748	0748	0817	0846t	0916	0946t	1046t	1146t	1246t	1346t	1446t	1546t	1646t	1746t	1846t	1946t	2048	2148	2248	2348
30	Doetinchem d.	0037	...	0637	0707	0737	0807	0807	0807	0837	0907	0937	1007	1107	1207	1307	1407	1507	1607	1707	1807	1907	2007	2107	2207	2307	0007
64	**Winterswijk** a.	0110	...	0710	0740	0810	0840	0840	0840	0910	0940	1010	1040	1140	1240	1340	1440	1540	1640	1740	1840	1940	2040	2140	2240	2342	0040

	⑦w		Ⓐ	Ⓐ	Ⓐ		Ⓐ		Ⓐ		Ⓐ														Ⓐ
Winterswijk d.	0020	...	0520	0550	0620	0650	0720	0750	0820	0850	0920	0950	1050	1150	1250	1350	1450	1550	1650	1750	1850	1950	2050	2150	2250	2320
Doetinchem d.	0052	...	0552	0622	0652	0722	0752	0822	0852	0922	0952	1022	1122	1222	1322	1422	1522	1622	1722	1822	1922	2022	2122	2222	2322	2352
Zevenaar d.	0111	...	0611	0641	0711	0741	0811	0841	0911	0941	1011	1041	1141	1241	1341	1441	1541	1641	1741	1841	1941	2041	2141	2241	2341	0011
Arnhem a.	0126	...	0626	0656	0726	0756	0825	0856	0926	0956	1025	1056	1156	1256	1356	1456	1556	1656	1756	1856	1956	2055	2156	2256	2356	0026

Zutphen - Winterswijk

km		H		Ⓐ	⑥k	Ⓐ	Ⓐ	©	Ⓐ			
0	**Zutphen** d.	0006	...	0702	0706	0732	0802	0806	0832	0906	and	2306
22	Ruurlo d.	0022	...	0718	0722	0748	0818	0822	0848	0922	hourly	2322
43	**Winterswijk** a.	0040	...	0736	0740	0806	0836	0840	0910	0940	until	2340

	Ⓐ	Ⓐ	⑥k	Ⓐ	Ⓐ	©				⑥k
Winterswijk d.	0616	0646	0650	0716	0746	0750	0850	and	2250	2350
Ruurlo d.	0634	0704	0708	0734	0804	0808	0908	hourly	2308	0008
Zutphen a.	0650	0720	0723	0750	0820	0823	0923	until	2323	0023

H – ②–⑦ (not Dec. 27, Apr. 18).
k – Also Apr. 27, May 25, June 5.
t – 2 minutes later on ©.
w – Also Apr. 28, May 26, June 6.
☛ Additional trains run on ⚒.

477 NIJMEGEN - VENLO - ROERMOND

Operated by **Arriva** (NS tickets valid)

km		Ⓐh	Ⓐh	⚒d	⚒d						
0	**Nijmegen** d.	0538	0608	0638	0708	0738	0808	and every 30 minutes until	2238	2308	2338
24	Boxmeer d.	0600	0630	0700	0730	0800	0830		2300	2330	0000
39	Venray d.	0615	0645	0715	0745	0815	0845		2315	2345	0015
61	**Venlo** d.	0633	0703	0733	0803	0833	0903		2333	0003	0031
84	**Roermond** a.	0655	0725	0755	0825	0855	0925		2355	0025	...

	⚒	⚒								
Roermond d.	...	0605a	0635a	0705r	0735r	0805	0835	and every 30 minutes until	2235	2305
Venlo d.	0559	0629v	0659	0729z	0759	0829	0859		2259	2329
Venray d.	0616	0646	0716	0746	0816	0846	0916		2316	2346
Boxmeer d.	0629	0659	0729	0759	0829	0859	0929		2329	2359
Nijmegen a.	0652	0722	0752	0822	0852	0922	0952		2352	0022

☛ Additional journeys: **Venlo** → **Roermond** at 0533 Ⓐ, 0603 Ⓐ; **Nijmegen** → **Venlo** at 0008; **Venlo** → **Nijmegen** at 0459 Ⓐ, 0529 Ⓐ; **Roermond** → **Venlo** at 2335, 0005, 0035.

a – Ⓐ only. **d** – Runs daily Venlo - Roermond. **h** – Also runs on ⑥ Venlo - Roermond. **r** – ⚒ only. **v** – 0628 on ⑥ (also Apr. 27, May 25, June 5). **z** – 0728 on †.

478 ARNHEM - TIEL - GELDERMALSEN - UTRECHT and 's-HERTOGENBOSCH

km		Ⓐ	Ⓐ	Ⓐ	Ⓐ	⚒	⚒	⚒															
0	**Tiel** d.	0547	...	0617	...	0647	...	0717	...	0747	...	0817	and at the same minutes past each hour until	...	2147	...	2217	2247	...	2317	2347	...	0017
	's-Hertogenbosch d.	|	0556	|	0626	|	0656	|	0726	|	0756	|		2126	|	2156	|	|	2256	|	|	2356	|
12	Geldermalsen a.	0559	0611	0629	0641	0659	0711	0729	0741	0759	0811	0829		2141	2159	2211	2229	2259	2311	2329	2359	0011	0029
38	**Utrecht** Centraal a.	0625	0638	0655	0708	0725	0738	0755	0808	0825	0838	0855		2208	2225	2238	2255	2325	2338	2355	0025	0038	0055

km		Ⓐ	Ⓐ	Ⓐ	Ⓐ	Ⓐ	⚒	⚒															
0	**Utrecht** Centraal d.	0535	0552	0605	0622	0635	0652	0705	0722	0735	0752	0805	and at the same minutes past each hour until	2122	2135	2152	2205	2235	2252	2305	2335	2352	0005
26	Geldermalsen d.	0600	0618	0630	0648	0700	0718	0730	0748	0800	0818	0830		2148	2200	2218	2230	2300	2318	2330	0000	0018	0030
48	**'s-Hertogenbosch** a.	|	0634	|	0704	|	0734	|	0804	|	0834	|		2204	|	2234	|	|	2334	|	|	0034	|
	Tiel a.	0612	...	0642	...	0712	...	0742	...	0812	...	0842		...	2212	...	2242	2312	...	2342	0012	...	0042

ARNHEM - TIEL and v.v. Operated by ***Arriva*** (NS tickets valid). 2nd class only. *44 km.* Journey time: 35 – 36 minutes.

From Arnhem at 0638 Ⓐ, 0708 Ⓐ, 0738 Ⓐ, 0808 Ⓐ, 0838 ⚒, 0908 Ⓐ, 0938, 1038, 1138, 1238, 1338, 1438, 1508 Ⓐ, 1538, 1608 Ⓐ, 1638, 1708 Ⓐ, 1738, 1808 Ⓐ, 1838, 1938, 2038, 2138, 2238 and 2338. **From Tiel** at 0617 Ⓐ, 0647 Ⓐ, 0717 Ⓐ, 0747 ⚒, 0817 Ⓐ, 0847, 0947, 1047, 1147, 1247, 1347, 1417 Ⓐ, 1447, 1517 Ⓐ, 1547, 1617 Ⓐ, 1647, 1717 Ⓐ, 1747, 1817 Ⓐ, 1847, 1947, 2047, 2147 and 2247.

479 DORDRECHT - GELDERMALSEN

Operated by **Arriva** (NS tickets valid); 2nd class only

km					Ⓐ	Ⓐ	⑥k	Ⓐ	⑥k	Ⓐ	Ⓒ	Ⓐ	Ⓒ	Ⓐ	Ⓒ	Ⓐ	Ⓒ	Ⓐ	Ⓒ						
0	**Dordrecht** d.	0011	0041	0111	0442	0509	0512	0539	0541	0609	0611	0639	0641	0709	0711	0739	0741	0809	0811	0841	0911	0941	and every 30 minutes until	2311	2341
10	Sliedrecht d.	0023	0053	0122	0453	0521	0523	0551	0553	0621	0623	0651	0653	0721	0723	0751	0753	0821	0823	0853	0923	0953		2323	2353
24	Gorinchem d.	0038	0107	0138	0509	0539	0539	0609	0609	0639	0639	0709	0709	0739	0739	0809	0809	0839	0839	0909	0939	1009		2339	0009
49	**Geldermalsen** a.	0101	...	...	0534	0604	0604	0634	0634	0704	0704	0734	0734	0804	0804	0834	0834	0904	0904	0934	1004	1034		0004	0034

					Ⓐ	Ⓐ	Ⓐ	⑥k	Ⓐ	⑥k	Ⓒ	Ⓐ	Ⓒ	Ⓐ	Ⓒ									
Geldermalsen d.	0009	0039	0105	...	...	0539	0609	0609	0639	0639	...	0709	0709	0739	0739	...	0809	0839	and every 30 minutes until	2309	2339	...	...	...	...
Gorinchem d.	0039	0107	0127	...	0537	0607	0637	0639	0707	0709	0709	0737	0739	0807	0809	...	0839	0909		2339	0009	...	...	...	...
Sliedrecht d.	0053	0122	0141	...	0551	0621	0651	0653	0721	0723	0723	0751	0753	0821	0823	...	0853	0923		2353	0023	...	...	...	...
Dordrecht a.	0105	0133	0151	...	0602	0633	0703	0705	0733	0735	0735	0804	0805	0833	0835	...	0905	0935		0005	0035	...	...	...	...

k – Also Apr. 27, May 25, June 5.

480 AMSTERDAM and SCHIPHOL ✈ - AMERSFOORT - DEVENTER - ENSCHEDE

SCHIPHOL ✈ - AMSTERDAM CENTRAAL - AMERSFOORT

km		Ⓐ	Ⓐ	Ⓐ	⚒	v		Ⓐ		⚒													D	B🚌	⑥⑦c
0	**Schiphol** ✈ d.	...	0541	...	0611	...	0641	...	0711	...	0741	...	0811	...	0841	and at the same minutes past each hour until	...	2241	...	2311	2341	2341	...	...
17	**Amsterdam** Centraal d.	0600	0611	0630	0641	0700	0711	0730	0741	0800	0811	0830	0841	0900	0911		2300	2311	2330	2341	0011	0011	...	0030
31	Weesp d.	|	0629	|	0659	|	0729	|	0759	|	0829	|	0859	|	0929		|	2329	|	2359	0027	0028	0032	|
40	Naarden-Bussum d.	|	0636	|	0706	|	0736	|	0806	|	0836	|	0906	|	0936		|	2336	|	0006	...	0035	0047	|
46	Hilversum d.	0622	0646	0652	0716	0722	0746	0752	0816	0822	0846	0852	0916	0922	0946		2322	2346	2352	0016	...	0046	0102	0052
53	Baarn d.	|	0652	|	0722	|	0752	|	0822	|	0852	|	0922	|	0952		|	2352	|	0022	...	0052	0117	|
62	**Amersfoort** a.	0634	0659	0704	0729	0734	0759	0804	0829	0834	0859	0904	0929	0934	0959		2334	2359	0004	0029	...	0059	0132	0104

		Ⓐ	Ⓐ	Ⓐ		Ⓐ		⚒		⚒		⚒										⑤⑥k		
Amersfoort d.	0448	0531	0601	0626	0631	0656	0701	0726	0731	0756	0801	0826	0831	0856	0901	0926	and at the same minutes past each hour until	2231	2256	2301	2326	2331	2356	0001
Baarn d.	0455	0538	0608	|	0638	|	0708	|	0738	|	0808	|	0838	|	0908	|		2238	|	2308	|	2338	|	0008
Hilversum d.	0502	0545	0615	0639	0645	0709	0715	0739	0745	0809	0815	0839	0845	0909	0915	0939		2245	2309	2315	2339	2345	0009	0015
Naarden-Bussum d.	0510	0553	0623	|	0653	|	0723	|	0753	|	0823	|	0853	|	0923	|		2253	|	2323	|	2353	|	0023
Weesp d.	0521	0604	0634	|	0704	|	0734	|	0804	|	0834	|	0904	|	0934	|		2304	|	2334	|	0004	|	0034
Amsterdam Centraal a.	0538	0620	0650	0700	0720	0731	0750	0800	0820	0831	0850	0901	0920	0930	0950	1000		2320	2330	2350	2400	0020	0030	0050
Schiphol ✈ a.	...	0648	0718	...	0748	...	0818	...	0848	...	0918	...	0948	...	1018	...		2348	...	0018	...	0048	...	0118c

SCHIPHOL ✈ - AMSTERDAM ZUID - AMERSFOORT - ENSCHEDE

km		Ⓐ	Ⓐ	⚒H	⚒	⚒	H			H			H				H			H			H		⑤⑥k
0	**Schiphol** ✈ d.	0536	0606	...	0636	0706	...	0736	0806	...	0836	0906	...	0936	and at the same minutes past each hour until	2106	...	2136	2206	...	2236	2306	...	2336	2336
9	Amsterdam Zuid d.	0545	0615	...	0645	0715	...	0745	0815	...	0845	0915	...	0945		2115	...	2145	2215	...	2245	2315	...	2345	2345
14	Duivendrecht d.	0550	0620	...	0650	0720	...	0750	0820	...	0850	0920	...	0950		2120	...	2150	2220	...	2250	2320	...	2350	2350
37	Hilversum d.	0608	0638	...	0708	0738	...	0808	0838	...	0908	0938	...	1008		2138	...	2208	2238	...	2308	2338	...	0008	0008
53	**Amersfoort** d.	0622	0650	0652	0722	0750	0752	0822	0850	0852	0922	0950	0952	1022		2150	2152	2222	2250	2252	2322	2350	2352	0020	0022
96	Apeldoorn d.	0647	...	0717	0747	...	0817	0847	...	0917	0947	...	1017	1047		...	2217	2247	...	2317	2347	...	0017	...	0047
111	**Deventer** d.	0700	...	0730	0800	...	0830	0900	...	0930	1000	...	1030	1100		...	2230	2300	...	2330	0000	...	0030	...	0100
149	Almelo 492 d.	0725	...	0755	0825	...	0855	0925	...	0955	1025	...	1055	1125		...	2255	2325	...	2355	0025	...	0055	...	0125
164	**Hengelo** 492 a.	0735	...	0805	0835	...	0905	0935	...	1005	1035	...	1105	1135		...	2305	2335	...	0005	0035	...	0105	...	0135
172	**Enschede** 492 a.	0744	...	0814	0844	...	0914	0944	...	1014	1044	...	1114	1144		...	2314	2344	...	0014	0044	...	0114	...	0144

	ⒶH	Ⓐ	Ⓐ	⚒	ⒶH	⚒H		⚒		H			H				H			H			U	
Enschede 492 d.	0446	...	0516	...	0546	...	...	0616	...	0646r	...	0716r	0746	...	0816	and at the same minutes past each hour until	2046	...	2116	2146	...	2216	2246	...
Hengelo 492 d.	0454	...	0524	...	0554	...	...	0624	...	0654r	...	0724r	0754	...	0824		2054	...	2124	2154	...	2224	2254	...
Almelo 492 d.	0506	...	0536	...	0606	...	...	0636	...	0706r	...	0736r	0806	...	0836		2106	...	2136	2206	...	2236	2306	...
Deventer d.	0533	...	0603	...	0633	0633	...	0703	...	0733	...	0803	0833	...	0903		2133	...	2203	2233	...	2303	2333	...
Apeldoorn d.	0544	...	0614	...	0644	0644	...	0714	...	0744	...	0814	0844	...	0914		2144	...	2214	2244	...	2314	2344	...
Amersfoort d.	0608	0610	0640	0640	0708	0708	0710	0740	0740	0808	0810	0840	0908	0910	0940		2208	2210	2240	2308	2310	2340	0008	0010
Hilversum d.	...	0623	0653	0653	...	...	0723	0753	0753	...	0823	0853	...	0923	0953		...	2223	2253	...	2323	2353	...	0023
Duivendrecht d.	...	0640	0710	0710	...	...	0740	0810	0810	...	0840	0910	...	0940	1010		...	2240	2310	...	2340	0010	...	0040
Amsterdam Zuid d.	...	0647	0717	0717	...	...	0747	0817	0817	...	0847	0917	...	0947	1017		...	2247	2317	...	2347	0017	...	0047
Schiphol ✈ a.	...	0653	0723	0723	...	...	0753	0823	0823	...	0853	0923	...	0953	1023		...	2253	2323	...	2353	0023	...	0053

Through trains AMSTERDAM CENTRAAL - DEVENTER - HENGELO

	F♥	v♥	Ⓐ	♥	Ⓐ	♥	Ⓐ	♥	Ⓐ	♥	Ⓐ	♥	Ⓐ	⑥k	E♥
Amsterdam Centraal d.	0502	0700	0800	0900	1000	1100	1200	1300	1400	1500	1600	1700	1800	1900	1900
Hilversum d.	0526	0722	0822	0922	1022	1122	1222	1322	1422	1522	1622	1722	1822	1922	1922
Amersfoort d.	0538	0736	0836	0936	1036	1136	1236	1336	1436	1536	1636	1736	1836	1936	1936
Apeldoorn d.	0603	0802	0902	1002	1102	1202	1302	1402	1502	1602	1702	1802	1902	2002	2002
Deventer d.	0615	0819	0912	1019	1112	1219	1312	1419	1512	1619	1712	1819	1912	2019	2019
Almelo d.	0640	0846	...	1046	...	1246	...	1446	...	1646	...	1846	...	2046	2046
Hengelo a.	0652	0857	...	1057	...	1257	...	1457	...	1657	...	1857	...	2057	2057

	Ⓐ	G♥	A♥	†	Ⓐ	♥	Ⓐ	♥	Ⓐ	♥	Ⓐ	♥	Ⓐ	♥	z♥
Hengelo d.	...	0803	0903	0903	...	1103	...	1303	...	1503	...	1703	...	1903	2103
Almelo d.	...	0816	0916	0916	...	1116	...	1316	...	1516	...	1716	...	1916	2116
Deventer d.	0648	0848	0948	0948	1048	1148	1248	1348	1448	1548	1648	1748	1818	1948	2148
Apeldoorn d.	0700	0900	1000	1000	1100	1200	1300	1400	1500	1600	1700	1800	1830	2000	2200
Amersfoort d.	0726	0926	1026	1026	1126	1226	1326	1426	1526	1626	1726	1826	1856	2026	2226
Hilversum d.	0739	0939	1039	1039	1139	1239	1339	1439	1539	1639	1739	1839	1909	2039	2239
Amsterdam Centraal a.	0800	1000	1100	1100	1200	1300	1400	1500	1600	1701	1801	1901	1930	2101	2301

A – ①–⑥ (not Dec. 26, Apr. 17, June 5, Oct. 2).
B – Mornings of ②③ (not Dec. 27, Apr. 18, June 6).
D – ③–⑦ (also Dec. 26, Apr. 17, June 5).
E – ⑧ to Apr. 6 / from Nov. 5 (not Dec. 25); ⑦ Apr. 9 - Oct. 29 (also Apr. 17, June 5; not Apr. 16, June 4).
F – ①–⑥ Apr. 8 - Nov. 4 (not Apr. 17, June 5, Oct. 2).
G – ① Apr. 10 - Oct. 30 (also Apr. 18, June 6; not Apr. 17, June 5).
H – From / to Den Haag (Table **481**).
U – 🚌12 Enschede - Utrecht (- Den Haag ⑤⑥ **k**).

c – Mornings of ⑥⑦ (also Apr. 28, May 26, June 6).
k – Also Apr. 27, May 25, June 5.
r – ⚒ only.
v – Not Dec. 25, Jan. 1.
z – Not Dec. 24, 31.
♥ – *IC* service to / from Germany via Bad Bentheim. Conveys 🍸. See Table **22** for further details.

ROTTERDAM and DEN HAAG - UTRECHT - ZWOLLE 481

km		Ⓐ	Ⓐ	⚒		Ⓐ	Ⓐ	⚒		Ⓐ	Ⓐ	⚒	⚒	⚒	⚒	⚒	⚒	⚒		⚒	⚒	⚒		⚒	
0	**Rotterdam** Centraal d.	...	...	...	...	...	0605	...	...	0620	...	...	...	0635	0650	...	...	0705	...	0720	...	...	0735	0750	...
10	Rotterdam Alexander d.	...	...	...	...	...	0613	...	...	0628	...	...	...	0643	0658	...	...	0713	...	0728	...	...	0743	0758	...
	Den Haag Centraal d.	...	0553	...	...	0608	|	...	...	|	0623	...	0638	|	|	0653	0708	|	...	|	0723	0738	|	|	0753
24	Gouda d.	...	0612	...	...	0627	0624	...	...	0639	0642	...	0657	0654	0709	0712	0727	0724	...	0739	0742	0757	0754	0809	0812
56	**Utrecht** Centraal a.	...	0630	...	...	0645	0642	...	...	0657	0700	...	0715	0712	0727	0730	0745	0742	...	0757	0800	0815	0812	0827	0830
56	**Utrecht** Centraal d.	0618	0636	0636	...	...	0648	0648	...	...	0706	0706	...	0718	...	0736	...	0748	...	...	0806	...	0818	...	0836
77	**Amersfoort** a.	0632	0650	0650	...	...	0702	0702	...	...	0720	0720	...	0732	...	0750	...	0802	...	...	0820	...	0832	...	0850
77	**Amersfoort** d.	0635	0652	0652	...	...	0705	0705	...	...	...	...	...	0735	...	0752	...	0805	0805	...	...	...	0835	...	0852
	Deventer **480** a.	|	0727	0727	...	...	|	|	...	...	...	...	...	|	...	0827	...	|	|	...	...	...	|	...	0927
	Enschede **480** a.	|	0814	0814	...	...	|	|	...	...	...	...	...	|	...	0914	...	|	|	...	...	...	|	...	1014
144	**Zwolle** a.	0710	...	...	...	...	0740	0740	...	...	...	...	...	0810	...	...	...	0840	0840	...	...	...	0910	...	...
	Leeuwarden **482** a.	0826	...	...	...	...	|	|	...	...	...	...	...	0917t	...	...	...	|	|	...	...	...	1013	...	...
	Groningen **482** a.	...	...	...	...	...	0843	0843	...	...	...	...	...	...	...	...	...	0943	0943	...	...	...	...	...	...

	⚒			⚒		⚒		⚒		⚒		⚒		⚒		⚒		⚒		⚒		⚒		⚒	
Rotterdam Centraal d.	...	0805	...	0820	...	...	0835	0850	...	...	0905	0920	...	...	0935	0950	...	...	1005	1020	...	...	1035	1050	...
Rotterdam Alexander d.	...	0813	...	0828	...	...	0843	0858	...	...	0913	0928	...	...	0943	0958	...	...	1013	1028	...	...	1043	1058	...
Den Haag Centraal d.	0808	|	...	|	0823	0838	|	|	0853	0908	|	|	0923	0938	|	|	0953	1008	|	|	1023	1038	|	|	1053
Gouda d.	0827	0824	...	0839	0842	0857	0854	0909	0912	0927	0924	0939	0942	0957	0954	1009	1012	1027	1024	1039	1042	1057	1054	1109	1112
Utrecht Centraal a.	0845	0842	...	0857	0900	0915	0912	0927	0930	0945	0942	0957	1000	1015	1012	1027	1030	1045	1042	1057	1100	1115	1112	1127	1130
Utrecht Centraal d.	...	0848	...	...	0906	...	0918	...	0936	...	0948	...	1006	...	1018	...	1036	...	1048	...	1106	...	1118	...	1136
Amersfoort a.	...	0902	...	...	0920	...	0932	...	0950	...	1002	...	1020	...	1032	...	1050	...	1102	...	1120	...	1132	...	1150
Amersfoort d.	...	0905	...	...	...	...	0935	...	0952	...	1005	...	...	...	1035	...	1052	...	1105	...	...	...	1135	...	1152
Deventer **480** a.	...	|	...	...	...	...	|	...	1027	...	|	...	...	...	|	...	1127	...	|	...	...	...	|	...	1227
Enschede **480** a.	...	|	...	...	...	...	|	...	1114	...	|	...	...	...	|	...	1214	...	|	...	...	...	|	...	1314
Zwolle a.	...	0940	...	...	...	...	1010	...	...	...	1040	...	...	...	1110	...	...	...	1140	...	...	...	1210	...	...
Leeuwarden **482** a.	...	|	...	...	...	...	1113	...	...	...	|	...	...	...	1213	...	...	...	|	...	...	...	1313	...	...
Groningen **482** a.	...	1043	...	...	...	...	...	...	...	...	1143	...	...	...	...	...	...	...	1243	...	...	...	...	...	...

Rotterdam Centraal d.	...	1105	1120	...	...	1135	1150	...	and at the same minutes past each hour until	...	2005	2020	...	...	2035	2050	...	2105	...	2135	...	2205	...	2235
Rotterdam Alexander d.	...	1113	1128	...	...	1143	1158	...		...	2013	2028	...	...	2043	2058	...	2113	...	2143	...	2213	...	2243
Den Haag Centraal d.	1108	|	|	1123	1138	|	|	1153		2008	|	|	2023	2038	|	|	2053	|	2123	|	2153	|	2223	|
Gouda d.	1127	1124	1139	1142	1157	1154	1209	1212		2027	2024	2039	2042	2057	2054	2109	2112	2124	2142	2154	2212	2224	2242	2254
Utrecht Centraal a.	1145	1142	1157	1200	1215	1212	1227	1230		2045	2042	2057	2100	2115	2112	2127	2130	2142	2200	2212	2230	2242	2300	2312
Utrecht Centraal d.	...	1148	...	1206	...	1218	...	1236		...	2048	...	2106	...	2118	...	2136	2148	2206	2218	2236	2248	2306	2318
Amersfoort a.	...	1202	...	1220	...	1232	...	1250		...	2102	...	2120	...	2132	...	2150	2202	2220	2232	2250	2302	2320	2332
Amersfoort d.	...	1205	...	...	...	1235	...	1252		...	2105	...	...	...	2135	...	2152	2205	...	2235	2252	2305	...	2335
Deventer **480** a.	...	|	...	...	...	|	...	1327		...	|	...	...	...	|	...	2227	|	...	|	2327	|	...	|
Enschede **480** a.	...	|	...	...	...	|	...	1414		...	|	...	...	...	|	...	2314	|	...	|	0014	|	...	|
Zwolle a.	...	1240	...	...	...	1310	...	...		...	2140	...	...	...	2210	...	...	2240	...	2310	...	2340	...	0010
Leeuwarden **482** a.	...	|	...	...	...	1413	...	...		...	|	...	...	...	2314	...	...	|	...	0016	...	|	...	...
Groningen **482** a.	...	1343	...	...	...	...	...	...		...	2243	...	...	...	...	...	...	2343	...	...	...	0043	...	...

			⚒					⑥⑦c	
Rotterdam Centraal d.	...	2305	2305	...	2335	...	0005	0005	...
Rotterdam Alexander d.	...	2313	2313	...	2343	...	0013	0013	...
Den Haag Centraal d.	2253	|	|	2323	|	2353	|	|	...
Gouda d.	2312	2324	2324	2342	2354	0012	0024	0024	...
Utrecht Centraal a.	2330	2342	2342	2400	0012	0030	0042	0042	...
Utrecht Centraal d.	2336	2348	2348	0006	0018	0036	0048	0048	...
Amersfoort a.	2350	0002	0002	0020	0032	0050	0102	0102	...
Amersfoort d.	2352	0005	0005	...	...	...	...	0106	...
Deventer **480** a.	0027	|	|	...	...	...	...	|	...
Enschede **480** a.	0114	|	|	...	...	...	...	|	...
Zwolle a.	...	0046	0046	...	...	...	...	0141	...
Leeuwarden **482** a.	...	...	|	...	...	...	...	|	...
Groningen **482** a.	...	...	0203	...	...	...	...	0254k	...

km		Ⓐ	Ⓐ	Ⓐ	Ⓐ	Ⓐ	Ⓐ	Ⓐ	Ⓐ	⚒	⚒
	Groningen **482** d.	...	...	...	...	...	...	...	...	...	...
	Leeuwarden **482** d.	...	...	...	...	...	...	...	...	...	...
	Zwolle d.	...	...	...	...	...	...	...	0550	...	...
	Enschede **480** d.	...	...	...	...	0446	...	...	|	...	...
	Deventer **480** d.	...	...	...	...	0533	...	...	|	...	...
	Amersfoort a.	...	...	...	...	0608	...	...	0625	...	...
	Amersfoort d.	...	...	...	...	0610	...	...	0628	0640a	...
	Utrecht Centraal a.	...	...	...	...	0624	...	...	0642	0654a	...
0	**Utrecht** Centraal d.	0600	0603	0614	0618	0630	0633	0644	0648	0700	0703
32	Gouda d.	0619	0622	0634	0637	0649	0652	0704	0707	0719	0722
60	**Den Haag** Centraal a.	0637	|	0652	|	0707	|	0722	|	0737	|
	Rotterdam Alexander d.	...	0632	...	0646	...	0702	...	0716	...	0732
	Rotterdam Centraal a.	...	0640	...	0655	...	0710	...	0725	...	0740

	⚒	⚒	Ⓐ	⚒	⚒	⚒	⚒	⚒	⚒	⚒		⚒		⚒	⚒			⚒	⚒			⚒	⚒		
Groningen **482** d.	...	...	0500j	...	...	...	...	...	...	...	...	0604	...	...	...	...	...	...	...	0716y	...	...	...	...	...
Leeuwarden **482** d.	...	...	|	...	...	...	0544a	...	...	...	...	|	...	...	...	0644h	...	...	...	|	...	...	...	0747v	...
Zwolle d.	...	...	0620	...	...	...	0650	...	...	...	...	0720	...	...	...	0750	...	...	...	0820	...	...	...	0850	...
Enschede **480** d.	...	...	|	0546a	...	...	|	...	...	...	...	|	0646r	...	...	|	...	...	...	|	0746	...	...	|	...
Deventer **480** d.	...	...	|	0633	...	...	|	...	...	...	...	|	0733	...	...	|	...	...	...	|	0833	...	...	|	...
Amersfoort a.	...	...	0655	0708	...	...	0725	...	...	...	...	0755	0808	...	...	0825	...	...	...	0855	0908	...	...	0925	...
Amersfoort d.	...	...	0658	0710	...	...	0728	0740	...	...	...	0758	0810	...	...	0828	0840	...	...	0858	0910	...	...	0928	0940
Utrecht Centraal a.	...	...	0712	0724	...	...	0742	0754	...	...	...	0812	0824	...	...	0842	0854	...	...	0912	0924	...	...	0942	0954
Utrecht Centraal d.	0714	0718	0718	0730	0733	0744	0748	0800	0803	0814	0818	0818	0830	0833	0844	0848	0900	0903	0914	0918	0930	0933	0944	0948	1000
Gouda d.	0734	0737	0737	0749	0752	0804	0807	0819	0822	0834	0837	0837	0849	0852	0904	0907	0919	0922	0934	0937	0949	0952	1004	1007	1019
Den Haag Centraal a.	0752	|	|	0807	|	0822	|	0837	|	0852	|	|	0907	|	0922	|	0937	|	0952	|	1007	|	1022	|	1037
Rotterdam Alexander d.	...	0746	0746	...	0802	...	0816	...	0832	...	0846	0846	...	0902	...	0916	...	0932	...	0946	...	1002	...	1016	...
Rotterdam Centraal a.	...	0755	0755	...	0810	...	0825	...	0840	...	0855	0855	...	0910	...	0925	...	0940	...	0955	...	1010	...	1025	...

	⚒	⚒			⚒	⚒			⚒														
Groningen **482** d.	...	...	0817	...	...	...	...	...	...	...	0918	...	...	...	...	...	...	and at the same minutes past each hour until	...	1718	...	...	...	...
Leeuwarden **482** d.	...	...	|	...	...	...	0847	...	...	...	|	...	...	...	0947	...	...		...	|	...	...	...	1747
Zwolle d.	...	...	0920	...	...	...	0950	...	...	...	1020	...	...	...	1050	...	...		...	1820	...	...	...	1850
Enschede **480** d.	...	...	|	0846	...	...	|	...	...	...	|	0946	...	...	|	...	...		...	|	1746	...	...	|
Deventer **480** d.	...	...	|	0933	...	...	|	...	...	...	|	1033	...	...	|	...	...		...	|	1833	...	...	|
Amersfoort a.	...	...	0955	1008	...	...	1025	...	...	...	1055	1108	...	...	1125	...	...		...	1855	1908	...	...	1925
Amersfoort d.	...	...	0958	1010	...	...	1028	1040	...	...	1058	1110	...	...	1128	1140	...		...	1858	1910	...	...	1928
Utrecht Centraal a.	...	...	1012	1024	...	...	1042	1054	...	...	1112	1124	...	...	1142	1154	...		...	1912	1924	...	...	1942
Utrecht Centraal d.	1003	1014	1018	1030	1033	1044	1048	1100	1103	1114	1118	1130	1133	1144	1148	1200	1203		1914	1918	1930	1933	1944	1948
Gouda d.	1022	1034	1037	1049	1052	1104	1107	1119	1122	1134	1137	1149	1152	1204	1207	1219	1222		1934	1937	1949	1952	2004	2007
Den Haag Centraal a.	|	1052	|	1107	|	1122	|	1137	|	1152	|	1207	|	1222	|	1237	|		1952	|	2007	|	2022	|
Rotterdam Alexander d.	1032	...	1046	...	1102	...	1116	...	1132	...	1146	...	1202	...	1216	...	1232		...	1946	...	2002	...	2016
Rotterdam Centraal a.	1040	...	1055	...	1110	...	1125	...	1140	...	1155	...	1210	...	1225	...	1240		...	1955	...	2011	...	2025

																								⑤⑥f	
Groningen **482** d.	...	...	...	1804z	...	...	...	...	...	1918	...	...	...	2018	...	...	...	2118	...	...	...	2218	...	...	...
Leeuwarden **482** d.	...	...	...	|	...	...	...	1847	...	|	...	1947	...	|	...	2047	...	|	...	2147	...	|	...	...	2236
Zwolle d.	...	...	...	1920	...	...	...	1950	...	2020	...	2050	...	2120	...	2150	...	2220	...	2250	...	2320	...	...	2350
Enschede **480** d.	...	...	...	|	1846	...	...	|	...	|	1946	|	...	|	2046	|	...	|	2146	|	...	|	2246	2246	|
Deventer **480** d.	...	...	...	|	1933	...	...	|	...	|	2033	|	...	|	2133	|	...	|	2233	|	...	|	2333	2333	|
Amersfoort a.	...	...	...	1955	2008	...	...	2025	...	2055	2108	2125	...	2155	2208	2225	...	2255	2308	2325	...	2355	0008	0008	0025
Amersfoort d.	1940	...	...	1958	2010	...	...	2028	2040	2058	2110	2128	2140	2158	2210	2228	2240	2258	2310	2328	2340	2358	0010	0010	0028
Utrecht Centraal a.	1954	...	...	2012	2024	...	...	2042	2054	2112	2124	2142	2154	2212	2224	2242	2254	2312	2324	2342	2354	0012	0024	0024	0042
Utrecht Centraal d.	2000	2003	2014	2018	2030	2033	2044	2048	2100	2118	2130	2148	2200	2218	2230	2248	2300	2318	2330	2348	0000	0018	...	0030	...
Gouda d.	2019	2022	2034	2037	2049	2052	2104	2107	2119	2137	2149	2207	2219	2237	2249	2307	2319	2337	2349	0007	0019	0037	...	0049	...
Den Haag Centraal a.	2037	|	2052	|	2107	|	2122	|	2137	|	2207	|	2237	|	2307	|	2337	|	0007	|	0037	|	...	0107	...
Rotterdam Alexander d.	...	2032	...	2046	...	2102	...	2116	...	2146	...	2216	...	2246	...	2316	...	2346	...	0016	...	0046	...	...	...
Rotterdam Centraal a.	...	2040	...	2055	...	2110	...	2125	...	2155	...	2225	...	2255	...	2325	...	2355	...	0025	...	0055	...	...	...

a – Ⓐ only.
c – Also Apr. 28, May 26, June 6.
f – Also Apr. 27, May 25, June 5.
h – ⚒ only. Departs 0636 on ⑥ (also Apr. 27, May 25, June 5).
j – 0504 on ①④⑤.
k – ⑥ only.
r – ⚒ only.
t – 0913 on ⑥ (also Apr. 27, May 25, June 5).
v – 0736 on †.
y – 0704 on ©.
z – 1818 on ©.

482 ZWOLLE - GRONINGEN and LEEUWARDEN

km		⑥		Ⓐ	Ⓐ	ⒶL	Ⓐ	Ⓐ	⑥k	Ⓐ	⚒L	Ⓐ	Ⓐ	⑥kL	⑥k	Ⓐ	Ⓐ	⚒		Ⓒ	Ⓐ		⚒	†M
	Rotterdam Centraal **481** d.	0005	...	...	...	...	...	...	...	...	...	...	...	...	...	...	...	0605a	...	...	...	...	...	...
	Utrecht Centraal **481** d.	0048	...	...	...	...	...	...	...	...	...	...	...	...	...	0618	...	0648	...	...	...	...	...	...
	Amersfoort **481** d.	0106	...	...	...	...	...	...	...	...	...	...	...	...	...	0635	...	0705	...	...	...	...	...	...
	Den Haag Centraal **460** d.	|	...	...	...	...	...	...	...	...	...	...	0533	...	...	|	...	|	...	0603k	0603	...	0633	...
	Schiphol + **460** d.	|	...	...	...	...	...	...	...	...	...	...	0603	...	...	|	...	|	...	0633k	0633	...	0703	...
	Amsterdam Zuid **460** d.	|	...	...	...	...	...	...	...	...	...	...	0612	...	...	|	...	|	...	0642k	0642	...	0712	...
	Zwolle **460 481** a.	0141	...	...	...	...	...	...	...	...	...	...	0713	...	...	0710	...	0740	...	0743k	0743	...	0813	...
0	**Zwolle** d.	0144	...	0544	0548	0614	0618	0624	0644	0645	0648	0654	0715	0715	0718	0721	0724	0745	0745	0748	0751	0754	0815	0815
27	Meppel d.	0200	...	0600	0604	0630	0634	0641	0700	|	0704	0711	|	0731	0735	0737	0741	|	|	0804	0807	0811	|	|
	Steenwijk d.	|	...	|	0613	|	0644	|	|	|	0713	|	|	|	0745	0747	|	|	|	0813	0816	|	|	|
	Heerenveen d.	|	...	|	0629	|	0700	|	|	|	0729	|	|	|	0801	0803	|	|	|	0829	0832	|	|	|
	Leeuwarden a.	|	...	|	0651	|	0723	|	|	|	0751	|	|	|	0824	0826	|	|	|	0851	0855	|	|	|
47	Hoogeveen d.	0213	...	0613	...	0642	...	0653	0713	|	...	0723	|	0743	...	...	0753	|	|	...	...	0823	|	|
77	Assen d.	0233	...	0633	...	0701	...	0712	0733	0725	...	0742	0755	0808	...	...	0812	0825	0825	...	...	0842	0855	0855
104	**Groningen** a.	0254	...	0656	...	0722	...	0733	0754	0743	...	0803	0813	0829	...	...	0833	0843	0843	...	...	0903	0913	0913

	Ⓒ	Ⓐ				⚒						⚒◐											
Rotterdam Centraal **481** d.	0635k	0635	...	0705r	...	...	...	0735	...	0805	...	...	...	0835	...	and at	1805	...	...	...	1835	...	1905
Utrecht Centraal **481** d.	0718k	0718	...	0748r	...	...	...	0818	...	0848	...	...	...	0918	...	the	1848	...	...	...	1918	...	1948
Amersfoort **481** d.	0735k	0735	...	0805	...	...	...	0835	...	0905	...	...	...	0935	...	same	1905	...	...	...	1935	...	2005
Den Haag Centraal **460** d.	|	|	...	|	0703	...	0733	|	...	|	0803	...	0833	|	...	minutes	|	1803	...	1833	|	...	|
Schiphol + **460** d.	|	|	...	|	0733	...	0803	|	...	|	0833	...	0903	|	...	past	|	1833	...	1903	|	...	|
Amsterdam Zuid **460** d.	|	|	...	|	0742	...	0812	|	...	|	0842	...	0912	|	...	each	|	1842	...	1912	|	...	|
Zwolle **460 481** a.	0810k	0810	...	0840	0843	...	0913	0910	...	0940	0943	...	1013	1010	...	hour	1940	1943	...	2013	2010	...	2040
Zwolle d.	0818	0821	0824	0845	0848	0854	0915	0918	0924	0945	0948	0954	1015	1018	1024	until	1945	1948	1954	2015	2018	2024	2045
Meppel d.	|	|	0841	|	0904	0911	|	|	0941	|	1004	1011	|	|	1041		|	2004	2011	|	|	2041	|
Steenwijk d.	0842	0845	|	|	0913	|	|	0942	|	|	1013	|	|	1042	|		|	2013	|	|	2042	|	|
Heerenveen d.	0857	0900	|	|	0929	|	|	0957	|	|	1029	|	|	1057	|		|	2029	|	|	2057	|	|
Leeuwarden a.	0913	0917	|	|	0951	|	|	1013	|	|	1051	|	|	1113	|		|	2051	|	|	2113	|	|
Hoogeveen d.	...	...	0853	|	...	0923	|	...	0953	|	...	1023	|	...	1053		|	...	2023	|	...	2053	|
Assen d.	...	...	0912	0925	...	0942	0955	...	1012	1025	...	1042	1055	...	1112		2025	...	2042	2055	...	2112	2125
Groningen a.	...	...	0933	0943	...	1003	1013	...	1033	1043	...	1103	1113	...	1133		2043	...	2103	2113	...	2133	2143

																							⚒⊖	⑤⑥f
Rotterdam Centraal **481** d.	...	...	...	1935	...	2005	...	...	...	2035	...	2105	...	...	...	2135	...	2205	...	...	...	...	2305	...
Utrecht Centraal **481** d.	...	...	...	2018	...	2048	...	...	...	2118	...	2148	...	...	...	2218	...	2248	...	...	...	...	2348	...
Amersfoort **481** d.	...	...	...	2035	...	2105	...	...	...	2135	...	2205	...	...	...	2235	...	2305	...	...	...	...	0005	...
Den Haag Centraal **460** d.	1903	...	1933	|	...	|	2003	...	2033	|	...	|	2103	...	2133	|	...	|	2203	...	2233	...	|	2303
Schiphol + **460** d.	1933	...	2003	|	...	|	2033	...	2103	|	...	|	2133	...	2203	|	...	|	2233	...	2303	...	|	2333
Amsterdam Zuid **460** d.	1942	...	2012	|	...	|	2042	...	2112	|	...	|	2142	...	2212	|	...	|	2242	...	2312	...	|	2342
Zwolle **460 481** a.	2043	...	2113	2110	...	2140	2143	...	2213	2210	...	2240	2243	...	2313	2310	...	2340	2343	...	0013	...	0046	0043
Zwolle d.	2048	2054	2115	2118	2124	2145	2148	2154	2215	2218	2224	2245	2248	...	2315	2318	...	2345	2348	...	0015	...	0049	0048
Meppel d.	2104	2111	|	|	2141	|	2204	2211	|	2234	2241	|	2304	...	2331	|	...	|	0004	...	0031	...	0105	0104
Steenwijk d.	2113	|	|	2142	|	|	2213	|	|	2243	|	|	2313	...	|	2344	...	|	0013	...	|	...	|	0113
Heerenveen d.	2129	|	|	2157	|	|	2229	|	|	2257	|	|	2329	...	|	2359	...	|	0029	...	|	...	|	0129
Leeuwarden a.	2151	|	|	2213	|	|	2251	|	|	2314	|	|	2351	...	|	0016	...	|	0051	...	|	...	|	0151
Hoogeveen d.	...	2123	|	...	2153	|	...	2223	|	...	2253	|	...	...	2343	...	...	|	...	...	0043	...	0118	...
Assen d.	...	2142	2155	...	2212	2225	...	2242	2255	...	2312	2325	...	...	0002	...	...	0025	...	...	0102j	...	0137	...
Groningen a.	...	2203	2213	...	2233	2243	...	2304	2313	...	2333	2343	...	...	0023	...	...	0043	...	...	0123j	...	0203	...

km		⑥	Ⓐ	Ⓐ	Ⓐ	Ⓐ	⑥k	Ⓐ	⚒	Ⓐ	⑥k	Ⓐ	⑥k	Ⓑb	Ⓐ	Ⓒ	Ⓐ	Ⓒ	Ⓐ	⚒	†	⚒	†	⚒
	Groningen d.	0026	...	0500t	...	0532t	0548	...	0604	0623	...	...	0636	0648	0653	...	...	0704	0716	0723	...	...	0732	0748
	Assen d.	0048	...	0524t	...	0555t	0605	...	0626	0645	...	...	0658	0705	0715	...	...	0726	0735	0745	...	...	0758	0805
	Hoogeveen d.	0107	...	0546	...	0617	|	...	0646	0705	...	...	0717	|	0735	...	...	0746	|	0805	...	...	0817	|
0	**Leeuwarden** d.	|	0507	|	0544	|	|	0607	|	|	0636	0644	|	|	|	0707	0708	|	|	|	0736	0747	|	|
29	Heerenveen d.	|	0528	|	0600	|	|	0628	|	|	0659	0701	|	|	|	0728	0729	|	|	|	0759	0803	|	|
53	Steenwijk d.	|	0545	|	0615	|	|	0645	|	|	0715	0715	|	|	|	0745	0746	|	|	|	0815	0819	|	|
67	Meppel d.	0119	0555	0559	0625	0629	|	0655	0659	0717	0725	0725	0729	|	0747	0755	0756	0759	|	0817	0825	|	0829	|
94	**Zwolle** a.	0135	0612	0615	0642	0645	0645	0712	0715	0733	0742	0742	0745	0745	0803	0812	0812	0815	0815	0833	0842	0842	0845	0845
	Zwolle **460 481** d.	...	0617	0620	0650	0647	0647	0717	0720	...	0750	0750	0747	0747	...	0817	0817	0820	0820	...	0850	0850	0847	0847
	Amsterdam Zuid **460** a.	...	0719	|	|	0750	0750	0819	|	...	|	|	0850	0850	...	0919	0919	|	|	...	|	|	0950	0950
	Schiphol + **460** a.	...	0725	|	|	0756	0756	0825	|	...	|	|	0856	0856	...	0925	0925	|	|	...	|	|	0956	0956
	Den Haag Centraal **460** a.	...	0756	|	|	0826	0826	0856	|	...	|	|	0926	0926	...	0956	0956	|	|	...	|	|	1026	1026
	Amersfoort **481** a.	...	...	0655	0725	...	...	...	0755	...	0825	0825	...	...	...	...	...	0855	0855	...	0925	0925	...	...
	Utrecht Centraal **481** a.	...	...	0712	0742	...	...	...	0812	...	0842	0842	...	...	...	...	...	0912	0912	...	0942	0942	...	...
	Rotterdam Centraal **481** a.	...	...	0755	0825	...	...	...	0855	...	0925	0925	...	...	...	...	...	0955	0955	...	1025	1025	...	...

	⚒◧															Ⓐ	Ⓒ						
Groningen d.	0753	...	0817	0823	...	0848	and at	1653	...	1718	1723	...	1748	1753	...	1804	1818	1823	...	1848	1853	...	1918
Assen d.	0815	...	0835	0845	...	0905	the	1715	...	1735	1745	...	1805	1815	...	1826	1835	1845	...	1905	1915	...	1935
Hoogeveen d.	0835	...	|	0905	...	|	same	1735	...	|	1805	...	|	1835	...	1846	|	1905	...	|	1935	...	|
Leeuwarden d.	|	0808	|	|	0847	|	minutes	|	1708	|	|	1747	|	|	1807	|	|	|	1847	|	|	1908	|
Heerenveen d.	|	0829	|	|	0903	|	past	|	1729	|	|	1803	|	|	1828	|	|	|	1903	|	|	1929	|
Steenwijk d.	|	0846	|	|	0919	|	each	|	1746	|	|	1819	|	|	1845	|	|	|	1919	|	|	1946	|
Meppel d.	0847	0856	|	0917	|	|	hour	1747	1756	|	1817	|	|	1847	1855	1859	|	1917	|	|	1947	1956	|
Zwolle a.	0904	0912	0915	0933	0942	0945	until	1803	1812	1815	1833	1842	1845	1903	1912	1915	1915	1933	1942	1945	2003	2012	2015
Zwolle **460 481** d.	...	0917	0920	...	0950	0947		...	1817	1820	...	1850	1847	...	1917	1920	1920	...	1950	1947	...	2017	2020
Amsterdam Zuid **460** a.	...	1019	|	...	|	1050		...	1919	|	...	|	1950	...	2019	|	|	...	|	2050	...	2119	|
Schiphol + **460** a.	...	1025	|	...	|	1056		...	1925	|	...	|	1956	...	2025	|	|	...	|	2056	...	2125	|
Den Haag Centraal **460** a.	...	1056	|	...	|	1126		...	1956	|	...	|	2026	...	2056	|	|	...	|	2126	...	2156	|
Amersfoort **481** a.	...	...	0955	...	1025	...		...	...	1855	...	1925	...	...	...	1955	1955	...	2025	...	...	...	2055
Utrecht Centraal **481** a.	...	...	1012	...	1042	...		...	...	1912	...	1942	...	...	...	2012	2012	...	2042	...	...	...	2112
Rotterdam Centraal **481** a.	...	...	1055	...	1125	...		...	...	1955	...	2025	...	...	...	2055	2055	...	2125	...	...	...	2155

	Ⓐ																							⊡
Groningen d.	...	1923	...	1948	1953	...	2018	2023	...	2048	2053	...	2118	2123	...	2148	2153	...	2218	2223	...	2248	...	2323
Assen d.	...	1945	...	2005	2015	...	2035	2045	...	2105	2115	...	2135	2145	...	2205	2215	...	2235	2245	...	2305	...	2345
Hoogeveen d.	...	2005	...	|	2035	...	|	2105	...	|	2135	...	|	2205	...	|	2235	...	|	2305	...	|	...	0005
Leeuwarden d.	1920	|	1947	|	|	2008	|	|	2047	|	|	2108	|	|	2147	|	|	2208	|	|	2236	|	2324	|
Heerenveen d.	1941	|	2003	|	|	2029	|	|	2103	|	|	2129	|	|	2203	|	|	2229	|	|	2259	|	2347	|
Steenwijk d.	1957	|	2019	|	|	2046	|	|	2119	|	|	2146	|	|	2219	|	|	2246	|	|	2315	|	0003	|
Meppel d.	2008	2017	|	|	2047	2056	|	2117	|	|	2147	2156	|	2217	|	|	2247	2256	|	2317	2325	|	0013	0017
Zwolle a.	...	2033	2042	2045	2103	2112	2115	2133	2142	2145	2203	2212	2215	2233	2242	2245	2303	2312	2315	2333	2342	2345	0030	0033
Zwolle **460 481** d.	...	...	2050	2047	...	2117	2120	...	2150	2147	...	2217	2220	...	2250	2247	...	2317	2320	...	2350	2347	...	...
Amsterdam Zuid **460** a.	...	...	|	2150	...	2219	|	...	|	2250	...	2319	|	...	|	2350	...	0019	|	...	|	0050	...	...
Schiphol + **460** a.	...	...	|	2156	...	2225	|	...	|	2256	...	2325	|	...	|	2356	...	0025	|	...	|	0056	...	...
Den Haag Centraal **460** a.	...	...	|	2226	...	2256	|	...	|	2326	...	2356	|	...	|	0026	...	0056	|	...	|	0126c	...	...
Amersfoort **481** a.	...	...	2125	...	...	...	2155	...	2225	...	...	...	2255	...	2325	...	...	...	2355	...	0025	...	...	...
Utrecht Centraal **481** a.	...	...	2142	...	...	...	2212	...	2242	...	...	...	2312	...	2342	...	...	...	0012	...	0042	...	...	...
Rotterdam Centraal **481** a.	...	...	2225	...	...	...	2255	...	2325	...	...	...	2355	...	0025	...	...	...	0055	...	...	...	...	...

L – From Lelystadt Centrum (Table **460**).
M – From Lelystadt Centrum (d. 0742).

a – Ⓐ only.
b – Not Apr. 27, May 25, June 5.
c – Mornings of ⑥⑦ (also Apr. 28, May 26, June 6).
f – Also Apr. 27, May 25, June 5.
j – 5–6 minutes later on the mornings of ④⑤ (not Apr. 28, May 26).

k – ⑥ (also Apr. 27, May 25, June 5).
t – 2–4 minutes later on ①④⑤.
r – ⚒ only.

⊡ – On ⑤⑥ (also Apr. 27, May 25, June 5) runs 2–3 minutes later and continues to Almere (Table **460**).
⊖ – Timings Zwolle - Groningen may vary by up to 4 minutes.
◐ – The 1554, 1654, 1754 and 1854 from Zwolle run daily.
◧ – The 1553 from Groningen runs daily.

OLDENZAAL - HENGELO - ZUTPHEN — 488

Operated by **Syntus** (NS tickets valid). 2nd class only

km		H			Ⓐ	Ⓐ	Ⓑb	⚒			⚒					Ⓑb				⚒	†		⚒		†
0	**Oldenzaal** d.	0002	0032	...	0602	0632	...	0702	0732	and at	1402	1432	1502	1532	and	2032	2102	2132	2132	2202	2232	2232	2302	2332	2332
11	**Hengelo** a.	0012	0042	...	0612	0642	...	0712	0742	the same	1412	1442	1512	1542	every 30	2042	2112	2142	2142	2212	2242	2242	2312	2342	2342
11	**Hengelo** d.	0016	0046	...	0616	0646	...	0716	0746	minutes	1416	1446	1516	1546	minutes	2046	2116	2146	...	2216	2246	...	2316	...	2346
26	Goor d.	0031	0100	...	0631	0701	0701	0731	0801	past each	1431	1501	1531	1601	until	2101	2131	2201	...	2231	2301	...	2331	...	2400
39	Lochem d.	0039	...	...	0639	0709	0709	0739	0809	hour until	1439	1509	1539	1609		2109	2139	2209	...	2239	2309	...	2339	...	...
56	**Zutphen** a.	0052	...	...	0653	0723	0723	0753	0823		1453	1523	1553	1623		2123	2153	2223	...	2253	2323	...	2353	...	...

	Ⓐ	Ⓐ	Ⓐ	⚒	Ⓐ		⚒		⚒			⚒							Ⓐ	⚒		⚒		⚒	
Zutphen d.	...	...	0608	...	0636	...	0706f	0736j	0806	0836j	and at	1306	1336j	1406	1436	and	2006	2036	2106	...	2136	...	2236	...	2336
Lochem d.	...	...	0621	...	0651	...	0721	0751	0821	0851	the same	1321	1351	1421	1451	every 30	2021	2051	2121	...	2151	...	2251	...	2351
Goor d.	0530	0600	0630	0630	0700	0700	0730	0800	0830	0900	minutes	1330	1400	1430	1500	minutes	2030	2100	2130	...	2200	...	2300	...	0000
Hengelo a.	0544	0614	0644	0644	0714	0714	0744	0814	0844	0914	past each	1344	1414	1444	1514	until	2044	2114	2144	...	2214	...	2314	...	0014
Hengelo d.	0548	0618	0648	0648	0718	0718	0748	0818	0848	0918	hour until	1348	1418	1448	1518		2048	2118	2148	2148	2218	2248	2318	2348	0018
Oldenzaal a.	0558	0628	0658	0658	0728	0728	0758	0828	0858	0928		1358	1428	1458	1528		2058	2128	2158	2158	2228	2258	2328	2358	0028

H – ②–⑦ (not Dec. 27, Apr. 18). b – Not Apr. 27, May 25, June 5. f – 0708 on ⑥ (also Apr. 27, May 25, June 5). j – 2 minutes later on †.

ZWOLLE - ENSCHEDE — 492

km		Ⓐ	Ⓐ	⚒	⚒						
0	**Zwolle** d.	0548	0618	0648	0718	0748	0818	and	2248	2318	2348
18	Raalte d.	0604	0634	0704	0734	0804	0834	every 30	2304	2334	0004
32	Nijverdal d.	0616	0646	0716	0746	0816	0846	minutes	2316	2346	0016
44	Almelo 480 d.	0630	0700	0730	0800	0830	0900	until	2330	0000	0030
59	Hengelo 480 d.	0647	0717	0747	0817	0847	0917		2347	0017	0047
67	**Enschede** 480 a.	0657	0727	0757	0827	0857	0927		2357	0027	0057

	Ⓐ	Ⓐ	Ⓐ	⚒	⚒					
Enschede 480 d.	*0446*	*0516*	0604	0634	0704	0734	0804	and	2234	2304
Hengelo 480 d.	0514	0545	0615	0645	0715	0745	0815	every 30	2245	2315
Almelo 480 d.	0530	0600	0630	0700	0730	0800	0830	minutes	2300	2330
Nijverdal d.	0544	0614	0644	0714	0744	0814	0844	until	2314	2344
Raalte d.	0553	0623	0653	0723	0753	0823	0853		2323	2353
Zwolle a.	0611	0641	0711	0741	0811	0841	0911		2341	0011

ZWOLLE - EMMEN — 493

Operated by **Arriva** (NS tickets valid)

km		⚒								⚒	⚒
0	**Zwolle** d.	0651	0748t	0818t	0851	0921	and at	2221	2251	2321	2351
23	Ommen d.	0708	0808	0838	0908	0938	the same	2238	2308	2338	0008
34	Mariënberg d.	0715	0815	0845	0915	0945	minutes	2245	2315	2345	0015
55	Coevorden d.	0734	0834	0900	0934	1000	past each	2300	2334	0000	0036
75	**Emmen** a.	0753	0853	0915	0953	1015	hour until	2315	2353	0015	0053

	Ⓐ	Ⓐ	⚒	⚒						⚒	⚒
Emmen d.	0539	0615	0638	0715	0738	0815	and at	2215	2238	2315	2338
Coevorden d.	0559	0631	0659	0731	0759	0831	the same	2231	2259	2331	2359
Mariënberg d.	0616	0646	0716	0746	0816	0846	minutes	2246	2316	2346	0016
Ommen d.	0623	0653	0723	0753	0823	0853	past each	2253	2323	2353	0023
Zwolle a.	0639	0709	0739	0810	0839	0909	hour until	2309	2339	0009	0039

t – 3 minutes later on Ⓒ.

☛ Other journeys Zwolle - Emmen and v.v.: **From Zwolle** at 0551Ⓐ, 0621Ⓐ and 0718Ⓐ. **From Emmen** at 0512Ⓐ.

LEEUWARDEN - GRONINGEN — 494

Operated by **Arriva** (NS tickets valid)

km				Ⓐ	Ⓐ	⑥k	Ⓐ	⚒	Ⓐ	Ⓐ	⚒		Ⓐ	⚒		⚒	⚒		⚒	⚒			⚒	
0	**Leeuwarden** d.	0020	...	0550	0618	0620	0643	0650	0720	0743	0750	0820	0843	0850	0920	0943	0950	1020	1043	1050	1120	1143	1150	and at the same
25	Buitenpost d.	0045	...	0615	0645	0645	0659	0715	0745	0759	0815	0845	0859	0915	0945	0959	1015	1045	1059	1115	1145	1159	1215	minutes past
54	**Groningen** a.	0108	...	0639	0709	0709	0718	0739	0809	0818	0839	0909	0918	0939	1009	1018	1039	1109	1118	1139	1209	1218	1239	each hour until

			⚒						†		
Leeuwarden d.	1820	1843	1850	1920	1943	2020	2043	2120	2143	2220	2320
Buitenpost d.	1845	1859	1915	1945	1959	2045	2059	2145	2159	2245	2345
Groningen a.	1909	1918	1939	2009	2018	2109	2118	2209	2218	2309	0008

			Ⓐ	⚒	Ⓐ	Ⓐ	⑥k	Ⓐ	Ⓐ		⚒
Groningen d.	0029	...	0550	0620	0641	0648	0650	0720	0741	0748r	0820
Buitenpost d.	0051	...	0612	0644	0659	0714	0714	0744	0759	0814	0844
Leeuwarden a.	0116	...	0637	0709	0715	0739	0739	0809	0815	0839	0909

	Ⓐ		⚒	⚒		⚒	⚒		†	⚒		⚒		†	⚒	⚒		†	⚒	⚒				
Groningen d.	0841	0848r	0920	0941	0950	1020	1041	1050	1120	1120	and at the same	1841	1850	1920	1920	1941	1950	2020	2020	2041	2050	2120	2220	2320
Buitenpost d.	0859	0914	0944	0959	1014	1044	1059	1114	1139	1144	minutes past	1859	1914	1939	1944	1959	2014	2039	2044	2059	2114	2143	2243	2343
Leeuwarden a.	0915	0939	1009	1015	1039	1109	1115	1139	1200	1209	each hour until	1915	1939	2000	2009	2015	2039	2100	2109	2115	2139	2208	2308	0008

k – Also Apr. 27, May 25, June 5. r – 2 minutes later on Ⓒ.

GRONINGEN - BAD NIEUWESCHANS - LEER — 495

Operated by **Arriva** (NS tickets valid)

km			Ⓐ	⑥k	Ⓐ	Ⓐ	Ⓐ	Ⓒ	Ⓒ	Ⓐ	⚒	⚒				⚒		⚒						
0	**Groningen** 498 d.	0022	0506	0546	0550	0619	0650	0652	0722	0723	0752	0822	0852	and at the same	1722	1752	1822	1852	1922	2022	2122	2222	2322
15	Hoogezand-Sappemeer 498 d.	0037	0521	0601	0605	0634	0704	0707	0737	0737	0807	0837	0907	minutes past	1737	1807	1837	1907	1937	2037	2137	2237	2337
34	Winschoten a.	0056	0540	0621	0624	0653	0723	0726	0756	0756	0826	0856	0926	each hour until	1756	1826	1856	1926	1956	2056	2156	2256	2357
46	**Bad Nieuweschans** a.	0106	0550	0633	0642	...	*0742*	0742k	0810j	...	0842r	0910j	0942		1810j	1842	1910	...	2010	2110	2210	2312	0006

			Ⓐ	Ⓐ	⑥k	Ⓐ	Ⓐ	Ⓒ	⚒			⚒			⚒		⚒				⚒		
Bad Nieuweschans d.	0010	0110	...	0616	...	...	*0711*	0716k	...	0816‡	0849j	0916	0949j	and at the same	1816	1849j	1913	1949	2049	2149	2219	2249	2319
Winschoten d.	0019	0119	0554	0627	0628	0658	0727	0731	0801	0831	0901	0931	1001	minutes past	1831	1901	1931	2001	2101	2201	2231	2301	2331
Hoogezand-Sappemeer 498 d.	0039	0138	0613	0646	0647	0717	0746	0750	0820	0850	0920	0950	1020	each hour until	1850	1920	1950	2020	2120	2220	2250	2320	2350
Groningen a.	0056	0155	0630	0703	0703	0734	0803	0807	0837	0907	0937	1007	1037		1907	1937	2007	2037	2137	2237	2307	2337	0007

Service to/from Leer (operates until further notice). Dutch holiday dates apply (see page 248). See panel above for full service Groningen - Bad Nieuweschans and v.v.

	Ⓐ	⑥h	Ⓐ	Ⓐ	⑥h	⑦t	Ⓐ	⑥h	⑦t	⊡		⑦t	⊡						⊡🚌	🚌	🚌	🚌	🚌	🚌	🚌
Groningen d.	0506	0546	0550	0650v	0652	0722	0752v	0752	0822	0852	and at	1722	1752	1822	1922	2022	2122	ALSO	0630	0830	1030	1230	1430	1630	1830
Bad Nieuweschans 🏛 d.	0551	0634	0643	0743	0743	0811	0843	0843	0911	0943	the same	1811	1843	1911	2011	2111	2211		|	|	|	|	|	|	|
Weener a.	0601	0643	0653	0753	0753	0820	0853	0853	0920	0953	minutes past each	1820	1853	1920	2020	2120	2220		|	|	|	|	|	|	|
Leer a.	*0627**	*0710**	*0723**	*0823**	*0823**	*0850**	*0923**	*0923**	*0950**	*1023**	hour until	*1830**	*1923**	*1950**	*2050**	*2150**	*2250**		0725	0925	1125	1325	1525	1725	1925

	Ⓐ	Ⓐ	⑥h	Ⓐ	⑥h		⑦t	⊡		⑦t	⊡								⊡🚌						
Leer d.	*0530**	*0630**	*0630**	*0730**	*0730**	...	*0808**	*0830**	and at	*1808**	*1830**	*1908**	*2008**	*2108**	*2208**	...	...	ALSO	0730	0930	1130	1330	1530	1730	1930
Weener d.	0605	0700	0705	0805	0805	...	0839	0905	the same	1839	1900	1939	2039	2139	2239	...	...		|	|	|	|	|	|	|
Bad Nieuweschans 🏛 a.	0615	0710	0715	0815	0815	...	0849	0915	minutes past each	1849	1910	1949	2049	2149	2249				|	|	|	|	|	|	|
Groningen a.	0703	0803v	0807	0907v	0907	...	0937	1007	hour until	1937	2007	2037	2137	2237	2337				0825	1025	1225	1425	1625	1825	2025

h – ⑥ (also Apr. 27, May 25).
j – † only.
k – ⑥ (also Apr. 27, May 25, June 5).
r – Change trains at Winschoten on Ⓐ.
t – ⑦ (also Dec. 26, Apr. 17, June 5).
v – Change trains at Winschoten (see upper panel).
* – By 🚌.
‡ – 0819 on †. Change trains at Winschoten on Ⓐ.
⊡ – ①–⑥ (not Dec. 26, Apr. 17, June 5).

LEEUWARDEN - STAVOREN — 496

Operated by **Arriva** (NS tickets valid); 2nd class only

km		Ⓐ	Ⓐ	⚒	Ⓐ	⚒	Ⓐ	⑥k	†	Ⓐ	⚒	⚒	†	Ⓐ	⚒	⚒	†	Ⓐ	⚒	⚒	†	Ⓐ	⚒	
0	**Leeuwarden** d.	0531	0541	0601	0621	0641	0701	0701	0721	0721	0741	0801	0808	0821	0841	0901	0908	0921	0941	1001	1008	1021	1041	and at the same
22	Sneek a.	0550	0600	0620	0640	0700	0720	0720	0739	0740	0800	0820	0827	0840	0900	0920	0927	0940	1000	1020	1027	1040	1100	minutes past
22	Sneek d.	0551	...	0622	0653	...	0724	0728	...	...	...	0828	0830	...	...	0928	0930	...	...	1028	1030	...	...	each hour until
51	**Stavoren** a.	0618	...	0649	0720	...	0751	0755	...	...	...	0855	0857	...	...	0955	0957	...	...	1055	1057	...	...	

	⚒	†	Ⓐ	⚒	Ⓐ					⑤⑥k	
Leeuwarden d.	1801	1808	1821	1841	1901	1921	2021	2121	2221	2221	2321
Sneek a.	1820	1827	1840	1900	1920	1940	2040	2140	2240	2240	2340
Sneek d.	1828	1830	...	...	...	1941	2041	2141	...	2241	...
Stavoren a.	1855	1857	...	...	...	2007	2107	2207	...	2307	...

	Ⓐ	Ⓐ	Ⓐ	⚒	⚒	†	Ⓐ	⚒	†	Ⓐ	⑥k
Stavoren d.	...	...	0623	...	0654	...	0725	...	...	0801	0802
Sneek a.	...	...	0651	...	0720	...	0751	...	...	0827	0828
Sneek d.	0615	0635	0655	0715	0735	0744	0755	0815	0832	0834	0835
Leeuwarden a.	0636	0656	0716	0736	0756	0803	0816	0836	0853	0856	0856

	Ⓐ	⚒	†	⚒	Ⓐ		⚒	†	⚒	Ⓐ	⚒	Ⓐ	⑥k	†	Ⓐ	⚒	†	⚒	†	⚒	†			⑤⑥k
Stavoren d.	...	...	0904	0902	...	and at the same	...	1804	1802	...	...	...	1907	1907	1915	2012	2013	2112	2113	2212	2213	...	...	2312
Sneek a.	...	...	0930	0928	...	minutes past	...	1830	1828	...	...	...	1933	1933	1941	2038	2039	2138	2139	2238	2239	...	...	2338
Sneek d.	0855	0915	0932	0935	0955	each hour until	1815	1832	1835	1855	1915	1934	1934	1935	1948	2040	2040	2140	2140	2240	2240	...	2345	2345
Leeuwarden a.	0916	0936	0953	0956	1016		1836	1853	1856	1916	1936	1954	1955	1956	2008	2101	2101	2201	2201	2301	2301	...	0005	0005

k – Also Apr. 27, May 25, June 5.

497   ROTTERDAM - HOEK VAN HOLLAND

Service until March 31. Line closed from April 1, for at least five months, and will reopen as an extension of the Rotterdam Metro lines A and B.

km			Ⓐ	🚻	Ⓐ	🚻	Ⓐ		Ⓐ		Ⓐ							
0	Rotterdam Centraal ....d.	0002	...	0532	0602	0617	0632	0647	0702	0717	0732	0747		0802 0832			2302 2332	...	...	...
4	Schiedam Centrum ....d.	0007	...	0537	0607	0622	0637	0652	0707	0722	0737	0752	and every 30	0807 0837			2307 2337	...	...	...
10	Vlaardingen Centrum ....d.	0015	...	0545	0615	0630	0645	0700	0715	0730	0745	0800	minutes until	0815 0845			2315 2345	...	...	...
27	Hoek van Holland Haven ....a.	0032	...	0602	0632	0648	0702	0718	0732	0748	0802	0818		0832 0902			2332 0002	...	...	...
	Hoek van Holland Haven...........d.	0026	...	0556	0626	0641	0656	0711	0726	0741	0756	0811		0826 0856			2326 2356	...	...	...
	Vlaardingen Centrum ....d.	0043	...	0613	0643	0658	0713	0728	0743	0758	0813	0828	and every 30	0843 0913			2343 0013	...	...	...
	Schiedam Centrum ....a.	0051	...	0621	0651	0707	0721	0737	0751	0807	0821	0837	minutes until	0851 0921			2351 0021	...	...	...
	Rotterdam Centraal ....a.	0057	...	0627	0657	0712	0727	0742	0757	0812	0827	0842		0857 0927			2357 0027	...	...	...

498   OTHER BRANCH LINES

ALMELO – MARIËNBERG   Operated by **Arriva** (NS tickets valid)   *19 km.*   Journey time: 17 – 19 minutes.

From Almelo:
0618 Ⓐ, 0648 Ⓐ, 0718 Ⓐ, 0748 🚻, 0818 Ⓐ, 0848, 0948, 1048, 1148, 1248, 1318 🚻, 1348, 1418 🚻, 1448, 1518 🚻, 1548, 1618 🚻, 1648, 1718 🚻, 1748, 1818 🚻, 1848, 1948, 2048, 2148, 2248 and 2357.

From Mariënberg:
0554 🚻, 0624 Ⓐ, 0654 Ⓐ, 0724 🚻, 0754 Ⓐ, 0824, 0854 Ⓐ, 0924, 1024, 1124, 1224, 1324, 1354 🚻, 1424, 1454 🚻, 1524, 1554 🚻, 1624, 1654 🚻, 1724, 1754 🚻, 1824, 1924, 2024, 2124, 2224 and 2324.

AMERSFOORT – EDE-WAGENINGEN   Operated by **Connexxion** (NS tickets valid)   *34 km.*   Journey time: 35 – 39 minutes.

From Amersfoort:
0009 L, 0039 ⑦ c, 0109 ⑦ c, 0511 Ⓐ, 0541 🚻, 0609 🚻, 0639 🚻, 0709, 0739, 0809, 0839 and every 30 minutes until 2339.

All trains call at Barneveld Centrum (17 minutes from Amersfoort)

From Ede-Wageningen:
0022, 0052 L, 0122 ⑦ c, 0152 ⑦ c, 0552 Ⓐ, 0622 🚻, 0652 🚻, 0723 🚻, 0752, 0822, 0852 and every 30 minutes until 2352.

All trains call at Barneveld Centrum (21 minutes from Ede-Wageningen)

APELDOORN – ZUTPHEN   Operated by **Arriva** (NS tickets valid)   *18 km.*   Journey time: 19 – 20 minutes.

From Apeldoorn:
0005, 0635 Ⓐ, 0705 Ⓐ, 0735 Ⓐ, 0805 🚻, 0835, 0905 and every 30 minutes until 2335.

From Zutphen:
0606 Ⓐ, 0636 Ⓐ, 0706 Ⓐ, 0736 🚻, 0806, 0836 and every 30 minutes until 2336.

GRONINGEN – DELFZIJL   Operated by **Arriva** (NS tickets valid)   *38 km.*   Journey time: 37 – 39 minutes.

From Groningen:
0033, 0518 Ⓐ, 0548 🚻, 0618, 0648 🚻, 0718, 0748 🚻 and at 18 and 48 🚻 minutes past each hour until 1718, 1748 🚻; then 1818, 1848 Ⓐ, 1918, 2018, 2048 ④ d, 2118, 2218 and 2318.

From Delfzijl:
0004, 0113, 0530 ① m, 0600 Ⓐ, 0630 🚻, 0700, 0730 🚻, 0800, 0830 🚻 and at 00 and 30 🚻 minutes past each hour until 1800, 1830 🚻; then 1900, 1930 Ⓐ, 2000, 2100, 2200 and 2300.

GRONINGEN – VEENDAM 🚂   Operated by **Arriva** (NS tickets valid)   *29 km.*   Journey time: 30 – 32 minutes.

From Groningen:
0008, 0456 Ⓐ, 0535 Ⓐ, 0606 🚻, 0635 Ⓐ, 0656 †, 0708 🚻, 0738 🚻, 0750 †, 0808 🚻, 0838 🚻, 0850 †, 0908 🚻, 0938 🚻, 0952 † and at 08 🚻, 38 🚻 and 52 † minutes past each hour until 1808 🚻, 1838 🚻, 1852 †; then 1908 🚻, 1952, 2052, 2152 and 2250.

All trains call at Hoogezand-Sappemeer (15 minutes from Groningen)

From Veendam:
0048, 0530 🚻, 0615 Ⓐ, 0646 🚻, 0716 Ⓐ, 0730 †, 0746 🚻, 0818 🚻, 0830 †, 0848 🚻, 0918 🚻, 0935 †, 0948 🚻 and at 18 🚻, 35 † and 48 🚻 minutes past each hour until 1918 🚻, 1935 †, 1948 🚻; then 2035, 2135, 2230 and 2332.

All trains call at Hoogezand-Sappemeer (15 minutes from Veendam)

LEEUWARDEN – HARLINGEN Haven ★   Operated by **Arriva** (NS tickets valid)   *26 km.*   Journey time: 25 – 26 minutes.   2nd class.

From Leeuwarden:
0544 🚻, 0619 🚻, 0644 🚻, 0719 🚻, 0744, 0819, 0844, 0919, 0944 🚻, 1019, 1044 🚻, 1119, 1144, 1219, 1244 🚻, 1319, 1344, 1419, 1444, 1519, 1544 🚻, 1619, 1644, 1719, 1744 🚻, 1819, 1844, 1919, 1944, 2019, 2119, 2219 and 2319.

From Harlingen Haven:
0613 🚻, 0648 🚻, 0713 Ⓐ, 0748 🚻, 0813, 0848, 0913, 0948 🚻, 1013, 1048 🚻, 1113, 1148, 1213, 1248 🚻, 1313, 1348, 1413, 1448, 1513, 1548 🚻, 1613, 1648, 1713, 1748 🚻, 1813, 1848, 1913, 1948, 2013, 2048, 2148, 2248 and 2348.

ZWOLLE – KAMPEN   *13 km.*   Journey time: 10 minutes.

From Zwolle:
0548 Ⓐ, 0618 Ⓐ, 0648 🚻, 0718 🚻, 0748 🚻, 0818, 0848 🚻 and at 18 and 48 🚻 minutes past each hour until 1218, 1248 🚻; then 1318, 1348 and every 30 minutes until 2348.

From Kampen:
0002, 0602 Ⓐ, 0632 Ⓐ, 0702 🚻, 0732 🚻, 0802 🚻, 0832 and at 02 🚻 and 32 minutes past each hour until 1302 🚻, 1332; then 1402, 1432 and every 30 minutes until 2332.

L –   ④–⑦ (also June 6).

c –   Also Apr. 28, May 26, June 6.
d –   Not Apr. 27, May 25.
m –   Not Dec. 26, Apr. 17, June 5.

★ –   For 🚢 to / from Terschelling and Vlieland. All trains also call at Harlingen (station for the town centre), 3 minutes from Harlingen Haven.
🚂 –   Station for *Museumspoorlijn S.T.A.R.* Steam trains operate to / from Stadskanaal on ⑦ May - September. www.stadskanaalrail.nl

499   OTHER 🚌 and 🚢 LINES   *Subject to confirmation*

ALKMAAR – LEEUWARDEN 🚌 *Arriva Qliner* route **350**

From Alkmaar rail station:
On Ⓐ at 0521, 0621, 0735, 0835, 0939, 1039, 1139, 1239, 1339, 1435, 1535, 1630, 1730, 1839, 1939, 2039 and 2139.
On ⑥ at 0639 and hourly until 2139.   On † at 0839 and hourly until 2239.

From Leeuwarden bus station:
On Ⓐ at 0602, 0720, 0820 and hourly until 1820; then 1921, 2022, 2122 and 2222.
On ⑥ at 0720 and hourly until 1820; then 1921, 2022, 2122 and 2222.
On † at 0820 and hourly until 1820; then 1921, 2022, 2122 and 2222.

Journey time: 1 hr 54 m – 2 hrs 10 m

DEN HELDER – TEXEL 🚢 *TESO* : ✆ +31 (0) 222 36 96 00
🚌 route 33 : Den Helder rail station (departs 18 minutes before ships sail) to Havenhoofd.
From Den Helder Havenhoofd: 0630 🚻, 0730 🚻 d, 0830 and hourly until 2030; 2130 n.

Journey time: 20 minutes
From Texel ('t Horntje ferryport): 0600 🚻, 0700 🚻 d, 0800 and hourly until 2000; 2100 n.
🚌 route 33 : Den Helder Havenhoofd to rail station (journey: 7 minutes).

ENKHUIZEN – STAVOREN 🚢 *Rederij V & O* ▲ : ✆ +31 (0) 228 32 66 67
From Enkuizen Spoorhaven: 0830 A, 1230 B, 1530 C, 1630 B.

Journey time: ± 90 minutes
From Stavoren: 1010 A, 1410 B, 1710 C, 1810 B.

VLISSINGEN – BRESKENS 🚢 *Westerschelde Ferry* ▲ Journey time: 20 minutes
0603 Ⓐ, 0703 Ⓐ, 0803, 0903 and hourly until 2103; then 2203 Ⓐ.
Additional sailings operate June - August.

BRESKENS ferryport – **BRUGGE** rail station 🚌 *Connexxion* 42 Journey time: 80 minutes
0632 Ⓐ, 0732 🚻, 0832 🚻, 0932, 1032 and hourly until 1932; then 2032 🚻.

BRUGGE rail station – **BRESKENS** ferryport 🚌 *Connexxion* 42 Journey time: 80 minutes
0705 🚻, 0805 🚻, 0905, 1005 and hourly until 2005; then 2105 🚻.

BRESKENS – VLISSINGEN 🚢 *Westerschelde Ferry* ▲ Journey time: 20 minutes
0633 Ⓐ, 0733 Ⓐ, 0833, 0933 and hourly until 2133; then 2233 Ⓐ.
Additional sailings operate June - August.

A –   Daily Apr. 28 - Oct. 1 (also Apr. 15, 16, 22, 23, 25, 26); ⑦ Oct. 7 – 29 (also Oct. 24 – 27).
B –   Daily May 1 - Sept. 30.
C –   Apr. 15, 16, 22, 23, 25, 26, 28, 29, 30, Oct. 1, 7, 8, 14, 15, 21, 22, 24 – 29.

d –   Runs daily Mar. 27 - Oct. 7.
n –   Not Dec. 31.

▲ –   Conveys foot passengers, cycles and mopeds only.

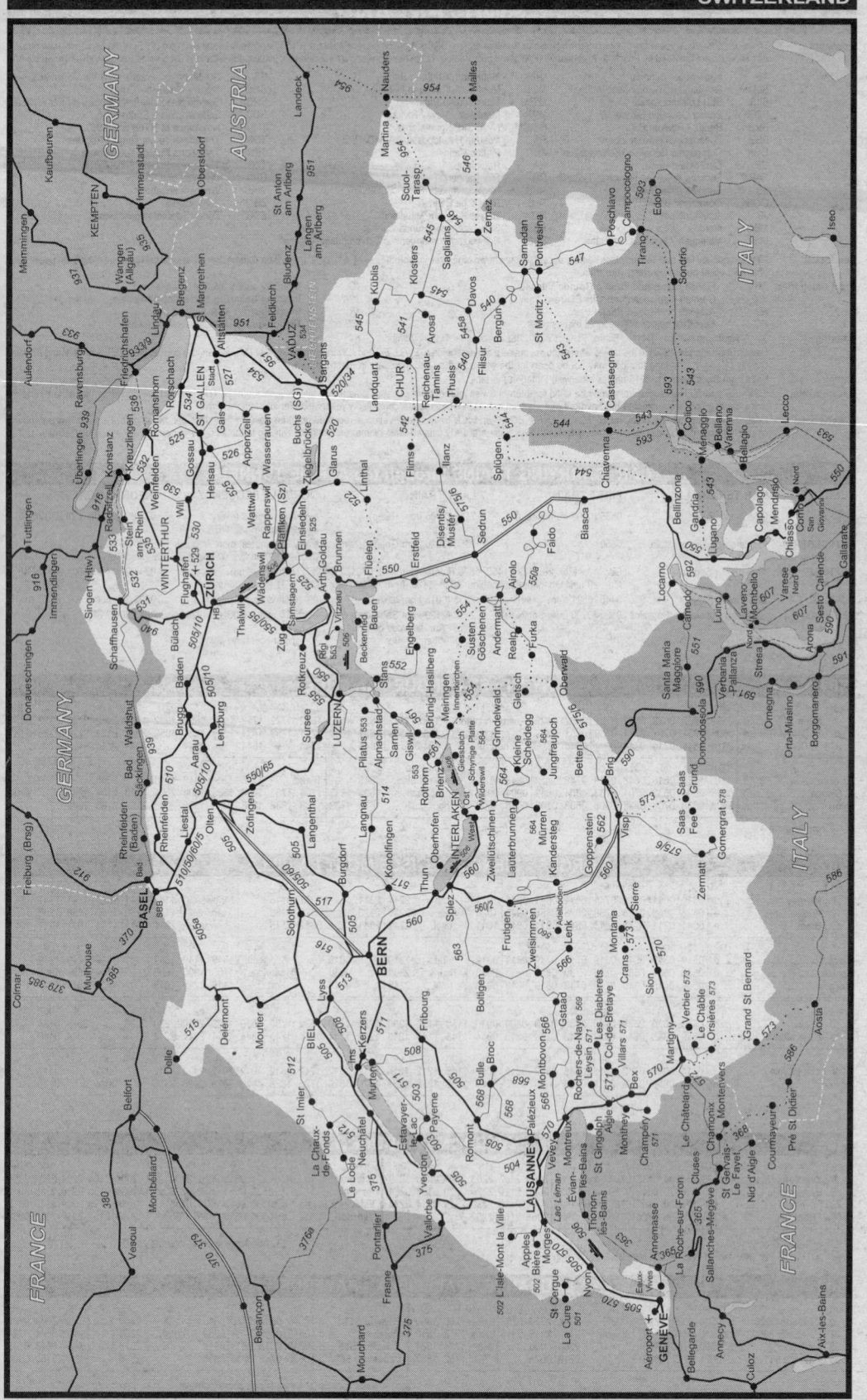

SWITZERLAND

Operators: There are numerous operators of which Schweizerische Bundesbahnen (SBB)/Chemins de fer Fédéraux (CFF)/Ferrovie Federali Svizzere (FFS) is the principal: www.sbb.ch.
Bus services are provided by PostAuto/Autopostale (PA): www.postauto.ch. Table headings show the operators' initials; abbreviations used in the European Rail Timetable are:

AB	Appenzeller Bahnen	MGB	Matterhorn Gotthard Bahn	SGV	Schifffahrtsgesellschaft des Vierwaldstättersees
BLM	Bergbahn Lauterbrunnen - Mürren	MOB	Montreux - Oberland Bernois	SMC	Sierre - Montana - Crans
BLS	BLS Lötschbergbahn	MThB	Mittelthurgau Bahn	SNCF	Société Nationale des Chemins de Fer Francais
BOB	Berner Oberland Bahnen	MVR	Montreux - Vevey Riviera	SOB	Schweizerische Südostbahn
BRB	Brienz - Rothorn Bahn	NStCM	Nyon-St Cergue-Morez	THURBO	an alliance of MThB and SBB
BSB	Bodensee-Schiffsbetriebe	PA	PostAuto / Autopostale / AutoDaPosta	TMR	Transports de Martigny et Régions
CGN	Compagnie Générale de Navigation	PB	Pilatus Bahn	TPC	Transports Publics du Chablais
CP	CarPostal Suisse	RA	RegionAlps	TPF	Transports Publics Fribourgeois
FART	Ferrovie Autolinee Regionali Ticinesi	RB	Rigi Bahnen	URh	Untersee und Rhein
FS	Ferrovie dello Stato	RBS	Regionalverkehr Bern - Solothurn	WAB	Wengernalpbahn
GGB	Gornergrat Bahn	RhB	Rhätische Bahn	ZB	Zentralbahn
JB	Jungfraubahn	RM	Regionalverkehr Mittelland	ZSG	Zürich Schifffahrtsgesellschaft
MBC	Morges - Bière - Cossonay	SBB	Schweizerische Bundesbahnen		
MIB	Meiringen - Innertkirchen Bahn	SBS	Schweizerische Bodensee-Schifffahrtsgesellschaft		

Services: All trains convey first and second class seating except where shown otherwise in footnotes or by a '1' or '2' in the train column. For most local services you must be in possession of a valid ticket before boarding your train.

Train Categories:
TGV	French high-speed **Train à Grande Vitesse**;	IC	**InterCity** quality internal express train;
ICE	German high-speed **InterCity Express** train;	ICN	**InterCity Neigezug** high-speed tilting train;
RJ	Austrian high-speed **Railjet** train;	IR	**InterRegio** fast inter-regional trains;
EC	**EuroCity** quality international express train;	RE	**RegioExpress** semi-fast regional trains.

Catering: ✗ – Restaurant; (✗) – Bistro; (⏲) – Bar coach; ⏲ – Minibar.
Details of catering is shown in the tables where known, but as a general guide ICE, RJ, EC and ICN trains convey ✗ or (✗), IC services convey ✗ or (⏲), and TGV and IR trains convey (⏲) or ⏲. Catering facilities may not be open for the whole journey and may vary from that shown.

Timings: Valid from **December 11, 2016** unless otherwise stated in the table.

Supplements: TGV, ICE and RJ high-speed trains may be used for internal Swiss journeys without supplement. For international journeys TGV services are priced as 'global' fare, and EC trains serving Italy are subject to the payment of a supplement; both types require compulsory reservation for international travel.

Reservations: Seat reservations may be made on all TGV, ICE, RJ, EC, IC and ICN trains. Reservation is recommended for travel in first class panorama cars. Fares in Switzerland are calculated according to distance and many Swiss railways use artificially inflated tariff-kilometres. Distances shown in tables below, however, are actual kilometres.

CAR-CARRYING TRAINS through the ALPINE TUNNELS

TUNNEL	CAR TERMINALS	FIRST TRAIN*	LAST TRAIN*	NORMAL FREQUENCY	INFORMATION ✆
FURKA:	Oberwald - Realp	0535 (0605 from Realp)	2135 (2205 from Realp)	every 60 minutes (every 30 minutes on ①⑤⑥⑦).	027 927 76 66, 027 927 76 76
LÖTSCHBERG:	Kandersteg - Goppenstein	0550	2350 (2320 from Goppenstein)	every 30 minutes, more frequent 0805–2120 on ⑤⑥⑦ and mid-June – mid-Oct.	0900 55 33 33
OBERALP:	Andermatt - Sedrun	Dec. 13 - Mar. 28: 0950, 1450, 1828 (from Andermatt); 0731, 1150, 1725 (from Sedrun). Mar. 29 until Oberalppass opening: 0828, 1728 (from Andermatt); 0731, 1731 (from Sedrun)			027 927 77 07, 027 927 77 40
SIMPLON:	Brig - Iselle (Italy)	0445 (0521 from Iselle)	2336 (0018 from Iselle)	9 – 10 services per day	0900 300 300
VEREINA:	Selfranga (Klosters) - Sagliains	0520 (0550 from Sagliains)	2050 (2120 from Sagliains) Dec. - Apr. services continue for a further 2 hours	every 30 minutes 0620 – 1920	081 288 37 37

*– Not necessarily daily.

---

501 NYON - ST CERGUE - LA CURE
Narrow gauge 2nd class only NStCM

km			Ⓐj	✗	✗		Ⓐj										✗				Ⓐj					k
0	Nyon............d.	0522	0552	0622	0652	0722	0752	0822	and at the same minutes past each hour until	1452	1522	1552	1622	1652	1722	1752	1822	1852	1922	1952	2052	2152	2322	0057
19	St Cergue......d.	0601	0631	0701	0731	0759	0831	0859		1531	1559	1631	1659	1731	1759	1831	1859	1931	1959	2031	2131	2226	2356	0131
27	La Cure ....a.	0614	0644	0714	0744	...	0844	...		1544	...	1644	...	1744	...	1844	...	1944	...	2044	2144	...	...	...

		Ⓐj		Ⓐj	✗		Ⓐj											Ⓐj			
La Cure.............d.			0616	0648	0716	0748		0848	and at the same minutes past each hour until	1548	...	1648	...	1748	...	1848	1948		2048	
St Cergue ....d.	0533	0604	0633	0704	0733	0804	0833	0904	0933	1604	1633	1704	1733	1804	1833	1904	2004	2033	2104	2233	0004
Nyon..................a.	0608	0638	0708	0738	0808	0838	0908	0938	1008	1638	1708	1738	1808	1838	1908	1938	2038	2108	2138	2308	0038

j – Not Sept. 18.　　　　k – ⑥⑦ (not Apr. 15).

---

502 MORGES - BIÈRE and L'ISLE MONT LA VILLE
Narrow gauge 2nd class only MBC

km		✗	✗												X		Ⓐ	Ⓐ	Ⓐ	Ⓐ	Ⓐ	Ⓐ
0	Morges ....d.	0611	0641	0711	0741	0811	0841	0911	1011	and	2211	2311	...	0011	0116	Additional services on Ⓐ	1141	1241	1641	1741	1841	1941
12	Apples ....a.	0628	0658	0728	0758	0828	0858	0928	1028	hourly	2228	2328	...	0028	0133		1158	1258	1658	1758	1858	1958
19	Bière ....a.	0641	0711	0741	0811	0841	0911	0941	1041	until	2241	2341	...	0041	0145		1211	1311	1711	1811	1911	2011

		✗	✗		✗		✗								X		Ⓐ	Ⓐ	Ⓐ	Ⓐ	Ⓐ	Ⓐ
Bière ....d.		0519	0549	0619	0649	0719	0749	0819	0919	and	2319	...	0019		Additional services on Ⓐ	1049	1149	1549		1649	1749	1849
Apples ....d.	0530	0600	0630	0700	0730	0800	0830	0930	hourly	2330	...	0030			1100	1200	1600		1700	1800	1900
Morges ....d.	0549	0619	0649	0719	0749	0819	0849	0949	until	2349	...	0049			1119	1219	1619		1719	1819	1919

km		Ⓐ	Ⓒ	Ⓐ	Ⓐ	Ⓐ	Ⓐ	Ⓐ	Ⓐ	Ⓒ	Ⓐ								X	X
0	Apples ....d.	0556	0630	0630	0700	0730	0730	0803	0930	1130	1130	1230	1430	1630	1630	1830	1930	2030	2230	2330	...	0030	0134
11	L'Isle Mont la Ville .. d.	0610	0643	0644	0713	0743	0744	0813	0944	1143	1144	1213	1244	1444	1644	1744	1844	1944	2044	2244	2344	...	0044	0148

		Ⓐ	Ⓒ	Ⓐ	Ⓐ	Ⓐ	Ⓐ	Ⓐ	Ⓒ	Ⓐ								X	X
L'Isle Mont la Ville .... d.	0614	0645	0712	0715	0745	0812	0815	1012	1145	1212	1215	1312	1512	1712	1812	1912	2012	2112	2312	...	0012	0112
Apples ....a.	0628	0658	0726	0728	0758	0826	0828	1026	1159	1226	1228	1326	1526	1726	1826	1926	2026	2126	2326	...	0026	0126

X – ⑥⑦ (not Apr. 15).

---

503 YVERDON - FRIBOURG
SBB

km		Ⓐ	Ⓐ	Ⓐ	Ⓐ								Ⓐ			Ⓐ			G	Ⓐ
0	Yverdon ....d.	0504	0604	0633	0704	and	1904	2003	2103	2203	2303	0048	0208		Fribourg ....d.	...	0535	0601	0704	and	2004	2104	2204	2304	2338
18	Estavayer-le-Lac......d.	0520	0620	0649	0720	hourly	1920	2020	2120	2220	2320	0104	0224		Payerne ....d.	0530	0601	0630	0730	hourly	2030	2130	2230	2330	0010
28	Payerne ....d.	0530	0630	0700	0730	until	1930	2030	2130	2230	2329	0114	0234		Estavayer-le-Lac......d.	0539	0610	0639	0739	until	2039	2139	2239	2339	0019
50	Fribourg ....a.	0556	0656	0726	0756		1956	2056	2156	2257	...				Yverdon ....a.	0555	0628	0655	0755		2055	2157	2257	2357	0035

G – ①②③④⑦ only.
K – ⑥⑦ (also Dec. 26, Jan. 2, Apr. 14, 17, May 25, June 5, Aug. 1).

Additional services operate on Ⓐ.

---

504 LAUSANNE - PALÉZIEUX - PAYERNE
SBB

km									⑥⑦											
0	Lausanne 505 .... d.	0524	0624	0724	and	2124	2324	0253	Extra	1700	1800		Payerne 511 ..... d.	0540	0640	0738	0840	and	2240	...	Extra	0608	0708
21	Palézieux 505 .... d.	0540	0640	0740	hourly	2140	2346	0315	trains	1718	1818		Moudon............ d.	0559	0659	0759	0859	hourly	2259	...	trains	0624	0724
38	Moudon ....d.	0600	0700	0800	until	2200	0006	...	▶▶	1734	1834		Palézieux 505 .... d.	0618	0718	0818	0918	until	2318	...	▶▶	0643	0743
58	Payerne 511 .....a.	0621	0722	0819		2219	0025	...		1752	1852		Lausanne 505 ..... a.	0636	0736	0836	0936		2336	...		0700	0800

▲ – Times vary by ± 4 minutes on some journeys.

12

km		IR 2155	IR 2155	IR 2355	IC 703	ICN 1507	IR 2159	ICN 507	IR 2357	IC 2505	IC 805	RE 3859	IC 705	ICN 1509	RE 3205	ICN 509	IR 2359	IR 2507	RE 3861	IC 1411	ICN 1511	IC 707	IR 2163	RE 3107
		y	z						Ⓐ		R									Ⓐ				
0	Genève Aéroport ✈ …… 570 d.																							
6	Genève …… 570 d.														0417							0542		0549
27	Nyon …… 570 d.														0435							0605		0605
53	Morges …… 570 d.														0456							0618		0626
66	Lausanne …… 570 a.														0509 ▬							0618		0639
	Lausanne …… d.					0445e						0543		0545						0615	0620	0642		
	Yverdon …… d.											0606								0639				
	Neuchâtel …… d.											0626								0659				
87	Palézieux …… 504 d.					0501e								0601										0658
106	Romont …… 568 d.					0516e						IR		0616										0721r
132	Fribourg …… 508 568 d.					0534			0604			2161		0634							0704			0739a
163	Bern …… 568 a.					0556			0626					0656							0726			
	Bern …… 560 d.	0407	0421	0440	0529p		0539	0600	0602	0607	0632		0634		0639		0707	0707	0711		0732	0734		
	Biel / Bienne …… a.												0642				0715							
	Biel / Bienne …… d.			0516			0543						0616	0644			0717							
186	Burgdorf …… d.			0454				0553			0621			0653		0721								
210	Langenthal …… d.			0513				0612			0641			0712		0741								
	Solothurn …… d.				0533			0601					0633	0701			0734							
230	Olten …… a.	0446	0446	0525	0555	0557		0624		0628	0652		0657	0700	0718	0724		0754		0757		0800		
	Olten …… d.	0448	0448	0535	0557	0559	0602	0620		0631 ▬			0659	0702	0720	0730		0759		0802				
243	Aarau …… d.	0459	0459	0547		0615	0632			0653			0715	0732		0753		0815						
253	Lenzburg …… d.	0506	0506	0554						0700						0800								
	Brugg …… d.					0630							0730				0830							
	Baden …… a.					0638							0738				0838							
285	Zürich HB …… 560 a.	0527	0527	0620	0628	0630	0654	0656		0702	0722	0728	0732	0754	0756	0805		0822	0810	0830	0828	0854		
	Zürich Flughafen ✈ 530/5 a.	0539	0539		0642	0649				0716		0742	0749					0849	0842					
	St Gallen 530 …… a.			0735	0748					0835	0848				0800			0948	0935					
	Luzern …… a.							0700									0800							

km		IR 2361	IR 2509	ICN 511	RE 3863	ICN 1513	IC 709	IR 2165	RE 3109	IR 2363	IR 2511	ICN 513	RE 3865	ICN 1515	IC 711	IR 2167	RE 3111	IR 2365	IR 2513	IC 515	RE 3867	ICN 1517	IC 713	IR 2169
	Genève Aéroport ✈ …… 570 d.		0550	0602			0632			0702	0705			0732				0802	0805			0832		
	Genève …… 570 d.		0600	0612			0642		0649	0712	0715			0742		0749		0812	0815			0842		
	Nyon …… 570 d.		0614	0625					0705							0805								
0	Morges …… 570 d.		0630	0642					0726		0742					0826			0842					
	Lausanne …… 570 a.		0642				0718	0739	0748				0818	0839	0848						0915	0918		
0	Lausanne …… d.		0647			0715	0720	0742	0750			0815	0820	0842	0850					0915	0920			
39	Yverdon …… d.			0707		0739						0807	0839					0907	0939					
75	Neuchâtel …… d.			0727		0759						0827	0859					0927	0959					
	Palézieux …… 504 d.		0703					0758						0858										
	Romont …… 568 d.		0756					0813						0913										
	Fribourg …… 508 568 d.		0734				0804				0834			0904				0934				1004		
	Bern …… 568 a.		0756				0826				0856			0926				0956				1026		
105	Bern …… 560 d.	0739	0800		0807		0832	0834		0839	0900		0907	0932	0934		0939	1000		1007	1032	1034		
	Biel / Bienne …… a.			0743	0815							0843	0915						0943	1015				
	Biel / Bienne …… d.			0746	0817							0846	0917						0946	1017				
	Burgdorf …… d.	0753			0821				0853				0921				0953				1021			
	Langenthal …… d.	0812			0841				0912				0941				1012				1041			
130	Solothurn …… d.			0801	0834				0901				0934				1001				1034			
165	Olten …… a.	0824	0818	0854	0857		0900		0924	0918	0954	0957		1000		1024	1018	1054	1057		1100			
	Olten …… d.	0830	0820		0859	0902	0915		0930	0920 ▬		0959	1002	1030		1020		1059	1102					
178	Aarau …… d.			0832	0853	0915			0932	0953	1015			1032	1053	1115								
	Lenzburg …… d.			0900					1000					1100										
196	Brugg …… d.					0930							1030				1130							
205	Baden …… a.					0938							1038				1138							
227	Zürich HB …… 560 a.	0905	0856	0922	0930	0928	0954		1005		0956	1022	1030	1028	1054		1105		1056	1122	1130	1128	1154	
	Zürich Flughafen ✈ 530/5 a.				0949	0942							1049	1042						1149	1142			
	St Gallen 530 …… a.				1050	1035							1148	1135						1248	1235			
	Luzern …… a.		0900							1000							1100							

		RE 3113	IR 2367	IR 2515	ICN 517	RE 3869	ICN 1519	IC 715	IR 2171	RE 3115	IR 2369	IR 2517	IC 519	RE 3871	ICN 1521	IC 717	IR 2173	RE 3117	IR 2371	IR 2519	IC 521	RE 3873	ICN 1523	IC 719	IR 2175
	Genève Aéroport ✈ …… 570 d.			0902	0905			0932				1002	1005			1032				1102	1105			1132	
	Genève …… 570 d.	0849		0912	0915			0942		0949		1012	1015			1042		1049		1112	1115			1142	
	Nyon …… 570 d.	0905								1005								1105							
	Morges …… 570 d.	0926			0942					1026			1042					1126			1142				
	Lausanne …… 570 a.	0939	0948				1018	1039	1048				1118	1139	1148						1218				
	Lausanne …… d.	0942	0950			1015	1020	1042	1050				1115	1120	1142	1150				1215	1220				
	Yverdon …… d.			1007		1039						1107	1139					1207	1239						
	Neuchâtel …… d.			1027		1059						1127	1159					1227	1259						
	Palézieux …… 504 d.	0958						1058						1158											
	Romont …… 568 d.	1013						1113						1213											
	Fribourg …… 508 568 d.		1034				1104				1134			1204				1234				1304			
	Bern …… 568 a.		1056				1126				1156			1226				1256				1326			
	Bern …… 560 d.	1039	1100		1107		1132	1134		1139	1200		1207	1232	1234		1239	1300		1307	1332	1334			
	Biel / Bienne …… a.			1043	1115							1143	1215						1243	1315					
	Biel / Bienne …… d.			1046	1117							1146	1217						1246	1317					
	Burgdorf …… d.	1053			1121				1153				1221				1253				1321				
	Langenthal …… d.	1112			1141				1212				1241				1312				1341				
	Solothurn …… d.			1101	1134				1201				1234				1301				1334				
	Olten …… a.	1124	1118	1154	1157		1200		1224	1218	1254	1257		1300		1324	1318	1354	1357		1400				
	Olten …… d.	1130	1120		1159	1202	1215		1230	1220 ▬		1259	1302	1330		1320		1359	1402						
	Aarau …… d.			1132	1153	1215			1232	1253	1315			1332	1353	1415									
	Lenzburg …… d.			1200					1300					1400											
	Brugg …… d.					1230							1330				1430								
	Baden …… a.					1238							1338				1438								
	Zürich HB …… 560 a.	1205	1156	1222	1230	1228	1254		1305		1256	1322	1330	1328	1354		1405		1356	1422	1430	1428	1454		
	Zürich Flughafen ✈ 530/5 a.				1249	1242							1349	1342						1449	1442				
	St Gallen 530 …… a.				1348	1335							1448	1435						1550	1535				
	Luzern …… a.		1200							1300							1400								

R – To Romanshorn (Table 535).
a – Ⓐ only.
e – ① (not Jan. 2).
p – Depart 0513 on dates in note y.
r – Arrive 0713.
y – Feb. 6, 11-13, 20, 27, Mar. 25-27, May 1-5, 8-12, 22, June 3-5, 12, July 17, Aug. 5-12, 14-19, Sept. 4, 18-22, 25-29, Oct. 14-16, 28-30, Nov. 6, 13, 27.
z – Daily (not Feb. 6, 11-13, 20, 27, Mar. 25-27, May 1-5, 8-12, 22, June 3-5, 12, July 17, Aug. 5-12, 14-19, Sept. 4, 18-22, 25-29, Oct. 14-16, 28-30, Nov. 6, 13, 27).

505 — GENÈVE - LAUSANNE - BERN / BIEL - ZÜRICH — SBB

Table 1

Station	RE 3119	IR 2373	IR 2521	ICN 523	RE 3875	ICN 1525	IC 721	IR 2177	RE 3121	IR 2375	IR 2523	ICN 525	RE 3877	ICN 1527	IC 723	IR 2179	RE 3123	IR 2377	IR 2525	ICN 527	RE 3879	IC 1429	ICN 1529	IC 725 Ⓐ
Genève Aéroport ✈ 570 d.			1202	1205			1232			1302	1305			1332					1402	1405				1432
Genève 570 d.	1149		1212	1215			1242		1249	1312	1315			1342			1349		1412	1415				1442
Nyon 570 d.	1205								1305								1405							
Morges 570 d.	1226		1242				1326				1342						1426						1442	
Lausanne 570 a.	1239	1248					1318		1339	1348			1418			1439	1439	1448						
Lausanne 570 d.	1242	1250		1315	1320		1342			1350		1415	1420	1442		1442	1450						1515	1520
Yverdon d.			1307		1339							1407		1439						1507			1539	
Neuchâtel d.			1327		1359							1427		1459						1527			1559	
Palézieux 504 d.	1258							1358							1458									
Romont 568 d.	1313							1413							1513									
Fribourg 508 568 d.			1334				1404				1434				1504				1534					1604
Bern 568 a.			1356				1426				1456				1526				1556					1626
Bern 560 d.		1339	1400		1407		1432	1434		1439	1500		1507	1532	1534		1539	1600		1607	1611			1632
Biel / Bienne a.				1343	1415						1443	1515							1543			1615		
Biel / Bienne d.				1346	1417						1446	1517							1546			1617		
Burgdorf d.		1353		1421				1453			1521				1553				1621					
Langenthal d.		1412		1441				1512			1541				1612				1641					
Solothurn d.			1401	1434				1501	1534						1601				1634					
Olten a.		1424	1418	1454	1457		1500		1524		1518	1554	1557		1600		1624		1618	1654		1657		
Olten d.		1430	1420		1459		1502	1530		1520		1559		1602	1630		1620		1659					
Aarau d.			1432	1453			1515			1532	1553		1615				1632	1653						
Lenzburg d.				1500								1600							1700					
Brugg a.						1530								1630										
Baden a.						1538								1638										
Zürich HB 560 a.		1505		1456	1522	1530	1528	1554		1605		1556	1622	1630	1628	1654		1705		1656	1722	1710	1730	1728
Zürich Flughafen ✈ 530/5 a.					1549	1542							1649	1642							1749		1742	
St Gallen 530 a.					1648	1635							1748	1735							1848		1835	
Luzern a.			1500								1600							1700						

Table 2

Station	IR 2181	RE 3125	IR 2379	IR 2527	ICN 529	RE 3881	IC 1431	ICN 1531	IC 727 Ⓐ	IR 2183	RE 3127	IR 2381	IR 2529	ICN 531	RE 3883	ICN 1533	IC 729	IR 2185	RE 3129	IR 2383	IR 2531	ICN 533	RE 3885	ICN 1535
Genève Aéroport ✈ 570 d.				1502	1505			1532				1602	1605			1632				1702	1705			
Genève 570 d.		1449		1512	1515			1542			1549	1612	1615			1632			1649	1712	1715			
Nyon 570 d.		1505						1605											1705					
Morges 570 d.		1526		1542				1626				1642						1726			1742			
Lausanne 570 a.		1539	1548				1618			1639	1648						1718	1739	1748					
Lausanne 570 d.		1542	1550				1615	1620		1642	1650				1715	1720	1742	1750						1815
Yverdon d.			1607		1639							1707		1739						1807		1839		
Neuchâtel d.			1627		1659							1727		1759						1827		1859		
Palézieux 504 d.	1558							1658								1758								
Romont 568 d.	1613							1713								1813								
Fribourg 508 568 d.			1634				1704				1734				1804				1834					
Bern 568 a.			1656				1726				1756				1826				1856					
Bern 560 d.	1634		1639	1700		1707	1711			1732	1734		1739	1800		1807		1832	1834		1839	1900		1907
Biel / Bienne a.					1643	1715							1743	1815							1843			1915
Biel / Bienne d.					1646	1717							1746	1817							1846			1917
Burgdorf d.			1653		1721							1753		1821						1853		1921		
Langenthal d.			1712		1741							1812		1841						1912		1941		
Solothurn d.			1701	1734						1801	1834						1901							1934
Olten a.	1700		1724	1718	1754	1757		1800		1824		1818	1854	1857		1900		1924		1918	1954			1957
Olten d.	1702		1730	1720		1759		1802	1830		1820		1859	1902	1930		1920				1959			
Aarau d.	1715			1732	1753			1815			1832	1853			1915				1932	1953				
Lenzburg d.					1800									1900					2000					
Brugg a.	1730							1830						1930										
Baden a.	1738							1838						1938										
Zürich HB 560 a.	1754		1805		1756	1822	1810	1830	1828	1854		1856	1922	1930	1928	1954		1956			2022			2030
Zürich Flughafen ✈ 530/5 a.						1849	1842							1949	1942									2049
St Gallen 530 a.						1950	1935							2048	2035									2150
Luzern a.				1800								1900							2000					2150

Table 3

Station	IC 731	IR 2187	RE 3131	IR 2385	IR 2533	ICN 535	RE 3887	ICN 1537	IC 733	IR 2189	IR 2387	RE 3133	IR 2535	ICN 537	RE 3889	ICN 1539	IC 735	IR 2191	IR 2389	RE 3135	IR 2537	ICN 539	IC 837 R	RE 3891
Genève Aéroport ✈ 570 d.	1732			1802	1805			1832				1902	1905			1932				2002	2005			
Genève 570 d.	1742	1749		1812	1815			1842			1849	1912	1915			1942			1949	2012	2015			
Nyon 570 d.			1805					1905								2005								
Morges 570 d.			1826		1842			1926					1942			2026					2042			
Lausanne 570 a.	1818		1839		1848			1918			1939	1948				2018			2039	2048				
Lausanne 570 d.	1820		1842		1850			1915	1920		1942	1950			2015	2020			2042	2050				
Yverdon d.				1907		1939							2007		2039					2107		2127		
Neuchâtel d.				1927		1959							2027		2059					2127				
Palézieux 504 d.		1858						1958								2058								
Romont 568 d.		1913						2013								2113								
Fribourg 508 568 d.	1904			1934				2004				2034				2104				2134				
Bern 568 a.	1926			1956				2026				2056				2126				2156				
Bern 560 d.	1932	1934		1939	2000		2007		2032	2034	2039		2100		2107		2132	2134	2138		2200		2202	2207
Biel / Bienne a.					1943	2015							2043	2115						2143				
Biel / Bienne d.					1946	2017							2046	2117						2146				
Burgdorf d.			1953		2021						2053		2121						2154		2212			2223
Langenthal d.			2012		2041						2112		2141						2212		2201			2242
Solothurn d.				2001	2034						2101	2134					2201							
Olten a.	2000		2024	2018	2054	2057		2100	2124		2118	2154	2157		2200	2225		2218	2228					2255
Olten d.	2002		2030	2020		2059		2102		2120		2159		2202	2220		2230							
Aarau d.	2015			2032	2053			2115			2132	2153			2215			2232	2253					
Lenzburg d.					2100									2200					2300					
Brugg a.	2030							2130						2230										
Baden a.	2038							2138						2238										
Zürich HB 560 a.	2028	2054		2105		2056	2122	2130	2128	2154		2156	2222	2230	2228	2254		2256	2302					2322
Zürich Flughafen ✈ 530/5 a.						2149								2249					2316					
St Gallen 530 a.						2248								2348										
Luzern a.					2100							2200							2300					

R – To Romanshorn (Table 535).

SBB — GENÈVE - LAUSANNE - BERN / BIEL - ZÜRICH — 505

	ICN 1541	IC 737	IR 2193	RE 3137	IR 2539	IC 839	ICN 541	RE 3893	ICN 1543	IC 739	RE 3139	IC 2541	IC 841	ICN 543	RE 3241	ICN 1545	IR 2543	IC 843	ICN 1547	ICN 1547	RE 3143	RE 3147	RE 3147	IR 2503
															D			g	y	z	g	w	h	
Genève Aéroport + 570 d.		2032				2102				2132											2339	0021	0028	
Genève 570 d.		2042	2049	2100	2112		2125		2142	2147					2219						2349	0031	0038	
Nyon 570 d.			2105	2114	2125		2142			2205					2235						0005	0047	0054	
Morges 570 d.			2126	2130	2142					2226					2256						0026	0108	0115	
Lausanne 570 a.	2115	2118	2139	2142					2218	2239					2309						0039	0121	0128	
Lausanne d.	2115	2120		2145				2215	2220		2245				2315	2347		0015	0022					0130
Yverdon d.	2139							2207	2239						2339			0039	0046					
Neuchâtel d.	2159							2227	2259						2359			0059	0106					
Paléizieux 504 d.				2201							2301							0003						0146
Romont 568 d.				2216							2316							0018						0201
Fribourg 508 568 d.		2204		2234						2304	2334				RE			0036						0218
Bern 568 a.		2226		2256						2326	2356				3895			0101						
Bern 560 d.		2232		2300	2302				2307	2332			0002		0007			0104						
Biel/Bienne a.	2215							2243	2315						0015			0115	0122					
Biel/Bienne d.	2217							2246	2317					2346										
Burgdorf d.									2323						0023									
Langenthal d.									2342						0042									
Solothurn d.	2234							2305	2334					0005										
Olten a.	2257					2328	2330	2355	2357	2358			0028		0055			0130						
Olten d.		2300	2302			2330	2335			0002			0033	0035				0133						
Aarau d.			2315			2347	2353			0014			0047					0145						
Lenzburg d.							0000						0053											
Brugg a.		2330																						
Baden a.		2338																						
Zürich HB 560 a.		2331	2354			0001	0010	0022		0037			0104	0112				0207						
Zürich Flughafen + 530/5 a.																								
St Gallen 530 a.																								
Luzern a.					2400																			

km (via hsl)	RE 3102	IR 2504	ICN 504	RE 3104	IC 702	ICN 1504	RE 3856	IR 2506	ICN 1606	RE 3106	IR 2354	IC 704	ICN 1506	RE 3858	IR 2508	ICN 2356	IR 508	IR 2158	RE 3108	ICN 1508	IR 706	RE 4808	IC 1408
						Ⓐ			D														Ⓐ
Luzern d.													0600										
St Gallen 530 d.																				0509			
Zürich Flughafen + 530/5 d.																				0613			
Zürich HB 560 d.										0519					0555	0603	0606			0630	0632	0638	0649
Baden d.																0622							
Brugg d.																0632							
Lenzburg d.										0540											0658		
Aarau d.										0548					0629	0646					0705		
Olten a.										0557					0626	0638	0657		0700				
0 Olten d.						0506				0536	0602	0602	0606		0636	0640	0659		0702				
Solothurn d.											0626					0658			0726				
Langenthal d.						0518				0548			0618	0648									
Burgdorf d.						0538				0607			0638	0707									
Biel/Bienne a.											0643		0713						0743				
Biel/Bienne d.			0516			0545			0616		0645		0716						0745				
62 Bern 560 a.						0553				0621	0628		0653	0700	0721		0726			0728			0750
Bern 568 d.		0459			0534		0604			0634			0704							0734			
Fribourg 508 568 d.		0521			0556		0626			0656			0726						0756				
Romont 568 d.		0539							0647										0747				
Paléizieux 504 d.		0554							0702										0802				
Neuchâtel d.			0534			0603			0634				0703						0734			0803	
Yverdon d.			0553			0622			0653				0722						0753			0822	
Lausanne a.		0610			0640	0645		0710		0717			0740	0745		0810			0817	0845	0840		
Lausanne 570 d.	0521	0612		0621	0642			0712		0721			0742			0812			0821		0842		
Morges 570 d.	0534		0618	0634				0718		0734						0818			0834				
Nyon 570 d.	0555			0655						0755									0855				
Genève 570 a.	0611	0648	0645	0711	0718			0748	0745	0811			0818			0848			0845	0911		0918	
Genève Aéroport + 570 a.	0620	0657	0654	0720	0727			0757	0754	0827			0857			0854				0927			

km (via hsl)	RE 3860	IR 2510	IR 2358	ICN 510	IR 2160	RE 3110	ICN 1510	IC 708	RE 4810	IC 1410	RE 3862	IR 2512	ICN 2360	IC 512	IR 2162	RE 3112	ICN 1512	IC 710	RE 4812	ICN 2514	IR 2362	ICN 514	IR 2164
							Ⓐ																
Luzern d.		0700								0800										0900			
St Gallen 530 d.						0612	0625									0712	0725						
Zürich Flughafen + 530/5 d.						0713	0718									0813	0818						
Zürich HB 560 d.			0655	0703	0706	0730	0732	0738		0749			0755	0803	0806	0830	0832	0838		0855	0903	0906	
Baden d.					0722										0822							0922	
Brugg d.					0732										0832							0932	
Lenzburg d.								0758										0858					
Aarau d.				0729	0746			0805						0829	0846			0905			0929		0946
Olten a.			0726	0738	0757		0800						0826	0838	0857		0900			0926	0938		0957
0 Olten d.	0706		0736	0740	0759	0802		0806					0836	0840	0859	0902		0906		0936	0940		0959
Solothurn d.				0758			0826							0858			0926				0958		
Langenthal d.	0718		0748			0818					0818	0848				0918				0948			
Burgdorf d.	0738		0807			0838					0838	0907				0938				1007			
Biel/Bienne a.			0813			0843					0913					0943				1013			
Biel/Bienne d.			0816			0845					0916					0945				1016			
61 Bern 560 a.	0753	0800	0821		0826		0828		0850	0853	0900	0921		0926		0928		0953	1000	1021		1026
Bern 568 d.		0804			0834						0904			0934						1004			
Fribourg 508 568 d.		0826			0856						0926			0956						1026			
Romont 568 d.					0847									0947									
Paléizieux 504 d.					0902									1002									
Neuchâtel d.			0834			0903					0934			1003						1034			
Yverdon d.			0853			0922					0953			1022						1053			
Lausanne a.			0917			0945	0940				1017	1045	1040			1110					1034		
Lausanne 570 d.		0912			0921		0942				1012	1021		1042		1112				1118			
Morges 570 d.			0918		0934						1018	1034									1118		
Nyon 570 d.					0955						1055												
Genève 570 a.		0948	0945		1011				1048	1045	1111			1118				1148	1145				
Genève Aéroport + 570 a.		0957	0954		1027				1057	1054	1127			1157					1154				

D – From/to Delémont (Table 505a).

g – ⑥⑦ (not Apr. 15).
h – ⑥⑦ (also Jan. 2, Aug. 1; not Apr. 15).
w – ①–⑤ (also Apr. 15).

y – ①⑦ (also Dec. 27, Jan. 3, Apr. 15,18, May 26, June 6, Aug. 2).
z – ②–⑥ (not Dec. 27, Jan. 3, Apr. 15,18, May 26, June 6, Aug. 2).

505 — ZÜRICH - BIEL / BERN - LAUSANNE - GENÈVE · SBB

Part 1

	RE 3114	ICN 1514	IC 712	RE 4814	IR 2516	IR 2364	ICN 516	IR 2166	RE 3116	ICN 1516	IC 714	RE 4816	IR 2518	IR 2366	ICN 518	IR 2168	RE 3118	ICN 1518	IC 716	RE 4818	IR 2520	IR 2368	ICN 520	IR 2170
Luzern ....d.				1000								1100								1200				
St Gallen 530 ....d.		0812	0825							0912	0925							1012	1025					
Zürich Flughafen + 530/5 .d.		0913	0918							1013	1018							1113	1118					
Zürich HB ....560 d.		0930	0932	0938		0955	1003	1006		1030	1032	1038		1055	1103	1106		1130	1132	1138		1155	1203	1206
Baden ....d.								1022								1122								1222
Brugg ....d.								1032								1132								1232
Lenzburg ....d.			0958								1058								1158					
Aarau ....d.			1005				1029	1046			1105				1129	1146			1205				1229	1246
Olten ....a.		1000	1005			1026	1038	1057		1100				1126	1138	1157		1200				1226	1238	1257
Olten ....d.		1002	1006			1036	1040	1059		1102	1106			1136	1140	1159		1202	1206			1236	1240	1259
Solothurn ....d.		1026					1058			1126					1158			1226					1258	
Langenthal ....d.			1018			1048					1118			1148					1218			1248		
Burgdorf ....d.			1038			1107					1138			1207					1238			1307		
Biel / Bienne ....a.		1043					1113			1143					1213			1243					1313	
Biel / Bienne ....d.		1045					1116			1145					1216			1245					1316	
Bern ....560 a.			1028	1053	1100	1121		1126			1128	1153	1200	1221		1226			1253	1300		1321		
Bern ....568 d.			1034		1104						1134		1204						1234		1304			
Fribourg ......508 568 d.			1056		1126						1156		1226						1256		1326			
Romont ....568 d.	1047																1147							
Palézieux ....504 d.	1102																1202							
Neuchâtel ....d.		1103			1122		1134		1153	1203			1222		1234		1253	1303			1322		1334	1353
Yverdon ....d.		1122					1153			1222					1253			1322					1353	
Lausanne ....a.	1117	1145	1140			1210	1217			1245	1240			1310	1317			1340				1410		
Lausanne ....570 d.	1121	1142				1212	1221			1242				1312	1321			1342				1412		
Morges ....570 d.	1134					1218	1234							1318	1334							1418		
Nyon ....570 d.	1155						1255								1355									
Genève ....570 a.	1211		1218			1248	1245			1311				1318				1345				1411	1418	1448 1445
Genève Aéroport + 570 a.			1227			1257	1254			1327				1327				1357	1354			1427	1457	1454

Part 2

	RE 3120	ICN 1520	IC 718	RE 4820	IR 2522	IR 2370	ICN 522	IR 2172	RE 3122	ICN 1522	IC 720	RE 4822	IR 2524	IR 2372	ICN 524	IR 2174	RE 3124	ICN 1524	IC 722	RE 4824	IR 2526	IR 2374	ICN 526
Luzern ....d.				1300								1400								1500			
St Gallen 530 ....d.		1112	1125							1212	1225							1312	1325				
Zürich Flughafen + 530/5 .d.		1213	1218							1313	1318							1413	1418				
Zürich HB ....560 d.		1230	1232	1238		1255	1303	1306		1330	1332	1338		1355	1403	1406		1430	1432	1438		1455	1503
Baden ....d.								1322								1422							
Brugg ....d.								1332								1432							
Lenzburg ....d.			1258								1358								1458				
Aarau ....d.			1305				1329	1346			1405				1429	1446			1505				1529
Olten ....a.		1300	1305			1326	1338	1357		1400				1426	1438	1457		1500				1526	1538
Olten ....d.		1302	1306			1336	1340	1359		1402	1406			1436	1440	1459		1502	1506			1536	1540
Solothurn ....d.		1326					1358			1426					1458			1526					1558
Langenthal ....d.			1318			1348					1418			1448					1518			1548	
Burgdorf ....d.			1338			1407					1438			1507					1538			1607	
Biel / Bienne ....a.		1343					1413			1443					1513			1543					1613
Biel / Bienne ....d.		1345					1416			1445					1516			1545					1616
Bern ....560 a.			1328	1353	1400	1421		1426			1428	1453	1500	1521		1526			1553	1600		1621	
Bern ....568 d.			1334		1404						1434		1504						1534		1604		
Fribourg ......508 568 d.			1356		1426						1456		1526						1556		1626		
Romont ....568 d.	1347																1547						
Palézieux ....504 d.	1402																1602						
Neuchâtel ....d.		1403			1422		1434		1453	1503			1522		1534		1553	1603			1622		1634
Yverdon ....d.		1422					1453			1522					1553			1622					1653
Lausanne ....a.	1417	1445	1440			1510	1517			1545	1540			1610	1617			1640				1710	
Lausanne ....570 d.	1421	1442				1512	1521			1542				1612	1621			1642				1712	
Morges ....570 d.	1434					1518	1534							1618	1634							1718	
Nyon ....570 d.	1455						1555								1655								
Genève ....570 a.	1511		1518			1548	1545			1611				1618				1645				1711	1748 1745
Genève Aéroport + 570 a.			1527			1557	1554			1627				1627				1657	1654			1727	1757 1754

Part 3

	IR 2176	RE 3126	ICN 1526	IC 724	RE 4826	IR 2528	IR 2376	ICN 528	IR 2178	RE 3128	ICN 1528	IC 726	RE 4828	IR 2530	IR 2378	ICN 530	IR 2180	RE 3130	ICN 1530	IC 728	RE 4830	IR 2532	IR 2380
Luzern ....d.					1600							1700								1800			
St Gallen 530 ....d.			1412	1425							1512	1525							1612	1625			
Zürich Flughafen + 530/5 .d.			1513	1518							1613	1618							1713	1718			
Zürich HB ....560 d.	1506		1530	1532	1538		1555	1603	1606		1630	1632	1638		1655	1703	1706		1730	1732	1738		1755
Baden ....d.	1522								1622								1722						
Brugg ....d.	1532								1632								1732						
Lenzburg ....d.				1558								1658								1758			
Aarau ....d.	1546			1605				1629	1646			1705				1729	1746			1805			
Olten ....a.	1557		1600				1626	1638	1657		1700				1726	1738	1757		1800				1826
Olten ....d.	1559		1602	1606			1636	1640	1659		1702	1706			1736	1740	1759		1802	1806			1836
Solothurn ....d.			1626					1658			1726					1758			1826				1848
Langenthal ....d.				1618			1648					1718			1748					1818			
Burgdorf ....d.				1638			1707					1738			1807					1838			1907
Biel / Bienne ....a.			1643					1713			1743					1813			1843				
Biel / Bienne ....d.			1645					1716			1745					1816			1845				
Bern ....560 a.	1626			1628	1653	1700	1721		1726			1728	1753	1800	1821		1826			1853	1900	1921	
Bern ....568 d.				1634		1704						1734		1804						1834		1904	
Fribourg ......508 568 d.				1656		1726						1756		1826						1856		1926	
Romont ....568 d.		1647							1747								1847						
Palézieux ....504 d.		1702							1802								1902						
Neuchâtel ....d.			1703			1734			1803			1834					1903						
Yverdon ....d.			1722			1753			1822			1853					1922						
Lausanne ....a.		1717	1745	1740		1810	1817			1845	1840		1910	1917			1940				2010		
Lausanne ....570 d.		1721		1742		1812	1821			1842			1912	1921			1942				2012		
Morges ....570 d.		1734					1818	1834						1918	1934								
Nyon ....570 d.		1755						1855							1955								
Genève ....570 a.		1811		1818		1848	1845			1911				1918	1948			1945		2011		2018	2048
Genève Aéroport + 570 a.				1827		1857	1854			1927				1927	1957			1954		2027			

SBB ZÜRICH - BIEL / BERN - LAUSANNE - GENÈVE — 505

	ICN 532	IR 2182	RE 3132	ICN 1532	IC 730	RE 4832	IR 2534	IR 2382	ICN 534	IR 2184	RE 3134	ICN 1534	IC 732	RE 4834	IR 2536	IR 2384	ICN 536	IR 2186	ICN 1536	IC 734	RE 4836	IR 2538	IR 2386	ICN 538
Luzern ....d.							1900	...						2000								2100	...	
St Gallen **530**...............d.			1712	1725							1812	1825							1912	1925				
Zürich Flughafen ✈ 530/5.d.			1813	1818							1913	1918							2013	2018				
Zürich HB.............**560** d.	1803	1806	1830	1832	1838			1855	1903	1906		1930	1932	1938			1955	2003	2006	2030	2032	2038		2055	2103
Baden ....d.		1822								1922								2022						
Brugg ....d.		1832								1932								2032						
Lenzburg ....d.				1858								1958							2058					
Aarau ....d.	1829	1846		1905				1929	1946			2005				2029	2046			2105				2129
Olten ....a.	1838	1857	1900				1926	1938	1957		2000				2026	2038	2057	2100			2105		2126	2138
Olten ....d.	1840	1859	1902	1906		1936	1940	1959		2002	2006			2036	2040	2059	2102		2106			2136	2140
Solothurn ....d.	1858		1926				1958			2026				2058			2126						2158
Langenthal ....d.			1918	1948						2018	2048						2118	2149				
Burgdorf ....d.			1938	2007						2038	2107						2138	2209				
Biel / Bienne ....a.	1913		1943				2013			2043				2113	2143				2213
Biel / Bienne ....d.	1916		1945				2016			2045				2116	2145				
Bern ....**560** a.		1926	1928	1953	2000	2021		2026		2028	2053	2100	2121		2126	2128	2153	2200	2226	
Bern ....**568** d.			1934	2004						2034	2104					2134	2204			
Fribourg ....**508 568** d.			1956	2026						2056	2126					2156	2226			
Romont ....**568** d.		1947						2047			2144						2244			
Palézieux ....**504** d.		2002						2102			2159						2259			
Neuchâtel ....d.	1934		2003				2034		2103			2134		2203				
Yverdon ....d.	1953		2022				2053		2122			2153		2222				
Lausanne ....a.		2017	2045	2040	2110		2117	2145	2140	2215		2245	2240	2315	
Lausanne ....**570** d.		2021		2042	2112		2121		2142				2242	
Morges ....**570** d.	2018	2034			2118		2134				2218	
Nyon ....**570** d.		2055					2155				2233	
Genève ....**570** a.	2045	2111	2118	2148	2145	2211	2218	2247	2318	
Genève Aéroport ✈ ..**570** a.	2054		2127	2157	2154		2227	2256	2327	

	IR 2188	ICN 1538	IC 736	RE 4838	IR 2540	IC 836	IR 2544	IR 2388	ICN 540	IR 2190	IC 738	RE 4840	IR 2542	IC 838	IR 2502	IR 2390	IC 542	IR 2192	IC 740	RE 4842	IC 842	IR 2194	IR 2392	IC 844
				R									**R**	**y**									**g**	**g**
Luzern ....d.				2200								2300											
St Gallen **530**...............d.		2012				2140								2240									
Zürich Flughafen ✈ 530/5.d.		2113																						
Zürich HB.............**560** d.	2106	2130	2132	2138		2202			2203	2206	2232	2238		2302			2303	2306	2332	2338	0002	0006		0102
Baden ....d.	2122									2222									2322			0022		
Brugg ....d.	2132				2158					2232			2258						2332			0030		
Lenzburg ....d.					2205				2229	2246			2305						2358			0005		
Aarau ....d.	2146						2229	2246			2305			2329	2346			0005				
Olten ....a.	2157	2200			2232		2238	2257	2302			2332			2338	2357	0002		0032			0132
Olten ....d.	2159	2202			2235		2237	2240		2304			2335		2337	2340	0004		0035		0037	0135
Solothurn ....d.		2226						2257							0005						
Langenthal ....d.				2249							2349						0049			
Burgdorf ....d.				2309							0009						0109			
Biel / Bienne ....a.		2243					2314				0022						0022			
Biel / Bienne ....d.		2245					2316				0025g									
Bern ....**560** a.	2226		2228		2300	2302		2326		2331	2400	0002		0023		0031		0102			0123	0202
Bern ....**568** d.			2234			2308						0008										
Fribourg ....**508 568** d.			2255			2330						0032										
Romont ....**568** d.						2349						0050										
Palézieux ....**504** d.						0004						0105										
Neuchâtel ....d.		2303	*RE*				2334		*RE*				0043g		*RE*			
Yverdon ....d.		2322	3238				2353		3240				0102g		3100			
Lausanne ....a.		2345			0020		0016				0121		0124g		g	
Lausanne ....**570** d.			2351						0051					0133	
Morges ....**570** d.			0004						0104					0146	
Nyon ....**570** d.			0025						0125					0207	
Genève ....**570** a.			0041						0143					0225	
Genève Aéroport ✈ ..**570** a.			0050g												

R – From Romanshorn (Table **535**). g – ⑥⑦ (not Apr. 15). y – ①⑥⑦ (also Aug. 1; not Apr. 15).

SBB BIEL - BASEL — 505a

km		ICN 1607	RE 3159	ICN 1609		RE 3161	ICN 1611	RE 3163		ICN 1613	RE 3165		ICN 1615	RE 3167	and at the same minutes past each hour until		ICN 1641	RE 3193		ICN 1545 L		RE 3151 ⑦	RE 3151 ⑥			
0	**Biel / Bienne**.....**515** d.	0549	0619	0649		0719	0749	0819		0849	0919		0949	1019			2249	2319		0019		0119	0126			
24	Moutier.............**515** d.	0608	0639	0708		0739	0808	0839		0908	0939		1008	1039			2308	2339		0039		0139	0146			
35	Delémont........**515** d.	0623	0648	0723		0748	0823	0848		0923	0948		1023	1048			2318	2348		0048		0148	0155			
74	**Basel** ....a.	0653		0753			0853			0953			1053				2353								

		RE 3154 G	ICN 1606	RE 3156	ICN 1608	RE 3158		ICN 1610	RE 3160	and at the same minutes past each hour until		ICN 1630	RE 3180		ICN 1632	IC 2232 x	IC 2234 w	RE 3182		ICN 1634	RE 3184	ICN 1636	RE 3186	ICN 1638	RE 3188		ICN 1640	ICN 1642
Basel ....d.		0457		0603		0703			minutes		1703			1803	1816	1827			1903		2003		2103			2203	2303
Delémont............**515** d.	0512	0542	0612	0642	0712		0742	0812	past each	1742	1812		1842	1900	1911	1912		1942	2012	2042	2112	2142	2212		2242	2337
Moutier...............**515** d.	0523	0552	0623	0652	0723		0752	0823	hour	1752	1823		1852			1923		1952	2023	2052	2123	2152	2223		2252	
Biel / Bienne ......**515** d.	0541	0610	0640	0710	0741		0810	0841	until	1810	1841		1910			1941		2010	2041	2110	2141	2210	2241		2310	

G – To Genève Aéroport (Table **505**). w – Ⓐ Jan. 9 - June 16.
L – From Lausanne (Table **505**). x – Ⓐ Dec. 12 - Jan. 6, June 19 - Dec. 8.

✗ – Restaurant (✗) – Bistro (⚱) – Bar coach ⚱ – Minibar

506   SWISS LAKES

LAC LÉMAN
December 11 - April 13   Operator: CGN

✕q	✕q	✕q				†r								d. Genève ⊗ .... a.	↑	✕q	✕q	✕q				†r				
...	...	...	...	1220	...	...	...	...	...	...			d. Genève ⊗ .... a.	↑	...	...	...	...	1455	...	...	...	...	
...	...	...	...	1305	...	...	...	...	...	...		↓	d. Coppet............... d.	↑	...	...	...	...	1405	...	...	...	...	
...	...	...	...	1330	...	...	...	...	...	...		↓	d. Nyon................. d.	↑	...	...	...	...	1340	...	...	...	...	
...	...	...	...	...	...	...	...	...	...	...		↓	d. Yvoire............... d.	↑	...	...	...	...	...	...	...	...	...	
...	...	...	...	...	...	...	...	...	...	...		↓	d. Thonon-les-Bains..... d.	↑	...	...	...	...	...	...	...	...	...	
0540	0700	0820	1005	1145	...	1315	1445	1615	1800	1920	2045	↓	d. Évian-les-Bains...... d.	↑	0530	0655	0815	1000	1135	1305	...	1435	1605	1750	1915	2035
...	...	...	...	...	...	...	...	...	...	...		↓	d. Morges.............. d.	↑	...	...	...	...	...	...	...	...	...	
0615	0735	0855	1040	1220	...	1350	1520	1650	1835	1955	2120		a. Lausanne-Ouchy...... d.	↑	0455	0620	0740	0925	1100	1230	...	1400	1530	1715	1840	2000

†r	†r	†r	†r			d. Lausanne-Ouchy...... a.	↑	†r	†r	†r	†r
...	...	1230	...	...	...	d. Lausanne-Ouchy...... a.		...	...	...	1615	...
...	1205	1335	...	1405	...	1605	↓ d. Vevey-Marché........ d. ↑	...	1200	...	1400	...	1515	...	1600
...	1210	1340	...	1410	...	1610	↓ d. Vevey-La Tour....... d. ↑	...					1507	
...	1240	1405	...	1440	...	1640	d. Montreux............ d.	...					1445	
...	1247	1412	...	1447	...	1647	↓ d. Territet............ d. ↑	...					1432	
...	1255	1420	...	1455	...	1655	d. Château-de-Chillon.. d.	...					1425	
...	1303	...	...	1503	...	1703	↓ d. Villeneuve......... d. ↑	...						
...	...	...	...	...	...	...	d. St Gingolph......... d.	...	1138	...	1338	...	...	1538
...	1325	...	...	1525	...	1725	↓ d. Bouveret........... d. ↑	...	1125	...	1325	...	...	1525
...	1338	...	...	1538	...	...	a. St Gingolph......... d.	...	...	...	...	...	...	...

VIERWALDSTÄTTERSEE
December 11 - April 13   Operator: SGV

	✕	†			†			Ⓐ			d. Luzern (Bahnhofquai).. a.	Ⓐ	✕	†				
...	0912	0912	1012	1112	1200	1312	1412	1512	1612	1718	d. Luzern (Bahnhofquai).. a.	0739	1141	1247	1347	1447	1547	...	1647	1747	1841
...	0922	0922	1022	1122	1210	1322	1422	1522	1622		d. Verkehrshaus Lido..... d.			1335	1435	1535		...	1635	1735	
...	0943	0943	1043	1143	1230	1343	1443	1543	1643	1743	↑ d. Hertenstein.......... d.	0712	1114	1221		1414	1514	...	1614	1714	1814
...	0953	0953	1053	1153	1240	1353	1453	1553	1653	1753	↑ d. Weggis.............. d.	0704	1105	1212	1312	1405	1505	...	1605	1705	1805
...	1009	1009	1109	1209	1254	1409	1509	1609	1709		d. Vitznau............. d.		1049		1256	1349	1449	...	1549	1649	1749
...	1027	1027	1127			1427	1526	1626	1727		d. Beckenried.......... d.		1032	1147		1332	1432	...	1532	1632	1732
...	1045	1045	1145			1445			1745		↑ d. Gersau.............. d.		1014			1314	1414	...			1714
...	1102	1102	1202			1502			1802		↑ d. Treib.............. d.		0957	1121		1257	1357	...			1657
...	1109	1114	1211			1511			1809		↑ d. Brunnen............ d.		0949	1114		1249	1349	...			1649
...			1221			1521					d. Rütli.............. d.					1236	1336	...			1636
...	1136					1532					↑ d. Sisikon............ d.					1324		...			
...	1143					1539					d. Tellsplatte......... d.					1316		...			
...		1235									↑ d. Bauen.............. d.					1221		...			1621
...		1243									d. Isleten-Isenthal.... d.					1212		...			1612
...	1158	1255				1555					a. Flüelen............ d.					1200	1300	...			1600

THUNERSEE
Operator: BLS   December 11 - March 31

⑦	H		H	C				⑦	H		H	C
0940	1010	1140	1240	1440	↓	d. Thun........... a.	↑	1120	1220	1620	1720	1750
0951		1151	1251	1451	↓	d. Hünibach....... d.	↑	1109	1209	1609	1709	1740
1003		1203	1303	1503	↓	d. Oberhofen...... d.	↑	1057	1157	1557	1657	1729
1016		1216	1316	1535	↓	d. Gunten........ d.	↑	1044	1144	1544	1644	1658
1026	1038	1228	1328	1547	↓	d. Spiez......... d.	↑	1034	1134	1534	1634	1648
...	...	1240	1340	1559	↓	d. Faulensee...... d.	↑	...	1120	1520	1620	1637
...	...	1255	1355	1614	↓	d. Merligen....... d.	↑	...	1105	1505	1605	...
...	1057	1302	1402	1621	↓	d. Beatenbucht.... d.	↑	...	1058	1458	1558	1622
...	...	1349	1449	...	↓	a. Interlaken West..... d.	↑	...	...	1410	1510	...

BRIENZERSEE
Operator: BLS   December 11 - March 31

NO SERVICE	↓ d. Interlaken Ost.. a. ↑	NO SERVICE	
	↓ d. Bönigen...... d. ↑		
	d. Iseltwald..... d.		
	d. Giessbach..... d.		
	↓ a. Brienz........ d. ↑		

ZÜRICHSEE
Operator: ZSG   December 11 - April 1

Ⓒ	Ⓒ			Ⓐ	Ⓒ	Ⓒ					Ⓒ			Ⓒ			
0940	1110	1240	1330	1410	1540	1540	1710	↓ d. Zürich (Bürkliplatz).. a. ↑	1105	1235	1405	1535	1705	1725	1835	...
1020	1157t	1320		1457t		1620	1757t	d. Erlenbach........ d.	1020t	1157	1320t	1457	1620t	1653	1757	
1028	1150	1328	1400	1450	1619	1628	1750	↓ d. Thalwil......... d. ↑	1030	1150	1330	1450	1630		1750	...
...	...	...	1407	...	...	...	...	d. Oberrieden....... d.	...	...	...	...	...	...	...	
...	...	...	...	...	...	...	...	↓ d. Wädenswil........ d. ↑	...	...	...	...	...	1612	...	
...	...	1520	...	...	...	...	...	a. Rapperswil........ d.	...	...	...	...	1530	...	...	

C – March 18 - 31.
H – Dec. 25 - Jan. 2. Normally operated by ⚓ historic Steamship.
q – Also Dec. 26.
r – Not Dec. 26.
t – Via Thalwill.
⊗ – Genève has landing stages at Mont-Blanc, Jardin-Anglais, Pâquis and Eaux-Vives. Services do not call at all landing stages.

Operators:
BLS – Schifffahrt Berner Oberland: ✆ +41 (0)33 334 52 11. (www.bls.ch)
CGN – Compagnie Générale de Navigation: ✆ +41 (0)848 811 848. (www.cgn.ch)
SGV – Schifffahrtsgesellschaft Vierwaldstättersee: ✆ +41 (0)41 367 67 67. (www.lakelucerne.ch)
ZSG – Zürichsee Schifffahrtsgesellschaft: ✆ +41 (0)44 487 13 33. (www.zsg.ch)

508   FRIBOURG - MURTEN - INS   TPF
Fribourg - Murten and v.v. subject to replacement by 🚌 July 8 - August 20

km			✕	✕	†					▲			⑤⑥					✕	✕	✕	▲				⑥⑦
0	Fribourg 505 ...... d.		0500	0530	0600	0630	and at the	2130	...	2230	2330		Neuchâtel 511... d.		0636d	0736	and at the	2136		2236	...		⑥⑦
22	Murten .... d.		0530	0600	0630	0700	same minutes	2200		2300	0000		Ins 511 .... d.		0548	0648	0748	same minutes	2148	...	2248	2320	0028
32	Ins 511 .... a.		0540	0610	0640	0710	past each	2210	...	2310	0010		Murten .... d.		0601	0701	0801	past each	2201	...	2301	2333	0041
45	Neuchâtel 511..... a.		...	0624	...	0724	hour until	2224					Fribourg 505 ... a.		0630	0730	0830	hour until	2230	...	2330	0001	0108

d – ✕ only.

▲ – Departures from Fribourg at 1030, 1130; from Neuchâtel at 0936, 1036 do not operate Fribourg - Murten and v.v. on Oct. 1.

SBB

BASEL - ZÜRICH 510

Via Lenzburg

km		IC	EC	IR	ICE	IC	IR	IC	ICE	ICE	IC	EC		ICE	IC	IC	IR	ICE	IC	IC	IR		IC	TGV	IC	IR	EC	IC
		551	191	2247	1251	559	2259	761	1253	1255	561	193		3	3	563	2263	271	271	565	2265		767	9203	553	2267	207	569
			Mq	p				Ⓐ	Ⓒ	Ⓐ	Ⓒ	M		ⒶA	Ⓒ			⚒H	†					♦	y		F	
0	Basel SBB d.	0533	0547	0547	0607	0633	0647	0707	0707	0733	0733	0747	...	0807	0807	0833	0847	0907	0907	0933	0947	...	1007	1033	1033	1047	1107	1133
14	Liestal d.	|	0557	0557	|	|	0657	|	|	|	|	0757	...	|	|	|	0857	|	|	|	0957	...	|	|	|	1057	|	|
50	Aarau d.	|	0624	0624	|	|	0724	|	|	|	|	0824	...	|	|	|	0924	|	|	|	1024	...	|	|	|	1124	|	|
59	Lenzburg d.	|	0631	0631	|	|	0731	|	|	|	|	0831	...	|	|	|	0931	|	|	|	1031	...	|	|	|	1131	|	|
91	Zürich HB a.	0626	0652	0652	0700	0726	0752	0800	0800	0826	0826	0852	...	0900	0900	0926	0952	1000	1000	1026	1052	...	1100	1126	1126	1152	1200	1226
	St Gallen 530 a.	...	0818	0818	...	|	...	...	|	|	|	1018	...	...	...	|	1118	|	|	|	1218	...	...	...	...	1318	...	|
	Chur 520 a.	...	...	...	...	0852	...	...	0922	0952	0952	...	...	...	...	1052	...	1122	1122	1152	...	...	...	...	...	...	...	1352

	IR	IC	IC	IR	ICE	ICE	TGV	IR	IC	IC	IR	ICE	TGV	IR	EC	IC	IR		ICE	IC	IR	IC	IC	IR	ICE	TGV	IR
	2269	771	571	2271	71	1271	9211	2273	775	575	2275	73	9213	2277	9	579	2279		75	581	2281	783	583	2283	77	9219	2285
					Hw	Hx	P					H‡	P		H				H‡						H‡	P	
Basel SBB d.	1147	1207	1233	1247	1307	1307	1333	1347	1407	1433	1447	1507	1533	1547	1607	1633	1647	...	1707	1733	1747	1807	1833	1847	1907	1933	1947
Liestal d.	1157	|	|	1257	|	|	|	1357	|	|	1457	|	|	1557	|	|	1657	...	|	|	1757	|	|	1857	|	|	1957
Aarau d.	1224	|	|	1324	|	|	|	1424	|	|	1524	|	|	1624	|	|	1724	...	|	|	1824	|	|	1924	|	|	2024
Lenzburg d.	1231	|	|	1331	|	|	|	1431	|	|	1531	|	|	1631	|	|	1731	...	|	|	1831	|	|	1931	|	|	2031
Zürich HB a.	1252	1300	1326	1352	1400	1400	1426	1452	1500	1526	1552	1600	1626	1652	1700	1726	1752	...	1800	1826	1852	1900	1926	1952	2000	2026	2052
St Gallen 530 a.	...	...	|	1518	|	|	...	1618	...	|	1718	...	...	1818	...	|	...	...	|	|	2018	...	|	2118	...	...	2218
Chur 520 a.	...	...	1452	...	1522	1522	...	...	...	1652	...	...	...	...	...	1852	...	...	1922	1952	...	...	2052b	...	...	...	...

	IC	IC	ICE	IR	ICE	TGV	IR	IC	IR	IC	
	787	587	1261	2287	79	9223	2289	791	2291	793	
		m	n		H‡	P					
Basel SBB d.	2007	2033	2033	2047	2107	2133	2147	2207	2247	2307	...
Liestal d.	|	|	|	2057	|	|	2157	|	2257	|	...
Aarau d.	|	|	|	2124	|	|	2224	|	2324	|	...
Lenzburg d.	|	|	|	2131	|	|	2231	|	2331	|	...
Zürich HB a.	2100	2126	2126	2152	2200	2226	2252	2300	2352	2400	...
St Gallen 530 a.	...	|	...	2318	...	...	0018	...	...	...	...
Chur 520 a.	...	2252	...	...	...	...	...	...	...	...	...

	IR	ICE	IR	IC	IC	IR	TGV	ICE	IR	IC	IC
	2252	78	2254	556	760	2256	9206	76	2258	560	764
		H‡					P	H‡			
Chur 520 d.	...	...	...	0509d	...	...	...	...	...	0709	...
St Gallen 530 a.	...	...	...	|	...	0542	...	...	...	|	...
Zürich HB d.	0508	0600	0608	0634	0700	0708	0734	0800	0808	0834	0900
Lenzburg d.	0528	|	0628	|	|	0728	|	|	0828	|	|
Aarau d.	0536	|	0636	|	|	0736	|	|	0836	|	|
Liestal d.	0601	|	0701	|	|	0801	|	|	0901	|	|
Basel SBB a.	0612	0652	0712	0727	0753	0812	0827	0853	0912	0927	0953

	IR	TGV	IC	ICE	IR	IC	EC	IR	TGV		ICE	IR	IC	IC	IR	TGV	ICE	IR	IC		EC	IR	TGV	IC	IC	IR	IC
	2260	9210	562	74	2262	564	8	2264	9218		72	2266	568	772	2268	9222	70	2270	572		206	2272	9226	590	778	2274	576
		Pj	k	H‡			H		P		H‡					P	H‡						♦	z			
Chur 520 d.	...	...	0809	...	...	0909	...	...	...	...	1039	...	1109	...	...	...	1239	...	1309	...	...	...	...	...	...	...	1509
St Gallen 530 a.	0742	...	|	...	0842	|	...	0942	...	...	|	...	|	...	1142	...	|	1242	|	...	...	1342	...	...	...	1442	|
Zürich HB d.	0908	0934	0934	1000	1008	1034	1100	1108	1134	...	1200	1208	1234	1300	1308	1334	1400	1408	1434	...	1500	1508	1534	1534	1600	1608	1634
Lenzburg d.	0928	|	|	|	1028	|	|	1128	|	...	|	1228	|	|	1328	|	|	1428	|	...	|	1528	|	|	|	1628	|
Aarau d.	0936	|	|	|	1036	|	|	1136	|	...	|	1236	|	|	1336	|	|	1436	|	...	|	1536	|	|	|	1636	|
Liestal d.	1001	|	|	|	1101	|	|	1201	|	...	|	1301	|	|	1401	|	|	1501	|	...	|	1601	|	|	|	1701	|
Basel SBB a.	1012	1027	1027	1053	1112	1127	1153	1212	1227	...	1253	1312	1327	1353	1412	1427	1453	1512	1527	...	1553	1612	1627	1627	1653	1712	1727

	ICE	ICE	ICE	IR	IC	ICE	IC		IR	IC	ICE	IR	IC	IR	IC		ICE	EC	ICE	ICE	IC	IR	IC	IR	IR	IR	
	272	1172	292	2276	578	1256	782		2278	580	4	2280	582	2282	584		1260	192	1262	1258	790	2286	792	2288	2292	2296	
	♦	♦	♦			n	m				F							M	n	m						t	
Chur 520 d.	...	...	...	...	1609	1639	...	...	...	1709	...	...	1809	...	1909	...	...	...	...	2009	...	...	...	...	...	...	...
St Gallen 530 a.	...	...	...	...	|	|	...	...	1642	|	...	1742	|	1842	|	...	...	1945	...	|	...	2042	...	...	...	...	...
Zürich HB d.	1700	1700	1700	1708	1734	1800	1800	...	1808	1834	1900	1908	1934	2008	2034	...	2100	2108	2134	2134	2200	2208	2300	2308	0008	0108	...
Lenzburg d.	|	|	|	1728	|	|	|	...	1828	|	|	1928	|	2028	|	...	|	2128	|	|	|	2228	|	2328	0028	0128	...
Aarau d.	|	|	|	1736	|	|	|	...	1836	|	|	1936	|	2036	|	...	|	2136	|	|	|	2236	|	2336	0036	0136	...
Liestal d.	|	|	|	1801	|	|	|	...	1901	|	|	2001	|	2101	|	...	|	2201	|	|	|	2301	|	0001	0101	0201	...
Basel SBB a.	1753	1753	1753	1812	1827	1853	1853	...	1912	1927	1953	2012	2027	2112	2127	...	2153	2212	2227	2227	2253	2312	0001	0012	0112	0212	...

Via Baden

km		IR	IR	IR	IR	IR	IR	IR	IR	IR	IR	IR	IR	IR	IR	IR	IR	IR	IR	IR	IR	IR	IR	IR	IR	IR
		2055	1957	2057	1959	2059	1961	2061	1963	2063	1965	2065	1967	2067	1969	2069	1971	2071	1973	2073	1975	2075	1977	2077	1979	2079
0	Basel SBB d.	0437	0513	0537	0613	0637	0713	0737	0813	0837	0913	0937	1013	1037	1113	1137	1213	1237	1313	1337	1413	1437	1513	1537	1613	1637
17	Rheinfelden d.	0449	0525	0549	0625	0649	0725	0749	0825	0849	0925	0949	1025	1049	1125	1149	1225	1249	1325	1349	1425	1449	1525	1549	1625	1649
57	Brugg d.	0520	0600	0620	0700	0720	0800	0820	0900	0920	1000	1020	1100	1120	1200	1220	1300	1320	1400	1420	1500	1520	1600	1620	1700	1720
66	Baden d.	0529	0608	0629	0708	0729	0808	0829	0908	0929	1008	1029	1108	1129	1208	1229	1308	1329	1408	1429	1508	1529	1608	1629	1708	1729
88	Zürich HB a.	0549	0624	0649	0724	0749	0824	0849	0924	0949	1024	1049	1124	1149	1224	1249	1324	1349	1424	1449	1524	1549	1624	1649	1724	1749
	Zürich Flug ✈ 530/5 a.	0604	...	0704	...	0804	...	0904	...	1004	...	1104	...	1204	...	1304	...	1404	...	1504	...	1604	...	1704	...	1804

	IR	IR	IR	IR	IR	IR	IR	IR	IR	IR	IR
	1981	2081	1983	2083	1985	2085	1987	1989	1991	1993	1995
Basel SBB d.	1713	1737	1813	1837	1913	1937	2013	2113	2213	2313	0013
Rheinfelden d.	1725	1749	1825	1849	1925	1949	2025	2125	2225	2325	0025
Brugg d.	1800	1820	1900	1920	2000	2020	2100	2200	2300	0000	0100
Baden d.	1808	1829	1908	1929	2008	2029	2108	2208	2308	0008	0108
Zürich HB a.	1824	1849	1924	1949	2024	2049	2124	2224	2324	0024	0124
Zürich Flug ✈ 530/5 a.	...	1904	...	2004	...	2104	...	...	...	...	...

	IR	IR	IR	IR	IR	IR	IR	IR	IR	IR
	1956	2058	1958	2060	1960	2062	1962	2064	1964	2066
Zürich Flug ✈ 530/5 d.	...	0556	...	0656	...	0756	...	0856	...	0956
Zürich HB d.	0536	0610	0636	0710	0736	0810	0836	0910	0936	1010
Baden d.	0552	0632	0652	0732	0752	0832	0852	0932	0952	1032
Brugg d.	0601	0641	0702	0741	0802	0841	0902	0941	1002	1041
Rheinfelden d.	0635	0713	0734	0810	0834	0910	0934	1010	1034	1110
Basel SBB a.	0650	0731	0747	0824	0847	0924	0947	1024	1047	1124

	IR	IR	IR	IR	IR	IR	IR	IR	IR	IR	IR		IR	IR	IR	IR	IR	IR	IR	IR	IR	IR	IR	IR	IR	IR
	1966	2068	1968	2070	1970	2072	1972	2074	1974	2076	1976		2078	1978	2080	1980	2082	1982	2084	1984	2086	1986	2088	1988	1990	1992
Zürich Flug ✈ 530/5 d.	...	1056	...	1156	...	1256	...	1356	...	1456	...	...	1556	...	1656	...	1756	...	1856	...	1956	...	2056	...	...	...
Zürich HB d.	1036	1110	1136	1210	1236	1310	1336	1410	1436	1510	1536	...	1610	1636	1710	1736	1810	1836	1910	1936	2010	2036	2110	2136	2236	2336
Baden d.	1052	1132	1152	1232	1252	1332	1352	1432	1452	1532	1552	...	1632	1652	1732	1752	1832	1852	1932	1952	2032	2052	2132	2152	2252	2352
Brugg d.	1102	1141	1202	1241	1302	1341	1402	1441	1502	1541	1602	...	1641	1702	1741	1802	1841	1902	1941	2002	2041	2102	2141	2202	2302	0002
Rheinfelden d.	1134	1210	1234	1310	1334	1410	1434	1510	1534	1610	1634	...	1710	1734	1810	1834	1910	1934	2010	2034	2110	2134	2210	2234	2334	0034
Basel SBB a.	1147	1224	1247	1324	1347	1424	1447	1524	1547	1624	1647	...	1724	1747	1824	1847	1924	1947	2024	2047	2124	2147	2224	2247	2347	0047

♦ – **NOTES** (LISTED BY TRAIN NUMBER)

272 – ①–⑤ (not Dec. 26, Apr. 17, May 1, June 5, Oct. 3, 31): [12] and ✕ Zürich - Basel - Hamburg.
292 – ⑦ (also Dec. 26, Apr. 17, May 1, June 5, Oct. 3, 31; not Dec. 25, Apr. 16, 30, June 4, Oct. 1, 29): [12] and ✕ Zürich - Basel - Berlin Ost.
1172 – ⑥ (also Dec. 25, Apr. 16, 30, June 4, Oct. 1, 29): [12] and ✕ Zürich - Basel - Hamburg.
1295 – ⑦ Feb. 12 - Apr. 16, July 2 - Aug. 13 (also Apr. 17; not Apr. 9): [12] and ✕ Kiel - Hamburg - Basel - Zürich.
9203 – ①–⑥ Dec. 12 - Apr. 29; ②–⑥ May 2 - 13; ①–⑥ May 15 - Dec. 9 (not Apr. 17, June 5, Aug. 15): [12] and (🍸) Paris Lyon - Basel - Zürich.
9226 – ⑧ (not May 25, July 14): [12] and (🍸) Zürich - Basel - Paris Lyon.

A – [12] and ✕ Karlsruhe - Basel - Zürich.
F – [12] and ✕ Frankfurt (Main) - Basel - Zürich and v.v.
H – [12] and ✕ Kiel / Hamburg - Basel - Zürich / Chur and v.v.
M – [12] and ✕ München - St Gallen - Basel and v.v.
P – [12] and (🍸) Paris Lyon - Basel - Zürich and v.v.

b – ⑧ only.
d – ⚒ only.
j – Apr. 3 - July 31, Aug. 28 - Dec. 9.
k – Dec. 11 - Apr. 2, Aug. 1 - 27.
m – ①–⑥ (not Dec. 26, Jan. 2, Apr. 17).
n – ⑦ (also Dec. 26, Jan. 2, Apr. 17).
p – Jan. 1 only.
q – Not Jan. 1.
t – ⑥⑦ (not Apr. 15).
w – Daily Dec. 11 - Feb. 10; Ⓐ Feb. 13 - Apr. 21; daily Apr. 22 - June 30, Aug. 14 - Dec. 9 (also Apr. 8, 9).
x – Ⓒ Feb. 11 - Apr. 16; daily July 1 - Aug. 13 (also Apr. 17; not Apr. 8, 9).
y – ⑦ Dec. 11 - Apr. 30; ①⑦ May 1 - 14; ⑦ May 21 - Dec. 3 (also Apr. 17, June 5, Aug. 15).
z – ⑥ (also May 25, July 14).

‡ – Train number varies on some days / dates:
70 runs as **1270**;
72 runs as **1272**;
73 runs as **1173 / 1273 / 1293**;
74 runs as **1274**;
75 runs as **1175 / 1275 / 1295**;
76 runs as **1276**;
77 runs as **1277**;
78 runs as **1278**;
79 runs as **1279**.

511 BERN - PAYERNE and NEUCHÂTEL — BLS

km												⊡				n					m
0	Bern .... d.	0553	0608	...	...	0653	0708	...	...	and at	2053	2108	...	...	2153	2208	...	2253	2308	...	2337	0008	...	m
22	Kerzers .... ▲ d.	0610	0631	0634	...	0710	0731	0734	...	the same	2110	2131	2134	...	2210	2231	2234	...	2310	2331	2334	0003	0034	0036	...
	Murten .... d.		0643	0703	...		0743	0803	minutes			2143	2203				2243	2303				2343			0045	0048
	Avenches .... d.		0649d	0711	...			0811	past each				2211					2311				2350			0056
	Payerne 504 ..... a.		0657d	0723	...			0823	hour				2223					2323				0002			0108
30	Ins 508 .... d.	0617	0638	...		0717	0738	...	until		2117	2138	...		2217	2238	...		2317	2338	...	0013	0041	...
43	Neuchâtel 508 ... a.	0627	0657	...		0727	0757	...			2127	2157	...		2227	2257	...		2327	2357	...	0026	0056	...

km												⊡								
	Neuchâtel 508 ... d.	0536	...	0601	0633	...	...	0701	0733	...	...	0801	0833	and at	...	2201	2233	...	2301	2333	...	...	0009
	Ins 508 .... d.	0552	...	0617	0643	...	...	0717	0743	...	...	0817	0843	the same	...	2217	2243	...	2317	2343	...	...	0025
0	Payerne 504 ..... d.		0556d		0634	0701d		0736			minutes	2136			2236			0006	
11	Avenches .... d.		0609d		0648	0710d		0748			past each	2148			2248			0017	
18	Murten .... d.		0617		0656	0717		0756	0817		hour	2156	2217		2256	2317		0025	
26	Kerzers .... ▲ d.	0600	0626	0630	0649	...	0726	0730	0749	...	until	2226	2230	2249	...	2326	2330	2349	...	0034	0038
	Bern .... a.	0626	0652d	0707	...	0752d	0807	...		0852	0907	...	2252	2307	...	2352	0012	...	0103

d – ⊗ only.
m – ⑥⑦ (also Dec. 26, Jan. 2, Apr. 14, 17, May 25, June 5, Aug. 1).
n – ①②③④⑦ (also Apr. 14).
⊡ – Times may vary ± 2 minutes.

▲ – Rail service KERZERS - LYSS and v.v.: 17 km, journey 20 minutes.
From Kerzers: 0606 and hourly until 2306.   From Lyss: 0535 and hourly until 2335, then 0009.

512 BIEL and NEUCHÂTEL - LA CHAUX DE FONDS - LE LOCLE — SBB

km																		
0	Biel / Bienne .... d.	0547	...	0647	...	...	0747	...	and at	1847	...	...	1947	...	2047	...	2147	...	2247	...	2347	...
28	St Imier .... d.	0613	...	0713	...	...	0813	...	the same	1913	...	...	2017	...	2117	...	2217	...	2317	...	0017	...
	Neuchâtel .... d.		0600		0700	...		0800	minutes		...	1900		2000		2100		2200		2300		0000
44	La Chaux de Fonds ... d.	0628	0631	0728	0731	...	0828	0831	past each	1928	1931	...	2034	2037	2134	2137	2234	2237	2334	2337	0034	0037
52	Le Locle .... a.		0639		0739	...		0839	hour until		1939			2045		2145		2245		2345		0045

km																m	n
0	Le Locle .... d.	0521	...	0621	...	0721	...		0821	and at	1921	...	2021	...	2113	...	2221	...	2321	...
8	La Chaux de Fonds ... d.	0529	0532	0629	0632	0729	0732		0829	0832	the same	1929	1932	1944	2029	2044	2121	2144	2229	2244	2329	2344	2344
37	Neuchâtel .... a.		0600		0700		0800			0900	minutes	2000		2100		2200		2300		2400	
	St Imier .... d.		0545		0645		0745	...		0845	past each	1945	2000	2100	2200	2300	0000	0000
	Biel / Bienne .... a.		0612		0712		0812	...		0912	hour until	2012	2040	2140	2240	2340	0040	0046

m – ①②③④⑦ (also Apr. 15).
n – ⑤⑥ (not Apr. 15).

Additional services operate.

513 BERN - BIEL — SBB

km		Ⓐ																												y
0	Bern .... d.	0500	0530	0600	0613	0630	0643	and at the	2000	2013	2030	2043	...	2100	2113	2132	2200	2213	2232	2300	2313	2332	0013	0015	0113
23	Lyss .... d.	0522	0552	0622	0630	0652	0700	same minutes	2022	2030	2052	2100	...	2122	2130	2154	2222	2230	2254	2322	2330	2354	0030	0037	0134
34	Biel / Bienne ... a.	0535	0605	0635	0638	0705	0708	past each hour until	2035	2038	2105	2108	...	2135	2138	2207	2235	2238	2307	2335	2338	0007	0038	0050	0142

																							y
Biel / Bienne ..... d.	0518	...	0552	0554	0622	0624	and at the same minutes	1952	1954	2022	2024	...	2052	2054	2122	2124	2154	2222	2224	2254	2322	2324	2354	0026
Lyss .... d.	0531	...	0601	0607	0631	0637	past each	2001	2007	2031	2037	...	2101	2107	2131	2137	2207	2231	2237	2307	2331	2337	0007	0035
Bern .... a.	0554	...	0617	0630	0647	0700	hour until	2017	2030	2047	2100	...	2117	2130	2147	2200	2230	2247	2300	2330	2347	2400	0030	0051

y – ⑥⑦ (not Apr. 15).

514 BERN - LUZERN via Langnau — BLS

For faster services Bern - (Olten -) Luzern see Tables 505/565

km															Ⓐ								
0	Bern .... d.	0536a	0612	0636	0712	and at	2136	2212	2236	2312	2342	0012		Luzern .... d.	...	0557	and at	2057	...	2157	2216	...	...
21	Konolfingen ... d.	0552a	0634	0652	0734	the same	2152	2234	2252	2334	2356	0034		Wolhusen .... d.	...	0615	the same	2115	...	2215	2240	2244	...
38	Langnau .... d.	0605	0652	0705	0752	minutes	2205	2252	2305	2352	0008	0052		Langnau .... d.	0553	0653	0707	minutes	2153	2207	2253	...	2321	2307	0008
75	Wolhusen ...... d.	0645	...	0745	...	past each	2245	...	2345	...			Konolfingen ... d.	0607	0707	0725	past each	2207	2225	2307	...	2325	0026
96	Luzern .... a.	0703	...	0803	...	hour until	2303	...	0010	...			Bern .... a.	0626	0726	0748	hour until	2226	2248	2326	...	2348	0049

a – Ⓐ only.

Additional services operate.

515 DELÉMONT - DELLE — SBB

Boncourt - Delle and v.v. (3 km) subject to 🚌 replacement October 1 - December 9

km																⊡			
0	Biel / Bienne ..... 505a d.	0619	...	0719	and at	2119	...	2219	2319		Delle 🚇 .... ▲ d.	...	0519	0619	...	0719	and at	2019	...	2119
24	Moutier .... 505a d.	0639	...	0739	the same	2139	...	2239	2339		Porrentruy .... d.	0435	0542	0642	...	0742	the same	2042	...	2142
35	Delémont .... 505a d.	0650	...	0750	minutes	2150	...	2250	2350		Delémont .... 505a d.	0512	0612	0712	...	0812	minutes	2112	...	2212
63	Porrentruy .... d.	0722	...	0822	past each	2222	...	2322	0017		Moutier .... 505a d.	0522	0622	0722	...	0822	past each	2122	...	2222
75	Delle 🚇 .... ▲ a.	0740	...	0840	hour until	2240	...	2340			Biel / Bienne .... 505a a.	0541	0640	0741	...	0841	hour until	2141	...	2241

⊡ – 13xx service from Delle departs 1302Ⓐ, 1319Ⓒ.

▲ – 🚌 connection available Delle - Belfort Montbéliard TGV and v.v.

516 BERN - SOLOTHURN — Narrow gauge. RBS

km		⊗	⊗			and at the same														y
0	Bern RBS .... d.	0513	0550	...	0605	0635	minutes past	1905	1935	...	2005	2035	...	2105	...	2137	2207	2237	2308	2337	...	0011	...
34	Solothurn .... a.	0556	0627	...	0642	0712	each hour until	1942	2012	...	2042	2112	...	2142	...	2220	2250	2320	2350	0020	...	0053	...

						and at the same												🚌 y
Solothurn .... d.	0519	0549	...	0619	0649	minutes past	1919	1949	...	2019	...	2049	2119	...	2141	2211	...	2241	2311	...	2341	...	0010
Bern RBS .... a.	0556	0626	...	0656	0726	each hour until	1956	2026	...	2056	...	2126	2156	...	2223	2253	...	2323	2353	...	0023	...	0100

y – ⑥⑦ only.

Additional services operate on Ⓐ.

BLS SOLOTHURN - BURGDORF - THUN 517

km																						
0	**Solothurn** d.	0545	0645	0745	0845	...	0945	1016	...		1845	1916	...	...	2016	...	2116	...	2216	...	2316	...
5	Biberist Ost d.	0550	0650	0750	0850	...	0950	1021	...	and at	1850	1921	...	...	2021	...	2121	...	2221	...	2321	...
21	**Burgdorf** a.	0612	0712	0812	0912	...	1012	1045	...	the same	1912	1945	...	...	2045	...	2145	...	2245	...	2345	...
21	**Burgdorf** d.	0625	0725	0825	0925	...	1025	*1049*	...	minutes	1925	*1949*	...	...	*2049*	...	*2149*	...	*2249*	...	*2349*	...
28	Hasle-Rüegsau d.	0638	0738	0838	0938	...	1038	*1057*	1102	past each	1938	*1957*	2002	...	*2057*	2101	*2157*	2201	*2257*	2301	*2357*	0001
46	Konolfingen a.	0700	0800	0900	1000	...	1100	...	1122	hour	2000	...	2022	...	...	2122	...	2222	...	2322	...	0022
46	Konolfingen d.	0701	0801	0901	1001	...	1101	...	1135	until	2001	...	2035	...	...	2136	...	2236	...	2336	...	0036
61	**Thun** a.	0719	0819	0919	1019	...	1119	...	1156		2019	...	2056	...	...	2156	...	2256	...	2356	...	0056

Solothurn d.	0009	...	
Biberist Ost d.	0014	...	
Burgdorf a.	0038	...	
Burgdorf d.	*0049*	...	
Hasle-Rüegsau d.	*0057*	...	
Konolfingen a.	...	...	
Konolfingen d.	...	...	
Thun a.	...	...	

Thun d.	0532a	0639	0739	0839	0939	...	1039	1103	...		1839	1903	...	...	1939	2009	...	2109	...	2209	...	2309	...	0009
Konolfingen a.	0553a	0658	0758	0858	0958	...	1058	1124	...	and at	1858	1924	...	...	1958	2030	...	2130	...	2230	...	2330	...	0030
Konolfingen d.	0600a	0700	0800	0900	1000	...	1100	1136	...	the same	1900	1936	...	...	2000	2036	...	2136	...	2236	...	2336	...	0036
Hasle-Rüegsau d.	0622a	0722	0822	0922	1022	...	1122	1156	*1201*	minutes	1922	1956	*2001*	...	2022	2057	*2101*	2157	*2201*	2257	*2301*	2357	*0001*	0057
Burgdorf a.	0632a	0732	0832	0932	1032	...	1132	...	*1211*	past each	1932	...	*2011*	...	2032	...	*2111*	...	*2211*	...	*2311*	...	*0011*	0106
Burgdorf d.	0647	0747	0847	0947	1047	...	1147	...	1215	hour	1947	...	2015	...	...	...	2115	...	2215	...	2315	...	0015	...
Biberist Ost a.	0706	0806	0906	1006	1106	...	1206	...	1236	until	2006	...	2036	...	...	...	2136	...	2236	...	2336	...	0036	...
Solothurn a.	0713	0813	0913	1013	1113	...	1213	...	1243		2013	...	2043	...	...	...	2143	...	2243	...	2343	...	0043	...

a – Ⓐ only.

Additional services operate

SBB ZÜRICH - SARGANS - CHUR 520

km		RE 4857	RE 5059	IC 557	RJ 161 F	IC 911	RE 5061	IC 559	IC 913 Ⓐ	ICE 1253 Ⓒ	RE 5063	ICE 1255 Ⓐ	IC 561	EC 163 T	RE 5065	IC 563	IC 271 Gp	ICE 271 Gq	RE 5067	IC 565	RJ 165 B	IC 919 g	RE 5069	IC 567	IC 921
	Basel SBB **510** d.	...	...	...	...	...	...	0633	...	0707	...	0733	0733	...	...	0833	0907	0907	...	0933	...	...	...	...	...
0	**Zürich** HB d.	...	0612	0637	0640	0707	0712	0737	0807	0807	0812	0837	0837	0840	0912	0937	1007	1007	1012	1037	1040	1107	1112	1137	1207
12	Thalwil d.	...	0621	|	|	|	0721	|	|	|	0821	|	|	|	0921	|	|	|	1021	|	|	|	1121	|	|
24	Wädenswil d.	...	0632	|	|	|	0732	|	|	|	0832	|	|	|	0932	|	|	|	1032	|	|	|	1132	|	|
33	Pfäffikon d.	...	0641	|	|	|	0741	|	|	|	0841	|	|	|	0941	|	|	|	1041	|	|	|	1141	|	|
57	Ziegelbrücke d.	...	0659	|	|	|	0759	|	|	|	0859	|	|	|	0959	|	|	|	1059	|	|	|	1159	|	|
90	**Sargans 534** d.	0627	0723	0733	0737	0803	0823	0833	0903	0903	0923	0933	0933	0937	1023	1033	1103	1103	1123	1133	1137	1203	1223	1233	1303
106	Buchs **534** a.	|	|	|	0748	|	|	|	|	|	|	|	|	0948	|	|	|	|	|	|	1148	|	|	|	|
103	Landquart d.	0640	0734	0743	...	0812	0834	0843	0912	0912	0934	0943	0943	...	1034	1043	1112	1112	1134	1143	...	1212	1234	1243	1312
116	**Chur 540** a.	0649	0743	0752	...	0822	0843	0852	0922	0922	0943	0952	0952	...	1043	1052	1122	1122	1143	1152	...	1222	1243	1252	1322

	RE 5071	IC 569	RJ 167 W	RE 5073	IC 571	ICE 1271 Gj	ICE 71 Gk	RE 5075	IC 573	RJ 169 W	RE 5077	IC 575	IC 929	RE 5079	IC 577	RJ 361 W		RE 5081	IC 579	ICE 75 Gz‡	IC 933 y	RE 5083	IC 581	RJ 363 N	RE 5085
Basel SBB **510** d.	...	1133	...	...	1233	1307	1307	...	...	...	...	1433	...	...	...	...	...	...	1633	1707	...	...	1733	...	...
Zürich HB d.	1212	1237	1240	1312	1337	1407	1407	1412	1437	1440	1512	1537	1607	1612	1637	1640	...	1712	1737	1807	1807	1812	1837	1840	1912
Thalwil d.	1221	|	|	1321	|	|	|	1421	|	|	1521	|	|	1621	|	|	...	1721	|	|	|	1821	|	|	1921
Wädenswil d.	1232	|	|	1332	|	|	|	1432	|	|	1532	|	|	1632	|	|	...	1732	|	|	|	1832	|	|	1932
Pfäffikon d.	1241	|	|	1341	|	|	|	1441	|	|	1541	|	|	1641	|	|	...	1741	|	|	|	1841	|	|	1941
Ziegelbrücke d.	1259	|	|	1359	|	|	|	1459	|	|	1559	|	|	1659	|	|	...	1759	|	|	|	1859	|	|	1959
Sargans 534 d.	1323	1333	1337	1423	1433	1503	1503	1523	1533	1537	1623	1633	1703	1723	1733	1737	...	1823	1833	1903	1903	1923	1933	1937	2023
Buchs **534** a.	|	|	1348	|	|	|	|	|	|	1548	|	|	|	|	|	1748	...	|	|	|	|	|	|	1948	|
Landquart d.	1334	1343	...	1434	1443	1512	1512	1534	1543	...	1634	1643	1712	1734	1743	...	...	1834	1843	1912	1912	1934	1943	...	2034
Chur 540 a.	1343	1352	...	1443	1452	1522	1522	1543	1552	...	1643	1652	1722	1743	1752	...	...	1843	1852	1922	1922	1943	1952	...	2043

	IC 583 Ⓑ	IC 593 ⑥	RE 5087	IC 585	RE 5089	IC 587 n	IC 597 m	RE 5091	RE 5093	RE 5095 x
Basel SBB **510** d.	1833	...	...	...	...	2033	...	...	...	...
Zürich HB d.	1937	1937	2012	2037	2112	2137	2137	2212	2312	0020
Thalwil d.	|	|	2021	|	2121	|	|	2221	2321	0028
Wädenswil d.	|	|	2032	|	2132	|	|	2232	2332	0037
Pfäffikon d.	|	|	2041	|	2141	|	|	2241	2341	0045
Ziegelbrücke d.	|	|	2059	|	2159	|	|	2259	0000	|
Sargans 534 d.	2033	2033	2124	2133	2224	2233	2233	2324	0028	0118
Buchs **534** a.	|	|	|	|	|	|	|	|	|	|
Landquart d.	2043	2043	2135	2143	2235	2243	2243	2336	0038	0128
Chur 540 a.	2052	2052	2144	2152	2243	2252	2252	2345	0047	0136

	IC 556 ⚒	RE 5056	IC 558	RE 5058	IC 912 Ⓐ	IC 560	RE 5060		IC 562	RE 5062
Chur 540 d.	0509	0516	0609	0616	0639	0709	0716	...	0809	0816
Landquart d.	0519	0525	0619	0625	0649	0719	0725	...	0819	0825
Buchs **534** d.	|	|	|	|	|	|	|	...	|	|
Sargans 534 d.	0528	0537	0628	0637	0658	0728	0737	...	0828	0837
Ziegelbrücke d.	|	0600	|	0700	|	|	0800	...	|	0900
Pfäffikon d.	|	0619	|	0719	|	|	0819	...	|	0919
Wädenswil d.	|	0629	|	0729	|	|	0829	...	|	0929
Thalwil d.	|	0639	|	0739	|	|	0839	...	|	0939
Zürich HB a.	0623	0648	0723	0748	0753	0823	0848	...	0923	0948
Basel SBB **510** a.	0727	...	...	...	...	0927	...	...	1027e	...

	IC 916	IC 564	RE 5064		RJ 360 N	IC 566	RE 5066		ICE 72 G‡	IC 568	RE 5068		RJ 362 W	IC 570	RE 5070	ICE 70 G‡		IC 572	RE 5072	RJ 160 W	IC 574		RE 5074	IC 928	IC 576
Chur 540 d.	0839	0909	0916	...	...	1009	1016	...	1039	1109	1116	...	...	1209	1216	1239	...	1309	1316	...	1409	...	1416	1439	1509
Landquart d.	0849	0919	0925	...	...	1019	1025	...	1049	1119	1125	...	...	1219	1225	1249	...	1319	1325	...	1419	...	1425	1449	1519
Buchs **534** d.	|	|	|	...	1012	|	|	...	|	|	|	...	1212	|	|	|	...	|	|	1412	|	...	|	|	|
Sargans 534 d.	0858	0928	0937	...	1025	1028	1037	...	1058	1128	1137	...	1225	1228	1237	1258	...	1328	1337	1425	1428	...	1437	1458	1528
Ziegelbrücke d.	|	|	1000	...	|	|	1100	...	|	|	1200	...	|	|	1300	|	...	|	1400	|	|	...	1500	|	|
Pfäffikon d.	|	|	1019	...	|	|	1119	...	|	|	1219	...	|	|	1319	|	...	|	1419	|	|	...	1519	|	|
Wädenswil d.	|	|	1029	...	|	|	1129	...	|	|	1229	...	|	|	1329	|	...	|	1429	|	|	...	1529	|	|
Thalwil d.	|	|	1039	...	|	|	1139	...	|	|	1239	...	|	|	1339	|	...	|	1439	|	|	...	1539	|	|
Zürich HB a.	0953	1023	1048	...	1120	1123	1148	...	1153	1223	1248	...	1320	1323	1348	1353	...	1423	1448	1520	1523	...	1548	1553	1623
Basel SBB **510** a.	...	1127	...	...	...	...	...	...	1253	1327	...	...	...	...	...	1453	...	1527	...	...	...	...	...	...	1727

	RE 5076	RJ 162 B	IC 578	RE 5078	ICE 1256		IC 580	RE 5080	IC 934 h	EC 164 T	IC 582	RE 5082	IC 936	IC 584	RE 5084	RJ 166 W	ICE 1258 z	IC 586 y		RE 5086	IC 588 †v	RE 5088	RJ 168 W	RE 5090	RE 5092 r
Chur 540 d.	1516	...	1609	1616	1639	...	1709	1716	1739	...	1809	1816	1839	1909	1916	...	2009	2009	...	2016	2109	2116	...	2214	2314
Landquart d.	1525	...	1619	1625	1649	...	1719	1725	1749	...	1819	1825	1849	1919	1925	...	2019	2019	...	2025	2119	2122	...	2222	2322
Buchs **534** d.	|	1612	|	|	|	...	|	|	|	1812	|	|	|	|	|	2012	|	|	...	|	|	|	2212	|	|
Sargans 534 d.	1537	1625	1628	1637	1658	...	1728	1737	1758	1825	1828	1837	1858	1928	1937	2025	2028	2028	...	2037	2128	2137	2225	2237	2337
Ziegelbrücke d.	1600	|	|	1700	|	...	|	1800	|	|	|	1900	|	|	2000	|	|	|	...	2100	|	2200	|	2300	0000
Pfäffikon d.	1619	|	|	1719	|	...	|	1819	|	|	|	1919	|	|	2019	|	|	|	...	2119	|	2219	|	2319	0019
Wädenswil d.	1629	|	|	1729	|	...	|	1829	|	|	|	1929	|	|	2029	|	|	|	...	2129	|	2229	|	2329	0029
Thalwil d.	1639	|	|	1739	|	...	|	1839	|	|	|	1939	|	|	2039	|	|	|	...	2139	|	2239	|	2339	0039
Zürich HB a.	1648	1720	1723	1748	1753	...	1823	1848	1853	1920	1923	1948	1953	2023	2048	2120	2123	2123	...	2148	2223	2248	2320	2348	0048
Basel SBB **510** a.	...	...	1827	...	1853y	...	1927	...	...	...	2027	...	...	2127	...	...	2227	...	...	...	...	...	...	...	...

Additional services SARGANS - BUCHS and v.v.

Sargans d.	0500 0536	0600 0636	and at the same minutes past	2200 2236	2300 0000 ...	Buchs d.	⚒ 0515 0615 0648	0715 0748	and at the same minutes past 2315 2348	0015 0048
Buchs a.	0512 0544	0612 0644	each hour until	2212 2244	2312 0012 ...	Sargans a.	0525 0624 0659	0724 0759	each hour until 2324 2359	0024 0059

B – 12 and ✕ Budapest - Wien - Zürich and v.v.
F – 12 and ✕ Feldkirch - Zürich and v.v.
G – 12 and ✕ Kiel / Hamburg / Frankfurt - Basel - Zürich - Chur.
N – 12 and ✕ Innsbruck - Zürich and v.v.
T – TRANSALPIN – 12 and ✕ Zürich - Graz and v.v.
W – 12 and ✕ Wien - Salzburg - Zürich and v.v.

e – Dec. 11 - Apr. 2, Aug. 1 - 27.
g – ⑥ Jan. 28 - Mar. 11.
h – ⑦ Jan. 29 - Mar. 12.

j – Ⓒ Feb. 11 - Apr. 16; daily July 1 - Aug. 13 (also Apr. 17; not Apr. 8, 9).
k – Daily Dec. 11 - Feb. 10; Ⓐ Feb. 13 - Apr. 21; daily Apr. 22 - June 30, Aug. 14 - Dec. 9 (also Apr. 8, 9).
m – ⑤–⑦ (also Dec. 26, Jan. 2, Apr. 17).
n – ①–④ (not Dec. 26, Jan. 2, Apr. 17).
p – ⑦ (also Dec. 26, Apr. 15, 17, May 1, June 5).
q – ①–⑥ (not Dec. 26, Apr. 15, 17, May 1, June 5).
r – ⑤⑥ (not Apr. 14).

v – Not Dec. 25, Apr. 14, 16, May 25, June 4, Aug. 1.
x – ⑥⑦ (not Apr. 15).
y – ⑦ (also Dec. 26, Jan. 2, Apr. 17).
z – ①–⑥ (not Dec. 26, Jan. 2, Apr. 17).

‡ – Train number varies on some days / dates:
70 runs as **1270**;
72 runs as **1272**;
75 runs as **1175** / **1275**.

12 ✕ – Restaurant (✕) – Bistro (🍸) – Bar coach 🍸 – Minibar 269

522 ZIEGELBRÜCKE - LINTHAL SBB

km											
	Zürich HB d.	...	...	...	0643		1743	...		...	...
0	Ziegelbrücke d.	0430	0530	0630	0730	and	1830	1903	and	2303	0003
11	Glarus d.	0444	0544	0644	0744	hourly	1844	1918	hourly	2318	0018
16	Schwanden d.	0500	0600	0700	0800	until	1900	1929	until	2329	0025
27	Linthal ▲ a.	0517	0617	0717	0817		1917	1946		2346	...

	Ⓐ										
Linthal ▲ d.	0443	0543		1843	...	1946	2011		2311	0011
Schwanden d.	0504	0607	and	1907	...	2007	2033	and	2333	0033
Glarus d.	0513	0616	hourly	1916	...	2016	2043	hourly	2343	0043
Ziegelbrücke a.	0526	0629	until	1929	...	2029	2056	until	2356	0056
Zürich HB a.	0617	0717		2017	...	...	...		...	...

h – Also Aug. 15.
x – Change required at either Balm (Klausen) or Klausen Passhöhe; 68/70 minutes respectively.

▲ – 🚌 service **Linthal - Flüelen** Bahnhof (Table **550**) and v.v. operates **June 24 - September 24, 2017** over the Klausenpass. [R]. Journey time: ± 2 hours 45 minutes. **NO WINTER SERVICE**.
From **Linthal**: 0827Ⓒ **h**, 0927, 1027, 1527, 1727Ⓒ **h**. From **Flüelen**: 0600Ⓒ **h**, 0730 **x**, 0930 **x**, 1500Ⓒ **h**, 1530.
Operator: PostAuto Zentralschweiz, Luzern. ✆ (Luzern) 058 448 06 22, fax: 058 667 34 33.

525 ARTH GOLDAU - ST GALLEN - ROMANSHORN SBB, SOB*

km				2561 S		Ⓐ	Ⓒ	2563 S			2565 S		2567 S			2591 S			2593 S			2595 S		
	Luzern **550** d.	...	...	...	...	...	...	...	...	...	...	...	0739	...		1939	...	...	...	...	...	...	...	...
0	**Arth Goldau** d.	...	...	...	...	*0519*	...	...	...	*0619*	...	...	0814	...		2014	...	2113	...	...	2213	...	...	2313
20	Biberbrugg ◐ ● d.	...	...	...	...	0550	0553	...	...	0653	...	...	0837	...		2037	...	2137	...	...	2237	...	...	2337
26	Samstagern ◐ ● d.	...	...	...	...	0601	0601	...	...	0701	...	...	|	...	and at	|	...	2145	...	...	2245	...	...	2345
34	Pfäffikon ● d.	...	...	...	...	0617	0617	...	...	0717	...	...	0854	...	the same	2054	...	2157	...	...	2257	...	...	2357
38	Rapperswil ● a.	...	...	...	...	0622	0622	...	...	0722	...	...	0859	...	minutes	2102	...	2202	...	...	2302	...	...	0002
38	Rapperswil d.	...	...	0603	...	...	...	0703	...	...	0803	...	0903	...	past each	2103	...	...	2203	...	...	2303	...	...
66	Wattwil d.	*0459*	*0559*	0628	0629	...	...	0728	0729	...	0828	0829	0928	0929	hour	2128	2129	...	2228	*2229*	...	2328	...	...
89	Herisau d.	*0524*	*0624*	0647	0654	...	...	0747	0754	...	0847	0854	0947	0954	until	2147	2154	...	2247	*2254*	...	2349	...	...
97	**St Gallen** a.	*0533*	*0633*	0655	0704	...	...	0755	0804	...	0855	0904	0955	1004		2155	2204	...	2255	*2303*	...	2357	...	...
97	**St Gallen 532** d.	0535	0635	...	0704	...	...	...	0804	...	...	0904	...	1004		...	2204	...	...	2305	...	...	0004	...
119	**Romanshorn 532** a.	0559	0659	...	0729	...	...	...	0829	...	...	0929	...	1029		...	2229	...	...	2329	...	...	0029	...

		2560 S	Ⓒ	Ⓐ		2562 S			2564 S			2588 S		2590 S				2592 S		2594 S		2596 S		2598 S
Romanshorn 532 d.	...	...	...	...	0529	...	...	0629	...		1829	...	1929	...	...	2029	...	2129	...	2229	...	2329	...
St Gallen 532 a.	...	...	...	...	0555	...	...	0655	...		1855	...	1955	...	...	2055	...	2155	...	2255	...	2355	...
St Gallen d.	...	...	...	...	0556	0605	...	0656	0705		1856	1905	1956	2005	...	2056	2105	—	2205	—	2305	—	0005
Herisau d.	...	0513	...	...	0606	0613	...	0706	0713	and at	1906	1913	2006	2013	...	2106	2113	...	2213	...	2313	...	0013
Wattwil d.	...	0533	...	...	0630	0633	...	0730	0733	the same	1930	1933	2030	2033	...	2130	2133	...	2233	...	2333	...	0033
Rapperswil a.	...	0557	...	...	...	0657	...	...	0757	minutes	...	1957	...	2057	...	...	2157	...	2257	...	2357	...	0057t
Rapperswil ● d.	0544	...	0636	0636	...	...	0659	...	0759	past each	...	1959	...	...	2057	...	...	2157	...	2257	...	0003	...
Pfäffikon ● d.	0549	...	0642	0642	...	...	0704	...	0804	hour	...	2004	...	...	2102	...	...	2202	...	2302	...	0007	...
Samstagern ◐ ● d.	0559	...	0654	0658	...	...	0714	...	|	until	...	|	...	...	2113	...	...	2213	...	2313	...	0019	...
Biberbrugg ◐ ● d.	0616	...	0702	0705	...	...	0721	...	0820		...	2020	...	...	2121	...	...	2221	...	2321	...	...	...
Arth Goldau a.	0641	...	...	...	...	...	0743	...	0844		...	2044	...	...	2146	...	...	2246	...	2346	...	...	...
Luzern **550** a.	...	...	...	...	...	...	...	...	0921		...	2121	...	...	...	...	...	...	...	...	...	...	...

km		Ⓐ			and at						v
0	**Wädenswil** d.	0541	0609	0634	the same	2209	2234	2309	2334	0015	0050
6	Samstagern ● d.	0549	0617	0642	minutes	2217	2242	2317	2342	0023	0057
11	Biberbrugg ● d.	0558	0625	0651	past each	2225	2251	2325	2351	0031	0106
17	**Einsiedeln** ● a.	0605	0632	0658	hour until	2232	2258	2332	2358	0038	0114

	Ⓐ			and at					w
Einsiedeln ● d.	0454	0525	0558	the same	2225	2258	2325	...	2358
Biberbrugg ● d.	0501	0532	0607	minutes	2232	2307	2332	...	0004
Samstagern ● d.	0510	0541	0617	past each	2241	2317	2341	...	0012
Wädenswil a.	0518	0549	0625	hour until	2249	2325	2349	...	0023

S – VORALPEN EXPRESS – [12] Luzern / Arth Goldau / Rapperswil - St Gallen and v.v. Also conveys (🍸) on most services.
t – ⑥⑦ (also Jan. 1, Apr. 14, 17, May 1, 25, 26, June 5, Aug. 1, Nov. 1; not Dec. 25).
v – ⑥⑦ (also Apr. 14, 17, May 1, 25, 26, June 5, Aug. 1; not Dec. 25).
w – ⑤⑥ (also Apr. 13, 16, 30, May 24, 25, June 4, July 31; not Dec. 24).
◐ – For service to Einsiedeln – see panel.
● – Additional services run Einsiedeln - Biberbrugg - Samstagern - Pfäffikon - Rapperswil and v.v.
* – Operated by SOB, except Rapperswil - Wattwil (SBB).

526 GOSSAU - APPENZELL - WASSERAUEN Narrow gauge. AB

km		⚒	Ⓐ																				🚌 j			
0	**Gossau** d.	0547	...	0647	0747	0851	0951	1051	1121	1151	1221	1251	1321	1421	1521	1551	1621	1721	1751	1851	1951	2051	...	2151	2251	2351
5	Herisau d.	0554	0554	0658	0758	0858	0958	1058	1128	1158	1228	1258	1328	1428	1528	1558	1628	1728	1758	1858	1958	2058	...	2158	2258	2358
15	Urnäsch d.	...	0609	0713	0813	0913	1013	1113	1143	1213	1243	1313	1343	1443	1543	1613	1643	1743	1813	1913	2013	2113	...	2213	2313	0013
26	**Appenzell** d.	...	0631	0731	0831	0931	1031	1131	1201	1231	1301	1330	1401	1501	1601	1631	1701	1801	1831	1930	2030	2130	2132	2230	2330	0030
32	**Wasserauen** a.	...	0642	0742	0842	0942	1042	1142	1212	1242	1312	...	1412	1512	1612	1642	1712	1812	1842	*1942*y	*2042*y	...	2142	...	...	...

																						🚌 j		
Wasserauen d.	...	...	0648a	0748	0848	0948	1048	1148	1218	1248	1318	...	1418	1518	1618	1648	1718	1818	1848	...	*1942*y	*2042*y	2142	...	...
Appenzell d.	0530a	0630	0700	0800	0900	1000	1100	1200	1230	1300	1330	1400	1430	1530	1630	1700	1730	1830	1900	1930	2000	2100	2153	2200	2300
Urnäsch d.	0545a	0645	0715	0815	0915	1015	1115	1215	1245	1315	1345	1415	1445	1545	1645	1715	1745	1845	1915	1945	2015	2115	...	2215	2315
Herisau d.	0601	0701	0731	0831	0931	1031	1131	1231	1301	1331	1401	1431	1501	1601	1701	1731	1801	1901	1931	2001	2031	2131	...	2231	2331
Gossau a.	0607	0707	0737	0837	0937	1037	1137	1237	1307	1337	1407	1437	1507	1607	1707	1737	1807	1907	1937	2007	2037	2137	...	2237	2337

a – Ⓐ only. j – Apr. 30 - Oct. 29. y – Connection by 🚌. Additional services operate Apr. 30 - Oct. 29.

527 ST GALLEN - APPENZELL Narrow gauge rack railway. AB

km		⚒	⚒	Ⓐ			⚒			and				Ⓐ								Ⓐ		🚌	🚌	🚌 y	🚌 z	🚌 z
0	**St Gallen** d.	0603	0637a	0703	0734d	0807	0837	0907	0937	every	1607	1637	1707	1728	1740	1810	1840	1910	1940	2010	2110	2140	2230	2330	0030	0135	0240
7	Teufen d.	0624	0654a	0724	0754d	0824	0854	0924	0954	30	1624	1654	1724	1743	1756	1826	1856	1926	1956	2026	2126	2156	2242	2342	0042	0147	0252
14	Gais ▲ d.	0640	0710	0740	0810	0840	0910	0940	1010	mins.	1640	1710	1740	1756	1812	1842	1912	1942	2012	2042	2142	2212	2252	2352	0052	0157	0302
20	**Appenzell** a.	0651	0721	0751	0821	0851	0921	0951	1021	until	1651	1721	1751	1808	1823	1853	1923	1953	2023	2053	2153	2223	2302	0002	0102	0207	0312

	⚒	Ⓐ	⚒	Ⓐ		⚒				and					Ⓒ	Ⓐ					Ⓐ		🚌	🚌	🚌	🚌 k
Appenzell d.	0515	0608	0638	0708	0708c	0738	0808	0838	0908	every	1538	1608	1638	1708	1738	1738	1810	1840	1910	1940	2010	2040	2105	2155	2249	2349
Gais ▲ d.	0527	0620	0650	0720	0720	0750	0820	0850	0920	30	1550	1620	1650	1720	1752	1756	1822	1852	1922	1952	2022	2052	2114	2204	2258	2358
Teufen d.	0540	0633	0703	0731	0733	0803	0833	0903	0933	mins.	1603	1633	1703	1733	1805	1809	1835	1905	1935	2005	2035	2105	2124	2214	2308	0008
St Gallen a.	0558	0651	0721	0748	0755	0821	0851	0921	0951	until	1621	1651	1721	1753	1823	1827	1853	1923	1953	2023	2053	2123	2137	2228	2321	0021

a – Ⓐ only.
c – Ⓒ only.
d – ⚒ only.
k – ⑤⑥ (also Apr. 13, 16, 30, May 24, 25, June 4, July 31, Oct. 31; not Dec. 24).
y – ⑥⑦ (also Apr. 14, 17, May 1, 25, 26, June 5, Aug. 1, Nov. 1; not Dec. 25).
z – ⑥⑦ (also Apr. 14, 17, May 1, 25, 26, June 5, Aug. 1, Nov. 1; not Dec. 25). Supplement payable.

▲ – Rail service **Gais - Altstätten Stadt** and v.v. *8 km*. Journey time: 19 - 22 minutes. **Operator**: AB.
From **Gais**: 0621Ⓐ, 0721 and hourly until 1821, then 1921🚌, 2021🚌.
From **Altstätten Stadt**: 0648Ⓐ, 0748 and hourly until 1848, then 1948🚌, 2048🚌.
A bus connects Altstätten Stadt with Altstätten SBB station (Table **534**). Journey time: 6 minutes.

529 ZÜRICH - ZÜRICH FLUGHAFEN ✈ SBB

Journey time: 9 - 13 minutes

From **Zürich** HB:
0502, 0514, 0529, 0533, 0544, 0546, 0552, 0601, 0607, 0609, 0614, 0616, 0633, 0637, 0639, 0644, 0646, 0652, 0707, 0709, 0714, 0716, 0733, 0737, 0739, 0744, 0746, 0752, then 10 - 13 trains per hour until 2052, then 2107, 2109, 2114, 2116, 2137, 2139, 2144, 2146, 2207, 2209, 2214, 2216, 2237, 2239, 2244, 2246, 2307, 2309, 2314, 2316, 2338, 2344, 2346, 0014, 0017.

From **Zürich** Flughafen:
0500, 0533, 0540, 0556, 0601, 0603, 0606, 0610, 0613, 0631, 0633, 0636, 0640, 0643, 0647, 0656, 0701, 0703, 0706, 0710, 0713, 0718, 0731, 0733, 0736, 0740, 0743, 0756, then 10 - 13 trains per hour until 2056, then 2101, 2103, 2106, 2110, 2113, 2131, 2133, 2136, 2140, 2143, 2201, 2203, 2210, 2213, 2231, 2233, 2236, 2240, 2301, 2303, 2313, 2331, 2333, 2336, 2340, 2343, 0003, 0005, 0013, 0033, 0043.

SBB — ZÜRICH - ST GALLEN — 530

km		IC 701	IR 2255	IC 703	ICN 1507	EC 2247 h	IC 191 Mj	IC 705 F	ICN 1509	IR 2251	EC 707	IC 1511	ICN 193 M	IR 709	IC 1513	ICN 2263	IR 711	IC 1515	ICN 2265	IR 713	IC 1517	ICN 2267	IR 715	1519
	Genève Aéroport + 505 d.												0632		0732			0832			0932			
	Genève 505 d.							0542			0642			0742			0842			0942				
	Lausanne 505 d.							0620	0615		0720	0715		0820	0815		0920	0915		1020	1015			
	Biel 505 d.				0516				0616			0717			0817			0917			1017			1117
	Bern 505 d.			0529p		0547	0632			0732			0832			0932			1032			1132		
	Basel 510 d.				0547			0616			0732		0747			0832			0932			1047		
0	Zürich HB 535 d.	0533	0609	0633	0639	0709	0709	0733	0739	0809	0833	0839	0909	0933	0939	1009	1033	1039	1109	1133	1139	1209	1233	1239
10	Zürich Flughafen + 535 d.	0544	0621	0644	0651	0721	0721	0744	0751	0821	0844	0851	0921	0944	0951	1021	1044	1051	1121	1144	1151	1221	1244	1251
30	Winterthur 535 d.	0559	0637	0659	0707	0737	0737	0759	0807	0837	0859	0907	0937	0959	1007	1037	1059	1107	1137	1159	1207	1237	1259	1307
57	Wil 539 d.	0620	0655		0723	0755	0755		0823	0855		0923	0955		1023	1055		1123	1155		1223	1255		1323
78	Gossau d.	0640	0710		0740	0810	0810		0840	0910		0940	1010		1040	1110		1140	1210		1240	1310		1340
87	St Gallen a.	0648	0718	0735	0748	0818	0818	0835	0855	0918	0935	0948	1018	1035	1118	1135	1148	1218	1235	1248	1318	1335	1348	

	EC 195 M	IC 717	ICN 1521	IR 2271	IC 719	ICN 1523	IR 2273	IC 721	ICN 1525	IC 2275	ICN 723	1527	IR 2277	IC 725	ICN 1529	EC 2249 w	IC 197 Mx	ICN 727	IC 1531	ICN 2281	IC 729	ICN 1533	IR 2283
Genève Aéroport + 505 d.		1032			1132			1232			1332			1432			1532			1632			
Genève 505 d.		1042			1142			1242			1342			1442			1542			1642			
Lausanne 505 d.		1120	1115		1220	1215		1320	1315		1420	1415		1520	1515		1620	1615		1720	1715		
Biel 505 d.			1217			1317			1417			1517			1617			1717			1817		
Bern 505 d.		1232			1332			1432			1532			1632			1732			1832			
Basel 510 d.				1247			1347			1447			1547				1747						
Zürich HB 535 d.	1309	1333	1339	1409	1433	1439	1509	1533	1539	1609	1633	1639	1709	1733	1739	1809	1809	1833	1839	1909	1933	1939	2009
Zürich Flughafen + 535 d.	1321	1344	1351	1421	1444	1451	1521	1544	1551	1621	1644	1651	1721	1744	1751	1821	1821	1844	1851	1921	1944	1951	2021
Winterthur 535 d.	1337	1359	1407	1437	1459	1507	1537	1559	1607	1637	1659	1707	1737	1759	1807	1837	1837	1859	1907	1937	1959	2007	2037
Wil 539 d.	1355		1423	1455		1523	1555		1623	1655		1723	1755		1823	1855		1923	1955		2023	2055	
Gossau d.	1410		1440	1510		1540	1610		1640	1710		1740	1810		1840	1910	1910		1940	2010		2040	2110
St Gallen a.	1418	1435	1448	1518	1535	1550	1618	1635	1648	1718	1735	1748	1818	1835	1848	1918	1918	1935	1950	2018	2035	2048	2118

	ICN 1535	IR 2285	ICN 1537	IR 2287	ICN 1539	IR 2289	IR 2293
Genève Aéroport + 505 d.							
Genève 505 d.							
Lausanne 505 d.	1815		1915		2015		
Biel 505 d.	1917		2017		2117		
Bern 505 d.							
Basel 510 d.		1947		2047		2147	
Zürich HB 535 d.	2039	2109	2139	2209	2239	2309	2338 0017
Zürich Flughafen + 535 d.	2051	2121	2151	2221	2251	2321	2348 0028
Winterthur 535 d.	2107	2137	2207	2237	2307	2337	0003 0043
Wil 539 d.	2123	2155	2223	2255	2323	2355	0025 0101
Gossau d.	2140	2210	2240	2310	2340	0010	0041 0121
St Gallen a.	2148	2218	2248	2318	2348	0018	0051 0129

	IC 706	IR 2256	IC 1510	IC 708	IR 2250	ICN 1512	IC 710	ICN 2260	ICN 1514
St Gallen d.	0509	0542	0612	0625	0642	0712	0725	0742	0812
Gossau d.	0518	0550	0620		0650	0720		0750	0820
Wil 539 d.	0539	0608	0640		0708	0740		0808	0840
Winterthur 535 d.	0558	0628	0658	0703	0728	0758	0803	0828	0858
Zürich Flughafen + 535 d.	0613	0643	0713		0743	0813		0843	0913
Zürich HB 535 a.	0623	0653	0723	0727	0753	0823	0827	0853	0923
Basel 510 a.		0812				1012			
Bern 505 a.	0728			0828			0928		
Biel 505 a.		0843			0943			1043	
Lausanne 505 a.	0840	0945	0940		1045	1040		1145	
Genève 505 a.	0918			1018			1118		
Genève Aéroport + 505 a.	0927			1027			1127		

	IC 712	IR 2262	ICN 1516	IC 714	IR 2264	ICN 1518	IC 716	EC 196	ICN 1520	IC 718	IR 2268	ICN 1522	IC 720	IR 2270	ICN 1524	IC 722	IR 2272	ICN 1526	IC 724	IR 2274	ICN 1528	IC 726
St Gallen d.	0825	0842	0912	0925	0942	1012	1025	1045	1112	1125	1142	1212	1225	1242	1312	1325	1342	1412	1425	1442	1512	1525
Gossau d.		0850	0920		0950	1020		1053	1120		1150	1220		1250	1320		1350	1420		1450	1520	
Wil 539 d.		0908	0940		1008	1040		1108	1140		1208	1240		1308	1340		1408	1440		1508	1540	
Winterthur 535 d.	0903	0928	0958	1003	1028	1058	1103	1128	1203	1228	1303	1328	1403	1428	1458	1503	1528	1558	1603			
Zürich Flughafen + 535 d.	0918	0943	1013	1018	1043	1113	1118	1143	1213	1218	1243	1313	1318	1343	1413	1418	1443	1513	1518	1543	1613	1618
Zürich HB 535 a.	0927	0953	1023	1027	1053	1123	1127	1153	1223	1227	1253	1323	1327	1353	1423	1427	1453	1523	1527	1553	1623	1627
Basel 510 a.			1112			1212			1412			1512			1612			1712				
Bern 505 a.	1028		1128			1228		1328			1428		1528			1628			1728			
Biel 505 a.			1143			1243		1343			1443		1543			1643			1743			
Lausanne 505 a.	1140		1245	1240		1345	1340		1445	1440		1545	1540		1645	1640		1745	1740		1845	1840
Genève 505 a.	1218		1318			1418			1518			1618			1718			1818			1918	
Genève Aéroport + 505 a.	1227		1327			1427			1527			1627			1727			1827			1927	

	EC 194 M	ICN 1530	IC 728	IR 2278	ICN 1532	IC 730	IR 2280	ICN 1534	IC 732	IR 2282	ICN 1536	IC 734	EC 192 M	ICN 2286	IC 1540	IR 2248 y	ICN 190 Mk	IR 23094	EC 2292	RE 2294
St Gallen d.	1545	1612	1625	1642	1712	1725	1742	1812	1825	1842	1912	1925	1945	2012	2042	2112	2142	2212	2242	2342
Gossau d.	1553	1620		1650	1720		1750	1820		1850	1920		1953	2020	2050	2120	2150	2153	2220	2250	2350
Wil 539 d.	1608	1640		1708	1740		1808	1840		1908	1940		2008	2040	2108	2140	2208	2240	2308	0008
Winterthur 535 d.	1628	1658	1703	1718	1758	1803	1828	1858	1903	1928	1958	2003	2028	2058	2128	2158	2228	2238	2328	0028
Zürich Flughafen + 535 d.	1643	1713	1718	1743	1813	1818	1843	1913	1918	2003	2018	2043	2113	2143	2213	2243	2313	2353	0043
Zürich HB 535 a.	1653	1723	1727	1753	1823	1827	1853	1923	1927	1953	2023	2053	2123	2153	2223	2253	2323	2353	0112	0053
Basel 510 a.			1912			2012			2112			2212		2312					0112	
Bern 505 a.		1828			1928			2028			2128									
Biel 505 a.	1843			1943			2043			2143			2243							
Lausanne 505 a.	1945	1940		2045	2040		2145	2140		2245	2240		2345							
Genève 505 a.	2018			2118			2218			2318										
Genève Aéroport + 505 a.	2027			2127			2227			2327										

F – From / to Fribourg.
M – From / to München.

h – Jan. 1 only.
j – Not Jan. 1.
k – Not Dec. 24, 31.

w – Dec. 24 only.
x – Not Dec. 24.
y – Dec. 24, 31 only.

p – Depart 0513 on Feb. 6, 11 - 13, 20, 27, Mar. 25 - 27, May 1 - 5, 8 - 12, 22, June 3 - 5, 12, July 17, Aug. 5 - 12, 14 - 19, Sept. 4, 18 - 22, 25 - 29, Oct. 14 - 16, 28 - 30, Nov. 6, 13, 27.

SBB — WINTERTHUR - SCHAFFHAUSEN — 531

km						and at the same minutes past each hour until																	
0	Winterthur d.	0542	0606	0619	0642		1806	1819	1842	1906	1919	1942	2006	2019	2042	...	2106	2119	2142	2206	2242	2306	2342 ... 0012
30	Schaffhausen a.	0613	0638	0646	0713		1838	1846	1913	1938	1946	2013	2038	2046	2113	...	2138	2146	2213	2238	2313	2338	0013 ... 0041

														and at the same minutes past each hour until								
Schaffhausen d.	0514	0521	0546	0614	0621	Ⓐn 0631	0646	0700	0714	0721	Ⓐn 0731	0746	0814	0821	Ⓐn 0846		2014	2021	2046	2121	2146	2221 2246 2321 2346
Winterthur a.	0541	0554	0619	0641	0654	0659	0719	0729	0741	0754	0759	0819	0841	0854	0919		2041	2054	2119	2154	2219	2254 2319 2354 0023

n – Not May 1.

SBB, THURBO* — SCHAFFHAUSEN - ROMANSHORN - RORSCHACH — 532

Temporarily relocated to page 280

533 SCHAFFHAUSEN - KREUZLINGEN

Valid Apr. 14 - Oct. 15, 2017 (no winter service) URh

	✕A		✕C		✕A		✕A		
Schaffhausen d.	0910	...	1110	...	1318	...	1518	...	...
Stein am Rhein d.	1115	...	1315	...	1523	...	1723	...	...
Kreuzlingen Hafen a.	1355	...	1555	...	1805	...	2005y	...	...

	✕A		✕B		✕A		✕D		
Kreuzlingen Hafen d.	0900	...	1100	...	1427	...	1627	...	...
Stein am Rhein d.	1130	...	1330	...	1657	...	1857	...	...
Schaffhausen a.	1245	...	1445	...	1815	...	2015y	...	...

A – ④⑤⑥† Apr. 14-30; daily May 1 - Oct. 1.
B – ④⑤⑥† Apr. 14-30; daily May 1 - Oct. 15.
C – † Apr. 14 - June 18; daily June 24 - Sept. 10, Oct. 1-15 (also May 1, June 15, Sept. 17, 24).
D – † Apr. 14 - June 18; daily June 24 - Sept. 10 (also May 1, June 15, Sept. 17, 24, Oct. 1).
y – Not Aug. 12.

534 WIL - ST GALLEN - BUCHS - CHUR

SBB

km		RE 4857	RE 4859	RE 4861	EC 191	RE 4863	RE 4865	EC 193	RE 4867	RE 4869	RE 4871	RE 4873	EC 195	RE 4875	RE 4877		RE 4879	RE 4881	RE 4883	EC 197	RE 4885	RE 4887	IC 585				RE 5093
		R	R	R	Mj	R	R	B	R	R	R	R	M	R	R		R	R	R	Mn	R	R					
	Wil 530 d.	0500	0601	0701	0755	0801	0901	0955	1001	1101	1201	1301	1355	1401	1501	...	1601	1701	1801	1855	1901	2001	...	2101	2201	2301	...
0	**St Gallen** d.	0526	0626	0726	0819	0826	0926	1019	1026	1126	1226	1326	1419	1426	1526	...	1626	1726	1826	1920	1926	2026	...	2126	2226	2326	...
16	Rorschach d.	0540	0640	0740	|	0840	0940	|	1040	1140	1240	1340	|	1440	1540	...	1640	1740	1840	|	1940	2040	...	2140	2240	2340	...
27	**St Margrethen** d.	0547	0647	0747	0840	0847	0947	1040	1047	1147	1247	1347	1440	1447	1547	...	1647	1747	1847	1941	1947	2047	...	2147	2247	2347	...
39	Altstätten 527 d.	0600	0700	0800	...	0900	1000	...	1100	1200	1300	1400	...	1500	1600	...	1700	1800	1900	...	2000	2100	...	2200	2300	0000	...
65	**Buchs 520** ⊖ d.	0615	0715	0815	...	0915	1015	...	1115	1215	1315	1415	...	1515	1615	...	1715	1815	1915	...	2015	2115	...	2215	2315	0015	...
81	Sargans **520** ⊖ d.	0627	0727	0827	...	0927	1027	...	1127	1227	1327	1427	...	1527	1627	...	1727	1827	1927	...	2027	2124	2133	2224	2324	0024	0028
93	Landquart **520** a.	0638	0736	0836	...	0936	1036	...	1136	1236	1336	1436	...	1536	1636	...	1736	1836	1936	...	2036	...	2141	*2246*	*2346*	...	0037
107	**Chur 520** a.	0649	0748	0848	...	0948	1048	...	1148	1248	1348	1448	...	1548	1648	...	1748	1848	1948	...	2048	...	2152	*2256*	*2356*	...	0047

	IC 556	RE 4858	RE 4860	RE 4862	RE 4864	RE 4866	EC 196	RE 4868	RE 4870	RE 4872	RE 4874	RE 4876	EC 194	RE 4878	RE 4880	RE 4882	RE 4884	EC 192	RE 4886	RE 4888	EC 190	RE 5088		RE 5090			
	⚒	R	R	R	R	R	M	R	R	R	R	R	M	R	R	R	R	B	R	R	Mk						
Chur 520 d.	0509	...	0612	0712	0812	0912	...	1012	1112	1212	1312	1412	...	1512	1612	1712	1812	...	1912	2012	...	2114	...	2214	...	*2231*	...
Landquart **520** d.	0519	...	0622	0722	0822	0922	...	1022	1122	1222	1322	1422	...	1522	1622	1722	1822	...	1922	2022	...	2122	...	2222	...	*2239*	...
Sargans **520** ⊖ d.	0527	0536	0636	0736	0836	0936	...	1036	1136	1236	1336	1436	...	1536	1636	1736	1836	...	1936	2036	...	2132	2136	2232	2236	2300	...
Buchs 520 ⊖ d.	...	0545	0645	0745	0845	0945	...	1045	1145	1245	1345	1445	...	1545	1645	1745	1845	...	1945	2045	...	...	2145	...	2245	2315	...
Altstätten **527** d.	...	0601	0701	0801	0901	1001	...	1101	1201	1301	1401	1501	...	1601	1701	1801	1901	...	2001	2101	...	...	2201	...	2301	2338	...
St Margrethen d.	...	0613	0713	0813	0913	1013	1024	1113	1213	1313	1413	1513	1524	1613	1713	1813	1913	1924	2013	2113	2124	...	2213	...	2313	2352	...
Rorschach d.	...	0620	0720	0820	0920	1020	|	1120	1220	1320	1420	1520	|	1620	1720	1820	1920	|	2020	2120	|	...	2220	...	2320	0002	...
St Gallen a.	...	0633	0733	0833	0933	1033	1043	1133	1233	1333	1433	1533	1543	1633	1733	1833	1933	1943	2033	2133	2143	...	2233	...	2333	0020	...
Wil 530 a.	...	0658	0758	0858	0958	1058	1106	1158	1258	1358	1458	1558	1606	1658	1758	1858	1958	2006	2058	2158	2206	...	2258	...	2358	...	...

⊖ – 🚌 services to **VADUZ (LIECHTENSTEIN)**

[line 11]	Ⓐ	Ⓐ	Ⓐ						and at the													f
Feldkirch (Bahnhof) d.	...	...	...	...	0624a	0654	0724	0754	same minutes	1724	1754	1824	1854	1924	1954	2024	2054	2124	2154	2224	2254	2324
Schaan (Bahnhof) d.	0515	0530	0600	0630	0700	0730	0800	0830	past each	1800	1830	1900	1930	2000	2030	2100	2130	2200	2230	2300	2330	0000
Vaduz Post d.	0524	0541	0611	0641	0711	0741	0811	0841	hour until	1811	1841	1908	1941	2008	2041	2108	2141	2208	2241	2308	2338	0008
Sargans (Bahnhof) a.	0554	0612	0642	0712	0742	0812	0842	0912		1842	1912	...	2012	...	2112	...	2212	...	2312f	...	...	...

[line 11]	Ⓐ	Ⓐ							and at the													f
Sargans (Bahnhof) d.	...	...	0544a	0614a	0644	0714a	0744	0814	same minutes	1844	1914	1944	2014	2044	...	...	2144	...	...	2244	...	2344
Vaduz Post d.	0520	0548	0618	0648	0718	0748	0818	0848	past each	1918	1948	2018	2048	2118	2148	...	2218	2248	...	2318	...	0018
Schaan (Bahnhof) d.	0530	0600	0630	0700	0730	0800	0830	0900	hour until	1930	2000	2030	2100	2130	2200	...	2230	2300	...	2328	...	0030
Feldkirch (Bahnhof) a.	0606	0636	0706	0736	0806	0836	0906	0936		2006	2036	2106	2136	2206	2236	...	2306	2336	...	...	...	...

🚌 [line 12] **Buchs** (Bahnhof) - **Vaduz** (Post) and v.v. Journey time: ± 15 minutes. **Service shown operates on Ⓐ only**. Regular services also operate between Buchs and Schaan. Operator: LIEmobil, Postplatz 7, FL-9494 Schaan. ✆ +423 237 94 94, fax +423 237 94 99, (www.liemobil.li).
From **Buchs**: 0630, 0700, 0730, 0748, 1200, 1230, 1300, 1630, 1700, 1730, 1800.
From **Vaduz**: 0639, 0709, 0739, 0749, 1209, 1239, 1309, 1639, 1709, 1739, 1809, 1839.

B – 🚃12 and ✕ Basel - Zürich - München and v.v.
M – 🚃12 and ✕ Zürich - München and v.v.
R – RHEINTAL EXPRESS.
a – Ⓐ only.
f – ⑤⑥ (subject to alteration on and around holidays).
j – Not Jan. 1.
k – Not Dec. 24, 31.
n – Not Dec. 24.

535 ZÜRICH - KONSTANZ and ROMANSHORN

SBB

km		IC 803	IR 2107	IC 805	IR 2109	IC 807	IR 2111	IC 809	IR 2113	IC 811	IR 2115	IC 813	IR 2117	IC 815	IR 2119	IC 817	IR 2121	IC 819	IR 2123	IC 821	IR 2125	IC 823	IR 2127	IC 825	IR 2129	IC 827	IR 2131
	Brig 560 d.	...	...	...	...	0546	...	0649	...	0749	...	0849	...	0949	...	1049	...	1149	...	1249	...	1349	...	1449	...	1549	...
	Bern 505 560 d.	...	...	0602	...	0702	...	0802	...	0902	...	1002	...	1102	...	1202	...	1302	...	1402	...	1502	...	1602	...	1702	...
0	**Zürich HB 530** d.	0607	0637	0707	0737	0807	0837	0907	0937	1007	1037	1107	1137	1207	1237	1307	1337	1407	1437	1507	1537	1607	1637	1707	1737	1807	1837
10	**Zürich Flug** ✈ **530** d.	0618	0648	0718	0748	0818	0848	0918	0948	1018	1048	1118	1148	1218	1248	1318	1348	1418	1448	1518	1548	1618	1648	1718	1748	1818	1848
30	Winterthur **530** d.	0634	0704	0734	0804	0834	0904	0934	1004	1034	1104	1134	1204	1234	1304	1334	1404	1434	1504	1534	1604	1634	1704	1734	1804	1834	1904
46	Frauenfeld d.	0646	0716	0746	0816	0846	0916	0946	1016	1046	1116	1146	1216	1246	1316	1346	1416	1446	1516	1546	1616	1646	1716	1746	1816	1846	1916
64	Weinfelden **539** ▲ d.	0700	0730	0800	0830	0900	0930	1000	1030	1100	1130	1200	1230	1300	1330	1400	1430	1500	1530	1600	1630	1700	1730	1800	1830	1900	1930
	Kreuzlingen ▲ a.	|	0751	|	0851	|	0951	|	1051	|	1151	|	1251	|	1351	|	1451	|	1551	|	1651	|	1751	|	1851	|	1951
	Konstanz ▲ a.	|	0754	|	0854	|	0954	|	1054	|	1154	|	1254	|	1354	|	1454	|	1554	|	1654	|	1754	|	1854	|	1954
86	**Romanshorn** a.	0718	...	0818	...	0918	...	1018	...	1118	...	1218	...	1318	...	1418	...	1518	...	1618	...	1718	...	1818	...	1918	...

	IC 829	IR 2133	IC 831	IR 2135	IC 833	IR 2137	IC 835	IR 2139 ‡	IC 837	RE 2143	IC 845 Y
Brig 560 d.	1649	...	1749	...	1849	...	1949	...	...	...	...
Bern 505 560 d.	1802	...	1902	...	2002	...	2102	...	2202	...	...
Zürich HB 530 d.	1907	1937	2007	2037	2107	2137	2207	2237	2307	2338	0008
Zürich Flug ✈ **530** d.	1918	1948	2018	2048	2118	2148	2218	2248	2318	2348	0021
Winterthur **530** d.	1934	2004	2034	2104	2134	2204	2234	2304	2334	0005	0036
Frauenfeld d.	1946	2016	2046	2116	2146	2216	2246	2316	2346	0016	0047
Weinfelden **539** ▲ d.	2000	2030	2100	2130	2200	2230	2300	2330	0000	0030	0058
Kreuzlingen ▲ a.	|	2051	|	2151	|	2251	|	2351	|	0051	|
Konstanz ▲ a.	|	2054	|	2155	|	2255	|	2354	|	0054	|
Romanshorn a.	2018	...	2118	...	2218	...	2318	...	0018	...	0116

	IR 2106	IC 806	IR 2108	IC 808	IR 2110	IC 810	IR 2112	IC 812	IR 2114	IC 814	IR 2116
Romanshorn d.	...	0538	...	0638	...	0741	...	0841	...	0941	...
Konstanz ▲ d.	0503	|	0603	|	0703	|	0803	|	0903	|	1003
Kreuzlingen ▲ d.	0506	|	0606	|	0706	|	0806	|	0906	|	1006
Weinfelden **539** ▲ d.	0529	0558	0629	0658	0729	0758	0829	0858	0929	0958	1029
Frauenfeld d.	0542	0612	0642	0712	0742	0812	0842	0912	0942	1012	1042
Winterthur **530** d.	0555	0625	0655	0725	0755	0825	0855	0925	0955	1025	1055
Zürich Flughafen ✈ **530** a.	0608	0638	0708	0738	0808	0838	0908	0938	1008	1038	1108
Zürich HB **530** a.	0621	0651	0721	0751	0821	0851	0921	0951	1021	1051	1121
Bern 505 560 a.	...	0758	...	0858	...	0958	...	1058	...	1158	...
Brig 560 a.	...	0911	...	1011	...	1111	...	1211	...	1311	...

km		IC 816	IR 2118	IC 818	IR 2120	IC 820	IR 2122	IC 822	IR 2124	IC 824	IR 2126	IC 826	IR 2128	IC 828	IR 2130	IC 830	IR 2132	IC 832	IR 2134	IC 834	IR 2136	IC 836	IR 2138 ‡	IC 838	RE 2142	IC 840	RE 2146
	Romanshorn d.	1041	...	1141	...	1241	...	1341	...	1441	...	1541	...	1641	...	1741	...	1841	...	1941	...	2041	...	2141	...	2241	...
0	**Konstanz** ▲ d.	|	1103	|	1203	|	1303	|	1403	|	1503	|	1603	|	1703	|	1803	|	1903	|	2003	|	2103	|	2203	|	2303
1	Kreuzlingen ▲ d.	|	1106	|	1206	|	1306	|	1406	|	1506	|	1606	|	1706	|	1806	|	1906	|	2006	|	2106	|	2206	|	2306
24	Weinfelden **539** ▲ d.	1058	1129	1158	1229	1258	1329	1358	1429	1458	1529	1558	1629	1658	1729	1758	1829	1858	1929	1958	2029	2058	2129	2158	2229	2258	2329
	Frauenfeld d.	1112	1142	1212	1242	1312	1342	1412	1442	1512	1542	1612	1642	1712	1742	1812	1842	1912	1942	2012	2042	2112	2142	2212	2242	2312	2342
	Winterthur **530** d.	1125	1155	1225	1255	1325	1355	1425	1455	1525	1555	1625	1655	1725	1755	1825	1855	1925	1955	2025	2055	2125	2155	2225	2258	2325	2353
	Zürich Flug ✈ **530** a.	1138	1208	1238	1308	1338	1408	1438	1508	1538	1608	1638	1708	1738	1808	1838	1908	1938	2008	2038	2108	2138	2208	2238	2311	2338	...
	Zürich HB 530 a.	1151	1221	1251	1321	1351	1421	1451	1521	1551	1621	1651	1721	1751	1821	1851	1921	1951	2021	2051	2121	2151	2221	2251	2323	2351	...
	Bern 505 560 a.	1258	...	1358	...	1458	...	1558	...	1658	...	1758	...	1858	...	1958	...	2058	...	2158	...	2302	...	0002	...	...	...
	Brig 560 a.	1411	...	1511	...	1611	...	1711	...	1811	...	1911	...	2011	...	2111	...	...	...	...	...	...	...	...	...	...	...

Y – ⑥⑦ (not Apr. 15).
n – Not May 1.
‡ – Runs as *RE* train on ①②③④⑦ (also Apr. 14).

▲ – Additional services operate **Weinfelden - Konstanz and v.v.** journey time: 30–36 minutes. A change of trains may be necessary at Kreuzlingen.
From **Weinfelden**: 0528Ⓐn, 0602, 0628Ⓐn, 0702, 0735Ⓐn, 0802, 0902, 1002, 1102, 1202, 1302, 1402, 1502, 1602, 1635Ⓐn, 1702, 1735Ⓐn, 1802, 1835Ⓐn, 1902, 1935Ⓐn, 2002, 2102, 2202, 2302, 0002.
From **Konstanz**: 0522, 0550Ⓐn, 0622, 0648Ⓐn, 0722, 0748Ⓐn, 0822, 0922, 1022, 1122, 1222, 1322, 1422, 1522, 1548Ⓐn, 1622, 1648Ⓐn, 1722, 1748Ⓐn, 1822, 1848Ⓐn, 1922, 2022, 2122, 2222, 2322.

ROMANSHORN - FRIEDRICHSHAFEN car ferry service — 536

BSB/SBS

		p	p	q	q		and		r	x	x
Romanshorn ☐ 535......d.		0536	0636	0736	0836	0936	and hourly	1636	1736 1836 1936 2036
Friedrichshafen ☐ 933..a.		0617	0717	0817	0917	1017	until	1717	1817 1917 2017 2117

		p	p	q	q		and		r	x	x
Friedrichshafen ☐ 933.d.		0540	0640	0740	0840	0940	and hourly	1640	1740 1840 1940 2040
Romanshorn ☐ 535.....a.		0621	0721	0821	0921	1021	until	1721	1821 1921 2021 2121

p – Ⓐ Dec. 12 - 23, Jan. 9 - Dec. 8 (not May 1, 25, June 15, Oct. 3, Nov. 1).
q – Ⓧ Dec. 12 - Mar. 18, Nov. 6 - Dec. 3 (not Dec. 24, 27 - 31).
r – Daily (not Dec. 24 - 26, Jan. 1, 2, 6).

x – Ⓐ Dec. 12 - 23, Jan. 9 - Mar. 17; daily Mar. 20 - Nov. 5; Ⓧ Nov. 6 - Dec. 8).
☐ – Autoquai.

Ⓧ available 0836 - 2036 from Romanshorn; 0840 - 2040 from Friedrichshafen. ⓨ on other sailings.
Operator: BSB/SBS ℰ 071 466 78 88.

WEINFELDEN - WIL — 539

THURBO

km		Ⓐ	Ⓐ	Ⓐ	Ⓐ	Ⓐ		and		
0	Weinfelden 535...d.	0505	0531	0601	0631	0701 0731 0801	...	0831 hourly	2331	
19	Wil 530 ....a.	0529	0555	0629	0655	0729 0755 0829	...	0855 until	2355	

		Ⓐ	Ⓐ	Ⓐ	Ⓐ	Ⓐ		and		
	Wil 530 .... d.	0532	0601	0632	0701	0732 0801 0832	0901	hourly	2301	0001
	Weinfelden 535 ... a.	0557	0625	0657	0725	0757 0825 0857	0925	until	2325	0025

Additional services operate on Ⓐ:
Weinfelden depart 1601, 1701, 1801, 1901; Wil depart 1632, 1732, 1832, 1932.

CHUR - ST MORITZ — 540

RhB. Narrow gauge

Thusis - Tiefencastel and v.v. subject to 🚌 replacement Oct. 30 - Nov. 17. For *Glacier Express* services see Table 575

km		2 Ⓧ			△	951 ♦Ⓡ✔	△	953 ♦Ⓡ✔	961 ♦Ⓡ✔		△	△	△	△	△	△		△	△	△	△	△	△
0	Chur 575..........d.	0510		0658	0758		0832	0858	0858	...	0958	1058	1158	1258	1358	1458	...	1558	1658	1758	1858	1958	2056
10	Reichenau-Tamins 575 ....d.			0710	0808			0908	0908u	...	1008	1108	1208	1308	1408	1508	...	1608	1708	1808	1908	2008	2107
27	Thusis ....d.	0541		0730	0830			0930	0930u	...	1030	1130	1230	1330	1430	1530	...	1630	1730	1830	1930	2030	2133
41	Tiefencastel ....d.	0558		0747	0847		0918	0947	0947u	...	1047	1147	1247	1347	1447	1547	...	1647	1747	1847	1947	2047	2149
	Davos Platz ...d.								0953														
51	Filisur 545a ......d.	0613		0802	0902		0933u	1002	1002u 1016u	...	1102	1202	1302	1402	1502	1602	...	1702	1802	1902	2002	2102	2205
59	Bergün/Bravuogn ...d.	0630		0814	0914		0947u	1014	1014u 1029u	...	1114	1214	1314	1414	1514	1614	...	1714	1814	1914	2014	2114	2217
72	Preda ....d.	0645x		0830	0930			1030		...	1130	1230	1330	1430	1530	1630	...	1730	1830	1930	2030	2130	2232
84	Samedan ....a.	0700		0845	0945			1045	1048u 1109u	...	1145	1245	1345	1445	1545	1645	...	1745	1846	1946	2046	2147	2248
84	Samedan 546 ......d.	...	0702	0849	0949			1049		...	1149	1249	1349	1449	1549	1649	...	1749	1849	1949	2049	2149	2251
89	Pontresina 546/7 ....a.					1019		1055															
87	Celerina 546/7 .....a.	...	0705	0852	0952			1052		...	1152	1252	1352	1452	1552	1652	...	1752	1852	1952	2052	2152	2254
89	St Moritz 546/7 ....a.	...	0709	0858	0958			1058		...	1158	1258	1358	1458	1558	1658	...	1758	1858	1958	2058	2158	2258

		w	Ⓐ	Ⓧ	†	△	△	△	△	△	△	△	950 ♦Ⓡ✔	954 ♦Ⓡ✔		960 ♦Ⓡ✔		△	△	△
St Moritz 546/7 ....d.				0541	0602	0702	0802	0902	1002	1102	1202	1302	1402	1502	1602		1702		1802	1902	2002
Celerina 546/7 ....d.				0544	0605	0705	0805	0905	1005	1105	1205	1305	1405	1505	1605		1705		1805	1905	2005
Pontresina 546/7 ......d.														1621s		1722s				
Samedan 546 ....a.				0550	0609	0709	0809	0909	1009	1109	1209	1309	1409	1509	1609		1708s 1709 1727s		1809	1909	2009
Samedan ....d.		0452	0511v	0550	0611	0717	0817	0917	1017	1117	1217	1317	1417	1517	1617			1717		1817	1917	2017
Preda ....d.				0555	0623	0730	0830	0930	1030	1130	1230	1330	1430	1530	1630			1730		1830	1930	2030
Bergün/Bravuogn ......d.		0518	0537v	0619	0640	0747	0847	0947	1047	1147	1247	1347	1447	1547	1647		1704s 1747s 1747 1804s		1847	1948	2048
Filisur 545a ....d.		0535	0554v	0635	0656	0801	0901	1001	1101	1201	1301	1401	1501	1601	1701		1717s 1759s 1801 1818s		1901	2001	2101
Davos Platz ....a.																		1846		
Tiefencastel ....d.		0550	0610v	0651	0711	0815	0915	1015	1115	1215	1315	1415	1515	1615	1715		1731s 1815s 1815		1915	2015	2116
Thusis ....d.		0607v	0627	0709	0728	0833	0933	1033	1133	1233	1333	1433	1533	1633	1733		1750s 1830s 1833		1933	2033	2133
Reichenau-Tamins 575 ....a.				0652		0752	0853	0953	1053	1153	1253	1353	1453	1553	1653		1753	1851s 1853		1953	2053	2156
Chur 575 ....a.				0705	0742	0805	0903	1003	1103	1203	1303	1403	1503	1603	1703		1803	1820 1903 1903		2003	2103	2209

♦ – NOTES (LISTED BY TRAIN NUMBER)

950/1 – BERNINA EXPRESS – Ⓒ Dec. 11 - May 14; daily May 15 - Oct. 29; ⑥⑦ Nov. 18 - Dec. 9 (also Dec. 27 - 30); 🚃 [panorama car] and ⓨ Tirano - Pontresina - Chur and v.v.

953/4 – BERNINA EXPRESS – Ⓐ Dec. 12 - May 12; daily Oct. 30 - Nov. 17; ①-⑤ Nov. 20 - Dec. 8 (not Dec. 27 - 30); 🚃 [panorama car] (also ⓨ, except Oct. 30 - Nov. 17) Chur - Pontresina - Tirano and v.v.

960/1 – BERNINA EXPRESS – May 25 - Oct. 22: 🚃 [panorama car] and ⓨ Tirano - Davos and v.v.

s – Stops to set down only.
u – Stops to pick up only.
v – Ⓐ Dec. 12 - Oct. 27; ①-⑤ Nov. 20 - Dec. 8.
w – ①-⑤ Oct. 30 - Nov. 17.
x – Stops only on request.
y – Connection by 🚌.
△ – Nominally conveys 🚃 [panorama car] Dec. 11 - Apr. 17, Ⓡ, ✔.
✔ – Supplement payable.

Catering (Ⓧ and/or ⓨ) available on most services.

CHUR - AROSA — 541

RhB. Narrow gauge

km								and			q	
0	Chur ....d.	0508	0620	0808	0908	...	1008	and hourly	1908	2006	2106	2300
18	Langwies ....d.	0549	0706	0849	0949	...	1049	hourly 1949	2044	2143	2340x
26	Arosa...............a.	0609	0723	0909	1009	...	1109	until 2009	2103	2206	2358

		Ⓧ	Ⓐ	Ⓒ				and			t	
Arosa...............d.		0548	0625	0648	0748	...	0848	and hourly	1948	2108	...	0003
Langwies ....d.		0604	0641	0704	0804	...	0904	hourly	2004	2123	...	0017x
Chur ....a.		0651	0723	0751	0851	...	0951	until	2051	2207	...	0059

q – Runs daily. Operated by 🚌 ①-④ Apr. 18 - Nov. 16 (not May 24, 25, June 5, July 31, Aug. 1).
t – Runs daily. Operated by 🚌 ②-⑤ Apr. 19 - Nov. 17 (not May 25, 26, June 6, Aug. 1, 2).

x – Stops only on request.

CHUR - FLIMS — 542

🚌 Chur (Postautostation) - Flims Dorf (Post), ± 35 minutes, and Flims Waldhaus (Caumasee), ± 40 minutes.

From Chur:
0603Ⓧ, 0638Ⓐ, 0658, 0758 and hourly until 1758, then 1828Ⓐ, 1858, 1928Ⓐ, 2000, 2100, 2200, 2300.

From Flims Waldhaus (± 5 minutes from Flims Dorf):
0516Ⓧ, 0613, 0700Ⓐ, 0714, 0814, 0914 and hourly until 1914, then 2013, 2113, 2213, 2313.

Additional services available

ST MORITZ and TIRANO - CHIAVENNA - LUGANO — 543

PA, RhB*

		P Ⓡ	B Ⓡ											
St Moritz, Bahnhof ....§ d.		0725	0915	1115	1220		1315	1415	1515	1715	1915			
Silvaplana, Post.........§ d.		0737	0923	1123	1232u		1323	1423	1523	1723	1927			
Sils / Segl Maria, Posta .§ d.		0744	0931	1131	1239u		1331	1431	1531	1731	1934			
Maloja, Posta............§ d.		0756	0946	1146	1250u		1346	1446	1554	1746	1946			
Castasegna 🚏..........§ d.		0835	1030	1230	1327u		1430	1530	1638	1830	2025			
Tirano, Stazione.........d.					1420									
Chiavenna, Stazione ...§ d.		0858	1053	1253	1410		1453	1553	1701	1853	2048			
Menaggio ....d.		...	...	...	1505x		...	...	...	...	...			
Lugano, Stazione ◎......a.		...	...	...	1620s	1730	...	...	...	...	...			
Lugano, Autosilo Balestra .a.		...	...	...	1630		...	...	...	...	...			

				B Ⓡ	Q Ⓡ						
Lugano, Autosilo Balestra . d.					1145						
Lugano, Stazione ◎.......d.				1000	1205u						
Menaggio ....d.					1255x						
Chiavenna, Stazione ...§ d.		0706	0906	1106	1306		1420	1506	1706	1606	1915
Tirano, Stazione.........d.					1300						
Castasegna 🚏..........§ d.		0726	0926	1126	1326		1436s	1526	1726	1626	1933
Maloja, Posta............§ d.		0812	1012	1212	1412		1510s	1611	1814	1712	2014
Sils / Segl Maria, Posta .§ d.		0825	1025	1225	1425		1521s	1622	1827	1725	2027
Silvaplana, Post.........§ d.		0833	1033	1233	1433		1529s	1629	1836	1733	2036
St Moritz, Bahnhof ....§ a.		0842	1042	1242	1442		1545	1638	1851	1742	2051

B – Bernina Express service. Runs Apr. 14 - Oct. 29.
P – Palm Express service. Runs ⑤⑥⑦ (daily Dec. 26 - Jan. 8, June 12 - Oct. 22).
Q – Palm Express service. Runs ①⑥⑦ (daily Dec. 27 - Jan. 9, June 13 - Oct. 23).
s – Stops to set down only.
u – Stops to pick up only.
x – Calls only if advance reservation is made.

§ – Additional services operate St Moritz - Chiavenna and v.v.
◎ – is at Gandria.
* – Operators:
Tirano - Lugano: RhB, Reservation: ℰ (081) 288 65 65;
St Moritz - Chiavenna - Lugano: PA, Reservation: ℰ St Moritz (058) 341 34 92; fax (058) 667 49 81.

Ⓧ – Restaurant (Ⓧ) – Bistro (ⓨ) – Bar coach ⓨ – Minibar

544   🚌 CHUR - BELLINZONA and CHIAVENNA   PA

km				S	Bj	Bh	B		S	B	Bh		B	Bh		B	B		B	S	Bh		B		ℝ✗g ℝ✗g
0	Chur Postautostation 540 ...d.	...	...	0808	0813	0913	...	...	1008	1113	...	1208	1313	...	1408	1513	...	1608	...	1713	...	1808	...	...
40	Thusis Bahnhof 540 ...... ⊡ d.	...	0735	...	0835	0840	0940	0935	...	1035	1140	1135	1235	1335	1435	1540	1535	1635	...	1740	1735	1835	1835	2250 2359
64	Splügen Dorf ....d.	0809	0820	0904	0904	1004	1009	1020	1104	1204	1209	1304	1404	1409	1504	1604	1609	1704	1715	1804	1809	1904	2009	2330 0040
	San Bernardino Posta ...... a.	0829		0923	0923	1023	1029		1123	1223	1229	1323	1423	1429	1523	1623	1629	1723		1823	1829	1923	2029	...
	Chiavenna Stazione ⦵......a.		1015				1215											1910			1923		...
179	Bellinzona Stazione ....a.	0950		1020	1013	1113	1150		1220	1313	1350	1420	1513	1550	1620	1713	1750	1820		1913	1951	2020	2151	...

		Ⓐ		S		B	B		Bh	B		B	Bh	B		S	B	Bh		S	B		B		ℝ✗g ℝ✗n
Bellinzona Stazione ....d.		0707		0807	0845	0940	1007	1045	1140	1207	1245	1340	1407	1445		1540	1607	1645		1740	1807	1845r			
Chiavenna Stazione ⦵...........d.			0750									1440					1640							
San Bernardino Posta ....d.	0600	0823		0923	0935	1031	1123	1135	1231	1335	1431	1523	1535		1631	1723	1735		1831	1923	1940			
Splügen Dorf ....d.	0622	0845	0940	0945	0953	1051	1145	1153	1251	1345	1353	1451	1553	1630	1651	1745	1753	1830	1851	1945	1958	2351	0056
Thusis Bahnhof 540 ...... ⦵ d.	0704	0924		1021	1020	1125	1224	1220	1325	1424	1420	1525	1624	1620		1725	1824	1820		1925	2024	2025	0016	0121
Chur Postautostation 540 ....a.				1045	1150		1245	1350		1445	1550		1645		1750		1845		1950		2050			

B – San Bernardino Route Express. ℝ.
S – Splügen Pass service. Runs June 10 - Oct. 22. Supplement payable.
g – ⑤⑥ (not Apr. 14). Operated by Bustaxi. ☏ (081) 651 55 77.
h – June 10 - Oct. 22.
j – Dec. 11 - June 9, Oct. 23 - Dec. 9.

n – ⑥⑦ (not Apr. 15). Operated by Bustaxi. ☏ (081) 651 55 77.
r – Depart 1855 on 🚌.
⦵ – Stops to set down only.
⊡ – Stops to pick up only.
❶ – 🚌 is at Splügen Pass.

✗ – Supplement payable.
Reservations:
☏ Chur (058) 386 31 66;
Thusis (058) 341 34 89.

545   CHUR - LANDQUART - KLOSTERS - DAVOS / SCUOL TARASP   Narrow gauge. RhB

km		Ⓐ L	✗		L		L				✣ L		✣ L			
	Chur 520/534 ....d.	...	0601	...	0731	...	0831	...	0931	1031	...	1731	...	1831	...
	Landquart 520/534 ......a.	...	0609	...	0739	...	0839	...	0939	1039	and at	1739	...	1839	...
0	Landquart ....d.	0456 0512 0534	0540	0747 0747	0750 0820	0847 0850	0920	0947 0950	1047 1050 1120	the same	1720 1747 1750	1847 1850 1920
21	Küblis ....d.	0515 0535x 0605	0645	0712	0810 0814	0844	0910 0914	0944	1010 1014	1110 1114 1144	minutes	1744 1810 1814	1910 1914 1944
30	Klosters Dorf ....d.	0553x 0618	0658	0724 0821		1021		1121		past each	1821	1921
32	Klosters Platz 🚗 ....d.	0530 0559 0629	0703 0734	0829 0833 0859	0929 0933 0959	1029 1033	1129 1133 1159	hour	1759 1829 1833	1929 1933 2001
	Sagliains 546 🚗 § a.	0653	0752	0851	0951	1051	1151	until	1851	1951
	Ardez ....a.	0705	0807	0903	1003	1103	1203		1903	2003
	Scuol-Tarasp 546 ....a.	0716	0819	0915	1015	1115	1215		1915	2015
47	Davos Dorf ....d.	0621	0723	0850	0950	1050	1150		1850	1950 2021
50	Davos Platz 545a .....a.	0633	0729	0856	0956	1056	1156		1856	1956 2029

					z					✗	✗	Ⓐ	✗						✣ L			
Chur 520/534 ....d.	1931	2031	2131	2231		Davos Platz 545a .....d.	0500		0600 0626		0700 0730		0802		0902	
Landquart 520/534 ....a.	1939	2039	2139	2239		Davos Dorf ....d.	0503		0603 0629		0703 0733		0806		0906	
Landquart ....d.	1947	2047	2147	2247		Scuol-Tarasp 546 ....d.		0541		0641		0741		0841		
Küblis ....d.	2013	2113	2213	2313		Ardez ....d.		0548		0648		0748		0848		
Klosters Dorf ....d.	2025	2125	2225	2325		Sagliains 546 🚗 § d.		0603		0703		0803		0903		
Klosters Platz 🚗 .....d.	2030 2034 2130 2134 2230 2234 2330 2332		Klosters Platz 🚗 .....d.	0528 0623 0628 0654 0723 0728 0758 0825 0831 0925 0931 0957
Sagliains 546 🚗 ....§ a.	2052	2152	2252			Klosters Dorf ....d.	0530	0630 0658		0730		0833		0933		
Ardez ....a.	2107	2207	2312	2356		Küblis ....d.	0544	0644 0711		0744 0813 0843 0910 0943 0950 1013
Scuol-Tarasp 546 ....a.	2119	2219	2319	0007		Landquart ....a.	0613	0713 0737		0813 0836 0910 0913 1010 1013 1036
Davos Dorf ....d.	2051	2151	2251	2351		Landquart 520/534 ....a.		0718		0818		0918		1018		
Davos Platz 545a .....a.	2057	2157	2257	2357		Chur 520/534 ....a.		0726		0826		0926		1026		

km				✣ L			L		L								z	
	Davos Platz 545a ....d.		1502		1602		1702		1802	1902	2000		2100	2150	...
0	Davos Dorf..................d.	and at	1506		1606		1706		1806	1906	2003		2103	2154	...
	Scuol-Tarasp 546 .....d.	the same	1441		1541		1641	1741	1841		1941 2041	2141		2241
17	Ardez ....d.	minutes	1448		1548		1648	1748	1848		1948 2048	2148		2248
39	Sagliains 546 🚗 § d.	past each	1503		1603		1703	1803	1903		2003 2103	2203		2303
	Klosters Platz 🚗 .....d.	hour	1525 1531 1557	1625 1631 1657 1725 1731 1757 1825 1831 1925 1931	2027 2029 2122 2129	2217 2223 2321
	Klosters Dorf ....d.	until	1533		1633		1733		1833	1933		2031	2131		2225
	Küblis ....d.		1543 1550 1613 1643 1650 1713 1743 1750 1813 1843 1943 1950	2045	2145	2239
	Landquart ....a.		1610 1613 1636 1710 1713 1736 1810 1813 1836 1910 1913 2010 2013	2113	2213	2305
	Landquart 520/534 ....a.		1618		1718		1818		1918	2018		2118	2218	...
	Chur 520/534 ....a.		1626		1726		1826		1926	2026		2126	2226	...

L – 🚗 Landquart - St Moritz and v.v.
x – Stops only on request.
z – ⑤⑥ (also Dec. 25, 26, Apr. 13, May 24; not Apr. 14).
✣ – Every two hours.
§ – Sagliains station can only be used for changing trains.
🚗 – Car-carrying shuttle available (see page 260).

545a   DAVOS - FILISUR   Narrow gauge. RhB

For *Glacier Express* services see Table 575

km		✗		961 ♦			and				✗		and		960 ♦			
0	Davos Platz 545....d.	0605 0731 0831 0931 0953	1031	hourly	1931 2031	...	Filisur 540................d.	0634 0804	hourly	1804	1819 1904 2004 2104
16	Filisur 540 ....a.	0630 0756 0856 0956 1015	1056	until	1956 2056	...	Davos Platz 545.....a.	0658 0829	until	1829	1846 1929 2029 2129

960/1 – BERNINA EXPRESS – May 25 - Oct. 22: 🚗 [panorama car] and ⚑ Tirano - Davos and v.v. ℝ ✗.
✗ – Supplement payable.

546   PONTRESINA / ST MORITZ - SCUOL TARASP   Narrow gauge. RhB

km		✗	✗	✗	✗	†	†			✣ L			✣ L		L		L	
0	Pontresina 540/7 ...d.		0535		0602		0702		0802			1402		1502		1602		1702
	St Moritz 540/7 .....d.	0502	0541 0602	0602	0702 0723		0802 0847	and at	1402 1447	1502 1538	1602 1647	1702
5	Samedan 540 ....a.	0509 0542 0548 0609 0608 0609k 0708 0709k 0729	0808 0809k 0855	the same	1408 1409k 1455	1508 1509k 1545	1608 1609k 1651 1708 1709k
5	Samedan ....d.	0513	0600 0609 0613	0713	0813	0858	minutes	1413	1458 1513	1545 1613	1658 1713
12	Zuoz ....d.	0527	0614 0622 0627	0727	0827	0910	past each	1427	1510 1527	1559 1627	1710 1727
32	Zernez ....⦵ ...d.	0547	0635	0647	0747	0849	hour	1449	1529 1549	1628 1649	1729 1749
38	Susch ....d.	0553	0641	0653	0753	0855	until	1455	1535 1555	1634 1655	1735 1755
40	Sagliains 545 ....§ a.	0558	0645 0653 0656	0756 0758	0900	1500	1600	1700	1800
	Klosters Platz 545..a.		0722			0955	1555	1655	1755	♦
57	Scuol-Tarasp 545 ...a.	0625	0716	0819	0923	1523	1623	1723	1823

L – 🚗 St Moritz - Landquart.
k – Connects with train in previous column.
✣ – Every two hours.
§ – Sagliains station can only be used for changing trains.
⦵ – For 🚌 service Zernez - Malles and v.v. – see next page.

Pontresina 540/7 ....d.	1802	...	1902	...	2002	...	2102	...	2202	...	Scuol-Tarasp 545 ....d.	0541	⚒ Ⓐ	...	⚒ †	...	0607 0641	...	0741	...	0834	...
St Moritz 540/7 ....d.		1802		1902		2002		2102		2202	Klosters Platz 545 ....d.		0530								
Samedan 540 ....a.	1808 1809k	1908 1909k	2008 2009k	2108 2109k	2208 2209k	Sagliains 545 .... § d.	0601	...	...	0703	...	0801 0803 0855	...
Samedan ....d.	1813	1913	2013	2113	2213	Susch ....d.		0552	0626 0705	...	0805 0857	...
Zuoz ....d.	1827	1927	2027	2127	2227	Zernez ....⊖ d.		0602	0607 0713	...	0813 0907	...
Zernez ....⊖ d.	1849	1949	2047	2147	2247	Zuoz ....d.		0622 0633d	0657 0733 0757d	...	0833 0927	...
Susch ....d.	1855	1955	2053	2153	2253	Samedan ....a.	0633 0646d	0731 0747 0811d	...	0847k 0942	...
Sagliains 545 .... § a.	1900	2000	2056 2058	2156 2158	2256 2258	Samedan 540 ....d.	0635 0648	0712 0748 0812	0849 0849 0948 0948
Klosters Platz 545 ....a.						St Moritz 540/7 ....a.	0643	0719	0819 0858		0958
Scuol-Tarasp 545 ......a.	1923	2023	2119	2219	2319	Pontresina 540/7 ....a.	0655	0755	0856 0955	

		❖			❖											z	
	L		L			L			1734	...	1834	...	1934 1941 2041	...	2141	...	2241	...
Scuol-Tarasp 545 ....d.	L	0934	L	1034		L	1634	Klosters Platz 545 ....d.	0901		1001			1601			1801		1934 1941 2041	2141	2241
Klosters Platz 545 ....d.	0901		1001		and at	1601		Sagliains 545 .... § d.	0955		1055	1755	1855	1955 2001 2101 2103	2203	2301 2302
Sagliains 545 .... § d.	0955		1055		the same	1655	Susch ....d.	0918 0957	1017 1057	1617 1657	1757	1817 1857	1957	2105	2205	2304
Susch ....d.	0918 0957	1017 1057	minutes	1617 1657	Zernez ....⊖ d.	0929 1007	1027 1107	1627 1707	1807	1827 1907	2007	2113	2213	2312
Zernez ....⊖ d.	0929 1007	1027 1107	past each	1627 1707	Zuoz ....d.	0953 1027	1046 1127	1646 1727	1827	1846 1927	2027	2133	2233	2331
Zuoz ....d.	0953 1027	1046 1127	hour	1646 1727	Samedan ....a.	1006 1042	1057 1142	1657 1742	1842	1857 1942	2042	2145	2245	2345
Samedan ....a.	1006 1042	1057 1142	until	1657 1742	Samedan 540 ....d.	1009 1043 1049	1100 1148 1149	1700 1748 1749	1848 1849	1900 1948	1949 2048 2049	2150 2149 2250 2251	2345
Samedan 540 ....d.	1009 1043 1049	1100 1148 1149	1700 1748 1749	St Moritz 540/7 ....a.	1016	1058	1109	1158	1709	1758	1858 1909	1958	2058	2158	2258	2352
St Moritz 540/7 ....a.	1016	1058	1109	1158	1709	1758	Pontresina 540/7 ....a.		1055		1155	1755	1855	1955	2055	2156	2256	
Pontresina 540/7 ....a.		1055		1155	1755													

L – 🚋 Landquart - St Moritz.
d – ✗ only.
k – Connects with train in previous column.
v – May 6 - Oct. 22.
z – ⑤⑥ (also Dec. 25, 26, Apr. 13, May 24; not Apr. 14).

❖ – Every two hours.

§ – Sagliains station can only be used for changing trains.

⊖ – 🚌 service Zernez - Malles and v.v. (journey ±1 h 35 minutes):
From **Zernez**: 0715, 0815, 0915, 1015v, 1032, 1115, 1215v, 1315, 1415v, 1515, 1615, 1715.
From **Malles/Mals** bahnhof: 0610v, 0657✗, 0803, 0903, 1003v, 1103, 1203v, 1303, 1403v, 1503, 1545v, 1603, 1703, 1803, 1903.

Operator: AutoDaPosta (PA); ✆ +41 (0)81 856 10 90.

---

km					973 ® w		951 ®	▷	953 ®✗	961 ®		w				975 ®		▷
0	St Moritz ....d.	...	...	0748 0848	0930	...	0948	...	1048	...	...	1148 1248	1348 1448	...	1512 1548	1648
2	Celerina Staz ⊡ d.		0751 0851		0951	1051		1151 1251	1351 1451		1551	1651
6	Pontresina ....a.		0758 0858		0958	1058		1158 1258	1358 1458		1558	1658
6	Pontresina 540 ....d.	0704d 0808 0904	0941u	1008 1021	1104 1104u1117u		1208 1304	1408 1504	1521u 1608	1704
12	Morteratsch ....⊡ d.	0712d 0816 0912		1016	1112		1216 1312	1416 1512		1616	1712
17	Bernina Diavolezza ⊡ d.	0719d 0823 0919		1023	1119		1223 1319	1423 1519		1623	1719
18	Bernina Lagalb ....⊡ d.	0722d 0826 0921		1025	1121		1225 1321	1425 1521		1625	1721
22	Ospizio Bernina ....d.	0729d 0837 0929		1033	1129 1129s		1233 1329	1433 1529	1551	1633	1731
27	Alp Grüm ....d.	0745d 0853 0944	1013s	1051 1057s	1144 1140s1157s		1251 1344	1451 1544	1601	1651	1744
44	Poschiavo ....a.	0756 0906 1022	1112s	1132 1200	1222 1222s1248s		1332 1422	1532 1622	1648s 1732	1822
44	Poschiavo ....d.	0610 0620 0736 0833 0938 1023		1134 1136v 1208 1223		1334 1336v	1423 1536 1623		1736	1823
48	Le Prese ....d.	0616 0627x0744x 0840 0945 1029	1131s	1139 1143v1216s 1229 1230s1301s		1339 1343v	1429 1543 1629	1701s 1743 1829
51	Miralago ....d.	0620 0632 0749 0844 0949 1034		1142 1147v	1234		1342 1347v	1434 1547 1634		1747	1834
54	Brusio ....⊡ d.	0624 0639 0757 0851 0956 1041		1146 1154v	1241		1346 1354v	1441 1554 1641		1754	1841
58	Campocologno 🏛 ....d.	0629 0650 0807 0908 1012 1049		1151 1203v	1249		1351 1403v	1449 1603 1649		1803	1849
61	Tirano ....a.	0638 0703 0823 0916 1021 1100		1200 1157 1219v 1245	1300 1300 1332		1357 1419v	1500 1619 1700		1732 1819	1900

	🚐		🚐		🚐								976 ◆® ✗	
			Ⓐ			h								
St Moritz ....d.	1748	1848	1948 2020		Tirano ....d.		0655	0740	...	0900 0940	...	1003
Celerina Staz ⊡ d.	1751	1851	1951 2023		Campocologno 🏛 d.		0702	0752		0908 0952
Pontresina ....a.	1758	1858	1958 2030	m	Brusio ....⊡ d.		0706	0759		0915 0959
Pontresina 540 ....d.	1808	1908	2014	2057	Miralago ....d.		0711	0805		0920 1005
Morteratsch ....⊡ d.	1816	1916	2022		Le Prese ....d.		0714	0810		0925 1010	1041u
Bernina Diavolezza ....d.	1823	1923	2029		Poschiavo ....a.		0730		0820		0935 1020	1048
Bernina Lagalb ....d.	1825	1925	2031		Poschiavo ....d.	0627	0732 0825		0937 1024	1049
Ospizio Bernina ....d.	1833x	1933x	2038x		Alp Grüm ....d.	0706	0814 0905		1014 1105	1125s
Alp Grüm ....a.	1851	1951	2054		Ospizio Bernina ....d.	0712x	0821 0912		1021 1112	1148s
Poschiavo ....a.	1932	2032	2132	2133	Bernina Lagalb ....d.	0722	0831 0922		1029 1121
Poschiavo ....d.		1934	2034		2134	Bernina Diavolezza ....⊡ d.	0724	0833 0924		1031 1124
Le Prese ....d.		1939	2039		2139	Morteratsch ....⊡ d.	0734	0844 0936		1039 1136
Miralago ....d.		1943	2043		2143	Pontresina 540 ....a.	0749	0857 0950	1052 1150	1224s
Brusio ....⊡ d.		1946	2046		2146	Pontresina ....d.	0801 0801	0901 1001	1101 1201
Campocologno 🏛 d.		1952	2052		2152	Celerina Staz ....⊡ d.	0806 0806	0906 1006	1106 1206
Tirano ....a.		1959	2059		2159	St Moritz ....a.	0811 0811	0911 1011	1111 1211	1236

	△	▷	🚐		◇	🚐	974 ◆®✗	950		954 ◆®	960 ✗			△	🚐	h			△	🚐 🚐	🚐
Tirano ....d.	1100 1140v 1159	1300 1340v 1359	1403 1426		1500	1500 1512	...	1540 1700 1740		1900 1940 2002 2102 2202
Campocologno 🏛 d.	1108 1152v 1205	1308 1352v 1405		1508		1552 1708 1750		1910 1950 2010x 2110x 2210x
Brusio ....⊡ d.	1115 1159v 1209	1315 1359v 1409		1515		1559 1715 1757		1917 1957 2016 2116 2216
Miralago ....d.	1120 1205v 1213	1320 1405v 1413		1520		1605 1720 1803		1923 2003 2019 2119 2219
Le Prese ....d.	1125 1210v 1216	1325 1410v 1416	1441u1455u	1525	1526u1539u		1610 1725 1807x		1927x2007x2023x2123x2223x
Poschiavo ....a.	1135 1220v 1221k	1335 1420v 1421k		1535	1547		1620 1735 1820		1940 2020 2029 2129 2229
Poschiavo ....d.	1137 1224	1337 1424	1449u1509u	1537	1537u 1557		1624 1737 1824 1905
Alp Grüm ....d.	1214 1305	1414 1505	1524u1544u	1614	1614		1705 1814 1905
Ospizio Bernina ....d.	1221 1312	1421 1512	1533u	1621	1621u1650u		1712 1821 1911x
Bernina Lagalb ....d.	1229 1321	1429 1521		1629		1721 1829 1919
Bernina Diavolezza ....⊡ d.	1231 1324	1431 1524		1631		1724 1831 1921
Morteratsch ....⊡ d.	1239 1336	1439 1536		1639		1736 1839 1931
Pontresina 540 ....a.	1252 1350	1452 1550	1602s 1616s	1652	1652s 1719s		1750 1852 1950 2000
Pontresina ....d.	1301 1401	1501 1601		1701		1801 1901 2001	n
Celerina Staz ....⊡ d.	1306 1406	1506 1606		1706		1806 1906 2006
St Moritz ....a.	1311 1411	1511 1611		1620	1711		1811 1911 2011

◆ – NOTES (LISTED BY TRAIN NUMBER)

950/1 – BERNINA EXPRESS – Ⓒ Dec. 11 - May 14; daily May 15 - Oct. 29; ⑥⑦ Nov. 18 - Dec. 9 (also Dec. 27 - 30): 🚋 [panorama car] and ⓨ Tirano - Chur and v.v.

953/4 – BERNINA EXPRESS – Ⓐ Dec. 12 - May 12; daily Oct. 30 - Nov. 17; ①–⑤ Nov. 20 - Dec. 8 (not Dec. 27 - 30): 🚋 [panorama car] (also ⓨ, except Oct. 30 - Nov. 17) Chur - Pontresina - Tirano and v.v.

960/1 – BERNINA EXPRESS – May 25 - Oct. 22: 🚋 [panorama car] and ⓨ Tirano - Davos and v.v.

973/4 – BERNINA EXPRESS – May 13 - Oct. 29: 🚋 [panorama car] and ⓨ Tirano - St Moritz and v.v.

975/6 – BERNINA EXPRESS – May 13 - Oct. 29: 🚋 [panorama car] and ⓨ Tirano - St Moritz and v.v.

d – ✗ only.
h – ⑤⑥⑦ (also Dec. 26, Jan. 2, Apr. 13, 17, May 24, 25, June 5, Aug. 1).
k – Connects with train in previous column.
m – From Samedan (d. 2050).
n – To Samedan (a. 2008).
s – Stops to set down only.
u – Stops to pick up only.
v – May 13 - Oct. 29.
w – Dec. 11 - May 12, Oct. 30 - Dec. 9.
x – Stops only on request.

△ – Conveys 🚋 [panorama car] Dec. 11 - Apr. 17, ®, ✗.
▽ – Conveys 🚋 [panorama car] Dec. 11 - May 12, Oct. 30 - Dec. 9, ®, ✗.
▷ – Conveys open panorama car July 1 - Aug. 31, ®, ✗. Subject to good weather.
◇ – Conveys open panorama car Poschiavo - St Moritz July 1 - Aug. 31, ®, ✗. Subject to good weather.
⊡ – Request stop.
✗ – Supplement payable.

550 LUZERN and ZÜRICH - ERSTFELD, LUGANO and MILANO

SBB, FS

km		RE 25509	RE 25511	EC 11	IR 2309	RE 4313	EC 13	IR 2311	2567	IC 861	IR 2891	IC 863	IR 2313	2569	IC 865		EC 15	IR 2315	2571	IC 867	ICN 667	IR 2417	2573	IC 869	EC 17
		B	A	✖ ◧		A	✖ ◧		(🍷) S		△ h		N	(🍷) S	Ⓒ		✖ ◧		(🍷) S				(🍷) S	Ⓒ	✖ ◧
	Basel SBB **565** d.	...	...	...	0504	...	...	0604	...	...	...	...	0704	...	...	...	...	0804	...	...	0904	...	...	...	...
	Luzern 565 d.	...	...	...	0618	...	...	0718	0739	...	...	...	0818	0839	...	...	...	0918	0939	...	1018	...	1039	...	...
	Küssnacht am Rigi d.	...	...	...	|	...	...	|	0758	...	...	...	|	0858	...	...	...	|	0958	...	|	...	1058	...	...
0	**Zürich** HB d.	...	...	0609	|	...	0709	|	|	0732	0740	0809	|	|	0832	...	0909	|	|	0932	|	1009	|	1032	1109
29	Zug d.	...	...	0631	|	...	0731	|	|	0800	|	0831	|	|	0900	...	0931	|	|	1000	|	1031	|	1100	1131
45	**Arth-Goldau** a.	...	...	0646	0646k	...	0746	0746k	0811	0815	0833	0846	0846k	0911	0915	...	0946	0946k	1011	1015	1046	1046k	1111	1115	1146
45	**Arth-Goldau** d.	...	...	0650	0653	...	0750	0753	...	0818	0835	0850	0853	...	0918	...	0950	0953	...	1018	1050	1053	...	1118	1150
53	Schwyz d.	...	...	|	0701	...	|	0801	...	|	0843	|	0901	...	|	...	|	1001	...	|	|	1101	...	|	|
56	Brunnen d.	...	...	|	0706	...	|	0806	...	|	|	|	0906	...	|	...	|	1006	...	|	|	1106	...	|	|
68	Flüelen d.	...	...	|	0716	...	|	0816	...	|	0859	|	0916	...	|	...	|	1016	...	|	|	1116	...	|	|
77	**Erstfeld** d.	...	...	|	0724	...	|	0824	...	|	0907	|	0924	...	|	...	|	1024	...	|	|	1124	...	|	|
165	Bellinzona ▲ a.	...	...	0747	...	...	0847	...	...	0918	1044	0947	...	...	1018	...	1047	...	...	1118	1147	...	...	1218	1247
165	Bellinzona ‡ d.	0614	0714	0750	...	0814	0850	...	...	0921	...	0950	...	...	1021	...	1050	...	...	1121	1150	...	...	1221	1250
194	**Lugano** ‡ d.	0642	0742	0818	...	0842	0918	...	...	0948	...	1017	...	...	1048	...	1118	...	...	1148	1217	...	...	1248	1318
213	Mendrisio ‡ d.	0658	0758	|	...	0858	|	...	...	...	...	...	...	...	...	...	|	...	...	...	...	...	...	...	|
220	**Chiasso** ‡ a.	0705	0805	0846	...	0905	0946	...	...	...	...	...	...	...	...	...	1146	...	...	...	...	...	...	...	1346
220	**Chiasso** 🏛 § d.	0708	0808	0852	...	0908	0952	...	...	...	...	...	...	...	...	...	1152	...	...	...	...	...	...	...	1352
224	Como San Giovanni § a.	0713	0813	|	...	0912	0956	...	...	...	...	...	...	...	...	...	|	...	...	...	...	...	...	...	1356
271	**Milano** Centrale § a.	0750	0850	0935	...	0950	1035	...	...	...	...	...	...	...	...	...	1235	...	...	...	...	...	...	...	1435

km		IR 2319	2575	IC 871	ICN 667	IR 2421	2577		EC 19	IR 2323	2579	IC 875	ICN 675	IR 2893	RE 4329	IR 2425	2581	IC 877		EC 21	RE 4331	IR 2327	2583	IC 879	EC 153
			(🍷) S				(🍷) S		✖ ◧		(🍷) S			△ G m			(🍷) S	†n		✖ ◧			(🍷) S		✖ ◧
	Basel SBB **565** d.	1004	...	...	1104	...	...	...	...	1204	...	...	1304	...	...	...	...	...	...	...	...	1404	...	...	1504
0	**Luzern 565** d.	1118	1139	...	1218	...	1239	...	...	1318	1339	...	1418	...	...	...	1439	...	...	...	...	1518	1539	...	1618
16	Küssnacht am Rigi d.	|	1158	...	|	...	1258	...	...	|	1358	...	|	...	...	...	1458	...	...	...	...	|	1558	...	|
	Zürich HB d.	|	|	1132	|	1209	|	...	1309	|	|	1332	|	...	...	1409	|	1432	...	1509	...	|	|	1532	|
	Zug d.	|	|	1200	|	1231	|	...	1331	|	|	1400	|	...	...	1431	|	1500	...	1531	...	|	|	1600	|
28	**Arth-Goldau** a.	1146k	1211	1215	1246	1246k	1311	...	1346	1346k	1411	1415	1446	...	...	1446k	1511	1515	...	1546	...	1546k	1611	1615	1646
	Arth-Goldau d.	1153	...	1218	1250	1253	...	...	1350	1353	...	1418	1450	...	...	1453	...	1518	...	1550	...	1553	...	1618	1650
	Schwyz d.	1201	...	|	|	1301	...	...	|	1401	...	|	|	...	...	1501	...	|	...	|	...	1601	...	|	|
	Brunnen d.	1206	...	|	|	1306	...	...	|	1406	...	|	|	...	...	1506	...	|	...	|	...	1606	...	|	|
	Flüelen d.	1216	...	|	|	1316	...	...	|	1416	...	|	|	1410	...	1516	...	|	...	|	...	1616	...	|	|
	Erstfeld d.	1224	...	|	|	1324	...	...	|	1424	...	|	|	|	1430	1524	...	|	...	|	1530	1624	...	|	|
	Bellinzona ▲ a.	...	...	1318	1347	...	...	...	1447	...	...	1518	1547	1554	1609	...	...	1618	...	1647	1709	...	...	1718	1747
	Bellinzona ‡ d.	...	...	1321	1350	...	...	...	1450	...	...	1521	1550	1610p	1614	...	...	1621	...	1650	1714	...	...	1721	1750
	Lugano ‡ d.	...	...	1348	1417	...	...	...	1518	...	...	1548	1617	1638p	1642	...	...	1648	...	1718	1742	...	...	1748	1818
	Mendrisio ‡ d.	...	...	...	...	...	...	...	|	...	...	...	...	...	1658	...	...	...	...	|	1758	...	...	...	|
	Chiasso ‡ a.	...	...	...	...	...	...	...	1546	...	...	...	...	...	1705	...	...	...	...	1746	1805	...	...	...	1846
	Chiasso 🏛 § d.	...	...	...	...	...	...	...	1552	...	...	...	...	...	1708	...	...	...	...	1752	1808	...	...	...	1852
	Como San Giovanni § a.	...	...	...	...	...	...	...	|	...	...	...	...	...	1712	...	...	...	...	1756	1812	...	...	...	1856
	Milano Centrale § a.	...	...	...	...	...	...	...	1635	...	...	...	...	...	1750	...	...	...	...	1835	1850	...	...	...	1945

	RE 4333	IR 2429	2585	EC 23		IR 2331	2587	IC 883	ICN 683	IR 2433	2589	EC 25		IR 2335	2591	IC 887	ICN 687	IR 2437	IC 889	IR 2339	IC 889	ICN 691	IR 2441	RE 2443	
		N	(🍷) S	✖ ◧			(🍷) S				(🍷) S	✖ ◧			(🍷) S				①–⑤		⑥⑦				
Basel SBB **565** d.	...	...	...	...	...	1604	...	...	1704	...	...	...	...	1804	...	...	1904	...	...	2004	...	2104	...	...	...
Luzern 565 d.	...	...	1639	...	...	1718	1739	...	1818	...	1839	...	...	1918	1939	...	2018	...	...	2118	...	2218	...	...	...
Küssnacht am Rigi d.	...	...	1658	...	...	|	1758	...	|	...	1858	...	...	|	1958	...	|	...	...	|	...	|	...	...	...
Zürich HB d.	...	1609	|	1709	...	|	|	1732	|	1809	|	1909	...	|	|	1932	|	2009	2109	|	2132	|	2209	2309	...
Zug d.	...	1631	|	1731	...	|	|	1800	|	1831	|	1931	...	|	|	2000	|	2031	2131	|	2200	|	2231	2331	...
Arth-Goldau a.	...	1646k	1711	1746	...	1746k	1811	1815	1846	1846k	1911	1946	...	1946k	2011	2015	2046	2046k	2146	2146k	2215	2246	2246k	2346	...
Arth-Goldau d.	...	1653	...	1750	...	1753	...	1818	1850	1853	...	1950	...	1953	...	2018	2050	2053	2150	2153	2218	2250	2253	...	...
Schwyz d.	...	1701	...	|	...	1801	...	|	|	1901	...	|	...	2001	...	|	|	2101	|	2201	|	|	2301	...	...
Brunnen d.	...	1706	...	|	...	1806	...	|	|	1906	...	|	...	2006	...	|	|	2106	|	2206	|	|	2306	...	...
Flüelen d.	...	1716	...	|	...	1816	...	|	|	1916	...	|	...	2016	...	|	|	2116	|	2216	|	|	2316	...	...
Erstfeld d.	1630	1724	...	|	...	1824	...	|	|	1924	...	|	...	2024	...	|	|	2124	|	2226	|	|	2326	...	...
Bellinzona ▲ a.	1809	...	...	1847	...	...	...	1918	1947	...	...	2047	...	...	...	2118	2147	...	2247	...	2323	2347	...	...	...
Bellinzona ‡ d.	1814	...	...	1850	...	...	...	1921	1950	...	...	2050	...	...	...	2121	2150	...	2250	...	2325	2350	...	...	...
Lugano ‡ d.	1842	...	...	1924	...	...	...	1948	2017	...	...	2118	...	...	...	2148	2217	...	2318	...	2355	0018	...	...	...
Mendrisio ‡ d.	1858	...	...	|	...	...	...	...	...	...	...	|	...	...	...	...	...	...	2335	...	0012	0035	...	...	...
Chiasso ‡ a.	1905	...	...	1948	...	...	...	...	...	...	...	2146	...	...	...	...	...	...	2344	...	0021	0044	...	...	...
Chiasso 🏛 § d.	1908	...	...	1952	...	...	...	...	...	...	...	2152	...	...	...	...	...	...	...	...	...	...	...	...	...
Como San Giovanni § a.	1912	...	...	|	...	...	...	...	...	...	...	2156	...	...	...	...	...	...	...	...	...	...	...	...	...
Milano Centrale § a.	1950	...	...	2035	...	...	...	...	...	...	...	2235	...	...	...	...	...	...	...	...	...	...	...	...	...

	RE 2408	IR 2308	IR 2310	IC 856	IR 2312	IC 858	2564	IR 2412	RE 4304	ICN 668	IC 866	2566	IR 2316		EC 12	2568	IR 2416	RE 4308	ICN 672	IC 868	2570		IR 2320	EC 14	2572
							(🍷) S					(🍷) S			✖◧	(🍷) S					(🍷) S			✖ ◧	(🍷) S
Milano Centrale § d.	...	...	...	...	...	...	...	...	...	...	...	...	...	...	0725	...	...	0810	...	...	...	...	...	0925	...
Como San Giovanni § d.	...	...	...	...	...	...	...	...	...	...	...	...	...	...	|	...	...	0847	...	...	...	...	...	1003	...
Chiasso 🏛 § a.	...	...	...	...	...	...	...	...	...	...	...	...	...	...	0808	...	...	0852	...	...	...	...	...	1008	...
Chiasso ‡ d.	...	...	...	0515	...	0615	...	...	0655	0712	0739	...	...	...	0815	...	...	0855	...	...	...	...	...	1015	...
Mendrisio ‡ d.	...	...	...	0524	...	0624	...	...	0702	0724	0746	...	...	...	|	...	...	0902	...	...	...	...	...	|	...
Lugano ‡ d.	...	...	...	0543	...	0643	...	...	0719	0743	0811	...	...	...	0843	...	...	0919	0943	1011	...	...	...	1043	...
Bellinzona ‡ a.	...	...	...	0610	...	0710	...	...	0748	0810	0838	...	...	...	0910	...	...	0948	1010	1038	...	...	...	1110	...
Bellinzona ▲ d.	...	...	...	0613	...	0713	...	...	0751	0813	0840	...	...	...	0913	...	...	0951	1013	1040	...	...	...	1113	...
Erstfeld d.	...	...	0627	|	0734	|	...	0834	0925	|	|	...	0934	...	|	...	1034	1125	|	|	...	...	1134	|	...
Flüelen d.	...	...	0637	0651	0742	|	...	0842	...	|	|	...	0942	...	|	...	1042	...	|	|	...	...	1142	|	...
Brunnen d.	0555a	...	0651	|	0753	|	...	0853	...	|	|	...	0953	...	|	...	1053	...	|	|	...	...	1153	|	...
Schwyz d.	0600a	...	0655	|	0758	|	...	0858	...	|	|	...	0958	...	|	...	1058	...	|	|	...	...	1158	|	...
Arth-Goldau a.	0609a	...	0706	0709k	0806	0809k	...	0906	...	0909k	0939	...	1006	...	1009k	...	1106	...	1109k	1139	...	...	1206	1209k	...
Arth-Goldau d.	0611	0614	0714	0713	0814	0813	0848	0913	...	0914	0944	0948	1014	...	1013	1048	1113	...	1114	1144	1148	...	1214	1213	1248
Zug d.	0629	|	|	0729	|	0829	|	0929	...	|	1001	|	|	...	1029	|	1129	...	|	1201	|	...	|	1229	|
Zürich HB a.	0651	|	|	0751	|	0851	|	0951	...	|	1028	|	|	...	1051	|	1151	...	|	1228	|	...	|	1251	|
Küssnacht am Rigi d.	...	|	|	...	|	...	0900	...	...	|	...	1000	|	...	...	1100	...	...	|	...	1200	...	|	...	1300
Luzern 565 a.	...	0641	0741	...	0841	...	0921	...	...	0941	...	1021	1041	...	...	1121	...	...	1141	...	1221	...	1241	...	1321
Basel SBB **565** a.	...	0755	0855	...	0955	...	...	...	...	1055	...	...	1155	...	...	...	...	...	1255	...	...	...	1355	...	...

▲ – Local services **BELLINZONA - LOCARNO and v.v.**:

km							②–⑦	⑥⑦							②–⑦	⑥⑦
0	Bellinzona d.	0500	0530	and at the same minutes past	2300	2330	0000	0030	0330	Locarno d.	0535	0605	and at the same minutes past	2335	0005	0035	0135	0305
21	Locarno a.	0527	0557	each hour until	2327	2357	0027	0057	0357	Bellinzona a.	0559	0629	each hour until	2359	0029	0059	0159	0329

A – From Airolo.
B – From Biasca.
G – GOTTHARD PANORAMA EXPRESS – 🚂 Flüelen - Bellinzona / Lugano and v.v.
N – Extended to Göschenen on Ⓒ Dec. 17 - Apr. 16; ⑥⑦ July 1 - Oct. 22 (also Apr. 17).
S – VORALPEN EXPRESS – 🚂 Luzern - Arth Goldau - Rapperswil - St Gallen and v.v.

a – Ⓐ only.
h – Ⓒ Apr. 15 - Oct. 22 (also Apr. 14; not Aug. 1).
k – Connects with a train in previous column(s).
m – Ⓒ Apr. 15 - July 2; daily July 3 - Oct. 22 (also Apr. 14).
n – Not Aug. 1.
p – ①–⑤ July 3 - Oct. 20.

◧ – Supplement payable in Italy and for international journeys.
▲ – For local services Bellinzona - Locarno and v.v. see panel above.
‡ – Local services operate every 30 minutes Bellinzona - Chiasso and v.v. (journey time 1 hour).
§ – Local services operate every 30 minutes Chiasso - Como San Giovanni - Milano Porta Garibaldi and v.v. (journey time 68 minutes).

550 — SBB, FS — MILANO, LUGANO and ERSTFELD - ZÜRICH and LUZERN

	IC 872	IR 2420	IR 2892	EC 158	IC 870	IR 2574	EC 2324	EC 16	IR 2576	ICN 2424	IC 680	IC 878	IR 2578	ICN 2328	EC 18	IC 880	IR 2580	ICN 2428	IR 684	IR 2582	IR 2894	IC 882
	†n		Gm	✕ D			(Y) S	✕ D	(Y) S				S		✕ D	©	S			(Y) S	△	Zh
Milano Centrale § d.				1015				1125					1325									
Como San Giovanni § d.				1103				1203					1403									
Chiasso 🚏 § a.				1108				1208					1408									
Chiasso ‡ d.				1115				1215					1415									
Mendrisio ‡ d.																						
Lugano ‡ a.	1111		1111p	1143	1211			1243		1343	1411		1443			1511			1543			1611
Bellinzona ‡ a.	1138		1137p	1210	1238			1310		1410	1438		1510			1538			1610			1638
Bellinzona ▲ d.	1140		1137	1213	1240			1313		1413	1440		1513			1540			1613		1618	1640
Erstfeld d.		1234						1334			1434			1534					1634		1758	
Flüelen d.		1242	1344					1342			1442			1542					1642		→	
Brunnen d.		1253						1353			1453			1553					1653			
Schwyz d.		1258						1358			1458			1558					1658			
Arth-Goldau a.	1239	1306		1309k	1339			1406	1409k		1506	1509k	1539	1606	1609k	1639			1706	1709		1739
Arth-Goldau d.	1244	1313		1314	1344	1348	1414	1413		1448	1513	1514	1544	1548	1614	1613		1644	1648	1713	1714	1748	1744
Zug d.	1301	1329			1401			1429			1529		1601	1629		1701			1729			1801
Zürich HB a.	1328	1351			1428			1451			1551		1628	1651		1728			1751			1828
Küssnacht am Rigi d.						1400				1500					1600			1700			1800	
Luzern 565 a.				1341		1421	1441			1521			1541		1621	1641		1721		1741	1821	
Basel SBB 565 a.				1455			1555						1655			1755					1855	

	IR 2332	EC 20	IR 2894	IC 884	IR 2584		IR 2432	ICN 688	IC 886	IR 2586	IR 2336	EC 22		IR 2588	IR 2338	EC 10		IC 890	RE 2238	IR 2340	EC 24		IR 2440	ICN 696
		✕ D Zh	©	©	(Y) S					(Y) S		✕ D		(Y) S		✕ D					✕ D			
Milano Centrale § d.		1525										1725				1825							1925	
Como San Giovanni § d.		1603										1803						1908					2003	
Chiasso 🚏 § a.		1608										1808				1908							2008	
Chiasso ‡ d.		1615										1815				1915							2015	
Mendrisio ‡ d.																								
Lugano ‡ a.		1643		1711				1743	1811		1843					1943		2011			2043		2143	
Bellinzona ‡ a.		1710		1738				1810	1838		1910					2010		2038			2110		2210	
Bellinzona ▲ d.		1713	←	1740				1813	1840		1913					2013		2040			2113		2213	
Erstfeld d.	1734		1758					1834			1934				2034					2134			2234	
Flüelen d.	1742		1805					1842			1942				2042					2142			2242	
Brunnen d.	1753							1853			1953				2053					2153			2253	
Schwyz d.	1758		1820					1858			1958				2058					2158			2258	
Arth-Goldau a.	1806	1809k	1828	1839				1906	1909k	1939	2006	2009k		2106	2109k	2139			2206	2209k	2306		2309	
Arth-Goldau d.	1814	1813	1830	1844	1848		1913	1914	1944	1948	2014	2013		2048	2114	2113		2144	2148	2214	2213		2313	2314
Zug d.		1829	1901				1929	2001			2029				2129			2201			2229			2329
Zürich HB a.		1851	1942	1928			1951	2028			2051				2151			2228			2251			2351
Küssnacht am Rigi d.					1900					2000						2100						2200		
Luzern 565 a.	1841				1921					1941			2021	2041			2121	2141				2221	2241	2341
Basel SBB 565 a.	1955													2059				2259						0102

B – From Basel.
C – From Chiasso.
G – GOTTHARD PANORAMA EXPRESS – 🚋 Flüelen - Bellinzona/Lugano and v.v.
M – From/to Milano.
S – VORALPEN EXPRESS – 🚋 Luzern - Arth Goldau - Rapperswil - St Gallen and v.v.
Z – From/to Zürich.

h – © Apr. 15 - Oct. 22 (also Apr. 14; not Aug. 1).
j – © Dec. 17 - Apr. 16; ⑥⑦ July 1 - Oct. 22 (also Apr. 17).
k – Connects with a train in previous column(s).
m – © Apr. 15 - June 11; daily June 12 - Oct. 29 (also Apr. 1).
n – Not Aug. 1.
p – ①–⑤ July 3 - Oct. 20.

D – Supplement payable in Italy and for international journeys.
▲ – For local services Bellinzona - Locarno and v.v. see previous page.
‡ – Local services operate every 30 minutes Bellinzona - Chiasso and v.v. (journey time 1 hour).
§ – Local services operate every 30 minutes Chiasso - Como San Giovanni - Milano Porta Garibaldi and v.v. (journey time 68 minutes).

550a — ERSTFELD - LUGANO (via Gotthard pass) — SBB, FS

km		RE 25509	RE 25511	RE 4313	RE 4315	RE 4317	IR 2891	RE 2313	RE 4319	RE 4321	RE 4323	RE 4325	RE 4327	IR 2893	RE 4329	RE 4331	RE 4333	IR 2429	RE 4335	RE 4337	RE 4339	RE 4341	RE 4343
		M	M	M			Zh Bj							Gm	M	M	Zj						⑤–⑦
0	Erstfeld d.				0730	0830	0907	0925	0930	1030	1130		1230	1330		1430	1530	1630	1725	1730	1830		1930	2030	2130
29	Göschenen d.				0755	0855	0933	0950	0955	1055	1155		1255	1355	1443	1455	1555	1655	1750	1755	1855		1955	2055	2155
45	Airolo d.		0614	0714	0814	0914	0948		1014	1114	1214		1314	1414	1501	1514	1614	1714		1814	1914		2014	2114	2214
65	Faido d.		0632	0732	0832	0932	1008		1032	1132	1232		1332	1432		1532	1632	1732		1832	1932		2032	2132	2232
91	Biasca d.		0654	0754	0854	0954	1030		1054	1154	1254		1354	1454		1554	1654	1754	1834	1854	1954		2054	2154	2254
110	Bellinzona a.		0609	0709	0809	0909	1009	1045		1109	1209	1309		1409	1509	1554	1609	1709	1809		1909	2009	2109	2209	2309
110	Bellinzona d.		0614	0714	0814		1041			1214			1414		1610p	1614	1714	1814			2014			
139	Lugano a.		0641	0741	0841		1041			1241			1441		1638p	1641	1741	1841			2041			

		RE 4300	RE 4302	RE 4304	RE 4306	IR 2416	RE 4308	RE 4310	IR 2892	RE 4312	RE 4314	RE 4316	RE 4318	RE 4320	IR 2894	RE 4322	IR 2432	RE 4324	RE 4326	RE 4328	RE 25534
				C		Zj		M	Gm						Zh		Zj		M	M	
Lugano d.				0719			0919		1111p	1119		1319		1519					1719		1819	
Bellinzona a.				0748			0948		1138p	1148		1348		1548					1748		1848	
Bellinzona d.		0551	0651	0751	0851		0951	1051	1137	1151	1251	1351	1451	1551	1618	1651		1751	1851	1951	2051
Biasca d.		0605	0705	0805	0905		1005	1105		1205	1305	1405	1505	1605	1633	1705		1805	1905	2005	2105
Faido d.		0627	0727	0827	0927		1027	1127		1227	1327	1427	1527	1627	1655	1727		1827	1927	2027	2127
Airolo d.		0646	0746	0846	0946		1046	1146		1246	1346	1446	1546	1646	1716	1746		1846	1946	2046	2144
Göschenen d.		0700	0800	0900	1000	1005	1100	1200	1307	1300	1400	1500	1600	1700	1732	1800		1900	2000	2100	
Erstfeld a.		0725	0825	0925	1025	1030	1125	1225	1325	1325	1425	1525	1625	1725	1756	1825	1830	1925	2025	2125	

B – From Basel.
C – From Chiasso.
G – GOTTHARD PANORAMA EXPRESS – 🚋 Flüelen - Bellinzona/Lugano and v.v.
M – From/to Milano.
Z – From/to Zürich.

h – © Apr. 15 - Oct. 22 (also Apr. 14; not Aug. 1).
j – © Dec. 17 - Apr. 16; ⑥⑦ July 1 - Oct. 22 (also Apr. 17).
m – © Apr. 15 - June 11; daily June 12 - Oct. 29 (also Apr. 14).
p – ①–⑤ July 3 - Oct. 20.
△ – Conveys panorama car.

551 — LOCARNO - DOMODOSSOLA — FART

km		C	V	C	V	V	C	V	C	C						C	V	V	V	C	C	C
0	Locarno 550 d.	0647	0749	0849	1049	1149	1249	1449	1549	1649	1748	1848	Domodossola 590 d.	0530a	0825	0925	1025	1125	1240	1325	1525	1625	1725	2025
20	Camedo 🚏 d.	0724	0824	0924	1124	1224	1324	1524	1624	1724	1824	1924	S. M. Maggiore § d.	0612a	0910x	1010x	1110x	1210x	1324	1410x	1610x	1710x	1810	2109
26	Re d.	0740	0840x	0940x	1140x	1240x	1340x	1540x	1640	1740x	1840x	1940	Re d.	0625	0922x	1022x	1122x	1222x	1339	1422x	1622x	1722x	1822	2122
34	S. M. Maggiore § d.	0753	0853x	0953x	1153x	1253x	1353x	1553x	1653	1753x	1853x	1953	Camedo 🚏 d.	0639	0940	1040	1140	1240	1355	1440	1640	1740	1840	2138
53	Domodossola 590 a.	0836	0936	1036	1236	1336	1436	1636	1736	1836	1936	2036	Locarno 550 a.	0720	1019	1119	1219	1319	1432	1519	1719	1819	1919	2215

C – CENTOVALLI EXPRESS.
V – TRENO PANORAMICO VIGEZZO VISION – Conveys panorama car (supplement payable).
a – ①–⑤ only.
u – Stops to pick up only.
x – Stops only on request.
§ – Full name is Santa Maria Maggiore.

552 LUZERN - STANS - ENGELBERG

Narrow gauge rack railway. ZB

km		E		E				E			E		🚌			🚌			🚌					T	T
0	**Luzern 561** d.	0505	0527	0610	0627	0657	and at	2010	2027	2057	2110	2127	...	2157	2227	...	2257	2327	...	2357	0032	0057		0836	0936
9	Hergiswil **561** .. d.	0517	0540	|	0640	0710	the same	|	2040	2110	|	2140	...	2210	2240	...	2310	2340	...	0010	0047	0110	EXTRA	0847	0947
11	Stansstad d.	0520	0544	|	0644	0714	minutes	|	2044	2114	|	2144	...	2214	2244	...	2314	2344	...	0014	0050	0114	SERVICES	0851	0951
15	Stans d.	0524	0548	0624	0648	0718	past each	2024	2048	2118	2124	2148	...	2218	2248	...	2318	2348	...	0018	0054	0118	▶▶▶	0854	0954
19	Dallenwil d.	0529	0552	0629	0652	...	hour until	2029	2052	...	2129	2152	2155	2222	2252	2255	2322	2352	2355	0022	0059	...		|	|
34	**Engelberg** ⊡ a.	0553	...	0653	...	...		2053	...	...	2153	...	2216	...	...	2316	...	...	0016	...	...	...		0921	1021

		🚌		E				E			E		🚌				🚌				🚌		T	T
Engelberg ⊡ d.	...	0535	...	0601	...	...	and at	2101	...	...	2201	...	2230	...	...	...	2330	...	...	...	0018		1631	1731
Dallenwil d.	0504	0558	0604	0629	...	0704	the same	2129	...	2204	2229	2234	2253	2304	...	2334	2353	...	0004	0034	0038	EXTRA	|	|
Stans d.	0510	...	0610	0634	0640	0710	minutes	2134	2140	2210	2234	2240	...	2310	...	2340	...	...	0010	0040	0046	SERVICES	1704	1804
Stansstad d.	0514	...	0614	|	0644	0714	past each	|	2144	2214	|	2244	...	2314	...	2344	...	...	0014	0044	...	▶▶▶	1707	1807
Hergiswil **561** d.	0518	...	0618	|	0648	0718	hour until	|	2148	2218	|	2248	...	2318	...	2348	...	...	0018	0048	...		1710	1810
Luzern 561 a.	0531	...	0632	0649	0702	0732		2149	2202	2232	2249	2302	...	2332	...	0002	...	...	0032	0102	...		1724	1824

E – LUZERN - ENGELBERG EXPRESS. Conveys panorama car.
T – Ⓒ Dec. 11 - Mar. 26, July 8 - Oct. 29 (also Dec. 27-30).
⊡ – Station for Titlis, accessible by cable car system (including the world's first revolving cable car).

553 MOUNTAIN RAILWAYS IN CENTRAL SWITZERLAND

2nd class only. RB

km			p			f ⫽		and		p	q	
0	Arth-Goldau d.	0800	0910	1010	...	1015	1110	hourly	1610	1710	1810	...
9	Rigi Kulm a.	0845	0947	1047	...	1215	1147	until	1647	1747	1847	...

		p				g		and		p	q
Rigi Kulm d.	0900	1004	1104	1204	1304	1401	1404	hourly	1704	1804	1904
Arth-Goldau a.	0948	1048	1148	1248	1348	1535	1448	until	1748	1848	1948

December 11 - April 13 and October 23 - December 9

km			and			f						
0	Rigi Kulm d.	1000	hourly	1400	...	1430	...	1500	1600	...	1700	...
7	Vitznau a.	1040	until	1440	...	1539	...	1540	1640	...	1740	...

				g ⫽			and		n		x ♧
Vitznau d.	0915	1015	1115	1116	...	1215	hourly	1615	1740	...	1915
Rigi Kulm a.	0947	1047	1147	1242	...	1247	until	1647	1812	...	1947

April 14 - May 24 and September 11 - October 22

						🚂			and		⑤⑥
Rigi Kulm d.	1000	1100	1200	1300	1400	1430	...	1500	hourly	2000	2240
Vitznau a.	1040	1140	1240	1340	1440	1539	...	1540	until	2040	2320

					🚂 ⫽			and			⑤⑥
Vitznau d.	0915	1015	1115	...	1116	...	1215	hourly	1915	...	2205
Rigi Kulm a.	0947	1047	1147	...	1242	...	1247	until	1947	...	2237

May 25 - September 10

		†	⚒				🚂		and		
Rigi Kulm d.	1000	1057	1100	1200	1300	1400	1430	1500	hourly	2000	2240
Vitznau a.	1040	1140	1140	1240	1340	1440	1539	1540	until	2040	2320

			†		🚂 ⫽		and				
Vitznau d.	0915	1015	1050	1115	1116	1215	hourly	1915	...	2205	...
Rigi Kulm a.	0947	1047	1122	1147	1242	1247	until	1947	...	2237	...

ALPNACHSTAD - PILATUS KULM. Narrow gauge rack railway. *5 km*. Journey time: 30 minutes uphill, 40 minutes downhill. **Operator**: PB, ✆ 041 329 11 11.
Services run daily **early May - November 19** (weather permitting). **No winter service** (December - April).

From **Alpnachstad**: 0810 **j**, 0850, 0935, 1015, 1055, 1135, 1220, 1300, 1345, 1425, 1505, 1550, 1630 **j**, 1710 **j**, 1750 **k**.

From **Pilatus Kulm**: 0845 **j**, 0930, 1010, 1050, 1130, 1215, 1255, 1340, 1420, 1500, 1545, 1625, 1705 **j**, 1745 **j**, 1845 **k**.

BRIENZ - BRIENZER ROTHORN. Narrow gauge rack railway. *8 km*. Most services operated by 🚂. Journey time: 55–60 minutes uphill, 60–70 minutes downhill.
Operator: BRB, ✆ 033 952 22 22. Service valid **June 3 - October 22**, and is subject to weather conditions on the mountain and demand. Extra trains may run at busy times. **No winter service**.

From **Brienz**: 0730 **h**, 0836, 0940, 1000③, 1045, 1145, 1258, 1358, 1458, 1636.

From **Brienzer Rothorn**: 0830 **h**, 0938, 1115, 1220, 1328, 1428, 1528, 1628, 1740.

f – Jan. 29, Feb. 26 only. Operated by 🚂.
g – Jan. 28, Feb. 25 only. Operated by 🚂.
h – ⑦ Sept. 3-24.
j – Until Oct. 28.
k – June 18 - Aug. 20.
n – Not Dec. 12-25.

p – Daily Dec. 17 - Mar. 12; Ⓒ Mar. 18 - Apr. 30; daily May 1 - Oct. 29; ⑥⑦ Nov. 4 - Dec. 3 (also Dec. 11, Nov. 1, Dec. 8, 9).
q – ⑤ Dec. 16 - Apr. 21; ⑤⑥⑦ Apr. 28 - June 25; daily June 26 - Sept. 3; ⑤⑥⑦ Sept. 8 - Oct. 29; ⑤ Nov. 3 - Dec. 8 (also Apr. 13, May 24, June 14).
x – ⑤⑥ Dec. 30 - Mar. 11, Oct. 27 - Dec. 9.

🚂 – June 4, 18, July 2, 16, Aug. 1, 6, 20, Sept. 3, 17. Reservations: ✆ 041 399 87 87.
⫽ – Supplement payable.
♧ – Subject to favourable weather conditions.

554 🚌 MEIRINGEN - ANDERMATT

Service June 24 - Oct. 15 (no winter service) PA

							Ⓒ				
Meiringen Bahnhof d.	...	0850	0925	...	...	1050	1055	1325	1325	1520	...
Steingletscher, Susten d.	...	0944	|	1000	...	|	1149	|	1425	|	...
Susten Passhöhe d.	...	...	|	1010	...	|	...	|	1435	|	...
Göschenen Bahnhof d.	...	...	|	1049	...	|	...	|	1514	|	...
Grimsel Passhöhe d.	0912	...	1100	|	...	1204	...	1439	|	1634	...
Gletsch Post d.	0922	...	1110	|	...	1215	...	1450	|	1645	...
Oberwald Bahnhof a.	0937	...	1125	|	...	1230	...	1505	|	1700	...
Oberwald Bahnhof d.	...	...	...	|	1220	...	...	...	|	...	*1704*
Gletsch Post d.	...	...	...	|	1233	...	...	...	|	...	1720
Furka Passhöhe d.	...	...	...	|	1354	...	...	...	|	...	1743
Realp Post d.	...	...	...	|	1420	...	...	...	|	...	1809
Andermatt Bahnhof a.	...	...	...	1104	1439	...	...	...	1529	...	1828

						Ⓒ					
Andermatt Bahnhof d.	...	...	...	0830	...	...	...	...	1534	1545	...
Realp Post d.	...	...	...	0842	...	...	...	...	1546	|	...
Furka Passhöhe d.	...	...	...	0906	...	...	...	...	1610	|	...
Gletsch Post d.	...	...	...	1005	...	...	...	...	1639	|	...
Oberwald Bahnhof a.	...	...	...	1020	...	...	...	...	*1700*	|	...
Oberwald Bahnhof d.	...	...	0845	...	1030	...	1250	1530	...	|	1704
Gletsch Post d.	...	...	0857	...	1046	...	1302	1542	...	|	1716
Grimsel Passhöhe d.	...	...	0911	...	1125	...	1330	1610	...	|	1732
Göschenen Bahnhof d.	0905	...	...	...	|	...	|	|	...	1605	|
Susten Passhöhe d.	0940	...	...	...	|	...	|	|	...	1640	|
Steingletscher, Susten d.	0950	1000	...	...	|	1150	|	|	...	1720	|
Meiringen Bahnhof a.	...	1050	...	...	1225	1240	1434	1714	...	1810	1835

Reservations: ✆ +41 (0)58 448 20 08.

555 ZÜRICH FLUGHAFEN ✈ - ZÜRICH - LUZERN

All trains *IR* SBB

km																	Ⓐ			Ⓐ							
0	**Zürich** Flughafen ✈ **530/5** d.	...	...	...	...	...	...	...	0847	...	and at	1547	...	...	...	1647	...	...	1747	...	...	1847	...	1947	...
10	**Zürich** HB **530/5** d.	0535	0604	0635	0704	0735	0804	0835	0904	0935	the same	1604	1635	...	1639	1704	1735	1739	1804	1835	...	1904	1935	2004	2035
22	Thalwil d.	0545	0614	0645	0714	0745	0814	0845	0914	0945	minutes	1614	1645	...	|	1714	1745	|	1814	1845	...	1914	1945	2014	2045
39	Zug d.	0602	0629	0702	0729	0802	0829	0902	0929	1002	past each	1629	1702	...	1712	1729	1802	1812	1829	1902	...	1929	2002	2029	2102
49	Rotkreuz d.	0610	|	0710	|	0810	|	0910	|	1010	hour	|	1710	...	1721	|	1810	1821	|	1910	...	|	2010	|	2110
67	**Luzern** a.	0625	0649	0725	0749	0825	0849	0925	0949	1025	until	1649	1725	...	1739	1749	1825	1839	1849	1925	...	1949	2025	2049	2125

									x ⫽	x ⫽	x ⫽
Zürich Flughafen ✈ **530/5** d.	2047	...	...	...	...	...	...	...	...	...	...
Zürich HB **530/5** d.	2104	2135	2204	2235	2304	2335	...	0008	0135	0235	0335
Thalwil d.	2114	2145	2214	2245	2314	2345	...	0017	|	|	|
Zug d.	2129	2202	2229	2302	2329	0002	...	0035	0155	0255	0355
Rotkreuz d.	|	2210	|	2310	|	0010	...	0046	0202	0302	0402
Luzern a.	2149	2225	2249	2325	2349	0025	...	0107	0225	0325	0425

				Ⓐ				Ⓐ	
Luzern d.	0455	0528	0610	0620	0635	...	0710	0720	0735
Rotkreuz d.	0513	0548	|	0636	0648	...	|	0736	0748
Zug d.	0526	0558	0631	0647	0658	...	0731	0747	0758
Thalwil d.	0542	0615	0646	|	0715	...	0746	|	0815
Zürich HB **530/5** a.	0555	0625	0656	0720	0725	...	0756	0820	0825
Zürich Flughafen ✈ **530/5** a.	0613	...	...	...	...	...	0813	...	...

																								x	x ⫽	x ⫽
Luzern d.	0810	0835	and at	1510	1535	...	1610	1635	1710	1735	1810	1835	1910	1935	2010	2035	2110	2135	2210	2235	2310	2335	0035	0135	0235
Rotkreuz d.	|	0848	the same	|	1548	...	|	1648	|	1748	|	1848	|	1948	|	2048	|	2148	|	2248	|	2348	0048	0146	0246
Zug d.	0831	0858	minutes	1531	1558	...	1631	1658	1731	1758	1831	1858	1931	1958	2031	2058	2131	2158	2231	2258	2331	2358	0058	0155	0255
Thalwil d.	0846	0915	past each	1546	1615	...	1646	1715	1746	1815	1846	1915	1946	2015	2046	2115	2146	2215	2246	2315	2346	0015	0116	0211	0311
Zürich HB **530/5** a.	0856	0925	hour	1556	1625	...	1656	1725	1756	1825	1856	1925	1956	2025	2056	2125	2156	2225	2256	2325	2356	0025	0125	0225	0325
Zürich Flughafen ✈ **530/5** a.	0913	...	until	1613	...	...	1713	...	1813	...	1913	...	2013	...	...	...	...	...	...	...	...	...	...	...	...

x – ⑥⑦ (also Apr. 14, 17, May 25, 26, June 5, Aug. 1; not Dec. 25).
⫽ – Supplement payable.

SBB — BASEL - BERN - INTERLAKEN and BRIG — 560

km		IC 955	IC 802	IC 1057	IC 957	IC 804	EC 51	IC 959	IC 806	ICE 1061	IC 961	IC 808	IC 1063	IC 963	IC 810	IC 1065	IC 965	IC 812	IC 1067	IC 967	IC 814	IC 1069	ICE 275	IC 816	EC 57
			(✕)			✕	✕ ◧		(✕)			✕	✕		(✕)			✕	✕ D		✕		G	✕	✕ ◧
	Romanshorn **535** d.	...	...	...	...	...	...	...	0538	...	...	0638	...	...	0741	...	...	0841	...	...	0941	...	...	1041	...
	Zürich Flug ✈ **535** d.	...	...	...	...	...	...	...	0640	...	...	0740	...	...	0840	...	...	0940	...	...	1040	...	...	1140	...
	Zürich HB **505** d.	...	...	...	...	0602	...	...	0702	...	...	0802	...	...	0902	...	...	1002	...	...	1102	...	...	1202	...
0	**Basel** SBB d.	...	...	0524	0559	|	0631	0659	|	0731	0759	|	0831	0859	|	0931	0959	|	1031	1059	|	1131	1159	|	1231
39	Olten d.	...	...	0557	0629	|	0657	0729	|	0757	0829	|	0857	0929	|	0957	1029	|	1057	1129	|	1157	1229	|	1257
101	**Bern** **505** a.	...	...	0624	0656	0658k	0724	0756	0758k	0824	0856	0858k	0924	0956	0958k	1024	1056	1058k	1124	1156	1158k	1224	1256	1258k	1324
101	**Bern** d.	0604	0606	0634	0704	0706	0734	0804	0806	0834	0904	0906	0934	1004	1006	1034	1104	1106	1134	1204	1206	1234	1304	1306	1334
132	Thun d.	0623	0625	0654	0723	0725	0754	0823	0825	0854	0923	0925	0954	1023	1025	1054	1123	1125	1154	1223	1225	1254	1323	1325	1354
142	**Spiez** a.	0632	0634	0702	0732	0734	0802	0832	0834	0902	0932	0934	1002	1032	1034	1102	1132	1134	1202	1232	1234	1302	1332	1334	1402
142	**Spiez** d.	0633	0636	0703	0733	0736	0805	0833	0836	0903	0933	0936	1005	1033	1036	1103	1133	1136	1205	1233	1236	1303	1333	1336	1405
	Interlaken West d.	0652	|	0723	0752	|	*0824*	0852	|	0923	0952	|	*1024*	1053	|	1123	1153	|	*1224*	1252	|	1323	1353	|	*1424*
	Interlaken Ost a.	0657	|	0728	0757	|	*0828*	0857	|	0928	0957	|	*1028*	1057	|	1128	1157	|	*1228*	1257	|	1328	1357	|	*1428*
197	Visp d.	...	0703	...	...	0803	0832	...	0903	...	...	1003	1032	...	1103	...	...	1203	1232	...	1303	...	...	1403	1432
206	**Brig** a.	...	0711	...	...	0811	0840	...	0911	...	...	1011	1040	...	1111	...	...	1211	1240	...	1311	...	...	1411	1440
	Milano C **590** a.	...	...	...	...	...	1037	...	...	...	...	...	...	...	...	...	...	...	...	...	...	...	...	...	1637

	IC 971	IC 818	IC 1073	EC 7	IC 820	IC 1075	IC 975	IC 822	IC 1077	IC 977	IC 824	IC 1079	IC 979	IC 826		EC 59	ICE 371	IC 828	IC 1083	IC 983	IC 830	IC 1085	ICE 373	IC 1087	IC 1089
		(✕)		G	✕	✕		(✕)			✕	(✕)		(✕)		✕ ◧	G	✕			✕	✕	G	①–⑥	⑦
Romanshorn **535** d.	...	1141	...	...	1241	...	...	1341	...	...	1441	...	...	1541	...	...	...	1641	...	...	1741	...	...	...	...
Zürich Flug ✈ **535** d.	...	1240	...	...	1340	...	...	1440	...	...	1540	...	...	1640	...	...	...	1740	...	...	1840	...	...	...	...
Zürich HB **505** d.	...	1302	...	...	1402	...	...	1502	...	...	1602	...	...	1702	...	...	...	1802	...	...	1902	...	...	...	...
Basel SBB d.	1259	|	1331	1359	|	1431	1459	|	1531	1559	|	1631	1659	|	...	1731	1759	|	1831	1859	|	1931	1959	2031	2031
Olten d.	1329	|	1357	1429	|	1457	1529	|	1557	1629	|	1657	1729	|	...	1757	1829	|	1857	1929	|	1957	2029	2057	2057
Bern **505** a.	1356	1358k	1424	1456	1458k	1524	1556	1558k	1624	1656	1658k	1724	1756	1758k	...	1824	1856	1858k	1924	1956	1958k	2024	2056	2124	2124
Bern d.	1404	1406	1434	1504	1506	1534	1604	1606	1634	1704	1706	1734	1804	1806	...	1834	1904	1906	1934	2004	2006	2034	2107	2134	2134
Thun d.	1423	1425	1454	1523	1525	1554	1623	1625	1654	1723	1725	1754	1823	1825	...	1854	1923	1925	1954	2023	2025	2054	2126	2154	2154
Spiez a.	1432	1434	1502	1532	1534	1602	1632	1634	1702	1732	1734	1802	1832	1834	...	1902	1932	1934	2002	2032	2034	2102	2135	2202	2202
Spiez d.	1433	1436	1503	1533	1536	1605	1633	1636	1703	1733	1736	1805	1833	1836	...	1905	1933	1936	2003	2033	2036	2105	2136	2205	2205
Interlaken West d.	1453	|	1523	1553	|	*1624*	1652	|	1723	1753	|	*1824*	1852	|	...	*1924*	1952	|	2023	2050	|	|	2152	|	|
Interlaken Ost a.	1457	|	1528	1557	|	*1628*	1657	|	1728	1757	|	*1828*	1857	|	...	*1928*	1957	|	2028	2054	|	|	2157	|	|
Visp d.	...	1503	...	...	1603	1632	...	1703	...	...	1803	1832	...	1903	...	1932	...	2003	...	...	2103	2132	...	2232	|
Brig a.	...	1511	...	...	1611	1640	...	1711	...	...	1811	1840	...	1911	...	1940	...	2011	...	...	2111	2140	...	2240	2301
Milano C **590** a.	...	...	...	...	...	...	...	...	...	...	...	...	...	...	...	2137	...	...	...	...	...	...	...	...	...

	IC 987	IC 1091	TGV 9225	IC 989	IC 1093	IC 1095	IC 1097	RE 4293	IC 991	IC 993
			(🍸) P		①–⑥	⑦				w
Romanshorn **535** d.	...	...	...	...	...	...	...	...	...	...
Zürich Flug ✈ **535** d.	...	...	...	...	...	...	...	...	...	...
Zürich HB **505** d.	...	...	...	...	...	...	...	...	...	...
Basel SBB d.	2059	2131	2136	...	...	...	2231	...	...	...
Olten d.	2129	2157	2202	...	...	...	2257	...	...	...
Bern **505** a.	2156	2224	2250	...	...	...	2326	...	...	...
Bern d.	2207	...	2302	2308	2234	2234	2339	...	0008	0108
Thun d.	2226	...	|	2327	2254	2254	0000	...	0029	0134
Spiez a.	2235	...	|	2336	2302	2302	0009	...	0038	0143
Spiez d.	2236	...	|	2337	2305	2305	...	0013	0038	0143
Interlaken West d.	2252	...	2349	2356	|	|	...	|	0054	0201
Interlaken Ost a.	2257	...	2353	0001	f	f	...	f	0100	0205
Visp d.	...	...	...	...	2335	|	...	|	...	...
Brig a.	...	...	...	...	2344	0011	...	0120	...	...
Milano C **590** a.	...	...	...	...	...	...	...	...	...	...

	IC 956	IC 805	IC 1056	ICE 372	IC 807	IC 1058	IC 960	IC 809	IC 1060	IC 962
				G	✕			✕	✕	
Milano C **590** d.	...	...	...	...	...	...	...	...	...	...
Brig d.	...	...	...	...	0546	...	...	0649	0720	...
Visp d.	...	...	...	...	0554	...	...	0657	0728	...
Interlaken Ost d.	...	...	0521	0600	f	0627	0700	|	*0729*	0800
Interlaken West d.	...	...	0526	0605	|	0632	0705	|	*0733*	0805
Spiez a.	...	...	0548	0621	0624	0652	0721	0724	0753	0821
Spiez d.	0520	...	0550	0622	0625	0654	0722	0725	0754	0822
Thun d.	0530	...	0601	0633	0636	0704	0733	0736	0804	0833
Bern a.	0552	...	0623	0652	0654k	0723	0752	0754k	0823	0852
Bern **505** d.	0604	0602	0636	0704	0702	0736	0804	0802	0836	0904
Olten d.	0632	0631	0705	0732	|	0805	0832	|	0905	0932
Basel SBB a.	0659	|	0729	0759	|	0829	0859	|	0929	0959
Zürich HB **505** a.	...	0702	...	...	0758	...	...	0858	...	...
Zürich Flug ✈ **535** a.	...	0716	...	...	0816	...	...	0916	...	...
Romanshorn **535** a.	...	0818	...	...	0918	...	...	1018	...	...

km		IC 811	TGV 9214	IC 1062	IC 964	IC 813	EC 50	ICE 278	IC 815	IC 1066	IC 968	IC 817	IC 1068	EC 6	IC 819	IC 1070	IC 972	IC 821	EC 52	IC 974	IC 823	IC 1074	ICE 376	IC 825	IC 1076
		(✕)	(🍸) P			✕	✕ ◧	G	(✕)			✕	✕	G	(✕)			✕	✕ ◧		✕		G‡	✕	✕ D
	Milano C **590** d.	...	...	...	...	...	0723	...	...	...	...	...	...	...	...	...	...	...	1123	...	...	...	...	...	...
	Brig d.	0749	...	...	...	0849	0920	...	0949	...	...	1049	1120	...	1149	...	...	1249	1320	...	1349	...	...	1449	1520
	Visp d.	0757	...	...	...	0857	0928	...	0957	...	...	1057	1128	...	1157	...	...	1257	1328	...	1357	...	...	1457	1528
0	**Interlaken** Ost d.	|	...	0830	0900	|	*0929*	1000	|	1030	1100	|	*1129*	1200	|	1230	1300	|	*1329*	1400	|	1430	1500	|	*1529*
2	Interlaken West d.	|	...	0835	0905	|	*0933*	1005	|	1035	1105	|	*1133*	1205	|	1235	1305	|	*1333*	1405	|	1435	1505	|	*1533*
18	**Spiez** a.	0824	...	0852	0921	0924	0953	1021	1024	1052	1121	1124	1153	1221	1224	1252	1321	1324	1353	1421	1424	1452	1521	1524	1553
	Spiez d.	0825	...	0854	0922	0925	0954	1022	1025	1054	1122	1125	1154	1222	1225	1254	1322	1325	1354	1422	1425	1454	1522	1525	1554
	Thun d.	0836	...	0904	0933	0936	1004	1033	1036	1104	1133	1136	1204	1233	1236	1304	1333	1336	1404	1433	1436	1504	1533	1536	1604
	Bern a.	0854k	...	0923	0952	0954k	1023	1052	1054k	1123	1152	1154k	1223	1252	1254k	1323	1352	1354k	1423	1452	1454k	1523	1552	1554k	1623
	Bern **505** d.	0902	0910	0936	1004	1002	1036	1104	1102	1136	1204	1202	1236	1304	1302	1336	1404	1402	1436	1504	1502	1536	1604	1602	1636
	Olten d.	|	|	1005	1032	|	1105	1132	|	1205	1232	|	1305	1332	|	1405	1432	|	1505	1532	|	1605	1632	|	1705
	Basel SBB a.	|	1023	1029	1059	|	1129	1159	|	1229	1259	|	1329	1359	|	1429	1459	|	1529	1559	|	1629	1659	|	1729
	Zürich HB **505** a.	0958	...	...	...	1058	...	...	1158	...	...	1258	...	...	1358	...	...	1458	...	...	1558	...	...	1658	...
	Zürich Flug ✈ **535** a.	1016	...	...	...	1116	...	...	1216	...	...	1316	...	...	1416	...	...	1516	...	...	1616	...	...	1716	...
	Romanshorn **535** a.	1118	...	...	...	1218	...	...	1318	...	...	1418	...	...	1518	...	...	1618	...	...	1718	...	...	1818	...

	IC 978	IC 827	IC 1078	IC 980	IC 829	IC 1080	IC 982	IC 831	IC 1082	IC 984	IC 833	IC 1084	IC 986	IC 835	EC 56	ICE 336	IC 837	IC 1088	ICE 338	IC 990	IC 1090	IC 1096	IC 992	IC 1092	IC 1094
		(✕)			✕	✕		(✕)			✕	(✕)		(✕)	✕ ◧						①–⑥			⑦	v
Milano C **590** d.	...	...	...	...	...	...	...	...	...	...	...	...	...	...	1823	...	...	...	...	...	...	...	...	...	...
Brig d.	...	1549	...	...	1649	1720	...	1749	...	...	1849	1920	...	1949	2020	...	...	2120	...	...	2220	...	...	2226	...
Visp d.	...	1557	...	...	1657	1728	...	1757	...	...	1857	1928	...	1957	2028	...	...	2128	...	...	2228	...	...	|	...
Interlaken Ost d.	1600	|	1630	1700	|	*1729*	1800	|	1830	1900	|	*1929*	2000	|	|	2100	...	|	...	2200	|	...	2300	|	2333
Interlaken West d.	1605	|	1635	1705	|	*1733*	1805	|	1835	1905	|	*1933*	2005	|	|	2105	...	|	...	2205	|	...	2305	|	2338
Spiez a.	1621	1624	1652	1721	1724	1753	1821	1824	1852	1921	1924	1953	2021	2024	2053	2121	...	2153	...	2221	2253	...	2321	2322	2356
Spiez d.	1622	1625	1654	1722	1725	1754	1822	1825	1854	1922	1925	1954	2022	2025	2054	2122	...	2154	...	2222	2254	...	2322	2325	2357
Thun d.	1633	1636	1704	1733	1736	1804	1833	1836	1904	1933	1936	2004	2033	2036	2104	2133	...	2204	...	2233	2304	...	2333	2336	0007
Bern a.	1652	1654k	1723	1752	1754k	1823	1852	1854k	1923	1952	1954k	2023	2052	2054k	2123	2152	...	2223	...	2252	2323	...	2352	2354	0026
Bern **505** d.	1704	1702	1736	1804	1802	1836	1904	1902	1936	2004	2002	2036	2104	2102	2136	...	2202	...	2236	...	...	2336	...	...	...
Olten d.	1732	|	1805	1832	|	1905	1932	|	2005	2032	|	2105	2132	|	2205	...	2230	...	2307	...	...	0007	...	...	...
Basel SBB a.	1759	|	1829	1859	|	1929	1959	|	2029	2059	|	2129	2159	|	2229	...	|	...	2330	...	...	0033	...	...	...
Zürich HB **505** a.	...	1758	...	...	1858	...	...	1958	...	...	2058	...	...	2158	...	...	2301	...	...	...	...	...	...	...	...
Zürich Flug ✈ **535** a.	...	1816	...	...	1916	...	...	2016	...	...	2116	...	...	2216	...	...	2316	...	...	...	...	...	...	...	...
Romanshorn **535** a.	...	1918	...	...	2018	...	...	2118	...	...	2218	...	...	2318	...	...	0018	...	...	...	...	...	...	...	...

D – 12 and ✕ Basel - Brig - Domodossola and v.v.
G – 12 and ✕ Interlaken - Basel - Frankfurt / Berlin / Hamburg and v.v.
P – 12 and (🍸) Paris Lyon - Basel - Bern / Interlaken and v.v.

f – Via Frutigen.
k – Connects with train in previous column.
v – ⑤⑥ (not Apr. 14).
w – ⑥⑦ (not Apr. 15).

◧ – Supplement payable for journeys from / to Italy.
‡ – Train number **396** on some days / dates.

12 ✕ – Restaurant (✕) – Bistro (🍸) – Bar coach 🍸 – Minibar 279

561 LUZERN - INTERLAKEN

Narrow gauge rack railway. ZB

km																								
		Ⓐ	Ⓐ	L		L			L				L			L			L			L		
0	**Luzern 552** d.	...	...	...	0542	0605	0612	0642	0705	0712	0742		1705	1712	1742	1805	1812	1842	1905	1912	1942	2005	2012	2042
9	Hergiswil **552** d.	...	...	...	0554	|	0624	0654	|	0724	0754		|	1724	1754	|	1824	1854	|	1924	1954	|	2024	2054
13	Alpnachstad d.	...	...	...	0559	|	0629	0659	|	0729	0759		|	1729	1759	|	1829	1859	|	1929	1959	|	2029	2059
15	Alpnach Dorf d.	...	...	...	0601	|	0631	0701	|	0731	0801	and at	|	1731	1801	|	1831	1901	|	1931	2001	|	2031	2101
21	Sarnen d.	...	...	...	0609	0624	0639	0709	0724	0739	0809	the same	1724	1739	1809	1824	1839	1909	1924	1939	2009	2024	2039	2109
23	Sachseln d.	...	...	...	0613	0628	0643	0713	0728	0743	0813	minutes	1728	1743	1813	1828	1843	1913	1928	1943	2013	2028	2043	2113
29	Giswil d.	...	...	...	0621	0638	0651	0721	0738	0751	0821	past each	1738	1751	1821	1838	1851	1921	1938	1951	2021	2038	2051	2121
36	Lungern d.	...	...	...	▬	0652	...	▬	0752	...	▬	hour	1752	...	▬	1852	...	...	1952	▬	...	2052	▬	...
40	Brünig Hasliberg d.	...	...	...	...	0704	...	...	0804	...	...	until	1804	...	...	1904	...	...	2004	...	...	2104	...	...
45	**Meiringen** ● a.	...	...	...	...	0716	...	...	0816	...	...		1816	...	...	1916	...	...	2016	...	...	2116	...	...
45	**Meiringen** ● d.	0515	0545	0614	0651	0722	...	0751	0822	...	0851		1822	...	1851	1922	...	...	...	2020	...	...	2120	...
58	**Brienz** d.	0527	0558	0628	0702	0733	...	0802	0837	...	0902		1837	...	1902	1935	...	...	...	2033	...	...	2132	...
65	Oberried d.	0537	0609	0639	0712	0744	...	0812	|	...	0912		|	...	1912	1944	...	...	...	2043	...	...	2142	...
74	**Interlaken** Ost a.	0550	0621	0651	0724	0754	...	0824	0855	...	0924		1855	...	1924	1955	...	...	...	2055	...	...	2155	...

	L								
Luzern 552 d.	2105	2112	2142	2212	2242	2312	2342	0012	0042
Hergiswil **552** d.	|	2124	2154	2224	2254	2324	2354	0024	0054
Alpnachstad d.	|	2129	2159	2229	2259	2329	2359	0029	0059
Alpnach Dorf d.	|	2131	2201	2231	2301	2331	0001	0031	0101
Sarnen d.	2124	2139	2209	2239	2309	2339	0009	0039	0109
Sachseln d.	2128	2143	2213	2243	2313	2343	0013	0043	0113
Giswil d.	2138	2151	2221	2251	2321	2351	0021	0051	0121
Lungern d.	2152	▬	...	▬	...	...	...	...	...
Brünig Hasliberg d.	2204	...	...	...	...	...	...	...	...
Meiringen ● a.	2216	...	...	y	...	...	...	...	...
Meiringen ● d.	...	2220	...	2320	...	...	...	...	...
Brienz d.	...	2232	...	2332	...	...	...	...	...
Oberried d.	...	2242	...	2342	...	...	...	...	...
Interlaken Ost a.	...	2255	...	2355	...	...	...	...	...

				L		Ⓐ		L	Ⓐ	
Interlaken Ost d.	...	...	...	...	...	0554	...	...	0627	...
Oberried d.	...	...	...	...	...	0608	...	...	0640	...
Brienz d.	...	...	...	...	...	0618	...	...	0650	...
Meiringen ● a.	...	...	...	...	...	0631	...	...	0703	...
Meiringen ● d.	...	...	...	0542	...	...	...	0642	▬	...
Brünig Hasliberg d.	...	...	...	0552	...	...	...	0652	...	...
Lungern d.	...	...	...	0605	...	...	...	0705	...	...
Giswil d.	0505	0535	0605	0622	0635	...	0705	0722	0735	0805
Sachseln d.	0513	0543	0613	0629	0643	...	0713	0729	0743	0813
Sarnen d.	0519	0549	0619	0635	0649	...	0719	0735	0749	0819
Alpnach Dorf d.	0524	0554	0624	|	0654	...	0724	|	0754	0824
Alpnachstad d.	0529	0559	0629	|	0659	...	0729	|	0759	0829
Hergiswil **552** d.	0534	0604	0634	|	0704	...	0734	|	0804	0834
Luzern 552 a.	0547	0617	0647	0655	0717	...	0747	0755	0817	0847

	L			L				L				L			Lv	Lw							z
Interlaken Ost d.	0704	...	0733	0804	...	0833		1804	...	1833	...	1904	...	1933	2004	...	...	2104	...	2204	...	2304	0006
Oberried d.	0714	...	0745	|	...	0844		|	...	1844	...	|	...	1946	2015	...	...	2115	...	2215	...	2315	0017
Brienz d.	0725	...	0754	0825	...	0854		1825	...	1854	...	1925	...	1956	2025	...	...	2124	...	2224	...	2324	0026
Meiringen ● a.	0736	...	0807	0836	...	0907	and at	1836	...	1907	...	1936	...	2009	2036	...	...	2137	...	2237	...	2337	0039
Meiringen ● d.	0742	...	▬	0842	...	▬	the same	1842	...	▬	...	1942	...	▬	2042	2042	...	▬	...	▬	...	▬	...
Brünig Hasliberg d.	0752	...	...	0852	...	...	minutes	1852	...	...	...	1952	...	...	2052	2052	...	...	...	...	...	...	...
Lungern d.	0805	...	...	0905	...	...	past each	1905	...	...	...	2005	...	...	2105	2105	...	...	...	...	...	...	...
Giswil d.	0822	0835	0905	0922	0935	1005	hour	1922	1935	2005	...	2022	2035	2105	2122	2122	2135	2205	2235	2305	2335	0005	...
Sachseln d.	0829	0843	0913	0929	0943	1013	until	1929	1943	2013	...	2029	2043	2113	2129	2129	2143	2213	2243	2313	2343	0013	...
Sarnen d.	0835	0849	0919	0935	0949	1019		1935	1949	2019	...	2035	2049	2119	2135	2135	2149	2219	2249	2319	2349	0019	...
Alpnach Dorf d.	|	0854	0924	|	0954	1024		|	1954	2024	...	|	2054	2124	|	|	2154	2224	2254	2324	2354	0024	...
Alpnachstad d.	|	0859	0929	|	0959	1029		|	1959	2029	...	|	2059	2129	|	|	2159	2229	2259	2329	2359	0029	...
Hergiswil **552** d.	|	0904	0934	|	1004	1034		|	2004	2034	...	|	2104	2134	|	|	2204	2234	2304	2334	0004	0034	...
Luzern 552 a.	0855	0917	0947	0955	1017	1047		1955	2017	2047	...	2055	2117	2147	2155	2155	2217	2247	2317	2347	0017	0047	...

L – LUZERN - INTERLAKEN EXPRESS. Conveys [panorama car] (reservation recommended). Also conveys ✕ on most services.

v – ①②③⑤⑥⑦ (also May 25).
w – ④ (not May 25).
y – ⑤⑥ (not Apr. 14).
z – ⑥⑦ (not Apr. 15).

● – Rail service **Meiringen** - **Innertkirchen** and v.v. Narrow gauge. 2nd class only. *5 km*. Journey time: 11 minutes. **Operator**: MIB.

From **Meiringen**: 0612Ⓐ, 0634Ⓐ, 0656, 0718Ⓒ, 0745, 0815Ⓒ, 0845, 0945, 1045, 1115Ⓒ, 1145, 1215Ⓒ, 1245, 1315Ⓒ, 1345, 1445, 1545, 1615Ⓒ, 1645, 1715Ⓐ, 1745, 1815Ⓐ, 1845, 1915Ⓒ, 1945, 2045, 2145, 2245**y**.

From **Innertkirchen**: 0558Ⓐ, 0623Ⓐ, 0629Ⓒ, 0645Ⓐ, 0707, 0729Ⓒ, 0802, 0827Ⓒ, 0902, 1002, 1102, 1127Ⓒ, 1202, 1227Ⓒ, 1302, 1327Ⓒ, 1402, 1502, 1602, 1627Ⓒ, 1702, 1727Ⓐ, 1802, 1827Ⓐ, 1902, 1927Ⓒ, 2002, 2102, 2202**y**.

562 SPIEZ - BRIG (via Lötschberg pass)

BLS

km									IC 1093	IC 1095	
			T		and at				①-⑥	⑦	
	Bern d.	...	...	0739	the same	1939	...	...	2234	2234	...
0	**Spiez** d.	0612	0712	0812	minutes	2012	2112	2212	2305	2305	0013
14	Frutigen ● d.	0625	0725	0825	past each	2025	2125	2225	2317	2317	0025
31	Kandersteg d.	0642	0742	0842	hour	2042	2142	2242	|	2335	0042
48	Goppenstein d.	0654	0754	0854	until	2054	2154	2254	|	2348	0053
74	**Brig** a.	0720	0820	0920		2120	2220	2320	2344	0011	0120

		IC 807								
		R			and at					
Brig d.	0516	0546	...	0636	the same	1736	1836	1936	2036	2207
Goppenstein d.	0542	|	...	0702	minutes	1802	1902	2002	2102	2232
Kandersteg d.	0554	|	←	0713	past each	1813	1913	2013	2113	2243
Frutigen ● d.	0609	0612	0631	0731	hour	1831	1931	2031	2131	2300
Spiez a.	→	0624	0644	0744	until	1844	1944	2044	2144	2313
Bern a.	...	0654	0720	0820		1920	...	...	...	...

R – Brig - Romanshorn.
T – From Thun.

– Car-carrying shuttle available (see page 260).

● – **SERVICE FRUTIGEN - ADELBODEN and v.v.:** 20 km, journey ±32 minutes. Operator: AFA, 3715 Adelboden. ✆ +41 (0)33 673 74 74, fax +41 (0)33 673 74 70.
From **Frutigen**: 0615Ⓐ, 0631, 0700Ⓐ, 0731, 0800, 0831, 0900Ⓒ, 0931, 1000Ⓒ, 1031, 1131 and hourly until 1631, then 1700, 1731, 1800, 1831, 1900Ⓐ, 1931, 2031, 2131, 2231, 2331.
From **Adelboden** (Post): 0535Ⓐ, 0550, 0622Ⓐ, 0650, 0725, 0750, 0825Ⓒ, 0850, 0925Ⓒ, 0950, 1050 and hourly until 1550, then 1625, 1650, 1725, 1750, 1825Ⓐ, 1850, 1950, 2050, 2150, 2225.

532 SCHAFFHAUSEN - ROMANSHORN - RORSCHACH

SBB, THURBO*

km																						X	Y		
0	**Schaffhausen 939/40** d.	...	...	...	...	0503		0531	...	0601	...		2031	...	2101	...	2131	...	2201	...	2231	2301	2301	2331	0001
20	Stein am Rhein d.	...	...	...	...	0526		0556	...	0626	...		2056	...	2126	...	2156	...	2226	...	2256	2326	2326	2356	0026
46	**Kreuzlingen** d.	0500	...	0530	...	0600	...	0630	...	0700	...	and at	2130	...	2200	...	2230	...	2300	...	2330	0000	0000	0026	0056
47	Kreuzlingen Hafen d.	0502	...	0532	...	0602	...	0632	...	0702	...	the same	2132	...	2202	...	2232	...	2302	...	2332	0002	0002	▬	...
65	**Romanshorn** a.	0526	...	0556	...	0626	...	0656	...	0726	...	minutes	2156	...	2226	...	2256	...	2326	...	2356	0026	0026	...	...
65	**Romanshorn** d.	0529	0531	0559	0601	0629	0631	0659	0701	0729	0731	past each	2159	2201	2229	2231	2259	2301	2329	2331	*0001*	0029	...	0031	...
	St Gallen **525** a.	0555	|	0624	|	0655	|	0724	|	0755	|	hour	2224	|	2255	|	2324	|	2355	|	|	0055	...	|	...
73	Arbon a.	...	0540	...	0610	...	0640	...	0710	...	0740	until	...	2210	...	2240	...	2310	...	2340	*0010*	...	...	0040	...
79	Rorschach Hafen a.	...	0547	...	0617	...	0647	...	0717	...	0747		...	2217	...	2247	...	2317	...	2347	*0017*	...	...	0047	...
80	**Rorschach** a.	...	0550	...	0620	...	0650	...	0720	...	0750		...	2220	...	2250	...	2320	...	2350	*0020*	...	...	0050	...

Rorschach d.	...	...	0508	...	0538	...	0608	...	0638	...		2108	...	2138	...	2208	...	2238	...	2308	...	2338	...	0008	...
Rorschach Hafen d.	...	...	0510	...	0540	...	0610	...	0640	...		2110	...	2140	...	2210	...	2240	...	2310	...	2340	...	0010	...
Arbon d.	...	...	0517	...	0547	...	0617	...	0647	...	and at	2117	...	2147	...	2217	...	2247	...	2317	...	2347	...	0017	...
St Gallen **525** d.	...	...	|	...	|	0535	|	0604	|	0635	the same	|	2104	|	2135	|	2204	|	2235	|	2305	|	2335	|	0004
Romanshorn a.	...	...	0527	...	0557	0559	0627	0629	0657	0659	minutes	2127	2129	2157	2159	2227	2229	2257	2259	2327	2329	2357	2359	0027	0029
Romanshorn d.	...	0501	...	0531	...	0601	...	0631	...	0701	past each	...	2131	...	2201	...	2231	...	2301	...	2331	...	0001	...	0031
Kreuzlingen Hafen d.	...	0524	...	0554	...	0624	...	0654	...	0724	hour	...	2154	...	2224	...	2254	...	2324	...	2354	...	0024	...	0054
Kreuzlingen d.	0500	0530	...	0600	...	0630	...	0700	...	0730	until	...	2200	...	2230	...	2300	...	2330	...	0000	...	0027	...	0057
Stein am Rhein d.	0530	0600	...	0630	...	0700	...	0730	...	0800		...	2230	...	2300	...	2330	...	0000	...	0030	...	...	...	...
Schaffhausen 939/40 a.	0556	0626	...	0656	...	0726	...	0756	...	0826		...	2256	...	2326	...	2356	...	0026	...	0053	...	...	...	...

X – ⑤⑥ Dec. 10 - Aug. 12, Aug. 25 - Dec. 8 (also Apr. 13, 16, 30, May 24, 25, June 4, July 31, Oct. 31; not Dec. 24).
Y – Daily **except** days/dates in note **X**.

* – SBB Romanshorn - Rorschach; THURBO Schaffhausen - Romanshorn.

BLS — SPIEZ - ZWEISIMMEN — 563

Spiez - Zweisimmen and v.v. subject to 🚌 replacement October 16 - 22

km																								
						Ⓒ											Ⓐ	Ⓒ	Ⓐ	Ⓒ		Ⓐ	Ⓐ	Ⓒ
	Interlaken Ost **560** d.	...	...	...	...	...	...	0908	...	...	...	...	...	...	1308	...	...	...	1508	1508	...	...	...	...
0	**Spiez 560** d.	0605	0712	0736	0818	0846	0912	0936	1018	1112	1136	1218	1312	...	1336	1418	1512	1512	1536	1536	1618	1641	1712	1712
11	Erlenbach im Simmental d.	0624	0729	0750	0833	|	0929	0950	1033	1129	1150	1233	1329	...	1350	1433	1529	1529	1550	1550	1633	1655	1729	1729
26	Boltigen d.	0642	0746	0810	0850	0911	0946	1010	1050	1146	1210	1250	1346	...	1410	1450	1546	1546	1608	1610	1650	1711	1746	1746
35	**Zweisimmen** a.	0653	0757	0819	0859	0920	0957	1019	1059	1157	1219	1259	1357	...	1419	1459	1556	1557	1617	1619	1659	1720	1756	1757

	Ⓐ	Ⓒ		Ⓐ					
Interlaken Ost **560** d.	1708	1708	...	...	...	...	...	...	...
Spiez 560 d.	1736	1736	1818	1841	1912	2012	2107	2207	2340
Erlenbach im Simmental d.	1750	1750	1833	1855	1929	2029	2121	2221	2355
Boltigen d.	1808	1810	1850	1911	1946	2046	2140	2240	0013
Zweisimmen a.	1817	1819	1859	1920	1957	2057	2150	2250	0023

	Ⓐ		Ⓐ		Ⓐ					
Zweisimmen d.	0538	0557	0633	0701	0738	...	0801	0903	0938	1001
Boltigen d.	0546	0606	0642	0710	0746	...	0810	0910	0946	1010
Erlenbach im Simmental d.	0603	0625	0657	0729	0803	...	0832	0930	1003	1032
Spiez 560 a.	0618	0640	0712	0747	0818	...	0847	0947	1018	1047
Interlaken Ost **560** a.	...	...	...	...	...	...	...	...	...	...

										Ⓐ	Ⓒ	Ⓒ			Ⓐ	Ⓒ							
Zweisimmen d.	1103	1138	1201	1303	1338	1401	1503	1538	...	1600	1601	1629	1703	1738	1800	1801	...	1903	2001	2106	...	2206	2306	...
Boltigen d.	1110	1146	1210	1310	1346	1410	1510	1546	...	1608	1610	1636	1710	1746	1808	1810	...	1910	2010	2115	...	2215	2315	...
Erlenbach im Simmental d.	1130	1203	1232	1330	1403	1432	1530	1603	...	1626	1632	1655	1730	1803	1826	1832	...	1929	2030	2134	...	2234	2334	...
Spiez 560 a.	1147	1218	1247	1347	1418	1447	1547	1618	...	1641	1647	1710	1747	1818	1841	1847	...	1945	2045	2149	...	2249	2352	...
Interlaken Ost **560** a.	...	1249	...	...	1449	...	...	1649	...	...	...	...	...	1849	...	...	...	...	...	...	...	...	...	...

Narrow gauge rack railway: BOB, WAB, JB — INTERLAKEN - KLEINE SCHEIDEGG - JUNGFRAUJOCH — 564

km																											
						r	v			r	r			r	r			r	r			r	r			r	
0	**Interlaken Ost** d.	0635	0635	0705	0705	0735	0735	0805	0805	0835	0835	0905	0905	0935	0935	1005	1005	1035	1035	1105	1105	1135	1135	1205	1205	1235	1305
3	Wilderswil ▲ d.	0640	0640	0710	0710	0740	0740	0810	0810	0840	0840	0910	0910	0940	0940	1010	1010	1040	1040	1110	1110	1140	1140	1210	1210	1240	1310
8	Zweilütschinen d.	0646	0647	0716	0717	0746	0747	0816	0817	0846	0847	0916	0917	0946	0947	1016	1017	1046	1047	1116	1117	1146	1147	1216	1217	1246	1317
12	**Lauterbrunnen** ● a.	0655		0725		0755		0825		0855		0925		0955		1025		1055		1125		1155		1225		1255	
	change trains																										
12	**Lauterbrunnen** d.	0707		0737		0807		0837		0907		0937		1007		1037		1107		1137		1207		1237		1307	
16	Wengen a.	0721		0751		0821		0851		0921		0951		1021		1051		1121		1151		1221		1251		1321	
16	Wengen d.	0724		0754		0824r		0854		0924r		0954		1024r		1054		1124r		1154		1224r		1254		1324r	
19	Grindelwald a.		0709		0739		0809		0839		0909		0939		1009		1039		1109		1139		1209		1239		1339
	change trains																										
19	Grindelwald d.		0717		0747		0817		0847		0917		0947		1017		1047		1117		1147		1217		1247		1347
20	Grindelwald Grund d.		0725		0755		0825		0855		0925		0955		1025		1055		1125		1155		1225		1255		1355
23*	**Kleine Scheidegg** a.	0750	0750	0820	0820	0850r	0850	0920	0920	0950r	0950	1020	1020	1050r	1050	1120	1120	1150r	1150	1220	1220	1250r	1250	1320	1320	1350r	1420

				r			r	r			r	r			v			v	v		j						
Interlaken Ost d.	1305	1405	1405	1435	1505	1505	1535	1535	1605	1605	1635	1635	1705	1705	1735	1805	1805	1835	1835	1905	1935	2002	2005	2102	2105	2202	2205
Wilderswil ▲ d.	1310	1410	1410	1440	1510	1510	1540	1540	1610	1610	1640	1640	1710	1710	1740	1810	1810	1840	1840	1910	1940	2007	2010	2107	2110	2207	2210
Zweilütschinen d.	1316	1417	1416	1447	1516	1517	1546	1547	1616	1617	1646	1647	1716	1717	1746	1816	1817	1846	1847	1917	1946	2013	2017	2113	2117	2213	2217
Lauterbrunnen ● a.	1325		1425		1525		1555		1625		1655		1725		1755	1825		1855			1955	2022		2122		2222	
change trains																					r						
Lauterbrunnen d.	1337		1437		1537		1607		1637		1707		1737		1807	1837		1907			2007	2030		2130		2230	
Wengen a.	1351		1451		1551		1621		1651		1721		1751		1821	1851		1921			2021	2044		2144		2244	
Wengen d.	1354		1454		1554		1624r		1654		1724t		1754r		1824j	1854j		...			...	...		...		...	
Grindelwald a.		1439		1509		1539		1609		1639		1709		1739			1839	...	1909	1939	...	...	2039	...	2139	...	2239
change trains												t		r			j		r	j							
Grindelwald d.		1447		1517		1547		1617		1647		1717		1747			1847	...	1917	1947	...	...	...	...	...	...	...
Grindelwald Grund d.		1455		1525		1555		1625		1655		1725		1755			1855	...	1922	1952	...	...	...	...	...	...	...
Kleine Scheidegg a.	1420	1520	1520	1550	1620	1620	1650r	1650	1720	1720	1750t	1750	1820r	1820	1850j	1920j	1920	...	...	...	...	...	...	...	...	...	...

Kleine Scheidegg d.	...	...	...	...	...	...	...	...	...	...	...	...	0801	0803	0831	0833	0901r	0903	0931	0933	1001r	1003	1031	1033	1101r	1103	1131
Grindelwald Grund d.	...	...	...	...	...	...	...	0708	...	0738	...	0808		0838		0908		0938		1008		1038		1108		1138	
Grindelwald a.	...	...	...	...	...	...	...	0712	...	0742	...	0812		0842		0912		0942		1012		1042		1112		1142	
change trains			⚒							v				r				r				r				r	
Grindelwald d.	0519	...	0547	...	0619	...	...	0719	...	0749	...	0819		0849		0919		0949		1019		1049		1119		1149	
Wengen a.		...		...		...	...		...		...		0830		0900		0930r		1000		1030r		1100		1130r		1200
Wengen d.		0512		0605		0642	0703		0733		0803		0833		0903		0933		1003		1033		1103		1133		1203
Lauterbrunnen a.		0529		0622		0659	0721		0751		0821		0851		0921		0951		1021		1051		1121		1151		1221
change trains						v			r				r				r				r				r		
Lauterbrunnen ● d.		0533		0633		0703	0733		0803		0833		0903		0933		1003		1033		1103		1133		1203		1233
Zweilütschinen d.	0537	0543	0611	0643	0643	0713	0743	0743	0813	0813	0843	0843	0913	0913	0943	0943	1013	1013	1043	1043	1113	1113	1143	1143	1213	1213	1243
Wilderswil ▲ d.	0543	0549	0617	0649	0649	0719	0749	0749	0819	0819	0849	0849	0919	0919	0949	0949	1019	1019	1049	1049	1119	1119	1149	1149	1219	1219	1249
Interlaken Ost a.	0549	0554	0622	0654	0654	0724	0754	0754	0824	0824	0854	0854	0924	0924	0954	0954	1024	1024	1054	1054	1124	1124	1154	1154	1224	1224	1254

																					r		j			
Kleine Scheidegg d.	1201r	1133	1231	1233	1331	1333	1401r	1403	1431	1433	1501r	1503	1531	1533	1603	1631	1633	1701r	1703	1731	1733	1833	1831r	1933	1931j	...	...
Grindelwald Grund d.		1208		1308		1408		1438		1508		1538		1608	1638		1708		1738		1808	1908		2008		...	...
Grindelwald a.		1212		1312		1412		1442		1512		1542		1612	1642		1712		1742		1812	1912		2012		...	...
change trains								r				r							v								
Grindelwald d.		1219		1319		1419		1449		1519		1549		1619	1649r		1719		1749		1819	1919		2019		2119	...
Wengen a.	1230r		1300		1400		1430r		1500		1530r		1600			1700		1730r		1800			1900r		2000j		...
Wengen d.	1233		1303		1403		1433		1503		1533		1603			1703		1733		1803			1903		2003		2103
Lauterbrunnen a.	1251		1321		1421		1451		1521		1551		1621			1721		1751		1821			1921		2021		2120
change trains	r						r				r							v									
Lauterbrunnen ● d.	1303		1333		1433		1503		1533		1603		1633			1733		1803		1833			1933		2033		2133
Zweilütschinen d.	1313	1243	1343	1343	1443	1443	1513	1513	1543	1543	1613	1613	1643	1643	1713r	1743	1743	1813	1813	1843	1843	1940	1943	2040	2043	2140	2143
Wilderswil ▲ d.	1319	1249	1349	1349	1449	1449	1519	1519	1549	1549	1619	1619	1649	1649	1719v	1749	1749	1819	1819	1849	1849	1946	1949	2046	2049	2146	2149
Interlaken Ost a.	1324	1254	1354	1354	1454	1454	1524	1524	1554	1554	1624	1624	1654	1654	1724v	1754	1754	1824	1824	1854	1854	1950	1954	2050	2054	2150	2154

At times of heavy snowfall (November 1 - April 30) the Eigergletscher - Jungfraujoch service is subject to cancellation

km																								
																				t	t	j	j
0	**Kleine Scheidegg** d.	0800	0830	0900	0930	1000	1030	1100	1130	...	1200	1230	1300	1330	1400	1430	...	1500	1530	1600	1630	1700	1730	1800
2	Eigergletscher d.	0810	0840	0910	0940	1010	1040	1110	1140	...	1210	1240	1310	1340	1410	1440	...	1510	1540	1610	1640	1710	1740	1810
9	**Jungfraujoch** a.	0835	0905	0935	1005	1035	1105	1135	1205	...	1235	1305	1335	1405	1435	1505	...	1535	1605	1635	1705	1735	1805	1835

																			t	t	j	j	
Jungfraujoch d.	0843	0913	0943	1013	1043	1113	1143	1213	1243	1313	...	1343	1413	1443	1513	1543	1613	1643	1713	1743	1813	1843	...
Eigergletscher d.	0910	0940	1010	1040	1110	1140	1210	1240	1310	1340	...	1410	1440	1510	1540	1610	1640	1710	1740	1810	1840	1910	...
Kleine Scheidegg a.	0918	0948	1018	1048	1118	1148	1218	1248	1318	1348	...	1418	1448	1518	1548	1618	1648	1718	1748	1818	1848	1918	...

j – May 13 - Sept. 3.
n – Dec. 17 - Apr. 2, May 13 - Oct. 22.
q – June 24 - Oct. 22.
r – Dec. 17 - Oct. 22.
t – Apr. 3 - Oct. 22.
v – Daily Dec. 11 - Oct. 28; ①–⑥ Oct. 30 - Dec. 9.
◆ – Additional services available Dec. 17 - Apr. 2, May 13 - Oct. 22.
* – Via Wengen (*28 km* via Grindelwald).

● – Cableway operates **Lauterbrunnen - Grütschalp**, and narrow gauge railway **Grütschalp - Mürren**, *total: 5 km*. **Operator**: BLM. Journey time: 20 minutes allowing for the connection.
From **Lauterbrunnen**: 0613, 0631, 0701, 0731, 0801, 0838, 0908, and every 30 minutes◆ until 1908, then 1938, 2035**n**.
From **Mürren**: 0606, 0636, 0706, 0736, 0806, 0828, 0858, and every 30 minutes◆ until 1858, then 1958**n**.

Cableway operates **Mürren - Schilthorn and v.v. Dec. 14 - Apr. 23, Apr. 29 - Nov. 12 (also Dec. 9)**.
From **Mürren**: 0810, 0840, 0910 and every 30 minutes until 1610. From **Schilthorn**: 0903, 0933 and every 30 minutes until 1633, then 1655. Additional services available Apr. 20 - Nov. 12. Operator: Schilthornbahn, ✆ +41 33 826 00 07.

▲ – Narrow gauge rack railway operates **May 27 - Oct. 22 Wilderswil - Schynige Platte**. *7 km*. Journey time: 52 minutes. **Operator**: BOB. Service may be reduced In bad weather.
From **Wilderswil**: 0725, 0805**q**, 0845, 0925, 1005, 1045, 1125, 1205, 1245, 1325, 1405, 1445, 1525, 1605, 1645.
From **Schynige Platte**: 0821, 0901**q**, 0941, 1021, 1101, 1141, 1221, 1301, 1341, 1421, 1501, 1541, 1621, 1701, 1753.

565 BASEL, OLTEN and BERN - LUZERN SBB

km		IR 2309	IR 2457	RE 4709	IR 2505	IR 2311	IR 2459	RE 4711	IR 2507	IR 2313	IR 2461	RE 4713	IR 2509	IR 2315	IR 2463	RE 4715		IR 2511	ICN 667	IR 2465	RE 4717	IR 2513	IR 2319	IR 2467	RE 4719	IR 2515	ICN 671
		E	Ⓐ			E				E				E					G				E				G
	Genève Aéroport ✈ **505** d.	...	...	...	...	...	...	...	...	...	...	...	0550	...	...	...	...	0702	...	...	...	0802	...	...	...	0902	...
	Genève **505** d.	...	...	...	...	...	...	...	...	...	...	...	0600	...	...	...	...	0712	...	...	...	0812	...	...	...	0912	...
	Lausanne **505** d.	...	...	...	0445e	...	...	...	0545	...	...	...	0647	...	...	...	...	0750	...	...	...	0850	...	...	...	0950	...
0	**Basel** SBB d.	0504	...	...	|	0604	0617	...	|	0704	0717	...	|	0804	0817	...	...	|	0904	0917	...	|	1004	1017	...	|	1104
14	Liestal d.	|	...	...	|	|	0627	...	|	|	0727	...	|	|	0827	...	...	|	|	0927	...	|	|	1027	...	|	|
21	Sissach d.	|	...	...	|	|	0633	...	|	|	0733	...	|	|	0833	...	...	|	|	0933	...	|	|	1033	...	|	|
39	**Olten** a.	0528	...	...	|	0628	0647	...	|	0728	0747	...	|	0828	0847	...	...	|	0928	0947	...	|	1028	1047	...	|	1128
39	**Olten** d.	0530	0549	0606	|	0630	0649	0706	|	0730	0749	0806	|	0830	0849	0906	...	|	0930	0949	1006	|	1030	1049	1106	|	1130
	Bern d.	|	|	|	0600	|	|	|	0700	|	|	|	0800	|	|	|	...	0900	|	|	|	1000	|	|	|	1100	|
47	Zofingen d.	|	0558	0613	0628	|	0658	0713	0728	|	0758	0813	0828	|	0858	0913	...	0928	|	0958	1013	1028	|	1058	1113	1128	|
69	Sursee d.	|	0611	0632	0641	|	0711	0732	0741	|	0811	0832	0841	|	0911	0932	...	0941	|	1011	1032	1041	|	1111	1132	1141	|
95	**Luzern** a.	0605	0630	0655	0700	0705	0730	0755	0800	0805	0830	0855	0900	0905	0930	0955	...	1000	1005	1030	1055	1100	1105	1130	1155	1200	1205

	IR 2469	RE 4721	IR 2517	IR 2323	IR 2471	RE 4723	IR 2519	ICN 675	IR 2473	RE 4725	IR 2521		IR 2327	IR 2475	RE 4727	IR 2523	EC 153	IR 2477	RE 4729	IR 2525	IR 2331	IR 2479	RE 4731	IR 2527	ICN 683	IR 2481	RE 4733
				E				G					E				◧ M				E				G		
Genève Aéroport ✈ **505** d.	...	...	1002	...	...	...	1102	...	...	...	1202	...	...	...	...	1302	...	...	...	1402	...	...	...	1502	...	...	...
Genève **505** d.	...	...	1012	...	...	...	1112	...	...	...	1212	...	...	...	...	1312	...	...	...	1412	...	...	...	1512	...	...	...
Lausanne **505** d.	...	...	1050	...	...	...	1150	...	...	...	1250	...	...	...	...	1350	...	...	...	1450	...	...	...	1550	...	...	...
Basel SBB d.	1117	...	|	1204	1217	...	|	1304	1317	...	|	...	1404	1417	...	|	1504	1517	...	|	1604	1617	...	|	1704	1717	...
Liestal d.	1127	...	|	|	1227	...	|	|	1327	...	|	...	|	1427	...	|	|	1527	...	|	|	1627	...	|	|	1727	...
Sissach d.	1133	...	|	|	1233	...	|	|	1333	...	|	...	|	1433	...	|	|	1533	...	|	|	1633	...	|	|	1733	...
Olten a.	1147	...	|	1228	1247	...	|	1328	1347	...	|	...	1428	1447	...	|	1528	1547	...	|	1628	1647	...	|	1728	1747	...
Olten d.	1149	1206	|	1230	1249	1306	|	1330	1349	1406	|	...	1430	1449	1506	|	1530	1549	1606	|	1630	1649	1706	|	1730	1749	1806
Bern d.	|	|	1200	|	|	|	1300	|	|	|	1400	...	|	|	|	1500	|	|	|	1600	|	|	|	1700	|	|	|
Zofingen d.	1158	1213	1228	|	1258	1313	1328	|	1358	1413	1428	...	|	1458	1513	1528	|	1558	1613	1628	|	1658	1713	1728	|	1758	1813
Sursee d.	1211	1232	1241	|	1311	1332	1341	|	1411	1432	1441	...	|	1511	1532	1541	|	1611	1632	1641	|	1711	1732	1741	|	1811	1832
Luzern a.	1230	1255	1300	1305	1330	1355	1400	1405	1430	1455	1500	...	1505	1530	1555	1600	1605	1630	1655	1700	1705	1730	1755	1800	1805	1830	1855

	IR 2529	IR 2335	IR 2483	RE 4735	IR 2531	ICN 687	IR 2485	RE 4737	IR 2533	IR 2339	IR 2487	RE 4739	IR 2535	ICN 691	IR 2489	RE 4741	IR 2537	IR 2343	IR 2491	RE 4743	IR 2539	IR 2345	IR 2493	RE 4745		IR 2347	IR 2349
		E				G				E				C													q
Genève Aéroport ✈ **505** d.	1602	...	...	...	1702	...	...	...	1802	...	...	...	1902	...	...	...	2002	...	...	...	...	...	...	...	...	...	...
Genève **505** d.	1612	...	...	...	1712	...	...	...	1812	...	...	...	1912	...	...	...	2012	...	...	...	2100	...	...	...	...	...	...
Lausanne **505** d.	1650	...	...	...	1750	...	...	...	1850	...	...	...	1950	...	...	...	2050	...	...	...	2145	...	...	...	...	...	...
Basel SBB d.	|	1804	1817	...	|	1904	1917	...	|	2004	2017	...	|	2104	2117	...	|	2202	2217	...	|	2302	2317	...	...	0002	0101
Liestal d.	|	|	1827	...	|	|	1927	...	|	|	2027	...	|	|	2127	...	|	2211	2227	...	|	2311	2327	...	...	0011	0110
Sissach d.	|	|	1833	...	|	|	1933	...	|	|	2033	...	|	|	2133	...	|	|	2233	...	|	|	2333	...	...	|	0116
Olten a.	|	1828	1847	...	|	1928	1947	...	|	2028	2047	...	|	2127	2147	...	|	2228	2247	...	|	2328	2347	...	...	0028	0128
Olten d.	|	1830	1849	1906	|	1930	1949	2006	|	2030	2049	2106	|	2130	2149	2206	|	2230	2249	2307	|	2330	...	0007	...	0035	0137
Bern d.	1800	|	|	|	1900	|	|	|	2000	|	|	|	2100	|	|	|	2200	|	|	|	2300	|	...	|	...	|	|
Zofingen d.	1828	|	1858	1913	1928	|	1958	2013	2028	|	2058	2113	2128	|	2158	2213	2228	|	2256	2314	2328	|	...	0014	...	0042	0144
Sursee d.	1841	|	1911	1932	1941	|	2011	2032	2041	|	2111	2132	2141	|	2211	2232	2241	|	...	2332	2341	|	...	0034	...	0056	0158
Luzern a.	1900	1905	1930	1955	2000	2005	2030	2055	2100	2105	2130	2155	2200	2205	2230	2255	2300	2305	...	2355	2400	0005	...	0056	...	0116	0216

km (via hsl)		RE 4706	IR 2456	IR 2456	IR 2306	IR 2508	RE 4708	IR 2458	IR 2308	IR 2510	RE 4710	IR 2460	IR 2310	IR 2512	RE 4712	IR 2462	IR 2312	IR 2514	RE 4714	IR 2464	ICN 668	IR 2516	RE 4716	IR 2466	IR 2316	IR 2518	RE 4718
			Ⓐ	Ⓒ					A				E				E				C				E		
	Luzern d.	0456	0530	...	0554	0600	0605	0630	0654	0700	0705	0730	0754	0800	0805	0830	0854	0900	0905	0930	0954	1000	1005	1030	1054	1100	1105
	Sursee d.	0521	0548	...	|	0618	0626	0648	|	0718	0726	0748	|	0818	0826	0848	|	0918	0926	0948	|	1018	1026	1048	|	1118	1126
0	Zofingen d.	0543	0602	...	|	0632	0643	0702	|	0732	0743	0802	|	0832	0843	0902	|	0932	0943	1002	|	1032	1043	1102	|	1132	1143
63	**Bern** a.	|	|	...	|	0700	|	|	|	0800	|	|	|	0900	|	|	|	1000	|	|	|	1100	|	|	|	1200	|
	Olten a.	0552	0610	...	0627	|	0652	0710	0727	|	0752	0810	0827	|	0852	0910	0927	|	0952	1010	1027	|	1052	1110	1127	|	1152
	Olten d.	...	0612	0612	0630	|	...	0712	0730	|	...	0812	0830	|	...	0912	0930	|	...	1012	1030	|	...	1112	1130	|	...
	Sissach d.	...	0627	0627	|	|	...	0727	|	|	...	0827	|	|	...	0927	|	|	...	1027	|	|	...	1127	|	|	...
	Liestal d.	...	0633	0633	|	|	...	0733	|	|	...	0833	|	|	...	0933	|	|	...	1033	|	|	...	1133	|	|	...
	Basel SBB a.	...	0644	0644	0655	|	...	0744	0755	|	...	0844	0855	|	...	0944	0955	|	...	1044	1055	|	...	1144	1155	|	...
	Lausanne **505** a.	...	...	...	...	0810	...	...	...	0910	...	...	...	1010	...	...	...	1110	...	...	...	1210	...	...	...	1310	...
	Genève **505** a.	...	...	...	...	0848	...	...	...	0948	...	...	...	1048	...	...	...	1148	...	...	...	1248	...	...	...	1348	...
	Genève Aéroport ✈ **505** a.	...	...	...	...	0857	...	...	...	0957	...	...	...	1057	...	...	...	1157	...	...	...	1257	...	...	...	1357	...

	IR 2468	ICN 672	IR 2520	RE 4720	IR 2470	IR 2320		IR 2522	RE 4722	IR 2472	EC 158	IR 2524	RE 4724	IR 2474	IR 2324		IR 2526	RE 4726	IR 2476	ICN 680	IR 2528	RE 4728	IR 2478	IR 2328	IR 2530	RE 4730	IR 2480
		G				E					◧ M				E					G				E			
Luzern d.	1130	1154	1200	1205	1230	1254	...	1300	1305	1330	1354	1400	1405	1430	1454	...	1500	1505	1530	1554	1600	1605	1630	1654	1700	1705	1730
Sursee d.	1148	|	1218	1226	1248	|	...	1318	1326	1348	|	1418	1426	1448	|	...	1518	1526	1548	|	1618	1626	1648	|	1718	1726	1748
Zofingen d.	1202	|	1232	1243	1302	|	...	1332	1343	1402	|	1432	1443	1502	|	...	1532	1543	1602	|	1632	1643	1702	|	1732	1743	1802
Bern a.	|	|	1300	|	|	|	...	1400	|	|	|	1500	|	|	|	...	1600	|	|	|	1700	|	|	|	1800	|	|
Olten a.	1210	1227	|	1252	1310	1327	...	|	1352	1410	1427	|	1452	1510	1527	...	|	1552	1610	1627	|	1652	1710	1727	|	1752	1810
Olten d.	1212	1230	|	...	1312	1330	...	|	...	1412	1430	|	...	1512	1530	...	|	...	1612	1630	|	...	1712	1730	|	...	1812
Sissach d.	1227	|	|	...	1327	|	...	|	...	1427	|	|	...	1527	|	...	|	...	1627	|	|	...	1727	|	|	...	1827
Liestal d.	1233	|	|	...	1333	|	...	|	...	1433	|	|	...	1533	|	...	|	...	1633	|	|	...	1733	|	|	...	1833
Basel SBB a.	1244	1255	|	...	1344	1355	...	|	...	1444	1455	|	...	1544	1555	...	|	...	1644	1655	|	...	1744	1755	|	...	1844
Lausanne **505** a.	...	...	1410	...	...	...	...	1510	...	...	...	1610	...	...	...	...	1710	...	...	...	1810	...	...	...	1910	...	...
Genève **505** a.	...	...	1448	...	...	...	...	1548	...	...	...	1648	...	...	...	...	1748	...	...	...	1848	...	...	...	1948	...	...
Genève Aéroport ✈ **505** a.	...	...	1457	...	...	...	...	1557	...	...	...	1657	...	...	...	...	1757	...	...	...	1857	...	...	...	1957	...	...

	ICN 684	IR 2532	RE 4732	IR 2482	IR 2332	IR 2534	RE 4734	IR 2484	ICN 688	IR 2536	RE 4736	IR 2486	IR 2336	IR 2538	RE 4738	IR 2488	IR 2338	IR 2540	RE 4740	IR 2490	IR 2340	IR 2542	RE 4742	ICN 696	RE 4744	IR 2344	
	G				E				G				E				E				E			G		q	
Luzern d.	1754	1800	1805	1830	1854	1900	1905	1930	1954	2000	2005	2030	2054	2100	2105	2130	2154	2200	2205	...	2254	2300	2305	2354	0005	0049	...
Sursee d.	|	1818	1826	1848	|	1918	1926	1948	|	2018	2026	2048	|	2118	2126	2148	|	2218	2226	...	|	2318	2326	|	0026	0108	...
Zofingen d.	|	1832	1843	1902	|	1932	1943	2002	|	2032	2043	2102	|	2132	2143	2202	|	2232	2243	2302	|	2332	2343	|	0043	0121	...
Bern a.	|	1900	|	|	|	2000	|	|	|	2100	|	|	|	2200	|	|	|	2300	|	|	|	2400	|	|	|	|	...
Olten a.	1827	|	1852	1910	1927	|	1952	2010	2027	|	2052	2110	2127	|	2152	2210	2227	...	2252	2310	2327	...	2352	0027	0052	0128	...
Olten d.	1830	|	...	1912	1930	|	...	2012	2030	|	...	2112	2130	|	...	2212	2233	...	...	2312	2333	...	...	0035	...	0137	...
Sissach d.	|	|	...	1927	|	|	...	2027	|	|	...	2127	|	|	...	2227	|	...	...	2327	|	...	...	|	...	|	...
Liestal d.	|	|	...	1933	|	|	...	2033	|	|	...	2133	|	|	...	2233	2249	...	...	2333	2349	...	...	0052	...	0153	...
Basel SBB a.	1855	|	...	1944	1955	|	...	2044	2055	|	...	2144	2155	|	...	2244	2259	...	...	2344	2359	...	...	0102	...	0203	...
Lausanne **505** a.	...	2010	...	...	...	2110	...	...	...	2215	...	...	...	2315	...	...	...	...	...	...	...	...	...	...	...	...	...
Genève **505** a.	...	2048	...	...	...	2148	...	...	...	...	...	...	...	...	...	...	...	...	...	...	...	...	...	...	...	...	...
Genève Aéroport ✈ **505** a.	...	...	...	...	...	2157	...	...	...	...	...	...	...	...	...	...	...	...	...	...	...	...	...	...	...	...	...

A – 🚃12 Basel - Arth-Goldau and v.v.
C – 🚃12 Basel - Chiasso and v.v.
E – 🚃12 Basel - Erstfeld / Göschenen and v.v.
G – 🚃12 Basel - Lugano and v.v.
M – 🚃12 Basel - Luzern - Arth-Goldau - Milano and v.v.

e – ① (not Jan. 2).
q – ⑥⑦ (not Apr. 15).
◧ – Supplement payable in Italy and for international journeys.

LENK - ZWEISIMMEN - MONTREUX 566

Narrow gauge. MOB

km		Ⓐ		Ⓐ				©		©										Ⓐ		Ⓐ					⑤⑥
0	**Lenk** d.	0611	0634	0703	0737	0837	0937	1003	1037	1103	1137	1237	1303	1337	1437	1537	1603	1637	1737	1803	1842	1903	1937	2037	2132	2232	2326
13	**Zweisimmen** a.	0629	0652	0721	0755	0855	0955	1021	1055	1121	1155	1255	1321	1355	1455	1555	1621	1655	1755	1821	1900	1921	1955	2055	2150	2250	2344

km			©	Ⓐ	Ⓐ	©		2111 G			3115 🍸 G	2217 (✕) C		2119 🍸 G★			3123 🍸 G			2127 (✕) C	2229 G	Ⓐ	2131 G★				
0	**Zweisimmen** d.	0411	0505	0505	0608	0617	0700	0825	0905	1005	1025	1105	1205	1225	1305	1405	1425	1505	1605	1625	1705	1805	1825	1905	2005	2102	2200
9	Saanenmöser d.	0426	0519	0519	0622	0631	0714	0839	0919	1019	1039	1119	1219	1239	1319	1419	1439	1519	1619	1639	1719	1819	1839	1919	2019	2116	2213
11	Schönried d.	0431	0524	0524	0626	0635	0719	0843	0924	1024	1043	1124	1224	1243	1324	1424	1443	1524	1624	1643	1724	1824	1843	1924	2024	2121	2218
16	**Gstaad** d.	0440	0533	0533	0635	0644	0730	0853	0937	1034	1053	1137	1234	1253	1337	1434	1453	1537	1634	1653	1737	1834	1853	1937	2037	2130	2232
19	Saanen d.	0444	0537	0537	0639	0648	0735	0858	0942	1038	1058	1142	1238	1258	1342	1438	1458	1542	1638	1658	1742	1838	1858	1942	2042	2135	2236
23	Rougemont d.	0450	0555	0555	0644	0653	0741	0903	0948	1044	1103	1148	1244	1303	1348	1444	1503	1548	1644	1703	1748	...	1903	1948	2048	2141	2241
29	Châteaux d'Oex d.	0503	0607	0607	0703	0703	0806t	0913	1006	...	1113	1206	...	1313	1406	...	1513	1606	...	1713	1806	...	1913	2006	2101	2152	2252
40	**Montbovon** d.	0522	0623	0623	0723	0723	0826	0928	1026	...	1128	1226	...	1328	1426	...	1528	1626	...	1728	1826	...	1928	2026	2116	2208	2307f
51	Les Avants § d.	0543	0644	0644	0744	0744	0847	0948	1047	...	1148	1247	...	1348	1447	...	1548	1647	...	1748	1847	...	1948	2047	2135	2228	2327f
55	Chamby ⊙ § d.	0551	0651	0651	0751	0751	0855	0955	1055	...	1155	1255	...	1355	1455	...	1555	1655	...	1755	1855	...	1955	2054	2142	2235	2334f
58	Chernex § d.	0600	0658	0658	0758	0758	0904	1004	1104	...	1204	1304	...	1404	1504	...	1604	1704	...	1804	1904	...	2004	2059	2147	2241	2339f
62	**Montreux** § a.	0610	0707	0707	0807	0807	0913	1013	1113	...	1213	1313	...	1413	1513	...	1613	1713	...	1813	1913	...	2013	2107	2158	2249	2348f

	Ⓐ	Ⓐ	©			2112 G	2216 (✕) C	2118 🍸 Ⓡ T	3118 🍸 G★		🍸	2124 🍸 G			3126 (✕) C		2228 🍸 G	2128 🍸 G★			Ⓐ	2234 G					
Montreux § d.	...	...	...	0537	0638	0744	0844	0857	0944	...	1044	1144	...	1244	1344	...	1444	1544	...	1644	...	1744	...	1844	1944	2113	2213
Chernex § d.	...	...	...	0548	0648	0753	0853	|	0953	...	1053	1153	...	1253	1353	...	1453	1553	...	1653	...	1753	...	1853	1953	2122	2222
Chamby ⊙ § d.	...	...	...	0556	0653	0758	0858	|	0958	...	1058	1158	...	1258	1358	...	1458	1558	...	1658	...	1758	...	1858	1958	2127	2225
Les Avants § d.	...	...	...	0604	0701	0807	0907	|	1007	...	1107	1207	...	1307	1407	...	1507	1607	...	1707	...	1807	...	1907	2007	2134	2239
Montbovon d.	...	0521	0548	0622	0722	0828	0927	0946	1028	...	1127	1228	...	1327	1428	...	1527	1628	...	1727	...	1827	...	1927	2029	2154	2259
Châteaux d'Oex d.	...	0539	0606	0639	0737	0843	0944	...	1043	...	1144	1243	...	1344	1443	...	1544	1643	...	1744	...	1844	...	1944	2045	2213	2315
Rougemont d.	...	0549	0616	0653	0750	0853	0959	...	1053	1111	1159	1253	1311	1359	1453	1511	1559	1653	1711	1759	...	1903	...	2005	2057	2224	2327
Saanen d.	0500	0554	0621	0659	0756	0859	1005	...	1059	1117	1205	1259	1317	1405	1459	1517	1605	1659	1717	1805	1845	1908	...	2010	2103	2229	2333
Gstaad d.	0505	0559	0625	0703	0803	0905	1023j	...	1105	1123	1223j	1305	1323	1423j	1505	1523	1623j	1705	1723	1823j	1851	1923j	...	2023r	2115r	2233	2339
Schönried d.	0513	0607	0635	0711	0812	0914	1032	...	1114	1132	1232	1314	1332	1432	1514	1532	1632	1714	1732	1832	1900	1932	...	2032	2122	2241	2347
Saanenmöser d.	0518	0611	0639	0715	0817	0918	1038	...	1118	1138	1238	1318	1338	1438	1518	1538	1638	1718	1738	1838	1905	1938	...	2038	2126	2246	2351
Zweisimmen a.	0535	0625	0653	0729	0834	0932	1052	...	1132	1152	1252	1332	1352	1452	1532	1552	1652	1732	1752	1852	1921	1952	...	2052	2142	2300	0005

	Ⓐ		Ⓐ				©		©				Ⓐ							Ⓐ		Ⓐ					⑤⑥
Zweisimmen d.	0550	0611	0634	0703	0803	0903	0937	1003	1037	1103	1137	1203	1237	1303	1403	1503	1537	1603	1703	1737	1803	1824	1903	2003	2103	2200	2306
Lenk a.	0608	0629	0652	0721	0821	0921	0956	1021	1056	1121	1156	1221	1256	1321	1421	1521	1556	1621	1721	1756	1821	1842	1921	2021	2121	2218	2324

§ – ADDITIONAL SERVICES LES AVANTS - MONTREUX and v.v. (2nd class only):

	Ⓐ	Ⓐ	Ⓐ		Ⓐ		Ⓐ	Ⓐ			
Les Avants d.	0620	0718	0813	...	1319	...	1713	1813	...	2320	...
Chamby ⊙ d.	0629	0725	0820	...	1326	...	1720	1820	...	2327	...
Chernex d.	0634	0731	0832	...	1332	...	1732	1832	...	2332	...
Montreux a.	0646	0741	0841	...	1341	...	1741	1841	...	2342	...

	Ⓐ	Ⓐ	Ⓐ		Ⓐ	Ⓐ	Ⓐ	Ⓐ			
Montreux d.	0549	0610	0715	...	1215	1615	1715	1815	2150	2250	...
Chernex d.	0558	0619	0730	...	1224	1624	1724	1824	2159	2259	...
Chamby ⊙ d.	0603	0627	0735	...	1229	1629	1729	1829	2204	2304	...
Les Avants a.	0610	0634	0742	...	1236	1636	1736	1836	2211	2311	...

C – GOLDEN PASS CLASSIC – [12] and (✕).
G – GOLDEN PASS PANORAMIC – conveys [12] [panorama car].
T – TRAIN DU CHOCOLAT – ①②③④ May 1 - June 29; daily July 1 - Aug. 31; ①③④ Sept. 4 - Oct. 30. Conveys [1] only.

f – ⑤⑥ only.
j – Arrive 12–14 minutes earlier.
r – Arrive 8–9 minutes earlier.
t – Arrive 16 minutes earlier.

★ – Also conveys VIP accommodation. Ⓡ
⊙ – Chamby is a request stop.

MONTBOVON - BULLE - PALÉZIEUX, BROC and BERN 568

Narrow gauge. 2nd class only. TPF

km		⚒		Ⓐ		⚒			Ⓐ	©				♣			♣						
0	**Montbovon** d.	...	...	0540	...	0640	...	...	0723	0740	...	...	...	0840	...		1840	...	...	1940	...	2040	...
13	Gruyères d.	...	...	0600	...	0700	...	...	0745	0800	...	...	...	0900	...	and at	1900	...	...	2000	...	2100	...
17	**Bulle** ▲ a.	...	...	0608	...	0708	...	...	0753	0808	...	...	...	0908	...	the same	1908	...	...	2008	...	2108	...
17	**Bulle** d.	0513	0554	0612	0613	...	0712	0733	...	...	0812	0833	...	0912	0933	minutes	1912	1933	...	...	2033	...	2118
	Châtel-St Denis d.	0539	0629	|	0643	...	|	0759	...	...	|	0859	...	|	0959	past each	|	1959	...	...	2059	...	2144
	Palézieux a.	0550	0640	|	0655	...	|	0810	...	...	|	0910	...	|	1010	hour until	|	2010	...	...	2110	...	2155
22	**Broc**-Fabrique a.	...	...	0624	...	...	0724	...	...	...	0824	...	...	0924	...		1924	...	...	...	...	...	...

km		Ⓐ	⚒	⚒	Ⓐ																		
	Broc-Fabrique d.	...	...	...	0636	...	...	0736	...	...	...	...	0836		...	1836	...	1936	...	...	...	...	...
0	**Palézieux** d.	...	...	0605	|	...	0646	|	0706	...	...	0746	|	and at	1746	|	1846	|	1946	2046	2115	2205	...
7	Châtel-St Denis d.	...	...	0618	|	...	0700	|	0722	...	...	0800	|	the same	1800	|	1900	|	2000	2100	2128	2218	...
27	**Bulle** a.	...	...	0644	0647	...	0727	0747	0749a	...	...	0827	0847	minutes	1827	1847	1927	1947	2027	2127	2153	2243	...
	Bulle ▲ d.	0450	0551	...	...	0651	...	...	...	0753	...	...	0851	past each	...	1851	...	1951	...	...	...	...	...
	Gruyères d.	0458	0559	...	...	0659	...	...	...	0801	...	...	0859	hour until	...	1859	...	1959	...	...	...	...	...
	Montbovon a.	0518	0620	...	...	0720	...	...	...	0822	...	...	0920		...	1920	...	2020	...	...	...	...	...

▲ – **BULLE - FRIBOURG - BERN and v.v.**: Operator: TPF

km				and at									
0	Bulle d.	0552	0620	the same	1852	1920	1952	2020	2052	2120	2220	2320	...
18	Romont d.	0611	0638	minutes	1911	1938	2011	2038	2111	2138	2238	2338	...
44	Fribourg **505** d.	0629	0655	past each	1929	1955	2028	2055	2129	2155	2255	2355	...
75	**Bern 505** a.	0651	...	hour until	1951	...	...	...	2151	...	...	...	...

			and at						g
Bern 505 d.	...	0609	the same	...	2009	...	...	...	...
Fribourg **505** d.	0604	0631	minutes	2004	2031	2104	2204	2304	0006
Romont d.	0623	0649	past each	2023	2049	2123	2223	2323	0024
Bulle a.	0642	0708	hour until	2042	2108	2142	2242	2342	0041

a – Ⓐ only.
g – ②–⑥ (not Dec. 27, Jan. 3, Apr. 15, 18, May 26, June 6, Aug. 2).

♣ – On 1540 departure, change trains at Bulle.

Operator: Transports Publics Fribourgeois (TPF), ✆ +41 26 351 02 00, fax +41 26 351 02 90.

MONTREUX - CAUX - ROCHERS DE NAYE 569

Narrow gauge rack railway. 2nd class only. MVR

Caux - Rochers de Naye and v.v.: no service during bad weather

km																									
0	**Montreux** d.	0547	0644	0744	...	0817	0917	1017	1117	...	1217	1317	1417	1517	...	1617	1717	...	1817	...	1917	2017	2117	2217	...
3	Glion ▲ d.	0558	0655	0755	...	0829	0929	1029	1129	...	1229	1329	1429	1529	...	1629	1729	...	1829	...	1927	2027	2127	2227	...
5	Caux a.	0607	0704	0804	...	0839	0939	1039	1139	...	1239	1339	1439	1539	...	1639	1739	...	1839	...	1936	2036	2136	2236	...
10	**Rochers de Naye** a.	...	...	...	...	0906	1006	1106	1206	...	1306	1406	1506	1606	...	1706t	1806t	...	1906v	...	...	...	...	...	...

																					v		
Rochers de Naye d.	...	...	...	...	0911	1011	1111	1211	...	1311	1411	1511	1611	...	1711t	1811t	...	...	...	...	...	2213	...	...
Caux d.	0612	0712	0812	...	0941	1041	1141	1241	...	1341	1441	1541	1641	...	1741	1841	...	1946	2046	2146	...	2242	...	2250
Glion ▲ d.	0625	0725	0829	...	0953	1053	1153	1253	...	1353	1453	1553	1653	...	1753	1853	...	1958	2058	2158	...	2252s	...	2302
Montreux a.	0637	0737	0841	...	1006	1106	1206	1306	...	1406	1506	1606	1706	...	1806	1906	...	2011	2111	2211	...	2307	...	2315

n – Not Aug. 20.
s – Stops to set down only.
t – May 6 - Oct. 15.
v – ⑤⑥ June 30 - Oct. 14.

▲ – Funicular railway operates **Glion** - **Territet** and v.v. (no service Aug. 14-19): From **Glion** and **Territet**: 0515, 0530, 0545, 0557, 0615, 0630, 0645, 0700 and every 15 minutes until 2100, then 2120, 2145, 2220, 2245, 2320, 2350, 0020, 0050, 0130⑥⑦ **n**.

Operator: MVR, ✆ 021 989 81 90.

12 ✕ – Restaurant (✕) – Bistro (🍸) – Bar coach 🍸 – Minibar 283

570 GENÈVE - LAUSANNE - SION - BRIG *SBB*

For *TGV Lyria* services Paris - Lausanne - Montreux - Brig and v.v. – see Table 42

km		*IR* 1705	*IR* 1805	*IR* 1707	*EC* 35	*IR* 1807	*IR* 1709	*IR* 1809	*IR* 1711	*EC* 37	*IR* 1811	*IR* 1713	*IR* 1813	*IR* 1715	*IR* 1815	*IR* 1717	*IR* 1817	*IR* 1719	*IR* 1819	*IR* 1721	*IR* 1821	*IR* 1723	*EC* 39	*IR* 1823	*IR* 1725	*IR* 1825
					◧					◧V													◧			
0	Genève Aéroport ✈ 505 d.	...	...	0520	...	...	0620	0650	0720	...	0750	0820	0850	0920	0950	1020	1050	1120	1150	1220	1250	1320	...	1350	1420	1450
6	**Genève 505** d.	...	0453	0530	0539	0609	0630	0700	0730	0739	0800	0830	0900	0930	1000	1030	1100	1130	1200	1230	1300	1330	1339	1400	1430	1500
27	Nyon **505** d.	...	0507	0544	|	|	0644	0714	0744	|	0814	0844	0914	0944	1014	1044	1114	1144	1214	1244	1314	1344	|	1414	1444	1514
53	Morges **505** d.	...	0525	0600	|	|	0700	0730	0800	|	0830	0900	0930	1000	1030	1100	1130	1200	1230	1300	1330	1400	|	1430	1500	1530
66	**Lausanne 505** a.	...	0539	0612	0615**k**	0648	0712	0742	0812	0815**k**	0842	0912	0942	1012	1042	1112	1142	1212	1242	1312	1342	1412	1415**k**	1442	1512	1542
66	**Lausanne** ▲ d.	...	0545	0621	0618	0650	0717	0750	0821	0818	0850	0917	0950	1017	1050	1117	1150	1217	1250	1317	1350	1421	1418	1450	1517	1550
84	Vevey ▲ d.	...	0559	0635	|	0704	0731	0804	0835	|	0904	0931	1004	1031	1104	1131	1204	1231	1304	1331	1404	1435	|	1504	1531	1604
92	**Montreux** ▲ d.	...	0606	0642	0637	0711	0738	0811	0842	0837	0911	0938	1011	1038	1111	1138	1211	1238	1311	1338	1411	1442	1437	1511	1538	1611
105	Aigle d.	...	0617	0653	|	0722	0749	0822	0853	|	0922	0949	1022	1049	1122	1149	1222	1249	1322	1349	1422	1453	|	1522	1549	1622
114	Bex d.	...	0624	|	|	|	0756	|	|	|	|	0956	|	1056	|	1156	|	1256	|	1356	|	|	|	|	1556	|
118	St Maurice d.	...	0629	|	|	0732	|	0832	|	|	0932	|	1032	|	1132	|	1232	|	1332	|	1432	|	|	1532	|	1632
133	Martigny d.	0609	0640	0711	|	0743	0809	0843	0911	|	0943	1009	1043	1109	1143	1209	1243	1309	1343	1409	1443	1511	|	1543	1609	1643
158	**Sion** d.	0624	0655	0726	0713	0758	0824	0858	0926	0913	0958	1024	1058	1124	1158	1224	1258	1324	1358	1424	1458	1526	1513	1558	1624	1658
174	Sierre d.	0634	0705	0736	|	0808	0834	0908	0936	|	1008	1034	1108	1134	1208	1234	1308	1334	1408	1434	1508	1536	|	1608	1634	1708
184	Leuk d.	0642	0713	|	|	|	0842	|	|	|	|	1042	|	1142	|	1242	|	1342	|	1442	|	|	|	|	1642	|
203	Visp d.	0655	0725	0755	|	0825	0855	0925	0955	|	1025	1055	1125	1155	1225	1255	1325	1355	1425	1455	1525	1555	|	1625	1655	1725
212	**Brig** a.	0702	0732	0802	0740	0832	0902	0932	1002	0940	1032	1102	1132	1202	1232	1302	1332	1402	1432	1502	1532	1602	1540	1632	1702	1732
	Milano Centrale **590** a.	...	...	...	0937	...	...	...	...	1137	...	...	...	...	...	...	...	...	...	...	...	...	1737	...	...	...

	IR 1727	*IR* 1827	*IR* 1729	*IR* 1729	*IR* 1927	*IR* 1829	*IR* 1929	*IR* 1731	*IR* 1731	*IR* 1931	*IR* 1831	*IR* 1733	*EC* 41	*IR* 1833	*IR* 1735	*IR* 1835	*IR* 1737	*IR* 1837	*IR* 1739	*IR* 1839	*IR* 1741	*IR* 1841	*RE* 3591	*IR* 1743	*RE* 3147	*RE* 3595
			Ⓐ	Ⓒ	Ⓐ		Ⓐ	Ⓐ	Ⓒ	Ⓐ			◧										⑤⑥		y	⑥⑦
Genève Aéroport ✈ 505 d.	1520	1550	1629	1620	1620	1650	1657	1729	1720	1720	1750	1820	...	1850	1920	1950	2020	2059	2120	2150	2220	2247	...	*2309*	0021	...
Genève 505 d.	1530	1600	1639	1630	1630	1700	1707	1739	1730	1730	1800	1830	1839	1900	1930	2000	2030	2109	2130	2200	2230	2257	...	*2319*	0031	...
Nyon **505** d.	1544	1614	|	1644	1644	1714	|	|	1744	1744	1814	1844	|	1914	1944	2014	2044	|	2144	2214	2244	2314	...	*2335*	0047	...
Morges **505** d.	1600	1630	|	1700	1700	1730	1734	|	1800	1800	1830	1900	|	1930	2000	2030	2100	|	2200	2230	2300	2330	...	*2356*	0108	...
Lausanne 505 a.	1612	1642	1715	1712	1712	1742	1751	1815	1812	1812	1842	1912	1915**k**	1942	2012	2042	2112	2148	2212	2242	2312	2342	...	*0009*	0121	...
Lausanne ▲ d.	1617	1650	1717	1717	1721	1750	1756	1817	1817	1821	1850	1921	1918	1950	2017	2050	2117	2150	2220	...	2320	...	2350	0025	...	0130
Vevey ▲ d.	1631	1704	|	1731	1735	1804	1810	|	1831	1835	1904	1935	|	2004	2031	2104	2131	2204	2234	...	2334	...	0004	0039	...	0145
Montreux ▲ d.	1638	1711	1736	1738	1742	1811	1817	1836	1838	1842	1911	1942	1937	2011	2038	2111	2138	2211	2241	...	2341	...	0011	0046	...	0152
Aigle d.	1649	1722	1747	1749	1753	1822	1831	1847	1849	1853	1922	1953	|	2022	2049	2122	2149	2222	2252	...	2352	...	0022	0057	...	0204
Bex d.	1656	|	|	1756	1800	|	1838	|	1856	1900	|	2000	|	|	2056	|	2156	|	2259	...	2359	...	0029	0104	...	0211
St Maurice d.	|	1732	|	|	1806	1832	1843	|	|	1906	1932	|	|	2032	|	2132	|	2232	2304	...	0004	...	0033	0109	...	0216
Martigny d.	1709	1743	1804	1809	1817	1843	...	1904	1909	1917	1943	2013	|	2043	2109	2143	2209	2242	2315	...	0015	...	...	0120	...	...
Sion d.	1724	1758	1819	1824	1832	1858	...	1919	1924	1932	1958	2028	2013	2058	2124	2158	2224	...	2330	...	0030	...	...	0134	...	...
Sierre d.	1734	1808	1829	1834	...	1908	...	1929	1934	...	2008	2038	|	2108	2134	2208	2234	...	2340	...	0040	...	...	...	...	...
Leuk d.	1742	|	1837	1842	...	|	...	1937	1942	...	|	2046	|	|	2142	|	2242	...	2348	...	0048	...	...	...	...	...
Visp d.	1755	1825	1850	1855	...	1925	...	1950	1955	...	2025	2058	|	2125	2155	2225	2255	...	0001	...	0101	...	...	...	...	...
Brig a.	1802	1832	1857	1902	...	1932	...	1957	2002	...	2032	2106	2040	2132	2202	2232	2302	...	0008	...	0108	...	...	...	...	...
Milano Centrale **590** a.	...	...	...	...	...	...	...	...	...	...	...	...	2237	...	...	...	...	...	...	...	...	...	...	...	...	...

	IR 1702	*IR* 1804	*IR* 1704	*IR* 1904	*IR* 1806	*IR* 1806	*IR* 1706	*IR* 1706	*IR* 1906	*IR* 1908	*IR* 1808	*IR* 1808	*IR* 1708	*IR* 1810	*IR* 1710	*IR* 1812	*IR* 1712	*IR* 1814	*IR* 1714	*IR* 1714	*EC* 32	*IR* 1816	*IR* 1716	*IR* 1818	*IR* 1718	*IR* 1820
				Ⓐ	Ⓒ	Ⓐ	Ⓐ	Ⓒ	Ⓐ	Ⓐ	Ⓒ	Ⓐ							Ⓐ	Ⓒ	◧					
Milano Centrale **590** d.	...	...	...	...	...	...	...	...	...	...	...	...	...	...	...	...	...	...	...	...	0823	...	...	...	...	...
Brig d.	...	0423	...	...	0525	0528	0552	0558	...	...	0625	0629	0658	0728	0758	0828	0858	0928	0958	0958	1020	1028	1058	1128	1158	1228
Visp d.	...	0430	...	...	0532	0535	0600	0606	...	...	0632	0636	0706	0735	0806	0835	0906	0935	1006	1006	|	1035	1106	1135	1206	1235
Leuk d.	...	0441	...	...	0543	0546	0611	0617	...	...	0643	0647	0717	|	0817	|	0917	|	|	1017	|	|	1117	|	1217	|
Sierre d.	...	0449	...	...	0551	0555	0619	0625	...	...	0651	0655	0725	0751	0825	0851	0925	0951	1023	1025	|	1051	1125	1151	1225	1251
Sion d.	0429	0501	0533	0553	0603	0607	0631	0637	0639	...	0703	0707	0737	0803	0837	0903	0937	1003	1035	1036	1048	1103	1137	1203	1237	1303
Martigny d.	0442	0514	0546	0609	0616	0620	0644	0650	0654	...	0716	0720	0750	0816	0850	0916	0950	1016	1048	1050	|	1116	1150	1216	1250	1316
St Maurice d.	0453	0525	0557	0620	0627	0631	0655	|	|	0718	0727	0731	|	0827	|	0927	|	1027	|	|	|	1127	|	1227	|	1327
Bex d.	0458	0530	0602	0625	|	|	0700	0703	|	0725	|	|	0803	|	0903	|	1003	|	|	|	|	|	1203	|	1303	|
Aigle d.	0505	0537	0609	0633	0637	0641	0707	0710	0712	0733	0737	0741	0810	0837	0910	0937	1010	1037	1106	1107	|	1137	1210	1237	1310	1337
Montreux ▲ d.	0516	0548	0620	0644	0648	0652	0718	0721	0723	0744	0748	0752	0821	0848	0921	0948	1021	1048	1117	1118	1123	1148	1221	1248	1321	1348
Vevey ▲ d.	0523	0555	0627	0652	0655	0659	0725	0728	|	0752	0755	0759	0828	0855	0928	0955	1028	1055	1124	1125	|	1155	1228	1255	1328	1355
Lausanne ▲ a.	0538	0610	0642	0707	0710	0714	0740	0743	0743	0807	0810	0814	0843	0910	0943	1010	1043	1110	1139	1139	1142**k**	1210	1243	1310	1343	1410
Lausanne 505 d.	0547	0617	0647	0709	0717	0717	0747	0747	0745	0809	0817	0817	0847	0917	0947	1017	1047	1117	1147	1147	1145	1217	1247	1317	1347	1417
Morges **505** d.	0558	0628	0658	0720	0728	0728	0758	0758	|	0820	0828	0828	0858	0928	0958	1028	1058	1128	1158	1158	|	1228	1258	1328	1358	1428
Nyon **505** d.	0615	0645	0715	|	0745	0745	0815	0815	|	|	0845	0845	0915	0945	1015	1045	1115	1145	1215	1215	|	1245	1315	1345	1415	1445
Genève 505 a.	0630	0700	0730	0751	0800	0800	0830	0830	0821	0851	0900	0900	0930	1000	1030	1100	1130	1200	1230	1230	1221	1300	1330	1400	1430	1500
Genève Aéroport ✈ 505 a.	0639	0709	0739	0800	0809	0809	0839	0839	0830	0900	0909	0909	0939	1009	1039	1109	1139	1209	1239	1239	...	1309	1339	1409	1439	1509

	IR 1720	*IR* 1822	*IR* 1722	*EC* 34	*IR* 1824	*IR* 1724	*IR* 1826	*IR* 1726	*IR* 1828	*IR* 1728	*IR* 1830	*IR* 1730	*IR* 1832	*IR* 1732	*EC* 36	*IR* 1834	*IR* 1734	*IR* 1836	*IR* 1736	*EC* 42	*IR* 1838	*RE* 3586	*RE* 3238	*IR* 1840	*IR* 1840	*RE* 3590
				◧											◧					◧V		⑤⑥		p	q	⑥⑦
Milano Centrale **590** d.	...	...	...	1223	...	...	...	...	...	...	...	...	...	...	1723	...	...	...	...	1923	...	...	...	...	...	...
Brig d.	1258	1328	1358	1420	1428	1458	1528	1558	1628	1658	1728	1758	1828	1858	1918	1928	1958	2023	2058	2118	2128	...	...	2228	2228	...
Visp d.	1306	1335	1406	|	1435	1506	1535	1606	1635	1706	1735	1806	1835	1906	|	1935	2006	2030	2106	|	2135	...	...	2235	2235	...
Leuk d.	1317	|	|	|	|	1517	|	1617	|	1717	|	1817	|	|	|	|	2017	2041	|	|	|	...	...	|	2246	...
Sierre d.	1325	1351	1423	|	1451	1525	1551	1625	1651	1725	1751	1825	1851	1923	|	1951	2025	2049	2123	|	2151	...	...	2251	2254	...
Sion d.	1337	1403	1435	1448	1503	1537	1603	1637	1703	1737	1803	1837	1903	1935	1948	2003	2037	2101	2135	2148	2203	...	...	2303	2306	...
Martigny d.	1350	1416	1448	|	1516	1550	1616	1650	1716	1750	1816	1850	1916	1948	|	2016	2050	2114	2148	|	2216	...	...	2316	2319	...
St Maurice d.	|	1427	|	|	1527	|	1627	|	1727	|	1827	|	1927	|	|	2027	|	2125	|	|	2227	2259	...	2327	2330	0039
Bex d.	1403	|	|	|	|	1603	|	1703	|	1803	|	1903	|	|	|	|	2103	2130	|	|	|	2304	...	|	|	0043
Aigle d.	1410	1437	1506	|	1537	1610	1637	1710	1737	1810	1837	1910	1937	2006	|	2037	2110	2137	2206	|	2237	2310	...	2337	2340	0049
Montreux ▲ d.	1421	1448	1517	1523	1548	1621	1648	1721	1748	1821	1848	1921	1948	2017	2023	2048	2121	2148	2217	2223	2248	2321	...	2348	2351	0101
Vevey ▲ d.	1428	1455	1524	|	1555	1628	1655	1728	1755	1828	1855	1928	1955	2024	|	2055	2128	2155	2224	|	2255	2327	...	2355	2358	0107
Lausanne ▲ a.	1443	1510	1539	1542**k**	1610	1643	1710	1743	1810	1843	1910	1943	2010	2039	2042**k**	2110	2143	2210	2239	2242**k**	2310	2342	...	0010	0017	0122
Lausanne 505 d.	1447	1517	1547	1545	1617	1647	1717	1747	1817	1847	1917	1947	2017	2047	2045	2117	2147	2221	2247	2245	2321	...	2351	0025	0025	...
Morges **505** d.	1458	1528	1558	|	1628	1658	1728	1758	1828	1858	1928	1958	2028	2058	|	2128	2158	2233	2258	|	2333	...	0004	0037	0037	...
Nyon **505** d.	1515	1545	1615	|	1645	1715	1745	1815	1845	1915	1945	2015	2045	2115	|	2145	2215	2252	2315	|	2352	...	0025	0056	0056	...
Genève 505 a.	1530	1600	1630	1621	1700	1730	1800	1830	1900	1930	2000	2030	2100	2130	2121	2200	2230	2307	2330	2321	0007	...	0041	0111	0111	...
Genève Aéroport ✈ 505 a.	1539	1609	1639	...	1710	1739	1809	1839	1910	1939	2009	2039	2109	2139	...	2209	2239	2316	2339	...	0016	...	0050**y**	0122	0122	...

▲ – Local services **Lausanne - Montreux - Villeneuve and v.v.**

Lausanne d.	0600	0636	0700	0736	and at	2000	2036	2100	2200	2300	0000
Vevey d.	0622	0653	0722	0753	the same	2022	2053	2122	2222	2322	0022
Montreux d.	0631	0702	0731	0802	minutes	2031	2102	2131	2231	2331	0031
Territet d.	0632	|	0732	|	past each	2032	|	2132	2232	2332	0032
Veytaux-Chillon d.	|	0704	|	0804	hour until	|	2104	|	|	|	|
Villeneuve a.	0637	0708	0737	0808		2037	2108	2137	2237	2337	0037

Villeneuve d.	0522	0549	0622	0651	and at	2022	2051	2122	2222	2322
Veytaux-Chillon d.	|	0551	|	0653	the same	|	2053	|	|	|
Territet d.	0524	|	0625	|	minutes past	2025	|	2125	2225	2325
Montreux d.	0527	0554	0627	0656	each	2027	2056	2127	2227	2327
Vevey d.	0537	0604	0637	0706	hour until	2037	2106	2137	2237	2337
Lausanne a.	0559	0624	0659	0723		2059	2123	2159	2259	2359

V – (12) Genève - Milano - Venezia and v.v.

k – Connects with train in previous column.
p – ⑥⑦ (also Dec. 26, Jan. 2, Apr. 14, 17, May 25, June 5, Aug. 1).
q – ①–⑤ (not Dec. 26, Jan. 2, Apr. 14, 17, May 25, June 5, Aug. 1).
y – ⑥⑦ (not Apr. 15).

◧ – Supplement payable for journeys from / to Italy.

VEVEY - BLONAY: Narrow gauge. 6 km. Journey time: 14–16 minutes. **Operator**: MVR.

From **Vevey**: 0610✗, 0629Ⓐ, 0640Ⓒ, 0649Ⓐ, 0710✗, 0727Ⓐ, 0740Ⓒ, 0747Ⓐ, 0810✗, 0829Ⓐ, 0840Ⓒ, 0850Ⓐ, 0910✗, 0940, 1010✗, 1040, 1110✗, 1140, 1210✗, 1240, 1310✗, 1340, 1410✗, 1440, 1510✗, 1540, 1610✗, 1629Ⓐ, 1640Ⓒ, 1649Ⓐ, 1710✗, 1729Ⓐ, 1740Ⓒ, 1749Ⓐ, 1810✗, 1829Ⓐ, 1840Ⓒ, 1849Ⓐ, 1910✗, 1940, 2010✗, 2040, 2140, 2240, 2340, 0045ⒼⓄ.

From **Blonay**: 0533✗, 0604, 0631Ⓐ, 0634Ⓖ, 0651Ⓐ, 0704, 0729Ⓐ, 0734Ⓖ, 0749Ⓐ, 0804, 0831Ⓐ, 0834Ⓖ, 0852Ⓐ, 0904, 0934✗, 1004, 1034✗, 1104, 1134✗, 1204, 1234✗, 1304, 1334✗, 1404, 1434✗, 1504, 1534✗, 1604, 1631Ⓐ, 1634Ⓖ, 1651Ⓐ, 1704, 1731Ⓐ, 1734Ⓖ, 1751Ⓐ, 1804, 1831Ⓐ, 1834Ⓖ, 1852Ⓐ, 1904, 1934✗, 2004, 2104, 2204, 2304, 0004ⓖⓄ.

AIGLE - LEYSIN: Narrow gauge rack railway. 6 km. Journey time: 29–39 minutes. **Operator**: TPC.

From **Aigle**: 0547Ⓐ, 0608Ⓐ, 0623Ⓒ, 0655Ⓒ, 0724Ⓐ, 0755, 0855 and hourly until 2255.

From **Leysin** Grand Hotel: 0522, 0619Ⓐ, 0640Ⓐ, 0655Ⓒ, 0755, 0852 and hourly until 2252, then 2327.

AIGLE - LES DIABLERETS: Narrow gauge. 23 km. Journey time: 45–55 minutes. **Operator**: TPC.

From **Aigle**: 0601, 0705, 0827, 0925, 1056, 1156 and hourly until 1856, then 2056, 2156.

From **Les Diablerets**: 0609, 0710, 0807, 0936, 1136, 1236, 1333, 1436 and hourly until 1836, then 1908, 2039, 2204.

AIGLE - CHAMPÉRY: Narrow gauge rack railway. 2nd class only. **Operator**: TPC.   Additional services operate Aigle - Monthey Ville and v.v.

km		✗		✗		✗		✗		✗		✗								⑥h	
0	Aigle .... d.	0511	0620	0730	0754	0825	0925	1033	1056	1125	1154	1225	1254	1325	1433	1525	1625	1654	1725	1825	1933	2025	2133	2225	2303	...	2355
11	Monthey Ville .. d.	0539	0642	0753	0813	0851	0948	1056	1115	1151	1213	1251	1313	1348	1456	1554	1651	1713	1751	1848	1956	2048	2156	2244	2322	2330	0014
23	Champéry ...... a.	0612	0717	0826	...	0924	1021	1129	...	1224	...	1324	...	1421	1529	1627	1724	...	1824	1921	2029	2121	2229	...	...	0003	...

		Ⓐ		✗		✗		✗		✗		✗		✗							⑦g	
Champéry ......d.	...	...	0552	0628a	0657d	0806	0904	...	1001	...	1109	...	1204	1304	1401	1509	1607	...	1704	...	1804	1901	2009	2101	2142	2232	0007
Monthey Ville .. d.	0544	0604	0644	0707	0738	0846	0946	1007	1040	1124	1146	1224	1246	1346	1440	1546	1646	1724	1746	1824	1846	1940	2046	2140	2224	2310	0042
Aigle ....a.	0604	0624	0707	0730	0801	0906	1006	1027	1100	1144	1206	1244	1306	1406	1500	1606	1706	1744	1806	1844	1906	2000	2106	2200	2244	2330	...

BEX - VILLARS-SUR-OLLON: 12 km. Journey time: 40–46 minutes. All trains call at Bex (Place du Marché), and Bévieux (3 km and 4 minutes from Bex). **Operator**: TPC.

From **Bex**: 0631, 0718, 0801, 0909, 1001, 1115, 1201, 1301, 1401, 1509, 1601, 1701, 1802, 1907, 2015, 2107.

From **Villars**: 0534, 0624, 0712, 0811, 0903, 0954, 1108, 1211, 1311, 1354, 1503, 1554, 1711, 1811, 1901, 2008, 2101.

VILLARS-SUR-OLLON - COL-DE-BRETAYE: 5 km. Journey time: 18–20 minutes. **Operator**: TPC.

From **Villars**:
Dec. 11 - 16, Apr. 18 - June 16, Sept. 11 - Dec. 9: 0900, 1100j, 1200, 1300j, 1500j, 1600.
Dec. 17 - Apr. 17: 0805, 0830, 0900, 0930 and every 30 minutes until 1730.
June 17 - Sept. 10: 0815, 0900, 1000 and hourly until 1700.

From **Col-de-Bretaye**:
Dec. 11 - 16, Apr. 18 - June 16, Sept. 11 - Dec. 9: 0930, 1130j, 1230, 1330j, 1530j, 1630.
Dec. 17 - Apr. 17: 0840, 0855, 0925, 0955 and every 30 minutes until 1725, then 1815.
June 17 - Sept. 10: 0837, 0930, 1030 and hourly until 1730.

a –	Ⓐ only.	d –	✗ only.	g –	Also Aug. 2.	h –	Also Aug. 1.	j –	Dec. 11-16, June 3-16, Sept. 11 - Oct. 29.

---

km				Ⓐ	Ⓒ																			♣	♣y
0	Martigny.................. d.	0604	...			0653	0746	0846	0946	1046	1146	1246	1346	1446	1546	...	1646	1746	1846	1946	2046	2146	...	2246	2346
7	Salvan..................... d.	0618	...			0707	0800	0900	1000	1100	1200	1300	1400	1500	1600	...	1700	1800	1900	2000	2100	2200	...	2300	0000
9	Les Marécottes............ d.	0622	...			0711	0804	0904	1004	1104	1204	1304	1404	1504	1604	...	1704	1804	1904	2004	2104	2204	...	2304	0004
14	Finhaut..................... d.	0635	...			0724	0817	0917	1017	1117	1217	1317	1417	1517	1617	...	1717	1817	1917	2017	2117	2217	...	2317s	0017s
18	Le Châtelard Frontière ⛰ a.	0645	...			0734	0827	0927	1027	1127	1227	1327	1427	1527	1627	...	1727	1827	1927	2027	2127	2227	...	2327	0027
18	Le Châtelard Frontière ⛰ d.						0827	0927	1027	1127	1227	1327	1427	1527	1627	...	1727	1827	1927	2027					
21	Vallorcine................. a.						0834	0934	1034	1134	1234	1334	1434	1534	1634	...	1734	1834	1934	2034					
21	Vallorcine................. d.		0638	0708	0738		0838	0938	1038	1138	1238	1338	1438	1538	1638	1708	1738	1838	1938						
28	Argentière Haute Savoie........... d.		0654	0724	0754		0854	0954	1054	1154	1254	1354	1454	1554	1654	1724	1754	1854	1954						
32	Les Tines..................... d.		0705	0734	0805		0905	1005	1105	1205	1305	1405	1505	1605	1705	1734	1805	1905	2005						
36	Chamonix.................. a.		0712	0742	0812		0912	1012	1112	1212	1312	1412	1512	1612	1712	1742	1812	1912	2012						
	St Gervais 365a......... a.		0757	0857	0857		0957	1057	...	1257	1357	1457	1557	1657	1757	...	1857	1957	2057						

		Ⓐ																		
	St Gervais 365a......... d.				0705	0805	0905		1005	...	1205	1305	1405	1505	...	1605	1705	1805	1905
	Chamonix.................. d.				0754	0854	0954		1054	1154	1254	1354	1454	1554	1654	1654	1754	1854	1954
	Les Tines..................... d.				0804	0904	1004		1104	1204	1304	1404	1504	1604	1634	1704	1804	1904	2004
	Argentière Haute Savoie......... d.				0812	0912	1012		1112	1212	1312	1412	1512	1612	1643	1712	1812	1912	2012
	Vallorcine................. a.				0831	0931	1031		1131	1231	1331	1431	1531	1631	1701	1731	1831	1931	2031
	Vallorcine................. d.					0845	0945	1045		1145	1245	1345	1445	1545	1645		1745	1845	1945	2045
	Le Châtelard Frontière ⛰ a.					0851	0951	1051		1151	1251	1351	1451	1551	1651		1751	1851	1951	2051
	Le Châtelard Frontière ⛰ d.	0529	0650	0752		0852	0952	1052		1152	1252	1352	1452	1552	1652		1752	1852	1952	2052	2152	2252	2334
	Finhaut..................... d.	0538	0659	0801		0901	1001	1101		1201	1301	1401	1501	1601	1701		1801	1901	2001	2101	2201	2301	2343
	Les Marécottes............ d.	0551	0712	0814		0914	1014	1114		1214	1314	1414	1514	1614	1714		1814	1914	2014	2114	2214	2314	2356
	Salvan..................... d.	0555	0716	0818		0918	1018	1118		1218	1318	1418	1518	1618	1718		1818	1918	2018	2118	2218	2318	0000
	Martigny.................. a.	0615	0736	0838		0938	1038	1138		1238	1338	1438	1538	1638	1738		1838	1938	2038	2138	2238	2338	0020

s –	Stops to set down only.	y –	⑤⑥ only.	♣ –	Runs only by prior reservation ✆ 027 764 12 71.

MARTIGNY - ORSIÈRES▲ and LE CHÂBLE: 19 km. Journey time: 26 minutes to both resorts.   ▲ – A change of train is necessary at Sembrancher.   **Operator**: RA.

From **Martigny**: 0605Ⓐ, 0717, 0817, 0917, 1017, 1145, 1223, 1317, 1417, 1517, 1645, 1723, 1817, 1917, 2017, 2123, 2317⑤⑥.

From **Orsières and Le Châble**: 0531Ⓐ, 0636, 0710, 0810, 0910, 1010, 1110, 1217, 1310, 1410, 1510, 1610, 1717, 1810, 1910, 2048, 2241⑤⑥.

LE CHÂBLE - VERBIER: 🚌 service. Journey time: ± 25 minutes. **Operator**: PA.

From **Le Châble** Gare: 0645✗, 0750, 0855, 0955, 1055⑥, 1255, 1355, 1455✗, 1610, 1715, 1755✗, 1806†, 1900, 1955, 2055.

From **Verbier** Post: 0608✗, 0715⑥, 0825†, 0840✗, 0925, 1025, 1230, 1330, 1430✗, 1525, 1640, 1740, 1835, 1930, 2020, 2120.

MARTIGNY - AOSTA: 🚌 service via Grand St Bernard tunnel. Service runs daily throughout the year (**not Dec. 25**). Journey time: ± 1 hour 45 minutes. **Operator**: TMR / SAVDA.

From **Martigny** Gare: 0825, 1830.

From **Aosta** Stazione: 1100, 1600.

SION - CRANS-SUR-SIERRE: 🚌 service. Journey time: ± 45 minutes. **Operator**: PA.

From **Sion** Gare: 0645✗, 0745, 0840✗, 1000, 1045✗, 1150, 1230✗, 1345, 1510Ⓒ, 1540Ⓐz, 1650✗, 1710†, 1810, 1910.

From **Crans-sur-Sierre** Post: 0643, 0740✗, 0835, 0930✗, 1050, 1135✗, 1245, 1335✗, 1545, 1635, 1805, 1905.

SIERRE - CRANS-SUR-SIERRE - MONTANA: 🚌 service. Principal stop in **Crans-sur-Sierre** is Hotel Scandia (± 40 minutes from Sierre, ± 8 minutes from Montana). **Operator**: SMC.

From **Sierre** Gare: 0745, 0845, 0945✗, 1045✗, 1145, 1231✗, 1340, 1440✗, 1546, 1652✗z, 1715, 1745, 1845✗, 1945, 2042, 2215.

From **Montana** Gare: 0602✗, 0622Ⓐz, 0632, 0736†, 0839✗, 0958, 1037✗, 1133✗, 1226, 1334✗, 1435, 1558, 1603Ⓐz, 1646, 1733✗, 1833, 1907, 2058.

BRIG - SAAS-FEE: 🚌 service. Journey time: 50–70 minutes. All services call at Visp (Bahnhof Süd) ± 20 minutes from Brig, and Saas Grund (Post) ± 10 minutes from Saas-Fee.

From **Brig** (Bahnhof): 0420, 0545, 0615, 0645 and every 30 minutes until 1045, then 1115, 1140, 1215, 1250, 1315, 1345 and every 30 minutes until 1845, then 1945, 2045, 2215.

From **Saas-Fee**: 0530, 0600, 0630, 0700, 0730, 0752, 0822, 0852, 0922, 0952 and every 30 minutes until 1852, then 1930, 2030.

Operator: PA.   Seat reservation recommended on Ⓒ from Saas Fee to Brig. ✆ 058 454 26 16.

z – Also Apr. 14; not June 15, Aug. 15, Nov. 1.

✗ – Restaurant	(✗) – Bistro	(⊤) – Bar coach	⊤ – Minibar

575 GLACIER EXPRESS — MGB, RhB*

Glacier Express through services (compulsory reservation). **No service Oct. 23 - Dec. 9, 2017.** For local services see Table **576**. Narrow gauge railway (part rack).

km		WINTER SERVICE ▶▶▶	902 ® ✕		SUMMER SERVICE ▶▶▶	900 ® T ✕	902 ® ✕	904 ® S ✕	
0	**Zermatt** d.		0852	...		0752	0852	0952	...
21	St Niklaus △ d.		|	...		|	|	1027	...
36	Visp △ d.		|	...		|	|	|	...
45	**Brig** △ d.		1018	...		0918	1018	1118	...
62	Fiesch △ d.		1042	...		0942	1042	1142	...
113	**Andermatt** a.	Dec. 11	1146	...	May 13	1046	1146	1246	...
113	**Andermatt** d.	to	1154	...	to	1054	1154	1254	...
142	**Disentis / Mustér** a.	May 12	1255	...	Oct. 22	1155	1255	1355	...
142	**Disentis / Mustér** d.		1328	...		1228	1328	1428	...
201	**Chur** ▽ a.		1435	...		1335	1435	1535	...
228	Thusis ▽ a.		1528	...		1428	1528	1628	...
242	Tiefencastel ▽ a.		1547	...		1447	1547	1647	...
252	**Filisur 545a** ▽ a.		1600	...		1500	1600	1700	...
260	Bergün / Bravuogn ▽ a.		1614	...		1514	1614	1714	...
285	**Samedan 546** ▽ a.		1645	...		1545	1645	1745	...
288	Celerina **546/7** ▽ a.		1654	...		1554	1654	1754	...
290	**St Moritz 546/7** a.		1658	...		1558	1658	1758	...

	WINTER SERVICE ▶▶▶	903 ® ✕		SUMMER SERVICE ▶▶▶	901 ® T ✕	903 ® ✕	905 ® S ✕	
St Moritz 546/7 d.		0902	...		0802	0902	1002	...
Celerina **546/7** △ d.		0905	...		0805	0905	1005	...
Samedan 546 △ d.		0917	...		0817	0917	1017	...
Bergün / Bravuogn △ d.		0947	...		0847	0947	1047	...
Filisur 545a △ d.		1001	...		0901	1001	1101	...
Tiefencastel △ d.	Dec. 11	1015	...	May 13	0915	1015	1115	...
Thusis △ d.	to	1033	...	to	0933	1033	1133	...
Chur △ d.	May 12	1126	...	Oct. 22	1026	1126	1226	...
Disentis / Mustér a.		1227	...		1127	1227	1327	...
Disentis / Mustér d.		1237	...		1137	1237	1337	...
Andermatt a.		1350	...		1255	1350	1450	...
Andermatt d.		1354	...		1308	1408	1508	...
Fiesch ▽ a.		1510	...		1410	1510	1610	...
Brig ▽ a.		1540	...		1440	1540	1640	...
Visp ▽ a.		|	...		|	|	|	...
St Niklaus ▽ a.		|	...		1524	|	|	...
Zermatt a.		1710	...		1610	1710	1810	...

All Glacier Express trains convey (12) [panorama cars]. Reservations can be made at any Swiss station. Reservations for ✕ are obligatory in advance; RhB, ✆ 081 288 65 65. Meals are served between 1100 and 1330 at your seat. Further information: www.glacierexpress.ch

S – May 25 - Sept. 17.
T – May 13 - Oct. 15.
△ – Calls to pick up only.
▽ – Calls to set down only.

* – Operators: MGB, Zermatt - Andermatt / Göschenen - Disentis; RhB, Disentis - Chur.

576 ZERMATT - BRIG - ANDERMATT (- GÖSCHENEN) - DISENTIS - CHUR local services — MGB, RhB*

Narrow gauge railway (part rack). For *Glacier Express* through services see Table 575

ZERMATT - BRIG

km													
0	**Zermatt** d.	0537	0613	0637	0813		1813	1837	1913	1937	2013	2113	2213
8	Täsch d.	0548	0625	0648	0825	and	1825	1848	1925	1948	2025	2125	2223
21	St Niklaus d.	0613	0650	0713	0850	every	1850	1913	1950	2013	2050	2150	2244
29	Stalden-Saas d.	0635	0710	0735	0910	hour	1910	1935	2010	2035	2110	2210	2305
36	Visp a.	0646	0722	0746	0922	until	1922	1946	2022	2046	2122	2222	2316
36	Visp d.	0650	0725	0750	0925	△	1925	1950	2025	2050	2125	2225	2318
45	**Brig** a.	0702	0737	0802	0937		1937	2002	2037	2102	2137	2237	2327

										①–⑥	⑦	
Brig d.	0520	0552	0627	0652	0727		1827	1952	2052	2227	2308	...
Visp a.	0531	0603	0638	0703	0738	and	1838	2003	2103	2238	2318	...
Visp d.	0533	0608	0641	0708	0741	every	1841	2008	2108	2241	2323	...
Stalden-Saas d.	0542	0618	0651	0718	0751	hour	1851	2018	2118	2249	2331	...
St Niklaus d.	0559	0636	0713	0736	0813	until	1913	2036	2136	2306	2347	...
Täsch d.	0621	0700	0736	0800	0836	▽	1936	2100	2200	2330	0007	...
Zermatt a.	0633	0714	0751	0814	0851		1951	2114	2214	2341	0018	...

VISP - BRIG - ANDERMATT

km										①–⑥	①–⑥	⑦
	Visp d.	...	0708	0808		1908	...	2008	2108	2238	...	2255
0	**Brig** d.	0623	0723	0823	and	1923	...	2023	2123	2249	2250	2312
7	Mörel d.	0633	0733	0833	every	1933	...	2033	2133	...	2300	2320
10	Betten d.	0639	0739	0839	hour	1939	...	2039	2139	...	2306	2326
17	Fiesch d.	0656	0756	0856	until	1956	...	2056	2155	...	2322	2343
41	Oberwald 🚗 d.	0742	0842	0942		2042	...	2139	*2237*z	...	...	...
59	Realp ▲ 🚗 § d.	0805	0905	1005		2105	...	...	...	...	...	...
68	**Andermatt** a.	0820	0920	1020		2120	...	...	...	...	...	...

											①–⑥	⑦
Andermatt d.	...	...	0737	0837		1737	1837	1937	2025	...	...
Realp ▲ 🚗 § d.	...	...	0750	0850	and	1750	1850	1950	2036	...	...
Oberwald 🚗 d.	*0612*z	0712	0812	0912	every	1812	1912	2012	2056	*2250*z	*2250*z
Fiesch d.	0656	0756	0856	0956	hour	1856	1956	2056	2131	2326	2346
Betten d.	0715	0815	0915	1015	until	1915	2015	2115	2147	2344	0004
Mörel d.	0722	0822	0922	1022		1922	2022	2122	2157	2351	0011
Brig a.	0733	0833	0933	1033		1933	2033	2133	2206	0001	0021
Visp a.	0750	0850	0950	1050		1950	*2103*	2150	...	...	...

ANDERMATT - GÖSCHENEN

km													
0	**Andermatt** d.	0638	0725	0741	0829	and hourly	1741	1829	1937	2037	2153	2253	
4	**Göschenen** a.	0652	0740	0756	0844	until	1756	1844	1952	2052	2208	2308	

Göschenen d.	0703	0759	0811	and hourly	1759	1811	1911	2011	2111	2211	2311
Andermatt a.	0713	0809	0821	until	1809	1821	1921	2021	2121	2221	2321

ANDERMATT - DISENTIS

km		🚌Ⓐ	🚌		w◇		w◇		w◇			w◇				w◇								🚌	🚌v	🚌v
0	**Andermatt** 🚗 d.	...	...	0728	0755	0828	0855	0928	0955	...	1028	1055	1128	1228	1328	1355	...	1428	1528	1628	1728	1828	...	...	...	...
10	Oberalppass d.	...	...	0750	0814	0850	0914	0950	1014	...	1050	1114	1150	1250	1350	1414	...	1450	1550	1650	1750	1850	...	...	...	...
19	Sedrun 🚗 d.	0616	0705	0816	...	0916	...	1016	...	...	1116	...	1216	1316	1416	...	...	1516	1616	1716	1816	1916	...	2001	2101	2201
29	**Disentis / Mustér** a.	0634	0725	0839	...	0939	...	1039	...	...	1139	...	1239	1339	1439	...	...	1539	1639	1739	1839	1939	...	2018	2118	2218

	🚌	n	r												w◇						🚌	🚌	🚌v	🚌v	🚌q
Disentis / Mustér d.	0640	0708	0714	0814	0914	...	1014	1114	1214	...	1314	1414	1514	...	...	...	1614	1714	1814	...	1922	2022	2122	2222	0015
Sedrun 🚗 d.	0650	0731	0731	0831	0931	...	1031	1131	1231	...	1331	1431	1531	...	...	...	1631	1731	1831	...	1940	2040	2140	2240	0033
Oberalppass d.	...	0753	0753	0853	0953	...	1053	1153	1253	...	1353	1453	1553	...	1625	...	1653	1753	1853	...	...	...	...	...	...
Andermatt 🚗 a.	...	0819	0819	0919	1019	...	1119	1219	1319	...	1419	1519	1619	...	1654	...	1719	1819	1919	...	...	...	...	...	...

DISENTIS - CHUR

km			⚒								
0	**Disentis / Mustér** d.	0544	0615	0644	0744	and	1744	1844	1944	2044	...
12	Trun d.	0600	0629	0700	0800	every	1800	1900	2000	2100	...
30	Ilanz d.	0624	0653	0724	0824	hour	1824	1924	2024	2123	...
49	Reichenau-Tamins d.	0649	0716x	0749	0849	until	1849	1949	2049	2149	...
59	**Chur** a.	0702	0732	0802	0901		1901	2001	2101	2202	...

	⚒									
Chur d.	0609	0654	0756	0856	and	1856	1956	2059	2259	...
Reichenau-Tamins d.	0621	0703	0805	0905	every	1905	2005	2113	2311	...
Ilanz d.	0654	0733	0833	0933	hour	1933	2033	2140	2333	...
Trun d.	0714	0754	0854	0954	until	1954	2054	2158	2351	...
Disentis / Mustér a.	0730	0811	0911	1011		2011	2111	2216	0009	...

n – Dec. 11 - May 12, Oct. 23 - Dec. 9.
q – ⑥⑦ Dec. 17 - Mar. 26.
r – May 13 - Oct. 22.
v – Dec. 16 - Mar. 26.
w – Dec. 17 - Mar. 26.
x – Stops only on request.
z – Connection by 🚌.

◇ – Subject to favourable weather conditions.
§ – Realp is a request stop.
△ – Additional services Zermatt - Visp: 0737, 0837, and hourly until 1737.
▽ – Additional services Visp - Zermatt: 0808, 0908, and hourly until 1908.

▲ – 🚂 service (summer only, not daily) runs Realp - Furka - Gletsch - Oberwald and v.v. Operator: Dampfbahn Furka-Bergstrecke ✆ 0848 000 144.
🚗 – Car-carrying shuttle available (see page 260).
* – Operators: MGB, Zermatt - Andermatt / Göschenen - Disentis; RhB, Disentis - Chur.

578 ZERMATT - GORNERGRAT — Narrow gauge rack railway. GGB

Journey 33 minutes uphill, 44 minutes downhill, *9 km. Services are liable to be suspended in bad weather*

Dec. 11 - Apr. 23, June 3 - Oct. 15, Nov. 25 - Dec. 9:
From Zermatt: 0700**s**, 0800, 0824, 0848, 0912*, 0936*, 1000*, 1024*, 1048*, 1112*, 1136, 1200, 1224, 1248, 1312, 1336, 1400, 1424, 1448, 1512, 1536, 1600, 1624, 1724, 1824**m**, 1924**p**.
From Gornergrat: 0735, 0843, 0907, 0931, 0955, 1019, 1043, 1107, 1131, 1155, 1219, 1243, 1307, 1331, 1355, 1419, 1443, 1507, 1531, 1555, 1619, 1638, 1718, 1818, 1918**m**, 2007**p**.

Apr. 24 - June 2, Oct. 16 - Nov. 24:
From Zermatt: 0700**r**, 0824, 0936**q**, 1024, 1136, 1224, 1336, 1424, 1536**q**, 1624, 1724**q**, 1824**q**.
From Gornergrat: 0735**r**, 0931, 1019**q**, 1131, 1219, 1331, 1419, 1531, 1619**q**, 1718, 1818**q**, 1918**q**.

m – Dec. 11 - Apr. 23, June 3 - Oct. 15.
p – Dec. 14 - Apr. 17, June 17 - Sept. 24.
q – Apr. 24 - June 2, Oct. 16 - 29.
r – Daily Apr. 24 - June 2, Oct. 16 - 31; ①–⑤ Nov. 2 - 24.
s – June 3 - Oct. 15.
* – Duplicated by non-stop journeys Dec. 24 - Apr. 1 (journey time 29 minutes).

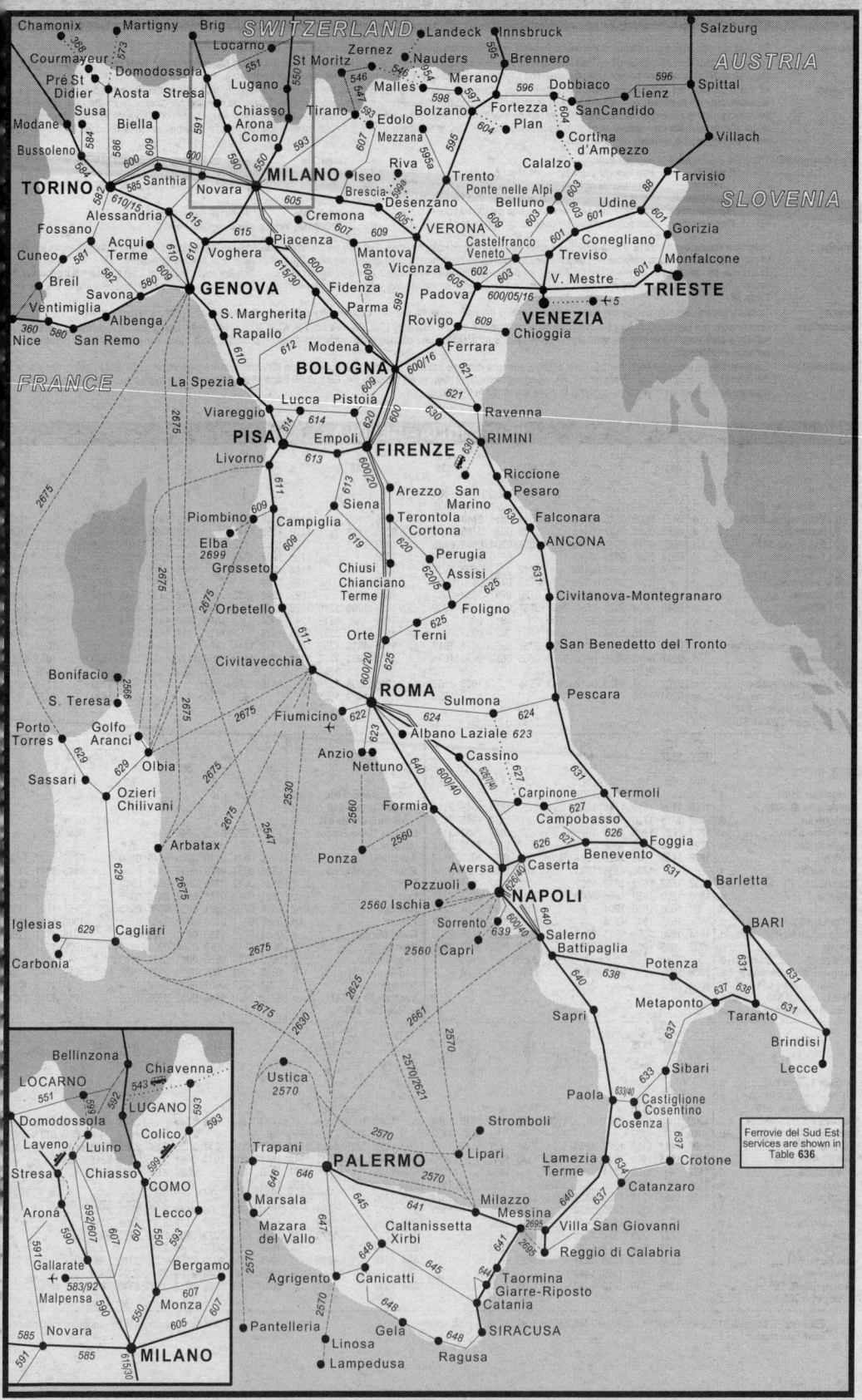

A list of Scenic Rail Routes appears elsewhere in the timetable – see Contents page

Ferrovie del Sud Est services are shown in Table **636**

ITALY

Operator: Services are operated by Trenitalia, a division of Ferrovie dello Stato Italiane S.p.a. (FS), unless otherwise noted: www.trenitalia.com.
Trenord is a joint venture between Trenitalia and Ferrovie Nord Milano (LeNord) that operates local services, mainly in the Lombardia region: www.trenord.it. Nuovo Trasporto Viaggiatori (NTV) is an open-access operator providing alternative services over the high-speed network: www.italotreno.it.

Services: All trains convey First and Second classes of travel unless otherwise shown by a figure "2" at the top of the column, or in a note in the Table heading. Four classes of accommodation is available on Frecciarossa (*FR*) services: Executive, Business, Premium and Standard class. Overnight sleeping car (🛏) or couchette (🛏) trains do not necessarily convey seating accommodation or may convey only second class seats - refer to individual footnotes. Excelsior sleeping cars offer en-suite facilities. Descriptions of sleeping and couchette cars appear on page 8. Refreshment services (✕ or 🍷) where known, may only be available for part of the journey, and may be added to or taken away from trains during the currency of the timetable.

Train Categories: There are 8 categories of express train:

EC	**EuroCity**	international express; supplement payable.
EN	**EuroNight**	international night express.
FA	**Frecciargento**	tilting trains used on both high-speed and traditional lines.
FB	**Frecciabianca**	fast premium fare services using traditional lines.
FR	**Frecciarossa**	fast premium fare services using high-speed lines.
IC	**InterCity**	internal day express; supplement payable.
ICN	**InterCity Notte**	internal night express.
ITA	**.italo**	high-speed service (operated by NTV).

Other services are classified:

R	**Regionale**	Regional (local) train.
RV	**Regionale Veloce**	Fast regional train.

Timings: Valid from **December 11, 2016** unless stated otherwise. Readers should note, however, that only partial information was available at press date and further changes are likely. In particular, details of local services and accommodation conveyed on domestic night trains may alter. Dates may refer to last year's schedules.
Trains may be cancelled or altered at holiday times – for public holiday dates see page 2. Some international trains which are not available for local travel are not shown in this section; these include some sleeper services from Austria, France and Germany – see International pages. Trains and international buses operating via Tarvisio are shown in Table **88**.

Tickets: Tickets must be date-stamped by the holder before boarding the train using the self-service validating machines – this applies to all tickets except passes.

Reservations: Reservations are **compulsory** for all journeys by services for which a **train category** (*EC, EN, FA, FB, FR, IC, ICN*) is shown in the timing column and passengers boarding without a prior reservation may be surcharged. Reservations for sleeping and couchette car accommodation on domestic night trains are valid only when presented with personal identification.

Supplements Supplements are calculated according to class of travel and total distance travelled (minimum 10km, maximum 3000km), and are payable on all *EC* and *IC* trains, regardless of the number of changes of train. A higher fare (including supplement) is payable for travel by *FA, FB* and *FR* trains. Some trains are only available to passengers holding long distance tickets and the restrictions applying to these are noted in the tables.

580 VENTIMIGLIA - GENOVA

km		*IC* **655** ⚒		Ⓐ 2	⚒ 2	Ⓐ 2	*IC* **505** ⚒	2	2	*EC* **139** 🍷 N		2	*IC* **745**	Ⓒ	2	2	*IC* **1539** †	Ⓒ	⚒ 2	† 2	2	*EC* **145** 🍷 N		Ⓒ	2
	Nice Ville **360/1** d.	...	...	...	...	...	...	...	...	0808	...	...	...	...	...	...	...	...	...	...	...	1408	...	...	...
0	**Ventimiglia** 🏛 **581** d.	0451	0500	0515	0535a	...	0641	0646	0748	|	...	0948	1105	...	1110	1148	1305	...	1313	1313	1348	1512	...	...	1548
5	Bordighera d.	0458	0507	0522	0544a	...	0649	0655	0755	|	...	0955	1113	...	1120	1155	1313	...	1320	1323	1355	|	...	...	1555
16	**San Remo 581** d.	0508	0515	0530	0553a	...	0658	0704	0803	0925	...	1003	1122	...	1128	1203	1322	...	1328	1331	1403	1525	...	...	1603
24	Taggia-Arma d.	0514	0520	0536	0558a	...	|	0710	0808	|	...	1008	|	...	1135	1208	1328	...	1334	1336	1408	|	...	...	1608
39	Imperia d.	0524	0532	0549	0610a	...	0712	0723	0820	0937	...	1022	1134	...	1148	1220	1338	...	1346	1348	1421	1537	...	...	1620
46	Diano Marina d.	|	0543	0602	0622a	...	0718	0736	0830	0943	...	1034	1140	...	1158	1234	|	...	1356	1355	1434	1543	...	...	1635
61	Alassio d.	0537	0558	0623	0643a	0650	0729	0757	0850	0952	...	1051	1152	...	1222	1248	1352	...	1422	1422	1448	1552	...	1605	1651
67	**Albenga** d.	0545	0604	0629	0650	0658	0737	0804	0856	1000	...	1057	1200	1210	1228	1257	1400	1406	1428	1428	1454	1600	...	1611	1657
76	Loano d.	|	0611	0648	0701	0709	|	0817	0903	|	...	1104	|	1218	1240	1304	|	1414	1440	1440	1504	|	...	1623	1704
79	Pietra Ligure d.	|	0616	0654	|	0713	|	0822	0907	|	...	1108	|	1222	1248	1308	|	1418	1447	1447	1508	|	...	1627	1708
85	Finale Ligure Marina d.	0600	0623	0701	0710	0724	0752	0831	0914	1017	...	1115	1214	1230	1258	1315	1414	1429	1458	1458	1515	1617	...	1634	1715
108	**Savona** d.	0617	0645	0719	0726	0745	0805	0852	0933	1033	...	1133	1233	1248	1322	1333	1432	1450	1522	1522	1533	1633	...	1651	1733
120	Varazze d.	|	0653	|	0734	0757	|	...	|	|	...	|	|	1259	...	|	|	1458	...	...	|	|	...	1659	|
151	**Genova** Piazza Principe § a.	0702	0737	0803	0812	0841	0848	...	1017	1108	...	1216	1308	1328	...	1416	1504	1532	...	...	1616	1708	...	1730	1816
	Milano Centrale **610** a.	0900	0945	...	...	...	|	...	...	1250	...	...	1450	1535	...	...	1650	1735	...	...	...	1850	...	1937	...
	Pisa Centrale **610** a.	...	...	...	...	...	1056	...	...	...	...	...	...	...	...	...	...	...	...	...	...	...	...	...	...
	Roma Termini **610** a.	...	...	...	...	...	1433	...	...	...	...	...	...	...	...	...	...	...	...	...	...	...	...	...	...

	IC **681** Ⓐ	*IC* **1537** Ⓒ	T2	2	*EC* **147** 🍷 N		2	T2	2	2
Nice Ville **360/1** d.	...	...	...	...	1807	...	...	...	...	...
Ventimiglia 🏛 **581** d.	1705	1705	1710	1748	1912	...	...	1916	1948	2110
Bordighera d.	1713	1713	1720	1755	|	...	...	1924	1955	2120
San Remo 581 d.	1722	1722	1728	1803	1925	...	...	1932	2003	2128
Taggia-Arma d.	1728	1728	1735	1808	|	...	...	1937	2008	2135
Imperia d.	1738	1738	1748	1820	1937	...	...	1950	2020	2148
Diano Marina d.	|	|	1756	1834	1943	...	...	1958	2034	2158
Alassio d.	1752	1752	1822	1848	1952	...	...	2022	2047	2223
Albenga d.	1800	1800	1828	1854	2000	...	2010	2028	2053	2231
Loano d.	|	1808	1839	1904	|	...	2019	2039	2104	2249
Pietra Ligure d.	|	1813	1847	1908	|	...	2023	2047	2108	2254
Finale Ligure Marina d.	1814	1820	1858	1915	2017	...	2030	2058	2115	2303
Savona d.	1833	1835	1922	1933	2033	...	2048	2122	2133	2326
Varazze d.	|	1843	...	|	|	...	2056	...	2146	...
Genova Piazza Principe § a.	1908	1908	...	2016	2108	...	2134	...	2224	...
Milano Centrale **610** a.	2050	2050	...	...	2250	...	...	...	...	...
Pisa Centrale **610** a.	...	...	...	...	...	...	...	...	...	...
Roma Termini **610** a.	...	...	...	...	...	...	...	...	...	...

	Ⓐ 2	2	2	⚒ 2	† 2	T2		*EC* **142** 🍷 N	2	T2
Roma Termini **610** d.	...	...	...	...	...	...	...	...	...	...
Pisa Centrale **610** d.	...	...	...	...	...	...	...	...	...	...
Milano Centrale **610** d.	...	...	...	...	...	...	...	0710	...	...
Genova Piazza Principe § d.	...	0522	0606	0646	...	...	...	0856	0935a	...
Varazze d.	...	0605	0653	0729	...	...	...	|	|	...
Savona d.	0515	0621	0710	0745	0745	0850	...	0931	1027	1050
Finale Ligure Marina d.	0530	0636	0728	0801	0801	0909	...	0943	1041	1109
Pietra Ligure d.	0536	0642	0736	0807	0807	0918	...	|	1050	1118
Loano d.	0541	0648	0741	0812	0812	0925	...	|	1055	1125
Albenga d.	0548	0702	0801	0824	0824	0943	...	0957	1102	1143
Alassio d.	0555	0711	0808	0832	0832	0951	...	1006	1109	1151
Diano Marina d.	0631	0733	0833	0851	0851	1009	...	1019	1121	1209
Imperia d.	0641	0748	0843	0904	0904	1019	...	1026	1131	1217
Taggia-Arma d.	0653	0759	0855	0921	0921	1030	...	|	1144	1228
San Remo 581 d.	0658	0804	0901	0929	0929	1036	...	1039	1149	1234
Bordighera d.	0707	0812	0909	0939	0939	1044	...	|	1159	1242
Ventimiglia 🏛 **581** a.	0719	0820	0918	0953	0953	1055	...	1051	1212	1255
Nice Ville **360/1** a.	...	...	...	...	...	...	...	1152	...	...

	⑥	*IC* **660** Ⓐ	*IC* **1536** Ⓒ	2	2	Ⓒ 2	*EC* **144** 🍷 N	2	Ⓐ 2	Ⓒ 2	2	2		*EC* **160** 🍷 N		2	2	*IC* **676**	2	2	*IC* **518**	*IC* **690**	2	2	
Roma Termini **610** d.	...	...	...	...	...	...	...	...	...	...	...	...	...	...	...	...	...	...	...	...	1557	...	...	...	...
Pisa Centrale **610** d.	...	...	...	...	...	...	...	...	...	...	...	...	...	...	...	...	...	...	...	...	1903	...	...	...	...
Milano Centrale **610** d.	...	0910	0910	...	...	...	1110	...	...	...	...	...	1425	1510	...	...	...	1705	...	...	|	2000	...	...	...
Genova Piazza Principe § d.	1000	1058	1058	1143	...	1200	1258	1343	1340	1354	...	1543	1626	1658	...	1743	...	1858	1943	...	2135	2201	2316	0043	...
Varazze d.	1049	|	1123	|	...	1244	|	|	1431	1432	...	|	1712	|	←	|	...	|	|	...	|	|	0002	0131	...
Savona d.	1108	1131	1131	1227	1250	1304	1331	1427	1445	1440	1450	1627	1725	1731	1734	1827	1850	1931	2026	2050	2206	2233	0015	0149	...
Finale Ligure Marina d.	1124	1143	1144	1241	1312	1320	1343	1441	...	1455	1509	1641	→	1743	1749	1841	1909	1943	2041	2112	2219	2245	...	...	...
Pietra Ligure d.	1132	|	1153	1251	1320	1328	|	1450	...	1505	1518	1648	...	|	1757	1850	1918	|	2050	2121	|	|	...	...	...
Loano d.	1137	|	1159	1256	1325	1334	|	1455	...	1511	1525	1653	...	|	1802	1855	1925	|	2055	2126	|	|	...	...	...
Albenga d.	1150	1157	1211	1303	1337	1345	1357	1502	...	1524	1543	1700	...	1757	1815	1902	1943	1957	2102	2138	2235	2259	...	...	...
Alassio d.	...	1206	1224	1310	1350	...	1406	1509	...	1535	1551	1707	...	1806	...	1909	1951	2006	2109	2151	2243	2307	...	...	...
Diano Marina d.	...	|	|	1322	1407	...	1419	1522	...	...	1609	1721	...	1819	...	1922	2009	|	2122	2211	2255	2319	...	...	...
Imperia d.	...	1221	1238	1332	1417	...	1426	1532	...	...	1617	1731	...	1826	...	1932	2017	2022	2134	2221	2302	2326	...	...	...
Taggia-Arma d.	...	1232	1248	1344	1428	...	|	1544	...	...	1628	1743	...	|	...	1944	2028	2032	2146	2232	|	|	...	...	...
San Remo 581 d.	...	1239	1255	1349	1434	...	1439	1551	...	...	1634	1749	...	1839	...	1951	2034	2039	2151	2238	2315	2339	...	...	...
Bordighera d.	...	1249	1304	1359	1442	...	|	1559	...	...	1642	1759	...	|	...	1959	2042	2049	2159	2246	2324	2349	...	...	...
Ventimiglia 🏛 **581** a.	...	1256	1310	1412	1453	...	1451	1612	...	...	1656	1812	...	1851	...	2012	2055	2056	2212	2300	2330	2356	...	...	...
Nice Ville **360/1** a.	...	...	...	...	...	...	1600	...	...	...	...	...	...	1952	...	...	...	...	...	...	...	...	...	...	...

N – 12 and 🍷 Marseille / Nice - Ventimiglia - Genova - Milano and v.v.
T – From / to Torino.
a – Ⓐ only.
§ – Local services may use the underground platforms.

VENTIMIGLIA and NICE - CUNEO 581

2nd class only

km		d	e										e	d	A			e		
	Ventimiglia ....d.	...	...	...	...	...	...	...	1037	...	...	...	...	1729	...	...	1837	...	...	...
0	Nice Ville ....d.	...	0543	...	...	0735	0833	...	0923	...	1240	...	1500	...	1637	...	1723	...	1803	...	1905	1951
34	Sospel.................d.	...	0635	...	...	0825	0928	...	1012		1330	...	1551	...	1727	...	1817	...	1858	...	1957	2041
43	Breil sur Roya........a.	...	0647	...	...	0837	0940	...	1024	1108	1342	...	1603	...	1739	...	1758	1829	...	1908	1910	...	2009	2053
	Breil sur Roya........d.	...	...	...	...	0842	...	...	1029	1109	1344	...	1608	...	...	...	1805	...	...	1917	...	...	...
	Tende ....d.	...	...	...	...	0939	...	...	1124	1201	1439	...	1704	...	...	...	1852	...	...	2009	...	...	...
	Limone ....d.	0640	...	0732	0932	...	...	1132	...	1232	1332	...	1532	...	1732	...	1840	1921	...	1932	2040	...	2132	...
	Cuneo ....a.	0719	...	0811	1011	...	...	1211	...	1311	1411	...	1611	...	1811	...	1919	1947	...	2011	2115	...	2211	...
	Fossano 582 ....d.	...	...	0835	1035	...	...	1235	...	...	1435	...	1635	...	1835	...	...	2120	...	2035	...	...	2235	...

km		f		e		f	A	⑧												d	
	Fossano 582 ....d.	...	...	...	...	...	...	0725	...	0925	...	1125	...	1325	...	...	1525	...	1725	...	1925
0	Cuneo ....d.	...	...	0550	...	0641	...	0750	0841	0950	...	1150	...	1350	1441	...	1550	...	1750	1841	1950
29	Limone ....d.	...	...	0628	...	0720	...	0830	0919	1028	...	1228	...	1428	1517	...	1628	...	1828	1919	2028
47	Tende ....d.	...	...	...	...	0747	...	0859	...	1001	...	1202	1447	...	1544	...	1712	...	...	...	...
75	Breil sur Roya........a.	...	...	...	...	0836	...	0954	...	1058	...	1252	1537	...	1638	...	1802	...	...	...	...
75	Breil sur Roya........d.	0540	0621	...	0704	0837	0733	0851	0955	...	1101	...	1254	1539	...	1642	1650	1804	...	1920	...
	Sospel................d.	0553	0635	...	0717		0745	0903	...	...	1114	...	1306	1551	...	...	1702	1817	...	1932	...
*	Nice Ville ....a.	0640	0724	...	0807		0837	0954	...	...	1203	...	1356	1641	...	...	1754	1906	...	2023	...
96	Ventimiglia ....a.	...	...	...	...	0909	...	1027	...	...	...	...	...	1720	...	...	...	...	...	...	...

A – ⑥⑦ July 9 - Aug. 28 (also Italian public holidays).
d – ①–⑥ (not Italian public holidays).
e – ①–⑤ (not French public holidays).
f – ①–⑥ (not French public holidays).

TORINO - CUNEO and SAVONA 582

Most trains 2nd class only

km			†A	V			†A		⚡	†A													
0	Torino Porta Nuova....d.	0525	...	0610	0625	...	0655	0725	...	0750	...	0825	...	0925	...	1025	...	1125	...	1225	...	1325	...
52	Savigliano..............d.	0603	...	0654	0703	...	0739	0803	...	0837	...	0903	...	1003	...	1103	...	1203	...	1303	...	1403	...
64	Fossano ....d.	0612	0622	0703	0713	0725	0748	0812	0822	0847	...	0913	0925	1012	1022	1113	1125	1212	1222	1313	1325	1412	1422
90	Cuneo ....a.	0636		...	0749	...	0836		...	0949	1036	...	1149	1236	...	1349	...	1436	...
83	Mondovi................d.	...	0640	0715	0728	...	0800	...	0840	0902	...	0928	...	1040	1128	...	1240	1328	...	...	1440
103	Ceva ....d.	...	0700	0729	0743	...	0817	...	0900	0921	...	0943	...	1100	1143	...	1300	1342	...	...	1500
153	Savona ....a.	...	0752d	0818	0836	...	0911	...	1004	1036	...	...	1236	...	...	1436	...	...	...

		⑧h		⑧j			⚡k														
Torino Porta Nuova..............d.	1425	...	1525	...	1625	...	1725	...	1750	...	1825	...	1855	1925	1955	2025	...	2125	...	2325	...
Savigliano.......................d.	1503	...	1603	...	1703	...	1803	...	1829	...	1903	...	1931	2003	2032	2103	...	2203	...	0014	...
Fossano ....d.	1513	1525	1612	1622	1713	1725	1812	1822	1837	1845	1913	1925	1941	2012	2041	2113	2125	2212	2217	0022	...
Cuneo ....a.	...	1549	1636	...	...	1749	1836	...	1901	...	1949	...	2036	...	2150	...	2236	...	0046	...
Mondovi.........................d.	1528	...	...	1640	1728	...	1840	...	1858	1928	...	1956	...	2100	2128	...	2235	...	...
Ceva ....d.	1543	...	...	1700	1743	...	1900	...	1912	1943	...	2018	...	2120	2143	...	2253	...	...
Savona ....a.	1636	...	...	1836	...	2036	...	2112	...	2236	...	...

		⑧h		†	⚡		⚡	⚡k			⚡k							⚡				
Savona ....d.	...	...	...	...	0530	...	...	...	0730	0808d	...	0930	...	1130	...
Ceva ....d.	...	0502	0520	...	0617	...	0650	...	0700	...	0817	0900	...	1017	1100	...	1217	1300	...
Mondovi.........................d.	...	0522	0540	...	0632	...	0706	...	0720	...	0832	0920	...	1032	1120	...	1232	1320	...
Cuneo ....d.	0421	0524	...	0612		0654		...	0724	0751	0812		0924	1012		1124	1212		1324
Fossano ....d.	0441	0544	0540	0558	0635	0644	0714	0723	...	0738	0744	0814	0835	0844	0938	0944	1035	1044	1138	1144	1235	1244	1338	1344
Savigliano.......................d.	0449	0552	...	0652	0722	0733	...	0752	0822	0852	...	0952	...	1052	...	1152	...	1252	...	1352
Torino Porta Nuova..............a.	0535	0635	...	0735	0805	0815	...	0835	0905	0935	...	1035	...	1135	...	1235	...	1335	...	1435

		†A		V	†A		†A		V		†A		V		†A		V	
Savona ....d.	...	1328	...	1530	...	1635	...	1730	1754	...	1800d	...	1845	...	1930	...	2028	...	2130	...
Ceva ....d.	...	1417	1500	...	1617	1700	...	1736	...	1817	1837	...	1900	...	1938	...	2017	2100	...	2115	...	2217	...
Mondovi.........................d.	...	1432	1520	...	1632	1720	...	1750	...	1832	1851	...	1920	...	1953	...	2032	2120	...	2133	...	2232	...
Cuneo ....d.	1412			1524	1612		1724		1812		1924		2012		2124		2212	
Fossano ....d.	1435	1444	1538	1544	1635	1644	1738	1744	1803	1835	1844	1903	...	1938	1944	2011	2035	2044	2138	2144	2155	2235	2244
Savigliano.......................d.	...	1452	1552	...	1652	...	1752	1812	...	1852	1912	...	1952	2020	...	2052	...	2152	2205	...	2252	...
Torino Porta Nuova..............a.	...	1535	1635	...	1735	...	1835	1850	...	1935	1955	...	2035	2110	...	2135	...	2235	2250	...	2335	...

A – Until Sept. 4.
V – From / to Ventimiglia.
d – ⚡ only.
h – Not Aug. 1 - 28.
j – Not July 30 - Aug. 28.
k – Not July 31 - Aug. 28.

MILANO MALPENSA AEROPORTO ✈ 583

LeNord

		X	and at	X						X	and at	X			
Milano Centrale................d.	0525	0555	the same	1925	1955	2025	2125	2225	2325	Malpensa Aeroporto ✈. d.	0543	...	0613	0643	the same	2113	2143	...	2243
Milano Porta Garibaldi.... d.	0535	0605	minutes	1935	2005	2035	2135	2235	2335	Milano Bovisa.............a.	0618	...	0648	0718	minutes	2148	2218	...	2318
Milano Bovisa................d.	0542	0612	past each	1942	2012	2042	2142	2242	2342	Milano Porta Garibaldi.... a.	0624	...	0654	0724	past each	2154	2224	...	2324
Malpensa Aeroporto ✈ ... a.	0616	0646	hour until	2016	2046	2116	2216	2316	0016	Milano Centrale............a.	0635	...	0705	0735	hour until	2205	2235	...	2335

All services below operate as *Malpensa Express*. Special fare payable.

Milano Cadorna ....d.	0427	0457	...	0527	0557	and	2227	2257	...	2327	Malpensa Aeroporto ✈. d.	0526	0556	...	0626	0656	and	2326	2356	...	0026
Milano Bovisa ....d.	0433	0503	...	0533	0603	each hour	2233	2303	...	2333	Milano Bovisa.............a.	0556	0626	...	0656	0726	each hour	2356	0026	...	0056
Malpensa Aeroporto ✈ ... a.	0504	0534	...	0604	0634	until	2304	2334	...	0004	Milano Cadorna............a.	0603	0633	...	0703	0733	until	0003	0033	...	0103

X – *Malpensa Express*. Special fare payable.

Operator: Ferrovie Nord Milano (LeNord), Piazzale Cadorna 14, 20123 Milano.
✆ + 39 02 85 111, fax: + 39 02 85 11 708, www.trenord.it

584 TORINO - OULX - BARDONECCHIA

2nd class only

For Italy-France services via Oulx and Modane – see Table 44

km																									
		⚒	⚒	†	⚒	⚒		⚒	†	⚒	⚒		⚒	†	⚒	⚒		⚒	†	⚒	⚒		⚒	†	⚒
0	**Torino** Porta Nuova d.	0445	0515	0545	0545	0615	0645	0715	0745	0745	0815	0845	0915	0945	0945	1015	1045	1115	1145	1145	1215	1245	1315	1345	1345
46	Bussoleno d.	0543	0559	0632	0643	0659	0743	0759	0832	0843	0859	0943	0959	1032	1043	1059	1143	1159	1232	1243	1259	1343	1359	1432	1443
	Susa a.	0553	|	|	0653	|	0753	|	|	0853	|	0953	|	|	1053	|	1153	|	|	1253	|	1353	|	|	1453
76	Oulx-Claviere-Sestriere ▲ d.	...	0628	0701	...	0728	...	0828	0901	...	0928	...	1028	1101	...	1128	...	1228	1301	...	1328	...	1428	1501	...
87	Bardonecchia ♣ d.	...	0641	0714	...	0741	...	0841	0914	...	0941	...	1041	1114	...	1141	...	1241	1314	...	1341	...	1441	1514	...

km																									
		⚒		⚒	†	⚒	⚒		⚒	†	⚒	⚒		⚒	†	⚒	⚒			⚒	†	⚒	⚒		
	Torino Porta Nuova d.	1415	1445	1515	1545	1545	1615	1645	1715	1745	1745	1815	1845	1915	1945	1945	2015	2045	...	2115	2145	2145	2215	2245	...
0	Bussoleno d.	1459	1543	1559	1632	1643	1659	1743	1759	1832	1843	1859	1943	1959	2032	2043	2059	2143	...	2159	2232	2243	2259	2342	...
8	Susa a.	|	1553	|	|	1653	|	1753	|	|	1853	|	1953	|	|	2053	|	2153	...	|	|	2253	|	...	...
	Oulx-Claviere-Sestriere ▲ d.	1528	...	1628	1701	...	1728	...	1828	1901	...	1928	...	2028	2101	...	2128	...	...	2228	2301	...	2328	...	...
	Bardonecchia ♣ d.	1541	...	1641	1714	...	1741	...	1841	1914	...	1941	...	2041	2114	...	2141	...	...	2241	2314	...	2341	...	...

	⚒	†	⚒	†	⚒	⚒	⚒	⚒	†	⚒		⚒	⚒	†		⚒		⚒	⚒	†	⚒		⚒	⚒	†
Bardonecchia ♣ d.	...	...	...	0509	0521	...	0621	...	0648	0721	...	0821	...	0848	...	0921	...	1021	...	1048	1121	...	1221	...	1248
Oulx-Claviere-Sestriere ▲ d.	...	...	...	0522	0534	...	0634	...	0701	0734	...	0834	...	0901	...	0934	...	1034	...	1101	1134	...	1234	...	1301
Susa d.	...	0439	0509	|	|	0609	|	0709	|	|	0809	|	0909	|	...	|	1009	|	1109	|	|	1209	|	1309	|
Bussoleno d.	0419	0449	0519	0549	0601	0619	0701	0719	0728	0801	0819	0901	0919	0928	...	1001	1019	1101	1119	1128	1201	1219	1301	1319	1328
Torino Porta Nuova a.	0515	0545	0615	0645	0645	0715	0745	0815	0815	0845	0915	0945	1015	1015	...	1045	1115	1145	1215	1215	1245	1315	1345	1415	1415

	⚒		⚒	⚒	†	⚒		⚒	⚒	†	⚒			⚒	⚒	†	⚒		⚒	⚒	†	⚒		⚒	
Bardonecchia ♣ d.	1321	...	1421	...	1448	1521	...	1621	...	1648	1721	...	...	1821	...	1848	1921	...	2021	...	2048	2121	...	2221	...
Oulx-Claviere-Sestriere ▲ d.	1334	...	1434	...	1501	1534	...	1634	...	1701	1734	...	...	1834	...	1901	1934	...	2034	...	2101	2134	...	2234	...
Susa d.	|	1409	|	1509	|	|	1609	|	1709	|	|	...	1809	|	1909	|	|	2009	|	2109	|	|	2209	|	...
Bussoleno d.	1401	1419	1501	1519	1528	1601	1619	1701	1719	1728	1801	...	1819	1901	1919	1928	2001	2019	2101	2119	2128	2201	2219	2301	...
Torino Porta Nuova a.	1445	1515	1545	1615	1615	1645	1715	1745	1815	1815	1845	...	1915	1945	2015	2015	2045	2115	2145	2215	2215	2245	2317	2345	...

▲ – Station for the resorts of Cesana, Claviere and Sestriere.

♣ – A cross-border 🚌 service is available Bardonecchia - Modane (Table **367**) and v.v.: 4 services on ⚒, 3 on †. See www.bardonecchia.it

585 TORINO - MILANO

For high-speed services – see Table 600. For Italy-France *TGV* service – see Table 44. *FB* and *FR* services convey 🍷

km																								
				FB	*FR*		*FB*			*FR*	*FR*				*FB*		*ICN*			*FR*		*FR*		*FB*
				8707	**9707**		**8709**			**9717**	**9723**				**8721**		**795**			**9737**		**9747**		**8731**
					Ⓐ T					Ⓒ		p					♦			T		T		
0	**Torino** Porta Nuova **586** d.	0454	0554	0610	0635	0650	0710	0754	0854	0905	1033	1054	1154	1254	1310	...	1335	1354	1450	1505	1554	1608	1654	1710
6	**Torino** Porta Susa **586** d.	0505	0605	0619**u**	0647**u**	0701	0719**u**	0805	0905	0915**u**	1045**u**	1105	1205	1305	1319**u**	...	1348**u**	1405	1501	1515**u**	1605	1615**u**	1705	1719**u**
29	Chivasso **586** d.	0520	0620	|	|	0716	|	0820	0920	|	|	1120	1220	1320	|	...	|	1420	1516	|	1620	|	1720	|
60	Santhià d.	0538	0638	|	|	0734	|	0838	0938	|	|	1138	1238	1338	|	...	|	1438	1534	|	1638	|	1738	|
79	Vercelli d.	0549	0649	0657	|	0745	0757	0849	0949	|	|	1149	1249	1349	1357	...	1425	1449	1545	|	1649	|	1749	1757
101	Novara d.	0604	0704	0713	|	0802	0813	0904	1004	|	|	1204	1304	1404	1413	...	1443	1504	1602	|	1704	|	1804	1813
153*	**Milano** Centrale **605** a.	0646	0746	0754	0735	0842	0846	0946	1046	1005	1133	1246	1346	1446	1450	...	1542**g**	1546	1642	1605	1746	1705	1846	1854
	Venezia SL **605** a.	...	...	1040	0958**v**	...	1140	...	...	1228**v**	1410	...	...	...	1740	...	...	...	...	1840	...	1928**v**	...	2140

			FR				*ICN*		
		2	**9757**				**797**		
		Ⓐ	T				♦	2	
Torino Porta Nuova **586** d.	1754	1820	1835	1854	1954	2054	2125	2154	2254
Torino Porta Susa **586** d.	1805	1829	1845**u**	1905	2005	2105	2140**u**	2205	2305
Chivasso **586** d.	1820	1842	|	1920	2020	2120	|	2220	2320
Santhià d.	1838	1904	|	1938	2038	2138	|	2238	2338
Vercelli d.	1849	1916	|	1949	2049	2149	2222	2249	2349
Novara d.	1904	1937	|	2004	2104	2204	2238	2304	0004
Milano Centrale **605** a.	1946	2020**g**	1935	2046	2146	2246	2315**g**	2346	0046
Venezia SL **605** a.	...	...	2145**v**	...	...	...	...	...	...

				ICN					*FR*
			2	**798**					**9710**
			Ⓐ	♦			p		T
Venezia SL **605** d.	...	...	...	...	...	...	...	...	0750**v**
Milano Centrale d.	0518	0618	0640**g**	0713**g**	0718	0818	0918	...	1000
Novara d.	0558	0658	0718	0805	0758	0858	0958	...	|
Vercelli d.	0612	0712	0735	0821	0812	0912	1012	...	|
Santhià d.	0624	0724	0747	|	0824	0924	1024	...	|
Chivasso **586** d.	0643	0743	0812	|	0843	0943	1043	...	|
Torino Porta Susa **586** a.	0658	0758	0829	0910**s**	0858	0958	1058	...	1050**s**
Torino Porta Nuova **586** a.	0710	0810	0840	0920	0910	1010	1110	...	1100

	FR					*ICN*		*FB*			*FB*		*FB*				*FB*				*FR*			
	9714					**794**		**8716**			**8718**		**8720**				**8724**				**9762**		2	
						♦																⚒	①	
Venezia SL **605** d.	0820	...	...	...	...	...	...	1320	...	...	1420	...	1520	...	...	...	1720	...	...	...	1950	...	...	...
Milano Centrale d.	1055	1118	1218	1318	1418	1444**g**	1518	1610	...	1618	1710	1718	1810	...	1818	1913	2006	2015	2115	2218	2230	2318	0018	...
Novara d.	|	1158	1258	1358	1458	1521	1558	1648	...	1658	1748	1758	1848	...	1858	1953	2048	2055	2155	2258	|	2358	0058	...
Vercelli d.	|	1212	1312	1412	1512	1536	1612	1701	...	1712	1801	1812	1901	...	1912	2009	2101	2109	2209	2312	|	0012	0112	...
Santhià d.	|	1224	1324	1424	1524	|	1624	|	...	1724	|	1824	|	...	1924	2021	|	2121	2221	2324	|	0024	0126	...
Chivasso **586** d.	|	1243	1343	1443	1543	|	1643	|	...	1743	|	1843	|	...	1943	2039	|	2140	2240	2343	|	0043	0147	...
Torino Porta Susa **586** a.	1143**s**	1258	1358	1458	1558	1630**s**	1658	1740**s**	...	1758	1840**s**	1858	1940**s**	...	1958	2053	2140**s**	2155	2255	2358	2319**s**	0058	0203	...
Torino Porta Nuova **586** a.	1155	1310	1410	1510	1610	1640	1710	1750	...	1810	1850	1910	1950	...	2010	2105	2150	2207	2307	0010	2330	0110	0215	...

♦ – **NOTES** (LISTED BY TRAIN NUMBER)

794 – 🛏 1, 2 cl., 🛌 2 cl. (4 berth) and (2) Reggio di Calabria - Milano - Torino.
795 – 🛏 1, 2 cl., 🛌 2 cl. (4 berth) and (2) Torino - Milano - Reggio di Calabria.
797 – 🛏 1, 2 cl., 🛌 2 cl. (4 berth) and (2) Torino - Milano - Napoli - Salerno.
798 – 🛏 1, 2 cl., 🛌 2 cl. (4 berth) and (2) Salerno - Napoli - Milano - Torino.

T – (12) and 🍷 Torino - Milano - Venezia Mestre - Trieste and v.v.

g – Milano **Porta Garibaldi**.
s – Stops to set down only.
u – Stops to pick up only.
v – Venezia **Mestre**.

* – Milano Porta Garibaldi: *149 km*.

586 TORINO - AOSTA

Most trains 2nd class only

km																									
						†	⚒	†	⚒	⚒		⚒	†	⚒			⚒				⚒		†	⚒	
0	**Torino** Porta Nuova **585** d.	...	0530	0730	0830	0930	1130	1130	*1130*	1230	1330	1430	1430	...	...	1630	...	1730	*1735*	1830	...	1930	2030	...	2230
6	**Torino** Porta Susa **585** d.	...	0539	0739	0839	0939	1139	1139	*1139*	1239	1339	1439	1439	...	...	1639	...	1739	*1743*	1839	...	1939	2039	...	2239
29	Chivasso **585** d.	0525	0605	0805	0905	1005	1205	1205	1225	1305	1405	1505	1505	1525	...	1705	...	1805	1825	1905	...	2005	2105	2125	2305
62	Ivrea a.	0607	0638	0831	0931	1031	1231	1231	1307	1331	1431	1531	1531	1607	...	1731	...	1831	1907	1931	...	2031	2131	2207	2331
	Change trains																								
62	Ivrea d.	0616	0647	0837	0937	1038	1237	1247	1312	1341	1447	1537	1547	...	1643	1747	1800	1847	1912	1947	2000	2047	2138	2212	2338
79	Pont Saint Martin d.	0629	0700	0849	0949	1050	1249	1300	1332	1354	1500	1550	1600	...	1656	1800	1829	1900	1929	2000	2029	2100	2150	2229	2350
91	Verrès d.	0644	0715	0900	0959	1106	1300	1315	1346	1415	1515	1600	1615	...	1715	1815	1844	1915	1944	2015	2044	2115	2200	2244	0000
104	Chatillon-Saint Vincent d.	0703	0726	0912	1010	1117	1311	1326	1402	1426	1526	1611	1626	...	1726	1826	1903	1926	2003	2026	2103	2126	2212	2303	0012
129	**Aosta** a.	0723	0753	0933	1031	1138	1333	1353	1423	1453	1553	1635	1653	...	1753	1853	1923	1953	2023	2053	2123	2153	2234	2323	0033

		⚒						⚒	†		⚒			⚒		†	⚒				⚒				
Aosta d.	0518	0540	0628	...	0728	0828	1034	1134	1140	1228	...	1340	1428	1503	1528	1628	1640	1705	1728	1828	1859	1928	2028	2128	...
Chatillon-Saint Vincent d.	0539	0603	0649	...	0749	0849	1055	1155	1203	1249	...	1401	1449	1526	1549	1649	1701	1726	1749	1849	1926	1949	2049	2149	...
Verrès d.	0550	0615	0700	...	0800	0900	1106	1206	1216	1300	...	1415	1500	1536	1600	1700	1715	1737	1800	1900	1944	2000	2100	2200	...
Pont Saint Martin d.	0601	0629	0713	...	0813	0913	1116	1220	1232	1313	...	1429	1513	1550	1613	1713	1730	1801	1813	1913	2000	2013	2113	2213	...
Ivrea a.	0614	0644	0726	...	0826	0926	1128	1235	1244	1326	...	1444	1526	1608	1626	1728	1744	1816	1826	1926	2014	2026	2126	2226	...
Change trains																									
Ivrea d.	0623	0650	0732	0750	0834	0934	1134	1250	1250	1334	1434	1450	1534	...	1634	1734	1750	...	1834	1934	...	2034	2134	...	2232
Chivasso **585** a.	0656	0737	0756	0837	0856	0956	1156	1337	1337	1356	1456	1537	1556	...	1656	1756	1837	...	1856	1956	...	2056	2156	...	2303
Torino Porta Susa **585** a.	0724	*0758*	0824	*0858*	0924	1024	1224	*1358*	*1358*	1424	1524	*1558*	1624	...	1724	1824	*1858*	...	1924	2024	...	2124	2224	...	*2358*
Torino Porta Nuova **585** a.	0735	*0810*	0835	*0910*	0935	1035	1235	*1410*	*1410*	1435	1535	*1610*	1635	...	1735	1835	*1910*	...	1935	2035	...	2135	2235	...	*0010*

BRIG - STRESA - MILANO   590

km				EC 35		EC 51		EC 37					EC 57		EC 39					EC 59	EC 41
		♠	2	♠ 2		2	2	2	2		♠	♠	♠ 2	2	♠ 2	2		♠ 2	2	♠	♠
	Genève 570 ....d.			0539			0739							1339						1839
	Lausanne 570 .....d.			0618			0818							1418						1918
	Basel 560 ....d.				0631								1231				1731			
	Bern 560 ....d.				0734								1334				1834			
0	Brig ▥ ....d.			0744	0844		0944						1444	1544				1944		2044
42	Domodossola ▥ § ....a.			0812			1012						1512	1612				2012		2112
42	Domodossola 551 ....d.	0453	0553	0603	0651	0720	0817	0853	0917	0958	1017	1158	1253	1358	1453	1517	1558	1617	1653	1758	1853	1958	2017	2053	2117
72	Verbània-Pallanza ....d.	0513	0613	0629	0713	0743		0913		1024		1224		1313	1424	1513		1624		1713	1824	1913	2024	2113
77	Baveno..........d.			0634					1029		1229			1429			1629			1829	2029
81	Stresa..........d.	0521	0621	0639	0721	0751	0840	0921	0940	1035		1235		1321	1435	1521	1540	1635	1640	1721	1835	1921	2035		2121	2140
98	Arona...........d.	0535	0635	0701	0735	0806		0935		1106		1306		1335	1506	1535		1706		1735	1906	1935	2106		2135
124	Gallarate.......▲ d.	0558	0658	0731	0758	0834		0958		1134	1104	1334		1358	1534	1558		1734		1758	1934	1958	2134	2105	2158
150	Rho Fiera Milano......d.	0619	0719	0800	0823	0900		1019		1200		1400		1419	1600	1619		1800		1819	2000	2019	2200		2219
165	Milano Porta Garibaldi .. a.			0811		0911				1211		1411			1611			1811			2011		2211
167	Milano Centrale.......a.	0631	0731		0835		0937	1031	1037		1137			1431		1631	1637		1737	1831		2031		2137	2231	2237

		EC 50			EC 32		EC 52		EC 34					EC 36	EC 56		EC 42					
		2	♠ 2	♠ 2	♠ 2	♠	2	2	2	♠	2		♠ 2	♠ 2	♠ 2		♠ 2	2	♠	♠ 2	♠ 2	♠ 2	♠ 2
	Milano Centrale.........d.		0723	0729		0823	0829	0929	1123		1223	1329		1529		1723	1729	1823		1829	1923	1929		2129
	Milano Porta Garibaldi......d.	0612			0749			1149		1349		1549			1749			1949	2049		2149	2249
	Rho Fiera Milano........d.	0622		0740	0759		0840	0940	1159		1340	1359	1540	1559		1740		1759	1840		1940	1959	2059	2140	2159	2259
	Gallarate............▲ a.	0649	0757	0802	0826		0902	1002	1226		1426	1602	1626		1826	1910	1902	1957	2002	2026	2126	2202	2226	2326
	Arona.............d.	0721		0823	0854		0923	1023		1254		1423	1454	1623	1654		1823		1854	1923		2023	2054	2154	2223	2254	2354
	Stresa.............d.	0742		0838	0916	0921	0938	1038	1221	1316	1321	1438	1516	1638	1716	1821	1838	1921	1916	1938		2038	2116		2238
	Baveno.............d.	0746			0921			1321		1521		1721		1921		2121
	Verbània-Pallanza ....d.	0751		0846	0926		0945	1045		1336		1445	1526	1645	1726		1845		1926	1945		2045	2126		2245
	Domodossola 551 ....a.	0820	0843	0907	1002	0943	1007	1107	1243	1402	1343	1507	1602	1707	1802	1843	1907	1943	2002	2007	2043	2107	2202	2307
	Domodossola ▥ § ....d.		0848		0948		1248	1348			1848	1948		2048
	Brig ▥ ....a.		0916		1016		1316	1416			1916	2016		2116
	Bern 560 ....a.		1023			1423				2123
	Basel 560 ....a.		1129			1529				2229
	Lausanne 570 ....a.				1142			1542				2042		2242
	Genève 570 ....a.				1221			1621				2121		2321

Additional services BRIG - DOMODOSSOLA and v.v.

km		Ⓐ h		Ⓒ	B	⑥	Ⓐ			Domodossola	Ⓐ		⑥	⑥	B	⑥
0	Brig ....d.	0607	0840	0940	1044	1145	1244	1344	1644	1745	1844	0026	Domodossola ......d.	0356	0456	0615	0655	1048	1148	1258	1448	1548	1648	1748
23	Iselle di Trasquera § .d.	0625				1203				1803	1902	0044	Iselle di Trasquera § d.	0418	0518	0638	0717		1320					
42	Domodossola ....a.	0643	0907	1008	1112	1222	1312	1412	1712	1822	1920	0102	Brig ....a.	0433	0533	0652	0732	1116	1216	1335	1516	1616	1716	1816

B –   IC service. 🛏 and ✗ Basel - Brig - Domodossola and v.v.
V –   🛏 and ♀ Genève - Milano - Venezia Santa Lucia and v.v.
h –   Also Mar. 25, May 5.
j –   Sept. 3 - 9, 16 - 19, Oct. 4 - 8, Nov. 8 - 13, Dec. 3 - 10.
k –   Operates during school terms only.
▥ –   ⒝ inclusive of supplement.

♠ –   Operator: Trenord.
§ –   Ticket point is **Iselle**.
▲ –   🚌 service operates Gallarate - Milano Malpensa Aeroporto and v.v. Journey time 25 minutes; operator: S.A.C.O. ✆ 0331 25 84 11.

DOMODOSSOLA and ARONA - NOVARA   591

2nd class only

km		✗	✗	✗	✗		✗	†	†	†	✗	B	A	✗B	✗A	†	✗	†		✗	✗		†	✗		†
0	Domodossola ....d.	0520		0620		0648	0800						1245	1245	1343	1343			1543		1747			1848
38	Omegna...............d.	0614		0657		0752	0850						1337	1337	1444	1444			1641		1842			1940
44	Pettenasco.............d.	0621		0704		0759	0856						1343	1343					1648		1849			1947
47	Orta-Miasino............d.	0626		0712		0804	0904						1351	1351	1453	1453			1653		1854			1952
60	Borgomanero............d.	0641		0724		0815	0917						1406	1406	1504	1504			1704		1905			2004
	Arona.................d.		0648		0748			0915	1115	1315	1348				1515	1548	1715		1748	1848		1915	1948		2115
	Oleggio................d.		0712		0812			0932	1132	1332	1412				1532	1612	1732		1812	1912		1932	2012		2132
90	Novara................a.	0716j	0732	0754j	0832	0842r	0945j	0948	1148	1348	1432	1437	1446r	1535	1542j	1548	1632	1748	1740r	1832	1932	1943r	1948	2032	2039r	2148

km		✗	✗	✗	✗	†	†	†	✗	✗	†	†	✗	✗	Ⓐ	✗	†	Ⓐ	✗		†	✗
0	Novara................d.	0546j	0645r	0650	0750	0812	1012	1212	1223r	1345j	1412	1423	1516r	1535	1612	1619t	1723	1734r		1812	1818t	1823	1915r	1923	2012
17	Oleggio................d.			0713	0813	0826	1026	1226			1426	1441		1541	1626		1741			1826		1841		1941	2026
37	Arona.................a.			0739	0839	0845	1045	1245			1445	1512		1612	1645		1812			1845		1912		2012	2045
	Borgomanero............d.	0621	0725						1249	1420			1552			1650		1811			1851		1950
	Orta-Miasino............d.	0645	0740						1306	1432			1608			1711		1826			1911		2006
	Pettenasco.............d.	0649	0744						1311	1436			1612			1715		1831			1915		2011
	Omegna...............d.	0656	0751						1318	1443			1619			1722		1843			1922		2018
93	Domodossola ....a.	0748	0849						1417	1542			1714			1804		1938			2004		2114

2nd class only   **Local services NOVARA - ALESSANDRIA and v.v.**

km		✗		✗y	†	✗		✗			✗				✗ y		♠ ✗	✗
0	Novara ....▲ d.	0608	0708	0808		0908	1408	1423	1608	1708	1908	2008	Alessandria........▲ d.	0645		1245	1345	1645	1745	1845	1945	2045
67	Alessandria........▲ a.	0715	0815	0915	1015	1015	1515	1532	1715	1815	2015	2125	Novara.............▲ a.	0753		1353	1453	1753	1853	1957	2053	2153

A –   Until Aug. 31.
B –   From Sept. 1.

j –   Not Aug. 14 - 21.
r –   Not Aug. 14 - 20.

t –   Not Aug. 13 - 21.
y –   Not July 31 - Aug. 28.

♠ –   Operator: Trenord.
▲ –   Additional journeys available by changing trains at Mortara (25 km from Novara).

Operator: Trenord.   2nd class only

BELLINZONA - LUINO - MILANO MALPENSA ✈   592

km					IR 2319 B	IR 2323 B	IR 2327 B				IR 2332 B	IR 2336 B	IR 2340 B	
0	Bellinzona 550 ....d.	0554	0754		1352	1552	1752		Milano Malpensa Aeroporto ✈ d.	0750		1350	1550	1750	1950
9	Cadenazzo............d.	0608	0808		1400	1408	1600	1608	1800	1808	Gallarate..............d.	0819		1419		1619	1819	2019
27	Pino-Tronzano ▥ ....d.	0628	0828		1428		1628		1828	Laveno Mombello ....d.	0901		1501		1701	1901	2101
40	Luino 608 ....d.	0645	0845		1445		1645		1845	Luino 608 ....d.	0918		1518		1715	1918	2118
55	Laveno Mombello ......d.	0705	0900		1500		1700		1900	Pino-Tronzano ▥ ....d.	0932		1532		1732	1932	2132
86	Gallarate.............d.	0746	0946		1546		1746		1946	Cadenazzo............d.	0956		1552	1559	1752	1759	1952	1958	2154
111	Milano Malpensa Aeroporto ✈ a.	0811	1011		1611		1811		2011	Bellinzona 550 ....a.	1005		1605		1805	2005	2204

B –   🛏 Basel - Locarno and v.v. Operator: SBB / CFF / FFS.   Additional services operate Bellinzona - Cadenazzo - Luino and v.v.

593 MILANO - COLICO - TIRANO

Operator: Trenord

km																									
		2							2		2		2	2			2				2	2	2	2
				†C		y										⚒								
0	**Milano** Centrale ▷ d.	...	0620	0720	0722p	0820	0920	1020	1220	1252p	1320	1352p	1420	1452p	1552p	1620	1720	1752p	1820	1920	2020	2120	2252	2322	2352
12	Monza ▷ d.	...	0632	0732	0739	0832	0932	1032	1232	1309	1332	1409	1432	1509	1609	1632	1732	1809	1832	1932	2032	2132	2309	2339	0009
50	Lecco ▷ d.	...	0702	0802	0815	0902	1002	1102	1302	1353	1402	1453	1502	1553	1653	1702	1802	1853	1902	2002	2102	2202	2353	0023	0055
72	Varenna-Esino d.	...	0724	0824	0853	0924	1024	1124	1324	...	1424	...	1524	...	...	1724	1824	...	|	2024	2124	2236	...	...	...
75	Bellano-Tartavalle Terme d.	...	0729	0829	0858	0929	1029	1129	1329	...	1429	...	1529	...	...	1729	1829	...	1929	2029	2129	2241	...	...	...
89	**Colico** ▲ a.	...	0747	0847	0923	0947	1047	1147	1347	...	1447	...	1547	...	...	1747	1847	...	1947	2047	2147	2258	...	...	...
130	Sondrio a.	0533	0820	0920	...	1020	1120	1220	1420	...	1520	...	1620	...	...	1820	1921	...	2020	2120	2221	2334	...	...	...
156	**Tirano** ♣ a.	0607	0852	0952	...	1052	1205	1252	1452	...	1552	...	1652	...	...	1852	...	...	2052	2152	...	...	...	...	...

	2	2	2	2				2			2		2	2			2		2			2		2	2
	j	k									⚒		⚒				⚒		†C	y					
Tirano ♣ d.	...	...	...	...	0612	0712	0908	...	1108	1208	...	1308	...	...	1508	1608	...	1708	...	1808	1908	...	2008	...	...
Sondrio d.	0432	0441	0532	...	0641	0741	0941	...	1141	1241	...	1341	...	...	1541	1641	...	1741	...	1841	1941	...	2041	2122	...
Colico ▲ d.	0503	0516	0603	...	0716	0816	1016	...	1216	1316	...	1416	...	...	1616	1716	...	1816	1837	1916	2016	...	2116	2200	...
Bellano-Tartavalle Terme d.	0518	0532	0618	...	0732	0832	1032	...	1232	1332	...	1432	...	...	1632	1732	...	1832	1901	1932	2032	...	2132	2215	...
Varenna-Esino d.	0523	0537	0623	...	0737	0837	1037	...	1237	1337	...	1437	...	...	1637	1737	...	1837	1906	1937	2037	...	2137	2220	...
Lecco ▽ d.	0549	0601	0652	0707	0759	0901	1101	1207	1301	1401	1437	1501	1537	1607	1701	1801	1837	1901	1946	2001	2101	2137	2201	2243	2307
Monza ▽ a.	0622	0626	0724	0749	0824	0926	1126	1249	1326	1426	1519	1526	1619	1649	1726	1826	1919	1926	2019	2026	2126	2219	2226	2315	2349
Milano Centrale ▽ a.	0640	0640	0738	0808p	0838	0940	1140	1308p	1340	1440	1538p	1540	1638p	1708p	1740	1840	1938p	1940	2038p	2040	2140	2238p	2240	2330	0008p

▲ – COLICO - CHIAVENNA and v.v.: 2nd class only

km																									
			h		⚒z	h	⚒z		†C		⚒z		⚒z		⚒z			⚒z	h		⚒z		🚌†	⚒z	
0	Colico d.	0548	0706	...	0810	0810	0845	...	0925	1004	1045	1204	1245	1404	1445	...	1604	1645	1730	1804	1852	2004	2100	2114	...
27	Chiavenna a.	0618	0730	...	0834	0840	0916	...	0955	1034	1116	1234	1316	1434	1516	...	1634	1716	1755	1834	1922	2034	2135	2144	...

	🚌Ⓐ		⚒z	h	⚒z				⚒z			⚒z		⚒z		†	z⚒		†C		⚒z	h	⚒z		
Chiavenna d.	0512	0626	0704	0738	0745	...	0844	0926	1044	1126	...	1244	1326	1444	1526	1638	1644	1726	1805	...	1848	1926	1932	...	2042
Colico a.	0548	0656	0735	0802	0809	...	0915	0956	1115	1156	...	1315	1356	1515	1556	1702	1715	1756	1835	...	1919	1956	2002	...	2112

C – †: (12) Milano - Colico - Chiavenna and v.v.
h – † (daily July 31 - Aug. 28).
j – Daily until Sept. 11; † Sept. 12 - Dec. 10.
k – ⚒ from Sept. 12.
p – Milano **Porta Garibaldi**.
y – Ⓒ (daily June 13 - Sept. 10).
z – Not July 31 - Aug. 28.
▷ – Local trains run Milano Porta Garibaldi - Lecco hourly 0652 - 2152.
▽ – Local trains run Lecco - Milano Porta Garibaldi hourly 0607 - 2207.

♣ – 🚌 TIRANO - EDOLO and v.v.

				⚒		
Tirano Stazione d.	0840	1040	...	1235	1435	1635
Aprica S Pietro a.	0920	1120	...	1320	1515	1720
Edolo a.	0945	1145	...	...	1540	1745

	⚒					
Edolo d.	...	0915	1115	1515	1715	...
Aprica S Pietro d.	0650	0940	1140	1540	1740	...
Tirano Stazione a.	0730	1020	1220	1620	1820	...

♣ – For 🚌 service Tirano - Edolo and v.v. – see panel.
Operator: Automobilistica Perego (AP): ✆ (0342) 701 200; fax (0342) 704 400.

595 INNSBRUCK - BOLZANO / BOZEN - VERONA - BOLOGNA

km																											
			FA	*FA*			*FA*								*FA*				*EC*	*EC*					*FA*	*EC*	
			8503	**8505**			**8507**				§				**8513**				**1289**	**81**					**8519**	**85**	
		2	🍷	🍷	2	2	🍷	2	2	2	2	2	2	2	🍷	2	2	2	✕	✕	2	2	2	2	🍷	✕	2
				♦	⚒	⚒	♦	⚒M		M		Ⓐ	M	Ⓐ		Ⓒ	ⒸM	Mp	♠f	♠a			M	M		♠	
	München Hbf **951** d.	...	...	...	...	...	...	...	...	...	...	...	...	...	...	...	...	...	0734	0734	...	...	...	...	...	0934	...
0	**Innsbruck** Hbf ▲ d.	...	...	...	...	...	...	...	...	...	0622	...	...	...	...	...	...	...	0924	0924	...	...	...	...	...	1124	...
37	**Brennero / Brenner** 🛃 ▲ a.	...	...	...	...	...	...	...	...	...	0659	...	...	...	...	...	...	...	1000	1000	...	...	...	...	...	1200	...
37	**Brennero / Brenner** 🛃 d.	...	...	...	...	...	...	0536	0608	0638	0702	...	0738	0808	...	...	0838	0938	1010	1014	...	...	1038	1138	...	1214	...
60	Vipiteno / Sterzing d.	...	...	...	...	...	...	0555	0627	0657	0723	...	0757	0827	...	...	0857	0957	|	|	...	...	1057	1157	...	|	...
78	Fortezza / Franzensfeste d.	...	...	...	0540	...	...	0613	0645	0715	0739	0745	0815	0845	...	...	0915	1015	1041	1046	...	...	1115	1215	...	1246	...
89	Bressanone / Brixen d.	...	...	...	0549	...	...	0623	0655	0725	0749	0755	0825	0855	...	...	0925	1025	1050	1056	...	...	1125	1225	...	1256	...
99	Chiusa / Klausen d.	...	...	...	0557	...	...	0631	0703	0733	0758	0803	0833	0903	...	...	0933	1033	|	|	...	...	1133	1233	...	|	...
127	**Bolzano / Bozen** a.	...	...	...	0621	...	...	0655	0729	0759	0823	0829	0859	0929	...	...	0959	1059	1115	1127	...	...	1159	1259	...	1327	...
					|				|	2		|	2⑥	2Ⓒ			2Ⓒ	2	|	|			2			|	
127	**Bolzano / Bozen** d.	0500	0516	...	0624	0636	0716	...	0731	0736	...	0831	0831	...	...	0936	1031	...	1117	1131	...	1136	1231	...	1316r	1331	1336
143	Ora / Auer d.	0512	|	...	0637	0655	|	...	0743	0755	...	0843	0843	...	...	0955	1043	...	|	|	...	1155	1243	...	|	|	1355
165	Mezzocorona d.	0525	|	...	0654	0716	|	...	0756	0816	...	0856	0856	...	...	1016	1056	...	|	|	...	1216	1256	...	|	|	1416
182	**Trento** **595a** d.	0537	0547	...	0710	0733	0747	...	0810	0833	...	0910	0910	...	...	1033	1110	...	1150	1204	...	1233	1310	...	1347r	1404	1433
206	Rovereto d.	0551	0602	...	0725	0747	0802	...	0825	0847	...	0925	0925	...	...	1047	1125	...	|	1219	...	1247	1325	...	1402r	1419	1447
274	**Verona** Porta Nuova **605** a.	0640	0642	...	0814	0854	0842	...	0914	0951	...	1014	1014	...	...	1151	1214	...	1237	1256	...	1351	1414	...	1442r	1458	1551
274	**Verona** Porta Nuova d.	0701	0652	0752	...	...	0852	...	...	...	...	...	...	1026	1152	...	...	1226	1239	1313	1326	...	1426	...	1452	1515	...
388	**Bologna** Centrale a.	0825	0742	0842	...	...	0942	...	...	...	...	...	...	1150	1242	...	...	1355	|	1407	1450	...	1554	...	1542	1620	...
	Milano Centrale **615** a.	...	|	|	...	...	|	...	...	...	...	...	...	...	|	...	...	...	|	...	...	...	...	...	|	...	...
	Venezia S L **605** a.	...	|	|	...	...	|	...	...	...	...	...	...	...	|	...	...	...	1356	...	...	...	...	...	|	...	...
	Firenze SMN **620** a.	...	0825c	0925c	...	...	1025c	...	...	...	...	...	...	...	1325c	...	...	...	...	...	...	...	...	...	1625c	...	...
	Roma Termini **620** a.	...	0945	1045	...	...	1145	...	...	...	...	...	...	...	1445	...	...	...	...	...	...	...	...	...	1745	...	...

				FA		*EC*	*FA*					*FA*		*EC*						*EC*				*ICN*			
				8523		**87**	**8525**					**8527**		**89**						**83**				**763**		§	
	2	2	2	🍷		✕	🍷	2	2	2	2	🍷		✕	2	2	2	2	2	✕	2	2	2		2	2	
	M		M			♠	♦	M		Ⓐ	M	♦		♠		M		Ⓐ	M	♠	M		M	♦			
München Hbf **951** d.	...	...	...	...	...	1134	...	...	...	...	...	...	...	1334	...	...	...	...	...	1534	...	...	...	...	...	...	...
Innsbruck Hbf ▲ d.	...	...	...	...	...	1324	...	...	...	...	...	...	...	1524	...	...	...	...	...	1724	...	...	...	...	...	2100	...
Brennero / Brenner 🛃 ▲ a.	...	...	...	...	...	1400	...	...	...	...	...	...	...	1600	...	...	...	...	...	1800	...	...	...	...	...	2137	...
Brennero / Brenner 🛃 d.	1238	1308	1338	...	...	1414	...	1438	1508	...	1538	...	...	1614	...	1638	1708	...	1738	1814	1838	1908	1938	...	...	2143	...
Vipiteno / Sterzing d.	1257	1327	1357	...	...	|	...	1457	1527	...	1557	...	...	|	...	1657	1727	...	1757	|	1857	1927	1957	...	...	2202	...
Fortezza / Franzensfeste d.	1315	1345	1415	...	...	1446	...	1515	1545	...	1615	...	...	1646	...	1715	1745	...	1815	1846	1915	1945	2015	...	...	2220	...
Bressanone / Brixen d.	1325	1355	1425	...	...	1456	...	1525	1555	...	1625	...	...	1656	...	1725	1755	...	1825	1856	1925	1955	2025	...	...	2230	...
Chiusa / Klausen d.	1333	1403	1433	...	...	|	...	1533	1603	...	1633	...	...	|	...	1733	1803	...	1833	|	1933	2003	2033	...	...	2238	...
Bolzano / Bozen a.	1359	1429	1459	...	...	1527	...	1559	1629	...	1659	...	...	1727	...	1759	1829	...	1859	1927	1959	2029	2059	...	...	2303	...
		|	2Ⓐ			|		2	|		2Ⓐ			|		2Ⓐ	|		2Ⓐ	|	2	|	2Ⓐ			2	
Bolzano / Bozen d.	...	1431	1436	1516	...	1531	...	1536	1631	1636	1704	1716	...	1731	1736	1806	1831	1836	1906	1931	1936	2031	2036	2130	2136	2308	...
Ora / Auer d.	...	1443	1455	|	...	|	...	1555	1643	1655	1720	|	...	|	1755	1822	1843	1855	1922	|	1955	2043	2055	2144	2155	2324	...
Mezzocorona d.	...	1456	1516	|	...	|	...	1616	1656	1716	1740	|	...	|	1816	1842	1856	1916	1942	|	2016	2056	2116	2200	2216	2344	...
Trento **595a** d.	...	1510	1533	1547	...	1604	...	1633	1710	1733	1758	1747	...	1804	1833	1855	1910	1933	1955	2004	2033	2110	2133	2216	2233	2357	...
Rovereto d.	...	1525	1547	1602	...	1619	...	1647	1725	1747	1812	1802	...	1819	1847	1910	1925	1947	2010	2019	2047	2125	2147	2232	2247e	...	...
Verona Porta Nuova **605** a.	...	1614	1654	1642	...	1658	...	1751	1814	1854	...	1842	...	1858	1951	...	2014	2051	2108	2056	2151	2214	2251	2316	2348e	...	...
Verona Porta Nuova d.	...	1626	...	1652	...	1700	1752	...	1826	...	...	1852	...	...	...	...	2104	...	...	...	...	...	...	2336	...	...	...
Bologna Centrale a.	...	1754	...	1742	...	|	1842	...	1954	...	...	1942	...	...	...	...	2225	...	...	...	...	...	...	0101	...	...	...
Milano Centrale **615** a.	...	...	...	|	...	|	|	...	...	...	...	|	...	...	...	...	...	...	...	...	...	...	...	|	...	...	...
Venezia S.L. **605** a.	...	...	...	|	...	1810	|	...	...	...	...	|	...	...	...	...	...	...	...	...	...	...	...	|	...	...	...
Firenze SMN **620** a.	...	...	...	1825c	...	...	1925c	...	...	...	...	2025c	...	...	...	...	...	...	...	...	...	...	...	|	...	...	...
Roma Termini **620** a.	...	...	...	1948	...	...	2045	...	...	...	...	2145	...	...	...	...	...	...	...	...	...	...	...	0600	...	...	...

♦ – NOTES (LISTED BY TRAIN NUMBER)
763 – ⑤⑥: 🛏 1, 2 cl., 🛌 2 cl. (4 berth) and (2) Bolzano - Roma.
8505 – (12) and 🍷 Brescia - Verona - Roma.
8507 – (12) and 🍷 Bolzano - Bologna - Roma - Napoli.
8525 – (12) and 🍷 Brescia - Verona - Roma.
8527 – (12) and 🍷 Bolzano - Bologna - Roma - Napoli.

M – To Merano. See Table **597**.
a – Ⓐ only.
c – Firenze **Campo di Marte**.
e – † only.
f – Ⓒ only.
p – Ⓒ (daily Sept. 3 - Dec. 10).
r – ⑤⑥⑦ only.

§ – Operated by *SAD* (for contact details see Table **598**).
♠ – Also available to passengers without reservation. Operator within Italy: LeNord.
▲ – For additional trains Innsbruck - Brennero / Brenner – see page 293. Austrian holiday dates apply Innsbruck - Brennero / Brenner.

BOLOGNA - VERONA - BOLZANO / BOZEN - INNSBRUCK — 595

			ICN 764								EC 88	FA 8502			EC 80	FA 8508		FA 8510	EC 84	FA 8512		
Roma Termini 620 .... d.	...	...	...	2300	...	...	...	...	...	...	...	0645	...	...	...	0845	...	...	0945	...	1045	...
Firenze SMN 620 .... d.													0803c				1003c			1103c	1203c	
Venezia SL 605 .... d.																						
Milano Centrale 615 ... d.																						
Bologna Centrale .... d.	...	...	...	0400	...	0613	...	0710	...	0845	...	...	1045	1010f	1145	1152	1245	...				1210
Verona Porta Nuova 605 .. a.	...	...	...	0530	...	0752	...	0832	...	0937	...	...	1137	1132f	1237	1247	1337	...				1332
Verona Porta Nuova ...... d.	...	0525	0600	0609	0709	0750	▬	0809	...	0850	0904	0947r	0950	1102	1147	1109d	1150	1209	...	1304	1347	1309	1350
Rovereto ...... d.	...	0613	0701	0714	0814	0839		0914	...	0937	0943	1002r	1039	1143	1226	1211d	1239	1314	...	1343	1426	1411	1439
Trento .... 595a d.	0602	0630	0717	0732	0832	0854		0932	...	0952	0959	1041r	1054	1159	1241	1225	1254	1332	...	1359	1441	1425	1454
Mezzocorona .... d.	0617	0644	0730	0746	0846	0905		0946	...	1005			1105		1239	1305	1346		...			1439	1505
Ora / Auer .... d.	0636	0706	0747	0806	0906	0919		1006	...	1020			1119		1300	1319	1406		...			1500	1519
Bolzano / Bozen .... a.	0652	0724	0805	0822	0922	0930		1022	...	1039	1031	1114r	1130	1231	1314	1322	1330	1422	...	1431	1514	1522	1530

	2M				2M		2M	2M				2Mp	2M			2M			2M
Bolzano / Bozen .... d.	0601	0701	0701	0732	0801	...	0901	...	0932	1001	...	1034	...	1101	1201	1234	1301	...	1332	...	1401	1434	1501	...	1532
Chiusa / Klausen .... d.	0626	0726	0726	0755	0826	...	0926	...	0955	1026	...		1126	1226		1326	...	1355	...	1426		1526	...	1555
Bressanone / Brixen .... d.	0635	0735	0735	0804	0835	...	0935	...	1004	1035	...	1104	1135	1235	1304	1335	...	1404	...	1435	1504	1535	...	1604
Fortezza / Franzensfeste ... d.	0645	0745	0745	0815	0845	...	0945	...	1015	1045	...	1115	1145	1245	1315	1345	...	1415	...	1445	1515	1545	...	1615
Vipiteno / Sterzing .... d.	0703	0803	0803	0833	0903	...	1003	...	1033	1103	...		1203	1303		1403	...	1433	...	1503		1603	...	1633
Brennero / Brenner ▓ ..... a.	0722	0822	0822	0852	0922	...	1022	...	1052	1122	...	1148	1222	1322	1348	1422	...	1452	...	1522	1548	1622	...	1652
Brennero / Brenner ▓ ▲ d.	...	0902									...	1200		1400						1600
Innsbruck Hbf ▲ a.	...	0938									...	1236		1436						1636					1827
München Hbf 951 ... a.											...	1426		1625											1827

	EC 86			EC 82	EC 1288							§	FA 8524		FA 8526	§	FA 8528		
	2		2		2		2	2	2	2	2	2	2	2	2	2	2	2	2
	M		(A)		(A)		♠a	♠f		M	(A)						(A)	♦	
Roma Termini 620 .... d.	...	...	...	...	...	...	...	...	...	...	...	1645	...	1745	...	1845	...	...
Firenze SMN 620 .... d.												1803c		1903c		2003c		
Venezia SL 605 .... d.		1350			1550													
Milano Centrale 615 ... d.																		
Bologna Centrale .... d.	...	...	1410	...	1552	...	...	1610	...	...	1810	1845	...	1945	...	2045	2010	2110
Verona Porta Nuova 605 .. a.	...	...	1500	1532	...	1645	1700	1732	...	1932	1937	...	2037	2137	2132	2240
Verona Porta Nuova ...... d.	1409	1502	1550	1609	1702	1702	1709	1750	1809	1950	1947	2009	2047	2109	2150	2250
Rovereto ...... d.	1514	1543	1550	1639	1743	1743	1814	1839	1914	2039	2026	2111	2126	2214	2239	2339
Trento .... 595a d.	1532	1559	1605	1654	1705	1732	1759	1759	1832	1854	1932	2054	2041	2125	2141	2232	2254	2352
Mezzocorona .... d.	1546		1616	1705	1716	1746		1846	1905	1946	2105		2139		2246	2305
Ora / Auer .... d.	1606		1636	1719	1736	1806		1906	1919	2006	2119		2200		2306	2319
Bolzano / Bozen .... a.	1622	1631	1652	1730	1752	1822	1831	1831	1922	1930	2022	2130	2114	2222	2214	2322	2332

			2M		2M			
Bolzano / Bozen .... d.	1601	1634	1701	1732	1801	1824a	1834	1834	1901	1932	2002	2032	2132	...	2232
Chiusa / Klausen .... d.	1626		1722	1755	1826	1847a		1926	1955	2026	2055	2155	...	2256
Bressanone / Brixen .... d.	1635	1704	1730	1804	1835	1856a	1904	1904	1935	2004	2035	2104	2204	...	2305
Fortezza / Franzensfeste ... d.	1645	1715	1745	1815	1845	1905a	1915	1915	1945	2015	2045	2115	2215	...	2314
Vipiteno / Sterzing .... d.	1703	1803	1833	1903	1923a		2003	2033	2103	2133	2233
Brennero / Brenner ▓ ..... a.	1722	1748	1822	1852	1922	1944a	1948	1948	2022	2052	2122	2151	2252
Brennero / Brenner ▓ ▲ d.	...	1800			2000	2000				2154
Innsbruck Hbf ▲ a.	...	1836			2036	2036				2230
München Hbf 951 ... a.	...	2025			2227	2227				

▲ — INNSBRUCK - BRENNERO / BRENNER and v.v. stopping services: 2nd class only

km																							
0	Innsbruck Hbf .... d.	0522	0552	0622	0652	0752	0822	0852	0952	1052	1152	1252	1352	1452	1552	1652	1752	...	1852	1952	2100	2200	2257	2352	...
18	Matrei .... d.	0540	0610	0640	0710	0810	0840	0910	1010	1111	1210	1310	1411	1510	1610	1710	1811	...	1910	2010	2118	2218	2315	0010	...
23	Steinach in Tirol .... d.	0545	0615	0645	0715	0815	0845	0915	1015	1116	1215	...	1315	1416	1515	1615	1715	1816	...	1915	2015	2123	2223	2320	0015	...
37	Brennero / Brenner ▓ ..... a.	0602	0632	0659	0732	0832	0902	0932	1032	1132	1232	...	1332	1432	1532	1632	1732	1832	...	1932	2032	2137	2240	2337	0032	...

Brennero / Brenner ▓ .... d.	0528	0558	0628	...	0658	0728	0828	0902	0928	...	1028	1128	1228	1328	...	1428	1528	...	1628	1728	...	1828	1928	...	2128	2304
Steinach in Tirol .... d.	0547	0617	0647	...	0717	0746	0846	0917	0947	...	1047	1147	1247	1347	...	1447	1547	...	1647	1747	...	1847	1947	...	2147	2323
Matrei .... d.	0551	0621	0651	...	0721	0750	0850	0921	0951	...	1051	1151	1251	1351	...	1451	1551	...	1651	1751	...	1851	1951	...	2151	2327
Innsbruck Hbf .... a.	0608	0638	0708	...	0739	0808	0908	0938	1008	...	1108	1208	1308	1408	...	1508	1608	...	1708	1808	...	1908	2008	...	2208	2344

♦ — **NOTES** (LISTED BY TRAIN NUMBER)

764 – ⑤⑥ ⚟ 1,2 cl., ▬ 2 cl. (4 berth) and ⚟ Roma - Bologna.
8508 – ⚟ and ♟ Napoli - Roma - Bologna - Bolzano.
8510 – ⚟ and ♟ Roma - Verona - Brescia.
8524 – ⚟ and ♟ Napoli - Roma - Bologna - Bolzano.
8528 – ⚟ and ♟ Roma - Verona - Brescia.

M – From Merano. See Table **597**.

a – Ⓐ only.
c – Firenze **Campo di Marte**.
d – ❊ only.
f – Ⓒ only.
p – Ⓒ (daily Sept. 3 - Dec. 10).
r – ⑤⑥⑦ only.

§ – Operated by *SAD* (for contact details see Table **598**).
♠ – Also available to passengers without reservation. Operator within Italy: LeNord.
▲ – For additional trains Brennero / Brenner - Innsbruck – see panel above. Austrian holiday dates apply Brennero / Brenner - Innsbruck.

TRENTO - MALÉ - MEZZANA — 595a

Trentino Trasporti

km		†	❊	❊	†	❊	†	❊							❊	†	❊		❊		❊	❊	†	❊	❊	†	†
0	Trento .... 595 d.	0602	0611	0710	0812	0931	1027	1031	1100	1106	1202	1233	1324	1343	1342	1454	1456	1554	1625	1634	1718	1722	1727	1809	1835	1836	1932	1933
56	Malé .... d.	0738	0752	0859	0947	0953	1107	1205	1206	1250	1347	1409	1421	1519	1524	1638	1631	1736	1800	1810	1839	1858	1905	1935	2009	2012	2104	2105
68	Mezzana .... d.	0754		0915	1003	1009	1123	1221	1222	1307	1406	1425		1535	1542	1654	1647	1752		1856				

	❊	†	❊	❊	❊	❊	❊	†	❊	❊						❊		❊	❊	❊	†	❊		
Mezzana .... d.			0611		0656		0814	0925	1021	1023		1136	1231	1245	1345	1422		1444		1614	1619	1713	1716	1808		1940	
Malé .... d.	0528	0555	0630	0644	0716	0823	0832	0943	1039	1041	1152	1154	1252	1303	1407	1440	1509	1503	1530	1633	1639	1731	1735	1825	1829	1958	2001
Trento .... 595 a.	0700	0729	0748	0826	0907	1002	1006	1121	1216	1215	1327	1338	1436	1437	1545	1623	1703	1908	2005	2004	2132	2135

Operator: Trentino Trasporti Esercizio S.p.a, Via Innsbruck 65, 38121 Trento.
✆ +39 0 461 821000, fax +39 0 461 031407.

596 — FORTEZZA / FRANZENSFESTE - S. CANDIDO / INNICHEN - LIENZ — 2nd class only

km			Ⓐ								Ⓐ	Ⓒ		Ⓐ				Ⓐ				Ⓐ	Ⓐ		
0	Fortezza / Franzensfeste....d.	0547	0617	0650	0750	0850	0950	1050	1120	1150	1220	1250	1320	1350	1420	1450	1520	1550	1650	1750	1820	1850	1920	1950	2050
33	Brunico / Bruneck..............d.	0630	0700	0730	0830	0930	1030	1130	1200	1230	1300	1330	1400	1430	1500	1530	1600	1630	1730	1830	1900	1930	2000	2030	2130
61	Dobbiaco / Toblach.............d.	0706	0736	0806	0906	1006	1106	1206	1236	1306	1336	1406	1436	1506	1536	1606	1636	1706	1806	1906	1936	2006	2036	2106	2206
65	S. Candido / Innichen.........a.	0710	0740	0810	0910	1010	1110	1210	1240	1310	1340	1410	1440	1510	1540	1610	1640	1710	1810	1910	1940	2010	2040	2110	2210
65	S. Candido / Innichen 🚲......d.	0716	...	0816	0916	1016	1116	1216	...	1316	...	...	...	1516	...	1616	...	1716	1816	1916c	...	2016a	...	...	...
78	Sillian 🚲 ....d.	0730	...	0830	0930	1030	1130	1230	...	1330	...	...	...	1530	...	1630	...	1730	1830	1930c	...	2030a	...	...	...
108	Lienz 971 ....a.	0809	...	0909	1009	1109	1209	1309	...	1409	...	...	...	1609	...	1709	...	1809	1909	2009c	...	2109a	...	...	...

		Ⓐ	✗		Ⓐ				Ⓐ					Ⓐ	Ⓒ		Ⓐ			Ⓐ				
Lienz 971 ....d.	...	...	0550	...	Ⓐ	0750	0850	...	...	0950	1050	...	...	1150	...	1250	...	...	1450	...	...	1650	1750	1850	1950
Sillian ....d.	...	...	0630	...		0830	0930	...	...	1030	1130	...	...	1230	...	1330	...	...	1530	...	...	1730	1830	1930	2030
S. Candido / Innichen 🚲....a.	...	...	0643	...		0843	0943	...	...	1043	1143	...	...	1243	...	1343	...	...	1543	...	...	1743	1843	1943	2043
S. Candido / Innichen 🚲....d.	0521	0550	0650	0720	0750	0850	0950	1020	1050	1150	1220	1250	1320	1350	1420	1450	1520	1550	1650	1750	1850	1950	2050		
Dobbiaco / Toblach............d.	0526	0555	0655	0725	0755	0855	0955	1025	1055	1155	1225	1255	1325	1355	1425	1455	1525	1555	1655	1755	1855	1955	2055		
Brunico / Bruneck.............d.	0600	0631	0731	0801	0831	0931	1031	1101	1131	1231	1301	1331	1401	1431	1501	1531	1601	1631	1731	1831	1931	2031	2131		
Fortezza / Franzensfeste....a.	0634	0710	0810	0840	0910	1010	1110	1140	1210	1310	1340	1410	1410	1440	1510	1540	1610	1640	1740	1810	1910	2010	2110	2210	

a – Ⓐ only.
c – Ⓒ only.

Operators:
SAD Fortezza - S. Candido; *ÖBB* S. Candido - Lienz.

597 — BOLZANO / BOZEN - MERANO / MERAN — 2nd class only

km		✗	✗		✗	✗§		✗		Ⓐ	Ⓒ		✗§		✗		✗		✗§		✗§
	Brennero 595.................d.	...	...	0536d	...	0638	0702	0738	...	...	0838	...	0938	...	...	1038	...	1138	...	1238	...	1338	...	1438	...
0	Bolzano / Bozen ....d.	0547	0626	0657	0735	0801	0835	0901	0935	1001	1001	1035	1101	...	1135	1201	1235	1301	1335	1401	...	1501	1535	1601	1635
32	Merano / Meran ....a.	0633	0707	0743	0815	0845	0915	0945	1014	1045	1045	1115	1145	...	1215	1245	1315	1345	1415	1445	...	1545	1615	1645	1715

		✗§		✗§		✗§	§							✗	✗		✗		✗		✗§	Ⓒ	✗
Brennero 595.................d.	1538	...	1638	...	1738	...	1838	1938			Merano / Meran ....d.	0602	0635	0713	0745	0816	0846	0916	0946	1016	1046
Bolzano / Bozen ....d.	1701	1735	1801	1835	1901	1935	2001	2101	2203		Bolzano / Bozen ....d.	0648	0720	0759	0826	0859	0926	0959	1026	1059	1126
Merano / Meran ....a.	1745	1815	1845	1914	1944	2014	2044	2144	2247		Brennero 595.................a.	0822	...	0922	...	1022	...	1122	...	1222	...

		✗§		✗§			✗§		✗§		✗§		✗§		✗§		✗§		✗	†	✗
Merano / Meran ....d.	1116	1146	1216	1246	...	1316	1346	1416	1446	1516	1546	...	1616	1646	1716	1746	1816	1846	1916	1946	...	2046	2046	2146
Bolzano / Bozen ....a.	1159	1226	1259	1326	...	1359	1426	1459	1526	1559	1626	...	1659	1726	1759	1826	1859	1926	1957	2027	...	2126	2126	2227
Brennero 595.................a.	1322	...	1422	...	...	1522	...	1622	...	1722	...	...	1822	...	1922	...	2022	...	2151	...	...	...	...	...

d – ✗ only.
§ – Operated by SAD (for contact details see Table **598**). Additional services operate on ✗.

598 — MERANO / MERAN - MALLES / MALS — 2nd class only — SAD

km		✗			and								✗			and				
0	Merano / Meran ....d.	0538	0638	0716	hourly	1916	1946	2046	2146	2250	...	Malles / Mals 546 / 954.. d.	0520	0542	0616	0720	hourly	1820	1920	2020	2120	...
60	Malles / Mals 546 / 954.....a.	0654	0754	0838	until	2038	2055	2155	2255	2358	...	Merano / Meran ....a.	0630	0654	0732	0843	until	1943	2039	2139	2239	...

Additional services operate.

Trains call at Silandro / Schlanders 46–54 minutes after leaving Merano,
24–28 minutes after leaving Malles.

Ferrovia della Val Venosta Operator: Servizi Autobus Dolomiti (SAD), Via Conciapelli 60, I - 39100 Bolzano.
✆ +39 0471 97 12 59, fax +39 0471 97 00 42.

599 — ITALIAN LAKES (LAGO MAGGIORE, GARDA, COMO)

Lago Maggiore: 🚢 services link Arona, Stresa, Baveno, Laveno, Luino and Locarno throughout the year on an irregular schedule.
Operator: Navigazione sul Lago Maggiore, P. le Baracca 1, 28041 Arona, Italy. ✆ +39 (0)322 233 200, fax: +39 (0)322 249 530. www.navigazionelaghi.it

Lago di Garda: 🚢 services link Desenzano, Peschiera, Garda, Salo, Gardone and Riva, (April to September only) on an irregular schedule.
Operator: Navigazione sul Lago di Garda, Piazza Matteotti 1, 25015 Desenzano del Garda, Italy. ✆ +39 (0)30 914 9511, fax: +39 (0)30 914 9520. www.navigazionelaghi.it

Lago di Como: 🚢 services link Como, Bellagio, Menaggio, Varenna, Bellano and Colico (April to September only) on an irregular schedule.
Operator: Navigazione Lago di Como, Via Per Cernobbio 18, 22100 Como, Italy. ✆ +39 (0)31 579 211, fax: +39 (0)31 570 080. www.navigazionelaghi.it

Hydrofoil service **subject to alteration**:

		✗	✗		†	✗		†	✗	✗	✗			✗	✗	†	✗			✗	†	✗			†	✗	
Como ....d.	0733	0900	1110	1225	1330	1400	1420	1615	1710	1810	1920		Colico ....d.	0606	...	0707	...	1035	...	1356	...	1604	1741	...
Tremezzo ....d.	0819r	0939	1153	1302	1419	1445	1457	1652	1746	1857	1957		Bellano ....d.	0630	...	0738	...	1106	...	1424	...	1644	1608	1808
Bellagio ....d.	0813r	0946	1200	1309	1439r	1452	1504	1658	1752	1904	2003		Menaggio ....d.	0641	0703	0748	0808	1117	1335	1435	1511	1654	1814	1832
Menaggio ....d.	0808	0954	1207	1316	1430	1500	1511	1704	1758	1919	2009		Bellagio ....a.	0647	0712	0757	0814	1127	1330	1442	1525	1704	1820	1839
Bellano ....d.	...	1004	1216	...	1455	1516	...	1713	1808	...	2021		Tremezzo ....d.	0653	0718	0803	0820	1134	1336	1448	1531	1710	1826	1845
Colico ....a.	...	1034	1243	...	1528	1549	...	1740	...	...	2044		Como ....a.	0730	0805	0850	0857	1220	1412	1525	1607	1800	1905	1916

r – Via Menaggio.

599a — LAKE GARDA 🚌 services — Valid from June 13, 2016

Desenzano FS → Salo +0h33 → Gardone +0h38 → Maderno +0h46 → Toscolano
+0h49 → Gargnano +1h00 → Limone +1h32 → **Riva** +1h50.
Route LN027. From Desenzano: 0600, 0810, 1135, 1330, 1620, 1830.

Riva → Limone +0h18 → Gargnano +0h50 → Toscolano +1h01 → Maderno +1h04 →
Gardone +1h12 → Salo +1h17 → **Desenzano** FS +1h50.
Route LN027. From Riva: 0540, 0810, 0910, 1245, 1510, 1710.

Verona P N → **Peschiera** FS +0h53 → Lazise +1h17 → Bardolino +1h29 → **Garda**
+1h39.
Route 164. From Verona: 0541, 0741, 0841 and hourly until 2041.

Garda → Bardolino +0h10 → Lazise +0h22 → **Peschiera** FS +0h46 → **Verona P N**
+1h34.
Route 164. From Garda: 0620, 0810, 0910 and hourly until 2010.

Verona P N → Lazise +0h54 → Bardolino +1h06 → **Garda** +1h16.
Route 163. From Verona: 0641, 1011, 1211, 1411, 1611, 1811, 2011.

Garda → Bardolino +0h10 → Lazise +0h22 → **Verona P N** +1h16.
Route 163. From Garda: 0615, 0645, 0840, 1040, 1240, 1440, 1640, 1840, 2040.

Garda → Torri del Benaco +0h14 → Porto Brenzone +0h35 → Malcesine +0h46 →
Torbole +1h06 → **Riva** +1h18.
Route 484. From Garda: 0625, 0725 and hourly until 2025.

Riva → Torbole +0h15 → Malcesine +0h35 → Porto Brenzone +0h48 → Torri del
Benaco +1h09 → **Garda** +1h22.
Route 484. From Riva: 0510, 0616, 0746, 0843, 0943 and hourly until 1743, then 1913, 2013

Services from Verona Porta Nuova bus station, and Peschiera and Desenzano railway stations
(Table **605**).

Operator: Azienda Trasporti Verona s.r.l., Lungadige Galtarossa 5, 37133 Verona.
✆ 045 8057811, fax 045 8057800.

Additional local services run serving the lakeside resorts.

Other operators: Brescia Transporti ✆ 030 44061, fax 030 3754505;
Trentino Transporti ✆ 0461 821000, fax 0461 031407.

HIGH-SPEED SERVICES – southbound 600

Operator: Trenitalia

Trenitalia high-speed services

All trains 🅁 and 🍸

km	km		FR 9601	FR 9501 ⚒ A	FR 9801 © L	FR 9605 Ⓐ	FA 8401 8402	FR 9403 ⚒	FR 9503 9505	FA 8503 Y	FR 9607	FR 9507 M	FR 9509	FR 9609 Ⓐ	FR 9561 Ⓐ	FR 9803 Ⓐ R	FA 8505 B	FR 9611 Ⓐ	FR 9407	FR 9513	FR 9613 Ⓐ	FR 9563 9565	FA 8507 Y	FR 9615	FA 8413 T	FA 8415 U	FR 9517	FR 9567
	0	**Venezia** Santa Lucia ♣ d.	...	...	...	...	...	0606	...	...	...	...	...	...	...	...	...	...	0725	...	...	...	...	...	...	...	...	...
	9	**Venezia** Mestre ♣ d.	...	...	...	...	0537	0618	...	...	...	...	...	...	...	...	...	...	0737	...	...	...	...	...	0837	0847	...	...
	37	Padova d.	...	...	...	...	0553	0632	...	...	...	...	...	...	...	...	...	...	0753	...	...	...	...	...	0853	0903	...	...
0		**Torino** Porta Nuova d.	...	...	...	...	|	|	...	...	0550	...	...	...	0620	...	...	...	|	0700	...	0720	...	0750	|	|	0810	0820
6		**Torino** Porta Susa d.	...	...	...	...	|	|	...	...	0600	...	...	...	0630	...	...	...	|	0710	...	0730	...	0800	|	|	0822	0830
		Verona Porta Nuova d.	...	...	...	...	|	|	...	0652	|	...	...	...	|	...	0752	...	|	|	...	|	0852	|	|	|	|	|
148		**Milano** Centrale a.	...	...	...	...	|	|	...	|	0650	...	...	...	0715g	...	|	...	|	0800	...	0815g	|	0850	|	|	0910	0915g
148		**Milano** Centrale d.	...	...	0600	0608	|	|	0615	|	0700	0542	0720	0730	0718g	0745	|	0800	|	0820	0830	0818g	|	0900	|	|	0920	0918g
158		**Milano** Rogoredo d.	...	...	|	|	|	|	|	|	0709	|	|	|	0735	|	|	|	|	|	|	0835	|	|	|	|	|	0935
299		Reggio Emilia AV d.	...	...	0647	0654	|	|	0701	|	|	|	|	|	0811	0830	|	|	|	|	|	0911	|	|	|	|	|	1011
363	160	**Bologna** Centrale ✣ d.	...	0600	0713	|	0653	|	0725	0745	|	0755	0825	0835	0840	0855	0845	|	0853	0925	0935	0940	0945	|	0953	1003	1025	1040
455	—	**Firenze** SMN a.	...	0641	...	|	0730	|	0759	0825c	|	0830	0859	|	0915	...	0925c	|	0930	0959	|	1015	1025c	|	1030	1040	1059	1115
455	0	**Firenze** SMN d.	...	0650	...	|	0738	|	0808	0827c	|	0839	0908	|	0924	...	0927c	|	0938	1008	|	1024	1027c	|	1038	1048	1108	1124
	257	**Roma** Tiburtina a.	...	0824	...	|	0858	|	0928	|	0948	0958	1028	|	1043	...	|	|	1058	1128	|	1143	|	|	|	1208	1228	1243
716	261	**Roma** Termini a.	...	0835	...	0910	0910	0930	0940	0945	0959	1010	1040	1029	1055	...	1045	1055	1110	1140	1128	|	1145	1155	1210	1220	1240	1255
716		**Roma** Termini d.	0735	0848	...	0920	0920	...	0953	...	1010	...	1053	1040	...	...	...	...	1123	1153	1140	|	1158	...	...	...	1253	...
		Roma Fiumicino ✈ a.	|	|	...	|	0952	...	|	...	|	...	|	|	...	...	...	...	|	|	|	|	|	...	...	...	|	...
938		**Napoli** Centrale a.	0845	0955	...	1032	...	...	1100	...	1120	...	1200	1148	...	...	...	...	1235	1300	1248	1253	1310	...	...	...	1400	...
988		Salerno a.	...	...	...	...	...	...	1154	...	...	...	...	...	...	...	...	...	...	...	...	1340	...	...	...	...	...	...

	FR 9619	FA 8419 8420	FR 9521 9523	FR 9623 Ⓐ	FR 9419	FR 9525	FR 9625 Ⓐ	FA 8513 B	FR 9627 Ⓐ	FA 8427	FR 9425	FR 9529	FR 9631 Ⓐ	FR 9427	FR 9533	FR 9633 Ⓐ	FR 9635	FA 8435	FR 9583 ⑤	FR 9537	FR 9569 9571 Ⓑ	FA 8519 Y	FR 9639	FR 9435	FR 9437	FR 9541 9543	FR 9573	FR 9641 Ⓑ
Venezia Santa Lucia ♣ d.	...	0925	...	...	1025	...	...	...	...	1125	1135	...	...	1225	...	...	...	1325	...	...	...	...	...	1425	1435	...	...	...
Venezia Mestre ♣ d.	...	0937	...	...	1037	...	...	...	...	1137	1147	...	...	1237	...	...	...	1337	...	...	...	...	...	1437	1447	...	...	...
Padova d.	...	0953	...	...	1053	...	...	...	...	1153	1203	...	...	1253	...	...	...	1353	...	...	...	...	...	1453	1503	...	...	...
Torino Porta Nuova d.	...	|	...	0950	|	...	...	...	...	|	|	...	1150	|	...	...	...	|	...	...	1320	...	...	|	|	...	1420	...
Torino Porta Susa d.	...	|	...	1000	|	...	...	...	...	|	|	...	1200	|	...	...	...	|	...	...	1330	...	...	|	|	...	1430	...
Verona Porta Nuova d.	...	|	...	|	|	...	...	1152	...	|	|	...	|	|	...	...	...	|	...	...	|	1452	...	|	|	...	|	...
Milano Centrale a.	...	|	...	1050	|	...	...	|	...	|	|	...	1250	|	...	...	...	|	...	...	1415g	|	...	|	|	...	1515g	...
Milano Centrale d.	1000	|	1020	1100	|	1120	1130	|	1200	|	|	1220	1300	|	1320	1330	1400	|	1405	1420	1418g	|	1500	|	|	1520	1518g	1530
Milano Rogoredo d.	|	|	|	|	|	|	|	|	|	|	|	|	|	|	|	|	|	|	|	|	1435	|	|	|	|	|	1535	|
Reggio Emilia AV d.	|	|	|	|	|	|	|	|	|	|	|	|	|	|	|	|	|	|	|	|	1511	|	|	|	|	|	1611	|
Bologna Centrale ✣ d.	|	1053	1125	|	1153	1225	1235	1245	|	1253	1303	1325	|	1353	1425	1435	|	1453	1510	1525	1540	1545	|	1553	1603	1625	1640	1635
Firenze SMN a.	|	1130	1159	|	1230	1259	|	1325c	|	1330	1340	1359	|	1430	1459	|	|	1530	1545	1559	1615	1625c	|	1630	1640	1659	1715	|
Firenze SMN d.	|	1138	1208	|	1238	1308	|	1327c	|	1338	1348	1408	|	1438	1508	|	|	1538	1554	1608	1624	1627c	|	1638	1648	1708	1724	|
Roma Tiburtina a.	|	1258	1328	|	1358	1428	|	|	|	1458	1508	1528	|	1558	1628	|	|	1658	1713	1728	1743	|	|	1758	1808	1828	1843	|
Roma Termini a.	1255	1310	1340	1355	1410	1440	1429	1445	1455	1510	1520	1540	1555	1610	1640	1629	1655	1710	1725	1740	|	1745	1755	1810	1820	1840	1855	1828
Roma Termini d.	1305	1320	1353	...	1424	1450	1440	...	...	...	...	1553	1605	1625	1650	...	1705	...	...	1753	|	...	...	...	1833	1850	...	1840
Roma Fiumicino ✈ a.	|	1352	|	...	|	|	|	...	...	...	...	|	|	|	|	...	|	...	...	|	|	...	...	...	|	|	...	|
Napoli Centrale a.	1415	...	1500	...	1535	1602	1550	...	...	...	...	1700	1713	1735	1800	...	1815	...	...	1900	1855	...	...	...	1940	2000	...	1950
Salerno a.	...	...	1550	...	...	...	...	...	...	...	...	...	...	...	...	...	...	...	...	...	1942	...	...	...	...	2047	...	...

	FR 9643 ⑤	FR 9439 9441	FR 9585 ⑤	FR 9545	FR 9645 Ⓑ	FA 8523 Y	FR 9647	FR 9443	FA 8447	FR 9549 9551	FR 9575	FA 8525 B	FR 9811 N	FR 9651	FA 8451	FR 9553	FR 9653 Ⓑ	FA 8527 Y	FR 9555 Ⓑ A	FR 9655	FR 9451	FR 9587 ⑤	FR 9557	FR 9657 Ⓑ	FR 9659 Ⓑ	FA 8459	FR 9559	FR 9663 †
Venezia Santa Lucia ♣ d.	...	1525	...	...	...	...	...	1625	1635	...	...	...	...	...	1725	...	...	...	...	...	1825	...	...	...	...	1925	...	...
Venezia Mestre ♣ d.	...	1537	...	...	...	...	...	1637	1647	...	...	...	...	...	1737	...	...	...	...	...	1837	...	...	...	...	1937	...	...
Padova d.	...	1553	...	...	...	...	...	1653	1703	...	...	...	...	...	1753	...	...	...	...	...	1853	...	...	...	...	1953	...	...
Torino Porta Nuova d.	...	|	...	...	...	...	1550	|	|	...	1620	...	...	...	|	...	...	...	...	1750	|	...	1810	...	...	|	1910	1950
Torino Porta Susa d.	...	|	...	...	...	...	1600	|	|	...	1630	...	...	...	|	...	...	...	...	1800	|	...	1822	...	...	|	1922	2000
Verona Porta Nuova d.	...	|	...	...	...	1652	|	|	|	...	|	1752	...	...	|	...	...	1852	...	|	|	...	|	...	...	|	|	|
Milano Centrale a.	...	|	...	...	...	|	1650	|	|	...	1715g	|	...	...	|	...	...	|	...	1850	|	...	1910	...	...	|	2010	2050
Milano Centrale d.	1600	|	1605	1620	1630	|	1700	|	|	1720	1718g	|	1740	1800	|	1820	1830	|	1850	1900	|	1901	1920	1930	2000	|	2020	2100
Milano Rogoredo d.	|	|	|	|	|	|	1709	|	|	|	1735	|	|	|	|	|	|	|	|	|	|	|	|	|	|	|	|	|
Reggio Emilia AV d.	|	|	|	|	|	|	|	|	|	|	1813	|	1826	|	|	|	|	|	1938	|	|	|	|	|	|	|	|	|
Bologna Centrale ✣ d.	|	1653	1710	1725	1735	1745	|	1753	1803	1825	1840	1845	1855	|	1853	1925	1935	1945	2005	|	1953	2010	2025	2035	|	2053	2125	|
Firenze SMN a.	|	1730	1745	1759	|	1825c	|	1830	1840	1859	1915	1925c	...	|	1930	1959	|	2025c	2040	|	2030	2045	2059	|	|	2130	2159	|
Firenze SMN d.	|	1738	1754	1808	|	1827c	|	1838	1848	1908	1924	1927c	...	|	1938	2008	|	2027c	...	|	2038	2054	2108	|	|	2138	2208	|
Roma Tiburtina a.	|	1858	|	1928	|	|	1948	1958	2008	2028	2043	|	...	|	2058	2128	|	|	...	|	2158	|	2228	|	|	2258	2328	|
Roma Termini a.	1855	1910	1920	1940	1929	1948	1958	2010	2020	2040	2055	2045	...	2055	2110	2140	2129	2145	...	2155	2210	2220	2240	2229	2255	2310	2340	2355
Roma Termini d.	1910	1925	1933	1953	1940	...	...	2025	...	2053	...	...	...	2105	...	2150	...	2155	...	2205	...	...	...	2240	...	...	...	...
Roma Fiumicino ✈ a.	|	|	|	|	|	...	...	|	...	|	...	...	...	|	...	|	...	|	...	|	...	...	...	|	...	...	...	...
Napoli Centrale a.	2025	2035	2040	2100	2050	...	...	2135	...	2200	...	...	...	2215	...	2300	...	2307	...	2317	...	...	...	2350	...	...	...	...
Salerno a.	...	2124	...	...	...	...	...	...	...	2247	...	...	...	...	...	...	...	...	...	...	...	...	...	...	...	...	...	...

A – Also calls at Arezzo (Table **620**).
B – From Brescia (Table **605**).
L – From Lecce (Table **631**).
M – Via Modena (Table **615**).
N – To Ancona (Table **630**).
R – To Bari (Table **631**).
T – From Trieste (Table **601**).
U – From Udine (Table **601**).
Y – From Bolzano (Table **595**).
c – Firenze **Campo di Marte**.
g – Milano **Porta Garibaldi**.
♣ – No local journeys permitted between Venezia Santa Lucia - Mestre and Torino Porta Nuova - Porta Susa.
✣ – Most services use underground platforms 16 – 19; allow a minimum of 10 mins. for connecting services.

Operator: Nuovo Trasporto Viaggiatori (NTV)

Italo high-speed services

Club, Prima, Smart XL and Smart class

All trains 🅁 — *Trenitalia* tickets and passes not valid — www.italotreno.it

	ITA 9901 9903	ITA 9961 ①-⑥	ITA 9991	ITA 9905	ITA 9965	ITA 9993	ITA 9907 9909	ITA 9967	ITA 9981	ITA 9911	ITA 9913 9915	ITA 9917	ITA 9995	ITA 9921	ITA 9969 x	ITA 9983	ITA 9923	ITA 9925 9927	ITA 9973	ITA 9985	ITA 9929	ITA 9975 9979	ITA 9933	ITA 9977	ITA 9999	ITA 9939	ITA 9989 y	ITA 9941 Ⓑ
Torino Porta Nuova d.	...	0605	...	...	...	...	0725	...	...	...	0925	...	...	1120	...	...	...	1325	...	...	1525	...	1625	1700	...	...	...	...
Torino Porta Susa d.	...	0615	...	...	...	...	0735	...	...	...	0935	...	...	1130	...	...	...	1335	...	...	1535	...	1635	1712	...	...	...	...
Milano Centrale d.	0535	0715	...	0735	0815	...	0835	0915	...	0935	1035	1135	...	1235	1315	...	1335	1435	1610	...	1635	1710	1745	1815	...	1835	...	1955
Milano Rogoredo d.	0545	0724	...	0745	0824	...	0845	0924	...	0945	1045	1145	...	1245	1324	...	1345	1445	1623	...	1645	1723	|	1824	...	1845	...	2005
Reggio Emilia ⊖ d.	0623	|	...	0823	|	...	0923	|	...	1023	1123	1223	...	1323	|	...	1423	1523	|	...	1723	|	|	|	...	1923	...	2040
Venezia Santa Lucia d.	|	|	...	|	|	...	|	|	0900	|	|	|	...	|	|	1300	|	|	|	1600	|	|	|	|	...	|	1900	|
Venezia Mestre d.	|	|	...	|	|	...	|	|	0912	|	|	|	...	|	|	1312	|	|	|	1612	|	|	|	|	...	|	1912	|
Padova d.	|	|	...	|	|	...	|	|	0927	|	|	|	...	|	|	1328	|	|	|	1627	|	|	|	|	...	|	1928	|
Brescia d.	|	|	0627	|	|	0727	|	|	|	|	|	|	...	|	|	|	|	|	|	|	|	|	|	|	1727	|	|	|
Verona Porta Nuova d.	|	|	0717	|	|	0817	|	|	|	|	|	|	1217	|	|	|	|	|	|	|	|	|	|	|	1817	|	|	|
Bologna Centrale ✣ d.	0650	|	0810	0850	|	0910	0950	|	1028	1050	1150	1250	1310	1350	|	1428	1450	1550	|	1728	1750	|	1850	|	1910	1950	2028	2110
Firenze SMN d.	0733	|	0852	0933	|	0952	1033	|	1113	1133	1233	1333	1352	1433	|	1513	1533	1633	|	1813	1833	|	1933	|	1952	2033	2113	2153
Roma Tiburtina a.	0853	1004	1017	1053	1104	1113	1153	1204	1233	1253	1353	1453	1513	1553	1604	1633	1653	1753	|	1933	1953	|	2053	2104	2117	2153	2233	2316
Roma Termini a.	0905	1014	1025	1105	1113	1125	1205	1214	1245	1305	1405	1505	1525	1605	1614	1645	1705	1805	1910	1945	2005	2010	2105	2114	2125	2205	2245	2325
Roma Termini d.	0925	...	1035	1115	...	...	1215	...	...	1315	1415	1515	...	...	...	...	1715	1815	1920	1958	2015	2030	...	2124b	2135	2215	2255	...
Napoli Centrale a.	1037	...	1143	1224	...	...	1322	...	...	1426	1523	1630	...	...	...	...	1823	1925	2030	2105	2125	2140	...	2235b	2245	2325	0005	...
Salerno a.	1135	...	...	...	...	...	1416	...	...	...	1616	...	...	...	...	...	...	2016	...	...	...	2229	...	...	...	...	...	...

b – Ⓑ only.
x – Not Dec. 25.
y – Not Dec. 31.
⊖ – Reggio Emilia Mediopadana.
✣ – Most services use underground platforms 16 – 19; allow a minimum of 10 minutes for connecting services from / to the main station.

600 HIGH-SPEED SERVICES – northbound

Trenitalia high-speed services

All trains 🅁 and 🍸 — Operator: Trenitalia

km		FR 9596 ⚒	FR 9500 ⚒ A	FR 9600 ⚒	FR 9502 ⚒	FR 9802 N	FR 9504 ⚒	FR 9602 Ⓐ	FA 8502 Y	FA 8408	FR 9606	FR 9566	FR 9608 Ⓐ	FR 9508	FR 9406	FR 9610	FR 9512 9514	FA 8416	FA 8508 Y	FR 9410 9412	FR 9614	FR 9518	FR 9568 9570 ⚒	FA 8510 B	FR 9616 Ⓐ	FR 9414	FR 9618 Ⓐ	FR 9572 ⚒
	Salerno d.	...	...	...	...	...	...	...	...	...	...	...	...	...	...	...	0612	...	...	0636	...	...	0717	...	...	...	...	...
	Napoli Centrale d.	...	...	...	...	...	...	...	...	...	...	...	0610	...	...	0640	0700	...	0708	0730	0740	0800	0805	...	0810	0830	0840	...
	Roma Fiumicino ✈ d.	...	...	...	...	...	...	...	...	...	...	...	|	...	...	|	|	...	|	|	|	|	|	...	|	|	|	...
	Roma Termini a.	...	...	...	...	...	...	...	...	...	...	...	0720	...	...	0750	0810	...	0823	0840	0850	0907	|	...	0920	0940	0947	...
	Roma Termini d.	...	...	0600	...	...	0620	0630	0645	0650	0700	0705	0730	0720	0750	0800	0820	0835	0845	0850	0900	0920	|	0945	0930	0950	1000	1005
	Roma Tiburtina d.	...	...	|	...	...	0629	|	|	0700	0707	0715	|	0729	0800	|	0829	0845	|	0900	|	0929	0915	|	|	1000	|	1015
	Firenze SMN a.	...	...	|	...	...	0751	|	0801c	0822	|	0836	|	0851	0922	|	0951	1007	1001c	1022	|	1051	1036	1101c	|	1122	|	1136
	Firenze SMN d.	...	0653	|	0730	...	0800	|	0803c	0830	|	0845	|	0900	0930	|	1000	1015	1003c	1030	|	1100	1045	1103c	|	1130	|	1145
0	**Bologna** Centrale ✥ d.	...	0731	|	0808	0810	0838	0828	0845	0910	|	0923	0928	0938	1010	|	1038	1055	1045	1110	|	1138	1123	1145	1128	1210	|	1223
	Reggio Emilia AV d.	...	0752	|	|	0835	|	|	|	|	|	0944	|	|	|	|	|	|	|	|	|	|	1144	|	|	|	|	1244
	Milano Rogoredo a.	...	|	|	|	|	|	|	|	|	0947	1024	|	|	|	|	|	|	|	|	|	|	1224	|	|	|	|	1324
	Milano Centrale a.	...	0840	0855	0910	0920	0942	0929	|	|	0959	1042g	1029	1040	|	1055	1140	|	|	|	1155	1240	1242g	|	1229	|	1255	1342g
	Milano Centrale d.	0800	...	0905	...	...	...	...	|	|	...	1045g	...	...	|	1105	...	|	|	|	...	...	1245g	|	...	|	...	1345g
114	**Verona** Porta Nuova a.	|	...	|	...	...	...	...	0937	|	...	|	...	...	|	|	...	|	1137	|	...	...	|	1237	...	|	...	|
	Torino Porta Susa a.	0848	...	0952	...	...	...	...	...	|	...	1130	...	...	|	1152	...	|	...	|	...	...	1330	...	...	|	...	1430
	Torino Porta Nuova a.	0900	...	1005	...	...	...	...	...	|	...	1140	...	...	|	1205	...	|	...	|	...	...	1340	...	...	|	...	1440
	Padova d.	...	...	...	...	...	...	...	...	1009	...	...	...	...	1109	...	...	1154	...	1209	...	...	...	...	...	1309	...	...
	Venezia Mestre ♣ a.	...	...	...	...	...	...	...	...	1023	...	...	...	...	1123	...	...	1208	...	1223	...	...	...	...	...	1323	...	...
	Venezia Santa Lucia ♣ a.	...	...	...	...	...	...	...	...	1035	...	...	...	...	1135	...	...	1220	...	1235	...	...	...	...	...	1335	...	...

	FR 9520	FR 9416	FA 8512 Y	FR 9418	FR 9622 ⚒	FR 9524 9526	FR 9624 Ⓐ	FR 9420	FA 8431 8432	FR 9626 Ⓐ	FR 9528	FA 8434	FR 9630 Ⓐ	FR 9532	FR 9430		FR 9634 Ⓑ	FR 9536	FA 8520 B	FA 8442	FR 9638	FR 9574 9576 Ⓑ	FR 9540	FR 9640 Ⓑ	FA 8445 8446	FR 9642 Ⓑ	FR 9578	FR 9544
Salerno d.	...	...	...	...	...	0914	...	...	...	...	...	...	...	...	...	...	...	...	...	...	...	1312	...	...	...	...	...	...
Napoli Centrale d.	0900	0915	...	0930	0940	1000	1005	...	...	...	1100	...	...	1200	1230	...	...	1300	...	...	...	1405	1400	1410	...	1440	...	1500
Roma Fiumicino ✈ d.	|	|	...	|	|	|	|	...	1108	...	|	...	...	|	|	...	...	|	...	...	...	|	|	|	1508	|	...	|
Roma Termini a.	1010	1022	...	1040	1050	1110	1115	...	1140	...	1210	...	...	1308	1337	...	...	1410	...	...	...	|	1510	1520	1540	1547	...	1610
Roma Termini d.	1020	1035	1045	1050	1100	1120	1130	1135	1150	1200	1220	1250	1300	1320	1350	...	1400	1420	1445	1450	1500	|	1520	1530	1550	1600	1605	1620
Roma Tiburtina d.	1029	1045	|	1100	|	1129	|	1145	1200	|	1229	1300	|	1329	1400	...	|	1429	|	1500	|	1515	1529	|	1600	|	1615	1629
Firenze SMN a.	1151	1207	1201c	1222	|	1251	|	1307	1322	|	1351	1422	|	1451	1522	...	|	1551	1601c	1622	|	1636	1651	|	1722	|	1736	1751
Firenze SMN d.	1200	1215	1203c	1230	|	1300	|	1315	1330	|	1400	1430	|	1500	1530	...	|	1600	1603c	1630	|	1645	1700	|	1730	|	1745	1800
Bologna Centrale ✥ d.	1238	1255	1245	1310	|	1338	1328	1355	1410	|	1438	1510	|	1538	1610	...	|	1638	1645	1710	|	1723	1738	1728	1810	|	1823	1838
Reggio Emilia AV d.	|	|	|	|	|	|	|	|	|	|	|	|	|	|	|	...	|	|	|	|	|	1744	|	|	|	|	1844	|
Milano Rogoredo a.	|	|	|	|	|	|	|	|	|	|	|	|	|	|	|	...	|	|	|	|	|	1822	|	|	|	|	1924	|
Milano Centrale a.	1340	|	|	|	1355	1440	1429	|	|	1455	1540	|	1555	1640	|	...	1655	1740	|	|	1755	1842g	1842	1829	|	1855	1942g	1940
Milano Centrale d.	...	|	|	|	1405	...	...	|	|	...	1550	|	...	...	|	...	1705	...	|	|	1805	1845g	1900	...	|	...	1945g	...
Verona Porta Nuova a.	...	|	1337	|	|	...	...	|	|	...	|	|	...	...	|	...	|	...	1737	|	|	|	|	...	|	...	|	...
Torino Porta Susa a.	...	|	...	|	1452	...	...	|	|	...	1636	|	...	...	|	...	1752	...	...	|	1852	1930	1948	...	|	...	2030	...
Torino Porta Nuova a.	...	|	...	|	1505	...	...	|	|	...	1650	|	...	...	|	...	1805	...	...	|	1905	1940	2000	...	|	...	2040	...
Padova d.	...	1354	...	1409	...	...	...	1454	1509	...	...	1609	...	...	1709	...	...	...	...	1809	...	...	...	...	1909	...	...	...
Venezia Mestre ♣ a.	...	1408	...	1423	...	...	...	1508	1523	...	...	1623	...	...	1723	...	...	...	...	1823	...	...	...	...	1923	...	...	...
Venezia Santa Lucia ♣ a.	...	1420	...	1435	...	...	...	1520	1535	...	...	1635	...	...	1735	...	...	...	...	1835	...	...	...	...	1935	...	...	...

	FR 9644 Ⓑ	FA 8448 9449 T	FA 8524 Y	FA 8450 U	FR 9646	FR 9548 9550	FR 9444 Ⓑ	FR 9648 Ⓑ	FA 8526 Y	FR 9446	FR 9650	FR 9580	FR 9552	FR 9652 Ⓑ	FA 8528 B	FR 9450 A	FR 9654	FR 9556 9558	FR 9814 Ⓐ R	FR 9584 ⑤	FR 9560 M	FA 8464	FR 9660 Ⓑ	FR 9562 Ⓑ	FR 9816 Ⓒ L	FR 9564 Ⓑ A	FR 9662 †	
Salerno d.	...	...	...	...	...	1510	...	...	...	...	...	...	...	...	...	...	...	1712	...	...	...	...	...	...	...	...	...	...
Napoli Centrale d.	1505	...	1520	...	...	1600	...	1605	...	1630	1640	...	1700	1710	...	...	...	1800	...	...	...	...	1840	1900	...	1930	1940	...
Roma Fiumicino ✈ d.	|	...	|	...	...	|	...	|	...	|	|	...	|	|	...	...	...	|	...	...	...	...	|	|	...	|	|	...
Roma Termini a.	1615	...	1635	...	...	1710	...	1715	...	1740	1750	...	1810	1820	...	...	...	1907	...	...	...	...	1948	2010	...	2040	2050	...
Roma Termini d.	1630	1635	1645	1650	1700	1720	1730	1730	1745	1750	1800	1805	1820	1830	1845	1850	1900	1920	...	1929	1935	1950	2000	2020	...	2050	2100	...
Roma Tiburtina d.	|	|	|	1700	1707	1729	|	|	|	1800	|	1815	1829	|	|	1900	|	1929	...	1939	1945	2000	|	2029	...	2100	|	...
Firenze SMN a.	|	1807	1801c	1822	|	1851	|	|	1901c	1922	|	1936	1951	|	2001c	2035	|	2051	...	2102	2107	2122	|	2151	...	2235	|	...
Firenze SMN d.	|	1815	1803c	1830	|	1900	|	|	1903c	1930	|	1945	2000	|	2003c	2043	|	2100	...	2111	2116	2130	|	2200	...	...	|	...
Bologna Centrale ✥ d.	1828	1855	1845	1910	|	1938	|	1928	1945	2010	|	2023	2038	2028	2045	2126	|	2138	2140	2150	2155	2210	|	2238	2240	...	|	...
Reggio Emilia AV d.	|	|	|	|	|	|	|	|	|	|	|	2044	|	|	|	|	2116	|	2204	2214	|	|	|	|	2306	...	|	...
Milano Rogoredo a.	|	|	|	|	1949	|	|	|	|	|	|	2124	|	|	|	|	|	|	|	|	|	|	|	|	|	...	|	...
Milano Centrale a.	1929	|	|	|	1959	2040	|	2029	|	|	2055	2142g	2140	2129	|	|	2202	2240	2250	2300	2345	|	2255	2340	2350	...	2355	...
Milano Centrale d.	...	|	|	|	2010	...	|	...	|	|	...	2145g	...	...	|	|	2212	...	...	...	...	|	...	...	...	...	...	...
Verona Porta Nuova a.	...	|	1937	|	|	...	|	...	2037	|	...	|	...	...	2137	|	|	...	...	...	...	|	...	...	...	...	...	...
Torino Porta Susa a.	...	|	...	|	2059	...	|	...	...	|	...	2230	...	...	...	|	2302	...	...	...	...	|	...	...	...	...	...	...
Torino Porta Nuova a.	...	|	...	|	2110	...	|	...	...	|	...	2240	...	...	...	|	2312	...	...	...	...	|	...	...	...	...	...	...
Padova d.	...	1954	...	2009	...	...	2029	...	...	2109	...	...	...	...	...	2224	...	...	...	...	...	2309	...	...	...	...	...	...
Venezia Mestre ♣ a.	...	2008	...	2021	...	...	2042	...	...	2123	...	...	...	...	...	2238	...	...	...	...	...	2323	...	...	...	...	...	...
Venezia Santa Lucia ♣ a.	...	...	...	...	...	...	2054	...	...	2135	...	...	...	...	...	2250	...	...	...	...	...	2335	...	...	...	...	...	...

A – Also calls at Arezzo (Table **620**).
B – To Brescia (Table **605**).
L – From Lecce (Table **631**).
M – Via Modena (Table **615**).
N – From Ancona (Table **630**).
R – From Bari (Table **631**).
T – From Trieste (Table **601**).
U – To Udine (Table **601**).
Y – To Bolzano (Table **595**).
c – Firenze **Campo di Marte**.
g – Milano **Porta Garibaldi**.
♣ – Local journeys are not permitted between Venezia Mestre - Santa Lucia and Torino Porta Susa - Porta Nuova.
✥ – Most services use underground platforms 16 – 19; allow a minimum of 10 mins. for connecting services.

Italo high-speed services

Club, Prima, Smart XL and Smart class — Operator: Nuovo Trasporto Viaggiatori (NTV)

All trains 🅁 — *Trenitalia* tickets and passes not valid — www.italotreno.it

	ITA 9900 ①-⑥	ITA 9960	ITA 9990 z	ITA 9902	ITA 9962	ITA 9980	ITA 9904	ITA 9964	ITA 9908 9910	ITA 9984	ITA 9912	ITA 9914	ITA 9992	ITA 9966 x	ITA 9986	ITA 9922	ITA 9996	ITA 9928 9930	ITA 9968	ITA 9988	ITA 9932	ITA 9970	ITA 9934 9936	ITA 9972	ITA 9940	ITA 9998 w	ITA 9976 9978	ITA 9948 Ⓑ
Salerno d.	...	...	...	...	...	...	...	...	0737	...	...	...	...	...	...	...	...	1334	...	...	...	...	1530	...	...	...	1759	...
Napoli Centrale d.	...	...	0555	0625	0655	0644	0720	0745	0825	0850	...	...	...	...	1255	...	1355	1420	1455	...	...	...	1625	...	1725	1755	1845	1920
Roma Termini a.	...	...	0705	0735	0805	0755	0830	0855	0935	1005	...	...	...	...	1403	...	1502	1530	1605	...	...	...	1735	...	1835	1902	2000	2028
Roma Termini d.	0545	0710	0715	0745	0815	0815	0845	0910	0945	1015	1045	1145	1215	1310	1415	1345	1515	1545	1615	1615	1645	1715	1745	1810	1845	1915	2010	2045
Roma Tiburtina d.	0553	0719	0725	0755	|	0825	0855	0919	0955	1025	1055	1155	1225	1318	1425	1355	1525	1555	|	1625	1655	|	1755	1819	1855	1925	2018	2055
Firenze SMN d.	0725	|	0854	0925	|	0954	1025	|	1125	1154	1225	1325	1354	|	1554	1525	1654	1725	|	1754	1825	|	1925	|	2025	2054	|	2225
Bologna Centrale ✥ d.	0803	|	0933	1003	|	1035	1103	|	1203	1235	1303	1403	1433	|	1635	1603	1733	1803	|	1835	1903	|	2003	|	2103	2133	|	2303
Verona Porta Nuova a.	|	|	1023	|	|	|	|	|	|	|	|	|	1526	|	|	|	1823	|	|	|	|	|	|	|	|	2223	|	|
Brescia a.	|	|	...	|	|	|	|	|	|	|	|	|	1616	|	|	|	1916	|	|	|	|	|	|	|	|	2316	|	|
Padova a.	|	|	...	|	|	1132	|	|	|	1333	|	|	...	|	1732	|	...	|	|	1933	|	|	|	|	|	...	|	|
Venezia Mestre a.	|	|	...	|	|	1148	|	|	|	1348	|	|	...	|	1748	|	...	|	|	1948	|	|	|	|	|	...	|	|
Venezia Santa Lucia a.	|	|	...	|	|	1200	|	|	|	1400	|	|	...	|	1800	|	...	|	|	2000	|	|	|	|	|	...	|	|
Reggio Emilia ⊖ d.	0824	|	...	1024	|	...	1124	|	1224	...	1324	1424	...	|	...	1624	...	1824	|	...	1924	|	2024	|	2124	...	|	2324
Milano Rogoredo a.	0905	0957	...	1103	|	...	1203	1157	1303	...	1403	1503	...	1558	...	1703	...	1903	|	...	2003	|	2103	2057	2203	...	2258	0003
Milano Centrale a.	0917	1009	...	1115	1110	...	1215	1209	1315	...	1415	1515	...	1609	...	1715	...	1917	1910	...	2017	2010	2115	2109	2215	...	2309	0015
Torino Porta Susa a.	1013	...	...	1215	...	...	1316	...	1413	...	...	1613	...	...	...	...	...	...	...	...	2113	...	2213	...	2313	...	...	...
Torino Porta Nuova a.	1025	...	...	1227	...	...	1328	...	1425	...	...	1625	...	...	...	...	...	...	...	...	2125	...	2225	...	2325	...	...	...

w – Not Dec. 24, 31.
x – Not Dec. 25.
z – Not Dec. 25, Jan. 1.
⊖ – Reggio Emilia Mediopadana.
✥ – Most services use underground platforms 16 – 19 allow a minimum of 10 minutes for connecting services from / to the main station.

VENEZIA - UDINE - TRIESTE   601

Venezia - Trieste direct services

km		IC 735	FR 9707 ⊛T	FR 9717 ©T		IC 589			FR 9747 T	FA 8449 ♦	FB 8727 M	IC 593	FR 9757 T
	Roma Termini 616 ....d.	…	0641	0741	0941	1030	1241 1341 1441 1541	1641 1741 1841	1941	1635		1540	2241
0	**Venezia** Santa Lucia 605 ..d.	0550	0653	0753	0953	1053	1247 1253 1353 1453 1553	1646 1653 1753 1853	1949 1953	2021	2046	2138	2155 2253
9	**Venezia** Mestre 605 ....d.	0617	0707	0817	1017	1046 1117	1305 1317 1417 1517 1617	1708 1717 1817 1917		2017		2216	2317
42	S. Dona di Piave-Jesolo ▯ d.	0635	0737	0817	1017	1046 1117 1305	1317 1417 1437 1537 1637	1717 1717 1917	1917	2017	2129	2234	2337
69	Portogruaro-Caorle ....d.	0635	0737	0837	1104	1137 1321	1337 1437 1537 1637 1730	1737 1837 1937	2037	2037		2234	2337
83	Latisana-Lignano-Bibione ..d.	0648	0748	0848	1048	1114 1148	1330 1348 1448 1548 1648	1740 1748 1848 1948		2048		2244	2348
101	S. Giorgio di Nogaro ...d.	0700	0800	0900	1100	1200	1346 1409 1500 1600 1700	1800 1900 2000	2101				0000
112	Cervignano-Aquileia-Grado ..d.	0709	0809	0909	1109	1209 1346	1409 1509 1609 1709 1800	1809 1909 2009 2110				2301 2252	0009
129	Monfalcone ....d.	0723	0823	0923	1123	1145 1223 1359	1423 1523 1623 1736 1816	1823 1923 2023 2059	2123		2159	2314 2305	0023
157	**Trieste** Centrale ....⊛ a.	0746	0846	0946	1146	1208 1242 1446 1446	1546 1646 1746 1839 1846	1946 2046 2122 2146 2222				2337 2328	0046

		FR 9710 T	FA 8412 ♦	FR 9716		IC 584		FB 8712 T	IC 594			FR 9758 M		IC 734
	Trieste Centrale ....⊛ d.	…	0515	0615	0608	0652 0708	0715 0721 0815 0915	0938	1215 1302 1315 1415 1515	1615 1702 1715 1815	1915 2115	2206
	Monfalcone ....d.	…	0539	0639	0632	0733	0739 0746 0839 0939	1003 1239	1327 1339 1439 1539	1639 1727 1739 1839	1939 2139	2230
	Cervignano-Aquileia-Grado ..d.	…	0551	0651	0643		0751 0758 0851 0951	1251 1337	1351 1451 1551 1651	1737 1751 1851	1951 2151	2242
	S. Giorgio di Nogaro ....d.	…	0600	0700			0800 0900 1000	1300	1400 1500 1600 1700	1800 1900	2000 2200	2251
	Latisana-Lignano-Bibione ..d.	0538	0613	0713			0813 0821 0913 1013	1313 1351	1413 1513 1613 1713	1751 1813 1913	2013 2213	2304
	Portogruaro-Caorle ....d.	0538	0624	0724		0806	0824 0832 0924 1024	1033 1324 1401	1424 1524 1624 1724	1801 1824 1924	2024 2224	2315
	S. Dona di Piave-Jesolo ▯ d.	0601	0640	0742			0842 0850 0942 1042	1342 1419	1442 1542 1642 1742	1817 1842 1942	2042	2337
	Venezia Mestre 605 ....a.	0636	0708	0808	0740	0824 0851	0908 0912 1008 1108	1114 1408 1452	1508 1608 1708 1808	1842 1908 2008	2108	0005
	Venezia Santa Lucia 605 ..a.	0650	0720	0820			0920 1020 1120	1424	1524 1620 1720 1820	1920 2020 2120		
	Roma Termini 616 ....a.	…			1210		1527	2042				

Venezia - Trieste via Udine

km		ICN 774							FR 9704									
0	**Venezia** Santa Lucia ..d.	0504	0515	0536	0602	0615	0704	0715 0715 0804 0804		0915 1004 1115 1204	1215 1304 1315 1404
9	**Venezia** Mestre ..d.	0516	0529		0616	0629	0716	0729 0729 0816 0816	0913	0929 1016 1129 1216	1229 1316 1329 1416
30	Treviso Centrale ..d.	0536	0554	0614	0636	0654	0736	0754 0754 0836 0836	0930	0954 1036 1154 1236	1254 1336 1354 1436
57	Conegliano 603 ..d.	0555	0622	0638	0655	0722	0755	0822 0822 0855 0855	0948	1022 1055 1222 1255	1322 1355 1422 1455
74	Sacile ..d.	0607	0638	0652	0707	0738	0807	0838 0838 0907 0907		1038 1117 1238 1307	1338 1407 1438 1507
87	Pordenone ..d.	0617	0650	0704	0717	0750	0817	0850 0850 0917 0917	1008	1050 1117 1250 1317	1350 1417 1450 1517
136	Udine ..a.	0653	0730	0740	0753	0830	0853	0930 0930 0953 0953	1037	1130 1153 1330 1353	1430 1453 1530 1553
136	Udine ..d.	0655	0736	0755			0853 0909	0932	0955	1109 1155 1355	1555
169	Gorizia Centrale ♣ d.	0719	0807	0828			0919 0940	1003	1019	1140 1219 1419	1619
192	Monfalcone ..d.	0740	0831	0855			0940 1004	1027	1040	1204 1240 1440	1640
219	**Trieste** Centrale ..⊛ a.	0803	0900	0920			1003 1033	1056	1103	1233 1303 1503	1703

				EC 30 ♦											FA 8450 ♦	FR 9752	
	Venezia Santa Lucia ..d.	1504	1515	1555	1604	1615 1704 1704	1715 1804 1815 1904 1904	1915 2004		2115 2204 2304
	Venezia Mestre ..d.	1516	1529	1607	1616	1629 1716 1716	1729 1816 1829 1916 1916	1929 2016 2040	2110 2129	2216 2316
	Treviso Centrale ..d.	1536	1554	1630	1636	1654 1736 1736	1754 1836 1854 1936 1936	1954 2036 2056	2130 2154	2236 2336
	Conegliano 603 ..d.	1555	1622		1655	1722 1755 1755	1822 1855 1922 1955 1955	2022 2055 2115	2148 2222	2255 2355
	Sacile ..d.	1607	1638		1707	1738 1807 1807	1838 1907 1938 2007 2007	2038 2107		2238 2307 0007
	Pordenone ..d.	1617	1650	1717	1717	1750 1817 1817	1850 1917 1950 2017 2017	2050 2117 2136	2208 2250	2317 0017
	Udine ..a.	1653	1730	1742	1753	1830 1853 1853	1930 1953 2030 2053 2053	2130 2153 2205	2237 2330	2353 0053
	Udine ..d.	1655	1709		1755	1809 1855 1909 1916	1955	2120 2120 2155		2355
	Gorizia Centrale ♣ d.	1719	1740		1819	1840 1919 1941 1947	2019	2151 2151 2219		0026
	Monfalcone ..d.	1740	1804		1840	1904 1940 1952 2011	2040	2215 2215 2240		0049
	Trieste Centrale ..⊛ a.	1803	1833		1903	1933 2003 2015 2040	2103	2244 2244 2303		0118

		FR 9791		FA 8415								EC 31 ♦			FR 9739		
	Trieste Centrale ..⊛ d.			0527	0555 0622	0657	0727 0857	0927	1057	1127 1127	1227 1257
	Monfalcone ..d.			0557	0625 0646	0721	0757 0921	0957	1121	1157 1157	1257 1321
	Gorizia Centrale ♣ d.			0619	0647	0742	0819 0942	1019	1205	1219 1219	1319 1342
	Udine ..a.			0651	0719 0721	0805	0851 1005	1051	1205	1251 1251	1351 1405
	Udine ..d.	0507	0607 0615	0631	0655 0701 0731	0807	0831 1007	1107 1207 1218 1231	1307	1325 1331	1407
	Pordenone ..d.	0542	0642 0644	0710	0729 0740 0810	0842	0910 1042	1142 1242 1251 1310	1342	1354 1410	1442
	Sacile ..d.	0552	0652	0724	0752 0824	0852	0924 1052	1152 1252 1324	1352	1424	1452
	Conegliano 603 ..d.	0605	0705 0710	0740	0752 0805 0840	0905	0940 1105	1205 1305 1340 1405	1413	1440	1505
	Treviso Centrale ..d.	0625	0725 0730	0807	0814 0825 0907	0925	1007 1144	1225 1325 1332 1407 1425	1432	1507	1525
	Venezia Mestre ..a.	0644	0744 0749	0832	0837 0844 0932	0944	1032 1144	1244 1344 1353 1432 1444	1449 1522	1544
	Venezia Santa Lucia ..a.	0656	0756	0846	0900 0946	0956	1046 1156	1256 1356 1405 1446 1456	1546	1556

															ICN 771 ♦		
	Trieste Centrale ..⊛ d.	1327	1327	1427 1457	1527	1630 1657	1727 1757	1857	2031 2040	2222
	Monfalcone ..d.	1357	1357	1457 1521	1557	1700 1721	1757 1821	1921	2057 2106	2246
	Gorizia Centrale ♣ d.	1419	1419	1519 1542	1619	1722 1742	1819 1842	1942	2119 2131	2308
	Udine ..a.	1451	1451	1551 1605	1651	1754 1805	1851 1905	2005	2151 2156 ←	2340
	Udine ..d.	1431 1507	1531	1607	1631	1707 1731	1807 1831	1907 1907 1931 2007	→ 2158 2207	
	Pordenone ..d.	1510 1542	1610	1642	1710	1742 1810	1842 1910	1942 1910 2010 2042	2234 2242	
	Sacile ..d.	1524 1552	1624	1652	1724	1752 1824	1852 1924	1952 1952 2024 2052	2246 2252	
	Conegliano 603 ..d.	1540 1605	1640	1705 1731 1740	1805 1840	1905 1940	2005 2005 2040 2105	2258 2305	
	Treviso Centrale ..d.	1607 1625	1707	1725 1754 1807	1825 1907	1925 2007	2025 2025 2107 2125	2317 2325	
	Venezia Mestre ..a.	1632 1644	1732	1744 1818 1832	1844 1932	1944 2032	2044 2044 2132 2144	2344	
	Venezia Santa Lucia ..a.	1646 1656	1746	1756 1830 1846	1856 1946	1956 2046	2058 2058 2146 2156	2345 2356	

♦ –   NOTES (LISTED BY TRAIN NUMBER)

30/1 – 🛏 and ✕ Wien - Villach - Udine - Venezia and v.v.
771 – 🛏 1,2 cl., 🛏 2 cl. (4 berth) and 🍴 Trieste (770) - Udine - Venezia - Roma.
774 – 🛏 1,2 cl., 🛏 2 cl (4 berth) and 🍴 Roma - Venezia - Udine (775) - Trieste.
8412 – 🍴 and 🍴 Trieste - Venezia Mestre (8413) - Trieste.
8415/50 – 🍴 and 🍴 Udine - Venezia Mestre - Roma and v.v.
8449 – 🍴 and 🍴 Roma (8448) - Venezia Mestre - Trieste.
9704/39 – 🍴 and 🍴 Udine - Venezia Mestre (9703/40) - Milano and v.v.

M – 🍴 and 🍴 Milano - Trieste and v.v.
T – 🍴 and 🍴 Torino - Milano - Trieste and v.v.

j – Until Sept. 18.	**w –** From Sept. 12.	**z –** © (daily June 13 - Sept. 10).
k – From Sept. 19.	**y –** From Sept. 11.	

▯ – A frequent 🚌 service operates 0600 - 1930 to Lido di Jesolo; 1–2 per hour, journey time 35 minutes.

♣ – Line 1 🚌 service operates between Gorizia Centrale and Nova Gorica (Slovenia; bus stop 100 metres from station on Italian side) stations. Total journey time ± 20 minutes.

⊛ – 🚋 service **Trieste** (Piazza Oberdan) - **Villa Opicina** (Stazione Trenovia) and v.v. Linea Tranviaria. Operator: Trieste Trasporti S.p.A.
From **Trieste**: 0711, 0731, 0751 and every 20 minutes until 2011.
From **Villa Opicina**: 0700, 0720, 0740 and every 20 minutes until 2000.
Walking times: Trieste Centrale railway station - Piazza Oberdan ± 10 minutes; Villa Opicina Stazione Trenovia - Villa Opicina railway station ± 20 minutes.

602 VICENZA - TREVISO

2nd class only except where shown

km		✕	✕	✕	†	Ⓐq		✕		✕		✕	✕	✕		✕		✕		
0	Vicenza................d.	0614	0714	0814	...	0914	...	1114	1214	...	1314	1414	...	1514	...	1614	1714	1814	...	1914	...	2014	...	...
24	Cittadella................d.	0639	0739	0839	...	0939	...	1139	1239	...	1339	1439	...	1539	...	1639	1739	1839	...	1939	...	2039	...
36	Castelfranco Veneto ....d.	0655	0755	0855	...	0955	...	1155	1255	...	1355	1455	...	1555	...	1655	1755	1855	...	1955	...	2055	...
60	Treviso Centrale ....a.	0721	0821	0921	...	1021	...	1221	1321	...	1421	1521	...	1621	...	1721	1821	1921	...	2021	...	2121	...

		✕	✕		y	†		z			†		✕		✕		✕			✕		
Treviso Centrale ....d.		0539	0639	...	0739	0839	...	0939	...	1139	1239	...	1339	...	1439	1539	...	1639	...	1739	...	1839	...	2039
Castelfranco Veneto ....d.		0607	0707	...	0807	0907	...	1007	...	1207	1307	...	1407	...	1507	1607	...	1707	...	1807	...	1907	...	2107
Cittadella................d.		0621	0721	...	0821	0921	...	1021	...	1221	1321	...	1421	...	1521	1621	...	1721	...	1821	...	1921	...	2121
Vicenza................a.		0646	0746	...	0846	0946	...	1046	...	1246	1346	...	1446	...	1546	1646	...	1746	...	1846	...	1946	...	2146

q – From Sept. 11.
y – ✕ until Sept. 10; Ⓐ from Sept. 12.

z – † until Sept. 4; Ⓑ from Sept. 11.

603 CONEGLIANO and PADOVA - BELLUNO and CALALZO

2nd class only

km		✕	✕	✕		✕	†	Ⓐ	Ⓒ	Ⓐ	P		Ⓒ			†	✕		✕	✕	✕	✕		✕	
0	Conegliano 601 ....d.	0641	...	0741	...	...	0841	0841	...	0941	...	1241	...	1341	...	1441	...	...	1641	...
14	Vittorio Veneto ....d.	0702	...	0802	...	...	0902	0902	...	1002	...	1302	...	1402	...	1502	...	...	1702	...
	Padova ....d.				0707	0723					0907	...	1107	1125		1207		1307	1407	1507
	Castelfranco Veneto ....d.				0736	0752					0936	...	1136	1152		1236		1336	1436	1536
	Montebelluna ....d.		0600		0753	0806					0953	...	1153	1206		1253		1353	1453	1553
	Feltre ....d.		0639		0839	0839					1039	...	1239	1239		1339		1439	1539	1639
	Belluno ....d.		0715	0730	0830	0915	0910			0930		1030	1115		1315	1315	1330		1415	1430		1515	1530	1615		1715
41	Ponte nelle Alpi-Polpet.. a.	0731	...	0738	0831	0838	...	0919	0931	0931	0938	1031	1038	...	1331	...	1338	1431	...	1438	1531	...	1538	...	1731	...
41	Ponte nelle Alpi-Polpet.. § d.	0739	...	0739	0839	0839	...	0920	0939	0939	0939	1039	1039	...	1339	...	1339	1439	...	1439	1539	...	1539	...	1739	...
	Belluno ....§ a.	0747	...		0847	...	...	0947			1047		...	1347	...		1447	...		1547	...	...	1747	...
78	Calalzo ▲ ....a.		...	0827	...	0927	...	1010	...	1027	1027	...	1127	...	1427	...		1527	...		1627	...

		✕	Ⓐ				Ⓑ	Ⓑ				✕	✕			✕	✕				✕	
Conegliano 601 ....d.		1741	...	1841	...	...			...	2041	2141
Vittorio Veneto ....d.		1802	...	1902	...	...			...	2102	2202
Padova ....d.			1625		1707		1807	1907	2125
Castelfranco Veneto ......d.			1652		1736		1836	1936	2153
Montebelluna ....d.			1706		1753		1853	1953	2207
Feltre ....d.			1739		1839		1939	2039	2246
Belluno ....d.		1730		1815		1915	1930	2015	2030	2115		2322
Ponte nelle Alpi-Polpet.. a.		1738	1831		1931		1938	2038	...	2131	2231
Ponte nelle Alpi-Polpet.. § d.		1739	1839		1939		1939	2039	...	2139	2239
Belluno ....§ a.		1847		1947					2147	2247
Calalzo ▲ ....a.		1827					2027		2127

		✕		Calalzo ▲ ....d.	...		✕		0628		✕		0728			0928
	Belluno ....§ d.		0520		0620		0720		0820	
	Ponte nelle Alpi-Polpet § a.		0528		0628	0708		0728	0808		0828	1008
	Ponte nelle Alpi-Polpet.. d.		0533		0633	0710		0733	0810		0833	1010
	Belluno ....d.		0534		0718	0734		0818	0844		1018
	Feltre ....d.		0613		0813			0923	
	Montebelluna ....d.		0707		0907			0957	
	Castelfranco Veneto ......d.		0725		0925			1010	
	Padova ....a.		0753		0953			1034	
	Vittorio Veneto ....d.	0601		0701			0801		0901	
	Conegliano 601 ....a.	0618		0718			0818		0918	

km			✕	✕		✕			✕	Ⓑ	Ⓑ	Ⓖ		✕		Ⓑ		H		Ⓒ	†		✕	
0	Calalzo ▲ ....d.	...		1228		1328			1528	1628		1728		1740	1758	1828			1928	
37	Ponte nelle Alpi-Polpet.. § a.		1020		1308		1328	1408		1428	1528	1608		1708		1728	1808		1828	1825	1842	1908		1928	2008	2028
37	Ponte nelle Alpi-Polpet.. § a.		1033		1310		1333	1410		1433	1533	1610		1711		1733	1810		1833	1833	1843	1910		1933	2010	2033
44	Belluno ....d.		1034		1234	1318	1334		1418	1434		1534		1618	1634	1718	1734		1818	1834		1853	1918	1934		2018	
75	Feltre ....d.		1113		1313		1413			1513	1613		1713		1813		1913		1932		2013	
110	Montebelluna ....d.		1207		1407		1457			1607	1707		1807		1907		2007		2017		2107	
127	Castelfranco Veneto ......d.		1225		1425		1510			1625	1725		1825		1925		2025		2032		2125	
158	Padova ....d.		1253		1453	1534			1653	1753		1853		1953		2053		2100		2153	
	Vittorio Veneto ....d.	...	1101			1401			1501	1601			1801		1901	1901			2001	2101
	Conegliano 601 ....a.	...	1118			1418			1518	1618			1818		1918	1918			2018	2118

H – Ⓐ from Sept. 12.
P – Ⓒ (daily from Sept. 10).
j – Arrive 1923 on †.

§ – See other direction of table for further connections.
▲ – Full name of station is Calalzo-Pieve di Cadore-Cortina.

604 VAL GARDENA / GRÖDNERTAL and CORTINA 🚌 services

Service 445/446		✕												Service 445/446										
S. Candido / Innichen ....d.		...	0839	...	1039	...	1339	...	1539	...	1739	...	Cortina ....d.	0805	...	1005	...	1305	...	1505	...	1705	...	1905
Dobbiaco / Toblach ♣ ....d.		0705	0849	0905	1049	1105	1349	1405	1549	1605	1749	1805	Dobbiaco / Toblach ♣ ....d.	0850	0910	1050	1110	1350	1410	1550	1610	1750	1810	1950
Cortina ....a.		0755	...	0955	...	1155	...	1455	...	1655	...	1855	S. Candido / Innichen ....a.	...	0920	...	1120	...	1420	...	1620	...	1820	...

♣ – Dobbiaco bus station. Services also call at Dobbiaco railway station en route between Dobbiaco town and Cortina (5 minutes from town stop).

Service 350		✕								Service 350		✕							
Bolzano / Bozen ♦ ....d.		0644	0826	...	1126	...	1526	...	1726	...	1926	Plan ▲ ....d.	0604	0704	0834	0904	1034	1304	1334	1504	1704	1734	1904
Ponte Gardena / Waidbruck ..d.		0715	0857	1057	1157	1257	1357	1557	1657	1757	1857	1957	Selva / Wolkenstein ▲ ....d.	0607	0707	0837	0907	1037	1307	1337	1507	1707	1737	1907
Ortisei / St Ulrich ▲ ....d.		0747	0927	1127	1227	1327	1427	1627	1727	1827	1927	2027	Santa / St Cristina ▲ ....d.	0616	0716	0846	0916	1046	1316	1346	1516	1716	1746	1916
Santa / St Cristina ▲ ....d.		0800	0940	1140	1240	1340	1440	1640	1740	1840	1940	2040	Ortisei / St Ulrich ▲ ....d.	0631	0731	0901	0931	1101	1331	1401	1531	1731	1801	1931
Selva / Wolkenstein ▲ ....a.		0808	0948	1148	1248	1348	1448	1648	1748	1848	1948	2048	Ponte Gardena / Waidbruck..d.	0659	0759	0931	0959	1131	1359	1431	1559	1759	1831	2001
Plan ▲ ....a.		0812	0952	1152	1252	1352	1452	1652	1752	1852	1952	2052	Bolzano / Bozen ♦ ....a.	0730	0830	1002	...	1202	...	1430	...	1630	...	1902

♦ – Bolzano / Bozen town. Services also call at railway station (2 minutes from town stop).

▲ – Extra buses run Ortisei/St Ulrich - Plan and v.v. in summer.

Valid until December 10, 2016.
Operator: Servizi Autobus Dolomiti, Via Conciapelli 60, 39100, Bolzano / Bozen. ✆ : + 39 0471 450111 Fax: + 39 0471 970042.

🚌 service 30 Cortina - Calalzo. 35 km. Journey time: 55 minutes.
Valid September 12, 2016 - June 11, 2017.

Operator: Dolomitibus, via Col Da Ren 14, 32100, Belluno, Italy.
✆ +39 00 437 217 111, fax +39 00 437 940 522.

From **Cortina Autostazione** (Bus Station):
0535✕, 0625, 0650✕, 0720 S, 0800†, 0930✕, 1115, 1220✕, 1240✕, 1240†y,
1315✕, 1402, 1620✕, 1705, 1755✕, 1920✕, 1940✕, 1940†p, 2010✕, 2010†y.

From **Calalzo Stazione** (FS rail station):
0625✕, 0647 S, 0658, 0720†w, 0740✕, 0820, 0935, 1100✕, 1215✕, 1215†x,
1310✕, 1310†p, 1400✕, 1400†y, 1450, 1635, 1740✕, 1850†, 1900✕.

S – Schooldays only.

p – Not Dec. 8 - Mar. 26.
w – Dec. 18 - Feb. 12.

x – Dec. 18 - Mar. 12.
y – Dec. 8 - Mar. 26.

12

MILANO - VERONA - VENEZIA 605

km					FA	FR	FR		FR	FB		FR	FB		FR	FR	FA		EC	FR	EC		FR	FB
					8505	9703	9705		9707	8707		9711	8709		9715	9717	8513		1289	9723	37		9727	8717
					🍷	🍷	🍷		🍷	🍷		🍷	🍷		🍷	🍷	🍷		✕	🍷	🍷		🍷	🍷
			⚒	†	R	♦			ⒶT	V		Ⓐ	V	Ⓐm		TⒸ	R		♦		♦			
0	**Milano** Centrale d.	...	...	...	...	0645	0715	...	0745	0805	...	0835	0905	...	0945	1015	...	...	...	1145	1205	...	1245	1305
4	**Milano** Lambrate d.	...	...	...	...	|	|	...	|	|	...	|	|	...	|	|	...	...	...	|	|	...	|	|
34	Treviglio d.	...	...	...	...	|	|	...	|	|	...	|	|	...	|	|	...	...	...	|	|	...	|	|
83	Brescia d.	...	0629	...	0708	0723	0753	...	0823	0853	...	0923	0953	...	1023	1053	1102	...	...	1223	1253	...	1323	1353
111	Desenzano-Sirmione **599a** d.	...	0652	...	|	0738	|	...	|	0908	...	|	1008	...	|	|	|	...	...	1238	|	...	1338	|
125	Peschiera del Garda **599a** ‡ d.	...	0701	...	|	|	0814	...	0844	|	...	0944	|	...	1044	1114	|	...	...	|	1314	...	|	1414
148	**Verona** Porta Nuova **599a** a.	...	0719	...	0741	0758	0828	...	0858	0928	...	0958	1028	...	1058	1128	1141	...	...	1258	1328	...	1358	1428
148	**Verona** Porta Nuova **595** d.	0621	0721	0721	...	0800	0830	0821	0900	0930	0921	1000	1030	1021	1100	1130	...	...	1239	1300	1330	1321	1400	1430
200	Vicenza d.	0702	0802	0802	...	0826	0856	0902	0926	0956	1002	1026	1056	1102	1126	1156	...	...	1311	1326	1356	1402	1426	1456
230	Padova **616** d.	0721	0821	0821	...	0844	0914	0921	0944	1014	1021	1044	1114	1121	1144	1214	...	...	1328	1344	1414	1421	1444	1514
258	**Venezia** Mestre **616** a.	0736	0836	0836	...	0858	0928s	0936	0958	1028s	1036	1058s	1128s	1136	1158s	1228	...	...	1344	1358s	1428s	1436	1458s	1528s
258	**Venezia** Mestre **616** d.	0738	0838	0838	...	...	|	0938	1020	|	1038	|	|	1138	|	1247	...	...	1346	|	|	1438	|	|
267	**Venezia** Santa Lucia **616** a.	0748	0848	0848	...	...	0940	0948	|	1040	1048	1110	1140	1148	1210	|	...	...	1356	1410	1440	1448	1510	1540
	Trieste Centrale **601** a.	...	...	...	...	...	...	...	1208	...	...	...	...	...	...	1422	...	...	...	...	...	...	...	...

			FR	FB		EC	FB		FA	FR			FR	FR		FB		FB	FR		FR	FB	FR	
			9733	8721		87	9743		8525	9745			9747	9749		8727		8731	9757		9759	8735	9649	
			🍷	🍷		✕	🍷		🍷	🍷			🍷	🍷	2	🍷		🍷	🍷	2	🍷	🍷	🍷	
	Ⓐm			V		♦◧	V		R				T					V					Ⓑ	
Milano Centrale d.	...	...	1445	1505	...	...	1615	...	...	1645	...	...	1715	1745	...	1805	...	1905	1945	...	2015	2035	2040	...
Milano Lambrate d.	...	...	|	|	...	...	|	...	...	|	...	...	|	|	...	|	...	|	|	...	|	|	|	...
Treviglio d.	...	...	|	|	...	...	|	...	...	|	...	...	|	|	...	|	...	|	|	...	|	|	|	...
Brescia d.	...	...	1523	1553	...	...	1653	...	1702	1723	...	...	1753	1823	...	1853	...	1953	2023	...	2053	2123	2116	...
Desenzano-Sirmione **599a** d.	...	...	1538	|	...	...	1708	...	|	1738	...	...	|	1838	...	1908	...	2008	|	...	|	2138	...	...
Peschiera del Garda **599a** ‡ d.	...	...	|	1614	...	...	|	...	|	|	...	...	1814	|	...	|	...	|	|	...	2114	|	...	...
Verona Porta Nuova **599a** a.	...	...	1558	1628	...	...	1728	...	1741	1758	...	...	1828	1858	...	1928	...	2028	2053	...	2128	2158	...	...
Verona Porta Nuova **595** d.	1421	1521	1600	1630	1621	1700	1730	1721	...	1800	...	1821	1830	1900	1921	1930	...	2030	2055	2042	2130	2200	...	2221
Vicenza d.	1502	1602	1626	1656	1702	1727	1756	1802	...	1826	...	1902	1856	1926	2002	1956	...	2056	|	2138	2156	2226	...	2302
Padova **616** d.	1521	1621	1644	1714	1721	1744	1814	1821	...	1844	...	1921	1914	1944	2021	2014	...	2114	|	2205	2214	2244	...	2321
Venezia Mestre **616** a.	1536	1636	1658s	1728s	1736	1758	1828s	1836	...	1858s	...	1936	1928	1958s	2036	2028	...	2128s	2145	2241	2228s	2258s	...	2336
Venezia Mestre **616** d.	1538	1638	|	|	1738	1801	|	1838	...	|	...	1938	1949	|	2038	2046	...	|	2155	2243	|	|	...	2338
Venezia Santa Lucia **616** a.	1548	1648	1710	1740	1748	1810	1840	1848	...	1910	...	1948	|	2010	2048	|	...	2140	|	2255	2240	2310	...	2348
Trieste Centrale **601** a.	...	...	...	...	...	...	...	...	...	...	...	...	2122	...	...	2222	...	...	2328	...	...	...	...	...

	FR	FB		FR	FR			FB	FR	FR		FR	FR	FR	FR	FA	FB		FR		FR		FB	EC
	9604	8700		9702	9706			8706	9710	9712		9712	9716	9720	9724	8510	8712		9728		9732		8716	86
	🍷	🍷		🍷	🍷			🍷	🍷	🍷		🍷	🍷	🍷	🍷	🍷	🍷		🍷		🍷		🍷	✕
	Ⓐ									Ⓐ		V		Ⓒ		R	T			Ⓐm			V	♦◧
Trieste Centrale **601** d.	...	...	...	...	...	...	...	...	0608	...	...	...	0708	...	...	...	0938	...	...	...	...	...	...	...
Venezia Santa Lucia **616** d.	...	0540	0612	0620	0650	...	0712	0720	|	...	0812	0820	|	0950	1050	...	|	1112	1150	1212	1250	1312	1320	1350
Venezia Mestre **616** a.	...	|	0622	|	|	...	0722	0730	0740	...	0822	|	0851	|	|	...	1114	1122	|	1222	|	1322	|	1400
Venezia Mestre **616** d.	...	0552u	0624	0632u	0702u	...	0724	0732	0750	0802	0824	0832u	0902	1002u	1102u	...	1132	1124	1202u	1224	1302u	1324	1332u	1402
Padova **616** d.	...	0607	0640	0648	0718	...	0740	0748	|	0818	0840	0848	0918	1018	1118	...	1148	1140	1218	1240	1318	1340	1348	1418
Vicenza d.	...	0625	0659	0705	0735	...	0759	0805	|	0835	0859	0905	0935	1035	1135	...	1205	1159	1235	1259	1335	1359	1405	1435
Verona Porta Nuova **595** a.	...	0650	0739	0730	0800	...	0839	0830	0843	0900	0939	0930	1000	1100	1200	...	1230	1239	1300	1339	1400	1439	1430	1500
Verona Porta Nuova **599a** d.	...	0652	...	0732	0802	...	...	0832	0845	0902	...	0932	1002	1102	1202	1251	1232	...	1302	...	1402	...	1432	...
Peschiera del Garda **599a** ‡ d.	...	0707	...	0748	|	...	...	0848	|	|	...	0947	|	1118	|	|	|	...	1318	...	|	...	1448	...
Desenzano-Sirmione **599a** d.	...	0716	...	|	0823	...	...	|	|	0923	...	|	1023	|	1223	|	1253	...	|	...	1423	...	|	...
Brescia d.	0519	0734	...	0809	0839	...	...	0909	|	0939	...	1009	1039	1139	1239	1330	1309	...	1339	...	1439	...	1509	...
Treviglio d.	|	|	...	|	|	...	...	|	|	|	...	|	|	|	|	...	|	...	|	...	|	...	|	...
Milano Lambrate d.	|	|	...	|	|	...	...	|	|	|	...	|	|	|	|	...	|	...	|	...	|	...	|	...
Milano Centrale a.	0555	0825	...	0845	0915	...	...	0955	0950	1015	...	1045	1115	1215	1315	...	1355	...	1415	...	1515	...	1555	...

		FB	FR		FB	EC	FR			EC	FA	FR		FB		FR		FR		FR		FA		
		8718	9740		8720	1288	9744			42	8520	9748		8724		9754		9758		9762		8528		
	2	🍷	🍷		🍷	✕	🍷			🍷	🍷	🍷		🍷		🍷		🍷		🍷		🍷		2
	⑥	V	♦		V	♦	Ⓐ	†	⚒	♦	R			V						V	Ⓐ	R		Ⓒ
Trieste Centrale **601** d.	...	...	...	...	...	...	...	...	...	...	...	...	...	...	...	...	...	1702	...	...	...	...	...	...
Venezia Santa Lucia **616** d.	1412	1420	...	1512	1520	1550	1550	1612	1612	1620	...	1650	1712	1720	...	1750	1812	|	1912	1950	2012	...	2112	0003
Venezia Mestre **616** a.	1422	|	...	1522	|	1600	|	1622	1622	1630	...	|	1722	|	...	|	1822	1842	1922	|	2022	...	2122	0013
Venezia Mestre **616** d.	1424	1432u	1502	1524	1532u	1602	1602u	1624	1624	1632	...	1702u	1724	1732u	...	1802u	1824	1902	1924	2002u	2024	...	2124	0015
Padova **616** d.	1440	1448	1518	1540	1548	1618	1618	1640	1640	1648	...	1718	1740	1748	...	1818	1840	1918	1940	2018	2040	...	2140	0038
Vicenza d.	1459	1505	1535	1559	1605	1635	1635	1659	1659	1705	...	1735	1759	1805	...	1835	1859	1935	1959	2035	2059	...	2159	0100
Verona Porta Nuova **595** a.	1539	1530	1600	1639	1630	1700	1700	1739	1739	1730	...	1800	1839	1830	...	1900	1939	2000	2039	2100	2139	...	2239	0134
Verona Porta Nuova **599a** d.	...	1532	1602	...	1632	...	1702	...	1744	1732	1751	1802	...	1832	...	1902	...	2002	...	2102	...	2151	...	...
Peschiera del Garda **599a** ‡ d.	...	|	|	...	1648	...	|	...	1802	1748	|	|	...	1848	...	1918	...	2018	...	|	...	|	...	...
Desenzano-Sirmione **599a** d.	...	1553	1623	...	|	...	1723	...	1811	|	|	1823	...	|	...	|	...	|	...	2123	...	|	...	...
Brescia d.	...	1609	1639	...	1709	...	1739	...	1834	1809	1830	1839	...	1909	...	1939	...	2039	...	2139	...	2232	...	...
Treviglio d.	...	|	|	...	|	...	|	...	...	|	...	|	...	|	...	|	...	|	...	|	...	...	...	...
Milano Lambrate d.	...	|	|	...	|	...	|	...	...	|	...	|	...	|	...	|	...	|	...	|	...	...	...	...
Milano Centrale a.	...	1655	1715	...	1755	...	1815	...	...	1855	...	1915	...	1955	...	2015	...	2115	...	2215	...	...	...	...

MILANO - VERONA and v.v. local services : Operator: Trenord

					Ⓐn	†																		
Milano Centrale d.	0625	0725	0825	...	0850	0925	...	1125	1225	1325	1425	...	1525	1625	1725	1825	...	1925	2025	...	2125	2225	...	0015
Milano Lambrate d.	0633	0733	0833	...	0900	0933	...	1133	1233	1333	1433	...	1533	1633	1733	1833	...	1933	2033	...	2133	2233	...	0022
Treviglio d.	0656	0756	0856	...	0926	0956	...	1156	1256	1356	1456	...	1556	1656	1756	1856	...	1956	2056	...	2156	2256	...	0049
Brescia d.	0735	0835	0935	...	1016	1035	...	1235	1335	1435	1535	...	1635	1735	1835	1935	...	2035	2135	...	2235	2335	...	0135
Desenzano-Sirmione **599a** d.	0751	0851	0951	...	...	1051	...	1251	1351	1451	1551	...	1651	1751	1851	1951	...	2051	2151	...	2251	2351	...	0151
Peschiera del Garda **599a** ‡ d.	0801	0901	1001	...	...	1101	...	1301	1401	1501	1601	...	1701	1801	1901	2001	...	2101	2201	...	2301	0001	...	0201
Verona Porta Nuova **599a** a.	0820	0920	1020	...	...	1120	...	1320	1420	1520	1620	...	1720	1820	1920	2020	...	2120	2220	...	2320	0020	...	0220

			Ⓐn														†							
Verona Porta Nuova **599a** d.	0540	0640	0655	0740	...	0836	0940	...	...	1236	1340	1440	1540	...	1640	1740	1810	1842	...	1940	2040	...	2140	...
Peschiera del Garda **599a** ‡ d.	0555	0655	0712	0755	...	0852	0955	...	...	1252	1355	1455	1555	...	1655	1755	1825	1857	...	1955	2055	...	2155	...
Desenzano-Sirmione **599a** d.	0605	0705	0721	0805	...	0902	1005	...	...	1302	1405	1505	1605	...	1705	1805	1835	1906	...	2005	2105	...	2205	...
Brescia d.	0625	0725	0740	0825	...	0925	1025	1244	...	1325	1425	1525	1625	...	1725	1825	1855	1925	...	2025	2125	...	2225	...
Treviglio d.	0702	0802	0813	0902	...	1002	1102	1332	...	1402	1502	1602	1702	...	1802	1902	1932	2002	...	2102	2202	...	2302	...
Milano Lambrate d.	0728	0828	0837	0928	...	1028	1128	1358	...	1428	1528	1628	1728	...	1828	1928	1958	2028	...	2128	2228	...	2328	...
Milano Centrale a.	0735	0835	0845	0935	...	1035	1135	1405	...	1435	1535	1635	1735	...	1835	1935	2005	2035	...	2135	2235	...	2335	...

♦ – **NOTES** (LISTED BY TRAIN NUMBER)

37/42 – [12] and 🍷 Genève - Milano - Venezia and v.v. [R] inclusive of supplement.
86/7 – [12] and ✕ Venezia - Verona - München and v.v. Operator within Italy: LeNord.
1288/9 – Ⓒ: [12] and ✕ Venezia - Verona - München and v.v. Operator within Italy: LeNord.
9703 – [12] and 🍷 Milano - Venezia Mestre (**9704**) - Udine.
9740 – [12] and 🍷 Udine (**9739**) - Venezia Mestre - Milano.

R – [12] and 🍷 Roma - Brescia and v.v.
T – [12] and 🍷 Trieste - Venezia Mestre - Milano - Torino and v.v.
V – [12] and 🍷 Torino - Milano - Venezia and v.v.

j – Until Sept. 18.
k – From Sept. 19.
m – Not July 24 - Sept. 11.

n – Not July 30 - Aug. 28.
s – Stops to set down only.
u – Stops to pick up only.

♠ – Operator: Trenord.
◧ – Also available to passengers without reservation. Operator within Italy: LeNord.
‡ – Station for Gardaland Park. Free shuttle bus available.

607 MILANO LOCAL SERVICES

Operator: Trenord

MILANO - BERGAMO: Some services 2nd class only

km							Ⓐ	Ⓒ	Ⓐ	Ⓒ															
0	**Milano** Centrale ◇ d.	0540	0610	0710	0810	0910	1010	1010	1110	1110	...	1210	1310	1410	1510	1610	1710	...	1810	1910	2010	2110	2210	2340	...
56	**Bergamo** a.	0628	0658	0758	0858	0958	1100	1103	1158	1203	...	1258	1358	1458	1558	1658	1758	...	1858	1958	2058	2158	2300	0050	...

				Ⓐ				Ⓒ	Ⓐ	Ⓒ	Ⓐ															
Bergamo d.	0500	0602	0702	0735	...	0802	0902	0957	1002	1057	1102	...	1202	1302	1402	1502	1602	1702	...	1802	1902	2002	2102	2202	2300
Milano Centrale ◇ a.	0550	0650	0750	0830	...	0850	0950	1050	1050	1150	1150	...	1250	1350	1450	1550	1650	1750	...	1850	1950	2050	2150	2250	2350

Additional trains run approximately hourly Milano Porta Garibaldi - Bergamo via Monza, journey 64 minutes, *43 km*.

MILANO - COMO LAGO: *46 km* Journey: 52–65 minutes 2nd class only

From **Milano** Cadorna: 0613⚒, 0643, 0713⚒, 0743, 0800Ⓐ, 0843, 0900, 0943, 1043, 1143, 1213⚒, 1243, 1313⚒, 1343, 1400†, 1413Ⓐ, 1443, 1513Ⓐ, 1543, 1613Ⓐ, 1643, 1700Ⓐ, 1713⚒, 1743, 1800Ⓐ, 1813, 1843, 1900Ⓐ, 1913⚒, 1943, 2013⚒, 2043, 2113Ⓐ, 2143, 2243.

From **Como Nord Lago**: 0546⚒, 0616, 0635Ⓐ, 0646⚒, 0716, 0735Ⓐ, 0746⚒, 0816, 0835⚒, 0916, 0935Ⓐ, 1016, 1116, 1216, 1246⚒, 1316, 1346⚒, 1416, 1446Ⓐ, 1516, 1546Ⓐ, 1616, 1646Ⓐ, 1716, 1746, 1816, 1835†, 1846⚒, 1916, 1946, 2016, 2046⚒, 2116.

A reduced service operates July 31 - Aug. 28.

MILANO - VARESE - LAVENO: *72 km* Journey: 87–107 mins 2nd class only

From **Milano** Cadorna: 0609⚒, 0639, 0709Ⓐ, 0752, 0852, 0939, 1039, 1139, 1209⚒, 1252, 1352, 1439Ⓒ, 1452Ⓐ, 1539, 1609Ⓐ, 1652, 1722Ⓐ, 1752, 1822Ⓐ, 1852, 1922Ⓐ, 1939Ⓒ, 2022Ⓐ, 2039Ⓒ.

From **Laveno-Mombello** FN: 0538Ⓐ, 0608⚒, 0638, 0708⚒, 0738, 0808Ⓐ, 0838, 0938, 1038, 1138, 1238, 1308⚒, 1338, 1438, 1538, 1638, 1738, 1808Ⓐ, 1838, 1938, 2038.

Additional journeys run Milano Cadorna - Varese (journey 63 minutes).

A reduced service operates July 31 - Aug. 28.

MILANO - LUINO: *91 km* 2nd class only

	ⒶB			†						ⒶB	ⒶB		
Milano P Garibaldi d.	*0632*	*0732*	0806	*0932*	*1232*	*1332*	*1432*	*1532*	*1632*	1806	1906	*2032*	2236
Gallarate **590** d.	0719	0819	0842	1019	1319	1419	1519	1619	1719	1842	1942	2119	2307
Laveno-Mombello d.	0801	0901	0922	1101	1401	1501	1601	1701	1801	1922	2022	2201	2341
Luino 592 a.	0816	0915	*0958*j	1116	1416	1515	1616	1715	1816	1941	2041	2216	2359

	Ⓒ	ⒶB	ⒶB	Ⓒ		†							
Luino 592 d.	0604	0619	0720	0744	0845	1044	1344	1445	1544	1645	1744	1944	2045
Laveno-Mombello d.	0620	0642	0736	0800	0900	1100	1400	1500	1600	1700	1800	2000	2100
Gallarate **590** a.	0652	0718	0805	0841	0941	1141	1441	1541	1641	1741	1841	2041	2141
Milano P Garibaldi a.	0728	0757	0844	*0928*	*1028*	*1228*	*1528*	*1628*	*1728*	*1828*	*1928*	*2128*	2228

Additional journeys are available by changing at Gallarate.

MILANO - CREMONA - MANTOVA:

km											
0	**Milano** C d.	0620	0820	1020	1220	...	1420	1620	1715	1820	1915	2020
60	Codogno d.	0702	0902	1102	1302	...	1502	1702	1758	1902	1958	2102
88	Cremona d.	0732	0930	1130	1330	...	1530	1730	1820	1930	2020	2130
151	**Mantova** a.	0814	1010	1210	1410	...	1610	1810	1910	2019	2110	2210

Mantova d.	0518	0610	0641	0850	1050	1250	1450	1650	1850	2050	...
Cremona d.	0617	0656	0732	0930	1130	1330	1530	1730	1930	2130	...
Codogno d.	0638	0717	0752	0952	1152	1352	1552	1752	1952	2152	...
Milano Centrale a.	0730	0810	0840	1040	1240	1440	1640	1840	2040	2240	...

BRESCIA - EDOLO: 2nd class only

km		⚒B	A							ⒶB		
0	**Brescia** d.	0555	0707	0907	1107	...	1307	1507	1707	1758	...	1907
103	Edolo a.	0834	0907	1107	1307	...	1507	1707	1907	2018	...	2107

	⚒B	⚒B								A	
Edolo d.	0554	0647	0754	0954	1154	...	1354	1554	1754	1954	...
Brescia a.	0754	0903	0954	1154	1354	...	1554	1754	1954	2200	...

For 🚌 Edolo - Tirano see Table **593**.

A – † (daily July 31 - Aug. 28).
B – Not July 31 - Aug. 28.
j – Connection by 🚌.

609 Local services in NORTHERN and CENTRAL ITALY

2nd class only

ALESSANDRIA - ACQUI TERME: *34 km* Journey 28–38 minutes

From **Alessandria**: 0643, 0743, 0938, 1043⚒, 1143, 1343, 1543, 1743, 1943.

From **Acqui Terme**: 0646⚒, 0737, 0942, 1137, 1337, 1437⚒, 1537, 1737, 1937.

BOLOGNA - PORRETTA TERME: *59 km* Journey 60–72 minutes

From **Bologna** Centrale: 0552⚒§, 0630⚒, 0704, 0804⚒, 0904⚒§, 0904†, 1004⚒, 1104, 1204⚒§, 1204†, 1304, 1404, 1504, 1604§, 1704, 1734, 1804, 1904Ⓐ, 1904Ⓒ§, 1934Ⓐd§, 2004, 2104, 2204.

From **Porretta Terme**: 0500⚒, 0550, 0608, 0640, 0718⚒§, 0718†, 0750⚒, 0822, 0922⚒, 1022⚒§, 1022†, 1122⚒, 1222, 1322, 1422⚒§, 1422†, 1522, 1622, 1722§, 1821, 1921, 2021Ⓐ, 2021Ⓒ§, 2050Ⓐ**d**, 2122Ⓐ**d**§.

CAMPIGLIA - PIOMBINO: *16 km* Journey 22–30 minutes

From **Campiglia Marittima**: 0556⚒, 1008**p**, 1336⚒, 1533, 1640, 1736**q**, 1806, 1839Ⓒ**r**.

From **Piombino Marittima**: 0632⚒, 0915Ⓒ, 0920Ⓐ, 1053**p**, 1140Ⓒ**r**, 1527⚒, 1608, 1724, 1812**q**, 1845.

GENOVA - ACQUI TERME: *58 km* Journey 65–81 minutes

From **Genova** Piazza Principe: 0612Ⓐ**a**, 0714**b**, 0921**c**, 1021⚒**c**, 1121**c**, 1221Ⓐ**c**, 1321**c**, 1421Ⓐ**c**, 1621**c**, 1721Ⓐ**c**, 1821**c**, 1921**c**, 2043**b**.

From **Acqui Terme**: 0520Ⓐ**a**, 0610**b**, 0703⚒**c**, 0740Ⓐ**a**, 0917**c**, 1117**c**, 1217**c**, 1317**b**, 1417Ⓐ**c**, 1617**c**, 1717Ⓐ**c**, 1817**c**, 2040**b**.

PORRETTA TERME - PISTOIA: *40 km* Journey 60–75 minutes

From **Porretta Terme**: 0655⚒**e**, 0717**f**, 0926⚒**e**, 1022**n**, 1324**f**, 1524**f**, 1824**f**.

From **Pistoia**: 0600**f**, 0825⚒**e**, 0921**n**, 1222**f**, 1422**f**, 1721**f**, 1926**f**.

ROVIGO - CHIOGGIA:

km		⚒t	m	⚒t	Ⓑx	†v		⚒t	⚒t	†v	⚒t	Ⓑx	x
0	**Rovigo** d.	0615	0715	0815	0915	1115	...	1315	1415	1515	1615	1715	1915
25	Adria d.	0642	0742	0842	0942	1142	...	1342	1442	1542	1642	1742	1942
57	**Chioggia** a.	0725	0825	0925	1025	1225	...	1425	1525	1625	1725	1825	2025

	⚒t	x	Ⓑx		⚒t	†v	⚒t	Ⓐy	x	Ⓑx	⑥z	
Chioggia d.	0635	0735	0935	...	1235	1335	1435	1535	1735	1935	2035	...
Adria d.	0714	0814	1014	...	1314	1414	1514	1614	1814	2014	2114	...
Rovigo a.	0745	0845	1045	...	1345	1445	1545	1645	1845	2045	2145	...

SANTHIÀ - BIELLA S. PAOLO: *27 km* Journey 20–35 minutes

From **Santhià**: 0548⚒, 0648⚒, 0748⚒, 0751†, 0848⚒, 0948⚒, 0951†, 1148⚒, 1151†, 1248⚒, 1348⚒, 1351†, 1448⚒, 1548⚒, 1551†, 1648⚒, 1748⚒, 1751†, 1848⚒, 1913Ⓐ**d**, 1948⚒, 1951†, 2048⚒, 2051†, 2148⚒, 2151†.

From **Biella S. Paolo**: 0548⚒, 0648, 0718Ⓐ**d**, 0748⚒, 0848, 0948⚒, 1048†, 1148⚒, 1248, 1348⚒, 1448, 1548⚒, 1648, 1748⚒, 1848, 1943†, 1948⚒, 2048, 2148⚒.

SIENA - GROSSETO:

km		⚒	†	⚒w	†	⚒	†	⚒	⚒	†	†	⚒		
0	**Siena** d.	0555	0748	0809	0946	1215	1245	1327	1545	1552	1740	1746	1843	1943
29	Buonconvento d.	0630	0818	0839	1011	1240	1311	1352	1610	1616	1814	1812	1909	2009
102	**Grosseto** a.	0734	0920	0941	1120	1340	1417	1510	1722	1722	1920	1921	2009	2113

	⚒	†	⚒		⚒w	†		†	⚒	⚒			
Grosseto d.	0500	0500	0610	0719	0952	1002	...	1322	1336	1500	1632	1755	1945
Buonconvento d.	0555	0559	0719	0817	1059	1105	...	1432	1443	1611	1732	1910	2056
Siena a.	0622	0625	0744	0840	1132	1132	...	1500	1511	1636	1806	1935	2117

TRENTO - BASSANO DEL GRAPPA: *97 km* Journey 120–130 minutes

From **Trento**: 0505⚒‡, 0605, 0705⚒, 0805, 0905‡, 1005⚒‡, 1105, 1205⚒, 1305, 1405⚒, 1505⚒‡, 1505†, 1605⚒, 1705, 1805⚒, 1905‡.

From **Bassano del Grappa**: 0502Ⓐ, 0625⚒‡, 0725‡, 0825⚒, 0925, 1025⑥, 1125⚒, 1125†‡, 1225⚒‡, 1325, 1425⚒‡, 1525, 1625⚒, 1725†, 1825⚒‡, 1925, 2025⚒, 2125.

All services stop at Levico Terme and Borgo Valsugana Centro (*31*/*44 km*, ± 50/65 minutes from Trento, respectively).

VENEZIA - BASSANO DEL GRAPPA:

km		⚒								
0	**Venezia** Santa Lucia d.	0556	0656	0756	...	0856	and	2056	...	2156
9	Venezia Mestre d.	0608	0708	0808	...	0908	hourly	2108	...	2210
45	Castelfranco Veneto d.	0646	0746	0846	...	0946	until	2146	...	2252
64	**Bassano del Grappa** a.	0707	0807	0907	...	1007		2207	...	2313

	⚒								
Bassano del Grappa d.	0523	0623	0723	...	0823	and	2023	...	2123
Castelfranco Veneto d.	0546	0646	0746	...	0846	hourly	2046	...	2146
Venezia Mestre a.	0622	0722	0822	...	0922	until	2122	...	2226
Venezia Santa Lucia a.	0634	0734	0834	...	0934		2134	...	2240

Additional services operate on ⚒.

VERONA PORTA NUOVA - MANTOVA: *37 km* Journey 45–50 minutes

From **Verona** PN: 0630⚒, 0730⚒, 0830⚒, 0930, 1230⚒, 1330, 1430⚒, 1530, 1630⚒, 1730, 1830⚒, 1930, 2030⚒, 2130†.

From **Mantova**: 0628⚒, 0728⚒, 0828, 0928⚒, 1228, 1328⚒, 1428, 1528⚒, 1628, 1728⚒, 1828, 1928⚒, 2028.

MANTOVA - MODENA: *Services operated by TPER on some days*

km		⚒		⚒						⚒			
0	**Mantova** d.	0535	0628	0730	0830	0930	1130	1330	1530	1630	1730	1930	2130
19	Suzzara d.	0554	0654	0756	0856	0956	1156	1356	1556	1656	1756	1956	2156
61	**Modena** a.	0647	0740	0842	0942	1046	1242	1442	1642	1740	1842	2042	2242

	⚒			†	⚒		⚒		⚒				
Modena d.	0603	0707	0907	1107	1207	1307	1407	1507	1607	1707	1907	2007	2207
Suzzara d.	0655	0755	0955	1155	1255	1355	1455	1555	1655	1755	1955	2055	2255
Mantova d.	0716	0816	1016	1216	1316	1416	1516	1616	1716	1816	2016	2116	2316

a – Not Aug. 6 - Sept. 4.
b – Not Aug. 8 - Sept. 4.
c – From Sept. 5.
d – Not July 30 - Aug. 28.
e – Not Aug. 21 - Sept. 11.
f – Not Aug. 22 - Sept. 10.
m – † until Aug. 28; daily from Sept. 12.
n – † until Sept. 11 (not Aug. 28, Sept. 4).
p – From Aug. 20.
q – Ⓐ (also † until Sept. 4).
r – Until Aug. 15.
t – Not Aug. 28 - Sept. 11.
v – Not Sept. 4, 11.
w – From Aug. 1.
x – Not Aug. 29 - Sept. 11.
y – Not Aug. 27 - Sept. 10.
z – Not Sept. 3, 10.

‡ – Operator: *TTE* ✆ contact centre 0461 821000; www.ttesercizio.it
§ – Operator: *TPER*. Trenitalia tickets valid.

Part 1

km		IC 501	FB 9601	FB 8605		IC 651	IC 503		EC 141	IC 505		IC 657	IC 1533		IC 659
		2	◆	2 ⟊	2	2 ⟊	2 y	2	N ◆	2	2	y ◆	◆	2 y	Ⓐ V
0	**Torino** Porta Nuova 615 ..d.	...	...	...	...	0530	0605		0630	...		0730			0820
56	Asti 615 ...d.	...	...	...	...	0607	..		0641	0707		0807			0904
91	Alessandria 615 ...d.	...	...	...	...	0631			0702	0731		0831			0931
112	Novi Ligure ...d.	...	...	...	...	0644			0718	0744		0844			0944
	Milano Centrale ...d.					0610	0625			0710		0725	0810 0810		0910
	Milano Rogoredo ...d.						0638					0738			
	Pavia ...d.					0635	0659		0735			0759	0835 0835		0935
	Voghera 615 ...d.						0714		0751			0814	0851 0851		
	Tortona 615 ...d.					0659	0725					0825			0959
166	**Genova** Piazza Principe ...a.					0735	0744	0803	0818	0835	0840	0912 0933	0944 0944		1034 1042
166	**Genova** Piazza Principe ...d.			0510	0606 0710	0711	0737	0747	0820		0851	0912 0935	0947 0947		1036
169	**Genova** Brignole ...d.		0500 0517u	0615 0717u	0720	0743	0756		0826	0900	0921	0941 0956	0956	1035	1042
194	S. Margherita-Portofino ...d.		0529		0647	0759	0820			0955		1016	1101 1105		
196	Rapallo ...d.		0533		0652 0741	0803	0825		0922	0959		1021 1021	1109		
205	Chiavari ...d.		0541 0546		0701	0811	0834		0931	1007		1030 1030	1117		
212	Sestri Levante ...d.	0505 0550			0710	0820	0842			1030		1038 1038	1124		
235	Levanto ...d.	0522 0614			0730	0844	0901					1100 1100	1148		
240	Monterosso ...d.	0528 0619			0735	0849	0907		2			1107 1107			
249	Riomaggiore ...d.	0631				0901	†								
256	**La Spezia** Centrale ...d.	0443 0544 0644	0616	0707	0750	0816 0909	0913 0923		1006 1017			1123 1123	1213 1215		
272	Sarzana ...d.	0459 0557		0728		0931			1032				1228		
282	Carrara-Avenza ...d.	0507 0606		0738		0939			1040			1141	1236		
289	Massa Centro ...d.	0513 0614	0636	0745	0836	0946 0945			1028 1046			1145 1148	1242		
310	Viareggio ...d.	0530 0628	0648 0806		0848	1011 1000			1041 1109			1200 1209	1259		
331	**Pisa** Centrale 611 ...a.	0551 0644	0704 0827		0904	1038 1017			1056 1139			1217 1223	1322		
	Livorno Centrale 611 ...a.	0701 0720		0920		1035			1119			1235 1240			
	Roma Termini 611 ...a.	1018o 1003		1203					1433						

Part 2

	IC 1535	FB 8613		EC 143	IC 511		IC 665		FB 8619		IC 669	IC 515		EC 159		FB 8623		IC 673
	©V	⟊	2 2 2	N	◆ y	2	y	2	y	⟊ †	2	N	2 ⟊	2	A N	⟊ y	2 2	©S
Torino Porta Nuova 615 ..d.				1030	1040 1130				1230			1330	1405			1520 1530		
Asti 615 ...d.		1107			1113 1207				1307			1407	1443			1600 1607		
Alessandria 615 ...d.		1128			1136 1231				1331			1431	1502			1616 1631		
Novi Ligure ...d.		1141			1244				1344			1444	1516			1644		
Milano Centrale ...d.	0910		1110			1210 1225		1310				1405	1425 1510				1605 1625
Milano Rogoredo ...d.						1238						1416	1438				1616 1638
Pavia ...d.	0935		1135			1235 1259		1335				1435	1459 1535				1635 1659
Voghera 615 ...d.			1151			1314						1451	1514 1551				1651 1714
Tortona 615 ...d.	0959					1259 1325							1525				1725
Genova Piazza Principe ...a.	1042		1230 1242		1221	1335 1344	1418	1434 1455		1534 1544	1550		1610 1642		1654 1734	1744 1819
Genova Piazza Principe ...d.		1210	1232		1224	1337 1347	1420	1436 1510		1536 1547	1553				1710 1736	1747
Genova Brignole ...d.		1217u	1235 1238		1233	1343 1356	1428	1442 1517		1542 1556	1559	1635			1717 1742	1756
S. Margherita-Portofino ...d.			1309			1416						1705				1816
Rapallo ...d.			1314		1304	1421			1541		1621	1709				1821
Chiavari ...d.		1246	1323		1313	1430					1630	1717			1746	1830
Sestri Levante ...d.			1333		1321	1438					1638	1724				1838
Levanto ...d.			1348			1500					1700	1744				1900
Monterosso ...d.						1507		2			1707					1907
Riomaggiore ...d.								2		Ⓐ						
La Spezia Centrale ...d.	1316 1319	1413			1352	1414 1521	1540	1616 1640	1715	1721	1814			1816	1923
Sarzana ...d.		1334				1429	1600		1700 1730							1941
Carrara-Avenza ...d.		1342			1411	1439	1608		1708 1738							
Massa Centro ...d.	1336 1348				1419	1445	1614		1636 1714	1744				1836	1949
Viareggio ...d.	1348 1406				1434	1502	1633		1648 1733	1803				1848	2002
Pisa Centrale 611 ...a.	1404 1427				1447	1526	1651		1704 1751	1825				1904	2017
Livorno Centrale 611 ...a.	1420				1502				1720					1920	2035
Roma Termini 611 ...a.	1703				1803				2003					2203	

Part 3

	IC 675	FB 8627 8629		IC 679	IC 519		IC 521	IC 685		IC 689	ICN 1963			IC 687		ICN 799
	Ⓐ	V	2 2	y	2	2	y	®	2	y V	V k j	2 A	2	y	2	◆
Torino Porta Nuova 615 ..d.				1730	1805		1830 1840			1930				2130 2155		
Asti 615 ...d.				1807	1843		1907 1921			2007				2207 2236		
Alessandria 615 ...d.				1831	1902		1931 1947			2031				2231 2259		
Novi Ligure ...d.				1844	1916		1944			2044				2244		
Milano Centrale ...d.	1625	1705			1805	1825		1905		2000 2010				2025 2110		
Milano Rogoredo ...d.	1638	1716			1816	1838		1916		2012				2038		
Pavia ...d.	1659	1735			1835	1859		1935		2032 2038				2059 2135		
Voghera 615 ...d.	1714	1751			1851	1914		1951		2049 2056				2114 2151		
Tortona 615 ...d.	1725				1902	1925				2108				2125		
Genova Piazza Principe ...a.	1821	1842	1934	1944 1952	2021	2034 2035	2044	2134 2145	2153		2219 2240	2332 2350
Genova Piazza Principe ...d.	1821	1852	1936	1947 1954		2036 2037	2047	2136	2156		2243	2334 2353
Genova Brignole ...d.	1830 1835	1859u 1920	1942	1956 2001	2035	2042 2044	2056	2142	2238 2238		2252 2340	0002
S. Margherita-Portofino ...d.	1905	1954		2016			2105				2321 2319		2315	
Rapallo ...d.	1909	1958		2021		2109	2126			2325 2320		2320		0028
Chiavari ...d.	1917	2006		2030		2117	2135			2334 2334		2329		0038
Sestri Levante ...d.	1924	2016		2038		2124				2345 2346		2341		
Levanto ...d.	1944	2035		2100		2148				0006 0010		2357		
Monterosso ...d.	1949	2041		2107		2153				0011 0016		0003		
Riomaggiore ...d.		2053				2204		2		0026 0036				
La Spezia Centrale ...d.	2013	2003 2101		2123		2213		2223 2226	2309	0035 0048		0018		0127
Sarzana ...d.								2235 2241						
Carrara-Avenza ...d.								2243 2249						
Massa Centro ...d.		2023		2145				2250 2256						
Viareggio ...d.				2200				2303 2317	2343					0216
Pisa Centrale 611 ...a.		2046		2217				2317 2337	2359					0237
Livorno Centrale 611 ...a.				2235				2335	0016					
Roma Termini 611 ...a.		2259							0313o					0549o

◆ — **NOTES** (LISTED BY TRAIN NUMBER)

501 – [train] Sestri Levante - Napoli.
505 – ⟊ [train] Ventimiglia - Genova - Roma.
511 – [train] Torino - Salerno.
657 – Ⓐ: [train] Milano - Livorno - Grosseto.
799 – 1,2 cl., and 2 cl. (4 berth) [train] Torino - Napoli - Salerno.
1533 – ©: [train] Milano - Livorno - Grosseto.
1963 – 1,2 cl., 1,2 cl. (T2) and 2 cl. (4 berth) Milano - Genova - Siracusa;
     1,2 cl. and 2 cl. (4 berth) Milano - Messina (**1965**) - Palermo.

A – To Albenga.
B – Sept. 19, 23, 26, 30, Oct. 1 - 3, Oct. 7 - Dec. 10.
C – Runs on dates not in note **B**.
N – [train] and ⟊ Milano - Genova - Nice / Marseille.
S – To Savona.
V – To Ventimiglia.

j – Until Sept. 18.
k – From Sept. 19.
o – Roma **Ostiense**.
r – Not Sept. 10 - 13, 24 - 27.
s – Stops to set down only.
u – Stops to pick up only.
y – Not Aug. 7.
z – Not Aug. 7, 14.

610 PISA - GENOVA - MILANO and TORINO

km			ICN 796		IC 652	IC 500	IC 656	IC 502					IC 658		ICN 1962	IC 662	IC 504		FB 8602/8604
		2 y	◆	2	y	2※	※V	V	2	Ⓐ	†	Ⓐ		2 jy	◆	k	2	2	2 y
	Roma Termini 611 ....d.		0006o				2※	※V	V							0243o				0605
	Livorno Centrale ....d.		0309t											0524		0543	0624			
	Pisa Centrale ....d.		0326											0542		0600	0642			0828
	Viareggio ....d.													0557		0619	0657			
	Massa Centro ....d.													0612			0709			0851
	Carrara-Avenza ....d.																0716			
	Sarzana ....d.																0724			
	La Spezia Centrale ......d.		0425		0459	0538	0600	0625						0638		0656	0738	0745		0913
	Riomaggiore ....d.						0547	0608												
	Monterosso ....d.					0517	0602	0623						0654						
	Levanto ....d.					0524	0607	0628	0642	0700						0757	0805			
	Sestri Levante ....d.	0432				0540	0634	0659	0659	0716						0814	0820			
	Chiavari ....d.	0443	0512			0552	0644	0708	0708	0724						0824	0830			
	Rapallo ....d.	0451	0521			0601	0655	0717		0733						0833	0838			
	S. Margherita-Portofino ...d.	0455				0607	0659	0721		0739										
	Genova Brignole ....d.	0520	0534	0555	0620	0633	0657	0750	0756	0757	0745	0809	0815	0822	0833	0909	0915	1013s	1020	
	Genova Piazza Principe ..a.	0528	0542	0601	0628	0641	0703	0756	0802	0803	0751	0815	0821	0828	0839	0915		1021	1028	
0	**Genova** Piazza Principe ..d.	0528	0542	0606	0628	0644	0708	0721	0750	0808		0818	0823	0830	0842	0918	0924	0930		1030
72	Tortona 615 ....d.		0632						0832				0859			0924				
89	Voghera 615 ....d.		0643				0734		0808	0843			0911			0937	1008			
115	Pavia ....d.		0701				0751		0825	0901			0927			1000	1025			
144	Milano Rogoredo ....a.		0720				0810		0848	0920										
154	**Milano** Centrale ....a.		0735				0823		0900	0945			0955			1045	1055			
	Novi Ligure ....d.	0614				0714	0741			0841			0914	0914				1014		1114
	Alessandria 615 ....d.	0631	0657			0731	0757			0857			0931	0931			1010	1031		1131
	Asti 615 ....d.	0654	0723			0754	0818			0918			0954	0954			1029	1054		1154
	Torino Porta Nuova 615 ..a.	0730	0810			0830	0855			0955			1030	1030			1110	1130		1230

		EC 140	FB 8606	IC 666	IC 746		IC 670	IC 1540		IC 510		IC 674		IC 512	FB 8616	EC
		2	Ⓨ N	Ⓨ	2	y	V y	2	2	Ⓐ	2	y †V	2	◆ ©ⒶⒶS	2	† 2※	y
	Roma Termini 611 ....d.		0657			y			1124		0957				1157
	Livorno Centrale ....d.		0940					1124		1245		1324	1419		1440
	Pisa Centrale ....d.		0956				1105	1142		1302		1342	1435		1456
	Viareggio ....d.		1012				1122	1200		1317		1402	1454		1512
	Massa Centro ....d.		1025				1143	1212		1330		1414	1512		1525
	Carrara-Avenza ....d.						1149	1219		1339			1518		
	Sarzana ....d.						1157						1531		
	La Spezia Centrale ......d.		1046	1035	1145		1220	1238	1345	1405		1438	1550		1546
	Riomaggiore ....d.							1353							
	Monterosso ....d.			1055			1255					1455			
	Levanto ....d.			1102		1207	1302		1407			1502			
	Sestri Levante ....d.	0955		1124		1221	1324		1421	1443		1524			
	Chiavari ....d.	1006	1116	1132		1230	1332		1430	1451		1532			
	Rapallo ....d.	1017		1141		1240	1341		1440	1500		1541		1622	
	S. Margherita-Portofino ...d.	1021				1244			1452			1546	2 y		
	Genova Brignole ....d.	1108	1145	1209	1220	1320	1325	1335	©	1409	1417	1525	1530	1609	1620	1640	1645
	Genova Piazza Principe ..a.	1114	1150	1215	1228	1328	1343 Ⓐ	1415	1425	1536		1628	1646	1650
	Genova Piazza Principe ..d.		1123	1159	1218	1228	1322	1328	1343	1342	1418	1425	1520	1539	1541	1542	1618	1630	1649	1723
	Tortona 615 ....d.							1432	1432				1632	1632	1700
	Voghera 615 ....d.		1208		1308	1408		1443	1443	1508	1608		1643	1643	1700		1810
	Pavia ....d.		1225		1325	1425		1501	1501	1525	1625		1701	1701	1725		1826
	Milano Rogoredo ....a.							1520	1520				1720	1720	
	Milano Centrale ....a.		1250		1350	1450		1535	1535	1550	1650		1735	1735	1750		1850
	Novi Ligure ....d.				1314	1414				1514			1714	1722	
	Alessandria 615 ....d.			1244	1331	1431				1531		1636	1731	1736	
	Asti 615 ....d.			1302	1354	1454				1554		1700	1754	1800	
	Torino Porta Nuova 615 ..a.			1340	1430	1530				1630		1740	1830	1840	

		IC 680	FB 8620	IC 682	IC 1538		IC 1534	IC 684		EC 148	IC 518		FB 8626	FB 8630		IC 522
		2	2 y	Ⓐ	Ⓨ	2 y	ⒶV ©V	◆	2	Ⓨ N	2		2	2	©	2	y
	Roma Termini 611 ....d.		y	Ⓐ	Ⓨ	1357					1557	1657	1827		1941o
	Livorno Centrale ....d.					1640		1718	1724		1846	1940	2107		2236
	Pisa Centrale ....d.		1505			1656		1736	1742	1834	1903	1956	2042	2123	2253
	Viareggio ....d.		1521			1712		1753	1800	1856	1919	2012	2102	2140	2310
	Massa Centro ....d.		1543			1725		1814	1814	1913	1932	2025	2119	2154	2323
	Carrara-Avenza ....d.		1549					1821	1919			2130		2331
	Sarzana ....d.		1557					1926			2143		2340
	La Spezia Centrale ......d.		1545	1621	1638	1746		1745	1838	1838	1947	1945	1953	2046	2158	2216	2150	2310	0008
	Riomaggiore ....d.		1553				1753			1953			2158	2319
	Monterosso ....d.		1601		1655			1855	1855	2001			2206	2335	0024
	Levanto ....d.		1607		1702		1807	1902	1902	2007			2212	2340	0031
	Sestri Levante ....d.		1621		1724		1821	1924	1924	2021			2226	0005	0049
	Chiavari ....d.		1630		1732	1816	1830	1932	1932	2038	2033		2246	2233	0014
	Rapallo ....d.		1640		1741	1824	1841	1941	1941	2	2047	2042	2122	2241	0025
	S. Margherita-Portofino ...d.				1746		1844	1946	1946	y	2051		2245	0029
	Genova Brignole ....d.	1720	1725	A	1809	1845	1820	1925	2009	2009	2020	2125	2126	2120	2145	Ⓑz	2315	2328	0123
	Genova Piazza Principe ..a.	1728	©	1815	1850	1828	2015	2015	2028	2132	2128	2150	A	2320
	Genova Piazza Principe ..d.	1728	1740	1740	1818	1852	1828	1922	1922	2018	2018	2028	2122	2128	2146
	Tortona 615 ....d.		1832	1832	1900		2000	2000			2232
	Voghera 615 ....d.		1843	1843			2108	2108		2208	2243
	Pavia ....d.		1901	1901	1925	2006	2025	2025	2125	2125	2225	2301
	Milano Rogoredo ....a.		1920	1920	1943						2320
	Milano Centrale ....a.		1937	1937	2000	2035	2050	2050	2150	2150	2250	2340
	Novi Ligure ....d.	1814			1914				2114			2214
	Alessandria 615 ....d.	1831			1931				2131			2231
	Asti 615 ....d.	1854			1954				2154			2254
	Torino Porta Nuova 615 ..a.	1930			2030				2230			2340

NOTES (LISTED BY TRAIN NUMBER)

510 – ⛌ Salerno - Torino.
518 – ⛌ Roma - Genova - Ventimiglia.
522 – ⛌ Napoli - Sestri Levante.
684 – Ⓐ: ⛌ Grosseto - Livorno - Milano.
796 – ⇌1,2 cl., ⇌2 cl.(4 berth) and ⛌ Salerno - Napoli - Torino.
1534 – ©: ⛌ Grosseto - Livorno - Milano.
1962 – ⇌1,2 cl., ⇌1,2 cl.(T2) and ⇌2 cl.(4 berth) Siracusa - Genova - Milano; ⇌1,2 cl. and ⇌2 cl.(4 berth) Palermo (**1964**) - Messina - Milano.

A – From Albenga.
B – Sept. 19, 23, 26, 30, Oct. 1 - 3, Oct. 7 - Dec. 10.
N – ⛌ and Ⓨ Marseille/Nice - Genova - Milano.
S – From Savona.
V – From Ventimiglia.

j – Until Sept. 18.
k – From Sept. 19.
o – Roma Ostiense.
r – Not ①⑤⑥⑦ Oct. 1 - Nov. 6.
s – Stops to set down only.
t – Not ② from Nov. 8.
y – Not Aug. 7.
z – Not Aug. 14.

PISA - ROMA 611

km		ICN 1963 ♦	ICN 799 ♦	2 ⚒	2 ⚒		IC 501 ♦	FB 8601 🍷		FB 8605 🍷	IC 505 ♦		IC 1533 ♦	IC 657 ♦		FB 8613 🍷		IC 511 ♦	2		FB 8619 🍷		FB 8623 🍷	2	2 Ⓑz
	Torino P N **610** d.	...	2155	...	...	...	...	...	...	...	...	...	...	...	...	...	...	1040	...	...	...	...	1520	...	...
	Milano Centrale **610** d.	2010	|	...	...	...	...	...	...	...	...	...	0810	0810	...	...	...	|	...	...	1310	...	|	...	...
	Genova P P **610** d.	2156	2353	...	...	...	...	0510	...	0710	0851	...	0947	0947	...	1210	...	1224	...	...	1510	...	1710	...	...
0	**Pisa** Centrale **610** d.	0002	0221	...	...	0545	0647	0707	0745	0907	1106	1145	1226	1220	...	1407	1343	1450	...	1545	1707	1745	1907	1945	2150
20	**Livorno** Centrale d.	0019	0240	...	...	0603	0703	0722	0803	0922	1121	1203	1255	1255	...	1422	1400	1504	...	1603	1722	1803	1922	2003	2209
43	Rosignano d.	|	|	...	...	0620	|	|	0820	|	|	1220	|	|	...	|	1416	|	...	1620	|	1820	|	2020	2230
54	Cecina d.	|	|	...	...	0629	0728	|	0829	|	1144	1229	1323	1326	...	|	1424	|	...	1629	|	1829	|	2029	2238
89	Campiglia Marittima d.	|	|	...	...	0650	0747	0757	0851	0957	|	1251	1341	1350	...	1457	1452	1540	...	1651	1757	1851	1957	2051	2306
106	Follonica d.	|	|	...	...	0700	0758	|	0902	|	1207	1302	1352	1401	...	|	1503	1552	...	1702	|	1902	|	2102	2318
148	Grosseto d.	|	0357	0419	0523	0728	0819	0824	0930	1024	1230	1330	1425	1433	...	1524	1530	1614	1629	1730	1824	1930	2024	2130	2343
186	Orbetello-Monte Argentario d.	|	|	0444	0549	0751	0838	|	0953	|	|	1353	...	...	...	|	1553	|	1655	1753	|	1953	|	2153	...
225	Tarquinia d.	|	|	0518	0622	0827	|	|	1029	|	|	1429	...	...	...	|	1629	|	1729	1829	|	2029	|	2229	...
255	**Civitavecchia** d.	|	0500	0532	0636	0842	0924	0916	1044	1116	1323	1444	...	...	...	1616	1644	1708	1743	1844	1916	2044	2116	2244	...
264	S. Marinella d.	|	|	0539	0643	0849	|	|	1051	|	|	1451	...	...	...	|	1651	|	1750	1851	|	2051	|	2251	...
286	Ladispoli-Cerveteri d.	|	|	0555	0700	0905	|	|	1105	|	|	1505	...	...	...	|	1705	|	1805	1905	|	2105	|	2305	...
329	**Roma** Ostiense a.	0313	0549	0633	0739	0936	1018	|	1139	|	1420	1536	...	...	...	|	1736	1752	1838	1936	|	2136	|	2336	...
336	**Roma** Termini **640** a.	...	|	0648	0750	0948	|	1003	1150	1203	1433	1548	...	...	...	1703	1747	1803	1848	1948	2003	2148	2203	2348	...
	Napoli Centrale **640** a.	...	0817	...	...	...	1229	...	...	...	...	...	...	...	...	...	...	2029	...	...	...	...	...	...	...

	ICN 796 ♦	ICN 1962 ♦	2 ⚒	2 †	2	FB 8606 🍷	IC 510 ♦		FB 8616 🍷		FB 9774 🍷		IC 1534 Ⓒ	IC 684 Ⓐ		IC 518 ♦		FB 8626 🍷	FB 8630 🍷		IC 522 ♦		2	2 †	
Napoli Centrale **640** d.	2146	...	...	...	...	...	0731	...	...	...	...	...	...	...	...	...	...	...	...	...	1731	...	...	...	...
Roma Termini **640** d.	|	...	...	...	0612	0657	0957	1012	1157	1212	1357	...	...	...	1412	1557	1612	1657	1827	1812	|	2012	2112	2212	...
Roma Ostiense d.	0006	0243	...	...	0623	|	1007	1023	|	1223	|	...	...	...	1423	1607	1623	|	|	1823	1941	2023	2121	2223	...
Ladispoli-Cerveteri d.	|	|	...	...	0651	|	|	1051	|	1251	|	...	...	...	1451	|	1651	|	|	1855	|	2051	2155	2300	...
S. Marinella d.	|	|	...	...	0706	|	|	1107	|	1307	|	...	...	...	1506	|	1706	|	|	1910	|	2106	2211	2315	...
Civitavecchia d.	0053	|	...	...	0715	0746	1047	1115	1246	1315	1446	...	...	...	1515	1647	1715	1746	1916	1924	2023	2115	2220	2324	...
Tarquinia d.	|	|	...	...	0729	|	|	1129	|	1328	|	...	...	...	1528	|	1728	|	|	1937	|	2128	2233	2336	...
Orbetello-Monte Argentario d.	|	|	0602	...	0801	|	|	1202	|	1400	|	...	...	...	1600	|	1800	|	|	2009	2102	2200	2306	0009	...
Grosseto d.	0153	0431	0628	0647	0826	0839	1139	1227	1339	1427	1539	...	1604	1610	1625	1739	1825	1839	2007	2033	2121	2227	2330	0034	...
Follonica d.	|	|	0652	0710	0859	|	1158	1254	|	1453	|	...	1624	1631	1653	1759	1857	|	|	2057	2141	2253	...	...	...
Campiglia Marittima d.	|	|	0704	0722	0908	0905	1209	1305	1405	1504	1605	...	1636	1642	1704	|	1906	1905	2032	2108	2151	2304	...	...	...
Cecina d.	|	|	0729	0746	0930	|	|	1327	|	1527	|	...	1655	1700	1727	1823	1928	|	|	2128	2210	2327	...	...	...
Rosignano d.	|	|	0737	0754	0939	|	|	1336	|	1536	|	...	|	|	1736	|	1936	|	|	2136	|	2336	...	...	...
Livorno Centrale d.	0309	0540	0755	0812	1001	0940	1245	1358	1440	1558	1640	...	1718	1724	1758	1846	1958	1940	2107	2158	2236	2358	...	...	...
Pisa Centrale **610** a.	0323	0557	0811	0829	1018	0953	1259	1415	1453	1615	1653	...	1733	1739	1815	1900	2015	1953	2120	2215	2250	0015	...	...	...
Genova P P **610** a.	0601	0839	...	...	...	1150	1536	...	1650	...	1850	...	2015	2015	...	2132	...	2150	2320	...	...	...	...	...	...
Milano Centrale **610** a.	|	1045	...	...	...	|	|	...	...	...	2035	...	2150	2150	...	...	...	...	...	...	...	...	...	...	...
Torino P N **610** a.	0810	...	...	...	...	1340	1740	...	...	...	...	...	...	...	...	...	...	...	...	...	...	...	...	...	...

♦ – **NOTES** (LISTED BY TRAIN NUMBER)

501 – 12 Sestri Levante - Napoli.
505 – ⚒: 12 Ventimiglia - Genova - Roma.
510 – 12 Salerno - Torino.
511 – 12 Torino - Salerno.
518 – 12 Roma - Genova - Ventimiglia.
522 – 12 Napoli - Sestri Levante.
657 – Ⓐ: 12 Milano - Livorno - Grosseto.
684 – Ⓐ: 12 Grosseto - Livorno - Milano.
796 – 1,2 cl., 2 cl. (4 berth) and 2 Salerno - Napoli - Torino.
799 – 1,2 cl., 2 cl. (4 berth) and 2 Torino - Napoli - Salerno.
1533 – Ⓒ: 12 Milano - Livorno - Grosseto.
1534 – Ⓒ: 12 Grosseto - Livorno - Milano.
1962 – 1,2 cl., 1,2 cl. (T2) and 2 cl. (4 berth) Siracusa - Genova - Milano; 1,2 cl. and 2 cl. (4 berth) Palermo (**1964**) - Messina - Milano.
1963 – 1,2 cl., 1,2 cl. (T2) and 2 cl. (4 berth) Milano - Genova - Siracusa; 1,2 cl. and 2 cl. (4 berth) Milano - Messina (**1965**) - Palermo.

f – Not Sept. 10 - 13, 24 - 27.
j – Until Sept. 18.
k – From Sept. 19.
r – Departs 2156 on Sept. 19, 23, 26, 30, Oct. 1 - 3, Oct. 7 - Dec. 10.
s – Stops to set down only.
u – Stops to pick up only.
y – Not Aug. 7.
z – Not Aug. 14.

PARMA and FIDENZA - SARZANA and LA SPEZIA 612

Most services 2nd class only

km		⚒						B		⚒	r	⚒		⚒	r	⚒		r				⚒	⑤n		⚒r	⚒r	†
	Milano Centrale d.	...	...	...	...	...	0645j	...	...	...	...	...	...	...	...	...	...	...	...	...	1705	...	1857g	...	...	...	...
0	**Parma** d.	...	...	0517j	0625j	0748j	|	...	...	1228r	1256	...	1344r	...	1442	...	1549r	1645	...	1747r	|	1947r	|	2057t	2140	2240	2240f
*	**Fidenza** d.	...	...	|	|	|	0824j	0913j	...	|	|	...	|	...	|	...	|	|	...	|	1830t	|	2030	|	|	|	|
23	Fornovo d.	...	...	0534j	0648j	0813j	0843j	0930j	...	1249r	1322	...	1407r	...	1506	...	1612r	1708	...	1812r	1851t	2014r	2047	2124t	2208	2309	2310f
61	Borgo Val di Taro d.	...	0544j	0605j	0725j	0846j	0931j	0959j	...	1322r	1359	...	1444r	...	1549	...	1644r	1747	...	1848r	1936t	2045r	2135	2157t	2240	2342	2343f
79	Pontremoli d.	0545	0601	0627	0743	0903	0953	1018	1216	1342	1416	1421	1503	1542	1607	1621	1700	1803	1822	1903	1957	2101	2152	2213	2255	2357	2359
100	Aulla Lunigiana d.	0608	0623	0657	0813	0922	1021	1035	1238	1410	...	1443	1522	1610	...	1643	1721	...	1843	1922	2027	2121	2211	2231	...	...	0019
108	S. Stefano di Magra d.	0615	0631	0704	0820	0930	1028	1042	1246	1416	...	1451	1531	1616	...	1651	1729	...	1851	1929	2034	2130	2219	2238	...	...	0026
116	**Sarzana** a.	|	0638	|	|	|	1042	1056	1255	|	...	1459	|	|	...	1659	|	...	1900	|	2042	|	2227	|	...	...	|
	Pisa C **611** a.	|	0736	|	|	|	1145	1200	1345	|	...	1551	|	|	...	1751	|	...	1951	|	2138	|	2322	|	...	...	|
	Livorno **611** a.	|	...	|	|	|	...	...	...	|	...	...	|	|	...	...	|	...	...	|	2155	|	2340	|	...	...	|
120	**La Spezia** Centrale a.	0631	...	0722	0838	0946	...	...	...	1432	...	...	1550	1633	...	...	1746	...	...	1947	...	2148	...	2256	...	...	0042

	j	⚒j			⚒	⚒			⚒r			⚒	r	⚒		⚒	⚒r	⚒	⑦h		B	⚒				G	
La Spezia Centrale d.	...	...	0615	...	0810	0927	1012	1226	...	1325	1419	...	...	1527	1610	...	...	1729	...	1809	...	1927	...	2011	...	2103	...
Livorno **611** d.	...	...	|	0552	|	|	|	|	...	|	|	...	...	|	|	...	...	|	1703	|	...	|	...	|	...	|	...
Pisa C **611** a.	...	...	|	0610	|	|	|	|	...	|	|	1405	...	|	|	1605	...	|	1720	|	1822	|	1909	|	2006	|	...
Sarzana d.	...	...	|	0701	|	|	|	|	...	|	|	1457	...	|	|	1657	...	|	1807	|	1915	|	1959	|	2058	|	...
S. Stefano di Magra d.	...	...	0631	0711	0829	0945	1030	1242	...	1343	1436	1509	...	1544	1629	1712	...	1747	1815	1828	1926	1943	2015	2029	2109	2118	...
Aulla Lunigiana d.	...	...	0638	0718	0838	0952	1038	1249	...	1351	1443	1516	...	1551	1637	1718	...	1754	1823	1836	1932	1950	2025	2038	2116	2126	...
Pontremoli d.	0413	0556	0658	0740	0858	1015	1058	1308	1351	1413	1501	1539	1550	1612	1656	1739	1750	1820	1844	1858	1952	2015	2042	2057	2139	2148	...
Borgo Val di Taro d.	0429	0613	0714j	0800j	0914j	...	1114r	1323r	1407	...	1516r	...	1607	...	1711r	...	1807	...	1859	1914t	2008t	...	2057t	2114r	...	2205t	...
Fornovo d.	0504	0649	0744j	0843j	0953j	...	1147r	1402r	1446	...	1550r	...	1644	...	1746r	...	1847	...	1936	1946t	2047t	...	2131t	2148r	...	2241t	...
Fidenza a.	|	|	|	0903j	|	...	|	|	|	...	|	...	|	...	|	...	|	...	2000	|	2103t	...	2156t	|	...	|	...
Parma a.	0530	0710	0805j	|	1013j	...	1206r	1428r	1510	...	1613r	...	1710	...	1804r	...	1917	...	|	2004t	...	...	|	2209r	...	2305t	...
Milano Centrale a.	...	...	...	1020j	...	...	...	...	...	...	...	...	...	...	...	...	...	...	2133g	...	...	...	2320t	...	...	...	...

B – 2 Bergamo - Pisa and v.v.
G – 2 Genova - La Spezia - Parma.

f – Not Aug. 14, 15.
g – Milano **Porta Garibaldi**.
h – Not Aug. 14, 21.
j – Not Aug. 12 - 21.

n – Not Aug. 12, 19.
r – Not Aug. 11 - 21.
t – Not Aug. 11 - 20.

* – Fidenza - Fornovo is *25 km*.

613 — FIRENZE - SIENA, PISA, PISA AEROPORTO + and LIVORNO
Most services 2nd class only

FB 8603

km																								
0	Firenze SMN 614....d.	0430	0535		0620	0653	0700			0733	0738c	0753	0810	0828	0910	0928	0953	1010	1028	1053	1100	1110	1128	...
34	Empoli....d.	0506	0601	0621	0650	0730	0722	0726		0806	0808		0827	0840	0858	0940	0958	1027	1040	1058	1127		1140	1157 1208
	Poggibonsi ▲....d.			0702	0724j			0811		0848				0915		1015			1115			1215		1249
81	Siena 609 619....a.			0731	0747j			0840		0915				0938		1038			1138			1238		1314
	Pisa Centrale 614....d.	0555	0637			0809	0752			0852	0826	0903		0932		1032	1103		1132	1203	1153		1227	...
101	Livorno Centrale....a.	0616	0651			0824	0808							0948		1048			1148		1208		1244	

km																						
0	Firenze SMN 614....d.	1138	1210	1228	1253	1300	1310	1328	1338	1353	1410	1428	1453	1500	1510	1528	1538	1546	1610	1628	...
38	Empoli....d.	1213	1240	1258	1308	1327	1340	1358	1408	1413	1427	1440	1458	1508	1527	1540	1558	1608	1613	1626	1640 1658 1708
	Poggibonsi ▲....d.			1315		1349		1415	1449			1514	1549		1615		1649		1715		1749
63	Siena 609 619....a.			1338		1414		1438	1517			1537	1614		1638		1714		1738		1814
	Pisa Centrale 614....d.	1259		1332		1403	1401		1432		1529	1503		1532		1603	1553		1632		1659 1703	1732
	Livorno Centrale....a.			1348		1416			1448		1526			1548		1612			1648		1748

Firenze SMN 614....d.	1653	1700	1710	1728	1738	1753	1810	1828	1853	1900	1910	1928	1953	2010	2028	2038	2053	2128	2157	2307
Empoli....d.	1727		1740	1758	1813	1827	1840	1858	1927		1940	1958	2008	2027	2040	2058	2108	2113	2127	2158	2208 2233 2343
Poggibonsi ▲....d.			1815			1915					2015	2049	2115		2152			2250
Siena 609 619....a.			1838			1938					2038		2114		2144		2216		2314
Pisa Centrale 614....d.	1803	1753		1832	1858	1904		1932	2003	1949		2032		2103		2128		2158	2205 2232j	2327 0035
Livorno Centrale....a.		1808		1846	1912			1948				2048						2224 2248j	2344 0050

Livorno Centrale....d.		0500	0519		0610			0710			0730	0740		0812		0852		0912	0912		1012	...
Pisa Centrale 614....d.	0415	0519	0539		0629			0732	0732		0754	0801		0832		0912		0932	0932		1032 1054
Siena 609 619....d.				0543		0625	0636	0636		0702	0715		0732		0818		0847		0918	
Poggibonsi ▲....d.				0606		0658	0659			0728	0745		0805		0846		0909		0946	
Empoli....d.	0453	0602	0618	0645	0659	0709	0735	0750	0804	0804	0820	0832	0847	0852	0904	0921	0940	1004	1017	1021	1104 1132
Firenze SMN 614....a.	0527	0638	0652	0721	0727	0734	0802	0827	0832	0832	0855	0855	0907	0922	0932	0950	1000	1005	1032	1046	1050 1132 1207

Livorno Centrale....d.			1112			1212			1252	1312		1343	1409		1452	1512		1540	1608		1652
Pisa Centrale 614....d.	1112		1132		1154		1232		1254	1312	1332		1354	1401	1432		1454	1512	1532	1601	1632	1654 1712
Siena 609 619....d.		1041	1118		1141		1218			1318			1418			1518		1618	
Poggibonsi ▲....d.		1112	1146		1212		1246			1346			1446			1546		1646	
Empoli....d.		1152	1204	1221	1232	1252	1304	1321	1332		1404	1421	1432	1447	1504	1521	1532		1604	1621	1647 1704	1721 1732 1737
Firenze SMN 614....a.	1200		1232	1250	1307		1332	1350	1407	1400	1432	1450	1507	1524	1532	1550	1607	1600	1632	1650	1724 1732	1750 1807 1801

FB 8628

		Ⓑ	⑥	Ⓑ									Ⓐ				
Livorno Centrale....d.	1712					1812		1852				2012			2112	
Pisa Centrale 614....d.	1732	1754	1754	1801		1832		1854	1912		1932		2001	2032	2048	2101	2132	2230
Siena 609 619....d.	1719			1741	1818		1841	1847		1918	1941		2018		2126
Poggibonsi ▲....d.	1746			1812	1846		1912	1912		1946	2012		2046		2150
Empoli....d.	1804	1821	1832	1836	1847	1852	1904	1921	1932		1952	1952	2004	2021	2047	2052	2104	2121 2147 2204 2221 2315
Firenze SMN 614....a.	1832	1850	1907	1915	1922		1932	1950	2007	2000		2032		2050	2121	2132 2140c	2150 2222 2232 2253 2350

c – Firenze **Campo di Marte**.
j – 5–7 minutes later on ☆.
r – Arrive 0821 Oct. 9 - Nov. 5.

▲ – Poggibonsi-S. Gimignano.

614 — FIRENZE - LUCCA - VIAREGGIO and PISA
Most services 2nd class only

km																			
0	Firenze SMN 613....d.		0510			0603		0710			0738	0810		0910		1010		1210	and at	1610
17	Prato Centrale....d.		0533			0623		0729			0759	0831		0931		1031		1231	the same	1631
34	Pistoia....d.		0551			0640		0745			0816	0844		0944		1044		1244	minutes	1644
47	Montecatini Centro....d.		0604			0658		0801			0832	0901		1001		1101		1301	past each	1701
78	Lucca....a.	0537	0646	0652	0708	0755		0830	0842	0850	0923	0930	0942	1030	1042	1130	1242	1312	1330 1342	hour	1730 1742
101	Viareggio....a.		0707j					0850j				0950j		1053j		1150j		1350j	until	1750j
	Pisa Centrale 613....a.	0602		0716	0741	0825			0913	0916			1013		1109		1313	1343	1413		1813

Firenze SMN 613....d.	1710		1810		1910		2010		2110	2210
Prato Centrale....d.	1731		1831		1931		2031		2131	2231
Pistoia....d.	1744		1844		1944		2044		2144	2246
Montecatini Centro....d.	1801		1901		2001		2101		2200	2301
Lucca....a.	1830	1842	1912	1930	1942	2030	2042	2130	2142	2249 2330
Viareggio....a.	1850j		1950j		2050j		2150j		2309j	2350j
Pisa Centrale 613....a.		1913	1943		2014		2113		2213

Pisa Centrale 613....d.			0613			0702	
Viareggio....d.	0545j		0628j	0710j			
Lucca....d.	0505	0609	0639	0648	0727	0736	0740
Montecatini Centro....d.	0533	0641		0715	0753		0821
Pistoia....d.	0551	0708		0732	0812		0841
Prato Centrale....d.	0611	0727		0747	0827		0900
Firenze SMN 613....a.	0637	0750		0806	0850		0922

km																				
0	Pisa Centrale 613....d.	0749		0850		0950		1020			1250		1342		1450	and at	1950		2050	2150
	Viareggio....d.		0810j		0910j		1010j		1207j		1310j		1410j		1510j	the same		2010j		2110j	2210j
24	Lucca....d.	0823	0831	0920	0931	1017	1031	1047	1231	1317	1331	1412	1431	1517	1531	minutes	2017	2031	2117	2131 2217 2231
	Montecatini Centro....d.		0857		0957		1057		1257		1357		1457		1557	past each		2057		2157	2257
	Pistoia....d.		0912		1012		1112		1312		1412		1512		1612	hour		2112		2212	2312
	Prato Centrale....d.		0929		1030		1128		1329		1430		1529		1629	until		2129		2229	2329
	Firenze SMN 613....a.		0950		1100		1150		1350		1450		1550		1650			2150		2250	2350

j – Not Nov. 7 - Dec. 3.

☑ – Additional services operate Lucca - Pisa Centrale and v.v. on ☆.

MILANO and TORINO - BOLOGNA — 615

For high-speed services – see Table 600.

Block 1 — Milano/Torino → Bologna

Trains: FR 9507 (⚏), IC 583 (A), P, IC 1589 (N), R, 2n, ◆, IC 605 (T), IC 8803 (⚏C), 2, A, A, FB 8807 (⚏C), IC 1545 (◆), A, FB 8809 (⚏T), FB 8811 (⚏C)

km	Station	Times
0	Milano Centrale d.	0515 0542 … 0620 0650 … 0645 0645 … 0705 0715 0735 … 0920 … 1000 1035 1120 1135
10	Milano Rogoredo d.	0527 … 0702 … 0700 0656u … 0717 0727 … 0932 … 1012u … 1132	
	Torino PN 610 d.	… 0832
	Asti 610 d.	… 0908
	Alessandria 610 d.	… 0924
	Tortona 610 d.	…
	Voghera 610 d.	… 0700 … 0804 …
72	Piacenza d.	0609 0624 0652 0715 0740 0752 0759 0734 … 0810 0814 0820 … 0844 0852 0952 1014 1020 ← 1048 1052 1120 1214 1220 ←
107	Fidenza d.	0632 … 0715 0739 0758 0815 0821 0809 … 0827 0841 … 0843 … 0915 1015 1041 … 1043 1105 1115 … 1241 … 1243
129	Parma d.	0646 0654 0730 0754 0811 0830 … 0823 … 0840 → 0846 0856 … 0930 1030 → 1046 1056 1121 1130 1146 → 1246 1256
157	Reggio Emilia d.	0704 0712 0747 0810 0830 0847 … 0839 … 0855 … 0900 0914 … 0947 1047 … 1100 1114 1138 1147 1200 … 1300 1314
182	Modena d.	0721 0730 0801 0826 0848 0901 … 0856 … 0915 0932 … 1001 1101 … 1115 1132 1153 1201 1215 … 1315 1332
219	Bologna Centrale 620 a.	0802 0752 0828 0902 0914 0928 … 0933 … 0954 1008 … 1028 1138 … 1138 1208 1219 1228 1238 … 1338 1408
	Roma Termini 620 a.	… 1010 … 1317t … 1311t

Block 2

Trains: FB 8813 (A ⚏C‡ R), FB (⚏C), IC 597 (A N A), IC 613 (E ⚏B), FB 8819 (A), ICN 795 (◆), 2 A R, FB 8823 (2m ⚏E), IC 599 (◆ 2 A), FB 8825 (⚏A)

Station	Times
Milano Centrale d.	1235 … 1320 1335 … 1450 … 1520 1510 1535 … 1544g … 1705 1720 1735 … 1740 … 1815 1835
Milano Rogoredo d.	… 1332 … 1501 1532 1522 … … 1717 1732 … 1800 … 1827
Torino PN 610 d.	…
Asti 610 d.	…
Alessandria 610 d.	…
Tortona 610 d.	…
Voghera 610 d.	… 1607 … 1807
Piacenza d.	1252 1320 1346 1414 1420 ← 1452 1545 1552 1614 1610 1620 … 1630 1647 1652 1752 1805 1814 1820 … 1845 1847 1852 1909 1922
Fidenza d.	1315 … 1415 1441 … 1443 1515 1603 1615 1641 1627 … 1643 … 1715 1815 1826 1841 … 1843 1903 … 1915 1931
Parma d.	1330 1346 1430 → 1446 1456 1530 1616 1630 → 1640 1646 1656 1705 … 1730 1830 → 1856 1916 … 1930 → 1948
Reggio Emilia d.	1347 1400 1447 … 1500 1514 1547 1633 1647 … 1655 1700 1714 1722 … 1747 1847 … 1900 1914 1933 … 1947 … 2002
Modena d.	1401 1415 1501 … 1515 1532 1601 1651 1701 … 1724 1715 1732 1741 … 1801 1901 … 1915 1932 1950 … 2001 … 2017
Bologna Centrale 620 a.	1428 1438 1528 … 1538 1608 1628 1714 1728 … 1746 1738 1808 … 1828 1928 … 1938 2008 2014 … 2028 … 2038
Roma Termini 620 a.	… 2112t … 2311t

Block 3 (left)

Trains: Rx, 2 ⑤y, FB 8829 (⚏A), ICN 765 (◆), ICN 755 (◆), 2, 757 (◆ 2), § 797 (2 ◆)

Station	Times
Milano Centrale d.	… 1857g 1920 1935 1950 … 2050 … 2120 … 2215 2317g
Milano Rogoredo d.	… 1918 1932 … … 2132 … 2228
Torino PN 610 d.	… 2020
Asti 610 d.	… 2101
Alessandria 610 d.	… 2122
Tortona 610 d.	1850 … 2139
Voghera 610 d.	1903 … 2007 … 2153
Piacenza d.	← 1952 2006 2014 2020 … 2052 2135 2152 2214 2230 2305 0011
Fidenza d.	1933 2015 2028 2043 … 2115 … 2215 2242
Parma d.	1956 2030 … 2056 2046 … 2130 2206 2230 2257 … 2332 0101
Reggio Emilia d.	2016 2047 … 2114 2100 … 2147 2224 2247 … 2347
Modena d.	2034 2101 … 2134 2115 … 2201 2240 2301 … 0001
Bologna Centrale 620 a.	2108 2128 … 2208 2138 2155 2230 2305 2328 … 2347 0030
Roma Termini 620 a.	… 0717t

Block 3 (right) — Bologna → Milano/Torino

Trains: ICN 1580 (◆), ICN 798 (◆), ICN 758 (◆), ICN 752 (◆)

Station	Times
Roma Termini 620 d.	… 2315t
Bologna Centrale 620 d.	0357 … 0432 0500 … 0528 0552 0620
Modena d.	… 0524 … 0555 0625 0645
Reggio Emilia d.	… 0538 … 0610 0642 0702
Parma d.	… 0521 … 0553 0610 0627 0705 0724
Fidenza d.	… 0607 0624 0639 0726
Piacenza d.	0516 0602 … 0638 0650 0706 0755 0816
Voghera 610 d.	0552 … 0718
Tortona 610 d.	0604
Alessandria 610 d.	0624
Asti 610 d.	0646
Torino PN 610 a.	0740
Milano Rogoredo a.	… 0733 0746 0838
Milano Centrale a.	… 0711g 0712 … 0745 0800 0850 0930

Block 4 — Bologna → Milano/Torino

Trains: § FB 8802 (2), ICN 754 (2 ⚏A A), FB 8804 (◆ 2n), FB 8806 (⚏A A A), IC 580 (⚏E A 2), IC 604/8810 (A E ⚏B A), ICN 794 (2), FB 8814 (R 2 ⚏C A), A

Station	Times
Roma Termini 620 d.	… 0639t
Bologna Centrale 620 d.	0700 0705 0728 0734 … 0752 0818 0828 0918 0928 … 0946 0952 1028 1105 1118 1128 1142 1152 1228 … 1318 1328 1352 1428
Modena d.	0737 0725 0756 … 0825 0840 0856 0941 0956 … 1007 1025 1056 1136 1141 1156 1217 1225 1256 … 1341 1356 1425 1456
Reggio Emilia d.	0755 0738 0810 … 0842 0853 0910 0954 1010 … 1021 1042 1110 1201 1154 1210 1234 1242 1310 … 1354 1410 1442 1510
Parma d.	0816 0753 0825 … 0905 0908 0925 1010 1025 … 1036 1105 1125 1218 1210 1225 1256 1305 1325 … 1410 1425 1505 1525
Fidenza d.	0831 … 0837 … 0905 0923 … 0937 … 1054 1117 1137 1230 … 1237 … 1326 1337 … 1437 1517 1537
Piacenza d.	0817 0858 0824 0905 0911 0930 0937 1005 1041 1105 1119 1150 1205 1252 1241 1305 1328 1350 1405 1423 1441 1505 1550 1605
Voghera 610 d.	0855 … 0944 … 1155 … 1504
Tortona 610 d.	0908 … 0954 … 1516
Alessandria 610 d.	… 1015
Asti 610 d.	… 1041
Torino PN 610 a.	… 1120
Milano Rogoredo a.	0936 0856s … 1007 1033 1012s … 1204 1233 1332 … 1433 … 1633
Milano Centrale a.	0950 0910 … 1020 1045 1025 … 1125 … 1215 1245 1345 1325 1442g 1445 … 1525 … 1645

Block 5 — Bologna → Milano/Torino

Trains: FB 8818 (⚏C‡ A), IC 590 (A), FB 8822 (R N ⚏T A), FB 8824 (A), IC 612 (⚏C R), IC 8826 (◆), IC 596 (T ⚏C A), 2 (N m), FB 8830 (P ⚏C Ax), IC 1588 / FR 9560 (◆ R)

km	Station	Times
	Roma Termini 620 d.	… 1240t … … 1639t … 1710t 1935
	Bologna Centrale 620 d.	1518 1528 1552 1628 1644 1718 1728 1752 1818 1828 1840 1905 1918 1928 1952 2028 2046 … 2052 2118 2128 2135 2155 2219
	Modena d.	1541 1556 1625 1656 1707 1741 1756 1818 1825 1841 1856 1921 1941 1956 2025 2056 2108 … 2116 2141 2156 2202 2217 2245
	Reggio Emilia d.	1554 1610 1642 1710 1721 1810 1810 1842 1854 1910 1924 2001 1954 2010 2042 2110 2122 … 2132 2154 2210 2217 2231 2258
	Parma d.	1610 1625 1705 1725 1736 1810 1825 1910 1925 1910 1925 2010 2010 2025 2105 2125 2138 … 2149 2210 2225 2235 2247 2325
	Fidenza d.	… 1637 1717 1737 1754 … 1837 1923 … 1937 1954 2030 … 2037 2124 2137 2154 2158 2205 … 2237 2249
0	Piacenza d.	1641 1705 1750 1805 1819 1841 1909 1950 1941 2005 2019 2051 2041 2105 2150 2205 2219 2226 2232 2241 2305 2311 2317
58	Voghera 610 d.	… 1955
75	Tortona 610 d.	…
97	Alessandria 610 d.	… 2044
132	Asti 610 d.	… 2102
188	Torino PN 610 a.	… 2140
	Milano Rogoredo a.	… 1833 … 1904 … 2033 … 2104 2134 … 2233 … 2306 2308 2315 … 2352s
	Milano Centrale a.	1725 … 1845 … 1917 1925 … 2045 … 2124 2125 … 2245 … 2315 2320 2325 2325 … 0005 2345

Notes

◆ — NOTES (LISTED BY TRAIN NUMBER)

580 – 🍴 Terni - Milano.
599 – 🍴 Milano - Terni.
752 – 🛏 1, 2 cl., 🛏 2 cl. (4 berth) and 🍴 Lecce - Bologna - Milano.
754 – ①–⑥: 🛏 1, 2 cl., 🛏 2 cl. (4 berth) and 🍴 Lecce - Bologna - Torino.
755 – ①–⑥: 🛏 1, 2 cl., 🛏 2 cl. (4 berth) and 🍴 Milano - Bologna - Lecce.
757 – 🛏 1, 2 cl., 🛏 2 cl. (4 berth) and 🍴 Torino - Bologna - Lecce.
758 – 🛏 1, 2 cl., 🛏 2 cl. (4 berth) and 🍴 Lecce - Bologna - Milano.
765 – 🛏 1, 2 cl., 🛏 2 cl. (4 berth) and 🍴 Milano - Bologna - Lecce.
794 – 🛏 1, 2 cl., 🛏 2 cl. (4 berth) and 🍴 Reggio di Calabria - Milano - Torino.
795 – 🛏 1, 2 cl., 🛏 2 cl. (4 berth) and 🍴 Torino - Milano - Reggio di Calabria.
797 – 🛏 1, 2 cl., 🛏 2 cl. (4 berth) and 🍴 Torino - Milano - Napoli - Salerno.
798 – 🛏 1, 2 cl., 🛏 2 cl. (4 berth) and 🍴 Salerno - Napoli - Milano - Torino.
1545 – ⑥: 🍴 Milano - Lecce.
1546 – ⑦: 🍴 Lecce - Milano.
1580 – ⑦: 🛏 1, 2 cl., 🛏 2 cl. (4 berth) and 🍴 Lecce - Bologna - Torino.
1588 – ⑦: 🍴 Reggio di Calabria - Milano.
1589 – ⑥: 🍴 Milano - Reggio di Calabria.

A – From / to Ancona.
B – From / to Bari.
C – From / to Lecce.
E – From / to Pescara.
N – From / to Napoli.
P – ⑥⑦: 🍴 Milano - Pescara and v.v.
R – From / to Rimini.
T – From / to Taranto.
g – Milano **Porta Garibaldi**.
m – Not Aug. 11 - 20.
n – Not Aug. 12 - 21.
s – Stops to set down only.
u – Stops to pick up only.
x – Not Sept. 24, 25.
y – Not Aug. 12, 19.

‡ – Train number variations:
8813 runs as 8893 on ©.
8818 runs as 8880 on ©.
§ – Operator: *TPER*. Trenitalia tickets valid.

616   VENEZIA - BOLOGNA

For additional high-speed trains Venezia - Padova - Bologna - Roma see Table **600** (only trains calling at Rovigo or Ferrara are included below)

km			FA 8401 ♦	✠	FB 8801	FA 8413 ♦ T	IC 585									FB 8817 ♦	IC 595		FA 8447	FA 8451						ICN 771 ♦
0	**Venezia** Santa Lucia 605	d.	...	...	0642	0657	0742	...	0842	...	1042	1142	1242	1342	1442	1457	...	1542	1635	1642	1725	1742	1842	1942	2142	0008
9	**Venezia** Mestre 605	d.	0537	0554	0654	0709u	0754	0837	0854	0929	1054	1154	1254	1354	1454	1509u	1514	1554	1647u	1654	1737u	1754	1854	1954	2154	0021
37	Padova 605	d.	0553	0610	0710	0724	0810	0853	0910	0945	1110	1210	1310	1410	1510	1524	1532	1610	1703	1710	1753	1810	1910	2010	2210	0045
81	Rovigo	d.	0613	0650	0750	0746	0850		0950	1022	1150	1250	1350	1450	1550	1546	1600	1650	1725	1750		1850	1950	2050	2248	0119
113	Ferrara	d.		0712	0811	0803	0911	0925	1011	1042	1211	1311	1411	1511	1611	1603	1621	1711		1811	1825	1910	2014	2111	...	0141
160	**Bologna** Centrale	a.	0650	0743	0843	0835	0940	0950	1040	1108	1240	1340	1441	1540	1640	1633	1645	1740	1800	1840	1850	1940	2044	2140	...	0212
	Roma Termini 600 620	a.	0910	...	...	...	1210	...	1527	...	...	...	...	...	...	2042	...	2020	...	2110	...	...	...	...	...	0635

			ICN 774 ♦	✠		FA 8408	FA 8416		FB 8816 ♦	IC 588					FA 8450 ♦ U	IC 592 ♦		FB 8828 ♦	FA 8464	
	Roma Termini 600 620	d.	2235			0650		0835		1030				1650	1540		1950		
	Bologna Centrale	d.	0318	0620	0720	0820	0910	0920	1018	1055	1220	1320	1416	1427	1452	1520	1618	1718	1820	1910	1920	1952	...	2016	2120	2210	...
	Ferrara	d.	0349	0651	0751	0851	0932	0951	1051		1251	1351	1443	1457	1518	1551	1651	1751	1851		1951	2018	...	2043	2151	2232	...
	Rovigo	d.	0411	0710	0810	0910		1010	1110	1132	1310	1410	1500	1515	1534	1610	1710	1810	1910	1946	2010	2035	...	2100	2210		...
	Padova 605	d.	0450	0751	0851	1009	1051	1009	1147	1154	1347	1447	1532	1601	1602	1651	1751	1851	2000	2009	2051	2102	...	2132	2251	2309	...
	Venezia Mestre 605	a.	0508	0806	0906	1006	1023s	1106	1203	1208s	1403	1503	1548s	1606	1619	1706	1806	1906	2014	2021	2106	2118	...	2148s	2306	2323s	...
	Venezia Santa Lucia 605	a.	0520	0818	0918	1018	1035	1118	1218	1220	1418	1518	1600	1618	...	1718	1818	1918	2026	...	2118	...	...	2200	2318	2335	...

♦ —   **NOTES** (LISTED BY TRAIN NUMBER)

585 –	🚻 Trieste (**584**) - Venezia Mestre - Roma.
588 –	🚻 Roma - Venezia Mestre (**589**) - Trieste.
592 –	🚻 Roma - Venezia Mestre (**593**) - Trieste.
595 –	🚻 Trieste (**594**) - Venezia Mestre - Roma.
771 –	🛏 1, 2 cl., 🛏 2 cl. (4 berth) and 🚻 Trieste (**770**) - Udine - Venezia - Roma.
774 –	🛏 1, 2 cl., 🛏 2 cl. (4 berth) and 🚻 Roma - Venezia - Udine (**775**) - Trieste.
8401 –	🚻 and ⛽ Venezia Mestre - Roma Termini (**9402**) - Roma Fiumicino Aeroporto.
8801 –	🚻 and ⛽ Venezia - Bologna - Lecce.
8816 –	🚻 and ⛽ Lecce - Bologna - Venezia.
8817 –	🚻 and ⛽ Venezia - Bologna - Lecce.
8828 –	🚻 and ⛽ Lecce - Bologna - Venezia.

T –	To / from Trieste (Table **601**).
U –	To / from Udine (Table **601**).
s –	Stops to set down only.
u –	Stops to pick up only.

619   SIENA - CHIUSI-CHIANCIANO TERME   2nd class only

km			✠	†	†	✠	†		✠	✠	✠	†	✠		†	✠	✠		✠	†	✠		✠	†	✠	
0	Siena 609 613	d.	0554	0600	0802	0804	1002	...	1215	1328	1357	1402	1443	...	1602	1604	1655	...	1743	1802	1815	...	1927	2002	2024	...
89	Chiusi-Chianciano Terme 620	a.	0715	0721	0927	0923	1127	...	1330	1448	1523	1523	1615	...	1727	1719	1820	...	1851	1927	1942	...	2053	2127	2142	...

			✠	†	†	✠	✠	†		✠	✠	✠		†	✠	✠	†	✠		✠	†	✠	✠	
	Chiusi-Chianciano Terme 620	d.	0430	0600	0627		0645	0707	0830	...	0914	1030	1045	...	1230	1348	1510	1630	1706	...	1830	1840	1955	2030	2151	...
	Siena 609 613	a.	0546	0723	0745	...	0750	0826	0950	...	1035	1150	1157	...	1350	1519	1632	1750	1836	...	1950	2003	2122	2150	2303	...

European Rail Timetable Subscription

Keep up to date with the latest changes to European rail schedules with a subscription.

See page 10 for details of our various subscription options

Order on-line at **www.europeanrailtimetable.eu**

✆ +44 (0) 1832 270198 (Monday to Friday 0900 – 1700)

BOLOGNA - FIRENZE (- PERUGIA - FOLIGNO) - ROMA — 620

For high-speed services – see Table 600

km		ICN 763 ♦	ICN 771 ♦	IC 581 ✕	FR 9501 ✕	2 ✕			IC 583	IC 1589	2		IC 585 ♦	2	2	2	2	2	IC 595 ♦	2
	Milano Centrale 615 .... d.	·							0650	0645										
0	Bologna Centrale 615 .... d.	0118	0217	0600					0918	0937			1118						1648	
81	Prato Centrale .... d.								1004	1044			1208						1732	
97	Firenze S M Novella .... d.			0641					1011r	1052r			1217r						1745r	
97	Firenze S M Novella .... d.			0550	0650	0640	0734	0802	0910	1014r	1055r	1113	1213	1220r	1313	1413	1513	1613	1713	1748r
185	Arezzo .... d.		0425	0630	0725	0743	0855	0913	1007	1109	1216	1316	1302	1416	1516	1616	1716	1816	1828	
203	Castiglion Fiorentino .... d.			0755	0907	0924	1020			1227	1327		1427	1527	1627	1727	1827			
219	Terontola-Cortona .... d.		0445	0609	0650	0808	0921	0941	1035	1240	1341	1440	1541	1640	1741	1840	1847			
	Passignano sul Trasimeno .... d.						0950			1021	1349			1550	1750					
	Perugia 625 .... d.						1021				1424			1624	1825					
	Assisi 625 .... d.						1050				1447			1649	1846					
	Foligno 625 .... a.						1106				1501			1703	1901					
230	Castiglione del Lago .... d.			0617			0815	0930	1042		1247		1447	1647		1847			←	
248	Chiusi-Chianciano Terme 619 .... d.		0507	0629	0710	0831	0943	1054	1145	1207	1259	1345	1459	1659	1858	1904	1912			
288	Orvieto .... d.	0500		0657	0731	0859		1120	1210		1325	1410	1525	1725	→	1929	1938			
330	Orte 625 .... d.			0731		0941		1155	1245		1400		1449	1600	1800	2002	2016			
408	**Roma Tiburtina 625** .... a.			0809		0824		1237	1317	1311	1436		1642	1837		2025				
413	**Roma Termini 625 640** .... a.	0600	0635	0821	0826	0835	0955	1248			1446		1527	1656	1850	2042	2126			
	Napoli Centrale 640 .... a.							1529	1547											

		IC 597 ♦	2	ICN 795	2	FR 9555 ®	2	IC 599 ♦				FR 9500 ✕	2 ✕	2 ✕		IC 580 ♦	2	ICN 794 ♦	2	2
	Milano Centrale 615 .... d.	1450		1544g		1850		1740			Napoli Centrale 640 .... d.						0603		0421	0728	0900
	Bologna Centrale 615 .... d.	1718				2005		2018			Roma Termini 625 640 .... d.						0603	0639	0737	0728	0908
	Prato Centrale .... d.	1808		1910				2108			Roma Tiburtina 625 .... d.						0612	0639	0737		0908
	Firenze S M Novella .... d.	1817r		1929c		2040		2120			Orte 625 .... d.						0647		0811		0942
	Firenze S M Novella .... d.	1813	1820r	1913	1932c	2049	2113	2142			Orvieto .... d.						0721		0844		1015
	Arezzo .... d.	1916	1902	2017		2116	2122	2216	2224		Chiusi-Chianciano Terme 619 .... d.		0543				0758t		0909		1058v
	Castiglion Fiorentino .... d.	1927		2029		2127		2227			Castiglione del Lago .... d.		0556				0809		0920		1109
	Terontola-Cortona .... d.	1941	1924	2042		2141		2240	2249		Foligno 625 .... d.		0515		0555					0912	
	Passignano sul Trasimeno .... d.	1950				2150					Assisi 625 .... d.		0530		0608					0925	
	Perugia 625 .... d.	2028		2221				2318			**Perugia 625** .... d.		0600		0635					0952	
	Assisi 625 .... d.	2053		2242				2339			Passignano sul Trasimeno .... d.		0636							1024	
	Foligno 625 .... a.	2110		2257				2350			Terontola-Cortona .... d.		0604	0656t			0710	0819		0927 1036	1119
	Castiglione del Lago .... d.			2049				2247			Castiglion Fiorentino .... d.		0618	0710				0831		0940	1131
	Chiusi-Chianciano Terme 619 .... d.		1945	2101				2259			Arezzo .... d.	0611	0632	0725		0732	0844		0953 1100	1145
	Orvieto .... d.		2010	2127				2325			Firenze S M Novella .... a.	0644	0738	0835		0806	0948	1006c	1057 1157	1250
	Orte 625 .... d.		2046	2202				2358			Firenze S M Novella .... d.	0653				0821		1008c		
	Roma Tiburtina 625 .... a.		2112	2243	2311			0032			Prato Centrale .... d.						0837		1030		
	Roma Termini 625 640 .... a.			2254				0045			Bologna Centrale 615 .... a.	0728					0942		1138		
	Napoli Centrale 640 .... a.	2329									Milano Centrale 615 .... a.	0840					1215		1442g	

km		IC 588 ♦	2	IC 590	2		IC 592	2	IC 596	IC 1588 ♦	2	IC 598 ®	2	FR 9564 ®	ICN 774 ♦	ICN 764 ♦	ICN 798 ♦	
	Napoli Centrale 640 .... d.			1031					1431	1452					1930			2101	
	Roma Termini 625 640 .... d.		1030		1300		1458	1540			1712	1816	2005	2050	2235	2300			
	Roma Tiburtina 625 .... d.			1240		1309	1507		1639		1710	1722	2015	2100				2315	
	Orte 625 .... d.		1110	1147	1314	1347	1542	1617	1715		1756	1854	2045				2341	2347	
	Orvieto .... d.		1145	1221	1345	1421	1616	1645	1745		1811	1829	1923	2119			0011		
	Chiusi-Chianciano Terme 619 .... d.		1210	1258t	1410	1458t	1658v	1710	1810		1835	1858	1946	2147		0007			
	Castiglione del Lago .... d.			1309		1509	1709				1909			2158					
	Foligno 625 .... d.	1108		1303		1503		1708				1903	2050						
	Assisi 625 .... d.	1122		1317		1517		1721				1917	2110						
0	**Perugia 625** .... d.	1144		1339		1539		1744				1941	2134						
31	Passignano sul Trasimeno .... d.	1212		1408		1609		1810				2009	2206						
43	Terontola-Cortona .... d.	1222	1319	1419	1519	1719	1719	1730	1819	1830	1853	1919	2004	2019	2205	2218		0025	
	Castiglion Fiorentino .... d.	1234	1331		1431	1531	1631	1731		1831		1931	2031	2218			0047		
	Arezzo .... d.	1245	1255	1344	1455	1444	1544	1644	1744	1755	1919	1944	2044	2231	2202				
	Firenze S M Novella .... a.	1348	1336r	1448	1536r	1548	1648	1748	1836r	1751	1936r	2005r	2048	2111	2148	2335	2235	0144c	
	Firenze S M Novella .... d.		1339r		1539r			1839r		1939r	2008r							0147c	
	Prato Centrale .... d.		1352		1552			1852		1952	2026								
	Bologna Centrale 615 .... a.		1443		1640			1948		2038	2130						0313	0342	
	Milano Centrale 615 .... a.				1917					2315	0005							0711g	

♦ — **NOTES** (LISTED BY TRAIN NUMBER)

580/99 –	🛏 Terni - Milano and v.v.
585/92 –	🛏 Trieste (584/593) - Venezia Mestre - Roma and v.v.
588/95 –	🛏 Roma - Venezia Mestre (589/594) - Trieste and v.v.
763 –	⑤⑥ (from Bolzano): 🛏 1,2 cl., 🛏 2 cl. (4 berth) and 🛏 Bolzano - Roma.
764 –	⑤⑥: 🛏 1,2 cl., 🛏 2 cl. (4 berth) and 🛏 Roma - Bolzano.
771 –	🛏 1,2 cl., 🛏 2 cl. (4 berth) and 🛏 Trieste (770) - Udine - Venezia - Roma.
774 –	🛏 1,2 cl., 🛏 2 cl. (4 berth) and 🛏 Roma - Venezia - Udine (775) - Trieste.
794 –	🛏 1,2 cl., 🛏 2 cl. (4 berth) and 🛏 Reggio di Calabria - Milano - Torino.
795 –	🛏 1,2 cl., 🛏 2 cl. (4 berth) and 🛏 Torino - Milano - Reggio di Calabria.
798 –	🛏 1,2 cl., 🛏 2 cl. (4 berth) and 🛏 Salerno - Napoli - Milano - Torino.
1588 –	⑦: 🛏 Reggio di Calabria - Milano.
1589 –	⑥: 🛏 Milano - Reggio di Calabria.

c –	Firenze **Campo di Marte**.
g –	Milano **Porta Garibaldi**.
h –	Also Aug. 7, 14.
p –	Also Aug. 13, 20.
r –	Firenze **Rifredi**.
t –	Arrive 9–13 minutes earlier.
v –	Arrive 14–18 minutes earlier.
w –	Not Aug. 14, Oct. 30, Dec. 7.
y –	Not Aug. 14.

FERRARA and BOLOGNA - RAVENNA - RIMINI — 621

2nd class only except where shown

For express services Bologna - Faenza - Rimini and v.v. – see Table 630

km		8851 ✕ R	⊙	⊙	⊙	✕v	✕w	✕	✕	†		⊙	✕	✕w		✕	†h	†n	†h		✕	✕w	⊙
0	Ferrara .... d.			0516		0545	0609			0710		0816			0817			0922	0939	1004				1215
	Bologna Centrale 630 .... d.							0650						075x		0852	0906x				1006	1106x	1206	
	Imola .... d.							0712				0826			0914	0936			1033	1136			1235	
	Castelbolognese-Riolo Terme d.							0719				0832			0942				1038	1142			1242	
	Lugo .... d.							0734				0847		0931	0958				1056	1200			1300	
74	Ravenna .... a.			0619		0702	0724		0805	0830		0921		0917	0925	0951	1030	1030	1052	1114	1118	1227		1327 1329
74	Ravenna .... d.	0525	0600		0628		0752			0836			0924	0934			1053	1116	1119		1245		1336
95	Cervia-Milano Marittima .... d.	0537		0650		0811			0900			0943	0958			1114	1134	1138		1307			1400
103	Cesenatico .... d.	0546		0657		0817			0906			0949	1005			1132	1142	1145		1313			1410
124	Rimini 630 .... a.	0605	0636	0727		0850			0932			1015	1027			1200	1216	1217		1345			1447

FOR NOTES SEE NEXT PAGE →

Compulsory reservation is required on all EC, EN, FA, FB, FR, IC and ICN trains in Italy

621 — FERRARA and BOLOGNA - RAVENNA - RIMINI

2nd class only except where shown

For express services Bologna - Faenza - Rimini and v.v. – see Table 630

				☼w	x	☼w	☼	☼	☼w	☼jw		☼w		☼	j	☼		☼	j	h	
Ferrara	d.	...	...	1309	1423			1615				1701		1814		2050					
Bologna Centrale 630	d.	1252	1306			1406x	1506		1606x	1652		1706x	1752	1806	1906	2006x		2116x	2206z
Imola	d.	1314	1336			1436	1536		1636	1714		1734		1838	1939	2036		2146	2238
Castelbolognese-Riolo Terme	d.		1342			1442	1542		1642			1742	1817	1844	1945	2042		2152	2244
Lugo	d.	1331	1358			1458	1600		1700	1731		1800	1831	1858	1959	2058		2208	2258
Ravenna	a.	1351	1427		1441	1530	1527	1627	1723	1727		1751	1814	1827		1851	1926	1928	2029	2127	2150	2237	2322
Ravenna	d.	...	1435			1532		1635		1735			1835		1935			2155	2257
Cervia-Milano Marittima	d.	...	1502			1554		1654		1754			1857		1956			2213	2313
Cesenatico	d.	...	1508			1603		1702		1803			1904		2006			2220	2320
Rimini 630	a.	...	1535			1630		1730		1835			1935		2034			2248	2343

km			☼	x	☼x	x	☼		☼v	☼w	☼	†	☼	☼jw		†	☼w	†	☼			☼		
	Rimini 630	d.	...	0520		x	0613		0658	0736		0820	0900			1036			1230	
	Cesenatico	d.	...	0545			0642		0724	0801		0852	0935			1104			1300	
	Cervia-Milano Marittima	d.	...	0551			0650		0730	0812		0859	0942			1113			1306	
	Ravenna	a.	...	0615			0712		0751	0827		0921	1003			1140			1325	
0	Ravenna	d.	0503		0621	0628	...	0726	0755	0753		0833	0849	0931	0932		1009	1032		1131	1133		1143	1227	1233		1331
28	Lugo	d.	0528			0657			0815			0901	0958		1031		1200	1200		1300	1358
42	Castelbolognese-Riolo Terme	d.	0544			0714						0916	1014			1214	1216		1316	1414
50	Imola	d.	0551			0721						0923	1021		1046		1221	1223		1323	1421
84	Bologna Centrale 630	a.	0621			0743			0854x			0954	1053x		1108		1251	1254		1354x	1454x
	Ferrara				0736			0847		0914			1005		1053		1142			1250	1348	

		☼		☼	☼w	☼		y	☼jw	☼w			☼		†h	☼w	☼		☼		☼		☼			☼	†	☼		☼	8852 R	
Rimini 630	d.	...	1318		1418		1508			1632		1703		1733	1837		1939		2037	2037	2127
Cesenatico	d.	...	1350		1451		1535			1701		1732		1802	1905		2006		2105	2105	
Cervia-Milano Marittima	d.	...	1359		1501		1541			1708		1740		1808	1912		2012		2113	2121	
Ravenna	a.	...	1418		1523		1604			1733		1759		1826	1929		2028		2131	2137	2200
Ravenna	d.	1341		1431	1453	1533	1540		1633		1733	1735		1801	1809	1824		1831	1931	1957		2033		2200	
Lugo	d.			1458		1600			1700		1800			1827	1831			1858	1958		2058	
Castelbolognese-Riolo Terme	d.			1514		1616			1716		1816			1837			1914	2014		2114	
Imola	d.			1521		1623			1723		1822			1843	1846			1920	2021		2122	
Bologna Centrale 630	a.			1554		1654x			1754		1854x			1908	1908			1954x	2054x		2154x	
Ferrara	a.	1501			1611		1651			1849		1936			2109			2300	

R – FB train. 🚌 and ⚹ Roma - Rimini - Ravenna and v.v.

h – Until Aug. 28.
j – From Aug. 29.
n – From Sept. 4.
p – Until Sept. 19.

q – From Sept. 20.
v – Not July 31 - Aug. 28.
w – Not Sept. 24.

x – Not Sept. 24, 25.
y – Not † Aug. 7 - 28.
z – Not Sept. 25.

☼ – Operated by *TPER*. Trenitalia tickets valid.

---

622 — ROMA AIRPORTS ✈

ROMA FIUMICINO AIRPORT ✈

Leonardo Express rail service Roma Termini - Roma Fiumicino ✈. 31 km Journey time: 32 minutes. Special fare payable.

From **Roma** Termini: 0535, 0605, 0635, 0705, 0735, 0805, 0835, 0850, 0905, 0935, 1005, 1035, 1050, 1105, 1135, 1205, 1220, 1235, 1250, 1305, 1335, 1405, 1435, 1450, 1505, 1535, 1605, 1620, 1635, 1650, 1705, 1735, 1750, 1805, 1820, 1835, 1905, 1935, 2005, 2035, 2105, 2135, 2205, 2235.

From **Roma** Fiumicino: 0623, 0653, 0723, 0753, 0823, 0853, 0923, 0938, 0953, 1023, 1053, 1123, 1138, 1153, 1223, 1253, 1308, 1323, 1338, 1353, 1423, 1453, 1523, 1538, 1553, 1623, 1653, 1708, 1723, 1738, 1753, 1823, 1838, 1853, 1908, 1923, 1953, 2023, 2053, 2123, 2153, 2223, 2253, 2323.

Additional rail service (2nd class only) operates from Roma Tiburtina **and** Roma Ostiense - Roma Fiumicino ✈. 39 km Journey times: Tiburtina - ✈ ± 45 minutes; Ostiense - ✈ ± 30 minutes.

From **Roma** Tiburtina (Ostiense 15 minutes later): ☾
0501, 0546⚹, 0601, 0616Ⓐ, 0631, 0646Ⓐ, 0701, 0716Ⓐ, 0731, 0746⚹, 0801, 0816⚹, 0831, 0846Ⓐ, 0901, 0916⚹, 0931, 0946Ⓐ, 1001, 1016Ⓐ, 1031, 1046Ⓐ, 1101, 1116Ⓐ, 1131⚹, 1146Ⓐ, 1201⚹, 1216Ⓐ, 1231⚹, 1246Ⓐ, 1301, 1316Ⓐ, 1331, 1346⚹, 1401, 1416Ⓐ, 1431, 1446Ⓐ, 1501, 1516Ⓐ, 1531, 1546Ⓐ, 1601, 1616⚹, 1631, 1646⚹, 1701, 1716⚹, 1731, 1746Ⓐ, 1801, 1816Ⓐ, 1831, 1846Ⓐ, 1901, 1916Ⓐ, 1931, 2001, 2031, 2101, 2146, 2201.

From **Roma** Fiumicino ✈: ☾
0557, 0627, 0642⚹, 0657, 0712Ⓐ, 0727, 0742Ⓐ, 0757, 0812Ⓐ, 0827, 0842Ⓐ, 0857⚹, 0912⚹, 0927⚹, 0942Ⓐ, 0957⚹, 1012⚹, 1027, 1042Ⓐ, 1057, 1112Ⓐ, 1127, 1142Ⓐ, 1157, 1212⚹, 1227, 1242Ⓐ, 1257, 1312Ⓐ, 1327, 1342Ⓐ, 1357, 1412⚹, 1427, 1442⚹, 1457, 1512⚹, 1527, 1542Ⓐ, 1557, 1612Ⓐ, 1627, 1642Ⓐ, 1657, 1712⚹, 1727, 1742⚹, 1757, 1812⚹, 1827, 1842Ⓐ, 1857, 1912Ⓐ, 1927, 1942Ⓐ, 1957, 2012Ⓐ, 2042, 2112, 2142, 2212, 2242.

ROMA CIAMPINO AIRPORT ✈

Frequent services operate Roma Termini - Ciampino and v.v., journey approximately 15 minutes. There is a 🚌 service between Ciampino station and airport.

☾ – A reduced service operates in July and August.

---

623 — ROMA - ANZIO and ALBANO LAZIALE

ROMA - ANZIO 57 km Journey time: 56 – 68 minutes. 2nd class only. All services continue to Nettuno (3 km and 4 – 6 minutes from Anzio).

From **Roma** Termini:
⚹: 0507, 0607, 0714, 0821, 0942, 1042, 1142, 1242, 1342, 1406Ⓐ, 1442, 1542, 1642, 1742, 1806⚹, 1842, 1906Ⓐ, 1942, 2042, 2136.
†: 0714, 0821, 0942, 1142, 1342, 1442, 1642, 1842, 1942, 2136.

From **Anzio**:
⚹: 0455, 0559, 0635, 0703Ⓐ, 0735, 0800, 0912, 1014, 1112, 1212, 1312, 1412, 1512Ⓖ, 1514Ⓐ, 1612, 1630Ⓐ, 1712, 1812, 1917, 2012, 2113Ⓐ, 2202.
†: 0635, 0735, 0912, 1014, 1312, 1512, 1712, 1812, 2012, 2202.

ROMA - ALBANO LAZIALE 29 km Journey time: 40 – 58 minutes. 2nd class only.

From **Roma** Termini: 0542⚹, 0721, 0821, 0900⚹, 1221, 1321⚹, 1421, 1521⚹, 1621, 1721⚹, 1821, 1921⚹, 2021, 2121⚹.

From **Albano** Laziale: 0629⚹, 0700⚹, 0743⚹, 0838, 1023, 1144⚹, 1343, 1443⚹, 1543, 1643⚹, 1743, 1843⚹, 1943, 2043⚹, 2140⚹, 2145†.

All trains call at Marino Laziale and Castel Gandolfo approximately 35 and 40 minutes from Roma, 7 and 15 minutes from Albano Laziale respectively.

---

624 — ROMA - PESCARA

2nd class only

km			†	⚹	†	⚹	†	⚹		†	⚹	†		Ⓖ	Ⓑ	Ⓐ	†	⚹	†	⚹		⚹	Ⓐ	
0	Roma Tiburtina § ▲	d.	...	...	...	0742	0742	0857		1033		1233		1433	1433	1527	1533		1633	1630	1733	1833	1833	1939	1938	2045
40	Tivoli ▲	d.	...	...	...	0833	0832	1000		1124		1308		1510	1510	1613	1614		1703	1723	1828	1906	1907	2019	2036	2137
108	Avezzano	d.	0615	0612	0730	0941	0945	1110		1256	1300	1409		1613	1617	1720	1720		1804	1823	1935	2011	2019	2126	2121	
172	Sulmona 627	d.	0747	0747	0844	1049	1049		1230	1410	1410	1536	1613	1705	1728	1740			1812	1913	1931		2126	2121	
226	Chieti	d.	0840	0854	0935	1127	1128		1337	1516	1510	1627	1708	1759	1812	1832			1903	2004	2016		2212	2212	
240	Pescara Centrale	a.	0858	0910	0955	1145	1145		1400	1540	1525	1650	1734	1820	1836	1850			1922	2020	2030		2230	2230	

		⚹		⚹		⚹		Ⓐ	Ⓐ	Ⓖ	†	⚹	Ⓐ	⚹	⚹	†	Ⓐ	Ⓖ	†	⚹	†	†	⚹	†	Ⓐ	
Pescara Centrale	d.			0615	0701	0921			1146	1334	1406	1410		1610	1655		1800	1846	1910	1957	2125
Chieti	d.			0628	0718	0938			1202	1353	1422	1425		1624	1712		1816	1901	1932	2014	2144
Sulmona 627	d.			0557	0724	0825	1025			1259	1450	1513	1513		1727	1811		1912	2002	2035	2119	2235
Avezzano	d.	0508	0530	0629	0654	0814	0920	1121	1155	1259	1259	1307	1425	1430		1615	1614	1721	1711	1840	1907	1910	2018	2100	
Tivoli ▲	d.	0614	0640	0736	0759	0921	1022	1225	1309	1417	1417	1416	1555		1722	1728	1827	1827		2020	2018	2131	2203	
Roma Tiburtina § ▲	a.	0700	0731	0830	0845t	1004	1104	1306	1359	1459	1515	1459	1654		1804	1803	1900	1912		2059	2100	2225t	2255t	

t – Roma **Termini**.

§ – Roma Tiburtina **Piazzale Est**.

▲ – Additional services operate Roma Tiburtina (Piazzale Est) - Tivoli and v.v., journey 60 – 75 minutes.

12

ROMA - PERUGIA and ANCONA — 625

km		2 Ⓐ	2 ⚒	2 ⚒	*IC* 580 T	2 †	2 ⚒q		⚒	*IC* 534		⚒	2 ⚒			*IC* 540		Ⓐ	*FB* 8852 R	2 Ⓐ	Ⓑy		⚒	*IC* 546 Ⓑ		
0	**Roma** Termini **620** d.	...	...	...	...	...	...	0545	0653	0740	0758	1128	1158	1328	1428	1535	1558	1700	1738	...	1758	1835	1858	1958	2058	2240
5	**Roma** Tiburtina **620** d.	...	...	...	...	...	...	0555	0702	|	0807	1137	1208	1337	1439	|	1607	1710	|	...	1807	1845	1907	2008	2109	2249
83	Orte **620** d.	...	...	...	...	...	...	0634	0739	0817	0840	1211	1240	1410	1511	|	1640	|	|	...	1840	1917	1941	2037	2141	2321
112	Terni d.	...	...	...	0505	...	...	0654	0800	0835	0901	1235	1305	1432	1531	1629	1704	1802	1827	...	1902	1943	2006	2054	2204	2339
141	Spoleto d.	...	...	...	0532	...	...	0716	0831	0915	0933	1259	1329	1457	1555	1659	1733	1825	|	...	1932	2008	2029	2121	2226	...
167	**Foligno** a.	...	...	...	0553	...	...	0740	0853	0929	0949	1319	1350	1516	1612	1715	1752	1844	1859	...	1953	2029	2048	2136	2242	...
167	**Foligno** d.	...	...	0545	0555	0622	0640	0742	...	0931	0953	1321	*1416*	1518	1614	1717	1754	...	1901	...	1955	2031	2050	2138	2244	...
	Spello d.	...	...	|	|	|	|	|	...	|	|	|	|	|	1619	|	|	...	|	...	2001	|	2059	|	|	...
	Assisi d.	...	...	|	0608	|	|	|	...	|	1008	|	|	|	1627	|	|	...	|	...	2010	|	2110	2151	|	...
	Perugia Ponte SG ▲ d.	...	...	|	0623	|	|	|	...	|	1018	|	|	|	1638	|	|	...	|	...	2021	|	2124	2202	|	...
	Perugia 620 a.	...	...	|	0633	|	|	|	...	|	1028	|	|	|	1655	|	|	...	|	...	2032	|	2132	2213	|	...
224	Fabriano d.	0500	0600	0646	...	0713	0732	0847	...	1021	...	1414	*1522*	1620	...	1806	1846	...	1942	1945	...	2122	...	...	2333	...
268	Jesi d.	0539	0641	0733	...	0758	0827	0924	...	1050	...	1501	*1605*	1704	...	1836	1922	...	2015	2028	...	2156	...	...	0010	...
286	Falconara Marittima **630** d.	0555	0700	0749	...	0818	0845	0940	...	1103	...	1523	*1625*	1721	...	1850	1941	...	2028	2046	...	2210	...	...	0025	...
295	**Ancona 630/2** a.	0604	0712	0802	...	0834	0856	0955	...	1113	...	1535	*1638*	1735	...	1859	1953	...	...	2054	...	2222	...	...	0040	...

km		⚒		⚒z	2 ⚒	*IC* 531 ⚒	†	*IC* 533	2 Ⓐ	*FB* 8851 R			2 ⚒	Ⓐ		⚒	*IC* 541	2 ⚒		2	†	⚒		2 Ⓐ	2	*IC* 599 T
	Ancona 630/2 d.	...	0350	...	0505	...	...	0625	0651	...	0845	...	...	...	1344	...	1532	1545	...	1733	1815	1825	1942	2015	2130	...
	Falconara Marittima **630** d.	...	0403	...	0513	...	...	0639	0701	0737	0855	...	...	...	1354	...	1542	1556	...	1745	1824	1835	1951	2025	2139	...
	Jesi d.	...	0415	...	0526	...	...	0656	0720	0750	0910	...	...	...	1409	...	1554	1614	...	1801	1848	1851	2004	2041	2153	...
	Fabriano d.	...	0451	...	0604	...	...	0732	0808	0824	0949	...	...	...	1450	...	1628	1710	...	1855	1939	1940	2038	2120	2235	...
0	**Perugia 620** d.	...	|	0554	|	0640	0712	|	...	|	|	1105	1226	1348	|	1556	|	...	1805	...	|	|	|	...	|	2318
11	Perugia Ponte SG ▲ d.	...	|	0603	|	0651	0721	|	...	|	|	1114	1235	1357	|	1605	|	...	1815	...	|	|	|	...	|	2328
24	Assisi d.	...	|	0618	|	0703	0732	|	...	|	|	1130	1246	1412	|	1624	|	...	1827	...	|	|	|	...	|	2339
35	Spello d.	...	|	0628	|	|	0741	|	...	|	|	1141	1255	1424	|	1636	|	...	1836	...	|	|	|	...	|	|
40	**Foligno** a.	...	0537	0634	0700	0715	0748	0818	...	0901	1039	1146	1301	1434	1543	1640	1714	...	1843	...	2029	2029	2134	...	2334	2350
	Foligno d.	...	0539	0636	...	0717	0749	0820	...	0903	1041	1148	...	1436	1545	1642	1716	...	1846	...	2031	2031	2136	...	...	2354
	Spoleto d.	...	0555	0653	...	0733	0809	0836	...	|	1057	1206	...	1455	1607	1658	1734	...	1901	...	2048	2048	2152	...	...	0011
	Terni d.	0540	0625	0732	...	0758	0833	0900	...	0936	1122	1235	...	1524	1630	1728	1800	...	1925	...	2118	2118	2225	...	...	0035
	Orte **620** d.	0600	0651	0801	...	0816	0854	0918	...	|	1149	1305	...	1547	1657	1749	|	...	1949	...	2140	2140	2246	...	...	...
	Roma Tiburtina **620** a.	0630	0723	0836	...	0847	0926	|	...	|	1221	1337	...	1618	1724	1817	|	...	2019	...	2209	2209	2318	...	...	...
	Roma Termini **620** a.	0640	0737	0850	...	0858	0939	0956	...	1020	1235	1356	...	1633	1742	1835	1902	...	2032	...	2225	2225	2330	...	...	...

R – [12] and 🍷 Ravenna - Rimini - Roma and v.v.
T – [12] Terni - Perugia - Milano and v.v.

q – From Sept. 5.
y – Not Aug. 14.

▲ – Perugia Ponte San Giovanni.

ROMA - CASERTA - NAPOLI and FOGGIA — 626

km		2 ⚒	2 ⚒	2 ⚒	2 ⚒	2 ⚒	2	*FA* 8303 🍷		*IC* 703 2	2 †	2 ⚒	2 †	2 ⚒	2	*FA* 8315 🍷	2	*IC* 705 T	2	2 †	2 ⚒	2 Ⓐ	2	*FA* 8323 🍷	2 †z	2	*ICN* 789 ♦
0	**Roma** Termini d.	...	...	...	...	0535	0621	0805	...	0728	1014	1014	...	1235	1242	1455	1542	1601	...	1642	1642	1707	1742	1800	1807	1942	2358
138	Cassino d.	0510	0550	...	0705	0736	0827	|	...	0912	1227	1245	1317	1406	1441	|	1742	|	1810	1845	1858	1844	1940	|	1946	2140	0140
170	Vairano-Caianello d.	0541	0621	0706	0737	...	...	|	...	0935	...	...	1350	1430	...	|	...	|	1842	1918	1928	...	...	|	2008	...	|
216	Caserta d.	0625	0705	0755	0822	...	...	0915	...	1011	...	...	1434	1512	...	1613	...	1801	1929	2000	2014	...	...	1914	2045	...	0236
	Napoli Centrale a.	0707	0746	0836	0903	...	...	|	...	|	...	...	1515	|	...	|	...	|	2012	...	...	...	...	|	...	...	|
279	Benevento d.	...	...	...	...	...	...	0952	...	1059	...	...	...	1615	...	1651	...	1848	...	...	...	...	...	1952	...	...	0324
380	**Foggia 631** a.	...	...	...	...	...	...	1056	...	1223	...	...	...	...	...	1752	...	2018	...	...	...	...	...	2056	...	...	0449
	Bari Centrale **631** a.	...	...	...	...	...	...	1204	...	1400	...	...	...	...	...	1900	...	2143	...	...	...	...	...	2204	...	...	0623
	Lecce **631** a.	...	...	...	...	...	...	1328	...	...	...	...	...	...	...	2024	...	...	...	...	...	...	...	2328	...	...	0809

km		2 ⚒	*ICN* 788 ♦	2 ⚒	2 †	2 ⚒	2 ⚒	2 ⚒	2 ⚒	2	*FA* 8302 🍷	2	2 ⚒h	2 ⚒h	2 ⚒	2 ⚒	*FA* 8314 🍷	2 †	2 †	2 Ⓐh	2 ⚒	2	*IC* 704 2	2 Ⓐh	*IC* 710 R	*FA* 8326 🍷	
	Lecce **631** d.	...	2230	...	...	...	...	...	...	...	0550	...	...	...	...	...	1150	...	...	...	...	...	...	...	...	1665	...
	Bari Centrale **631** d.	...	0015	...	...	...	...	...	...	...	0714	...	...	...	...	...	1314	...	...	...	...	...	1555	...	1714	1814	...
	Foggia 631 d.	...	0200	...	...	...	...	...	...	...	0822	...	...	...	...	...	1422	...	...	...	...	...	1741	...	1839	1922	...
	Benevento d.	...	0321	...	...	0520	...	...	0632	...	0925	...	...	...	...	...	1525	...	...	...	...	...	1900	...	2001	2031	...
0	**Napoli** Centrale d.	...	|	...	...	|	0450	...	|	0750	|	...	1150	...	1340	...	|	1550	...	1656	1750	...	|	1950	|	|	...
34	Caserta d.	0410	0413	0500	0512	0611	0530	0610	0730	0830	1010	...	1230	1330	1420	1530	1602	1630	...	1736	1830	...	1958	2030	2051	2110	...
80	Vairano-Caianello d.	0455	|	0547	0557	|	0615	0646	0808	0912	|	...	1312	1413	1506	1613	|	1713	...	1816	1912	...	2025	2112	|	|	...
112	Cassino d.	0530	|	0618	0627	|	...	0711	0837	0947	|	1025	1347	1446	...	1648	|	1747	1822	1853	1947	2020	2048	2147	|	|	...
250	**Roma** Termini a.	...	0634	0820	0834	0827	...	0848	1013	...	1123	1227	...	...	...	...	1720	...	2020	...	...	2241	2220	...	2311	2220	...

♦ – **NOTES** (LISTED BY TRAIN NUMBER)

788 – ⑦: 🛏 1, 2 cl., 🛌 2 cl. (4 berth) and [2] Lecce - Roma.
789 – ⑤ (from Roma): 🛏 1, 2 cl., 🛌 2 cl. (4 berth) and [2] Roma - Lecce.

R – ⑦: [12] Taranto - Roma.
T – ⑤: [12] Roma - Taranto.

h – Not July 31 - Aug. 28.
p – Until Sept. 18.

q – From Sept. 19.
z – Until Sept. 4.

ROMA and NAPOLI - CAMPOBASSO - TERMOLI — 627

2nd class only

km		⚒		⚒		⚒	⚒	†			⚒	⚒	†	⚒		⚒	†	⚒	Ⓑn		†	🚌		⚒	†	⚒
0	**Roma** Termini d.	...	...	...	0615	...	...	...	0907	...	...	...	...	1307	...	...	1435	1435	...	...	1740	...	...	1935	2014	2035
138	Cassino d.	...	...	...	0742	...	...	...	1033	...	...	...	...	1445	...	...	1602	1603	...	...	|	...	...	|	|	|
	Napoli Centrale d.	...	...	...	|	...	...	...	|	...	...	1210	...	|	1410	...	|	|	...	1713	|	...	1930	|	|	|
	Caserta d.	...	...	...	|	...	0805	0837	|	...	...	1245	...	|	1440	...	|	|	...	1745	|	...	2004	|	|	|
	Vairano-Caianello d.	...	...	...	|	...	0850	0922	|	...	...	1320	...	|	1516	...	|	|	...	1821	|	...	2040	|	|	|
187	Isernia d.	...	...	0646	0828	...	0934	1012	1116	...	...	1408	...	1528	1557	...	1641	1650	...	1901	1949	...	2126	2148	2226	2238
198	Carpinone ♣ d.	...	...	0657	0839	...	|	|	1128	...	...	1420	...	1540	1610	...	|	|	...	1913	2000	...	2138	|	|	|
246	**Campobasso** ▲ a.	0553	0646	0751	0924	0940	1036	1110	1212	1218	1414	1519	1525	1633	1709	1720	1742	1749	1828	2007	2052	2100	2227	2243	2325	2338
333	Termoli a.	0743	0835	...	...	1118	...	...	...	1409	1553	...	1708	...	...	1908	...	...	2009	...	...	2245	...	...	...	...

km		⚒		⚒	⚒	†	⚒			⚒	†			⚒	†	⚒	⚒	†	⚒	⚒			⚒		🚌	🚌
	Termoli d.	...	...	...	...	...	0548	0645	...	...		...	1220	...	...	1317	...	...	1500	...	1616	...	1728	...	1855	2045
	Campobasso ▲ d.	0513	0550	0628	0653	0727	0743	0825	0836	1232	1232	1316	1400	1415	1421	1501	1528	1621	1645	1650	1753	1758	1918	1938	2040	2230
	Carpinone ♣ d.	0554	|	0716	|	0811	...	...	0926	1315	1317	1359	...	|	|	...	1613	1712	...	1736	...	1845	...	|	...	...
0	Isernia d.	0607	0644	0727	0745	0825	...	...	0937	1328	1330	1411	...	1510	1515	...	1627	1724	...	1749	...	1858	...	2033	...	...
46	Vairano-Caianello d.	0648	|	0809	|	0909	...	...	|	|	1412	1459	...	|	|	...	1718	|	...	|	...	1949	...	|	...	...
92	Caserta a.	0715	|	0846	|	0937	...	...	|	|	1449	1534	...	|	|	...	1756	|	...	|	...	2025	...	|	...	...
126	**Napoli** Centrale a.	0752	|	0925	|	1008	...	...	|	|	...	1608	...	|	|	...	...	|	...	|	...	2100	...	|	...	...
	Cassino a.	...	0726	...	|	...	...	...	1017	1416	...	...	...	1549	1557	...	...	1804	...	1829	...	...	...	2115	...	...
	Roma Termini a.	...	0853	...	0959	...	...	...	1147	...	...	...	...	1727	1727	...	...	1934	...	1953	...	...	...	2254	...	...

♣ – 🚌 SULMONA - CASTEL DI SANGRO - CARPINONE

	⚒	⚒		⚒	⚒	⚒
Sulmona **624** d.	...	...	1110	...	...	1932
Castel di Sangro d.	0615	0805	1210	1240	1830	2032
Carpinone a.	0718	0908	...	1343	1933	...

	⚒	⚒	⚒	⚒		⚒
Carpinone d.	...	0653	0853	1433	...	2038
Castel di Sangro d.	0610	0758	0958	1538	1710	2143
Sulmona **624** a.	0720	...	...	...	1820	...

▲ – 🚌 **CAMPOBASSO - BENEVENTO and v.v.**:
(*67 km*, journey time 70 minutes).
From Campobasso: 0620⚒, 1305⚒, 1416⚒, 1750⚒.
From Benevento: 0640⚒, 0740⚒, 1420⚒, 1740⚒.

n – Not Aug. 14.

629 SARDINIA

Some trains 2nd class only

km		⚒		⚒	⚒	†	†	†	†	⚒	⚒	†	⚒	⚒	⚒	†	†	†	⚒	†	⚒	⚒W	†	⚒	⚒	⚒	†	†
0	**Cagliari** d.	...	...	...	...	...	...	...	0624	0632	...	...	0722	0840	...	...	...	0914	0918	1013	1040	...	1113	1118	...	1222	1222	...
17	Decimomannu d.	...	...	...	...	...	...	...	0638	0643	...	...	0737	|	...	...	...	0929	0932	1032	|	...	1132	1137	...	1237	1238	...
95	**Oristano** d.	...	...	...	...	...	...	...	0730	0728	...	...	0829	0930	...	...	...	1030	1038	1129	1130	...	1229	1244	...	1329	1330	...
154	Macomer d.	...	...	...	...	...	...	...	0815	0817	...	...	...	1017	...	...	...	1122	1128	—	1217	...	...	—	...	—	1421	...
214	Ozieri-Chilivani a.	...	...	...	...	...	...	...	0858	0855	...	...	...	1055	...	...	...	—	...	⚒	|	...	...	⚒	...	...	1505	...
214	Ozieri-Chilivani d.	...	...	0652	0656	0757	0805	...	0906	0858	0900	0904	...	1058	1100	1101	1105	...	...	1243	|	...	...	1431	...	⚒W	1507	1510
	Sassari d.	...	0650	|	0743	0843	|	0848	0945	|	0939	|	...	|	1139	|	1145	...	...	|	1328	1333	...	1515	...	1426	|	1551
	Porto Torres a.	...	0705	|	0756	...	|	0901	...	|	...	|	...	|	...	|	...	...	...	|	...	1348	...	...	...	1441	|	...
	Porto Torres M a.	...	0708	|	0759	...	|	0905	...	|	...	|	...	|	...	|	...	...	...	|	...	1351	...	...	...	1444	|	...
285	Olbia a.	0645	...	0750	...	...	0908	...	...	0951	...	1000	...	1151	...	1201	...	1300	...	1349	...	...	...	...	1430	...	1602	...
306	Golfo Aranci a.	0708	...	...	...	...	...	...	...	...	...	...	...	...	...	...	...	1325	...	...	...	...	...	...	1455	...	...	...

km		⚒	⚒		⚒	⚒	⚒	†	†	⚒	†	⚒	⚒	†	†	†	⚒	†	⚒	†	⚒	†	⚒	⚒	⚒	⚒	†	
	Cagliari d.	...	...	...	1322	1430	...	1413	...	1522	1638	1640	...	...	...	1713	1720	1822	1834	...	...	1913	...	1920	🚌	2035	2035	...
	Decimomannu d.	...	...	...	1338	|	...	1428	...	1537	|	|	...	...	...	1732	1739	1837	|	...	...	1932	...	1938	...	2050	2050	...
	Oristano d.	1334	...	...	1431	1529	...	1531	...	1632	1730	1730	...	...	...	1829	1845	1930	1930	...	...	2029	...	2045	2050	2149	2159	...
	Macomer d.	1426	...	...	1520	1619	...	1629	...	...	1815	1817	...	...	...	...	...	2022	2017	...	...	...	2032	...	2158	...	...	...
	Ozieri-Chilivani a.	1509	...	...	...	1656	...	1711	...	...	1853	1855	...	...	...	...	...	2106	|	...	...	...	2115	...	...	...	...	...
0	Ozieri-Chilivani d.	1514	1514	...	...	1703	1701	1719	1716	...	1900	1858	1900	1905	2006	...	...	2108	|	2108	2120	...	2117	...	...	...	...	...
47	**Sassari** d.	|	1553	...	...	1742	|	1758	|	...	1946	|	1939	|	2050	...	...	|	2128	2148	2200	...	|	...	...	...	...	...
66	Porto Torres a.	|	...	...	...	1754	|	1810	|	...	...	|	...	|	...	...	...	|	...	...	...	...	|	...	...	...	...	...
67	Porto Torres M a.	|	...	...	...	1759	|	1814	|	...	...	|	...	|	...	...	...	|	...	...	...	...	|	...	...	...	...	...
	Olbia a.	1619	...	1626	...	...	1757	...	1814	...	...	1951	...	2002	...	...	...	2203	...	...	...	...	2214	...	...	...	...	...
	Golfo Aranci a.	...	...	1651	...	...	...	...	...	...	...	...	...	...	...	...	...	...	...	...	...	...	...	...	...	...	...	...

		⚒	⚒	⚒	⚒	†	⚒	⚒	⚒	†	†	⚒		⚒	†	⚒	†	†	⚒	⚒	⚒	†	†	⚒	⚒	⚒	⚒
Golfo Aranci d.	...	🚌	...	🚌	...	...	...	...	...	...	...	...	...	0715	...	...	...	...	...	...	...	...	...	...	...	...	...
Olbia d.	...	...	...	...	...	...	...	0600	...	0651	...	...	...	0738	...	0800	0802	...	...	1000	...	1002	...	...	...	...	1329
Porto Torres M d.	...	...	...	...	...	...	...	|	...	|	...	...	0718	—	...	|	|	...	0952	|	...	|	1001	...	...	...	|
Porto Torres d.	...	...	...	...	...	...	...	|	...	|	...	...	0721	⚒	...	|	|	...	0955	|	...	|	1004	...	...	...	|
Sassari d.	...	...	...	...	...	...	0610	|	0640	|	0715	...	0736	0815	0816	|	|	0917	1010	|	1015	|	1018	...	1202	...	|
Ozieri-Chilivani a.	...	...	...	...	...	...	0649	0651	|	0751	0754	...	...	0853	0855	0855	0901	1004	...	1053	1051	1059	1056	...	1241	...	1429
Ozieri-Chilivani d.	...	...	...	...	...	...	...	0654	|	...	0801	...	...	...	...	0858	0903	...	...	...	1058	...	1104	...	...	...	...
Macomer d.	...	0525	...	0620	...	...	...	0738	0753	...	0848	...	...	...	...	0938	0946	...	...	...	1138	...	1147	...	...	1339	...
Oristano d.	0530	0620	0630	0725	0730	0730	...	...	0835	...	0930	0930	...	...	...	1020	1030	...	...	...	1220	...	1230	1330	...	1430	...
Decimomannu d.	0629	...	0721	...	0821	0828	...	...	|	...	1018	1030	...	...	...	|	1129	...	...	...	|	...	1327	1422	...	1521	...
Cagliari a.	0643	...	0737	...	0837	0841	...	...	0927	...	1031	1051	...	...	...	1117	1144	...	...	...	1311	...	1343	1438	...	1537	...

	†	⚒W		†	†	⚒	⚒	⚒	⚒W	†	⚒	⚒	†	†		⚒	†	⚒	⚒	⚒	†	†	†	†	⚒	†	⚒
Golfo Aranci d.	...	...	1335	...	...	...	...	...	...	...	1525	...	...	...	1731	...	...	...	...	...	...	...	...	...	...	...	...
Olbia d.	...	...	1359	1401	...	1410	...	...	...	...	1550	1600	...	1614	1755	...	...	...	1800	...	...	1852	...	...	...	2007	2015
Porto Torres M d.	...	1400	—	|	...	|	...	...	1552	...	—	|	...	|	...	...	...	...	|	1813	1850	|	...	...	...	|	|
Porto Torres d.	...	1403	...	|	...	|	...	...	1555	...	⚒	|	...	|	...	...	...	...	|	1816	1853	|	...	...	...	|	|
Sassari d.	...	1418	...	|	1422	|	1430	...	1610	...	1615	|	1629	|	...	1651	...	1815	|	1831	1908	|	1921	2025	2025	|	|
Ozieri-Chilivani a.	...	...	...	1503	1500	1510	1508	...	...	...	1653	1655	1708	1714	...	1733	...	1853	1854	...	—	1958	2001	2103	2112	2106	2115
Ozieri-Chilivani d.	...	...	...	...	1508	...	1515	...	...	...	...	1658	...	...	...	1741	...	...	1858	...	...	...	2009	...	...	...	...
Macomer d.	...	...	†	...	1546	...	1554	1638	...	1731	...	1738	...	...	...	1836	...	...	1938	...	⚒	...	2057	...	...	...	...
Oristano d.	1430	...	1530	...	1630	...	1634	1730	...	1830	...	1820	...	...	...	1930	1930	...	2020	...	2130	...	2143	...	...	...	...
Decimomannu d.	1530	...	1629	...	1723	...	|	1829	...	1930	...	|	...	...	...	2030	2030	...	|	...	2237	...	2241	...	...	...	...
Cagliari a.	1552	...	1650	...	1738	...	1725	1849	...	1945	...	1911	...	...	...	2052	2052	...	2116	...	2250	...	2255	...	...	...	...

km		⚒	⚒	⚒	ⒶW	T	T			⚒	⚒	S	R	⚒	⚒	S	R	⚒	⚒		T	⚒W		⚒	⚒		Ⓐ
0	**Cagliari** d.	0526	0545	...	0615	0645	...	0745	...	0845	...	0945	...	1045	...	1145	...	1245	...	1345	...	1418	...	1445	...	1545	1645
17	Decimomannu d.	0541	0604	...	0635	0705	...	0804	...	0904	...	1004	...	1105	...	1204	...	1304	...	1404	...	1432	...	1504	...	1604	1705
46	Villamassargia a.	0601	0629	0639	0701	0729	0734	0829	0834	0929	0934	1029	1034	1129	1134	1229	1234	1329	1334	1429	1434	1457	...	1529	1534	1629	1729
	Carbonia Serbariu a.	|	0652	|	|	|	0751	0847	|	|	0951	1047	|	|	1150	1247	|	|	1350	1447	|	|	...	|	1550	1647	|
55	**Iglesias** a.	0611	...	0648	0712	0739	...	...	0848	0939	...	...	1043	1139	...	...	1243	1339	...	...	1443	1506	...	1539	...	...	1739

	V	N		A	Ⓐ	Ⓐ		A		🚌	
Cagliari d.	1645	...	1745	...	1845	...	1945	...	2045	...	...
Decimomannu d.	1704	...	1804	...	1904	...	2004	...	2105	...	...
Villamassargia a.	1729	1734	1829	1834	1929	1934	2029	2034	2129	2135	...
Carbonia Serbariu a.	|	1750	1847	|	|	1950	2047	|	|	2158	...
Iglesias a.	1739	...	...	1843	1939	...	...	2043	2138	...	...

	⚒	⚒	⚒	†	⚒	T	T	ⒶW	A		⚒
Iglesias d.	0554	0626	...	0630	0654	...	0722	0754	0819	...	...
Carbonia Serbariu d.	|	|	0616	|	|	0710	|	|	|	0810	0910
Villamassargia d.	0603	0633	0638	0638	0703	0726	0731	0803	0826	0831	0926
Decimomannu d.	0632	...	0702	0703	0732	...	0755	0831	...	0855	...
Cagliari a.	0651	...	0723	0723	0750	...	0812	0850	...	0915	...

km		⚒	ⒷV	ⒶW	†	⚒	⚒	ⒷV	†	ⒶW	⚒	⚒	T	†	⚒	⚒	⚒	⚒W	T		N	N	P		Ⓐ	Ⓐ	A	
	Iglesias d.	0922	1019	...	...	...	1122	1219	...	...	...	1322	1419	...	...	...	1522	1554	1619	...	...	1722	1819	...	...	1922	2019	...
0	**Carbonia** Serbariu d.	|	|	1010	1010	1110	|	|	1210	1210	1310	|	|	1410	1410	1510	|	|	|	1610	1710	|	|	1810	1910	|	|	2010
23	Villamassargia d.	0931	1026	1031	1031	1126	1131	1226	1231	1231	1326	1331	1426	1431	1431	1526	1531	1602	1626	1631	1726	1731	1826	1831	1926	1931	2026	2031
	Decimomannu d.	0955	...	1055	1055	...	1156	...	1255	1300	...	1355	...	1454	1500	...	1555	1631	...	1655	...	1755	...	1855	...	1955	...	2054
	Cagliari a.	1015	...	1114	1115	...	1214	...	1315	1319	...	1413	...	1512	1519	...	1612	1645	...	1716	...	1812	...	1919	...	2013	...	2112

A – Daily until Sept. 3; ⚒ from Sept. 5.
N – Ⓐ (Ⓑ from Sept. 11).
P – ⚒ (daily from Sept. 11).
R – Ⓑ from Sept. 11.
S – † (Ⓑ from Sept. 11).
T – ⚒ until Sept. 3; daily from Sept. 5.
V – From Sept. 11.
W – From Sept. 12.

Narrow gauge services on Sardinia are operated by ARST Gestione FdS, Via Zagabria 54, 09129 Cagliari. ✆ +39 070 4098 1, fax +39 070 4098 220, www.arst.sardegna.it.

Regular services operate on the following routes to differing frequencies: Monserrato Gottardo - Isili (*71 km*); Macomer - Nuoro (*61 km*); Sassari - Alghero (*30 km*); Sassari - Sorso (*11 km*). Tram connections are available at Monserrato Gottardo to / from Cagliari (Repubblica).

Additionally, summer only tourist services operate on the following routes: Sassari - Tempio (*91 km*); Tempio - Palau Marina (*59 km*); Macomer - Bosa Marina (*46 km*); Mandas - Arbatax (*159 km*); Isili - Sorgono (*83 km*).

See www.treninoverde.com.

MILANO - BOLOGNA - RIMINI - ANCONA 630

km		2 ⚒	2 ⚒	2 †	2 t	FB 8851 🍷 R		FR 9801 🍷 Ⓒ		IC 603	FB 8801 🍷 V		FR 9803 🍷 Ⓐ	2 ⑥⑦	FB 8803 🍷	2	IC 605 T	Ⓒ	Ⓐ	FB 8807 🍷		IC 607	FB 8809 🍷 T	IC 1545 ◆	
	Torino Porta Nuova 615 d.	...	...	...	...	...	...	...	...	...	...	...	...	...	...	...	...	...	...	0832	...	...	...	...	...
0	**Milano Centrale 600/15** d.	...	...	...	...	...	...	0600	...	...	...	...	0745	0620	0735	...	0705	...	...	|	...	...	1035	1000	...
219	**Bologna Centrale** d.	...	...	...	0500	...	0635	0719	0735	0800	0842	0835	0858	0911	0942	0935t	0958	1035	1035	1142	1135	1200	1242	1223	1235
254	Imola d.	...	...	...	0526	...	0701	|	0801	|	|	0901	|	0945	|	1001	|	1101	1101	|	1201	|	|	|	1301
261	Castelbolognese-Riolo Terme d.	...	...	...	0532	...	0709	|	0809	|	|	0909	|	|	|	1009	|	1109	1109	|	1209	|	|	|	1309
269	Faenza d.	...	...	...	0538	...	0716	|	0816	0827	|	0916	|	0954	|	1016	1025	1116	1124	|	1216	1225	|	1256	1316
284	Forlì d.	...	...	...	0547	...	0727	|	0827	0837	|	0927	|	1003	|	1027	1036	1127	1142	|	1227	1236	|	1306	1327
302	Cesena d.	...	...	...	0602	...	0742	|	0842	0849	|	0945	|	1014	|	1042	1048	1142	1205	|	1243	1248	|	1328	1342
331	**Rimini 621** ● ⊖ d.	0547	0610	0645	0629	0638	0803	0814	0903	0910	0936	1005	0957	1042	1036	1103	1110	1203	1232	1236	1315	1310	1336	1352	1403
340	Riccione d.	0558	0620	0653	...	|	0813	|	0911	0919	|	1014	|	1052	|	...	1119	1213	1242	|	1325	1319	|	1400	1413
349	Cattolica-Gabicce d.	0606	0629	0659	...	|	0822	|	0918	|	|	1023	|	1059	|	...	|	1223	1255	|	1335	|	|	|	1423
364	Pesaro d.	0617	0640	0710	...	0659	0834	|	0929	0937	0958	1034	|	1111	1058	...	1137	1234	1309	1258	1347	1337	1358	1415	1434
376	Fano d.	0625	0648	0718	...	|	0842	|	0937	0946	|	1042	|	|	|	...	1146	1242	1317	|	1355	1346	|	1424	1442
398	Senigallia d.	0640	0702	0732	...	|	0857	|	0952	0958	|	1057	|	1130	|	...	1158	1257	1331	|	1410	1358	|	1438	1457
415	Falconara Marittima 625 d.	0654	0717	0744	...	0727	0908	|	1002	|	|	1108	|	|	|	...	|	1308	1347	|	1429	|	|	|	1508
423	**Ancona 625** a.	0707	0730	0757	...	...	0925	0900	1012	1017	1029	1119	1042	1150	1129	...	1217	1319	1400	1329	1445	1417	1429	1459	1519
	Pescara Centrale 631 a.	...	...	...	...	...	...	1008	...	1159	1140	...	1151	1345	1240	...	1352	...	...	1440	...	1552	1540	1655	...
	Bari Centrale 631 a.	...	...	...	...	...	...	1239	...	1511	1432	...	1425	...	1521	...	1700	...	...	1721	...	1852	1821	2019	...
	Lecce 631 a.	...	...	...	...	...	...	1406	...	1706	1555	...	...	...	1648	...	...	...	...	1848	...	...	...	2215	...

	FB 8811 🍷		IC 609	FB 8813 🍷 Ⓐ	FB 8893 🍷 Ⓒ		FB 8815 🍷		IC 611	FB 8817 🍷 V		FB 8819 🍷		IC 613		FR 9811 🍷	FB 8823 🍷		FB 8825 🍷		FB 8829 🍷	2	ICN 765 ◆	ICN 755 ◆	ICN 757 ◆
Torino Porta Nuova 615 d.	...	...	...	...	...	...	...	...	...	...	...	...	...	...	...	...	...	...	...	...	...	...	...	...	2020
Milano Centrale 600/15 d.	1135	...	...	1235	1235	...	1335	...	...	...	...	1535	...	1510	...	1740	1735	...	1835	...	1935	...	1950	2050	|
Bologna Centrale d.	1342	1335	1400	1442	1442	1435	1542	1535	1600	1642	1635	1742	1735	1758	1835	1858	1942	1935t	2042	2035	2142	2135	2200	2310	2352
Imola d.	|	1401	|	|	|	1501	|	1601	|	|	1701	|	1801	|	1901	|	|	2001	|	2101	|	2201	|	|	|
Castelbolognese-Riolo Terme d.	|	1409	|	|	|	1509	|	1609	|	|	1709	|	1809	|	1909	|	|	2009	|	2109	|	2209	|	|	|
Faenza d.	|	1416	1425	|	|	1516	|	1616	1625	|	1716	1807	1816	1825	1916	|	2007	2016	2107	2116	|	2216	2234	2337	|
Forlì d.	|	1427	1436	|	|	1527	|	1627	1636	|	1727	1817	1827	1836	1927	1931	2017	2027	2117	2127	|	2227	2246	2348	|
Cesena d.	|	1442	1448	|	|	1542	|	1642	1648	|	1742	1829	1842	1848	1945	|	2029	2043	2129	2142	|	2242	2300	0002	|
Rimini 621 ● ⊖ d.	1436	1503	1510	1536	1536	1603	1636	1712	1710	1736	1803	1848	1903	1910	2005	1956	2048	2110	2148	2203	2236	2320	2330	0025	0058
Riccione d.	|	1510	1519	|	|	1613	|	1723	1719	|	1813	|	1911	1919	2014	|	|	...	|	2213	|	...	|	|	|
Cattolica-Gabicce d.	|	1517	|	|	|	1622	|	1733	|	|	1823	|	1923	|	2023	|	|	...	|	2223	|	...	|	|	|
Pesaro d.	1455	1528	1537	1558	1558	1633	1658	1745	1737	1758	1834	1910	1939	1937	2034	2017	2110	...	2210	2234	2258	...	2358	|	|
Fano d.	|	1536	1546	|	|	1641	|	...	1746	|	1842	|	1951	1946	2042	|	|	...	|	2242	|	...	|	|	|
Senigallia d.	|	1550	1558	|	|	1655	|	...	1758	|	1857	|	2005	1958	2057	|	|	...	|	2257	|	...	|	|	|
Falconara Marittima 625 d.	|	1604	|	|	|	1705	|	...	|	|	1908	|	2021	|	2108	|	|	...	|	2308	|	...	|	|	|
Ancona 625 a.	1529	1625	1617	1629	1629	1719	1729	...	1817	1829	1919	1941	2033	2017	2119	2046	2141	...	2241	2319	2329	...	0048	0130	0206
Pescara Centrale 631 a.	1640	...	1752	1740	1740	...	1840	...	1952	1940	...	2057	...	2152	...	...	2258	...	...	...	...	...	0228	0313	0338
Bari Centrale 631 a.	1940	...	2100	2021	2028	...	2121	...	2300	2221	...	2338	...	...	...	...	...	...	...	...	...	...	0611	0644	0654
Lecce 631 a.	2055	...	2256	2148	2155	...	2248	...	...	2348	...	...	...	...	...	...	...	...	...	...	...	...	0919	0830	0852

	ICN 1580 ◆	ICN 758 ◆	ICN 752 ◆		FB 8802 🍷	ICN 754 ◆		FR 9802 🍷	FB 8804 🍷		FB 8806 🍷		Ⓐ	IC 604	Ⓒ	FB 8810 🍷			IC 606		FB 8814 🍷		FB 8816 🍷 V	IC 608	
Lecce 631 d.	1835	1823	2120	...	...	2210	...	...	...	...	...	...	...	...	...	...	...	...	...	...	0603	...	0703	0626	...
Bari Centrale 631 d.	2030	2133	2309	...	...	0001	...	...	...	...	...	...	...	...	...	0530	...	...	0555	...	0730	...	0830	0807	...
Pescara Centrale 631 d.	0006	0103	0236	...	...	0323	...	...	...	...	0600	...	...	0710	...	0811	...	...	0902	...	1011	...	1111	1102	...
Ancona 625 d.	0139	0228	0403	0435	0500	0511	0533	0610	0620	0640	0716	0740	0825	0836	0850	0922	...	...	1036	1040	1122	1140	1222	1236	1240
Falconara Marittima 625 d.	|	|	|	0444	|	|	0541	|	|	0651	|	0753	0834	|	0901	|	...	...	|	1051	|	1151	|	|	1253
Senigallia d.	|	|	|	0457	|	|	0551	|	|	0705	|	0805	0844	0854	0911	|	...	...	1054	1101	|	1205	|	1254	1303
Fano d.	|	|	|	0512	|	|	0606	|	|	0721	|	0820	0858	0907	0925	|	...	...	1107	1115	|	1221	|	1307	1318
Pesaro d.	|	|	|	0520	0528	0545	0615	0638	0649	0729	0745	0828	0906	0917	0934	0955	...	...	1117	1124	1155	1229	1255	1317	1326
Cattolica-Gabicce d.	|	|	|	0534	|	|	0626	|	|	0740	|	0839	0917	|	0945	|	...	...	|	1135	|	1240	|	|	1337
Riccione d.	|	|	|	0547	|	|	0633	|	|	0749	|	0847	0926	0934	0954	|	...	...	1134	1144	|	1249	|	1334	1346
Rimini 621 ● ⊖ d.	0245	0324	0459	0600	0550	0610	0645	0700	0709	0800	0806	0857	0940	0947	1007	1017	...	1041	1147	1157	1217	1300	1317	1347	1357
Cesena d.	|	|	|	0618	0607	0628	0706	|	0725	0816	0824	0916	1001	1009	1025	|	...	1108	1207	1216	|	1318	|	1407	1416
Forlì d.	|	|	|	0631	0620	0640	0724	0724	0736	0827	0836	0927	1023	1021	1036	|	...	1123	1219	1227	|	1329	|	1419	1427
Faenza d.	|	|	|	0642	0629	0650	0735	|	0746	0838	0846	0937	1034	1031	1046	|	...	1133	1229	1237	|	1339	|	1429	1438
Castelbolognese-Riolo Terme d.	|	|	|	0649	|	|	0743	|	|	0844	|	0944	1044	|	1058	|	...	1140	|	1244	|	1345	|	|	1444
Imola d.	|	|	|	0656	|	|	0756	|	|	0856	|	0956	1056	|	1104	|	...	1146	|	1256	|	1356	|	|	1456
Bologna Centrale a.	0352	0427	0615	0722	0701	0727	0821	0807	0814	0921	0914	1021	1121	1101	1129	1114	...	1221t	1300	1321	1314	1421	1412	1500	1521t
Milano Centrale 600/15 a.	|	0712	0930	...	0910	|	...	0920	1025	...	1125	...	...	1345	...	1325	...	...	...	...	1525	...	...	...	...
Torino Porta Nuova 615 a.	0740	...	...	...	...	1120	...	...	...	...	...	...	...	...	...	...	...	...	...	...	...	...	...	...	...

	FB 8880 🍷 Ⓒ	FB 8818 🍷 Ⓐ	2	IC 610		FB 8822 🍷 T		FB 8824 🍷	IC 1546 ◆	IC 612 T		FB 8826 🍷		FB 8828 🍷 V	2 ⑥⑦	IC 614		FB 8830 🍷	FR 9814 🍷 Ⓐ	2	FB 9852 🍷R	FR 9816 🍷 Ⓒ	Ⓐ	Ⓒ	2
Lecce 631 d.	0756	0803	...	0820	...	...	...	1103	1005	...	...	1203	...	1303	...	...	...	1403	...	...	...	1540	...	...	...
Bari Centrale 631 d.	0923	0930	...	0955	...	1130	...	1230	1142	1155	...	1330	...	1430	...	1355	...	1530	1615	...	...	1704	...	...	...
Pescara Centrale 631 d.	1211	1211	...	1302	...	1411	...	1511	1445	1502	...	1611	...	1711	1620	1702	...	1811	1848	...	...	1938	...	...	...
Ancona 625 d.	1322	1322	...	1436	1440	1522	...	1622	1616	1636	1640	1722	...	1822	1810	1836	1840	1922	1956	...	...	2049	2040	2040	2240
Falconara Marittima 625 d.	|	|	...	|	1451	|	...	|	|	|	1651	|	...	|	1818	|	1853	|	|	...	2038	|	2051	2052	2249
Senigallia d.	|	|	...	1454	1501	|	...	|	1631	1654	1704	|	...	|	1833	1854	1903	|	|	...	|	|	2104	2108	2301
Fano d.	|	|	...	1507	1515	|	...	|	1647	1707	1718	|	...	|	1851	1907	1918	|	|	...	|	|	2118	2126	2315
Pesaro d.	1355	1355	...	1517	1524	1555	...	1655	1700	1717	1727	1758	1817	1855	1901	1917	1926	1955	|	...	2102	|	2127	2135	2323
Cattolica-Gabicce d.	|	|	...	|	1535	|	...	|	|	|	1738	|	1828	|	1912	|	1937	|	|	...	|	|	2138	2146	2334
Riccione d.	|	|	...	1534	1544	|	...	|	1717	1734	1745	|	1837	|	1919	1934	1946	|	|	...	|	|	2145	2154	2341
Rimini 621 ● ⊖ d.	1417	1417	1444	1547	1557	1617	1644	1717	1727	1747	1757	1817	1847	1917	1927	1947	1957	2017	2042	2050	2125	2142	2157	2206	2355
Cesena d.	|	|	1509	1607	1616	|	1709	|	1744	1807	1816	|	1912	|	1944	2007	2016	|	|	2111	...	|	2216	2225	...
Forlì d.	|	|	1527	1619	1627	|	1727	|	1757	1819	1827	|	1926	|	1956	2019	2027	|	|	2125	...	|	2227	2236	...
Faenza d.	|	|	1537	1629	1638	|	1736	|	1807	1829	1837	|	1937	|	2007	2029	2037	|	|	2135	...	|	2238	2247	...
Castelbolognese-Riolo Terme d.	|	|	1544	|	1644	|	1744	|	|	|	1844	|	1945	|	|	|	2044	|	|	2142	...	|	2244	2253	..
Imola d.	|	|	1556	|	1656	|	1756	|	|	|	1856	|	1956	|	2017	|	2056	|	|	2148	...	|	2256	2300	...
Bologna Centrale a.	1514	1514	1621t	1700	1721	1714	1821t	1814	1833	1901	1921	1914	2021	2012	2047	2100	2121t	2114	2137	2214t	...	2237	2321	2325	...
Milano Centrale 600/15 a.	1725	1725	...	...	...	1925	...	|	2115	2145	...	2125	...	...	2325	...	...	2325	2250	...	...	2350	...	...	...
Torino Porta Nuova 615 a.	...	...	...	...	...	...	...	2140	...	...	...	...	...	...	...	...	...	...	...	...	...	...	...	...	...

◆ – NOTES (LISTED BY TRAIN NUMBER)

- **752** – 🛏 1, 2 cl., ▬ 2 cl. (4 berth) and (2) Lecce - Bologna - Milano.
- **754** – ①–⑥: 🛏 1, 2 cl., ▬ 2 cl. (4 berth) and (2) Lecce - Bologna - Torino.
- **755** – 🛏 1, 2 cl., ▬ 2 cl. (4 berth) and (2) Milano - Bologna - Lecce.
- **757** – 🛏 1, 2 cl., ▬ 2 cl. (4 berth) and (2) Torino - Bologna - Lecce.
- **758** – 🛏 1, 2 cl., ▬ 2 cl. (4 berth) and (2) Lecce - Bologna - Milano.
- **765** – 🛏 1, 2 cl., ▬ 2 cl. (4 berth) and (2) Milano - Bologna - Lecce.
- **1545** – ⑥: (12) Milano - Lecce.
- **1546** – ⑦: (12) Lecce - Milano.
- **1580** – ⑦: 🛏 1, 2 cl., ▬ 2 cl. (4 berth) and (2) Lecce - Bologna - Torino.

- **R** – From/to Ravenna.
- **T** – From/to Taranto.
- **V** – From/to Venezia.

- **e** – Arrive 1210 on Aug. 7.
- **f** – Depart 0735 on Aug. 7 (train number **35805**).
- **g** – Arrive 2230 on Aug. 7.
- **j** – June 13 - Sept. 18.
- **k** – June 15 - Sept. 7.

- **p** – July 31 - Dec. 4.
- **q** – June 26 - July 24.
- **r** – ⑤⑥⑦ only.
- **t** – Not Sept. 24, 25.
- **w** – Until Nov. 20.
- **x** – From Nov. 21.
- **y** – Until Sept. 19.
- **z** – From Sept. 20.

⊖ – Connections may be available to service(s) in previous column(s).
● – For 🚌 service Rimini - San Marino and v.v. – see page 312.

12 *Compulsory reservation is required on all EC, EN, FA, FB, FR, IC and ICN trains in Italy* 311

631 ANCONA - BARI - LECCE

km		ICN 765	ICN 789	ICN 755	ICN 757				FA 8303	FR 9801	IC 703	FB 8801	FR 9803		IC 603	FB 8803
		2	2	2	2	2	2	2	⚊		2	⚊		2		2
		⚊	⚊	⚊	⚊	⚊	⚊		⚊	⚊	⚊	V	Ⓐ			⚊
Torino Porta Nuova 615......d.		...	...	...	2020	...	...	...	...	...	...	...	...	...	...
Milano Centrale 615/30 ....d.		...	1950	...	2050	...	...	...	0600	...	...	0745	...	0735	...
Bologna Centrale 615/30 ....d.		2200	2200	2310	2352	...	...	0719	0842	0858	...	0800	0942
Ancona 625/30 ....d.	0	0051		0133	0209			0903		1032	1045	1020	1132
Civitanova Marche-Montegranaro . d.	43											1042	...
S. Benedetto del Tronto .... d.	85											1116	...
Pescara Centrale ....a.	146	0228		0313	0338			1008		1140	1151	1159	1240
Pescara Centrale ....d.	146	0233		0315	0340			1011		1143	1154	1201	1243
Termoli ....d.	236							1059		1231	1242	1255	1331
Roma Termini 626 ....d.		2358			0805		0728						
Foggia 626 ....a.	323	0449	0449	0515	0535			1056	1142	1223	1315	1325	1352	1415
Foggia ....d.	323	0453	0504	0519	0539	0606	0710	1105	1145	1318	1328	1355	1418	1452
Barletta ....d.	391	0528	0537	0554	0615	0650	0754	1136		1310	1351	1428	1447	1508
Bari Centrale ....a.	446	0611	0623	0640	0654	0740	0844	1204	1239	1400	1432	1425	1511	1521	1556
Bari Centrale ....▲ d.	446	0500	0542	0610	0641	0627	0648	0658	0744	0846	0940	1208	1215	1242	1257	1405	1436	1442	1515	1525	1558
Gioia del Colle ....▲ d.		0717										
Taranto 637/8 ....▲ a.		0755										
Monopoli ....d.	487	0534	0616	0638	0651	0713	0727	0820	0915	1014	1241	1331	1435	1516	1556	1630
Fasano ....d.	501	0542	0624	0646	0702	0724	0740	0829	0923	1022	1249	1339	1444	1524	1607	1638
Ostuni ....d.	521	0555	0637	0657	0716	0739	0754	0840	0936	1035	1350	1455	1537	1620	1651
Brindisi ♣ ....d.	557	0620	0702	0717	0854	0739	0803	0820	0906	1003	1058	1303	1320	1340	1411	1518	1530	1603	1642	1619	1714
Lecce ....a.	596	0652	0735	0745	0919	0809	0830	0852	0935	1034	1130	1328	1345	1406	1443	1548	1555	1634	1706	1648	1745

		IC 605	FB 8807		FB 8809	IC 607	FA 8315	FB 8811		IC 1545	FB 8813	FB 8893		IC 609	FB 8815		IC 705	FA 8323	FB 8817		IC 611	FB 8819	IC 613	FB 8823
		2	⚊	2	⚊	⚊	⚊	⚊			⚊	⚊	2	⚊		2	⚊		⚊	⚊	2		⚊	⚊	⚊
		⑥⑦								♦	Ⓐ	Ⓒ	⚊			⑤		V						
Torino Porta Nuova 615....d.			0832																	
Milano Centrale 615/30 ....d.		0620	0705		1035			1135		1000	1235	1235			1335					1535	1510	1735
Bologna Centrale 615/30 ...d.		0911	0958	1142	1242	1200		1342		1223	1442	1442		1400	1542			1642		1600	1742	1758	1942
Ancona 625/30 ....d.		1152	1220	1332	1432	1420		1532		1501	1632	1632		1620	1732			1832		1820	1944	2020	2144
Civitanova-Montegranaro...d.		1227	1242			1442				1527				1642						1842		2042
S. Benedetto del Tronto....d.		1256	1316			1516				1555				1716						1916	2023	2116	2223
Pescara Centrale.............a.		1345	1352	1440	1540	1552		1640		1655	1740	1740		1752	1840			1940		1952	2057	2152	2258
Pescara Centrale.............d.		1354	1443		1543	1554		1643		1659	1743	1743		1754	1843			1943		1954	2100		
Termoli ....d.		1447	1531		1631	1647		1731		1759	1831	1831		1848	1931			2031		2047	2148	
Roma Termini 626.........d.							1455									1601	1800				
Foggia 626 ....a.		1535	1615		1715	1735	1752	1821		1851	1915	1924		1935	2015		2018	2056	2115		2135	2232
Foggia ....d.		1538	1618		1718	1738	1801	1824		1854	1918	1927		1938	2018		2036	2105	2118		2138	2235
Barletta ....d.		1610	1647		1747	1810	1829	1852		1930	1947	1956		2010	2047		2110	2136	2147		2210	2304
Bari Centrale ....a.		1700	1721		1821	1852	1900	1930		2019	2021	2043		2100	2121		2143	2204	2221		2300	2338
Bari Centrale ....▲ d.		1715	1725	1815	1836		1904	1934		2023	2025	2032	2040	2104	2125		2201	2208	2225	2240		
Gioia del Colle ....▲ d.		1747			1908											2233		
Taranto 637/8 ....▲ a.		1820			1942											2310		
Monopoli ....d.			1850						2100		2114	2130				2314		
Fasano ....d.			1859						2110		2123	2156				2322		
Ostuni ....d.			1912						2123		2137	2209				2335		
Brindisi ♣ ....d.			1819	1934			2001	2030		2147	2121	2126	2201	2231	2219		2303	2319	2357	
Lecce ....a.			1848	2005			2024	2055		2215	2148	2155	2233	2256	2248		2328	2348	0030	

		FB 8806	IC 604	FB 8810	IC 606			FA 8302	FB 8814		IC 608	FB 8816		FB 8880	FB 8818	IC 610			FB 8822	IC 1546		IC 612		FB 8824	FA 8314	FB 8826
		⚊		⚊		2	2	⚊	⚊		⚊	⚊	2	⚊	⚊	⚊	2			⚊	♦	2		2		⚊	⚊	⚊
											⚊			V	Ⓒ	Ⓐ					V				
Lecce ....d.			0450	0507	0550	0603	0555	0626	0703	0710	0756	0803	0820		0810		1005	1000		1040	1103	1150	1203
Brindisi ♣ ....d.			0522	0535	0611	0626	0635	0650	0726	0739	0819	0826	0842		0845		1029	1031		1109	1126	1211	1226
Ostuni ....d.			0544	0601		0659	0713			0904		0914		1050	1052		1131
Fasano ....d.			0558	0616		0713	0726		0810		0917			1103	1104		1145
Monopoli ....d.			0607	0624		0722	0736		0820		0927		0934	1114	1113		1153
Taranto 637/8 ....▲ d.													1010		1025		
Gioia del Colle ....▲ d.													1041		1059		
Bari Centrale ....▲ a.			0643	0700	0710	0726	0756	0803	0826	0919	0926	0951	1000	1115	1139	1153	1130	1236	1226	1310	1326
Bari Centrale ....d.			0530	0555	0645	0714	0730	0758	0807	0830	0923	0930	0955	1130	1142	1155	1240	1230	1314	1330
Barletta ....a.			0602	0643	0732	0745	0802	0859	0850	0902	0955	1002	1043	1202	1224	1243	1326	1302	1345	1402
Foggia ....a.			0633	0713		0813	0803	0949	0920	0933	1026	1033	1115	1233	1252	1315	1410	1333	1413	1432
Foggia 626 ....d.			0636	0716		0822	0836		0923	0936	1029	1036	1118	1236	1254	1318		1336	1422	1436
Roma Termini 626.........d.						1123									1720		
Termoli ....d.			0722	0806			0921		1010	1022		1122	1122	1206	1322	1353		1406	1422		1522
Pescara Centrale.............a.			0808	0900			1008		1100	1108		1208	1208	1303	1408	1443		1500	1508		1608
Pescara Centrale.............d.		0600	0710	0811	0902		1011		1102	1111		1211	1211	1302	1411	1445		1502	1511		1611
S. Benedetto del Tronto....d.		0630	0745	0840	0941				1141			1341		1520	1541		
Civitanova-Montegranaro...d.			0810		1010				1210			1410		1545	1610		
Ancona 625/30 ....a.		0713	0833	0919	1033		1119		1233	1219		1319	1319	1433	1519	1613		1619		1719
Bologna Centrale 615/30 ...a.		0914	1101	1114	1300		1314		1500	1412		1514	1514	1700	1714	1833		1901	1814		1914
Milano Centrale 615/30 ....a.		1125	1345	1325			1525					1725	1725		1925	2115		2145		2125
Torino Porta Nuova 615 ...a.															2140		

♦ — **NOTES** (LISTED BY TRAIN NUMBER)

755 – 🛏 1, 2 cl., 🚃 2 cl. (4 berth) and 🚃 Milano - Bologna - Lecce.
757 – 🛏 1, 2 cl., 🚃 2 cl. (4 berth) and 🚃 Torino - Bologna - Lecce.
765 – 🛏 1, 2 cl., 🚃 2 cl. (4 berth) and 🚃 Milano - Bologna - Lecce.
789 – ⑤ (from Roma): 🛏 1, 2 cl., 🚃 2 cl. (4 berth) and 🚃 Roma - Lecce.
1545 – ⑥: 🚃 Milano - Lecce.
1546 – ⑦: 🚃 Lecce - Milano.

V – From/to Venezia.
f – Depart 0735 on Aug. 7.
j – Depart 0009 on Aug. 8 (Aug. 7 departure from Torino).
p – Until Sept. 18.
q – From Sept. 19.
v – Also Dec. 8; not Dec. 9.
w – Until Nov. 20.
x – From Nov. 21.
y – Until Sept. 19.
z – From Sept. 20.

▲ – For additional services Bari - Taranto and v.v. – see page 313.
♣ – For additional services Brindisi - Taranto and v.v. – see panel.
● – For 🚌 service Rimini - San Marino and v.v. – see panel.

BRINDISI - TARANTO No service on †

		⚊	⚊		⚊		⚊	⚊		⚊	⚊
Brindisi ....d.		0651	0744		1045		1521	1646	...	1804	2001
Francavilla Fontana 636 d.		0726	0819		1121		1601	1726	...	1838	2036
Taranto ....a.		0755	0853		1148		1629	1755	...	1913	2103

		⚊	⚊	⚊		⚊	⚊	⚊		⚊
Taranto ....d.		0545	0616	0856		1244	1455	1648	...	1849
Francavilla Fontana 636 d.		0611	0643	0923		1311	1522	1715	...	1915
Brindisi ....a.		0647	0726	0959		1347	1557	1752	...	1958

● – 🚌 service **RIMINI - SAN MARINO and v.v.**: Valid June 7 - Sept. 14, 2016
27 km, journey 50 – 55 minutes.
From **Rimini** (FS railway station): 0655, 0810, 0925, 1040, 1155, 1310, 1425, 1540, 1655, 1810, 1925, 2040.
From **San Marino**: 0645, 0800, 0915, 1030, 1145, 1300, 1415, 1530, 1645, 1800, 1915, 2030.
Operator: BonelliBus s.a.s., Via Murano 47838, Riccione ✆ +39 0541 662.069.

LECCE - BARI - ANCONA   631

		IC 614	FB 8828			FB 8830	IC 704	FR 9814		IC 710	FR 9816			FA 8326			ICN 1580	ICN 758		ICN 752	ICN 754	ICN 788
		2 ⑥⑦	2	V	2	⚒	2	†		⚒ Ⓐ	2 ⚒	⑦	2 Ⓒ	2 ⚒	2 ⚒	2 ⚒	◆	◆	2	◆	◆	◆
Lecce........................d.	...	1210	1303	1323	1340	1403	...	...	1430	...	1540	1610	1630	1650	1710	1835	1835	1823	1911	2120	2210	2230
Brindisi ♣...............d.	...	1238	1326	1348	1410	1426	...	...	1500	...	1605	1633	1652	1711	1739	1858	1904	1852	1935	2148	2238	2255
Ostuni.....................d.	...	1300			1409	1432	...	...	1522	...		1655		1803	1919	1928		1956		2211	2301	2317
Fasano.....................d.	...	1314			1420	1446	...	...	1536	...		1707	1722	1817	1931	1943		2008		2226	2316	2330
Monopoli...................d.	...	1322			1430	1455	...	...	1544	...		1717	1731	1827	1940	1955		2023		2237	2327	2341
Taranto 637 / 8 ......▲ d.	...						...	1540	...	...							1949					
Gioia del Colle ....▲ d.	...						...	1612	...	...							2023					
Bari Centrale.........▲ a.	...	1358		1426	1508	1545	1526	...	1622	1649	1701	1753	1800	1810	1905	2015	2026	2108	2045	2305	2357	0010
Bari Centrale............d.	...		1355	1430	...	...	1530	1555	1615	...	1714	1704	...	1814	...	...	2030	2133	...	2309	0001	0015
Barletta...................d.	...		1443	1502	...	...	1602	1648		...	1746	...	...	1845	...	...	2121	2221	...	2357	0034	0103
Foggia.....................a.	...		1515	1533	...	...	1633	1725	1711	...	1819	1801	...	1913	...	...	2200	2302	...	0037	0111	0145
Foggia 626................d.	...		1518	1536	...	...	1636	1741	1714	...	1839	1804	...	1922	...	...	2203	2306	...	0041	0115	0200
Roma Termini 626 ....a.	...				...	...	2220			...	2311		...	2220	...	...			...			0634
Termoli....................a.	...		1606	1622	...	...	1722		1758	...	1850		...		...	...	2304		...			
Pescara Centrale......a.	...		1700	1708	...	...	1808		1845	...	1935		...		...	...	0003	0101	...	0234	0321	
Pescara Centrale......d.	1620		1702	1711	...	...	1811		1848	...	1938		...		...	...	0006	0103	...	0236	0323	
S. Benedetto del Tronto..d.	1708		1741		...	...				...			...		...	...			...			
Civitanova Marche-Montegranaro..d.	1736		1810		...	...				...			...		...	...			...			
Ancona 625 / 30 ....a.	1808		1833	1819	...	...	1919		1953	...	2046		...		...	...	0135	0224	...	0359	0508	
Bologna Centrale 615 / 30..a.	2047		2100	2012	...	...	2114		2137	...	2237		...		...	...	0352	0427	...	0615	0727	
Milano Centrale 615 / 30..a.	2325				...	...	2325		2250	...	2350		...		...	...		0712	...	0930		
Torino Porta Nuova 615..a.	...				...	...				...			...		...	...	0740		...		1120	

▲ – BARI - TARANTO and v.v. local services:
2nd class only

km																			
0	Bari...............d.	⚒ 0530	⚒ 0624		⚒ 0715	† 0815	...	⚒ 1020	...	⚒ 1308	⚒ 1335	...	† 1443	⚒ 1510	...	† 1600	⚒ 1615	...	⚒ 1744
54	Gioia del Colle..d.	0610	0706		0802	0856	...	1101	...	1342	1418	...	1524	1543	...	1640	1657	...	1817
115	Taranto..........a.	0650	0746		0843	0938	...	1143	...	1415	1500	...	1603	1624	...	1720	1734	...	1856

Bari...............d.	⚒ 1815	...	⚒ 1932	...	2040								
Gioia del Colle..d.	1855	...	2013	...	2123								
Taranto..........a.	1950	...	2056	...	2207								

Taranto..........d.	⚒ 0525	⚒ 0609		0630	0630		⚒ 0720	0814	...	† 1040	⚒ 1220	...	⚒ 1345	† 1352	⚒ 1433		⚒ 1537	...	⚒ 1700	† 1700	⚒ 1911	⚒ 1910	†	2006
Gioia del Colle..d.	0601	0650		0709	0713		0759	0853	...	1119	1301	...	1425	1431	1511		1617	...	1739	1739	1942	1950		2043
Bari...............a.	0640	0732		0751	0755		0841	0933	...	1200	1351	...	1506	1519	1543		1658	...	1811	1812	2025	2033		2125

◆ – NOTES (LISTED BY TRAIN NUMBER)

752 – 🛏 1, 2 cl., 🛏 2 cl. (4 berth) and 🍽 Lecce - Bologna - Milano.
754 – ①–⑥: 🛏 1, 2 cl., 🛏 2 cl. (4 berth) and 🍽 Lecce - Bologna - Torino.
758 – 🛏 1, 2 cl., 🛏 2 cl. (4 berth) and 🍽 Lecce - Bologna - Milano.
788 – ⑦: 🛏 1, 2 cl., 🛏 2 cl. (4 berth) and 🍽 Lecce - Bologna - Torino.
1580 – ⑦: 🛏 1, 2 cl., 🛏 2 cl. (4 berth) and 🍽 Lecce - Roma.

V – From / to Venezia.
p – Until Sept. 18.
q – From Sept. 19.
r – June 27 - July 25: Bologna a. 0443, Torino Porta Nuova a. 0916.
t – Arrive 1210 on Aug. 7.
v – Also Aug. 15, Nov. 1; not Aug. 14, Oct. 30.
y – Until Sept. 19.
z – From Sept. 20.

▲ – For additional services Bari - Taranto and v.v. – see panel.
♣ – For additional services Brindisi - Taranto and v.v. – see page 312.

PAOLA - COSENZA - SIBARI   633
2nd class only

km																			
	Napoli Centrale 640.....d.	⚒	⚒	⚒	⚒		Ⓒ 0650	0855		⚒	⚒	A	⚒		1225	⚒	⚒	⚒		1925
0	Paola 640.........d.	0527		0727	0827		0927		1051	1302		1404	1427		1527	1621		1727	1827		1927		2027	2127	2307
	Cosenza............d.		0545			0845				1345			1445				1845		1945		
21	Castiglione Cosentino..d.	0540	0550	0740	0840	0851	0940		1105	1316	1351	1417	1440	1451	1540	1634		1740	1840	1851	1940	1951	2040	2141	2321
21	Castiglione Cosentino..a.	0541	0550	0741	0841	0851	0941		1106	1317	1351	1418	1441	1451	1541	1635		1741	1841	1851	1941	1954	2041	2142	2322
26	Cosenza 640......a.	0549		0749	0849		0949		1114	1324		1426	1449		1549	1643		1749	1849		1949		2049	2159	2329
	Sibari 637........a.		0654			0948			1440			1546						1942		2050		2254

km																			
0	Sibari 637........d.		⚒ 0543		⚒ 0630		⚒ 0843			⚒ 1243			⚒ 1520		⚒ 1643			⚒ 1958		
	Cosenza 640......d.	0537	0555		0630	0637		0737		0937	1237		1324		1337	1437	1502		1702		1737	1837	1900	2002	...
62	Castiglione Cosentino..d.	0543	0601	0630	0636	0643	0718	0743	0931	0943	1243		1330	1330	1343	1443	1508	1610	1708	1730	1743	1843	1906	2008	2048
62	Castiglione Cosentino..a.	0543	0601	0630	0636	0643	0719	0743	0932	0943	1243		1330	1331	1343	1443	1508	1610	1708	1731	1743	1843	1906	2008	2049
67	Cosenza............a.		0638			0725		0938			1338			1616		1738			2055
	Paola 640.........a.	0559	0617		0652	0659	0759	0759		0959	1259		1347		1359	1459	1524		1724		1759	1859	1922	2024	...
	Napoli Centrale 640.....a.		1010								1740			1920					2312		

A – ⚒ until Sept. 16; Ⓐ from Sept. 19.

CATANZARO LIDO - LAMEZIA TERME   634
2nd class only

km																
0	Catanzaro Lido 637 ......d.	⚒ 0547	...	0640	...	⚒ 0747	...	0947	...	⚒ 1047	...	1140	...	1340	...
9	Catanzaro..........d.	0555	...	0648	...	0755	...	0955	...	1055	...	1148	...	1348	...
47	Lamezia Terme Centrale 640..a.	0630	...	0730	...	0830	...	1030	...	1130	...	1230	...	1430	...

Catanzaro Lido 637 ......d.	⚒ 1440	...	1540	...	1640	...	1947	...
Catanzaro..........d.	1448	...	1548	...	1648	...	1955	...
Lamezia Terme Centrale 640..a.	1530	...	1630	...	1730	...	2030	...

Lamezia Terme Centrale 640..d.	0655	...	0850	...	1155	...	1255	...	1355	...	⚒ 1455	...	1555	...	1655	...	1755	...	1855	...	⚒ 2140	...
Catanzaro..........d.	0729	...	0925	...	1229	...	1329	...	1429	...	1529	...	1629	...	1729	...	1829	...	1929	...	2213	...
Catanzaro Lido 637 ......a.	0737	...	0932	...	1237	...	1432	...	1437	...	1537	...	1637	...	1737	...	1837	...	1937	...	2221	...

636 SUD EST services

Valid until June 3, 2017. No service on †

Line 1: BARI - TARANTO

km																									
														W			W			W		W		W	
0	Bari Centrale ♣ d.	...	...	...	...	...	...	0559	0624	0644	0714	0805	0814	0928	0946	1030	1053	...	1133	...	1201	1236	...	1248	1340
1	Bari Sud Est d.	0421	...	...	0518	0525	...	0602	0627	0647	0718	0810	0817	0932	0950	1033	1056	...	1137	...	1204	1239	...	1252	1343
4	Mungivacca d.	0427	...	...	0524	0531	...	0608	0634	0653	0724	0817	0823	0938	0956	1040	1102	...	1143	...	1211	1245	...	1258	1349
	Casamassima d.	|	...	...	0555	|	...	0641	|	0726	|	0851	|	1010	|	1111	|	...	1215	...	|	1317	...	|	1421
43	Putignano d.	0513	...	...	0627	0628	...	0713	0740	0759	0824	0922	0918	1041	1052	1143	1155	...	1247	...	1308	1349	...	1403	1453
78	Martina Franca 2 d.	0556	0606	0651	...	0713	0743	...	0825	...	0909	...	1000	...	1133	...	1239	1242	...	1327	1350	...	1414	1448	...
113	Taranto ♣ a.	...	0644	0730	...	...	0823	...	...	...	...	...	...	...	...	...	...	1321	...	1407	...	...	1454	...	...

km																									
																	W								
	Bari Centrale ♣ d.	1343	1426	1429	...	1529	1533	1613	...	1616	...	1712	1722	...	1745	...	1830	1838	...	1929	1933	2037	2040	2120	...
	Bari Sud Est d.	1346	1429	1432	...	1532	1536	1616	...	1619	...	1716	1725	...	1749	...	1834	1842	...	1933	1937	2040	2044	2124	...
0	Mungivacca d.	1352	1435	1438	...	1539	1543	1623	...	1625	...	1723	1731	...	1755	...	1840	1848	...	1939	1943	2046	2050	2131	...
20	Casamassima d.	|	1507	|	...	1614	|	|	...	1656	...	|	1803	...	|	...	1911	|	...	2011	|	2117	|	|	...
44	Putignano d.	1459	1539	1531	...	1647	1641	1717	...	1727	...	1809	1834	1812	1847	1908	1943	1940	...	2042	2036	2149	2138	2218	...
	Martina Franca 2 d.	1542	...	1618	1639	...	1723	1759	1822	...	...	...	...	1854	...	1949	...	...	...	...	2119	...	...	...	...
	Taranto ♣ a.	...	...	...	1717	...	...	...	1900	...	...	...	...	...	...	...	...	...	...	...	...	...	...	...	...

												W							W	W		W		
Taranto ♣ d.	...	...	...	...	...	...	...	...	...	...	0650	...	...	0743	...	...	0836	...	...	...	...	...	...	...
Martina Franca 2 d.	...	0456	...	0541	...	0612	0638	...	0724	...	0731	...	...	0832	...	...	0915	0925	1008	...	...	1137	...	1224
Putignano d.	0444	0544	0546	0625	0632	0655	0734	0736	0810	0819	...	0836	...	0917	0927	0936	...	1010	1053	1100	1116	1222	1222	1310
Casamassima d.	0516	|	0620	|	0705	|	|	0809	|	0852	...	|	...	|	|	1009	...	|	|	1133	|	|	1255	|
Mungivacca d.	0546	0633	0654	0712	0739	0736	0836	0840	0859	0921	...	0928	...	0953	1018	1041	...	1058	1134	1205	1210	1312	1328	1404
Bari Sud Est a.	0552	0639	0700	0719	0746	0742	0842	0846	0906	0931	...	0936	...	1000	1024	1047	...	1105	1140	1211	1216	1318	1334	1411
Bari Centrale ♣ a.	0554	0641	0702	0721	0748	0744	0844	0848	0908	0933	...	0938	...	1002	1026	1049	...	1107	1142	1213	1218	1320	1336	1413

		W			W		W				W				W									
Taranto ♣ d.	...	...	...	1327	...	...	1412	...	...	...	...	1529	...	...	...	1726	...	...	...	...	1922	...	...	...
Martina Franca 2 d.	...	...	1315	1408	1411	...	1453	...	1509	...	1545	1608	1624	...	1726	1806	1819	...	...	...	2001	2020	2123	...
Putignano d.	1308	1411	1408	...	1456	1456	...	1542	1557	1622	1634	...	1718	1731	1811	...	1905	1918	1955	2106	...	2105	2204	2207
Casamassima d.	1341	1445	|	...	|	1529	...	1615	|	1657	|	...	|	1804	|	...	|	1951	|	2139	...	|	...	2239
Mungivacca d.	1413	1517	1500	...	1544	1601	...	1649	1645	1731	1724	...	1807	1836	1902	...	1955	2023	2046	2209	...	2153	...	2307
Bari Sud Est a.	1419	1523	1507	...	1550	1607	...	1656	1651	1737	1730	...	1814	1843	1908	...	2002	2030	2052	2215	...	2159	...	2313
Bari Centrale ♣ a.	1421	1525	1509	...	1552	1609	...	1658	1653	1739	1732	...	1816	1845	1910	...	2004	2032	2054	2217	...	2201	...	2315

Line 2: MARTINA FRANCA - LECCE

km																									
					W	S											W								
0	Martina Franca 1 d.	0523	0621	...	0727	0733	...	...	...	...	1025	...	1242	...	1349	...	1454	...	...	1623	...	...	1829	...	...
41	Francavilla Fontana ♣ d.	0605	0707	...	0811	0811	...	...	...	...	1104	...	1325	...	1432	...	1537	...	...	1701	...	...	1910	...	...
92	Novoli 3 d.	0712	0815	...	0907	0907	0921	...	1017	1149	1202	...	1418	1512	1529	...	1630	1643	...	1752	1808	...	2003	2016	...
103	Lecce 5 ♣ a.	0724	0827	...	0919	0919	0933	...	1026	1201	1211	...	1427	1524	1541	...	1642	1652	...	1804	1820	...	2015	2028	...

										W														
Lecce 5 ♣ d.	0528	...	0617	0655	...	0759	...	1028	...	1244	...	1307	1341	...	1431	...	1619	1659	...	1833	...	1902	...	...
Novoli 3 d.	0538	...	0626	0715	...	0818	...	1038	...	1254	...	1316	1352	...	1442	...	1636	1708	...	1843	...	1911	...	...
Francavilla Fontana ♣ d.	0632	...	...	0810	...	0912	...	1130	...	1356	...	...	1501	...	1538	...	1729	...	...	1937	...	...	...	...
Martina Franca 1 a.	0716	...	...	0851	...	0952	...	1208	...	1440	...	...	1544	...	1621	...	1811	...	...	2017	...	...	...	...

Line 3: NOVOLI - GAGLIANO

km												
0	Novoli 2 d.	0628	0716	0818	...	1042	1321	1441	...	1710	1914	...
25	Nardò Centrale 5 d.	0659	0745	0847	...	1116	1350	1511	...	1740	1945	...
49	Casarano 4 d.	0728	0813	0918	...	1144	1419	1540	...	1808	2013	...
74	Gagliano Leuca 6 a.	0802	0846	0951	...	1218	1452	1613	...	1841	2046	...

Gagliano Leuca 6 d.	...	0642	0737	0847	1013	1151	1243	1333	1504	1633	1842
Casarano 4 d.	0603	0716	0815	0917	1047	1224	1317	1407	1539	1707	1916
Nardò Centrale 5 d.	0631	0746	0848	0944	1118	1252	1351	1439	1608	1738	1946
Novoli 2 a.	0659	0813	0915	1012	1147	1320	1415	1510	1635	1805	2013

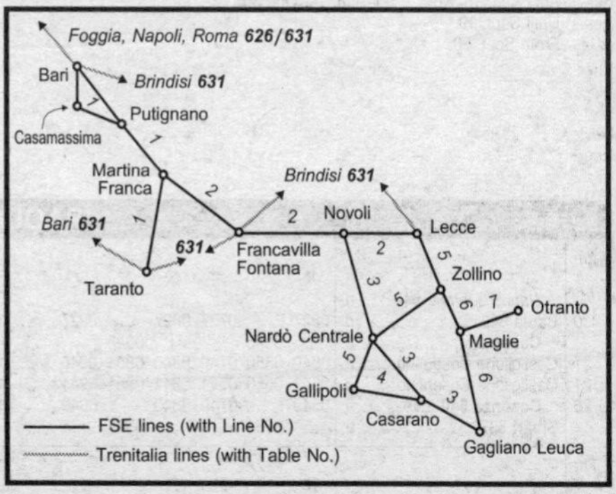

Foggia, Napoli, Roma 626/631
Bari
Brindisi 631
Putignano
Casamassima
Martina Franca
Brindisi 631
Bari 631
631
Taranto
Francavilla Fontana
Novoli
Lecce
Zollino
Otranto
Nardò Centrale
Maglie
Gallipoli
Casarano
Gagliano Leuca
FSE lines (with Line No.)
Trenitalia lines (with Table No.)

Line 4: CASARANO - GALLIPOLI

km												
		S	W									
0	Casarano 3 d.	0717	0735	...	0817	...	1259	1422	...	1541	1647	...
22	Gallipoli 5 a.	0742	0801	...	0842	...	1324	1447	...	1606	1712	...

				W	S						
Gallipoli 5 d.	0536	...	0645	0736	0745	...	1226	1335	...	1500	1619
Casarano 3 a.	0601	...	0710	0802	0810	...	1251	1401	...	1525	1644

Line 5: LECCE - GALLIPOLI

km																									
						W	S	S	W	S	W					W	W	S	S	W		S	S	W	S
0	Lecce 2 ♣ d.	0554	0612	0655	0758	0936	0937	0956	1044	1052	1140	...	1300	1341	1432	1530	1653	1705	1726	1752	1859	2016	2051	2104	2115
19	Zollino 6 d.	0617	0636	0723	0825	1009	0955	1011	1111	1118	1210	...	1327	1414	1455	1553	1718	1721	1741	1818	1924	2033	2106	2128	2132
36	Nardò Centrale 3 d.	...	0700	0748	0850	1031	1012	...	1129	1136	1230	...	1351	1436	1513	...	1741	1739	...	1838	1947	...	...	2147	2149
53	Gallipoli 4 a.	...	0717	0806	0908	1049	1025	...	1148	1155	1250	...	1409	1454	1531	...	1759	1752	...	1856	2005	...	...	2205	2202

						W	S	S	W	W		W		S	W	W	W	S	S	S		S	S	
Gallipoli 4 d.	0611	0637	0724	0826	...	0924	0940	...	1108	...	1225	1328	1412	1531	1546	...	1717	1723	...	...	1922	...	2117	...
Nardò Centrale 3 d.	0634	0702	0746	0849	...	0945	0954	...	1128	...	1246	1349	1437	1551	1607	...	1739	1739	...	...	1944	...	2131	...
Zollino 6 d.	0700	0722	0806	0908	0924	1006	1012	1035	1147	1112	1307	1408	1457	1610	1625	1608	1759	1754	1804	1906	2004	2131	2148	...
Lecce 2 ♣ a.	0725	0742	0829	0931	0947	1029	1027	1050	1211	1135	1331	1430	1520	1633	1648	1631	1823	1809	1819	1923	2027	2146	2203	...

Line 6: ZOLLINO - GAGLIANO

km																									
					W	S	S			W				W		W	S	S	W			S		S	
0	Zollino 5 d.	0618	0728	0823	1008	1013	...	1116	...	1205	1326	1412	1502	1554	...	1720	1742	...	1819	...	1928	2034	...	2107	...
10	Maglie 7 d.	0633	0750	0837	1023	1022	1024	1134	...	1219	1352	1437	1520	1611	...	1739	1751	1753	1834	...	1949	2043	...	2119	...
47	Gagliano Leuca 3 a.	0728	0844	0932	1117	...	1056	1228	...	1314	1446	1530	1613	1704	...	1832	...	1825	1927	...	2042	...	...	2151	...

							S	S	W			W			W		S	S			S	S	S	
Gagliano Leuca 3 d.	0540	0611	0654	0812	0858	...	0951	...	1001	1154	...	1242	1330	1457	1633	...	1720	...	1854	...	...	2046	...	...
Maglie 7 d.	0642	0705	0749	0908	0952	...	1023	1025	1056	1250	...	1350	1438	1553	1741	...	1752	1754	1948	...	1856	2118	2120	...
Zollino 5 d.	0655	0718	0802	0921	1005	...	...	1034	1109	1303	...	1404	1451	1607	1754	...	...	1803	2001	...	1905	...	2129	...

Line 7: MAGLIE - OTRANTO

km														
				W	S	W	W				W	W	S	S
0	Maglie 6 d.	0643	0751	0856	1026	1135	1249	1343	1439	...	1612	1737	1755	2044
18	Otranto a.	0709	0817	0922	1041	1201	1315	1409	1505	...	1638	1803	1810	2059

		W	W	S		W		W		S	W	S	S
Otranto d.	0715	0828	0924	1006	1220	1316	1410	1522	1706	1735	1805	1840	2102
Maglie 6 a.	0741	0854	0950	1021	1246	1342	1436	1548	1732	1750	1831	1855	2117

S – July 1 - Aug. 31.
W – Not July 1 - Aug. 31.
♣ – Connections into *Trenitalia* services possible.

Operator: Ferrovie Del Sud Est E Servizi Automobilistici S.R.L., Sede via Giovanni Amendola, 106/D, 70126 Bari. ✆ +39 080 546 2111, fax +39 080 546 2376. Call centre ✆ 800 079 090.

REGGIO DI CALABRIA - SIBARI - TARANTO 637

2nd class only

km		🚌 ⚒	🚌 ⚒	⚒	🚌 ⚒	⚒	⚒	🚌 ⚒	⚒		Ⓑ		Ⓐ	Ⓐ	🚌 ⚒				🚌 ⚒	IC 562/3		⚒	🚌 ⚒	
0	**Reggio di Calabria** Centrale **640** d.	...	...	...	...	...	0518	...	0618	0718	...	...	...	0818	...	0918	1018	...	...	1155	1318	1418	...	...
30	Melito di Porto Salvo d.	...	...	...	...	...	0541	...	0641	0741	...	...	...	0841	...	0941	1041	...	...	1219	1341	1441	...	...
96	Locri d.	...	...	...	...	...	0627	...	0802	0827	...	...	...	0957	...	1027	1151	...	...	1315	1428	1559	...	...
101	Siderno d.	...	...	...	...	...	0634	...	0808	0834	...	...	...	1003	...	1034	1157	...	...	1323	1434	1604	...	...
112	Roccella Jonica d.	...	...	...	...	...	0648	...	0816	0848	...	...	...	1016	...	1048	1210	...	...	1340	1448	1618	...	...
160	Soverato d.	...	...	...	...	...	0720	...	...	0920	...	...	...	...	...	1120	...	...	...	1425	1520	...	...	...
178	Catanzaro Lido a.	...	...	...	...	...	0735	...	...	0935	...	...	...	...	...	1135	...	...	...	1439	1535	...	...	...
178	Catanzaro Lido **634** d.	...	...	0540	...	0640	...	...	...	...	0940	...	1040	...	...	...	...	1340	...	1441	...	...	...	1640
238	**Crotone** d.	...	...	0634	...	0734	...	...	...	...	1034	...	1140	...	...	...	...	1434	...	1551	...	...	...	1725
325	Rossano d.	...	...	0751	...	0848	...	...	...	...	1142	...	1301	...	...	...	...	1542	...	1657	...	...	...	1841
336	Corigliano Calabro d.	...	...	0800	...	0857	...	...	...	...	1150	...	1310	...	...	...	...	1551	...	1711	...	...	...	1850
351	**Sibari 633** a.	...	...	0814	...	0914	...	...	...	...	1204	...	1324	...	...	...	...	1605	...	1727	...	...	...	1905
351	**Sibari** d.	0500	0720	...	...	...	...	0957	...	...	...	...	...	...	1403	...	...	...	1620	1729	...	...	1843	...
366	Trebisacce d.	0514	0734	...	...	...	...	1011	...	...	...	...	...	...	1417	...	...	...	1634	1743	...	...	1857	...
430	Metaponto **638** d.	0632	0850	...	0944	...	...	1129	...	...	...	...	...	...	1530	...	...	...	1752	1835	...	...	2015	...
473	**Taranto 631/8** a.	0727	...	...	1034	...	...	1239	...	...	...	...	...	...	1640	...	...	...	1847	1907	...	...	2110	...

	⚒	⚒		🚌 ⚒	⚒	⚒			
Reggio di Calabria Centrale **640** d.	1518	...	1718	...	1818	1918	...	2018	...
Melito di Porto Salvo d.	1542	...	1741	...	1841	1941	...	2041	...
Locri d.	1627	...	1827	...	1952	2027	...	2152	...
Siderno d.	1634	...	1834	...	1958	2034	...	2157	...
Roccella Jonica d.	1648	...	1848	...	2013	2048	...	2210	...
Soverato d.	1720	...	1920	...	...	2120	...	...	...
Catanzaro Lido a.	1735	...	1935	...	...	2135	...	...	...
Catanzaro Lido **634** d.	...	1840	...	...	...	...	...	...	...
Crotone d.	...	1934	...	2040	...	...	...	...	...
Rossano d.	...	2040	...	2208	...	...	...	...	...
Corigliano Calabro d.	...	2048	...	2226	...	...	...	...	...
Sibari 633 a.	...	2105	...	2246	...	...	...	...	...
Sibari d.	...	...	...	2246	...	...	...	...	...
Trebisacce d.	...	...	...	2311	...	...	...	...	...
Metaponto **638** d.	...	...	...	...	...	...	...	...	...
Taranto 631/8 a.	...	...	...	...	...	...	...	...	...

	⚒	⚒		⚒		⚒			🚌 ⚒
Taranto 631/8 d.	...	...	...	...	...	...	...	...	0515
Metaponto **638** d.	...	...	...	...	...	...	...	...	0627
Trebisacce d.	...	...	...	...	...	...	...	...	0743
Sibari 633 a.	...	...	...	...	...	...	...	...	0757
Sibari d.	...	...	...	0525	...	0620	...	...	...
Corigliano Calabro d.	...	...	...	0537	...	0633	...	...	...
Rossano d.	...	...	...	0546	...	0641	...	...	...
Crotone d.	...	...	...	0650	...	0750	...	...	...
Catanzaro Lido a.	...	...	...	0737	...	0837	...	...	...
Catanzaro Lido **634** d.	...	0545	...	...	0745	...	...	0945	...
Soverato d.	...	0559	...	...	0758	...	...	0958	...
Roccella Jonica d.	0533	0631	0703	...	0831	...	...	1031	...
Siderno d.	0545	0647	0715	...	0847	...	...	1047	...
Locri d.	0550	0652	0720	...	0852	...	...	1052	...
Melito di Porto Salvo d.	0656	0737	0837	...	0937	...	...	1137	...
Reggio di Calabria Cle **640** a.	0730	0805	0905	...	1005	...	...	1205	...

		⚒	IC 558/9 ‡	Ⓐ	🚌 ⚒	🚌 ⚒		Ⓐ	⚒		⚒		🚌 ⚒			Ⓐ	⚒	🚌 ⚒	⚒		🚌 ⚒	🚌 ⚒	
Taranto 631/8 d.	...	...	0820	...	0835	0900	...	...	...	...	...	...	1235	...	...	...	...	1425	...	...	1800	1918	...
Metaponto **638** d.	...	...	0856	...	0915	0957	...	...	...	...	...	...	1313	...	...	...	...	1517	...	...	1857	2015	...
Trebisacce d.	...	...	0944	...	...	1116	...	...	...	...	...	...	...	...	...	...	...	1625	...	...	2013	2129	...
Sibari 633 a.	...	...	0958	...	...	1135	...	...	...	...	...	...	...	...	...	...	...	1640	...	...	2027	2143	...
Sibari d.	0825	...	1000	1025	...	...	...	...	1215	...	...	...	...	1425	...	1620	...	...	1716	1818	...	...	...
Corigliano Calabro d.	0838	...	1016	1037	...	...	...	...	1228	...	...	...	...	1438	...	1634	...	...	1728	1831	...	...	...
Rossano d.	0847	...	1028	1046	...	...	...	...	1237	...	...	...	...	1447	...	1648	...	...	1741	1840	...	...	...
Crotone d.	0950	...	1141	1158	...	...	...	...	1350	...	...	...	...	1554	...	1752	...	...	1850	1950	...	...	...
Catanzaro Lido a.	1037	...	1238	1258	...	...	...	...	1437	...	...	...	...	1637	...	1837	...	...	1937	2037	...	...	...
Catanzaro Lido **634** d.	...	...	1240	...	...	...	1345	...	...	...	1545	...	...	...	1745	...	1945	...	...	...	...	...	...
Soverato d.	...	...	1258	...	...	...	1358	...	...	...	1558	...	...	...	1758	...	1958	...	...	...	...	...	...
Roccella Jonica d.	...	1253	1339	...	...	...	1431	1503	...	...	1631	1703	...	...	1830	...	2031	...	...	...	...	...	...
Siderno d.	...	1304	1357	...	...	...	1447	1515	...	...	1647	1715	...	...	1847	...	2047	...	...	...	...	...	...
Locri d.	...	1313	1405	...	...	...	1452	1520	...	...	1652	1721	...	...	1853	...	2052	...	...	...	...	...	...
Melito di Porto Salvo d.	...	1437	1502	...	...	...	1539	1637	...	...	1737	1837	...	...	1937	...	2137	...	...	...	...	...	...
Reggio di Calabria Centrale **640** a.	...	1505	1530	...	...	...	1605	1705	...	...	1805	1905	...	...	2005	...	2205	...	...	...	...	...	...

‡ – Subject to confirmation.

NAPOLI - POTENZA - TARANTO 638

2nd class only

km		🚌 ⚒	🚌 ⚒	IC 701	🚌 j	†k	🚌 ⚒	⚒k	⚒k	k	j	IC 707 §	🚌 m	🚌
	Roma T **640** d.	...	...	0626	...	...	...	...	...	...	...	1526	...	...
0	**Napoli** C **640** d.	...	...	0845	...	...	...	...	...	1617	...	1750	...	...
54	Salerno d.	0650	0750	0924	0935	0956	1135	1357	...	1659	1706	1824	1835	2115
74	Battipaglia **640** d.	|	|	0939	1003	1012	|	1412	...	1720	1732	1840	1903	|
166	**Potenza** Centrale d.	0812	0915	1059	1126	1146	1310	1540	1715	1848	1846	2004	2026	2240
273	Metaponto **637** d.	0944	...	1218	1245	...	1443	...	1847	2007	2012	2124	2145	2355
317	**Taranto 637** a.	1034	...	1253	1326	...	1523	...	1922	2045	2057	2156	2226	0035

	q	⚒k	🚌 p	IC 700 §	🚌 ⚒	🚌 j	k	k	🚌 j	IC 702	†k	🚌 ⚒	⚒k
Taranto 637 d.	...	0517	0700	0805	0835	0930	0941	...	1300	1400	...	1800	...
Metaponto **637** d.	...	0556	0741	0838	0918	1025	1016	...	1341	1433	...	1841	...
Potenza Centrale d.	0715	0730	0900	0958	1055	1150	1147	1325	1500	1557	1928	2015	2104
Battipaglia **640** d.	0841	...	1023	1124	|	|	1312	1459	1623	1721	2103	...	2233
Salerno d.	0857	...	1100	1138	1222	1345	1327	1518	1700	1737	2119	...	2247
Napoli C **640** a.	...	...	...	1215	...	...	1405	...	...	1810	...	...	...
Roma T **640** a.	...	...	...	1434	...	...	...	...	...	2034	...	...	...

j – July 18 - Aug. 14.
k – Not July 18 - Aug. 14.
m – July 17 - Aug. 14.
n – Not July 17 - Aug. 14.
p – July 18 - Aug. 15.
q – Not July 18 - Aug. 15.
§ – Also conveys 1st class.

NAPOLI - SORRENTO, BAIANO and SARNO 639

Circumvesuviana Ferrovia 2nd class only

km																											
0	**Napoli** P. Garibaldi ▲ d.	0611	0642	0711	0741	0813	0841	0911	and	1311	1343	1411	1441	1513	1541	1611	1641	1711	1743	1811	1841	1913	1941	2011	and	2141	...
10	Ercolano Scavi d.	0628	0652	0728	0758	0823	0858	0928	every	1328	1353	1428	1458	1523	1558	1628	1658	1728	1753	1828	1858	1923	1958	2028	every	2158	...
23	Pompei S. Villa Misteri d.	0647	0705	0747	0817	0836	0917	0947	30	1347	1406	1447	1517	1536	1617	1647	1717	1747	1806	1847	1917	1936	2017	2047	30	2217	...
29	Castellammare d.	0657	0715	0757	0827	0846	0927	0957	minutes	1357	1416	1457	1527	1546	1627	1657	1727	1757	1816	1857	1927	1946	2027	2057	minutes	2227	...
42	**Sorrento** a.	0717	0732	0817	0847	0903	0947	1017	until	1417	1433	1517	1547	1603	1647	1717	1747	1817	1833	1917	1947	2003	2047	2117	until	2247	...

Sorrento d.	0601	0625	0722	0755	0826	0852	0907	0937	1037	and	1307	1325	1356	1422	1455	1526	1607	1637	1707	1725	1756	1822	1855	1926	2007	2037	2107	2137
Castellammare d.	0621	0645	0739	0815	0845	0909	0927	0957	1057	every	1327	1345	1415	1439	1515	1545	1627	1657	1727	1745	1815	1839	1915	1945	2027	2057	2127	2156
Pompei S. Villa Misteri d.	0631	0655	0748	0825	0853	0918	0937	1007	1107	30	1337	1356	1423	1448	1525	1553	1637	1707	1737	1755	1823	1848	1925	1953	2037	2107	2137	2205
Ercolano Scavi d.	0649	0713	0807	0843	0906	0937	0955	1025	1125	minutes	1355	1414	1436	1507	1543	1606	1655	1725	1755	1813	1836	1907	1943	2006	2055	2125	2155	2222
Napoli P. Garibaldi ▲ a.	0707	0731	0826	0901	0916	0956	1013	1043	1143	until	1413	1431	1446	1526	1601	1616	1713	1743	1813	1831	1846	1926	2001	2016	2113	2143	2213	2239

NAPOLI (Porta Nolana) ▲ **- BAIANO and v.v.** Journey 60 minutes.

From **Napoli:** 0618, 0648⚒, 0718, 0748, 0818, 0918, 1018, 1118, 1148⚒, 1218, 1318, 1418, 1448⚒, 1518, 1618, 1718, 1748Ⓐ, 1818, 1848, 1918, 1948.

From **Baiano:** 0602, 0632⚒, 0700, 0730, 0802, 0832, 0902, 0932, 1002, 1102, 1202, 1302, 1332⚒, 1402, 1502, 1602, 1632⚒, 1702, 1802, 1902, 1932Ⓐ, 2002.

NAPOLI (Porta Nolana) ▲ **- SARNO and v.v.** Journey 65 minutes. All services call at Poggiomarino (49 minutes from Napoli, 12 minutes from Sarno).

From **Napoli:** 0632, 0651 **p**, 0722, 0802, 0902, 1002, 1102, 1132⚒, 1202, 1302, 1402, 1432⚒, 1502, 1602, 1702, 1732Ⓐ, 1802, 1832, 1932, 2002 **p**.

From **Sarno:** 0619, 0649, 0719, 0759, 0819, 0849, 0949, 1049, 1149, 1249, 1349, 1449, 1549, 1619⚒, 1649, 1749, 1849, 1919Ⓐ, 1949.

p – To Poggiomarino only.

▲ – Services originate / terminate at Napoli Porta Nolana station (journey time: 1 – 2 minutes).

Operator: Circumvesuviana Ferrovia ✆ +39 081 77 22 444, fax +39 081 77 22 450.

A reduced service operates in peak summer.

Frequent 🚌 services operate along the Amalfi Coast between Sorrento and Salerno. Up to 20 services on ⚒, less frequent on †. Change of buses at Amalfi is necessary. Operator: SITA, Via G. Pastore 28/30, 84131 Salerno. ✆ +39 089 3866 701, fax +39 089 3856 494.

ROMA - NAPOLI - COSENZA and REGGIO DI CALABRIA

For high-speed services – see Table 600

Panel 1

km	Station	2	2	2	2	ICN 799	IC 701	2	ICN 797	IC 723	IC 721	FB 8873	2	2	IC 551	2	2	2	2
						◆	◆			◆	K	双	双			双	双		†
	Torino P N 610 d.	…	…	…	…	2155	…	…	2125	…	…	…	…	…	…	…	…	…	…
	Milano C 615 d.	…	…	…	…	…	…	…	2317g	…	…	…	…	…	…	…	…	…	…
	Venezia SL 616 d.	…	…	…	…	…	…	…	…	…	…	…	…	…	…	…	…	…	…
	Bologna C 620 d.	…	…	…	…	…	…	…	…	…	…	…	…	…	…	…	…	…	…
0	Roma Termini 620 d.	…	…	…	0536	0552o	0626	…	0725t	0726	0726	0814	…	0849	0926	…	…	…	…
62	Latina d.	…	…	…	0612	0637	0700	…	…	0800	0800	…	…	0850	1000	…	…	…	…
129	Formia-Gaeta d.	…	…	…	0702	0717	0735	…	…	0835	0835	…	…	0937	1035	…	…	…	…
195	Aversa d.	…	…	…	0748	0758	0811	…	…	0911	0911	1025	…	…	1111	…	…	…	…
	Caserta 626 d.	…	…	…	0812	0817	0829	…	…	…	…	…	…	…	…	…	…	…	…
214	Napoli Centrale 626 a.	…	…	…	…	…	…	…	0938	0929	0929	1044	…	1036	1129	…	…	…	…
214	Napoli Centrale d.	0540	…	0650	0755	0835	0845	0855	0955	0950	0950	…	1046	…	1145	…	…	1207	1225
268	Salerno d.	0637	…	0737	0806	0912	0924	0937	1032	1029	1029	…	1120	…	1222	…	…	1247	1312
288	Battipaglia 638 d.	0652	…	0754	0824	…	0937	0952	…	…	…	…	…	…	1237	…	…	1305	1327
318	Agropoli-Castellabate d.	0714	…	0816	0848	…	…	1014	…	…	…	…	…	…	1257	…	…	1327	1350
349	Ascea d.	0743	…	0842	0914	…	…	1041	…	…	…	…	…	…	…	…	…	1351	1419
395	Sapri d.	0825	…	0927	1000	…	…	1120	…	1135	1135	…	1237	1241	1344	…	1358	1431	1459
407	Maratea d.	…	…	0943	…	…	…	1133	…	…	…	…	1257	…	1357	…	1414	1442	1511
455	Belvedere Marittimo d.	…	…	1016	…	…	…	1208	…	…	…	…	1334	…	…	…	1451	1519	1547
	Cosenza 633 a.	…	0937	…	…	…	…	…	…	1237	…	…	…	1337	1437	…	…	…	…
489	Paola 633 d.	…	1009	1051	…	…	…	1302	…	1231	1231	1309	1330	1404	1409	1445	1509	1522	1550 1621
	Cosenza 633 a.	…	…	1114c	…	…	…	1324	…	…	…	…	…	1426	…	…	…	…	1643
546	Lamezia Terme Centrale a.	1040	…	…	…	…	…	…	…	1259	1259	1340	1355	…	1440	…	1517	1540	
546	Lamezia Terme Centrale 634 d.	1042	…	…	…	…	…	…	…	1302	1302	1342	1358	…	1442	…	1520	1542	
616	Gioia Tauro d.	1120	…	…	…	…	…	…	…	…	…	1420	1436	…	1520	…	1602	1620	
652	Villa S. Giovanni 641 a.	1151	…	…	…	…	…	…	…	1405	1405	1451	1459	…	1551	…	1628	1651	
652	Villa S. Giovanni d.	1153	…	…	…	…	…	…	…	1425	1425	1453	1502	…	…	…	1631	1653	
667	Reggio di Calabria C 637 a.	1210	…	…	…	…	…	…	…	…	…	1510	1515	…	1610	…	1648	1710	
	Siracusa 641 a.	…	…	…	…	…	…	…	…	1829	…	…	…	…	…	…	…	…	
	Palermo C 641 a.	…	…	…	…	…	…	…	…	1905	…	…	…	…	…	…	…	…	

Panel 2

Station	IC 501	IC 727	IC 729	IC 553	2	2	IC 583	IC 1589	2	FB 8877	2	IC 555	2	IC 707	IC 705	IC 561	FA 8353	IC 561
	◆		◆	L		双		双	◆	⑥	双	双		◆	◆		双	
Torino P N 610 d.	…	…	…	…	…	…	…	…	…	…	…	…	…	…	…	…	…	…
Milano C 615 d.	…	…	…	…	…	…	0650	0645	…	…	…	…	…	…	…	…	…	…
Venezia SL 616 d.	…	…	…	…	…	…	0918	0937	…	…	…	…	…	…	…	…	…	…
Bologna C 620 d.	…	…	…	…	…	…	…	…	…	…	…	…	…	…	…	…	…	…
Roma Termini 620 d.	1021o	1106	1126	1126	…	1226	1236	1322t	1314t	…	…	1336	1356	1426	1436	1526	1601 1626 1636	1730
Latina d.	1057	1143	1200	1200	…	1300	1312	1400	1406	…	1413	…	1500	1512	1600	…	1700	1718
Formia-Gaeta d.	1134	1241	1235	1235	…	1335	1400	1435	1444	…	1509	…	1535	1603	1635	…	1735	1807
Aversa d.	1209	1321	1311	1311	…	1411	1449	1511	1523	…	1554	…	1611	1651	1711	…	1811	1858
Caserta 626 d.	…	…	…	…	…	…	…	…	…	…	…	…	…	…	…	1758	←	
Napoli Centrale 626 a.	1229	1343	1329	1329	…	1429	1511	1529	1547	…	1616	1541	1629	1715	1729	1829 1918		1829
Napoli Centrale d.	…	1345	1345	…	…	1448	…	1530	1610	…	1551	…	1645	1715	1750	1850		1850
Salerno d.	…	1424	1424	…	…	1526	…	1613	1653	…	1628	…	1729	1757	1824	→		1859 1923
Battipaglia 638 d.	…	…	…	…	…	1540	…	1628	…	…	…	…	1743	1815	1838			1940
Agropoli-Castellabate d.	…	…	…	…	…	1600	…	2 1656	…	…	…	…	1804	1838	…			
Ascea d.	…	…	1532	1532	…	1644	…	双 1725	1739	…	1732	…	1832	1903	…			2048
Sapri d.	…	…	…	…	…	…	1745	1805	1816	…	…	…	1905	1943	…			2102
Maratea d.	…	…	…	…	…	…	1758	…	…	…	…	…	…	…	…			
Belvedere Marittimo d.	…	…	…	…	…	…	1833	…	…	…	…	…	…	…	…			
Cosenza 633 a.	…	…	…	…	1737	…	…	…	…	…	1837	…	…	…	…			
Paola 633 d.	…	…	1625	1625	…	1743	1809	1903	…	1915	…	1821	1909	2003	…		2035	2147
Cosenza 633 a.	…	…	…	…	…	…	…	…	…	…	…	…	…	…	…			
Lamezia Terme Centrale a.	…	…	1652	1652	…	1814	1840	…	…	1946	…	1848	1940	2034	…		2101	2218
Lamezia Terme Centrale 634 d.	…	…	1655	1655	…	1817	1842	…	…	1949	…	1851	1942	2037	…		2104	2221
Gioia Tauro d.	…	…	…	…	…	1857	1922	…	…	2033	…	1931	2020	2117	…			2302
Villa S. Giovanni 641 a.	…	…	1800	1800	…	1923	2001	…	…	2058	…	1953	2051	2143	…		2156	2328
Villa S. Giovanni d.	…	…	1820	1820	…	1926	2003	…	…	2101	…	1956	2053	2146	…		2159	2331
Reggio di Calabria C 637 a.	…	…	…	…	…	1945	2019	…	…	2120	…	2013	2110	2203	…		2213	2345
Siracusa 641 a.	…	…	2245	…	…	…	…	…	…	…	…	…	…	…	…			
Palermo C 641 a.	…	…	…	2305	…	…	…	…	…	…	…	…	…	…	…			

Panel 3

km	Station	IC 591	IC 511	2	2 ⑦	2 ①–⑤	2 ⑧	2	2 ①–⑥	IC 597	ICN 1955 D	ICN 1957	ICN 1959 C	ICN 1961	ICN 795	2	ICN 789	2	2	ICN 1963	ICN 1965 A
	Torino P N 610 d.	…	…	1040	…	…	…	…	…	…	…	…	…	…	1335	…	…	双	…	…	…
	Milano C 615 d.	…	…	…	…	…	…	…	1450	…	…	…	…	…	1544g	…	…	…	…	2010	2010
	Venezia SL 616 d.	…	…	…	…	…	…	…	1718	…	…	…	…	…	…	…	…	…	…	…	…
	Bologna C 620 d.	…	…	…	…	…	…	…	…	…	…	…	…	…	…	…	…	…	…	…	…
0	Roma Termini 620 d.	1726	…	1826	1836	1836	…	1931	2056	2122t	2131	2131	2300	2300	2317t	…	2358	…	…	0316o	0316o
	Latina d.	1800	…	1900	1916	1916	…	2006	2132	2200	2207	2207	…	…	…	…	…	…	…	…	…
	Formia-Gaeta d.	1835	…	1935	2006	2007	…	2042	2220	2235	2244	2244	…	…	…	…	…	…	…	…	…
216	Caserta 626 d.	1911	…	2011	2052	2058	…	2139	…	…	0115	0115	…	…	…	…	0232	…	…	…	…
	Napoli Centrale 626 a.	…	1929	2029	2113	2118	…	2220	2325	2329	2337	2337	…	…	…	…	…	…	…	…	…
287	Napoli Centrale d.	1925	1950	2028	2053	…	2122	…	…	…	2358	2358	…	…	…	…	…	…	…	…	…
	Salerno d.	2010	2027	2111	2130	…	2205	…	…	…	0208	0208	0221	…	…	…	…	…	0551	0559	0559
	Battipaglia 638 d.	2025	…	2129	…	…	2222	…	…	…	…	…	…	…	…	…	…	…	0610	0618	0618
	Agropoli-Castellabate d.	2044	…	2153	…	…	2241	…	…	…	…	…	…	…	…	…	…	…	0632	0639	0639
	Ascea d.	2111	…	2218	…	…	2302	…	…	…	…	…	…	…	…	…	…	…	0657	0705	0705
	Sapri d.	2149	…	2255	…	…	2340	…	…	…	0343	…	…	…	…	…	…	…	0747	0737	0737
	Maratea d.	2201	…	…	…	…	…	…	…	…	双 2	…	…	…	…	…	…	…	0759	0751	0751
	Belvedere Marittimo d.	2232	…	…	…	…	…	…	…	…	0537	0637	…	…	…	…	0832	…	…	…	…
0	Cosenza 633 a.	…	…	…	…	…	…	…	…	…	…	…	…	…	…	…	…	…	…	…	…
26	Paola 633 d.	2307	…	…	…	…	…	…	…	0248	0248	0428	0428	0441	0530	0609	0709	0809	0903	0840	0840
	Cosenza 633 a.	2329	…	…	…	…	…	…	…	…	…	…	…	…	…	…	…	…	…	…	…
	Lamezia Terme Centrale a.	…	…	…	…	…	…	…	…	0516	0602	0640	0640	0740	0840	…	…	…	…	0916	0916
	Lamezia Terme Centrale 634 d.	…	…	…	…	…	…	…	…	0519	0604	0642	0742	0842	…	…	…	…	…	0919	0919
	Gioia Tauro d.	…	…	…	…	…	…	…	…	0700	0642	0720	0820	0920	…	…	…	…	…	1006	1006
	Villa S. Giovanni 641 a.	…	…	…	…	…	…	…	…	0425	0425	0610	0610	0735	0715	0751	0851	0951	…	1040	1040
	Villa S. Giovanni d.	…	…	…	…	…	…	…	…	0445	0445	0635	0635	0738	0717	0753	0853	0953	…	1105	1105
	Reggio di Calabria C 637 a.	…	…	…	…	…	…	…	…	…	…	0805	0741	0810	0910	1010	…	…	…	…	…
	Siracusa 641 a.	…	…	…	…	…	…	…	…	0936	…	1121	…	…	…	…	…	…	…	1548	…
	Palermo C 641 a.	…	…	…	…	…	…	…	…	1003	…	1155	…	…	…	…	…	…	…	…	1653

FOR NOTES SEE PAGE 318

REGGIO DI CALABRIA and COSENZA - NAPOLI - ROMA — 640

For high-speed services – see Table 600

Band 1

	IC 582			IC 510	ICN 1960	ICN 1958			IC 590			IC 550	FA 8352	IC 550	IC 700		IC 552
	2 ①–⑥	2 ①–⑥	2 ⑦	2 ⑦	①–⑥	♦	2 ♦	2 W	♦	2 %	2 %		Ⴧ	Ⴧ	♦	2	2 ①–⑥
Palermo C **641** ...... d.						2055											
Siracusa **641** ...... d.					2145												
Reggio di Calabria C **637** ... d.												0515	0610	0615 0648	0715		0810
Villa S. Giovanni **641** ... a.					0200	0200						0530	0626	0632 0701	0730		0825
Villa S. Giovanni ... d.					0230	0230						0532	0629	0634 0704	0732		0828
Gioia Tauro ... d.												0604	0652	0704	0804		0852
Lamezia Terme Centrale ... a.												0642	0732	0742 0753	0842		0935
Lamezia Terme Centrale **634** d.												0644	0735	0744 0756	0844		0938
Cosenza **633** ... d.									0555	0630							
Paola **633** ... d.				0429	0429				0620	0655	0727	0810	0827	0826	0927		1013
Cosenza **633** ... a.									0647	0726					0949		
Belvedere Marittimo ... d.									0725	0806		0903					
Maratea ... d.									0547	0640 0739		0820		0912			1109
Sapri ... d.			0438						0624	0712 0821							
Ascea ... d.			0514						0650	0734 0847							1157
Agropoli-Castellabate ... d.			0540						0711	0756 0911		1011			1124		1222
Battipaglia **638** ... d.			0603						0729	0817 0930		1000	1033	1138			1237
Salerno ... d.			0528	0621	0630 0642 0640				0808	0900 1010		1115	1215		1239		1315
Napoli Centrale ... a.			0605	0701	0707 0718 0718						1031						1331
Napoli Centrale **626** ... d.	0512	0517	0532	0631	0636		0731 0739 0739				1049	1131	1231		1349	
Caserta **626** ... d.																	
Aversa ... d.	0529	0542	0550 0648 0654		0748					1149	1248		1258	1349		
Formia-Gaeta ... d.	0611	0631	0638 0722 0740			0822 0833 0833			1122	1222	1322		1349	1422		
Latina ... d.	0653	0724	0722 0800 0825			0900 0912 0912			1200	1300	1400		1438	1500		
Roma Termini **620** ... a.	0734	0806	0806 0834 0904			0934 0951 0951			1237	1135	1334		1434	1524		1534
Bologna C **620** ... a.									1640								
Venezia SL **616** ... a.									1917								
Milano C **615** ... a.					1740												
Torino PN **610** ... a.																	

Band 2

	FB 8872	IC 596	IC 1588		IC 556	IC 728	IC 722	IC 522		IC 702			IC 724	IC 730	
	Ⴧ		♦	2 †	2 %	♦	N	♦	2	2 %	2 %	2 ♦	2 %	P	2
Palermo C **641** ... d.						0700								0955	
Siracusa **641** ... d.							0732						1025		
Reggio di Calabria C **637** ... d.	0840		0925		1010	1125	1125			1215	1315		1415	1425	1425
Villa S. Giovanni **641** ... a.	0852		0938		1025	1155	1155			1230	1330		1430	1455	1455
Villa S. Giovanni ... d.	0855		0941		1028	1155	1155			1232	1332		1432	1455	1455
Gioia Tauro ... d.	0918		1009		1052					1304	1404		1504		
Lamezia Terme Centrale ... a.	0957		1052		1135	1253	1253			1342	1442		1542	1556	1556
Lamezia Terme Centrale **634** d.	1000		1055		1138	1256	1256			1344	1444		1544	1559	1559
Cosenza **633** ... d.								1324c				1502			
Paola **633** ... d.	1028		1135		1213	1230	1330	1330		1350	1427 1527	1528	1615	1631	1631
Cosenza **633** ... a.								1449 1549							
Belvedere Marittimo ... d.						1257		1336		1421		1558			
Maratea ... d.								1458				1643			
Sapri ... d.	1116		1228		1250	1309	1347	1420 1420		1513		1655		1720	1720
Ascea ... d.			1300		1330	1337	1426			1554		1730			
Agropoli-Castellabate ... d.					1356	1357	1454			1619		1756			1756
Battipaglia **638** ... d.	1229		1351		1428	1421	1519			1644		1721			1820
Salerno ... d.	1229		1351		1446	1438	1545 1536 1536			1702	1737		1836	1836	1843
Napoli Centrale ... a.	1305		1433		1525	1515	1623 1615 1615			1740	1810		1912	1912	1920
Napoli Centrale **626** ... d.	1319	1431	1452	1442	1446	1531	1631 1631 1637	1731		1831	1839		1931	1931	
Caserta **626** ... d.															
Aversa ... d.		1449	1510	1500	1505	1549	1649 1649 1702	1748		1849	1904		1949	1949	
Formia-Gaeta ... d.		1522	1548	1558	1557	1622	1722 1722 1758	1822		1922	2001		2022	2022	
Latina ... d.		1600	1625	1644	1644	1700	1800 1800 1846	1859		2000	2047		2100	2100	
Roma Termini **620** ... a.	1504	1637t	1706t	1727	1724	1734	1834 1834 1927	1939o		2034	2129		2134	2134	
Bologna C **620** ... a.		2038	2130												
Venezia SL **616** ... a.															
Milano C **615** ... a.		2315	0005												
Torino PN **610** ... a.															

Band 3

	IC 560	IC 710	ICN 798	FB 8878	ICN 796			ICN 1962	ICN 1964			ICN 788	ICN 794	ICN 1956	ICN 1954
	2	♦	2	Ⴧ	2 † %	♦	2	♦ Z	2 %	2	2	♦	♦	♦	X
Palermo C **641** ... d.								1250							1830
Siracusa **641** ... d.								1335						1910	
Reggio di Calabria C **637** ... d.		1510		1600		1615 1715		1815 1815	1830 1930			2135		2335	2335
Villa S. Giovanni **641** ... a.		1525		1611		1630 1730		1815 1815	1845 1845	1832 1932		2155	0005	0005	
Villa S. Giovanni ... d.		1528		1614		1632 1732		1845 1845		1832 1932		2155	0005	0005	
Gioia Tauro ... d.		1552				1707 1804		1921 1921	1904 2004			2237			
Lamezia Terme Centrale ... a.		1637		1716		1743 1842		2007 2007	1942 2042			0009			
Lamezia Terme Centrale **634** d.		1640		1719		1745 1844		2010 2010	1944 2044			0012			
Cosenza **633** ... d.							1900 2002								
Paola **633** ... d.		1713		1748	1715	1827 1915	2027	2047 2047	2027 2115			0052	0143	0143	
Cosenza **633** ... a.						1849		2049							
Belvedere Marittimo ... d.				1741			1954 2055								
Maratea ... d.		1757		1818			2032 2131	2143 2143							
Sapri ... d.	1729	1809		1836	1842 1842		2045 2142	2156 2156				0153			
Ascea ... d.	1809			1917	1917		2123	2226 2226							
Agropoli-Castellabate ... d.	1833	1857		1946	1946		2149	2254 2254							
Battipaglia **638** ... d.	1857	1923		2012	2012		2214	2315 2315							
Salerno ... d.	1915	1937	2006	1946	2032 2032 2052		2232	2333 2333			0325	0405	0405		
Napoli Centrale ... a.	1955	2015	2045	2020	2110 2110 2130		2312				0405				
Napoli Centrale **626** ... d.		2031	2045	2101	2036	2146						0404	0421		
Caserta **626** ... d.			2051										0413		
Aversa ... d.		2053	2103			2205						0427	0440		
Formia-Gaeta ... d.		2128	2155			2243						0511	0518	0551	0551
Latina ... d.		2205	2243			2321						0547	0555	0632	0632
Roma Termini **620** ... a.		2241	2311	2324	2310t	2221 0003o		0240o 0240o				0627	0634	0631t	0713 0713
Bologna C **620** ... a.															
Venezia SL **616** ... a.															
Milano C **615** ... a.			0711g			0810		1045 1045					1138	1442g	
Torino PN **610** ... a.			0920					1640							

FOR NOTES SEE PAGE 318

641 VILLA SAN GIOVANNI - MESSINA - SIRACUSA and PALERMO

km				*ICN* 1955	*ICN* 1957				*ICN* 1961	*ICN* 1959							*ICN* 1963		*ICN* 1965					*IC* 721	*IC* 723
		2 ⚒	2 ⚒	♦	D	2	2 Ⓑ	2 ⚒	C	♦	2	2 ⚒	2	2 ⚒	2 ⚒		♦	2 ⚒	A	2 Ⓐ	2 ⚒	2	2	K	♦
0	**Villa S. Giovanni 640** ▲ d.	...	...	0445	0445	...	...	...	0635	0635	...	...	...	...	...	...	1105	...	1105	...	...	...	...	1425	1425
9	**Messina** Centrale ▲ a.	...	...	0610	0610	...	...	...	0805	0805	...	...	...	...	...	...	1245	...	1245	...	...	...	...	1530	1530
9	**Messina** Centrale d.	0500	0513	0640	0645	0655	0703	0726	0837	0840	0915	1115	1122	1220	1230	...	1310	1318	1320	1355	1415	1423	1546	1555	1605
	Taormina-Giardini d.	|	0552	0731	|	0756	|	0806	|	0932	1001	1154	|	1319	|	...	1355	1405	|	|	1505	|	|	1636	|
	Giarre-Riposto **644** d.	|	0610	0748	|	0823	|	0820	|	0948	1014	1210	|	1339	|	...	1409	1419	|	|	1532	|	|	1652	|
	Catania Centrale a.	|	0631	0818	|	0855	|	0840	|	1011	1036	1233	|	1408	|	...	1432	1441	|	|	1603	|	|	1719	|
	Catania Centrale d.	|	0635	0825	|	...	|	0842	|	1014	1038	1235	|	...	|	...	1436	1507	|	|	...	|	|	1722	|
	Augusta d.	|	0730	0913	|	...	|	0927	|	1103	1128	1319	|	...	|	...	1526	1557	|	|	...	|	|	1810	|
	Siracusa 648 a.	|	0755	0936	|	...	|	0950	|	1121	1150	1342	|	...	|	...	1548	1625	|	|	...	|	|	1829	|
45	Milazzo d.	0521	...	...	0708	...	0723	...	0859	...	...	...	1156	...	1300	...	...	...	1343	1415	...	1454	1618	...	1628
174	Cefalù d.	0702	...	...	0911	...	0909	...	1046	...	...	...	1402	...	1507	...	...	...	1540	1625	...	1709	1838	...	1816
204	Termini Imerese **645/7** d.	0732	...	...	0933	...	0927	...	1114	...	...	...	1427	...	1534	...	...	...	1619	1703	...	1736	1902	...	1837
241	**Palermo** C **645/7** a.	0800	...	...	1003	...	0957	...	1155	...	...	...	1500	...	1601	...	...	...	1653	1729	...	1800	1930	...	1905

							IC 729	*IC* 727		
	2 Ⓐ	2	2 ⚒	2	2	2	L	♦	2	2
Villa S. Giovanni 640 ▲ d.	...	...	...	...	...	...	1820	1820	...	...
Messina Centrale ▲ a.	...	...	...	...	...	...	1930	1930	...	...
Messina Centrale d.	1713	1715	1725	1825	...	1910	1955	2005	2018	2120
Taormina-Giardini d.	|	1758	|	1929	...	|	|	2045	2123	2232
Giarre-Riposto **644** d.	|	1812	|	1947	...	|	|	2102	2147	2251
Catania Centrale a.	|	1833	|	2014	...	|	|	2126	2216	2320
Catania Centrale d.	|	1835	|	...	2036	|	|	2129	...	...
Augusta d.	|	1933	|	...	2120	|	|	2222	...	...
Siracusa 648 a.	|	1958	|	...	2140	|	|	2245	...	...
Milazzo d.	1736	...	1758	...	...	1932	2017	...	...	...
Cefalù d.	1906	...	2007	...	...	2116	2216	...	...	...
Termini Imerese **645/7** d.	1929	...	2035	...	...	2138	2238	...	...	...
Palermo C **645/7** a.	2000	...	2100	...	...	2206	2305	...	...	...

							IC 722	*IC* 728		
	2 ⚒	2 ⚒	2 Ⓐ	2	2 ⚒	2 ⚒	N	♦	2	2
Palermo C **645/7** d.	...	...	0508	...	0606	...	...	0700	0804	0903
Termini Imerese **645/7** d.	...	...	0535	...	0634	...	...	0728	0830	0931
Cefalù d.	...	...	0600	...	0701	...	...	0753	0850	1009
Milazzo d.	...	...	0739	...	0843	...	...	0937	1037	1201
Siracusa 648 d.	...	0515	|	...	|	0640	0732	|	|	|
Augusta d.	...	0535	|	...	|	0703	0753	|	|	|
Catania Centrale a.	...	0617	|	...	|	0758	0838	|	|	|
Catania Centrale d.	0510	0619	|	0633	|	0800	0841	|	|	|
Giarre-Riposto **644** d.	0534	0640	|	0653	|	0830	0904	|	|	|
Taormina-Giardini d.	0552	0659	|	0716	|	0850	0919	|	|	|
Messina Centrale a.	0655	0753	0800	0833	0903	0942	0956	1000	1104	1230
Messina Centrale ▲ d.	...	...	...	...	...	...	1015	1015	...	...
Villa S. Giovanni 640 ▲ a.	...	...	...	...	...	...	1125	1125	...	...

km		*IC* 730	*IC* 724				*ICN* 1964	*ICN* 1962												*ICN* 1956	*ICN* 1954			*ICN* 1960	*ICN* 1958
		P	♦	2 ⚒	2 ⚒	2 ⚒	Z	♦	2	2 ⚒	2 ⚒	2	2	2 Ⓐ	2	2 ⚒	2	2 †	2 Ⓐ	♦	X	2 ⚒	2	♦	W
	Palermo C **645/7** d.	0955	...	...	1108	....	1250	...	1306	...	1405	1506	...	1605	...	...	...	1704	1805	...	1830	...	2006	...	2055
	Termini Imerese **645/7** d.	1028	...	...	1137	...	1318	...	1334	...	1437	1535	...	1632	...	...	...	1730	1832	...	1900u	...	2033	...	2122
	Cefalù d.	1047	...	...	1206	...	1344	...	1402	...	1506	1602	...	1652	...	...	...	1802	1907	...	1937u	...	2055	...	2143
	Milazzo d.	1232	...	...	1411	...	1558	...	1609	...	1657	1803	...	1831	...	...	...	2013	2037	...	2126u	...	2238	...	2350
0	**Siracusa 648** d.	|	1025	...	|	1253	|	1335	|	1415	|	|	1615	|	...	1714	1820	|	|	1910	|	1930	|	2145	|
31	Augusta d.	|	1046	...	|	1320	|	1400	|	1435	|	|	1634	|	...	1738	1841	|	|	1932	|	1954	|	2206	|
87	**Catania** Centrale a.	|	1136	...	|	1407	|	1447	|	1523	|	|	1720	|	...	1834	1925	|	|	2019	|	2044	|	2251	|
87	**Catania** Centrale d.	|	1139	1220	|	1411	|	1456	|	1525	|	|	1722	|	1745	1836	1927	|	|	2026	|	2046	|	2254	|
117	Giarre-Riposto **644** d.	|	1205	1253	|	1431	|	1522	|	1545	|	|	1743	|	1815	1900	1947	|	|	2051	|	2115	|	2318	|
135	Taormina-Giardini d.	|	1220	1319	|	1448	|	1539	|	1602	|	|	1758	|	1838	1919	2000	|	|	2107	|	2135	|	2333	|
182	**Messina** Centrale a.	1255	1300	1430	1445	1539	1620	1625	1643	1649	1717	1833	1840	1858	1949	2000	2045	2051	2101	2150	2155	2225	2303	0015	0020
182	**Messina** Centrale ▲ d.	1315	1315	...	...	...	1640	1640	...	...	...	...	...	...	...	...	...	...	...	2210	2210	...	...	0035	0035
191	**Villa S. Giovanni 640** ▲ a.	1425	1425	...	...	...	1815	1815	...	...	...	...	...	...	...	...	...	...	...	2335	2335	...	...	0200	0200

♦ – **NOTES FOR TABLES 640/641**

501 – [12] Sestri Levante - Napoli.
510 – [12] Salerno - Torino.
511 – [12] Torino - Salerno.
522 – [12] Napoli - Sestri Levante.
590 – [12] Napoli - Firenze - Milano.
597 – [12] Milano - Firenze - Napoli.
700 – [12] Taranto - Roma.
701 – [2] Roma - Taranto.
702 – [2] Taranto - Roma.
705 – ⑤: [12] Roma - Taranto.
707 – [12] Roma - Salerno - Taranto.
710 – ⑦: [12] Taranto - Roma.
723 – [12] Roma - Palermo; [12] Roma - Messina (**721**) - Siracusa.
724 – [12] Siracusa - Roma; [12] Palermo (**730**) - Messina - Roma.
727 – [12] Roma - Siracusa; [12] Roma - Messina (**729**) - Palermo.
728 – [12] Palermo - Roma; [12] Siracusa (**722**) - Messina - Roma.
788 – ⑦: 🛏 1,2 cl., ▬ 2 cl. (4 berth) and [2] Lecce - Roma.
789 – ⑤ (from Roma): 🛏 1,2 cl., ▬ 2 cl. (4 berth) and [2] Roma - Lecce.
794 – 🛏 1,2 cl., ▬ 2 cl. (4 berth) and [2] Reggio di Calabria - Milano - Torino.
795 – 🛏 1,2 cl., ▬ 2 cl. (4 berth) and [2] Torino - Milano - Reggio di Calabria.
796 – 🛏 1,2 cl., ▬ 2 cl. (4 berth) and [2] Salerno - Napoli - Torino.
797 – 🛏 1,2 cl., ▬ 2 cl. (4 berth) and [2] Torino - Milano - Napoli - Salerno.
798 – 🛏 1,2 cl., ▬ 2 cl. (4 berth) and [2] Salerno - Napoli - Milano - Torino.
799 – 🛏 1,2 cl., ▬ 2 cl. (4 berth) and [2] Torino - Napoli - Salerno.
1588 – ⑦: [12] Reggio di Calabria - Milano.
1589 – ⑥: [12] Milano - Reggio di Calabria.
1955 – 🛏 1,2 cl. and ▬ 2 cl. (4 berth) Roma - Siracusa; 🛏 1,2 cl. and ▬ 2 cl. (4 berth) Roma - Messina (**1957**) - Palermo.
1956 – 🛏 1,2 cl. and ▬ 2 cl. (4 berth) Siracusa - Roma; 🛏 1,2 cl. and ▬ 2 cl. (4 berth) Palermo (**1954**) - Messina - Roma.
1959 – 🛏 1,2 cl. and ▬ 2 cl. (4 berth) Roma - Siracusa; 🛏 1,2 cl. and ▬ 2 cl. (4 berth) Roma - Messina (**1961**) - Palermo. Train number **1559** on ①.
1960 – 🛏 1,2 cl. and ▬ 2 cl. (4 berth) Siracusa - Roma; 🛏 1,2 cl. and ▬ 2 cl. (4 berth) Palermo (**1958**) - Messina - Roma.
1962 – 🛏 1,2 cl., 🛏 1,2 cl. (T2) and ▬ 2 cl. (4 berth) Siracusa - Genova - Milano; 🛏 1,2 cl. and ▬ 2 cl. (4 berth) Palermo (**1964**) - Messina - Milano. Train number **1584** on some dates.
1963 – 🛏 1,2 cl., 🛏 1,2 cl. (T2) and ▬ 2 cl. (4 berth) Milano - Genova - Siracusa; 🛏 1,2 cl. and ▬ 2 cl. (4 berth) Milano - Messina (**1965**) - Palermo.

A – 🛏 1,2 cl. and ▬ 2 cl. (4 berth) Milano (**1963**) - Genova - Messina - Palermo.
C – 🛏 1,2 cl. and ▬ 2 cl. (4 berth) Roma (**1959**) - Messina - Palermo.
D – 🛏 1,2 cl. and ▬ 2 cl. (4 berth) Roma (**1955**) - Messina - Palermo.
K – [12] Roma (**723**) - Messina - Siracusa.
L – [12] Roma (**727**) - Messina - Palermo.
N – [12] Siracusa - Messina (**728**) - Roma.
P – [12] Palermo - Messina (**724**) - Roma.
W – 🛏 1,2 cl. and ▬ 2 cl. (4 berth) Palermo - Messina (**1960**) - Roma.
X – 🛏 1,2 cl. and ▬ 2 cl. (4 berth) Palermo - Messina (**1956**) - Roma.
Z – 🛏 1,2 cl. and ▬ 2 cl. (4 berth) Palermo - Messina (**1962**) - Genova - Milano.

‡ – Time varies – see main table.
▲ – Through trains are conveyed by ⛴ Villa S. Giovanni - Messina and v.v. See **Table 2695** for other available sailings.

c – Ⓒ only.
g – Milano **Porta Garibaldi**.
j – Not July 17 - Aug. 14.
k – Not July 18 - Aug. 14.
m – Until Sept. 10.
n – From Sept. 11.
o – Roma **Ostiense**.
q – Not July 18 - Aug. 15.
s – Stops to set down only.
t – Roma **Tiburtina**.
u – Stops to pick up only.
y – Arrive 1000 on Aug. 7.
z – Arrive 1800 on Aug. 7.

644 CATANIA - RANDAZZO - RIPOSTO

Ferrovia Circumetnea

Winter service valid September 12, 2016 - June 10, 2017. No service on †

km		⚒	⚒	⚒	⚒	⚒	⚒	⚒	⚒	⚒	⚒	⚒	⚒	Ⓐw	⚒
0	**Catania** ▲ d.	...	0536	0641	0757	0943	1135	1235	1348	1512	1642	1735	1843	1940	2008
20	Paternò d.	...	0608	0718	0832	1016	1212	1311	1423	1545	1718	1810	1919	2013	2042
36	Adrano N. d.	...	0636	0755	0858	1040	1240	1341	1452	1612	1747	1833	1946	2040	...
52	Bronte d.	...	0701	0818	0921	1100	1303	1404	1512	1635	1811	1854	2008	...	...
71	Randazzo a.	...	0732	0846	0948	1126	1331	1431	1537	1701	1838	1920	2036	...	...
71	Randazzo d.	0632	0750	...	1021	...	1333	...	...	1715	...	...	...	...	...
109	Giarre **640** a.	0746	0854	...	1125	...	1439	...	...	1819	...	...	...	...	...
111	**Riposto** a.	0750	0858	...	1129	...	1443	...	...	1823	...	...	...	...	...

	⚒	⚒	⚒	⚒	⚒	⚒	⚒	⚒	⚒	⚒	⚒	⚒	⚒	⑥y
Riposto d.	...	...	...	0636	0910	...	1132	1252	1412	1455	...	...	...	...
Giarre **640** d.	...	...	...	0641	0915	...	1137	1257	1419	1500	...	...	...	...
Randazzo a.	...	...	...	0744	1018	...	1240	1402	1530	1603	...	...	...	...
Randazzo d.	0525	0603	0701	0816	1033	1233	1335	1443	...	...	1742	1851	...	...
Bronte d.	0550	0629	0730	0846	1101	1303	1403	1513	...	...	1810	1921	...	...
Adrano N. d.	0610	0651	0753	0912	1125	1326	1426	1537	...	...	1834	1945	2045	...
Paternò d.	0638	0719	0815	0939	1153	1354	1455	1600	...	...	1901	2013	2111	2050
Catania ▲ a.	0711	0752	0858	1012	1227	1427	1528	1632	...	...	1935	2045	2143	2124

w – Ⓐ (not Dec. 23 - Jan. 7, Apr. 14 - 18).
y – ⑥ (daily Dec. 23 - Jan. 7, Apr. 14 - 18).
▲ – Catania Borgo station. The Metropolitana di Catania operates a metro service Borgo - Porto and v.v. (3.8 km) via Catania Centrale station. Weekdays only, every 15 minutes 0700 – 2045.

PALERMO and AGRIGENTO - CATANIA　645

2nd class only except where shown

km		⚒	0500	⚒	⚒		0736		0938			⚒		1338			⚒		A		1538		1736				⚒		1938
0	**Palermo** Centrale 647 ....d.	...	0500	...	...	...	0736	...	0938	...	...	⚒	...	1338	...	...	...	...	...	...	1538	...	1736	...	...	...	...	...	1938
37	Termini Imerese 647 ....d.	...	0525		...	...	0759						...								1759		...					
70	Roccapalumba-Alia 647 ......d.	...		...	0640							1435		1549								1949					
	Agrigento Centrale 647 ...d.	...	0505						1254		1357							1912							
	Aragona-Caldare 647 ....d.	...	0522						1311		1415							1930							
	Canicattì 648 ....d.	...	0601						1349		1452							2008							
	Caltanissetta Xirbi 648 ......a.	...	0626	0740		0900		1100		1500		1537		1641	1700		1900			2047	2100				
	Caltanissetta Centrale 648..d.	0525		0635	0757	0800			1357	1415		1521	1555		1657		1757			2035	2104				
127	Caltanissetta Xirbi 648 ....d.	0534	0627			0809	0901		1101	1407		1501			1701	1805	1901		2043		2101				
154	Enna 648 ....d.	0607	0647			0842	0921		1121	1442		1521			1721	1842	1921				2121				
243	**Catania** Centrale ....a.	0733	0750			1005	1025		1225	1605		1625			1825	2005	2026				2225				

km		⚒		⚒	B		⚒	⚒			⚒	⚒		1449		A	⚒	⚒	⚒		⚒	⚒	
	Catania Centrale ....d.	...	0503		0737	0849	0932			1338	1449		1532			1647	1732			1849	1932	...
	Enna 648 ....d.	...	0606		0841	1011	1041			1441	1611		1641			1811	1841			2011	2041	...
0	Caltanissetta Xirbi 648 ......a.	...	0626		0900	1035	1100			1500	1634		1700			1836	1900			2038	2100	...
6	Caltanissetta Centrale 648..d.	0500	0558		0645		1044		1305	1409		1644		1732	1745	1900		1930	2053		...
	Caltanissetta Xirbi 648 ....d.	0515		0627		0901		1101	1320	1424	1501			1701		1801		1901			2101	...
35	Canicattì 648 ....d.		0633		0720						1813				2012				
65	Aragona-Caldare 647 ....d.		0705		0751						1847				2046				
78	**Agrigento** Centrale 647 ....a.		0725		0808						1905				2104				
	Roccapalumba-Alia 647 ......d.	0616						1415	1529			1908							
	Termini Imerese 647 ....d.		0727		1006					1627		1827			2006				
	Palermo Centrale 647 ......a.		0752		1029		1227			1627		1827			2029			2227	

A – Ⓐ until Sept. 2; Ⓑ from Sept. 5.　　　　　　　　　　　　　B – ⚒ from Sept. 12.

PALERMO - TRAPANI　646

2nd class only

km		⚒	⚒	⚒	⚒	⚒q	⚒	⚒p	†	⚒p	⚒q	†	⚒	⚒	⚒	⚒q	⚒q	⚒p	⚒q	q§	§
0	**Palermo** Centrale ....d.	...	...	...	...	0600	...	0705	...	1002	1007	...	...	...	1257	...	1435t	1510	1639t	1843	...
	Fiera.................................d.															1510		1712			
32	Piraineto ....d.			0721	0745	0825	0835	1123	1128	1135				1417		1621	1621	1715	1823	1915	2003	...
73	Castellammare del Golfo ..d.				0831		0914			1216	1225			1549			1755		2001		2116
79	Alcamo Diramazione ....d.				0839		0921			1223	1233		1534	1600			1802		2016		2124
121	Castelvetrano ....d.	0530	0619	0640	0722	0830		0920		0958		1300	1316	1400	1611	1655	1713		1838		2052	2205
144	Mazara del Vallo ....d.	0550	0638	0706	0748	0856		0939		1018			1336	1410	1630		1735		1858		2111
165	Marsala ....d.	0613	0658	0729	0808	0914		0956		1035			1356	1446	1648		1758		1915		2128
196	**Trapani** ....a.	0644	0739	0755	0841	0943		1020		1105			1430	1520	1716		1825		1940		2200

km		⚒	⚒	†	⚒	⚒p		⚒	⚒	†	⚒	⚒	⚒		⚒	⚒q	⚒p		⚒p	⚒q	Ⓐz	⚒
0	**Trapani** ....d.	...	0543	0543	...	...	...	0654	0800	0830	...	1200	1240	1342	...	1435	...	...	1601	...	1726	1830	1945	2035
	Marsala ....d.		0612	0612				0728	0837	0909		1234	1313	1422		1513			1627		1757	1856	2018	2106
	Mazara del Vallo ....d.		0640	0640				0747	0855	0930		1253	1337	1442		1534			1650		1815	1918	2041	2131
	Castelvetrano ....d.	0500	0700	0701		0705		0810	0921	0959		1315	1359	1505	1538	1555			1710		1835	1938	2110	2155
47	Alcamo Diramazione ....d.	0540		0738		0806			0959	1037			1440		1621				1803			2015		
53	Castellammare del Golfo ..d.	0547		0745		0817			1006	1045					1628				1811			2023		
94	Piraineto ....d.	0630		0825	0833	0955			1125	1215			1707		1715	1815	1855	1915	1915					
	Fiera.................................d.														1825			2026					
126	**Palermo** Centrale ....a.				0944		1157		1326						1857t	1926		2026	2102t					

p – Until Aug. 28.　　t – Connection by train.　　§ – Connection available between services at Partinico (a. 2043, d. 2055).
q – Until Sept. 3.　　z – Not days before holidays.

PALERMO - AGRIGENTO　647

2nd class only

km		⚒	⚒	⚒	⚒		⚒	⚒	⚒	⚒		⚒	⚒	⚒	⚒	†
0	**Palermo** Centrale 645..d.	0548	0743	0841	1143	1243	1343	1443	1543	1643	1743	1841	2022		**Agrigento** C 645........d.	0520	0614	0814	1014	1214	1314	1414	1514	1615	1714	1814	2014
37	Termini Imerese 645.....d.	0616	0810	0906	1209	1309	1409	1509	1608	1709	1810	1908	2050		Aragona-Caldare 645...d.	0536	0630	0831	1034	1231	1331	1434	1534	1634	1734	1834	2034
70	Roccapalumba-Alia 645....d.	0651	0842	0941	1241	1342	1441	1541	1642	1742	1844	1940	2123		Roccapalumba-Alia 645.d.	0624	0725	0922	1121	1319	1423	1522	1623	1723	1824	1920	2124
125	Aragona-Caldare 645...d.	0744	0933	1033	1334	1435	1535	1635	1735	1835	1936	2035	2210		Termini Imerese 645....d.	0658	0752	0951	1152	1351	1452	1552	1652	1753	1852	1950	2152
139	**Agrigento** C 645..........a.	0758	0954	1052	1354	1453	1554	1654	1754	1854	1954	2052	2226		**Palermo** C 645..........a.	0722	0816	1016	1216	1416	1516	1616	1716	1822	1916	2016	2216

SIRACUSA - GELA - CALTANISSETTA　648

2nd class only

km		B	⚒	⚒		⚒		⚒	⚒		⚒	
0	**Siracusa** 640........d.	...	1010	...	1356	...	1425	1735	...	1922		**Caltanissetta** C 645 d.	...	...	...	0500	...	1120	...	1419	...
62	Pozzallo ....d.	...	1113		1508		1530	1846		2031		Canicattì 645 ....d.	...	...	...	0541		1205		1505	...
92	Modica ....d.	0515	1200	1415	1604		1926	1932	2110		Licata ....d.	...	...	...	0621		1250		1550	...
112	Ragusa ....d.	0543	1223	1441	1630			2002		**Gela** 645 ....d.	...	...	...	0700		1324	1426	1640	1758
153	Vittoria ....d.	0622	1309	1541	1721			2042		Vittoria ....d.	...	0638		0748			1457		1829
183	**Gela** 645..........d.		1340	1457	1631	1748	1748		2130		Ragusa ....d.	...	0727		0828			1541		1918
218	Licata ....d.		1542	1721	1838					Modica ....d.	0541	0612	0748	0821	0858		1601		1938
264	Canicattì 645 ....d.		1638	1805	1922					Pozzallo ....d.	0614	0644		0854		1540			2010
293	**Caltanissetta** C 645..d.		1728	1858	2003					**Siracusa** 640.........a.	0717	0747		0957		1645			2115

B – ⚒ from Sept. 12.

Frequent bus services throughout Malta and Gozo are operated by Malta Public Transport www.publictransport.com.mt. Travellers will also find useful information on the unofficial website www.maltabybus.com.

MALTA

PRINCIPAL BUS SERVICES　649

Routes from Valletta: X4 Airport - Hal Far, 1 L'Isla (Senglea), 2/4 Birgu (Vittoriosa), 3 Birgu - Smart City - Rinella - Kalkara, 13-15 Sliema - San Giljan (St Julian's), 13 Bahar ic-Caghaq, 31/45/48 Mosta - Bugibba (45 via Qawra seafront), 31/43/45 Naxxar, 41/42 Mosta - St Paul's Bay - Mellieha - Ghadira - Cirkewwa (for Gozo ferry), 44 Ghajn Tuffieha (Golden Bay), 49 Armier Bay (summer), 51-53 Rabat / Mdina, 52/56 Dingli, 61 Zebbug, 62 Siggiewi, 71/73 Zurrieq, 72 Qrendi, 74 Hagar Qim - Blue Grotto, 80/82/X4 Birzebbuga, 81/85 Marsaxlokk, 91-93 Marsaskala, 94 Xghajra.
Other routes: X1 Airport - Cirkewwa, X2 Airport - Sliema, X3 Airport - Rabat - Bugibba, 186 Bugibba - Ta' Qali - Rabat, 202 Sliema - Naxxar - Mosta - Rabat, 203 Sliema - Naxxar - Mosta - Bugibba, 212 Sliema - San Giljan - Bugibba, 221 Bugibba - Mellieha - Cirkewwa, 222 Sliema - St Paul's Bay - Mellieha - Cirkewwa, 223 Bugibba - Ghajn Tuffieha, 225 Sliema - St Paul's Bay - Ghajn Tuffieha.
Gozo: routes from Rabat (Victoria): 301/303 Mgarr (for Cirkewwa ferry), 302 Ramla, 305 Sannat, 306/330 Xlendi, 307 Xaghra, 308 Ta' Pinu - Ghasri, 309 Zebbug, 310 Marsalforn, 311 Dwejra.

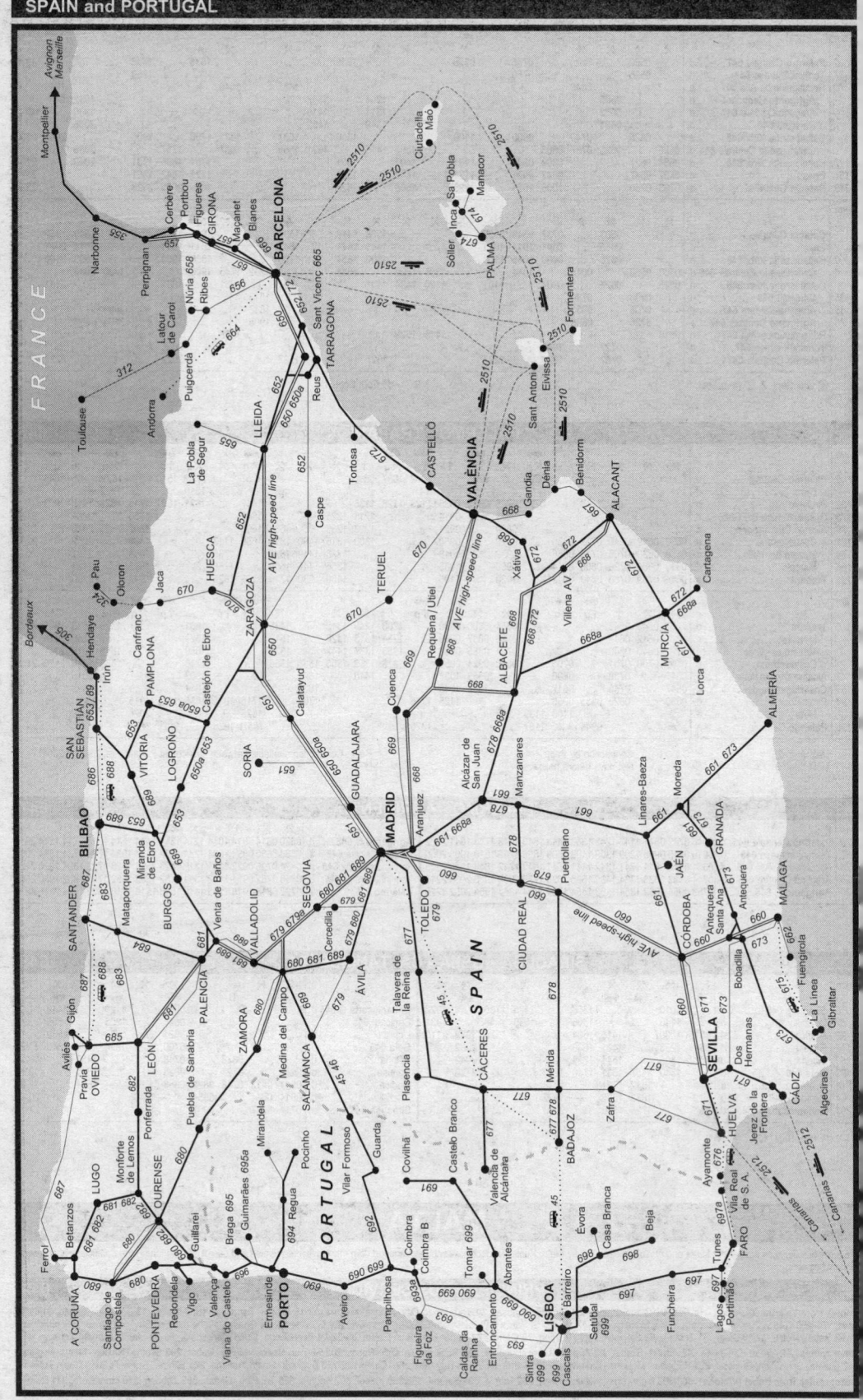

SPAIN

Operator: **Renfe Operadora** – unless otherwise indicated. www.renfe.es

Services: On long-distance trains first class is known as *Preferente* and second class as *Turista*. Unless otherwise indicated (by '2' in the train column or 🚃2 in the notes), all trains convey both first- and second-class seating accommodation.

🍸 indicates a buffet car (*cafetería*) or a mobile trolley service. 🍴 indicates a full restaurant car service or the availability of hot meals served from the buffet car. Meals are served free of extra charge, on Mondays to Fridays, to holders of *Preferente* tickets on all *AVE* and *Euromed* trains. Note that catering services may not be available throughout a train's journey, particularly in the case of trains with multiple origins / destinations.

▬ indicates coaches equipped with couchettes: for occupancy of these a standard supplement is payable in addition to the normal *Turista* fare. 🛏 indicates sleeping-cars with single, double, and 3- or 4-berth compartments. The *Turista* fare is payable plus a sleeping-car supplement corresponding to the type and standard of accommodation. ***Trenhotel*** services additionally convey *Gran Clase* accommodation: *de luxe* single- and double-occupancy compartments with *en suite* shower and toilet. *Preferente* fare is payable for travel in *Gran Clase* plus a sleeping-car supplement corresponding to the type and standard of accommodation.

Local (*Media Distancia*) and suburban (*Cercanías*) trains are shown without an indication of category except for some fast ***Media Distancia*** (*MD*).

Train categories:

Altaria (*Alta*): Talgo trains which can change gauge and run on the high-speed lines as well as the broad-gauge system.
Alta Velocidad Española (*AVE*): High-speed trains running on the standard-gauge lines.
Alvia: High-speed gauge-changing trains.
Avant (*Av*): Medium-distance high-speed trains on the standard-gauge lines.
Euromed (*Em*): *AVE*-like trains running on the broad-gauge Barcelona - València - Alacant route.
Intercity (*IC*): *Alvia*-like trains offering *Turista* class only.
Media Distancia (*MD*): Medium distance regional trains.
Regional Exprés (*RE*): Medium distance regional trains.
Talgo: Quality express trains using light, articulated stock.
Train à Grande Vitesse (*TGV*): French High-speed trains.
Trenhotel (*Hotel*): Quality night express trains (see Services, above).

Reservations: Reservations are compulsory for all journeys by services for which a train category (e.g. *AVE, RE*) is shown in the timing column. Advance purchase of tickets is also available for travel by services for which a train number is shown.

Supplements: Higher fares, incorporating a supplement, are payable for travel by *Altaria, Alvia, AVE, Euromed, InterCity, Talgo, TGV* and *Trenhotel* services.

Timings: Timings have been compiled from the latest information supplied by operators.

High-speed services — MADRID - ZARAGOZA - BARCELONA — 650

km		*AVE*	*AVE*	*AVE*	*Av*	*AVE*	*AVE*	*AVE*	*AVE*	*AVE*	*AVE*	*AVE*	*AVE*	*AVE*	*AVE*	*AVE*	*AVE*	*AVE*	*AVE*	*AVE*	*AVE*	*AVE*	*AVE*	*AVE*	*Av*	*AVE*
		3263	**3053**	**3061**	**8087**	**3463**	**3063**	**3071**	**3271**	**3483**	**3073**	**3073**	**3081**	**3283**	**3083**	**3293**	**3093**	**3103**	**3993**	**3943**	**3113**	**3123**	**9724**	**3141**	**8167**	**3143**
		①–⑤	①④⑤	①–④		⑥⑦	①–⑤	①–⑤	①–④	⑥⑦	①–⑤	⑥⑦	①–⑤	①–④		②③							**19725** **M**	Ⓑ	Ⓑ	Ⓑ
	Sevilla **660** d.	...	...	...	...	...	...	...	...	...	...	...	...	...	...	...	...	...	...	0850	...	...	...	...	...	...
	Málaga **660** d.	...	...	...	...	...	...	...	...	...	...	...	...	...	...	...	...	...	0840	|	...	...	...	...	...	...
0	**Madrid** Puerta de Atocha d.	...	0550	0610	...	0620	0630	0700	0720	...	0730	0730	0800	0820	0830	0900	0930	1030	|	|	1130	1230	1325	1400	...	1430
64	Guadalajara - Yebes d.	...	|	|	...	|	|	|	|	...	0754	0754	|	|	|	|	|	|	|	|	|	|	1350	|	...	|
221	Calatayud d.	...	|	|	...	0716	0726	|	|	...	|	|	|	|	|	|	|	|	|	|	1226	|	|	|	...	1526
307	**Zaragoza** Delicias d.	0620	0706	|	...	0742	0752	|	|	0800	0852	0852	|	0936	0946	1016	1046	1146	1236	1236	1252	1346	1452	|	...	1552
447	Lleida d.	0705	0750	|	0800	0826	|	|	|	0855	0937	0937	|	|	|	|	1131	|	1322	1322	1337	1431	|	|	1600	|
526	Camp de Tarragona d.	0735	0819	|	0832	0854	|	|	|	0923	1005	1005	|	|	|	|	1159	|	1351	1351	1405	|	1547	|	1632	|
621	**Barcelona** Sants a.	0810	0855	0840	0908	0929	0920	0930	0950	0958	1040	1040	1030	1105	1115	1145	1234	1315	1425	1425	1440	1530	1624	1630	1708	1721
	Girona **657** a.	...	...	...	...	1023	...	1023	...	...	...	1128	...	...	...	...	1322	...	...	...	1529f	1618v	1723	...	...	1815
	Figueres Vilafant **657** a.	...	...	...	...	1040	...	1040	...	...	...	1145	...	...	...	...	1339	...	...	...	1545f	1635v	1740	...	...	1832

	AVE	*AVE*	*AVE*	*Av*	*AVE*	*AVE*	*Av*	*AVE*	*Av*	*AVE*	*AVE*	*AVE*	*AVE*	*AVE*	*AVE*	*AVE*	*AVE*	*AVE*	*Av*	*AVE*	*AVE*	*AVE*	*AVE*	*AVE*		
	3151	**3153**	**3161**	**8187**	**3163**	**3163**	**3563**	**3171**	**3793**	**3991**	**3941**	**3173**	**3181**	**3995**	**3945**	**3183**	**3183**	**3191**	**8207**	**3193**	**3201**	**3203**	**3211**	**3593**		
	①–⑤		Ⓑ		①–⑤	⑥⑦	④⑤⑦	Ⓑ	⑤⑦				Ⓑ	⑦	⑦	⑥	Ⓑ	Ⓑ			Ⓑ		Ⓑ	Ⓑ		
Sevilla **660** d.	...	...	...	...	...	...	...	...	...	...	1450	...	...	...	1555	...	...	...	...	...	...	...	...	...	...	...
Málaga **660** d.	...	...	...	...	...	...	...	...	...	1435	|	...	...	1555	|	...	...	...	...	...	...	...	...	...	...	...
Madrid Puerta de Atocha d.	1500	1530	1600	...	1630	1630	1635	1700	...	|	|	1730	1800	|	|	1830	1830	1900	...	1930	2000	2030	2125	2130	...	...
Guadalajara - Yebes d.	|	|	|	...	|	|	|	|	...	|	|	1754	|	|	|	|	|	|	...	|	|	2054	|	2155	...	...
Calatayud d.	|	1626	|	...	|	|	|	|	...	|	|	|	|	|	|	|	|	|	...	|	|	|	|	2235	...	...
Zaragoza Delicias d.	|	1652	|	...	1746	1746	1756	|	1805	1831	1831	1852	|	1935	1935	1946	1946	|	...	2046	|	2152	|	2300	...	...
Lleida d.	|	1737	|	1800	|	|	...	|	1848	1918	1918	1937	|	|	|	|	|	|	2040	2131	|	2237	|	...	...	...
Camp de Tarragona d.	|	1805	|	1832	|	|	...	|	1916	1947	1947	2005	|	2039	2039	2045	2045	|	2112	2206	|	2305	|	...	...	...
Barcelona Sants a.	1730	1840	1830	1908	1915	1915	...	1930	1951	2022	2022	2040	2030	2115	2115	2120	2120	2130	2148	2240	2230	2340	2355	...	...	...
Girona **657** a.	...	1928	...	...	2003	...	...	...	...	...	...	...	...	...	...	2208	...	2218	...	...	...	...	...	...	...	...
Figueres Vilafant **657** a.	...	1945	...	...	2020	...	...	...	...	...	...	...	...	...	...	2225	...	2235	...	...	...	...	...	...	...	...

	AVE	*AVE*	*AVE*	*AVE*	*AVE*	*AVE*	*AVE*	*AVE*	*AVE*	*AVE*	*AVE*	*AVE*	*AVE*	*AVE*	*AVE*	*AVE*	*Av*	*AVE*	*AVE*	*AVE*	*AVE*	*AVE*	*AVE*	*AVE*	*AVE*	*AVE*
	3252	**3772**	**3062**	**3260**	**3462**	**3270**	**3072**	**3070**	**3662**	**3082**	**3082**	**3080**	**3940**	**3990**	**3092**	**3092**	**8096**	**3944**	**3994**	**3102**	**3112**	**3122**	**9731**	**3132**	**3142**	**3152**
	①–④	①–⑥	①–⑥	①–⑤	①–④	①–④		①–④	①–⑤	①–⑤	⑥⑦	①–⑥			①–⑥	⑦		⑥	⑥				**19730** **M**	①–⑥		
Figueres Vilafant **657** d.	...	...	...	...	...	...	...	...	0630	0655	...	...	...	...	0755	...	...	...	...	0855	...	...	1143	...	...	...
Girona **657** d.	...	...	...	...	...	...	...	...	0646	0711	...	...	...	...	0811	...	...	...	...	0911	...	...	1200	...	...	...
Barcelona Sants d.	0550	...	0605	0625	0640	0700	0705	0725	0740	0800	0800	0825	0830	0830	0900	0900	0910	0940	0940	1000	1100	1200	1250	1325	1400	1500
Camp de Tarragona d.	|	...	0638	|	|	|	|	0757	|	0833	0833	|	0905	0905	|	|	0947	1015	1015	1033	|	1233	1322	|	1433	|
Lleida d.	|	...	0704	|	|	|	|	|	|	0859	0859	|	0934	0934	|	|	1018	|	|	1059	|	1259	|	|	1459	|
Zaragoza Delicias d.	|	0705	0748	|	0806	|	0831	|	|	0943	0943	|	1020	1020	1026	1026	...	1114	1114	1143	1226	1343	1425	1451	1543	1626
Calatayud d.	|	0732	|	|	|	|	|	|	|	1008	1008	|	|	|	|	|	...	|	|	|	|	|	|	|	1608	|
Guadalajara - Yebes d.	|	0813	0845	|	|	|	|	|	|	|	|	|	|	|	|	|	...	|	|	1243	|	1443	|	|	|	|
Madrid Puerta de Atocha a.	0820	0840	0915	0855	0925	0930	0950	1001	1010	1110	1110	1055	|	|	1145	1145	...	|	|	1310	1345	1510	1545	1610	1710	1745
Málaga **660** a.	...	...	...	...	...	...	...	...	...	...	...	...	|	1424	...	...	...	|	1516	...	...	...	...	...	...	...
Sevilla **660** a.	...	...	...	...	...	...	...	...	...	...	...	...	1402	...	...	...	...	1455	...	...	...	...	...	...	...	...

	Av	*AVE*	*AVE*	*AVE*	*AVE*	*AVE*	*Av*	*AVE*	*AVE*	*AVE*	*AVE*	*AVE*	*Av*	*AVE*	*Av*	*AVE*	*AVE*	*AVE*	*AVE*	*AVE*	*Av*	*AVE*	*AVE*	*AVE*	*AVE*	
	3562	**3150**	**3942**	**3992**	**3162**	**3162**	**8166**	**3160**	**3946**	**3172**	**3172**	**3170**	**3792** **10792**	**3182**	**8186**	**3180**	**3180**	**3192**	**3190**	**3202**	**8206**	**3212**	**3412**	**3610**	**3222**	
	⑤⑦	①–⑤			①–⑥	⑦	Ⓑ	Ⓑ	⑤	①–⑥	⑦	Ⓑ	④⑤⑦			①–⑤	⑦		Ⓑ			⑤⑦	**A**	⑤⑦		
Figueres Vilafant **657** d.	...	...	...	...	1455	...	...	...	...	...	1545	...		1655	...	...	1720	1755	...	...	...	...	...	...	...	...
Girona **657** d.	...	...	...	...	1511	...	...	...	...	...	1601	...	...	1711	...	...	1736	1811	...	...	...	...	...	...	...	...
Barcelona Sants d.	1515	1525	1550	1550	1600	1600	1605	1625	1632	1700	1700	1725	...	1800	1805	1825	1825	1900	1925	2000	2010	2100	2115	2125	2150	...
Camp de Tarragona d.	1548	|	1623	1623	1633	1633	1642	|	1705	|	|	|	...	1833	1842	|	|	1932	|	2033	2047	2133	|	|	2223	...
Lleida d.	1614	|	1649	1649	1659	1659	1713	|	|	|	|	|	...	1859	1913	|	|	1958	|	2059	2118	2159	|	|	2250	...
Zaragoza Delicias d.	1655	|	1733	1733	1743	1743	...	|	1804	1826	1826	|	1900	1943	...	|	|	2041	|	2143	...	2243	2243	|	2335	...
Calatayud d.	...	|	|	|	1808	1808	...	|	|	|	|	|	|	2008	...	|	|	|	|	|	...	|	|	|	...	...
Guadalajara - Yebes d.	...	|	|	|	|	|	...	|	|	|	|	|	|	|	...	|	|	|	|	2243	...	|	|	|	...	...
Madrid Puerta de Atocha a.	...	1755	|	|	1910	1910	...	1855	|	1945	1945	1955	2030	2110	...	2055	2055	2200	2155	2310	...	0002	0002	2355	...	...
Málaga **660** a.	...	...	|	2140	...	...	...	...	|	...	...	...	...	...	...	...	...	...	...	...	...	...	...	...	...	...
Sevilla **660** a.	...	...	2115	...	...	...	...	...	2143	...	...	...	...	...	...	...	...	...	...	...	...	...	...	...	...	...

A – ①②③④⑥. **M** – To / from Marseille (Table **13**). **f** – ①–⑤. **v** – Not ⑥. ☛ *AVE* trains convey 🍴 and 🍸. *Avant* trains (*Av*) are *Turista* class only.

650a — MADRID – LOGROÑO, PAMPLONA/IRUÑA, HUESCA – BARCELONA

	Hotel 921 ☾ A	IC 635 ①–⑤ y	IC 10655 ⑥	Alvia 533 K	Alvia 433 F	Alvia 601	IC 631 ①–⑤–⑥ B	Alvia 603	Alvia 605	IC 633 B	Alvia 661 G	AVE 3363 ⑤⑦	IC 10657 625 b	Alvia 621 J	Alvia 537 K	Alvia 437 F	Alvia 609	Alvia 613	Alvia 613 ⑤	AVE 701 ④⑦ b	Alvia 3393 ⑥	Alvia 801 ⑧
Madrid Puerta de Atocha ....d.	...	...	...	...	...	0735	...	0940	1135	...	1605	...	...	...	...	...	1505	1735	1735	1835	1905	1935	...
Guadalajara-Yebes ....d.	...	...	...	...	...		...	1007	1202	...		...	...	...	...	...	1532			1901	1928		...
Calatayud ....d.	...	...	...	...	...		...	1055	1250	...		...	...	...	...	...	1620			1948	2007		...
Logroño 653 ....a.	0403	...	...	...	0904		1021			1434		...	...	...	...	1753				2158			...
Pamplona/Iruña 653 ....a.	...	0625	0812	0913		1038		1252	1440		1508	...	1625	1724	1754		1826	2043	2043			2240	...
Zaragoza Delicias.......................a.	0632	0810	1003	1113	1113		1215			1628	1701	1727	1811	1918	1952	1952					2034		...
Huesca 670...............................a.	...	...	...	...	...		...	...	...		1810	...					...	...	...		2118		...
Lleida ....d.	0730	0900	1056	1203	1203		1313			1722	1754		2013	2051	2051		...	...	...				...
Camp de Tarragona........................d.	0804	0930	1127	1238	1238		1343			1753	1827		1924	2050	2128	2128	...	...	...				...
Barcelona Sants............................a.	0849	1010	1205	1320	1320		1420			1835	1903		2000	2125	2209	2209	...	...	...				...

	Alvia 802 ①–⑤	AVE 3272	Alvia 702 ①–⑥	Alvia 800 ① b	Alvia 600 ⑥	Alvia 534 K	Alvia 434 F	Alvia 602 ①–⑥	Alvia 622 626 J	IC 10560 ⑥	Alvia 606	Alvia 664 G	IC 632 B	Alvia 612	Alvia 612 b	Alvia 530 K	Alvia 430 F	AVE 3592 ⑤⑦	Alvia 610 ⑧	IC 562 ①–⑤ w	IC 562 ⑥ w	Hotel 922 ☾ A
Barcelona Sants............................d.	...	...	...	0730	0730	...	...	0930	1005	...	1210	1410	...	...	1530	1530	...	...	1840	1930	2020
Camp de Tarragona........................d.	...	...	...	0808	0808	...	...	1007	1043	...	1248	1447	...	...	1608	1608	...	...	1918	2008	2103
Lleida ....d.	...	...	...	0844	0844	...	...	1037	1115	...	1322	1517	...	...	1639	1639	...	...	1950	2041	2142
Huesca 670...............................d.	...	0815	...	...	...	...	...	...	...	...	...	...	...	...	...	...	1935	...	...	...	...
Zaragoza Delicias........................d.	...	0900	...	0810	0900	0934	0934		1128	1204	1414	1608	...	1729	1729	2020	...	2102	2134	2250
Pamplona/Iruña 653 ....d.	0635	...	...	0810	0900	1117		1130	1315	1354	1535	1606		1807	1807	1922		1935	2244	2328
Logroño 653 ....d.	...	...	0735			1123						1750			1936					0102
Calatayud ....d.	...	0925	0936		1101		1324									2134		
Guadalajara-Yebes ....d.	...	1005	1022		1150		1412									2224		
Madrid Puerta de Atocha ....a.	0945	1035	1050	1120	1218		1440			1838			2125	2125			2140	2253	

A – ⑧: GALICIA *Trenhotel* – 🛏, 🛋 (reclining)
    Barcelona - Logroño - A Coruña and Vigo and v.v.
B – 🍴 Valladolid - Barcelona and v.v. (Tables 653, 689).
F – 🍴 Bilbao - Barcelona and v.v. (Table 653).

G – 🍴 Gijón - Barcelona and v.v. (Table 685).
J – 🍴 Vigo/A Coruña - Barcelona and v.v. (Table 680).
K – 🍴 Irún - Barcelona and v.v. (Table 653).

b – From/to Irún (Table 653).
w – To Vitoria/Gasteiz on ⑤ (Table 653).
y – From Vitoria/Gasteiz (Table 653).

651 — MADRID - SORIA and ZARAGOZA

km	For high-speed trains see Tables 650 and 650a		2 Ⓐ		2 Ⓐ H	2 Ⓐ	2 Ⓒ	2 Ⓒ		2 ⑤	2 ⑤	2 w		2 Ⓐ	2 ⑦	2 Ⓐ ✧	
0	Madrid Chamartín.....................d.	...	...	...	0715	0745	0814	0915	...	1432	1540	1545	...	1900	1935	2002	2007
55	Guadalajara................................d.	...	...	...	0756	0823	0854	0959	...	1509	1624	1638	...	1940	2025	2038	2117
138	Sigüenza ....d.	...	...	...	0858	0915	0944	1102	...	1612	1713	1740	...	2032	2128	2142	...
248	Soria ....a.	...	...	...		1042	1110		...		1840		...	2158			...
178	Arcos de Jalón............................d.	0650	...	0850	0936	...		1140	...	...		1814	...	...	...	...	...
241	Calatayud ....d.	0736	...	0936	1016	...		1221	1321	...		1859	...	...	...	...	...
339	Zaragoza Delicias ♣ ....a.	0855	...	1101	1114	...		1325	1438	...		2011	...	...	...	...	...

	For high-speed trains see Tables 650 and 650a		2 Ⓐ		2 Ⓐ	2 Ⓒ		2 f	2 H		2 ⑤	2 ⑧	2 ⑦			2 ⑦	2
	Zaragoza Delicias ♥ ....d.	...	...	...	...	...	...	0857	1359	...	1620	...	...	...	...	2036	...
	Calatayud ....d.	...	...	...	...	...	...	1018	1458	...	1742	...	...	...	...	2157	...
	Arcos de Jalón............................d.	...	...	...	...	...	...	1104	1535	...		...	...	...	...	2244	...
	Soria ....d.	...	...	0750	...	0845	...			...	1657	1906	...	...	...		...
	Sigüenza ....d.	0650	...	0914	...	1009	1140	...	1612	1700	1817	2033	2150	...	...	...	...
	Guadalajara................................d.	0800	...	1006	...	1057	1244	...	1716	1758	1908	2126	2248	...	...	...	...
	Madrid Chamartín.....................a.	0913	...	1045	...	1136	1329	...	1807	1837	1948	2206	2327	...	...	...	...

H – To/from Barcelona (Table 652).
f – From Lleida on Ⓐ (Table 652).
w – To Lleida (Table 652).

♥ – All services call 7 – 8 minutes earlier at Zaragoza **Goya** and 5 minutes earlier at Zaragoza **Portillo**.
♣ – All services call 4 – 5 minutes later at Zaragoza **Portillo** and 6 – 8 minutes later at Zaragoza **Goya**.
✧ – Subject to confirmation.

652 — ZARAGOZA - BARCELONA

km	For high-speed trains see Tables 650 and 650a		2 ⚒	2	2	Hotel 921 ¶ G ☾	2	2 Ⓐ	2	2	2 ⑥	2 ⑦	2 Ⓐ	2 Ⓒ		2 Ⓐ	2 ⚒	2 ⑦	2	2	2
	Madrid Chamartín 651 ....d.	...	...	...	...	0632	...	0610	...	...	0857	1027	...	...	0715	...	...	...	...	1621	1545
0	Zaragoza Delicias ♣ ....d.	...	...	...		0632		0610	...	...	0857	1027	1116	1116		...	1515	...	...	1621	2015	2012
114	Caspe ....d.	...	...	...			0655		...	...			1250	1250		...		...	...	1755	2155	
★	Lleida ....d.	...	...	0715	0730		0820		...	1121	1237	1310			1545	...	1727	1748	1748			2240
239	Reus ....d.	0537	0641	0734		0906		1107	1206	1308		1437	1500	1500	1714	1837				2007		...
257	Tarragona ....672 d.	0555	0659	0749		0804t	0927		1125	1225	1326		1455	1517	1517	1730	1859			2030		...
282	Sant Vicenç de Calders....672 d.	0616	0719	0810	0847		0949		1145	1246	1347		1517	1541	1541	1750	1920	1913	1923	2050		...
342	Barcelona Sants ....672 a.	0718	0807	0907	0939	0849	1037		1237	1337	1437		1610	1637	1637	1840	2010	2010	2019	2137		...
345	Barcelona Pass. de Gràcia ...a.	0724	0813	0913	0944		1045		1244	1346	1444		1615	1645	1645	1845	2017	2015	2024	2144		...
350	Barcelona França ....a.	0735	0824	0925	0954		1055		1255	1357	1455		1625	1655	1655	1855	2028	2025	2034	2154		...

	For high-speed trains see Tables 650 and 650a		2 Ⓐ	2 Ⓐ	2	2 Ⓒ	2 ⑥	2	2	2	2	2	2	2	2 ⑦	2 Ⓐ		2	2	2	2	2 ⑧	Hotel 922 ¶ G ☾	2
	Barcelona França.................d.	...	...	0610	...	...	0647	0713	0843	0943	1143	...	1313	1343	...	...	1543	1643	1713	1843	1847	1943	2013	...	2113
	Barcelona Pass. de Gràcia....d.	...	...	0621	...	...	0658	0724	0854	0954	1154	...	1323	1354	...	...	1554	1654	1724	1854	1859	1954	2024	...	2124
	Barcelona Sants ....672 d.	...	...	0630	...	...	0706	0733	0903	1003	1203	...	1333	1403	...	...	1603	1703	1733	1903	1906	2003	2033	2020	2133
	Sant Vicenç de Calders..672 d.	...	...	0719	...	0807	0820	0950	1046	1248	...	1419	1449	...	...	1648	1747	1819	1948	2005	2049	2119	...	2222
	Tarragona ....672 d.	...	...	0741	...		0844	1101	1108	1308	...	1442	1511	...	...	1710	1809	1841		2037	2110	2140	2103t	2241
	Reus ....d.	...	...	0757	...		0900	1028	1326	...	1459	1531	...	...	1727	1827	1858		2052	2126	2156		2259
	Lleida ....d.	...	0625		...	1025	0956		1455	1515	...	1650	1803	1836	...	1955		2112				2142		...
	Caspe ....d.	0651		...	1040		1232			...		1943			2117								...
	Zaragoza Delicias ♥ ....d.	0823	0856		1212	1253	1407			1729	...	2023	2044	2115								2238		...
	Madrid Chamartín 651 ....a.	...	1329				1807				...													...

G – ⑧: GALICIA *Trenhotel* – 🛏, 🛋 (reclining)
    Barcelona - A Coruña and Vigo and v.v.
¶ – Via high speed line.
t – **Camp** de Tarragona.

★ – Leida - Reus: 90 km. Zaragoza - Lleida: 189 km. Lleida - Sant Vicenç: 106 km.
♥ – All trains (except *Hotel* 922) call 5 – 8 minutes earlier at Zaragoza **Goya** and 3 – 5 minutes earlier at Zaragoza **Portillo**.
♣ – All trains (except *Hotel* 921) call 4 – 5 minutes later at Zaragoza **Portillo** and 6 – 8 minutes later at Zaragoza **Goya**.

ZARAGOZA - IRÚN and BILBAO 653

km				Alvia	Alvia	Alvia	Alvia	Alvia	Alvia	IC		Alvia			IC	Alvia		Alvia		Alvia	Alvia				IC	Alvia	Alvia		Hotel
		18071	16071	601	603	534	434	622	605	10560	18021	664	18073	16015	632	609	18023	530	16017	430	613	18075	16027	18077	562	701	801	18079	922
		2	2				B	626			2	A	2	2	V		2		2			2	2	2	S			2	G 🍸
		①–⑥	①–⑤	①–⑤	⑥			J	Ⓑ	⑥							⑤		①–⑥		④⑤⑦		⑦		Ⓑ	Ⓑ	Ⓑ	⑤⑥⑦	¶
	Barcelona Sants **652** d.	...	...	...	...	0730	0730	0930	...	1005	...	1210	...	...	1410	...	...	1530	...	1530	...	...	...	...	1840	...	...	...	2020
	Madrid PA ‡ **650a** d.	...	...	0735	0940	|	|	|	1135	|	...	|	...	...	|	1505	...	|	...	|	1735	...	...	...	|	1835	1935	...	|
0	**Zaragoza** Delicias d.	0625	...	|	|	0934	0934	1128	|	1204	1309	1414	1435	...	1608	|	1652	1729	...	1729	|	1742	...	1921	2102	|	|	2109	2250
94	Castejón de Ebro ★ d.	0729	0730	0945	1159	1028	1031	1224	|	1259	1417	|	1540	...	1702	|	1748	1833	...	1845	|	1849	1852	2031	|	|	|	2215	0014
182	**Pamplona / Iruña** d.	0837	|	1038	1252	1119	|	1317	1440	1356	1526	1608	|	1642	|	1826	1859	1924	1930	|	2044	|	2005	2138	2244a	|	2240	|	|
234	Altsasu **689** d.	0918t	|	...	...	1150	|	|	...	|	...	|	|	1718t	|	...	...	1953	2004t	|	|	|	2046t	...	|	|	...	|	|
275	Vitoria / Gasteiz **689** d.	0950	|	...	...	|	|	1410	...	|	...	1702	|	1753	|	...	...	|	2037	|	|	|	2118	...	2337r	|	...	|	|
321	San Seb / Don ❖ d.	|	|	...	...	1305	|	|	...	1550	...	|	|	|	|	...	...	2112	...	|	2227x	|	|	...	...	|	...	|	|
337	**Irún** **689** a.	|	|	...	...	1328	|	|	...	1611	...	|	|	|	|	...	...	2135	...	|	2245x	|	|	...	...	|	...	|	|
171	**Logroño 650a** d.	|	0829	...	...	...	1125	|	...	...	...	|	1635	|	1751	...	...	...	...	1938	...	1945	|	...	...	2158	...	2312	0102
242	Miranda de Ebro **689** d.	1016	...	...	...	...	1225	1431	...	...	...	1722	...	1820	1851	...	...	...	...	2032	...	...	2143	...	...	...	...	...	...
347	**Bilbao** Abando **689** a.	...	...	...	...	...	1404	...	...	...	...	...	...	...	...	...	...	...	...	2209	...	...	...	...	...	...	...	...	...

		IC		Alvia	Alvia	Alvia		IC	Alvia	Alvia	Alvia		Alvia	IC		Alvia	Alvia	IC			Alvia	Alvia	Alvia	Alvia	Alvia				Hotel
	18068	635	18072	802	800	702	18074	10655	600	533	433	16019	602	631	18076	661	606	10657	18070	18029	621	537	437	612	610	16111	16011	18078	921
	2		2		11616		2					2		V	2	A			2	2	625	M	P			2	2	2	G 🍸
	①–⑤	①–⑤	①–⑤	①–⑤	①	①–⑥		⑥	⑥				Ⓑ			①–⑥		⑦	⑤⑥⑦	b	J			⑤⑦	Ⓑ	①–⑥	⑦	❦	¶
Bilbao Abando **689** d.	...	...	...	...	...	...	...	...	...	...	0630	...	...	...	...	...	...	...	...	...	...	...	1520	...	...	...	...	...	...
Miranda de Ebro **689** d.	...	...	...	...	...	...	...	...	...	...	0805	0940	...	0921	...	1325	...	...	...	1501	1605	...	1652	...	...	...	...	...	...
Logroño 650a d.	...	...	0615	...	...	0735	...	...	...	...	0904	|	...	1021	1415	|	...	...	1642	|	|	...	1753	...	...	...	...	2018	0403
Irún **689** d.	...	...	|	...	0605	|	...	...	...	0710	|	|	...	|	|	|	...	1420	|	|	|	1552	|	1600r	...	...	...	|	|
San Seb / Don ❖ d.	...	...	|	...	0624	|	...	...	...	0728	|	|	...	|	|	|	...	1437	|	|	|	1610	|	1619r	...	...	...	|	|
Vitoria / Gasteiz **689** d.	...	...	|	...	|	|	...	0718	...	|	|	1005	...	|	|	1350	...	|	|	1530	1627	|	|	|	...	1900	1921	|	|
Altsasu **689** d.	...	...	|	...	|	|	...	|	...	0842	|	1038t	...	|	|	|	|	|	|	1601t	|	1722	|	|	...	1931t	1952t	|	|
Pamplona / Iruña d.	...	0625	|	0635	0810	|	0743z	0812	0900	0913	|	1110	1130	|	|	1447	1535	1625	|	1638	1724	1754	|	1807	1935	2015	2026	|	|
Castejón de Ebro d.	0605	0717	0720e	0725	|	|	0850	|	0952	1010	1010	...	|	1114	1510	|	|	|	1741	1744	1818	1854	1854	|	|	2121	2123	2121	0456
Zaragoza Delicias a.	0715	0807	0836	|	|	|	0956	1000	|	1110	1110	...	|	1212	1611	1635	|	1808	...	1851	1916	1950	1950	|	|	2229	2217	2229	0629
Madrid PA ‡ **650a** a.	...	|	...	0945	1120	1050	...	|	1218	|	|	...	1440	|	...	|	1838	|	...	...	|	|	|	2125	2253	...	...	...	|
Barcelona Sants **652** a.	...	1010	...	...	...	...	...	1205	...	1320	1320	...	...	1420	...	1850	...	2000	...	...	2125	2209	2209	...	...	...	...	...	0849

A – 🚃12 Barcelona - Gijón and v.v. (Table **685**).

B – ①–⑥ (daily June 21 - Sept. 13).

G – Ⓑ: GALICIA *Trenhotel* – 🛏, 🚃1 (reclining) Barcelona - A Coruña and Vigo and v.v.

J – 🚃12 🍸 Barcelona - Vigo / A Coruña and v.v. (Table **680**).

P – Ⓑ (daily June 20 - Sept. 12).

S – On ⑦ departs Barcelona 1930, Zaragoza 2134, arrives Pamplona 2328.

V – 🚃12 Barcelona - Valladolid and v.v. (Tables **650a**, **689**). On ⑦ *IC* **631** runs as *IC* **633**, departs Miranda de Ebro 1337, Logroño 1434, Castejón de Ebro 1527, arrives Zaragoza 1626, Barcelona 1835.

a – Arrival time.

b – From Burgos Rosa de Lima on ①–⑥ (Table **689**).

e – Arrive 0709.

r – ⑤ only.

t – Altsasu Pueblo (*230 km*).

x – ④⑦.

z – ①–⑤.

❦ – On ⑦ runs 13 - 18 minutes earlier.

¶ – Via high speed line.

★ – Calatayud - Castejón: *140 km*.

‡ – Full name is Madrid Puerta de Atocha.

❖ – Full name is San Sebastián / Donostia.

FGC 2nd class — LLEIDA - LA POBLA DE SEGUR 655

km		Ⓐ			A	†	Ⓐ		⑥	†	①–④	⑤	
0	**Lleida** d.	0525	0620	0750	1030	1045	1045	1305	1505	1715	1730	1930	...
27	Balaguer d.	0550	0644	0819	1100	1114	1114	1329	1529	1739	1754	1954	...
77	Tremp d.	0648	...	0917	|	1212	1212	...	1627	1837	1852	2052	...
90	**La Pobla de Segur** a.	0701	...	0930	1230	1225	1225	...	1640	1850	1905	2105	...

	Ⓐ	Ⓑ	⑥	Ⓑ	Ⓑ	⑥	A	Ⓒ	①–④	⑥	Ⓑ	⑤
La Pobla de Segur d.	0710	1005	1300	...	1530	...	1730	1900	1930	...	...	2120
Tremp d.	0722	1017	1312	...	1542	...	|	1912	1942	...	...	2132
Balaguer d.	0820	1115	1410	1410	1640	1640	1900	2010	2040	2145	2200	2230
Lleida a.	0845	1140	1435	1435	1705	1705	1930	2035	2105	2210	2225	2255

A – Tren dels Llacs: ⑥ Apr. 1 - July 8, Aug. 19 - Oct. 28.

2nd class — BARCELONA - PUIGCERDÀ - LATOUR DE CAROL 656

km		Ⓐ ❖	Ⓐ	Ⓐ	Ⓐ	Ⓒ	Ⓐ	Ⓒ	Ⓐ	Ⓒ	Ⓐ	Ⓐ	Ⓒ	Ⓐ	Ⓒ	Ⓐ	Ⓐ	Ⓒ	Ⓐ	Ⓒ	Ⓐ	Ⓒ	Ⓐ	Ⓒ	Ⓐ	Ⓒ	Ⓐ
0	**Barcelona** Sants d.	...	0511	0602	0622	0701	0701	0749	0752	0936	0951	1022	1109	1122	1207	1233	1303	1317	1402	1408	1501	1510	1549	1623	1702	1717	1732
	La Sagrera-Meridiana d.	...	0524	0615	0636	0714	0714	0802	0805	0949	1004	1035	1122	1135	1220	1246	1316	1330	1415	1421	1514	1523	1602	1637	1715	1730	1745
	Sant Andreu Arenal d.	...	0526	0617	0639	0717	0716	0804	0807	0951	1006	1037	1124	1137	1222	1248	1318	1332	1417	1423	1516	1525	1604	1639	1717	1732	1747
33	Granollers - Canovelles d.	...	0556	0645	0706	0743	0744	0833	0837	1017	1033	1108	1153	1209	1248	1315	1347	1406	1444	1450	1542	1550	1633	1708	1741	1759	1817
74	Vic d.	...	0638	0722	0743	0816	0824	0914	0924	1051	1115	1147	1232	1252	1326	1353	1426	1445	1519	1521	1617	1623	1714	1755	1813	1832	1900
90	Torelló d.	...	...	0736	0805	0831	...	0927	0938	1105	1129	1202	1246	1305	1340	1408	1441	1501	1535	1536	1632	1636	1730	1809	1827	1847	1916
110	Ripoll d.	...	...	0801	0829	0856	...	0953	1006	1130	1156	1228	1313	1330	1404	1436	1513	1531	1559	1600	1658	1700	1757	1835	1856	1914	1942
124	Ribes de Freser **658** a.	...	...	...	0847	0914	...	1013	1023	1147	1214	...	...	...	1421	1458	...	1548	...	...	1715	1718	...	...	1916	1931	...
145	La Molina a.	...	...	...	0912	0947	...	...	...	1212	1240	...	...	...	1448	1523	...	...	...	...	1740	1751	...	...	1949	1958	...
159	Puigcerdà a.	0801	...	...	0934	1007	...	...	...	1232	1259	...	...	...	1508	1542	...	...	...	...	1800	1811	...	...	2007	2017	...
163	**Latour de Carol** 🏛 **312** a.	0807	...	...	0940	1013	...	...	...	1238	1305	...	...	...	1514	1548	...	...	...	...	1806	1817	...	...	...	...	...

	Ⓐ	Ⓐ	Ⓒ	Ⓐ	Ⓒ	Ⓐ	Ⓐ	Ⓐ	Ⓒ	Ⓐ	
Barcelona Sants d.	1827	1857	1857	2012	2015	2054	2102	2132	2207	2230	...
La Sagrera-Meridiana d.	1840	1910	1910	2025	2028	2107	2115	2145	2220	2243	...
Sant Andreu Arenal d.	1842	1912	1912	2027	2030	2109	2117	2147	2222	2245	...
Granollers - Canovelles d.	|	1939	1941	2054	2055	2139	2145	2217	2251	2312	...
Vic d.	1935	2017	2019	2128	2131	2218	2223	2256	2328	2349	...
Torelló d.	|	2036	2033	2143	2145	...	...	...	...	...	...
Ripoll d.	2010	2102	2059	2208	2210	...	...	...	...	...	...
Ribes de Freser **658** a.	|	2119	2116	...	...	...	...	...	...	...	...
La Molina a.	|	2143	2141	...	...	...	...	...	...	...	...
Puigcerdà a.	2106	2201	2200	...	...	...	...	...	...	...	...
Latour de Carol 🏛 **312** a.	...	...	...	...	...	...	...	...	...	...	...

			Ⓐ	Ⓒ	Ⓐ	Ⓐ	Ⓒ	Ⓐ	Ⓐ	Ⓒ	Ⓐ
Latour de Carol 🏛 **312** d.	...	...	...	...	...	...	...	...	...	...	...
Puigcerdà d.	...	...	...	...	...	0617	0652	0729	...	...	...
La Molina d.	...	...	...	...	...	|	0710	0747	...	...	...
Ribes de Freser **658** d.	...	...	...	...	...	|	0735	0812	...	...	...
Ripoll d.	...	...	0625	...	...	0713	0753	0830	...	...	0913
Torelló d.	...	...	0651	...	...	|	0817	0854	...	...	0940
Vic d.	0548	0641	0705	0723	0726	0750	0831	0908	0925	0917	0955
Granollers - Canovelles d.	0625	0720	0744	0801	0803	|	0902	0942	1002	0956	1034
Sant Andreu Arenal a.	0651	0750	0809	0830	0832	0843	0930	1010	1029	1024	1059
La Sagrera-Meridiana a.	0654	0753	0812	0833	0835	0847	0933	1013	1032	1027	1102
Barcelona Sants a.	0707	0806	0825	0846	0850	0902	0946	1026	1045	1040	1115

	Ⓒ	Ⓒ	Ⓐ	Ⓐ	Ⓒ	Ⓐ	Ⓒ	Ⓐ	Ⓒ	Ⓒ	Ⓐ	Ⓐ	Ⓒ	Ⓐ	Ⓐ	Ⓒ	Ⓒ	Ⓐ	Ⓒ	Ⓐ	Ⓐ	Ⓒ		Ⓒ	Ⓐ	Ⓐ	Ⓒ
Latour de Carol 🏛 **312** d.	...	0848	0850	...	...	...	...	1048	1113	...	...	1334	1347	...	...	...	...	...	...	...	1713	1652	...	1859	1852	...	...
Puigcerdà d.	...	0855	0856	...	...	...	...	1055	1120	...	...	1341	1354	...	...	...	...	...	...	...	1720	1659	...	1906	1859	...	...
La Molina d.	...	0913	0915	...	...	...	...	1113	1138	...	...	1359	1412	...	...	...	...	...	...	...	1739	1717	...	1924	1917	...	...
Ribes de Freser **658** d.	...	0938	0944	...	...	1103	1111	1137	1205	...	...	1423	1439	...	...	...	1640	...	...	...	1805	1744	...	1951	1943	...	...
Ripoll d.	0919	0956	1004	1036	...	1121	1129	1155	1223	1407	1342	1441	1457	...	1604	...	1658	1705	...	...	1823	1802	1906	2009	2004	2104	...
Torelló d.	0946	1020	1028	1102	...	1149	1156	1222	1247	1431	1410	1507	1522	...	1631	...	1724	1732	...	...	1848	1828	1933	2035	2035	2130	...
Vic d.	1001	1034	1041	1117	1121	1203	1211	1236	1301	1446	1425	1521	1536	1601	1646	1650	1739	1746	1806	1823	1902	1846	1949	2051	2049	2145	2140
Granollers - Canovelles d.	1044	1110	1115	1155	1201	1243	1256	1312	1332	1529	1505	1558	1608	1640	1727	1728	1817	1826	1850	1904	1938	1918	2033	2123	2124	2227	2219
Sant Andreu Arenal a.	1112	1135	1141	1221	1230	1310	1328	1339	1357	1557	1536	1627	1638	1708	1754	1757	1851	1851	1918	1937	2009	1942	2058	2150	2151	2253	2247
La Sagrera-Meridiana a.	1115	1138	1144	1223	1233	1312	1331	1342	1400	1600	1538	1630	1638	1711	1756	1800	1854	1853	1921	1940	2012	1945	2101	2153	2154	2256	2250
Barcelona Sants a.	1128	1150	1157	1236	1246	1325	1344	1355	1412	1613	1551	1644	1650	1724	1809	1813	1907	1906	1934	1954	2025	1958	2114	2206	2207	2309	2303

❖ – Timing subject to confirmation. Please check locally.

657   BARCELONA - GIRONA - FIGUERES - PORTBOU / PERPIGNAN

Reservations are not compulsory on *Media Distancia* (*MD*) services on the Barcelona - Girona - Portbou - Cebère route. All stopping services convey 2nd class only.

Block 1 (train type / number — symbols)

km	km	Station	MD 15900 Ⓐ	TGV 9700 34700* Ⓐ GP	⑥	Ⓐ	AVE 9734 Ⓒ L	MD 15056 Ⓐ	MD 15076 Ⓐ	Ⓒ	TGV 9702 Ⓐ P	AVE 3071 34071* Ⓐ	MD 15908 Ⓒ	MD 15094 Ⓐ	Ⓒ	AVE 3073 34073* Ⓐ ⑥⑦	Ⓒ	MD 15078 Ⓐ	MD 15078 Ⓒ	AVE 3093 34093* Ⓐ	MD 15004 Ⓒ
		Madrid ⊠ 630 .... d.									0700x					0730				0930	
0	0	Barcelona Sants .... 666 d.	0556	0610	0616	0646	0716	0720	0746	0816	0846	0916	0925	0945 0946	1016	1046	1116 1146	1146	1244	1246 1246	1316
3		Barcelona P de G ¶ .... d.	0601		0620	0650	0720		0751	0821	0850	0920		0951 1021	1050		1120 1151	1151		1251 1250	1320
31		Granollers Centre .... d.			0646	0716	0752			0917		0946					1116 1146				1316 1346
72		Maçanet - Massanes .. 666 d.	0651		0722	0752	0832	0843	0913	0957	1022	1043	1113	1152	1222	1243 1243	1343		1353	1422
86		Caldes de Malavella .... d.	0702		0733	0803	0843	0854	0924	1007	1033	1054	1124	1203	1233	1254 1253	1353		1403	1433
102	95	Girona .... d.	0713	0651	0748	0818	0858 0801	0905	0935	1023 1049	1006 1026	1105	1135 1218	1130	1248	1305 1305	1324	1404 1419	1448
118		Flaçà .... d.	0713 0726		0802	0832	0912	0915	0948	1038	1104	1118	1148	1232	1302	1318 1318	1417			1502
143		Figueres .... § d.	0744		0827	0857	0937	0957	1007	1102	1129	1137	1207	1257	1327	1336 1337	1437	1458		1527
	129	Figueres Vilafant .... d.		0708			0818		1023 1040					1145		1339			
162		Llançà .... d.			0842	0912	0952		0950	1020	1116 1143		1150	1312	1342	1350		1512	1542
169		Portbou 🚇 .... 355 a.			0852	0922	1002		0957	1027	1126 1153	1157	1227	1323	1352	1357		1521	1557
171		Cerbère 🚇 .... 355 a.			0857	0927	1007				1130	1157		1327		1357		1526	1557
177		Perpignan .... 355 a.		0731							0843					1046			

Block 2

Station	TGV 9704 P	MD 15910 ⑤⑦	MD 15096 ①–⑥	AVE 3113 34113* ①–⑤		AVE 3123 34123* Ⓑ	MD 15098	TGV 9706 34707*		AVE 3143 19725* CP✤	TGV 9724 M		MD 15080 Ⓐ	AVE 15082 3143 Ⓒ	MD 15922 34727* ET✤	AVE 9726 Ⓐ	MD 15084 ①–⑤	AVE 3153 34153*		AVE 3163 31163*	MD 31399* ⑦	MD 15086 Ⓐ	MD 15088 Ⓒ	AVE 15006 3191 31162* Ⓑ	TGV 9713 34712* P	MD 15916 ⑨
Madrid ⊠ 630 .... d.				1130			1230				1325	1430					1530		1630					1900		
Barcelona Sants .... 666 d.	1320	1346	1416	1450	1516	1540	1616	1620	1716	1645	1737	1746	1816	1819	1830	1846	1850	1916 1925z	1945	1946	2016	2046	2140	2146		
Barcelona P de G ¶ .... d.		1351	1421		1520		1621		1720		1751	1821	1824		1851		1920			1951	2021	2051		2151		
Granollers Centre .... d.					1546			1746								1947									
Maçanet - Massanes .... 666 d.		1443	1513		1622		1713		1822		1843	1913			1945		2043		2113	2157		2250		
Caldes de Malavella .... d.		1454	1524		1633		1724		1833		1854	1924	1931		1956		2054		2124	2301				
Girona .... d.	1401	1505	1535	1531	1648	1620	1735	1701	1848	1726	1817	1905	1935	1942	1911	2007	1930	2054 2005z	2025	2105	2135	2217	2220	2311
Flaçà .... d.		1518t	1548		1702		1748		1902		1918	1948	1955		2020		2108		2118	2148		2229		2323
Figueres .... § d.		1537t	1607		1727		1806		1927		1937	2006	2013		2038		2130		2138	2206	2246			
Figueres Vilafant .... § d.	1418			1545		1635		1718		1743	1832				1928		1945		2020z 2040				2235	
Llançà .... d.		1550t	1620f		1742				1942			1950				2145							
Portbou 🚇 .... 355 a.		1557t	1627f		1751				1952			1957				2155							
Cerbère 🚇 .... 355 a.					1757				1957														
Perpignan .... 355 a.	1443						1742		1806						1951								

Block 3

Station	MD 15010 Ⓐ	MD 15046 ①–⑥	AVE 3662 34662* ①–⑤	AVE 3082 31082* Ⓐ	MD 15060 Ⓒ	MD 15060 ①–⑤	Av 31472* ①–⑥		AVE 3092 31092* ⑦	MD 15064 ①–⑤	MD 15066 31102* Ⓒ	AVE 3102 Ⓐ		MD 15068 BT✤	AVE 9729 34728* M		AVE 9731 19730* CP✤	MD 15070 Ⓐ	TGV 9711 34710* P		MD 15090 Ⓐ	AVE 15002 3162 31162* Ⓒ		TGV 9713 34712* P
Perpignan .... 355 d.														1000			1117		1212				1513
Portbou 🚇 .... 355 d.					0623			0703				0833			1033		1127	1235 1327			1433	
Llançà .... d.					0630			0712				0842			1042		1135	1244 1335			1442	
Figueres Vilafant .... d.			0630	0655			0720		0755		0855			1026		1143	1239			1455	1539
Figueres .... § d.	0544	0555			0643	0643		0728		0749	0819		0858	0949		1058		1149	1300 1349	1419		1458
Flaçà .... d.	0600	0615			0659	0659		0750		0805	0835		0920	1005		1120		1205	1323 1405	1435		1520
Girona .... d.	0614	0629	0646	0711	0713	0713	0736	0806	0811	0819	0849	0919	0936	1019	1043	1136	1200	1219 1256	1339 1419	1449	1511 1536	1556
Caldes de Malavella .... d.	0624	0640			0724	0724		0820		0829	0859		0950	1029		1150		1229	1353 1429	1459		1550
Maçanet - Massanes .... 666 d.	0635	0651			0735	0735		0831		0839	0909		1001	1039		1201		1239	1404 1439	1509		1601
Granollers Centre .... d.								0905					1035			1235			1437			1635
Barcelona P de G ¶ .... a.	0735	0749			0835	0835		0934		0935	1005		1105	1135		1305		1335	1505 1535	1605		1705
Barcelona Sants .... 666 a.	0739	0753	0725	0750	0839	0839	0815	0939	0850	0939	1009	0950	1109	1139	1121	1309	1238	1334 1339	1509 1539	1609	1550 1709	1634
Madrid ⊠ 630 .... a.			1010	1110				1145				1310			1545				1910			

Block 4

Station	AVE 3172 ⑦	MD 15072 Ⓑ		AVE 3182 34182* ⑦	AVE 3180 ⑥		MD 15018 Ⓐ	MD 15018 ⑦	AVE 3192 Ⓐ	MD 15092 Ⓒ		MD 15918 Ⓐ	AVE 9743 34742* L	MD 15074 Ⓑ	AVE 15920 ⑥		TGV 9715 P		MD 15000 Ⓐ	AVE 3222 34222* Ⓒ	TGV 9717 AP	MD 15904 Ⓒ
Perpignan .... 355 d.												1810					1913				2125	
Portbou 🚇 .... 355 d.		1527j	1603		1633				1727	1733	1757		1839		1903	1941					2028	2028
Llançà .... d.		1535j	1612		1642				1735	1742	1805		1848		1912	1950				2045	2036	2036
Figueres Vilafant .... § d.	1545			1655	1720			1755			1836			1939					2150		
Figueres .... § d.		1549	1628		1658	1719			1749	1758	1819		1849	1856	1904		1928	2006	2029		2050	2049
Flaçà .... d.		1605	1650		1720	1735			1805	1820	1835		1905	1912	1926		1950	2030	2045		2106	2107
Girona .... d.	1601	1619	1706	1711	1736	1736	1749	1749	1811	1819	1836	1849	1853	1919	1926	1942	1956	2006 2046	2059	2101	2207	2121 2121
Caldes de Malavella .... d.		1629	1720		1750	1759	1759		1829	1839	1850		1929	1936	1956		2020	2100	2109		2129	2134
Maçanet - Massanes .... 666 d.		1639	1731		1801	1809	1809		1839	1839	1901	1909		1939	1946	2007		2031	2111	2119		2139	2145
Granollers Centre .... d.					1835					1935						2105	2145				2219
Barcelona P de G ¶ .... a.		1735	1835		1905	1905	1905		1935	1935	2004	2005		2035	2042	2105		2135	2215	2215		2235	2237
Barcelona Sants .... 666 a.	1640	1739	1839	1750	1905	1909	1909	1850	1939	1939	2009	1931	2039	2039	2044	2139	2129	2140	2246	2239	2251
Madrid ⊠ 630 .... a.	1945z		2110	2055				2200												

A – July 3 - Aug. 28.
B – Apr. 2 - Sept. 26.
C – June 2 - Aug. 28.
E – Apr. 3 - Sept. 25.
G – July 4 - Aug. 28.

L – To/from Lyon (Table 13).
M – To/from Marseille (Table 13).
P – To/from Paris (Table 13).
T – To/from Toulouse (Table 13).
⊠ – Madrid Puerta de Atocha.

t – ⑦ only.
x – 0620 on ⑥⑦.
z – 3 - 5 minutes later June 12 - Sept. 11.

✤ – Service runs Barcelona - Girona - Figueres and v.v. when International service does not run.
⬇ – On ⑥, as train number **3183**, depart Madrid 1830, Barcelona 2130, Girona 2210, arrive Figueres 2225.
* – Train number for *Turista* class (classified Av).
¶ – Barcelona Passeig de Gràcia.

§ – **FIGUERES VILAFANT - FIGUERES BUS STATION** (150m from Figueres). *5 km.* By 🚌. Journey time: 15 - 20 minutes.

From **Figueres Vilafant**: 0835 ①, 1020, 1050, 1125, 1150, 1255, 1345, 1550 Ⓐ, 1645 Ⓑ, 1725, 1830, 1935, 1955, 2035 Ⓐ, 2240.

From **Figueres Bus Station**: 0600 Ⓐ, 0625 Ⓐ, 0725 ✕, 0815, 0945, 1030, 1105, 1215, 1425 ✕, 1515 ⑦, 1625, 1740, 1815, 1915, 2015, 2205.

---

658   VALL DE NÚRIA   2nd class

Ribes Enllaç - **Ribes** Vila - **Queralbs** - **Núria** rack railway

HIGH SEASON:

⑥⑦ (daily July 15 - Sept. 11), also Apr. 1, May 1, 20, June 24, Nov. 1:
From **Ribes** Enllaç: 0735 v, 0830 n, 0920 and hourly until 1730, also 1840 c.
From **Núria**: 0830, 0920 n, 1020 and hourly until 1820, also 1930 c.

LOW SEASON:

①–⑤ (except dates above). No service from Nov. 4 (resumes early December).
From **Ribes** Enllaç: 0730 v, 0910, 1110, 1250, 1440, 1630, 1820 ⑤.
From **Núria**: 0820, 1000, 1200, 1345, 1530, 1720, 1910 ⑤.

Journey times **Ribes – Queralbs** (6 km) 24 minutes, **Ribes – Núria** (12 km) 44 minutes.
Ferrocarrils de la Generalitat de Catalunya (FGC) ✆ +34 972 73 20 20. www.valldenuria.cat

c – ⑤ (also July 27, Aug. 3 - 31, Sept. 1, 7, 11).
n – Ski season only, also ⑥⑦ in June and July (daily July 29 - Sept. 1).
v – From Ribes Vila.

---

659   AEROPORT BARCELONA   2nd class

Local rail service *Cercanías* (suburban) line **R2 Nord**. *14 km*
Aeroport - Barcelona Sants - Barcelona Passeig de Gràcia
Journey time: 19 minutes Sants, 26 minutes Passeig de Gràcia

From Aeroport del Prat:
0542, 0608, 0638, 0708, 0738 and every 30 minutes until 2208, 2238, 2308, 2338.

From Barcelona Sants:
0513, 0535, 0609, 0639, 0709 and every 30 minutes until 2139, 2209, 2239, 2314.

✕ – Daily except Sundays and holidays   † – Sundays and holidays   Ⓐ – Mondays to Fridays, except holidays   Ⓑ – Daily except Saturdays

High-speed services — MADRID - CÓRDOBA - SEVILLA and MÁLAGA — 660

Buses replace trains between Antequera - Santa Ana and Granada until Autumn 2017

km		*Av*	*AVE*	*AVE*	*AVE*	*AVE*	*AVE*	*AVE*	*Alvia*	*Alta*	*AVE*	*AVE*	*AVE*	*Alvia*	*AVE*	*AVE*	*AVE*	*AVE*	*AVE*	*AVE*	*AVE*	*AVE*	*AVE*	*AVE*	*AVE*	*Alvia*	*AVE*	*AVE*	*AVE*
		2260	**2070**	**2270**	**2072**	**2072**	**2080**	**2082**	**2084**	**9366**	**2090**	**3982**	**2092**	**2294**	**2100**	**2102**	**2110**	**3940**	**3990**	**2112**	**2120**	**3944**	**3994**	**2130**	**2122**	**2134**	**2140**	**2142**	**2142**
		①–⑤	①–⑤	①–④	①–⑤	⑥⑦	①–⑥	①–④				①–⑥		⑥	①–⑥	①–⑤						⑥	⑥					Ⓑ	⑥
		D ❦	**D**	**D**								**V**												**C**					
	Barcelona Sants **650** . d.	...	...	...	...	...	...	...	...	...	...	...	...	...	...	...	...	0830	0830	...	...	0940	0940	...	...	...	...	...	...
0	**Madrid** Puerta de Atocha d.	0620	0700	0730	0720	0735	0800	0825	0830	0835	0900	...	0935	0945	1000	1035	1100	|	|	1135	1200	|	|	1300	1300	1330	1400	1435	1435
171	Ciudad Real .... d.	0720	|	|	|	|	|	|	0922	0937	0951	1021	1026	|	|	|	|	1213	1213	|	|	|	|	1351	1351	1421	|	|	|
210	Puertollano .... d.	0738	|	|	|	|	|	|	0937	0953	1007	1037	1044	|	|	|	|	1229	1229	|	|	|	|	1407	1407	1435	|	|	|
345	**Córdoba** .... d.	0830	0844	|	0902	0917	0944	|	1020	1039	1052	1121	1127	1132	1144	|	1244	1319	1330	1324	1344	1406	1416	1452	1505	1517	1544	1619	1619
470	**Sevilla** .... a.	0916	0930	0950	|	|	1030	|	1106	|	1135	1205	|	|	1230	|	1330	1402	|	|	1430	1455	|	1540	|	1605	1630	|	|
	Cádiz **671** .... a.	...	...	...	|	|	...	|	1238	|	...	...	|	|	...	|	...	...	|	|	...	...	|	...	|	1740	...	|	|
	Huelva **671** .... a.	...	...	...	|	|	...	|	...	|	...	...	|	1320	...	|	...	...	|	|	...	...	|	...	|	...	...	|	|
419	Puente Genil - Herrera ¶ a.	...	...	...	0923	0938	...	|	...	|	...	...	|	...	...	|	...	...	1351	|	...	...	1438	...	1526	...	...	|	|
455	Antequera - Santa Ana § a.	...	...	...	0937	0952	...	|	...	1117	...	...	1155	...	...	|	...	...	1402	1352	...	...	1452	...	1539	...	...	1654	1654
	Algeciras **673** .... a.	...	...	...	|	|	...	|	...	1348	...	...	|	...	...	|	...	...	|	|	...	...	|	...	|	...	...	|	|
	Granada **673** .... a.	...	...	...	*1130*¦	*1130*¦	...	|	...	...	...	...	*1330*¦	...	...	|	...	...	*1610*¦	|	...	...	*1630*¦	...	|	...	...	*1820*¦	|
513	**Málaga** María Zambrano . a.	...	...	...	1035	1020	...	1045	...	...	...	...	1222	...	...	1255	...	...	1424	1417	...	...	1516	...	1605	...	...	1718	1718

	AVE	*Alta*	*AVE*	*AVE*	*Alvia*	*IC*	*AVE*	*AVE*	*AVE*	*AVE*	*AVE*	*Alvia*	*AVE*	*AVE*	*AVE*	*AVE*	*Alvia*	*AVE*	*AVE*	*AVE*	*AVE*	*AVE*	*AVE*	*Av*	*AVE*				
	2150	**9330**	**2152**	**2160**	**2164**	**2364**	**2360**	**2162**	**2170**	**2172**	**2180**	**2384**	**2182**	**3942**	**3992**	**3974**	**2184**	**2190**	**3946**	**2390**	**2192**	**2200**	**2202**	**2410**	**2212**				
	Ⓑ		④⑤⑦			⑤	④⑤⑦					Ⓑ	Ⓑ			①⑤⑦	⑤⑦	Ⓑ	⑤						⑤⑦				
	D	◐					**M**									**E**			**K**	**H**				❦					
Barcelona Sants **650** .. d.	...	...	...	...	...	...	...	...	...	...	...	...	...	1550	1550	...	...	...	1632	...	...	...	...	...	...	...	...	...	...
Madrid Puerta de Atocha d.	1500	1505	1535	1600	1615	1620	1630	1635	1700	1735	1800	1805	1830	|	|	...	1835	1900	|	1930	1930	2035	2035	2125	2120	...	...	...	...
Ciudad Real .... d.	|	|	|	|	|	|	|	|	1751	1826	|	|	|	1936	1936	1942	|	1951	|	|	|	2126	2126	2219	|	...	...	...	...
Puertollano .... d.	|	|	|	|	|	|	|	|	1807	1842	|	|	|	|	|	1957	|	2007	|	|	|	2142	2142	2234	|	...	...	...	...
Córdoba .... d.	|	1708	|	1744	|	|	|	1819	1852	1925	1944	1952	|	2030	2040	2045	2016	2052	2056	2114	2114	2227	2227	2324	|	...	...	...	...
Sevilla .... a.	1720	|	|	1830	|	1852	1855	|	1935	|	2030	|	|	2115	|	|	2106	2135	2143	2205	|	2315	|	0010	|	...	...	...	...
Cádiz **671** .... a.	...	|	|	...	2010	|	...	|	...	|	...	|	|	...	|	|	2239	...	...	...	|	...	|	...	|	...	...	...	...
Huelva **671** .... a.	...	|	|	...	...	2026	...	|	...	|	...	2145	|	...	|	|	...	...	...	...	|	...	|	...	|	...	...	...	...
Puente Genil - Herrera ¶. a.	...	|	|	...	...	...	...	|	...	1946	...	...	|	...	2104	2110	...	...	...	...	|	...	2302	...	|	...	...	...	...
Antequera - Santa Ana §. a.	...	1753	|	...	...	...	...	|	...	1959	...	...	|	...	2117	2125	...	...	...	...	|	...	2315	...	|	...	...	...	...
Algeciras **673** .... a.	...	2030	|	...	...	...	...	|	...	|	...	...	|	...	|	|	...	...	...	...	|	...	|	...	|	...	...	...	...
Granada **673** .... a.	...	...	|	...	...	...	...	|	...	*2130*¦	...	...	|	...	*2300*¦	*2300*¦	...	...	...	...	|	...	|	...	|	...	...	...	...
Málaga María Zambrano . a.	...	...	1806	...	...	...	...	1907	...	2025	...	...	2053	...	2140	2151	...	...	...	...	2218	...	2340	...	2343	...	...	...	...

	Av	*AVE*	*AVE*	*AVE*	*AVE*	*AVE*	*AVE*	*AVE*	*AVE*	*AVE*	*AVE*	*Alvia*	*AVE*	*AVE*	*Alvia*	*AVE*	*AVE*	*AVE*	*Alta*	*Alvia*	*AVE*	*AVE*	*AVE*	*AVE*	*AVE*	*AVE*	*AVE*	*AVE*	*AVE*
	2261	**2063**	**2061**	**2073**	**2471**	**2271**	**2071**	**2083**	**2081**	**3993**	**3943**	**2285**	**2093**	**2091**	**2085**	**3971**	**2101**	**2113**	**9367**	**2205**	**2111**	**2123**	**2121**	**2131**	**2143**	**2141**	**3991**	**3941**	**2153**
	①–⑤	①–④	①–⑤	①–④	⑥⑦	①–④	①–⑥					①–⑤		①–⑥		⑤⑥				⑥			Ⓑ						④⑤⑦
	D ★	**D**	**D**	**D**	**P**	**D**										**U**										**W**			
Málaga María Zambrano . d.	...	0620	...	0710	...	...	...	0800	...	0840	...	...	0900	...	...	0945	...	1055	...	...	...	1205	...	...	1405	...	1435	...	1500
Granada **673** .... d.	...	|	...	|	...	...	...	*0655*¦	...	*0645*¦	...	...	|	...	...	*0830*¦	...	*1000*¦	...	...	...	|	...	...	|	...	*1245*¦	...	|
Algeciras **673** .... d.	...	|	...	|	...	...	...	|	...	|	...	...	|	...	...	|	...	|	0843	...	...	|	...	...	|	...	|	...	|
Antequera - Santa Ana §. d.	...	0644	...	|	...	...	...	0823	...	0902	...	...	0926	...	...	1008	...	1123	|	...	...	|	...	...	1429	...	1500	...	|
Puente Genil - Herrera ¶. d.	...	0657	...	|	...	...	...	|	...	0916	...	...	|	...	...	1021	...	|	|	...	...	|	...	...	1442	...	1513	...	|
Huelva **671** .... d.	...	|	...	|	...	...	...	|	...	|	...	0800	|	...	...	|	...	|	|	1025	...	|	...	...	|	...	|	...	|
Cádiz **671** .... d.	...	|	...	|	...	...	...	|	...	|	...	|	|	...	0815	|	...	|	|	|	...	|	...	...	|	...	|	...	|
Sevilla .... d.	0610	|	0645	|	0700	0715	0745	|	0845	|	0850	|	|	0945	0950	|	1045	|	|	|	1145	|	1245	1345	|	1445	|	1450	|
Córdoba .... d.	0653	0722	0729	|	0750	0803	|	0856	0929	0943	0943	0950	0959	1028	1042	1051	1129	1156	1202	1218	1229	1256	1328	|	1506	1529	1542	1542	|
Puertollano .... d.	0744	|	|	|	0841	0845	|	|	|	|	|	|	1041	1110	1125	1135	|	|	|	|	|	|	1413	|	1548	|	1625	1625	|
Ciudad Real .... d.	0759	|	|	|	0858	0859	|	|	|	1039	1039	|	1057	1124	1140	1149	|	|	|	|	|	|	1427	|	1603	|	1639	1639	|
Madrid Puerta de Atocha a.	0857	0905	0915	0938	1002	0955	1005	1040	1115	|	|	1141	1150	1220	1236	...	1315	1340	1405	1410	1415	1440	1520	1605	1655	1715	|	|	1740
Barcelona Sants **650** .. a.	...	...	...	...	...	...	...	...	...	1425	1425	...	...	...	...	...	...	...	...	...	...	...	...	...	...	...	2022	2022	...

	Alvia	*AVE*	*AVE*	*AVE*	*AVE*	*AVE*	*AVE*	*AVE*	*AVE*	*AVE*	*Alvia*	*Alta*	*AVE*	*AVE*	*AVE*	*AVE*	*IC*	*Alvia*	*AVE*	*AVE*	*AVE*	*AVE*	*Alvia*	*Av*	*AVE*				
	2135	**2151**	**3995**	**3945**	**2163**	**2163**	**2361**	**2161**	**3973**	**2173**	**2365**	**9331**	**2171**	**2183**	**3981**	**2181**	**2375**	**2175**	**2391**	**2193**	**2191**	**2203**	**2195**	**2411**	**2213**				
			⑦	⑦	Ⓑ	⑥	④⑤⑦		⑦		⑦			Ⓑ	Ⓑ	Ⓑ	⑦						⑤⑦		⑤⑦				
							M		**F**			★			**V**				**H**					★	**X**				
Málaga María Zambrano . d.	...	...	1535	...	1555	1555	...	...	1635	1700	...	...	...	1810	...	...	...	...	...	1905	...	2005	...	...	2120	...	...	...	...
Granada **673** .... d.	...	...	*1400*¦	...	*1500*¦	|	...	...	*1520*¦	|	...	...	...	|	...	...	...	...	...	|	...	*1900*¦	...	...	|	...	...	...	...
Algeciras **673** .... d.	...	...	|	...	|	|	...	...	|	|	...	1503	...	|	...	...	...	...	...	|	...	|	...	...	|	...	...	...	...
Antequera - Santa Ana §. d.	...	...	1557	...	1623	1623	...	...	1658	1724	...	1733	...	|	...	...	...	...	...	1929	...	2030	...	...	|	...	...	...	...
Puente Genil - Herrera ¶. d.	...	...	1611	...	|	|	...	...	1711	1737	...	|	...	|	...	...	...	...	...	|	...	2044	...	...	|	...	...	...	...
Huelva **671** .... d.	...	...	|	...	|	|	...	...	|	|	1620	|	...	|	...	...	1750	...	...	|	...	|	...	...	|	...	...	...	...
Cádiz **671** .... d.	1330	...	|	...	|	|	...	...	|	|	|	|	...	|	...	...	|	1728	...	|	...	|	1855	...	|	...	...	...	...
Sevilla .... d.	1500	1545	|	1555	|	|	1625	1645	|	|	|	|	1745	|	1830	1845	|	|	1915	|	1945	|	2036	2100	|	...	...	...	...
Córdoba .... d.	1554	1629	1641	1641	1656	1656	1710	1729	1740	1802	1810	1815	1829	1900	1914	1929	1919	|	|	2001	2029	2110	2127	2149	2208	...	...	...	...
Puertollano .... d.	1637	|	|	|	|	|	1752	|	1823	|	|	1919	|	|	1957	|	|	|	|	|	|	2153	|	2239	|	...	...	...	...
Ciudad Real .... d.	1653	|	|	|	|	|	1806	|	1837	|	|	1936	|	|	2010	|	|	|	|	|	|	2208	|	2255	|	...	...	...	...
Madrid Puerta de Atocha a.	1748	1815	|	|	1841	1841	1903	1915	...	1945	2001	2035	2015	2045	...	2113	2159	2127	2135	2145	2215	2306	2314	2350	2355	...	...	...	...
Barcelona Sants **650** .. a.	...	...	2115	2115	...	...	...	...	...	...	...	...	...	...	...	...	...	...	...	...	...	...	...	...	...	...	...	...	...

C – ①④⑤⑦.
D – Not July 25 - Sept. 4.
E – ①⑤⑦ From València, dep. 1712.
F – ⑦ (To València, arr. 2105).
H – ③④⑤⑦.
K – Not July 8 - Sept 9.
M – Not July 20 - Sept. 4.

P – ⑥⑦ (daily July 25 - Sept. 4).
U – ⑤⑥ To València, arr. 1418.
V – From / to València (Table **668**).
W – ①④⑤⑦ (not July 25 - Sept. 4).
X – ⑤⑦ (Ⓑ July 25 - Sept. 4).

§ – ± *17 km* from Antequera.
‡ – Antequera - Ciudad.

★ – Also calls at Villanueva de CLP (⊠), 23 - 24 mins. after departing Córdoba.
◐ – Also calls at Villanueva de CLP (⊠), 100 mins. after departing Madrid.
❦ – Also calls at Villanueva de CLP (⊠), 25 - 28 mins. after departing Puertollano.
⊠ – Full name: Villanueva de Córdoba-Los Pedroches.
¦ – 🚌 Antequera-Santa Ana - Granada and v.v. Subject to alteration until Autumn 2017.
☛ All trains convey 🍷. *AVE* trains also convey ✕.

Turista class; 🍷 — Málaga – Córdoba – Sevilla — *Avant* high-speed shuttle services

	8654	**8664**	**8664**	**8694**	**8714**	**8744**	**8764**	**8784**	**8804**
	①–⑤	①–⑤			①–⑤		①–⑤		
Málaga María Zambrano .... d.	...	0645	...	0915	...	1415	1615	1820	2015
Antequera - Santa Ana § .... d.	...	0711	...	0941	...	1441	1641	1844	2041
Puente Genil - Herrera ¶ .... d.	...	0725	...	0955	...	1455	1655	1858	2055
Córdoba .... a.	...	0750	...	1020	...	1520	1720	1922	2120
Córdoba .... d.	0650	0755	0755	1025	1300	1525	1725	1930	2125
Sevilla .... a.	0735	0840	0840	1110	1345	1610	1810	2015	2210

	8075	**8085**	**8095**	**8095**	**8125**	**8155**	**8175**	**8195**	**8215**	
	①–⑤	①–⑤	⑥⑦				①–⑤			
Sevilla .... d.	0650	0800	0920	0920	1250	1540	1755	1935	2135	...
Córdoba .... a.	0735	0845	1005	1005	1335	1625	1840	2020	2220	...
Córdoba .... d.	0740	0850	1010	...	1340	1630	1845	2025	...	...
Puente Genil - Herrera ¶ ..... d.	0803	0913	1033	...	1403	1653	1908	2048	...	...
Antequera - Santa Ana § ..... d.	0817	0927	1047	...	1417	1707	1922	2102	...	...
Málaga María Zambrano .... a.	0845	0955	1115	...	1445	1735	1950	2130	...	...

§ – ± *17 km* from Antequera.

¶ – ± *8 km* from Puente Genil.

Turista class; 🍷 — Madrid – Puertollano — *Avant* high-speed shuttle services

		8260		**8080**		**8100**			**8130**	**8140**		**8150**		**8170**	**8180**	**8190**	**8200**		**8220**					
		①–⑤		①–⑥						①–⑤		①–⑥			①–⑤		Ⓑ							
Madrid Puerta de Atocha ...... d.	...	0640	...	0805	...	1015	...	...	1315	1415	...	1545	...	1715	1815	1915	2015	...	2215	...	...	...	...	...
Ciudad Real ...... d.	...	0736	...	0901	...	1111	...	...	1411	1511	...	1641	...	1812	1911	2011	2111	...	2311	...	...	...	...	...
Puertollano ...... a.	...	0753	...	0918	...	1128	...	...	1428	1528	...	1658	...	1828	1928	2028	2128	...	2328	...	...	...	...	...

		8261		**8271**	**8471**	**8081**		**8101**		**8121**			**8151**	**8161**	**8171**	**8181**	**8191**		**8211**					
		①–⑤		①–⑤	①–⑤	①–⑥							①–⑥	①–⑤		⑦								
Puertollano ...... d.	...	0625	...	0700	0750	0815	...	1015	...	1215	...	...	1515	1615	1715	1815	1915	...	2115	...	...	...	...	...
Ciudad Real ...... d.	...	0642	...	0717	0807	0832	...	1032	...	1232	...	...	1532	1632	1732	1832	1932	...	2132	...	...	...	...	...
Madrid Puerta de Atocha ...... a.	...	0742	...	0813	0903	0928	...	1128	...	1329	...	...	1628	1728	1828	1928	2028	...	2228	...	...	...	...	...

661 — MADRID - ALMERÍA and JAÉN

For other trains Madrid – Córdoba – Granada / Málaga and v.v. via the AVE high-speed line, see Table 660

km		MD 17008 2 ①–⑤	MD 13079 2 E	Talgo 276 ⚓	MD 18030 2	MD 18170 2 C	MD 13083 2 E	MD 13035 2 E	Talgo 697 ⚓ N	MD 13073 2 E	Talgo 278 ⚓ ①–⑤	MD 18032 2	MD 18034 2 ⑧	MD 18036 2	MD 17000 2
0	Madrid Chamartín .... 668a 669 d.	...	...	0800	0916	1258	...	...	...	...	1456	1545	1720	1918	2114
8	Madrid Atocha Cercanías 668a 669 d.	0713	...	0819	0929	1310	...	...	...	...	1513	1559	1734	1932	2128
57	Aranjuez.................. 668a 669 d.	0751	...		1004	1342	...	...	...	...		1634		2010	2207
	Barcelona Sants 672 .... d.	...	...				...	...	0930	...					
	València Nord 668 .... d.	...	...				...	...	1255	...					
157	Alcázar de San Juan .... 678 d.	0840	...	0937	1101	1435	...	...	1603	...	1634	1723	1854	2101	2301
206	Manzanares.................. 678 d.	...	...		1125	1459	...	...	1626	...	1657	1747	1918	2124	...
323	Linares - Baeza .... a.	...	...	1117	1249		...	...	1745	...	1811	1911	2039	2241	...
323	Linares - Baeza .... d.	...	...	1119	1250		...	...	1747	...	1813	1912	2040	2242	...
441	Moreda .... d.	...	...				...	...		...	1951				...
499	Granada .... 673 a.	...	...				...	...		...					...
466	Guadix .... 673 d.	...	...	1309			...	...		...	2013				...
565	Almería .... 673 a.	...	...	1422			...	...		...	2129				...
¶	Jaén .... d.	...	0637		1333		1430	1650		1830	1955		2125	2325	...
371	Andújar...................... d.	...	0720				1514	1737	1831	1913					...
450	Córdoba .... a.	...	0810				1610	1828	1926	2007					...

		MD 18047 2 ①–⑤	MD 18031 2 ①–⑤	MD 18033 2	Talgo 277 ⚓	MD 13001 2 E	Talgo 694 ⚓ N	MD 18171 2	MD 13003 2 C	MD 17041 2 ⑥⑦	MD 18035 2 E	MD 13009 2	MD 18037 2 T	MD 13011 2	Talgo 279 ⚓ E	MD 13017 2 E
	Córdoba ....d.	...	...			0906	0950		1002	...	...	1451	1626		2105	...
	Andújar........................d.	...	...			0959	1040		1056	...	...	1544	1720		2157	...
	Jaén .... d.	...	0610	0830		1049			1143	...	1520	1629	1718	1811	2245	...
	Almería .... 673 d.	...			0730					...				1605		...
	Guadix .... 673 d.	...			0848					...				1719		...
	Granada .... 673 d.	...			0910					...						...
	Moreda .... d.	...								...						...
	Linares - Baeza .... a.	...	0650	0912	1040		1117			...	1602		1800		1914	...
	Linares - Baeza .... d.	...	0651	0913	1045		1120			...	1603		1801		1916	...
	Manzanares.................. 678 d.	...	0807	1032			1237			1520	1723		1921		2035	...
	Alcázar de San Juan......... 678 d.	0527	0832	1055	1223		1315	1355		1546	1745		1946		2059	...
	València Nord 668 .... a.	...						1602								...
	Barcelona Sants 672 .... a.	...						2000								...
	Aranjuez.................. 668a 669 a.	0621	0918	1143				1447		1643	1830		2032			...
	Madrid Atocha Cercanías 668a 669 a.	0656	0959	1214	1343			1526		1717	1905	2109		2219		...
	Madrid Chamartín .... 668a 669 a.	...	1013	1228	1358			1541		1731	1919	2122		2233		...

C – To / from Ciudad Real (Table 678).
E – To / from Cádiz (Table 671).

N – TORRE DEL ORO – 🛏 ⚓ Barcelona - Córdoba - Sevilla and v.v. (Tables 668a, 671, 672).

T – Daily from Sevilla. From Cádiz on ①–⑤. Table 671.
¶ – Linares - Jaen : 59 km. Jaen - Andújar : 54 km.

662 — MÁLAGA - TORREMOLINOS - FUENGIROLA — 2nd class

km												
0	Málaga María Zambrano.d.	0523	0558	0633	0653 and	2133	2203	2233	2303	2333	...
8	Málaga Aeropuerto ✈...d.	0532	0607	0642	0702 every	2142	2212	2242	2312	2342	...
16	Torremolinos ....d.	0543	0618	0653	0713 20	2153	2223	2253	2323	2353	...
20	Benalmádena ....d.	0554	0629	0704	0724 mins.	2204	2234	2304	2334	0004	...
31	Fuengirola ....a.	0606	0641	0716	0736 until	2216	2246	2316	2346	0016	...

Fuengirola ....d.	0610	0645	0720	0740 and	2220	2250	2320	2350	0020	...
Benalmádena ....d.	0624	0659	0734	0754 every	2234	2304	2334	0004	0034	...
Torremolinos ....d.	0633	0708	0743	0803 20	2243	2313	2343	0013	0043	...
Málaga Aeropuerto ✈...d.	0644	0719	0754	0814 mins.	2254	2324	2354	0024	0054	...
Málaga María Zambrano a.	0652	0727	0802	0822 until	2302	2332	0002	0032	0102	...

♨ – 0653, 0733, 0813 from Málaga and 0740, 0820, 0900 from Fuengirola do not run on ⑥⑦.

664 — 🚌 BARCELONA - ANDORRA

From **Barcelona** Nord bus station : 0630*, 0700, 0730*, 1030, 1500, 1700*, 1900.
From **Andorra la Vella** bus station : 0600, 0815*, 1100, 1500, 1700*, 1915.
Journey 3 hr 15 min (*4 hours). Operator: Alsina Graells, Barcelona (ALSA) ☎ (+34) 91 327 05 40.

From **Barcelona** Airport ✈ (T1 and T2): 0730, 1100, 1300, 1500, 1730, 2000, 2300.
From **Barcelona** Sants railway station : 0615, 0815, 1145, 1345, 1545, 1815, 2045, 2345.
From **Andorra la Vella** bus station : 0615, 0815, 1115, 1315, 1515, 1815, 2015, 2215.
Journey 3 hours (3 hrs 30 mins to / from Barcelona ✈). Operator: Autocars Nadal ☎ + 376 805 151.

665 — BARCELONA - SITGES - SANT V de CALDERS — 2nd class

Local rail service **Barcelona - Sitges - Sant Vicenç de Calders**.
From **Barcelona** Sants: 0606, 0636 and every 30 minutes until 2206; then 2306.
From **Sant Vicenç**: 0600, 0615⚡, 0632 Ⓐ, 0643 Ⓐ, 0658, 0732, 0751, 0816, 0831, 0903, 0933 and every 30 minutes until 2103, 2133 Ⓐ, then 2200.

Additional trains operate **Barcelona - Sitges** and v.v.

Journey times: **Barcelona – Sitges** (34 km) 30 minutes,
Barcelona – Sant Vicenç (60 km) 57 minutes.

666 — BARCELONA - MATARÓ, BLANES and MAÇANET — 2nd class

Cercanías (suburban) line R1. For faster services Barcelona - Maçanet via Granollers, see Table 657.
Approximate journey times (in mins) to / from **Barcelona** Sants: Mataró (46), Arenys de Mar (57), Calella (69), Pineda de Mar (73), Malgrat de Mar (79), Blanes (84), Maçanet-Massanes (97).

Barcelona Sants – **Mataró** and v.v.   35 km
Ⓐ : 4 – 6 trains per hour.
From Barcelona 0546 – 2354; from Mataró 0450 – 2313.
Ⓒ : 2 – 4 trains per hour.
From Barcelona 0612 – 0010; from Mataró 0457 – 2220.

Barcelona Sants – **Blanes**   67 km
0612, 0642 and every 30 mins. until 2042, then 2112 Ⓒ, 2124 Ⓐ, 2142 Ⓒ, 2154 Ⓐ, 2213 Ⓒ, 2224 Ⓐ.
Blanes - Barcelona Sants
Ⓐ : 2 trains per hour, 0617 – 2115, 2155
Ⓒ : 2 trains per hour; 0603 – 2103, 2144.

Barcelona Sants – **Blanes** – **Maçanet - Massanes**   82 km
Ⓐ : 0546 and hourly until 2012, then 2042, 2142.
Ⓒ : 0612 and hourly until 2012, then 2042, 2142.
Maçanet - Massanes – Blanes – **Barcelona** Sants
Ⓐ : 0605, 0636, 0704, 0734, 0804 and hourly until 2103
Ⓒ : 0620, 0650, 0720 and hourly until 2020, then 2130.

667 — ALACANT - BENIDORM - DÉNIA — 2nd class

☀ By tram (route L1)		①–⑤								
Alacant Luceros ☉ .....d.	...	0541	0611	0711	every	1911	2011	2111	2211	
El Campello............d.	...	0609	0639	0739	hour	1939	2039	2139	2239	
La Vila Joiosa...........d.	0612	0635	0705	0805	◖	2005	2105	2205	2305	
Benidorm..............a.	0630	0653	0723	0823	until	2023	2123	2223	2323	

☀ By tram (route L1)	①–⑤									
Benidorm...............d.	0635	0705	0805	every	1905	2005	2105	2205	2235	
La Vila Joiosa..........d.	0653	0723	0823	hour	1923	2023	2123	2223	2253	
El Campello.............d.	0723	0753	0853	◖	1953	2053	2153	2253	...	
Alacant Luceros ☉.......a.	0751	0821	0921	until	2021	2121	2221	2321	...	

By train (route L9)										
Benidorm...............d.	0601	0701	0801	0901		1901	2001	2101	2201	
Altea..................d.	0615	0715	0815	0915	every	1915	2015	2115	2215	
Calpe.................d.	0636	0736	0836	0936	hour	1936	2036	2136	...	
Calpe........🚌.......d.	0641	0741	0841	0941	◖	1941	2041	2141	...	
Gata.........🚌.......d.	0714	0814	0914	1014	until	2014	2114	2214	...	
Dénia........🚌.......a.	0741	0841	0941	1041		2041	2141	2241	...	

By train (route L9)										
Dénia........🚌.......d.	0545	0645	0745	0845		1845	1945	2045	...	
Gata.........🚌.......d.	0612	0712	0812	0912	every	1912	2012	2112	...	
Calpe........🚌.......d.	0645	0745	0845	0945	hour	1945	2045	2145	...	
Calpe.................d.	0652	0752	0852	0952	◖	1952	2052	2152	...	
Altea..................d.	0714	0814	0914	1014	until	2014	2114	2214	2228	
Benidorm...............a.	0727	0827	0927	1027		2027	2127	2227	2241	

◖ – Alacant - Benidorm runs every 30 minutes 0641 - 2141 (also 0025, 0155 night of ⑤⑥ July 2 - Aug. 28).
❖ – Benidorm - Alacant runs every 30 minutes 0635 - 2205 (also 0211, 0441 night of ⑤⑥ July 2 - Aug. 28).
☉ – ± 400 m from Alacant Renfe station.
Operator : Tram Metropolitano / FGV ☎ 900 72 04 72 www.fgvalicante.com

MADRID - ALBACETE, ALACANT and VALÈNCIA — 668

km		AVE 5270 ①-⑤ c	AVE 18024 B	AVE 18018 ⑥⑦	AVE 5072 ①-⑥	AVE 5070 ①-⑤ D	AVE 5080 ①-⑤	AVE 5290 ①-⑥	AVE 5090 ①-⑥ c	MD 14404 ⑦	AVE 5302 h	AVE 5100 ①-⑤	MD 18081 ⑦	AVE 5310	AVE 5110 ①-⑤	AVE 5320 ⑦	Alvia 4072 ①-⑤ S	AVE 5122 ①-⑤	AVE 3971 ⑤⑥ M	AVE 5120 ①-⑤ c	Talgo 694 T	AVE 5340 ⑥⑦ S	Alvia 4092	AVE 5142 ①-⑤
0	Madrid Puerta de Atocha d.	0645	...	...	0745	0740	0840	0910	0940	...	1010	1040	...	1110	1140	1210	1215	1230	...	1240	...	1410	1420	1445
189	Cuenca Fernando Zóbel d.	0737	...	...	0842	...	0936	1002	...	...	1103	...	...	1202	1236	1302	1325	...	1319	...	...	...	1526	1542
321	Requena/Utiel d.	0811	...	...	...	...	1036	...	...	...	...	...	1236	1310	...	...	...	...	...	...	1529	...	...	...
322*	Albacete d.	...	0806	0918	0918	...	...	...	...	1100	1139	...	1229	...	...	1405	1356	...	...	1420	...	...	1605	1618
436	Villena AV d.	...	...	0953	...	...	...	...	...	1214	...	...	...	...	...	1449	1431	...	...	...	...	...	1652	1653
486	Alacant Terminal a.	...	...	1014	...	...	...	...	...	1235	1412	...	...	...	...	1512	1452	...	...	...	...	...	1715	1714
477	Xátiva d.	...	0928	1039	...	...	...	...	...	1206	...	...	...	...	...	...	...	...	...	...	1524	...	...	...
391	València Joaquín Sorolla § a.	0839	...	...	...	0922	1029	1104	1124	...	1222	...	...	1304	1334	1359	...	1418	1422	...	...	1554	...	...
	València Nord § a.	...	1011	1115	...	...	...	...	...	1245	...	...	...	...	...	...	...	...	...	...	...	1602	...	...
	Sagunt a.																							
	Castelló de la Plana 672 a.																					1703		

	AVE 5150 ⑥ W	MD 14406 ⑥	Alvia 4584 R	AVE 5162	AVE 4110 ⑧ G	Alvia 18181 h	MD 5570 2V	IC 5170 J	AVE 5172	IC 5036 K	AVE 5180	AVE 3973	AVE 5392 G	AVE 5190 ⑧ P	AVE 4140 ⑧	Alvia 3981	AVE 5212 ⑧	AVE 5410
Madrid Puerta de Atocha d.	1540	...	1555	1625	1640	1645	...	1710	1740	1745	1748	1840	...	1920	1940	2010	...	2105 2110
Cuenca Fernando Zóbel d.	1636	...	1657	...	1752	...	1822	...	...	2005	2017	...	2130	2202	2203	...		
Requena/Utiel d.	...	...	...	...	...	...	...	...	...	...	...	...	2238	...				
Albacete d.	...	1650	1740	...	1831	1849	...	1911	2012	...	2053	...	2238	...				
Villena AV d.	...	...	1824	...	1914	...	...	...	2128	...	2313	...						
Alacant Terminal a.	...	...	1846	1834	...	1936	2032	...	2001	...	2149	...	2334	...				
Xátiva d.	...	1757	...	...	...	...	2115	...										
València Joaquín Sorolla § a.	1729	...	...	1822	...	1929	1922	...	2022	2105	...	2122	2210	2224	...	2304		
València Nord § a.	...	1837	...	...	...	...	2153	...										
Sagunt a.	...	...	...	...	2006	...	2247	...										
Castelló de la Plana 672 a.	...	...	...	...	2037	...	2320	...										

	AVE 5261 ①-⑤ c	AVE 5063 ①-⑤	IC 5035 ①-⑤	AVE 5071 ①-⑤	AVE 5081 ⑥ D	AVE 5081 ①-⑤	AVE 3982 ⑥ P	AVE 5073 ①-⑥ G	AVE 4111 ①-⑥	AVE 5281 ⑦	AVE 5091 ①-⑥	AVE 5293 ①-⑤	AVE 5301 ⑥⑦	AVE 5301 2	MD 18183 ⑦	Alvia 4143 h	Alvia 4345 S	Alvia 4143 F	AVE 5321 S	AVE 5123 U	Talgo 697 T	MD 14405	AVE 5141	Alvia 4181 4381 G
Castelló de la Plana 672 d.	...	...	...	...	...	...	0717	...	...	...	...	...	...	...	...	...	...	...	...	1158	...			
Sagunt d.	...	...	...	...	...	...	0743	...																
València Nord § d.	...	...	...	...	...	...	...	...	...	...	...	...	...	...	1255	1345	...							
València Joaquín Sorolla § d.	0645	...	0620	0710	0800	0800	0807	...	0820	0840	...	1040	1045	...	1240	...	1337	1426	...	1410	...			
Xátiva d.	...	...	0659	...	...	...	...	...																
Alacant Terminal d.	...	0615	...	...	...	...	...	0720	...	...	0905	...	1012	1020	1020	1035	1240	...	1445					
Villena AV d.	...	0636	...	...	...	...	...	...	0926	...	1043	1043	1058	1301	...	1508								
Albacete d.	...	0712	0803	...	...	0810	...	...	1002	...	1146	1125	1125	1140	1337	1439	1534	...	1553					
Requena/Utiel d.	0708	...	...	...	0823	...	0903	...	1103	...	2133	...												
Cuenca Fernando Zóbel d.	0743	0748	...	...	0855	0858	0902	...	0939	...	1038	1138	1140	...	1204	1204	...	1413	...	1630				
Madrid Puerta de Atocha a.	0838	0845	1020	0851	0948	0953	...	0935	1020	1033	1056	1135	1233	1233	...	1310	1310	1320	1421	1510	...	1548		1735

	AVE 5151 b	AVE 5161	AVE 5163	AVE 5171	AVE 3974 ①⑤⑦ C	MD 18083 2	18027	IC 5481 A	AVE 5181 2V	AVE 5183	AVE 5193	AVE 5201 R	AVE 5211 b	Alvia 5203	MD 14407 ①-⑥	AVE 5213 ⑦
Castelló de la Plana 672 d.	...	...	...	...	...	1625	...									
Sagunt d.	...	...	...	...	1651	...										
València Nord § d.	...	...	...	...	1730	...	2045	...								
València Joaquín Sorolla § d.	1510	1615	...	1710	1712	...	1730	1810	...	1940	2015	2110	...			
Xátiva d.	...	...	...	...	1806	...	2124	...								
Alacant Terminal d.	...	...	1610	...	1705	...	1810	1905	...	2010	2115	...				
Villena AV d.	...	...	1631	...	...	2031	...									
Albacete d.	...	...	1707	...	1840	1924	...	1900	...	2107	2232	...				
Requena/Utiel d.	1533	...	...	...	2133	...										
Cuenca Fernando Zóbel d.	1607	...	1743	...	1812	...	1834	...	2207	2143	...					
Madrid Puerta de Atocha a.	1703	1756	1838	1851	...	1943	1951	2025	2116	2124	2156	2303	2241	...		2323

A – To Ciudad Real on ⑦ (Table **678**).
B – From Ciudad Real on ① (Table **678**).
C – ①⑤⑦. To Málaga (Table **660**).
D – ①–④ (①–⑤ July 18 - Sept. 11).
F – To Ferrol (Table **682**).
G – From/to Gijón (Table **685**).
J – Daily not ⑥ July 23 - Sept. 10).
K – ⑦. From Málaga (Table **660**).
M – ⑤⑥. From Málaga (Table **660**).
P – From/to Sevilla (Table **660**).
R – ⑤⑦ (⑧ June 12 - Sept. 11).
S – From/to Santander (Table **684**).
T – TORRE DEL ORO – ▢. ⏍ Barcelona - Sevilla and v.v. (Table **672**).
U – ①–⑤ (daily June 1 - Sept. 11).
V – To/from Vinaròs (Table **672**). Conveys ▢ to/from Gandia.
W – From Pontevedra (Table **680**).
e – Not ⑥⑦.
h – From/to Ciudad Real (Table **678**).
y – ⑥ only.
b – Not July 18 - Sept. 11.
c – Not July 17 - Sept. 11.
§ – Free ▢ between València Joaquín Sorolla and València Nord, 0615 - 2330, every ± 10 minutes.
* – Albacete - Xátiva - València: 203 km.

△ – Cercanías (suburban) line **C1**: **València - Gandia** and v.v. 62 km 2nd class. Journey time: 54 - 60 minutes.

From **València** Nord
Ⓐ: 0611, 0641 and every 30 minutes until 1941; then 1956, 2033, 2041, 2111, 2141, 2211, 2241.
Ⓒ: 0641, 0741 and hourly until 2241.

From **Gandia**
Ⓐ: 0605, 0640, 0655, 0710, 0725, 0740, 0755, 0825, 0840, 0855, 0915, 0925, 0955 and every 30 minutes until 2225.
Ⓒ: 0655, 0755 and hourly until 2055; then 2225.

MADRID - CARTAGENA — 668a

km		Alta 18024 ①-⑤ w	Alta 220 ①-⑤	Talgo 222	Alta 694	MD 228 ⑧ A	IC 18040	Alta 10146 B	MD 224 ⑧	Alta 18042 ⑧	Alta 226
0	Madrid Chamartín ‡ d.	...	0713	0900	...	1234	1419	1555	1629	1818	1900
8	Madrid Atocha C ▯ ‡ d.	...	0730	0921	...	1251	1432	1609	1648	1832	1919
57	Aranjuez d.	...	...	...	...	1509	1649	...	1908	...	
157	Alcázar de San Juan ‡ d.	0645	0849	...	1315	1404	1604	...	2000	2034	
288	Albacete d.	0805	0947	1132	1418	1502	1715	1827	1856	2106	2135
354	Hellín d.	...	1023	...	...	...	...	2215	...		
466	Murcia 672 d.	...	1144	1326	...	1645	...	2006	2050	...	2331
531	Cartagena 672 a.	...	...	1412	1424	...	1728	...	2138	...	0017

		MD 18047 ①-⑤	MD 18041 ①-⑤	MD 18049 ⑥⑦	Alta 221 ①-⑤	Alta 223	Talgo 697	Alta 229 A	MD 18043	Alta 225 D	IC 10418 18027	Alta 227 w
	Cartagena 672 d.	...	...	0530	0850	...	1215†	...	1600	...		1820
	Murcia 672 d.	...	0610	0936	...	1258	...	1647	1713	...		1905
	Hellín d.	...	...	1049	...	...	...	...				2026
	Albacete d.	0412f	0605	0730c	0753	1129	1441	1446	1740	1834q	1955 2106	2107
	Alcázar de San Juan ‡ d.	0527	0711	0837	...	1235	1548	...	1851	1929q	1955 2106	2204
	Aranjuez d.	0621	0807	0903	...	...	...	1948	...	2042		
	Madrid Atocha C ▯ ‡ a.	0656	0844	1008	1008	1402	...	1704	2020	2045	2125	2325
	Madrid Chamartín ‡ a.	...	0858	1022	1025	1416	...	1718	2034	2100	2140	2340

A – TORRE DEL ORO – ▢. ⏍ Sevilla - Alcázar - Albacete - Barcelona and v.v. (Tables **661, 671, 672**).
B – ⑤. ▢ Madrid - Murcia - Aguilas (arrive 2150).
D – ⑦. ▢ Aguilas (depart 1533) - Murcia - Madrid.
c – ⑥ only.
f – ① only.
k – Not ⑤.
q – Not ⑦.
t – ⑦ only.
‡ – See also Table **661**.
w – To/from València Nord (Table **668**).
▯ – Madrid **Atocha Cercanías**.

669 MADRID - CUENCA - VALÈNCIA

2nd class

km		18160 ①-⑤	18160 ⑦	18160 ⑥	18162 ①-⑤	18162 ⑦	14162 ⑦	18164 ①-④	18164 ⑤⑥⑦	18768 ⑤
0	**Madrid** Chamartín d.	0554	...	...	1207	...	...	1607	...	...
8	**Madrid** Atocha Cercanías d.	0607	0620	0800	1221	1242	...	1621	1630	1754
16	Villaverde Bajo **677** d.	0616	0630	0808	1229	1250	...	1629	1640	1803
57	Aranjuez **661 668a** a.	0652	0700	0836	1305	1318	...	1705	1708	1832
	change trains on certain services	|	|	|	|	|		|	|	|
57	Aranjuez **661 668a** d.	0702	0702	0837	1322	1322	...	1709	1709	1833
209	**Cuenca** d.	0918	0918	1044	1537	1537	1740	1921	1921	2055
335	Requena d.	1152	1152	1303	1756	1756	2010	2145	2145	...
407	**València** Nord a.	1320	1320	1433	1925	1925	2143	2307	2307	...

	18161 ⑥⑦	18161 ①-⑤	18163 ⑤⑦	18163 ①-④	18765 ⑦	18165 ⑤	18165 ①-④	18165 ⑥⑦	14163 ⑤
València Nord d.	0638	0638	0950	0950	...	1451	1451	1454	1641
Requena d.	0818	0818	1126	1126	...	1638	1638	1639	1814
Cuenca d.	1045	1045	1405	1405	1745	1914	1914	1914	2045
Aranjuez **661 668a** a.	1254	1254	1618	1618	1954	2123	2123	2126	...
change trains on certain services	|	|	|	|	|	|	|	|	
Aranjuez **661 668a** d.	1255	1312	1619	1630	1955	2125	2132	2128	...
Villaverde Bajo **677** a.	1328	1348	1649	1706	2027	2156	2208	2209	...
Madrid Atocha Cercanías a.	1337	1357	1657	1715	2035	2204	2216	2217	...
Madrid Chamartín a.	...	1410	...	1728	...	...	2230	...	...

670 VALÈNCIA - TERUEL - ZARAGOZA - HUESCA - CANFRANC

2nd class (except *AVE* trains)

km		Ⓒ	Ⓐ	Ⓒ	18500	MD 18502		MD 18504 C	AVE 3363 ⑤⑦	AVE 3393		MD 18506	14530 A
0	**València** Nord d.	...	...	...	...	0917	...	1220	...	...	...	1735	1911
34	Sagunt d.	...	...	...	...	0950	...	1254	...	...	...	1810	1946
65	Segorbe d.	...	...	...	...	1017	...	1324	...	...	...	1839	2022
171	**Teruel** d.	...	...	...	0630	1157	...	1503	...	...	...	2024	2218
242	Calamocha d.	...	...	...	0719	|	...	1547	...	...	...	2106	...
305	Cariñena d.	...	...	...	0817	1339	...	1637	...	...	...	2205	...
	Madrid ◇ **650** d.	...	...	...	|	|	...	|	1605	1905	...	|	...
359	**Zaragoza** Delicias d.	0640	0840	0847	0905	1426	1541	1719	1727	2034	2140	2252	...
361	**Zaragoza** Portillo d.	0643	0843	0851	0910	1429	1545	1722	|	|	2143	2255	...
363	**Zaragoza** Goya d.	0645	0845	0855	0914	1433	1549	1726	|	|	2145	2257	...
417	Tardienta d.	0727	0932	0936	▬	...	1629	...	|	2105	2227	...	...
439	**Huesca** d.	0748	0953	0959	...	...	1652	...	1810	2118	2242	...	...
474	Ayerbe d.	0831	1036	1047	...	...	1738	...	...	...	...	...	...
533	Sabiñánigo d.	0937	1143	1157	🚌	...	1841	...	...	...	...	...	...
549	Jaca d.	0953	1159	1214	1450	...	1902	...	...	...	...	...	...
574	**Canfranc 324** a.	1026	1232	...	1515	...	1937	...	...	...	...	...	...

	Ⓐ	MD 18511	AVE 3272	Ⓒ	Ⓐ	MD 18523 w	Ⓒ	MD 18515	🚌	Ⓒ	AVE 3592 ⑤⑦	
Canfranc 324 d.	...	...	...	...	0600	...	0845	...	1310	...	...	1753
Jaca d.	...	...	...	...	0635	...	0920	...	1340	1610	...	1828
Sabiñánigo d.	...	...	...	...	0650	...	0934	...	▬	1625	...	1844
Ayerbe d.	...	...	...	...	0757	...	1045	...	...	1737	...	1953
Huesca d.	0640	...	0815	0829	0845	...	1138	...	...	1827	1935	2041
Tardienta d.	0656	...	0827	0845	0859	...	1152	...	**18517**	1842	|	2055
Zaragoza Goya d.	0738	0806	|	0933	0940	1058	1234	1658	1923	1935	|	2139
Zaragoza Portillo d.	0740	0809	|	0935	0942	1101	1236	1701	1926	1939	|	2142
Zaragoza Delicias d.	0744	0814	0900	0938	0945	1107	1240	1705	1932	1943	2020	2148
Madrid ◇ **650** a.	▬	|	1035	...	...	|	...	|	|	...	2140	...
Cariñena d.	**14531**	0905	...	...	...	1154	...	1752	2022	...	...	...
Calamocha d.	**B**	0958	...	...	...	1253	...	1851	2129	...	...	...
Teruel d.	0725	1044	...	...	...	1336	...	1932	2219	...	...	...
Segorbe d.	0912	1218	...	...	...	1510	...	2117	...	...	...	...
Sagunt d.	0950	1249	...	...	...	1543	...	2148	...	...	...	...
València Nord a.	1024	1321	...	...	...	1615	...	2223	...	...	...	...

A – ②④⑥⑦.
B – ①③⑤⑦.
C – From Cartagena on ①–⑤. From Murcia on ⑥ (Table **672**).
w – To Cartagena (Table **672**).
◇ – Madrid Puerta de Atocha.
🚌 Jaca - Canfranc (- Astun). See Table **324** for 🚌 Canfranc - Bedous.

671 CÓRDOBA - SEVILLA - HUELVA and CÁDIZ

km		MD 13000 2 ①-⑤	MD 13002 2 ①-⑥	MD 13030 2 ①-⑤	MD 13030 2 ⑥⑦	MD 13099 2 ⑥⑦		MD 13079 2 J	MD 13037 2 ①-⑤	MD 13020 2	Alvia 2084	Alvia 2294 ⑥	MD 13008 2 ①-⑤
	Madrid PA ✣ **660** d.	...	...	...	...	...	...	...	...	...	0830	0945	...
0	**Córdoba 660** d.	...	...	0700	...	...	...	0812	...	0908	1020	1132	...
51	Palma del Río d.	...	...	0729	...	...	...	0845	...	0940	|	|	...
129	**Sevilla 660** a.	...	...	0821	...	...	...	0937	...	1029	1106	|	...
129	**Sevilla 673** § d.	0640	0745	0830	0830	0845	...	0945	1000	1045	1109	|	1245
204	La Palma del Condado d.	|	|	|	|	0949	...	|	1108	|	|	1254	|
244	**Huelva** a.	|	|	|	|	1020	...	|	1138	|	|	1320	|
145	Dos Hermanas **673** § d.	0654	0758	0843	0843	...	...	0958	...	1058	|	...	1258
162	Utrera § d.	0705	|	0854	0854	...	...	|	...	1108	|	...	1308
224	Aeropuerto de Jerez ▲ d.	0739	|	0929	0929	...	...	|	...	1143	|	...	1345
236	Jerez de la Frontera ▲ d.	0746	0846	0936	0936	...	...	1047	...	1151	1204	...	1353
251	Puerto de Santa María d.	0756	0855	0946	0946	...	...	1057	...	1200	1213	...	1402
270	San Fernando - Bahía Sur d.	0809	0911	1002	1002	...	...	1112	...	1214	1228	...	1418
285	**Cádiz** a.	0826	0923	1013	1013	...	...	1126	...	1226	1238	...	1430

		MD 13010 2	MD 13032 2 ⑥⑦	MD 13032 2 ①-⑤	Alvia 2134	MD 13014 2	MD 13039 2	MD 13083 2 J	Alvia 2164	IC 2364 ⑤	Alvia 2384 Ⓑ	MD 13035 2 J
Madrid PA ✣ **660** d.	...	...	...	...	1330	...	...	...	1615	1620	1805	...
Córdoba 660 d.	...	...	1400	1400	1517	...	...	1612	|	|	1952	1830
Palma del Río d.	...	...	1431	1431	|	...	...	1643	|	|	|	1905
Sevilla 660 a.	...	...	1520	1520	1605	...	...	1730	|	1852	|	1956
Sevilla 673 § d.	...	1445	...	1545	1608	1645	1700	1745	|	1902	|	2010
La Palma del Condado d.	...	|	...	|	|	|	1758	|	|	2000	2120	|
Huelva a.	...	|	...	|	|	|	1834	|	|	2026	2145	|
Dos Hermanas **673** § d.	...	1500	...	1559	|	1658	...	1758	|	...	...	2023
Utrera § d.	...	|	...	1609	|	|	...	1808	|	...	...	|
Aeropuerto de Jerez ▲ d.	...	1540	...	|	|	1741	...	1844	|	...	...	|
Jerez de la Frontera ▲ d.	...	1548	...	1651	1705	1749	...	1852	1934	...	...	2113
Puerto de Santa María d.	...	1558	...	1700	1714	1758	...	1901	1943	...	...	2122
San Fernando - Bahía Sur d.	...	1615	...	1714	1729	1813	...	1917	1958	...	...	2137
Cádiz a.	...	1627	...	1726	1740	1825	...	1930	2010	...	...	2150

	Talgo 697 G	MD 13394 2	Alvia 2384 Ⓑ	MD 13095 2	MD 13073 2 J	Alvia 2184 ⑤⑦					
Madrid PA ✣ **660** d.	...	...	1805	...	...	1835	...	...	...	...	...
Córdoba 660 d.	1931	...	1952	...	2010	2016	...	...	...	...	...
Palma del Río d.	|	...	|	...	2042	|	...	...	...	...	...
Sevilla 660 a.	2051	...	|	...	2128	2106	...	...	...	...	...
Sevilla 673 § d.	...	2045	|	2050	2150	2109	...	...	...	...	...
La Palma del Condado d.	...	|	2120	2149	|	|	...	...	...	...	...
Huelva a.	...	|	2145	2218	|	|	...	...	...	...	...
Dos Hermanas **673** § d.	...	2058	...	...	2203	|	...	...	...	...	...
Utrera § d.	...	2109	...	...	2213	|	...	...	...	...	...
Aeropuerto de Jerez ▲ d.	...	|	...	...	2248	|	...	...	...	...	...
Jerez de la Frontera ▲ d.	...	2148	...	...	2256	2204	...	...	...	...	...
Puerto de Santa María d.	...	2157	...	...	2305	2213	...	...	...	...	...
San Fernando - Bahía Sur d.	...	2212	...	...	2321	2228	...	...	...	...	...
Cádiz a.	...	2223	...	...	2335	2239	...	...	...	...	...

	MD 13001 2J ①-⑤	MD 13041 2	Talgo 694 G	Alvia 2285 ①-⑤	MD 13003 2 M		Alvia 2085	MD 13005 2	MD 13007 2 ①-⑤
Cádiz d.	0540	...	...	...	0630	...	0815	0840	0940
San Fernando - Bahía Sur d.	0553	...	...	...	0641	...	0827	0851	0951
Puerto de Santa María d.	0608	...	...	...	0656	...	0840	0905	1006
Jerez de la Frontera ▲ d.	0617	...	...	...	0705	...	0850	0914	1015
Aeropuerto de Jerez ▲ d.	0624	...	...	...	0713	...	|	|	1023
Utrera § d.	0702	...	...	...	0751	...	|	|	|
Dos Hermanas **673** § d.	0712	...	...	...	0801	...	|	1005	1107
Huelva d.	|	0655	...	0800	|	...	|	|	|
La Palma del Condado d.	|	0725	...	0824	|	...	|	|	|
Sevilla 673 § a.	0728	0825	...	|	0816	...	0947	1020	1120
Sevilla 660 d.	0740	...	0835	|	0838	...	0950	...	...
Palma del Río d.	0828	...	|	|	0926	...	|	...	...
Córdoba 660 a.	0904	...	0945	0948	1000	...	1040	...	...
Madrid PA ✣ **660** a.	...	...	...	1141	...	...	1236	...	...

	Alvia 2205 ⑥	MD 13009 2 J	MD 13011 2J ①-⑤	MD 13011 2J ⑥⑦	Alvia 2135	MD 13393 2	MD 13013 2 ①-⑤	MD 13043 2	Alvia 2365 ⑦	MD 13015 2	
Cádiz d.	...	1140	1240	...	1330	1412	1440	...	...	1540	...
San Fernando - Bahía Sur d.	...	1151	1251	...	1342	1423	1451	...	...	1551	...
Puerto de Santa María d.	...	1206	1306	...	1355	1436	1506	...	...	1606	...
Jerez de la Frontera ▲ d.	...	1215	1315	...	1405	1445	1515	...	...	1615	...
Aeropuerto de Jerez ▲ d.	...	1223	|	...	|	|	1523	...	...	1623	...
Utrera § d.	...	|	1356	...	|	1525	|	...	...	1700	...
Dos Hermanas **673** § d.	...	1306	1406	...	|	1535	1606	...	...	1710	...
Huelva d.	1025	|	|	...	|	|	|	1500	1620	|	...
La Palma del Condado d.	1047	|	|	...	|	|	|	1530	1647	|	...
Sevilla 673 § a.	|	1320	1420	...	1458	1549	1620	1627	|	1725	...
Sevilla 660 d.	|	1330	1503	1503	1500	...	...	...	|	1735	...
Palma del Río d.	|	1415	1551	1551	|	...	...	...	|	1824	...
Córdoba 660 a.	1216	1449	1624	1624	1552	...	...	...	1808	1857	...
Madrid PA ✣ **660** a.	1410	...	...	...	1748	...	...	...	2001	...	...

	Alvia 2175	IC 2375 ⑦	MD 13017 2 J	MD 13031 2	MD 13049 2	Alvia 2195 ⑤⑦	MD 13019 2	MD 13021 2						
Cádiz d.	1728	...	1740	1840	...	1855	1940	2040	...	...	...	...	...	...
San Fernando - Bahía Sur d.	1740	...	1751	1851	...	1907	1951	2052	...	...	...	...	...	...
Puerto de Santa María d.	1754	...	1805	1905	...	1921	2006	2106	...	...	...	...	...	...
Jerez de la Frontera ▲ d.	1805	...	1814	1914	...	1931	2015	2115	...	...	...	...	...	...
Aeropuerto de Jerez ▲ d.	|	...	1822	1921	...	|	|	|	...	...	...	...	...	...
Utrera § d.	|	...	|	|	...	|	2102	2156	...	...	...	...	...	...
Dos Hermanas **673** § d.	|	...	1906	2005	...	|	2112	2206	...	...	...	...	...	...
Huelva d.	|	1750	|	|	1900	|	|	|	...	...	...	...	...	...
La Palma del Condado d.	|	1817	|	|	1930	|	|	|	...	...	...	...	...	...
Sevilla 673 § a.	|	1911	1920	2017	2030	2033	2128	2220	...	...	...	...	...	...
Sevilla 660 d.	|	1919	1940	2030	...	2036	...	...	...	...	...	...	...	...
Palma del Río d.	|	|	2027	2117	...	|	...	...	...	...	...	...	...	...
Córdoba 660 a.	|	|	2102	2148	...	2125	...	...	...	...	...	...	...	...
Madrid PA ✣ **660** a.	2127	2159	...	...	...	2314	...	...	...	...	...	...	...	...

G – TORRE DEL ORO – (12) 🍸 Barcelona - València - Córdoba - Sevilla and v.v. (Tables **661**, **668a**, **672**).
J – From / to Jaén (Table **661**).
M – To Jaén on ⑥⑦ (Table **661**).
t – ①–⑤.
✣ – Madrid Puerta de Atocha.
§ – Frequent suburban services operate Sevilla - Utrera and v.v.
▲ – Additional suburban services operate Jerez de la Frontera - Aeropuerto de Jerez and v.v.: depart Aeropuerto 0720 Ⓐ, 0820 Ⓒ, 1325, 1920; depart Jerez 0657 Ⓐ, 0757 Ⓒ, 1257, 1857.

BARCELONA - VALÈNCIA - ALACANT - CARTAGENA 672

km		MD 14123 2	Alvia 4111 ①-⑤ G			Em 1071 ①-⑤ 2	Em 1081 ①-⑥①-④ 2		Em 1091 2	Talgo 697 ⑤⑥⑦	Em 1101 2		Talgo 1111 2		Talgo 463 Ⓨ 2		MD 18523 Ⓟ 2	IC 5481 ⑦ 2	Em 1341 2	Talgo 165 ⑤		Talgo 10541 2	Em 1161 ⑤
0	Barcelona França....d.	...	...	0543	0634	0734	0743	0833	0904	0933	0913	...	1043	...	1243	...	...	1403	...	1443	...	1533
5	Barcelona Passeig de Gràcia d.			0556		0756				0926		...	1054	...	1256			1456			
8	Barcelona Sants....652 d.			0603	0700	0800	0803	0900	0930	1000	0933	1100	1103	1200	1303	...	...	1430	1500	1503	1530	1600
68	Sant Vicenç de Calders 652 d.			0649		0848				1019			1347			1547							
82	Altafulla - Tamarit......d.			0700		0901				1030			1400			1558							
93	Tarragona......652 d.			0710	0754	0843	0911	0956	1029	1034	1041	1155	1201	1254	1410	...	...	1524	1554	1607	1625	1654
103	Port Aventura......d.			0719		0920				1051		1214			1420			1616			
105	Salou......d.			0724		0924		1041		1055	1206	1218	1312	1424			1606	1620			
	Tortosa......d.		0645											1330							
163	L'Aldea - Amposta......d.		0658	0811		0933	1012	1036	1109		1145	1244	1304	1340	1345	1510	...	...	1602	1635	1713	
176	Tortosa......a.		0822			1022				1159		1316		1523				1722			
202	Vinaròs......d.	0720				1124				1239	1301	1355	1407			1543		1651			
208	Benicarló - Peñiscola......d.	0726				1131				1245	1306	1400	1413			1548		1657			
268	Benicàssim......d.	0804								1322	1337	1423	1450			1616		1724			
280	Castelló de la Plana......d.	0717	0815		0917	1020		1121	1200	1218	1331	1348	Ⓑ	1431	1459			1625	1646	1733		1816
353	València Nord......a.	0814r	0920		1005r	1112r		1212r	1250	1306r	1432	1438	2	1525	1602			1722r	1740r	1828		1906r
353	València Nord......668 d.	0717	0820r		1015r				1255	1314r		1448	1502	1538			1635	1705	1730r		1838		1920r
409	Xàtiva......668 a.	0753					1337			1529	1539	1616		1711	1744			1913		1933	
	Madrid P de Atocha..668 a.	1020									1943									
	Sevilla 671......a.					2051														
495	Elda - Petrer......a.	0840							1623	1632	1658		1757	1839			1954			
536	Alacant......a.	0908			1156				1455	1658	1704	1727		1823	1914			2020		2041	2055
536	Alacant......⁝ d.	0916									1745		1830			2035			
614	Murcia......668a ⁝ a.	1043									1859		1941			2147			
677	Lorca Sutullena......⁝ a.										2004								
679	Cartagena......668a ⁝ a.												2036			2245			

	Talgo 1171 ①-⑤ 2	Em 2	Em 1181 Ⓑ	Talgo 1391 2	Em 1401 Ⓑ 2		2				Em 1262 2	Em 1472 ①-⑤ 2	Em 1282 2
Barcelona França......d.	1613	...	...	1734	1743	...	1913	2004	2043	Cartagena......668a ⁝ d.	...	...	...
Barcelona Passeig de Gràcia d.	1625	...	...	1755	...	1921	2031	2056		Murcia......668a ⁝ d.	...	...	...
Barcelona Sants......652 d.	1633	1700	...	1730	1800	1803	1930	1933	2030	2103	Alacant......d.	...	...	...
Sant Vicenç de Calders 652 d.				1847		2017		2148	Alacant......d.	...	...	0650	...
Altafulla - Tamarit......d.				1859		2029		2201	Elda - Petrer......d.	...	...	...
Tarragona......652 d.	1728	1754	...	1824	1854	1909	2024	2041	2125	2212	Xàtiva......d.	...	...	0802r
Port Aventura......d.	1735			1917		2051		2222	València Nord......668 a.	...	...	0830r
Salou......d.	1740	1807	...	1921	2037	2055		2226	València Nord......d.	...	0625r	0730r	0830r 0805
Tortosa......d.		1858							Castelló de la Plana......d.	...	0705	0810	0910 0917
L'Aldea - Amposta......d.	1822	1846	1915	1902	2016	2109	2143	2211	2314	Benicàssim......d.				0930
Tortosa......a.	1832				2027		2200		2325	Benicarló - Peñiscola......d.				1007
Vinaròs......d.		1902	1938			2125	2240		Vinaròs......d.				1013
Benicarló - Peñiscola......d.		1907	1943		2131				Tortosa......d.	0600	0605	0745	0910		1045
Benicàssim......d.		1936	2028		2159			L'Aldea - Amposta......d.	0612	0618	0750	0800	0854	0923	1039 1056
Castelló de la Plana......d.	1945	2038	1955	2022		2208	2258		Tortosa......d.							1055
València Nord......a.	2034	2138	2042r	2110r		2302	2343r		Salou......d.	0657	0707		0843	1014		1143
València Nord......668 d.	2046		2120r						Port Aventura......d.	0700	0710	0845	1017		1146
Xàtiva......668 d.	2123								Tarragona......652 d.	0711	0725	0837	0856	0936	1027	1033	1156
Elda - Petrer......d.	2207								Altafulla - Tamarit......d.		0732		0904	1035		
Alacant......a.	2235		2257						Sant Vicenç de Calders......652 d.		0746		0917	1049		1221
Alacant......⁝ d.	2250								Barcelona Sants......652 d.	0810	0835	0939	1005	1040	1138	1141	1307
Murcia......668a ⁝ a.	2355								Barcelona Passeig de Gràcia......d.	0816	0841		1014		1144		1314
Cartagena......668a ⁝ a.									Barcelona França......a.	0827	0852	1005	1023		1157	1205	1326

	Talgo 1102 ①-⑥ 2	Em 1112 2	MD 18504 Ⓨ 2 f	Talgo 460 Ⓒ m		Talgo 1142 Ⓑ 2	Em 1152 2		Em 1162 2		Talgo 694 T	Em 264 2			Em 1182 2	Talgo 10458 ⑦	Em 1192 ①-④⑤⑥⑦ 2	Talgo 1392 ⑦ 2		IC 5570 ①-⑥ 2	Talgo 1202 ⑦ 2	Em 1202 2	MD 14202 Ⓑ 2	Alvia 4140 Ⓑ G
Cartagena......668a ⁝ d.	...	...	0740z						...	1255						1638			
Lorca Sutullena......⁝ d.	...	...	0828															
Murcia......668a ⁝ d.	0630k	0838	0934						1354					1647	1735			
Alacant......a.	0744k	0955	1052						1502					1804	1846			
Alacant......d.	0800	0920	1003	1108			1402		1516	1610	1708			1838	1838	1856	1930	
Elda - Petrer......d.	0828		1032	1137				1542					1905	1905	1925	2004	
Madrid P de Atocha.. 668 d.	...						0835				1710						2010
Sevilla 671......d.	...																
Xàtiva......668 d.	0917		1120	1216				1524	1620		1815			1945	1945	2014	2103	
València Nord......668 a.	0954	1052r	1156	1253			1545r	1602	1658	1749r			1929r	2021	2021	2048	2143	2210r
València Nord......d.	1005	1011r		1305		1400	1455r	1442	1555r	1610	1710	1635	1800r	1855r	1925r	1943r	2005	2035	2035		2220r
Castelló de la Plana......d.	1050	1140		1345		1445	1535	1551	1635	1649	1750	1747	1840	1935	2005	2039	2107	2120	2120		2320
Benicàssim......d.	1100		1356		1452		1605		1758	1755			2046	2115	2130	2130		
Benicarló - Peñiscola......d.	1133		①-⑤ 1426		1521		1646		1721	1825	1834		2114	2151	2202	2202		
Vinaròs......d.	1139		2	1431		1526		1651		1727	1831	1840		2118	2157	2208	2208		
Tortosa......d.			1336		1548			1715		1935			2057					
L'Aldea - Amposta......d.	1156		1347	1449	1559	1541	1625	1718		1726	1743	1847	1947		2020	2051	2111		2219	2226	2226	
Tortosa......a.							1738						2233					
Salou......d.	1228		1428	1524	1646	1617		1811	1823	1919	2037		2159			2258	2258		
Port Aventura......d.	1231		1431		1649			1815		2041		2203					
Tarragona......652 d.	1241	1312	1442	1539	1658	1636	1712		1800	1825	1837	1933	2057	2104	2132	2215		2310	2310		
Altafulla - Tamarit......d.			1706			1834		2105									
Sant Vicenç de Calders 652 d.			1719			1848		2116		2235							
Barcelona Sants......652 a.	1340	1409	1542	1640	1807	1740	1810		1909	1937	2000	2040	2207	2110	2210	2210	2237	2322		2359	2359		
Barcelona Passeig de Gràcia a.			1547	1814		1944		2216		2328							
Barcelona França......a.	...	1435	1557	1825		1836		1935	1955	2034		2225	2137		2237	2306	2341				

Murcia – Cartagena

		Alta Ⓐ 2 m	Alta 222 Ⓐ 2 m		Alta 228 Ⓐ 2	MD 18523 Ⓒ p	Alta 224 2 m	Talgo 165	Alta 226 Ⓑ m			Alta 221 Ⓐ m	MD 18504 Ⓐ f	Alta 223 2 m		Alta 229 Ⓐ ⑦ m	Talgo 264 2		Alta 225 Ⓐ 2	MD 14202 Ⓑ m	Alta 227 Ⓐ 2			
Murcia......d.		0745	0950	1150	1326	1443	1645	1745	1948	2050	2202	2331	...	Cartagena....d.	0530	0740	0850	1050	1215	1255	1438	1600	1638	1820	1938	2110	2205
Cartagena......d.		0834	1040	1240	1412	1536	1728	1840	2033	2138	2245	0017	...	Murcia......a.	0608	0830	0934	1140	1256	1340	1528	1645	1726	1902	2030	2205	2257

C – Ⓑ (daily Aug. 1 - 29).

G – To/from Gijón (Tables 681, 685).

K – June 22 - Sept. 12.

T – TORRE DEL ORO – 🚃 Ⓨ Barcelona -
Sevilla and v.v. (Tables 661, 668a, 671).

f – To Zaragoza (Table 670).

k – ①-⑥.

m – From/to Madrid (Table 668a).

p – From Zaragoza (Table 670).

r – València Joaquín Sorolla.
Free 🚌 to València Nord.

x – Also ⑥ Aug. 1 - 29.

z – ①-⑤.

⁝ – Additional local trains operate
between these stations.

673 SEVILLA and ALGECIRAS - MÁLAGA, GRANADA and ALMERÍA *2nd class*

For trains **Sevilla – Málaga** and v.v. via **Córdoba**, see Table **660**. **Buses replace trains between Antequera-Santa Ana and Granada until Autumn 2017**

km		MD	MD	MD	Alta		MD	MD	MD	MD	MD	Alta	MD	MD	MD	MD	MD		MD		
		13920	**13063**	**13900**	**9367**		**13902**	**13922**	**13065**	**13904**	**13906** ⑤⑦	**9331**	**13924**	**13061**	**13077**	**13908**	**13926**		**13910**		
0	**Sevilla** ¶ d.	0635	...	0740	...	...	1100	1145	...	1308	1510	...	1555	...	...	1725	1756	...	2005	...	...
15	Dos Hermanas ¶ d.	0650u	...	0754u	...	...	1114u	1159u	...	1322u	1524u	...	1612u	...	...	1739u	1812u	...	2019u	...	...
	Algeciras d.	|	0615	|	0843	...	|	|	1145	|	|	1503	|	...	1530	|	|	...	|	...	...
	San Roque-La Línea d.	|	0630	|	0858	...	|	|	1201	|	|	1518	|	...	1546	|	|	...	|	...	...
	Ronda d.	|	0753	|	1009	...	|	|	1336	|	|	1631	|	1650	1713	|	|	...	|	...	...
167	Bobadilla **661** d.	|	0846	0919	|	...	1243	|	1429	1448	1645	|	|	1739	1801	1905	|	...	2145	...	...
236	**Málaga** M. Zambrano **661** a.	|	|	1015	|	...	1336	|	|	1547	1736	|	|	1850	|	1955	|	...	2236	...	...
	Antequera-Santa Ana § a.	0817	0856	...	|	...	...	1336	1440	...	...	1733	1737	...	1811	...	1940	...	...	...	...
	Madrid Pta de Atocha **660** a.	|	|	...	1405	...	...	|	|	...	...	2035	|	...	|	...	|	...	...	...	...
183	Antequera-Ciudad d.	*0836*¦	*0915*¦	...	...	...	...	*1356*¦	*1459*¦	...	...	...	*1757*¦	...	*1828*¦	...	*2000*¦	...	...	...	...
290	**Granada** **661** a.	*1002*¦	*1055*¦	...	...	...	...	*1512*¦	*1610*¦	...	...	...	*1915*¦	...	*1945*¦	...	*2116*¦	...	...	...	...
372	Guadix **661** d.	1111	...	...	...	...	...	1621	...	...	...	...	2019	...	...	...	2224	...	...	...	...
471	**Almería** **661** a.	1223	...	...	...	...	...	1746	...	...	...	...	2136	...	...	...	2343	...	...	...	...

km		MD	MD	MD	MD	Alta	MD	MD		MD	MD		MD	Alta	MD	MD	MD	MD	MD		
		13062	**13901**	**13941**	**13057**	**9366**	**13903**	**13943**		**13064**	**13905**		**13907**	**9330**	**13076**	**13945**	**13909** ⑤⑦	**13911**	**13947**		
0	**Almería** **661** d.	...	...	0615	...	...	...	0900	...	...	...	...	...	...	...	1500	...	...	1815	...	...
99	Guadix **661** d.	...	...	0735	...	...	...	1014	...	...	...	...	...	...	...	1616	...	...	1939	...	...
181	**Granada** d.	*0645*¦	...	*0843*¦	...	...	...	*1124*¦	...	*1245*¦	...	...	...	...	*1700*¦	*1732*¦	...	...	*2056*¦	...	...
288	Antequera-Ciudad d.	*0750*¦	...	*0955*¦	...	...	...	*1236*¦	...	*1402*¦	...	...	...	...	*1807*¦	*1841*¦	...	...	*2202*¦	...	...
	Madrid Pta de Atocha **660** d.	|	...	|	...	0835	...	|	...	|	...	...	...	1505	|	|	...	...	|	...	...
	Antequera-Santa Ana § d.	0818	...	1018	...	1118	...	1259	...	1440	...	...	...	1754	1840	1902	...	...	2225	...	...
	Málaga M. Zambrano **661** d.	|	0740	|	1005	|	1040	|	...	|	1408	...	1648	|	|	|	1900	2005	|	...	...
304	Bobadilla **661** d.	0826	0835	|	1104	|	1129	|	...	1452	1502	...	1747	|	1847	|	1956	2057	|	...	...
376	Ronda d.	0918	|	|	1156	1221	|	|	...	1546	|	...	|	1858	1940	|	|	|	|	...	...
468	San Roque-La Línea d.	1045	|	|	...	1335	|	|	...	1725	|	...	|	2016	2102	|	|	|	|	...	...
480	**Algeciras** a.	1100	|	|	...	1348	|	|	...	1740	|	...	|	2030	2117	|	|	|	|	...	...
456	Dos Hermanas ¶ a.	...	1002s	1147s	...	...	1252s	1423s	...	...	1626s	...	1917s	...	...	2028s	2118s	2226s	2352s	...	...
471	**Sevilla** ¶ a.	...	1019	1207	...	...	1310	1443	...	...	1641	...	1933	...	...	2044	2135	2241	0008	...	...

s – Calls to set down only.
u – Calls to pick up only.
§ – ± *17 km* from Antequera.
¦ – 🚌 Antequera-Santa Ana - Antequera-Ciudad - Granada and v.v. Until Autumn 2017.
¶ – Frequent suburban services run Sevilla - Dos Hermanas and v.v.

674 PALMA DE MALLORCA - INCA - SA POBLA and MANACOR *SFM 2nd class*

For services between Inca and sa Pobla, and Inca and Manacor change at Enllaç (5 *km* from Inca, 34 *km* from Palma)

km		Ⓐ ◧	Ⓐ ◧		Ⓐ	Ⓒ	Ⓐ ◧		Ⓐ	Ⓒ	Ⓐ ◧		Ⓐ	Ⓒ	Ⓐ		and at the same minutes past each hour until		Ⓐ	Ⓒ	Ⓐ		Ⓐ	Ⓒ	Ⓒ	Ⓐ
0	**Palma** d.	0545	0607	0615x	0635	0640	0650	0715x	0735	0740	0750	0815x	0835	0840	0855	0915x		2015x	2035	2040	2055	2115x	2135	2140	2210	2215
7	Marratxi d.	0600	0615	0623	0643	0655	0658	0723	0743	0754	0758	0823	0843	0854	0903	0923		2023	2043	2054	2103	2123	2143	2154	2225	2229
29	**Inca** d.	0625	0632	0644	0704	0720	0715	0744	0804	0815	0815	0844	0904	0915	0923	0944		2044	2104	2115	2123	2144	2204	2215	2250	2250
***	sa Pobla a.	0642	...	|	*0723*	0736	...	|	*0823*	*0834*	...	|	*0923*	*0934*	...	|		|	*2123*	*2134*	...	|	*2223*	*2234*	|	|
64	**Manacor** a.	...	...	*0718*	...	...	...	*0818*	...	...	...	*0916*	...	...	...	*1016*		*2116*	...	...	...	*2216*	...	...	2320	2325

	Ⓐ	Ⓐ ◧		Ⓐ	Ⓐ ◧		Ⓐ	Ⓒ	Ⓐ ◧		Ⓐ	Ⓒ	Ⓐ		Ⓐ	Ⓒ	and at the same minutes past each hour until	Ⓐ		Ⓐ	Ⓒ	Ⓐ		Ⓐ	Ⓒ	
Manacor d.	...	...	*0623*	...	*0659*	*0723*	...	...	...	*0823*	...	...	...	*0923*	...	...		...	*2023*	...	...	...	*2123*	...	...	2223
sa Pobla d.	...	...	|	*0656*	|	|	*0756*	*0807*	...	|	*0856*	*0907*	...	|	*0956*	*1007*		...	|	*2056*	*2107*	...	|	*2156*	*2207*	|
Inca d.	0621	0650	0656	0716	0733	0756	0816	0827	0833	0856	0916	0927	0936	0956	1016	1027		2036	2056	2116	2127	2136	2156	2216	2227	2254
Marratxi d.	0645	0707	0716	0736	0750	0816	0836	0847	0850	0916	0936	0947	0956	1016	1036	1047		2056	2116	2136	2147	2156	2216	2236	2247	2318
Palma a.	0653	0715	0724z	0744	0758	0824z	0844	0901	0858	0924z	0944	1001	1004	1024z	1044	1101		2104	2124z	2144	2201	2204	2224z	2253	2301	2333

x – 5 minutes earlier on Ⓒ.
z – 7 minutes later on Ⓒ.
◧ – Incaexprés.
*** – *19 km* Inca - sa Pobla.
Operator: Serveis Ferroviaris de Mallorca (SFM) ✆ +34 971 752 245.

PALMA DE MALLORCA - SÓLLER *28 km* Journey time: 55 minutes. **Operator**: Ferrocarril de Sóller (FS) ✆ +34 971 752 051. **SÓLLER - PALMA DE MALLORCA**

The main tunnel between Palma and Sóller requires attention and therefore it closed on November 7, 2016 and is due to reopen on February 1, 2017

Palma de Mallorca - Sóller: Nov. - Mar.: 1030, 1250, 1510, 1800. Apr. - Oct.: 1010, 1050, 1215, 1330, 1510, 1930.

Sóller - Palma de Mallorca: Nov. - Mar.: 0900, 1140, 1400, 1700. Apr. - Oct.: 0900, 1050, 1215, 1400, 1830.

A connecting tram service operates **Sóller - Port de Sóller**. *5 km.* Journey time: 15–20 minutes. Not all services shown.

From Sóller: 0800, 0900, 1000, 1100, 1200, 1300, 1400, 1500, 1600, 1700, 1800, 1900.
From Port de Sóller: 0830, 0930, 1025, 1130, 1230, 1325, 1430, 1530, 1630, 1730, 1830, 1930.

675 🚌 MÁLAGA and ALGECIRAS - LA LÍNEA (for Gibraltar)

There are no cross-border 🚌 services: passengers to / from Gibraltar must cross the frontier on foot (walking-time about 5 minutes) and transfer to / from Gibraltar local 🚌 services

🚌 **MÁLAGA** bus stn – **LA LÍNEA** bus station (for **Gibraltar**)

From Málaga: 0700, 1130 ▽, 1400, 1630, 1915 ⑦.
From La Línea: 0850, 1030, 1630 ▽, 1900, 2045 ⑦.
Journey time: 3 hours. Operator: Automóviles Portillo, Málaga ✆ (+34) 902 020 052.
▽ – Journey operated by Alsina Graells (see Table **664** for contact details).

🚌 **ALGECIRAS** bus station - **LA LÍNEA** bus station (for **Gibraltar**) Route M-120

From Algeciras: Ⓐ: 0700 and every 30 minutes until 2130, also 2230.
⑥: every 45 mins 0700 – 2115, also 2230. †: every 45 mins 0800 – 2130, also 2230.
From La Línea: Ⓐ: 0700, 0745 and every 30 minutes until 2215, also 2315.
⑥: every 45 mins 0700 – 2200, also 2315. †: 0700, 0845 then every 45 mins until 2215, also 2315.
Journey time: 45 mins. Operator: Transportes Generales Comes SA, Algeciras ✆ (+34) 902 450 550.

676 🚌 SEVILLA - AYAMONTE - FARO - LAGOS *DAMAS ☆*

	Summer				Ⓐ	Ⓒ		Ⓐ	†	⑥	Ⓐ	Winter	Ⓐ	Ⓒ	⚒		⑥	Ⓐ		†	Ⓐ	⑥	†	⚒
Sevilla ⊖ d.	July 1 -	0730	0930	1130	*1230*	*1330*	1530	1800	1900	2000	2030	Sept. 1 -	0730	*0730*	0930	1130	1300	*1300*	1530	*1630*	*1730*	1730	1900	1930
Huelva d.	Aug. 31	0900	1100	1300	1400	1500	1700	1930	2030	2130	2200	June 30,	0900	0900	1100	1300	1430	1530	1700	1900	1900	1900	2030	2100
Ayamonte a.		1015	1215	1415	1500	1600	1815	2045	2145	2245	2315	2016	1000	1000	1200	1400	1530	1630	1800	2000	2000	2000	2130	2200

	Summer	⚒	Ⓑ		⚒	Ⓐ	⑥	†	Ⓐ	⑦		Winter	⚒	Ⓐ			Ⓐ	⑥	†	Ⓐ	⑥	⑥	Ⓑ	
Ayamonte d.	June 28 -	0640	0830	0930	1145	1400	1515	1615	1715	1730	1945	Sept. 1 -	0645	0830	0930	1145	1400	1500	1515	1545	1615	1715	1730	1930
Huelva d.	Aug. 31	0740	0930	1030z	1245	1500	1645	1715	1815	1830	2045	June 30,	0745	0945	1030	1245	1500	1600	1615	1645	1715	1815	1830	2045
Sevilla ⊖ a.		0910	*1115*	1215z	*1515*	1645	1815	1845	1945	*2015*	2215	2016	0915	*1115*	1215	*1415*	*1645*	1715	1745	1815	1845	1945	*2045*	2215

⛴ **Ayamonte - Vila Real de Santo António Guadiana** Journey time: 10 minutes. ✆ (+34) 959 470 617. Sept. 16 - Mar. 31: hourly (from Ayamonte 1000 - 1900 ⚒, 1100 - 1700, 1815 †). Apr. 1 - June 30: hourly (from Ayamonte 1000 - 2000 ⚒, 1100 - 1700, 1815 †). July 1 - Sept. 15: every 30 mins (from Ayamonte 0930 - 2100 ⚒, 1000 - 1900, 2015 †).

INTERNATIONAL 🚌 SERVICE Joint EVA △ / DAMAS ☆ service *for international journeys only* No service Dec. 25, Jan. 1

	→ Winter Sept. 5 - June 30, 2017			→ Summer July 1 - Sept. 4			
Sevilla, Plaza de Armas ⊖ d.	0730	1615		0730	0930	1445	1615
Huelva d.	0845	1730		0845	1100	1600	1730
Ayamonte 🏛 ES d.	0930	|		|	1200	|	
Vila Real de Santo António 🏛 PT a.	|	1740		|	|	|	1740
Faro, Av. da República a.	1020	1850		0920	1240	1615	1850
Albufeira, Alto dos Caliços a.	1120	1940		1015	1340	1715	1940
Portimão, Largo do Dique a.	1215	2015		|	1415	|	2015
Lagos, Rossio de S. João a.	1245	2045		1100	1445	1800	2045

	→ Winter Sept. 5 - June 30, 2017			→ Summer July 1 - Sept. 4			
Lagos, Rossio de S. João d.	0620	1345		0620	0800	1230	1515
Portimão, Largo do Dique d.	0650	1415		0650	|	|	1545
Albufeira, Alto dos Caliços d.	0725	1450		0725	0845	1315	1620
Faro, Av. da República d.	0810	1535		0810	0930	1355	1705
Vila Real de Santo António 🏛 PT d.	0935	|		0935	|	|	|
Ayamonte 🏛 ES a.	|	1830		|	|	|	2000
Huelva a.	1145	1930		1145	1200	1645	2115
Sevilla, Plaza de Armas ⊖ a.	1300	2045		1300	1315	1800	2230

r – 30 minutes later on ⚒.
z – 30 minutes later on Ⓒ.
☆ – DAMAS, Huelva ✆ +34 959 256 900. www.damas-sa.es
△ – EVA, Faro ✆ +351 289 899 700. www.eva-bus.com
⊖ – Sevilla Plaza de Armas bus station (± 2 km from Santa Justa rail station).
ES – Spain (Central European Time).
PT – Portugal (West European Time).
Huelva bus station is ± 1 km from the rail station.
Ayamonte bus station is ± 1.5 km from the ferry terminal.

MADRID - CÁCERES - BADAJOZ — 677

km	Station		MD 13084	17905	17014	17028	MD 17900	MD 17902	17702	MD 17012	17194	MD 18330	17018	17706
		class	2	2	2	2	2	2	2	2	2	2	2	2
		notes	①–⑥	Ⓐ	Ⓐ	Ⓒ	Ⓐ	①–⑥	T	⑤⑥⑦	①–④	Ⓐ	Ⓑ	Ⓑ
0	Madrid Chamartín	d.										1604		
8	Madrid Atocha Cercanías	d.					0807	1018	1228	1430	1623		1827	2043
16	Villaverde Bajo 669	d.							1236					2051
146	Talavera de la Reina	d.					0937	1154	1408	1614	1755		2004	2218
	Navalmoral de La Mata	d.					1016	1230		1652	1833		2039	
278	Plasencia	a.					1107	1310	1310	1740			2123	
278	Plasencia	d.				0708	1110	1313	1313	1743z			2126	
343*	Cáceres	d.		0650	0805	0818	1219	1416	1416	1640	1843z	2003	2235	
	San Vicente de Alcántara	d.							1333					
430	Valencia de Alcántara	d.							1348					
409	Mérida	a.		0746	0901	0921	1317	1517	1517	1733			2100	
409	Mérida 678	d.		0754	0754	0910	0910 1320	1522	1522	1524 1741	1751		2105	2105
469	Badajoz 678	a.		0841		1006	1405	1603		1842			2145	2145
475	Zafra	d.		0843	0959				1615 1614	1829				
649	Sevilla	a.		1133	1247									
521	Fregenal de la Sierra	a.							1655					
	Jabugo-Galaroza	d.	0735						1738					
660	Huelva	a.	0932						1934					

	Station		17703	17705	17021	MD 18331	MD 17197	MD 17199	17707	17026	17709	17029	MD 17907	MD2 17907	17025			MD 13089
		class	2	2	2	2	2	2	2	2	2	2	2	2	2	2	2	2
		notes	Ⓐ	Ⓒ	①–⑥	Ⓐ			Ⓐ		Ⓒ	T	⑤⑥⑦	①–④	Ⓑ			Ⓑ
	Huelva	d.											1055					1940
	Jabugo-Galaroza	d.											1252					2133
	Fregenal de la Sierra	d.											1335					
	Sevilla	d.														1720		
	Zafra	d.			0655								1418	1418				2002
	Badajoz 678	d.				0656	0717	0845		1225		1425			1705	2010		
	Mérida 678	d.			0742	0741	0753	0924		1311		1510	1507	1507	1744	2055	2053	
	Mérida	d.				0758	0930			1316			1518	1518	1750		2101	
	Valencia de Alcántara	d.									1425							
	San Vicente de Alcántara	d.									1439							
	Cáceres	d.		0715		0854	1027		1416		1557	1616	1616	1850		2200		
	Plasencia	a.		0821					1529			1718	1718	2004				
	Plasencia	d.		0825					1531			1721	1721	2007				
	Navalmoral de La Mata	d.		0907		1020	1154		1616			1801	1801	2049				
	Talavera de la Reina	d.	0650	0840	0940	1056	1234	1510	1657	1755		1840	1840	2124				
	Villaverde Bajo 669	a.	0814	1008				1636	1918									
	Madrid Atocha Cercanías	a.	0827	1018	1107	1226	1353	1646	1828	1927	2009	2009	2258					
	Madrid Chamartín	a.				1242	1411											

T – Not ②.   z – ⑤ only.   * – Madrid - Cáceres via Plasencia 363 km.

ALCÁZAR DE SAN JUAN - BADAJOZ — 678

km	Station		MD 17042		Ⓑ	MD 18183	MD 18170	MD 18330	18027 A		Station		18024 B	MD 18081	18331	MD 17041	18181		MD 17043
		class	2	2	2	2	2	2	2			class	①	2	2	2	2	2	2
		notes				h	f	h	⑦			notes		h		f	h		
	Madrid AC § 661 668	d.				1310			1842 1926		Badajoz 677	d.		0656			1425		2010
	Albacete 668a	d.				1148			1842 1926		Mérida 677	d.		0750			1520		2104
0	Alcázar de San Juan 661	d.	0715			1300	1435	1610	1954 2050		Cabeza del Buey	d.		0935			1707		2256
50	Manzanares 661	d.	0740			1325	1500	1633	2021 2117		Puertollano 660	d.		1118			1854		
114	Ciudad Real 660	d.	0820			1406	1546	1720	2102 2157		Ciudad Real 660	d.	0536	1012	1158	1440	1625		2222
265	Cabeza del Buey	d.		0720x		1323	1545z		1949		Manzanares 661	d.	0614	1052	1243	1520	1712		2300
392	Mérida 677	d.		0910		1524	1751		2145		Alcázar de San Juan 661	a.	0642	1117	1309	1545	1735		2327
451	Badajoz 677	a.		1006		1603	1842		2227		Albacete 668a	a.	0805	1227			1847		
											Madrid AC § 661 668	a.			1717				

A – ⑦. �car València - Albacete - Ciudad Real (Table 668).   f – From/to Madrid Chamartín (Table 661).   x – ①–⑥.   § – Madrid Atocha Cercanías.
B – ①. 🚗 Ciudad Real - Albacete - València (Table 668).   h – From/to Alacant (Table 668).   z – ⑦ only.

679 — MADRID - TOLEDO, SEGOVIA, VALLADOLID, SALAMANCA and EL ESCORIAL · 2nd class

km		Av 8062	Av 8072	Av 8082	Av 8292	Av 8102	Av 8312	Av 8322		Av 8132 ①–⑤	Av 8142 ①–⑤	Av 8152	Av 8162	Av 8172 ①–⑤	Av 8182 ①–⑤	Av 8192		Av 8212		
0	Madrid Puerta de Atocha .....d.	0650	0750	0850	0920	1020	1120	1220	...	1350	1450	1550	1650	1750	1850	1950	...	2150	...	...
75	Toledo ....a.	0723	0823	0923	0953	1051	1153	1253	...	1423	1523	1623	1723	1823	1923	2023	...	2223	...	...

		Av 8063 ①–⑤	Av 8273 ①–⑤	Av 8073 ①–⑤	Av 8283 ①–⑤		Av 8093	Av 8103		Av 8123	Av 8133		Av 8153 ①–⑤	Av 8163 ①–⑤	Av 8173	Av 8183	Av 8193	Av 8203	Av 8213
	Toledo ....d.	0625	0650	0725	0755	...	0925	1025	...	1225	1325	...	1525	1618	1725	1825	1920	2025	2130
	Madrid Puerta de Atocha ....a.	0658	0723	0758	0828	...	0958	1058	...	1258	1358	...	1558	1651	1758	1858	1953	2058	2203

km	km		Av 8069 ①–⑤	Av 8079 ①–⑤	Alvia 4899	Av 8109		Av 8129 ①–⑤	Alvia 34149 ⑤	Av 8159 ①–⑤	Alvia 8359 ⑤	Av 4969	IC 10167 A	Av 8169 ①–⑤	Av 8179 ①–⑤	Av 8189	Av 8199	Av 8209 ⑤	Alvia 34209 ⑥	Av 4909	Av 8219
0	0	Madrid Chamartín ....d.	0640	0730	0855	1015	...	1200	1245	1440	1510	1540	1555	1605	1635	1700	1840	1925	2000	2025	2035	2130
68	68	Segovia AV ....d.	0708	0758	0923	1043	...	1228	1313	1508	1538	1608	1623	1635	1703	1728	1908	1952	2028	...	2103	2158
180		Valladolid ⊠ ....a.	0745	0835		1120	...	1305		1541	1615	1645		1721	1740	1805	1945	...	2105	2119		2235
	230	Salamanca ....a.	...	...	1031	...	...	1421				1731							2211			

		Av 8058 ①–⑤	Av 8068 ①–⑤	Av 8078 ①–⑤	Av 4868	Av 8278 ①–⑤	Alvia 34078	Av 8088 ①–⑤	Alvia 8098 ⑤⑦	Av 4918 ①–⑤	Av 8108 ①–⑤	IC 10086	Av 8148	Alvia 4958		Av 8178	Alvia 34178	Av 4988	Av 8198	Av 8208
Salamanca ....d.		...	...	...	0650		...		0845		...	1050		1530		...	1820	...		
Valladolid ⊠ ....d.		...	0645	0715		0750	0811	0845		0935		1130	1311	1410	1520		1745	1836		1946	2035
Segovia AV ....d.		0700	0722	0752	0759	0827		0922	0954	1012	1159	1207	1359	1447	1557	1639		1822	1912	1929	2023	2112
Madrid Chamartín ....a.		0728	0750	0820	0826	0855	0907	0950	1021	1040	1226	1235	1428	1515	1625	1706		1850	1939	1956	2051	2140

km			①–⑤	⑥⑦	⑥⑦	①–⑤	⑥⑦		⑤	⑥⑦	①–⑤	⑥⑦			①–⑤	⑥⑦	⑥⑦			⑤	⑥⑦	①–⑤	⑥⑦
0	Madrid Chamartín .... d.		0845	1015	1116	1216		1547	1616	1846	1916		Segovia ....d.		0750	1050	1250	1450		1750	1850	2050	2120
58	Cercedilla .... d.		0700	0947	1132	1230	1332		1700	1732	2000	2032		Cercedilla ....a.		0828	1128	1326	1527		1826	1926	2127	2157
100	Segovia ....a.		0737	1024	1208	1307	1409		1736	1808	2039	2110		Madrid Chamartín .....a.		0935	1234	1435	1635		1935	2036	2235	2254

km			MD 18601 ①–⑤	MD 18921 ⑥⑦	MD 18903	MD 18905	MD 18907 Ⓑ	MD 18913	MD 18909	MD 18911				MD 18920 ①–⑤	MD 18900 ①–⑥	MD 18912	MD 18902	MD 18904	MD 18906 ①–⑤	MD 18006	MD 18908
0	Madrid Chamartín ..Ⅱ d.		0733	0830	1108	1335	1530	1757	1930	2112	...	...	Salamanca ....d.		0543	0732	0950	1233	1649	1738		2003
122	Ávila ....Ⅱ d.		0913	1001	1244	1511	1719	1934	2112	2243	...	...	Ávila ....Ⅱ d.		0555	0650	0840	1100	1343	1817	1851	1900	2111
233	Salamanca ....a.		1041	1125	1358	1619	1826	2048	2222	2351	...	...	Madrid Chamartín ..Ⅱ a.		0743	0832	1016	1237	1519	2009	...	2056	2248

MADRID ATOCHA CERCANÍAS - VILLALBA - EL ESCORIAL. 45 km. Line C8. Journey time: Villalba, 53 minutes; El Escorial, 66-67 minutes. Depart 14 minutes later from Madrid Chamartín; arrive 15 minutes earlier at Madrid Charmartin. Additional services operate.

From **Madrid Atocha Cercanías:** 0621 Ⓐ, 0635 Ⓒ, 0651 Ⓐ, 0709 Ⓐ, 0723 Ⓐ, 0737 Ⓒ, 0750 Ⓐ, 0835 Ⓒ, 0839 Ⓐ, 0935 Ⓒ, 0941 Ⓐ, 1036, 1135, 1235, 1335, 1407 Ⓐ, 1436 Ⓒ, 1450 Ⓐ, 1521 Ⓐ, 1536 Ⓒ, 1547 Ⓐ, 1635, 1715 Ⓐ, 1736 Ⓒ, 1745 Ⓐ, 1827 Ⓐ, 1836 Ⓒ, 1847 Ⓐ, 1920, 1936, Ⓒ, 1944 Ⓐ, 2036 Ⓐ, 2042 Ⓒ, 2139, 2236, 2334.
From **El Escorial:** 0548, 0616 Ⓒ, 0631 Ⓐ, 0658 Ⓐ, 0706 Ⓐ, 0716 Ⓒ, 0736 Ⓐ, 0802 Ⓒ, 0817 Ⓒ, 0831 Ⓐ, 0915, 1015, 1115, 1315, 1414, 1515, 1601 Ⓒ, 1615 Ⓒ, 1624 Ⓐ, 1713, 1815, 1858 Ⓐ, 1912 Ⓐ, 1915 Ⓒ, 1930 Ⓐ, 1959 Ⓐ, 2013 Ⓒ, 2029 Ⓐ, 2115, 2215.

A –	①②③④⑥.	Av –	**Avant** high-speed services. Single class.	⊠ –	Full name is Valladolid Campo Grande.	Ⅱ –	See also Tables **680, 681, 689.**

MD – Medium Distance Plus.

679a — MADRID - VALLADOLID

High-speed services. For Avant high-speed services, see Table **679.**

		Alvia 4071 ①–⑥	Alvia 4275 ①–⑤	Alvia 4073 ①–⑥	Alvia 4087	Alvia 4187 ①–⑥	AVE 4099 4299 L	Alvia 4111 V		Alvia 4143 Ⓑ	Alvia 4543 ⑥	Alvia 4141 ⑦ L S 1035c	Alvia 4345 ⑤ F	Alvia 4145 ⑥ F 1020	Alvia 4143 ①	Alvia 4167 2	Alvia 4267 ⑦
0	Alacant Terminal 668 ....d.	...	...	...	...	...	...	...	...	1035c	...	...	1020	...	...	...	...
	Madrid Chamartín.............d.	0705	0720	0745	0800	0800	...	1105		1420	1440	1440	1450	1500	1500	1525	1605	1605
68	Segovia AV ....d.		0750		0830	0830	0958	1137			1508			1531	1531		1635	1635
	A Coruña 680 ....a.													2052	2052			
	Pontevedra 680 ....a.		1353															
180	Valladolid ⊠ ....a.	0808	...	0843	0916	0916	1033	1214		1520	1541	1539	1549		1626	1721	1721	
	Gijón Cercanías 681 ....a.	1158						1604			1938	1922						
	Santander 681 ....a.		1209							1815				1947				
	Bilbao Abando 689 ....a.				1304											2116		
	Hendaye 689 ....a.					1355									2158			

		Alvia 4179 Ⓑ 2P	IC 4177 ⑤ 2Q	Alvia 4377 ⑦ 2Q	Alvia 4181 4381	Alvia 4193 ①④ T	Alvia 4197 L	AVE 4209			Irún 689 LS	Alvia 4088 ①–⑤ 2P	Alvia 4076 T	Alvia 4072 ①–⑤	Alvia 4070 ①–⑥	Alvia 4270 ①–⑥	Alvia 4064 F	Alvia 4092 ⑥⑦	Alvia 4086 ①–⑥	Alvia 4186
	Alacant Terminal 668 .....d.	...	...	...	1445	...	...	...		Irún 689 ....d.	...	...	...	...	...	...	...	0840	...	
	Madrid Chamartín ....d.	1730	1740	1740	1830	1900	1915	2025		Bilbao Abando 689 ....d.									0920	
	Segovia AV ....d.	1758				1929				Santander 681 ....d.			0705			0910				
	A Coruña 680 ....a.									Gijón Cercanías 681 ....d.				0700	0700					
	Pontevedra 680 ....a.									Valladolid ⊠ ....d.	0811	0910	0916	1011	1035	1055		1216	1311	1311
	Valladolid ⊠ ....a.	1833	1848	1848	1930	2005	2023	2119		Pontevedra 680 ....a.						0715				
	Gijón Cercanías 681 ....a.	...		2322r						A Coruña 680 ....a.		0947		1051			1237	1256	1359	1359
	Santander 681 ....a.				2312					Segovia AV ....d.	0910	1015	1030	1121	1138	1158	1306	1326	1428	1428
	Bilbao Abando 689 ....a.									Madrid Chamartín ....a.				1512			1715			
	Hendaye 689 ....a.									Alacant Terminal 668 .....a.										

		AVE 4128 ①–⑤ 2LS	Alvia 4084 ⑥	Alvia 4584	Alvia 4110		Alvia 4142 V	Alvia 4140 LS	AVE 4176 ⑤ 2L	AVE 4162 ⑥ 2Q	IC 4198 ⑥	Alvia 4166 Ⓑ LW	AVE 4266 ⑤	Alvia 4398 Ⓑ L	Alvia 4354 ⑥	Alvia 4180 ⑦	Alvia 4380 Ⓑ	Alvia 4208 ⑦ 2P	Alvia 4192
	Irún 689 ....d.	...	...	...	...		...	...	...	...	1615	...	...	...	...	...	...	...	...
	Bilbao Abando 689 ....d.											1700							
	Santander 681 ....d.				1400					1610						1900			
	Gijón Cercanías 681 ....d.			1100		1425							1800	1810					
	Valladolid ⊠ ....d.	1341		1450		1704	1813	1836	1901	1914	1930	2005	2050	2050	2106		2145	2145	2156	2207
	Pontevedra 680 ....a.		0818	0818								1546							
	A Coruña 680 ....a.																		
	Segovia AV ....d.	1421				1853	1915	1941				2137	2137	2145	2216				
	Madrid Chamartín ....a.	1448	1504	1506	1557	1807	1926	1942	2020	2027	2040	2110	2206	2214	2245	2253	2253	2303	2310
	Alacant Terminal 668 .....a.			1846	1936														

F –	To / from Ferrol (Table **682**).	T –	To and from Vitoria / Gasteiz (Table **689**).	c –	1020 on ⑦.
L –	To / from Leon (Table **681**).	U –	⑥ (daily July 30 - Aug. 28).	r –	2305 on ⑤.
P –	To / from Ponferrada (Tables **681, 682**).	V –	From / to Castelló de la Plana and València on dates shown in Table **668**.		
Q –	To / from Irún (Table **689**).	W –	⑥ (①–⑥ July 30 - Aug. 28).	⊠ –	Full name is Valladolid Campo Grande.
S –	Not July 30 - Aug. 28.			☛ –	All trains convey ⟐. AVE trains also convey ✗.

MADRID - ZAMORA - VIGO, PONTEVEDRA and A CORUÑA

For services to/ from A Coruña via León, see Table 682

Additional connections between Vigo and Ourense can be made by changing trains at Santiago de Compostela

km		Av 12512 ①–⑤ 2	MD 9470 ②①–⑤	Av 9072 ②	MD 12480 ②	Av 9480 ①–⑤	MD 12584 ②	MD 9082 ②	Av 12526 ②	MD 9112 ②	Hotel 922 G	Av 12586 2	MD 12528 ①–⑤	Alvia 4275 ①–⑤	Av 9520 ②	MD 9132 ②	Alvia 12960 ②	MD 4095 ①–⑤	Av 9142 ①–⑤	MD 9550 ①–⑤	MD 12538 b 2	Av 9162 ②	MD 9172 ②
0	Madrid Chamartín..681 689 d.													0715						0915			
75	Segovia AV........679 679a d.													0745									
	Irún 689...............d.																						
	Barcelona Sants 652.......d.							2020							◨								
207*	Medina AV.........681 689 d.													0815									
297	Zamora................d.													0853				1044					
404	Puebla de Sanabria....d.																						
547	Ourense................d.		0650			0755						0938		1148	1208	1210		1330	1336		1530		
641	Guillarei.................d.											1109		1251	1333								
	Vigo Urzáiz..............d.	0513c		0640	0658c		0725c	0850	0945c	1115			1210c	1230c			1340		1435		1510c	1635	1715
666	Redondela AV...........d.	0526r		0648	0711r		0737r		0958r				1130	1222r	1243r	1310r	1357r		1348		1521r		
678	Vigo Guixar.............a.									1141				1320	1412		◨						
684	Pontevedra.............d.	0544		0659	0729		0758	0905	1017	1130			1243	1302	1353			1401		1450		1542	1650	1730
717	Vilagarcía de Arousa...d.	0602		0716	0747			0920	1035	1145			1320							1505		1600	1705	1745
677§	Santiago de Compostela..a.	0648	0730	0742	0828	0835		0942	1122	1207			1405		1250	1444	1515	1417		1527	1610	1644	1727	1807
751§	A Coruña................a.	0727	0758	0813		0903		1010	1158	1235			1442		1318	1512		1448		1555	1638	1721	1755	1835

	Alvia 4325 q	Av 9570 2	MD 12588 ②①–⑤	MD 9182 ②	MD 12488 2	IC 283 B	IC 283 A	Alvia 4145 4345 ⑧	MD 9192 ②	Av 9590 ②	Alvia 12554 2	Alvia 4165 ②		Alvia 622 ⓠ h	Alvia 626 ⓠ P	MD 9212 ②	MD 12560 ②	RE 18322 ⑧	Alvia 4185 2	Hotel 751 ⁂ C ⑧	Hotel 851 ⁂ D ⑧
							b d													
Madrid Chamartín..681 689 d.	1305					1500			1625									1850	2214	2214	
Segovia AV..........679 679a d.	1337					1531															
Irún 689.............d.					0915																
Barcelona Sants 652.......d.	◨					◨					0930	0930									
Miranda de Ebro 681 689 d.					1140	1140					1432	1432									
Medina AV.........681 689 d.	1408					1602												1805x		0030x	0030x
Zamora.............d.	1441					1636					1752							1858	2019		
Puebla de Sanabria d.	1556					1755												2024	2135		
Ourense.............d.	1742	1800				1913	1918	1939		2010		2045	2100	2125	2120			2319		0655	
Guillarei.............d.						2027							2218							0808	
Vigo Urzáiz..........d.			1725c	1815	1820c				1935		2030c				2135						0834r
Redondela AV........d.			1739r		1833r	2051r				2043r		2239r	2252		2143						
Vigo Guixar.........a.						2104	◨	◨			2214	2249	2303	◨						0846	
Pontevedra.........d.	1801		1830	1852				1950		2102	2246				2156					0933	
Vilagarcía de Arousa d.		1845	1914					2005		2122					2213						
Santiago de Compostela a.	1840	1907	1956			2001	2021	2027	2050	2207			2200	2229	2239	2255	2359				
A Coruña...........a.	1908	1935				2033	2052	2055	2118	2243			2230	2307	2331			0841			

km		RE 18321 J	Alvia 4344 ①–⑤	Alvia 4254 ⑥⑦	Av 12411 ①–⑤	MD 12585 ①–⑤	MD 9073 2	Alvia 4064 ①–⑤		Alvia 621 ⓠ h	Alvia 625 R	Alvia 4484 ①–⑥	MD 9083 2	MD 9093 2	Av 9581 ① –⑤	IC 280 A	IC 280 B	MD 12421 2	Av 9113 ①–⑤	Av 9111 q	Alvia 4114 ②	MD 9123 ②①–⑤	MD 12587 ②①–⑤
					b																	
0	A Coruña.............d.			0515	0538	0630		0700	0715		0805		0800	0900	0910	0930		1000	1100	1140		1200	
74	Santiago de Compostela d.		0515	0600	0617	0700		0730	0748		0834		0830	0930	0939	1006		1042	1130	1210		1230	
116	Vilagarcía de Arousa d.				0654		0756						0850	0950				1120	1150			1250	
149	Pontevedra..........d.			0714		0805	0813			0818	0906	1006						1138	1206			1306	1350
167	Vigo Guixar.........d.							◨	0705	0745	◨	0849			◨	◨	0916						
179	Redondela AV........d.			0733r		0823r			0716r	0756		0901r			0920			0927	1156r			1408r	
192	Vigo Urzáiz.........d.			0744c		0835c	0833			0920	1020							1209c	1220			1320	1420c
	Guillarei............d.							0735		0920							0947						
	Ourense............d.		0555	0640		0738			0829	0855	0916	0916	1027		1016	1113	1113		1248	1303			
	Puebla de Sanabria d.	0702	0733	0818				1007											1451			
	Zamora.............d.	0826	0850	0940		1130				1333									1616			
	Medina AV.........681 689 d.	0919x				1205													1655			
	Miranda de Ebro 681 689 a.							1603	1603					1842	1842							
	Barcelona Sants 652......a.	◨		◨				2125	2125		◨						◨						
	Hendaye 689........a.										2115											
	Segovia AV.........679 679a d.		1023	1109		1237				1504									1725			
	Madrid Chamartín 681 689 a.		1048	1134		1306				1504									1754			

	MD 9133 ②①–⑤	Av 12453 2	Alvia 9141 ①–⑤	MD 12455 b 2	Av 4134 h	MD 9153 ②		Av 9161 ⑧	Alvia 4354 2	MD 12431 ①–⑤	MD 12967 2	Hotel 921 G	MD 9173 ②	MD 12589 ①–⑤	MD 9183 2	MD 12441 ②	Av 9201 2	Hotel 852 ⁂ D	MD 12459 ⑧	Av 9213 2	MD 12461 2	Hotel 752 ⁂ C	MD 12561 ⑧ 2
A Coruña.............d.	1300	1315	1400		1440	1500		1630		1545		1700		1800	1908	2000			2100		2225	2210	
Santiago de Compostela d.	1330	1357	1430	1435	1512	1530		1700	1627	1725		1730		1830	1950	2030			2040	2132	2200		2248
Vilagarcía de Arousa d.	1355	1433		1516		1550		1704		1750		1850	2033			2118	2158	2241				
Pontevedra..........d.	1412		1534		1606			1546	1722		1806	1840	1906	2054			2128	2136	2216	2259		
Vigo Guixar.........d.				1430	◨	1619		1755			◨						2215					
Redondela AV........d.	1422		1554r		1443r			1630r	1740r		1805		1858r		2115r			2226r	2156r	2228	2319r	
Vigo Urzáiz.........d.	1429		1607c		1620			1753c			1820	1910c	1920	2126c			2209c	2236	2332c	
Guillarei............d.				1504		1647			1825						2251					
Ourense............d.		1508		1550		1629	1738	1753		1911	1933			2108	2359					
Puebla de Sanabria d.							1947											
Zamora.............d.			1844				2108											
Medina AV.........681 689 d.							2144					0650x		0650x				
Miranda de Ebro 681 689 a.									0849								
Barcelona Sants 652......a.							2216											
Hendaye 689........a.																	
Segovia AV.........679 679a d.			2017				2216					0931		0931				
Madrid Chamartín 681 689 a.			2017				2245					0931		0931				

A — CAMINO DE SANTIAGO – ◨ ⓨ Irún/Hendaye - Miranda de Ebro - A Coruña and v.v.

B — CAMINO DE SANTIAGO – ◨ Bilbao - Miranda de Ebro - Ourense - Vigo and v.v.

C — ⑧: ATLÁNTICO Trenhotel – ◾, ◨. Madrid - A Coruña - Ferrol and v.v.

D — ⑧: RÍAS GALLEGAS Trenhotel – ◾, ◨. Madrid - Pontevedra and v.v.

G — ⑧ (daily June 17 - Sept. 16): GALICIA Trenhotel – ◾, ◨ (reclining) Barcelona - Vigo and v.v.

J — ◨ Valladolid - Medina del Campo - Puebla de Sanabria and v.v. (Table 689).

P — ③⑤⑦ ◨ ⓨ Barcelona - Ourense - Vigo ⁂.

Q — ①②④⑥ ◨ ⓨ Barcelona - Ourense - A Coruña ⁂.

R — ①④⑥ ◨ ⓨ Vigo - Ourense - Barcelona ⁂.

S — ②③⑤⑦ ◨ ⓨ A Coruña - Ourense - Barcelona ⁂.

b — To/from Ferrol (Table 682).

c — Vigo Guixar.

d — From Alacant on ⑦ (Table 668).

h — To/from León (Table 682).

q — To/from Lugo (Table 682).

r — Redondela de Galica.

x — Medina del Campo.

y — To Alacant on ⑥ (Table 668).

* — 153 km Madrid - Medina del Campo via high-speed line.

§ — 636 km Madrid - Santiago de Compostela via high-speed line. 697 km Madrid - A Coruña via high-speed line.

⁂ — On days of indirect service, connections are available between Ourense and Vigo/ A Coruña and v.v. in the same timings.

◑ – Via Lugo (Table 682).

◨ – Via high-speed line.

681 MADRID - LEÓN

km	km via HSL			Alvia	Alvia		AVE	Alvia	IC	IC	Alvia	Alvia	AVE	Alvia	Alvia	Alvia	MD	Alvia	Alvia	MD	Alvia	AVE	Hotel	Hotel		
				4071	4073	18101	4099	4111	283	283	4143	622	4149	4541	4141	664	18003	4179	4181	18005	4193	4209	751	922		
				①–⑥	①–⑥		4299		2 🍷	2		626	Ⓑ	⑥	Ⓑ		2	Ⓑ	4381	2			Ⓑ			
			2			2		P	B	K	E	L	S	U	S			2	m				C	G		
0	0	**Madrid** Chamartín ... 680 689 d.	...	0705	0745	...	0930	1105	...	...	1420	...	1440	1440	1450	...	1620	1730	1830	1820	1900	2025	2214	...	...	...
121		Ávila ... 680 689 d.	...	◧	◧	...	◧	◧	...	...	◧	...	◧	◧	◧	...	1759	◧	◧	2009	◧	◧	2344	...	...	...
207		Medina del Campo .. 680 689 d.	...	|	|	...	|	|	...	...	|	...	|	|	|	...	1845	|	|	2054	|	|	0030	...	...	...
249	180	**Valladolid** C. Grande ... 689 d.	0700	0810	0845	0955	1035	1216	...	...	1522	...	1543	1541	1551	...	1913	1835	1932	2120	2007	2121	0058	...	...	...
286		Venta de Baños ... 689 d.	0732	|	|	1027	|	|	...	...	|	...	|	|	|	...	1938	|	|	2147	|	|	0126	...	...	...
		Barcelona Sants **652** ... d.	|	|	|	|	|	|	...	...	|	0930	|	|	|	1210	|	|	|	|	|	|	|	2020	...	...
		Irún **689** ... d.	|	|	|	|	|	|	0915	...	|	|	|	|	|	|	|	|	|	|	|	|	|	|	...	...
		Bilbao Abando **689** ... d.	|	|	|	|	|	|	|	0942	|	|	|	|	|	|	|	|	|	|	|	|	|	|	...	...
		Miranda de Ebro ... 689 d.	|	|	|	|	|	|	1140	1140	|	1432	|	|	|	1723	|	|	|	|	|	|	|	|	...	...
		Burgos Rosa de Lima . 689 d.	|	|	|	|	|	|	1233	1233	|	1525	|	|	|	1816	|	|	|	|	|	|	|	0249	...	...
297	233	Palencia ... 689 d.	0746	0838	0917	1038	1102	1243	1323	1323	1552	1613	1610	|	|	1906	1949	1902	1959	2158	2039	2148	0139	0342	...	...
		Santander **684** ... a.	|	|	1209	1341	|	|	|	|	1815	|	|	|	|	|	|	|	|	|	2312	|	|	|	...	...
420	345	**León** ... a.	0913	0921	...	...	1145	1330	1428	1428	...	1721	1653	1651	|	2014	2102	1945	2043e	2307	...	2231	0246	0450	...	...
		Gijón Cercanías **685** ... a.	1227	1158	...	...	...	1604	|	|	...	|	...	1938	1922	2300x	...	|	2322z	...	...	...	|	|	...	...
		Ponferrada **682** ... a.	...	...	...	...	...	...	1612	1612	...	1852	...	...	...	...	...	2133	...	...	...	...	0431	0649	...	...
		Vigo Guixar **682** ... a.	...	...	...	...	...	...	|	2104	...	2303	...	...	...	...	...	...	...	...	...	...	|	1141	...	...
		A Coruña **682** ... a.	...	...	...	...	...	...	2033	...	...	2230	...	...	...	...	...	...	...	...	...	...	0841	1114	...	...
		Ferrol **682** ... a.	...	...	...	...	...	...	...	...	...	...	...	...	...	...	...	...	...	...	...	...	1025	...	...	...

	MD	AVE	Alvia	Alvia	AVE	Alvia	Alvia	Alvia	AVE	Alvia	Alvia	IC	IC	Alvia	MD	Alvia	AVE		AVE		Alvia	Alvia	Alvia	Hotel	Hotel	
	18002	4078	4088	4072	4288	4070	4092	661	4128	4110	625	280	280	4142	18006	4140	4178	18104	4198		4180	4380	4192	921	752	
	2	①–⑤	①–⑤	①–⑤	⑥⑦	4270	⑥⑦	①–⑥	①–⑤		621	2 🍷	2		2		Ⓑ	2	⑥	✣	①–⑤	⑦	Ⓑ		Ⓑ	
		S	2	E	T		E		S	m	L	B	K			P	S		W	2				G	C	
Ferrol **682** ... d.	...	...	...	...	...	...	...	...	...	...	...	...	...	...	...	...	...	...	...	...	...	...	...	...	2040	...
A Coruña **682** ... d.	...	...	...	...	...	...	...	...	...	...	0805	0930	...	...	...	...	...	...	...	...	...	...	...	1749	2225	...
Vigo Guixar **682** ... d.	...	...	...	...	...	...	...	...	...	...	0745	|	0916	...	...	...	...	...	...	...	...	...	...	1755	|	...
Ponferrada **682** ... d.	...	...	0611	...	...	...	...	...	...	...	1128	1344	1344	...	...	...	...	...	...	...	...	...	...	2222	0236	...
Gijón Cercanías **685** ... d.	...	...	|	...	...	0700	...	0805	...	1100	|	|	|	...	...	1425	...	...	...	1627t	1800	1810	...	|	|	...
León ... d.	0650	0700	0750	...	0840	0931j	...	1044	1230	1336	1310	1544	1544	...	1550	1659	1725	...	1850	1945	2031	|	...	0012	0425	...
Santander **684** ... d.	|	|	|	0705	|	|	0910	|	|	|	|	|	|	1400	|	|	|	1538	|	|	|	|	1900	|	|	...
Palencia ... 689 d.	0800	0744	0834	0935	0924	|	1140	1157	1314	1420	1419	1655	1655	1628	1702	1743	1809	1844	1935	2109	2115	2115	2131	0124	0536	...
Burgos Rosa de Lima ... 689 d.	|	|	|	|	|	|	|	1252	|	|	1508	1746	1746	|	|	|	|	|	|	|	|	|	|	0217	|	...
Miranda de Ebro ... 689 a.	|	|	|	|	|	|	|	1345	|	|	1603	1842	1842	|	|	|	|	|	|	|	|	|	|	|	|	...
Bilbao Abando **689** ... a.	|	|	|	|	|	|	|	|	|	|	|	|	2032	|	|	|	|	|	|	|	|	|	|	|	|	...
Hendaye **689** ... a.	|	|	|	|	|	|	|	|	|	|	|	2115	...	|	|	|	|	|	|	|	|	|	|	|	|	...
Barcelona Sants **652** ... a.	|	|	|	|	|	|	|	1903	|	|	2125	...	...	|	|	|	|	|	|	|	|	|	|	0849	|	...
Venta de Baños ... 689 d.	0813	|	|	|	|	|	|	...	|	|	...	...	...	|	1717	|	|	1855	|	2122	|	|	|	...	0548	...
Valladolid C. Grande ... 689 d.	0843	0811	0910	1011	0951	1035v	1216	...	1341	1450	...	...	...	1704	1747	1813	1836	1927	2005	2156	2145	2145	2207	...	0618	...
Medina del Campo ... 680 689 a.	0909	|	|	|	|	|	|	...	|	|	...	...	...	|	1812	|	|	...	|	...	|	|	|	...	0648	...
Ávila ... 680 689 a.	0943	◧	◧	◧	◧	◧	◧	...	◧	◧	...	...	...	◧	1858	◧	◧	...	◧	...	◧	◧	◧	...	0738	...
Madrid Chamartín ... 680 689 a.	1145	0910	1015	1121	1050	1138v	1326	...	1448	1557	...	...	...	1807	2056	1926	1942	...	2114	...	2253	2253	2310	...	0931	...

☛ **FOR NOTES**, SEE TABLE **682** BELOW.

682 LEÓN - VIGO, FERROL and A CORUÑA

km		MD	MD	Hotel	Hotel	MD		Alvia	Alvia	MD	MD	IC	IC	Alvia	MD	Alvia		MD	Alvia	Alvia	MD	Alvia	Hotel	Hotel	
		37064	12641	922	922	12741		4134	4095	12685	12687	283	283	4325	12691	4145		37752	626	622	12647	4179	751	851	
		2	2	🍷		2	2		①–⑥	2	2	2 🍷	2		2	4345	2	2			2	2	Ⓑ	Ⓑ	
		①–⑤	①–⑤	G	G	⑥⑦		A	A			B	K	M		Ⓑ A g		Ⓑ	L	L	R	Ⓑ	C	D	
	Madrid Chamartín ‡ d.	...	...	...	...	...	...	...	0915	...	...	...	...	1305	...	1500	...	...	...	...	...	1730	2214	2214	...
	Barcelona Sants ... ‡ d.	...	...	2020	2020	...	...	...	|	...	...	...	...	|	...	|	...	...	0930	0930	...	|	|	|	...
	Irún ... ‡ d.	...	...	|	|	...	...	...	|	...	...	0915	...	|	...	|	...	...	|	|	...	|	|	|	...
	Bilbao Abando ... ‡ d.	...	...	|	|	...	...	...	|	...	...	|	0942	|	...	|	...	...	|	|	...	|	|	|	...
0	**León** ... d.	...	...	0505	0505	...	0710	...	|	...	...	1443	1443	|	...	|	1700	...	1726	1726	...	1950	0301	0301	...
52	Astorga ... d.	...	...	0541	0541	...	0754	...	|	...	...	1515	1515	|	...	|	1733	...	1756	1756	...	2026	0335	0335	...
128	**Ponferrada** ... d.	...	...	0651	0651	...	0910	...	|	...	...	1614	1614	|	...	|	1834	...	1853	1853	...	2133	0432	0432	...
238	Monforte de Lemos ... a.	...	...	0822	0822	...	1105	...	|	...	...	1749	1749	1831	...	|	2016	...	2022	2022	...	...	0559	0559	...
238	Monforte de Lemos ... d.	...	0730	0835	0842	0900	1110	...	|	...	...	1805	1805	1833	...	|	2021	...	2027	2027	2042	...	0614	0615	...
285	Ourense ... 680 d.	...	|	|	0938	|	1208	...	1336	...	...	1918	1913	1752	...	1939	2100	...	2120	2125	1950	...	|	0655	...
416	**Vigo** Guixar ... 680 a.	...	|	|	1141	|	1412	...	|	...	...	|	2104	|	...	|	2249	...	|	2303	|	...	|	0846	...
309	Lugo ... d.	...	0824	0935	...	0956	...	...	|	...	...	|	...	1926	1945	|	...	...	|	...	2134	...	0710	...	...
445	**Ferrol** ... d.	0555	|	|	...	|	...	1325	|	1718	1915	▲	...	...	|	|	...	2040	▲	...	|	...	|	...	...
402	Betanzos - Infesta ... d.	0641	0950	1052	...	1127	...	1408	1526	1811	2004	|	...	...	2056	2127	...	2225f	|	...	2246	...	0818	...	...
428	**A Coruña** ... 680 a.	0705	1016	1114	...	1151	...	1430	1448	1835	2030	2033	...	...	2125	2059	...	2207	2230	...	2315	...	0841	...	...
445	**Ferrol** ... a.	...	...	...	...	...	...	...	1604	...	...	...	...	...	...	2209	...	...	...	...	...	...	1025	...	...

	Alvia		MD	MD	Alvia	Alvia	Alvia	MD	MD	Alvia	IC	IC	MD	Alvia	Alvia		MD	Alvia	MD	Hotel	Hotel	MD	MD	Hotel	Hotel
	4088		12644	12680	4064	621	625	37751	12686	4114	280	280	12682	4134	4208		12684	4095	12696	921	921	12642	37145	752	852
	2	2	2	2	A			2	2		2 🍷	2	2		2	2	2	A	2		🍷	2	12692	Ⓑ	Ⓑ
	①–⑤		R	①–⑥	①–⑤	L	L	①–⑥		M	B	K	⑥⑦	A	⑦			①–⑥		G	G		2	C	D
Ferrol ... d.	...	...	...	...	0555	...	...	...	...	...	...	...	...	1325	...	...	...	...	...	...	...	...	...	2040	...
A Coruña ... 680 d.	...	...	0638	0706	0715	...	0805	0845	0920	...	0930	...	1050	1440	...	...	1431	1458	1720	...	1749	1930	2059	2225	...
Betanzos - Infesta ... d.	...	...	0708	0738	0641	...	|	0947f	0949	...	|	...	1123	1408	...	...	1459	1526	1751	...	1811	2001	2127	2249	...
Ferrol ... a.	...	...	|	0820	|	...	▲	1025	|	...	▲	...	1207	|	...	...	1545	1604	1838	...	|	|	2209	|	...
Lugo ... d.	...	...	0826	...	|	...	|	...	1056	1110	|	...	▬	|	...	...	...	...	...	...	1924	2135	...	2356	...
Vigo Guixar ... 680 d.	...	0705	|	...	|	0745	|	...	...	|	|	0916	...	|	...	1430	...	...	...	1755	|	|	...	|	2215
Ourense ... 680 d.	...	0858	1020	...	0829	0916	0916	...	...	1303	1113	1113	...	1550	...	1630	...	...	...	1933	|	|	...	|	2359
Monforte de Lemos ... a.	...	0946	0929	...	|	0953	0953	...	...	1203	1150	1150	...	|	...	1720	...	...	...	2013	2021	2228	...	0048	0038
Monforte de Lemos ... d.	...	0951	...	...	|	0958	0958	...	...	1206	1208	1208	2	|	...	1726	...	...	...	2041	2041	...	...	0108	0108
Ponferrada ... d.	0611	1144	...	...	|	1128	1128	...	...	|	1344	1344	1755	|	1855	1925	...	...	...	2222	2222	...	...	0236	0236
Astorga ... d.	0708	1247	...	...	|	1228	1228	...	...	|	1453	1453	1920	|	1957	...	...	...	...	2325	2325	...	...	0332	0332
León ... a.	0745	1323	...	...	|	1302	1302	...	...	|	1528	1528	2017	|	2035	...	...	...	...	2357	2357	...	...	0410	0410
Bilbao Abando ... ‡ a.	|	...	...	...	|	|	|	...	...	|	|	2032	...	|	|	...	...	...	...	|	|	...	...	|	|
Hendaye ... ‡ a.	|	...	...	...	|	|	|	...	...	|	2115	...	...	|	|	...	...	...	...	|	|	...	...	|	|
Barcelona Sants ... ‡ a.	|	...	...	...	|	2125	2125	...	...	|	...	...	...	|	|	...	...	...	...	0849	0849	...	...	|	|
Madrid Chamartín .. ‡ a.	1015	...	...	...	1306	...	...	...	...	1754	...	...	...	2017	2303	...	...	...	...	...	...	...	...	0931	0931

A – [12] Madrid - Zamora - Ourense - A Coruña - Betanzos - Ferrol and v.v. (Table **680**).
B – CAMINO DE SANTIAGO – [2] 🍷 Irún / Hendaye - Monforte de Lemos - Santiago - A Coruña and v.v.
C – Ⓑ: ATLÁNTICO *Trenhotel* – 🛏, [1] (reclining) Madrid - A Coruña - Ferrol and v.v.
D – Ⓑ: RÍAS GALLEGAS *Trenhotel* – 🛏, [2] Madrid - Vigo - Pontevedra and v.v.
E – [12] Alacant - Madrid - Santander and v.v.
G – Ⓑ (daily June 17 - Sept. 16): GALICIA *Trenhotel* – 🛏, [1] (reclining) Barcelona - A Coruña and Vigo and v.v.
K – CAMINO DE SANTIAGO – [2] Bilbao - Monforte de Lemos - Vigo and v.v.
L – [12] 🍷 Barcelona - A Coruña and Vigo and v.v. For days of running see Table **680**.
M – [12] Madrid - Zamora - Ourense - Monforte de Lemos - Lugo and v.v. (Table **680**).

P – From / to Castelló de la Plana and València on dates shown in Table **668**.
R – Routeing is A Coruña - Lugo - Monforte de Lemos - Ourense and v.v., with connections at Ourense to and from Madrid (Table **680**).
S – Not July 30 - Aug. 28.
T – ⑥⑦ (daily July 30 - Aug. 28).
U – ⑥ (daily July 30 - Aug. 28).
W – ⑥ (①–⑥ July 30 - Aug. 28).

e – Not ⑤.
f – Betanzos - **Cidade**.

g – From Alicant on ⑦.
j – ⑦ only.
m – From / to Alacant (Table **668**).
t – ①–⑥.
v – 20 minutes later on ⑦.
x – Not ⑥.
z – 2305 on ⑤.

▲ – Via Santiago (Table **680**).
‡ – See Table **681**.
◧ – Via high-speed line (Table **663**).
✣ – On ⑦ runs 4 - 11 minutes later.

683 LEÓN - BILBAO

FEVE narrow-gauge

1350 ✣ →	1410 →	1445 →	1535 →	1636 →	1717 →	1801 →	1935 →	2044 →	2130
León	San Feliz	La Vecilla	Cistierna	Guardo	Vado Cervera	Mataporquera	Espinosa	Balmaseda	**Bilbao** Concordia
2200 ✣	← 2138	← 2059	← 2018	← 1921	← 1841	← 1800	← 1623	← 1520	← 1430

✣ – Journey may be by 🚌 between León and Asunción-Universidad y León, due to construction of a new tunnel.

PALENCIA - SANTANDER 684

km		Alvia 4073 ①–⑥	2		Alvia 4143 A	Alvia 4153 ⑤ 2	2 C	⑤ 2	Alvia 4193	
	Madrid Chamartín **681 689** d.	0745	...	...	1420	1525	...	...	1900	...
	Valladolid C G **681 689** d.	0845	0955	...	1522	1628	1654	1829	2007	...
0	**Palencia** d.	0917	1038	...	1552	1706	1736	1915	2039	...
98	Aguilar de Campoo d.	1030	1152	...	|	1805	1750	2028	2132	...
110	Mataporquera **683** ‡ d.	|	1201	...	|	1815	1901	2042	|	...
129	Reinosa § d.	1053	1216	...	|	1831	1917	2058	2157	...
188	Torrelavega § d.	1145	1312	...	1751	1921	2020	2153	2246	...
218	**Santander** § a.	1209	1341	...	1815	1947	2102	2222	2312	...

	⑥⑦ 2	Alvia 4072 ①–⑤ A	Alvia 4092 ⑥⑦ A	①–⑤ 2	Alvia 4142	2	Alvia 4162 ⑦ 2	Alvia 4192 Ⓑ	
Santander § d.	0700	0705	0910	0919	1400	1538	1610	1900	...
Torrelavega § d.	0729	0729	0934	0953	1424	1609	1633	1923	...
Reinosa § d.	0823	0816	1021	1056	|	1702	1729	2010	...
Mataporquera **683** ‡ d.	0838	|	|	1112	|	1723	1745	|	...
Aguilar de Campoo d.	0848	0838	1047	1122	|	1733	1754	2032	...
Palencia a.	1001	0933	1138	1234	1626	1843	1854	2129	...
Valladolid C G **681 689** a.	1047	1006	1211	1320	1659	1927	1928	2202	...
Madrid Chamartín **681 689** a.	...	1121	1326	...	1807	...	2040	2310	...

A – From/to Alacant (Table **668**). C – ①②③④⑥⑦. ‡ – Narrow gauge station is 600 metres. § – Additional local services operate between these stations.

LEÓN - OVIEDO - GIJÓN 685

km		2 Y	Alvia 4071 ①–⑥	Alvia 4111 V	Alvia 4541 ⑥ U	Alvia 4141 Ⓑ S	Alvia 4171 ⑤ 2	Alvia 664 A	Alvia 4381 ⑤ C	Alvia 4181 CZ
	Barcelona Sants **681** d.	...	...	...	...	...	...	1210	...	...
	Madrid Chamartín **681** d.	...	0705	1105	1440	1450	1715	|	1830	1830
0	**León** d.	0918	0926	1335	1656	|	|	2019	|	2048
109	Pola de Lena § a.	1121	|	1508	|	|	|	2155x	|	|
140	**Oviedo** ▽ § a.	1154	1128	1536	1905	1850	2117	2227x	2233	2253
172	**Gijón** Cercanias § a.	1227	1158	1604	1938	1922	2150	2300x	2305	2322

	Alvia 4070	Alvia 661 ①–⑥ A	Alvia 4110 C	Alvia 4140 W	Alvia 4160 ⑦ 2	2 ①–⑥ Y	Alvia 4180 ①–⑤	Alvia 4380 ⑦	⑦
Gijón Cercanias § d.	0700	0805	1100	1425	1626	1627	1800	1810	2025
Oviedo ▽ § d.	0727	0831	1127	1451	1653	1658	1827	1837	2055
Pola de Lena § d.	|	0900	1158	1520	|	1735	|	|	2127
León a.	|	1039	1331	1654	|	1940	2026	|	2352
Madrid Chamartín **681** a.	1138f	|	1557	1926	2106	...	2253	2253	...
Barcelona Sants **681** a.	...	1903	...	...	...	...	...	...	...

A – (12) Gijón - Barcelona and v.v. (Table **681**).
C – From/to Alacant (Table **668**).
S – Not July 30 - Aug. 28.
U – ⑥ (daily July 30 - Aug. 28).
V – From Castelló de la Plana and València on ①–⑥ (Table **668**).
W – To València and Castelló de la Plana on Ⓑ (Table **668**).
Y – From/to Valladolid (Table **681**).
Z – ①②③④⑥⑦.
f – 1158 on ⑦.
x – Not ⑥.

▽ – **OVIEDO – AVILÉS** and v.v. ***Renfe Cercanías*** (suburban) service. *31 km.* Journey time: ± 38 minutes. **Additional services on** Ⓐ.
From Oviedo: Approximately 1 train each hour 0550 Ⓐ, 0616 Ⓐ, then 0716 until 2216. **From Avilés**: Approximately 1 train each hour 0641 Ⓐ, 0741 Ⓐ, then 0841 until 2311.

§ – **GIJÓN – OVIEDO – POLA de LENA** and v.v. ***Renfe Cercanías*** (suburban) service. *63 km.* Journey time: ± 78 minutes.
From Pola de Lena: Approximately 1–2 trains each hour from 0630 until 2200. **From Gijón**: Approximately 1–2 trains each hour from 0600 until 2230.

SAN SEBASTIÁN - BILBAO 686

EuskoTren (narrow gauge)

	Ⓐ	Ⓐ	Ⓒ					
San Sebastián ⊡ Amara d.	0550	0650	...	0750	0850		1950	2050
Zarautz d.	0620	0720	...	0820	0920		2020	2120
Zumaia d.	0629	0729	...	0829	0929	and	2029	2129
Eibar d.	0711	0811	0811	0911	1011	hourly	2111	2211
Durango d.	0742	0842	0842	0942	1042	until	2142	2241
Bilbao Bolueta ⊖ a.	0818	0918	0918	1018	1118		2218	...
Bilbao Atxuri § a.	0822	0922	0922	1022	1122		2222	...

	Ⓐ	Ⓐ	Ⓒ					
Bilbao Atxuri § d.	...	0600	...	0700	0800		2000	2100
Bilbao Bolueta ⊖ d.	...	0603	...	0703	0803		2003	2103
Durango d.	0540	0640	...	0740	0840	and	2040	2140
Eibar d.	0614	0714	...	0814	0914	hourly	2114	2214
Zumaia d.	0700	0800	0800	0900	1000	until	2200	...
Zarautz d.	0708	0808	0808	0908	1008		2208	...
San Sebastián ⊡ Amara a.	0738	0838	0838	0938	1038		2238	...

⊡ – San Sebastián/Donostia.
⊖ – Metro interchange.
§ – Bilbao Atxuri ⇆ Bilbao Concordia: ± *1000 m.* Linked by tram approx every 10 minutes, journey 6 minutes. Bilbao Concordia is adjacent to Bilbao Abando (*Renfe*).
Operator: EuskoTren. 2nd class, narrow gauge. Distance: San Sebastian - Bilbao *108* km.

BILBAO - SANTANDER - OVIEDO - FERROL 687

FEVE (narrow gauge)

		Ⓐ			Ⓐ					
Bilbao Concordia § d.	...	...	...	0800	...	1300	...	...	1930	...
Marrón d.	...	0715	...	0943	...	1440	...	...	2112	...
Treto d.	...	0726	...	0955	...	1451	...	...	2124	...
Santander a.	...	0825	...	1101	...	1600	...	...	2225	...
Santander ▽ d.	...	...	0910	...	...	...	1610	...	...	...
Torrelavega ▽ d.	...	...	0937	...	...	...	1637	...	...	...
Cabezón de la Sal ▽ d.	...	...	1007	...	...	...	1707	...	...	...
Unquera d.	...	...	1049	...	...	...	1749	...	...	...
Llanes d.	0740	...	1121	...	1420	...	1826	...	...	...
Ribadesella d.	0821	...	1200	...	1500	...	1905	...	...	...
Oviedo a.	1037	...	1410	...	1713	...	2109	...	...	...

					Ⓐ			Ⓐ		
Oviedo d.	...	...	0835	...	1045	...	1535	...	1855	...
Ribadesella d.	...	...	1041	...	1256	...	1746	...	2104	...
Llanes d.	...	...	1121	...	1333	...	1826	...	2141	...
Unquera d.	...	...	1151	...	...	...	1855	...	...	...
Cabezón de la Sal ▽ d.	...	...	1233	...	...	...	1936	...	...	...
Torrelavega ▽ d.	...	...	1303	...	...	...	2005	...	...	...
Santander ▽ a.	...	...	1333	...	...	...	2033	...	...	...
Santander d.	0800	...	...	1400	...	1900	...	2045	...	...
Treto d.	0858	...	...	1507	...	2001	...	2144	...	...
Marrón d.	0910	...	...	1519	...	2013	...	2155	...	...
Bilbao Concordia § a.	1053	...	...	1658	...	2158	...	...	...	...

					Ⓐ					
Oviedo △ d.	...	...	0730	...	...	...	...	...	1430	...
Gijón Sanz Crespo △ d.	...	0701	|	0931	...	...	1131	1421	|	1831
Avilés △ d.	...	0740	|	1018	...	...	1218	1500	|	1918
Pravia △ d.	...	0812	0833	1048	...	...	1248	1529	1534	1948
Luarca d.	...	...	1004	...	...	...	...	...	1708	...
Navia d.	...	...	1034	...	...	...	...	...	1739	...
Ribadeo d.	0655	...	1134	...	...	1500	...	...	1840	...
Viveiro d.	0803	...	1244	...	...	1609	...	...	1948	...
Ortigueira d.	0843	...	1324	...	1505	1650	...	...	2028	...
Ferrol a.	1000	...	1444	...	1624	1810	...	...	2144	...

							Ⓐ			
Ferrol d.	...	...	0820	...	1045	...	1300	1530	...	1905
Ortigueira d.	...	...	0938	...	1204	...	1420	1649	...	2027
Viveiro d.	...	...	1018	...	1245	...	...	1729	...	2106
Ribadeo d.	...	...	1130	...	1353	...	...	1841	...	2215
Navia d.	...	...	1226	...	...	...	...	1939	...	...
Luarca d.	...	...	1256	...	...	...	...	2011	...	...
Pravia △ d.	0848	1148	1429	1448	...	1648	...	2151	2155	...
Avilés △ d.	0926	1226	|	1526	...	1726	...	|	2229	...
Gijón Sanz Crespo △ a.	1008	1308	|	1608	...	1808	...	|	2309	...
Oviedo △ a.	...	...	1530	...	...	...	...	2253	...	...

▽ – Additional trains run Santander - Cabezón de al Sal and v.v.
△ – Additional trains run Oviedo/Gijón - Pravia and v.v.
§ – Bilbao Concordia is adjacent to Bilbao Abando (*Renfe*).
Operator: FEVE. 2nd class, narrow gauge.

IRÚN - BILBAO - SANTANDER - GIJÓN 688

ALSA ★

	▽ ①–⑥			♡ Ⓑ	♡ ⑥	①–⑥	⑦				♡ Ⓑ	⑥		♡ Ⓑ		♡	⑤⑦					⊖ ⑤⑦		⑦	
Irún RENFE rail station d.	...	...	...	0645	...	0745	...	...	0845	...	...	...	1100	...	1345	1445	...	...	1615	...	1830	...	2045	2115	2355
San Sebastián/Donostia d.	...	...	...	0710	...	0810	...	...	0910	...	...	...	1125	...	1410	1510	...	...	1640	...	1855	...	2110	2140	0020
Bilbao TermiBus d.	0600	...	0700	0830	0830	0930	0930	1000	1030	1130	1230	1230	1330	1430	1530	1630	1730	1730	1800	1845	2030	2115	2230	2300	0145
Santander d.	0715	0830	0830	0950	0950	1100	1115	1130	1215	1300	1350	1400	1530	1550	1700	1750	1900	1900	1930	2015	2200	2235	2350	0020	0330
Oviedo a.	1000*	1145	...	1205	1205	...	...	...	1530	...	1605	...	1845	1805	...	2005	2145	...	2230	2230	...	0050	...	...	0600
Gijón a.	0930	1215	...	1230	1230	...	...	...	1600	...	1635	...	1915	1835	...	2030	2215	...	2300	2300	...	0120	...	...	0700

		①–⑥			①–⑥	♡	♡ ①–⑥	⑤	⑦	①–⑥	♡ ①–⑥		⑤⑦	♡			⑥	♡ Ⓑ				▽ Ⓑ	⑤⑦	▽ ⑤	▽ ⑦
Gijón d.	0014	...	...	...	...	0715	...	...	0815	0815	0915	1130	...	1315	...	1515	1545	1630	...	1715	...	1915	2015	2115	2115
Oviedo d.	0100	...	...	...	...	0745	...	...	0845	0845	0945	|	...	1345	...	|	1615	1700	...	1745	...	1945	2045	2145	2145
Santander d.	0345	0600	0700	0800	0930	1005	1200	...	1200	1230	1200	1400	1545	1605	1700	1900	1900	1920	...	2030	2100	2205	2340	0005	2359
Bilbao TermiBus d.	0515	0730	0840	0930	1100	1120	1315	1400	1400	1415	1315	1530	1745	1720	1830	2045	2030	2035	2045	2200	2230	2320	...	0120	0115
San Sebastián/Donostia a.	0640	0845	1000	...	1210	1230	...	1510	1600	1615	...	...	1855	1830z	1940	2155	...	2145r	2155	2310	...	...	...	...	0225
Irún RENFE rail station a.	0700	0915	1030	...	1240	1305	...	1545	1630	1645	...	...	1925	1905z	2010	2225	...	2220r	2225	2340	...	...	...	...	0300

♡ – *Clase Supra+* luxury coach.
▽ – *Clase Supra Economy* luxury coach.
⊖ – *Supra+ on* ⑤, *Supra Economy* on ⑦.
r – ①–④ only.
z – ⑥ only.
* – Calls after Gijon.
★ – ALSA: ✆ +34 913 270 540 www.alsa.es
Frequent services operate Bilbao - Santander and Oviedo - Gijon.

12 *La explicación de los signos convencionales se da en la página 4* 335

689 — MADRID and SALAMANCA - BILBAO and IRÚN

km △		RE 16001 2 ①-⑤	Hotel 310 ✕ B	MD 18316 ①-⑥	IC 631 ①-⑥	16019 2 N	17227 2	17201 2	RE 18302 2 ①-⑤	Alvia 4087	Alvia 4187	MD 18001 2 ①-⑥	RE 18321 2 Y	18203 2 ⑥⑦	MD 18324 2 ⑦	IC 633 ⑦	Alvia 661 2 ①-⑥	MD 18061 2 A	18029 2 Z	2	Alvia 621 2 625 Q	MD 18011 2 ⑥⑦
0	Madrid Chamartín 680 681 d.									0800	0800				0800	0621		0900				1021
121	Ávila 680 681 d.							0645				0808	0905		0954			1038				1208
	Salamanca d.			0456	0600				0712							0954						
207	Medina del Campo 680 681 d.		0600	0639			0655	0733	0802			0856	0920	0954	1042			1125				1256
250	Valladolid Campo Grande 681 d.		0629	0705	0716		0730	0807	0830	0918	0918	0925	0955	1022	1108	1132		1150	1220			1325
286	Venta de Baños 681 d.																	1215	1300			
298	Palencia 681 d.														1157	1229			1313	1419		
371	Burgos Rosa de Lima 681 d.		0748		0821					1028	1028				1240	1252	1320	1405j		1508		
460	Miranda de Ebro 653 d.	0720	0830	0848		0921	0940			1128	1135				1337	1347	1417	1501		1605		
565	Bilbao Abando 653 d.										1304											
494	Vitoria / Gasteiz 653 d.	0747	0902	0912			1005			1151						1411	1440	1530		1627		
	Barcelona Sants 653 a.					1420										1835	1903			2125		
537	Altsasu 653 d.		0931				1038n									1509	1601n					
624	San Sebastián / Donostia ▲ 653 d.		1049	1055						1326						1629						
641	Irún ▲ 653 a.		1113	1117s						1348s						1651						
643	Hendaye ▲ 653 a.		1128							1355												

		MD 18063 2 ⑧	MD 18063 2 ⑥	MD 18306 2	IC 280 2 D	IC 280 2 E	MD 18314 2	16111 2 Z	16011 2 Z	RE 18009 2 ①-⑥	Alvia 4167 ⑦	Alvia 4177 g	IC 4377 2 ①-④	Alvia 4177 ⑦	Alvia 18065 ⑧	MD 18312 2 ⑧	RE 18007 2 ⑧	Hotel 921 ⛾ G
	Madrid Chamartín 680 681 d.	1212	1212							1541	1605	1605	1740	1740	1915	1700		2020
	Ávila 680 681 d.	1405	1405		1510					1641					1850			2209
	Salamanca d.			1400		1555											2040	
	Medina del Campo 680 681 d.	1452	1452	1504		1559	1635			1734					1938	2135	2256	
	Valladolid Campo Grande 681 d.	1517	1517	1529		1632	1703			1806	1723	1723	1850	1850	2006	2209	2321	
	Venta de Baños 681 d.	1542	1542	1605						1834					2034		2347	
	Palencia 681 d.	1557	1557	1617	1655	1655									2050		2358	0124
	Burgos Rosa de Lima 681 d.	1645	1652		1746	1746				1927	1833	1833	1959	1959	2134	2143		0217
	Miranda de Ebro 653 d.	1741	1747		1850	1858				2027	1935	1948	2054	2054	2230	2239		
	Bilbao Abando 653 a.					2032					2116							
	Vitoria / Gasteiz 653 d.	1802	1807		1911		1900	1921	2050	1956		2117	2117	2300			0849	
	Barcelona Sants 653 a.	1829	1836	1934														
	Altsasu 653 d.						1931n	1952n										
	San Sebastián / Donostia ▲ 653 d.	1949	2000	2051						2130		2252	2250					
	Irún ▲ 653 a.	2011	2022	2109s						2151s		2310	2312t					
	Hendaye ▲ 653 a.			2115						2158								

km		MD 18066 2 ①-⑥	RE 18300 2 ①-⑤	Alvia 4056 K	Alvia 4076 2 ②-⑤	MD 18304 2 ①-⑥	MD 18010 2	17218 2 ①-⑥	16000 2 Z	18071 2 Z	Alvia 4086 ①-⑥	Alvia 4186 k	IC 283 2 E	IC 283 2 D	MD 18308 2	MD 18004 2 ①-⑥	MD 18070 2 ⑦	MD 18012 2 Q	MD 18012 2 ①-⑤	Alvia 622 2 Y	RE 18322 2 Y
0	Irún ▲ 653 d.		0450					0600	0840		0915				1100	1100					
17	San Sebastián / Donostia ▲ 653 d.		0510				0619	0857		0933				1119	1119						
104	Altsasu 653 d.					0736	0918n			1046				1237	1237				0930		
	Barcelona Sants 653 d.		0645	0645		0745		0803	0950	1033		1108			1307	1307	1410	1430			
147	Vitoria / Gasteiz 653 d.									0920	0942										
	Bilbao Abando 653 d.		0706	0706	0806			1016	1058	1058	1140	1140			1245	1327	1327	1432	1457		
180	Miranda de Ebro 681 d.		0800	0800	0903		1156	1156	1233	1233			1347	1424	1424	1525					
270	Burgos Rosa de Lima 681 d.	0550			1002					1321	1321	1335		1516	1522	1611		1638			
353	Palencia 681 d.	0603			1013							1348		1527	1533		1652				
355	Venta de Baños 681 d.	0636	0735	0916	0916	0940	1039	1205		1311	1311		1419	1435		1554	1600		1735	1740	
391	Valladolid Campo Grande 681 d.	0702	0812			1007	1105	1243				1448	1511		1620	1626		1804			
434	Medina del Campo 680 681 d.		0903			1046							1548								
511	Salamanca a.		0750				1155	1334							1600	1710	1715				
	Ávila 680 681 d.	0942		1030	1030		1339				1428	1428			1747	1900	1900				

		MD 18014 2 ⑦	RE 18318 2	IC 4176 2 A	Alvia 664 2 ⑦	17200 2 N	RE 18008 2 ⑧	Alvia 18015 2	4166 2	Alvia 4266 2	IC 632 2	MD 18310 2 C	17226 ①-⑥	Hotel 313 ✕ 2 N	16017 2b	16027 2	RE 16004 2	Hotel 922 ⛾ G
	Irún ▲ 653 d.	1350		1450					1615				1850				1937	
	San Sebastián / Donostia ▲ 653 d.	1408		1509					1633				1910				1957	
	Altsasu 653 d.	1527				1718n								2004n	2046n	2116		
	Barcelona Sants 653 d.				1210					1410							2020	
	Vitoria / Gasteiz 653 d.	1557	1644	1702		1715	1753	1809					2046	2037	2118	2150		
	Bilbao Abando 653 d.							1700										
	Miranda de Ebro 681 d.	1617	1705	1723	1739	1820	1835	1835	1856			2108		2143	2215			
	Burgos Rosa de Lima 681 d.	1714	1759	1816	1838		1933	1933	1948			2200					0249	
	Palencia 681 d.	1806		1904													0339	
	Venta de Baños 681 d.	1817			1929													
	Valladolid Campo Grande 681 d.	1845	1905	1914		2030	2005		2050	2050	2058	2135	2230					
	Medina del Campo 680 681 d.	1912	1933		2107	2038						2210	2306	0011				
	Salamanca a.		2021										2252	0057				
	Ávila 680 681 d.	2000			2157	2133												
	Madrid Chamartín 680 681 a.	2201		2027		2330			2206	2206								

A – 🚃 Gijón - Barcelona and v.v. (Table 685).
B – SUD EXPRESSO / SUREX Trenhotel – 🛏 Gran Clase / Gran Classe (1, 2 berths), 🛏 Preferente (1, 2 berths), 🛏 Turista (4 berths), ✕ Lisboa (310) - Vilar Formoso (311) - Salamanca - Hendaye (Table 45).
C – SUREX / SUD EXPRESSO Trenhotel – 🛏 Gran Clase / Gran Classe (1, 2 berths), 🛏 Preferente (1, 2 berths), 🛏 Turista (4 berths), ✕ Irún (312) - Salamanca - Vilar Formoso (313) - Lisboa (Table 45).
D – CAMINO DE SANTIAGO – 🚃 A Coruña - Palencia - Miranda de Ebro - Irún / Hendaye and v.v.
E – CAMINO DE SANTIAGO – 🚃 Vigo - Palencia - Miranda de Ebro - Bilbao and v.v.
G – ⑧ (daily June 18 - Sept. 17): GALICIA Trenhotel – 🛏, 🚃 (reclining) ⛾ Barcelona - A Coruña and Vigo and v.v.
K – ① June 27 - Aug. 29.
N – To / from Pamplona (Table 653).
Q – 🚃 Vigo / A Coruña - Palencia - Barcelona and v.v. (Table 680).
Y – 🚃 Puebla de Sanabria - Medina del Campo - Valladolid and v.v. (Table 680).
Z – To / from Pamplona and Zaragoza (Table 653).

b – From / to Castejón de Ebro and Pamplona / Iruña (Table 653).
g – Daily June 20 - Oct. 17.
j – ①-⑥.
k – Daily June 21 - Oct. 18.
n – Altsasu Pueblo.
s – Calls to set down only.
t – June 28 - Aug. 30.
🔲 – Via high-speed line (Table 663).
△ – Via Ávila.

▲ – SAN SEBASTIÁN - IRÚN and v.v. Renfe Cercanías (suburban) service.
From San Sebastián: Approximately 2-3 trains each hour from 0630 until 2300. From Irún: Approximately 2-3 trains each hour from 0522 until 2222.
17 km. Journey time: ± 23 minutes.

▲ – SAN SEBASTIÁN (Amara) - IRÚN (Colón, near Renfe station) - HENDAYE (SNCF station) and v.v. EuskoTren (narrow-gauge) service. 22 km. Journey time: ± 37 minutes.
From San Sebastián: 0555 Ⓐ, 0615 Ⓑ, 0645 Ⓐ, 0715, 0745 and every 30 mins until 2145, also 2315 Ⓑ s. On ⑦ also 0015, 0115 s, 0215, 0315 s, 0415, 0515 s.
From Hendaye (A): 0647 Ⓐ, 0703 Ⓐ, 0733 Ⓐ, 0803, 0833 and every 30 mins until 2233. On ⑦ also 0003 s, 0103, 0203 s, 0303, 0403 s, 0503.
A – 4 minutes later from Irún. s – Summer only (late-June to mid-Sept).

PORTUGAL

SEE MAP PAGE 320

Operator: CP – Comboios de Portugal (www.cp.pt).

Train categories: *Alfa Pendular* – *AP* – high-quality tilting express trains. *Intercidades* – *IC* – high-quality express trains linking the main cities of Portugal to Lisboa and Porto. *Interregional* – *IR* – 'semi-fast' links usually calling at principal stations only. *Celta* – International services between Porto and Vigo. *Regional* and *Suburbano* – local stopping trains (shown without train numbers).
Higher fares are payable for travel by *AP* and *IC* trains, also the international **Sud Expresso** service (Lisboa - Hendaye / Irún - Lisboa), and there is an additional supplement for travel by *AP* trains. The **Lusitania** *Hotel Train* service (Lisboa - Madrid and v.v.) is shown in Table **46**, special fares apply.

Services: Valid from **December 11, 2016**. All services shown with a train number convey first and second class accommodation (on *Alfa Pendular* trains termed, respectively, *Conforto* and *Turística*) unless otherwise indicated. *Regional* and *Suburbano* trains convey second-class seating only.
AP, *IC*, *IR* and international trains convey a buffet car (*carruagem-bar*) and there is an at-seat service of meals to passengers in 1st class on *AP* and certain *IC* trains. Sleeping (🛏) and couchette (▬) cars are of the normal European types described on page 8.

Reservations: Reservations are **compulsory** for travel by *AP*, *IC* and international trains. Seat reservation is not normally available on other services.

Timings: Timings shown are the most recent available. Amendments to timetables may come into effect at short notice, especially during the Christmas and New Year period.

LISBOA - COIMBRA - PORTO 690

Reservations compulsory on *AP* and *IC* trains. For local trains Entroncamento - Coimbra / Coimbra - Aveiro see Table **699**. Local trains Aveiro - Porto run approx hourly.

km		*IR* 823	*AP* 121 Ⓐ	*AP* 131 △	*IC* 521 ①–⑥ n	*AP* 141 ☆	*IC* 511 ◇	*IC* 721 △	*AP* 182	*IC* 523	*AP* 125 ⚒	*IC* 513 ◇	*AP* 133 △	*IC* 525	*AP* 135 Ⓑ h△	*AP* 127	*IC* 621 ☆‡	*AP* 184	*IC* 515 ◇	*AP* 137 △	*IC* 723 △	*AP* 129	Ⓑ	310 335 S Ⓡ	*IC* 527
	Faro **697** d.	...	...	...	...	...	...	...	0700	...	...	...	...	...	...	...	...	1505	...	...	...	...	...	...	...
0	**Lisboa** S Apolónia ▷ d.	...	0600	0700	0730	0800	0830	0930	|	1130	1200	1330	1400	1530	1600	1700	1730	|	1830	1900	1930	2000	...	2125	2200
7	**Lisboa** Oriente ▷ d.	...	0609	0709	0739	0809	0839	0939	1009	1139	1209	1339	1409	1539	1609	1709	1739	1809	1839	1909	1939	2009	...	2134	2209
31	Vila Franca de Xira ▷ d.	...	|	|	0752	|	0852	0952	|	1152	|	1352	|	1552	|	|	1752	|	1852	|	1952	|	...	|	2222
75	Santarém ▷ d.	...	|	|	0813	0839	0913	1013	|	1213	|	1413	|	1613	|	|	1813	|	1913	|	2013	2039	...	|	2243
107	**Entroncamento** ▷ d.	...	|	|	0831	0856	0932	1031	|	1231	|	1432	|	1631	|	|	1831	|	1932	|	2031	2056	2136	2230	2301
131	Fátima ⊙ d.	...	|	|	|	|	0948	|	|	|	|	1448	|	|	|	|	|	|	1948	|	|	|	2157	|	|
140	Caxarias ⊖ d.	...	|	|	|	|	0955	1051	|	|	|	1455	|	|	|	|	1850	|	1955	|	|	|	2206	2249	2321
171	Pombal d.	...	|	|	0905	0926	1011	1107	|	1305	|	1511	|	1705	|	|	1907	|	2011	|	2105	2126	2229	2306	2337
199	Alfarelos d.	...	|	|	|	|	1025	|	|	1319	|	1525	|	1719	|	|	|	|	2025	|	|	|	2252	|	|
218	**Coimbra** B ▶ d.	0520	0745	0845	0930	0950	1039	1133	1145	1332	1345	1539	1545	1732	1745	1845	1932	1945	2039	2045	2130	2150	2316	2332	0003
232	Pampilhosa d.	0533	|	|	|	|	1050	|	|	1343	|	1550	|	1743	|	|	|	|	2050	|	|	|	2327	...	|
273	Aveiro d.	0601	0812	0912	1001	1016	...	1201	1212	1402	1412	...	1612	1802	1812	1912	2000	2012	...	2112	2201	2216	0000	...	0031
318	Espinho d.	0633	|	|	1024	1036	...	1224	|	1424	|	...	|	1824	|	|	2024	|	...	|	2224	2236	0029	...	0054
334	Vila Nova de Gaia d.	0644	0838	0939	1034	1046	...	1234	1238	1433	1438	...	1639	1833	1839	1938	2034	2038	...	2139	2235	2245	0039	...	0103
337	**Porto** Campanhã ▽ a.	0650	0844	0944	1039	1052	...	1239	1244	1439	1444	...	1644	1839	1844	1944	2039	2044	...	2144	2239	2252	0045	...	0109

	①–⑥	313 332 S Ⓡ	*AP* 180	*AP* 130 △	*IC* 520 ①–⑥ n	*AP* 120 ①–⑥ n	*IC* 510 ◇	*IC* 620 ☆	*AP* 122 ⚒	*IC* 720 △	*AP* 124 Ⓑ b	*IC* 522	*AP* 132 △	*IC* 512 ◇	*IC* 722 △	*AP* 186	*AP* 126	*IC* 524	*AP* 140 ☆	*IC* 20532 ⑦ h	*AP* 134 △	*IC* 514 ◇	*IC* 526	*AP* 136 Ⓑ h△	*IR* 822
Porto Campanhã ▽ d.	0055	...	0547	0647	0652	0745	...	0852	0947	1052	1147	1252	1347	...	1452	1547	1647	1652	1745	1752	1847	...	1952	2047	2155
Vila Nova de Gaia d.	0101	...	0552	0652	0657	0750	...	0857	0952	1057	1152	1257	1352	...	1457	1552	1652	1657	1750	1757	1852	...	1957	2052	2201
Espinho d.	0113	...	|	|	0707	0800	...	0908	|	1107	|	1307	|	...	1507	|	|	1707	1800	1808	|	...	2007	|	2212
Aveiro d.	0151	...	0621	0721	0731	0821	...	0932	1021	1129	1221	1331	1421	...	1529	1621	1721	1731	1821	1832	1921	...	2031	2121	2245
Pampilhosa d.	0225	...	|	|	|	|	0907	|	|	1146	|	|	|	1510	1546	|	|	|	|	|	|	2010	|	|	2314
Coimbra B ▶ d.	0238	0447	0646	0746	0800	0846	0921	0959	1046	1157	1246	1357	1446	1521	1557	1646	1746	1757	1846	1859	1946	2021	2057	2146	2325
Alfarelos d.	0254	|	|	|	|	|	0934	|	|	1210	|	|	|	1534	1610	|	|	|	|	|	|	2034	|	|	...
Pombal d.	0315	0522	|	|	0826	0910	0949	1024	|	1226	|	1423	|	1549	1626	|	|	1823	1910	1925	|	2049	2123	|	...
Caxarias ⊖ d.	0337	0543	|	|	|	|	1005	1040	|	|	|	1439	|	1605	|	|	|	1839	|	1941	|	2105	2139	|	...
Fátima ⊙ d.	0345	|	|	|	|	|	1012	|	|	|	|	|	|	1612	|	|	|	|	|	|	|	2112	|	|	...
Entroncamento ▷ d.	0410	0606	|	|	0858	0939	1027	1059	|	1258	|	1458	|	1627	1658	|	|	1858	1939	2000	|	2127	2158	|	...
Santarém ▷ d.	0440	|	|	|	0916	0955	1046	1117	|	1316	|	1516	|	1646	1716	|	|	1916	1955	2018	|	2146	2216	|	...
Vila Franca de Xira ▷ d.	0524	|	|	|	0939	|	1109	1139	|	1339	|	1539	|	1709	1739	|	|	1939	|	|	|	2209	2239	|	...
Lisboa Oriente ▷ a.	0550	0720	0823	0922	0952	1031	1122	1152	1222	1352	1422	1552	1622	1722	1752	1823	1922	1952	2031	2052	2122	2222	2252	2322	...
Lisboa S Apolónia ▷ a.	0559	0730	|	0930	1000	1040	1130	1200	1230	1400	1430	1600	1630	1730	1800	|	1930	2000	2040	2100	2130	2230	2300	2330	...
Faro **697** a.	...	...	1123	...	...	...	...	...	...	...	...	...	...	...	...	2123	...	...	...	...	...	...	...	...	...

S – SUD EXPRESSO / LUSITANIA – see Tables **45** / **692**. International journeys only.
b – Not public holidays.
h – Not ⑦ if the following day is a public holiday. Not ⑤ if it is a public holiday.
n – Not ① if it is a public holiday. Not ⑥ if the day before is a public holiday.
⊙ – *20 km* from Fátima (full name of station is Chão de Maçãs - Fátima).
◇ – Lisboa - Guarda and v.v. (Table **692**).
☆ – Lisboa - Porto - Guimarães and v.v. (Table **695a**).
△ – Lisboa - Porto - Braga and v.v. (Table **695**).
▷ – For other fast trains see Table **691**, for local trains see Table **699**.
▽ – Local services run Porto Campanhã - Porto São Bento.
▶ – Local trains run Coimbra B - Coimbra and v.v.
⊖ – 🚌 available Caxarias - Fátima. See www.rodotejo.pt for details.
‡ – Departs Lisboa 5 minutes earlier on ⑤ (not calling at Vila Franca de Xira).

LISBOA - ENTRONCAMENTO - COVILHÃ 691

km		Ⓐ		⚒	*IC* 541		*IC* 543			*IC* 545	
0	**Lisboa** Sta Apolónia ▷ d.	0545	...	0645	0815	*0945*	1315	1615	*1745*	1915	1945
7	**Lisboa** Oriente ▷ d.	0553	...	0653	0823	*0953*	1323	1623	*1753*	1923	1953
31	Vila Franca de Xira ▷ d.	0611	...	0711	0838	*1011*	1338	1639	*1811*	1938	2011
75	Santarém ▷ d.	0655	...	0755	0905	*1055*	1405	1706	*1855*	2005	2055
107	**Entroncamento** ▷ a.	0719	...	0819	0925	*1119*	1425	1726	*1919*	2025	2119
107	**Entroncamento** d.	▬	0748	...	0926	1152	1426	1727	1943	2026	*2154*
135	Abrantes d.	...	0820	...	0950	1224	1450	1758	2021	2050	*2235*
199	Ródão d.	...	0928	...	1042	1323	1548	1904	2126	2142	...
229	Castelo Branco a.	⚒	0957	...	1105	1352	1611	1948	2154	2206	...
229	Castelo Branco d.	0625	1000	...	1106	1420	1612	1951	...	2207	...
283	Fundaõ d.	0713	1048	...	1142	1513	1648	2039	...	2243	...
301	**Covilhã** a.	0729	1104	...	1156	1529	1702	2055	...	2257	...

	①–⑥	*IC* 540		Ⓐ			*IC* 542		*IC* 544	
Covilhã d.	*0450*r	0731	0850	...	...	*1300*	1431	...	1831	1841
Fundaõ d.	*0506*r	0746	0906	...	...	*1316*	1446	...	1846	1857
Castelo Branco a.	*0553*r	0820	0953	...	...	*1404*	1521	...	1920	1944
Castelo Branco d.	0556	0821	1009	...	...	*1408*	1522	*1817*	1921	...
Ródão d.	0624	0845	1042	...	...	*1436*	1548	*1845*	1945	...
Abrantes d.	0723	0937	1141	...	...	*1541*	1639	*1946*	2037	...
Entroncamento a.	0800	1006	1216	...	...	*1611*	1703	*2015*	2106	...
Entroncamento ▷ d.	0808	1007	...	1238	1342	1638	1704	2042	2107	...
Santarém ▷ d.	0827	1026	...	1302	1406	1702	1726	2106	2126	...
Vila Franca de Xira ▷ d.	0856	1055	...	1347	1447	1747	1755	2147	2155	...
Lisboa Oriente ▷ a.	0911	1111	...	1405	1505	1805	1811	2205	2211	...
Lisboa Sta Apolónia ▷ a.	0920	1120	...	1413	1513	1813	1820	2213	2220	...

r – ① (not public holidays).
▷ – For other fast trains see Table **690**, for local trains see Table **699**.

(LISBOA -) COIMBRA - GUARDA - VILAR FORMOSO 692

km		*IC* 511			*IC** 513		Ⓑ		Ⓑ	*IC** 515	*IN* 311 S Ⓡ
	Lisboa Sta Apolónia **690** d.	0830	...	...	1330	...	...	...	...	1830	2125
	Lisboa Oriente **690** d.	0839	...	...	1339	...	...	...	...	1839	2134
0	**Coimbra** ▶ d.	*1014*	...	1221	*1453*	...	1624	1824	2014	|	|
2	**Coimbra** B d.	1039	...	1227	1539	...	1630	1828	2017	2039	2332
16	Pampilhosa d.	1050	...	1242	1550	...	1648	1848	...	2050	|
51	Santa Comba Dão d.	1122	...	1317	1622	...	1726	1937	...	2122	0016
83	Nelas d.	1144	...	1342	1644	...	1800	2008	...	2144	|
95	Mangualde d.	1152	...	1351	1652	...	1810	2018	...	2152	0046
171	**Guarda** a.	1251	1305	1501	1751	1805	1921	2128	...	2251	0144
218	Vilar Formoso 🛃 a.	...	1348	...	...	1848	...	...	...	...	0220

	IN 312 S Ⓡ	⚒	*IC* 510	⑦h		*IC** 512	⚒b	⑦z	⚒b	*IC** 514
Vilar Formoso 🛃 d.	0150	...	*0615*r	0917	...	...	...	*1530*	1710	...
Guarda d.	0223	0500	0707	1000	1010	1309	1625	1625	1755	1809
Mangualde d.	0324	0559	0804	...	1118	1408	1733	1733	...	1908
Nelas d.	|	0609	0812	...	1128	1416	1744	1744	...	1916
Santa Comba Dão d.	0355	0636	0834	...	1202	1437	1812	1812	...	1937
Pampilhosa d.	|	0718	0907	...	1242	1510	1851	1851	...	2010
Coimbra B a.	0447	0731	0921	...	1256	1520	1902	1903	...	2020
Coimbra ▶ a.	|	0736	*0946*a	...	1302	*1551*a	1908	*1914*	...	*2041*a
Lisboa Oriente **690** a.	0720	...	1122	...	...	1722	...	2142	...	2222
Lisboa Sta Apolónia **690** a.	0730	...	1130	...	...	1730	...	2150	...	2230

S – SUD EXPRESSO / LUSITANIA – see Tables **45** / **690**.
a – Ⓐ only.
b – ①–⑥ (if ① is a public holiday runs previous day instead).
h – Also public holidays if they fall on ①–④ or ⑥.
r – ⚒ only.
z – If the following day is a public holiday runs ① instead.
▶ – Local trains run Coimbra B - Coimbra and v.v.
* – On ⑤ **513** and **515** are numbered **517** and **519**; on ⑦ **512** and **514** are numbered **516** and **518**.

693 LISBOA - CALDAS DA RAINHA - FIGUEIRA DA FOZ / COIMBRA *Linha do Oeste*

km										
				Ⓐ	◇				⊡	◇
	Lisboa Santa Apolonia .... d.	...	0541	...	...	1150	1350	1630	...	...
0	**Lisboa** Rossio .... ▷ d.	...	|	*0701*	*0831*	|	|	|	*1731*	*1831*
7	Entrecampos .... ▷ d.	...	0555	|	|	1201	1401	1641	|	|
9	Sete Rios .... ▷ d.	...	0558	|	|	1204	1404	1644	|	|
22	Agualva - Cacém .... ⊙ ▷ d.	...	0613	*0727*	*0857*	1221	1421	1700	*1757*	*1857*
26	Mira Sintra - Meleças .... ▷ a.	...	0617	*0730*	*0900*	1226	1426	1704	*1800*	*1900*
26	Mira Sintra - Meleças .... d.	...	0618	0735	0925	1227	1427	1705	1835	1930
72	Torres Vedras .... d.	0619	0715	0835	1023	1326	1525	1813	1936	2030
95	Bombarral .... d.	0644	0741	0859	1047	1354	1547	1836	2001	...
114	**Caldas da Rainha** .... a.	0706	0803	0921	1109	1416	1609	1858	2023	...
	Leiria (below) .... a.	...	0929	...	...	1529	...	2029	...	...

	Ⓐ			Ⓐ			⊖		
Leiria (below) .... d.	...	...	...	...	*1009*	1213	*1509*	...	1813
Caldas da Rainha .... d.	...	0606	0721	0816	1116	1316	1616	1730	1923
Bombarral .... d.	...	0627	0742	0838	1137	1338	1637	1750	1945
Torres Vedras .... d.	0603	0651	0807	0904	1159	1400	1659	1814	2009
Mira Sintra - Meleças .... a.	0705	0753	0915	...	1301	1501	1758	1913	2108
Mira Sintra - Meleças ..... ▷ d.	*0710*	0754	*0930*	...	1302	1502	*1810*	*1930*	2109
Agualva - Cacém .... ⊙ ▷ a.	*0713*	0757	*0933*	...	1306	1506	*1813*	*1933*	2113
Sete Rios .... ▷ a.	|	0813	|	...	1323	1523	|	|	2128
Entrecampos .... ▷ a.	|	0816	|	...	1327	1527	|	|	2132
Lisboa Rossio .... ▷ a.	*0739*	|	*0959*	...	|	|	*1839*	*1959*	|
Lisboa Santa Apolónia ...... a.	...	0830	...	...	1341	1541	...	...	2142

km		*IR* 801			*IR* 803			*IR* 805		
		①–⑥								
	Lisboa S Apolónia (above). d.	...	...	0541	...	...	1150	*1350*	...	1630
0	**Caldas da Rainha** .... d.	0615	...	0830	1115	...	1430	1615	...	1930
13	São Martinho do Porto .... d.	0623	...	0842	1123	...	1442	1623	...	1942
47	Marinha Grande .... d.	0652	...	0920	1152	...	1520	1652	...	2020
57	Leiria .... d.	0700	...	0929	1200	...	1529	1700	...	2029
110	Verride .... d.	0748	0756	...	1248	1249	...	1748	1749	...
104	Bifurcação de Lares ..... ▽ a.	|	0803	...	|	1256	...	|	1756	...
111	**Figueira da Foz** .... a.	|	0815	...	|	1309	...	|	1809	...
118	Alfarelos .... ▽ d.	0756	...	...	1256	...	...	1756	...	...
138	**Coimbra** B .... ▽ a.	0810	...	...	1310	...	...	1810	...	...

			IR 802			*IR* 804			*IR* 806
									Ⓑ
Coimbra B .... ▽ d.	...	...	0851	...	...	1351	...	...	1851
Alfarelos .... ▽ d.	...	...	0905	...	...	1405	...	...	1905
Figueira da Foz .... d.	...	0858	|	...	1358	|	...	1858	|
Bifurcação de Lares ... ▽ d.	...	0911	|	...	1411	|	...	1911	|
Verride .... d.	...	0918	0921	...	1418	1421	...	1918	1921
Leiria .... d.	0713	...	1009	1213	...	1509	1813	...	2009
Marinha Grande .... d.	0723	...	1019	1223	...	1519	1823	...	2019
São Martinho do Porto .... d.	0756	...	1046	1256	...	1546	1856	...	2046
Caldas da Rainha .... a.	0808	...	1055	1308	...	1555	1908	...	2055
Lisboa S Apol. (above) ... a.	...	...	*1341*	1541	...	...	2142	...	...

▷ – For suburban services see Table **699** (including connections from / to Oriente).
▽ – See Table **693a**.
⊙ – Connections to / from Lisboa Rossio every 20 - 30 minutes (see Table **699**).
◇ – On Ⓐ there is a connection 20 minutes later Lisboa Rossio - Mira Sintra-Meleças.
⊡ – On Ⓐ there is a connection 30 minutes later Lisboa Rossio - Mira Sintra-Meleças.
⊖ – On Ⓒ connection Mira Sintra-Meleças - Lisboa Rossio runs 20 minutes later.

693a FIGUEIRA DA FOZ - COIMBRA

km																								
		⚒	⚒	Ⓐ																				
0	**Figueira da Foz** .... d.	0558	0658	0740	...	0858	...	0958	1058	...	1158	1258	...	1358	1458	1558	...	1658	1758	...	1858	1958	...	2158
8	Bifurcação de Lares .... d.	0611	0711	0750	...	0911	...	1011	1111	...	1211	1311	...	1411	1511	1611	...	1711	1811	...	1911	2011	...	2211
20	Verride .... d.	0620	0720	0757	...	0920	...	1020	1120	...	1220	1320	...	1420	1520	1620	...	1720	1820	...	1920	2020	...	2220
28	Alfarelos .... d.	0633	0733	0806	0812	0938	1031	1033	1133	1212	1238	1333	1412	1433	1538	1633	1704	1738	1838	1903	1933	2038	2119	2233
47	**Coimbra** B .... a.	0700	0800	0824	0832	1005	1052	1104	1200	1232	1305	1400	1432	1500	1605	1700	1725	1805	1905	1924	2000	2105	2142	2300
49	**Coimbra** .... a.	0710	0814	0837	0841	1014	1103	1113	1210	1241	1314	1410	1441	1510	1614	1710	1735	1814	1914	1938	2010	2114	2157	2310

		⚒	⚒											Ⓐ			Ⓐ	Ⓑ		Ⓐ			Ⓑ	
Coimbra .... d.	0017	0523	0553	0659	0814	0853	0953	1014	1159	1253	1314	1359	1453	1559	1614	1659	1714	1756	1814	1900	1914	1953	2014	2232
Coimbra B .... d.	0026	0531	0601	0707	0822	0901	1001	1022	1207	1301	1322	1407	1501	1607	1622	1707	1722	1807	1822	1908	1922	2001	2022	2242
Alfarelos .... d.	0055	0606	0636	0736	0844	0938	1036	1044	1236	1336	1344	1436	1536	1636	1644	1736	1744	1836	1844	1932	1944	2036	2044	2311
Verride .... d.	0106	0619	0649	0756	...	0949	1049	...	1249	1349	...	1449	1549	1649	...	1749	...	1849	...	1940	...	2049	...	2323
Bifurcação de Lares .... d.	0114	0626	0656	0803	...	0956	1056	...	1256	1356	...	1456	1556	1656	...	1756	...	1856	...	|	...	2056	...	2330
Figueira da Foz .... a.	0126	0639	0709	0815	...	1009	1109	...	1309	1409	...	1509	1609	1709	...	1809	...	1909	...	1955	...	2109	...	2342

For main line trains calling at Alfarelos see Table **690**. Other trains : Coimbra - Alfarelos Table **699**, Figueira da Foz - Bifurcação de Lares Table **693**.

694 PORTO - RÉGUA - POCINHO

km		*IR* 861	*IR* 863	*IR* 865	*IR* 867	*IR* 869	*IR* 871	*IR* 875			
									Ⓐ		
0	**Porto** São Bento .... d.	...	0910	...	...	1510	...	1925	*1930*	...	*2300*
3	**Porto** Campanhã .... d.	0715	0915	1115	1315	1515	1715	1930	*1935*	2156	*2305*
12	Ermesinde .... d.	0727	0927	1127	1327	1527	1727	1941	*1947*	2205	*2317*
50	Caíde .... d.	0807	1007	1207	1407	1607	1807	2014	2040	2237	0008
59	Livração .... d.	0816	1016	1216	1416	1616	1816	2022	2053	2251	0022
64	Marco de Canaveses .... d.	0824	1024	1224	1424	1624	1824	2030	2101	2259	0029
107	**Régua** .... a.	0908	1108	1309	1508	1709	1908	2115	2200	2354	...
	Pocinho (below) ...... a.	1034	1241	...	1634	*1846*	2033	...	...	...	...

	IR 860	*IR* 864	*IR* 868	*IR* 870	*IR* 872	*IR* 874	*IR* 878	*IR* 960		
					Ⓐ	Ⓒ				
Pocinho (below) ..... d.	...	*0718*	...	1119	1326	...	...	1722	*1908*	...
Régua .... d.	0648	0848	1048	1248	1448	1448	1648	1848	2050	...
Marco de Canaveses .. d.	0735	0935	1135	1335	1535	1535	1735	1935	2150	...
Livração .... d.	0741	0941	1141	1341	1541	1541	1741	1941	2156	...
Caíde .... d.	0754	0954	1154	1354	1554	1554	1754	1954	2214	...
Ermesinde .... d.	0826	1026	1226	1426	1626	1626	1826	2026	*2304*	...
Porto Campanhã ...... a.	0835	1035	1235	1435	1635	1635	1835	2035	*2315*	...
Porto São Bento .... a.	0850	...	...	1450	...	...	1850	...	*2320*	...

km		*IR* 861	*IR* 863			*IR* 867		*IR* 873		*IR* 871	
				△							△
	Porto São Bento ...... d.	...	0910	...	...	...	...	*1510*	...	...	...
	Porto Campanhã ..... d.	0715	0915	...	...	1315	...	*1515*	...	1715	...
0	**Régua** .... d.	0909	1114	...	...	1509	...	1720	...	1909	...
23	Pinhão .... d.	0937	1142	...	...	1537	...	1746	...	1935	...
36	Tua .... a.	0951	1156	1205	...	1551	...	1801	...	1950	1955
90	Mirandela .... a.	|	|	1335	...	|	...	|	...	|	2115
68	**Pocinho** .... a.	1034	1241	...	...	1634	...	1846	...	2033	...

	IR 862		*IR* 870		*IR* 872	*IR* 876	*IR* 960			
		△			Ⓐ	Ⓒ			△	
Pocinho .... d.	0718	...	1119	...	1326	1508	1722	...	...	1908
Mirandela .... d.	|	0955	|	...	|	|	|	...	1800	|
Tua .... d.	0759	1142	1202	...	1407	1553	1804	...	1943	1951
Pinhão .... d.	0814	...	1217	...	1422	1608	1819	...	...	2006
Régua .... a.	0840	...	1243	...	1447	1635	1845	...	...	2032
Porto Campanhã ... a.	*1035*	...	1435	...	1635	*1835*	2035	...	...	...
Porto São Bento .... a.	...	...	1450	...	...	*1850*	...	...	...	...

△ – By Taxi Tua - Mirandela and v.v. (Auto Tuela ✆ 917 534 718). *Subject to confirmation.*

🚂 steam-hauled tourist train Regua - Tua and v.v. : ⑥ June 4 - Oct. 22, 2016 (also ⑦ July 3 - Sept. 25 and ③ Aug. 3 - 31, also Aug. 15). Régua d. 1521 → Tua a. 1640 / d. 1724 → Régua a. 1839.

695 PORTO - BRAGA

km					*AP* 131				*IC* 721					*AP* 133				*AP* 135					*AP* 137		*IC* 723	
																	Ⓐ	Ⓑ h						Ⓐ		
	Lisboa Sta Ap. **690**. d.	...	...	...	0700	...	...	...	0930	...	...	...	...	1400	...	...	...	1600	...	...	...	...	1900	...	2000	...
0	**Porto** São Bento ... △ d.	0645	0745	0845	|	0945	1045	1145	|	1245	1345	1445	1545	|	1645	1745	1815	|	1845	1915	1945	2045	|	2145	|	2245
3	**Porto** Campanhã ... △ d.	0650	0750	0850	0946	0950	1050	1150	1246	1250	1350	1450	1550	1646	1650	1750	1820	1846	1850	1920	1950	2050	2146	2150	2246	2250
12	Ermesinde .... △ d.	0702	0802	0902	|	1002	1102	1202	|	1302	1402	1502	1602	|	1702	1802	1832	|	1902	1932	2002	2102	|	2202	|	2302
26	Trofa .... △ d.	0716	0816	0916	|	1016	1116	1216	|	1316	1416	1516	1616	|	1716	1816	1844	|	1916	1944	2016	2116	|	2216	|	2316
35	Famalicão .... △ d.	0727	0827	0927	1009	1027	1127	1227	1309	1327	1427	1527	1627	1709	1727	1827	1852	1909	1927	1952	2027	2127	2209	2227	2309	2327
42	Nine .... △ d.	0735	0835	0935	1015	1035	1135	1235	1315	1335	1435	1535	1635	1715	1735	1835	1857	1915	1935	1957	2035	2135	2215	2235	2315	2335
57	**Braga** .... △ a.	0756	0856	0956	1025	1056	1156	1256	1325	1356	1456	1556	1656	1725	1756	1856	1909	1925	1956	2009	2056	2156	2225	2256	2325	2356

		AP 130							*IC* 720				*AP* 132		*IC* 722						*AP* 134				*AP* 136	
	⚒			Ⓐ	Ⓒ														Ⓐ			Ⓐ			Ⓑ h	
Braga .... ▽ d.	0534	0607	0634	0721	0734	0804	0834	0934	1005	1039	1134	1234	1307	1334	1405	1434	1534	1634	1721	1734	1807	1821	1834	1934	2007	2034
Nine .... ▽ d.	0554	0618	0654	0733	0754	0824	0854	0954	1016	1059	1154	1254	1318	1354	1416	1454	1554	1654	1733	1754	1818	1833	1854	1954	2018	2054
Famalicão .... ▽ d.	0602	0623	0702	0738	0802	0832	0902	1002	1021	1107	1202	1302	1323	1402	1421	1502	1602	1702	1738	1802	1823	1838	1902	2002	2023	2102
Trofa .... ▽ d.	0613	|	0713	0746	0813	0843	0913	1013	|	1118	1213	1313	|	1413	|	1513	1613	1713	1746	1813	|	1846	1913	2013	|	2113
Ermesinde .... ▽ d.	0629	|	0729	0759	0829	0859	0929	1029	|	1134	1229	1329	|	1429	|	1529	1629	1729	1759	1829	|	1859	1929	2029	|	2129
Porto Campanhã ... ▽ a.	0641	0647	0741	0811	0841	0911	0941	1041	1052	1146	1241	1341	1347	1441	1752	1541	1641	1741	1811	1841	1847	1911	1941	2041	2047	2141
Porto São Bento ... ▽ a.	0645	|	0745	0815	0845	0915	0945	1045	|	1150	1245	1345	|	1445	|	1545	1645	1745	1815	1845	|	1915	1945	2045	|	2145
Lisboa Sta Ap. **690**. a.	...	0930	...	...	...	...	...	...	1400	...	...	...	1630	...	1800	...	...	...	...	...	2130	...	...	...	2330	...

d – Journey 55 minutes.
h – Not ⑦ if ① is a public holiday. Not ⑤ if it is a public holiday.
△ – Additional journeys : 0115, 0615Ⓐ**d**, 0715Ⓐ, 0815Ⓐ**d**, 1215Ⓐ**d**, 1615Ⓐ**d**, 1715Ⓐ**d**. For other trains Porto - Nine see Table **696**.
▽ – Additional journeys : 0434, 0621Ⓐ**d**, 0745Ⓐ, 1321Ⓐ**d**, 2134Ⓒ, 2234Ⓐ, 2332. For other trains Nine - Porto see Table **696**.

338 *Reservations are compulsory for travel by AP and IC trains (also Sud Expresso and Lusitania)* 12

PORTO - GUIMARÃES 695a

60 km

	AP141											IC621
					Ⓐ					Ⓐ		
Lisboa Sta Ap. **690** d.	...	...	...	0800	...	...	...	...	...	...	...	1730
Porto São Bento ▷ d.	0720	0820	1020	|	1120	1220	1420	1620	1820	1855	2020	|
Porto Campanhã ▷ d.	0725	0825	1025	1100	1125	1225	1425	1625	1825	1900	2025	2041
Ermesinde ▷ d.	0737	0837	1037	|	1137	1237	1437	1637	1837	1910	2037	|
Trofa ▷ d.	0752	0852	1052	1121	1152	1252	1452	1652	1852	1921	2052	2100
Guimarães a.	0836	0936	1133	1153	1236	1336	1533	1736	1937	1954	2133	2138

		IC620						AP140				
	Ⓐ								Ⓐ	Ⓐ	Ⓐ	
Guimarães d.	0706	0743	0848	0948	1159	1348	1548	1655	1712	1812	2012	2148
Trofa ▷ d.	0739	0824	0933	1033	1243	1433	1633	1727	1801	1901	2104	2233
Ermesinde ▷ d.	0751	|	0949	1049	1259	1449	1649	|	1819	1919	2119	2249
Porto Campanhã ▷ a.	0801	0852	1001	1101	1311	1501	1701	1744	1831	1931	2131	2301
Porto São Bento ▷ a.	0805	|	1005	1105	1315	1505	1705	|	1835	1935	2135	2305
Lisboa Sta Ap. **690** a.	...	1200	...	...	...	...	...	2040	...	...	...	...

ALSO: **Porto - Guimarães** 0620Ⓐ, 1720Ⓐ, 1920Ⓐ; 2120Ⓒ, 2220Ⓐ, 2320; **Guimarães - Porto** 0548Ⓐ, 0648Ⓒ, 0748Ⓐ, 1248Ⓐ, 1748Ⓒ, 1916Ⓐ, 1948Ⓒ, 2248. ▷ – See also **695**, **696**.

PORTO - VIANA DO CASTELO - VALENÇA - VIGO 696

km		IR851				421*						IR853				IR855			IR857		423*	IR859		
		Ⓐ	Ⓐ		⚒	2 [R]			Ⓐ					Ⓐ							2 [R]	Ⓐ		
0	**Porto** Campanhã ▷ d.	0610	0620	...	*0650*	0815	...	...	0820	...	*0950*	1300	1250	...	*1350*	1615	*1650*	...	1815	*1850*	1910	2015	2210	...
12	Ermesinde ▷ d.	0619	0632	...	*0702*	|	...	...	0832	...	*1002*	1311	1302	...	*1402*	1627	*1702*	...	1827	*1902*	|	2026	2221	...
23	Trofa ▷ d.	0630	0644	...	*0716*	|	...	...	0844	...	*1016*	1323	1316	...	*1416*	1638	*1716*	...	1838	*1916*	|	2038	2232	...
32	Famalicão ▷ d.	0638	0652	...	*0727*	|	...	...	0852	...	*1027*	1332	1327	...	*1427*	1646	*1727*	...	1846	*1927*	|	2047	2241	...
39	**Nine** ▷ a.	0644	0656	...	*0735*	0842	...	...	0857	...	*1035*	1339	1335	...	*1435*	1652	*1735*	...	1852	*1935*	1939	2054	2247	...
39	**Nine** d.	0644	...	0701	0747	0843	...	...	...	0905	1104	1340	...	1358	1500	1655	1737	...	1853	2001	1939	2056	2248	...
51	Barcelos d.	0654	...	0716	0804	|	...	...	...	0918	1117	1350	...	1411	1513	1705	1750	...	1903	2014	|	2106	2302	...
82	**Viana do Castelo** a.	0734	...	0802	0851	0922	...	...	...	1004	1202	1423	...	1456	1600	1738	1834	...	1936	2104	2014	2140	2345	...
82	**Viana do Castelo** d.	0736	...	0820	...	0923	...	...	...	1012	...	1425	...	...	1615	1739	1839	...	1937	...	2016	2141	...	...
116	Vila Nova de Cerveira d.	0804	...	0908	...	|	...	...	...	1055	...	1457	...	...	1657	1807	1921	...	2009	...	|	2209	...	...
130	**Valença** 🏛 PT d.	0816	...	0924	...	0957	1000	...	...	1110	...	1508	...	...	1712	1819	1936	1944	2020	...	2050	2220	...	...
134	Tui 🏛 ES d.	...	...	...	...	|	1107	...	...	...	...	...	...	...	...	...	...	2051	...	...	|	...	...	...
162	Redondela **680** d.	...	...	...	...	|	1139	...	...	...	...	...	...	...	...	...	...	2124	...	...	|	...	...	...
174	**Vigo** Guixar ◐ **680** a.	...	...	...	...	1135	1150	...	...	...	...	...	...	...	...	...	...	2135	...	...	2234	...	...	...

					IR850	420*					IR852				IR854					IR856	422*			
		Ⓐ	Ⓐ	Ⓐ		2 [R]							Ⓐ				Ⓐ				2 [R]			
Vigo Guixar ◐ **680** d.	...	...	...	...	...	0858	...	...	...	0920	...	...	...	...	...	...	...	...	...	...	1956	1812	...	...
Redondela **680** d.	...	...	...	...	...	|	...	...	...	0931	...	...	...	...	...	...	...	...	...	...	|	1824	...	...
Tui 🏛 ES d.	...	...	...	...	...	|	...	...	...	1003	...	...	...	...	...	...	...	...	...	...	|	1858	...	...
Valença 🏛 PT d.	...	...	0535	0617	0736	0836	...	...	...	0911	0911	1116	...	...	1425	1517	...	...	...	1752	1937	1806	1834	...
Vila Nova de Cerveira d.	...	...	0548	0632	0747	|	...	...	...	...	0926	1131	...	...	1435	1532	...	...	...	1806	|	...	1849	...
Viana do Castelo a.	...	...	0625	0715	0814	0908	...	...	...	...	1006	1214	...	...	1505	1614	...	...	...	1838	2011	...	1934	...
Viana do Castelo d.	0511	...	0627	0718	0816	0909	...	0944	...	...	1010	1215	1349	...	1508	1620	...	...	1748	1840	2014	...	...	2022
Barcelos d.	0553	...	0717	0803	0853	|	...	1027	...	...	1043	1258	1436	...	1538	1706	...	...	1835	1922	|	...	...	2105
Nine a.	0608	...	0732	0819	0904	0949	...	1042	...	...	1053	1313	1452	...	1548	1721	...	...	1850	1933	2049	...	...	2120
Nine ▷ d.	...	0633	0735	*0824*	0905	0950	...	...	1059	...	1054	*1354*	...	1454	1549	...	1733	...	*1854*	1935	2050	...	...	2120
Famalicão ▷ d.	...	0638	0743	*0832*	0913	|	...	...	1107	...	1102	*1402*	...	1502	1557	...	1738	...	*1902*	1942	|	...	...	2128
Trofa ▷ d.	...	0646	0751	*0843*	0921	|	...	...	1118	...	1109	*1413*	...	1513	1605	...	1746	...	*1913*	1949	|	...	...	2135
Ermesinde ▷ d.	...	0659	0807	*0859*	0935	|	...	...	1134	...	1121	*1429*	...	1529	1619	...	1759	...	*1929*	2001	|	...	...	2147
Porto Campanhã ▷ a.	...	0710	0819	*0910*	0945	1018	...	...	1145	...	1130	*1440*	...	1540	1630	...	1810	...	*1940*	2010	2118	...	...	2156

◐ – New terminus (1 km from Vigo Urzaiz).
▷ – See also Table **695**.
* – Trains **420 - 423** are branded *Celta*.
ES – Spain (Central European Time).
PT – Portugal (West European Time).

LISBOA - PINHAL NOVO - TUNES - FARO 697

km		AP 180	IC 21180	IC 570		IC 572		IC 574	AP 186	IC 576
			⑥S							⑤R
	Porto Campanhã **690** d.	0547	...	...	...	...	...	...	1547	...
	Coimbra B **690** d.	0646	...	...	...	...	...	...	1646	...
0	**Lisboa** Oriente ⊙ d.	0823	0830	1002	...	1402	...	1732	1823	1932
7	Entrecampos ⊙ d.	0831	0840	1010	...	1410	...	1740	1831	1940
9	Sete Rios ⊙ d.	|	|	1014	...	1414	...	1744	|	1944
18	Pragal ⊙ d.	|	|	1026	...	1426	...	1756	|	1956
47	Pinhal Novo ⊙ d.	0906	0917	1048	...	1448	...	1818	1906	2018
118	Grândola d.	|	|	1119	...	1516	...	1846	|	2103
180	Funcheira d.	|	|	1155	...	1552	...	1929	|	2138
264	**Tunes** ▷ d.	1054	1122	1302	...	1704	...	2034	2055	2245
269	Albufeira ▷ d.	1101	1129	1307	...	1710	...	2039	2102	2250
286	Loulé ▷ d.	1113	1141	1319	...	1722	...	2051	2114	2302
302	**Faro** ▷ a.	1123	1150	1330	...	1732	...	2102	2123	2312

	AP 182	IC 670		IC 672	AP 184	IC 21184		IC 674	IC 676
						⑥S			⑦R
Faro ▷ d.	0700	0824	...	1354	1505	1515	...	1756	1850
Loulé ▷ d.	0710	0835	...	1405	1516	1526	...	1806	1900
Albufeira ▷ d.	0723	0847	...	1417	1529	1544	...	1818	1912
Tunes ▷ d.	0729	0853	...	1423	1535	1550	...	1825	1918
Funcheira d.	0823	1000	...	1526	|	|	...	1929	2035
Grândola d.	0854	1037	...	1604	|	|	...	2008	2111
Pinhal Novo ⊙ d.	0923	1107	...	1637	1723	1745	...	2040	2154
Pragal ⊙ a.	|	1130	...	1704	|	|	...	2104	2214
Sete Rios ⊙ a.	|	1143	...	1714	|	|	...	2114	2224
Entrecampos ⊙ a.	0957	1146	...	1717	1757	1817	...	2117	2227
Lisboa Oriente ⊙ a.	1005	1156	...	1726	1805	1825	...	2126	2236
Coimbra B **690** a.	1145	...	...	...	1945	...	...	...	...
Porto Campanhã **690** a.	1244	...	...	...	2044	...	...	...	...

LOCAL TRAINS LAGOS - TUNES - FARO

km			⚒		Ⓐ					Ⓐ	⑦R	
0	**Lagos** d.	0616	0659	0748	0903	1114	1310	1418	1705	1813	1813	2001
18	Portimão d.	0634	0718	0807	0922	1133	1329	1437	1724	1832	1832	2020
29	Silves d.	0650	0734	0824	...	1150	1350	1454	1745	1849	1849	2037
42	Algoz d.	0705	0749	0840	...	1206	1409	1510	1801	1912	1907	2054
46	**Tunes** ▷ d.	0711	0755	0853	...	1212	1423	1516	1807	1918	1913	2107
52	Albufeira ▷ d.	0722	0801	0859	...	1218	1429	1528	1818	1925	...	2114
69	Loulé ▷ d.	0743	0816	0919	...	1239	1444	1543	1834	1941	...	2130
85	**Faro** ▷ a.	0759	0837	0934	...	1254	1459	1559	1849	1956	...	2145

	⚒	Ⓐ				Ⓐ					
Faro ▷ d.	0711	...	0902	1023	1222	...	1619	1715	1812	1938	2018
Loulé ▷ d.	0728	...	0919	1039	1239	...	1636	1737	1834	2002	2035
Albufeira ▷ d.	0743	...	0935	1100	1307	...	1652	1755	1850	2021	2101
Tunes ▷ d.	0755	...	0942	1106	1313	...	1706	1807	1857	2035	2107
Algoz d.	0801	...	0947	1112	1319	...	1712	1812	1902	2040	2112
Silves d.	0824	...	1003	1130	1335	...	1729	1830	1918	2058	2128
Portimão d.	0837	0931	1018	1150	1350	1545	1745	1849	1932	2111	2143
Lagos a.	0856	0950	1036	1208	1408	1604	1803	1907	1951	2128	2201

R – July 1 - Sept. 4.
S – ⑥ July 16 - Aug. 27.
▷ – Also see other section of table above or below.
⊙ – See Table **698** for other fast trains, Table **699** for local services, including connections Barreiro - Pinhal Novo.

FARO - VILA REAL DE SANTO ANTÓNIO 697a

km									Ⓐ			
0	**Faro** d.	0744	0955	1134	1355	1500	1624	1751	1828	1927	2106	2151
10	Olhão d.	0759	1006	1145	1406	1511	1635	1802	1840	1938	2118	2203
32	Tavira d.	0824	1031	1210	1436	1536	1705	1832	1905	2008	2143	2228
56	**Vila Real** § a.	0852	1100	1238	1505	1605	1733	1900	1938	2036	2212	2257

								Ⓐ		⊡	
Vila Real § d.	0548	0705	0722	0908	1113	1239	1333	1533	1635	1803	2042
Tavira d.	0613	0734	0751	0938	1139	1308	1407	1607	1705	1832	2110
Olhão d.	0634	0759	0821	1006	1206	1332	1432	1635	1729	1901	2139
Faro a.	0644	0810	0831	1017	1217	1343	1443	1646	1739	1912	2150

ALSO: Faro - Villa Real at 0857Ⓐ, 1255Ⓐ; Villa Real - Faro at 0626Ⓐ, 1910Ⓐ.

⊡ – On ⑦ July 3 - Sept. 4 departs 1740 (Faro arrive 1845).
§ – Vila Real de Santo António (± *1500m* from bus station/ferry terminal).

LISBOA - PINHAL NOVO - ÉVORA and BEJA 698

km		IC 590	IC 581	IC 592	IC 583	IC 594	IC 585	IC 596	IC 587	IC 598	IC 589
		Ⓐ	Ⓐ	Ⓐ	Ⓐ	Ⓒ	Ⓒ				
0	**Lisboa** Oriente ▷ d.	0702	...	0902	...	0952	...	1702	...	1902	...
7	Entrecampos ▷ d.	0710	...	0910	...	1000	...	1710	...	1910	...
9	Sete Rios ▷ d.	0714	...	0914	...	1004	...	1714	...	1914	...
18	Pragal ▷ d.	0726	...	0926	...	1015	...	1726	...	1926	...
47	**Pinhal Novo** ▷ d.	0748	...	0948	...	1032	...	1748	...	1948	...
88	Vendas Novas d.	0818	...	1010	...	1102	...	1810	...	2010	...
122	Casa Branca a.	0831	...	1023	...	1115	...	1823	...	2023	...
122	Casa Branca d.	0832	0835	1024	1030	1116	1119	1824	1829	2024	2025
148	Évora a.	0842	|	1035	|	1126	|	1835	|	2035	|
185	**Beja** a.	...	0926	...	1121	...	1210	...	1920	...	2115

	IC 580	IC 690		IC 582	IC 692		IC 584	IC 694		IC 586	IC 696
	Ⓐ	Ⓐ									
Beja d.	0623	...	...	0822	...	...	1611	...	...	1815	...
Évora d.	|	0706	...	|	0906	...	|	1657	...	|	1906
Casa Branca a.	0711	0716	...	0914	0916	...	1700	1707	...	1908	1916
Casa Branca d.	...	0717	...	...	0917	...	...	1708	...	...	1917
Vendas Novas d.	...	0731	...	...	0931	...	...	1722	...	...	1931
Pinhal Novo ▷ d.	...	0753	...	...	0953	...	...	1751	...	...	1953
Pragal ▷ a.	...	0814	...	...	1014	...	...	1814	...	...	2014
Sete Rios ▷ a.	...	0824	...	...	1024	...	...	1824	...	...	2024
Entrecampos ▷ a.	...	0828	...	...	1028	...	...	1828	...	...	2028
Lisboa Oriente ▷ a.	...	0836	...	...	1036	...	...	1836	...	...	2036

▷ – See Table **697** for other fast trains and Table **699** for local services, including connections Barreiro - Pinhal Novo.

12 *Reservations are compulsory for travel by AP and IC trains (also Sud Expresso and Lusitania)* 339

699 OTHER LOCAL SERVICES

LISBOA - ESTORIL - CASCAIS

km																									
0	**Lisboa** Cais do Sodre d.	Ⓐ	0530	every	0700	every	1000	every	1700	every	2012	every	2132	2200	every	0130	Ⓒ	0530	every	0800	every	1900	every	0130
24	Estoril d.		0606	30	0729	12	1036	20	1729	12	2048	20	2208	2236	30	0206		0606	30	0836	20	1936	30	0206
26	**Cascais** a.		0610	mins	0733	mins	1040	mins	1733	mins	2052	mins	2212	2240	mins	0210		0610	mins	0840	mins	1940	mins	0210

Cascais d.	Ⓐ	0530	0600	0630	0652	every	2104	2130	every	0130	...	Ⓒ	0530	every	0630	0704	every	1904	every	2104	2130	every	0130
Estoril d.		0534	0604	0634	0656	12-20 ◧	2108	2134	30	0134	...		0534	30	0634	0708	20	1908	30	2108	2134	30	0134
Lisboa Cais do Sodre a.		0610	0640	0710	0725	mins	2144	2210	mins	0210	...		0610	mins	0710	0744	mins	1944	mins	2144	2210	mins	0210

◧ – Every 12 minutes 0704 - 1004 and 1704 - 2004; every 20 minutes 1004 - 1704.

LISBOA ORIENTE - SINTRA

		Ⓐ		Ⓐ		Ⓒ		Ⓒ
Lisboa Oriente d.	Ⓐ	0558		0108	Ⓒ	0608		0108
Roma Areeiro d.		0605	See	0115		0615	every	0115
Entrecampos d.		0607	note	0117		0617	30	0117
Sete Rios d.		0610	△	0120		0620	mins	0120
Monte Abraão d.		0625		0135		0635	until	0135
Agualva - Cacém d.		0631		0141		0641		0141
Sintra a.		0645		0155		0655		0155

		Ⓐ		Ⓐ		Ⓒ		Ⓒ
Sintra d.	Ⓐ	0506		0006	Ⓒ	0506		0006
Agualva - Cacém d.		0519	See	0019		0519	every	0019
Monte Abraão d.		0524	note	0024		0524	30	0024
Sete Rios d.		0539	▽	0039		0539	mins	0039
Entrecampos d.		0542		0042		0542	until	0042
Roma Areeiro d.		0544		0044		0544		0044
Lisboa Oriente a.		0552		0052		0552		0052

△ – 0558, 0618, every 10 mins 0638 - 0938, every 20 mins 0958 - 1638, every 10 mins 1648 - 1958, 2018, every 30 mins 2038 - 0108.

▽ – 0506, 0536, 0606, every 10 mins 0626 - 0936, every 20 mins 0956 - 1556, every 10 mins 1616 - 1936, 1956, 2016, every 30 mins 2036 - 0006.

LISBOA ROSSIO - SINTRA and MIRA SINTRA-MELEÇAS

	Ⓒ	Ⓐ			n		n
Lisboa Rossio d.	0601	0641		0101	0621	and	2021
Monte Abraão d.	0621	0701	See	0121	0641	hourly	2041
Agualva - Cacém d.	0627	0707	note	0127	0647	until	2047
Mira Sintra - Meleças a.	|	|	△	|	0650	⊡	2050
Sintra a.	0641	0721		0141	...		...

Sintra d.	0520		0020	...		...	...
Mira Sintra - Meleças d.	|	See	|	0730	and	2030	...
Agualva - Cacém d.	0533	note	0033	0733	hourly	2033	...
Monte Abraão d.	0539	▽	0039	0739	until	2039	...
Lisboa Rossio a.	0559		0059	0759	⊡	2059	...

n – On Ⓒ runs 10 minutes later.

△ – Ⓐ: every 30 mins 0641 - 2011 (◧) and 2031 - 0101.
Ⓒ: hourly 0601 - 2001, every 30 mins 2101 - 0101.

▽ – Ⓐ: every 30 mins 0520 - 0620, 0640 - 2010 (◐), 2050 - 0020.
Ⓒ: 0520, hourly 0550 - 2050, every 30 mins 2120 - 0020.

⊡ – Additional services operate during peak hours on Ⓐ.

◧ – Between 0941Ⓐ and 1641Ⓐ runs at xx41, xx01.

◐ – Between 0940Ⓐ and 1640Ⓐ runs at xx40, xx00.

LISBOA - PINHAL NOVO - SETÚBAL

Operator: Fertagus. CP tickets not valid.

								Ⓒ			
Roma Areeiro d.	Ⓐ	0043	0543		2243	2358	Ⓒ	0643		2343
Entrecampos d.		0045	0545	and	2245	0000		0645	and	2345
Sete Rios d.		0049	0549	every	2249	0004		0649	every	2349
Pragal d.		0100	0600	hour	2300	0015		0700	hour	0000
Pinhal Novo d.		0128	0628	until	2328	0043		0728	until	0028
Setúbal a.		0141	0641		2341	0056		0741		0041

Setúbal d.	Ⓐ	0548	0658		1858	1928	2018		0018	Ⓒ	0558		2258
Pinhal Novo d.		0602	0712	and	1912	1942	2032	and	0032		0612	and	2312
Pragal d.		0629	0739	every	1939	2009	2059	every	0059		0639	every	2339
Sete Rios d.		0640	0750	hour	1950	2020	2110	hour	0110		0650	hour	2350
Entrecampos d.		0644	0754	until	1954	2024	2114	until	0114		0654	until	2354
Roma Areeiro a.		0646	0756		1956	2026	2116		0116		0656		2356

Additional journeys on Ⓐ: from Roma Areeiro 1813, 1913, 2013, from Setúbal 0628, 0728, 0828. Trains run every 10 – 20 minutes (every 30 mins evenings and Ⓒ) Roma Areeiro - Pragal - Coina.

Catamaran LISBOA - BARREIRO

Transtejo — *Certain Ⓐ peak journeys do not run in July / August*

From Lisboa Terreiro do Paço: By ⛴ journey time 20 - 25 minutes. *10* km

Ⓐ: 0545, 0610, 0640, 0700 and every 10 minutes until 0920, 0940, 0955 and every 30 minutes until 1555, 1615, 1630, 1650 and every 10 minutes 2010, 2030, 2050, 2110, 2125, 2155, 2225, 2255, 2330, 0000, 0100, 0200.

Ⓒ: 0545, 0615, 0645, 0715, 0755, 0825⑥, 0855, 0925⑥, 0955, 1025⑥, 1055, 1155, 1255, 1355, 1455, 1525, 1625, 1655, 1725, 1755, 1825, 1855, 1925, 1955, 2055, 2125, 2155, 2225, 0000, 0100, 0200.

From Barreiro Barcos: By ⛴ journey time 20 - 25 minutes. *10* km

Ⓐ: 0515, 0545, 0615, 0635 and every 10 minutes until 0855, 0900, 0910, 0925, 0940, 0955 and every 30 minutes until 1525, 1545, 1600, 1620 and every 10 minutes until 1940, 2005, 2020, 2040, 2100, 2125, 2155, 2225, 2300, 2330, 0030, 0130.

Ⓒ: 0515, 0545, 0620, 0650, 0725, 0755⑥, 0825, 0855⑥, 0925, 0955⑥, 1025, 1125, 1225, 1325, 1425, 1455, 1525, 1555, 1625, 1655, 1725, 1755, 1825, 1855, 1925, 2025, 2055, 2125, 2225, 2330, 0030, 0130.

BARREIRO - SETÚBAL

km		Ⓐ						
0	**Barreiro** d.	0555	0625	every 30 mins	2125	2232	2325	0029
15	Pinhal Novo d.	0614	0644	(hourly on Ⓒ)	2144	2251	2344	0048
28	**Setúbal** a.	0626	0656	until	2156	2303	2356	0100

	Ⓐ	Ⓒ	Ⓐ				Ⓐ			
Setúbal d.	0508	0548	0618	0648	every 30 mins	2048	2122	2151	2248	2348
Pinhal Novo d.	0520	0600	0630	0700	(hourly on Ⓒ)	2100	2136	2202	2300	0000
Barreiro a.	0538	0618	0648	0718	until	2118	2154	2220	2318	0018

Most journeys continue to / from Praias do Sado A (8 minutes from Setúbal).

LISBOA - ENTRONCAMENTO - TOMAR

km			Ⓐ	⚒		Ⓐ		Ⓐ	Ⓐ		Ⓐ		Ⓐ			Ⓐ§		Ⓐ§				Ⓐ		
0	**Lisboa** Santa Apolónia ▷ d.	0015	0545	0645	0745	0845	0945	1045	1145	1245	1345	1445	1545	1615	1645	1715	1745	1815	1845	1945	2045	2145	2245	...
7	**Lisboa** Oriente ▷ d.	0025	0553	0653	0753	0853	0953	1053	1153	1253	1353	1453	1553	1623	1653	1723	1753	1823	1853	1953	2053	2153	2253	...
31	Vila Franca de Xira d.	0051	0611	0711	0811	0911	1011	1111	1211	1311	1411	1511	1611	1639	1711	1739	1811	1838	1911	2011	2111	2211	2311	...
75	Santarém d.	0135	0655	0755	0855	0949	1055	1148	1255	1348	1455	1549	1655	1706	1756	1806	1855	1907	1955	2055	2149	2259	2348	...
107	Entroncamento a.	0159	0719	0819	0919	1013	1119	1212	1319	1412	1519	1614	1719	1726	1820	1826	1919	1927	2019	2119	2214	2323	0012	...
130	**Tomar** a.	...	0751	0847	0947	...	1151	1247	...	1440	1551	1651	1751	...	1853	1900	1951	2000	2051	2147	2251	2351	0040	...

	①–⑥	Ⓐ	Ⓐ§		Ⓐ§		①–⑥		Ⓐ			Ⓐ		Ⓐ					Ⓐ	⑦d		Ⓐ	⑦d	
Tomar d.	...	0515	0605	0615r	0650	0711r	...	0802	...	1011	1111r	...	1315	...	1511	1611	1711	1811	1911	...	2011	...	...	2211
Entroncamento d.	0410	0542	0626	0642	0711	0742	0808	0838	0942	1038	1142	1238	1342	1438	1542	1638	1742	1841	1944	2037	2042	2145	2226	2241
Santarém d.	0440	0606	0645	0706	0731	0806	0827	0902	1006	1102	1206	1302	1406	1502	1606	1702	1806	1906	2008	2057	2106	2205	2245	2305
Vila Franca de Xira d.	0524	0647	0717	0747	0802	0847	0856	0947	1047	1147	1247	1347	1447	1547	1647	1747	1847	1955	2047	2126	2147	2247	2326	2344
Lisboa Oriente ▷ d.	0550	0705	0733	0805	0818	0905	0911	1005	1105	1205	1305	1405	1505	1605	1705	1805	1905	2012	2105	2142	2205	2305	2342	0002
Lisboa Santa Apolónia ▷ a.	0559	0713	0741	0813	0828	0913	0920	1013	1113	1213	1313	1413	1513	1613	1713	1813	1913	2020	2113	2150	2213	2313	2350	0010

▷ – Additional local trains are available.

d – If ⑦ is a public holiday runs next day instead.

r – ⚒ only.

§ – *IR* train.

ENTRONCAMENTO - COIMBRA

km		†	Ⓐ		Ⓐ						Ⓐ		Ⓑ
0	**Entroncamento** d.	...	0555	0655	0755	0905	1055	1255	1547	1740	1855	1955	2136
24	Fátima ⊙ d.	...	0616	0716	0816	0926	1116	1316	1608	1807	1916	2016	2157
64	Pombal d.	...	0648	0748	0848	0958	1148	1348	1640	1839	1948	2048	2229
91	Alfarelos d.	0710	0712	0812	0919	1031	1212	1412	1704	1903	2012	2119	2252
111	**Coimbra B** a.	0732	0732	0832	0941	1052	1232	1432	1725	1924	2032	2142	2314
111	**Coimbra B** d.	0737	0737	0837	0949	1059	1237	1437	1731	1935	2038	2153	...
113	**Coimbra** a.	0741	0741	0841	0953	1103	1241	1441	1735	1938	2041	2157	...

	⚒	Ⓐ					Ⓐ			Ⓑ
Coimbra d.	0604	0714	0814	1014	1314	1614	1714	1814	1914	2014
Coimbra B a.	0607	0717	0817	1017	1317	1617	1717	1817	1917	2017
Coimbra B d.	0612	0722	0822	1022	1322	1622	1722	1822	1922	2022
Alfarelos d.	0635	0745	0845	1045	1345	1645	1745	1845	1945	2045
Pombal d.	0710	0818	0918	1118	1410	1718	1818	1918	2018	2110
Fátima ⊙ d.	0744	0901	0950	1150	1450	1750	1901	2001	2050	2150
Entroncamento a.	0804	0921	1011	1211	1511	1811	1921	2021	2111	2211

r – Ⓐ only.

⊙ – Station is *20 km* from Fátima (full name of station is Chão de Maçãs - Fátima).

*For fast trains Entroncamento - Coimbra B see Table **690**.*

AVEIRO - COIMBRA

km					Ⓐ		Ⓐ		Ⓐ				
0	**Aveiro** d.	0650	0750	0950	1050	1134	1224	1350	1450	1534	1750	1950	2150
41	Pampilhosa d.	0726	0826	1026	1126	1210	1300	1426	1526	1610	1826	2026	2226
55	**Coimbra B** a.	0740	0840	1040	1140	1224	1314	1440	1540	1626	1840	2040	2240
57	**Coimbra** a.	0753	0846	1046	1151	1231	1324	1446	1551	1633	1852	2052	2246

		⚒								
Coimbra d.	0630	0743	0846	1053	1343	1449	1643	1829	1943	2208
Coimbra B d.	0634	0748	0850	1058	1348	1454	1648	1833	1949	2213
Pampilhosa d.	0652	0804	0908	1115	1405	1512	1704	1856	2012	2230
Aveiro a.	0729	0841	0943	1152	1442	1548	1741	1935	2048	2307

Additional trains: **Aveiro - Coimbra**: 0550⚒, 0734Ⓐ, 0850Ⓐ, 1648Ⓐ, 1850Ⓐ, 2050Ⓐ. **Coimbra - Aveiro**: 0538Ⓐ, 1005Ⓐ, 1143Ⓐ, 1243Ⓐ, 1542Ⓐ, 1743Ⓐ, 2043Ⓐ.

340 *Reservations are compulsory for travel by AP and IC trains (also Sud Expresso and Lusitania)* 12

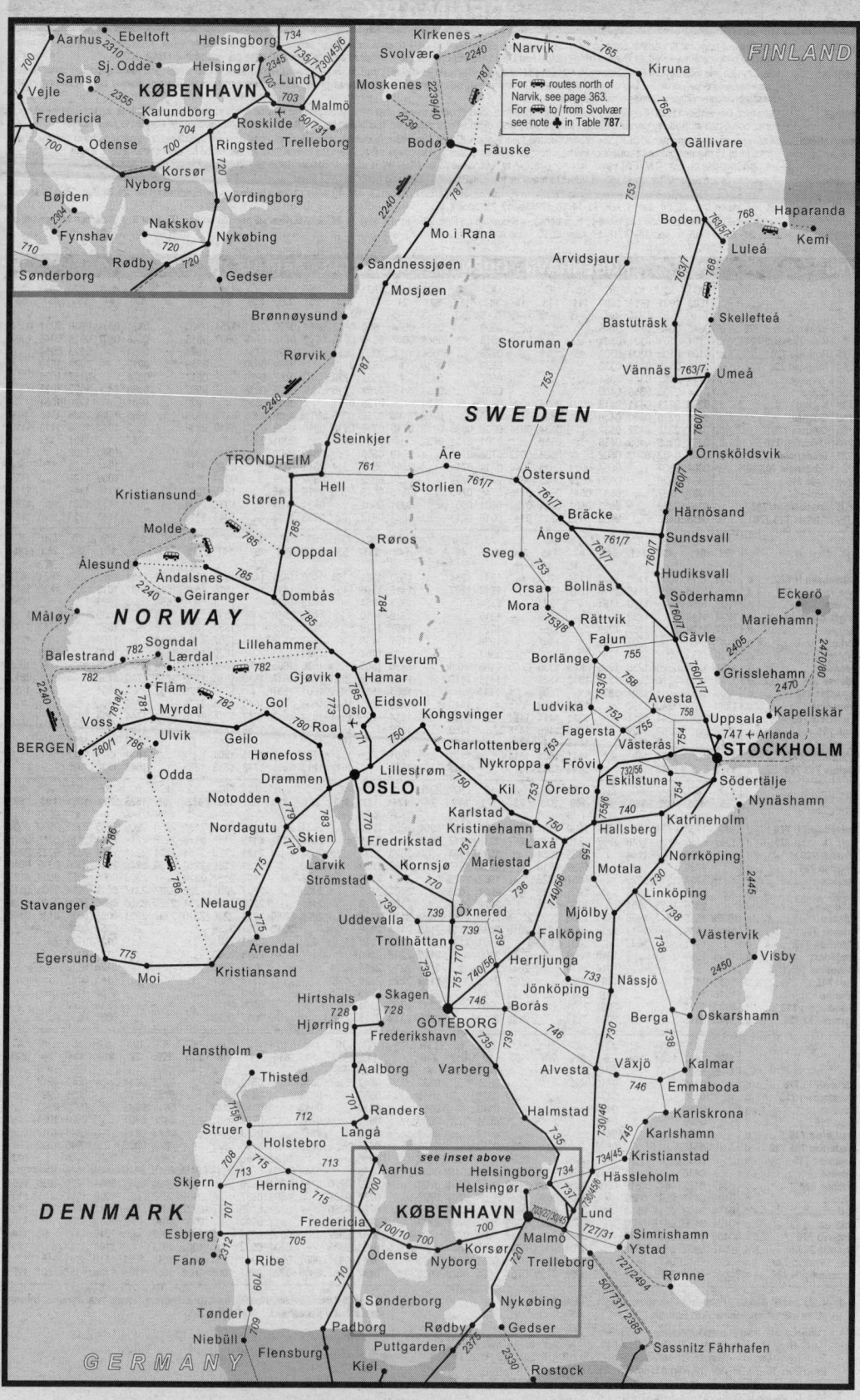

DENMARK

Operators: The principal operator is Danske Statsbaner (*DSB*): www.dsb.dk. Arriva Tog (*AT*) operate many local services in Jutland: www.arriva.dk. Additionally, local trains over the Øresund bridge are marketed as Øresundståg (*Øtåg*), and DSB Øresund operate the *Kystbanen* service between Helsingør and Malmö (Table 703).

Services: InterCity (*IC*) and InterCityLyn (*Lyn*) trains offer *Business* (1st class), *Standard* (2nd class), and on some services *Hvilepladser* ('quiet' seats) and *Familiepladser* ('family' seats). These services often consist of two or more portions for different destinations and care should be taken to join the correct portion. Other trains convey 1st and 2nd (standard) classes of accommodation unless otherwise shown.

Timings: Valid from **December 11, 2016** unless otherwise stated. Readers should note, however, that minor amendments may be made at any time, especially on and around the dates of public holidays (see **Holiday periods** below). Engineering work often affects schedules (particularly during the summer) and readers are advised to check locally.

Reservations: Seat reservations (currently 30 DKK) are recommended for travel on *IC* and *Lyn* trains (especially at peak times) and may be purchased a maximum of two months and a minimum of 15 minutes before departure of the train from its *originating* station. Passengers may board the train without a reservation but are not guaranteed a seat. Reservations are also available on EuroCity (*EC*) trains. It is not possible to reserve seats on other types of train. Special reservation rules may apply during holiday periods.

Supplements: Supplements are payable for travel to and from Germany by InterCityExpress (*ICE*) and EuroCity (*EC*) trains.

Holiday periods: Danske Statsbaner services will be amended as follows: a ⑤ service will operate on Dec. 23, Apr. 12, May 11, 24; a ⑥ service will operate on Dec. 24, 31, Apr. 15; a ⑦ service will operate on Dec. 25, 26, Jan. 1, Apr. 13, 14, 16, 17, May 12, 25, June 4, 5.

Arriva services will be amended as follows: a ⑤ service will operate on Dec. 23, Apr. 12, May 11, 24; a ⑥ service will operate on Apr. 15, June 3; a ⑦ service will operate on Dec. 24 - 26, 31, Jan. 1, Apr. 13, 14, 16, 17, May 12, 25, June 4, 5.

700 KØBENHAVN - ODENSE - FREDERICIA - AARHUS

km		*IC*	*IC*	*IC*	*IC*	*IC*	*IC*	*Lyn*	*IC*	*IC*	*IC*	*Lyn*	*IC*	*IC*	*Lyn*	*IC*	*IC*	*Lyn*	*IC*		*IC*	*Lyn*	*IC*	*IC*	*Lyn*
		1603	**1601**	**1611**	**1609**	**111**	**113**	**17**	**117**	**117**	**821**	**21**	**121**	**821**	**25**	**125**	**829**	**29**	**129**		**833**	**41**	**133**	**837**	**43**
0		①–⑤	⑥⑦	①–⑤	⑥⑦	①–⑤	①–⑤	①–⑤	①–⑤	⑥⑦	①–⑤	①–⑤		①–⑤											
0	**København** H **720** .. § d.	0045	0045	0245	0245	...	...	...	0500	...	0531	0554	0600	0631	0654	0700	0731	0754	0800	...	0831	0854	0900	0931	0954
20	Høje Taastrup **720** ... § d.	0101	0101	0301	0301	...	...	...	0515	...	0546	0607	0615	0646	0707	0715	0746	0807	0815	...	0846	0907	0915	0946	1007
31	Roskilde **720** .... § d.	0109	0109	0309	0309	...	...	...	0523	...	0554	|	0623	0654	|	0723	0754	|	0823	...	0854	|	0923	0954	|
64	Ringsted **720** .... d.	0125	0132	0325	0332	...	...	...	0539	...	0610	|	0639	0710	|	0739	0810	|	0839	...	0910	|	0939	1010	|
93	Slagelse .... d.	0144	0151	0344	0351	...	...	...	0557	...	0628	|	0657	0728	|	0757	0828	|	0857	...	0928	|	0957	1028	|
108	Korsør .... d.	0154	0200	0358	0400	...	...	...	0607	...	0638	|	0707	0738	|	0807	0838	|	0907	...	0938	|	1007	1038	|
132	Nyborg .... d.	0207	0213	0411	0413	...	0516	...	0620	...	0651	|	0720	0751	|	0820	0851	|	0920	...	0951	|	1020	1051	|
160	**Odense** .... a.	0230	0230	0430	0430	...	0532	...	0636	...	0705	0708**k**	0736	0805	0808**k**	0836	0905	0908**k**	0936	...	1005	1008**k**	1036	1105	1108**k**
160	**Odense 728** .... d.	0232	0232	0432	0432	...	0534	0614	0638	0638	0713	0710	0738	0813	0810	0838	0913	0910	0938	...	1013	1010	1038	1113	1110
210	Middelfart **710** .... d.	0255	0255	0455	0455	...	0557	|	0701	0701	0737	|	0801	0837	|	0901	0937	|	1001	...	1037	|	1101	1137	|
220	**Fredericia** .... a.	0302	0302	0502	0502	...	0604	0642	0708	0708	...	0740	0808	...	0840	0908	...	0940	1008	...	...	1040	1108	...	1140
220	**Fredericia 705/10/5** .... d.	0304	0304	...	0504	0514	0614	0644	0714	0714	...	0744	0814	...	0844	0914	...	0944	1014	...	...	1044	1114	...	1144
246	Vejle **715** .... d.	0320	0320	...	0520	0529	0629	0659	0729	0729	...	0759	0829	...	0859	0929	...	0959	1029	...	...	1059	1129	...	1159
277	Horsens .... d.	0337	0337	...	0537	0545	0645	0715	0745	0745	...	0815	0845	...	0915	0945	...	1015	1045	...	...	1115	1145	...	1215
306	Skanderborg **713** .... d.	0353	0353	...	0553	0601	0701	0731	0801	0801	...	0831	0901	...	0931	1001	...	1031	1101	...	...	1131	1201	...	1231
329	**Aarhus 713 728** .... a.	0413	0406	...	0606	0613	0713	0743	0813	0813	...	0843	0913	...	0943	1013	...	1043	1113	...	...	1143	1213	...	1243

	IC	*IC*	*Lyn*	*IC*	*IC*	*Lyn*	*IC*	*IC*	*IC*	*Lyn*		*IC*	*IC*	*Lyn*	*IC*	*IC*	*Lyn*	*IC*	*Lyn*	*IC*	*Lyn*	*IC*	*IC*	*Lyn*	*IC*
	137	**841**	**45**	**141**	**845**	**47**	**145**	**386**	**849**	**49**		**149**	**853**	**53**	**153**	**857**	**57**	**157**	**259**	**861**	**61**	**161**	**384**	**263**	**865**
								H											**w**				**H**	**w**	
København H **720** .... § d.	1000	1031	1054	1100	1131	1154	1200	...	1231	1254	...	1300	1331	1354	1400	1431	1454	1500	1524	1531	1554	1600	...	1624	1631
Høje Taastrup **720** .... § d.	1015	1046	1107	1115	1146	1207	1215	...	1246	1307	...	1315	1346	1407	1415	1446	1507	1515	1536	1546	1607	1615	...	1636	1646
Roskilde **720** .... § d.	1023	1054	|	1123	1154	|	1223	...	1254	|	...	1323	1354	|	1423	1454	|	1523	|	1554	|	1623	...	|	1654
Ringsted **720** .... d.	1039	1110	|	1139	1210	|	1239	...	1310	|	...	1339	1410	|	1439	1510	|	1539	|	1610	|	1639	...	|	1710
Slagelse .... d.	1057	1128	|	1157	1228	|	1257	...	1328	|	...	1357	1428	|	1457	1528	|	1557	1613	1628	|	1657	...	1713	1728
Korsør .... d.	1107	1138	|	1207	1238	|	1307	...	1338	|	...	1407	1438	|	1507	1538	|	1607	|	1638	|	1707	...	|	1738
Nyborg .... d.	1120	1151	|	1220	1251	|	1320	...	1351	|	...	1420	1451	|	1520	1551	|	1620	1635	1651	|	1720	...	1733	1751
Odense .... a.	1136	1205	1208**k**	1236	1305	1308**k**	1336	...	1405	1408**k**	...	1436	1505	1508**k**	1536	1605	1608**k**	1636	1650	1705	1708**k**	1736	...	1747	1805
Odense 728 .... d.	1138	1213	1210	1238	1313	1310	1338	...	1413	1410	...	1438	1513	1510	1538	1613	1610	1638	1700	1713	1710	1738	...	...	1813
Middelfart **710** .... d.	1201	1237	|	1301	1337	|	1401	...	1437	|	...	1501	1537	|	1601	1637	|	1701	1726	1737	|	1801	...	...	1837
Fredericia .... a.	1208	...	1240	1308	...	1340	1408	...	...	1440	...	1508	...	1540	1608	...	1640	1708	1734	...	1740	1808	...	...	...
Fredericia 705/10/5 ..... d.	1214	...	1244	1314	...	1344	1414	1421	...	1444	...	1514	...	1544	1614	...	1644	1714	1736	...	1744	1814	1821	...	...
Vejle **715** .... d.	1229	...	1259	1329	...	1359	1429	1436	...	1459	...	1529	...	1559	1629	...	1659	1729	|	...	1759	1829	1836	...	...
Horsens .... d.	1245	...	1315	1345	...	1415	1445	1455	...	1515	...	1545	...	1615	1645	...	1715	1745	|	...	1815	1845	1855	...	...
Skanderborg **713** .... d.	1301	...	1331	1401	...	1431	1501	1511	...	1531	...	1601	...	1631	1701	...	1731	1801	|	...	1831	1901	1911	...	...
Aarhus 713 728 .... a.	1313	...	1343	1413	...	1443	1513	1525	...	1543	...	1613	...	1643	1713	...	1743	1813	1829	...	1843	1913	1925	...	...

	Lyn	*IC*	*Lyn*	*IC*	*Lyn*	*IC*	*IC*	*Lyn*	*IC*	*IC*	*Lyn*	*IC*	*IC*	*IC*	*IC*	*Lyn*	*IC*	*IC*	*IC*	*IC*	*IC*	*IC*	*IC*	*IC*	*IC*
	65	**165**	**267**	**869**	**69**	**169**	**873**	**73**	**173**	**877**	**77**	**177**	**177**	**382**	**881**	**81**	**183**	**1681**	**885**	**185**	**1685**	**230**	**1691**	**193**	**1693**
			w									⑦–④	⑤⑥	**H**			⑤⑥	⑦–④		⑤⑥	⑦–④	**y**	**z**	⑥⑦	⑦–④
København H **720** .... § d.	1654	1700	1724	1731	1754	1800	1831	1854	1900	1931	1954	2000	2000	...	2031	2054	2100	2100	2131	2200	2200	2255	2300	0000	0000
Høje Taastrup **720** .... § d.	1707	1715	1736	1746	1807	1815	1846	1907	1915	1946	2007	2015	2015	...	2046	2107	2115	2115	2146	2216	2216	2311	2316	0015	0015
Roskilde **720** .... § d.	|	1723	|	1754	|	1823	1854	|	1923	1954	|	2023	2023	...	2054	|	2123	2123	2154	2224	2224	2324	2324	0023	0023
Ringsted **720** .... d.	|	1739	|	1810	|	1839	1910	|	1939	2010	|	2039	2039	...	2110	|	2139	2139	2210	2239	2248	2348	2340	0039	0045
Slagelse .... d.	|	1757	1813	1828	|	1857	1928	|	1957	2028	|	2057	2057	...	2128	|	2157	2157	2228	2257	2308	0008	2358	0057	0103
Korsør .... d.	|	1807	|	1838	|	1907	1938	|	2007	2038	|	2107	2107	...	2138	|	2207	2207	2238	2307	2317	0017	0008	0106	0113
Nyborg .... d.	|	1820	1833	1851	|	1920	1951	|	2020	2051	|	2120	2120	...	2151	|	2220	2220	2251	2320	2330	0030	0021	0119	0126
Odense .... a.	1808**k**	1836	1847	1905	1908**k**	1936	2005	2008**k**	2036	2105	2108**k**	2136	2136	...	2205	2208**k**	2236	2236	2310	2337	2351	0051	0038	0135	0148
Odense 728 .... d.	1810	1838	...	1913	1910	1938	2013	2010	2038	2113	2110	2138	2138	...	...	2210	2238	2238	...	...	...	0053	0040	...	...
Middelfart **710** .... d.	|	1901	...	1937	|	2001	2037	|	2101	2137	|	2201	2201	...	...	|	2301	2301	...	...	...	0117	0103	...	...
Fredericia .... a.	1840	1908	...	...	1940	2008	...	2040	2108	...	2140	2208	2208	...	...	2240	2308	2308	...	...	...	0124	0110	...	...
Fredericia 705/10/5 ..... d.	1844	1914	...	...	1944	2014	...	2044	2114	...	2144	2210	2214	2221	...	...	2318	2318	...	...	...	0126	0112	...	...
Vejle **715** .... d.	1859	1929	...	...	1959	2029	...	2059	2129	...	2159	2225	2229	2236	...	...	2333	2337	...	...	...	0141	0127	...	...
Horsens .... d.	1915	1945	...	...	2015	2045	...	2115	2145	...	2215	2245	2245	2255	...	...	2349	2357	...	...	...	0158	0144	...	...
Skanderborg **713** .... d.	1931	2001	...	...	2031	2101	...	2131	2201	...	2231	2300	2301	2311	...	...	0005	0012	...	...	...	0214	0200	...	...
Aarhus 713 728 .... a.	1943	2013	...	...	2043	2113	...	2143	2213	...	2243	2319	2318	2325	...	...	0017	0028	...	...	...	0232	0213	...	...

		IC	*IC*	*IC*	*Lyn*	*IC*	*Lyn*	*IC*	*Lyn*	*IC*	*Lyn*		*IC*	*IC*	*Lyn*	*IC*	*IC*	*Lyn*	*IC*	*IC*	*Lyn*	*IC*	*IC*	*Lyn*	*IC*
	1600	**1602**	**1604**	**104**	**6**	**808**	**206**	**108**	**10**	**812**	**210**		**112**	**112**	**14**	**816**	**116**	**18**	**820**	**120**	**22**	**824**	**124**	**26**	**828**
	①–⑤	⑥⑦	①–⑤		①–⑤	①–⑤	**w**		①–⑤	①–⑤	**w**		①–⑤	⑥⑦											
Aarhus 713 728 .... d.	...	0242	...	...	0410	...	...	...	0515	...	0522	...	0542	...	0614	...	0642	0714	...	0742	0814	...	0842	0914	...
Skanderborg **713** .... d.	...	0255	...	...	0424	...	...	...	0528	...	0536	...	0555	...	0628	...	0655	0728	...	0755	0828	...	0855	0928	...
Horsens .... d.	...	0310	...	...	0439	...	...	...	0543	...	0551	...	0610	...	0643	...	0710	0743	...	0810	0843	...	0910	0943	...
Vejle **715** .... d.	...	0328	...	...	0501	...	...	...	0601	...	0609	...	0628	...	0701	...	0728	0801	...	0828	0901	...	0928	1001	...
Fredericia 715 .... a.	...	0343	...	...	0517	...	...	...	0617	...	0623	...	0643	...	0717	...	0743	0817	...	0843	0917	...	0943	1017	...
Fredericia 705 710 ...... d.	...	0348	...	...	0522	...	...	0548	0622	...	0625	...	0648	...	0722	...	0748	0822	...	0848	0922	...	0948	1022	...
Middelfart **710** .... d.	...	0355	...	...	|	0520	...	0556	|	0620	0632	...	0656	...	|	0720	0756	|	0820	0856	|	0920	0956	|	1020
Odense .... a.	...	0418	...	...	0549	0545**k**	...	0618	0649	0645**k**	0659	...	0718	...	0749	0745**k**	0818	0849	0845**k**	0918	0949	0945**k**	1018	1049	1045**k**
Odense 728 .... d.	0347	0422	0442	0519	0551	0554	0609	0620	0651	0654	0709	...	0720	0720	0751	0754	0820	0851	0854	0920	0951	0954	1020	1051	1054
Nyborg .... d.	0401	0437	0501	0537	|	0609	0626	0637	|	0709	0726	...	0737	0737	|	0809	0837	|	0909	0937	|	1009	1037	|	1109
Korsør .... d.	0414	0450	0514	0550	|	0622	|	0650	|	0722	|	...	0750	0750	|	0822	0850	|	0922	0950	|	1022	1050	|	1122
Slagelse .... d.	0424	0500	0523	0600	|	0631	0647	0700	|	0731	0747	...	0800	0800	|	0831	0900	|	0931	1000	|	1031	1100	|	1131
Ringsted **720** .... a.	0450	0518	0540	0617	|	0648	|	0717	|	0748	|	...	0817	0817	|	0848	0917	|	0948	1017	|	1048	1117	|	1148
Roskilde **720** .... § a.	0512	0533	0602	0632	|	0704	|	0733	|	0804	|	...	0833	0833	|	0904	0933	|	1004	1033	|	1104	1133	|	1204
Høje Taastrup **720** .... § a.	0524	0542	0611	0641	0651	0712	0721	0741	0751	0812	0821	...	0841	0841	0851	0912	0941	0951	1012	1041	1051	1112	1141	1151	1212
København H **720** .... § a.	0540	0557	0627	0657	0705	0728	0735	0757	0805	0828	0835	...	0857	0857	0905	0928	0957	1005	1028	1057	1105	1128	1157	1205	1228

H – (12) and 🍸 Aarhus / Fredericia - Hamburg and v.v. (Table **710**). Ⓡ for international journeys in summer.

k – Connects with train in previous column.

w – ①–⑤ Dec. 12 - June 23, Aug. 7 - Dec. 8 (not Dec. 27 - 30, Apr. 10 - 12, May 26).

y – ①②③④⑦ Dec. 11 - May 18; Ⓑ May 21 - Sept. 7; ①②③④⑦ Sept. 10 - Dec. 7 (also Dec. 16 - 23, 30, Apr. 12, May 11; not Apr. 13 - 17, May 12).

z – ⑤⑥ Dec. 24 - May 27; ⑥ June 3 - Aug. 26; ⑤⑥ Sept. 2 - Dec. 9 (also Apr. 13 - 17, May 12, 25; not Dec. 30, Apr. 12, May 11, 24).

§ – *IC* and *Lyn* trains are not available for local journeys. Frequent local trains run between Roskilde and København.

AARHUS - FREDERICIA - ODENSE - KØBENHAVN 700

	IC 383 Ha	*IC* 1183 Hc	*IC* 128	*Lyn* 40	*IC* 832	*IC* 132	*Lyn* 42	*IC* 836	*IC* 136	*Lyn* 44	*IC* 840	*IC* 140	*Lyn* 46	*IC* 844	*IC* 385 Ha	*IC* 1185 Hc	*IC* 144	*Lyn* 48	*IC* 848	*IC* 148	*Lyn* 50	*IC* 852	*IC* 152	*Lyn* 54	*IC* 856
Aarhus 713 728 d.	0926	0932	0942	1014	...	1042	1114	...	1142	1214	...	1242	1314	...	1326	1332	1342	1414	...	1442	1514	...	1542	1614	...
Skanderborg **713** d.	0942	0948	0955	1028	...	1055	1128	...	1155	1228	...	1255	1328	...	1342	1348	1355	1428	...	1455	1528	...	1555	1628	...
Horsens d.	0958	1003	1010	1043	...	1110	1143	...	1210	1243	...	1310	1343	...	1358	1403	1410	1443	...	1510	1543	...	1610	1643	...
Vejle **715** d.	1016	1021	1028	1101	...	1128	1201	...	1228	1301	...	1328	1401	...	1416	1421	1428	1501	...	1528	1601	...	1628	1701	...
Fredericia 715 a.	1031	1035	1043	1117	...	1143	1217	...	1243	1317	...	1343	1417	...	1431	1435	1443	1517	...	1543	1617	...	1643	1717	...
Fredericia 705 710 d.	...	...	1048	1122	...	1148	1222	...	1248	1322	...	1348	1422	...	...	...	1448	1522	...	1548	1622	...	1648	1722	...
Middelfart **710** d.	...	...	1056	|	1120	1156	|	1220	1256	|	1320	1356	|	1420	...	...	1456	|	1520	1556	|	1620	1656	|	1720
Odense a.	...	...	1118	1149	1145**k**	1218	1249	1245**k**	1318	1349	1345**k**	1418	1449	1445**k**	...	...	1518	1549	1545**k**	1618	1649	1645**k**	1718	1749	1745**k**
Odense 728 d.	...	...	1120	1151	1154	1220	1251	1254	1320	1351	1354	1420	1451	1454	...	...	1520	1551	1554	1620	1651	1654	1720	1751	1754
Nyborg d.	...	...	1137	|	1209	1237	|	1309	1337	|	1409	1437	|	1509	...	...	1537	|	1609	1637	|	1709	1737	|	1809
Korsør d.	...	...	1150	|	1222	1250	|	1322	1350	|	1422	1450	|	1522	...	...	1550	|	1622	1650	|	1722	1750	|	1822
Slagelse d.	...	...	1200	|	1231	1300	|	1331	1400	|	1431	1500	|	1531	...	...	1600	|	1631	1700	|	1731	1800	|	1831
Ringsted **720** a.	...	...	1217	|	1248	1317	|	1348	1417	|	1448	1517	|	1548	...	...	1617	|	1648	1717	|	1748	1817	|	1848
Roskilde **720** § a.	...	...	1233	|	1304	1333	|	1404	1433	|	1504	1533	|	1604	...	...	1633	|	1704	1733	|	1804	1837	|	1904
Høje Taastrup **720** § a.	...	...	1241	1251	1312	1341	1351	1412	1441	1451	1512	1541	1551	1612	...	...	1641	1651	1712	1741	1751	1812	1841	1851	1912
København H **720** § a.	...	...	1257	1305	1328	1357	1405	1428	1457	1505	1528	1557	1605	1628	...	...	1657	1705	1728	1757	1805	1828	1857	1905	1928

	IC 156	*Lyn* 58	*IC* 860	*IC* 387 Ha	*IC* 387 Hc	*IC* 160	*Lyn* 62	*IC* 864	*IC* 164	*Lyn* 66	*IC* 868		*IC* 168 ⑤⑥	*IC* 1668 ⑦–④	*Lyn* 70 ⑤⑥	*Lyn* 72 ⑦–④	*IC* 172 ⑤⑥	*IC* 1672 ⑦–④	*IC* 176 ⑤⑥	*IC* 1676 ⑦–④	*IC* 1680 ⑤⑥	*IC* 1680 ⑦–④	*IC* 186	*IC* 188	
Aarhus 713 728 d.	1642	1714	...	1726	1732	1742	1814	...	1842	1914	...	...	1942	1942	2014	2014	2042	2042	2142	2142	2245	2245	2350	0050	...
Skanderborg **713** d.	1655	1728	...	1742	1748	1755	1828	...	1855	1928	...	...	1955	1955	2028	2028	2055	2055	2155	2156	2258	2258	0004	0104	...
Horsens d.	1710	1743	...	1758	1803	1810	1843	...	1910	1943	...	...	2010	2010	2043	2043	2110	2110	2210	2210	2313	2313	0019	0118	...
Vejle **715** d.	1728	1801	...	1816	1821	1828	1901	...	1928	2001	...	...	2028	2028	2101	2101	2128	2128	2228	2230	2333	2333	0038	0135	...
Fredericia 715 a.	1743	1817	...	1831	1835	1843	1917	...	1943	2017	...	...	2043	2043	2117	2117	2143	2143	2243	2246	2356	2356	0058	0150	...
Fredericia 705 710 d.	1748	1822	...	...	...	1848	1922	...	1948	2022	...	...	2048	2048	2122	2122	2148	2148	2250	2250	2358	2358	...	0158	...
Middelfart **710** d.	1756	|	1820	...	...	1856	|	1920	1956	|	2020	...	2056	2055	|	|	2155	2155	2258	2258	0006	0006	...	0206	...
Odense a.	1818	1849	1845**k**	...	...	1918	1949	1945**k**	2018	2049	2045**k**	...	2118	2117	2149	2149	2218	2217	2329	2329	0035	0035	...	0235	...
Odense 728 d.	1820	1851	1854	...	...	1920	1951	1954	2020	2051	2054	...	2120	2119	2151	2151	2220	2219	2331	2333	0037	...	...	0237	...
Nyborg d.	1837	|	1909	...	...	1937	|	2009	2037	|	2109	...	2137	2137	|	|	2237	2237	2348	2352	0051	...	...	0251	...
Korsør d.	1850	|	1922	...	...	1950	|	2022	2050	|	2122	...	2150	2150	|	|	2250	2250	0002	0006	0104	...	...	0304	...
Slagelse d.	1900	|	1931	...	...	2000	|	2031	2100	|	2131	...	2200	2200	|	|	2300	2300	0011	0015	0114	...	...	0314	...
Ringsted **720** a.	1917	|	1948	...	...	2017	|	2048	2117	|	2148	...	2217	2220	|	|	2317	2320	0029	0035	0131	...	...	0331	...
Roskilde **720** § a.	1933	|	2004	...	...	2033	|	2104	2133	|	2204	...	2233	2245	|	|	2333	2345	0044	0100	0147	...	...	0347	...
Høje Taastrup **720** § a.	1941	1951	2012	...	...	2041	2051	2112	2141	2151	2212	...	2241	2254	2251	2259	2341	2358	0053	0108	0155	...	...	0355	...
København H **720** § a.	1957	2005	2028	...	...	2057	2105	2128	2157	2205	2228	...	2257	2314	2305	2317	0005	0020	0114	0129	0216	...	...	0416	...

H – 12 and 🍸 Aarhus / Fredericia - Hamburg and v.v. (Table **710**). R for international journeys in summer.

a – ①–⑤ only.
c – ⑥⑦ only.
k – Connects with train in previous column.

§ – *IC* and *Lyn* trains are not available for local journeys. Frequent local trains run between Roskilde and København.

2nd class only (*IC* & *Lyn* 1st & 2nd class) AARHUS - AALBORG - FREDERIKSHAVN 701

A change of train may be necessary at Aalborg

km		W	①–⑤		①–⑤	A	①–⑤	B	①–⑤	A		⑥⑦	①–⑤		⑥⑦	①–⑤										⑥⑦	①–⑤
0	**Aarhus 712** d.	...	...	0421	...	...	0521	...	0551	...	0621	...	0651	0721	...	0751	0821	0851	0921	0951	1021	1051	1121	1151	1221	1251	1251
46	Langå **712** d.	...	...	0447	...	...	0547	...	|	...	0647	...	|	0747	...	|	0847	|	0947	|	1047	|	1147	|	1247	|	|
59	Randers d.	...	...	0456	...	...	0556	...	0622	...	0656	...	0722	0756	...	0822	0856	0922	0956	1022	1056	1122	1156	1222	1256	1322	1322
91	Hobro d.	...	...	0512	...	...	0612	...	0638	...	0712	...	0738	0812	...	0838	0912	0938	1012	1038	1112	1138	1212	1238	1312	1338	1338
140	**Aalborg** a.	...	...	0552	...	...	0651	...	0709	...	0752	...	0809	0851	...	0907	0951	1007	1051	1107	1151	1207	1251	1307	1351	1407	1407
140	**Aalborg** d.	0411	0512	...	0612	0642	...	0712	0712	0742	...	0812	0812	...	0912	0912	...	1012	...	1112	...	1212	...	1312	...	1412	1412
188	Hjørring **702** d.	0458	0600	...	0700	0734	...	0756	0803	0837	...	0900	0900	...	0957	0957	...	1101	...	1157	...	1301	...	1400	...	1459	1504
225	**Frederikshavn** a.	0522	0629	...	0729	0805	...	0823	0828	0908	...	0923	0923	...	1024	1024	...	1124	...	1224	...	1324	...	1427	...	1523	1527

	A		G	A			A																⑤⑥ D	E	F	H
Aarhus 712 d.	...	1321	1351	...	1421	1451	...	1521	1551	1621	1651	1721	1751	1821	1851	1921	1951	2021	2051	2121	...	2221	2326	0025	0036	0221	0240
Langå **712** d.	...	1347	|	...	1447	|	...	1547	|	1647	|	1747	|	1847	|	1947	|	2047	|	2147	...	2247	2352	0051	0102	0248	0307
Randers d.	...	1356	1422	...	1456	1522	...	1556	1622	1656	1722	1756	1822	1856	1922	1956	2022	2056	2122	2156	...	2256	0001	0100	0111	0257	0316
Hobro d.	...	1412	1438	...	1512	1538	...	1612	1638	1712	1738	1812	1838	1912	1938	2012	2038	2112	2138	2212	...	2312	0017	0116	0127	0313	0332
Aalborg a.	...	1451	1507	...	1551	1607	...	1651	1707	1751	1807	1851	1907	1951	2007	2051	2107	2151	2207	2251	...	2358	0103	0155	0206	0350	0409
Aalborg d.	1442	...	1512	1542	...	1612	1642	...	1712	...	1812	...	1912	...	2012	...	2112	...	2212	...	2312	...	...	...	...	...	...
Hjørring **702** d.	1533	...	1559	1633	...	1659	1733	...	1757	...	1901	...	1957	...	2101	...	2157	...	2301	...	2355	...	...	...	...	...	...
Frederikshavn a.	1604	...	1627	1704	...	1723	1804	...	1824	...	1924	...	2024	...	2124	...	2224	...	2324	...	0022	...	...	...	...	...	...

	①–⑤	①–⑤	①–⑤		J			A	B	A		A															A
Frederikshavn d.	...	...	0438	...	0538	...	...	0547	0630	0634	...	0647	0731	...	0831	...	0933	...	1033	...	1133	...	1233	...	1333	...	1347
Hjørring **702** d.	...	...	0506	...	0606	...	...	0633	0703	0703	...	0733	0803	...	0903	...	1003	...	1103	...	1203	...	1303	...	1403	...	1433
Aalborg a.	...	...	0543	...	0643	...	...	0713	0743	0743	...	0813	0843	...	0943	...	1043	...	1143	...	1243	...	1343	...	1443	...	1513
Aalborg d.	0447	0503	0547	0603	0647	0647	0703	...	0747	0747	0803	...	0847	0903	0947	1003	1047	1103	1147	1203	1247	1303	1347	1403	1447	1503	...
Hobro d.	0517	0542	0617	0642	0717	0717	0742	...	0817	0817	0842	...	0917	0942	1017	1042	1117	1142	1217	1242	1317	1342	1417	1442	1517	1542	...
Randers d.	0533	0558	0633	0658	0733	0733	0758	...	0833	0833	0858	...	0933	0958	1033	1058	1133	1158	1233	1258	1333	1358	1433	1458	1533	1558	...
Langå **712** d.	|	0606	|	0706	|	|	0806	...	|	|	0906	...	|	1006	|	1106	|	1206	|	1306	|	1406	|	1506	|	1606	...
Aarhus 712 a.	0606	0635	0706	0735	0806	0806	0835	...	0906	0906	0935	...	1006	1035	1106	1135	1206	1235	1306	1335	1406	1435	1805	1535	1606	1635	...

	C	A		A	①–⑤	⑥⑦		A	A	K		①–⑤	⑥⑦		V	W										⑤⑥	
Frederikshavn d.	1430	1435	...	1451	1530	1534	...	1547	1630	1630	...	1725	1732	...	1832	1837	...	1933	...	2033	...	2133	...	2233	...	...	...
Hjørring **702** d.	1503	1503	...	1533	1603	1603	...	1633	1703	1703	...	1806	1806	...	1905	1903	...	2006	...	2106	...	2206	...	2306	...	...	...
Aalborg a.	1543	1543	...	1613	1643	1643	...	1713	1743	1743	...	1843	1843	...	1943	1943	...	2043	...	2143	...	2243	...	2343	...	...	...
Aalborg d.	1547	1547	1603	...	1647	1647	1703	...	1747	1747	1803	1847	1847	1903	1947	1947	2003	...	2103	...	2207	...	2307	...	0007	0203	...
Hobro d.	1617	1617	1642	...	1717	1717	1742	...	1817	1817	1842	1917	1917	1942	2017	2017	2042	...	2142	...	2245	...	2347	...	0048	0242	...
Randers d.	1633	1633	1658	...	1733	1733	1758	...	1833	1833	1858	1933	1933	1958	2033	2033	2058	...	2158	...	2302	...	0002	...	0104	0258	...
Langå **712** d.	|	|	1706	...	|	|	1806	...	|	|	1906	|	|	2006	|	|	2106	...	2206	...	2311	...	0011	...	0113	0306	...
Aarhus 712 a.	1706	1706	1735	...	1806	1806	1835	...	1906	1906	1935	2006	2006	2035	2106	2106	2135	...	2238	...	2343	...	0043	...	0145	0335	...

A – ①–⑤ Dec. 12 - June 23, Aug. 7 - Dec. 8 (not Dec. 27 - 30, Apr. 10 - 12, May 26).
B – ⑥⑦ (also Dec. 27 - 30, Apr. 10 - 12, May 26, June 26 - Aug. 4).
C – ⑥⑦ (also Dec. 27 - 30, May 26, June 26 - Aug. 4).
D – Not Feb. 4, 11, 18, 25, Apr. 8 - 15, 22.
E – Dec. 25, Apr. 13, 14, 16, May 12, June 4.
F – ⑤⑥ Dec. 24 - May 27; ⑥ June 3 - Aug. 26; ⑤⑥ Sept. 2 - Dec. 8 (also Apr. 13 - 16, May 12; not Dec. 30, Apr. 12, May 11, 24).
G – Not Apr. 10 - 12.
H – ⑤ Apr. 12 - Sept. 1 (also Dec. 16, 17, 23, 25, 30, June 4; not Apr. 21 - May 5, 19, 26).
J – ①–⑤ Dec. 12 - Aug. 4; daily Aug. 6 - Dec. 9.
K – ⑥⑦ (also Dec. 27 - 29, May 26, June 26 - Aug. 4).
V – Dec. 11 - Aug. 5.
W – Aug. 6 - Dec. 9.

703 HELSINGØR - KØBENHAVN - KØBENHAVN LUFTHAVN (KASTRUP) ✈ - MALMÖ

EASTBOUND

Services operate every 20 minutes (less frequent 0000 - 0400 hours) **Helsingør** - Østerport - København H - **København Lufthavn (Kastrup)** ✈.

A change of train is necessary for Malmö passengers.

Journey times:
Helsingør - København H: 46 minutes;
København H - København Lufthavn (Kastrup) ✈: 12 minutes;
København Lufthavn (Kastrup) ✈ - Malmö C: 27 minutes.

Connection time between trains at København Lufthavn (Kastrup) ✈: 18 minutes (minimum).

WESTBOUND

Services operate every 20 minutes (less frequent 0000 - 0400 hours) **Malmö C** - København Lufthavn (Kastrup) ✈ - København H - Østerport - **Helsingør**.

Journey times:
Malmö C - København Lufthavn (Kastrup) ✈: 21 minutes;
København Lufthavn (Kastrup) ✈ - København H: 14 minutes;
København H - Helsingør: 45 minutes.

704 KØBENHAVN - KALUNDBORG

km		①–⑤	①–⑤	①–⑤	①–⑤		①–⑤	①–⑤		①–⑤	①–⑤				①–⑤			①–⑤							
0	**København** H........... d.	0457	0527	0545	0557	0627	0645	0657	0727	0745	0757	0827	0845	and at	1657	1727	1745	1757	1827	1845	1927	1945	2027	2045	2127
20	Høje Taastrup........... d.	0512	0542	0559	0612	0642	0659	0712	0742	0759	0812	0842	0859	the same	1712	1742	1759	1812	1842	1859	1942	1959	2042	2059	2142
31	**Roskilde**.................. d.	0524	0554	0609	0624	0654	0709	0724	0754	0809	0824	0854	0909	minutes	1724	1754	1809	1824	1854	1909	1954	2009	2054	2109	2154
67	Holbæk..................... a.	0555	0625	0628	0655	0725	0728	0755	0825	0828	0855	0925	0930	past	1755	1825	1830	1855	1925	1930	2025	2030	2125	2130	2225
67	Holbæk..................... d.	...	...	0630	...	0730**c**	0730	...	0830**c**	0830	...	...	0930	each hour	...	...	1830	...	...	1930	...	2030	...	2130	2231**j**
111	**Kalundborg 2355**..... a.	...	...	0710	...	0810**c**	0810	...	0910**c**	0910	...	...	1010	until	...	...	1910	...	...	2010	...	2110	...	2210	2310**j**

	⑤⑥				⑥⑦					
København H .... d.	2145	2227	2327	0027	0227	...	EXTRA	1515	1615	1715
Høje Taastrup............ d.	2159	2242	2342	0042	0242	...	SERVICES	1528	1628	1728
Roskilde .... d.	2209	2256	2356	0056	0254	...	▶▶▶	1537	1637	1737
Holbæk...................... a.	2230	2326	0031	0131	0325	...	(see note **z**)	1559	1659	1759
Holbæk...................... d.	2231	2330	0033	0132**c**	...	...		1600	1700	1800
Kalundborg 2355...... a.	2310	0010	0110	0210**c**	...	...		1634	1734	1834

	①–⑤		①–⑤	①–⑤		①–⑤	①–⑤		①–⑤	①–⑤	
Kalundborg 2355.. d.	...	0446	...	0548	0546**c**	...	0646	0646**c**	...	0746	0746**c**
Holbæk.................. a.	...	0528	...	0628	0628**c**	...	0728	0728**c**	...	0828	0828**c**
Holbæk.................. d.	0505	0535	0605	0629	0635	0703	0729	0735	0805	0829	0835
Roskilde .... d.	0536	0606	0636	0649	0706	0734	0749	0806	0835	0849	0906
Høje Taastrup........ d.	0546	0616	0646	0658	0716	0744	0758	0816	0836	0858	0916
København H........ a.	0600	0632	0702	0712	0732	0801	0812	0832	0902	0912	0932

	①–⑤				①–⑤									⑤⑥				⑥⑦						
Kalundborg 2355...... d.	...	0846	...	and at	...	1846	...	...	1946	...	2046	...	...	2146	2146**j**	2246	...	...	...	EXTRA	0524	0622	0722	...
Holbæk...................... a.	...	0928	...	the same	...	1928	...	...	2027	...	2127	...	...	2227	2227**j**	2327	...	...	...	SERVICES	0555	0655	0755	...
Holbæk...................... d.	0905	0928	0935	minutes	1905	1928	1935	...	2028	2035	2128	2135	...	2228	2235	2335	...	0333	...	▶▶▶	0556	0656	0756	...
Roskilde .... d.	0936	0949	1006	past	1936	1949	2006	...	2051	2106	2151	2206	...	2251	2306	0006	...	0404	...	(see note **z**)	0619	0719	0819	...
Høje Taastrup............ d.	0946	0958	1016	each hour	1946	1957	2016	...	2058	2116	2158	2216	...	2258	2316	0018	...	0414	...		0628	0728	0828	...
København H .... a.	1002	1012	1032	until	2002	2012	2032	...	2112	2132	2212	2232	...	2312	2338	0038	...	0430	...		0642	0742	0842	...

c – ⑥⑦ only.　**j** – ①②③④⑦ only.　**z** – ①–⑤ Dec. 12 - June 23, Aug. 7 - Dec. 8 (not Dec. 27 - 30, Apr. 10 - 12, May 26).

705 FREDERICIA - ESBJERG

2nd class only (*IC* & *Lyn* 1st & 2nd class)

km						*IC*		*IC*		*IC*		*IC*		*IC*		*IC*		*IC*		*IC*		*IC*		*IC*		*IC*
				617		**821**		**825**		**829**		**833**		**837**		**841**		**845**		**849**		**853**		**857**		**861**
		①–⑤		①–⑤		①–⑤		‡																		
	København H **700**.. d.	...	...	...	...	0531	...	0631	...	0731	...	0831	...	0931	...	1031	...	1131	...	1231	...	1331	...	1431	...	1531
	Odense **700**........... d.	...	...	0608	...	0713	...	0813	...	0913	...	1013	...	1113	...	1213	...	1313	...	1413	...	1513	...	1613	...	1713
	Middelfart **700**........ d.	...	...	0632	...	0737	...	0837	...	0937	...	1037	...	1137	...	1237	...	1337	...	1437	...	1537	...	1637	...	1737
	Aarhus **700** .... d.	...	...	|	0556**a**	|	0656	|	0756	|	0856	|	0956	|	1056	|	1156	|	1256	|	1356	|	1456	|	1556	|
0	**Fredericia 700/10**..... d.	0511	0614	|	0714	|	0814	|	0914	|	1014	|	1114	|	1214	|	1314	|	1414	|	1514	|	1614	|	1714	|
20	Kolding **710**.............. d.	0525	0628	0645	0728	0751	0828	0851	0928	0951	1028	1051	1128	1151	1228	1251	1328	1351	1428	1451	1528	1551	1628	1651	1728	1751
33	Lunderskov **710** .... d.	0533	0636	0654	0736	0759	0836	0859	0936	0959	1036	1059	1136	1159	1236	1259	1336	1359	1436	1459	1536	1559	1636	1659	1736	1759
44	Vejen .... d.	0541	0644	0702	0744	0807	0844	0907	0944	1007	1044	1107	1144	1207	1244	1307	1344	1407	1444	1507	1544	1607	1644	1707	1744	1807
72	Bramming **709** .... a.	0602	0705	0723	0805	0821	0905	0921	1005	1021	1105	1121	1205	1221	1305	1321	1405	1421	1505	1521	1605	1621	1705	1721	1805	1821
88	**Esbjerg 709** .... a.	0614	0717	0735	0817	0832	0917	0932	1017	1032	1117	1132	1217	1232	1317	1332	1417	1432	1517	1532	1617	1632	1717	1732	1817	1832

		IC		*IC*		*IC*		*IC*		
		865		**869**		**873**		**877**		
København H **700** .... d.	...	1631	...	1731	...	1831	...	1931	...	...
Odense **700** .... d.	...	1813	...	1913	...	2013	...	2113	...	...
Middelfart **700** .... d.	...	1837	...	1937	...	2037	...	2137	...	...
Aarhus **700** .... d.	1656	|	1756	|	1856	|	1956	|	...	...
Fredericia 700/10............... d.	1814	|	1914	|	2014	|	2114	|	2214	2328
Kolding **710** .... d.	1828	1851	1928	1951	2028	2051	2128	2151	2228	2341
Lunderskov **710** .... d.	1836	1859	1936	1959	2036	2059	2136	2159	2236	2349
Vejen...................................... d.	1844	1907	1944	2007	2044	2107	2144	2207	2244	2357
Bramming **709** .... a.	1905	1921	2005	2021	2105	2121	2205	2221	2305	0017
Esbjerg 709 .... a.	1917	1932	2017	2032	2117	2132	2217	2232	2321	0034

	IC	*IC*		*IC*			*IC*		*IC*	
	808	**812**		**816**			**820**		**824**	
	①–⑤	①–⑤	①–⑤		⑥⑦	①–⑤				
Esbjerg 709 .... d.	...	0525	0539	0625**a**	0630	0639	0725	0739	0825	0839
Bramming **709** .... d.	...	0536	0550	0636**a**	0641	0650	0736	0751	0836	0850
Vejen .... d.	...	0550	0611	0650**a**	0702	0711	0750	0812	0850	0911
Lunderskov **710** .... d.	...	0557	0619	0657**a**	0710	0719	0857	0820	0857	0919
Kolding **710**......................... d.	0506	0606	0628	0706	0719	0728	0806	0829	0906	0928
Fredericia 700/10............ a.	|	|	0642	|	0733	0742	|	0843	|	0942
Aarhus **700** .... a.	|	|	0801	|	...	0901	|	1001	|	1101
Middelfart **700**............... a.	0520	0620	...	0720	...	...	0820	...	0920	...
Odense **700**..................... a.	0545	0645	...	0745	...	...	0845	...	0945	...
København H **700**......... a.	0728	0828	...	0928	...	...	1028	...	1128	...

	IC		*IC*		*IC*		*IC*		*IC*		*IC*		*IC*		*IC*		*IC*		*IC*		*IC*		*IC*				
	828		**832**		**836**		**840**		**844**		**848**		**852**		**856**		**860**		**864**		**868**		**872**				
Esbjerg 709 .... d.	0925	0939	1025	1039	1125	1139	1225	1239	1325	1339	1425	1439	1525	1539	1625	1639	1725	1739	1825	1839	1925	1939	2025	2036	2136	2245	2347
Bramming **709** .... d.	0936	0950	1036	1050	1136	1150	1236	1250	1336	1350	1436	1450	1536	1550	1636	1650	1736	1750	1836	1850	1936	1950	2036	2047	2147	2256	2357
Vejen......................... d.	0950	1011	1050	1111	1150	1211	1250	1311	1350	1411	1450	1511	1549	1611	1650	1711	1750	1811	1850	1911	1950	2011	2050	2108	2208	2318	0019
Lunderskov **710** .... d.	0957	1019	1057	1119	1157	1219	1257	1319	1357	1419	1457	1519	1557	1619	1657	1719	1757	1819	1857	1919	1957	2019	2057	2116	2216	2325	0026
Kolding **710** .... d.	1006	1028	1106	1128	1206	1228	1306	1328	1406	1428	1506	1528	1606	1628	1706	1728	1806	1828	1906	1928	2006	2028	2106	2125	2225	2334	0034
Fredericia 700/10..... a.	|	1042	|	1142	|	1242	|	1342	|	1442	|	1542	|	1642	|	1742	|	1842	|	1942	|	2042	|	2139	2239	2352	0053
Aarhus **700** .... a.	|	1201	|	1301	|	1401	|	1501	|	1601	|	1701	|	1801	|	1903	|	2001	|	2101	|	2201	|	...	...	...	...
Middelfart **700** .... a.	1020	....	1120	...	1220	....	1320	...	1420	...	1520	...	1620	...	1720	...	1820	...	1920	...	2020	...	2120	...	...	...	...
Odense **700** .... a.	1045	....	1145	...	1245	...	1345	...	1445	...	1545	...	1645	...	1745	...	1845	...	1945	...	2145	...	2145	...	...	...	...
København H **700** . a.	1228	...	1328	...	1428	...	1528	...	1628	...	1728	...	1828	...	1928	...	2028	...	2128	...	2228	...	...	...	...	...	...

a – ①–⑤ only.　‡ – Train runs as *Lyn* **25** on ⑥⑦ (København H depart 0654).

707 ESBJERG - SKJERN

2nd class only.　Operator: *AT*

km																		⑥	⑥		†					
0	**Esbjerg 705**........ ⊗ d.	Ⓐ	0457	0549	0647	*0730*	0834	0932	and	1732	1933	2033	2133	2233	2333	Ⓒ	0444	0552	...	0642	0751	...	0951	and every	2151
17	Varde.................. ⊗ d.		0515	0613	0707	0802	0857	0958	hourly	1758	1958	2051	2158	2251	2351		0503	0612	...	0702	0814	...	1014	two hours	2214
60	**Skjern 708/13** ....a.		0552	0651	0748	0841	0935	1037	until	1837	2037	...	2237	...	...		0539	0648	...	0738	0850	...	1050	until	2250

															⑥	⑥	†							
Skjern 708/13........... d.	Ⓐ	0503	0605	0659	0813	...	0950	and	1750	1853	...	2053	...	2253	Ⓒ	0600	0717	0802	0917	...	1117	and every	2317	...	...
Varde .... ⊗ d.		0552	0650	0739	0855	...	1031	hourly	1831	1931	2031	2131	2231	2331		0638	0755	0848	0955	...	1155	two hours	2355	...	...
Esbjerg 705 .... ⊗ a.		0610	0708	0801	0917	...	1052	until	1852	1953	2053	2153	2253	2353		0656	0813	0910	1013	...	1213	until	0013	...	...

⊗ – Additional services operate Esbjerg - Varde and v.v.

SKJERN - STRUER 708

Operator: *AT* 2nd class only

km																							
																	Ⓒ	⑥	⑥	†				
0	**Skjern 707/13** d.	Ⓐ	0504	0616	0713	0801	0847	0947	1047		1547	1647	1850	2053	2253	...		0540	0654	0740	...	0854		2054	2254
23	Ringkøbing a.		0522	0637	0731	0819	0905	1005	1105	and	1605	1705	1907	2111	2311	...		0602	0711	0802	...	0911	and every	2111	2311
23	Ringkøbing d.		0525	0642	0734	0823	0907	1007	1107	hourly	1607	1707	1908	2112	2312	...		0604	0712	0804	...	0912	two hours	2112	2312
71	Holstebro a.		0605	0722	0814	0903	0946	1046	1146	until	1646	1746	1948	2154	2354	...		0649	0752	0849	...	0952	until	2152	2352
71	Holstebro 715 d.		0606	0723	0824	0905	0947	1047	1147		1647	1748	1949	2155	2355	...		0651	0754	0851	...	0954		2154	2354
86	**Struer 715** a.		0621	0736	0837	0921	1000	1100	1200		1700	1801	2002	2208	0008	...		0702	0805	0902	...	1005		2205	0005

																Ⓒ	⑥	⑥	†	†	⑥			
Struer 715 d.	Ⓐ	0433	0521	0632	0723	0851	1001	1101		1501	1601	1732	1932	2110	2310	...		0446	0552	0647	0752	0752	0952		2152
Holstebro 715 a.		0445	0533	0648	0736	0903	1013	1113	and	1513	1613	1747	1947	2122	2322	...		0458	0604	0659	0804	0806	1006	and every	2206
Holstebro d.		0445	0533	0650	0739	0913	1014	1114	hourly	1514	1614	1748	1950	2123	2323	...		0500	0606	0701	0806	0808	1008	two hours	2208
Ringkøbing a.		0525	0616	0733	0823	0956	1058	1158	until	1558	1658	1827	2029	2206	0003	...		0539	0645	0740	0845	0847	1047	until	2247
Ringkøbing d.		0525	0616	0734	0824	1007	1109	1209		1609	1709	1828	2030	2207	0004	...		0540	0647	0741	0847	0849	1049		2249
Skjern 707/13 a.		0544	0634	0752	0842	1026	1128	1228		1628	1728	1846	2048	2226	0023	...		0558	0712	0759	0912	0912	1112		2312

ESBJERG - TØNDER - NIEBÜLL 709

Operator: *AT* 2nd class only

km																											
																			Ⓒ	⑥							
0	**Esbjerg 705** ⊗ d.	Ⓐ	0500	0615	0758	0859	0959	1059	1159	1259	1359	1459	1559	1659	1759	1859	1959	2159		0517	0717	0917		1717	1917	2017	2232
16	Bramming 705 ⊗ d.		0513	0629	0811	0912	1012	1112	1212	1312	1412	1512	1612	1712	1812	1912	2012	2212		0531	0731	0931		1731	1931	2031	2246
33	Ribe ⊗ d.		0539	0648	0832	0932	1032	1132	1232	1332	1432	1532	1632	1732	1832	1932	2032	2232		0601	0801	1001	and every	1801	2001	2053	2315
80	**Tønder** a.		0630	0736	0923	1023	1123	1223	1323	1423	1523	1623	1723	1823	1923	2023	2123	2323		0649	0849	1049	two hours	1849	2049	2145	0003
			y																				until				
80	**Tønder** d.		0706	0832	...	1032	...	1232	1340	1432	1532	1632	...	1832	...	2032	...	...		...	0932e	1132		1932	2106	2232t	...
97	Niebüll 821 a.		0725	0851	...	1051	...	1251	1402	1451	1551	1651	...	1851	...	2051	...	...		...	0951e	1151		1951	2125	2251t	...

			y																Ⓒ	⑥							
Niebüll 821 d.	Ⓐ	...	0639	0733	...	1007	...	1207	1320	1407	1507	1607	...	1807	...	2007	2207v	...		...	...	0809e	1009		2009	...	2207t
Tønder a.		...	0656	0750	...	1025	...	1225	1337	1425	1525	1625	...	1825	...	2025	2224v	...		...	...	0826e	1026	and every two hours	2026	...	2224t
Tønder d.		0558	0639	0827	0927	1027	1127	1227	1327	1427	1527	1627	1727	1827	1927	2027	2227	...		0513	0713	0913	1113	until	2113	...	2227
Ribe ⊗ d.		0650	0730	0915	1015	1115	1215	1315	1415	1515	1615	1715	1815	1915	2015	2115	2315	...		0607	0807	1007	1207		2207	...	2315
Bramming 705 ⊗ a.		0711	0750	0936	1036	1136	1236	1336	1436	1536	1636	1736	1836	1936	2036	2136	2336	...		0629	0829	1029	1229		2229	...	2334
Esbjerg 705 ⊗ a.		0724	0803	0949	1049	1149	1249	1349	1449	1549	1649	1749	1849	1949	2049	2149	2349	...		0643	0843	1043	1243		2243	...	2348

e – ⑥ only.
t – Ⓒ Apr. 8 - Oct. 29.
v – ⑤ Apr. 7 - Oct. 27.
y – Also Apr. 13, May 12.
⊗ – Additional services operate Esbjerg - Ribe and v.v.

FREDERICIA - SØNDERBORG and FLENSBURG (- HAMBURG) 710

km		IC 5744		IC 5722	IC 821		Lyn 921	IC 825	IC 5720	IC 829	Lyn 929	Lyn 41	IC 383	IC 837	Lyn 943	Lyn 45	IC 5736	IC 845	Lyn 947	Lyn 49	IC 385	IC 853	Lyn 953	IC 5752	IC 861	Lyn 961	Lyn 65	IC 387
		①–⑥	①–⑤		①–⑤	⑥⑦	①–⑤	①–⑤					H‡								H‡							H‡
	København H 700 d.	...	...	...	0531	...	0554	0631	...	0731	0754	0854	...	0931	0954	1054	...	1131	1154	1254	...	1331	1354	...	1531	1554	1654	...
	Odense 700 d.	...	0510	...	0713	0641	0710	0813	...	0913	0910	1010	...	1113	1110	1210	...	1313	1310	1410	...	1513	1510	...	1713	1710	1810	...
	Aarhus 700 d.	...	|	0527k	|	|	|	|	...	|	|	|	0926	|	|	|	...	|	|	|	1326	|	|	...	|	|	|	1726
0	**Fredericia 700** d.	...	0549	0646d	|	0749	0749	|	0846	|	0949	1040	1046	|	1149	1240	1246	|	1349	1440	1446	|	1549	1646	|	1749	1840	1846
*	Middelfart 700 d.	...	|	|	0737	|	|	0837	|	0937	|	...	|	1137	|	...	|	1337	|	...	|	1537	|	|	1737	|	...	|
20	Kolding 705 d.	...	0601	0658d	0751	0801	0801	0851	0858	0951	1001	...	1058	1151	1201	...	1258	1351	1401	...	1458	1551	1601	1658	1751	1801	...	1858
33	Lunderskov 705 d.	...	0608	0706d	0759	0808	0808	0859	0906	0959	1008	...	1106	1159	1208	...	1306	1359	1408	...	1506	1559	1608	1706	1759	1808	...	1906
60	Vojens d.	...	0625	0723d	...	0825	0825	...	0923	...	1025	...	1123	...	1224	...	1323	...	1425	...	1523	...	1625	1723	...	1825	...	1923
95	Tinglev d.	0610	0646	0744	...	0846	0846	...	0944	...	1046	...	1144	...	1246	...	1344	...	1446	...	1544	...	1646	1744	...	1845	...	1944
136	**Sønderborg** a.	|	0719	|	...	0919	0919	...	|	...	1119	...	|	...	1319	...	|	...	1519	...	|	...	1719	|	...	1919	...	|
110	Padborg 🏛 a.	0620	...	0754	...	...	...	...	0954	...	...	...	1154	...	...	...	1354	...	...	...	1554	...	...	1754	...	...	...	1954
122	**Flensburg** 🏛 **823** a.	0635	...	0807	...	...	...	...	1007	...	...	...	1207	...	...	...	1407	...	...	...	1607	...	...	1807	...	...	...	2007
302	*Hamburg Hbf* 823 a.	...	...	...	...	...	...	...	...	...	...	...	1402	...	...	...	...	...	...	...	1803	...	...	...	...	...	...	2211h

	IC 869	Lyn 969	Lyn 73	IC 5768	Lyn 977	Lyn 81	2375	IC 1681		IC 230	IC 1130
										Ky	Kz
København H 700 d.	1731	1754	1854	...	1954	2054	...	2100	...	2255	2300
Odense 700 d.	1913	1910	2010	...	2110	2210	...	2238	...	0053	0040
Aarhus 700 d.	|	|	|	...	|	|	...	|	...	|	|
Fredericia 700 d.	|	1949	2040	2046	2149	2240	2258	2328	0006	|	|
Middelfart 700 d.	1937	|	...	|	|	...	|	|	|	0120	0106
Kolding 705 d.	1951	2001	...	2058	2201	...	2310	2341	0018	0135	0135
Lunderskov 705 d.	1959	2008	...	2106	2209	...	2318	2349	0026	|	|
Vojens d.	...	2025	...	2123	2226	...	2335	...	0043	|	|
Tinglev d.	...	2046	...	2144	2248	...	2358	...	0104	|	|
Sønderborg a.	...	2119	...	|	2321	...	...	...	0138	|	|
Padborg 🏛 a.	...	...	...	2154	...	...	...	...	...	|	|
Flensburg 🏛 **823** a.	...	...	...	2207	...	...	...	...	...	|	|
Hamburg Hbf 823 a.	...	...	...	...	...	...	...	...	...	0528	0541

	2316	Lyn 10	IC 812	Lyn 914	IC 816	IC 5721	Lyn 18	Lyn 922	IC 824	IC 5729	Lyn 26	Lyn 940
	①–⑤	①–⑤	①–⑤	①–⑤								
Hamburg Hbf 823 d.	...	...	...	...	...	...	...	...	...	...	...	...
Flensburg 🏛 **823** d.	...	...	...	...	...	0648d	...	...	...	0848	...	...
Padborg 🏛 d.	...	...	...	...	...	0704d	...	...	...	0904	...	...
Sønderborg d.	...	...	...	0536	...	|	...	0736	...	|	...	0936
Tinglev d.	0513	...	...	0612	...	0715	...	0812	...	0915	...	1012
Vojens d.	0532	...	...	0631	...	0735	...	0831	...	0935	...	1031
Lunderskov 705 d.	0548	...	0557	0648	0657a	0751	...	0848	0857	0951	...	1048
Kolding 705 d.	0556	...	0606	0656	0706	0800	...	0856	0906	1000	...	1056
Middelfart 700 a.	|	...	0620	|	0720	|	...	|	0920	|	...	|
Fredericia 700 a.	0608	0622	|	0708	|	0812	0822	0908	|	1012	1022	1108
Aarhus 700 a.	...	|	|	|	|	...	|	|	|	1125	|	|
Odense 700 a.	...	0649	0645	0749	0745	...	0849	0949	0945	...	1049	1149
København H 700 a.	...	0805	0828	0905	0928	...	1005	1105	1128	...	1205	1305

	IC 832	IC 5737	Lyn 42	Lyn 944	IC 840	IC 386	Lyn 46	Lyn 948	IC 848	IC 5753	Lyn 50	Lyn 954	IC 856	IC 384	Lyn 58	Lyn 962	IC 864	IC 5769	Lyn 66	Lyn 970	IC 872	IC 382	IC 676	IC 1676		IC 5745		
						H								H								H	⑤⑥	⑦–④				
Hamburg Hbf 823 d.	...	...	...	...	...	1053	...	...	...	...	...	...	...	1450	...	...	...	...	...	...	...	1901h	...	...	...	...	...	...
Flensburg 🏛 **823** d.	...	1048	...	...	...	1250	...	...	...	1450	...	...	...	1650	...	...	...	1848	...	...	...	2048	...	...	...	2248	...	...
Padborg 🏛 d.	...	1104	...	...	...	1305	...	...	...	1504	...	...	...	1705	...	...	...	1904	...	...	...	2104	...	...	...	2304	...	...
Sønderborg d.	...	|	...	1136	...	|	...	1336	...	|	...	1536	...	|	...	1736	...	|	...	1936	...	|	...	...	2135	|	2338	...
Tinglev d.	...	1115	...	1212	...	1316	...	1412	...	1515	...	1612	...	1716	...	1812	...	1915	...	2012	...	2115	...	...	2210	2315	0012	...
Vojens d.	...	1135	...	1231	...	1336	...	1431	...	1535	...	1631	...	1736	...	1831	...	1935	...	2031	...	2135	...	...	2229	2335	...	...
Lunderskov 705 d.	1057	1151	...	1248	1257	1352	...	1448	1457	1551	...	1648	1657	1752	...	1848	1857	1951	...	2048	2057	2151	2216	2216	2247	2351	...	...
Kolding 705 d.	1106	1200	...	1256	1306	1401	...	1456	1506	1600	...	1656	1706	1801	...	1856	1906	2000	...	2056	2106	2200	2225	2225	2256	0000	...	...
Middelfart 700 a.	1120	|	...	|	1320	|	...	|	1520	|	...	|	1720	|	...	|	1920	|	...	|	2120	|	|	|	|	|	...	...
Fredericia 700 a.	|	1212	1222	1308	|	1414	1422	1508	|	1612	1622	1708	|	1814	1822	1908	|	2012	2022	2108	|	2212	2239	2239	2312	0012	...	...
Aarhus 700 a.	|	...	|	|	|	1525	|	|	|	...	|	|	|	1925	|	|	|	...	|	|	|	2325	|	|	|	...	...	...
Odense 700 a.	1145	...	1249	1349	1345	...	1449	1549	1545	...	1649	1749	1745	...	1849	1949	1945	...	2049	2149	2145	...	2329	2329	2356	...	...	...
København H 700 a.	1328	...	1405	1505	1528	...	1605	1705	1728	...	1805	1905	1928	...	2005	2105	2128	...	2205	2305j	...	...	0114	0129	...	...	...	...

H – (12) and 🍸 Aarhus / Fredericia - Hamburg and v.v. Ⓡ for international journeys in summer.
K – (12) København - Hamburg. Ⓡ for international journeys in summer.

a – ①–⑤ only.
d – ①–⑥ only.
h – June 2 - Sept. 3.
j – Arrive 2317 on ①②③④⑦.
k – ①–⑥ only (depart 0542 on ⑥).
y – Daily Dec. 16 - 30; Ⓑ June 2 - Sept. 1 (not Dec. 24).
z – ⑥ June 3 - Sept. 2.

‡ – Variations on ⑥⑦:
Train **383** runs as **1183** (Aarhus d. 0932);
train **385** runs as **1185** (Aarhus d. 1332);
train **387** runs as **1187** (Aarhus d. 1732).

* – Middelfart - Kolding: *23 km*.

DENMARK

712 AARHUS - VIBORG - STRUER

2nd class only (*IC* & *Lyn* 1st & 2nd class). Operator: *AT*

km																										
											♣								♣					⑥	⑥	†	
	København H **700** d.	Ⓐ	...	...	...	...	...	...	...	...	...	...	...	...	...	...	...	...	...	...	...	...	Ⓒ	...	...	...	...
0	**Aarhus 700** ⊗ d.		0440	0525	0625	0654	0754	0854	0954	1054	1154	1254	1354	1454	1554	1654	1754	1854	1954	2054	2154	2329		...	0554	...	0654
46	Langå **701** ⊗ a.		0510	0555	0655	0724	0824	0924	1024	1122	1224	1324	1424	1524	1624	1724	1824	1922	2024	2124	2224	2359		...	0624	...	0724
46	Langå ⊗ d.		0514	0559	0659	0728	0828	0928	1028	1128	1228	1328	1428	1528	1628	1728	1828	1928	2028	2128	2228	0003		...	0628	...	0728
86	Viborg ⊗ d.		0549	0649	0731	0806	0906	1006	1106	1206	1306	1406	1506	1606	1706	1806	1906	2006	2106	2206	2306	0033		0559	0659	0659	0759
116	Skive d.		0614	0713	0754	0828	0928	1028	1128	1228	1328	1428	1528	1628	1728	1828	1928	2028	2127	2228	2328	...		0621	0721	0721	0821
148	**Struer 715 716** a.		0636	0738	0818	0855	0955	1055	1155	1255	1355	1455	1555	1655	1755	1855	1955	2055	...	2255	2351			0644	0744	0744	0844

																					629	**643**	**645**	**661**	**663**	
						♣	♣					♣				†	⑥	⑥		♣	①–⑤	⑥	⑦	⑥⑦	①–⑤	
København H **700** d.	...	...	...	...	...	...	...	...	...	...	...	...	...	...	...	...	...	...	...		0754	0954	1054	1554	1554	...
Aarhus 700 ⊗ d.	0754	0854	0954	1054	1154	1254	1354	1454	1554	1654	1754	1854	1954	2054	2154	2254	2254	2354	...	DSB	1054	1254	1354	1854	1854	...
Langå **701** ⊗ a.	0824	0924	1024	1124	1224	1324	1424	1524	1624	1724	1824	1922	2024	2124	2224	2324	2324	0024	...	*IC/Lyn*	1122	1324	1422	1922	1922	...
Langå ⊗ d.	0828	0928	1028	1128	1228	1328	1428	1528	1628	1728	1828	1928	2028	2128	2228	2328	2328	0028	...	services	1128	1328	1428	1928	1928	...
Viborg ⊗ d.	0859	0959	1059	1159	1259	1359	1459	1559	1659	1759	1859	1959	2059	2159	2259	2358	2359	0058	...	►►►►	1206	1359	1459	1959	2006	...
Skive d.	0921	1021	1121	1221	1321	1421	1521	1621	1721	1821	1921	2021	2121	2222	2321	...	0021	...	...		1228	1421	1521	2021	2028	...
Struer 715 716 a.	0944	1044	1144r	1244	1344	1444	1544	1644	1744t	1844	1944	2044	2144	2245	2344	...	0044	...	...		1255	1444	1544	2044	2055	...

						♣						♣										⑥	⑥	⑥	†	♣
Struer 715 716 d.	Ⓐ	0447	0509	0550	0640	0718	0820	0920	1020	1120	1220	1320	1420	1520	1620	1720	1820	1920	2020	...	2220	Ⓒ	...	0522	0622	...	0722
Skive d.		0510	0532	0613	0703	0741	0843	0943	1043	1143	1243	1343	1443	1543	1643	1743	1843	1943	2043	2143	2243		...	0555	0655	...	0755
Viborg ⊗ d.		0534	0608	0638	0738	0808	0908	1008	1108	1208	1308	1408	1508	1608	1708	1808	1908	2008	2108	2208	2308		0522	0622	0722	0722	0822
Langå ⊗ a.		0612	0641	0711	0811	0841	0941	1041	1141	1241	1341	1441	1541	1641	1741	1841	1941	2041	2141	2241	2341		0553	0653	0753	0753	0853
Langå **701** ⊗ d.		0616	0647	0718	0816	0847	0947	1047	1147	1247	1347	1447	1547	1647	1747	1847	1947	2047	2147	2247	2347		0557	0657	0757	0757	0859
Aarhus 700 ⊗ a.		0648	0719	0750	0849	0919	1019	1119	1219	1319	1419	1519	1619	1719	1819	1919	2019	2119	2219	2319	0019		0629	0729	0829	0829	0929
København H **700** a.		...	...	...	...	...	...	...	...	...	...	...	...	...	...	...	...	...	...	...	...		...	...	...	...	...

																					626	**628**	**652**	**660**	**664**	
				⑥	†				♣	♣	⑥	†								♣	①–⑤	⑥⑦	①–⑤	⑥	⑦	
Struer 715 716 d.	0822	0922	1022	1122	...	1222	1322	1422	1522	1622	...	1722	1822	1922	2022	2122	2223	2322	...		0718	0722	1320	1522	1622	...
Skive d.	0855	0955	1055	1155	1155	1255	1355	1455	1555	1655	1655	1755	1855	1955	2055	2155	2255	2355	...	DSB	0741	0755	1343	1555	1655	...
Viborg ⊗ d.	0922	1022	1122	1222	1222	1322	1422	1522	1622	1722	1722	1822	1922	2022	2122	2222	2322	0021	...	*IC/Lyn*	0808	0822	1408	1622	1722	...
Langå ⊗ a.	0953	1053	1153	1253	1253	1353	1453	1553	1653	1753	1853	1853	1953	2053	2153	2253	2353	...	...	services	0841	0853	1441	1653	1753	...
Langå **701** ⊗ d.	0957	1057	1157	1257	1257	1357	1457	1557	1657	1757	1857	1857	1957	2057	2157	2257	2357	...	...	►►►►	0847	0859	1447	1659	1757	...
Aarhus 700 ⊗ a.	1029	1129	1229	1329	1329	1429	1529	1629	1729	1829	1929	1929	2029	2129	2229	2329	0029	...	...		0919	0929	1519	1729	1829	...
København H **700** a.	...	...	...	...	...	...	...	...	...	...	...	...	...	...	...	...	...	...	...		1257	1257	1857	2057	2157	...

r – ⑥ only.
t – † only.

♣ – Runs as DSB *Lyn* service on some days / dates – see panel (and heading).
⊗ – Additional services operate Aarhus - Viborg and v.v.

☛ See Table **715** below for direct services Struer - Herning - København and v.v.

713 AARHUS - HERNING - SKJERN

2nd class only. Operator: *AT*

km																											
																			⑥								
0	**Aarhus 700** ⊗ d.	Ⓐ	0530	0633	0800	0830	0930	1000	and at	1630	1700	1730	1819	2019	2119	2219	2332	Ⓒ	0625	0725	0825	and	1925	2025	2125	2225	2340
23	Skanderborg **700** ⊗ d.		0551	0655	0820	0851	0951	1020	the same	1651	1720	1751	1839	2039	2139	2239	2354		0645	0745	0845	every	1945	2045	2145	2245	2359
53	Silkeborg ⊗ d.		0616	0722	0849	0912	1012	1049	minutes	1712	1749	1817	1909	2109	2209	2305	0021		0712	0812	0912	two	2012	2112	2212	2311	0026
94	**Herning** ⊗ a.		0646	0754	0931	0946	1046	1131	past	1746	1834	1848	1948	2148	2248	2341	0057		0748	0848	0948	hours	2048	2148	2248	2349	0102
94	**Herning 715** d.		0705	0822	0938	...	1108	...	each hour	1808	...	...	2006	2206	2325	...	...		0806	...	1006	until	...	2206	2325	...	...
136	**Skjern 707 708** a.		0742	0857	1013	...	1143	...	until	1845	...	...	2041	2241	2400	...	...		0844	...	1041		...	2241	2400	...	...

																			⑥								
Skjern 707 708 d.	Ⓐ	0509	0559	0659	0812	...	0954	and at	...	1557	...	1657	...	1757	1917	2117	2246	Ⓒ	0517	...	0717	...	and	1917	...	2117	2246
Herning 715 a.		0548	0635	0734	0850	...	1036	the same	...	1636	...	1736	...	1836	1952	2152	2321		0552	...	0752	...	every	1952	...	2152	2321
Herning ⊗ d.		0554	0647	0755	0854	1007	1054	minutes	1607	1654	1707	1746	1809	1911	2011	2211	2325		0608	0708	0808	0908	two	2008	2108	2208	2325
Silkeborg ⊗ d.		0629	0728	0828	0929	1051	1129	past	1651	1729	1751	1818	1851	1951	2051	2251	0005		0647	0747	0847	0947	hours	2047	2147	2247	0001
Skanderborg **700** ⊗ a.		0650	0749	0849	0950	1120	1150	each hour	1720	1750	1820	1839	1920	2020	2120	2320	0035		0715	0815	0915	1015	until	2115	2215	2315	0029
Aarhus 700 ⊗ a.		0710	0809	0909	1010	1140	1210	until	1740	1810	1840	1859	1940	2040	2140	2340	0055		0735	0835	0935	1035		2135	2235	2335	0049

A change of train may be necessary at Herning.

⊗ – Additional services operate Aarhus - Herning and v.v

715 FREDERICIA - HERNING - STRUER

2nd class only (*IC* & *Lyn* 1st & 2nd class)

km		*IC*		*IC*			*IC*	*Lyn*		*Lyn*	*IC*	*Lyn*		*Lyn*	*IC*	*Lyn*		*Lyn*	*Lyn*		*Lyn*	*Lyn*		*Lyn*	*Lyn*	*Lyn*		*Lyn*
		1603		**1611**			**117**	**21**		**725**	**125**	**29**		**741**	**133**	**43**		**745**	**47**		**749**	**53**		**757**	**761**	**61**		**765**
		①–⑤	①–⑤	①–⑤	①–⑤			①–⑤																	①–⑤	⑥⑦	⑥⑦	⑥⑦
	København H **700** d.	0045	...	0245	...	...	...	0554	...	0654	0700	0754	...	0854	0900	0954	...	1054	1154	...	1254	1354	...	1454	1554	1554	...	1654
	Odense **700** d.	0232	...	0432	...	...	0638	0710	...	0810	0838	0910	...	1010	1038	1110	...	1210	1310	...	1410	1510	...	1610	1710	1710	...	1810
0	**Fredericia 700** d.	0304	0447	0502	0547	0647	0714	0744	0747	0847	0914	0944	0947	1047	1114	1144	1147	1247	1344	1347	1447	1544	1547	1647	1747	1740	1747	1847
26	Vejle **700** d.	0318	0502	...	0602	0702	0727	0757	0802	0902	0927	0957	1002	1102	1127	1157	1202	1302	1357	1402	1502	1557	1602	1702	1802	...	1802	1902
99	Herning a.	...	0558	...	0658	0758	...	...	0858	0958	...	...	1058	1158	...	...	1258	1358	...	1458	1558	...	1658	1758	1858	...	1858	1958
99	Herning **713** d.	...	0600	...	0700	0804	...	...	0900	1000	...	...	1100	1200	...	...	1300	1400	...	1500	1600	...	1700	1800	1900	...	1900	2000
140	Holstebro **708** d.	...	0636	...	0737	0839	...	...	0935	1035	...	...	1135	1235	...	...	1335	1435	...	1535	1635	...	1735	1835	1935	...	1935	2035
155	**Struer 708** a.	...	0647	...	0748	0850	...	...	0946	1046	...	...	1146	1246	...	...	1346	1446	...	1546	1646	...	1746	1846	1946	...	1946	2046
229	*Thisted* **716** a.	...	...	...	...	...	...	...	...	...	...	...	...	1411c	...	...	...	...	...	...	...	...	...	...	...	...	...	...

	Lyn	*Lyn*		*Lyn*	*Lyn*	*Lyn*			*Lyn*
	765	**69**		**769**	**773**	**77**			**781**
	①–⑤		⑥–④	⑤			⑤⑥	⑦–④	
København H **700** d.	1654	1754	...	1754	1854	1954	...	...	2054
Odense **700** d.	1810	1910	...	1910	2010	2110	...	...	2210
Fredericia 700 d.	1847	1940	1947	1947	2047	2144	2147	2148	2247
Vejle **700** d.	1902	...	2002	2002	2102	2157	2202	2208	2302
Herning a.	1958	...	2058	2058	2158	...	2258	2313	2358
Herning **713** d.	2000	...	2100	2100	2200	...	2300	2314	0000
Holstebro **708** d.	2035	...	2135	2135	2233	...	2336	2346	0035
Struer 708 a.	2046	...	2146	2146	2246	...	2347	2358	0046
Thisted **716** a.	...	...	...	...	...	...	...	...	...

	Lyn	*Lyn*	*Lyn*		*Lyn*	*IC*	*Lyn*		*Lyn*	*IC*	*Lyn*	*Lyn*		*Lyn*
	710	**714**	**718**		**22**	**124**	**726**		**40**	**132**	**742**	**744**		**44**
	①–⑤	①–⑤										⑤⑦	**G**	
Thisted **716** d.	...	...	...	...	...	...	0653	...	...	...	...	...	...	...
Struer 708 d.	0415	0515	0609	0706	...	...	0812	0908	...	...	1008	1108	1108	...
Holstebro **708** d.	0427	0527	0621	0720	...	...	0824	0920	...	...	1020	1120	1120	...
Herning **713** a.	0456	0556	0650	0749	...	...	0853	0949	...	...	1049	1149	1149	...
Herning d.	0458	0558	0658	0758	...	...	0858	0958	...	...	1058	1158	1158	...
Vejle **700** d.	0556	0656	0756	0857	0901	0928	0956	1057	1101	1128	1156	1256	1257	...
Fredericia 700 a.	0612	0712	0812	0912	0917	0943	1012	1112	1117	1143	1212	1312	1312	1322
Odense **700** a.	0649	0749	0849	...	0949	1018	1049	...	1149	1218	1249	1349	...	1349
København H **700** a.	0805	0905	1005	...	1105	1157	1205	...	1305	1357	1405	1505	...	1505

	IC	*Lyn*	*Lyn*		*Lyn*	*IC*	*Lyn*		*Lyn*	*IC*	*Lyn*		*Lyn*	*IC*	*Lyn*		*Lyn*	*Lyn*	*IC*	*IC*		*IC*	*IC*		*IC*		*IC*	
	140	**746**	**748**		**48**	**148**	**750**		**54**	**156**	**758**		**62**	**164**	**766**		**70**	**72**	**172**	**1672**		**176**	**1676**		**1680**		**188**	
			①–⑤	⑥⑦													⑤⑥	⑦–④	⑤⑥	⑦–④		⑤⑥	⑦–④					
Thisted **716** d.	...	...	...	...	...	...	...	...	...	...	1422c	...	...	...	...	...	...	...	...	...	...	...	...	...	...	...	...	...
Struer 708 d.	...	1208	1308	1308	...	...	1408	1508	...	...	1608	1708	...	...	1808	1908	...	...	...	...	2008	...	...	2103	...	2303	...	...
Holstebro **708** d.	...	1220	1320	1320	...	...	1420	1520	...	...	1620	1720	...	...	1820	1920	...	...	...	...	2020	...	...	2120	...	2321	...	...
Herning **713** a.	...	1249	1349	1349	...	...	1449	1549	...	...	1649	1749	...	...	1850	1949	...	...	...	...	2049	...	...	2149	...	2351	...	...
Herning d.	...	1258	1358	1358	...	...	1458	1558	...	...	1658	1758	...	...	1858	1958	...	...	...	...	2058	...	...	2158	...	2358	...	...
Vejle **700** d.	1328	1354	1456	1457	...	1528	1556	1657	1701	1728	1756	1857	1901	1928	1956	2057	2101	2101	2128	2128	2157	2228	2230	2257	2333	0057	0135	...
Fredericia 700 a.	1343	1412	1512	1512	1522	1543	1612	1712	1717	1743	1812	1912	1917	1943	2012	2112	2117	2117	2143	2143	2212	2243	2246	2318	2356	0112	0150	...
Odense **700** a.	1418	1449	1549	...	1549	1618	1649	...	1749	1818	1849	...	1949	2018	2049	...	2149	2149	2218	2217	...	2329	2329	...	0035	...	0235	...
København H **700** a.	1557	1605	1705	...	1705	1757	1805	...	1905	1957	2005	...	2105	2157	2205	...	2305	2317	0005	0020	...	0114	0129	...	0216j	...	0416	...

G – ①②③④⑥ only.
c – ⑥⑦ only.
j – ⑤⑥ only.

STRUER - THISTED | 716

Operator: *AT* (*Lyn* trains: *DSB*). 2nd class only (*Lyn* 1st & 2nd class)

															741 K‡						
0	Struer 708/12/5 .....d.	Ⓐ	0438	0536	0722	1005	1204	1305	1405	1505	1605	1705	1905	2100	2300	Ⓒ	⑥ 0528	0645	0854	1054	1254
74	Thisted ....a.		0600	0723	0912	1122	1322	1424	1524	1624	1724	1824	2022	2217	0017		0646	0804	1011	1211	1411

		‡									
			...	1454	1654	1854	2054	2254
			...	1611	1811	2011	2211	0011

			726 K‡														726 K‡					
Thisted ....d.	Ⓐ	0605	0653	0744	0931	1131	1328	1428	1528	1628	1728	1828	2027	2227	Ⓒ	⑥ 0456	0653	0822	1022	1222	1422
Struer 708/12/5 ....a.		0721	0810	0903	1053	1253	1453	1552	1652	1752	1852	1952	2147	2347		0616	0810	0941	1141	1341	1541

1622	1822	2022	2222	...
1741	1941	2141	2341	...

K – ⚏ København - Struer - Thisted and v.v. InterCityLyn (*Lyn*) service (see Table 715). ‡ – Operated by *DSB*.

KØBENHAVN - RØDBY - PUTTGARDEN (- HAMBURG) | 720

km			1213 A	1217 q	EC 238 ①–⑤		①–⑤	EC 38 ✕		①–⑤	EC 36 ✕		①–⑤	EC 34 ✕		①–⑤	EC 232 ✕s	1253
0	København H 700/4 ....d.				0510	0537	...	0610	0637	0710	0737	0810	0837	0910	0937	1010	1037	1110	1137	1210	1237	1310	1337	1337
20	Høje Taastrup 700/4 ....d.				0526	0551	...	0626	0651	0726	0751	0826	0851	0926	0951	1026	1051	1126	1151	1226	1251	1326	1351	1351
31	Roskilde 700/4 ....d.				0535	0600	...	0635	0700	0735	0800	0835	0900	0935	1000	1035	1100	1135	1200	1235	1300	1335	1400	1400
64	Ringsted 700 ....d.				0553		...	0653		0753		0853		0953		1053		1153		1253		1353		
91	Næstved ....d.				0612	0631	...	0712	0731	0812	0831	0912	0931	1012	1031	1112	1131	1212	1231	1312	1331	1412	1431	1431
118	Vordingborg ....d.				0631	0646	...	0731	0746	0831	0846	0931	0946	1031	1046	1131	1146	1231	1246	1331	1346	1431	1446	1446
147	Nykøbing (Falster) ....☉ d.		0544	0644	0658	0714	0744	0758	0810	0858	0914	0958	1010	1058	1114	1158	1210	1258	1314	1358	1410	1458	1514	1514
183	Rødby ....⚓▲a.		0606	0706	...	0735	0806	...	...	0935	...	...	1135	...	...	1335	...	...	1535	1535
202	Puttgarden ....⚓▲a.		...	...	0836	...	...	...	...	1036	...	...	1236	...	...	1436	...	...	1636	...
291	Lübeck 825 ....a.		...	...	0937	...	...	...	...	1137	...	...	1337y	...	...	1537	...	...	1737	...
353	Hamburg Hbf 825 ....a.		...	...	1020	...	...	...	...	1220	...	...	1421y	...	...	1622	...	...	1821	...

		ICE 1232 ✕s	ICE 32 ✕B	1261 L	①–⑤		①–⑤	EC 30 ✕F	①–⑤		2277	⑦–④ ✕	⑤⑥	M ✕	⑤⑥	⑦–④ ✕	⑤⑥
København H § 700/4 ....d.		1410	1437	1510	1537	1537	1537	1541	1610	1637	1710	1737	1810	1837	1910	2010	2110	2200	2210	2255	2310	...	0000	0010
Høje Taastrup § 700/4 ....d.		1426	1451	1526	1551	1551	1551	1556	1626	1651	1726	1751	1826	1851	1926	2026	2126	2216	2226	2311	2326	...	0015	0026
Roskilde § 700/4 ....d.		1435	1500	1535	1600	1600	1600	1608	1635	1700	1735	1800	1835	1900	1935	2035	2135	2224	2235	2324	2335	...	0023	0035
Ringsted § 700 ....d.		1453		1553				1625	1653		1752		1853		1953	2053	2153	2253	2252	2359		...	0048	0059
Næstved § ....d.		1512	1531	1612	1631	1631	1631	1644	1712	1731	1812	1831	1912	1931	2012	2112	2212	2312	2312	0011	0018	...	0107	0118
Vordingborg § ....d.		1531	1546	1631	1646	1646	1646	1709	1731	1746	1831	1846	1931	1946	2031	2131	2231	2331	2331	0037	0037	...	0130	0137
Nykøbing (Falster) ....☉ d.		1558	1610	1658	1714	1714	1714	1741	1755	1810	1858	1914	1955	2010	2058	2157	2258	2355	2355	0101	0101	...	0154	0201
Rødby ....⚓▲a.		...	...	1735	1735	1735	1803s	...	1935	...	...	2219	...	...	...	...
Puttgarden ....⚓▲a.		...	...	1836	1836	1836	...	...	2036	...	...	...
Lübeck 825 ....a.		...	...	1937	1937	1937	...	...	2137z	...	...
Hamburg Hbf 825 ....a.		...	...	2021	2021	2021	...	...	2223z	...	...

				1212 G	1216 H	1220 ①–⑤	①–⑤					EC 31 ✕J					EC 33 ✕
Hamburg Hbf 825 ....d.		①–⑤	①–⑤			①–⑤	①–⑤					0724	①–⑤			0928
Lübeck 825 ....d.											0806			1006
Puttgarden ....⚓▲d.											0908			1108
Rødby ....⚓▲d.						0620r	...	0720q	...	0820		1020	1020			1220
Nykøbing (Falster) ....☉ d.		0434	0503	0548	0603	0619	0628	0647	0709	0747	0759	0843	0847	0859	0947	0959		1047	1047	1059	1147	1159	1247	1259
Vordingborg ....d.		0458	0528	0609	0628	0658	0658	0709	0728	0809	0828		0909	0928	1009	1028		1109	1109	1128	1209	1228	1309	1328
Næstved ....d.		0517	0547	0627	0647	0717	0717	0727	0747	0827	0847		0927	0947	1027	1047		1127	1127	1147	1227	1247	1327	1347
Ringsted 700 ....d.		0536	0605		0705	0736	0736		0805		0905			1005		1105			1205		1305		1405
Roskilde 700 ....d.		0553	0624	0657	0724	0753	0753	0757	0824	0857	0924		0957	1024	1057	1124		1157	1157	1224	1257	1324	1357	1424
Høje Taastrup 700/4 ....d.		0605	0632	0707	0732	0805	0805	0807	0832	0906	0932		1006	1032	1106	1132		1206	1206	1232	1306	1332	1406	1432
København H 700/4 ....a.		0622	0649	0724	0749	0822	0822	0824	0849	0922	0949		1022	1049	1122	1149		1222	1222	1249	1322	1349	1422	1449

		EC 233 ✕s	①–⑤		①–⑤	EC 35 ✕	①–⑤	EC 37 ✕	①–⑤	EC 39 ✕	⑤⑥	⑦–④	⑤⑥	⑦–④	EC 239 ✕s	4274	⑤⑥	⑦–④
Hamburg Hbf 825 ....d.		1128	①–⑤	...	1328	①–⑤	1528j	✕	1728	⑤⑥⑦–④	1928	⑤⑥⑦–④
Lübeck 825 ....d.		1206		...	1406		1606j		1806		2006
Puttgarden ....⚓▲d.		1308		...	1508		1708		1908		2108
Rødby ....⚓▲d.		1420	1420	...	1620		1820		2020		2220	2238
Nykøbing (Falster) ....☉ d.		1347	1359	1447	1447	1459	1547	1559	1647	1659	1759	1847	1859	1959	2047	2103	2107	2203	2207	2247	2301	2326	2326
Vordingborg ....d.		1409	1428	1509	1509	1528	1609	1628	1709	1728	1828	1909	1928	2028	2109	2128	2133	2228	2309		2330	2352
Næstved ....d.		1427	1447	1527	1527	1547	1627	1647	1727	1747	1847	1927	1947	2047	2127	2147	2156	2247	2255	2350	0012
Ringsted 700 ....d.			1505			1605		1705		1805	1905		2005	2105		2215	2305	2315		0007	0030
Roskilde 700 ....d.		1457	1524	1557	1557	1624	1657	1724	1757	1824	1924	2024	2127	2224	2245	2324	2332	2345	0006		0041	0108
Høje Taastrup 700/4 ....d.		1506	1532	1606	1606	1632	1706	1732	1806	1832	1932	2006	2032	2132	2206	2232	2254	2332	2345	0006		0041	0108
København H 700/4 ....a.		1522	1549	1622	1622	1649	1722	1749	1819	1849	1949	2022	2049	2149	2219	2249	2314	2354	0020	0022		0102	0129

A – ①–⑤ June 23 - Aug. 11.
B – Dec. 16 - 23, 25, 27 - 30, Jan. 1, Mar. 31 - June 22, Aug. 14 - Dec. 9.
G – June 23, Aug. 7 - 11.
H – ⑥ Dec. 12 - June 23, Aug. 7 - Dec. 8 (not Dec. 27 - 30, Apr. 10 - 12, May 26, Oct. 16 - 20).
J – Dec. 17 - 31, Apr. 1 - Oct. 1 (not Dec. 25).
L – Dec. 11 - Mar. 30 (not Dec. 16 - 23, 25, 30, Jan. 1).
M – ①②③④⑦ Dec. 11 - June 1, Sept. 3 - Dec. 7 (not Apr. 13 - 17, May 12, 25).
¶ – Dec. 17 - 23, 25, 27 - 30, Jan. 1.
q – ⑥ Dec. 12 - June 22, Aug. 14 - Dec. 8.
r – June 23 - Aug. 12.
s – June 23 - Aug. 13.

y – Dec. 17 - 31 (not Dec. 25).
z – Dec. 11 - Oct. 1.

☉ – Trains run approximately hourly (more frequent on ①–⑤) Nykøbing (Falster) -
Nakskov and v.v., journey 45 minutes. Operator: Lokaltog A/S.

▲ – Through trains are conveyed by ⚓ Rødby - Puttgarden and v.v. ✕ on board
ship. Passengers to/from Rødby or Puttgarden may be required to leave or join
the train on board the train-ferry. See Table 2375 for other available sailings.

✕ – ℝ for international journeys in summer.

KØBENHAVN - YSTAD - RØNNE | 727

Valid until March 31

km		A	B	C		D	E		F	G			A	B	C		D	E		F	G
0	København H ....d.	0632		1043	1443	...	1643	1843	...	2043	2243	Rønne ⚓ ....d.	0630		1030	1430	...	1630	1830	...	2030	2230
12	Kastrup ✈ ....d.											Ystad ⚓ ....a.	0750		1150	1550	...	1750	1950	...	2150	2350
94	Ystad ....a.	0747		1147	1547	...	1747	1947	...	2147	2347	Ystad ....d.	0809		1209	1609	...	1809	2009	...	2209	0009
	Ystad ⚓ ....d.	0830		1230	1630	...	1830	2030	...	2230	0020	Kastrup ✈ ....a.										
	Rønne ⚓ ....a.	0950		1350	1750	...	1950	2150	...	2350	0140	København H ....a.	0922		1322	1722	...	1922	2122	...	2322	0116

A – Daily (not Jan. 1).
B – Dec. 17, 22 - 24, 26, 31, Jan. 1; ⑥ Jan. 7 - Mar. 25.
C – Dec. 11, 16 - 18, 22, 23, 25, 30, Jan. 1, 6, 8, 13, 15, 20, 22, 27, 29, Feb. 3, 5, 10,
12, 17, 19, 24, 26, Mar. 3, 5, 10, 12, 17, 19, 24, 26, 31.
D – Dec. 12 - 15, 19 - 21, 27 - 29, Jan. 2 - 5, 9 - 12, 16 - 19, 23 - 26, 30, 31, Feb. 1, 2, 6 - 9,
13 - 16, 20 - 23, 27, 28, Mar. 1, 2, 6 - 9, 13 - 16, 20 - 23, 27 - 30.

E – Dec. 11, 16 - 18, 22, 23, 25, 26, 30, Jan. 1, 6, 7, 8, 13 - 15, 20 - 22, 27 - 29, Feb. 3 - 5, 10 - 12,
17 - 19, 24 - 26, Mar. 3 - 5, 10 - 12, 17 - 19, 24 - 26, 31.
F – Dec. 12 - 15, 19 - 21, 27 - 29, Jan. 2 - 5, 9 - 12, 16 - 19, 23 - 26, 30, 31, Feb. 1, 2, 6 - 9, 13 - 16,
20 - 23, 27, 28, Mar. 1, 2, 6 - 9, 13 - 16.
G – Summer only.

DENMARK and ICELAND

728 Valid until August 5 — Northern SECONDARY LINES

Nordjyske Jernbaner A/S. 2nd class only

From **Frederikshavn**:
①-⑤: 0604, 0642, 0700, 0745, 0838, 0938, 1038, 1150, 1250, 1337, 1404, 1442, 1507, 1544, 1610, 1647, 1712, 1751, 1838, 1938, 2038, 2138, 2238, 2338.
⑥⑦: 0737⑥, 0837⑦, 0937, 1037 and hourly until 1737, then 1837⑥, 1937, 2037⑥, 2137, 2237⑥, 2337.

From **Hjørring**:
①-⑤: 0500, 0522, 0600, 0629, 0700, 0732, 0801, 0831, 0903, 1003, 1103, 1203, 1303, 1331, 1402, 1431, 1502, 1531, 1602, 1631, 1702, 0731, 1802, 1903, 2103, 2203, 2303.
⑥⑦: 0703, 0803 and hourly until 1903, then 2103, 2203, 2303.

From **Skagen**: *40 km* Journey 36 minutes
①-⑤: 0522, 0542, 0620, 0658, 0723, 0748, 0827, 0951, 1051, 1151, 1251, 1352, 1419, 1444, 1522, 1546, 1623, 1701, 1752, 1851, 1951, 2051, 2151, 2253.
⑥⑦: 0651⑥, 0750⑦, 0850, 0950 and hourly until 1550, then 1650⑥, 1653⑦, 1753⑥, 1850, 1950⑥, 2050, 2150⑥, 2250.

From **Hirtshals / Color Line**: *18 km* Journey 22 minutes
①-⑤: 0525, 0603, 0630, 0659, 0733, 0804, 0834, 0905, 0930, 1030, 1130, 1230, 1334, 1405, 1434, 1505, 1534, 1605, 1634, 1705, 1734, 1805, 1830, 2010, 2130, 2230, 2330.
⑥⑦: 0730, 0830 and hourly until 1830, then 2010, 2130, 2230, 2330.

Minor time variations are possible.

ICELAND

There are no railways in Iceland but bus services serve most major settlements. Principal services enabling a circuit of the country (along road number 1) and some other important routes are shown below. Additional information may be obtained from the websites of the operators. For a complete listing of all routes, including local services and ferries, see www.publictransport.is. Buses have scheduled stops in all settlements (often at N1 filling stations) but may also stop on demand at any point along the route (confirm with operator).

Winter timings: Only *STR* and a few shorter routes shown in 'Other Services' below operate. No long-distance services on Dec. 24, 25, 31, Jan. 1.
Summer timings: In addition to *STR* services, many more routes are run by private operators, with bus passes available for the *STA / SBA* and *RE / SBA* networks, respectively. Timings shown are for summer 2016; comparable services are expected for summer 2017.

Tourist excursions are also available all year. All schedules may change at short notice - contact operators for latest timings. Confirm timings, particularly in winter, as in adverse weather conditions buses may be advanced, delayed or cancelled.

Public holidays in 2016: Jan. 1, Mar. 24, 25, 27, 28, Apr. 21, May 1, 5, 15, 16, June 17, Dec. 25, 26. **Public holidays in 2017**: Jan. 1, Apr. 13, 14, 16, 17, 20, May 1, 25, June 4, 5, 17, Dec. 25, 26

729 PRINCIPAL BUS SERVICES

KEFLAVÍK - REYKJAVÍK - AKUREYRI

km	operator	WINTER	*STR*	*STR*	*STR*	SUMMER	*STR*	*GL*	*STR*	*STR*	*STA*
	route number		57	57	57		57	North	57	57	60
			VX	**Ⓐ V**	**† V**		**N**	**T**	**Ⓐ N**	**Ⓒ N**	**R**
	Keflavík Airport d.		...	...	...		...	1700	...	...	...
0	Reykjavík (BSÍ terminal) ■ d.		0840**z**	*1657***d**	*1703***d**		0840**z**	1745**g**	*1658***d**	*1702***d**	2345**h**
7	Reykjavík (Mjódd) ■ d.		0900	1730	1730		0900	|	1730	1730	|
•426	Akureyri (Hof) a.		1529**y**	2359	2359		1529**y**	2300**r**	2359	2359	0550**r**

operator	WINTER	*STR*	*STR*	SUMMER	*STA*	*STR*	*STR*	*GL*
route number		57	57		60a	57	57	South
		Ⓑ V	**V**		**R**	**N**	**N**	**T**
Akureyri (Hof) d.		1015	1620		0730**r**	1015	1620	2315
Reykjavík (Mjódd) ■ a.		1644	2249		|	1644	2249	|
Reykjavík (BSÍ terminal) ■ a.		*1703***e**	*2302***e**		1310**h**	*1703***e**	*2302***e**	0410**g**
Keflavík Airport a.		...	...		...	...	...	0500

Additional local *STR* services operate Reykjavík (Mjódd) - Borgarnes (Hyrnan) (82 *km*, journey ± 1h 23 mins.) and v.v. 3 - 8 services per day; no services on Dec. 25, Jan. 1. On Dec. 24, 31 only first morning services operate.

Reykjavík - Keflavík Airport: 50 *km*, local services. From BSÍ terminal ■: *flybus*, operator *RE*, journey ± 45 minutes. From Holtagardar terminal ■: *airportexpress*, operator *GL*, journey ± 45 minutes. *GL* shuttle bus from Laekjartorg departs 30 minutes earlier. *RE* and *GL* both offer departures in connection with all flights. Optional hotel transfer available.
Additional stopping services operated by *STR* route 55 (Reykjavík BSÍ terminal (Umferdarmidstödin) during Ⓐ peak hours only) - Hafnarfjördur (Fjördur) - Keflavík Airport (FLE) and v.v. During off peak hours and on Ⓒ use *STR* city route 1 Hlemmur via city bus stop at BSÍ (direction Hfj. Vellir); change to route 55 in Hafnarfjördur (Fjördur). 7 - 13 services per day, total journey time 75 - 90 minutes.

AKUREYRI - EGILSSTADIR - HÖFN

km	operator	WINTER	*STR*		SUMMER	*STA*	*SBA*	*STA*	*STR*	*STR*
	route number		56			70	62	78	56	56
			Y			**S**§	**F**§	**S**§	**D**	**D**
0	Akureyri (Hof) d.		1535**y**	...		0730**r**	0800**r**	...	1150	1535**y**
103	Reykjahlíd (Mývatn) (N1) d.		1705	...		0945	1000	...	1320	1705
266	Egilsstadir (Campsite) ❄ d.		1906	...		1400**s**	1300	1610	...	1906
533	Höfn í Hornafirdi (N1) ❄ a.		...	...		...	1730	2030**t**	...	...

operator	WINTER	*STR*		SUMMER	*STA*	*STR*	*STR*	*SBA*	*STA*
route number		56			70a	56	56	62a	78a
		Y			**S**§	**D**	**D**	**F**§	**R**§
Höfn í Hornafirdi (N1) ❄ d.		...	...		...	...	...	0800	1745**t**
Egilsstadir (Campsite) ❄ d.		0909	...		0900	0909	...	1300	2205
Reykjahlíd (Mývatn) (N1) d.		1110	...		1400**s**	1110	1325	1525	...
Akureyri (Hof) a.		1240	...		1710**r**	1240	1455	1715**r**	...

❄ – No through service in winter. Additional local services run all year on separate routes Egilsstadir - Reydarfjördur (299 *km*) - *Breiddalsvík* (365 *km*) and v.v. (2 - 3 services per day), and Djúpivogur (430 *km*) - Höfn and v.v. (5 services per week). Operator: *SVA*.

HÖFN - REYKJAVÍK

km	operator	WINTER	*STR*	*STR*	*STR*	SUMMER	*STR*	*STA*	*RE*	*RE*	*STR*	*RE*
	route number		51	51	51		51	12a	19	20a	51	21a
			wW	**†W**	**Ⓐ W**		**C**	**G**§	**L**§	**K**§	**C**	**P**§
0	Höfn í Hornafirdi (N1) d.		...	1025**v**	1155**v**		0735**v**	0755**t**	0800	...	1605**v**	...
135	Skaftafell d.		...	1220	1350		0935	1125	1215	1230	1805	...
275	Vík í Mýrdal (N1) d.		1442	1442**c**	1600**c**		1200**c**	1420	...	1530	2030**c**	2030
456	Reykjavík (Mjódd) ■ a.		1724	1724	1845		1445**f**	|	...	|	2315	|
461	Reykjavík (BSÍ) ■ a.		*1733***e**	*1733***e**	*1902***e**		*1503***e**	1810**h**	...	1935	*2332***e**	2345

operator	WINTER	*STR*	*STR*	*STR*	SUMMER	*STA*	*RE*	*STR*	*RE*	*STR*	*RE*
route number		51	51	51		12	20	51	19	51	21
		wW	**†W**	**Ⓐ W**		**G**§	**L**§	**C**	**L**§	**C**	**P**§
Reykjavík (BSÍ) ■ d.		*1101***d**	*1101***d**	*1231***d**		0730**h**	0800	*0840***z**	...	*1657***d**	1600
Reykjavík (Mjódd) ■ d.		1130	1130	1300		|	|	0900	...	1730	|
Vík í Mýrdal (N1) d.		1412	1445**c**	1615**c**		1150	1400	1200**c**	...	2030**c**	1940
Skaftafell d.		...	1650	1820		1420	1600	1410	1730	2240	...
Höfn í Hornafirdi (N1) a.		...	1835**v**	2005**v**		1700**t**	...	1555**v**	1930	0025**v**	...

Additional local *STR* services operate (Hvolsvöllur (N1) -) Selfoss (N1) - Reykjavík (Mjódd) and v.v. Hvolsvöllur - Selfoss - Mjódd (100 *km*), journey ± 1h 40 mins., 3 - 8 services per day. Selfoss - Mjódd (52 *km*), journey 53 mins., 8 - 12 services per day. No services on Dec. 25, Jan. 1. On Dec. 24, 31 only first morning services operate.

OTHER SERVICES

Egilsstadir - Seydisfjördur: 27 *km*, journey ± 35 minutes, operator *FAS*. Services connect with Smyril Line ferry (Table **2285**). Confirm departure point with operator.
Summer (June 10 - Aug. 29, 2016): From **Egilsstadir** (Campsite): 0900Ⓐ, 1020④, 1305⑥⑦, 1640Ⓐ. From **Seydisfjördur**: 0750Ⓐ **m**, 0930④ **n**, 1215⑥⑦ **m**, 1545Ⓐ **m**.
Winter (Aug. 30, 2016 - June 14, 2017): From **Egilsstadir** (Campsite): 0900Ⓐ, 1030⑥, 1050② **U**, 1640Ⓐ. From **Seydisfjördur**: 0750Ⓐ **m**, 0930⑥ **m**, 1000② **U n**, 1545Ⓐ **m**.

Reykjavík - Blue Lagoon: 48 *km*, journey ± 45 minutes. From BSÍ terminal ■: operator *RE*. From Holtagardar terminal ■: operator *GL*. Departures several times per day, also infrequent departures from Keflavík airport.

INTERIOR HIGHLAND ROUTE: Reykjavík - Akureyri via Selfoss - Geysir§ - Gulfoss§ - Kjölur§ (448 *km*).
Reykjavík BSÍ ■ d. 0800 ⟶ Akureyri (**r**) a. 1830. Akureyri (**r**) d. 0800 ⟶ Reykjavík BSÍ ■ a. 1830. Daily June 18 - Sept. 10, 2016, depending on road opening dates, §. Operator: *SBA* route 610 / 610a.

Reykjavík BSÍ - Thingvellir - Geysir - Gullfoss (Golden Circle): operator *RE* route 6 / 6a (with sightseeing stops). Departures June 13 - Sept. 14, 2016 from Reykjavík at 1000, arriving back in Reykjavík at 1845. Geysir / Gullfoss also served by *SBA* and *STA* Reykjavík - Kjölur - Akureyri services (see above). *Daily excursions also available from different operators, including during winter.*

C – May 15 - Sept. 10, 2016.
D – May 29 - Aug. 27, 2016.
F – June 1 - Sept. 10, 2016.
G – June 1 - Sept. 9, 2016.
K – June 1 - Sept. 8, 2016.
L – June 1 - Sept. 7, 2016.
N – June 5 - Sept. 10, 2016.
P – June 1 - Aug. 31, 2016.
R – June 20 - Sept. 2, 2016.
S – June 22 - Sept. 4, 2016.

T – ②④⑦ Apr. 1 - May 31; daily June 1 - Sept. 30, 2016.
U – ② Aug. 30 - Oct. 25, 2016 and Apr. 4 - June 14, 2017.
V – Sept. 11, 2016 - circa June 4, 2017 (not Dec. 24, 25, 31, Jan. 1).
W – Sept. 11, 2016 - circa May 14, 2017 (not Dec. 24, 25, 31, Jan. 1).
X – On Dec. 24, 31 only to Borgarnes (a. 1023).
Y – ①③⑤† Aug. 28, 2016 - circa May 28, 2017 (not Dec. 24, 25, 31, Jan. 1).

c – Change bus in Vík í Mýrdal.
d – *STR* city route 3 to Mjódd (direction Sel/Fell).
e – *STR* city route 3 from Mjódd (direction Hlemmur); departures at xx21 and xx51 minutes past each hour.
f – Change to route 52 at Selfoss N1 (a. 1348 / d. 1352).
g – Reykjavík Holtagardar.
h – Reykjavík Harpa concert hall.
m – Seydisfjördur Herdubreid.
n – Seydisfjördur Smyril Line terminal.
r – Akureyri Hafnarstraeti 77 / 82 (500 metres south of *STR* bus stop at Hof concert hall).
s – Via Dettifoss§ (48 *km* detour). Change bus at Dettifoss (a. 1120, d. 1200).
t – Höfn campsite (opposite of N1).
v – Höfn STR bus stop at Víkurbraut / Heppuskóli (600 metres south of N1).
w – ⑥ only (not holidays).
y – For connection between *STR* services 57 and 56 d. 1535 to Mývatn / Egilsstadir contact operator / bus driver.
z – † only; *STR* route 57 from BSÍ terminal; change bus in Mjódd. On other days connection with *STR* city route 3, d. *0831* from city bus stop near BSÍ.
§ – With sightseeing stops.
N1 – Bus stop is at N1 filling station.
• – *389 km* by *STA* services, *439 km* by *GL*.

■ Reykjavík terminals

Located around city centre: Harpa concert hall (*STA*); Laekjartorg (*GL*); BSÍ bus terminal (*RE*, also some *STR* services on routes 52, 55, 57). Holtagardar terminal (*GL*) is 5 *km* east of city centre; connections by *GL* shuttle bus from Laekjartorg. Mjódd bus terminal (*STR*) is 7 *km* southeast of city centre.
STR city service 3 connects Hlemmur - Sel / Fell via Harpa, Laekjartorg, city bus stop near BSÍ and Mjódd every 15 - 30 minutes. Journey time to Mjódd 28 - 32 minutes from Hlemmur, 18 - 23 minutes from BSÍ; no city services on † mornings before 0950. Tickets valid on connecting *STR* services.

Operators:

FAS	Ferdathjónusta Austurlands + 354 472 1515	www.visitseydisfjordur.com
GL	Gray Line Iceland + 354 540 1313	www.airportexpress.is
RE	Reykjavík Excursions + 354 580 5400	www.re.is
SBA	SBA - Nordurleid + 354 550 0700	www.sba.is
STA	Sterna + 354 551 1166	www.sterna.is
STR	Straetó + 354 540 2700	www.straeto.is
SVA	Straetisvagnar Austurlands + 354 471 2320	www.svaust.is

SWEDEN

SEE MAP PAGE 341

Operators: Most services are operated by **SJ AB** (*SJ*) - Swedish State Railways - formerly part of Statens Järnvägar: www.sj.se. There is, however, a number of other operators that run services shown within the European Rail Timetable; these are indicated by their initials in the relevant table heading, or at the top of each train column where more than one operator runs services on the same route.

AEX – Arlanda Express (A - Train AB)　　　IB – Inlandsbanan AB　　　　　MTR – MTR Nordic　　　　　　　NSB – Norges Statsbaner
NT – Norrtåg　　　　　　　　　　　　　　　Øtåg – Øresundståg　　　　　SKJB – Skandinaviska Jernbanor　　Tågab – Tågkeriet i Bergslagen AB
VEO – Veolia Transport (Snälltåget)

The Regional Public Transport Authority is responsible for many local services, known collectively as Länstrafik (*LT*). Those shown within these pages are abbreviated as follows:

JLT – Jönköpings Länstrafik　　　　KLT/ÖT – Kalmar Läns Trafik / ÖstgötaTrafiken　　　Skåne – Skånetrafiken
V – Västtrafik　　　　　　　　　VTAB – Värmlandstrafik　　　　　　　　　　　　　　XT – X-Trafik

Services: Trains convey first and second classes of accommodation, unless otherwise shown. The fastest trains are classified Snabbtåg (*Sn*) and InterCity (*IC*). Sleeping cars (🛏) are of two basic types with a range of supplements: older cars (those without showers) have one berth in first class, two or three berths in second class. Newer cars either have compartments with shower and WC (one or two berth, first class only) or have shower and WC available in the car (one or two berths in first class, two berths in second class). Couchette cars (🛌) have six berths and are second class only. Refreshment services (✗, ♟, 🍴 or 🍴) may be available for part of the journey only.

Timings: Valid **December 11, 2016 - June 10, 2017** except where shown otherwise. Alterations and cancellations may be made on and around the dates of public holidays.

Reservations: Seat reservation is compulsory on all Snabbtåg and night trains, and for through journeys to København (excluding local and Skåne services). Reserved seats are not labelled and, if occupied, must be claimed by presenting the seat ticket on the train.

Supplements: Special supplements are payable for travel on Snabbtåg high-speed trains.

STOCKHOLM - MALMÖ - KØBENHAVN   730

km		Sn 21519	Sn 21521		VEO 10523	VEO 3933	VEO 3933	21525		VEO 10527	VEO 3941	VEO 3941	Sn 21529		Sn 10531		Sn 21533	VEO 3931	Sn 10535		Sn 21537	Sn 21537
0	Stockholm Central ‡ d.	0521	0621	0651	0721	0735	0736	0821	0844	0921	0929	0930	0940	1021	1040	1044	1121	1140	1221	1244	1244	1321	1340	1421	1421
15	Flemingsberg d.			0702							0952		1051		1151		1221		1351	
36	Södertälje Syd ‡ d.	0539	0639	0714	0739	0755	0806	0839	0906	0939		1003	1103	1103	1108	1139	1203	1239	1307	1306	1339	1403	1439	1439
103	Nyköping d.			0759							1047		1147		1247		1347	
162	Norrköping d.	0635	0735	0838	0835	0900	0911	0935	1011	1035	1048	1055	1126	1135	1227	1213	1235	1326	1335	1414	1421	1435	1528	1535	1535
209	Linköping d.	0659	0759		0859	0927	0938	0959	1036	1059	1115	1122		1159		1239	1259		1359	1439	1500	1459		1559	1559
241	Mjölby 755 d.		0814					1014				1214			1414				1614	1614
277	Tranås d.			0928														
329	Nässjö 733 d.	0749	0852		0952	1026	1043	1052		1149	1210	1217		1252		1349		1452		1607	1549		1652	1652
416	Alvesta d.	0822	0925		1025	1106	1128	1125		1222	1246	1253		1325		1422		1525		1654	1622		1725	1725
514	Hässleholm 745/6 a.	0910	1010		1110	1203s	1223s	1210		1310	1340s	1345s		1410		1510		1610		1754s	1710		1810	1810
581	Lund 745/6 § a.	0942s	1042		1142s	1158s	1316s	1242		1342s	1425s	1425s		1442		1542s		1642		1830s	1742s		1842s	1842
597	Malmö C 745/6 § a.	0954	1054		1143	1228	1254	1254		1354	1440	1440		1454		1554		1654		1843	1754		1854	1854
597	Malmö C 703 d.		1059			1259				1359			1459		1659			1859
632	København (Kastrup) ✈ 703 a.		1118s			1318s				1518s			1718s			1918s
644	København H 703 a.		1132			1332				1532			1732			1932

		Sn 21539	IC 10207		Sn 10541	Sn 10551	VEO 3943	VEO 3943	Sn 513		Sn 10505	Sn 21543		Sn 10545		Sn 10547		Sn 10549			1
	Stockholm Central ‡ d.	1440	1444	1521	1514	1544	1614	1621	1630	1630	1640	1644	1655	1706	1721	1740	1821	1844	1921	1940	2021	2044	2136	2140	2314
	Flemingsberg d.	1451							1706		1751		1952		2147	2151	
	Södertälje Syd ‡ d.	1503	1506	1533	1606	1633	1639		1659	1704	1718		1739	1803	1839	1907	1939	2004	2039	2107	2158	2203	2338u
	Nyköping d.	1547						1801		1846		2047		2242	2246	
	Norrköping d.	1627	1611	1635	1653	1709	1735	1735	1755	1755	1804	1809	1842		1835	1927	1935	2012	2035	2126	2135	2211	2328	2334	0105
	Linköping d.		1636	1659	1723	1736	1759	1759	1822	1822	1840	1834	1907		1859		1959	2038	2059		2159	2237	2353	2359	0147
	Mjölby 755 d.				1814	1814							2014			2214	
	Tranås d.								1911								
	Nässjö 733 d.		1749	1821		1852	1852	1919	1919	1937			1949		2052		2149		2252		0351j
	Alvesta d.		1822	1902		1925	1925	2001	2002			1956	2022		2125		2222		2325		0445
	Hässleholm 745/6 a.		1910	1948		2010	2010	2054s	2047s			2039	2107		2210		2310		0010		0553s
	Lund 745/6 § a.		1942	2024s		2042s	2042s	2126s	2214s			2113s	2138		2242s		2342s		0042s		0636s
	Malmö C 745/6 § a.		1954	2040		2054	2054	2140	2225			2125	2154		2254		2354		0054		0655
	Malmö C 703 d.		1959									2159					
	København (Kastrup) ✈ 703 a.		2017s									2217s					
	København H 703 a.		2032									2232					

		Sn 512				Sn 10522	Sn 500	Sn 516	Sn 10524		Sn 21526	Sn 21526		Sn 10528		VEO 3940	Sn 21530		VEO 3940	VEO 3940	Sn 10532		Sn 10534
	København H 703 d.										0620			0820				
	København Kastrup ✈ 703 d.										0632u			0832u				
	Malmö C 703 d.										0656			0856				
	Malmö C 745/6 § d.					0458	0520		0658	0658		0758		0805	0958		0920	0920	0958		1058
	Lund 745/6 § d.					0510u	0532u		0610u		0710	0710u		0810u		0814u	0910		0930u	0930u	1010u		1110u
	Hässleholm 745/6 d.					0542	0602		0642		0742	0742		0842		1006u	0942		1006	1006u	1042		1142
	Alvesta 746 d.					0630		0730		0830	0830		0930		1049	1030		1049	1049	1130		1230
	Nässjö 733 d.			0626		0704		0738	0804		0904	0904		1004		1128	1104		1128	1128	1204		1304
	Tranås d.			0653				0804									
	Mjölby 755 d.					0743				0943	0943			1143						1343
	Linköping d.	0521	0600	0611		0727		0758	0809	0837	0858	0917	0958	0958		1058	1121	1226	1158		1226	1225	1258	1312	1358
	Norrköping 754 d.	0549	0627	0642	0718	0742	0822		0904	0922	0945	1022	1122	1148	1252	1222	1230	1252	1251	1322	1346	1422	1430
	Nyköping d.			0727	0800	0754	0823					1116			1315			1515
	Södertälje Syd ‡ a.	0652	0729	0806	0841	0900	0905	0920		1009	1019	1018	1118	1155	1219	1251		1319	1353		1418	1450	1519	1555
	Flemingsberg d.			0817	0852		0916						1206			1404				1606
	Stockholm Central ‡ a.	0716	0749	0831	0905	0920	0931	0939	0946	1039	1116	1139	1139	1220	1239	1435	1339	1417	1420	1439	1516	1539	1620

♦ – **NOTES** (LISTED BY TRAIN NUMBER)

1 – 　 Ⓑ, 🛏, 🛌, 🍴 and ♟ Stockholm - Malmö.
512 – 　 Ⓐ (not Dec. 24 - Jan. 8); 🍴 and ✗ Jönköping - Nässjö - Stockholm.
513 – 　 Ⓑ (not Dec. 25 - Jan. 6); 🍴 and ✗ Stockholm - Nässjö - Jönköping.
516 – 　 ⑥ (not Dec. 31, Jan. 7); 🍴 and ✗ Jönköping - Nässjö - Stockholm.

A – ④⑤ Dec. 30 - Jan. 5; Ⓑ Mar. 13 - June 9.
B – Ⓒ Dec. 11 - 18; daily Dec. 25 - Jan. 8; Ⓒ Jan. 14 - June 10.
C – ⑥ Feb. 18 - Mar. 4.
D – ③⑥ Dec. 21 - Jan. 7.
E – ①②⑥ Dec. 12 - Jan. 3; ✗ Apr. 18 - June 10.
F – † Apr. 23 - June 10.
G – ④⑤† Apr. 20 - June 10.
H – Dec. 11, 18, Jan. 28, 29, Mar. 11, 12, Apr. 15, 16, May 27, 28.
J – From Jan. 23.
K – ⑤† Dec. 11 - Jan. 15; Ⓑ Jan. 20 - June 9.

L – Daily Dec. 11 - Apr. 19; ①②③⑥ Apr. 22 - June 10.
N – Dec. 11, 17, 18, Jan. 28, 29, Mar. 11, 12, Apr. 15, 16, May 27, 28.
P – † Dec. 26 - Apr. 17; daily Apr. 18 - June 10.
Q – ①②③④† only.
U – Until Apr. 13.

j – Arrive 0307.
s – Stops to set down only.
u – Stops to pick up only.
w – Not Dec. 24 - Jan. 7.
x – Not Dec. 24 - Jan. 8.

‡ – Most trains on this table may not be used for local journeys between Stockholm and Södertälje Syd or v.v. Local trains run every 30 mins Stockholm Central - Södertälje Hamn - Södertälje Centrum and v.v. (journey 42 mins). 🚌 Södertälje Syd - Södertälje Centrum runs every 30 mins.
§ – Frequent local trains run Lund - Malmö and v.v.

730 KØBENHAVN - MALMÖ - STOCKHOLM

	Sn 502 🄁✕ †	Sn 21536 🄁✕ Ⓑ	Ⓐ		VEO 3930 ✕ F	VEO 3930 ✕ R	VEO 3930 ✕ S	Sn 21538 🄁✕		Sn 10540 🄁✕ Ⓑ	Ⓐ		Sn 21542 🄁✕		IC 10204 ④⑤†	Sn 10544 🄁✕	Ⓐ	VEO 3942 ✕ T	Sn 21546 🄁✕	Ⓑ	Sn 10548 🄁✕ ⒷM	Sn 506 🄁✕ †v	Sn 21550 🄁✕ Ⓑ		2 🄁 ◆
København H **703** d.	...	...	...	...	...	...	...	1220	...	...	...	...	1420	...	...	...	...	...	1620	...	...	...	1820	...	...
København Kastrup ✈ **703** d.	...	...	...	...	...	...	...	1232u	...	...	...	...	1432u	...	...	...	...	...	1632u	...	...	...	1832u	...	...
Malmö C **703** a.	...	...	...	...	...	...	...	1256	...	...	...	...	1456	...	...	...	...	...	1656	...	...	...	1856	...	...
Malmö C **745/6** § d.	1120	1158	...	...	1204	1204	1204	1258	...	1358	...	...	1458	...	1452	1558	...	1620	1658	...	1758	1836	1858	...	2208
Lund **745/6** § d.	1132u	1210u	...	...	1214u	1214u	1214u	1310	...	1410u	...	...	1510	...	1506u	1610u	...	1642u	1710	...	1810u	1848u	1910	...	2224u
Hässleholm **745/6** d.	1209	1242	...	...	1258u	1258u	1258u	1342	...	1442	...	...	1542	...	1548	1642	...	1717u	1742	...	1842	1921	1942	...	2308u
Alvesta **746** d.	1253	1330	...	...	1359	1359	1359	1430	...	1530	...	...	1630	...	1638	1730	...	1802	1830	...	1930	2008	2030	...	0016
Nässjö 733 d.	1329	1404	...	...	|	|	|	1504	...	1604	...	...	1704	...	1718	1804	...	1838	1904	...	2004	2042	2104	...	0111
Tranås d.	|	|	...	...	|	|	|	|	...	1630	...	...	|	...	|	|	...	|	|	...	|	|	2130	...	|
Mjölby 755 d.	|	|	...	...	|	|	|	1543	...	|	...	...	1743	...	|	|	...	|	1943	...	|	|	|	...	|
Linköping d.	1422	1458	...	1520	1549	1549	1549	1558	...	1658	...	1711	1758	...	1818	1858	...	1935	1958	...	2058	2133	2158	...	0229
Norrköping 754 d.	1447	1522	1530	1548	|	|	|	1622	1629	1722	1730	1743	1822	1852	1847	1922	1952	2002	2022	2051	2122	2157	2222	...	0345
Nyköping d.	|	|	1615	|	|	|	|	|	1715	|	1815	|	|	1940	|	|	2033	|	|	2135	|	|	|	...	|
Södertälje Syd ‡ a.	1546	1619	1656	1650	1738	1746	1746	1719	1754	1819	1855	1851	1918	2024	2009	2019	2125	|	2119	2220	2218	|	2319	...	0525s
Flemingsberg ‡ a.	|	|	1707	|	|	|	|	|	1805	|	1906	|	|	2035	|	|	2136	|	|	2233	|	|	|	...	|
Stockholm Central ‡ a.	1609	1639	1720	1709	1803	1816	1816	1739	1820	1839	1920	1916	1939	2048	2031	2039	2150	2130	2139	2246	2239	2312	2339	...	0554

◆ – **NOTES** (LISTED BY TRAIN NUMBER)

2 – Ⓑ: 🛏, 🛏, 2 and 🍷 Malmö - Stockholm.

M – From Mar. 13.
R – ④⑤ from Apr. 20.
S – ⑤ Feb. 17 - Mar. 3.
T – ①⑤† Dec. 16 - Jan. 3; daily Apr. 17 - June 10.

u – Stops to pick up only.
v – Not Dec. 19 - Jan. 7.

‡ – Most trains on this table may not be used for local journeys between Stockholm and Södertälje Syd or v.v. Local trains run every 30 mins Stockholm Central - Södertälje Hamn - Södertälje Centrum and v.v. (journey 42 mins). 🚌 Södertälje Syd - Södertälje Centrum runs every 30 mins.
§ – Frequent local trains run Malmö - Lund.

731 MALMÖ - YSTAD - SIMRISHAMN and TRELLEBORG

Operator: *Skåne*

km		Ⓒ	Ⓐ	Ⓐ	⑥	Ⓐ		Ⓐ		⚒		❖			❖		⚒	†	⚒	⚒	†	⑤⑥	G		⚒	Ⓒ🚌
0	**Malmö** C d.	0107	...	0507	...	0537	0607	0637	0707	0727	0807	0837	and at the same mins.	2107	2138	...	2204	2207	2237	2307	2307	2337	2343	...	0007	...
70	Ystad ◧ a.	0156	0458	0556	0558	0628	0656	0728	0756	0826	0856	0928	past each	2156	2228	...	2256	2256	2328	2356	2356	0028	0028	...	0056	0102
116	Simrishamn a.	...	0538	0638	0638	...	0738	...	0838	...	0938	...	hour until	2238	...	...	2338	...	...	0038	...	...	...	...	...	0204

	②-⑤	Ⓒ	Ⓐ	Ⓐ		Ⓐ		Ⓐ		Ⓐ								⚒		⚒		⚒		Ⓒ	⚒
Simrishamn d.	0047	0047	...	...	...	...	0547a	...	0647d	...	0747	...	and at the same mins.	1847	...	...	1947	...	2047	...	2147	...	2247	...	2347
Ystad ◧ d.	0126	0130	0430	0500	0530	0600	0630	0700	0730	0800	0830	0900	past each	1930	2000	...	2030	2100	2130	2200	2230	2300	2330	0000	0030
Malmö C a.	...	0221	0521	0551	0621	0651	0721	0751	0821	0851	0921	0951	hour until	2021	2051	...	2121	2151	2221	2251	2321r	2350	0021d	0051	0121

km							⑤⑥	⑦-④		⑤⑥	⑤⑥
0	**Malmö** C d.	0550	0620	0650	and hourly	2250	2320	2327	2350	0020	0050
44	Trelleborg C ... **2380/5/90** a.	0622	0652	0722	until	2322	2352	2352	0022	0052	0122

										Ⓒ
Trelleborg C **2380/5/90** d.	0505	0535	and hourly	2135	2205	2235	2305	2335	...	0005
Malmö C a.	0539	0609	until	2209	2239	2259j	2332j	2359j	...	0039

G – ①②③④† only.
a – Ⓐ only.
d – ⚒ only.
f – ⑥⑦ only.
j – 7–10 minutes later on ⑤⑥.
r – Arrive 2314 on ①②③④†.
❖ – 2037 and 2137 departures from Malmö run ⚒ only.
◧ – For direct services Ystad - København and v.v. see Table **727**.

732 STOCKHOLM - ESKILSTUNA - ARBOGA

km		Ⓐ	Ⓐ		Ⓐ		Ⓐ			Ⓐ		Ⓐ		Ⓐ	Ⓐ			Ⓐ	Ⓐ		Ⓐ			G	⑤⑥
0	**Stockholm** C d.	...	0514	0640	0751	0851	0951	1051	...	1151	1251	1351	1451	1551	1629	...	1651	1729	1751	1851	1951	2051	...	2251	2329
36	Södertälje Syd d.	...	0547	0702	0813	0913	1013	1113	...	1213	1313	1413	1513	1613	1651	...	1713	1751	1813	1913	2013	2113	...	2313	2351
67	Läggesta ● d.	...	0605	0726	0831	0931	1031	1131	...	1231	1331	1431	1531	1631	1709	...	1731	1809	1831	1931	2031	2131	...	2331	0009
83	Strängnäs d.	0512	0622	0742	0841	0941	1041	1141	...	1241	1341	1441	1541	1641	1727	...	1741	1827	1841	1941	2041	2141	...	2341	0019
115	Eskilstuna a.	0535	0645	0801	0859	0959	1059	1159	...	1259	1359	1459	1559	1659	1746	...	1759	1846	1859	1959	2059	2159	...	2359	0037
115	Eskilstuna d.	0538	0648	0804	...	1002	...	1202	...	...	1402	1502	1602	1702	...	...	1808	...	1902	2002	...	2202	...	...	...
141	Kungsör d.	0555	0702	0818	...	1016	...	1216	...	...	1416	1516	1616	1716	...	...	1822	...	1916	2016	...	2216	...	...	...
159	**Arboga 756** a.	0606	0713	0829	...	1027	...	1227	...	...	1427	1527	1627	1727	...	...	1833	...	1927	2027	...	2227	...	...	...
	Örebro **756** a.	0636	0737	...	...	...	...	...	...	...	...	1551	1652a	1751	...	...	1905a	...	1951	...	...	...	...	...	...

	Ⓐ	Ⓐ	Ⓐ	Ⓒ	Ⓐ		Ⓑ	⑥	⚒		Ⓐ			Ⓐ		Ⓐ		Ⓐ		Ⓐ				
Örebro **756** d.	...	0504	0602	...	...	...	0705a	...	0808a	...	...	...	...	...	...	...	...	1607	1706a	1807	...	...	...	...
Arboga 756 d.	...	0527	0625	...	...	...	0728	0831	0831	0931	...	1131	...	...	1331	...	1531	1630	1729	1830	...	1931	2131	2236
Kungsör d.	...	0536	0635	...	...	...	0738	0841	0841	0941	...	1141	...	...	1341	...	1540	1640	1739	1840	...	1941	2144	2246
Eskilstuna a.	...	0554	0652	...	...	...	0755	0858	0858	0958	...	1158	...	...	1358	...	1558	1657	1756	1857	...	1958	2200	2303
Eskilstuna d.	0517	0556	0657	0657	0716	...	0801	0901	0901	1001	1101	1201	...	1301	1401	1501	1604	1701	1801	1901	...	2001	2201	...
Strängnäs d.	0535	0614	0715	0715	0734	...	0819	0919	0919	1019	1119	1219	...	1319	1419	1519	1622	1719	1819	1919	...	2019	2219	...
Läggesta ● d.	0545	0624	0725	0725	0744	...	0829	0929	0929	1029	1129	1229	...	1329	1429	1529	1632	1729	1829	1929	...	2029	2229	...
Södertälje Syd d.	0602	0641	0742	0742	0801	...	0846	0946	0946	1046	1146	1246	...	1346	1446	1546	1653	1746	1846	1946	...	2046	2246	...
Stockholm C a.	0624	0705	0805	0805	0824	...	0909	1009	1009	1109	1209	1309	...	1409	1509	1609	1716	1809	1909	2009	...	2109	2309	...

G – ①②③④† only.
a – Ⓐ only.

● – Summer only narrow gauge service operates Mariefred - Läggesta (nedre) - Taxinge-Näsby and v.v. Operator: Östra Södermanlands Järnväg, Box 53, SE-647 22 Mariefred. ✆ +46 (0)159 210 00, fax +46 (0)159 211 15

733 SKÖVDE - JÖNKÖPING - NÄSSJÖ

2nd class only. Operator: *V* (except *Sn* trains)

km		Sn 512 ◆	Ⓐ	Sn 516 ◆	Ⓐ	⚒	Ⓐ		Ⓐ	⑥		Ⓐ			Ⓑ	⑥		Ⓑ	⑥		Ⓑ		Ⓐ	†	⑥
0	**Skövde 740** d.	...	0444	...	0549	0650	0757	0853	0952	...	1052	...	1253	...	...	...	1453	...	1554	1653	...	1854	1952	2056	2154
30	Falköping **740** d.	...	0509	...	0614	0716	0820	0916	1015	1015	1116	1217	1316	...	1414	1415	1516	1617	1617	1717	1819	1917	2015	2119	2216
100	Jönköping a.	...	0552	...	0700	0758	0902	1000	1100	1100	1200	1301	1400	...	1459	1500	1603	1702	1702	1801	1902	2001	2100	2203	2303
100	Jönköping d.	0545	0555	0700	0702	0806	0904	1004	1103	1103	1205	1306	1405	...	1502	1502	1605	1706	1706	1806	1905	2003	2106	2208	2307
143	**Nässjö 730** a.	0615	0632	0728	0738	0842	0940	1041	1139	1139	1242	1343	1439	...	1541	1541	1640	1741	1741	1842	1939	2037	2140	2240	2342

	Ⓐ	Ⓐ	Ⓐ	Ⓐ	⑥	⚒		Ⓐ			⑥	Ⓐ		Ⓑ		⑥		Ⓑ	Ⓒ	Sn 513 ◆		Ⓐ	G	⑤⑥
Nässjö 730 d.	0443	0550	...	0714	0729	0818	0919	1020	1115	...	1219	1219	1316	1416	1528	1620	1717	1818	1916	1944	...	2022	2120	2120
Jönköping a.	0514	0627	...	0750	0802	0851	0956	1055	1152	...	1252	1252	1349	1448	1601	1653	1753	1851	1956	2014	...	2058	2151	2151
Jönköping d.	0521	0630	0728	0758	0806	0916	1000	1116	1200	...	1254	1301	1400	1502	1604	1702	1801	1902	2002	...	...	2100	2204	2204
Falköping **740** a.	0606	0714	0812	0845	0850	1000	1046	1200	1245	...	1342	1344	1443	1545	1647	1744	1845	1944	2045	...	...	2146	2247	2247
Skövde 740 a.	0626	...	0841	0905	0910	...	1106	...	1306	...	...	1404	1503	1604	1707	1803	1906	...	2107	...	...	...	2312	2314

◆ – **NOTES** (LISTED BY TRAIN NUMBER)

512 – Ⓐ (not Dec. 24 - Jan. 8): 12 and ✕ Jönköping - Nässjö - Stockholm.
513 – Ⓑ (not Dec. 24 - Jan. 7): 12 and ✕ Stockholm - Nässjö - Jönköping.
516 – ⑥ (not Dec. 31, Jan. 7): 12 and ✕ Jönköping - Nässjö - Stockholm.

G – ①②③④† only.

KRISTIANSTAD - HÄSSLEHOLM - HELSINGBORG 734

Operator: *Skåne* 2nd class only

km		Ⓐ	Ⓐ	Ⓐ		⚒	Ⓐ		Ⓐ		Ⓐ					Ⓐ			Ⓐ								Ⓒ
0	**Kristianstad 745** d.	...	...	0538	0603	...	0638	*0703*	0738	*0803*	0838	...	*0903*	and at	*1403*	1438	*1503*	and at	1738	*1803*	...	*1903*	*2003*	*2103*	*2138*	*2243*	*0003*
30	**Hässleholm 745** a.	...	...	0557	0624	...	0657	*0724*	0757	*0824*	0859	...	*0924*	the same	*1424*	1457	*1524*	the same	1757	*1824*	...	*1924*	*2024*	*2124*	*2159*	*2304*	*0024*
30	Hässleholm d.	0501	0531	0601	...	0631	0701	0731	0801	0831	0901	...	0931	minutes	1431	1501	1531	minutes	1801	1831	...	1931	2031	2131	2231	2331	0031
83	Åstorp d.	0542	0612	0640	...	0712	0740	0812	0840	0912	0940	...	1012	past each	1512	1540	1612	past each	1840	1912	...	2012	2112	2212	2312	0012	0112
107	**Helsingborg** a.	0605	0635	0703	...	0735	0803	0835	0903	0935	1003	...	1035	hour until	1535	1603	1635	hour until	1903	1935	...	2035	2135	2235	2335	0035	0135

	Ⓐ	Ⓐ	Ⓐ	⚒	Ⓐ	Ⓐ		Ⓐ		Ⓐ				Ⓐ			Ⓐ							⚒	Ⓒ
elsingborg d.	0417	...	0447	0517	...	0547	0617	0647	0717	0747	0817	and at	1317	1347	1417	and at	1647	1717	...	1817	and at	2217	...	2317	0017
storp d.	0440	...	0511	0540	...	0611	0640	0711	0740	0811	0840	the same	1340	1411	1440	the same	1711	1740	...	1840	the same	2240	...	2340	0040
ässleholm a.	0518	...	0551	0618	...	0651	0718	0751	0818	0848	0918	minutes	1418	1451	1518	minutes	1751	1818	...	1918	minutes	2318	...	0018	0118
ässleholm 745 d.	...	0531	0557	...	0631	0657	*0731*	0757	*0831*	0850	*0931*	past each	*1431*	1457	*1531*	past each	1757	*1831*	...	*1931*	past each	*2331*	...	...	...
ristianstad 745 a.	...	0552	0618	...	0652	0718	*0752*	0818	*0852*	0920	*0952*	hour until	*1452*	1518	*1552*	hour until	1818	*1852*	...	*1952*	hour until	*2352*	...	...	...

GÖTEBORG - MALMÖ - KØBENHAVN 735

Operator: *Øtåg* (except *Sn* trains)

km				*Sn* 481		*Sn* 483		*Sn* 485				*Sn* 487			*Sn* 489				*Sn* 491			*Sn* 493		*Sn* 495	
		Ⓐ	Ⓐ	Ⓐ	⚒	Ⓐ		⑥							Ⓑ							Ⓑ			
0	**Göteborg C** ▲ d.	...	...	0540	0555a	0640	0655	0735	0755	0855	0955	1010	1055	...	1140	1155	1255	1355	1410	1455	1555	1610	1655	1740	1755
28	Kungsbacka ▲ d.	...	...	|	0613a	|	0713	|	0813	0913	1013	|	1113	...	|	1213	1313	1413	|	1513	1613	|	1713	|	1813
76	Varberg ▲ d.	...	...	|	0634a	|	0734	|	0834	0934	1034	|	1134	...	|	1234	1334	1434	|	1534	1634	|	1734	|	1834
106	Falkenberg ▲ d.	...	...	|	0648a	|	0748	|	0848	0948	1048	|	1148	...	|	1248	1348	1448	|	1548	1648	|	1748	|	1848
150	**Halmstad** ▲ d.	0512	0612	0641	0712	0740	0812	0833	0912	1012	1112	1110	1212	...	1239	1312	1412	1512	1511	1612	1715	1710	1812	1840	1912
173	Laholm d.	0522	0622	|	0722	|	0822	|	0922	1022	1125	|	1222	...	|	1322	1422	1526	|	1622	1725	|	1822	|	1922
185	Båstad d.	0528	0628	|	0728	|	0828	|	0928	1028	1131	|	1228	...	|	1328	1428	1532	|	1628	1731	|	1828	|	1928
210	Ängelholm d.	0541	0641	|	0741	|	0841	|	0941	1041	1142	|	1241	...	|	1341	1441	1544	|	1641	1742	|	1841	|	1941
237	**Helsingborg** a.	0608	0708	0719	0808	0818	0908	0911	1008	1108	1208	1147	1308	...	1319	1408	1508	1608	1549	1708	1811	1756	1908	1919	2008
237	**Helsingborg 737** d.	0612	0712	0721	0812	0820	0912	0915	1012	1112	1212	1149	1312	...	1321	1412	1512	1612	1551	1712	1812	1758	1912	1921	2012
259	Landskrona **737** d.	0623	0723	|	0823	|	0923	|	1023	1123	1223	|	1323	...	|	1423	1523	1623	|	1723	1823	|	1923	|	2023
290	Lund **737** d.	0641	0741	0747s	0841	0847s	0941	0942s	1041	1141	1241	1212s	1341	...	1344s	1441	1541	1641	1614s	1741	1841	1821s	1941	1944s	2041
306	**Malmö C 737** a.	0651	0751	0800	0851	0901	0951	0954	1051	1151	1251	1227	1351	...	1356	1451	1551	1651	1627	1751	1851	1837	1951	1957	2051
306	**Malmö C 703** d.	0653	0753	...	0853	...	0953	...	1053	1153	1253	...	1353	...	...	1453	1553	1653	...	1753	1853	...	1953	...	2053
341	København (Kastrup) ✈ **703** a.	0713	0813	...	0913	...	1013	...	1113	1213	1313	...	1413	...	...	1513	1613	1713	...	1813	1913	...	2013	...	2113
353	**København H 703** a.	0728	0828	...	0928	...	1028	...	1128	1228	1328	...	1428	...	...	1528	1628	1728	...	1828	1928	...	2028	...	2128

	Sn 439 ⒷS								
öteborg C ▲ d.	1840	1855	...	1955	2055	2155	...	2255	2355
ungsbacka ▲ d.	|	1913	...	2013	2113	2213	...	2313	0013
arberg ▲ d.	|	1934	...	2034	2134	2235	...	2335	0035
alkenberg ▲ d.	|	1948	...	2048	2148	2249	...	2349	0049
almstad ▲ d.	1940	2012	...	2112	2212	2312	...	0007	0107
aholm d.	|	2022	...	2122	2222	2322	...	...	...
åstad d.	|	2028	...	2128	2228	2328	...	...	...
ngelholm d.	|	2041	...	2141	2241	2341	...	...	...
elsingborg a.	2019	2108	...	2208	2308	0004	...	...	...
elsingborg 737 d.	2021	2112	...	2212	2312	...	...	...	...
andskrona **737** d.	|	2123	...	2223	2323	...	...	...	...
und **737** a.	2044s	2141	...	2241	2341	...	...	...	...
almö C 737 a.	2057	2151	...	2251	2351	...	...	...	...
almö C 703 d.	...	2153	...	2253	...	...	...	...	...
øbenhavn (Kastrup) ✈ **703** a.	...	2213	...	2313	...	...	...	...	...
øbenhavn H 703 a.	...	2228	...	2328	...	...	...	...	...

						Sn 426		*Sn* 482	*Sn* 418
	Ⓐ	Ⓐ	Ⓐ	Ⓐ	⚒	ⒶS	⚒	Ⓐ	⑥S
København H 703 ♣ d.	...	...	...	...	...	...	...	...	...
København (Kastrup) ✈ **703** d.	...	...	...	...	...	...	...	...	...
Malmö C 703 a.	...	...	...	...	...	...	...	...	...
Malmö C **737** d.	...	...	...	...	0508a	0602	0608	0702	0702
Lund **737** d.	...	...	...	...	0520a	0614u	0620	0714u	0714u
Landskrona **737** d.	...	...	...	...	0535a	|	0635	|	|
Helsingborg 737 a.	...	...	...	...	0548a	0640	0648	0740	0740
Helsingborg d.	...	...	0453	...	0553a	0642	0653	0742	0742
Ängelholm d.	...	...	0516	...	0616a	|	0716	|	|
Båstad d.	...	...	0526	...	0626a	|	0726	|	|
Laholm d.	...	...	0532	...	0632a	|	0732	|	|
Halmstad ▲ d.	0451	0521	0551	0621	0652	0718	0752	0818	0818
Falkenberg ▲ d.	0507	0537	0607	0637	0708	|	0808	|	|
Varberg ▲ d.	0522	0552	0623	0652	0724	|	0824	|	|
Kungsbacka ▲ d.	0545	0615	0645	0715	0745	|	0845	|	|
Göteborg C ▲ a.	0605	0635	0705	0735	0805	0820	0905	0920	0920

			Sn 484 ⚒			*Sn* 486			*Sn* 488			*Sn* 490 Ⓑ				*Sn* 492			*Sn* 494 Ⓑ					
øbenhavn H **703** ♣ d.	*0556*	*0656*	...	*0756*	*0856*	...	*0956*	*1056*	...	*1156*	*1256*	...	*1356*	...	*1456*	...	*1556*	*1656*	...	*1756*	*1856*	*1956*	...	*2156*
øbenhavn (Kastrup) ✈ **703** d.	0626	0726	...	0826	0926	...	1026	1126	...	1226	1326	...	1426	...	1526	...	1626	1726	...	1826	1926	2026	...	2226
almö C 703 a.	0653	0753	...	0853	0953	...	1053	1153	...	1253	1353	...	1453	...	1553	...	1653	1753	...	1853	1953	2053	...	2253
almö C **737** d.	0708	0808	0835	0908	1008	1102	1108	1208	1302	1308	1408	1435	1508	...	1608	1659	1708	1808	1902	1908	2008	2108	...	2308
und **737** d.	0720	0820	0848u	0920	1020	1114u	1120	1220	1314u	1320	1420	1447u	1520	...	1620	1711u	1720	1820	1914u	1920	2020	2120	...	2320
andskrona **737** d.	0735	0835	|	0935	1035	|	1135	1235	|	1335	1435	|	1535	...	1635	|	1735	1835	|	1935	2035	2135	...	2335
elsingborg 737 a.	0748	0848	0913	0948	1048	1140	1148	1248	1340	1348	1448	1510	1548	...	1648	1740	1748	1848	1940	1948	2048	2148	...	2348
elsingborg d.	0753	0853	0915	0953	1053	1147	1153	1253	1342	1353	1453	1512	1553	...	1653	1742	1753	1853	1942	1953	2053	2153	...	2353
ngelholm d.	0816	0916	|	1016	1116	|	1216	1316	|	1416	1516	|	1616	...	1716	|	1816	1916	|	2016	2116	2216	...	0016
åstad d.	0826	0926	|	1026	1126	|	1226	1326	|	1426	1526	|	1626	...	1726	|	1826	1926	|	2026	2126	2226	...	0026
aholm d.	0832	0932	|	1032	1132	|	1232	1332	|	1432	1532	|	1632	...	1732	|	1832	1932	|	2032	2132	2232	...	0032
almstad ▲ d.	0852	0952	0951	1052	1152	1225	1252	1346	1417	1452	1552	1548	1652	...	1752	1818	1852	1952	2018	2052	2152	2252	...	0046
alkenberg ▲ d.	0908	1010	|	1108	1208	|	1308	1352	|	1508	1608	|	1708	...	1808	|	1908	2008	|	2108	2208	2308	...	...
arberg ▲ d.	0924	1025	|	1126	1224	|	1324	1424	|	1524	1624	|	1724	...	1824	|	1924	2024	|	2125	2224	2324	...	...
ungsbacka ▲ d.	0945	1045	|	1145	1245	|	1345	1445	|	1545	1645	|	1745	...	1845	|	1945	2045	|	2145	2245	2345	...	...
öteborg C ▲ a.	1005	1105	1100	1205	1305	1325	1405	1505	1520	1605	1705	1650	1805	...	1905	1920	2005	2105	2120	2205	2305	0005	...	...

– From / to Stockholm.

a – Ⓐ only.
s – Stops to set down only.
u – Stops to pick up only.

♣ – By connecting service to Kastrup ✈.
▲ – Additional services operate on Ⓐ Göteborg - Halmstad and v.v.
All *Sn* trains convey ✕ and require compulsory reservation Ⓡ.

HALLSBERG - LIDKÖPING - HERRLJUNGA 736

Operator: *V* 2nd class only

km		Ⓐ	Ⓐ	Ⓐ	Ⓐ	†	⑥		Ⓐ	Ⓐ	†	⑥	Ⓐ	Ⓐ	†	†	⑥	Ⓐ	Ⓐ	†	⑥	Ⓐ		Ⓐ	†	Ⓐ
	Örebro C **755/6** d.	...	...	...	...	...	...	...	0745	...	...	...	...	...	...	...	...	...	...	...	...	1630	...	...	...	...
0	**Hallsberg 740** d.	...	...	...	...	...	...	...	0806	...	...	...	...	...	1236	...	...	...	...	...	1555	1651	...	...	1910	1938
30	Laxå **740** d.	...	...	...	...	...	...	...	0825	...	...	...	...	1220	1255	...	...	...	...	...	1615	1710	...	...	1929	1957
92	Mariestad d.	...	0526	0705	0800	0830	0845	...	0913	1011	...	1205	1221	1318	1341	1400	1431	...	1546	1707	1754j	1757	...	...	2024	2042
146	Lidköping a.	...	0610	0756	0857	0914	0928	...	1004	1107	...	1255	1309	1414	...	1444	1514	...	1642	1751	1844	1845	...	...	2114	...
146	Lidköping d.	0515	0613	0759	0900	0916	0930	...	1008	1111	1142	1259	...	1444	...	1446	1517	1515	1704	1754	...	...	...	2005	...	...
201	**Herrljunga 740** a.	0605	0659	0850	0954	1002	1013	...	1111	1157	1235	1352	...	1533	...	1529	1601	1601	1751	1836	...	...	...	2052	...	...
	Göteborg C **740** a.	...	0755	...	...	1055	1100	...	1200	...	1325	1455	...	1635	...	1635	1705	...	...	1930	...	...	...	...	...	...

	Ⓐ	Ⓐ	⑥	Ⓐ	Ⓐ	†	⑥	Ⓐ	⑥	⑥	Ⓐ	†	Ⓐ	Ⓐ	Ⓐ	Ⓐ	†	†	Ⓐ	⑥	Ⓐ	⑥	Ⓐ	†	†	Ⓐ
Göteborg C **740** d.	...	...	...	...	...	...	...	0930	...	1120	...	1130	...	...	1255	...	1355	...	...	1525	1655	1720	...	1755	1955	...
errljunga 740 d.	...	...	...	0700	0905	...	0955	1019	...	1209	1208	1219	...	1248	1355	...	1457	...	1611	1615	1757	1810	1852	1854	2052	2057
idköping a.	...	...	...	0750	1001	...	1045	1103	...	1249	1253	1257	...	1332	1439	...	1542	...	1656	1659	1836	1853	1938	1935	2130	2143
dköping d.	...	0612	...	0758	1007	1008	1047	1109	...	1257	...	1259	1315	...	1441	1543	1545	...	1658	1703	1847	1855	...	1937	...	...
ariestad d.	0550	0657	0838	0851	1102	1100	1138	1154	1303	1344	...	1346	1407	...	1531	1634	1636	1648	1755	1752	1935	1941	...	2022	...	...
axå **740** d.	0641	...	0924	...	1148	1147	...	...	1349	...	...	...	1454	...	...	...	...	1735	1841	...	...	...	...	...	...	...
allsberg 740 a.	0700	...	0943	...	...	1206	...	...	1408	...	...	...	1526	...	...	...	...	1753	1909	...	...	...	...	...	...	...
Örebro C **755/6** a.	0725	...	...	...	...	...	...	...	...	...	...	...	1548	...	...	...	...	...	...	...	...	...	...	...	...	...

– Arrive 1659.

737 KØBENHAVN - LUFTHAVN (KASTRUP) ✈ - MALMÖ - HELSINGBORG — Operator: Skåne (Ø – Øtåg)

km		Ø	Ø(A)(A)2 2	Ø (A)2 2	Ø (A)2 2	Ø (A)2 2 2	Ø 2 2	Ø
0	København H 703 ♣ d.	0356	... 0456 ...	0556 ...	0656 ...	0756 ...	0856 ...	0956 ... 1056
12	Lufthavn (Kastrup) ✈ 703 d.	0426	... 0526 ...	0626 ...	0726 ...	0826 ...	0926 ...	1026 ... 1126
47	Malmö C 703 735 d.	0448 0508 0511 0541	0548 0608 0611 0641	0708 0711 0741 ...	0808 0811 0841 0908 0911 0941 1008	... 1011 1041 1108 1111 1141 1208		
63	Lund 735 d.	0458 0520 0526 0556	0558 0620 0626 0656	0720 0726 0756 ...	0820 0826 0856 0920 0926 0956 1020	... 1026 1056 1120 1126 1156 1220		
95	Landskrona 735 d.	... 0535 0550 0620	... 0635 0650 0720	0735 0750 0820 ...	0835 0850 0920 0935 0950 1020 1035	... 1050 1120 1135 1150 1220 1235		
116	Helsingborg 735 a.	... 0548 0607 0638	... 0648 0707 0738	0748 0807 0838 ...	0848 0907 0938 0948 1007 1038 1048	... 1107 1138 1148 1207 1238 1248		

		©2 2 Ø	©2 2 Ø	2 2 Ø	2 2 Ø	2 2 Ø	Ø (A)2 2	Ø Ø 2 2
	København H 703 ♣ d.	... 1156 ...	1256 ...	1356 ...	1456 ...	1556 ...	1656 ...	1756 ...
	Lufthavn (Kastrup) ✈ 703 d.	... 1226 ...	1326 ...	1426 ...	1526 ...	1626 ...	1726 ...	1826 ...
	Malmö C 703 735 d.	1211 1241 1308 1311 1341	... 1408 1411 1441 1508 1511 1541	1608 1611 1641 ...	1708 1711 1741 1808 1811 1841	... 1908 1911 1941		
	Lund 735 d.	1226 1256 1320 1326 1356	... 1420 1426 1456 1520 1526 1556	1620 1626 1656 ...	1720 1726 1756 1820 1826 1856	... 1920 1926 1956		
	Landskrona 735 d.	1250 1320 1335 1350 1420	... 1435 1450 1520 1535 1550 1620	1635 1650 1720 ...	1735 1750 1820 1835 1850 1920	... 1935 1950 2020		
	Helsingborg 735 a.	1307 1338 1348 1407 1438	... 1448 1507 1538 1548 1607 1638	1648 1707 1738 ...	1748 1807 1838 1848 1907 1938	... 1948 2007 2038		

		2 Ø 2 Ø	2 Ø 2	※2 Ø				
	København H 703 ♣ d.	1856 ... 1956 ...	2056 ... 2156 ...	2256 ...				
	Lufthavn (Kastrup) ✈ 703 d.	1926 ... 2026 ...	2126 ... 2226 ...	2326 ...				
	Malmö C 703 735 d.	2008 2041 2108 2141	2208 2241 2308 2341	0008 ...				
	Lund 735 d.	2020 2056 2120 2156	2220 2256 2320 2356	0020 ...				
	Landskrona 735 d.	2035 2120 2135	2220 2235 2320	2335 0020 0035 ...				
	Helsingborg 735 a.	2048 2138 2148	2238 2248 2338	2348 0038 0048				

		(A)2 Ø	(A)2 2 Ø	(A)2 2 Ø	(A)2 2 Ø			
	Helsingborg 735 d.	0454 0512 0524	0554 0612 0624	0654 0712 0724	0754			
	Landskrona 735 d.	0511 0524 0541	0611 0623 0641	0711 0723 0741	0811			
	Lund 735 d.	0535 0541 0605	0635 0641 0705	0735 0741 0805	0835			
	Malmö C 703 735 d.	0548 0551 0618	0648 0651 0718	0748 0751 0818	0848			
	Lufthavn (Kastrup) ✈ 703 a.	... 0613 ...	0713 ...	0813 ...				
	København H 703 a.	... 0628 ...	0728 ...	0828 ...				

		Ø (A)2 2	Ø ©2 2	Ø 2 2	Ø ©2 2	Ø ©2 2	Ø 2 2	Ø
	Helsingborg 735 d.	0812 0824 0854	0912 0924 0954 1012	... 1024 1054 1112 1124 1154 1212	... 1224 1254 1312 1324 1354 1412	... 1424 1454 1512 1524		
	Landskrona 735 d.	0823 0841 0911	0923 0941 1011 1023	... 1041 1111 1123 1141 1211 1223	... 1241 1311 1323 1341 1411 1423	... 1441 1511 1523 1541		
	Lund 735 d.	0841 0905 0935	0941 1005 1035 1041	... 1105 1135 1141 1205 1235 1241	... 1305 1335 1341 1405 1435 1441	... 1505 1535 1541 1605		
	Malmö C 703 735 d.	0851 0918 0948	0951 1018 1048 1051	... 1118 1148 1151 1218 1248 1251	... 1318 1348 1351 1418 1448 1451	... 1518 1548 1551 1618		
	Lufthavn (Kastrup) ✈ 703 a.	0913 ...	1013 ...	1113 ... 1213 ...	1313 ...	1413 ...	1513 ...	1613
	København H 703 a.	0928 ...	1028 ...	1128 ... 1228 ...	1328 ...	1428 ...	1528 ...	1628

		2 2 Ø	2 2 Ø	2 2 Ø	(A)2 2 Ø	2 2 Ø	2 2 Ø	※2 ©2 Ø
	Helsingborg 735 d.	1554 1612 1624 1654	1712 1724 1749 1812 1824 1854	... 1912 1924 1954 2012 2054 2112 2154 2212	... 2254 2312 2354 0054 0154			
	Landskrona 735 d.	1611 1623 1641 1711	1723 1741 1811 1823 1841 1911	... 1923 1941 2011 2023 2111 2123 2211 2223	... 2311 2323 0011 0111 0211			
	Lund 735 d.	1635 1641 1705 1735	1741 1805 1835 1841 1905 1935	... 1941 2005 2035 2041 2135 2141 2235 2241	... 2335 2341 0035 0135 0235			
	Malmö C 703 735 d.	1648 1651 1718 1748	1751 1818 1848 1851 1918 1948	... 1951 2018 2048 2051 2148 2151 2248 2251	... 2348 2351 0048 0148 0248			
	Lufthavn (Kastrup) ✈ 703 a.	... 1713 ...	1813 ... 1913 ...	2013 ... 2113 ...	2213 ... 2313 ...			
	København H 703 a.	... 1728 ...	1828 ... 1928 ...	2028 ... 2128 ...	2228 ... 2328 ...			

♣ – By connecting service to Kastrup ✈.   Ø – Operated by Øtåg.

---

738 South-eastern SECONDARY LINES — Operator: KLT/ÖT

km		(A)					B			
0	Västervik d.	0541 0737	... 1007 1203	... 1405 1605 1807 2005						
77	Åtvidaberg d.	0647 0844	... 1114 1310	... 1512 1714 1915 2112						
116	Linköping a.	0727 0921	... 1152 1352	... 1549 1750 1952 2152						

		(A)					B			
Linköping d.	0541	... 0808 1010 1210	... 1410 1610 1810	... 2010						
Åtvidaberg d.	0615	... 0843 1043 1241	... 1443 1644 1845	... 2042						
Västervik a.	0726	... 0950 1150 1348	... 1550 1752 1951	... 2149						

km		(A)	(A)	⑥							B	⑤
0	Linköping d.	... 0534	... 0827	1026 1224 1423 1624 1818 2024								
41	Rimforsa d.	... 0610	... 0904	1100 1300 1500 1706 1900 2105								
123	Hultsfred d.	0609 0709	0709 1003	1203 1403 1603 1803 2003 2202								
159	Berga d.	0634 0736	0736 1032	1233 1433 1633 1833 2033 2227								
159	Berga d.	0639 0741	0741 1037	1238 1438 1638 1838 2038 2227								
188	Oskarshamn a.	| |	| |	| | | | | 2249								
235	Kalmar 746 a.	0738 0840	0844 1138	1338 1538 1738 1938 2138 ...								

		(A)		(A)	(A)						B	⑤
Kalmar 746 d.	... 0541	... 0637 0837	1036 1236 1436 1636 1836 2034									
Oskarshamn a.	0450 ...	0625 |	...									
Berga d.	0510 0638	0645 0734 0934	1133 1333 1533 1733 1933 2133									
Berga d.	0511 0646	0645 0739 0939	1138 1338 1538 1738 1938 2138									
Hultsfred d.	0535 0710	0710 0803 1003	1202 1402 1602 1802 2000 2202									
Rimforsa d.	0641 0811	0811 0902 1102	1302 1502 1703 1902 2102 2308									
Linköping a.	0719 0850	0850 0939 1139	1338 1540 1741 1943 2139 2349									

Additional services operate on (A) Berga - Oskarshamn and v.v. (journey 20 minutes):
From Berga: 1038, 1238, 1438, 1638, 1838.
From Oskarshamn: 1112, 1312, 1512, 1712, 2010.

---

739 VARBERG - UDDEVALLA — 2nd class only   Operator: V (except Sn trains)

km											Sn 467 S(A)j	Sn 457 S†z	Sn 10467 S(A)k		†		†	†
		(A)	(A)	(A)	†	(A)	©	©		(A)	(A)	©	†		(A)	⑥		
0	Varberg 735 d.		... 0608	... 0708		... 1037											... 1741
84	Borås d.	0545	0654 0730 0749	0913 0945 1145	... 1214	1345 1350 1448	... 1744 1744	... 1744 1945 1945									
127	Herrljunga 740 d.	0632	0739 0816 0831	0957 1031 1232	... 1256	1433 1433 1531	... 1831 1831	... 1831 2031 2031									
127	Herrljunga d.	0644	0800 0900 0933	1034 1134 1334	... 1334	1534 1534 1634	... 1837 1858	... 1923 1923 1930 ... 1950 2058 2102									
191	Vänersborg d.	0733	0851 0952 1024	1123 1223 1423	... 1423	1624 1623 1730	... 1928 1956	... 2012 2012 2014 ... 2041 2151 2154									
195	Öxnered 750 d.	0740	0857 0959 1030	1129 1229 1429	... 1429	1630 1630 1737	... 1934 2003	... 2047 2157 2201									
217	Uddevalla C a.	0756	0913 1013 1045	1146 1245 1445	... 1445	1646 1646 1754	... 1945 2017	... 2036 2036 2038 ... 2101 2211 2216									

		Sn 462 S(A)x		Sn 460 S©y										†		†	†
		(A)	(A)	(A)	S©y (A)	©	©		(A)	©	(A)	©	(A)		(A)	⑥	
Uddevalla C d.	0511 0528	... 0620 0658	... 0659 0717 0814	... 0919 1019	... 1115 1148 1317 1317 1517	... 1615 1718	... 1718 1910									
Öxnered 750 d.	0527 ...	0645 |	... 0715 0734 0830	... 0935 1035	... 1131 1204 1333 1335 1533	... 1631 1734	... 1734 1926									
Vänersborg d.	0534 0549	... 0651 0719	... 0721 0740 0836	... 0941 1041	... 1137 1210 1341 1341 1539	... 1637 1740	... 1740 1932									
Herrljunga 746 d.	0626 0635	... 0740 0802	... 0818 0829 0930	... 1032 1132	... 1229 1300 1430 1434 1635	... 1730 1831	... 1831 2030									
Herrljunga d.	0642 ...	0753 ...	0855 0935 1035	... 1134 ...	1258 1306 1534 1534 1734	... 1835 1858	... 1935 2102									
Borås 746 a.	0725 ...	0836 ...	0941 1015 1116	... 1217 ...	1340 1348 1616 1616 1816	... 1920 1940	... 2016 2144									
Varberg 735 a.	0852 ...	0958 ...	1117 ...	1322 ...	... 2125	...										

GÖTEBORG - UDDEVALLA - STRÖMSTAD

km		※		B				※		B		
0	Göteborg C ▲ d.	0640	... 1040	... 1240	... 1440	... 1840	Strömstad d.	0641	... 1031	... 1427	... 1626 ... 1835
89	Uddevalla C ▲ a.	0753	... 1153	... 1353	... 1553	... 1953	Skee d.	0649	... 1039	... 1435	... 1634 ... 1843
89	Uddevalla C d.	0804	... 1202	... 1403	... 1600	... 2000	Uddevalla C a.	0800	... 1152	... 1550	... 1751 ... 1953
173	Skee d.	0918	... 1314	... 1520	... 1718	... 2112	Uddevalla C d.	0807	... 1207	... 1607	... 1807 ... 2007
180	Strömstad a.	0925	... 1322	... 1530	... 1726	... 2120	Göteborg C ▲ a.	0920	... 1320	... 1720	... 1920 ... 2120

S – 🚲 and ✗ Stockholm - Herrljunga - Uddevalla and v.v. Ⓡ.
j – Dec. 12-23, May 29 - June 9.
k – Jan. 9 - May 24.
x – Not Dec. 24 - Jan. 8.
y – Not Dec. 31, Jan. 7.
z – Not Dec. 25, Jan. 1.

▲ – Additional services Göteborg - Uddevalla and v.v.:
From Göteborg C: 0040©, 0525(A), 0740(A), 0840, 0940※, 1140※, 1240⑥, 1340※, 154C 1640, 1645(A), 1710※, 1740, 1940, 2040, 2140※, 2240, 2340(A).
From Uddevalla: 0007©, 0507(A), 0534(A), 0607(A), 0637(A), 0647(A), 0707※, 0807↑ 0907※, 1007, 1107※, 1307※, 1407, 1507, 1707, 1807⑥, 1907, 2107, 2207, 2307(A).
Operator: Västtrafik.

For additional services Stockholm - Hallsberg and v.v. see Table 750 (also Table 756 via Västerås). For long distance sleeper trains see Table 767

km		MTR	Sn 401	Sn 421	MTR	Sn 423	Sn 12023	Sn 425	MTR	MTR	Sn 427	MTR	MTR	Sn 419	Sn 429	MTR	Sn 431	MTR	SKJB	IC 103	SKJB		Sn 433	MTR	SKJB	Sn 435	Sn 415
			①-③	Ⓐx	Ⓐ	④⑤	Ⓐ	①-③		M	Ⓐ	⑥	Ⓒ	Ⓐ	Ⓐ	Ⓑ	†	P	†	Ⓐ		Ⓐ	⑥	Ⓐ	†
0	Stockholm C730/50/6 d.	0528	0551		0606	0626	0710	0725	0810	0825	0914	0920	1010	1014	1026	1114	1126	1129	1136	1159	...	1214	1226	1259	1314	1314
36	Södertälje Syd ..... 750 d.			0625u	0644u		0744u	0829u	0844u			0926	1010	1014	1028u		1044u		1144u		1156u			1244u			
131	Katrineholm .... 750 d.			0703		0806		0906		1006		1106	1106		1206					1306			1406	1406
197	Hallsberg .... 750/55/6 a.					0830										1258	1306	1326				1427	
	Örebro C 755/6 ....d.																						
197	Hallsberg .... 756 d.					0832										1300	1306	1334				1429	
272	Töreboda .... 756 d.																						
311	Skövde .... 756 d.			0809	0833	0914	0933	1011	1033	1112	1133	1210		1233	1311	1333	1353	1353	1429		1411	1433	1522	1511
341	Falköping .... 756 d.																						
375	Herrljunga ... 736/9/56 d.	0803s		0845	0908		1008		1108		1208	1247	1245	1308		1408				...		1508		1544	
	Uddevalla C 739......a.																						
410	Alingsås .... 756 a.			0906s											1454s		1535s				1615s		
455	Göteborg C .... 756 a.	0855	0900	0935	1000	1030	1055	1130	1155	1230	1255	1335	1330	1430	1455	1535	1540	1610		1530	1555	1700	1630	1630

		IC 107	MTR	Sn 417	Sn 437	SKJB	SKJB		Sn 439	MTR	Sn 405	Sn 441	Sn 411	Sn 10441		Sn 467	Sn 10467	Sn 457	SKJB 7083	Sn 473	Sn 407	Sn 443	Sn 10443	IC 109
		⑤	Ⓒ	Ⓐ	Ⓐ	N	Q		Ⓑ	B	Ⓐ	Ⓑ	†	Ⓑ		♦	♦	♦	†	Ⓐ	Ⓒ	E	F	†
	Stockholm C 730/50/6 d.	1324	1326	1410	1414	1506	1506	...	1510	1526	1559	1606	1610	1610	1621		1625	1625	1629	1655	1659	1710	1714	1714	1736	1755
	Södertälje Syd ..... 750 d.	1345u	1344u	1429u	1433u			...		1544u		1624u	1629u	1629u	1639u						1718u		1733u	1733u	1744u	1816u
	Katrineholm .... 750 d.			1506	1511						1706	1706	1706							1759		1811	1811	
	Hallsberg ..... 750/5/6 a.	1456				1656	1656		1624											1904				1939
	Örebro C 755/6 ......d.																						
	Hallsberg ....756 d.	1458				1659	1659		1624											1906				1940
	Töreboda .... 756 d.																1824	1824	1824				
	Skövde .... 756 d.	1551	1533	1611	1615	1803	1817		1708	1733		1810	1810	1833		1839	1846	1839	1959	1909	1915	1916	1933	2040
	Falköping .... 756 d.															1859	1906	1859				
	Herrljunga ... 736/9/56 d.	1632	1608			1808				1847		1908		1923	1930	1923			2008	
	Uddevalla C 739.....a.													2036	2038	2036			
	Alingsås .... 756 a.			1853s	1907s				1901s		1904s						2055s		
	Göteborg C .... 756 a.	1730	1655	1730	1735	1930	2000		1825	1855	1905	1935	1935	1935	1955		2130	2030	2015	2035	2035	2055	2200

		Sn 455	Sn 445	Sn 10445	MTR 447	MTR	Sn 471	Sn 449	Sn 10449			Sn 420	MTR 400	Sn 402		Sn 462	MTR 422	Sn 424
		Ⓐ	Ⓐ	Ⓐ	Ⓒ	Ⓐ	Ⓐ	J	H	D			Ⓐ	①-③	Ⓐx	B	♦	※	Ⓐx
	Stockholm C 730/50/6 d.	1810	1814	1814	1826	1914	1926	2006	2014	2014	Göteborg C.........756 d.	0500	0530	0550	0555		0600	0625	0700	0725
	Södertälje Syd ..... 750 d.	1828u		1844u	1933u	1944u				Alingsås .... 756 d.	0525u							0750u
	Katrineholm .... 750 d.	1906	1906	1906		2106	2106	2106	Uddevalla C 739 .... d.			0528			
	Hallsberg ..... 750/5/6 d.								Herrljunga .... 736/9/56 d.	0545		0640	0645	0747
	Örebro C 755/6 ......d.								Falköping .... 756 d.	0600		0655	
	Hallsberg ....756 d.								Skövde .... 756 d.	0616		0711	0715	0728	0815	0833
	Töreboda .... 756 d.								Töreboda .... 756 d.	0633		
	Skövde .... 756 d.	2010	2011	2011	2033	2111	2133	2215	2211	2228	Hallsberg ....756 a.	0705		0759
	Falköping .... 756 d.								Örebro C 755/6 ......a.			
	Herrljunga ... 736/9/56 d.	2047	2047	2108	2208	Hallsberg ..... 750/5/6 d.	0708		0801
	Uddevalla C 739.....a.					Katrineholm .... 750 d.	0734		
	Alingsås .... 756 a.	2104s	Södertälje Syd ..... 750 a.	0812s		0911s 0915s 1004s
	Göteborg C.........756 a.	2135	2135	2135	2155	2230	2300	2335	2330	2345	Stockholm C 730/50/6 a.	0835	0846	0850	0854		0924	0931	0935	1024	1031

		Sn 460	SKJB	MTR	Sn 416	Sn 426		Sn 428	Sn 418	Sn 430	IC 102	SKJB 7076	MTR 432		Sn 434	Sn 414	MTR	MTR	MTR 436	MTR	IC 104
		♦	⑥	K	⑥	Ⓐ		Ⓐ	⑥	L	⑥	†	Ⓐ	†	Ⓑ	†	Ⓐ	Ⓒ	T	R	†	Ⓑ	Ⓒ	⑤
	Göteborg C.........756 d.	...	0740	0800	0825	0830	...	0850	0900	0925	0930	1025	1030	1100	1100	1125	1200		1225	1230	1300	1300	1325	1400	1400
	Alingsås .... 756 d.		0807u		0850u			0920u						1130u				
	Uddevalla C 739 .... d.	0658														
	Herrljunga .... 736/9/56 d.	0811		0847	0910			0947	1007			1147			1247		1305	1310	1347	1347	1347		1447	1447
	Falköping .... 756 d.	0826													
	Skövde .... 756 d.	0842	0855	0915	0937	0934		1007	1015		1033	1128	1139	1215	1217	1228	1315		1337	1415		1415	1428	1515	1519
	Töreboda .... 756 d.														
	Hallsberg ....756 a.	0930	0948		1020			1058		1120		1246	1309							1626
	Örebro C 755/6 ......a.														
	Hallsberg ..... 750/5/6 d.	0932	0950		1022			1100		1122		1250	1317							1626
	Katrineholm .... 750 d.			1049	1049		1139		1237				1437	1446			1537
	Södertälje Syd ..... 750 d.	1037s		1104s 1124s			1204s			1402s 1404s		1410s 1504s		1525s 1604s 1604s 1604s		1704s 1740s
	Stockholm C 730/50/6 a.	1101	1131	1124	1146	1146		1246	1224	1233	1246	1331	1424	1424	1446	1431	1524		1533	1546	1624	1624	1624	1631	1724	1802

		Sn 438	MTR 470	Sn 440	MTR 410	Sn 442		Sn 408	IC 108	MTR 444	IC		MTR 446	Sn 2048	Sn 450	Sn 10450	Sn 472
		Ⓐ	⑥	Ⓐ	†	†		P	Ⓒ	Ⓐ	Ⓑ	†		Ⓐ	Ⓒ	H	V	J
	Göteborg C.........756 d.	1425	1500	1520		1525	1525	1600	1625		1645	1650	1700		1720	1725	1730		1800	1825	2000	2025	2025	2025	...
	Alingsås .... 756 d.							1650u		1720u				1755u				
	Uddevalla C 739 .... d.														
	Herrljunga .... 736/9/56 d.		1547			1647	1709		1747					1847	2046			
	Falköping .... 756 d.														
	Skövde .... 756 d.	1528	1615	1633		1628	1628	1715	1736		1807		1815		1844	1828	1843		1915	1928	2115		2128	2132	2133
	Töreboda .... 756 d.														
	Hallsberg ....756 a.							1922			1936	1915	1938			2215	2216	2222
	Örebro C 755/6 ......a.														
	Hallsberg ..... 750/5/6 d.	1638						1924			1938	1915	1940			2215	2216	2222
	Katrineholm .... 750 d.			1737	1737	1846							2037			
	Södertälje Syd ..... 750 d.	1714s 1803s 1827s			1904s 1924s			2004s		2014s 2049s		2104s	2304s			2330s
	Stockholm C 730/50/6 a.	1735	1824	1848		1833	1831	1924	1940		2051	1952	2024		2112	2035	2112		2124	2131	2324		2331	2331	2351

♦ – NOTES (LISTED BY TRAIN NUMBER)

457 – † : 🚃 and ✕ Stockholm - Herrljunga - Uddevalla.
460 – ⑥ : 🚃 and ✕ Uddevalla - Herrljunga - Stockholm.
462 – Ⓐ Dec. 12 - 23, Jan. 9 - June 9: 🚃 and ✕ Uddevalla - Herrljunga - Stockholm.
467 – Ⓐ Dec. 12 - 23, May 29 - June 9: 🚃 and ✕ Stockholm - Herrljunga - Uddevalla.
10467 – Ⓐ Jan. 9 - May 24: 🚃 and ✕ Stockholm - Herrljunga - Uddevalla.

A – ②-⑥ Dec. 17-27; ※ Jan. 7 - June 10.
B – ①②③④ Dec. 12-15, Jan. 16 - Apr. 6, Apr. 24 - June 8.
C – ①②③④ Dec. 12-15, Jan. 16 - June 8.
D – Ⓐ Jan. 9 - May 26.
E – Ⓑ Dec. 11 - Jan. 5; † Jan. 8 - May 28; Ⓑ May 29 - June 9.

F – Ⓐ Jan. 9 - May 24.
G – † Dec. 11 - Jan. 1; Ⓑ Jan. 22 - June 9.
H – Ⓑ Dec. 11 - 23; † Jan. 8 - May 25; Ⓑ May 28 - June 9.
J – Ⓑ Dec. 25 - Jan. 6.
K – ④⑤⑥† only.
L – ②③④⑤ Dec. 21-27; Ⓐ Jan. 16 - Dec. 9.
M – ④⑤⑥† Dec. 15 - Mar. 12; ④⑤⑥ Mar. 16 - June 10.
N – ⑤ Dec. 16 - May 19; Ⓐ May 24 - June 9.
P – † Dec. 11 - June 8.
Q – ①②③④ Jan. 9 - Mar. 6; ①③④ Mar. 8 - May 24.
R – Ⓐ Jan. 9 - June 9.
T – Ⓐ Dec. 12 - Jan. 5.
V – Ⓐ Jan. 23 - May 26.

s – Stops to set down only.
u – Stops to pick up only.
x – Not Dec. 24 - Jan. 8.

Sn – High speed train. Special supplement payable.

745 KØBENHAVN - MALMÖ - KRISTIANSTAD - KARLSKRONA

Operator: *Øtåg*

km																									
0	**København** H **703/30** ♣ d.	0616	0636	0716	0736	0816	0836	0916	0936	1016	1036	1116	1136	1216	1236	1316	1336	1416	1436	1516	1536	1616	1636	1716	1736
12	Kastrup ✈ **703/30** d.	0646	0706	0746	0806	0846	0906	0946	1006	1046	1106	1146	1206	1246	1306	1346	1406	1446	1506	1546	1606	1646	1706	1746	1806
47	**Malmö** C **703** a.	0713	0733	0813	0833	0913	0933	1013	1033	1113	1133	1213	1233	1313	1333	1413	1433	1513	1533	1613	1633	1713	1733	1813	1833
47	**Malmö** C **730/46** d.	0729	0748	0829	0848	0929	0948	1029	1048	1129	1148	1229	1248	1329	1348	1429	1448	1529	1548	1629	1648	1729	1748	1829	1848
63	Lund **730/46** d.	0741	0800	0841	0900	0941	1000	1041	1100	1141	1200	1241	1300	1341	1400	1441	1500	1541	1600	1641	1700	1741	1800	1841	1900
81	Eslöv **746** d.	|	0810	|	0910	|	1010	|	1110	|	1210	|	1310	|	1410	|	1510	|	1610	|	1710	|	1810	|	1910
130	Hässleholm **730/4/46** d.	0812	0838	0912	0938	1012	1036	1112	1136	1212	1236	1312	1336	1412	1436	1512	1536	1612	1636	1712	1736	1812	1836	1912	1936
160	**Kristianstad 734** a.	0832	...	0932	...	1032	...	1132	...	1232	...	1332	...	1432	...	1532	...	1632	...	1732	...	1832	...	1932	...
160	**Kristianstad** d.	0838	...	0938a	...	1038	...	1138d	...	1238	...	1338	...	1438	...	1538	...	1638	...	1738	...	1838	...	1938b	...
191	Sölvesborg d.	0858	...	0958a	...	1058	...	1158d	...	1258	...	1358	...	1458	...	1558	...	1658	...	1758	...	1858	...	1958b	...
222	**Karlshamn** d.	0919	...	1019a	...	1119	...	1219d	...	1319	...	1419	...	1519	...	1619	...	1719	...	1819	...	1919	...	2019b	...
260	Ronneby d.	0946	...	1046a	...	1146	...	1246d	...	1346	...	1446	...	1546	...	1646	...	1746	...	1846	...	1946	...	2046b	...
290	**Karlskrona** a.	1012	...	1112a	...	1212	...	1312d	...	1412	...	1512	...	1612	...	1712	...	1812	...	1912	...	2012	...	2112b	...

								Ⓐ		
København H **703/30** ♣ d.	1816	1836	1916	1936	2016	2036	2116	2136	2216	2236
Kastrup ✈ **703/30** d.	1846	1906	1946	2006	2046	2106	2146	2206	2246	2306
Malmö C **703** a.	1913	1933	2013	2033	2113	2133	2213	2233	2307	2328
Malmö C **730/46** d.	1929	1948	2029	2048	2129	2148	2229	2248	2329	2348
Lund **730/46** d.	1941	2000	2041	2100	2141	2200	2241	2300	2341	2358
Eslöv **746** d.	|	2010	|	2110	|	2210	|	2310	|	...
Hässleholm **730/4/46** d.	2012	2036	2112	2136	2212	2238	2312	2338	0012	...
Kristianstad 734 a.	2032	...	2132	...	2232	...	2332	...	0032	...
Kristianstad d.	2038	...	2138b	...	2238	...	...	...	...	...
Sölvesborg d.	2058	...	2158b	...	2258	...	...	...	...	...
Karlshamn d.	2119	...	2219b	...	2319	...	...	...	...	...
Ronneby d.	2146	...	2246b	...	2346	...	...	...	...	...
Karlskrona a.	2212	...	2312b	...	0012	...	...	...	...	...

		Ⓐ		⚒		Ⓐ				⚒
Karlskrona d.	...	0447	...	0547	...	0647	...	0747	...	0847
Ronneby d.	...	0508	...	0608	...	0708	...	0808	...	0908
Karlshamn d.	...	0535	...	0635	...	0735	...	0835	...	0935
Sölvesborg d.	...	0557	...	0657	...	0757	...	0857	...	0957
Kristianstad a.	...	0618	...	0718	...	0818	...	0918	...	1018
Kristianstad 734 d.	...	0624	...	0724	...	0824	...	0924	...	1024
Hässleholm **730/4/46** d.	0623	0644	0720	0744	0820	0844	0923	0944	1023	1044
Eslöv **746** d.	0647	|	0747	|	0847	|	0947	|	1047	|
Lund **730/46** d.	0701	0719	0801	0819	0901	0919	1001	1019	1101	1119
Malmö C **730/46** a.	0711	0729	0811	0829	0911	0929	1011	1029	1111	1129
Malmö C **703** d.	0713	0733	0813	0833	0913	0933	1013	1033	1113	1133
Kastrup ✈ **703/30** a.	0733	0753	0833	0853	0933	0953	1033	1053	1133	1153
København H **703/30** a.	0748	0808	0848	0908	0948	1008	1048	1108	1148	1208

				⚒													Ⓑ				Ⓑ				Ⓑ	
Karlskrona d.	...	0947	...	1047	...	1147	...	1247	...	1347	...	1447	...	1547	...	1647	...	1747	...	1847	...	1947	...	2047	2147
Ronneby d.	...	1008	...	1108	...	1208	...	1308	...	1408	...	1508	...	1608	...	1708	...	1808	...	1908	...	2008	...	2108	2208
Karlshamn d.	...	1035	...	1135	...	1235	...	1335	...	1435	...	1535	...	1635	...	1735	...	1835	...	1935	...	2035	...	2135	2235
Sölvesborg d.	...	1057	...	1157	...	1257	...	1357	...	1457	...	1557	...	1657	...	1757	...	1857	...	1957	...	2057	...	2157	2257
Kristianstad a.	...	1118	...	1218	...	1318	...	1418	...	1518	...	1618	...	1718	...	1818	...	1918	...	2018	...	2118	...	2218	2318
Kristianstad 734 d.	...	1124	...	1224	...	1324	...	1424	...	1524	...	1624	...	1724	...	1824	...	1924	...	2024	...	2124	...	2224	2324
Hässleholm **730/4/46** d.	1123	1144	1223	1244	1323	1344	1423	1444	1523	1544	1623	1644	1723	1744	1823	1844	1923	1944	2023	2044	2120	2144	2220	2244	2344
Eslöv **746** d.	1147	|	1247	|	1347	|	1447	|	1547	|	1647	|	1747	|	1847	|	1947	|	2047	|	2148	|	2248	|	|
Lund **730/46** d.	1201	1219	1301	1319	1401	1419	1501	1519	1601	1619	1701	1719	1801	1819	1901	1919	2001	2019	2101	2119	2201	2219	2301	2319	0019
Malmö C **730/46** a.	1211	1229	1311	1329	1411	1429	1511	1529	1611	1629	1711	1729	1811	1829	1911	1929	2011	2029	2111	2129	2211	2229	2311	2329	0029
Malmö C **703** d.	1213	1233	1313	1333	1413	1433	1513	1533	1613	1633	1713	1733	1813	1833	1913	1933	2013	2033	2113	2133	2213	2233	2313	2333	0033
Kastrup ✈ **703/30** a.	1233	1253	1333	1353	1433	1453	1533	1553	1633	1653	1733	1753	1833	1853	1933	1953	2033	2053	2133	2153	2233	2253	2333	2353	0053
København H **703/30** a.	1248	1308	1348	1408	1448	1508	1548	1608	1648	1708	1748	1808	1848	1908	1948	2008	2048	2108	2148	2208	2248	2308	2348	0008	0108

a – Ⓐ only. b – Ⓑ only. d – ⚒ only. ♣ – By connecting service to Kastrup ✈.

746 KØBENHAVN, MALMÖ and GÖTEBORG - KALMAR

km		Øtåg	Øtåg	Øtåg		Øtåg	Øtåg	Øtåg	Øtåg		Øtåg	Øtåg		Øtåg	Øtåg	Øtåg		Øtåg	Øtåg		Øtåg	Øtåg		Øtåg	Øtåg	Øtåg
		Ⓐ	Ⓐ	Ⓐ	Ⓐ					⚒			†		Ⓒ	Ⓐ	⑥			Ⓑ			Ⓑ			
0	**København** H **703** ♣ d.	...	0456	0536	...	0636	0736	0836	0936	...	1036	1136	...	1236	1336	1336	...	1436	1536	...	1636	1736	...	1836	1936	2036
12	Kastrup ✈ **703** d.	...	0526	0606	...	0706	0806	0906	1006	...	1106	1206	...	1306	1406	1406	...	1506	1606	...	1706	1806	...	1906	2006	2106
47	**Malmö** C **703** a.	...	0546	0633	...	0733	0833	0933	1033	...	1133	1233	...	1333	1433	1433	...	1533	1633	...	1733	1833	...	1933	2033	2133
47	**Malmö** C **730/45** d.	...	0548	0648	...	0748	0848	0948	1048	...	1148	1248	...	1348	1448	1448	...	1548	1648	...	1748	1848	...	1948	2048	2148
63	Lund **730/45** d.	...	0600	0700	...	0800	0900	1000	1100	...	1200	1300	...	1400	1500	1500	...	1600	1700	...	1800	1900	...	2000	2100	2200
80	Eslöv **745** d.	...	0610	0710	...	0810	0910	1010	1110	...	1210	1310	...	1410	1510	1510	...	1610	1710	...	1810	1910	...	2010	2110	2210
130	Hässleholm **730/45** d.	...	0644	0744	...	0844	0944	1044	1144	...	1244	1344	...	1444	1544	1544	...	1644	1744	...	1844	1944	...	2044	2144	2244
181	Älmhult d.	...	0710	0810	...	0910	1010a	1110	1210a	...	1310	1410a	...	1510	1610	1610	...	1710	1810b	...	1910	2010b	...	2110	2210b	2310
	Göteborg C ▲ d.	...	|	|	0605	|	|	|	|	1005	|	|	1200	|	|	|	1405	|	|	1605	|	|	1805	|	|	|
	Borås ▲ d.	...	|	|	0659	|	|	|	|	1059	|	|	1257	|	|	|	1459	|	|	1705	|	|	1859	|	|	|
	Limmared d.	...	|	|	0727	|	|	|	|	1128	|	|	1325	|	|	|	1527	|	|	1733	|	|	1927	|	|	|
	Värnamo d.	...	|	|	0808	|	|	|	|	1210	|	|	1406	|	|	|	1609	|	|	1818	|	|	2013	|	|	|
228	Alvesta **730** a.	...	0735	0835	0835	0935	1035a	1135	1235a	1235	1335	1435a	1434	1535	1633	1633	1636	1735	1835b	1845	1935	2035b	2039	2135	2235b	2335
228	Alvesta ▲ d.	0632	0737	0843	0838	0937	1037a	1137	1242a	1236	1337	1437a	1438	1537	1635	1637	1638	1737	1837b	1848	1937	2037b	2042	2138	2237b	2337
245	**Växjö** ▲ d.	0648	0748	0853	0852	0948	1048a	1148	1253a	1248	1348	1448a	1451	1548	1646	1648	1651	1750	1847b	1902	1948	2047b	2056	2148	2247b	2347
302	Emmaboda a.	0725	0825	...	0927	1025	1125a	1225	...	1323	1425	1525a	1527	1628	...	1725	1726	1825	...	1936	2028	...	2130	2225	...	...
302	Emmaboda ► d.	0730	0830	...	0929	1030	1130a	1230	...	1330	1430	1530a	1530	1630	...	1730	1730	1830	...	1937	2035	...	2132	2230	...	...
330	Nybro d.	0743	0843	...	0943	1043	1143a	1243	...	1344	1443	1548a	1544	1645	...	1743	1744	1843	...	1951	2048	...	2146	2243	...	...
359	**Kalmar** a.	0759	0859	...	1001	1059	1159a	1259	...	1405	1459	1604a	1601	1701	...	1759	1801	1859	...	2009	2104	...	2203	2259	...	...

km		Øtåg		Øtåg	Øtåg	Øtåg	Øtåg		Øtåg	Øtåg		Øtåg	Øtåg		Øtåg	Øtåg	Øtåg	Øtåg		Øtåg	Øtåg		Øtåg	Øtåg	Øtåg	Øtåg
		Ⓐ	Ⓐ	Ⓐ	Ⓐ	Ⓒ		⑥			Ⓑ	Ⓐ		Ⓑ					⚒			†			Ⓑ	Ⓐ
	Kalmar d.	...	0500	...	0600	...	0700	0757	0800a	0900	0955	...	1100	1151	...	1300	1400a	1500	1557	...	1655	1756	1800a	1906	2005a	2100
	Nybro d.	...	0517	...	0614	...	0714	0814	0814a	0914	1012	...	1114	1211	...	1314	1414a	1514	1618	...	1714	1813	1814a	1920	2020a	2114
	Emmaboda ► a.	...	0531	...	0629	...	0729	0829	0829a	0929	1027	...	1129	1225	...	1329	1429a	1529	1632	...	1729	1827	1829a	1935	2035a	2129
	Emmaboda d.	...	0533	...	0630	...	0730	0831	0830a	0930	1030	...	1130	1227	...	1330	1430a	1530	1633	...	1730	1828	1830a	1936	2035a	2130
	Växjö ▲ d.	0515	0607	0615	0710	0715t	0810	0905	0910a	1010	1105	1111	1210	1302	1315a	1410	1510b	1610	1706	1712a	1810	1902	1910b	2010	2116	2205
	Alvesta ▲ a.	0526	0620	0626	0720	0726t	0820	0918	0920a	1020	1118	1122	1220	1314	1326a	1420	1520b	1620	1719	1723a	1820	1915	1920b	2020	2126	...
0	Alvesta **730** d.	0528	0622	0628	0728	0728t	0828	0922	0928a	1028	1120	1128	1228	1316	1328a	1428	1528b	1628	1722	1728a	1828	1922	1928b	2028	2128	...
49	Värnamo d.	|	0647	|	|	|	|	0947	|	|	1145	|	|	1340	|	|	|	|	1749	|	|	1947	|	|	|	...
110	Limmared d.	|	0727	|	|	|	|	1028	|	|	1228	|	|	1420	|	|	|	|	1828	|	|	2030	|	|	|	...
149	Borås ▲ a.	|	0757	|	|	|	|	1058	|	|	1256	|	|	1449	|	|	|	|	1857	|	|	2058	|	|	|	...
222	**Göteborg** C ▲ a.	|	0855	|	|	|	|	1155	|	|	1350	|	|	1550	|	|	|	|	1955	|	|	2155	|	|	|	...
	Älmhult d.	0547	...	0647	0747	0747t	0847	...	0947a	1047	...	1147	1247	...	1347a	1447	1547b	1647	...	1747a	1847	...	1947b	2047	2147	...
	Hässleholm **730/45** d.	0623	...	0723	0823	0820	0923	...	1023	1123	...	1223	1323	...	1423	1523	1623	1723	...	1823	1923	...	2023	2120	2220	...
	Eslöv **745** a.	0647	...	0747	0847	0848	0947	...	1047	1147	...	1247	1347	...	1447	1547	1647	1747	...	1847	1947	...	2047	2148	2248	...
	Lund **730/45** d.	0701	...	0801	0901	0901	1001	...	1101	1201	...	1301	1401	...	1501	1601	1701	1801	...	1901	2001	...	2101	2201	2301	...
	Malmö C **730/45** a.	0711	...	0811	0911	0911	1011	...	1111	1211	...	1311	1411	...	1511	1611	1711	1811	...	1911	2011	...	2111	2211	2311	...
	Malmö C **703** d.	0713	...	0813	0913	0913	1013	...	1113	1213	...	1313	1413	...	1513	1613	1713	1813	...	1913	2013	...	2113	2213	2313	...
	Kastrup ✈ **703** a.	0733	...	0833	0933	0933	1033	...	1133	1233	...	1333	1433	...	1533	1633	1733	1833	...	1933	2033	...	2133	2233	2333	...
	København H **703** a.	0748	...	0848	0948	0948	1048	...	1148	1248	...	1348	1448	...	1548	1648	1748	1848	...	1948	2048	...	2148	2248	2348	...

► – CONNECTING SERVICES **Emmaboda - Karlskrona and v.v.** (2nd class only) : Operator: *LT*

km		Ⓐ	⚒	⚒	⚒		⚒				Ⓑ		Ⓑ		Ⓑ		Ⓑ
0	Emmaboda d.	0634	0734	0834	0934	1034	1146	1234	1334	1434	1534	1636	1734	1834	1953	2034	2135
57	Karlskrona a.	0717	0817	0917	1017	1117	1229	1317	1417	1517	1617	1719	1817	1917	2036	2117	2218

	Ⓐ	⚒	⚒	⚒		⚒				Ⓑ		Ⓑ		Ⓑ		Ⓑ
Karlskrona a.	0542	0642	0742	0842	0942	1042	1135	1242	1342	1442	1542	1640	1742	1842	1942	2042
Emmaboda d.	0624	0724	0824	0924	1024	1124	1217	1324	1424	1524	1624	1726	1824	1924	2024	2124

a – Ⓐ only.
b – Ⓑ only.
t – ⑥ only.

♣ – By connecting service to Kastrup ✈.

▲ – Additional trains run Göteborg - Borås and v.v., and Alvesta - Växjö and v.v.

Operator: A -Train AB (*AEX*) Arlanda Express	STOCKHOLM - STOCKHOLM ARLANDA ✈	747

Journey time: 20 minutes. All services stop at Arlanda Södra (17 minutes from Stockholm, 2 minutes from Arlanda Norra). Södra serves terminals 2, 3 and 4; Norra serves terminal 5.

From **Stockholm** Central : 0435, 0505, 0520, 0535, 0550, 0605, 0620, 0635, 0650 and at the same minutes past each hour until 2205, then 2220, 2235, 2305, 2335, 0005, 0035.

From **Arlanda** Norra : 0505, 0535, 0550, 0605, 0620, 0635, 0650 and at the same minutes past each hour until 2205, then 2220, 2235, 2250, 2305, 2335, 0005, 0035, 0105.

Minor alterations to schedules are possible at peak times

STOCKHOLM - HALLSBERG - KARLSTAD - OSLO 750

km		VTAB	Sn 615	VTAB	ST 619	VTAB	Sn 623	VTAB	Sn 625	VTAB VTAB	Sn Sn 629 633	VTAB	ST	VTAB VTAB 635	Sn 657	Sn 637	Tågab	VTAB VTAB	VTAB 641	Sn 631
			2 ⓇⓍ	2	ⓇⓍ	2	2 ⓇⓍ	2	2 ⓇⓍ	Ⓐ ⑥	2 2 ⓇⓍ ⓇⓍ	2	Ⓐ †	2 2 ⓇⓍ ⓇⓍ	ⓇⓍ	Ⓐ ⑥ †		Ⓐ ⑥	2 2 ⓇⓍ	ⓇⓍ
0	Stockholm C 730/40 ▲ d.	... Ⓐ x		Ⓐ	Ⓒ	Ⓐ	0540		0714		0814	...	1036 1106		1336 1414	1425	1425			1610	1614
36	Södertälje Syd 730/40 ▲ d.								0833u		1055u		1354u 1433u	1443u					1629u	1633u
131	Katrineholm 740 ▲ d.					0811		0911		1133 1204		1434 1511	1524	1525					1711u	1711u
197	Hallsberg 740 ▲ d.		0610 0655	0712g	0838		0937		1157 1233 1320		1503 1537	1552	1556			1722 1737	1737
261	Degerfors d.		0648	0743g	0919		1008		1229 1305 1352		1537 1607	1626 1633			1757	
287	Kristinehamn d.		0702	0801g	0935		1022 1212		1242 1319 1409		1520 1615 1551	1621 1640 1656			1715 1811	
327	Karlstad 751 a.		0730 0758	0829g	0956		1043 1237		1304 1342 1437		1544 1650 1614	1642 1703 1716			1751 1836	1842 1842
327	Karlstad d.	0529 0558	0731 0803 0801	0845	0902 0959	1025 1045	1240 1242 1310		1443 1518 1543	1645			1726 1753		1845 1845
347	Kil d.	0544	0745	0904 0920	1042		1256 1254		1455 1535 1604	1718			1744 1805		
395	Arvika d.	0618 0637	0821 0842	0939 0956	1040 1120 1122		1331 1332 1352		1530 1617 1641	1756	1721			1821 1840		1923 1923
430	Charlottenberg 🚊 d.	0639	0843	1002 1019	1141		1352 1353		1553 1639 1703	1819			1846		
472	Kongsvinger d.		0727	0928 1039	1125		1441		1706			1804			2007 2007
572	**Oslo** Sentral a.		0844	1030 1210	1229		1324		1610			1914			2129 2129

		Sn 639	VTAB	Tågab 643	Sn	VTAB 645	Sn	VTAB VTAB Tågab VTAB	Sn 649			VTAB	Sn 620	Tågab	Sn 622	VTAB	Sn VTAB Tågab Tågab	Sn 624	VTAB	VTAB Sn 626
		ⓇⓍ	2		ⓇⓍ	2		2	ⓇⓍ			2	ⓇⓍ	2	ⓇⓍ	2	2	ⓇⓍ		2	ⓇⓍ
		Ⓐ y	⑥	⑥	Ⓑ	†	⑥	Ⓐ ⑥	†	Ⓑ			Ⓐ	Ⓐ	Ⓐ	Ⓐ	⑥	†	Ⓐ	Ⓐ	⑥
Stockholm C 730/40 ▲ d.		1614	1627 1736		1810		1936		2025		Oslo Sentral d.			0550					0550		
Södertälje Syd 730/40 ▲ d.		1633u		1755u		1833u			2043u		Kongsvinger d.			0659						
Katrineholm 740 ▲ d.		1711u	1727 1832u		1911		2035		2125		Charlottenberg 🚊 d.				0556		0732 0748			
Hallsberg 740 ▲ d.		1737	1808 1858		1937		2106		2153		Arvika d.		0512		0619		0741 0755 0811			
Degerfors d.			1842 1929		2006		2140		2228		Kil d.		0545		0658		0837 0851			
Kristinehamn d.			1856 1944		2020 2019		2204		2245		Karlstad 751 a.		0557		0715		0818 0849 0907			
Karlstad 751 a.		1842	1917 2006		2042 2047		2226		2307		Karlstad d.		0610 0653 0710 0730 0750 0800 0821 0851						0930		
Karlstad d.		1845 1858	2010e 2040		2049 2133		2228				Kristinehamn d.		0630 0716 0732 0758 0814 0820 0840 0915						0949		
Kil d.			1915	2101		2106 2150		2240			Degerfors d.		0646 0734 0750	0827 0835 0856					1005		
Arvika d.		1923 1951	2047e 2141		2144 2222		2319			Hallsberg 740 ▲ a.			0813 0824	0903 0910 0927				1040		
Charlottenberg 🚊 a.			2013e	2202		2207 2246		2341			Katrineholm 740 ▲ a.			0847 0851	0931		0959		1104		
Kongsvinger a.		2007		2144e							Södertälje Syd 730/40 ▲ a.			0933s					1143s		
Oslo Sentral a.		2129		2304e							Stockholm C 730/40 ▲ a.		0839 1001 0954		1035		1046		1205		

		VTAB	Sn 630	Sn 630	Sn 632	Sn 632	VTAB	Sn 634	Sn 636	Sn 656		VTAB 640	Tågab 650	VTAB VTAB	Sn 642	Sn 644	VTAB	Sn 646	VTAB VTAB	ST Tågab
		2	ⓇⓍ	ⓇⓍ	ⓇⓍ	ⓇⓍ	2	ⓇⓍ	ⓇⓍ	ⓇⓍ		ⓇⓍ	ⓇⓍ		2	ⓇⓍ	2	ⓇⓍ	2	2
		Ⓐ	†	⑥	Ⓐ y	Ⓐ	⑥	†	Ⓐ	†	Ⓐ		⑥	†	Ⓒ	⑥	Ⓐ †	Ⓒ	Ⓐ ⑥	Ⓐ †
Oslo Sentral d.			0550	0932		1056 1132				1332 1332		1346		1456		1656		1936		
Kongsvinger d.			1004	1036		1213 1238				1440 1440		1502		1603		1805		2055		
Charlottenberg 🚊 d.	0934			1157			1333		1421 1425		1531 1532		1615		1925		2119		
Arvika d.	0956		1045	1120 1219 1252 1331		1356		1444 1447	1528 1531		1553 1557 1645		1641 1846 1950 2032 2141				
Kil d.	1033			1253		1430 1428 1520 1522			1627 1631		1715		2022 2107 2218 2251				
Karlstad 751 a.	1045		1128	1209 1306 1332 1410		1442 1441 1532 1540 1609 1611		1639 1645 1726		1728 1927 2034 2119 2238 2305				
Karlstad d.	1050 1131 1131 1218		1335 1413 1415 1446 1447 1546		1614 1614		1642e 1658 1730 1735 1751 1928		2311				
Kristinehamn d.	1114 1152 1152 1243 1243		1356 1433 1436 1510 1519 1612		1636 1638		1714e 1729 1750 1756 1824 1956		2332				
Degerfors d.	1129 1205 1205 1258 1258		1410 1447 1451		1533		1652 1654		1729e 1744 1804 1814		2010				
Hallsberg 740 ▲ a.	1200 1242 1242 1334 1334		1443 1521 1525		1609		1727 1729		1804e 1819 1835 1851		2042				
Katrineholm 740 ▲ a.		1306 1306		1555		1646		1753 1756		1859 1917		2106				
Södertälje Syd 730/40 ▲ a.		1345s 1345s		1541s		1635s				1959s						
Stockholm C 730/40 ▲ a.		1405 1405 1501 1501		1602 1646 1701		1748		1854 1854		1954 2020	2201			

▲ – Regional services STOCKHOLM - HALLSBERG and v.v. (2nd class only):

		Ⓐ	Ⓐ	⅀	Ⓑ		Ⓐ	Ⓐ	Ⓐ	Ⓐ	Ⓐ	Ⓐ	Ⓐ	Ⓐ
Stockholm C d.	0629 0729 0829 1029 1229 1429 1529 1706 1729 1744 1857 2036 2206	
Flemingsberg d.	0640 0741 0840 1040 1240 1440 1542 1717 1740 1756 1908 2047 2217	
Södertälje Syd d.	0653 0753 0852 1055 1251 1452 1555 1729 1757 1809 1919 2058 2228	
Flen d.	0731 0830 0927 1132 1328 1527 1629 1804 1832 1854 2131 2303	
Katrineholm d.	0744 0842 0941 1146 1440 1543 1643 1818 1850 1859 2007 2144 2317	
Hallsberg a.	0818 0914 1014 1218 1410 1620 1721 1851 1921 1941 2042 2214 2347	

		Ⓐ	Ⓐ	⅀	†	Ⓐ	Ⓐ	Ⓐ	Ⓐ	Ⓐ	Ⓐ	Ⓐ	Ⓐ
Hallsberg d.	0628 0730 0940 1140 1318 1324 1433 1542 1546 1640 1740 1922 2046	
Katrineholm d.	0702 0801 1012 1212 1350 1356 1505 1614 1619 1711 1812 1954 2119	
Flen d.	0719 0814 1024 1224 1402 1408 1516 1626 1631 1722 1824 2005 2130	
Södertälje Syd d.	0756 0850 1100j 1302 1443 1443 1550 1705 1705 1805 1905 2041 2206	
Flemingsberg d.	0808 0901 1110j 1312 1453 1453 1602 1718 1718 1818 1917 2052 2218	
Stockholm C a.	0820 0916 1121j 1324 1505 1505 1616 1731 1731 1831 1931 2105 2231	

e – † only.
g – ⑥ only.
j – On ⑥: Södertälje Syd d. 1106, Flemingsberg d. 1121, Stockholm C a. 1133.
s – Stops to set down only.

u – Stops to pick up only.
x – Not Dec. 24 - Jan. 8.
y – Dec. 27 - Jan. 5.

Sn – High speed train. Special supplement payable.
▲ – For regional services Stockholm - Hallsberg and v.v. – see panel above.

KARLSTAD - GÖTEBORG 751

km			Tågab Tågab				Tågab Tågab		H					Tågab		Tågab			Tågab Tågab		Tågab
		Ⓐ	Ⓐ	Ⓐ	⑥	Ⓐ			Ⓑ	†			Ⓐ	Ⓐ	⑥	⅀	†	Ⓐ	Ⓒ	⑥		Ⓐ
0	Karlstad 750 d.	0613 0818 0932 1005 1012 1214 1416 1611 1701 1715 1815 2224		Göteborg C d.	0510 0615 0715 0835 0915 1115 1315 1345 1405 1515 1715 1915 2045
19	Kil d.	0628 0830 0948 1020 1027 1229 1428 1629 1713 1732 1829 2237		Trollhättan d.	0544 0650 0752 0914 0952 1152 1352 1419 1445 1552 1751 1952 2119
70	Säffle d.	0659 0901 1018 1053 1059 1300 1500 1701 1749 1800 1901 2308		Öxnered d.	0549 0656 0800 0921 1000 1200 1400 1425 1451 1600 1800 2000 2125
87	Åmål d.	0709 0911 1030 1105 1109 1310 1510 1710 1801 1812 1912 2314		Mellerud d.	0610 0716 0821 0946 1021 1220 1421	1509 1620 1819 2019 2144
128	Mellerud d.	0741 0936 1057 1132 1135 1335 1537 1736 1824	1938 2342		Åmål d.	0633 0740 0845 1012 1044 1244 1444 1510 1537 1644 1846 2043 2206
169	Öxnered d.	0802 0956 1120 1151 1155 1359 1556 1759 1851 1857 1958 0002		Säffle d.	0644 0750 0901 1022 1059 1300 1500 1547 1659 1902 2056 2216
179	Trollhättan d.	0808 1002 1127 1159 1205 1405 1602 1805 1857 1903 2005 0008		Kil a.	0720 0819 0932 1053 1130 1331 1531 1547 1615 1730 1932 2129 2251
251	Göteborg C a.	0845 1035 1205 1235 1240 1440 1645 1845 1945 1940 2040 0040		Karlstad 750 a.	0733 0836 0951 1110 1147 1346 1546 1605 1629 1746 1945 2145 2305

H – ①②③④† only.

VÄSTERÅS - LUDVIKA 752

2nd class only

km		Ⓐ	Ⓐ	Ⓐ	Ⓐ x	Ⓐ	Ⓐ	Ⓐ x	Ⓐ x		Ⓐ	Ⓐ x	Ⓐ	Ⓐ	Ⓐ	Ⓐ	Ⓐ x		Ⓒ	Ⓐ	Ⓐ	Ⓐ x
	Stockholm C 756 d.																1707			2025	
0	Västerås 756 d.	0615 0715 0815 0829 0915 1015 1029 1115 1215	1229 1315 1415 1429 1515 1615 1629 1715 1815		1815 1915 2015 2127 2227
80	Fagersta C d.	0712 0810 0910 0929 1010 1112 1129 1210 1310	1329 1412 1510 1529 1612 1710 1729 1812 1910		1914 2012 2110 2227 2322
129	Ludvika a.	0754	0954 1018	1154 1218		1418 1454	1618 1854		1956 2054	2309

		Ⓐ	Ⓐ	Ⓐ	Ⓐ	Ⓐ	Ⓐ	Ⓐ		Ⓐ	Ⓐ	Ⓐ	Ⓐ	Ⓐ	Ⓐ	Ⓐ	Ⓐ x		Ⓐ	Ⓐ x	Ⓐ
Ludvika d.		0607	0802 0807 0948		1007 1148		1307 1348		1507 1548	1707 1748		1907	2107
Fagersta C d.	0530 0645 0802 0845 0850 1032		1050 1232		1350 1432 1450 1632 1650 1750 1832		1850 1950 2050 2150
Västerås 756 a.	0625 0745 0845 0945 0945 1132		1145 1332		1445 1532 1545 1732 1745 1845 1930		1945 2045 2145 2245
Stockholm C 756 a.		0905	1052										

x – Not Dec. 24 - Jan. 8.

753 KRISTINEHAMN - MORA - ÖSTERSUND - GÄLLIVARE   INLANDSBANAN

Temporarily relocated on page 358

754 NORRKÖPING - VÄSTERÅS - SALA   2nd class only

km		Ⓐ	Ⓐ	✕							
	Linköping 730...d.	...	0506	0604a	0811c	1007	1207	1407	1607	1807	2007
0	Norrköping 730...d.	...	0533	0632a	0838	1034	1234	1434	1636	1834	2034
48	Katrineholm...d.	...	0559	0656a	0904	1100	1300	1500	1702	1900	2100
71	Flen 730...d.	...	0612	0709a	0917	1113	1313	1513	1717	1917	2113
112	Eskilstuna...d.	0546	0652	0752	0952	1152	1352	1552	1752	1952	2152
160	Västerås...a.	0619	0725	0825	1025	1225	1425	1625	1825	2025	2225
160	Västerås...d.	0622	0728	0828	1028	1228	1428	1628	1828	2028	...
199	Sala 758...a.	0647	0753	0853	1053	1253	1453	1653	1853	2053	...

	Ⓐ	Ⓐ									
Sala 758...d.	...	0708	0808	0908	1108	1308	1508	1708	1908	2110
Västerås...a.	...	0732	0832	0932	1132	1332	1532	1732	1932	2133
Västerås...d.	0529	0735	0835	0935	1135	1335	1535	1735	1935	2135
Eskilstuna...d.	0604	0809	0909	1009	1209	1409	1609	1809	2009	2209
Flen 730...d.	...	0640	0844	0943	1044	1244	1444	1644	1844	2044	2246a
Katrineholm...d.	...	0654	0858	0958	1058	1258	1459	1658	1858	2058	2301a
Norrköping 730...a.	...	0718	0922	1022	1122	1322	1525	1722	1922	2122	2330a
Linköping 730...a.	...	0749	0950	1050	1149	1349	1552	1748	1949	2149	2359a

a – Ⓐ only.   c – Ⓒ only.

755 MJÖLBY - HALLSBERG - ÖREBRO - GÄVLE

km		Ⓐ	Ⓐ	Ⓐ	✕	✕x	Ⓐ	Ⓐ	Ⓐ	⑥	Ⓐx	Ⓐx	Ⓐx	⑥	Ⓐx	Ⓐx	Ⓑ	Ⓐx	Ⓑ	†	Ⓐ	Ⓑ
0	Mjölby 730...d.				0551			0806d		1006			1206		1406			1606		1806		2006
27	Motala...d.				0606			0821d		1021			1221		1421			1621		1821		2021
96	Hallsberg...a.				0653			0906d		1106			1306		1506			1706		1906		2106
	Hallsberg 736/56...d.			0532a	0637	0658	0734	0830		0919d		1119		1248	1317		1518	1637	1648a	1716	1838 1925 1940 1940 2115
121	Örebro C 736/56...d.			0551a	0656	0717	0753	0849		0938d		1138		1307	1336		1537	1656	1707a	1735	1857 1944 2000 2000 2134
	Örebro C...d.			0555a	0659	0721	0759	0853	0853	0859	0914	1309	1309	1359	1459	1559	1659	1719	1759	1957 2003 2013 2139
146	Frövi...d.			0610a	0714	0736	0814	0908	0908	0914	1013d	1114	1214	1314	1324	1414	1514	1614	1714	1725 1814 1914 2014 2020 2018 2205
204	Kopparberg...d.			0657a	0758		0858		0957	1056d	1203	1259	1400		1501	1600	1700	1759	1858	1958 2057 2246
232	Grängesberg...d.			0717a	0818		0918		1017	1120d	1223	1318	1419		1521	1620	1719	1819	1918	2018 2117 2305
247	Ludvika...d.		0631	0731a	0831		0930		1028	1133d	1234	1330	1431		1532	1632	1731	1831	1930	2030 2130 2317
295	Borlänge...d.		0658	0758a	0859			1111	1204	1301	1359	1501		1601	1659	1758	1858	1957	2057 2203 2348
295	Borlänge 758...d.	0558		0703	0809	0904a	1004		1113	1203	1308	1404	1508		1608j	1706	1802	1910	2012	2210
317	Falun 758...d.	0617		0721	0829	0927a	1022		1132	1226	1329	1422	1529		1633j	1727	1824	1946	2029	2226
	Fagersta...d.		0601		0821		0954	0954					1409 1409			1810		2110 2119
	Avesta Krylbo...d.		0627		0846		1019	1019			1434 1434			1835		2135 2147
371	Storvik...d.	0657	0704	0802	0905	1006a	0927	1104	1055	1055	1211	1307	1405	1503	1604	1511 1519 1711j	1804	1905	1912 2109 2218 2240
385	Sandviken...d.	0708	0715	0813	0916	1017a	0937	1117	1106	1106	1223	1322	1416	1514	1615	1522 1536 1723j	1815	1915	1923 2120 2228 2253
408	Gävle 760...a.	0723	0735	0828	0931	1037a	0955	1135	1121	1121	1238	1335	1436	1534	1635	1539 1552 1738j	1835	1933	1943 2135 2244 2309

km		Ⓐ	Ⓐ	Ⓐ	✕	Ⓐx	Ⓐx	⑥	✕	Ⓐx	†	Ⓐx	Ⓐ	Ⓐ	Ⓐx	Ⓑ	Ⓐx	Ⓑ	†	Ⓐ	Ⓑ
0	Gävle 760...d.	0430		0514	0617d	0722	0822	0822	0827	0925	1024	1030	1122	1222	1238	1423	1430	1622 1638 1708 1822 1830 1903 2025
23	Sandviken...d.	0446		0530	0633d	0738	0838	0838	0844	0941	1040	1046	1138	1243	1254	1439	1446	1638 1654 1724 1838 1846 1920 2041
37	Storvik...d.	0456		0540	0643d	0748	0848	0848	0853	0952	1050	1056	1148	1253	1304	1449	1458	1648 1704 1734 1848 1856 1932 2051
95	Avesta Krylbo...d.	0535						0931		1135		1342		1536		1742		1935 2010
130	Fagersta...d.	0600						0956		1200		1408		1600		1808		1957 2034
	Falun 758...d.			0619	0725d	0825	0930	0930		1036	1129		1234	1331		1529		1726 1826 1934 2140
	Borlänge 758...a.			0634	0741d	0841	0946	0946		1052	1145		1254	1347		1545		1742 1842 1950 2156
	Borlänge...d.		0518	0555	0658	0800d	0859		0958		1058	1201		1301	1359		1600	1700 1800b 1859 1958
	Ludvika...d.		0548	0624	0729	0829d	0928		1027		1132	1230		1331	1429		1630	1729 1839b 1929 2028
	Grängesberg...d.		0558	0634	0739	0839d	0938		1037		1142	1240		1341	1439		1640	1739 1839b 1939 2038
	Kopparberg...d.		0607	0658	0758	0858d	0957		1056		1203	1259		1400	1501		1659	1759 1858b 1958 2057
202	Frövi...d.		0644	0703	0743	0843	0943d	1015		1143	1240 1246 1346 1244 1446 1542 1745 1648 1843 1943b 1855 2044 2141
228	Örebro C...a.		0654	0713	0753	0853d	0954	1100		1158	1054 1302 1403 1259 1500 1600 1506 1759 1704 1858 1957b 1909 2059 2156
	Örebro C 736/56...d.	0615	0700	0721	0815	0900	1013		1216	1056a		1413		1609 1508 1808 1706 2004b 1911 2158
252	Hallsberg 736/56...d.	0634	0719	0740	0835	0919	1033		1235	1115a		1433		1628 1527 1829 1725 2023b 1930 2217
	Hallsberg...d.	0647		0847		1047		1247		1447		1647	1847b	2047b
	Motala...d.	0726		0926		1126		1326		1526		1726	1926b	2126b
	Mjölby 730...a.	0744		0944		1144		1344		1544		1744	1944b	2144b

a – Ⓐ only.   b – Ⓑ only.   d – ✕ only.   j – By connecting train on ✕.   x – Not Dec. 24 - Jan. 8.

756 STOCKHOLM - VÄSTERÅS - ÖREBRO - HALLSBERG - GÖTEBORG

km		Ⓐj	⑥	Ⓐ	Ⓐ	Ⓐ	Ⓐ	Ⓐ	✕	©	Ⓐ	Ⓐ	K Ⓐ	Ⓑ							
0	Stockholm C...d.		0555	0725d	0825	0925	1007	1125	1225	1325	1351	1425	1525	1525	1551	1625	1655	1724	1751	1825	1925 2225
72	Enköping...d.		0636	0806d	0906	1006	1054	1206	1306	1406		1506	1606	1606		1706	1738	1806		1906	2006 2306
107	Västerås 752...d.	0520	0623		0659	0824d	0941	1024	1110	1224	1325	1424		1525	1624	1624		1724	1800	1824	1923 2025 2340
141	Köping...d.	0536	0639		0715	0841d	0941	1041	1041	1241	1341	1441		1541	1641	1641		1741	1818	1841	1939 2041 2340
159	Arboga 757...d.	0548	0651		0727	0853d	0953	1053	1142	1253	1353	1453	1523	1653	1653	1723	1753	1830	1853	1928 1951 2053 2352
205	Örebro C 736/40/55...d.	0620	0730	0730	0750	0930	1018	1127	1205	1330	1417	1526	1551	1616	1730	1730	1751	1815	1855	1930 1953 2116 0015
230	Hallsberg 736/40/55...a.	0642	0753	0753	0810	0953	1038	1153	1226	1353	1437	1548		1636	1753	1756		1835	1915	1953 2013 2035 2136 0030
260	Laxå...736 d.		0809j	0809		1009		1209		1409		1604			1809	1812			2009
305	Töreboda...740 d.		0823j	0828		1028		1228		1428		1624			1828	1831			2028
344	Skövde...740 d.	0729	0844j	0844		1044		1244		1444		1644			1844	1920			2045
374	Falköping...740 d.	0753	0907j	0907		1107		1307		1507		1705			1907	1941			2107
408	Herrljunga...736/9/40 d.		0926j	0926		1126		1326		1526		1724			1926	2000			2126
443	Alingsås...740 d.		0949j	0949		1149		1349		1549		1747			1949	2032			2149
488	Göteborg C...740 a.	0905	1025j	1025		1225		1425		1625		1830			2025	2100			2225

	Ⓐ	Ⓐ	Ⓐ	Ⓐ	Ⓐ	⑥	†	✕	Ⓐ	Ⓐ	†	✕	Ⓐ	Ⓐ	Ⓑ	G
Göteborg C...740 d.				0540j	0545		0750		0950		1150	1150		1350	1350		1550 1750 1750 1850
Alingsås...740 d.				0608j	0613		0818		1018		1218	1218		1418	1418		1618 1818 1818 1919
Herrljunga...736/9/40 d.				0652j	0656		0839		1041		1239	1239		1441	1442		1641 1839 1839 1940
Falköping...740 d.				0706j	0651		0856		1056		1256	1256		1456	1456		1656 1856 1856 2002
Skövde...740 d.				0722j	0708		0916		1113		1317	1313		1518	1513		1718 1912 1917 2020
Töreboda...740 d.				0739j	0726		0936		1131		1331	1331		1531	1531		1735 1930 1935 2039
Laxå...736 d.				0758j	0746		0955		1156		1356	1356		1556	1556		1755 1956 1956 2101
Hallsberg 736/40/55...d.	0518	0544	0620	0725		0823	0812	0823	0924	1015	1133	1223	1323	1416	1423	1523	1623 1623 1722 1815 2023 2023 2120
Örebro C 757...d.	0541	0607	0643	0748	0808	0846	0846	0846	0946	1046	1156	1246	1346	1446	1446	1546	1607 1646 1646 1745 1838 2046 2046 2143
Arboga 757...d.	0602	0630	0704	0809	0831	0907	0907	0907	1007	1107	1218	1309	1407	1507	1507	1630	1707 1707 1806 1907 2107 2107 2204
Köping...d.	0612	0640	0715	0819		0917	0917	0917	1017	1117	1228	1320	1417	1517	1517	1617	1717 1717 1816 1917 2117 2117 2212
Västerås 752...d.	0638	0703	0739	0840		0940	0940	0940	1040	1140	1253	1340	1440	1540	1540	1640	1740 1740 1840 1940 2140 2140 2232
Enköping...d.	0652	0720	0753	0854		0954	0954	0954	1054	1154	1307	1354	1454	1554	1554	1654	1754 1754 1854 1954 2154 2154
Stockholm C...a.	0735	0805	0835	0935		1035	1035	1035	1135	1235	1353	1435	1535	1635	1635	1735	1809 1835 1835 1935 2035 2235 2235

G – ①②③④† only.
K – Jan. 9 - May 26.
d – ✕ only.
j – Not Jan. 9 - May 26.
☐ – Additional services operate Stockholm - Västerås and v.v.

STOCKHOLM - BORLÄNGE - FALUN and MORA — 758

km		IC 660 Ⓐ	IC 14 Ⓐx	IC 662 Ⓐp	IC 662 ⑥	IC 42	IC 670 Ⓐx		IC 18 ⑥	IC 672 †		IC 674 Ⓐ	IC 20 ⑥J	IC 46 †		IC 22 Ⓐx	IC 678 Ⓐp	IC 678 Ⓒ		IC 680 Ⓐx	IC 48 Ⓑ	IC 696 ⑥		IC 26 Ⓑ
0	**Stockholm** C **760** ♠ d.	0615	0745	0745	0745	0945	1115	...	1145	1145	...	1345	1345	1345	...	1545	1545	1545	...	1646	1745	1745	...	1945
39	Arlanda C ✈ **760** ◧ ♠ d.	0634	0806	0806	0806	1006	1136	...	1206	1206	...	1406	1406	1406	...	1606	1606	1606	...	1705	1806	1806	...	2006
69	Uppsala **760** ◧ ♠ d.	0653	0824	0824	0824	1024	1154	...	1224	1224	...	1424	1424	1424	...	1624	1624	1624	...	1724	1824	1824	...	2024
131	Sala **754** d.	0739	0900	0900	0900	1100	1230	...	1300	1300	...	1500	1500	1500	...	1700	1700	1700	...	1805	1900	1900	...	2100
164	Avesta Krylbo d.	0759	0921	0921	0921	1121	1258	...	1321	1321	...	1521	1521	1521	...	1720	1720	1720	...	1823	1921	1921	...	2121
229	**Borlänge 755** ▲ ● a.	0840	1008	1008	1008	1209	1339	...	1409	1409	...	1609	1609	1609	...	1804	1804	1804	...	1900	2002	2002	...	2202
253	Falun **755** ● a.	0900	1027	1027	1027	|	...	...	1434	1434	...	1630	1630	|	...	1825	1825	1825	...	1920	|	|	...	2221
	Leksand ▲ d.	...	...	...	...	1251	...	...	...	...	...	...	...	1653	...	...	...	...	...	...	2043	2043	...	...
	Rättvik ▲ d.	...	...	...	...	1309	...	...	...	...	...	...	...	1711	...	...	...	...	...	...	2101	2101	...	...
	Mora 753 ▲ a.	...	...	...	...	1334	...	...	...	...	...	...	...	1736	...	...	...	...	...	...	2126	2126	...	...

	IC 13 Ⓐ	IC 661 Ⓐx	IC 41 Ⓐ	IC 15 ⑥		IC 43 ⑥	IC 669 Ⓑ		IC 19 Ⓐx	IC 673 Ⓐp	IC 673 ⑥	IC 691 †		IC 21 †	IC 677 ⑥	IC 677 Ⓐx		IC 47	IC 685 Ⓑ	IC 25 ⑥J		IC 49 †	IC 27 Ⓐ
Mora 753 ▲ d.	...	...	0629	...	...	0831	...	...	...	...	...	1034	...	...	...	...	...	1434	...	...	...	1823	...
Rättvik ▲ d.	...	...	0653	...	...	0855	...	...	...	...	...	1058	...	...	...	...	...	1458	...	...	...	1847	...
Leksand ▲ d.	...	...	0712	...	...	0914	...	...	...	...	...	1117	...	...	...	...	...	1517	...	...	...	1908	...
Falun **755** ● d.	0531	0614	|	0739	...	|	0937	...	1136	1136	1136	|	...	1338	1338	...	...	|	1734	1734	...	|	1928
Borlänge 755 ▲ ● d.	0550	0633	0752	0758	...	0956	0956	...	1157	1157	1157	1157	...	1357	1357	1357	...	1557	1752	1753	...	1948	1948
Avesta Krylbo d.	0633	0708	0839	0840	...	1039	1039	...	1239	1239	1239	1239	...	1439	1439	1439	...	1639	1841	1841	...	2039	2039
Sala **754** d.	0653	|	0900	0900	...	1100	1100	...	1300	1300	1300	1300	...	1500	1500	1500	...	1700	1900	1900	...	2100	2100
Uppsala **760** ◧ ♠ a.	0728	0801	0934	0934	...	1134	1134	...	1334	1334	1334	1334	...	1534	1534	1534	...	1734	1934	1934	...	2134	2134
Arlanda C ✈ **760** ◧ ♠ a.	0751	0821	0952	0952	...	1152	1152	...	1352	1352	1352	1352	...	1552	1552	1552	...	1752	1952	1952	...	2152	2152
Stockholm C **760** ♠ a.	0815	0844	1015	1015	...	1215	1215	...	1415	1415	1415	1415	...	1615	1615	1615	...	1815	2015	2015	...	2215	2215

▲ – Local services BORLÄNGE - MORA and v.v.

km		Ⓐ	⚒					⚒			Ⓑ
0	**Borlänge** d.	0636	0851	...	1020	...	1422	1624	1815	...	2213
43	Leksand d.	0708	0926	...	1052	...	1454	1656	1852	...	2245
63	Rättvik d.	0726	0941	...	1107	...	1515	1713	1907	...	2300
103	**Mora 753** ♣ a.	0749	1004	...	1130	...	1538	1736	1930	...	2323
104	Morastrand ♣ a.	0753	1008	...	1134	...	1542	1740	1934	...	2327

	Ⓐ	⑥	Ⓑ		⚒				⚒	Ⓑ
Morastrand ♣ d.	0503	0627	0831	...	1021	1220	...	1622	1820	2030
Mora 753 ♣ d.	0508	0632	0836	...	1026	1225	...	1627	1825	2035
Rättvik d.	0531	0655	0859	...	1049	1248	...	1650	1848	2058
Leksand d.	0546	0710	0914	...	1106	1306	...	1710	1906	2116
Borlänge 755 a.	0618	0742	0946	...	1140	1338	...	1742	1938	2148

J – From Jan. 7.

p – Dec. 27 - Jan. 5.
x – Not Dec. 24 - Jan. 8.

Sn – High speed train. Special supplement payable.

♠ – Frequent local services operate Stockholm - Uppsala and v.v.
● – Additional services operate Borlänge - Falun and v.v.
♣ – Local journeys are not permitted Mora - Morastrand and v.v.
▲ – For Borlänge - Mora and v.v. local services – see panel above.
◧ – Stops to pick up / set down only from / to Stockholm.

STOCKHOLM - SUNDSVALL - UMEÅ — 760

For additional services Stockholm - Gävle and v.v. see Table 761. For sleeper services see Table 767.

km		NT 2 Ⓐ	NT 2 Ⓐ	NT 2	Sn 560 🅁✕ Ⓐ	Sn 566 🅁✕ †	Sn 564 🅁✕ Ⓐ	Sn 564 🅁✕ ⑥	NT 2 Ⓑ	Sn 568 🅁✕	NT 2	NT 2 Ⓐ	Sn 572 🅁✕	NT 2 Ⓑ	Sn 576 🅁✕ Ⓑ	Sn 10574 🅁✕ ⑥	NT 2 ⑥	IC 60 ⑤	NT 2 Ⓐx	Sn 580 🅁✕ Ⓑ	Sn 582 🅁✕ Ⓐ	NT 2 Ⓐ	Sn 586 🅁✕ †	Sn 584 🅁✕ ⚒	Sn 588 🅁✕ †
0	**Stockholm** C d.	...	...	...	0622	0822	0822	0822	...	1022	...	...	1222	...	1422	1422	...	1445	...	1622	1722	...	1822	1822	2022
39	Arlanda C ✈ ‡ d.	...	...	...	0641	0841	0841	0841	...	1041	...	...	1241	...	1441	1441	...	1506	...	1641	1741	...	1841	1841	2041
69	Uppsala ‡ d.	...	...	...	0700	0900	0900	0900	...	1100	...	...	1300	...	1500	1500	...	1528	...	1700	1800	...	1900	1900	2100
182	**Gävle** C ▲ d.	...	...	...	0748	0948	0948	0948	...	1148	...	...	1348	...	1548	1548	...	1626	...	1748	1848	...	1948	1948	2148
260	Söderhamn ▲ d.	...	...	...	0834	1034	1034	1034	...	1234	...	...	1434	...	1634	1634	...	1713	...	1834	1927	...	2034	2034	2234
314	Hudiksvall ▲ d.	...	...	...	0900	1100	1100	1100	...	1300	...	...	1500	...	1700	1700	...	1759	...	1900	1952	...	2100	2100	2300
402	**Sundsvall** ▲ a.	...	...	...	0956	1149	1156	1156	...	1356	...	...	1556	...	1757	1757	...	1900	...	1956	2041	...	2149	2156	2356
					|		NT 2 ⑥	|					|		|					|					
402	**Sundsvall** d.	0551	0755	0903	1007	...	1109	1207	1208	...	1429	1526	1607	1640	1807	...	1807	...	1933	2007	...	2051	...	...	...
470	Härnösand d.	0642	0849	0957	1100	...	1206	1300	1259	...	1522	1620	1700	1736	1900	...	1859	...	2025	2100	...	2142	...	...	...
516	Kramfors d.	0710	0917	1020	1123	...	1247	1324	1324	...	1545	1646	1723	1804	1923	...	1924	...	2048	2123	...	...	...	...	...
603	Örnsköldsvik C d.	0753	0955	1101	1158	...	1326	1400	1404	...	1630	1734	1757	1849	1957	...	2003	...	2128	2157	...	...	...	...	...
713	**Umeå** Östra ♠ a.	0847	1048	1201	1241	...	1421	1443	1458	...	1728	1833	1842	1944	2041	...	2054	...	2220	2241	...	...	...	...	...
715	**Umeå** C ♠ a.	0850	1051	1204	1245	...	1424	1447	1502	...	1732	1836	1846	1947	2045	...	2057	...	2223	2245	...	...	...	...	...

	Sn 561 🅁✕ Ⓐ	Sn 563 🅁✕ Ⓐ	NT 2 Ⓐ	Sn 567 🅁✕ Ⓐ	Sn 567 🅁✕ †	Sn 569 🅁✕ ⑥	NT 2 Ⓐ	NT 2 Ⓑ	Sn 571 🅁✕ ⚒	Sn 573 🅁✕ †	NT 2 ⑥	NT 2 Ⓐx	Sn 575 🅁✕ Ⓑ	Sn 575 🅁✕ ⑥	NT 2	Sn 579 🅁✕ ⑥	Sn 579 🅁✕ Ⓐ	Sn 581 🅁✕ †	NT 2	Sn 583 🅁✕ Ⓑ	IC 61 †	Sn 587 🅁✕	NT 2 Ⓐx	NT 2	NT 2
Umeå C ♠ d.	...	...	0441	0515	...	...	0550	0640	0715	...	0730	0756	0915	...	1053	1113	...	...	1254	...	...	1515	1528	1618	1714
Umeå Östra ♠ d.	...	...	0444	0518	...	...	0554	0644	0718	...	0734	0800	0918	...	1057	1116	...	...	1258	...	...	1518	1532	1622	1718
Örnsköldsvik C d.	...	...	0539	0601	...	...	0654	0741	0801	...	0827	0857	1001	...	1150	1201	...	...	1352	...	...	1601	1628	1715	1815
Kramfors d.	...	...	0617	0637	...	...	0732	0824	0837	...	0909	0939	1042	...	1232	1237	...	...	1434	...	...	1637	1707	1756	1853
Härnösand d.	...	...	0641	0700	...	...	0755	0848	0900	...	0932	1005	1109	...	1255	1303	...	...	1457	...	...	1700	1733	1819	1918
Sundsvall a.	...	...	0735	0753	...	...	0846	0939	0953	...	1025	1057	1200	...	1347	1356	...	...	1549	...	...	1753	1828	1914	2007
				|					|				|			|						|			
Sundsvall ▲ d.	0506	0618	...	0804	0804	0818	...	...	1004	1004	...	...	1204	1204	...	1404	1404	1411	...	1604	1640	1804	...	...	...
Hudiksvall ▲ d.	0559	0705	...	0900	0900	0905	...	...	1100	1100	...	...	1300	1300	...	1500	1500	1500	...	1700	1734	1900	...	...	...
Söderhamn ▲ d.	0628	0731	...	0927	0927	0931	...	...	1127	1127	...	...	1327	1327	...	1527	1527	1527	...	1727	1809	1927	...	...	...
Gävle C ▲ d.	0714	0814	...	1014	1014	1014	...	...	1214	1214	...	...	1414	1414	...	1614	1614	1614	...	1814	1903	2014	...	...	...
Uppsala ‡ a.	0759	0859	...	1059	1059	1059	...	...	1259	1259	...	...	1459	1459	...	1659	1659	1659	...	1859	2003	2059	...	...	...
Arlanda C ✈ ‡ a.	0817	0917	...	1117	1117	1117	...	...	1317	1317	...	...	1517	1517	...	1717	1717	1717	...	1917	2022	2117	...	...	...
Stockholm C a.	0838	0938	...	1138	1138	1138	...	...	1338	1338	...	...	1538	1538	...	1738	1738	1738	...	1938	2045	2138	...	...	...

Operator: *XT*

▲ – Local services GÄVLE - SUNDSVALL and v.v. (2nd class only):

	Ⓐ	Ⓒ	Ⓐ		Ⓐ	Ⓒ	Ⓐ	⑥	Ⓐ	Ⓑ	†	Ⓐ
Gävle C d.	0520	0836	0913	...	1204	1230	1405	1508	1610	1710	1907	2110
Söderhamn d.	0602	0918	0956	...	1245	1312	1446	1555	1652	1754	1954	2205
Hudiksvall d.	0634	0959	1024	...	1318	1346	1514	1623	1733	1825	2022	2232
Sundsvall a.	0733	1059	1123	...	1419	1451	1619	1720	1833	1923	2115	2326

	Ⓐ	⚒	Ⓐ	Ⓒ	Ⓐ	⑥	Ⓐ	†		⚒	Ⓐ	†
Sundsvall d.	0538	0834	1219	1244	1439	1610	1640	1657	...	1924	2023	2031
Hudiksvall d.	0633	0934	1319	1346	1535	1706	1734	1757	...	2034	2125	2144
Söderhamn d.	0702	1004	1347	1414	1603	1735	1803	1831	...	2111	2154	2213
Gävle C a.	0744	1048	1439	1459	1652	1819	1854	1921	...	2157	2240	2257

Sn – High speed train. Special supplement payable.

‡ – From Stockholm stops to pick up only; to Stockholm stops to set down only.
♠ – Local journeys are not permitted Umeå C - Umeå Östra and v.v.
▲ – For Gävle - Sundsvall and v.v. local services – see panel above.

761 STOCKHOLM and SUNDSVALL - ÖSTERSUND - TRONDHEIM

For additional services Stockholm - Gävle and v.v. see Table 760. For sleeper services see Table 767

km		NT	NSB	NT	NT	NT	IC	IC	IC	IC	NT	NT	NT	NSB	NT	Sn	IC	IC		Sn	NT	Sn	Sn	NT	NT
							80	80	80	82						594	84	84		10574		598	598		
		2	2	2	2	2					2	2	2	2	2	[R]✕				[R]✕	2	[R]✕	[R]✕	2	2
				Ⓐ	Ⓐ		⑥G	ⒷE	⑥C	ⒶC	Ⓑ	⑥			Ⓐ	⑥	H	⑤†J		⑥C	Ⓑ	K	ⒷG	Ⓑ	⚒
0	**Stockholm** C .... ▲ d.	...	...	...	...	...	0800	0800	0800	0800	...	...	...	...	...	1415	1415	1415	...	1422	...	1652	1652	...	...
39	Arlanda C ✈ .... ▲ d.	...	...	...	...	...	0823u	0823u	0823u	0823u	...	...	...	...	...	1436u	1436u	1436u	...	1441u	...	1711u	1711u	...	...
69	Uppsala .... ▲ d.	...	...	...	...	...	0850u	0850u	0850u	0850u	...	...	...	...	...	1455u	1505u	1505u	...	1500u	...	1730u	1730u	...	...
182	**Gävle** C .... ▲ d.	...	...	...	...	...	0956	0956	0956	0956	...	...	...	...	...	1544	1558	1558	...	1548	...	1826	1826	...	...
281	Bollnäs .... d.	...	...	...	...	...	1051	1051	1051	1051	...	...	...	...	...	1635	1654	1654	...	|	...	1922	1922	...	...
344	Ljusdal .... d.	...	...	...	...	...	1134	1134	1134	1134	...	...	...	...	...	1715	1735	1735	...	|	...	1958	1958	...	...
	Sundsvall .... d.	0503	...	0606	0805	1011	|	|	|	|	1205	1205	1408	...	1627	|	|	|	...	1800	1813	|	|	2021	2213
450	Ånge .... d.	0618	...	0725	0923	1129	1233	1233	1233	1233	1323	1323	1523	...	1744	1838	1838	1838	...	1921	1932	2055	2055	2136	2334
480	Bräcke .... d.	0635	...	0742	0940	1146	1254	1254	1254	1254	1340	1340	1540	...	1800	1856	1857	1857	...	1941	1949	2113	2113	2154	...
551	**Östersund** C .... a.	0722	...	0831	1029	1237	1344	1344	1344	1344	1427	1427	1631	...	1854	1943	1952	1952	...	2025	2040	2155	2155	2241	...
551	**Östersund** C **753** .... d.	0724	...	...	1031	1239	1349	1349	...	...	...	1429	1633	...	...	1953	1955	...	...	...	2042	...	2158	...	...
656	Åre .... d.	0837	...	...	1144	1355	1507s	1507	...	...	...	1543	1744	...	...	2105s	2112s	...	...	...	2152	...	2300s	...	...
665	Duved .... d.	0845	...	...	...	1402	1530	...	...	...	...	1550	1752	...	...	2122	2131	...	...	...	2159	...	2312	...	...
713	Storlien 🏛 .... a.	0917	0928	...	...	...	...	...	...	...	...	...	1825	1830	...	...	...	...	...	...	...	...	...	...	...
819	**Trondheim 787** .... a.	...	1056	...	...	...	...	...	...	...	...	...	...	2000	...	...	...	...	...	...	...	...	...	...	...

km		NT	Sn	NT	NT	Sn	Sn	Sn		NT	NT	Sn	NSB	NT	NT	IC	NT	NT	IC	IC	IC	NT	NSB	NT	
			591			597	593	573				595				83			85	85	85				
		2	[R]✕	2	2	[R]✕	[R]✕	[R]✕		2	2	[R]✕	2	2	2		2	2				2	2	2	
		Ⓐ	Ⓐx	†	⚒	ⒶD	⑥C	†C		†	⚒	ⒸE			Ⓐ	†E	Ⓑ		⑥G	ⒷE	F	Ⓐx			
	Trondheim 787 .... d.	...	...	...	...	...	...	...	...	...	...	...	0750	...	...	...	...	...	...	...	...	...	1650	...	...
	Storlien 🏛 .... d.	...	...	...	...	...	...	...	...	...	...	...	0922	0942	...	...	...	...	...	...	...	...	1822	1847	...
	Duved .... d.	...	...	...	0611	...	...	...	...	0747	...	0818	...	1016	...	1248	...	1512	1530	...	...	...	...	1922	...
	Åre .... d.	...	...	...	0620	...	...	...	...	0756	...	0830u	...	1025	1212	1306	...	1521	1548u	1548	...	...	...	1930	...
	Östersund C .... a.	...	...	...	0727	...	...	...	...	0908	...	0937	...	1133	1320	1430	...	1628	1715	1715	...	...	...	2037	...
	Östersund C **753** .... d.	0503	0546	...	0729	0746	0753	0746	...	0910	0924	0940	...	1135	1322	1443	1527	1635	1720	1720	1720	1913	...	2040	...
	Bräcke .... d.	0600	0626	...	0817	0835	0833	0826	...	0957	1013	1020	...	1223	1411	|	1615	1723	1804	1804	1804	2006	...	2131	...
0	Ånge .... d.	0618	0644	0835	0835	0852	0851	0843	...	1015	1031	1038	...	1239	1429	|	1633	1741	1823	1823	1823	2024	...	2149	...
94	**Sundsvall** .... a.	0735	|	0953	0953	|	|	1004	...	1136	1147	|	...	1353	1553	|	1754	1859	|	|	|	2147	...	2305	...
	Ljusdal .... d.	...	0742	...	...	0954	0955	|	...	...	...	1136	...	...	...	|	...	...	1922	1922	1922	...	...	...	...
	Bollnäs .... a.	...	0818	...	...	1029	1029	|	...	...	...	1218	...	...	...	1728	...	...	2004	2004	2004	...	...	...	...
	Gävle C .... ▲ d.	...	0914	...	...	1133	1133	1214	...	...	...	1319	...	...	...	1830s	...	...	2106	2106	2106	...	...	...	...
	Uppsala .... ▲ a.	...	0959s	...	...	1226s	1226s	1259s	...	...	...	1404s	...	...	...	1926s	...	...	2204s	2204s	2204s	...	...	...	...
	Arlanda C ✈ .... ▲ a.	...	1017s	...	...	1247s	1247s	1317s	...	...	...	1424s	...	...	...	1958s	...	...	2223s	2223s	2223s	...	...	...	...
	Stockholm C .... ▲ a.	...	1038	...	...	1308	1308	1338	...	...	...	1445	...	...	...	2022	...	...	2245	2245	2245	...	...	...	...

▲ – Regional services STOCKHOLM - GÄVLE and v.v.

km		Ⓐ	⚒					Ⓑ		Ⓐ	†	A
0	**Stockholm** C .... d.	0722	0922	1122	...	1322	1522	1615	...	1715	1722	1922
39	Arlanda C ✈ .... d.	0741	0941	1141	...	1341	1541	1634	...	1734	1741	1941
69	Uppsala .... d.	0803	1000	1200	...	1400	1600	1654	...	1754	1800	2000
182	**Gävle** C .... a.	0851	1048	1249	...	1445	1649	1741	...	1851	1849	2047

	Ⓐ	⑥	Ⓐ	⑥					⑤⑥†	Ⓑ	
Gävle C .... d.	0611	0710	0710	0914	1114	...	1314	1509	1714	1914	...
Uppsala .... d.	0701	0801	0806	1001	1201	...	1401	1601	1801	2001	...
Arlanda C ✈ .... a.	0717	0817	0827	1017	1217	...	1417	1617	1817	2017	...
Stockholm C .... a.	0738	0838	0846	1038	1238	...	1438	1638	1838	2038	...

A – Daily until May 7; † from May 14.
C – From May 6.
D – Dec. 27 - Jan. 5.
E – Until May 1.
F – From May 2.
G – Until Apr. 29.
H – ④⑤† until Apr. 28.
J – From May 1.
K – ①②③† until Apr. 26; Ⓑ from May 1.
s – Stops to set down only.
u – Stops to pick up only.
x – Not Dec. 24 - Jan. 8.
Sn – High speed train. Special supplement payable.

763 UMEÅ - LULEÅ

2nd class only. Operator: *NT*

km		Ⓐ	Ⓐ	Ⓐ	Ⓐ	Ⓐ	⑥	Ⓐ	Ⓐ	Ⓐ	†	Ⓐ	Ⓐ
0	**Umeå** Östra **760** .. ♣ d.	0635	0745	0900	1209	1428	1508	1606	1614	1726	1745	1841	2100
2	**Umeå** C **760** .... ♣ d.	0639	0749	0904	1224	1432	1513	1611	1618	1730	1750	1844	2104
33	Vännäs .... ♣ d.	0701	0811	0926	1247	1455	1541	|	1640	1752	1818	1907	2126
142	Bastuträsk .... d.	...	...	...	...	...	1653	1749	...	...	1927	...	...
269	Älvsbyn .... d.	...	...	...	...	...	1807	1902	...	...	2045	...	...
315	Boden **765** .... a.	...	...	...	...	...	1836	1927	...	...	2113	...	...
351	**Luleå 765** .... a.	...	...	...	...	...	1906	2005	...	...	2153	...	...

	Ⓐ	Ⓐ	Ⓐ	⑥	Ⓐ	Ⓐ	†	Ⓐ	Ⓐ	Ⓐ	Ⓐ	Ⓐ
Luleå 765 .... d.	...	...	0542	0640	...	...	1029	...	...	...	...	...
Boden **765** .... d.	...	...	0616	0711	...	...	1101	...	...	...	...	...
Älvsbyn .... d.	...	...	0641	0736	...	...	1126	...	...	...	...	...
Bastuträsk .... d.	...	...	0800	0901	...	...	1242	...	...	...	...	...
Vännäs .... ♣ d.	0708	0828	|	1017	1130	1342	1407	1532	1648	1801	1916	2017
Umeå C **760** ..... ♣ a.	0730	0850	0949	1039	1152	1404	1429	1554	1710	1823	1938	2038
Umeå Östra **760** ♣ a.	0735	0854	0954	1043	1157	1408	1434	1558	1714	1827	1942	2042

♣ – Additional services operate Umeå - Vännäs and v.v., journey 22 minutes; all services commence from / continue to Umeå Östra (2–4 minutes earlier):

From **Umeå C**: 0520Ⓐ, 0942†, 1119⑥, 1219†, 1548⑥, 1634†, 1646Ⓐ, 1820⑥, 2133†.
From **Vännäs**: 0555Ⓐ, 1137†, 1308⑥, 1545†, 1736⑥, 2014⑥, 2017†.

765 LULEÅ - NARVIK

km					NT		IC		NT		NT	
		3964	94				96					
		[R]	[R]		2		2		2		2	
		♦	♦		⚒				Ⓑ			
0	**Luleå 763** .... d.	0506	...	...	0629	...	1000	...	1232	...	1630	...
36	Boden **763** .... d.	0534	0551	...	0657	...	1035	...	1302	...	1703	...
204	Gällivare **753** .... d.	...	0824	...	0858	...	1246	...	1504	...	1851	...
304	**Kiruna** .... a.	...	0936	...	1000	...	1419	...	1607	...	2007	...
304	**Kiruna** .... d.	...	0954	...	...	...	1445	...	...	...	...	...
397	Abisko Östra .... d.	...	1057	...	...	...	1554	...	...	...	...	...
406	Björkliden .... d.	...	1112	...	...	...	1608	...	...	...	...	...
426	Vassijaure .... ◇ d.	...	|	...	...	...	1641	...	...	...	...	...
433	Riksgränsen 🏛 .... d.	...	1141	...	...	...	1652	...	...	...	...	...
473	**Narvik 787** .... a.	...	1231	...	...	...	1745	...	...	...	...	...

	NT		NT		IC		NT				
					95				93	3963	
	2		2		2		2		[R]	[R]	
			⚒				Ⓑ		♦	♦	
Narvik 787 .... d.	...	...	...	...	1100	...	...	...	1515	...	...
Riksgränsen 🏛 . d.	...	...	...	...	1149	...	...	...	1604	...	...
Vassijaure ..... ◇ d.	...	...	...	...	1202	...	...	...	|	...	...
Björkliden .... d.	...	...	...	...	1220	...	...	...	1631	...	...
Abisko Östra ..... d.	...	...	...	...	1235	...	...	...	1647	...	...
Kiruna .... a.	...	...	...	...	1343	...	...	...	1758	...	...
Kiruna .... d.	0620	...	1109	...	1402	...	1639	...	1825	...	...
Gällivare **753** ..... d.	0732	...	1214	...	1520	...	1756	...	1934	...	...
Boden 763 .... a.	0927	...	1412	...	1742	...	2008	...	2138	2141	...
Luleå 763 .... a.	0952	...	1439	...	1822	...	2034	...	...	2206	...

FOR NOTES – SEE TABLE 767

753 KRISTINEHAMN - MORA - ÖSTERSUND - GÄLLIVARE

INLANDSBANAN

Service from December 11, 2016. Summer service (from June 12, 2017) is subject to alteration

km		W		♠	C
0	**Kristinehamn 750** ... d.	...	...	1037	...
40	Nykroppa .... d.	...	...	1111	...
131	Grängesberg .... d.	...	...	1218	...
146	Ludvika .... d.	...	...	1231	...
296	**Mora 758** .... d.	1342	...	1416t	1451
310	Orsa .... d.	1355	...	...	1505
433	Sveg .... d.	1530	...	...	1656
617	**Östersund** C .... a.	1818	...	...	2103

	W		C	♠
Östersund C .... d.	0738	...	0825	...
Sveg .... d.	1010	...	1128	...
Orsa .... d.	1155	...	1348	...
Mora 758 .... d.	1214	...	1402	1505j
Ludvika .... d.	...	...	...	1650
Grängesberg .... d.	...	...	...	1700
Nykroppa .... d.	...	...	...	1810
Kristinehamn 750 a.	...	...	...	1849

km		D	
0	**Östersund** C .... d.	0720	...
115	Ulriksfors .... d.	0907	...
244	Vilhelmina .... d.	1106	...
312	Storuman .... d.	1307	...
384	Sorsele .... d.	1425	...
473	Arvidsjaur .... d.	1555	...
646	Jokkmokk .... d.	1851	...
746	**Gällivare** .... a.	2102	...

	E	
Gällivare .... d.	0750	...
Jokkmokk .... d.	0915	...
Arvidsjaur .... d.	1243	...
Sorsele .... d.	1418	...
Storuman .... d.	1520	...
Vilhelmina .... d.	1709	...
Ulriksfors .... d.	1907	...
Östersund C .... a.	2049	...

All rail services operated by Railbus.

C – June 12 - Aug. 20.
D – June 12 - Aug. 19.
E – June 13 - Aug. 20.
W – Dec. 22 - June 11 (not Dec. 24).

j – Depart 1447 on ⑥⑦.
t – Arrive 1427 on ⑥⑦.
♠ – July 3 - Aug. 12: [12] Göteborg - Mora and v.v. – see Tables **750/1/8**. Operated by *Tågab*.

🚂 – Steam train operates ⑤⑥ July 15 - 30, 2016 Arvidsjaur - Slagnäs and v.v. (*53 km*); depart 1745, arrive back 2200 (approximate timings). Contact: Arvidsjaur Järnvägsförening ✆ +46 (0)730 81 93 69.

Operator: Inlandsbanan AB, Box 561, 831 27, Östersund. ✆ +46 (0)771 53 53 53, fax +46 (0)63 19 44 06.

LONG DISTANCE SLEEPER TRAINS — 767

	94 ◆	3965	92 ◆	VEO 3900 ◆	74 ◆	76 ◆
Malmö C 730 .... d.				1640		
Göteborg .... d.			1830			
Herrljunga .... d.						
Skövde .... d.			1951			
Hallsberg .... d.			2055			
Stockholm C .... a.			2235			
Stockholm C .... d.	1729		2240	2300	2344	2358
Arlanda C ✦ .... d.	1753u		2304		0007u	0102u
Uppsala .... d.	1821u		2326	2352u	0029u	0124u
Gävle .... a.	1923		0023		0129	
Gävle .... d.	1926		0023		0136	0230u
Söderhamn .... d.	2023		0110			
Hudiksvall .... d.	2121		0143			
Sundsvall .... a.	2219		0247			
Sundsvall .... d.	2234		0258			
Härnösand .... d.	2323		0352			
Kramfors .... d.	2352		0421			
Ånge .... d.						
Bräcke .... d.						
Östersund C .... a.				0620s	0642	0642s
Östersund C .... d.					0647	
Åre .... a.				0750s	0816s	0816s
Duved .... a.				0825	0831	0834
Storlien ⊞ .... a.						
Örnsköldsvik .... d.	0044		0507			
Umeå C .... a.	0140		0625			
Umeå C .... d.	0150		0630			
Bastuträsk .... d.	0323		0828			
Älvsbyn .... d.	0446		0952			
Boden .... a.	0524	0558	1022			
Luleå .... a.		0630	1111			
Narvik 765 .... a.	1231					

	VEO 3901 ◆	77 ◆	91 ◆	3962 ◆	93 ◆
Narvik 765 .... d.					1515
Luleå .... d.			1731	2105	
Boden .... d.			1825	2128	2155
Älvsbyn .... d.			1901		2224
Bastuträsk .... d.			2034		2348
Umeå C .... a.			2221		0115
Umeå C .... d.			2226		0119
Örnsköldsvik .... d.			2334		0217
Storlien ⊞ .... d.					
Duved .... d.	1545	1730			
Åre .... d.	1615u	1751u			
Östersund C .... a.		1920			
Östersund C .... d.	1755u	1927			
Bräcke .... d.					
Ånge .... d.					
Kramfors .... d.			0021		0303
Härnösand .... d.			0050		0331
Sundsvall .... a.			0147		0424
Sundsvall .... d.			0152		0435
Hudiksvall .... d.			0252		0539
Söderhamn .... d.			0326		0629
Gävle .... a.		2347	0427		0725
Gävle .... d.		0012	0430		0727
Uppsala .... a.	2301s	0126s	0543		0826s
Arlanda C ✦ .... a.		0147s	0606		0851s
Stockholm C .... a.	2340	0213	0631		0915
Stockholm C .... d.			0641		
Hallsberg .... d.			0900		
Skövde .... d.			0956		
Herrljunga .... d.					
Göteborg .... a.			1135		
Malmö C 730 .... a.	0645				

NOTES (LISTED BY TRAIN NUMBER)

74 – ⑤⑥ Feb. 24 - Mar. 4: ⇌ and ⇌ Stockholm - Östersund - Duved.
76 – ②③④⑤⑥† Dec. 21 - Jan. 5; ③⑥ Jan. 7-28; ③④⑤⑥ Feb. 1 - Apr. 13 (also Jan. 2; not Dec. 24, 31, Feb. 8, 24, 25, Mar. 3, 4): ⇌ and ⇌ Stockholm - Östersund - Duved.
77 – ④† Dec. 22 - Apr. 23 (also Dec. 23, 27-30, Jan. 2-7; not Feb. 2, 9, Mar. 2, 4, 5, Apr. 13, 21, 22): ⇌ and ⇌ Duved - Östersund - Stockholm.
91 – Not Dec. 24, 31: ⇌, ⇌, 🛏 and ✗ Luleå - Stockholm - Göteborg.
92 – Not Dec. 24, 31: ⇌, ⇌, 🛏 and ✗ Göteborg - Stockholm - Luleå.
93 – Not Dec. 24, 31: ⇌, ⇌, 🛏 and ✗/ 🍴 Narvik - Boden - Stockholm; ⇌, ⇌, 🛏 and ✗/🍴 Luleå (3962) - Boden - Stockholm; 🛏 Narvik (3963) - Boden - Luleå.
94 – Not Dec. 24, 31 (from Stockholm, one day later from Boden): ⇌, ⇌, 🛏 and ✗/🍴 Stockholm - Boden - Narvik; ⇌, ⇌, 🛏 and ✗/🍴 Stockholm - Boden (3965) - Luleå; 🛏 Luleå (3964) - Boden - Narvik.
3900 – ③⑥ Dec. 21 - Apr. 15 (not Dec. 24, 31): ⇌, ⇌ and ✗/🍴 Malmö - Östersund - Duved.
3901 – ④⑦ Dec. 22 - Apr. 16 (not Dec. 25, Jan. 1): ⇌, ⇌ and ✗/🍴 Duved - Östersund - Malmö.
3962 – Not Dec. 24, 31: ⇌, ⇌ and ✗/🍴 Luleå - Boden (93) - Stockholm.
3963 – 🛏 Narvik (93) - Boden - Luleå.
3964 – 🛏 Luleå - Boden (94) - Narvik.
3965 – Not Dec. 24, 31: (from Stockholm, one day later from Boden): ⇌, ⇌ and ✗/🍴 Stockholm (94) - Boden - Luleå.

s – Stops to set down only.
u – Stops to pick up only.

◇ – Ticket point.

🚌 UMEÅ - LULEÅ - HAPARANDA - KEMI — 768

UMEÅ - LULEÅ - HAPARANDA / TORNIO and v.v.   Valid June 20 - Dec. 10, 2016   Länstrafiken Norrbotten, routes 20/100

	①-⑤	①-⑤ ①-⑤ ⑥⑦	⑥⑦ ①-⑤	⑦	①-⑥	①-⑤	⑥⑦ ⑦	①-⑤	①-⑤
Umeå .... d.		0515 0545	0730 0730		0900 0900		1315 1430	1525 1630	1725 1930 2100
Umeå Universitetssjukhuset ♣ a.		0520 0550	0735 0735		0905 0905		1320 1435	1530 1635	1730 1935 2105
Skellefteå .... d.		0535 0635 0740 0800	0950 0955		1115 1125		1520 1635	1755 1835	1955 2135 2300
Piteå .... d.		0700 0805 0905 0925	1115 1120		1240 1250		1635 1750	1925 1950	2120 2250
Luleå .... a.		0800 0905 1005 1025	1210 1215		1335 1345		1725 1840	2015 2040	2215 2340
Luleå .... d.	0515	0830 0950 1050 1050	1230 1245		1350 1400	1510 1735	1855	2110	
Haparanda / Tornio ⊞ § d.	0755	1035 1215 1320 1315	1500 1520		1635 1950	1745 1950	2110	2325	

	①-⑤ ⑥⑦	①-⑤ ⑥	⑥⑦	⑦	①-⑤ ⑥⑦	①-⑤ ①-⑤ ①-⑤	⑥⑦ ①-⑤	⑦	①-⑤
Haparanda / Tornio ⊞ § d.		0530	0650 0725 0810 0955		1050 1230	1340 1345 1510	1610	1710 1720 1810 2015	
Luleå .... a.		0750	0945 0950 1030 1235		1310 1450	1605 1610 1750	1845	1940 1955 2040 2230	
Luleå .... d.	0540 0800 0800	1000	1040 1300		1320 1500	1635 1635 1810	1910	2005 2010 2055 2230	
Skellefteå .... d.	0635 0855 0855	1105	1135 1405	1830	1415 1555	1750 1750 1915	2010	2105 2110 2150 2300	
Umeå Universitetssjukhuset ♣ a.	0750 1015 1015	1230	1425 1535		1715 1900 2035	2120 2120 2225	2330	0025	
Umeå .... a.	0935 1200 1200	1435	1445 1740		1725 1910 2035	2130 2130 2235	2340	0035	

HAPARANDA / TORNIO - KEMI and v.v.   Valid August 8, 2016 - June 2, 2017   NET-Matkat, route 70

	①-⑤	①-⑤	①-⑤	①-⑤	①-⑥	①-⑤	①-⑥	①-⑤	①-⑤	①-⑤	①-⑤	①-⑤
Haparanda / Tornio ⊞ § ⊡ d.	0605	0705	0805	0905	1005	1105	1205	1305	1405	1505	1605	1705
Kemi ⊡ a.	0645	0745	0845	0945	1045	1145	1245	1345	1445	1545	1645	1745

	①-⑤ ①-⑤	①-⑤	①-⑤	①-⑤	①-⑥	①-⑤	①-⑥	①-⑤	①-⑤	①-⑤	①-⑥	①-⑤	⑥
Kemi ⊡ d.	0605 0705	0805	0905	1005	1105	1205	1305	1405	1505	1605	1705	1805	
Haparanda / Tornio ⊞ § ⊡ a.	0645 0745	0845	0945	1045	1145	1245	1345	1445	1545	1645	1745	1845	

No services on ⑦. From Kemi services call at Kemi railway station 1 minute later; from Haparanda / Tornio services continue to Kemi railway station upon request.
Other services operated by NorthBus; www.northbus.fi. For all other departures by other operators see www.matkahuolto.fi
For additional departures by other operators see www.matkahuolto.fi

All stops refer to bus stations except where shown otherwise.
⊡ – Finnish time, one hour later than Swedish time.
♣ – Change for Umeå Östra railway station (200 metres approx.).
§ – Swedish name: Haparanda / Tornio; Finnish name: Tornio / Haaparanta.

Haparanda / Tornio bus station is located on the Swedish side of the border (100 metres approx.).
Operators:
LN – Länstrafiken Norrbotten: www.ltnbd.se
NET – NET-Matkat: www.netmatkat.com
See also www.matkahuolto.fi

NORWAY

SEE MAP PAGE 341

Operator: Norges Statsbaner (NSB) www.nsb.no

Services: All trains convey second class seating accommodation. Many services, as identified in the notes, also convey *NSB Komfort* accommodation (see below). Sleeping-cars (🛏) have one- and two-berth compartments; the sleeper supplement is 900 NOK per compartment (for two people travelling together, or sole use for single travellers). Most long distance express trains convey a bistro car (✕) serving hot and cold meals, drinks and snacks. 🍸 indicates that drinks and light refreshments are available from automatic vending machines.

Timings: NSB services are valid **December 11**, 2016 - **June 18**, 2017. (unless otherwise stated). Dec. 25, 26, Jan. 1, Apr. 13, 14, 16, 17, May 1, 17, 25, June 4, 5 are Norwegian public holidays and services are subject to alteration on and around these dates. Alterations to internal Norwegian services during holiday periods are not usually shown in the tables and readers are advised to confirm timings before travelling (✆ +47 815 00 888).

Reservations: Seat reservation is highly recommended on long-distance routes Oslo - Kristiansand - Stavanger (Table **775**), Oslo - Bergen (Table **780**), Oslo - Trondheim / Åndalsnes (Table **785**) and Trondheim - Bodø (Table **787**).

NSB Komfort: *NSB Komfort* is a dedicated area provided on many trains with complimentary tea / coffee and newspapers; a supplement of 90 NOK is payable per single journey.

770 OSLO - HALDEN - GÖTEBORG

All trains convey *NSB Komfort* and 🍸

km	Norwegian train number	139			103	105	107	109	111	113	115	117	119	121	141	123	143	125	127	129	131	133	135	137
	Swedish train number					391						395							399					
					Ⓐ	⚒		⚒		⚒					Ⓐ		Ⓐ			Ⓑ		Ⓑ		Ⓑ
0	**Oslo** Sentral d.	0001	...	...	0601	0701	0802	0901	1001	1101	1201	1301	1401	1501	1528	1601	1628	1702	1802	1901	2001	2101	2201	2301
60	Moss d.	0052	...	...	0644	0745	0844	0944	1044	1144	1244	1344	1444	1546	1614	1645	1713	1746	1844	1944	2044	2144	2244	2344
69	Rygge ✈ d.	0059	...	...	0651	0752	0851	0951	1051	1151	1251	1351	1451	1553	1621	1652	1720	1753	1851	1951	2051	2151	2251	2351
94	Fredrikstad d.	0119	...	...	0711	0812	0911	1016	1112	1211	1311	1411	1511	1616	1642	1713	1741	1813	1911	2011	2112	2211	2311	0011
109	Sarpsborg d.	0133	...	...	0729	0825	0929	1033	1126	1225	1325	1425	1529	1633	1656	1727	1755	1827	1925	2028	2126	2225	2325	0025
137	**Halden** ★ d.	0152	...	...	0748	0846	0948	1052	1145	1244	1344	1446	1548	1652	1720	1746	1820	1846	2002z	2047	2145	2244	2344	0044
268	Öxnered **751** d.	...	...	...	...	1002	...	...	...	...	...	1602	...	...	...	...	...	...	2117	...	...	...	...	...
278	Trollhättan **751** d.	...	...	...	...	1008	...	...	...	...	...	1609	...	...	...	...	...	...	2123	...	...	...	...	...
350	**Göteborg 751** a.	...	...	...	...	1040	...	...	...	...	...	1650	...	...	...	...	...	...	2200	...	...	...	...	...

Swedish train number										390						394					398			
Norwegian train number	102	154	104	142	156	106	144	108	110	112	114	116	118	120	122	124	126	128	130	132	134	136		138
	Ⓐ	⑥	Ⓐ	Ⓐ	⑦	⚒	Ⓐ	⚒		⚒		⚒								Ⓑ		Ⓑ		
Göteborg 751 d.	...	...	...	...	...	...	...	...	...	0655	...	...	...	...	...	1300	...	...	...	...	1755	...	...	...
Trollhättan **751** d.	...	...	...	...	...	...	...	...	...	0735	...	...	...	...	...	1336	...	...	...	...	1834	...	...	...
Öxnered **751** d.	...	...	...	...	...	...	...	...	...	0742	...	...	...	...	...	1342	...	...	...	...	1840	...	...	...
Halden ★ d.	0400	0500	0502	0533	0600	0602	0633	0700	0802	0910	1005	1103	1202	1302	1402	1510	1605	1703	1802	1902	2005	2102	...	2202
Sarpsborg d.	0422	0520	0524	0553	0620	0624	0654	0721	0824	0930	1026	1125	1224	1324	1424	1530	1626	1725	1825	1924	2026	2124	...	2224
Fredrikstad d.	0436	0534	0538	0608	0634	0638	0709	0736	0838	0944	1040	1139	1238	1338	1438	1544	1640	1739	1839	1938	2040	2138	...	2238
Rygge ✈ d.	0454	0552	0556	0626	0652	0656	0727	0756	0856	1002	1058	1157	1256	1356	1456	1602	1658	1757	1857	1956	2058	2156	...	2256
Moss d.	0503	0601	0608	0635	0701	0708	0736	0808	0908	1012	1108	1208	1308	1408	1508	1612	1711	1808	1908	2008	2108	2208	...	2308
Oslo Sentral a.	0552	0651	0651	0722	0751	0751	0822	0851	0949	1052	1149	1249	1349	1449	1549	1652	1751	1849	1949	2049	2149	2249	...	2349

z – Arrives 1944.

★ – 🛃 at Kornsjø (*km169*).

☛ Norwegian holiday dates apply for international journeys.

771 OSLO - OSLO GARDERMOEN ✈

See also Tables 783 and 785

Operated by Flytoget AS.
Special fares apply.
✆ +47 815 00 777.

Daily services (journey time: 22 minutes)
Trains call at Lillestrøm 10 minutes from Oslo
From Oslo Sentral every 20 minutes 0440 - 0000.
From Gardermoen every 20 minutes 0530 - 0050.

Additional services on Ⓑ (journey time: 19 minutes)
Non-stop services
From Oslo Sentral every 20 minutes: 0610 - 2230 on Ⓐ, 1210 - 2310 on ⑦.
From Gardermoen every 20 minutes: 0640 - 2300 on Ⓐ, 1240 - 2340 on ⑦.

773 OSLO - GJØVIK

All trains convey *NSB Komfort* and 🍸

km								Ⓐ				Ⓐ
0	**Oslo** S d.	0002	0702	0902	1102	1302	1502	1612	1702	1902	2102	2302
56	Roa d.	0103	0800	0959	1158	1358	1600	1705	1803	1959	2158	0003
70	Jaren d.	0119	0816	1015	1214	1414	1616	1722	1819	2015	2214	0019
99	Eina d.	0142x	0840	1039	1238	1437	1639	1750	1842	2039	2238	0042
110	Raufoss d.	0152	0850	1049	1248	1447	1649	1801	1852	2049	2248	0052
122	**Gjøvik** a.	0202	0900	1059	1258	1457	1659	1811	1902	2059	2258	0102

	Ⓐ	⑥⑦	Ⓐ	Ⓐ								
Gjøvik d.	0431	0528	0543	0631	0733	0932	1131	1327	1530	1729	1932	2131
Raufoss d.	0442	0539	0554	0641	0744	0943	1142	1338	1541	1740	1943	2142
Eina d.	0452x	0549	0604	0650	0754	0953	1152	1348	1551	1751	1953	2152
Jaren d.	0515	0612	0627	0713	0817	1016	1215	1412	1615	1818	2016	2215
Roa d.	0531	0628	0644	0730	0833	1032	1231	1429	1631	1834	2032	2231
Oslo S a.	0628	0728	0744	0830	0930	1128	1330	1530	1730	1930	2130	2328

x – Stops on request only.

775 OSLO - KRISTIANSAND - STAVANGER

Long distance services are not available for local journeys Oslo - Drammen and v.v. or Sandnes - Stavanger and v.v.

km		701	709	715	719	719	723	729	733	733	737	745
		Ⓐ	Ⓐ D		Ⓐ	Ⓑ			Ⓑ		Ⓑ	Ⓑ
		✕ ⊡	✕ ⊡	✕ ⊡	✕ ⊡	✕ ⊡	✕ ⊡	✕ ⊡	✕ ⊡	✕ ⊡	✕ ⊡	♣ ✕
0	**Oslo** Sentral § d.	...	0419	0725	0925	...	1125	1425	1625	1625	1825	2225
41	Drammen § d.	...	0454	0800	1000	...	1200	1500	1700	1700	1900	2300
87	Kongsberg § d.	...	0530	0836	1036	...	1236	1547	1747	1747	1946	2344
134	Nordagutu d.	...	0604	0911	1114	...	|	1620	1822	1822	2022	0020x
151	Bø d.	...	0619	0925	1128	...	1327	1638	1841	1841	2037	0036
209	Neslandsvatn d.	...	0712	1010	1212	...	1412	1720	1924	1924	2124	0125x
225	Gjerstad d.	...	0725x	1023x	1225x	...	|	1734x	1937x	1937x	2137x	0139x
270	Nelaug d.	...	0800	1055	1257	...	1459	1806	2012	2012	2210	0221x
353	**Kristiansand** a.	...	0856	1153	1358	...	1601	1903	2108	2108	2309	0330
353	**Kristiansand** d.	0502	0909	1203	1408	1408	1615	1910	2115	...	...	0347
457	Sira d.	0624	1028	1326	1526	1526	1743	2028	2237	...	...	0512x
465	Moi d.	0631x	1035x	1333x	1533x	1533x	1751	2035x	2244x	...	...	0520x
514	Egersund ◇ d.	0706	1113	1407	1607	1607	1830	2111	2318	...	...	0605
573	Sandnes S ▲◇ a.	0752	1152	1452	1702	1702	1922	2149	2359	...	...	0702
587	**Stavanger** ◇ a.	0805	1205	1505	1719	1719	1935	2204	0012	...	...	0720

	702	708	708	712	716	720	724	730	730	734	744
	Ⓐ	Ⓐ	⚒				Ⓑ	Ⓑ		Ⓑ	Ⓑ
	✕ ⊡	✕ ⊡	✕ ⊡	✕ ⊡	✕ ⊡	✕ ⊡	✕ ⊡	✕ ⊡	✕ ⊡	✕ ⊡	♣ ✕
Stavanger ◐ d.	...	0422	...	0648	0849	1017	1249	1533	1533	1749	2237
Sandnes S ▲ ◐ d.	...	0436	...	0702	0903	1031	1303	1550	1550	1803	2252
Egersund ◐ d.	...	0532	...	0746	0944	1115	1343	1646	1646	1844	2347
Moi d.	...	0615x	...	0823x	1020x	1158	1424x	1723x	1723x	1921x	0032x
Sira d.	...	0623	...	0830	1028	1206	1431	1730	1730	1928	0040x
Kristiansand a.	...	0742	...	0946	1145	1333	1547	1846	1846	2047	0205
Kristiansand d.	0445	0754	0754	0956	1155	1350	1603	1853	...	...	0218
Nelaug d.	0545	0858	0858	1056	1256	1457	1702	1957	...	...	0337x
Gjerstad d.	0618x	0930x	0930x	1129x	1328x	|	1735x	2029x	...	...	0412x
Neslandsvatn d.	0631	0943	0943	1143	1343	|	|	2043	...	...	0426x
Bø d.	0714	1027	1027	1227	1429	1624	1827	2127	...	...	0514
Nordagutu d.	0728	1041	1041	1241	1444	1641	1842	2142	...	...	0528x
Kongsberg ‡ d.	0802	1117	1117	1317	1519	1717	1917	2217	...	...	0608
Drammen ‡ a.	0851	1151	1151	1350	1551	1751	1951	2251	...	...	0650
Oslo S ‡ a.	0925	1225	1225	1425	1625	1825	2025	2325	...	...	0725

Nelaug - Arendal

km		Ⓐ		⚒							⑦	
0	Nelaug d.	0700	...	0905	1104	1304	1505	...	1815	2020	2218	...
36	Arendal a.	0737	...	0942	1141	1341	1542	...	1852	2057	2255	...

	Ⓐ		⚒				Ⓑ	⑥			⑦
Arendal d.	0503	...	0811	1008	1209	1408	1615	1720	1911	...	2123
Nelaug a.	0540	...	0848	1045	1246	1445	1652	1757	1948	...	2200

D – Runs daily Kristiansand - Stavanager.

x – Stops on request.

▲ – Long distance trains call at Sandnes on request only.

♣ – Conveys 🛏 and 🛋. Reservation recommended.

⊡ – Reservation recommended. Conveys *NSB Komfort*.

§ – Other local trains **Oslo** S - **Drammen** (35 minutes) - **Kongsberg** (75–81 minutes): 0009, 0609 Ⓐ, 0709, 0809 and hourly until 2309.

‡ – Other local trains **Kongsberg** - **Drammen** (43–44 minutes) - **Oslo** S (77–78 minutes): 0434 Ⓐ, 0534, 0634, 0734, 0834, 0934, 1034, 1133, 1234, 1334, 1434, 1534, 1633, 1734, 1834, 1933, 2033, 2134 and 2234.

◇ – Other local trains **Egersund** - **Sandnes** S (51–58 minutes) - **Stavanger** (67–74 minutes): 0453 Ⓐ, 0518 Ⓐ, 0551 Ⓐ, 0621 ⚒, 0650 Ⓐ, 0720 ⚒, 0818 ⚒, 0918, 1019, 1116, 1221, 1317, 1419, 1450 Ⓐ, 1520, 1550 Ⓐ, 1620, 1650 Ⓐ, 1721, 1818, 1921, 2020, 2123, 2223 and 2321.

◐ – Other local trains **Stavanger** - **Sandnes** S (16 minutes) - **Egersund** (69–78 minutes): 0447 Ⓐ, 0524 Ⓐ, 0554 ⚒, 0654 ⚒, 0754 ⚒, 0854, 0954, 1054, 1154, 1254, 1324 Ⓐ, 1354, 1424 Ⓐ, 1454, 1524 Ⓐ, 1554, 1624 Ⓐ, 1654, 1754, 1854, 1954, 2054, 2154, 2254 Ⓑ and 2324

Warning! Subject to alteration on and around public holiday dates

NORWAY

km			Ⓐ	Ⓐ	Ⓐ	Ⓐ	Ⓐ	Ⓐ	Ⓐ	Ⓐ				Ⓐ	Ⓐ	Ⓐ	Ⓐ	Ⓐ	Ⓐ	Ⓐ	Ⓐ
0	Porsgrunn. 783 d.		0633	0751	1151	1334	1433	1556	1750	Notodden......... d.		0643	0809	0900	1302	1450	1614	1812	2010
9	Skien......... 783 d.	0530	0646	0800	1200	1352	1454	1605	1759	Nordagutu......... a.		0701	0827	0919	1321	1508	1632	1830	2028
43	Nordagutu ...... a.	0559	0721	0830	1230	1421	1528	1635	1828	Nordagutu......... d.		0702	0831	0920	1321	1509	1636	1831	2029
43	Nordagutu ...... d.	0606	0722	0832	1231	1422	1529	1636	1831	Skien......... 783 a.		0732	0902	0951	1350	1539	1706	1901	2059
62	Notodden ...... a.	0625	0740	0851	1250	1441	1548	1655	1850	Porsgrunn......783 a.		0741	0911	1000	1359	1547	1722	1922	...

km			609	61		601	607	63		605				62		602		64	610	604		606
			B				⑦C			ℬ									B	⑤C		ℬ
			✗⬚	✗⬚		✗⬚	✗⬚	✗⬚		N✗				✗⬚		✗⬚		✗⬚	✗⬚	✗⬚		N✗
0	Oslo Sentral .... 783 d.		0625	0825		1203		1543		2325		Bergen .... 781 d.		0757		1159		1559		1705		2259
41	Drammen .... 783 d.		0700u	0900u		1238u		1618u		0003u		Arna .... 781 d.		0807		1209		1609u		1717u		2310
112	Hønefoss .... d.		0757	0954		1333		1712		0103		Dale .... 781 d.		0839		1242						2347
208	Nesbyen .... d.		0909	1103		1444		1822		0219		Voss .... 781 d.		0908		1313		1711	1745	1828		0021
225	Gol .... d.		0923	1116		1500		1836		0234		Myrdal .... 781 d.		0950		1406		1754	1834	1911		0106
250	Ål .... d.		0943	1135		1520	1541	1855		0300		Finse .... d.		1016		1434		1820	1912	1941		0138
275	Geilo .... d.		1009	1156		1541	1602	1921		0322		Ustaoset .... d.		1042		1503		1846	1952	2016		0210
286	Ustaoset .... d.		1021	1207		1553	1615	1932		0334		Geilo .... d.		1055		1516		1858	2006	2030		0224
324	Finse .... d.		1104	1234		1623	1648	2000		0407		Ål .... d.		1115		1540		1918	2028	2049		0255
354	Myrdal .... 781 d.		1134r	1258		1648	1714	2024		0435		Gol .... d.		1139		1600		1939	2049			0318
403	Voss .... 781 a.		1300	1334		1736	1804	2111		0524		Nesbyen .... d.		1152		1613		1954	2104			0332
443	Dale .... 781 a.		...	1412		1812		2139		0556		Hønefoss .... d.		1304		1732		2107	2231			0454
480	Arna .... 781 a.		...	1446		1844	1904s	2218		0637s		Drammen .... 783 a.		1407s		1833s		2157s	2326s			0551s
489	Bergen .... 781 a.		...	1455		1858	1916	2230		0649		Oslo Sentral .... 783 a.		1445		1913		2235	0005			0625

B – From May 22.
C – Until Apr. 23.

N – Conveys 🛏 and 🛒. Reservation recommended.
r – Departs 1206.

s – Trains stop to set down only.
u – Trains stop to pick up only.

⬚ – Reservation recommended.
Conveys NSB Komfort.

SERVICE UNTIL APRIL 30

km			605								61			601	607		63			
			Ⓐ	①–⑥	Ⓐ	Ⓐ	Ⓒ	Ⓐ			Ⓐ			Ⓐ	⑦		Ⓐ	⑤	⑥	ℬ
			✗⬚								✗⬚			✗⬚	A✗		✗⬚			
	Oslo Sentral 780.... d.		2325p		...	...	...	...			0825			1203			1543			
0	Myrdal .... d.		0436		...	...	...	...		1111	1300		1543	1650	1717		2026	2036		
18	Mjølfjell .... d.				0747					1130			1601				2053x			
49	Voss .... a.		0524		0821					1207	1342		1635	1736	1804		2111	2132		
49	Voss .... d.		0507	0529	0610	0720	0834	0836	0921	1040	1121	1238	1346	1438	1539	1637	1741	1807	1839	1938	2113	2145	2239
89	Dale .... d.		0538	0558	0645	0751	0908	0910	0958	1114	1202	1312	1414	1513	1614	1714	1814		1913	2016	2141	2216	2314
104	Vaksdal .... d.		0553		0700	0806	0930	0931	1013	1129	1227	1327	1429	1528	1630	1730			1928	2034		2235	2331
126	Arna .... ‡ d.		0612	0637s	0721	0831	0948	0949	1034	1148	1245	1347	1446s	1548	1648	1748	1904s	1947	2052	2221	2255	2349
135	Bergen .... ‡ a.		0621	0649	0730	0840	0957	0959	1043	1157	1254	1356	1455	1557	1657	1757	1858	1916	1956	2101	2230	2304	2358

			62						602				64					604					606		
			①–⑥	Ⓐ				Ⓐ			Ⓐ				64	⑤G	⑤	⑤F						606	ℬ	⑥
			✗⬚								✗⬚				✗⬚		A✗							ℬ	
Bergen .... ‡ d.		0009		0535	0652	0757	0843	0959	1058	1159	1256	1358		1514	1559	1615	1658		1705		1758	1858		2040	2144	2259	2320
Arna .... ‡ d.		0018		0549	0701	0807	0852	1008	1107	1209	1305	1407		1524	1609u	1625	1707		1717u		1807	1907		2052	2156	2310	2329
Vaksdal .... d.		0036		0615	0719	...	0910	1029	1128		1326	1428		1545		1645	1729				1828	1928		2109	2217		2347
Dale .... d.		0054		0630	0734	0839	0925	1044	1142	1242	1341	1443		1600		1700	1744				1843	1943		2123	2234	2347	0002
Voss .... a.		0125		0703	0809	0906	0956	1115	1216	1310	1415	1514		1631	1709	1734	1818		1826		1914	2014		2158	2311	0018	0033
Voss .... d.				0705		0908	1001		1313	1442				1711						1820	1828	1902				0021	
Mjølfjell .... d.				0737		...	1033x		1514											1853x		1940x					
Myrdal .... a.						0948	1051		1403	1532				1752						1912	1909	1959			0103		
Oslo Sentral 780 ... a.						1445			1913					2235							0625						

MYRDAL - FLÅM *Service until March 31* ⊠

0	Myrdal .... d.	1005	...	1305	...	1550	...	1805	...	Flåm .... d.	0900	...	1150	...	1440	...	1650	...
20	Flåm .... a.	1055	...	1355	...	1635	...	1850	...	Myrdal .... a.	0940	...	1235	...	1530	...	1740	...

MYRDAL - FLÅM *Service from April 1* ⊠

					T	V	T	V	T	V	T	T							T	V	T	T	V	T	T
0	Myrdal ..... d.	0940	1058	1213	1327	1443	1550	1559	1715	1805	1835	1948		Flåm ..... d.	0835	0945	1105	1220	1335	1440	1450	1605	1650	1725	1840
20	Flåm ..... a.	1035	1155	1310	1425	1540	1635	1655	1810	1850	1930	2045		Myrdal ..... a.	0928	1043	1201	1315	1431	1530	1546	1703	1740	1817	1936

A – Until Apr. 23. To/ from Ål (Table 780).
F – Until Apr. 21.
G – From Apr. 28.
T – From May 1.
V – Apr. 1 – 30 only.

p – Previous day.
s – Stops to set down only.
u – Stops to pick up only.
x – Stops on request.

◇ – Reservation recommended.
‡ – Additional local services operate.
⊠ – Operator: Flåm Utvikling AS. ✆ + 47 57 63 21 00. 30% discount for rail pass holders.
Subject to alteration on Dec. 24, 25, 31.

			🚢	🚢	🚢			🚌	🚌	🚌	
			B						Ⓐ		A
Flåm .... d.		0930	...	1500	...	Voss .... d.	1010	...	1610	...
Gudvangen .... a.		1125	...	1700	...	Gudvangen .... a.	1105	...	1710	...
Gudvangen .... d.		...	1200	...	1725	Gudvangen .... d.	...	1200	...	1730
Voss .... a.		...	1255	...	1820	Flåm .... a.	...	1400	...	1930

B – Oct. 1–31 only.

🚢 operators : Skyss ✆ + 47 55 55 90 70.
🚌 operator : Fjord1 AS ✆ + 47 57 57 75 72 00.

		🚌	🚌	🚌	🚌		🚌	🚌	🚌						🚌	🚌	🚌	🚌		🚌	🚌	🚌	🚌	
		🍴	Ⓐ	ℬ	⑦		1030	h	Ⓑ	v	s		Bergen ▢...... d.		s	0845	0845		1140	🍴	Ⓐ	Ⓑ		1350	1415	1525	1630	1715
Lillehammer skysst. d.						1030						Voss .... d.		1035	1035		1325		1540		1720		1905
Sogndal ⊕ ...... d.		0755	1130		1430		1715				Balestrand ...... d.	1005			1315				1820		2025	
Kaupangersenteret d.		0810	1145		1445		1730				Leikanger ◇ ...... d.	1055			1355				1835		2045	
Øvre Årdal ◇ ... d.		0740	1135		1430		1705	1850			Flåm .... a.		1145	1145		1440		1653		1830		2015
Fodnes ...... d.		0835		1215		1515		1755	1940		Sogndal ⊕ ...... d.	1130			1430	1430			1900		2120	
Gol Skysstasjon ... d.					1320				1900		Kaupangersenteret... d.	1145			1445	1445						
Lærdal Rådhuset..... d.		0845	1225	1225		1525	1525	1805		2105		Lærdal Rådhuset..... a.	1225	1245		1525		1530	1605	1745		1920		2105
Kaupangersenteret... d.					1600			2000	2140		Gol skysstasjon...... a.	1415			1715							
Sogndal ⊕ ...... d.		0705			1540			2015	2205		Fodnes .... a.		1300			1515	1540	1615	1755		1935		2115
Flåm .... d.			0930		1310		1620	1620		1850		Øvre Årdal ◇ ...... a.		1345		1600		1655	1840		2025		2200
Leikanger ◇ ...... d.		0730			1605			1645		2230		Kaupangersenteret a.		1320			1600		1820		2000		2140
Balestrand ...... d.		0750			1625			1735		2310		Sogndal ⊕ ...... a.		1335			1615		1835		2015		2155
Voss .... d.			1035		1420	1730	1730		1955		Lillehammer skysst. a.				1735							
Bergen ▢ ...... a.		1150	1225		1605	2015	1915	1915		2145													

h – Change 🚌 at Håbakken (a. 1535, d. 1545).
k – Change 🚌 at Håbakken (a. 1225, d. 1235).
s – Change 🚌 at Sogndal.
v – Not Nov. 27 - Dec. 21.
z – Not Dec. 10 – 21.

⊕ – 🚌: Sogndal skysstasjon. ⚓: Sogndal kai.
▢ – Bus station. ⚓: Strandkaiterminal.
◇ – Øvre Årdal Farnes.

🚌 operators : Nettbuss Sogn Billag ✆ + 47 57 67 66 00.
NOR-WAY Bussekspress ✆ + 47 815 44 444.
⚓ operator : Norled AS ✆ + 47 5186 8700.

NORWAY *Warning! Subject to alteration on and around public holiday dates*

783 EIDSVOLL - OSLO - SKIEN

All trains convey *NSB Komfort* and 🍷

km		Ⓐ	⚒	Ⓒ	Ⓐ	⚒	Ⓑ	⑥	⚒	Ⓑ	⑥		Ⓑ	⑥		Ⓐ		Ⓐ			Ⓑ	Ⓐ	Ⓒ	Ⓑ		Ⓑ	
0	**Eidsvoll** .... 785 d.	0501	0601	0701	0701	0801	0901	0901	1001	1101	1101	1201	1301	1301	1401	1452	1501	1552	1601	1701	1801	1901	1901	2001	2101	2201	2301
16	Oslo ✈ ● .785 d.	0513	0613	0713	0713	0813	0913	0913	1013	1113	1113	1213	1313	1313	1413	1503	1513	1603	1613	1713	1813	1913	1913	2013	2113	2213	2313
47	Lillestrøm .. 785 d.	0526	0626	0726	0726	0826	0926	0926	1026	1126	1126	1226	1326	1326	1426	1516	1526	1616	1626	1726	1826	1926	1926	2026	2126	2226	2326
68	**Oslo** S ...... 785 d.	0539	0639	0739	0739	0839	0939	0939	1039	1139	1139	1239	1339	1339	1439	1533	1539	1633	1639	1739	1839	1939	1939	2039	2139	2239	2339
108	Drammen .... d.	0614	0714	0814	0815	0914	1014	1014	1114	1214	1214	1314	1414	1414	1514	|	1614	|	1714	1814	1914	2014	2014	2114	2214	2314	0014
142	Holmestrand ... d.	0638	0733	0833	0833	0933	1033	1033	1133	1233	1233	1333	1433	1433	1533	|	1633	|	1733	1833	1933	2033	2033	2133	2233	2333	0033
156	Skoppum .... d.	0650	0741	0841	0841	0941	1041	1041	1141	1241	1241	1341	1441	1441	1541	|	1641	|	1741	1841	1941	2041	2041	2141	2241	2341	0041
172	Tønsberg .... d.	0702	0752	0852	0852	0952	1052	1052	1152	1252	1252	1352	1452	1452	1552	1643	1652	1743	1752	1852	1952	2052	2052	2152	2252	2352	0052
191	Torp ✈ .... d.	0721	0812	0912	0912	1012	1112	1112	1212	1312	1312	1412	1512	1512	1612	|	1712	|	1812	1912	2012	2112	2112	2212	2312	0007	|
196	**Sandefjord** ..... d.	0727	0818	0918	0918	1018	1118	1118	1218	1318	1318	1418	1518	1518	1618	1705	1718	1805	1818	1918	2018	2118	2118	2218	2318	0012	0111
215	Larvik .... a.	0745	0831	0931	0931	1031	1131	1131	1231	1331	1331	1431	1531	1531	1631	1718	1731	1818	1831	1931	2031	2131	2131	2231	2331	0025	0124
215	Larvik .... d.	0749*	0835*	0935*	0939	1039j	1135*	1134	1235*	1335*	1339	1435*	1535*	1534	1639r	1719	1739t	1819	1839	1939	2035*	2135*	2139	2233	2332	0026	0125
249	Porsgrunn .779 d.	0813*	0859*	0959*	1016	1116j	1159*	1212	1259*	1359*	1417	1459*	1559*	1611	1716r	1756	1817t	1856	1916	2018	2059*	2159*	2216	2310	0009	0103	0202
258	**Skien** .... 779 a.	0835*	0921*	1021*	1024	1124j	1221*	1220	1321*	1421*	1425	1521*	1621*	1619	1724r	1804	1825t	1904	1924	2026	2121*	2221*	2224	2318	0017	0111	0210

	Ⓐ	⚒	Ⓐ		Ⓐ	⚒	Ⓐ	Ⓒ	⚒	Ⓑ	⑥	Ⓐ	Ⓒ			⑥	Ⓑ		⚒	†	Ⓐ	Ⓒ		Ⓑ		Ⓑ	
Skien .... 779 d.	0346	0446	0519	0538	0552	0642	0730*	0744	0833	0930*	0935	1030*	1044	1130*	1234v	1330*	1335	1435	1525*	1535	1625*	1635	1730*	1830*	1930*	2030*	2130*
Porsgrunn .. 779 d.	0354	0454	0527	0546	0600	0650	0748*	0752	0841	0948*	0943	1048*	1052	1148*	1242v	1348*	1343	1443	1548*	1543	1648*	1643	1748*	1848*	1948*	2048*	2148*
Larvik .... a.	0431	0531	0604	0624	0638	0729	0817*	0829	0920	1017*	1020	1117*	1129	1217*	1320v	1417*	1420	1520	1617*	1620	1717*	1720	1817*	1917*	2017*	2117*	2217*
Larvik .... d.	0432	0532	0606	0629	0640	0732	0832	0832	0932	1032	1032	1132	1132	1232	1332	1432	1432	1532	1632	1632	1732	1732	1832	1932	2032	2132	2232
Sandefjord .... d.	0447	0547	0621	0643	0654	0747	0847	0847	0947	1047	1047	1147	1147	1247	1347	1447	1447	1547	1647	1647	1747	1747	1847	1947	2047	2147	2247
Torp ✈ .... d.	0451	0551	|	0647	|	0751	0851	0851	0951	1051	1051	1151	1151	1251	1351	1451	1451	1551	1651	1651	1751	1751	1851	1951	2051	2151	2251
Tønsberg .... d.	0508	0608	0640	0708	0721	0808	0908	0908	1008	1108	1108	1208	1208	1308	1408	1508	1508	1608	1708	1708	1808	1808	1908	2008	2108	2208	2308
Skoppum .... d.	0518	0618	|	0718	|	0818	0918	0918	1018	1118	1118	1218	1218	1318	1418	1518	1518	1618	1718	1718	1818	1818	1918	2018	2118	2218	2318
Holmestrand ..... d.	0526	0626	|	0726	|	0826	0926	0926	1026	1126	1126	1226	1226	1326	1426	1526	1526	1626	1726	1726	1826	1826	1926	2026	2126	2226	2326
Drammen .... d.	0547	0647	|	0747	|	0847	0947	0947	1047	1147	1147	1247	1247	1347	1447	1547	1547	1647	1747	1747	1847	1847	1947	2047	2147	2247	2347
Oslo S ...... 785 d.	0624	0724	0752	0824	0825	0924	1024	1024	1124	1224	1224	1324	1324	1424	1524	1624	1624	1724	1824	1824	1924	1924	2024	2124	2224	2324	0024
Lillestrøm ... 785 d.	0635	0735	0802	0835	0845	0935	1035	1035	1135	1235	1235	1335	1335	1435	1535	1635	1635	1735	1835	1835	1935	1935	2035	2135	2235	2335	0035
Oslo ✈ ● .785 d.	0649	0749	...	0849	0859	0949	1049	1049	1149	1249	1249	1349	1349	1449	1549	1649	1649	1749	1849	1849	1949	1949	2049	2149	2249	2349	0049
Eidsvoll ... 785 a.	0659	0759	...	0859	0908	0959	1059	1059	1159	1259	1259	1359	1359	1459	1559	1659	1659	1759	1859	1859	1959	1959	2059	2159	2259	2359	0059

j – By 🚌 on ⑥ (Larvik d. 1035, Porsgrunn d. 1059, Skien a. 1121).
r – By 🚌 on Ⓒ (Larvik d. 1635, Porsgrunn d. 1659, Skien a. 1721).
t – By 🚌 on † (Larvik d. 1735, Porsgrunn d. 1759, Skien a. 1821).
v – By 🚌 on ⑥ (Skien d. 1230, Porsgrunn d. 1248, Larvik a. 1317).
* – By 🚌 Larvik - Skien and v.v.
● – Oslo Lufthavn Gardermoen.

784 HAMAR - RØROS - TRONDHEIM

km		Ⓐ	⑥	Ⓐ	⚒	Ⓑ	Ⓐ	Ⓒ		Ⓑ	Ⓑ	
0	**Hamar** .... d.	...	...	0810	1011	1210	1210	...	1607	1811	2017	...
32	Elverum .... d.	...	...	0833	1036	1235	1235	...	1633	1834	2042	...
64	Rena .... d.	...	...	0855	1059	1257	1257	...	1656	1859	2104	...
120	Koppang .... d.	...	...	0937	1141	1339	1339	...	1739	1941	2146	...
273	**Røros** .... d.	0505	0700	1130	1337	1531	1537	1630	1937	2133	2339	...
384	Støren .... 785 d.	0640	0830	...	...	...	1710	1802	2108	...	...	...
435	**Trondheim** S ...... 785 a.	0735	0925	...	...	...	1802	1855	2200	...	...	...

	Ⓐ	⚒	Ⓐ		Ⓑ	⑦		Ⓐ	⑦
Trondheim S .... 785 d.	...	...	0545	0945	...	1352	...	1615	2040
Støren .... 785 d.	...	...	0640	1039	...	1447	...	1712	2133
Røros .... d.	0419	0617	0818	1217	1410	1620	1620	1847	2305
Koppang .... d.	0611	0809	1015	1416	1605	1817	1817	...	...
Rena .... d.	0653	0854	1059	1458	1656	1859	1859	...	...
Elverum .... d.	0715	0916	1121	1520	1718	1921	1921	...	...
Hamar .... a.	0740	0941	1146	1545	1743	1946	1946	...	...

785 OSLO - LILLEHAMMER - ÅNDALSNES and TRONDHEIM

km		407	41	2341	311	2343	45	2345	47	2347	329	405	
		Ⓐ				Ⓐ			Ⓑ	Ⓑ	Ⓑ	Ⓑ	
			R	R		R	R	R	R	R		R	
			✕⊡	🍷	🍷⊡	🍷	✕⊡	🍷	✕⊡	🍷	🍷⊡	✕N	
0	**Oslo** Sentral .... ★ d.	...	0802	...	0934	...	1402	...	1602	...	1834	2246	...
21	Lillestrøm .... ★ d.	...	0813u	...	0945	...	1414u	...	1613u	...	1845	2321u	...
52	Oslo ✈ ⊖ .... ★ d.	...	0828u	...	0959	...	1429u	...	1629u	...	1859	2340u	...
127	**Hamar** .... ★ d.	...	0921	...	1052	...	1522	...	1722	...	1952	0033	...
185	**Lillehammer** .... ★ d.	...	1010	...	1140	1150	1610	...	1812	...	2048	0122	...
243	Ringebu .... d.	...	1052	...	...	1248	1652	...	1856	...	2129	0211	...
267	Vinstra .... d.	...	1108	...	...	1305	1713	...	1919	...	2145	0229	...
298	Otta .... d.	...	1131	...	...	1328	1735	...	1942	...	2206	0259	...
344	Dombås .... d.	...	1203	1205	...	1407	1808	1810	2013	2016	2235	0343	...
458	**Åndalsnes** .... a.	...	|	1323	...	1535	|	1930	|	2134	...	|	...
430	Oppdal .... d.	0645	1301	...	...	...	1905	...	2110	...	...	0446	...
502	Støren .... 784 d.	0735	1349	...	...	...	1957	...	2204	...	...	0540	...
553	**Trondheim** S .... 784 a.	0830	1431	...	...	...	2045	...	2249	...	...	0640	...

	308	2340	316	2342	42	2344	44	2346	46	406
	⚒	Ⓐ				Ⓑ	Ⓑ			Ⓑ
		R		R	R	R	R	R	R	R
	🍷⊡	🍷	🍷⊡	🍷	✕⊡	🍷	✕⊡	🍷	✕⊡	✕N
Trondheim S . 784 d.	...	...	...	...	0818	...	1320	...	1530	2320
Støren .... 784 d.	...	...	...	...	0905	...	1409	...	1615	0010
Oppdal .... d.	...	...	...	...	0958	...	1501	...	1706	0109
Åndalsnes .... d.	...	0738	...	0932	|	1434	|	1637	|	|
Dombås .... d.	0517	0859	...	1052	1057	1554	1559	1757	1808	0221
Otta .... d.	0549	0930	...	...	1129	...	1630	...	1838	0257
Vinstra .... d.	0613	0953	...	...	1150	...	1652	...	1859	0320
Ringebu .... d.	0629	1010	...	...	1207	...	1709	...	1916	0337
Lillehammer .... ★ d.	0714	1055	1114	...	1248	...	1751	...	1958	0422
Hamar .... ★ d.	0807	...	1208	...	1334	...	1841	...	2042	0515
Oslo ✈ ⊖ .... ★ a.	0901	...	1301	...	1432s	...	1933s	...	2133s	0616s
Lillestrøm .... ★ a.	0915	...	1315	...	1449s	...	1949s	...	2149s	0635s
Oslo Sentral ..... ★ a.	0926	...	1326	...	1503	...	2004	...	2204	0650

🚌 ✣					Ⓐ	Ⓐ	Ⓑ			Ⓑ¶	⑦	Ⓐ
Åndalsnes .... d.	0620z	1000	1340	1345	1550	1550	1800	1945	1945	2135	2135	2200
Molde .... a.	0750	1125	|	1510	|	1715	1925	|	2110	|	2250	2325
Ålesund .... a.	...	...	1540	...	1750	...	...	2145	...	2345	...	...

🚌 ✣	Ⓐ			⚒	⑦	Ⓐ	Ⓑ	v		
Ålesund .... d.	...	0705	...	...	1155	1215	...	1400	...	...
Molde .... d.	0610	|	0755	1000	|	|	1300	|	1440	2200
Åndalsnes .... a.	0735	0910	0920	1120	1405	1420	1420	1605	1605	2315

🚌 ✣	⚒		Ⓐ				⑤⑦		Ⓑ			
Oppdal skysstasjon .... d.	0530	...	1050	...	1315	...	1810	...	2120	...	...	...
Kristiansund .... a.	0915	...	1425	...	1635	...	2125	...	0030	...	...	...

🚌 ✣	Ⓐ		Ⓐ				⑤⑦		Ⓑ	
Kristiansund .... d.	0630	...	1040	...	1315	...	1635	...	2120	...
Oppdal skysstasjon a.	0940	...	1445	...	1645	...	2010	...	0035	...

	Ⓐ	Ⓐ		⚒		⚒		⚒						Ⓑ		Ⓑ		Ⓑ	
Oslo Sentral 771 783 d.	...	0634	0734	0834	0934	1034	1134	1234	1334	1434	1534	1634	1734	1834	1934	2034	2134	2234	2334
Lillestrøm .... 783 d.	...	0645	0745	0845	0945	1045	1145	1245	1345	1445	1545	1645	1745	1845	1945	2045	2145	2245	2345
Oslo ✈ ⊖ ... 771 783 d.	...	0659	0759	0859	0959	1059	1159	1259	1359	1459	1559	1659	1759	1859	1959	2059	2159	2259	2359
Eidsvoll .... 783 d.	...	0709	0809	0909	1009	1109	1209	1309	1409	1509	1609	1709	1809	1909	2009	2109	2209	2309	0009
Hamar .... a.	...	0750	0850	0950	1050	1150	1250	1350	1450	1550	1650	1750	1852	1950	2053	2150	2251	2350	0050
Hamar .... d.	0652	0752	0852	0952	1052	1152	1252	1352	1452	1552	1652	1752	1853	1952	2054	2152	2253	2352	0052
Lillehammer .... a.	0740	0840	0937	1040	1140	1238	1341	1441	1536	1640	1736	1840	1940	2040	2140	2236	2337	0036	0136

	Ⓐ			⚒		⚒		⚒								Ⓑ		Ⓑ	
Lillehammer .... d.	0414	...	0524	0614	0714	0814	0907	1014	1114	1208	1311	1415	1508	1614	1708	1810	1910	2007	2114
Hamar .... a.	0459	...	0611	0705	0805	0905	1005	1105	1205	1305	1405	1505	1605	1705	1805	1906	2005	2106	2205
Hamar .... d.	0501	...	0613	0708	0807	0907	1008	1108	1208	1308	1407	1507	1607	1707	1807	1908	2008	2108	2207
Eidsvoll .... 783 d.	0541	...	0652	0752	0852	0952	1052	1152	1252	1352	1452	1552	1652	1752	1852	1952	2052	2152	2252
Oslo ✈ ⊖ ... 771 783 d.	0603	...	0703	0803	0903	1003	1103	1203	1303	1403	1503	1603	1703	1803	1903	2003	2103	2203	2303
Lillestrøm .... 783 d.	0616	...	0716	0816	0916	1016	1116	1216	1316	1416	1516	1616	1716	1816	1916	2016	2116	2216	2316
Oslo Sentral 771 783 a.	0626	...	0726	0826	0926	1026	1126	1226	1326	1426	1526	1626	1726	1826	1926	2026	2126	2226	2326

N – Conveys 🛏 and 2nd class seats.
R – Reservation recommended.

s – Stops to set down only.
u – Stops to pick up only.
v – 10 minutes later on ⑥.
z – 0630 on ⑥⑦.

⊡ – Conveys *NSB Komfort*.
⊖ – Oslo Lufthavn Gardermoen.
¶ – Journey is by taxi and is only available for passengers from train **2347** (please inform the on train staff).
★ – See also panel below main table.
✣ – 🚌 services are subject to confirmation.

786 SOUTHWEST NORWAY 🚌 LINKS

BERGEN - TRONDHEIM (Operator: NOR-WAY Bussekspress ✆ +47 815 44 444)
Bergen ⊡ d. 1630 → Oppdal a. 0440 → Trondheim a. 0642.
Trondheim d. 2230 → Oppdal d. 0032 → Bergen ⊡ a. 1220.

BERGEN - ÅLESUND (Operator: NOR-WAY Bussekspress ✆ +47 815 44 444)
From Bergen ⊡ at 0800 daily (Ålesund a. 1745) and 1230 Ⓑ § (Ålesund a. 2215 ①–⑤ / 2245 ⑦).
From Ålesund at 0810 Ⓐ § / 0815 ⑥ § (Bergen a. 1820) and 1110 daily (Bergen a. 2025).

BERGEN - KRISTIANSAND (Operator: NOR-WAY Bussekspress ✆ +47 815 44 444)
Bergen ⊡ d. 0820 → Odda d. 1120 → Haukeli a. 1300, d. 1455 → Kristiansand ⊡ a. 1900.
Kristiansand ⊡ d. 0845 → Haukeli a. 1250, d. 1455 → Odda a. 1645 → Bergen ⊡ a. 2005.

BERGEN - STAVANGER (Operator: NOR-WAY Bussekspress ✆ +47 815 44 444)
Journey time: 4 hrs 30 m – 5 hrs 30 m. From Bergen ⊡ at 0900, 1040 ⑦, 1100 Ⓐ, 1130 ⑥, 1300, 1445 Ⓐ, 1500 ⑦, 1600 Ⓒ, 1615 Ⓐ, 1700 Ⓑ and 1900. From Stavanger ⊙ at 0715 Ⓐ, 0845 ⑥, 0915 Ⓑ, 1015 Ⓐ, 1045 Ⓒ, 1245 ⑥, 1315 Ⓑ, 1510 Ⓐ, 1515 Ⓒ, 1715 Ⓑ, 1835 Ⓑ and 1845 ⑥.

BERGEN - ODDA ★ 🚌/⛴ *Journey time: 2 hrs 40 m – 2 hrs 55 m.*
From Bergen ⊡ at 0820, 1150 Ⓑ and 2055 Ⓑ. From Odda ⊡ at 0530 ⚒ and 1710.

VOSS - ODDA ★ *Journey time: 1 hr 55 m – 2 hrs 10 m.*
From Voss at 0920, 1125 ⚒, 1250, 1550 ⚒, 1745 and 2205 Ⓑ.
From Odda ⊡ at 0620 ⚒, 0720, 1225, 1410 ⚒ ‡, 1700 and 2035 Ⓑ.

VOSS - ULVIK ★ *Journey time: 55 – 65 minutes. A change of bus may be required.*
From Voss at 0755 Ⓐ, 0920 Ⓐ, 1005, 1125 ⚒, 1440 Ⓐ, 1550 ⚒, 1745, 1905 Ⓑ and 2205 Ⓑ.
From Ulvik ⊡ at 0610 Ⓐ, 0725 Ⓐ, 0830, 1045, 1330 Ⓐ, 1515, 1740, 2130 ⑦ and 2135 Ⓐ.

‡ – 1405 on schooldays.
§ – Change bus at Førde.
⊡ – Bus station.
⊙ – Stavanger Byterminalen.
★ – Operator: Tide Buss AS / Skyss ✆ +47 55 55 90 70.

Warning! Subject to alteration on and around public holiday dates

NORWAY / FINLAND

TRONDHEIM - BODØ and NARVIK — 787

km		1781 Ⓐ Ⓨ	1783 Ⓐ Ⓨ	475 N R	◇	473 ⓎR	473 ⓎR	1785 ⋇	471 Ⓐ Ⓨ	1791 ◇	479 Ⓑ ⓎR	477 Ⓑ ⓎR
0	Trondheim S ...d.			2340				0738				1600
33	Værnes ✈ ‡ ●..d.		0006					0811				1630u
34	Stjørdal.....d.		0011					0817				1636u
126	Steinkjer.....d.		0129					0947				1801u
220	Grong.....d.		0240					1055				1909
406	Mosjøen.....d.		0458		0655	0655		1314		1655	2130
498	Mo i Rana.....d.		0610		0757	0800		1424		1757	2238
648	Rognan.....d.	0542	0642	0806			0953	1125	1616	1745	1941	...
	Bodø ⊖......d.				0715					1645		
674	Fauske.....d.	0601	0701	0828	0820		1013	1144	1637	1804	1750	1959
674	Fauske.....d.	0602	0702	0831	0850		1015	1145	1646	1812	1810	2000
	Narvik ⊡ ♣..a.				1330					2300		...
729	Bodø.....a.	0642	0742	0915			1055	1225	1728	1850		2040

		478 Ⓐ ⓎR	470 Ⓐ Ⓨ	1784 Ⓐ	472 ◇	1790 Ⓐ ⋇R	474 Ⓐ ⓎR	476 ◇	1792 ②-⑥ N R
	Bodø.....d.		0745	1012		1227	1605	1730	...	2110	2355
	Narvik ⊡ ♣..d.			0700				1610		...
	Fauske.....d.		0825	1058	1155	1314	1644	1809	2110	2156	0035
	Fauske.....d.		0830	1059	1210	1316	1646	1810	2125	2200	0036
	Bodø ⊖.....a.			1320				2230		...
	Rognan.....d.		0848	1119		1336	1705	1833		2221	0055
	Mo i Rana.....d.	0815	1032			1535		2024		0020	...
	Mosjøen.....d.	0927	1138			1645		2128		0150	...
	Grong.....d.	1149				1907				0426	
	Steinkjer.....d.	1252				2016				0540	
	Stjørdal.....d.	1404				2133				0705	
	Værnes ✈ ‡..d.	1406				2135				0707	
	Trondheim.....a.	1437				2205				0747	

Local services Trondheim - Steinkjer and v.v.

km		Ⓐ	⋇				Ⓐ					Ⓐ
0	Trondheim S ...d.	0610	0710	0910	1110	1310	1510	1610	1710	1810	1910	2110	2310
31	Hell ●.....d.	0643	0743	0942	1141	1341	1541	1641	1741	1841	1943	2141	2341
33	Værnes ✈ ‡ ●..d.	0645	0745	0944	1143	1343	1543	1643	1743	1843	1945	2143	2343
34	Stjørdal.....d.	0652	0752	0952	1152	1352	1552	1652	1752	1852	1952	2152	2347
126	Steinkjer.....d.	0819	0916	1116	1321	1516	1716	1816	1916	2016	2116	2313	0105

		Ⓐ					Ⓐ					Ⓐ
	Steinkjer.....d.	0528	0728	0928	1128	1328	1528	1728	1925	2028	2128
	Stjørdal.....d.	0652	0852	1052	1252	1452	1652	1852	2052	2152	2252
	Værnes ✈ ‡ ●..d.	0654	0854	1054	1254	1454	1654	1854	2054	2154	2254
	Hell ●.....d.	0657	0857	1057	1257	1457	1657	1857	2057	2157	2257
	Trondheim S.a.	0732	0932	1132	1332	1532	1732	1932	2132	2227	2332

N – Conveys ⌖, ⌂ and ⋇.
R – Reservation recommended.

u – Stops to pick up only.

● – Trains stop on request.
⊡ – Bus station.
⊖ – Bodø Sentrumsterminalen.
‡ – Station for Trondheim Airport.
◇ – Operator: Saltens Bilruter Nordlandsbuss.
Subject to confirmation.

▶ – Additional services on Ⓐ Trondheim - Stjørdal - Steinkjer and v.v.:
From Trondheim at 0515, 0810, 1010, 1210, 1410, 1445 and 1545.
From Steinkjer at 0500, 0600, 0628, 0828, 1028, 1228, 1428, 1628 and 1828.
♣ – 🚌 **Narvik - Svolvær** (Lofoten). Operator: Veolia Transport. 253km.
Journey time: 4 hrs 5 m - 4 hrs 30 m. **From Narvik** at 0920 ⑥, 0940 Ⓐ, 1145 ⑦ and 1530.
From Svolvær sentrum at 0950, 1510 ⋇ and 1655 ⑦.

Norwegian routes show 2016 timings

Narvik – Tromsø – Alta
Operator: Torghatten

km		①–⑤ ①–⑥		Ⓑ			⑦	
0	Narvik bus station ....d.	0520		1250			1520	1840	...
	Narvik rail station...d.					←		1845	
181	Nordkjosbotn.....d.	0825	0825		1615	1620		1620	1845	2200	...
252	Tromsø Prostneset..d.	0930	0930		→		1600	1730	1950	2305	...
241	Lyngseidet.....d.					1731	1745		
465	Alta.....a.						2223		

km		①–⑤	Ⓑ ①–⑤			⑦	⑦
0	Alta.....d.				1055		1410	...
224	Lyngseidet.....d.				1545	1545		1915	1915	...
293	Tromsø Prostneset.d.	0610	1000		1725		1600	2055		1920
	Nordkjosbotn.....d.	0725	1105			1653	1705		2023	2025
	Narvik rail station ......a.								
	Narvik bus station ......a.	1030	1415			2010			2330

Alta – Hammerfest – Karasjok – Kirkenes
Operator: Snelandia

km		①–⑤	Ⓑ	Ⓑ	⑦	①–⑤	①–⑤	Ⓑ		⑤⑦	Ⓑ	⑤⑦
			N		N								
0	Alta.....d.		0900			1145		1430	1605	1950		
	Hammerfest.....d.	0720		1220	1225		1515				2040
87	Skaidi.....d.	0820	1045	1145	1320	1325	1330	1615	1630		2120	2140
144	Hammerfest.....d.		1245			1			2220		
112	Olderfjord.....d.	0845	1115		1345	1400	1400	1655	1655		2220
212	Honningsvåg ★..a.		1255			1545		1835			
	Nordkapp.....d.		1340k								
174	Lakselv.....d.	0955			1450	1515		1750			2320
248	Karasjok.....d.				1625		1900		1927		0030
429	Tanabru.....d.	1400		1845					2335		
571	Kirkenes ♦.....a.	1630		2105							

		①–⑤	①–⑤	Ⓑ		Ⓑ	①–⑤		Ⓑ	⑦	⑤⑦	⑤⑦
				N			N					
	Kirkenes ♦.....d.			0630				1120	1510		
	Tanabru.....d.			0855				1355			
	Karasjok.....d.		0615			1430			1928	2000
	Lakselv.....d.		0730			1245		1545		1745		2115
	Nordkapp.....d.				1440k						
	Honningsvåg ★..d.	0655			0935		1520				
	Olderfjord.....d.	0845	0845		1115	1345	1655	1655		1845		2220
	Hammerfest.....d.		1040				1640			
	Skaidi.....d.	0910	0915	1140	1145	1405	1725	1725	1739	1905		2250
	Hammerfest.....d.	1015			1505		1825		2005		2350
	Alta.....a.	1050		1320		1900		1900		2240	...

Rovaniemi – Muonio – Tromsø
Service from Jan. 1, 2017

km	Operator:	G	G	G
0	Rovaniemi bus station d.	0800	1140	1720
	Rovaniemi rail station d.	0820	1100	1730
157	Kittilä.....d.	1040	1340	1935
238	Muonio.....d.	1300z	1505	2045
327	Karesuvanto.....d.	1435	1625b	...
440	Kilpisjärvi ⊡ .... FI d.	1625	1810b	...
535	Nordkjosbotn ..... NO d.		1830b	...
608	Tromsø Prostneset ...a.		1930b	...

		G	E	G
	Tromsø Prostneset ..d.		0730e	...
	Nordkjosbotn ..... NO d.		0830e	...
	Kilpisjärvi ⊡ .... FI d.		1110e	1315
	Karesuvanto.....d.		1240e	1515
	Muonio.....d.	0840	1405	1700f
	Kittilä.....d.	1000	1530	1835
	Rovaniemi rail station a.	1204x	1725	2035x
	Rovaniemi bus station a.	1205	1735	2040

Rovaniemi – Karasjok, Nordkapp and Tanabru
Service from Jan. 1, 2017

km	Operator:	J ①–⑤	G	J ⑥⑦	J ①–⑤	E D✧	E 1145		P ①–⑤	E	G/L Ⓑ
0	Rovaniemi bus station d.		0800			1145	1145		1520	1720	2100
	Rovaniemi rail station d.		0820			1100	1100		1525	1725	2115
130	Sodankylä.....d.		1020			1345	1345		1730	1910	2305
305	Ivalo.....FI d.	1100	1250	1400	1525f	1625f		1935	2115	0115
345	Inari.....FI d.	1135		1440	1610	1655	1655		2150		...
461	Karasjok ⊖.....NO a.				1740	1740				
536	Lakselv, Statoil .....a.					1855				
	Honningsvåg ◇.....a.					2135x				
735	Nordkapp.....a.					2215				
	Tanabru ⊙.....NO a.						2340r			

	Operator:	P ①–⑤	E	J ①–⑤	G/L ①–⑥	E A✧	E ⑥⑦	J ①–⑤	G
	Tanabru ⊙.....NO d.		0320t						
	Nordkapp.....d.			0100					
	Honningsvåg ◇.....d.			0510g					
	Lakselv, Statoil .....d.			0810					
	Karasjok ⊖.....d.			0915	0915				
	Inari.....FI d.		0705	1100		1210	1210	1415	1500	...
	Ivalo.....FI d.	0430	0750	1140	1215	1315f	1315f	1450	1535	1615
	Sodankylä.....d.	0650	1005		1500	1545	1545			1845
	Rovaniemi rail station a.	0835	1140		1715	1725	1725			2030
	Rovaniemi bus station .....a.	0840	1150		1710	1730	1730			2035

Operator codes
E – Eskelisen Lapin Linjat.
G – Gold Line.
J – Jbus.
P – Pikakuljetus Rovaniemi.
L – Liikenne O. Niemelä.

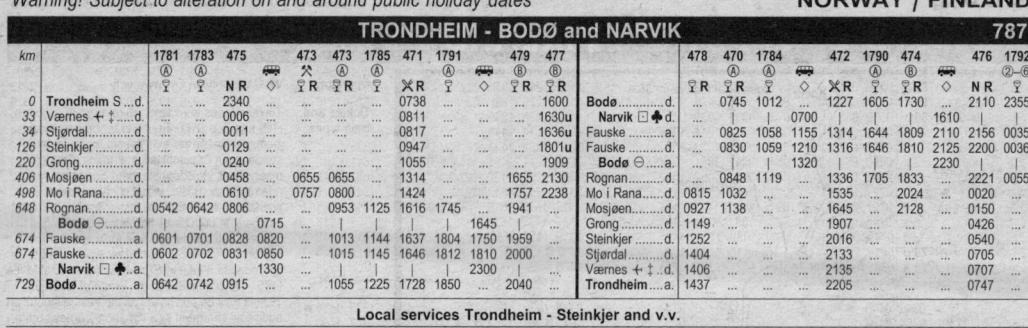

A – June 2 - Aug. 21.
B – May 1 - Sept. 30.
C – May 2 - Oct. 1.
D – June 1 - Aug. 20.
N – From May 1.
b – Runs Muonio - Tromsø summer only (2017 dates not yet available).
e – Summer only (2017 dates not yet available).
f – Arrives 30 - 35 minutes earlier.
g – Arrives 0140. Stops to pick up only.
k – May 1 - Sept. 30.
r – ④⑤⑦.
t – ①⑤⑥.
x – Stops on request.
z – Arrives 1200.

✧ – Trekking centre (Retkeilykeskus).
⊖ – Karasjok, Scandic Hotel.
✧ – 2017 running dates not yet available.
★ – **Honningsvåg - Nordkapp** and v.v. 34 km. Journey time: 45 minutes.
From Honningsvåg (Nordkapphuset) at 0745 B, 1130, 1550 B, 1840 B and 2130 B. **From Nordkapp** at 0015 C, 0840 B, 1345, 1640 B and 1935 B.
♦ – **Kirkenes - Murmansk** (RU) and v.v. Journey time: 4 hours. Operated by Pasvikturist AS. www.pasvikturist.no Please check visa requirements. **From Kirkenes** at 1500 (1400 during winter time). **From Murmansk** at 0700.

FI – Finland (East European Time).
NO – Norway (Central European Time).
RU – Russia (Moskva Time).

FINLAND

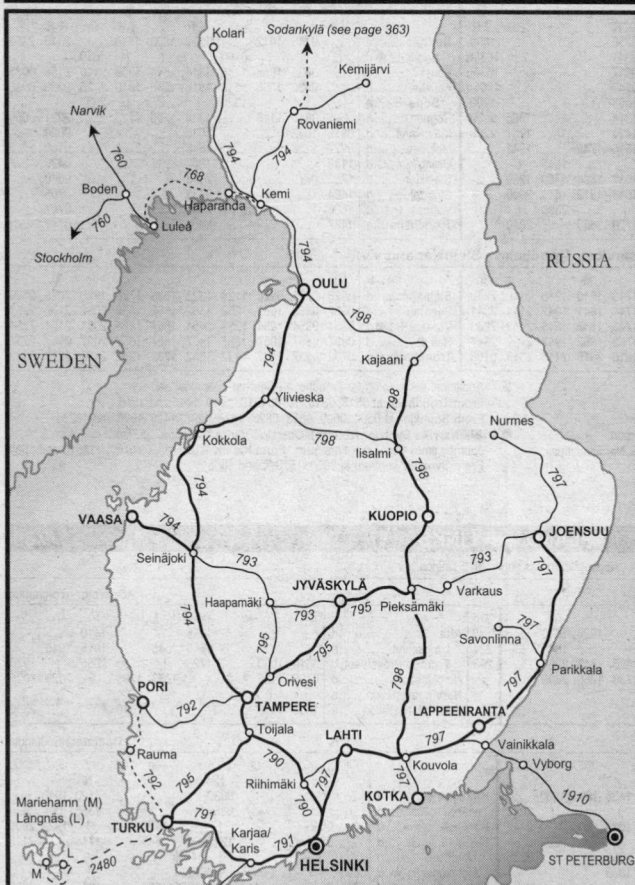

Operator: **VR** – VR-Yhtymä Oy   www.vr.fi

Tickets and train types: Travel classes in Finland are referred to as *Extra* (1st) and *Eco* (2nd). For all except purely local journeys, tickets are always sold for travel by a specific train or combination of trains with seat reservations included. Standard *Eco* fares are referred to as 'Basic', whilst cheaper advance puchase 'Saver' fares are also available in limited numbers. In both cases tickets can be changed to a different date / departure time for a €5 fee (plus any price difference). Both ticket types can be upgraded to a seat in *Extra* class for a variable fee (€5 – 17, dependent on the length of journey). Tickets may be purchased on the train, although an additional charge of €3 (for short journeys up to 76km) or €6 (for journeys over 76km) will be added to the 'Basic' fare.

▶ **S Pendolino** (e.g. S123) – high-speed tilting trains, with *Extra* and *Eco* class seats, all reservable.

▶ **InterCity** (e.g. IC124) – quality fast trains between major centres, with *Eco* class seats (most also convey *Extra* class seats), all reservable.

▶ **Express**, *pikajunat* (train number only shown, e.g. 128) – other fast trains, with *Eco* class seats, all reservable. Night expresses convey sleeping-cars and *Eco* class seats only (marked ★ in the tables).

▶ **Regional**, *taajamajunat* (no train number shown) – stopping-trains, normally with *Eco* class seats only. Regional fares apply.

Rail tickets are **not** valid on 🚌 services (except Kemi - Tornio). However, special combined train / bus fares are available on certain routes.

Services: ✕ indicates a train with a restaurant car.

Trains marked ⟲ convey a *MiniBistro* trolley service.

A variable supplement is payable for travel in sleeping-cars (🛏) in addition to the relevant *Eco* class fare – the price to be paid depends on the date of travel and the type of accommodation required. A higher supplement is charged for occupancy of a single-berth cabin.

Timings: Timings are valid, unless otherwise indicated, **December 11, 2016 - June 18, 2017**.

In these tables Ⓐ = ①–⑤, ✕ = ①–⑥.

Changes to the normal service pattern are likely to occur on and around the dates of public holidays (see page 2).

---

790   HELSINKI - TAMPERE

For through journeys to / from **Oulu** and **Rovaniemi**, see Table **794**. For through journeys to / from **Jyväskylä** and **Pieksämäki**, see Table **795**.

km		IC81 ✕ 2 Ⓐ	IC21 ✕ Ⓐ	IC141 ⟲	IC41 ⟲ 2 Ⓐ		IC165 ✕ 2 Ⓐ	IC167 ⟲	IC23 ✕	S143 2	IC43 ✕	S169 2		IC25 ⟲ Ⓐ	IC173 ⟲ 𝖯	S145 ✕		S45 ✕ Ⓐ	IC151 ⟲		IC27 ✕ Ⓐ	IC147 ⟲ 𝖯	S47 ✕	IC177 ⟲		S49 ✕
0	Helsinki...........d.	0527	0542	0627	0706	0727	0742	0827	0906	0927	1006	1027	1127	1142	1227	1306	1327	1342	1427	1506	1512	1527	1606	1627	1706	1712	1727
6	Pasila............d.	0533	0547	0633	0712	0733	0747	0833	0912	0933	1012	1033	1133	1147	1233	1312	1333	1347	1433	1512	1517	1533	1612	1633	1712	1717	1733
16	Tikkurila ⊙......d.	0543	0556	0643	0722	0743	0756	0843	0922	0943	1012	1043	1143	1156	1243	1322	1343	1356	1443	1522	1526	1543	1622	1643	1722	1726	1743
71	Riihimäki........d.		0640		0752		0840		0952		1052			1240		1352		1440		1552	1613		1652		1752	1813	
108	Hämeenlinna....d.		0702		0811		0902		1011		1111			1302		1411		1502		1611	1636		1711		1811	1836	
147	Toijala............d.		0725		0831		0925		1031		1131			1325		1431		1525		1631	1659		1731		1831	1859	
187	Tampere..........a.	0656	0748	0756	0852	0856	0948	0956	1052	1056	1152	1156	1256	1348	1356	1452	1456	1548	1556	1652	1722	1656	1752	1756	1852	1922	1856

	IC179 ✕	IC29 ✕ Ⓐ	IC149 ⟲	IC265 2	S53 ✕ ★	269 N	IC187 ✕ 2	S91 ★ ⑦	S273 2			IC266 ★ Ⓐ	IC160 ⟲ Ⓐ	270 ✕ Ⓑ	IC162 ⟲ Ⓐ	S274 2	272	S40 ✕ 𝖯	IC164 ⟲	S42 ✕	IC150 ⟲ Ⓐ	S44 ✕	IC140 ⟲	IC20
Helsinki ....d.	1806	1827	1906	1852	1942	2027	2052	2206	2206	2152	2342	Tampere ......d.	0430	0520	0543	0604	0612	0622	0702	0707	0802	0807	0902	0907	1002
Pasila............d.	1812	1833	1912	1900	1947	2033	2100	2212	2212	2200	2347	Toijala.........d.	0457	0541	0610	0627	0640	0701		0728		0828		0928	
Tikkurila ⊙......d.	1822	1843	1922	1944	1956	2043	2144	2222	2222	2244	2356	Hämeenlinna..d.	0524	0601	0630	0648	0709	0753		0749		0849		0949	
Riihimäki........d.	1852		1952	2022	2043		2222	2252	2252	2322	0040	Riihimäki......d.	0548	0620	0702	0708	0736	0818		0809		0909		1009	
Hämeenlinna....d.	1911		2011	2048	2106		2248	2311	2311	2348	0102	Tikkurila ⊙....a.	0625	0647	0746	0737			0858	0818	0837	0918	0937	1018	1037	1118
Toijala............d.	1931		2031		2129			2331	2331		0125	Pasila............a.	0658	0656	0824	0746	0829	0827	0846	0927	0846	0927	0946	1027	1046	1127
Tampere..........a.	1952	1956	2052	2138	2152	2156	2336	2352	2352	0040	0148	Helsinki ....a.	0706	0702	0832	0752	0900	0837	0852	0933	0952	0933	0952	1033	1052	1133

	S54 ✕ ⑦		S170 2	S46 ✕	IC142 ⟲	IC22 ✕	IC174 ⟲	S172 ✕	S178 L ⑤		IC48 ✕	IC144 ⟲	IC24 ✕		IC86 ✕ Ⓑ	S84 ✕ ⑥	IC180 ⟲ 𝖯 Ⓑ		IC50 ✕	S146 ✕	IC26 ✕	S88 ✕ ⑤⑦	IC184 ⟲ 𝖯	S56 ✕ ⑤⑦	IC148 ⟲	IC28 ✕	S152 ⑦
Tampere ....d.	1002		1006	1102	1202	1207	1302	1307	1307	1402	1411	1502	1507	1602	1611	1702	1702	1707	1737	1737	1802	1807	1902	2002	2007	2102	2107	2202	2302
Toijala............d.			1029		1228		1328	1328		1434		1528		1634			1728	1800		1828			2028		2128			
Hämeenlinna....d.			1052		1249		1349	1349		1457		1549		1657			1749	1823		1849			2049		2149			
Riihimäki........d.			1114		1309		1409	1409		1519		1609		1719			1809	1845		1909			2109		2209			
Tikkurila ⊙......a.	1118		1203	1218	1318	1337	1418	1437	1437	1518	1603	1618	1637	1718	1803	1818	1818	1837	1933	1918	1937	2018	2118	2137	2218	2237	2318	0018
Pasila............a.	1127		1212	1227	1327	1346	1427	1446	1446	1527	1612	1627	1646	1727	1812	1827	1827	1846	1942	1927	1946	2027	2127	2146	2227	2246	2327	0027
Helsinki ....a.	1133		1217	1233	1333	1352	1433	1452	1452	1533	1617	1633	1652	1733	1817	1833	1833	1852	1947	1933	1952	2033	2133	2152	2233	2252	2333	0033

Regional trains (2nd class only) HELSINKI - RIIHIMÄKI and v.v. See also note ⊠.

km		Ⓐ														Ⓐ															
0	Helsinki..........d.	0042	...	0512	0612	0712	0812	0912	0942			2342	Riihimäki.....d.		⑥⑦ 0412	0512	0525	0555		0625				2025	2055	2155	2255	2355
3	Pasila............d.	0047	...	0517	0617	0717	0817	0917	0947	and		2347	Hyvinkää.....d.		0421	0521	0533	0603	0633		and		2033	2103	2203	2303	0003
16	Tikkurila ⊙......d.	0056	...	0526	0626	0726	0826	0926	0956	hourly		2356	Järvenpää....d.		0438	0538	0547	0617			hourly		2047	2117	2217	2317	0017
37	Järvenpää........d.	0111	...	0541	0641	0741	0841	0941	1011	until		0011	Tikkurila ⊙....a.		0503	0603	0603	0633		0703	until		2103	2133	2233	2333	0033
59	Hyvinkää..........d.	0127	...	0557	0657	0757	0857	0957	1027			0027	Pasila.........a.		0518	0618	0612	0647		0717			2112	2142	2242	2342	0042
71	Riihimäki........a.	0135	...	0605	0705	0805	0905	1005	1035				Helsinki.......a.		0523	0623	0617	0647		0717			2117	2147	2247	2347	0047

L – Not ⑤.   ⊙ – For Helsinki ✈ Vantaa.

N – ①②③④⑦.   ★ – Overnight train to / from northern Finland. Conveys 🛏, 🚗

𝖯 – To / from Pori (Table 792).   and ✕. For through cars and days of running see Table 794.

⊠ – Additional journeys: **From Helsinki** at 0442 Ⓐ, 0542 Ⓐ, 0642 ✕, 0742 ✕, 0842 ✕, 1012 Ⓐ and hourly until 2112. **From Riihimäki** at 0455 Ⓐ, 0655 Ⓐ, 0755 ✕, Ⓐ and hourly until 1955.

HELSINKI - TURKU and HANKO　　791

km		IC941	IC943			IC979	IC981	IC945	S947	IC951				IC955	IC957	IC989	IC959	S975	IC924	IC961			IC963	IC965	S985	IC977	S967
		✕	⟟	2	🚌	✕	✕	✕	✕	✕		2		✕	⟟	✕	✕	✕	✕	✕		2	🚌	✕	✕	✕	✕	✕
		Ⓐ	Ⓐ	Ⓐ					Ⓐ					Ⓐ	Ⓑ	Ⓐ	⑥⑦	Ⓑ	Ⓐ	⑦			Ⓐ			⑥	⑥	⑥
0	Helsinki..............d.	0517	0627	0635		0730	0737	0837	0937	1137	1243			1337	1437	1532	1537	1610		1637	1643			1737	1837	1837	2037	2037
3	Pasila................d.	0523	0633	0639		0736	0743	0843	0943	1147	1247			1343	1443	1538	1543	1616		1643	1647			1743	1843	1843	2043	2043
38	Kirkkonummi........d.	0548	0658	0716	0730					1324	1330										1724	1730				1939		
87	Karjaa / Karis ★.d.	0615	0725		0820	0832	0832	0932	1032	1232			1420	1432	1532	1627	1632			1732				1832	1932	1932	2132	2132
138	Salo.................d.	0657	0800			0900	0900	1000	1100	1300				1500	1600	1654	1700			1800				1900	2000	2000	2200	2200
194	Turku................a.	0739	0830			0930	0930	1030	1130	1330				1530	1630	1726	1730	1748	1812	1830				1930	2030	2030	2230	2230
197	Turku satama.....a.	0748																	1819					1939				

		IC942			IC944	S976	IC946	IC948	IC950		IC954				S958	IC960	IC982	IC962			IC984	S964	IC986	IC966	IC968		IC972
		⟟	🚌	2	✕	✕	⟟	✕	✕		⟟		2		S	IC	IC	✕	🚌	2	✕	S	✕	IC	IC		✕
		Ⓐ		Ⓐ	Ⓐ		Ⓐ	✕			Ⓐ				Ⓐ	Ⓑ	⑥⑦	Ⓐ			Ⓐ	⑦	Ⓑ	⑥⑦	Ⓑ		
	Turku satama ....d.						0810																					
	Turku.................d.	0532			0622	0708	0740	0830	0930		1130				1330	1430	1521	1530			1621	1630	1717	1730	1830		2020
	Salo...................d.	0603			0653		0801	0901	1001		1201				1401	1501	1557	1601			1653	1701	1801	1801	1901		2030
	Karjaa / Karis ★.d.	0630	0633		0720		0828	0928	1028		1228	1233			1428	1528	1623	1628	1633		1728	1728	1828	1828	1928		2101
	Kirkkonummi........d.		0723	0728							1323	1338					1723	1736			1855	1855					2128
	Pasila.................a.	0719		0806	0809	0840	0917	1017	1117		1317			1414	1517	1617	1717	1717			1814	1817	1817	1920	1920	2017		2155
	Helsinki...............a.	0725		0811	0815	0846	0923	1023	1123		1323			1419	1523	1623	1723	1723			1819	1823	1823	1926	1926	2023		2220
																												2226

★ – **KARJAA / KARIS - HANKO** and v.v. *50 km.* 2nd class only. Journey: 40 minutes.
　From Karjaa at 0730 Ⓐ, 0939, 1239, 1439, 1639, 1839 and 2139.
　From Hanko at 0632 Ⓐ, 0840, 1140, 1340, 1535, 1740 and 2040.

TAMPERE and TURKU - PORI　　792

Most trains convey ✕

km		477	IC461	IC465	IC467	IC469	IC471	IC473	IC475						IC164	IC462	IC466		IC464	478	IC468	IC470	IC472	IC186
							Ⓑ	Ⓑ							✕	✕	✕			Ⓐ				
	Helsinki 790........d.							1606*				**Pori................d.**		0520	0615	0715		1010	1215	1415	1615	1815	1815
0	**Tampere................d.**	0603	0807	1215	1415	1615	1815	1815	2007	2207		**Tampere.............d.**		0650	0745	0850		1140	1351	1545	1747	1945	1945
135	**Pori.....................a.**	0748	0937	1347	1547	1747	1947	1947	2137	2337		*Helsinki 790........a.*		0852									2152

🚌 TURKU - RAUMA - PORI ⊠

km		🚌	🚌	🚌	🚌		🚌	🚌		🚌	🚌				🚌	🚌		🚌	🚌		🚌	🚌	🚌	🚌
		Ⓐ					Ⓑ			Ⓑ					Ⓐ	💥		Ⓑ						
0	**Turku bus station....d.**	0600	0815	1100	1500		1630	1800		1830	2030		**Pori bus station....d.**	0530	0700		0830	0900		1200	1700	1900	2005
90	**Rauma bus station.....d.**					1615	1805		1915	2010		**Rauma bus station.....d.**			0850	0940		1040	1250	1800		2100
139	**Pori bus station.......a.**	0815	1035	1320	1715	1715		2015	2015	2235		**Turku bus station......a.**	0740	0915	1000		1115	1220	1415	1925	2115	

* – Train number **147** Helsinki - Tampere.　　　　　　　　　　　　⊠ – Selected journeys only (many additional services operate).

JOENSUU - PIEKSÄMÄKI - JYVÄSKYLÄ - SEINÄJOKI　　793

km			IC142	S146		S148				IC159	IC141		S143	S145		IC151
		💥2				2						2			⑥2	Ⓑ2	Ⓑ2
0	**Joensuu ....d.**		0700			1550		**Seinäjoki ....d.**			1034					1941
134	Varkaus ....d.		0837			1727		Alavus..................d.			1107					2014
183	**Pieksämäki 795 d.**		0912	0923	1527	1802	1818	Haapamäki...........d.			1217					2121
263	**Jyväskylä 795 d.**	0600		1009	1613	1625	1909	**Jyväskylä 795 d.**	0802	1039		1322	1339	1644	1838	2226
341	Haapamäki ....d.	0707				1741		**Pieksämäki 795 d.**	0848	1125	1142		1425	1730	1817 1925 1938	
414	Alavus ....d.	0813				1842		Varkaus ....d.			1219				1854	2015
459	**Seinäjoki ....d.**	0845				1913		**Joensuu ....a.**			1353				2028	2149

TAMPERE - VAASA, OULU, KOLARI and ROVANIEMI　　794

km		IC273	S455	IC21	IC711		IC41	IC41	IC23	IC413	IC43	IC25	IC415	441	S45	IC27		S47	S51	S51	S49	IC29	S457	S53	IC265	269
		★⊕	✕	✕	✕		✕	✕	✕	2⟟	✕	✕	✕	2	✕	✕		✕	✕	✕	✕	✕	✕	★	★	⊕
			Ⓐ		K	Ⓐ	⑥⑦	Ⓐ				Ⓑ	⑤			Ⓐ			Ⓑ	④⑤	Ⓑ		⑤	Ⓖ	A	A
	Helsinki 790 ...d.	2152		0627			0706	0727	0927		1027	1227		1327	1427	1527		1627	1627	1627	1727	1827		2027	1852	2052
0	**Tampere...........d.**	0115		0800			0900	0900	1100		1200	1400		1512	1600	1700		1800	1800	1800	1900	2000		2200	2211	2359
75	Parkano ....d.	0211					0943	0943			1243			1602				1842	1842	1842				2234	2303	
159	Seinäjoki ....a.	0301		0904			1016	1016	1204		1316	1504		1649	1717	1804		1916	1916	1916	2004	2104		2308	0008	0153
159	**Seinäjoki ....d.**	0304	0656	0908		0915	1028	1028	1208		1328	1508		1720	1808	1815		1920	1925	1925	2008	2108	2112	2310	0011	0156
	Vaasa.............a.		0749			1035	1115	1115			1415				1807		1930	2007		2055		2159	2357			
292	Kokkola ....d.	0443		1017					1305			1617			1905			2035	2037		2210			0151	0339	
371	Ylivieska ....d.	0538		1106					1351			1705			1951				2124		2257			0250	0432	
493	Oulu ....a.	0719		1218					1455			1822			2052				2250		0010			0450	0552	
493	**Oulu ....d.**	0743			1227				1503			1830			2056									0457	0622	
599	Kemi ....d.	0851			1327				1603			1931			2157									0607	0748	
808	**Kolari ....a.**																									1048
713	**Rovaniemi ⊡ a.**	1040			1440				1717			2044			2334									0728		
796	Kemijärvi ⊡ a.																								0845	

		S40	S52	S42	S44		IC20	S54	S46	IC22	IC48	IC414	IC24	IC24	IC50	IC416	IC26	442	S456	S56	IC710	S458	IC28	IC266	270	272	IC274
		✕	①–④	✕	✕		Ⓐ	✕	⑦		✕		✕	✕	✕	2⟟	✕	2		✕	K	①–④	★	★⊕	★	★	✕
		Ⓐ									💥		⑦			Ⓐ			⑤	⑤⑦	⑤⑦				B	C	
	Kemijärvi...... ⊡ d.																										1945
	Rovaniemi ...... ⊡ d.						0555r			0927	0927			1209						1518			1803				2115
	Kolari...........d.																							1820	1820		
	Kemi.............d.						0711r			1045	1045			1325						1640			1930	2120	2120	2233	
	Oulu.............a.						0815r			1150	1150			1423						1737			2055	2238	2238	2336	
	Oulu.............d.					0529			0833			1155	1155			1434			1604			1804	2123	2310	2310	2342	
	Ylivieska ....d.					0650			0952			1307	1307			1552			1723			1907	2318	0046	0046	0115	
	Kokkola ....d.		0532			0750			1042			1353	1353			1642			1816			1953	0018	0149	0149	0207	
	Vaasa...........d.	0455		0554	0650	0720		0804	0940		1240				1548	1620			1830		1934						
	Seinäjoki ....a.	0542	0637	0641	0737	0840	0848	0851	1027	1149	1327		1450	1450	1635	1740	1749		1917	1930		2048	0150	0328	0328	0358	
	Seinäjoki ....d.	0545	0649	0649	0739		0853	0853	1037	1153	1337		1453	1453	1638		1753	1810	1934			2053	0155	0331	0331	0402	
	Parkano ....d.	0620	0724	0724	0814				1112		1412			1713			1858		2014			0306					
	Tampere ....a.	0654	0758	0758	0855		0958	0958	1155	1258	1455		1558	1558	1755		1858	1950		2055		2158	0355	0535	0535	0546	
	Helsinki 790 ......a.	0833	0933	0933	1033		1133	1133	1333	1433	1633		1733	2133	1933		2133	2233		2233		2333	0706	0832	0937	0900	

A – Dec. 14 - Apr. 29 (also June 14, 16, 17; not Dec. 15, 18,
　Jan. 9, 10, 12, 15, 16, 17, 19, 22, 23, 30, Apr. 23, 24, 25, 27).
B – ⑤⑥ Dec. 17 - Apr. 28 (also June 17; not Dec. 15, 18).
C – ①②③④⑦ Dec. 15 - Apr. 30 (also June 15, 18;
　not Jan. 9, 10, 11, 16, 17, 18, 24, 31, Apr. 24, 25, 26).
G – ①②③④⑦.
H – Daily until Apr. 28; Ⓑ from Apr. 30.
K – From / to Kuopio (Table **798**).

r – Not ⑦.
z – Not Dec. 25, Jan. 1.

★ – Conveys 🛏, �car and ✕.
⊕ – Conveys 🛏 Turku - Tampere - Rovaniemi and v.v. See Table **795**.
⊡ – Other 🚌 services Rovaniemi rail station - Kemijärvi bus station and v.v.
　Journey time: 70 - 80 minutes. **Service until June 2.**
　From Rovaniemi rail station at 1130 Ⓐ, 1520 Ⓐ, 1755 H and 2100 ⑦ z.
　From Kemijärvi bus station at 0510 Ⓐ, 0830 Ⓐ, 1020 ⑥, 1035 H, 1540 H and 1915 ⑦ z.

FINLAND

Warning! Subject to alteration on and around public holiday dates

795 TURKU - TAMPERE - PIEKSÄMÄKI

km		*IC* 81	*IC* 905	*IC* 141	*IC* 909	*S* 143	*IC* 917	*S* 145	*S* 87	*IC* 921	*IC* 151	*IC* 923	*IC* 147	*S* 89	*S* 89	*IC* 927	*IC* 149	*IC* 931	*IC* 933	*S* 91
		✕	✕	✕	✕	✕	✕	✕	✕	✕	✕	✕	✕	✕	✕	✕	✕	✕	✕	✕
		Ⓐ	Ⓐ						⑤⑦	⑤⑦	Ⓑ			Ⓑ	⑦K	⑤⑦			R	⑦
	Turku satama .. d.	...	...	...	*0810*	...	...	...	...	...	...	...	...	...	...	...	...	1945	...	...
0	**Turku** .... d.	...	0700	...	0905	...	1305	...	...	1505	...	1605	...	...	...	1805	...	2005	2125	...
66	Loimaa .... d.	...	0741	...	0944	...	1344	...	...	1544	...	1644	...	...	...	1844	...	2044	2212	...
86	Humppila ...... d.	...	0754	...	0959	...	1359	...	...	1559	...	1659	...	...	...	1859	...	2059	2227	...
	Helsinki **790**. d.	0527	|	0706	|	1006	|	1327	1427	|	1506	|	1606	1727	1727	|	1906	|	|	2206
128	Toijala .... **790** d.	|	0820	0831	1025	1131	1425	|	|	1625	1631	1725	1731	|	|	1925	2031	2125	2256	2331
168	**Tampere**... **790** a.	0656	0842	0852	1047	1152	1447	1456	1556	1647	1652	1747	1752	1856	1856	1947	2052	2147	2322	2352
168	**Tampere** ...... d.	0709	...	0905	...	1205	...	1505	1609	...	1705	...	1805	1913	1913	...	2105	...	...	2359
210	Orivesi .... d.	0734	...	0930	...	1230	...	1530	1634	...	1730	...	1830	1938	1938	...	|	...	...	|
266	Jämsä .... d.	0815	...	1005	...	1305	...	1610	1716	...	1805	...	1913	2020	2020	...	2200	...	...	0055
323	Jyväskylä .... ▶ d.	0845	...	1039	...	1339	...	1644	1746	...	1838	...	1943	2050	2052	...	2235	...	...	0130
403	**Pieksämäki** ▶ a.	...	...	1125	...	1425	...	1730	...	...	1925	...	...	...	2135	...	...	...	...	...

	IC 904	*S* 80	*IC* 150	*IC* 140	*IC* 910	*IC* 142	*IC* 916		*IC* 144	*IC* 922	*IC* 924	*IC* 86	*S* 84	*S* 146	*IC* 928	*IC* 930	*S* 88	*IC* 148	*IC* 934	*S* 152
	✕	✕	✕	✕	✕	✕	✕		✕	✕	✕	✕	✕	✕	✕	✕	✕	✕	✕	✕
	T	Ⓐ	⚒	⚒						⑤⑦		Ⓑ	⑥			⑦	⑤⑦		Ⓑ	⑦K
Pieksämäki ...... d.	...	...	...	0630	...	0923	...	...	1223	...	...	...	...	1527	...	...	...	1818	...	2035
Jyväskylä .... d.	...	0525	0620	0720	...	1013	...	...	1313	...	...	1515	1515	1617	...	...	1813	1920j	...	2126
Jämsä .... d.	...	0556	0651	0751	...	1051	...	...	1351	...	...	1546	1546	1652	...	...	1849	1956	...	2159
Orivesi .... d.	...	|	0726	0826	...	1126	...	...	1426	...	...	1626	1626	1727	...	...	|	2031	...	|
Tampere .... a.	...	0650	0750	0850	...	1150	...	...	1450	...	...	1650	1650	1750	...	...	1944	2054	...	2254
Tampere ... **790** d.	0556	0702	0807	0907	0911	1207	1211	...	1507	1511	1606	1702	1702	1807	1811	1911	2002	2107	2111	2302
Toijala .... **790** d.	0623	|	0828	0928	0935	1228	1235	...	1528	1535	1635	|	|	1828	1835	1935	|	2128	2135	|
Helsinki **790**.... a.	|	0833	0952	1052	|	1352	|	...	1652	|	|	1833	1833	1952	|	|	2133	2252	|	0033
Humppila .... d.	0652	...	...	...	1000	...	1300	...	...	1600	1700	...	...	...	1900	2000	...	...	2200	...
Loimaa .... d.	0706	...	...	...	1013	...	1313	...	...	1613	1713	...	...	...	1915	2013	...	...	2213	...
Turku .... a.	0750	...	...	...	1050	...	1355	...	...	1655	1750	...	...	...	1955	2055	...	...	2250	...
Turku satama ... a.	0809	...	...	...	...	...	...	...	...	...	1819	...	...	...	2007	...	...	...	...	...

TAMPERE - HAAPAMÄKI

km		2	2	Ⓑ2
	Tampere ..... d.	1005	1617	2019
0	Orivesi .... d.	1031	1643	2045
47	Vilppula .... d.	1106	1718	2119
72	**Haapamäki**.. a.	1124	1736	...

	Ⓐ2	⑥2	2	2
Haapamäki .. d.	...	...	1224	1833
Vilppula .... d.	0640	0850	1245	1854
Orivesi .... d.	0715	0925	1320	1929
Tampere ...... a.	0740	0950	1345	1954

K – To / from Kuopio (Table **798**).

R – (12) Turku - Tampere; conveys 🛏 Turku - Tampere (**273**) - Rovaniemi.

T – (12) Tampere - Turku; conveys 🛏 Rovaniemi (**266**) - Tampere - Turku.

j – Arrives 1909.

▶ – Additional journey (daily): *IC* **159** departs Jyväskylä 0802, arrives Pieksämäki 0848.

797 HELSINKI - KOUVOLA - JOENSUU - NURMES

km			*IC* 1			*IC* 63	*IC* 3		*IC* 65	*IC* 5			*S* 67	*S* 109	*IC* 7	*S* 9	*S* 9		*S* 69		*IC* 111	*IC* 11		*IC* 73	*IC* 115	*S* 113
		2	✕	2	2	✕	✕	2	✕	✕	2	2	✕	✕	✕	✕	✕	2	✕	2	✕	✕	2	✕	✕	✕
		⚒				K			O			Ⓑ	L	Ⓑ	Ⓑ		Ⓑ	Ⓑ	ⒷJ	Ⓐ	Ⓑ			K	Ⓑ	⑥
0	**Helsinki** .... ⊡ d.	...	0723	...	...	0817	1017	...	1117	1317	...	...	1417	1417	1517	1617	1617	...	1617	1635	1717	1817	...	1917	2017	2017
3	Pasila .... ⊡ d.	...	0729	...	...	0823	1023	...	1123	1323	...	...	1423	1423	1523	1623	1623	...	1623	1641	1723	1823	...	1926	2023	2023
16	Tikkurila ⊙ ... ⊡ d.	...	0738	...	...	0833	1033	...	1133	1333	...	...	1433	1433	1533	1633	1633	...	1633	1650	1733	1833	...	1935	2033	2033
104	**Lahti** .... ⊡ d.	...	0812	...	...	0908	1108	...	1213	1408	...	...	1508	1508	1608	1708	1708	...	1708	1745	1808	1908	...	2009	2108	2108
166	**Kouvola** .... a.	...	0839	...	...	0935	1135	...	1242	1435	...	...	1535	1535	1635	1735	1735	...	1735	1829	1835	1935	...	2036	2135	2135
166	**Kouvola** .... d.	...	0841	...	...	...	1137	...	...	1437	...	...	...	1539	1637	1739	1739	...	...	...	1827	1937	...	...	2137	2137
252	Lappeenranta .... d.	...	0921	...	...	...	1219	...	...	1519	...	...	...	1616	1717	1820	1820	...	...	...	1917	2017	...	...	2217	2217
288	Imatra .... d.	...	0947	...	...	...	1246	...	...	1546	...	...	...	...	1740	1844	1846	...	...	...	1941	2043	...	...	2241	2241
352	Parikkala .... d.	0734	1029	1034	...	...	1329	1334	...	1629	1634	...	...	...	|	...	1931	1936	...	...	...	2125	2130	...	...	...
411	Savonlinna ..... a.	0827	|	1127	...	...	|	1427	...	|	1727	...	...	...	|	...	|	2027	...	...	...	|	2223	...	...	...
482	**Joensuu** .... d.	...	1140	...	1147	...	1440	...	...	1740	...	1800	...	...	1923	...	2042	...	...	...	...	2236	...	...	...	...
586	Lieksa .... d.	...	...	...	1308	...	...	...	...	...	...	1921	...	...	...	...	...	...	...	...	...	...	...	...	...	...
642	**Nurmes** .... a.	...	...	...	1353	...	...	...	...	...	...	2006	...	...	...	...	...	...	...	...	...	...	...	...	...	...

		IC 102	*IC* 102		*IC* 104		*S* 2	*IC* 62	*IC* 4	*S* 100	*S* 64	*IC* 74			*IC* 6	*S* 66		*IC* 8	*S* 114	*IC* 68		*IC* 10			*IC* 12	
	2	✕	✕	2	✕	2	✕	✕	✕	✕	✕	✕	2	2	✕	✕	2	✕	✕	✕	2	✕	2	2	✕	2
	Ⓐ	Ⓐ	⚒	Ⓐ	⚒	⚒	⚒	⚒K	⚒	⑦	⚒J	⑦K	⚒			M			Ⓑ	K						Ⓑ
Nurmes .... d.	...	...	...	...	...	...	...	...	...	...	...	...	0635	...	...	...	...	...	...	...	...	...	1540	...	...	...
Lieksa .... d.	...	...	...	...	...	...	...	...	...	...	...	...	0722	...	...	...	...	...	...	...	...	...	1626	...	...	...
Joensuu .... d.	...	...	...	...	...	...	0518	...	0617	...	...	...	0850	...	0917	...	...	1217	...	...	...	1517	1745	...	1817	...
Savonlinna ..... d.	...	...	...	...	...	0530	|	...	|	...	...	...	...	0930	|	...	1230	|	...	...	1530	|	▬	1830	|	2035
Parikkala .... d.	...	...	...	...	...	0623	0628	...	0731	...	...	...	...	1023	1031	...	1323	1331	...	...	1623	1631	*IC*	1923	1933	2120
Imatra .... d.	...	0515	...	...	0615	...	0705	...	0812	0812	...	...	...	...	1112	...	...	1412	...	...	...	1712	**70**	...	2014	...
Lappeenranta ..... d.	...	0542	...	...	0642	...	0728	...	0840	0840	...	...	...	...	1140	...	...	1440	1628	...	...	1742	✕	...	2043	...
Kouvola .... a.	...	0620	...	...	0720	...	0806	...	0918	0918	...	...	...	...	1218	...	...	1518	1706	...	...	1820	**O**	...	2121	...
Kouvola .... d.	0529	0623	0623	0626	0723	...	0808	0823	0923	0923	1123	1123	...	...	1223	1420	...	1523	1708	1723	...	1823	2016	...	2123	...
Lahti .... ⊡ d.	0615	0652	0652	0712	0752	...	0837	0852	0952	0952	1152	1152	...	...	1252	1449	...	1552	1737	1752	...	1852	2048	...	2152	...
Tikkurila ⊙ ... ⊡ a.	0711	0726	0726	0808	0826	...	0911	0926	1026	1026	1226	1226	...	...	1326	1523	...	1626	1811	1826	...	1926	2126	...	2226	...
Pasila .... ⊡ a.	0721	0735	0735	0818	0835	...	0920	0935	1035	1035	1235	1235	...	...	1335	1532	...	1635	1820	1835	...	1935	2135	...	2235	...
Helsinki .... ⊡ a.	0727	0742	0742	0824	0842	...	0927	0942	1042	1042	1242	1242	...	...	1342	1539	...	1642	1827	1842	...	1942	2142	...	2242	...

Local trains **KOUVOLA - KOTKA** and v.v. 2nd class only.

km		⚒	Ⓐ	⑥⑦			
0	**Kouvola** .... d.	0609	0800	0850	1253	1541	1752
51	**Kotka** .... a.	0644	0844	0934	1337	1623	1836
52	**Kotka** satama ... a.	0647	0847	0937	1340	1625	1839

	⚒				
Kotka satama .... d.	0654	1015	1425	1630	1920
Kotka .... d.	0657	1018	1428	1633	1923
Kouvola .... a.	0742	1103	1513	1715	2008

Local trains **RIIHIMÄKI - LAHTI** and v.v.
59 km. Journey time: 40 – 41 minutes. 2nd class only.
From Riihimäki at 0615 ⚒, 0715 ⚒, 0815 and hourly until 1915; then 2115 and 2215. **From Lahti** at 0546 Ⓐ, 0627 ⑥, 0706 ⚒, 0806 and hourly until 2006; then 2206.

J – To / from Kajaani (Table **798**).

K – To / from Kuopio (Table **798**).

L – (12) Helsinki - Kouvola - Kuopio (- Kajaani ⚒) (- Oulu Ⓐ). See Table **798**.

M – (12) (Oulu ②–⑥ -) (Kajaani ②–⑦ -) Kuopio - Kouvola - Helsinki.

O – To / from Oulu via Kuopio (Table **798**).

⊙ – For Helsinki ✈ Vantaa.

⊡ – Other local journeys Helsinki - Lahti and v.v. (journey time 61 – 70 minutes): **From Helsinki** at 0635 and hourly until 1435; then 1533 Ⓐ, 1535 ⑥⑦, 1635, 1735, 1835, 1935, 2035, 2135 and 2312. **From Lahti** at 0530 Ⓐ, 0621 ⑥⑦, 0721 ⑥⑦, 0802, 0912, 1021, 1121 and hourly until 2321.

798 KOUVOLA - KUOPIO - OULU

km		*IC* 711		*IC* 63	*IC* 713		*IC* 65		*S* 67	*S* 67	*S* 67	*IC* 717		701	*S* 69		*S* 89		*IC* 73
		✕		✕	2🍷		✕		✕	✕	✕	2🍷		2	✕		✕		✕
		R								⚒	Ⓐ	⑦		Ⓑ	Ⓑ		⑦		
	Helsinki **797** ... d.	...	...	0817	...	...	1117	...	1417	1417	1417	...	...	*1517*	1617	...	1727	...	1917
0	**Kouvola** .... d.	...	...	0945	...	...	1255	...	1548	1548	1548	...	...	1649	1747	...	|	...	2047
113	Mikkeli .... d.	...	...	1051	...	...	1359	...	1655	1655	1655	...	...	1752	1851	...	◇	...	2150
184	Pieksämäki .... d.	...	...	1131	...	...	1438	...	1738	1738	1738	...	...	1837	1932	...	2137	...	2229
273	**Kuopio** .... a.	...	...	1220	...	...	1528	...	1832	1832	1832	...	...	1927	2023	...	2225	...	2321
273	**Kuopio** .... d.	0753	...	...	1245	...	1543	...	...	1838	1838	1838	...	...	2027	...	...	...	...
358	Iisalmi .... d.	0857	...	...	1344	...	1643	...	...	1937	1937	1937	...	...	2131	...	...	...	...
441	**Kajaani** .... a.	0950	...	...	1432	...	1731	...	...	2032	2032	2032	...	...	2220	...	...	...	...
441	**Kajaani** .... d.	0957	...	...	1434	...	1748	...	...	...	2115	2115	...	...	...	...	...	...	...
484	Paltamo .... d.	1028	...	...	1505	...	1819	...	...	...	2149	2149	...	...	...	...	...	...	...
633	**Oulu** .... a.	1224	...	...	1651	...	2010	...	...	...	2330	2330	...	...	...	...	...	...	...

	700	*IC* 62		*S* 64	*IC* 74		*IC* 714	*S* 66	*S* 66	*S* 66		*IC* 716	*IC* 68		*IC* 70		*S* 152		*IC* 710
	2	✕		✕	✕		2🍷	✕	✕	✕		2🍷	✕		✕		✕		✕
	⚒	⚒		⚒	⑦		①	②–⑥	②–⑦								⑦		V
Oulu .... d.	...	...	...	...	...	...	0655	0655	...	...	...	1000	...	...	1246	...	...	...	1742
Paltamo .... d.	...	...	...	...	...	...	0839	0839	...	...	...	1146	...	...	1434	...	...	...	1930
Kajaani .... a.	...	...	...	...	...	...	0909	0909	...	...	...	1215	...	...	1514	...	...	...	2000
Kajaani .... d.	...	...	...	0633	...	...	0923	0923	0923	...	...	1217	...	...	1517	...	...	...	2006
Iisalmi .... d.	...	...	...	0725	...	...	1017	1017	1017	...	...	1308	...	...	1611	...	...	...	2057
Kuopio .... a.	...	...	...	0821	...	...	1115	1115	1115	...	...	1407	...	...	1708	...	...	...	2153
Kuopio .... d.	0440	0535	...	0826	0826	...	...	1123	1123	1123	...	...	1430	...	1712	...	1938	...	...
Pieksämäki .... d.	0533	0629	...	0922	0922	...	...	1226t	1226t	1226t	...	...	1526	...	1814	...	2035	...	...
Mikkeli .... d.	0613	0709	...	1002	1002	...	...	1306	1306	1306	...	...	1606	...	1854	...	◇	...	...
Kouvola .... a.	0715	0811	...	1106	1106	...	...	1409	1409	1409	...	...	1712	...	1956	...	|	...	...
Helsinki **797** ... a.	*0842*	0942	...	1242	1242	...	...	1539	1539	1539	...	...	1842	...	2142	...	0033	...	...

IISALMI - YLIVIESKA

km		⚒2	2
0	**Iisalmi** .... d.	0737	1647
99	Haapajärvi .... d.	0847	1753
154	**Ylivieska** .... a.	0923	1829

	2		Ⓑ2
Ylivieska .... d.	1414	...	2022
Haapajärvi .... d.	1450	...	2058
Iisalmi .... a.	1600	...	2209

R – To Rovaniemi (Table **794**).

V – From Rovaniemi on ①③④⑤⑦ (Table **794**). Runs as *IC* **708** on ②⑥.

t – Arrives 1216.

◇ – Via Tampere (Table **795**).

366 *Please check times locally if planning to travel on or around the dates of public holidays* 12

GERMANY

Operator: Principal operator is Deutsche Bahn AG (DB) www.bahn.de
Many regional services are run by private operators – these are specified in the table heading (or by footnotes for individual trains).

Services: Trains convey first- and second-class seating accommodation unless otherwise shown (by '2' in the column heading, a footnote or a general note in the table heading).
Overnight sleeping car (🛏) and couchette (🛌) trains do not necessarily convey seating accommodation - refer to individual footnotes for details. Descriptions of sleeping and couchette cars appear on page 8.

There are various categories of trains in Germany. The type of train is indicated by the following letter codes above each column (or by a general note in the table heading):

ICE	**InterCity Express**	German high-speed (230 – 320 km/h) train.	IRE	**InterRegio Express**	Regional express train.
EC	**EuroCity**	International express train.	RE	**Regional Express**	Regional semi-fast train.
IC	**InterCity**	Internal express train.	RB	**Regional Bahn**	Regional stopping train.
TGV	**Train à Grande Vitesse**	French high-speed (320 km/h) train.	S-Bahn		Suburban stopping train.
RJ	**Railjet**	Austrian high-speed train.			

Overnight services:

EN	**EuroNight** ÖBB nightjet	Quality overnight express train operated by Austrian Railways. All services convey *Deluxe* sleeping cars (1/2/3 berth) with en-suite shower and WC, standard sleeping cars (1/2/3 berth), couchettes (4/6 berth) and 2nd class seats (in a compartment). **Reservation compulsory.** For further details see pages 8 and 33.
EN	**EuroNight**	Other international overnight express train. See also pages 8 and 33.
D	**Durchgangszug**	Or **Schnellzug** – other express train (day or night); rarely used nowadays.

Other long-distance service operators:

ALX	**alex**	Regional express train operated by *Vogtlandbahn* on the routes München - Oberstdorf/Lindau and München - Regensburg - Hof (also international services München - Regensburg - Schwandorf - Furth im Wald - Praha).
HKX	**Hamburg-Köln-Express**	Operates a limited number of fast services on the Hamburg - Köln route. DB tickets are **not** valid.

Timings: Valid **December 11, 2016 - June 10, 2017** (except where shown otherwise).

Many long distance trains operate on selected days only for part of the journey. These are often indicated in the train composition footnote by showing the dated journey segment within brackets. For example '🔲 Leipzig - Hannover (- Dortmund ⑦)' means that the train runs daily (or as shown in the column heading) between Leipzig and Hannover, but only continues to Dortmund on Sundays. Additional footnotes/symbols are often used to show more complex running dates, e.g. '🔲 (München ⊡ -) Nürnberg - Hamburg' means that the train runs only on dates in note ⊡ between München and Nürnberg, but runs daily (or as shown in the column heading) between Nürnberg and Hamburg. Please note that international overnight trains that are not intended for internal German journeys are not usually shown in the German section (refer to the International section).

Engineering work may occasionally disrupt services at short notice (especially at weekends and during holiday periods), so it is advisable to check timings locally before travelling. Please see panel below for information regarding major engineering work alterations affecting long-distance services during this timetable period.

Tickets: There are three standard levels of fares, corresponding to travel by (in ascending order of price): ○ Regional trains. ○ *IC/EC* trains. ○ High-speed *ICE* (also *TGV/RJ*) trains. A variable supplement is payable for sleeping car and couchette accommodation (and sometimes seating) on overnight *EN* trains, the cost of which depends on the type required. Please note that Interrail and Eurail pass holders may have to pay a special fare on overnight *EN* trains.

Catering: Two types of catering are indicated in the tables: ☕ Bordbistro – hot and cold drinks, snacks and light meals; ✕ Bordrestaurant – full restaurant car service (bordbistro also available). First class passengers on *ICE* and *IC* trains benefit from an at-seat service. On overnight trains ☕ indicates that drinks and light snacks are available, usually from the sleeping or couchette car attendant (the refreshment service may only be available to sleeping and couchette car passengers).

Reservations: Reservation compulsory for travel in sleeping and couchette accommodation on overnight *EN* trains (also in the seating accommodation of ÖBB *nightjet* services). Optional reservations are available on *ICE/IC* trains (€ 4,50).

Holidays: Jan. 1, Apr. 14, 17, May 1, 25, June 5, Oct. 3, Dec. 25, 26 are German national public holidays (trains marked ✗ or Ⓐ do not run). In addition there are other regional holidays as follows: Jan. 6 – Heilige Drei Könige (Epiphany), June 15 – Fronleichnam (Corpus Christi), Aug. 15 – Mariä Himmelfahrt (Assumption), Oct. 31 – Reformationstag (Reformation Day), Nov. 1 – Allerheiligen (All Saints Day) and Nov. 22 – Buß und Bettag. On these days the regional service is usually that applicable on ⑦ (please refer to individual footnotes). **Please see panel below for information regarding Christmas/New Year holidays.**

CHRISTMAS/NEW YEAR HOLIDAY VARIATIONS IN GERMANY

Owing to the complex nature of running dates over the Christmas/New Year period we will not be showing full details of variations to running dates during the period **December 23 to January 2**. This should drastically reduce the number of notes in some of our tables and hopefully make them easier to read. Holiday variations in April, May and June are shown, although these are subject to alteration.

There are a few general rules for **long-distance trains** which are outlined below (other variations are possible and readers are advised to check before travelling during this period):

☐ Trains shown as running on ①–⑥ do not usually run on Dec. 26.
☐ Trains shown as running on ①–⑤ do not usually run on Dec. 26.
☐ Trains shown as running on ①–④ do not usually run on Dec. 26.
☐ Trains shown as running on ① may not run on Dec. 26; may also run on Dec. 27.

☐ Trains shown as running on ⑧ do not usually run on Dec. 25.
☐ Trains shown as running on ⑤⑦ may not run on Dec. 25; may also run on Dec. 26.
☐ Trains shown as running on ⑦ may not run on Dec. 25; may also run on Dec. 26.
☐ Trains may also be cancelled on certain other days over the Christmas/New Year period, particularly on Dec. 24, 25, 26, 31, Jan. 1 (even if shown as running daily).

Running dates of **regional trains** are usually shown in our tables using the standard symbols ✗, Ⓐ, Ⓒ and ✝. On Dec. 26 trains marked ✗ and Ⓐ do not run, but trains marked Ⓒ and ✝ do. **On most regional routes services will shut down earlier than normal on Dec. 24, 31 and early morning trains may not run on Dec. 25, Jan. 1.**

MAJOR ENGINEERING WORK ALTERATIONS AFFECTING LONG DISTANCE SERVICES

☐ ⑥⑦ Feb. 11 - Apr. 2 (also Apr. 14–17). Major alterations in the Frankfurt area affecting services that use the Frankfurt - Fulda/Würzburg routes. Earlier departures/later arrivals at Frankfurt (Main) Hbf possible (timing variations may also occur at Frankfurt Flughafen, Hanau and Fulda). Many services call at Frankfurt (Main) **Süd** instead of Frankfurt (Main) Hbf and some do not call at Hanau Hbf. Fast *ICE Sprinter* services between Frankfurt and Berlin via Erfurt do not run between Frankfurt and Erfurt. Please note that, in many cases, different train numbers apply on these dates. Late evening services on ⑤ Feb. 10 - Mar. 31 (also Apr. 13) may also be affected. Readers travelling to or from Frankfurt on these dates are strongly advised to check timings beforehand.

☐ Major work to upgrade the line between Eisenach and Bebra/Bad Hersfeld will affect services in Table 850 from February 11 to May 22. A special version of the table will be found on page 560 to help show alternative schedules during the period from March 11 to May 22 when the most significant alterations are in place. Timings between Erfurt and Berlin will also be subject to change during certain periods owing to work in the Halle area, further complicating services in this particular table. The weekend changes in the Frankfurt area, mentioned above, also affect journeys from/to Frankfurt. Unfortunately it is not possible for us to show all variations on this route and so readers intending to use services in Table 850 are strongly advised to confirm timings before travelling.

☐ From March 6 to June 25 all services between Nürnberg and Würzburg are subject to alteration. Timings München - Nürnberg - Würzburg and v.v. may vary by up to 40 minutes (earlier departures/later arrivals possible) and the following trains do not run between München and Nürnberg: 523, 526, 527/1127, 620, 621, 624/1124, 625, 628, 629 and 722/1122. Certain services do not call at Ingolstadt or Nürnberg. Other services between München and Nürnberg may also be retimed by a few minutes. Updated timings will be shown in the March edition.

☐ Timings in the Berlin area (also at Stendal) of services using the high-speed line via Wolfsburg are subject to alteration from May 13 to Aug. 31. Timings may vary by up to 30 minutes (earlier departures/later arrivals possible). *IC* services to/from Amsterdam and Osnabrück do not call at Berlin Spandau. Other *IC* services running to/from/via Dortmund are subject to considerably extended journey times with some services diverted via Magdeburg (meaning calls at Berlin Spandau and Wolfsburg may be omitted). Please note that certain *ICE* services are diverted in the Berlin area and do not serve Berlin Ostbahnhof.

☐ From February 9 all services between Berlin and Eberswalde (Table 845) are diverted via an alternative route with extended journey times. Most regional services between Berlin and Stralsund run from/to Berlin Lichtenberg. Regional services between Berlin and Lutherstadt Wittenberg/Falkenberg continue to run from/to Berlin Hbf, so not connecting with the Stralsund trains. A special version of Table 845 will be found on page 559 with full details of amended timings from February 9 for both long-distance and regional services.

For more detail of the Ruhr area see inset

Table 800 shows all long-distance trains which pass through the Ruhr area below. Local RE and S-Bahn services are shown in Table 802.

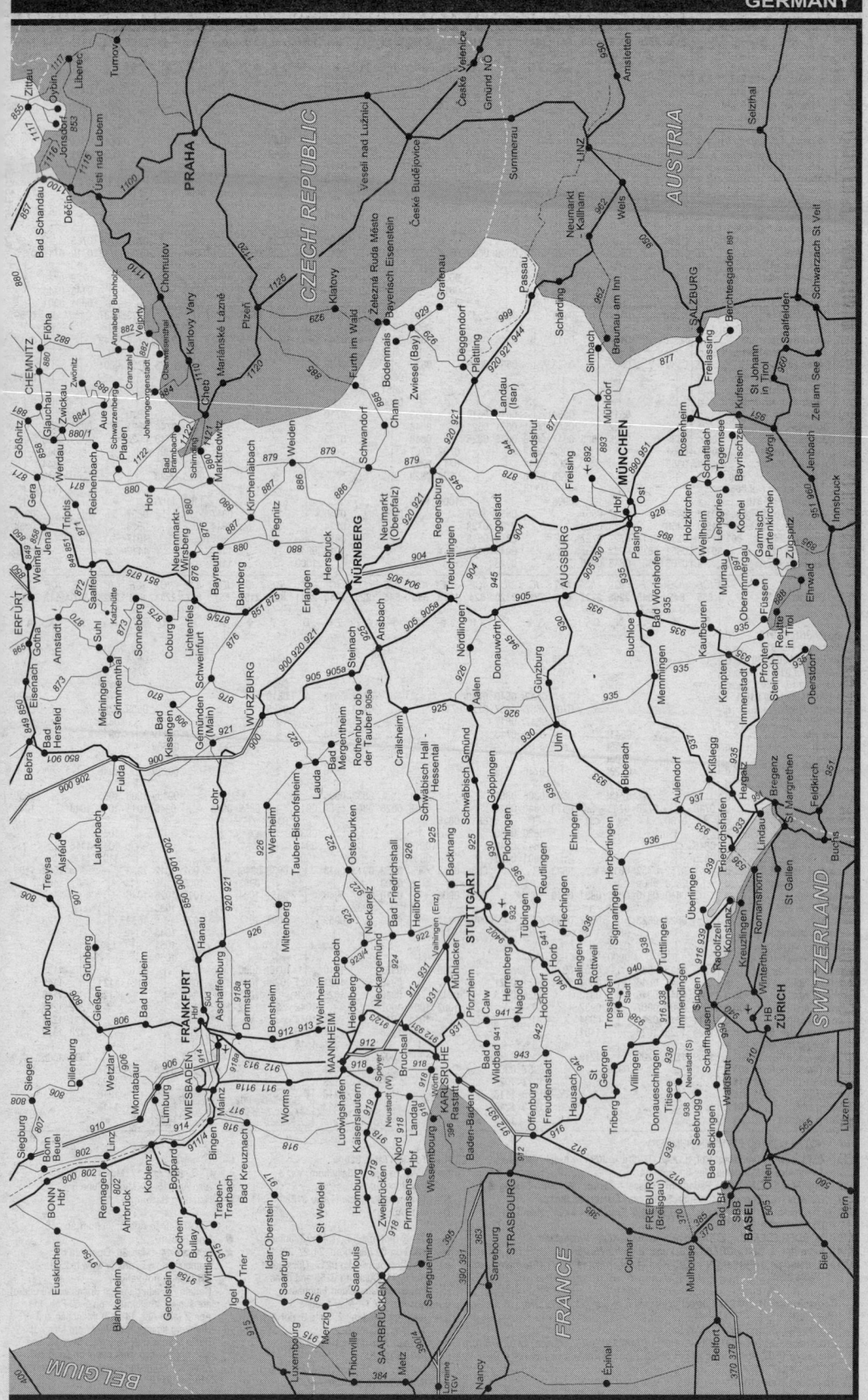

See page 367 for a summary of Christmas / New Year alterations

800 KOBLENZ - KÖLN - DORTMUND - HAMBURG

km	SEE NOTE ⊠	IC 2020	IC 2326	IC 2228	IC 2228	ICE 541	IC 2445	IC 2214	IC 2314	ICE 853	ICE 843	IC 2208	ICE 543	IC 208	ICE 1098	ICE 222	ICE 222	HKX 1800	ICE 553	ICE 543	IC 2212	ICE 618	ICE 1018	IC 2443	IC 2410
			Ⓐ	①g	①–⑤	①–⑥	①–⑥	Q		①–⑥		⑥B			①–④	①–⑤		⑥	①–⑥			①–⑥	⑦w	①–⑥	⑥
				🍷	a🍷	e✕	eD	🍷	🍷♦	e✕	✕	N	✕	K	m✕	aA	A🍷	★	e✕	✕	🍷♦	e🍷	🍷	eD	♦
	Basel SBB 🏛 **912** d.	...	...	...	...	...	...	...	...	...	...	...	...	2313	...	🍷	...	🍷	...	...	...	...	...	...	...
	Karlsruhe Hbf **912** d.	...	...	...	...	...	...	...	...	...	...	...	...	0130	...	...	...	...	...	...	...	0349	0349	...	...
	München Hbf **904 930** d.	...	...	...	...	...	...	...	...	...	...	...	...	|	...	...	...	...	...	...	...	0001	0001	...	...
	Stuttgart Hbf **912** d.	...	...	...	...	...	...	...	...	...	...	...	...	|	...	...	...	...	...	...	...	0230	0230	...	...
	Nürnberg Hbf **920** d.	...	...	...	...	...	...	...	...	...	...	...	...	|	...	...	...	...	...	...	...	|	|	...	...
	Frankfurt (Main) Hbf **910/1** d.	2324	...	...	...	...	...	...	...	...	...	...	...	0342	...	0456	...	...	...	...	...	0544	0544	...	...
	Frankfurt Flughafen ✈ § d.	2339	...	...	...	...	...	...	...	...	...	...	...	0357	...	0512	...	...	...	...	...	0601	0601	...	...
	Mainz Hbf **911** d.	0001	...	...	...	...	...	...	...	...	...	...	...	0417	...	|	...	...	...	...	...	|	|	...	...
0	**Koblenz** Hbf d.	0058	...	...	...	...	...	...	...	...	...	...	...	0513	...	|	...	...	0545	...	0605	|	|	...	...
18	Andernach d.	0110	...	...	...	...	...	...	...	...	...	...	...	|	...	|	...	...	0558	...	0618	|	|	...	...
39	Remagen d.	0122	...	...	...	...	...	...	...	...	...	...	...	|	...	|	...	...	|	...	0631	|	|	...	...
59	**Bonn** Hbf d.	0138	...	...	...	...	...	...	...	...	...	...	...	0546	...	|	...	...	0622	...	0646	|	|	...	...
	Köln/Bonn Flughafen ✈ d.	|	...	...	...	...	...	...	...	...	...	...	...	|	...	|	...	...	|	...	|	|	|	...	...
93	**Köln** Hbf a.	0159b	...	...	...	...	...	...	...	...	...	...	...	0605	...	0621	...	...	0643	...	0705	0706	0705	...	...
93	**Köln** Hbf d.	0213c	...	0408	...	0429	0512	0509	0509	0544	0528	0541	0600	0610	0615	0628	0628	0701	0648	...	0709	0713	0710	0712	0720
94	**Köln** Messe/Deutz d.	|	...	|	...	|	|	|	|	|	|	|	|	|	|	|	|	|	|	...	|	|	|	|	|
	Solingen Hbf d.	|	...	|	...	|	0530	|	|	0603	|	|	|	|	|	|	|	|	|	...	|	|	0728	0730	|
	Wuppertal Hbf d.	|	...	|	...	|	0544	|	|	0616	|	|	|	|	|	|	|	|	0716	...	|	|	0743	0744	|
	Hagen Hbf d.	|	...	|	...	|	0601	|	|	0635	|	|	|	|	|	|	|	|	0735	...	|	|	0801	0801	|
133	**Düsseldorf** Hbf d.	0236c	...	0432	...	0453	|	0533	0533	|	0552	0606	0627	0633	0638	0656	0656	0727	|	←	0733	0737	|	|	0759
140	Düsseldorf Flughafen ✈ d.	0243c	...	|	...	0501	|	|	|	|	0600	0613	0635	|	|	|	|	|	|	0646	|	|	|	|	|
157	**Duisburg** Hbf d.	0253c	...	0447	...	0511	|	0546	0546	|	0610	0626	→	0646	0651	0713	0713	0742	|	0701	0746	0749	|	|	0817
165	Oberhausen Hbf d.	|	...	|	...	|	|	|	|	|	|	0633	...	|	|	0719	0719	|	|	|	|	|	|	|	|
176	**Essen** Hbf d.	0309	...	0500	...	0523	|	0559	0559	|	0623	|	...	0659	0703	...	...	0755	|	0723	0759	0801	|	|	|
	Gelsenkirchen Hbf d.	|	...	|	...	|	|	|	|	|	|	0645	...	|	|	...	...	0805	|	|	|	...	|	|	0839
	Wanne-Eickel Hbf d.	|	...	|	...	|	|	|	|	|	|	0651	...	|	|	...	...	|	|	|	|	...	|	|	|
	Recklinghausen Hbf d.	|	...	|	...	|	|	|	|	|	|	0700	...	|	|	...	...	|	|	|	|	...	|	|	|
192	Bochum Hbf d.	0319	...	0511	...	0534	|	0610	0610	|	0635	|	...	0710	|	...	...	|	|	0735	0810	...	|	|	|
210	**Dortmund** Hbf a.	0329	...	0522	...	0545	0621	0621	0621	|	0646	|	...	0721	|	...	...	|	|	0746	0821	...	0821	0821	|
210	**Dortmund** Hbf **805** d.	0332	...	0525	0525	0547	0628	0625	0625	|	0648	|	...	0725	|	...	...	|	|	0748	0825	...	...	0828	|
	Hamm (Westf) **805** a.	0351	...	|	|	0602	0642	|	|	0702	0707	|	...	|	|	...	...	|	0802	0807	|	...	...	0842	|
	Hamm (Westf) d.	0353	...	|	|	0604	0644	|	|	0711	0711	|	...	|	|	...	...	|	0811	0811	|	...	...	0844	|
	Hannover Hbf **810** a.	|	...	|	|	0728	0818	|	|	0828	0828	|	...	|	|	...	...	|	0928	0928	|	...	...	1018	|
	Leipzig Hbf **866** a.	|	...	|	|	|	1118	|	|	|	|	|	...	|	|	...	...	|	|	|	|	...	...	1318	|
	Berlin Hbf **810** a.	|	...	|	|	0906	...	|	|	1009	1009	|	...	|	|	...	...	|	1106	1106	|	...	...	...	|
266	Münster (Westf) Hbf **801** d.	0417	...	0557	0557	...	...	0657	0657	...	...	0728	...	0758	|	...	...	0847	...	...	0857	...	...	...	0929
316	Osnabrück Hbf **801 815** d.	0450	...	0623	0623	...	...	0723	0723	...	...	...	...	0824	|	...	...	0914	...	...	0923	...	...	...	0954
438	**Bremen** Hbf **801 815** d.	0555	0717	0727	0727	...	...	0818	0818	...	...	...	...	0918	|	...	...	|	...	...	1017	...	...	...	|
553	**Hamburg** Hbf **801** a.	0651	0812	0832	0832	...	...	0913	0913	...	...	...	...	1013	0945	...	...	1107	...	...	1112	...	...	...	1138z
560	**Hamburg** Altona a.	0706	0827	0848	0848	...	...	0928	...	...	...	...	...	...	1000	...	...	1123	...	...	...	...	...	...	...

SEE NOTE ⊠	ICE 855	ICE 845	ICE 1045	IC 2206	IC 2222	ICE 616	IC 2220	IC 2320	ICE 824	ICE 1223	ICE 555	ICE 545	ICE 220	IC 2310	IC 2441	ICE 822	IC 2155	ICE 857	ICE 847	IC 2204	ICE 614	IC 2028	ICE 557	ICE 547	ICE 128
		①–⑤	⑥⑦	L	Ⓐ			⊡	①–⑤							①–⑥									
	✕	✕	✕	N	C🍷	🍷	🍷♦	🍷	aH	🍷♦	✕	✕	A🍷	🍷♦	D	e🍷	♦	✕	✕	E	🍷	K🍷	✕	✕	A🍷
Basel SBB 🏛 **912** d.	...	...	...	...	...	...	...	...	🍷	...	...	...	...	...	...	...	...	...	...	...	...	...	...	...	...
Karlsruhe Hbf **912** d.	...	...	...	...	...	...	...	...	...	...	...	...	...	...	...	...	...	...	...	...	...	...	...	...	...
München Hbf **904 930** d.	...	...	...	...	...	0324	...	...	...	...	...	...	...	...	...	0449	...	...	...	...	0524	...	...	...	...
Stuttgart Hbf **912** d.	...	...	...	...	...	0551	...	...	...	...	...	...	...	...	...	|	...	...	...	...	0751	...	...	...	...
Nürnberg Hbf **920** d.	...	...	...	...	...	|	...	...	...	...	...	...	...	...	...	0600	...	...	...	...	|	0527	...	...	...
Frankfurt (Main) Hbf **910/1** d.	...	...	...	...	...	|	0542r	0542	0710	...	...	...	0727	0638	...	0810	...	...	...	...	|	0742	...	...	0929
Frankfurt Flughafen ✈ § d.	...	...	...	...	...	0709	0557r	0557	0725	0714a	...	...	0743	0657	...	0825	...	...	...	...	0909	0758	...	...	0943
Mainz Hbf **911** d.	...	...	...	...	...	|	0617r	0617	|	|	...	...	|	0717	...	|	...	...	...	...	|	0820	...	...	|
Koblenz Hbf d.	...	...	...	0641t	...	|	0713	0713	|	|	...	...	|	0813	...	|	...	...	...	0841v	|	0913	...	...	|
Andernach d.	...	...	...	0656t	...	|	|	|	|	|	...	...	|	|	...	|	...	...	...	0856v	|	|	...	...	|
Remagen d.	...	...	...	0708t	...	|	|	|	|	|	...	...	|	|	...	|	...	...	...	0908v	|	|	...	...	|
Bonn Hbf d.	...	...	...	0723t	...	|	0746	0746	|	|	...	...	|	0846	...	|	...	...	...	0923v	|	0946	...	...	|
Köln/Bonn Flughafen ✈ d.	...	0712	...	|	...	|	|	|	|	|	...	...	|	|	...	|	...	...	...	|	|	|	...	...	|
Köln Hbf a.	...	|	...	0743t	...	0805	0805	0805	|	|	...	...	0833	0905	...	|	...	...	...	0943v	1005	1005	...	...	1032
Köln Hbf d.	0748	|	0728	0746	...	0810	0810	0810	|	|	0848	0828	0844	0909	0912	|	0859	0948	...	0946	1011	1010	1048	...	1041
Köln Messe/Deutz d.	|	0730	|	|	...	|	|	|	0817	0825	|	|	|	|	|	0917	|	|	...	|	|	|	|	...	|
Solingen Hbf d.	|	|	|	|	...	|	0830	0830	|	|	|	|	|	|	0930	|	|	|	...	|	|	1030	|	...	|
Wuppertal Hbf d.	0816	|	|	|	...	|	0843	0843	|	|	0916	|	|	|	0944	|	|	1016	...	|	|	1043	1116	...	|
Hagen Hbf d.	0835	|	|	|	...	|	0901	0901	|	|	0935	|	|	|	1001	|	|	1035	...	|	|	1101	1135	...	|
Düsseldorf Hbf d.	|	0752	0752	0812	...	0833	|	|	0838	0848	|	0852	0913	0933	|	0938	0946j	|	0952	1012	1033	|	|	1052	1109
Düsseldorf Flughafen ✈ d.	|	0800	0800	|	...	|	|	|	|	|	|	0900	|	|	|	|	0953	|	1000	|	|	|	|	1100	|
Duisburg Hbf d.	|	0810	0810	0826	0831	0846	|	|	0851	0903	|	0910	0927	0946	|	0951	1004	|	1010	1026	1046	|	|	1110	1126
Oberhausen Hbf d.	|	|	|	0834	|	|	|	|	|	|	|	|	0932	|	|	|	|	|	|	1033	|	|	|	|	1132
Essen Hbf d.	|	0823	0823	|	0847	0859	|	|	0902	0917	|	0923	...	0959	|	1004	1017	|	1023	|	1059	|	|	1123	...
Gelsenkirchen Hbf d.	|	|	|	0846	|	|	|	|	...	|	|	|	...	|	|	|	|	|	|	1045	|	|	|	|	...
Wanne-Eickel Hbf d.	|	|	|	0852	|	|	|	|	...	|	|	|	...	|	|	|	|	|	|	1051	|	|	|	|	...
Recklinghausen Hbf d.	|	|	|	0900	|	|	|	|	...	|	|	|	...	|	|	|	|	|	|	1059	|	|	|	|	...
Bochum Hbf d.	|	0835	0835	|	0857	0910	|	|	...	0930	|	0935	...	1010	|	1016h	1030	|	1035	|	1110	|	|	1135	...
Dortmund Hbf a.	|	0846	0846	|	0909	0921	0921	0921	...	0940	|	0946	...	1021	1021	1029h	1041	|	1046	|	1121	1121	|	1146	...
Dortmund Hbf **805** d.	|	0848	0848	|	0912	...	0925	0925	...	0942	|	0948	...	1025	1028	...	1043	|	1048	|	...	1125	|	1148	...
Hamm (Westf) **805** a.	0902	0907	0907	|	0932	...	|	|	...	1002	1002	1007	...	|	1042	...	1102	1102	1107	|	...	|	1202	1207	...
Hamm (Westf) d.	0911	0911	0911	|	0934	...	|	|	...	...	1011	1011	...	|	1044	...	...	1111	1111	|	...	|	1211	1211	...
Hannover Hbf **810** a.	1028	1028	1028	|	1101	...	|	|	...	...	1128	1128	...	|	1218	...	...	1228	1228	|	...	|	1328	1328	...
Leipzig Hbf **866** a.	|	|	|	|	|	...	|	|	...	...	|	|	...	|	1518	...	...	|	|	|	...	|	|	|	...
Berlin Hbf **810** a.	1209	1209	1209	|	1249	...	|	|	...	...	1307	1307	...	|	...	...	...	1409	1409	|	...	|	1506	1506	...
Münster (Westf) Hbf **801** d.	...	...	...	0930	...	...	0957	0957	...	...	...	...	...	1057	...	...	...	...	...	1128	...	1157	...	...	...
Osnabrück Hbf **801 815** d.	...	...	...	...	...	...	1023	1023	...	...	...	...	...	1123	...	...	...	...	...	...	...	1223	...	...	...
Bremen Hbf **801 815** d.	...	...	...	...	...	...	1118	1118	...	...	...	...	...	1218							...	1318	...	...	...
Hamburg Hbf **801** a.	...	...	...	...	...	...	1213	1213	...	...	...	...	...	1313							...	1413	...	...	...
Hamburg Altona a.	...	...	...	...	...	...	...	1228	...	...	...	...	...	...							...	...	...	...	...

*See Table **802** for Rhein-Ruhr local RE and S-Bahn services*

♦ – **NOTES** (LISTED BY TRAIN NUMBER)

1223 – [12] and 🍷 (Darmstadt Hbf, d. 0648 ①–⑤**a** -) Köln - Kassel - München. Terminates at Dortmund May 6 - June 14.
2155 – Until May 5. [12] Köln - Paderborn - Kassel (- Erfurt - Weimar - Leipzig ●).
2212 – RÜGEN – [12] and 🍷 Koblenz - Stralsund - Ostseebad Binz.
2220 – ⑤⑦ to Apr. 2; ⑧ from Apr. 7. [12] and 🍷 Frankfurt - K]öln - Hamburg - Lübeck Hbf (a. 1300).
2310 – NORDFRIESLAND – [12] and 🍷 Frankfurt - Köln - Westerland.
2314 – From Apr. 7. DEICHGRAF – [12] and 🍷 Köln - Westerland.
2410 – ⑥ from Apr. 8. FEHMARN – [12] Köln - Lübeck Hbf (a. 1237) - Fehmarn-Burg (Table **825**).

A – To Amsterdam (Table **28**). Subject to alteration on Jan. 21, 22, 29, Mar. 18, 19, May 20, 21.
B – ⑥ from Apr. 8 (also Apr. 13, May 25).
C – From Aachen Hbf (d. 0707), Rheydt Hbf (d. 0748), Mönchengladbach Hbf (d. 0755), Viersen (d. 0803) and Krefeld Hbf (d. 0816). Also calls at Mülheim (Ruhr), d. 0839.
D – To Dresden (Table **842**).
E – To Emden (Table **812**).
H – From Würzburg (Table **920**) on ①–④ (not Apr. 13, May 25).
K – To Kiel (Table **820**).
L – ①–⑥ to Apr. 1; daily from Apr. 3 (not June 5).
N – To Norddeich Mole (Table **812**).
Q – Until Apr. 6.

a – ①–⑤ (not Apr. 14, 17, May 1, June 5).
b – 0206 on © (also Feb. 24, 27, 28).
c – On ⑥ departs Köln 0217, Düsseldorf Hbf 0241, Duisburg 0255 and does **not** call at Düsseldorf Flughafen.
e – Not Apr. 15, 17, May 1, June 5.
g – Also Apr. 18, May 2, June 6; not Apr. 17, May 1, June 5.
h – ⑥ (also Apr. 14; not Apr. 15).
j – Arrives 0925.
m – Not Apr. 13, 17, May 1, 24, 25, June 5.
r – ⑤ to Mar. 31; ⑧ from Apr. 7.
t – Ⓐ only.
v – ①–⑥ (not Apr. 17, May 1, June 5).
w – Also Apr. 15, 17, May 1, June 5.
z – Hamburg **Harburg**.

⊡ – ①②③④⑥ to Apr. 8; ⑥ from Apr. 15.
● – Until Feb. 10.
★ – Not Jan. 14 - Mar. 25. Operated by Hamburg-Köln-Express. www.hkx.de. **DB tickets not valid**.
⊠ – Certain Frankfurt timings (trains via Nürnberg) are subject to alteration on ⑥⑦ Feb. 11 - Apr. 2 (also Apr. 14 – 17). München and Nürnberg timings may vary from March 6. Berlin timings may vary from May 13. See also engineering work panel on page 367.
§ – Frankfurt Flughafen Fernbahnhof (Tables **910** and **911**).

KOBLENZ - KÖLN - DORTMUND - HAMBURG 800

SEE NOTE ⊠	ICE 916	IC 1959	IC 2010	IC 2010	IC 2010	IC 2018	HKX 1802	IC 2216	ICE 202	IC 2049	ICE 728	ICE 859	ICE 849	IC 2202	ICE 612	IC 2226	ICE 726	ICE 559	ICE 549	ICE 126	ICE 914	IC 2218	ICE 200	IC 2047	ICE 724
	Q	⑤⑦	Ⓐ	⑤f	⑦b	⑥	⑤⑦		①–④	⑤–⑦							①–⑥				①–⑥		⑥k	Ⓑq	
	✕	♦	T🍷	🍷		♦	★🍷	🍷♦	m🍷	vD	🍷	✕	✕	N	🍷	🍷♦	e🍷	✕	✕	A🍷	e🍷	🍷	🍷	D	🍷
Basel SBB ▦ **912** d.	...	...	...	...	...	...	...	...	0713	...	...	...	...	...	...	...	...	...	...	...	...	...	0913	...	...
Karlsruhe Hbf **912** d.	...	...	...	...	...	...	...	...	0900	...	...	...	...	...	...	...	...	...	...	...	...	...	1100	...	...
München Hbf **904 930** d.	...	...	...	...	...	...	...	...	│	...	0652	...	...	...	0727	...	0755	...	...	...	...	...	│	...	0852
Stuttgart Hbf **912** d.	0837	...	0714	0714	...	0712	...	0737	│	...	│	...	...	...	0951	...	│	...	...	...	1041	0937	│	...	│
Nürnberg Hbf **920** d.	│	...	│	│	...	│	...	│	│	...	0800	...	...	...	│	0729d	0900	...	...	...	│	│	│	...	1000
Frankfurt (Main) Hbf **910/1** d.	│	...	│	│	...	│	...	│	│	...	1010	...	...	...	│	0942	1110	...	...	1129	│	│	│	...	1210
Frankfurt Flughafen ✈ § d.	0955	...	│	│	...	│	...	│	1009	...	1025	...	...	...	1109	0958	1122	...	...	1143	1155	│	1209	...	1225
Mainz Hbf **911** d.	│	...	0848	0848	...	0848	...	0920	│	...	│	...	...	...	│	1020	│	...	...	│	│	1120	│	...	│
Koblenz Hbf d.	│	...	0943	0943	...	0943	...	1013	│	...	│	...	...	...	│	1113	│	...	...	│	│	1213	│	...	│
Andernach d.	│	...	0956	0956	...	0956	...	│	│	...	│	...	...	...	│	│	│	...	...	│	│	│	│	...	│
Remagen d.	│	...	1008	1008	...	1008	...	│	│	...	│	...	...	...	│	│	│	...	...	│	│	│	│	...	│
Bonn Hbf d.	│	...	1023	1023	...	1023	...	1046	│	...	│	...	...	...	│	1146	│	1222e	...	│	│	1246	│	...	│
Köln/Bonn Flughafen ✈ d.	│	...	│	│	...	│	...	│	│	...	│	...	...	...	│	│	│	│	...	│	│	│	│	...	1314
Köln Hbf a.	│	...	1043	1043	...	1043	...	1105	1105	...	│	...	...	...	1205	1205	│	1243e	...	1232	│	1305	1305	...	│
Köln Hbf d.	│	...	1046	1046	1046	1046	1100	1109	1111	1113	│	1148	...	1146	1211	1210	│	1248	...	1241	│	1309	1311	1312	│
Köln Messe/Deutz d.	1046	...	│	│	│	│	│	│	│	│	1117	│	...	│	│	│	1228	│	...	│	1247	│	│	│	1327
Solingen Hbf d.	│	...	│	│	│	│	│	│	1129	1131	│	│	...	│	│	1230	│	│	...	│	│	│	1329	1330	│
Wuppertal Hbf d.	│	...	│	│	│	│	│	│	1143	1145	│	1216	...	│	│	1243	│	1316	...	│	│	│	1343	1344	│
Hagen Hbf d.	│	...	│	│	│	│	│	│	1201	1202	│	1235	...	│	│	1301	│	1335	...	│	│	│	1401	1401	│
Düsseldorf Hbf d.	1113	1113	1113	1118	1118	1118	1127	1133	│	│	1138	│	1152	1212	1233	│	1250	│	1254	1309	1313	1333	│	│	1348
Düsseldorf Flughafen ✈ d.	│	│	...	│	│	│	│	│	│	│	│	│	1200	│	│	│	│	│	│	│	│	│	│	│	│
Duisburg Hbf d.	1128	1129	...	1133	1133	│	1142	1146	│	│	1151	│	1210	1226	1246	│	1303	│	1310	1326	1328	1346	│	│	1402
Oberhausen Hbf d.	│	│	...	│	│	│	│	│	│	│	│	│	│	1234	│	│	│	│	│	1332	│	│	│	│	│
Essen Hbf d.	1141	1141	...	1147	1147	│	1155	1159	│	│	1204	│	1223	│	1259	│	1317	│	1323	...	1341	1359	│	│	1417
Gelsenkirchen Hbf d.	│	│	...	│	│	1148	1205	│	│	│	│	│	│	1246	│	│	│	│	│	...	│	│	│	│	│
Wanne-Eickel Hbf d.	│	│	...	│	│	│	│	│	│	│	│	│	│	1252	│	│	│	│	│	...	│	│	│	│	│
Recklinghausen Hbf d.	│	│	...	│	│	1159	│	│	│	│	│	│	│	1300	│	│	│	│	│	...	│	│	│	│	│
Bochum Hbf d.	1152	1152	...	1158	1158	│	│	1210	│	│	1216	│	1235	│	1310	│	1329h	│	1335	...	1352	1410	│	│	1429k
Dortmund Hbf a.	1203	1203	...	1209	1209	│	│	1221	1221	1222	1230	│	1246	│	1321	1321	1342h	│	1346	...	1403	1421	1421	1421	1442k
Dortmund Hbf **805** d.	...	1207	...	1212	1212	│	│	1225	...	1228	...	│	1248	│	...	1325	...	│	1348	...	...	1425	...	1428	...
Hamm (Westf) **805** a.	...	1228	...	1232	1232	│	│	│	...	1242	...	1302	1307	│	...	│	...	1402	1407	...	...	│	...	1442	...
Hamm (Westf) d.	...	1234	...	1234	1234	│	│	│	...	1244	...	1311	1311	│	...	│	...	1411	1411	...	...	│	...	1444	...
Hannover Hbf **810** a.	...	│	...	1401	1401	│	│	│	...	1418	...	1428	1428	│	...	│	...	1528	1528	...	...	│	...	1618	...
Leipzig Hbf **866** a.	...	│	...	│	│	│	│	│	...	1718	...	│	│	│	...	│	...	│	│	...	...	│	...	1918	...
Berlin Hbf **810** a.	...	1843	...	1553	1550	│	│	│	...	...	...	1609	1609	│	...	│	...	1706	1706	...	...	│	...	...	...
Münster (Westf) Hbf **801** d.	...	...	...	...	...	1228	1249	1257	...	...	...	...	...	1328	...	1357	...	...	...	...	...	1457	...	...	...
Osnabrück Hbf **801 815** d.	...	...	...	...	...	...	1316	1323	...	...	...	...	...	...	...	1423	...	...	...	...	...	1523	...	...	...
Bremen Hbf **801 815** d.	...	...	...	...	...	...	│	1417	...	...	...	...	...	...	...	1518	...	...	...	...	...	1618	...	...	...
Hamburg Hbf **801** a.	...	...	...	...	...	...	1507	1511	...	...	...	...	...	...	...	1613	...	...	...	...	...	1713	...	...	...
Hamburg Altona a.	...	...	...	...	...	...	1521	...	...	...	...	...	...	...	...	1628	...	...	...	...	...	1728	...	...	...

SEE NOTE ⊠	IC 2200	ICE 951	ICE 941	ICE 610	IC 2024	ICE 722	ICE 1122	ICE 651	ICE 641	IC 1926	ICE 124	IC 1920	IC 1216	IC 2312	ICE 108	IC 2045	ICE 720	IC 2157	ICE 953	ICE 943	IC 2006	IC 2014	IC 2004	ICE 518	IC 2026
						①–⑤	⑥⑦			①–④		⑦w	⑤f		⑥k	Ⓑq		Ⓑ	Ⓑq		⑥k	⑤f			
	N	✕	✕	🍷	P🍷	a🍷	c🍷	✕	✕	B	A🍷	🍷	S🍷	🍷	🍷	D	🍷	♦	✕	✕	🍷♦	🍷♦	🍷♦	🍷	🍷
Basel SBB ▦ **912** d.	...	...	...	...	...	...	...	...	...	...	...	...	...	...	1113	...	...	...	...	...	...	...	...	...	...
Karlsruhe Hbf **912** d.	...	...	...	...	...	...	...	...	...	...	...	...	...	...	1300	...	...	...	...	...	1221	...	1221y	...	...
München Hbf **904 930** d.	...	...	...	0928	...	0955	0955	...	...	...	...	...	0847	...	│	...	1055	...	...	...	│	...	│	1128	...
Stuttgart Hbf **912** d.	...	...	...	1151	...	│	│	...	...	...	...	...	1114	1137	│	...	│	...	...	...	│	1209	│	1351	...
Nürnberg Hbf **920** d.	...	...	...	│	0929	1100	1100	...	...	...	...	...	│	│	│	...	1200	...	...	...	│	│	│	│	...
Frankfurt (Main) Hbf **910/1** d.	...	...	...	│	1142	1310	1310	...	...	...	1329	1215	│	│	│	...	1410	...	...	...	│	│	│	│	1344
Frankfurt Flughafen ✈ § d.	...	...	...	1309	1158	1325	1322	...	...	...	1343	1228	│	│	1409	...	1425	...	...	...	│	│	│	1509	1358
Mainz Hbf **911** d.	...	...	...	│	1220	│	│	...	...	...	│	1248	1248	1320	│	...	│	...	...	...	1344	1344	1344y	│	1420
Koblenz Hbf d.	...	...	...	│	1313	│	│	...	...	...	│	1343	1343	1413	│	...	│	...	...	...	1443	1443	1443	│	1513
Andernach d.	...	...	...	│	│	│	│	...	...	...	│	1356	1356	│	│	...	│	...	...	...	1456	1456	1456	│	│
Remagen d.	...	...	...	│	│	│	│	...	...	...	│	1408	1408	│	│	...	│	...	...	...	1508	1508	1508	│	│
Bonn Hbf d.	...	...	...	│	1346	│	│	...	...	...	│	1423	1423	1446	│	...	│	...	...	...	1523	1523	1523	│	1546
Köln/Bonn Flughafen ✈ d.	...	...	...	│	│	│	│	...	...	...	│	│	│	│	│	...	│	...	...	...	│	│	│	│	│
Köln Hbf a.	...	...	...	1405	1405	│	│	...	...	...	1433	1442	1442	1505	1505	...	│	...	...	...	1543	1543	1543	1605	1605
Köln Hbf d.	1346	1348	...	1411	1410	│	│	1448	...	1438	1446	1445	1445	1509	1511	1512	│	1520	1548	...	1546	1546	1546	1610	1610
Köln Messe/Deutz d.	│	│	...	│	│	1417	1427	│	...	│	│	│	│	│	│	│	1517	│	│	...	│	│	│	│	│
Solingen Hbf d.	│	│	...	│	1430	│	│	│	...	│	│	│	│	│	1529	1530	│	│	│	...	│	│	│	│	1630
Wuppertal Hbf d.	│	1416	...	│	1443	│	│	1516	...	│	│	│	│	│	1543	1544	│	│	1616	...	│	│	│	│	1643
Hagen Hbf d.	│	1435	...	│	1501	│	│	1535	...	│	│	│	│	│	1601	1601	│	│	1635	...	│	│	│	│	1701
Düsseldorf Hbf d.	1414	│	1352	1433	│	1438	1448	│	1452	1509	1513	1518	1518	1533	│	│	1538	1546	│	1552	1611	1612	1612	1633	│
Düsseldorf Flughafen ✈ d.	│	│	1400	│	│	│	│	│	1500	│	│	│	│	│	│	│	│	1553	│	1600	│	│	│	│	│
Duisburg Hbf d.	1428	│	1410	1446	│	1454	1502	│	1510	1524	1529	1533	1533	1546	│	│	1551	1604	│	1610	1624	1626	1626	1646	│
Oberhausen Hbf d.	1435	│	│	│	│	│	│	│	│	│	1534	│	│	│	│	│	│	│	│	│	│	1634	1634	│	│
Essen Hbf d.	│	│	1423	1459	│	1505	1517	│	1523	1537	...	1545	1545	1559	│	│	1604	1617	│	1623	1639	│	│	1659	│
Gelsenkirchen Hbf d.	1446	│	│	│	│	...	│	│	│	1548	...	│	│	│	│	│	│	│	│	│	│	1646	1646	│	│
Wanne-Eickel Hbf d.	1452	│	│	│	│	...	│	│	│	│	...	│	│	│	│	│	│	│	│	│	│	1652	1652	│	│
Recklinghausen Hbf d.	1500	│	│	│	│	...	│	│	│	1559	...	│	│	│	│	│	│	│	│	│	│	1700	1700	│	│
Bochum Hbf d.	│	│	1435	1510	│	...	1529j	│	1535	│	...	1556	1556	1610	│	│	1616k	1630	│	1635	1652	│	│	1710	│
Dortmund Hbf a.	│	│	1446	1521	1521	...	1542j	│	1546	│	...	1608	1608	1621	1621	1621	1630k	1641	│	1646	1702	│	│	1721	1721
Dortmund Hbf **805** d.	│	│	1448	...	1525	...	...	│	1548	│	...	1612	1612	1625	...	1628	...	1643	│	1648	...	│	│	...	1725
Hamm (Westf) **805** a.	│	1502	1507	...	│	...	...	1602	1607	│	...	1632	1632	│	...	1642	...	1702	1702	1707	...	│	│	...	│
Hamm (Westf) d.	│	1511	1511	...	│	...	...	1611	1611	│	...	1634	1634	│	...	1644	...	...	1711	1711	...	│	│	...	│
Hannover Hbf **810** a.	│	1628	1628	...	│	...	...	1728	1728	│	...	1801	1801	│	...	1818	...	...	1828	1828	...	│	│	...	│
Leipzig Hbf **866** a.	│	│	│	...	│	...	...	│	│	│	...	│	│	│	...	2118r	...	...	│	│	...	│	│	...	│
Berlin Hbf **810** a.	│	1809	1809	...	│	...	...	1906	1906	│	...	1958	1958	│	...	...	...	...	2009	2009	...	│	│	...	│
Münster (Westf) Hbf **801** d.	1528	...	...	...	1557	...	...	...	...	1630	...	...	...	1657	...	...	...	...	...	...	...	1728	1728	...	1757
Osnabrück Hbf **801 815** d.	...	...	...	...	1623	...	...	...	...	1655	...	...	...	1723	...	...	...	...	...	...	...	...	...	...	1823
Bremen Hbf **801 815** d.	...	...	...	...	1718	...	...	...	...	...	...	...	...	1818	...	...	...							...	1918
Hamburg Hbf **801** a.	...	...	...	...	1813	...	...	...	...	...	...	...	...	1913	...	...	...							...	2013
Hamburg Altona a.	...	...	...	...	1828	...	...	...	...	...	...	...	...	1928	...	...	...							...	2028

*See Table **802** for Rhein - Ruhr local RE and S-Bahn services*

♦ – **NOTES** (LISTED BY TRAIN NUMBER)

1959 – ⑤⑦ to May 5 (also Apr. 13, 17, May 1; not Apr. 14, 16, 30). [12] Düsseldorf - Kassel - Halle - Berlin. Train number **1969** Feb. 12 - May 5.

2004 – ①②③④⑦ (also May 26; not Apr. 13, 16, 30, May 24, June 4). [12] and 🍷 (Konstanz - Karlsruhe ⑦**y** -) Koblenz - Emden.

2006 – [12] and 🍷 Konstanz - Karlsruhe - Mannheim - Dortmund.

2014 – [12] and 🍷 Stuttgart - Mannheim - Münster - Emden.

2018 – ⑥ from Apr. 8. [12] Stuttgart - Münster - Emden - Norddeich Mole.

2157 – Ⓑ to May 5 (not Apr. 14, 16, 19, 26, 30). [12] Köln - Kassel - Halle.

2216 – [12] and 🍷 Stuttgart - Köln - Hamburg - Stralsund (- Greifswald Ⓐ**u**).

2226 – [12] and 🍷 (Passau ● -) (Regensburg ①–⑥**d** -) Frankfurt - Hamburg.

A – To Amsterdam (Table **28**). Subject to alteration on Jan. 21, 22, 29, Mar. 18, 19, May 20, 21.

B – ①–④ (not Apr. 13, 17, May 1, 24, June 5). To Berlin (Table **810**).

D – To Dresden (Table **842**).

N – To Norddeich Mole (Table **812**).

P – From Passau (Table **920**).

Q – ①②③④⑥ (also Apr. 14, May 26; not Apr. 13, 15, 17, May 1, 24, June 5).

S – From Salzburg (Table **890**).

T – Ⓐ (not Dec. 27–30, May 26). From Tübingen (d. 0611).

a – Not Apr. 14, 17, May 1, June 5.

b – Also June 5; not Apr. 16, 30, June 4.

c – Also Apr. 14, 17, May 1, June 5.

d – ①–⑥ (also Apr. 16, 30, June 4; not Apr. 13, 17, May 1, 24, June 5).

e – ①–⑥ (not Apr. 15, 17, May 1, June 5).

f – Also Apr. 13, May 24; not Apr. 14, May 26.

h – ⑥ (also Apr. 14; not Apr. 15).

j – ⑥ (also Apr. 14, 16, 17, 30, May 1, June 4, 5).

k – ⑥ (also Apr. 14, 16, 30, June 4).

m – Not Apr. 13, 17, May 1, 24, 25, June 5.

q – Not Apr. 14, 16, 30, June 4.

r – 2134 on on ①② Jan. 9 - Mar. 14, ①② May 15–30 (also June 6).

u – Not May 26.

v – Also Apr. 13, 17, May 1, 24, 25, June 5; not Apr. 16, May 26, 27.

w – ⑦ (also Apr. 17, May 1, June 5; not Apr. 16, 30, June 4).

y – ⑦ (also Apr. 17, May 1, 25, 26, June 5; not Apr. 16, 30, June 4).

● – ①⑤⑥ (also Apr. 16, 30, June 4; not Apr. 15, 17, May 1, June 5).

★ – Operated by Hamburg-Köln-Express. www.hkx.de. **DB tickets not valid**.

⊠ – Certain Frankfurt timings (trains via Nürnberg) are subject to alteration on ⑥⑦ Feb. 11 - Apr. 2 (also Apr. 14–17). München and Nürnberg timings may vary from March 6. Berlin timings may vary from May 13. See also engineering work panel on page 367.

§ – Frankfurt Flughafen Fernbahnhof (Tables **910** and **911**).

800

KOBLENZ - KÖLN - DORTMUND - HAMBURG

SEE NOTE ⊠	IC 2196 ⑧q	ICE 628	ICE 653	ICE 643	IC 2012	EC 8	ICE 106	ICE 626	ICE 122	ICE 955	ICE 945 ⑧q	IC 2002	ICE 516	ICE 2022 Ⓐ	ICE 624 Ⓒ	ICE 1124	ICE 655	ICE 645	IC 118	EC 6	EC 6 ⑧q	ICE 504	ICE 104	IC 2041	ICE 622
Basel SBB 912 ...d.					1220	1313														1427	1427	1513	1513		
Karlsruhe Hbf 912 ...d.					1412	1500														1612	1612	1700	1700		
München Hbf 904 930 ...d.		1155							1255			1328			1355	1355						1512			1455
Stuttgart Hbf 912 ...d.					1312								1551												
Nürnberg Hbf 920 ...d.		1300							1400				1500	1500											1600
Frankfurt (Main) Hbf 910/1 ...d.		1510					1609		1629			1544			1710	1710								1810	
Frankfurt Flughafen + § ...d.		1525					1609	1626	1643				1709	1558	1725	1722						1809	1809	1825	
Mainz Hbf 911 ...d.				1448	1520							1620	1713				1648	1720	1720						
Koblenz Hbf ...d.				1543	1613							1713					1743			1813	1813				
Andernach ...d.				1556														1756							
Remagen ...d.				1608							1701n	1723							1808						
Bonn Hbf ...d.				1623	1646							1723					1746			1823		1846	1846		
Köln/Bonn Flughafen + ...d.																									
Köln Hbf ...a.				1643			1705	1705			1739	1742			1805	1805				1843		1905	1905	1905	1905
Köln Hbf ...d.	1614		1648	1646			1710	1711		1746	1748	1745	1810	1810			1848			1846		1910	1910	1911 1914 1913	1924
Köln Messe/Deutz ...d.		1619					1717						1816	1828											1924
Solingen Hbf ...d.							1729						1830									1929	1931		
Wuppertal Hbf ...d.			1716				1743		1816				1843		1916							1943	1945		
Hagen Hbf ...d.			1735				1801		1835				1901		1935							2001	2002		
Düsseldorf Hbf ...d.	1637	1641		1652	1715	1733		1738	1814		1752	1817z	1833		1837	1850		1846	1910	1933	1933			1938	1946
Düsseldorf Flughafen + ...d.				1700							1800					1900									
Duisburg Hbf ...d.	1650	1654		1710	1729x	1746		1751	1827		1810	1830	1846		1850	1903		1910	1924	1946	1946			1951	2003
Oberhausen Hbf ...d.									1833			1837												1956	
Essen Hbf ...d.	1702	1717z		1723	1745	1759		1804			1823		1859		1904	1917		1923	1936	1959	1959				2017
Gelsenkirchen Hbf ...d.									1849										1946						
Wanne-Eickel Hbf ...d.											1852								1952						
Recklinghausen Hbf ...d.											1900								2000						
Bochum Hbf ...d.		1730k		1735	1756	1810		1815k			1835		1910		1916	1930		1935		2010	2010			2022	2029
Dortmund Hbf ...a.		1742k		1746	1808	1821	1821	1829k			1846		1921	1921	1930	1943		1946		2021	2021	2021		2028	2042
Dortmund Hbf 805 ...d.				1748	1828	1825					1848		1925					1948		2025				2028	
Hamm (Westf) 805 ...a.				1802	1807	1843			1902	1907								2002	2007					2042	
Hamm (Westf) ...d.				1811	1811	1845			1911	1911								2011	2011					2044	
Hannover Hbf 810 ...a.				1928	1928	2018			2028	2028								2128	2128					2218	
Leipzig Hbf 866 ...a.					2325w																				
Berlin Hbf 810 ...a.				2106	2106				2223	2223								2306	2306						
Münster (Westf) Hbf 801 ...a.						1857						1928					1957			2030			2057		
Osnabrück Hbf 801 815 ...a.						1923											2023						2123		
Bremen Hbf 801 815 ...a.						2018											2118						2219		
Hamburg Hbf 801 ...a.	1946					2113											2213						2314		
Hamburg Altona ...a.	2001					2128											2228						2329		

SEE NOTE ⊠	ICE 957 ⑦v	ICE 947	EC 114	ICE 26	ICE 514	ICE 620	ICE 120 G	ICE 912 A	ICE 657	IC 2318 ⑧q	IC 2318 ⑦w	ICE 1102	IC 102 ⑥k	IC 528 ⑧q	ICE 1522	ICE 512	ICE 526	ICE 1910 ⑧q ⑦w	ICE 2210 ⑧q	IC 447	IC 100	IC 524	ICE 22	ICE 522
Basel SBB 912 ...d.												1713	1713									1913		
Karlsruhe Hbf 912 ...d.												1900	1900									2101		
München Hbf 904 930 ...d.			1346		1528	1555								1652	1618	1727	1755	1619				1855		1952
Stuttgart Hbf 912 ...d.			1609		1751			1837				1737	1737			1951		1914	1918p					
Nürnberg Hbf 920 ...d.				1529	1700							1800	1733	1901						2000		1929		2100
Frankfurt (Main) Hbf 910/1 ...d.				1742		1910	1929					2010	1944	2110					2210			2146y	2310
Frankfurt Flughafen + § ...d.				1758	1909	1922	1943	1955				2009	2009	2025	1758	2109	2125			2209	2225	2159	2325
Mainz Hbf 911 ...d.			1744	1820					1920	1920				2020			2048	2120			2220		
Koblenz Hbf ...d.			1843	1913					2013	2013				2113			2143	2213			2313		
Andernach ...d.			1856														2156						
Remagen ...d.			1908														2208						
Bonn Hbf ...d.			1923	1946				2024	2046	2046				2146			2223	2246			2329	2346		
Köln/Bonn Flughafen + ...d.																								
Köln Hbf ...a.			1943	2005	2005		2033	2045	2105	2105	2105	2105			2206	2205	2243	2305	2307			0006	0045
Köln Hbf ...d.	1948		1946	2010	2011		2042	2048		2110	2111	2111			2210	2211	2246		2312	2316		0011	0045
Köln Messe/Deutz ...d.						2029	2047				2117			2217				2341					
Solingen Hbf ...d.	2016			2030							2129	2230											
Wuppertal Hbf ...d.				2043			2116				2143	2243											
Hagen Hbf ...d.	2035			2101			2135				2201	2302											
Düsseldorf Hbf ...d.		1952	2011		2033	2050	2109	2113		2133	2133			2138		2233	2238	2309		2336	2340	0003	0034	0109
Düsseldorf Flughafen + ...d.		2000																	2348					0116
Duisburg Hbf ...d.		2010	2024		2046	2103	2126	2129		2146	2146			2151		2246	2251	2321	2352	2357	0016		0047	0126
Oberhausen Hbf ...d.						2132																		
Essen Hbf ...d.		2023	2039		2059	2117		2139		2159	2159			2204		2307z	2304	2337		0005	0010	0029	0059	0138
Gelsenkirchen Hbf ...d.																								
Wanne-Eickel Hbf ...d.																								
Recklinghausen Hbf ...d.														2327										
Bochum Hbf ...d.		2035	2050		2110	2130				2210	2210			2216		2316	2347		0016	0021	0039		0110	0148
Dortmund Hbf ...a.		2046	2101	2122	2121	2142				2221	2221	2221		2230	2321	2327	2359		0028	0031	0050		0121	0159
Dortmund Hbf 805 ...d.		2048		2125						2225w	2228	2228						2356		0031				
Hamm (Westf) 805 ...a.	2102	2107					2202			2247	2247									0047				
Hamm (Westf) ...d.	2111	2111					2209			2249	2249									0049				
Hannover Hbf 810 ...a.	2228	2228					2328			0018	0018									0223				
Leipzig Hbf 866 ...a.																								
Berlin Hbf 810 ...a.	0009	0009					0110													0533				
Münster (Westf) Hbf 801 ...a.				2157						2254w							2356							
Osnabrück Hbf 801 815 ...a.				2224																				
Bremen Hbf 801 815 ...a.				2319																				
Hamburg Hbf 801 ...a.				0014																				
Hamburg Altona ...a.																								

See Table 802 for Rhein - Ruhr local RE and S-Bahn services

♦ — **NOTES** (LISTED BY TRAIN NUMBER)

6 – ⬚ and ✗ Interlaken - Bern - Basel - Dortmund (- Hamburg ⑧q).
8 – ⬚ and ✗ Zürich - Basel - Hamburg.
114 – WÖRTHERSEE – ⬚ and ⟐ Klagenfurt - Salzburg - München - Dortmund.
118 – ⬚ Innsbruck - Bregenz - Lindau - Ulm - Münster.
2002 – ⬚ Bonn - Münster (- Emden ●).
2012 – ALLGÄU – ⬚ and ⟐ Oberstdorf - Stuttgart - Köln - Hannover (- Magdeburg ⊖) (- Leipzig ⑦ w).

A – To Amsterdam (Table 28). Subject to alteration on Jan. 21, 22, 29, Mar. 18, 19, May 20, 21.
B – From Wien (Tables 950/920).
G – From Garmisch on ⑥ to Mar. 4 (Table 895).

b – Not Dec. 25 – 30, Apr. 14, 16, 30, May 25, 26, June 4.
k – ⑥ (also Apr. 14, 16, 30, June 4).
n – ⑥ from Apr. 8.
p – 1937 on ⑤⑦ (also ①–④ Mar. 13 - Apr. 20).
q – Not Apr. 14, 16, 30, June 4.

t – Not Apr. 17, May 1, 5.
v – Apr. 15, 17, May 1, June 5.
w – ⑦ (also Apr. 17, May 1, June 5; not Apr. 16, 30, June 4).
x – 1733 on ④⑤⑦ (also Apr. 12, 17, 24, May 1, 23, 24, June 5; not Apr. 14, 30, May 26, June 4).
y – Calls at Frankfurt (Main) Süd (not Hbf) on ⑥⑦ Feb. 11 - Apr. 2 (also Apr. 14 – 17).
z – Arrives 9 – 10 minutes earlier.

⊖ – ①④⑤⑦ (also Apr. 12, 18, May 2, 23, 24, June 6; not Apr. 14, 16, 30, May 25, 26, June 4).
● – ⑧ to Mar. 31; daily from Apr. 2.
⊠ – Certain Frankfurt timings (trains via Nürnberg) are subject to alteration on ⑥⑦ Feb. 11 - Apr. 2 (also Apr. 14 – 17). München and Nürnberg timings may vary from March 6. Berlin timings may vary from May 13. See also engineering work panel on page 367.
§ – Frankfurt Flughafen Fernbahnhof (Tables 910 and 911).

HAMBURG - DORTMUND - KÖLN - KOBLENZ 800

km	SEE NOTE ⊠	ICE 523	ICE 511	ICE 23	ICE 1125	ICE 525	ICE 101	IC 2319	IC 2319	IC 446	ICE 913	IC 2003	ICE 813	ICE 1127	ICE 527	ICE 1521	ICE 513	ICE 815	EC 115	ICE 529	ICE 103	EC 7	EC 7	IC 119	ICE 121
		①–⑥	① g		⑦ y	①–⑥		① g	①–⑥		①–⑥	Ⓐ	Ⓐ	⑥	Ⓐ			Ⓐ				①–⑥			①–⑥
		e 🍷	🍷	🍴♦	🍷	d 🍷	🍷	🍷	e 🍷		e 🍷		🍷	G 🍷	🍷	🍴	🍷	🍴	🍷♦	🍷	🍷	e ♦	🍴♦	♦	e A
	Hamburg Altona d.	...	...	...	...	...	...	...	...	...	...	...	...	...	...	...	...	...	...	...	...	0428	...	...	🍷
	Hamburg Hbf 801 d.	...	...	...	...	...	...	...	...	...	...	...	...	...	...	...	...	...	...	...	...	0442	...	...	...
	Bremen Hbf 801 815 d.	...	...	...	...	...	...	...	...	...	...	...	...	...	...	...	...	...	...	...	...	0540	...	...	...
	Osnabrück Hbf 801 815 d.	...	...	...	...	...	...	...	...	...	...	...	...	...	...	...	...	...	...	...	...	0637	...	...	...
	Münster (Westf) Hbf 801 d.	...	...	...	...	...	...	0503	...	...	...	...	...	...	...	...	0601	...	0631	...	...	0703	...	0727	...
	Berlin Hbf 810 d.	...	...	...	...	...	...	|	...	2353	...	...	...	...	...	...	|	...	|	...	...	|	...	|	...
	Leipzig Hbf 866 d.	...	...	...	...	...	...	|	...	|	...	...	...	...	...	...	|	...	|	...	...	|	...	|	...
	Hannover Hbf 810 d.	...	...	...	...	...	...	|	...	0340	...	...	...	...	...	...	|	...	|	...	0540	|	...	|	...
	Hamm (Westf) a.	...	...	...	...	...	...	|	...	0510	...	...	...	...	...	...	|	...	|	...	0713	|	...	|	...
0	Hamm (Westf) 805 d.	...	...	...	...	...	...	|	...	0512	...	...	...	...	...	...	|	...	|	...	0715	|	...	|	...
	Dortmund Hbf 805 a.	...	...	...	...	...	...	0533	...	0530	...	...	...	...	...	...	0632	...	|	...	0732	0733	...	|	...
	Dortmund Hbf d.	0406	0437	0437	0514	0525	0537	0537	0537	0534	0552	0549	0600	0614	0624	0636	0637	0652	|	0725	0737	0737	0737	|	...
	Bochum Hbf d.	0417	|	0449	0526	0538	|	0549	0549	|	0604	|	|	0627	0638	|	0649	0704	|	0738	|	0749	0749	|	...
	Recklinghausen Hbf d.	|	|	|	|	|	|	|	|	|	|	|	|	|	|	|	|	|	0700	|	|	|	|	0758	...
	Wanne-Eickel Hbf d.	|	|	|	|	|	|	|	|	|	|	0606	|	|	|	|	|	|	0708	|	|	|	|	0806	...
	Gelsenkirchen Hbf d.	|	|	|	|	|	|	|	|	|	|	0612	|	|	|	|	|	|	0714	|	|	|	|	0812	...
	Essen Hbf d.	0428	|	0500	0538	0553	|	0600	0600	0604	0615	|	|	0639	0653	|	0700	0715	|	0754	|	0800	0800	0823	...
	Oberhausen Hbf d.	|	|	|	|	|	|	|	|	|	|	0626	|	|	|	|	|	|	0726	|	|	|	|	|	0826
	Duisburg Hbf d.	0441	|	0512	0550	0607	|	0613	0613	0618	0628	0633	|	0652	0707	|	0713	0729	0734	0808	|	0813	0813	0838	0834
	Düsseldorf Flughafen ✈ d.	|	|	|	|	|	|	|	|	|	|	|	|	|	|	|	|	|	|	|	|	|	|	|	|
	Düsseldorf Hbf d.	0455	|	0527	0605	0621	|	0627	0627	0633	0648	0652	|	0707	0721	|	0727	0747	0751	0822	|	0827	0827	0852	0848
48	**Hagen** Hbf d.	|	0457	|	|	|	0557	|	|	|	|	|	0621	|	|	0657	|	|	|	|	0757	|	|	|	|
75	Wuppertal Hbf d.	|	0515	|	|	|	0615	|	|	|	|	|	0637	|	|	0714	|	|	|	|	0815	|	|	|	|
93	Solingen Hbf d.	|	0527	|	|	|	0627	|	|	|	|	|	0650	|	|	0727	|	|	|	|	0827	|	|	|	|
120	**Köln** Messe/Deutz a.	0515	|	|	0626	0642	|	|	|	|	0710	|	|	0728	0742	|	|	0809	|	0842	|	|	|	|	|
121	**Köln** Hbf a.	|	0546	0549	|	|	0646	0650	0650	0657	|	0715	0709	|	|	0747	0749	|	0815	|	0846	0850	0850	0915	0912
	Köln Hbf d.	|	0555	0553	|	|	0654	0653	0653	...	|	0718	0720	|	|	0753	0755	|	0818	|	0855	0853	0853	0918	0927
	Köln/Bonn Flughafen ✈ a.	0529	|	|	|	|	|	|	|	...	|	|	|	|	|	|	|	0820	|	|	|	|	|	|	|
	Bonn Hbf d.	|	|	0614	|	|	|	0714	0714	...	|	0738	|	|	|	0814	|	|	0838	|	|	0914	0914	0938	|
	Remagen d.	|	|	|	|	|	|	|	|	...	|	0751	|	|	|	|	|	|	0851	|	|	|	|	0951	|
	Andernach d.	|	|	|	|	|	|	|	|	...	|	0804	|	|	|	|	|	|	0904	|	|	|	|	1004	|
	Koblenz Hbf a.	|	|	0646	|	|	|	0746	0746	...	|	0816	|	|	|	0846	|	|	0915	|	|	0946	0946	1015	|
	Mainz Hbf 911 a.	|	|	0738	|	|	|	0838	0838	...	|	...	|	|	|	0938	|	|	1015	|	|	1038	1038	1110	|
	Frankfurt Flughafen ✈ § a.	0633	0649	0759	0733	0733	0749	|	|	...	0807	...	0826	0833	0833	0959	0849	0926	|	0933	0949	|	|	|	1016
	Frankfurt (Main) Hbf 910/1 a.	0648	|	0813	0748	0748	|	|	|	...	|	...	0841	0848	0848	1013	|	0941	|	0948	|	|	|	|	1030
	Nürnberg Hbf 920 a.	0859	|	1027	0959	0959	|	|	|	...	|	...	...	1059	1059	1224	|	...	|	1159	|	|	|	|	...
	Stuttgart Hbf 912 a.	|	0808	...	|	|	|	1024	1024	...	0924	...	...	|	|	|	1008	...	1153	|	|	|	|	1246	...
	München Hbf 904 930 a.	1004	1027	...	1107	1107	|	...	...	...	...	...	...	1204	1204	1339	1227	...	1411	1304	|	|	|	...	...
	Karlsruhe Hbf 912 a.	...	...	...	...	...	0858	...	...	...	...	...	...	...	...	...	...	...	...	...	1058	1147	1147	...	...
	Basel SBB 🏛 912 a.	...	...	...	...	...	1047	...	...	...	...	...	...	...	...	...	...	...	...	...	1247	1330	1330	...	...

SEE NOTE ⊠	ICE 646	ICE 656	ICE 621	ICE 1099	IC 2401	ICE 515	ICE 27	IC 2005	IC 2005	ICE 623	ICE 946	ICE 956	ICE 105	EC 9	IC 2013	ICE 644	ICE 654	ICE 625	IC 2023	ICE 517	IC 1927	IC 2009	ICE 944	ICE 954	IC 2156
	Ⓐ	Ⓐ		①–④	⑤ f			①–⑥	⑤⑥		①–⑥	①–⑥				①–⑥					⑤			①–⑥	①–⑥
	🍴	🍴	🍷	m 🍴		🍷	🍴♦	t E	J 🍷	🍷	e 🍴	e 🍴	A 🍷	Z 🍴	🍷♦	e 🍴	🍴	🍷	🍷	🍷	♦	♦	🍴	e 🍴	H
Hamburg Altona d.	...	...	...	0558	0558	...	...	🍷	...	...	...	...	...	0631	...	...	...	...	0730	...	...	...	...	...	...
Hamburg Hbf 801 d.	...	...	...	0612	0612	...	0546	...	...	...	...	...	...	0646	...	...	...	...	0746	...	...	...	...	...	...
Bremen Hbf 801 815 d.	...	...	...	|	|	...	0644	...	...	...	...	...	...	0744	...	...	...	...	0844	...	...	...	...	...	...
Osnabrück Hbf 801 815 d.	...	...	...	|	|	...	0737	...	...	...	...	...	...	0837	...	...	...	...	0937	...	...	...	...	...	...
Münster (Westf) Hbf 801 d.	...	...	...	|	|	...	0802	0832	0832	...	...	...	...	0903	...	...	...	...	1003	...	...	1032	...	...	...
Berlin Hbf 810 d.	0430	0430	...	|	|	...	|	|	|	...	0538	0538	...	|	...	0652	0652	...	|	...	0701	|	0749	0749	...
Leipzig Hbf 866 d.	|	|	...	|	|	...	|	|	|	...	|	|	...	|	0442g	|	|	...	|	...	|	|	|	|	...
Hannover Hbf 810 d.	0621	0621	...	|	|	...	|	|	|	...	0731	0731	...	|	0740	0831	0831	...	|	...	0856	|	0931	0931	...
Hamm (Westf) a.	0748	0748	...	|	|	...	|	|	|	...	0848	0848	...	|	0913	0948	0948	...	|	...	1024	|	1048	1048	...
Hamm (Westf) 805 d.	0752	0754	...	|	|	...	|	|	|	...	0852	0854	...	|	0915	0952	0954	...	|	...	1026	|	1052	1054	1056
Dortmund Hbf 805 a.	0809	|	...	|	|	...	0833	|	|	...	0909	|	...	0933	0931	1009	|	...	1033	...	1048	|	1109	|	1114
Dortmund Hbf d.	0812	|	0815c	|	|	0837	0838	|	|	0916c	0912	|	...	0937	0952	1012	|	1016c	1036	1037	1052	|	1112	|	1116
Bochum Hbf d.	0824	|	0827c	|	|	|	0849	|	|	0929c	0924	|	...	0949	1003	1024	|	1029c	|	1049	1103	|	1124	|	1129
Recklinghausen Hbf d.	|	|	|	|	|	|	|	0901	0901	|	|	|	...	|	|	|	|	|	|	|	|	1101	|	|	|
Wanne-Eickel Hbf d.	|	|	|	|	|	|	|	0909	0909	|	|	|	...	|	|	|	|	|	|	|	|	1109	|	|	|
Gelsenkirchen Hbf d.	|	|	|	|	|	|	|	0915	0915	|	|	|	...	|	|	|	|	|	|	|	|	1115	|	|	|
Essen Hbf d.	0836	|	0840	0854	0854	|	0900	|	|	0941	0936	|	...	1000	1014	1036	|	1040	|	1100	1114	|	1136	|	1140
Oberhausen Hbf d.	|	|	|	|	|	|	|	0927	0927	|	|	|	1000	|	|	|	|	|	|	|	|	1127	|	|	|
Duisburg Hbf d.	0849	|	0855	0907	0907	|	0912	0934	0934	0955	0949	|	1008	1013	1030	1049	|	1055	|	1112	1130	1134	1149	|	1155
Düsseldorf Flughafen ✈ d.	0859	|	|	|	|	|	|	|	|	|	0957s	|	|	|	1040	1057s	|	|	|	|	|	|	1157s	|	1206
Düsseldorf Hbf d.	0906	|	0913	0921	0921	|	0927	0949	0949	1012	1006	|	1022	1027	1048	1111	|	1108	|	1127	1145	1149	1206	|	1216
Hagen Hbf d.	...	0823	|	|	|	0857	|	|	|	|	...	0923	|	|	|	...	1024	|	1057	|	|	|	...	1123	|
Wuppertal Hbf d.	...	0840	|	|	|	0915	|	|	|	|	...	0940	|	|	|	...	1041	|	1115	|	|	|	...	1140	|
Solingen Hbf d.	...	|	|	|	|	0927	|	|	|	|	...	|	|	|	|	...	|	|	1127	|	|	|	...	|	|
Köln Messe/Deutz a.	...	|	0933	|	|	|	|	|	|	1031	...	|	|	|	|	...	|	1128	|	|	|	|	...	|	|
Köln Hbf a.	...	0909	|	0945	0945	0946	0950	1015	1015	|	...	1009	1045	1050	1112	...	1109	|	1147	1149	1212	1215	...	1209	1239
Köln Hbf d.	...	...	|	...	...	0955	0953	1018	1018	|	...	...	1055	1053	1117	...	...	|	1153	1155	...	...	...	...	...
Köln/Bonn Flughafen ✈ a.	...	...	|	...	...	|	|	|	|	1043	...	...	|	|	|	...	...	|	|	|	...	...	...	...	...
Bonn Hbf d.	...	...	|	...	...	|	1014	1037	1037	|	...	...	|	1114	1137	...	...	|	1214	|	...	...	...	...	...
Remagen d.	...	...	|	...	...	|	|	1051	1051	|	...	...	|	|	1151	...	...	|	|	|	...	...	...	...	...
Andernach d.	...	...	|	...	...	|	|	1103	1103	|	...	...	|	|	1203	...	...	|	|	|	...	...	...	...	...
Koblenz Hbf a.	...	...	|	...	...	|	1046	1115	1115	|	...	...	|	1146	1215	...	...	|	1246	|	...	...	...	...	...
Mainz Hbf 911 a.	...	...	|	...	...	|	1138	...	1215	|	...	...	|	1238	1310	...	...	|	1338	|	...	...	...	...	...
Frankfurt Flughafen ✈ § a.	...	...	1033	...	...	1049	1159	...	|	1133	...	...	1149	|	|	...	...	1233	1359	1249	...	...	...	...	...
Frankfurt (Main) Hbf 910/1 a.	...	...	1048	...	...	|	1213	...	|	1148	...	...	|	|	|	...	...	1248	1412	|	...	...	...	...	...
Nürnberg Hbf 920 a.	...	...	1259	...	...	|	1427	...	|	1403	...	...	|	|	|	...	...	1459	...	|	...	...	...	...	...
Stuttgart Hbf 912 a.	...	...	|	...	...	1208	...	...	|	|	...	...	|	|	1446	...	...	|	...	1408	...	...	...	...	...
München Hbf 904 930 a.	...	...	1404	...	...	1427	...	...	|	1508	...	...	|	|	...	...	...	1606	...	1627r	...	...	...	...	...
Karlsruhe Hbf 912 a.	...	...	...	...	...	...	...	...	1334	...	...	...	1258	1347	...	...	...	...	...	...	...	...	...	...	...
Basel SBB 🏛 912 a.	...	...	...	...	...	...	...	...	...	...	...	...	1447	1535	...	...	...	...	...	...	...	...	...	...	...

♦ – **NOTES** (LISTED BY TRAIN NUMBER)

7 – 🛏 and 🍴 (Hamburg ①–⑥ **e** -) Dortmund - Basel - Bern - Interlaken.
23 – 🛏 and 🍴 Dortmund - Regensburg - Passau - Linz - Wien.
27 – 🛏 and 🍴 Hamburg - Dortmund - Regensburg - Passau - Linz - Wien.
115 – WÖRTHERSEE – 🛏 and 🍷 Münster - München - Salzburg - Klagenfurt.
119 – 🛏 Münster - Ulm - Lindau - Bregenz - Innsbruck.
1927 – ⑤ (also Apr. 13, May 24; not Apr. 14, May 26). 🛏 Berlin - Köln - Aachen Hbf (a. 1312).
2009 – 🛏 (Emden ● -) Münster - Köln.
2013 – ALLGÄU – 🛏 and 🍷 (Leipzig ① **g** -) (Magdeburg ①–⑥ **e** -) Braunschweig - Hannover - Köln - Mannheim - Stuttgart - Ulm - Oberstdorf.

A – From Amsterdam (Table **28**). Subject to alteration on Jan. 21, 22, 29, Mar. 18, 19, May 20, 21.
E – From Emden (Table **812**).
G – ⑥ (also Apr. 14, May 25; not Apr. 15, May 27). To Garmisch on ⑥ to Mar. 4 (Table **895**).
H – ①–⑥ to Feb. 10. 🛏 Halle - Kassel - Paderborn - Köln.
J – ⑤⑥ (also Apr. 13, 16, 30, May 24, 25, June 4). 🛏 and 🍷 Emden - Mannheim - Karlsruhe - Konstanz.
Z – To Zürich (Tables **510**).

c – ⑥⑦ (also Apr. 14, 17, May 1, June 5).
d – Not Apr. 15, 17, May 1, 25, June 5.
e – Not Apr. 15, 17, May 1, June 5.
f – Also Apr. 13, May 24; not Apr. 14, May 26.
g – ① (also Apr. 18, May 2, June 6; not Apr. 17, May 1, June 5).
m – Not Apr. 13, 17, May 1, 24, 25, June 5.
r – 1635 from Mar. 30.
s – Stops to set down only.
t – Also Apr. 16, 30, June 4; not Apr. 17, May 1, June 5.
y – Also Apr. 15, 17, May 1, 25, June 5.

● – ①–⑥ to Mar. 25; daily from Mar. 27.
⊠ – Certain Frankfurt timings (trains via Nürnberg) are subject to alteration on ⑥⑦ Feb. 11 - Apr. 2 (also Apr. 14 – 17). Nürnberg and München timings may vary from March 6. Berlin timings may vary from May 13. See also engineering work panel on page 367.
§ – Frankfurt Flughafen Fernbahnhof (Tables **910** and **911**).

800   HAMBURG - DORTMUND - KÖLN - KOBLENZ

SEE NOTE ⊠	ICE 627	IC 2044	ICE 107	IC 2313	IC 1911	IC 123	IC 1929	ICE 642	ICE 652	IC 2025	IC 1929	ICE 519	IC 2201	IC 942	IC 952	ICE 721	IC 2046	IC 109	IC 2217	IC 2411	IC 2011	IC 2011	IC 2017	ICE 915	ICE 125
notes	①-⑥	eD	⑦v	⑤⑦r	A	B	①-④				①-④		N				⑥h	⑧b		C	⑥w	⑤f		F	A
Hamburg Altona d.			0830						0930									1046	1120x						
Hamburg Hbf 801 d.			0846						0946									1046		1144					
Bremen Hbf 801 815 d.			0943						1044											1144					
Osnabrück Hbf 801 815 d.			1036			1108			1137											1237					
Münster (Westf) Hbf 801 d.			1103			1132			1203					1232						1303					
Berlin Hbf 810 d.								0852	0852					0949	0949								1001		
Leipzig Hbf 866 d.		0643																0843							
Hannover Hbf 810 d.		0940				1031	1031							1131	1131		1140				1156	1156			
Hamm (Westf) a.		1114				1148	1148							1248	1248		1314				1324	1324			
Hamm (Westf) 805 d.		1116				1152	1154							1252	1254		1316				1326	1326			
Dortmund Hbf 805 a.		1132		1133			1209			1233				1309			1332		1333					1347	1348
Dortmund Hbf d.	1125c	1137	1137	1137	1152		1212		1236		1237			1312	1325t	1337	1337	1337			1349		1352		1354
Bochum Hbf d.	1138c			1149	1203		1224		1249					1324			1338t		1349		1402	1403			1406
Recklinghausen Hbf d.							1206						1300						1338						
Wanne-Eickel Hbf d.							1214						1308						1346						
Gelsenkirchen Hbf d.							1220						1314						1352						
Essen Hbf d.	1153		1200	1214			1236						1300			1336	1353		1400	1404	1413	1414			1417
Oberhausen Hbf d.					1226	1238			←				1327												1426
Duisburg Hbf d.	1207			1213	1230	1234	1244		1249		1255	1312	1334			1349	1407				1428	1430	1432		1438
Düsseldorf Flughafen + d.							→			1259		1306				1359									
Düsseldorf Hbf d.	1221		1227	1244	1248		1306			1323j	1327	1348	1406			1421			1427	1433	1446	1446	1446		1454
Hagen Hbf d.		1158	1157						1223	1257				1323				1358	1357						
Wuppertal Hbf d.		1214	1215						1240	1315				1340				1414	1415						
Solingen Hbf d.		1227	1227							1327								1427	1427						
Köln Messe/Deutz a.	1242															1442									1512
Köln Hbf a.		1246	1246	1250	1312	1315			1309	1347	1357	1349	1413	1409		1446	1446	1450	1459		1512	1512	1512		1518
Köln Hbf d.				1255	1253	1317	1328			1353		1355	1418n					1455	1453		1517	1517	1517		1529
Köln/Bonn Flughafen + a.																									
Bonn Hbf d.				1314	1337					1414			1438n					1514			1537	1537	1537		
Remagen d.					1351								1459n								1551	1551	1551		
Andernach d.					1403																1603	1603	1603		
Koblenz Hbf a.				1346	1415					1446			1538					1546			1615	1615	1615		
Mainz Hbf 911 a.				1438	1510					1538								1638			1710	1710	1710		
Frankfurt Flughafen + § a.	1333		1349		1416					1559	1549			1533		1549								1607	1616
Frankfurt (Main) Hbf 910/1 a.	1348				1430					1613				1548											1630
Nürnberg Hbf 920 a.	1559													1759											
Stuttgart Hbf 912 a.				1622	1646					1608								1825			1846	1846	1846	1719	
München Hbf 904 930 a.	1704									1827				1907											2118
Karlsruhe Hbf 912 a.			1456											1658											
Basel SBB 🚲 912 a.			1647											1847											

SEE NOTE ⊠	ICE 640	ICE 650	ICE 723	IC 2027	ICE 611	IC 2019	IC 2203	ICE 940	ICE 950	ICE 725	IC 2048	IC 2311	HKX 1805	ICE 1915	ICE 917	IC 127	IC 548	IC 558	IC 1228	IC 1224	ICE 727	IC 2229	ICE 613	IC 2205	IC 2205
notes			⑧q	P		⑥H	J					D	★	U	⑤⑦r ⑧q	A			⑤⑦(A)	C	⑧q		N	N	⑧z
Hamburg Altona d.				1130									1236												
Hamburg Hbf 801 d.				1146							1246	1249											1346		
Bremen Hbf 801 815 d.				1244							1344												1444		
Osnabrück Hbf 801 815 d.				1337							1437	1444											1537		
Münster (Westf) Hbf 801 d.				1403		1432	1432				1503	1509											1603		
Berlin Hbf 810 d.	1052	1052						1149	1149					1202					1252	1252					
Leipzig Hbf 866 d.										1043															
Hannover Hbf 810 d.	1231	1231						1331	1331	1340				1356					1431	1431					
Hamm (Westf) a.	1348	1348						1448	1448	1514				1524					1548	1548					
Hamm (Westf) 805 d.	1352	1354						1452	1454	1516				1524					1552	1554	1556	1556			
Dortmund Hbf 805 a.	1409			1433				1509		1532	1533			1547					1609	1614	1614		1633		
Dortmund Hbf d.	1412	1425g	1436	1437				1512	1525k	1537	1537	1549		1556					1612	1616	1616		1636	1637	
Bochum Hbf d.	1424	1438g		1449				1524	1538k	1549		1601	1607						1624	1629	1629		1649		
Recklinghausen Hbf d.					1500	1500																		1700	1700
Wanne-Eickel Hbf d.					1508	1508																		1708	1708
Gelsenkirchen Hbf d.					1514	1515							1550											1714	1714
Essen Hbf d.	1436		1453	1500				1536		1554		1600	1604		1617			1636	1640	1640	1653		1700		
Oberhausen Hbf d.						1527	1527						1626										1727	1727	
Duisburg Hbf d.	1449		1507	1513		1534	1534	1549		1608		1613	1618	1627	1633	1638y	1649		1655	1655	1707		1712	1734	1734
Düsseldorf Flughafen + d.	1459						1557s									1657s									
Düsseldorf Hbf d.	1506		1520	1527	1548	1548	1606			1622	1627	1633	1644	1648	1653y	1710		1708	1708	1721	1727		1748	1748	
Hagen Hbf d.		1423		1457					1523		1558						1623				1657				
Wuppertal Hbf d.		1440		1515					1540		1615						1640				1715				
Solingen Hbf d.				1527							1627										1727				
Köln Messe/Deutz a.			1542						1642									1728			1742				
Köln Hbf a.		1509		1547	1549	1613	1613		1609		1646	1650	1657	1712	1718y	1709		1733		1747	1749		1813	1813	
Köln Hbf d.				1553	1555	1618	1618				1653	1717	1717	1728				1753	1755				1818		
Bonn Hbf d.				1614	1638	1636					1714	1737						1814					1837		
Remagen d.					1651							1751											1851		
Andernach d.					1704							1803											1903		
Koblenz Hbf a.				1646	1715						1746	1815						1846					1916		
Mainz Hbf 911 a.				1738	1815						1838	1910						1938							
Frankfurt Flughafen + § a.		1633	1659	1649						1733					1807	1816		1915	1959	1849					
Frankfurt (Main) Hbf 910/1 a.		1648	1813							1748					1830			1933	1848	2013					
Nürnberg Hbf 920 a.		1859	2027							1959								2059	2226q						
Stuttgart Hbf 912 a.				1808	1958						2024	2046	1924							2008					
München Hbf 904 930 a.		2004		2027														2205	2226						
Karlsruhe Hbf 912 a.									*See Table 802 for Rhein-Ruhr*																
Basel SBB 🚲 912 a.									*local RE and S-Bahn services*																

♦ – NOTES (LISTED BY TRAIN NUMBER)

1224 – ⓒ (also May 26). [🍴] and ♈ München - Kassel - Paderborn - Köln. Starts from Dortmund May 6 - June 11.

1228 – Ⓐ (not May 26). [🍴] and ♈ München - Kassel - Paderborn - Köln - Wiesbaden - Frankfurt. Starts from Dortmund May 8 - June 14.

2217 – [🍴] and ♈ München - Kassel - Paderborn - Köln.

2229 – [🍴] and ♈ Kiel - Köln - Frankfurt (- Nürnberg Ⓑq) (- Passau ●).

2311 – NORDFRIESLAND – [🍴] and ♈ Westerland - Heidelberg - Stuttgart.

2411 – ⑥ from Apr. 8. FEHMARN – [🍴]. Fehmarn-Burg - Lübeck - Köln.

A – From Amsterdam (Table 28). Subject to alteration on Jan. 21, 22, 29, Mar. 18, 19, May 20, 21.
B – ①-④ (not Apr. 13, 17, May 1, 24, June 5). From Berlin (Table 810).
C – ①②③④⑦ (not Apr. 13, 16, 30, May 24, June 4). On ①-④ (not Apr. 13, May 24) continues to Tübingen Hbf (a. 1950).
D – From Dresden (Table 841).
F – From Wolfsburg (Table 810).
H – ⑥ from Apr. 8.
J – Daily to Apr. 7; ⑧ from Apr. 9.
N – From Norddeich Mole (Table 812).

P – To Passau (Table 920).
U – To Tübingen Hbf on ⑦w (a. 2150).
b – Not Apr. 14, 16, 30, May 25, June 4.
c – ⑥⑦ (also Apr. 14, 17, May 1, June 5).
e – Not Apr. 15, 17, May 1, June 5.
f – Also Apr. 13, May 24; not Apr. 14, May 26.
g – ①②③④⑦ (not Apr. 13, 16, 30, June 4).
h – Also Apr. 24; not May 25; not Apr. 15, May 27.
j – Arrives 1313.
k – ⑥ (also May 14, 16, 30, June 4).
m – ⑥ from Apr. 8 (also Apr. 14, May 25).
q – ⑧ (not Apr. 14, 16, 30, June 4).
r – Also May 13, 17, May 1, 24, June 5; not Apr. 14, 16, 30, May 26, June 4.
s – Stops to set down only.
t – ⑤-⑦ (also Apr. 13, 17, May 1, June 5).
u – Not May 26.
v – Also Apr. 15, 17, May 1, June 5.

w – ⑦ (also Apr. 17, May 1, June 5; not Apr. 16, 30, June 4).
y – Hamburg Harburg.
x – On Apr. 8, 14, 15, 22, June 3 departs Duisburg 1634, Düsseldorf 1648, arrives Köln 1712.
z – Not Apr. 16, 30, June 4.
● – ④⑤⑦ (also Apr. 17, May 1, 24, June 5; not Apr. 16, 30, May 25, June 4).
▢ – ①②③④⑦ (not Apr. 13, 16, 30, May 24, June 4).
★ – Not Jan. 14 - Mar. 25. Operated by Hamburg-Köln-Express. www.hkx.de. ♈ DB tickets not valid.
⊠ – Certain Frankfurt timings (via Nürnberg) are subject to alteration on ⑥⑦ Feb. 11 - Apr. 2 (Feb. 14 - 17). Nürnberg and München timings may vary from March 6. Berlin timings may vary from May 13. See engineering work panel on page 366.
§ – Frankfurt Flughafen + Fernbahnhof (Tables 910 and 911).

SEE NOTE ⊠	ICE 848	ICE 858	ICE 2152	IC 729	ICE 2440	IC 2213	ICE 2223	ICE 129	IC 821	ICE 546	ICE 556	ICE 556	ICE 2195	ICE 2197	ICE 2029	ICE 615	ICE 2207	ICE 846	ICE 1046	ICE 856	IC 605	IC 2442	IC 2215	ICE 2315	HKX 1807
	✗	✗	♦	☕	D	♦	C	A☕	☕	♦	✗	✗	✗ (A)	☕ (A d)	L (⑦w)	☕	E	☕ (Q)	✗ (⑤B)	✗	✗ (Bq)	☕ (T)	D♦	♦ (⑤⑦)	★
Hamburg Altona d.													1557	1557	1530								1630		1636
Hamburg Hbf 801 d.						1446							1611	1611	1546								1646	1646	1649
Bremen Hbf 801 815 d.				1544										1644									1744	1744	
Osnabrück Hbf 801 815 d.				1637										1737									1837	1837	1844
Münster (Westf) Hbf 801 d.				1703										1803				1832					1903	1903	1909
Berlin Hbf 810 d.	1349	1349					1357			1452	1452	1452						1549	1549	1549					
Leipzig Hbf 866 d.				1243																			1443		
Hannover Hbf 810 d.	1531	1531				1540		1631	1631	1631								1731	1731	1731	1740				
Hamm (Westf) a.	1648	1648				1714		1724	1748	1748	1748							1848	1848	1854	1914				
Hamm (Westf) 805 d.	1652	1654	1656			1716		1726	1752	1754	1754							1852	1853	1854	1916				
Dortmund Hbf 805 a.	1709		1714			1732	1733	1748	1809							1833		1909	1909		1932	1933	1933		
Dortmund Hbf d.	1712		1716	1725k	1737	1737	1752		1812							1836	1837	1912	1912		1924k	1937	1937		
Bochum Hbf d.	1724		1729		1738k		1749	1803	1824								1849	1924	1924			1938k	1949	1949	
Recklinghausen Hbf d.																	1900								
Wanne-Eickel Hbf d.																	1909								
Gelsenkirchen Hbf d.																	1915								1950
Essen Hbf d.	1736				1740	1754		1800	1814		1841	1836	1854	1854		1900	1927	1936	1936			1950	2000	2000	2004
Oberhausen Hbf d.					1826																				
Duisburg Hbf d.	1749		1755		1808	1813		1828	1834	1855	1849		1907	1907		1912	1934	1949	1951			2004	2013	2013	2018
Düsseldorf Flughafen + d.	1759						1857s							1959											
Düsseldorf Hbf d.	1806		1810		1822	1827		1848	1908	1910			1921	1921		1927	1948	2008	2016			2018	2027	2027	2033
Hagen Hbf d.			1723				1758								1857	1823	1823		1923			1958			
Wuppertal Hbf d.			1740				1814								1915	1840	1840		1940			2014			
Solingen Hbf d.							1827								1927							2027			
Köln Messe/Deutz a.				1842					1928																
Köln Hbf a.		1809				1846	1850	1912		1909	1909	1945	1945	1947	1949	2013	2039		2009	2041	2046	2050	2050		2057
Köln Hbf d.						1853	1921				1912			1953	1957					2046		2053	2053		
Köln/Bonn Flughafen + a.																									
Bonn Hbf d.						1914					1934			2014								2114	2114		
Remagen a.											2001														
Andernach a.											2011														
Koblenz Hbf a.						1946								2046								2146	2146		
Mainz Hbf 911 a.						2038								2141								2238	2238		
Frankfurt Flughafen + § a.				1933				2010	2033					2200	2049					2151		2259	2259		
Frankfurt (Main) Hbf 910/1. a.				1948				2025	2048					2213								2311	2311		
Nürnberg Hbf 920 a.				2159					2259h						0042										
Stuttgart Hbf 912 a.						2224											2208								
München Hbf 904 930 a.				2307				0007h									0027								
Karlsruhe Hbf 912 a.																					2300				
Basel SBB 912 a.																					0056r				

SEE NOTE ⊠	ICE 221	ICE 544	ICE 554	IC 2321	IC 2221	IC 2209	ICE 619	ICE 844	ICE 854	IC 854	ICE 2307	IC 2444	ICE 1952	ICE 542	IC 552	ICE 209	ICE 842	ICE 852	IC 2446	IC 2309	IC 2309	ICE 540	IC 2021
	A☕	✗	✗	☕ (H)	♦ (R)	N	✗	✗	☕ (⑧w)	K (⑧q)	♦	✗ (⑤⑦)	✗	☕	✗	☕	✗	☕ (⑦b)	D (J)	f	☕ (⑤–⑦)	p✗	
Hamburg Altona d.					1730								1930				2030	2030					2230
Hamburg Hbf 801 d.				1746	1746						1846		1946				2046	2046					2246
Bremen Hbf 801 815 d.				1844	1844						1944		2044				2144	2144				2344	
Osnabrück Hbf 801 815 d.				1937	1937						2037		2137				2238	2238					0037
Münster (Westf) Hbf 801 d.				2003	2003	2032					2103		2203				2304	2304					0105
Berlin Hbf 810 d.		1652	1652					1749	1749	1749			1534y	1852	1852		1949	1949				2107	
Leipzig Hbf 866 d.												1643						1843					
Hannover Hbf 810 d.		1831	1831					1931	1931	1931	1940		2031	2031			2131	2131	2140			2301	
Hamm (Westf) a.		1948	1948					2048	2048	2048	2110	2135	2148	2148			2248	2248	2310			0028	0123
Hamm (Westf) 805 d.		1952	1954					2052	2054	2054	2112	2140	2152	2154			2252	2254	2312			0030	0125
Dortmund Hbf 805 a.		2009		2033	2033			2109			2133	2156	2209			2233	2309		2332	2334	2334	0048	0141
Dortmund Hbf d.		2012		2037	2037			2058	2112		2137	2137	2200	2212		2237	2312		2337		2337	0052	0144
Bochum Hbf d.		2024		2049	2049			2111	2124		2149		2211	2222		2249	2324			2349		0104	0155
Recklinghausen Hbf d.				2100																			
Wanne-Eickel Hbf d.				2109																			
Gelsenkirchen Hbf d.				2115																			
Essen Hbf d.	2036				2100	2100		2125	2136		2200		2225	2236		2300	2336			0000		0115	0206
Oberhausen Hbf d.	2026				2127																		
Duisburg Hbf d.	2034	2049		2113	2113	2134	2139	2149			2213		2242	2249		2313	2349			0013		0129	0219
Düsseldorf Flughafen + d.			2059				2159						2259				2359				0137s		0229
Düsseldorf Hbf d.	2048	2108		2127	2127	2148	2155	2208			2227		2300	2308		2327	0008			0027		0148	0240
Hagen Hbf d.			2023					2123	2123		2158		2223					2323	2358				
Wuppertal Hbf d.			2040					2140	2140		2214		2240					2340	0014				
Solingen Hbf d.											2227		2253						0027				
Köln Messe/Deutz a.																2128							
Köln Hbf a.	2112	2133	2109	2150	2150	2213	2219	2230	2209	2209	2250	2246	2325	2330	2314	2350	0030	0010	0046		0050	0211	0302
Köln Hbf d.	2126	▽		2153	2153		2230		2217	2253						2353			0352				
Köln/Bonn Flughafen + a.					2240																		
Bonn Hbf a.				2214	2214				2237		2314						0014						0416
Remagen a.											2328												0431
Andernach a.											2341												0446
Koblenz Hbf a.				2246	2246				2313		2354						0046						0458
Mainz Hbf 911 a.				2338z	2338												0138						0626
Frankfurt Flughafen + § a.	2216			2359z	2359												0159			2347			0646
Frankfurt (Main) Hbf 910/1. a.	2230			0013z	0013												0213			2400			0702
Nürnberg Hbf 920 a.																							
Stuttgart Hbf 912 a.					0320																		
München Hbf 904 930 a.					0602																		
Karlsruhe Hbf 912 a.					0156																	0401	
Basel SBB 912 a.																						0622	

♦ – **NOTES** (LISTED BY TRAIN NUMBER)

821 – [IC] Essen - Frankfurt - Würzburg (- München ④⑤⑦ h).
1952 – ⑤⑦ to Apr. 28 (also Apr. 13, 17, May 1; not Apr. 14, 16). [IC] Berlin - Kassel - Paderborn - Köln. Train number **1962** Feb. 12 - May 1.
2152 – Until May 5. [IC] (Leipzig - Weimar - Erfurt ♥ -) Kassel - Düsseldorf.
2213 – ⑦ (①②③④⑤⑥⑦ also Apr. 14, May 26; not Apr. 13, May 24).
2221 – ⑤⑦ to Apr. 2; ⑧ from Apr. 7. [IC] and ☕ Lübeck Hbf (d. 1637) - Hamburg - Frankfurt.
2315 – From Apr. 7. DEICHGRAF – [IC] and ☕ Westerland - Frankfurt.

A – From Amsterdam (Table 28). Subject to alteration on Jan. 21, 22, 29, Mar. 18, 19, May 20, 21.
B – ⑤ (also Apr. 13, May 24; not Apr. 14, May 26). To Neuss Hbf (a. 2029) and Mönchengladbach Hbf (a. 2043).
C – To Krefeld Hbf (a. 1843), Viersen (a. 1856), Mönchengladbach Hbf (a. 1905), Rheydt Hbf (a. 1910) and Aachen Hbf (a. 1950).
D – From Dresden (Table 842).
E – ⑧ to Mar. 31; daily from Apr. 2. From Emden (Table 812).
H – ①②③④⑥ to Apr. 8; ⑥ from Apr. 15.
H – ⑧ to May 26 (not Apr. 14, 16, 30); daily from May 28.

K – From Kiel (Table 820).
L – From Flensburg (d. 1352), Schleswig (d. 1415), Rendsburg (d. 1433) and Neumünster (d. 1459).
N – From Norddeich Mole (Table 912).
Q – ⑧ ①②③④⑤⑥⑦ (also Apr. 14, May 26; not Apr. 13, May 24).
R – ⑦ to Apr. 2; ⑤–⑦ from Apr 7 (also Apr. 12, 13, 17, May 1, 24, June 5).
T – Until Apr. 6.
b – Also Apr. 15, 17, May 1, June 5.
d – Not Dec. 27–30, May 26.
f – Also Apr. 13, 17, May 1, 24, June 3, 5, 10; not Apr. 14, 16, 30, June 4.
h – Würzburg - Nürnberg - München on ④⑤⑦ (also Apr. 17; not Apr. 14, 16, 30, June 4).
k – Also Apr. 14, 16, 30, June 4.
p – Also Apr. 13, 17, May 1.
q – ⑧ (not Apr. 14, 16, 30, June 4).

r – Karlsruhe - Basel on ①②③④⑦ (not Apr. 9, 13, 16, 30, June 4). Basel **Badischer Bf**.
s – Stops to set down only.
w – ⑦ (also Apr. 17, May 1, June 5; not Apr. 16, 30, June 4).
y – Subject to alteration (see Table 850).
z – ①–④ to Apr. 6; ⑥ from Apr. 8.
∇ – Continues to Aachen Hbf (a. 2219) on ⑦ w.
♥ – Until Feb. 10.
★ – Operated by Hamburg-Köln-Express. www.hkx.de. **DB tickets not valid.**
⊠ – Certain Frankfurt timings (trains via Nürnberg) are subject to alteration on ⑥⑦ Feb. 11 - Apr. 2 (also Apr. 14–17). Nürnberg and München timings may vary from March 6. Berlin timings may vary from May 13. See also engineering work panel on page 367.
§ – Frankfurt Flughafen Fernbf (Tables 910/911).

GERMANY *See page 367 for a summary of Christmas / New Year alterations*

801 Local services MÜNSTER - OSNABRÜCK and BREMEN - HAMBURG

See Table **800** for fast trains

MÜNSTER - OSNABRÜCK and v.v. Operated by WestfalenBahn. Journey time: 36 minutes. Trains call at **Lengerich** (Westf), 21 – 22 minutes from Münster, 14 minutes from Osnabrück. **From Münster** (Westf) Hbf at 0503 Ⓐ, 0603 ⚒, 0634 Ⓐ, 0703, 0734 Ⓐ, 0803, 0834 Ⓐ, 0903, 1003, 1103, 1203, 1303, 1334 Ⓐ, 1403, 1503, 1534 Ⓐ, 1603, 1634 Ⓐ, 1703, 1734 Ⓐ, 1803, 1834 Ⓐ, 1903, 2003, 2103, 2203 and 2303. **From Osnabrück** Hbf at 0519 Ⓐ, 0549 Ⓐ, 0619 ⚒, 0649 Ⓐ, 0719, 0749 Ⓐ, 0819, 0849 Ⓐ, 0919, 1019, 1119, 1219, 1319, 1419, 1447 Ⓐ, 1519, 1549 Ⓐ, 1619, 1649 Ⓐ, 1719, 1749 Ⓐ, 1819, 1919, 2016, 2119, 2219 and 2319.

BREMEN - HAMBURG and v.v. Operated by *metronom*. Journey time: 69 – 90 minutes. Trains call at **Rotenburg** (Wümme), 21 – 30 minutes from Bremen, 47 – 56 minutes from Hamburg. **From Bremen** Hbf at 0015 Ⓒ, 0115 Ⓒ, 0433 Ⓐ, 0459, 0528 Ⓐ, 0559, 0626 Ⓐ, 0633 Ⓒ, 0659, 0733, 0759, 0833, 0859 and at 33 and 59 minutes past each hour until 1633, 1659; then 1733, 1800, 1833, 1859, 1933, 1959, 2033, 2100, 2133 ⑤⑥ **b**, 2159 and 2315. **From Hamburg** Hbf at 0048 Ⓒ, 0315 Ⓒ, 0515 Ⓒ, 0538 ⚒, 0559 Ⓐ, 0615 Ⓒ, 0638, 0715, 0738, 0815, 0838 and at 15 and 38 minutes past each hour until 2115, 2138; then 2238 and 2338.

b – Also Apr. 13, 16, 30, May 24, June 4.

802 RHEIN – RUHR LOCAL SERVICES

RE / RB services

Services in this table (pages 376 – 378) are shown route by route. Sub-headings indicate the route number and principal stations served.

RE1 / RE11 Aachen - Köln - Düsseldorf - Dortmund - Hamm (- Kassel: Table 805) ⊡ *RE6* Köln - Neuss - Düsseldorf - Bielefeld (- Minden) ⊡

km		m		Ⓐk	m		m		k	m			m	❖		k	m		m					
0	**Aachen** Hbf .... **807** d.	...	...	...	...	0451e	...	0551	...	...	0651	...	...		1751	...	...	1851	...	1951	...	2051	2151	2251
31	Düren .... **807** d.	...	...	...	...	0517e	...	0617	...	...	0717	...	...		1817	...	...	1917	...	2017	...	2117	2217	2317
	Köln/Bonn Flugh ✈ .d.	...	...	...	0449e	|	0549e	|	...	0649r	|	...	0749		|	...	1849	|	1949	|	2049	|	|	|
70	**Köln** Hbf .... **807** a.	...	...	...	0502e	0544e	0602e	0644	...	0702r	0744	...	0802		1844	...	1902	1944	2002	2044	2102	2144	2244	2344
70	**Köln** Hbf ....d.	...	...	...	0508e	0549	0608e	0649	...	0708r	0749	...	0808	and at	1849	...	1908	1949	2008	2049	2108	2149	2249	2349
71	**Köln** Messe/Deutz......d.	...	...	...	|	0552	|	0652	...	|	0752	...	|		1852	...	|	1952	|	2052	|	2152	2252	2352
83	Leverkusen Mitte ....d.	...	...	...	|	0604	|	0704	...	|	0804	...	|	the same	1904	...	|	2004	|	2104	|	2204	2304	0004
	Neuss Hbf...............d.	...	...	...	0536e	|	0636e	|	...	0736r	|	...	0836		|	...	1936	|	2036	|	2136	|	|	|
110	**Düsseldorf** Hbf ....d.	...	0521	0536	0554e	0621	0654e	0721	0736	0754r	0821	0836	0854	minutes	1921	1936	1954	2021	2054	2121	2154	2221	2321	0021
117	Düsseldorf Flughafen ✈ d.	...	0528	0542	0602e	0628	0702e	0728	0742	0802r	0828	0842	0902		1928	1942	2002	2028	2102	2128	2202	2228	2328	0028
134	**Duisburg** Hbf ....d.	...	0538	0557	0615e	0638	0715e	0738	0757	0815r	0838	0857	0915	past each	1938	1959	2015	2038	2115	2138	2215	2238	2338	0038
144	Mülheim (Ruhr) Hbf......d.	...	0544	0603	0621e	0644	0721e	0744	0803	0821r	0844	0903	0921		1944	2005	2021	2044	2121	2144	2221	2244	2344	0044
153	**Essen** Hbf ....d.	...	0552	0613	0629e	0652	0729e	0752	0813	0829r	0852	0913	0929	hour until	1952	2013	2029	2052	2129	2152	2229	2252	2352	0052
169	Bochum Hbf.................d.	...	0603	0626	0642e	0703	0742e	0803	0826	0842r	0903	0926	0942		2003	2026	2042	2103	2142	2203	2242	2303	0003	0103
187	**Dortmund** Hbf............d.	0554	0616	0642	0654	0716	0754	0816	0839	0854	0916	0939	0954		2016	2039	2054	2116	2154	2216	2254	2316	0016	0116
218	**Hamm** (Westf) . **810** ★d.	0615	0639	0702	0715	0739	0815	0839	0902	0915	0939	0958	1015		2039	2102	2115	2144	2215	2244	2315	2344	0044	0144
268	Gütersloh Hbf .. **810** ★d.	0649	...	...	0749	...	0849	...	...	0949	...	...	1049		...	...	2149	...	2249	...	2349	...	...	...
285	**Bielefeld** Hbf... **810** ★a.	0658	...	...	0758	...	0858	...	...	0958	...	...	1058		...	...	2158	...	2258	...	0003	...	...	...

				Ⓐ				m	⚒m	k		m	▲	k		m	k		m		m	⑤⑥v	⊖	m
Bielefeld Hbf.... **810** ★d.	...	...	...	0458	...	...	...	0558	0558	...	...	0658		...	...	1958	...	...	2058	...	2158	...	...	2258
Gütersloh Hbf ... **810** ★d.	...	...	...	0508	...	...	...	0608	0608	...	...	0708		...	...	2008	...	...	2108	...	2208	...	...	2308
Hamm (Westf)... **810** ★d.	0415	...	0515	0544	...	0557e	0620	0644	0644	0657	0720	0744		1957	2020	2044	2057	2115	2144	2215	2244	2315	2315	2344
Dortmund Hbf.............d.	0445	...	0545	0606	...	0621	0645	0704	0706	0721	0745	0806		2021	2045	2106	2121	2145	2206	2245	2304	2345	2345	0004
Bochum Hbf..................d.	0455	...	0555	0619	...	0633	0655	▬	0719	0733	0755	0819	and at	2033	2055	2119	2133	2155	2219	2255	▬	2355	2355	...
Essen Hbf ....d.	0509	...	0609	0632	...	0647	0709	...	0732	0746	0809	0832		2046	2109	2132	2147	2209	2232	2309	...	0009	0009	...
Mülheim (Ruhr) Hbf.......d.	0515	...	0615	0638	...	0654	0715	...	0738	0752	0815	0838	the same	2052	2115	2138	2154	2215	2238	2315	...	0015	0015	...
Duisburg Hbf ....d.	0522	...	0622	0648	...	0708	0722	...	0748	0808	0822	0848		2108	2122	2148	2208	2222	2248	2322	...	0022	0020	...
Düsseldorf Flughafen ✈ d.	0532	...	0632	0657	...	0717	0732	...	0757	0817	0832	0857	minutes	2117	2132	2157	2217	2232	2257	2332	...	0032	...	...
Düsseldorf Hbf ....d.	0539	0614	0639	0714j	0714	0724	0739	0814	0814j	0824	0839	0914j		2124	2139	2214j	2224	2239	2314j	2339	...	0039	...	...
Neuss Hbf.................d.	|	0624	|	0724	0724	...	|	0824	0824	...	|	0924	past each	...	|	2224	...	|	2324	|	...	|	...	...
Leverkusen Mitte ....d.	0555	|	0655	|	|	...	0755	|	|	...	0855	|		...	2155	|	...	2255	|	2355	...	0055	...	...
Köln Messe/Deutz........d.	0608	|	0708	|	|	...	0808	|	|	...	0908	|	hour until	...	2208	|	...	2308	|	0008	0037	0108	...	...
Köln Hbf ....a.	0612	0652	0712	0752	0752	...	0812	0852	0852	...	0912	0952		...	2212	2252	...	2312	2352	0012	0039	0112	...	...
Köln Hbf .... **807** d.	0615	0658	0715	0758	0758	...	0815	0858	0858	...	0915	0958		...	2215	2258	...	2315	2358	0015	0040	0115	...	...
Köln/Bonn Flugh ✈ ..a.	|	0711	|	0811	0811	...	|	0911	0911	...	|	1011		...	|	2311	...	|	0011	|	|	|	...	...
Düren .... **807** d.	0639	...	0739	...	...	...	0839	...	...	...	0939	...		...	2239	...	...	2339	...	0039	0118	0139	...	...
Aachen Hbf.......... **807** a.	0707	...	0807	...	...	...	0907	...	...	...	1007	...		...	2307	...	...	0008	...	0108	0144	0207	...	...

RE2 Düsseldorf - Essen - Gelsenkirchen - Münster ⊡ *RE42* Mönchengladbach - Essen - Münster

km		⚒	Ⓐ		⚒	⚒							●											
0	**Düsseldorf** Hbf ....d.	...	...	...	0506	...	0606r	...	0706	...	0806	...		1806	...	1906	...	2006	...	2106	...	2206	...	2306
7	Düsseldorf Flughafen ✈ d.	...	...	...	0513	...	0613r	...	0713	...	0813	...		1813	...	1913	...	2013	...	2113	...	2213	...	2313
	Mönchengladbach .d.	...	...	...	|	0522	|	0622	|	0722	|	0822	and at	|	1822	|	1922	|	2022	|	2122	|	2222	|
	Viersen ....d.	...	...	...	|	0530	|	0630	|	0730	|	0830	the same	|	1830	|	1930	|	2030	|	2130	|	2230	|
	Krefeld Hbf...............d.	...	...	...	|	0542	|	0642	|	0742	|	0842		|	1842	|	1942	|	2042	|	2142	|	2242	|
24	**Duisburg** Hbf ....d.	...	...	...	0524	0602	0624r	0702	0724	0802	0824	0902	minutes	1824	1902	1927	2002	2027	2102	2124	2202	2224	2302	2324f
34	Mülheim (Ruhr) Hbf......d.	...	...	...	0530	0610	0630r	0710	0730	0810	0830	0910		1830	1910	1934	2010	2036	2110	2130	2210	2230	2310	2330f
43	**Essen** Hbf ....d.	0444	0518	...	0544	0618	0644	0718	0744	0818	0844	0918	past each	1844	1918	1944	2018	2044	2118	2144	2218	2244	2318	2344
53	Gelsenkirchen Hbf ....d.	0453	0526	...	0553	0626	0653	0726	0753	0826	0853	0926	hour until	1853	1926	1953	2026	2053	2126	2153	2226	2253	2326	2353
58	Wanne-Eickel Hbf ....d.	0458	0531	...	0558	0631	0658	0731	0758	0833	0858	0931		1858	1931	1958	2031	2058	2131	2158	2231	2258	2331	2358
68	Recklinghausen Hbf.....d.	0506	0539	...	0605	0639	0705	0739	0805	0841	0905	0939		1905	1939	2005	2039	2105	2139	2205	2239	2305	2339	0006
84	Haltern am See ....d.	0517	0550	...	0616	0650	0716	0750	0816	0852	0916	0950		1916	1950	2016	2050	2116	2150	2216	2250	2316	2350	0017
97	Dülmen.......................d.	0526	0559	...	0625	0659	0725	0759	0825	0901	0925	0959		1925	1959	2025	2059	2125	...	2225	...	2325	...	0026
126	**Münster** (Westf) Hbf....a.	0550	0622	...	0650	0722	0750	0822	0852	0924	0950	1022		1950	2022	2052	2122	2150	...	2250	...	2350	...	0050

		Ⓒ	Ⓒ			⚒	⚒	⚒								♥								⑤⑥
Münster (Westf) Hbf.....d.	0010	0010	0110	0210	...	0410	...	0510	0536e	0610	0636r	0709	0736r	0810	0836		2010	2036	2110	...	2212	...	2310	2310
Dülmen.........................d.	0033	0033	0133	0233	...	0433	...	0533	0558e	0633	0658r	0732	0758r	0833	0858		2033	2058	2133	...	2234	...	2333	2333
Haltern am See ....d.	0042	0043	0143	0243	...	0443	0507	0543	0607	0643	0707	0742	0807	0843	0907	and at	2043	2107	2143	2207	2244	...	2343	2343
Recklinghausen Hbf.....d.	...	0054	0154	0254	...	0454	0518	0554	0618	0654	0718	0753	0818	0854	0918		2054	2118	2154	2218	2255	...	2354	2354
Wanne-Eickel Hbf ....d.	...	0103	0203	0303	...	0502	0527	0602	0627	0702	0727	0801	0827	0902	0927	the same	2102	2127	2202	2227	2304	...	0003	0003
Gelsenkirchen Hbf ....d.	...	0108	0208	0308	...	0508	0532	0608	0632	0708	0732	0807	0832	0908	0932		2108	2132	2208	2232	2310	...	0008	0008
Essen Hbf ....d.	...	0117	0217	0317	...	0521	0544	0621	0644	0721	0744	0820	0844	0921	0944	minutes	2121	2144	2221	2244	2321	...	0017	0021
Mülheim (Ruhr) Hbf.......d.	...	...	...	...	...	0527	0551	0627	0651	0727	0751	0826	0851	0927	0951	past each	2127	2151	2227	2251	2327	...	...	0027
Duisburg Hbf ....d.	...	...	...	...	...	0536	0600	0636	0700	0736	0800	0836	0900	0936	1000	hour until	2136	2200	2236	2300	2336	...	...	0036
Krefeld Hbf..................d.	...	...	...	...	...	|	0618	|	0718	|	0818	|	0918	|	1018		|	2218	|	2318	|	...	...	|
Viersen.........................d.	...	...	...	...	...	|	0633	|	0732	|	0832	|	0932	|	1032		|	2232	|	2332	|	...	...	|
Mönchengladbach ..a.	...	...	...	...	...	|	0641	|	0741	|	0841	|	0941	|	1041		|	2241	|	2341	|	...	...	|
Düsseldorf Flughafen ✈.a.	...	...	...	...	...	0545	...	0645	...	0745	...	0845	...	0945	...		2145	...	2245	...	2345	...	...	0045
Düsseldorf Hbf ....a.	...	...	...	...	...	0553	...	0653	...	0753	...	0853	...	0953	...		2153	...	2253	...	2353	...	...	0053

RE3 Düsseldorf - Duisburg - Gelsenkirchen - Dortmund - Hamm ⊡ ◇

km		Ⓐ									
0	**Düsseldorf** Hbf ....d.	0445	0545	0645		1845	1945	2045	2145	2245	2345
7	Düsseldorf Flughafen ✈ ..d.	0453	0553	0653		1853	1953	2053	2153	2253	2353
24	**Duisburg** Hbf .... d.	0510	0610	0710	and	1910	2010	2110	2210	2310	0010
32	Oberhausen Hbf ....d.	0516	0616	0716	hourly	1916	2016	2116	2216	2316	0016
48	Gelsenkirchen Hbf ....d.	0529	0629	0729		1929	2029	2129	2229	2329	0029
53	Wanne-Eickel Hbf...........d.	0534	0634	0734	until	1934	2034	2134	2234	2334	0034
57	Herne ....d.	0538	0638	0738		1938	2038	2138	2238	2338	0038
78	**Dortmund** Hbf................a.	0557	0657	0757		1957	2057	2157	2257	2357	0057
109	**Hamm** (Westf) ....a.	0629	0729r	0829		2029	*2144*	*2244*	*2344*	*0044*	*0144*

Hamm (Westf)................d.	*0215*z	0530e	0630e	0730r	0830		2030	*2115*	*2215*
Dortmund Hbf...............d.	0303	0603	0703	0803	0903		2103	2203	2303
Herne ....d.	0320	0620	0720	0820	0920	and	2120	2220	2320
Wanne-Eickel Hbf ....d.	0324	0624	0724	0824	0924	hourly	2124	2224	2324
Gelsenkirchen Hbf ....d.	0329	0629	0729	0829	0929		2129	2229	2329
Oberhausen Hbf ....d.	0343	0643	0743	0843	0943	until	2143	2243	2343
Duisburg Hbf ....a.	0350	0650	0750	0850	0950		2150	2250	2350
Düsseldorf Flughafen .....a.	0402	0702	0802	0902	1002		2202	2302	0002
Düsseldorf Hbf ....a.	0412	0712	0812	0912	1012		2212	2312	0012

e – Ⓐ only.
f – 4 minutes later on †.
j – Arrives 10 minutes earlier.
k – To / from stations in Table **805**.
m – To / from Minden (Table **811**).
r – ⚒ only.
v – Also Apr. 13, 16, 30, May 24, June 4.
z – Ⓒ only.

⊖ – ①②③④⑦ (not Apr. 13, 16, 30, May 24, June 4).
❖ – Köln/Bonn Flughafen d. 1741 (not 1749).
▲ – The 1158, 1258 and 1358 from Bielefeld run 6 minutes earlier Köln Hbf - Köln/Bonn Flughafen.
♥ – Certain trains run 2 minutes later Münster - Essen.
● – Trains may depart Duisburg / Mülheim up to 6 minutes later on certain days. Certain Münster arrivals are 2 minutes earlier.

★ – Other local journeys (◇) Hamm - Bielefeld and v.v. (journey 43 minutes): **From Hamm** at 0549 Ⓐ, 0649 Ⓐ, 0749 ⚒, 0849 and hourly until 2049. **From Bielefeld** at 0527 Ⓐ, 0627 Ⓐ, 0727 Ⓐ, 0827 ⚒, 0927 and hourly until 2027.
◇ – Operated by **eurobahn** Keolis Deutschland GmbH & Co. KG.
⊡ – See note and shaded panel on page 377.

RE/RB services — RHEIN – RUHR LOCAL SERVICES — 802

RE4 Aachen - Mönchengladbach - Düsseldorf - Wuppertal - Dortmund ⊡ RE13 Venlo - Mönchengladbach - Düsseldorf - Wuppertal - Hamm ⊡ ◇

km			Ⓐ	⚒	Ⓐ	⚒	⚒		⚒															
0	**Aachen** Hbf 473 d.	0253	0413	0413	...	...	0513	0513	...	0613	...	0713	...	and at	...	1813	...	1913	...	2013	...	2113	...	2237
14	Herzogenrath 473 d.	0307	0427	0427	...	...	0527	0527	...	0627	...	0727	...		...	1827	...	1927	...	2027	...	2127	...	2252
58	Rheydt Hbf d.	0341	0503	0503	...	...	0603	0603	...	0703	...	0803	...		...	1903	...	2003	...	2103	...	2203	...	2330
	Venlo 🏛 d.	|	|	|	0505	0505	|	|	0605	|	0705	|	0805		1805	|	1905	|	2005	|	2105	|	2205	|
	Kaldenkirchen d.	|	|	|	0510	0510	|	|	0610	|	0710	|	0810		1810	|	1910	|	2010	|	2110	|	2210	|
	Viersen d.	|	|	|	0527	0527	|	|	0627	|	0727	|	0827	the same	1827	|	1927	|	2027	|	2127	|	2227	|
62	**Mönchengladbach** Hbf d.	0349	0510	0510	0545j	0545j	0610	0610	0645j	0710	0745j	0810	0845j		1845j	1910	1945j	2010	2045j	2110	2145j	2210	2236	2336
79	Neuss Hbf d.	0403	0524	0524	0557	0557	0624	0624	0657	0724	0757	0824	0857	minutes	1857	1924	1957	2024	2057	2124	2157	2224	...	...
90	**Düsseldorf** Hbf a.	0413	0534	0534	0608	0608	0634	0634	0708	0734	0808	0834	0908		1908	1934	2008	2034	2108	2134	2208	2234	...	...
90	**Düsseldorf** Hbf d.	d	0540	...	0612	...	0640	...	0712	0740	0812	0840	0912	past each	1912	1940	2012	2040	...	2140	...	2240	...	...
117	**Wuppertal** Hbf d.	...	0602	...	0632	...	0702	...	0732	0802	0832	0902	0932		1932	2002	2032	2102	...	2202	...	2302	...	...
144	**Hagen** Hbf 804 d.	...	0630	...	0658	...	0730	...	0758	0830	0858	0930	0958	hour until	1958	2030	2055	2130	...	2230	...	2330	...	...
159	Witten d.	...	0641	...	|	...	0741	...	|	0841	|	0941	|		|	2041	|	2141	...	2241	...	2341	...	...
175	**Dortmund** Hbf d.	...	0651	...	|	...	0751	...	|	0851	|	0951	|		|	2051	|	2151	...	2251	...	2351	...	...
	Schwerte (Ruhr) 804 d.	...	...	...	0708	...	...	...	0808e	...	0908r	...	1008		2008	...	*2133*	...	...	...	...	...	...	...
	Unna d.	...	...	...	0720	...	...	...	0820e	...	0920r	...	1020		2020	...	*2144*	...	...	...	...	...	...	...
	Hamm (Westf) d.	...	...	...	0734	...	...	...	0834e	...	0934r	...	1034		2034	...	*2157*	...	...	...	...	...	...	...

km		⚒	⚒	⚒		Ⓐ		⚒		⚒r														
0	**Hamm** (Westf) d.	...	...	...	...	...	...	0625e	...	...	...	0725e	...	0825e	...	0925r	...	1025		1925	...	...	...	...
19	Unna d.	...	...	...	...	...	...	0637e	...	...	...	0737e	...	0837e	...	0937r	...	1037		1937	...	...	...	...
35	Schwerte (Ruhr) 804 d.	...	...	...	...	...	...	0649e	...	...	...	0749e	...	0849e	...	0949r	...	1049		1949	...	...	...	...
	Dortmund Hbf d.	...	...	...	...	0609	...	|	...	0709	...	|	0809	|	0909	|	1009	|	and at	|	2009	...	2109	2209
	Witten d.	...	...	...	...	0619	...	|	...	0719	...	|	0819	|	0919	|	1019	|		|	2019	...	2119	2219
48	**Hagen** Hbf 804 d.	...	...	0602e	...	0632	...	0702	...	0732	...	0802	0832	0902	0932	1002	1032	1102	the same	2002	2032	...	2132	2232
75	**Wuppertal** Hbf d.	...	...	0625e	...	0658	...	0725	...	0758	...	0825	0858	0925	0958	1025	1058	1125		2025	2058	...	2158	2258
102	**Düsseldorf** Hbf a.	...	...	0646e	...	0719	...	0746	...	0819	...	0846	0919	0946	1019	1046	1119	1146	minutes	2046	2119	...	2219	2319
102	**Düsseldorf** Hbf d.	0548	0622	0649	...	0722	0722	0749	0749	0822	0822	0849	0922	0949	1022	1049	1122	1149		2049	2122	2149	2222	2322
113	Neuss Hbf d.	0601	0636	0701	...	0736	0736	0801	0801	0836	0836	0901	0936	1001	1036	1101	1136	1201	past each	2101	2136	2201	2236	2336
130	**Mönchengladbach** Hbf d.	0625j	0649	0725j	0725	0749	0749	0825j	0825j	0849	0849	0925j	0949	1025j	1049	1125j	1149	1225j		2125j	2149	2225j	2249	2349
139	Viersen d.	0633	|	0733	0733	|	|	0833	0833	|	|	0933	|	1033	|	1133	|	1233	hour until	2133	|	2233	|	|
157	Kaldenkirchen a.	0650	|	0750	0750	|	|	0850	0850	|	|	0950	|	1050	|	1150	|	1250		2150	|	2250	|	|
167	**Venlo** 🏛 a.	0656	|	0756	0756	|	|	0856	0856	|	|	0956	|	1056	|	1156	|	1256		2156	|	2256	|	|
	Rheydt Hbf d.	...	0654	...	...	0754	0754	...	...	0854	0854	...	0954	...	1054	...	1154	...		...	2154	...	2254	2354
	Herzogenrath 473 d.	...	0729	...	...	0829	0829	...	...	0929	0929	...	1029	...	1129	...	1229	...		...	2229	...	2329	0029
	Aachen Hbf 473 a.	...	0745	...	...	0845	0845	...	...	0945	0945	...	1045	...	1145	...	1245	...		...	2245	...	2345	0045

RE5 Koblenz - Bonn - Köln - Düsseldorf - Duisburg - Wesel ⊡ RE19 Düsseldorf - Emmerich - Arnhem ⊙

km		①–⑥	⑦		⚒◐	Ⓐ	⚒b		◐	⚒b		◐△				◐			◐		◐		◐	◐
0	**Koblenz** Hbf d.	...	...	...	0426	0516	...	...	0526	0616	...	0626	0716		...	1930	2016	...	2030	...	2130	...	2230	2330
18	Andernach d.	...	...	...	0444	0528	...	...	0544	0628	...	0644	0728		...	1945	2028	...	2045	...	2145	...	2245	2345
29	Bad Breisig d.	...	...	...	0454	0535	...	...	0554	0635	...	0654	0735	and at	...	1955	2035	...	2055	...	2155	...	2255	2355
39	Remagen d.	...	...	...	0511j	0543	...	...	0611j	0643	...	0711j	0743		...	2011j	2043	...	2111j	...	2211j	...	2311j	0011j
59	**Bonn** Hbf d.	...	...	...	0532	0601	...	...	0632	0701	...	0732	0801	the same	...	2032	2101	...	2132	...	2232	...	2332	0032
93	**Köln** Hbf d.	...	...	*0549*	0602	0631	0631	*0649*	0702	0731	*0749*	0802	0831		*2049*	2102	2131	*2149*	2202	*2249*	2302	2349	0002	0102
106	Leverkusen Mitte d.	...	...	*0604*	...	0645	0645	*0704*	...	0745	*0804*	...	0845	minutes	*2104*	...	2145	*2204*	...	*2304*	...	0004	▬	...
133	**Düsseldorf** Hbf d.	...	...	0626	...	0703	0703	0726	...	0803	0826	...	0903		2126	...	2203	2226	...	2326	...	0021	...	...
140	Düsseldorf Flughafen ✈ d.	...	...	0633	...	0709	0709	0733	...	0809	0833	...	0909	past each	2133	...	2209	2233	...	2333	...	0028	...	...
157	**Duisburg** Hbf d.	0544	0544	0644	...	0720	0720	0744	...	0820	0844	...	0920		2144	...	2220	2244	...	2344	...	0036	0044	...
165	Oberhausen Hbf d.	0550	0550	0650	...	0727	0727	0750	...	0827	0850	...	0927	hour until	2150	...	2227	2250	...	2350	...	...	0050	...
192	Wesel d.	0617	0617	0717	...	0755	0755	0817	...	0855	0917	...	0955		2217	...	2255	2317	...	0017	...	...	0117	...
226	**Emmerich** a.	0645	0645	0745	...	...	...	0845	...	...	0945	...	...		2245	...	...	2345	...	0045	...	...	0145	...
	Arnhem ‡ a.	0715‡	0726‡	0815‡	...	...	...	0915‡	...	...	1015‡	...	...		2315‡	...	...	0015‡	...	...	...	...	...	...

	Ⓐ	◐	⚒	◐			⚒	◐		▽	◐				◐			◐		◐				
Arnhem ‡ d.	...	...	...	...	...	...	...	...	...	...	...	0644‡		...	...	1844‡	...	...	1944‡	...	2044‡	2144‡	...	2244‡
Emmerich d.	...	...	...	...	0508	...	...	...	0608	...	...	0708		...	...	1908	...	...	2008	...	2108	2208	...	2308
Wesel d.	...	...	0506e	...	0543	0606	0606	...	0643	0706	...	0743	and at	1906	...	1943	2011	...	2043	...	2143	2245	...	2343
Oberhausen Hbf d.	...	...	0533e	...	0608	0633	0633	...	0708	0733	...	0808		1933	...	2008	2033	...	2108	...	2208	2310	...	0008
Duisburg Hbf d.	...	...	0542	...	0616	0640	0642	...	0716	0742	...	0816	the same	1942	...	2016	2042	...	2116	...	2216	2317	2322	0015
Düsseldorf Flughafen ✈ d.	...	...	0550	...	0625	▬	0650	...	0725	0750	...	0825		1950	...	2025	2050	...	2025	...	2225	▬	2332	...
Düsseldorf Hbf d.	...	...	0558	...	0633	...	0658	...	0733	0758	...	0833	minutes	1958	...	2033	2058	...	2133	...	2233	...	2339	...
Leverkusen Mitte d.	...	...	0614	...	*0655*	...	0714	...	*0755*	0814	...	*0855*		2014	...	*2055*	2114	...	*2155*	...	*2255*	◐	2355	...
Köln Hbf d.	0532	0556	0632	0656	*0712*	0732	0732	0756	*0812*	0832	0856	*0912*	past each	2032	2056	*2112*	2129	2156	*2212*	2256	*2312*	2356	0012	...
Bonn Hbf d.	0557	0627	0657	0727	...	0757	0757	0827	...	0857	0927	...		2057	2127	...	...	2227	...	2327	...	0027	...	...
Remagen d.	0615	0654j	0715	0754j	...	0815	0815	0854j	...	0915	0954j	...	hour until	2115	2157j	...	...	2254j	...	2354j	...	0054j	...	...
Bad Breisig d.	0623	0702	0723	0802	...	0823	0823	0902	...	0923	1002	...		2123	2205	...	...	2302	...	0002	...	0102	...	...
Andernach d.	0630	0712	0730	0813	...	0830	0830	0912	...	0930	1012	...		2130	2215	...	...	2312	...	0012	...	0112	...	...
Koblenz Hbf a.	0642	0727	0742	0828	...	0842	0842	0927	...	0942	1027	...		2142	2234	...	...	2330	...	0028	...	0131	...	...

RE7 Köln - Wuppertal - Hagen - Hamm - Münster (- Rheine: Table 812) ⊡

km		Ⓐ									
0	**Köln** Hbf ♥ d.	...	0521e	0621r	0721		1921	2021	2121	2221	2352
28	Solingen Hbf d.	...	0543e	0643r	0743	and	1943	2043	2143	2243	0020
46	**Wuppertal** Hbf d.	...	0556e	0656r	0756		1956	2056	2156	2256	0037
73	**Hagen** Hbf d.	0522	0622	0722	0822	hourly	2022	2122	2222	2322	...
86	Schwerte (Ruhr) d.	0533	0633	0733	0833		2033	2133	2233	2333	...
102	Unna d.	0544	0644	0744	0844	until	2044	2144	2244	2344	...
121	**Hamm** (Westf) d.	0559	0659	0759	0859		2059	2159	2259	2357	...
157	**Münster** (Westf) Hbf a.	0622	0722	0822	0922		2122	2229	2329	*0040*	...

	Ⓐ	⚒							v	⑤⑥t
Münster (Westf) d.	...	...	0529e	0634		2034	...	2134	2234	2234
Hamm (Westf) d.	...	0500	0600	0700	and	2100	...	2200	2300	2300
Unna d.	...	0513	0613	0713		2113	...	2213	2313	2313
Schwerte (Ruhr) d.	...	0525	0625	0725	hourly	2125	...	2225	2325	2325
Hagen Hbf d.	0439	0539	0639	0739		2139	...	2236	2336	2339
Wuppertal Hbf d.	0504	0604	0704	0804	until	2204	2320	...	...	0003
Solingen Hbf d.	0515	0615	0715	0815		2215	2337	...	...	...
Köln Hbf ★ a.	0538	0638	0738	0839		2238	0005	...	...	...

Düsseldorf and Köln - Krefeld - Kleve ⊖

km		⚒	⚒							
0	**Düsseldorf** Hbf d.	...	0609	...	0709		...	2209	...	2309
•	**Köln** Hbf d.	0542	|	0642	|	and at	2142	|	2242	|
•	Neuss Hbf d.	0607	|	0707	|	the same	2207	|	2307	|
27•	**Krefeld** Hbf d.	0624	0636	0724	0736		2224	2236	2324	2336
57	Geldern d.	...	0702	...	0802	minutes	...	2302	...	0002
66	Kevelaer d.	...	0708	...	0808	past each	...	2308	...	0008
72	Weeze d.	...	0717	...	0817		...	2317	...	0014
79	Goch d.	...	0723	...	0823	hour until	...	2323	...	0020
92	**Kleve** a.	...	0735	...	0835		...	2335	...	0032

	⚒								
Kleve d.	0525	...	0625	...	0721	...		2221	...
Goch d.	0538	...	0638	...	0738	...	and at	2238	...
Weeze d.	0545	...	0645	...	0745	...	the same	2245	...
Kevelaer d.	0551	...	0651	...	0751	...		2251	...
Geldern d.	0558	...	0658	...	0758	...	minutes	2258	...
Krefeld Hbf d.	0626	0635	0726	0735	0826	0835	past each	2326	2335
Neuss Hbf d.	|	0653	|	0753	|	0853		|	2353
Köln Hbf a.	|	0718	|	0818	|	0918	hour until	|	0018
Düsseldorf Hbf a.	0652	...	0752	...	0852	...		2352	...

b – Runs daily Duisburg - Wesel.
d – To Düsseldorf Flughafen Terminal (a. 0425).
e – Ⓐ only.
f – Arrives 2146. Departs 2157 on ⚒.
j – Arrives 7–11 minutes earlier.
r – ⚒ only.
t – Also Apr. 13, 16, 30, May 24, June 4; not Apr. 14.
v – Terminates at Hamm on Apr. 14.
△ – Subsequent trains depart Koblenz at 0726, 0830 and then at 30 mins past each hour.
▽ – Certain later services depart Emmerich at 11 minutes past the hour.

‡ – Services to / from Arnhem are expected to start running from Apr. 6.
• – Distance from Köln Hbf: Neuss *36 km*, Krefeld *54 km*.
◐ – Operated by Mittelrheinbahn.
◇ – *RE13* services operated by **eurobahn** Keolis Deutschland GmbH & Co. KG.
⊖ – Düsseldorf - Kleve is operated by Nord West Bahn GmbH.
⊙ – Düsseldorf - Emmerich - Arnhem operated by Abellio Rail NRW.
⊡ – See shaded panel for a summary of the principal Rhein – Ruhr *RE* routes.

	RE1	*RE2*	*RE3*	*RE4*	*RE5*	*RE6*	*RE7*	*RE11*	*RE13*	*RE42*
Aachen Hbf	●	...	...	●	...	...	...	...	...	...
Köln Hbf	●	...	...	|	●	●	●	...	...	...
Mönchengladbach Hbf	|	...	...	●	|	|	|	...	●	●
Düsseldorf Hbf	●	●	●	●	●	●	|	●	●	|
Duisburg Hbf	●	●	●	|	●	●	|	●	|	●
Essen Hbf	●	●	|	|	...	●	|	●	|	●
via Gelsenkirchen	|	●	●	|	...	|	|	|	|	●
via Wuppertal and Hagen	|	|	|	●	...	|	●	|	●	|
Dortmund Hbf	●	|	●	●	...	●	|	●	|	|
Hamm (Westf)	●	|	●	...	...	●	●	●	●	|
Münster (Westf) Hbf	...	●	...	...	...	...	●	...	...	●

GERMANY *See page 367 for a summary of Christmas / New Year alterations*

802 RHEIN – RUHR LOCAL SERVICES *RE / RB services*

RE8 / RB27 Mönchengladbach - Köln - Königswinter - Koblenz

km		Ⓐ	⚒	⚒		⚒						▲								Ⓑ				
0	**Mönchengladbach** ⊖ d.	0440	0503e	0540	0603e	0640	0703e	0740	0803e	0840	...		1340	...	1440	1503e		1740	1803e	1840	1903e	*1940*	*2040*	*2140*
3	Rheydt Hbf ⊖ d.	0444	0507e	0544	0607e	0644	0707e	0744	0807e	0844	...		1344	...	1444	1507e		1744	1807e	1844	1907e	*1944*	*2044*	*2144*
22	Grevenbroich ⊖ d.	0502	0528e	0602	0628e	0702	0728e	0802	0828e	0902	...	and at	1402	...	1502	1528e	and at	1802	1828e	1902	1928e	*2002*	*2102*	*2202*
56	**Köln** Hbf ⊖ a.	0535	0600e	0635	0700e	0735	0800e	0835	0900e	0935	...		1435	...	1535	1600e		1835	1900e	1935	2000e	*2035*	*2135*	*2235*
56	**Köln** Hbf 807 d.	0538	0601t	0638	0701t	0738	0801t	0838	0901t	0938	1001t	the same	1438	1501t	1538	1601t	the same	1838	1901t	1938	2001t	2101	2201	2301
57	**Köln** Messe/Deutz d.	0541	0604t	0641	0704t	0741	0804t	0841	0904t	0941	1004t		1441	1504t	1541	1604t		1841	1904t	1941	2004t	2104	2204	2304
71	Köln/Bonn Flughafen ✈ d.	0551	|	0651	|	0751	|	0851	|	0951	|	minutes	1451	|	1551	|	minutes	1851	|	1951	|	|	|	|
83	Troisdorf 807 d.	0601	0623	0701	0723	0801	0823	0901	0923	1001	1023		1501	1523	1601	1623		1901	1923	2001	2023	2123	2223	2323
92	**Bonn** Beuel d.	0611	0633	0711	0733	0811	0833	0911	0933	1011	1033	past each	1511	1533	1611	1633	past each	1911	1933	2011	2033	2133	2233	2333
100	Königswinter d.	0620	0643	0720	0743	0820	0843	0920	0943	1020	1043		1520	1543	1620	1643		1920	1943	2020	2043	2143	2243	2343
105	Bad Honnef d.	0626	0649	0726	0749	0826	0849	0926	0949	1026	1049	hour until	1526	1549	1626	1649	hour until	1926	1949	2026	2049	2149	2249	2349
115	Linz (Rhein) d.	0637	0702	0735t	0802	0835	0902	0935	1002	1035	1102		1535	1602	1635	1702		1935	2002	2035	2102	2202	2302	0002
122	Bad Hönningen d.	0642	0709	0740t	0809	0840	0909	0940	1009	1040	1109		1540	1609	1640	1709		1940	2009	2040	2109	2209	2309	...
138	Neuwied 914 d.	0655	0724	0751t	0824	0851	0924	0951	1024	1051	1124		1551	1624	1651	1724		1951	2024	2051	2124	2224	2324	...
◊153	**Koblenz** Hbf 914 a.	0715	0740	0813t	0840	0913	0940	1013	1040	1113	1140		1613	1640	1713	1740		2013	2040	2113	2140	2240	2340	...

	⚒			Ⓐ		Ⓐ	⑥		⚒													Ⓑ		
Koblenz Hbf 914 d.	...	...	0518r	0537	0618r	0637	0647	0718	0747	0818	0847		1147	1218	1246	1318	1347		1818	1847	1918	1947	2018	2118
Neuwied 914 d.	...	...	0533r	0557	0633r	0657	0708	0733	0808	0833	0908		1208	1233	1306	1333	1408		1833	1908	1933	2008	2033	2133
Bad Hönningen d.	...	...	0546r	0611	0646r	0711	0719	0746	0819	0846	0919	and at	1219	1246	1317	1346	1419	and at	1846	1919	1946	2019	2046	2146
Linz (Rhein) d.	0453	...	0553	0618	0653	0718	0724	0753	0824	0853	0924		1224	1253	1322	1353	1424		1853	1924	1953	2024	2053	2153
Bad Honnef d.	0503	...	0603	0629	0703	0729	0733	0803	0833	0903	0933	the same	1233	1303	1333	1403	1433	the same	1903	1933	2003	2033	2103	2203
Königswinter d.	0509	...	0609	0635	0709	0735	0739	0809	0839	0909	0939		1239	1309	1339	1409	1439		1909	1939	2009	2039	2109	2209
Bonn Beuel d.	0518	...	0618	0646	0718	0746	0749	0818	0849	0918	0949	minutes	1249	1318	1349	1418	1449	minutes	1918	1949	2018	2049	2118	2218
Troisdorf 807 d.	0528	...	0628	0659	0728	0759	0759	0828	0859	0928	0959		1259	1328	1359	1428	1459		1928	1959	2028	2059	2128	2228
Köln/Bonn Flughafen ✈ d.	|	...	|	0708	|	0808	0808	|	0908	|	1008	past each	1308	|	1408	|	1508	past each	|	2008	|	2108	|	|
Köln Messe/Deutz d.	0550	0619	0650	0719	0750	0819	0819	0850	0919	0950	1019		1319	1350	1419	1450	1519		1950	2019	2050	2119	2150	2250
Köln Hbf 807 a.	0553	0622	0653	0722	0753	0822	0822	0853	0922	0953	1022	hour until	1322	1353	1422	1453	1522	hour until	1953	2022	2053	2122	2153	2253
Köln Hbf ⊖ d.	0559e	0625	0659e	0725	0759e	0825	0825	...	0925	...	1025		1325	...	1425	1459e	1525		1959e	2025	...	2125	*2225*	*2325*
Grevenbroich ⊖ d.	0630e	0655	0730e	0755	0830e	0855	0855	...	0955	...	1055		1355	...	1455	1530e	1555		2030e	2055	...	2155	*2255*	*2355*
Rheydt Hbf ⊖ d.	0651e	0715	0751e	0815	0851e	0915	0915	...	1015	...	1115		1415	...	1515	1551e	1615		2051e	2115	...	2215	*2315*	*0015*
Mönchengladbach ⊖ a.	0656e	0720	0756e	0820	0856e	0920	0920	...	1020	...	1120		1420	...	1520	1556e	1620		2056e	2120	...	2220	*2320*	*0020*

S-Bahn 13 Köln - Köln/Bonn Flughafen ✈ - Troisdorf

			Ⓒz	Ⓐv	Ⓒz	Ⓐv	Ⓐ		Ⓐ	Ⓒ	Ⓐ			Ⓐ	Ⓒ	Ⓐ							
Köln Hbf d.	0011	0041	0241	0245	0341	0345	0421	0441	0501	0511	0521	0541	and at the same	2001	2011	2021	2041	2111	2141	2211	2241	2311	2341
Köln Messe/Deutz d.	0013	0043	0243	0247	0343	0347	0423	0443	0503	0513	0523	0543	minutes past	2003	2013	2023	2043	2113	2143	2213	2243	2313	2343
Köln/Bonn Flughafen ✈ d.	0026	0056	0256	0259	0356	0359	0436	0456	0516	0526	0536	0556	each hour until	2016	2026	2036	2056	2126	2156	2226	2256	2326	2356
Troisdorf a.	0036	0108	0308	...	0408	...	0446	0508	0528	0536	0547	0607		2027	2036	2048	2108	2136	2208	2236	2308	2336	0008

				Ⓒz		Ⓒz		Ⓐ		Ⓐ	Ⓒ	Ⓐ			Ⓐ	Ⓒ	Ⓐ						
Troisdorf d.	0013	0043	0113	0313	...	0413	...	...	0513	0533	0543	0553	and at the same	2013	2033	2043	2053	2113	2143	2213	2243	2313	2343
Köln/Bonn Flughafen ✈ d.	0024	0054	0124	0324	0324	0424	0424	0444	0524	0544	0554	0604	minutes past	2024	2044	2054	2104	2124	2154	2224	2254	2324	2354
Köln Messe/Deutz a.	0036	0106	0136	0336	0336	0436	0436	0456	0536	0556	0606	0616	each hour until	2036	2056	2106	2116	2136	2206	2236	2306	2336	0006
Köln Hbf a.	0039	0109	0139	0339	0339	0439	0439	0459	0539	0559	0609	0619		2039	2059	2109	2119	2139	2209	2239	2309	2339	0009

Dortmund - Unna - Soest ✣

km			Ⓒ	⚒	⚒	Ⓐ	Ⓐ	Ⓐ	Ⓐ	Ⓐ		Ⓐh			Ⓐh		Ⓐh		Ⓐh				
0	**Dortmund** Hbf 805 d.	0007	0107	0507	0607	0637	0707	0737	0807	0837	0907	0937	and at the same	1707	1737	1807	1837	1907	1937	2007	2107	2207	2307
23	Unna d.	0032	0132	0532	0632	0702	0732	0802	0832	0902	0932	1002	minutes past	1732	1802	1832	1902	1932	2002	2032	2132	2232	2332
53	**Soest** 805 a.	0054	0154	0554	0654	0724	0754	0824	0854	0924	0954	1024	each hour until	1754	1824	1854	1924	1954	2024	2054	2154	2254	2354

		Ⓒ	Ⓒ	⚒	Ⓐ	⚒	Ⓐ		Ⓐ		Ⓐ		Ⓐh			Ⓐh		Ⓐh					
Soest 805 d.	0003	0103	...	0503	0533	0603	0633	0703	0733	0803	0833	0903	0933	and at the same	1703	1733	1803	1833	1903	2003	2103	2203	2303
Unna d.	0027	0127	0237	0527	0557	0627	0657	0727	0757	0827	0857	0927	0957	minutes past	1727	1757	1827	1857	1927	2027	2127	2227	2327
Dortmund Hbf 805 a.	0051	0151	0302	0551	0621	0651	0721	0751	0821	0851	0921	0951	1021	each hour until	1751	1821	1851	1921	1951	2051	2151	2251	2351

RB 53 Dortmund - Schwerte - Iserlohn

km		Ⓐ	Ⓐ		Ⓐ		Ⓐ		Ⓐ					Ⓐ		Ⓐ		Ⓐ								
0	**Dortmund** Hbf d.	0523	0553	0623	0653	0723	0753	0823	0853	0923	and	1323	1423	1453	1523	1553	1623	1653	1723	1823	1923	2023	2123	2223	2323
18	Schwerte (Ruhr) d.	0545	0615	0645	0715	0745	0815	0845	0915	0945	hourly	1345	1445	1515	1545	1615	1645	1715	1745	1845	1945	2045	2145	2245	2345
38	**Iserlohn** a.	0609	0638	0709e	0739	0809r	0839	0909	0939	1009	until	1409	1509	1539	1609	1639	1709	1739	1809	1909	2009	2109	2209	2309	0009

	Ⓐ	Ⓐ	Ⓐ	Ⓐ		Ⓐ		Ⓐ		Ⓐ						Ⓐ		Ⓐ		Ⓐ						
Iserlohn d.	...	0521	...	0621	0651e	0721	0751r	0821	0851	0921	0951	and	1351	1451	1521	1551	1621	1651	1721	1751	1851	1951	2051	2151	2251
Schwerte (Ruhr) d.	0520	0550	0620	0650	0720	0750	0820	0850	0920	0950	1020	hourly	1420	1520	1550	1620	1650	1720	1750	1820	1920	2020	2120	2220	2320
Dortmund Hbf a.	0838	0608	0638	0708	0738	0808	0838	0908	0938	1008	1038	until	1438	1538	1608	1638	1708	1738	1808	1838	1938	2038	2138	2238	2338

BONN - REMAGEN (*20 km*) - AHRBRÜCK (*48 km*) and v.v.

From Bonn Hbf at 0749⚒r, 0849 and hourly until 2049; then 2149⑤⑥**k**.
Trains depart Remagen 22 minutes later. Journey time from Bonn: 67 minutes.

From Ahrbrück at 0703⚒, 0803 and hourly until 2003 (also 2103 and 2203 to Remagen only). Journey time to Remagen 44 minutes, Bonn 66 minutes.

DUISBURG - MOERS - XANTEN and v.v. (45 km, journey time: 45 – 57 minutes) ⊠

From Duisburg Hbf at: 0555⚒, 0655⚒, 0810, 0910 and hourly until 2310.

From Xanten at: 0458⚒, 0558⚒, 0658, 0801, 0901 and hourly until 1601; then 1702, 1802, 1901, 2001, 2101 and 2201.

Trains call at Moers, 18 minutes from Duisburg, 27 – 29 minutes from Xanten.

OTHER USEFUL S-BAHN LINKS

Services operate every 20 minutes (every 30 minutes evenings and weekends)

Service	*Route (journey time in minutes)*
S1	Solingen Hbf - Düsseldorf Hbf (22) - Düsseldorf Flughafen ✈ (35) - Duisburg Hbf (53) - Essen Hbf (72) - Bochum Hbf (90) - Dortmund Hbf (113)
S3	Oberhausen Hbf - Mülheim Hbf (8) - Essen Hbf (17).
S9	Essen Hbf - Wuppertal Hbf (46).
S11	Düsseldorf Flughafen Terminal ✈ - Düsseldorf Hbf (12) - Neuss Hbf (31) - Köln Hbf (82).

e – Ⓐ only.
h – Also Dec. 17.
k – Also Apr. 13, 16, 30, May 24, June 4.
r – ⚒ only.
t – 2 – 4 minutes later on Ⓐ.
v – Not Feb. 24, 27, 28.

z – Also Feb. 24, 27, 28.

▲ – On Ⓐ the 1040, 1140 and 1240 from Mönchengladbach run 2 – 6 minutes later Linz (Rhein) - Koblenz Hbf.

⊠ – Operated by Nord West Bahn GmbH.

✣ – Operated by **eurobahn** Keolis Deutschland GmbH & Co. KG (2nd class only).

◊ – Via Koblenz-Lützel (*159 km* via Ehrenbreitstein).

⊖ – Additional journeys Mönchengladbach Hbf - Köln Hbf and v.v.:
From Mönchengladbach at 0040Ⓒ, 0440⑥, 0540†, 0627Ⓐ, 0640†, 1840⑥, 2240 and 2340. **From Köln** at 0025, 0125Ⓒ, 0525⚒, 0725Ⓒ, 0825†, 0925† and 2125⑥.

803 DORTMUND and MÜNSTER - ENSCHEDE *2nd class only*

km	△	Ⓐ	⚒									△	Ⓐ	⚒	⚒	Ⓐ	Ⓒ				
0	**Dortmund** Hbf d.	0552	0652	0752r	0852		1852	1952	2052	2152		**Enschede** d.	...	...	0556e	0656	0702j	0802		2002	2102
44	Dülmen d.	0640	0740	0840r	0940	and	1940	2040	2140	2240		Gronau (Westf) d.	...	0524e	0620	0708	0720j	0820	and	2020	2113
61	Coesfeld (Westf) d.	0705	0800	0900	1000	hourly	2000	2100	2153	2253		Coesfeld (Westf) d.	0506	0603	0703	0803	0803	0903	hourly	2103	...
96	Gronau (Westf) d.	0745	0845	0945	1045	until	2045	2145q	...	...		Dülmen d.	0520	0617	0717	0817	0817	0917	until	2117	...
103	**Enschede** a.	0756	0856	0956	1056		2056	2156q	...	...		**Dortmund** Hbf a.	0607	0707	0807	0907	0907	1007		2207	...

km	△	Ⓐ	Ⓐ	⚒								△	⚒	⚒							⑤⑥s
0	**Münster** (Westf) Hbf d.	0508	0608	0708	...	0808	and	2108	2208	2308		**Enschede** d.	...	0626	0732v	...	0832	and	2132	2232	2332
56	Gronau (Westf) d.	0609	0715	0815	0815	0915	hourly	2215	2315	0004		Gronau (Westf) d.	0544	0644	0744	...	0844	hourly	2144	2244	2344
63	**Enschede** a.	0620	0726	0826	0826	0926	until	2226	2326	...		**Münster** (Westf) Hbf a.	0644	0744	0844	...	0944	until	2244	2344	0044

e – Ⓐ only.
j – ⑥ only.
q – Coesfeld - Enschede on †.
r – ⚒ only.
s – Also Apr. 13, 16, 30, May 24; not Apr. 14.
v – ①-⑥ (not Apr. 17, May 25, June 5).
△ – German holiday dates apply.

HAGEN - KASSEL — 804

RE services

km		Ⓐf	Ⓐ	⚒	Ⓐ	⑥	f												⑥				d	d	d
0	**Hagen** Hbf 802 d.	...	0503	...	0556	0617	...	0717	0817	0917	1017	1117	1217	1317	1417	1517	1617	1717	1717	1817	1917	2017	*2122*	*2222*	*2322*
14	Schwerte (Ruhr) 802 d.	...	0513	...	0606	0628	...	0728	0828	0928	1028	1128	1228	1328	1428	1528	1628	1728	1728	1828	1928	2028	2149	2249	2349
57	Arnsberg (Westf) d.	...	0542	...	0639	0658	...	0758	0858	0958	1058	1158	1258	1358	1458	1558	1658	1758	1758	1858	1958	2058	2219	2321	0021
77	Meschede d.	...	0601	...	0657	0716	...	0816	0916	1016	1116	1216	1316	1416	1516	1616	1716	1816	1816	1916	2016	2116	2237	2339	0039
85	Bestwig d.	...	0608	...	0706	0723	...	0823	0923	1023	1123	1223	1323	1423	1523	1623	1723	1823	1823	1923	2022	2123	2246	2345	0045
100	Brilon Wald d.	...	0622	...	0732j	0737	...	0837	0937	1037	1137	1237	1337	1437	1537	1637	1737	1837	1837	1937	...	2137	2259	...	...
126	Marsberg d.	...	0650	...	0759	0800	...	0900	1000	1100	1200	1300	1400	1500	1600	1700	1800	1900	1900	2000	...	2200	...	...	...
151	Warburg (Westf) a.	...	0709	...	0818	0819	...	0919	1019	1119	1219	1319	1419	1519	1619	1719	1819	1919	1919	2019	...	2219	...	...	...
151	Warburg (Westf) 805 d.	0621	0723	0723	...	...	0824	0923	*1024*f	...	...	...	*1424*f	1523	*1624*f	1723	...	...	1923	*2024*f	...	*2224*t	...	...	...
177	Hofgeismar d.	0637	0739	0739	...	...	0838	0939	*1038*f	...	...	...	*1438*f	1539	*1638*f	1739	...	...	1939	*2038*f	...	*2239*t	...	...	...
202	**Kassel** Wilhelmshöhe 805 a.	0653	0758	0758	...	...	0857	0958	*1056*f	...	...	...	*1456*f	1558	*1656*f	1757	...	...	1956	*2055*f	...	*2258*t	...	...	...

	⚒	⚒	Ⓐ	⑥		Ⓐ	⑥						⑦b												
Kassel Wilhelmshöhe 805 d.	...	...	...	...	...	*0555*f	...	...	...	*0702*f	0802	...	1002	...	*1102*f	1202	*1302*f	...	...	1602	*1703*f	1802	*1903*f	...	*2102*t
Hofgeismar d.	...	...	...	...	...	*0611*f	...	...	...	*0719*f	0820	...	1020	...	*1119*f	1220	*1319*f	...	...	1620	*1719*f	1820	*1919*f	...	*2119*t
Warburg (Westf) 805 a.	...	...	...	...	...	*0625*f	...	...	...	*0733*f	0836	...	1036	...	*1133*f	1236	*1333*f	...	...	1636	*1733*f	1836	*1933*f	...	*2133*t
Warburg (Westf) d.	...	...	0530	0538	...	0630	0638	...	...	0738	0838	0938	1038	1038	1138	1238	1338	1438	1538	1638	1738	1838	1938	...	2138
Marsberg d.	...	...	0550	0559	...	0650	0659	...	...	0759	0859	0959	1059	1059	1159	1259	1359	1459	1559	1659	1759	1859	1959	...	2159
Brilon Wald d.	...	...	0616	0621	...	0718	0721	...	...	0821	0921	1021	1121	1121	1221	1321	1421	1521	1621	1721	1821	1921	2021	...	2221
Bestwig d.	0434	0534	0634	0634	0634	0734	0734	0734	...	0834	0934	1034	1134	1134	1234	1334	1434	1534	1634	1734	1834	1934	2034	...	2234
Meschede d.	0441	0541	0641	0641	0641	0741	0741	0741	...	0841	0941	1041	1141	1141	1241	1341	1441	1541	1641	1741	1841	1941	2041	...	2241
Arnsberg (Westf) d.	0459	0559	0659	0659	0659	0759	0759	0759	...	0859	0959	1059	1159	1159	1259	1359	1459	1559	1659	1759	1859	1959	2059	...	2259
Schwerte (Ruhr) 802 a.	0528	0628	0728	0728	0728	0828	0828	0828	...	0928	1028	1128	1228	1228	1328	1428	1528	1628	1728	1828	1928	2028	2128	...	2328
Hagen Hbf 802 a.	0542	0642	0742	0742	0742	0842	0842	0842	...	0942	1042	1142	1242	1242	1342	1442	1542	1642	1742	1842	1942	2042	2142	...	2342

b – Also Apr. 14, 15, May 25, June 5.
d – From Dortmund Hbf (departs 26 minutes before Schwerte departures time).
f – Until May 5.
j – Arrives 0722.
t – Until May 4.

DORTMUND and MÜNSTER - PADERBORN - KASSEL — 805

SERVICE UNTIL MAY 5 (subject to alteration late evening on May 5)

km								*RE*						*RE*			*ICE*			*IC*			*IC*		
			◇	◇	◇	◇		**10001**	◇	◇	◇	◇		**10005**	◇	◇	**1223**	◇	◇	**2155**	◇	◇	**1959**	◇	◇
		Ⓐ	Ⓐ	⑥	Ⓐ	Ⓒ			Ⓐ	Ⓒ	Ⓐ	Ⓒ			Ⓐ	Ⓒ		Ⓐ	Ⓒ		Ⓐ	Ⓒ	⑤⑦	Ⓐ	Ⓒ
																	E 🍷			**X**			**B**		
	Köln Hbf 800 802 d.	...	...	...	...	...	...	...	...	...	...	...	...	...	...	...	0825d	...	...	0859	...	...	...	...	...
	Düsseldorf Hbf 800 802 d.	...	...	...	...	...	...	0536a	...	...	...	...	...	0736	...	...	0848	...	...	0946	...	...	1113	...	...
0	**Dortmund** Hbf 802 d.	*0441*	...	...	...	...	...	0642a	...	...	...	...	...	0839	...	...	0942	...	...	1043	...	...	1207	...	...
	Münster (Westf) Hbf 802 d.	|	0510	0510	0610	0610	0634	|	0710	0710	0810	0810	0834	|	0910	0910	|	1010	1010	|	1110	1110	|	1210	1210
31	Hamm (Westf) 802 a.	*0457*	0537	0537	0637	0637	0657	0702a	0737	0737	0837	0837	0857	0902	0937	0937	1002	1037	1037	1102	1137	1137	1228	1237	1237
31	Hamm (Westf) d.	0503	0546	0552	0646	0652	...	0708	0746	0752	0846	0852	...	0908	0946	0952	1007	1046	1052	1107	1146	1152	1234	1246	1252
57	Soest 802 d.	0517	0602	0608	0702	0708	...	0722	0802	0808	0902	0908	...	0922	1002	1008	1022	1102	1108	1122	1202	1208	1248	1302	1308
77	Lippstadt d.	0528	0614	0620	0714	0720	...	0733	0814	0820	0914	0920	...	0933	1014	1020	1033	1114	1120	1133	1214	1220	1259	1314	1320
109	**Paderborn** Hbf 809 811 d.	0544	0642	0642	0739	0744	...	0750	0842	0842	0939	0940	...	0950	1042	1042	1049	1139	1140	1149	1242	1242	1317	1339	1340
126	Altenbeken 809 811 d.	0557	0654	0654	...	...	...	0801	0854	0854	...	...	...	1001	1054	1054	1103	...	...	1204	1254	1254	1330	...	...
163	Warburg (Westf) 804 d.	0621	0716	0716	...	...	...	0824	0916	0916	...	...	...	1024	1116	1116	1125	...	...	1226	1316	1316	|	...	...
214	**Kassel** Wilhelmshöhe 804 a.	0653	*0758*	*0758*	...	...	...	0857	*0958*	*0958*	...	...	...	1056	...	...	1156	...	...	1257	...	...	1419	...	...

		RE						*RE*					*IC*			*RE*				*RE*			*RE*		
		10013	◇	◇	◇	◇		**10017**	◇	◇	◇	◇	**2157**	◇	◇	**10023**	◇	◇		**10025**	◇		**10029**	◇	◇
			Ⓐ	Ⓒ	Ⓐ	Ⓒ			Ⓐ	Ⓒ	Ⓐ	Ⓒ	Ⓑ	Ⓐ	Ⓒ		Ⓐ	Ⓒ							
													D												
Köln Hbf 800 802 d.	...	...	...	...	...	...	...	...	...	...	...	...	1520	...	...	...	...	...	...	...	...	...	...	...	...
Düsseldorf Hbf 800 802 d.	...	1136	...	...	...	...	...	1336	...	...	...	...	1546	...	...	1636	...	...	...	1736	...	...	1936	...	...
Dortmund Hbf 802 d.	...	1239	...	...	...	...	...	1439	...	...	...	...	1643	...	...	1739	...	...	...	1839	...	...	2039	...	...
Münster (Westf) Hbf 802 d.	1234	|	1310	1310	1410	1410	1434	|	1510	1510	1610	1610	|	1710	1710	|	1810	1810	1834	|	*1934*	2034	|	*2134*	*2234*
Hamm (Westf) 802 a.	1257	1302	1337	1337	1437	1437	1457	1502	1537	1537	1637	1637	1702	1737	1737	1802	1837	1837	1857	1902	*1957*	2057	2102	*2157*	*2257*
Hamm (Westf) d.	...	1308	1346	1352	1446	1452	...	1508	1546	1552	1646	1652	1707	1746	1752	1808	1846	1852	...	1908	2007	...	2108	2207	2307
Soest 802 d.	...	1322	1402	1408	1502	1508	...	1522	1602	1608	1702	1708	1722	1802	1808	1822	1902	1908	...	1922	2023	...	2122	2223	2323
Lippstadt d.	...	1333	1414	1420	1514	1520	...	1533	1614	1620	1714	1720	1733	1814	1820	1833	1914	1920	...	1933	2035	...	2133	2235	2335
Paderborn Hbf 809 811 d.	...	1350	1442	1442	1539	1540	...	1550	1642	1642	1739	1740	1749	1842	1842	1849	1938	1940	...	1950	2059	...	2150	2300	0002
Altenbeken 809 811 d.	...	1401	1454	1454	...	...	...	1601	1654	1654	...	...	1804	1854	1854	...	...	...	...	2001	2111	...	2201	...	0014c
Warburg (Westf) 804 d.	...	1424	1516	1516	...	...	...	1624	1716	1716	...	...	1826	1916	1916	...	...	...	...	2024	2133	...	2224	...	0037c
Kassel Wilhelmshöhe 804 a.	...	1456	*1558*	*1558*	...	...	...	1656	*1757*	*1757*	...	...	1857	...	*1956*k	...	...	...	...	2055	...	...	2258	...	...

			RE			*RE*		*RE*						*IC*					*RE*						*RE*
	◇	◇	**10004**	◇	◇	**10006**	◇	**10008**		◇	◇	◇	◇	**2156**	◇	◇	◇	◇	**10016**		◇	◇	◇	◇	**10020**
	⑥	Ⓐ	Ⓐ		Ⓐ	⚒				Ⓒ	Ⓐ	Ⓒ	Ⓐ	①–⑥	Ⓒ	Ⓐ	Ⓒ	Ⓐ			Ⓒ	Ⓐ	Ⓒ	Ⓐ	
										¶				**H**											
Kassel Wilhelmshöhe 804 d.	...	...	...	...	...	0555a	...	0702	...	...	...	*0802*	*0802*	0902	...	...	*1002*v	...	1102	...	...	...	*1202*	*1202*	1302
Warburg (Westf) 804 d.	...	...	0534	...	0614	0634a	...	0734	...	...	...	0839	0839	0935	...	...	1039	1039	1134	...	...	...	1239	1239	1334
Altenbeken 809 811 d.	...	...	0559	...	0638	0659a	...	0759	...	...	...	0902	0902	0956	...	...	1102	1102	1159	...	...	...	1302	1302	1359
Paderborn Hbf 809 811 d.	0513	0544	0611	0621	0651	0711	0721	0811	...	0816	0821	0916	0921j	1010	1016	1021	1116	1121j	1211	...	1216	1221	1316	1321j	1411
Lippstadt d.	0536	0607	0627	0644	0714	0727	0744	0827	...	0836	0844	0936	0944	1026	1036	1044	1136	1144	1227	...	1236	1244	1336	1344	1427
Soest 802 d.	0548	0619	0638	0656	0726	0738	0756	0838	...	0848	0856	0948	0956	1037	1048	1056	1148	1156	1238	...	1248	1256	1348	1356	1438
Hamm (Westf) a.	0606	0637	0652	0714	0744	0752	0814	0852	...	0906	0914	1006	1014	1052	1106	1114	1206	1214	1252	...	1306	1314	1406	1414	1452
Hamm (Westf) 802 d.	0620	0650	0657	0720	0750	0757	0820	0857	0859	0920	0920	1020	1020	1056	1120	1120	1220	1220	1257	1259	1320	1320	1420	1420	1457
Münster (Westf) Hbf 802 a.	0647	0717	|	0747	0817	|	0847	|	0922	0947	0947	1047	1047	|	1147	1147	1247	1247	|	1322	1347	1347	1447	1447	|
Dortmund Hbf 802 a.	...	...	0717	...	...	0817	...	0917	...	...	...	...	...	1114	...	...	...	...	1317	...	...	...	...	...	1517
Düsseldorf Hbf 800 802 a.	...	...	0824	...	...	0924	...	1024	...	...	...	...	...	1212	...	...	...	...	1424	...	...	...	...	...	1624
Köln Hbf 800 802 a.	...	...	...	...	...	...	...	...	...	...	...	...	...	1239	...	...	...	...	...	...	...	...	...	...	...

				ICE	*ICE*			*IC*					*RE*				*RE*			*RE*		*IC*			
		◇	◇	**1224**	**1228**	◇	◇	**2152**	◇	◇	◇	◇	**10028**		◇	◇	**10030**	◇	◇	**10032**		**1952**	◇		◇
		Ⓒ	Ⓐ	Ⓒ	Ⓐ	Ⓒ	Ⓐ		Ⓒ	Ⓐ	Ⓒ	Ⓐ			Ⓒ	Ⓐ		Ⓒ	Ⓐ			⑤⑦			
				M 🍷	**A** 🍷			**L**														**G**			
Kassel Wilhelmshöhe 804 d.	...	...	...	1402	1402	...	...	1502	...	...	*1602*	*1602*	1703	...	...	...	...	*1802*	*1802*	1903	...	1943	...	2102	...
Warburg (Westf) 804 d.	...	...	...	1433	1433	1438	1438	1535	...	...	1639	1639	1734	...	...	...	...	1839	1839	1934	...	2018	2039	2134	...
Altenbeken 809 811 d.	...	...	...	1456	1456	1502	1502	1556	...	...	1702	1702	1759	...	...	...	...	1902	1902	1959	...	2040	2102	2159	...
Paderborn Hbf 809 811 d.	...	1416	1421	1510	1510	1516	1521j	1610	1616	1621	1716	1721j	1811	...	1816	1821	1911	1916	1921j	2011	...	2054	2116	2211	2311
Lippstadt d.	...	1436	1444	1526	1526	1536	1544	1626	1636	1644	1736	1744	1827	...	1836	1844	1927	1936	1944	2027	...	2110	2139	2227	2334
Soest 802 d.	...	1448	1456	1537	1537	1548	1556	1637	1648	1656	1748	1756	1838	...	1848	1856	1938	1948	1956	2038	...	2121	2151	2238	2346
Hamm (Westf) a.	...	1506	1514	1551	1551	1606	1614	1652	1706	1714	1806	1814	1852	...	1906	1914	1952	2006	2014	2052	...	2135	2211	2252	0004
Hamm (Westf) 802 d.	1459	1520	1520	1556	1556	1620	1620	1656	1720	1720	1820	1820	1857	1859	1920	1920	1957	2020	2020	2057	2059	2140	2220	2259	0010
Münster (Westf) Hbf 802 a.	1522	1547	1547	|	|	1647	1647	|	1747	1747	1847	1847	|	1922	1947	1947	|	2047	2047	|	2122	|	2247	*2329*	0040
Dortmund Hbf 802 a.	...	...	...	1614	1614	...	...	1714	...	...	...	...	1919	...	...	...	2017	...	...	2117	...	2156	...	...	...
Düsseldorf Hbf 800 802 a.	...	...	...	1706	1706	...	...	1810	...	...	...	...	1624	...	...	...	2124	...	...	2224	...	2256	...	...	...
Köln Hbf 800 802 a.	...	...	...	1733	1728d	...	...	...	...	...	...	...	...	...	...	...	...	...	...	...	...	2325	...	...	...

A – [12] and 🍷 München - Kassel - Düsseldorf - Wiesbaden - Frankfurt.
B – ⑤⑦ (also Apr. 13, 17, May 1; not Apr. 14, 16, 30). [12] Düsseldorf - Kassel - Halle - Berlin. Train number **1969** Feb. 12 - May 5.
D – Ⓑ (not Apr. 14, 16, 19, 26, 30). [12] Köln - Kassel - Halle.
E – [12] and 🍷 (Darmstadt Ⓐ -) Köln - Kassel - Nürnberg - München.
G – ⑤⑦ (also Apr. 13, 17, May 1; not Apr. 14, 16, 30, May 5). [12] Berlin - Halle - Erfurt - Kassel - Köln. Train number **1962** Feb. 12 - May 1.
H – ①–⑥ to Feb. 10. [12] Halle - Kassel - Köln.
L – [12] (Leipzig - Weimar - Erfurt ● -) Kassel - Düsseldorf.
M – [12] and 🍷 München - Nürnberg - Kassel - Köln.
X – [12] Köln - Kassel (- Erfurt - Weimar - Leipzig ●).

a – Ⓐ only.
c – Runs Paderborn - Warburg on the mornings of ⑥⑦ (also Apr. 14).
d – Köln **Messe/Deutz**.
j – Arrives 6 minutes earlier.
k – ⑥ only.
v – ⑦ (also Apr. 14, 15, May 25, June 5).

¶ – Change trains at Hamm on ⑥.
● – Until Feb. 10.
◇ – Operated by **eurobahn** Keolis Deutschland (2nd class only).

806 FRANKFURT - GIESSEN - KASSEL and SIEGEN

FRANKFURT - GIESSEN - KASSEL

km	SEE NOTE ⊖	*RE* 4170 †	*RE* 4150 ⚒	*IC* 2378 ①–⑥ e🍷	*RE* 4152	◇	*IC* 2376 O🍷	*RE* 4154	◇	*IC* 2374 A🍷	*RE* 4156	◇	*IC* 2372 🍷	*RE* 4158	*IC* 2370 ◧ 🍷	*RE* 4160	*IC* 2276 🍷	*RE* 4162	◇	*IC* 2274 🍷	*RE* 4164	◇	*IC* 2272 ①–⑤ d🍷	*IC* 2172 ⑦w S🍷	*RE* 4166
	Karlsruhe Hbf **912** d.	...	...	...	...	...	0702	...	...	0905	...	...	1110k	...	1310	...	1510	...	...	1710	...	...	1910	...	...
	Heidelberg Hbf **912** d.	...	...	...	...	...	0746	...	...	0946	...	...	1146k	...	1346	...	1546	...	...	1746	...	...	1946	1946	...
0	**Frankfurt (Main)** Hbf ¶ d.	0508	0522	0649	0718	0814j	0852	0922	1022	1052	1122	1222	1252	1322	1450	1522	1650	1720	1822	1849	1922	2021	2052	2052	2122
34	Friedberg (Hess) ¶ d.	0530	0545	0715	0745	0845	0916	0945	1045	1116	1145	1245	1316	1345	1516	1545	1716	1745	1845	1916	1945	2045	2116	2116	2145
66	**Gießen** ¶ d.	0604	0604	0735	0804	0905	0935	1004	1105	1136	1204	1305	1335	1404	1535	1604	1735	1804	1905	1935	2004	2105	2135	2135	2204
96	Marburg (Lahn) ¶ d.	0620	0620	0751	0820	0920	0951	1020	1120	1152	1220	1320	1351	1420	1551	1620	1751	1820	1920	1951	2020	2120	2151	2151	2220
118	Stadtallendorf d.	0634	0634	0805	0834	0938	1005	1034	1138	1206	1234	1338	1405	1434	1605	1634	1805	1835	1938	2005	2034	2138	2205	2205	2234
138	Treysa ¶ d.	0649	0649	0818	0849	0955	1018	1049	1155	1219	1249	1355	1418	1449	1618	1649	1818	1849	1955	2018	2049	2155	2218	2218	2249
166	Wabern d.	0707	0707	|	0907	1017	|	1107	1217	|	1307	1417	|	1507	|	1707	1835	1907	2017	2035y	2107	2217	|	|	2307
196	**Kassel** Wilhelmshöhe a.	0726	0726	0852	0926	1047	1053	1126	1247	1254	1326	1447	1453	1526	1652	1726	1855	1926	2048	2055	2126	2247	2256	2256	2326
200	**Kassel** Hbf a.	0734	0734	|	0934	1055	|	1134	1255	|	1334	1455	|	1534	|	1734	|	1934	2055	|	2134	2253	...	...	2334
	Hannover Hbf **900** a.	...	...	0956	...	...	1156	...	...	1356	...	...	1556	...	1756	...	1956	...	...	2156v	...	...	...	...	...
	Hamburg Hbf **900** a.	...	...	1128	...	...	1328	...	...	1529	...	...	1732	...	1928	...	2128p	...	...	2328w	...	...	...	...	...
	Stralsund Hbf **830** a.	...	...	...	...	...	1630	...	...	...	...	...	2028	...	2228w	...	...	...	...	...	...	...	...	...	...

SEE NOTE ⊖	*RE* 4171 Ⓐ	*RE* 4151 ⑥	*IC* 2273 Ⓐ 🍷	*RE* 4173 Ⓐ	*RE* 4153 Ⓒ	*IC* 2271 ①–⑥ e🍷	*RE* 4155	*IC* 2277 ①–⑥ u🍷	◇	*RE* 4157	*IC* 2279 🍷	◇	*RE* 4159	*IC* 2371 🍷	*RE* 4161	*IC* 2373 🍷	*RE* 4163	*IC* 2375 B🍷	◇	*IC* 1995 ⑦w S🍷	*RE* 4165	*IC* 2377 O🍷	*RE* 4167	*IC* 2379 ⑤⑦ n🍷	*RE* 4169
Stralsund Hbf **830** d.	...	...	...	...	...	...	...	...	...	...	0524e	...	...	...	...	0927	...	...	...	...	...	1327	...	1527	...
Hamburg Hbf **900** d.	...	...	...	...	...	...	...	0625	...	...	0828e	...	...	1028	...	1228	...	1428	...	...	...	1627	...	1828	...
Hannover Hbf **900** d.	...	...	...	...	...	0558a	...	0801	...	...	1001e	...	...	1201	...	1401	...	1601	...	1703	...	1801	...	2001	...
Kassel Hbf d.	0400	0423	...	0611	0615	|	0823	|	0903	1023	|	1103	1223	|	1423	|	1623	|	1703	|	1823	|	2023	|	2223
Kassel Wilhelmshöhe d.	0405	0429	0459	0617	0621	0700	0829	0903	0908	1029	1103	1108	1229	1303	1429	1503	1629	1703	1709	1809	1829	1903	2029	2103	2229
Wabern d.	0423	0448	0520	0639	0645	0720	0848	|	0938	1048	|	1138	1248	|	1448	|	1648	|	1738	|	1848	|	2048	|	2252
Treysa ¶ d.	0441	0506	0537	0700	0703	0737	0906	0937	1005	1106	1137	1205	1306	1337	1506	1537	1706	1737	1805	|	1906	1937	2106	2137	2310
Stadtallendorf d.	0455	0519	0550	0716	0718	0750	0919	0950	1019	1119	1150	1219	1319	1350	1519	1550	1719	1750	1819	|	1919	1950	2119	2150	2323
Marburg (Lahn) ¶ d.	0512	0535	0605	0734	0734	0805	0935	1005	1035	1135	1205	1235	1335	1405	1535	1605	1735	1805	1835	1906	1935	2005	2135	2205	2339
Gießen ¶ d.	0536	0553	0623	0753	0753	0823	0953	1023	1054	1153	1223	1254	1353	1423	1553	1623	1753	1823	1854	1926	1953	2023	2153	2223	0008
Friedberg (Hess) ¶ d.	0600	0612	0642	0812	0812	0842	1012	1042	1112	1212	1242	1312	1412	1442	1612	1642	1812	1842	1912	|	2012	2042	2212	2242	0036
Frankfurt (Main) Hbf ¶ a.	0626	0635	0708	0838	0838	0908	1035	1108	1135	1235	1308	1335	1435	1508	1638	1708	1837	1908	1935	2012	2035	2108	2235	2304	0100
Heidelberg Hbf **912** a.	...	...	0812	...	...	1012	...	1212h	...	...	1412	...	...	1612	...	1812	...	2012	...	2112	...	2247f	...	...	...
Karlsruhe Hbf **912** a.	...	...	0850	...	...	1050	...	1250h	...	...	1450	...	...	1650	...	1852	...	2052	...	...	...	2327f	...	...	...

FRANKFURT - GIESSEN - SIEGEN

km		†	◇ ⚒	Ⓐ	◇ Ⓐ	◇ Ⓐ	◇ Ⓒ	◇ Ⓒ	Ⓐ	◇ ⚒		◇ Ⓐ	◇ Ⓒ		◇ ⚒		◇		◇		◇		◇		◇	◇
0	**Frankfurt** (Main) Hbf ‡ d.	0508	*0522*	0552	...	0615	0622	0622	0630	*0718*	0745	0814	*0822*	0831	*0922*	0952	1022	1031	*1122*	1152	1222	1231	*1322*	1352	1422	1422
34	Friedberg (Hess) ‡ d.	0530	*0545*	0615	...	0646	0645	0645	0657	*0745*	0815	0845	*0845*	0859	*0945*	1015	1045	1059	*1145*	1215	1245	1259	*1345*	1415	1445	1445
38	Bad Nauheim ‡ d.	0535	|	0619	...	|	|	|	0701	|	0819	|	|	0903	|	1019	|	1103	|	1219	|	1303	|	1419	|	|
66	**Gießen** ‡ a.	0602	*0602*	0635	...	0702	0702	0702	0724	*0802*	0835	0902	*0902*	0928	*1002*	1035	1102	1128	*1202*	1235	1302	1328	*1402*	1435	1502	1502
66	**Gießen** **906** d.	0604	0609	0640	0652	0705	0705	0709	0740	0809	0839	0909	0909	0940	1009	1039	1109	1140	1209	1239	1309	1340	1409	1439	1505	1509
	Marburg (Lahn) ‡ a.	0619	|	|	|	0720	0719	|	|	|	0904	|	|	|	|	1104	|	|	|	1304	|	|	|	1504	1519	|
	Treysa ‡ a.	0649	|	|	|	0753	0753	|	|	|	...	|	|	|	|	...	|	|	|	...	|	|	|	...	1553	|
79	Wetzlar **906** d.	...	0618	0650	0703	...	...	0718	0750	0818	...	0918	0918	0950	1018	...	1118	1150	1218	...	1318	1350	1418	...	...	1518
101	Herborn d.	...	0631	0712	0730	...	...	0733	0812	0833	...	0933	0933	1012	1033	...	1133	1212	1233	...	1333	1412	1433	...	...	1533
107	Dillenburg d.	...	0637	0722	0738	...	...	0738	0822	0838	...	0938	0938	1022	1038	...	1138	1222	1238	...	1338	1422	1438	...	...	1538
139	**Siegen** a.	...	0705	...	0805	...	...	0805	...	0905	...	1005	1005	...	1105	...	1205	...	1305	...	1405	...	1505	...	...	1605

		◇		◇ Ⓒ	◇	Ⓐ		Ⓐ	◇ Ⓒ	◇ Ⓐ		◇		◇		◇		◇			◇	◇			◇	
Frankfurt (Main) Hbf ‡ d.	1431	*1522*	1552	1622	1622	1631	1631	1701	*1720*	1730	1752	1822	1831	*1922*	1952	2021	2031	*2122*	2152	2152	2222	2222	2231	2324	...	0031
Friedberg (Hess) ‡ d.	1459	*1545*	1615	1645	1645	1659	1659	1725	*1745*	|	1815	1845	1859	*1945*	2015	2045	2059	*2145*	2215	2215	2245	2245	2259	2345	...	0059
Bad Nauheim ‡ d.	1503	|	1619	|	|	1703	1703	1730	|	1758	1819	|	1903	|	2019	|	2103	|	2219	2219	|	|	2303	|	...	0103
Gießen ‡ a.	1528	*1602*	1635	1702	1702	1728	1728	1748	*1802*	|	1835	1902	1928	*2002*	2035	2102	2128	*2202*	2235	2235	2302	2302	2328	0004	...	0128
Gießen **906** d.	1540	1609	1639	1705	1709	1739	1740	1749	1809	|	1839	1909	1940	2009	2039	2109	2139	2209	2240	2243	2305	2309	2333	0007	0011	0132
Marburg (Lahn) ‡ a.	|	|	1704	1719	|	1804	|	1815	|	|	1904	|	|	|	2104	|	2206	|	|	2309	2319	|	|	0031	|	0159
Treysa ‡ a.	|	|	1742a	1753	|	1840	|	...	|	|	1939r	|	|	|	...	|	...	|	|	...	2355	|	|	0101	|	...
Wetzlar **906** d.	1550	1618	...	...	1718	...	1750	...	1818	1821	...	1918	1950	2018	...	2118	...	2218	2250	...	...	2318	2343	...	0021	...
Herborn d.	1612	1633	...	...	1733	...	1812	...	1833	1835	...	1933	2012	2033	...	2133	...	2233	2312	...	...	2333	0005	...	0043	...
Dillenburg d.	1622	1638	...	...	1738	...	1822	...	1838	1839	...	1938	2022	2038	...	2138	...	2238	2322	...	...	2338	0015	...	0050	...
Siegen a.	...	1705	...	...	1805	...	...	...	1905	1905	...	2005	...	2105	...	2205	...	2305	...	...	...	0005	...	...	0120	...

		Ⓐ	⚒z	◇ Ⓐ	Ⓐ	†	†	Ⓐ	◇ ⑥	◇ ⑥	◇ Ⓐ	Ⓐ	◇ ⚒	Ⓐ		⚒	◇	◇ ⚒		◇ ⚒		◇		◇		◇
Siegen d.	...	...	...	0457	...	...	...	...	...	0554	0600	...	0654	...	...	...	0754	...	...	0854	...	0954	...	1054	...	1154
Dillenburg d.	...	...	0503	0525	...	0552	...	...	...	0617	0626	...	0728	...	0733	...	0817	...	...	0917	0933	1017	...	1117	1133	1217
Herborn d.	...	...	0511	0530	...	0600	...	...	...	0622	0631	...	0734	...	0740	...	0822	...	...	0922	0940	1022	...	1122	1140	1222
Wetzlar **906** d.	...	...	0533	0547	...	0621	...	...	...	0637	0649	...	0751	...	0802	...	0837	...	...	0937	1002	1037	...	1137	1202	1237
Treysa ‡ d.	...	...	|	|	...	|	...	0600	0559	|	|	...	|	...	|	0715a	|	0803b	0815a	|	|	|	...	|	|	|
Marburg (Lahn) ‡ d.	0359	0440	|	|	0538	|	0608	0634	0635	|	|	0702	|	...	|	0748	|	0835	0849a	|	|	|	1049	|	|	|
Gießen **906** ‡ a.	0427	0510	0544	|	0604	0632	0637	0651	0651	0646	0658	0732	0801	...	0814	0818	0846	0851	0918a	0946	1014	1046	1118	1146	1214	1246
Gießen ‡ d.	0428	0514	...	|	0607	...	0639	0652	0654	0654	0706	0736	...	0809	0828	0828	0854	0854	0922	*0953*	1028	1054	1122	*1153*	1228	1254
Bad Nauheim ‡ d.	0453	0538	...	0611	0624	...	0705	|	|	|	0724	0754	...	0826	0853	0853	|	|	0938	|	1053	|	1138	|	1253	|
Friedberg (Hess) ‡ d.	0458	0542	...	|	0630	...	0710	0712	0712	0712	0732	0800	...	0830	0858	0858	0912	0912	0942	*1012*	1058	1112	1142	*1212*	1258	1312
Frankfurt (Main) Hbf ‡ a.	0527	0607	...	0641	0659	...	0737	0738	0735	0735	0757	0826	...	0859	0927	0927	0935	0935	1007	*1035*	1127	1135	1207	*1235*	1327	1335

		◇			◇	◇		◇		◇	◇		◇		◇		◇		◇	◇		◇	◇		◇	
Siegen d.	...	1254	...	...	1354	...	...	1454	...	1554	...	...	1654	...	1754	...	1854	...	1954	...	...	2054	2154	...	2311	...
Dillenburg d.	...	1317	1333	...	1417	...	...	1517	1533	1617	...	...	1717	1733	1817	...	1917	1933	2017	...	...	2117	2217	...	2334	...
Herborn d.	...	1322	1340	...	1422	...	...	1522	1540	1622	...	...	1722	1740	1822	...	1922	1940	2022	...	...	2122	2222	...	2339	...
Wetzlar **906** d.	...	1337	1402	...	1437	...	...	1537	1602	1637	...	...	1737	1802	1837	...	1937	2002	2037	...	...	2137	2237	...	2352	...
Treysa ‡ d.	...	|	|	1315a	|	1405	...	|	|	|	1605	...	|	|	|	...	|	|	|	2005	...	|	|	...	|	2310
Marburg (Lahn) ‡ d.	1249	|	|	1348	|	1435	1449	|	|	|	1635	1649	|	|	|	1849	|	|	|	2035	2048	|	|	2243	|	2339
Gießen **906** ‡ a.	1318	1346	1414	1418	1446	1451	1518	1546	1614	1646	1651	1718	1746	1814	1846	1918	1946	2014	2046	2051	2118	2146	2246	2312	0001	0004
Gießen ‡ d.	1322	*1353*	1428	1428	1454	1454	1522	*1553*	1628	1654	1654	1722	*1753*	1828	1854	1922	*1953*	2030	2055	2055	2122	*2153*	2255	2315	...	0008
Bad Nauheim ‡ d.	1338	|	1453	1453	|	|	1538	|	1653	|	|	1738	|	1853	|	1938	|	2054	|	|	2138	|	|	2338	...	0031
Friedberg (Hess) ‡ d.	1342	*1412*	1458	1458	1512	1512	1542	*1612*	1658	1712	1712	1742	*1812*	1858	1912	1942	*2012*	2059	2112	2112	2142	*2212*	2312	2342	...	0036
Frankfurt (Main) Hbf ‡ a.	1407	*1435*	1527	1527	1535	1535	1607	*1638*	1727	1735	1735	1807	*1838*	1927	1935	2007	*2035*	2127	2135	2135	2207	*2235*	2335	0005	...	0100

A – WATTENMEER – Continues to Westerland on ④–⑦ to Apr. 2, daily from Apr. 6 (Table **821**).
B – WATTENMEER – Starts from Westerland on ①⑤⑥⑦ to Apr. 3, daily from Apr. 7 (Table **821**).
O – To / from Ostseebad Binz on dates in Table **844**.
S – From / to Stuttgart (Table **912**).

a – Ⓐ only.
b – 0800 on ⑥.
d – Not Apr. 14, 17, May 1, June 5.
e – ①–⑥ (not Apr. 15, 17, May 1, June 5).
f – ⑤ (also Apr. 13, May 24; not Apr. 14, May 26).
h – ⑤⑥ (also Apr. 13, May 24; not Apr. 15).

j – 0822 on Ⓒ.
k – ⑤–⑦ (also Apr. 13, 17, May 1, 24, 25, June 5).
n – Also Apr. 13, 17, May 1, 24, June 5; not Apr. 14, 16, 30, June 4.
p – ⑤–⑦ (also Apr. 13, 17, May 1, 24, June 5).
r – ⚒ only.
u – Not Apr. 15, 17, May 1, 25, June 5.
v – ⑤⑦ (also Apr. 13, 17, May 1, 24, June 5; not Apr. 14, 16, 30, May 26, June 4).
w – ⑦ (also Apr. 17, May 1, June 5; not Apr. 16, 30, June 4).
y – ①–⑥ (also Apr. 16, 30, June 4; not Apr. 17, May 1, June 5).
z – Runs 7 minutes later on Ⓐ.

◧ – Train number **2270** on ⑦ **w**.
◇ – Operated by Hessische Landesbahn.
¶ – See also Frankfurt - Siegen panel.
‡ – See also Frankfurt - Kassel panel. Services to / from Treysa also call at Stadtallendorf.
⊖ – Additional journeys (◇) Frankfurt - Kassel and v.v.: **From Frankfurt** Hbf at 0615 Ⓐ, 0622 Ⓒ, 1422 and 1622 Ⓒ. **From Kassel** Hbf at 0703 ⚒, 1303, 1503 and 1903.

AACHEN - KÖLN - SIEGEN — 807

RE / RB services

km		Ⓒ	2	⚒¶	Ⓒ2	Ⓐ2	Ⓐ¶	Ⓐ¶	⑥¶	⚒														
0	**Aachen** Hbf ... 802 910 d.	...	...	...	...	...	...	...	...	0518e	0618e	0718e	0818r	0918		1418	1518	1618	1718	1818	1918	...	...	...
31	Düren ... 802 d.	...	0003	...	0303	...	...	...	...	0545e	0645e	0745e	0845r	0945		1445	1545	1645	1745	1845	1945	...	...	...
70	**Köln** Hbf ... 802 910 a.	...	0040	...	0340	...	...	...	...	0612e	0712e	0812e	0912r	1012		1512	1612	1712	1812	1912	2012	...	...	...
70	**Köln** Hbf ... 802 910 d.	0023	0041	...	0341	0431	...	...	...	0623	0723	0823	0923	1023	and	1523	1623	1723	1823	1924	2023	2123	2223	2323
71	**Köln** Messe/Deutz 802 910 d.	0026	0043	...	0343	0433	...	...	...	0626	0726	0826	0926	1026		1526	1626	1726	1826	1927	2026	2126	2226	2326
91	Troisdorf ... 802 d.	0041	0109	...	0409	0454	...	...	...	0641	0741	0841	0941	1041	hourly	1541	1641	1741	1841	1941	2041	2141	2241	2341
95	Siegburg/Bonn ... 910 d.	0046	0114	...	0414	0500	...	...	...	0646	0746	0846	0946	1046		1546	1646	1746	1846	1946	2046	2146	2246	2346
102	Hennef (Sieg) ... d.	0050	0119	...	0419	0506	...	...	...	0650	0750	0850	0950	1050	until	1550	1650	1750	1850	1950	2050	2150	2250	2350
114	Eitorf ... d.	0059	0132	...	0432	0518	...	...	...	0659	0759	0859	0959	1059		1559	1659	1759	1859	1959	2059	2159	2259	2359
136	Au (Sieg) ... d.	0116	0154	0448	0454	0541	0543	0610	0612	0716	0816	0916	1016	1116		1616	1716	1816	1916	2016	2116	2216	2316	0016
142	Wissen (Sieg) ... d.	0124	...	0455	...	...	0550	0617	0619	0721	0821	0921	1021	1121		1621	1721	1821	1921	2021	2121	2224	2324	0024
154	Betzdorf (Sieg) ... d.	0138	...	0509	...	...	0603	0629	0632	0730	0830	0930	1030	1130		1630	1730	1830	1930	2030	2130	2238	2338	0038
171	**Siegen** ... a.	0200	...	0532	...	...	0629	0651	0655	0750	0850	0950	1050	1150		1650	1750	1850	1950	2050	2150	2300	2400	0100

	Ⓐ	⚒	Ⓐ							Ⓐ				2	2	⚒¶
Siegen ... d.	...	0454	0526	0610	0710	0810		1810	1910	...	2010	2110	2210	...	...	2311
Betzdorf (Sieg) ... d.	...	0515	0546	0628	0728	0828		1828	1928	...	2028	2128	2228	...	...	2335
Wissen (Sieg) ... d.	...	0528	0558	0637	0737	0837		1837	1937	...	2037	2137	2237	...	...	2347
Au (Sieg) ... d.	...	0537	0604	0643	0743	0843	and	1843	1943	...	2043	2143	2243	2320	...	2355
Eitorf ... d.	...	0557	0624	0700	0800	0900		1900	2000	...	2100	2200	2300	2339	...	...
Hennef (Sieg) ... d.	...	0609	0637	0709	0809	0909	hourly	1909	2009	...	2109	2209	2309	2353	...	...
Siegburg/Bonn ... 910 d.	...	0614	0641	0714	0814	0914		1914	2014	...	2114	2214	2314	2357	...	...
Troisdorf ... 802 d.	...	0618	0647	0718	0818	0918	until	1918	2018	...	2118	2218	2318	0003	0013	...
Köln Messe/Deutz ... 802 910 d.	0533	0633	0709	0733	0833	0933		1933	2033	2041	2133	2233	2333	0027	0037	...
Köln Hbf ... 802 910 a.	0536	0636	0712	0736	0836	0936		1936	2036	2044	2136	2236	2336	0029	0039	...
Köln Hbf ... 802 910 d.	0547	0648e	...	0747e	0848r	0947		1947	...	2047	...	...	...	...	0040	...
Düren ... 802 d.	0614	0714e	...	0814e	0914r	1014		2014	...	2114	...	...	...	...	0118	...
Aachen Hbf ... 802 910 a.	0644	0744e	...	0844e	0944r	1044		2044	...	2145	...	...	...	...	0144	...

e – Ⓐ only.
r – ⚒ only.

¶ – Operated by Hessische Landesbahn.

ESSEN - HAGEN - SIEGEN — 808

ABELLIO Rail NRW SEE NOTE ✣

km		Ⓒ	Ⓐ	Ⓐ	Ⓐ	Ⓐ	Ⓒ	Ⓐ		⚒				⚒		★	⚒				⚒				
0	**Essen** Hbf ... ⊡ d.	...	...	...	...	...	...	...	0634e	...	0734e	...	0834r	...	0934		...	1734	...	1834	...	1934	...	...	...
16	**Bochum** Hbf ... ⊡ d.	...	...	...	...	...	...	...	0647e	...	0747e	...	0847r	...	0947	and at	...	1747	...	1847	...	1947	...	...	...
30	**Witten** Hbf ... ⊡ d.	...	...	...	...	...	...	...	0657e	...	0757e	...	0857r	...	0957		...	1757	...	1857	...	1957	...	...	...
45	**Hagen** Hbf ... ⊡ a.	...	...	...	...	...	...	...	0709e	...	0809e	...	0909r	...	1009	the same	...	1809	...	1909	...	2009	...	...	...
45	**Hagen** Hbf ... d.	0025	...	...	0540	0610	0615	0640	0715	0740	0815	0840	0915	0940	1015		1740	1815	1840	1915	1940	2015	2115	2215	2315
75	Altena (Westf) ... d.	0051	...	...	0605	0636	0640	0705	0740	0805	0840	0905	0940	1005	1040	minutes	1805	1840	1905	1940	2005	2040	2140	2240	2340
84	Werdohl ... d.	0100	...	...	0614	0645	0649	0714	0749	0814	0849	0914	0949	1014	1049		1814	1849	1914	1949	2014	2049	2149	2249	2349
106	Finnentrop ... d.	0118	0502	0558	0631	0703	0707	0731	0807	0831	0907	0931	1007	1031	1107	past each	1831	1907	1931	2007	2031	2110	2207	2307	0007
119	Lennestadt ♥ ... d.	0130	0515	0610	0643	0715	0718	0743	0818	0843	0918	0943	1018	1043	1118		1843	1918	1943	2018	2043	2121	2219	2319	0019
141	Kreuztal ... d.	0153	0537	0633	0706	0738	0737	0806	0837	0906	0937	1006	1037	1106	1137	hour until	1906	1937	2006	2037	2106	2143	2242	2342	0042
152	**Siegen** ... a.	0205	0550	0644	0719	0750	0748	0819	0848	0919	0948	1019	1048	1119	1148		1919	1948	2020	2048	2121	2154	2254	2354	0054

	⚒	Ⓐ	⚒		Ⓐ		Ⓐ			⚒		♣	⚒					⚒							
Siegen ... d.	...	0402	0503	...	0543	0612	0635	0712	...	0743	0812		1543	1612	...	1643	1712	1744	1812	1844	1912	2011	2111	2211	2311
Kreuztal ... d.	...	0413	0514	...	0554	0622	0647	0722	...	0754	0822	and at	1554	1622	...	1654	1722	1755	1822	1855	1922	2022	2122	2222	2323
Lennestadt ♥ ... d.	...	0436	0537	...	0617	0641	0710	0741	...	0817	0841		1617	1641	...	1717	1741	1818	1841	1918	1941	2045	2145	2245	2347
Finnentrop ... d.	0453	0453	0553	0553	0630	0653	0730	0754	...	0830	0853	the same	1630	1653	...	1730	1753	1831	1853	1931	1953	2058	2158	2258	2400
Werdohl ... d.	0510	0510	0610	0610	0647	0710	0747	0810	...	0847	0910		1647	1710	...	1747	1810	1848	1910	1948	2010	2115	2215	2315	...
Altena (Westf) ... d.	0518	0518	0618	0618	0655	0718	0755	0818	...	0855	0918	minutes	1655	1718	...	1755	1818	1856	1918	1956	2018	2123	2223	2323	...
Hagen Hbf ... a.	0546	0546	0646	0646	0724	0746	0824	0846	...	0924	0946		1724	1746	...	1824	1846	1924	1946	2024	2046	2152	2252	2352	...
Hagen Hbf ... ⊡ d.	...	...	0651e	...	...	0751e	...	0851r	...	...	0951	past each	...	1751	...	...	1851	...	1951	...	...	...	...	...	...
Witten Hbf ... ⊡ d.	...	...	0702e	...	...	0802e	...	0902r	...	...	1002		...	1802	...	...	1902	...	2002	...	...	...	...	...	...
Bochum Hbf ... ⊡ d.	...	...	0714e	...	...	0814e	...	0914r	...	...	1014	hour until	...	1814	...	...	1914	...	2014	...	...	...	...	...	...
Essen Hbf ... ⊡ a.	...	...	0729e	...	...	0829e	...	0929r	...	...	1029		...	1829	...	...	1929	...	2029	...	...	...	...	...	...

	⚒									
Essen Hbf ... d.	0507	0607	0707	and	1907	2007	2107	2207	2307	...
Bochum Hbf ... d.	0521	0621	0721	hourly	1921	2021	2121	2221	2321	...
Witten Hbf ... d.	0533	0633	0733	until	1933	2033	2133	2233	2333	...
Hagen Hbf ... a.	0547	0647	0747		1947	2047	2147	2247	2347	...

	⚒								
Hagen Hbf ... d.	0517	0617	0717	and	1917	2017	2117	2217	2317
Witten Hbf ... d.	0531	0631	0731	hourly	1931	2031	2131	2231	2331
Bochum Hbf ... d.	0542	0642	0742	until	1942	2042	2142	2242	2342
Essen Hbf ... a.	0557	0657	0757		1957	2057	2157	2257	2357

e – Ⓐ only.
r – ⚒ only.
★ – The 1040, 1240, 1440 and 1640 from Hagen run daily.
♣ – The 0843, 1043, 1243 and 1443 from Siegen run daily.
⊡ – See also panel below main table.
♥ – Lennestadt - Altenhundem.
✣ – Services Hagen - Siegen and v.v. are subject to alteration on ⑥⑦ Jan. 7 - Mar. 26 (also from approximately 2100 on ⑤ Jan. 6 - Mar. 24).

PADERBORN - HAMELN - HANNOVER - HANNOVER FLUGHAFEN ✈ — 809

S-Bahn 5

km									Ⓐ	⑥			⚒	†				⚒	†						
0	**Paderborn** Hbf ▲. 805 811 d.	...	...	...	...	...	...	...	0512	...	...	...	0615	...	...	0715	...	0815	...	...	0915	...	1015	...	1115
17	Altenbeken ... 805 811 d.	...	...	...	...	...	...	...	0524	...	...	...	0627	...	...	0727	...	0827	...	...	0927	...	1027	...	1127
56	Bad Pyrmont ... d.	...	...	...	...	...	0505r	...	0602	0605	...	0635e	0702	0705	0735e	0802	...	0902	0905	...	1002	...	1102	...	1202
75	Hameln ... a.	...	...	...	...	...	0519r	...	0616	0618	...	0649e	0716	0718	0749e	0816	...	0916	0918	...	1016	...	1116	...	1216
75	Hameln ... d.	...	...	...	0420e	0450r	0520	0550r	0620	0620	0620	0650r	0720	0720	0750r	0820	0850r	0920	0920	0950r	1020	1050r	1120	1150r	1220
133	**Hannover** Hbf ... a.	...	...	...	0503e	0533r	0603	0633r	0703	0703	0703	0733r	0803	0803	0833r	0903	0933r	1003	1003	1033r	1103	1133r	1203	1233r	1303
133	**Hannover** Hbf ... d.	0335	0411	0435	0505	0535	0605	0635	0705	0705	0705	0735	0805	0805	0835	0905	0935	1005	1005	1035	1105	1135	1205	1235	1305
148	**Hannover** Flughafen ✈ ... a.	0353	0429	0453	0523	0553	0623	0653	0723	0723	0723	0753	0823	0823	0853	0923	0953	1023	1023	1053	1123	1153	1223	1253	1323

																								⑤⑥f	A
Paderborn Hbf ▲ .. 805 811 d.	...	1215	...	1313	...	1415	...	1515	...	1615	...	1715	...	1815	...	1915	...	2015	...	2115	...	2215	...	2310	...
Altenbeken ... 805 811 d.	...	1227	...	1327	...	1427	...	1527	...	1627	...	1727	...	1827	...	1927	...	2027	...	2127	...	2227	...	2322	...
Bad Pyrmont ... d.	...	1302	1335e	1402	...	1502	...	1602	1635e	1702	1735e	1802	1835e	1902	...	2002	...	2102	...	2202	...	2302	...	2357	0005
Hameln ... a.	...	1316	1349e	1416	...	1516	...	1616	1649e	1716	1749e	1816	1849e	1916	...	2016	...	2116	...	2216	...	2316	...	0011	0019
Hameln ... d.	1250r	1320	1350r	1420	1450r	1520	1550	1620	1650	1720	1750	1820	1850	1920	1950	2020	2050e	2120	...	2220	...	2320	...	0020	0020
Hannover Hbf ... a.	1333r	1403	1433r	1503	1533r	1603	1633	1703	1733	1803	1833	1903	1933	2003	2033	2103	2133e	2203	...	2303	...	0003	...	0103	0103
Hannover Hbf ... d.	1335	1405	1435	1505	1535	1605	1635	1705	1735	1805	1835	1905	1935	2005	2035	2105	2135	2205	2235	2305	2335	0005	0035	0105	0105
Hannover Flughafen ✈ ... a.	1353	1423	1453	1523	1553	1623	1653	1723	1753	1823	1853	1923	1953	2023	2053	2123	2153	2223	2253	2323	2353	0023	0053	0123	0123

			Ⓐ					⚒		Ⓐ		⚒													
Hannover Flughafen ✈ ... d.	0006	0036	0036	0106	0136	...	0406	0436	0436	0506	0506	0536	0536	0606	0636	0706	0736	0806	0836	0906	0936	1006	1036	1106	1136
Hannover Hbf ... a.	0024	0053	0053	0123	0154	...	0424	0453	0453	0523	0523	0553	0553	0623	0653	0723	0753	0823	0853	0923	0953	1023	1053	1123	1153
Hannover Hbf ... d.	...	...	0055	...	...	...	...	0455	...	0525	...	0555	...	0625r	0655	0725r	0755	0825r	0855	0925r	0955	1025r	1055	1125r	1155
Hameln ... a.	...	...	0140	...	...	...	...	0540	...	0610	...	0640	...	0710r	0740	0810r	0840	0910r	0940	1010r	1040	1110r	1140	1210r	1240
Hameln ... d.	...	...	...	...	...	...	...	0544	...	0611	...	0644	...	0711e	0744	...	0844	...	0944	...	1044	...	1144	...	1244
Bad Pyrmont ... d.	...	...	...	...	...	...	...	0600	...	0625	...	0700	...	0725e	0800	...	0900	...	1000	...	1100	...	1200	...	1300
Altenbeken ... 805 811 d.	...	...	...	...	...	...	...	0633	...	...	...	0733	...	...	0833	...	0933	...	1033	...	1133	...	1233	...	1333
Paderborn Hbf ▲ .. 805 811 a.	...	...	...	...	...	...	...	0646	...	...	...	0746	...	...	0846	...	0946	...	1046	...	1146	...	1246	...	1346

																					B	⑤⑥f		
Hannover Flughafen ✈ ... d.	1206	1236	1306	1336	1406	1436	1506	1536	1606	1636	1706	1736	1806	1836	1906	1936	2006	2036	2106	2136	2206	2236	2236	2306	2336
Hannover Hbf ... a.	1223	1253	1323	1353	1423	1453	1523	1553	1623	1653	1723	1753	1823	1853	1923	1953	2023	2053	2123	2153	2223	2253	2253	2323	2353
Hannover Hbf ... d.	1225r	1255	1325r	1355	1425r	1455	1525	1555	1625	1655	1725	1755	1825	1855	1925	1955	2025r	2055	2125e	2155	...	2255	2255	...	2355
Hameln ... a.	1310r	1340	1410r	1440	1510r	1540	1610	1640	1710	1740	1810	1840	1910	1940	2010	2040	2110r	2140	2210e	2240	...	2340	2340	...	0040
Hameln ... d.	1311e	1344	...	1444	...	1544	1611e	1644	1711e	1744	1811e	1844	...	1944	...	2044	...	2144	...	2244	...	2341	2344	...	...
Bad Pyrmont ... d.	1325e	1400	...	1500	...	1600	1625e	1700	1725e	1800	1825e	1900	...	2000	...	2100	...	2200	...	2300	...	2355	0000	...	...
Altenbeken ... 805 811 d.	...	1433	...	1533	...	1633	...	1733	...	1833	...	1933	...	2033	...	2133	...	2233	...	2333	...	...	0033	...	...
Paderborn Hbf ▲ .. 805 811 a.	...	1446	...	1546	...	1646	...	1746	...	1846	...	1946	...	2046	...	2146	...	2246	...	2346	...	...	0046	...	...

A – Mornings of ①–⑤ (not Apr. 14, 17, May 1, 25, June 5).
B – ①②③④⑦ (not Apr. 13, 16, 30, May 24, June 4).
e – Ⓐ only.
f – Also Apr. 13, 16, 30, May 24, June 4.
r – ⚒ only.
▲ – Paderborn timings are subject to alteration May 6 - June 14.

810 HAMM and BAD BENTHEIM - HANNOVER - BERLIN

Warning! *Stendal and Berlin timings are subject to alteration from May 13. See engineering work summary panel on page 367.*

km		IC	ICE	IC	ICE	IC	IC	ICE	ICE	IC	ICE	ICE	IC	IC	ICE	ICE	IC	ICE	ICE	ICE
		447	**649**	**2447**	**841**	**2179**	**2241**	**541**	**1041**	**2445**	**843**	**853**	**2343**	**245**	**543**	**553**	**2443**	**845**	**1045**	**855**
			①–⑤	①g	①–⑥	Ⓐ	①–⑥	①–⑥	⑦z	①–⑥		①–⑥	⑦	①–⑥		①–⑥	①–⑥	①–⑤	⑥⑦	
		♥	¶✕	D	L✕	H	eM 🍷	e✕	✕	eD	✕	e✕	N	C🍷	✕	eK	eD	✕	✕	✕
	Bonn Hbf **800** d.	...	...	...	...	...		...	...	...	...	...	...	...	...	0622	...	...	...	...
	Köln Hbf **800** d.	2312	...	...	...	...	...	0429	...	0512	0528	0544	...	...	...	0648	0712	...	0728	0748
	Wuppertal Hbf **800** d.	|	...	...	...	...	...	|	...	0544	|	0616	...	...	...	0716	0744	...	|	0816
	Düsseldorf Hbf **800** d.	2336	...	...	...	...	...	0453	...	|	0552	|	...	...	0627	|	|	0752	0752	|
	Dortmund Hbf **800** d.	0031	...	...	...	...	...	0547	...	0628	0648	|	...	...	0748	|	0828	0848	0848	|
0	**Hamm** (Westf) **802** d.	0049	...	...	...	...	...	0604	...	0644	0711	0711	...	...	0811	0811	0844	0911	0911	0911
50	Gütersloh Hbf **802** d.	0112	...	...	...	...	...	0629	...	0707	|	|	...	...	|	|	0907	|	|	|
67	**Bielefeld** Hbf **802 811** d.	0124	...	0518	...	...	...	0640	...	0719	0738	0738	...	...	0838	0838	0919	0938	0938	0938
81	Herford **811** d.	|	...	0527	...	...	...	|	...	0728	|	|	...	...	|	|	0928	|	|	|
	Amsterdam C **22** △ d.	|	...	|	...	...	...	|	...	|	|	|	...	0502	|	|	|	|	|	|
	Bad Bentheim 🏛 **811** d.	|	...	|	...	...	...	|	...	|	|	|	...	0721	|	|	|	|	|	|
	Rheine **811** d.	|	...	|	...	...	...	|	...	|	|	|	...	0735	|	|	|	|	|	|
	Osnabrück Hbf **811** d.	|	...	|	...	...	0604	|	...	|	|	|	0804	0805	|	|	|	|	|	|
	Bünde (Westf) **811** d.	|	...	|	...	...	0627	|	...	|	|	|	0827	0826	|	|	|	|	|	|
97	Bad Oeynhausen **811** d.	|	...	|	...	...	0639	|	...	|	|	|	0839	0839	|	|	|	|	|	|
112	Minden (Westf) **811** d.	0152	...	0548	...	...	0649	|	...	0748	|	|	0849	0849	|	|	0948	|	|	|
177	**Hannover** Hbf **811** a.	0223	...	0618	...	...	0718	0728	...	0818	0828	0828	0918	0918	0928	0928	1018	1028	1028	1028
177	**Hannover** Hbf d.	0240	0527	0636	0631	0704	0721	0731	0731	0836	0831	0831	0921	0922	0931	0931	1036	1031	1031	1031
	Magdeburg Hbf **866** a.	0402	▽	0755	|	|	|	|	|	0955	|	|	|	|	|	|	1155	|	|	|
	Leipzig Hbf **866** a.	|	|	0918	|	|	|	|	|	1118	|	|	|	|	|	|	1318	|	|	|
252	Wolfsburg **902** d.	|	0620	...	0704	0735	0755	|	0804	...	0905	0905	0955	0955	|	|	...	1105	1105	1105
327	Stendal **838** d.	|	0647	...	0734	...	0827	|	0833	...	|	|	1027	1027	|	|	...	|	|	|
419	**Berlin** Spandau **838 902** a.	|	0721	...	0809	...	0904	0854	0906	...	0958	0958	1104	1104	1054	1054	...	1158	1158	1158
435	**Berlin** Hbf **838 902** a.	0533	0732	...	0824	...	0922	0906	0918	...	1009	1009	1122	1122	1106	1106	...	1209	1209	1209
440	**Berlin** Ostbahnhof **838 902** a.	0544	...	...	...	...	0934	...	...	...	...	...	1134	1134	...	...	...	...	...	...

	IC	IC	ICE	ICE	IC	ICE	ICE	IC	ICE	ICE	IC	IC	IC	ICE	ICE	IC	ICE	ICE	IC	ICE	ICE	IC	ICE	ICE
	2222	**141**	**545**	**555**	**2441**	**847**	**857**	**143**	**547**	**557**	**2010**	**2010**	**2049**	**849**	**859**	**145**	**549**	**559**	**2047**	**941**	**951**	**147**	**641**	**651**
	Ⓐ										⑦b	⑤f	⑤–⑦						Ⓑq					
	V🍷	🍷	✕	✕	D	✕	✕	🍷	✕	✕		T🍷	sD	✕	✕	🍷	✕	✕	D	✕	✕	🍷	◐✕	✕
Bonn Hbf **800** d.	...	...	...	...	...	...	...	...	...	...	...	1023	...	...	...	...	...	1222e	...	...	...	...	...	...
Köln Hbf **800** d.	...	...	0828	0848	0912	...	0948	...	...	1048	1046	1046	1113	...	1148	...	...	1248	1312	...	1348	...	...	1448
Wuppertal Hbf **800** d.	...	...	|	0916	0944	...	1016	...	...	1116	|	|	1145	...	1216	...	...	1316	1344	...	1416	...	...	1516
Düsseldorf Hbf **800** d.	...	...	0852	|	|	0952	|	...	1052	|	1118	1118	|	1152	|	...	1254	|	|	1352	|	...	1452	|
Dortmund Hbf **800** d.	0912	...	0948	|	1028	1048	|	...	1148	|	1212	1212	1228	1248	|	...	1348	|	1428	1448	|	...	1548	|
Hamm (Westf) **802** d.	0934	...	1011	1011	1044	1111	1111	...	1211	1211	1234	1234	1244	1311	1311	...	1411	1411	1444	1511	1511	...	1611	1611
Gütersloh Hbf **802** d.	0955	...	|	|	1107	|	|	...	|	|	1255	1255	1307	|	|	...	|	|	1507	|	|	...	|	|
Bielefeld Hbf **802 811** d.	1006	...	1038	1038	1119	1138	1138	...	1238	1238	1306	1306	1319	1338	1338	...	1438	1438	1519	1538	1538	...	1638	1638
Herford **811** d.	1015	...	|	|	1128	|	|	...	|	|	1315	1315	1328	|	|	...	|	|	1528	|	|	...	|	|
Amsterdam C **22** △ d.	|	0700	|	|	|	|	|	0900	|	|	|	|	|	|	|	1100	|	|	|	|	|	1300	|	|
Bad Bentheim 🏛 **811** d.	|	0928	|	|	|	|	|	1128	|	|	|	|	|	|	|	1328	|	|	|	|	|	1528	|	|
Rheine **811** d.	|	0942	|	|	|	|	|	1142	|	|	|	|	|	|	|	1342	|	|	|	|	|	1542	|	|
Osnabrück Hbf **811** d.	|	1008	|	|	|	|	|	1208	|	|	|	|	|	|	|	1408	|	|	|	|	|	1608	|	|
Bünde (Westf) **811** d.	|	|	|	|	|	|	|	1229	|	|	|	|	|	|	|	|	|	|	|	|	|	1629	|	|
Bad Oeynhausen **811** d.	|	1039	|	|	|	|	|	|	|	|	|	|	|	|	|	1439	|	|	|	|	|	|	|	|
Minden (Westf) **811** d.	|	1049	|	|	1148	|	|	1249	|	|	|	|	1348	|	|	1449	|	|	1548	|	|	1649	|	|
Hannover Hbf **811** a.	1101	1118	1128	1128	1218	1228	1228	1318	1328	1328	1401	1401	1418	1428	1428	1518	1528	1528	1618	1628	1628	1718	1728	1728
Hannover Hbf d.	1104	1122	1131	1131	1236	1231	1231	1322	1331	1331	1404	1404	1436	1431	1431	1522	1531	1531	1636	1631	1631	1722	1731	1731
Magdeburg Hbf **866** a.	|	|	|	|	1355	|	|	|	|	|	|	|	1555	|	|	|	|	|	1755	|	|	|	|	|
Leipzig Hbf **866** a.	|	|	|	|	1518	|	|	|	|	|	|	|	1718	|	|	|	|	|	1918	|	|	|	|	|
Wolfsburg **902** d.	1138	1155	|	|	...	1305	1305	1355	|	|	1438	1438	...	1505	1505	1555	|	|	...	1705	1705	1755	|	|
Stendal **838** d.	|	1227	|	|	...	|	|	1427	|	|	|	|	...	|	|	1627	|	|	...	|	|	1827	|	|
Berlin Spandau **838 902** a.	1239	1304	1254	1254	...	1358	1358	1504	1454	1454	1539	1539	...	1558	1558	1704	1654	1654	...	1758	1758	1904	1854	1854
Berlin Hbf **838 902** a.	1249	1322	1307	1307	...	1409	1409	1522	1506	1506	1550	1553	...	1609	1609	1722	1706	1706	...	1809	1809	1922	1906	1906
Berlin Ostbahnhof **838 902** a.	...	1334	...	...	...	...	...	1534	...	...	...	1608	...	...	...	1734	...	...	...	...	...	1934	...	...

	IC	IC	IC	IC	ICE	ICE	IC	ICE	ICE	IC	ICE	ICE	IC	IC	ICE	ICE	IC	ICE	ICE	IC	ICE	ICE	ICE
	1926	**1216**	**1920**	**2045**	**943**	**953**	**149**	**643**	**653**	**2012**	**945**	**955**	**241**	**241**	**645**	**655**	**2041**	**947**	**957**	**243**	**657**	**102**	**1102**
	①–④	⑤f	⑦w	Ⓑq		Ⓑq					Ⓑq		B	⑦w			⑦w		⑦z	⑦v	⑦w	Ⓑq	⑥h
	m	J🍷	R🍷	D	✕	✕	🍷	✕	✕	A🍷	✕	✕	🍷	🍷	✕	✕		✕	✕	🍷	✕	Q🍷	Q🍷
Bonn Hbf **800** d.	...	1423	1423	...	...	...	...	...	...	1623	...	...	...	...	...	...	...	...	...	...	2024	...	...
Köln Hbf **800** d.	1438	1445	1445	1512	...	1548	...	...	1648	1646	...	1748	...	...	...	1848	1913	...	1948	...	2048	2111	2111
Wuppertal Hbf **800** d.	|	|	|	1544	...	1616	...	...	1716	|	...	1816	...	...	...	1916	1945	...	2016	...	2116	2143	|
Düsseldorf Hbf **800** d.	1509	1518	1518	|	1552	|	...	1652	|	1715	1752	|	...	...	1846	|	|	1952	|	...	|	|	2133
Dortmund Hbf **800** d.	|	1612	1612	1628	1648	|	...	1748	|	1828	1848	|	...	...	1948	|	2028	2048	|	...	|	2228	2228
Hamm (Westf) **802** d.	|	1634	1634	1644	1711	1711	...	1811	1811	1845	1911	1911	...	...	2011	2011	2044	2111	2111	...	2209	2249	2249
Gütersloh Hbf **802** d.	|	1655	1655	1707	|	|	...	|	|	1905	|	|	...	...	|	|	2107	|	|	...	|	2311	2311
Bielefeld Hbf **802 811** d.	|	1706	1706	1719	1738	1738	...	1838	1838	1916	1938	1938	...	...	2038	2038	2119	2138	2138	...	2237	2321	2321
Herford **811** d.	|	1715	1715	1728	|	|	...	|	|	1927	|	|	...	...	|	|	2128	|	|	...	|	2330	2330
Amsterdam C **22** △ d.	|	|	|	|	|	|	1500	|	|	|	|	|	1700	1700	|	|	|	|	|	1900	|	|	|
Bad Bentheim 🏛 **811** d.	|	|	|	|	|	|	1728	|	|	|	|	|	1928	1928	|	|	|	|	|	2128	|	|	|
Rheine **811** d.	|	|	|	|	|	|	1742	|	|	|	|	|	1942	1942	|	|	|	|	|	2142	|	|	|
Osnabrück Hbf **811** d.	1657	|	|	|	|	|	1808	|	|	|	|	|	2008	2008	|	|	|	|	|	2208	|	|	|
Bünde (Westf) **811** d.	|	|	|	|	|	|	|	|	|	|	|	|	2029	2029	|	|	|	|	|	|	|	|	|
Bad Oeynhausen **811** d.	|	|	|	|	|	|	1839	|	|	1937	|	|	|	|	|	|	|	|	|	2240	|	|	|
Minden (Westf) **811** d.	|	|	|	1748	|	|	1849	|	|	1949	|	|	2049	2049	|	|	2148	|	|	2252	|	2347	2347
Hannover Hbf **811** a.	1802	1801	1801	1818	1828	1828	1918	1928	1928	2018	2028	2028	2118	2118	2128	2128	2218	2228	2228	2324	2328	0018	0018
Hannover Hbf d.	1805	1804	1804	1836	1831	1831	1922	1931	1931	2036p	2031	2031	...	2122	2131	2131	...	2231	2231	...	2331	...	...
Magdeburg Hbf **866** a.	|	|	|	1955	|	|	|	|	|	2155p	|	|	...	|	|	|	...	|	|	...	|	...	...
Leipzig Hbf **866** a.	|	|	|	2118r	|	|	|	|	|	2325w	|	|	...	|	|	|	...	|	|	...	|	...	...
Wolfsburg **902** d.	1839	1838	1838	...	1905	1905	1955	|	|	...	2105	2105	...	2155	|	|	...	2305	2305	...	0004	...	...
Stendal **838** d.	|	|	|	...	|	|	2027	|	|	...	2134	2134	...	2227	|	|	...	|	|	...	|	...	...
Berlin Spandau **838 902** a.	1944	1944	1944	...	1958	1958	2104	2054	2054	...	2207	2207	...	2304	2254	2254	...	2358	2358	...	0058	...	...
Berlin Hbf **838 902** a.	1958	1958	1958	...	2009	2009	2122	2106	2106	...	2223	2223	...	2322	2306	2306	...	0009	0009	...	0110	...	...
Berlin Ostbahnhof **838 902** a.	2009	2009	2009	...	...	...	2134	...	...	...	...	...	...	2334	...	...	...	...	...	...	...	...	...

A – ALLGÄU – 12 and 🍷 Oberstdorf - Ulm - Stuttgart - Mannheim - Koblenz - Köln - Hannover (- Magdeburg ①④⑤⑦ **p**) (- Leipzig ⑦ **w**).
B – Ⓑ (daily from Apr. 2; not Apr. 30).
C – ①–⑥ from Apr. 8 (not Apr. 17, June 5).
D – To Dresden (Table **842**).
H – Ⓐ (not May 26). From Hamburg (Table **900**).
J – 12 and 🍷 Salzburg - München - Stuttgart - Köln - Berlin.
K – 12 and ✕ Koblenz Hbf (d. 0545) - Köln - Berlin.
L – ①–⑥ (not Apr. 14, 17, May 1, June 5). 12 and ✕ (Oldenburg - Bremen Ⓐ -) Hannover - Berlin.
M – From Münster (Westf) Hbf (d. 0538).
N – ⑦ (also Apr. 17, June 5). From Münster (Westf) Hbf (d. 0738).
Q – 12 and 🍷 Basel - Karlsruhe - Köln - Hannover.
R – From Frankfurt (Table **911**).
T – From Tübingen via Stuttgart (Tables **911** and **912**).
V – From Aachen Hbf (d. 0707), Rheydt Hbf (d. 0748), Mönchengladbach Hbf (d. 0755), Viersen (d. 0803) and Krefeld Hbf (d. 0816).

b – Also June 5; not Apr. 16, 30, June 4.
e – ①–⑥ (not Apr. 15, 17, May 1, June 5).
f – Also Apr. 13, May 24; not Apr. 14, May 26.
g – Also Apr. 18, May 2, June 6; not Apr. 17, May 1, June 5.
h – Also Apr. 14, 16, 30, June 4.
m – Not Apr. 13, 17, May 1, 24, June 5.
p – ①④⑤⑦ (also Apr. 12, 18, May 2, 23, 24, June 6; not Apr. 14, 16, 30, May 25, 26, June 4).
q – Not Apr. 14, 16, 30, June 4.
r – 2134 on ①② Jan. 9 - Mar. 14, ①② May 15–30 (also June 6).
s – Also Apr. 13, 17, May 1, 24, 25, June 5; not Apr. 16, May 26, 27.
v – Also Apr. 17, June 5; not Apr. 16, June 4.
w – ⑦ (also Apr. 17, May 1, June 5; not Apr. 16, 30, June 4).
z – Also Apr. 15, 17, May 1, June 5.

▽ – Via Braunschweig Hbf (d. 0601).
¶ – ①–⑤ (not Apr. 14, 17, May 1, June 5). From May 15 departs Hannover 0518, Braunschweig 0551, Wolfsburg 0610 and does not call at Stendal.
△ – Amsterdam timings are subject to alteration on Apr. 27.
♥ – Also calls at Braunschweig Hbf (a. 0313), Brandenburg Hbf (a. 0444), Potsdam Hbf (a. 0504) and Berlin Wannsee (a. 0513).

BERLIN - HANNOVER - HAMM and BAD BENTHEIM 810

Warning! Berlin and Stendal timings are subject to alteration from May 13. See engineering work summary panel on page 367.

km		ICE 103 L 🍷		ICE 656 Ⓐ ✕	ICE 646 Ⓐ ✕	IC 242 ①–⑥ r 🍷	ICE 956 ①–⑥ e ✕	ICE 946 ①–⑥ e ✕	IC 2013 A 🍷	ICE 654 ✕	ICE 644 ①–⑥ e ✕	IC 240 ①–⑥ d 🍷	IC 240 E 🍷	IC 1927 ⑤f C	ICE 954 ①–⑥ e ✕	ICE 944 ✕	IC 2044 ①–⑥ e D	IC 1929 ①–④ m 🍷	ICE 652 ✕	ICE 642 ✕	IC 148 🍷	ICE 952 ✕	ICE 942 ✕	IC 2046 ⑥k D
0	**Berlin** Ostbahnhof 838 902 d.	...	...	...	...	...	...	...	...	...	...	0623	...	0650	...	...	...	0749	...	...	0823	...	...	...
5	**Berlin** Hbf 838 902 d.	...	...	0430	0430	...	0538	0538	...	0652	0652	0634	...	0701	0749	0749	...	0800	0852	0852	0834	0949	0949	...
21	**Berlin** Spandau 838 902 d.	...	...	0442	0442	...	0550	0550	...	0703	0703	0651	...	0715	0801	0801	...	0814	0903	0903	0851	1001	1001	...
113	Stendal 838 d.	...	...	0515	0515	...	0626	0626	...	|	|	0734	...	|	|	|	...	|	|	|	0934	|	|	...
188	Wolfsburg 902 d.	...	...	0548	0548	...	0656	0656	...	0753	0753	0804	...	0820	0853	0853	...	0920	|	|	1004	1053	1053	...
	Leipzig Hbf **866** d.	...	...	|	|	...	|	|	0442g	|	|	|	...	|	|	|	0643	|	|	|	|	|	|	0843
	Magdeburg Hbf **866** d.	...	...	|	|	...	|	|	0601e	|	|	|	...	|	|	|	0804	|	|	|	|	|	|	1004
263	**Hannover** Hbf a.	...	...	0618	0618	...	0728	0728	0723e	0828	0828	0836	...	0853	0928	0928	0923	0953	1028	1028	1036	1128	1128	1123
263	**Hannover** Hbf 811 d.	0540	...	0621	0621	0640	0731	0731	0740	0831	0831	0840	0840	0856	0931	0931	0940	0956	1031	1031	1040	1131	1131	1140
328	Minden (Westf) 811 d.	0612	...	0651	0651	0712	|	|	0812	|	|	0912	0912	|	|	|	1014	|	|	|	1112	|	|	1214
343	Bad Oeynhausen 811 d.	|	...	|	|	0722	|	|	0822	|	|	|	|	|	|	|	|	|	|	|	1122	|	|	|
359	Bünde (Westf) 811 d.	|	...	|	|	|	|	|	|	|	|	0932	0932	|	|	|	|	|	|	|	|	|	|	|
396	**Osnabrück** Hbf 811 d.	|	...	|	|	0753	|	|	|	|	|	0953	0953	|	|	|	|	1106	|	|	1153	|	|	|
444	Rheine 811 d.	|	...	|	|	0821	|	|	|	|	|	1021	1021	|	|	|	|	|	|	|	1221	|	|	|
465	Bad Bentheim 🏛 811 a.	|	...	|	|	0834	|	|	|	|	|	1034	1034	|	|	|	|	|	|	|	1234	|	|	|
655	*Amsterdam C* **22** △ a.	|	...	|	|	1100	|	|	|	|	|	1300	1300	|	|	|	|	|	|	|	1500	|	|	|
	Herford 811 d.	0632	...	0711	0711	...	|	|	0832	|	|	...	...	0944	|	|	1032	|	|	|	...	|	|	1232
	Bielefeld Hbf 802 811 d.	0641	...	0721	0721	...	0822	0822	0842	0922	0922	...	...	0953	1022	1022	1041	|	1122	1122	...	1222	1222	1241
	Gütersloh Hbf 802 d.	0651	...	|	|	...	|	|	0852	|	|	...	...	1003	|	|	1052	|	|	|	...	|	|	1252
	Hamm (Westf) 802 a.	0713	...	0748	0748	...	0848	0848	0913	0948	0948	...	...	1024	1048	1048	1114	|	1148	1148	...	1248	1248	1314
	Dortmund Hbf **800** a.	0732	...	|	0809	...	|	0909	0931	|	1009	...	...	1048	|	1109	1132	|	|	1209	...	|	1309	1332
	Düsseldorf Hbf **800** a.	|	...	|	0906	...	|	1006	1046	|	1111	...	...	1142	|	1206	|	1313	|	1306	...	|	1406	|
	Wuppertal Hbf **800** a.	0813	...	0838	...	...	0938	...	|	1039	...	...	...	|	1138	...	1212	|	1238	...	...	1338	...	1412
	Köln Hbf **800** a.	0846	...	0909	...	...	1009	...	1112	1109	...	...	...	1212	1209	...	1246	1357	1309	...	...	1409	...	1446
	Bonn Hbf **800** a.	...	...	...	...	...	...	...	1135	...	...	...	...	...	...	...	...	...	...	...	...	...	...	...

	IC 2011 ⑦w S 🍷	IC 2017 ⑤f Y	ICE 650 ✕	ICE 640 ✕	IC 146 🍷	ICE 950 ✕	ICE 940 ✕	IC 2048 D	IC 1915 ⑤⑦v S 🍷	ICE 558 ✕	ICE 548 ✕	IC 144 🍷	ICE 858 ✕	ICE 848 ✕	IC 2440 D	IC 2223 Ⓐ ⊡ 🍷	ICE 556 U ✕	ICE 546 ✕	IC 142 🍷		ICE 856 ✕	ICE 846 ♣ ✕	ICE 1046 ⑤f G ✕	IC 2442 Ⓑq D
Berlin Ostbahnhof 838 902 d.	0950	...	...	...	1023	...	...	...	1151	...	...	1223	...	...	...	...	...	...	1423	...	...	...	...	...
Berlin Hbf 838 902 d.	1001	...	1052	1052	1034	1149	1149	...	1202	1252	1252	1234	1349	1349	...	1357	1452	1452	1434	...	1549	1549	1549	...
Berlin Spandau 838 902 d.	1015	...	1103	1103	1051	1201	1201	...	1216	1303	1303	1251	1401	1401	...	1407	1503	1503	1451	...	1601	1601	1601	...
Stendal 838 d.	|	...	|	|	1134	|	|	...	|	|	|	1334	|	|	...	1447	|	|	1534	...	|	|	|	...
Wolfsburg 902 d.	1120	1120	|	|	1204	1253	1253	...	1321	|	|	1404	1453	1453	...	1520	|	|	1604	...	1653	1653	1653	...
Leipzig Hbf **866** d.	|	|	|	|	|	|	|	1043	|	|	|	|	|	|	1243	|	|	|	|	...	|	|	|	1443
Magdeburg Hbf **866** d.	|	|	|	|	|	|	|	1204	|	|	|	|	|	|	1404	|	|	|	|	...	|	|	|	1604
Hannover Hbf a.	1153	1153	1228	1228	1236	1328	1328	1323	1353	1428	1428	1436	1528	1528	1523	1553	1628	1628	1636	...	1728	1728	1728	1723
Hannover Hbf 811 d.	1156	1156	1231	1231	1240	1331	1331	1340	1356	1431	1431	1440	1531	1531	1540	1556	1631	1631	1640	...	1731	1731	1731	1740
Minden (Westf) 811 d.	|	|	|	|	1312	|	|	1414	|	|	|	1512	|	|	1614	|	|	|	1712	...	|	|	|	1814
Bad Oeynhausen 811 d.	|	|	|	|	|	|	|	|	|	|	|	1522	|	|	|	1634	|	|	|	...	|	|	|	|
Bünde (Westf) 811 d.	|	|	|	|	1332	|	|	|	|	|	|	|	|	|	|	|	|	|	1732	...	|	|	|	|
Osnabrück Hbf 811 d.	|	|	|	|	1353	|	|	|	|	|	|	1553	|	|	|	|	|	|	1753	...	|	|	|	|
Rheine 811 d.	|	|	|	|	1421	|	|	|	|	|	|	1621	|	|	|	|	|	|	1821	...	|	|	|	|
Bad Bentheim 🏛 811 a.	|	|	|	|	1434	|	|	|	|	|	|	1634	|	|	|	|	|	|	1834	...	|	|	|	|
Amsterdam C **22** △ a.	|	|	|	|	1701	|	|	|	|	|	|	1901	|	|	|	|	|	|	2101	...	|	|	|	|
Herford 811 d.	1244	1244	|	|	...	|	|	1432	1444	|	|	...	|	|	1632	|	|	|	...	...	|	|	|	1832
Bielefeld Hbf 802 811 d.	1253	1253	1322	1322	...	1422	1422	1441	1453	1522	1522	...	1622	1622	1641	1653	1722	1722	...	...	1822	1822	1822	1841
Gütersloh Hbf 802 d.	1303	1303	|	|	...	|	|	1452	1503	|	|	...	|	|	1652	1703	|	|	...	...	|	|	|	1852
Hamm (Westf) 802 a.	1324	1324	1348	1348	...	1448	1448	1514	1524	1548	1548	...	1648	1648	1714	1724	1748	1748	...	...	1848	1848	1848	1914
Dortmund Hbf **800** a.	1347	1348	|	1409	...	|	1509	1532	1547	|	1609	...	|	1709	1732	1748	|	1809	...	...	|	1909	1909	1932
Düsseldorf Hbf **800** a.	1442	1442	|	1506	...	|	1606	|	1642	|	1710	...	|	1806	|	...	|	1910	...	...	|	2006	2016	|
Wuppertal Hbf **800** a.	|	|	1438	...	...	1538	...	1613	|	1638	...	...	1738	...	1812	...	1838	...	...	...	1938	|	...	2012
Köln Hbf **800** a.	1512	1512	1509	...	...	1609	...	1646	1712	1709	...	...	1809	...	1846	...	1909	...	...	...	2009	2039	...	2046
Bonn Hbf **800** a.	1535	1535	...	...	...	...	...	...	1735	...	...	...	...	...	...	...	1932a	...	...	...	...	...	...	...

	ICE 554 ✕	ICE 544 ✕	IC 140 🍷	ICE 854 Ⓑ T ✕	ICE 844 ✕	IC 2444 Ⓑq D	ICE 552 ✕	ICE 542 ✕	IC 2242 M			IC 1932 ⑦w R 🍷	ICE 852 ⑦h ✕	ICE 842 ✕	ICE 832 ①–⑥ e O ✕	IC 2446 ⑦w D	IC 1932 ⑦w R 🍷		IC 2240 ⑦w N 🍷	ICE 540 ✕	ICE 540 ⑤–⑦ p ✕	ICE 850 ⑦h O ✕		IC 446 ♥
Berlin Ostbahnhof 838 902 d.	...	...	1623	...	...	...	...	...	1823	...	...	...	...	...		...	...	...	2023	...	...	...	...	2343
Berlin Hbf 838 902 d.	1652	1652	1634	1749	1749	...	1852	1852	1834	...	...	...	1949	1949	1949	...	...	...	2034	2107	2107	2154	...	2353
Berlin Spandau 838 902 d.	1703	1703	1651	1801	1801	...	1903	1903	1851	...	...	1948	2001	2001	2001	...	←	...	2051	2118	2118	2207	...	|
Stendal 838 d.	|	|	1734	|	|	...	|	|	1934	...	...	2025	|	|	|	...	2031	...	2134	2153	2153	2243	...	|
Wolfsburg 902 d.	|	|	1804	1853	1853	...	|	|	2004	...	...	→	2053	2053	2053	...	2104	...	2204	2223	2223	2313	...	|
Leipzig Hbf **866** d.	|	|	|	|	|	1643	|	|	|	...	...	...	|	|	|	1843	|	...	|	|	|	|	...	|
Magdeburg Hbf **866** d.	|	|	|	|	|	1804	|	|	|	...	...	...	|	|	|	2004	|	...	|	|	|	|	...	0130
Hannover Hbf a.	1828	1828	1836	1928	1928	1923	2028	2028	2036	...	...	...	2128	2128	2128	2123	2140	...	2236	2256	2256	2344	...	0303
Hannover Hbf 811 d.	1831	1831	1840	1931	1931	1940	2031	2031	2040	...	...	...	2131	2131	...	2140	...	...	2240	...	2301	...	...	0340
Minden (Westf) 811 d.	|	|	1912	|	|	2014	|	|	2112	...	...	...	|	|	...	2214	...	...	2312	...	|	...	...	0412
Bad Oeynhausen 811 d.	|	|	1922	|	|	|	|	|	2122	...	...	...	|	|	...	|	...	...	2322	...	|	...	...	|
Bünde (Westf) 811 d.	|	|	|	|	|	|	|	|	2135	2146	...	...	|	|	...	|	...	...	2335	...	|	...	...	|
Osnabrück Hbf 811 d.	|	|	1953	|	|	|	|	|	2159	2214	...	...	|	|	...	|	...	...	2358	...	|	...	...	|
Rheine 811 d.	|	|	2021	|	|	|	|	|	...	2248	...	...	|	|	...	|	...	...	...	...	|	...	...	|
Bad Bentheim 🏛 811 a.	|	|	2034	|	|	|	|	|	...	2303	...	...	|	|	...	|	...	...	...	...	|	...	...	|
Amsterdam C **22** △ a.	|	|	2301	|	|	|	|	|	...	...	...	...	|	|	...	|	...	...	...	...	|	...	...	|
Herford 811 d.	|	|	...	|	|	2032	|	|	...	...	...	...	|	|	...	2232	...	...	...	...	2346	...	...	|
Bielefeld Hbf 802 811 d.	1922	1922	...	2022	2022	2041	2122	2122	...	...	...	...	2222	2222	...	2241	...	...	...	...	2357	...	...	0436
Gütersloh Hbf 802 d.	|	|	...	|	|	|	|	|	...	...	...	...	|	|	...	|	...	...	...	...	0008	...	...	0447
Hamm (Westf) 802 a.	1948	1948	...	2048	2048	2110	2148	2148	...	...	...	...	2248	2248	...	2310	...	...	...	...	0028	...	...	0510
Dortmund Hbf **800** a.	|	2009	...	|	2109	2132	|	2209	...	...	...	...	|	2309	...	2332	...	...	...	...	0048	...	...	0530
Düsseldorf Hbf **800** a.	|	2106	...	|	2206	|	|	2306	...	...	...	...	|	0006	...	|	...	...	...	...	0146	...	...	0631
Wuppertal Hbf **800** a.	2038	|	...	2138	|	2212	2238	|	...	...	...	...	2338	|	...	0012	...	...	...	...	|	...	...	|
Köln Hbf **800** a.	2109	2133	...	2209	2230	2246	2314	2330	...	...	...	...	0010	0030	...	0046	...	...	...	...	0211	...	...	0657
Bonn Hbf **800** a.	...	▽	...	2235w	...	...	...	...	...	...	...	...	...	...	...	...	...	...	...	...	...	...	...	...

A – ALLGÄU – [12] and 🍷 (Leipzig ① **g** -) (Magdeburg ①–⑥ **e** -) Braunschweig - Hannover - Köln - Stuttgart - Oberstdorf.
C – To Aachen Hbf (a. 1312).
D – From Dresden (Table **842**).
E – ①–⑥ (daily from Apr. 3).
G – To Neuss Hbf (a. 2029) and Mönchengladbach Hbf (a. 2043).
L – To Basel (Table **912**).
M – To Münster (Westf) Hbf (a. 2225). Conveys 🍷 on Ⓑ.
N – To Münster (Westf) Hbf (a. 0024).
O – To Oldenburg via Bremen (Table **813**).
R – [12] and 🍷 Stralsund - Berlin - Bremen - Oldenburg.
S – To Stuttgart (Tables **911** and **912**).
T – To Koblenz Hbf (a. 2313) on ⑦ **w**.
U – To Koblenz Hbf (a. 2011) on Ⓐ.
Y – [12] Wolfsburg - Köln - Stuttgart - München.

a – Ⓐ only.
d – Not Apr. 15, 17, June 5.
e – ①–⑥ (not Apr. 15, 17, May 1, June 5).
f – Also Apr. 13, May 24; not Apr. 14, May 26.
g – ① (also Apr. 18, May 2, June 6; not Apr. 17, May 1, June 5).
h – Also Apr. 15, 17, May 1, June 5.
k – Also Apr. 14, May 25; not Apr. 15, May 27.
m – Not Apr. 13, 17, May 1, 24, June 5.
p – Also Apr. 13, 17, May 1.
q – Ⓑ (not Apr. 14, 16, 30, June 4).
r – Not Apr. 17, June 5.
v – Also Apr. 13, 17, May 1, 24, June 5; not Apr. 14, 16, 30, May 26, June 4.
w – ⑦ (also Apr. 17, May 1, June 5; not Apr. 16, 30, June 4).

♣ – ①②③④⑥⑦ (also Apr. 14, May 26; not Apr. 13, May 24).
⊡ – To Krefeld Hbf (a. 1843), Viersen (a. 1856), Mönchengladbach Hbf (a. 1905), Rheydt Hbf (a. 1910) and Aachen Hbf (a. 1950).
♥ – Also calls at Berlin Zoo (d. 0000), Berlin Wannsee (d. 0012), Potsdam Hbf (d. 0021), Brandenburg Hbf (d. 0048) and Braunschweig Hbf (d. 0224).
▽ – Continues to Aachen Hbf (a. 2219) on ⑦ **w**.
△ – Amsterdam timings are subject to alteration on Apr. 27.

12 *For explanation of standard symbols see page 4* 383

811 Regional services BIELEFELD and BAD BENTHEIM - HANNOVER and PADERBORN

See Table **810** for faster *ICE / IC* services Bielefeld / Bad Bentheim - Hannover and v.v.

km		⚒¶	⚒¶	⚒¶	⚒¶	¶	⚒	¶	¶		¶	¶		¶	¶	A	A¶	B¶	A	A¶	B¶			¶
0	Bad Bentheim ... d.	...	...	...	...	...	...	0557e	...	...	0657r	...	...	0757r	...	...	0857	...	...	0957	...	and in	...	1857
21	**Rheine** ... d.	...	...	...	0514	...	...	0614e	0638	...	0714r	...	...	0814	0838	...	0914	...	...	1014	1038	the same	...	1914
43	Ibbenbüren ... d.	...	...	...	0528	...	...	0628e	0654	...	0728r	...	...	0828	0854	...	0928	...	...	1028	1054	pattern	...	1928
69	**Osnabrück** Hbf ... d.	...	0448	0516	0548	...	...	0648	0716	...	0748	...	...	0848	0916	...	0948	...	...	1048	1116	every	...	1948
106	Bünde (Westf) ... d.	...	0512	0539	0612	...	D	0712	0739	K	0812	...	K	0912	0939	K	1012	...	K	1112	1139	two hours	K	2012
	Bielefeld Hbf ... d.	0424	|	|	|	0624	0659	|	|	0759	|	0824	0859	|	|	0959	|	1024	1059	|	|	until	1959	|
120	Herford ... a.	0431	0526	|	0626	0631	0707	0726	|	0807	0826	0831	0907	0926	|	1007	1026	1031	1107	1126	|		2007	2026
120	Herford ... d.	0433	0537	|	0637	0633	0708	0737	|	0808	0837	0833	0908	0937	|	1008	1037	1033	1108	1137	|		2008	2037
134	**Bielefeld** Hbf ... a.	|	0548	|	0648	|	|	0748	|	|	0848	|	|	0948	|	|	1048	|	|	1148	|		|	2048
	Löhne ... d.	0440	...	0551	...	0640	0714	...	0751	0814	...	0840	0914	...	0951	1014	...	1040	1114	...	1151		2014	...
	Bad Oeynhausen ... d.	0445	...	0557	...	0645	0719	...	0757	0819	...	0845	0919	...	0957	1019	...	1045	1119	...	1157		2019	...
	Minden (Westf) ... a.	0457	...	0607	...	0657	0730	...	0807	0830	...	0857	0930	...	1007	1030	...	1057	1130	...	1207		2030	...
	Minden (Westf) ... d.	0507	...	0608	...	0707	*0735*	...	0808	*0835*	...	0907	*0935*	...	1008	*1035*	...	1107	*1135*	...	1208		*2035*	...
	Hannover Hbf ... a.	0550	...	0650	...	0750	*0830*	...	0850	*0930*	...	0950	*1030*	...	1050	*1130*	...	1150	*1230*	...	1250		*2130*	...
	Braunschweig Hbf **866** ... a.	0641	...	0741	...	0841	...	...	0941	...	...	1041	...	...	1141	...	...	1241	...	...	1341		...	...

	¶		¶	¶	⚒	¶	¶	Ⓑ	¶		¶
Bad Bentheim ... d.	...	...	1957	...	...	2057	...	...	2157	...	2312
Rheine ... d.	...	...	2014	2038	...	2114	...	...	2214	...	2329
Ibbenbüren ... d.	...	...	2028	2054	...	2128	...	...	2228	...	2344
Osnabrück Hbf ... d.	...	...	2048	2116	...	2148	...	...	2248	...	0002
Bünde (Westf) ... d.	...	K	2112	2139	K	2212	...	K	2312	...	...
Bielefeld Hbf ... d.	2024	2059	|	|	2159	|	2224	2259	|	2327	...
Herford ... a.	2031	2107	2126	|	2207	2226	2231	2307	2326	2335	...
Herford ... d.	2033	2108	2137	|	2208	2237	2233	2308	2337	2336	...
Bielefeld Hbf ... a.	|	|	2148	|	|	*2248*	|	|	2348	|	...
Löhne ... d.	2040	2114	...	2151	2214	▬	2240	2314	▬	2343	...
Bad Oeynhausen ... d.	2045	2119	...	2157	2219	...	2245	2319	...	2348	...
Minden (Westf) ... a.	2057	2130	...	2207	2230	...	2257	2330	...	2400	...
Minden (Westf) ... d.	2107	*2135*	...	2208	...	2235	2307h	...	2335	...	...
Hannover Hbf ... a.	2150	*2230*	...	2250	...	2330	2350h	...	0030	...	...
Braunschweig Hbf **866** ... a.	2241	...	...	2341	...	...	...	...	...	...	...

km			Ⓒ		Ⓐ¶	Ⓐ	⚒¶	⚒¶	⚒¶
	Braunschweig Hbf **866** ... d.	...	...	...	...	...	...	0420	...
0	**Hannover** Hbf ... d.	0028	...	...	...	...	...	0509	...
65	Minden (Westf) ... a.	0123	...	...	...	...	...	0553	...
65	Minden (Westf) ... d.	...	0127	...	...	0528	...	0555	...
80	Bad Oeynhausen ... d.	...	0138	...	...	0539	...	0605	...
86	Löhne ... d.	...	0143	...	...	0544	...	0611	...
	Bielefeld Hbf ... d.	...	|	...	...	|	0509	|	0609
96	Herford ... a.	...	0149	...	...	0549	0520	|	0620
96	Herford ... d.	...	0150	...	...	0550	0533	|	0633
110	**Bielefeld** Hbf ... a.	...	0201	...	...	0557	|	|	|
	Bünde (Westf) ... d.	...	...	...	...	K	0546	0621	0646
	Osnabrück Hbf ... d.	...	...	...	0514	...	0614	0646	0714
	Ibbenbüren ... d.	...	...	...	0530	...	0630	0703	0730
	Rheine ... d.	...	...	...	0548	...	0648	0721	0748
	Bad Bentheim ... a.	...	...	...	0603	...	0703	...	0803

	⚒	¶	¶	⚒	B¶	A¶	A	B¶	A¶	A		¶	¶		¶	¶		¶	¶	⚒	¶	¶	¶	
Braunschweig Hbf **866** ... d.	...	0520	...	...	0620	...	...	0720	...	...	and in	1820	...	...	1920	...	...	2020	...	...	2120	...	2222	...
Hannover Hbf ... d.	*0528*	0609	...	*0628*	0709	...	*0728*	0809	...	*0828*	the same	1909	...	*1928*	2009	...	*2028*	2109	...	*2128*	2209	...	2309	*2328*
Minden (Westf) ... a.	*0623*	0659	...	*0723*	0751	...	*0823*	0853	...	*0923*	pattern	1951	...	*2023*	2053	...	*2123*	2151	...	*2223*	2253	...	2351	*0023*
Minden (Westf) ... d.	0628	0702	...	0728	0752	...	0828	0902	...	0928	every	1952	...	2028	2102	...	2128	2152	...	2228	2302	...	2352	0030
Bad Oeynhausen ... d.	0639	0714	...	0739	0803	...	0839	0914	...	0939	two hours	2003	...	2039	2114	...	2139	2203	...	2239	2314	...	0003	0042
Löhne ... d.	0644	0719	...	0744	0809	...	0844	0919	...	0944	until	2009	...	2044	2119	...	2144	2209	...	2244	2319	...	0009	0047
Bielefeld Hbf ... d.	|	|	0709	|	|	0809	|	|	0909	|		|	2009	|	|	2109	|	|	2209	|	|	2309	|	|
Herford ... a.	0649	0725	0720	0749	|	0820	0849	0925	0920	0949		|	2020	2049	2125	2120	2149	|	2220	2249	2325	2320	|	0053
Herford ... d.	0650	0727	0733	0750	|	0833	0850	0927	0933	0950		|	2033	2050	2127	2133	2150	|	2233	2250	2327	2333	|	0054
Bielefeld Hbf ... a.	0657	0739j	|	0757	|	|	0857	0936	|	0957		|	|	2057	2136	|	2157	|	|	2257	2336	|	|	0105
Bünde (Westf) ... d.	K	...	0746	K	0819	0846	K	...	0946	K		2019	2046	K	...	2146	D	2219	2246	D	...	2346	0019	...
Osnabrück Hbf ... d.	...	...	0814	...	0846	0914	...	...	1014	...		2046	2114	...	...	2214	...	2246	2314	...	...	0012	0041	...
Ibbenbüren ... d.	...	...	0830	...	0903	0930	...	...	1030	...		2103	2130	...	...	2230	...	2303h	2330	...	...	...	...	...
Rheine ... d.	...	...	0848	...	0921	0948	...	...	1048	...		2121	2148	...	...	2248	...	2321h	2346	...	...	...	...	...
Bad Bentheim ... a.	...	...	0903	...	...	1003	...	...	1103	...		...	2203	...	...	2303	...	...	...	...	...	...	...	...

BIELEFELD - PADERBORN - HOLZMINDEN - KREIENSEN ⊖ △ and OTTBERGEN - GÖTTINGEN ★ ⊖

km			Ⓐ		⚒	⚒	⚒																		
0	**Bielefeld** Hbf ... § d.	...	0434	...	0534	0634	0734	0834	0934	1034	1134	1234	1334	1434	1534	...	1634	1734	1834	1934	...	2034	2134	2234	2334
44	**Paderborn** Hbf ... § a.	...	0527	...	0627	0727	0827	0927	1027	1127	1227	1327	1427	1527	1627	...	1727	1827	1927	2027	...	2127	2227	2327	0027
	Change trains	Ⓐ	⚒	Ⓐ	d	⚒	d								Ⓐ	Ⓒ					†		P		
44	**Paderborn** Hbf . **805 809** △ d.	0453	0553	...	0653	0753	0853	0953	1053	1153	1253	1353	1453	1553	1653	1653	1753	1853	1953	2053	2053	2206	2315	...	...
61	Altenbeken ... **805 809** d.	0507	0607	...	0707	0807	0907	1007	1107	1207	1307	1407	1507	1607	1707	1707	1807	1907	2007	2107	2107	2219	2329	...	...
92	Ottbergen ... ★ d.	0536	0636	...	0736	0836	0936	1036	1136	1236	1336	1436	1536	1636	1736	1736	1836	1936	2036	2136	2136	2245	2355	...	...
102	Höxter Rathaus ... d.	0545	0645	...	0745	0845	0945	1045	1145	1245	1345	1445	1545	1645	1745	1745	1845	1945	2045	2145	2145	2253	0003	...	...
110	Holzminden ... a.	0554	0654	...	0754	0854	0954	1054	1154	1254	1354	1454	1554	1654	1754	1754	1854	1954	2054	2154	2154	2302	0012	...	...
110	Holzminden ... d.	*0629*	...	0711	0758	...	0958	...	1158	...	1358	...	1558	1654e	1754	1758	...	1958	...	...	2158	...	...	...	...
154	**Kreiensen** ... a.	*0703*	...	0745	0832	...	1032	...	1232	...	1432	...	1632	1728e	1828	1832	...	2032	...	...	2232	...	...	...	...

		Ⓐ	⚒	⚒	Ⓐ	⑥											Ⓐ	Ⓒ		Ⓐ					†
Kreiensen ... d.	...	...	...	0627e	0709	0723	...	0754e	0923	...	1123	...	1323	...	1523	...	1652	1723	...	1828	...	1923	...	2125	2241
Holzminden ... a.	...	...	...	0700e	0742	0756	...	0827e	0956	...	1156	...	1356	...	1556	...	1725	1756	...	1900	...	1956	...	2158	2314
Holzminden ... d.	...	0501	0601	0701	0801	0801	0801	0901	1001	1101	1201	1301	1401	1501	1601	1701	...	1801	1801	1901	1901	2001	2101	2201	2316
Höxter Rathaus ... d.	...	0510	0610	0710	0810	0810	0810	0910	1010	1110	1210	1310	1410	1510	1610	1710	...	1810	1810	1910	1910	2010	2110	2210	2325
Ottbergen ... ★ d.	...	0526	0626	0726	0826	0826	0826	0926	1026	1126	1226	1326	1426	1526	1626	1726	...	1826	1826	1926	1926	2026	2126	2226	2335
Altenbeken ... **805 809** d.	...	0552	0652	0752	0852	0852	0852	0952	1052	1152	1252	1352	1452	1552	1652	1752	...	1852	1852	1952	1952	2052	2152	2252	0001
Paderborn Hbf ... **805 809** △ a.	...	0605	0705	0805	0905	0905	0905	1005	1105	1205	1305	1405	1505	1605	1705	1805	...	1905	1905	2005	2005	2105	2205	2305	0015
Change trains	⚒	⚒	⚒																						
Paderborn Hbf ... § d.	0513	0613	0713	0813	...	...	0913	1013	1113	1213	1313	1413	1513	1613	1713	1813	...	...	1913	...	2013	2113	2213	2313	...
Bielefeld Hbf ... § a.	0607	0707	0807	0907	...	...	1007	1107	1207	1307	1407	1507	1607	1707	1807	1907	...	...	2007	...	2107	2207	2307	0007	...

MÜNSTER - BIELEFELD ⊡ ♠ and BIELEFELD - DETMOLD - ALTENBEKEN ⊡

km		⚒		⚒			⚒				
0	**Bielefeld** Hbf ... ♠ d.	0749	0849	0949	1049	1249	1349	1449	1649	1849	2049
11	Oerlinghausen ... d.	0803	0903	1003	1103	1303	1403	1503	1703	1903	2103
22	Lage (Lippe) ... d.	0813	0913	1013	1113	1313	1413	1513	1713	1913	2113
31	Detmold ... a.	0820	0920	1020	1120	1320	1420	1520	1720	1920	2120
60	**Altenbeken** ... a.	...	0949	1049	1149	1349	1449	1549	1749	1949	2146r

	⚒			⚒			⚒				⚒
Altenbeken ... d.	0713e	0813e	1013	1113	1213	1413	1513	1613	1813	2013	2213
Detmold ... d.	0740	0840	1040	1140	1240	1440	1540	1640	1840	2040	2240
Lage (Lippe) ... d.	0750	0850	1050	1150	1250	1450	1550	1650	1850	2050	2250
Oerlinghausen ... d.	0800	0900	1100	1200	1300	1500	1600	1700	1900	2100	2300
Bielefeld Hbf ... ♠ a.	0811	0911	1111	1211	1311	1511	1611	1711	1911	2111	2311

HERFORD - PADERBORN ¶ △

km		Ⓐ		⚒					N
0	**Herford** ... d.	0530	...	0633	0733	and	2133	2233	2233
8	Bad Salzuflen ... d.	0537	...	0640	0740	hourly	2140	2240	2240
19	Lage (Lippe) ... d.	0549	...	0652	0752	until	2152	2252	2252
28	Detmold ... d.	0559	...	0702	0802		2202	2258	2302
57	Altenbeken ... **805 809** a.	0624	...	0727	0827		2227	...	2327
74	**Paderborn** Hbf . **805 809** △ a.	0638	...	0741	0841		2241	...	2341

	Ⓐ	⚒			✣		L		
Paderborn Hbf **805 809** △ d.	...	0518	...	0621	and	2021	2121	...	...
Altenbeken ... **805 809** d.	...	0530	...	0633	hourly	2033	2133	...	...
Detmold ... d.	0458	0558	...	0701	until	2101	2201	...	...
Lage (Lippe) ... d.	0506	0606	...	0709		2109	2209	...	...
Bad Salzuflen ... d.	0517	0617	...	0720		2120	2220	...	...
Herford ... a.	0524	0624	...	0727		2127	2227	...	...

A – Train runs hourly.
B – Train runs every **two** hours.
D – From / to Dortmund (Table **802**).
K – From / to Köln/Bonn Flughafen via Dortmund (Table **802**).
L – To Bielefeld Hbf (a. 2248).
N – ⑤–⑦ (also Dec. 26, Apr. 13, 17, May 1, 24, 25, June 5).
P – ⑤–⑦ (also Dec. 26, Apr. 17, May 1, 25, June 5).

d – Daily.
e – Ⓐ only.
h – ⑤⑥ (not Apr. 14).
j – 0736 on Ⓒ.
r – ⚒ only.
✣ – The 1221 from Paderborn runs 3–4 minutes later Detmold - Herford on Ⓐ.
△ – Paderborn timings are subject to alteration from May 5.

§ – Additional trains run on Ⓐ.
¶ – Operated by Westfalen Bahn.

⊖ – Operated by NordWestBahn. 2nd class only.
⊡ – Operated by **eurobahn** Keolis Deutschland.

★ – **OTTBERGEN - GÖTTINGEN** ⊖. *63 km.* Journey: 73–81 minutes (103 minutes for train marked ‡). Most trains run from / to Paderborn, attached to Holzminden trains shown in the main table above. **From Ottbergen** at 0534 ⚒, 0634 ⚒, 0734, 0834 ⚒, 0934, 1034 ⚒, 1134, 1234 ⑥, 1234 Ⓐ ‡, 1334 Ⓒ 1534, 1634 Ⓐ, 1734, 1834 Ⓐ, 1934 and 2034. **From Göttingen** at 0603 ⚒, 0711, 0803 ⚒, 0911 1003 ⚒, 1111, 1203 ⚒, 1311 Ⓒ, 1403 ⑥, 1511, 1603 Ⓐ, 1711, 1803 Ⓐ, 1911, 2003 Ⓐ and 2111.

♠ – **MÜNSTER - BIELEFELD** ⊡. *76 km.* Journey: 91–102 minutes. **From Münster (Westf)** at 0607 Ⓐ 0717 ⚒, 0817, 0917 ⚒, 1017, 1117 ⚒, 1217, 1317 ⑥, 1417, 1517 ⚒, 1617, 1717 ⚒, 1817, 1917 ⚒, 2017, 2117 ⚒ and 2217 ⑥. **From Bielefeld Hbf** at 0608 ⑥, 0614 Ⓐ, 0709 ⚒, 0814, 0914 ⚒, 1014, 1114 ⚒, 1214, 1314 ⚒, 1414, 1514 ⚒, 1614, 1714 ⚒, 1814, 1914 ⚒, 2014 and 2114.

MÜNSTER - EMDEN - NORDDEICH — 812

RE services except where shown

km		◇ Ⓐ	◇ ⚒	IC 2438 ①–⑥ e	◇ ⚒	Ⓐ	◇	Ⓐ	IC 2208 ⑥C	◇		◇	Ⓐ	IC 2206 Q	◇		◇	Ⓐ	IC 2204	◇ Ⓒ	◇ Ⓐ		IC 2018 ⑥ ♦		◇	Ⓐ
	Koblenz Hbf **800** d.	...	...	...	...	...	...	...	...	...	...	...	...	0641t	...	...	...	...	0841v	...	...	...	0943	...	...	...
	Köln Hbf **800 802** d.	...	...	...	...	...	...	0521	0541	...	0621r	...	0721	0746	...	0821	...	0921	0946	...	...	1021	1046	...	...	1121
	Düsseldorf Hbf **800** d.	...	...	...	...	...	...	|	0606	...	|	...	|	0812	...	|	...	|	1012	...	...	|	1118	...	...	|
	Hagen Hbf **802** d.	...	...	...	...	0522	...	0622	|	...	0722	...	0822	|	...	0922	...	1022	|	...	...	1122	|	...	...	1222
0	**Münster** (Westf) Hbf d.	0502	...	...	0602	0624	0702	0724	0731	0805	0824	0905	0924	0932	1005	1024	1105	1124	1131	1205	1205	1224	1231	...	1305	1324
15	Greven d.	0513	...	...	0613	0637	0713	0733	|	0814	0833	0914	0933	|	1014	1033	1114	1133	|	1214	1214	1233	|	...	1314	1333
26	Emsdetten d.	0522	...	...	0622	0646	0722	0740	|	0822	0840	0922	0940	|	1022	1040	1122	1141	|	1222	1222	1240	|	...	1322	1340
39	**Rheine** d.	0534	0534	...	0634	0658	0734	0749	0756	0834	0851	0934	0949	0956	1034	1051	1134	1150	1156	1234	1234	1251	1256	...	1334	1349
70	Lingen (Ems) d.	0555	0555	...	0655	—	0755	...	0815	0855	—	0955	...	1015	1055	—	1155	...	1215	1255	1255	...	|	...	1355	...
90	Meppen d.	0609	0609	...	0709	...	0809	...	0829	0909	...	1009	...	1029	1109	...	1209	...	1229	1309	1328z	...	|	...	1409	...
136	Papenburg (Ems) d.	0642	0642	...	0742	...	0842	...	0856	0942	...	1042	...	1056	1142	...	1242	...	1256	1342	1404	...	|	...	1442	...
153	Leer (Ostfriesl) **813** d.	0653	0653	0715	0753	0824	0853	...	0909	0953	1024	1053	...	1109	1153	1224	1253	...	1309	1353	1417	...	|	1424	1453	...
180	**Emden** Hbf ◧ **813** a.	0709	0709	0731	0809	0840	0909	...	0925	1009	1040	1109	...	1125	1209	1240	1309	...	1325	1409	1432	...	1416	1440	1509	...
180	**Emden** Hbf **813** d.	...	...	0742	...	0842	...	...	0942	...	1042	...	...	1142	...	1242	...	...	...	...	...	...	1421	1442	...	...
209	Norden **813** d.	...	...	0808	...	0906	...	...	1005	...	1106	...	...	1205	...	1306	...	...	...	...	...	...	1447	1506	...	...
215	**Norddeich** **813** a.	...	...	0814	...	0912	...	...	1011	...	1112	...	...	1211	...	1312	...	...	...	...	...	...	1453	1512	...	...
	Norddeich Mole ‡ **813** a.	...	...	0819	...	0916	...	...	1016	...	1116	...	...	1216	...	1316	...	...	...	...	...	...	1500	1516	...	...

	IC 2202	◇		◇	Ⓐ	IC 2200	◇		◇	Ⓐ	IC 2014 ⑤ 🍷♦	IC 2004 🍷♦	IC 2036 Ⓑq	◇	⑥		◇	Ⓐ	IC 2002 N B	IC 2034	◇		◇	◇	◇	◇
Koblenz Hbf **800** d.	...	...	...	...	...	...	...	...	...	...	1443	1443	...	...	...	...	...	...	...	...	...	...	...	...	...	...
Köln Hbf **800 802** d.	1146	...	1221	...	1321	1346	...	1421	...	1521	1546	1546	...	...	...	1621	...	1721	1745	...	...	1821	...	...	...	...
Düsseldorf Hbf **800** d.	1212	...	|	...	|	1414	...	|	...	|	1612	1612	...	...	...	|	...	|	1817	...	...	|	...	...	...	...
Hagen Hbf **802** d.	|	...	1322	...	1422	|	...	1522	...	1622	|	|	...	...	...	1722	...	1822	|	...	...	1922	...	...	...	...
Münster (Westf) Hbf d.	1331	1405	1424	1505	1524	1531	1605	1624	1705	1724	1731	1731	...	1805	...	1824	1905	1924	1931	...	2005	2024	2105	2211	2313	0013
Greven d.	|	1414	1433	1514	1533	|	1614	1633	1714	1733	|	|	...	1814	...	1833	1914	1933	|	...	2014	2033	2114	2222	2326	0026
Emsdetten d.	|	1422	1440	1522	1540	|	1622	1640	1722	1740	|	|	...	1822	...	1840	1922	1940	|	...	2022	2040	2122	2231	2335	0035
Rheine d.	1356	1434	1451	1534	1549	1556	1634	1649	1734	1749	1756	1756	...	1834	...	1851	1934	1949	1956	...	2034	2051	2134	2252j	2346	0046
Lingen (Ems) d.	1415	1455	—	1555	...	1615	1655	—	1755	...	1815	1815	...	1855	...	...	1955	...	2015	...	2055	—	2155	2313	...	...
Meppen d.	1429	1509	...	1609	...	1629	1709	...	1809	...	1829	1829	...	1909	...	...	2009	...	2029	...	2109	...	2209	2327	...	...
Papenburg (Ems) d.	1456	1542	...	1642	...	1656	1742	...	1842	...	1856	1856	...	1942	...	...	2042	...	2056	...	2142	...	2242	0000	...	...
Leer (Ostfriesl) **813** d.	1509	1553	1624	1653	...	1709	1753	1824	1853	...	1909	1909	1922	1953	2024	...	2053	...	2109	2122	2153	2224	2253	0012	...	...
Emden Hbf ◧ **813** a.	1525	1609	1640	1709	...	1725	1809	1840	1909	...	1925	1925	1938	2009	2040	...	2109	...	2125	2138	2209	2240	2309	0028	...	...
Emden Hbf **813** d.	1542	...	1642	...	...	1728	...	1842	...	...	...	...	1942	...	2042	...	...	...	...	2142	...	2242	...	...	...	...
Norden **813** d.	1605	...	1706	...	...	1751	...	1906	...	...	...	...	2008	...	2106	...	...	...	...	2208	...	2306	...	...	...	...
Norddeich **813** a.	1611	...	1712	...	...	1757	...	1912	...	...	...	...	2014	...	2112	...	...	...	...	2214	...	2312	...	...	...	...
Norddeich Mole ‡ **813** a.	1616	...	1716	...	...	1804	...	1916	...	...	...	...	2020	...	2116	...	...	...	...	...	...	...	...	...	...	...

	⊙ ⚒	Ⓐ	◇ ⚒		◇	IC 2035 ①–⑥ e	IC 2005 ①–⑥ 🍷♦	Ⓐ	◇ Ⓐ	◇ Ⓒ		◇	IC 2037 ①–⑥ h	IC 2009 P	Ⓐ	◇		◇	IC 2201	Ⓐ	◇		◇ Ⓐ	◇ Ⓒ	◇ Ⓐ	IC 2019 ⑥ ♦
Norddeich Mole ‡ **813** d.	...	...	...	...	...	...	...	...	...	...	...	...	0736	...	...	...	0839	...	0952	...	...	1039	...	...	...	1136
Norddeich **813** d.	...	...	...	...	...	0536	...	...	...	...	0641	...	0739	...	...	...	0841	...	0955	...	...	1041	...	...	...	1139
Norden **813** d.	...	...	...	...	...	0543	...	...	...	...	0647	...	0746	...	...	...	0847	...	1004	...	...	1047	...	...	...	1146
Emden Hbf **813** a.	...	...	...	...	...	0607	...	...	...	...	0715	...	0814	...	...	...	0915	...	1026	...	...	1115	...	...	...	1214
Emden Hbf ◧ **813** d.	...	...	0452	...	0552r	0609	0634	...	0642	0652	0717	0752	0816	0833	...	0852	0917	0952	1034	...	1052	1117	1152	1152	1224	1234
Leer (Ostfriesland) **813** d.	...	...	0509	...	0609r	0626	0653	...	0659	0709	0733	0809	0833	0853	...	0909	0933	1009	1053	...	1109	1133	1209	1209	1241	1253
Papenburg (Ems) d.	...	...	0519	...	0619r	...	0704	...	0709	0719	—	0819	...	0904	...	0919	—	1019	1104	...	1119	—	1219	1219	1251	1304
Meppen d.	...	...	0550	...	0650	...	0731	...	0750j	0750	...	0850	...	0931	...	0950	...	1050	1131	...	1150	...	1250	1250	1325	1331
Lingen (Ems) d.	...	...	0604	...	0704	...	0744	...	0804	0804	...	0904	...	0944	...	1004	...	1104	1144	...	1204	...	1304	1304	→	1344
Rheine d.	0453	0608	0628	0708	0729	...	0804	0808	0829	0829	0908	0929	...	1004	1008	1029	1108	1129	1204	1208	1229	1308	1327	1329	...	1404
Emsdetten d.	0502	0616	0636	0716	0737	...	|	0816	0837	0837	0916	0937	...	|	1016	1037	1116	1137	|	1216	1237	1316	1337	1337	...	|
Greven d.	0511	0623	0644	0723	0745	...	|	0823	0845	0845	0923	0945	...	|	1023	1045	1123	1145	|	1223	1245	1323	1346	1345	...	|
Münster (Westf) Hbf a.	0525	0633	0654	0733	0756	...	0829	0833	0856	0856	0933	0956	...	1029	1033	1056	1133	1156	1230	1233	1256	1333	1356	1356	...	1429
Hagen Hbf **802** a.	...	0736	...	0836	...	...	|	0936	...	...	1036	...	...	|	1136	...	1236	...	|	1336	...	1436	...	...	...	|
Düsseldorf Hbf **800** a.	...	|	...	|	...	...	0946	|	...	...	|	...	...	1146	|	...	|	...	1346	|	...	|	...	...	...	1546
Köln Hbf **800 802** a.	...	0839	...	0938	...	...	1015	1038	...	...	1138	...	...	1215	1238	...	1338	...	1413	1438	...	1538	...	...	...	1613
Koblenz Hbf **800** a.	...	...	...	...	...	...	1115	...	...	...	...	...	...	...	...	...	...	...	...	...	...	...	...	...	...	1715

	IC 2203 E B	Ⓐ	◇ Ⓐ	◇ Ⓒ		◇	IC 2205	Ⓐ	◇		◇	IC 2207 N	Ⓐ	◇		◇	IC 2209 D	Ⓐ	◇		◇	◇	◇		◇ ⑤⑥ f	◇
Norddeich Mole ‡ **813** d.	1136	...	...	...	1239	...	1351k	...	...	1439	...	...	...	...	1639	...	1758	...	...	1839	...	...	...	2039	...	...
Norddeich **813** d.	1139	...	...	...	1241	...	1357k	...	...	1441	...	...	...	...	1641	...	1801	...	...	1841	...	...	...	2041	...	...
Norden **813** d.	1146	...	...	...	1247	...	1407k	...	...	1447	...	...	...	...	1647	...	1808	...	...	1847	...	...	...	2047	...	...
Emden Hbf **813** a.	1214	...	...	...	1315	...	1429k	...	...	1515	...	...	...	...	1715	...	1830	...	...	1915	...	...	...	2115	...	...
Emden Hbf ◧ **813** d.	1234	...	...	1252	1317	1352	1434	...	1452	1517	1552	1634	...	1652	1717	1752	1834	...	1852	1917	1952	2052	...	2117	2214	...
Leer (Ostfriesland) **813** d.	1253	...	...	1309	1333	1409	1453	...	1509	1533	1609	1653	...	1709	1733	1809	1853	...	1909	1933	2009	2109	...	2133	2231	...
Papenburg (Ems) d.	1304	...	←	1319	—	1419	1504	...	1519	—	1619	1704	...	1719	—	1819	1904	...	1919	...	2019	2119	...	...	2240	...
Meppen d.	1331	...	1337	1350	...	1450	1531	...	1550	...	1650	1731	...	1750	...	1850	1931	...	1950	...	2050	2150	...	...	2313	...
Lingen (Ems) d.	1344	...	1351	1404	...	1504	1544	...	1604	...	1704	1744	...	1804	...	1904	1944	...	2004	...	2104	2204	...	...	2327	...
Rheine d.	1404	1408	1429j	1429	1508	1529	1604	1608	1629	1708	1729	1804	1808	1829	1908	1929	2004	2008	2029	...	2129	2229	2253	...	2349	2353
Emsdetten d.	|	1416	1437	1437	1516	1537	|	1616	1637	1716	1737	|	1816	1837	1916	1937	|	2016	2037	...	2137	2237	2302	...	...	0002
Greven d.	|	1423	1445	1445	1523	1545	|	1623	1645	1723	1745	|	1823	1845	1923	1945	|	2023	2046	...	2146	2245	2311	...	...	0011
Münster (Westf) Hbf a.	1429	1433	1456	1456	1533	1556	1629	1633	1656	1733	1756	1829	1833	1856	1933	1956	2029	2033	2056	...	2156	2256	2325	...	...	0025
Hagen Hbf **802** a.	|	1536	...	...	1636	...	|	1736	...	1836	...	|	1936	...	2036	...	|	2136	...	...	...	...	...	...	...	...
Düsseldorf Hbf **800** a.	1546	|	...	...	|	...	1746	|	...	|	...	1946	|	...	|	...	2146	|	...	...	...	...	...	...	...	...
Köln Hbf **800 802** a.	1613	1638	...	...	1738	...	1813	1838	...	1938	...	2013	2038	...	2138	...	2213	2238	...	...	...	...	...	...	...	...
Koblenz Hbf **800** a.	...	...	...	...	...	...	1916b	...	...	...	...	...	...	...	...	...	...	...	...	...	...	...	...	...	...	...

♦ – **NOTES** (LISTED BY TRAIN NUMBER)

2004 – ①②③④⑦ (also May 26; not Apr. 13, 16, 30, May 24, June 4). [12] and 🍷 (Konstanz - Karlsruhe ⑦**w** -) Koblenz - Münster - Emden.

2005 – ①–⑥ (also Apr. 16, 30, June 4; not Apr. 17, May 1, June 5). [12] and 🍷 Emden - Münster - Koblenz (- Karlsruhe - Konstanz ⑤⑥**s**).

2014 – ⑤ (also Apr. 13, May 24; not Apr. 14, May 26). [12] and 🍷 Stuttgart - Mannheim - Münster - Emden.

2018 – ⑥ from Apr. 8. [12] Stuttgart - Mannheim - Münster - Norddeich Mole.

2019 – ⑥ from Apr. 8. [12] Norddeich Mole - Münster - Mannheim - Stuttgart.

B – From / to Bonn (Table **800**).
C – ⑥ from Apr. 8 (also Apr. 13, May 25).
D – ⑦ to Apr. 2; ⑤–⑦ from Apr. 7 (also Apr. 12, 13, 17, May 1, 24, June 5).
E – Daily to Apr. 7; Ⓑ from Apr. 9.
N – Ⓑ to Mar. 31; daily from Apr. 2.
P – ①–⑥ to Mar. 25; daily from Mar. 27.
Q – ①–⑥ to Apr. 1; daily from Apr. 3 (not June 5).

b – Ⓑ (not Apr. 16, 30, June 4).
e – Not Apr. 15, 17, May 1, June 5.
f – Not Apr. 14.
h – Not Apr. 15.
j – Arrives 9–11 minutes earlier.
k – On ⑥ from Apr. 8 (also Apr. 14) departs Norddeich Mole 1337, Norddeich 1340, Norden 1347, arrives Emden 1414.
q – Not Apr. 14, 16, 30, June 4.
r – ⚒ only.
s – Also Apr. 13, 16, 30, May 24, 25, June 4.
t – Ⓐ only.
v – ①–⑥ (not Apr. 17, May 1, June 5).
w – Also Apr. 17, May 1, 25, 26, June 5; not Apr. 16, 30, June 4.
z – Arrives 1307.

◇ – Operated by WestfalenBahn.
⊙ – Operated by WestfalenBahn on ⑥.
‡ – For ⛴ to / from Juist and Norderney.
◧ – For train / 🚌 / ⛴ connections to / from Borkum via Emden Außenhafen (certain Emden trains may be extended to / from Emden Außenhafen to connect with sailings).

813 NORDDEICH - EMDEN - BREMEN - HANNOVER

km	SEE NOTE ⊠	RE 4441	ICE 841	RE 4443	IC 2033	IC 2033	RE 4405	RE 4407	ICE 533	RE 4407	IC 2035	IC 2035	RE 4409	ICE 535	ICE 535	RE 4411	IC 2037	RE 4413	ICE 537	ICE 537	RE 4415	IC 2039	RE 4417	ICE 1139	RE 4419
			Ⓐd ✕		①–⑥ e		B		①–⑥ e✕		①–⑥ e		B	Ⓒm ✕	✕			B	⑦w n✕	n ✕			B	n 🍸	
	Norddeich Mole ‡ **812** d.	...	...	...	...	...	...	...	...	...	...	...	...	...	...	...	0736t	...	...	...	0839	0936	...	...	1039
0	**Norddeich** **812** d.	...	...	...	...	...	...	...	...	...	0536	...	...	...	...	0641	0739t	...	...	...	0841	0939	...	...	1041
6	Norden **812** d.	...	...	...	...	...	...	...	...	...	0543	...	...	...	...	0647	0746t	...	...	...	0847	0946	...	...	1047
35	**Emden** Hbf ◧ **812** d.	...	...	...	0416	...	...	0517	...	...	0609	...	...	...	...	0717	0816	...	...	...	0917	1016	...	...	1117
62	Leer (Ostfriesland) **812** a.	...	...	...	0433	...	...	0533	...	...	0626	...	...	...	...	0733	0833	...	...	...	0933	1033	...	...	1133
62	Leer (Ostfriesland) d.	...	...	...	0441	...	...	0541	...	...	0634	...	...	...	...	0741	0841	...	...	...	0941	1041	...	...	1141
101	Bad Zwischenahn d.	...	...	...	0513	...	...	0612	...	...	0712	...	...	...	...	0812	0913	...	...	...	1012	1113	...	...	1212
116	**Oldenburg** (Oldb) a.	...	...	...	0523	...	...	0623	...	...	0723	...	...	...	...	0823	0923	...	...	...	1023	1123	...	...	1223
116	**Oldenburg** (Oldb) d.	...	0440	...	0535	...	...	0635	0641	...	0735	0735	...	0841	...	0835	0935	...	1041	...	1035	1135	...	...	1235
147	Delmenhorst d.	...	0458	...	0554	...	...	0654	0659	...	0754	0754	...	0859	...	0854	0954	...	1059	...	1054	1154	...	...	1254
161	**Bremen** Hbf a.	...	0508	...	0605	...	...	0705	0709	←	0805	0805	...	0909	...	0905*	1005	...	1109	...	1105*	1205	...	...	1305*
161	**Bremen** Hbf d.	0408	0510	0517	0609	0609	0617	→	0714	0717	0809	0809	0817	0914	0914	0917	1009	1017	1114	1114	1117	1209	1217	1314	1317
196	Verden (Aller) d.	0441	0531	0541	0630	0630	0641	...	|	0741	0830	0830	0841	|	|	0941	1030	1041	|	|	1141	1230	1241	|	1341
227	Nienburg (Weser) d.	0503	|	0603	0646	0646	0703	...	|	0803	0846	0846	0903	|	|	1003	1046	1103	|	|	1203	1246	1303	|	1403
283	**Hannover** Hbf a.	0538	0614	0638	0713	0713	0738	...	0814	0838	0913	0913	0938	1014	1014	1038	1113	1138	1214	1214	1238	1313	1338	1414	1438
	Magdeburg Hbf **866** a.	...	|	...	0856	0856	...	...	|	...	1056	...	...	|	|	...	1256	...	|	|	...	1456	...	|	...
	Berlin Hbf **810** a.	...	0824	...	|	|	...	...	|	...	|	...	...	|	|	...	|	...	|	|	...	|	...	|	...
	Leipzig Hbf **866** a.	...	...	...	1019	1019	...	...	|	...	1219	...	...	|	|	...	1419	...	|	|	...	1619	...	|	...
	Nürnberg Hbf **900** a.	...	...	...	...	...	...	...	1124	...	...	...	...	1324	1324	...	...	...	|	|	...	...	...	1724	...
	München Hbf **900** a.	...	...	...	...	...	...	...	1239	...	...	...	...	1441	1441	...	...	...	1701	1701	...	...	...	1843	...

SEE NOTE ⊠	IC 2431	RE 4421	ICE 631	RE 4423	IC 2433	RE 4425	ICE 633	RE 4427	IC 2435	RE 4429	ICE 635	ICE 635	ICE 1135	RE 4431	IC 2437	IC 2437	RE 4433	RE 4435	IC 2439	RE 4437	♣	RE 4439		RE 4445	♣
	C	B	n ✕			B	✕			B	Ⓑq ✕	⑤⑦r ✕	⑥k ✕			Ⓑq	B			B					
Norddeich Mole ‡ **812** d.	...	...	...	1239	...	...	...	1439	...	...	...	...	...	1639	...	...	...	1839	...	...	...	2039	...	...	...
Norddeich **812** d.	...	...	...	1241	...	...	...	1441	...	...	...	...	...	1641	...	...	...	1841	...	...	...	2041	...	...	...
Norden **812** d.	...	...	...	1247	...	...	...	1447	...	...	...	...	...	1647	...	...	...	1847	...	...	...	2047	...	...	...
Emden Hbf ◧ **812** d.	1218	...	...	1317	1416f	...	...	1517	1616	...	...	...	...	1717	1816	1816	...	1917	2016	...	...	2117	...	...	...
Leer (Ostfriesland) **812** a.	1235	...	...	1333	1433f	...	...	1533	1633	...	...	...	...	1733	1833	1833	...	1933	2033	...	...	2133	...	...	...
Leer (Ostfriesland) d.	1241	...	...	1341	1441	...	...	1541	1641	...	...	...	...	1741	1841	1841	...	1941	2041	...	...	2141	...	...	...
Bad Zwischenahn d.	1313	...	...	1412	1513	...	...	1612	1713	...	...	...	...	1812	1913	1913	...	2012	2113	...	2145	2212	...	...	2345
Oldenburg (Oldb) a.	1323	...	...	1423	1523	...	...	1623	1723	...	...	...	...	1823	1923	1923	...	2023	2123	...	2157	2223	...	...	2357
Oldenburg (Oldb) d.	1335	...	...	1435	1535	...	...	1635	1735	...	...	...	...	1835	1935	1935	...	2035	2135	...	2206	2235	...	...	0006
Delmenhorst d.	1354	...	...	1454	1554	...	...	1654	1754	...	...	...	...	1854	1954	1954	...	2054	2154	...	2231	2254	...	...	0031
Bremen Hbf a.	1405	...	...	1505*	1605	...	...	1705*	1805	...	...	...	...	1905*	2005	2005	...	2105*	2205	...	2244	2305	...	...	0044
Bremen Hbf d.	1409	1417	1514	1517	1609	1617	1714	1717	1809	1817	1914	1914	1914	1917	...	2009	2017	2117	...	2217	...	2313	...	0013	...
Verden (Aller) d.	1430	1441	|	1541	1630	1642	|	1741	1830	1841	|	|	|	1941	...	2030	2041	2141	...	2241	...	2346	...	0046	...
Nienburg (Weser) d.	1446	1503	|	1603	1646	1704	|	1803	1846	1903	|	|	|	2003	...	2046	2103	2203	...	2303	...	0008	...	0108	...
Hannover Hbf a.	1513	1538	1614	1638	1713	1738	1814	1838	1913	1938	2014	2014	2014	2038	...	2113	2138	2238	...	2338	...	0040	...	0140	...
Magdeburg Hbf **866** a.	1657	...	|	...	1856	...	|	...	2056	...	|	|	...	...	...	2301	...	...	...	...	...	...	...	...	...
Berlin Hbf **810** a.	1822	...	|	...	|	...	|	...	|	...	|	|	...	...	...	...	...	...	...	...	...	...	...	...	...
Leipzig Hbf **866** a.	...	...	|	...	2019	...	|	...	2223j	...	|	|	...	...	...	...	...	...	...	...	...	...	...	...	...
Nürnberg Hbf **900** a.	...	...	1924	...	...	...	2124	...	...	...	2324	2324	...	...	...	...	...	...	...	...	...	...	...	...	...
München Hbf **900** a.	...	...	2038	...	...	...	2314	...	...	...	...	0040	...	...	...	...	...	...	...	...	...	...	...	...	...

SEE NOTE ⊠	♣	RE 4438	RE 4440	IC 2438	RE 4402	RE 4404	RE 4404	IC 2436	RE 4406	ICE 636	RE 4408	IC 2434	RE 4410	ICE 634	RE 4412	IC 2432	RE 4414	ICE 1132	RE 4416	IC 2430	RE 4418	ICE 630	RE 4420	IC 2038	RE 4422
	Ⓐ	⚒	B	①–⑥ e		Ⓐ B	Ⓒ B			Ⓐd ✕	B			①–⑥ en✕	B	C		n 🍸	B			n ✕	B		
München Hbf **900** d.	...	...	...	...	...	...	...	...	...	...	...	...	...	0520a	...	...	...	0641	...	...	...	0905	...	...	...
Nürnberg Hbf **900** d.	...	...	...	...	...	...	...	...	...	...	...	...	...	0634	...	...	...	0834	...	...	...	|	...	...	...
Leipzig Hbf **866** d.	...	...	...	...	...	...	...	...	...	...	...	0536e	...	|	...	...	...	|	...	0938	...	|	...	1138	...
Berlin Hbf **810** d.	...	...	...	...	...	...	...	...	...	...	...	|	...	|	...	0731	...	|	...	|	...	|	...	|	...
Magdeburg Hbf **866** d.	...	...	...	...	...	...	...	0501e	...	...	...	0659e	...	|	...	0901	...	|	...	1059	...	|	...	1259	...
Hannover Hbf d.	...	...	0420	...	0520	0618	0620	0645e	0720	0745	0820	0845	0920	0945	1020	1045	1120	1145	1220	1245	1320	1345	1420	1445	1520
Nienburg (Weser) d.	...	...	0454	...	0554	0654	0654	0713e	0754	|	0854	0913	0954	|	1054	1113	1154	|	1254	1313	1354	|	1454	1513	1554
Verden (Aller) d.	...	...	0516	...	0616	0716	0716	0730e	0816	|	0916	0930	1016	|	1116	1130	1216	|	1316	1330	1416	|	1516	1530	1616
Bremen Hbf a.	...	...	0539	...	0639	0739	0739	0750e	0839	0844*	0939	0950	1039	1044*	1139	1150	1239	1244*	1339	1350	1439	1444*	1539	1550	1639
Bremen Hbf d.	0415	...	...	0553	0653	...	...	0753	0853	...	...	0953	1053	...	...	1153	1253	...	...	1353	1453	...	...	1553	1653
Delmenhorst d.	0428	...	...	0604	0703	...	...	0804	0903	...	...	1004	1103	...	...	1204	1303	...	...	1404	1503	...	...	1604	1703
Oldenburg (Oldb) a.	0453	...	...	0623	0723	...	...	0823	0923	...	...	1023	1123	...	...	1223	1323	...	...	1423	1523	...	...	1623	1723
Oldenburg (Oldb) d.	0458	0533	...	0626	0733	...	...	0833	0933	...	...	1033	1133	...	...	1233	1333	...	...	1433	1533	...	...	1633	1733
Bad Zwischenahn d.	0510	0544	...	0637	0744	...	...	0844	0944	...	...	1044	1144	...	...	1244	1344	...	...	1444	1544	...	...	1644	1744
Leer (Ostfriesland) a.	...	0613	...	0707	0813	...	...	0914	1013	...	...	1114	1213	...	...	1314	1413	...	...	1514	1613	...	...	1714	1813
Leer (Ostfriesland) **812** d.	...	0624	...	0715	0824	...	...	0922	1024	...	...	1122	1224	...	...	1322	1424	...	...	1522	1624	...	...	1722	1824
Emden Hbf ◧ **812** d.	...	0642	...	0742	0842	...	...	0938	1042	...	...	1138	1242	...	...	1338	1442	...	...	1538	1642	...	...	1738	1842
Norden **812** d.	...	0706	...	0808	0906	...	...	...	1106	...	...	...	1306	...	...	...	1506	...	...	...	1706	...	...	...	1906
Norddeich **812** a.	...	0712	...	0814	0912	...	...	...	1112	...	...	...	1312	...	...	...	1512	...	...	...	1712	...	...	...	1912
Norddeich Mole ‡ **812** a.	...	0716	...	0819	0916	...	...	...	1116	...	...	...	1316	...	...	...	1516	...	...	...	1716	...	...	...	1916

SEE NOTE ⊠	ICE 538	RE 4424	IC 2036	RE 4426	RE 4426	ICE 536	RE 4428	IC 2034	IC 1934	RE 4430	ICE 776	RE 4430	RE 4432	IC 2032	IC 2032	RE 4434	ICE 832	IC 1932	RE 4434	RE 4434	RE 4442	ICE 1032	ICE 732	RE 4444	ICE 850
	n H✕	B			⑥	✕	B		⑦w		Ⓑ F✕		B	Ⓑq			①–⑥ e✕	⑦w S🍸		⑥		⑦v ✕	①–⑥ eG		⑦h
München Hbf **900** d.	1122	...	...	...	...	1322	...	...	...	...	...	...	...	...	...	...	...	...	...	...	...	1820	1820	...	...
Nürnberg Hbf **900** d.	1234	...	...	...	...	1434	...	...	...	...	...	...	...	...	...	...	...	...	...	...	...	1934	1934	...	...
Leipzig Hbf **866** d.	|	...	1338p	...	...	|	...	1538b	1558	...	...	...	...	1738	...	...	...	...	...	...	...	|	|	...	...
Berlin Hbf **810** d.	|	...	|	...	...	|	...	|	|	...	...	...	...	|	...	...	1949	1948z	...	...	...	|	|	...	2154
Magdeburg Hbf **866** d.	|	...	1459p	...	...	|	...	1659b	1724	...	...	...	...	1859	...	...	|	|	...	...	...	|	|	...	|
Hannover Hbf d.	1545	1620	1645	1720	1720	1745	1820	1845	1901	1920	1950	...	2020	2045	2045	2120	2140	2143	...	...	2222	2244	2250	2322	2349
Nienburg (Weser) d.	|	1654	1713	1754	1754	|	1854	1913	1929	1954	|	...	2054	2113	2113	2154	2209	2211	...	...	2255	2313	2319	2355	0017
Verden (Aller) d.	|	1716	1730	1816	1816	|	1916	1930	1948	2016	|	...	2116	2130	2130	2216	2228	2229	...	...	2316	2331	2337	0016	0035
Bremen Hbf a.	1644*	1739	1750	1839	1839	1844*	1939	1950	2009	2039	2047	←	2139	2150	2150	2239	2247	2247	←	←	2349	2350	2356	0049	0056
Bremen Hbf d.	...	...	1753	1853	1853	...	...	1953	2013	→	2050	2054	...	2153	2153	→	2249	2249	2253	2253	...	2352	2358	...	0058
Delmenhorst d.	...	...	1804	1903	1903	...	...	2004	2024	...	|	2104	...	2204	2204	...	2300	2300	2304	2304	...	0004	0010	...	0110
Oldenburg (Oldb) a.	...	...	1823	1923	1923	...	...	2023	2040	...	2117	2123	...	2223	2223	...	2318	2318	2323	2323	...	0021	0028	...	0128
Oldenburg (Oldb) d.	...	...	1833	1933	1933	...	...	2033	2042	...	...	2133	...	2233	...	...	...	...	...	2333	...	...	...	...	...
Bad Zwischenahn d.	...	...	1844	1944	1944	...	...	2044	2055	...	...	2144	...	2244	...	...	...	...	...	2344	...	...	...	...	...
Leer (Ostfriesland) a.	...	...	1914	2013	2013	...	...	2114	2128	...	...	2213	...	2314	...	...	...	...	...	0013	...	...	...	...	...
Leer (Ostfriesland) **812** d.	...	...	1922	2024	2024	...	...	2122	2136	...	...	2224	...	2322	...	...	...	...	...	0024	...	...	...	...	...
Emden Hbf ◧ **812** d.	...	...	1942	2040	2042	...	...	2142	2152	...	...	2242	...	2338	...	...	...	...	...	0040	...	...	...	...	...
Norden **812** d.	...	...	2008q	...	2106	...	...	2208	...	...	...	2306	...	...	...	...	...	...	...	...	...	...	...	...	...
Norddeich **812** a.	...	...	2014q	...	2112	...	...	2214	...	...	...	2312	...	...	...	...	...	...	...	...	...	...	...	...	...
Norddeich Mole ‡ **812** a.	...	...	2020q	...	2116	...	...	...	...	...	...	...	...	...	...	...	...	...	...	...	...	...	...	...	...

B – To / from Bremerhaven (Table **815**).
C – To / from Cottbus on dates in Table **838**.
F – Ⓑ (not Apr. 14, 16, 30, May 26, June 4). From Frankfurt (Table **900**).
G – From Garmisch (Table **895**) on ⑥ to Mar. 4. Conveys ✕.
H – From Garmisch (Table **895**) on ⑥ to Feb. 18.
S – From Stralsund (Table **845**).

a – ①–⑤ (not Apr. 17, May 1, June 5).
b – Ⓑ (not Apr. 14, 16).
d – Not May 26.
e – ①–⑥ (not Apr. 15, 17, May 1, June 5).
f – 2 minutes later on ⑥ from Apr. 8 (also Apr. 14).
h – Also Apr. 15, 17, May 1, June 5.
j – 2233 on certain dates (see Table **866**).
k – Also Apr. 14, 16, 30, June 4.
m – Also May 26.
n – Not Feb. 20 - Apr. 12.
p – Ⓑ (not Apr. 14).
q – Ⓑ (not Apr. 14, 16, 30, June 4).
r – Also Apr. 13, 17, May 1, June 5; not Apr. 14, 16, 30, June 4.
t – ①–⑥ (not Apr. 15).
v – Also Apr. 15, 17, May 1, June 5.
w – Also Apr. 17, May 1, June 5; not Apr. 16, 30, June 4.
z – Berlin **Spandau**.

♣ – Operated by Nord West Bahn (2nd class only).
‡ – For sailings from / to Juist and Norderney.
◧ – For train / 🚌 / ⛴ connections from / to Borkum via Emden Außenhafen.
* – Connects with train in previous column.
⊠ – Nürnberg and München timings are subject to alteration from March 6. Berlin timings are subject to alteration from May 13. See engineering work summary panel on page 367.

GERMANY

Nord West Bahn — OSNABRÜCK - OLDENBURG - WILHELMSHAVEN — 814

Journeys Varel - Wilhelmshaven and v.v. are operated by 🚌 on ⑥⑦ from Mar. 4 (also late evenings on ⑤ from Mar. 3; extended journey time of up to 40 minutes with earlier departures ✤).

km		⚒	Ⓐ					†	
0	**Osnabrück** Hbf .... d.	...	0459	0601	and	2201	2253	2253	...
20	Bramsche .... d.	...	0518	0618	hourly	2218	2318	2318	...
50	Quakenbrück .... d.	...	0540	0640	until	2240	2340	2340	...
72	Cloppenburg .... d.	...	0556	0656		2256	2356	2356	...
113	**Oldenburg** (Oldb) ..... a.	...	0629	0729		2329	0029	0029	...
113	**Oldenburg** (Oldb) ..... d.	0536	0636	0736		2336	...	0036	...
143	Varel (Oldb) .... d.	0559	0659	0759		2359	...	0059	...
165	**Wilhelmshaven** Hbf . a.	0619	0719	0819		0019	...	0119	...

	Ⓐ		⚒	⚒	Ⓐ		⊠			
Wilhelmshaven Hbf .... d.	...	...	0444	0544	0613	0644	and	2144	...	...
Varel (Oldb) .... d.	...	...	0503	0603	0632	0703	hourly	2203	...	...
Oldenburg (Oldb) .... a.	...	...	0525	0625	0652	0725	until	2225	...	...
Oldenburg (Oldb) .... d.	0406	...	0529	0629	0659	0729		2229	...	...
Cloppenburg .... d.	0438	...	0606	0706	0736	0806		2306	...	...
Quakenbrück .... d.	0453	...	0621	0721	0751	0821		2321	...	...
Bramsche .... d.	0516	...	0642	0741	0812	0841		2341	...	...
Osnabrück Hbf .... a.	0534	...	0658	0758	0830	0858		2358	...	...

⊠ – On ⑥ until Feb. 25 depart Wilhelmshaven Hbf at *1329* (not 1344) and change trains at Sande (a. *1336*, d. 1350).

✤ – Earlier southbound departures from Wilhelmshaven and Varel.

RE services — OSNABRÜCK - BREMEN - BREMERHAVEN - CUXHAVEN — 815

km		⚒¶	⚒	ⒶH	¶	⚒	H		H		H		H		H		H		H		H		¶	Ⓒ	Ⓐ	¶
0	**Osnabrück** Hbf.. **800** d.	...	0417	...	...	0534	*0634*r	0734	*0834*	0934	*1034*	1134	*1234*	1334	*1434*	1534	*1634*	1734	*1834*	1934	*2034*	2134	...	2234	2252	...
53	Diepholz .... d.	...	0450	...	...	0604	*0704*r	0804	*0904*	1004	*1104*	1204	*1304*	1404	*1504*	1604	*1704*	1804	*1904*	2004	*2104*	2204	...	2304	2321	...
122	**Bremen** Hbf .... **800** a.	...	0546	...	...	0651	*0751*r	0851	*0951*	1051	*1151*	1251	*1351*	1451	*1551*	1651	*1751*	1851	*1951*	2051	*2151*	2251	...	2351	0008	...
122	**Bremen** Hbf .... d.	0540	...	0556	0640	0656	0756	0856	0956	1056	1156	1256	1356	1456	1556	1656	1756	1856	1956	2056	2156	...	2312	...	...	0012
143	Osterholz-Scharmbeck d.	0556	...	0610	0656	0710	0810	0910	1010	1110	1210	1310	1410	1510	1610	1710	1810	1910	2010	2110	2210	...	2328	...	...	0028
185	**Bremerhaven** Hbf ..... a.	0625	...	0630	0725	0730	0830	0930	1030	1130	1230	1330	1430	1530	1630	1730	1830	1930	2030	2130	2230	...	2357	...	...	0057
188	**Bremerhaven**-Lehe .. a.	0630	...	0635	0730	0735	0835	0935	1035	1135	1235	1335	1435	1535	1635	1735	1835	1945j	2035	2135	2235	...	0002	...	...	0102

	Ⓒ¶		⚒	⚒¶	ⒶH	⚒	⚒		H		H		H		H		H		H		H		H	¶		¶
Bremerhaven-Lehe ... d.	0008	...	...	0407	0523	...	0623	...	0723	0823	0923	1023	1123	1223	1323	1423	1523	1623	1723	1823	1923	2023	2123	2158	...	2258
Bremerhaven Hbf ..... d.	0012	...	...	0412	0528	...	0628	...	0728	0828	0928	1028	1128	1228	1328	1428	1528	1628	1728	1828	1928	2028	2128	2203	...	2303
Osterholz-Scharmbeck. d.	0043	...	...	0444	0550	...	0650	...	0750	0850	0950	1050	1150	1250	1350	1450	1550	1650	1750	1850	1950	2050	2150	2233	...	2333
Bremen Hbf .... a.	0100	...	...	0504	0603	...	0703	...	0803	0903	1003	1103	1203	1303	1403	1503	1603	1703	1803	1903	2003	2103	2203	2250	...	2350
Bremen Hbf .... **800** d.	...	...	0507	...	...	0607	0707	0707	*0807*	0907	*1007*	1107	*1207*	1307	*1407*	1507	*1607*	1707	*1807*	1907	*2007*	2107	*2207*	...	2313	...
Diepholz .... d.	...	...	0550	...	...	0650	0750	0750	*0850*	0950	*1050*	1150	*1250*	1350	*1450*	1551	*1651*	1750	*1850*	1950	*2050*	2150	*2254*	...	0001	...
Osnabrück Hbf ... **800** a.	...	...	0622	...	...	0722	0822	0822	*0922*	1022	*1122*	1222	*1322*	1422	*1522*	1623	*1723*	1822	*1922*	2022	*2122*	2222	*2326*	...	0033	...

BREMERHAVEN - CUXHAVEN

km	⊡	Ⓐ	⚒					Ⓐ		
0	**Bremerhaven** Hbf ..... d.	0506	0636	0736	0836	and	2036	2136	2236	...
3	Bremerhaven-Lehe .... d.	0511	0641	0741	0841	hourly	2041	2141	2241	...
43	**Cuxhaven** .... a.	0557	0727	0827	0927	until	2127	2227	2327	...

⊡	Ⓐ	⚒						Ⓐ	
Cuxhaven .... d.	0509	0639	0739	0839	and	1939	2039	2139	2239
Bremerhaven-Lehe .... d.	0549	0719	0819	0919	hourly	2019	2119	2219	2319
Bremerhaven Hbf .... a.	0553	0723	0823	0923	until	2023	2123	2223	2323

H – From / to Hannover (Table **813**).

j – 1935 on Ⓒ.

r – ⚒ only.

⊡ – Operated by Elbe-Weser.

¶ – Operated by Nord West Bahn (2nd class only).

☛ Additional stopping trains operate Bremen Hbf - Bremerhaven-Lehe (operated by Nord West Bahn):
From Bremen Hbf at 0740, 0841, 0940, 1040 and hourly until 1840; then 1941, 2041 and 2141.
From Bremerhaven-Lehe at 0453 Ⓐ, 0537 ⚒, 0556 Ⓐ, 0637, 0656 Ⓐ, 0737, 0837 and hourly until 2037.

metronom; Elbe-Weser — HAMBURG - CUXHAVEN and BREMERHAVEN — 818

km	✤	‡	Ⓐ‡	⚒◧	‡	Ⓐ	⚒	‡	⚒																	
0	**Hamburg** Hbf .... ⊖ d.	0028	0448	...	0528	*0602*	...	0628	0706	...	0806	0906	1006	1106	1206	1306	1406	1506	1606	1706	1806	1906	2006	2106	2206	2306
12	**Hamburg** Harburg ⊖ d.	0041	0501	...	0541	0624	...	0641	0724	...	0824	0924	1024	1124	1224	1324	1424	1524	1624	1724	1824	1924	2024	2124	2224	2324
33	**Buxtehude** .... ⊖ d.	0106	0526	...	0606	0641	...	0706	0741	...	0841	0941	1041	1141	1241	1341	1441	1541	1641	1741	1841	1941	2041	2141	2241	2341
54	Stade .... ⊖ d.	0127	0547	0550	0627	0657	0657	0727	0757	0757	0857	0957	1057	1157	1257	1357	1457	1557	1657	1757	1857	1957	2057	2157	2257	2357
102	Otterndorf .... d.	...	...	0632	...	0737	0737	...	0837	0837	0937	1037	1137	1237	1337	1437	1537	1637	1737	1837	1937	2037	2137	2237	2337	0037
116	**Cuxhaven** .... a.	...	...	0645	...	0750	0750	...	0850	0850	0950	1050	1150	1250	1350	1450	1550	1650	1750	1850	1950	2050	2150	2250	2350	0050

✤	Ⓐ	⚒	Ⓐ		Ⓐ	Ⓒ								†	⚒								‡	⑤⑥f	‡	★
Cuxhaven .... d.	0432	0509	0549	0609	0650	0709	0809	0909	1009	1109	1209	1309	1409	1509	1509	1609	1709	1809	1909	2009	2109	...	...	2209	...	2237
Otterndorf .... d.	0444	0521	0601	0621	0701	0721	0821	0921	1021	1121	1221	1321	1421	1521	1521	1621	1721	1821	1921	2021	2121	...	...	2221	...	2250
Stade .... ⊖ d.	0526	0603	0643	0703	0743	0803	0903	1003	1103	1203	1303	1403	1503	1603	1603	1703	1803	1903	2003	2103	2203	...	2234	2303	2334	2332
Buxtehude .... ⊖ d.	0544	0621	0701	0721	0801	0821	0921	1021	1121	1221	1321	1421	1521	1621	1621	1721	1821	1921	2021	2121	2221	...	2254	2321	2354	...
Hamburg Harburg . ⊖ a.	0559	0638	0716	0736	0817	0836	0937	1036	1136	1236	1336	1436	1536	1636	1636	1736	1836	1937	2036	2136	2236	...	2320	2336	0020	...
Hamburg Hbf .... ⊖ a.	*0620*	0658	0734	0756	0835	0853	0957	1058	1154	1256	1356	1453	1558	1657	1659	1756	1900	1957	2055	2157	2257	...	2335	2355	0035	...

km	△		Ⓐ	Ⓐ	Ⓐ	Ⓒ	Ⓐ	Ⓐ	Ⓒ	Ⓐ	Ⓐ	Ⓒ	Ⓐ	Ⓐ	Ⓒ	Ⓐ	Ⓒ	Ⓐ	Ⓐ	Ⓒ	Ⓐ	Ⓐ	Ⓒ	Ⓐ	Ⓒ	Ⓐ
	Hamburg Hbf ..... ¶ d.	...	*0448*	*0548*	*0628*	*0648*	*0748*	*0848*	*0858*	*0948*	*1048*	*1058*	*1148*	*1248*	*1258*	*1408*	*1458*	*1508*	*1608*	*1658*	*1708*	*1808*	*1858*	*1908*	*2058*	*2108*
0	**Buxtehude** .... d.	...	0537	0637	0717	0737c	0837	0937	0945	1037	1137	1145	1237	1337	1345	1451	1545	1551	1651	1745	1751	1851	1945	1951	2145	2151
39	Bremervörde .... a.	...	0621	0723	0823	0822c	0923	1023	1027	1123	1223	1227	1323	1423	1427	1532	1627	1632	1732	1827	1832	1932	2027	2032	2226	2232
39	Bremervörde .... d.	0638	0638	0738	0838	0838	0938	1038	1038	1138	1238	1238	1338	1438	1438	1538	1638	1638	1738	1838	1838	1938	2038	2038	...	...
78	**Bremerhaven** Hbf a.	0720	0720	0820	0920	0920	1020	1120	1120	1220	1320	1320	1420	1520	1520	1620	1720	1720	1820	1920	1920	2020	2120	2120	...	...

△	⚒	†	⚒	Ⓐ	Ⓒ	Ⓐ	Ⓐ	Ⓒ	Ⓐ	Ⓐ	Ⓒ	Ⓐ	Ⓒ	Ⓐ	Ⓐ	Ⓒ	Ⓐ	Ⓐ	Ⓒ	Ⓐ	Ⓐ	Ⓒ		⚒	Ⓑ	
Bremerhaven Hbf . d.	0536e	...	0636	0736	0736	0836	0936	0936	1036	1136	1136	1236	1336	1336	1436	1536	1536	1636	1736	1736	1836	1936	1936	2036	2136	2354
Bremervörde .... a.	0620e	...	0720	0820	0820	0920	1020	1020	1120	1220	1220	1320	1420	1420	1520	1620	1620	1720	1820	1820	1920	2020	2020	2120	2220	0036
Bremervörde .... d.	0625	0632	0725	0825	0832	0925	1025	1032	1125	1225	1232	1325	1432	1439	1539	1632	1639	1739	1832	1839	1939	2032	...	...	...	...
Buxtehude .... a.	0709	0716	0809	0909	0916	1009	1109	1116	1209	1309	1316	1409	1516	1526	1626	1716	1726	1826	1916	1926	2026	2116	...	...	...	...
Hamburg Hbf ...... ¶ a.	*0755*	*0756*	*0855*	*0955*	*1005*	*1055*	*1155*	*1205*	*1255*	*1355*	*1405*	*1455*	*1605*	*1615*	*1715*	*1805*	*1815*	*1915*	*2005*	*2015*	*2115*	*2205*	...	...	...	...

c – On † Buxtehude d. 0745, Bremervörde a. 0827.

e – Ⓐ only.

f – Also Apr. 13, 16, 30, May 24, June 4.

★ – ①②③④⑦ (not Apr. 13, 16, 30, May 24, June 4).

◧ – Runs 6 minutes later on ⑥.

‡ – Hamburg S-Bahn (2nd class only).

⊖ – Additional S-Bahn trains operate.

✤ – Hamburg - Cuxhaven operated by *metronom*.

△ – Buxtehude - Bremerhaven operated by Elbe-Weser.

¶ – Connections shown are Hamburg S-Bahn services. Faster connections, operated by *metronom*, may be available (see Hamburg - Cuxhaven panel).

RE services except where shown — HAMBURG - KIEL — 820

km				⚒	†		Ⓐ	Ⓒ	⚒										*ICE* 1188 ①–⑤ a Y	*IC* 208 B	*ICE* 906 ①–⑥ r D	*IC* 2028 F	*ICE* 74 Z	*EC* 378 L	*ICE* 1094 Ⓑ b S	*ICE* 1206 ⑦ w K
0	**Hamburg** Hbf **823** d.	0045	0143	0430	0443	0532	0615	0626	0717	0821	0921	and	2121	2146	2221	2322	2345		0900	1016	1127t	1416	1738	1913	2032	2127t
37	Elmshorn .... **823** d.	0115	0213	0500	0513	0602	0647	0656	0747	0847	0947	hourly	2147	2216	2247	2348	0015	also	|	|	|	|	|	|	|	|
73	Neumünster .. **823** d.	0142	0240	0530	0540	0630	0717	0733	0817	0917	1017	until	2217	2240	2317	0018	0040		0951	1104	1226	1503	1826	2001	2123	2232
111	**Kiel** Hbf .... a.	0209	0307	0557	0607	0657	0738	0800	0838	0938	1038		2237	2307	2338	0039	0107		1009	1121	1244	1521	1844	2018	2144	2249

			Ⓒ	Ⓐ	Ⓐ	Ⓒ	⚒	†	⚒									*ICE* 1207 ① g K	*ICE* 973 ①–⑥ h S	*ICE* 73 ①–⑥ e Z	*EC* 379 L	*ICE* 1175 ⑦ d Z	*ICE* 77 Z	*IC* 2229 F	*ICE* 801 ①–⑥ r A	*ICE* 885 M	*IC* 2307 N
Kiel Hbf .... d.	0002	0102	0311	0359	0402	0445	0459	0521	0621	and	2021	2102	2121	2202	2302		0513	0613	0713	0742	0911	1113	1233	1413	1639	1733
Neumünster ... **823** d.	0028	0128	0331	0425	0428	0511	0525	0542	0642	hourly	2042	2129	2142	2232	2332	also	0531	0632	0732	0800	0930	1132	1252	1432	1657	1752
Elmshorn .... **823** d.	0057	0155	0400	0454	0455	0536	0548	0611	0711	until	2111	2152	2211	2301	0001		|	|	|	|	|	|	|	|	|	|
Hamburg Hbf **823** a.	0127	0224	0427	0520	0524	0601	0617	0637	0737		2137	2221	2237	2331	0031		0632v	0719	0820	0848	1020	1219	1342	1532v	1750	1842

A – (12) and ✕ Kiel - Berlin.

B – (12) Basel - Frankfurt - Köln - Kiel.

D – (12) and ✕ Leipzig - Berlin - Kiel.

F – (12) and 🍷 Kiel - Köln - Frankfurt and v.v.

K – (12) and ✕ München - Leipzig - Berlin - Kiel and v.v.

L – (12) and ✕ Praha - Dresden - Berlin - Kiel and v.v.

M – (12) and ✕ Kiel - Hannover - München.

N – (12) and 🍷 Kiel - Köln - Koblenz.

S – (12) and ✕ Kiel - Frankfurt - Stuttgart and v.v.

Y – (12) and ✕ Frankfurt - Hannover - Kiel.

Z – (12) and ✕ Kiel - Frankfurt - Basel - Zürich and v.v.

a – Not Apr. 14, 17, May 1, June 5.

b – Not Apr. 14, 16, 30, May 25, 26, June 4.

d – Also Apr. 17, May 1, June 5.

e – Not Apr. 15, 17, May 1, June 5.

g – Also Apr. 18, May 2, June 6; not Apr. 17, May 1, June 5.

h – Not Apr. 15, 17, May 1, 26, 27, June 5.

r – Also Apr. 16, 30, June 4; not Apr. 17, May 1, June 5.

t – Also calls at Hamburg Altona (departs 19 – 24 minutes later).

v – Also calls at Hamburg Altona (arrives 21 minutes earlier).

w – Also Apr. 17, May 1, June 5; not Apr. 16, 30, June 4.

12 German national public holidays are on Dec. 25, 26, Jan. 1, Apr. 14, 17, May 1, 25, June 5 and Oct. 3 387

GERMANY

See page 367 for a summary of Christmas / New Year alterations

821 HAMBURG - WESTERLAND

See Tables **820** and **823** for connecting *RE* services Hamburg Hbf - Elmshorn and v.v. Frequent S-Bahn services operate Hamburg Hbf - Altona and v.v.

km														*IC*• 2314				*IC*• 2072			*IC*• 2310				*IC*• 2374
		L		① g	②–⑥ p		L	Ⓐ		Ⓒ z	Ⓐ			S 🍷	W	S		D 🍷			F 🍷				Q K 🍷
	Köln Hbf **800** d.	...	...	...	...	...	...	...	...	...	...	...	...	0509	...	...	...	...	...	...	0909	...	...	...	...
	Berlin Hbf **840** d.	...	...	...	...	...	...	...	...	...	...	...	...	|	...	...	...	0906	...	...	|	...	...	...	...
	Hamburg Hbf ... **820** d.	...	...	...	...	...	...	...	...	...	...	...	...	0916	...	...	...	1116	...	...	1316	...	...	...	1532
0	**Hamburg** Altona d.	...	...	0425	...	...	...	0529	...	0629	0640	0740	0840	|	0940	0940	1040	|	1140	1240	|	1340	1440	1540	|
30	Elmshorn **820** d.	...	...	0445	...	...	...	0549	...	0649	0701	0801	0901	|	1001	1001	1101	|	1201	1301	|	1401	1501	1601	|
64	Itzehoe d.	...	...	0508	0511	...	...	0612	...	0714	0724	0824	0924	1014t	1024	1024	1124	1214t	1224	1324	1414t	1424	1524	1624	1642t
123	Heide (Holst) a.	...	...	0552	0552	...	...	0656	...	0758	0758	0858	0958	1050	1058	1058	1158	1250	1258	1358	1450	1458	1558	1658	1717
123	Heide (Holst) d.	...	...	0553	0553	...	...	0702	...	0802	0802	0902	1002	1052	1102	1102	1202	1252	1302	1402	1452	1502	1602	1702	1719
157	Husum d.	0458	0600	0630t	0617	0630	0700	0730	0730	0830	0830	0930	1030	1118	1130	1130	1230	1318	1330	1430	1518	1530	1630	1730	1742
197	Niebüll a.	0528	0628	0658	...	0658	0728	0758	0758	0858	0858	0958	1058	1145	1158	1206	1258	1345	1406	1458	1545	1606	1658	1758	1809
197	Niebüll d.	0531	0631	0701	...	0701	0731	0801	0801	0901	0901	1001	1101	1201	1201	1216	1301	1401	1431	1501	1601	1616	1701	1801	1831
237	**Westerland** (Sylt) a.	0605	0705	0735	...	0735	0805	0835	0835	0937	0937	1035	1135	1234	1235	1251	1335	1434	1505	1537	1634	1651	1735	1835	1904

						⑥ h	Y	④ X	④ X		⑤–⑦ m	
Köln Hbf **800** d.	...	...	...	...	...	...	...	...	...	...	...	...
Berlin Hbf **840** d.	...	...	...	...	...	...	...	...	...	...	...	...
Hamburg Hbf ... **820** d.	...	...	...	...	...	...	...	...	...	...	...	...
Hamburg Altona d.	1640	1740	1840	1940	2040	2140	2140	2140	...	2240	2345	...
Elmshorn **820** d.	1701	1801	1901	2001	2101	2201	2201	2201	...	2301	0005	...
Itzehoe d.	1724	1824	1926	2026	2126	2226	2226	2226	...	2326	0030	...
Heide (Holst) a.	1758	1858	2000	2100	2200	2310	2310	2310	...	0010	0113	...
Heide (Holst) d.	1802	1902	2002	2102	2202	2311	2311	2311	...	0011	0114	...
Husum d.	1830	1930	2030	2130	2230	2339	2339	2337	2348	0037	0140	...
Niebüll a.	1858	1958	2058	2158	2258	0007	0007	...	0016	...	...	...
Niebüll d.	1901	2001	2101	2201	2301	0008	0008	...	0017	...	...	...
Westerland (Sylt) a.	1935	2035	2135	2235	2335	0041	0050	...	0050	...	...	...

			Ⓐ	Ⓐ			⚒	†	
Westerland (Sylt) d.	0002	...	...	0422	...	0522	0622	0622	0722
Niebüll a.	0033j	...	...	0453	...	0559	0659	0659	0759
Niebüll d.	0034j	...	...	0454	...	0601	0701	0701	0801
Husum d.	0102j	...	0424	0524	0524	0631	0731	0731	0831
Heide (Holst) a.	...	...	0449	0549	0549	0656	0756	0754	0856
Heide (Holst) d.	...	...	0450	0550	0550	0657	0802	0755	0902
Itzehoe d.	...	...	0534	0634	0634	0734	0837	0837	0937
Elmshorn **820** d.	...	...	0600	0700	0700	0800	0900	0900	1000
Hamburg Altona a.	...	...	0621	0721	0721	0821	0921	0921	1021
Hamburg Hbf **820** a.	...	...	...	...	...	...	...	...	...
Berlin Hbf **840** a.	...	...	...	...	...	...	...	...	...
Köln Hbf **800** a.	...	...	...	...	...	...	...	...	...

			IC• 2311		*IC*• 2375					*IC*• 2315			*IC*• 2073											△	
			H 🍷		R K 🍷			S	W	S G 🍷			D 🍷		Ⓐ		Ⓐ					⑤†	N		
Westerland (Sylt) d.	0822	0910	0926	1022	1056	1122	1222	1310	1322	1326	1422	1452	1526	1622	1652	1722	1752	1822	1922	2022	2122	2122	...	...	2222
Niebüll a.	0859	0944	0959	1059	1129	1159	1259	1343	1359	1359	1459	1529	1559	1659	1729	1759	1829	1859	1959	2059	2159	2159	...	...	2255
Niebüll d.	0901	1000	1013	1101	1145	1201	1301	1355	1401	1413	1501	1555	1613	1701	1731	1801	1831	1901	2001	2101	2201	2201	...	...	2301
Husum d.	0931	1031	1042	1131	1212	1231	1331	1431	1431	1442	1531	1631	1642	1731	1808	1831	1859	1931	2031	2131	2229	2231t	2248	...	2329
Heide (Holst) a.	0956	1056	1106	1156	1233	1256	1356	1456	1456	1506	1556	1656	1706	1756	...	1856	...	1956	2056	2156	...	2256	2312	...	...
Heide (Holst) d.	1002	1102	1108	1202	1235	1302	1402	1502	1502	1508	1602	1702	1708	1802	...	1902	...	2002	2104	2204	...	2304	2313	...	...
Itzehoe d.	1037	1137	1155t	1237	1326r	1337	1437	1537	1537	1555t	1637	1737	1755t	1837	...	1937	...	2037	2139	2247	...	2347	2353	*0002*	...
Elmshorn **820** d.	1100	1200	|	1300	|	1400	1500	1600	1600	|	1700	1800	|	1900	...	2000	...	2100	2202	2310	...	0012	...	0033	...
Hamburg Altona a.	1121	1221	|	1321	|	1421	1521	1621	1621	|	1721	1821	|	1921	...	2021	...	2121	2223	2331	...	0033	...	0057	...
Hamburg Hbf ... **820** a.	...	...	1242	...	1424	...	...	...	...	1642	...	...	1848	...	...	...	...	...	...	...	...	...	...	...	...
Berlin Hbf **840** a.	...	...	|	...	...	...	...	...	...	|	...	...	2055	...	...	...	...	...	...	...	...	...	...	...	...
Köln Hbf **800** a.	...	...	1650	...	...	...	...	...	...	2050	...	...	...	...	...	...	...	...	...	...	...	...	...	...	...

D – UTHLANDE – From / to Dresden on dates in Table **840**.
F – NORDFRIESLAND – (12) and 🍷 Frankfurt - Köln - Westerland.
G – DEICHGRAF – (12) and 🍷 Westerland - Köln - Frankfurt.
H – NORDFRIESLAND – (12) and 🍷 Westerland - Köln - Stuttgart.
K – WATTENMEER – (12) and 🍷 Karlsruhe - Frankfurt - Hamburg - Westerland and v.v.
L – Ⓐ (daily from Apr. 3).
N – ①②③④⑥ (not Apr. 17, May 1, 25, June 5).
Q – ④–⑦ to Apr. 2; daily from Apr. 6.
R – ①⑤⑥⑦ to Apr. 3; daily from Apr. 7.
S – From Apr. 7.
W – Until Apr. 6.
X – ④ from Apr. 6 (also Apr. 12, May 23; not Apr. 13, May 25).
Y – Ⓑ to Apr. 5; ①②③⑤⑦ from Apr. 7 (also May 25; not Apr. 12, 16, 30, May 23, 24, June 4).

g – Also Apr. 18, May 2, 26, June 6; not Apr. 17, May 1, June 5.
h – Also Apr. 13, 16, 30, May 24, June 4.
j – 6 minutes later on ⑤ from Apr. 7 (also Apr. 13, May 24; not Apr. 14, May 26).
m – Also Apr. 17, May 1, 25, June 5.
p – Not Apr. 14, 15, 18, May 2, 25, 26, June 6.
r – Arrives 1310.
t – Arrives 11–12 minutes earlier.
z – Not Apr. 15.

• – Conveys (2) to / from Dagebüll Mole on dates in Table **822**.
△ – Operated by *nordbahn*.

822 SCHLESWIG-HOLSTEIN BRANCH LINES

NEUMÜNSTER - HEIDE - BÜSUM (Operated by *nordbahn*)

km		⚒	⚒	†	⚒	⑥	Ⓐ																		
0	Neumünster d.	...	...	...	...	0532	0532	...	0739	...	0939	...	1139	...	1339	...	1539	...	1739	...	1939	...	...	...	2139
63	Heide a.	...	...	...	...	0643	0710	...	0847	...	1047	...	1247	...	1447	...	1647	...	1847	...	2047	...	...	...	2247
63	Heide d.	0449	0556	0654	0701	0701	...	0801	0901	1001	1101	1201	1301	1401	1501	1601	1701	1801	1901	2003	...	2103	2203	...	...
87	Büsum a.	0515	0622	0720	0727	0727	...	0827	0927	1027	1127	1227	1327	1427	1527	1627	1727	1827	1927	2029	...	2129	2229	...	...

	⚒	⚒	⚒	⑥		†	⚒																		
Büsum d.	...	0519	0626	0626	...	0724	0731	0831	0931	1031	1131	1231	1331	1431	1531	1631	1731	1831	1931	2033	...	...	2133	...	2233
Heide a.	...	0545	0652	0652	...	0750	0757	0857	0957	1057	1157	1257	1357	1457	1557	1657	1757	1857	1957	2059	...	...	2159	...	2259
Heide d.	0514	...	...	0718	0718	...	...	0918	...	1118	...	1318	...	1518	...	1718	...	1918	...	...	2118	...	...	...	2318
Neumünster a.	0622	...	...	0828	0828	...	...	1028	...	1228	...	1428	...	1628	...	1828	...	2028	...	...	2228	...	...	...	0025

HUSUM - BAD ST PETER ORDING

km		Ⓐ									
0	Husum d.	0436	0536	0636	and	1836	1936	2036	2136	2236
21	Tönning d.	0501	0601	0701	hourly	1901	2001	2101	2201	2301
43	Bad St Peter Ording a.	0527	0627	0727	until	1927	2027	2127	2227	2327

	Ⓐ								
Bad St Peter Ording d.	0533	0633	0733	and	1933	2033	2133	2233	2333
Tönning d.	0604	0704	0804	hourly	2004	2104	2204	2304	0004
Husum a.	0625	0725	0825	until	2025	2125	2225	2325	0025

NIEBÜLL - DAGEBÜLL MOLE *See note* ⊡

km	*Until Apr. 6*	♥	Ⓐ		Ⓐ		Ⓐ					⑤–⑦
0	Niebüll neg d.	0635	0735	0905	1010	1125	1235	1335	1440	1603	1815	1910
14	Dagebüll Mole a.	0655	0754	0924	1029	1144	1254	1354	1459	1619	1832	1929

Until Apr. 6	♥	Ⓐ		Ⓐ		Ⓐ		J			♣
Dagebüll Mole d.	0705	0815	0930	1035	1150	1305	1410	1505	1625	1835	1935
Niebüll neg a.	0724	0834	0949	1054	1209	1324	1429	1524	1644	1854	1955

km	*From Apr. 7*				⊗	★			★	★		★
	Hamburg Hbf a.	...	...	...	...	0916	...	...	1116	1316	...	1532
	Niebüll a.	...	...	...	...	1145	...	...	1345	1545	...	1809
0	Niebüll neg d.	0735	0905	1010	1135	1205	1310	1335	1440	1605	1710	1825
14	Dagebüll Mole a.	0754	0924	1029	1154	1224	1329	1354	1459	1624	1729	1844

From Apr. 7		★		★ ⑤–⑦		★	★				E
Dagebüll Mole d.	0815	0930	1035	1110	1200	1340	1505	1635	1735	1850	1940
Niebüll neg a.	0834	0949	1054	1127	1227	1357	1524	1654	1754	1909	1956
Niebüll d.	...	1013k	...	1145k	...	1413	1613	...	...	...	...
Hamburg Hbf a.	...	1242k	...	1424k	...	1642	1848	...	...	...	...

E – ⑤–⑦ (also Apr. 13, 17, May 24, June 5).
J – Runs 10 minutes later Jan. 2–5.
k – Not Apr. 7.
t – Not Apr. 13, 17, May 24, June 5.
♥ – Daily. By 🚌 on Ⓒ.
♣ – By 🚌 on ①–④.

★ – Conveys (2) (*IC*) from / to Hamburg and beyond (Table **821**).
⊗ – On ⑤ Niebüll d. 1105, Dagebüll Mole a. 1124.
⊡ – **Operator**: Norddeutsche Eisenbahngesellschaft Niebüll GmbH. ✆ +49 (0) 4661 980 880. Niebüll neg station is situated a short distance from the Niebüll DB station forecourt. Dagebüll Mole is the station for ferries to / from the islands of Föhr and Amrum.
Additional journeys from Apr. 7:
Niebüll neg → Dagebüll Mole at 0635 Ⓐ, 0635 Ⓒ 🚌, 1025 ⑤–⑦ and 1915 **E**.
Dagebüll Mole → Niebüll neg at 0705 Ⓐ, 0705 Ⓒ 🚌, 1245, 1400, 1935 ①–④ t 🚌.

388 *For explanation of standard symbols see page 4* 12

823 — HAMBURG - NEUMÜNSTER - FLENSBURG

RE/ RB services except where shown

km															IC 386							IC 384					IC 382	IC 1284						
			�couteau ①–⑥		�couteau										A							A					A	⑦w ①–⑥ ⑦w R M t						
			k																															
0	Hamburg Hbf	820 d.	0430	0532	0615q	0740	0843	0943	1043	1143	1243	1343	1443	1450	1543	1643	1747	1843	1901	1943	2041	2043	2046	2146	2243
37	Elmshorn	820 d.	0500	0602	0647q	0809	0909	1009	1109		1209	1309	1409	1509		1609	1709	1813	1909		2009		2109	2112	2216	2313
73	Neumünster	820 d.	0530	0643	0733	0833	0933	1033	1133		1233	1333	1433	1533		1633	1733	1842j	1933		2033		2130	2133	2136	2242	2336
112	Rendsburg	824 d.	0558	0712	0801	0901	1001	1101	1201	1213	1301	1401	1501	1601	1616	1701	1801	1912	2001	2013	2101	2156	2201	2212	2310	0004
136	Schleswig	824 d.	0616	0730	0819	0919	1016	1119	1216		1319	1416	1519	1616		1719	1816	1930	2016		2119	2211	2216	2230	2328	0022
174	Flensburg	a.	0645	0758	0844	0948	1042	1148	1242	1248	1343	1442	1548	1642	1648	1748	1842	1958	2042	2048	2148	2233	2242	2255	2357	0051

										IC 1981 383 ⑤f	IC 383 1183				IC 385					IC 387 1187				
			�couteau	①–⑥	①–⑥	⑦S				M	A				A					RA				
Flensburg	d.	0409	0509	0609	0621	0709	0815	0909	1015	1109	1130	1209	1215	1309	1415	1509	1609	1615	1709	1815	1909	2009	2015	2109	2212	2309
Schleswig	824 d.	0436	0536	0636	0648	0736	0839	0936	1039	1136	1151		1239	1336	1439	1536		1639	1736	1839	1936		2039	2136	2239	2336
Rendsburg	824 d.	0457	0557	0657	0709	0757	0857	0957	1057	1157	1207	1243	1257	1357	1457	1557	1643	1657	1757	1857	1957	2043	2057	2157	2300	2357
Neumünster	820 a.	0523	0623	0723	0735	0823	0923	1023	1123	1223	1231		1323	1423	1523	1623		1723	1823	1923	2023		2124	2224	2327	0023
Elmshorn	820 a.	0610	0647	0747		0847	0947	1047	1147	1247			1347	1447	1547	1647		1747	1847	1947	2047		2151	2300	2400	0056
Hamburg Hbf	820 a.	0637	0715	0815	0826	0915	1015	1115	1215	1315	1317	1402	1415	1516	1615	1715	1803	1815	1916	2016	2116	2156	2221	2331	0031	0127

A – 🚃 Aarhus - Fredericia - Padborg - Flensburg - Hamburg and v.v.
M – From/ to München (Table 900).
R – From June 2.
S – From Jan. 8.

f – Also Apr. 13, May 24; not Apr. 14, May 26.
h – Also Dec. 11, 18.
j – Arrives 1835.
k – Also Dec. 11, 18, 25, Jan. 1.

q – On ⓒ departs Hamburg 0626, Elmshorn 0656.
t – Also Apr. 16, 30, June 4; not Apr. 17, May 1, June 5.
w – Also Apr. 17, May 1, June 5; not Apr. 16, 30, June 4.

---

824 — KIEL - HUSUM and FLENSBURG

RB services

km			�couteau	D	E								
0	Kiel Hbf	d.	0348	0503	0603	0703	and	2103	2203	2303	0003	...
40	Rendsburg. 823	d.	0435v	0535	0635	0735	hourly	2135	2235	2343	0043	...
65	Schleswig ..823	d.	0453	0553	0653	0753	until	2153	2253	0001	0101	...
102	Husum	a.	0525	0625	0725	0825		2225	2325	0033	0133	...

			�couteau	D								
	Husum	d.	0430	0535	...	0635	and	2035	2135	2235	2335
	Schleswig ..823	d.	0502	0607	...	0707	hourly	2107	2207	2307	0007
	Rendsburg .. 823	d.	0521	0626	...	0726	until	2126	2226	2329	0030
	Kiel Hbf	a.	0554	0657	...	0757		2157	2257	2400	0113

km			Ⓐ	�couteau	Ⓐ	ⓒ						
0	Kiel Hbf	d.	0413	0517	0617	0640	0742	and	2042	2142	2247	2347
29	Eckernförde	d.	0448	0548	0648	0710	0810	hourly	2110	2215	2320	0020
50	Süderbrarup	d.	0506	0606	0706	0730	0830	until	2130	2239	2339	0039
81	Flensburg	a.	0536	0636	0736	0756	0856		2156	2305	0005	0106

			�couteau									
	Flensburg	d.	0529	0603	0703	0803	and	2003	2103	2212	2312
	Süderbrarup	d.	0549	0629	0729	0829	hourly	2029	2129	2239	2339
	Eckernförde	d.	0549	0649	0749	0849	until	2049	2154	2259	2359
	Kiel Hbf	a.	0615	0715	0816	0916		2116	2224	2329	0029

D – ①–⑥ (also Dec. 11, 18).
E – ①–⑥ (also Dec. 11, 18, 25, Jan. 1).
v – Arrives 0419.

---

825 — HAMBURG - LÜBECK - PUTTGARDEN and TRAVEMÜNDE

RB/RE services

HAMBURG - LÜBECK

km						ⓒ		�couteau		Ⓐ				Ⓐ					D	F	⑥H
0	Hamburg Hbf	d.	0024	0055	0255	...	0504	0604	0634	and at the same	2004	2034	...	2108	2208	...	2323	...	1100	1218	2103
40	Bad Oldesloe	d.	0050	0137	0337	...	0530	0630	0702	minutes past	2030	2102	...	2132	2232	...	2347	also			
63	Lübeck Hbf	a.	0108	0155	0355	...	0548	0648	0720	each hour until	2048	2120	...	2150	2250	...	0005	...	1138	1300	2142

			ⓒ			Ⓐ			Ⓐ	Ⓐ	Ⓐ							J	E	G
Lübeck Hbf	d.	0017	0207	0417	0508	0541	0608	0641	0708	0741	...	0808	0843	and at the same	1908	1943	2008	2108	2208	2308	...	0816	1416	1637
Bad Oldesloe	d.	0034	0224	0434	0525	0558	0625	0658	0725	0758	...	0825	0900	minutes past	1925	2000	2025	2125	2225	2325	...	also			
Hamburg Hbf	a.	0107	0307	0517	0551	0626	0653t	0724	0751	0824	...	0851	0926	each hour until	1951	2026	2051	2151	2251	2351	...	0856	1456	1732

LÜBECK - TRAVEMÜNDE STRAND

km			Ⓐ	�couteau				Ⓐ					Ⓐ	�couteau						
0	Lübeck Hbf	d.	0503	0603	0703	0803r	and	2203r	2303	...		Travemünde Strand	d.	0534	0634	0734	...	0834	and	2234	2334
18	Travemünde Skandinavienkai	a.	0519	0619	0719	0819	hourly	2219	2319	...		Travemünde Skandinavienkai	d.	0539	0639	0739	...	0839	hourly	2239	2339
21	Travemünde Strand	a.	0525	0625	0725	0825	until	2225	2325	...		Lübeck Hbf	a.	0556	0656	0756	...	0858	until	2258	2356

HAMBURG - LÜBECK - PUTTGARDEN (- KØBENHAVN)

km				EC 31 Y		ⓒ	ICE 1233 N ⎚			⑥		IC 2410 N	EC 35 Q ⑥L		ⓒ	EC 37 T		EC 39 U				
0	Hamburg Hbf	d.	...	...	0724	...	0821	0928	...	...	...	1140x	1328	...	...	1426	1528	...	1728	...	...	...	...
63	Lübeck Hbf	☐ d.	0512	...	0712	0806	0912	0915	1006	1112	...	1308	1312	1314	1406	...	1512	1515	1606	1712	1806	1912	...	2112	...	2312
93	Neustadt (Holst)	☐ d.	...	...	...	...	...	...	...	...	...	...	...	...	...	...	...	...	...	...	...	...	...	2345
115	Oldenburg (Holst)	d.	0616	...	0816	0839	1016	1016	1039	1216	...	1405	1416	1417	1439	...	1616	1616	1639	1816	1839	2016	...	2216	...	0017
144	Fehmarn-Burg	d.	0643	...	0840	...	1040	1042	...	1240	...	1428	1440	1442	...	...	1640	1642	...	2040	...	2240	...	0040
151	Puttgarden 🚢	d.	0656	...	0855h	0905	1055p	1058	1105	1105z	...	1440	1455b	...	1505	...	1655f	1658	1705	1855	1905	2055z	...	2255	...	0055
	København H 720 ●	a.	...	...	1222	...	...	1422	...	...	...	...	...	1819	...	...	...	2022	...	2219	...	...	...	...

			IC 2411 ⑥L		EC 38 N	ⓒ		EC 36 W ⑥	⑥ N		EC 34 Q	EC 2413 ⑥M		ⓒ N	EC 32 T X		ICE 1230 ⎚	
København H 720 ●	a.	...	...	...	0737	...	...	0937	...	...	1137	...	...	...	1537	...	1737	...
Puttgarden 🚢	d.	0519	0620	0720	...	0915h	...	1042	1110	1115p	...	1242	1310	1315b	1442	...	1515z	...	1710	1715f	1842	1915	...	2042	2115z
Fehmarn-Burg	d.	0530	0631	0731	0824	...	0931	...	1125	1131	...	1321	1331	1510	1531	...	1725	1731	...	1931	...	2131
Oldenburg (Holst)	d.	0553	0654	0754	0916	...	0954	...	1107	1154	1154	...	1307	1344	1354	1507	1534	1554	...	1751	1754	1907	1954	...	2107	2154
Neustadt (Holst)	d.	0623	...	...	...	...	...	...	...	...	...	...	...	...	...	...	...	...	...	...
Lübeck Hbf	☐ d.	0654	0754	0854	1004	...	1054	...	1137	1242	1254	...	1337	1454	1454	1537	1635	1654	...	1842	1854	1937	2054	...	2137	2254
Hamburg Hbf	a.	...	...	1114x	...	...	...	1220	1337	...	...	1421	...	...	1622	1732	...	1938	...	2021	...	2223

O – ICE 784. From München (Table 900).
E – ICE 681. To München (Table 900).
F – ⑤⑦ to Apr. 2; ⑧ from Apr. 7. IC 2220. From Frankfurt via Köln (Tables 800/911).
G – ⑤⑦ to Apr. 2; ⑧ from Apr. 7. IC 2221. To Frankfurt via Köln (Tables 800/911).
H – ⑧ (not Apr. 14, 30, June 4). ICE 584. From München (Table 900).
J – ①–⑥ (not Apr. 15, 17, May 1, June 5). ICE 585. To München (Table 900).
L – ⑥ from Apr. 8. FEHMARN – 🚃 Köln - Hamburg Harburg - Fehmarn-Burg and v.v.
M – ⑥ from Apr. 8. LÜBECKER BUCHT.
N – From Apr. 8.
Q – Daily to Apr. 7; ⑧ from Apr. 9.
T – Daily to Apr. 7; Ⓐ from Apr. 10.
U – Dec. 17 - Jan. 1 (not Dec. 24, 31).
W – Dec. 17–24, 26–31.
X – Dec. 16 - Jan. 1 (not Dec. 24, 31); from Mar. 31.
Y – Dec. 17–24, 26–31 and from Apr. 1.

b – ⑧ from Apr. 7.
f – Ⓐ from Apr. 7.
h – Ⓐ (daily from Apr. 3).
p – ⓒ to Apr. 2; Ⓐ from Apr. 7.
r – 2 minutes earlier on ⓒ from Apr. 8.
t – 0651 on ⓒ.
x – Hamburg Harburg.
z – From Apr. 7.

● – København timings are subject to alteration Apr. 8–17.
☐ – Full service Lübeck - Neustadt (Holst) and v.v. (journey time 31–46 minutes):
   From Lübeck Hbf at 0442 Ⓐ, 0512 Ⓐ, 0612, 0712, 0812, 0912 T, 0912 ⓒ N, 1012, 1112, 1212, 1308 ⑥ N, 1312 Q, 1412, 1508 ⓒ N, 1512 T, 1612, 1712, 1812, 1912, 2012, 2112, 2212 and 2312.
   From Neustadt (Holst) at 0523 Ⓐ, 0623, 0653 Ⓐ, 0717 Ⓐ, 0723 ⓒ, 0817, 0919 ⓒ N, 0923 T, 1017, 1114 ⓒ N, 1123 T, 1217 T, 1223 ⓒ N, 1317 ⑥ N, 1323 Q, 1417, 1514 ⓒ N, 1523 T, 1617, 1714 ⓒ N, 1723 T, 1817 T, 1823 ⓒ N, 1923, 2017, 2123, 2217 and 2317.

GERMANY

See page 367 for a summary of Christmas / New Year alterations

826 KIEL - LÜBECK

RE / RB services

km		Ⓒ	Ⓐ	Ⓒ	Ⓐ							
0	**Kiel** Hbf d.	0543	0544	0643	0644	0744	and	1944	2044	2143	2243	2343
33	Plön d.	0615	0615	0713	0715	0815	hourly	2015	2115	2215	2315	0015
47	Eutin d.	0629	0629	0727	0729	0829	until	2029	2131	2229	2329	0029
80	**Lübeck** Hbf a.	0658	0652	0752	0752	0852		2052	2153	2258	2358	0058

	⑥	Ⓐ	Ⓒ	Ⓐ							
Lübeck Hbf d.	0501	0504	0601	0606	0704	0806	and	2006	2106	2201	2301
Eutin d.	0529	0529	0629	0629	0729	0829	hourly	2029	2131	2229	2329
Plön d.	0544	0544	0643	0645	0745	0845	until	2045	2145	2244	2344
Kiel Hbf a.	0617	0615	0715	0715	0815	0915		2115	2215	2317	0017

Other stopping trains Kiel - Lübeck and v.v. (journey 87 – 88 minutes): **From Kiel** Hbf at 0436 Ⓐ, 0444 Ⓒ, 0515 Ⓐ, 0604 Ⓐ, 0704 and hourly until 2004.
From Lübeck Hbf at 0017, 0356 Ⓐ, 0401 Ⓒ, 0528 Ⓐ, 0628 Ⓐ, 0728 and hourly until 2028.

827 LÜBECK - BÜCHEN - LÜNEBURG

RB services

km		Ⓐ																	D	E	
0	**Lübeck** Hbf d.	0505	0605	0707	0809	0909	1009	1109	1209	1309	1409	1509	1609	1709	1809	1909	2009	2109	2219	2219	2325
9	Lübeck Flughafen ✈ d.	0514	0614	0716	0819	0919	1019	1119	1219	1319	1419	1519	1619	1719	1819	1919	2019	2119	2229	2229	2335
22	Ratzeburg d.	0527	0627	0730	0830	0930	1030	1130	1230	1330	1430	1530	1630	1730	1830	1930	2030	2130	2243	2243	2345j
31	Mölln (Lauenburg) d.	0534	0634	0737	0837	0937	1037	1137	1237	1337	1437	1537	1637	1737	1837	1937	2037	2137	2250	2250	2352j
50	Büchen a.	0546	0646	0748	0848	0948	1048	1148	1248	1348	1448	1548	1648	1748	1848	1948	2048	2148	2302	2302	0003j
50	Büchen d.	0555	0655	0750	0858	0950	1107	1150	1307	1350	1507	1550	1707	1750	1907	1950	2107	2201	2303	2333	...
79	**Lüneburg** a.	0618	0718	0815	0921	1015	1130	1215	1330	1415	1530	1615	1730	1815	1930	2015	2130	2224	2326	2356	...

	Ⓐ	Ⓐ	⑥	Ⓐ																D	E
Lüneburg d.	0431	0526	0545	0628	0631c	0745	0831	0945	1031	1145	1231	1345	1431	1545	1631	1745	1831	1945	2031	2238	2245
Büchen a.	0453	0548	0607	0650	0653c	0808	0853	1008	1053	1208	1253	1408	1453	1608	1653	1808	1853	2008	2053	2300	2308
Büchen d.	0455	0555	0608	0657	0709	0809	0909	1009	1109	1209	1309	1409	1509	1609	1709	1809	1909	2009	2109	2309	2333
Mölln (Lauenburg) d.	0509	0609	0620	0709	0722	0822	0922	1022	1122	1222	1322	1422	1522	1622	1722	1822	1922	2022	2122	2322	2345
Ratzeburg d.	0517	0617	0632	0717	0732	0832	0932	1032	1132	1232	1332	1432	1532	1632	1732	1832	1932	2032	2132	2332	2352
Lübeck Flughafen ✈ d.	0525	0625	0641	0726	0741	0841	0941	1041	1141	1241	1341	1441	1541	1641	1741	1841	1941	2041	2141	2346	0001
Lübeck Hbf a.	0536	0636	0652	0736	0752	0852	0952	1052	1152	1252	1352	1452	1552	1652	1752	1852	1952	2052	2154	2357	0011

D – ①–④ (not Apr. 17, May 1, June 5).
E – ⑤–⑦ (also Apr. 17, May 1, June 5).

c – Ⓒ only.
j – On ⑤–⑦ (also Apr. 17, May 1, June 5) runs 7 – 10 minutes later Ratzeburg - Büchen.

828 LÜBECK - BAD KLEINEN

RE / RB services

km			Ⓐ S		S		S		S		S		S		P		N		G	A
0	**Lübeck** Hbf d.	0502	0602	0703	0802	0903	1002	1103	1202	1303	1402	1503	1602	1703	1802	1903	2002	2103	2206	2307
39	Grevesmühlen d.	0537	0637	0740	0837	0940	1037	1140	1237	1340	1437	1540	1637	1740	1837	1940	2037	2140	2242	2340
62	**Bad Kleinen** a.	0551	0653	0754	0853	0954	1053	1154	1253	1354	1453	1554	1654	1754	1854	1954	2053	2154	2300	2359

	Ⓐ A	Ⓐ T		N		S		S		S		S		S		S		S		
Bad Kleinen d.	0432	0518	0603	0702	0803	0902	1003	1102	1203	1302	1403	1502	1603	1702	1803	1902	2003	2102	...	2203
Grevesmühlen d.	0446	0539	0617	0721	0817	0921	1017	1121	1217	1321	1417	1521	1617	1721	1817	1921	2017	2121	...	2221
Lübeck Hbf a.	0525	0624	0656	0757	0856	0957	1056	1157	1256	1357	1456	1557	1656	1757	1856	1957	2056	2157	...	2301

A – From / to Schwerin (Table **830**).
G – To Güstrow (Table **836**).
N – To / from Neubrandenburg (Table **836**).
P – To Pasewalk (Table **836**).
S – To / from Szczecin (Table **836**).
T – From Szczecin (Table **836**) on ①.

830 HAMBURG - ROSTOCK - STRALSUND

Subject to alteration from May 28

km		*RE* 13001	*RE* 13003	*RE* 13190	*RE* 4301	*RE* 13005	*RE* 4331	*RB* 13944	*RE* 4305	*RE* 4305	*RE* 13007	*IC* 2184	*RE* 4307	*RE* 13009	*IC* 2182	*IC* 2238	*RE* 4309	*RE* 13011	*IC* 2212	*RE* 4311	*RE* 13013	*IC* 2376	*RE* 4313	*RE* 13015	*IC* 2216	*RE* 4315
			Ⓐ	Ⓐ			Ⓐ	Ⓐ	Ⓐ	Ⓒ																
		S	S	L		S					S	🍷♦		S	🍷♦	♦		S	🍷♦		S	🍷♦		S	🍷♦	
0	**Hamburg** Hbf d.	...	...	...	...	...	0450	...	0613	0618	...	0733	0819	...	0944	...	1017	...	1142c	1223	...	1344	1421	...	1517	1611
47	Büchen d.	...	...	...	0458a	...	0524	...	0658t	0658t	...	|	0858t	...	|	...	1058t	...	|	1258	...	|	1458t	...	|	1659p
123	**Schwerin** Hbf 836 837 d.	...	...	0413	0547	...	0622	0645	0747	0747	...	0837	0947	...	1037	1055	1147	...	1237c	1347	...	1437	1548	...	1614	1747
140	Bad Kleinen 836 837 d.	...	...	0425	0603	...	...	0703	0803	0803	...	|	1003	...	|	1111	1203	...	|	1403	...	|	1603	...	|	1803
181	Bützow 836 d.	...	...	...	0629	...	...	0730	0829	0829	...	0911	1029	...	1111	1136	1229	...	1311	1429	...	1511	1629	...	1648b	1829
211	**Rostock** Hbf a.	...	...	...	0650	...	...	0751	0850	0850	...	0932	1050	...	1132	1155	1253	...	1332	1450	...	1532	1650	...	1706	1850
211	**Rostock** Hbf d.	0456	0554	...	...	0700	...	...	...	...	0901	0938	...	1101	1138	...	...	1301	1338	...	1501	1538	...	1701	1717	...
240	Ribnitz-D'garten West d.	0517	0618	...	...	0723	...	...	...	...	0922	1000	...	1122	1200	...	...	1322	1400	...	1522	1600	...	1722	1739	...
265	Velgast d.	0539	0639	...	...	0741	...	...	...	...	0940	1016	...	1140	1216	...	...	1340	1416	...	1540	1616	...	1740	1754	...
283	**Stralsund** Hbf a.	0554	0655	...	...	0756	...	...	...	...	0955	1028	...	1157	1228	...	...	1355	1431	...	1555	1630	...	1755	1811	...
	Ostseebad Binz 844 a.	...	...	...	...	...	...	...	...	...	...	1132v	...	...	...	...	...	...	1529	...	...	1720k	...	...	...	...

	RE 13017	*IC* 2372	*RE* 4317	*RE* 4317	*RE* 13019	*IC* 2188	*IC* 2270	*IC* 2404	*RE* 4319	*RE* 4329	*RE* 4321
			Ⓐ	Ⓒ		①–④	⑦w	⑤f		①–④	⑤–⑦
	S	🍷♦			S	m🍷	A🍷			h	j
Hamburg Hbf d.	...	1742	1813	1823	...	1944	1944	1944	2021	2215	2257
Büchen d.	...	|	1858p	1858	...	|	|	|	2058t	2247	2329
Schwerin Hbf 836 837 d.	...	1837	1947	1947	...	2037	2037	2037	2147	2335	0017
Bad Kleinen 836 837 d.	...	1850	2003	2003	...	|	|	|	2203	2347	0030
Bützow 836 d.	...	1913	2029	2029	...	2111	2111	2111	2229	0013	0055
Rostock Hbf a.	...	1933	2050	2050	...	2132	2132	2130	2250	0033	0115
Rostock Hbf d.	1901	1938	...	...	2101	...	2138	2138	...	...	...
Ribnitz-Damgarten West d.	1922	2000	...	...	2122	...	2200	2200	...	...	...
Velgast d.	1940	2016	...	...	2140	...	2216	2216	...	...	...
Stralsund Hbf a.	1955	2028	...	...	2155	...	2228	2228	...	...	...
Ostseebad Binz 844 a.	...	...	...	...	...	...	...	...	...	...	...

	RE 4300	*RE* 4338	*RE* 4330	*IC* 2189	*IC* 2189	*RE* 4302	*RE* 13000	*IC* 2279	*RE* 13002	*RE* 4304
	Ⓐ	Ⓒ	Ⓐ	B	①–⑤		Ⓐ	①–⑥		
				🍷	d🍷		S	eA 🍷	S	
Ostseebad Binz 844 d.	...	...	...	...	...	...	...	...	...	...
Stralsund Hbf d.	...	...	...	0405	...	...	0454	0524	0557	...
Velgast d.	...	...	...	0419	...	...	0508	0539	0614	...
Ribnitz-Damgarten West d.	...	...	...	0433	...	...	0526	0553	0632	...
Rostock Hbf a.	...	...	...	0452	...	...	0548	0615	0654	...
Rostock Hbf d.	...	...	...	0458	0458	0507	...	0625	...	0707
Bützow 836 d.	...	...	...	0519	0519	0529	...	0646	...	0729
Bad Kleinen 836 837 d.	...	...	...	0545	0545	0559	...	|	...	0759
Schwerin Hbf 836 837 d.	0350	0444	0455	0558	0558	0613	...	0722	...	0813
Büchen d.	0446	0540	0553	0634	0634	0707	...	|	...	0907
Hamburg Hbf a.	0516	0611	0625	0703	0703	0738	...	0816	...	0936

	IC 2217	*RE* 13004	*RE* 4306	*IC* 2373	*RE* 13006	*RE* 4308	*IC* 2213	*RE* 13008	*RE* 4310	*IC* 2239	*IC* 2377	*RE* 13010	*RE* 4312	*IC* 2379	*RE* 13012	*RE* 4314	*RE* 13030	*RB* 13963	*IC* 1989	*RE* 13014	*RE* 4316	*RE* 13016	*RE* 4318	*RE* 13018	*RE* 4320	*RE* 13099
																	①–④	E	⑦w							
	🍷♦	S		A🍷	S		🍷♦	S		♦	🍷♦	S		🍷♦	S		g		🍷			S		S		L‡
Ostseebad Binz 844 d.	...	...	...	...	...	...	1026	...	...	...	1227z	...	...	...	...	...	1604	...	...	1704	...	...	...	...	...	...
Stralsund Hbf d.	0727	0801	...	0927	1001	...	1127	1201	...	...	1327	1401	...	1527	1601	...	1700	...	1727	1801	...	2001	...	2201	...	...
Velgast d.	0741	0815	...	0941	1015	...	1141	1215	...	...	1341	1415	...	1541	1615	...	1712	...	1741	1815	...	2015	...	2215	...	...
Ribnitz-Damgarten West d.	0755	0833	...	0955	1033	...	1155	1233	...	...	1355	1433	...	1555	1633	...	1738	...	1801	1833	...	2033	...	2233	...	...
Rostock Hbf a.	0815	0855	...	1019	1055	...	1219	1255	...	...	1419	1455	...	1619	1655	...	1758	...	1820	1855	...	2055	...	2255	...	...
Rostock Hbf d.	0825	...	0907	1025	...	1107	1244	...	1307	1405	1425	...	1507	1625	...	1707	...	1808	1825	...	1907	...	2107	...	2307	...
Bützow 836 d.	0846	...	0929	1046	...	1129	1304	...	1329	1425	1446	...	1529	1646	...	1729	...	1830	1846	...	1929	...	2129	...	2329	...
Bad Kleinen 836 837 d.	|	...	0959	|	...	1159	|	...	1359	1449	|	...	1559	|	...	1759	...	1904t	|	...	1959	...	2159	...	2355	0000
Schwerin Hbf 836 837 d.	0922	...	1013	1122	...	1213	1338	...	1413	1501	1522	...	1613	1722	...	1813	...	1916	1922	...	2013	...	2211	...	0007	0011
Büchen d.	|	...	1107	|	...	1307	|	...	1512p	...	|	...	1712p	|	...	1912p	...	...	|	...	2107	...	...	...	...	...
Hamburg Hbf a.	1015	...	1141	1215	...	1336	1432	...	1549	...	1616	...	1749	1816	...	1949	...	...	2016	...	2141	...	...	...	...	...

♦ – **NOTES** (LISTED BY TRAIN NUMBER)

2182 – ①–⑥ to Apr. 29 (also Apr. 9, 23; not Apr. 15); daily from May 1. [12] and 🍷 (Kassel Ⓐ -) (Hannover ①–⑥ **e** -) Hamburg - Stralsund.
2184 – Ⓐ to Mar. 31; ①–⑥ from Apr. 3 (not Apr. 17, May 1, June 5). [12] and 🍷 (Hannover Ⓐ -) Hamburg - Stralsund (- Ostseebad Binz on dates in note **v**). Departs Hamburg 0743 on ⑥ (also Apr. 14, May 25).
2212 – RÜGEN – [12] and 🍷 Koblenz - Köln - Hamburg - Ostseebad Binz.
2213 – RÜGEN – [12] and 🍷 Ostseebad Binz - Hamburg - Köln - Koblenz - Stuttgart.
2216 – [12] and 🍷 Stuttgart - Koblenz - Köln - Hamburg - Stralsund (- Greifswald Ⓐ **n**).
2217 – [12] and 🍷 (Greifswald Ⓐ **n** -) Stralsund - Hamburg - Köln - Koblenz - Stuttgart.
2238/9 – ⑤ to Mar. 31; ⑤–⑦ from Apr. 7 (also May 1, 24, 25). WARNOW – [12] Leipzig - Magdeburg - Rostock (- Warnemünde from Apr. 7 ●) and v.v.
2372 – [12] and 🍷 (Karlsruhe ⑤–⑦ **u** -) Frankfurt - Hannover - Hamburg - Stralsund.
2376 – [12] and 🍷 Karlsruhe - Frankfurt - Hamburg - Stralsund (- Ostseebad Binz ⑥ **k**).
2377 – [12] and 🍷 (Ostseebad Binz **z** -) Stralsund - Hamburg - Hannover - Frankfurt (- Karlsruhe ⑤ **f**).
2379 – Ⓑ to Mar 31; daily from Apr. 2 (not Apr. 16, 29, June 4). [12] and 🍷 Stralsund - Hamburg (- Hannover Ⓑ **q**) (- Frankfurt ⑤⑦ **y**).

A – [12] and 🍷 Karlsruhe - Frankfurt - Hannover - Hamburg - Stralsund and v.v.
B – Runs on Apr. 10, 18, 24, May 2, 8, 15, 22, 29, June 6 only.
E – ①②③④⑥ (not Apr. 15, 17, May 1, 25, June 5).
L – To / from Lübeck (Table **828**).
S – To / from Sassnitz (Table **844**).

a – Ⓐ only.
b – Ⓑ (also Apr. 15, May 27; not Apr. 14, May 25).
c – On ⑥ Hamburg d. 1117, Schwerin a. 1210, d. 1237.
d – Not Apr. 17, May 1, 25, 26, June 5.
e – Not Apr. 15, 17, May 1, June 5.
f – Also Apr. 13, May 24; not Apr. 14, May 26.
g – Not Apr. 13, 17, May 1, 25, June 5.
h – Not Apr. 17, May 1, June 5.
j – Also Apr. 17, May 1, June 5.
k – ⑥ (also Apr. 14, May 25).
m – Not Apr. 13, 17, May 1, 24, 25, June 5
n – Not May 26.
p – Arrives 10 – 13 minutes earlier.
q – Not Apr. 14, 16, 30, June 4.
t – Arrives 6 – 7 minutes earlier.
u – Also Apr. 13, 17, May 1, 24, 25, June 5
v – ①–⑥ from May 2 (also Apr. 8, 14, 15 22, 29; not June 5).
w – Also Apr. 17, May 1, June 5; not Apr. 16, 30, June 4.
y – Also Apr. 13, 17, May 1, 24, June 5 not Apr. 14, 16, 30, June 4.
z – ⑦ to Apr. 23 (also Apr. 8, 14, 15, 17, 22); daily from Apr. 29.
‡ – Runs 9 minutes later on the mornings of ①⑥⑦.
● – **2238** arrives Warnemünde 1213. **2239** departs Warnemünde 1343.

ROSTOCK - WARNEMÜNDE 831

S-Bahn

ROSTOCK - WARNEMÜNDE and v.v. *13 km*. Journey time: 21 minutes. Additional services run at peak times on Ⓐ.

From Rostock Hbf at 0433, 0448 Ⓐ, 0503, 0518 Ⓐ, 0533, 0548 Ⓐ, 0603, 0618 Ⓐ, 0633, 0648 Ⓐ, 0703, 0718 Ⓐ, 0733, 0748 Ⓐ, 0803, 0818, 0833, 0848, 0903, 0918, 0933, 0948 and at 03, 18, 33 and 48 minutes past each hour until 2003, 2018, 2033, 2048; then 2103, 2133, 2203, 2233, 2303, 2333 and 0003.

From Warnemünde at 0403, 0430, 0448 Ⓐ, 0503, 0518 Ⓐ, 0533, 0548 Ⓐ, 0603, 0618 Ⓐ, 0633, 0648 Ⓐ, 0703, 0718 Ⓐ, 0733, 0748 Ⓐ, 0803, 0818 Ⓐ, 0833, 0848, 0903, 0918, 0933, 0948 and at 03, 18, 33 and 48 minutes past each hour until 2003, 2018, 2033, 2048; then 2103, 2133, 2203, 2233, 2303, 2333 and 0003.

BERLIN - KOSTRZYN 832

Niederbarnimer Eisenbahn (2nd class only)

km																								
			Ⓒ	Ⓐ								Ⓒ	Ⓐ				Ⓐ	Ⓒ						
0	**Berlin** Lichtenberg d.	0537	0637	0637	0737	0837	0937	1037	1137	1237	1337	1437	1437	1537	1637	1737	1837	1837	1937	2037	2137	...	2337	...
23	Strausberg d.	0555	0655	0655	0755	0855	0955	1055	1155	1255	1355	1455	1455	1555	1655	1755	1855	1855	1955	2055	2155	...	2355	...
47	Müncheberg (Mark) ¶ d.	0613	0713	0722	0813	0913	1013	1113	1213	1313	1413	1513	1517	1613	1717	1813	1913	1917	2013	2113	2213	...	0013	...
80	**Kostrzyn** 🏛 a.	0654	0744	0753	0854	0944	1054	1144	1254	1344	1454	1544	1548	1654	1748	1854	1944	1948	2054	2144	2254	...	0054	...

				Ⓐ	Ⓐ	Ⓒ								Ⓐ	Ⓒ				Ⓒ	Ⓐ				
Kostrzyn 🏛 d.	0411	0508	0602	0617	0702	0711	0802	0911	1002	1111	1202	1311	1402	1505	1511	1602	1705	1802	1905	1911	2002	...	2202	...
Müncheberg (Mark) ¶ d.	0453	0549	0649	0700	0749	0749	0849	0949	1049	1149	1249	1349	1449	1549	1549	1649	1749	1849	1949	1949	2049	...	2249	...
Strausberg d.	0510	0610	0710	0716	0810	0810	0910	1010	1110	1210	1310	1410	1510	1610	1610	1710	1810	1910	2010	2010	2110	...	2310	...
Berlin Lichtenberg a.	0528	0628	0728	0738	0828	0828	0928	1028	1128	1228	1328	1428	1528	1628	1628	1728	1828	1928	2028	2028	2128	...	2328	...

¶ – Station for the Buckower Kleinbahn (operates Ⓒ May - September).

WISMAR - ROSTOCK 833

RE services

km		⚒	Ⓐ				
0	**Wismar** d.	0442	0542	0642	and	2042	2142
22	Neubukow d.	0511	0611	0711	hourly	2111	2211
41	Bad Doberan ▲ d.	0530	0630	0730	until	2130	2230
57	**Rostock** Hbf a.	0551	0651	0751		2151	2251

	Ⓐ		⚒				
Rostock Hbf d.	0412	0506	0606	0706	and	2006	2106
Bad Doberan ▲ d.	0432	0532	0632	0732	hourly	2032	2132
Neubukow d.	0451	0551	0651	0751	until	2051	2151
Wismar a.	0515	0615	0715	0815		2115	2215

▲ – **BAD DOBERAN - OSTSEEBAD KÜHLUNGSBORN WEST**. All services worked by steam locomotive. 2nd class only. Journey time: 43 minutes.
Operator: Mecklenburgische Bäderbahn Molli GmbH, Am Bahnhof, 18209 Bad Doberan. ✆ +49 (0) 38293 431331, Fax +49 (0) 38293 431332. **Service until Apr. 12.**
From **Bad Doberan** at 0835 Ⓐ, 1035, 1235, 1435 and 1640. From **Kühlungsborn West** at 0640 Ⓐ, 0935, 1135, 1342 and 1535.

STRALSUND - NEUBRANDENBURG - NEUSTRELITZ 834

km																									
		Ⓐ	Ⓐ			Ⓐ									Ⓑn			Ⓑn			Ⓑn				
0	**Stralsund** Hbf d.	...	0406	...	0502	0604	...	0702	0804r	0902	1004r	1102	1204r	1302	1404	...	1502	1604	...	1702	1804	...	1902	...	2106
23	Grimmen d.	...	0424	...	0523	0624	...	0723	0824r	0923	1024r	1123	1224r	1323	1424	...	1523	1624	...	1723	1824	...	1923	...	2128
47	Demmin d.	...	0445	...	0546	0646	...	0746	0846r	0946	1046r	1146	1246r	1346	1446	...	1546	1646	...	1746	1846	...	1946	...	2146
89	**Neubrandenburg** a.	...	0529	...	0629	0729	...	0829	0929r	1029	1129r	1229	1329r	1429	1529	...	1629	1729	...	1829	1929	...	2029	...	2229
89	**Neubrandenburg** d.	0429	0530	0530	0630	0730	0730	0830	0930	1030	1130	1230	1330	1430	1530	1530	1630	1730	1730	1830	1930	1930	2030	2130	2230
124	**Neustrelitz** Hbf a.	0458	0557	0557	0659	0756	0756	0859	0956	1059	1156	1259	1356	1459	1556	1556	1659	1756	1756	1859	1956	1956	2059	2156	2259
	Berlin Hbf **835** a.	0614	...	...	0816	...	...	1014	...	1216	...	1414	...	1616	...	...	1814	...	...	2014	...	...	2216	...	0014v

	Ⓐ	Ⓐ		Ⓐ									Ⓑn			Ⓑn			Ⓑn						
Berlin Hbf **835** d.	...	...	...	...	...	0541	...	0741	...	0941	...	1141	...	...	1341	...	...	1541	...	...	1741	...	1941	...	2141
Neustrelitz Hbf d.	...	0501	...	0603	0603	0701	0803	0901	1003	1101	1203	1301	1403	1403	1501	1603	1603	1701	1803	1803	1901	2003	2101	2203	2301
Neubrandenburg a.	...	0529	...	0630	0630	0729	0828	0929	1028	1129	1228	1329	1428	1428	1529	1628	1628	1729	1828	1828	1929	2028	2129	2228	2329
Neubrandenburg d.	0431	0531	0531	0631	...	0731	0831r	0931	1031r	1131	1231r	1331	1431	...	1531	1631	...	1731	1831	...	1931	...	2131	...	...
Demmin d.	0510	0610	0610	0710	...	0810	0910r	1010	1110r	1210	1310r	1410	1510	...	1610	1710	...	1810	1910	...	2010	...	2210	...	...
Grimmen d.	0529	0629	0629	0729	...	0829	0929r	1029	1129r	1229	1329r	1429	1529	...	1629	1729	...	1829	1929	...	2029	...	2229	...	...
Stralsund Hbf a.	0551	0651	0651	0751	...	0851	0951r	1051	1151r	1251	1351r	1451	1551	...	1651	1751	...	1851	1951	...	2051	...	2251	...	...

n – Not Apr. 14. r – ①–⑥ (not Apr. 17, May 1, June 5). v – Neustrelitz - Berlin on ⑤⑥ (also Apr. 13, 16, 30, May 24; not May 27, June 3, 10).

ROSTOCK - BERLIN - ELSTERWERDA 835

km	SEE NOTE ⊠	*RE* 3503	*RE* 4353	*RE* 3505	*RE* 4355	*IC* 2355	*RE* 3507	*RE* 4357	*RE* 3509	*RE* 4359	*IC* 2301	*RE* 3511	*RE* 4361	*RE* 3513	*RE* 4363	*RE* 3515	*RE* 4365	*RE* 3517	*RE* 18497	*RE* 4367	*RE* 18491	*RE* 3519	*RE* 4369	*RE* 3521	*RE* 3525
						①–⑤ a M 🍷					⑥⑦j M 🍷								† D		⑥ D			⑤⑥ v	
	Warnemünde 831 d.	...	...	...	...	...	...	...	...	...	1059	...	...	...	...	...	...	...	1736	...	1844	...	...	...	...
0	**Rostock** Hbf 831 d.	...	0434e	...	0634	0722	...	0834	...	1034	1121	...	1234	...	1434	...	1634	...	1759	1834	1910	...	2034	...	2334
34	Güstrow d.	...	0456e	...	0656	|	...	0856	...	1056	|	...	1256	...	1456	...	1656	...	|	1856	|	...	2056	...	2356
85	Waren (Müritz) d.	...	0535e	...	0735	0800	...	0935	...	1135	1159	...	1335	...	1535	...	1735	...	1844	1935	1954	...	2135	...	0028
	Stralsund Hbf **834** d.	...	|	0502	|	|	0702	|	0902	|	|	1102	|	1302	|	1502	|	1702	|	|	|	1902	|	2106	|
	Neubrandenburg **834** d.	0429e	|	0630	|	|	0830	|	1030	|	|	1230	|	1430	|	1630	|	1830	|	|	|	2030	|	2230	|
120	**Neustrelitz** Hbf a.	0458e	0556e	0659	0756	0817	0859	0956	1059	1156	1216	1259	1356	1459	1558	1659	1756	1859	1905	1958	2015	2059	2156	2259	0049
120	**Neustrelitz** Hbf d.	0500	0600	0700	0800	0829	0900	1000	1100	1200	1218	1300	1400	1500	1600	1700	1800	1900	1907	2000	2017	2100	2200	2300	...
141	Fürstenberg (Havel) d.	0511	0612	0711	0811	|	0911	1011	1111	1211	|	1311	1411	1511	1611	1711	1811	1911	1920	2011	2031	2111	2211	2311	...
162	Gransee d.	0525	0625	0723	0825	|	0923	1025	1123	1225	|	1323	1425	1523	1625	1723	1825	1923	|	2024	|	2123	2225	2323	...
191	Oranienburg d.	0545	0644	0744	0844	|	0944	1044	1144	1244	|	1344	1444	1544	1644	1744	1844	1944	1952	2044	2104	2144	2244	2344	...
223	**Berlin** Gesundbrunnen d.	0610	0712	0812	0912	0920	1010	1112	1212	1312	1319	1410	1513	1612	1709	1810	1912	2010	2018	2110	2135	2212	2309	0010	...
227	**Berlin** Hbf a.	0614	0717	0816	0916	0925	1014	1116	1216	1316	1324	1414	1517	1616	1715	1814	1916	2014	2022	2115	2140	2216	2313	0014	...
227	**Berlin** Hbf ▶ d.	0618	0719	0818	0918	0930	1018	1118	1218	1318	1330	1418	1519	1618	1718	1818	1918	2018	...	2117	...	2218	2318f	...	...
233	**Berlin** Südkreuz ▶ d.	0627	0725	0827	0925	0935	1027	1125	1227	1325	1335	1427	1525	1627	1725	1827	1925	2025	...	2124	...	2225	2325f	...	...
347	Doberlug-Kirchhain d.	*0851**	...	*1051**	...	...	*1251**	...	*1451**	...	...	*1651**	...	*1851**	...	*2051**	...	*2251**	...	*0008**	...	...	...	...	...
367	**Elsterwerda** ▶ a.	*0931**	...	*1131**	...	...	*1331**	...	*1531**	...	...	*1731**	...	*1931**	...	*2131**	...	*2331**	...	*0048**	...	...	...	...	...

km		*RE* 4350	*RE* 3504	*RE* 4352	*RE* 3506	*RE* 18490	*RE* 4354	*RE* 3508	*RE* 4356	*RE* 3510	*RE* 4358	*RE* 3512	*IC* 2300	*RE* 4360	*RE* 3514	*RE* 4362	*RE* 3516	*IC* 2356	*RE* 4364	*RE* 3518	*RE* 4366	*RE* 3520	*RE* 4368	*RE* 3522	*RE* 3526
		Ⓐ				Ⓒ D				◇			⑥h M 🍷					Ⓑq M 🍷					❦		⑤⑥ v
	Elsterwerda ▶ d.	...	...	...	*0421**	...	...	*0621**	...	*0821**	...	*1021**	...	...	*1221**	...	*1421**	...	...	*1621**	...	*1821**	...	*2021**	*2021**
	Doberlug-Kirchhain d.	...	...	...	*0503**	...	...	*0703**	...	*0903**	...	*1103**	...	...	*1303**	...	*1503**	...	...	*1703**	...	*1903**	...	*2103**	*2103**
	Berlin Südkreuz ▶ d.	...	0533e	0633	0733	...	0833	0933	1033	1133	1233	1333	1424	1433	1533	1633	1733	1824	1833	1933	2033	2133	2233	2333	2333
	Berlin Hbf ▶ a.	...	0539e	0639	0739	...	0839	0939	1039	1139	1239	1339	1430	1439	1539	1639	1739	1830	1839	1939	2039	2139	2239	2342	2342
	Berlin Hbf d.	0442	0541	0641	0741	0807	0841	0941	1041	1141	1241	1341	1435	1441	1541	1641	1741	1835	1841	1941	2041	2141	2241	...	2344
	Berlin Gesundbrunnen d.	0447	0547	0647	0747	0817	0847	0947	1047	1147	1247	1347	1441	1447	1547	1647	1747	1841	1847	1947	2047	2147	2247	...	2350
	Oranienburg d.	0510	0609	0709	0809	0840	0909	1009	1109	1209	1309	1409	|	1510	1609	1709	1809	|	1910	2009	2109	2209	2309	...	0012
	Gransee d.	0530	0632	0730	0832	|	0930	1032	1130	1232	1330	1432	|	1530	1632	1730	1832	|	1930	2032	2130	2232	2330	...	0034
	Fürstenberg (Havel) d.	0546	0645	0745	0845	0913	0945	1045	1145	1245	1345	1445	|	1545	1645	1745	1845	|	1945	2045	2145	2245	2345	...	0050
	Neustrelitz Hbf a.	0558	0658	0758	0858	0927	0958	1058	1158	1258	1358	1458	1539	1558	1658	1758	1858	1939	1958	2058	2158	2258	2358	...	0103
	Neustrelitz Hbf d.	0605	0701	0805	0901	0929	1005	1101	1205	1301	1405	1501	1541	1605	1701	1805	1901	1941	2005	2101	2205	2301	0005	...	...
	Neubrandenburg **834** a.	|	0729	|	0929	|	|	1129	|	1329	|	1529	|	|	1729	|	1929	|	|	2129	|	2329	|	...	...
	Stralsund Hbf **834** a.	|	0851	|	1051	|	|	1251	|	1451	|	1651	|	|	1851	|	2051	|	|	2251	|	...	|	...	...
0	Waren (Müritz) d.	0630	...	0830	...	0951	1030	...	1230	...	1430	...	1559	1630	...	1830	...	1959	2030	...	2230	...	0028	...	...
	Güstrow d.	0701	...	0901	...	|	1101	...	1301	...	1501	...	|	1701	...	1901	...	|	2101	...	2301	...	0058	...	...
78	**Rostock** Hbf 831 a.	0723	...	0923	...	1036	1123	...	1323	...	1523	...	1637	1723	...	1923	...	2037	2123	...	2323	...	0122	...	...
	Warnemünde 831 a.	...	...	...	...	1057	...	...	...	...	...	...	1706	...	...	...	...	...	...	...	...	...	...	...	...

A – ①②③④⑥ (not May 24).
B – ⑤⑦ (also May 24).
D – From Apr. 14.
M – To/from München (Table **851**).
a – Not Apr. 14, 17, May 1, June 5.
e – Ⓐ only.
f – From Feb. 9.
h – Also Apr. 14, 16.
j – Also Apr. 14, 17.
q – Not Apr. 14, 16, 30, June 4.
v – Also Apr. 13, 16, 30, May 24; not May 27, June 3, 10.
⊠ – Timings between Neustrelitz and Berlin may vary by 1 – 2 minutes until Feb. 8.
* – By 🚌 Wünstdorf-Waldstadt - Elsterwerda and v.v. Wünstdorf-Waldstadt is located 50 km (approximately 50 minutes) south of Berlin Südkreuz. Other rail connections are available via Falkenberg or Cottbus (see country map on page 368 for relevant table numbers).
▶ – A limited number of direct rail services run Berlin Hbf - Elsterwerda-**Biehla** (via Falkenberg; journey 2 hrs 5 mins southbound, 2 hrs 11 mins northbound): From Berlin Hbf 1331, 1531 **A**, 1534 **B** and 1731. From Elsterwerda-Biehla at 0616 Ⓐ, 1216 Ⓒ, 1616, 1816 and 2016.
◇ – Change trains at Berlin Hbf on Ⓐ to Feb. 8.
❦ – Subject to alteration on ⑥⑦ from May 27.

836 LÜBECK - PASEWALK - SZCZECIN

RE services

Timings at Bad Kleinen are subject to alteration from May 28

km		Ⓑ	Ⓐ			Ⓐ	Ⓒ														B	⑤			
0	**Lübeck** Hbf .... **828** d.	...	...	...	...	0602	...	...	0802	...	1002	...	1202	...	1402	...	1602	...	1802	...	...	...	2002	...	2206
62	Bad Kleinen .. **828 830** d.	...	...	...	...	0656	0703	...	0903	...	1103	...	1303	...	1503	...	1657b	...	1903	...	...	...	2103	...	2303
103	Bützow .... **830** d.	...	...	0534	0634	0734	0734	0834	0934	1034	1138	1234	1334	1434	1534	1634	1734	1834	1934	2034	2034	2034	2134	2234	2334
117	Güstrow .... a.	...	...	0543	0643	0743	0743	0843	0943	1043	1147	1243	1343	1443	1543	1643	1743	1843	1943	2043	2043	2043	2143	2243	2343
117	Güstrow .... d.	...	...	0605	0705	0805	0805	0905	1005	1105	1205	1305	1405	1505	1605	1705	1805	1905	2005	2105	2105	2105	2205	2305	...
146	Teterow .... d.	...	...	0632	0732	0832	0832	0932	1032	1132	1232	1332	1432	1532	1632	1732	1832	1932	2032	2132	2132	2132	2232	2328	...
160	Malchin .... d.	...	0529	0642	0742	0842	0842	0942	1042	1142	1242	1342	1442	1542	1642	1742	1842	1942	2042	2142	2142	2142	2242	2338	...
204	**Neubrandenburg** .... a.	...	0601	0714	0814	0914	0914	1014	1114	1214	1314	1414	1514	1614	1714	1814	1914	2014	2114	2214	2214	2214	2314	0011	...
204	**Neubrandenburg** .... d.	0513a	0606	0718	0818r	0918	0918	1018	1118	1218	1318	1418	1518	1618	1718	1818	1918	2018	2118	...	2218	2218	...	...	...
257	**Pasewalk** ⊙ .... a.	0559a	0652	0813	0910r	1010	1010	1110	1210	1310	1410	1510	1614	1710	1813	1910	2010	2110	2210	...	2306	2306	...	...	...
257	**Pasewalk** ⊙ .... d.	0615	...	0815	...	1015	1015	...	1215	...	1415	...	1615	...	1815	...	2015	...	...	...	...	2315	...	...	...
284	Grambow .... d.	0637	...	0837	...	1037	1037	...	1237	...	1437	...	1637	...	1837	...	2037	...	...	...	...	2337	...	...	...
294	Szczecin Gumience 🚌 d.	0648	...	0848	...	1048	1048	...	1248	...	1448	...	1648	...	1848	...	2048	...	...	...	...	2348	...	...	...
299	**Szczecin** Glowny .... a.	0654	...	0854	...	1054	1054	...	1254	...	1454	...	1654	...	1854	...	2054	...	...	...	...	2354	...	...	...

	①m				Ⓐ		Ⓐ												A		⑦w				
Szczecin Glowny .... d.	0226	...	...	...	0500	...	...	...	0700	...	0900	...	1100	...	1300	...	1500	...	1700	...	1730	...	1900	...	2100
Szczecin Gumience 🚌 d.	0232	...	...	...	0506	...	...	...	0706	...	0906	...	1106	...	1306	...	1506	...	1706	...	1736	...	1906	...	2106
Grambow .... d.	|	...	...	...	0517	...	...	...	0717	...	0917	...	1117	...	1317	...	1517	...	1717	...	1747	...	1917	...	2117
Pasewalk ⊙ .... a.	0300	...	...	...	0539	...	...	...	0739	...	0939	...	1139	...	1339	...	1539	...	1739	...	1809	...	1939	...	2139
Pasewalk ⊙ .... d.	0301	...	...	...	0541	0541	0652	...	0752	0852r	0952	1052	1152	1252	1352	1452	1552	1652	1752	1752	1852	1852	1952	2052	2152
Neubrandenburg .... a.	0338	...	...	...	0622	0622	0735	...	0835	0935r	1035	1135	1235	1335	1435	1535	1635	1735	1835	1835	1935	1935	2035	2135	2236
Neubrandenburg .... d.	0340	...	0447	0544	0624	0624	0744	0744	0844	0944	1044	1144	1244	1344	1444	1544	1644	1744	1844	1844	1944	1944	2044	2144	...
Malchin .... d.	0410	...	0531j	0620	0708	0708	0820	0820	0920	1020	1120	1220	1320	1420	1520	1620	1720	1820	1920	1920	2020	2020	2120	2220	...
Teterow .... d.	0421	...	0541	0630	0730j	0730j	0830	0830	0930	1030	1130	1230	1330	1430	1530	1630	1730	1830	1930	1930	2030	2030	2130	2230	...
Güstrow .... a.	0439	...	0603	0653	0753	0753	0853	0853	0953	1053	1153	1253	1353	1453	1553	1653	1753	1853	1953	1953	2053	2053	2153	2253	...
Güstrow .... d.	0440	0502	0608	0708	0808	0808	0908	0908	1008	1108	1208	1308	1408	1508	1608	1708	1808	1908	2008	2008	2108	2108	2208	2308	...
Bützow .... **830** a.	0450	0512	0618	0718	0818	0818	0918	0918	1018	1118	1218	1318	1418	1518	1618	1718	1818	1918	2018	2018	2118	2118	2218	2318	...
Bad Kleinen ... **828 830** a.	0517	...	0646	...	0846	0846	...	...	1046	...	1246	...	1454	...	1646	...	1846	...	2046	2046	...	...	2246	...	...
Lübeck Hbf .... **828** a.	0624	...	0757	...	0957	0957	...	...	1157	...	1357	...	1557	...	1757	...	1957	...	2157	2157	...	...	...	...	...

A – ①–⑥ (also Apr. 16, 30, June 4; not Apr. 17, May 1, June 5).
B – ⑤–⑦ (also Apr. 13, 17, May 1, 24, June 5).

a – Ⓐ only.
b – 1703 on Ⓒ.
h – 1427 on ⑤ (also Apr. 13, May 24; not Apr. 14).

j – Arrives 12 – 13 minutes earlier.
m – Also Apr. 18, May 2, June 6; not Apr. 17, May 1, June 5.
r – ⚒ only.
w – Also Apr. 17, May 1, June 5; not Apr. 16, 30, June 4.

⊙ – **PASEWALK - UECKERMÜNDE** (30 km, journey 31 – 35 minutes).
From Pasewalk at 0518 Ⓐ, 0610 ⚒, 0701 Ⓐ, 0822, 1022, 1222, 1422h, 1515 Ⓐ, 1619 (change trains at Jatznick), 1822 and 2022.
From Ueckermünde Stadthafen at 0601 Ⓐ, 0701 ⚒, 0738 Ⓐ, 0901, 1101, 1301, 1501 Ⓒ, 1517 Ⓐ, 1601 Ⓐ, 1701, 1901 and 2101.

837 WISMAR - BERLIN - COTTBUS

Ostdeutsche Eisenbahn (IC trains operated by DB)

Services on the Wismar - Wittenberge - Berlin - Cottbus route are subject to alteration Feb. 14 - Mar. 18. Timings Wismar - Schwerin and v.v. are subject to alteration from May 28.

km			⚒		Ⓐ		⚒										2239 L		2431 ⒷE							
0	**Wismar** .... ‡ d.	...	...	...	0424	...	0522	...	...	0734	...	0924	...	1124	...	1323	*1424*	...	...	1523	...	1724	...	1924	...	2124
16	Bad Kleinen .. **830/6** ‡ d.	...	...	...	0439	...	0537	...	...	0748	...	0939	...	1142	...	1339	1449	...	...	1539	...	1739	...	1939	...	2139
32	**Schwerin Hbf 830/6** ‡ a.	...	...	...	0451	...	0549	...	...	0800	...	0951	...	1154	...	1351	1501	...	...	1551	...	1751	...	1951	...	2151
32	**Schwerin** Hbf .... ‡ d.	...	...	...	0500	0500	0601	...	...	0802	...	1000	...	1200	...	1400	1503	...	...	1600	...	1800	...	2000	...	2200
72	Ludwigslust .... **840** ‡ d.	...	...	...	0534	0534	0635	...	...	0835	...	1034	...	1234	...	1434	1527	...	...	1634	...	1834	...	2034	...	2234
116	Wittenberge .... **840** d.	0406	0506	...	0606j	0606j	0704	0704	0806	0904	1006	1104	1206	1304	1406	1504	1545	1606	...	1704	1806	1904	2006	2104	...	2307j
207	Nauen .... d.	0501	0601	...	0704	0704	0804	0804	0904	1004	1104	1204	1304	1404	1504	1604	...	1704	...	1804	1904	2004	2104	2204	...	0003
229	**Berlin** Spandau .. **840** d.	0517	0617	...	0721	0721	0821	0821	0921	1021	1121	1221	1321	1421	1521	1621	...	1721	...	1821	1921	2021	2121	2221	...	0019
241	**Berlin** Zoo .... d.	0526	0626	0626	0730	0730	0830	0830	0930	1030	1130	1230	1330	1430	1530	1630	...	1730	...	1830	1930	2030	2130	2230	...	0035j
245	**Berlin** Hbf .... **840** d.	0531	0631	0631	0735	0735	0835	0835	0935	1035	1135	1235	1335	1435	1535	1635	...	1735	1826	1835	1935	2035	2135	2235	...	0043
250	**Berlin** Ostbahnhof .... d.	0542	0642	0642	0746	0746	0846	0846	0946	1046	1146	1246	1346	1446	1546	1646	...	1746	1839	1846	1946	2046	2146	2246	2346	0055
283	Königs Wusterhausen d.	0608	0708	0708	0811	0811	0911	0911	1011	1111	1211	1311	1411	1511	1611	1711	...	1811	1904	1911	2011	2111	2211	2311	0012	0120
329	Lübben (Spreewald) ... d.	0631	0731	0731	0834	0834	0934	0934	1034	1134	1234	1334	1434	1534	1634	1734	...	1834	1927	1934	2034	2134	2234	2346	0047	0155
340	Lübbenau (Spreew) .... d.	0638	0737	0737	0841	0841	0941	0941	1041	1141	1241	1341	1441	1541	1641	1741	...	1841	1935	1941	2041	2141	2241	2353	0054	0202
370	**Cottbus** .... a.	0701	0759	0759	0859	0859	0959	0959	1059	1159	1259	1359	1459	1559	1659	1759	...	1859	1951	1959	2059	2159	2304	0015	0117	0224

			⚒		S	⑦w	2432 G		2238 L																V	T
Cottbus .... d.	...	0357	0357	0456	0533	0557	0604	0701	...	0801	0901	1001	1101	1201	1301	1401	1501	1601	1701	1801	1901	2001	2101	2201	2301	2301
Lübbenau (Spreew) .... d.	...	0420	0420	0520	0556	0620	0621	0720	...	0820	0920	1020	1120	1220	1320	1420	1520	1620	1720	1820	1920	2020	2120	2224	2324	2324
Lübben (Spreewald) ... d.	...	0427	0427	0527	0602	0627	0629	0727	...	0827	0927	1027	1127	1227	1327	1427	1527	1627	1727	1827	1927	2027	2127	2231	2331	2331
Königs Wusterhausen . d.	...	0451	0451	0551	0627	0651	0652	0751	...	0851	0951	1051	1151	1251	1351	1451	1551	1651	1751	1851	1951	2051	2151	2255	0007	0007
Berlin Ostbahnhof ..... d.	0406	0514	0514	0614	0654	0714	0719	0814	...	0914	1014	1114	1214	1314	1414	1514	1614	1714	1814	1914	2014	2114	2214	2319	0033	0033
Berlin Hbf .... **840** d.	0421	0525	0526	0625	0705	0725	0727	0825	...	0925	1025	1125	1225	1325	1425	1525	1625	1725	1825	1925	2025	2125	2225	...	0044	0057
Berlin Zoo .... d.	0426	0531	0532	0631	0731e	0731	...	0831	...	0931	1031	1131	1231	1331	1431	1531	1631	1731	1831	1931	2031	2131	2231	...	0050	0103
Berlin Spandau ...... **840** d.	0435	...	0541	0640	0740	0740	...	0840	...	0940	1040	1140	1240	1340	1440	1540	1640	1740	1840	1940	2040	2140	2240	...	0058	0111
Nauen .... d.	0459	...	0559	0700	0803j	0803j	...	0900	...	1003j	1100	1203j	1300	1403j	1500	1603j	1700	1803j	1900	2003j	2100	2203j	2300	...	...	...
Wittenberge .... **840** d.	0603j	...	0701	0757	0901	0901	...	0957	1012	1101	1157	1301	1357	1501	1557	1701	1757	1901	1957	2101	2157	2301	2357	...	...	...
Ludwigslust .... **840** ‡ d.	0628	...	0726	...	0926	0926	...	...	1031	1126	...	1326	...	1526	...	1728	...	1926	...	2126	...	2326	...	...	...	...
Schwerin Hbf .... ‡ a.	0657	...	0757	...	0957	0957	...	...	1053	1157	...	1357	...	1557	...	1759	...	1957	...	2157	...	2357	...	...	...	...
Schwerin Hbf 830/6 ‡ d.	0658	...	0806	...	1006	1006	...	...	1055	1206	...	1406	...	1606	...	1806	...	2006	...	2206	...	...	...	...	...	...
Bad Kleinen ... **830/6** ‡ d.	0713	...	0819	...	1019	1019	...	...	1108	1219	...	1419	...	1619	...	1819	...	2019	...	2219	...	...	...	...	...	...
Wismar .... ‡ a.	0727	...	0837	...	1037	1037	...	...	*1138*	1237	...	1437	...	1637	...	1837	...	2037	...	2237	...	...	...	...	...	...

STENDAL - RATHENOW - BERLIN ⊡

km		Ⓐ	⚒		Ⓐ	†		⚒															N	P	
0	**Stendal** .... d.	...	0444k	...	0524	0542	...	0631	...	...	*0831*	...	*1031*	...	*1231*	...	*1431*	...	*1631*	...	*1831*	...	*2031*	...	...	*2231*
34	Rathenow .... d.	0401	0503	0503	0549	0603	0603	0656	0704	0803	0908	1003	1108	1203	1308	1403	1508	1603	1708	1803	1909	2003	2108	2203	2209	2306
92	**Berlin** Spandau .... d.	0449	0551	0551	...	0651	0651	...	0751	0851	0951	1051	1151	1251	1351	1451	1551	1650	1751	1851	1951	2051	2151	2251	2252	2349
104	**Berlin** Hbf .... a.	0459	0601	0601	...	0701	0701	...	0801	0901	1001	1101	1201	1301	1401	1501	1601	1700	1801	1901	2001	2101	2201	2301	2302	2400
110	**Berlin** Südkreuz .... a.	0511	0610	0610	...	0713	0713	...	0813	0913	1013	1113	1213	1313	1413	1513	1610	1713	1813	1913	2013	2117	...	...	...	...

	Q	R		Ⓐ	Ⓐ	⚒		⚒		†																
Berlin Südkreuz .... d.	...	...	...	...	...	...	0549	...	0649	...	0752	0849	0949	1049	1149	1249	1349	1449	1549	1649	1750	1849	1949	2049	2149	...
Berlin Hbf .... d.	0044	0057	...	...	0458	...	0558	...	0658	...	0800	0858	0958	1058	1158	1258	1400	1458	1600	1658	1800	1858	1958	2058	2158	2308
Berlin Spandau .... d.	0059	0112	...	...	0510	...	0610	...	0710	...	0812	0910	1010	1111	1210	1310	1412	1510	1612	1710	1812	1910	2010	2110	2210	2320
Rathenow .... a.	0137	0149	...	0442	0552	0555	0657	0702	0756	0800	0859	0957	1051	1157	1253	1356	1458	1556	1657	1757	1857	1958	2057	2157	2250	0002
Stendal .... a.	...	...	...	0507	...	0620	...	0725	...	0825	*0925*	...	*1125*	...	*1325*	...	*1525*	...	*1725*	...	*1926*	...	*2125*	...	...	0022

E – Ⓑ (not Apr. 14, 16, 30, June 4). *IC* **2431**. (12) Emden - Bremen - Hannover - Magdeburg - Berlin - Cottbus.
G – ①–⑥ (not Apr. 15, 17, May 1, June 5. *IC* **2432**. (12) Cottbus - Berlin - Magdeburg - Hannover - Bremen - Norddeich Mole.
L – ⑤ to Mar. 31; ⑤–⑦ from Apr. 7 (also May 1, 24, 25). *IC* **2238/9**. WARNOW – (12) Leipzig - Magdeburg - Stendal - Rostock (- Warnemünde from Apr. 7) and v.v.
N – Until May 12.
P – From May 13.
Q – ①⑤⑥⑦ (also May 25).
R – ②–④ (not May 25).
S – ①–⑥ (not Apr. 15, 17, May 1, June 5).
T – ①–③ (not May 24). To Rathenow (see panel below main table).
V – ④–⑦ (also May 24). To Rathenow (see panel below main table).

e – Arrives 0709.
j – Arrives 8 – 10 minutes earlier.
k – 0437 from May 13.
t – Ⓐ only.
w – Also Apr. 15, 17, May 1, June 5.

⊡ – See Table **810** for fast *IC* / *ICE* trains Stendal - Berlin and v.v.
‡ – See panel below main table for other local trains Wismar - Ludwigslust and v.v.

Other local trains WISMAR - LUDWIGSLUST (operated by DB)

Wismar .... d.	0626	...	0824	1024	and every two hours until	2024	...	2224
Bad Kleinen ...... d.	0642	...	0840	1040		2040	...	2240
Schwerin Hbf .. a.	0654	...	0852	1052		2052	...	2252
Schwerin Hbf .. d.	0700	...	0900	1100		2100	...	...
Ludwigslust ..... a.	0734	...	0934	1134		2134	...	...

		Ⓑ						
Ludwigslust ..... d.	0459t	0649t	0826	1036	1226	and every two hours until	2026	2256
Schwerin Hbf .. a.	0531t	0721t	0858	1108	1258		2058	2328
Schwerin Hbf .. d.	0532	0732	0904	1109	1304		2104	...
Bad Kleinen ...... d.	0545	0758	0917	1122	1317		2117	...
Wismar .... a.	0600	0803	0937	1138	1337		2137	...

MAGDEBURG - BERLIN - FRANKFURT (ODER) - COTTBUS — 839

RE services

km																							
														P				B	W♣			△	△	
0	**Magdeburg** Hbf ... d.	...	...	0429a	...	0523	0605	...	0708	...	and at	1608	...	1659	1708	...	1808	...	1854	1908	2008	2108	2208	2323
79	**Brandenburg** Hbf ... d.	0423	0500	0525	0600	0625j	0700	0725j	0800	0825		1700	1725	1739	1800	1825	1900	1925	|	2000	2100	2158	2258	0019
114	Potsdam Hbf ... d.	0452	0525	0555	0625	0655	0725	0755	0825	0855	the same	1725	1755	1800	1825	1855	1925	1955	2011	2025	2125	2225	2325	0048
123	Berlin Wannsee ... d.	0459	0532	0602	0632	0702	0732	0802	0832	0902	minutes	1732	1802	1808	1832	1902	1932	2002	2021	2032	2132	2232	2332	0055
138	**Berlin** Zoo ... d.	0512	0545	0615	0645	0715	0745	0815	0845	0915		1745	1815	|	1845	1915	1945	2015	2033	2045	2145	2245	2345	0107
142	**Berlin** Hbf ... **1001** d.	0518	0551	0621	0651	0721	0751	0821	0851	0921	past each	1751	1821	1826	1851	1921	1951	2021	2038	2051	2151	2251	2351	...
147	**Berlin** Ostbahnhof ... **1001** d.	0531	0604	0634	0704	0734	0804	0834	0904	0934	hour until	1804	1834	1834	1904	1934	2004	2034	2049	2104	2204	2304	0004	...
194	Fürstenwalde (Spree) ... d.	0609	0642	0714	0742	0814	0842	0914	0942	1014		1842	1914	...	1942	2014	2042	2114	...	2144	2245	2346	0045	...
228	**Frankfurt (Oder)** ... **1001** a.	0626	0708	0731	0808	0831	0908	0931	1008	1031		1908	1931	...	2008	2031	2108	2131	...	2211	2312	0013	0112	...

	Y	©						B		©♣	N		D										B⊖	
Frankfurt (Oder) ... **1001** d.	0027	...	...	...	0350c	...	0450	0533	0558	...	...	0633	0658	0733	0758	and at	1833	1858	1933	1958	2033	2127	2230r	2327r
Fürstenwalde (Spree) ... d.	0052	...	...	...	0416c	...	0516	0550	0625	...	...	0650	0725	0750	0825		1850	1925	1950	2025	2050	2152	2255r	2352r
Berlin Ostbahnhof ... **1001** d.	0129		...	...	0459	0529	0559	0629	0659	0707	0719	0729	0759	0829	0859	the same	1929	1959	2029	2059	2129	2229	2333	0029
Berlin Hbf ... **1001** d.	0141	0241	...	...	0511	0541	0611	0641	0711	0720	0731	0741	0811	0841	0911		1941	2011	2041	2111	2141	2241	2345	0041
Berlin Zoo ... d.	0147	0247	...	...	0517	0547	0617	0647	0717	0727	|	0747	0817	0847	0917	minutes	1947	2017	2047	2116	2147	2247	2351	0047
Berlin Wannsee ... d.	0200	0300	...	...	0530	0600	0630	0700	0730	0738	0746	0800	0830	0900	0930	past each	2000	2030	2100	...	2200	2300	0004	0100
Potsdam Hbf ... d.	0209	0309	...	...	0539	0609	0639	0709	0739	0746	0755	0809	0839	0909	0939		2009	2039	2109	...	2209	2309	0013	0109
Brandenburg Hbf ... d.	0235	0335	0420	...	0600	0636	0700	0736	0800	|	0814	0836	0900	0936	1000	hour until	2036	2100	2138	...	2236	2338	0040	0137
Magdeburg Hbf ... a.	...	...	0517	...	0649	...	0749	...	0849	0902	0858	...	0949	...	1049		...	2149	2234	...	...	0027	...	0225z

FRANKFURT (ODER) - COTTBUS

km		Ⓐ		Ⓐ				B		
0	**Frankfurt (Oder)** ... d.	0411	0537	0604	0637	0737	and	2037	2133	2316
23	Eisenhüttenstadt ... d.	0431	0558	0619	0658	0758	hourly	2058	2153	2337
48	Guben ... d.	0452	0618	0636	0718	0818	until	2118	2213	2357
86	**Cottbus** ... a.	0530	0656	0700	0756	0856		2156	2249	0033

	⚒B		ⒶD						B	
Cottbus ... d.	0414	0506	0551	0606	0706	and	1906	2006	2110	2306
Guben ... d.	0450	0544	0615	0644	0744	hourly	1944	2043	2146	2343
Eisenhüttenstadt ... d.	0510	0604	0635	0704	0804	until	2004	2104	2206	0004
Frankfurt (Oder) ... a.	0531	0626	0655	0726	0826		2026	2124	2228	0024

B – [12] Brandenburg - Berlin - Frankfurt (Oder) - Cottbus and v.v.
D – [12] Cottbus - Frankfurt (Oder) - Berlin - Magdeburg.
N – *IC* **2432**. [12] (Cottbus ①–⑥ **e** -) Berlin - Hannover - Bremen - Emden.
P – *IC* **2431**. [12] Emden - Bremen - Hannover - Berlin (- Cottbus Ⓑ **q**).
W – ⑤–⑦ (also Apr. 13, 17, May 1, 24, 25, June 5).
Y – ⑥⑦ only. Runs daily Frankfurt (Oder) - Berlin Zoo until Jan. 8. Also runs Berlin Ostbahnhof - Brandenburg on Apr. 14, 17, May 1, 25, June 5.

a – Ⓐ only.
c – ⑥⑦ (daily to Jan. 8).
e – Not Apr. 15, 17, May 1, June 5.
j – 5 minutes later on Ⓐ.
q – Not Apr. 14, 16, 30, June 4.
r – ⑤⑥ (daily to Jan. 7).
z – Mornings of © only.

△ – Magdeburg - Berlin Ostbahnhof daily; Magdeburg - Frankfurt (Oder) on ⑤⑥ (daily to Jan. 7).
⊖ – Runs 12 – 13 minutes later Berlin Ostbahnhof - Brandenburg on ①–③.
♣ – *HARZ-BERLIN-EXPRESS.* [2] Berlin - Halberstadt - Thale (Table **862**) / Goslar (Table **860**) and v.v. Operated by Transdev Sachsen-Anhalt. **DB tickets not valid**.

HAMBURG - BERLIN - DRESDEN — 840

km		*EC* 171	*ICE* 701	*ICE* 1207	*EC* 173	*ICE* 703	*ICE* 1509	*EC* 379	*ICE* 1609	*ICE* 1511	*EC* 175	*ICE* 707	*ICE* 901	*EC* 177	*ICE* 709	*ICE* 1613	*ICE* 1515	*EC* 179	*ICE* 801	*ICE* 803	*IC* 1918	*ICE* 1517	*IC* 2071	*IC* 2079	*ICE* 1717
			Ⓐ	①–⑥											⑤⑦	R				⑤f	⑤T				¶
		P✕	✕	jKM	H✕	✕	M✕	L✕	M✕	M✕	P✕	✕	✕	P✕	v✕	M✕	M✕	P✕	K✕	✕	🍷	M✕	✕	✕	E✕
0	**Hamburg** Altona ... d.	...	0512	0621	0636	0721	0819	...	0921	1020	...	1121	1221	1239	1321	1321	1420	1437	1519	1553	...	1618	1639	...	1720
7	**Hamburg** Hbf ... **830** d.	...	0527	0636	0648	0738	0836t	0851	0938	1036	...	1138	1236	1251	1338	1338	1436	1451	1538	1605	...	1636	1651	...	1735
54	Büchen ... **830** d.	...	|	|	0715	|	|	0915	|	|	...	|	|	1315	|	|	|	1515	|	|	...	|	1715	...	|
122	Ludwigslust ... **837** d.	...	0613	|	0742	|	|	0942	|	|	...	|	|	1342	|	|	|	1542	|	|	...	|	1742	...	1819
167	Wittenberge ... **837** d.	...	0631	|	0802	|	|	1002	|	|	...	|	|	1402	|	|	|	1602	|	|	...	|	1802	...	|
280	**Berlin** Spandau ... **837** d.	...	0711	0810	0846	0912	1010	1046	1112	1210	...	1312	1410	1446	1512	1512	1610	1646	1712	1747	...	1810	1846	...	1913
293	**Berlin** Hbf ... **837** a.	...	0720	0819	0855	0921	1019	1055	1121	1219	...	1320	1419	1455	1520	1521	1619	1655	1720	1756	...	1819	1855	...	1922
293	**Berlin** Hbf ... **835** d.	0703	|	0828	0904	|	1027	1104	1130	1227	1303	|	|	1504	|	1530	1628	1704	|	|	1802	1827	|	1901	1927
299	**Berlin** Südkreuz ... **835** d.	0710	0728	0835	0910	0929	1034	1110	1137	1234	1310	1329	1428	1510	1529	1537	1635	1710	1729	1805	1809	1834	1903	1907	1934
	Leipzig Hbf **851** ... a.	|	...	0943	|	...	1143	|	1243	1343	|	...	...	|	...	1643	1743	|	...	...	|	1943	...	|	2044
433	Elsterwerda ... **843 835** d.	|	...	...	|	...	...	|	...	...	|	...	...	|	...	...	...	|	...	...	|	...	...	|	...
486	**Dresden** Neustadt ... a.	|	...	...	|	...	...	|	...	...	|	...	...	|	...	...	...	|	...	...	2019	...	...	|	...
490	**Dresden** Hbf ... **843** a.	0856	...	...	1056	...	...	1256	...	...	1456	...	...	1656	...	...	...	1856	...	...	2026	...	...	2056	...

	ICE 903	*IC* 2073	*IC* 2073	*IC* 2077	*ICE* 805	*ICE* 1701	*ICE* 905	*ICE* 1703	*ICE* 907	
	Ⓑq		⊡	②		Ⓑq		⑤f	⑦w	
	✕	D🍷	D🍷	🍷	✕	✕	✕	✕	✕	
Hamburg Altona ... d.	1819	...	...	...	1921	2020	2137	2237	2237	...
Hamburg Hbf ... **830** d.	1836	1851	1851	...	1938	2036	2151	2251	2251	...
Büchen ... **830** d.	|	1915	1915	...	|	|	2215	2315	2315	...
Ludwigslust ... **837** d.	|	1942	1942	...	|	|	2242	2342	2342	...
Wittenberge ... **837** d.	|	2002	2002	...	|	|	2303	0002	0002	...
Berlin Spandau ... **837** d.	2010	2046	2046	...	2112	2210	2345	0044	0044	...
Berlin Hbf ... **837** a.	2019	2055	2055	...	2121	2219	2354	0053	0053	...
Berlin Hbf ... **835** d.	2027	...	2102	2102	2130	2227	|	|	|	...
Berlin Südkreuz ... **835** d.	2034	...	2109	2109	2137	2234	0002	0101	0101	...
Leipzig Hbf **851** ... a.	2143z	...	|	|	2248z	2346v	...	...	...	...
Elsterwerda ... **843 835** d.	...	...	|	|	...	...	...	...	...	...
Dresden Neustadt ... a.	...	...	2255	2255	...	...	...	...	...	...
Dresden Hbf ... **843** a.	...	...	2302	2302	...	...	...	...	...	...

	IC 1978	*ICE* 1708	*IC* 1974	*ICE* 1618	*IC* 2070	*ICE* 908	*IC* 2078	*ICE* 806	*IC* 2076	*IC* 2072
	①g	Ⓐ◧	⑥h	①–⑥		①–⑥	①–⑥		③⑦	⊖
		✕	🍷	e✕	✕	e✕	e✕	✕	s🍷	D🍷
Dresden Hbf ... **843** d.	...	...	...	...	...	...	0606	...	0654	0654
Dresden Neustadt ... d.	...	...	...	...	...	...	0613	...	0701	0701
Elsterwerda ... **843 835** d.	...	...	...	...	...	...	|	...	|	|
Leipzig Hbf **851** ... d.	...	...	...	0510a	...	0615	|	...	|	|
Berlin Südkreuz ... **835** d.	0458	0519	0519	0624	0657	0728	0811	0829	0850	0855
Berlin Hbf ... **835** a.	|	|	|	0629	|	0733	0818	|	0857	0900
Berlin Hbf ... **837** d.	0506	0527	0527	0638	0706	0742	...	0839	...	0906
Berlin Spandau ... **837** d.	0516	0537	0537	0648	0717	0752	...	0849	...	0917
Wittenberge ... **837** d.	0601	0621	0620	|	0802	|	...	|	...	1002
Ludwigslust ... **837** d.	0621	0641	0641	0741	0821	|	...	|	...	1021
Büchen ... **830** d.	0649	|	|	|	0849	|	...	|	...	1049
Hamburg Hbf ... **830** a.	0711	0724	0725	0824	0911	0924	...	1021	...	1111
Hamburg Altona ... a.	0725	0739	0740	0840	0923	0942	...	1037	...	...

	IC 2072	*ICE* 906	*ICE* 1616	*ICE* 1626	*EC* 178	*ICE* 1514	*ICE* 1614	*EC* 176	*ICE* 1512	*ICE* 800	*EC* 174	*ICE* 900	*IC* 2015	*ICE* 1610	*EC* 378	*ICE* 1508	*ICE* 706	*EC* 172	*ICE* 1206	*ICE* 704	*EC* 170	*ICE* 1504		*ICE* 898	*ICE* 1604
			①–⑥	⑦s									⑦w				Ⓑq			Ⓑq				Q	⑤f
	D🍷	K✕	eN ✕	E✕	P✕	M✕	M✕	P✕	M✕	✕	P✕	✕	⊙🍷	M✕	L✕	M✕	✕	H✕	MK ✕	M✕	P✕	M✕		✕	M✕
Dresden Hbf ... **843** d.	...	...		...	0855	...	...	1055	...	...	1255	...	1339	...	1455	...	...	1655		...	1855	...	...	...	...
Dresden Neustadt ... d.	...	...	...	...	|	...	...	|	...	...	|	...	1346	...	|	...	...	|	...	...	|	...	...	...	...
Elsterwerda ... **843 835** d.	...	...	...	...	|	...	...	|	...	...	|	...	|	...	|	...	...	|	...	...	|	...	...	...	...
Leipzig Hbf **851** ... d.	...	0815	0915	0915	|	1015q	1115	|	1215	...	|	...	|	1515	|	1615	...	|	1815	1915v	|	2015	...	...	2115
Berlin Südkreuz ... **835** d.	0855	0928	1024	1024	1050	1128	1224	1252	1328	1423	1452	1524	1539	1624	1652	1728	1829	1852	1928	2024	2050	2128	...	2229	2224
Berlin Hbf ... **835** a.	0900	0933	1030	1030	1057	1133	1230	1257	1333	|	1457	|	1548	1630	1657	1733	|	1857	1933	2030	2057	2133	...	|	2230
Berlin Hbf ... **837** d.	0906	0942	1039	1039	...	1142	1239	1307	1342	1439	1506	1542	...	1639	1706	1742	1839	1906	1942	2039	...	2142	...	2239	2239
Berlin Spandau ... **837** d.	0917	0952	1049	1049	...	1152	1249	1317	1352	1449	1517	1552	...	1649	1717	1752	1849	1917	1952	2049	...	2152	...	2249	2249
Wittenberge ... **837** d.	1002	|	|	|	...	|	|	1402	|	|	1602	|	...	|	1802	|	|	2002	|	|	...	2232	...	2329	2329
Ludwigslust ... **837** d.	1021	|	|	|	...	|	|	1421	|	|	1621	|	...	|	1821	|	|	2021	|	|	...	2250	...	2347	2347
Büchen ... **830** d.	1049	|	|	|	...	|	|	1449	|	|	1649	|	...	|	1849	|	|	2049	|	|	...	|	...	|	|
Hamburg Hbf ... **830** a.	1111	1124	1221	1221	...	1324	1422	1511	1524	1621	1711	1724	...	1823	1911	1924	2021	2115	2124	2221	...	2333	...	0030	0030
Hamburg Altona ... a.	...	1139	1237	1237	...	1339	1439	1527	1539	1638	1724	1743	...	1840	...	1939	2039	2136	2138	2238	...	2349	...	0046	0046

D – UTHLANDE – To / from Westerland (Table **821**).
E – To / from Eisenach (Table **850**).
H – [12] and ✕ Budapest - Bratislava - Praha - Dresden - Hamburg and v.v.
K – From / to Kiel on dates on Table **820**.
L – [12] and ✕ Praha - Dresden - Hamburg - Kiel and v.v.
M – [12] and ✕ Hamburg - Berlin - Nürnberg - München and v.v. See also Table **851**.
N – [12] and ✕ (Nürnberg - Saalfeld ● -) Leipzig - Hamburg.
P – To / from Praha (Tables **60/1100**).
Q – ①②③④⑥⑦ (also Apr. 14, May 26; not Apr. 13, May 24).
R – ①②③④⑥ (also Apr. 14, 16, 30, May 26, June 4; not Apr. 13, 17, May 1, 24, June 5).
T – ⑤ to May 12 (also Apr. 13; not Apr. 14).

a – ①–⑤ (not Apr. 14, 17, May 1, June 5).
e – Not Apr. 15, 17, May 1, June 5.
f – Also Apr. 13, May 24; not Apr. 14, May 26.
g – Also Apr. 18, May 2, June 6; not Apr. 17, May 1, June 5.
h – Also Apr. 14, May 25; not Apr. 15, May 27.
j – Also Apr. 16, 30, June 4; not Apr. 17, May 1, June 5.
q – Ⓑ (not Apr. 14, 16, 30, June 4).
s – Also Apr. 15, 17, May 1, June 5.
t – 0835 Feb. 10 - Apr. 16.
v – ⑤⑦ (also Apr. 13, 17, May 1, 24, June 5; not Apr. 14, 16, 30, May 26, June 4).
w – Also Apr. 17, May 1, June 5; not Apr. 16, 30, June 4.
z – 22 – 29 minutes later on ①② Jan. 9 - Mar. 14, ①② from May 15 (not June 5).

⊡ – ①③④⑤⑦ (not Apr. 14, 16, 30, June 4).
⊖ – ①②④⑤⑥ (not Apr. 15, 17, May 1, June 5).
¶ – On ⑤⑦ (also Apr. 13, 17, May 1, 24, June 5; not Apr. 30, May 26, June 4) conveys [12] (**1617**) Hamburg - Berlin - Leipzig - Jena - Nürnberg - München.
● – See Table **851** for running dates from Nürnberg and Saalfeld.
◧ – Train number **808** on ① (also Apr. 18, May 2, June 6).
⊙ – From May 14 Dresden Hbf d. 1336, Dresden Neustadt d. 1343, Berlin Südkreuz a. 1529, Berlin Hbf a. 1536.

12 *For explanation of standard symbols see page 4* 393

GERMANY

See page 367 for a summary of Christmas / New Year alterations

841 MAGDEBURG - STENDAL - UELZEN and WITTENBERGE

RE / RB services except where shown

km																											
		⚒	Ⓐe		H		Ⓐe			A												Ⓑb					
0	**Magdeburg** Hbf ... d.	0348	...	0508	0554	0608	*0638*	0708	0808	0857	0903	0908	1008	1103	1108	1208	1303	1308	1408	1503	1508	1603	1608	1703	1708	1808	1903
58	Stendal ... a.	0433	...	0556	0633	0656	*0726*	0756	0856	0932	0942	0956	1056	1142	1156	1256	1342	1356	1456	1542	1556	1642	1656	1741	1756	1856	1942
58	Stendal ... d.	0440	0500	0600	0634	0700e	0729	0800	0900r	0934	0944	1000	...	1144	1200	1300e	1344	1400	1510e	1544	1600	1644	1700e	1743	1800	1900e	1944
113	**Wittenberge** ... a.	|	0542	0642	|	0742e	|	0842	0942r	1010	|	1042	...	|	1242	1342e	|	1442	1552e	|	1642	|	1742e	|	1842	1942e	|
116	Salzwedel ... d.	0519	...	...	0714	...	0806	...	...	...	1015	...	...	1214	...	...	1414	...	...	1614	...	1714	...	1814	...	...	2014
167	**Uelzen** ... a.	0550	...	...	0746	...	...	...	...	...	1046	...	...	1246	...	...	1446	...	...	1646	...	1747	...	1847	...	...	2046

							⑦z
Magdeburg Hbf ... d.	1908	2008	2108	2139	2212	2312	...
Stendal ... a.	1956	2056	2156	2218	2300	2400	...
Stendal ... d.	2000	2100b	2200	2232d	...	...	0030
Wittenberge ... a.	2042	2142b	2242	|	...	...	|
Salzwedel ... d.	...	...	...	2310d	...	...	0112
Uelzen ... a.	...	...	...	...	...	...	...

				Ⓐ	⚒		⚒				r					
Uelzen ... d.	...	...	...	...	0619	...	0700	...	...	0902	...	...	...	1102	...	...
Salzwedel ... d.	...	0555	...	...	0652	...	0746	...	...	0934	...	1010	...	1135	...	...
Wittenberge ... d.	0500e	|	0610e	0637	|	0710	|	0806e	0910	|	1010	|	1110	|	...	1310
Stendal ... a.	0540e	0633	0650e	0713	0722	0750	0827	0847e	0950	1007	1051	1053	1150	1207	...	1351
Stendal ... d.	0556	0641	0657	0716	*0725e*	0756	...	0856	0956	1010	...	*1056*	1156	1210	1256	1356
Magdeburg Hbf ... a.	0643	0727	0743	0757	*0813e*	0843	...	0943	1043	1050	...	*1143*	1243	1250	1343	1443

					A					Ⓑb			Ⓐe			H	Ⓑb	
Uelzen ... d.	1302	...	...	1502	...	...	...	1702	...	1802	...	1902	...	...	...	2103	...	...
Salzwedel ... d.	1335	...	...	1535	...	...	...	1735	...	1836	...	1935	...	2013	...	2136	...	...
Wittenberge ... d.	|	1410e	1510	|	1547	1610e	1710	|	1810e	|	1910	|	2010	|	2110	|	2210	2310
Stendal ... a.	1406	1451e	1551	1607	1621	1650e	1750	1808	1850e	1917	1950	2007	2051	2053	2150	2214	2251	2351
Stendal ... d.	1410	1456	1556	1610	1623	1656	1756	1810	1856	...	1956	2010	...	*2056*	2156	2215	...	2352
Magdeburg Hbf ... a.	1450	1543	1643	1650	1658	1743	1843	1850	1943	...	2043	2050	...	*2146*	2243	2256	...	0037

2nd class only ❦	*IRE* 4276		*IRE* 4278	*IRE* 4272
	E		⑦w	
Berlin Hbf ... d.	0803‡	...	1320‡	1701‡
Rathenow ... d.	0842	...	|	|
Stendal ... d.	0903	...	1418	1808
Salzwedel ... d.	0934	...	1455	1838
Uelzen ... a.	1003s	...	1529s	1902s
Lüneburg ... a.	1029s	...	1548s	1930s
Hamburg Hbf ... a.	1104	...	1621	2004

2nd class only ❦	*IRE* 4273	*IRE* 4275	*IRE* 4277	*IRE* 4279
	D	⑦w	④⑤f	Ⓒ
Hamburg Hbf ... d.	0655	1241	1642	1931
Lüneburg ... d.	0735u	1313u	1715u	2005u
Uelzen ... d.	0756u	1331u	1733u	2024u
Salzwedel ... d.	0821	1356	1810	2057
Stendal ... a.	0850	1444	1842	2125
Rathenow ... a.	|	|	1900	|
Berlin Hbf ... a.	0942*	1542*	1952*	2219*

A – *IC* **2238/9**. ⑤ to Mar. 31; ⑤–⑦ from Apr. 7 (also May 1, 24, 25). [12] Leipzig - Schwerin - Rostock (- Warnemünde from Apr. 7) and v.v.
D – ①–⑥ (also Apr. 16, 30; not Apr. 17, May 1).
E – ④–⑥ (also Dec. 19, 20, 21, 27, 28, Jan. 2, 16, Apr. 16, 30).
H – From / to Halle (Table **866**).

b – Ⓑ (not Apr. 14, 16, 30, June 4).
d – Ⓑ (not Jan. 6, Apr. 14, 16, 30, June 4).
e – Ⓐ (not Jan. 6).

f – Also Dec. 19, 20, 21, 27, 28, Jan. 2; not Apr. 14.
r – ①–⑥ (not Apr. 15, 17, May 1, 25, June 5).
s – Calls to set down only.
u – Calls to pick up only.
w – Also Apr. 17, May 1; not Apr. 16, 30.
z – Also Jan. 7, Apr. 15, 17, May 1, June 5.

* – Also calls at Berlin Spandau, Zoo and Ostbahnhof.
‡ – Also calls at Berlin Ostbahnhof, Zoo and Spandau.
❦ – Subject to alteration from May 13.

842 LEIPZIG - DRESDEN

km	SEE NOTE ⊠	*ICE* **1659**		*RE* **16501**		*RE* **16503**	*RE* **16503**		*EC* **259**		*RE* **16505**	*RE* **16507**	*IC* **2043**	*RE* **16509**	*ICE* **1553**	*RE* **16511**	*IC* **2447**	*RE* **16513**	*ICE* **1555**	*RE* **16515**	*IC* **2445**	*RE* **16517**	*ICE* **1597**	*ICE* **1557**
		①g ▲		⚒		⚒			①–⑥ zT		⚒		①–⑤ aG		①–⑥ A✕		D		▲✕		①–⑥ eK		⑦s ¶✕	①–⑥ eR ▲✕
	Frankfurt Flughafen § **850** .. d.	2101p	...	...	...	...	...	...	...	...	...	...	...	...	...	...	...	...	...	...	...	...	0901	
	Frankfurt (Main) Hbf **850** ... d.	2119p	...	...	...	...	...	...	...	...	...	...	...	...	0458g	...	...	...	0718	...	...	...	0919	0919
0	**Leipzig** Hbf ... d.	0031	...	...	...	0500	...	...	0555	...	0600	0700	0732	0800	0831	0900	0932	1000	1031	1100	1132	1200	1231	1231
26	Wurzen ... d.	|	...	...	...	0518	...	...	|	...	0618	0718	|	0818	|	0918	|	1018	|	1118	|	1218	|	|
53	Oschatz ... d.	|	...	...	...	0536	...	...	|	...	0636	0736	|	0836	|	0936	|	1036	|	1136	|	1236	|	|
66	Riesa ... d.	0101	...	0445	...	0545	0545	...	0632	...	0645	0745	0803	0845	0901	0945	1003	1045	1101	1145	1203	1245	1301	1301
102	Coswig ... **843 856 857** d.	|	...	0513	...	0613	0613	...	|	...	0713	0813	|	0913	|	1013	|	1113	|	1213	|	1313	|	|
110	Radebeul Ost ... **857** d.	|	...	0519	...	0619	0619	...	|	...	0719	0819	|	0919	|	1019	|	1119	|	1219	|	1319	|	|
116	**Dresden** Neustadt ... **856/7** a.	0128	...	0524	...	0624	0624	...	0659	...	0724	0824	0829	0924	0928	1024	1029	1124	1128	1224	1229	1324	1328	1328
120	**Dresden** Hbf ... **843 856 857** a.	0135	...	0531	...	0631	0631	...	0706	...	0731	0831	0836	0931	0935	1031	1036	1131	1135	1231	1236	1331	1335	1335

SEE NOTE ⊠	*RE* **16519**	*IC* **2443**	*RE* **16521**	*ICE* **1559**	*RE* **16523**	*IC* **2441**	*RE* **16525**	*ICE* **1651**	*RE* **16527**	*IC* **2049**	*RE* **16529**	*ICE* **1653**	*RE* **16531**	*IC* **2047**	*RE* **16533**	*ICE* **1655**	*RE* **16535**	*IC* **2045**		*ICE* **1697**	*ICE* **1657**	*IC* **2435**	*RE* **16539**	
		K		¶ ▲✕		K		¶ ▲✕		K		¶ ▲✕		Ⓑq K		¶ ▲✕		Ⓑq ◊K		①② ⊕🍷	Ⓑx ¶▲	⑥ B		
Frankfurt Flughafen § **850** ... d.	...	...	...	1101	...	...	...	1301	...	...	...	1501	...	...	...	1701	...	...	...	...	1901	...	...	...
Frankfurt (Main) Hbf **850** ... d.	...	...	...	1119	...	...	...	1319	...	...	...	1520	...	...	...	1720	...	...	...	...	1919	...	...	...
Leipzig Hbf ... d.	1300	1332	1400	1431	1500	1532	1600	1631	1700	1732	1800	1831	1900	1932	2000	2031	2100	2132	...	2235	2238	2238	2300	...
Wurzen ... d.	1318	|	1418	|	1518	|	1618	|	1718	|	1818	|	1918	|	2018	|	2118	|	...	|	|	|	2318	...
Oschatz ... d.	1336	|	1436	|	1536	|	1636	|	1736	|	1836	|	1936	|	2036	|	2136	|	...	|	|	|	2336	...
Riesa ... d.	1345	1403	1445	1501	1545	1603	1645	1701	1745	1803	1845	1901	1945	2003	2045	2101	2145	2203	...	2308	2308	2308	2345	...
Coswig ... **843 856 857** d.	1413	|	1513	|	1613	|	1713	|	1813	|	1913	|	2013	|	2113	|	2213	|	...	|	|	|	0013	...
Radebeul Ost ... **857** d.	1419	|	1519	|	1619	|	1719	|	1819	|	1919	|	2019	|	2119	|	2219	|	...	|	|	|	0019	...
Dresden Neustadt ... **856/7** a.	1424	1429	1524	1528	1624	1629	1724	1728	1824	1829	1924	1928	2024	2029	2124	2128	2224	2229	...	2335	2335	2335	0024	...
Dresden Hbf ... **843 856 857** a.	1431	1436	1531	1535	1631	1636	1731	1735	1831	1836	1931	1935	2031	2036	2131	2135	2231	2236	...	2342	2342	2342	0031	...

SEE NOTE ⊠	*RE* **16500**	*IC* **2044**	*RE* **16502**	*ICE* **1654**	*RE* **16504**	*IC* **2046**	*RE* **16506**	*ICE* **1652**	*RE* **16508**	*IC* **2048**	*RE* **16510**	*ICE* **1650**	*RE* **16512**	*IC* **2440**	*RE* **16514**	*ICE* **1558**	*RE* **16516**	*IC* **2442**	*RE* **16518**	*ICE* **1556**	*RE* **16520**	*IC* **2444**	*RE* **16522**	*ICE* **1594**
	⚒	①–⑤ aK		①–⑥ e¶✕	⚒	①–⑥ eK		¶✕		K		¶✕		K		¶✕		K		¶✕		K		⑥h ¶✕
Dresden Hbf ... **843 856 857** d.	0417	0513	0517	0613	0617	0713	0717	0813	0817	0913	0917	1013	1017	1113	1117	1213	1217	1313	1317	1413	1417	1513	1517	1613
Dresden Neustadt ... **856/7** d.	0425	0520	0525	0620	0625	0720	0725	0820	0825	0920	0925	1020	1025	1120	1125	1220	1225	1320	1325	1420	1425	1520	1525	1620
Radebeul Ost ... **857** d.	0431	|	0531	|	0631	|	0731	|	0831	|	0931	|	1031	|	1131	|	1231	|	1331	|	1431	|	1531	|
Coswig ... **843 856 857** d.	0437	|	0537	|	0637	|	0737	|	0837	|	0937	|	1037	|	1137	|	1237	|	1337	|	1437	|	1537	|
Riesa ... d.	0505	0550	0605	0650	0705	0750	0805	0850	0905	0950	1005	1050	1105	1150	1205	1250	1305	1350	1405	1450	1505	1550	1605	1650
Oschatz ... d.	0514	|	0614	|	0714	|	0814	|	0914	|	1014	|	1114	|	1214	|	1314	|	1414	|	1514	|	1614	|
Wurzen ... d.	0531	|	0631	|	0731	|	0831	|	0931	|	1031	|	1131	|	1231	|	1331	|	1431	|	1531	|	1631	|
Leipzig Hbf ... a.	0550	0619	0650	0718	0750	0819	0850	0918	0950	1019	1050	1118	1150	1219	1250	1318	1350	1419	1450	1518	1550	1619	1650	1718
Frankfurt (Main) Hbf **850** ... a.	...	...	...	1037	...	...	...	1237	...	...	...	1437	...	...	...	1637	...	...	...	1837	...	...	...	2036
Frankfurt Flughafen § **850** ... a.	...	...	...	1055	...	...	...	1255	...	...	...	1455	...	...	...	1655	...	...	...	1855	...	...	...	2057

SEE NOTE ⊠	*ICE* **1554**	*RE* **16524**	*IC* **2446**	*RE* **16526**	*ICE* **1552**	*RE* **16528**	*IC* **2030**	*RE* **16530**	*ICE* **1550**	*RE* **16532**	*EC* **258**	*RE* **16536**	*RE* **16538**
	Ⓑq R✕		K		✕		Ⓑq H		⑦w ✕		Ⓑb T		
Dresden Hbf ... **843 856 857** d.	1613	1617	1713	1717	1813	1817	1913	1917	2013	2017	2047	2217	2317
Dresden Neustadt ... **856/7** d.	1620	1625	1720	1725	1820	1825	1920	1925	2020	2025	|	2225	2325
Radebeul Ost ... **857** d.	|	1631	|	1731	|	1831	|	1931	|	2031	|	2231	2331
Coswig ... **843 856 857** d.	|	1637	|	1737	|	1837	|	1937	|	2037	|	2237	2337
Riesa ... d.	1650	1705	1750	1805	1850	1905	1950	2005	2050	2105	2124	2305	0005
Oschatz ... d.	|	1714	|	1814	|	1914	|	2014	|	2114	|	2314	...
Wurzen ... d.	|	1731	|	1831	|	1931	|	2031	|	2131	|	2331	...
Leipzig Hbf ... a.	1718	1750	1819	1850	1918	1950	2019j	2050	2118	2150	2203	2350	...
Frankfurt (Main) Hbf **850** ... a.	2036	...	...	...	2254	...	...	...	0037	...	...	...	...
Frankfurt Flughafen § **850** ... a.	...	...	...	...	...	...	...	...	...	...	...	...	...

A – [12] and ✕ (Frankfurt ①**g** -) Eisenach - Leipzig - Dresden. Runs 4–5 minutes later Leipzig - Dresden on ②–⑥ Feb. 11 - Mar. 9. Departs Frankfurt 0437 from Mar. 13.
B – ⑥ (also Apr. 14, 16, 30, May 25, June 5; not Apr. 15). [12] Emden - Bremen - Hannover - Magdeburg - Dresden.
D – [12] (Bielefeld ①**g** -) (Hannover ①–⑥**e** -) Leipzig - Dresden.
G – From Magdeburg (Table **866**).
H – To Hannover (Table **866**).
K – [12] Köln - Dortmund - Hannover - Magdeburg - Dresden and v.v.
R – [12] and ✕ Saarbrücken - Mannheim - Frankfurt - Dresden and v.v.
T – [12] Praha - Dresden - Leipzig and v.v.

a – Not Apr. 14, 17, May 1, June 5.
b – Not Apr. 16.
e – Not Apr. 15, 17, May 1, June 5.
g – ① (also Apr. 18, May 2, June 6; not Apr. 17, May 1, June 5).
h – Also Apr. 14, 16, 30, June 4.
j – 2027 on ①② Jan. 9 - Mar. 14, ①② May 15 – 30 (also June 6)
p – Previous day.
q – Not Apr. 14, 16, 30, June 4.
s – Also Apr. 15, 17, May 1, June 5.
w – Also Apr. 17, May 1, June 5; not Apr. 16, 30, June 4.
x – Not ①② Jan. 9 - Mar. 14, Apr. 14, 16, 30, May 15, 16, 22, 23, 29, 30, June 4, 6.
z – Not Apr. 17.

⊕ – ①② Jan. 9 - Mar. 14; ①② from May 15 (not June 5).
¶ – To / from Wiesbaden (Table **911**).
§ – Frankfurt Flughafen Fernbahnhof ✈.
◊ – Runs up to 30 minutes later on on ①② Jan. 9 - Mar. 14, ①② May 15 – 30 (also June 6).
▲ – Mar. 11 - May 22 runs 16 – 22 minutes later Leipzig - Dresden.
⊠ – Frankfurt timings are subject to alteration on ⑥⑦ Feb. 11 - Apr. 2 (also Apr. 14 – 17). See engineering work panel on page 367.

ELSTERWERDA - CHEMNITZ and DRESDEN; DÖBELN - LEIPZIG — 843

RE/ RB services

km			Ⓐ		Ⓐ		Ⓐ		Ⓐ		Ⓐ		Ⓐ		Ⓐ		Ⓐ		Ⓐ		Ⓐ		†	Ⓑ	✗
0	Elsterwerda ....d.		0514		0614		0714	0814		1014		1214		1414	1514	1614	1714		1814	1914	2014	2114		2226	
24	Riesa ....a.		0539		0639		0739	0839		1039		1239		1439	1539	1639	1739		1839	1939	2039	2139		2251	
24	Riesa ....d.	0449	0549	0549	0649	0649	0749	0849	0949	1049	1149	1249	1349	1449	1549	1649	1749	1749	1849	1949	2049	2149	2149	2252	2252
50	Döbeln Hbf ....d.	0511	0611	0611	0711	0711	0811	0911	1011	1111	1211	1311	1411	1511	1611	1711	1811	1811	1911	2011	2111	2211	2211	2317	2317
91	Chemnitz Hbf ....a.	0551	0649	0649	0749	0749	0849	0949	1049	1149	1249	1349	1449	1549	1649	1749	1849	1849	1949	2049	2149	2253	2253	2358	2358

			Ⓐ		Ⓐ		Ⓐ	Ⓐ	Ⓐ		Ⓐ		Ⓐ		Ⓐ		Ⓐ		Ⓐ		Ⓐ	Ⓒ		Ⓐ	
	Chemnitz Hbf ....d.	0409	0509	0509	0609	0707	0809	0909	1009	1109	1209	1309	1409	1509	1509	1609	1709	1809	1909	2009	2009		2136	2236	
	Döbeln Hbf ....d.	0445	0545	0545	0645	0747	0845	0945	1045	1145	1245	1345	1445	1545	1545	1645	1745	1845	1945	2045	2045		2217	2317	
	Riesa ....a.	0509	0609	0609	0709	0810	0909	1009	1109	1209	1309	1409	1509	1609	1609	1709	1809	1909	2009	2109	2109		2240	2340	
	Riesa ....d.	0515		0615	0715		0915		1115		1315	1415	1515		1615	1715	1815	1915	2015		2115		2244		
	Elsterwerda ....a.	0537		0637	0737		0937		1137		1337	1437	1537		1637	1737	1837	1937	2037		2137		2306		

km			Ⓐ							Ⓐ										Ⓐ		
0	Elsterwerda-Biehla ....d.	0440	0540e	0640	0740	and every	2140	2321	Dresden Hbf ....▷ d.	0508	0608	0708	0908	1108	1308	1508	1608	1708	1908	2108	2308
2	Elsterwerda ....d.	0444		0644	0744	two hours	2144	2344	Coswig ....▷ d.	0531	0631	0731	0931	1131	1331	1531	1631	1731	1931	2131	2331
41	Coswig ....d.	0523		0623	0723	until	2223	0023	Elsterwerda ....d.	0609	0709	0809	1009	1209	1409	1609	1709	1809	2009	2209	0009
59	Dresden Hbf ....▷ a.	0544		0644	0744	0844	2244	0044	Esterwerda-Biehla ....a.	0613	0713	0813	1013	1213	1413	1613	1713	1813	2013		

km			Ⓐ						Leipzig Hbf	Ⓐ							
0	Döbeln Hbf ....d.	0450	0550	0650	and hourly	2050			Leipzig Hbf ....d.	0506	0606	and hourly	2006	2206		
13	Leisnig ....d.	0502	0602	0702	on Ⓐ,	2102			Grimma ob Bf ....d.	0541	0641	on Ⓐ,	2041	2240		
28	Großbothen ....d.	0517	0617	0717	every two	2117			Großbothen ....d.	0547	0647	every two	2047	2246		
35	Grimma ob Bf ....d.	0527	0627	0727	hours on	2127	2227	2306	Leisnig ....d.	0604	0704	hours on	2104	2300		
66	Leipzig ....a.	0600	0700	0800	Ⓒ until	2200	2300	2339	Döbeln Hbf ....a.	0617	0717	Ⓒ until	2117	2213		

e – Ⓐ only.

Ⓓ – Mitteldeutsche Regiobahn.

▷ – See also Tables 842, 856, 857.

STRALSUND - OSTSEEBAD BINZ / SASSNITZ — 844

RE/ RB services except where shown

											IC 2184			ICE 1731			ICE 1731				
km			Ⓐ	Ⓐ	Ⓐ	Ad	A		Ad	A		Ⓐ♦		Ad	A		⑥P	Ad	A		
	Rostock Hbf 830 ....d.		0456		0554		0700			0901	0938			1101			1301		
0	Stralsund Hbf ....d.	0501	0600		0700	0700		0800		1000	1038	1101		1154	1200		1237	1301		1400
29	Bergen auf Rügen ....d.	0530	0630		0730	0730		0830		0930	1030	1106	1130		1218	1230		1302	1330		1430
39	Lietzow (Rügen) ....d.	0538	0638	0641	0738	0738	0741	0838	0841	0938	0941	1038	1041		1138	1141		1238	1341v		1341	1438	1441
	Ostseebad Binz ....a.			0655			0755		0855	0953		1055	1132	1153		1239		1257	1333	1355		1455
51	Sassnitz ....a.	0552	0652		0752	0752		0852			0955	1052			1155		1252			1355	1452

		IC 2212	ICE 1524			IC 2376	ICE 1712			IC 2424				IC 1970				
		Ⓐ♦	⑥k M	Ad	A	⑥♦	Ad	B	Ad	A	B	Ad	A	⑤f	Ad	A		Ⓑ
	Rostock Hbf 830 ....d.	1338			1501	1538			1701		1901			1901			2101		
	Stralsund Hbf ....d.	1439	1453	1501		1600	1632	1648	1701		1800		1847	1901		2000	2101	2117	2201		2301
	Bergen auf Rügen ....d.	1504	1518	1530		1630		1657	1712	1730		1830		1918r	1930		2030	2130	2143	2230		2330
	Lietzow (Rügen) ....d.			1538	1541	1638	1641		1738	1741	1838	1841		1938	1941	2038	2041	2138	2141		2238	2241
	Ostseebad Binz ....a.	1529	1538	1553			1655	1720	1738	1755		1855	1942r	1953		2055	2153		2204	2255	
	Sassnitz ....a.				1555	1652			1755	1852			1955	2052			2155		2252	

								IC 2425				ICE 1513	IC 2213				ICE 1715	IC 2377
km			Ⓐ		Ⓐ	✗		A	Ad	B		A	Ad	M	Ⓐ♦		A	Ad	⑦	A	Ad
0	Sassnitz ....d.	0400		0503		0603		0703		0803		0903	1000			1103	1200			
12	Ostseebad Binz ....d.				0602		0702		0802	0819	0902		1004	1016	1026	1102		1204	1212	1227
22	Lietzow (Rügen) ....d.	0414		0518	0615	0618	0715	0718	0815	0818		0915	0914	1018		1115	1118	1214	1218		
22	Bergen auf Rügen ....d.	0423		0527		0627		0727		0827	0842	0927	1027	1038	1055		1127		1227	1242	1256
51	Stralsund Hbf ....a.	0451		0555		0655		0755		0855	0906	0955	1055	1106	1119	1155t		1255	1307	1320
	Rostock Hbf 830 ....a.	0548				0755				0855			1055		1219			1255		1419

		ICE 1536														
		⑥♦	A	Ad		A	Ad		A	Ad		A	Ad		A	Ad
	Sassnitz ....d.	1303		1400		1503	1600		1700		1800		1903	2000		2106	2200
	Ostseebad Binz ....d.	1302		1316	1404	1502		1604	1704		1804	1902		2004	2105		2204
	Lietzow (Rügen) ....d.	1315	1318		1414	1418	1515	1518	1614	1618	1714	1721	1814	1818	1915	1918	2014	2118	2121	2214	2218
	Bergen auf Rügen ....d.		1327	1338		1427		1527		1627		1730		1827	1927		2027		2130		2227
	Stralsund Hbf ....a.		1355	1401		1455		1555		1655		1758		1855	1955		2055		2158		2255
	Rostock Hbf 830 ....a.		1455					1655				1758h		1855	2055				2255		

♦ – **NOTES** (LISTED BY TRAIN NUMBER)

1536 – ⑥ to Feb. 4. ⓒ and ✗ Ostseebad Binz - Berlin - Erfurt - Frankfurt.

1715 – ⑦ (also Apr. 15, 17, May 1, June 5). ⓒ and ✗ Ostseebad Binz - Berlin - Leipzig - München. Until Feb. 5 Ostseebad Binz d. 1242, Bergen d. 1307, Stralsund a. 1332.

2184 – ①–⑥ from May 2 (also Apr. 8, 14, 15, 22, 29; not June 5). ⓒ and ♀ (Hannover Ⓐ -) Hamburg - Ostseebad Binz.

2212 – RÜGEN – ⓒ and ♀ Koblenz - Köln - Hamburg - Ostseebad Binz.

2213 – RÜGEN – ⓒ and ♀ Ostseebad Binz - Hamburg - Köln - Stuttgart.

2376 – ⑥ (also Apr. 14, May 25). ⓒ and ♀ Karlsruhe - Frankfurt - Hannover - Hamburg - Ostseebad Binz.

2377 – ⑦ (also Apr. 8, 14, 15, 17, 22); daily from Apr. 29. ⓒ and ♀ Ostseebad Binz - Hamburg - Hannover - Frankfurt.

A – Ⓐ (daily from May 22).

B – From/ to Berlin (Table 845).

M – ⓒ and ✗ Ostseebad Binz - Berlin - Leipzig - München.

P – ⑥ from Apr. 22 (also May 25; not May 27). ⓒ and ✗ Erfurt - Berlin - Ostseebad Binz.

Q – ⑥ to Feb. 4. ⓒ and ✗ Eisenach - Berlin - Ostseebad Binz.

d – Runs daily Stralsund - Bergen auf Rügen and v.v.

f – Also Apr. 13, May 24; not Apr. 14, May 26.

h – ①–④ (not Apr. 13, 17, May 1, 25, June 5).

k – Also Apr. 14, 16, 30, June 4.

r – Until Feb. 8 Bergen d. 1915, Ostseebad Binz a. 1934.

t – 1200 on ⑥ to Feb. 4.

v – 1243 from Feb. 6.

BERGEN AUF RÜGEN - PUTBUS - LAUTERBACH and RÜGENSCHE BÄDERBAHN — 844a

Preßnitztalbahn

km	SEE NOTE ★		r							r		SEE NOTE ★		Ⓐ	Ⓒ		r					
0	Bergen auf Rügen ....d.	0740	0840	0940	1040	1140	1340	1540	1740	1940	2040	Lauterbach Mole........d.	0604	0704	0800		1000	1104	1304	1504	1704	1904
9	Putbus ....d.	0749	0849	0949	1049	1149	1349	1549	1749	1949	2049	Putbus ....d.	0611	0711	0811	0854	1011	1111	1311	1511	1711	1911
12	Lauterbach Mole........a.	0754		0954	1054	1154	1354	1554	1754	1954r		Bergen auf Rügen ....a.	0620	0720	0820	0903	1020	1120	1320	1520	1720	1920

RÜGENSCHE BÄDERBAHN   **SERVICE UNTIL MAY 24, 2017**   Please note that Binz Lokalbahn station is situated 2½ km from Ostseebad Binz DB station.

km											Göhren (Rügen) ....d.	0953	1153	1353	1553	1753	1953		
0	Lauterbach Mole ....d.											Sellin (Rügen) Ost........d.	1011	1211	1411	1611	1811	2011		
2	Putbus ....d.											Binz Lokalbahn ....d.	1040	1240	1440	1640	1840	2040		
2	Putbus ....d.	0808	1008	1208	1408	1608	1808					Putbus ....a.	1106	1306	1506	1706	1906	2106		
14	Binz Lokalbahn ....d.	0840	1040	1240	1440	1640	1840					Putbus ....d.								
22	Sellin (Rügen) Ost ....d.	0909	1109	1309	1509	1709	1909					Lauterbach Mole........a.								
27	Göhren (Rügen) ....a.	0923	1123	1323	1523	1723	1923													

r – From May 25.

★ – Additional journeys **from May 25** Bergen - Putbus - Lauterbach and v.v.:
From Bergen auf Rügen at 1240, 1440, 1640 and 1840.
From Lauterbach at 1200, 1400, 1600, 1800 and 2000.

See page 367 for a summary of Christmas / New Year alterations

845 **LUTHERSTADT WITTENBERG - BERLIN - STRALSUND** RE services except where shown

SERVICE UNTIL FEBRUARY 8 (see page 560 for service from February 9)

km				IC 2217 N						S	ICE 1731 ⑥ L✕			ICE 1524 ⑥ C✕			ICE 1712 O✕		S	
		ⓒ	✕			Ⓐ														
0	Lutherstadt Wittenberg.. 851 d.	0024						0449		0613		0643		0812	1012	1052	1212		1412
	Falkenberg (Elster) .... d.												0843			1043		1243	
32	Jüterbog .... d.	0053			0433		0533	0641		0733		0837e	0936	1037e		1136	1237e	1336	1437e
45	Luckenwalde .... d.	0100			0441		0545	0649		0740		0846e	0944	1046e		1144	1246e	1344	1446e
91	Berlin Südkreuz .... 851 d.	0148			0522		0620	0721		0821		0921	1020	1121	1128	1220	1321	1420	1521
97	Berlin Hbf .... 851 d.	0154		0421	0531		0632	0734		0830	0919	0932	1032	1132	1146	1232	1332	1432	1532
101	Berlin Gesundbrunnen .... d.			0427	0537		0638	0740	0805	0838	0925	0939	1038	1139	1153	1238	1339	1359	1438	1451	1539
122	Bernau (b. Berlin) .... d.			0442	0551		0654	0755	0822	0854		0954	1054	1154		1254	1354		1454	1509	1554
144	Eberswalde Hbf .... d.			0507	0607		0709	0810	0838	0909		1009	1109	1209	1220	1309	1409	1428	1509	1527	1609
170	Angermünde .... a.			0526	0626		0728	0830	0853	0928		1028	1128	1228	1236	1328	1428	1443	1528	1543	1628
170	Angermünde .... d.			0533	0634c	0634	0731	0834		0933		1034	1133	1235	1238	1333	1434	1445	1533		1634
193	Schwedt (Oder) .... a.				0656c	0656		0856				1056		1258		1456				1656
	Prenzlau .... d.				0601		0759		1001			1201	1302	1401		1508	1601	
	Pasewalk .... d.		0419		0620		0817		1019			1219	1318	1419		1526	1619	
	Anklam .... d.		0450		0652		0849		1051			1251	1344	1451		1552	1651	
	Züssow .... 846 d.		0504		0706		0903	1105	1116		1305	1356	1505		1605	1705	
	Greifswald .... 846 d.		0520	0701	0721		0919	1121	1130		1321	1409	1521		1620	1721	
	Stralsund Hbf .... 846 a.		0541	0722	0744		0940	1142	1149		1342	1435	1542		1641	1742	

	IC 2424 O	IC 2428 ①–④ S	IC 1970 ⑤ O	IC 1924 ⑦			ⓒ	Ⓐ		⑤ S		①–④	⑥	⑤	⑦	⑧	⑦		⑤⑥ k
Lutherstadt Wittenberg .. 851 d.			1612				1812	1812		2012								2225	2225
Falkenberg (Elster) .... d.	1443				1643				1843		2043	2043	2043					2225	2225
Jüterbog .... d.	1536		1637e		1736	1837e	1837e	1936		2037e	2136	2136	2136				2252	2252
Luckenwalde .... d.	1544		1646e		1744	1846e	1846e	1944		2046e	2144	2144	2144				2300	2300
Berlin Südkreuz .... 851 d.	1531	1620	1723	1721		1820	1921	1921	2020		2121	2220	2220	2220				2348	2348
Berlin Hbf .... 851 d.	1546	1632	1737	1732	1818	1822	1832	1930	1932	1933	2031		2133	2233	2233	2235	2235		2356	2356
Berlin Gesundbrunnen .... d.	1552	1638	1720	1743	1739	1828	1838		1939	1939	2038	2105	2139		2239	2239	2240	2240		0002	0002
Bernau (b. Berlin) .... d.		1654	1737	1801	1754	1843	1843	1854		1954	1954	2054	2123	2154		2254	2254	2256	2256		0017	0017
Eberswalde Hbf .... d.	1623	1709	1752	1817	1809	1902	1909	1909		2009	2009	2109	2137	2214		2313	2313	2316	2316		0036	0038
Angermünde .... d.	1637	1728	1807	1837	1828	1917	1917	1928		2028	2028	2128	2153	2233		2332	2332	2338			0058
Angermünde .... d.	1639	1733		1840	1834	1919	1919	1933		2036	2036	2133		2234		2334	2345		2340	2345	2345		0059
Schwedt (Oder) .... a.				1856					2058	2058		2256		2356		0002			0120
Prenzlau .... d.	1702	1801		1903		1942	1942	2001		2201			0013		0013	0013		0147
Pasewalk .... d.	1717	1819		1919		1958	1959	2019		2219			0029		0029	0030		
Anklam .... d.	1743	1851		1944		2024	2024	2051		2251					0100		
Züssow .... 846 d.	1755	1905		1956		2036	2037	2105		2305					0112		
Greifswald .... 846 d.	1808	1921		2010		2050	2049	2121		2321					0127		
Stralsund Hbf .... 846 a.	1836	1942		2030		2110	2109	2142		2342					0147		

km							✕		Ⓐ		S		Ⓐ		IC 2429 ①–④	· IC 2425 O		ICE 1513 C✕	
0	Stralsund Hbf .... 846 d.	¶				0406		0416					0616	0708		0816	0911		1016	1111	1216
31	Greifswald .... 846 d.					0425		0437					0637	0729		0837	0931		1037	1134	1237
49	Züssow .... 846 d.					0438		0453					0653	0749		0853	0951		1053	1149	1253
66	Anklam .... d.					0449		0505					0705	0800		0905	1005		1105	1200	1305
109	Pasewalk .... d.			0519	0519	0544j	0544				0744j	0837		0944j	1039		1144j	1239	1344j
133	Prenzlau .... d.			0537	0537	0602	0602				0802	0852		1002	1054		1202	1255	1402
	Schwedt (Oder) .... d.		0506					0701	0704c		0906			1106			1306	
170	Angermünde .... a.			0528	0603	0603	0629	0629		0723	0726c	0829	0913	0928	1029		1115	1128	1229	1316	1328	1429
170	Angermünde .... d.		0427		0533	0605	0605	0633	0633	0707		0733	0833	0915	0933	1033	1107	1117	1133	1233	1318	1333	1433
196	Eberswalde Hbf .... d.		0448	0448	0554	0628	0628	0654	0654	0724		0754	0854	0932	0954	1054	1124	1134	1154	1254	1335	1354	1454
218	Bernau (b. Berlin) .... d.		0509	0509	0609	0644	0644	0709	0709	0741		0809	0909	0947	1009	1109	1140		1209	1309		1409	1509
239	Berlin Gesundbrunnen .... d.		0524	0524	0625	0700	0700	0725	0725	0756		0825	0925	1004a	1025	1125	1156	1159a	1225	1325	1425	1525
243	Berlin Hbf .... 851 d.	0044	0532	0532	0631	0709	0709	0731	0731		0831	0931	1007a	1031	1131		1206	1231	1331	1407a	1431	1531z
249	Berlin Südkreuz .... 851 d.	0053	0540	0540	0640	0717	0717	0740	0740		0840	0940	1016a	1040	1140			1240	1340	1432a	1440	1540z
295	Luckenwalde .... d.	0133		0614	0614	0711r		0814	0814		0911r	1014		1111r	1214		1311r	1414		1511r	1614z
308	Jüterbog .... d.	0141		0625	0625	0719r		0825	0825		0919r	1025		1119r	1225		1319r	1425		1519r	1625
357	Falkenberg (Elster) .... a.			0707	0707			0907	0907		1107			1307			1507		1707
	Lutherstadt Wittenberg.. 851 d.	0157c				0748					0948		1148			1348	1507	1548	

	IC 2325 ⑤	ICE 1715 J✕	ICE 1536 ⑥ H✕			⑤ f		ⓒ	IC 1932 ⑦ A	IC 2216 Ⓐ N	S		♠			✕	⑤⑥	
Stralsund Hbf .... 846 d.	1310	1340		1406	1419		1619	1619		1704	1813	1825		2016		2216	2216	2237
Greifswald .... 846 d.	1331			1427	1440		1641	1641		1724	1833	1846		2037		2237	2237	2258
Züssow .... 846 d.	1349	1413		1440	1456		1657	1657			1902		2053		2253	2253	2314
Anklam .... d.	1401	1424			1508		1709	1709	1746		1915		2105		2305	2305	2329
Pasewalk .... d.	1431	1450			1544		1744	1744	1812		1946		2144j		2336	2344	2351
Prenzlau .... d.	1450	1506			1602		1802	1802	1827		2003		2202		0002	
Schwedt (Oder) .... d.			1506		1706				1906		2106	2106		2307		
Angermünde .... a.	1512	1528		1629	1728		1829	1829		1928		2030	2128	2128		2229	2328		0029
Angermünde .... d.	1514	1533		1633	1733	1808	1833	1833		1933		2033	2046	2133	2133		2233	2333		0033
Eberswalde Hbf .... d.	1532	1542	1554	1654	1754	1825	1854	1854	1903	1954		2054	2104	2154	2154		2254	2354		0054
Bernau (b. Berlin) .... d.	1547		1609	1709	1809	1841	1908	1908	1920	2009		2109	2119	2209	2209		2314	0009		0114
Berlin Gesundbrunnen .... d.	1600a	1617	1625	1629a	1725	1821	1857	1922	1922	1934	2024		2125	2140	2224	2224		2328	0024		0128
Berlin Hbf .... 851 d.	1607a	1622a	1631	1638	1731	1831		1926	1935	1935		2031		2131		2228	2236	2236	2333	0028		0136
Berlin Südkreuz .... 851 d.	1615	1633a	1640		1740	1840		1944	1944		2040		2140		2246	2246			
Luckenwalde .... d.			1711r		1814	1911r		2017	2017		2111		2214		2328	2328			
Jüterbog .... d.			1719r		1825	1919r		2025	2025		2119		2226		2336	2336			
Falkenberg (Elster) .... d.			1907					2107	2107		2310					
Lutherstadt Wittenberg .. 851 a.		1707	1748		1946					2142				0003	0003		

A – 🚃 and ♀ Stralsund - Berlin - Hannover - Bremen - Oldenburg.
C – 🚃 and ✕ Ostseebad Binz - Berlin - Leipzig - München and v.v.
H – 🚃 and ✕ Ostseebad Binz - Berlin - Erfurt - Frankfurt.
J – 🚃 and ✕ Ostseebad Binz - Stralsund - Berlin - Leipzig - München.
L – 🚃 and ✕ Eisenach / Erfurt - Berlin - Stralsund - Ostseebad Binz.
N – 🚃 and ♀ Greifswald - Hamburg - Köln - Stuttgart and v.v.
O – To / from Ostseebad Binz (Table 844).
S – To / from Szczecin (Table 949).

a – Arrival time.
c – ⓒ only.
e – 3–4 minutes later until Jan. 6.
f – Subject to alteration Jan. 13 - Feb. 3.
j – Arrives 8 minutes earlier.
r – 3–4 minutes later from Jan. 7.
z – 3–4 minutes later on ⑤⑦.

♠ – ①②③④⑥.
¶ – From / to Halle on ⓒ (Tables 848).

846 STRALSUND - ZÜSSOW - ŚWINOUJŚCIE

Usedomer Bäderbahn (2nd class only) — *Service until May 19*

km																		
0	Stralsund Hbf 845 d.	0521e	0616	0721	0816	0914	1016	1121	1216	1321	1419	1521	1619	1721	1825	1921	2016	2122
31	Greifswald 845 d.	0545e	0637	0745	0837	0938	1037	1145	1237	1345	1440	1545	1641	1745	1846	1945	2037	2146
49	Züssow 845 d.	0607e	0707	0807	0907	1007	1107	1205	1307	1407	1507	1607	1707	1807	1907	2007	2107	2207
67	Wolgast d.	0630	0730	0830	0930	1030	1130	1230	1330	1430	1530	1630	1730	1830	1930	2030	2130	2230
77	Zinnowitz ▲ d.	0649	0749	0849	0949	1049	1149	1249	1349	1449	1549	1649	1749	1849	1949	2049	2149	2249
104	Seebad Heringsdorf d.	0730	0830	0930	1030	1130	1230	1330	1430	1530	1630	1730	1830	1930	2030	2130	2230	2324
106	Seebad Ahlbeck d.	0735	0835	0935	1035	1135	1235	1335	1435	1535	1635	1735	1835	1935	2035	2135	2235	...
110	Świnoujście Centrum a.	0740	0840	0940	1040	1140	1240	1340	1440	1540	1640	1740	1840	1940	2040	2140	2240	...

	Ⓐ		Ⓐ	Ⓒ														
Świnoujście Centrum d.	0421	0518	0554	0618	0718	0818	0918	1018	1118	1218	1318	1418	1518	1618	1718	1818	1918	2118
Seebad Ahlbeck d.	0426	0523	0600	0623	0723	0823	0923	1023	1123	1223	1323	1423	1523	1623	1723	1823	1923	2123
Seebad Heringsdorf d.	0436	0533	0609	0633	0733	0833	0933	1033	1133	1233	1333	1433	1533	1633	1733	1833	1933	2133
Zinnowitz ▲ d.	0511	0611	0648	0711	0811	0911	1011	1111	1211	1311	1411	1511	1611	1711	1811	1911	2011	2211
Wolgast d.	0528	0628	0708	0728	0828	0928	1028	1128	1228	1328	1428	1528	1628	1728	1828	1928	2028	2228
Züssow 845 a.	0546	0646	0746	0746	0846	0946	1046	1146	1246	1346	1446	1546	1646	1746	1846	1946	2046	2246
Greifswald 845 a.	0619	0720	0819	0819	0915	1021	1120	1219	1320	1419	1520	1619	1720	1822	1920	2019	2120	2320
Stralsund Hbf 845 a.	0644	0744	0844	0844	0940	1046	1142	1244	1342	1444	1542	1644	1742	1847	1942	2044	2142	2342

e – Ⓐ only.
t – Not Dec. 22 - Jan. 2, Feb. 6–17, Apr. 10–19, June 2–6.
z – Daily Dec. 22 - Jan. 2, Feb. 4–19, Apr. 8–19 and June 2–6.

▲ – **Zinnowitz - Peenemünde** and v.v. (*12 km*, journey 14 minutes).
From Zinnowitz at 0431 Ⓐ, 0513 Ⓐ, 0613, 0659 Ⓐ t, 0713 Ⓒ z, 0813, 0913 and hourly until 2113.
From Peenemünde at 0452 Ⓐ, 0531 Ⓐ, 0631, 0717 Ⓐ t, 0731 Ⓒ z, 0831, 0931 and hourly until 2131.

847 BERLIN SCHÖNEFELD ✈ - BERLIN - DESSAU

RE services

km			Ⓐ																	†		A				
0	Berlin Schönefeld ✈ d.	0444	0544	0644	0744	0844	0944	1044	1144	1244	1344	1444	1544	1644	1744	1844	1944	2044	2144	2144	2244	2244	also	0503	and	2303
19	Berlin Ostbahnhof d.	0503	0603	0703	0803	0903	1003	1103	1203	1303	1403	1503	1603	1703	1803	1903	2003	2103	2203	2203	2305	2305		0526	hourly	2325
24	Berlin Hbf d.	0515	0615	0715	0815	0915	1015	1115	1215	1315	1415	1515	1615	1715	1815	1915	2015	2115	2215	2215	2316	2316		0537	until	2337
28	Berlin Zoo d.	0521	0621	0721	0821	0921	1021	1121	1221	1321	1421	1521	1621	1721	1821	1921	2021	2121	2221	2221	2322	2322		0543		2344
	Berlin Spandau a.	|	|	|	|	|	|	|	|	|	|	|	|	|	|	|	|	|	|	|	|	|		0554		2354
43	Berlin Wannsee d.	0534	0634	0734	0834	0934	1034	1134	1234	1334	1434	1534	1634	1734	1834	1934	2034	2134	2234	2234	2335	2335		...		...
95	Bad Belzig a.	0615	0715	0815	0915	1015	1115	1215	1315	1415	1515	1615	1715	1815	1915	2015	2115	2215	2315	2315	0016	0016		...		...
139	Roßlau (Elbe) 848 a.	0648	0749	0848	0949e	1048	1149e	1248	1349e	1448	1549e	1648	1749e	1848	1949e	2048	2149e	2248	...	2349	...	0048		...		...
144	Dessau Hbf 848 a.	0653	0754	0853	0954e	1053	1154e	1253	1354e	1453	1554e	1653	1754e	1853	1954e	2053	2154e	2253	...	2354	...	0053		...		...

																			B	D	Ⓒ				
Dessau Hbf 848 d.	...	0407e	0507h	0607e	0707	0808e	0907	1008e	1107	1208e	1307	1408e	1507	1608e	1707	1808e	1907	2008e	2107	2217	2217	2317		...		...
Roßlau (Elbe) 848 d.	...	0412e	0512h	0612e	0712	0813e	0912	1013e	1112	1213e	1312	1413e	1512	1613e	1712	1813e	1912	2013e	2112	2222	2222	2322		...		...
Bad Belzig d.	0345e	0445	0545	0645	0745	0845	0945	1045	1145	1245	1345	1445	1545	1645	1745	1845	1945	2045	2145	2254	2254	2354		...		...
Berlin Wannsee d.	0428e	0528	0628	0728	0828	0928	1028	1128	1228	1328	1428	1528	1628	1728	1828	1928	2028	2128	2228	2338	2339	0038		...	▲	...
Berlin Spandau d.	|	|	|	|	|	|	|	|	|	|	|	|	|	|	|	|	|	|	|	|	|	|		0559		2059
Berlin Zoo d.	0443	0541	0641	0741	0841	0941	1041	1141	1241	1341	1441	1541	1641	1741	1841	1941	2041	2141	2241	2353	0001	0054		0610	and	2110
Berlin Hbf d.	0449	0547	0647	0747	0847	0947	1047	1147	1247	1347	1447	1547	1647	1747	1847	1947	2047	2147	2247	2359	0005	0100	also	0616	hourly	2116
Berlin Ostbahnhof d.	0501	0558	0658	0758	0858	0958	1058	1158	1258	1358	1458	1558	1658	1758	1858	1958	2058	2158	2256	0008	...	0109		0627	until	2127
Berlin Schönefeld ✈ a.	0520	0620	0720	0820	0920	1020	1120	1220	1320	1420	1520	1620	1720	1820	1920	2020	2120	2220	...	...	...	...		0648		2148

A – ①②③④⑦ (not Apr. 13, 16, 30, May 24, June 4).
B – ④⑤ (also May 24; not Apr. 14, May 25).
D – ①–③ (not Apr. 17, May 1, 24, June 5).
e – Ⓐ only.
h – ①–⑥ only.
▲ – Berlin Spandau d. 1755 (not 1759).

848 MAGDEBURG - DESSAU - LEIPZIG and HALLE (SAALE)

RE / RB / S-Bahn services

Subject to alteration Dec. 27 - Jan. 6. Late evening services in the Leipzig area (from approx. 2100) are subject to alteration on ①② Jan. 9 - Mar. 14 and ①② from May 15.

km			🚌	Ⓐ e L		🚌		🚌			Ⓐ e	🚌			🚌		🚌				🚌		🚌	
0	Magdeburg Hbf d.	...	...	...	0434	...	...	...	0533r	...	0620	...	0703	...	...	0804	...	0904	and in	...	...	1604	...	1704	...
56	Roßlau (Elbe) 847 d.	...	...	...	0523	...	...	...	0623r	...	0709	...	0746	...	...	0858	...	0946	the same	...	...	1658	...	1746	...
61	Dessau Hbf 847 a.	...	...	...	0526	...	...	...	0627r	...	0714	...	0749	...	...	0901	...	0949	pattern	...	...	1701	...	1749	...
61	Dessau Hbf d.	0445	...	...	0528	...	0606	...	0628	0706	0716	...	0751	0806	...	0906	...	0951	every	1606	...	1706	...	1751	1806
87	Bitterfeld a.	0508	...	...	0551	...	0629	...	0647	0729	0733	...	0808	0829	...	0929	...	1008	two hours	1629	...	1729	...	1808	1829
87	Bitterfeld ▷ d.	0513	0515	0546	...	0556	0631	0635	0648	0731	0735	0735	0809	0831	0835	0931	0935	1009	until	1631	1635	1731	1735	1809	1831
	Halle (Saale) Hbf ▷ a.	|	0555	|	...	0636	|	0715	|	|	0805	0815	|	|	0915	|	1015	|		|	1715	|	1815	|	|
120	Leipzig Hbf a.	0543	...	0613	...	...	0658	...	0713	0758	...	...	0836	0858	...	0958	...	1035		1658	...	1758	...	1835	1858
125	Leipzig-Connewitz a.	0554	...	0626	...	...	0709	...	...	0809	...	...	...	0909	...	1009	...	...		1709	...	1809	...	...	1909

	🚌		🚌		🚌				L				
Magdeburg Hbf d.	...	1804	...	1904	...	2004	...	2104	...	...	2142	...	2314
Roßlau (Elbe) 847 d.	...	1858	...	1946	...	2058	...	2146	...	...	2232	...	0005
Dessau Hbf 847 a.	...	1901	...	1949	...	2104	...	2149	...	...	2236	...	0009
Dessau Hbf d.	...	1906	...	1951	...	2106	...	2150	...	2204	...	2257	▬
Bitterfeld a.	...	1929	...	2008	...	2129	...	2212	...	2227	...	2317	...
Bitterfeld ▷ d.	1835	1931	1935	2009	2035	2131	2135	2213	2219	2237	...	2319	2331
Halle (Saale) Hbf. ▷ a.	1915	|	2015	|	2115	|	2207	|	|	2303	...	|	0005
Leipzig Hbf a.	...	1958	...	2030	...	2158	...	2236	2245	...	...	2343k	...
Leipzig-Connewitz a.	...	2009	...	...	...	2210	...	...	2256	...	...	2355v	...

		Ⓐ e	⚒ r	Ⓐ e				🚌	
Leipzig-Connewitz d.	...	...	...	...	...	...	0553	...	0653
Leipzig Hbf d.	...	...	...	...	0545	...	0603	...	0703
Halle (Saale) Hbf ▷ d.	...	0409	...	0450	|	0554	|	0640	|
Bitterfeld ▷ a.	...	0442	...	0523	0607	0625	0629	0725	0729
Bitterfeld d.	...	0446	...	0535	0608	...	0632	▬	0732
Dessau Hbf a.	...	0510	...	0558	0628	...	0655	...	0755
Dessau Hbf 847 d.	0432	0519	0600	0600	0630	...	...	0700	...
Roßlau (Elbe) 847 d.	0437	0523	0603	0603	0634	...	...	0703	...
Magdeburg Hbf a.	0527	0614	0653	0653	0723	...	...	0755	...

		🚌		🚌				🚌		🚌			🚌		🚌			🚌							
Leipzig-Connewitz d.	...	...	0753	...	0853	...	and in	...	1553	...	1653	...	...	1753	...	1853	...	...	1953	...	...	2107	2207	...	2307
Leipzig Hbf d.	0719	...	0803	...	0903	0919	the same	...	1603	...	1703	1719	...	1803	...	1903	1919	...	2003	...	...	2117	2217	...	2317
Halle (Saale) Hbf. ▷ d.	|	0740	|	0840	|	|	pattern	1540	|	1640	|	|	1740	|	1840	|	|	1940	|	...	2122	|	|	2321	|
Bitterfeld ▷ a.	0745	0825	0829	0925	0929	0945	every	1625	1629	1725	1729	1745	1825	1829	1925	1929	1945	2025	2029	...	2148	2145	2245	2348	2345
Bitterfeld d.	0746	...	0832	...	0932	0946	two hours	...	1632	...	1732	1746	...	1832	...	1932	1946	...	2032	...	...	2151	2249	...	2351
Dessau Hbf a.	0803	...	0855	...	0955	1003	until	...	1655	...	1755	1803	...	1855	...	1955	2003	...	2055	...	...	2212	2312	...	0012
Dessau Hbf 847 d.	0806	...	0900	...	...	1006		...	1700	...	...	1806	...	1900	...	...	2006	...	2057	2100	...	2214	2314	...	...
Roßlau (Elbe) 847 d.	0810	...	0903	...	...	1010		...	1703	...	...	1810	...	1903	...	...	2010	...	2100	2105	...	2218	2317	...	...
Magdeburg Hbf a.	0853	...	0955	...	...	1053		...	1755	...	...	1853	...	1955	...	...	2053	...	...	2155	...	2302	0008	...	...

km		Ⓒ H	Ⓐ e	⚒ r	Ⓐ e	Ⓐ e		Ⓐ e							Ⓐ e			Ⓐ e			Ⓐ e				
0	Falkenberg (Elster) d.	...	...	...	0536	0620	...	...	...	...	...	...	...	...	...	...	...	1608	...	...	1813	...	...	...	2119
54	Lutherstadt Wittenberg d.	0157	0403	0514	0623	0706	0723	0823	0923	1023	1123	1223	1323	1423	1455	1523	1623	1655	1723	1823	1857	1923	2023	...	2205
86	Roßlau (Elbe) d.	|	0432	0545	0653	0734	0753	0853	0953	1053	1153	1253	1353	1453	1522	1553	1653	1722	1753	1853	...	1953	2053	...	2236
91	Dessau Hbf a.	0223	0436	0548	0657	0738	0757	0857	0957	1057	1157	1257	1357	1457	1527	1557	1657	1727	1757	1857	...	1957	2057	...	2240

	Ⓐ e		⚒ r	Ⓐ e		⚒ r		⚒ r					Ⓐ e		Ⓐ e		Ⓐ e							Ⓐ e	Ⓒ z
Dessau Hbf d.	0424	0527	0527	0624	0713	0803	0903	1003	1103	1203	1303	1403	1434	1503	1532	1603	1634	1703	1803	1903	2003	2057	...	2231	2321
Roßlau (Elbe) d.	0429	0532	0532	0629	0718	0807	0907	1007	1107	1207	1307	1407	1439	1507	1537	1607	1639	1707	1807	1907	2007	2101	...	2236	2326
Lutherstadt Wittenberg d.	0500	0601	0603	0658	0749	0837	0937	1037	1137	1237	1337	1437	1506	1537	1602	1637	1706	1737	1837	1937	2037	2131	2136	2306	2356
Falkenberg (Elster) a.	0544	...	0647	...	0833	...	...	...	...	...	...	...	1550	...	...	...	1750	...	...	...	...	...	2220	...	...

km		Ⓒ H			Ⓐ e L	Ⓐ e			◇					Ⓐ e	Ⓒ z						Ⓐ d		L		
	Falkenberg (Elster) d.	...	...	...	...	...	...	0706	...	0906	...	1106	...	...	1306	...	1506	...	1706	...	1906	...	...	...	...
0	Lutherstadt Wittenberg d.	0157	...	0440	0514	0626	0645	0753	0849	0953	1045	1153	1245	1353	1353	1445	1553	1645	1753	1845	1953	2052	2148	...	2245
37	Bitterfeld a.	0239	...	0509	0543	0654	0715	0821	0918	1021	1115	1221	1315	1421	1421	1515	1621	1715	1821	1915	2021	2120	2217	...	2315
67	Halle (Saale) Hbf ▷ a.	0307	...	...	...	...	...	...	...	...	...	...	...	...	...	...	1649e	...	...	...	...	2207	...	...	0005

	Ⓐ e	Ⓒ S							Ⓒ z				Ⓐ			⊙									
Halle (Saale) Hbf ▷ d.	...	0450	...	...	...	...	...	...	...	...	...	...	...	...	...	...	...	...	...	...	2122	...	2321	...	...
Bitterfeld d.	0538	0538	0639	0737	0845	0937	1045	1137	1137	1245	1337	1445	1502	1537	1645	1737	1845	1936	2045	...	2149	2249	2349	...	...
Lutherstadt Wittenberg d.	0608	0610	0710	0807	0917	1007	1117	1207	1207	1325	1407	1517	1526	1607	1723	1807	1917	2007	2136j	...	2219	2319	0019	...	...
Falkenberg (Elster) a.	...	...	...	...	...	1050	...	...	1250	...	1450	...	...	1650	...	1850	...	2050	2220	...	...	...	...	...	...

H – 🚆12 Berlin - Lutherstadt - Dessau - Halle (Table **845**).
L – 🚆12 Lutherstadt Wittenberg - Bitterfeld - Leipzig.
S – To Berlin (also Schwedt until Feb. 5) (Table **845**).
d – Runs daily Dec. 27 - Apr. 21.
e – Ⓐ (not Jan. 6).
j – Arrives 2117.
k – 2347 on ①–④.
r – ⚒ (not Jan. 6).
v – ⑤–⑦ only.
z – Also Jan. 6.
⊙ – Runs 2 minutes later on ⑦ from May 7 (also June 5; not June 4).
◇ – 3–8 minutes earlier to Dec. 26 and from Apr. 18.
▷ – Timings Bitterfeld - Halle and v.v. are valid Jan. 7 - Apr. 17.

GERMANY *See page 367 for a summary of Christmas / New Year alterations*

849 Local services LEIPZIG and HALLE - EISENACH and SAALFELD

Operated by ABELLIO Rail Mitteldeutschland. See Tables **850** and **851** for faster *ICE* and *IC* trains.

Warning! Services on the Halle - Naumburg - Erfurt - Eisenach route are subject to alteration from February 11 (services on the Leipzig - Naumburg - Erfurt / Saalfeld routes are unaffected).

km			Ⓐ		Ⓒ	Ⓐ			A		✣			A					A					⑤⑥	
0	**Halle** (Saale) Hbf .... d.	0424	0526	...	...	...	0624	...	0724	...	...	0824	...	0924		...	1824	...	1924	...	2024	2125	2228	2228	2325
	Leipzig Hbf .... d.	|	0455t	...	0552	0552	|	0652	|	...	0752	|	0852	|	and in	1752	|	1852	|	1952	|	|	2213t	2213t	2307
32	Weißenfels .... d.	0453	0555	...	0629	0629	0654	0729	0754	...	0829	0854	0929	0954	the same	1829	1854	1929	1954	2029	2054	2154	2259	2259	2355
46	Naumburg (Saale) Hbf a.	0503	0606	...	0639	0637	0705	0737	0804	...	0837	0904	0937	1004	pattern	1837	1904	1937	2004	2037	2104	2204	2309	2309	0004
46	Naumburg (Saale) Hbf d.	0505	0607	...	0643	0643	0706	0738	0806	...	0844	0906	0938	1006		1844	1906	1938	2006	2044	2106	2206	2310	2310	0006
72	Apolda .... d.	0527	0628	...	0702	0702	0728	0757	0828	...	0903	0928	0957	1028	every	1903	1928	1957	2028	2103	2128	2228	2331	2331	0029
87	Weimar .... **858** d.	0539	0641	...	0713	0713	0741	0807	0841	0841	0914	0941	1007	1041	**two** hours	1914	1941	2007	2041	2114	2141	2241	2343	2343	0044
108	**Erfurt** Hbf .... **858** a.	0554	0657	...	0728	0728	0756	0821	0857	0857	0930	0956	1021	1057		1930	1956	2022	2057	2127	2156	2256	2358	2358	0059
108	**Erfurt** Hbf .... d.	0555	0700	0700	...	...	0800	...	0900	0900	...	1000	...	1100	until	...	2000	...	2100	...	2218	2318	...	0010	...
136	Gotha .... d.	0617	0721	0721	...	...	0825	...	0921	0921	...	1025	...	1121		...	2025	...	2127	...	2242	2340	...	0032	...
165	**Eisenach** .... a.	0640	0744	0744	...	...	0846	...	0944	0944	...	1046	...	1144		...	2047	...	2149	...	2304	0002	...	0054	...

	Ⓐ	Ⓐ				Ⓐ		Ⓐ				A					A			⊖	Ⓐ				
Eisenach .... d.	0410	...	...	0502	...	0608	0646	0711	...	...	...	0813	...	0911	and in	...	1813	...	1911	...	2013	2013	2113	...	2219
Gotha .... d.	0435	...	...	0525	...	0631	0713	0733	...	...	...	0835	...	0933		...	1835	...	1933	...	2035	2035	2135	...	2241
Erfurt Hbf .... a.	0456	...	...	0548	...	0653	0735	0756	...	...	...	0858	...	0956	the same	...	1858	...	1956	...	2058	2058	2158	...	2304
Erfurt Hbf .... **858** d.	0458	...	0531	0601	0620	0701	0737	0801	0801	...	0831	0901	0937	1001		1831	1901	1937	2001	2033	2101	...	2201	...	2314
Weimar .... **858** d.	0514	...	0545	0618	0633	0718	0751	0818	0818	...	0844	0918	0951	1018	pattern	1845	1918	1951	2018	2046	2118	...	2218	...	2331
Apolda .... d.	0525	...	0555	0629	0643	0729	0801	0829	0829	...	0854	0929	1001	1029	every	1856	1929	2001	2029	2056	2129	...	2229	...	2342
Naumburg (Saale) Hbf a.	0545	...	0615	0650	0701	0751	0818	0850	0850	...	0913	0950	1018	1050	**two** hours	1913	1950	2018	2050	2120	2150	...	2253	...	0003
Naumburg (Saale) Hbf d.	0546	...	0616	0652	0724	0752	0819	0852	0852	...	0920	0952	1019	1052		1920	1952	2019	2052	2122	2152	...	2255	...	0004
Weißenfels .... d.	0556	0604	0626	0702	0734	0802	0829	0902	0902	...	0929	1002	1029	1102	until	1929	2002	2029	2102	2133	2202	...	2305	2317	0014
Leipzig Hbf .... a.	|	0640	0705g	|	0810	|	0904	|	|	...	1004	|	1104	|		2004	|	2104	|	2208	|	...	|	2354	|
Halle (Saale) Hbf .... a.	0621	...	0655	0733	...	0833	...	0933	0933	...	...	1033	...	1133		...	2033	...	2133	...	2235	...	2336	...	0043

LEIPZIG / HALLE - JENA - SAALFELD

km			N	Ⓐ		N	z			N		z			N	z			N	z					x
0	**Leipzig** Hbf .... d.	...	...	0552	...	...	...	0752	...	...		...	1552	...	...	...	1752	...	...	...	1952	2052	2213	..	2307
	Halle (Saale) Hbf .... d.	0424y	...	|	0624x	...	0747	|	0847z	...	and in	1547	|	1647n	...	1747	|	1847z	...	1947	|	|	|	2228k	2325
40	Weißenfels .... d.	0453	...	0629	0654x	...	0810	0829	0910z	...	the same	1610	1629	1710n	...	1810	1829	1910z	...	2010	2029	2129	2250	2259	2355
56	Naumburg (Saale) Hbf a.	0503	...	0637	0705x	...	0821	0837	0921z	...		1621	1637	1721n	...	1821	1837	1921z	...	2021	2037	2137	...	2309	0004
56	Naumburg (Saale) Hbf d.	0505	...	0638	0711	...	...	0838	0931	...	pattern	...	1638	1731	...	...	1838	1931	...	...	2038	2138	...	2315	0006
	Großheringen .... d.	0520	...	|	|	...	...	|	|	...	every	...	|	|	...	...	|	|	...	...	|	|	...	|	0020
95	**Jena** Paradies ... **875** d.	0544	0618	0711	0743	0818	...	0911	1003	1018	**two** hours	...	1711	1803	1818	...	1911	2003	2018	...	2111	2211	...	2348	0044
100	Jena-Göschwitz .. **875** d.	0549	0622	0716	0759	0822	...	0916	1008	1022		...	1716	1808	1822	...	1916	2008	2022	...	2116	2221	...	2353	0049
132	Rudolstadt (Thür) **875** d.	0615	0644	0742	0827	0844	...	0942	1035	1044	until	...	1742	1835	1844	...	1942	2035	2044	...	2142	2247	...	0019	...
142	**Saalfeld** (Saale) . **875** a.	0625	0651	0751	0836	0851	...	0951	1044	1051		...	1751	1844	1851	...	1951	2044	2051	...	2151	2256	...	0028	...

	Ⓐ		z		z		M		z	N				z	N			z	N			N		z	
Saalfeld (Saale) ... **875** d.	0431	0451‡	...	0609	...	0646	0659	0807	...	0906	0911		1607	...	1706	1711	1807	...	1908	1912	2000	2106	2123v	...	2243
Rudolstadt (Thür) . **875** d.	0440	0500‡	...	0618	...	0655	0707	0816	...	0913	0920	and in	1616	...	1713	1720	1816	...	1915	1921	2009	2113	2132v	...	2252
Jena-Göschwitz ... **875** d.	0502	0526‡	...	0644	...	0722	0729	0842	...	0935	0947	the same	1642	...	1735	1747	1842	...	1937	1948	2035	2135	2210	...	2319
Jena Paradies ..... **875** d.	0507	0531‡	...	0651	...	0727	0734	0847	...	0939	0952		1647	...	1739	1752	1847	...	1941	1953	2040	2139	2216	...	2325
Großheringen .... a.	|	|	...	|	...	|	—	|	...	...	|	pattern	|	...	...	|	|	...	...	|	2104	...	2240	2244	2350
Naumburg (Saale) Hbf a.	0539	0602‡	...	0722	...	0812	z	0918	...	...	1025	every	1718	...	...	1825	1918	...	...	2025	2120	...	...	2253	0003
Naumburg (Saale) Hbf d.	0551	0612	0616	0724	0738	0819	0838	0920	0938	...	1038z		1720	1738	...	1838z	1920	1938	...	2052z	2122	...	...	2255	0004
Weißenfels .... d.	0601	0621	0626	0734	0747	0829	0847	0929	0947	...	1047z	**two** hours	1729	1747	...	1847z	1929	1947	...	2102z	2133	...	...	2305	0014
Halle (Saale) Hbf ..... a.	|	|	0655	|	0812	|	0912	|	1012	...	1112z	until	|	1812	...	1912z	|	2012	...	2133z	|	...	...	2336	0043z
Leipzig Hbf .... a.	0640	0705	...	0810	...	0904	...	1004	...	...	...		1804	...	...	...	2004	...	...	...	2208	...	...	2354t	...

EISENACH - BEBRA Journey time: 34 – 47 minutes. Operated by CANTUS Verkehrsgesellschaft (2nd class only).

TO MARCH 10 AND FROM MAY 23:

From Eisenach at 0436 Ⓐ, 0530 Ⓐ, 0613 ⚒, 0713 ⚒, 0813, 0903 ⚒ **Q**, 0914 ⚒ **R**, 1014, 1114 Ⓐ, 1214, 1303 Ⓐ **Q**, 1314 Ⓐ **R**, 1414, 1503 Ⓐ **Q**, 1514 Ⓐ **R**, 1614, 1703 Ⓐ **Q**, 1714 Ⓐ **R**, 1814 1903 Ⓐ **Q**, 1914 Ⓐ **R**, 2014, 2114 Ⓐ and 2214 Ⓒ.

From Bebra at 0504 Ⓐ, 0559 ⑥, 0604 Ⓐ, 0659 Ⓐ, 0704 Ⓒ, 0723 Ⓐ, 0804 ⑥, 0904, 1004 Ⓐ, 1104, 1204 Ⓐ, 1304 Ⓒ, 1315 Ⓐ, 1404 Ⓐ, 1507, 1604 Ⓐ, 1704, 1804 Ⓐ, 1904, 2004 Ⓐ and 2104

MARCH 11 - MAY 22:

From Eisenach at 0434 Ⓐ, 0530 Ⓐ, 0611 **S**, 0706 Ⓐ, 0711 ⑥, 0813, 0912 ⚒, 1014, 1112 Ⓐ, 1214, 1312 Ⓐ, 1414, 1512 Ⓐ, 1614, 1712 Ⓐ, 1814, 1912 Ⓐ, 2014, 2114 Ⓐ and 2214 Ⓒ.

From Bebra at 0504 Ⓐ, 0559 ⑥ ¶, 0609 **T**, 0659 Ⓐ ¶, 0709 Ⓒ, 0723 Ⓐ ¶, 0809 ⑥, 0909, 1009 Ⓐ, 1107, 1209 Ⓐ, 1309, 1409 Ⓐ, 1509, 1609 Ⓐ, 1709, 1807 Ⓐ, 1909, 2009 Ⓐ and 2109.

A – ①–⑤ (also Dec. 17; not Dec. 26); runs daily Weimar - Eisenach and v.v.
M – From Bamberg (Table **875**).
N – To / from Nürnberg (Table **875**).
Q – To Feb. 10.
R – From Feb. 11.
S – ②–⑥ (not Apr. 14, 18, May 2).
T – ②–⑤ (not Apr. 14, 18, May 2).

g – Change trains at Großkorbetha (a. 0631, d. 0635).

k – Departs 2210 Mar. 26 - May 20.
n – Not Mar. 26 - May 20. On ⑤⑦ to Feb. 10 (also Dec. 26; not Dec. 25) departs Halle 1642, Weißenfels 1712, arrives Naumburg a. 1721.
r – 0648 on †.
t – Change trains at Weißenfels.
v – 10 minutes later on ①②③④⑥ (also Dec. 25, Apr. 14, 16, 30, May 26, June 4; not Dec. 26, Apr. 13, 17, May 1, 24, June 5).
x – Not Mar. 26 - May 20.
y – Departs 0405 Mar. 27 - May 21.

z – Subject to alteration Mar. 26 - May 20 (journey time extended by up to 37 minutes; earlier departures possible).

‡ – 9 minutes later on Ⓒ.
¶ – Extended journey: 50 – 61 minutes.
⊖ – Change trains at Großheringen (a. 2105, d. 2110).
✣ – Timings of subsequent trains may vary by up to 4 minutes Naumburg - Erfurt.

850 BERLIN and LEIPZIG - ERFURT - KASSEL and FRANKFURT

Other regional services: Table **845** Berlin - Lutherstadt Wittenberg. Table **848** Lutherstadt Wittenberg - Halle. Table **849** Leipzig / Halle - Erfurt - Eisenach - Bebra.

SERVICE UNTIL MARCH 10 (see page 561 for service from March 11). *Subject to alteration – see engineering work panel on page 367.*

km		IC	IC		ICE		ICE	IC	ICE	IC		ICE	ICE	ICE	ICE	ICE	ICE	ICE		ICE	ICE		ICE	IC
		1950	**1950**		**1646**		**1656**	**2156**	**1644**	**2156**		**1654**	**1636**	**1642**	**1734**	**1652**	**1634**	**1640**		**1650**	**1632**		**1548**	**2152**
	SEE NOTE ⊠	①	Ⓐ		Ⓐ		①–⑥	①–⑥	①–⑥	①–⑥			①–⑤				⑥⑦							
			d		⊙			**X**		**X**					**R**		**X**							**X**
					✗		✗	**P**	✗	**P**		✗	✗	✗	✗	✗	✗	✗		✗	✗		✗	**U**
	Berlin Hbf .... **851 902** d.	0029	...	...	...	...	...	...	...	...	...	...	0659	...	0815	...	0900	...	...	...	1100	...	...	...
	Berlin Südkreuz .... **851** d.	0036	...	...	...	...	...	...	...	...	...	...	0707	...	0822	...	0907	...	...	...	1107	...	...	...
	Lutherstadt Wittenberg ... **851** d.	0113	...	...	...	...	...	...	...	...	...	...	|	...	|	...	|	...	...	...	|	...	...	...
	Bitterfeld .... **851** d.	0129	...	...	...	...	...	...	...	...	...	...	|	...	|	...	|	...	...	...	|	...	...	...
	Halle (Saale) Hbf .... **851** d.	0154	...	...	...	...	...	0552	...	...	...	...	0814	...	0932	...	1014	...	...	...	1214	...	...	...
	Dresden Hbf **842** .... d.	|	...	...	...	...	...	|	...	...	...	0613e	|	...	|	0813	|	...	...	1013	|	...	...	...
0	**Leipzig** Hbf .... **851** d.	0238	...	...	0425	...	0529	|	0631	...	...	0729	|	0835	|	0929	|	1035	...	1129	|	...	1235	1201
	Naumburg (Saale) Hbf .... d.	|	...	...	|	...	|	0630	|	...	...	|	|	|	|	|	|	|	...	|	|	...	|	1244
	Weimar .... d.	0336	...	...	|	...	|	0657	|	←	...	|	|	|	|	|	|	|	...	|	|	...	|	1312
120	**Erfurt** Hbf .... d.	0353	...	...	0514	...	0618	0710	0716	0725	...	0818	0849	0920	1005	1018	1049	1120	...	1218	1249	...	1320	1327
147	Gotha .... d.	0408	...	...	0531	...	0635	→	0733	0743	...	0835	|	|	...	1035	|	|	...	1235	|	...	|	1343
176	**Eisenach** .... d.	0426	...	...	0549	...	0651	...	0749	0758	...	0851	|	0949	...	1051	|	1149	...	1251	|	...	1349	1359
	Bebra .... **901** d.	0500	0500	...	|	...	|	...	|	0822	...	|	|	|	...	|	|	|	...	|	|	...	|	1423
	Kassel Wilhelmshöhe. **901** a.	|	|	...	|	...	|	...	|	0857	...	|	|	|	...	|	|	|	...	|	|	...	|	1458
233	Bad Hersfeld .... **901** d.	0511	0511	...	0618	...	|	...	0818	...	...	|	|	1018	...	|	|	1218	...	|	|	...	1418	...
275	Fulda .... **900/1/2** d.	0541	0541	...	0645	...	0744	...	0845	...	...	0944	|	1045	...	1144	|	1245	...	1344	|	...	1445	...
356	Hanau Hbf .... **900/1/2** d.	0624	0624	...	|	...	|	...	|	...	...	|	|	|	...	|	|	|	...	|	|	...	|	...
375	**Frankfurt** (Main) Süd .... a.	|	|	...	0737	...	|	...	0937	...	...	|	|	1137	...	|	|	1337	...	|	|	...	1537	...
379	**Frankfurt** (Main) Hbf **900/1/2** a.	0642	0642	...	|	...	0837	...	|	...	...	1037	1056	|	...	1237	1256	|	...	1437	1456	...	|	...
	Frankfurt Flughafen ✈ § ... a.	...	...	...	0751	...	0855	...	0949	...	...	1055	...	1149	...	1255	...	1349	...	1455	...	...	1549	...
	Wiesbaden Hbf **911** .... a.	...	...	...	...	...	0933	...	...	...	...	1133	...	...	...	1333	...	...	...	1533	...	...	...	...

FOR NOTES SEE NEXT PAGE →

398 *German national public holidays are on Dec. 25, 26, Jan. 1, Apr. 14, 17, May 1, 25, June 5 and Oct. 3* 12

BERLIN and LEIPZIG - ERFURT - KASSEL and FRANKFURT   850

Other regional services: Table 845 Berlin - Lutherstadt Wittenberg. Table 848 Lutherstadt Wittenberg - Halle. Table 849 Leipzig / Halle - Erfurt - Eisenach - Bebra.
SERVICE UNTIL MARCH 10 (see page 561 for service from March 11)

SEE NOTE ⊠	ICE 1730	ICE 1558	ICE 1630	ICE 1546	IC 1956	ICE 1556	ICE 1538	IC 1958	ICE 1544	IC 1962	ICE 1952	ICE 1594	ICE 1554	ICE 1536	ICE 1542	ICE 1552	ICE 1572	ICE 1534	IC 1938	ICE 1717	ICE 1550	EN 471
			⑤–⑦		⑥			⑧		⑤⑦	⑤⑦		⑥		⑤	⑤	⑦				⑦	ᴿ
	G		X		M			X			V		U	U	S	T	K	K		H X		A
	✕	✕	✕	✕	✕	✕	✕		✕		✕	⊤¶▯			✕		✕	✕		H✕	✕	
Berlin Hbf .... 851 902 d.	1215	...	1300	...	...	1500	...	...	1500	1534	...	...	1700	...	...	...	1903	1903	1927	...	...	2259
Berlin Südkreuz .... 851 d.	1222	...	1307	...	...	1507	...	...	1507	1541	...	...	1707	...	...	...	1911	1911	1934	...	...	2307
Lutherstadt Wittenberg .... 851 d.									1545	1619									2009			
Bitterfeld .... 851 d.																			2026			
Halle (Saale) Hbf .... 851 d.	1333	...	1414	...	...	1614	...	...	1636	1648	...	...	1814	...	...	2017	2022	...	...	...	0022
Dresden Hbf 842 ....d.	...	1213	...	...	1413	...	...	...	...	1613h	1613	...	...	1813	...	...	...	2013	...	
Leipzig Hbf .... 851 d.	...	1329	...	1435	1407	1529	...	1538	1635	...	1729	1729	...	1835	1941	1941	...	...	2051	2133	
Naumburg (Saale) Hbf ....d.					1451			...		1718										0051
Weimar ....d.					1517			1650		1746										
Erfurt Hbf ....d.	1406	1418	1449	1520	1531	1618	1648	1710	1720	...	1801	1818	1818	1849	1920	2026	2026	2052	...	2139	2218	0130
Gotha ....d.	...	1435	...	...	1547	1635	...	1728	...	...	1817	1835	1835	...	...	2043	2043	2108X	...	2154	2235	
Eisenach ....d.	...	1451	...	1549	1603	1651	...	1744	1749	...	1832	1851	1851	...	1949	2059	2059	2122X	...	2210	2252	
Bebra .... 901 d.											1903									
Kassel Wilhelmshöhe . 901 a.											1929	1940								
Bad Hersfeld .... 901 a.				1618				1818							2018					
Fulda .... 900/1/2 d.	...	1544	...	1645	1659	1744	...	1837	1845	...	...	1944	1944	...	2045	2158	2158	...	...	2344	0300
Hanau Hbf .... 900/1/2 d.								1915							2125	2239	2239			
Frankfurt (Main) Süd ....a.				1737				1929							2138					0359
Frankfurt (Main) Hbf . 900/1/2 a.	...	1637	1656	...	1752	1837	1856	...	1940	...	...	2036	2036	2056	...	2254	2254	...	...	0037	...
Frankfurt Flughafen ✈ § ....a.			1655		1749		1855		1949				2057			2149				
Wiesbaden Hbf 911 ....a.			1733				1933						2133							

km	SEE NOTE ⊠	EN 470	ICE 1531	ICE 1716	ICE 1731	ICE 1553	ICE 1553		ICE 1626	ICE 1543	ICE 1533	IC 1937	ICE 1555	ICE 1545	ICE 1535	ICE 1557	ICE 1597	ICE 1735	ICE 1547	ICE 1537	ICE 1559	IC 2155	ICE 1549
		ᴿ	Ⓐ	Ⓐ	⑥	①	①–⑥		⑦	①–⑥	♣	⑥			⑥⑦	①–⑤							
		B	¶		J									X	S	⊤○	R		K		X	
			¶	✕	T✕	✕	✕		H✕	✕	✕	○	✕	✕	✕	✕	✕	✕	✕	✕	U	✕
	Wiesbaden Hbf 911 ....d.	...	...	...	...	...	...		...	...	0811		...	...	0824z	...	...	1024	...	...	
0	Frankfurt Flughafen ✈ § ..d.	...	...	...	...	0458	...		...	0617	0702	...	0718	...	0901	...	1011	...	1101	...	1211
11	Frankfurt (Main) Süd ......d.	0054	...	...	...	...	...		...	...	...	...	0822	...	0902	0919	0919	...	1102	1119	...	1222
	Hanau Hbf .... 900/1/2 d.								0633									1022			
	Fulda .... 900/1/2 d.	0209	...	...	...	0554	...		...	0714	...	...	0814	0914	...	1014	1014	...	1114	...	1214	...	1314
	Bad Hersfeld .... 901 d.					0621			0740				0940					1140			1340
0	Kassel Wilhelmshöhe . 901 d.																		1259		
54	Bebra .... 901 d.																		1335		
99	Eisenach ....d.	...	...	0550t	0640X	0651	0651		0754t	0809	...	...	0907	1009	...	1107	1107	...	1209	...	1307	1400	1409
128	Gotha ....d.	...	...	0609t	0655X	0708	0707		0810t	...	...	...	0923	...	...	1123	1123	...	...	1323	...	...	
155	Erfurt Hbf ....d.	0339	...	0627	0712	0727	0727		0827	0839	0912	...	0939	1037	1112	1139	1139	1146	1239	1312	1339	1428	1439
	Weimar ....a.																		1440		
	Naumburg (Saale) Hbf ....a.	0414																		1508	
	Leipzig Hbf .... 851 a.	...	...	0709	...	0810	0810		0910	0923	...	...	1022	1123	...	1222	1222	...	1323	...	1422	1551	1523
	Dresden Hbf 842 ....a.					0935	0935			...	...	1135		...	...	1335	1337j	...	1535		
249	Halle (Saale) Hbf .... 851 a.	...	...	0646	...	0748	...		...	0948	0948	...	...	1148	...	1222	...	1348	...	
279	Bitterfeld .... 851 a.	0510																	
316	Lutherstadt Wittenberg .. 851 a.	...	...	...	0748				0948											
406	Berlin Südkreuz .... 851 a.	0559	...	0754	0822	0854			...	1022	...	1054	1054	...	1254	...	1340	...	1454	...	
414	Berlin Hbf .... 851 902 a.	0606	...	0801	0829	0901			...	1030	...	1101	1102	...	1301	...	1347	...	1501	...	

SEE NOTE ⊠	ICE 1539	ICE 1651	ICE 1739	IC 1959	IC 1969	ICE 1641	IC 1955	ICE 1631	ICE 1653	IC 1957	ICE 1643	ICE 2398	ICE 1633	ICE 1655	ICE 2157	ICE 1645	IC 2157	ICE 2157	ICE 1635	ICE 1657	ICE 1647	ICE 1659	ICE 1659
	⑤–⑦			⑤⑦	⑤⑦		⑤					①–④			⑧		⑧	⑧				⑧	⑦
	X		Q	V	U		X			X		m			X		P		X	V	X		
	✕	✕	✕	U	U	✕		✕		✕		✕		✕	P	✕	P		✕	✕	✕	✕	✕
Wiesbaden Hbf 911 ....d.	...	1224	...	...	...	...	1424	...	...	...	1624	...	...	...	...	1824	...	2024	2024	2024
Frankfurt Flughafen ✈ § ....d.	...	1301	...	...	1411	...	1501	...	1610	...	1701	...	1811	...	...	1901	...	2101	2102	2102
Frankfurt (Main) Hbf . 900/1/2 d.	1302	1319	...	...	1417	1502	1520	1546	...	1617	1702	1720	...	...	1902	1919	2022	2119	2119	2119
Frankfurt (Main) Süd ....d.	...	...	...	1422	...	...	...	1622	...	...	1822	...	...	2038	...	
Hanau Hbf .... 900/1/2 d.	...	...	...	1438	...	...	1641	...	...	...	...	...	
Fulda .... 900/1/2 d.	...	1414	...	1514	1525	1614	1658	1714	1723	...	1814	...	1914	...	2014	2118	2214	2214	2214
Bad Hersfeld .... 901 d.				1540			1725	1740	1753			1940			2144	2239	2239	2239
Kassel Wilhelmshöhe . 901 d.	...	...	1419	1425	...	...	...	...	1859	...	1909		
Bebra .... 901 d.			1503				1803		1935			
Eisenach ....d.	...	1507	1527	1609	...	1707	1754	1809	...	1907	1959	2009	...	2107	2215	2309	2309	2309
Gotha ....d.	...	1523	1542	...	1633	...	1723	1809	...	1923	2015	2027	←	2123	2230	2325	2325	2325
Erfurt Hbf ....d.	1512	1539	1546	1557	1639	1656	1712	1739	1826	1841	1912	1939	2030	2043	2046	2114	2139	2250	2341	2343	2343
Weimar ....a.	...	...	1611	...	1709	...	1838	...	2058	...	→	
Naumburg (Saale) Hbf ....a.	...	...	1641	...	1739	...	1907	...	2136		
Leipzig Hbf .... 851 a.	...	1622	...	1723	1822	...	1822	1943	1925	...	2022	2123‡	...	2222‡	2340	...	0026	0026
Dresden Hbf 842 ....a.	...	1735	...	1935	...	2135	...	2342b	...	0135
Halle (Saale) Hbf .... 851 d.	1548	...	1622	1716	1716	...	1748	...	...	1948	...	2206	2206	2150		
Bitterfeld .... 851 d.				1757									
Lutherstadt Wittenberg .. 851 d.	...	...	...	...	1748	...	...	...	...	...	2255	...	
Berlin Südkreuz .... 851 a.	1654	...	1734	1835	1854	...	1854	...	...	2054	...	2255	...	
Berlin Hbf .... 851 902 a.	1701	...	1741	1843	1903	...	1901	...	...	2102	...	2303	...	

A – ÖBB nitejtet. ⎚ 1, 2 cl., ⎚ 2 cl. and ⎌ Hamburg Hbf (d. 2052) - Berlin - Basel - Zürich.
B – ÖBB nitejtet. ⎚ 1, 2 cl., ⎚ 2 cl. and ⎌ Zürich - Basel - Berlin - Hamburg Hbf (a. 0831).
H – From / to Hamburg (Table 840).
J – Not Mar. 9. From Jena (Table 851). From Jan. 9 arrives Berlin Südkreuz 0829, Berlin Hbf 0837.
K – To / from Stuttgart on dates in Table 912.
M – To Karlsruhe (Table 912).
P – ⎌ Halle - Kassel - Hamm - Köln and v.v.
Q – ①–④ (daily Feb. 11 - Mar. 10).
R – Ⓐ (daily Feb. 6 - Mar. 10).
S – To / from Saarbrücken (Table 919).
T – From / to Seebad Binz and Stralsund on dates in Tables 844 and 845.
U – To / from Düsseldorf (Tables 800/805).
V – From Feb. 12.
X – Until Feb. 10.

b – ⑧ to Jan. 8; ③④⑤⑦ from Jan. 11.
d – Not Dec. 27 - 30.
e – ①–⑥ only.
h – ⑥ only.
j – ⑦ only.
m – Not Dec. 26 - 29.
t – 5 - 10 minutes earlier from Feb. 12.
z – ⑥ only.

‡ – Arrives up to 36 minutes later on ①② from Jan. 9.
♣ – From Darmstadt Hbf (d. 0637).
◨ – Conveys ✕ on ⑥.
◗ – Conveys ✕ on ⑦.
○ – Also calls at Leipzig/Halle Flughafen (d. 0438).
⊠ – **WARNING!** Berlin timings may vary by up to 25 minutes Jan. 7 - Feb. 10 (earlier departures / later arrivals possible; certain trains may not call at Berlin Südkreuz or Lutherstadt Wittenberg). All timings are subject to alteration Feb. 11 - Mar. 10 with earlier departures / later arrivals possible (please confirm timings locally). Timings at Frankfurt Flughafen, Frankfurt (Main) Hbf and Hanau are subject to alteration on ⑥⑦ Feb. 11 - Apr. 2 (also Apr. 14 - 17). See also engineering work panel on page 367.
§ – Frankfurt Flughafen Fernbahnhof.

See page 367 for a summary of Christmas / New Year alterations

851 BERLIN - LEIPZIG - SAALFELD - NÜRNBERG

Other regional services: Table 835 Berlin - Lutherstadt Wittenberg. Table 848 Lutherstadt Wittenberg - Leipzig. Table 849 Leipzig / Halle - Saalfeld.

Timings at München and Ingolstadt may vary by up to 10 minutes from March 6.

km		ICE 985 Ⓐr	ICE 1501 Ⓐt	ICE 705 ⑥h	ICE 1503 Ⓐ	ICE 1505 e	ICE 1005 ①–⑥☐	IC 2355 KⓇ	ICE 1509	ICE 1609	ICE 1511	IC 2301 R	ICE 1513 S	ICE 1613	ICE 1515	ICE 1715 ⑦b O	ICE 1615 Ⓑq	ICE 1615 ⑤⑦	ICE 1615 u
	Berlin Gesundbrunnen d.				0416	0619	0718		0920				1319			1617y	1718	1718	1718
	Hamburg Hbf 840 d.							0636n		0836j	0938	1036			1338A	1436			
0	Berlin Hbf 850 d.			0427	0427	0627	0730	0828	0930	1027	1130	1227	1330	1427	1530	1628	1730	1730	1730
6	Berlin Südkreuz 850 d.			0434	0434	0634	0737	0835	0937	1034	1137	1234	1337	1434	1537	1635	1737	1737	1737
97	Lutherstadt Wittenberg 850 d.			0509	0509	0709	0812	0909	1012	1109	1212	1309	1412	1509	1612	1709	1812	1812	1812
134	Bitterfeld 850 d.			0526	0526			0926		1126		1326							
	Halle (Saale) Hbf d.																		
167	Leipzig Hbf a.			0543	0543	0743	0843	0943	1043	1143	1243	1343	1443	1543	1643	1743	1843	1843	1843
167	Leipzig Hbf 850 d.			0548	0548	0748	0848	0948	1048	1148	1248	1348	1448	1548	1648	1748	1848	1848	1848
221	Naumburg (Saale) Hbf 850 d.			0626	0626	0826	0926	1026	1126	1226	1326	1426	1526	1626	1726	1826	1926	1926	1926
260	Jena Paradies d.			0651	0651	0851	0951	1051	1151	1251	1351	1451	1551	1651	1751	1851	1951	1951	1951
307	Saalfeld (Saale) 875 d.			0723	0723			1024		1224		1424		1624		1824	2022		2024
394	Lichtenfels 875 d.		0627	0828	0828		1028	1228		1428		1628		1828		2028			2131
426	Bamberg 875 d.		0645	0846	0846	1046	1148	1246	1346	1446	1548	1646	1748	1846	1948	2046	2046		2148
464	Erlangen 875 d.	0607	0709	0909	0909	1109		1309		1509		1709		1909		2109			2210
488	Nürnberg Hbf 875 a.	0625	0725	0925	0925	1124	1223	1324	1423	1525	1623	1724	1823	1924	2023	2124	2124		2226
	Ingolstadt Hbf 904 a.	0659	0800	1000	1000					1559						2159	2159		2301
	Augsburg Hbf 905 a.					1334‡		1534‡		1744*		1944*			2145*				2342
	München Hbf 904 905 a.	0737	0841	1039	1039	1243	1416‡	1446	1606‡	1638	1815*	1838	2016*	2043	2220	2239	2239		2342

	ICE 1517 Ⓑ	ICE 1517 ⑥	ICE 1717 EⒶ	ICE 1617 ⑤⑦w		ICE 903 Ⓑq	ICE 805	ICE 1701 ⑤⑦
Berlin Gesundbrunnen d.			1717					
Hamburg Hbf 840 d.	1636	1636	1735	1735		1836	1938	2036
Berlin Hbf 850 d.	1827	1827	1927	1927		2027	2130	2227
Berlin Südkreuz 850 d.	1834	1834	1934	1934		2034	2137	2234
Lutherstadt Wittenberg 850 d.	1909	1909	2009	2009		2109	2212	2309
Bitterfeld 850 d.	1926	1926	2026	2026		2126	2230	2326
Halle (Saale) Hbf d.								
Leipzig Hbf a.	1943	1943	2044	2044		2143z	2248z	2349
Leipzig Hbf 850 d.	1948	1948		2048				
Naumburg (Saale) Hbf 850 d.	2026	2026		2126				
Jena Paradies d.	2051	2051		2151				
Saalfeld (Saale) 875 d.	2123	2123		2224				
Lichtenfels 875 d.	2228	2228		2331				
Bamberg 875 d.	2246	2246		2350				
Erlangen 875 d.	2309	2309		0012				
Nürnberg Hbf 875 d.	2324	2324		0028				
Ingolstadt Hbf 904 a.	0006	0010		0103				
Augsburg Hbf 905 a.								
München Hbf 904 905 a.	0044	0048		0143				

	ICE 1618 ①–⑤①–⑥ ⒶⒸ	ICE 908 Ⓐ	ICE 1531	ICE 1531 Ⓐ	ICE 1716 Ⓑ①–⑥ gE	ICE 906 KⓍ	ICE 1616 D	ICE 1616 T	ICE 1616 ①–⑥	ICE 1626 ⑦b EⓍ
München Hbf 904 905 d.										
Augsburg Hbf 905 d.										
Ingolstadt Hbf 904 d.										
Nürnberg Hbf 875 d.							0531			
Erlangen 875 d.							0547			
Bamberg 875 d.							0610			
Lichtenfels 875 d.							0628			
Saalfeld (Saale) 875 d.							0736	0736		
Jena Paradies d.			0502	0542			0809	0809		
Naumburg (Saale) Hbf 850 d.			0532	0607			0834	0834		
Leipzig Hbf a.	0510	0615					0910	0910		
Leipzig Hbf 850 d.	0510	0615			0715	0815	0915	0915	0915	0915
Halle (Saale) Hbf d.			0646	0646						
Bitterfeld 850 d.	0532	0634					0834			
Lutherstadt Wittenberg 850 d.	0548	0652			0748	0852	0948	0948	0948	0948
Berlin Südkreuz 850 a.	0622	0726	0754	0754	0822	0926	1022	1022	1022	1022
Berlin Hbf 850 a.	0629	0733	0801	0801	0829	0933	1030	1030	1030	1030
Hamburg Hbf 840 a.	0824	0924					1124	1221	1221	1221 1221
Berlin Gesundbrunnen a.						0842				

	ICE 1514 ①–⑤ aⓍ	ICE 1514 Ⓑq	ICE 1524 ⑥k SⓍ		ICE 1614	ICE 1512	IC 2300 RⓉ	ICE 1510	ICE 1610	ICE 1508	IC 2356 RⓉ	ICE 1206 KⓍ	ICE 704 A vⓍ	ICE 804	ICE 1504	ICE 1604	ICE 1604 ⑤f m	ICE 1002 ①–④–⑤ pⓉ	ICE 1000 vⓍ	ICE 1602		ICE 1500	ICE 1500 ⑤⑦ dⓍ
München Hbf 904 905 d.	0515		0515		0538●		0718	0739§	0918	0920‡	1117	1139	1317	1420	1420	1516	1618	1618	1640	1716	1739¶	1922	1922
Augsburg Hbf 905 d.					0612●			0814§	1022◊		1214						1714x			1813¶			
Ingolstadt Hbf 904 d.	0552		0552			0756		0956				1459	1459	1657	1657					2000	2000		
Nürnberg Hbf 875 d.	0630	0630		0734		0831	0934	1031	1134	1231	1334	1431	1534	1534	1631	1736	1736	1833	1833	1935		2034	2034
Erlangen 875 d.	0646	0646				0848		1048		1248		1448		1648		1848	1848					2049	2049
Bamberg 875 d.	0707	0707		0809		0909	1009	1109	1209	1309	1409	1509	1609	1609	1709	1809	1809	1909	1909	2009		2109	2109
Lichtenfels 875 d.	0733	0733				0931		1131		1331		1531		1731		1931	1931					2131	2131
Saalfeld (Saale) 875 d.	0838	0838		0936		1136		1336		1536		1736	1736	1936	1936	2038	2038		2136			2238	2238
Jena Paradies d.	0908	0908		1008		1108	1208	1308	1408	1508	1608	1708	1808	1808	1908	2009	2009	2108	2108	2208		2308	2308
Naumburg (Saale) Hbf 850 d.	0934	0934		1034		1134	1234	1334	1434	1534	1634	1734	1834	1834	1934	2034	2034	2134	2134	2234		2334	2334
Leipzig Hbf a.	1010	1010		1110		1210	1310	1410	1510	1610	1710	1810	1910	1910	2010	2110	2110	2210	2210	2308		0010	0010
Leipzig Hbf 850 d.	1015	1015	1015		1115	1215	1315	1415	1515	1615	1715	1815	1915	1915	2015	2115‡	2115	2215‡	2215	2314			0015
Halle (Saale) Hbf d.																							
Bitterfeld 850 d.	1034	1034	1034			1234		1434		1634		1834						2234‡					0034
Lutherstadt Wittenberg 850 d.	1052	1052	1052		1148	1252	1348	1452	1548	1652	1748	1852	1948	1948	2052	2148‡	2148	2252‡	2252	2348			0052
Berlin Südkreuz 850 a.	1126	1126	1126		1222	1326	1422	1526	1622	1726	1822	1926	2022	2022	2126	2226‡	2126	2326‡	2326	0021			0126
Berlin Hbf 850 a.	1133	1133	1133		1230	1333	1430	1533	1630	1733	1830	1933	2030	2031	2133	2230‡	2230	2333‡	2333	0029			0133
Hamburg Hbf 840 a.	1324	1324			1422	1524		1823	1924		2124	2221		2333		0036							
Berlin Gesundbrunnen a.			1151y			1439			1839			2039		2343‡									

A – ①②③④⑥ (also Apr. 14, 16, 30, May 26, June 4; not Apr. 13, 17, May 1, 24, June 5).
B – Ⓐ to Mar. 24 (not Mar. 9, 16, 23); Ⓐ from May 22. Jan. 9 - Mar. 24 arrives Berlin Südkreuz 0829, Berlin Hbf 0837.
C – Ⓐ Mar. 27 - May 19 (not Mar. 30, Apr. 6, 13). Mar. 27 - Apr. 12 arrives Berlin Südkreuz 0829, Berlin Hbf 0837.
D – ① to Mar. 27; ①–⑥ from Mar. 30 (not Apr. 15, 17, May 1, June 5).
E – To / from Eisenach (Table 850).
K – From / to Kiel on dates in Table 820.
O – From Ostseebad Binz (Tables 844 and 845).
R – From / to Rostock / Warnemünde on dates in Table 835.
S – From / to Ostseebad Binz or Stralsund on dates in Tables 844 and 845.
T – Ⓐ to Mar. 24; ①–⑥ from Mar. 27 (not Apr. 15, 17, May 1, June 5).

a – Not Apr. 14, 17, May 1, June 5.
b – Also Apr. 15, 17, May 1, June 5.
d – Also Apr. 13, 17, May 1, 24, June 3, 5; not May 26, June 4.
e – Not Apr. 15, 17, May 1, June 5.
f – Also Apr. 13, May 24; not Apr. 14, May 26.
g – Not Apr. 15, 17, May 1, 25, June 5.
h – Also Apr. 14, May 25; not Apr. 15, May 27.
j – 0835 Feb. 10 - Apr. 16.
k – ⑥ (also Apr. 14, 16, 30, June 4).

m – Not Apr. 13, May 1, June 5.
n – ①–⑥ (also Apr. 16, 30, June 4; not Apr. 17, May 1, June 5).
p – Also Apr. 13, 17, May 1, June 5.
q – Not Apr. 14, 16, 30, June 4.
r – Not Jan. 6, May 26.
t – Not Jan. 6.
u – Also Apr. 13, 17, May 1, 24, June 5; not Apr. 14, 16, 30, June 4.
v – Also Apr. 13, 17, May 1, 24, June 5; not Apr. 14, 16, 30, May 26, June 4.
w – Also Apr. 13, 17, May 1, 24, June 5; not Apr. 30, May 26, June 4.
x – 1710 from Mar. 30.
y – Until Feb. 5.
z – 22 – 29 minutes later on ①② Jan. 9 - Mar. 14, ①② from May 15 (not June 5).

‡ – On ①② Jan. 9 - Mar. 14, ①② from May 15 (not June 5) departs Leipzig 2–3 minutes later and then runs up to 40 minutes later to Berlin.
* – 1–2 minutes later from Mar. 30.
! – 9–28 minutes later from Mar. 30 (see Table 905).
● – From Mar. 30 departs München 0537, Augsburg 0607.
§ – From Mar. 30 departs München 0741, Augsburg 0809.
◊ – From Mar. 30 departs München 0941, Augsburg 1014.
¶ – From Mar. 30 departs München 1720, Augsburg 1755.
☐ – To / from Mittenwald / Innsbruck on dates in Table 895.

German national public holidays are on Dec. 25, 26, Jan. 1, Apr. 14, 17, May 1, 25, June 5 and Oct. 3

12

COTTBUS - LEIPZIG — 852

RE / RB services

km		⚒									
0	**Cottbus** d.	0505	0705	0905	1105	1305	1505	1705	1905	2104	2309
24	Calau (Niederl) d.	0522	0722	0922	1122	1322	1522	1722	1922	2122	2327
46	Finsterwalde d.	0535	0735	0935	1135	1335	1535	1735	1935	2137	2342
56	Doberlug-Kirchhain d.	0543	0743	0943	1143	1343	1543	1743	1943	2145	2351
79	Falkenberg **856** d.	0600	0800	1000	1200	1400	1600	1800	2000	2212	0018
97	Torgau **856** d.	0612	0812	1012	1212	1412	1612	1812	2012	...	...
124	Eilenburg **856** d.	0634	0834	1034	1234	1434	1634	1834	2034	...	...
149	**Leipzig** Hbf **856** a.	0655	0855	1055	1255	1455	1655	1855	2101	...	...

			⚒							
Leipzig Hbf **856** d.	...	...	0703	0903	1103	1303	1503	1703	1903	2103
Eilenburg **856** d.	...	...	0725	0925	1125	1325	1525	1725	1925	2125
Torgau **856** d.	...	...	0745	0945	1145	1345	1545	1745	1945	2145
Falkenberg **856** d.	0443	0652	0801	1001	1201	1401	1601	1801	2001	2201
Doberlug-Kirchhain d.	0507	0716	0815	1015	1215	1415	1615	1815	2015	2215
Finsterwalde d.	0516	0724	0823	1023	1223	1423	1623	1823	2023	2223
Calau (Niederl) d.	0539	0739	0837	1037	1237	1437	1637	1837	2037	2237
Cottbus a.	0558	0758	0854	1054	1254	1454	1654	1854	2054	2254

Other stopping trains: Cottbus → Falkenberg at 0600 Ⓐ, 0804, 1204, 1404, 1604, 1804, 2004. Falkenberg → Cottbus at 0351 Ⓐ, 0552 Ⓐ, 0852 Ⓒ, 0855 Ⓐ, 1255, 1455, 1652, 1852.

STEAM TRAINS IN SACHSEN — 853

km	⊠	Ⓐe							A	
0	Radebeul Ost **842 857** d.	0456	...	0826	1021	1256	1426	1726	1856	...
8	Moritzburg d.	0525	...	0853	1051	1323	1456	1754	1923	...
16	Radeburg a.	0546	...	...	1112	...	1517	...	...	...

⊠	Ⓐe								A
Radeburg d.	0611	...	...	1136	...	1541	...	...	...
Moritzburg d.	0634	...	0903	1203	1333	1607	1803	...	1933
Radebeul Ost **842 857** a.	0701	...	0930	1230	1400	1633	1830	...	2000

km			🍷		C	🍷		C d		🍷		C d		🍷		C d		C		🍷	🍷	🍷	🍷	🍷	🍷
0	Zittau d.	High season	0905	...	1016	1105	...	1216	...	1309	...	1413	...	1505	...	1613	...	...	Low season	0902	...	...	1302	...	...
9	Bertsdorf d.	♥	0940	0940	1047	1140	1140	1245	1247	1342	1342	1445	1447	1540	1540	1645	1645	1743	♣	0935	1027	1135	1335	1427	1535
12	Kurort Oybin a.	→	0951	|	1058	1151	|	|	1258	1352	|	|	1458	1551	|	1655	|	1754	→	0944	|	1144	1344	|	1544
13	Kurort Jonsdorf a.		...	0952	*1059*z	...	1152	1258	...	...	1354	1458	...	...	1552	...	1658	...		...	1038	...	...	1438	...

			🍷		C d		🍷		C d		🍷		C d		🍷	C d	h	C		🍷	🍷	🍷	🍷	🍷	🍷
Kurort Jonsdorf d.	High season	1002	...	...	1111	1202	...	...	1311	1402	...	...	1511	1602	...	...	1719	...	Low season	...	1052	...	...	1452	...
Kurort Oybin d.	♥	|	1003	1108	|	|	1203	1308	|	|	1403	1508	|	|	1603	1719	|	1803	♣	1000	|	1200	1400	|	1600
Bertsdorf d.	→	1013	1015	1119	1123	1213	1215	1319	1323	1413	1415	1519	1523	1613	1615	1730	1730	1815	→	1009	1102	1211	1409	1502	1611
Zittau a.		...	1045	...	1154	...	1245	...	1354	...	1445	...	1554	...	1645	1756	1756	1845		...	...	1236	...	...	1636

Operators: Radebeul – SDG Sächsische Dampfeisenbahngesellschaft mbH, Lößnitzgrundbahn, Am Bahnhof 1, 01468 Moritzburg. ✆ +49 (0) 35207 89290. www.loessnitzgrundbahn.de
Zittau – SOEG - Sächisch Oberlausitzer Eisenbahngesellschaft mbH, Bahnhofstraße 41, 02763 Zittau. ✆ +49 (0) 3583 540540. www.soeg-zittau.de

A – Apr. 1 - Oct. 31 only.
C – Ⓒ Apr. 29 - Nov. 5 (also May 26, Aug. 14, 15, Oct. 2, 30, 31).
d – Diesel train.
e – Not Dec. 23 - Jan. 2, Feb. 13–24, Apr. 13–21, May 26, June 26 - Aug. 4, Oct. 2–13, 30, 31, Nov. 22.
h – Change trains at Bertsdorf on dates in note **C**.
z – Change trains at Bertsdorf.
♥ – Dec. 23 - Jan. 2, Jan. 28 - Feb. 5, Feb. 11–26, Apr. 1 - Nov. 5.
♣ – Low season: Dec. 11–22, Jan. 3–27, Feb. 6–10, Feb. 27 - Mar. 31, Dec. 2–9. **No service Nov. 6 - Dec. 1, 2017.**
⊠ – No service Nov. 1–17.

SEUSSLITZ - DRESDEN - BAD SCHANDAU — 853a

Apr. 7 - Nov. 5, 2017

Subject to alteration on May 1, 18, 19, Aug. 18, 19, 20. Contact the operator for service details on these dates.

	A			J	K				A	H	
Seußlitz d.	...	...	...	...	...	...	...	...	...	1330	...
Meißen d.	...	...	...	...	...	...	...	...	...	1500	...
Radebeul d.	...	...	...	...	...	...	...	...	...	1645	...
Dresden Terrassenufer d.	...	0930	1000	1015	...	1200	1400	...	1700	1815	...
Pillnitz d.	...	1100	1150	|	1245	1350	1550	...	1830	...	...
Pirna d.	0930	1200	...	1240	1345	...	...	...	1930	...	...
Königstein d.	1130	1410	...	1445	1545	...	...	...	...	...	...
Bad Schandau a.	1230	...	...	1545	1630	...	...	...	...	...	...

	H					K	A				J
Bad Schandau d.	...	...	0930	...	...	...	1300	...	...	...	1615
Königstein d.	...	...	1000	...	...	...	1330	...	1450	...	1645
Pirna d.	...	...	1120	...	...	...	1450	...	1610	...	1805
Pillnitz d.	...	...	1200	1210	...	1410	1530	1610	1650	...	1845
Dresden Terrassenufer d.	0945	...	...	1310	...	1510	1630	1710	1750	...	1945
Radebeul d.	1045	...	...	...	...	...	...	...	...	...	...
Meißen d.	1145	...	...	...	...	...	...	...	...	...	...
Seußlitz a.	1240	...	...	...	...	...	...	...	...	...	...

A – May 2 - Oct. 15.
H – ②–⑦ May 2 - Oct. 15 (also June 5).
J – ⑤–⑦ May 5 - Oct. 15 (also May 25, June 5, Oct. 3).
K – ⑤–⑦ Apr. 7–30 (also Apr. 14, 17); daily May 2 - Oct. 15; ⑤–⑦ Oct. 20 - Nov. 5.

Operator: Sächsische Dampfschiffahrts GmbH & Co. Conti Elbschiffahrts KG. Georg-Treu-Platz 3, 01067 Dresden. ✆ +49 (0) 351 866 090.

FORST - COTTBUS - GÖRLITZ - ZITTAU — 854

ODEG ★ 2nd class only

km		Ⓐ	Ⓐ	⚒							Ⓐ											Ⓐ				
0	**Cottbus** d.	...	0504	...	0604	0704	0804	0904	1004	1104	1104	1204	1304	1404	1504	1604	1704	1804	1904	2004	2104	2204	...	2309	...	...
24	Spremberg d.	...	0522	...	0622	0722	0822	0922	1022	1121	1122	1222	1322	1422	1522	1622	1722	1822	1922	2022	2122	2222	...	2326	...	...
42	Weißwasser d.	0436	0536	0536	0636	0736	0836	0936	1036	...	1136	1236	1336	1436	1536	1636	1736	1836	1936	2036	2136	2236	...	2344	...	...
72	Horka d.	0500	0600	0600	0700	0800	0900	1000	1100	...	1200	1300	1400	1500	1600	1700	1800	1900	2000	2100	2200	2300	...	0005	...	...
93	**Görlitz** a.	0515	0615	0615	0715	0815	0915	1015	1115	...	1215	1315	1415	1515	1615	1715	1815	1915	2015	2115	2215	2315	...	0020	...	...
93	**Görlitz** d.	0519	0619	0619	0719	0819	0919	1019	1119	...	1219	1319	1419	1519	1619	1719	1819	1919	2018	...	2219	...	...	...	...	...
127	**Zittau** a.	0555	0655	0655	0755	0855	0955	1055	1155	...	1255	1355	1455	1555	1655	1755	1857	1955	2053	...	2255	...	...	...	...	...

	Ⓐ	A	⑦w						Ⓐd											Ⓐ
Zittau d.	...	...	...	0501r	0601	0701	0801	0901	1003	1101	1201	1301	1401	1501	1601	1701	1803	1901	2104	2201
Görlitz a.	...	...	...	0540r	0640	0740	0840	0940	1039	1140	1240	1340	1440	1540	1640	1740	1840	1940	2140	2240
Görlitz d.	0344	0444	0445	0544	0644	0744	0844	0944	1045	1144	1244	1344	1444	1544	1644	1744	1844	1944	2144	2244
Horka d.	0358	0500	0500	0600	0700	0800	0900	1000	1101	1200	1300	1400	1500	1600	1700	1800	1900	2000	2200	2300
Weißwasser d.	0423	0521j	0521	0621	0721	0821	0921	1021	1121	1221	1321	1421	1521	1621	1721	1821	1921	2021	2221	2321
Spremberg d.	0436	0538	0534	0638	0738	0838	0938	1038	1138	1238	1338	1438	1538	1638	1738	1838	1938	2038	2238	...
Cottbus a.	0453	0556	0554	0656	0756	0856	0956	1056	1156	1256	1356	1456	1556	1656	1756	1856	1956	2056	2256	...

A – ①–⑥ (not Apr. 15, 17, May 1, June 5).
d – Runs daily Spremberg - Cottbus.
j – 0524 on ⑥.
r – ⚒ only.
w – Also Apr. 15, 17, May 1, June 5.
★ – Ostdeutsche Eisenbahn. ✆ +49 (0) 30 514 88 88 88. www.odeg.de

FORST (Lausitz) - **COTTBUS** and v.v. *22 km.* Journey time: 18–19 minutes.
From Forst at 0431 Ⓐ, 0533, 0633 and hourly until 2133. **From Cottbus** at 0507 Ⓐ, 0607, 0707 and hourly until 2107; then 2312.

DRESDEN - GÖRLITZ and ZITTAU — 855

Trilex (2nd class only)

km		Ⓒ	Ⓒ		⚒w							w						w								
0	**Dresden** Hbf d.	0048	0533	0533j	0608	0635	0708	0808	0908	1008	1108	1208	1308	1408	1508	1608	1708	1808	1908	2008	2035	2135	2235	2235	2335	2335
4	Dresden Neustadt d.	0054	0539	0539j	0615	0642	0715	0815	0915	1015	1115	1215	1315	1415	1515	1615	1715	1815	1915	2015	2042	2142	2242	2242	2342	2342
41	Bischofswerda d.	0129	0616	0620	0644	0717	0744	0844	0944	1044	1144	1244	1344	1444	1544	1644	1744	1844	1944	2044	2117	2214	2320	2323	0020	0023
79	Ebersbach (Sachs) d.	|	|	0701	|	|	0815	|	1015	|	1215	|	1415	|	1615	|	1815	|	2015	|	|	2244	2356	|	0049	|
83	Neugersdorf d.	|	|	0705	|	|	0819	|	1019	|	1219	|	1419	|	1619	|	1819	|	2019	|	|	2248	0000	|	0053	|
105	**Zittau** a.	|	|	0728	|	|	0839	|	1039	|	1239	|	1439	|	1639	|	1839	|	2039	|	|	2307	0023	|	0112	|
	Liberec **1117** a.	|	|	*0824*	|	|	0915	|	1127v	|	*1355*	|	1524v	|	1716f	|	1920	|	*2115*	|	|	...	...	|	...	|
	Bautzen d.	0144	0631	...	0656	0732	...	0856	...	1056	...	1256	...	1456	...	1656	...	1856	...	2056	2132	...	...	2337	...	0037
	Löbau (Sachs) d.	0201	0650	...	0710	0751	...	0910	...	1110	...	1310	...	1510	...	1710	...	1910	...	2110	2151	...	...	2356	...	0056
	Görlitz a.	0220	0710	...	0726	0812	...	0926	...	1126	...	1326	...	1526	...	1726	...	1926	...	2126	2212	...	...	0017	...	0117

km		⚒				⚒			w									w					w			
0	**Görlitz** d.	...	0446	...	0545	0643	...	0745	0845	...	0945	1045	...	1245	...	1445	...	1645	...	1845	...	1945	2045	...	...	2245
24	Löbau (Sachs) d.	...	0507	...	0600	0658	...	0806	0900	...	1006	1100	...	1300	...	1500	...	1700	...	1900	...	2006	2100	...	...	2306
46	Bautzen d.	...	0525	...	0614	0714	...	0824	0914	...	1024	1114	...	1314	...	1514	...	1714	...	1914	...	2024	2114	...	...	2324
	Liberec **1117** d.	...	|	...	|	|	*0602*	|	|	0838	|	|	1038v	|	*1231*	|	1433c	|	1633v	|	1838	|	|	*2005*	...	|
	Zittau d.	0352	|	0510	|	|	0719	|	|	0919	|	|	1119	|	1319	|	1519	|	1719	|	1919	|	|	2119	2212	|
	Neugersdorf d.	0415	|	0530	|	|	0739	|	|	0939	|	|	1139	|	1339	|	1539	|	1739	|	1939	|	|	2139	2235	|
	Ebersbach (Sachs) d.	0420	|	0535	|	|	0743	|	|	0943	|	|	1143	|	1343	|	1543	|	1743	|	1943	|	|	2143	2244	|
65	Bischofswerda d.	0501	0540	0605	0626	0726	0814	0839	0926	1014	1039	1126	1214	1326	1414	1526	1614	1726	1814	1926	2014	2039	2126	2214	2345k	2345
102	Dresden Neustadt a.	0535	0614	0634	0653	0753	0842	0912	0953	1042	1112	1153	1242	1353	1442	1553	1642	1753	1842	1953	2042	2112	2153	2242	0018	0018
106	**Dresden** Hbf a.	0542	0621	0640	0700	0800	0849	0921	1000	1049	1121	1200	1249	1400	1449	1600	1649	1800	1849	2000	2049	2121	2200	2249	0025	0025

c – Daily to Jan. 8; ⑥⑦ from Jan. 14 (also Apr. 14, 17, May 1, 8, 25, June 5). Change trains at Zittau from Jan. 8.
f – Until Jan. 7. From Jan. 8 connection arrives *1755*.
j – 2–3 minutes later on Ⓐ.
k – Arrives 2319.
v – Change trains at Zittau from Jan. 8.
w – To / from Wrocław (Table **1085**).

☛ **Other stopping trains**: Dresden Hbf → Görlitz at 0408 Ⓐ, 0535 Ⓐ, 0835, 1035, 1235, 1435, 1635 and 1835. Görlitz → Dresden Hbf at 0606, 1145, 1345, 1545 and 1745. Dresden Hbf → Zittau at 0408 Ⓐ, 0735, 0935, 1135, 1335, 1535, 1735 and 1935. Zittau → Dresden Hbf at 0632, 0832, 1032, 1232, 1432, 1632, 1832 and 2032.

12 *Les signes conventionnels sont expliqués à la page 4* 401

GERMANY
See page 367 for a summary of Christmas / New Year alterations

856 DRESDEN and LEIPZIG - RUHLAND - COTTBUS and HOYERSWERDA *RE / RB services*

See Tables **842**, **843** and **857** for other services Dresden - Coswig. See Table **852** for other direct services Leipzig - Falkenberg - Cottbus.

km																								
0	**Dresden** Hbf d.	...	...	0550	...	0650	...	and in	1550	...	1650	...	1750	...	1850	...	1950	...	2050	...	2150	...	...	...
4	**Dresden** Neustadt d.	...	...	0556	...	0656	...	the same	1556	...	1656	...	1756	...	1856	...	1956	...	2056	...	2156	...	...	...
18	Coswig d.	...	...	0607	...	0707	...	pattern	1607	...	1707	...	1807	...	1907	...	2007	...	2107	...	2207	...	...	...
73	Ruhland a.	...	...	0655	...	0757	...	every **two**	1655	...	1757	...	1855	...	1957	...	2055	...	2157	...	2255	...	...	...
73	Ruhland d.	0505	0559	0656	0705	*0802*	0800	hours until	1656	1705	*1802*	1800	1856	1905	*2002*	2000	2056	2105	2200	2202	2256	...	...	...
	Hoyerswerda a.	|	|	0718	|	*0823*	|		1718	|	*1823*	|	1918	|	*2022*	|	2119	|	|	2223	2319	...	...	...
86	Senftenberg d.	0516	0610	...	0716	...	0810		...	1716	...	1810	...	1916	...	2010	...	2116	2210	...	...	...	...	...
120	**Cottbus** a.	0547	0642	...	0748	...	0839		...	1748	...	1839	...	1948	...	2039	...	2148	2239	...	...	...	...	...

	Ⓐ																			L				
Cottbus d.	0415	...	0516	...	0607	...	0716	...	0807	...	and in	1716	...	1807	...	1916	...	2007	...	2207	2309	...	...	...
Senftenberg d.	0445	...	0544	...	0638	...	0744	...	0838	...	the same	1744	...	1838	...	1944	...	2038	...	2238	2339	...	...	...
Hoyerswerda d.	|	0439	|	*0534*	|	0639	|	*0734*	|	0840	pattern	|	*1734*	|	1840	|	*1934*	|	2039	|	...	...	...	...
Ruhland a.	0457	0501	0554	*0556*	0650	0701	0754	*0755*	0850	0901	every **two**	1754	*1755*	1850	1901	1954	*1955*	2050	2101	2250	...	...	...	...
Ruhland d.	...	0502	...	0602	...	0702	...	0802	...	0902	hours until	...	1802	...	1902	...	2002	...	2102	...	...	...	...	...
Coswig d.	...	0550	...	0650	...	0750	...	0850	...	0950		...	1850	...	1950	...	2050	...	2150	...	...	...	...	...
Dresden Neustadt d.	...	0600	...	0704	...	0800	...	0900	...	1000		...	1900	...	2000	...	2100	...	2200	...	...	...	...	...
Dresden Hbf a.	...	0606	...	0711	...	0806	...	0906	...	1006		...	1906	...	2006	...	2106	...	2206	...	...	...	...	...

km		Ⓐ	E	Ⓐ		⚒		⚒	Ⓒ	Ⓐ					Ⓑ		Ⓑ		Ⓐ						
0	Leipzig-Stötteritz ★ d.	...	...	...	0545	...	0745	...	0945	0945	...	1145	...	1345	...	1545	...	1745	...	1945	...	...	...	...	...
7	**Leipzig** Hbf ★ d.	...	...	...	0558	...	0758	...	0958	0958	...	1158	...	1358	...	1558	...	1758	...	1958	...	...	...	...	...
32	Eilenburg d.	...	...	...	0628	...	0828	...	1028	1028	...	1228	...	1428	...	1628	...	1828	...	2028	...	...	...	...	...
59	Torgau d.	...	...	...	0649	...	0849	...	1049	1049	...	1249	...	1449	...	1649	...	1849	...	2049	...	...	...	...	...
77	Falkenberg (Elster) a.	...	...	...	0704	...	0904	...	1104	1104	...	1304	...	1504	...	1704	...	1904	...	2104	...	...	...	...	...
77	Falkenberg (Elster) d.	0417	...	0608	0712	0812	0912	1012	1105	1112	1208	1312	1412	1505	1608	1705	1808	1905	2008	2112	...	...	...	...	...
101	Elsterwerda-Biehla d.	0435	0522	0630	0733	0830	0933	1030	1126	1133	1230	1333	1430	1526	1630	1726	1830	1926	2030	2133	...	...	...	...	...
127	Ruhland a.	0457	0553	0652	0754	0852	0954	1052	1147	1154	1252	1354	1452	1547	1652	1747	1852	1947	2052	2154	...	...	...	...	...
127	Ruhland d.	...	...	...	0802	...	1002	...	1202	1202	...	1402	...	1602	...	1802	...	2002	...	2202	...	...	...	...	...
152	**Hoyerswerda** a.	...	...	...	0823	...	1023	...	1223	1223	...	1423	...	1623	...	1823	...	2022	...	2223	...	...	...	...	...

	Ⓐ		Ⓐ		⚒		Ⓐ	⑥						Ⓑ		Ⓑ		Ⓐ		L					
Hoyerswerda d.	...	0534	...	0734	...	0934	...	...	1134	...	1334	...	1534	...	1734	...	1934	...	...	...	...	...	...	...	...
Ruhland a.	...	0556	...	0755	...	0955	...	...	1155	...	1355	...	1555	...	1755	...	1955	...	...	...	...	...	...	...	...
Ruhland d.	0505	0602	0705	0802	0905	1002	1105	1105	1202	1305	1402	1505	1602	1705	1802	1905	2002	2105	...	2259	...	...	...	...	...
Elsterwerda-Biehla d.	0527	0624	0727	0824	0927	1024	1127	1131	1224	1327	1424	1531	1624	1731	1824	1931	2024	2127	...	2321	...	...	...	...	...
Falkenberg (Elster) a.	0546	0646	0746	0846	0946	1046	1146	1150	1246	1346	1446	1550	1646	1750	1846	1950	2046	2146	...	...	...	...	...	...	...
Falkenberg (Elster) d.	...	0657	...	0857	...	1057	...	...	1257	...	1457	...	1657	...	1857	...	2057	...	...	...	...	...	...	...	...
Torgau d.	...	0712	...	0912	...	1112	...	...	1312	...	1512	...	1712	...	1912	...	2112	...	...	...	...	...	...	...	...
Eilenburg d.	...	0735	...	0935	...	1135	...	...	1335	...	1535	...	1735	...	1935	...	2135	...	...	...	...	...	...	...	...
Leipzig Hbf ★ a.	...	0803	...	1003	...	1203	...	...	1403	...	1603	...	1803	...	2003	...	2203	...	...	...	...	...	...	...	...
Leipzig-Stötteritz ★ a.	...	0815	...	1015	...	1215	...	...	1415	...	1615	...	1815	...	2015	...	2215	...	...	...	...	...	...	...	...

E – From Elsterwerda (d. 0519).
L – 12 Cottbus - Ruhland - Elsterwerda (a. 2324).
★ – Trains also call City Tunnel stations Leipzig MDR, Bayerischer Bahnhof, Wilhelm-Leuschner-Platz and Markt.

857 BAD SCHANDAU - DRESDEN - MEISSEN *S-Bahn*

km	*S-Bahn*					Ⓐ			⚒		✣											
0	**Bad Schandau** ⊡ 1100 d.	0015	...	...	...	0445	...	0515	0545	...	0611	0645		2011	2045	2115	2145	2215	...	2315	...	...
23	Pirna d.	0037	...	...	0437	0507	0507	0537	0607	0607	0637	0707	and at	2037	2107	2137	2207	2237	2307	2337	...	...
40	**Dresden** Hbf 842/3 856 1100 d.	0058	...	0430	0500	0530	0530	0600	0630	0630	0700	0730	the same	2100	2130	2200	2230	2300	2330	0000	...	...
44	**Dresden** Neustadt 842 856 d.	...	...	0437	0507	0537	0537	0607	0637	0637	0707	0737	minutes	2107	2137	2207	2237	2307	2337	0007	...	...
50	Radebeul Ost d.	...	...	0446	0516	0546	0546	0616	0646	0646	0716	0746	past each	2116	2146	2216	2246	2316	2346	0016	...	...
58	Coswig 842/3 856 d.	...	...	0456	0526	0556	0556	0626	0656	0656	0726	0756	hour until	2126	2156	2226	2256	2326	2356	0026	...	...
68	**Meißen** a.	...	...	0504	0534	0604	0604	0634	0704	0704	0734	0804		2134	2204	2234	2304	2334	0004	0034	...	...

S-Bahn	Ⓐ			⚒																		
Meißen d.	...	0421	0451	0451	0521	0551		2021	2051	2121	2151	2221	2251	2321	...	...	...	...	...	...	...	...
Coswig 842/3 856 d.	...	0430	0500	0500	0530	0600	and at	2030	2100	2130	2200	2230	2300	2330	...	...	...	...	...	...	...	...
Radebeul Ost d.	...	0440	0510	0510	0540	0610	the same	2040	2110	2140	2210	2240	2310	2340	...	...	...	...	...	...	...	...
Dresden Neustadt 842 856 d.	...	0450	0520	0520	0550	0620	minutes	2050	2120	2150	2220	2250	2320	2350	...	...	...	...	...	...	...	...
Dresden Hbf 842/3 856 1100 d.	0429	0459	0529	0529	0559	0629	past each	2059	2129	2159	2229	2259	2329	0012f	...	...	...	...	...	...	...	...
Pirna d.	0451	0521	0550	0551	0621	0651	hour until	2121	2151	2221	2250	2321	2350	0034	...	...	...	...	...	...	...	...
Bad Schandau ⊡ 1100 a.	0513	0543	...	0613	0643	0713		2143	2213	2243	...	2143	...	0056	...	...	...	...	...	...	...	...

f – Arrives 2357.

✣ – Subsequent trains depart Bad Schandau 0715, 0811, 0915, 1011, 1115, 1211, 1315, 1411, 1515, 1611, 1715, 1811 and 1915 (other timings follow the same pattern).

⊡ – A frequent ferry services links the railway station with Bad Schandau town centre. **Operator**: Oberelbische Verkehrsgesellschaft Pirna - Sebnitz mbH. ✆ +49 (0) 3501 7920.

857a DRESDEN - DRESDEN FLUGHAFEN ✈ *S-Bahn*

km										
0	**Dresden** Hbf d.	0418	0448	and every	2218	2248	2318	...	...	...
4	**Dresden** Neustadt d.	0425	0455	30 minutes	2225	2255	2325	...	...	...
15	**Dresden** Flughafen ✈ a.	0439	0509	until	2239	2309	2339	...	...	...

Dresden Flughafen ✈ d.	0447	0517	and every	2247	2317	2347	...	...	...
Dresden Neustadt a.	0500	0530	30 minutes	2300	2330	2400	...	...	...
Dresden Hbf a.	0509	0539	until	2309	2339	0009	...	...	...

858 GLAUCHAU and ALTENBURG - GERA - ERFURT *RB / RE services*

km		Ⓒ‡	⚒‡	⚒		Ⓐ	⚒																‡	‡
0	**Glauchau** (Sachs) d.	...	...	...	...	...	0607	...	...	0807	...	1007	...	1207	...	1407	...	1607	...	1807	...	2007	...	...
16	Gößnitz a.	...	...	...	...	...	0620	...	...	0820	...	1020	...	1220	...	1420	...	1620	...	1820	...	2020	...	...
16	Gößnitz d.	...	...	...	...	...	0628	0628	...	0828	...	1028	...	1228	...	1428	...	1628	...	1828	...	2028	...	...
	Altenburg d.	...	...	*0414*e	0507r	...	|	|	0714	|	0914	|	1114	|	1314	|	1514	|	1714	|	1914	|	*2114*	...
51	**Gera** Hbf a.	...	...	*0452*e	0545r	...	0659	0659	0750	0859	0950	1059	1150	1259	1350	1459	1550	1659	1750	1859	1950	2059	*2150*	...
51	**Gera** Hbf d.	...	0436	0507	0600	0626	0705	0705	0805	0905	1005	1105	1205	1305	1405	1505	1605	1705	1805	1905	2005	2105	2205	2344
91	Jena-Göschwitz d.	0413	0509	0536	0628	0654	0732	0732	0832	0932	1032	1132	1232	1332	1432	1532	1632	1732	1832	1932	2032	2132	2235	0017
96	**Jena** West d.	0418	0515	0541	0634	0700	0738	0738	0838	0938	1038	1138	1238	1338	1438	1538	1638	1738	1838	1938	2038	2138	2241	0022
119	Weimar 849 850 d.	0436	0534	0558	0651	0717	0755	0755	0855	0955	1055	1155	1255	1355	1455	1555	1655	1755	1855	1955	2055	2155	2257	0041
140	**Erfurt** Hbf 849 850 a.	0449	*0554*	0610	0706	0731	0808	0808	0908	1007	1108	1207	1308	1407	1508	1607	1708	1807	1908	2007	2108	2208	2310	...
	Göttingen **865** a.	...	...	0751	...	...	0951	0951	...	1151	...	1351	...	1551	...	1751	...	1951	...	2150	...	...	...	...

km		‡		Ⓐ																Ⓑ				‡
	Göttingen **865** d.	...	...	...	...	...	0604	...	0808	...	1008	...	1208	...	1408	...	1608	...	1808	1808	...	2008	2108	...
	Erfurt Hbf 849 850 d.	0031	0439	0540	...	0652	0752	0852	0952	1052	1152	1252	1352	1452	1552	1652	1752	1852	1952	1952	2052	2152	2256	2349
	Weimar 849 850 d.	0049	0452	0554	...	0707	0807	0907	1007	1107	1207	1307	1407	1507	1607	1707	1807	1907	2007	2007	2107	2207	2309	0005
	Jena West d.	0109	0507	0610	...	0723	0823	0923	1023	1123	1223	1323	1423	1523	1623	1723	1823	1923	2023	2023	2123	2223	2324	0025
	Jena-Göschwitz d.	0116	0512	0618	...	0728	0828	0928	1028	1128	1228	1328	1428	1528	1628	1728	1828	1928	2028	2028	2128	2228	2329	0031
	Gera Hbf a.	0145c	0542	0648	...	0756	0856	0956	1056	1156	1256	1356	1456	1556	1656	1756	1856	1956	2056	2056	2156	2256	2358	0102
0	**Gera** Hbf d.	...	0546	0658	0658	0806	0858	1006	1058	1206	1258	1406	1458	1606	1658	1806	1858	2006	...	2058	...	...	...	...
50	**Altenburg** a.	...	0624	|	|	0844	|	1044	|	1244	|	1444	|	1644	|	1844	|	2044	...	|	...	...	...	...
	Gößnitz a.	...	...	0728	0728	...	0928	...	1128	...	1328	...	1528	...	1728	...	1928	...	...	2128	...	...	...	...
	Gößnitz d.	...	...	0736	0736	...	0936	...	1136	...	1336	...	1536	...	1736	...	1936	...	...	2136	...	...	...	...
	Glauchau (Sachs) a.	...	...	0749	0749	...	0949	...	1149	...	1349	...	1549	...	1749	...	1949	...	...	2149	...	...	...	...

c – Ⓒ only. e – Ⓐ only. r – ⚒ only. ‡ – Operated by Erfurter Bahn.

402 *German national public holidays are on Dec. 25, 26, Jan. 1, Apr. 14, 17, May 1, 25, June 5 and Oct. 3* 12

DB (*RB* services); erixx ⊠ — BRAUNSCHWEIG - BAD HARZBURG, GOSLAR and HERZBERG — 859

km		Ⓐ	Ⓐ	⚒	⚒							⑥												
0	**Braunschweig** Hbf d.	0524	0524	0624	0624	0724	0724	and	2124	2124	2224	...	...	...	...	...	...	...	...	...	...	...	...	...
12	Wolfenbüttel d.	0533	0533	0633	0633	0733	0733	hourly	2133	2133	2233	...	...	...	...	...	...	...	...	...	...	...	...	...
39	Vienenburg 860 d.	0600	0602	0700	0702	0800	0802	until	2200	2202	2300	2302	...	...	...	...	...	...	...	...	...	...	...	...
47	**Bad Harzburg** 860 a.	|	0611	|	0711	|	0811		|	2211	|	2311	...	...	...	...	...	...	...	...	...	...	...	...
	Goslar 860 a.	0610	...	0712	...	0812	...		2212	...	2312	...	...	...	...	...	...	...	...	...	...	...	...	...

km		Ⓐ	Ⓐ	⚒	Ⓐ	Ⓐ	Ⓒ	⑥						⑥	⑥									
0	**Goslar** 860 d.	0445	...	0545	...	0645	0645	...	...	0745	and	...	2145	...	2245	...	...	...	...	...	...	...	...	...
	Bad Harzburg 860 d.	|	0545	|	0626	|	|	0645	0745	|	hourly	2145	|	2245	|	...	...	...	...	...	...	...	...	...
13	Vienenburg 860 d.	0503	0603	0603	0635	0700	0703	0703	0803	0803	until	2203	2203	2303	2303	...	...	...	...	...	...	...	...	...
40	Wolfenbüttel d.	0526	0626	0626	0659	0726	0726	0726	0826	0826		2226	2226	2326	2326	...	...	...	...	...	...	...	...	...
52	**Braunschweig** Hbf a.	0535	0635	0635	0708	0735	0735	0735	0835	0835		2235	2235	2335	2335	...	...	...	...	...	...	...	...	...

km		Ⓐ	Ⓐd		⚒d		⚒d		⚒d		⚒d		⚒d		⚒d		⚒d		⚒B						
0	**Braunschweig** Hbf d.	0503	0603	0703	0803	0903	1003	1103	1203	1303	1403	1503	1603	1703	1803	1903	2003	2103	2203	...	...	...	...	...	...
31	Salzgitter-Ringelheim d.	0529	0629	0729	0829	0929	1029	1129	1229	1329	1429	1529	1629	1729	1829	1929	2029	2129	2229	...	...	...	...	...	...
52	Seesen d.	0545	0645	0745	0845	0945	1045	1145	1245	1345	1445	1545	1645	1745	1845	1945	2045	2145	2244	...	...	...	...	...	...
71	Osterode (Harz) Mitte d.	0607	0707	0807	0907	1007	1107	1207	1307	1407	1507	1607	1707	1807	1907	2007	2107	2207	...	...	...	...	...	...	...
83	**Herzberg** (Harz) a.	0621	0721	0821	0921	1021	1121	1221	1321	1421	1521	1621	1721	1821	1921	2021	2121	2221	...	...	...	...	...	...	...

	ⒶB	Ⓐ	⑥B	Ⓐd	Ⓐ	Ⓒ	⚒d		⚒d		⚒d		⚒d		⚒d		⚒d		⚒d						
Herzberg (Harz) d.	...	0534	...	0634	0730	0734	0834	0934	1034	1134	1234	1334	1434	1534	1634	1734	1834	1934	2034	2134	...	...	...	...	...
Osterode (Harz) Mitte d.	...	0547	...	0647	0745	0747	0847	0947	1047	1147	1247	1347	1447	1547	1647	1747	1847	1947	2047	2147	...	...	...	...	...
Seesen d.	0513	0613	0613	0713	0813	0813	0913	1013	1113	1213	1313	1413	1513	1613	1713	1813	1913	2013	2113	2213	...	...	...	...	...
Salzgitter-Ringelheim d.	0529	0629	0629	0729	0829	0829	0929	1029	1129	1229	1329	1429	1529	1629	1729	1829	1929	2029	2129	2229	...	...	...	...	...
Braunschweig Hbf a.	0551	0651	0651	0751	0851	0851	0951	1051	1151	1251	1351	1451	1551	1651	1751	1851	1951	2051	2151	2251	...	...	...	...	...

km		Ⓐ	Ⓒ	Ⓐ			Ⓒ														⚒B		
0	**Bad Harzburg** 860 d.	...	...	0630	0734	0748	0821	...	0934	1022	1134	1222	1334	1422	1534	1622	1734	1822	1934	2022	2134	...	...	...
11	Goslar 860 d.	0544	0636	0643	0758	0800	0836	0836	0958	1038	1158	1236	1358	1436	1556	1636	1758	1836	1958	2036	2158	...	...	...
34	Seesen d.	0603	0654	0702	0817	...	0854	0854	1017	1056	1217	1254	1417	1454	1617	1654	1817	1854	2017	2055	2217	2245	...	...
48	Bad Gandersheim d.	0613	0705	0713	0827	...	0905	0905	1027	1106	1227	1305	1427	1505	1627	1705	1827	1905	2027	2105	2227	2255	...	...
54	**Kreiensen** a.	0618	0711	0718	0832	...	0911	0911	1032	1111	1232	1311	1432	1511	1632	1711	1832	1911	2032	2111	2232	2301	...	...
54	**Kreiensen** 903 d.	*0623*	*0719*	*0723*	0839	...	*0919*	*0919*	1039	*1119*	1239	*1319*	1439	*1519*	1639	*1719*	1839	*1919*	2039	*2119*	2239	*2319*	...	...
73	Northeim (Han) 903 d.	*0636*	*0733*	*0736*	0855	...	*0935*	*0935*	1055	*1133*	1255	*1333*	1455	*1533*	1655	*1733*	1855	*1933*	2055	*2133*	2255	*2333*	...	...
93	**Göttingen** 903 a.	*0649*	*0747*	*0749*	0910	...	*0949*	*0949*	1110	*1147*	1310	*1347*	1510	*1547*	1710	*1747*	1910	*1947*	2110	*2147*	2309	*2347*	...	...

	ⒶB			Ⓐ	⑥B		Ⓐ	Ⓒ	Ⓒ	Ⓐ															
Göttingen 903 d.	*0409*	...	0504	...	...	0607	...	...	0648	0719	...	*0809*	0848	*1009*	1048	*1209*	1248	*1409*	1448	*1609*	1648	*1809*	1848	*2009*	2051
Northeim (Han) 903 d.	*0422*	...	0517	...	...	0620	...	...	0702	0734	...	*0822*	0902	*1022*	1102	*1222*	1302	*1422*	1502	*1622*	1702	*1822*	1902	*2022*	2105
Kreiensen 903 a.	*0436*	...	0530	...	...	0633	...	...	0718	0749	...	*0836*	0918	*1036*	1118	*1236*	1318	*1436*	1518	*1636*	1717	*1836*	1918	*2036*	2120
Kreiensen d.	0456	...	...	0535	0556	...	0640	0642	0723	0750	...	0842	0923	1042	1123	1242	1323	1442	1523	1642	1722	1842	1923	2042	2123
Bad Gandersheim d.	0501	...	...	0540	0601	...	0645	0647	0729	0756	...	0847	0929	1047	1129	1247	1329	1447	1529	1647	1728	1847	1929	2047	2129
Seesen d.	0511	...	...	0551	0611	...	0656	0658	0739	0806	...	0858	0939	1058	1139	1258	1339	1458	1539	1658	1738	1858	1939	2058	2139
Goslar 860 d.	...	...	...	0611	...	...	0718	0718	0801	0826	0856	0917	1001	1117	1201	1317	1401	1517	1601	1717	1800	1917	2001	2117	2158
Bad Harzburg 860 a.	...	...	...	0623	...	...	0729	0729	0813	...	0906	0929	1013	1129	1213	1329	1413	1529	1613	1729	1813	1929	2013	2129	...

B – [12] Braunschweig - Seesen - Kreiensen and v.v.
d – Runs daily Braunschweig - Seesen and v.v.
⊠ – Braunschweig - Goslar / Bad Harzburg operated by erixx GmbH.

erixx; HEX ◇ — HANNOVER - BAD HARZBURG and GOSLAR - HALLE — 860

HANNOVER - BAD HARZBURG ⊠

km		⚒								
0	**Hannover** Hbf d.	0548	0648	0748	and	1748	1848	1948	2048	2148	2248
36	**Hildesheim** Hbf d.	0614	0714	0814	hourly	1814	1914	2014	2114	2214	2314
70	Salzgitter-Ringelheim d.	0641	0741	0841	until	1841	1941	2041	2141	2241	2341
89	Goslar 859 d.	0656	0756	0856		1856	1956	2056	2156	2256	2356
100	**Bad Harzburg** 859 a.	0706	0806	0906		1906	2006	2106	2206	2306	0006

		⚒							
Bad Harzburg 859 d.	...	0548r	0648	and	1748	1848	1948	2048	2148
Goslar 859 d.	0503	0603	0703	hourly	1803	1903	2003	2103	2203
Salzgitter-Ringelheim d.	0516	0616	0716	until	1816	1916	2016	2116	2216
Hildesheim Hbf d.	0544	0644	0744		1844	1944	2044	2144	2244
Hannover Hbf a.	0610	0710	0810		1910	2010	2110	2210	2310

GOSLAR - HALBERSTADT - HALLE ◇

km		⚒		Ⓐ	Ⓐ	Ⓒ	Ⓐ		Ⓒ	Ⓐ	Ⓒ	Ⓐ														
0	**Goslar 859** d.	...	...	...	...	...	...	...	...	...	...	0605	0704	...	0805	0904	...	1005	1104	...	1205	1304	...	1405	1504	...
13	Vienenburg **859** d.	...	...	...	...	...	...	...	...	...	...	0615	0715	...	0816	0915	...	1016	1115	...	1216	1315	...	1416	1515	...
29	Ilsenburg d.	...	...	0411	...	...	...	0529	...	...	0629	0629	0731	...	0831	0931	...	1031	1131	...	1231	1331	...	1431	1531	...
38	Wernigerode d.	...	...	0422	...	...	...	0540	...	...	0640	0640	0742	...	0840	0942	...	1040	1142	...	1240	1342	...	1440	1542	...
62	**Halberstadt** a.	...	...	0438	...	...	...	0556	...	...	0656	0656	0756	...	0856	0956	...	1056	1156	...	1256	1356	...	1456	1556	...
62	**Halberstadt** d.	0331	...	...	0446	0446	0528	...	0607	0607	0657	0701	...	0802	0901	...	1002	1101	...	1202	1301	...	1402	1501	...	1602
94	Aschersleben d.	0359	0359	...	0521	0521	0557	...	0641	0641	0726	0726	...	0824	0926	...	1024	1126	...	1224	1326	...	1424	1526	...	1624
105	Sandersleben (Anh) d.	0419	0419	...	0536	0536	0606	...	0656	0656	0737	0737	...	0836	0937	...	1036	1137	...	1236	1337	...	1436	1537	...	1636
122	Könnern d.	0432	0432	...	0551	0550	0618	...	0709	0709	0749	0749	...	0849	0949	...	1049	1149	...	1249	1349	...	1449	1549	...	1650
152	**Halle** (Saale) Hbf a.	0501	0501	...	0612	0622	0639	...	0738	0741	0814	0814	...	0914	1014	...	1114	1214	...	1314	1414	...	1514	1614	...	1714

									⑥		
Goslar 859 d.	1605	1704	...	1805	1904	...	2005	2104	2205	2304	...	...
Vienenburg **859** d.	1616	1715	...	1816	1915	...	2016	2115	2216	2315	...	...
Ilsenburg d.	1631	1731	...	1831	1931	...	2031	2131	2232	2331	2331	...
Wernigerode d.	1640	1742	...	1840	1942	...	2040	2142	2243	2342	2342	...
Halberstadt a.	1656	1756	...	1856	1956	...	2056	2156	2258	2356	2356	...
Halberstadt d.	1701	**A**	1802	1901	...	2002	2101	...	2305	...	...	...
Aschersleben d.	1726	...	1824	1926	...	2024	2126	...	2333	...	...	...
Sandersleben (Anh) d.	1737	...	1836	1937	...	2036	2137	...	2347	...	...	...
Könnern d.	1749	...	1849	1949	...	2049	2149	...	0000	...	...	...
Halle (Saale) Hbf a.	1814	...	1914	2014	...	2114	2212	...	0029	...	...	...

	Ⓒ	Ⓐ	Ⓐ						
Halle (Saale) Hbf d.	...	0345	...	...	0526	0632	...	0749	0849
Könnern d.	...	0406	...	...	0551	0710	...	0810	0910
Sandersleben (Anh) d.	...	0418	0454	...	0606	0724	...	0822	0924
Aschersleben d.	...	0429	0507	...	0627	0737	...	0835	0937
Halberstadt a.	...	0458	0537	...	0656	0757	...	0859	0957
Halberstadt d.	0457	0459	...	0559	0704	...	0804	0904	...
Wernigerode d.	0514	0516	...	0616	0721	...	0818	0921	...
Ilsenburg d.	0525	0530	...	0630	0730	...	0830	0930	...
Vienenburg **859** d.	...	0542	...	0643	0742	...	0843	0942	...
Goslar 859 a.	...	0553	...	0654	0753	...	0854	0953	...

																			⑤⑥f	⑥					
Halle (Saale) Hbf d.	...	0949	1049	...	1149	1249	...	1349	1449	...	1549	1649	...	1749	1849	...	1949	...	2049	2049	2049	...	...	2307	...	2316
Könnern d.	...	1010	1110	...	1210	1310	...	1410	1510	...	1610	1710	...	1810	1910	...	2010	...	2110	2110	2110	...	...	2330	...	2350
Sandersleben (Anh) d.	...	1022	1124	...	1222	1324	...	1422	1524	...	1622	1724	...	1822	1924	...	2022	...	2124	2124	2124	...	...	2346	...	|
Aschersleben d.	...	1035	1137	...	1235	1337	...	1435	1537	...	1635	1737	...	1835	1937	...	2035	...	2137	2137	2137	...	...	0005	...	0040
Halberstadt a.	**B**	1059	1157	...	1259	1357	...	1459	1557	...	1659	1757	...	1859	1957	...	2104	...	2159	2159	2159	...	...	0034	...	0110
Halberstadt d.	1004	1104	...	1204	1304	...	1404	1504	...	1604	1704	...	1804	1904	...	2004	2105	...	...	2205	2205	2205	...	...	0038	...
Wernigerode d.	1018	1121	...	1218	1321	...	1418	1521	...	1618	1721	...	1818	1921	...	2018	2121	...	...	2219	2219	2219	...	...	0055	...
Ilsenburg d.	1030	1130	...	1230	1330	...	1430	1530	...	1630	1730	...	1830	1930	...	2030	2130	...	...	2230	2230	2230	...	...	0106	...
Vienenburg **859** d.	1043	1142	...	1243	1342	...	1443	1541	...	1643	1742	...	1843	1942	...	2043	2142	...	...	...	2243	...	...	...	...	...
Goslar 859 a.	1054	1153	...	1254	1353	...	1454	1552	...	1654	1753	...	1854	1953	...	2054	2153	...	...	...	2254	...	...	...	...	...

BERNBURG - HALLE ◇ ◧

	Ⓐ	⚒								
Bernburg d.	0447	0612	0722	0819	1055	1219	1419	1623	1819	2100
Könnern a.	0510	0636	0745	0842	1118	1242	1442	1646	1842	2123
Halle (Saale) Hbf a.	0546	0714	*0814*	*0914*	1156	*1314*	*1514*	*1714*	*1914*	2158

	⚒	⚒					Ⓐ					
Halle (Saale) Hbf d.	0506	0605c	0807	1007	1207	1407	1507	1607	1807	2007	2220	2316
Könnern d.	0539	0639	0844	1041	1244	1444	1553	1648	1844	2044	2256	2350
Bernburg a.	0605	0705	0908	1105	1308	1508	1617	1712	1908	2108	2320	0014

A – To Berlin via Magdeburg on ⑤-⑦ (also Apr. 13, 17, May 1, 24, 25, June 5). See Tables **862** / **839**.
B – From Berlin via Magdeburg on Ⓒ. See Tables **839** / **862**.
c – 0559 on ⑥.
f – Not Apr. 14.
r – ⚒ only.
⊠ – Operated by erixx GmbH.
◇ – *Harz Elbe Express*. Operated by Transdev Sachsen-Anhalt.
◧ – Bernburg to Könnern is *16 km*.

861 MAGDEBURG - SANGERHAUSEN - ERFURT and DESSAU - ASCHERSLEBEN

RE / RB services

Magdeburg - Erfurt and Aschersleben

km		Ⓐ¶		Ⓐ	Ⓐt										Ⓐt	Ⓒz	Ⓐt			Ⓐt	¶					
0	**Magdeburg** Hbf d.	...	...	0437	0512	0609k	0712	0826	0912	1026	1112	1226	1312	1426	1457	1512	1533	1626	1712	1712	...	1826	1912	2026	2112	2250
17	Schönebeck (Elbe) d.	...	...	0450	0528	0622	0726	0838	0926	1038	1126	1238	1325	1438	1508	1526	1545	1638	1726	1726	...	1838	1926	2038	2126	2310
37	Staßfurt d.	...	...	0509	0550	0648	0750	0852	0950	1052	1150	1252	1350	1452	1534	1550	1608	1652	1750	1750	...	1852	1950	2052	2150	2332
44	Güsten d.	...	...	0515	0558	0658	0758	0858	0958	1058	1158	1258	1358	1458	1541	1558	1615	1658	1759	1803	...	1858	1958	2058	2158	2339
	Aschersleben a.	...	...	|	0610	|	0810	|	1010	|	1210	|	1410	|	|	1610	1627	|	1810	|	...	|	2010	|	2210	2351
60	Sandersleben d.	...	...	0546	▬	0711	▬	0911	▬	1111	▬	1311	▬	1511	1554	▬	...	1711	...	1816	...	1911	▬	2111	...	...
66	Hettstedt d.	...	...	0554	...	0718	...	0918	...	1118	...	1318	...	1518	1601	...	...	1718	...	1823	...	1918	...	2118	...	...
75	Klostermansfeld d.	...	...	0603	¶	0728	¶	0928	¶	1128	¶	1328	¶	1528	1610	¶	...	1728	...	1832	...	1928	¶	2128	...	...
97	**Sangerhausen** d.	0348	0547	0623	0642	0748	0852	0948	1052	1148	1252	1348	1452	1548	1629	1652	...	1748	...	1856	1911	1947	2052	2158j	...	...
142	Sömmerda d.	0431	0633	0702	0731	0829	0931	1029	1131	1229	1331	1429	1531	1629	...	1731	...	1829	...	...	1958	2029	2137	2242	...	...
167	**Erfurt** Hbf a.	0451	0654	0724	0751	0850	0952	1050	1152	1250	1352	1451	1552	1650	...	1752	...	1850	...	...	2019	2050	2159	2303	...	...

	Ⓐt	Ⓐt	Ⓒz	Ⓐt	Ⓐt		Ⓒz	Ⓐt	Ⓐ¶		¶		¶		¶		¶		¶		¶			¶		¶
Erfurt Hbf d.	...	...	...	...	...	0506	...	...	0612	0705	0809	0910	1009	1110	1209	1310	1409	1509	1609	1710	1809	1910	...	2031	2114	2317
Sömmerda d.	...	...	...	...	...	0524	...	...	0634	0730	0829	0932	1029	1132	1229	1332	1429	1532	1629	1732	1829	1932	...	2051	2138	2337
Sangerhausen d.	...	...	...	0510	...	0615	...	...	0721	0818	0909	1018	1109	1218	1309	1418	1509	1618	1709	1818	1909	2018	...	2135	2226	0022
Klostermansfeld d.	...	...	...	0529	...	0635	...	...	...	0837	▬	1037	▬	1237	▬	1437	▬	1637	▬	1837	▬	2037	...	...	...	...
Hettstedt d.	...	...	...	0538	...	0645	...	...	...	0846	...	1046	...	1246	...	1446	...	1646	...	1846	...	2046	...	...	...	...
Sandersleben d.	...	...	...	0545	...	0653	...	...	...	0853	...	1053	...	1253	...	1453	...	1653	...	1853	...	2053	...	...	...	...
Aschersleben d.	0449	0530	0544	|	0621	|	0744	0746	...	|	0946	|	1146	|	1346	|	1546	|	1746	|	1946	|	2144	...	...	...
Güsten d.	0501	0542	0556	0559	0633	0707	0758	0758	...	0907	0958	1107	1158	1307	1358	1507	1558	1707	1758	1907	1958	2107	2158	...	...	...
Staßfurt d.	0510	0552	0604	0609	0641	0714	0808	0808	...	0914	1008	1114	1208	1314	1408	1514	1608	1714	1808	1914	2008	2114	2208	...	...	...
Schönebeck (Elbe) d.	0531	0613	0626	0626	0703	0729	0829	0829	...	0929	1029	1129	1229	1329	1429	1529	1629	1729	1829	1929	2029	2129	2230	...	...	...
Magdeburg Hbf a.	0542	0625	0637	0639	0715	0740	0840	0840	...	0940	1040	1140	1240	1340	1440	1540	1640	1740	1840	1940	2040	2140	2247	...	...	...

Dessau - Aschersleben

km		Ⓐt	Ⓒz	Ⓐt	Ⓐt	Ⓒz	Ⓐt	Ⓒz	Ⓐt								Ⓐt	Ⓒz								
0	**Dessau** Hbf d.	0424	0453	0516	0553	0600	0642	0710	0731	0804	0902	1004	1102	1204	1302	1404	1502	1502	1604	1702	1804	1902	2004	2114	2147	2318
21	Köthen a.	0447	0516	0537	0620	0620	0711	0732	0754	0825	0922	1025	1122	1225	1323	1425	1522	1522	1625	1722	1825	1922	2025	2136	2215	2340
21	Köthen d.	0448	0517	0538	0630	0630	0722	0733	0754	0827	0923	1027	1123	1227	1323	1427	1523	1523	1627	1723	1827	1923	2027	2137	...	2341
42	Bernburg d.	0509	0539	0558	0652	0652	0743	0755	0812	0852	0943	1052	1143	1252	1343	1452	1543	1543	1652	1743	1852	1943	2052	2202	...	0002
54	Güsten d.	0520	0550	0610	0703	0703	0754	0810	0823	0903	0954	1103	1154	1303	1354	1503	1554	1554	1703	1754	1903	1954	2103	2213	...	0014
66	**Aschersleben** a.	0532	0602	0621	0714	0714	*0810*	0821	0831	0914	*1010*	1114	*1210*	1314	*1410*	1514	1606	*1610*	1714	*1810*	1914	*2010*	2114	2224	...	0026

	Ⓒz	Ⓐt	Ⓐt			Ⓒz	Ⓐt								Ⓐt	Ⓒz									
Aschersleben d.	0431	0431	0516	0557	0648	0744	*0746*	0848	*0946*	1048	*1146*	1248	*1346*	1448	1536	*1546*	1648	*1746*	1848	*1946*	2041	...	...	...	2144
Güsten d.	0442	0442	0527	0608	0701	0801	0801	0901	1001	1101	1201	1301	1401	1501	1550	1601	1701	1801	1901	2001	2052	2110	...	...	2201
Bernburg d.	0454	0454	0538	0618	0712	0812	0812	0912	1012	1112	1212	1312	1412	1512	1601	1612	1712	1812	1912	2012	...	2122	...	...	2212
Köthen a.	0516	0516	0600	0637	0735	0833	0833	0935	1033	1135	1233	1335	1433	1535	1624	1633	1735	1833	1935	2033	...	2143	...	...	2234
Köthen d.	0517	0517	0601	0638	0736	0835	0835	0936	1035	1136	1235	1336	1435	1536	1635	1635	1736	1835	1936	2035	...	2144	...	2221	2235
Dessau Hbf a.	0540	0544	0623	0701	0757	0855	0855	0957	1055	1157	1255	1357	1455	1557	1655	1655	1757	1855	1957	2055	...	2206	...	2243	2251

j – Arrives 2146.
k – 0607 on Ⓐ from Apr. 3.
t – Not Jan. 6.
z – Also Jan. 6.
¶ – Operated by Abellio Rail Mitteldeutschland.

862 MAGDEBURG - HALBERSTADT - THALE

HEX ◇

km		Ⓐ t							Ⓒ ▲																
	Berlin Ostbf **839** d.	...	...	...	...	...	...	...	0707	...	...	...	...	...	...	...	...	...	...	...	...	...	...	...	...
0	**Magdeburg** Hbf d.	0429	...	...	0544	0709	0809	0909	0909	1009	1109	1209	1309	1409	1509	1609	1709	1809	1844	1909	2007	2107	2207	2317	...
39	Oschersleben (Bode) d.	0507	...	...	0625	0742	0842	0942	0942	1042	1142	1242	1342	1442	1542	1642	1742	1842	1925	1942	2045	2145	2247	2354	...
59	**Halberstadt** a.	0524	...	...	0642	0758	0858	0958	0958	1058	1158	1258	1358	1458	1558	1658	1758	1858	1942	1958	2101	2201	2302	0010	...
59	**Halberstadt** d.	0537	0537	0606	0706	0806	0906	1006	1006	1106	1206	1306	1406	1506	1606	1706	1806	1906	...	2006	2106	2203	...	...	0023
77	Quedlinburg a.	0553	0553	0623	0723	0823	0923	1023	1023	1123	1223	1323	1423	1523	1623	1723	1823	1923	...	2023	2123	2220	...	...	0040
77	Quedlinburg d.	0554	0554	0630	0730	0830	0930	1030	1030	1130	1230	1330	1430	1530	1630	1730	1830	1930	...	2030	2130	2221	...	...	0041
87	**Thale** Hbf a.	0606	0606	0642	0742	0842	0942	1042	1042	1142	1242	1342	1442	1542	1642	1742	1842	1942	...	2042	2142	2232	...	...	0052

	Ⓐ t				Ⓐ t						⊕							⑤–⑦ b▲							
Thale Hbf d.	...	...	...	0522	...	0617	0717	0817	0917	1017	1117	1217	1317	1417	1517	1617	1717	1717	1817	1917	2017	2117	...	2233	2343
Quedlinburg a.	...	...	...	0532	...	0628	0728	0828	0928	1028	1128	1228	1328	1428	1528	1628	1728	1728	1828	1928	2028	2128	...	2243	2353
Quedlinburg d.	...	...	...	0533	...	0633	0733	0833	0933	1033	1133	1233	1333	1433	1533	1633	1733	1733	1833	1933	2033	2133	...	2244	2354
Halberstadt a.	...	...	...	0549	...	0649	0749	0849	0949	1049	1149	1249	1349	1449	1549	1649	1749	1749	1849	1949	2049	2149	...	2300	0010
Halberstadt d.	0330	0443	0540	0601	0618	0701	0801	0901	1001	1101	1201	1301	1401	1501	1601	1701	1801	1801	1901	2001	2103	...	2203	...	...
Oschersleben (Bode) d.	0346	0459	0556	0617	0635	0717	0817	0917	1017	1117	1217	1317	1417	1517	1617	1717	1817	1817	1917	2017	2119	...	2219	...	...
Magdeburg Hbf a.	0423	0537	0637	0644	0715	0744	0844	0944	1044	1144	1244	1344	1444	1544	1644	1744	1844	1844	1944	2056	2149	...	2257	...	...
Berlin Ostbf **839** a.	...	...	...	...	...	...	...	...	...	...	...	...	...	...	...	...	...	2049	...	...	...	...	...	...	...

b – Also Apr. 13, 17, May 1, 24, 25, June 5.
t – Not Jan. 6.
⊕ – Change trains at Halberstadt on Ⓒ.
◇ – *Harz Elbe Express.* Operated by Transdev Sachsen-Anhalt.
▲ – *HARZ-BERLIN-EXPRESS.* DB tickets not valid for journeys from / to Berlin. Conveys 2 Berlin - Halberstadt - Goslar and v.v. (Table **860**).

863 BRAUNSCHWEIG - HILDESHEIM - HAMELN - BÜNDE

Nord West Bahn ★

km		Ⓐ	⚒	⑥	Ⓐ			Ⓐ			Ⓐ			Ⓐ			Ⓐ			Ⓐ			Ⓐ			
0	**Hildesheim** Hbf d.	...	0537	0634	0637	0737	0834	0834	0937	1034	1034	1137	1234	1234	1337	1434	1434	1537	1634	1634	1737	1834	1834	1937	2034	2137
18	Elze a.	...	0553	0650	0653	0753	0850	0850	0953	1050	1050	1153	1250	1250	1353	1450	1450	1553	1650	1650	1753	1850	1850	1953	2050	2153
18	Elze d.	...	0602	0702	0702	0802	0902	0902	1002	1102	1102	1202	1302	1302	1402	1502	1502	1602	1702	1702	1802	1902	1902	2002	2102	2202
47	**Hameln** d.	0529	0629	0727	0729	0829	0927	0929	1029	1127	1129	1229	1327	1329	1429	1527	1529	1629	1727	1729	1829	1927	1929	2029	2127	2227
71	Rinteln d.	0546	0646	...	0746	0846	...	0946	1046	...	1146	1246	...	1346	1446	...	1546	1646	...	1746	1846	...	1946	2046	...	...
88	Vlotho d.	0601	0701	...	0801	0901	...	1001	1101	...	1201	1301	...	1401	1501	...	1601	1701	...	1801	1901	...	2001	2101	...	...
100	Löhne (Westf) **811** a.	0614	0714	...	0814	0914	...	1014	1114	...	1214	1314	...	1414	1514	...	1614	1714	...	1814	1914	...	2014	2114	...	...
110	**Bünde** (Westf) **811** a.	0625	0725e	...	0825	...	...	1025	...	...	1225	1325e	...	1425	...	...	1625	1725e	...	1825	...	...	...	...	...	...

	⚒	Ⓐ	⚒	⚒		Ⓐ			Ⓐ			Ⓐ			Ⓐ			Ⓐ			Ⓐ			Ⓐ		
Bünde (Westf) **811** d.	...	...	...	0632e	...	0732	...	0832e	...	...	1032e	...	...	1232e	1332	...	1432e	...	...	1632e	1732	...	1832e	...	...	...
Löhne (Westf) **811** d.	...	0545	...	0645	...	0745	...	0845	0945	...	1045	1145	...	1245	1345	...	1445	1545	...	1645	1745	...	1845	1945	...	2045
Vlotho d.	...	0559	...	0659	...	0759	...	0859	0959	...	1059	1159	...	1259	1359	...	1459	1559	...	1659	1759	...	1859	1959	...	2059
Rinteln d.	...	0610	...	0710	...	0810	...	0910	1010	...	1110	1210	...	1310	1410	...	1510	1610	...	1710	1810	...	1910	2010	...	2110
Hameln d.	0528	0628	0628	0728	0728	0828	0828	0928	1028	1028	1128	1228	1228	1328r	1428	1428	1528	1628	1628	1728	1828	1828	1928	2028	2028	2128
Elze a.	0553	0652	0652	0753	0753	0852	0852	0953	1052	1052	1153	1252	1252	1353r	1452	1452	1553	1652	1652	1753	1852	1852	1953	2052	2052	2153
Elze d.	0602	0702	0702	0802	0802	0907	0907	1002	1107	1107	1202	1307	1307	1402	1507	1507	1602	1707	1707	1802	1907	1907	2002	2107	2107	2202
Hildesheim Hbf a.	0620	0720	0720	0820	0820	0925	0925	1020	1125	1125	1220	1325	1325	1420	1525	1525	1620	1725	1725	1820	1925	1925	2020	2125	2125	2220

Regional trains WOLFSBURG - BRAUNSCHWEIG - HILDESHEIM ⊠

km		Ⓐ	⚒						
0	**Wolfsburg** Hbf d.	0514	0614	0714	0814	and	2214	2314	...
32	**Braunschweig** Hbf d.	0535	0635	0735	0835	hourly	2235	2335	...
75	**Hildesheim** Hbf a.	0602	0702	0802	0902	until	2302	0002	...

	Ⓐ	⚒	⚒								
Hildesheim Hbf d.	0455	...	0555	...	0655	0755	and	1955	2109	2155	2255
Braunschweig Hbf d.	0526	0526	0626	0626	0726	0826	hourly	2026	2136	2226	2326
Wolfsburg Hbf a.	0545	0545	0645	0645	0745	0845	until	2045	2200	2245	2345

e – Ⓐ only.
r – On Ⓐ (not Dec. 21 - Jan. 6, Jan. 30, 31, Apr. 10–21, May 26, June 6) Hameln d. 1335, Elze a. 1401.
★ – Bünde - Hildesheim operated by Nord West Bahn.
⊠ – Operated by *enno*. See Table **902** for faster *ICE* trains operated by DB.

GÖTTINGEN - KASSEL local services — 864

CANTUS Verkehrsgesellschaft (2nd class only)

km		Ⓐ	⑥	⑥	Ⓐ	Ⓒ	Ⓐ	⚒		⚒			Ⓒ	Ⓐ				Ⓑ	Ⓐ	Ⓒ	Ⓑ	⚒	Ⓑ	Ⓐ	⑥	Ⓒ
0	**Göttingen** .... 908 d.	0442	0444	0543	0600	0703	0714	0814	0914	1018	1114	1218	1314	1335	1418	1514	1614z	1714	1814	1818	1914	2014	2118	2214	2219	2359
20	Eichenberg......... 908 a.	0456	0458	0557	0613	0717	0728	0828	0928	1032	1128	1232	1328	1350	1432	1528	1628z	1728	1828	1832	1928	2028	2132	2228	2233	0013
20	Eichenberg......... 865 d.	0508	0502	0603	0623	0723	0733	0833	0933	1033	1133	1233	1333	1356	1433	1533	1633	1733	1833	1833	1933	2033	2133	2234	2239	0014
43	Hann Münden .... 865 d.	0528	0523	0623	0644	0743	0753	0853	0953	1053	1153	1253	1353	1416	1453	1553	1653	1753	1853	1853	1953	2053	2153	2254	2301	0033
67	**Kassel** Hbf ⊡.... 865 a.	0549	0543	0643	0703	0803	0813	0913	1013	1113	1213	1313	1413	1437	1513	1614	1713	1813	1913	1913	2013	2113	2213	2319	2324	0054

	Ⓐ		Ⓐ	⑥	Ⓐ	Ⓒ		⚒	†	⚒	⚒						Ⓑ				Ⓑ	⚒			Ⓐ	Ⓒ
Kassel Hbf ⊡......865 d.	0415	...	0534	0546	0625	0636	...	0746	0846	0846	0946	1046	1146	1246	1346	1446	1546	1646	1746	1846	1946	2046	2146	...	2314	2346
Hann Münden......865 d.	0435	...	0554	0606	0645	0656	...	0806	0906	0906	1006	1106	1206	1306	1406	1506	1606	1706	1806	1906	2006	2106	2206	...	2334	0006
Eichenberg ....865 a.	0455	...	0614	0626	0705	0715	...	0826	0926	0926	1026	1126	1226	1326	1426	1526	1626	1726	1825	1926	2026	2126	2226	...	2355	0026
Eichenberg ....908 d.	0502	...	0624	0627	0707	0722	...	0832	0927	0932	1032	1127	1232	1327	1432	1527	1632	1727	1832	1927	2032	2127	2227	...	0003	0027
Göttingen ....908 a.	0515	...	0637	0640	0721	0735	...	0845	0940	0945	1045	1140	1245	1340	1445	1540	1645	1740	1845	1940	2045	2140	2240	...	0018	0040

z – 4 minutes later on Ⓒ.

⊡ – See Tables **804**, **806** and **901** for connecting trains to / from Kassel Wilhelmshöhe.

ERFURT and HALLE - LEINEFELDE - KASSEL and GÖTTINGEN — 865

DB (RE / RB services); Abellio

km		Ⓐ‡	Ⓐ	Ⓐ‡	Ⓐ		Ⓐ	‡	‡	G	Ⓐ‡			‡	A	⚒‡⊕			‡	A	⊕‡			‡	A
0	**Erfurt** Hbf .... 849 850 d.	...	...	...	...	0430	0502	...	...	0613v	...	0623	0709	...	0811v	...	0829	0909	...	1011v	...	1029	1109	...	1211v
27	Gotha .... 849 850 d.	...	...	...	...	0500	◇	...	...	0637x	...	|	◇	...	0839x	...	|	◇	...	1039x	...	|	◇	...	1239x
48	Bad Langensalza ....d.	...	...	...	0450	0512	0555	...	...	0648	...	0710	0800	...	0850	...	0914	0959	...	1050	...	1114	1159	...	1250
67	Mühlhausen (Thür) ....d.	...	...	...	0506	0526	0611	...	...	0700	...	0726	0815	...	0900	...	0926	1015	...	1100	...	1126	1215	...	1300
	Bitterfeld .... 848 ◧ d.	...	...	...	|	|	|	...	...	|	...	|	|	...	|	0737k	|	|	0837k	|	0937k	|	|	1037k	|
	Halle (Saale) Hbf... 848 ◧ d.	...	...	...	|	|	|	0446b	...	|	0534	|	|	0704	|	0804	|	|	0904	|	1004	|	|	1104	|
	Lutherstadt Eisleben .... ◧ d.	...	...	...	|	|	|	0526	...	|	0614	|	|	0733	|	0833	|	|	0933	|	1033	|	|	1133	|
	Sangerhausen .... ◧ d.	...	...	0415	|	|	|	0545	...	|	0634	|	|	0752	|	0855	|	|	0952	|	1055	|	|	1152	|
	Nordhausen .... ◧ d.	...	...	0448	|	|	|	0622	0632	|	0707	|	|	0825	|	0921	|	|	1025	|	1121	|	|	1225	|
94	**Leinefelde** ....a.	...	...	0528	0532	0545	0634	0653	0712	0717	0747	0750	0839	0856	0917	0952	0949	1039	1056	1117	1152	1149	1239	1256	1317
94	**Leinefelde** ....d.	0425	0502	...	0533	0548	...	0654	...	0718	...	0751	...	0857	0918	...	0955	...	1057	1118	...	1155	...	1257	1318
110	Heilbad Heiligenstadt..........d.	0439	0513	...	0547	0559	...	0705	...	0729	...	0801	...	0907	0929	...	1005	...	1107	1129	...	1205	...	1307	1329
144	**Göttingen** ....a.	|	0539	...	|	0625	...	|	...	0751	...	|	...	|	0951	...	|	...	|	1151	...	|	...	|	1351
125	Eichenberg.................. 864 d.	0452	...	...	0602	...	...	0719	...	...	...	0816	...	0919	...	...	1019	...	1119	...	...	1219	...	1319	...
148	Hann Münden .... 864 d.	*0528*	...	...	0622	...	...	0736	...	...	...	0833	...	0936	...	...	1036	...	1136	...	...	1236	...	1336	...
172	**Kassel** Hbf .... 864 a.	*0549*	...	...	0643	...	...	|	...	...	...	|	...	|	...	...	|	...	|	...	...	|	...	|	...
176	**Kassel** Wilhelmshöhe .. 864 a.	...	...	...	0657	...	...	0754	...	...	...	0852	...	0954	...	...	1053	...	1153	...	...	1253	...	1355	...

	⊕‡			‡	A	⊕‡			‡	A	‡			‡	A	‡			‡	A			⑥		
Erfurt Hbf..............849 850 d.	...	1229	1309	...	1411v	...	1429	1509	...	1611v	...	1629	1709	...	1811v	...	1829	1909	...	2011v	2029	...	...	2113	2245
Gotha................849 850 d.	...	|	◇	...	1439x	...	|	◇	...	1639x	...	|	◇	...	1839x	...	|	◇	...	2039x	|	...	...	2138	◇
Bad Langensalza ....d.	...	1313	1359	...	1450	...	1514	1559	...	1650	...	1714	1759	...	1850	...	1914	1959	...	2050	2112	...	...	2151	2332
Mühlhausen (Thür) ....d.	...	1325	1415	...	1500	...	1526	1615	...	1700	...	1726	1815	...	1900	...	1926	2015	...	2100	2124	...	...	2204	2348
Bitterfeld ....848 ◧ d.	1137k	|	|	1237k	|	1337k	|	|	1437c	|	1537k	|	|	1637c	|	1737k	|	...	1837k	|	|	2037k	...	|	...
Halle (Saale) Hbf.....848 ◧ d.	1204	|	|	1304	|	1404	|	|	1504	|	1604	|	|	1704	|	1804	|	...	1904	|	|	2104	...	|	...
Lutherstadt Eisleben......◧ d.	1233	|	|	1333	|	1433	|	|	1533	|	1633	|	|	1733	|	1833	|	...	1933	|	|	2133	...	|	...
Sangerhausen.................◧ d.	1255	|	|	1352	|	1455	|	|	1552	|	1655	|	|	1752	|	1855	|	...	1952	|	|	2152	...	|	...
Nordhausen ....◧ d.	1321	|	|	1425	|	1521	|	|	1625	|	1721	|	|	1825	|	1921	|	...	2025	|	|	2225	...	|	...
Leinefelde.............................a.	1352	1349	1439	1456	1517	1552	1549	1639	1656	1717	1752	1749	1839	1856	1917	1952	1949	...	2056	2117	2144	▬	...	2222	...
Leinefelde.............................d.	...	1355	...	1457	1518	...	1555	...	1657	1718	...	1755	...	1857	1918	...	1955	...	2057	2119	2150	...	...	2224	...
Heilbad Heiligenstadt ....d.	...	1405	...	1507	1529	...	1605	...	1707	1729	...	1805	...	1907	1929	...	2005	...	2107	2130	2201	...	...	2234	...
Göttingen.........................a.	...	|	...	|	1551	...	|	...	|	1751	...	|	...	|	1951	...	|	...	|	2150	|	Ⓐ	...	2256	...
Eichenberg .... 864 d.	...	1419	...	1519	...	...	1620	...	1719	...	...	1820	...	1919	...	...	2019	...	2119	...	2212	2234	2239	...	...
Hann Münden............... 864 d.	...	1436	...	1536	...	...	1637	...	1736	...	...	1837	...	1936	...	...	2036	...	2136	...	...	2254	2301	...	...
Kassel Hbf .... 864 a.	...	|	...	|	...	...	|	...	|	...	...	|	...	|	...	...	|	...	2154	...	...	2319	2324	...	...
Kassel Wilhelmshöhe ... 864 a.	...	1453	...	1553	...	...	1656	...	1754	...	...	1856	...	1954	...	...	2053	...	...	...	...	...	...	...	...

km			Ⓐ‡	Ⓐ	A	Ⓐ‡	Ⓒ‡		Ⓐ		Ⓐ‡	A	‡			⚒‡⊕	A	‡			⊕‡	A	‡		
0	**Kassel** Wilhelmshöhe .. 864 d.	...	...	...	...	...	...	...	0704	...	...	...	0806	...	0906	...	...	1006	...	1106	...	...	1206	...	1306
	Kassel Hbf .... 864 d.	...	*0415*	...	...	0559	0606	...	|	...	...	...	|	...	|	...	...	|	...	|	...	...	|	...	|
23	Hann Münden .... 864 d.	...	*0435*	...	...	0615	0623	...	0724	...	...	...	0823	...	0922	...	...	1023	...	1122	...	...	1223	...	1322
46	Eichenberg.................. 864 d.	...	0501	...	...	0633	0640	...	0744	...	...	...	0840	...	0941	...	...	1040	...	1141	...	...	1240	...	1341
	Göttingen ....d.	...	|	...	0604	|	|	...	|	...	...	0808	|	...	|	...	1008	|	...	|	...	1208	|	...	|
61	Heilbad Heiligenstadt..........d.	0444t	0514	...	0628	0647	0652	...	0758	...	...	0831	0852	...	0955	...	1031	1052	...	1155	...	1231	1252	...	1355
77	**Leinefelde** ....a.	0459t	0527	...	0639	0701	0702	...	0807	...	...	0841	0902	...	1005	...	1041	1102	...	1205	...	1241	1302	...	1405
77	**Leinefelde** ....d.	0501	0527	0547	0640	0702	0703	0719t	0808	0808	*0811*	0843	0903	0919	1007	1010	1043	1103	1119	1207	1209	1243	1303	1319	1407
119	**Nordhausen** .... ◧ d.	|	0601	|	|	0734	0734	|	|	|	*0841*	|	0934	|	|	1040	|	1134	|	|	1240	|	1334	|	|
157	Sangerhausen .... ◧ d.	|	0633	|	|	0809	0809	|	|	|	0912	|	1009	|	|	1112	|	1209	|	|	1312	|	1409	|	|
179	Lutherstadt Eisleben .... ◧ d.	|	0651	|	|	0828	0828	|	|	|	0928	|	1028	|	|	1128	|	1228	|	|	1328	|	1428	|	|
217	**Halle** (Saale) Hbf... 848 ◧ a.	|	0728	|	|	0857	0857	|	|	|	0958	|	1057	|	|	1158	|	1257	|	|	1358	|	1457	|	|
—	**Bitterfeld** .... 848 ◧ a.	|	...	|	|	0925k	0925k	|	|	|	1025k	|	1125k	|	|	1225k	|	1325k	|	|	1425k	|	1525c	|	|
	Mühlhausen (Thür) ....d.	0524	...	0612	0659	...	...	0742	0832	0832	...	0901	...	0942	1032	...	1101	...	1142	1232	...	1301	...	1342	1432
0	Bad Langensalza ....d.	0536	...	0628	0709	...	...	0759	0844	0844	...	0911	...	0959	1044	...	1111	...	1159	1244	...	1311	...	1359	1444
	Gotha .... 849 850 a.	0552	...	⊙	0721x	...	...	⊙	|	|	...	0923x	...	⊙	|	...	1123x	...	⊙	|	...	1323x	...	⊙	|
38	**Erfurt** Hbf .... 849 850 a.	0617	...	0723	0745v	...	...	0848	0928	0928	...	0946v	...	1048	1128	...	1146v	...	1248	1328	...	1346v	...	1448	1528

	⊕‡	A	‡			⊕‡	A	‡			⊕‡	A	‡			‡	‡	G	‡	G		‡			
Kassel Wilhelmshöhe ... 864 d.	...	...	1406	...	1506	...	...	1606	...	1706	...	...	1805	...	1906	...	...	...	2006	...	2106	...	...	...	...
Kassel Hbf .... 864 d.	...	...	|	...	|	...	...	|	...	|	...	...	|	...	|	...	...	...	|	...	|	...	2146	...	...
Hann Münden............... 864 d.	...	...	1423	...	1522	...	...	1623	...	1722	...	...	1823	...	1922	...	...	...	2023	...	2122	...	2206	...	...
Eichenberg .... 864 d.	...	...	1440	...	1541	...	...	1640	...	1741	...	...	1840	...	1941	...	...	...	2040	...	2141	...	2226	2241	...
Göttingen........................d.	...	1408	|	...	|	...	1608	|	...	|	...	1808	|	...	|	...	...	2008	|	2108	|	...	...	|	2308
Heilbad Heiligenstadt ....d.	...	1431	1452	...	1555	...	1631	1652	...	1755	...	1831	1852	...	1955	...	...	2031	2052	2132	2155	...	...	2253	2332
Leinefelde.............................a.	...	1441	1502	...	1605	...	1641	1702	...	1805	...	1841	1902	...	2005	...	...	2041	2102	2142	2205	...	...	2303	2343
Leinefelde.............................d.	1410	1443	1503	1519	1607	1609	1643	1703	1719	1807	1810	1843	1903	1919	2007	2010	...	2043	2103	2145	2223	2226	...	...	...
Nordhausen ....◧ d.	1440	|	1534	|	|	1640	|	1734	|	|	1840	|	1934	|	|	2040	2056	|	2137	|	|	2306	...	...	...
Sangerhausen.................◧ d.	1512	|	1609	|	|	1712	|	1809	|	|	1912	|	2009	|	|	...	2130	|	2211	|	|	2337	...	...	...
Lutherstadt Eisleben......◧ d.	1528	|	1628	|	|	1728	|	1828	|	|	1928	|	2028	|	|	...	2149	|	2230	|	|	2356	...	...	...
Halle (Saale) Hbf.....848 ◧ a.	1558	|	1657	|	|	1759	|	1857	|	|	1958	|	2057	|	|	...	2228	|	2259	|	|	0034	...	...	...
Bitterfeld ....848 ◧ a.	1625k	|	1725c	|	|	1825k	|	1925k	|	|	2026k	|	...	|	|	...	...	|	...	|	|	...	...	...	...
Mühlhausen (Thür) ....d.	...	1501	...	1542	1632	...	1701	...	1742	1832	...	1901	...	1942	2027	...	...	2101	...	2203	2242	...	...	...	...
Bad Langensalza ....d.	...	1511	...	1559	1644	...	1711	...	1759	1844	...	1911	...	1959	2038	...	...	2111	...	2213	2258	...	...	...	...
Gotha................849 850 a.	...	1523x	...	⊙	|	...	1723x	...	⊙	|	...	1923x	...	⊙	|	...	...	2122x	...	2224x	|	...	...	...	...
Erfurt Hbf..............849 850 a.	...	1546v	...	1648	1728	...	1746v	...	1848	1928	...	1946v	...	2048	2123	...	...	2146	...	2254	2340	...	...	...	...

Other services **BITTERFELD - HALLE - NORDHAUSEN - LEINEFELDE** (operated by Abellio Rail Mitteldeutschland)

			Ⓐ	Ⓐ	Ⓐ			Ⓐ		
Bitterfeld............................d.	...	...	...	...	...	1937k	...	...	...	...
Halle (Saale) Hbf ....d.	0011	...	...	0629	1231	2004	2034	2142	2234	2313
Lutherstadt Eisleben ....d.	0054	...	...	0704	1309	2033	2116	2224	2316	2342
Sangerhausen ....d.	0114	...	0524	0725	1327	2050	2136	2244	2336	0001
Nordhausen...........................a.	...	...	0556	0757	1400	...	...	...	...	0034
Leinefelde............................a.	...	...	0636	0839	1443	...	...	...	...	...

		⚒	Ⓐ		⚒	Ⓒ	†	Ⓐ	Ⓐ	Ⓐ
Leinefelde ....d.	...	...	0445	...	0549h	...	...	...	...	...
Nordhausen ....d.	...	0427	0524	0533	0632	...	...	1256	1456	...
Sangerhausen.........................d.	0427	0501	...	0611	0709	0912	1112	1330	1530	1629
Lutherstadt Eisleben.........d.	0448	0520	...	0630	0728	0928	1128	1349	1549	1649
Halle (Saale) Hbf ....a.	0527	0549	...	0700	0757	0959	1158	1428	1628j	1728
Bitterfeld.............................a.	...	...	...	0725k	0825k	1025k	1225k	...	...	...

A – From / to Glauchau (Table **858**).
G – From / to Gera (Table **858**).

b – 0455 until Feb. 10.
c – Ⓒ (not Jan. 7 - Apr. 17).
h – 0600 on ⑥.

j – 1631 on ⑤ Feb. 17 - May 5 (also Apr. 13).
k – Not Jan. 7 - Apr. 17.
t – Ⓐ only.
v – 3–5 minutes later from Feb. 11.
x – Not Apr. 19 - June 16.

⊕ – Change trains at Sangerhausen on Ⓐ.
◇ – Connecting trains Gotha - Bad Langensalza (journey time: 18 minutes). **From Gotha** at 0531 Ⓐ, 0737, 0937, 1137, 1337, 1537, 1737, 1937 and 2245.
⊙ – Connecting trains Bad Langensalza - Gotha (journey time: 19 minutes). **From Bad Langensalza** at 0650, 0801, 1001, 1201, 1401, 1601, 1801 and 2001.
◧ – See panel below main table for other services Bitterfeld - Halle - Nordhausen - Leinefelde.
‡ – Operated by Abellio Rail Mitteldeutschland.

866 HANNOVER - MAGDEBURG - LEIPZIG

See panels below main table for regional / S-Bahn trains. See Table **848** for other regional trains between Magdeburg and Leipzig via Dessau.

km		IC	IC	IC	IC	IC	IC	IC	IC	IC	IC	IC	IC	IC	IC	IC	IC	IC	IC	IC	IC	IC	RE	IC	RE
		2043	**2031**	**2447**	**2033**	**2445**	**2035**	**2443**	**2037**	**2441**	**2039**	**2049**	**2049**	**1949**	**2431**	**2239**	**2047**	**2433**	**2045**	**2435**	**2012**	**2012**	**16339**	**2437**	**16341**
		①–⑤	①–⑤	①–⑥		①–⑥	①–⑥						⑤–⑦	⑤			Ⓑ		Ⓑ		T	⑦		Ⓑ	
		a	a	e		e	e						d	f	C	A	q		q		D 🍷	w D 🍷		q	
	Köln Hbf **800** d.	...	...	...	...	0512	...	0712e	...	0912	...	...	1113	...	...	...	1312	...	1512	...	1646	1646	...	...	...
	Dortmund Hbf **800** d.	...	...	...	...	0628	...	0828e	...	1028	...	...	1228	...	...	...	1428	...	1628	...	1828	1828	...	...	...
	Bielefeld Hbf **810** d.	...	...	0518g	...	0719	...	0919e	...	1119	...	...	1319	...	...	...	1519	...	1719	...	1916	1916	...	...	...
	Norddeich **813** d.	...	...	|	...	|	0536	|	0739j	|	0939	...	|	...	...	...	|	...	|	...	|	|	...	...	...
	Emden Hbf **813** d.	...	...	|	0416e	|	0609	|	0816	|	1016	...	|	...	1218	...	|	1416f	|	1616	|	|	...	1816	...
	Oldenburg (Oldb) **813** d.	...	...	|	0535e	|	0735	|	0935	|	1135	...	|	...	1335	...	|	1535	|	1735	|	|	...	1935	...
	Bremen Hbf **813** d.	...	...	|	0609	|	0809	|	1009	|	1209	...	|	...	1409	...	|	1609	|	1809	|	|	...	2009	...
0	**Hannover** Hbf d.	...	0531	0636	0736	0836	0936	1036	1136	1236	1336	1436	1436	1509	1536	...	1636	1736	1836	1936	2036	2036	...	2136	...
35	Peine d.	...	0553	|	|	|	|	|	|	|	|	|	|	1533	|	...	|	|	|	|	|	|	...	2157	...
61	**Braunschweig** Hbf d.	...	0610	0711	0810	0911	1010	1111	1210	1311	1410	1511	1511	1548	1610	...	1711	1810	1911	2010	2111	2111	...	2213	...
97	Helmstedt d.	...	0632	|	0832	|	1032	|	1232	|	1432	|	|	1610	1632	...	|	1832	|	2032	|	|	...	2235	...
145	**Magdeburg** Hbf a.	...	0656	0755	0856	0955	1056	1155	1256	1355	1456	1555	1555	1634	1657	...	1755	1856	1955	2056	2155	2155	...	2301	...
145	**Magdeburg** Hbf d.	0558	0702	0801	0902	1001	1102	1201	1302	1401	1502	1601	1601	1636	1659	1700	1801	1902	2001	2103	...	2201	2207	...	2308
	Berlin Hbf **839** a.	|	|	|	|	|	|	|	|	|	|	|	|	|	1822	|	|	|	|	|	...	|	|	...	|
195	Köthen d.	0628	|	0831	|	1031	|	1231	|	1431	|	1631	1631	|	...	1729	1831	|	2031	2132	...	|	2247	...	2348
231	**Halle** (Saale) Hbf a.	0652	0750	0852	0950	1052	1150	1252	1350	1452	1550	1652	1652	◐	...	1750	1852	1950	2052	2151	...	⊖	2317	...	0015
231	**Halle** (Saale) Hbf d.	0654	0752	0854	0952	1054	1152	1254	1352	1454	1552	1654	1654	|	...	1752	1854	1952	2054	2153	...	|	*2347*	...	*0023*
249	Leipzig/Halle Flughafen ✈ a.	|	0804	|	1004	|	1204	|	1404	|	1604	|	|	|	...	1804	|	2004	|	2205‡	...	|	*2358*⁝	...	|
268	**Leipzig** Hbf a.	0718	0819	0918	1019	1118	1219	1318	1419	1518	1619	1718	1718	1815	...	1819	1918	2019	2118x	2223x	...	2325	*0016*	...	*0100*
	Dresden Hbf **842** a.	0836	...	1036	...	1236	...	1436	...	1636	...	1836	1836	...	...	...	2036	...	2236x	2342h	...	...	...	...	...

	IC	IC	IC	IC		IC	IC	IC	IC	IC	IC	IC	IC	IC	IC	IC	IC	IC	IC	IC	IC	IC	IC	IC	IC
	2436	**2013**	**2013**	**2013**		**2434**	**2044**	**2238**	**2432**	**2046**	**2046**	**2430**	**2048**	**2038**	**2440**	**2036**	**2442**	**2034**	**1934**	**2444**	**2032**	**2446**	**2446**	**2030**	**2448**
	①–⑥	①	①–⑥	⑦		①–⑥	①–⑥			①–⑥	⑥					Ⓑ		Ⓑ	⑦		Ⓑ		⑦		Ⓑ
	e	g E 🍷	e E 🍷	s E 🍷		e	e	A	C	e	k					b		r	w		q		w	R	q
Dresden Hbf **842** d.	...	...	...	...	...	...	0513a	...	...	0713	0713	...	0913	...	1113	...	1313	...	...	1513	...	1713	1713	...	1913
Leipzig Hbf d.	...	0442	...	...	...	0536	0643	0738	...	0843	0843	0938	1043	1138	1243	1338	1443	1538	1558	1643	1738	1843	1843	1936	2043p
Leipzig/Halle Flughafen ✈ d.	...	|	...	...	...	0549	|	0751	...	|	|	0951	|	1151	|	1351	|	1551	|	|	1751	|	|	1955	|
Halle (Saale) Hbf a.	...	|	...	...	...	0602	0706	0804	...	0906	0906	1004	1106	1204	1306	1404	1506	1604	|	1706	1804	1906	1906	2007	2106
Halle (Saale) Hbf d.	...	⊕	...	...	...	0604	0708	0806	...	0908	0908	1006	1108	1206	1308	1406	1508	1606	◧	1708	1806	1908	1908	2009	2108
Köthen d.	...	|	...	...	...	0626	0729	0827	...	0929	0929	|	1129	|	1329	|	1529	|	|	1729	|	1929	1929	2031	2129
Berlin Hbf **839** d.	...	|	...	...	...	|	|	|	0731	|	|	|	|	|	|	|	|	|	|	|	|	|	|	|	|
Magdeburg Hbf a.	...	0557	...	...	...	0653	0758	0855	0858	0958	0958	1053	1158	1253	1358	1453	1558	1653	1720	1758	1853	1958	1958	2101	2158
Magdeburg Hbf d.	0501	0601	0601	...	...	0659	0804	...	0901	1004	1004	1059	1204	1259	1404	1459	1604	1659	1724	1804	1859	2004	2004	...	2204
Helmstedt d.	0528	0628	0628	...	...	0728	|	...	0928	|	|	1128	|	1328	|	1528	|	1728	|	|	1928	|	|	...	2231
Braunschweig Hbf d.	0551	0651	0651	0704	...	0751	0851	...	0951	1051	1051	1151	1251	1351	1451	1551	1651	1751	1816	1851	1951	2051	2051	...	2254
Peine d.	0606	|	|	|	...	|	|	...	|	|	|	|	|	|	|	|	|	|	|	|	|	|	|	...	|
Hannover Hbf a.	0626	0723	0723	0737	...	0823	0923	...	1023	1123	1123	1223	1323	1423	1523	1623	1723	1823	1851	1923	2023	2123	2123	...	2326
Bremen Hbf **813** a.	0750	|	|	|	...	0950	|	...	1150	...	|	1350	|	1550	|	1750	|	1950	2009	|	2150	...	|	...	...
Oldenburg (Oldb) **813** a.	0823	|	|	|	...	1023	|	...	1223	...	|	1423	|	1623	|	1823	|	2023	2040	|	2223	...	|	...	...
Emden Hbf **813** a.	0938	|	|	|	...	1138	|	...	1338	...	|	1538	|	1738	|	1938	|	2138	2152	|	2338	...	|	...	...
Norddeich **813** a.	...	|	|	|	...	...	|	...	...	...	|	...	|	...	|	2014q	|	2214	...	|	...	...	|	...	...
Bielefeld Hbf **810** a.	...	0840	0840	0840	...	...	1039	...	...	...	1239	...	1439	...	1639	...	1839q	...	...	2039q	...	...	2239	...	...
Dortmund Hbf **800** a.	...	0931	0931	0931	...	...	1132	...	...	...	1332	...	1532	...	1732	...	1932q	...	...	2132q	...	...	2332	...	...
Köln Hbf **800** a.	...	1112	1112	1112	...	...	1246	...	...	...	1446	...	1646	...	1846	...	2046q	...	...	2246q	...	...	0046	...	...

Other regional trains **HANNOVER - BRAUNSCHWEIG** (operated by WestfalenBahn; most trains start from / continue to Bielefeld or Rheine – see Table **811**)

				⚒							⚒								
Hannover Hbf d.	0013	...	...	0454	0555	and	2255	...	...	**Braunschweig** Hbf d.	0420	...	0520	and	2120	...	2222	2320	...
Peine d.	0039	...	...	0523	0624	hourly	2324	...	...	Peine d.	0438	...	0538	hourly	2138	...	2240	2338	...
Braunschweig Hbf a.	0056	...	...	0539	0641	until	2341	...	...	**Hannover** Hbf a.	0505	...	0605	until	2205	...	2307	0005	...

Other regional trains **BRAUNSCHWEIG - MAGDEBURG** (calling at all stations)

	⑦s		Ⓒ		Ⓐ	Ⓐ		Ⓐ		Ⓐ		Ⓐ	Ⓒ	Ⓐ	Ⓐ		Ⓐ		Ⓐ			Ⓑq	⑥m	Ⓑq	
Braunschweig Hbf d.	0107	...	0541	...	0542	0617	0717	0817	0917	1017	1117	1217	1317	1320	1417	1517	1617	1717	1817	1917	2017	2117	2147	2217	2347
Helmstedt d.	0136	...	0610	0610	0616	0646	0746	0846	0946	1046	1146	1246	1346	1348	1446	1546	1646	1746	1846	1946	2046	2146	2216	2246	0017
Magdeburg Hbf a.	0218	...	0652	0652	...	0729	0829	0929	1029	1129	1229	1329	1429	1429	1528	1629	1729	1829	1929	2029	2129	2229	2300	2328	...

	⑥y	Ⓐ					Ⓐ			Ⓐ		Ⓐ			Ⓐ			Ⓐ			Ⓐ				
Magdeburg Hbf d.	0253	0433	0533	0633	0733	...	0833	0933	...	1033	1133	1233	1333	...	1433	1533	...	1633	1733	...	1833	1933	2033	2204	2313
Helmstedt d.	0333	0513	0613	0713	0813	0913	0913	1013	1113	1113	1213	1313	1413	1513	1513	1613	1713	1713	1813	1913	1913	2013	2113	2244	2354
Braunschweig Hbf a.	0403	0542	0642	0742	0842	0942	0942	1042	1142	1142	1242	1342	1442	1542	1542	1642	1742	1742	1842	1942	1942	2042	2142	2313	...

Other regional / S-Bahn trains **MAGDEBURG - HALLE - LEIPZIG**. SEE NOTE ★.

				Ⓐt																		U		
Magdeburg Hbf d.	...	0415	...	0500	...	...	...	0537	...	...	and at	1937	...	...	...	2037	...	...	...	2207	...	2308	...	...
Schönebeck (Elbe) d.	...	0425	...	0513	...	...	...	0550	...	...	the same	1951	...	...	...	2050	...	...	...	2220	...	2321	...	...
Köthen d.	...	0452	...	0537	...	...	...	0617	...	...	minutes	2017	...	...	...	2117	...	...	...	2247	...	2348	...	...
Halle (Saale) Hbf a.	...	0521	...	0602	...	...	...	0645	...	...	past each	2045	...	...	...	2147	...	...	...	2317	...	0015	...	...
Halle (Saale) Hbf ■ d.	0413	...	0536	...	0616	0636	...	...	0716	0736	hour until	...	2116	2136	...	...	2216	2250	...	...	2347	...	0023	0053
Leipzig/Halle Flughafen ✈ ■ a.	0424	...	0547	...	|	0647	...	...	|	0746		...	|	2146	...	...	|	2301	...	...	2358	...	|	0105
Leipzig Hbf ■ a.	0438	...	0608	...	0653	0708	...	...	0753	0808		...	2153	2208	...	...	2254	2317	...	...	0016	...	0100	0120

		U	Ⓐ	Ⓐt	Ⓒz		Ⓐt																	
Leipzig Hbf ■ d.	0404	...	0438	...	...	0523	...	0553	0608	...	0653	0708	...	and at	1853	1908	...	2053	...	2152	...	...	2327	...
Leipzig/Halle Flughafen ✈ ■ d.	0420	...	|	...	...	0535	...	0609	|	...	0709	|	...	the same	1909	|	...	2110	...	2209	...	...	2343	...
Halle (Saale) Hbf ■ a.	0435	...	0514	...	...	0554	...	0624	0644	...	0724	0744	...	minutes	1924	1944	...	2125	...	2224	...	...	2358	...
Halle (Saale) Hb d.	...	0441t	...	0541	0542	...	0613	...	...	0716	...	...	0813	past each	...	...	2013	...	2130	...	2250	...	...	0013
Köthen d.	...	0511	...	0611	0611	...	0643	...	...	0744	...	...	0843	hour until	...	...	2043	...	2159	...	2319	...	...	0043
Schönebeck (Elbe) d.	...	0538	...	0637	0637	...	0708	...	...	0809	...	...	0908		...	...	2108	...	2224	...	2344	...	...	0108
Magdeburg Hbf a.	...	0551	...	0652	0652	...	0724	...	...	0823	...	...	0922		...	...	2122	...	2238	...	2358	...	...	0122

A – WARNOW – 12 Leipzig - Magdeburg (- Schwerin - Rostock ♣) (- Warnemünde ♥) and v.v.
C – To / from Cottbus on dates in Table **838**.
D – ALLGÄU – 12 and 🍷 Oberstdorf - Stuttgart - Köln - Hannover - Magdeburg (- Leipzig ⑦**w**).
E – ALLGÄU – 12 and 🍷 (Leipzig ①**g** -) (Magdeburg ⚒ -) Braunschweig - Hannover - Köln - Stuttgart - Oberstdorf.
R – ①②③④⑦ (not Apr. 13, 16, 30, June 4).
T – ①④⑤⑦ (also Apr. 12, 18, May 2, 23, 24, June 6; not Apr. 14, 16, 30, May 25, 26, June 4).
U – From / to Uelzen (Table **841**).

a – ①–⑤ (not Apr. 14, 17, May 1, June 5).
b – Not Apr. 14.
d – Also Apr. 13, 17, May 1, 24, 25, June 5; not Apr. 16, May 26, 27.
e – ①–⑥ (not Apr. 15, 17, May 1, June 5).
f – Also Apr. 13, May 24; not Apr. 14, May 26.
g – ① (also Apr. 18, May 2, June 6; not Apr. 17, May 1, June 5).
h – ⑥ (also Apr. 14, 16, 30, May 25, June 5; not Apr. 15).
j – ①–⑥ (not Apr. 15).
k – Also Apr. 14, May 25; not Apr. 15, May 27.
m – Also Apr. 14, 16, 30, June 4.
p – 2029 on ①② Jan. 9 - Mar. 14, ①② May 15 – 30 (also June 6).
q – Ⓑ (not Apr. 14, 16, 30, June 4).
r – Not Apr. 14, 16.
s – Also Apr. 15, 17, May 1, June 5.
t – Ⓐ (not Jan. 6).
v – 1418 on ⑥ from Apr. 8 (also Apr. 14).
w – Also Apr. 17, May 1, June 5; not Apr. 16, 30, June 4.
x – 10 – 30 minutes later on ①② Jan. 9 - Mar. 14, ①② May 15 – 30 (also June 6).
y – Also Apr. 14.
z – Also Jan. 6.

◐ – Via Dessau Hbf (d. 1728) and Bitterfeld (d. 1746).
◧ – Via Bitterfeld (d. 1622) and Dessau Hbf (d. 1640).
⊖ – Via Dessau Hbf (d. 2246).
⊕ – Via Dessau Hbf (d. 0516).
‡ – Not ①② Jan. 9 - Mar. 14, ①② May 15 – 30, June 6.
⁝ – Not ①② Jan. 9 - Mar. 14, ①② from May 15.
♣ – ⑤ to Mar. 31; ⑤–⑦ from Apr. 7 (also May 1, 24, 25).
♥ – ⑤–⑦ from Apr. 7 (also May 1, 24, 25).
■ – See also Table **881**.
★ – Late evening services (from approx. 2000) between Halle and Leipzig via Leipzig/Halle Flughafen are subject to alteration on ①② Jan. 9 - Mar. 14 and ①② from May 15 (also during the early hours of the following morning).

867 HARZER SCHMALSPURBAHNEN

2nd class only

WINTER SERVICE DECEMBER 17, 2016 - APRIL 28, 2017. The origin / destination of certain trains may vary on Dec. 24, 31.

km		v	G 🚂	🚂	🚂	🚂	B 🚂	r 🚂	r 🚂	r 🚂	n 🚂	n
0	**Wernigerode** § ¶ d.	0725	0855	0940	1025	1155	...	...	...	1455	B	1625
15	Drei Annen Hohne ¶ a.	0802	0932	1017	1102	1232	...	...	...	1532	...	1702
15	Drei Annen Hohne ¶ d.	0810	0945	1030	1115	1240	1245	1339	1506	1546	1540	1718
20	Schierke ¶ d.	|	1005	1050	1135	|	1313	1358	1539	1621	|	|
34	**Brocken** ¶ a.	|	1036	1121	1206	|	1344	1428	1609	1652	|	|
19	Elend d.	0822	—	...	...	1252	—	...	...	...	1552	1730
28	Sorge d.	0841	...	...	...	1311	...	...	...	...	1611	1749
31	Benneckenstein d.	0850	...	...	...	1320	...	...	...	...	1620	1758
44	Eisfelder Talmühle a.	0918	v ⊕	...	...	1348	...	...	...	...	1649	1826
44	Eisfelder Talmühle d.	...	0943	...	...	...	1402	...	...	...	1702	1833
50	Ilfeld d.	...	0959	...	...	...	1417	...	...	...	1717	1850
61	**Nordhausen** Nord § a.	...	1023*	...	...	...	1439*	...	...	...	1739	1913

	v	B 🚂	🚂	🚂	G 🚂	🚂	n	n 🚂	r 🚂	n	n
Nordhausen Nord § d.	0825	1024	...	...	...	...	1325	...	...	1754*	...
Ilfeld d.	0849	1047	...	...	...	...	1346	...	...	1817	...
Eisfelder Talmühle a.	0903	1101	...	...	...	...	1400	...	...	1831	...
Eisfelder Talmühle d.	0938	1108	...	...	...	...	—	1408	...	—	1838
Benneckenstein d.	1007	1137	...	...	...	...	...	1437	...	...	1907
Sorge d.	1015	1145	...	...	...	...	...	1445	...	...	1915
Elend d.	1035	1205	...	...	...	...	🚂 B	1505	...	r 🚂	1935
Brocken ¶ d.	|	|	1136	1221	1314	1359	1451	|	1622	1707	|
Schierke ¶ d.	|	|	1224	1312	1355	1439	1522	|	1703	1737	|
Drei Annen Hohne ¶ a.	1046	1216	1236	1324	1407	1451	1533	1516	1714	1749	1946
Drei Annen Hohne ¶ d.	1108	...	1253	...	1423	...	...	1553	1723	1808	1954
Wernigerode § ¶ a.	1145	...	1333	...	1503	...	...	1633	1800	1845	2030

km		v 🚂		🚂	n	n 🚂	n	n	n	n	n	n 🚂
0	**Quedlinburg** § d.	...	0830v	1030v	1339	...	...	...	1530	...	1752	1943
8	**Gernrode** a.	...	0845v	1045v	1354	...	...	...	1545	...	1808	1958
8	**Gernrode** d.	0734	0846	1046	—	1357	1501	...	1546	...	1809	—
18	Mägdesprung d.	0805	0918	1117	...	1428	1532	...	1618	...	1842	n
	Harzgerode d.	|	|	|	1211	|	|	1620	|	...	|	1840
23	Alexisbad a.	0819	0932	1131	1221	1442	1546	1630	1632	...	1856	1850
23	Alexisbad d.	0826	0939	1133	1229	1455	1548	—	1633	1634	1903	1858
26	**Harzgerode** a.	0835	|	1143	|	|	1558	...	|	1643	1913	|
26	Silberhütte d.	—	0950	—	1240	1506	—	...	1644	—	—	1909
30	Straßberg (Harz) d.	...	1001	...	1251	1520	...	...	1655	...	...	1921
35	Güntersberge d.	...	1010	...	1300	1529	n 🚂	...	1704	n	...	1930
	Hasselfelde d.	1012	|	...	|	|	1609	...	|	1758	...	|
44	Stiege a.	1025	1026	...	1316	1545	1622	...	1720	1811	...	1946
44	Stiege d.	...	1027	...	1326	1546	1623	...	1734	1812	...	1947
48	**Hasselfelde** a.	...	|	v	|	1559	|	n 🚂	1747	|	n	|
53	Eisfelder Talmühle d.	...	1050	1103	1402f	...	1643	1702	...	1833	1915	2015
59	Ilfeld d.	...	...	1118	1417	...	...	1717	...	1850	1929	2029
70	**Nordhausen** Nord § a.	...	...	1139	1439*	...	...	1739	...	1913	1952	2053*

	⊕	v		🚂		n	n	n	n	n 🚂	n
Nordhausen Nord § d.	0854*	0925	...	1024	...	1225	1325	...	1625	...	...
Ilfeld d.	0917	0959	...	1047	...	1246	1346	...	1646	...	...
Eisfelder Talmühle d.	0932	1013	...	1101	1105	1301	1401	...	1700	1702	...
Hasselfelde d.	|	—	1012	—	|	|	|	1439	—	|	...
Stiege a.	0952	...	1025	...	1125	1321	1421	1452	...	1722	...
Stiege d.	0953	...	1031	...	1126	1322	1422	1453	...	1732	1734
Hasselfelde a.	1006	...	|	...	|	|	1435	|	...	|	1747
Güntersberge d.	—	...	1047	...	1144	1340	...	1509	...	1748	—
Straßberg (Harz) d.	...	...	1057	...	1154	1350	...	1519	...	1758	...
Silberhütte d.	...	v 🚂	1109	...	1205	1401	...	1531	...	1809	n
Harzgerode d.	...	0845	|	...	|	|	...	|	...	⊙	1923
Alexisbad a.	...	0855	1119	🚂	1216	1412	...	1541	n	1820	1933
Alexisbad d.	...	0902	1133	1146	1223	1413	...	1548	1602	1827	1940
Harzgerode a.	...	|	1143	|	|	|	...	1558	|	⊙	|
Mägdesprung d.	...	0919	...	1201	1237	1429	...	...	1619	1841	1954
Gernrode a.	v	0950	...	1231	1307	1459	...	...	1649	1911	2024
Gernrode d.	0800	0959	...	...	1308n	1500	...	...	1659	1912	...
Quedlinburg § a.	0815	1015	...	...	1324n	1516	...	...	1715	1928	...

B – 🚂 (2) Brocken - Nordhausen and v.v.
G – Dec. 17 - Jan. 8, Jan. 28 - Mar. 5 and Apr. 1 – 23.

f – Arrives 1348.
n – Not Dec. 24, 31.
r – Not Dec. 24.
v – Not Jan. 1.

⊕ – Change trains at Ilfeld on Ⓐ, through train on Ⓒ.

¶ – Additional journeys Apr. 1 – 23 (🚂): Wernigerode d. 1325 → Drei Annen Hohne d. 1415 → Brocken a. 1530; Brocken d. 1540 → Drei Annen Hohne a. 1632 → Wernigerode a. 1721.
⊙ – Harzgerode connections (not Dec. 24, 31): Harzgerode d. 1811 → Alexisbad a. 1821; Alexisbad d. 1825 → Harzgerode a. 1835.
🚂 – Steam train.
* – Nordhausen **Bahnhofsplatz**.
§ – Adjacent to DB station.

Operator: Harzer Schmalspurbahnen GmbH, Friedrichstrasse 151, 38855 Wernigerode. ✆ + 49 (0) 3943 558 0. Fax + 49 (0) 3943 558 148.

868 ERFURT - NORDHAUSEN

RE / RB services

km		Ⓐ																	
0	**Erfurt** Hbf d.	0450	0602	0702	0802	0902	1002	1102	1202	1302	1402	1502	1602	1702	1802	1902	2002	...	2217
27	Straußfurt d.	0516	0625	0729	0823	0929	1024	1129	1224	1329	1424	1529	1624	1729	1824	1929	2024	...	2243
60	Sondershausen d.	0553	0657	0804	0857	0957	1057	1157	1257	1357	1457	1557	1657	1757	1857	1957	2057	...	2315
80	**Nordhausen** a.	0615	0715	0825	0920	1015	1120	1215	1320	1415	1520	1615	1720	1815	1920	2015	2120	...	2336

	Ⓐ	Ⓐ																	
Nordhausen d.	0422	0530	...	0639	0724	0832	0935	1030	1135	1230	1335	1430	1535	1630	1735	1830	1935	...	2137
Sondershausen d.	0445	0552	...	0657	0747	0857	0957	1057	1157	1257	1357	1457	1557	1657	1757	1857	1957	...	2158
Straußfurt d.	0516	0625	...	0729	0824	0929	1024	1129	1224	1329	1424	1529	1624	1729	1824	1929	2024	...	2228
Erfurt Hbf a.	0542	0651	...	0751	0855	0951	1055	1151	1255	1351	1455	1551	1655	1751	1855	1951	2055	...	2259

869 NORDHAUSEN - GÖTTINGEN

RB services

km		Ⓐ	⚒																	
0	**Nordhausen** d.	...	0539	0639	0739	0839	0939	1039	1139	1239	1339	1439	1539	1639	1739	1839	1939	2039	2139
20	Walkenried d.	...	0603	0703	0803	0903	1003	1103	1203	1303	1403	1503	1603	1703	1803	1903	2003	2103	2203
23	Bad Sachsa d.	...	0608	0708	0808	0908	1008	1108	1208	1308	1408	1508	1608	1708	1808	1908	2008	2108	2208
37	Bad Lauterberg ⊡ d.	...	0619	0719	0819	0919	1019	1119	1219	1319	1419	1519	1619	1719	1819	1919	2019	2119	2219
43	Herzberg (Harz) d.	0523	0626	0726	0826	0926	1026	1126	1226	1326	1426	1526	1626	1726	1826	1926	2026	2126	2226
70	Northeim (Han) 903 a.	0547	0650	0750	0850	0950	1050	1150	1250	1350	1450	1550	1650	1750	1850	1950	2050	2150	2250
90	**Göttingen** 903 a.	0605	0710	0808j	0910	1008	1110	1208	1310	1408	1510	1608	1710	1808	1910	2008	2110	2208	2309

	Ⓐ	⚒	Ⓐ	Ⓒ														⑤⑥ f
Göttingen 903 d.	0409	0549	0638	0648	0749	0848	0949	1048	1149	1248	1349	1448	1549	1648	1749	1848	1949	2051	2149
Northeim (Han) 903 d.	0506	0606	0702	0707	0806	0906	1006	1106	1206	1306	1406	1506	1606	1706	1806	1906	2006	2108	2206
Herzberg (Harz) d.	0530	0630	0730	0731	0830	0930	1030	1130	1230	1330	1430	1530	1630	1730	1830	1930	2030	2132	2230
Bad Lauterberg ⊡ d.	0536	0636	0736	0737	0836	0936	1036	1136	1236	1336	1436	1536	1636	1736	1836	1936	2036	2138	2236
Bad Sachsa d.	0547	0647	0747	0748	0847	0947	1047	1147	1247	1347	1447	1547	1647	1747	1847	1947	2047	2149	2247
Walkenried d.	0552	0652	0752	0752	0852	0952	1052	1152	1252	1352	1452	1552	1652	1752	1852	1952	2052	2153	2252
Nordhausen a.	0615	0715	0815	0815	0915	1015	1115	1215	1315	1414	1515	1615	1715	1815	1915	2015	2115	2215	2315

f – ⑤⑥ (not Apr. 14); runs daily Göttingen - Herzberg.
j – 0810 on ①.

⊡ – Bad Lauterberg im Harz Barbis.

870 ERFURT - MEININGEN - SCHWEINFURT - WÜRZBURG

DB (RE services); STB; EB

km		▽			▽ Ⓐ		▽		▽		▽		▽		▽		▽		▽			▽		▽	
0	**Erfurt** Hbf 872 d.	0010	...	...	0400	0500	...	...	0645	0734	0846	0934	1046	1134	1245	1334	1446	1534	1646	1734	1829	1846	1934	2048	2213
23	Arnstadt Hbf 872 d.	0031	...	...	0416	0516	...	...	0706	0751	0906	0951	1106	1151	1306	1351	1506	1551	1706	1751	1846	1906	1951	2106	2231
31	Plaue (Thür) d.	0042	...	...	0424	0523	...	...	0724v	0758	0919j	0958	1119j	1158	1319j	1358	1519j	1558	1719j	1758	1853	1919j	1958	2119j	2241
37	Gräfenroda d.	0047	...	...	0428	0528	...	...	0729	0803	0924	1003	1124	1203	1324	1403	1524	1603	1724	1803	1858	1924	2003	2124	2246
53	Oberhof (Thür) d.	0101	...	...	0443	0540	...	...	0744	0815	0943	1015	1143	1215	1343	1415	1543	1615	1743	1815	1909	1943	2015	2145j	2257
58	Zella-Mehlis d.	0107	...	...	0450	0545	...	...	0751	0819	0950	1019	1150	1219	1350	1419	1550	1619	1750	1819	1914	1950	2019	2151	2302
64	Suhl d.	0113	...	...	0511v	0551	...	...	0757	0825	0957	1025	1157	1225	1357	1425	1557	1625	1757	1825	1920	1957	2025	2201	2307
84	Grimmenthal 873 a.	0129	...	...	0532	0603	0624	...	0813	0836	1013	1036	1213	1236	1413	1436	1613	1636	1813	1836	1937	2013	2036	2217	2318
92	**Meiningen** 873 a.	0137	...	...	0541	|	0630	...	0821	0848	1021	1048	1221	1248	1421	1448	1621	1648	1821	1848	1948	2021	2048	2225	2325
		◇ Ⓐe	◇ Ⓐe	◇	▽ Ⓐ	|	◇ Ⓐe	◇ ⑥	◇	|	◇	|	◇	|	◇	|	◇	|	◇	|	◇		|	◇	◇
	Meiningen 873 d.	0414	...	0524	0544	|	0642	...	0720k	0822	0924	1022	1124	1222	1324	1422	1541	1622	1724	1822	1924	...	2022	2124	...
84	Grimmenthal 873 d.	|	...	|	0550	0605	|	...	|	0836	|	1036	|	1236	|	1436	|	1636	|	1836	|	...	2036	|	...
110	Mellrichstadt d.	0438	0507	0548	...	0623	0709	0709	0748	0849	0948	1049	1148	1249	1348	1449	1608	1649	1748	1849	1948	...	2049	2148	...
124	Bad Neustadt (Saale) d.	0447	0515	0601	...	0637	0718	0718	0800	0857	0959	1057	1159	1257	1359	1457	1620	1657	1759	1857	1959	...	2057	2159	2259
134	Münnerstadt d.	0455	0523	0609	...	0645	0728	0728	0808	0904	1007	1104	1207	1305	1407	1505	1628	1704	1807	1904	2007	...	2104	2207	2307
149	Ebenhausen (Unterfr) d.	0506	0540j	0625	...	0659	0739	0739	0825j	0916	1025j	1116	1225j	1316	1425j	1516	1639	1716	1825j	1916	2025j	...	2116	2228v	2325j
163	**Schweinfurt** Hbf 876 a.	...	0553	0636	...	0716	0751	0752	0841	0926	1041	1125	1241	1326	1441	1526	1652	1726	1840	1926	2040	...	2126	2239	2337
206	**Würzburg** Hbf 876 a.	...	...	0722	...	0746	0820	0820	0922	0955	1122	1155	1319	1355	1521	1555	1721	1755	1921	1955	2122	...	2157	...	0016

e – Not Jan. 6.
j – Arrives 6 – 8 minutes earlier.
k – 0724 on Ⓒ (also Jan. 6).
v – Arrives 11 – 16 minutes earlier.
▽ – Operated by Süd Thüringen Bahn (2nd class only).
◇ – Operated by Erfurter Bahn (2nd class only).

GERMANY

See page 367 for a summary of Christmas / New Year alterations

870 WÜRZBURG - SCHWEINFURT - MEININGEN - ERFURT

DB (*RE* services); *STB*; *EB*

					◇	◇	◇	◇	◇		◇		◇		◇	◇		◇		◇		◇		◇	◇
					⚒r	Ⓐe	Ⓐe	†z	⑥						Ⓐe	Ⓒz									
Würzburg Hbf ...... 876 d.	...	...	*0454*r	...	...	...	*0635*	*0604*	*0604*	0801	*0835*	1001	*1035*	1201	*1207*	*1235*	1401	*1435*	1601	*1636*	1801	*1836*	2001	*2139*	*2236*
Schweinfurt Hbf .... 876 d.	...	...	0530	...	0611	0611	0703f	0716	0716	0830	0911	1030	1111	1230	1243	1311	1430	1511	1630	1711	1830	1911	2030	2214	2347
Ebenhausen (Unterf) .... d.	...	...	0541	...	0629	0629	0717	0732	0740v	0840	0932	1040	1132	1240	1253	1332	1441	1532	1640	1732	1840	1932	2040	2231	0001
Münnerstadt .... d.	...	...	0550	...	0646	0646	0728	0744	0751	0849	0944	1049	1144	1249	1305	1344	1450	1545	1649	1744	1849	1944	2049	2242	0012
Bad Neustadt (Saale) ... d.	...	...	0557	...	0654	0654	0737	0758	0800	0857	0958	1057	1158	1257	1319	1358	1457	1558	1657	1758	1857	1958	2057	2251	0020
Mellrichstadt .... d.	...	...	0606	...	0703	0707	0746	0807	0809	0906	1007	1106	1207	1306	1328	1407	1506	1607	1706	1807	1906	2007	2106	2259	▬
Grimmenthal .... 873 a.	...	...	0621	...	▬	|	|	|	|	0919	|	1119	|	1319	|	|	1519	|	1719	|	1919	|	2120	|	...
Meiningen .... 873 a.	...	...	|	...	...	0734	0810	0831	0833	*0932*	1031	*1132*	1231	*1332*	1358	1431	*1532*	1631	*1732*	1831	*1932*	2031	*2135*	2323	...
		▽			▽	◇					▽		▽		▽			▽		▽		▽		▽	▽
						Ⓐe																			⑤⑥
Meiningen .... 873 d.	0506	0525	*0611*	0711	0733	0805	...	...	...	*0906*	0933	*1106*	1133	*1306*	1333	...	*1506*	1533	*1706*	1733	*1906*	1933	*2106*	2136	2326
Grimmenthal .... 873 d.	0512	0533	0621	0718	0740	|	...	...	...	0919	0940	1119	1140	1319	1340	...	1519	1540	1719	1740	1919	1940	2121	2143	2332
Suhl .... d.	0524	0550	0633	0731	0758	0838	...	...	...	0931	0958	1131	1158	1331	1358	...	1531	1558	1731	1758	1931	1958	2133	2200	2348
Zella-Mehlis .... d.	0532	0559	0639	0737	0808	0846	...	...	...	0937	1008	1137	1208	1337	1408	...	1537	1608	1737	1808	1937	2008	2139	2208	2354
Oberhof (Thür) .... d.	0537	0604	0644	0742	0815	|	...	...	...	0942	1015	1142	1215	1342	1415	...	1542	1615	1742	1815	1942	2015	2144	2215	2359
Gräfenroda .... d.	0549	0619	0654	0752	0829	|	...	...	...	0952	1029	1152	1229	1352	1429	...	1552	1629	1752	1829	1952	2029	2154	2229	0010
Plaue (Thür) .... d.	0553	0631j	0659	0757	0842j	|	...	...	...	0957	1042j	1157	1242j	1357	1442j	...	1557	1642j	1757	1842j	1957	2042j	2159	2242j	0018
Arnstadt Hbf .... 872 d.	0601	0639	0706	0805	0850	0913	...	...	...	1006	1050	1206	1250	1406	1450	...	1606	1650	1806	1850	2006	2050	2206	2250	0026
Erfurt Hbf .... 872 a.	0619	0656	0721	0821	0905	0928	...	...	...	1023	1105	1223	1305	1423	1505	...	1623	1705	1821	1905	2023	2105	2223	2310	0046

e – Not Jan. 6.
f – 0706 from Mar. 6.
j – Arrives 7 – 8 minutes earlier.
r – ⚒ (not Jan. 6).
v – Arrives 0728.
z – Also Jan. 6.
▽ – Operated by Süd Thüringen Bahn (2nd class only).
◇ – Operated by Erfurter Bahn (2nd class only).

871 LEIPZIG - GERA - SAALFELD

Erfurter Bahn; 2nd class only

km																									
				Ⓐ	Ⓐ		Ⓐ		Ⓐ◧		◧		◧		◧		◧		◧						⑤⑥
0	**Leipzig** Hbf .... d.	0009	...	...	...	...	0507	0609	0656	0756	0856	0956	1056	1156	1256	1356	1456	1556	1656	1756	1856	1956	2056	2153	2311
45	Zeitz .... d.	0050	...	...	0437	...	0548	0655	0735	0835	0935	1035	1135	1235	1335	1435	1535	1635	1735	1835	1935	2035	2135	2235	2352
72	**Gera** Hbf .... a.	0114	...	...	0501	...	0616	0725	0759	0858	0958	1058	1158	1258	1358	1458	1558	1658	1758	1858	1958	2059	2206	2259	0015
72	**Gera** Hbf .... d.	...	...	0453	0524	0617	0617	0730	0801	0901	1001	1101	1201	1301	1401	1501	1601	1701	1801	1901	2001	2110	...	2301	...
84	Weida .... d.	...	...	0505	0537	0628	0628	0746	0812	0913	1014	1113	1214	1313	1414	1513	1614	1713	1814	1913	2014	2122	...	2313	...
99	Triptis .... d.	...	...	0518	0550	0642	0642	0759	...	0928	1030	1128	1230	1328	1430	1528	1630	1728	1830	1928	2030	2140	...	2331	...
108	Neustadt (Orla) .... d.	...	...	0525	0557	0649	0649	0806	...	0935	1037	1135	1237	1335	1437	1535	1637	1735	1837	1935	2037	2147	...	2338	...
139	**Saalfeld** (Saale) .... a.	...	...	0555	0624	0716	0716	0836	...	1002	1058	1202	1258	1402	1458	1602	1700	1802	1858	2002	2058	2214	...	0005	...

	Ⓐ		Ⓐ	⚒		Ⓐ				◧		◧		◧		◧		◧		◧			◧	⑤⑥	
Saalfeld (Saale) .... d.	...	...	...	0514	...	0549	...	0656	0755	0858	0955	1058	1155	1258	1355	1458	1555	1658	1755	1858	2007	2051	...	...	2242
Neustadt (Orla) .... d.	...	...	...	0541	...	0620	...	0724	0822	0919	1022	1119	1222	1319	1422	1519	1622	1719	1822	1919	2038	2118	...	...	2308
Triptis .... d.	...	...	...	0552	...	0627	...	0732	0830	0927	1030	1127	1230	1327	1430	1527	1630	1727	1830	1927	2046	2126	...	...	2315
Weida .... d.	...	...	...	0611	...	0643	...	0745b	0843	0946	1043	1146	1243	1346	1443	1546	1643	1746	1843	1946	2059	2138	2141	...	2328
Gera Hbf .... a.	...	...	...	0623	...	0654	...	0756b	0855	0957	1055	1157	1255	1357	1455	1557	1655	1757	1855	1957	2111	...	2151	...	2339
Gera Hbf .... d.	0350	0500	0538	0629	0629	0701	0701	0801	0901	1001	1101	1201	1301	1401	1501	1601	1701	1801	1901	2001	...	...	2153	2245	...
Zeitz .... d.	0415	0526	0606	0653	0653	0726	0726	0825	0925	1025	1125	1225	1325	1425	1525	1625	1725	1825	1925	2025	...	...	2216	2312	...
Leipzig Hbf .... a.	0453	0604	0647	0731	0731	0803	0803	0906	1006	1106	1206	1306	1406	1506	1606	1706	1806	1906	2006	2106	...	...	2253	2350	...

km									
			Ⓐ						
	Leipzig Hbf .... d.	...	0656	...	0856	1056	1256	1456	1656
0	**Gera** Hbf .... d.	0554	0801	0801	1001	1201	1401	1601	1801
12	Weida .... d.	0609	0814	0814	1016	1216	1416	1616	1816
84	**Hof** Hbf .... a.	0725	0925	0925	1125	1325	1525	1725	1925

Hof Hbf .... d.	0833	1033	1233	1433	1633	1833	2036
Weida .... a.	0942	1142	1342	1542	1742	1942	2141
Gera Hbf .... a.	0957	1157	1357	1557	1757	1957	2151
Leipzig Hbf a.	1106	1306	1506	1706	1906	2106	2253

b – 3 minutes later on Ⓒ.

◧ – Conveys (12) Leipzig - Weida - Hof and v.v. (see panel below main table).

872 ERFURT - SAALFELD and ROTTENBACH - KATZHÜTTE

DB; Erfurter Bahn★; 2nd class only

km											
		Ⓐ									
0	**Erfurt** Hbf .... 870 d.	*0528*	0630	*0734*	0841	and in	*1934*	2041	*2213*	*2317*	...
23	Arnstadt Hbf .... 870 d.	0552	0646	0802	0902	the same	2002	2102	2235	2340	...
38	Stadtilm .... d.	0605	0658	0815	0915	pattern	2015	2115	2248	2353	...
54	Rottenbach .... d.	0619	0711	0829	0929	every	2029	2129	2302	0005	...
62	Bad Blankenburg .... d.	0627	0718	0837	0937	**two** hours	2037	2137	2309	0012	...
70	**Saalfeld** (Saale) .... a.	0635	0725	0845	0945	until	2045	2144	2318	0020	...

Saalfeld (Saale) ..... d.	0604	0656	0814	0914	and in	1814	1914	2014	2246
Bad Blankenburg .... d.	0611	0703	0821	0921	the same	1821	1921	2021	2253
Rottenbach .... d.	0619	0712	0829	0929	pattern	1829	1929	2029	2302
Stadtilm .... d.	0631	0726	0842	0942	every	1842	1942	2042	2314
Arnstadt Hbf .... 870 a.	0644	0739	0855	0955	**two** hours	1855	1955	2055	2327
Erfurt Hbf .... 870 a.	0707	*0810*	0917	*1023*	until	1917	*2023*	2117	2345

km											
		Ⓐ									⑤⑦j
0	Rottenbach .... d.	0541	0631	0721	0841	and	1641	1741	1841	1941	2041
15	Obstfelderschmiede .. a.	0604	0655	0744	0905	hourly	1705	1805	1905	2005	2105
25	Katzhütte .... a.	0620	0712	0802	0922	until	1722	1822	1922	2022	2122

	Ⓐ								⑤⑦j
Katzhütte .... d.	0535	0626	...	0736	0836	0936	and	1936	2036
Obstfelderschmiede d.	0552	0643	...	0754	0853	0953	hourly	1953	2053
Rottenbach .... a.	0614	0705	...	0817	0917	1017	until	2017	2117

j – Also Apr. 17, June 5; not Apr. 16, June 4.

★ – Erfurt - Saalfeld operated by Erfurter Bahn. Rottenbach - Katzhütte operated by DB.

☛ **Oberweißbacher Bergbahn**. Obstfelderschmiede - Lichtenhain - Cursdorf. Journey: 26 – 44 minutes. **Subject to confirmation**.
From Obstfelderschmiede at 0625, 0700, 0730 and every 30 minutes until 1730; then 1808, 1830, 1908, 1930. **From Cursdorf** at 0614, 0640, 0706, 0734, 0814, 0844 and every 30 minutes until 1944.

873 EISENACH - MEININGEN - SONNEBERG

Süd Thüringen Bahn (2nd class only)

km																										
		Ⓐ	Ⓐ	Ⓐ		Ⓒ	Ⓐ								Ⓒ	Ⓐ		Ⓒ	Ⓐ							
0	**Eisenach** .... d.	...	*0355*	0450	...	0604	0604	0715	0815	0915	1015	1115	1215	1315	1415	1415	1515	1615	1615	1715	1815	1915	2015	2115	2220	2312
27	Bad Salzungen .... d.	...	*0420*	0522	...	0635	0635	0742	0842	0942	1042	1142	1242	1342	1442	1442	1542	1642	1642	1742	1842	1942	2042	2142	2250	2337
41	Wernshausen .... d.	...	*0438*	0537	...	0651	0651	0758	0858	0958	1058	1158	1258	1358	1458	1458	1558	1658	1658	1758	1858	1958	2058	2158	2306	...
61	**Meiningen** .... a.	...	*0501*	0559	...	0707	0707	0814	0914	1014	1114	1214	1314	1414	1514	1514	1614	1714	1714	1814	1914	2014	2115	2215	2323	...
61	**Meiningen** .... 870 d.	0429	0544	0611	0611	0719	0719	0822	0919	1022	1119	1222	1319	1422	1519	1519	1622	1719	1719	1822	1919	2022	...	2227	...	...
68	Grimmenthal ...... 870 d.	0440	0551	0625n	0625n	0731	0742k	0831	0931	1031	1131	1231	1331	1431	1531	1542k	1631	1731	1742k	1831	1942k	2040n	...	2234	...	...
82	Themar .... d.	0452	0605	0637	0637	0743	0754	0843	0943	1043	1143	1243	1343	1443	1543	1554	1643	1743	1754	1843	1954	2052	...	2246	...	...
94	Hildburghausen .... d.	0504	0616	0653	0653	0801	0804	0901	1001	1101	1201	1301	1401	1501	1601	1604	1701	1801	1804	1901	2004	2103	...	2257	...	...
109	**Eisfeld** .... d.	0520	0643n	0716n	0716n	0815	0820	0916	1015	1116	1215	1316	1415	1516	1615	1620	1716	1815	1820	1916	2020	2118	...	2313	...	...
141	**Sonneberg** (Thür) Hbf a.	0607	0727	0759	0759	...	...	0959	...	1159	...	1359	...	1559	...	...	1759	...	...	1959	...	...	...	...	...	...

	Ⓐ	Ⓒ	Ⓐ	Ⓐ																
Sonneberg (Thür) Hbf d.	...	...	...	...	...	0546	...	0802	...	1002	...	1202	...	1402	...	1602	...	1802	...	2002
Eisfeld .... d.	0401	...	...	0536	...	0636	0745	0845	0945	1045	1145	1245	1345	1445	1545	1645	1745	1845	1945	2045
Hildburghausen .... d.	0416	...	...	0551	...	0651	0759j	0859	0959	1059	1159	1259	1359	1459	1559j	1659	1759j	1859	2006	2105
Themar .... d.	0426	...	...	0605	...	0702	0811j	0911	1011	1111	1211	1311	1411	1511	1611j	1711	1811j	1911	2017	2116
Grimmenthal .... 870 d.	0440	...	...	0624	0624	0726n	0829	0926	1029	1126	1229	1326	1429	1526	1629	1726	1829	1926	2029	2129
Meiningen .... 870 a.	0446	...	...	0630	0630	0732	0835	0932	1035	1132	1235	1332	1435	1532	1635	1732	1835	1932	2035	2135
Meiningen .... d.	0447	0526	0546	0632	0632	0739	0839	0939	1039	1139	1239	1339	1439	1539	1639	1739	1839	1939	2039	2139
Wernshausen .... d.	0506	0544	0605	0652	0652	0758	0858	0958	1058	1158	1258	1358	1458	1558	1658	1758	1858	1958	2058	2158
Bad Salzungen .... d.	0520	0558	0618	0710	0710	0811	0911	1011	1111	1211	1311	1411	1511	1611	1711	1811	1911	2011	2111	2211
Eisenach .... a.	0544	0629	0643	0741	0741	0841	0941	1041	1141	1241	1341	1441	1541	1641	1741	1841	1941	2041	2141	2236

j – 6 – 7 minutes later on Ⓐ.
k – Arrives 17 minutes earlier.
n – Arrives 8 – 12 minutes earlier.

874 LEIPZIG - CHEMNITZ

km							
			⚒				
0	**Leipzig** Hbf .... d.	0518	0620	0720		2120	2329
33	Bad Lausick .... d.	0547	0647	0747	and	2147	2353
44	Geithain .... d.	0556	0656	0756	hourly	2156	0002
66	Burgstädt .... d.	0613	0713	0813	until	2213	0020
81	**Chemnitz** Hbf .... a.	0625	0725	0825		2225	0031

		⚒				
Chemnitz Hbf .... d.	0421	0531	0631		2031	2244
Burgstädt .... d.	0433	0543	0643	and	2043	2256
Geithain .... d.	0451	0600	0700	hourly	2100	2313
Bad Lausick .... d.	0500	0609	0709	until	2109	2322
Leipzig Hbf .... a.	0525	0630	0730		2130	2352

Operator: Mitteldeutsche Regiobahn.

RE / RB services — Regional services NÜRNBERG - LICHTENFELS - SONNEBERG and JENA — 875

See Table **851** for faster *ICE* and *IC* services Nürnberg - Erlangen - Bamberg - Lichtenfels - Saalfeld - Jena and v.v.

km		2	Ⓐe	W	J	Ⓐe S	W	J	W	J	W	J	W	J	Ⓐe S	W	Ⓐe	J	W	J	W	L		⑥	
0	**Nürnberg** Hbf .... 921 d.	0049	*0449*	0540	0642	0706	0740	0840	0940	1040	1140	1240	1340	1441	1510	1540	1608	1641	1740	1840	1940	2041	2140	2247	2247	2346
8	Fürth (Bay) Hbf ... 921 d.	0057	*0457*	0547	0650	0713	0746	0847	0947	1047	1147	1247	1347	1448	1517	1547	1615	1648	1747	1847	1947	2048	2147	2253	2253	2352
24	Erlangen .... d.	0113	*0513*	0559	0701	0725	0759	0900	0959	1059	1159	1259	1359	1459	1527	1559	1627	1659	1759	1859	1959	2059	2159	2304	2304	0003
39	Forchheim (Oberfr) .... d.	0127	*0527*	0608	0709	0735	0808	0908	1008	1108	1208	1308	1408	1508	1536	1608	1636	1708	1808	1908	2008	2108	2208	2314	2314	0012
62	**Bamberg** .... a.	0146	*0546*	0623	0730b	0752	0823	0923	1023	1123	1223	1323	1423	1523	1554	1623	1651	1723	1823	1923	2023	2123	2223	2329	2329	0027
62	**Bamberg** .... 876 d.	...	0552	0625	0736	0756	0835	0936	1035	1136	1235	1336	1435	1536	1556	1635	1653	1736	1835	1936	2033	2135	2238	2346	2346	0029
94	Lichtenfels .... 876 a.	...	0617	0651	0754	0822	0853	0954	1053	1154	1253	1358	1453	1554	1622	1653	1719	1754	1853	1954	2053	2200	2303	0010	0010	0056
94	Lichtenfels .... d.	...	0618	0659	0803	...	0903	1003	1103	1203	1303	1403	1503	1603	1626	1703	1722	1803	1903	2003	2103	2205	2309	0012	0012	...
114	**Coburg** .... d.	...	0643	0720	0820	...	0920	1020	1120	1220	1320	1420	1520	1620	1645	1721	1742	1821	1920	2020	2120	2221	2329	0031	0032	...
135	**Sonneberg** (Thür) Hbf a.	...	0705	0744	0842	...	0942	1042	1142	1242	1342	1442	1542	1642	1706	1743	1805	1843	1942	2042	2142	2243	2350	...	0053	...

			Ⓐe	K	Ⓐe K	Ⓐe W	Ⓒz S	Ⓐe S	J	W	J	W	J	W	J	W	Ⓐe S	J	W	J	W	J	W	J		2
Sonneberg (Thür) Hbf d.	...	0411e	...	0509	...	0611	0611	...	0712	0811	0911	1011	1111	1211	1311	1411	...	1511	1611	1711	1811	1911	2011	2111	2212	...
Coburg .... d.	0400h	0433e	0508	0530	0612	0632	0633	...	0740	0839	0939	1039	1139	1239	1340	1439	...	1539	1638	1740	1840	1938	2039	2139	2239	...
Lichtenfels .... a.	0416h	0454e	0529	0551	0637	0650	0650	...	0757	0857	0957	1056	1157	1256	1357	1456	...	1557	1656	1757	1856	1957	2056	2159	2300	...
Lichtenfels .... 876 d.	0417r	0455	0533	0557	0640	0657	0703	0728	0804	0903	1004	1103	1204	1303	1404	1503	1536	1604	1703	1804	1903	2004	2103	2207	*2322*	...
Bamberg .... 876 a.	0441r	0522	0559	0623	0700	0720	0729	0754	0820	0921	1020	1121	1220	1321	1420	1521	1601	1620	1721	1820	1921	2020	2121	2232	*2346*	...
Bamberg .... d.	0444	0524c	0601	0628	0702	0733	0733	0758	0836	0936	1036	1136	1236	1336	1436	1536	1602	1636	1736	1836	1936	2036	2136	2236	...	0020
Forchheim (Oberfr) ..... d.	0457	0543	0616	0647	0720	0747	0747	0815	0850	0950	1050	1150	1250	1350	1450	1550	1616	1650	1750	1850	1950	2050	2150	2249	...	0038
Erlangen .... d.	0509	0555	0628	0659	0731	0759	0759	0826	0901	1001	1101	1201	1301	1402	1501	1601	1629	1701	1801	1902	2001	2101	2201	2259	...	0053
Fürth (Bay) Hbf..... 921 d.	0522	0608	0641	0709	0744	0811	0811	0839	0911	1011	1111	1211	1311	1412	1511	1611	1642	1711	1811	1912	2011	2111	2213	2310	...	0110
Nürnberg Hbf...... 921 a.	0529	0615	0649	0716	0751	0819	0819	0847	0919	1019	1119	1219	1319	1419	1519	1619	1648	1719	1819	1919	2019	2119	2220	2319	...	0118

BAMBERG - SAALFELD - JENA

km			Ⓐe							Ⓒz	Ⓐe				Ⓒz	Ⓐe						Y	⑥p	⑤⑦j	⑤f
	Nürnberg Hbf (see above) d.	...	...	...	0642	0706e	0840	...	1040	...	...	1240	...	1441	...	1510	1641	...	1840	...	...	2041	2041	2041	2041
0	**Bamberg** .... d.	0504	0552	...	0736	0756	0936	0956	1136	1156	1156	1336	1356	1536	1554	1556	1736	1813	1936	2013	...	2135	2135	2135	2135
32	Lichtenfels......................... d.	0540	0617	0640	0800	0829	1000	1029	1200	1229	1240	1400	1429	1600	1628	1628	1800	1841	2000	2041	...	2202	2202	2214	2214
56	Kronach .... d.	0601	...	0702	0812	0850	1012	1050	1212	1248	1303	1412	1450	1612	1650	1650	1812	1901	2012	2101	...	2222	2223	2234	2235
119	**Saalfeld** (Saale) .... 849 d.	0659	...	0759	0906	0949	1106	1149	1306	1347	1403	1506	1549	1706	1749	1749	1908	1959	2106	2159	...	...	2319	...	2331
129	Rudolstadt (Thür).......... 849 d.	0707	...	...	0913	...	1113	...	1313	...	...	1513	...	1713	...	...	1915	...	2113	...	...	...	...	...	...
161	Jena-Göschwitz............. 849 d.	0729	...	...	0935	...	1135	...	1335	...	...	1535	...	1735	...	...	1937	...	2135	...	...	...	...	...	...
166	**Jena** Paradies .... 849 a.	0734	...	...	0939	...	1139	...	1339	...	...	1539	...	1739	...	...	1941	...	2139	...	...	...	...	...	...

	Ⓐe	Ⓐe	Ⓐe	Ⓒz	Ⓐe								Ⓒz	Ⓐe											
Jena Paradies .... 849 d.	...	...	...	...	...	0618	...	0818	...	1018	...	1218	...	...	1418	...	1618	...	1818	...	2018	...	...	...	...
Jena-Göschwitz .... 849 d.	...	...	...	...	...	0622	...	0822	...	1022	...	1222	...	...	1422	...	1622	...	1822	...	2022	...	...	...	...
Rudolstadt (Thür) .... 849 d.	...	...	...	...	...	0644	...	0844	...	1044	...	1244	...	...	1444	...	1644	...	1844	...	2044	...	...	...	...
Saalfeld (Saale)........... 849 d.	...	...	...	0535	0609	0652	0805	0852	1005	1052	1205	1252	1405	1412	1452	1605	1652	1805	1852	2005	2052	...	2206	...	...
Kronach .... d.	0534	0613	0633	0633	0708	0747	0901	0947	1101	1147	1301	1347	1501	1510	1547	1701	1747	1901	1947	2101	2147	...	2302	...	...
Lichtenfels .... a.	0554	0633	0653	0653	0726	0800	0918	1000	1118	1200	1318	1400	1518	1535	1600	1718	1800	1918	2000	2118	2201	...	2321	...	...
Bamberg .... a.	0623	0700	...	0729	0754	0820	0944	1020	1144	1220	1344	1420	1544	1601	1620	1744	1820	1944	2020	2144	2232	...	2346	...	...
Nürnberg Hbf (see above) . a.	0716	0751	...	0819	0847	0919	...	1119	...	1319	...	1519	...	1648	1719	...	1919	...	2119	...	2319	...	...	...	...

J – Conveys 🚲 Nürnberg - Lichtenfels - Jena and v.v. See panel below main table.
K – Conveys 🚲 Kronach - Lichtenfels - Nürnberg. See panel below main table.
L – Conveys 🚲 Nürnberg - Lichtenfels - Kronach (- Saalfeld ⑤⑥ t). See panel below main table.
S – Conveys 🚲 Nürnberg - Lichtenfels - Saalfeld and v.v. See panel below main table.
W – Conveys 🚲 Nürnberg - Bamberg - Würzburg and v.v. See Table **876**.
Y – ①②③④⑥ (also Jan. 6, Apr. 14, 16, 30, June 4; not Jan. 5, Apr. 13, 17, May 1, 24, 25, June 5).

b – 0727 on Ⓒ (also Jan. 6).
c – 0530 on Ⓒ (also Jan. 6).
e – Ⓐ (not Jan. 6).
f – Also Jan. 5, Apr. 13, May 24; not Jan. 6, Apr. 14.
h – ⑥ only.

j – Also Jan. 5, Apr. 13, 17, May 1, 24, 25, June 5; not Jan. 6, Apr. 14, 16, 30, June 4.
p – Also Jan. 6, Apr. 14, 16, 30, June 4.
r – ⚒ (not Jan. 6).
t – Also Jan. 5, Apr. 13, May 24, June 4.
z – Also Jan. 6.

RE / RB services — WÜRZBURG - BAMBERG - HOF — 876

km		‡Ⓐe				⊕		N				N				N				N				N		
0	**Bamberg**..... 851 875 d.	...	*0504*	...	*0625*	*0625*	*0736*	*0736*	0838	0838	*0936*	*0936*	1038	1038	*1136*	*1136*	1238	1238	*1336*	*1336*	1438	1438	*1536*	*1536*	1638	1638
32	Lichtenfels.... 851 875 d.	0512	0549	...	0656	0656	0806	0806	0900	0900	1006	1006	1059	1059	1206	1206	1259	1259	1406	1406	1459	1459	1606	1606	1659	1659
62	Kulmbach .... d.	0536	0611	...	0718	0718	0826	0826	0919	0919	1026	1026	1118	1118	1226	1226	1318	1318	1426	1426	1518	1518	1626	1626	1718	1718
74	Neuenmarkt-Wirsberg a.	0547	0625	...	0726	0726	0833	0833	0927	0927	1033	1033	1126	1126	1233	1233	1326	1326	1433	1433	1526	1526	1633	1633	1726	1726
74	Neuenmarkt-Wirsberg d.	0547	0626	0634	0728	0732	0835	0838	0929	0932	1035	1038	1128	1132	1235	1238	1327	1332	1435	1438	1528	1532	1635	1638	1728	1732
96	**Bayreuth** Hbf .... a.	0608	|	0657	|	0757	|	0856	|	0956	|	1056	|	1156	|	1256	|	1356	|	1456	|	1556	|	1656	|	1756
103	Münchberg .... 880 d.	...	0652	...	0755	...	0900	...	0955	...	1100	...	1155	...	1300	...	1355	...	1500	...	1555	...	1700	...	1755	...
116	Schwarzenbach.......... d.	...	0704	...	0806	...	0909	...	|	...	1109	...	|	...	1309	...	|	...	1509	...	|	...	1709	...	|	...
127	**Hof** Hbf............... 880 a.	...	0716	...	0818	...	0920	...	1018	...	1120	...	1218	...	1320	...	1418	...	1520	...	1618	...	1720	...	1818	...

						N			‡		T	
Bamberg...... 851 875 d.	*1736*	*1736*	1838	1838	*1936*	*1936*	2038	2038	*2135*	2241	2241	...
Lichtenfels .... 851 875 d.	1806	1806	1859	1859	2006	2006	2059	2059	2209	2312	2312	...
Kulmbach .... d.	1826	1826	1918	1918	2026	2026	2119	2119	2232	2337	2337	...
Neuenmarkt-Wirsberg a.	1833	1833	1926	1926	2033	2033	2128	2128	2243	2349	2349	...
Neuenmarkt-Wirsberg d.	1835	1838	1928	1932	2035	2038	2130	2132	2244	2350	2350	...
Bayreuth Hbf......... a.	|	1856	|	1956	|	2058	|	2152	2303	0016	|	...
Münchberg .... 880 d.	1900	...	1955	...	2100	...	2157	...	...	...	0037	...
Schwarzenbach .... d.	1909	...	|	...	2109	...	2209	...	...	...	0046	...
Hof Hbf .... 880 a.	1920	...	2019	...	2119	...	2222	...	...	...	0058	...

		Ⓐe	Ⓒz				N		
Hof Hbf .... 880 d.	...	0527	0535	...	0636	0736j	...	...	0836
Schwarzenbach .... d.	...	0537	0543	...	0645	|	...	...	0845
Münchberg .... 880 d.	...	0546	0553	...	0656	0754j	...	...	0856
Bayreuth Hbf .... d.	0545	|	|	0701	|	|	0801	0902	|
Neuenmarkt-Wirsberg....... a.	0608	0615	0615	0720	0725	0823	0828	0920	0925
Neuenmarkt-Wirsberg........ d.	...	0616	0616	0727	0727	0831	0831	0927	0927
Kulmbach .... d.	...	0626	0626	0736	0736	0839	0839	0936	0936
Lichtenfels .... 851 875 a.	...	0648	0648	0755	0755	0900	0900	0955	0955
Bamberg .... 851 875 a.	...	*0720*	*0729*	0818	0818	*0921*	*0921*	1018	1018

		N				N				N				N				N				N			R	
Hof Hbf .... 880 d.	0936	...	...	1036	1136	...	...	1236	1337	...	...	1436	1536	...	...	1636	1736	...	...	1835	1936	...	...	2036	2136	...
Schwarzenbach .... d.	|	...	...	1045	|	...	...	1245	|	...	...	1445	|	...	...	1645	|	...	...	1844	|	...	...	2047	|	...
Münchberg .... 880 d.	0954	...	...	1056	1154	...	...	1256	1354	...	...	1456	1554	...	...	1656	1754	...	...	1855	1954	...	...	2058	2153	...
Bayreuth Hbf......... d.	|	1001	1102	|	|	1201	1259	|	|	1401	1502	|	|	1602	1702	|	|	1801	1902	|	|	2001	2103	|	|	2204
Neuenmarkt-Wirsberg a.	1021	1026	1120	1125	1221	1226	1320	1325	1421	1426	1520	1525	1621	1626	1720	1725	1821	1826	1920	1925	2021	2026	2121	2125	2230	2230
Neuenmarkt-Wirsberg d.	1031	1031	1127	1127	1231	1231	1327	1327	1431	1431	1527	1527	1631	1631	1727	1727	1831	1831	1927	1927	2031	2031		2127	2233	2233
Kulmbach .... d.	1039	1039	1136	1136	1239	1239	1336	1336	1439	1439	1536	1536	1639	1639	1736	1736	1839	1839	1936	1936	2039	2039		2136	2246	2246
Lichtenfels .... 851 875 a.	1059	1059	1155	1155	1259	1259	1355	1355	1459	1459	1555	1555	1659	1659	1755	1755	1859	1859	1955	1955	2059	2059		2156	2306	2306
Bamberg...... 851 875 a.	*1121*	*1121*	1218	1218	*1321*	*1321*	1418	1418	*1521*	*1521*	1618	1618	*1721*	*1721*	1818	1818	*1921*	*1921*	2018	2018	*2121*	*2121*		2219	*2346*	*2346*

WÜRZBURG - BAMBERG

km			Ⓒz		Ⓐe	⚒r		Ⓐe																		Ⓒz
0	**Würzburg** Hbf ... 870 d.	0036	0036	...	...	0454	0604	0635	0738	0835	0935	1035	1135	1235	1338	1435	1538	1636	1738	1836	1938	2035	2139	2236	2336	2336
43	Schweinfurt Hbf.. 870 d.	0106	0107	...	0436	0543f	0636	0658	0802	0900	1000	1100	1201	1300	1402	1500	1602	1702	1802	1901	2002	2100	2202	2300	0009	0010
68	Haßfurt........................ d.	...	0126	...	0455	0601	0654	0711	0815	0913	1014	1113	1215	1314	1415	1513	1615	1714	1815	1914	2015	2113	2216	2317	...	0029
100	**Bamberg** .... a.	...	0147	...	0520	0621	0717	0730	0832	0930	1032	1130	1232	1330	1432	1530	1632	1730	1832	1930	2032	2129	2232	2340	...	0054
	Nürnberg Hbf 875 .. a.	...	...	...	...	...	...	0819	...	1019	...	1219	...	1419	...	1619	...	1819	...	2019	...	2220	...	...	...	...

	Ⓐe	Ⓒz		Ⓐe	Ⓒz	Ⓐe				Ⓐe																
Nürnberg Hbf 875.... d.	...	...	...	...	...	...	0540	...	0740	...	...	0940	...	1140	...	1340	...	1540	...	1740	...	1940	...	...	...	...
Bamberg .... d.	0034	0104	...	0445	0445	0552	0627	0725	0826	0838	0925	1026	1125	1226	1326	1426	1525	1626	1725	1826	1925	2026	2038	2138	...	2304
Haßfurt......................... d.	0055	0126	...	0506	0506	0615	0643	0742	0842	0900	0942	1042	1142	1242	1342	1442	1542	1642	1742	1842	1942	2042	2100	2159	...	2326
Schweinfurt Hbf ....870 d.	0113	0144	...	0525	0525	0641	0657	0757	0857	0918	0956	1057	1156	1257	1356	1457	1556	1657	1756	1857	1956	2057	2118	2218	...	2344
Würzburg Hbf.....870 a.	...	0215	...	0548	0557	0718	0722	0820	0922	0951	1020	1122	1220	1319	1420	1521	1620	1721	1820	1921	2020	2122	2150	2251	...	0016

N – To / from Nürnberg via Pegnitz (Table **880**).
R – Change trains at Trebgast (a. 2215, d. 2225).
T – Change trains at Trebgast (a. 2354, d. 0011).

e – Ⓐ (not Jan. 6).
f – Arrives 0525.

j – On † (also Jan. 6) departs Hof 0744, Münchberg 0802.

r – Not Jan. 6.
z – Also Jan. 6.

⊕ – Change trains at Neuenmarkt on Ⓒz.
‡ – Operated by *agilis* (2nd class only).

GERMANY *See page 367 for a summary of Christmas / New Year alterations*

877 LANDSHUT - MÜHLDORF - SALZBURG
RB services

km		Ⓐe	⑥								
0	**Landshut** (Bay) Hbf .... d.	...	...	*0609*r	0836	1036	1236	1436	1636	1836	2036
55	Mühldorf (Oberbay) ..... a.	...	...	*0712*r	0928	1128	1328	1528	1728	1928	2128
55	Mühldorf (Oberbay) ..... d.	0556	0617	0741	0943	1143	1343	1544	1743	1943	2146
120	Freilassing .... 890/1 a.	0704	0711	0840	1043	1244	1444	1644	1844	2046	2245
126	**Salzburg** Hbf .... 890/1 a.	*0719*	*0728*	0855	1055	*1319*	1455	1655	1855	2057	2256

	Ⓐe	①–⑥								
Salzburg Hbf. 890/1 d.	*0515*	...	*0703*q	0909	1109	*1313*	1509	1709	1909	2109
Freilassing ..... 890/1 d.	0535	...	0718	0924	1124	1324	1524	1724	1926	2124
Mühldorf (Oberbay) ... a.	0628	...	0814	1017	1217	1418	1617	1817	2018	2224
Mühldorf (Oberbay) ... d.	...	0633	0830	1030	1230	1430	1630	1830	2032	2240
Landshut (Bay) Hbf .. a.	...	0723	0921	1121	1321	1521	1721	1921	2121	2329

e – Not Jan. 6. q – *0650* on ⑥; *0642* on ⑦ (also Jan. 6, Apr. 14, 17, May 1, 25, June 5). r – ⚒ (not Jan. 6).

878 MÜNCHEN - REGENSBURG
DB (*RE* services); *ALX*

km		*ALX* ⚒rP	N	*ALX*	N	*ALX*	*ALX* P	N	*ALX*	N	*ALX* P	*ALX* ⑤f	N	*ALX*	N	*ALX*	*ALX* P	N	*ALX*	N	*ALX*	*ALX* ⑦w		*ALX*	*ALX*
0	**München** Hbf ...... 944 d.	0455	0544	0644	0744	0844	0901	0944	1044	1144	1244	1244	1343	1444	1544	1604	1702	1744	1844	1944	2044	2044	2144	2244	0004
42	Freising .... 944 d.	0518	0608	0709	0808	0909	|	1008	1109	1208	1309	1309	1408	1509	1608	1629	1728	1808	1909	2008	2109	2109	2208	2309	0028
76	Landshut (Bay) Hbf 944 d.	0538	0632	0731	0832	0931	0944	1032	1132	1232	1332	1332	1432	1531	1632	1650	1749	1832	1932	2032	2132	2132	2232	2335	0050
99	Neufahrn (Niederbay) .. d.	|	0649	0748	0849	0948	|	1049	1148	1249	1348	1348	1449	1548	1649	|	|	1849	1948	2049	2148	2148	2249	2351	0106
138	**Regensburg** Hbf .... a.	0614	0717	0811	0914	1011	1020	1115	1211	1314	1411	1411	1514	1611	1715	1726	1825	1916	2012	2116	2211	2211	2320	0017	0133
	Schwandorf 879 885 a.	0649	...	0846	...	1050	1059	...	1247	...	1447	1447	...	1647	...	1802	1902	...	2102	...	2252	2252	...	...	...
	Hof Hbf 879 .... a.	...	...	1019	...	1220	...	...	1420	...	...	1619	...	1819	...	1933	...	...	2235	...	...	0026	...	...	...

	ALX ⚒r	*ALX*	Ⓐe	*ALX* Ⓒz	*ALX* Ⓐe	ⒶeN	*ALX*	N	*ALX* P	*ALX*	N	*ALX*	N	*ALX* P	*ALX*	N	*ALX*	N	*ALX* P	N	*ALX*	*ALX*	N	*ALX* P	N
Hof Hbf 879 .... d.	...	...	...	...	...	...	0531	...	...	0740	...	0940	...	...	1140	...	1340	...	...	...	1740	1841w	...	...	
Schwandorf 879 885 .d.	...	0501r	...	...	...	...	0703	...	0902	0909	...	1109	...	1302	1309	...	1510	...	1708	...	1909	2009w	...	2104	
Regensburg Hbf .... d.	0442	0546	0622	0646	0650	0702	0747	0844	0951	0951	1044	1146	1244	1342	1346	1444	1546	1644	1746	1844	1946	2046	2050	2141	2245
Neufahrn (Niederbay) ... d.	0508	0610	0647	0711	|	0728	0811	0911	1014	1014	1111	1211	1311	|	1411	1511	1611	1711	1811	1911	2011	2111	2120	|	2317
Landshut (Bay) Hbf 944 d.	0527	0628	0706	0729	0732	0747	0827	0929	1030	1030	1130	1227	1329	1419	1428	1529	1627	1729	1827	1929	2027	2127	2139	2220	2335
Freising .... 944 d.	0548	0649	0730	0751	|	0810	0848	0951	1050	1050	1150	1248	1349	|	1449	1549	1648	1749	1849	1951	2048	2147	*2210*	2241	2357
München Hbf .... 944 a.	0615	0717	0757	0819	0819	0835	0917	1018	1118	1118	1217	1317	1417	1505	1516	1617	1717	1817	1915	2017	2116	2217	*2235*	2305	0023

N – To / from Nürnberg (Table **921**).
P – 12 München - Schwandorf - Furth im Wald 🚌 - Praha and v.v. See also Tables **57** and **885**.
e – Not Jan. 6.
f – Also Jan. 5, Apr. 13, May 24; not Jan. 6, Apr. 14, May 26.
r – ⚒ (not Jan. 6).
w – ⑦ (also Apr. 17, May. 1, June 5; not Apr. 16, 30, June 4).
z – Also Jan. 6.
ALX – Operated by Vogtlandbahn. 🍸.

879 REGENSBURG - HOF
DB (*RE* services); *ALX*; Oberpfalzbahn

km		2 Ⓐe		2	*ALX*	2	*ALX*	2	*ALX*	2	2	*ALX* ⑤f	D	2	*ALX*	2	*ALX*		2	2	*ALX*	2	*ALX*	*ALX* ⑦w	2	2
	München Hbf 878 .. d.	...	...	...	0644	...	0844	...	1044	...	...	1244	...	...	1444	...	1604	...	...	...	1844	...	2044	2044	...	
0	**Regensburg** Hbf 885 d.	*0512*	0628	0703	0821	0857	1021	1057	1221	1257	1357	1419	1431	1457	1621	1657	1734	1828	1857	1957	2031	2138	2221	2221	...	233
42	Schwandorf .... 885 a.	*0541*	0654	0732	0846	0925	1050	1125	1247	1325	1425	1447	1458	1525	1647	1726	1802	1855	1926	2025	2102	2207	2252	2252	...	000
42	Schwandorf .... d.	0552	0656	0733	0847	0926	1051	1126	1247	1326	1426	1451	1459	1526	1647	1727	1803	1905	1927	2026	2103	2209	...	2256	2315	000
86	Weiden (Oberpf) .... d.	0630	0721	0809	0914	1002	1117	1202	1314	1402	1502	1517	1521	1602	1714	1803	1831	1928	2003	2108	2130	2248	...	2322	2350	004
137	Marktredwitz ...... 880 a.	0711	0753	0850z	0951	1044	1152	1244	1351	1444	1544	1552	1552	1644	1751	1844	1906	2001	2044	2149	2208	2327	...	2357	...	...
179	**Hof** Hbf .... 880 a.	*0754*	0819	*0924*z	1019	*1124*	1220	*1324*	1420	*1524*	...	1619	1619	*1724*	1819	*1924*	1933	2025	*2125*	...	2235	*0004*	...	0026	...	...

	ALX ⚒r	Ⓐe	2 Ⓒz	*ALX*	2	*ALX*	2	*ALX*	2	*ALX*	2	*ALX*	2	*ALX* ⑤f	2		2	2 ⑦v	2	*ALX*	2	*ALX* ⑦w			2	2
Hof Hbf .... 880 d.	...	0420	...	0531	*0629*	0740	*0840*	0940	*1040*	1140	*1240*	1340	...	1447	*1440*	1540	...	*1640*	*1640*h	1740	...	1841	1940	2040	...	*223*
Marktredwitz .... 880 d.	...	0447	...	0557	0704	0806	0915	1006	1115	1206	1315	1406	1415	1513	1516	1604	1615	1705	1715h	1806	1815	1910	2004	2104	2132	233
Weiden (Oberpf) .... d.	*0414*e	0524	0519	0636	0742	0842	0956	1042	1156	1242	1356	1442	1456	1545	1556	1638	1656	1742	1756	1842	1856	1944	2035	▬	2222j	001
Schwandorf .... a.	*0451*e	0545	0556	0701	0807	0908	1031	1108	1231	1308	1431	1509	1531	1612	1632	1700	1730	1806	1831	1908	1930	2008	2056	2	2257	...
Schwandorf .... 885 d.	0501	0548	0604	0703	0808	0909	1032	1109	1232	1309	1432	1510	1532	1613	1633	1702	1733	1808	1832	1909	1933	2009	2057	2207	*2313*	...
Regensburg Hbf .885 a.	0536	0615	0635	0737	0837	0938	1104	1137	1304	1338	1504	1537	1604	1642	1704	1731	1804	1837	1904	1937	2004	2038	2127	2238	*2341*	...
München Hbf 878 ... a.	0717	...	...	0917	...	1118	...	1317	...	1516	...	1717	...	...	...	...	...	...	...	2116	...	2217	...	...	...	...

D – ①②③④⑥⑦ (also Jan. 6, Apr. 14, May 26; not Jan. 5, Apr. 13, May 24).
e – Ⓐ (not Jan. 6).
f – Also Jan. 5, Apr. 13, May 24; not Jan. 6, Apr. 14, May 26.
h – ①–⑥ (not Apr. 17, May 1, June 5).
j – Arrives 2211.
r – Not Jan. 6.
v – Also Apr. 17, May 1, June 5.
w – Also Apr. 17, May. 1, June 5; not Apr. 16, 30, June
z – Ⓒ (also Jan. 6).
ALX – Operated by Vogtlandbahn. 🍸.

880 NÜRNBERG - HOF - DRESDEN
IRE / *RE* / *RB* services

NÜRNBERG - HOF

km				Ⓒz	Ⓒz	Ⓐe	Ⓐe	L			Ⓐe		L			Ⓐe			L			Ⓐe			L
0	**Nürnberg** Hbf .... ● d.	0535	0535	0631	0631	0637	0637	0656	0738	0738	0758	0837	0905	0938	0938	1005	1037	1037	1105	1138	1138	1205	1237	1237	130
28	Hersbruck (r Pegnitz) .... ● d.	0555	0555	0652	0652	|	|	0715	0754	0754	0815	|	0920	|	|	1019	|	|	1120	|	|	1219	|	|	132
67	Pegnitz .... ● a.	0619	0619	0713	0713	0714	0714	0738	0822	0822	0839	0914	0942	1015	1015	1042	1114	1114	1142	1215	1215	1242	1314	1314	134
67	Pegnitz .... d.	0628	0624	0715	0721	0715	0721	0739	0824	0828	0841	0916	0943	1017	1021	1043	1116	1121	1143	1217	1221	1243	1316	1321	134
	Bayreuth Hbf .... d.	|	0647	0732	|	0732	|	0758	0847	|	0855	0932	1000	1042	|	1058	1132	|	1200	1242	|	1258	1332	|	140
	Münchberg .... 876 d.	|	▬	0805	|	0805	|	...	...	|	▬	1005	...	...	|	▬	1205	|	...	...	|	▬	1405	|	...
94	Kirchenlaibach .... 887 d.	0643	⊖	|	0736	|	0736	...	...	0845	⊖	|	...	...	1042t	⊖	|	1136	...	...	1242t	⊖	|	1336	...
125	Marktredwitz ...... 879 1121 d.	0700	0712	|	0802r	|	0802r	...	...	0901	0908	|	...	...	1058	1108	|	1202r	...	...	1258	1308	|	1402r	...
	Cheb .... 1121 a.	|	0737	|	0822	|	0822	...	...	|	0933	|	...	...	|	1133	|	1222	...	...	|	1333	|	1422	...
167	**Hof** Hbf .... 876 879 887 a.	0723	...	0823	...	0823	...	...	...	0924	...	1023	...	...	1124	...	1223	...	...	...	1324	...	1423	...	...

			Ⓐe			L			Ⓐe			L			Ⓐe			L							
Nürnberg Hbf .... ● d.	1338	1338	1405	1437	1437	1505	1538	1538	1605	1637	1637	1705	1738	1738	1805	1837	1837	1905	1938	1938	2055	2055	2206	2206	225
Hersbruck (r Pegnitz) .... ● d.	|	|	1420	|	|	1520	|	|	1620	|	|	1720	|	|	1820	|	|	1920	1954	1954	2112	2112	2223	2223	231
Pegnitz .... ● a.	1415	1415	1442	1514	1514	1542	1615	1615	1642	1714	1714	1742	1815	1815	1842	1914	1914	1942	2021	2021	2137	2137	2248	2248	233
Pegnitz .... d.	1417	1421	1443	1516	1521	1543	1617	1621	1643	1716	1721	1743	1817	1821	1843	1916	1920	1943	2023	2028	2139	2144	2250	2255	233
Bayreuth Hbf .... d.	1442	|	1458	1532	|	1601	1642	|	1658	1732	|	1800	1842	|	1858	1932	|	2000	2049	|	2158	|	2310	|	235
Münchberg .... 876 d.	...	|	▬	1605	|	...	...	|	▬	1805	|	...	...	|	▬	2005	|	...	...	|	...	|	▬	|	003
Kirchenlaibach .... 887 d.	...	1442t	⊖	|	1536	...	...	1642t	⊖	|	1736	...	...	1842t	⊖	|	1935	...	...	2044	...	2158	⊖	2309	|
Marktredwitz .... 879 1121 d.	...	1459	1508	|	1602r	...	...	1658	1708	|	1802r	...	...	1858	1911	|	2001	...	...	2100	...	2216	2218	2333	|
Cheb .... 1121 a.	...	|	1533	|	1622	...	...	|	1733	|	1822	...	...	|	1936	|	...	...	...	|	...	|	2243	|	|
Hof Hbf .... 876 879 887 a.	...	1524	...	1623	...	...	...	1724	...	1823	...	...	...	1924	...	2024	...	...	...	2125	...	2242	...	0004	005

HOF - DRESDEN ⊠

km		Ⓒ																						◇
0	**Hof** Hbf .... 881 d.	...	...	...	...	0427	...	0527	...		1727	...	1827	...	1936	...	2030	...	...	...	...	...	...	224
48	Plauen (Vogtl) ob Bf ..... 881 d.	...	...	...	...	0459	...	0559	...	and at	1759	...	1859	...	2008	...	2102	...	...	...	...	...	...	232
73	Reichenbach (Vogtl) ob Bf 881 d.	...	...	...	...	0515	...	0615	...	the same	1815	...	1915	...	2024	...	2118	...	...	...	...	...	...	234
96	**Zwickau** (Sachs) Hbf .... d.	0343	...	...	0439	0531	0539	0631	0639	minutes	1831	1839	1931	1939	2040	2045	2134	2139	...	2243	...	2343	...	000
112	Glauchau (Sachs) .... 858 d.	0359	...	...	0455	0541	0555	0641	0655	past each	1841	1855	1941	1955	2050	2101	2144	2155	...	2258	...	2358	...	...
144	**Chemnitz** Hbf .... 858 d.	0430	0430	0503	0530	0603	0630	0703	0730	hour until	1903	1930	2003	2030	2112	2132	2205	2230	...	2330	...	0029	...	...
157	Flöha .... d.	0443	0443	0513	0543	0613	0643	0713	0743		1913	1943	2013	2043	2121	2144	...	2243	...	2343	...	...	...	...
183	Freiberg (Sachs) .... d.	0508	0508	0531	0608	0631	0708	0731	0808		1931	2008	2031	2108	2139	2208	...	2308	...	0008	...	...	...	...
223	**Dresden** Hbf .... a.	0551	0551	0605	0651	0705	0751	0805	0851		2005	2051	2105	2151	2211	2251	...	2351	...	0051	...	...	...	...

L – To Lichtenfels (Table **876**).
e – Ⓐ (not Jan. 6).
r – Arrives 8 minutes earlier.
t – Arrives 6 minutes earlier.
z – Also Jan. 6.
⊖ – Operated by Oberpfalzbahn.
◇ – Operated by Vogtlandbahn.
⊠ – Operated by Mitteldeutsche Regiobahn (2nd class only).
● – Certain trains between Nürnberg and Pegnitz convey portions for two separate destinations. Passengers should take care to join the correct portion for their destination.

IRE / RE services

DRESDEN - HOF - NÜRNBERG 880

DRESDEN - HOF ⊠

	Ⓐ◇	©																			◇			
resden Hbf d.	...	...	...	...	0452	0506	0552	0606	0652		1606	1652	1706	1752	1806	1852	1906	1952	2006	2052	...	2106	2206	2306
reiberg (Sachs) d.	...	...	...	...	0525	0550	0625	0650	0725	and at	1650	1725	1750	1825	1850	1925	1950	2025	2050	2125	...	2150	2250	2350
löha d.	...	...	...	...	0544	0613	0644	0713	0744	the same	1713	1744	1813	1844	1913	1944	2013	2044	2113	2144	...	2213	2313	0013
hemnitz Hbf 858 d.	...	0250	0410	...	0555	0631	0655	0731	0755	minutes	1731	1755	1831	1855	1931	1955	2031	2055	2131	2155	...	2231	2331	0025
lauchau (Sachs) 858 d.	...	0321	0441	...	0617	0702	0717	0802	0817	past each	1802	1817	1902	1917	2002	2017	2102	2117	2202	2217	...	2302	0002	...
wickau (Sachs) Hbf d.	0401	0337	0457	0510	0628	0718	0728	0818	0828	hour until	1818	1828	1918	1928	2018	2028	2118	2128	2218	2228	2240	2318	0018	...
eichenbach (Vogtl) ob Bf. 881 d.	0420	...	...	0527	0643	...	0743	...	0843		...	1843	...	1943	...	2043	...	2143	...	...	2309	...	...	...
lauen (Vogtl) ob Bf 881 d.	0442	...	...	0546	0700	...	0800	...	0900		...	1900	...	2000	...	2100	...	2200	...	...	2330	...	...	...
of Hbf 881 a.	0521	...	...	0618	0732	...	0832	...	0932		...	1932	...	2032	...	2132	...	2232	...	...	...	...	...	...

HOF - NÜRNBERG

km			Ⓐe	Ⓐe	Ⓐe	©z	©z	Ⓐe	⊖				⚒e	ⒶeL	⊖					ⒶeL	⊖				⊖
0	Hof Hbf 876 879 887 d.	...	0420	...	...	...	*0531*	0527	...	0629	...	...	0736	...	...	0840	...	...	0936	...	...	1040	...	1136	...
	Cheb 1121 d.	...	|	...	...	...	|	|	0629	|	...	...	|	...	0829	|	...	0938	|	...	1027	|	...	|	1227
	Marktredwitz 879 1121 d.	...	0442	0547	...	...	0600	|	0654	0657	...	...	|	...	0854	0902	...	1001	|	...	1052	1102	...	|	1252
	Kirchenlaibach 887 d.	...	0506	0608	...	...	0616	|	▬	0713	...	...	|	...	▬	0923t	...	1023	|	...	▬	1123t	...	|	▬
24	Münchberg 876 d.	...	|	|	...	...	|	0546	Ⓐe	|	...	...	0754	...	...	|	...	|	0954	...	...	|	...	1154	ⒶeL
72	Bayreuth Hbf d.	0500	|	|	0605	0605	|	0627	0703	|	0712	0800	0830	0903	0915	|	1001	|	1029	1103	1115	|	1201	1229	1303
99	Pegnitz a.	0521	0527	0622	0626	0626	0630	0642	0717	0731	0735	0817	0844	0918	0941	0937	1018	1038	1044	1118	1141	1137	1219	1243	1318
99	Pegnitz d.	0529	0529	0630	0630	0633	0633	0642	0718	0738	0738	0818	0845	0919	0944	0944	1019	1046	1046	1119	1144	1144	1219	1246	1319
138	Hersbruck (r Pegnitz) d.	0552	0552	0654	0654	0656	0656	|	0742	0802	0802	0839	|	0939	|	|	1039	|	|	1139	|	|	1241	|	|
166	Nürnberg Hbf a.	0607	0607	0710	0710	0712	0712	0718	0757	0819	0819	0857	0922	0955	1020	1020	1056	1122	1122	1155	1220	1220	1256	1322	1355

						ⒶeL	⊖					ⒶeL	⊖					⊖					⊖		
lof Hbf 876 879 887 d.	1240	...	...	...	1337	...	...	1440	...	...	1536	...	...	1640	...	...	1736	...	1839	...	...	1936	...	2040	2136
Cheb 1121 d.	|	...	...	1338	|	...	1427	|	...	1538	|	...	1627	|	...	1738	|	1827	|	...	1938	|	2027	|	|
larktredwitz 879 1121 d.	1302	...	...	1401	|	...	1452	1502	...	1601	|	...	1652	1702	...	1801	|	1852	1901	...	2009r	|	2052	2105	|
irchenlaibach 887 d.	1323t	...	...	1423	|	...	▬	1523t	...	1623	|	...	▬	1723t	...	1823	|	▬	1923t	...	2025	|	▬	2121	|
Münchberg 876 d.	|	...	...	|	1354	...	...	|	...	|	1554	...	...	|	...	|	1754	...	|	...	|	1954	L	|	2153
Bayreuth Hbf d.	|	1315	1401	|	1429	1503	1515	|	1601	|	1629	1703	1715	|	1801	|	1829	1915	|	2001	|	2029	2113	|	2227
egnitz a.	1337	1341	1419	1438	1444	1518	1541	1537	1619	1638	1644	1718	1741	1737	1819	1838	1844	1941	1937	2019	2039	2044	2133	2138	2246
egnitz d.	1344	1344	1419	1446	1446	1519	1544	1544	1619	1646	1646	1719	1744	1744	1819	1846	1846	1944	1944	2019	2047	2047	2141	2141	2247
ersbruck (r Pegnitz) d.	1405	1405	1440	|	|	1539	|	|	1640	|	|	1739	|	|	1840	|	|	2007	2007	2040	|	|	2207	2207	2314
ürnberg Hbf a.	1420	1420	1456	1522	1522	1555	1620	1620	1656	1722	1722	1755	1820	1820	1856	1922	1922	2022	2022	2056	2122	2122	2222	2222	2329

. – From Lichtenfels (Table 876).
– Not Jan. 6.
r – Arrives 2000.
t – Arrives 6 minutes earlier.
z – Also Jan. 6.
⊖ – Operated by Oberpfalzbahn.
◇ – Operated by Vogtlandbahn.
⊠ – Operated by Mitteldeutsche Regiobahn (2nd class only).

S-Bahn 5

ZWICKAU - LEIPZIG - HALLE 881

ate evening services Leipzig - Halle and v.v (from approx. 2000) are subject to alteration on ①② Jan. 9 - Mar. 14 and ①② from May 15 (also during the early hours of the following morning).

km			Ⓐ	©											❖								
0	Zwickau (Sachs) Hbf 858 d.	...	0335	0344	...	0505e	0514	0605	...	0705e	0713	0805	...	0905		1905	1913	2005	...	2105e	2113	...	2213
9	Werdau 858 d.	...	0344	0355	...	0513e	0524	0613	...	0713e	0724	0813	...	0913	and in	1913	1924	2013	...	2113e	2124	...	2223
29	Gößnitz 858 d.	...	0401	0415	...	0526e	0543	0626	...	0726e	0743	0826	...	0926	the same	1926	1943	2026	...	2126e	2143	...	2243
44	Altenburg d.	...	0433t	0433	0503	0538	0603	0638	0703	0738	0803	0838	0903	0938	pattern	1938	2003	2038	2103	2138	2155	...	2258
80	Leipzig-Connewitz ★ d.	0017r	0509	0509	0539	0611	0639	0711	0739	0811	0839	0911	0939	1011	every	2011	2039	2111	2139	2211	2246	2317	2346
85	Leipzig Hbf ★ 866 d.	0023‡	0523	0523	0553	0623	0653	0723	0753	0823	0853	0923	0953	1023	two hours	2023	2053	2122	2152	2223	2308k	2327	0008k
104	Leipzig/Halle Flughafen ✈ 866 d.	0038‡	0535	0535	0609	0636	0709	0736	0809	0836	0909	0936	1009	1036	until	2036	2110	2136	2209	2236	|	2343	|
122	Halle (Saale) Hbf 866 a.	0052	0554	0554	0624	...	0724	...	0824	...	0924	...	1024	...		...	2125	...	2224	...	2344	2358	0044

										❖													
lalle (Saale) Hbf 866 d.	0413	...	...	0536	...	0636	...	0736	...		1836	...	1936	...	2036	...	2136	...	2216	2250	2316	2347	0053
eipzig/Halle Flughafen ✈ 866 d.	0425	0449	0525	0549	0625	0649	0725	0749	0825	and in	1849	1926	1949	2025	2049	2122	2149	2225	|	2302	|	2359	0104
eipzig Hbf ★ 866 d.	0439	0509	0539	0609	0639	0709	0739	0809	0839	the same	1909	1939	2009	2039	2109	2139	2209	2239	2304	2318	0004	0017	0121
eipzig-Connewitz ★ d.	0449	0519	0549	0619	0649	0719	0749	0819	0849	pattern	1919	1949	2019	2049	2119	2149	2219	2249	2314	2327	0014	0028r	0130r
ltenburg d.	0522e	0600	0622	0657	0722	0800	0822	0857	0922	every	2000	2022	2057	2122	2200	2223	2257	...	0002	...	0101	...	...
ößnitz 858 d.	0535e	0615	0635e	...	0735	0815	0835	...	0935	two hours	2015	2035	...	2135	2215	2236	...	...	0016	...	...	...	...
Verdau 858 d.	0548e	0632	0648e	...	0750	0832	0848	...	0950	until	2032	2048	...	2148	2232	2253	...	...	0035	...	...	...	...
wickau (Sachs) Hbf 858 a.	0558e	0645	0658e	...	0758	0845	0858	...	0958		2045	2058	...	2158	2245	2304	...	...	0045	...	...	...	...

PLAUEN - WERDAU ◇

km		Ⓐ								Ⓐ
	Cheb 1122 d.	...	...	...	1005	1205	...	1605	1805	...
	Plauen (Vogt) ob Bf d.	0528	0728	0928	1128	1328	1528	1728	1928	2030
0	Reichenbach (Vogt) ob Bf d.	0550	0750	0950	1150	1350	1550	1750	1950	2052
17	Werdau a.	0603	0803	1003	1203	1403	1603	1803	2003	2104
	Zwickau (Sachs) Hbf a.	0617	0817	1017	1217	1417	1617	1817	2017	2119

									H	
Zwickau (Sachs) Hbf d.	0537	0737	0937	1137	1337	1537	1737	1937	2034	2240
Werdau d.	0553	0753	0953	1153	1353	1553	1753	1953	2053	2256
Reichenbach (Vogt) ob Bf a.	0606	0806	1006	1206	1406	1606	1806	2006	2105	2308
Plauen (Vogt) ob Bf a.	0629	0829	1029	1229	1429	1629	1829	2029	2127	2330
Cheb 1122 a.	...	0952	1152	...	1552	1752	...	...	...	...

H – To Hof Hbf (a. 2209).
– Ⓐ only.
k – Arrives 13 minutes earlier.
r – Mornings of ①⑥⑦ only.
t – Arrives 0412.
★ – All trains also call at Leipzig MDR, Leipzig Bayerischer Bahnhof, Leipzig Wilhelm-Leuschner-Platz and Leipzig Markt.
◇ – Operated by Vogtlandbahn (2nd class only).
❖ – Timings may vary by 1–2 minutes.
‡ – 3–4 minutes later on ①⑥⑦.

DB (RB services); ČD

CHEMNITZ - CRANZAHL - VEJPRTY - CHOMUTOV 882

km										C		
0	Chemnitz Hbf 880 d.	0636	0836	0936	1136	1236	1336	1436	1636	...	1836	2036
13	Flöha 880 d.	0647	0847	0947	1147	1247	1347	1447	1647	...	1847	2047
31	Zschopau d.	0708	0908	1008	1208	1308	1410	1508	1708	...	1910	2108
57	Annaberg-Buchholz ¶ d.	0743	0943	1048	1243	1348	1445	1543	1743	...	1945	2143
64	Cranzahl ⊖ d.	...	0955	1102	1255	1400	1501	1555z	1755	1804r	...	...
74	Bärenstein d.	...	...	1114v	▬	...	...	...	...	1816r	...	...
75	Vejprty 🏛 a.	...	...	1118v	C	...	...	...	...	1820r	...	...
75	Vejprty 🏛 d.	...	...	...	1150	...	...	...	...	1822	...	...
133	Chomutov a.	...	...	...	1310	...	...	...	...	1944	...	...

		C						C		
Chomutov d.	...	0952	...	...	...	...	...	1609	...	...
Vejprty 🏛 a.	...	1123	...	...	...	...	...	1740	...	...
Vejprty 🏛 d.	...	▬	1137v	...	...	...	...	1742r	...	...
Bärenstein d.	...	...	1141v	...	...	...	...	1746r	...	...
Cranzahl ⊖ d.	...	1001	1155	1301	1445	1557	1655z	1758r	1801	...
Annaberg-Buchholz ¶ d.	0807	1013	1207	1313	1507	1609	1707	...	1813	2007
Zschopau d.	0844	1047	1244	1347	1544	1644	1744	...	1847	2044
Flöha 880 a.	0908	1108	1308	1408	1608	1708	1808	...	1908	2108
Chemnitz Hbf. 880 a.	0920	1120	1320	1420	1620	1720	1820	...	1920	2120

⊖ – **Cranzahl - Kurort Oberwiesenthal** *Fichtelbergbahn* (17 km, narrow gauge steam). Journey: 57–64 minutes.
Operator: SDG Sächsische Dampfeisenbahngesellschaft GmbH, Bahnhofstraße 7, 09484 Kurort Oberwiesenthal. ✆ + 49 (0) 37348 151 0.
From **Cranzahl** at 0959 **E**, 1015 **D**, 1137 **E**, 1315 **E**, 1316 **D**, 1504 **E**, 1640 ⊡, 1641 **D** and 1813 **E**.
From **Kurort Oberwiesenthal** at 0825 **E**, 0850 **D**, 1014 **E**, 1152 **E**, 1157 **D**, 1330 **E**, 1519 ⊡, 1523 **D** and 1655 **E**.

C – ⑥⑦ from Apr. 29 (also May 1, 8).
D – Mar. 6 - Apr. 7.
E – To Mar. 5 and from Apr. 8.
r – Not May 1, 8.
v – ⑥⑦ from Apr. 29 (also May 1).
z – © only.
⊡ – © (also May 26; runs daily Dec. 17 - Jan. 1, Apr. 13–23).
¶ – Annaberg-Buchholz unterer Bf.

RB services

CHEMNITZ - AUE 883

km											
0	Chemnitz Hbf d.	0605	0810	0910	1110	1310	1510	1710	1910	2116	2245
27	Thalheim d.	0658	0857	0958	1157	1357	1557	1757	1957	2157	2325
36	Zwönitz d.	0709	0908	1009	1208	1408	1608	1808	2008	2208	2336
47	Lößnitz unt Bf. ⊗ d.	0719	0918	1019	1218	1418	1618	1818	2018	2218	2347
51	Aue (Sachs) a.	0724	0923	1024	1223	1423	1623	1823	2023	2223	2352

		Ⓐ								©	Ⓐ	©	
Aue (Sachs) d.	0410	0526	0629	0828	0929	1128	1328	1528	1728	1829	1928	2035	2125
Lößnitz unt Bf ⊗ d.	0415	0531	0634	0833	0934	1133	1333	1533	1733	1834	1933	2040	2130
Zwönitz d.	0427	0543	0646	0845	0946	1145	1345	1545	1745	1846	1945	2052	2142
Thalheim d.	0438	0558	0658	0858	0958	1158	1358	1558	1758	1858	1958	2104	2158
Chemnitz Hbf a.	0516	0636	0741	0941	1041	1241	1441	1641	1841	1941	2041	2147	2237

⊗ – Trains stop on request only.

884 ZWICKAU - JOHANNGEORGENSTADT - KARLOVY VARY

DB; ČD (2nd class only)

km		Ⓐ									⑤⑥f
0	**Zwickau** (Sachs) Hbf . d.	0509	...	0609	and	1909	2009	2109	2209	2309
27	Aue (Sachs) d.	0541	0541	0641	hourly	1941	2041	2141	2241	2342
37	Schwarzenberg (Erzg) . d.	0555	0555	0655	until	1955	2055	2154	...	2354
56	**Johanngeorgenstadt**. a.	0620	0620	0720		2020	2120	...	...	...

	Ⓐ								⑤⑥
Johanngeorgenstadt d.	0429	...	0529	0629	and	1829	1929	2029	...
Schwarzenberg (Erzg) d.	0456	0456	0556	0656	hourly	1856	1956	2056	2200
Aue (Sachs) d.	0509	0509	0609	0709	until	1909	2009	2109	2214
Zwickau (Sachs) Hbf a.	0541	0541	0641	0741		1941	2041	2141	2246

km	See note ▶	Ⓐ	⊗	Ⓐ	Ⓒ					Ⓒ	
0	**Johanngeorgenstadt**. d.	...	0726	0928	1028	1238	1447	1627	2040	2040	...
1	Potůčky 🏛 d.	0600	0730	0932	1032	1242	1451	1631	2050	2050	...
28	Nejdek d.	0700	0816	1016	1116	1328	1541	1716	2132	2138	2226
44	**Karlovy Vary** a.	0726	0840	1040	1141	1352	1605	1741	...	2202	2251
47	**Karlovy Vary** dolní a.	0734	0848	1048	1147	1358	1613z	1749	...	2208	...

See note ▶					Ⓐ	Ⓒ	Ⓐ	Ⓒ		
Karlovy Vary dolní d.	0540e	0743	0943	1255	1405	1433	1705	1807	2105	...
Karlovy Vary d.	0545	0749	0949	1301	1411	1447	1715	1813	2112	...
Nejdek d.	0618	0815	1017	1328	1438	1513	1741	1839	2137	2221
Potůčky 🏛 d.	0708	0901	1104	1415	1524	1600	1824	1924	...	2303
Johanngeorgenstadt a.	0710	0903	1106	1417	1526	1602	1826	1926	...	...

e – Ⓐ only. f – Also Apr. 13, 16, June 4. z – Change trains at Karlovy Vary on Ⓐ. ⊗ – Change trains at Nejdek on Ⓐ. ▶ – Czech holiday dates apply (see page 2).

885 REGENSBURG - SCHWANDORF - FURTH IM WALD - PLZEŇ

km			◇	◇	351	◇		◇	◇	353	◇	◇	◇	◇	355	◇	◇		◇		◇	357	◇		◇
			Ⓐe		‡					‡					‡🍷					A¶		‡🍷		¶	B
	München Hbf 878 d.	...	...	...	0455r	...	...	0644	...	0901	...	...	1044	...	1244	...	...	...	1444	...	1604	1702	...	1844	...
0	**Regensburg** Hbf . 879 d.	...	0512	...	0623r	0732e	...	0821	0932	1031	...	1132	1221	1332	1419	...	1532	...	1621	1657	1734	1835	1932	2031	2136
42	**Schwandorf** 879 d.	...	0550	0630	0705	0802	...	0904	1004	1107	1114	1202	1304	1404	1507	1514	1602	...	1704	1735	1805	1909	2007	2108	2210
90	Cham (Oberpf) d.	...	0628	0715	0736	0846	...	0942	1039	1135	1152	1245	1342	1439	1535	1552	1645	...	1740	1821	1840	1938	2047	2143	2246
109	**Furth im Wald** 🏛 d.	...	0644	0732	0750	0906	...	0959	1055	1150	1209	1301	1358z	1456	1550	1609	1706	...	1756	1833	1856	1952	2104	2159	2302
131	Domažlice ⊠ d.	0532	...	...	0810	0928	0939	...	...	1210	...	...	...	...	1610	...	1728	1739	...	...	...	2012	...	...	...
190	**Plzeň** Hlavni ⊠ a.	0642	...	...	0857	...	1048	...	...	1257	...	...	...	...	1657	...	...	1848	...	...	...	2059	...	...	...
–	Praha Hlavní 1120 a.	...	...	...	1041	...	...	...	...	1441	...	...	...	...	1841	...	...	...	...	...	...	2241	...	...	...

				◇	◇	356	◇		◇	◇	354	◇	◇	◇	◇	352	◇		◇			350	◇		
	Ⓐe¶	¶	‡🍷			‡🍷					‡🍷	Ⓒz				‡		Ⓐ				‡			
Praha Hlavní 1120 d.	...	...	...	...	...	0512	...	...	...	...	0912	...	...	...	...	1312	...	...	...	...	...	1712	...	...	...
Plzeň Hlavni ⊠ d.	...	...	...	...	...	0659	...	0810	...	...	1059	...	...	...	...	1459	...	1610	...	1710	...	1859	...	2110	2255
Domažlice ⊠ d.	...	...	...	...	...	0746	...	0925	0937	...	1146	...	...	...	...	1546	...	1727	1737t	1820	1837c	1946	...	2220	2355
Furth im Wald 🏛 d.	0446	0606	...	0657	0755	0812	0905	...	1002	1100	1212	1302	...	1402	1501	1612	1704	...	1804	...	1901	2014	2106	...	...
Cham (Oberpf) d.	0502	0624	...	0715	0812	0826	0922	...	1018	1117	1226	1322	1322	1418	1517	1626	1721	...	1821	...	1918	2028	2124	...	...
Schwandorf 879 a.	0534	0655	0703	0755	0844	0854	0955	...	1055	1154	1254	1356	1356	1455	1555	1655	1755	...	1857	...	1956	2056	2158	...	...
Regensburg Hbf 879 a.	0615	...	0737	0837	...	0929	1030	...	1137	1230	1330	1430	1430	1537	1630	1736	1832	...	1937	...	2030	2133	2238	...	...
München Hbf 878 a.	...	...	0917	...	...	1118	...	...	1317	...	1505	...	...	1717	...	1915	...	...	2116	...	...	2305	...	...	...

A – ①–④ (not Apr. 17, May 1, 25, June 5).
B – ⑤–⑦ (also Apr. 17, May 1, 25, June 5).
c – ⑥⑦ (also Apr. 14, 17, May 1, 8).
e – Ⓐ (not Jan. 6).
r – ⚒ (not Jan. 6).
t – ①–⑤ (not Apr. 14, 17, May 1, 8).
z – Ⓒ (also Jan. 6).
¶ – From / to Nürnberg (Table **886**).
◇ – Operated by Oberpfalzbahn (2nd class).
‡ – Train category *ALX* in Germany (operated by Vogtlandbahn).
⊠ – Other local trains Domažlice - Plzeň and v.v. (journey 68 – 80 minutes). **From Domažlice** at 0347, 0429 Ⓐ, 0614 Ⓐ, 0731, 1131, 1339, 1429 Ⓐ, 1531, 1629 Ⓐ and 1931. **From Plzeň Hlavni** at 0506 Ⓐ, 0606, 0710, 1110, 1310, 1410 Ⓐ, 1506, 1810 Ⓐ and 1910.

886 NÜRNBERG - SCHWANDORF and WEIDEN

RE services

km				Ⓐe		Ⓐe	Ⓒz										Ⓐef		⊡		⊡		f			
0	**Nürnberg** Hbf ◧ d.	0017	...	0434	0535	0624	0631	0738	0843	0943	1043	1143	1243	1343	1443	1543	1605	1643	1705	1743	1805	1843	1938	2055	2206	2257
28	Hersbruck (r Pegnitz) ◧ d.	0033	...	0449	0551	0652‡	0648	0757	0858	0958	1058	1158	1258	1358	1458	1558	1625	1658	1725	1758	1825	1858	1958	2117	2227	2316
56	Sulzbach-Rosenberg . d.	0059	...	0515	0619	0728	0728	0826	0925	1026	1126	1226	1326	1426	1526	1626	1649	1726	1749	1826	1852	1926	2026	2142	2251	2341
68	Amberg d.	0106	...	0526	0627	0736	0736	0833	0935	1033	1133	1233	1333	1433	1533	1633	1701	1736	1801	1833	1901	1933	2036	2150	2259	2348
94	**Schwandorf** a.	...	...	0543	0643	0757	0757	0848	0949	1048	1148	1248	1350	1448	1548	1650	1722	1751	1824	1848	1926	1947	2051	2204	2312	0002

	Ⓐe	⚒e	†z	Ⓐe	Ⓐef	Ⓒz	Ⓐe	f	Ⓐe																
Schwandorf d.	0407	0509	0516	0544	0558	0609	0644	0707	0740	0806	0906	1006	1106	1206	1306	1406	1504	1605	1705	1807	1908	2006	2107	2212	0010
Amberg d.	0423	0526	0532	0559	0615	0626	0700	0725	0756	0822	0921	1021	1121	1221	1321	1421	1521	1621	1721	1821	1922	2021	2121	2226	0025
Sulzbach-Rosenberg d.	0432	0535	0541	0607	0626	0634	0707	0732	0807	0829	0929	1029	1129	1229	1329	1429	1529	1629	1729	1829	1929	2029	2129	2234	...
Hersbruck (r pegnitz) d.	0503	0607	0607	|	0649	0707	|	0757	0841	0900	0959	1100	1159	1300	1359	1500	1559	1700	1759	1900	1959	2100	2207‡	2314‡	...
Nürnberg Hbf a.	0518	0621	0621	0651	0706	0722	0751	0814	0857	0915	1014	1115	1214	1316	1414	1515	1614	1715	1814	1916	2014	2116	2222	2329	...

NÜRNBERG - WEIDEN

km			Ⓐe	Ⓒz								
0	**Nürnberg** Hbf ◧ d.	0535	0624	0631	0738	0843	and	1843	1938	2055	2206	2257
28	Hersbruck (r Pegnitz) ◧ d.	0551	0643	0648	0757	0858	hourly	1858	1958	2117	2227	2316
97	**Weiden** (Oberpf) a.	0645	0734	0748	0852	0950	until	1950	2051	2214	2321	0008

	Ⓒz	Ⓐe			✣					
Weiden (Oberpf) d.	0610	0610	0657	0806	and	1703	1803	1906	2003	2215
Hersbruck (r Pegnitz) a.	0706	0707	0756	0859	hourly	1758	1859	1958	2059	2306
Nürnberg Hbf a.	0722	0724	0814	0915	until	1814	1916	2014	2116	2329

e – Not Jan. 6.
f – To / from Furth im Wald (Table **885**).
z – Also Jan. 6.
⊡ – ①–④ (not Apr. 17, May 1, 25, June 5).
‡ – Arrives 8 – 10 minutes earlier.
✣ – Weiden d. 1403 / 1603 (not 1406 / 1606).
◧ – Certain trains from Nürnberg and Hersbruck convey portions for two separate destinations. Passengers should take care to join the correct portion for their destination.

887 BAYREUTH - WEIDEN

Operated by *agilis* (2nd class only)

km		Ⓐe								Ⓒz	Ⓐe								
0	**Bayreuth** Hbf ★ d.	0507	0624	0805	0859	0959	1059	1159	1259	1359	1401	1459	1559	1659	1759	1859	2023	2203	0002
19	Kirchenlaibach ★ a.	0528	0639	0826	0915	1016	1115	1215	1315	1415	1417	1515	1616	1715	1816	1915	2039	2223	0018
19	Kirchenlaibach d.	0528	0652	0826	0920	1020	1120	1220	1320	1420	1420	1520	1620	1720	1820	1920	2048	2224	...
59	**Weiden** a.	0557	0726	0855	0950	1050	1150	1249	1353	1449	1449	1549	1649	1749	1849	1949	2117	2252	...

	Ⓐe	Ⓐe							Ⓒz	Ⓐe									
Weiden d.	...	0525	0638e	0734	0907	1007	1107	1207	1307	1323	1407	1507	1607	1707	1807	1907	2007	2134	...
Kirchenlaibach a.	...	0600	0707e	0803	0941	1041	1141	1241	1341	1354	1441	1541	1641	1741	1841	1940	2041	2204	...
Kirchenlaibach ★ d.	0509	0606	0720	0807	0942	1042	1142	1242	1342	1355	1442	1542	1642	1742	1842	1941	2044	2204	2337
Bayreuth Hbf ★ a.	0524	0622	0735	0823	0958	1058	1158	1258	1358	1415	1458	1558	1658	1758	1857	1957	2100	2220	2353

e – Ⓐ (not Jan. 6).
z – Also Jan. 6.
★ – **Additional journeys** Bayreuth - Kirchenlaibach and v.v. (journey: 16 – 22 minutes). **From Bayreuth** at 0718, 0919, 1119, 1319, 1519, 1719, 1824, 2005. **From Kirchenlaibach** at 0657, 0840, 0921, 1121, 1321, 1417, 1521, 1617, 1721, 1817, 2123.

888 KEMPTEN - REUTTE IN TIROL - GARMISCH-PARTENKIRCHEN

RE / *RB* services

km											
0	**Kempten** (Allgäu) Hbf d.	0540	0734	0934	1134	1334	1534	1634	1734	1951	2253
18	Oy-Mittelberg d.	0607	0801	1001	1201	1401	1601	1701	1801	2018	2323
24	Nesselwang d.	0620	0812	1012	1212	1412	1612	1712	1812	2029	2334
31	Pfronten-Ried d.	0629	0822	1022	1222	1422	1622	1722	1822	2038	2344
33	**Pfronten-Steinach** 🏛 d.	0634	0828	1031	1227	1427	1627	1731	1831	2042	2347
38	Vils in Tirol 🏛 d.	0643d	0837	1040	1236	1436	1636	1740	1840	2051	...
48	**Reutte in Tirol** a.	0657d	0851	1054	1250	1450	1650	1754	1854	2105	...

Reutte in Tirol d.	0709a	0804c	0907	1109	1309	1509	1707	1807	1903	2110
Vils in Tirol 🏛 d.	0723a	0818c	0921	1123	1323	1523	1721	1821	1917	2124
Pfronten-Steinach 🏛 d.	0734	0834	0934	1134	1334	1534	1734	1834	1927	2137
Pfronten-Ried d.	0738	0838	0938	1138	1338	1538	1738	1838	1931	2141
Nesselwang d.	0748	0848	0948	1148	1348	1548	1748	1848	1940	2151
Oy-Mittelberg d.	0801	0901	1001	1201	1401	1601	1801	1901	1950	2201
Kempten (Allgäu) Hbf a.	0828	0928	1028	1228	1428	1628	1828	1928	2018	2228

km		h		h			a			a	c		a	c		
0	**Reutte in Tirol** d.	0526	0701	0801	0901	1101	1158	1301	1501	1601	1626	1701	1801	1826	1901	2107
20	Lermoos d.	0550	0725	0825	0925	1125	1225	1325	1525	1625	1652	1725	1825	1852	1925	2131
23	Ehrwald Zugspitzbahn 🏛 d.	0556	0731	0831	0931	1131	1231	1331	1531	1631	1658	1731	1831	1858	1931	2137
45	**Garmisch**-Partenkirchen a.	0623	0757	0857r	0957	1157	1257	1357	1557	1657	1729	1757	1857	1929	1957	2203
	München Hbf 895 a.	...	0926z	1026e	1126	1326	1426	1526	1726z	1826	1847	1926	2026e	2046	2126	...

	h	c	a		a				a		c				Ⓑb	
München Hbf 895 d.	...	0532	...	0632z	0732	0832	...	1032	1132	1232	...	1432z	1532	1632	1732	1832
Garmisch-Partenkirchen d.	0637	0704	0722	0804	0904	1004	...	1204	1304	1404	1504	1604	1657v	1804	1904k	2004
Ehrwald Zugspitzbahn 🏛 d.	0702	0731	0752	0831	0931	1031	...	1231	1400j	1431	1531	1631	1731	1831	1931	2031
Lermoos d.	0706	0735	0756	0835	0935	1035	...	1235	1404	1435	1535	1635	1735	1835	1935	2035
Reutte in Tirol a.	0736	0800	0833	0900	1000	1100	...	1300	1431	1500	1600	1700	1800	1900	2000	2100

a – ①–⑤ (not Jan. 6, Apr. 17, May 1, 25, June 5).
b – Not Jan. 5, Apr. 16, 30, May 24, June 4.
c – ⑥⑦ (also Jan. 6, Apr. 17, May 1, 25, June 5).
d – ①–⑥ (not Jan. 6, Apr. 14, 17, May 1, 25, June 5).
e – ①–⑤ (not Jan. 6, Apr. 14, 17, May 1, 25, June 5).
h – ①–⑥ (not Jan. 6, Apr. 17, May 1, 25, June 5).
j – Arrives 1329.
k – 1856 on ⑦ (also Jan. 6, Apr. 17, May 1, 25, June 5).
r – 0901 on ⑥.
v – 1704 on dates in note **a**.
z – ⑥⑦ (also Jan. 6, Apr. 14, 17, May 1, 25, June 5).

MÜNCHEN - SALZBURG 890

Bayerische Oberlandbahn; DB

km		◇ Ⓐt		◇ Ⓒz	◇ Ⓐt	RJ 265 ✗	◇	RJ 61 B✗	◇	RJ 111 ◧ ✗♦	◇	RJ 63 Ⓒ B✗	RJ 63 B✗	◇	EC 217 L 🍷♦	◇	RJ 65 B✗	◇	EC 113 ◧ ✗♦	◇	RJ 67 B✗	◇	IC 2083 L 🍷♦	EC 115 ◧ 🍷♦
	Frankfurt (Main) Hbf **912** d.	...	...	...	...	...	...	...	...	...	...	0517	...	...	...	...	...	...	0822	...	...	...	...	...
	Stuttgart Hbf **930** d.	...	...	...	...	...	...	...	...	...	...	0658	...	...	0758	...	...	...	0958	...	...	...	...	1158
0	**München** Hbf **951** d.	...	...	0548	0552	0624**b**	0655	0725	0755	0818	0855	0930**b**	0930**b**	0955	1017	1055	1130**b**	1155	1217	1255	1330**b**	1355	...	1417
10	München Ost **951** d.	...	...	0557	0601	0633**b**	0704	|	0805	0827	0904	|	|	1004	1027	1104	|	1204	1227	1304	|	1404	1412	1427
65	Rosenheim **951** d.	0532	...	0635	0640	0703**b**	0735	0803	0835	0857	0935	|	|	1035	1057	1135	|	1235	1257	1335	|	1435	1441	1457
82	Bad Endorf d.	0543	...	0646	0652	|	0746	|	0846	|	0946	|	|	1046	|	1146	|	1246	|	1346	|	1446	1454	|
90	Prien am Chiemsee d.	0549	...	0652	0659	|	0752	|	0852	0913	0952	|	|	1052	1113	1152	|	1252	1313	1352	|	1452	1502	1513
118	Traunstein d.	0612	...	0716	0722	|	0816	|	0916	0933	1016	|	|	1116	1133	1216	|	1316	1333	1416	|	1516	1523	1533
147	Freilassing **891** d.	0633	...	0734	0744	|	0834	|	0934	0951	1034	|	|	1134	1151	1234	|	1334	1351	1434	|	1534	1540	1551
153	**Salzburg** Hbf 🏛 **891** a.	0640	...	0741	0751	0758	0841	0858	0941	0959	1041	1058	1058	1141	1159	1241	1258	1341	1359	1441	1458	1541	...	1559
	Wien Hbf **950** a.	...	...	...	...	1030	...	1130	...	...	...	1330	1330	...	...	...	1530	...	...	...	1730	...	...	...

	◇	◇ Ⓐt	RJ 69 ✗	◇	EC 219 L 🍷♦	◇ Ⓐt	◇	◇ Ⓐt	RJ 261 ✗	◇	EC 117 ⒷL 🍷♦	EC 1217 ⑥L 🍷♦	◇	IC 1269 ⒷL K🍷	NJ 295 [R] M♦	◇	NJ 295 [R] L♦	EC 391 ⒷL 🍷	◇	◇	◇	EN 463 [R] N 🍷♦	EN 499 [R] N 🍷♦	◇
Frankfurt (Main) Hbf **912** d.	...	...	...	...	1220	...	...	...	...	...	1420	...	...	...	...	...	...	1620	...	...	...	...	...	...
Stuttgart Hbf **930** d.	...	...	...	...	1358	...	...	...	...	...	1558	1558	...	1653	...	...	...	1758	...	...	...	...	...	...
nchen Hbf **951** d.	1455	1527	1530	1555	1617	1634	1655	1726	1730	1755	1817	1817	1856	1916	1917	1955	2010	2017	2044	2144	2244	2335	2335	2350
nchen Ost **951** d.	1504	1535	|	1604	1627	1643	1704	1734	|	1804	1827	1827	1905	1926	1927**u**	2004	2020**u**	2029	2052	2152	2252	2346**u**	2346**u**	2359
senheim **951** d.	1535	1613	|	1635	1657	1715	1735	1814	|	1835	1857	1857	1935	1956	2015**u**	2035	2050**u**	2058	2131	2231	2331	0018**u**	0018**u**	0035
d Endorf d.	1546	1626	|	1646	|	1726	1746	1826	|	1846	|	|	1946	2008	|	2046	|	2110	2142	2242	2342	|	|	0046
ien am Chiemsee d.	1552	1633	|	1652	1713	1733	1752	1833	|	1852	1913	1913	1952	2015	|	2052	|	2117	2148	2248	2348	|	|	0052
aunstein d.	1616	1656	|	1716	1733	1756	1816	1856	|	1916	1933	1933	2016	2035	|	2116	|	2136	2211	2311	0011	|	|	0116
eilassing **891** d.	1634	...	|	1734	1751	...	1834	...	|	1934	1951	1951	2034	2052	|	2134	|	2154	2230	2330	0030	|	|	0134
lzburg Hbf 🏛 **891** a.	1641	...	1658	1741	1759	...	1840	...	1858	1941	1959	1959	2041	2100	2125	2141	2152	2202	2237	2337	0037	0119	0119	0141
Wien Hbf **950** a.	...	...	1930	...	...	...	...	...	2130	...	...	...	...	...	...	...	...	...	...	...	...	0635	...	...

	◇ Ⓐt	EN 462 [R] 🍷♦	EN 498 [R] 🍷♦		◇ Ⓐt	◇	◇ Ⓐt	IC 1296 ①–⑥ L🍷	◇ Ⓐt	◇	NJ 294 [R] ♦	IC 1268 ⊡ K🍷	IC 1216 ⑤ 🍷♦	◇ Ⓐt	◇ Ⓒz	EC 390 L 🍷	◇	◇ Ⓐt	RJ 260 ✗	◇	IC 2082 L 🍷♦	EC 218 L 🍷♦	◇	RJ 262 ✗
Wien Hbf **950** d.	...	2325	...	...	...	...	...	...	...	...	...	...	...	...	...	...	...	...	0630	...	...	...	...	0830
lzburg Hbf 🏛 **891** d.	0400	0427	0427	...	...	0515	...	0545	0600	0615	0627	0642	0642	*0703*	0715	0800	0815	...	0900	0915	...	1000	1015	1100
eilassing **891** d.	0408	|	|	...	...	0524	...	0553	0608	0624	|	0650	0650	0724	0724	0808	0824	...	|	0924	0945	1008	1024	|
aunstein d.	0426	|	|	...	0516	0544	0600	0611	0627	0644	|	0708	0708	0744	0744	0825	0844	0905	|	0944	1003	1025	1044	|
ien am Chiemsee d.	0448	|	|	...	0538	0606	0622	0629	0650	0706	|	0727	0727	0806	0806	0844	0906	0927	|	1006	1025	1044	1106	|
d Endorf d.	0455	|	|	...	0544	0613	0629	0637	0656	0713	|	0735	0735	0813	0813	|	0913	0933	|	1013	1033	|	1113	|
senheim **951** d.	0508	0525**s**	0525**s**	...	0559	0629	0644	0652	0712	0729	0731**s**	0749	0749	0829	0829	0903	0929	0948	|	1029	1047	1103	1129	|
nchen Ost **951** a.	0535	0557**s**	0557**s**	...	0627	0656	0711	0719	0739	0756	|	0817	0817	0856	0856	0931	0956	1016	|	1056	1115	1131	1156	|
nchen Hbf **951** a.	0545	0610	0610	...	0640	0710	0721	0731	0749	0806	0819**c**	0828	0828	0906	0906	0941	1006	1025	1030**c**	1106	...	1141	1206	1230**c**
Stuttgart Hbf **930** a.	...	...	...	...	...	...	...	0959	...	...	...	1106	1107	...	...	1159	...	...	...	...	...	1359	...	...
Frankfurt (Main) Hbf **912** a.	...	...	...	...	...	...	...	1140	...	...	...	...	...	...	...	1340	...	...	...	...	...	1540	...	...

	◇	EC 114 🍷♦	◇	RJ 60 B✗	◇	EC 112 ✗♦	◇	RJ 62 B✗	◇	EC 216 L 🍷♦	◇	RJ 64 B✗	◇		◇	RJ 66 ⊖ B✗	RJ 1066 ⑤⑥v B✗	◇	RJ 110 ◐ ✗♦	◇	RJ 68 B✗	◇		◇
Wien Hbf **950** d.	...	...	...	1030	...	...	...	1230	...	...	...	1430	...	...	...	1630	1630	...	...	...	1830	...	...	...
lzburg Hbf 🏛 **891** d.	1115	1200	1215	1300	1313	1400	1415	1500	1515	1600	1615	1700	1715	...	1815	1856	1856	1915	2000	2020	2100	2115	...	2300
eilassing **891** d.	1124	1208	1224	|	1324	1408	1424	|	1524	1608	1624	|	1724	...	1824	|	|	1929	2008	2029	|	2129	...	2310
aunstein d.	1144	1225	1244	|	1344	1425	1444	|	1544	1625	1644	|	1744	...	1844	|	|	1949	2025	2049	|	2149	...	2329
en am Chiemsee d.	1206	1244	1306	|	1406	1444	1506	|	1606	1644	1706	|	1806	...	1906	|	|	2011	2044	2111	|	2211	...	2351
d Endorf d.	1213	|	1313	|	1413	|	1513	|	1613	|	1713	|	1813	...	1913	|	|	2018	|	2118	|	2218	...	2357
senheim **951** d.	1229	1303	1329	|	1429	1503	1529	|	1629	1703	1729	|	1829	...	1929	|	|	2032	2103	2133	2156	2232	...	0012
nchen Ost **951** a.	1256	1331	1356	|	1456	1531	1556	|	1656	1731	1756	|	1856	...	1956	|	|	2105	2131	2207	|	2305	...	0046
nchen Hbf **951** a.	1306	1341	1406	1430**c**	1505	1541	1606	1631**c**	1706	1741	1806	1831	1906	...	2006	2029**c**	2032**c**	2115	2142	2217	2232	2315	...	0057
Stuttgart Hbf **930** a.	...	1600	...	...	...	1759	...	...	...	2000	...	...	...	...	...	...	2259	...	...	...	...	...	...	...
Frankfurt (Main) Hbf **912** a.	...	...	...	...	...	1940	...	...	...	...	...	...	...	...	...	...	0042	...	...	...	...	...	...	...

– **NOTES** (LISTED BY TRAIN NUMBER)

0/1 – [12] and ✗ Klagenfurt - Villach - München and v.v.
2/3 – [12] and ✗ Klagenfurt - Villach - München - Frankfurt and v.v.; [12] Zagreb (**212/3**) - Ljubljana - Jesenice 🏛 - Villach - München - Frankfurt and v.v.
4 – WÖRTHERSEE – [12] and 🍷 Klagenfurt - München - Mannheim - Dortmund.
5 – WÖRTHERSEE – [12] and 🍷 Münster - Köln - Mannheim - München - Klagenfurt.
7 – [12] and 🍷 Frankfurt - Salzburg - Villach - Klagenfurt.
6/7 – [12] and 🍷 Graz - Bischofshofen - Salzburg - Mannheim - Saarbrücken and v.v.
3/9 – [12] and 🍷 Graz - Bischofshofen - Salzburg - Frankfurt and v.v.
4/5 – 🛏 1, 2 cl., ▬ 2 cl. and [2] Roma - Firenze - Bologna - München and v.v.
2/3 – KÁLMÁN IMRE – 🛏 1, 2 cl., ▬ 2 cl., [2] and 🍷 Budapest - München and v.v.
8/9 – LISINSKI – 🛏 1, 2 cl., ▬ 2 cl. and [2] Zagreb - Ljubljana - Jesenice 🏛 - Villach - München and v.v.
16 – ⑤ to Apr. 7 (also Apr. 13). [12] and 🍷 Salzburg - Mannheim - Mainz - Köln - Dortmund - Berlin.
17 – [12] and 🍷 Karlsruhe - Salzburg - Villach - Klagenfurt.
82/3 – KÖNIGSSEE – [12] and 🍷 Berchtesgaden - Augsburg - Hamburg and v.v.

– To / from Budapest (Table **1250**).
– To / from Karlsruhe (Table **931**).

L – Until Apr. 13.
M – From Apr. 14.
N – On ⑥⑦ from Apr. 15 (not May 20, 21) departs München Hbf 2154, München Ost 2204, Rosenheim 2256.

b – 1–2 minutes **earlier** from Apr. 14.
c – 3–10 minutes later from Apr. 14.
s – Calls to set down only.
t – Not Jan. 6.
u – Calls to pick up only.
v – Also Dec. 25, Apr. 13, 16, 30, May 24, June 4.
z – Also Jan. 6.

⊖ – ①②③④⑦ (not Dec. 25, Apr. 13, 16, 30, May 24, June 4).
⊡ – ①②③④⑥ to Apr. 12.
◧ – Timings may vary by up to 11 minutes Apr. 14 - July 16.
◐ – Timings may vary by up to 1–2 minutes Apr. 14 - July 16.
◇ – *Meridian* regional service (operated by Bayerische Oberlandbahn). German holiday dates apply. **Subject to alteration from Apr. 14**.

SALZBURG - FREILASSING - BERCHTESGADEN 891

erchtesgadener Land Bahn *

Subject to alteration from April 14

km		Ⓐ t	‡	Ⓐ t	Ⓒ z					⊡					A										
0	**Salzburg** Hbf **890** d.	0451	*0615*	*0703*	*0715*	*0815*	0842	*0915*	0942	and at	1342	*1415*	*1442*	1525	*1542*	*1615*	1642	*1715*	1742	*1815*	1842	*1915*	*2042*	*2142*	2229
6	Freilassing **890** a.	0503	*0622*	*0712*	*0722*	*0822*	0854	*0922*	0954	the same	1354	*1422*	*1454*	1537	*1554*	*1622*	1654	*1722*	1754	*1822*	1854	*1922*	*2054*	*2154*	2241
6	Freilassing d.	0505	0634	0718	0741	0841	0858	0941	1004	minutes	1404	1441	1502	1541	1604	1640	1704	1741	1804	1841	1904	1941	2059	2200	2246
21	Bad Reichenhall d.	0522	0655	0741	0759	0902	0920	1000	1022	past each	1422	1500	1520	1558	1624	1658	1722	1800	1822	1900	1922	2000	2118	2217	2305
39	**Berchtesgaden** Hbf a.	...	0726	0810	0827	0929	...	1028	...	hour until	...	1528	...	...	1656	1726	...	1828	...	1928	...	2028	2147	2245	2333

	Ⓐ t	① g	Ⓐ t		Ⓒ z		Ⓐ t	①–⑥ r		A			♥						‡						
rchtesgaden Hbf d.	...	0531	...	0621	...	0706	...	...	...	0828	...	0930	and at	...	1529	...	1618	...	1727	...	1829	...	1929	2029	2208
d Reichenhall d.	0528	0601	0601	0654	...	0740	0803	...	0839	0901	0939	0959	the same	1539	1601	1639	1657	1739	1759	1839	1859	1940	1959	2059	2242
ilassing a.	0545	0618	0618	0711	...	0757	0820	...	0857	0918	1000	1020	minutes	1600	1620	1700	1720	1800	1821	1900	1920	2000	2016	2115	2302
ilassing **890** d.	0547	0620	0620	*0717*r	0734	*0807*	...	0826	*0907*	*0934*	1007	*1034*	past each	1607	*1634*	1707	*1734*	1807	*1834*	*1907*	*1934*	2007	*2025*	*2134*	*2307*
lzburg Hbf **890** a.	0558	0631	0631	*0728*r	0741	*0819*	...	0837	*0919*	*0941*	1019	*1041*	hour until	1619	*1641*	1719	*1741*	1819	*1840*	*1919*	*1941*	2019	*2037*	*2141*	*2319*

– Until Apr. 13. *IC* **2082/3**: KÖNIGSSEE – [12] and 🍷 Berchtesgaden - München Ost - Hamburg and v.v. Train category *RE* Berchtesgaden - Freilassing and v.v. Operated by DB.

– Also Apr. 18, May 2, 26, June 6; not Apr. 17, May 1, June 5.
①–⑥ (not Jan. 6, Apr. 17, May 1, 25, June 5).

t – Not Jan. 6.
z – Also Jan. 6.

– The 1039, 1239 and 1439 from Bad Reichenhall require a change of trains at Freilassing.

⊡ – The 1042 and 1242 from Salzburg require a change of trains at Freilassing (and runs 2 minutes **earlier** Freilassing - Bad Reichenhall). Connection departs Salzburg *1313* (not *1315*).

* – Services to / from Bad Reichenhall or Berchtesgaden are operated by Berchtesgadener Land Bahn GmbH. 2nd class only. Other trains are operated by either DB or ÖBB. German holiday dates apply.

‡ – Operated by DB. Conveys 🍷.

GERMANY
See page 367 for a summary of Christmas / New Year alterations

892 FLUGHAFEN MÜNCHEN ✈ (S-Bahn services S1, S8) — 2nd class only

km		S8	S8	S8	S8		S8	S1	S8	S1	S8	S1	S8		S1	S8	S1	S8	S1	S8	S8
0	**München** Pasing d.	0005	0045	0125	0305	and every	0445	...	0505	...	0525	...	0545	and at the	...	2245	...	2305	...	2325	234
7	**München** Hbf (low level) d.	0015	0055	0135	0315	20 minutes	0455	0503	0515	0523	0535	0543	0555	same minutes	2243	2255	2303	2315	2323	2335	235
11	**München** Ost d.	0024	0104	0144	0324	until	0504	|	0524	|	0544	|	0604	past each	|	2304	|	2324	|	2344	000
44	**München Flughafen** Terminal ✈ a.	0055	0135	0215	0355		0535	0546	0555	0606	0615	0626	0635	hour until	2326	2335	2346	2355	0006	0015	003

km*		S8	S8	S8	S8		S8	S1	S8	S1	S8	S1	S8		S1	S8	S1	S8	S1	S8	S1
0	**München Flughafen** Terminal ✈ d.	0004	0044	0124	0404	and every	0544	0551	0604	0611	0624	0631	0644	and at the	2251	2304	2311	2324	2331	2344	235
	München Ost a.	0035	0115	0155	0435	20 minutes	0615	|	0635	|	0655	|	0715	same minutes	|	2335	|	2355	|	0015	|
41	**München** Hbf (low level) a.	0045	0125	0205	0445	until	0625	0637	0645	0657	0705	0717	0725	past each	2337	2345	2357	0005	0017	*0027*	003
	München Pasing a.	0055	0135	0215	0455		0635	...	0655	...	0715	...	0735	hour until	...	2355	...	0015	...	*0037*	...

* – Via Neufahrn (b Freising).

☛ Many **S1** trains from München Hbf are combined with a Freising service - travel in the rear portion for the Airport.

893 MÜNCHEN - MÜHLDORF - SIMBACH

km																										
				⚒e								Ⓐe		Ⓐe	Ⓒz	Ⓐe		Ⓐe		Ⓐe		Ⓐe		⊙		
0	**München** Hbf d.	...	0606	0706	0807z	0907	1007	1107	1207	1307	1407	1427	1506	1522	1607	1626	1707	1721	1806	1831	1907	1948	2027	2129	2228	232
10	**München** Ost d.	...	0616	0716	0816	0917	1017	1117	1217	1317	1417	1439	1515	1532	1617	1638	1717	1739	1817	1840	1917	1957	2038	2139	2238	233
85	**Mühldorf** (Oberbay) a.	...	0722	0818	0919	1016	1116	1216	1316	1417	1517	1535	1619	1630	1717	1731	1820r	1830	1919	1931	2020	2101	2140	2236	2336	003
			|	◇	¶	¶	¶	¶	¶	¶	¶	|	¶	|		◇	¶	|		◇	¶		¶	|	¶	
		⚒e	|									|	Ⓒz	|			Ⓒz	|						|		
85	**Mühldorf** (Oberbay) d.	0637	0737	0837	0937	1037	1137	1227‡	1337	1437	1538	1538	1637	1634	...	1737	1837	1833	...	1937	2037	...	2146	2247	2342	...
124	**Simbach** (Inn) 962 a.	0713	0813	0913	1013	1113	1213	1258‡	1413	1513	1614	1614	1713	1708	...	1813	1913	1907	...	2013	2113	...	2218	2318	0014	...

			Ⓐe	⑥	Ⓐe	Ⓐe	Ⓒz						Ⓒz	Ⓐe						Ⓐe	Ⓒz		Ⓐe	Ⓒz	⊙		
Simbach (Inn) 962 d.	...	...	0507	0543	0554	0648	0648	0749	0849	0949	1049	1149	1249	1259	1349	1449	1550	...	1639	1649	1749	1839	1849	1949	2049	215
Mühldorf (Oberbay) a.	...	...	0540	0614	0628	0722	0722	0822	0922	1022	1123	1222	1322	1332	1421	1525	1622	...	1718	1722	1822	1917	1922	2022	2125	222
			¶	¶	|	|	¶	¶	¶	¶	¶	¶		◇	¶	¶	¶			◇	¶		◇	|	|	|
	⚒e	⚒e	Ⓐe	Ⓒz	|	|	Ⓒz										Ⓒz	Ⓐe						|	|	
Mühldorf (Oberbay) d.	0429	0522	0546	0623	0637	0732	0731	0830	0937	1030	1138	1231	...	1340	1430	1538	1630	1634	...	1737	1842	...	1940	2034	2146	224
München Ost a.	0523	0625	0640	0724	0722	0822	0826	0926	1045	1127	1246	1327	...	1443	1525	1645	1725	1745	...	1845	1945	...	2043	2144	2247	235
München Hbf a.	0533	0637	0652	0736	0734	0833	0837	0935	1056	1138	1256	1337	...	1454	1536	1656	1737	1754	...	1855	1955	...	2055	2154	2257	000

e – Not Jan. 6.
r – 1816 on Ⓒ (also Jan. 6).
z – Ⓒ (also Jan. 6).
‡ – On Ⓒ (also Jan. 6) Mühldorf d. 1237, Simbach a. 1313.
⊙ – Change trains at Mühldorf on † (also Jan. 6).
◇ – Change trains. Daily from Mühldorf.
¶ – Change trains.

895 MÜNCHEN - GARMISCH - INNSBRUCK — DB; ÖBB (2nd class only in Austria)

km										ICE		ICE			ICE											
				◧	◧	◧	◧		◧	◧	1127	◧	583		◧	1207	◧	◧	◧	◧						
		Ⓐe		Ⓒz							⑥D		⑥L			QK										Ⓒz
0	**München** Hbf d.	0453	...	0532	0632	0732	0832	0932f	1032	1132	1213	1232	1252	1332	1432	1453j	1532	1632	1732	1832	1932	2032	2132	2232	2332	233
7	München Pasing d.	0500	...	0539	0639	0739	0839	0939f	1039	1139	|	1239	|	1339	1439	|	1539	1639	1739	1839	1939	2039	2139	2239	2339	233
40	Tutzing d.	0528	...	0601	0701	0801	0901	1001	1101	1201	1242	1301	1324	1401	1501	1522	1601	1700	1801	1901	2001	2101	2201	2301	0001	000
54	Weilheim (Oberbay) d.	0545	...	0612	0712	0812	0912	1012	1112	1212	|	1312	|	1412	1512	|	1612	1712	1812	1912	2012	2112	2212	2312	0012	001
75	Murnau d.	0605	...	0628	0728	0828	0928	1028	1128	1228	1311	1328	1357	1428	1528	1558	1628	1728	1828	1928	2028	2128	2228	2328	0028	002
101	**Garmisch**-Partenk. a.	0630	...	0654	0754	0854	0954	1054	1154	1254	1337	1354	1428	1454	1554	1622	1654	1755	1854	1954	2054	2154	2254	2354	0054	005
101	**Garmisch**-Partenk. d.	0632	0632	...	*0802*	0906	1002	1102	*1202*	1302	...	1402	...	1502	*1602*	1625	1702	1802	1902	*2002*	2102	2202	2302	0002	...	010
118	**Mittenwald** a.	0653	0653	...	*0823*	0927	1023	1123	*1223*	1323	...	1423	...	1523	*1623*	1653	1723	1823	1923	*2023*	2123	2223	2323	0023	...	012
118	**Mittenwald** 🏛 d.	0655	0655	...	*0826*	0936	1026	1136c	*1226*	1336c	...	1426	...	1536	*1626*	1715b	1736c	1826	1936	*2026*	...	...	...	...	...	...
125	Scharnitz 🏛 ⊡ d.	0703	0703	...	*0834*	0944	1034	1144c	*1234*	1344c	...	1434	...	1544	*1634*	|	1744c	1834	1944	*2034*	...	...	...	...	...	...
135	Seefeld in Tirol ⊡ d.	0716	0716	...	*0846*	0956	1046	1156c	*1246*	1356c	...	1446	...	1556	*1646*	1746b	1756c	1846	1956	*2046*	...	...	...	...	...	...
160	**Innsbruck** Hbf ⊡ a.	0753	0753	...	*0923*	*1053*t	1123	...	*1323*	...	...	1523	...	*1653*t	*1723*	1822b	...	1923	*2053*t	*2123*	...	...	...	...	...	...

									ICE			ICE				ICE			ICE							
						◧		◧	538	◧		1206	◧	◧	◧	620		◧	732	◧	◧	◧	◧			
	⚒e	Ⓐe	Ⓒz	Ⓐe	Ⓒz		Ⓒz	Ⓐe	⑥P			RK				⑥D			⑥B							
Innsbruck Hbf ⊡ d.	...	...	...	...	...	*0638*	...	...	...	0838	*0908*t	0939b	*1038*	...	1238	...	...	*1438*	...	*1508*t	1638	...	*1838*	*1908*t	2038	...
Seefeld in Tirol ⊡ d.	...	...	...	...	...	*0715*	...	...	...	0915	1004	1018b	*1115*	1204c	1315	...	1404c	*1515*	...	1604	1715	1804c	*1915*	2004	2115	...
Scharnitz 🏛 ⊡ d.	...	...	...	...	...	*0728*	...	...	...	0928	1016	|	*1128*	1216c	1328	...	1416c	*1528*	...	1616	1728	1816c	*1928*	2016	2128	...
Mittenwald 🏛 a.	...	...	...	...	...	*0735*	...	...	...	0935	1025	1042b	*1135*	1225c	1335	...	1425c	*1535*	...	1625	1735	1825c	*1935*	2025	2135	...
Mittenwald d.	...	0530	0536	0634	0634	*0736*	0836	0836	...	0936	1036	1054	*1136*	1236	1336	...	1436	*1536*	...	1636	1736	1836	*1936*	2036	2136	223
Garmisch-Partenk. a.	...	0551	0557	0700	0700	*0757*	0857	0900	...	1000	1057	1119	*1157*	1300	1400	...	1500	*1557*	...	1700	1800	1900	*1957*	2057	2157	225
Garmisch-Partenk. d.	0500	0559	0607	0702	0707	0807	0905	0907	0912	1007	1107	1121	1207	1307	1407	1413	1507	1607	1623	1705	1805	1905v	2005	2107	2207	230
Murnau d.	0524	0626	0632	0728	0732	0832	0932	0932	0943	1032	1132	1151	1231	1332	1432	1444	1532	1632	1652	1732	1832	1932	2031	2132	2232	233
Weilheim (Oberbay) d.	0541	0646	0649	0746	0749	0849	0949	0949	|	1049	1149	|	1249	1349	1449	|	1549	1649	|	1750	1850	1950	2049	2149	2249	234
Tutzing d.	0555	0700	0700	0800	0800	0900	1000	1000	1018	1100	1200	|	1300	1400	1500	1516	1600	1700	1721	1800	1900	2000	2100	2200	2300	000
München Pasing a.	0614	0719	0719	0819	0819	0919	1019	1019	|	1119	1219	1248	1319	1419	1519	|	1619	1719	|	1819	1919	2019	2119	2219	2319	001
München Hbf a.	0621	0726	0726	0826	0826	0926	1026	1026	1054	1126	1226	1257	1326	1426	1526	1544	1626	1726	1757	1826	1926	2026	2126	2226	2326	002

MÜNCHEN - TUTZING - KOCHEL

km																											
		Ⓐe	⚒e	Ⓐe						Ⓒz	Ⓐe				Ⓐe	Ⓒz	Ⓐe	Ⓒz	Ⓐe	Ⓒz	Ⓐe	Ⓒz		◇			
0	**München** Hbf d.	0532	0559‡	0632	0659	0759‡	0900	0959	1132	1159	*1232*	1259	1359	1459	1556	1559	1656	1659	1756	1759	1856	1859	1959	2032	*2132*	*2232*	*233*
7	München Pasing d.	0539	0605	0639	0705	0805	0906	1005	1139	1205	*1239*	1305	1405	1505	1604	1605	1704	1705	1804	1805	1904	1905	2005	2039	*2139*	*2239*	*233*
40	Tutzing d.	0601	0626	0703	0731	0828y	0933	1033	1203	1233	1310	1333	1433	1533	1630	1633	1730	1733	1830	1833	1930	1933	2030v	2103	2203	2303	000
75	**Kochel** a.	0636	0706	0738	0808	0908	1008	1108	1239	1308	1347	1412	1508	1608	1708	1708	1808	1808	1908	1908	2008	2008	2108	2138	2238	2338	003

	Ⓐe		⚒e	Ⓐe	Ⓐe	Ⓒz	Ⓐe	Ⓒz	Ⓐe					Ⓒz	Ⓐe	Ⓒz	Ⓐe			Ⓐe							
Kochel d.	0435	0510	0544	0614	0645	0645	0715	0745	0745	0845	0945	1045	1145	1245	1258	1345	1352	1445	1545	1615	1645	1745	1845	1945	2116	2216	231
Tutzing a.	0510	0547	0625	0652	0724	0724	0753	0825	0827	0924	1024	1124	1225	1324	1334	1424	1425	1524	1625	1653	1725	1825	1925	2025	2153	2253	235
München Pasing a.	*0535*	0614	0657	0719	0753	0800	0819	0902	0902	0952	1052	1152	1252	1352	1401	1452	1452	1552	1652	*1719*	1752	1852	1954	2052	*2219*	*2319*	*001*
München Hbf a.	*0544*	0621	0705	0726	0800	0808	0826	0909	0909	1000	1100	1200	1300	1400	1409	1501	1500	1600	1700	*1726*	1800	1900	2002	2100	*2226*	*2326*	*002*

B – ⑥ to Mar. 4. ZUGSPITZE – [12] and ✕ Garmisch - Nürnberg - Bremen.
D – ⑥ to Mar. 4. [12] and 🍷 Dortmund - Frankfurt - Nürnberg - Garmisch and v.v.
K – [12] and ✕ Berlin - Nürnberg - München - Innsbruck and v.v.
L – ⑥ to Mar. 4. [12] and ✕ Hamburg - Nürnberg - Garmisch.
P – ⑥ to Mar. 4. [12] and ✕ Garmisch - Hannover - Bremen.
Q – ⑥ (also Apr. 14, 16, 30, June 4).
R – ⑥⑦ (also Apr. 14, 17, May 1, June 5).

b – Dec. 17 - Mar. 26.
c – ⑥⑦ (also Jan. 6, Apr. 17, May 1, 25, June 5).
e – Not Jan. 6.
f – 1 minute earlier Mar. 4 - Apr. 24.
j – 1446 on Apr. 8, 14, 15, 16, 22.
t – ①–⑤ (not Jan. 6, Apr. 17, May 1, 25, June 5).
v – 2–3 minutes later on Ⓒ (also Jan. 6).
y – 0833 on Ⓒ (also Jan. 6).
z – Also Jan. 6.

‡ – 3–4 minutes earlier on Ⓐ Mar. 6 - Apr. 24.
◇ – Change trains at Tutzing on Ⓐ (not Jan. 6).
◧ – Conveys [12] München - Garmisch - Reutte in Tirol and v.v. on dates in Table **888**.
⊡ – Other journeys Scharnitz - Seefeld - Innsbruck and v.v. **From Scharnitz** at 0003, 0633, 0733 ⚒, 0803 ⚒, 090… 1303, 1403 Ⓐ, 1503, 1703, 1803 Ⓐ, 1903 and 2133. **From Innsbruck** Hbf at 0708 ⚒, 0808, 1208, 1308 Ⓐ, 1408, 1608, 1708 Ⓐ, 1808, 2008 and 2308.

A rack railway operates between Garmisch-Partenkirchen and the Zugspitz mountain: departures at 0815 and hourly to 1415, returning from Bf Zugspitzplatt at 0930 and hourly to 1630. All trains call at Eibsee (30 minutes from Garmisch, 45 minutes from Zugspitzplatt). Service may be suspended in bad weather conditions – please check locally before travelling. Cable cars r… between Eibsee and Zugspitzgipfel (Eibsee-Seilbahn) and between Zugspitzplatt and Zugspitzgipfel summit (Gletscherbahn). **Operator**: Bayerische Zugspitzbahn AG ✆ + 49 (0) 88 21 797…

897 MURNAU - OBERAMMERGAU — *RB* services

km		Ⓐe	⑥	Ⓐe													
0	**Murnau** d.	0512	0553	0600	0648	0742	0842	0942	1042	1142	1234	1334	1442	and	2242	...	2334
12	Bad Kohlgrub d.	0530	0611	0619	0706	0801	0901	1001	1101	1201	1253	1353	1501	hourly	2301	...	2353
24	**Oberammergau** ♥ a.	0550	0631	0638	0726	0821	0921	1021	1121	1221	1312	1412	1521	until	2321	...	0012

	Ⓐe	⑥	Ⓐe													
Oberammergau ♥ d.	0507	0548	0556	0643	0738	0838	0938	1038	1138	1229	1329	1438	and	2238	...	2329
Bad Kohlgrub d.	0529	0610	0618	0705	0800	0900	1000	1100	1200	1252	1352	1500	hourly	2300	...	2352
Murnau a.	0547	0628	0636	0723	0819	0919	1019	1119	1219	1310	1410	1519	until	2319	...	0010

e – Not Jan. 6.

♥ – All trains call at Unterammergau (*km 20*) 4–6 minutes from Oberammergau.

NÜRNBERG and FRANKFURT - HAMBURG 900

WARNING! Timings München - Nürnberg - Würzburg are subject to alteration from March 6. See Engineering Work Summary on page 367. SEE ALSO NOTE ⊠.

km	SEE NOTE ⊠	*ICE* 990		*IC* 2178	*IC* 2184		*IC* 2176	*EN* 40420	*EN* 490	*EN* 470		*ICE* 988	*ICE* 1188		*IC* 2182	*IC* 2182	*ICE* 672	*ICE* 888	*ICE* 774	*ICE* 784	*ICE* 634	*IC* 2378	*IC* 2378
		①g		Ⓐ	Ⓐ		Ⓐ	R	R	R		⑥h	①–⑤		Ⓐ	①–⑥		Ⓐ	①–⑥		①–⑥	①–⑥	
					🍷♦		🍷	B	♦	♦		✕	a K ✕		T 🍷	e T 🍷	Q ✕	✕	e ✕	◇ ✕	e n ✕	e 🍷	🍷
	Basel SBB **912** ▦ d.	...	...	...	...	...	...	...	...	2113	...	...		...	...		...	...	...	...		...	...
	Karlsruhe Hbf **912** d.	...	...	...	...	...	...	...	...	2304	...	...	...	...	...	...	...	...	...	...	...	...	...
	Stuttgart Hbf **912** d.	2305p	...	...	...	...	...	...	...	|	...	...	...	...	...	...	...	...	0502	...	...	...	...
	Mannheim Hbf **912** d.	2351p	...	...	...	...	...	...	...	2359	...	...	...	...	...	...	...	...	0605	...	...	...	...
	Frankfurt Flughafen Fernbf ✈ **912** d.	0031	...	...	...	...	...	...	...	|	...	...	...	...	...	...	0539	...	0641	...	...	...	...
	Frankfurt (Main) Hbf **850 901 902** d.	0055	...	...	...	...	...	...	...	0054x	...	0506	0506	...	...	...	0555	...	0658	...	...	0649	...
	Hanau Hbf **850 901 902** d.	0113	...	...	...	...	...	...	...	|	...	0522	0522	...	...	...	0611	...	|	...	...	|	...
	München Hbf **904 905** d.	|	...	...	...	...	...	2252	...	|	...	|	|	...	...	...	|	0415	|	0520t	0520r	|	...
	Augsburg Hbf **905** d.	|	...	...	...	...	...	2330‡	...	|	...	|	|	...	...	...	|	|	|	|	|	◧	...
0	**Nürnberg** Hbf **920 921** d.	|	...	...	...	...	...	0200	0200	|	...	|	|	...	...	...	|	0532	|	0634	0634	|	...
102	**Würzburg** Hbf **920 921** d.	|	...	...	...	...	...	0300	0300	|	...	|	|	...	...	...	|	0630	|	0729	0729	|	...
195	Fulda **850 901 902** d.	0158	...	...	...	...	...	|	|	|	...	0604	0604	...	...	...	0653	0707	|	0803	0803	|	...
285	**Kassel** Wilhelmshöhe **901 902** d.	|	...	...	...	...	...	|	|	|	...	0636	0636	...	0623	...	0724	0739	0821	0836	0836	0854	...
330	Göttingen **902 903** d.	0325	...	...	...	...	0546	0553	0553	|	...	0656	0656	...	0645	...	0743	0759	0840	0856	0856	0917	...
430	**Hannover** Hbf **903** a.	0421	...	...	...	...	0657	0649	0649	|	...	0732	0732	...	0756	...	0817	0833	0917	0932	0932	0956	...
430	**Hannover** Hbf **903** d.	0424	...	0511	0555	...	0701	0705	0705	|	...	0736	0736	...	0759	0759	0820	0836	0920	0936	0945	1000	1000
	Bremen Hbf **813** a.	|	...	|	|	...	|	|	|	|	...	|	|	...	|	|	|	|	|	|	1044	|	|
471	Celle **903** d.	|	...	0532	0619	...	0720	|	|	|	...	|	|	...	0819	0819	|	|	|	|	...	1020	1020
523	Uelzen **903** d.	|	...	0556	0642	...	0742	|	|	|	...	|	|	...	0842	0842	|	|	|	|	...	1042	1042
559	Lüneburg **903** d.	0515	...	0613	0658	...	0758	|	|	|	...	|	|	...	0902	0902	|	|	|	|	...	1058	1058
608	**Hamburg** Hbf **903** a.	0549	...	0643	0728	...	0828	0836	0836	0831	...	0856	0856	...	0933	0933	0935	0953	1035	1054	...	1128	1128
615	**Hamburg** Altona a.	...	...	0659	...	...	0844	0854	0854	0901	...	0914	...	...	...	...	0950	1008	1050	...	...	1144	1144

SEE NOTE ⊠	*ICE* 674	*ICE* 886	*ICE* 772	*ICE* 1082	*ICE* 1132	*IC* 2376	*ICE* 78	*ICE* 882		*ICE* 770	*ICE* 680	*ICE* 630	*IC* 2374	*ICE* 76	*ICE* 880	*IC* 1972	*ICE* 1224 1228	*ICE* 578	*ICE* 588	*ICE* 538	*IC* 2372	*ICE* 74	*ICE* 788
					n							n				⑤f				G			
	✕	✕	✕	✕	🍷	🍷♦	Z ✕	✕		✕	✕	✕	🍷♦	Z ✕	✕		H 🍷	✕	✕	✕	T 🍷	✕♦	✕
Basel SBB **912** ▦ d.	0511b	...	...	...	...	...	0706	...	...	...	...	...	...	0906	...	...	...	...	...	...	...	1106	...
Karlsruhe Hbf **912** d.	0651	...	...	...	...	0702	0851	...	...	...	...	...	0905	1051	...	...	...	...	...	...	1110v	1251	...
Stuttgart Hbf **912** d.	|	...	0725	...	...	|	|	...	...	0925	...	...	|	|	...	...	...	1125	...	...	|	|	...
Mannheim Hbf **912** d.	0716	...	0806	...	...	|	0916	...	...	1006	...	...	|	1116	...	...	...	1206	...	...	|	1316	...
Frankfurt Flughafen Fernbf ✈ **912** d.	|	...	0841	...	...	|	|	...	...	1041	...	...	|	|	...	...	...	1241	...	...	|	|	...
Frankfurt (Main) Hbf **850 901 902** d.	0758	...	0858	...	...	0852	0958	...	...	1058	...	...	1052	1158	...	1217	...	1258	...	...	1252	1358	...
Hanau Hbf **850 901 902** d.	|	...	|	...	...	|	|	...	...	|	...	...	|	|	...	1238	...	|	...	...	|	|	...
München Hbf **904 905** d.	|	0617	|	0641	0641	|	|	0822	...	|	0905	0905	|	|	1022	|	1055	|	1122	1122	|	|	1222
Augsburg Hbf **905** d.	|	|	|	0716	0716	◧	|	|	...	|	0938	0938	◧	|	|	|	|	|	|	|	◧	|	|
Nürnberg Hbf **920 921** d.	|	0734	|	0834	0834	|	|	0933	...	|	|	|	|	|	1133	|	1200	|	1234	1234	|	|	1333
Würzburg Hbf **920 921** d.	|	0830	|	0929	0929	|	|	1030	...	|	1129	1129	|	|	1230	|	1301j	|	1329	1329	|	|	1430
Fulda **850 901 902** d.	|	0904	|	1003	1003	|	|	1104	...	|	1203	1203	|	|	1304	1320	1332	|	1403	1403	|	|	1504
Kassel Wilhelmshöhe **901 902** d.	0921	0936	1021	1036	1036	1055	1121	1136	...	1221	1236	1236	1256	1321	1336	1359	1400	1421	1436	1436	1455	1521	1536
Göttingen **902 903** d.	0940	0956	1040	1056	1056	1117	1140	1156	...	1240	1256	1256	1318	1340	1356	1420	...	1440	1456	1456	1517	1540	1556
Hannover Hbf **903** a.	1017	1032	1117	1132	1132	1156	1217	1232	...	1317	1332	1332	1356	1417	1432	1459	...	1517	1532	1532	1556	1617	1632
Hannover Hbf **903** d.	1020	1036	1120	1136	1145	1159	1220	1236	...	1320	1336	1345	1359	1420	1436	1502	...	1520	1536	1545n	1559	1620	1636
Bremen Hbf **813** a.	|	|	|	|	1244	|	|	|	...	|	|	1444	|	|	|	|	...	|	|	1644n	|	|	|
Celle **903** d.	|	|	|	|	...	1219	|	|	...	|	|	...	1419	|	|	1522	...	|	|	...	1619	|	|
Uelzen **903** d.	|	|	|	|	...	1242	|	|	...	|	|	...	1442	|	|	1544	...	|	|	...	1642	|	|
Lüneburg **903** d.	|	1128	|	|	...	1259	|	|	...	|	|	...	1501	|	|	1600	...	|	|	...	1703	|	|
Hamburg Hbf **903** a.	1135	1156	1235	1253	...	1328	1335	1354	...	1435	1454	...	1529	1535	1554	1628	...	1635	1653	...	1732	1735	1753
Hamburg Altona a.	1150	1212	1250	1308	...	...	1350	1409	...	1450	1508	...	...	1550	1609	1644	...	1650	1709	...	...	...	1813

SEE NOTE ⊠	*IC* 2082	*ICE* 576	*ICE* 586	*ICE* 536	*IC* 2370	*IC* 2270	*ICE* 72	*ICE* 786	*IC* 1284	*ICE* 1094	*ICE* 574	*ICE* 584	*ICE* 984	*ICE* 1084	*ICE* 776	*IC* 2276	*IC* 2276	*IC* 2386	*ICE* 70	*ICE* 1090		*ICE* 1522	*ICE* 90
					①–⑥	⑦w			⑦w	Ⓑy	⑥d	Ⓑ	⑦w	⑥u	Ⓑ		⑤–⑦	①–④		Ⓑ			
	🍷♦	✕	✕	✕	s 🍷	T 🍷	✕♦	✕	F	K ✕	✕	L ✕	✕	✕	N ✕	🍷	c 🍷	m	✕♦	✕♦		✕	✕♦
Basel SBB **912** ▦ d.	...	...	...	...	...	...	1306	...	...	...	...	...	...	...	...	...	...	...	1506	...	...	...	...
Karlsruhe Hbf **912** d.	...	...	...	...	1310	1310	1451	...	...	...	...	...	...	...	...	1510	1510	...	1651	...	...	...	...
Stuttgart Hbf **912** d.	...	1325	...	...	|	|	|	...	...	1525	1525	...	...	...	...	|	|	...	|	1651	...	...	...
Mannheim Hbf **912** d.	...	1406	...	...	|	|	1516	...	...	1606	1606	...	...	...	...	|	|	...	1716	1732	...	...	...
Frankfurt Flughafen Fernbf ✈ **912** d.	...	1441	...	...	|	|	|	...	...	1641	1641	...	...	...	...	|	|	...	|	|	...	...	...
Frankfurt (Main) Hbf **850 901 902** d.	...	1458	...	...	1450	1450	1558	...	...	1658	1658	...	...	...	1716	1650	1650	...	1758	1813	...	...	...
Hanau Hbf **850 901 902** d.	...	|	...	...	|	|	|	...	...	|	|	...	...	...	|	|	|	...	|	|	...	...	...
München Hbf **904 905** d.	1117o	|	1322	1322	|	|	|	1340	1355	|	|	1522	1522	1522	|	|	|	...	|	|	...	1618	...
Augsburg Hbf **905** d.	1230	|	|	|	◧	◧	|	1413	1425	|	|	|	|	|	|	◧	◧	...	|	|	...	|	...
Nürnberg Hbf **920 921** d.	|	|	1434	1434	|	|	|	1534	|	|	|	1634	1634	1634	|	|	|	...	|	|	...	1733	1729
Würzburg Hbf **920 921** d.	1437	|	1529	1529	|	|	|	1630	1638	|	|	1729	1729	1729	|	|	|	...	|	|	...	1825	1830j
Fulda **850 901 902** d.	1518	|	1603	1603	|	|	|	1704	1717	|	|	1803	1803	1803	1818	|	|	...	|	|	...	...	1907
Kassel Wilhelmshöhe **901 902** d.	1553	1621	1636	1636	1654	1654	1721	1736	1758	|	1821	1836	1836	1836	1851	1857	1857	...	1921	|	...	...	1940
Göttingen **902 903** d.	1614	1640	1656	1656	1717	1717	1740	1756	1820	|	1840	1856	1856	1856	1912	1918	1918	...	1940	|	...	...	|
Hannover Hbf **903** a.	1653	1717	1732	1732	1756	1756	1817	1832	1859	1906	1917	1932	1932	1932	1947	1956	1956	...	2017	2021	...	...	2032
Hannover Hbf **903** d.	1657	1720	1736	1745	1759	1759	1820	1836	1905	1909	1920	1936	1936	1936	1950	...	1959	2000	2020	...	...	...	2036
Bremen Hbf **813** a.	|	|	|	1844	|	|	|	|	|	|	|	|	|	|	2047	...	|	|	|	...	...	...	|
Celle **903** d.	1718	|	|	...	1819	1819	|	|	1931	|	|	|	|	|	...	...	2019	2020	|	...	...	...	|
Uelzen **903** d.	1742	|	|	...	1842	1842	|	|	1955	|	|	|	|	|	...	...	2042	2042	|	...	...	...	|
Lüneburg **903** d.	1758	|	|	...	1858	1858	|	|	2011	|	2012	2028	2028	2028	...	...	2058	2058	|	...	...	...	|
Hamburg Hbf **903** a.	1829	1835	1853	...	1928	1928	1935	1953	2038	2024	2038	2058	2058	2058	...	...	2128	2128	2138	...	...	...	2153
Hamburg Altona a.	1844	1850	1908	...	1946	...	1950	2010	...	...	2101	...	2113	2114	...	...	2144	2144	2153	...	...	...	2211

– **NOTES** (LISTED BY TRAIN NUMBER)

/2 – 12 and ✕ Chur - Zürich - Basel - Hamburg.
– 12 and ✕ Zürich - Basel - Hamburg - Kiel.
– 12 and ✕ Wien - Linz - Passau - Regensburg - Hamburg.
0 – *ÖBB nightjet.* 1, 2 cl., 2 cl. and 2 Zürich - Basel - Berlin - Hamburg. Arrives Hamburg Hbf 0849, Altona 0901 Feb. 11 - Apr. 17.
0 – *ÖBB nightjet.* 1, 2 cl., 2 cl. and 2 Wien - Passau - Nürnberg - Hamburg.
90 – Ⓑ (not Dec. 25–30, ⑦ Feb. 12 - Apr. 2, Apr. 14, 16, 17, 30, June 4). To Berlin (Table **902**).
82 – KÖNIGSSEE – 12 and 🍷 Berchtesgaden - München - Hamburg (from Apr. 14 starts from München Hbf, d. 1120, not calling at München Ost); conveys 12 Oberstdorf (**2084**) - Augsburg (**2082**) - Hamburg.
84 – 12 and 🍷 Hannover - Hamburg - Stralsund (- Ostseebad Binz from May 2).
74 – WATTENMEER – 12 and 🍷 Karlsruhe - Frankfurt - Hamburg (- Westerland ♠).
76 – 12 and 🍷 Karlsruhe - Frankfurt - Hamburg - Stralsund (- Ostseebad Binz ⑥, also Apr. 14, May 25).

– *ÖBB nightjet.* 1, 2 cl., 2 cl. and 2 Innsbruck - München - Hamburg. Departs München 2249 on ⑦ from Apr. 2 (not Apr. 16, 30, June 4).
– WATTENMEER – Continues to Westerland on ④–⑦ to Apr. 2, daily from Apr. 6 (Table **821**).
– To Flensburg (Table **823**). From Schwarzach Jan. 8 - Mar. 26 (Table **960**).
– From Garmisch on dates in Table **895**.
– Not May 6 - June 14. 12 and 🍷 München - Kassel - Paderborn - Hamm - Düsseldorf.
– To Kiel (Table **820**).
– Ⓑ (not Apr. 14, 30, June 4). To Lübeck (Table **825**).

N – Ⓑ (not Apr. 14, 16, 30, May 26, June 4). To Oldenburg (Table **813**).
Q – From Wiesbaden (Table **911**).
T – To Stralsund (Table **830**).
Z – From Zürich (Table **510**).

a – Not Apr. 14, 17, May 1, June 5.
b – Ⓒ only. Basel **Badischer Bahnhof**.
c – ⑤–⑦ (also Apr. 13, 17, May 1, 24, June 5).
d – Also Apr. 14, 16, 30, May 25, 26, June 4.
e – ①–⑥ (not Apr. 15, 17, May 1, June 5).
f – Also Apr. 13, May 24; not Apr. 14, May 26.

g – Also May 2, June 6; not Apr. 17, May 1, June 5.
h – Also Apr. 14; not Apr. 15.
j – Arrives 8 minutes earlier.
m – Not Apr. 13, 17, May 1, 24, June 5.
n – Not Feb. 20 - Apr. 12.
o – München **Ost** until Apr. 13.
p – Previous day.
r – ①–⑤ (not Apr. 17, May 1, June 5).
s – Also Apr. 16, 30, June 4; not Apr. 17, May 1, June 5.
t – Ⓐ only.
u – Also Apr. 14, 30, June 4.
v – ⑤–⑦ (also Apr. 13, 17, May 1, 24, 25, June 5).
w – Also Apr. 17, May 1, June 5; not Apr. 16, 30, June 4.
x – Frankfurt (Main) **Süd**.
y – Not Apr. 14, 16, 30, May 25, 26, June 4.

‡ – Daily to Mar. 31, ①–⑤ from Apr. 3.
◧ – Via Gießen (Table **806**).
◇ – To Lübeck (Table **825**).
♠ – ④–⑦ to Apr. 2; daily from Apr. 6.
⊠ – Frankfurt, Hanau and Fulda timings are subject to alteration on ⑥⑦ Feb. 11 - Apr. 2 (also Apr. 14–17). See also engineering work panel on page 367.

GERMANY *See page 367 for a summary of Christmas / New Year alterations*

900 NÜRNBERG and FRANKFURT - HAMBURG

WARNING! Timings München - Nürnberg - Würzburg and v.v. are subject to alteration from March 6. See Engineering Work Summary on page 367. SEE ALSO NOTE ⊠.

SEE NOTE ⊠	IC 1980 ⑦w	ICE 572 ✕	ICE 582 ✕	IC 2274 ⑤⑦ v🍷	IC 2274 ⑦w 🍷	ICE 376 ⑤⑦ ✕♦	ICE 782 ♥ ✕	ICE 732 ★ G✕	ICE 592 ✕	ICE 782 ♥ ✕	ICE 732 ★ G✕		ICE 570 ⑦w ✕	ICE 580 ⑧q ✕	ICE 580 ⑦w ✕	ICE 292 ⑦w ✕♦	ICE 580 ⑦w ✕	ICE 1172 ⑥k Z✕	ICE 272 A Z✕		ICE 780 ⑦w ✕	ICE 992 ⑦w ✕	ICE 698 ⑤f ✕
Basel SBB 912 🚂 d.	...	...	...	...	...	1706	...	...	...	...	...	...	...	...	...	1813	...	1813	1813	...	...	...	...
Karlsruhe Hbf 912 d.	...	...	...	1710	1710	1851	...	...	...	...	...	...	...	...	...	2000	...	2000	2000	...	...	...	...
Stuttgart Hbf 912 d.	...	1725	...	|	|	|	...	...	1851	...	...	...	1925	...	...	|	...	|	|	...	...	2051	2051
Mannheim Hbf 912 d.	...	1806	...	|	|	1916	...	...	1932	...	...	...	2006	...	...	2032	...	2032	2032	...	...	2132	2132
Frankfurt Flughafen Fernbf ✈ *912* d.	...	1841	...	|	|	|	...	...	|	...	...	...	2041	...	...	|	...	|	|	...	...	|	|
Frankfurt (Main) Hbf ... 850 901 902 d.	...	1858	...	1849	1849	1958	...	...	2013	...	...	...	2058	...	...	2113	...	2113	2113	...	...	2217	2217
Hanau Hbf ... 850 901 902 d.	...	1914	...	|	|	|	...	...	2029	...	...	...	2114	...	...	2129	...	2129	2129	...	...	2234	2234
München Hbf 904 905 d.	1552	|	1721	|	|	|	1820	1820	|	...	...	...	|	1853	1853	|	...	|	|	...	2020	|	|
Augsburg Hbf 905 d.	1625	|	|	◧	◧	|	|	|	|	...	...	...	|	1932	1932	|	...	|	|	...	|	|	|
Nürnberg Hbf ... 920 921 d.	|	|	1834	|	|	|	1934	1934	|	...	...	...	|	|	|	|	...	|	|	...	2135	|	|
Würzburg Hbf ... 850 920 921 d.	1837	|	1929	|	|	|	2030	2030	|	...	...	...	|	2131	2131	|	...	|	|	...	2230	|	|
Fulda ... 850 901 902 d.	1916	|	2003	|	|	|	2103	2103	|	←	←	...	|	2204	2204	2211	...	2211	2211	...	2304	2320	2319
Kassel Wilhelmshöhe ... 901 902 d.	1952	2025	2036	2055	2055	2121	2135	2135	2138	2142	2142	...	2225	2234	2236	2243	←	2243	2243	...	2339	2354	0032
Göttingen ... 902 903 d.	2012	2046	2056	2118	2118	2140	→	→	...	2202	2202	...	2245	...	2255	2301	2306	2306	2305	...	...	0047	...
Hannover Hbf ... 903 a.	2051	2119	2132	2156	2156	2217	...	...	...	2240	2240	...	2318	...	→	...	2341	2341	0002	...	...	0146	...
Hannover Hbf ... 903 d.	2055	2122	2136	...	2159	2220	...	...	...	2244	2250	...	2321	...	...	...	2345	2344	0005	...	...	0149	...
Bremen Hbf 813 a.	|	|	|	...	|	|	...	...	...	|	2356	...	|	...	...	...	|	|	|	...	...	|	...
Celle ... 903 d.	2118	|	|	...	2219	2240	...	...	...	|	...	...	|	...	...	...	0005	|	0027	...	...	|	...
Uelzen ... 903 d.	2142	|	|	...	2242	2303	...	...	...	2322	...	...	|	...	...	...	0027	0023	0050	...	...	|	...
Lüneburg ... 903 d.	2158	2214	|	...	2258	2319	...	...	...	2339	...	...	0015	...	...	...	0044	0041	0106	...	...	|	...
Hamburg Hbf ... 903 a.	2227	2243	2254	...	2328	2351	...	...	...	0008	...	...	0044	...	...	...	0113	0111	0136	...	...	0308	...
Hamburg Altona ... a.	2245	2301	2310	...	2344	0006	...	...	...	0023	...	...	0102	...	...	...	0129	0126	0200	...	...	0324	...

SEE NOTE ⊠	ICE 271 ①g ♦		ICE 591 ①–⑤ a✕	ICE 591 ①–⑥ e✕	ICE 781 ①g B✕	ICE 781 ①–⑥ e✕		IC 2271 Ⓐ 🍷		ICE 581 ✕	ICE 571 ①–⑥ e✕	IC 2179 Ⓐb H	ICE 1097 Ⓐb D✕	ICE 783 ①–⑥ e✕	ICE 71 Ⓒc ✕♦	ICE 71 Ⓐb ✕♦	IC 2277 ①–⑥ p🍷	ICE 533 ①–⑥ eN	ICE 583 G✕	ICE 973 ①–⑥ sK	ICE 573 ⑦m ✕		IC 2083 🍷♦
Hamburg Altona ... d.	0030	...	0331	...	...	...	...	...	...	0441	0500	0505	0553	0540	0556	0603	0609	✕	0646	✕	0707	...	0713
Hamburg Hbf ... 903 d.	0045	...	0346	...	...	...	...	...	...	0456	0517	0524	0608	0555	0611	0618	0625	...	0701	0722	0722	...	0729
Lüneburg ... 903 d.	|	...	0418	...	...	...	...	...	...	0526	0547	0555	|	0626h	0642	0648	0655	...	|	|	|	...	0801
Uelzen ... 903 d.	|	...	0435	...	...	...	...	...	...	0542	|	0615	|	0642h	0659	|	0715	...	|	|	|	...	0817
Celle ... 903 d.	|	...	0457	...	...	...	...	...	...	|	|	0638	|	|	0721	|	0739	...	|	|	|	...	0840
Bremen Hbf 813 d.	|	...	|	...	...	...	...	...	...	|	|	|	|	|	|	|	|	0714	|	|	|	...	|
Hannover Hbf ... 903 a.	0207	...	0517	...	...	...	...	...	...	0620	0638	0657	0719	0723	0739	0738	0758	0814	0820	0838	0838	...	0859
Hannover Hbf ... 903 d.	0210	...	0520	0514	...	...	...	0558	...	0626	0641	...	0722	0726	0741	0741	0801	0826	0826	0841	0841	...	0903
Göttingen ... 902 903 d.	0307	...	0555	0555	0602	...	...	0637	...	0702	0716	...	|	0802	0816	0816	0840	0902	0902	0916	0916	...	0944
Kassel Wilhelmshöhe ... 901 902 d.	|	...	0616	0616	0623	0623	...	0700	...	0723	0737	...	|	0823	0837	0837	0903	0923	0923	0937	0937	...	1007
Fulda ... 850 901 902 d.	0434	...	0648	0648	0656	0656	...	|	...	0756	|	...	|	0856	|	|	|	0956	0956	|	|	...	1043
Würzburg Hbf ... 920 921 d.	|	...	|	|	0729	0729	...	|	...	0830	|	...	|	0929	|	|	|	1030	1030	|	|	...	1122
Nürnberg Hbf ... 920 921 a.	|	...	|	|	0824	0824	...	◧	...	0924	|	...	|	1024	|	|	◧	1124	1124	|	|	...	|
Augsburg Hbf 905 a.	|	...	|	|	|	|	...	|	...	1041	|	...	|	|	|	|	|	|	|	|	|	...	1331
München Hbf 904 905 a.	|	...	|	|	0939	0939	...	|	...	1116	|	...	|	1140	|	|	|	1239	1239	|	|	...	1410
Hanau Hbf ... 850 901 902 d.	0520	...	0730	0730	...	...	...	|	...	...	|	...	|	...	|	|	|	...	...	|	|	...	...
Frankfurt (Main) Hbf ... 850 901 902 a.	0537	...	0745	0745	...	...	...	0908	...	...	0900	...	0928	...	1000	1000	1108	...	...	1100	1100	...	...
Frankfurt Flughafen Fernbf ✈ *912* a.	|	...	|	|	...	...	...	|	...	...	0917	...	...	...	|	|	|	...	...	1117	1117	...	...
Mannheim Hbf 912 a.	0625	...	0827	0827	...	...	...	|	...	...	0954	...	...	...	1043	1043	|	...	...	1154	1154	...	...
Stuttgart Hbf 912 a.	|	...	0908	0908	...	...	...	|	...	...	1035	...	...	...	|	|	|	...	...	1235	1235	...	...
Karlsruhe Hbf 912 a.	0656	...	...	...	...	...	...	1050	...	...	...	...	...	...	1108	1108	1250j	...	...	...	...	...	...
Basel SBB 912 a.	0847	...	...	...	...	...	...	...	...	...	...	...	...	...	1254	1254	...	...	...	...	...	...	...

SEE NOTE ⊠	ICE 91 ✕♦	ICE 1521 ✕	ICE 91 ✕♦		ICE 73 ①–⑥ e♦	ICE 1173 ⑦d Z✕	IC 2279 ①–⑥ eT	ICE 585 ①–⑥ eL	ICE 1085 ⑦d ✕	ICE 535 N✕	ICE 575 ✕	ICE 1223 🍷♦		ICE 787 ✕	ICE 75 ①–⑥ e♦	ICE 1175 ⑦ ✕♦	IC 2371 🍷	ICE 537 n N✕	ICE 587 ✕	ICE 577 ✕	ICE 789 ✕	ICE 77 ✕♦	IC 2373 T🍷
Hamburg Altona ... d.	0747	...	...	...	✕	0807	🍷	✕	0846	...	0906	...	...	0946	1007	...	1013	...	1046	1107	1146	...	...
Hamburg Hbf ... 903 d.	0803	...	...	...	0824	0824	0828	0901	0901	...	0924	...	...	1001	1024	1024	1028	...	1101	1124	1201	1224	1228
Lüneburg ... 903 d.	|	...	...	...	|	|	0859	|	|	...	|	...	...	|	|	|	1059	...	|	|	|	|	1259
Uelzen ... 903 d.	|	...	...	...	|	|	0916	|	|	...	|	...	...	|	|	|	1115	...	|	|	|	|	1315
Celle ... 903 d.	|	...	...	...	|	|	0939	|	|	...	|	...	...	|	|	|	1139	...	|	|	|	|	1338
Bremen Hbf 813 d.	|	...	...	...	|	|	|	|	|	0914	|	...	...	|	|	|	|	1114	|	|	|	|	|
Hannover Hbf ... 903 a.	0921	...	...	...	0938	0938	0958	1022	1022	1014	1038	...	...	1120	1138	1138	1158	1214	1222	1238	1320	1338	1354
Hannover Hbf ... 903 d.	0926	...	...	...	0941	0941	1001	1026	1026	1026	1041	...	...	1126	1141	1141	1201	1226	1226	1241	1326	1341	1401
Göttingen ... 902 903 d.	1003	...	...	...	1016	1016	1040	1102	1102	1102	1116	...	...	1202	1216	1216	1240	1302	1302	1316	1402	1416	1440
Kassel Wilhelmshöhe ... 901 902 d.	1025	...	...	...	1037	1037	1103	1123	1123	1123	1137	1158	...	1223	1237	1237	1303	1323	1323	1337	1423	1437	1503
Fulda ... 850 901 902 d.	1057	...	←	...	|	|	|	1156	1156	1156	|	1228	...	1256	|	|	|	1356	1356	|	1456	|	|
Würzburg Hbf ... 920 921 d.	1128	1132	1135	...	|	|	|	1230	1230	1230	|	1310	...	1329	|	|	|	1430	1430	|	1529	|	|
Nürnberg Hbf ... 920 921 a.	→	1224	1227	...	|	|	◧	1324	1324	1324	|	1403	...	1424	|	|	◧	|	|	|	1624	|	◧
Augsburg Hbf 905 a.	...	|	...	...	|	|	|	|	|	|	|	|	...	|	|	|	|	1626	1626	|	|	|	|
München Hbf 904 905 a.	...	1339	...	...	|	|	|	1441	1441	1441	|	1508	...	1541	|	|	|	1701	1701	|	1738	|	|
Hanau Hbf ... 850 901 902 d.	...	...	...	...	|	|	|	...	...	...	|	...	...	...	|	|	|	...	...	|	...	|	|
Frankfurt (Main) Hbf ... 850 901 902 a.	...	...	...	...	1200	1200	1308	...	...	...	1300	...	...	...	1400	1400	1508	...	...	1500	...	1600	1700
Frankfurt Flughafen Fernbf ✈ *912* a.	...	...	...	...	|	|	|	...	...	...	1317	...	...	...	|	|	|	...	...	1517	...	|	|
Mannheim Hbf 912 a.	...	...	...	...	1243	1243	|	...	...	...	1354	...	...	...	1443	1443	|	...	...	1554	...	1643	|
Stuttgart Hbf 912 a.	...	...	...	...	|	|	|	...	...	...	1435	...	...	...	|	|	|	...	...	1635	...	|	|
Karlsruhe Hbf 912 a.	...	...	...	...	1308	1308	1450	...	...	...	...	...	...	...	1508	1508	1650	...	...	...	...	1708	185[illegible]
Basel SBB 912 a.	...	...	...	...	1454	1454	...	...	...	...	...	...	...	...	1654	1654	...	...	...	...	...	1854	...

♦ – **NOTES** (LISTED BY TRAIN NUMBER)

71 – [12] and ✕ Hamburg - Basel - Zürich - Chur.
73/7 – [12] and ✕ Kiel - Hamburg - Basel - Zürich.
75 – ①–⑥ (not Apr. 17, May 1, June 5). [12] and ✕ Hamburg - Basel - Zürich - Chur.
91 – [12] and ✕ Hamburg - Regensburg - Passau - Linz - Wien.
271 – [12] Hamburg - Basel - Zürich - Chur. ✕ Frankfurt - Chur.
292 – [12] and ✕ Zürich - Basel - Berlin.
376 – ⑤⑦ (also Apr. 13, 17, May 1, 24, June 5; not Apr. 14, 16, 30, May 26, June 4). [12] and ✕ Interlaken - Bern - Basel - Hamburg.
1175 – ⑦ (also Apr. 17, May 1, June 5). [12] and ✕ Kiel - Hamburg - Basel - Zürich. Continues to Chur on May 1, June 5.
1223 – Not May 6 - June 14. [12] and 🍷 Köln - Paderborn - Kassel - München.
2083 – KÖNIGSSEE – [12] and 🍷 Hamburg - München - Berchtesgaden (from Apr. 14 terminates at München Hbf, a. 1406, not calling at München Ost); conveys [12] Hamburg - Augsburg (**2085**) - Oberstdorf.

A – ①–⑤ (not Apr. 17, May 1, June 5).
B – From Berlin (Table **902**).
D – To Darmstadt Hbf (a. 0953).
G – From / to Garmisch on dates in Table **895**.
H – To Wolfsburg (Table **810**).
K – From Kiel (Table **820**).
L – From Lübeck (Table **825**).
N – From Oldenburg on dates in Table **813**.

T – From Stralsund (Table **830**).
Z – From / to Zürich (Table **510**).

a – Not Apr. 14, 17, May 1, June 5.
b – Not May 26.
c – Also May 26.
d – Also Apr. 15, 17, May 1, June 5.
e – Not Apr. 15, 17, May 1, June 5.
f – Also Apr. 13, May 24; not Apr. 14, May 26.
g – Also Apr. 18, May 2, June 6; not Apr. 17, May 1, June 5.
h – ⑥ (not Apr. 15).
j – ⑤⑥ (also Apr. 13, May 24; not Apr. 15).
k – Also Apr. 16, 30, June 4.
m – Also Apr. 15, 17, May 1, 26, 27, June 5.
n – Not Feb. 20 - Apr. 12.
o – München **Ost** until Apr. 13.
p – Not Apr. 15, 17, May 1, 25, June 5.
q – Not Apr. 14, 16, 30, June 4.
s – Not Apr. 15, 17, May 1, 26, 27, June 5.
v – Also Apr. 13, 17, May 1, 24, June 5; not Apr. 14, 16, 30, May 26, June 4.
w – Also Apr. 17, May 1, June 5; not Apr. 16, 30, June 4.

♥ – On ⑦ (also Apr. 15, 17, May 1, June 5) service is retimed from Kassel, d. 2137 (connection at Kassel with train **592** not available), then Göttingen d. 2157, Hannover a. 2232, d. 2236, Uelzen d. 2314, Lüneburg d. 2333, Hamburg Hbf a. 000[illegible] Hamburg Altona a. 0016. Train number **1182** on ⑥ (also Apr. 14, May 25).
★ – To Oldenburg (Table **813**). On ⑦ (also Apr. 15, 17, May 1, June 5) runs with train number **1032** and is retimed from Kassel, d. 2137 (connection at Kassel with train 5[illegible] not available), then Göttingen d. 2157, Hannover a. 2232, d. 2244, Bremen a. 235[illegible]
⊠ – Frankfurt, Hanau and Fulda timings are subject to alteration on ⑥⑦ Feb. 11 - Apr. [illegible] (also Apr. 14 – 17). See also engineering work panel on page 367.
◧ – Via Gießen (Table **806**).

HAMBURG - FRANKFURT and NÜRNBERG — 900

WARNING! Timings Würzburg - Nürnberg - München are subject to alteration from March 6. See Engineering Work Summary on page 367. SEE ALSO NOTE ⊠.

SEE NOTE ⊠	ICE 1139 n ⚑	ICE 1189	IC 579	IC 1981 r♣	ICE 881	ICE 79 Z♣	IC 2375 L⚑	IC 631	IC 681	ICE 771 ◇♣	IC 1995 ⑦w ⑤⑦ r⚑	IC 2171 ①–④ m⚑	IC 2281	ICE 883	IC 1171	ICE 2377 O⚑	ICE 633	ICE 683 ⑧q	IC 773 ⑧q ⚑	IC 2173 ⑦w	IC 2173	ICE 885 K⚑
Hamburg Altona.............d.		1246	1309		1346	1407				1507		1513	1513	1546	1607		1646	1707	1713	1713		
Hamburg Hbf.........903 d.		1301	1324	1328	1401	1424	1428		1501	1524		1528	1528	1601	1627	1627	1701	1724	1728	1728		1801
Lüneburg...........903 d.				1359	1429		1459					1558	1558			1659		1757	1757			
Uelzen..............903 d.			1414			1515						1619	1619			1715		1819	1819			
Celle...............903 d.					1539							1641	1641			1738		1841	1841			
Bremen Hbf 813.......d.	1314					1514										1714n						
Hannover Hbf.......903 a.	1414	1420	1438	1451	1522	1538	1558	1614	1622	1638		1700	1700	1720	1738	1757	1814n	1822	1838	1905	1905	1921
Hannover Hbf.......903 d.	1426	1426	1441	1454	1526	1541	1601	1626	1626	1641	1703	1707	1703	1726	1741	1801	1826	1826	1841		1909	1926
Göttingen.......902 903 d.	1503	1503	1516	1534	1602	1616	1641	1702	1702	1716	1744	1748	1814	1802	1816	1840	1902	1902	1916		2022	2002
Kassel Wilhelmshöhe..901 902 d.	1525	1525	1537	1558	1623	1637	1703	1723	1723	1737	1809	1810		1823	1837	1903	1923	1923	1937		2049	2027
Fulda..........850 901 902 d.	1557	1557		1633	1656			1756	1756			1852		1856			1956	1956				2100
Würzburg Hbf......920 921 d.	1631	1631		1713	1729			1830	1830				1929				2030	2030				2134
Nürnberg Hbf......920 921 a.	1724	1724		1824			◘	1924	1924		◘		2024		◘		2124	2124				2228
Augsburg Hbf 905........a.				1929													2240	2240				
München Hbf 904 905.......a.	1843	1843		2002	1940			2038	2038				2140				2314	2314				2346
Hanau Hbf........850 901 902 a.											1935											
Frankfurt (Main) Hbf..850 901 902 a.			1700		1800	1908				1900	2012	1950			2000	2108		2100				
Frankfurt Flughafen Fernbf ✈ 912 a.			1717								1917							2117				
Mannheim Hbf 912..........a.			1754		1843						1954					2043		2154				
Stuttgart Hbf 912...........a.			1835								2035	2156	2155f					2250				
Karlsruhe Hbf 912..........a.					1908	2052					2054					2108	2327f					
Basel SBB 912..............a.						2054											2300c					

SEE NOTE ⊠	ICE 273 ⑤⑥ s♣	ICE 273	IC 2379 ⑥ q♣	IC 2379 yT	ICE 635	ICE 685	ICE 635 ⑤⑦	IC 635 ⑤⑥⑦	ICE 775 ⑧q t♣	ICE 887 ⑧q ♣	IC 1087 ⑥h N♣	EN 471 Ⓡ D	EN 491 Ⓡ H	EN 40491 Ⓡ C	IC 1985 ⑦w
Hamburg Altona.............d.	1806	1806	⚑	yT		1846		1846	1908	1946	1946z	2014	2014	2014	2114
Hamburg Hbf.........903 d.	1824	1824	1828	1828		1901		1901	1924	2001	2001	2052	2029	2029	2128
Lüneburg...........903 d.			1859	1859						2028	2028				2200
Uelzen..............903 d.			1915	1915						2044	2044				2216
Celle...............903 d.			1939	1939											2239
Bremen Hbf 813.......d.					1914		1914								
Hannover Hbf.......903 a.	1938	1938	1958	1958	2014	2020	2014	2023	2038	2123	2123		2154	2154	2258
Hannover Hbf.......903 d.	1941	1941	2001	2001	2026	2026	2026	2041	2126	2137		2157	2157	2301
Göttingen.......902 903 d.	2016	2016	2040	2102	2102	2102	2116	2202	2213		2259	2259	2339
Kassel Wilhelmshöhe..901 902 d.	2037	2037	2103	2123	2123	2123	2123	2137	2223	2234				
Fulda..........850 901 902 d.				2156	2156	2156	2156		2256	2306				
Würzburg Hbf......920 921 d.			2229	2229	2229	2229				0133	0133	
Nürnberg Hbf......920 921 a.			◘	2324	2324	2324	2324				0232	0232	
Augsburg Hbf 905........a.												0626	
München Hbf 904 905.......a.					0040	0040						0705	
Hanau Hbf........850 901 902 a.									2339	2351				
Frankfurt (Main) Hbf..850 901 902 a.	2200	2200		2304				2300	2355	0008	0359x			
Frankfurt Flughafen Fernbf ✈ 912 a.									0024	0024				
Mannheim Hbf 912..........a.	2243	2243									0440			
Stuttgart Hbf 912...........a.														
Karlsruhe Hbf 912..........a.	2308	2308									0507			
Basel SBB 912..............a.		0100									0720			

C – ÖBB nightjet. 🛏 1, 2 cl., 🛏 2 cl. and 🚲 Hamburg - München - Innsbruck.
D – ÖBB nightjet. 🛏 1, 2 cl., 🛏 2 cl. and 🚲 Hamburg - Berlin - Basel - Zürich.
From Feb. 11 departs Hamburg Altona 1939, Hamburg Hbf 1956.
H – ÖBB nightjet. 🛏 1, 2 cl., 🛏 2 cl. and 🚲 Hamburg - Passau - Wien.
K – From Kiel (Table 820).
L – WATTENMEER – 🚲 and ⚑ (Westerland ♠ -) Hamburg - Frankfurt - Karlsruhe.
N – To Wiesbaden (Table 911).
O – From Stralsund (Table 830), also Ostseebad Binz on dates in Table 845.
T – From Stralsund (Table 830).
Z – To Zürich (Table 510).

c – ⑥⑦ (also Apr. 14, 17, May 1, June 5).
f – ⑤ (also May 24; not Apr. 14, May 26).
h – Also Apr. 14, 16, 30, June 4.
m – Not Apr. 13, 17, May 1, 24, 25, June 5.
n – Not Feb. 20 - Apr. 12.

q – Not Apr. 14, 16, 30, June 4.
r – Also Apr. 13, 17, May 1, 24, June 5; not Apr. 14, 16, 30, May 26, June 4.
s – Also Apr. 13, 16, 30, June 4.
t – Also Apr. 13, 17, May 1, June 5.
v – Also Apr. 13, 17, May 1, June 5; not Apr. 14, 16, 30, June 4.
w – Also Apr. 17, May 1, June 5; not Apr. 16, 30, June 4.
x – Frankfurt (Main) Süd.
y – Also Apr. 13, 17, May 1, 24, June 5; not Apr. 14, 16, 30, June 4.
z – Not Feb. 11 - Apr. 1, Apr. 14 – 16.

◇ – From Lübeck (Table 825).
♣ – From Flensburg (Table 823) on ⑤ (also Apr. 13, May 24).
♠ – ①⑤⑥⑦ to Apr. 3; daily from Apr. 7.
⊠ – Frankfurt, Hanau and Fulda timings are subject to alteration on ⑥⑦ Feb. 11 - Apr. 2 (also Apr. 14 – 17). See also engineering work panel on page 367.

Other *ICE/IC* services: Table 850 for Bebra - Kassel Wilhelmshöhe and v.v., also Frankfurt - Fulda - Bad Hersfeld and v.v. Tables 900/902 for Frankfurt - Fulda - Kassel Wilhelmshöhe and v.v.

Warning! Services between Frankfurt and Fulda are subject to alteration on ⑥⑦ Feb. 11 - Apr. 2 (also late evening on ⑤ Feb. 10 - Mar. 31).

km					A							
0	Frankfurt (Main) Hbf..921 d.	0524	0626		2126	2226	2326v					
4	Frankfurt (Main) Süd...921 d.	0530	0633	and	2133	2233	2333					
10	Offenbach (Main) Hbf...921 d.	0535	0638	hourly	2138	2238	2338					
23	Hanau Hbf.........921 d.	0545	0648	until	2148	2248	2348					
104	Fulda.............a.	0646	0749		2250	2349	0049					

		ⒶB	✝	☿	ⒶB							
Fulda.............d.	0401	0455	0505	0600	0608	0708	0808	0908			2309
Hanau Hbf.........921 d.	0500	0539	0609	0616	0655	0709	0809	0909	1009	and	0009
Offenbach (Main) Hbf...921 d.	0509	0548	0617	0624		0717	0817	0921t	1017	hourly	0017
Frankfurt (Main) Süd...921 d.	0515	0553	0623	0630	0710	0723	0823	0927t	1023	until	0023
Frankfurt (Main) Hbf..921 d.	0520	0558	0628	0636	0716	0728	0828	0932t	1028		0028

FULDA - KASSEL. Operated by CANTUS Verkehrsgesellschaft (except trains marked with note B). 2nd class only.

km		Ⓐ	Ⓐ	Ⓐ	Ⓐg																G	⑤⑦f				g	h	ⒶB
0	Fulda.............d.	0548	0616	0644	0656	0719	0819	0919	1019	1119	1219	1319	1419	1519	1619	1719	1819	1819	1919	1919	2019	2123e	2221	2301	2357
42	Bad Hersfeld.......d.	0505	0616	0644	0714	0721	0747	0847	0947	1047	1147	1247	1347	1447	1547	1647	1747	1847	1947	2047	2150	2250	2329	0027
56	Bebra.............d.	0520	0627	0657	0727	0731	0758	0857	0958	1057	1158	1257	1358	1457	1557	1657	1758	1857	1947	2058	2201	2301	2340	0041
62	Rotenburg (Fulda)....d.	0526	0633	0703	0733		0804	0903	1004	1103	1204	1303	1404	1503	1604	1703	1804	1903	1910	2004	2104	2206		
84	Melsungen.........d.	0545	0653	0723	0753		0824	0923	1024	1123	1224	1323	1424	1523	1624	1723	1824	1923	1929	2024	2225			
110	Kassel Wilhelmshöhe 804/6 a.	0611	0712	0742	0813		0843	0942	1042	1142	1242	1342	1442	1542	1642	1742	1842	1942	1949	2042	2146	2252		
114	Kassel Hbf.........804/6 a.	0616	0718	0748	0818		0849	0948	1048	1148	1248	1348	1448	1548	1648	1748	1848	1948	1954	2048	2150	2257		

		ⒶB	ⒶB	Ⓒ	Ⓐ		g																					ⒶB
Kassel Hbf.........804/6 d.			0506	0605	0626	0709		0810j	0910	1010	1110	1210	1310	1409	1510	1610	1710	1810	1910	2010	2010	2110	2210	2310
Kassel Wilhelmshöhe 804/6 d.			0510	0614	0630	0714		0814	0914	1014	1115	1214	1314	1413	1514	1614	1715	1814	1914	2014	2014	2115	2214	2316
Melsungen.........d.			0529	0634	0648	0733		0834	0934	1034	1134	1234	1334	1434	1534	1634	1734	1834	1933	2034	2034	2133	2233	2336
Rotenburg (Fulda)....d.			0549	0653	0708	0752		0852	0952	1052	1152	1252	1352	1452	1552	1652	1752	1852	1951	2052	2052	2151	2252	2355
Bebra.............d.	0315	0359	0522	0558	0700	0716	0800	0815	0859	0958	1051	1158	1259	1358	1459	1552	1659	1758	1859	2059	2059	2159	2304	0002
Bad Hersfeld.......d.	0325	0409	0531	0608	0709	0725	0811	0824	0908	1009	1108	1209	1308	1408	1508	1609	1708	1808	1908	2008	2108	2111	2209	2315	0012
Fulda.............a.	0354	0450	0558	0637	0737	0753		0852	0937	1035	1138	1137	1237	1337	1437	1537	1637	1737	1840	1937	2037	2137	2140	0027

A – To Bebra on Ⓐ.
B – 🚲 Bebra - Fulda - Frankfurt and v.v.
G – ①②③④⑥ (not Apr. 13, 17, May 1, 24, June 5).

e – Ⓐ only.
f – Also Apr. 13, 17, May 1, 24, 25, June 5.
g – To/from Göttingen (Table 908).

h – Runs 8 minutes later on ✝.
j – 0806 on ✝.
t – 4 minutes earlier on Ⓒ.

v – 2320 Jan. 2 - Apr. 5.

902 FRANKFURT - BRAUNSCHWEIG - BERLIN

See Table **850** for other fast services Frankfurt - Berlin via Erfurt. SEE NOTE ⊠.

km	SEE NOTE ⊠	*ICE*	*ICE*	*ICE*	*ICE*	*ICE*	*ICE*	*ICE*		*ICE*	*ICE*	*ICE*	*ICE*	*ICE*	*ICE*	*ICE*	*ICE*	*ICE*	*ICE*	*ICE*	*IC*	*IC*	*ICE*	*ICE*	*ICE*
		649	**1188**	**876**	**1092**	**696**	**874**	**694**	**1818**	**374**	**692**	**372**	**690**	**370**	**598**	**278**	**596**	**276**	**1090**	**594**	**1076**	**1998**	**274**	**592**	**292**
		①–⑤	①–⑥	①–⑥	①–④	①g			♥										⑧h	⑥k	⑤⑦	④v		s	⑦w
		a◇	e‡	d✕	m✕	✕	✕	✕	🍷	✕	✕	✕	✕	✕	✕	✕	✕	✕	✕	✕	r§🍷		✕	✕	Z✕
	Interlaken Ost **560** d.	✕	✕	...	...	...	...	...	...	...	...	0600	...	...	...	1000	...	...	...	...	...	...	...	...	...
	Bern **560** d.	...	...	...	...	...	...	...	...	...	...	0704	...	...	...	1104	...	...	...	...	...	...	...	...	...
	Basel SBB **912** d.	...	...	...	...	...	0412b	...	...	0608	...	0813	...	1013	...	1213	...	1413	...	...	...	...	1613	...	1813
	Karlsruhe Hbf **912** d.	...	...	...	0500g	...	0558	...	...	0800	...	1000	...	1200	...	1400	...	1601	...	...	...	...	1801	...	2000
	Ulm Hbf **930** d.	...	...	...	|	...	|	...	...	|	0751a	|	0951	|	1151	|	1351	|	1551	1551	...	...	|	1751	|
	Stuttgart Hbf **912** d.	...	...	...	|	...	|	0651	0621	|	0851	|	1051	|	1251	|	1451	|	1651	1651	...	...	|	1851	|
	Mannheim Hbf **912** d.	...	...	...	0528g	...	0632	0732	|	0832	0932	1032	1132	1232	1332	1432	1532	1632	1732	1732	...	...	1832	1932	2032
0	**Frankfurt** (Main) Hbf **850 900** d.	...	0506	0513g	0613	...	0713	0813	0830⁝	0913	1013	1113	1213	1313	1413	1513	1613	1713	1813	1813	1817	1817	1913	2013	2113
23	Hanau Hbf **850 900** d.	...	0522	0529g	|	...	0729	0829	0842	0929	1029	1129	1229	1329	1429	1529	1629	1729	|	1829	1837	1838	1929	2029	2129
104	Fulda **850 900** d.	...	0604	0611g	|	...	0811	0911	0923	1011	1111	1211	1311	1411	1511	1611	1711	1811	|	1911	1920	1929	2011	|	2211
194	**Kassel** Wilhelmshöhe **900** d.	...	0636	0643	|	0743	0843	0943	0959	1043	1143	1243	1343	1443	1543	1643	1743	1843	|	1944x	1959	2008	2043	2146	2243
239	Göttingen **900** d.	...	0654	0702	|	0802	0902	1002	1020	1102	1202	1302	1402	1502	1602	1702	1802	1902	|	2003	2021	2029	2102	2205	2302
317	Hildesheim Hbf **863** d.	...	...	0732	|	0832	0932	1032	|	1132	1232	1332	1432	1532	1632	1732	1832	1932	|	2032	2059	2105	2132	2234	2332
360	**Braunschweig** Hbf **863** d.	0601	...	0759	|	0859	0959	1059	|	1159	1259	1359	1459	1559	1659	1759	1859	1959	|	2059	2124	2128	2159	2259	2359
392	Wolfsburg **810 863** d.	0620	...	0817	|	0917	1017	|	1148	1217	|	1417	|	1617	|	1817	|	2017	|	2117	2143	2148	2217	2317	0017
559	**Berlin** Spandau **810** a.	0721	...	0912	0940	1011	1111	1209	|	1312	1409	1512	1609	1712	1809	1912	2009	2112	2151	2212	2245	2248	2312	0020	0111
575	**Berlin** Hbf **850 810** a.	0732	...	0926	0955	1025	1128	1225	1306	1328	1425	1528	1625	1728	1825	1928	2025	2128	2205	2227	2300	2305	2330	0035	0126
580	**Berlin** Ostbahnhof **810** a.	...	...	0937	1006	1037	1139	1236	1318	1339	1437	1539	1637	1739	1837	1939	2037	2139	...	2238	2311	2316	2342	0046	0137

SEE NOTE ⊠	*ICE*		*ICE*	*ICE*	*ICE*	*ICE*	*ICE*	*ICE*	*ICE*	*ICE*	*ICE*	*ICE*	*ICE*	*ICE*		*ICE*	*ICE*	*ICE*	*ICE*	*ICE*		*ICE*	*ICE*	*ICE*	*ICE*
	781		**275**	**593**	**1091**	**277**	**595**	**279**	**597**	**371**	**599**	**373**	**691**	**375**	**1819**	**693**	**377**	**695**	**1093**	**877**		**697**	**997**	**887**	**879**
	①g		①–⑤	⑥⑦	①–⑤										♥			⑥k	⑧h			⑤⑦	①–④	⑧q	⑦w
	M✕		a✕	c✕	a✕	✕	✕	✕	✕	✕	✕	✕	✕	✕	🍷	✕	✕	✕	✕	✕		r✕	m✕	✕	✕
Berlin Ostbahnhof **810** d.	0232	...	0421	0520	0553	0619	0722	0819	0922	...	1122	1219	1322	1419	1442	1522	1619	1722	1752	1819	...	1919	...	...	2019
Berlin Hbf **850 810** d.	0244	...	0432	0531	0604	0630	0734	0830	0934	1034	1134	1230	1334	1430	1454	1534	1630	1734	1803	1830	...	1931	1935	...	2030
Berlin Spandau **810** d.	|	...	0446	0545	0618	0645	0748	0845	0948	1045	1148	1245	1348	1445	|	1548	1645	1748	1817	1845	...	1945	1945	...	2045
Wolfsburg **810 863** d.	|	...	0540	0641	|	0740	|	0940	|	1140	|	1340	|	1540	1611	|	1740	|	|	1940	...	|	|	...	2140
Braunschweig Hbf **863** d.	0454	...	0558	0700	|	0758	0858	0958	1058	1158	1258	1358	1458	1558	|	1658	1758	1858	|	1958	...	2058	2058	...	2158
Hildesheim Hbf **863** d.	0518	...	0625	0725	|	0825	0925	1025	1125	1225	1325	1425	1525	1625	|	1725	1825	1925	|	2025	...	2125	2125	...	2225
Göttingen **900** d.	0602	...	0655	0755	|	0855	0955	1055	1155	1255	1355	1455	1555	1655	1742	1755	1855	1955	|	2055	...	2155	2155	2202	2255
Kassel Wilhelmshöhe **900** d.	0623	...	0716	0816	|	0916	1016	1116	1216	1316	1416	1516	1616	1716	1804	1816	1916	2016	|	2116	...	2216	2215	2223	2316
Fulda **850 900** d.	0654	...	0748	0848	|	0948	1048	1148	1248	1348	1448	1548	1648	1748	1840	1848	1948	2048	|	2148	...	2248	...	2256	2348
Hanau Hbf **850 900** d.	...	...	0828	0928	|	1028	1128	1228	1328	1428	1528	1628	1728	1828	1920	1928	2028	|	|	2228	...	2328	...	2339	0028
Frankfurt (Main) Hbf **850 900** a.	...	...	0844	0944	0944	1044	1144	1244	1344	1444	1544	1644	1744	1844	1937⁝	1944	2044	2142	2142	2248	...	2344	...	2355	0048
Mannheim Hbf **912** a.	...	...	0927	1027	1027	1127	1227	1327	1427	1527	1627	1727	1827	1927	|	2027	2127	2228	2228	2353	...	...	...	...	0149
Stuttgart Hbf **912** a.	...	...	|	1108	1108	|	1308	|	1508	|	1708	|	1908	|	2120	2108	|	2308	2310	|	...	...	...	...	|
Ulm Hbf **930** a.	...	...	|	1207	1207	|	1407	|	1607	|	1807	|	2007	|	...	2207q	|	...	0011t	|	...	...	...	...	|
Karlsruhe Hbf **912** a.	...	...	0958	...	...	1158	...	1358	...	1558	...	1758	...	1958	...	...	2158	...	...	0022	...	...	...	...	0217
Basel SBB **912** a.	...	...	1147	...	...	1347	...	1547	...	1747	...	1947	...	2147	...	...	2354	...	...	...	...	...	...	...	...
Bern **560** a.	...	...	1256	...	...	...	...	...	...	1856	...	2056	...	...	...	...	...	...	...	...	...	...	...	...	...
Interlaken Ost **560** a.	...	...	1357	...	...	...	...	...	...	1957	...	2157	...	...	...	...	...	...	...	...	...	...	...	...	...

M – To München (Table **900**). Also calls at Potsdam Hbf (d. 0306), Brandenburg Hbf (d. 0325) and Magdeburg Hbf (d. 0406).
Z – From Zürich HB (d. 1700).

a – ①–⑤ (not Apr. 14, 17, May 1, June 5).
b – ① (also Apr. 18, May 2, June 6; not Apr. 17, May 1, June 5). Basel **Badischer Bahnhof**.
c – Also Apr. 14, 17, May 1, June 5.
d – Also Apr. 16, 30, June 4; not Apr. 17, May 1, June 5.
e – Not Apr. 15, 17, May 1, June 5.
g – ① (also Apr. 18, May 2, June 6; not Apr. 17, May 1, June 5).
h – Not Dec. 25 – 30, ⑦ Feb. 12 - Apr. 2, Apr. 14, 16, 17, 30, June 4.
k – Also Dec. 25 – 30, ⑦ Feb. 12 - Apr. 2, Apr. 14, 16, 17, 30, June 4.
m – Not Apr. 13, 17, May 1, 24, 25, June 5.

q – ⑧ (not Apr. 14, 16, 30, June 4).
r – Also Apr. 13, 17, May 1, 24, June 5; not Apr. 14, 16, 30, May 26, June 4.
s – Also calls at Stendal (d. 2346).
t – Stuttgart - Ulm on ⑦ (also May 1, June 5).
v – Also Apr. 12, May 23; not Apr. 13, May 25.
w – Also Apr. 17, May 1, June 5; not Apr. 16, 30, June 4.
x – Not ⑦ Feb. 12 - Apr. 2; not Apr. 17.
§ – Train number **1992** on ⑤ (also Apr. 13, May 24). Subject to alteration on ⑦ Feb. 12 - Apr. 9 (also Apr. 17). Berlin timings are subject to alteration on ⑦ from May 14 (also June 5).

‡ – Train number **988** on ⑥ (also Apr. 14).
⁝ – Frankfurt (Main) **Süd**.
♥ – From Dec. 14. Operated by Locomore. Special fares (DB tickets **not** valid). Also calls at Hannover Hbf (train **1818** at 1115; train **1819** at 1646).
◇ – From May 15 departs Braunschweig 0551, Wolfsburg 0610.
⊠ – Frankfurt, Hanau and Fulda timings are subject to alteration on ⑥⑦ Feb. 11 - Apr. 2 (also Apr. 14 – 17); many trains do not call at Hanau on these dates. Berlin timings are subject to alteration from May 13. See engineering work panel on page 367.

903 Local services GÖTTINGEN - HANNOVER - UELZEN - HAMBURG *metronom*

Services below are operated by ***metronom*** (except trains **A**, **B**, **D** and **E**). For faster *ICE* and *IC* services see Table **900**.

km																											
				⚒		Ⓐ		Ⓐ																			
						A🍷	h	B🍷																			L
0	**Göttingen** d.	...	...	0409	0504	0546	0607	0645	...	0707	0809	0907	1009	1107	1209	...	1307	1409	1507	1609	1707	1809	1907	2009	...	2107	2209
20	Northeim (Han) d.	...	...	0422	0517	0600	0620	0658	...	0720	0822	0920	1022	1120	1222	...	1320	1422	1520	1622	1720	1822	1920	2022	...	2120	2222
39	Kreiensen d.	...	...	0437	0533	0617	0633	0712	...	0733	0837	0933	1037	1133	1237	...	1333	1437	1533	1637	1733	1837	1933	2037	...	2133	2237
58	Alfeld (Leine) d.	...	...	0450	0546	0629	0646	0725	...	0746	0850	0946	1050	1146	1250	...	1346	1450	1546	1650	1746	1850	1946	2050	...	2146	2250
75	Elze (Han) d.	...	...	0503	0558	0640	0658	0736	...	0758	0903	0958	1103	1158	1303	...	1358	1503	1558	1703	1758	1903	1958	2103	...	2158	2303
108	**Hannover** Hbf. a.	...	...	0526	0623	0657	0723	0756	...	0823	0926	1023	1126	1223	1326	...	1423	1526	1623	1726	1823	1926	2025	2126	...	2223	2326
108	**Hannover** Hbf. d.	...	...	0540	0640	0701	0740	0759	...	0840	0940	1040	1140	1240	1340	...	1440	1540	1640	1740	1840	1940	2040	2140	...	2248	2340
149	Celle d.	...	...	0606	0706	0720	0806	0819	...	0906	1006	1106	1206	1306	1406	...	1506	1606	1706	1806	1906	2006	2106	2206	...	2315	0006
201	Uelzen a.	...	...	0638	0738	0740	0838	0840	...	0938	1038	1138	1238	1338	1438	...	1538	1638	1738	1838	1938	2038	2138	2238	...	2346	0038
					▬	|	▬	|							|						|						
				Ⓐ		|		|							|						|			N	⑦w	Ⓒ	
201	Uelzen d.	0501	0605	0647	0704	0742	0802	0842	0902	1002	1101	1201	1301	1401	1445f	1501	1601	1701	1801	1902	2001	2102	2201	2306	2306	0005	...
214	Bad Bevensen d.	0509	0614	0655	0713	|	0810	0850	0910	1010	1109	1209	1309	1409	1455f	1509	1609	1709	1809	1910	2009	2110	2209	2314	2315	0013	...
237	Lüneburg d.	0524	0629	0709	0728	0758	0828	0902	0928	1028	1131j	1228	1328	1428	1512f	1528	1628	1728	1828	1929	2031	2128	2228	2328	2336	0032	...
256	Winsen (Luhe) d.	0535	0640	0720	0740	|	0839	|	0939	1039	1142	1239	1339	1439	1523f	1539	1639	1739	1839	1940	2042	2139	2239	2344	2351	0047	...
286	**Hamburg** Hbf . a.	0556	0702	0741	0802	0828	0902	0933	1001	1101	1204	1301	1401	1502	1545f	1601	1701	1802	1902	2001	2102	2201	2301	0019	0024	0120	...

					①–⑤	⑥⑦									①–④			⑦									
															D🍷			E🍷									
Hamburg Hbf d.	...	...	...	...	0543	0601	0652	0757	0857	0957	1057	1157	1257	1357	1528	1457	1557	1728	1657	1757	1857	1957	2057	2158	2234	2334	0034
Winsen (Luhe) d.	...	...	...	...	0604	0622	0713	0819	0919	1019	1119	1219	1319	1419	|	1519	1619	|	1719	1819	1919	2019	2119	2220	2307	0008	0106
Lüneburg d.	...	...	...	...	0615	0633	0724	0834	0933	1033	1133	1233	1333	1433	1558	1533	1633	1757	1733	1833	1933	2033	2130	2231	2323	0023	0122
Bad Bevensen d.	...	...	...	...	0630	0647	0742	0848	0948	1048	1148	1248	1348	1448b	1610	1548	1648	1809	1748	1848	1948	2048	2145	2246	2337	0037	0137
Uelzen a.	...	...	...	...	0638	0655	0750	0856	0956	1056	1156	1256	1356	1456b	1617	1556	1656	1817	1756	1856	1956	2056	2153	2253	2348	0045	0146
															|			|						|			
	⚒	Ⓒ	Ⓐ	h	Ⓐ	Ⓒ																					
Uelzen d.	0413	0513	0513	0609	0651	0709	0809	0909	1009	1109	1209	1309	1409	1509	1619	1609	1709	1819	1809	1909	2009	2114	2209	2309	...	...	...
Celle d.	0447	0547	0547	0647	0747v	0747	0847	0947	1047	1147	1247	1347	1447	1547	1641	1647	1747	1841	1847	1950	2047	2147	2247	2347	...	...	...
Hannover Hbf a.	0514	0614	0614	0714	0814	0814	0914	1014	1114	1214	1314	1414	1514	1614	1700	1714	1814	1905	1914	2016	2114	2215	2316	0016	...	...	...
Hannover Hbf d.	0536	0633	0636	0736	0833	0833	0936	1033	1136	1233	1336	1433	1536	1633	1703	1736	1833	1909	1936	2033	2133k	2233	2336	...	...	...	...
Elze (Han) d.	0558	0655	0658	0758	0855	0855	0958	1055	1158	1255	1358	1455	1558	1655	1722	1758	1855	1929	1958	2055	2158	2255	2358	...	...	...	...
Alfeld (Leine) d.	0610	0706	0710	0810	0906	0906	1010	1106	1210	1306	1410	1506	1610	1706	1733	1810	1906	1940	2010	2106	2210	2306	0010	...	...	...	...
Kreiensen d.	0623	0719	0723	0823	0919	0919	1023	1119	1223	1319	1423	1519	1623	1719	1746	1823	1919	1953	2023	2119	2223	2319	0023	...	...	...	...
Northeim (Han) d.	0636	0733	0736	0836	0935	0935	1036	1133	1236	1333	1436	1533	1636	1733	1759	1836	1933	2007	2036	2133	2236	2333	0036	...	...	...	...
Göttingen a.	0649	0747	0749	0849	0949	0949	1049	1147	1249	1347	1449	1547	1649	1747	1814	1849	1947	2020	2049	2147	2249	2347	0049	...	...	...	...

A – *IC* **2176**. Operated by DB.
B – *IC* **2182**. Operated by DB. From Kassel Wilhelmshöhe (d. 0623).
D – ①–④ (not Apr. 13, 17, May 1, 24, 25, June 5). *IC* **2281**. Operated by DB.
E – ⑦ (also Apr. 17, May 1, June 5; not Apr. 16, 30, June 4). *IC* **2173**. Operated by DB. To Kassel Wilhelmshöhe (a. 2048).
L – On Ⓒ Hannover Hbf d. 2348, Celle d. 0015, Uelzen a. 0049.

N – ①–⑥ (not Apr. 17, May 1, June 5).
b – On ⑤ (also Apr. 13, May 24; not Apr. 14) Bad Bevensen d. 1452, Uelzen a. 1459.
f – ⑤ (not Apr. 14).
h – Change trains at Hannover on Ⓐ.

j – Arrives 1124.
k – 2136 on Ⓐ.
v – Arrives 0728.
w – Also Apr. 17, May 1, June 5.

MÜNCHEN - INGOLSTADT - NÜRNBERG 904

km		ICE 888	ICE 822	ICE 1514	ICE 1524	ICE 684	ICE 820	ICE 886	ICE 728	ICE 1512	ICE 726	ICE 882	ICE 724	ICE 1510	ICE 722	ICE 880	ICE 720	ICE 1508	ICE 588	ICE 628	ICE 788	ICE 626	ICE 1206	ICE 586
		Ⓐ	①-⑥	①-⑤	⑥p	Ⓐ	①-⑥				①-⑥				1122									
			eK	a	S	D	eK		K		eK		K		K		K♠		⊖	K		K	H	⊖
		✕	🍷	✕	✕	⊖✕	🍷	✕	🍷	✕	🍷	✕	🍷	✕	🍷	✕	🍷	✕	✕	🍷	✕	🍷	✕	✕
0	**München** Hbf d.	0415	0449	0515	0515	0520	0552	0617	0652	0718	0755	0822	0852	0918	0955	1022	1055	1117	1122	1155	1222	1255	1317	1322
81	**Ingolstadt** Hbf d.	0453	0528	0552	0552	0558	0630	0655	0730	0756	|	0900	0930	0956	|	1100	|	|	1200	|	1300	|	|	1400
171	**Nürnberg** Hbf a.	0523	0555	0625	0625	0629	0657	0725	0757	0828	0857	0930	0957	1028	1057	1130	1157	1227	1231	1257	1330	1357	1427	1431
	Würzburg Hbf **900 920** a.	0627	0653	|	|	0727	0753	0827	0853	|	0953	1027	1053	|	1153	1227	1253	|	1327	1353	1427	1453	|	1527
	Frankfurt (Main) Hbf **920** ⊠ a.	|	0804	|	|	|	0904	|	1004	|	1104	|	1204	|	1304	|	1404	|	|	1504	|	1604	|	|
	Leipzig Hbf **851** a.	|	...	1010	1010	|	...	|	...	1210	...	|	...	1410	...	|	...	1610	|	...	|	...	1810	|
	Berlin Hbf **851** a.	|	...	1133	1133	|	...	|	...	1333	...	|	...	1533	...	|	...	1733	|	...	|	...	1933	|
	Hamburg Hbf **900** a.	0953	...	...	...	1054	...	1156	...	...	...	1354	...	...	...	1554	...	...	1653	...	1753	...	...	1853

	ICE 624 1124	ICE 704 804	ICE 622	ICE 1504	ICE 584 1084	ICE 620	ICE 1522	ICE 1604	ICE 528	ICE 1000	ICE 582	ICE 526	ICE 782 1182	ICE 524	ICE 1500	ICE 1500	ICE 522	ICE 780	ICE 520	ICE 1620	ICE 922		ICE 920		
										⑤-⑦		Ⓑq				⑤⑦		⑦w	①-④	⑥	⑤⑦				
	K		K		D	GK	K		K	u		K	☆	K		n	K	A	m	g	v				
	🍷	✕	🍷	✕	✕	🍷	✕	✕	🍷	🍷	✕	🍷	✕	🍷	✕	✕	🍷	✕	🍷	✕	✕		✕		
München Hbf d.	1355	1420	1455	1516	1522	1555	1618	1618	1652	1716	1721	1755	1820	1855	1922	1922	1952	2020	2055	2055	2055	...	2255	...	...
Ingolstadt Hbf d.	|	1459	|	|	1600	|	1657	1657	1730	|	1800	|	1900	|	2000	2000	2030	2101	2132	|	2132	...	2334	...	...
Nürnberg Hbf a.	1457	1530	1557	1627	1631	1657	1729	1729	1757	1827	1831	1857	1931	1957	2031	2031	2057	2132	2201	2201	2201	...	0005	...	...
Würzburg Hbf **900 920** a.	1553	|	1653	|	1727	1753	1825	|	1853	|	1927	1953	2028	2053	|	|	2153	2228	2255	2255	2255	...	...	...	...
Frankfurt (Main) Hbf **920** ⊠ a.	1704	|	1804	|	|	1904	1936	|	2004	|	|	2104	|	2204	|	|	2305	...	0004	0004	0004	...	...	...	...
Leipzig Hbf **851** a.	...	1910	...	2010	|	...	...	2110	...	2210	|	...	|	...	0010	0010	...	...	...	...	...	...	...	...	...
Berlin Hbf **851** a.	...	2031	...	2133	|	...	...	2230	...	2333	|	...	|	...	...	0133	...	...	...	...	...	...	...	...	...
Hamburg Hbf **900** a.	...	...	...	...	2058	...	...	...	...	...	2254	...	0008	...	...	...	...	...	...	...	...	...	...	...	...

	ICE 823	ICE 985	ICE 827	ICE 1581	ICE 521	ICE 781	ICE 523	ICE 1503	ICE 705	ICE 525	ICE 783	ICE 527	ICE 1127	ICE 583	ICE 1505	ICE 529	ICE 1521	ICE 621	ICE 585	ICE 1207	ICE 623	ICE 787	ICE 625	ICE 1509
	Ⓐt	Ⓐt	①-⑤	Ⓐt		①-⑥	①-⑥	Ⓐ	⑥h	1125	①-⑥	Ⓐ	⑥h		①-⑥				1085					
		M	aK	E	K	eN	eK			K	e	K	KG	G⊖	e	K	K	K	⊖	H	K♠		K	
	🍷	✕	🍷	✕	🍷	✕	🍷	✕	✕	🍷	✕	🍷	🍷	✕	✕	🍷	✕	🍷	✕	✕	🍷	✕	🍷	✕
Hamburg Hbf **900** d.	...	...	...	...	...	...	...	...	...	...	0555	...	...	0701	...	...	...	...	0901	...	...	1001	...	...
Berlin Hbf **851** d.	...	...	...	...	...	...	...	0427	0427	...	|	...	...	|	0627	...	...	...	|	0828	...	|	...	1027
Leipzig Hbf **851** d.	...	...	...	...	...	...	...	0548	0548	...	|	...	...	|	0748	...	...	...	|	0948	...	|	...	1148
Frankfurt (Main) Hbf **920** ⊠ d.	...	...	0454	...	0551	...	0654	|	|	0754	|	0854	0854	|	|	0954	1018	1054	|	|	1154	|	1254	|
Würzburg Hbf **900 920** d.	...	...	0604	...	0704	0729	0804	|	|	0904	0929	1004	1004	1030	|	1104	1132	1204	1230	|	1310	1329	1404	|
Nürnberg Hbf d.	0558	0628	0702	0728	0802	0827	0902	0928	0928	1002	1027	1102	1102	1128	1132	1202	1227	1302	1328	1332	1406	1427	1502	1528
Ingolstadt Hbf d.	0627	0701	0731	0803	|	0901	|	1002	1002	1031	1101	|	|	1201	|	|	1301	|	1401	|	|	1501	|	1601
München Hbf a.	0703	0737	0808	0841	0905	0939	1004	1039	1039	1107	1140	1204	1204	1239	1243	1304	1339	1404	1441	1446	1508	1541	1606	1638

	ICE 627	ICE 789	ICE 629	ICE 1511	ICE 1189	ICE 721	ICE 881	ICE 723	ICE 681	ICE 1513	ICE 725	ICE 883	ICE 727	ICE 1515	ICE 729	ICE 1615	ICE 885	ICE 821	ICE 685	ICE 635	ICE 1517	ICE 1517		ICE 1617
								Ⓑq					Ⓑq			⑤⑦		Q	⑤-⑦	⑤⑦	Ⓑ	⑥		⑤⑦
	K		K		⊖	K		K	D⊖	S	K		K		K	b	L	K	u	¶				d
	🍷	✕	🍷	✕	✕	🍷	✕	🍷	✕	✕	🍷	✕	🍷	✕	🍷	✕	✕	🍷	✕	✕	✕	✕		✕
Hamburg Hbf **900** d.	...	1201	...	...	1301	...	1401	...	1501	...	...	1601	...	...	...	...	1801	...	1901	...	...	...	...	...
Berlin Hbf **851** d.	...	|	...	1227	|	...	|	...	|	1427	...	|	...	1628	...	1730	|	...	|	...	1827	1827	...	1927
Leipzig Hbf **851** d.	...	|	...	1348	|	...	|	...	|	1548	...	|	...	1748	...	1848	|	...	|	...	1948	1948	...	2048
Frankfurt (Main) Hbf **920** ⊠ d.	1354	|	1454	|	|	1554	|	1654	|	|	1754	|	1854	|	1954	|	|	2054	|	...	|	|	...	|
Würzburg Hbf **900 920** d.	1504	1529	1604	|	1631	1704	1729	1804	1830	|	1904	1929	2004	|	2104	|	2134	2205	2229	2229	|	|	...	|
Nürnberg Hbf d.	1602	1627	1702	1728	1732	1802	1827	1902	1928	1932	2002	2027	2103	2128	2202	2229	2233	2302	2328	2328	2334	2338	...	0031
Ingolstadt Hbf d.	|	1701	|	|	1805	1831	1901	|	2001	|	2031	2101	|	2201	2231	2303	2309	2331	0001	0001	0008	0012	...	0105
München Hbf a.	1704	1738	1804	1838	1843	1907	1940	2004	2038	2043	2107	2140	2205	2239	2307	2342	2346	0007	0040	0040	0044	0048	...	0143

RE services via the high-speed line (SEE NOTE ❖). **WARNING! Timings are subject to alteration from March 6.**

km		Ⓐt	⑥	†z	⚒t	Ⓐt	Ⓒz	⑥		Ⓒz	Ⓐt	⑤f	Ⓒz	Ⓒz	Ⓐt	Ⓒz	Ⓐt		Ⓐt	Ⓐt	Ⓒz	Ⓒz	Ⓐt	Y	X
0	**München** Hbf d.	0453	0521	0604	0704	0901	0905	1005	1104	1300	1304	1359	1402	1500	1504	1600	1600	1658	1712	1800	1806	1900	1908	2108	2129
50	Pfaffenhofen (Ilm) d.	0519	0547	0631	0731	0930	0932	1028	1131	1329	1331	1430	1429	1529	1531	1627	1629	1729	1744	1829	1829	1929	1935	2134	2205
81	**Ingolstadt** Hbf a.	0538	0606	0650	0751	0952	0952	1047	1151	1351	1351	1450	1448	1550	1551	1646	1650	1752	1805	1850	1848	1950	1955	2154	2228
81	**Ingolstadt** Hbf d.	0539	0608	0705	0805	1005	1005	1105	1205	1407	1407	1505	1505	1605	1605	1708	1708f	1807z	1807	...	1905	2005	2007	2156	2236
171	**Nürnberg Hbf** a.	0634	0652	0748	0848	1048	1048	1149	1248	1450	1450	1548	1548	1648	1648	1751	1751f	1852z	1852	...	1948	2048	2050	2240	2320

	Ⓐt	Ⓐt	Ⓒz	Ⓐt	⑥	Ⓒz	Ⓐt		⑥	Ⓐt	Ⓒz	⑤f	Ⓐt	Ⓒz	Ⓒz	Ⓐt	Ⓐt	Ⓒz	Ⓒz	Ⓐt	Ⓐt	Ⓒz	Y	X	⑤⑥r
Nürnberg Hbf d.	0510	0607	0632	0732	0809	0910	0910	1110	1210	1310	1310	1410	1510	1510	1610	1610f	1710	1710	1809	...	1910	1910	2110	2138	2342
Ingolstadt Hbf a.	0556	0655	0717	0817	0855	0955	0955	1155	1255	1355	1355	1456	1556	1556	1655	1656f	1755	1755	1855	...	1955	1955	2155	2224	0029
Ingolstadt Hbf d.	0600	0705	0719	0819	0905	1006	1011	1209	1305	1409	1411	1505	1605	1605	1705	1705	1809	1810	1905	1905	2008	2009	2207	2235	0030
Pfaffenhofen (Ilm) d.	0619	0727	0737	0838	0926	1027	1033	1230	1326	1430	1433	1527	1626	1627	1726	1727	1830	1832	1926	1927	2029	2031	2228	2259	0049
München Hbf a.	0646	0757	0804	0900	0954	1054	1103	1301	1354	1453	1500	1558	1653	1657	1753	1757	1857	1902	1953	1957	2057	2101	2256	2336	0116

RE services via EICHSTÄTT and TREUCHTLINGEN. **WARNING! Timings are subject to alteration from March 6.**

km		◧	Ⓐt		◧		◧		◧		◧		◐		◐		◐		Ⓐ	Ⓒ			⑥		
0	**München** Hbf d.	...	0526	...	0626	0728	0826	0929	1029	1129	1229	1329	1429	1529	1625	1729	1829	1927	2021	2029	2129	2227	2227	2329	0032
50	Pfaffenhofen (Ilm) d.	...	0602	...	0702	0805	0902	1006	1105	1205	1305	1405	1505	1605	1702	1806	1905	2003	2102	2105	2205	2304	2304	0005	0108
81	**Ingolstadt** Hbf d.	0528	0629	0629	0730	0830	0930	1030	1130	1230	1330	1430	1530	1630	1730	1830	1930	2030	2130	2130	2232	2328	2329	0028	0130
108	Eichstätt Bahnhof ♥ d.	0556	0656	0656	0757	0856	0956	1057	1156	1256	1356	1456	1556	1656	1756	1857	1956	2056	2156	2156	2258	...	2357	...	...
137	Treuchtlingen a.	0620	0719	0719	0820	0919	1020	1120	1220	1319	1420	1519	1620	1719	1820	1920	2020	2119	2220	2220	2321	...	0021	...	...
137	Treuchtlingen **905** d.	0623	0725	0725	0825c	0925	1025c	1125	1225c	1325	1425c	1525	1625	1725	1825	1925	2025	2125	2225	2225	2325	...	...	...	...
146	Weißenburg (Bay) **905** d.	0630	0732	0732	0832c	0932	1032c	1131	1232c	1332	1432c	1532	1632	1732	1832	1931	2032	2132	2232	2232	2332	...	...	...	...
199	**Nürnberg** Hbf **905** a.	0716	0817	0817	0917c	1017	1117c	1217	1318c	1417	1517c	1617	1717	1817	1917	2017	2117	2217	2317	2317	0017	...	...	...	...

	Ⓐt	Ⓒz	⚒t	†z	Ⓐt	Ⓒz	⚒t	†z		◧		◧	Ⓒz	Ⓐt	◧		◐		◐		◐		◐		
Nürnberg Hbf **905** d.	...	...	0435	0439	0523	0538	0629	0639	0738	0839	0938	1039	1138	1138	1239	1337	1439	1538	1639	1738	1839	1938	2039	2139	2342
Weißenburg (Bay) **905** d.	...	...	0518	0523	0607	0622	0716	0723	0822	0923	1022	1123	1222	1222	1323	1422	1523	1622	1723	1822	1923	2022	2123	2223	0027
Treuchtlingen **905** a.	...	...	0525	0530	0614	0629	0723	0730	0829	0930	1029	1130	1229	1229	1330	1429	1530	1630	1730	1830	1930	2030	2130	2230	0035
Treuchtlingen d.	0450	...	0532	0532	0630	0634	0735	0735	0835	0935	1035	1135	1235	1240	1336	1435	1535	1635	1735	1835	1935	2035	2135	2235	...
Eichstätt Bahnhof ♥ d.	0514	...	0556	0556	0654	0657	0759	0759	0900	0959	1059	1159	1259	1303	1400	1459	1559	1659	1759	1859	1959	2059	2159	2259	...
Ingolstadt Hbf d.	0533	0539	0631j	0631j	0734j	0734j	0833	0833	0931	1034j	1131	1231	1331	1335	1435j	1531	1631	1731	1834j	1931	2034j	2132	2235j	2334j	...
Pfaffenhofen (Ilm) d.	0556	0603	0655	0655	0758	0758	0857	0857	0955	1058	1155	1255	1355	1359	1459	1556	1655	1755	1858	1955	2058	2156	2259	2358	...
München Hbf a.	0634	0640	0734	0734	0836	0836	0934	0935	1033	1136	1235	1335	1435	1437	1537	1634	1735	1835	1936	2035	2136	2234	2336	0036	...

A – To Kassel (Table **900**).
D – To/from Lübeck on dates in Table **825**.
E – From Lichtenfels (Table **851**).
G – From/to Garmisch on dates in Table **895**.
H – To/from Mittenwald/Innsbruck on dates in Table **895**.
K – To/from Köln, Essen or Dortmund (Table **910**).
L – From Kiel (Table **820**).
M – From Erlangen (Table **851**).
N – From Kassel (also Berlin on ①). Tables **900/2**.
Q – ④⑤⑦ (also Apr. 17; not Apr. 14, 16, 30, June 4).
S – From/to Ostseebad Binz or Stralsund on dates in Tables **844** and **845**.
X – ①-④ (not Apr. 17, May 1, 25, June 5).
Y – ⑤-⑦ (also Apr. 17, May 1, 25, June 5).

a – Not Apr. 14, 17, May 1, June 5.
b – Also Apr. 13, 17, May 1, 24, June 5; not Apr. 14, 16, 30, June 4.
c – 2–4 minutes later on ⚒ (not Jan. 6).
d – Also Apr. 13, 17, May 1, 24, June 5; not Apr. 30, May 26, June 4.
e – Not Apr. 15, 17, May 1, June 5.
f – ⑤ (not Jan. 6, Apr. 14).
g – Also Apr. 30, June 4.
h – Also Apr. 14, May 25; not Apr. 15, May 27.
j – Arrives 9–14 minutes earlier.
m – Not Apr. 13, 17, May 1, June 5.
n – Also Apr. 13, 17, May 1, 24, June 3, 5; not May 26, June 4.
p – Also Apr. 14, 16, 30, June 4.
q – Not Apr. 14, 16, 30, June 4.
r – Also Jan. 5, Apr. 13, 16, 30, May 24, June 4.
t – Not Jan. 6.
u – Also Apr. 13, 17, May 1, June 5.
v – Also Apr. 13, 17, May 1, June 5; not Apr. 14, 16, 30, June 4.
w – Also Apr. 17, May 1, June 5; not Apr. 16, 30, June 4.
z – Ⓒ (also Jan. 6).

⊠ – Frankfurt timings are subject to alteration on ⑥⑦ Feb. 11 - Apr. 2 (also Apr. 14–17). See Engineering Work Summary on page 367.
¶ – ⑤⑦ (also Apr. 13, 17, May 1, June 5; not Apr. 14, 16, 30, June 4). From Bremen (Table **900**).
◧ – Change at Treuchtlingen on ⚒ (not Jan. 6).
◐ – Change at Treuchtlingen on Ⓐ (not Jan. 6).
☆ – Conveys on dates in Table **900**: [12] (*ICE* **732/1032**) Garmisch - München - Hannover - Bremen.
⊖ – Conveys [12] München - Hannover - Bremen and v.v. (Table **900**).
♠ – Conveys [12] Köln - Paderborn - Kassel - Würzburg - München and v.v. (Tables **805/900**).
♥ – Connecting trains run Eichstätt Bahnhof - Eichstätt Stadt (*5 km*; operated by Bayerische Regiobahn).
❖ – *RE* services via the high-speed line call at Kinding and Allersberg (located 112 and 146 km from München respectively).

905 MÜNCHEN - AUGSBURG - NÜRNBERG and WÜRZBURG

See Table **904** for services via Ingolstadt. See Table **905a** for local trains Treuchtlingen - Würzburg.

ICE and *IC* services. Services which call at both Nürnberg and Würzburg are subject to alteration from March 6 (see engineering work panel on page 367).

	ICE 1614	*ICE* 1614	*ICE* 1082	*IC* 2300	*IC* 2300	*ICE* 680	*ICE* 1610	*ICE* 1610	*IC* 2082	*IC* 2082	*IC* 2356	*IC* 2082	*ICE* 786	*IC* 1284	*IC* 2288	*IC* 2288	*IC* 1980	*ICE* 1002	*ICE* 1002	*ICE* 1602	*ICE* 1602	*ICE* 1602	*ICE* 1602	*ICE* 580	*ICE* 580
									L	M				⑦w	Ⓐt	Ⓐ	⑦w	①-④	①-④	Ⓑq	⑤⑦	Ⓑ	⑤⑦	Ⓑq	⑦w
	Y	T	⊖	TR	YR	⊖	Y	T	A	A	R	A		F	T	Y	G	T	Ym	Y	vY	T	T	Q	
	✕	✕	✕	🍷	🍷	✕	✕	✕	🍷	🍷	🍷	🍷	✕					🍷	🍷	✕	✕	✕	🍷	✕	✕
München Ost ... d.	...	...	...	...	...	...	...	...	1117	...	...	...	...	...	...	...	...	...	...	...	...	...	...	...	...
München Hbf ... **930** d.	0537	0538	0641	0739	0741	0905	0941	0952	|	1120	1139	...	1340	1355	1539	1540	1552	1640	1640	1720	1720	1739	1739	1853	1853
München Pasing ... **930** d.	|	0547	|	0748	|	0914	|	|	1130	1130	1148	←	|	|	1548	|	1600	1649	|	1729	1729	1748	1748	1902	1902
Augsburg Hbf ... **930** d.	0607	0612	0716	0814	0809	0938	1014	1022	1200	1200	1214	1230	1413	1425	1613	1610	1625	1714	1710	1755	1755	1813	1813	1932	1932
Donauwörth ... d.	0626	0630	0738	0838	0828	|	|	|	→	→	|	1249	|	1444	1633	1629	1645	1733	1729	1813	1813	1833	1833	1952	1952
Treuchtlingen ... d.	0648	0651	|	|	|	|	|	|	...	...	|	1310c	|	1506	1654	1654	1707	1754	1751	1834	1834	1855	1855	2012	2012
Nürnberg Hbf ... **900 920** a.	0726	0726	0829	0929	0926	|	1126	1129	...	...	1327	|	1526	|	1728	1735	|	1828	1828	1924	1924	1929	1929	|	|
Leipzig Hbf **851** ... a.	1110	1110	|	1310	1310	|	1510	1510	...	...	1710	|	|	|	...	...	|	2210	2210	...	2308	...	2308	|	|
Berlin Hbf **851** ... a.	1230	1230	|	1430	1430	|	1630	1630	...	...	1830	|	|	|	...	...	|	2333r	2333r	...	0029	...	0029	|	|
Würzburg Hbf ... **900 920** a.	...	...	0927	...	...	1127	...	...	...	...	...	1435	1628	1636	...	...	1835	...	...	...	...	...	...	2129	2129
Hamburg Hbf **900** ... a.	...	...	1253	...	...	1454	...	...	...	...	...	1829	1953	2038	...	...	2227	...	...	...	...	...	...	...	0113

	ICE 981	*IC* 2287	*IC* 2287	*ICE* 989	*ICE* 989		*ICE* 581		*IC* 2083	*IC* 2083	*ICE* 1005	*ICE* 1005	*IC* 2355	*IC* 2355	*ICE* 587	*ICE* 1609	*ICE* 1609	*IC* 1981	*IC* 2301	*IC* 2301		*ICE* 1613	*ICE* 1613	*ICE* 633	*ICE* 683
	Ⓐt	Ⓐ	Ⓐt	Ⓐ	Ⓐt				M	L								⑤⑦							Ⓑq
		Y	T	Y	T				A	A	T	Y	TR	YR	⊖	T	Y	vN	TR	YR		Y	T	E	
	✕			✕	✕		✕		🍷	🍷	🍷	🍷	🍷	🍷	✕	✕	✕		🍷	🍷		✕	✕	✕	✕
Hamburg Hbf **900** ... d.	...	...	...	...	...	...	0456	...	0729	0729	...	...	...	...	1101	...	...	1328	...	...	...	...	...	...	1701
Würzburg Hbf ... **900 920** d.	...	...	...	...	...	...	0830	...	1122	1122	...	...	...	...	1430	...	...	1713	...	...	...	...	...	2030	2030
Berlin Hbf **851** ... d.	...	...	...	...	...	...	|	...	|	|	0730	0730	0930	0930	|	1130	1130	|	1330	1330	...	1530	1530	|	|
Leipzig Hbf **851** ... d.	...	...	...	...	...	...	|	...	|	|	0848	0848	1048	1048	|	1248	1248	|	1448	1448	...	1648	1648	|	|
Nürnberg Hbf ... **900 920** d.	...	0535	0547	0603	0615	...	0930	...	|	|	1228	1231	1430	1428	|	1629	1628	|	1830	1829	...	2028	2033	2130	2130
Treuchtlingen ... d.	...	0615	0622	0646	0651	...	|	...	|	1250c	|	|	|	|	|	|	|	1844	|	|	...	|	|	|	|
Donauwörth ... d.	0557	0644	0644	0711	0711	...	1021	...	1305	1312x	|	|	|	|	1608	1725	1727	1907	1925	1928	...	2128	2125	2222	2222
Augsburg Hbf ... **930** a.	0618	0705	0705	0731	0731	...	1041	...	1330	1331x	1334	1402	1534	1544	1626	1744	1746	1929	1944	1946	...	2147	2145	2240	2240
München Pasing ... **930** a.	0645	0734	0734	0758	0758	...	1107	...	1357	1357	|	|	|	|	1650	|	|	1953	|	|	...	|	|	2303	2303
München Hbf ... **930** a.	0655	0743	0743	0808	0808	...	1116	...	1406	|	1416	1436	1606	1615	1701	1815	1817	2002	2016	2017	...	2220	2220	2314	2314
München Ost ... a.	...	...	...	...	...	...	...	...	...	1410	...	...	...	...	...	...	...	...	...	...	...	...	...	...	...

RE services. See Table **930** for other connecting trains München - Augsburg and v.v. **WARNING! Timings are subject to alteration from March 30.**

km																										
		Ⓒz	⚒s		⚒s		⚒s	⚒s		⚒s		⚒s		Ⓐt		Ⓐt	⑥		Ⓐt	Ⓐt		Ⓒz	Ⓐt			
							H										H		H			H				
0	**München** Hbf ... **930** d.	*0159*	...	0532	...	0734	...	...	0935	...	1134	...	1335	...	1534	...	...	1734	...	...	1935	...	...	2100	2201	2300
7	München Pasing **930** d.	*0206*	...	0538	...	0742	...	...	0943	...	1142	...	1343	...	1542	...	...	1742	...	...	1943	...	...	2107	2209	2307
62	**Augsburg** Hbf ... **930** a.	*0246*	...	0619	...	0819	...	...	1019	...	1219	...	1419	...	1619	...	...	1819	...	...	2019	...	...	2148	2244	2348
62	**Augsburg** Hbf ... d.	0315	0516	0628	0719	0828	0840	0923	1028	1126	1224	1327	1429	1526	1628	1726	1735	1828	1918	1921	2028	2118	2126	2154	2254	0001
103	Donauwörth ... d.	0358	0558k	0659	0758	0858	0905	1000	1059	1158	1259	1358	1459	1558	1659	1758	1757	1859	1940	1958	2059	2139	2158	2233	2332	0040
137	Treuchtlingen ... a.	0417	0620	0720	0820	0920	|	1020	1120	1220	1320	1420	1520	1620	1720	1820	1816	1920	|	2020	2120	2158	2220	2253	...	...
137	Treuchtlingen ... **904** d.	0418	0623	*0725*	0829	*0925*	|	1029	*1125*	1229	*1325*	1429	*1525*	1625	*1725*	1825	1817	*1925*	|	2025	*2125*	2200	2225	*2325*	...	...
146	Weißenburg (Bay) **904** d.	0424	0630	*0732*	0836	*0932*	|	1036	*1131*	1236	*1332*	1436	*1532*	1632	*1732*	1832	|	*1931*	|	2032	*2132*	|	2232	*2332*	...	...
199	**Nürnberg** Hbf ... **904** a.	0507	0716	*0817*	0920	*1017*	0954	1120	*1217*	1320	*1417*	1520	*1617*	1717	*1817*	1917	1848	*2017*	2028	2117	*2217*	2232	2317	*0017*	...	...

	Ⓒz	Ⓐt	Ⓒz	Ⓐt	⚒s		⚒s			⚒s		⚒s		⚒s		Ⓐt		Ⓐt			Ⓐt		Ⓐt		Ⓒz	
								H	D										H							
Nürnberg Hbf ... **904** d.	0053	...	...	...	0435	*0523*b	0629	0717	*0738*	0839	*0938*	1039	*1138*	1239	*1337*	1439	*1538*	1639	1732	*1738*	1839	*1938*	2039	2139	...	...
Weißenburg (Bay) **904** d.	0135	...	...	...	0518	*0607*b	0716	|	*0822*	0923	*1022*	1123	*1222*	1323	*1422*	1523	*1622*	1723	|	*1822*	1923	*2022*	2123	2223	...	...
Treuchtlingen ... **904** a.	0142	...	...	...	0525	*0614*b	0723	0748	*0829*	0930	*1029*	1130	*1229*	1330	*1429*	1530	*1630*	1730	|	*1830*	1930	*2030*	2130	2230	...	...
Treuchtlingen ... d.	0143	...	...	...	0526	0634	0731y	0749	0834	0935	1034	1135	1234	1335	1434	1535	1634	1735	|	1834	1935	2035	2135	...	2235	...
Donauwörth ... d.	0207	0414	0520	0527	0604j	0658	0754	0807	0858	0958	1058	1158	1258	1358	1458	1558	1658	1758	1818	1858	1958	2058	2158	...	2258	2328
Augsburg Hbf ... a.	0229	0453	0558	0612	0639	0728	0826	0828	0928	1031	1128	1229	1328	1432	1528	1638	1728	1832	1839	1928	2031	2128	2231	...	2328	0006
Augsburg Hbf ... **930** d.	...	0502	0606	0615	*0649*t	0739	...	...	0939	...	1139	...	1339	...	1539	...	1739	...	...	1939	...	2139	...	...	*2339*	...
München Pasing ... **930** a.	...	0541	0645	0653	*0729*t	0813	...	...	1013	...	1213	...	1413	...	1613	...	1813	...	...	2013	...	2222	...	...	*0022*	...
München Hbf ... **930** a.	...	0549	0652	0702	*0738*t	0821	...	...	1021	...	1221	...	1421	...	1621	...	1821	...	...	2021	...	2230	...	...	*0030*	...

A – KÖNIGSSEE – 🛏12 and 🍷 (Berchtesgaden - Freilassing until Apr. 13) - München - Augsburg - Hamburg and v.v.; 🛏12 Oberstdorf (**2084/5**) - Augsburg - Hamburg and v.v.
D – Change trains at Donauwörth on Ⓒ (also Jan. 6).
E – From Bremen (Table **900**).
F – To Flensburg (Table **823**). From Schwarzach (Tables **960/951**) Jan. 8 - Mar. 26. Also calls at Gunzenhausen (d. 1519) and Ansbach (d. 1536).
G – Also calls at Gunzenhausen (d. 1720) and Ansbach (d. 1736).
H – From / to Lindau and Oberstdorf (Table **935**).
L – Until Apr. 13.
M – From Apr. 14.
N – Also calls at Ansbach (d. 1814) and Gunzenhausen (d. 1830). From Flensburg (Table **823**) on ⑤ (also Apr. 13, May 24).
Q – To Kassel (Table **900**).
R – From / to Rostock / Warnemünde on dates in Table **835**.
T – Until Mar. 29.
Y – From Mar. 30.

b – 15 minutes later on Ⓒ (also Jan. 6).
c – Until Mar. 29.
j – Arrives 0550.
k – Arrives 0549.
m – Not Apr. 13, 17, May 1, June 5.
q – Not Apr. 14, 16, 30, June 4.
r – 36 minutes later on ①② Jan. 9 - Mar. 14, ①② from May 15 (not June 5).
s – Not Jan. 6.
t – Ⓐ (not Jan. 6).
v – Also Apr. 13, 17, May 1, 24, June 5; not Apr. 14, 16, 30, May 26, June 4.
w – Also Apr. 17, May 1, June 5; not Apr. 16, 30, June 4.
x – Mar. 30 - Apr. 13 Donauwörth d. 1305, Augsburg a. 1330.
y – 0725 on ⑥.
z – Also Jan. 6.

905a TREUCHTLINGEN - WÜRZBURG

RB services (except train **A**)

km																										
		⚒r	Ⓒz	Ⓐt	Ⓐt	Ⓐt	Ⓒz		⑥						Ⓐt	A🍷										
0	**Treuchtlingen** ... d.	...	0502	0512	0535	0614	0626	*0705*t	0725	0825	0925	1025	1125	1225	1306	1310c	1325z	1425	1525	1625	1725	1825	1925	2025	2125	2225
24	Gunzenhausen ... d.	...	0515	0527	0550	0626	0639	*0719*t	0739	0839	0939	1039	1139	1239	1318	1324	1339z	1439	1539	1639	1739	1839	1939	2038	2139	2239
51	Ansbach ... a.	...	0535	0547	0611	0645	0659	*0739*t	0759	0859	0959	1059	1159	1259	1339	1341	1359z	1459	1559	1659	1759	1859	1959	2058	2159	2259
51	Ansbach ... d.	0440	0536	0606	0627	0701	0710	0810	0810	0910	1010	1110	1210	1311	...	1343	1410	1510	1610	1710	1810	1910	2010	2110	...	2310
83	Steinach (b Rothenb) ◐ d.	0503	0559	0628	0650	0723	0732	0832	0832	0932	1032	1132	1232	1332	...	1403	1432	1532	1632	1732	1832	1932	2032	2132	...	2332
140	**Würzburg** Hbf ... a.	0547	0644	0713	0737	0810	0816	0918	0918	1016	1118	1216	1318	1416	...	1435	1518	1616	1718	1816	1915	2018	2116	2218	...	0016

	⚒r	Ⓐt	Ⓒz	Ⓐt	Ⓐt	Ⓒz					A🍷	Ⓒz	Ⓐt											†w	⚒r
Würzburg Hbf ... d.	0430	...	0531	0531	0632	0641	0738	0841	0941	1041	1122	1141	1141	1241	1341	1441	1541	1641	1741	1841	1941	2041	2142	2241	2304
Steinach (b Rothenb) ◐ ... d.	0512	...	0614	0614	0716	0724	0824	0924	1024	1124	1156	1224	1224	1326	1424	1524	1624	1724	1824	1924	2024	2124	2224	2324	2347
Ansbach ... a.	0535	...	0636	0636	0737	0746	0846	0946	1046	1146	1215	1246	1247	1347	1446	1546	1646	1746	1846	1946	2046	2146	2246	2347	0009
Ansbach ... d.	0537	0610	0654	0711	0754	0754	0854	0954	1054	1154	1217	1254	1317	1354	1454	1554	1654	1754	1854	1954	2054	2154	2247h	...	0010
Gunzenhausen ... d.	0556	0629	0715	0730	0815	0815	0915	1015	1115	1215	1234	1315	1336	1415	1515	1615	1715	1815	1915	2015	2115	2215	2306h	...	0029
Treuchtlingen ... a.	0609	0643	0730	0744	0829	0829	0929	1029	1129	1229	1248	1329	1350	1429	1529	1629	1729	1829	1929	2029	2129	2230	2321h	...	0043

◐ – Local trains **STEINACH** (b Rothenb) - **ROTHENBURG OB DER TAUBER** and v.v. 2nd class only *12 km* Journey time: 14 minutes.
From Steinach at 0519 ⚒r, 0617 Ⓒz, 0631 Ⓐt, 0726 Ⓐt, 0735 Ⓒz, 0835, 0935, 1035, 1135, 1235, 1335, 1435, 1535, 1635, 1735, 1835 Ⓒz, 1845 Ⓐt, 1935, 2035 and 2235.
From Rothenburg ob der Tauber at 0445 ⚒r, 0541 Ⓒz, 0556 Ⓐt, 0657 Ⓐt, 0706 Ⓒz, 0806, 0906, 1006, 1106, 1206, 1309, 1406, 1506, 1606, 1706, 1806, 1906, 2006 and 2206.

A – *IC* 2082/3. KÖNIGSSEE – 🛏12 and 🍷 (Berchtesgaden until Apr. 13) - München - Augsburg - Hamburg and v.v.; 🛏12 Oberstdorf (**2084/5**) - Augsburg - Hamburg and v.v.
c – Until Mar. 29.
h – 7 minutes later on ⑦.
r – Not Jan. 6.
t – Ⓐ (not Jan. 6).
w – Also Jan. 6.
z – Ⓒ (also Jan. 6).

906 GIESSEN - KOBLENZ; LIMBURG - FRANKFURT and WIESBADEN

DB (*RE* services); HLB★

km	⊠		⚒	⚒								⊙
0	**Gießen** .... **807** d.	...	0618	0716	0916	1116	1316	1516	1716	1916	2021	2116	2221
13	Wetzlar .... **807** d.	...	0630	0726	0926	1126	1326	1526	1726	1926	2033	2126	2233
36	Weilburg .... d.	...	0656	0742	0942	1142	1342	1542	1742	1942	2058	2142	2258
65	**Limburg** (Lahn) .. a.	...	0733	0807	1007	1207	1407	1607	1807	2007	2136	2207	2336
			◧ d	|	|	|	|	|	|	|	▬	|	▬
65	**Limburg** (Lahn) .. d.	0645	0745	0808	1008	1208	1408	1608	1808	2008	2045	2208	2245
68	Diez .... d.	0649	0749	0812	1012	1212	1412	1612	1812	2012	2049	2212	2249
91	Nassau (Lahn) .... d.	0715	0815	0832	1032	1232	1432	1632	1832	2032	2115	2232	2315
99	Bad Ems .... d.	0725	0825	0839	1039	1239	1439	1639	1839	2039	2125	2239	2325
112	Niederlahnstein... d.	0743	0843	0852	1052	1252	1452	1652	1852	2052	2143	2252	2343
117	**Koblenz** Hbf ...... a.	0750	0850	0859	1059	1259	1459	1659	1859	2059	2150	2259	2352

⊠	Ⓐ										
Koblenz Hbf .... d.	0509	0658	0858	1058	1258	1458	1658	1858	1909	2109	2209
Niederlahnstein .... d.	0516	0704	0904	1104	1304	1504	1704	1904	1916	2116	2216
Bad Ems .... d.	0533	0718	0918	1118	1318	1518	1718	1918	1933	2133	2233
Nassau (Lahn) ...... d.	0543	0726	0926	1126	1326	1526	1726	1926	1943	2143	2243
Diez .... d.	0609	0746	0946	1146	1346	1546	1746	1946	2009	2209	2309
Limburg (Lahn).... a.	0613	0749	0949	1149	1349	1549	1749	1949	2013	2213	2313
	◧ Ⓐ	|	|	|	|	|	|	|	◧	◧	
Limburg (Lahn).... d.	0618	0750	0950	1150	1350	1550	1750	1950	2023	2223	...
Weilburg .... d.	0655	0816	1016	1216	1416	1616	1816	2016	2100	2301	...
Wetzlar .... **807** d.	0720	0833	1033	1233	1433	1633	1833	2033	2126	2327	...
Gießen .... **807** a.	0731	0842	1042	1242	1442	1642	1842	2043	2138	2338	...

Limburg - Niedernhausen - Frankfurt and Wiesbaden

km		⚒	Ⓐ	Ⓐ	⑥	Ⓐ	©	Ⓐ	Ⓐ	Ⓐ	⚒	†	Ⓐ		⚒	†		⚒	†		⚒	†	Ⓐ		⚒	†
0	**Limburg** (Lahn)......... d.	0418	0448	0518	0518	0555	0618	0625	0638	0655	0718	0718	0755	0818	0918	0918	1018	1118	1118	1218	1318	1318	1355	1418	1518	1518
21	Bad Camberg............ d.	0442	0512	0542	0542	0614	0642	0644	0703	0714	0742	0742	0814	0842	0942	0942	1042	1142	1142	1242	1342	1342	1414	1442	1542	1542
30	Idstein...................... d.	0451	0521	0551	0551	0621	0651	0651	0713	0721	0751	0751	0821	0851	0951	0951	1051	1151	1151	1251	1351	1351	1421	1451	1551	1551
38	Niedernhausen........‡a.	0457	0527	0557	0559	0627	0657	0657	0722	0727	0757	0759	0827	0857	0957	0959	1057	1157	1159	1257	1357	1359	1427	1457	1557	1559
58	**Wiesbaden** Hbf..... a.	|	0555	0625	0625	0655	0725k	|	0744	|	0827	0825	0857	0925	1025	1025	1125	1225	1225	1325	1427	1425	1457	1527	1627	1625
70	**Frankfurt** (Main) Hbf ‡ a.	0528	0558	0628	...	0658	0728	0728	...	0758	0828	...	0858	0928	1028	...	1128	1228	...	1328	1428	...	1458	1528	1632c	...

	Ⓐ		Ⓐ	⚒	†	Ⓐ		⚒	†			
Limburg (Lahn) .... d.	1555	1618	1655	1718	1718	1755	1818	1918	1918	2018	2118	2218
Bad Camberg .... d.	1614	1642	1714	1742	1742	1814	1842	1942	1942	2042	2142	2242
Idstein .... d.	1621	1651	1721	1751	1751	1821	1851	1951	1951	2051	2151	2251
Niedernhausen ....‡ a.	1627	1657	1727	1757	1759	1827	1857	1957	1959	2057	2159	2258
Wiesbaden Hbf...... a.	1657	1727	1757	1827	1825	1857	1927	2027	2025	2125	2225	2325
Frankfurt (Main) Hbf ‡ a.	1658	1728	1758	1828	...	1858	1928	2028	...	2128	...	2333

		Ⓐ	©	Ⓐ	Ⓐ	©	Ⓐ		⚒	†
Frankfurt (M) Hbf . ‡ d.	...	0601	0631	0643	0731	...	...	0831	0931	...
Wiesbaden Hbf .. d.	0531v	0601	0636k	0650	0720	0736k	0806	0836	0936	0936
Niedernhausen..... ‡ d.	0601	0631	0701	0718	0801	0801	0831	0901	1001	1001
Idstein.................... d.	0608	0638	0708	0725	0808	0808	0838	0908	1008	1008
Bad Camberg......... d.	0617	0647	0717	0734	0817	0817	0847	0917	1017	1017
Limburg (Lahn)....... a.	0641	0711	0741	0801	0841	0841	0911	0941	1041	1041

		⚒	†		⚒	†		Ⓐ		Ⓐ	©	Ⓐ	Ⓐ	⚒	†	Ⓐ		Ⓐ	⚒	†		Ⓐ	©			
Frankfurt (Main) Hbf ‡ d.	1031	1131	...	1231	1331	...	1431	1501	1531k	1601	1631	...	1701	1731	...	1801	1831	1901	1931	...	2031	2131	...	2231	...	0028
Wiesbaden Hbf...... d.	1036	1136	1136	1236	1336	1336	1436	1506	1536b	1606	1636	1636	1706	1736	1736	1806	1834	1906	1936	1936	2036	2136	2136	2236	2336	|
Niedernhausen .... ‡ d.	1101	1201	1201	1301	1401	1401	1501	1531	1601	1631	1701	1701	1731	1801	1801	1831	1901	1931	2001	2001	2101	2201	2201	2301	0001	0101
Idstein .... d.	1108	1208	1208	1308	1408	1408	1508	1538	1608	1638	1708	1708	1738	1808	1808	1838	1908	1938	2008	2008	2108	2208	2208	2308	0008	0108
Bad Camberg .... d.	1117	1217	1217	1317	1417	1417	1517	1545	1617	1645	1717	1717	1745	1817	1817	1845	1917	1945	2017	2017	2117	2217	2217	2317	0017	0117
Limburg (Lahn) .... a.	1141	1241	1241	1341	1441	1441	1541	1604	1641	1704	1741	1741	1804	1841	1841	1904	1941	2004	2041	2041	2141	2241	2241	2341	0041	0141

b – Change trains at Niedernhausen on ⑥.
c – 1628 on ⑥.
d – Daily.
k – ⑥ only.
v – ⚒ only. 0536 on ⑥.

⊙ – Runs 26–27 minutes later on Ⓐ.
◧ – Change trains at Limburg.
★ – Hessische Landesbahn.
⊠ – Additional stopping trains operate.

‡ – **Additional S-Bahn** *S2* **services** Frankfurt - Niedernhausen and v.v. Journey: 35 minutes.
From Frankfurt (Main) Hbf: On ⚒ every 30 minutes 0452–2352; on † at 0452, 0521, 0552, 0621, 0652, 0721, 0752, 0822, 0852 and every 30 minutes 2352.
From Niedernhausen: On ⚒ every 30 minutes 0433–2333; on † at 0433, 0533, 0603, 0633 and every 30 minutes until 2333.

907 GIESSEN - FULDA

Hessische Landesbahn

km		Ⓐ	Ⓐ	⑥	⚒	©	Ⓐ						Ⓐ	©						©	Ⓐ	©w	Ⓐ	Ⓐ	©	©
0	**Gießen** .... d.	...	0524	...	0617e	0744k	0747	0844	0947	1044	1147	1241	1346	1347	1444t	1547	1644t	1747	1844t	1947	1947	2044	2055	2208	2209	2309
23	Grünberg (Oberhess). d.	...	0549	...	0709e	0811k	0816	0911	1013	1111	1213	1311	1411	1413	1511	1611v	1711	1811v	1911	2015	2015	2111	2119	2236	2234	2337
60	Alsfeld (Oberhess) ..... d.	0515	0633	0649	0749	0849	0849	0949	1049	1149	1249	1349	1449	1449	1549	1649	1749	1849	1949	2055	2054	2146	2210	2312	2310	0011
79	Lauterbach (Hess) ..... d.	0529	0649	0703	0803	0903	0903	1003	1103	1203	1303	1403	1503	1503	1603	1703	1803	1903	2003	2103	2107	...	...	...	...	...
106	**Fulda** .... a.	0602	0719	0729	0829	0929	0929	1029	1129	1229	1329	1429	1529	1529	1629	1729	1829	1929	2029	2128	2137	...	...	...	...	...

	Ⓐ	Ⓐ	Ⓐ	⑥	Ⓐ	⑥	Ⓐ	Ⓐ	†	⑥													©	Ⓐ		
Fulda .... d.	...	...	...	...	0535	...	0610	0653	...	0735	0835	0935	1035	1135	1235	1335	1435	1535	1635	1735	1835	1935	2035	2059	2159	2235
Lauterbach (Hess) ...... d.	...	...	...	...	0612j	...	0654j	0723	...	0805	0905	1005	1105	1205	1305	1405	1505	1605	1705	1805	1905	2005	2105	2124	2224	2300
Alsfeld (Oberhess) ...... d.	0415	0532	0556	0616	0631	0712	0719j	0757j	0814	0819	0919	1019	1119	1219	1319	1419	1519	1619	1719	1819	1919	2019	2122	2137	2238	2314
Grünberg (Oberhess).. d.	0456	0614	0639	0651	0705	0747	0753	0838	0848	0850	0953	1050	1153	1250t	1353	1450t	1553	1650t	1753	1850t	1953	2056	2202	2215	...	...
Gießen .... a.	0521	0640	0704	0716	0729	0816	0818	0906	0915	0915	1018	1115	1218	1315	1416v	1515	1616v	1715	1816v	1915	2018	2124	2232	2239	...	...

e – Ⓐ only.
j – Arrives 10–12 minutes earlier.
k – ⑥ only.
t – 3 minutes later on Ⓐ.
v – 2 minutes later on ©.
w – From May 1 departs Gießen 2055, Grünberg 2119, arrives Alsfeld 2154.

908 GÖTTINGEN - BEBRA

CANTUS Verkehrsgesellschaft (2nd class only)

km		Ⓐ	⑥	Ⓐ	ⒶF	©F	©	⚒		Ⓐ						Ⓐ	©	Ⓐ	©	ⒶH	Ⓐ	©		Ⓑ	⑥
0	**Göttingen** ....**864** d.	0442	0543	0600	0703	0703	...	0814	0914	1040	1114	1240	1314	1440	1514	1614	1640	1714	1714	1814	1914	1914	2014	2214	2219
20	Eichenberg ....**864** d.	0458	0558	0618	0718	0719	...	0830	0930	1054	1130	1254	1330	1454	1530	1630	1654	1730	1730	1830	1930	1930	2030	2229	2235
35	Bad Sooden Allendorf . d.	0509	0608	0628	0728	0729	...	0840	0940	1105	1140	1305	1340	1505	1540	1640	1705	1740	1740	1840	1940	1940	2040	2239	2244
49	Eschwege .... a.	0520	0619	0639	0739	0741	...	0852	0952	1116	1152	1316	1352	1516	1552	1651	1716	1751	1751	1851	1952	1952	2051	2250	2255
49	Eschwege .... d.	0525	0624	0644	0746	0746	0821	0921	1018	1121	1218	1321	1418	1521	1618	1656	1721	1756	1818	1856	1957	2018	2056	2256	2300
87	**Bebra** .... a.	0553	0652	0711	0814	0814	0849	0949	1047	1149	1247	1349	1447	1549	1647	1724	1751	1824	1847	1924	2027	2047	2124	2324	2328

	Ⓐ	Ⓐ	⑥	Ⓐ	G	⚒	Ⓐ	©	Ⓐ							Ⓐ	©		Ⓐ					©F	ⒶF
Bebra .... d.	0403	0518	0622	0633	0731	0832	0905	0932	1003	1105	1203	1305	1403	1505	1603	1705	1705	...	1803	1905	2003	2103	...	2303	2303
Eschwege .... a.	0432	0548	0650	0700	0800	0900	0934	1000	1031	1134	1231	1334	1431	1534	1631	1734	1734	...	1831	1934	2031	2131	...	2331	2331
Eschwege .... d.	0437	0555	0655	0705	0805	0905	1005	1005	1036	1205	1236	1405	1436	1605	1636	1739	1805	1805	1836	2005	2036	2136	...	2336	2336
Bad Sooden Allendorf .. d.	0449	0606	0707	0716	0816	0916	1016	1016	1047	1216	1247	1416	1447	1616	1647	1750	1816	1816	1847	2016	2047	2147	...	2347	2347
Eichenberg ....**864** d.	0502	0624	0722	0732	0832	0932	1032	1032	1100	1232	1301	1432	1500	1632	1700	1806	1832	1832	1900	2032	2100	2200	...	0003	2359
Göttingen ....**864** a.	0515	0637	0735	0745	0845	0945	1045	1045	1113	1245	1314	1445	1513	1645	1713	1820	1845	1845	1913	2045	2113	2215	...	0017	0018

F – To / from Fulda (Table **901**).
G – From Fulda (Table **901**) on ©.
H – To Bad Hersfeld (a. 1937).

909 WÜRZBURG - BAD KISSINGEN - GEMÜNDEN

DB (*RB* services); EB ★

km			⚒r						©z	Ⓐe															
0	**Würzburg** Hbf .... **870 876** ‡ d.	...	0454r	0738	0801	0835	0935	1001	1135	1135	1201	1338	1401	1435	1538	1601	1636	1738	1801	1836	1938	2001	2035	2139	2236
43	**Schweinfurt** Hbf. **870 876** ‡ d.	0450e	0611	0811	0830	0911	1011	1030	1205	1205	1230	1411	1430	1511	1612	1630	1711	1811	1830	1911	2012	2030	2111	2214	2347
57	Ebenhausen (Unterf)... **870** ‡ d.	0511e	0625	0825	0843	0930	1025	1043	1224	1224	1243	1425	1443	1530	1625	1643	1730	1825	1843	1930	2025	2043	2130	2228	0003
66	**Bad Kissingen** .... a.	0520e	0634	0834	0853	0939	1034	1053	1233	1233	1253	1434	1453	1539	1634	1653	1739	1834	1853	1939	2034	2053	2139	2237	0012
66	**Bad Kissingen** .... d.	0540	0640	0839	...	...	1039	...	1239	1239	1330e	1439	...	1544e	1639	...	1744e	1839	...	1944	2047	...	2144	...	...
85	Hammelburg .... d.	0607	0707	0908	...	...	1106	...	1308	1313	1400e	1506	...	1608e	1706	...	1808e	1906	...	2007	2114	...	2212	...	...
113	**Gemünden** (Main)............. a.	0639	0741	0942	...	...	1141	...	1341	1350	1441e	1541	...	1641e	1741	...	1841e	1941	...	2039	2151	...	...	...	...

	Ⓐe		©z	Ⓐe	Ⓐe							©z	Ⓐe												
Gemünden (Main) .... d.	...	...	...	0607	...	0707r	...	0812	...	1012	...	1212	1212	1320e	1412	1507e	...	1609	1707e	...	1809	1907e	...	2115	2211
Hammelburg .... d.	0546	0616e	0645	0645	0715	0746r	...	0844	...	1044	...	1244	1244	1358e	1444	1543e	...	1644	1743e	...	1844	1943e	...	2151	2248
Bad Kissingen .... a.	0609	0638e	0708	0708	0738	0808r	...	0907	...	1107	...	1307	1307	1420e	1507	1610e	...	1707	1809e	...	1907	2009e	...	2212	2309
Bad Kissingen .... d.	0614	0644	0720	...	0746	0814	0901	0919	1101	1119	1301	1319	1333	1501	1519	1615	1701	1719	1814	1901	1919	2014	2101	2217	2314
Ebenhausen (Unterf) ..... **870** a.	0623	0653	0729	...	0755	0823	0910	0928	1110	1128	1310	1328	1342	1510	1528	1624	1710	1728	1823	1910	1928	2023	2110	2226	2323
Schweinfurt Hbf ....**870 876** a.	0636	0716	0743	...	0809	0841	0926	0943	1125	1144	1326	1343	1357	1526	1543	1640	1726	1743	1840	1926	1943	2040	2126	2239	2337
Würzburg Hbf ....**870 876** a.	0718	0746	0820	...	0851	0922	0955	1020	1155	1220	1355	1420	1451	1555	1620	1721	1755	1820	1921	1955	2020	2122	2157	...	0016v

e – Ⓐ (not Jan. 6).
r – ⚒ (not Jan. 6).
v – Change trains at Schweinfurt.
z – © (also Jan. 6).

¶ – 3 minutes later from Mar. 6.
★ – Erfurter Bahn (2nd class only).
‡ – Trains between Würzburg, Schweinfurt and Ebenhausen are often combined with a service to Meiningen or Erfurt. Passengers should take care to join the correct portion for their destination.

☛ **Additional journeys** Schweinfurt - Bad Kissingen and v.v.:
From Schweinfurt at 0530, 0703 Ⓐ**e**¶, 0716 ©**z**, 0737 Ⓐ**e**, 1111, 1303 Ⓐ**e**¶, 1311 ©**z**, 1330 Ⓐ**e**, 1545 Ⓐ**e** and 1745 Ⓐ**e**.
From Bad Kissingen at 0458 Ⓐ, 0528 Ⓐ**e**, 0703 Ⓐ**e**, 1014, 1214, 1414, 1548 Ⓐ**e** and 1747 Ⓐ**e**.

See page 367 for a summary of Christmas/New Year alterations

910 AACHEN - KÖLN - FRANKFURT via high-speed line

See Tables 800/911 for services via Bonn and Koblenz. See Table 20 for *Thalys* services Paris - Brussels - Aachen - Köln. SEE NOTES ⊠ AND ❖.

km	SEE NOTES ⊠ AND ❖	ICE 827 ①–⑤ a	ICE 827	ICE 521 ①–⑥	ICE 523 e	ICE 511 ①g	ICE 511	ICE 711 Ⓐu	ICE 811 Ⓐ	ICE 1125 ⑦j	ICE 525 ①–⑥	ICE 101 Ⓐ h	ICE 913 ①–⑥	ICE 813	ICE 1127 Ⓐ G	ICE 527 Ⓐ	ICE 513	ICE 11 M	ICE 815 ①–⑥	ICE 529 Ⓐ	ICE 103 H	ICE 121	ICE 621
	Dortmund Hbf 800 d.				0406	0437				0514	0525	0537	0552	0600	0614	0624	0637		0652	0725	0737		0815
	Essen Hbf 800 d.				0428					0538	0553		0615		0639		0653	0700	0715		0754		0840
	Amsterdam Centraal 28 d.																					0637	
	Düsseldorf Hbf 800 d.				0455				◐	0605	0621	◐	0648	◐	0707	0721	0727		0747	0822	◐	0848	0913
	Brussels Midi/Zuid 21 d.											0625						0739					
	Aachen Hbf 802 807 a.					0546												0739					
	Köln Hbf 800 802 807 a.							0646				0709						0749			0846	0912	
0	Köln Hbf 802 807 d.	0317	0317	0418		0555	0555	0611	0620		0646	0654	0720			0755		0827			0855		0927
1	Köln Messe/Deutz 802 d.				0518					0629	0644		0713			0730	0744			0811	0844		0936
	Köln/Bonn Flughafen + 802 d.	0329	0329		0531														0822				
25	Siegburg/Bonn [tram] 807 d.	0340	0340	0433	0542	0610	0610	0626	0636	0643	0710		0736	0744		0810		0832			0910		
88	Montabaur d.	0403	0403	0453	0603			0646	0656	0703			0756		0804			0857					1005
110	Limburg Süd d.	0414	0414	0504	0614			0657	0707	0714			0807	0815				0908					1015
	Wiesbaden Hbf a.					0719																	
	Mainz Hbf a.					0744																	
169	Frankfurt Flughafen Fernbf + a.	0433	0433	0527	0633	0649	0649	0726	0733	0733	0749	0807	0826	0833	0833	0849	0916	0926	0933	0949	1016		1033
180	Frankfurt (Main) Hbf a.	0448	0448	0544	0648				0741	0748	0748		0841	0848	0848			0930	0941	0948	1030		1048
	Nürnberg Hbf 920 a.		0659		0759		0859			0959	0959		1059	1059					1159				1259
	Mannheim Hbf 912 d.					0723	0723	0824				0823	0840				0923				1023		
	Karlsruhe Hbf 912 d.											0858									1058		
	Basel SBB 912 d.											1047									1247		
	Stuttgart Hbf 912 d.												0924				1008						
	München Hbf 904 930 a.	0808		0905	1004	1027	1027			1107	1107		1204	1204	1227			1304					1404

	SEE NOTES ⊠ AND ❖	ICE 515	ICE 13	ICE 623	ICE 105	ICE 625	ICE 517	ICE 15	ICE 627 ⑦v	ICE 107	ICE 107	ICE 123	ICE 629	ICE 519 ⑤⑦	ICE 211 r	ICE 721	ICE 109 ⑧m	ICE 915 T	ICE 915	ICE 817 ⑥q	ICE 817	ICE 125	ICE 723 ⑥q	ICE 611
	Dortmund Hbf 800 d.	0837		0916c		1016c	1037		1125c	1137			1237		1325y	1337		1354					1425f	1437
	Essen Hbf 800 d.			0941		1040	1100		1153				1300		1353			1417					1453	1500
	Amsterdam Centraal 28 d.				0802‡				1037												1237			
	Düsseldorf Hbf 800 d.	◐	1012	1022	1108	1127		1221		1248	1308	1327		1421	◐	1450	1450	1454	1520	1527				
	Brussels Midi/Zuid 21 d.		0824x			1025						1225												
	Aachen Hbf 802 807 a.		0939			1139						1339												
	Köln Hbf 800 802 807 a.	0946	1015		1045	1149	1215	1246		1315	1349	1415		1446				1518					1549	
	Köln Hbf 802 807 d.	0955	1026	1055		1155	1218	1255	1255	1328	1355	1426	1455	1455	1458	1501		1529					1555	
	Köln Messe/Deutz 802 d.			1033	1130		1244			1333								1514	1514					
	Köln/Bonn Flughafen + 802 d.			1045	1231																			
	Siegburg/Bonn [tram] 807 d.	1010		1110	1144	1210		1310	1310	1347	1410					1517	1517						1610	
	Montabaur d.			1204						1407						1542	1542							
	Limburg Süd d.			1215						1418						1553	1553							
	Frankfurt Flughafen Fernbf + a.	1049	1116	1133	1149	1233	1249	1316	1333	1349	1349	1416	1436	1449	1516	1533	1549	1549	1607	1607	1612	1612	1616	1633	1649
	Frankfurt (Main) Hbf a.		1130	1148		1248		1330	1348			1430	1449		1530	1548			1625	1625	1630		1648
	Nürnberg Hbf 920 a.			1403		1459			1559				1659		1759								1859	
	Mannheim Hbf 912 d.	1123			1223		1323			1423	1423		1523			1623	1623	1639	1639				1723
	Karlsruhe Hbf 912 d.			1258						1456	1456					1658	1658						
	Basel SBB 912 d.			1447						1647	1647					1847	1847						
	Stuttgart Hbf 912 d.	1208				1408							1608					1719	1719				
	München Hbf 904 930 a.	1427		1508		1606	1627t		1704				1804		1827	1907							2004	2027

	SEE NOTES ⊠ AND ❖	ICE 17 Ⓐ	ICE 17 Ⓐ	ICE 725 X	ICE 819 Ⓐ	ICE 201 X	ICE 917 ⑥q	ICE 127	ICE 1228 Ⓐu L	ICE 727 ⑥q	ICE 613	ICE 215	ICE 729	ICE 911 ⑦v	ICE 1103 Q	ICE 203	ICE 129	ICE 821 ⑥q	ICE 615 Q	ICE 19	ICE 605 R	ICE 605	ICE 221	ICE 619
	Dortmund Hbf 800 d.			1525k		1556		1616		1637		1725k	1700	1754					1837	1924k				2058
	Essen Hbf 800 d.			1554		1617		1640	1653	1700		1754						1841	1900		1950	1950		
	Amsterdam Centraal 28 d.						1437							1632n									1837	
	Düsseldorf Hbf 800 d.			1622		1648	1653z	1708	1721	1727		1822			1848	1908	1908	1927		2018	2018	2048		2155
	Brussels Midi/Zuid 21 d.	1425	1425				1616p							1739						1825				
	Aachen Hbf 802 807 a.	1539	1539											1739						1939				
	Köln Hbf 800 802 807 a.	1615	1615			1718z			1749		1815			1912				1949	2015	2041	2041	2112	2219	
	Köln Hbf 802 807 d.	1620	1620	1628	1655	1728	1733	1744	1755	1819	1826	1855	1855	1921	1957	2028	2046	2046	2126	2230
	Köln Messe/Deutz 802 d.			1644		1713		1733	1744		1844				1930	1930								2242
	Köln/Bonn Flughafen + 802 d.		1636	1644	1710		1747			1844		1910	1910		1944	1944	2012			2101	2101		2253
	Siegburg/Bonn [tram] 807 d.		1636		1710		1747					1910	1910		1944	1944	2012			2101	2101			2253
	Montabaur d.		1656		1704		1812					1904			2004	2004				2121	2121			2313
	Limburg Süd d.		1707				1822					1918			2015	2015				2132	2132			2323
	Wiesbaden Hbf a.						1841																	
	Mainz Hbf a.						1854																	
	Frankfurt Flughafen Fernbf + a.	1709	1726	1733	1740	1749	1807	1816	1915	1833	1849	1909	1933	1940	1949	1949	2010	2033	2033	2049	2116	2151	2151	2216	2347
	Frankfurt (Main) Hbf a.	1722	1741	1748	1756			1830	1933	1848		1925	1940	1957	2025	2048	2048		2130			2230	2400
	Nürnberg Hbf 920 a.			1959						2059		2159					2259							
	Mannheim Hbf 912 d.				1823	1839				1923			2023	2023			2123			2224	2224		0104
	Karlsruhe Hbf 912 d.				1858							2100	2100						2300	2300		0156
	Basel SBB 912 d.				2047								2250	2300a									0056b
	Stuttgart Hbf 912 d.					1924							2008				2208						0320
	München Hbf 904 930 a.		2107						2205	2226		2307						0007	0027					0602

G – ⑥ (also Apr. 14, May 25; not Apr. 15, May 27). To Garmisch on ⑥ to Mar. 4 (Table 895).
H – From Hannover (Table 810).
L – [rail logo] and ⚋ Kassel - Paderborn - Dortmund - Mainz - Frankfurt. Starts from Dortmund May 8 - June 14.
M – From Münster (Table 800).
N – To Würzburg (Table 920).
Q – ④⑤⑦ (also Apr. 17; not Apr. 14, 16, 30, June 4).
R – ①②③④⑦ (not Apr. 9, 13, 16, 30, June 4).
T – ①②③④⑦ (not Apr. 13, 16, 30, May 24, June 4).

a – ①–⑤ (not Apr. 14, 17, May 1, June 5).
b – Basel **Badischer Bahnhof**.
c – ⑥⑦ (also Apr. 14, 17, May 1, June 5).
d – Not Apr. 17, May 1, June 5.
e – Not May 15, 17, May 1, June 5.
f – ①②③④⑦ (not Apr. 13, 16, 30, June 4).
g – Also Apr. 18, May 2, June 6; not Apr. 17, May 1, June 5.
h – Not Apr. 15, 17, May 1, 25, June 5.
j – Also Apr. 15, 17, May 1, 25, June 5.
k – ⑥ (also Apr. 14, 16, 30, June 4).
m – Not Apr. 14, 16, 30, May 25, June 4.
n – 1637 on ⑥⑦.

p – 1625 on ⑦ (also Apr. 17, May 1, 25, June 5).
q – Not Apr. 14, 16, 30, June 4.
r – Also Apr. 17, May 25, June 5; not Apr. 16, May 26, June 4.
s – Not May 25, June 15.
t – 1635 from Mar. 30.
u – Not May 26.
v – Also Apr. 15, 17, May 1, June 5.
x – 0825 on ⑥⑦ (also Apr. 17, May 1, 25, June 5).
y – ⑤–⑦ (also Apr. 13, 17, May 1, June 5).
z – On Apr. 8, 14, 15, 22, June 3 Düsseldorf d. 1648, Köln a. 1712.

‡ – 0805 on ⑥⑦.
◐ – Via Wuppertal (Table 800).
⊠ – Services from Amsterdam are subject to alteration on Jan. 21, 22, 29, Mar. 18, 19, May 20, 21. Amsterdam timings are subject to alteration on Apr. 27.
❖ – Certain Frankfurt timings (of trains via Nürnberg) are subject to alteration on ⑥⑦ Feb. 11 - Apr. 2 (also Apr. 14–17). Timings at Nürnberg and München may vary from March 6. See also engineering work panel on page 367.

[tram logo] – Frequent light-rail services operate from/to Bonn Hbf.

GERMANY

FRANKFURT - KÖLN - AACHEN via high-speed line   910

See Tables 800/911 for services via Koblenz and Bonn. See Table 20 for *Thalys* services Köln - Aachen - Brussels - Paris. SEE NOTES ※ AND ❖.

km	SEE NOTES ※ AND ❖	ICE 222	ICE 1018	ICE 618	ICE 712	ICE 18	ICE 616	ICE 824	ICE 1223	ICE 220	ICE 604	ICE 822	ICE 214	ICE 614	ICE 820	ICE 128	ICE 916	ICE 202	ICE 202	ICE 728	ICE 16	ICE 16	ICE 612	ICE 726
		①–⑤	⑦s	①–⑥	Ⓐu	①–⑤	①–⑥		①–⑤		①–⑥		①–⑥		①–⑥	①–④		①–⑥		⑦y	①–⑥		①–⑥	
		a⛵		e⛵		d⛵	⛵	aE	aD	⛵		⛵	⛵	⛵	e⛵	⛵	e✕	⛵	m⛵		d⛵	⛵		⛵
	München Hbf 904 930 ....d.	...	0001	0001	...	0324	...	...	...	...	0449	...	0524	0552	...	...	0652	...	...	0727	0755
	Stuttgart Hbf 912 ....d.	...	0230	0230	...	0551	...	...	...	...	...	0751	...	...	0837	...	...	...	...	0951
	Basel SBB 912 ....d.								0515b							0713e	0713			
	Karlsruhe Hbf 912 ....d.		0349	0349					0700						0900	0900			
	Mannheim Hbf 912 ....d.		0440	0440		0636			0736		0836			0921	0936	0936			1036
	Nürnberg Hbf 920 ....d.									0600			0700				0800			0900
0	Frankfurt (Main) Hbf...........d.	0456	0544	0544	...	0629		0710		0727	0810	0816		0909	0929			1010	1016	1029		1110
10	Frankfurt Flughafen Fernbf ✈ ...d.	0512	0601	0601	...	0643	0709	0725	0714	0743	0809	0825	0831	0909	0922	0943	0955	1009	1009	1025	1031	1043	1109	1122
	Mainz Hbf ....d.				0607																
	Wiesbaden Hbf...........d.				0623																
65	Limburg Süd ....d.	0533	0620	0620	0644			0733				0850		0941				1050		1141
87	Montabaur ....d.	0545	0631	0631	0655			0748				0901		0952				1101		1152
150	Siegburg/Bonn ⌷ 807 d.	0607	0650	0650		0748		0809		0848		0921	0948	1012		1048	1048			1148	1212
166	Köln/Bonn Flughafen ✈ ... 802 a.				0726													1114		
180	Köln Messe/Deutz... 802 a.						0814	0823			0914		1025		1041					1225
181	Köln Hbf...... 802 807 d.	0621	0705	0706	0728	0739	0805		0833	0905	0939	1005		1032		1105	1105	1133	1133	1205
181	Köln Hbf...... 800 802 807 a.	0628	0710	0713		0743	0810		0844		0943	1011		1041		1111		1143	1143	1211
251	Aachen Hbf ...... 802 807 a.					0816						1016						1216	1216	
	Brussels Midi/Zuid 21 ....a.					0935						1135						1335	1335	
	Düsseldorf Hbf .... 800 a.	0652	◐	0735			0831	0836	0846	0911		0936		1031	1048	1105	1109		◐	1136		1231	1248
	Amsterdam Centraal 28 .....a.	0928							1128								1328				
	Essen Hbf 800 ....a.			0801			0857	0902	0914			1002		1057			1139v			1202		1257	1314
	Dortmund Hbf 800 ....a.		0821				0921		0940			1029p		1121			1203v		1221	1230		1321	1342p

	SEE NOTES ※ AND ❖	ICE 126	ICE 914	ICE 200	ICE 724	ICE 210	ICE 610	ICE 722	ICE 1122	ICE 124	ICE 818	ICE 108	ICE 108	ICE 720	ICE 14	ICE 518	ICE 628	ICE 816	ICE 106	ICE 626	ICE 826	ICE 12	ICE 122	ICE 710	ICE 516
							⑤⑦		①–⑤		①–⑥		⑥h							Ⓐ	Ⓑ			
			e⛵	⛵	⛵	⛵	a⛵	c⛵	⛵		⛵		✕	⛵	⛵	⛵	⛵	⛵	⛵	⛵	⛵	⛵	⛵	✕	u
	München Hbf 904 930 ....d.	...	...	0852	...	0928	0955	0955		...	...	...	1055	...	1128	1155	...	...	1255	1255	...	...	...	1328
	Stuttgart Hbf 912 ....d.	...	1041		...	1151				...			...	1351			...	...		1433	1551
	Basel SBB 912 ....d.		0913							1113	1113			1313					1636
	Karlsruhe Hbf 912 ....d.		1100						1300	1300			1500					
	Mannheim Hbf 912 ....d.		1121	1136		1236				1336	1336		1436		1536			1533	1636
	Nürnberg Hbf 920 ....d.		1000		1100	1100			1200		1300		1400	1400			
	Frankfurt (Main) Hbf ....d.	1129		1210	1229		1310	1310	1329	1335		1410	1429		1510	1517		1609	1609	1629	1629		
	Frankfurt Flughafen Fernbf ✈ ...d.	1143	1155	1209	1225	1243	1309	1325	1343	1349	1409	1409	1425	1443	1509	1525	1531	1609	1626	1632	1643	1643		1709
	Mainz Hbf ....d.																			1622
	Wiesbaden Hbf ....d.																			1645
	Limburg Süd ....d.						1341		1408					1550				1702f	1702f	1708
	Montabaur ....d.						1352		1419					1601			1656			1719
	Siegburg/Bonn ⌷ 807 d.			1248	1303		1348		1412		1439	1448	1448		1548		1622	1648		1728z			1739	1748
	Köln/Bonn Flughafen ✈ ... 802 a.				1312														1747
	Köln Messe/Deutz... 802 a.			1241	1324				1414	1425			1514		1614		1714			
	Köln Hbf...... 802 807 d.	1232		1305		1332	1405		1433	1456	1505	1505		1533	1605	1639	1705		1741	1739	1739	1801	1805
	Köln Hbf...... 800 802 807 a.	1241		1311h		1343	1411		1446		1511		1542	1610		1711			1743	1746	1810
	Aachen Hbf ...... 802 807 a.					1416							1616						1816	
	Brussels Midi/Zuid 21 ....a.					1535							1735						1935	
	Düsseldorf Hbf .... 800 a.	1305	1310	◐	1346		1431	1436	1446	1511		◐	1536		1631	1635	◐		1736		1812	1831
	Amsterdam Centraal 28 .....a.	1528							1728										2026
	Essen Hbf 800 ....a.		1339		1414		1457	1505	1514			1602		1657	1707		1802			1857
	Dortmund Hbf 800 ....a.		1403	1421h	1442h		1521		1542k			1621	1630h		1721	1742h		1821	1829h		1921

	SEE NOTES ※ AND ❖	ICE 624	ICE 1124	ICE 814	ICE 504	ICE 104	ICE 622	ICE 812	ICE 10	ICE 812	ICE 514	ICE 620	ICE 120	ICE 102	ICE 1102	ICE 528	ICE 810	ICE 512	ICE 526	ICE 100	ICE 524	ICE 1110	ICE 522
		Ⓐ	Ⓐ		①–⑤	Ⓐ		Ⓑt		Ⓑt			Ⓑq	Ⓑq	Ⓑq	Ⓑ			Ⓑq			⑦w	
		⛵	⛵	⛵	d⛵	⛵	⛵	⛵	⛵	⛵	⛵	G⛵	⛵	H⛵	H⛵	⛵	⛵	M⛵	⛵	⛵	⛵	⛵	⛵
	München Hbf 904 930 ....d.	1355	1355	...	...	1455	...	...	...	...	1528	1555	...	...	1652	...	1727	1755	...	1855	...	1928	1952
	Stuttgart Hbf 912 ....d.	...	...	1513	1513						1751		1837			1951			1913		2151
	Basel SBB 912 ....d.			1700	1700								1713	1713			2101		
	Karlsruhe Hbf 912 ....d.			1736	1736					1836		1900	1900			2036		2136		2237
	Mannheim Hbf 912 ....d.											1921	1936	1936					
	Nürnberg Hbf 920 ....d.	1500	1500			1600					1700		1800		1901		2000		2100
	Frankfurt (Main) Hbf ....d.	1710	1710	1717			1810	1816	1829		1910	1929		2010	2031		2110		2210		2310
	Frankfurt Flughafen Fernbf ✈ ...d.	1725	1722	1731	1809	1809	1825	1831	1843		1909	1922	1943	1955	2009	2009	2025	2044	2109	2125	2209	2225	2311	2325
	Mainz Hbf ....d.																			
	Wiesbaden Hbf ....d.																			
	Limburg Süd ....d.		1741	1750			1850		←		1941			2103			2244		2344
	Montabaur ....d.		1752	1801			1859		1906		1952			2114			2255		2355
	Siegburg/Bonn ⌷ 807 d.		1812	1822	1848	1848		→	1922	1929	1948	2012		2048	2048		2134	2148		2252	2319	2352	0019
	Köln/Bonn Flughafen ✈ ... 802 a.							1937						2142			2327	
	Köln Messe/Deutz... 802 a.	1813	1826			1914					2025		2043			2113		2214		2339
	Köln Hbf...... 802 807 d.		1839	1905	1905		1939	1956	2005	2033	2105	2105		2156	2205	2205		2307		0007	0042
	Köln Hbf...... 800 802 807 a.		1911	1914		1943		2011	2042	2111	2111		2211	2316		0045
	Aachen Hbf ...... 802 807 a.						2016									
	Brussels Midi/Zuid 21 ....a.						2135									
	Düsseldorf Hbf .... 800 a.	1835	1848	◐	1936	1944			2031	2048	2105	2110	◐	2131	2136		2231	2236	2338	0001	◐	0107
	Amsterdam Centraal 28 .....a.		1914		2156					2326						
	Essen Hbf 800 ....a.	1901	1914		2015			2057	2115		2139		2157	2202		2257	2302	0008	0027		0136
	Dortmund Hbf 800 ....a.	1930	1943	2021		2042		2121	2142		2221	2221	2230		2327	2331	0031	0050		0159

⌷ and ⛵ Darmstadt Hbf (d. 0648) - Dortmund - Paderborn - Kassel. Terminates at Dortmund May 8 - June 14.		r –	Also Apr. 17, May 25, June 5; not Apr. 16, May 26, June 4.
e – From Würzburg (Table 920) on ①–④ (not Apr. 13, May 25).		s –	Also Apr. 15, 17, May 1, June 5.
g – From Garmisch on ⑥ to Mar. 4 (Table 895).		t –	Not Apr. 14, 16, 30, May 25, June 4.
H – To Hannover (Table 810).		u –	Not May 26.
M – To Münster (Table 800).		v –	①②③④⑤ (also Apr. 14, May 26; not Apr. 13, 15, 17, May 1, 24, June 5).
		w –	Also Apr. 17, May 1, June 5; not Apr. 16, 30, June 4.
Ⓐ – Not Apr. 14, 17, May 1, June 5.		y –	Also Apr. 17, May 1, June 5.
①–⑤ (not Apr. 14, 17, May 1, June 5). Basel **Badischer Bahnhof**.		z –	Arrives 1716.
b – Also Apr. 14, 17, May 1, June 5.			
c – Not Apr. 17, May 1, June 5.		◐ –	Via Wuppertal (Table 800).
d – ①–⑥ (not Apr. 15, 17, May 1, June 5).		※ –	Services to Amsterdam are subject to alteration on Jan. 21, 22, 29, Mar. 18, 19, May 20, 21. Amsterdam timings are subject to alteration on Apr. 27.
Ⓑ – Ⓐ only.			
⑥ (also Apr. 14, 16, 30, June 4).		❖ –	Certain Frankfurt timings (of trains via Nürnberg) are subject to alteration on ⑥⑦ Feb. 11 - Apr. 2 (also Apr. 14–17). Timings at München and Nürnberg may vary from March 6. See also engineering work panel on page 367.
f – ⑥ (also Apr. 14, 16, 17, 30, May 1, June 4, 5).			
h – Not Apr. 13, 17, May 1, 24, 25, June 5.			
k – ⑥ (also Apr. 14; not Apr. 15).		⌷ –	Frequent light-rail services operate from / to Bonn Hbf.
p – Not Apr. 14, 16, 30, June 4.			

911 KOBLENZ - MAINZ - MANNHEIM and FRANKFURT

km	SEE NOTE ⊠	IC 209		ICE 672	ICE 991	IC 2021	ICE 23	IC 2317	ICE 711	IC 2319	ICE 1597	ICE 1521	EC 115	EC 7	ICE 1559	IC 119	ICE 27	IC 2005	EC 9	ICE 1651	IC 2013	IC 2023	IC 2313	ICE 1653
				H	①–⑤			⑥h	Ⓐu	①–⑥								⑤⑥						
				✕	a✕	◇	✕♦		✕	e🍷	D🍷	✕	🍷♦	✕♦	D✕	♦	✕♦	🍷♦	Z✕	D✕	🍷♦	🍷	🍷	D✕
	Hamburg Hbf **800** d.	1946	...	...	...	2246	...	...	...	...	...	...	...	0442e	...	...	0546	...	0646	...	...	0746	0846	...
	Dortmund Hbf **800** d.	2237	...	...	...	0144	0437	...	...	0537	...	0636	...	0737	...	...	0838	...	0937	...	0952	1036	1137	...
	Köln Hbf **800** d.	2353	...	...	...	0352	0553	...	0611	0653	...	0753	0818	0853	...	0918	0953	1018	1053	...	1117	1153	1253	...
	Bonn Hbf **800** d.	0014	...	...	...	0416	0614	...	|	0714	...	0814	0838	0914	...	0938	1014	1037	1114	...	1137	1214	1314	...
0	**Koblenz** Hbf **914** d.	0048	...	...	...	0531	0648	...	|	0748	...	0848	0917	0948	...	1017	1048	1117	1148	...	1217	1248	1348	...
61	Bingen (Rhein) Hbf **914** d.	|	...	...	...	0609	|	...	|	|	...	|	0952	|	...	1052	|	1152	|	...	1252	|	|	...
	Wiesbaden Hbf **917a** d.	|	...	0500	0524	|	|	...	0732	|	0824c	|	|	|	1024	|	|	|	|	1224	|	|	|	1424
91	**Mainz** Hbf **914 917a** a.	0138	...	0510	0535	0626	0738	...	0744	0838	0835c	0938	1015	1038	1035	1110	1138	1215	1238	1235	1310	1338	1438	1435
91	**Mainz** Hbf **911a 917a** d.	0140	...	0512	0540	0628	0740	0743	0746	0840	0843	0940	1017	1040	1043	1112	1140	1217	1240	1243	1312	1340	1440	1443
117	**Frankfurt** Flughafen ✈ ◧ **917a** a.	0159	...	0530	|	0646	0759	|	|	|	0859	0959	|	|	1059	|	1159	|	|	1259	|	1359	|	1459
128	**Frankfurt** (Main) Hbf **917a** a.	0213	...	0550	|	0702	0813	|	|	|	0912	1013	|	|	1113	|	1213	|	|	1313	|	1412	|	1515
	Nürnberg Hbf **920** a.	|	...	...	|	...	1027	|	|	|	...	1224	|	|	...	|	1427	|	|	...	|	...	|	...
	Worms Hbf **911a** d.	|	...	...	0608	...	...	|	|	|	...	|	1045	|	...	|	...	1245	|	...	|	...	|	...
	Mannheim Hbf **911a** a.	0331	...	...	0623	...	...	0824	0824	0921	...	|	1100	1121	...	1152	...	1307	1321	...	1352	...	1521	...
	Stuttgart Hbf **912** a.	|	...	...	0708	...	...	0928	0928	1024	...	|	1153	|	...	1246	...	|	|	...	1446	...	1622	...
	München Hbf **930** a.	|	...	...	0927	...	...	...	...	...	...	1339	1411	|	...	...	...	|	|	...	...	...	...	...
	Karlsruhe Hbf **912** a.	0401	...	...	...	...	...	...	...	...	...	...	...	1147	...	...	...	1334	1347	...	...	...	...	...
	Basel SBB **912** a.	0622	...	...	...	...	...	...	...	...	...	...	...	1330	...	...	...	...	1535	...	...	...	...	...

SEE NOTE ⊠	IC 1911	IC 2025	IC 2217	ICE 1655	IC 2011	IC 2017	IC 2027	IC 2019	IC 2311	ICE 1657	ICE 1228	IC 1915	IC 2229	IC 2213	ICE 1659	ICE 1625		IC 2029		IC 2215	IC 2315		IC 2221	IC 2321
	⑤⑦					⑤f		⑥			Ⓐu	⑤⑦			Ⓑq	⑥k				T	S			R
	v🍷	🍷	🍷♦	D✕	🍷♦	N	P🍷	♦	G🍷	✕♦	🍷	v♦	🍷♦	🍷♦	✕♦	✕		🍷		🍷	G🍷		🍷♦	🍷
Hamburg Hbf **800** d.	...	0946	1046	...	...	...	1146	...	1246	...	...	🍷	1346	1446	...	...	...	1546	...	1646	1646	...	1746	1746
Dortmund Hbf **800** d.	1152	1236	1337	...	1349w	1352	1436	...	1537	...	1616	1549	1636	1737	...	...	...	1836	...	1937	1937	...	2037	2037
Köln Hbf **800** d.	1317	1353	1453	...	1517	1517	1553	1618	1653	...	|	1717	1753	1853	...	...	...	1953	...	2053	2053	...	2153	2153
Bonn Hbf **800** d.	1337	1414	1514	...	1537	1537	1614	1638	1714	...	|	1737	1814	1914	...	...	...	2014	...	2114	2114	...	2214	2214
Koblenz Hbf **914** d.	1417	1448	1548	...	1617	1617	1648	1717	1748	...	|	1817	1848	1948	...	...	...	2048	...	2148	2148	...	2248	2248
Bingen (Rhein) Hbf **914** d.	1452	|	|	...	1652	1652	|	1752	|	...	|	1852	|	|	...	...	...	2123	...	|	|	...	|	|
Wiesbaden Hbf **917a** d.	|	|	|	1624	|	|	|	|	|	1824	1846	|	|	|	2024	2024	...	|	...	|	|	...	|	|
Mainz Hbf **914 917a** a.	1510	1538	1638	1635	1710	1710	1738	1815	1838	1835	1854	1910	1938	2038	2035	2035	...	2141	...	2238	2238	...	2338	2338
Mainz Hbf **911a 917a** d.	1512	1540	1640	1643	1712	1712	1740	1817	1840	1843	1856	1912	1940	2040	2043	2043	...	2143	...	2240	2240	...	2340	2340
Frankfurt Flughafen ✈ ◧ **917a** a.	|	1559	|	1659	|	|	1759	|	|	1859	1915	|	1959	|	2059	2059	...	2200	...	2259	2259	...	2359	2359
Frankfurt (Main) Hbf **917a** a.	|	1613	|	1715	|	|	1813	|	|	1913	1933	|	2013	|	2113	2113	...	2213	...	2311	2311	...	0013	0013
Nürnberg Hbf **920** a.	|	...	|	...	|	|	2027	|	|	...	...	|	2226q	|	...	2329	...	0042	...	...	...	...	...	...
Worms Hbf **911a** d.	|	...	|	...	|	|	...	1845	|	...	...	|	...	|	...	...	...	...	...	...	...	...	...	...
Mannheim Hbf **911a** a.	1552	...	1721	...	1752	1752	...	1901	1921	...	...	1952	...	2121	...	...	...	...	...	...	...	...	...	...
Stuttgart Hbf **912** a.	1646	...	1825	...	1846	1846	...	1958	2024	...	...	2046	...	2224	...	...	...	...	...	...	...	...	...	...
München Hbf **930** a.	...	...	...	...	...	2118	...	...	...	...	...	...	...	...	...	...	...	...	...	...	...	...	...	...
Karlsruhe Hbf **912** a.	...	...	...	...	...	...	...	...	...	...	...	...	...	...	...	...	...	...	...	...	...	...	...	...
Basel SBB **912** a.	...	...	...	...	...	...	...	...	...	...	...	...	...	...	...	...	...	...	...	...	...	...	...	...

km	SEE NOTE ⊠	ICE 887 1087		IC 208	IC 2220	IC 2320	IC 2310	IC 1114	IC 2028	IC 2018	IC 2010	ICE 1656	IC 2216	IC 2226	ICE 1654	IC 2218	IC 2024	IC 1920	IC 1216	ICE 1652	IC 2312	IC 2006	IC 2004	IC 2014
						★	⊖	Ⓐ		⑥	Ⓐ							⑦w	⑤f			⑥	⑦	⑤f
		H		K	🍷♦	🍷	G🍷		K🍷	♦	🍷♦	✕♦	🍷♦	🍷♦	✕♦	🍷	P🍷	B🍷	🍷♦	D✕	🍷	🍷♦	🍷♦	🍷♦
	Basel SBB **912** d.	...	...	2313	...	...	...	...	...	...	...	...	...	...	...	...	...	...	...	...	...	...	...	...
	Karlsruhe Hbf **912** d.	...	...	0130	...	...	...	...	...	...	...	...	...	...	...	...	...	...	...	...	...	1221	1221	...
	München Hbf **930** d.	...	...	|	...	...	...	...	...	...	...	...	...	...	...	...	...	...	0847	...	...	|	|	...
	Stuttgart Hbf **912** d.	...	...	|	...	...	...	0630	...	0712	0714	...	0737	...	...	0937	...	...	1114	...	1137	|	|	1209
0	**Mannheim** Hbf **911a** d.	...	...	0216	...	...	...	0734	...	0808	0808	...	0839	...	...	1039	...	...	1208	...	1239	1258	1258	1258
24	Worms Hbf **911a** d.	...	...	|	...	...	...	|	...	|	|	...	|	...	...	|	...	...	|	...	|	1315	1315	1315
	Nürnberg Hbf **920** d.	...	...	|	...	...	...	|	0527	|	|	...	|	0729d	...	|	0929	...	|	...	|	|	|	|
	Frankfurt (Main) Hbf **917a** d.	0013	...	0342	0542	0542	0638	|	0742	|	|	0842	|	0942	1042	|	1142	1215	|	1242	|	|	|	|
	Frankfurt Flughafen ✈ ◧ **917a** d.	0027	...	0357	0557	0557	0657	|	0758	|	|	0858	|	0958	1058	|	1158	1228	|	1258	|	|	|	|
70	**Mainz** Hbf **911a 917a** a.	0045	...	0415	0615	0615	0715	0815	0818	0846	0846	0915	0918	1018	1115	1118	1218	1246	1246	1315	1318	1340	1340	1340
70	**Mainz** Hbf **914 917a** d.	0047	...	0417	0617	0617	0717	...	0820	0848	0848	0922	0920	1020	1122	1120	1220	1248	1248	1322	1320	1344	1344	1344
80	**Wiesbaden** Hbf **917a** a.	0057	...	|	|	|	|	...	|	|	|	0933	|	|	1133	|	|	|	|	1333	|	|	|	|
	Bingen (Rhein) Hbf **914 917a** d.	...	...	0435	0635	0635	|	...	|	0906	0906	...	|	|	...	|	|	1306	1306	...	|	1406	1406	1406
	Koblenz Hbf **914 917a** a.	...	...	0511	0711	0711	0811	...	0911	0941	0941	...	1011	1111	...	1211	1311	1341	1341	...	1411	1441	1441	1441
	Bonn Hbf **800** a.	...	...	0544	0744	0744	0844	...	0944	1021	1021	...	1044	1144	...	1244	1344	1421	1421	...	1444	1521	1521	1521
	Köln Hbf **800** a.	...	...	0605	0805	0805	0905	...	1005	1043	1043	...	1105	1205	...	1305	1405	1442	1442	...	1505	1543	1543	1543
	Dortmund Hbf **800** a.	...	...	0721	0921	0921	1021	...	1121	...	1209f	...	1221	1321	...	1421	1521	1608	1608	...	1621	1702	...	...
	Hamburg Hbf **800** a.	...	...	1013	1213	1213	1313	...	1413	...	...	...	1511	1613	...	1713	1813	...	...	...	1913	...	...	...

♦ – **NOTES** (LISTED BY TRAIN NUMBER)

6 – [12] and ✕ Interlaken - Bern - Basel - Dortmund (- Hamburg Ⓑ**q**).
7 – [12] and ✕ (Hamburg ①–⑥**e** -) Dortmund - Basel - Bern - Interlaken.
22/3 – [12] and ✕ Wien - Linz - Passau - Regensburg - Dortmund and v.v.
26/7 – [12] and ✕ Wien - Linz - Passau - Regensburg - Dortmund - Hamburg and v.v.
114 – WÖRTHERSEE – [12] and 🍷 Klagenfurt - Villach - Salzburg - München - Dortmund.
115 – WÖRTHERSEE – [12] and 🍷 Münster - München - Salzburg - Villach - Klagenfurt.
118/9 – [12] Innsbruck - Bregenz - Lindau - Stuttgart - Münster and v.v.
1216 – [12] and 🍷 Salzburg - München - Stuttgart - Dortmund - Berlin.
1654 – [12] and ✕ (Dresden ①–⑥**e** -) Leipzig - Frankfurt - Wiesbaden.
1656 – [12] and ✕ (Leipzig ①–⑥**e** -) Frankfurt - Wiesbaden.
1657 – [12] and ✕ Wiesbaden - Frankfurt - Leipzig (- Dresden Ⓑ**q**).
1659 – [12] and ✕ Wiesbaden - Frankfurt - Erfurt (- Leipzig ⑤⑦) (- Dresden ⑦).
1915 – [12] and 🍷 Berlin - Köln - Mannheim - Stuttgart (- Tübingen ⑦**w**).
2004 – ⑦ (also Apr. 17, May 1, 25, 26, June 5; not Apr. 16, 30, June 4). [12] and 🍷 Konstanz - Karlsruhe - Münster - Emden.
2005 – ⑤⑥ (also Apr. 13, 16, 30, May 24, 25, June 4). [12] and 🍷 Emden - Münster - Karlsruhe - Konstanz.
2006 – ⑥ (also Apr. 14, 16, 30, June 4). [12] and 🍷 Konstanz - Karlsruhe - Dortmund.
2010 – Ⓐ (not Dec. 27 – 30, May 26). [12] and 🍷 Tübingen - Stuttgart - Köln - Düsseldorf (- Berlin ⑤**f**).
2011 – ①②③④⑦ (not Apr. 13, 16, 30, May 24, June 4). [12] (Berlin ⑦**w** -) Düsseldorf - Koblenz - Stuttgart. On ①–④ (not Apr. 13, May 24) continues to Tübingen Hbf (a. 1950).
2012/3 – ALLGÄU – [12] and 🍷 Oberstdorf - Kempten - Ulm - Stuttgart - Köln - Dortmund - Hannover (- Magdeburg - Leipzig ♣) and v.v.
2014 – [12] and 🍷 Stuttgart - Münster - Emden.
2018/9 – ⑥ from Apr. 8. [12] Stuttgart - Münster - Norddeich Mole and v.v.
2213 – RÜGEN – [12] and 🍷 Ostseebad Binz - Stralsund - Rostock - Hamburg - Stuttgart.
2216/7 – [12] and 🍷 Stuttgart - Hamburg - Rostock - Stralsund (- Greifswald Ⓐ**u**) and v.v.
2220 – ⑤ to Mar. 31; Ⓑ from Apr. 7. [12] Frankfurt - Köln - Hamburg - Lübeck.
2221 – ⑤⑦ to Apr. 2; Ⓑ from Apr. 7. [12] Lübeck - Hamburg - Köln - Frankfurt.
2226 – [12] and 🍷 (Passau ● -) (Regensburg ①–⑥**d** -) Frankfurt - Köln - Hamburg.
2229 – [12] and 🍷 Kiel - Köln - Frankfurt (- Nürnberg Ⓑ**q**) (- Passau ●).
2318 – [12] and 🍷 Stuttgart - Köln (- Dortmund Ⓑ**q**) (- Münster ⑦**w**).

B – From / to Berlin (Table **810**).
D – To / from Dresden via Leipzig (Table **850**).
G – From / to Westerland (Table **821**).
H – To / from Hamburg (Table **900**).
K – To Kiel (Table **820**).
N – From Wolfsburg (Table **810**).
P – From / to Passau (Table **920**).
R – ①–④ to Apr. 6; ⑥ from Apr. 8.
S – From Apr. 7.
T – Until Apr. 6.
Z – To / from Zürich (Tables **510**).

a – Not Apr. 14, 17, May 1, June 5.
b – 0206 on the mornings of © (also Feb. 24, 27, 28).
c – © only.
d – ①–⑥ (also Apr. 16, 30, June 4; not Apr. 13, 17, May 1, 24, June 5).
e – ①–⑥ (not Apr. 15, 17, May 1, June 5).
f – ⑤ (also Apr. 13, May 24; not Apr. 14, May 26).
h – Also Apr. 14, May 1, 25; not Apr. 15.
k – Also Apr. 14; not Apr. 15.
q – Ⓑ (not Apr. 14, 16, 30, June 4).
r – 1937 on ⑤⑦ (also ①–④ Mar. 13 - Apr. 20).
u – Not May 26.
v – Also Apr. 13, 17, May 1, 24, June 5; not Apr. 14, 16, 30, May 26, June 4
w – ⑦ (also Apr. 17, May 1, June 5; not Apr. 16, 30, June 4).

⊠ – Frankfurt timings are subject to alteration on ⑥⑦ Feb. 11 - Apr. 2 (als Apr. 14 – 17). Timings at Nürnberg and München may vary from Marc 6. See Engineering Work Summary on page 367.
★ – ①②③④⑥ to Apr. 8; ⑥ from Apr. 15.
● – See Table **920** for days of running from / to Passau.
⊕ – Train number **1010** on ⑤⑥ (also Apr. 13, 16, 30, June 4), **1190** on (also Apr. 17, May 1, June 5; not Apr. 16, 30, June 4). Also conveys on ①–④ (not Apr. 13, 17, May 1, June 5).
◇ – Also calls at Boppard Hbf (d. 0544).
⊖ – Also calls at Boppard Hbf (d. 0758).
⊙ – Also calls at Boppard Hbf (d. 0043).
♣ – See Table **866** for running dates to / from Magdeburg and Leipzig.
◧ – Frankfurt Flughafen Fernbahnhof.

MANNHEIM and FRANKFURT - MAINZ - KOBLENZ 911

SEE NOTE ⊠	IC 2026	IC 2012	ICE 1650	EC 8	IC 2022	ICE 710	IC 118	ICE 1558	EC 6	EC 114	IC 2316	ICE 26	ICE 1556	IC 2318	ICE 1522	IC 1910		ICE 1594	IC 2210		ICE 22		ICE 510	IC 2020
						Ⓐu					Ⓑq					⑦w			Ⓑq				⊕	
	🍷	🍷♦	D✕	Z✕	🍷	✕	♦	D✕	✕♦	🍷♦		✕♦	D✕	🍷♦	✕	🍷		D🍷	🍷		✕♦		🍷	⊙
Basel SBB **912** d.	...	...	...	1220	...	...	...	...	1427	...	...	...	...	...	...	...	...	...	...	...	...	...	...	...
Karlsruhe Hbf **912** d.	...	...	...	1412	...	...	...	...	1612	...	...	...	...	...	...	...	...	...	...	...	...	...	...	...
München Hbf **930** d.	...	...	...	|	...	...	...	...	|	1346	...	...	...	...	1618	1619	...	...	...	...	...	...	1928	...
Stuttgart Hbf **912** d.	...	1312	...	|	...	1433	1512	...	|	1609	1636	...	...	1737	|	1914	...	...	1918r	...	...	...	2151	...
Mannheim Hbf **911a** d.	...	1408	...	1439	...	1533	1608	...	1639	1658	1738	...	...	1839	|	2008	...	...	2039	...	...	...	2237	...
Worms Hbf **911a** d.	...	|	...	|	...	|	|	...	|	1714	|	...	...	|	|	|	...	...	|	...	...	...	|	...
Nürnberg Hbf **920** d.	...	|	...	|	...	|	|	...	|	|	|	1529	...	|	1733	|	...	...	|	...	1929	...	|	...
Frankfurt (Main) Hbf **917a** d.	1344	|	1442	|	1544	|	|	1642	|	|	|	1742	1842	|	1944	|	...	2042	|	...	2146	...	|	2324
Frankfurt Flughafen ✈ ◨ **917a** d.	1358	|	1458	|	1558	|	|	1658	|	|	|	1758	1858	|	1958	|	...	2059	|	...	2159	...	2313	2339
Mainz Hbf **911a 917a** a.	1418	1446	1515	1518	1618	1615	1646	1715	1718	1740	1815	1818	1915	1918	2018	2046	...	2115	2118	...	2218	...	2330	2359
Mainz Hbf **914 917a** d.	1420	1448	1522	1520	1620	1622	1648	1722	1720	1744	...	1820	1922	1920	2020	2048	...	2122	2120	...	2220	...	2332	0001
Wiesbaden Hbf **917a** a.	|	|	1533	|	|	1633	|	1733	|	|	...	|	1933	|	|	|	...	2133	|	...	|	...	2344	|
Bingen (Rhein) Hbf **914 917a** d.	|	1506	...	|	|	|	1706	...	|	1806	...	|	...	|	|	2106	...	...	|	...	|	...	...	0018
Koblenz Hbf **914 917a** a.	1511	1541	...	1611	1711	|	1741	...	1811	1841	...	1911	...	2011	2111	2141	...	...	2211	...	2311	...	...	0056
Bonn Hbf **800** a.	1544	1621	...	1644	1744	|	1821	...	1844	1921	...	1944	...	2044	2144	2221	...	...	2244	...	2344	...	...	0136
Köln Hbf **800** a.	1605	1643	...	1705	1805	1801	1843	...	1905	1943	...	2005	...	2105	2206	2243	...	...	2305	...	0006	...	...	0159b
Dortmund Hbf **800** a.	1721	1808	...	1821	1921	...	...	...	2021	2101	...	2122	...	2221q	2321	2359	...	...	...	...	0121	...	...	0329
Hamburg Hbf **800** a.	2013	...	...	2113	2213	...	...	...	2314q	...	...	0014	...	...	...	...	...	...	...	...	...	...	...	0651

← FOR NOTES SEE PREVIOUS PAGE

RE / RB services — Local services MAINZ - MANNHEIM and MAINZ - SPEYER - KARLSUHE 911a

km																										
			Ⓐ	⚒	Ⓐ	Ⓐ		⚒	Ⓐ																	
0	**Mainz** Hbf **911** d.	0008	0456	0515	0545	...	0552b	0622	0652	0656	0722r	0752	0813	0913	0952	1013	1117	1152	1213	1317	1352	1413	1517	1553	1613	1625r
46	Worms Hbf **911** a.	0051	0540	0556	0614	...	0634b	0706	0719	0739	0806r	0836	0839	0940	1036	1039	1144	1236	1239	1344	1436	1439	1544	1636	1639	1718r
46	Worms Hbf **911** d.	...	0541	0556	0615	...	0635	0712	0720	0746	0816	0848	0840	0941	1048	1040	1145	1249	1240	1345	1448	1440	1545	1648	1640	1718
67	Ludwigshafen Hbf **918** d.	...	0558	0616	0637	0654	0653	0731	0736	0804	0837	0909	0857	0958t	1111	1057	1204t	1309	1257	1404t	1508	1457	1604t	1709	1656	1737
87	Speyer Hbf **918** d.	...	|	|	|	0712	|	|	|	|	|	|	0914	|	|	1114	|	|	1314	|	|	1514	|	|	1714	|
101	Germersheim **918** a.	...	|	|	|	0720	|	|	|	|	|	|	0922	|	|	1122	|	|	1322	|	|	1522	|	|	1722	|
138	**Karlsruhe** Hbf a.	...	|	|	|	0752	|	|	|	|	|	|	0952	|	|	1152	|	|	1352	|	|	1552	|	|	1753	|
70	**Mannheim** Hbf **911** a.	...	0603	0621	0641	...	0658	0736	0742	0811	0842	0915	...	1001	1116	...	1207	1314	...	1407	1514	...	1606	1714	...	1742

		Ⓒ	Ⓐ				Ⓐ					
Mainz Hbf **911** d.	1652	1717	1718	1752	1813	1917	1925	1952	2013	2052	2208	2308
Worms Hbf **911** a.	1736	1744	1744	1836	1839	1944	2008	2036	2039	2136	2251	2351
Worms Hbf **911** d.	1749	1745	1745	1848	1840	1945	2018	2048	2040	2148	2251	2351
Ludwigshafen Hbf **918** d.	1809	1806t	1800	1909	1857	2004t	2037	2111	2057	2209	2309	0008
Speyer Hbf **918** d.	|	|	1819	|	1914	|	|	|	2114	|	|	|
Germersheim **918** a.	|	|	1828	|	1922	|	|	|	2122	|	|	|
Karlsruhe Hbf a.	|	|	...	|	1952	|	|	|	2152	|	|	|
Mannheim Hbf **911** a.	1814	1810	...	1914	...	2007	2043	2115	...	2214	2314	0013

		⚒	Ⓐ	⚒		⚒	Ⓐ		Ⓐ
Mannheim Hbf **911** d.	0012	0430	0500	0530	0550e	0618	...	0650	...
Karlsruhe Hbf d.	|	|	|	|	|	|	...	|	...
Germersheim **918** d.	|	|	|	|	|	|	0620	|	0718
Speyer Hbf **918** d.	|	|	|	|	|	|	0632	|	0728
Ludwigshafen Hbf **918** d.	0017	0436	0505	0535	0558e	0624	0654	0659	0750
Worms Hbf **911** a.	0039	0454	0524	0552	0615e	0644	0712	0718	0804
Worms Hbf **911** d.	...	0455	0525	0555	0622	0655	0713	0725	0805
Mainz Hbf **911** a.	...	0537	0607	0637	0706	0737	0747	0807	0836

	Ⓐ	Ⓒ																								
Mannheim Hbf **911** d.	0748	0752	0844	...	0916	0944	0958	1044	...	1149	1244	...	1349	1444	...	1549	1644	...	1752	1844	...	1951	2044	...	2144	2248
Karlsruhe Hbf d.	|	|	|	0808	|	|	|	|	1008	|	|	1208	|	|	1408	|	|	1608	|	|	1808	|	|	2008	|	|
Germersheim **918** d.	|	|	|	0838	|	|	|	|	1038	|	|	1238	|	|	1438	|	|	1638	|	|	1838	|	|	2038	|	|
Speyer Hbf **918** d.	|	|	|	0847	|	|	|	|	1047	|	|	1247	|	|	1447	|	|	1647	|	|	1847	|	|	2047	|	|
Ludwigshafen Hbf **918** d.	0755	0755t	0850	0904	0921	0950	1000t	1050	1104	1152t	1250	1303	1352t	1450	1504	1552t	1650	1704	1754t	1850	1904	1954t	2050	2104	2150	2253
Worms Hbf **911** a.	0814	0816	0914	0919	0938	1014	1019	1111	1119	1216	1311	1319	1416	1514	1519	1616	1714	1719	1816	1913	1919	2016	2114	2119	2213	2312
Worms Hbf **911** d.	0825	0817	0925	0920	0955e	1025	1020	1125	1120	1217	1325	1320	1417	1525	1520	1617	1725	1720	1817	1925	1920	2017	2125	2120	2218	2315
Mainz Hbf **911** a.	0907	0843	1007	0947	1036e	1107	1046	1207	1147	1243	1407	1347	1443	1607	1547	1652	1807	1747	1843	2007	1947	2043	2207	2147	2300	2358

b – Not ⑥. e – Ⓐ only. r – ⚒ only. t – Ludwigshafen (Rhein) **Mitte**.

FRANKFURT - BASEL and STUTTGART 912

km	km	SEE NOTE ⊠	ICE 619	ICE 879		IC 209		EN 471	ICE 3			RJ 63	IC 2099	ICE 991	ICE 271	ICE 271		TGV 9578			ICE 977	EC 217	ICE 511	ICE 5	IC 1971
				①g				Ⓡ	Ⓐ		Ⓐ	Ⓒ	Ⓐt	①–⑤	①g	①–⑥		①–⑥	Ⓐ		①–⑥				Ⓐ
			♦					♦	✕	◐2	◐2	✕♦		G✕	H	eH	◐2	Ⓡ♦	◐2		e✕	🍷♦	🍷	✕	
		Hamburg Hbf **800 900** d.	...	...	...	1946	...	2052	...	...	...	...	...	...	0045	✕	...	...	...	...	...	...	...	...	...
		Berlin Hbf **810 902** d.	...	2030p	...	|	...	2259	...	...	...	...	...	...	|	...	...	...	...	...	...	...	...	...	...
		Hannover Hbf **810 900** d.	...	|	...	|	...	|	...	...	...	...	...	...	0210	...	...	...	...	...	...	...	...	...	...
		Dortmund Hbf **800** d.	2058	|	...	2237	...	|	...	...	...	...	...	...	|	...	...	...	...	...	...	...	0437g	...	...
		Köln Hbf **800 910** d.	2230	|	...	2353	...	|	...	...	...	...	...	...	|	...	...	...	...	...	...	...	0555	...	...
		Koblenz Hbf **911** d.	|	|	...	0048	...	|	...	...	...	...	...	...	|	...	...	...	...	...	...	...	|	...	...
		Mainz Hbf **911** d.	|	|	...	0140	...	|	...	...	...	...	...	0540	|	...	...	...	...	...	...	...	|	...	...
0	0	**Frankfurt** (Main) Hbf **913** d.	0009	0109	...	0248	...	0402x	...	...	...	0517	0520	|	0550	0550	...	...	...	...	0556	...	|	0650	0655
		Frankfurt Flughafen ✈ ◨ d.	0028	|	...	0202	...	|	...	...	...	0539	|	|	|	|	...	...	...	...	|	...	0652	|	|
78		**Mannheim** Hbf **913** a.	0104	0149	...	0331	...	0440	...	...	...	0610	|	0623	0625	0625	...	...	...	...	|	...	0723	0727	0751
78		**Mannheim** Hbf **913** d.	0106	0152	...	0333	...	0442	...	...	...	0612	|	0629	0633	0633	...	...	...	...	|	0712	0731	0736	0753
	28	Darmstadt Hbf **913** d.	|	|	...	|	...	|	...	...	...	|	0537	|	|	|	...	...	...	...	0613	|	|	|	|
	50	Bensheim **913** d.	|	|	...	|	...	|	...	...	...	|	0550	|	|	|	...	...	...	...	0625	|	|	|	|
	64	Weinheim **913** d.	|	|	...	|	...	|	...	...	...	|	0600	|	|	|	...	...	...	...	0636	|	|	|	|
	87	**Heidelberg** Hbf **913 931** d.	0119	|	...	|	...	|	...	...	...	|	0615	|	|	|	...	...	...	...	0652	|	|	|	0806
	120	Bruchsal **913 931** d.	0139	|	...	|	...	|	...	...	...	|	|	|	|	|	...	...	...	...	|	|	|	|	|
		Vaihingen (Enz) **931** d.	0248	|	...	|	...	|	...	...	...	|	|	|	|	|	...	...	...	...	|	|	|	|	|
		Stuttgart Hbf **931** a.	0320	|	...	|	...	|	...	...	...	0652	0700	0708	|	|	...	0654	...	...	0737	0754	0808	|	0846
		München Hbf **930** a.	0602	|	...	|	...	|	...	...	...	0910	...	0927	|	|	...	|	...	...	...	1011	1027	|	...
138	141	**Karlsruhe** Hbf **913 916** d.	0156a	0217	...	0403	...	0509	0555	...	...	...	...	...	0658	0658	...	0732	...	...	...	...	...	0800	...
169	172	Baden-Baden **916** d.	...	...	...	0426	...	0529	0613	...	...	...	...	...	0715	0715	...	|	...	...	...	...	...	|	...
209		Offenburg **916** ☆ d.	...	...	...	0451	...	0547	0629	0632	0705	...	...	...	0732	0732	0735	|	0805	...	...	...	...	0829	...
	217	Kehl 🏛 d.	...	...	...	|	...	|	|	0653	0722	...	...	...	|	|	0757	|	0827	...	...	...	...	|	...
	225	**Strasbourg** a.	...	...	...	|	...	|	|	0704	0734	...	...	...	|	|	0807	0811	0836	...	...	...	...	|	...
272		**Freiburg** (Brsg) Hbf ☆ d.	...	...	...	0531	...	0622	0702	...	...	...	...	...	0802	0802	...	...	...	...	...	...	...	0901	...
330*		**Basel** Bad Bf 🏛 ☆ a.	...	...	...	0609	...	0706	0735	...	...	...	...	...	0834	0834	...	...	...	...	...	...	...	0934	...
335*		**Basel** SBB ☆ a.	...	...	...	0622	...	0720	0747	...	...	...	...	...	0847	0847	...	...	...	...	...	...	...	0947	...
		Zürich HB **510** a.	...	...	...	...	...	0905	0900	...	...	...	...	...	1000	1000	...	...	...	...	...	...	...	...	...

♦ – **NOTES** (LISTED BY TRAIN NUMBER)

63 – 🚃12 and ✕ Frankfurt - Salzburg - Wien - Budapest.
217 – 🚃12 and 🍷 Saarbrücken - München - Salzburg - Bischofshofen - Graz. Terminates at München from Apr. 14.
471 – *ÖBB nightjet.* 🛏 1, 2 cl., 🛌 2 cl. and 🚃2 Hamburg - Berlin - Basel - Zürich. Feb. 11 - Apr. 17 departs Hamburg 1956, Berlin 2204. From Apr. 18 departs Hamburg 1956, Berlin 2212.
619 – 🚃12 Dortmund - Frankfurt - Mannheim - Karlsruhe - Stuttgart - München.
9578 – ①–⑥ (not Apr. 17, May 1, June 5). To Paris (Table **32**).

G – ①–⑤ (not Apr. 14, 17, May 1, June 5). From Wiesbaden Hbf (d. 0524).
H – To Chur (Table **520**).

a – Arrival time (calls before Vaihingen).
e – Not Apr. 15, 17, May 1, June 5.
g – ① (also Apr. 18, May 2, June 6; not Apr. 17, May 1, June 5).
p – Previous day from Berlin.
t – Not May 26.
x – Frankfurt (Main) **Süd**.

⊠ – Certain Frankfurt timings (mainly trains from Hamburg or Berlin via Fulda) are subject to alteration on ⑥⑦ Feb. 11 - Apr. 2 (also Apr. 14 – 17). Berlin timings are subject to alteration from May 13. See engineering work panel on page 367.
◐ – Operated by Südwestdeutsche Verkehrs. German holiday dates apply.
* – Distance via Katzenberg Tunnel (3 km further via the original route).
☆ – See also panel on page 426.
◨ – Frankfurt Flughafen Fernbahnhof.

See page 367 for a summary of Christmas/New Year alterations

912   FRANKFURT - BASEL and STUTTGART

Panel 1

SEE NOTE	ICE 9568	IC 2273	IC 2317	ICE 711	ICE 591	ICE 999	ICE 101	ICE 913	EC 207	TGV 9576	EC 113	IC 2319	ICE 513	ICE 275	ICE 9566	ICE 571	IC 2271	ICE 1091	ICE 593	ICE 103	ICE 71
	⑧n E⑬ ✗	◇2	Ⓐ ◇2	L⛾	⑥o	Ⓐ①-⑥ e✗	⑦v ✗	✗	e⛾	✗	⛾ R◆	◇2	✗◆	e⛾	⛾ M✗ N✗	E⑬ ✗	◇2	e✗ e◆	a✗	c✗ ⛾	C✗
Hamburg Hbf 800 900 ... d.	✗					0346a										0517					0618h
Berlin Hbf 810 902 ... d.															0432a		0604	0531			
Hannover Hbf 810 900 ... d.					0520						0537	0637				0641	0558g			0540	0741
Dortmund Hbf 800 ... d.							0537	0552			0537	0637								0737	
Köln Hbf 800 910 ... d.				0611			0654	0713d			0653	0755								0855	
Koblenz Hbf 911 ... d.											0748										
Mainz Hbf 911 ... d.				0743	0746						0840										
Frankfurt (Main) Hbf 913 ... d.	0658		0714		0750	0750		0801			0822		0850	0856		0905	0920	0950	0950		1005
Frankfurt Flughafen + 10. ... d.							0751	0809				0852				0921			0951		
Mannheim Hbf 913 ... d.	0737		0824	0824	0827	0827	0823	0840	0844		0921	0923	0927	0937		0954	1027	1027	1023		1043
Mannheim Hbf 913 ... d.	0739		0826	0826	0830	0830	0836	0842	0846		0923	0931	0936	0940		0956	1030	1030	1036		1045
Darmstadt Hbf 913 ... d.			0731								0838					0937					
Bensheim 913 ... d.			0746								0850					0950					
Weinheim 913 ... d.			0758								0900					1000					
Heidelberg Hbf 913 931 ... d.			0814	0838x	0838x						0914	0936x				1014					
Bruchsal 913 931 ... d.			0836													1036					
Vaihingen (Enz) 931 ... d.				0909	0909							1006									
Stuttgart Hbf 931 ... a.				0928	0928	0908	0908		0924		0854	1024	1008			1035		1108	1108		
München Hbf 930 ... a.				1127	1127						1211	1227						1327	1327		
Karlsruhe Hbf 913 916 ... d.	0807		0850			0900		0911	0932		1000	1006				1050				1100	1110
Baden-Baden 916 ... d.						0917		0927													1127
Offenburg 916 ☆ ... d.		0842	0905			0936					1005					1029	1035			1129	
Kehl ... d.		0900	0922								1022					1052					
Strasbourg ... a.	0847	0910	0934							1012	1034					1047	1104				
Freiburg (Brsg) Hbf ☆ ... d.						1007		1015			1101									1201	1212
Basel Bad Bf ☆ ... a.						1038		1045			1134									1234	1245
Basel SBB ☆ ... a.						1047		1054			1147									1247	1254
Zürich HB 510 ... a.								1200													1400

Panel 2

SEE NOTE	ICE 9574	IC 2293	EC 115	EC 515	ICE 277	ICE 119	ICE 973	IC 2277	ICE 595	ICE 105	ICE 73	EC 219	IC 2005	EC 9	ICE 517	ICE 279	IC 2013
	P R✗	◇2	Ⓒ ⛾	⛾	N✗ ⛾	◆ ◇2	⊖ ⑤-⑦ ✗	✗ ◇2	◆	Ⓐ ⛾	K✗ z⛾	Ⓐ ◇2	□ ✗	Ⓒ ⑤⑥	⛾	Ⓐ ◇2	◇2 ⛾
Hamburg Hbf 800 900 ... d.	R✗						0722	0625			0824				0646		
Berlin Hbf 810 902 ... d.			0442e							0734						0830	
Hannover Hbf 810 900 ... d.				0630			0841	0801			0941						0740
Dortmund Hbf 800 ... d.				0737	0837								0937	1037			0952
Köln Hbf 800 910 ... d.			0818	0853	0955			0918		1055			1018	1053	1155		1117
Koblenz Hbf 911 ... d.			0917	0948				1017					1148				1217
Mainz Hbf 911 ... d.			1017	1040				1112					1240				1312
Frankfurt (Main) Hbf 913 ... d.		1020			1050		1105	1120	1150		1205	1220			1250		
Frankfurt Flughafen + 10. ... d.				1052				1121		1151			1252				
Mannheim Hbf 913 ... d.		1100	1121	1123	1127		1152	1154	1227	1223	1245		1307	1321	1323	1327	1352
Mannheim Hbf 913 ... d.		1102	1123	1131	1136		1154	1156	1230	1236	1245		1309	1323	1331	1336	1354
Darmstadt Hbf 913 ... d.			1037					1137			1237						
Bensheim 913 ... d.			1056					1150			1250						
Weinheim 913 ... d.								1200			1300						
Heidelberg Hbf 913 931 ... d.		1110					1206x	1214			1314						1406x
Bruchsal 913 931 ... d.								1236									
Vaihingen (Enz) 931 ... d.			1137														
Stuttgart Hbf 931 ... a.	1054	1150	1153	1208			1246	1235	1308		1354			1408			1446
München Hbf 930 ... a.		1411	1427					1528			1611	1627t					
Karlsruhe Hbf 913 916 ... d.	1132		1149		1200			1250	1300	1310		1336	1349	1400			
Baden-Baden 916 ... d.				1218							1327	1356	1407				
Offenburg 916 ☆ ... d.		1205		1235	1234	1305			1329	1336	1405	1415		1429	1435	1505	
Kehl ... d.		1222		1252	1322				1354	1422				1452	1522		
Strasbourg ... a.	1213	1234		1304	1334				1404	1434				1504	1535		
Freiburg (Brsg) Hbf ☆ ... a.			1251		1306			1412			1455	1501					
Basel Bad Bf ☆ ... a.			1322	1338				1434	1445		1527	1534					
Basel SBB ☆ ... a.			1330	1347				1447	1454		1535	1547					
Zürich HB 510 ... a.								1600			1700						

Panel 3

SEE NOTE	ICE 575	IC 2279	ICE 597	ICE 107	TGV 9580	ICE 75	TGV 9580	ICE 9572	IC 2299	ICE 117	EC 2313	ICE 519	ICE 371	ICE 577	ICE 1911	ICE 2371	ICE 599	ICE 109	ICE 915	ICE 77	EC 391	IC 2217	ICE 611	ICE 373
	✗	⛾◆	✗	✗	R	⛾◆	X✗	R	⑥k	⑧q	✗	✗	N✗	✗	r⛾	⑦	✗	⛾	⑧q	K✗	⛾◆	⛾◆	⛾	N✗
Hamburg Hbf 800 900 ... d.	0924	0828e								0846				1124	1028					1224	1046			1230
Berlin Hbf 810 902 ... d.			0934									1034			1134									
Hannover Hbf 810 900 ... d.	1041	1001e				1141							1241	1201					1341					
Dortmund Hbf 800 ... d.				1137v						1137	1237			1152				1337	1354j	1337	1437			
Köln Hbf 800 910 ... d.				1255					1253	1355		1317			1455	1514d			1453	1555				
Koblenz Hbf 911 ... d.									1348					1417				1548						
Mainz Hbf 911 ... d.										1440				1512				1640						
Frankfurt (Main) Hbf 913 ... d.	1305	1320	1350		1358	1405			1420	1420		1450	1505	1520	1550	1551	1609			1605	1620			1650
Frankfurt Flughafen + 10. ... d.	1321		1351							1452		1521	1521	1609					1652					
Mannheim Hbf 913 ... d.	1354	1427	1423	1437		1443			1521	1523	1527	1554	1552	1627	1623	1639				1643	1721	1723	1727	
Mannheim Hbf 913 ... d.	1356	1430	1434	1439		1445			1523	1531	1536	1556	1554	1630	1636	1641				1645	1723	1731	1736	
Darmstadt Hbf 913 ... d.		1337								1437	1437			1537							1637			
Bensheim 913 ... d.		1350									1450			1550							1650			
Weinheim 913 ... d.		1400								1456	1500			1600							1700			
Heidelberg Hbf 913 931 ... d.		1414								1510	1514	1536x		1606x	1614						1714	1736x		
Bruchsal 913 931 ... d.		1436									1605				1636								1808	
Vaihingen (Enz) 931 ... d.																								
Stuttgart Hbf 931 ... a.	1435		1508				1454		1550	1554	1622	1608		1635	1646		1708		1719	1754	1825	1827		
München Hbf 930 ... a.			1727t						1811		1827			1927						2011	2027			
Karlsruhe Hbf 913 916 ... d.		1450		1458	1504	1510	1512	1532			1600		1650	1700			1710	1727		1800				
Baden-Baden 916 ... d.					1527	1534			◇2					◇2			1727							
Offenburg 916 ☆ ... d.				1529					1605			1629	1635	1705			1729	1735	1805				1829	
Kehl ... d.									1622			1652		1722			1753	1822						
Strasbourg ... a.							1600	1613	1634			1704		1734			1804	1834						
Freiburg (Brsg) Hbf ☆ ... a.				1601		1612						1701						1801		1812			1901	
Basel Bad Bf ☆ ... a.				1634		1645						1734						1834		1845			1934	
Basel SBB ☆ ... a.				1647		1654						1747						1847		1854			1947	
Zürich HB 510 ... a.				1800														2000						

Regional trains OFFENBURG - BASEL (German holiday dates apply). On Jan. 6 regional services between Offenburg and Basel Bad Bf run as on ⑦.

	†	Ⓐ	Ⓐ	✗			✗																	✗	
Offenburg ... d.	0049	0425	0522	...	0551	0632	...	0706	...	0807	0907	1007	1107	1204	1307	1404	1507	1607	1707	1807	1907	2007	...	2107	2244
Freiburg (Brsg) Hbf ... a.	0131	0525	0626	...	0649	0727	...	0756	...	0855	0955	1055	1155	1253	1355	1450	1555	1656	1756	1856	1955	2055	...	2202	2342
Freiburg (Brsg) Hbf ... d.	0132	0526	0628	0628	0710	0732	...	0815	0815	0915	1011	1115	1215	1315	1415	1515	1615	1715	1815	1915	2015	...	2145		2343
Müllheim (Baden) ... d.	0152	0547	0655	0655	0731	0749	...	0835	0835	1035	1135	1235	1337	1435	1535	1635	1735	1835	1935	2035	...	2212		0010
Basel Bad Bf ... a.	0220	0625	0732	0732	0745	0806	0811	0819	0911	0911	1011	1111	1211	1311	1412	1511	1611	1711	1811	1911	2011	2111	...	2249	2319	0046
Basel SBB ... a.	...	0650	...	...	0750	...	0820	0825	0925	0925	1025	1125	1225	1325	1425	1525	1620§	1720§	1820§	1925	2025	2125	...	...	2325	...

FOR NOTES SEE NEXT PAGE →

FRANKFURT - BASEL and STUTTGART 912

SEE NOTE ⊠	TGV 9560	ICE 579	IC 2011	IC 2017	IC 2373	IC 2283	ICE 691	ICE 201	ICE 917	ICE 79	TGV 9570		IC 1956	IC 2295	IC 2019	IC 2311	ICE 613	IC 2262	ICE 375	IC 2262	IC 1915	ICE 771	IC 2375	ICE 693	1819
	E			⑤f		①–④			Ⓑq		P		⑦	Ⓑq	⑥			Ⓑq		Ⓑq	⑤⑦				♥
	[R]🍷	✕	F🍷		A🍷	m	✕	🍷	✕	✕	[R]🍷	◐2	◆	🍷	◆	J🍷	🍷	🍷◆	✕	🍷◆	rT	✕	🍷◆	✕	🍷
Hamburg Hbf **800 900** d.	...	1324	...	...	1228	...	...	...	...	1424	...	...	...	...	...	1246	...	...	...	...	🍷	1524	1428	...	...
Berlin Hbf **810 902** d.	...	|	1001w	...	|	...	1334	...	...	|	...	...	...	...	...	|	...	...	1430	...	1202	|	|	1534	1454
Hannover Hbf **810 900** d.	...	1441	1156w	1156	1401	...	|	...	...	1541	...	...	...	...	...	|	...	...	|	...	1356	1641	1601	|	1646
Dortmund Hbf **800** d.	...	|	1349w	1352	|	...	|	...	1556	|	...	...	...	...	...	1537	1637	...	|	...	1549	|	|	|	|
Köln Hbf **800 910** d.	...	|	1517	1517	|	...	|	1655	1713d	|	...	...	...	...	1618	1653	1755	...	|	...	1717	|	|	|	|
Koblenz Hbf **911** d.	...	|	1617	1617	|	...	|	|	|	|	...	...	...	...	1717	1748	|	...	|	...	1817	|	|	|	|
Mainz Hbf **911** d.	...	|	1712	1712	|	...	|	|	|	|	...	...	...	...	1817	1840	|	...	|	...	1912	|	|	|	|
Frankfurt (Main) Hbf **913** d.	1658	1705	|	|	1720	1746	1750	|	|	1805	...	...	1759	1820	|	|	|	...	1850	...	|	1905	1920	1950	1937‡
Frankfurt Flughafen ✈ ◧ d.	|	1721	|	|	|	|	|	1751	1809	|	...	...	|	|	|	|	1852	...	|	...	|	1921	|	|	|
Mannheim Hbf **913** a.	1737	1754	1752	1752	|	|	1827	1823	1839	1843	...	...	|	|	1901	1921	1923	...	1927	...	1952	1954	|	2027	|
Mannheim Hbf **913** d.	1740	1756	1754	1754	|	|	1830	1836	1841	1845	...	...	|	|	1903	1923	1931	...	1936	...	1954	1956	|	2030	|
Darmstadt Hbf **913** d.	|	|	|	|	1737	1804	|	|	|	|	...	...	1821	1837	|	|	|	...	|	...	|	|	1937	|	1954
Bensheim **913** d.	|	|	|	|	1750	|	|	|	|	|	...	...	1835	1850	|	|	|	...	|	...	|	|	1950	|	|
Weinheim **913** d.	|	|	|	|	1800	1825	|	|	|	|	...	...	1848	1900	|	|	|	...	|	...	|	|	2000	|	|
Heidelberg Hbf **913 931** d.	|	|	1806x	1806x	1814	1843	|	|	|	|	...	...	1902	1914	1916x	1936x	|	...	|	...	2006x	|	2014	|	2033
Bruchsal **913 931** d.	|	|	|	|	1836	1901	|	|	|	|	...	...	|	|	|	|	|	...	|	...	|	|	2036	|	|
Vaihingen (Enz) **931** d.	|	|	|	|	|	|	|	|	|	|	...	...	|	|	|	2005	|	...	|	...	|	|	|	|	2103
Stuttgart Hbf **931** a.	|	1835	1846	1846	|	|	1908	|	1924	|	1854	...	|	1954	1958	2024	2008	...	|	...	2046	2035	|	2108	2120
München Hbf **930** a.	|	▬	▬	2118	|	|	2127	|	...	|	|	...	|	2215	...	...	2226	...	|	...	▬	2319f	|	2329q	...
Karlsruhe Hbf **913 916** d.	1807	...	Ⓐ	...	1852	1916	...	1900	...	1910	1932	...	1940	...	...	...	...	1955	2000	...	...	...	2052	...	...
Baden-Baden **916** d.	|	◐2	◐2	...	...	...	...	|	...	1927	|	...	...	...	...	...	...	|	2018	...	◐2	...	...	...	...
Offenburg **916** ☆ d.	|	1835	1905	...	...	...	...	1929	...	|	|	2005	...	...	...	...	...	2026	2034	...	2105	...	...	...	...
Kehl 🏛 d.	|	1852	1922	...	...	...	...	|	...	|	|	2022	...	...	...	...	...	|	|	...	2122	...	...	...	...
Strasbourg a.	1847	1904	1934	...	...	...	...	|	...	|	2013	2034	...	...	...	...	...	|	|	←	2134	...	...	...	...
Freiburg (Brsg) Hbf ☆ d.	...	...	...	...	...	...	...	2001	...	2012	...	...	...	...	...	...	...	2100	2106	2112	...	...	...	...	...
Basel Bad Bf 🏛 ☆ a.	...	...	...	...	...	...	...	2034	...	2045	...	...	...	...	...	...	...	→	2138	2155	...	...	...	...	...
Basel SBB ☆ a.	...	...	...	...	...	...	...	2047	...	2054	...	...	...	...	...	...	...	...	2147	...	...	...	...	...	...
Zürich HB **510** a.	...	...	...	...	...	...	...	...	...	2200	...	...	...	...	...	...	...	...	...	...	...	...	...	...	...

SEE NOTE ⊠	ICE 203	ICE 1103	ICE 1171	ICE 1171	ICE 203		IC 2171	IC 1995	IC 2297	IC 2213	ICE 615	ICE 377		ICE 773	ICE 695	ICE 1093	ICE 1093	ICE 605	IC 2377	IC 1973	ICE 273	ICE 273	ICE 605	ICE 877	ICE 1552
	①–⑥	⑦v		⑥⑦	①–⑤		⑤f	⑦w	2397						⑥¶	Ⓑb	⑦y		⑤f	⑦w		⑤⑥	⊙		⑥⑦
	e🍷	🍷	✕	c✕	a🍷	◐2	🍷	🍷	Y🍷	🍷◆	🍷	✕	◐2	✕	✕	✕	✕	🍷◆	A🍷	✕	✕	p✕	🍷◆	✕	⊕🍷
Hamburg Hbf **800 900** d.	...	...	1624	1624	...	...	1528	...	...	1446	...	...	...	1724	...	...	...	...	1627	...	1824	1824	...	...	...
Berlin Hbf **810 902** d.	...	...	|	|	...	...	|	...	...	|	...	1630	...	|	1734	1803	1803	...	|	...	|	|	...	1830	...
Hannover Hbf **810 900** d.	...	...	1741	1741	...	...	1707	1703	...	|	...	|	...	1841	|	|	|	...	1801	...	1941	1941	...	|	...
Dortmund Hbf **800** d.	...	...	|	|	...	...	|	|	...	1737	1837	|	...	|	|	|	|	1924k	|	...	|	|	...	|	...
Köln Hbf **800 910** d.	1855	1855	|	|	...	...	|	|	...	1853	1957	|	...	|	|	|	|	2046	|	...	|	|	...	|	...
Koblenz Hbf **911** d.	|	|	|	|	...	...	|	|	...	1948	|	|	...	|	|	|	|	|	|	...	|	|	...	|	...
Mainz Hbf **911** d.	|	|	|	|	...	...	|	|	...	2040	|	|	...	|	|	|	|	|	|	...	|	|	...	|	...
Frankfurt (Main) Hbf **913** d.	|	|	2005	2005	...	...	2015	2020	2020	|	|	2050	...	2105	2151	2151	2151	|	2155	2155	2205	2205	...	2300	2308
Frankfurt Flughafen ✈ ◧ d.	1951	1951	|	|	...	...	|	|	|	|	2052	|	...	2121	|	|	|	2153	|	|	|	|	...	2317	|
Mannheim Hbf **913** a.	2023	2023	2043	2043	...	...	|	|	|	2121	2123	2127	...	2154	2228	2228	2228	2224	|	|	2243	2243	...	2353	|
Mannheim Hbf **913** d.	2036	2036	2045	2045	...	...	|	|	|	2123	2131	2136	...	2156	2231	2231	2231	2236	|	|	2245	2245	...	2358	|
Darmstadt Hbf **913** d.	|	|	|	|	...	...	2037	2037	2037	|	|	|	...	|	|	|	|	|	2212	2212	|	|	...	|	2327
Bensheim **913** d.	|	|	|	|	...	...	2050	2050	2050	|	|	|	...	|	|	|	|	|	2224	2224	|	|	...	|	2341
Weinheim **913** d.	|	|	|	|	...	...	2100	2100	2100	|	|	|	...	|	|	|	|	|	2234	2234	|	|	...	|	|
Heidelberg Hbf **913 931** d.	|	|	|	|	...	...	2114	2114	2114	2136x	|	|	...	2210	|	|	|	|	2249	2249	|	|	...	|	0004
Bruchsal **913 931** d.	|	|	|	|	...	...	|	|	|	|	|	|	...	|	|	|	|	|	2311	|	|	|	...	|	|
Vaihingen (Enz) **931** d.	|	|	|	|	...	...	|	|	|	2205	|	|	...	|	|	|	|	|	|	2321	|	|	...	|	0033
Stuttgart Hbf **931** a.	|	|	|	|	...	...	2155	2156	2155	2224	2208	|	...	2250	2308	2310	2310	|	|	2338	|	|	...	|	0050
München Hbf **930** a.	|	|	|	|	←	...	...	...	...	...	0027	|	...	...	...	...	0133	|	|	...	|	|	←	|	...
Karlsruhe Hbf **913 916** d.	2100	2102	2108	2112	2112	...	...	...	...	...	...	2200	...	...	...	...	...	2300	2327	...	2308	2312	2312	0022	...
Baden-Baden **916** d.	→	2119	...	2129	2129	...	...	...	...	...	...	2218	...	...	...	...	...	→	...	...	...	2329	2331	...	...
Offenburg **916** ☆ d.	...	2135	...	2145	2145	2205	...	...	...	...	...	2237	2325	...	...	...	...	...	...	...	...	2345	2350	...	...
Kehl 🏛 d.	...	|	...	|	|	2222	...	...	...	...	...	|	2348	...	...	...	...	...	...	...	...	|	|	...	...
Strasbourg a.	...	|	...	|	|	2234	...	...	...	...	...	|	2400	...	...	...	...	...	...	...	...	|	|	...	...
Freiburg (Brsg) Hbf ☆ d.	...	2208	...	2217	2217	...	...	...	...	...	...	2311	...	...	...	...	...	...	...	...	...	0017	0022	...	...
Basel Bad Bf 🏛 ☆ a.	...	2242	...	2251	2251	...	...	...	...	...	...	2346	...	...	...	...	...	...	...	...	...	0050	0056	...	...
Basel SBB ☆ a.	...	2250	...	2300	2300	...	...	...	...	...	...	2354	...	...	...	...	...	...	...	...	...	0100	...	...	...
Zürich HB **510** a.	...	...	...	...	...	...	...	...	...	...	...	...	...	...	...	...	...	...	...	...	...	...	...	...	...

◆ – **NOTES** (LISTED BY TRAIN NUMBER) for pages 426 and 427

75 – [12] and ✕ Hamburg - Zürich (- Chur ①–⑥). On ⑦ (also Apr. 17, May 1, June 5) runs with train number **1175** and starts from Kiel (Table **820**).
105 – [12] and 🍷 Amsterdam - Köln - Basel.
113 – [12] and ✕ Frankfurt - Salzburg - Villach - Klagenfurt; conveys [12] Frankfurt - Villach (**213**) - Ljubljana - Zagreb.
115 – WÖRTHERSEE – [12] and 🍷 Münster - München - Salzburg - Villach - Klagenfurt.
117 – [12] and 🍷 Frankfurt - München - Salzburg - Klagenfurt. Terminates at München Apr. 14 - July 16.
119 – [12] Münster - Ulm - Lindau - Bregenz - Innsbruck.
219 – [12] and 🍷 Frankfurt - München - Salzburg - Bischofshofen - Selzthal - Graz. Terminates at München from Apr. 14.
391 – [12] and 🍷 Frankfurt - München (- Salzburg Ⓑ to Apr. 13).
605 – [12] and 🍷 (Dortmund ⑥**k** -) Essen - Karlsuhe (- Basel Bad Bf ⊙).
1956 – ⑦ to Feb. 5. [12] Leipzig - Erfurt - Frankurt - Karlsruhe.
2005 – ⑤⑥ (also Apr. 13, 16, 30, May 24, 25, June 4). [12] and 🍷 Emden - Münster - Konstanz.
2013 – ALLGÄU – [12] and 🍷 Hannover - Dortmund - Stuttgart - Ulm - Oberstdorf.
2019 – ⑥ from Apr. 8. [12] Norddeich Mole - Münster - Stuttgart.
2213 – RÜGEN – [12] and 🍷 Ostseebad Binz - Stralsund - Rostock - Hamburg - Stuttgart.
2217 – [12] and 🍷 (Greifswald Ⓐ**u** -) Stralsund - Rostock - Hamburg - Köln - Stuttgart. Vaihingen and Stuttgart timings are 3 minutes earlier Mar. 11 - Apr. 23.
2262 – [12] and 🍷 München - Stuttgart - Basel.
2271 – [12] and 🍷 (Hannover Ⓐ -) Kassel - Karlsruhe.
2279 – [12] and 🍷 (Stralsund - Hamburg ①–⑥**e** -) Kassel - Frankfurt - Karlsruhe.
2375 – WATTENMEER – [12] and 🍷 (Westerland ♠ -) Hamburg - Frankfurt - Karlsruhe.
9576 – [12] and 🍷 München - Stuttgart - Paris.
9580 – [12] and 🍷 Frankfurt - Strasbourg - Mulhouse - Lyon - Marseille.

A – From Stralsund (Table **830**).
C – To Chur (Table **520**).
E – [12] Frankfurt - Strasbourg - Paris.
F – ①②③④⑦ (not Apr. 13, 16, 30, May 24, June 4). On ①–④ (not Apr. 13, May 24) continues to Tübingen Hbf (a. 1950).
G – Runs as *TGV* **9592** on ⑥ (also Apr. 16, 30, June 4). *ICE* conveys ✕, *TGV* conveys 🍷.
J – From Westerland (Table **821**).
K – From Kiel (Table **820**).
L – From Kassel (Table **806**).
M – From Münster (Table **800**).
N – To Interlaken via Bern (Table **560**).
P – [12] Stuttgart - Paris (Table **32**).

T – To Tübingen (a. 2150) on ⑦**w**.
Y – ①②③④⑥ (also Apr. 14; not Jan. 5, Apr. 13, 15, 17, May 1, 24, 25, 27, June 5).

a – ①–⑤ (not Apr. 14, 17, May 1, June 5).
b – Not Dec. 25 – 30, ⑦ Feb. 12 - Apr. 2, Apr. 14, 16, 17, 30, June 4.
c – Also Apr. 14, 17, May 1, June 5.
d – Köln **Messe/Deutz**.
e – ①–⑥ (not Apr. 15, 17, May 1, June 5).
f – ⑤ (also Apr. 13, May 24; not Apr. 14, May 26).
g – Ⓐ only.
h – 0611 on ⓒ (also May 26).
j – ①②③④⑦ (not Apr. 13, 16, 30, May 24, June 4).
k – ⑥ (also Apr. 14, 16, 30, June 4).
m – Not Apr. 13, 17, May 1, 24, 25, June 5.
n – Not Apr. 16, 30, June 4.
o – Also Apr. 14, May 1, 25; not Apr. 15.
p – Also Apr. 13, 16, 30, June 4.
q – Ⓑ (not Apr. 14, 16, 30, June 4).
r – Also Apr. 13, 17, May 1, 24, June 5; not Apr. 14, 16, 30, May 26, June 4.
s – Also Apr. 16, 30, June 4.
t – 4 – 8 minutes later from Mar. 30.
u – Not May 26.
v – ⑦ (also Apr. 15, 17, May 1, June 5).
w – ⑦ (also Apr. 17, May 1, June 5; not Apr. 16, 30, June 4).
x – Not Mar. 11 - Apr. 23.
y – Also May 1, June 5; not Feb. 12 - Mar. 26, Apr. 2, 16, 30, June 4.
z – Also Apr. 13, 17, May 1, 24, 25, June 5.

◊ – ⑤⑥ (also Apr. 13, May 24; not Apr. 15).
⊙ – ①②③④⑦ (not Apr. 9, 13, 16, 30, June 4).
¶ – Also Dec. 25 – 30, ⑦ Feb. 12 - Apr. 2, Apr. 14, 16, 17, 30, June 4.
⁝ – Ⓑ (not Apr. 14, 16, 30, May 25, June 4).
‡ – Frankfurt (Main) **Süd**.
⊖ – Train number **573** on ⑦ (also Apr. 15, 17, May 1, 26, 27, June 5).
□ – Train number **1173** on ⑦ (also Apr. 15, 17, May 1, June 5).
⊕ – Also May 1, June 5; not ⑦ Feb. 12 - Mar. 26, Apr. 2, 16, 30, May 27, June 4. From Dresden / Leipzig (Table **850**). Train number **1572** on ⑦ (also May 1, June 5).
♠ – ①⑤⑥⑦ to Apr. 3; daily from Apr. 7.
▲ – Not Feb. 20 – 24, Apr. 18 – 21.
♥ – From Dec. 14. Operated by Locomore. Special fares payable (DB tickets **not** valid).
§ – On ⓒ change trains at Basel Badischer Bf (arrives Basel SBB 5 minutes later).
⊠ – Certain Frankfurt timings (mainly trains from Hamburg or Berlin via Fulda) are subject to alteration on ⑥⑦ Feb. 11 - Apr. 2 (also Apr. 14 – 17). Berlin timings are subject to alteration from May 13. See engineering work panel on page 367.
☆ – See panel on page 426 for other local services.
◐ – Operated by Südwestdeutsche Verkehrs. German holiday dates apply.
◧ – Frankfurt Flughafen Fernbahnhof.

See page 367 for a summary of Christmas / New Year alterations

912 — BASEL and STUTTGART - FRANKFURT

km	km	SEE NOTE ✕	ICE 618 1018 ①g ✕	ICE 1092 e✕	ICE 774 ①-⑥ ✕	ICE 874 ⬧Ⓨ	ICE 616 Ⓨ	IC 2278	ICE 674 Ⓐo ✕	ICE 674 ♥ ✕	IC 2396 ①-⑤ ✕	ICE 1818 Ⓐ aⓎ	IC 1818 Ⓐ Ⓨ	ICE 604 ✕	ICE 604 AⓎ	ICE 694 ◇2	IC 1114 Ⓐ	IC 2376 ✕	ICE 676 ✕	ICE 772 ◆	IC 2018 ⑥ Ⓨ◆	IC 2010 Ⓐ	IC 2392 e◆	IC 2261 ①g Ⓨ	ICE 374 Ⓐ ✕
		Zürich HB 510 d.																							0608
		Basel SBB ☆ d.																						0600	0618
		Basel Bad Bf ☆ d.			0412g			0511					0515						0549					0600	0618
		Freiburg (Brsg) Hbf ☆ d.			0447g			0546					0552						0622					0646	0652
	0	Strasbourg d.																	0622						
	8	Kehl d.																	0634						
	29	Offenburg 916 ☆ d.			0520g			0618					0626						0652	0657				0731	
		Baden-Baden 916 d.			0536g			0634					0641						0714					0749	0741
		Karlsruhe Hbf 913 916 d.	0349	0500		0558			0615	0651	0651			0700	0700			0702		0736				0806	0800
0	0	München Hbf 930 d.	0001				0324																		
29	29	Stuttgart Hbf 931 d.	0230	0502		0551			0602		0621						0651	0630							
		Vaihingen (Enz) 931 d.	0259	0519					0620		0640						0648								
		Bruchsal 913 931 d.	0405				0633										0724								
	92	Heidelberg Hbf 913 931 d.	0428			0547			0654	0658	0717						0720x	0746			0755x	0755x	0800		
		Weinheim 913 d.								0714								0800					0817		
		Bensheim 913 d.								0728								0809					0828		
		Darmstadt Hbf 913 d.								0742	0804							0824					0841		
107	109	Mannheim Hbf 913 a.	0438	0526	0559	0623	0628	0709	0714	0714				0723	0723	0729	0732		0800	0804	0806	0806			0823
107		Mannheim Hbf 913 d.	0440	0528	0605	0632	0636	0711	0716	0716				0736	0736	0732	0734		0806	0808	0808				0832
179		Frankfurt Flughafen + 🚇 a.	0512		0637		0706					0806	0806						0837						
		Frankfurt (Main) Hbf 913 a.	0533	0608	0652	0708		0752	0752	0752	0802	0830‡		0808			0840			0852			0902		0908
		Mainz Hbf 911 a.												0815					0846	0846					
		Koblenz Hbf 911 a.																	0941	0941					
		Köln Hbf 800 910 a.	0706			0805								0905	0905				1043	1043					
		Dortmund Hbf 800 a.	0821z			0921													1209f						
		Hannover Hbf 810 900 a.			0917				1017	1017			1115			1156				1117				1401f	
		Berlin Hbf 810 902 a.		0955		1128				1306			1225							1553f					
		Hamburg Hbf 800 900 a.			1035				1135	1135						1328				1235				1328	

	SEE NOTE ✕	ICE 614 Ⓨ	IC 2216 Ⓨ◆	IC 2294	ICE 78 ✕	ICE 916 ①-⑥ e✕	ICE 202 ◇2	ICE 202 ◇2	ICE 692 eⓎ	ICE 2374 Ⓨ◆	ICE 770 ✕	ICE 1537 Ⓒ Ⓨ◆	ICE 9571 Ⓐ ◇2	TGV 9561 P sD ℝ〼	IC 372 ①-⑥ N✕	ICE 612 Ⓨ◆	IC 2218	IC 1296 GⓎ	IC 76 ✕	ICE 914 ①-⑥ eⓎ	ICE 200 ◇2
	Zürich HB 510 d.					0600								0813		0906			0800		0913
	Basel SBB ☆ d.					0706						0713			0813	0906					0913
	Basel Bad Bf ☆ d.					0715						0722			0823	0915					0923
	Freiburg (Brsg) Hbf ☆ d.					0749						0755			0857	0949					0957
	Strasbourg d.				0722	0750					0820	0831		0852	0909				0922		
	Kehl d.				0734	0804					0831				0904				0934		
	Offenburg 916 ☆ d.				0752	0822		0827			0849				0922			0930	0952		1030
	Baden-Baden 916 d.					0834						0843									
	Karlsruhe Hbf 913 916 d.			0851				0900	0900			0905			0910			0955	1000		1100
	München Hbf 930 d.	0524		0536‡							0629a					0727			0746•		
	Stuttgart Hbf 931 d.	0751	0737	0805		0837					0851		0925	0904	0948	0951	0937	1004		1041	
	Vaihingen (Enz) 931 d.		0755								0928					0955					
	Bruchsal 913 931 d.										0923										
	Heidelberg Hbf 913 931 d.		0825x	0846						0946		0956					1025x	1046			
	Weinheim 913 d.			0900						1000		1001					1100				
	Bensheim 913 d.			0909						1009		1011					1109				
	Darmstadt Hbf 913 d.			0924						1024		1040					1124				
	Mannheim Hbf 913 a.	0828	0837		0914	0919	0924	0924	0929		1004		1018	1023	1028	1037		1114	1119	1124	
	Mannheim Hbf 913 d.	0836	0839		0916	0921	0936	0936	0932		1006		1021	1032	1036	1039		1116	1121	1136	
	Frankfurt Flughafen + 🚇 a.	0906			0953		1006	1006			1037					1106				1206	
	Frankfurt (Main) Hbf 913 a.				0940	0953				1008		1040	1052	1057	1108	1140			1153		
	Mainz Hbf 911 a.		0918												1118						
	Koblenz Hbf 911 a.		1011												1211						
	Köln Hbf 800 910 a.	1005	1105			1041d					1105	1105			1205	1305			1241d		1305
	Dortmund Hbf 800 a.	1121	1221			1203y					1221r					1321	1421			1403	1421h
	Hannover Hbf 810 900 a.				1217								1356	1317					1417		
	Berlin Hbf 810 902 a.										1425			1501							
	Hamburg Hbf 800 900 a.		1511		1335						1529	1435				1713			1535		

	SEE NOTE ✕	ICE 690 ✕	IC 2372 ⑤-⑦ mA	IC 1216 ⑤ GⓎ	ICE 578 ✕	ICE 370 ◇2	IC 610 ✕	IC 2312 Ⓨ	EC 390 Ⓨ	IC 2006 ⑥h GⓎ	IC 2014 ⑦ Ⓨ◆	ICE 74 K✕	IC 108 ✕	IC 598 ⑤f Ⓨ◆	IC 2370 ◇2	ICE 2012 ✕	IC 576 Ⓨ◆	ICE 9573 T P ℝ	ICE 278 ◇2	ICE 518 N✕	EC 8 Ⓨ	EC 218 ✕
	Zürich HB 510 d.											1000							1100			
	Basel SBB ☆ d.					1013						1106	1113						1213	1220		
	Basel Bad Bf ☆ d.					1023						1115	1123						1223	1230		
	Freiburg (Brsg) Hbf ☆ d.					1057						1149	1157						1257	1304		
	Strasbourg d.				1052													1246	1252			1322
	Kehl d.				1104													1304				1335
	Offenburg 916 ☆ d.				1122			1130					1230						1322	1330		1353
	Baden-Baden 916 d.									1202	1202	1234							1352		
	Karlsruhe Hbf 913 916 d.			1110			1200			1221	1221	1251	1300		1310	1328			1400	1412		
	München Hbf 930 d.	0828		0847				0928	0947				1028			1128						1147
	Stuttgart Hbf 931 d.	1051		1114	1125			1151	1204	1209			1251		1312	1325	1404		1351			1404
	Vaihingen (Enz) 931 d.								1155	1226												
	Bruchsal 913 931 d.			1124									1324									
	Heidelberg Hbf 913 931 d.			1146	1155x				1225x	1246			1346	1355x							1446	
	Weinheim 913 d.			1200						1300			1400								1500	
	Bensheim 913 d.			1209						1309			1409								1509	
	Darmstadt Hbf 913 d.			1224						1324			1424								1524	
	Mannheim Hbf 913 a.	1129		1206	1204	1224	1228	1237	1250	1250	1256	1314	1323	1329	1406	1404		1423	1428	1437		
	Mannheim Hbf 913 d.	1132		1208	1206	1232	1236	1239	1258	1258	1258	1316	1336	1332	1408	1406		1432	1436	1439		
	Frankfurt Flughafen + 🚇 a.				1237			1306				1406				1437					1506	
	Frankfurt (Main) Hbf 913 a.	1208	1240		1252	1308		1340			1353	1408	1440		1452	1508				1540		
	Mainz Hbf 911 a.		1246										1446							1518		
	Koblenz Hbf 911 a.		1341										1541							1611		
	Köln Hbf 800 910 a.		1442							1405	1505	1543	1543	1543	1643				1605	1705		
	Dortmund Hbf 800 a.		1608							1521	1621	1702			1808				1721	1821		
	Hannover Hbf 810 900 a.		1556	1801	1517							1617			1756	2018	1717					
	Berlin Hbf 810 902 a.	1625	1958			1728							1825						1928			
	Hamburg Hbf 800 900 a.		1732		1635				1913			1735			1928	1835						2113

Regional trains BASEL - OFFENBURG (German holiday dates apply). On Jan. 6 regional services between Basel Bad Bf and Offenburg run as on ⑦.

km		✕		Ⓐ												Ⓐ	Ⓒ	Ⓐ	⑥		✕			
0	Basel SBB d.	0532		0603		0736§	0836§	0934	1034	1134	1234	1334	1434	1534	1636§	1736§	1804	1836	1904		1934			2240
5	Basel Bad Bf d.	0538	0545	0625	0634	0748	0848	0948	1048	1148	1248	1348	1448	1545	1648	1748	1826	1848	1848	1926	1948	2110	2126	2258
37	Müllheim (Baden) d.	—	0616	0649	0707	0823	0923	1023	1123	1223	1323	1423	1523	1723	1823	1855	1923	1955		2023	2054	2158		2332
66	Freiburg (Brsg) Hbf d.		0642	0718	0736	0847	0944	1044	1144	1244	1344	1444	1544	1644	1744	1844	1923	1944	1944		2021	2219		0001
66	Freiburg (Brsg) Hbf d.	0555	0656	0722	0803	0903	1003	1103	1203	1307	1403	1500	1603	1706	1803	1903	1925	2003		2025	2025	2125	2225	0018
129	Offenburg a.	0645	0745	0814	0851	0953	1053	1153	1253	1353	1450	1553	1650	1753	1850	1949	2021	2050		2121	2121	2221	2318	0112

FOR NOTES SEE NEXT PAGE →

SEE NOTE ⊠	TGV 9583	ICE 72	TGV 9583	ICE 106	ICE 596	ICE 710 Ⓐu	IC 2276	IC 118	ICE 1094 Ⓑ◇	ICE 574 ⑥c	ICE 276	ICE 516	EC 6	IC 2292	EC 114	TGV 9575	ICE 70	ICE 104	ICE 504 ⑦b	ICE 1090 Ⓑb	ICE 594 ⑥j	IC 2316 Ⓑq
	ⓨ◆	H✗	ⓨ◆	ⓨ	✗	ⓨ	✗	◆	K✗	ⓨ◆	✗	ⓨ	N✗	ⓨ	ⓨ◆	H✗	ⓨ◆	ⓨ	n✗	ⓨ◆	✗	
Zürich HB 510 .... d.		1200														1400						
Basel SBB ....☆ d.		1306	1313								1413	1427				1506	1513	1513				
Basel Bad Bf ....☆ d.		1315	1323								1423	1435				1515	1523	1523				
Freiburg (Brsg) Hbf ..☆ d.		1349		1357							1455	1507				1549	1557	1557				
Strasbourg .... d.	1355								1422	1452						1522	1546					
Kehl .... d.									1434	1504						1534						
Offenburg ...916 ☆ d.				1430					1452	1522	1527					1552						
Baden-Baden .... d.	1425	1434←									1543					1634						
Karlsruhe Hbf ...913 916 d.	1446	1451	1454	1500			1510				1601		1612			1628	1651	1700	1700			
München Hbf 930 .... d.	→				1228						1328				1346					1428	1428	
Stuttgart Hbf 931 d.					1451	1433		1512	1525	1525	1551		1604		1609	1704				1651	1651	1636
Vaihingen (Enz) 931 d.						1454								1626								
Bruchsal ...913 931 d.							1524															
Heidelberg Hbf...913 931 d.							1520	1546	1555x					1646								1720x
Weinheim ...913 d.								1600						1700								
Bensheim ...913 d.								1609						1709								
Darmstadt Hbf ...913 d.								1624						1724								
Mannheim Hbf ...913 a.		1514		1518	1523	1529	1531		1606	1604	1604	1624	1628		1637	1656	1714	1723	1723	1729		1736
Mannheim Hbf ...913 d.		1516		1521	1536	1532	1533		1608	1606	1606	1632	1636		1639	1658	1716	1736	1736	1732	1732	1738
Frankfurt Flughafen ✈ a.						1606			1637	1637		1706							1806	1806		
Frankfurt (Main) ...913 a.	1553	1558			1608			1640	1652	1652	1708			1740		1753			1808	1808		1815
Mainz Hbf 911 .... a.						1615		1646					1718		1740							
Koblenz Hbf 911 .... a.						1741							1811		1841							
Köln Hbf 800 910 .... a.				1705					1801	1843	1805	1905	1943						1905	1905		
Dortmund Hbf 800 .... a.				1821							1921	2021	2101						2021			
Hannover Hbf 810 900 .... a.		1817				1956			1906	1917								2017			2021	
Berlin Hbf 810 902 .... a.						2025					2128								2138			
Hamburg Hbf 800 900 .... a.		1935						2128t	2024	2038					2314q			2138				

SEE NOTE ⊠	IC 2274	ICE 572	ICE 9563 Ⓐ D	ICE 274 Ⓐ ✗	ICE 514	IC 2318	EC 112	EC 206	ICE 912 Ⓑq	TGV 9577 Ⓑ⊗	ICE 376	ICE 102 ♥	ICE 592	ICE 2172 ⑦w	ICE 2272 ①–⑤	IC 570 ⑦w	IC 1910	IC 1172 ⑥	ICE 272 ①–⑤	ICE 292 ⑦w
	ⓨ◆	✗	❍2	❍2	H✗	✗	ⓨ	ⓨ◆	✗◆	E?	❍2	Y▯	N✗	❍2	✗	L?◆	a L		❍2	s✗
Zürich HB 510 .... d.																		1700	1700	1700
Basel SBB ....☆ d.				1613		1619					1706	1713						1813	1813	1813
Basel Bad Bf ....☆ d.				1623		1627					1715	1723						1823	1823	1823
Freiburg (Brsg) Hbf ..☆ d.				1655		1702					1749	1756						1857	1857	1857
Strasbourg .... d.					1622	1652	1713			1722	1746							1852		
Kehl .... d.					1634	1704				1734	1804							1904		
Offenburg ...916 ☆ d.					1652	1722	1727			1752	1822	1827						1922	1930	1930
Baden-Baden .... d.							1743			1752	1834	1843								
Karlsruhe Hbf ...913 916 d.	1710					1755	1801		1812		1828	1851				1910		2000	2000	2000
München Hbf 930 .... d.					1528			1547					1628				1619			
Stuttgart Hbf 931 d.		1725			1751	1737	1805	1837					1851	1903		1925	1914			
Vaihingen (Enz) 931 d.	1724					1755								1924						
Bruchsal ...913 931 d.	1724																			
Heidelberg Hbf...913 931 d.	1746						1825x	1846					1946	1946		1955x				
Weinheim ...913 d.	1800							1900					2000	2000						
Bensheim ...913 d.	1809							1909					2009	2009						
Darmstadt Hbf ...913 d.	1824							1924					2024	2024						
Mannheim Hbf ...913 a.		1804			1818	1824	1828		1837		1841	1919	1914	1924	1929	2004	2006	2024	2024	2024
Mannheim Hbf ...913 d.		1806			1821	1832	1836		1839		1843	1921	1916	1932		2006	2008	2032	2032	2032
Frankfurt Flughafen ✈ a.							1837				1906			1953		2037				
Frankfurt (Main) ...913 a.	1840	1852			1858	1908	1940	1942			1953		2008	2040	2040	2052		2108	2108	2108
Mainz Hbf 911 .... a.						1918		2011					2046					2141		
Koblenz Hbf 911 .... a.								2011										2141		
Köln Hbf 800 910 .... a.							2005	2105		2043d			2105					2243		2359
Dortmund Hbf 800 .... a.							2121	2221q					2221					2359		
Hannover Hbf 810 900 .... a.	2156v	2119								2217v			0018			2318		2341	0002	0126
Berlin Hbf 810 902 .... a.				2330									0035							
Hamburg Hbf 800 900 .... a.	2328w	2243								2351v			0044					0111	0136	

◆ – NOTES (LISTED BY TRAIN NUMBER)

▲04 – ▭ and ⓨ Basel - Köln - Amsterdam.
▲12 – ▭ and ✗ Klagenfurt - Villach - Salzburg - Frankfurt; ▭ Zagreb (212) - Ljubljana - Villach (112) - Frankfurt.
▲14 – WÖRTHERSEE – ▭ and ⓨ Klagenfurt - Villach - Salzburg - München - Dortmund.
▲18 – ▭ Innsbruck - Bregenz - Lindau - Ulm - Stuttgart - Münster.
218 – ▭ and ⓨ Graz - Selzthal - Bischofshofen - Salzburg - München - Frankfurt. Starts from München from Apr. 14.
▲537 – ⓒ (not June 5). ▭ and ✗ Stuttgart - Frankfurt - Erfurt - Berlin. Departs Stuttgart 0911 on certain dates. Berlin arrival time may vary. Runs as ICE 1637 and terminates at Frankfurt Feb. 11 - May 21.
▲004 – ⑦ (also Apr. 17, May 1, 25, 26, June 5; not Apr. 16, 30, June 4). ▭ and ⓨ Konstanz - Karlsruhe - Münster - Emden.
▲006 – ▭ and ⓨ Konstanz - Karlsruhe - Dortmund.
▲010 – Ⓐ (not Dec. 27–30, May 26). ▭ and ⓨ Tübingen Hbf (d. 0611) - Stuttgart - Düsseldorf (- Berlin ⑤f).
▲012 – ALLGÄU – ▭ and ⓨ Oberstdorf - Ulm - Stuttgart - Dortmund - Hannover.
▲014 – ▭ and ⓨ Stuttgart - Münster - Emden.
▲018 – ⑥ from Apr. 8. ▭ Stuttgart - Münster - Emden - Norddeich Mole.
▲216 – ▭ and ⓨ Stuttgart - Hamburg - Rostock - Stralsund (- Greifswald Ⓐu).
▲261 – ▭ and ⓨ Basel - Stuttgart - München.
▲274 – ▭ and ⓨ Karlsruhe - Frankfurt - Kassel (- Hannover ⑤⑦v) (- Hamburg ⑦w).
▲318 – ▭ and ⓨ Köln (- Dortmund Ⓑq) (- Münster ⑦w).
▲370 – ▭ and ⓨ Karlsruhe - Frankfurt - Hamburg. On ⑦w runs with train number 2270 and continues to Stralsund (Table 830).
▲374 – WATTENMEER – ▭ and ⓨ Karlsruhe - Frankfurt - Hamburg (- Westerland ♠).
▲583 – ▭ and ⓨ Marseille - Lyon - Mulhouse - Strasbourg - Frankfurt.

Ⓐ – To Stralsund (Table 830).
) – ▭ Paris - Strasbourg - Frankfurt.
E – To Essen (Table 800).
S – From Salzburg (Table 890).
C – From Chur (Table 520).
K – To Kiel (Table 820).
H – From Interlaken via Bern (Table 560).
~ – ▭ Paris - Strasbourg - Stuttgart (Table 32).
" – Runs as TGV 9593 on ⑥ (also Apr. 16, 30, June 4). ICE conveys ✗, TGV conveys ⓨ.
⊗ – ▭ and ⓨ Paris - Strasbourg - München.

a – ①–⑤ (not Apr. 14, 17, May 1, June 5).
b – Not Dec. 25–30, ⑦ Feb. 12 - Apr. 2, Apr. 14, 16, 17, 30, June 4.
c – Also Apr. 14, 16, 30, May 25, 26, June 4.
d – Köln Messe/Deutz.
e – Not Apr. 15, 17, May 1, June 5.
f – ⑤③, May 24; not Apr. 14, May 26.
g – ① (also Apr. 18, May 2, June 6; not Apr. 17, May 1, June 5).
h – ⑥ (also Apr. 14, 16, 30, June 4).
j – Also Dec. 25–30, ⑦ Feb. 12 - Apr. 2, Apr. 14, 16, 17, 30, June 4.
m – Also Apr. 13, 17, May 1, 24, 25, June 5.
n – Not Apr. 17, May 1, 5.
o – Not Jan. 6.
q – Not Apr. 14, 16, 30, June 4.
r – ①–④ (not Apr. 13, 17, May 1, 24, 25, June 5).
s – Not Apr. 17, May 5.
t – Also Apr. 13, 17, May 1, 24, June 5.
u – Not May 26.
v – ⑤⑦ (also Apr. 13, 17, May 1, 24, June 5; not Apr. 14, 16, 30, May 26, June 4).
w – Not Apr. 17, May 1, June 5; not Apr. 16, 30, June 4.
x – Not Mar. 11 - Apr. 23.
y – ①②③④⑥ (also Apr. 14, May 26; not Apr. 13, 15, 17, May 1, 24, June 5).
z – Not Apr. 15, 17, May 1, June 5.

● – ①–⑥ (also Apr. 16, 30, June 4; not Apr. 17, May 1, June 5).
◇ – Not Apr. 14, 16, 30, May 25, 26, June 4.
☉ – Not Apr. 16, 30, June 4.
⊗ – Not Apr. 16, 30, June 4.
♠ – ④–⑦ to Apr. 2; daily from Apr. 6.
! – Ⓐ (not May 26). 0542 from Mar. 30.
‡ – Frankfurt (Main) Süd.
§ – On ⓒ depart Basel SBB 2 minutes earlier and change trains at Basel Bad Bf.
♥ – From Dec. 14. Operated by Locomore. Special fares payable (DB tickets not valid).
⊠ – Certain Frankfurt timings (mainly trains to Hamburg or Berlin via Fulda) are subject to alteration on ⑥⑦ Feb. 11 - Apr. 2 (also Apr. 14–17). Berlin timings are subject to alteration from May 13. See engineering work panel on page 367.
☆ – See panel on page 428 for other local services.
Ⓞ – Operated by Südwestdeutsche Verkehrs. German holiday dates apply.
▯ – Frankfurt Flughafen Fernbahnhof.

GERMANY *See page 367 for a summary of Christmas / New Year alterations*

912 BASEL and STUTTGART - FRANKFURT

SEE NOTE ⊠	ICE 512	IC 2210	IC 2210	EC 216	IC 1976	ICE 978		TGV 9579	ICE 100	ICE 590		ICE 4	ICE 1110	ICE 510	ICE 976	ICE 990	ICE 990	RJ 1066			EN 470				IC 208
		①–④	⑤⑦		①–⑥	⑦w		H					⑦w		①–⑤	A	⑦z	⑤⑥			Ⓡ			△	
	M🍷	b🍷	c🍷	🍷♦	h	✕	◐2	Ⓡ🍷	🍷	✕♦	◐2	✕	🍷	🍷♦	a✕	✕	✕	✕♦		◐2	♦		◐2	◐2	K
Zürich HB **510** d.	...	...	...	...	...	...	...	...	...	...	...	1900	...	...	...	...	...	...	...	...	2000	...	...	...	...
Basel SBB ☆ d.	...	...	...	...	...	...	...	...	1913	...	...	2013	...	...	...	...	...	...	...	...	2113	...	...	...	2313
Basel Bad Bf 🚊 ☆ d.	...	...	...	...	...	...	...	...	1923	...	...	2023	...	...	...	...	...	...	...	...	2122	...	...	...	2323
Freiburg (Brsg) Hbf ☆ d.	...	...	...	...	...	...	...	...	1956	...	...	2055	...	...	...	...	...	...	...	...	2158	...	...	...	0005
Strasbourg d.	...	...	...	...	...	...	1922	1946	|	...	2022	|	...	...	...	...	...	...	...	2152	|	...	2252	0005	|
Kehl 🚊 d.	...	...	...	...	...	...	1934	|	|	...	2034	|	...	...	...	...	...	...	...	2204	|	...	2304	0016	|
Offenburg **916** ☆ d.	...	...	...	...	...	...	1952	|	2028	...	2052	2127	...	...	...	...	...	...	...	2222	2230	...	2322	0034	0044
Baden-Baden **916** d.	...	...	...	...	...	...	...	|	2044	...	...	2143	...	...	...	...	...	...	...	...	|	...	...	...	0108
Karlsruhe Hbf **913 916** d.	...	...	...	...	...	...	...	2028	2101	...	...	2201	...	...	...	...	...	...	...	...	2304	...	...	...	0130
München Hbf **930** d.	1727	...	...	1747	...	...	...	|	|	1828	...	|	1928	1928	...	2044	2044	2044	...	...	|	...	...	...	|
Stuttgart Hbf **931** d.	1951	1918	1937	2004	2009	2009	...	2104	|	2051	...	|	2151	2151	2155	2305	2305	2305	...	...	|	...	...	...	|
Vaihingen (Enz) **931** d.	|	|	1954	|	|	|	...	...	|	|	...	|	|	|	|	|	|	|	...	...	|	...	...	...	|
Bruchsal **913 931** d.	|	|	|	|	|	|	...	...	|	|	...	|	|	|	|	|	|	|	...	...	|	...	...	...	0143
Heidelberg Hbf **913 931** d.	|	2025t	2025x	|	2054	2054	...	...	|	|	...	|	|	|	2248	|	|	|	...	...	2333	...	...	...	0202
Weinheim **913** d.	|	|	|	|	2109	2109	...	...	|	|	...	|	|	|	2303	|	|	|	...	...	|	...	...	...	|
Bensheim **913** d.	|	|	|	|	2119	2119	...	...	|	|	...	|	|	|	2313	|	|	|	...	...	|	...	...	...	|
Darmstadt Hbf **913** d.	|	|	|	|	2133	2133	...	...	|	|	...	|	|	|	2327	|	|	|	...	...	|	...	...	...	|
Mannheim Hbf **913** a.	2028	2037	2037	2048	|	|	...	...	2124	2129	...	2224	2229	2229	|	2345	2345	2345	...	...	2346	...	...	...	0214
Mannheim Hbf **913** d.	2036	2039	2039	...	|	|	...	...	2136	2132	...	2233	2237	2237	|	2351	2351	2351	...	...	2359	...	...	...	0216
Frankfurt Flughafen ✈ ◧ a.	2106	|	|	...	|	|	...	...	2206	|	...	|	2308	2308	|	0023	0023	0023	...	...	|	...	...	...	0354
Frankfurt (Main) Hbf **913** a.	|	|	|	...	2152	2152	...	...	|	2208	...	2313j	|	|	2343	0042	0042	0042	...	...	0051r	...	...	...	0302
Mainz Hbf **911** a.	|	2118	2118	...	...	...	...	...	|	|	...	...	|	2330	...	...	|	...	...	...	|	...	...	...	0415
Koblenz Hbf **911** a.	|	2211	2211	...	...	...	...	...	|	|	...	...	|	...	...	...	|	...	...	...	|	...	...	...	0511
Köln Hbf **800 910** a.	2205	2305	2305	...	...	...	...	...	2307	|	...	...	0007	...	...	...	|	...	...	...	|	...	...	...	0605
Dortmund Hbf **800** a.	...	...	...	...	...	...	...	...	0031	|	...	...	...	...	...	...	|	...	...	...	|	...	...	...	0721
Hannover Hbf **810 900** a.	...	...	...	...	...	...	...	...	...	0146	...	...	...	...	...	...	0421	...	...	...	|	...	...	...	|
Berlin Hbf **810 902** a.	...	...	...	...	...	...	...	...	...	|	...	...	...	...	...	...	|	...	...	...	0606	...	...	...	|
Hamburg Hbf **800 900** a.	...	...	...	...	...	...	...	...	...	0308	...	...	...	...	...	...	0549	...	...	...	0831	...	...	...	1013

♦ – **NOTES** (LISTED BY TRAIN NUMBER)

216 – [12] and 🍷 Graz - Selzthal - Bischofshofen - Salzburg - München - Saarbrücken. Starts from München from Apr. 14.

470 – *ÖBB nightjet.* 🛏 1, 2 cl., couchette 2 cl. and [2] Zürich - Basel - Berlin - Hamburg. Arrives Berlin 0633, Hamburg 0849 Feb. 11 - Apr. 17. Arrives Berlin 0608 from Apr. 18.

510 – [12] and 🍷 München - Wiesbaden Hbf (a. 2344). Train number **1010** on ⑤⑥ (also Apr. 13, 16, 30, June 4), **1190** on ⑦ (also Apr. 17, May 1, June 5; not Apr. 16, 30, June 4). Also conveys ✕ on ①–④ (not Apr. 13, 17, May 1, June 5).

590 – [12] and ✕ München - Frankfurt (- Kassel ⑤⑦ v) (- Hannover - Hamburg ⑦ w). Train number **698** on ⑤ (also Apr. 13, May 24; not Apr. 14, May 26), **992** on ⑦ (also Apr. 17, May 1, June 5; not Apr. 16, 30, June 4).

1066 – ⑤⑥ (also Apr. 13, 16, 30, May 24, June 4). [12] and ✕ Budapest - Wien - Salzburg - Frankfurt.

A – ①②③④⑦ (not Apr. 13, 16, 30, May 24, June 4). Train number **1590** on ④ (also Apr. 12, May 23).
H – [12] and 🍷 Paris - Strasbourg - Stuttgart (- München ⑥, also Apr. 16, 30, June 4).
K – To Kiel (Table **820**).
M – To Münster (Table **800**).

a – Not Apr. 14, 17, May 1, June 5.
b – Not Mar. 13 - Apr. 20.
c – Also ①–④ Mar. 13 - Apr. 20; not Apr. 14, 16, 30, June 4.
h – Also Apr. 30, June 4; not Apr. 15, 17, May 1, 26, June 5. Conveys 🍷 on ⑥
j – 2318 on ⑤–⑦ Feb. 10 - Apr. 16 (also Apr. 13, 17; not Apr. 7, 8, 9).
r – Frankfurt (Main) **Süd**.
t – Arrives 2002.
v – Also Apr. 13, 17, May 1, 24 June 5; not Apr. 14, 16, 30, May 26, June 4.
w – Also Apr. 17, May 1, June 5; not Apr. 16, 30, June 4.
x – Not Mar. 12 - Apr. 23.
z – Also May 1, June 5; not Apr. 16, 30, June 4.

⊠ – Certain Frankfurt timings (mainly trains to Hamburg or Berlin via Fulda) are subject to alteration on ⑥⑦ Feb. 11 - Apr. 2 (also Apr. 14–17). Berlin timings are subject to alteration from May 13. See engineering work panel on page 367.
△ – Not the mornings of Feb. 22–25, Apr. 19–22.
☆ – See panel on page 428 for other local services.
◐ – Operated by Südwestdeutsche Verkehrs-AG.
◧ – Frankfurt Flughafen Fernbahnhof.

913 Local trains FRANKFURT - HEIDELBERG - KARLSRUHE

RE / RB / S-Bahn services

See Table **912** for *ICE / IC* services.

FRANKFURT - DARMSTADT - HEIDELBERG and MANNHEIM

	Ⓐ	Ⓐ		Ⓒ	Ⓐ	⑦	①–⑥		Ⓐ	⑦	①–⑥				Ⓐ		Ⓐ		Ⓒ	Ⓐ				
Frankfurt (Main) Hbf d.	...	0506	0606	...	0633	0706	0706	0806	0834	0906	0906	1006		1706	1734	1806	1833	1906	2006	2034	2106	2206	2312	0006
Darmstadt Hbf d.	0426	0530	0630	...	0653	0730	0734	0830	0853	0930	0930	1030	and	1730	1757	1830	1853	1930	2030	2054	2130	2230	2332	0030
Bensheim d.	0452	0557	0655	...	0709	0755	0757	0859	0909	0955	0959	1059	hourly	1759	1825	1859j	1909	1959	2059	2109	2155	2255	2355	0055
Weinheim (Bergstr) d.	0508	0612	0710	...	0722	0811	0811	0914	0922	1010	1014	1114	until	1814	1842	1914	1922	2017	2117	2122	2210	2310	0010	0110
Mannheim Friedrichsfeld a.	0521	0625	0723	0732	0732	0824	0824	0927	|	1023	1027	1127		1827	1856	1927	|	2031	2130	2131	2223	2323	0023	0123
Mannheim Hbf a.	0545	0644r	|	0743	0745	0842	0842	0942	0940	1042	1042	1142		1842	1910	1942	1940	2042	2143	2143	2242	2343	|	0138
Heidelberg Hbf a.	0532	0635	0736	...	...	0835	0834	0939	...	1037	1039	1139		1838	...	1939	...	2040	2141	2142	2237	2334	0035	...

	Ⓐ		Ⓐ		Ⓐ	Ⓒ	Ⓐ		Ⓐ						Ⓐ			Ⓐ						
Heidelberg Hbf d.	0422	0524	...	0625	...	...	...	0724	...	0821	0921		1421	1523	...	1621	1724	...	1821	1921	2021	2124	2221	2324
Mannheim Hbf d.	|	0515	0607	0612	0651	0716	0720	|	0820	0816	0916	and	1416	1516	1620	1616	1716	1820	1816	1916	2016	2116	2216	2316
Mannheim Friedrichsfeld d.	0432	0533	|	0635	0706	0726	0731	0734	|	0831	0932	hourly	1432	1532	|	1632	1734	|	1832	1932	2032	2134	2232	2334
Weinheim (Bergstr) d.	0446	0548	0626	0648	0719	...	...	0746	0839	0845	0945	until	1446	1545	1639	1645	1746	1839	1845	1945	2045	2149	2245	2349
Bensheim d.	0506	0603	0642	0703	0733	...	...	0800	0851	0900	1000		1500	1600	1652	1700	1800	1852	1900	2000	2100	2204	2300	0003
Darmstadt Hbf d.	0530	0630	0658	0730	0758	...	...	0830	0906	0930	1030		1530	1630	1706	1730	1830	1906	1930	2030	2130	2230	2330	0030
Frankfurt (Main) Hbf a.	0548	0648	0716	0748	0816	...	...	0848	0924	0948	1048		1548	1648	1724	1748	1848	1924	1948	2048	2148	2248	2348	0048

FRANKFURT - BIBLIS - WORMS and MANNHEIM

	⚒	⚒			⚒				⚒					Ⓐ				Ⓐ				Ⓐ		
Frankfurt (Main) Hbf d.	0607	...	0710	...	0807	...	0913	...	1010	...	and in the same	1713	...	1810	...	1913	...	2010	...	2113	...	2210	...	2314
Biblis d.	0656	0658	0758	0804	0858	0904	0958	1004	1058	1104	pattern every	1758	1804	1858	1904	1958	2004	2058	2104	2158	2204	2258	2304	2358
Worms Hbf a.	|	0708	|	0814	|	0914	|	1014	|	1114	**two** hours until	|	1814	|	1913	|	2014	|	2114	|	2214	|	2314	|
Mannheim Hbf a.	0719	...	0819	...	0919	...	1019	...	1119	...		1819	...	1919	...	2019	...	2119	...	2219	...	2319	...	0019

km				Ⓐ		⚒	⚒	⊖			⚒					Ⓐ				Ⓐ				Ⓐ
	Mannheim Hbf d.	0013	...	...	0532	...	0639	...	0739	...	0839	...	0939	and in the same	...	1839	...	1939	...	2039	...	2139	...	2240
0	**Worms** Hbf d.	|	...	0540	|	0640	|	0743	|	0843	|	0943	|	pattern every	1843	|	1943	|	2043	|	2143	|	2243	|
10	Biblis d.	0038	...	0550	0559	0650	0659	0753	0759	0853	0859	0953	0959	**two** hours until	1853	1859	1953	1959	2053	2059	2153	2159	2253	2302
63	**Frankfurt** (Main) Hbf a.	0134	...	...	0645	...	0747	...	0845	...	0947	...	1045		...	1947	...	2045	...	2147	...	2245	...	2349

MANNHEIM - HEIDELBERG - KARLSRUHE

S-Bahn					Ⓐt	Ⓒz	Ⓐt										Ⓒz	Ⓐt								
Mannheim Hbf ⊡ d.	0040	...	0457	0535	0615	0630	0646	0730	0830	0930	1030	1130	1230	1330	1430	1530	1630	1630	1730	1759	1830	1930	2030	2137	2237	2340
Heidelberg Hbf ⊡ d.	0057	...	0516	0559	0633	0706	0706	0748	0848	0948	1048	1148	1248	1348	1448	1548	1648	1648	1748	1818	1848	1948	2057f	2155	2255	2358
Bruchsal d.	0129	...	0548	0626	0700	0732	0733	0817	0915	1015	1115	1215	1315	1415	1515	1615	1715	1716	1815	1844	1915	2015	2123	2223	2333f	0032
Karlsruhe Hbf a.	0148	...	0604	0644	0718	0752	0750	0833	0936	1032	1132	1232	1332	1431	1536	1632	1732	1736	1832	1900	1932	2032	2137	2237	2351	0053

S-Bahn				Ⓐt	Ⓐt	Ⓒz	Ⓒz	Ⓐt		Ⓐt																
Karlsruhe Hbf d.	0013	...	0328	0419	0516	0520	0610	0620	0725v	0755	0828	0928	1028	1128	1228	1328	1428	1528	1628	1728	1828	1928	2028	2128	2228	2328
Bruchsal d.	0027	...	0345	0437	0534	0538	0629	0638	0744	0814	0844	0944	1044	1144	1244	1344	1444	1544	1644	1744	1844	1944	2044	2144	2244	2344
Heidelberg Hbf ⊡ d.	0055	...	0413	0505	0602	0608	0700	0709	0813	0843	0913	1013	1113	1213	1313	1413	1513	1613	1713	1813	1913	2013	2114	2214	2314	0014
Mannheim Hbf ⊡ a.	0115	...	0429	0522	0621	0625	0753	0726	0829	0901	0929	1029	1129	1229	1329	1429	1529	1629	1729	1829	1929	2029	2130	2230	2330	0030

f – Arrives 10–12 minutes earlier.
j – 1855 on ⑥.
r – *0648* on ⑥ (also Jan. 6).
t – Not Jan. 6.
v – 0728 on Ⓐ (not Jan. 6).
z – Also Jan. 6.
⊖ – Runs 2 minutes later on Ⓐ.
⊡ – See also Tables **918**, **919**, **923** and **924**.

430 *German national public holidays are on Dec. 25, 26, Jan. 1, Apr. 14, 17, May 1, 25, June 5 and Oct. 3* 12

Local trains KOBLENZ - WIESBADEN - FRANKFURT and KOBLENZ - MAINZ - FRANKFURT 914

Neuwied - Koblenz - St Goarshausen - Wiesbaden - Frankfurt *(Rechte Rheinstrecke)* ❖

km		Ⓐ	⚒	Ⓐ								Ⓐ		Ⓐ								Ⓒ	Ⓐ	Ⓒ	Ⓐ	
0	**Neuwied** .... **802** d.	0437	...	0537	...	0637z	0737	0837	0937	1037	1137	...	1237	...	1337	1437	1537	1637	1737	1837	1937	2037	2037	2137	2137	2237
15	**Koblenz** Hbf .**802 906** d.	0453	...	0553	...	0653	0753	0853	0953	1053	1153	1223	1253	1323	1353	1453	1553	1653	1753	1853	1953	2053	2053	2153	2153	2253
20	Niederlahnstein .. **906** d.	0459	...	0559	...	0659	0759	0859	0959	1059	1159	1229	1259	1329	1359	1459	1559	1659	1759	1859	1959	2059	2059	2159	2159	2259
26	Braubach .... d.	0506	...	0606	...	0706	0806	0906	1006	1106	1206	1236	1306	1336	1406	1506	1606	1706	1806	1906	2006	2106	2106	2206	2206	2306
38	Kamp-Bornhofen .... d.	0516	...	0616	...	0716	0816	0916	1016	1116	1216	1246	1316	1346	1416	1516	1616	1716	1816	1916	2016	2116	2116	2216	2216	2316
50	St Goarshausen .... d.	0526	...	0626	...	0726	0826	0926	1026	1126	1226	1256	1326	1356	1426	1526	1626	1726	1826	1926	2026	2126	2126	2226	2226	2326
61	Kaub .... d.	0536	...	0636	0636	0736	0836	0936	1036	1136	1236	1306	1336	1406	1436	1536	1636	1736	1836	1936	2036	2136	2136	2236	2236	2335
67	Lorch (Rhein) .... d.	0542	...	0642	0642	0742	0842	0942	1042	1142	1242	1312	1342	1412	1442	1542	1642	1742	1842	1942	2042	2142	2142	2242	2242	...
79	Rüdesheim (Rhein) .... d.	0553	0553	0653	0653	0753	0853	0953	1053	1153	1253	1323	1353	1423	1453	1553	1653	1753	1853	1953	2053	2153	2153	2253	2253	...
109	**Wiesbaden** Hbf .... a.	0625	0625	0725	0725	0825	0925	1025	1125	1225	1325	1355	1425	1455	1525	1625	1725	1825	1925	2025	2125	2225	2225	2325	2325	...
109	**Wiesbaden** Hbf .... d.	0632	...	0732	0732	0832	0932	1032	1132	1232	1332	...	1432	...	1532	1632	1732	1832	1932	2032	2132	2232	*2235*	2332	*2335*	...
150	**Frankfurt** (Main) Hbf .. a.	0705	...	0805	0805	0905	1005	1105	1205	1305	1405	...	1505	...	1605	1705	1805	1905	2005	2105	2205	2305	*2318*	0005	*0018*	...

	Ⓐ	Ⓐ		⚒										Ⓐ		Ⓐ		Ⓐ		Ⓐ					Ⓐ	Ⓒ
Frankfurt (Main) Hbf .. d.	...	...	...	0553e	0653	0753	0853	0953	1053	1153	1253	1353	1453	1523	1553	1622	1653	1723	1753	1823	1853	1953	2053	2153	...	2253
Wiesbaden Hbf .... a.	...	...	...	0628e	0728	0828	0928	1028	1128	1228	1328	1428	1528	1558	1628	1658	1728	1758	1828	1858	1928	2028	2128	2228	...	2328
Wiesbaden Hbf .... d.	...	...	0533e	0633	0733	0833	0933	1033	1133	1233	1333	1433	1533	1603	1633	1703	1733	1803	1833	1903	1933	2033	2133	2233	2333	2333
Rüdesheim (Rhein) ..... d.	...	0532	0606e	0706	0806	0906	1006	1106	1206	1306	1406	1506	1606	1636	1706	1736	1806	1836	1906	1936	2006	2106	2206	2306	0004	0004
Lorch (Rhein) .... d.	...	0541	0615e	0715	0815	0915	1015	1115	1215	1315	1415	1515	1615	1645	1715	1745	1815	1845	1915	1945	2015	2115	2215	2315	...	...
Kaub .... d.	0450	0550	0623	0723	0823	0923	1023	1123	1223	1323	1423	1523	1623	1653	1724	1753	1823	1854	1924	1954	2023	2123	2223	2323	...	...
St Goarshausen .... d.	0459	0559	0632	0732	0832	0932	1032	1132	1232	1332	1432	1532	1632	1702	1732	1802	1832	1902	1932	2002	2032	2132	2232	...	...	...
Kamp-Bornhofen .... d.	0510	0610	0643	0743	0843	0943	1043	1143	1243	1343	1443	1543	1643	1713	1743	1813	1843	1913	1943	2013	2043	2143	2243	...	...	...
Braubach .... d.	0521	0621	0654	0754	0854	0954	1054	1154	1254	1354	1454	1554	1654	1724	1754	1824	1854	1924	1954	2024	2054	2154	2254	...	...	...
Niederlahnstein .... **906** d.	0527	0627	0700	0800	0900	1000	1100	1200	1300	1400	1500	1600	1700	1730	1800	1830	1900	1930	2000	2030	2100	2200	2300	...	...	...
Koblenz Hbf. **802 906** a.	0533	0633	0706	0806	0906	1006	1106	1206	1306	1406	1506	1606	1706	1736	1806	1836	1906	1937	2006	2037	2106	2206	2306	...	...	...
Neuwied .... **802** a.	0556	...	0726	0826	0926	1026	1126	1226	1326	1426	1526	1626	1726	...	1826	...	1926	...	2026	...	2126	2226	2326	...	...	...

Koblenz - Bingen - Mainz - Frankfurt *(Linke Rheinstrecke)* ⊠

km			Ⓐ	Ⓐ										Ⓐ		⚒		⚒						
0	**Koblenz** Hbf .... d.	0507	0606	0617	0707	0904	1104	1304	1504	1704	1904	2104		0452	...	0552	...	0652	0730		1930	2030	2152	2252
19	Boppard Hbf .... d.	0519	0620	0632	0719	0916	1116	1316	1516	1716	1916	2116		0507	...	0607	...	0707	0744		1944	2044	2207	2307
24	Boppard-Bad Salzig .. d.	│	│	0636	│	│	│	│	│	│	│	│	Other	0511	...	0611	...	0711	0748		1948	2048	2211	2311
34	St Goar .... d.	│	│	0645	│	│	│	│	│	│	│	│		0519	...	0619	...	0719	0756	and	1956	2056	2219	2319
41	Oberwesel .... d.	0533	0635	0651	0733	0930	1130	1330	1530	1730	1930	2130	Stopping	0525	...	0625	...	0725	0801		2001	2101	2225	2325
47	Bacharach .... d.	0537	│	0656	0737	0936	1136	1336	1536	1736	1936	2136		0529	...	0629	...	0729	0806	hourly	2006	2106	2229	2329
61	Bingen (Rhein) Hbf ..... a.	0546	0647	0709	0746	0946	1146	1346	1546	1746	1946	2146	services	0543	...	0643	...	0743	0819		2019	2119	2243	2345
61	Bingen (Rhein) Hbf ..... d.	0547	0648	0713	0747	0947	1147	1347	1547	1747	1947	2147		0552	0552	0654	0654	0754	0824	until	2024	2127	2254	...
62	Bingen (Rhein) Stadt .. d.	│	│	0716	│	│	│	│	│	│	│	│	→	0555	0555	0657	0657	0757	0827		2027	2129	2257	...
73	Ingelheim .... d.	0556	0656	0722	0755	0955	1155	1355	1555	1755	1955	2155		0605	0605	0707	0707	0807	0837		2037	2139	2307	...
91	**Mainz** Hbf .... a.	0608	0708	0736	0808	1008	1208	1408	1608	1808	2008	2208	⊡	0624	0624	0725	0725	0825	0855		2055	2156	2325	...
119	Frankfurt Flughafen ◧ a.	0634	0734	0805	0835	1035	1235	1435	1635	1834	2034	2236		...	...	...	...	...	...		...	...	...	...
130	**Frankfurt** (Main) Hbf .. a.	0647	0751	0822	0849	1049	1249	1449	1648	1851	2051	2249		...	...	...	...	...	...		...	...	...	...

	Ⓐ						Ⓐ		Ⓐ					Ⓐ	Ⓒ	Ⓐ							⑤⑥d	
Frankfurt (Main) Hbf .. d.	0508	0706	0908	1108	1308	1508	1608	1708	1808	1908	2108	2308		...	...	...	...	...		...	...	...	...	...
Frankfurt Flughafen ◧ d.	0521	0721	0924	1123	1323	1524	1623	1724	1823	1923	2123	2323		...	...	...	...	...		...	...	...	...	...
Mainz Hbf .... d.	0544	0751	0951	1151	1351	1551	1651	1751	1851	1951	2151	2351	Other	0532	0538	0625	0701	0803		2103	2203	2303	2303	0008
Ingelheim .... d.	0556	0802	1002	1202	1402	1602	1703	1802	1903	2002	2202	0002		0550	0556	0643	0719	0821	and	2121	2221	2320	2320	0026
Bingen (Rhein) Stadt ... d.	│	│	│	│	│	│	│	│	│	│	│	│	Stopping	0600	0606	0653	0735	0831		2131	2231	2328	2328	0036
Bingen (Rhein) Hbf ..... a.	0606	0811	1011	1211	1411	1611	1714	1811	1911	2011	2211	0011		0604	0609	0657	0738	0834	hourly	2134	2234	2331	2331	0040
Bingen (Rhein) Hbf ..... d.	0607	0813	1013	1213	1413	1613	1717	1813	1912	2013	2216	0022	services	0610	0626	0700	0739	0839		2139	...	...	2332	...
Bacharach .... d.	0615	0821	1021	1221	1421	1621	1730	1821	1921	2021	2228	0034		0622	0638	0712	0750	0850	until	2150	...	...	2344	...
Oberwesel .... d.	0620	0826	1026	1226	1426	1626	1735	1826	1926	2026	2232	0038	→	0626	0649	0716	0754	0854		2154	...	...	2348	...
St Goar .... d.	│	│	│	│	│	│	1741	│	│	│	2238	0044		0632	0656	0722	0800	0900		2200	...	...	2354	...
Boppard-Bad Salzig ... d.	│	│	│	│	│	│	1748	│	│	│	2247	0053	⊡	0640	0704	0730	0808	0908		2208	...	...	0002	...
Boppard Hbf .... d.	0635	0840	1040	1240	1440	1640	1752	1840	1941	2040	2251	0057		0644	0708	0734	0812	0912		2212	...	...	0006	...
Koblenz Hbf .... a.	0651	0854	1054	1254	1454	1654	1809	1854	1957	2054	2309	0115		0702	0725	0751	0827	0927		2227	...	...	0023	...

– Also Apr. 13, 16, 30, May 24, June 4.
– Ⓐ only.
– Ⓒ only.

◧ – Frankfurt Flughafen Regionalbahnhof ✈.
❖ – Operated by VIAS GmbH.
⊡ – Stopping services are operated by Mittelrheinbahn.

⊠ – See Table **911** for long-distance *ICE* | *IC* services. See Table **917a** for S-Bahn service Mainz - Frankfurt Flughafen ✈ - Frankfurt (Main) Hbf and v.v.

Köln Düsseldorfer Deutsche Rheinschiffahrt — KÖLN - KOBLENZ - MAINZ — *2016 service* — 914a

◐		A	A ⛴	K◇	D	C	E⊠	F⊠	Q	R	H
750	**Köln** (Rheingarten) ...... d.	...	...	...	...	...	...	...	0930	0930	...
1600	**Bonn** .... d.	...	...	...	...	...	0730	0730	1230	1230	...
1300	Bad Godesberg .... d.	...	...	...	...	...	0800	0800	1300	1300	...
900	Königswinter Fähre ...... d.	...	...	...	...	...	0815	0815	1330	1330	...
750	Bad Honnef (Rhein) ...... d.	...	...	...	...	...	0835	0835	1350	1350	...
400	Remagen .... d.	...	...	...	...	...	0910	0910	1420	1420	...
750	Linz am Rhein .... d.	...	...	...	...	...	0930	0930	1450	1450	...
1500	Bad Breisig .... d.	...	...	...	...	...	1000	1000	▬	1520	...
400	Bad Hönningen .... d.	...	...	...	...	...	1005	1005	...	1525	...
1200	Andernach .... d.	...	...	...	...	...	1050	1050	A	...	...
2200	**Koblenz** ⊙ .... d.	...	0900	0945	...	...	1300	1300	1400	...	1810
600	Winningen (Mosel) ... a.	...	│	1055	...	...	1430	│	│	...	│
800	Cochem (Mosel) .... a.	...	│	1500	...	...	...	│	│	...	│
150	Oberlahnstein .... d.	...	0940	...	...	...	...	│	1440	...	1845
450	Braubach .... d.	...	1005	...	...	...	...	1345	1505	...	1910
400	**Boppard** .... d.	0900	1100	...	1300	1400	...	1430	1600	...	2000
400	Kamp-Bornhofen .... d.	0910	1110	...	1310	1410	...	...	1610	...	...
300	Bad Salzig .... d.	0925	1125	...	1325	1425	...	...	1625	...	...
450	**St Goarshausen** ... ★ d.	1010	1210	...	1410	1510	...	...	1710	...	...
250	**St Goar** .... ★ d.	1020	1220	...	1420	1520	...	...	1720	...	...
450	Oberwesel .... d.	1050	1250	...	1450	1550	...	...	1750	...	...
900	Kaub .... d.	1105	1305	...	1505	1605	...	...	1805	...	...
600	Bacharach .... d.	1130	1330	...	1530	1630	...	...	1830	...	...
900	Assmannshausen .... d.	1230	1430	...	1630	1730	...	...	1930	...	...
400	**Bingen** (Rhein) ...... ♥ d.	1300	1500	...	1700	1800	...	...	2000	...	...
900	**Rüdesheim** (Rhein) ♥ d.	1315	1515	...	1715	1815	...	...	2015	...	...
1500	Wiesbaden-Biebrich .... d.	...	...	...	1900	2000t	...	...	...	...	...
1600	**Mainz** .... a.	...	...	...	1930	2030t	...	...	...	...	...

	L	R	A	D	C	F⊠	A	H	K◇	A ⛴
Mainz .... d.	...	...	...	0830	0930v	...	...	...	...	...
Wiesbaden-Biebrich . d.	...	...	...	0845	0945v	...	...	...	...	...
Rüdesheim .... ♥ d.	...	...	0915	1015	1115	...	1415	1415	...	1615
Bingen (Rhein) ... ♥ d.	...	...	0930	1030	1130	...	1430	1430	...	1630
Assmannshausen ..... d.	...	...	0945	1045	1145	...	1445	1445	...	1645
Bacharach .... d.	...	...	1015	1115	1215	...	1515	1515	...	1715
Kaub .... d.	...	...	1025	1125	1225	...	1525	1525	...	1725
Oberwesel .... d.	...	...	1035	1135	1235	...	1535	1535	...	1735
St Goar .... ★ d.	...	...	1055	1155	1255	...	1555	1555	...	1755
St Goarshausen ★ d.	...	...	1105	1205	1305	...	1605	1605	...	1805
Bad Salzig .... d.	...	...	1130	│	│	...	1630	1630	...	1830
Kamp-Bornhofen ...... d.	...	...	1140	1240	1340	...	1640	1640	...	1840
Boppard .... d.	...	...	1150	1250	1350	1600	1650	1650	...	1850
Braubach .... d.	...	...	1220	...	...	1630	▬	1720	...	1920
Oberlahnstein .... d.	...	...	1240	...	...	│	...	1740	...	1940
Cochem (Mosel) .... d.	...	...	│	...	...	│	E⊠	│	1540	│
Winningen (Mosel) d.	...	...	│	...	...	│	1540	│	1845	│
Koblenz ⊙ .... d.	...	...	1310	...	...	1700	1700	1810	2000	2010
Andernach .... d.	...	...	...	...	...	1805s	1805s	...	...	...
Bad Hönningen .... d.	...	1615	...	...	...	1830s	1830s	...	...	...
Bad Breisig .... d.	...	1620	...	...	...	1840s	1840s	...	...	...
Linz am Rhein .... d.	1450	1650	...	...	...	1905s	1905s	...	...	...
Remagen .... d.	1500	1700	...	...	...	1915s	1915s	...	...	...
Bad Honnef (Rhein) .. d.	1525	1725	...	...	...	1940s	1940s	...	...	...
Königswinter Fähre .. d.	1540	1740	...	...	...	2000	2000	...	...	...
Bad Godesberg .... d.	1545	1745	...	...	...	2010	2010	...	...	...
Bonn .... d.	1615	1815	...	...	...	2030	2030	...	...	...
Köln (Rheingarten) ... a.	1800	2000	...	...	..	....	...	...	...	...

– Mar. 25 - Oct. 23.
– Apr. 23 - Oct. 23.
– Apr. 23 - Oct. 3.
– ① July 4 - Aug. 29.
– ③ July 6 - Aug. 31.
– ①⑤⑥⑦ Mar. 25 - Apr. 18; daily Apr. 22 - Oct. 3; ①⑤⑥⑦ Oct. 7 – 23.
– ⑤–⑦ June 10 - Oct. 2.
– ⑤⑥ Apr. 23 - Oct. 1; ⑤–⑦ Oct. 7 – 23.
– Daily Apr. 23 - Oct. 3; ⑤–⑦ Oct. 7 – 23.

R – ①②③④⑦ Apr. 24 - Oct. 3.

s – Sets down only.
t – Daily July 1 - Sept. 4; ④–⑦ Sept. 8 - Oct. 23.
v – Daily July 1 - Aug. 31; ①⑤⑥⑦ Sept. 2 - Oct. 23.

⛴ – Operated by paddlesteamer *Goethe* Apr. 23 - Oct. 3.
⊠ – Operated by Personenschifffahrt Siebengebirge.
◇ – Operated by Personenschifffahrt Gilles.
⊙ – Koblenz (Konrad-Adenauer-Ufer).

◐ – Distance in metres from rail station to river landing stage.
★ – A frequent ferry service operates St Goar - St Goarshausen and v.v. Operator: Rheinschifffahrt Goar. ✆ + 49 (0) 6771 26 20.
♥ – Passenger ferry Bingen - Rüdesheim and v.v. Operator: Bingen-Rüdesheimer Fahrgastschiffahrt. ✆ + 49 (0) 6721 30808 10. Service **May 1 - Oct. 31**: From Bingen at 0700 and hourly until 2100. From Rüdesheim at 0730 and hourly until 2130.

Operator: Köln Düsseldorfer Deutsche Rheinschiffahrt, Frankenwerft 35, D-50667 Köln. ✆ +49 (0) 221 20 88 318, Fax +49 (0) 221 20 88 345. A special service operates on "Rhein in Flammen" days.

915 KOBLENZ - TRIER - LUXEMBOURG and SAARBRÜCKEN

RE services except where shown

Many Saarbrücken services continue to / start from Mannheim (see Table **919**). ***Warning!*** *Services between Koblenz and Trier are subject to alteration May 6 - June 2.*

km			①-⑤ e	⑦ w	①-⑤ a	Ⓒ	①-⑤ a		①-⑤ a		①-⑤ a		①-⑤ e	①-⑤ e		①-⑤ e								
0	**Koblenz** Hbf d.	...	...	...	...	...	...	...	...	...	...	...	0603	0603	...	...	0617	0706	...	0806	0806		1806	1806
47	Cochem (Mosel) d.	...	...	...	...	...	...	...	...	...	...	...	0638	0638	...	...	0715	0741	...	0841	0841	and at	1841	1841
59	Bullay d.	...	...	...	...	...	...	...	...	...	...	...	0648	0648	...	...	0727	0751	...	0851	0851		1851	1851
76	Wittlich Hbf d.	...	...	...	...	...	...	...	0550	...	...	...	0700	0700	...	0705	0742	0803	...	0903	0903	the same	1903	1903
112	**Trier** Hbf a.	...	...	...	...	...	...	...	0627	...	...	...	0731	0731	...	0745	0819	0830	...	0930	0930		1930	1930
112	**Trier** Hbf d.	...	0456	0533	0536	0551	0607	0633	0637	0637	0713	0733	0733	0737	0737	0750	...	0833	0837	0933	0937	minutes	1933	1937
163	**Luxembourg** a.	...	|	|	0629	|	0709	|	0730	0730	0809	|	|	0829	0829	0850	...	|	0929	|	1029		|	2029
135	Saarburg d.	...	0514	0551	...	0618	...	0651	...	...	...	0751	0751	...	...	...	...	0851	...	0951	...	past each	1951	...
161	Merzig (Saar) d.	0435	0534	0610	...	0645	...	0710	...	...	...	0810	0810	...	...	...	...	0910	...	1010	...		2010	...
173	Dillingen (Saar) d.	0446	0543	0619	...	0656	...	0720	...	...	...	0820	0820	...	...	...	...	0920	...	1020	...	hour until	2020	...
177	Saarlouis Hbf d.	0450	0547	0623	...	0659	...	0724	...	...	...	0824	0824	...	...	...	...	0924	...	1024	...		2024	...
190	Völklingen d.	0500	0556	0632	...	0710	...	0732	...	...	...	0832	0832	...	...	...	...	0932	...	1032	...		2032	...
200	**Saarbrücken** Hbf a.	0513	0605	0641	...	0724	...	0741	...	...	...	0841	0841	...	...	...	...	0941	...	1041	...		2041	...

							Ⓐ	Ⓒ	◧	
Koblenz Hbf d.	1906	1906	2006	2006	2106	2106	2206	2206	2206	2318
Cochem (Mosel) d.	1941	1941	2041	2041	2141	2141	2241	2241	2241	2353
Bullay d.	1951	1951	2051	2051	2151	2151	2251	2251	2251	0004
Wittlich Hbf d.	2003	2003	2103	2103	2203	2203	2303	2303	2303	0016
Trier Hbf a.	2030	2030	2130	2130	2230	2230	2330	2330	2330	0042
Trier Hbf d.	2033	2037	2133	2137	2233	2237	2332	2332	2337	...
Luxembourg a.	|	2129	|	2229	|	2329	|	|	0031	...
Saarburg d.	2051	...	2151	...	2251	...	2356	2356	...	...
Merzig (Saar) d.	2110	...	2210	...	2310	...	0020	0022	...	...
Dillingen (Saar) d.	2120	...	2220	...	2320	...	0028	0034	...	...
Saarlouis Hbf d.	2124	...	2224	...	2324	...	0032	0038	...	...
Völklingen d.	2132	...	2232	...	2332	...	0041	0050	...	...
Saarbrücken Hbf a.	2141	...	2241	...	2341	...	0050	0103	...	...

	Ⓐ	Ⓐ	Ⓒ	Ⓐ	Ⓐ	⚒				①-⑤ a
Saarbrücken Hbf d.	...	...	...	...	0458	...	0520	...	0619	...
Völklingen d.	...	...	...	...	0507	...	0531	...	0627	...
Saarlouis Hbf d.	...	...	...	...	0515	...	0541	...	0636	...
Dillingen (Saar) d.	...	...	...	...	0519	...	0545	...	0640	...
Merzig (Saar) d.	...	...	...	...	0528	...	0555	...	0648	...
Saarburg d.	...	...	...	...	0548	...	0622h	...	0708	...
Luxembourg d.	...	...	...	0518	|	...	|	0612	|	0651
Trier Hbf a.	...	...	...	0604	0608	...	0652h	0707	0728	0806
Trier Hbf d.	0412	0512	0527	0612	0612	0627	...	0712	0732	...
Wittlich Hbf d.	0436	0536	0554	0636	0636	0702	...	0736	0756	...
Bullay d.	0449	0549	0607	0649	0649	0718	...	0749	0809	...
Cochem (Mosel) d.	0459	0559	0628j	0659	0659	0729	...	0759	0819	...
Koblenz Hbf a.	0535	0635	0721	0735	0735	0822	...	0835	0855	...

			✣									①-⑤ a									⑤⑥ k	⑤⑥ k			
Saarbrücken Hbf d.	...	0719		...	1519	...	1619	...	1719	...	1819	...	...	1919	...	2019	...	2119	...	...	2222	2222	...	2320
Völklingen d.	...	0727	and at	...	1527	...	1627	...	1727	...	1827	...	...	1927	...	2027	...	2127	...	...	2231	2231	...	2328
Saarlouis Hbf d.	...	0736		...	1536	...	1636	...	1736	...	1836	...	...	1936	...	2036	...	2136	...	...	2239	2239	...	2335
Dillingen (Saar) d.	...	0740	the same	...	1540	...	1640	...	1740	...	1840	...	...	1940	...	2040	...	2140	...	...	2242	2242	...	2339
Merzig (Saar) d.	...	0748		...	1548	...	1648	...	1748	...	1848	...	...	1948	...	2048	...	2148	...	...	2250	2250	...	2348
Saarburg d.	...	0808	minutes	...	1608	...	1708	...	1808	...	1908	...	...	2008	...	2108	...	2208	...	...	2309	2309	...	0008
Luxembourg ▷ d.	0731	|		1531	|	1631	|	1731	|	1831	|	1859	1931	|	2031	|	2131	|	2231	2231	|	|	2331	|
Trier Hbf ▷ a.	0825	0828	past each	1625	1628	1725	1728	1825	1828	1925	1928	2006	2025	2028	2125	2128	2225	2228	2325	2325	2328	2328	0025	0028
Trier Hbf d.	0832	0832		1632	1632	1732	1732	1832	1832	1932	1932	...	2032	2032	2132	2132	...	2232	...	2332	2332	...	...	...
Wittlich Hbf d.	0856	0856	hour until	1656	1656	1756	1756	1856	1856	1956	1956	...	2056	2056	2156	2156	...	2256	...	2356	2356	...	...	...
Bullay d.	0909	0909		1709	1709	1809	1809	1909	1909	2009	2009	...	2109	2109	2209	2209	...	2309	...	0009	0009	...	...	...
Cochem (Mosel) d.	0919	0919		1719	1719	1819	1819	1919	1919	2019	2019	...	2119	2119	2219	2219	...	2319	...	0019	0019	...	...	...
Koblenz Hbf a.	0955	0955		1755	1755	1855	1855	1955	1955	2055	2055	...	2155	2155	2255	2255	...	2355	...	0055	0055	...	...	...

D – Until June 2.
E – From June 3.

a – Not Apr. 17, May 1, 25, June 5.
e – Not Apr. 17, May 1, June 5.
h – On Ⓒ departs Saarburg 0631, arrives Trier 0658.
j – Arrives 0616.
k – Also Apr. 13, 16, 30, June 4.
w – Also Apr. 17, May 1, June 5.

✣ – The 0931 from Luxembourg requires a change of trains at Trier on Ⓒ.
◧ – Change trains at Trier on Apr. 14, 17, May 1, 25, June 5.
▷ – Additional journeys Luxembourg - Trier: 1659 ①-⑤ **a**, 1759 ①-⑤ **a**.

BULLAY - TRABEN-TRARBACH

13 km Journey time: 18 minutes

Operated by Rhenus Veniro. *Subject to alteration May 6 - June 2.*
From Bullay at 0558 ⚒, 0658, 0822, 0922 and hourly until 2122.
From Traben-Trarbach at 0621 ⚒, 0745, 0845 and hourly until 2145.

TRIER - PERL - METZ

Service suspended until July 2, 2017

km										
0	**Trier** Hbf d.	...	...	...	...	**Metz** d.	...	...	...	...
49	Perl 🚌 d.	...	...	...	...	Thionville d.	...	...	...	...
70	Thionville a.	...	...	...	...	Perl 🚌 d.	...	...	...	...
100	**Metz** a.	...	...	...	...	**Trier** Hbf a.	...	...	...	...

Other local *RB* services **Trier - Perl** and v.v. Journey time: 49–56 minutes.
From Trier Hbf at 0506 Ⓐ, 0623 Ⓐ, 0704 ⚒, 0746, 0846, 0946, 1046, 1146, 1246, 1323 Ⓐ, 1346 Ⓒ, 1446, 1605, 1646, 1746, 1850, 1946, 2046, 2217 **D** and 2221 **E**.
From Perl at 0505 Ⓐ, 0625 ⚒, 0649 Ⓐ, 0725 ⚒, 0825, 0925, 1025, 1125, 1225, 1325, 1425 Ⓒ, 1525, 1625, 1725, 1825, 1925, 2025 and 2125.

915a KÖLN - GEROLSTEIN - TRIER

RE / RB services

km		⑥	Ⓐ	Ⓐ	⑥	†	Ⓒ	Ⓐ		†	⚒	†	⚒		Ⓐ	Ⓒ	Ⓒ	Ⓐ			Ⓐ		Ⓒ		
0	**Köln** Messe/Deutz d.	...	...	...	...	...	...	...	0605	0705	0715	0805	0815	0856	0915	0915	1015	1015	1115	1215	1256	1315	1355	1415	1513
1	**Köln** Hbf d.	...	...	...	...	...	...	...	0611	0711	0721	0811	0821	0905	0921	0921	1021	1021	1121	1221	1305	1321	1405	1421	1521
41	Euskirchen d.	...	...	...	...	...	...	...	0656	0756	0800	0900	0900	0943	1000	1000	1100	1100	1200	1300	1343	1400	1443	1500	1600
56	Mechernich d.	...	...	...	...	...	...	...	0707	0807	0809	0909	0909	0952	1009	1009	1109	1109	1209	1309	1352	1409	1452	1509	1609
65	Kall d.	...	...	...	...	...	...	...	0717	0817	0817	0917	0917	1000	1017	1017	1117	1117	1217	1317	1400	1417	1500	1517	1617
81	Blankenheim d.	...	...	...	...	...	...	...	0732	0832	0832	0932	0932	|	1032	1032	1132	1132	1232	1332	|	1432	|	1532	1632
94	Jünkerath d.	...	0514	...	0546	...	...	0654	0746	0846	0846	0946	0946	1022	1046	1046	1146	1146	1246	1346	1422	1446	1522	1546	1646
113	**Gerolstein** d.	0508	0531	0559	0603	0611	0658	0712	0803	0903	0903	1003	1003	1035	1103	1103	1203	1203	1303	1403	1435	1503	1535	1603	1703
143	Bitburg-Erdorf d.	0541	0604	0633	0641	0644	0733	0758	0841	0941	0941	1041	1041	1100	1133	1141	1233	1241	1341	1441	1500	1541	1600	1641	1741
182	**Trier** Hbf a.	0627	0652	0717	0727	0727	0827	0839	0927	1027	1027	1127	1127	1140	1227	1227	1327	1327	1427	1527	1540	1627	1640	1727	1827

	Ⓒ	Ⓐ					†	⚒			
Köln Messe/Deutz d.	1615	1615	1713	1815	1915	1956	2005	2015	2105	2205	...
Köln Hbf d.	1621	1621	1721	1821	1921	2005	2011	2027	2111	2211	...
Euskirchen d.	1700	1700	1800	1900	2000	2043	2056	2111	2200	2300	...
Mechernich d.	1709	1709	1809	1909	2009	2052	2107	2122	2211	2311	...
Kall d.	1717	1717	1817	1917	2017	2100	2117	2132	2220	2320	...
Blankenheim d.	1732	1732	1832	1932	2032	|	2132	2147	2236	2336	...
Jünkerath d.	1746	1746	1846	1946	2046	2122	2146	2201	2250	2350	...
Gerolstein d.	1803	1803	1903	2003	2103	2135	2203	2225	2307	0007	...
Bitburg-Erdorf d.	1833	1841	1941	2041	2141	2200	2241	2258	...	...	...
Trier Hbf a.	1927	1927	2027	2127	2227	2240	2327	2345	...	...	...

	⚒	Ⓐ	⑥	Ⓐ	Ⓐ	⑥	Ⓐ	†	⑥	Ⓐ
Trier Hbf d.	...	...	...	...	...	...	...	...	0535	0615
Bitburg-Erdorf d.	...	...	...	...	...	...	...	...	0619	0658
Gerolstein d.	0441	0524	0542	0544	0614	0618	0651	0652	0656	0736
Jünkerath d.	0500	0543	0605	0601	0631	0635	0713	0709	0713	0813
Blankenheim d.	0514	0557	0619	0615	0645	0649	0727	0723	0727	0827
Kall d.	0531	0613	0635	0632	0702	0706	0742	0738	0742	0842
Mechernich d.	0540	0622	0644	0641	0711	0715	0749	0745	0749	0849
Euskirchen d.	0556	0639	0656	0656	0724	0729	0803	0756	0803	0903
Köln Hbf a.	0639	0715	0739	0739	0757	0812	0839	0839	0839	0939
Köln Messe/Deutz a.	0645	0721	0745	0745	0802	0818	0845	0845	0845	0946

	†	⑥						Ⓐ		Ⓒ						Ⓑ	⑥	Ⓒ	⑥	Ⓑ					
Trier Hbf d.	...	0635	0725	0735	0835	0935	1035	1125	1135	1225	1235	1335	1435	1535	1635	1735	1735	1825	1835	1835	1935	2035	2135	2235	2335
Bitburg-Erdorf d.	...	0719	0758	0819	0919	1019	1119	1158	1219	1258	1319	1419	1519	1619	1719	1819	1819	1858	1919	1919	2019	2119	2219	2319	0019
Gerolstein d.	0756	0756	0823	0856	0956	1056	1156	1223	1256	1323	1356	1456	1556	1656	1756	1856	1856	1923	1956	1956	2053	2156	2253	2353	0053
Jünkerath d.	0813	0813	0836	0913	1013	1113	1213	1236	1313	1336	1413	1513	1613	1713	1813	1913	1913	1936	2009	2013	...	2213	...	...	...
Blankenheim d.	0827	0827	|	0927	1027	1127	1227	|	1327	|	1427	1527	1627	1727	1827	1927	1927	|	2023	2027	...	2227	...	...	...
Kall d.	0842	0842	0859	0942	1042	1142	1242	1259	1342	1359	1442	1542	1642	1742	1842	1942	1942	1959	2039	2042	...	2242	...	...	...
Mechernich d.	0849	0849	0906	0949	1049	1149	1249	1306	1349	1406	1449	1549	1649	1749	1849	1949	1949	2006	2047	2049	...	2249	...	...	...
Euskirchen d.	0900	0903	0917	1003	1103	1203	1302	1317	1402	1417	1503	1603	1703	1803	1903	2003	2002	2017	2107j	2107j	...	2307j	...	...	...
Köln Hbf a.	0939	0939	0952	1039	1139	1239	1339	1352	1439	1452	1539	1639	1739	1839	1939	2039	2044	2052	2151	2151	...	2351	...	...	...
Köln Messe/Deutz a.	0946	0946	0958	1045	1145	1245	1345	1358	1445	1458	1545	1645	1745	1845	1945	2045	2050	2058	2158	2158	...	2358	...	...	...

j – Arrives 9 minutes earlier.

KARLSRUHE - OFFENBURG - KONSTANZ 916

RE services except where shown

km																									
												IC					*IC*								
												2005					2313								
		Ⓐ	Ⓒ	Ⓐ								⑤⑥ v					Ⓐ					Ⓑ		Ⓑ
		e	z	e U								E 🍷					S							d
0	**Karlsruhe** Hbf ...... 912 943 d.	*0403**	*0458*	...	0607	0704	0809h	0909	1009	1109	1209	1309	1336	1409	1509	1609	1709	1733	1809	1909	2009	2116	2116	2209	...
23	Rastatt .... 943 d.	|	*0511*	...	0619	0718	0823	0923	1023	1123	1223	1323	|	1423	1523	1623	1723	1746	1823	1923	2023	2129	2129	2228	...
31	Baden-Baden .... 912 d.	*0426**	*0517*	...	0625	0726	0830	0930	1030	1130	1230	1330	1356	1430	1530	1630	1730	1754	1830	1930	2030	2136	2136	2235	...
71	**Offenburg** .... 912 942 d.	0523	0554	...	0658	0759	0859	0959	1059	1159	1259	1359	1418	1459	1559	1659	1759	1814	1859	1959	2059	2205	2205	2301	2323
104	Hausach .... 942 d.	0548	0619	...	0722	0821	0921	1021	1121	1221	1321	1421	1439	1521	1621	1721	1821	...	1921	2021	2124	2229	2229	...	2348
114	Hornberg (Schwarzw) .... d.	0556	0627	...	0730	0829	0929	1029	1129	1229	1329	1429	1448	1529	1629	1729	1829	...	1929	2029	2132	2237	2237	...	2356
127	Triberg .... d.	0609	0640	0640	0744	0843	0943	1043	1143	1243	1343	1443	1503	1543	1643	1743	1843	...	1943	2043	2146	2250	2250	...	0010
142	St Georgen (Schwarzw) .... d.	0625	0655	0655	0758	0857	0957	1057	1157	1257	1357	1457	1520	1557	1657	1757	1857	...	1957	2057	2201	2305	2305	...	0024
157	Villingen (Schwarzw) .... 938 d.	0636	0705	0705	0807	0906	1006	1106	1206	1306	1406	1506	1531	1606	1706	1806	1906	...	2006	2106	2210	2313	2313	...	0032
171	Donaueschingen .... 938 d.	0654j	0714	0714	0818	0917	1017	1117	1217	1317	1417	1517	1542	1617	1717	1817	1917	...	2017	2117	2219	...	2323	...	...
190	Immendingen .... 938 d.	0706	0726	...	0829	0928	1028	1128	1228	1328	1428	1528	1554	1628	1728	1828	1928	...	2028	2128	2235	...	2335	...	...
206	Engen .... 940 d.	0719	0738	...	0842	0940	1040	1140	1240	1340	1440	1540	|	1640	1740	1840	1940	...	2040	2140	2248	...	|	...	...
220	**Singen** .... 939 940 d.	0735	0752	...	0853	0952	1052	1152	1252	1352	1452	1552	1618	1652	1752	1852	1952	...	2052	2152	2302	...	2356	...	...
230	Radolfzell .... 939 d.	0746	0800	...	0901	1000	1100	1200	1300	1400	1500	1600	1628	1700	1800	1900	2000	...	2100	2200	2311	...	0003	...	...
250	**Konstanz** .... a.	0810	0816	...	0918	1016	1116	1216	1316	1416	1516	1616	1645	1716	1816	1916	2016	...	2116	2216	2330	...	0018	...	...

	IC								*IC*	*IC*															
	2365								2004	2006															
	Ⓐ		⑥	Ⓐ					⑦ w	⑥															
	S		k	e					E 🍷	D 🍷							⊕								
Konstanz .... d.	...	...	0502	0502	0524	0640	0735	0840	0909	0909	0940	1040	1140	1240	1340	1440	1540	1640	1740	1840	1940	2040	...	2159	2322
Radolfzell .... 939 d.	...	...	0516	0516	0539	0656	0758j	0857	0923	0923	0957	1057	1157	1257	1357	1457	1557	1657	1757	1857	1957	2058	...	2223	2346
Singen .... 939 940 d.	...	...	0530j	0530j	0556j	0706	0806	0906	0932	0932	1006	1106	1206	1306	1406	1506	1606	1706	1806	1906	2006	2106	...	2234	0000
Engen .... 940 d.	...	...	0539	0539	|	0715	0815	0915	|	|	1015	1115	1215	1315	1415	1515	1615	1715	1815	1915	2015	2115	...	2250	0013
Immendingen .... 938 d.	...	...	0552	0552	0617	0728	0829	0929	0953	0953	1029	1129	1229	1329	1429	1529	1629	1729	1829	1929	2029	2128	...	2307	...
Donaueschingen .... 938 d.	...	*0510*r	0603	0607	0629	0740	0840	0940	1005	1005	1040	1140	1240	1340	1440	1540	1640	1740	1840	1940	2040	2140	...	2319	...
Villingen (Schwarzw) .... 938 d.	...	0535	0612	0616	0640	0750	0850	0950	1016	1016	1050	1150	1250	1350	1450	1550	1650	1750	1850	1950	2050	2150	...	2328	...
St Georgen (Schwarzw) .... d.	...	0544	0621	0626	0649	0759	0859	0959	1026	1026	1059	1159	1259	1359	1459	1559	1659	1759	1859	1959	2059	2159	...	...	...
Triberg .... d.	...	0558	0635	0641	0704	0814	0914	1014	1042	1042	1114	1214	1314	1414	1514	1614	1714	1814	1914	2014	2114	2213	...	...	...
Hornberg (Schwarzw) .... d.	...	0612	0649	0655	0717	0826	0926	1026	1056	1056	1126	1226	1326	1426	1526	1626	1726	1826	1926	2026	2128	2227	...	...	...
Hausach .... 942 d.	...	0621	0657	0705	0726	0837	0937	1037	1105	1105	1137	1237	1337	1437	1537	1637	1737	1837	1937	2037	2137	2235	...	...	...
Offenburg .... 912 942 a.	0558	0647	0719	0738	0746	0859	0959	1059	1125	1125	1158	1259	1358	1459	1558	1659	1758	1859	1958	2059	2158	2300	2323	...	...
Baden-Baden .... 912 a.	0616	0724	...	...	0819	0926	1027	1127	1200	1200	1227	1327	1427	1527	1627	1727	1827	1927	2027	2127	2227	...	2347	...	...
Rastatt .... 943 a.	0624	0731	...	...	0825	0933	1033	1133	|	|	1233	1333	1433	1533	1633	1733	1833	1933	2033	2133	2233	...	2353	...	...
Karlsruhe Hbf .... 912 943 a.	0635	0750	...	...	0839	0949	1049	1149	1219	1219	1249	1349	1449	1549	1649	1749	1849	1949	2049	2149	2249	...	0007	...	...

D – ⑥ (also Apr. 14, 16, 30, June 4). 🚃12 and 🍷 Konstanz - Mannheim - Köln - Dortmund.
E – 🚃12 and 🍷 Konstanz - Mannheim - Köln - Emden and v.v.
S – Ⓐ (not Jan. 6, May 26). From / to Stuttgart (Table **931**).
U – To Ulm (Table **938**).

d – Runs daily Offenburg - Hausach.
e – Not Jan. 6.
h – 0811 on † (also Jan. 6).
j – Arrives 8 – 10 minutes earlier.
k – Also Jan. 6, Apr. 14, 17, May 1, 25, June 5.
r – ⚒ (not Jan. 6).

v – Also Apr. 13, 16, 30, May 24, 25, June 4.
w – Also Apr. 17, May 1, 25, 26, June 5; not Apr. 16, 30, June 4.
z – Also Jan. 6.

* – Connection by *IC* train.
⊕ – Change trains at Offenburg on Ⓐ (not Jan. 6).

FRANKFURT - MAINZ - IDAR OBERSTEIN - SAARBRÜCKEN 917

Vlexx

km																									
		⚒¶	⚒¶	¶	Ⓐ	¶	⚒																		
0	**Frankfurt** (Main) Hbf .... ‡ d.	...	...	...	...	...	...	...	0725	0825	*0908*	1025	*1108*	1225	*1308*	1425	1524e	1625	1724e	1825	*1908*	2025	*2108*	...	2225
11	Frankfurt Flughafen ✈ § .... ‡ d.	...	...	...	...	...	...	...	0737	0837	*0924*	1037	*1123*	1237	*1323*	1437	1537e	1637	1737e	1837	*1923*	2037	*2123*	...	2237
39	**Mainz** Hbf .... ‡ d.	...	...	...	...	...	0556	0655	0800	0900	0956	1100	1156	1300	1356	1500	1600	1700	1800	1900	1956	2100	2156	...	2300
80	Bad Kreuznach .... d.	...	...	...	0514	...	0624	0724	0826	0926	1024	1126	1224	1326	1424	1526	1626	1726	1826	1926	2024	2126	2224	...	2326
102	Bad Sobernheim .... d.	...	...	...	0536	...	0644	0744	0846	0946	1044	1146	1244	1346	1444	1546	1646	1746	1846	1946	2044	2146	2244	...	2346
117	Kirn .... d.	...	...	...	0551	...	0654	0754	0856	0956	1054	1156	1254	1356	1454	1556	1656	1756	1856	1956	2054	2156	2254	...	2356
131	Idar-Oberstein .... d.	...	...	...	0606	...	0705	0807	0907	1007	1107	1207	1307	1407	1507	1607	1707	1807	1907	2007	2107	2207	2307	...	0007
155	Türkismühle .... d.	0409	0440	0541	0632	0642	0726	0826	0926	1026	1126	1226	1326	1426	1526	1626	1726	1826	1926	2026	2126	2226	2326	...	0026
170	St Wendel .... d.	0425	0457	0557	0651	0659	0739	0837	0937	1037	1137	1237	1337	1437	1537	1637	1737	1837	1937	2037	2137	2237	2337	...	0037
179	Ottweiler (Saar) .... d.	0434	0506	0606	0658	0708	0746	0844	0944	1044	1144	1244	1344	1444	1544	1644	1744	1844	1944	2044	2144	2244	2344	...	0044
184	Neunkirchen (Saar) .... d.	0445	0513	0613	0705	0717	0753	0852	0952	1052	1152	1252	1352	1452	1552	1652	1752	1852	1952	2052	2152	2252	2352	...	0052
205	**Saarbrücken** Hbf .... a.	0510	0540	0638	0723	0743	0812	0912	1012	1112	1212	1312	1412	1512	1612	1712	1812	1912	2012	2111	2212	2312	0012	...	0112

	¶									Ⓐ	Ⓒ		Ⓐ	Ⓒ							¶		¶	¶	¶
Saarbrücken Hbf .... d.	0122	0346	0446	0546	0651	0751	0851	0951	1051	1151	1151	1251	1351	1351	1451	1549	1651	1751	1851	1951	2035	2112	2135	2235	2335
Neunkirchen (Saar) .... d.	0148	0404	0504	0604	0710	0810	0910	1010	1110	1210	1210	1310	1410	1410	1510	1608	1710	1810	1910	2010	2100	2130	2214	2313j	0000
Ottweiler (Saar) .... d.	0155	0410	0510	0610	0715	0815	0915	1015	1115	1215	1215	1315	1415	1415	1515	1613	1715	1815	1915	2015	2107	2135	2221	2320	0007
St Wendel .... d.	0204	0417	0517	0617	0722	0822	0922	1022	1122	1222	1222	1322	1422	1422	1522	1620	1722	1822	1922	2022	2127	2143	2231	2330	0017
Türkismühle .... d.	...	0428	0528	0628	0732	0832	0932	1032	1132	1232	1232	1332	1432	1432	1532	1632	1732	1832	1932	2032	2142	2154	2247	2345	...
Idar-Oberstein .... d.	...	0449	0549	0649	0752	0852	0952	1052	1152	1252	1252	1352	1452	1452	1552	1652	1752	1852	1952	2052	...	2216	...	...	...
Kirn .... d.	...	0500	0600	0700	0803	0903	1003	1103	1203	1303	1303	1403	1503	1503	1603	1703	1803	1903	2003	2103	...	2227	...	...	...
Bad Sobernheim .... d.	...	0509	0610	0710	0812	0912	1012	1112	1212	1312	1312	1412	1512	1512	1612	1712	1812	1912	2012	2112	...	2236	...	...	...
Bad Kreuznach .... d.	...	0530	0631	0731	0832	0932	1032	1132	1232	1330	1332	1432	1530	1532	1632	1732	1832	1932	2032	2132	...	2300	...	...	...
Mainz Hbf .... ‡ a.	...	0558	0658	0758	0858	0959	1058	1159	1258	1359	1359	1458	1558	1559	1658	1759	1858	1959	2058	2159	...	2328	...	...	...
Frankfurt Flughafen ✈ § .... ‡ a.	...	0620	0720	0820e	0920	*1035*	1120	*1235*	1320	*1435*	*1435*	1520	1620	*1635*	1720	*1834*	1920	*2034*	2120	*2236*	...	...	...	...	...
Frankfurt (Main) Hbf .... ‡ a.	...	0636	0736	0836e	0936	*1049*	1136	*1249*	1336	*1449*	*1449*	1536	1636	*1648*	1736	*1851*	1936	*2051*	2136	*2249*	...	...	...	...	...

e – Ⓐ only.
j – Arrives 2259.

‡ – See also Tables **911** / **914** / **917a**.
§ – Frankfurt Flughafen Regionalbahnhof.
¶ – Operated by DB.

Operator: Vlexx GmbH (except trains marked ¶ which are operated by DB).

FRANKFURT - FRANKFURT FLUGHAFEN ✈ - MAINZ - WIESBADEN 917a

S-Bahn 8/9

Frankfurt (Main) Hbf ▽ d.	0002	0017	0047	0117	0215e	0315e	0346h	0415e	0447	0502	0517	0532	0547	and at	2102	2117	2132	2147	2202	2217	2232	2247	2302	2317	2347
Frankfurt Flughafen ★ d.	0013	0028	0101f	0131f	0231f	0331f	0402f	0428	0458	0514	0529	0544	0559	the same	2114	2129	2144	2159	2214	2229	2244	2258	2313	2328	2358
Mainz Hbf .... d.	|	0057	0127	0157	0257	0357	|	0457	0527	|	0557	|	0627	minutes	|	2157	|	2227	|	2257	|	2327	|	2357	0027
Mainz-Kastel .... d.	0039	|	|	|	|	|	0424	|	|	0539	|	0609	|	past each	2139	|	2209	|	2239	|	2309	|	2339	|	|
Wiesbaden Hbf .... a.	0048	0110	0140	0210	0310	0410	0433	0510	0540	0548	0610	0618	0640	hour until	2148	2210	2218	2240	2248	2310	2318	2340	2348	0010	0040

Wiesbaden Hbf .... d.	0019	0049	0149	0249	0349	0411	0419	0441	0449	0511	0519	0541	0549	and at	2111	2119	2141	2149	2211	2219	2241	2249	2311	2319	2349
Mainz-Kastel .... d.	|	|	|	|	|	0419	|	0449	|	0519	|	0549	|	the same	2119	|	2149	|	2219	|	2249	|	2319	|	|
Mainz Hbf .... d.	0033	0103	0203	0303	0403	|	0433	|	0503	|	0533	|	0603	minutes	|	2133	|	2203	|	2233	|	2303	|	2333	0003
Frankfurt Flughafen ★ d.	0101f	0132f	0232f	0332f	0431	0446	0501	0517	0532	0547	0602	0617	0632	past each	2147	2202	2217	2232	2247	2301	2316	2331	2346	0001	0031
Frankfurt (Main) Hbf .. a.	0113	0145	0245	0345	0443	0458	0513	0528	0543	0558	0613	0628	0643	hour until	2158	2213	2228	2243	2258	2313	2328	2343	2358	0013	0043

e – Not Jan. 3 - Apr. 6 (during this period calls at Frankfurt (Main) **Süd**, departing 6 – 10 minutes earlier).
f – Calls at Frankfurt Flughafen **Fernbahnhof** (not Regionalbahnhof).
h – Departs from the main station (not underground platforms).

▽ – From the underground platforms.
★ – Frankfurt Flughafen Regionalbahnhof ✈.

918 RHEINLAND-PFALZ LOCAL SERVICES

RB / S-Bahn services

PIRMASENS - SAARBRÜCKEN

km		Ⓐ	⚒	Ⓐ	⚒	†				
0	**Pirmasens** Hbf d.	0515	0552	*0622*	*0732*	0732	0832	and	1932	2032
7	Pirmasens Nord d.	0522	0559	0641	0743	0743	0843	hourly	1943	2043
31	Zweibrücken Hbf d.	0552	0640	0713	0813	0813	0913	until	2013	2113
67	**Saarbrücken** Hbf a.	0631	0723	0751	0851	0851	0951		2051	2151

	⚒	⑥	Ⓐ						
Saarbrücken Hbf d.	0602	...	0633	0705	0807	and	1907	2007	2107
Zweibrücken Hbf d.	0643	...	0713	0745	0845	hourly	1945	2045	2145
Pirmasens Nord a.	0715	0750	0741	0815	0915	until	2015	2115	2215
Pirmasens Hbf a.	0728e	0757	0753	0826	0926		2026	2126	2226

PIRMASENS - LANDAU (Pfalz)

km		Ⓐ	⑥	Ⓐ	Ⓐ					
0	**Pirmasens** Hbf d.	0440	0542	0544	0622	0702	and	1902	2002	...
7	Pirmasens Nord d.	0452	0555	0609	0634	0718	hourly	1918	2018	...
55	**Landau** (Pfalz) Hbf a.	0547	0658	0708	0734	0818	until	2018	2118	...

	Ⓐ	Ⓐ	⑥						
Landau (Pfalz) Hbf d.	0528	0608	0641	...	0741	and	1841	1941	2041
Pirmasens Nord a.	0632	0715	0740	...	0840	hourly	1940	2040	2140
Pirmasens Hbf a.	0657	0728	0757	...	0857	until	1957	2057	2157

BINGEN - KAISERSLAUTERN - PIRMASENS

km		Ⓐ	Ⓐ	⚒	⚒											Ⓐ	Ⓒ		Ⓐ				†	
0	**Bingen** (Rhein) Hbf d.	...	...	...	0546	...	0649	...	0755	...	0855	...		1655	...	1728	1755	...	1755	1855	...	1955	2102	...
16	Bad Kreuznach d.	...	0508	...	0607	...	0710	...	0816	...	0916	...	and at	1716	...	1752	1816	...	1832b	1916	...	2016	2132	...
43	Rockenhausen d.	...	0536	...	0635	...	0740	...	0855v	...	0955	...	the same	1755	...	1821	1855	...	1901	1955	...	2055	2159	...
79	**Kaiserslautern** Hbf a.	...	0611	...	0712	...	0812	...	0926v	...	1026	...	minutes	1826	...	1857	1928	...	1943	2026	...	2130	2239	...
79	**Kaiserslautern** Hbf d.	0516	...	0626	...	0735	...	0835	...	0935	...	1035	past each	...	1835	...	...	1935	...	...	2035	...	...	2300
108	Pirmasens Nord a.	0553	...	0707	...	0806	...	0906	...	1006	...	1106	hour until	...	1906	...	...	2006	...	...	2107	...	...	2332
115	**Pirmasens** Hbf a.	0608	...	0719	...	0818	...	0918	...	1018	...	1118		...	1918	...	...	2018	...	...	2118	...	...	2341

	⚒	⑥	Ⓐ	B																				
Pirmasens Hbf d.	...	...	*0531*	0640	...	0732t	...	0841	...		1441	...	1541	...	1641	...	1741	...	1841	...	1941	...	2041	...
Pirmasens Nord d.	...	...	*0538*	0648	...	0750	...	0850	...	and at	1450	...	1550	...	1650	...	1750	...	1850	...	1950	...	2050	...
Kaiserslautern Hbf a.	...	...	*0609*	0720	...	0826	...	0926	...	the same	1526	...	1626	...	1726	...	1826	...	1926	...	2026	...	2126	...
Kaiserslautern Hbf d.	0514	0624	0637	...	0735	...	0832	...	0932	minutes	...	1532	...	1636	...	1735	...	1838	...	1932	...	2032	...	2148
Rockenhausen d.	0549	0656	0711	...	0810	...	0901	...	1001	past each	...	1601	...	1709	...	1809	...	1911	...	2001	...	2101	...	2222
Bad Kreuznach d.	0621k	0743b	0743	...	0841	...	0941	...	1041	hour until	...	1641	...	1741	...	1841	...	1941	...	2041	...	2137	...	2305h
Bingen (Rhein) Hbf a.	0640k	0803	0803	...	0901	...	1001	...	1101		...	1701	...	1801	...	1901	...	2001	...	2101	...	2157	...	2326

NEUSTADT (Weinstr) - KARLSRUHE and WISSEMBOURG

km		Ⓐ	Ⓐ	Ⓐ	Ⓐ	⚒	⚒	⚒	Ⓐ	†	⑥							D	†E		D	†E			Ⓐ
0	**Neustadt** (Weinstr) Hbf d.	0422	...	*0506*	...	0529	0610	0636e	0659	0700	0709	0736	0809	0836	0909	0936	1009	1036	1045	1109	1136	1145	1209	1236	1305
18	Landau (Pfalz) Hbf d.	0449	...	0535	...	0555	0634	0658e	0713	0722	0722	0758	0822	0858	0922	0958	1022	1058	1058	1122	1158	1158	1222	1258	1319
31	Winden (Pfalz) d.	0503	0505	0549	0555	0603	0650	0708	0722	0731	0731	0809	0831	0909	0931	1009	1031	1109	1109	1131	1209	1209	1231	1309	1331
47	**Wissembourg** ▦ ◐ a.	|	0521	...	0615	|	|	0726	|	|	|	0827	|	0927	|	1028	|	1127	1127	|	1227	1227	|	1327	|
44	Wörth (Rhein) d.	0520	...	...	...	0617	0709	...	0735	0744	0744	...	0844	...	0944	...	1044	...	...	1144	...	...	1244	...	1344
58	**Karlsruhe** Hbf a.	0534	...	...	...	0636	0726	...	0753	0754	0754	...	0854	...	0954	...	1054	...	...	1154	...	...	1254	...	1354

	Ⓒ			✣							⑥
Neustadt (Weinstr) Hbf d.	1309	1336	1409	and at	1936	2009	2104	*2136*	2226	2335	2335
Landau (Pfalz) Hbf d.	1322	1358	1422	the same	1958	2022	2122	*2158*	2248	2356	2357
Winden (Pfalz) d.	1331	1409	1431	minutes	2009	2031	2131	2229	2304	...	0006
Wissembourg ▦ ◐ a.	|	1427	|	past each	2027	|	|	|	|	...	|
Wörth (Rhein) d.	1344	...	1444	hour until	...	2044	2144	2245	2320	...	0019
Karlsruhe Hbf a.	1354	...	1454		...	2054	2154	2257	2337	...	0029

	Ⓐ	Ⓐ	⚒	Ⓐ	Ⓒ	Ⓐ		Ⓐ
Karlsruhe Hbf d.	0430	...	0600	...	0705	0717	...	0805
Wörth (Rhein) d.	0447	...	0617	...	0715	0736	...	0816
Wissembourg ▦ ◐ d.	|	0526	|	0626	|	|	0733r	|
Winden (Pfalz) d.	0502	0553	0631	0647	0727	0748	0757r	0829
Landau (Pfalz) Hbf d.	0518	0607	0645	0701	0736	0757	0807	0838
Neustadt (Weinstr) Hbf a.	0540	0628	0705	0722	0750	0811	0826	0851

	Ⓒ						Ⓐ	Ⓒ	†E	D	Ⓐ	Ⓒ	†E	D							⑥			
Karlsruhe Hbf d.	0806	...	0906	and at	1506	...	1601	1606	...	...	1705	1706	...	...	1806	...	1906	...	2006	...	...	2106	2206	2311
Wörth (Rhein) d.	0816	...	0916	the same	1516	...	1616	1616	...	...	1716	1716	...	...	1816	...	1916	...	2016	...	...	2116	2216	2321
Wissembourg ▦ ◐ d.	|	0833	|	minutes	|	1533	|	|	1633	1633	|	|	1733	1733	|	1833	|	1933	|	2033	2103	|	|	|
Winden (Pfalz) d.	0829	0853	0929	past each	1529	1553	1629	1629	1653	1653	1729	1729	1753	1753	1829	1853	1929	1953	2029	2053	2123	2131	2229	2334
Landau (Pfalz) Hbf d.	0838	0903	0938	hour until	1538	1603	1638	1638	1701	1703	1738	1738	1801	1803	1838	1903	1938	2003	2038	2103	2131	2140	2237	2343
Neustadt (Weinstr) Hbf a.	0851	0924	0950		1551	1624	1651	1651	1712	1724	1751	1751	1816	1824	1851	1924	1951	2024	2051	2124	...	2202	2256	2359

GERMERSHEIM - SPEYER - MANNHEIM - HEIDELBERG

km			Ⓐ	Ⓐ	Ⓐ	⑥	Ⓐ	Ⓐ	Ⓒ	Ⓐ													⑥	Ⓑ
0	**Germersheim** ‡ d.	0410e	0517	0557	0620	0622	0643	0704	0704	0725	0749	0810	0849	0912	0949	and at	1512	1549	1612	1649	1712	1749	1812	1812
14	Speyer Hbf ‡ d.	0424	0533	0610	0632	0635	0659	0713	0717	0738	0802	0823	0902	0925	1002	the same	1525	1602	1625	1702	1725	1802	1825	1825
23	Schifferstadt ‡ d.	0437	0548	0627	0640	0647	0712	|	0729	0801h	0811	0835	0911	0935	1011	minutes	1535	1611	1635	1711	1735	1811	1835	1835
34	Ludwigshafen Hbf ‡ d.	0451	0604	0640	0649	0659	0725	0727	0742	0814	0821	0848	0921	0948	1021	past each	1548	1621	1648	1720	1749	1821	1848	1848
37	**Mannheim** Hbf ⊡ a.	0456	*0616*	0645	*0704*	0705	...	0732	0747	0819	0825	0853	0926	0953	1026	hour until	1553	1626	1653	1726	1753	1826	1853	1853
54	**Heidelberg** Hbf ⊡ a.	0515	...	0703j	*0723j*	0723	...	0754	*0823*	...	0845j	0916j	0944	1016	1044		1616	1645	1716	1745	1816	1845	1912	1916

Germersheim ‡ d.	1849	1912	1949	2014	2050	2114	2158	2256	2322	...
Speyer Hbf ‡ d.	1902	1925	2002	2027	2103	2127	2211	2309	2335	...
Schifferstadt ‡ d.	1911	1935	2011	2046	2112	2147	2229	2319	2350	...
Ludwigshafen Hbf ‡ d.	1921	1948	2021	2057	2123	2200	2241	2332	0001	...
Mannheim Hbf ⊡ a.	1926	1953	2026	2102	2130	2205	2251	2337	0007	...
Heidelberg Hbf ⊡ a.	1945	2016	2047	2123	2153	2223	2323	2356	0025	...

	Ⓐ	Ⓒ	Ⓐ	Ⓐ	Ⓒ	Ⓐ	Ⓐ	Ⓒ	Ⓐ	⚒	
Heidelberg Hbf ⊡ d.	0505j	0533	0535j	...	...	0602j	*0618j*	*0608*	0644j	0709a	0742a
Mannheim Hbf ⊡ d.	0526	0554	0554	...	...	0622	0647	0656	0706	0730	0804
Ludwigshafen Hbf ‡ d.	0531	0600	0600	0611	0612	0638	0654	0702	0712	0735	0810
Schifferstadt ‡ d.	0545	0611	0611	0626	0624	0650	0706	0717	0729	0755	0824
Speyer Hbf ‡ d.	0555	...	...	0634	0634	0659	0712	0726	0738	0805	0833
Germersheim ‡ a.	0610	...	...	0648	0647	0712	0720	0740	0752	0818	0845

Heidelberg Hbf ⊡ d.	0813j	0843a	0913	0943	1013	1043	and at	1513	1543	1613	1643	1713	1743	1813	1843	1913	1943	2013	...	2114	2144a	2214	2244	2314
Mannheim Hbf ⊡ d.	0831	0904	0931	1004	1031	1104	the same	1531	1605	1631	1704	1731	1804	1831	1904	1931	2004	2031	2056	2137	2210	2242	2315	2338
Ludwigshafen Hbf ‡ d.	0836	0910	0936	1009	1036	1110	minutes	1536	1610	1636	1710	1736	1810	1836	1910	1936	2010	2036	2103	2142	2216	2248	2320	2343
Schifferstadt ‡ d.	0847	0924	0947	1024	1047	1123	past each	1546	1624	1647	1724	1747	1823	1847	1924	1947	2023	2047	2120	2158	2233	2305	2332	0002
Speyer Hbf ‡ d.	0856	0932	0956	1033	1056	1132	hour until	1557	1633	1657	1733	1757	1833	1857	1933	1957	2032	2057	2129	2208	2242	2314	2342	0012
Germersheim ‡ a.	0909	0945	1009	1045	1109	1145		1609	1645	1709	1745	1809	1845	1909	1945	2009	2045	2109	2142	2221	2255	2327	2356	0025

WÖRTH (Rhein) - GERMERSHEIM

km		Ⓐ	Ⓐ	Ⓐ	Ⓐ	Ⓒ	Ⓐ	Ⓒ	Ⓐ	Ⓒ	Ⓐ	Ⓒ	Ⓐ	Ⓒ	Ⓐ		Ⓐ	Ⓒ	Ⓐ		Ⓐ	Ⓒ	Ⓐ
0	**Wörth** (Rhein) d.	0536	0609	0627	0712	0725	0731	0825	0835	0925	0935	1025	1035	1125	1135	...	1218	1225	1233	and at the same minutes past	1918	1925	1933
27	**Germersheim** a.	0603	0636	0659	0745	0757	0803	0857	0907	0957	1007	1057	1107	1157	1207	...	1244	1257	1307	each hour until	1944	1957	2007

	Ⓒ	Ⓐ					
Wörth (Rhein) d.	2025	2035	2122	2222	...	2329	...
Germersheim a.	2057	2107	2154	2254	...	0004	...

	⚒	⑥	Ⓐ	⑥	Ⓐ	Ⓐ	Ⓒ	Ⓐ	Ⓐ	Ⓒ	Ⓐ	Ⓒ	Ⓐ	Ⓒ
Germersheim d.	0437	0519	0550	0601	0616	0655	0701	0725	0756	0801	0850	0901	0950	1001
Wörth (Rhein) a.	0509	0551	0623	0634	0650	0727	0734	0758	0827	0834	0922	0934	1022	1034

	Ⓐ	Ⓒ	Ⓐ	Ⓒ	Ⓐ	Ⓐ		Ⓒ	Ⓐ	Ⓐ	Ⓒ	Ⓐ	Ⓐ	Ⓒ	Ⓐ	Ⓐ	Ⓒ						
Germersheim d.	1050	1101	1150	1201	1214	1250	and at the same minutes past	1601	1614	1650	1701	1714	1740	1801	1814	1850	1901	1950	2050	2150	2225	...	2335
Wörth (Rhein) a.	1122	1134	1222	1234	1240	1322	each hour until	1634	1640	1722	1734	1740	1815	1834	1840	1922	1934	2022	2122	2222	2256	...	0007

B – On † Pirmasens Hbf d. 0641, Pirmasens Nord d. 0652, Kaiserslautern a. 0724.
D – Daily to Apr. 30; ⚒ from May 2.
E – † from May 1.

a – Ⓐ (not Jan. 6).
b – Arrives 17 – 19 minutes earlier.
e – Ⓐ only.
h – Arrives 12 – 14 minutes earlier.
j – Not Jan. 6.

k – On ⑥ Bad Kreuznach a. 0620, d. 0643, Bingen a. 0702.
r – ⚒ only.
t – 0741 on †.
v – On † from May 1 Rockenhausen d. 0857, Kaiserslautern a. 0929.

✣ – Neustadt d. 1505 (not 1509) and 1705 (not 1709).
◐ – For Strasbourg connections see Table **396**.
⊡ – See also Tables **913**, **919**, **923** and **924**.
‡ – See also Table **911a**.

WIESBADEN - MAINZ - DARMSTADT - ASCHAFFENBURG — 918a

RB services

km					✕	✕	Ⓐ										Ⓐ	Ⓐ							
0	Wiesbaden Hbf	d.		0538	0608	0638	0702	0738	0838	0938	1038	1138	1238	1338	1438	1538	1602	1638	1702	1738	1802	1838	1938	2038	2138	2238	2338
10	Mainz Hbf	d.		0549	0619	0649	0715	0749	0849	0949	1049	1149	1249	1349	1449	1549	1615	1649	1715	1749	1815	1849	1949	2049	2149	2249	2349
43	Darmstadt Hbf	a.		0621	0656	0723	0750	0821	0921	1021	1121	1221	1321	1421	1521	1621	1650	1721	1750	1821	1850	1921	2021	2121	2221	2321	0021
43	Darmstadt Hbf	d.	0452	0632	0703	0732	0800	0832r	0932	1032r	1132	1232	1332	1432	1532	1632	1700	1732	1800	1832	1900	1932	2032	2132	...	...	...
87	Aschaffenburg Hbf	a.	0535	0713	0745	0813	0843	0913r	1013	1113r	1213	1313	1413	1513	1613	1713	1742	1813	1842	1913	1942	2013	2113	2213	...	...	...

			Ⓐ			Ⓐ												Ⓐ		Ⓐ							
Aschaffenburg Hbf	d.	...	0510	0542r	0610	0640r	0716	0746	0846r	0946	1046r	1146	1246	1346	1446	1516	1546	1616	1646	1716	1746	1816	1846	1946	2046	2146	...
Darmstadt Hbf	a.	...	0552	0623r	0651	0727r	0759	0827	0927r	1027	1127r	1227	1327	1427	1527	1559	1627	1659	1727	1759	1827	1859	1927	2027	2127	2227	...
Darmstadt Hbf	d.	0440	0610	0640	0706	0740	0810	0840	0940	1040	1140	1240	1340	1440	1540	1610	1640	1710	1740	1810	1840	1910	1940	2040	2140	2240	2338
Mainz Hbf	d.	0513	0645	0713	0740	0813	0845	0913	1013	1113	1213	1313	1413	1513	1613	1645	1713	1745	1813	1845	1913	1945	2013	2113	2213	2313	0013
Wiesbaden Hbf	a.	0525	0655	0725	0755	0825	0855	0925	1028	1125	1228	1325	1428	1525	1628	1655	1725	1755	1828	1855	1925	1955	2028	2125	2225	2325	0025

r – ✕ only.

SAARBRÜCKEN - MANNHEIM - FRANKFURT and STUTTGART — 919

RE services except where shown

Additional S-Bahn services run Kaiserslautern - Mannheim - Heidelberg and v.v.

km			EC 217		ICE 1557				IC 2059			TGV 9551		ICE 9553	
			·Ⓒ	Ⓐ	①–⑤	⑥	①–⑥	w		⑦	①–⑥		R ♀		R ✕
			G ♀		d		eL¶	w		w	e				
	Trier Hbf 915	d.	...	...	0456	...	...	0533	...	...	...	0833	0933	...	1033	1133	1233	...
0	Saarbrücken Hbf	d.	...	0444	0531	0552	0608	...	0642	0645	0700	0747	0847	0847	0851	0902	0947	1047	1058	1102	1147	1249	1347	1459	1503
31	Homburg (Saar) Hbf	d.	...	0505	0552	0623	0632	...	0703	0706	0727	0809	0909	0909	0917	0927	1009	1109	...	1127	1209	1310	1409	...	1527
67	Kaiserslautern Hbf	d.	0413	0511	0529	0617	0650	0654	0702	0726	0730	0738	0830	0929	0933	0937	1000	1030	1129	1136	1158	1230	1333	1430	1537	1538
100	Neustadt (Weinstr) Hbf	d.	0441	0544	0552	0641	...	0716	0733	0750	0758	0830	0853	...	1000	1001	1030	1055	...	1230	1253	1359	1455	...	1630
128	Ludwigshafen Hbf	d.	0500	0612	0610	0705	...	0734	0800	...	0857	...	...	1057	...	1257	...	...	...	1657
129	Ludwigshafen Mitte	d.	0503	0615	...	...	0802	...	0813	0900	0911	...	1019	...	1100	1113	...	1300	1311	1420	1513	...	1700
131	Mannheim 918	a.	0506	0618	0616	0709	...	0742	0805	0811	0816	0903	0914	...	1023	1021	1102	1116	1216	1303	1315	1424	1517	1617	1703
131	Mannheim Hbf 912 918 ▽ d.		0535	0630	0631	0712	...	0746t	0807	0813	0830	0907	0930	...	1030	1023	1107	1130	1219	1307	1330	1430	1530	1619	1707
	Heidelberg Hbf 912 918 d.		0552	0646	0644	...	...	0801t	0823	...	0845	0923	0944	...	1044	...	1123	1144	...	1323	1344	1444	1544	...	1723
	Stuttgart Hbf 912 a.		...	...	0754	...	...	...	...	...	...	...	...	1118	...	...	...	...	...	...	...	...	...
191	Darmstadt Hbf ▽ a.		...	...	...	...	...	0846	...	...	...	...	...	...	...	...	...	...	...
219▲	Frankfurt (Main) Hbf ▽ a.		...	...	...	...	...	0904	...	...	...	...	...	...	1258	...	...	1658	...

			ICE 9555		ICE 9557															ICE 9586	
			R ✕		R ✕			Frankfurt (Main) Hbf ▽ d.		✕	Ⓐ	Ⓒ	Ⓐ		⑥	Ⓑ	⑥	R ✕
									ICE 9558								
Trier Hbf 915	d.	1433	1533	1633	...	1833	...	2033	...	Frankfurt (Main) Hbf d.	...	...	0558	...	...	...	0658
Saarbrücken Hbf	d.	1547	1647	1747	1859	1903	1947	2059	...	2147	2202	Darmstadt Hbf ▽ d.	...	...	...	...	...	...	...
Homburg (Saar) Hbf	d.	1609	1709	1809	...	1927	2009	...	2209	2227	Stuttgart Hbf 912 d.	...	...	...	...	...	...	...
Kaiserslautern Hbf	d.	1630	1730	1830	1937	1958	2030	2137	2141	2236j	2302	Heidelberg Hbf 912 918 d.	0413	...	0553a	0554	...	0630a	0656	0713z
Neustadt (Weinstr) Hbf	d.	1652	1754	1853	...	2030	2053	...	2210	2300	2330	Mannheim Hbf 912 918 ▽ d.	0429	...	0606a	0611	0638	...	0650a	0712	0730z	0737
Ludwigshafen Hbf	d.	...	...	...	2057	...	...	2241	...	0001	Mannheim 918 d.	0430	...	0612	0612	0639	...	0656	0718	0736	0738
Ludwigshafen Mitte	d.	1711	1810	1914	...	2059	2111	...	2247	2323	0005	Ludwigshafen Mitte d.	0433	...	0614	0615	...	...	0658	0721	0739	
Mannheim 918	a.	1715	1820	1914	2017	2102	2115	2217	2251	2326	0007	Ludwigshafen Hbf 918 d.	0437	...	0617	0617	...	...	0702	...	...	
Mannheim Hbf 912 918 ▽ d.		1730	1830	1919	2019	2107	2137	2219	2305	2340	0009	Neustadt (Weinstr) Hbf d.	0505	...	0648	0655k	...	...	0731	0740	0758	
Heidelberg Hbf 912 918 d.		1745	1845	1945	...	2123	2153	...	2323	2356	0025	Kaiserslautern Hbf d.	0535	0624	0707	0723	0721	0731	0759	0803	0831j	0822
Stuttgart Hbf 912 a.		...	...	...	...	...	...	...	...	Homburg (Saar) Hbf d.	0606	0652	...	...	...	0752	...	0831	0852	
Darmstadt Hbf ▽ a.		...	...	...	...	...	...	...	Saarbrücken Hbf a.	0645	0715	...	...	0759	0816	...	0857	0915	0901
Frankfurt (Main) Hbf ▽ a.		...	...	2058	...	2258	...	...	Trier Hbf 915 a.	...	0828	...	...	...	0928	...	1028	1028	

			ICE 9556		ICE 9554		TGV 9552						IC 2058		ICE 9550		EC 216		ICE 1554	
			⑥⑦	Ⓐ		①–⑤	C							⑧ q		⑧ b	⑥ p		G ♀		⑧ q
			w	R ✕		d	R ✕							R ✕		R ✕					L ♀
Frankfurt (Main) Hbf ▽ d.		...	0856	...	1058	...	1258	...	...	...	...	...	1858	...	...	2054	...
Darmstadt Hbf ▽ d.		...	...	...	...	...	...	...	...	...	...	2111	...
Stuttgart Hbf 912 d.		...	...	...	...	...	...	...	1655	...	1858	...	2004	...
Heidelberg Hbf 912 918 d.		0813	0913	...	0933	1013	1113	...	1133	1213	...	1333	1413	1513	1613	1713	...	1813	1833	...	1913	1933	...	2033	...	2214
Mannheim Hbf 912 918 ▽ d.		0829	0929	0939	0951	1029	1129	1141	1151	1229	1338	1351	1429	1529	1629	1729	1745	1829	1851	1938	1929	1951	2048	2051	2146	2230
Mannheim 918 d.		0839	0939	0940	0964	1039	1139	1142	1156	1233	1340	1356	1439	1543	1636	1739	1747	1835	1856	1939	1939	1956	2050	2056	2148	2239
Ludwigshafen Mitte d.		0842	0942	...	0956	1042	1142	...	1158	1242	...	1358	1442	...	1742	...	1839	1858	...	1942	1958	...	2058	...	2242
Ludwigshafen Hbf 918 d.		...	...	1002	...	...	1203	...	1403	...	1548	1642	...	1903	...	2001	2103	
Neustadt (Weinstr) Hbf d.		0905	1000	...	1032	1100	1200	...	1232	1300	...	1432	1500	1605	1659	1800	1811	1900	1932	...	2000	2032	2112	2132	2212f	2303
Kaiserslautern Hbf d.		0931	1025	1022	1059	1131	1231j	1224	1258	1331j	1422	1459	1531j	1631	1731j	1831j	1835	1931j	2000	2022	2031j	2056	2135	2159	2235f	2329
Homburg (Saar) Hbf d.		0952	1052j	...	1130	1152	1252	...	1330	1352	...	1530	1552	1652	1752	1851	1952	...	2052	2130	2157	2228	2255	2356
Saarbrücken Hbf a.		1015	1115	1100	1156	1215	1315	1303	1356	1415	1500	1557	1615	1715	1815	1912	1918	2015	...	2100	2115	2156	2218	2304	2316	0019
Trier Hbf 915 a.		1128	1228	...	1328	1428	...	1528	...	1728	1828	1928	2028	...	2128	...	2228	...

A – ①–⑤ (not Apr. 17, May 1, June 5).
C – ⑥⑦ (also Apr. 17, May 1, June 5).
G – �car and ♀ Graz - Salzburg - München - Stuttgart - Saarbrücken and v.v. Does not run Graz - München and v.v. from Apr. 14.
L – 🚗 and ✕ Saarbrücken - Frankfurt - Erfurt - Leipzig - Dresden and v.v.
R – From / to Paris (Table 390). Ⓡ for international journeys.

a – Ⓐ (not Jan. 6).
b – Not Apr. 16, 30, June 4.
d – Not Apr. 17, May 1, June 5.
e – Not Apr. 15, 17, May 1, June 5.
f – 2 minutes earlier from May 7.
j – Arrives 6 – 7 minutes earlier.

k – Arrives 0643 until May 6.
p – Also Apr. 16, 30, June 4.
q – Not Apr. 14, 16, 30, June 4.
t – Not Apr. 14, May 25.
w – Also Apr. 17, May 1, June 5.
z – On Ⓒ (also Jan. 6) connection departs Heidelberg 0656, arrives Mannheim 0712.

¶ – Subject to alteration on ⑥⑦ Feb. 11 - Apr. 2 (also Apr. 14 – 17).
☐ – On ⑥ (also Apr. 16, 30, June 4) runs as TGV 9559 (conveys ♀, not ✕).
⊖ – From May 7 departs Mannheim Hbf 0622, Ludwigshafen Mitte 0625, Ludwigshafen Hbf 0627.
▽ – See also Table 912 (ICE trains) and Table 913 (local trains).
▲ – 209 km for trains running non-stop Mannheim - Frankfurt.

See page 367 for a summary of Christmas/New Year alterations

920 FRANKFURT - NÜRNBERG - PASSAU (- WIEN)

See Table 921 for other regional trains

km	SEE NOTE ⊠	⚒t ◐	Ⓐt	Ⓐt ◐		⚒t	Ⓒz ◐	RE 59493 Ⓐs	RE 59275 ⒸP	ICE 827 ①–⑤ a🍷	ICE 521 🍷	ICE 21 ✕	ICE 523 ①–⑥ e🍷	ICE 1125 ⑦j 🍷	ICE 525 ①–⑥ h🍷	ICE 23 ✕	ICE 1127 ⑥ G🍷	ICE 527 Ⓐ 🍷	ICE 529 🍷	ICE 91 ✕	ICE 1521 ✕	ICE 91 ✕	ICE 621 🍷	ICE 623 🍷
	Hamburg Hbf **800 900** d.	...	...	...	...	...	...	...	...	...	...	...	...	...	...	...	...	...	...	0803	...	...	...	...
	Dortmund Hbf **800** d.	...	...	...	...	...	...	...	...	...	...	...	0406	0514	0525	0437	0614	0624	0725	|	0636	...	0815c	0916c
	Essen Hbf **800** d.	...	...	...	...	...	...	...	...	...	...	...	0428	0538	0553	0500	0639	0653	0754	|	|	...	0840	0941
	Düsseldorf Hbf **800** d.	...	...	...	...	...	...	...	...	...	...	...	0455	0605	0621	0527	0707	0721	0822	|	|	...	0913	1012
	Köln Hbf **800 910** d.	...	...	...	...	...	...	...	...	0317	0418	...	|	|	|	0553	|	|	|	|	0753	...	|	|
	Köln Messe/Deutz **910** d.	...	...	...	...	...	...	...	...	|	|	...	0518	0629	0644	|	0730	0744	0844	|	|	...	0936	1033
	Bonn Hbf **800** d.	...	...	...	...	...	...	...	...	|	|	...	|	|	|	0614	|	|	|	|	0814	...	|	|
	Koblenz Hbf **911** d.	...	...	...	...	...	...	...	...	|	|	...	|	|	|	0648	|	|	|	|	0848	...	|	|
	Mainz Hbf **911** d.	...	...	...	...	...	...	...	...	|	|	...	|	|	|	0740	|	|	|	|	0940	...	|	|
0	**Frankfurt** Flughafen ✈ § d.	...	...	...	...	...	...	...	...	0435	0534	...	0635	0735	0735	0802	0835	0835	0935	|	1002	...	1035	1135
11	**Frankfurt** (Main) Hbf d.	...	...	...	...	...	...	...	...	0454	0551	0621	0654	0754	0754	0819*	0854	0854	0954	|	1018	...	1054	1154
35	Hanau Hbf d.	...	...	...	...	...	...	...	...	|	0608	0638	|	|	|	0836*	|	|	|	|	1035	...	|	|
57	Aschaffenburg Hbf d.	...	...	...	...	...	...	...	...	0524	0624	0652	0724	0824	0824	|	0924	0924	1024	|	|	←	1124	1224
136	**Würzburg** Hbf **900** d.	...	...	...	...	...	...	...	...	0604	0704	0733	0804	0904	0904	0933	1004	1004	1104	1128	1132f	1135	1204	1310f
238	**Nürnberg** Hbf **900** a.	...	...	...	...	...	...	...	...	0659	0759	0827	0859	0959	0959	1027	1059	1059	1159	→	1224	1227	1259	1403
238	**Nürnberg** Hbf d.	...	0501	...	0521	0541	...	0615	0705	0702	0802	0830	0902	1002	1002	1030	1102	1102	1202	...	1227	1230	1302	1406
	München Hbf **904** a.	...	|	...	|	|	...	|	|	0808	0905	|	1004	1107	1107	|	1204	1204	1304	...	1339	|	1404	1508
271	Neumarkt (Oberpf) d.	...	0534	0552	0555	0614	0620	0638	0726	...	...	|	...	...	...	|	...	...	...	...	...	|	...	...
335	**Regensburg** Hbf d.	0540	...	0654	...	...	0716	0725	0811	...	...	0927	...	...	...	1127	...	...	...	...	...	1327	...	...
375	Straubing d.	0607	...	0722	...	...	0741	...	0838	...	...	|	...	...	...	|	...	...	...	...	...	|	...	...
400	Plattling **944** d.	0623	...	0738	...	...	0756	...	0853	...	...	1000	...	...	...	1200	...	...	...	...	...	1400	...	...
452	**Passau** Hbf 🏨 **944** a.	*0718*	...	*0833*	...	...	*0836*	...	0930	...	...	1034	...	...	...	1234	...	...	...	...	...	1434	...	...
	Linz Hbf **950** a.	...	...	...	...	...	...	...	...	...	...	1143	...	...	...	1343	...	...	...	...	...	1543	...	...
	Wien Hbf **950** a.	...	...	...	...	...	...	...	...	...	...	1309	...	...	...	1509	...	...	...	...	...	1709	...	...

SEE NOTE ⊠	ICE 27 ✕	ICE 625 🍷	ICE 627 🍷	ICE 29 ✕	RE 59495 Ⓐt	ICE 629 🍷	ICE 721 🍷	ICE 229 ✕	ICE 723 Ⓑq 🍷	ICE 725 🍷	IC 2027 🍷	ICE 727 Ⓑq 🍷	ICE 729 🍷	IC 2229 Ⓑq 🍷	IC 2229 V 🍷	RE 59499	ICE 821 Ⓑq 🍷	ICE 821 T 🍷	ICE 1625 ⑥D ✕	IC 2029 🍷	EN 491 Ⓡ N	EN 40491 Ⓡ BN	EN 421 Ⓡ BN	EN 40421 Ⓡ N
Hamburg Hbf **800 900** d.	0546	...	...	...	...	...	...	...	...	...	1146	...	...	1346	1346	...	...	...	...	1546	2029	2029	...	...
Dortmund Hbf **800** d.	0838	1016c	1125c	...	...	...	1325n	...	1425g	1525k	1436	...	1725k	1636	1636	...	...	...	...	1836	|	|	...	...
Essen Hbf **800** d.	0900	1040	1153	...	...	...	1353	...	1453	1554	|	1653	1754	|	|	...	1841	1841	...	|	|	|	...	...
Düsseldorf Hbf **800** d.	0927	1108	1221	...	...	1308	1421	...	1520	1622	|	1721	1822	|	|	...	1908	1908	...	|	|	|	2054	2054
Köln Hbf **800 910** d.	0953	|	|	...	...	|	|	...	|	|	1553	|	|	1753	1753	...	|	|	...	1953	|	|	2121	2121
Köln Messe/Deutz **910** d.	|	1130	1244	...	...	1333	1444	...	1544	1644	|	1744	1844	|	|	...	1930	1930	...	|	|	|	|	|
Bonn Hbf **800** d.	1014	|	|	...	...	|	|	...	|	|	1614	|	|	1814	1814	...	|	|	...	2014	|	|	2143	2143
Koblenz Hbf **911** d.	1048	|	|	...	...	|	|	...	|	|	1648	|	|	1848	1848	...	|	|	...	2048	|	|	2217	2217
Mainz Hbf **911** d.	1140	|	|	...	...	|	|	...	|	|	1740	|	|	1940	1940	...	|	|	2043	2143	|	|	2311	2317
Frankfurt Flughafen ✈ § d.	1202	1235	1335	...	...	1438	1535	...	1635	1735	1802	1835	1935	2002	2002	...	2035	2035	2101	2202	|	|	2353r	2353r
Frankfurt (Main) Hbf d.	1221	1254	1354	1421⁝	...	1454	1554	1621	1654	1754	1821	1854	1954	2018	2018	...	2054	2054	2119	2221	|	|	0007x	0007x
Hanau Hbf d.	1237	|	|	1438⁝	...	|	|	1638	|	|	|	|	|	2035	2035	...	|	|	2135	2238	|	|	|	|
Aschaffenburg Hbf d.	|	1324	1424	|	...	1524	1624	1652	1724	1824	1849	1924	2024	2049	2049	...	2124	2124	2150	2253	|	|	|	|
Würzburg Hbf **900** d.	1333	1404	1504	1533⁝	...	1604	1704	1733	1804	1904	1933	2004	2104	2131	2131	...	2203	2205	2233	2346	0133	0133	0136	0136
Nürnberg Hbf **900** a.	1427	1459	1559	1627⁝	...	1659	1759	1827	1859	1959	2027	2059	2159	2226	2226	...	▬	2259	2329	0042	0232	0232	0237	0237
Nürnberg Hbf d.	1431	1502	1602	1630	1636	1702	1802	1830	1902	2002	2031	2103	2202	...	2237	2257	...	2302	...	...	0307	0342	0342	0307
München Hbf **904** a.	|	1606	1704	|	|	1804	1907	|	2004	2107	|	2205	2307	...	|	|	...	0007	...	...	|	0705	0705	|
Neumarkt (Oberpf) d.	|	...	...	|	1657	...	...	|	...	...	|	...	...	...	|	2319	◐	...	...	...	|	...	...	|
Regensburg Hbf d.	1527	...	...	1727	1747	...	...	1927	...	...	2133	...	...	...	2340	0005	0009	...	...	...	0413	...	...	0413
Straubing d.	|	...	...	|	...	...	...	|	...	...	2155	...	...	...	0003	...	0036	...	...	...	|	...	...	|
Plattling **944** d.	1600	...	...	1800	...	...	...	2000	...	...	2209	...	...	...	0018	...	0050	...	...	...	|	...	...	|
Passau Hbf 🏨 **944** a.	1634	...	...	1834	...	...	...	2034	...	...	2241	...	...	...	0049	...	*0130*	...	...	...	0518	...	...	0518
Linz Hbf **950** a.	1743	...	...	1943	...	...	...	2143	...	...	...	...	...	...	...	...	...	...	...	...	0633	...	...	0633
Wien Hbf **950** a.	1909	...	...	2109	...	...	...	2309	...	...	...	...	...	...	...	...	...	...	...	...	0819	...	...	0819

B – To Innsbruck (Table **951**). Also calls at Augsburg Hbf (a. 0626).
D – ⑥ (also Apr. 14; not Apr. 15). From Wiesbaden Hbf (d. 2024).
G – ⑥ (also Apr. 14, May 25; not Apr. 15, May 27). To Garmisch on ⑥ to Mar. 4 (Table **895**).
N – *ÖBB nightjet*. Conveys 🛏 1, 2 cl., 🛏 2 cl. and 🚃 (2 cl.).
P – Ⓒ from Apr. 1.
T – ④⑤⑦ (also Apr. 17; not Apr. 14, 16, 30, June 4).
V – ④⑤⑦ (also Apr. 17, May 1, 24, June 5; not Apr. 14, 16, 30, May 25, June 4).

a – Not Apr. 14, 17, May 1, June 5.
c – ⑥⑦ (also Apr. 14, 17, May 1, June 5).
e – Not Apr. 15, 17, May 1, June 5.
f – Arrives 7–9 minutes earlier.
g – ①②③④⑦ (not Apr. 13, 16, 30, June 4).
h – Not Apr. 15, 17, May 1, 25, June 5.
j – Also Apr. 15, 17, May 1, 25, June 5.
k – ⑥ (also Apr. 14, 16, 30, June 4).
n – ⑤–⑦ (also Apr. 13, 17, May 1, June 5).
q – Not Apr. 14, 16, 30, June 4.
r – Frankfurt Flughafen **Regionalbahnhof**.
t – Not Jan. 6.
x – Frankfurt (Main) **Süd**.
z – Also Jan. 6.

***** – On ⑦ departs Frankfurt 0821, Hanau 0837.
⊠ – Frankfurt timings are subject to alteration on ⑥⑦ Feb. 11 - Apr. 2 (also Apr. 14 – 17). Timings Würzburg - Nürnberg - München may vary from March 6. See engineering work panel on page 367.
⁝ – Not ⑥⑦ Feb. 11 - Apr. 2; not Apr. 14 – 17.
◐ – Operated by *agilis*.
§ – Frankfurt Flughafen Fernbahnhof.

921 Local trains FRANKFURT - WÜRZBURG - NÜRNBERG - REGENSBURG - PASSAU

RE / RB services

For faster *ICE / IC* trains see Table **920** above. Neumarkt - Regensburg - Plattling trains are operated by *agilis*.

Warnings! Frankfurt - Würzburg is subject to alteration on ⑥⑦ Feb. 11 - Apr. 2 (also late evening on ⑤ Feb. 10 - Mar. 31). Würzburg - Nürnberg is subject to alteration from March 6.

km					Ⓐ										Ⓒ	Ⓐ		Ⓒ	Ⓐ							
0	**Frankfurt** (Main) Hbf d.	...	0450	...	0520	0634	0730	0834	0930	1034	1130	1234	1330	1434	1530	1534	1634	1730	1734	1834	1930	2034	2130	2230k	2330k	0030k
4	**Frankfurt** (Main) Süd d.	...	0458	...	0526	0640	0736	0840	0936	1040	1136	1240	1336	1440	1536	1540	1640	1736	1740	1840	1936	2040	2136	2236	2336	0036
10	Offenbach (Main) Hbf d.	...	|	...	|	0645	|	0845	|	1045	|	1245	|	1445	|	1545	1645	|	1745	1845	|	2045	|	|	|	|
24	Hanau Hbf d.	...	0521	...	0550	0657	0759	0858	0959	1057	1159	1257	1359	1457	1559	1558	1657	1759	1757	1857	1959	2057	2159	2259	2359	0059
46	Aschaffenburg Hbf d.	0501	0545	0613	0613	0717	0817	0917	1017	1117	1217	1317	1417	1517	1617	1617	1717	1817	1817	1917	2017	2117	2219	2322	0022	0122
84	Lohr Bahnhof d.	0531	...	0643	0643	0743	0843	0943	1043	1143	1243	1343	1443	1543	1643	1643	1743	1843	1843	1943	2043	2143	2250	2353	0053h	...
96	Gemünden (Main) d.	0543	...	0656	0656	0756	0856	0957	1056	1156	1256	1357	1456	1556	1656	1656	1756	1856	1856	1956	2056	2156	2300	0004	0104h	...
109	Karlstadt (Main) d.	0554	...	0705	0705	0805	0905	1005	1105	1205	1305	1405	1505	1605	1705	1705	1805	1905	1905	2005	2105	2205	2310	0012	...	...
136	**Würzburg** Hbf a.	0617	...	0721	0721	0821	0921	1021	1121	1221	1321	1421	1521	1621	1721	1721	1821	1921	1921	2021	2121	2221	2332	0027	...	...

km				⚒r		⚒r	Ⓐt																			
0	**Würzburg** Hbf d.	0038	...	0438	...	0536	0607	...	0637	0741	0842	0942	1042	1142	1242	1342	1442	1542	1640	1742	1842	1942	2042	2148	...	2304
23	Kitzingen d.	0059	...	0456	...	0554	0623	...	0655	0801	0901	1001	1101	1201	1301	1401	1501	1601	1701	1801	1901	2001	2101	2208	...	2323
61	Neustadt (Aisch) Bf d.	...	...	0519	0546	0616	0648	0648	0717	0826	0926	1026	1126	1226	1324	1426	1526	1626	1726	1826	1926	2026	2126	2239	...	2346
94	Fürth (Bay) Hbf d.	...	...	0546	0614	0644	0711	0711	0740	0847	0947	1047	1147	1247	1347	1447	1547	1647	1747	1847	1947	2047	2147	2309	...	0016
102	**Nürnberg** Hbf a.	...	...	0553	0621	0652	0719	0719	0749	0854	0954	1054	1154	1254	1353	1454	1554	1654	1754	1854	1954	2054	2154	2316	...	0023

	Ⓐt					Ⓒz																L				
Nürnberg Hbf d.	0551	*0621*	0735	...	*0817*	...	0934	...	*1017*	1136	...	*1217c*	1336	...	*1417*	1536	...	*1617n*	1736	...	*1817*	1936	...	*2021*	2134	...
Neumarkt (Oberpf) d.	0619	0706	0759	0806	0906	...	0959	1006	1106	1159	1206	1306c	1359	1406	1506	1559	1606	1706	1759	1806	1906	1959	2006	2106	2159	2206
Regensburg Hbf a.	0659	0758	0838	0858	0957	...	1038	1058	1159	1238	1258	1358c	1438	1458	1558	1638	1658	1758	1838	1858	1958	2038	2058	2158	2238	2258
Regensburg Hbf d.	0702	0801	0844	0901	1001t	1001	1044	1101	1201	1244	1301	1401	1444	1501	1601	1644	1701	1801	1844	1901	2001	...	2101	2201	2245	2301
München Hbf **878** a.	0835	|	1018	|	|	|	1217	|	|	1417	|	|	1617	|	|	1817	|	|	2017	|	|	...	|	|	0023	|
Straubing d.	...	0827	...	0927	1027t	1027	▬	1127	1227	...	1327	1427	...	1527	1627	...	1727	1827	...	1927	2027	...	2128	2228	...	2327
Plattling a.	...	0844	...	0943	1044t	1042	...	1144	1244	...	1344	1444	...	1544	1644	...	1744	1844	...	1944	2044	...	2144	2244	...	2344
Plattling **944** d.	...	*0901*	...	*1004*	...	1046p	1102	*1204*	*1302*	...	*1404*	*1502*	...	*1604*	*1702*	...	*1804*	*1902*	...	*2004*	*2102*	...	*2157*	*2306*	...	...
Passau Hbf **944** a.	...	*0934*	...	*1038*	...	1131p	1136	*1239*	*1336*	...	*1439*	*1536*	...	*1639*	*1736*	...	*1839*	*1937*	...	*2039*	*2139*	...	*2232*	*2341*	...	...

L – To Landshut (Table **878**).

c – Ⓒ (daily Dec. 24 - Jan. 8, Feb. 25 - Mar. 5, Apr. 8 – 23, June 3 – 18).
h – Aschaffenburg - Gemünden on the mornings of ①⑦ (also Jan. 7, Apr. 15, 18, May 2, 26, June 6).
k – 6 – 11 minutes **earlier** Jan. 2 - Apr. 5.
n – *1636* on Ⓐ (not Jan. 6).
p – From Apr. 1.
r – Not Jan. 6.
t – Ⓐ (not Jan. 6).
z – Also Jan. 6.

GERMANY

(WIEN -) PASSAU - NÜRNBERG - FRANKFURT — 920

See Table 921 for other regional trains

SEE NOTE ⊠	ICE 824 ①–④ b🍷	IC 2028 🍷	ICE 822 ①–⑥ e🍷	RE 59496 Ⓒz	RE 59492 Ⓐt	ICE 820 ①–⑥ e🍷	IC 2226 A 🍷	IC 2226 ①–⑥ d🍷	ICE 728 🍷	◐	Ⓐt ◐	RE 4850	ICE 726 ①–⑥ e🍷	IC 2024 🍷	ICE 724 🍷	ICE 722 ①–⑤ a🍷	ICE 1122 ⑥⑦ c🍷	ICE 228 🍴	ICE 720 🍷	ICE 628 🍷	ICE 28 🍴	ICE 626 🍷	ICE 826 Ⓐ 🍷	ICE 624 Ⓐ 🍷
Wien Hbf **950** d.	...	...	...	...	...	...	...	...	...	...	...	...	...	...	...	...	...	0650	...	...	0850	...	...	...
Linz Hbf **950** d.	...	...	...	...	...	...	...	...	...	...	...	...	...	...	...	...	...	0817	...	...	1017	...	...	...
Passau Hbf 🏛 **944** d.	...	...	...	...	...	...	0511	...	...	0523	...	...	...	0717	...	...	...	0924	...	...	1124	...	...	...
Plattling **944** d.	...	...	...	...	...	...	0544	...	...	0609	0629	...	...	0751	...	...	...	0958	...	...	1158	...	...	...
Straubing d.	...	...	...	...	...	...	0558	...	...	0625	0645	...	...	0806	...	...	...	|	...	...	|	...	...	...
Regensburg Hbf d.	...	...	...	0530	0530	...	0622	0622	...	0656	0711	0719	...	0827	...	...	...	1029	...	...	1229	...	...	...
Neumarkt (Oberpf) d.	...	...	...	0618	0620	...	0700	0700	...	0750	...	0800	...	|	...	...	...	|	...	...	|	...	...	...
München Hbf **904** d.	...	...	0449	|	|	0552	|	|	0652	...	...	|	0755	|	0852	0955	0955	|	1055	1155	|	1255	1255	1355
Nürnberg Hbf a.	...	...	0555	0640	0642	0657	0721	0721	0757	...	...	0823	0857	0925	0957	1057	1057	1126	1157	1257	1326	1357	1357	1457
Nürnberg Hbf **900** d.	...	0527	0600	...	...	0700	0729	0729	0800	...	...	...	0900	0929	1000	1100	1100	1129	1200	1300	1329⁝	1400	1400	1500
Würzburg Hbf **900** d.	0555	0625	0655	...	...	0755	0826	0826	0855	...	...	...	0955	1026	1055	1155	1155	1227	1257	1355	1427⁝	1455	1455	1555
Aschaffenburg Hbf d.	0636	0708	0736	...	...	0836	|	|	0936	...	...	...	1036	|	1136	1236	1236	|	1336	1436	|	1536	1536	1636
Hanau Hbf d.	|	|	|	...	...	|	0920	0920	|	...	...	...	|	1120	|	|	|	1320	|	|	1520⁝	|	|	|
Frankfurt (Main) Hbf a.	0704	0736	0804	...	...	0904	0936	0936	1004	...	...	...	1104	1136	1204	1304	1304	1336	1404	1504	1536⁝	1604	1604	1704
Frankfurt Flughafen ✈ § a.	0722	0755	0822	...	...	0920	0955	0955	1022	...	...	...	1120	1155	1222	1322	1320	...	1422	1522	...	1622	1622	1722
Mainz Hbf **911** a.	|	0818	|	...	...	|	1018	1018	|	...	...	...	|	1218	|	|	|	...	|	|	...	|	|	|
Koblenz Hbf **911** a.	|	0911	|	...	...	|	1111	1111	|	...	...	...	|	1311	|	|	|	...	|	|	...	|	|	|
Bonn Hbf **800** a.	|	0944	|	...	...	|	1144	1144	|	...	...	...	|	1344	|	|	|	...	|	|	...	|	|	|
Köln Messe/Deutz **910** a.	0814	|	0914	...	...	1025	|	|	1114	...	...	...	1225	|	1324	1414	1425	...	1514	1614	...	1714	|	1813
Köln Hbf **800 910** a.	|	1005	|	...	...	|	1205	1205	|	...	...	...	|	1405	|	|	|	...	|	|	...	|	1741	|
Düsseldorf Hbf **800** a.	0836	|	0936	...	...	1048	|	|	1136	...	...	...	1248	|	1346	1436	1446	...	1536	1639	...	1736	...	1835
Essen Hbf **800** a.	0902	|	1002	...	...	...	|	|	1202	...	...	...	1314	|	1414	1505	1514	...	1602	1707	...	1802	...	1901
Dortmund Hbf **800** a.	...	1121	1029p	...	...	...	1321	1321	1230	...	...	...	1342p	1521	1442k	...	1542h	...	1630k	1742k	...	1829k	...	1930
Hamburg Hbf **800 900** a.	...	1413	...	...	...	...	1613	1613	...	...	...	...	...	1813	...	...	...	...	...	...	...	...	...	...

SEE NOTE ⊠	ICE 1124 Ⓒ 🍷	ICE 26 🍴	ICE 622 🍷	ICE 620 G🍷	ICE 90 🍴	ICE 1522 🍴	ICE 90 🍴	ICE 528 🍷	ICE 526 Ⓑq 🍷	ICE 22 🍴	ICE 524 🍷	RE 59272 ⒸP	ICE 522 🍷	ICE 20 🍴	ICE 520 ①–④ m🍷	ICE 1620 ⑥y 🍴	ICE 922 ⑤⑦ v🍴	◐	RB 59494	◐	EN 490 Ⓡ N	EN 40420 Ⓡ BN	EN 420 Ⓡ BN	EN 40490 Ⓡ N
Wien Hbf **950** d.	...	1050	...	...	1250	...	...	...	...	1450	...	...	...	1650	...	...	...	...	...	...	2039	...	...	2039
Linz Hbf **950** d.	...	1217	...	...	1417	...	...	...	...	1617	...	...	...	1817	...	...	...	...	...	...	2215	...	...	2215
Passau Hbf 🏛 **944** d.	...	1324	...	...	1524	...	...	...	...	1724	...	1831	...	1924	...	...	...	2128	...	...	2322	...	...	2322
Plattling **944** d.	...	1358	...	...	1558	...	...	...	...	1758	...	1903	...	1958	...	...	...	2210	...	2311	|	...	...	|
Straubing d.	...	|	...	...	|	...	...	...	...	|	...	1916	...	|	...	...	...	2226	...	2327	|	...	...	|
Regensburg Hbf d.	...	1429	...	...	1629	...	...	...	...	1830	...	1944	...	2029	...	...	...	2254	2324	2355	0027	...	...	0027
Neumarkt (Oberpf) d.	...	|	...	...	|	...	...	...	...	|	...	2032	...	|	...	...	...	...	0021	...	|	...	...	|
München Hbf **904** d.	1355	|	1455	1555	|	1618	...	1652	1755	|	1855	|	1952	|	2055	2055	2055	...	|	...	|	2252j	2252j	|
Nürnberg Hbf a.	1457	1526	1557	1657	1726	1729	...	1757	1857	1926	1957	2053	2057	2126	2201	2201	2201	...	0044	...	0127	0116	0116	0127
Nürnberg Hbf **900** d.	1500	1529	1600	1700	1729	1733	←	1800	1901	1929	2000	...	2100	2129	2204	2204	2204	...	...	...	0200	0200	0246	0246
Würzburg Hbf **900** d.	1555	1627	1655	1755	1822	1827	1830	1855	1955	2027	2055	...	2155	2227	2257	2257	2257	...	...	...	0300	0300	|	|
Aschaffenburg Hbf d.	1636	|	1736	1836	→	|	|	1936	2036	|	2136	...	2236	2308	2336	2336	2336	...	...	...	|	|	|	|
Hanau Hbf d.	|	1720	|	|	...	1920	|	|	|	2120	|	...	2250	2322	|	|	|	...	...	...	|	|	|	|
Frankfurt (Main) Hbf a.	1704	1736	1804	1904	...	1936	|	2004	2104	2136	2204	...	2305	2340	0004	0004	0004	...	...	...	|	|	0524x	0523x
Frankfurt Flughafen ✈ § a.	1720	1755	1822	1920	...	1956	|	2022	2122	2157	2222	...	2322	...	...	...	...	...	...	...	|	|	0536r	0536r
Mainz Hbf **911** a.	|	1818	|	|	...	2018	|	|	|	2218	|	...	|	...	...	...	...	...	...	...	|	|	0602	0602
Koblenz Hbf **911** a.	|	1911	|	|	...	2111	|	|	|	2311	|	...	|	...	...	...	...	...	...	...	|	|	0705	0705
Bonn Hbf **800** a.	|	1944	|	|	...	2144	|	|	|	2344	|	...	|	...	...	...	...	...	...	...	|	|	|	|
Köln Messe/Deutz **910** a.	1826	|	1914	2025	...	|	|	2113	2214	|	2339	...	|	...	...	...	...	...	...	...	|	|	|	|
Köln Hbf **800 910** a.	|	2005	|	|	...	2206	|	|	|	0006	|	...	0042	...	...	...	...	...	...	...	|	|	0815	0815
Düsseldorf Hbf **800** a.	1848	|	1944	2048	...	|	|	2136	2236	0032	0001	...	0107	...	...	...	...	...	...	...	|	|	0842	0841
Essen Hbf **800** a.	1914	|	2015	2115	...	|	|	2202	2302	0057	0027	...	0136	...	...	...	...	...	...	...	|	|	...	...
Dortmund Hbf **800** a.	1943	2122	2042	2142	...	2321	|	2230	2327	0121	0050	...	0159	...	...	...	...	...	...	...	|	|	...	...
Hamburg Hbf **800 900** a.	...	0014	...	...	...	...	2153	...	...	...	...	...	...	...	...	...	...	...	...	...	0836	0836	...	...

A – ①⑤⑥ (also Apr. 16, 30, June 4; not Apr. 15, 17, May 1, June 5).
B – From Innsbruck (Table **951**). Also calls at Augsburg Hbf daily to Mar. 31, ①–⑤ from Apr. 3 (d. 2330).
G – From Garmisch on ⑥ to Mar. 4 (Table **895**).
N – *ÖBB nightjet.* Conveys 🛏 1, 2 cl., 🛏 2 cl. and (2.).
P – Ⓒ from Apr. 1.

a – Not Apr. 14, 17, May 1, June 5.
b – Not Apr. 13, 17, May 1, 25, June 5.
c – Also Apr. 14, 17, May 1, June 5.
d – Also Apr. 16, 30, June 4; not Apr. 13, 17, May 1, 24, June 5.
e – Not Apr. 15, 17, May 1, June 5.

h – ⑥ (also Apr. 14, 16, 17, 30, May 1, June 4, 5).
j – 2249 on ⑦ from Apr. 2 (not Apr. 16, 30, June 4).
k – ⑥ (also Apr. 14, 16, 30, June 4).
m – Not Apr. 13, 17, May 1, June 5.
p – ⑥ (also Apr. 14; not Apr. 15).
q – Not Apr. 14, 16, 30, June 4.
r – Frankfurt Flughafen **Regionalbahnhof**.
t – Not Jan. 6.
v – Also Apr. 13, 17, May 1, June 5; not Apr. 14, 16, 30, June 4.
x – Frankfurt (Main) **Süd**.
y – Also Apr. 30, June 4.

z – Also Jan. 6.

⊠ – Frankfurt timings are subject to alteration on ⑥⑦ Feb. 11 - Apr. 2 (also Apr. 14 – 17). Timings München - Nürnberg - Würzburg may vary from March 6. See engineering work panel on page 367.
⁝ – Not ⑥⑦ Feb. 11 - Apr. 2; not Apr. 14 – 17.
§ – Frankfurt Flughafen Fernbahnhof ✈.
◐ – Operated by *agilis*.

Local trains PASSAU - REGENSBURG - NÜRNBERG - WÜRZBURG - FRANKFURT — 921

RE / RB services

For faster *ICE / IC* trains see Table **920** above. Plattling - Regensburg - Neumarkt trains are operated by *agilis*.

Warnings! Nürnberg - Würzburg is subject to alteration from March 6. Würzburg - Frankfurt is subject to alteration on ⑥⑦ Feb. 11 - Apr. 2 (also late evening on ⑤ Feb. 10 - Mar. 31).

		Ⓐt																Ⓐt	Ⓒz							
Passau Hbf **944** d.	...	0604	0627z	0725	...	0825	0916	...	1025	1116	...	1225	1316	...	1425	1516	1625	...	1632p	1715	...	1822	1916	...	2025	...
Plattling **944** a.	...	0640	0701z	0759	...	0900	0950	...	1100	1150	...	1259	1349	...	1459	1550	1659	...	1703p	1751	...	1857	1949	...	2058	...
Plattling d.	...	...	0707	0810	...	0910	1010	...	1110	1210	...	1310	1410	...	1510	1610	—	1710	1710	1810	...	1910	2010	...	2110	...
Straubing d.	...	...	0723	0826	...	0926	1026	...	1126	1226	...	1326	1426	...	1526	1626	...	1726	1726	1826	...	1926	2026	...	2126	...
München Hbf **878** d.	0544	...	|	|	0744	|	|	0944	|	|	1144	|	|	1343	|	|	1544	|	|	|	1744	|	|	1944	|	...
Regensburg Hbf a.	0717	...	0753	0852	0914	0952	1052	1115	1152	1252	1314	1352	1452	1514	1553	1653	1715	1752	1752	1852	1916	1952	2052	2116	2152	...
Regensburg Hbf d.	0719	...	0756	0856	0918	0956	1056	1118	1156	1256	1318	1356	1456	1518	1556	1656	1718	1756	...	1856	1918	1956	2056	2118	...	2156
Neumarkt (Oberpf) d.	0800	...	0852	0950	1000	1053	1150	1200	1253	1350	1400	1452	1550	1600	1652	1750	1800	1852	...	1950	2000	2050	2150	2200	...	2250
Nürnberg Hbf a.	0823	...	0942	...	1023	1142	...	1223	1342	...	1423	1542	...	1623	1742	...	1824	1942	...	...	2024	2142	...	2223	...	2338

				⚒t														Ⓐt								
Nürnberg Hbf d.	0101	...	...	0443	...	0605	0705	0805	0905	1005	1105	1205	1305	1405	1505	1605	1624	1705	1805	1905	2005	2105	2206	2239	...	2335
Fürth (Bay) Hbf d.	0109	...	...	0451	...	0611	0711	0811	0911	1011	1111	1211	1311	1411	1511	1611	1632	1711	1811	1911	2011	2111	2212	2247	...	2344
Neustadt (Aisch) Bf d.	0137	...	...	0521	...	0634	0734	0834	0934	1034	1134	1234	1334	1434	1534	1634	1701	1734	1834	1934	2034	2134	2235	2316	...	0013
Kitzingen d.	...	...	...	0543	...	0657	0757	0857	0957	1057	1157	1257	1357	1457	1557	1657	1725	1757	1857	1957	2057	2157	2258	...	...	0034
Würzburg Hbf a.	...	...	...	0603	...	0714	0817	0916	1016	1116	1216	1316	1416	1516	1616	1716	1747	1816	1916	2016	2116	2220	2316	...	...	0053

		Ⓐt			Ⓐ	Ⓒ										A	⑦w		A	⑦w					⚒t	†v
Würzburg Hbf d.	...	0419	...	0515	0637	0637	0737	0837	0937	1037	1137	1237	1337	1437	1537	1637	1637	1737	1837	1837	1937	2037	2133	2233	2339	2349
Karlstadt (Main) d.	...	0443	...	0538	0652	0652	0752	0852	0952	1052	1152	1252	1352	1452	1552	1652	1652	1752	1852	1852	1952	2052	2155	2256	0002	0012
Gemünden (Main) d.	...	0453	...	0549	0704	0704	0804	0904	1004	1104	1204	1304	1404	1504	1604	1704	1704	1804	1904	1904	2004	2104	2204	2306	0012	0022
Lohr Bahnhof d.	...	0504	...	0600	0715	0715	0815	0915	1015	1115	1215	1315	1415	1515	1615	1715	1715	1815	1915	1915	2015	2115	2214	2317	0023	0033
Aschaffenburg Hbf d.	0428	0540	0540	0640j	0743	0743	0843	0943	1043	1143	1243	1343	1443	1543	1643	1743	1743	1843	1943	1943	2043	2143	2244	2348	0057	0105
Hanau Hbf d.	0455	0602	0602	0702	0802	0803	0902	1003	1102	1203	1302	1403	1502	1603	1702	1803	1803	1902	2003	2003	2102	2209	2308	0015	...	...
Offenbach (Main) Hbf d.	|	0612	0612	0712	0812	|	0912	|	1112	|	1312	|	1512	|	1712	|	|	1912	|	|	2112	|	|	|	...	...
Frankfurt (Main) Süd a.	0517	0616	0616	0716	0816	0825	0916	1025	1116	1225	1316	1425	1516	1625	1716	1825	1825	1916	2025	2025	2116	2231	2330	0037	...	...
Frankfurt (Main) Hbf a.	0524	0624	0624	0724	0824	0832	0924	1032	1124	1232	1324	1432	1524	1632	1724	1832	1840	1924	2032	2040	2124	2239	2336	0044	...	...

A – ①–⑥ (also Apr. 30, June 4; not May 1, June 5).

j – Arrives 0631.
p – From Apr. 1.

t – Not Jan. 6.
v – Also Jan. 6.
w – Also May 1, June 5; not Apr. 30, June 4.
z – Ⓒ (also Jan. 6).

12 German national public holidays are on Dec. 25, 26, Jan. 1, Apr. 14, 17, May 1, 25, June 5 and Oct. 3 437

GERMANY *See page 367 for a summary of Christmas / New Year alterations*

922 WÜRZBURG - HEILBRONN - STUTTGART

RE services

km		Ⓒz	Ⓐe	Ⓐe				Ⓐe				⑤†						
0	**Würzburg** Hbf .... d.	...	...	...	0636	...	0837	0937	1037	1237	1438	1537	1637	1737	1837	1937	2037	2137
43	Lauda .... d.	...	...	*0525*	0707	0718**e**	0910	1008	1110	1310	1510	1608	1710	1807	1910	2007	2110	2207
78	Osterburken .... d.	...	0502	0616	0733	0802**e**	0933	1032	1133	1333	1533	1631	1733	1830	1933	2030	2133	2230
94	Möckmühl .... d.	...	0519	0632	0745	0819**e**	0945	1043	1145	1345	1545	1643	1745	1841	1945	2042	2145	2242
116	Bad Friedrichshall Hbf d.	...	0544	0658	0801	0845**e**	1001	1101	1201	1401	1601	1700	1801	1858	2001	2058	2202	2258
127	**Heilbronn** Hbf ...... ★ d.	0554	0559	0712	0812	0856	1012	1111	1212	1412	1612	1713	1812	1909	2012	2108	2211	2309
140	Lauffen (Neckar) ... ★ d.	0604	0610	|	|	0904	|	|	|	|	|	|	|	|	|	2117	2219	2318
180	**Stuttgart** Hbf .... ★ a.	0643	0651	0747	0853	0943	1053	1146	1253	1453	1653	1758	1853	1949	2053	2158	2254	2356

	Ⓐe	Ⓒz	Ⓐe					⑤†				Ⓒz	Ⓐe					D
Stuttgart Hbf .... ★ d.	0450	*0456*	0558	0659**h**	0907	1107	1307	1409	1504	1555	1704	1805	1809	1907	1942	2104	2315	...
Lauffen (Neckar) ...... ★ d.	0525	*0531*	|	0739	|	|	|	|	|	|	|	|	|	|	2017	2137	2351	...
Heilbronn Hbf .... ★ d.	0536	0544	0641	0749	0945	1145	1345	1446	1545	1645	1745	1845	1844	1945	2027	2150	0001	0005
Bad Friedrichshall Hbf d.	0549	0554	0650	0800	0955	1155	1355	1456	1555	1655	1755	1855	1854	1955	2036	2201	...	0026
Möckmühl .... d.	0605	0611	0713	0817	1012	1213	1413	1513	1612	1713	1812	1913	1918	2012	2059	2218	...	0051
Osterburken .... d.	0616	0622	0727	0828	1027	1227	1427	1527	1627	1727	1827	1927	1930	2027	2127**v**	2230	...	0108
Lauda .... d.	0643	0650	0750	0851	1050	1250	1450	1550	1650	1750	1850	1953	1953	2050	2156**p**	2254	...	...
Würzburg Hbf .... a.	0724	0720	0820	0921	1121	1321	1521	1621	1721	1821	1921	2024	2024	2121	...	2326	...	...

D – Mornings of ①⑥⑦ (also Jan. 6, Apr. 14, 18, May 2, 25, 26, June 6).

e – Ⓐ (not Jan. 6).

f – On Ⓐ (not Jan. 6) departs Heilbronn 1928, Lauffen 1938.

h – 0702 on Ⓐ (not Nov. 1).

p – ①②③④⑦ (not Jan. 5, Apr. 13, 16, 30, May 24, June 4).

v – Arrives 2116.

z – Also Jan. 6.

❖ – Timings may vary by up to 1 – 2 minutes.

★ – See also panel below main table.

OTHER TRAINS HEILBRONN - STUTTGART

	Ⓐe	Ⓒz	Ⓐe		Ⓐe				Ⓐe	Ⓒz	Ⓐe			Ⓐe			❖		Ⓐe					
Heilbronn Hbf .... d.	0435	0446	0627	0653	0725	0758	0826	0926	0956	1026	1029	1057	1126	1156	1227	1257	and in the same	1726	1754	1826	1857	1926**f**	2026	2126
Lauffen (Neckar) .... d.	0445	0456	0637	0704	0736	0806	0837	0937	1004	1037	1039	1105	1137	1204	1237	1305	pattern every	1737	1802	1837	1905	1937**f**	2037	2137
Stuttgart Hbf .... a.	0523	0535	0718	0743	0815	0843	0915	1015	1043	1115	1115	1146	1215	1243	1315	1343	**two** hours until	1815	1839	1915	1943	2015	2115	2215

			Ⓒz	Ⓐe	Ⓐe				Ⓐe					Ⓐe				Ⓐe				Ⓐe		
Stuttgart Hbf .... d.	0015	...	0545	0545	0634	0745	0815	0845	0915	0945	1015	1045	and in the same	1515	1545	1613	1645	1715	1745	1815	1845	1914	2015	2215
Lauffen (Neckar) .... d.	0051	...	0621	0623	0712	0820	0850	0920	0953	1020	1050	1120	pattern every	1553	1620	1650	1720	1753	1820	1850	1920	1953	2051	2251
Heilbronn Hbf .... a.	0101	...	0630	0632	0722	0829	0901	0929	1001	1029	1101	1129	**two** hours until	1601	1629	1701	1729	1801	1829	1901	1929	2001	2101	2301

923 MANNHEIM - EBERBACH - OSTERBURKEN

S-Bahn

km		Ⓐe		Ⓐe	Ⓒz	Ⓐe		Ⓐe											⚒e	†z				
0	**Mannheim** Hbf .... ¶ **924** d.	0421	0535	0602	0630	0634	0738	0807	0838	0907	and at	1938	2007	2038	2107	2142	...	...	2207	2207	...	2305	...	0009
17	**Heidelberg** Hbf......... ¶ **924** d.	0442	0555	0625	0655	0655	0755	0825	0855	0925		1955	2025	2055	2127	2158	...	...	2226	2235	...	2326	...	0026
28	Neckargemünd .... **924** d.	0456	0609	0640	0709	0709	0809	0839	0909	0939	the same	2009	2039	2109	2141	|	...	...	2241	2249	...	2341	...	0040
34	Neckarsteinach .... d.	0502	0615	0646	0715	0715	0815	0845	0915	0945	minutes	2015	2045	2115	2147	|	...	...	2247	2255	...	2347	...	0046
41	Hirschhorn (Neckar) .... d.	0509	0622	0653	0722	0722	0822	0852	0922	0952		2022	2052	2122	2154	|	...	...	2254	2302	...	2354	...	0053
50	Eberbach .... **924** d.	0516	0629	0713**f**	0729	0729	0829	0859	0929	0959	past each	2029	2059	2129	2201	2221	←	...	2301	2308	...	0001	...	0100
69	Mosbach-Neckarelz...... **924** d.	0535	0648	0735	0748	0748	0848	0918	0948	1018	hour until	2048	2118	2148	2219	2234	2244	...	2320	2327	...	0021	...	0119
72	Mosbach (Baden) .... d.	0540	0652	0740	0752	0752	0852	0923	0952	1023		2052	2123	2152	→	...	2249	...	2324	2331	...	0026	...	0124
101	**Osterburken** .... a.	0610	0723	...	0823	0823	0923	...	1023	...		2123	...	2223	...	...	2320	...	...	...	...	0056	...	...

	Ⓐe	Ⓒz	Ⓐe	Ⓐe	Ⓒz	Ⓐe	Ⓒz		Ⓐe														
Osterburken .... d.	...	...	...	0510	0529	0536	0636	...	0702	0733	...	0836	and at	...	1836	...	1938	...	2036	...	2138	...	2238
Mosbach (Baden) .... d.	0432	0456	0504	0539	0558	0605	0705	0705	0731	0802	0835	0905		1835	1905	1935	2007	...	2105	...	2207	...	2307
Mosbach-Neckarelz .... **924** d.	0437	0501	0523**g**	0548	0603	0610	0710	0710	0740	0810	0840	0910	the same	1840	1910	1940	2013	...	2110	...	2212	...	2312
Eberbach .... **924** d.	0456	0520	0542	0607	0622	0629	0729	0729	0759	0829	0859	0929		1859	1929	1959	2032	...	2129	...	2231	...	2331
Hirschhorn (Neckar) .... d.	0503	0527	0549	0614	0629	0636	0736	0736	0806	0836	0906	0936	minutes	1906	1936	2006	2039	...	2136	...	2238	...	2338
Neckarsteinach .... d.	0509	0534	0556	0620	0635	0642	0742	0742	0812	0842	0912	0942	past each	1912	1942	2012	2045	...	2142	...	2244	...	2344
Neckargemünd .... **924** d.	0516	0540	0603	0627	0642	0649	0749	0749	0819	0849	0919	0949	hour until	1919	1949	2019	2051	...	2149	...	2251	...	2351
Heidelberg Hbf .... ¶ **924** a.	0530	0553	0616	0641	0655	0702	0802	0802	0832	0902	0932	1002		1932	2002	2032	2105	...	2203	...	2305	...	0005
Mannheim Hbf .... ¶ **924** a.	0551	0611	0632	0701	0712	0719	0819	0819	0851	0920	0951	1019		1951	2020	2051	2130	...	2230	...	2330	...	0030

e – Not Jan. 6.

f – Arrives 0700.

g – Arrives 0508.

z – Also Jan. 6.

¶ – See also Tables **913**, **918**, **919**.

924 MANNHEIM - HEILBRONN

RE / RB / S-Bahn services

VIA EBERBACH

km		2	Ⓐe	Ⓒz2	Ⓐe	Ⓒz2	Ⓐe	Ⓐe	Ⓐe	Ⓒz	Ⓐe	Ⓒz	Ⓐe	Ⓒz	Ⓐe	Ⓒz	Ⓐe	Ⓒz	Ⓐe	Ⓒz			2		2
0	**Mannheim** Hbf .... ¶ **923** d.	...	...	...	...	...	...	0735	0935	0935	1135	1135	1335	1335	1535	1535	1735	1735	1935	1935	2142		...		...
17	**Heidelberg** Hbf......... ¶ **923** d.	...	...	...	...	...	...	0749	0949	0949	1149	1149	1349	1349	1549	1549	1749	1749	1949	1949	2158		...		...
50	Eberbach .... **923** d.	...	...	...	...	...	...	0814	1014	1018	1214	1218	1414	1418	1614	1618	1814	1818	2014	2018	2221	A	...		...
69	Mosbach-Neckarelz...... **923** d.	0510	0616	0650	0652	0750	0752	0829	1029	1032	1229	1232	1429	1432	1629	1632	1829	1832	2029	2032	2235	L	0850	and	2050
87	Bad Friedrichshall Hbf.... **922** d.	0528	0637	0708	0712	0808	0812	0842	1042	1045	1242	1245	1442	1445	1642	1645	1842	1845	2042	2045	2248	S	0908	hourly	2108
92	Neckarsulm......... **922** d.	0538	0643	0718	0717	0816	0817	0847	1047	1050	1247	1250	1447	1450	1647	1650	1847	1850	2047	2050	2255	O	0918	until	2118
98	**Heilbronn** Hbf .... **922** a.	0557	0650	0737	0724	*0824*	0824	0851	1051	1054	1251	1254	1451	1454	1651	1654	1851	1854	2052	2054	2259		0937		2137
	Stuttgart Hbf **922** .... a.	...	0743	...	0815	*0915*	0915	...	...	...	...	...	...	...	...	...	...	...	...	...	...		...		...

	Ⓐe		Ⓒz	Ⓐe	Ⓒz2					Ⓐe	Ⓒz	Ⓐe	Ⓒz					2		2	2	2	2	2	
Stuttgart Hbf **922** .... d.	...	...	0545	0545	...	...	...	...	...	...	...	...	...	...	...	...		...		...	...	...	...	...	...
Heilbronn Hbf .... **922** d.	0452	...	0631	0634	0618	0700	0906	1106	1306	1505	1506	1705	1706	1906	2105	...		0718		1918	2118	2218	2318	0018	...
Neckarsulm......... **922** d.	0456	...	0635	0640	0639	0705	0911	1111	1311	1511	1511	1711	1711	1911	2109	...	A	0739	and	1939	2139	2239	2339	0039	...
Bad Friedrichshall Hbf .... **922** d.	0501	...	...	0645	0648	0710	0916	1116	1316	1516	1516	1716	1716	1916	2113	...	L	0748	hourly	1948	2148	2248	2348	0048	...
Mosbach-Neckarelz...... **923** d.	0514	...	...	0703	0707	0729	0929	1129	1329	1529	1529	1729	1729	1929	2131	...	S	0807	until	2007	2207	2307	0007	0107	...
Eberbach......... **923** d.	0528	...	...	...	...	0743	0943	1143	1343	1543	1543	1743	1743	1943	2144	...	O	...		...	...	...	...	...	...
Heidelberg Hbf .... ¶ **923** a.	0552	...	...	...	...	0809	1009	1209	1409	1609	1609	1809	1809	2009	2208	...		...		...	...	...	...	...	...
Mannheim Hbf .... ¶ **923** a.	0606	...	...	...	...	0824	1024	1224	1424	1624	1624	1824	1824	2024	2224	...		...		...	...	...	...	...	...

VIA SINSHEIM

km		Ⓐe2	Ⓒz2	Ⓒz	Ⓐe	Ⓒz	Ⓒz	2		2		2		2		2		2		2		2			
0	**Mannheim** Hbf ★ ...... ¶ **923** d.	...	...	...	0631	...	...	...	0835	...	1035	...	1235	...	1435	...	1635	...	1835	...	2044	...	...	2313	...
17	**Heidelberg** Hbf......... ¶ **923** d.	...	...	0631	0645	...	0731	*0734e*	0849	*0931*	1049	*1131*	1249	*1331*	1449	*1531*	1649	*1731*	1849	*1931*	2059	*2131*	2231	2331	0032
29	Neckargemünd......... **923** d.	...	...	0645	0655	...	0745	*0745e*	|	*0945*	|	*1145*	|	*1345*	|	*1545*	|	*1745*	|	*1945*	|	*2145*	2245	2345	0046
49	Sinsheim (Elsenz) Hbf......... d.	0511	0611	0708	0710	0711	0808	0811	0913	1011	1113	1211	1313	1411	1513	1611	1713	1811	1913	2011	2125	2211	2308	0010	0108
66	Bad Rappenau......... d.	0530	0630		0727	0727	...	0830	0927	1030	1127	1230	1327	1430	1527	1630	1727	1830	1927	2030	2142	2230	...	0035	...
72	Bad Wimpfen......... d.	0542	0638	...	0732	0732	...	0839	0932	1039	1132	1239	1332	1439	1532	1639	1732	1839	1932	2042	2147	2238	...	0041	...
75	Bad Friedrichshall Hbf.... **922** d.	0548	0648	...	0741	0743	...	0848	0938	1048	1138	1248	1338	1448	1538	1648	1738	1848	1938	2048	2151	2243	...	0044	...
80	Neckarsulm......... **922** d.	0558	0658	...	0746	0750	...	0858	0944	1058	1144	1258	1344	1458	1544	1658	1744	1858	1944	2058	2157	2253	...	0053	...
86	**Heilbronn** Hbf .... **922** a.	0617	0717	...	0751	0755	...	0917	0951	1117	1151	1317	1351	1517	1551	1717	1751	1917	1951	2117	2201	2312	...	0058	...

	Ⓐe		Ⓒz2	Ⓐe2		2		2		2		2	Ⓐe	Ⓐe	Ⓒz	2	Ⓐe	Ⓒz	2	Ⓐe		2		2	2
Heilbronn Hbf .... **922** d.	0542	...	0636	0638	0806	0840	1006	1040	1206	1240	1406	1440	...	1605	1606	1640	1805	1806	1840	...	2006	2018	2206	*2301*	*0005*
Neckarsulm......... **922** d.	0547	...	0656	0657	0811	0859	1011	1059	1211	1259	1411	1459	...	1611	1611	1659	1811	1811	1859	...	2011	2039	2211	2313	0013
Bad Friedrichshall Hbf .... **922** d.	0553	...	0712	0710	0818	0912	1018	1112	1218	1312	1418	1512	...	1618	1618	1712	1818	1818	1912	...	2018	2051	2218	2322	0022
Bad Wimpfen......... d.	0556	...	0718	0718	0822	0918	1022	1118	1222	1318	1422	1518	...	1622	1622	1718	1822	1822	1918	...	2022	2056	2222	2327	0027
Bad Rappenau......... d.	0604	...	0727	0726	0830	0927	1030	1127	1230	1327	1430	1527	...	1630	1630	1727	1830	1830	1927	...	2030	2107	2230	2335	0035
Sinsheim (Elsenz) Hbf......... d.	0620	0645	0745	0745	0844	0945	1044	1145	1244	1345	1444	1545	1559	1644	1644	1745	1844	1844	1945	1959	2044	2130	2245	2354	0054
Neckargemünd .... **923** d.	|	0710	*0811*	*0813*	|	*1011*	|	*1211*	|	*1425*	|	*1611z*	1625	|	|	*1825*	|	|	*2011z*	2025	|	*2211*	*2311*	...	...
Heidelberg Hbf .... ¶ **923** a.	0648	0723	*0826*	*0828*	0909	*1026*	1109	*1226*	1309	*1437*	1509	*1626z*	1637	1709	1709	*1837*	1909	1909	*2026z*	2037	2109	*2226*	*2326*	...	...
Mannheim Hbf .... ¶ **923** a.	0706	...	...	...	0924	...	1124	...	1324	...	1524	...	...	1724	1724	...	1924	1924	...	...	2124	...	...	...	...

e – Ⓐ (not Jan. 6).

z – Ⓒ (also Jan. 6).

¶ – See also Tables **913**, **918**, **919**.

GERMANY

925 STUTTGART - BACKNANG / AALEN - NÜRNBERG

RE services except where shown

km																										
					IC 2061				*IC* 2063			*IC* 2065			*IC* 2067			*IC* 2069			*IC* 2161				*IC* 2163	
				Ⓐt g	Ⓐt	⚒v															Ⓑq		Ⓒz	Ⓐt		
	Karlsruhe Hbf **931** .. d.	...	...	...	...	...	...	...	0706e	...	...	0906	...	...	1106	...	...	1306	...	...	1506	...	...	...	1706	...
0	**Stuttgart** Hbf ‡ d.	0035	...	0543	0605	0620t	...	0643	0807	0822	0841f	1007	1022	1041f	1207	1222	1241f	1407	1422	1441f	1607	1621	1641	1657	1807	1821
31	Backnang d.	|	...	0607	|	|	...	0708	|	|	0906f	|	|	1106f	|	|	1306f	|	|	1506f	|	|	1706	1723	|	|
73	Schwäbisch H-H ⊡ a.	|	...	0653	|	|	...	0747f	|	|	0946f	|	|	1146f	|	|	1346f	|	|	1546f	|	|	1746	1758	|	|
73	Schwäbisch H-H ⊡ d.	|	...	0654	|	|	...	0759	|	|	0959	|	|	1159	|	|	1359	|	|	1559	|	|	1759	1759	|	|
	Schwäbisch Gmünd ‡ d.	0117	...	|	0643	0706	...	|	0842	0905	|	1040	1105	|	1240	1305	|	1440	1505	|	1640	1705	|	|	1840	1905
	Aalen ‡ a.	0138	...	|	0658	0725	...	|	0857	0925	|	1055	1125	|	1255	1325	|	1455	1525	|	1655	1725	|	|	1855	1925
	Aalen d.	...	...	|	0659	▬	0728	|	0859	*0928*	|	1057	*1128*	|	1257	*1328*	|	1457	*1528*	|	1657	*1728*	|	|	1857	*1928*
	Ellwangen d.	...	...	|	0710	...	0752	|	0910	*0952*	|	1108	*1152*	|	1308	*1352*	|	1508	*1552*	|	1708	*1752*	|	|	1908	*1952*
100	Crailsheim d.	...	0606	0714	0726	⚒v	0809	0818	0926	*1009*	1018	1125	*1209*	1218	1325	*1409*	1418	1525	*1609*	1618	1725	*1809*	1818	1818	1925	*2009*
146	Ansbach d.	...	0641	0745	0750	0754	...	0850	0950	...	1050	1150	...	1250	1350	...	1450	1550	...	1650	1750	...	1850	1850	1950	...
190	**Nürnberg** Hbf a.	...	0717	...	0818	0835	...	0925	1018	...	1125	1218	...	1325	1418	...	1525	1618	...	1725	1818	...	1925	1925	2018	...

					IC 2165						
		Ⓒz	Ⓒz	Ⓐt	A						
Karlsruhe Hbf **931** .. d.	...	...	...	...	1906	...	...	...	...	...	...
Stuttgart Hbf ‡ d.	1841f	*1945**	...	1958	2007	2022	2058	2228	2235	2335	2358
Backnang d.	1906f	2021	...	2025	|	|	2124	2252	|	|	0026
Schwäbisch H-H ⊡. a.	1946f	2055	...	2102	|	|	2202	2334	|	|	0102
Schwäbisch H-H ⊡. d.	1959	...	2059	2103	|	|	2203	2334	|	|	0103
Schwäbisch Gmünd ‡ d.	|	...	|	|	2040	2105	|	|	2316	0017	|
Aalen ‡ a.	|	...	|	|	2055	2125	|	|	2338	0038	|
Aalen d.	|	...	|	|	2057	*2128*	|	|	*2344*	...	|
Ellwangen d.	|	...	|	|	2108	*2152*	|	|	*0004*	...	|
Crailsheim d.	2018	...	2121	2121	2125	*2209*	2220	2353	*0020*	...	0120
Ansbach d.	2050	...	...	...	2150	...	...	...	...	...	...
Nürnberg Hbf a.	2125	...	...	...	2218	...	...	...	...	...	...

km											
						IC 2164					
			Ⓐt	Ⓐt	Ⓒz	Ⓐt	Ⓐt	Ⓒz	Ⓒz	Ⓐt	Ⓐt
0	**Nürnberg** Hbf d.	...	...	...	...	0538	...	...	...	...	...
44	Ansbach d.	...	...	...	...	0603	...	...	...	...	...
90	Crailsheim d.	0452	*0514*	0533	0552	0632	0634	0634	...	0701	*0646*
111	Ellwangen d.	|	*0530*	|	|	0648	|	|	...	|	*0710*
127	**Aalen** a.	|	*0550*	|	|	0659	|	|	...	|	*0727*
127	**Aalen** ‡ d.	|	0600	|	|	0701	|	|	...	|	0733
152	Schwäbisch Gmünd ‡ d.	|	0620	|	|	0718	|	|	...	|	0752
	Schwäbisch H-H ⊡ a.	0511	|	0551	0609	|	0652	0653	...	0716	|
	Schwäbisch H-H ⊡ d.	0512	|	0553	0613	|	0653	...	0700	0717	|
	Backnang d.	0549	|	0635	0650	|	0736	...	0737	0752	|
203	**Stuttgart** Hbf ‡ a.	0617	0714	0702	0717	0753	0803	...	*0815**	0818	0843
	Karlsruhe Hbf **931** .. a.	...	...	...	...	0853	...	...	...	...	...

				IC 2162			*IC* 2160			*IC* 2068			*IC* 2066			*IC* 2064				*IC* 2062			*IC* 2060			
	Ⓒz			①–⑥ e													Ⓐe	Ⓒz					A			
Nürnberg Hbf d.	...	0636	...	0739	0833k	...	0939	1036	...	1139	1236	...	1339	1436	...	1539	1636	1636	...	1739	1836	...	1939	...	2036	...
Ansbach d.	...	0707	...	0807	0907	...	1007	1107	...	1207	1307f	...	1407	1507	...	1607	1707	1707	...	1807	1907	...	2007	...	2107	...
Crailsheim d.	*0651*	0742	*0747*	0835	0942	*0947*	1035	1142	*1147*	1235	1342	*1347*	1435	1542	*1547*	1635	1742	1742	*1747*	1835	1942	*1947*	2035	*2042*z	2142	*2147*
Ellwangen d.	*0712*	|	*0813*	0851	|	*1012*	1051	|	*1212*	1251	|	*1412*	1451	|	*1612*	1651	|	|	*1812*	1851	|	*2012*	2051	*2112*	|	*2210*
Aalen a.	*0732*	|	*0832*	0901	|	*1032*	1101	|	*1232*	1301	|	*1432*	1501	|	*1632*	1701	|	|	*1832*	1901	|	*2032*	2101	*2132*	|	*2228*
Aalen ‡ d.	0735	|	0835	0903	|	1035	1103	|	1235	1303	|	1435	1503	|	1635	1703	|	|	1835	1903	|	2035	2103	2135	|	2235
Schwäbisch Gmünd ‡ d.	0754	|	0854	0919	|	1054	1119	|	1254	1319	|	1454	1519	|	1654	1719	|	|	1854	1919	|	2054	2119	2154	|	2254
Schwäbisch H-H ⊡. a.	|	0759	|	|	0959	|	|	1159	|	|	1359	|	|	1559	|	|	1758	1759	|	|	1959	|	|	|	2159	|
Schwäbisch H-H ⊡. d.	|	0810f	|	|	1010f	|	|	1210f	|	|	1410f	|	|	1610f	|	|	1800	1810	|	|	2003h	|	|	|	2203	|
Backnang d.	|	0851	|	|	1051	|	|	1251	|	|	1451	|	|	1651	|	|	1851	1851	|	|	2051	|	|	|	2251	|
Stuttgart Hbf ‡ a.	0836	0918	0937	0953	1118	1137	1153	1318	1337	1353	1518	1537	1553	1718	1739	1753	1915	1918	1943j	1953	2118	2137	2153	2237	2318	2337
Karlsruhe Hbf **931** .. a.	...	...	...	1053	...	...	1253	...	...	1453	...	...	1653	...	...	1853	...	...	...	2054	...	...	2259	...	...	...

A – ④⑤⑦ (also Jan. 4, Apr. 12, 17, May 23, 24, June 5; not Jan. 6, Apr. 14, 16, 30, May 25, 26, June 4).

– ①–⑥ (not Apr. 15, 17, May 1, June 5).
– 2–4 minutes later on Ⓐ (not Jan. 6).
– Change trains at Gaildorf West (a. 0640, d. 0643).
– 2010 on Ⓒ (also Jan. 6).
– 1937 on Ⓒ (also Jan. 6).

k – 0836 on Ⓒ (also Jan. 6).
q – Not Apr. 14, 16, 30, June 4.
t – Ⓐ (not Jan. 6).
v – Not Jan. 6.
z – Ⓒ (also Jan. 6).

* – S-Bahn (underground) platforms.
⊡ – Schwäbisch Hall-Hessental.

‡ – Other *RE* trains Stuttgart - Schwäbisch Gmünd - Aalen and v.v.
From Stuttgart Hbf at 0453 Ⓐ**t**, 0550 Ⓐ**t**, 0650 Ⓐ**t**, 0721, 0922, 1122, 1322, 1449 Ⓐ**t**, 1521 Ⓐ**t**, 1522 Ⓒ**z**, 1549 Ⓐ**t**, 1636 Ⓐ**t**, 1649 Ⓐ**t**, 1721 Ⓐ**t**, 1722 Ⓒ**z**, 1748 Ⓐ**t**, 1846 Ⓐ**t**, 1919 Ⓐ**t**, 1925 Ⓒ**z** and 2122.
From Aalen at 0426 Ⓐ**t**, 0503 Ⓐ**t**, 0518 Ⓐ**t**, 0533 Ⓐ**t**, 0535 Ⓒ**z**, 0625 Ⓐ**t**, 0635 Ⓒ**z**, 0706 Ⓐ**t**, 0805 Ⓐ**t**, 0935, 1135, 1335, 1535, 1605 Ⓐ**t**, 1708 Ⓐ**t**, 1735, 1805 Ⓐ**t** and 1935.

926 HEILBRONN / ASCHAFFENBURG - CRAILSHEIM and AALEN - DONAUWÖRTH / ULM

RE / *RB* services

ASCHAFFENBURG - LAUDA - CRAILSHEIM ⊠

km		Ⓐt	Ⓒz							
0	**Aschaffenburg** Hbf d.	...	...	0639f	0922	1123	1323	1523	1723	1923g
38	Miltenberg d.	...	...	0750	0959	1159	1359	1559	1759	1959
69	Wertheim d.	...	*0626*	0828j	1035	1235	1435	1635	1835	2035
93	Tauberbischofsheim d.	0545	*0653*	0900	1100	1300	1500	1700	1900	2101
100	**Lauda** a.	0555	*0702*	0906	1106	1306	1506	1706	1906	2106
100	**Lauda** d.	0608	0713	0913	1113	1313	1513	1713	1913	2113
110	Bad Mergentheim d.	0620	0725	0925	1125	1325	1525	1725	1925	2124
169	**Crailsheim** a.	0726	0830	1028	1228	1428	1628	1828	2028	...

	Ⓐt	Ⓒz	Ⓐt								
Crailsheim d.	...	...	*0520*	0731	0931	1131	1328s	1531	1731	1931	...
Bad Mergentheim d.	...	...	*0636*	0833f	1033	1233	1433	1633	1833	2033	2053t
Lauda a.	...	...	*0647*	0843f	1043	1243	1443	1643	1843	2043	2104t
Lauda d.	...	0614	0702	0853	1053	1253	1453	1653	1853	▬	2110
Tauberbischofsheim d.	...	0624	0712	0900	1059	1259	1459	1659	1859	...	2120
Wertheim d.	0600	0700	0800p	0921	1121	1321	1521	1721	1921	...	2147
Miltenberg d.	0636	0740	0840	0959	1159	1359	1559	1759	1959	2037	2222
Aschaffenburg Hbf a.	0712	0829	0930	1037	1237	1437	1637	1837	2034z	2121	2307

HEILBRONN - CRAILSHEIM ⊠

km		Ⓐt		Ⓒz	Ⓐt		Ⓒz	Ⓐt	Ⓒz	Ⓐt
0	**Heilbronn** Hbf d.	*0546*	0803	1003	1005	and every	1803	1805	2003	2005
27	Öhringen d.	0618	0825	1025	1027	**two** hours	1825	1827	2025	2027
54	Schwäbisch Hall d.	0642	0851	1051	1051	until	1851	1851	2051	2051
61	Schwäbisch Hall-H ⊡ a.	0649	0858	1058	1058		1858	1858	2058	2058
88	**Crailsheim** a.	*0713*	0921	1121	1121		1921	1921	2121	*2121*

	Ⓐt	Ⓒz	Ⓐt	Ⓒz		Ⓐt	Ⓒz	Ⓒz	Ⓐt
Crailsheim d.	*0634*	0634	0838	0838	and every	1838	1838	2038	2038
Schwäbisch Hall-H ⊡ d.	0658	0658	0858	0900	**two** hours	1858	1900	2103	2106
Schwäbisch Hall d.	0705	0704	0905	0906	until	1905	1906	2110	2112
Öhringen a.	0729	0729	0928	0930		1928	1930	2136	2136
Heilbronn Hbf a.	0752	0752	0951	0952		1951	1952	*2221*	*2221*

AALEN - DONAUWÖRTH

km		Ⓐt	Ⓐt	Ⓒz	Ⓐt	Ⓐt	Ⓐt			Ⓐt		Ⓐt	Ⓒz	Ⓐt	Ⓐt		Ⓐt		Ⓐt		Ⓐt					
0	**Aalen** d.	...	...	0531	...	0603	0625	...	0735	0835	0935	1035	1135	1135	1235	1335	1435	1535	1635	1735	1835	1935	2035	...	...	...
39	Nördlingen a.	...	...	0613	...	0638	0706	...	0813	0913	1013	1113	1213	1219	1313	1413	1513	1613	1713	1813	1913	2013	2113	...	...	...
39	Nördlingen d.	0518	0600	0616	0624	0639	0707	...	0816	0916	1016	1116	1216	1222	1316	1416	1516	1616	1716	1816	1916	2016	2116	...	...	...
68	**Donauwörth** a.	0546	0632	0648	0652	0706	0734	...	0848	0948	1048	1148	1244	1249	1348	1448	1548	1649	1747	1847	1948	2048	2148	...	...	...

	Ⓐt		Ⓐt		Ⓒz	Ⓐt	Ⓐt		Ⓐt		Ⓐt		Ⓐt		Ⓐt		Ⓐt	Ⓐt	Ⓐt		Ⓐt			Ⓐt	Ⓒz	
Donauwörth d.	...	...	0608	...	0706	0707	0806	0906	1006	1106	1206	1306	1406	1506	1606	1706	1747	1806	1847	1906	2006	2106	...	2212	2242	...
Nördlingen a.	...	...	0638	...	0734	0739	0834	0934	1034	1134	1238	1334	1434	1534	1634	1734	1815	1834	1915	1934	2034	2134	...	2239	2308	...
Nördlingen d.	0532	...	0641	0641	0744	0744	0844	0944	1044	1144	1244	1344	1444	1544	1644	1744	...	1844	...	1944	...	2134	...	...	...	...
Aalen a.	0614	...	0721	0721	0826	0826	0926	1026	1126	1226	1326	1426	1526	1626	1726	1826	...	1926	...	2026	...	2215	...	...	...	...

AALEN - ULM

km		Ⓐt	⑥	Ⓐt	Ⓐt	Ⓒz	Ⓐt																				
0	**Aalen** d.	0442	0525	0554	0625	0633	0702	0733	0834	0907	0933	1033	1107	1133	1307	1333	1507	1533	1633	1706	1733	1833	1907	1933	2035	2107	2137
23	Heidenheim d.	0506	0547	0613	0647	0656	0725	0756	0859	0923	0955	1059	1123	1154	1323	1354	1523	1554	1659	1722	1754	1859	1923	1953	2107	2124	2200
73	**Ulm** Hbf a.	0552	0642	0700	0743	0743	0756	0844	0944	0954	1044	1144	1154	1244	1354	1444	1554	1644	1744	1754	1844	1944	1954	2044	2150	2156	2249

	Ⓐt	Ⓐt	Ⓐt	Ⓒz	Ⓐt	Ⓒz																					
Ulm Hbf d.	0430	0539	0601	0606	0646	0705	0803	0813	0913	1000	1013	1113	1200	1213	1313	1400	1413	1513	1600	1613	1713	1800	1813	1913	2000	2013	2216
Heidenheim d.	0519	0628	0656	0657	0800	0800	0835	0859	1005	1032	1059	1205	1232	1259	1403	1432	1459	1605	1634	1659	1805	1832	1859	2003	2036	2059	2304
Aalen a.	0545	0651	0721	0720	0823	0822	0851	0924	1027	1050	1124	1227	1250	1324	1426	1450	1526	1627	1650	1724	1827	1850	1924	2026	2053	2124	2328

– 3 minutes later on Ⓐ (not Jan. 6).
– 1928 on Ⓒ (also Jan. 6).
– 0835 on Ⓐ (not Jan. 6).
– Arrives 0738.

s – 1331 on Ⓒ (also Jan. 6). 1334 on ①–⑤ Dec. 27 - Jan. 5, Ⓐ Apr. 10–21 and June 6–9.
t – Ⓐ (not Jan. 6).
z – Ⓒ (also Jan. 6).

⊠ – 2nd class only.
⊡ – Schwäbisch Hall-Hessental.

12 *German national public holidays are on Dec. 25, 26, Jan. 1, Apr. 14, 17, May 1, 25, June 5 and Oct. 3* 439

GERMANY

See page 367 for a summary of Christmas / New Year alterations

928 MÜNCHEN - BAYRISCHZELL, LENGGRIES and TEGERNSEE

Bayerische Oberlandbahn GmbH

On Jan. 6 services run as on ⑦. Most trains run combined München - Holzkirchen - Schaftlach (please make sure you join the correct portion for your journey).

km																											
				©	Ⓐ	Ⓐ	©		©						Ⓐ				Ⓐ								♥
0	**München** Hbf . d.	0004	...	0604	0629	0702	0704	0804	0827	0904	0924	1004	1104	1204	1229	1304	1404	1504	1527	1604	1704	1804	1904	2004	2104	2204	2304
37	Holzkirchen ..... d.	0032	...	0632	0701	0732	0732	0832	0855	0932	0956	1032	1132	1232	1302	1332	1432	1532	1555	1632	1732	1832	1932	2032	2132	2232	2332
61	Schliersee .... d.	0101	...	0701	0726	0801	0801	0901	0921	1001	1022	1101	1201	1301	1331	1401	1501	1601	1621	1701	1801	1901	2001	2101	2201	2301	0001
78	**Bayrischzell** ... a.	0124	...	0724	...	0824	0824	0925	...	1024	...	1124	1224	1324	1354	1424	1524	1624	...	1724	1824	1924	2024	2124	2224	2324	0024

km																											
					Ⓐ	Ⓐ	©		©						Ⓐ				Ⓐ								
0	**München** Hbf . d.	0004	...	0604	0629	0702	0704	0804	0827	0904	0924	1004	1104	1204	1229	1304	1404	1504	1527	1604	1704	1804	1904	2004	2104	2204	2304
37	Holzkirchen ..... d.	0035	...	0635	0705	0735	0735	0835	0858	0935	0958	1035	1135	1235	1305	1335	1435	1535	1558	1635	1735	1835	1935	2035	2135	2235	2335
47	Schaftlach .... d.	0048	...	0648	0717	0748	0748	0848	0915	0948	1015	1048	1148	1248	1318	1348	1448	1548	1615	1648	1748	1848	1948	2048	2148	2248	2348
57	Bad Tölz .... d.	0100	...	0700	0730	0800	0800	0900	0927	1000	1027	1100	1200	1300	1330	1400	1500	1600	1627	1700	1800	1900	2000	2100	2200	2300	0000
67	**Lenggries** ...... a.	0111	...	0711	0741	0811	0811	0911	0938	1011	1038	1111	1211	1311	1341	1411	1511	1611	1638	1711	1811	1911	2011	2111	2211	2311	0011

km																											
					Ⓐ	Ⓐ	©		©						Ⓐ				Ⓐ						⊡		
0	**München** Hbf . d.	*0004*	...	0604	0629	0702	0704	0804	0827	0904	0924	1004	1104	1204	*1229*	1304	1404	1504	1527	1604	1704	1804	1904	2004	2104	*2204*	*2304*
37	Holzkirchen ..... d.	*0035*	...	0635	0705	0735	0735	0835	0858	0935	0958	1035	1135	1235	*1305*	1335	1435	1535	1558	1635	1735	1835	1935	2035	2135	*2235*	*2335*
47	Schaftlach .... d.	0048	...	0648	0718	0748	0748	0848	0915	0948	1015	1048	1148	1248	1317	1348	1448	1548	1615	1648	1748	1848	1948	2048	2148	2248	2348
59	**Tegernsee** ...... a.	0109	...	0709	0739	0809	0809	0909	0936	1009	1036	1109	1209	1309	1338	1409	1509	1609	1636	1709	1809	1909	2009	2109	2209	2309	0009

	Ⓐ	⑥	Ⓐ		Ⓐ	©	Ⓐ	Ⓐ	⑥						©	Ⓐ					©						
Bayrischzell ..... d.	...	...	0449	0532	0607	0632	0634	0705	...	0732	0832	0932	1032	1132	1232	1232	1332z	1432	1532	1632	...	1732	1832	1932	2032	2132	2232
Schliersee .... d.	0444	0459	0516	0559	0635	0659	0702	0734	0734	0759	0859	0959	1059	1159	1259	1303	1359	1459	1559	1659	1734	1759	1859	1959	2059	2159	2259
Holzkirchen .... d.	0510	0528	0544	0628	0705	0728	0732	0804	0804	0828	0928	1028	1128	1228	1328	1332	1428	1528	1628	1728	1804	1828	1928	2028	2128	2228	2328
München Hbf ... a.	0535	0553	0612	0653	0735	0753	0758	0831	0832	0856j	0956j	1055j	1153	1254	1353	1357	1453	1556j	1656j	1756j	1831	1854	1953	2054	2153	2253	2353

	Ⓐ	⑥	Ⓐ		Ⓐ	©	Ⓐ	Ⓐ	⑥						©	Ⓐ					©				⊖		
Lenggries .... d.	0431	0447	0506	0547	0622	0647	0647	0718	0717	0747	0847	0947	1047	1147	1247	1247	1347	1447	1547	1647	1717	1747	1847	1947	2047	2147	2247
Bad Tölz .... d.	0443	0500	0518	0600	0634	0700	0700	0731	0730	0800	0900	1000	1100	1200	1300	1305	1400	1500	1600	1700	1730	1800	1900	2000	2100	2200	2300
Schaftlach .... d.	0454	0516	0531	0616	0647	0716	0716	0747	0747	0816	0916	1016	1116	1216	1316	1318	1416	1516	1616	1716	1747	1816	1916	2016	2116	2216	2316
Holzkirchen .... d.	0510	0528	0544	0628	0701	0728	0732	0804	0804	0828	0928	1028	1128	1228	1328	1332	1428	1528	1628	1728	1804	1828	1928	2028	2128	2228	2328
München Hbf ... a.	0535	0553	0612	0653	0731	0753	0758	0831	0832	0856j	0956j	1055j	1153	1254	1353	1357	1453	1556j	1656j	1756j	1831	1854	1953	2054	2153	2253	2353

		⑥	Ⓐ		Ⓐ	©	Ⓐ	Ⓐ	⑥						©	Ⓐ					©				⊡		⊕
Tegernsee .... d.	...	0452	0505	0552	0621	0652	0652	0722	0722	0752	0852	0952	1052	1152	1252	1252	1352	1452	1552	1652	1722	1752	1852	1952	2052	2152	2252
Schaftlach .... a.	...	0513	0525	0613	0641	0713	0713	0743	0743	0813	0913	1013	1113	1213	1313	1313	1413	1513	1613	1713	1743	1813	1913	2013	2113	2213	2313
Holzkirchen .... a.	...	0526	0541	0626	0656	0726	0726	0756	0756	0826	0926	1026	1126	1227	1326	1327	1426	1526	1626	1726	1757	1826	1926	2026	2126	*2226*	2326
München Hbf ... a.	...	0553	0612	0653	0731	0753	0758	0831	0832	0856j	0956j	1055j	1153	1254	1353	1357	1453	1556j	1656j	1756j	1831	1854	1953	2054	2153	*2253*	2353

j – 2–3 minutes earlier on ©.
z – © only.
⊖ – On ①②③④⑦ (also Jan. 6, Apr. 14) passengers travelling from Lenggries or Bad Tölz to München should change trains at Schaftlach.
♥ – Change trains at Schliersee on ①②③④⑦ (also Jan. 6, Apr. 14).
⊕ – Change trains at Schaftlach on ⑤⑥†.
⊡ – Change trains at Schaftlach on ⑥.

929 PLATTLING - BAYERISCH EISENSTEIN - PLZEŇ

Waldbahn ⊠; ČD; 2nd class only

km																									
			7511			**773**						**775**						**777**							**779**
			◇§	Ⓐ	©	◇		Ⓐ	Ⓐe	Ⓐe		◇			k			◇							◇
0	**Plattling** .... d.	0101	...	...	...	...	...	...	0520	0629	0659	...	0806	0906	...	1006	1106	...	1206	1306	...	1406	...	1506	...
9	Deggendorf Hbf .... d.	0110	...	...	...	...	...	...	0531	0638	0709	...	0816	0916	...	1016	1116	...	1216	1316	...	1416	...	1516	...
33	Gotteszell .... d.	0129	...	...	...	...	...	...	0554	0657	0733	...	0835	0935	...	1035	1135	...	1235	1335	...	1435	...	1535	...
48	Regen .... d.	0143	...	...	...	...	...	...	0609	0712	0748	...	0849	0949	...	1049	1149	...	1249	1349	...	1449	...	1549	...
58	Zwiesel (Bay) .... d.	0153	...	...	...	...	...	...	0623	0725	0800	...	0900	1000	...	1100	1200	...	1300	1400	...	1500	...	1600	...
72	**Bayerisch Eisenstein** ☆ 🏛 a.	...	...	...	...	...	...	...	0636	0738	0813	...	0913	1013	...	1113	1213	...	1313	1413	...	1513	...	1613	...
72	**Železná Ruda-Alžbětín** ☆ 🏛 d.	...	...	0408	0457	...	...	0608	▬	▬	...	0845	...	...	1045	▬	...	1245	▬	...	1445	...	1532j	...	1645
76	Železná Ruda Město ..... d.	...	...	0416	0505	...	...	0616	...	...	...	0853	...	...	1053	...	...	1253	...	...	1453	...	1541j	...	1653
79	Špičák .... d.	...	...	0421	0510	...	...	0621	...	...	...	0859	...	...	1059	...	...	1259	...	...	1459	...	1547j	...	1659
131	**Klatovy** .... a.	...	...	0516	0600	...	...	0716	Ⓐ	...	...	0953	...	...	1153	...	...	1353	...	...	1554	...	1639j	...	1753
131	**Klatovy** .... d.	...	0400	*0530*	...	0606	0646	...	0806	0846	...	1006	...	...	1206	1246	...	1406	1446	...	1606	...	1646	...	1806
141	Švihov u Klatov .... d.	...	0412	*0541*	...	0615	0658	...	0815	0858	...	1015	...	...	1215	1258	...	1415	1458	...	1615	...	1658	...	1815
170	**Plzeň** Hlavni .... a.	...	0459	*0630*	...	0656	0746	...	0856	0946	...	1056	...	...	1256	1346	...	1456	1546	...	1656	...	1746	...	1856
	Praha Hlavní **1120** ... a.	...	0641	...	...	0841	...	...	...	...	...	1241	...	...	...	...	...	1641	...	...	...	...	...	...	2041

Plattling .... d.	1606	...	1706	1806	...	1906	2006	2102	2213	2307
Deggendorf Hbf .... d.	1616	...	1716	1816	...	1916	2016	2111	2223	2318
Gotteszell .... d.	1635	...	1735	1835	...	1935	2035	2135	2241	2337
Regen .... d.	1649	...	1749	1849	...	1949	2049	2149	2255	2351
Zwiesel (Bay) .... d.	1700	...	1800	1900	...	2000	2100	2158	2304	0001
Bayerisch Eisenstein ☆ 🏛 a.	1713	...	1813	1913	...	2013	2113	...	...	...
Železná Ruda-Alžbětín ☆ 🏛 d.	...	1732	...	...	1932	...	...	...	...	...
Železná Ruda Město ..... d.	...	1741	...	...	1939	...	...	...	...	...
Špičák .... d.	...	1747	...	...	1944	...	...	...	...	...
Klatovy .... a.	...	1839	...	...	2039	...	...	...	...	...
Klatovy .... d.	...	1846	...	...	2046	...	...	...	...	...
Švihov u Klatov .... d.	...	1858	...	...	2058	...	...	...	...	...
Plzeň Hlavni .... a.	...	1946	...	...	2146	...	...	...	...	...
Praha Hlavní **1120** ... a.	...	...	...	...	...	...	...	...	...	...

	Ⓐe	Ⓐe	©z	Ⓐe	©z		Ⓐe		
Praha Hlavní **1120** ... d.	...	...	...	...	...	...	...	...	...
Plzeň Hlavni .... d.	...	...	...	...	...	...	...	...	0525
Švihov u Klatov .... d.	...	...	...	...	...	...	...	...	0615
Klatovy .... a.	...	...	...	...	...	...	...	...	0627
Klatovy .... d.	...	...	...	...	...	...	...	...	0656
Špičák .... d.	...	...	...	...	...	...	...	...	0753
Železná Ruda Město ..... d.	...	...	...	...	...	...	...	...	0758
Železná Ruda-Alžbětín ☆ 🏛 a.	...	...	...	...	...	...	...	...	0804
Bayerisch Eisenstein ☆ 🏛 d.	...	...	...	...	...	...	0705	0744e	...
Zwiesel (Bay) .... d.	0416	0529	0559	0621	0655	...	0722	0759	...
Regen .... d.	0426	0539	0608	0630	0705	...	0732	0808	...
Gotteszell .... d.	0440	0555	0622	0644	0721	...	0751	0822	...
Deggendorf Hbf .... d.	0501	0614	0645	0709	0739	0739	0815	0845	...
Plattling .... a.	0510	0623	0654	0718	0748	0748	0825	0854	...

						778						**776**							**774**					**772**	
	Ⓐ	k				◇		Ⓐ				◇		Ⓐ				Ⓑq	◇					◇	
Praha Hlavní **1120** ... d.	...	...	...	...	...	0712	...	...	...	...	...	1112	...	...	...	...	...	...	1512	...	...	...	...	1912	...
Plzeň Hlavni .... d.	0607	0702	...	0811	...	0902	...	1011	1102	1211	...	1302	...	*1411*	...	1502	...	1611	1702	...	...	1811	*1911*	2102	2255
Švihov u Klatov .... d.	0658	0743	...	0858	...	0943	...	1058	1143	1258	...	1343	...	*1458*	...	1544	...	1658	1743	...	...	1858	*1958*	2143	2342
Klatovy .... a.	0711	0752	...	0911	...	0952	...	1111	1152	1311	...	1352	...	*1511*	...	1553	...	1711	1752	...	...	1911	*2011*	2152	2354
Klatovy .... d.	▬	0804	...	0919j	...	1004	...	▬	1204	▬	...	1404	...	1514	...	1604	...	▬	...	1804	...	▬	2018	▬	▬
Špičák .... d.	...	0859	...	1016j	...	1059	...	...	1259	...	...	1459	...	1613	...	1659	...	...	...	1859	...	...	2115	...	...
Železná Ruda Město ..... d.	...	0905	...	1022j	...	1105	...	...	1305	...	...	1505	...	1618	...	1705	...	...	...	1905	...	...	2120	...	...
Železná Ruda-Alžbětín ☆ 🏛 a.	...	0912	...	1028j	...	1112	...	...	1312	w	...	1512	...	1624	...	1712	...	...	...	1912	...	...	2126	...	...
Bayerisch Eisenstein ☆ 🏛 d.	0841	...	0944	...	1041	...	1141	1241	...	1341	1444	...	1541	...	1641	...	1741	1841	...	...	1941	2041	...	2141	...
Zwiesel (Bay) .... d.	0859	...	0959	...	1059	...	1159	1259	...	1359	1459	...	1559	...	1659	...	1759	1859	...	...	1959	2059	...	2204r	...
Regen .... d.	0908	...	1008	...	1108	...	1208	1308	...	1408	1508	...	1608	...	1708	...	1808	1908	...	...	2008	2108	...	2214	...
Gotteszell .... d.	0922	...	1022	...	1122	...	1222	1322	...	1422	1522	...	1622	...	1722	...	1822	1922	...	...	2022	2122	...	2228	...
Deggendorf Hbf .... d.	0945	...	1045	...	1145	...	1245	1345	...	1445	1545	...	1645	...	1745	...	1845	1945	...	...	2045	2141	...	2251	2329
Plattling .... a.	0954	...	1054	...	1154	...	1254	1354	...	1454	1554	...	1654	...	1754	...	1854	1954	...	...	2054	2150	...	2300	2339

ZWIESEL - GRAFENAU and BODENMAIS ⊠

ZWIESEL - GRAFENAU *32 km.* Journey time: 47–49 minutes.

From Zwiesel (Bay) at 0702 © **z**, 0713 Ⓐ **e**, 0902, 1102, 1304, 1502, 1702 and 1902. **From Grafenau** at 0805, 1000, 1200, 1400, 1600, 1800 and 2000.

ZWIESEL - BODENMAIS *15 km.* Journey time: 20 minutes.

From Zwiesel at 0624 Ⓐ **e**, 0802 Ⓐ **e**, 0902, 1002 and hourly until 2002; then 2202. **From Bodenmais** at 0558 Ⓐ **e**, 0649 Ⓐ **e**, 0829, 0929 and hourly until 2029.

e – Ⓐ (not Jan. 6).
j – Dec. 11 - Mar. 12.
k – Change trains at Klatovy on Ⓐ.
r – Arrives 2154.
q – Not Apr. 14, 16, 30, May 7.
w – Change trains at Zwiesel on Ⓐ (not Jan. 6).
z – Also Jan. 6.
◇ – Also conveys 🚃 Praha - Klatovy and v.v.
§ – Train number **771** Plzeň - Praha.
⊠ – Operated by *Regentalbahn - Die Länderbahn* (under contract from *DB Regio*).
☆ – Bayerisch Eisenstein (German) / Železná Ruda-Alžbětín (Czech) is the same station.

440 *German national public holidays are on Dec. 25, 26, Jan. 1, Apr. 14, 17, May 1, 25, June 5 and Oct. 3* 12

STUTTGART - MÜNCHEN   930

km		ICE 619	IC 2097	IC 2095	IC 2291	IRE 4205	ICE 699	RJ 63	IRE 4207	ICE 991	EC 217	IRE 4209	ICE 511	IC 2261	IRE 4211	ICE 591	ICE 999	EC 113	IRE 4213	ICE 513	IC 2093	IRE 4215
		Ⓐd	②-⑥①-⑥		Ⓐt			Ⓒ		①-⑤								①-⑥⑦p			⑤f	
		u		h	L		✕	✕♦	L	a♦	Y♦	L	Y	Y♦	L	e♦	✕	✕♦	L	M✕	Y	L
	Dortmund Hbf 800 ...d.	2058										0437g				✕		0637				
	Köln Hbf 800 910 ...d.	2230											0555					0755				
	Frankfurt (Main) Hbf 912 ...d.	0009					0517									0750	0750			0822	0852	
	Frankfurt Flughafen ✈ 912 ...d.	0028					0539				0652					0830	0830				0931	
	Mannheim Hbf 912 ...d.	0106					0612	0629		0712	0731									0914	0931	
	Heidelberg Hbf 912 ...d.	0119																		0914		
	Karlsruhe Hbf 931 ...d.	0211			0455d								0806									
0	Stuttgart Hbf ...936 d.	0336		0515	0553	0557	0656	0658	0700	0713	0758	0801	0814	0853	0900	0913	0913	0958	1001	1014	1053	1100
22	Plochingen ...936 d.	0353		0534	0609	0611				0718			0818		0909	0918			1018		1109	1118
42	Göppingen ...d.			0547	0621	0624				0729			0829.		0921	0929			1029		1121	1129
61	Geislingen (Steige) ...d.			0600		0637				0740			0840			0941			1040			1140
94	Ulm Hbf ...945 d.	0442	0544	0625	0656	0703	0756	0756	0803	0809	0836	0903	0910	0956	1003	1009	1009	1057	1103	1110	1156	1203
118	Günzburg ...945 d.	0458	0601	0644	0710		0811						0910		1003					1110		
180	Augsburg Hbf ...905 d.	0532	0636	0715	0742		0842	0839		0855			0942	0955		1039	1056	1142		1155	1239	
235	München Pasing ...905 d.	0553	0703	0738	0804		0903	0901		0918			1018	1101		1118	1118	1218		1301		
242	München Hbf ...905 a.	0602	0712	0748	0804		0913	0910		0927	1011		1027	1111		1127	1127	1211		1227	1311	
	Salzburg Hbf 890 ...a.							1058			1159							1359				

km		ICE 1091	ICE 593	EC 115	IRE 4217	ICE 515	RB 19237	IC 2263	RB 19237	IC 119	EC 595	IC 219	IRE 4221	ICE 517	IC 4223	ICE 2013	ICE 597	IRE 1217	ICE 4225	IC 519	IRE 4227	ICE 599	EC 391
		①-⑤										△				Ⓑq	⑥			Ⓑq			△
		aB	cB	♦	L		Y		Y	♦	B✕	Y♦	L	Y	L	Y♦	B✕	Y♦	Y♦	L	Y♦	B✕	Y♦
	Dortmund Hbf 800 ...d.	✕	✕		0837									1037	0952				1237				
	Köln Hbf 800 910 ...d.			0818	0955					0918				1155	1117				1355				
	Frankfurt (Main) Hbf 912 ...d.	0950	0950								1150	1220				1350	1420				1550	1620	
	Frankfurt Flughafen ✈ 912 ...d.				1052									1252					1452				
	Mannheim Hbf 912 ...d.	1030	1030	1102	1131			1230			1314	1331			1430				1531			1630	1714
	Heidelberg Hbf 912 ...d.							1206x			1314				1406x		1514						
	Karlsruhe Hbf 931 ...d.						1205											1505		1605			
0	Stuttgart Hbf ...936 d.	1113	1113	1158	1201	1214	1231	1253	1257	1313	1358	1401	1414	1454	1458	1513	1558	1558	1601	1614	1653	1659	1712	1758
22	Plochingen ...936 d.				1218	1249	1309			1418			1509	1514				1618			1709	1718	
42	Göppingen ...d.				1229	1306	1321	←	1325				1429			1522	1528	1629			1721	1729	
61	Geislingen (Steige) ...d.				1240		1328	1335					1440			1533		1640			1740		
94	Ulm Hbf ...945 d.	1209	1209	1256	1303	1310		1356	1357	1401	1409	1456	1503	1510	1559	1613	1609	1656	1656	1703	1710	1756	1803	1809	1856
118	Günzburg ...945 d.			1310										1510				1710					1910
180	Augsburg Hbf ...905 d.	1255	1255	1342		1355		1439			1455	1542		1555*		1655*	1742	1742		1755	1839		1855	1942
235	München Pasing ...905 d.	1318	1318			1418		1501			1518			1618*		1718*	1818			1818	1901		1918	
242	München Hbf ...905 a.	1327	1327	1411		1427		1511			1528	1611		1627*		1727*	1811	1811		1827	1911		1927	2011
	Salzburg Hbf 890 ...a.		1559								1759						1959	1959			2100			2202

km		IRE 4229	ICE 611	IC 2267	IC 2011	IC 2017	IRE 4231	ICE 691	TGV 9577	IC 2295	IRE 4233	ICE 613	ICE 771	IC 2269	IC 2269	IRE 4235	TGV 9579	ICE 693	IRE 4237	ICE 615	RB 19283	ICE 1093	IRE 4239
					①-④	⑤f			Ⓑb	Ⓑq			⑦w	⑤f		⑦w	Ⓑq			⑥k		⑦n	
		L	Y	Y	Y♦		L	B✕	AY	Y		F		T	H✕		Y	L	AY	B✕		B✕	
	Dortmund Hbf 800 ...d.		1437			1352						1637	1549							1837			
	Köln Hbf 800 910 ...d.		1555		1517	1517						1755	1717							1957			
	Frankfurt (Main) Hbf 912 ...d.			1437				1750		1820				1905				1950				2151	
	Frankfurt Flughafen ✈ 912 ...d.		1652									1852		1921				2052					
	Mannheim Hbf 912 ...d.		1731		1754	1754		1830				1931	1954	1956				2030		2131		2231	
	Heidelberg Hbf 912 ...d.				1806x	1806x							1914	2006x									
	Karlsruhe Hbf 931 ...d.		1805					1828							2005	2005		2028					
0	Stuttgart Hbf ...936 d.	1802	1814	1853	1850	1856	1859	1913	1922	1958	2001	2014	2050	2054	2053	2101	2112	2113	2201	2214	2231	2315	2322
22	Plochingen ...936 d.	1818		1909	1904	1913	1918			2018			2106	2109	2109	2118			2218		2249		2339
42	Göppingen ...d.	1829		1921		1930				2029				2121	2121	2129			2229		2306		2350
61	Geislingen (Steige) ...d.	1840			1937	1942				2040				2134	2134	2140			2240		2328		0002
94	Ulm Hbf ...945 d.	1903	1910	1956	2001	2003	2009	2020		2056	2103	2110	2158	2155	2158	2203	2210	2209	2303	2310		0014	0032
118	Günzburg ...945 d.									2110				2215	2215								0030
180	Augsburg Hbf ...905 d.		1955	2039	2045			2055	2103	2143		2155		2247	2247		2258	2255		2355			0101
235	München Pasing ...905 d.		2018	2101	2108			2118		2216		2216		2309		2310		2320		2317		0017	0123
242	München Hbf ...905 a.		2027	2111	2118			2127	2136	2215		2223		2319	2319		2329	2329		2327		0027	0133
	Salzburg Hbf 890 ...a.																						

Regional trains ULM - MÜNCHEN

		Ⓐt		Ⓐt																		
Ulm Hbf ...d.			0446	0523	0621	0723	0823	0923	1023	1123	1223	1324	1423	1523	1623	1723	1824	1923	2023	2123	2223	2323
Günzburg ...d.		0504	0542	0640	0742	0842	0942	1042	1142	1242	1342	1442	1542	1642	1742	1842	1942	2042	2142	2242	2341
Augsburg Hbf ...a.		0559	0633	0733	0833	0933	1033	1133	1233	1333	1433	1533	1633	1733	1833	1933	2033	2133	2233	2333	
Augsburg Hbf ...d.	0439	0539	0605	0639	0739	0833	0839	0939	1039	1139	1239	1339	1439	1533	1639	1739	1839	1939	2039	2139	2239
München Pasing ...a.	0513	0613	0641	0714	0813	0913	1013	1113	1213	1313	1413	1514	1613	1713	1813	1913	2013	2114	2222	2315	0022
München Hbf ...a.	0521	0621	0649	0721	0821	0921	1021	1121	1221	1321	1421	1522	1621	1722	1821	1921	2021	2121	2230	2322	0030

♦ — **NOTES** (LISTED BY TRAIN NUMBER)

63 – ▢ and ✕ Frankfurt - Wien - Budapest.
113 – ▢ and ✕ Frankfurt - Salzburg - Villach - Klagenfurt; conveys ▢ Frankfurt - Villach (213) - Ljubljana - Zagreb.
115 – WÖRTHERSEE – ▢ and ✕ Münster - Köln - Koblenz - Salzburg - Villach - Klagenfurt.
117 – ▢ and ✕ Frankfurt - Salzburg - Villach - Klagenfurt. Terminates at München from Apr. 14.
119 – ▢ Münster - Köln - Koblenz - Ulm - Lindau - Bregenz - Innsbruck.
217 – ▢ and ✕ Saarbrücken - München - Salzburg - Bischofshofen - Selzthal - Graz.
219 – ▢ and ✕ Frankfurt - München - Salzburg - Bischofshofen - Selzthal - Graz.
391 – ▢ and ✕ Frankfurt - München (- Salzburg ⑧ to Apr. 13).
591 – ▢ and ✕ (Hamburg ①-⑤ a -) Hannover - Frankfurt - München.
991 – ▢ and ✕ Wiesbaden - Mainz - München.
1217 – ⑥ (also Apr. 14, 16, 30, June 4). ▢ and ✕ Karlsruhe - München - Salzburg - Villach - Klagenfurt. Terminates at München from Apr. 14.
2011 – ①-④ (not Apr. 13, May 24). ▢ and ✕ Düsseldorf - Stuttgart - Plochingen - Nürtingen (a. 1917) - Reutlingen Hbf (a. 1937) - Tübingen Hbf (a. 1950).
2013 – ALLGÄU – ▢ and ✕ Hannover - Dortmund - Köln - Koblenz - Ulm - Kempten - Oberstdorf.
2261 – ▢ and ✕ (Basel ①-⑥ e -) Karlsruhe - München.

A – ▢ and ✕ Paris - Strasbourg - München. ⑧ for international journeys.
B – From Berlin (Table 902).
F – To Friedrichshafen (Table 933).
H – From Hamburg (Table 900).
L – To Lindau (Table 933).
M – From Münster (Table 800).
T – To Nürtingen (a. 2118), Reutlingen Hbf (a. 2137) and Tübingen Hbf (a. 2150).
Y – ①②③④⑦ (not Apr. 13, 16, 30, May 24, 25, June 4).

a – Not Apr. 14, 17, May 1, June 5.
b – Not Apr. 16, 30, June 4.
c – Also Apr. 14, 17, May 1, June 5.
d – Ⓐ (not May 26).
e – Apr. 15, 17, May 1, June 5.
f – Also Apr. 13, May 24; not Apr. 14, May 26.
g – ① (also Apr. 18, May 2, June 6; not Apr. 17, May 1, June 5).
h – Not Apr. 15, 17, May 1, 25, 26, June 3, 5, 10.
k – Also Apr. 16, 30, June 4.
n – Also May 1, June 5; not Feb. 12 - Mar. 26, Apr. 2, 16, 30, June 4.
p – Apr. 15, 17, May 1, June 5.
q – Not Apr. 14, 16, 30, June 4.
t – Not Jan. 6.
u – Not Apr. 15, June 6.
w – Also Apr. 17, May 1, June 5; not Apr. 16, 30, June 4.
x – Not Mar. 11 - Apr. 23.

* – 3 - 8 minutes later from Mar. 30.
△ – Terminates at München from Apr. 14.

See page 367 for a summary of Christmas / New Year alterations

MÜNCHEN - STUTTGART

	ICE 618 ①-⑥ e E	ICE 1018 ⑦ v		ICE 616	RB 19204	IRE 4200	IC 2268 ⑨ g 🍴	IC 2268 Ⓐ d 🍴	IC 2010 Ⓒ z 🍴	RB 19210	IRE 4202 Ⓐ t	ICE 614 🍴	IRE 4204 L	IC 2294 Ⓐ d 🍴	RB 19214 Ⓐ t	TGV 9576 ①-⑤ ♦	TGV 9576 ⑥⑦ ✗	ICE 692 a B	IRE 4206/8 L	IC 2266 y🍴	ICE 612 🍴	IRE 4210 L	IC 1296 R△ 🍴	ICE 690 B✗
Salzburg Hbf 890 ......d.	...	...		...	...	...	...	...	...	...	...	...	...	...	...	...	...	...	...	...	...	...	0545	...
München Hbf ......905 d.	0001	0001		0324		0442						0524		0536k		0623	0628	0629		0646	0727		0746	0828
München Pasing ......905 d.	0009	0009		0333		0451						0533					0638			0655	0736			0837
Augsburg Hbf ......905 d.	0032	0032		0357		0516						0601		0611		0656	0705	0706		0721	0803		0817	0903
Günzburg ......945 d.	0102	0102				0546								0641									0848	
Ulm Hbf ......945 d.	0116	0116		0440	0500t	0522	0602	0602			0620	0650	0654	0659	0704	0742	0750	0751	0754	0804	0850	0854	0904	0951
Geislingen (Steige) ......d.				0529	0552	0625	0625		0629	0647		0717	0723	0730			0818			0918				
Göppingen ......d.				0550	0606	0639	0639		0650	0701		0729		0750			0829	0838		0929				
Plochingen ......936 d.	0201	0200		0607	0619	0651	0651	0655	0707	0718		0740	0746	0807			0840	0850		0940				
Stuttgart Hbf ......936 a.	0216	0216		0537	0624	.0637	0706	0706	0710	0724	0736	0745	0756	0800	0824	0839	0847	0846	0856	0906	0945	0956	0959	1046
Karlsruhe Hbf 931 ......a.	0335	0335			0753	0753								0930	0930			0953						
Heidelberg Hbf 912 ......a.	0426	0426					0753x					0844									1044			
Mannheim Hbf 912 ......a.	0438	0438		0628			0806				0828						0929			1028			1129	
Frankfurt Flughafen ✈ 912..a.	0512	0512		0706							0906									1106				
Frankfurt (Main) Hbf 912 ......a.	0533	0533												0940				1008				1140	1208	
Köln Hbf 800 910 ......a.	0706	0705		0805			1043			1005								1205						
Dortmund Hbf 800 ......a.		0821		0921			1209f			1121								1321						

	IRE 4212 L	IC 1268 Y 🍴	IC 1268 ⑤ f 🍴	ICE 610	IRE 4214 L	EC 390 △ 🍴	ICE 598 B✗	IRE 2012 L ♦	IC 518 🍴	ICE 4216	IRE 4218 L	EC 218 △ 🍴	ICE 596 B✗	IC 118 ♦	IC 2264 🍴	RB 19246	ICE 516 🍴	IRE 4222 L	IC 114 🍴	ICE 1090 ⑧ n B✗	ICE 594 ⑥ j B✗	IRE 4224 L	IC 2362 ⑤ f 🍴	ICE 514 🍴
Salzburg Hbf 890 ......d.		0642h	0642p			0800						1000								1200				
München Hbf ......905 d.		0847	0847	0928		0947	1028			1128		1147	1228		1247		1328		1346	1428	1428		1447	1528
München Pasing ......905 d.		0856	0856	0937			1037			1137			1237		1256		1337			1437	1437		1456	1537
Augsburg Hbf ......905 d.		0921	0921	1003		1017	1103			1203		1217	1303		1321		1403		1417	1503	1503		1521	1603
Günzburg ......945 d.						1048						1247							1448					
Ulm Hbf ......945 d.	0954	1004	1004	1050	1054	1104	1151	1154	1157	1250	1254	1304	1351	1356	1404		1409	1450	1454	1551	1551	1554	1604	1654
Geislingen (Steige) ......d.	1018			1118			1218		1318				1432				1518			1618				
Göppingen ......d.	1029			1129			1229	1235	1329			1433			1451		1529			1629				
Plochingen ......936 d.	1040	1050	1050	1140			1240	1248	1340			1449	1507		1540			1640						
Stuttgart Hbf ......936 a.	1056	1106	1107	1145	1156	1159	1246	1256	1304	1345	1356	1359	1446	1500	1504	1524	1545	1556	1600	1646	1646	1656	1704	1745
Karlsruhe Hbf 931 ......a.		1154												1550							1753			
Heidelberg Hbf 912 ......a.			1153x			1244			1353x				1444		1553x									
Mannheim Hbf 912 ......a.		1206	1228		1329		1406	1408			1529	1606			1628		1656	1729	1729				1828	
Frankfurt Flughafen ✈ 912 ......a.			1306					1506				1706						1808	1808				1906	
Frankfurt (Main) Hbf 912 ......a.		1340	1408					1540	1608														
Köln Hbf 800 910 ......a.		1442	1405					1643	1605				1843				1805		1943				2005	
Dortmund Hbf 800 ......a.		1608	1521					1808	1721								1921		2101				2121	

	IRE 4226 L	EC 112 ✗♦	IC 1910 ⑦w 🍴	ICE 592	IRE 4228 4230 L	IC 1910 ⑦w 🍴	IC 2262 🍴♦	IC 2094 ①-④ m	IC 512 M🍴	IRE 4232 L	IC 216 △ 🍴	ICE 590 □ B✗	IC 2234 ⑦w 🍴	IC 2092 ⑧q 🍴	IC 1110 🍴	IC 510 L	IRE 4236 L	ICE 4238	ICE 990 N	RJ 1066 ⑤⑥ ✗♦		RB 19282 19284 ⑧s	IC 2090 ⑧s 🍴	IC 19284
Salzburg Hbf 890 ......d.		1400									1600								1856			...	...	...
München Hbf ......905 d.		1547	1619	1628		1647	1709	1727		1747	1828		1845	1928	1928			2044	2044			2151		
München Pasing ......905 d.				1628	1637		1656	1718	1736		1837		1853	1937	1937			2053	2053			2200		
Augsburg Hbf ......905 d.		1617	1653	1703		1721	1745	1802		1817	1904		1918	2003	2003			2117	2117			2224		
Günzburg ......945 d.		1648	1728				1816			1847			1948					2147	2147			2255		
Ulm Hbf ......945 d.	1654	1703	1742	1751	1754		1804	1835	1850	1854	1904	1951	1954	2004	2050	2050	2054	2154	2204	2204		2252	2310	←
Geislingen (Steige) ......d.	1718		1806		1818		←	1918					2018			2118	2218			2320			2321	
Göppingen ......d.	1729		1818		1829	1832	1838		1929				2029	2038		2129	2229			→		2344	2350	
Plochingen ......936 d.	1740		→		1840		1850		1940				2040	2050		2140	2240					2357	0007	
Stuttgart Hbf ......936 a.	1756	1759		1846	1856	1859	1906		1945	1956	2000	2056	2126	2145	2145	2156	2256	2259	2259			0012	0024	
Karlsruhe Hbf 931 ......a.							1953					2153												
Heidelberg Hbf 912 ......a.		1844					1953x																	
Mannheim Hbf 912 ......a.			1929		2006			2028		2048	2129			2229	2229		2345	2345				0023	0023	
Frankfurt Flughafen ✈ 912 ......a.								2106						2308	2308							0042	0042	
Frankfurt (Main) Hbf 912 ......a.		1940		2008					2208															
Köln Hbf 800 910 ......a.							2243			2205						0007								
Dortmund Hbf 800 ......a.							2359																	

Regional trains MÜNCHEN - ULM

		Ⓒ z	✗ r																					
München Hbf ......d.	0008	0008	...	...	0531	0636	0734	0835	0935	1035	1134	1235	1335	1435	1534	1635	1734	1835	1935	2035	2100	2201	2300
München Pasing ......d.	0016	0016	...	...	0538	0644	0742	0843	0943	1043	1142	1243	1343	1443	1542	1643	1742	1843	1943	2043	2107	2209	2307
Augsburg Hbf ......d.	0051	0051	...	...	0619	0720	0819	0919	1019	1119	1219	1319	1419	1519	1619	1719	1819	1919	2019	2119	2148	2244	2348
Augsburg Hbf ......d.		0054	...	0521	0625	0725	0825	0925	1025	1125	1222	1325	1425	1525	1625	1725	1825	1925	2024	2125	2151	2251	2351
Günzburg ......d.		0147	0529	0614	0716	0819	0927b	1016	1116	1216	1321	1416	1516c	1616	1716	1821	1916	2017	2116	2216	2242	2342	0042
Ulm Hbf ......a.		0205	0547	0633	0735	0840	0946	1034	1134	1235	1339	1434	1535c	1635	1735	1839	1934	2037	2135	2235	2302	0002	0100

♦ — NOTES (LISTED BY TRAIN NUMBER)

112 – 🚃 and ✗ Klagenfurt - Villach - Salzburg - Frankfurt; conveys 🚃 Zagreb (212) - Ljubljana - Frankfurt.
114 – WÖRTHERSEE – 🚃 and 🍴 Klagenfurt - Villach - Salzburg - Koblenz - Köln - Dortmund.
118 – 🚃 Innsbruck - Bregenz - Lindau - Ulm - Koblenz - Köln - Münster.
216 – 🚃 and 🍴 Graz - Selzthal - Bischofshofen - Salzburg - München - Saarbrücken.
218 – 🚃 and 🍴 Graz - Selzthal - Bischofshofen - Salzburg - München - Frankfurt.
1066 – ⑤⑥ (also Apr. 13, 16, 30, May 24, June 4). 🚃 and ✗ Budapest - Wien - Frankfurt.
2010 – Ⓐ (not Dec. 27 - 30, May 26). 🚃 and 🍴 Tübingen Hbf (d. 0611) - Reutlingen (d. 0623) - Nürtingen (d. 0642) - Stuttgart - Düsseldorf (- Berlin ⑤ f).
2012 – ALLGÄU – 🚃 and 🍴 Oberstdorf - Kempten - Ulm - Köln - Dortmund - Hannover.
2262 – 🚃 and 🍴 München - Karlsruhe (- Basel ⑧ q).
9576 – 🚃 and 🍴 München - Strasbourg - Paris. 🖬 for international journeys.

B – To Berlin (Table 902).
D – To Wiesbaden (Table 911).
E – To Essen (Table 800).
L – From Lindau (Table 933).
M – To Münster (Table 800).
N – ①②③④⑦ (not Apr. 13, 16, 30, May 24, June 4). Train number 1590 on ④ (also Apr. 12, May 23).
R – ①-⑥ (also Apr. 16, 30, June 4; not Apr. 17, May 1, June 5).
Y – ①②③④⑥⑦ (also Apr. 14, May 26; not Apr. 13, May 24).

a – Not Apr. 14, 17, May 1, June 5.
b – Arrives 0916.
c – On Ⓒ (also Jan. 6) Günzburg d. 1519, Ulm a. 1539.
d – Not May 26.
e – Not Apr. 15, 17, May 1, June 5.

f – ⑤ (also Apr. 13, May 24; not Apr. 14, May 26).
g – Also Apr. 18, May 2, June 6; not Apr. 17, May 1, June 5.
h – ①②③④⑥ to Apr. 12.
j – Also Dec. 25 - 30, ⑦ Feb. 12 - Apr. 2, Apr. 14, 16, 17, 30, June 4.
k – 0542 from Mar. 30.
m – Not Apr. 13, 17, May 1, 24, 25, June 5.
n – Not Dec. 25 - 30, ⑦ Feb. 12 - Apr. 2, Apr. 14, 16, 17, 30, June 4.
p – Until Apr. 13.
q – Not Apr. 14, 16, 30, June 4.
r – Not Jan. 6.
s – Not Apr. 14, June 4.
t – Ⓐ (not Jan. 6).
v – Also Apr. 15, 17, May 1, June 5.
w – Also Apr. 17, May 1, June 5; not Apr. 16, 30, June 4.
x – Not Mar. 11 - Apr. 23.
y – Also Apr. 16, 30, June 4; not Apr. 17, May 1, June 5.
z – Also Jan. 6.

★ – Train number 1010 on ⑤⑥ (also Apr. 13, 16, 30, May 24, June 4), 1190 on ⑦ (also Apr. 17, May 1, June 5; not Apr. 16, 30, June 4). Also conveys ✗ on ①-④ (not Apr. 13, 17, May 1, June 5).
□ – On ⑤ (also Apr. 13, May 24; not Apr. 14, May 26) runs with train number 698 and continues to Kassel (Table 900). On ⑦ (also Apr. 17, May 1, June 5; not Apr. 16, 30, June 4) runs with train number 992 and continues to Hamburg (Table 900).
△ – Starts from München from Apr. 14.

KARLSRUHE - STUTTGART (also local trains HEIDELBERG - STUTTGART) 931

See Table **32** for full details of international *TGV* services from / to Paris. See Table **912** for fast trains Heidelberg - Stuttgart and v.v.

km	km		*ICE* 619		*IC* 2291	*IRE* 19011	*IC* 2363	*IRE* 4901	*RE* 19503	*IC* 2365	*IC* 2367	*IC* 2063	*RE* 19525	*IC* 2369	*IC* 2261	*IRE* 4903	*RE* 19505	*IC* 2065	*RE* 19527 19529	*IRE* 4905	*RE* 19507	*IC* 2067	*RE* 19531 19533	*IC* 2263	*IRE* 4907
			R		Ⓐn	Ⓐt	①–⑥ e🍷	Ⓐt	Ⓒz	Ⓐm O🍷	Ⓐt 🍷	①–⑥ eN	Ⓒz	Ⓐm	B🍷			N				N		🍷	
0		**Karlsruhe** Hbf d.	0211	...	0455	...	0559	0601	...	0637	0658	0706	0719	0741	0806	0805	...	0906	0919	1005	...	1106	1119	1205	1205
26		Pforzheim d.	|	...	|	0546	|	0624	...	|	|	0727	0743	|	|	0826	...	0927	0943	1026	...	1127	1143	|	1226
	0	**Heidelberg** Hbf 912 d.	|	...	|	|	|	|	0610	|	|	|	|	|	|	|	0810	|	|	|	1010	|	|	|	|
	33	Bruchsal 912 d.	|	...	0513	|	0617	|	0632	0654	0719	|	|	0758	0819	|	0833	|	|	|	1033	|	|	1219	|
39	65	Mühlacker d.	|	...	|	0555	|	0632	0656	|	|	0737	0755	|	|	0834	0859	0937	0955	1034	1059	1137	1155	|	1234
47	73	Vaihingen (Enz) 912 d.	0248	...	0532	0602	|	0639	0705	|	|	0746	0804	|	|	0841	0907	0946	1007	1041	1107	1146	1204	|	1241
86	112	**Stuttgart** Hbf 912 a.	0320	...	0549	0619	0648	0657	0740	0725	0750	0803	0839	0829	0849	0858	0939	1003	1039	1058	1139	1203	1239	1249	1258
		München Hbf 930 a.	0602	...	0814	...	...	...	...	...	...	...	...	...	1111	...	...	...	...	...	...	...	...	1511	...

	RE 19509	*IC* 2069	*IC* 2265	*IRE* 4909	*RE* 19511	*EC* 1217	*IC* 2161	*IC* 2361	*IC* 1269	*IRE* 4911	*RE* 19513	*IC* 2163	*IC* 2267	*IRE* 4913	*TGV* 9577	*RE* 19515	*IC* 2165	*RE* 19547 19549	*IC* 2269	*IRE* 4915	*TGV* 9579	*RE* 19517	*IC* 2167	*IRE* 4917	*RE* 19553
		N	⑤f 🍷			⑥k A🍷	Ⓑq N	⑤f	Ⓑq S🍷			N	🍷		Ⓑd P🍷		L		T G🍷		⑥c P🍷		Ⓑu		
Karlsruhe Hbf d.	...	1306	1405	1405	...	1505	1506	1544	1605	1605	...	1706	1805	1805	1828	...	1906	1919	2005	2005	2028	...	2106	2205	2321
Pforzheim d.	...	1327	|	1426	...	|	1527	|	|	1626	...	1727	|	1826	|	...	1927	1943	|	2026	|	...	2127	2226	2343
Heidelberg Hbf 912 d.	1210	|	|	|	1410	|	|	|	|	|	1610	|	|	|	|	1810	|	|	|	|	|	2010	|	|	|
Bruchsal 912 d.	1233	|	1419	|	1433	1518	|	1558	1619	|	1633	|	1819	|	|	1833	|	|	2019	|	|	2030	|	|	|
Mühlacker d.	1259	1337	|	1434	1459	|	1537	|	|	1634	1659	1737	|	1834	|	1859	1937	1955	|	2034	|	2055	2137	2234	2356
Vaihingen (Enz) 912 d.	1307	|	|	1441	1507	|	1546	|	|	1641	1707	1746	|	1841	|	1907	1946	2007	|	2041	|	2103	2146	2240	0005
Stuttgart Hbf 912 a.	1339	1359	1449	1458	1539	1554	1603	1629	1649	1658	1739	1803	1849	1858	1904	1939	2003	2039	2049	2058	2104	2137	2203	2258	0040
München Hbf 930 a.	...	...	...	...	...	1811	...	...	1911	...	...	...	2111	...	2136	...	...	...	2319w	...	2329	...	...	...	...

km		*RE* 19556		*ICE* 618 1018		*IC* 2368	*RE* 19500	*RE* 19522	*IC* 2268	*RE* 19524	*RE* 19526	*IC* 2164	*RE* 19502	*TGV* 9576	*IRE* 4902	*IC* 2266	*RE* 19528	*RE* 19530	*IC* 2162	*RE* 19504	*IRE* 4904	*IC* 1268	*IC* 2160	*RE* 19506	*IRE* 4906
				R		Ⓐm		Ⓐt	Ⓐn H🍷	Ⓒz	Ⓐt	①–⑥ eN△		P🍷		①–⑥ j🍷	Ⓒz	Ⓐt	①–⑥ eN			S🍷	N		
	München Hbf 930 d.	...	...	0001	...	...	...	...	0442g	...	...	...	...	0624b	...	0646	...	...	...	...	...	0847v	...	...	...
0	**Stuttgart** Hbf 912 d.	0019	...	0230	...	0546	0614	0626	0711	0717	0722	0759	0819	0854	0900	0911	0917	0919	0959	1019	1059	1111	1159	1219	1259
29	Vaihingen (Enz) 912 d.	0052	...	0259	...	0603	0645	0704	|	0750	0753	0816	0850	|	0916	|	0950	0952	1016	1050	1115	|	1216	1250	1315
	Mühlacker d.	0101	...	|	...	0611	0700	0714	|	0759	0801	0823	0900	|	0922	|	0959	1000	1023	1100	1121	|	1223	1300	1321
66	Bruchsal 912 d.	|	...	|	...	|	0728	|	0740	|	|	|	0929	|	|	0940	|	|	|	1129	|	1140	|	1329	|
	Heidelberg Hbf 912 a.	|	...	|	...	|	0748	|	|	|	|	|	0949	|	|	|	|	|	|	1149	|	|	|	1349	|
	Pforzheim d.	0114	...	|	...	0622	...	0729	|	0813	0814	0834	...	|	0930	|	1013	1013	1034	...	1130	|	1234	...	1330
87	**Karlsruhe** Hbf a.	0137	...	0335	...	0645	...	0753	0753	0838	0838	0853	...	0930	0953	0953	1038	1038	1053	...	1153	1154	1253	...	1353

	IC 2068	*RE* 19508	*IRE* 4908	*IC* 2264	*IC* 2066	*RE* 19510	*IC* 2313	*IRE* 4910	*IC* 2362	*IC* 2360	*IC* 2064	*RE* 19514	*IRE* 4912	*IC* 2262	*RE* 19548	*RE* 19550	*IC* 2062	*RE* 19516	*IRE* 4914	*IC* 2092	*RE* 19512	*IC* 2060	*RE* 19552 19554		*IC* 2260
	N△			🍷	N		Ⓐm O🍷		‡	①–⑤ a🍷	N			B🍷	Ⓒz	Ⓐt	N△			Ⓑq 🍷		Ⓑr L			⑦w 🍷
München Hbf 930 d.	...	...	...	1247	...	...	...	...	1447f	...	...	...	...	1647	...	...	...	...	...	1845	...	...	...	...	...
Stuttgart Hbf 912 d.	1359	1419	1459	1508	1559	1617	1641	1659	1708	1734	1759	1819	1859	1911	1918	1922	1959	2019	2059	2111	2120	2159	2219	...	2309
Vaihingen (Enz) 912 d.	1416	1450	1515	|	1616	1650	|	1715	|	|	1816	1850	1915	|	1950	1953	2016	2051	2115	|	2152	2216	2254	...	2326
Mühlacker d.	1423	1500	1521	|	1623	1700	|	1721	|	|	1823	1900	1921	|	1959	2001	2023	2100	2121	|	2201	2223	2303	...	2334
Bruchsal 912 d.	|	1529	|	1537	|	1729	1712	|	1737	1804	|	1929	|	1940	|	|	|	2129	|	2140	|	|	|	...	|
Heidelberg Hbf 912 a.	|	1549	|	|	|	1749	|	|	|	|	|	1949	|	|	|	|	|	2156	|	|	|	|	|	...	|
Pforzheim d.	1434	...	1530	|	1634	...	|	1730	|	|	1834	...	1930	|	2013	2014	2034	...	2130	|	2214	2234	2317	...	2344
Karlsruhe Hbf a.	1453	...	1553	1550	1653	...	1731	1753	1753	1821	1853	...	1953	1953	2038	2038	2054	...	2153	2153	2237	2259	2340	...	0008

A – [12] and 🍷 Karlsruhe - München - Salzburg - Klagenfurt. Terminates at München from Apr. 14.
B – From / to Basel on dates in Table **912**.
G – [12] Karlsruhe - Stuttgart - Ulm (- München ⑦**w**).
H – [12] (München ①**g** -) Ulm - Stuttgart - Karlsruhe.
L – [12] Karlsruhe - Stuttgart (- Nürnberg ♥) and v.v.
N – [12] Karlsruhe - Stuttgart - Nürnberg and v.v.
O – To / from Offenburg (Table **916**).
P – [12] and 🍷 München - Stuttgart - Paris and v.v. Ⓡ for international journeys.
R – From / to Dortmund or Essen (Tables **800**/**912**).
S – From / to Salzburg (Table **890**).
T – ①②③④⑦ (not Apr. 13, 16, 30, May 24, 25, June 4).

a – Not Apr. 14, 17, May 1, June 5.
b – 0629 on ⑥⑦.
c – Also Apr. 16, 30, June 4.
d – Not Apr. 16, 30, June 4.
e – Not Apr. 15, 17, May 1, June 5.
f – ⑤ (also Apr. 13, May 24; not Apr. 14, May 26).
g – ① (also Apr. 18, May 2, June 6; not Apr. 17, May 1, June 5).
j – Also Apr. 16, 30, June 4; not Apr. 17, May 1, June 5.
k – Also Apr. 14, 16, 30, June 4.
m – Not Jan. 6, May 26.
n – Not May 26.
q – Not Apr. 14, 16, 30, June 4.

r – Not Apr. 14, 16, 30, May 25, 26, June 4.
t – Not Jan. 6.
u – Not Jan. 6, Apr. 14, 16, 30, May 25, 26, June 4.
v – ①②③④⑥⑦ (also Apr. 14, May 26; not Apr. 13, May 24).
w – ⑦ (also Apr. 17, May 1, June 5; not Apr. 16, 30, June 4).
z – Also Jan. 6.

♥ – ④⑤⑦ (also Jan. 4, Apr. 12, 17, May 23, 24, June 5; not Jan. 6, Apr. 14, 16, 30, May 25, 26, June 4).
‡ – Train number **2366** on ⑦ (also Apr. 17, May 1, 25, 26, June 5; not Apr. 16, 30, June 4). Train number **2166** on ⑥ (also Apr. 14, 16, 30, June 4).
△ – Subject to alteration until Jan. 23.

STUTTGART - STUTTGART FLUGHAFEN / MESSE ✈ 932

S-Bahn 2 / 3

20 km. Journey time: 27 minutes. On Jan. 6 services run as on ⑦.

From Stuttgart Hbf: 0025, 0055, 0455 Ⓐ, 0515 Ⓐ, 0525, 0545 Ⓑ, 0555 ⚒, 0615 Ⓐ, 0625, 0645 Ⓑ, 0655 ⚒, 0715 Ⓐ, 0725, 0745, 0755, 0815, 0825, 0845, 0855 and at 15, 25, 45 and 55 minutes past each hour until 1815, 1825, 1845, 1855, 1915 Ⓐ, 1925, 1945 Ⓐ, 1955, 2015 Ⓐ, 2025, 2045 Ⓐ, 2055, 2115 Ⓐ, 2125, 2145 Ⓐ, 2155, 2215 Ⓐ, 2225, 2245 Ⓐ, 2255, 2315 Ⓐ, 2325, 2355.

From Stuttgart Flughafen ✈: 0008, 0038, 0508, 0518 Ⓐ, 0538 ⚒, 0548 Ⓑ, 0608, 0618 Ⓐ, 0638 ⚒, 0648 Ⓑ, 0708, 0718 Ⓐ, 0738 ⚒, 0748 Ⓑ, 0808, 0818, 0838, 0848 and at 08, 18, 38 and 48 minutes past each hour until 1808, 1818, 1838, 1848, 1908, 1918, 1938, 1948 Ⓐ, 2008, 2018 Ⓐ, 2038, 2048 Ⓐ, 2108, 2118 Ⓐ, 2138, 2148 Ⓐ, 2208, 2218 Ⓐ, 2238, 2248 Ⓐ, 2308, 2318 Ⓐ, 2338, 2348 Ⓐ. ***Warning!*** *Timings of late evening services (2200 to 0100 the following morning) may vary on ① (not Dec. 26, Jan. 2, Feb. 27, Mar. 13, Apr. 3, 17, 24, May 1, June 5).*

ULM - FRIEDRICHSHAFEN - LINDAU 933

IRE / RE services (except trains **C** and **D**)

km		F	F	B			B			B			B	C		B			B			B			
	Stuttgart Hbf 930 d.	...	0557e	...	0700	0801	...	0900	1001	...	1100	1201	...	1257	1401	...	1454	1601	...	1659	1802	...	1859	2001	2101
0	**Ulm** Hbf d.	0550	0712h	0805	0812	0912	1005	1012	1112	1205	1212	1312	1405	1411	1512	1605	1612	1712	1805	1812	1914	2005	2012	2112	2212
37	Biberach (Riß) d.	0619	0736	0825	0836	0936	1025	1036	1136	1225	1236	1336	1425	1433	1536	1625	1636	1736	1825	1836	1938	2025	2036	2136	2238
62	Aulendorf d.	0638	0755	|	0855	0955	|	1055	1155	|	1255	1355	1442	1451	1555	|	1655	1755	|	1855	2002	|	2055	2155	2258
84	Ravensburg d.	0652	0808	0852	0908	1008	1052	1108	1208	1252	1308	1408	1456	1505	1608	1652	1708	1808	1852	1908	2015	2052	2108	2208	2311
95	Meckenbeuren d.	0659	0816	|	0916	1016	|	1116	1216	|	1316	1416	1503	1513	1616	|	1716	1816	|	1916	2022	|	2116	2216	2318
99	Friedrichshafen Flughafen ✈ d.	0704	|	0901	|	|	1101	|	|	1301	|	|	|	|	|	1701	|	|	1901	|	|	2101	|	|	|
103	Friedrichshafen Stadt a.	0710	0823	0906	0923	1023	1106	1123	1223	1306	1323	1423	1511	1521	1623	1706	1723	1823	1906	1923	2030	2106	2123	2224	2326
103	Friedrichshafen Stadt d.	0727	0828	...	0928	1028	...	1128	1228	...	1328	1428	...	1535	1631t	...	1728	1828	...	1928	2035	...	2128	*2246*	2331
127	**Lindau** Hbf 🚢 a.	0752	0854	...	0952	1055	...	1152	1254	...	1352	1455	...	1554	1657	...	1752	1855	...	1952	2100	...	2156	*2319*	2359

	Ⓒz	Ⓐe		F		B			B		D	B			B		⊙	B			B			B	
Lindau Hbf 🚢 d.	...	0452	0559	0701v	0803	...	0904	1005	...	1104	1202	...	1305	1405	...	1505	1600	...	1705	1805	...	1905	2005	...	*2204*
Friedrichshafen Stadt a.	...	0524	0622	0726	0826	...	0926	1026	...	1126	1220	...	1326	1426	...	1527	1621	...	1726	1826	...	1926	2026	...	*2231*
Friedrichshafen Stadt d.	0521	0530	0628	0731	0831	0850	0931	1031	1049	1131	1233	1243	1331	1431	1450	1531	1625	1648	1731	1831	1850	1931	2031	2048	2235
Friedrichshafen Flughafen ✈ d.	|	|	0633z	|	|	0855	|	|	1054	|	|	|	|	|	1455	|	|	1655	|	|	1855	|	|	2053	2240
Meckenbeuren d.	0528	0538	0635k	0738	0838	|	0938	1038	|	1138	1241	1250	1338	1438	|	1538	1635	|	1738	1838	|	1938	2038	|	2245
Ravensburg d.	0537	0546	0643k	0746	0846	0905	0946	1046	1104	1146	1250	1258	1346	1446	1505	1546	1644	1704	1746	1846	1904	1946	2046	2102	2253
Aulendorf d.	0552	0601	0659k	0801	0901	|	1001	1101	|	1201	1306	1313	1401	1501	|	1601	1701	|	1801	1901	|	2001	2101	2117	2308
Biberach (Riß) d.	0610	0620	0720	0820	0920	0930	1019	1120	1129	1219	1322	1330	1420	1520	1530	1620	1719	1730	1820	1920	1930	2020	2120	2132	2326
Ulm Hbf a.	0641	0644	0744	0844	0944	0953	1044	1144	1153	1244	1345	1353	1444	1544	1553	1644	1744	1753	1844	1944	1952	2044	2144	2155	2357
Stuttgart Hbf 930 a.	...	0756	0856	0956	1056	...	1156	1256	...	1356	1500	...	1556	1656	...	1756	1856	...	1956	2056	...	2156	2256	...	...

B – To / from Basel Bad Bf (Table **939**).
C – *IC* **119**: [12] Münster - Lindau - Bregenz - Innsbruck.
D – *IC* **118**: [12] Innsbruck - Bregenz - Lindau - Münster.
F – Change trains at Friedrichshafen Stadt on Ⓒ**z**.

e – Ⓐ (not Jan. 6).
h – 0708 on Ⓒ (also Jan. 6).
k – 3 minutes later on Ⓒ (also Jan. 6).
t – 1628 on Ⓒ (also Jan. 6).
v – *0657* on Ⓒ (also Jan. 6).

z – Ⓒ (also Jan. 6).

⊙ – On Ⓒ (also Jan. 6) Lindau d. 1605, Friedrichshafen Stadt a. 1626, d. 1631, Meckenbeuren d. 1638, Ravensburg d. 1646 and then as shown.

See page 367 for a summary of Christmas / New Year alterations

935   MÜNCHEN, AUGSBURG and ULM - OBERSTDORF and LINDAU   RE/RB services except where shown

Subject to alteration Mar. 4 - Apr. 23 ⊗. For services to/from Bad Wörishofen see panel at foot of page (also on page 445). For regional services Memmingen - Lindau via Kißlegg see Table **937**.

km				ALX	ALX												EC 196	ALX				
			©z	Ⓐe	Ⓐe	⚒r‡	⚒r‡		Ⓐe		Ⓐe	Ⓐe	©z	©z		★	©z			Ⓐe	©z	©z
0	München Hbf ......⊡ d.		...	0448	0448	...	...	0552	0552	...	...	0653	...	...	...	...	0717	0720	...	0751
7	München Pasing........ d.		...	0455	0455	...	...	0600	0600	...	...	0700	...	...	...	...	0727	...	...	0800
42	Geltendorf.............. d.		...	0517	0517	...	...	0622	0622	...	...	0722	...	...	...	...	...	...	...	0822
56	Kaufering............... d.		...	0526	0526	...	...	0631	0631	...	...	0731	...	...	...	...	0756	...	...	0832
	Nürnberg Hbf **905**... d.																			
	Augsburg Hbf .... d.		0500	...	...	...	0548	...	...	0618	0618	...	0703	...	...	...	0730	0815	...
68	Buchloe.............. a.	0533	0534	0534	...	...	0621	0640	0639	0649	0649	0738	0735c	...	0756	0804	0759c	0843	0841
68	Buchloe.............. d.	▬	0536	0536	...	0615	...	0631	0641	0652	0642	0650	0650	0739	0749	...	0758	0807	0818	▬	0846
88	Kaufbeuren........... d.	0549	0549	0554	0628	...	0655	0700	0700	0752	0801	...	0821	...	0859
94	Biessenhofen......... d.	0554	0554	0600	0634	...	0701	0705	0705	0757v	0806	...	0905
100	Marktoberdorf........ d.	0610	0646	0712	0817	0915
131	Füssen.............. a.	0649	0726	0752	0855	0956
	Türkheim (Bay).......... d.	0638	0700t	0659	0825
	Mindelheim.............. d.	©z	0648	0713	0709	Ⓐe	0835
	Ulm Hbf................ d.	0511	0549	0618	0659	0659	0717	0717	0819
	Memmingen.......... a.	0555	Ⓐe	Ⓐe	0644	0709	0733	0729	0721	0759	0759	0800	0800	0855	0856
131	Memmingen **937** d.	0556	0559	0559	0646	0723	0723	0802	0802	0802	0802	0904
131	Kempten Hbf .... a.	0620	0621	0621	0633	0633	0717	0757	0726	0726	0757	0819v	0826	0826	0827	0827	0839	0848	0925
131	Kempten Hbf .... d.	0514	0526	0625	0625	0651	0651	0800	0729	0729	0800	0828	0828	0828	0828	0841	0852	ALX
152	Immenstadt........... a.	0526	0538	0641	0641	0708	0708	0814	0744	0744	0814	0842	0842	0842	0842	0907	0914
152	Immenstadt........... d.	0527	0539	0645	0656	0713	0719	0820	0747	0751	0820	0844	0850	0850	0844	0911	0914
	Sonthofen............ d.	0706	0730	0829	0801	0829	0900	0900	0922
	Oberstdorf........... a.	0729	0748	0851	0819	0851	0918	0918	0939
197	Hergatz......**937** d.	0600	0612	0725	0752	0819	0921	0916	0946
203	Wangen (Allgäu) **937** a.	0756	0926
220	Lindau Hbf .....**937** a.	0615	0626	0743	0834	0931	0946	1003

		ALX											ALX			EC 194			ALX	
		†z		◑						◑				◑			♥				
München Hbf........⊡ d.		0820	0840	0853	...	0919	...	0952	...	1020	1053	...	1119	...	1152	1220	1233	1253	...	1319
München Pasing........ d.		0827	0847	0900	...	0927	...	1000	...	1027	1100	...	1127	...	1200	1227	1300	...	1327
Geltendorf.............. d.		0849	0922	...	...	1022	...	1049	1122	...	1222	1249	1322	...
Kaufering............... d.		0900	0931	...	0955	...	1032	...	1059	1131	...	1155	...	1232	1259	1331	...	1355
Nürnberg Hbf **905**... d.	0717n
Augsburg Hbf .... d.	0830	0903	...	0930	1015	1030	...	1103	1130	1215	1230	...	1303	...	1329
Buchloe.............. a.	0851	0908	0930k	0935c	1003	0959c	1043	1041	1051	1108	1138	1135c	...	1203	1159c	1243	1241	1251	1308	1315	1338	1335c	...	1403	1401c
Buchloe.............. d.	0854	0911	0941k	0947	1005	1006	1046	1054	1111	1139	1147	1205	1206	1246	1254	1309	1317	1339	1347	1405	1406
Kaufbeuren........... d.	0906	0954k	1000	1018	1059	1106	1153	1200	1218	1259	1306	1353	1400	1418
Biessenhofen......... d.	1000	1006	1105	1159	1206	1305	1359v	1406
Marktoberdorf........ d.	0950	1016	1115	1216	1315v	1416
Füssen.............. a.	1027	1055	1155	1255	1355v	1455
Türkheim (Bay).......... d.	0918	1014	...	1118	...	1214	1316	...	1414
Mindelheim............. d.	0930	1032t	1130	Ⓐe	1232t	1335t	1430
Ulm Hbf................ d.	0919	1019	1119	1119	1219	1317	1317
Memmingen.......... a.	0951	0954	1053	1056	1151	1200	1200	1253	1256	1355	1344	1355	1355	1451
Memmingen.......**937** d.	1104	1202	1202	1304	1346	1402	1402
Kempten Hbf .... a.	0928	1025k	1026	1046	1126	1128	1221	1226	1226	1246	1326	1328	1421v	1426	1426	1446
Kempten Hbf .... d.	0931	1031	1047	ALX	1131	1231	1231	1247	ALX	1331	1431	1431	1447	ALX
Immenstadt........... a.	0945	◄	1045	1102	◄	1145	1245	1245	1302	◄	1345	◄	1445	1445	1502	◄
Immenstadt........... d.	0947	0951	1052	1106	1115	1147	1151	1247	1251	1306	1319	1347	1351	1447	1451	1506	1514
Sonthofen............ d.	1001	1102	1123	1201	1301	1330	1401	1501	1522
Oberstdorf........... a.	1023	1120	1140	1219	1319	1348	1419	1519	1539
Hergatz......**937** d.	1019	1144	1219	1323	1344	1419	1518	1544
Wangen (Allgäu) **937** a.	1328
Lindau Hbf .....**937** a.	1033	1200	1234	1400	1433	1447	1532	1600

		IC 2085 H				ALX	ALX	RE 2013 A Ⓨ						EC 192 ♥						ALX		ALX	
									◑						Ⓐe	©z	Ⓐe	©z		Ⓐe	◑	©z	
München Hbf........⊡ d.		...	1352	1420	1451	...	1519	...	...	1551	...	1620	1633	1651	1651	...	...	1713	...	1719
München Pasing........ d.		1400	1427	1459	...	1527	1559	1627	1659	1659	1720	1727
Geltendorf.............. d.		1422	1449	1522	1622	1651	1722	1722	...
Kaufering............... d.		1432	1459	1531	...	1555	1632	1700	1731	1732	1750	1755
Nürnberg Hbf **905**... d.	
Augsburg Hbf .... d.	1356	1415	1430	...	1503	...	1530	1615	1630	...	1703	...	1729	...	1815
Buchloe.............. a.	1421	1443	1441	1451	1508	1538	1535c	1603	1559c	1643	1641	1651	1708	1715	1735	1738	1741	1735c	...	1759	1759c	1803	1843
Buchloe.............. d.	1422	1446	1454	1511	1539	1547	1605	1606	1646	1654	1709	1717	1736	1739	1742	1747	1802	1806	1805	▬
Kaufbeuren........... d.	1438	1459	1506	1553	1600	1618	1659	1706	1749	1753	1756	1800	1816	1818
Biessenhofen......... d.	1505	1600	1606	1705	1806t	1801	1801	1806
Marktoberdorf........ d.	1515	1616	1715	1816	1818
Füssen.............. a.	1557	1655	1756	1856
Türkheim (Bay).......... d.	1518	...	1614	1716	1814
Mindelheim............. d.	1530	Ⓐe	1635t	1735t	1830
Ulm Hbf................ d.	1419	1519	1519	1615	1717	1717
Memmingen.......... a.	1456	1551	1555	1555	1643	1655	1755	1744	1757	1757	1851
Memmingen.......**937** d.	1504	1602	1602	1645	1746	1801	1801
Kempten Hbf .... a.	1509	1526	1528	...	1622	1626	1626	1646	1707	1728	1823	1829	1825	1825	1846	ALX	1846	ALX
Kempten Hbf .... d.	1511	1531	1631	1631	1647	1709	1731	1832	1832	1847	Ⓐe	1848	©z
Immenstadt........... a.	1527	1545	◄	1645	1645	1702	1724	1745	1846	1846	1902	◄	1903	◄
Immenstadt........... d.	1542	1547	1551	1647	1651	1706	1714	1740	1747	1751	1848	1852	1907	1915	1907	1915
Sonthofen............ d.	1552	1601	1701	1722	1752	1801	1902	1923	1923
Oberstdorf........... a.	1611	1619	1719	1739	1813	1819	1920	1940	1945
Hergatz......**937** d.	1619	1724	1744	1819	1922	1945	1945
Wangen (Allgäu) **937** a.	1729
Lindau Hbf .....**937** a.	1633	1800	1833	1847	1937	2001	2001

A – ALLGÄU – 🛏 (IC 2013) Hannover - Dortmund - Köln - Stuttgart - Ulm (RE 2013) - Oberstdorf.

H – NEBELHORN – 🛏 Hamburg (2083) - Augsburg (2085) - Oberstdorf.

R – ⑤–⑦ (also Apr. 17, May 1, 25, June 5).

c – Connects with train in preceding column.

e – Ⓐ (not Jan. 6).

k – On © (also Jan. 6): Buchloe a. 0938, d. 0939, Kaufbeuren d. 0953, Kempten a. 1022.

n – 0709 from Mar. 30.

r – Not Jan. 6.

t – Arrives 8 – 12 minutes earlier.

v – 2 – 3 minutes later on Ⓐ (not Jan. 6).

z – Also Jan. 6.

★ – Change trains at Immenstadt on Ⓐ (not Jan. 6).

♥ – 🛏 and ✗ München - Bregenz - St Gallen - Zürich (Table 75).

◑ – Conveys 🛏 Augsburg - Türkheim - Bad Wörishofen (see panel below).

‡ – Runs daily from Kempten.

⊗ – Services from München are subject to alteration Mar. 4 - Apr. 23.

♠ – Additional journeys Türkheim - Bad Wörishofen: 0525 Ⓐe, 0559 Ⓐe, 0627 Ⓐe, 0726 Ⓐe and 2247 R.

◄ – Detached from train in previous column at Immenstadt.

⊡ – Most trains in Table 935 use platforms 27 – 36 at München Hbf (minimum connecting time from other services is 10 minutes).

ALX – Operated by Vogtlandbahn. Ⓨ.

AUGSBURG - TÜRKHEIM - BAD WÖRISHOFEN

km			Ⓐe	©z																	R	
0	Augsburg Hbf .... d.		...	...	...	0930	...	1130	...	1329	...	1530	...	1729	...	1930	...	2131	...	2331
40	Buchloe............... d.		...	...	1006	1206	1406	1606	1806	2006	2209	0009
48	Türkheim (Bay)..... ♠ d.	0658	0702	0816	0847	0920	1017	1047	1120	1217	1247	1320	1417	1447	1520	1617	1647	1719	1817	1847	1920	2017	2047	2121	2219	2321	0027
53	Bad Wörishofen..... ♠ a.	0704	0708	0822	0853	0926	1023	1053	1126	1223	1253	1326	1423	1453	1526	1623	1653	1725	1823	1853	1926	2023	2053	2128	2226	2328	0032

| RE/RB services except where shown | MÜNCHEN, AUGSBURG and ULM - OBERSTDORF and LINDAU | 935 |

Subject to alteration Mar. 4 - Apr. 23 ⊗. For services to/from Bad Wörishofen see panel at foot of page (also on page 444). For regional services Memmingen - Lindau via Kißlegg see Table 937.

München, Augsburg, Ulm → Oberstdorf / Lindau

		EC 190 ♥	ALX			①						①			⑤-⑦ R	⑤-⑦ R		ALX		①
München Hbf ....☐ d.		1751	1820	...	1833	1851	...	1919	...	1952	2019	...	...	2119	...	...	2220	...	2319	...	0001
München Pasing .... d.		1759	1827	...	1859	1927	...	1959	2027	...	...	2127	...	...	2227	...	2327	...	0008
Geltendorf .... d.		1822	1849	...	1922	...	...	2022	2050	...	...	2148	...	...	2249	...	2348	...	0030
Kaufering .... d.		1832	1859	...	1931	...	1955	2032	2101	...	...	2158	...	...	2259	...	2358	...	0040
Nürnberg Hbf 905.. d.		...	...	1732n	1732n	...
Augsburg Hbf .... a.		...	1844	1844	...	1903	...	1930	2015	...	2050	2050	...	2131	...	2233	2233	...	...	2331	...
Buchloe		1841	1907	1904c	1904	1915	1939	1935c	2003	1959c	2043	2041	2110	2109c	2109	...	2203	2206c	...	2305	2305	...	2307c	...	0006	0003c	0049
Buchloe		1846	1909	1910	1910	1917	1941	1947	2005	2006 —	2050	2112	2114	2114	...	2209	2208	...	2310	2310	...	2312	...	0007	0009	...
Kaufbeuren		1859	1922	1922	...	1954	2000	2018	...	...	2103	...	2125	2125	...	2221	2227	2321	2321	2329	...	...	0020	...
Biessenhofen .... d.		1905	...	...	...	2000	2006	...	...	2109	...	2130	2130	...	...	2236	2325	2325	2334	...	...	0025	...
Marktoberdorf .... d.		1915	...	...	2016	...	...	2120	...	...	2246	...	2346	...
Füssen .... a.		1955	...	...	2055	...	...	2200	...	...	2326	...	0026	...
türkheim (Bay) .... d.		...	1916	...	...	...	2014	...	2119	...	...	2217	...	...	2319	...	0017	...
Mindelheim .... d.		...	1935j	...	...	2030	...	2130	...	...	2230	...	...	2330	...	0027	...
Ulm Hbf .... d.		1819	...	...	1919	...	2019	...	2119	...	2221	...	...	2323	...
Memmingen .... a.		1857	1955	...	1944	...	1955	2051	2057	...	2151	...	2159	2251	...	2254	...	2352	0003	...	0047
Memmingen ....937 d.		1903	2005	...	1946	...	2003	...	2105	...	...	2200	...	2256	...	...	0004	...
Kempten Hbf .... a.		1928	...	1947	1947	...	2025	2028	2046	...	2129	...	2152	2152	2230	...	2250	2320	2347	2347	...	...	0029	0052
Kempten Hbf .... d.		1933	...	1949	1949	...	...	2048	...	...	2154	2154	...	2254	2324	2349	...
Immenstadt .... a.		1947	◇	2003	2003	...	2103	...	2208	2208	...	2310	2340	...	0003
Immenstadt .... d.		1953	...	2005	2015	...	2106	2111	...	2211	2214	...	2311	2346	...	0005
Sonthofen .... d.		2003	...	2025	...	2121	...	2224	...	2356	...
Oberstdorf .... a.		2021	...	2049	...	2139	...	2242	...	0014
Hergatz ....937 a.		...	2103	2038	...	...	2144	...	...	2250	...	...	2348	...	0039
Wangen (Allgäu) 937 a.		...	2058	...
Lindau Hbf ....937 a.		...	2118	2053	2047	...	2201	...	...	2304	...	...	0005	...	0053

Lindau / Oberstdorf → München

km	km		ALX									ALX	ALX								
			Ⓐe	🍴r	Ⓐe		Ⓐe		Ⓐe	Ⓐe	Ⓐe		Ⓐe		🍴r	🍴r	🍴r	†z	†z	†z		†z
0		Lindau Hbf ....937 d.	...	...	...	...	0442e	...	...	...	...	0520	0610	...	0624	...	0707
		Wangen (Allgäu) 937 d.															0730
23	0	Hergatz ....937 d.					0456e					0537	0624		0639		0724
	0	Oberstdorf ....d.						0501				0542	0622		0631	
	13	Sonthofen ....d.						0520				0601	0641		0654	
	21	Immenstadt ....a.					0531e	0529				0610c	0616c	0650	0659		0706	0714
	21	Immenstadt ....d.					0532e	0536			0623	►	0629	►	0703		►	0717	◇
	42	Kempten Hbf ....a.					0545e	0552			0638	0646	0717		0731
	42	Kempten Hbf ....d.		0446	0529	0521	0548	0556	0601		0641	0648	0722		0734	0734	0736
85	77	Memmingen ....937 a.					0554				0708		0800	0800		0813
85	77	Memmingen ....a.	0451	0525	0556		0552	0622	0626		0647	0710		0739	0739		0804	0804		0815
129		Ulm Hbf ....a.				0643		0719		0743		0839	0839
112		Mindelheim ....d.	0513	0548		0613		0648	0713		0800	0800		0836
123		Türkheim (Bay) ....d.	0521	0557 Ⓐe		0622	0656h	0722		0810	0809	©z	Ⓐe		0844
		Füssen ....d.			0452		0600		0702	0704
		Marktoberdorf ....d.			0534		0644		0746	0749
		Biessenhofen ....d.		0513	0548	0615	0627	0652	0745	0754	0757	0801
		Kaufbeuren ....d.		0519	0547	0553	0620	0634	0657	0751	0759	0802	0807
131		Buchloe ....a.	0528	0530c	0604	0605c	0631	0629c	0647	0704h	0709c	0729	0730c	0802	0817	0817	0812c	0815c	0818c	0851
131		Buchloe ....d.	0535	0533	0609	0607	0633	0640	0648	0648	0711	0712	0739	0732	0805	0820	0820	0824	0824	0820	0853
171		Augsburg Hbf ....a.	0607		0640	0712	0716	0716	0744	0811	0829	0856	0856	0856
		Nürnberg Hbf 905... a.									0954p
		Kaufering ....d.		0541	0617	0641	0720	0741	0829	0829	0901
		Geltendorf ....d.			0628	0651	0730	0838	0838	0910
		München Pasing ....a.		0610	0651	0711	0756	0809	0857	0857	0933
		München Hbf ....☐ a.		0618	0658	0718	0804	0819	0904	0904	0941

	ALX	ALX		EC 191 ♥			IC 2084 H	IC 2012 Ⓐ🍴	ALX	ALX		EC 193 ♥	
		Ⓐe								©z			
indau Hbf ....937 d.	...	0725	...	0758	...	0912	0925			...	0958	1016	1112	1125
Wangen (Allgäu) 937 d.				0829
ergatz ....937 d.	...	0739	0814	0839	0941	1014	1031	1139
Oberstdorf ....d.	0734f		0822	0837	0904	0940	0948	1024	1039g	1142
Sonthofen ....d.	0801		0839	0901	0931	1001	1012	1041	1102	1201
Immenstadt ....a.	0810	0814	0847	0851	0910	0914	0940	1015	1009	1021	1049	1051	1108	1111	1210	1214
Immenstadt ....d.	►	0817	►	0900	0917	0917	1017	1027	1036	►	1100	1117	1117	►	1217
Kempten Hbf ....a.	0830		0914	0931	0931	1030	1043	1052	1114	1131	1131	1230
Kempten Hbf ....d.	0832	0835	0916	0934	0934	0941	1032	1045	1055	1116	1134	1134	1141	1232	1235
Memmingen ....937 a.	0857		0958	0958	1013	1123 Ⅱ	1158	1158	1213	1257
Memmingen ....a.	0904		0907	1002	1002	1015	1005	1127	1107	1204	1205	1215	1205	1304
Ulm Hbf ....a.	0939		1039	1039	1155	1239	1239	1339
Mindelheim ....d.	0932		1037j	1132	1237j
Türkheim (Bay) ....d.	0946		1045	1146	1245
Füssen ....d.	0806		0905	1006	1105	1206
Marktoberdorf ....d.	0849		0949	1049	1147	1249
Biessenhofen ....d.	0858		0957	1005	1058	1156	1205	1258
Kaufbeuren ....d.	0856	0903	0943	1002	1010	1056	1103	1115	1143	1201	1210	1256	1303
uchloe ....a.	0907	0915	0952	0954c	1016	1021c	1041	1052	1107	1115	1129	1152	1154c	1213	1221c	1241	1252	1307	1315
uchloe ....d.	0909	0918	0918	1000	0955	1022	1043	1053	1109	1118	1118	1131	1200	1155	1224	1242	1243	1253	1309	1318	1345
Augsburg Hbf ....a.	0930	0945	1029	1056	1130	1145	1156	1229	1256	1330	1345
Nürnberg Hbf 905... a.	
aufering ....d.	0928		1003	1029	1101	1128	1203	1230	1301	1328
eltendorf ....d.	0937		1038	1110	1137	1238	1310	1337
München Pasing ....a.	0958		1033	1058	1133	1158	1233	1305	1357
München Hbf ....☐ a.	1005		1041	1105	1128	1141	1205	1241	1305	1328	1343	1404

– ALLGÄU – 🚲 and 🍴 Oberstdorf - Stuttgart - Köln - Hannover.
– NEBELHORN – 🚲 Oberstdorf - Augsburg (2082) - Hamburg.
– ⑤-⑦ (also Apr. 17, May 1, 25, June 5).
– Change trains at Buchloe on ⑥.
– Connects with train in preceding column.
– Ⓐ (not Jan. 6).
– 0739 on ©️ (also Jan. 6).
– 1044 on Ⓐ (not Jan. 6).
– On ©️ (also Jan. 6) Türkheim d. 0659, Buchloe a. 0706.
– Arrives 11 minutes earlier.

n – 1701 from Mar. 30.
p – 0957 from Mar. 30.
r – Not Jan. 6.
z – Also Jan. 6.
①️ – Conveys 🚲 Augsburg - Türkheim - Bad Wörishofen (see panel page 444).
Ⅱ – Conveys 🚲 Bad Wörishofen - Türkheim - Augsburg (see panel below).
► – Attached to train in the next column at Immenstadt.
◇ – Via Kißlegg (Table 937).

♥ – 🚲 and ✗ München - Bregenz - St Gallen - Zürich and v.v. (Table 75).
⊗ – Services from/to München are subject to alteration Mar. 4 - Apr. 23.
♣ – Additional journeys Bad Wörishofen - Türkheim: 0611 Ⓐe, 0709 Ⓐe, 0758 Ⓐe and 2308 R.
☐ – Most trains in Table 935 use platforms 27 - 36 at München Hbf (minimum connecting time from/to other services is 10 minutes).

ALX – Operated by Vogtlandbahn. 🍴.

BAD WÖRISHOFEN - TÜRKHEIM - AUGSBURG

	Ⓐe	Ⓐe	©z																								R
ad Wörishofen ..♣ d.	0510	0544	0645	0739	0833	0907	0932	1034	1107	1132	1234	1302	1332	1428	1507	1532	1634	1705	1731	1828	1905	1932	2028	2108	2133	2231	2343
ürkheim (Bay) ..♣ a.	0517	0551	0652	0746	0840	0914	0939	1041	1114	1139	1241	1309	1339	1435	1514	1539	1641	1712	1737	1835	1912	1939	2035	2115	2139	2238	2349
uchloe .... a.	...	...	0753	...	0952	...	...	1152	...	...	1352	...	...	...	1752	...	...	...	1952	...	...	2151	...	0002
ugsburg Hbf ...... a.	...	...	0829b	...	1029	...	...	1229	...	...	1429	...	...	...	1629	...	...	...	1829	...	...	2029	...	2245	0049

935 LINDAU and OBERSTDORF - ULM, AUGSBURG and MÜNCHEN

RE / RB services except where shown

Subject to alteration Mar. 4 - Apr. 23 ⊗. For services from / to Bad Wörishofen see pages 444 and 445. For regional services Lindau - Memmingen via Kißlegg see Table 937.

	ALX	*ALX*	Ⓐe							*ALX*	*ALX*			*EC* 195 ♥					*ALX*	*ALX*			Ⓒz	Ⓐe	Ⓐe	Ⓒz¶
Lindau Hbf 937 d.	...	1158	...	...	...	...	1325	...	...	...	1358	...	...	1512	...	1525	...	...	...	1557	1624z	...	...	...	1657	1714
Wangen (Allgäu) 937 d.	...	|	1230	...	...	...	|	...	...	...	|	...	...	|	...	|	...	...	...	|	1630e	...	...	...	|	|
Hergatz 937 d.	...	1214	1239	...	...	...	1340	...	...	...	1414	...	...	|	...	1539	...	...	...	1614	1639	...	...	...	1711	1728
Oberstdorf d.	1222	|	|	1237f	...	1334	|	...	...	1422	|	1442	...	|	1540	|	...	...	1622	|	|	1637	...	1704	|	|
Sonthofen d.	1239	|	|	1301	...	1401	|	...	...	1439	|	1501	...	|	1601	|	...	...	1639	|	|	1701	...	1730	|	|
Immenstadt a.	1247	1251	1314	1310	...	1410	1414	...	...	1447	1451	1510	...	|	1610	1614	...	...	1647	1651	1714	1710	...	1739	1746	1803
Immenstadt d.	▶	1300	▶	1317	...	▶	1417	...	...	▶	1500	1517	...	|	▶	1617	...	...	▶	1700	▶	1717	...	▶	1749	▬
Kempten Hbf a.	▬	1314	▬	1331	...	▬	1430	...	...	▬	1514	1531	...	|	▬	1630	...	...	▬	1714	▬	1731	...	▬	1803	...
Kempten Hbf d.	...	1316	...	1334	1341	...	1432	1435	...	...	1516	1534	1541	|	...	1632	1635	...	...	1716	...	1734	1736	...	1809	...
Memmingen 937 a.	◧	|	...	1359	|	...	|	1456	...	◧	|	1558	|	1613	...	|	1704	...	...	|	◧	1759	|	...	|	...
Memmingen d.	1307	|	...	1404	|	1408	|	1504	...	1507	|	1602	|	1615	1605	|	1705	...	...	|	1707	1804	|	...	|	1807
Ulm Hbf a.	|	|	...	1439	|	|	|	1539	...	|	|	1641	|	|	|	|	1739	...	...	|	|	1840	|	...	|	|
Mindelheim d.	1332	|	...	▬	|	1430	|	▬	...	1532	|	▬	|	|	1637j	|	▬	...	...	|	1731	▬	|	...	|	1830
Türkheim (Bay) d.	1346	|	Ⓒz	Ⓐe	|	1439	|	...	...	1546	|	...	|	|	1645	|	...	...	†w	|	1746	...	|	...	|	1838
Füssen d.	|	|	1305	1305	|	|	|	1406	...	|	|	1505	|	|	|	|	1606	...	1634	|	|	1705	|	...	|	|
Marktoberdorf d.	|	|	1347	1351	|	|	|	1449	...	|	|	1548	|	|	|	|	1649	...	1718	|	|	1749	|	...	|	|
Biessenhofen d.	|	|	1356	1359	1405	|	|	1458	...	|	|	1557	1605	|	|	|	1658	...	|	|	|	1757	1804	...	1831	|
Kaufbeuren d.	|	1343	1401	1404	1410	|	1456	1503	...	|	1543	1602	1610	|	|	1656	1703	...	|	1743	|	1803	1809	...	1836	|
Buchloe a.	1352	1354c	1413	1417	1421c	1445	1507	1515	...	1552	1554c	1616	1621c	1641	1652	1707	1715	...	|	1754	1752c	1815	1820c	...	1848	1845c
Buchloe d.	1400	1355	1424	1424	1422	1453	1509	1518	1518	1600	1555	1624	1622	1643	1653	1709	1718	1719	|	1755	1800	1824	1821	1821	1849	1851
Augsburg Hbf a.	1429	|	1456	1456	|	|	1530	|	1545	1629	|	1656	|	|	|	1730	|	1746	|	|	1829	1856	|	|	1914	|
Nürnberg Hbf 905 a.	...	|	...	...	|	|	...	|	...	...	|	...	|	|	|	1848k	|	...	|	|	...	...	|	|	2028n	|
Kaufering d.	...	1403	...	...	1430	1501	...	1528	...	...	1603	...	1629	|	1701	...	1728	...	|	1803	...	...	1830	1830	...	1900
Geltendorf d.	...	|	...	...	1438	1510	...	1537	...	...	|	...	1638	|	1710	...	1737	...	|	|	...	...	1840	1840	...	1910
München Pasing a.	...	1433	...	...	1458	1533	...	1558	...	...	1633	...	1658	|	1733	...	1758	...	1811	1833	...	...	1910	1910	...	1933
München Hbf ⊡ a.	...	1441	...	...	1509	1541	...	1605	...	...	1641	...	1705	1728	1741	...	1805	...	1820	1841	...	...	1917	1917	...	1941

	†w	⑥		Ⓐe	*ALX*	*ALX*	Ⓐe					*ALX*	*ALX*	◧	*EC* 197 ♥			⑤–⑦ R	⑤–⑦ R		◧		*ALX*			
Lindau Hbf 937 d.	...	...	...	...	...	1757	...	...	...	1902	...	...	1954	...	2016	...	...	...	2107	...	...	...	2209	...	...	2310
Wangen (Allgäu) 937 d.	...	...	...	...	...	|	1819	...	...	|	...	...	|	...	|	...	...	...	|	...	...	...	|	...	...	|
Hergatz 937 d.	...	...	...	...	...	1813	1839	...	...	1917	...	...	2010	...	|	...	...	...	2121	...	...	...	2226	...	...	2324
Oberstdorf d.	1725	1740	...	1740	1823	|	|	1838	1906	|	1942	2020	|	...	|	...	2102	...	|	...	...	2228	|	...	2326	|
Sonthofen d.	1750	1801	...	1801	1840	|	|	1902	1933	|	2002	2037	|	...	|	...	2121	...	|	...	...	2252	|	...	2345	|
Immenstadt a.	1801	1810	...	1810	1848	1851	1914	1911	1942	1954	2011	2045	2047	...	|	...	2130	...	2156	...	...	2301	2305	...	2356	2359
Immenstadt d.	1807	1817	...	1817	▶	1857	▶	1917	▶	1957	2017	▶	2055	...	|	...	2136	...	2157	...	...	▬	2306	...	0003	0003
Kempten Hbf a.	1821	1831	...	1831	▬	1912	▬	1931	▬	2011	2031	▬	2110	...	2122	...	2150	...	2211	...	...	...	2323	...	0018	0018
Kempten Hbf d.	1829	1836	1834	1834	...	1914	...	1934	...	2012	2034	...	2114	...	2124	...	2155	...	2212	2212	...	...	2325	2334	...	...
Memmingen 937 a.	|	|	1856	1856	◧	|	...	1959	...	|	2058	...	|	...	|	...	2221	...	|	|	...	...	|	2400	...	...
Memmingen d.	|	|	1904	1904	1907	|	...	2004	2008	|	2105	...	|	2107	|	2208	2227	...	|	|	2317	...	|	0004	...	...
Ulm Hbf a.	|	|	1939	1939	|	|	...	2039	|	|	2155b	...	|	|	|	|	2315	...	|	|	|	...	|	0045	...	...
Mindelheim d.	|	|	▬	▬	1932	|	...	...	2030	|	...	...	|	2132	|	2233	...	...	|	|	2343	...	|	▬	...	...
Türkheim (Bay) d.	|	|	...	...	1946	|	...	...	2039	|	...	...	|	2145	|	2241	...	...	|	|	2356	...	|	...	...	...
Füssen d.	|	|	1806	...	|	|	1905	...	|	|	...	2033	|	|	|	|	...	2111	|	|	|	2238	|	...	...	...
Marktoberdorf d.	|	|	1849	...	|	|	1948	...	|	|	...	2118	|	|	|	|	...	2153	|	|	|	2320	|	...	...	...
Biessenhofen d.	|	|	1858	...	|	|	1956	...	|	|	...	2126	|	|	|	|	...	2201	2233	2233	|	2329	2351	...	...	...
Kaufbeuren d.	1852	1858	1903	...	|	1941	2010j	...	|	2038	...	2132	2141	|	|	|	...	2206	2238	2238	|	2334	2356	...	...	...
Buchloe a.	1902	1909	1915	...	1952	1953c	2022	...	2045	2048c	...	...	2153	2151c	2203c	2248	...	...	2248c	2248c	0002	...	0008	←	...	...
Buchloe d.	1903	1910	1918	1918	2000	1954	2024	...	2052	2052	...	...	2155	2215	2205	2251	...	...	2253	2253	→	...	0009	0016	...	...
Augsburg Hbf a.	1922	1930	|	1945	2029	|	2056	...	|	2121h	...	...	|	2245	|	|	...	...	2321	2321	...	...	|	0049	...	...
Nürnberg Hbf 905 a.	...	...	|	...	...	|	...	...	|	2232z	...	...	|	...	|	|	...	...	...	...	...	...	|	...	...	...
Kaufering d.	...	...	1928	...	...	2002	...	...	2101	...	...	...	2203	...	|	2301	...	...	...	...	...	...	0017	...	...	...
Geltendorf d.	...	...	1937	...	...	|	...	...	2110	...	...	...	|	...	|	2310	...	...	...	...	...	...	0027	...	...	...
München Pasing a.	...	...	1958	...	...	2033	...	...	2133	...	...	...	2233	...	|	2333	...	...	...	...	...	...	0049	...	...	...
München Hbf ⊡ a.	...	...	2005	...	...	2040	...	...	2141	...	...	...	2241	...	2245	2341	...	...	...	...	...	...	0057	...	...	...

R – ⑤–⑦ (also Apr. 17, May 1, 25, June 5).

b – 2139 on Ⓒ (also Jan. 6).
c – Connects with train in preceding column.
e – Ⓐ (not Jan. 6).
f – 1242 on Ⓒ (also Jan. 6).
h – 2116 on Ⓒ (also Jan. 6).

j – Arrives 10–11 minutes earlier.
k – ⑥ only. 1855 from Apr. 1.
n – 2036 from Mar. 30.
w – Also Jan. 6.
z – Ⓒ (also Jan. 6).

¶ – Runs 11 minutes later on ⑥.

♥ – 12 and ✕ Zürich - St Gallen - Bregenz - München (Table 75).
▶ – Attached to train in the next column at Immenstadt.
⊗ – Services to München are subject to alteration Mar. 4 - Apr. 23.
◧ – Conveys 12 Bad Wörishofen - Türkheim - Augsburg (see panel on page 445).
⊡ – Most trains in Table 935 use platforms 27–36 at München Hbf (minimum connecting time to other services is 10 minutes).
ALX – Operated by Vogtlandbahn. 🍷.

936 STUTTGART - TÜBINGEN - AULENDORF

DB (*IRE / RB* services); HzL ◇

km		Ⓐe2	2	Ⓐe	Ⓒz2		2		2	Ⓐe	Ⓒz	2	Ⓐe	Ⓒz	2	B	C	2		2		2		2	2	A2
0	**Stuttgart** Hbf ☆ d.	...	...	...	...	...	...	0817	...	1011	1016	...	1211	1216	...	1411	1416	...	1617	...	1817	...	2017	...	...	...
57	Reutlingen ☆ d.	...	...	...	...	0644e	...	0849	...	1050	1049	...	1250	1249	...	1450	1449	...	1649	...	1849	...	2049	...	...	...
71	**Tübingen** Hbf ☆ d.	...	...	*0546*	0612	0658	0727	0900	0928	1058	1100	1128	1258	1300	1328	1458	1500	1528	1700	1728	1900	1928	2100	2136	2236	2339
96	Hechingen d.	...	...	*0615*	0638	0719	0753	0920	0952	1120	1120	1152	1320	1320	1352	1520	1520	1552	1720	1752	1920	1952	2120	2204	2300	0004
113	Balingen (Württ) d.	...	...	*0637*	0652	0734	0808	0935	1007	1135	1135	1207	1335	1335	1407	1535	1535	1607r	1735	1807	1935	2007	2132	2219	2315	0019
131	Albstadt-Ebingen d.	...	...	0703	0710	0747	0832	0947	1032	1147	1147	1232	1347	1347	1432	1547	1547	1632	1747	1832	1948	2032	2149	2238	2333	0038
158	**Sigmaringen** a.	...	...	0725	...	0811	0856	1011	1056	1211	1211	1256	1411	1411	1456	1611	1611	1656	1811	1856	2011	2056	2210	...	...	...
158	**Sigmaringen** 938 d.	0538	0652	0727	...	0812	*0903*	1012	*1103*	1212	1212	*1303*	1412	1412	*1503*	1612	1612	*1703*	1812	*1903*	2013	*2108*	2212	...	...	...
175	Herbertingen 938 d.	0553	0708	0741	...	0825	*0917*	1024	*1117*	1224	1224	*1317*	1424	1424	*1517*	1624	1624	*1717*	1824	*1917*	2025	*2128*	2230	...	...	...
184	Bad Saulgau d.	0606	0724j	...	...	0834	*0929*	1033	*1129*	1233	1233	*1329*	1433	1433	*1529*	1633	1633	*1729*	1834	*1929*	2035	*2137*	2239	...	...	...
203	**Aulendorf** a.	0622	0740	...	...	0850	*0944*	1050	*1144*	1249	1249	*1344*	1449	1449	*1544*	1649	1649	*1744*	1850	*1944*	2050	*2152*	2254	...	...	...

	2	Ⓐe	⑥2	Ⓐe2	Ⓐe2	Ⓐe2	Ⓒz2	Ⓐe2		2		2		2		2		2		2		2	A2	2	2	2
Aulendorf d.	...	...	...	...	0549	...	...	0632	0706	*0812*	0912	*1012*	1112	*1212*	1312	*1412*	1512	*1612*	1712	*1812*	1912	*2012*	...	2119	2206	2313
Bad Saulgau d.	...	...	...	...	0605	...	...	0647	0722	*0834*	0928	*1033*	1128	*1233*	1328	*1433*	1528	*1633*	1728	*1833*	1928	*2035*	...	2138	2221	2334
Herbertingen 938 d.	...	...	...	...	0614	...	...	0656	0731	*0845*	0937	*1044*	1137	*1244*	1337	*1444*	1537	*1644*	1737	*1844*	1937	*2046*	...	2147	2230	2343
Sigmaringen 938 a.	...	...	...	...	0628	...	...	0715	0745	*0859*	0950	*1059*	1150	*1259*	1350	*1459*	1550	*1659*	1750	*1859*	1950	*2100*	...	2201	2248	2358
Sigmaringen d.	...	0542	...	...	0630	...	...	...	0750	0903	0951	1103	1151	1305	1351	1503	1551	1703	1751	1905	1951	2105	...	...	...	...
Albstadt-Ebingen d.	0503	0605	0622	0633	0655	0703	0727	...	0812	0928	1011	1128	1211	1329	1411	1528	1611	1728	1811	1929	2011	2129	2254	...	...	...
Balingen (Württ) d.	0521	0619	0638	0700	...	0734	0751	...	0827	0952	1027	1152	1227	1352	1427	1552	1627	1752	1827	1952	2027	2148	2315	...	...	...
Hechingen d.	0536	0634	0701	0718	...	0752	0807	...	0839	1007	1039	1207	1239	1407	1439	1607	1639	1807	1840	2007	2039	2204	2330	...	...	...
Tübingen Hbf ☆ a.	0601	0652	0726	0744	...	0818	0830	...	0857	1030	1057	1230	1257	1430	1457	1630	1657	1830	1857	2030	2057	2229	2356	...	...	...
Reutlingen ☆ a.	...	0707	...	*0806*	...	...	...	...	0908	...	1108	...	1308	...	1508	...	1708	...	1908	...	2108	...	...	...	...	...
Stuttgart Hbf ☆ a.	...	0743	...	*0843*	...	...	...	...	0943	...	1143	...	1343	...	1543	...	1743	...	1943	...	2143	...	...	...	...	...

Other services Stuttgart - Tübingen

km		②–⑦	①		Ⓐe	⑥	Ⓐe	Ⓒz				
0	**Stuttgart** Hbf 930 d.	0048	0057	...	0522	*0525*	0616	*0631*	0722	0822		2322
22	Plochingen 930 d.	0107	0117	...	0541	0611	0637	0659	0742	0844	and	2344
35	Nürtingen d.	0120	0130	...	0552	0622	0649	0711	0755	0855	hourly	2355
57	Reutlingen Hbf d.	0137	0146	...	0608	0641	0706	0729	0812	0912	until	0012
71	**Tübingen** Hbf a.	0151	0200	...	0619	0654	0719	0745	0823	0923		0023

	Ⓐe		Ⓒz	Ⓐe						
Tübingen Hbf d.	0506	0537	0622	0625	0737		2037	2136	2236	231
Reutlingen Hbf d.	0517	0547	0632	0636	0748	and	2048	2150	2250	233
Nürtingen d.	0533	0604	0649	0652	0804	hourly	2104	2206	2306	234
Plochingen 930 d.	0547	0618	0700	0704	0818	until	2118	2218	2319	000
Stuttgart Hbf 930 a.	0607	0638	0718	0723	0838		2138	2238	2339	*002*

A – ⑤⑥ (also Jan. 5, Apr. 13, 16, 30, May 24, June 4).
B – ①–④ (not Jan. 5, Apr. 13, 17, May 1, 24, 25, June 5).
C – ⑤–⑦ (also Jan. 5, Apr. 13, 17, May 1, 24, 25, June 5).

e – Ⓐ (not Jan. 6).
j – Arrives 0717.
r – 1611 on Ⓐ (not Jan. 6).
z – Also Jan. 6.

☆ – See panel below main table for other services.
◇ – Hohenzollerische Landesbahn.

RE / RB services; 2nd class only

MEMMINGEN - LINDAU and AULENDORF 937

km		Ⓐe	Ⓒz							M	
0	**Memmingen** 935 d.	0625	...	...	...	...	...	...	...	2005	2101
32	Leutkirch d.	0703	0725	...	...	...	...	...	...	2038	2139
	Aulendorf d.	|	|	0908	1108	1308	1508	1708	...	|	|
	Bad Waldsee d.	|	|	0916	1116	1316	1516	1716	...	|	|
	Kißlegg a.	0713	0734	0932	1132	1332	1532	1732	...	2047	2147
43	Kißlegg d.	0714	0741	0946	1145	1338	1546	1738	1938	2047	2148
56	Wangen (Allgäu) 935 d.	0731	0753	0959	1156	1352	1556	1751	1952	2058	2159
62	Hergatz 935 d.	0737	0759	1004	1201	1357	1601	1757	1957	2103	2204
85	**Lindau Hbf** 935 a.	0755	0816	1021	1218	1414	1618	1814	2014	2118	2222

	Ⓐe	⑥	M	N							Ⓐe	
Lindau Hbf 935 d.	...	0602	0707	0741	0941	1142	1339	1542	1736	1938	2040	*2310*
Hergatz 935 d.	0615	0618	0724	0759	1004	1201	1357	1601	1756	1957	2104	2328
Wangen 935 d.	0620	0623	0730	0804	1011	1208	1403	1608	1801	2003	2109	2333
Kißlegg a.	0630	0633	0740	0815	1022	1218	1414	1618	1811	2014	2120	2344
Kißlegg d.	0631	0633	0741	0826	1026	1226	1427	1626	1826	2050	2121	2346
Bad Waldsee d.	|	|	|	0843	1043	1243	1443	1643	1843	2106	|	|
Aulendorf a.	|	|	|	0851	1051	1251	1451	1651	1851	2114	|	|
Leutkirch d.	0640	0642	0750	...	...	...	...	...	...	...	2132	2355
Memmingen 935 a.	0707	0707	0813	...	...	...	...	...	...	...	...	...

km		Ⓐe	⑥	Ⓒz	Ⓐe						
0	**Memmingen** d.	...	...	...	...	0900	1059	1300	1500	1700	1900
32	Leutkirch d.	0540	0622	...	...	0924	1123	1324	1524	1724	1924
	Hergatz d.	|	|	0650	0656	|	|	|	|	|	|
	Wangen (Allgäu) d.	|	|	0655	0701	|	|	|	|	|	|
43	Kißlegg d.	0550	0636	0711	0716	0934	1134	1334	1534	1734	1934
63	Bad Waldsee d.	0615	0652	0733	0733	0950	1150	1350	1550	1750	1950
73	**Aulendorf** a.	0623	0659	0741	0741	0958	1158	1358	1558	1758	1958

	Ⓐe	Ⓒz			ⒸD	Ⓐt						
Aulendorf d.	0555	0712	0803e	1003	1203	1203	1403	1603	1803	1908	2003	2203
Bad Waldsee d.	0609	0720	0810e	1010	1210	1210	1410	1610	1810	1916	2010	2210
Kißlegg d.	0633	0736	0826	1026	1226	1226	1426	1626	1826	1935	2028	2232
Wangen (Allgäu) d.	0644	...	|	|	|	|	|	|	|	|	|	2243
Hergatz a.	0648	...	|	|	|	|	|	|	|	|	|	2247
Leutkirch d.	...	...	0835	1035	1235	1246	1435	1635	1835	1944e	2037	...
Memmingen a.	...	...	0859	1059	1259	1316	1500	1659	1859	...	2101	...

D – Runs daily Dec. 23 - Jan. 8, Apr. 8 – 23 and June 3 – 18.
M – 🚲12 München - Lindau and v.v. (Table **935**).
N – From Friedrichshafen Stadt (d. 0700) on Ⓐ (not Jan. 6).
e – Ⓐ (not Jan. 6).
t – Not Dec. 23 - Jan. 6, Apr. 10 – 21, June 5 – 16.
z – Ⓒ (also Jan. 6).

DB (*RE* / *RB* services); HzL ◇

ULM and ROTTWEIL - NEUSTADT (Schwarzw) - FREIBURG 938

km		Ⓒz	Ⓐe	Ⓐe2	Ⓒz		2		Ⓐe																
0	**Ulm** Hbf d.	...	...	...	...	...	...	0557	0706	0817	0916	1016	1116	1216	1316	1416	1516	1616	1716	1817	1917	...	2017	2117	2217
16	Blaubeuren d.	...	...	...	...	...	...	0612	0718	0829	0927	1028	1128	1228	1328	1428	1527	1628	1728	1829	1928	...	2029	2129	2235
34	Ehingen (Donau) d.	...	...	...	...	...	...	0630	0725	0842	0940	1044	1140	1244	1340	1444	1540	1644	1740	1844	1940	...	2045	2145	2251
76	Herbertingen 937 d.	...	...	...	...	...	...	0709	0813	0917	1008	1117	1208	1317	1408	1517	1608	1717	1808	1918	2008	...	2117	2214	2324
93	**Sigmaringen** 937 a.	...	...	...	...	...	...	0725	0829	0931	1027	1131	1227	1331	1427	1531	1627	1731	1827	1931	2027	...	2131	2230	2337
93	**Sigmaringen** d.	...	...	...	...	...	...	0730k	—	0934	—	1133	—	1334	—	1533	—	1734	—	1933	—	...	2134	—	—
135	Tuttlingen d.	...	...	...	...	...	...	0813	...	1013	...	1213	...	1413	...	1613	...	1813	...	2013	...	...	2213	...	...
145	Immendingen 916 d.	...	...	...	...	...	...	0821	...	1021	...	1221	...	1421	...	1621	...	1821	...	2021	2	...	2221	Ⓐe2	Ⓒz2
	Rottweil d.	...	...	0646	0702	...	0746	|	0909	|	1109	|	1309	|	1509	|	1710	|	1909	|	2055	...	|	2203	2252
	Trossingen Bahnhof ▲ d.	...	...	0658	0713	...	0759	|	0918	|	1118	|	1318	|	1518	|	1719	|	1918	|	2107	...	|	2214	2302
	Villingen (Schwarzw) 916 d.	0604	0620	0721	0737	0737	0823	|	0937	|	1137	|	1337	|	1537	|	1737	|	1937	|	2124	2210	|	2236	2326
164	Donaueschingen 916 a.	0614	0640	0739	0748	0748	0841	0834	0948	1034	1148	1234	1348	1434	1548	1634	1748	1834	1948	2034	...	2218	2234	2254	2343
164	Donaueschingen d.	0615	0642	...	0749	0749	...	0848	0949	1048	1149	1248	1349	1448	1549	1648	1749	1848	1949	2048	...	...	...	...	...
204	**Neustadt** (Schwarzw) a.	0652	0726	...	0825	0825	...	0925	1025	1125	1225	1325	1425	1525	1625	1725	1825	1925	2025	2125	...	...	...	...	...

km			⚒r2	Ⓐe	Ⓐe2	2	Ⓐe	Ⓒz													Ⓒz	Ⓐe	Ⓒz2	
0	**Neustadt** (Schwarzw) d.	...	...	...	0626	...	...	...	0732	0832	0932	1032	1132	1231	1330n	1432	1532	1632	1732	1832	1932	2032	2032	...	2201
40	Donaueschingen a.	...	...	...	0707	...	⊙	...	0808	0909	1008	1109	1208	1309	1408	1509	1608	1709	1808	1909	2008	2109	2109	...	2238
40	Donaueschingen 916 d.	...	0510	0514	0708	0714z	0717	0721	0809	0922	1010	1122	1209	1322	1409	1522	1609	1722	1809	1922	2009	2122	2110	2115	2239
54	Villingen (Schwarzw) 916 d.	...	0532	0504‡	0724	0734f	|	0711‡	0826j	|	1026	|	1226j	|	1426j	|	1623	|	1826j	|	2026j	|	2119	2139	2304
69	Trossingen Bahnhof ▲ d.	...	0550	|	—	0800	|	|	0839	|	1039	|	1239	|	1439	|	1636	|	1839	|	2039	|	*2146*	2200	2317z
81	**Rottweil** a.	...	0602	|	...	0810	|	|	0848	|	1048	|	1248	|	1448	|	1645	|	1848	|	2048	|	*2158*	2211	2328z
	Immendingen 916 d.	...	—	0529	...	...	0733	0735	—	0935	—	1135	—	1335	—	1535	—	1735	—	1935	...	2135	—	...	...
	Tuttlingen d.	...	...	0537	...	...	0750j	0745	...	0944	...	1144	...	1344	...	1544	...	1744	...	1944	...	2144	...	...	...
	Sigmaringen a.	...	...	0620	...	...	0828	0823	...	1027	...	1226	...	1427	...	1626	...	1827	...	2025	...	2226	...	...	...
	Sigmaringen 937 d.	0527	0630	0630	0727	...	0830	0830	0933	1030	1133	1230	1333	1430	1533	1630	1733	1830	1933	2032	...	2231	2231	...	...
	Herbertingen 937 d.	0541	0642	0642	0742	...	0845	0845	0949	1044	1149	1244	1349	1444	1549	1644	1749	1845	1949	2046	...	2244	2244	...	...
	Ehingen (Donau) d.	0611t	0716	0716	0814	...	0912	0912	1019	1112	1219	1312	1419	1512	1619	1712	1819	1912	2019	2117	...	2310	2310	...	...
	Blaubeuren d.	0626	0732	0732	0830	...	0928	0928	1031	1128	1231	1328	1431	1528	1631	1728	1831	1928	2031	2131	...	2324	2324	...	...
	Ulm Hbf a.	0637t	0744	0744	0842	...	0940	0940	1042	1140	1242	1340	1442	1540	1642	1740	1842	1940	2044	2147	...	2341	2341	...	...

km		e🚌	Ⓐe	⚒r	e🚌	Ⓐe	Ⓐe	Ⓒz	Ⓐe	Ⓒz	Ⓐe	Ⓑ											🚌	
0	**Neustadt** (Schwarzw) d.	△	0526	0555	△	0631	0642	0656	...	0708	...	0731	0801	...	0831	...	and at the same	1931	...	2031	...	2131	△	2223
	Seebrugg d.	0459	|	|	0601	|	|	|	0641	|	0705	|	|	...	|	0839*	minutes past	|	1939*	|	2021	|	2132	|
5	Titisee d.	0531	0533	0602	0633	0638	0649	0703	0708	0715	0731	0738	0808	...	0838	0908	each hour until	1938	2008	2038	2048	2138	2204	2230
36	**Freiburg** (Brsg) Hbf a.	...	0612	0640	...	0718	0738	0741	0748	...	...	0818	0848	...	0918	0948		2018	2048	2118	...	2218	...	2313

km		Ⓐe	Ⓐe	Ⓐe	Ⓐe	Ⓒz	Ⓒz	Ⓐe	Ⓐe											🚌				
0	**Freiburg** (Brsg) Hbf d.	...	0535	...	0640	0638	...	0710	...	0742	...	0810	0840	and at the same	1810	1840	1910	1940	2010	△	...	2110	2225	2325
31	Titisee d.	0608	0612	0630	0719	0722	0724	0749	0752	0819	...	0849	0919	minutes past	1849	1919	1949	2019	2049	2055	2058	2149	2301	0001
50	**Seebrugg** a.	0633	|	0658	|	0749	|	|	0818	|	...	0916	|	each hour until	1916	|	2015	|	|	2129	|	|	|	|
	Neustadt (Schwarzw) a.	...	0618	...	0725	...	0730	0755	...	0825	...	...	0925		...	1925	...	2025	2055	...	2104	2155	2307	0007

– Ⓐ (not Jan. 6).
– 0739 on Ⓒ (also Jan. 6).
– Arrives 8 – 10 minutes earlier.
– 0728 on Ⓒ (also Jan. 6).
n – 1332 on Ⓒ (also Nov. 1).
r – Not Jan. 6.
t – On Ⓒ (also Jan. 6) Ehingen 0609, Ulm 0643.
z – Ⓒ (also Jan. 6).
* – 3 minutes earlier on † (also Jan. 6).
⊙ – From Triberg (Table **916**).
‡ – Starts from Villingen, then Donaueschingen.
◇ – Hohenzollerische Landesbahn.
▲ – Connecting services run to / from Trossingen Stadt (operated by HzL). Journey time: 5 minutes.
△ – Subject to confirmation.

IRE / *RB* services

FRIEDRICHSHAFEN - SCHAFFHAUSEN - BASEL 939

km		Ⓐe		Ⓐe2	Ⓒz2	Ⓐe	Ⓒz	2		2		2		2		2		2		2	2		2	L2	2
	Ulm Hbf 933 d.	...	...	...	...	...	...	...	0805	...	1005	...	1205	...	1405	...	1605	...	1805	...	...	2005	...	...	...
0	**Friedrichshafen** Stadt d.	0430	...	0546	0636	0702	0713	0739	0913	0938	1113	1138	1313	1338	1513	1538	1713	1738	1913	1938	2032	2113	2138	2232	2335
34	Überlingen d.	0513	...	0621	0710	0730	0734	0813	0934	1013	1134	1213	1335	1413	1535	1613	1735	1813	1934	2013	2111	2134	2213	2315	0010
59	Radolfzell 916 d.	0543	...	0647	0732	0751	0753	0842	0953	1042	1153	1242	1353	1442	1553	1642	1753	1842	1953	2042	2139	2153	2246	2341	0033
69	**Singen** 916 a.	0554	...	*0703*	*0747*	0758	0800	*0855*	1000	*1055*	1200	*1255*	1400	*1455*	1600	*1655*	1800	*1855*	2000	*2055*	...	2200	...	2349	0041
		|				|	|		|		|		|		|		|		|		|				
69	**Singen** 🏛 940 d.	0559	0651	...	...	0802	0802	0902	1002	1102	1202	1302	1402	1502	1602	1702	1802	1902	2002	2102	...	2202	...	0006	...
88	**Schaffhausen** 🏛 940 d.	0612	0716	...	...	0816	0816	0916	1016	1116	1216	1316	1416	1516	1616	1716	1816	1916	2016	2116	...	2216	...	0024	...
107	Erzingen (Baden) 🏛 d.	0625	0729	...	...	0829	0829	0929	1029	1129	1229	1329	1429	1529	1629	1729	1829	1930	2029	2129	...	2232	...	...	...
127	Waldshut d.	0640	0742	...	...	0842	0842	0942	1042	1142	1242	1342	1442	1542	1642	1742	1842	1943	2042	2144	...	2248	...	...	...
150	Bad Säckingen d.	0653	0756	...	...	0856	0856	0956	1056	1156	1256	1356	1456	1556	1656	1756	1856	1956	2056	2158	...	2310	...	...	...
167	Rheinfelden (Baden) d.	0703	0806	...	...	0906	0906	1006	1106	1206	1306	1406	1506	1606	1706	1806	1906	2006	2106	2208	...	2325	...	...	...
182	**Basel** Bad Bf a.	0714	0816	...	...	0916	0916	1016	1116	1216	1316	1416	1516	1616	1716	1816	1916	2016	2116	2218	...	2340	...	...	...

						Ⓐe	Ⓒz	Ⓐe														N			2
asel Bad Bf d.	...	...	...	...	...	0510	0617	0635	0742	0842	0942	1042	1142	1242	1342	1442	1542	1642	1742	1842	1942	2042	...	2145	2152
heinfelden (Baden) d.	...	...	...	...	...	0525	0632	0645	0751	0851	0951	1051	1151	1251	1351	1451	1551	1651	1751	1851	1951	2051	...	2154	2206
ad Säckingen d.	...	...	...	...	...	0541	0648	0655	0801	0901	1001	1101	1201	1301	1401	1501	1601	1701	1801	1901	2001	2101	...	2204	2222
/aldshut d.	...	...	...	...	...	0604	0714	0711	0814	0914	1014	1114	1214	1314	1414	1514	1614	1714	1814	1914	2014	2114	...	2217	2252
rzingen (Baden) 🏛 d.	...	...	...	*0518*	*0548*	0629	0729	0729	0829	0929	1029	1129	1229	1329	1429	1529	1629	1729	1829	1929	2029	2129	...	2233	2311
chaffhausen 🏛 940 d.	...	...	0528	0551	0631	0643	0743	0743	0843	0943	1043	1143	1243	1343	1443	1543	1643	1743	1843	1943	2043	2143	...	2246	*2339*
ingen 🏛 940 a.	...	...	0547	0610	0650	0659	0756	0756	0856	0956	1056	1156	1256	1356	1456	1556	1656	1756	1856	1956	2056	2153	...	2258	...
	Ⓐe2	Ⓐe2	Ⓒz2	Ⓐe2	Ⓒz2		|	|	2	|	2	|	2	|	2	|	2	|	2	|	2	|	2	2	
ingen 916 d.	0422	0524	0613	0617	0700	...	0757	0757	*0902*	0957	*1102*	1157	*1302*	1357	*1502*	1557	*1702*	1757	*1902*	1957	*2102*	2157	*2210*	*2302*	...
adolfzell 916 d.	0430	0532	0621	0625	0709	...	0805	0805	0914	1005	1114	1205	1314	1405	1514	1605	1714	1806	1914	2005	2114	2205	2225	2315	...
berlingen d.	0453	0554	0644	0654	0740	...	0823	0823	0942	1023	1142	1222	1342	1423	1542	1623	1742	1823	1942	2023	2142	2222	2247	2343	...
riedrichshafen Stadt a.	0527	0624	0723	0737	0821	...	0842	0842	1021	1041	1221	1242	1421	1442	1621	1642	1821	1842	2021	2042	2221	2241	2321	0020	...
Ulm Hbf 933 a.	...	...	...	...	...	...	0953	0953	...	1153	...	1353	...	1553	...	1753	...	1952	...	2155	...	...	...	...	...

– From Lindau Hbf (d. 2204).
N – To Lindau Hbf (a. 2258).
e – Not Jan. 6.
z – Also Jan. 6.

GERMANY

See page 367 for a summary of Christmas / New Year alterations

940 STUTTGART - SINGEN - SCHAFFHAUSEN - ZÜRICH

Subject to alteration Apr. 8 – 14 and June 3 – 18.

km					IC 181			IC 183			IC 185		IC 187		IC 281		IC 283		IC 285				◇		
		Ⓐe	Ⓐe																Ⓑb			⚒r	†w		†w
0	**Stuttgart** Hbf .... 942 d.	0516	0548	0718	0829	0918	1018	1029	...	1118	1229	1318	1429	1518	1624t	1718	1829	1918	2029	2018	2118	2118	...	2225	2225
26	Böblingen .... 942 d.	0537	0608	0738	0850	0938	1038	1050	...	1138	1250	1338	1450	1538	1650	1738	1850	1938	2050	2038	2138	2138	...	2246	2246
42	Herrenberg .... 942 d.	0547	0619	0750	|	0950	1050	|	←	1150	|	1350	|	1550	|	1749	|	1950	|	2050	2149	2149	...	2256	2256
57	Eutingen im Gäu .. 942 d.	0600	0637	0806	|	1006	1103	|	1111	1206	|	1405	|	1605	|	1805	|	2006	|	2111	2207	2207	...	2313	2313
67	Horb .... d.	0607	0645	0814	0915	1014	→	1115	1121	1214	1315	1414	1515	1614	1715	1814	1915	2014	2115	2121	2215	2215	...	2321	2321
110	Rottweil .... d.	0642	0736v	0851	0944	1051	...	1144	1154	1251	1344	1451	1544	1651	1744	1851	1944	2051	2144	2154r	2245	2246	2253	2354	2355
138	Tuttlingen .... d.	0721	0759	0914	1000	1115	...	1200	...	1314	1400	1514	1600	1714	1800	1915	2000	2114	2200	...	...	2308	2318	...	0013
157	Engen .... 916 d.	0735	|	0930	|	1130	...	|	...	1330	|	1530	|	1730	|	1930	|	2130	|	...	...	2323	...	...	0028
172	**Singen** .... 916 a.	0746	0823	0942	1025	1142	...	1225	...	1342	1425	1542	1625	1742	1825	1942	2025	2142	2225	...	...	2333	...	...	0040
172	**Singen** .... 939 d.	0802	0828	1002	1032	1202	...	1232	...	1402	1432	1602	1632	1802	1832	2002	2032	2202	2232	...	...	2336	...	...	...
191	**Schaffhausen** 🛃 . 939 a.	0814	0843	1014	1045	1214	...	1245	...	1414	1445	1614	1645	1814	1845	2014	2045	2214	2245	...	...	2354	...	...	...
239	**Zürich** HB .... a.	...	...	...	1125	...	...	1325	...	...	1525	...	1725	...	1925	...	2125	...	2325	...	...	...	...	...	...

							◇		IC 284				IC 282		IC 280		IC 186		IC 184		IC 182		IC 180	
	Ⓐe	Ⓐe		Ⓐe	Ⓐe	Ⓒw	Ⓒw		★															
Zürich HB .... d.	...	...	...	...	...	...	...	...	0635	...	...	...	0835	...	1035	...	1235	...	1435	...	1635	...	1835	...
Schaffhausen 🛃 .... 939 d.	...	...	...	0528	0551	0551	...	...	0716	...	0743	0755e	0916	0943	1116	1143	1316	1343	1516	1543	1716	1743	1916	1943
Singen .... 939 a.	...	...	...	0547	0610	0610	...	...	0730	...	0756	0811e	0930	0956	1130	1156	1330	1356	1530	1556	1730	1756	1930	1956
Singen .... 916 d.	...	...	...	0551	0617	0618	...	...	0737	...	...	0818	0937	1018	1137	1218	1337	1418	1537	1618	1737	1818	1937	2018
Engen .... 916 d.	...	...	...	0600	0626	0627	...	...	|	...	...	0827	|	1027	|	1227	|	1427	|	1627	|	1827	|	2027
Tuttlingen .... d.	...	...	...	0615	0641	0643	0703	...	0800	...	...	0843	1000	1043	1200	1243	1400	1443	1600	1644	1800	1843	2000	2043
Rottweil .... d.	0508	0538	0608	0639	0705	0704	0741	0803	0817	...	...	0907	1017	1107	1217	1309	1417	1507	1617	1707	1817	1907	2017	2107
Horb .... d.	0546	0616	0646	0710	0745	0743	...	0837	0846	←	...	0946	1046	1146	1246	1346	1446	1546	1646	1746	1846	1946	2046	2146
Eutingen im Gäu .... 942 d.	0555	0625	0655	|	0756	0755	...	0847	|	0857	...	0955	|	1155	|	1355	|	1555	|	1755	|	1955	|	2155
Herrenberg .... 942 d.	0612	0642	0712	0727	0811	0811	...	→	|	0912	...	1012	|	1212	|	1412	|	1612	|	1812	|	2012	|	2212
Böblingen .... 942 d.	0622	0652	0722	0737	0822	0822	...	...	0911	0922	...	1022	1111	1222	1311	1422	1511	1622	1711	1822	1911	2022	2111	2222
Stuttgart Hbf .... 942 a.	0642	0712	0742	0757	0842	0842	...	...	0933	0942	...	1042	1133	1242	1333	1442	1536	1642	1736	1842	1933	2042	2133	2242

SCHAFFHAUSEN - ZÜRICH (operated by SBB)

km								
0	**Schaffhausen** .... d.	0547	0616	and at the same	2116	2147	2247	2327
28	Bülach .... d.	|	0638	minutes past	2138	|	|	2358
48	**Zürich** HB .... a.	0625	0655	each hour until	2155	2225	2325	0023

Zürich HB .... d.	0005	...	0605	0635	and at the same	2035	2105	2205	2305
Bülach .... d.	0023	...	0623	|	minutes past	|	2123	2223	2323
Schaffhausen .... a.	0043	...	0643	0713	each hour until	2113	2143	2243	2343

b – Also Dec. 17.
e – Ⓐ (not Jan. 6).
r – ⚒ (not Jan. 6).
t – 1629 on Ⓒ (also Jan. 6).
v – Arrives 0720.
w – Also Jan. 6.
★ – ①–⑥ (also Dec. 11, 18).
◇ – Operated by Hohenzollerische Landesbahn. 2nd class only.

941 TÜBINGEN - HORB - PFORZHEIM - BAD WILDBAD

RB services (2nd class only)

km		Ⓐe	⑥	Ⓐe			Ⓒz													
	Tübingen .... ⊡ d.	...	...	...	...	...	0727	...	0927	...	1127	...	1327	...	1527	...	1727	...	1927	2127
0	**Horb** .... ⊡ d.	0440	0600	0611	0651	0758	0758	0851	0958	1051	1158	1251	1358	1451	1558	1651	1758	1851	1959	2200
15	Hochdorf (b. Horb) ..... d.	0451	0610	0622	0702	0809	0809	0902	1009	1102	1209	1302	1409	1502	1609	1702	1809	1902	2009	2220
25	Nagold .... d.	0507	0622	0633	0719	0820	0820	0913	1020	1113	1220	1313	1420	1513	1620	1713	1820	1913	2021	2232
34	Wildberg (Württ) .... d.	0515	0629	0646	0730	0833	0833	0920	1028	1121	1228	1321	1428	1521	1628	1721	1828	1921	2029	2239
45	Calw .... d.	0525	0639	0656	0740	0843	0843	0934	1038	1134	1238	1334	1438	1534	1638	1734	1838	1934	2039	2249
52	Bad Liebenzell .... d.	0532	0647	0704	0750	0850	0850	0944	1046	1144	1246	1344	1446	1544	1646	1744	1846	1944	2047	2300
71	**Pforzheim** Hbf .... a.	0553	0708	0724	0810	0910	0910	1006	1107	1206	1307	1406	1507	1606	1707	1806	1907	2006	2111	2320

	Ⓐe	Ⓐe	Ⓒz	⚒r										Ⓐe		Ⓐe				
Pforzheim Hbf .... d.	0446	0637	0651	0753	0853	0950	1050	1149	1250	1350	1450	1550	1650	1720	1750	1823	1850	1950	2043	2238
Bad Liebenzell .... d.	0506	0708	0713	0816	0915	1011	1113	1211	1313	1411	1513	1611	1713	1743	1811	1848	1913	2011	2104	2258
Calw .... d.	0513	0715	0719	0823	0922	1018	1120	1218	1320	1418	1520	1618	1720	1750	1818	1855	1920	2018	2111	2305
Wildberg (Württ) .... d.	0526	0728	0730	0832	0932	1029	1132	1229	1332	1429	1532	1629	1732	1803	1829	1905	1932	2029	2121	2315
Nagold .... d.	0533	0739	0740	0840	0940	1039	1139	1239	1339	1439	1539	1639	1739	1821	1839	1914	1939	2037	2129	2323
Hochdorf (b. Horb) ...... d.	0544	0751	0751	0852	0951	1051	1151	1251	1351	1451	1551	1651	1751	1832	1851	1925	1951	2049	2148	2340
Horb .... ⊡ a.	...	0802	0802	0903	1002	1102	1202	1302	1402	1502	1602	1702	1802	1843	1902	1937	2003	2101	2159	2351
Tübingen .... ⊡ a.	...	...	0833	...	1033	...	1233	...	1433	...	1633z	1759e	1833z	...	...	...	2033	...	2232	...

e – Ⓐ (not Jan. 6).
r – ⚒ (not Jan. 6).
z – Ⓒ (also Jan. 6).
⊡ – See panel below main table for full service Tübingen - Horb and v.v.
⊠ – The 1235 from Bad Wildbad Kurpark runs only on Ⓒz (see also note ▶ below).
▶ – S-Bahn route **S6**. Additional journeys on Ⓐ (not Nov. 1): **From Pforzheim** Hbf at 0612, 0705, 1227, 1317, 1617, 1717, 1817 and 1917. **From Bad Wildbad** Kurpark at 0505, 0601, 0805, 0905, 1215, 1305, 1605, 1705 and 1805.

km		Ⓐe	Ⓐe	Ⓐe	Ⓐe	Ⓒz						Ⓐe					Ⓐe									
0	**Tübingen** Hbf .... d.	0535	0558	0630	0724	0727	0835	0927	1035	1127	1235	1304	1327	1435	1527	1636	1704	1727	1836	1927	2036	2127	2236	...	...	...
32	**Horb** .... a.	0603	0637	0706	0754	0754	0911	0954	1111	1154	1311	1336	1354	1511	1554	1711	1736	1754	1911	1955	2111	2156	2309	...	...	...

			Ⓐe	Ⓐe	Ⓒz	Ⓐe								Ⓐe		Ⓐe	Ⓒz		Ⓐe	Ⓐe	Ⓒz	Ⓐe				
Horb .... d.	0455	...	0617	0648	0652	0725	0806	0853	1006	1053	1206	1253	1406	1424	1453	1605	1606	1653	1717	1805	1806	1824	1853	2006	2053	2203
Tübingen Hbf .... a.	0526	...	0651	0723	0723	0801	0833	0924	1033	1124	1233	1324	1433	1455	1524	1632	1633	1724	1759	1832	1833	1855	1924	2033	2124	2232

km	*SEE NOTE* ▶	Ⓐe	Ⓐe	⑥						
0	**Pforzheim** Hbf .... d.	0514	0647	0647	0747	and	2147	2217	2321	0017
23	**Bad Wildbad** Bf .... a.	0545	0713	0718	0818	hourly	2218	2248	2350	0048
25	**Bad Wildbad** Kurpark a.	0547	0716	0722	0822	until	2222	2252	2353	0052

SEE NOTE ▶	Ⓐe	⚒e	Ⓐe		⊠			
Bad Wildbad Kurpark .... d.	0532	0635	0659	0735	and	2135	2245	2345
Bad Wildbad Bf .... d.	0536	0639	0703	0739	hourly	2139	2249	2351
Pforzheim Hbf .... a.	0609	0710	0731	0810	until	2210	2320	0020

942 STUTTGART - FREUDENSTADT - OFFENBURG

km		Ⓐe2		2		2		2		2		2		2		2		2			Ⓒz2	Ⓐe		
0	**Stuttgart** Hbf .... 940 d.	...	...	...	0818	...	1018	...	1218	...	1418	...	1618	...	1818	...	2018	...	...	2225	...	...	...	...
26	Böblingen .... 940 d.	...	...	...	0838	...	1038	...	1238	...	1438	...	1638	...	1838	...	2038	...	...	2246	...	...	...	...
42	Herrenberg .... 940 d.	...	...	...	0850	...	1050	...	1250	...	1450	...	1650	...	1850	...	2050	...	...	2256	2317	2317	...	...
57	Eutingen im Gäu .... 940 d.	0639	0709	0810	0909	1010	1109	1210	1309	1410	1509	1610	1709	1810	1909	2010	2109	2211	...	2312	2333	2333	...	...
62	Hochdorf (b. Horb) .... d.	0644	0713	0814	0913	1014	1113	1214	1313	1414	1513	1614	1713	1814	1913	2014	2113	2215	...	...	2337	2337	...	...
87	**Freudenstadt** Hbf .... a.	0711	0741	0841	0941	1041	1141	1241	1341	1441	1541	1641	1741	1841	1941	2041	2141	2241	...	...	0001	0003	...	...

	Ⓐe2	Ⓐe2	Ⓐe	Ⓒz	2		2		2		2		2		2		2		Ⓒz	2		2		
Freudenstadt Hbf .... d.	0519	...	0615	0619	0719	0819	0919	1019	1119	1219	1319	1419	1519	1619	1719	1819	1919	2019	2019	2119	2219	...	...	...
Hochdorf (b. Horb) .... d.	0544	0547	0644	0646	0744	0846	0944	1046	1144	1246	1344	1446	1544	1646	1744	1846	1944	2045	2045	2144	2246	...	...	...
Eutingen im Gäu .... 940 a.	...	0551	0648	0650	0749	0850	0949	1050	1149	1250	1349	1450	1549	1650	1749	1850	1949	2050	2050	2149	2250	...	...	...
Herrenberg .... 940 a.	...	...	...	...	...	0911	...	1111	...	1311	...	1511	...	1711	...	1911	...	...	2110	...	2311	2316	...	...
Böblingen .... 940 a.	...	...	...	...	...	0922	...	1122	...	1322	...	1522	...	1722	...	1922	...	...	...	...	...	2330	...	...
Stuttgart Hbf .... 940 a.	...	...	...	...	...	0942	...	1142	...	1342	...	1542	...	1742	...	1942	...	...	...	...	...	2355	...	...

FREUDENSTADT - OFFENBURG (operated by Südwestdeutsche Verkehrs-AG; 2nd class only)

km		Ⓐe	⚒e				❖		Ⓐe	
0	**Freudenstadt** Hbf ...... d.	0533	0643	0743	0843	0943	and	2043	2143	...
16	Alpirsbach .... d.	0552	0659	0759	0858	0959		2059	2159	...
25	Schiltach .... d.	0603	0710	0810	0910	1010	hourly	2110	2210	...
35	Wolfach .... d.	0613	0720	0820	0920	1020	until	2120	2221	...
39	Hausach .... 916 a.	0618	0725	0825	0925	1025		2125	2225	2235
72	**Offenburg** .... 916 a.	0647	0755	0855	0955	1055		2155	...	2300

	Ⓐe	⑥	Ⓐe						
Offenburg .... 916 d.	0458	0554	0558	0702	0804	and	2004	...	2226
Hausach .... 916 d.	0525	0627	0627	0732	0832		2032	...	2254
Wolfach .... d.	0530	0632	0632	0737	0837	hourly	2037	...	2259
Schiltach .... d.	0540	0643	0643	0747	0847	until	2047	...	2309
Alpirsbach .... d.	0551	0701	0701	0801	0901		2101	...	2323
Freudenstadt Hbf .... a.	0607	0717	0717	0817	0917		2117	...	2339

e – Not Jan. 6.
z – Also Jan. 6.

❖ – The 1243 from Freudenstadt runs on Ⓒ (also Feb. 27, 28; daily Dec. 23 - Jan. 8, Apr. 8 – 23 and June 3 – 18). On other dates service is retimed to run as follows: Freudenstadt d. 1220, Alpirsbach d. 1236, Schiltach d. 1254, Wolfach d. 1305, Hausach a. 1309, Offenburg a. 1345.

448 *For explanation of standard symbols see page 4* 12

S-Bahn (2nd class only)

KARLSRUHE - FREUDENSTADT 943

km		Ⓐe	Ⓐe	⑥	Ⓐe	Ⓒz		†w																
	Karlsruhe Bahnhofsvorplatz d.	0431	0509	0511	...	0611	0711z	...	0805j	0911	1011	1111		2011	2111	2211	2311		...	...	...	...	...
0	**Karlsruhe** Hbf......... **916** d.	|	|	|	0610	|	0707e	0806	|	|	|	|		|	|	|	|		1008	1210	1410	1610	1810
24	Rastatt......................... **916** d.	0503	0534	0538	0633	0638	0738	0829	0838	0938	1038	1138	and	2038	2138	2238	2338	also	1029	1229	1429	1629	1829
40	Gernsbach Bf.......................d.	0525	0556	0600	0656	0700	0800	0844	0900	1000	1100	1200		2100	2200	2300	0000	faster	1044	1244	1444	1644	1844
51	Forbach (Schwarzw)..............d.	0544	0613	0618	0718	0718	0818	0900	0918	1018	1118	1218	hourly	2118	2218	2318	0018		1100	1300	1500	1700	1900
61	Schönmünzach ....d.	0556	0624	0631	0729	0729	0829	0911	0929	1029	1129	1229		2129	2229	2329	0034	trains	1111	1311	1511	1711	1911
74	Baiersbronn Bf ....d.	0612	0642	0649	0750	0749	0849	0922	0949	1049	1149	1249	until	2149	2249	2346	0050		1122	1322	1522	1722	1922
79	**Freudenstadt** Stadt...........a.	0620	0650	0657	0758	0757	0857	0930	0957	1057	1157	1257		2157	2257	2354	0058	at	1130	1329	1530	1730	1929
82	**Freudenstadt** Hbf...............a.	0625	0705	0707	0807	0807	0907	0937	1007	1112	1215	1307		2207	2307	2400	0104		1137	1337	1537	1737	1937

	Ⓒz	Ⓐe	Ⓐe	Ⓒz	Ⓐe	Ⓐe	Ⓒz	Ⓐe	Ⓐe	Ⓒz	⚒r												Ⓒz
Freudenstadt Hbf ....d.	0006	0443	0524	0601	0614	0648	0653	0720	0745	0753	0823	0853		1953	2053	2153	2253		1023	1223	1423	1623	1823
Freudenstadt Stadt.............d.	0011	0449	0530	0607	0620	0654	0703	0730	0803	0803	0830	0903		2003	2103	2203	2306	also	1030	1230	1430	1630	1830
Baiersbronn Bf......................d.	0018	0458	0539	0616	0628	0702	0711	0738	0811	0811	0838	0911	and	2011	2111	2211	2314		1038	1238	1438	1638	1838
Schönmünzach......................d.	0034	0513	0555	0631	0645	0730	0729	0749	0829	0829	0849	0929		2029	2129	2229	2330	faster	1049	1249	1449	1649	1849
Forbach (Schwarzw)...............d.	0045	0525	0612	0643	0701	0742	0742	0801	0842	0842	0901	0942	hourly	2042	2153t	2300v	2341	trains	1101	1259	1501	1701	1901
Gernsbach Bf ....d.	0101	0541	0631	0659	0728	0800	0800	0815	0900	0900	0915	1000		2100	2211	2316	0000		1115	1315	1515	1715	1915
Rastatt................................ **916** d.	0122	0557	0706t	0722	0754	0822	0822	0830	0922	0922	0931	1022	until	2122	2232	2338	0022	at	1130	1330	1530	1731	1931
Karlsruhe Hbf........... **916** a.	0146	0614	0728	|	0816	|	|	0849	|	|	0949	|		|	|	|	|		1149	1349	1549	1749	1949
Karlsruhe Bahnhofsvorplatz a.	...	...	...	0746	...	0846	0846	...	0946	0946	...	1046		2146	2256	0002	0046		...	...	...	...	...

e – Ⓐ (not Jan. 6). j – 0811 on Ⓒ (also Jan. 6). r – Not Jan. 6. t – Arrives 13 minutes earlier. v – Arrives 2240. w – Also Jan. 6. z – Ⓒ (also Jan. 6).

RE services

MÜNCHEN - PASSAU 944

km		Ⓐe	⚒e	Ⓐe	Ⓐe	Ⓒz											Ⓐe	Ⓐe						
0	**München** Hbf............... **878** d.	...	0455	0524	0604	0624	0724	0824	0924	1024	1124	1224	1324	1424	1524	1622	1642	...	1723	1824	1924	2024	2124	2325
42	Freising .... **878** d.	...	0518	0549	0628	0651	0748	0848	0948	1048	1149	1249	1348	1448	1548	1648	1708	1713	1749	1848	1948	2048	2148	2349
76	Landshut (Bay) Hbf......... **878** d.	...	0543	0613	0650	0714	0809	0910	1014	1109	1212	1314	1414	1511	1613	1709	1730	1744	1815	1910	2013	2111	2212	0014
121	Landau (Isar)..............................d.	...	0625	0701v	0737n	0744	0845	0944	1048	1144	1244	1343	1449	1544	1648	1744	...	1823	1848	1941	2045	2143	2248	0044
139	Plattling ....a.	...	0640	0714	0750	0756	0857	0953	1100	1154	1256	1355	1500	1555	1700	1755	...	1835	1900	1953	2056	2155	2301	0055
139	Plattling .... **920** d.	0600	0642	0725	0800	0802	0901	1004	1102	1204	1302	1404	1502	1604	1702	1804	...	...	1902	2004	2102	2157	2306	0057
191	**Passau** Hbf.................. **920** a.	0633	0718	0800	0833	0836	0934	1038	1136	1239	1336	1439	1536	1639	1736	1839	...	...	1937	2039	2139	2232	2341	0130

	⚒e		Ⓐe	Ⓒz	Ⓐe																			
Passau Hbf.................... **920** d.	0442	0523	0604	0627	0646	...	0725	0825	0916	1025	1116	1225	1316	1425	1516	1625	1715	1822	1916	2025	...	2128	...	2313
Plattling .... **920** a.	0514	0558	0640	0701	0720	...	0759	0900	0950	1100	1150	1259	1349	1459	1550	1659	1751	1857	1949	2058	...	2200	...	2347
Plattling ....d.	0520	0600	0642	0702	0723	...	0802	0901	1002	1102	1202	1301	1402	1502	1602	1702	1801	1902	2002	2100	...	2202	...	2350
Landau (Isar)..............................d.	0532	0613	0656	0714	0735	...	0814	0913	1012	1114	1212	1313	1413	1515	1612	1714	1811	1915	2013	2112	...	2216	...	0003
Landshut (Bay) Hbf......... **878** d.	0608	0647	0727	0749	0807	...	0849	0947	1048	1148	1248	1349	1448	1548	1648	1748	1848	1949	2049	2149	...	2248	...	0038
Freising .... **878** d.	0630	0709	0748	0810	0830	...	0910	1009	1110	1210	1310	1410	1510	1610	1710	1810	1910	2011	2110	2210	...	2310	...	...
München Hbf................ **878** a.	0655	0736	0815	0836	0855	...	0937	1035	1135	1235	1335	1435	1535	1636	1735	1835	1935	2035	2135	2235	...	2336	...	...

e – Not Jan. 6. n – Arrives 0729. v – Arrives 0649. z – Also Jan. 6.

agilis

REGENSBURG - INGOLSTADT - DONAUWÖRTH - ULM 945

On Jan. 6 services run as on ⑦

km			Ⓐ		Ⓐ	Ⓐ	Ⓐ	Ⓐ	Ⓐ	Ⓐ	Ⓐ	Ⓐ	Ⓐ	Ⓐ	Ⓐ	Ⓐ	Ⓐ	Ⓐ	Ⓐ	Ⓐ	Ⓐ	Ⓐ	Ⓐ	Ⓐ	Ⓐ	Ⓐ
0	**Regensburg** Hbf ...... d.	Ⓐ	...	...	0405	0452	0508	0534	0609	...	0713	0745	0845	0945	1045	1145	1245	1345	1445	1545	1614	1645	1728	1745	1845	...
46	Neustadt (Donau) ...... d.		...	...	0442	0534	0556	0626	0656	...	0803	0830	0930	1028	1131	1229	1323	1427	1527	1629	1702	1731	1811	1830	1929	...
74	**Ingolstadt** Hbf.......... a.		...	...	0502	0554	0622	0652	0719	...	0826	0851	0954	1050	1153	1250	1349	1449	1548	1650	1733	1755	1835	1851	1950	...
74	**Ingolstadt** Hbf.......... d.		...	...	0509	0608	0633	0702	...	0807	...	0908	1009	1108	1209	1307	1407	1508	1607	1707	1740	1810	1841	1908	...	2047
95	Neuburg (Donau)....... d.		...	...	0528	0627	0647	0729	...	0828	...	0925	1028	1129	1228	1328	1428	1527	1628	1725	1802	1828	1855	1928	...	2108
127	**Donauwörth**............. a.		...	...	0553	0653	0725	0753	...	0852	...	0951	1053	1153	1253	1353	1453	1553	1653	1753	1834	1853	1920	1953	...	2136
127	**Donauwörth**............. d.		0500	...	0603	0703	...	0803	...	0901	...	1002	1101	1202	1302	1400	1503	1601	1702	1801	...	1901	...	2016	...	2139
153	Dillingen (Donau)....... d.		0524	...	0632	0723	...	0823	...	0925	...	1023	1121	1223	1330	1423	1525	1624	1725	1823	...	1922	...	2040	...	2204
176	Günzburg........... **930** a.		0541	...	0649	0740	...	0840	...	0940	...	1040	1140	1240	1347	1440	1540	1640	1740	1840	...	1940	...	2056	...	2221
200	**Ulm** Hbf............. **930** a.		0610	...	0710	0758	...	0858	...	0958	...	1058	1158	1310	1410	1458	1558	1658	1758	1858	...	1958	...	2115	...	2302

	Ⓐ	Ⓐ	Ⓐ	Ⓐ			Ⓒ		Ⓒ	Ⓒ	Ⓒ	Ⓒ	Ⓒ	Ⓒ	Ⓒ	Ⓒ	Ⓒ	Ⓒ	Ⓒ	Ⓒ	Ⓒ	Ⓒ	Ⓒ	⑥	Ⓒ	Ⓒ
Regensburg Hbf .... d.	1945	2011	2111	2222	...	Ⓒ	...	...	...	0557	0651	0759	0845	1000	1045	1200	1245	1358	1445	1600	1645	1800	1845	1947	2046	2222
Neustadt (Donau) .... d.	2027	2101	2207	2302	...		...	...	...	0638	0732	0838	0933	1038	1132	1238	1332	1438	1532	1638	1732	1838	1932	2029	2132	2302
Ingolstadt Hbf.......... a.	2053	2122	2227	2322	...		...	...	...	0654	0753	0854	0955	1054	1153	1254	1354	1454	1552	1654	1755	1854	1952	2050	2152	2322
Ingolstadt Hbf.......... d.	...	2143	2240	2336	...		...	...	0608	0708	0808	0907	1008	1107	1208	1307	1408	1507	1608	1707	1808	1907	2038	...	2240	2336
Neuburg (Donau)........ d.	...	2203	2257	2351	...		...	...	0627	0722	0824	0922	1024	1122	1224	1322	1424	1522	1624	1722	1824	1922	2059	...	2257	2351
Donauwörth............. a.	...	2228	2323	0021	...		...	...	0653	0747	0853	0947	1053	1147	1253	1347	1453	1547	1653	1747	1853	1947	2123	...	2323	0021
Donauwörth............. d.	...	2237	2337	...	...		0503	...	0703	0750	0901	0949	1101	1150	1303	1350	1503	1550	1702	1750	1901	1950	2138	...	2337	...
Dillingen (Donau)........ d.	...	2302	2358	...	...		0524	...	0723	0807	0925	1006	1121	1206	1324	1406	1525	1606	1725	1806	1922	2006	2159	...	2358	...
Günzburg............**930** a.	...	2319	0014	...	...		0541	...	0740	0824	0940	1022	1140	1222	1340	1422	1540	1622	1740	1825	1940	2023	2221	...	0014	...
Ulm Hbf..............**930** a.	...	2337	0033	...	...		0610	...	0758	0844	0958	1040	1158	1240	1358	1440	1558	1640	1758	1844	1958	2041	2302	...	0033	...

		Ⓐ	Ⓐ	Ⓐ	Ⓐ	Ⓐ	Ⓐ	Ⓐ	Ⓐ	Ⓐ	Ⓐ	Ⓐ	Ⓐ	Ⓐ	Ⓐ	Ⓐ	Ⓐ	Ⓐ	Ⓐ	Ⓐ	Ⓐ	Ⓐ	Ⓐ	Ⓐ	Ⓐ	Ⓐ
Ulm Hbf..............**930** d.	Ⓐ	...	...	...	0450	0533	...	0625	...	0745	0848	0948	1048	1148	1248	1348	...	1448	1548	1648	1744	1831	...	1944	...	2048
Günzburg............**930** d.		...	...	...	0509	0551	...	0645	...	0804	0913	1011	1115	1211	1314	1411	...	1513	1611	1713	1804	1851	...	2004	...	2115
Dillingen (Donau)........ d.		...	...	...	0524	0607	...	0701	...	0829	0933	1032	1132	1231	1331	1431	...	1533	1632	1733	1829	1907	...	2021	...	2131
Donauwörth............. a.		...	...	...	0545	0629	...	0729	...	0851	0953	1052	1153	1252	1352	1452	...	1553	1652	1753	1851	1932	...	2042	...	2153
Donauwörth............. d.		...	0502	...	0554	0631	0701	0731	0801	0859	1004	1102	1202	1302	1402	1501	...	1602	1702	1801	1901	1940	2005	2043	2138	...
Neuburg (Donau)........ d.		...	0527	...	0627	0704	0730	0804	0830	0930	1030	1130	1230	1329	1430	1535	...	1630	1734	1830	1930	2008	2029	2108	2205	...
Ingolstadt Hbf.......... a.		...	0544	...	0648	0723	0746	0833	0846	0949	1046	1146	1246	1346	1446	1553	...	1648	1750	1848	1946	2022	2046	2125	2222	...
Ingolstadt Hbf.......... d.		0521	0600	0628	0705	0730	0805	...	0905	1006	1105	1206	1318	1405	1505	1605	1622	1704	1805	1905	2007	2030	2108	2138	2236	...
Neustadt (Donau) .... d.		0545	0622	0656	0729	0752	0828	...	0928	1027	1127	1227	1339	1427	1527	1627	1651	1727	1827	1927	2027	2047	2133	2203	2302	...
Regensburg Hbf .... a.		0628	0707	0739	0811	0836	0910	...	1010	1110	1210	1310	1422	1510	1611	1711	1734	1810	1910	2011	2110	2129	2210	2252	2344	...

	Ⓐ	Ⓐ	Ⓐ			Ⓒ	Ⓒ	Ⓒ	Ⓒ	Ⓒ	Ⓒ	Ⓒ	Ⓒ	Ⓒ	Ⓒ	Ⓒ	Ⓒ	Ⓒ	Ⓒ	Ⓒ	Ⓒ	Ⓒ	Ⓒ		Ⓒ	Ⓒ
Ulm Hbf..............**930** d.	...	2223	2255	...	Ⓒ	...	0555	0718	0745	0918	0948	1118	1148	1318	1348	1518	1550	1718	1744	1918	...	1944	...	...	2223	2255
Günzburg............**930** d.	...	2244	2318	...		...	0614	0736	0804	0936	1011	1136	1211	1336	1411	1536	1611	1736	1812	1936	...	2004	...	...	2244	2318
Dillingen (Donau)........ d.	...	2301	2334	...		...	0630	0752	0829	0952	1032	1152	1231	1352	1431	1552	1632	1752	1831	1952	...	2029	...	...	2301	2334
Donauwörth............. a.	...	2323	2400	...		...	0653	0812	0851	1012	1052	1212	1252	1412	1452	1612	1652	1812	1853	2012	...	2051	...	...	2323	2400
Donauwörth............. d.	2238	2338	...	...		0502	0701	0814	0904	1014	1102	1214	1302	1414	1501	1614	1702	1814	1901	2014	...	2138	...	...	2338	...
Neuburg (Donau)........ d.	2308	0004	...	...		0527	0732	0838	0932	1037	1132	1237	1332	1437	1533	1637	1733	1837	1933	2037	...	2205	...	...	0004	...
Ingolstadt Hbf.......... a.	2326	0021	...	...		0544	0749	0851	0949	1051	1148	1251	1349	1451	1549	1651	1749	1851	1948	2056	...	2222	...	...	0021	...
Ingolstadt Hbf.......... d.	2338	...	...	...		0605	0805	0905	1005	1105	1205	1305	1405	1505	1605	1705	1805	1905	2005	2105	2206	...	2338	...	...	...
Neustadt (Donau) .... d.	2359	...	...	...		0627	0828	0921	1027	1121	1227	1321	1427	1521	1627	1721	1827	1921	2029	2121	2227	...	2359	...	...	...
Regensburg Hbf .... a.	0042	...	...	...		0708	0910	0953	1110	1155	1310	1355	1510	1555	1711	1756	1910	1955	2111	2155	2312	...	0042	...	...	...

ANGERMÜNDE - SZCZECIN 949

km		⚒							E	⑤f	
	Berlin Gesund. **845**..d.	...	0805g	...	...	1451g	1720g	...	...	2105g	...
0	**Angermünde** ....d.	0640	0855	1040	1345	1545	1808	1933	2133	2155	...
40	Tantow ....d.	0718	0928	1118	1425	1625	1847	2014	2211	2234	...
59	Szczecin Gumience ...d.	0732	0942	1132	1439	1639	1907	2028	2225	2248	...
64	**Szczecin** Główny.........a.	0738	0948	1138	1445	1645	1913	2034	2231	2254	...

		⚒				E	⑤f		
Szczecin Główny................d.	0605	0823	1006	1223	1403	1603	1707	1824	1951
Szczecin Gumience ....d.	0611	0829	1012	1229	1409	1609	1713	1830	1957
Tantow ....d.	0625	0843	1026	1243	1425	1625	1727	1847	2012
Angermünde.......................a.	0705	0922	1104	1322	1504	1704	1805	1926	2044
Berlin Gesund. **845**.........a.	0756h	...	1156h	...	...	...	1857h	...	2140h

E – ①②③④⑥⑦ (also Apr. 14; not Apr. 13).

f – Also Apr. 13; not Apr. 14.
g – Berlin **Lichtenberg** from Feb. 9 (departs 3–5 minutes **earlier**).
h – Berlin **Lichtenberg** from Feb. 9 (arrives 2–4 minutes later).

Countries: CZECH REPUBLIC, SLOVAKIA, HUNGARY, CROATIA, SLOVENIA, ITALY, SWITZERLAND, GERMANY

Cities and towns:
BRATISLAVA, WIEN, Marchegg, Schwechat, Bruck an der Leitha, Ebenfurth, Sopron, Deutschkreutz, Hegyeshalom, Kittsee, Budapest, Győr, Szentgotthárd, Szombathely, Fehring, MARIBOR, Zidani Most, Zagreb

Hohenau, Stockerau, Tulln, Baden, Wiener Neustadt, Puchberg, Hochschneeberg, Mürzzuschlag, Hartberg, Spielfeld-Straß, Bleiburg, LJUBLJANA

Brno, Bŕeclav, Znojmo, Retz, Sigmundsherberg, Absdorf, ST PÖLTEN, Hochschneeberg, Mariazell, Weißenbach, Bruck an der Mur, Leoben, St Michael, Zeltweg, GRAZ

Jihlava, Praha, Veselí nad Lužnicí, České Velenice, Gmünd NÖ, Schwarzenau, Krems an der Donau, Emmersdorf, Melk, Amstetten, Waidhofen a.d. Ybbs, Selzthal, Stainach-Irdning, Unzmarkt, Friesach, St Veit an der Glan, KLAGENFURT, Rosenbach, Jesenice

Plzeň, České Budějovice, Horní Dvořiště, Summerau, Sarmingstein, St Valentin, LINZ, Wels, Rohr, Kirchdorf, Bad Aussee, Bad Ischl, Radstadt, Schwarzach-St Veit, Spittal-Millstättersee, VILLACH, Tarvisio, UDINE

Bayerisch Eisenstein, Deggendorf, Passau, Neumarkt-Kallham, Attnang-Puchheim, Gmunden, St Wolfgang, St Gilgen, SALZBURG, Freilassing, Berchtesgaden, Bischofshofen, Bad Gastein, Lienz, San Candido, Fortezza, Venezia

Plattling, Landshut, Simbach, Braunau am Inn, Mühldorf, St Johann, Zell am See, Krimml, Mayrhofen, Brennero, BOLZANO, Verona

REGENSBURG, München Flughafen, Rosenheim, Kufstein, Wörgl, Ellmau, Kitzbühel, Jenbach, Hinterglemm, Zell am Ziller, Obergurgl, Merano

Nürnberg, MÜNCHEN, Weilheim, Achensee, Mittenwald, Seefeld, INNSBRUCK, Ötztal, Imst, Landeck, St Anton, Nauders, Malles

AUGSBURG, Buchloe, Garmisch-Partenkirchen, Ehrwald, Reutte, Lech, Langen, Scuol Tarasp

Stuttgart, ULM, Memmingen, Kempten, Immenstadt, Füssen, Oberstdorf, Pfronten, Bludenz, Schruns, Klosters, Davos, Zernez, St Moritz

BREGENZ, FELDKIRCH, Bludenz, Langwies, Landquart, Chur, Sargans, Buchs

Lindau, St Margrethen, St Gallen, Zürich, Bur, Friedrichshafen, Trano

Route numbers (selection): 1150, 1169, 1135, 1133, 1132, 1130, 1125, 990, 991, 983, 993, 666, 992, 950, 962, 963, 964, 961, 974, 976, 977, 975, 980, 086, 998, 971, 088, 595, 596, 597, 951, 953, 954, 955, 956, 957, 958, 959, 960, 540, 545, 546, 530, 935, 930, 893, 877, 944, 920/1, 929, 892, 888, 895, 868, 890, 891, 999, 984, 994, 978, 965, 985, 987, 986, 995, 1250, 1251, 1252, 1233, 1315, 1300/15, 1300

AUSTRIA

Operator: Except where otherwise stated, rail services are operated by Österreichische Bundesbahnen (**ÖBB**) www.oebb.at

Timings: Valid **December 11**, 2016 - **December 9**, 2017, unless stated otherwise in individual tables. See page 2 for public holiday dates.

Services: Trains convey both first- and second-class seating unless footnotes show otherwise or there is a '2' in the train column. Overnight sleeping car (🛏) or couchette (▬) trains do not necessarily convey seating accommodation - refer to individual footnotes for details. Descriptions of sleeping and couchette cars appear on page 8.

Train categories:

RJ	**Railjet**	Austrian high-speed train. Conveys first and economy (2nd) class. *Business class* also available to first class ticket holders (supplement payable).
ICE	**InterCity Express**	German high-speed train.
EC	**EuroCity**	International express train.
IC	**InterCity**	Internal or international express train.
D	**Schnellzug**	Ordinary fast train.
EN	**EuroNight**	(also *ÖBB nightjet*). Overnight express train - see page 8.
WB	**Westbahn**	Wien - Linz - Salzburg private operator (special fares – ÖBB tickets are not valid).
REX	**Regional Express**	Semi-fast regional train.
	Regional / S-Bahn	Local stopping trains – no category or train number shown.

Reservations: Seats may be reserved on all express trains (*RJ, ICE, EC, IC, NJ, D*).

Catering: Three types of catering are indicated in the tables: ✕ – Restaurant car; ⊗ – Bordbistro; 🍸 – At seat trolley service.

FLUGHAFEN WIEN - WIEN - LINZ - SALZBURG — 950

km		*REX* 5885	*RJ* 898	*RJ* 362	*RJ* 540	*RJ* 660	*RJ* 260	*ICE* 228	*RJ* 542	*IC* 942	*RJ* 160	*RJ* 560	*RJ* 662	*RJ* 262	*ICE* 28	*RJ* 596	*RJ* 162	*RJ* 562	*RJ* 548	*IC* 528	*RJ* 60	*RJ* 860	*ICE* 26	*RJ* 640	*RJ* 564	*RJ* 642
		⚒ F2	K✕	①–⑥ r✕	✕	✕	✕	Q✕	✕	Ⓒ G🍸	✕	✕	✕	✕	Q✕	K✕	B✕	✕	✕	Ⓒ △🍸	B✕	✕	R✕	✕	▽✕	✕
0	**Flughafen Wien** ✈ d.	...	...	...	...	...	...	...	*0633*	...	...	0703	0733	0803	...	0833	...	0903	*0933*	...	...	1003	...	1033	1103	*1133*
17	**Wien** Hbf d.	...	...	0530	0555	0630	0630	0650	0655	0714	0730	0730	0755	0830	0850	0855	0930	0930	0955	1015	1030	1030	1050	1055	1130	1155
21	**Wien** Meidling d.	...	...	0537	0602	0637	0637	0657	0702	0721	0737	0737	0802	0837	0857	0902	0937	0937	1002	1022	1037	1037	1057	1102	1137	1202
52	Tullnerfeld **993** d.	...	...	|	0617	|	|	|	0717	|	|	|	0817	|	|	0917	|	|	1017	|	|	|	|	1117	|	1217
82	**St Pölten** Hbf **993** d.	...	...	0600	0632	0700	0700	0723	0732	0753	0800	0800	0832	0900	0923	0932	1000	1000	1032	1047	1100	1100	1123	1132	1200	1232
142	Amstetten d.	...	...	|	0700	|	|	|	0800	0823	|	|	0900	|	|	1000	|	|	1100	|	|	|	|	1200	|	1300
179	St Valentin **976** d.	...	...	|	0716	|	|	|	0816	|	|	|	0916	|	|	1016	|	|	1116	|	|	|	|	1216	|	1316
204	**Linz** Hbf **976** a.	...	...	0646	0730	0746	0746	0813	0830	0851	0846	0846	0930	0946	1013	1030	1046	1046	1130	1135	1146	1146	1213	1230	1246	1330
204	**Linz** Hbf **962** d.	0504	0632	0648	0732	0748	0748	0817	0832	0853	0848	0848	0932	0948	1017	1032	1048	1048	1132	1137	1148	1148	1217	1232	1248	1332
229	**Wels** Hbf **962** d.	0520	0645	|	0745	|	|	0833	0845	0918	|	|	0945	|	1033	1045	|	|	1145	1150	|	|	1233	1245	|	1345
	Passau Hbf **962** 🏛 a.	|	|	|	|	|	|	0918	|	...	|	|	|	|	1118	|	|	|	|	|	|	|	1318	|	|	|
259	Attnang-Puchheim d.	0544	0700	|	0800	|	|	...	0900	...	|	|	1000	|	...	1100	|	|	1200	1203	|	|	...	1300	|	1400
264	Vöcklabruck d.	0549	0706	|	0806	|	|	...	0906	...	|	|	1006	|	...	1106	|	|	1206	...	|	|	...	1306	|	1406
329	**Salzburg** Hbf a.	0648	0748	0752	0848	0852	0852	...	0948	...	0952	0952	1048	1052	...	1148	1152	1152	1248	...	1252	1252	...	1348	1352	1448
	München Hbf **890** a.	...	...	|	...	|	1030t	...	...	...	|	|	|	1230t	...	...	|	|	...	...	1430t	|	...	...	|	...
	Innsbruck Hbf **951** a.	...	...	0944	...	1044	...	...	...	...	1144	1144	1244	...	...	...	1344	1344r	...	...	...	1444	...	...	1544	...
	Zürich HB **520** a.	...	...	1320	...	|	...	...	...	...	1520	...	|	...	...	...	1720	...	...	...	...	|	...	...	...	...
	Bregenz **951** a.	...	...	...	...	1317	...	...	...	...	...	...	1517	...	...	...	...	...	...	...	...	1717	...	...	...	...

	RJ 62	*RJ* 862	*ICE* 90	*RJ* 644	*RJ* 166	*RJ* 566	*RJ* 646	*RJ* 64	*RJ* 864	*ICE* 22	*RJ* 698	*RJ* 168	*RJ* 568	*D* 720	*RJ* 740	*RJ* 66	*RJ* 866	*ICE* 20	*RJ* 742	*RJ* 760	*RJ* 960	*RJ* 744	*RJ* 68	*RJ* 868	*RJ* 746	*RJ* 762
	B✕	✕	E✕	✕	✕	✕	✕	B✕	✕	R✕	K✕	✕	✕	Ⓐ	✕	N✕	✕	Q✕	✕	✕	✕	✕	B✕	✕	✕	✕
Flughafen Wien ✈ d.	...	1203	...	1233	...	1303	*1333*	...	1403	...	1433	...	1503	...	1533	*1603*	*1603*	...	1633	...	1703	*1733*	...	1803	*1833*	1903
Wien Hbf d.	1230	1230	1250	1255	1330	1330	1355	1430	1430	1450	1455	1530	1530	1550	1555	1630	1630	1650	1655	1730	1730	1755	1830	1830	1855	1930
Wien Meidling d.	1237	1237	1257	1302	1337	1337	1402	1437	1437	1457	1502	1537	1537	1557	1602	1637	1637	1657	1702	1737	1737	1802	1837	1837	1902	1937
Tullnerfeld **993** d.	|	|	|	1317	|	|	1417	|	|	|	1517	|	|	|	1617	|	|	|	1717	|	|	1817	|	|	1917	|
St Pölten Hbf **993** d.	1300	1300	1323	1332	1400	1400	1432	1500	1500	1523	1532	1600	1600	1622	1632	1700	1700	1723	1732	1800	1800	1832	1900	1900	1932	2000
Amstetten d.	|	|	|	1400	|	|	1500	|	|	|	1600	|	|	1647	1700	|	|	|	1800	|	|	1900	|	|	2000	|
St Valentin **976** d.	|	|	|	1416	|	|	1516	|	|	|	1616	|	|	|	1716	|	|	|	1816	|	|	1916	|	|	2016	|
Linz Hbf **976** a.	1346	1346	1413	1430	1446	1446	1530	1546	1546	1613	1630	1646	1646	1715	1730	1746	1746	1813	1830	1846	1846	1930	1946	1946	2030	2046
Linz Hbf **962** d.	1348	1348	1417	1432	1448	1448	1532	1548	1548	1617	1632	1648	1648	...	1732	1748	1748	1817	1832	1848	1848	1932	1948	1948	2032	2048
Wels Hbf **962** d.	|	|	1433	1445	|	|	1545	|	|	1633	1645	|	|	...	1745	|	|	1833	1845	|	|	1945	|	|	2045	|
Passau Hbf **962** 🏛 a.	|	|	1518	|	|	|	|	|	|	1718	|	|	|	...	|	|	|	1918	|	|	|	|	|	|	|	|
Attnang-Puchheim d.	|	|	...	1500	|	|	1600	|	|	...	1700	|	|	...	1800	|	|	...	1900	|	|	2000	|	|	2100	|
Vöcklabruck d.	|	|	...	1506	|	|	1606	|	|	...	1706	|	|	...	1806	|	|	...	1906	|	|	2006	|	|	2106	|
Salzburg Hbf a.	1452	1452	...	1548	1552	1552	1648	1652	1652	...	1748	1752	1752	...	1848	1852	1852	...	1948	1952	1952	2048	2052	2052	2148	2152
München Hbf **890** a.	1631t	|	...	...	|	|	...	1831	|	...	...	|	|	...	...	2029t	|	...	...	|	|	...	2232	|	...	|
Innsbruck Hbf **951** a.	...	1644	...	...	1744	1744	...	...	1844	...	...	1944	1944	...	...	...	2048	...	...	2144	2144h	...	...	2248b	...	2348
Zürich HB **520** a.	...	|	...	...	2120	|	...	...	|	...	...	2320	...	...	...	...	|	...	...	|	...	...	...	...	...	...
Bregenz **951** a.	...	1917	...	...	...	2017n	...	...	2117	...	...	...	...	...	...	...	...	...	...	0013	...	...	...	...	...	...

	RJ 748	*RJ* 42	*RJ* 664	*EN* 490	*RJ* 840	*EN* 466	*RJ* 820	*EN* 246	*EN* 462	*EN* 40462	
	✕	B✕	● ✕	H♣	✕	W	✕	♥	D♣	⊙	
Flughafen Wien ✈ d.	*1933*	...	2003	...	2033	...	2133	*2233*	...	...	...
Wien Hbf d.	1955	2030	2030	2039	2055	2127	2155	2255	2325	2325	...
Wien Meidling d.	2002	2037	2037	2047	2102	2135	2202	2303	2333	2333	...
Tullnerfeld **993** d.	2017	|	|	|	2117	|	2217	2323	|	|	...
St Pölten Hbf **993** d.	2032	2100	2100	2116	2132	2202	2232	2341	0000	0000	...
Amstetten d.	2100	|	|	|	2200	2229	2300	0014	|	|	...
St Valentin **976** d.	2116	|	|	|	2216	|	2316	0040	|	|	...
Linz Hbf **976** a.	2130	2146	2146	2213	2230	2257	2330	0056	0050	0050	...
Linz Hbf **962** d.	2132	2148	2148	2215	2232	2300	...	0058	0105	0105	...
Wels Hbf **962** d.	2145	|	|	2232	2245	2317	...	0118	|	|	...
Passau Hbf **962** 🏛 a.	|	|	|	2320	|	|	...	|	|	|	...
Attnang-Puchheim d.	2200	|	|	...	2300	2335	...	0137	|	|	...
Vöcklabruck d.	2206	|	|	...	2306	|	...	|	|	|	...
Salzburg Hbf a.	2248	2252	2252	...	2348	0022	...	0225	0210	0210	...
München Hbf **890** a.	...	...	...	...	...	|	...	|	0610	|	...
Innsbruck Hbf **951** a.	...	...	...	...	...	0423	...	0519	...	0423	...
Zürich HB **520** a.	...	...	...	...	...	0820	...	|	...	0820	...
Bregenz **951** a.	...	...	...	...	...	...	...	0823	...	...	...

	EN 247	*EN* 463	*EN* 40467	*EN* 247	*RJ* 821	*D* 621	*RJ* 823	*EN* 467	*RJ* 541	*EN* 491
	♥	D♣	⊖	♥	✕	Ⓐ	①–⑥ r✕	W	✕	H♣
Bregenz **951** d.	2146	...	...	...	...	...	...	...	...	...
Zürich HB **520** d.	|	...	2140	...	...	...	...	2140	...	...
Innsbruck Hbf **951** d.	0044	...	0128	...	...	...	...	0128	...	...
München Hbf **890** d.	|	2335x	|	...	...	...	...	|	...	...
Salzburg Hbf d.	0324	0350	0350	...	...	...	...	0438	0512	...
Vöcklabruck d.	|	|	|	...	...	...	...	|	0554	...
Attnang-Puchheim d.	0411	|	|	...	...	...	...	0527	0600	...
Passau Hbf **962** 🏛 d.	|	|	|	...	...	...	...	|	|	0524
Wels Hbf **962** d.	0429	|	|	...	...	...	...	0545	0616	0619
Linz Hbf **962** a.	0443	0455	0455	...	...	...	...	0601	0628	0633
Linz Hbf **976** d.	0445	0510	0510	...	0530	...	0610	0605	0630	0635
St Valentin **976** d.	0504	|	|	←	0545	...	|	|	0645	|
Amstetten d.	0524	|	|	0526	0602	0620	0637	0644	0702	0710
St Pölten Hbf **993** d.	→	0602	0602	0610	0630	0645	0702	0715	0730	0742
Tullnerfeld **993** a.	...	|	|	0626	0642	|	|	|	0742	|
Wien Meidling a.	...	0627	0627	0646	0658	0711	0723	0746	0758	0811
Wien Hbf a.	...	0635	0635	0654	0705	0718	0730	0755	0805	0819
Flughafen Wien ✈ a.	...	*0657*	*0657*	...	0727	...	0757	...	*0827*	...

	RJ 761	*RJ* 543	*RJ* 49	*RJ* 949	*RJ* 545	*RJ* 763	*RJ* 265	*RJ* 547	*RJ* 861	*RJ* 61	*RJ* 549	*RJ* 765 965	*RJ* 691	*ICE* 21	*RJ* 863	*RJ* 63	*RJ* 643	*RJ* 161	*RJ* 645	*ICE* 23	*RJ* 665	*RJ* 65	*RJ* 865	*RJ* 563	*RJ* 649	*ICE* 91
	✕	✕	①–⑥ sB✕	✕	✕	✕	✕	✕	✕	B✕	✕	✕	K✕	Q✕	✕	M✕	✕	✕	✕	R✕	⑥⑦ u✕	B✕	✕	✕	✕	E✕
Bregenz **951** d.	...	...	...	...	...	...	...	...	...	...	...	0548	...	...	0640	...	...	...	...	...	...	...	0840	...	...	...
Zürich HB **520** d.	...	...	...	...	...	...	...	...	...	...	...	|	...	...	|	...	...	0640	...	...	...	...	|	...	...	...
Innsbruck Hbf **951** d.	...	...	0510	0510y	...	0610	...	...	0713	...	...	0817	...	...	0914	...	...	1017	...	...	...	...	1114	1217	...	...
München Hbf **890** d.	...	...	|	|	...	|	0624v	...	|	0725	...	|	...	...	|	0930v	...	|	...	...	...	1130v	|	|	...	...
Salzburg Hbf d.	0605	0612	0708	0708	0712	0808	0808	0812	0908	0908	0912	1008	1012	...	1108	1108	1112	1208	1212	...	1308	1308	1312	1408	1412	...
Vöcklabruck d.	|	0654	|	|	0754	|	|	0854	|	|	0954	|	1054	...	|	|	1154	|	1254	...	|	|	1354	|	1454	...
Attnang-Puchheim d.	0650	0700	|	|	0800	|	|	0900	|	|	1000	|	1100	...	|	|	1200	|	1300	...	|	|	1400	|	1500	...
Passau Hbf **962** 🏛 d.	|	|	|	|	|	|	|	|	|	|	|	|	|	1040	|	|	|	|	|	1240	|	|	|	|	|	1440
Wels Hbf **962** d.	|	0716	|	|	0816	|	|	0916	|	|	1016	|	1116	1129	|	|	1216	|	1316	1329	|	|	1416	|	1516	1529
Linz Hbf **962** a.	0712	0728	0812	0812	0828	0912	0912	0928	1012	1012	1028	1112	1128	1143	1212	1212	1228	1312	1328	1343	1412	1412	1428	1512	1528	1543
Linz Hbf **976** d.	0714	0730	0814	0814	0830	0914	0914	0930	1014	1014	1030	1114	1130	1147	1214	1214	1230	1314	1330	1347	1414	1414	1430	1514	1530	1547
St Valentin **976** d.	|	0745	|	|	0845	|	|	0945	|	|	1045	|	1145	|	|	|	1245	|	1345	|	|	|	1445	|	1545	|
Amstetten d.	|	0802	|	|	0902	|	|	1002	|	|	1102	|	1202	|	|	|	1302	|	1402	|	|	|	1502	|	1602	|
St Pölten Hbf **993** d.	0802	0830	0902	0902	0930	1002	1002	1030	1102	1102	1130	1202	1230	1239	1302	1302	1330	1402	1430	1439	1502	1502	1530	1602	1630	1639
Tullnerfeld **993** a.	|	0842	|	|	0942	|	|	1042	|	|	1142	|	1242	|	|	|	1342	|	1442	|	|	|	1542	|	1642	|
Wien Meidling a.	0823	0858	0923	0923	0958	1023	1023	1058	1123	1123	1158	1223	1258	1302	1323	1323	1358	1423	1458	1502	1523	1523	1558	1623	1658	1702
Wien Hbf a.	0830	0905	0930	0930	1005	1030	1030	1105	1130	1130	1205	1230	1305	1309	1330	1330	1405	1430	1505	1509	1530	1530	1605	1630	1705	1709
Flughafen Wien ✈ a.	0857	0927	...	0957	*1027*	1057	...	1127	1157	...	*1227*	1257j	1327	...	1357	...	1427	1457	1527	...	1557	*1557*	*1627*	1657	1727	...

☛ See page 452 for regional trains Wien Westbf - St Pölten - Melk - Amstetten - Linz, also services Wien - Linz - Salzburg operated by *Westbahn*.

FOR NOTES SEE PAGE 452 →

950 SALZBURG - LINZ - WIEN

	RJ	RJ	RJ	RJ	RJ	RJ	ICE	RJ	RJ	IC	RJ	RJ	RJ	IC	RJ	ICE	RJ	RJ	RJ	RJ	RJ	ICE	RJ	RJ	RJ	RJ
	867	**67**	**741**	**565**	**165**	**793**	**27**	**869**	**69**	**725**	**745**	**167**	**567**	**947**	**797**	**29**	**661**	**261**	**749**	**169**	**841**	**229**	**663**	**843**	**361**	**845**
										Ⓒ			Ⓑq	Ⓒ												Ⓑq
	✕	B✕	✕	✕	B✕	K✕	R✕	✕	✕	△🍸	✕	✕	✕	G🍸	K✕	Q✕	✕	✕	✕	✕	✕	Q✕	✕	✕	✕	✕
Bregenz **951** d.	1040	...	...	...	...	...	...	1240	...	...	...	...	...	...	...	...	1440	...	...	...	...	...	...	...	...	...
Zürich HB **520** d.	|	...	...	...	1040	...	...	|	...	...	...	1240	...	...	...	...	|	...	...	1440	...	...	...	...	1640	...
Innsbruck Hbf **951** d.	1314	...	...	1417	1417	...	...	1514	...	...	...	1617	1617	...	...	...	1714	...	...	1817	...	...	1914	...	2017	...
München Hbf **890** d.	|	1330v	...	|	|	...	...	|	1530	...	...	|	|	...	...	...	|	1730	...	|	...	...	|	...	|	...
Salzburg Hbf d.	1508	1508	1512	1608	1608	1612	...	1708	1708	...	1712	1808	1808	...	1812	...	1908	1908	1912	2008	2012	...	2108	2112	2208	2212
Vöcklabruck d.	|	|	1554	|	|	1654	...	|	|	...	1754	|	|	...	1854	...	|	|	1954	|	2054	...	|	2154	|	2254
Attnang-Puchheim d.	|	|	1600	|	|	1700	...	|	|	1755	1800	|	|	...	1900	...	|	|	2000	|	2100	...	|	2200	|	2300
Passau Hbf **962** 🏛 d.	|	|	|	|	|	|	1640	|	|	|	|	|	|	...	|	1840	|	|	|	|	|	2040	|	|	|	|
Wels Hbf **962** d.	|	|	1616	|	|	1716	1729	|	|	1811	1816	|	|	1844	1916	1929	|	|	2016	|	2116	2129	|	2216	|	2316
Linz Hbf **962** a.	1612	1612	1628	1712	1712	1728	1743	1812	1812	1823	1828	1912	1912	1904	1928	1943	2012	2012	2028	2112	2128	2143	2212	2228	2312	2328
Linz Hbf **976** d.	1614	1614	1630	1714	1714	1730	1747	1814	1814	1826	1830	1914	1914	1906	1930	1947	2014	2014	2030	2114	2130	2147	2214	...	2314	...
St Valentin **976** d.	|	|	1645	|	|	1745	|	|	|	|	1845	|	|	|	1945	|	|	|	2045	|	2145	|	|	...	|	...
Amstetten d.	|	|	1702	|	|	1802	|	|	|	|	1902	|	|	1940	2002	|	|	|	2102	|	2202	|	|	...	|	...
St Pölten Hbf **993** d.	1702	1702	1730	1802	1802	1830	1839	1902	1902	1915	1930	2002	2002	2007	2030	2039	2102	2102	2130	2202	2230	2239	2302	...	0002	...
Tullnerfeld **993** a.	|	|	1742	|	|	1842	|	|	|	|	1942	|	|	|	2042	|	|	|	2142	|	2242	|	|	...	|	...
Wien Meidling a.	1723	1723	1758	1823	1823	1858	1902	1923	1923	1939	1958	2023	2023	2030	2058	2102	2123	2123	2158	2223	2258	2302	2323	...	0023	...
Wien Hbf a.	1730	1730	1805	1830	1830	1905	1909	1930	1930	1946	2005	2030	2030	2037	2105	2109	2130	2130	2205	2230	2305	2309	2330	...	0030	...
Flughafen Wien ✈ a.	1757	...	*1827*	1857	...	1927	...	1957	...	...	*2027*	2057z	2057	...	2127	...	2157	...	2227	...	...	...	...	...	...	...

Regional ÖBB trains **WIEN - MELK - AMSTETTEN - ST VALENTIN - LINZ** (2nd class only)

km ‡		⚒	ⒶT	⚒	Ⓐ		¶	P								Ⓒ	Ⓐ	Ⓒ	Ⓐ	Ⓒ	Ⓐ	Ⓒ	Ⓐ	⚒		
0	**Wien** Westbahnhof ◧ d.	...	0417	...	0620	0554c	0720	...	0820e	*0854*	*1054*	1220e	1320e	1420e	1520e	*1554*	1620	*1654*	1720	1754	1820	1854	1920	*1954*	*2054*	2354
6	**Wien** Hütteldorf ◧ d.	...	0423	...	0628	0600c	0728	...	0828e	*0900*	*1100*	1228e	1328e	1428e	1528e	*1600*	1628	*1700*	1728	1800	1828	1900	1928	*2000*	*2100*	0000
	Tullnerfeld d.	...	|	...	0640	|	0740	0810	0840e	|	|	1240e	1340e	1440e	1540e	|	1640	|	1740	|	1840	|	1940	|	|	|
61	**St Pölten** Hbf ◧ a.	...	0518	...	0653	0655c	0753	0850	0853e	*0955*	*1155*	1253e	1353e	1453e	1553e	*1655*	1653	*1755*	1753	1855	1853	1955	1953	*2055*	*2155*	0055
61	**St Pölten** Hbf d.	0435	0520	0550	...	0705	0805	0855	0905	1005	1205	1305	1405	1505	1605	1705	1705	1805	1805	1905	1905	2005	2005	2105	2235	0103
85	Melk d.	0457	0537	0612	...	0722	0822	0911	0922	1022	1222	1322	1422	1522	1622	1722	1722	1822	1822	1922	1922	2022	2022	2122	2257	0122
94	Pöchlarn d.	0507	0544	0619	...	0729	0829	0920	0929	1029	1229	1329	1429	1529	1629	1729	1729	1829	1829	1929	1929	2029	2029	2129	2304	0129
107	Ybbs an der Donau d.	0519	0552	0631	...	0740	0840	0931	0940	1040	1240	1340	1440	1540	1640	1740	1740	1840	1840	1940	1940	2040	2040	2140	2316	0138
124	Amstetten a.	0533	0607	0647	...	0755	0855	0942	0955	1055	1255	1355	1455	1555	1655	1755	1755	1855	1855	1955	1955	2055	2055	2155	2330	0153
163	**St Valentin** a.	0607	*0631*	...	...	...	...	1008	...	...	...	...	...	...	...	...	1839	...	1939	...	2039	...	...	...	...	...
188	**Linz** Hbf a.	*0636*	*0651*	...	...	...	...	1035	...	...	...	...	...	...	...	...	*1908*	...	*2008*	...	*2108*	...	...	...	...	...

		⚒	Ⓐ	Ⓐ	Ⓐ		Ⓐ	⚒T														Ⓒ	P		Ⓒ	⊗
Linz Hbf d.	...	...	...	...	*0430*	...	...	...	...	...	...	...	...	...	...	...	...	...	...	*1652*	*1752*	...	1925	...	...	...
St Valentin d.	...	*0353*e	...	0432	0501	...	0521	...	...	...	...	...	...	...	...	...	...	...	...	1721	1821	...	1948	...	...	...
Amstetten d.	0412	0431	0442	0507	0537	0553	0607	0616	0705	0805	0905	...	1105	1205	1305	1405	1505	1605	1705	1805	1905	2005	2015	...	2105	2205
Ybbs an der Donau d.	0426	0445	0456	0521	0551	0608	0621	0630	0719	0819	0919	...	1119	1219	1319	1419	1519	1619	1719	1819	1919	2019	2028	...	2119	2219
Pöchlarn d.	0435	0458	0505	0530	0600	0621	0630	0643	0730	0830	0930	1020	1130	1230	1330	1430	1530	1630	1730	1830	1930	2030	2039	2054	2130	2230
Melk d.	0441	0504	0511	0536	0606	0628	0636	0650	0736	0836	0936	1026	1136	1236	1336	1436	1536	1636	1736	1836	1936	2036	2048	2101	2136	2236
St Pölten Hbf a.	0500	0527	0530	0555	0625	0652	0655	0716	0755	0855	0955	1050	1155	1255	1355	1455	1555	1655	1755	1855	1955	2055	2106	2124	2155	2255
St Pölten Hbf ◧ d.	0502	0535	0532	0607	0637	*0705*	0707	*0735*	*0807*e	*0907*e	*1005*	*1105*	*1205*	*1305*	*1405*	1507e	1607e	1707e	1807e	1905	2005	2105	...	...	*2205*	2305
Tullnerfeld a.	0515	|	0545	0619	0649	|	0719	|	*0819*e	*0919*e	|	|	|	|	|	1519e	1619e	1719e	1819e	|	|	|	...	...	|	|
Wien Hütteldorf ◧ a.	0527	0628	0557	0631	0701	*0758*	0731	*0828*	*0831*e	*0931*e	*1058*	*1158*	*1259*	*1358*	*1459*	1531e	1631e	1731e	1831e	1958	2059	2158	...	...	*2323*	0023
Wien Westbahnhof ◧ a.	0536	0636	0606	0640	0710	*0806*	0740	*0836*	*0840*e	*0940*e	*1106*	*1206*	*1307*	*1406*	*1507*	1540e	1640e	1740e	1840e	2006	2107	2206	...	...	*2332*	0032

SERVICES OPERATED BY *WESTBAHN* **WIEN - LINZ - SALZBURG**. Special fares payable (ÖBB tickets not valid). All trains convey 🍸.

km		*WB*	*WB*		*WB*	*WB*		*WB*	*WB*	*WB*	*WB*	*WB*	*WB*	*WB*	*WB*	*WB*	*WB*	*WB*	*WB*	*WB*	*WB*	*WB*	*WB*	*WB*		
		900	**900**		**902**	**902**		**904**	**906**	**908**	**910**	**912**	**914**	**916**	**918**	**920**	**950**	**950**	**922**	**924**	**926**	**928**	**928**	**930**		
		①d	⚒		⚒												Ⓑ	⑤a					⊡	Ⓑ		
0	**Wien** Westbahnhof d.	0540	...	...	0640	...	...	0740	0840	0940	1040	1140	1240	1340	1440	1540	1616	1616	1640	1740	1840	1940	1940	2040	...	...
6	**Wien** Hütteldorf d.	0547	...	...	0647	...	...	0747	0847	0947	1047	1147	1247	1347	1447	1547	1622	1622	1647	1747	1847	1947	1947	2047	...	...
30	Tullnerfeld d.	0558	...	...	0658	...	...	0758	0858	0958	1058	1158	1258	1358	1458	1558	|	|	1658	1758	1858	1958	1958	2058	...	...
60	**St Pölten** Hbf d.	0611	...	...	0711	...	...	0811	0911	1011	1111	1211	1311	1411	1511	1611	1643	1643	1711	1811	1911	2011	2011	2111	...	...
120	Amstetten d.	0634	...	...	0734	...	...	0834	0934	1034	1134	1234	1334	1434	1534	1634	1709	1709	1734	1834	1934	2034	2034	2134	...	...
182	**Linz** Hbf **962** d.	0700	0700	...	0800	0800	...	0900	1000	1100	1200	1300	1400	1500	1600	1700	1735	1740	1800	1900	2000	2059	2100	2159	...	...
207	**Wels** Hbf **962** d.	0712	0712	...	0812	0812	...	0912	1012	1112	1212	1312	1412	1512	1612	1712	...	1753	1812	1912	2012	...	2112	...	...	...
237	Attnang-Puchheim d.	0729	0729	...	0825	0825	...	0925	1025	1125	1225	1325	1425	1525	1625	1725	...	1813	1825	1925	2025	...	2125	...	...	...
307	**Salzburg** Hbf a.	0812	0812	...	0908	0908	...	1008	1108	1208	1308	1408	1508	1608	1708	1808	...	...	1908	2008	2108	...	2208	...	...	...

	WB	*WB*	*WB*	*WB*	*WB*	*WB*	*WB*	*WB*	*WB*	*WB*	*WB*	*WB*	*WB*	*WB*	*WB*	*WB*	*WB*	*WB*	*WB*	*WB*						
	903	**905**	**941**	**907**	**907**	**909**	**911**	**913**	**915**	**917**	**919**	**921**	**923**	**925**	**951**	**927**	**929**	**931**	**933**	**933**						
	Ⓐ	⚒	⚒	†											†				⊡	♠						
Salzburg Hbf d.	...	0552	0700	0700	...	0752	0852	0952	1052	1152	1252	1352	1452	1552	...	1652	1752	1852	1952	1952	...	...	...	...	...	...
Attnang-Puchheim d.	...	0635	|	0744	0744	0835	0935	1035	1135	1235	1335	1435	1535	1635	...	1735	1835	1935	2035	2035	...	...	...	...	...	...
Wels Hbf **962** d.	...	0648	|	0757	0757	0848	0948	1048	1148	1248	1348	1448	1548	1648	...	1748	1848	1948	2048	2048	...	...	...	...	...	...
Linz Hbf **962** d.	0601	0701	0804	0809	0809	0901	1001	1101	1201	1301	1401	1501	1601	1701	1756	1801	1901	2001	2100	2101	...	...	...	...	...	...
Amstetten d.	0627	0727	|	0835	0835	0927	1027	1127	1227	1327	1427	1527	1627	1727	1822	1827	1927	2027	...	2127	...	...	...	...	...	...
St Pölten Hbf d.	0650	0750	|	0858	0858	0950	1050	1150	1250	1350	1450	1550	1650	1750	1845	1850	1950	2050	...	2150	...	...	...	...	...	...
Tullnerfeld d.	0702	0802	|	|	|	1002	1102	1202	1302	1402	1502	1602	1702	1802	|	1902	2002	2102	...	2202	...	...	...	...	...	...
Wien Hütteldorf a.	0713	0813	0909	0918	0918	1013	1113	1213	1313	1413	1513	1613	1713	1813	1905	1913	2013	2113	...	2213	...	...	...	...	...	...
Wien Westbahnhof a.	0720	0820	0916	0925	0925	1020	1120	1220	1320	1420	1520	1620	1720	1820	1912	1920	2020	2120	...	2220	...	...	...	...	...	...

B – From / to Budapest (Table **1250**).
D – KÁLMÁN IMRE – 🛏 1, 2 cl., ▬ 2 cl. and [2] Budapest - Wien - München and v.v.
E – [12] and ✕ Hamburg - Hannover - Nürnberg - Regensburg - Passau - Wien and v.v.
F – To Freilassing (a. 0707).
G – [12] and 🍸 Wien - Schwarzach - Zell am See - Wörgl and v.v.
H – *ÖBB nightjet.* 🛏 1, 2 cl., ▬ 2 cl. and [2] Wien - Hannover - Hamburg and v.v.; 🛏 1, 2 cl., ▬ 2 cl. and [2] (**40490/40421**) Wien - Köln - Düsseldorf and v.v.
K – To / from Klagenfurt (Table **970**).
M – [12] and ✕ (Frankfurt ⑥⑦ **k** -) München - Wien - Budapest.
N – [12] and ✕ Budapest - München (- Frankfurt ⑤⑥ **f**). Train number **1066** and arrives München 2032**t** on ⑤⑥ **f**.
P – May 1 - Oct. 26. [2] Wien Franz-Josefs-Bf - Passau and v.v.
Q – [12] and ✕ Frankfurt - Nürnberg - Regensburg - Passau 🏛 - Wien and v.v.
R – [12] and ✕ Dortmund - Frankfurt - Nürnberg - Regensburg - Passau 🏛 - Wien and v.v.
T – To / from Kleinreifling (Table **977**).
W – *ÖBB nightjet.* 🛏 1, 2 cl., ▬ 2 cl. and [2] Wien - Zürich and v.v.; conveys 🛏 1, 2 cl., ▬ 2 cl. and [2] (*EN* **237/236**) Wien - Salzburg - Villach - Tarvisio 🏛 - Venezia and v.v.

a – Not Jan. 6, Dec. 8.
b – Ⓑ (not Dec. 25, Apr. 16, 30, June 4, Aug. 13).
c – Ⓒ only.
d – Not Dec. 26, Apr. 17, May 1, June 5.
e – Ⓐ only.
f – ⑤⑥ (also Dec. 25, Apr. 13, 16, 30, May 24, June 4).
h – ⑦ (also Dec. 26, Apr. 17, May 1, June 5; not Dec. 25, Apr. 16, 30, June 4).
j – Change trains at Wien Hbf on ⑦ (also Jan. 7, Dec. 9; not Jan. 8).
k – ⑥⑦ (also Dec. 26, Apr. 14, 17, May 1, 25, June 5).
n – Ⓑ (also Jan. 7, Dec. 9; not Jan. 6, Dec. 8).
q – Not Dec. 25, Apr. 16, 30, June 4.
r – ①–⑥ (not Dec. 26, Apr. 17, May 1, June 5).
s – Not Dec. 26, Apr. 17, May 1, June 5, Aug. 14.
t – 3–10 minutes later Apr. 14 - July 16.
u – Also Dec. 26, Jan. 6, Apr. 17, May 1, June 5, Dec. 8; not Dec. 25, Jan. 7, Apr. 16, 30 June 4, Dec. 9.
v – 1–2 minutes **earlier** from Apr. 14 - July 16.
x – 2154 on ⑥⑦ Apr. 15 - July 16 (not May 20, 21).
y – ① (also Dec. 27, Apr. 18, May 2, June 6, Aug. 16; not Dec. 26, Apr. 17, May 1, June 5 Aug. 14).
z – ⑥ (also Dec. 25, Apr. 16, 30, June 4).

⊡ – ④–⑦ (also Dec. 26, Apr. 17, May 1, June 5, Aug. 15, Nov. 1).
♠ – ⑤–⑦ (also Dec. 26, Apr. 17, May 1, 25, June 5, 15, Aug. 15, Oct. 26, Nov. 1).
● – ①②③④⑦.
¶ – Change trains at St Pölten on Ⓐ.
⊗ – Change trains at St Pölten on Ⓒ.
⊙ – *ÖBB nightjet.* 🛏 1, 2 cl., ▬ 2 cl. and [2] Budapest (**462**) - Salzburg (**466**) - Zürich
⊖ – *ÖBB nightjet.* 🛏 1, 2 cl., ▬ 2 cl. and [2] Zürich (**467**) - Salzburg (**463**) - Budapest
♥ – *ÖBB nightjet.* Conveys 🛏 1, 2 cl., ▬ 2 cl. and [2].
△ – [12] Wien - Attnang-Puchheim and v.v.; [2] Wien - Attnang-Puchheim - Stainach-Irdning and v.v. (Table **961**).
▽ – On ⑥ conveys [12] (*RJ* **1264**) Wien Hbf - Salzburg - Zell am See.
♣ – Ⓡ for journeys to / from Germany.
‡ – Via the classic route. Trains calling at Tullnerfeld are classified *REX200* and use the high-speed line between Wien and St Pölten.
◧ – Full stopping service Wien - St Pölten and v.v.:
From Wien Westbahnhof at 0054 Ⓒ, 0417 Ⓐ, 0454, 0524 ⚒, 0554, 0624 ⚒, 0654, 0724 Ⓐ, 0754, 0854, 0954, 1054, 1124 Ⓐ, 1154 and at 24 Ⓐ and 54 minutes past each hour until 1824 Ⓐ, 1854; then 1954, 2054, 2128, 2228 and 2354.
From St Pölten at 0439 Ⓐ, 0509, 0535 ⚒, 0605, 0635 ⚒, 0705, 0735 ⚒, 0805, 0835 Ⓐ 0905, 1005, 1105, 1205, 1235 Ⓐ and at 05 and 35 Ⓐ minutes past each hour until 2005 2035 Ⓐ; then 2105, 2205 and 2305.

452 *Standard-Symbole sind auf Seite 4 erklärt* 12

SALZBURG and MÜNCHEN - INNSBRUCK - BREGENZ - LINDAU 951

km		*EN* 466	*EN* 60466		*EN* 464	*EN* 246		*RJ* 666	*IC* 1285			*RJ* 360	*RJ* 668	*IC* 118	*EN* 421	*EC* 81	*RJ* 362		*RJ* 660	*EC* 85	*RJ* 560	*RJ* 160		*RJ* 662	*EC* 87	*RJ* 562
									⑥	Ⓒ	Ⓐ				Ⓡ	¶										①–⑥
		N	⊙	2	♦	N	2	✕	♦	◇2	2	✕	✕	🍷♦	♦	A✕	✕	2▮	✕	A✕	F✕	✕	2▮	F✕	A✕	tF✕
	Wien Hbf **950** d.	2127	2325	...	...	2255	...	...	...	...	...	...	...	...	...	...	0530t	...	0630	...	0730	0730	...	0755	...	0930
	Linz Hbf **950** d.	2300	0105	...	...	0058	...	...	...	...	...	...	...	...	...	...	0648t	...	0748	...	0848	0848	...	0932	...	1048
0	**Salzburg** Hbf d.	0230	0230	...	...	0306	...	...	...	...	...	...	0656	...	...	...	0756	...	0856	...	0956	0956	...	1056	...	1156
	München Hbf **890** ‡ d.	|	|	...	...	|	...	...	0455	...	...	...	|	...	0717	0734	|	...	|	0934	|	|	...	|	1134	|
	München Ost **890** ‡ d.	|	|	...	...	|	...	...	0505	...	...	...	|	...	|	0744	|	...	|	0944	|	|	...	|	1144	|
	Rosenheim .. **890** ‡ d.	|	|	...	...	|	...	...	0537	...	...	...	|	...	|	0814	|	...	|	1014	|	|	...	|	1214	|
120	Kufstein 🏛 ‡ d.	|	|	...	...	|	0510	...	0559	0605	0641	...	|	...	0827	0836	0909	...	|	1036	1109	1109	...	|	1236	1309
134	Wörgl Hbf **960** d.	|	|	...	...	|	0524	...	0609	0622	0654	...	0817	...	0839	0846	0919	...	1015	1046	1119	1119	...	1215	1246	1319
159	Jenbach **960** d.	|	|	...	...	|	0546	...	...	0643	0710	...	0831	...	0855	0901	|	...	1029	1101	|	|	...	1229	1301	|
193	**Innsbruck** Hbf **960** a.	0423	0423	...	...	0519	0620	...	...	0713	0739	...	0846	...	0914	0918	0944	...	1044	1118	1144	1144	...	1244	1318	1344
193	**Innsbruck** Hbf d.	0431	0431	...	0453	0523	...	0642	...	...	...	0745	▬	0854	...	...	0948	0952	1048	...	...	1148	1152	1248	...	...
239	Ötztal d.	|	|	...	|	0551	...	0706	...	...	...	0809	...	0928	...	...	1012	1030	|	...	...	1212	1230	|	...	...
248	Imst-Pitztal d.	|	|	...	|	0602	...	0716	...	...	...	0819	...	0939	...	...	|	1041	1119	...	...	|	1241	1319	...	...
265	Landeck - Zams d.	|	|	...	0545	0622	...	0730	...	...	...	0833	...	0954	...	...	1033	1056	1133	...	...	1233	1256	1333	...	...
293	St Anton am Arlberg d.	|	|	...	0610	0648	...	0754	...	...	...	0857	...	1022	...	...	1057	▬	|	...	...	1257	▬	|	...	...
304	Langen am Arlberg d.	|	|	...	0620	0659	...	0804	...	...	...	|	...	1032	...	...	|	...	1204	...	...	|	...	1404	...	...
329	Bludenz **952** d.	0623	0623	0630	0706	0735	...	0831	...	...	...	0931	...	1102	...	...	1131	...	1231	...	...	1331	...	1431	...	...
350	**Feldkirch** **952** a.	0637	0637	0645	0721	0749	...	0842	...	...	...	0942	2	1113	...	...	1142	2	1248	...	...	1342	2	1442	...	...
350	**Feldkirch** **952** d.	0640	0640	0647	0738	0755	...	0848	...	...	...	0944	0947	1115	...	...	1147	1147	1248	...	...	1348	1347	1448	...	...
369	**Buchs** 🏛 **952** a.	0656	0656	|	0753	|	...	|	...	...	...	0959	|	|	...	...	1206	|	|	...	...	1406	|	|	...	...
	Zürich HB **520** a.	0820	0820	|	0920	|	...	|	...	...	...	1120	|	|	...	...	1320	|	|	...	...	1520	|	|	...	...
375	Dornbirn **952** d.	...	...	0709	...	0815	...	0908	...	...	...	...	1009	1132	...	...	...	1209	1308	...	...	...	1409	1508	...	...
387	**Bregenz** 🏛 **952** a.	...	...	0718	...	0823	...	0917	...	...	...	...	1018	1141	...	...	...	1218	1317	...	...	...	1418	1517	...	...
397	**Lindau** Hbf 🏛 **952** a.	...	...	0731	...	...	...	*0932*	...	...	...	...	1031	1153	...	...	...	1231	*1332*	...	...	...	1431	*1532*	...	...

	RJ 162		*RJ* 860	*EC* 89	*EC* 164	*RJ* 564		*RJ* 1287	*RJ* 862	*RJ* 1287	*IC* 1281	*EC* 83	*RJ* 166	*RJ* 566		*RJ* 864	*EC* 287	*RJ* 168	*RJ* 568	*RJ* 866	*EC* 289	*RJ* 760		*RJ* 868	*RJ* 762	
								⑥C		⑥C	⑥			S										⑧w		
	♥✕	2▮	F✕	A✕	✕♦	F✕	2▮		F✕		♦	A✕	✕	F✕	2	F✕	✕	✕	F✕	✕	✕	✕	2	F✕	F✕	2
Wien Hbf **950** d.	0930	...	1030	...	...	1130	...	...	1230	...	...	...	1330	1330	...	1430	...	1530	1530	1630	...	1730	...	1830	1930	...
Linz Hbf **950** d.	1048	...	1148	...	...	1248	...	...	1348	...	...	...	1448	1448	...	1548	...	1648	1648	1748	...	1848	...	1948	2048	...
Salzburg Hbf d.	1156	...	1256	...	...	1356	...	...	1456	...	...	...	1556	1556	...	1656	...	1756	1756	1900	...	1956	...	2056	2156	...
München Hbf **890** ‡ d.	|	...	|	1334	...	|	...	1430	|	...	1520	1534	|	|	...	|	1734	|	|	|	1934	|	...	|	|	...
München Ost **890** ‡ d.	|	...	|	1344	...	|	...	1439	|	...	|	1544	|	|	...	|	1744	|	|	|	1944	|	...	|	|	...
Rosenheim .... **890** ‡ d.	|	...	|	1414	...	|	...	1509	|	...	1600	1614	|	|	...	|	1814	|	|	|	2014	|	...	|	|	...
Kufstein 🏛 ‡ d.	1309	...	|	1436	...	1509	...	1530	|	...	1622	1636	1709	1709	...	|	1836	1909	1909	|	2036	2109	2112	2209	2309	...
Wörgl Hbf **960** d.	1319	...	1415	1446	1502	1519	...	1544	1615	...	1635	1646	1719	1719	...	1815	1846	1919	1919	2019	2046	2119	2129	2219	2319	...
Jenbach **960** d.	|	...	1429	1501	1518	|	...	1600	1629	...	...	1701	|	|	...	1829	1901	|	|	2033	2101	|	2151	2233	2333	...
Innsbruck Hbf **960** a.	1344	...	1444	1518	1540	1544p	...	1617	1644	...	...	1718	1744	1744	...	1844	1918	1944	1944	2048	2118	2144	2225	2248	2348	...
Innsbruck Hbf d.	1348	1352	1448	...	1548	...	1552	1624	1648	...	...	...	1748	1748	1752	1848	...	1948	▬	...	...	2148	2237r	...	...	2359
Ötztal d.	1412	1430	|	...	1612	...	1630	1703	|	←	...	...	1812	1812	1830	|	...	2012	...	...	...	2212	2316r	...	...	0057
Imst-Pitztal d.	|	1441	1519	...	|	...	1641	1712	1719	1723	...	...	|	|	1841	1919	...	2022	...	...	...	2222	2326r	...	...	0107
Landeck - Zams d.	1433	1456	1533	...	1633	...	1656	→	1733	1746	...	...	1833	1833	1856	1933	...	2036	...	...	...	2236	2341r	...	...	0123
St Anton am Arlberg d.	1457	▬	|	...	1657	...	▬	...	|	1817	...	...	1857	1857	...	|	...	2100	...	...	...	2300	...	...	...	...
Langen am Arlberg d.	|	...	1604	...	|	...	...	...	1804	1828	...	...	|	|	...	2004	...	|	...	...	...	2310	...	...	...	...
Bludenz **952** d.	1531	...	1631	...	1731	...	...	...	1831	1904	...	...	1931	1931	...	2031	...	2134	...	...	...	2337	...	...	...	...
Feldkirch **952** a.	1542	2	1642	...	1742	...	2	...	1842	1919	...	...	1942	1942	...	2042	...	2145	2	...	...	2348	...	...	...	...
Feldkirch **952** d.	1548	1547	1648	...	1744	...	1747	...	1848	...	...	...	1948	1950	...	2048	...	2148	2150	...	...	2350	...	...	...	...
Buchs 🏛 **952** a.	1606	|	|	...	1758	...	|	...	|	...	...	...	2006	|	...	|	...	2203	|	...	...	|	...	...	...	...
Zürich HB **520** a.	1720	|	|	...	1920	...	|	...	|	...	...	...	2120	|	...	|	...	2320	|	...	...	|	...	...	...	...
Dornbirn **952** d.	...	1609	1708	...	...	...	1809	...	1908	...	...	...	...	2008	...	2108	...	...	2212	...	...	0005	...	...	...	...
Bregenz 🏛 **952** a.	...	1618	1717	...	...	...	1818	...	1917	...	...	...	...	2017	...	2117	...	...	2221	...	...	0013	...	...	...	...
Lindau Hbf 🏛 **952** a.	...	1631	*1732*	...	...	...	1831	...	...	...	...	...	...	*2032*	...	*2132*	...	...	2234	...	...	...	...	...	...	...

km		*RJ* 49		*RJ* 763			*RJ* 861	*EC* 288	*RJ* 765 965	*RJ* 863	*IC* 1280		*RJ* 161	*EC* 286	*RJ* 1286	*RJ* 865	*RJ* 1286			*EC* 163	*RJ* 563	*EC* 88	*RJ* 867		*RJ* 165	*RJ* 565
		①–⑥			⑥	Ⓐ					⑥				⑥C		⑥C									
		d♥	2	F✕	2	2	F✕	✕	F✕	F✕	♦	2	F✕	✕		✕		2	2	✕♦	F✕	A✕	F✕	2	♥✕	F✕
	Lindau Hbf 🏛 **952** d.	✕	...	...	...	...	...	...	...	*0624*	...	0727	...	...	...	*0825*	...	0927	0927	...	...	...	*1025*	1127	...	...
	Bregenz 🏛 **952** d.	...	...	...	...	...	...	...	0548	0640	...	0740	...	...	...	0840	...	0940	0940	...	...	...	1040	1140	...	...
	Dornbirn **952** d.	...	...	...	...	...	...	...	0557	0652	...	0751	...	...	...	0852	...	0951	0951	...	...	...	1052	1151	...	...
	Zürich HB **520** d.	...	...	...	...	...	...	...	|	|	...	|	0640	...	...	|	...	|	|	0840	...	...	|	|	1040	...
	Buchs 🏛 **952** d.	...	...	...	...	...	...	...	|	|	...	|	0754	...	...	|	...	|	|	1000	...	...	|	|	1154	...
	Feldkirch **952** a.	...	...	...	...	...	...	...	0611	0709	...	0812	0809	...	...	0909	...	1012	1012	1015	...	...	1109	1212	1209	...
	Feldkirch **952** d.	...	...	...	...	...	...	...	0613	0717	...	▬	0817	...	0850	0917	...	▬	▬	1017	...	...	1117	▬	1217	...
	Bludenz **952** d.	...	...	...	...	...	...	...	0626	0730	...	...	0830	...	0905	0930	...	...	...	1030	...	...	1130	...	1230	...
	Langen am Arlberg d.	...	...	...	...	...	...	...	0652	0756	...	...	|	...	0937	0956	...	...	...	|	...	...	1156	...	|	...
	St Anton am Arlberg d.	...	...	...	...	...	...	...	0703	|	...	2△	0903	...	0948	|	...	...	2△	1103	...	...	|	2△	1303	...
	Landeck - Zams d.	...	0434	...	0604	0605	...	...	0727	0827	...	0901	0927	...	1017	1027	←	...	1101	1127	...	...	1227	1301	1327	...
	Imst-Pitztal d.	...	0451	...	0619	0620	...	...	0740	0840	...	0917	|	...	1033	1040	1046	...	1118	|	...	...	1240	1318	|	...
	Ötztal d.	...	0504	...	0631	0631	...	...	0751	|	...	0931	0948	...	→	|	1107	*IC*	1131	1148	...	...	|	1331	1348	...
	Innsbruck Hbf a.	...	0553	...	0702	0702	...	...	0814	0911	...	1006	1011	...	...	1111	1136	**1284**	1206	1211	...	...	1311	1406	1411	...
0	**Innsbruck** Hbf **960** d.	0510	...	0610	...	...	0713	0717	0817	0914	...	...	1017	1040	...	1114	1140	⑦	...	1221	1217	1240	1314	...	1417	1417
34	Jenbach **960** d.	0527	...	0627	...	...	0730	0735	|	0931	...	...	|	1101	...	1131	1201	♦	...	1244	|	1301	1331	...	|	|
59	Wörgl Hbf **960** d.	0541	...	0641	...	...	0745	0749	0843	0945	1024	...	1043	1116	...	1145	1220	1222	...	1258	1243	1316	1345	...	1443	1443
73	Kufstein 🏛 ‡ d.	0551	...	0651	...	...	|	0759	0853	|	1037	...	1053	1126	...	|	1232	1232	...	...	1253	1326	|	...	1453	1453
107	Rosenheim ... **890** ‡ a.	|	...	|	...	...	|	0818	|	|	1056	...	|	1145	...	|	|	1255	...	...	|	1345	|	...	|	|
162	**München** Ost **890** ‡ a.	|	...	|	...	...	|	0849	|	|	|	...	|	1216	...	|	1322	|	...	...	|	1416	|	...	|	|
172	**München** Hbf **890** ‡ a.	|	...	|	...	...	|	0901	|	|	1135	...	|	1227	...	|	1333	1345	...	...	|	1426	|	...	|	|
	Salzburg Hbf a.	0702	...	0802	...	...	0902	...	1003	1102	...	...	1203	...	...	1302	...	...	...	...	1403	...	1502	...	1603	1603
	Linz Hbf **950** a.	0812	...	0912	...	...	1012	...	1112	1212	...	...	1312	...	...	1428	...	...	...	...	1512	...	1612	...	1712	1712
	Wien Hbf **950** a.	0930	...	1030	...	...	1130	...	1230	1330	...	...	1430	...	...	1605	...	...	...	...	1630	...	1730	...	1830	1830

♦ – **NOTES** (LISTED BY TRAIN NUMBER)

118 – (12) Innsbruck - Lindau - Ulm - Stuttgart - Köln - Münster.

163/4 – TRANSALPIN – (12) and ✕ Zürich - Kitzbühel - Schwarzach - Selzthal - Graz and v.v.

421 – *ÖBB nightjet.* 🛏 1, 2 cl., ▬ 2 cl. and (2) Düsseldorf - Frankfurt - Innsbruck; conveys 🛏 1, 2 cl., ▬ 2 cl. and (2) (**40491**) Hamburg - Hannover - Innsbruck.

464 – *ÖBB nightjet.* 🛏 1, 2 cl., ▬ 2 cl. and (2) Graz - Schwarzach - Zürich; 🛏 1, 2 cl.*, ▬ 2 cl.* and (2) Beograd (**414**) - Zagreb - Ljubljana - Villach - Schwarzach (**464**) - Zürich.

1280 – ⑥ Jan. 7 - Mar. 25; ⑥ July 1 - Sept. 9. (12) Zell am See - Wörgl - München.

1281 – ⑥ Jan. 7 - Mar. 25 (also Dec. 25); ⑥ June 24 - Sept. 9. (12) München - Wörgl - Schwarzach.

1284 – ⑦ Jan. 8 - Mar. 26 (also Dec. 26); ⑦ June 25 - Sept. 10. (12) Schwarzach - Wörgl - München - Hamburg - Flensburg.

1285 ⑥ Jan. 7 - Mar. 25. (12) München - Wörgl - Zell am See.

A – To / from Verona, Bologna or Venezia via Brennero (Table **70**).

C – ⑥ Jan. 7 - Mar. 25; ⑥ July 1 - Sept. 9.

F – From / to Wien Flughafen ✈ (Table **950**).

N – *ÖBB nightjet.* Conveys 🛏 1, 2 cl., ▬ 2 cl. and (2).

R – ①–⑤ (not Dec. 26, Jan. 6, Apr. 14, 17, May 1, 25, June 5, 15, Aug. 15, Oct. 3, 31, Nov. 1).

S – Daily to Innsbruck; ⑧ (also Jan. 7, Dec. 9; not Jan. 6, Dec. 8) Innsbruck - Bregenz.

d – Not Dec. 26, Apr. 17, May 1, June 5, Aug. 14.

h – Not ①–④.

p – Connects with train in previous column.

r – ⚒ only.

t – ①–⑥ (not Dec. 26, Apr. 17, May 1, June 5).

w – Not Dec. 25, Apr. 16, 30, June 4, Aug. 13.

¶ – Train number **1289** on ⑥⑦.

♥ – From / to Budapest (Table **1250**).

▮ – On † departs Ötztal 2 minutes later, Imst-Pitztal 9 minutes later, arrives Landeck 10 minutes later.

△ – Runs 5–11 minutes **earlier** on †.

⊙ – *ÖBB nightjet.* 🛏 1, 2 cl., ▬ 2 cl. and (2) Budapest (**462**) - Salzburg (**466**) - Zürich.

◇ – On † departs Kufstein 0612, Wörgl 0629, Jenbach 0651, arrives Innsbruck 0725.

* – 🛏 1, 2 cl. and ▬ 2 cl. from Zagreb.

‡ – See panel below for *Meridian* regional services (operated by Bayerische Oberlandbahn) München - Kufstein and v.v. Subject to alteration from Apr. 14.

LOCAL TRAINS MÜNCHEN - KUFSTEIN

	R									
München Hbf d.	0515	0642	0744	0844	and	1844	1944	2044	*2144*	*2244*
München Ost d.	0525	0651	0752	0852	hourly	1852	1952	2052	*2152*	2252
Rosenheim d.	0606	0728	0830	0931	until	1931	2035	2135	2235	2335
Kufstein a.	0634	0756	0857	0958		1958	2102	2202	2303	0003

Kufstein d.	0602	0700	0802	0903	1002	and	1902	1959	2058	2158
Rosenheim d.	0632	0732	0832	0932	1032	hourly	1932	2026	2125	2225
München Ost a.	0705	0805	0905	1005	1105	until	2005	*2105*	*2207*	*2305*
München Hbf a.	0717	0815	0915	1015	1115		2016	*2115*	*2217*	*2315*

951 LINDAU - BREGENZ - INNSBRUCK - MÜNCHEN and SALZBURG

	EC 80	IC 1282 ⑥D	RJ 869		RJ 167	RJ 567 Ⓑq	EC 84	RJ 661		RJ 169	EC 86	IC 119	RJ 663		RJ 361	EC 82 ◧	EN 420 🅁	RJ 667		RJ 363		EN 247	EN 465		EN 40467	EN 467
	A✕		F✕	2	✕	F✕	A✕	F✕	2	✕	A✕	🍷♦	✕	2	✕	A✕	♦	✕	2	✕	2	N	♦	2	◇	N
Lindau Hbf 🏛 ..... 952 d.	...	...	*1225*	1327	...	...	...	*1425*	1525	...	...	1601	...	1727	...	...	...	*1825*	1927	...	...	...	...	2227	...	...
Bregenz 🏛 ..... 952 d.	...	...	1240	1340	...	...	...	1440	1540	...	...	1611	...	1740	...	...	...	1840	1940	...	...	2146	...	2240	...	...
Dornbirn ..... 952 d.	...	...	1252	1351	...	...	...	1452	1551	...	...	1621	...	1750	...	...	...	1852	1951	...	...	2156	...	2251	...	...
Zürich HB **520** ..... d.	...	...	|	|	1240	...	...	|	|	1440	...	|	...	|	1640	...	...	|	|	1840	...	|	2040	|	2140	2140
Buchs 🏛 ..... 952 d.	...	...	|	|	1354	...	...	|	|	1554	...	|	...	|	1759	...	...	|	|	1954	...	|	2205	|	2305	2305
Feldkirch ..... 952 a.	...	...	1309	1412	1409	...	...	1509	1612	1609	...	1638	...	1809	1814	...	...	1909	2012	2009	...	2212	2220	2312	2321	2321
Feldkirch ..... 952 d.	...	...	1317	—	1417	...	...	1517	—	1617	...	1640	...	—	1817	...	...	1917	—	2017	...	2227	2245	...	2324	2324
Bludenz ..... 952 d.	...	...	1330	...	1430	...	...	1530	...	1630	...	1656	...	...	1830	...	...	1930	...	2030	...	2242	2301	...	2340	2340
Langen am Arlberg ..... d.	...	...	1356	...	|	...	...	1556	...	|	...	1728	...	...	|	...	...	1956	...	|	...	2310	2335	...	|	|
St Anton am Arlberg .. d.	...	...	|	2△	1503	...	...	|	2△	1703	...	1738	...	2△	1903	...	...	2007	...	2103	...	2320	2345	...	|	|
Landeck-Zams ..... d.	...	...	1427	1501	1527	...	...	1627	1701	1727	...	1805	...	1901	1927	...	...	2031	...	2127	...	2348	0009	...	|	|
Imst-Pitztal ..... d.	...	...	1440	1518	|	...	...	1640	1718	|	...	1821	...	1918	1940	...	...	2044	...	2140	...	0002	|	...	|	|
Ötztal ..... d.	...	...	|	1531	1548	...	...	|	1731	1748	...	1835	...	1931	1951	...	...	2055	...	2151	...	0013	|	...	|	|
Innsbruck Hbf ..... a.	...	...	1511	1606	1611	...	...	1711	1806	1811	...	1905	...	2006	2014	...	...	2118	2	2214	...	0039	0054	...	0120	0120
Innsbruck Hbf ..... 960 d.	1440	1501	1514	...	1617	1617	1640	1714	...	1817	1840	...	1914	...	2017	2040	2044	...	2135	...	2235	0044	0056	...	0128	0128
Jenbach ..... 960 d.	1501	1523	1531	...	|	|	1701	1731	...	|	1901	...	1931	...	|	2101	2106	...	2209	...	2309	|	0119	...	|	|
Wörgl Hbf ..... 960 d.	1516	1547	1545	...	1643	1643	1716	1745	...	1843	1916	...	1945	...	2043	2116	2123	...	2235	...	2335	|	0136	...	|	|
Kufstein 🏛 ..... ‡ d.	1526	1559	|	...	1653	1653	1726	|	...	1853	1926	...	|	...	2053	2126	2135	...	2248	...	2348	|	...	...	|	|
Rosenheim .... 890 ‡ a.	1545	|	|	...	|	|	1745	|	...	|	1945	...	|	...	|	2145	2158	...	...	...	...	|	...	...	|	|
München Ost 890 ‡ a.	1615	|	|	...	|	|	1816	|	...	|	2016	...	|	...	|	2216	|	...	...	...	...	|	...	...	|	|
München Hbf 890 ‡ a.	1625	1650	|	...	|	|	1827	|	...	|	2026	...	|	...	|	2227	2238	...	...	...	...	|	...	...	|	|
Salzburg Hbf ..... a.	...	...	1702	...	1803	1803	...	1902	...	2003	...	...	2104	...	2206	...	...	...	...	...	...	0258	...	...	0323	0323
Linz Hbf **950** ..... a.	...	...	1812	...	1912	1912	...	2012	...	2112	...	...	2212	...	2312	...	...	...	...	...	...	0443	...	...	0455	0601
Wien Hbf **950** ..... a.	...	...	1930	...	2030	2030	...	2130	...	2230	...	...	2330	...	0030	...	...	...	...	...	...	0654	...	...	0635	0755

♦ – **NOTES** (LISTED BY TRAIN NUMBER)

119 – (12) Münster - Köln - Stuttgart - Ulm - Lindau - Innsbruck.
420 – *ÖBB nightjet.* 🛏 1, 2 cl., ▬ 2 cl. and (2) Innsbruck - Frankfurt - Düsseldorf; conveys 🛏 1, 2 cl., ▬ 2 cl. and (2) (**40420**) Innsbruck - Hannover - Hamburg.
465 – *ÖBB nightjet.* ZÜRICHSEE – 🛏 1, 2 cl., ▬ 2 cl. and (2) Zürich - Schwarzach - Graz; 🛏 1, 2 cl.*, ▬ 2 cl.* and (2) Zürich - Schwarzach (**415**) - Villach - Ljubljana - Zagreb - Beograd.

A – From Verona, Bologna or Venezia via Brennero (Table **70**).
D – ⑥ Jan. 7 - Mar. 25 (also Dec. 25, 30).

F – To Wien Flughafen ✈ (Table **950**).
N – *ÖBB nightjet.* Conveys 🛏 1, 2 cl., ▬ 2 cl. and (2).
q – Not Dec. 25, Apr. 16, 30, June 4.
* – 🛏 1, 2 cl. and ▬ 2 cl. to Zagreb.
◇ – *ÖBB nightjet.* 🛏 1, 2 cl., ▬ 2 cl. and (2) Zürich (**467**) - Salzburg (**463**) - Budapest.
△ – Runs 5–11 minutes **earlier** on †.
◧ – Train number **1288** on ⑥⑦.
‡ – See panel on page 453 for other regional services Kufstein - München.

952 VORARLBERG LOCAL SERVICES

2nd class only (except where shown)

BLUDENZ - BREGENZ - LINDAU ⊖ △

Bludenz ..... d.	0439	0600	0656	0730	0800	0900	1000	1009	1200	1209	1300	1400	1409	1500	1539	1600	1609	1700	1800	1809	1900	1909	1939	2009	2039	2209	2239
Feldkirch ..... d.	0500	0617	0715	0747	0817	0917	1017	1030	1217	1230	1317	1417	1430	1517	1600	1617	1630	1717	1817	1830	1917	1930	2000	2030	2100	2230	2300
Dornbirn ..... d.	0529	0639	0739	0809	0839	0939	1039	1059	1239	1259	1339	1439	1459	1539	1629	1639	1659	1739	1839	1859	1939	1959	2029	2059	2129	2259	2329
Bregenz 🏛 ..... d.	0545	0649	0748	0819	0849	0949	1049	1115	1249	1320	1349	1449	1520	1549	1645	1648	1720	1749	1849	1915	1948	2020	2045	2120	2145	2315	2344
Lindau Hbf 🏛 .. a.	0556	0658	...	0831	0901	1001	1101	1127	1301	1332	1401	1501	1532	1601	1657	...	1732	1801	1901	1927	...	2032	2057	2132	2157	2327	...

Lindau Hbf 🏛 .. d.	...	...	0624	0657	0757	0825	0857	...	1001	1053	1157	1225	1257	1357	1425	1459	1627	1701	1757	1825	1901	1957	2031	2104	2201	2301	0001
Bregenz 🏛 ..... d.	0514	0610	0644	0710	0810	0844	0910	1010	1014	1106	1210	1244	1310	1410	1444	1514	1640	1714	1810	1844	1914	2010	2044	2114	2214	2314	0014
Dornbirn ..... d.	0530	0621	0700	0721	0821	0900	0921	1021	1030	1117	1221	1300	1321	1421	1500	1530	1651	1730	1821	1900	1930	2021	2100	2130	2230	2330	0030
Feldkirch ..... d.	0601	0644	0731	0744	0844	0931	0944	1044	1101	1144	1244	1331	1344	1444	1531	1601	1714	1801	1844	1931	2001	2044	2131	2201	2301	0001	0101
Bludenz ..... a.	0621	0659	0751	0759	0859	0951	0959	1059	1121	1159	1259	1351	1359	1459	1551	1621	1729	1821	1859	1951	2021	2059	2151	2221	2321	0021	0121

ST MARGRETHEN - BREGENZ - LINDAU ⊡ △

km						EC 191			EC 193					EC 195							EC 197					
				Ⓐ		c♥			♥					♥					Ⓐ		d♥					
0	St Margrethen 🏛 ..... d.	0625	0655	0725	0755	0842	0855	0955	1042	1055	1155	1255	1355	1442	1455	1555	1655	1755	1825	1855	1942	1955	2055	2155	2255	2355
12	**Bregenz** 🏛 ..... a.	0640	0710	0740	0810	0853	0910	1010	1053	1110	1210	1310	1410	1453	1510	1610	1710	1810	1840	1910	1953	2010	2110	2210	2310	0010
22	**Lindau** Hbf 🏛 ..... a.	*0658*	*0731*	*0759*	*0831*	0905	*0932*	*1031*	1105	*1127*	*1231*	*1332*	*1431*	1505	*1532*	*1631*	*1732*	*1831*	*1901*	*1927*	2005	*2032*	*2132*	*2234*	*2327*	...

							EC 196						EC 194							EC 192			EC 190		
				Ⓐ				♥						♥		Ⓐ			Ⓐ		♥			e♥		
Lindau Hbf 🏛 ..... d.	...	...	*0624*	*0657*	*0727*	*0825*	*0927*	0954	*1025*	*1127*	*1225*	*1327*	*1425*	1454	*1525*	1605	*1627*	*1727*	*1757*	*1825*	1854	*1927*	*2031*	2054	*2131*	*2227*
Bregenz 🏛 ..... d.	0542	0617	0647	0717	0747	0849	0947	1006	1049	1147	1247	1347	1449	1506	1547	1617	1647	1747	1817	1847	1906	1949	2047	2106	2147	2247
St Margrethen 🏛 ..... a.	0558	0634	0704	0734	0804	0904	1004	1018	1104	1204	1304	1404	1504	1518	1604	1634	1704	1804	1834	1904	1918	2004	2104	2118	2204	2304

FELDKIRCH - BUCHS ⊖

km		A	A	AB	A	A		A	A	A	A	
0	**Feldkirch** ..... d.	0533	0649	0714	0745	0849	...	1612	1645	1715	1815	...
16	Schaan-Vaduz d.	0552	0708	0733	0806	0908	...	1634	1704	1734	1834	...
19	**Buchs** 🏛 ..... a.	0555	0711	0736	0809	0911	...	1637	1707	1737	1837	...

	A	A	A		A		A	A	A	A	A
Buchs 🏛 ..... d.	0617	0716	0819	...	1234	...	1619	1649	1719	1819	1849
Schaan-Vaduz ..... d.	0620	0719	0822	...	1237	...	1622	1652	1722	1822	1852
Feldkirch ..... a.	0639	0737	0841	...	1256	...	1641	1711	1741	1841	1911

BLUDENZ - SCHRUNS

Operated by Montafonerbahn. *12 km.* Journey time: 19 minutes.

From Bludenz at 0535 Ⓐ, 0632 ⚒, 0702, 0737, 0805, 0837, 0937, 1037, 1137, 1205 ⚒, 1237, 1305 ⚒, 1337, 1437, 1537, 1605, 1634, 1705, 1737, 1805, 1837, 1937, 2037, 2137, 2245, 2345

From Schruns at 0504 Ⓐ, 0534 ⚒, 0631, 0701, 0736, 0804, 0904, 1004, 1104, 1136 ⚒, 1204, 1236 ⚒, 1304, 1404, 1504, 1536, 1604, 1633, 1704, 1736, 1804, 1904, 2004, 2110, 2210, 2310

A – ①–⑤ (not Dec. 26, Apr. 17, May 1, 25, June 5, 15, Nov. 1, Dec. 8).
B – From Bludenz (d. 0647).
c – Not Jan. 1. **d** – Not Dec. 24. **e** – Not Dec. 24, 31.

♥ – (12) and ✕ Zürich - München and v.v. See Table **75**.
⊡ – Additional trains run on Ⓐ.
⊖ – Selected local trains. See also Table **951**.

△ – Austrian holiday dates apply.

953 🚌 IMST - ÖTZTAL - OBERGURGL, ST ANTON - LECH

SERVICE DECEMBER 17 - APRIL 23

km	🚌 Route **4194/8352**																							
										Ⓒ	Ⓐ	Ⓐ	Ⓒ	Ⓒ	Ⓐ	Ⓒ	Ⓐ	Ⓒ	Ⓐ					
0	**Imst** (Terminal Post) ..... d.	0605	0632	...	0805	0855	1000	1115	1155	1230	1235	1340	1400	1450	1510	1530	1600	1630	1645	1800	1830	1915	1950	2105
13	**Ötztal** (Bahnhof) ..... a.	0622	0649	...	0822	0909	1017	1132	1212	1247	1252	1357	1417	1507	1527	1544	1617	1647	1702	1817	1847	1932	2007	2127
13	**Ötztal** (Bahnhof) ..... d.	0623	0700	0800	0825	0910	1020	1135	1215	1248	1300	1400	1420	1510	1535	1545	1618	1648	1705	1818	1850	1935	2015	2130
21	Oetz (Posthotel Kassel) ..... d.	0637	0714	0813	0839	0924	1034	1149	1229	1302	1314	1414	1434	1524	1549	1559	1632	1702	1719	1832	1904	1949	2029	2144
54	Sölden (Postamt) ..... d.	0725	0802	0902	0927	1012	1122	1237	1317	1350	1402	1502	1522	1612	1637	1647	1720	1752	1809	1922	1952	2037	2117	2232
58	Zwieselstein (Gh Neue Post) . d.	0733	0810	0910	0935	1020	1130	1245	1325	1358	1410	1510	1530	1620	1645	1655	1728	1800	1817	1930	2000	2045	2125	2240
68	**Obergurgl** (Zentrum) ..... a.	0748	0825	0925	0950	1035	1145	1300	1340	1413	1425	1525	1545	1635	1700	1710	1743	1815	1832	1945	2015	2100	2140	2255

🚌 Route **4194/8352**	Ⓐ								Ⓐ	Ⓒ	Ⓐ	Ⓒ												
Obergurgl (Zentrum) ..... d.	...	...	...	0650	0750	0845	1015	1115	1205	1215	1305	1315	1345	1515	1545	1615	1645	1715	1745	1815	1915	2020	2200	2330
Zwieselstein (Gh Neue Post) .. d.	...	0548	...	0705	0805	0900	1030	1130	1220	1230	1320	1330	1400	1530	1600	1630	1700	1730	1800	1830	1930	2035	2215	2345
Sölden (Postamt) ..... d.	0525	0558	...	0715	0815	0910	1040	1140	1230	1240	1330	1340	1410	1540	1610	1640	1710	1740	1810	1840	1940	2045	2225	2355
Oetz (Posthotel Kassel) ..... d.	0612	0645	...	0807	0907	1002	1132	1232	1322	1332	1424	1432	1502	1632	1702	1732	1802	1834	1903	1934	2034	2137	2320	0050
Ötztal (Bahnhof) ..... a.	0622	0655	...	0817	0917	1012	1142	1242	1332	1342	1432	1442	1512	1642	1712	1742	1812	1844	1914	1944	2044	2147	2330	0100
Ötztal (Bahnhof) ..... d.	...	0700	...	0820	0920	1015	1145	1245	1335	1345	1435	1445	1515	1645	...	1745	...	1845	...	1945	2045	...	...	...
Imst (Terminal Post) ..... a.	...	0715	...	0835	0935	1030	1200	1300	1350	1400	1450	1500	1530	1700	...	1800	...	1900	...	2000	2100	...	...	...

🚌 Route **92**: **ST ANTON AM ARLBERG - LECH** *20 km.* Journey time: 36–40 minutes.

From St Anton a. A. Terminal West at 0735 ‡, 0910, 1010 ‡, 1110, 1210 ‡, 1310 ‡, 1410 ‡, 1510, 1610 ‡, 1710, 1810 ‡, 1910 ‡.

From Lech Postamt at 0816 ‡, 0906 ‡, 1006, 1106 ‡, 1206 ‡, 1306, 1406 ‡, 1506 ‡, 1606, 1706 ‡, 1806, 1906 ‡, 2006 ‡.

Winter service: **Valid until Apr. 23.**
☛ All services call at St Christoph am Arlberg and Zürs
‡ – Dec. 17 - Apr. 17.

🚌 LANDECK - NAUDERS - SCUOL and MALLES 954

Landeck - Nauders and Martina

Routes 4218/4220												Ⓐ												
Landeck-Zams Bahnhof d.	0650	0800	0855	1000	1055	1212	1255	1400	1455	1600	1647	1702	1805	1905	...	...	...	...	...	...	...	...	...	...
Ried im Oberinntal d.	0718	0828	0923	1028	1123	1240	1323	1428	1523	1628	1715	1730	1833	1933	...	...	...	...	...	...	...	...	...	...
Martina cunfin 🛃 a.	|	|	0956	|	1156	|	1356	|	1556	|	1756	|	|	|	...	...	...	...	...	...	...	...	...	...
Nauders Mühle a.	0800	0910	...	1110	...	1322	...	1510	...	1710	...	1812	1915	2015	...	...	...	...	...	...	...	...	...	...

Nauders Mühle d.	0607	0647	...	0847	...	1047	...	1247	...	1447	...	1647	...	1847	...	...	...	...	...	...	...	...	...	...
Martina cunfin 🛃 d.	|	|	...	|	1000	|	1200	|	1400	|	1600	|	1800	|	...	...	...	...	...	...	...	...	...	...
Ried im Oberinntal d.	0647	0727	...	0927	1032	1127	1232	1327	1432	1527	1632	1727	1832	1927	...	...	...	...	...	...	...	...	...	...
Landeck-Zams Bahnhof a.	0712	0752	...	0952	1057	1152	1257	1352	1457	1552	1657	1752	1857	1952	...	...	...	...	...	...	...	...	...	...

Scuol Tarasp - Nauders - Malles

	⚒	⚒											
Scuol Tarasp Staziun d.	0630	...	0730	...	and at	1730	...	1830	...	1930	...	...
Martina cunfin 🛃 d.	0655	0705	0755	0805	the same	1755	1805	1855	1910	2003	2010	...
Nauders Mühle 🛃 d.	...	0716	...	0816	minutes	...	1816	...	1921	...	2021	...
Reschenpass/Passo di Resia 🛃 d.	...	0720	...	0820	past each	...	1820	...	1925	...	2025	...
Resia d.	...	0723	...	0823	hour until	...	1823	...	1928	...	2028	...
Malles Stazione **597** a.	...	0753	...	0853		...	1853	...	1958	...	2058	...

	⚒	⚒								⚒		
Malles Stazione **597** d.	0601	...	0701	...	and at	1801	...	1901	...	2001	...	...
Resia d.	0631	...	0731	...	the same	1831	...	1931	...	2031	...	...
Passo di Resia/Reschenpass 🛃 d.	0634	...	0734	...	minutes	1834	...	1934	...	2034	...	...
Nauders Mühle 🛃 d.	0638	...	0738	...	past each	1838	...	1938	...	...	...	...
Martina cunfin 🛃 d.	0649	0701	0749	0801	hour until	1849	1901	1949	1952	...	...	...
Scuol Tarasp Staziun a.	...	0728	...	0828		...	1928	...	2028	...	...	...

Operators

Landeck - Nauders: ÖBB-Postbus GmbH, Landeck. ✆ +43 (0) 5442 64 422.

Scuol Tarasp - Martina: Auto Da Posta, Svizra. CH-7550 Scuol. ✆ +41 (0) 58 453 28 28.

Martina - Nauders - Malles: Servizi Autobus Dolomiti (SAD). Corso Italia 13N, I-39100 Bolzano. ✆ +39 0471 450 111.

JENBACH - MAYRHOFEN 955

2nd class only Narrow gauge Zillertalbahn *

km																🚂 A
0	**Jenbach** Zillertalbahnhof § d.	0630	0652	0746	0807	0834	and at	1707	1734	1821	1856	...	1956	...		1010
11	Fügen-Hart d.	0646	0709	0804	0822	0852	the same	1722	1752	1837	1912	...	2012	...		1040
17	Kaltenbach-Stumm d.	0656	0720	0815	0833	0903	minutes	1733	1803	1848	1923	...	2023	...	also	1057
21	Aschau im Zillertal d.	0703	0727	0821	0839	0909	past each	1739	1809	1854	1928	...	2028	...		1112
25	**Zell am Ziller** d.	0710	0735	0828	0846	0916	hour until	1746	1816	1900	1935	...	2035	...		1123
32	**Mayrhofen** a.	0722	0747	0839	0857	0927		1757	1827	1911	1946	...	2046	...		1142

	Ⓒ	Ⓐ															🚂 A
Mayrhofen d.	0546	0602	0609	0638	0731	0815	0845	and at	1615	1645	1715	1745	1847	1947		1301
Zell am Ziller d.	0557	0611x	0620	0650	0741	0827	0857	the same	1627	1657	1727	1757	1858	1958		1318
Aschau im Zillertal d.	0603	0617x	0626	0656	0747	0833	0903	minutes	1633	1703	1733	1803	1904	2004	also	1327
Kaltenbach-Stumm d.	0610	0622x	0633	0702	0754	0839	0909	past each	1639	1709	1739	1809	1910	2010		1343
Fügen-Hart d.	0620	0631x	0645	0716	0804	0850	0921	hour until	1650	1721	1750	1822	1922	2022		1404
Jenbach Zillertalbahnhof § a.	0637	0646	0703	0733	0820	0906	0940		1706	1740	1805	1841	1937	2037		1426

A – Ⓒ Apr. 29 - May 28; ③-⑦ May 31 - Oct. 15.

x – Stops on request only.

🚂 – Steam train. Special fares apply.

§ – Adjacent to ÖBB station.

* – Zillertaler Vehrkehrsbetriebe, Austraße 1, A-6200 Jenbach. ✆ +43 (0) 5244 606 0.

JENBACH - ACHENSEE 956

2nd class only *Achenseebahn*

Narrow gauge rack railway operated by steam locomotives (special fares apply). *7 km.* Journey time 42–50 minutes. **Service May 1 - Oct. 30, 2016.**

Operator: Achenseebahn AG, A-6200 Jenbach: ✆ +43 (0) 5244 62243, Fax +43 (0) 5244 622435. Jenbach Achensee Bf is adjacent to the ÖBB station.

May 1–27 and **Oct. 10–30**: **From Jenbach Achensee Bf** at 1100, 1300 and 1500. **From Achensee Seespitz Bahnstation** at 1200, 1400 and 1600.

May 28 - Oct. 9: **From Jenbach Achensee Bf** at 0815, 1000, 1045, 1200, 1345, 1500 and 1645. **From Achensee Seespitz Bahnstation** at 0915, 1105, 1220, 1405, 1520, 1600 and 1740.

ZELL AM SEE - KRIMML and 🚌 KRIMML - MAYRHOFEN 957

2nd class only

ZELL AM SEE - KRIMML ⊡

					🚂 S		🚂 S				Ⓐ				Ⓐ	Ⓒ
0	**Zell am See** Lokalbahn d.	0630	0800	0900	0920	1000	←	1100	and	1600	1650	1700	1800	1900	2000	2050
29	Mittersill d.	0723	0848	0948	1038	1048	1108	1148	hourly	1648	1729	1748	1848	1948	2048	2134
39	Bramberg d.	0737	0904	1004	→	1104	1131	1204	until	1704	1740	1804	1904	2004	2104	2148
53	**Krimml** a.	0755	0923	1023	...	1123	1202	1223		1723	1755	1823	1923	2023	2123	2205

		Ⓐ	Ⓐ					🚂 S		🚂 S					
Krimml d.	0533	0603	0628	0640	0733	and	1433	1455	1533	...	1633	1733	1833	...	...
Bramberg d.	0552	0621	0644	0658	0751	hourly	1451	1523	1551	←	1651	1751	1851	...	...
Mittersill d.	0608	0638	0656	0720	0808	until	1508	1545	1608	1615	1708	1808	1908	...	...
Zell am See Lokalbahn a.	0655	0725	0737	0805	0855		1555	→	1655	1728	1755	1855	1955	...	...

🚌 Krimml Bahnhof - Krimml Wasserfälle and v.v. Route **670**. *3 km.* Journey time: 5–8 minutes. **Subject to confirmation.**

From Krimml Bahnhof at 0757, 0929, 1029 and hourly until 1729; then 1829 **B**, 1844 and 1934.

From Krimml Wasserfälle at 0823, 1023, 1123 and hourly until 1723; then 1823 **B**.

🚌 routes **673** and **4094**: KRIMML - KÖNIGSLEITEN - MAYRHOFEN *Winter service valid until April 23*

km				A		A			A	
0	**Krimml** Bahnhof d.	...	...	...	...	...	...	...	...	...
3	Krimml Wasserfälle d.	...	...	...	...	...	...	...	...	...
16	Königsleiten Almdorf d.	...	1000	1028	1123	1323	1423	1523	...	1713
25	**Gerlos** Gasthaus Oberwirt d.	0701	1011	1046	1141	1341	1442	1542	1623	1733
45	Zell am Ziller Bf **955** a.	0735	1048	1120	1218	1418	1520	1620	1701	1813
53	**Mayrhofen** Bahnhof **955** a.	0745	...	...	...	1428	...	...	1711	1823

		A			A		A		
Mayrhofen Bahnhof **955** d.	0835	0910	0945	...	...	...	1445	...	1845
Zell am Ziller Bahnhof **955** d.	0850	0925	1000	1100	1200	1327	1500	1600	1900
Gerlos Gasthaus Oberwirt d.	0923	0958	1033	1138	1238	1405	1538	1638	1931
Königsleiten Almdorf d.	0943	1017	1051	1156	1256	1416	...	1649	...
Krimml Wasserfälle a.	...	...	...	...	...	...	...	...	...
Krimml Bahnhof a.	...	...	...	...	...	...	...	...	...

A – Dec. 23 - Apr. 2.
B – June 1 - Sept. 30.

S – ④⑤ May 26 - July 7; ②-④ July 12 - Aug. 31 (also Sept. 7, 9, 14, 21, 28). Steam train with special fares.

⊡ – Narrow gauge railway. **Operator**: Pinzgauer Lokalbahn. Trains call at Mittersill and Bramberg on request only.

🚌 WÖRGL - ELLMAU - KITZBÜHEL and ST JOHANN 958

ÖBB-Postbus routes **4006, 4060, 4902**

	⚒	Ⓐ¶	⑥	⚒	Ⓐ	⑥	⚒	†	⚒		⚒		Ⓐ	⑥	†	⚒	⚒	†		⚒	Ⓐ	⚒	Ⓐ	Ⓑ
Wörgl Hauptbahnhof d.	...	0545	...	0640	0743	0743	...	...	0905	...	1120	...	1210	1210	...	...	1405	...	...	1610	...	1750	1835	...
Söll (Dorf) ♥ d.	...	0605	0612	0659	0805	0810	...	0917	0937	...	1140	...	1240	1240	1240	...	1437	1545	...	1640	...	1820	1905	1905
Scheffau am Wilden Kaiser ★ d.	...	0612	0621	...	0812	0817	...	0927	0947	...	1150	...	1250	1250	1250	...	1447	1555	...	1650	...	1830	1913	1913
Ellmau (Dorf) d.	0622	0620	0633	...	0820	0825	0900	0940	1000	...	1203	...	1303	1305	1303	1315	1500	1608	...	1703	1715	1843	1923	1923
Kitzbühel Bahnhof a.	0650	|	|	...	|	|	0924	|	|	...	|	...	|	...	|	1345	|	|	...	|	1745	|	|	|
St Johann in Tirol Bahnhof a.	...	0641	0654	...	0841	0847	...	1004	1024	...	1227	...	1327	...	1327	...	1524	1632	...	1727	...	1907	1940	1940

	Ⓐ	⚒	Ⓐ	⚒	⚒	†	⚒	⚒		⚒	⚒	Ⓐ	⑥		⚒	⚒	Ⓐ	Ⓑ	Ⓐ	⚒	⚒	Ⓐ	Ⓐ	Ⓐ
St Johann in Tirol Bahnhof d.	...	0535	0535	...	0725	0750	...	0855	1055	1055	...	1235	...	1340	1340	1555	...	1655	1655	...	1755	1755	...	1907
Kitzbühel Bahnhof d.	...	|	|	...	|	|	0803	|	|	|	1215	|	...	|	|	|	1630	|	|	...	|	|	1830	|
Ellmau (Dorf) d.	...	0552	0552	...	0745	0810	0833	0915	1115	1115	1245	1300	1305	1400	1400	1615	1700	1715	1715	...	1815	1815	1858	1927
Scheffau am Wilden Kaiser ★ d.	...	0559	0559	...	0753	0818	...	0923	1123	1123	...	1308	1311	1408	1408	1623	...	1723	1723	...	1823	1823	...	1935
Söll (Dorf) ♥ d.	0550	0612	0615	0715	0810	0832	...	0940	1137	1140	...	1325	1325	1422	1425	1645e	...	1737	1745	1745	1837	1840	...	1952
Wörgl Hauptbahnhof a.	0620	...	0645	0750	0840	...	...	1010	...	1210	...	1355	1352	...	1455	1715	...	...	1808	1808	...	1903	...	2015

e – Arrives 1637.

★ – Scheffau am Wilden Kaiser Am Trattenbach.

¶ – Runs 5–11 minutes later during school holiday periods.

♥ – 🚌 **KUFSTEIN** Bahnhof → **SÖLL** Dorf (journey time: 27–29 minutes): 0540 ⚒, 0639 Ⓐ, 0735 Ⓐ, 0740 ⑥, 0840 Ⓐ, 0845 Ⓒ, 1010, 1110, 1210 Ⓐ, 1300 Ⓒ, 1310 Ⓐ, 1410 Ⓐ, 1510 Ⓒ, 1524 Ⓐ, 1610 ⚒, 1710 Ⓐ, 1740 Ⓒ, 1810 Ⓐ and 1907 Ⓐ.
🚌 **SÖLL** Dorf → **KUFSTEIN** Bahnhof (journey time: 25–29 minutes): 0610 ⚒, 0706 Ⓐ, 0812 ⚒, 0915 Ⓒ, 0940 Ⓐ, 1040, 1140, 1240 Ⓐ, 1330 Ⓒ, 1337 Ⓐ, 1440 Ⓐ, 1540 Ⓒ, 1551 Ⓐ, 1640 ⑥, 1642 Ⓐ, 1742 Ⓐ, 1810 †, 1840 ⚒ and 1934 Ⓐ.

959 🚌 ZELL AM SEE - HINTERGLEMM

ÖBB-Postbus Route **680**

km															
		⚒	E	E		E		E		A		A		A	
0	**Zell am See** Bahnhof .... d.	0610p	0656	0820	0920	1020	1120	1220	1320	1420	1520	1620	1720	1820	1920
20	Saalbach Schattberg .... a.	0637	0725	0852	0952	1052	1152	1252	1352	1452	1552	1652	1752	1852	1952
23	**Hinterglemm** Ellmauweg ...... a.	0643	0730	0857	0957	1057	1157	1257	1357	1457	1557	1657	1757	1857	1957

	⚒	E			E		E		E		A		A		A
Hinterglemm Ellmauweg .... d.	0611	0657	0750	...	0920	1020	1120	1220	1320	1420	1520	1620	1720	1820	1916
Saalbach Schattberg .... d.	0618	0703	0800	...	0930	1030	1130	1230	1330	1430	1530	1630	1730	1830	1922
Zell am See Bahnhof .... a.	0646	0732	0830	...	1000	1100	1200	1300	1400	1500	1600	1700	1800	1900	1950

A – Ⓐ (daily to Apr. 21, June 12 - Sept. 29 and Nov. 27 - Dec. 9).
E – ⚒ (daily to Apr. 22, June 12 - Sept. 30 and Nov. 27 - Dec. 9).
p – Zell am See Postplatz (not Bahnhof).
Information: ✆ +43 (0) 6542 5444-18

960 SALZBURG - SCHWARZACH - INNSBRUCK

km																									
		EN	*EN*								*IC*			*IC*			*RJ*		*IC*			*RJ*		*IC*	
		237	**464**								**590**			**1280**			**898**		**1284**			**111**		**942**	
						⚒		Ⓒ	Ⓐ	Ⓐ			Ⓐ	⑥**N**					⑦**M**	Ⓐ**d**			Ⓐ	Ⓒ	
		2⊖	**A**		2	2	2	2	2	2	🍷⊖	2	2		2	2	✕⊖	2		2	2	✕⊖	2	🍷	2
	Wien Hbf **950** .... d.	2128	...	...	...	...	...	...	...	...	...	...	...	...	...	...	...	...	...	...	...	...	...	0714	...
0	**Salzburg** Hbf **951 970 975** ‡ d.	0134	...	...	...	...	...	0421	0441	...	0612	...	...	...	0708	...	0812	...	...	0908	...	1012	...	|	1108
29	Golling-Abtenau .... **970** ‡ d.	|	...	...	...	...	...	0459	0505	...	0633	...	...	...	0734	...	0833	...	...	0934	...	1033	...	1041	1134
53	**Bischofshofen** ....**970 975** ‡ d.	|	0158	...	...	...	...	0524	0529	...	0654	...	...	...	0756	...	0854	...	...	0956	...	1054	...	1104	1156
61	St Johann im Pongau. **970** ‡ d.	|	|	...	...	...	...	0534	0539	...	0703	...	...	...	0804	...	0903	...	...	1004	...	1103	...	1113	1204
67	**Schwarzach - St Veit**. **970** ‡ a.	0223	0211	...	...	...	...	0539	0545	...	0709	...	...	...	0810	...	0909	...	...	1010	...	1109	...	1119	1210
67	**Schwarzach - St Veit** .... d.	...	0232	...	...	...	...	0541	0547	...	...	0712	...	...	0812	...	...	0912	0956	1012	...	...	1112	1121	1212
99	**Zell am See** .... d.	...	|	...	...	...	...	0616	0623	...	...	0745	...	0829	0845	...	...	0945	1027	1045	...	...	1145	1151	1245
113	Saalfelden .... d.	...	|	...	0401	0520	0550	0628	0636	...	...	0755	...	0840	0855	0914c	...	0955	1038	1055	...	...	1155	1201	1255
131	Hochfilzen .... d.	...	|	...	0418	0537	0610	...	0654	...	...	0813	0835	0856	0913	0933	...	1013	1055	1113	1133	...	1213	|	1313
148	St Johann in Tirol .... d.	...	|	...	0434	0553	0628	...	0711	0751	...	0828	0853	0913	0928	0951	...	1028	1112	1128	1151	...	1228	1231	1328
157	**Kitzbühel** .... d.	...	|	...	0442	0601	0637	...	0719	0800	...	0835	0902	0921	0935	1000	...	1035	1121	1135	1200	...	1235	1239	1335
166	Kirchberg in Tirol .... d.	...	|	...	0451	0612	0648	...	0728	0811	...	0843	0913	0934	0943	1011	...	1043	1133	1143	1211	...	1243	1247	1343
192	Wörgl Hbf .... **951** a.	...	|	...	0518	0637	0717	...	0753	0840	...	0908	0942	1003	1008	1040	...	1108	1202	1208	1240	...	1308	1309	1408
217	Jenbach .... **951** a.	...	|	...	0538	...	...	...	0815	...	...	...	...	...	...	...	...	...	...	...	...	...	...	...	...
251	**Innsbruck** Hbf .... **951** a.	...	0449	...	0607	...	...	...	0840	...	...	...	...	...	...	...	...	...	...	...	...	...	...	...	...

		RJ	*EC*			*EC*		*RJ*				*EC*	*IC*					*RJ*					*EC*		
		596	**164**			**113**		**1264**				**115**	**518**					**698**					**117**		
				Ⓐ**d**				⑥	Ⓐ					Ⓐ	Ⓐ**d**		Ⓐ			Ⓑ		⚒	**1217**		
	2	✕⊖	**Z**✕	2	2	✕⊖	2	✕	2	2	2	⊗⊖	**G**🍷	2	2	2	2	✕⊖	2	2	2	2	⊗§⊖	2	2
Wien Hbf **950** .... d.	...	0855	...	...	...	...	...	1130	...	...	...	...	...	...	...	...	...	1455	...	...	...	...	...	...	...
Salzburg Hbf. **951 970 975** ‡ d.	...	1212	...	1308	...	1412	...	1415	...	1508	...	1612	...	...	1708	...	1741	1812	...	...	1908	...	2012	...	2211
Golling-Abtenau ....**970** ‡ d.	...	1233	...	1334	...	1433	...	1443	...	1534	...	1633	...	...	1734	...	1810	1833	...	...	1934	...	2033	...	2239
Bischofshofen.....**970 975** ‡ d.	...	1254	1250	1356	...	1454	...	1507	...	1556	...	1654	1650	...	1756	...	1835	1854	...	...	1956	...	2054	...	2302
St Johann im Pongau ..**970** ‡ d.	...	1303	1259	1404	...	1503	...	1517	...	1604	...	1703	1659	...	1804	...	1845	1903	...	...	2004	...	2103	...	2311
Schwarzach - St Veit...**970** ‡ a.	...	1309	1305	1410	...	1509	...	1523	...	1610	...	1709	1705	...	1810	...	1850	1909	...	...	2010	...	2109	...	2317
Schwarzach - St Veit........... d.	...	...	1313	1412	...	...	1512	1525	...	1612	...	...	1713	...	1813	...	1853	...	1912	1912	2012	...	...	2112	2319
Zell am See .... d.	...	...	1344	1445	...	...	1545	1555	...	1645	...	...	1744	...	1846	...	1929	...	1946	1946	2046	...	...	2148	2356
Saalfelden .... d.	...	...	1354	1455	...	...	1555	...	...	1655	...	...	1754	...	1856	...	1941	...	1956	1957	2057	...	...	2200	0005
Hochfilzen .... d.	1333	...	|	1513	1533	...	1613	...	1635	1713	1733	...	|	1835	1913	1933	...	...	...	2016	2116	2205	...	...	...
St Johann in Tirol .... d.	1351	...	1422	1528	1551	...	1628	...	1653	1728	1751	...	1822	1853	1928	1951	...	...	...	2030	2130	2223	...	...	...
Kitzbühel .... d.	1400	...	1430	1535	1600	...	1635	...	1702	1735	1800	...	1830	1902	1935	2000	...	...	...	2038	2138	2232	...	...	...
Kirchberg in Tirol .... d.	1411	...	1438	1543	1611	...	1643	...	1713	1743	1811	...	1838	1913	1943	2011	...	...	...	2045	2145	2243	...	...	...
Wörgl Hbf .... **951** a.	1440	...	1500	1608	1640	...	1708	...	1742	1808	1840	...	1900	1942	2008	2040	...	...	...	2110	2210	2312	...	...	...
Jenbach .... **951** a.	...	...	1516	...	...	...	...	...	...	...	...	...	1916	...	...	...	...	...	...	...	...	...	...	...	...
Innsbruck Hbf .... **951** a.	...	...	1540	...	...	...	...	...	...	...	...	...	1939	...	...	...	...	...	...	...	...	...	...	...	...

	EN	*EN*								*IC*		*RJ*				*IC*	*EC*					*EC*			
	465	**236**								**1285**		**691**				**515**	**114**					**112**			
				⚒			⚒	Ⓑ		⑥**Q**			Ⓐ		Ⓐ				Ⓐ**d**	Ⓐ					Ⓐ
	A	2⊖		2	2	2	2	2	2		2	✕⊖	2	2	2	**G**🍷	⊗⊖	2	2	2	2	✕⊖	2	2	2
Innsbruck Hbf .... **951** d.	0056	...	...	...	...	...	...	...	...	...	...	...	...	...	...	0821	...	...	...	...	...	...	...	...	...
Jenbach .... **951** d.	0119	...	...	...	...	...	...	...	...	...	...	...	...	...	...	0844	...	...	...	...	...	...	...	...	...
Wörgl Hbf .... **951** d.	0138	...	...	...	...	...	0542	0605	...	0627	0652	...	0722	0752	0820	0900	...	0922	0952	1020	1052	...	1122	1152	1220
Kirchberg in Tirol .... d.	|	...	...	...	...	...	0609	0635	...	0701	0717	...	0752	0817	0850	0921	...	0952	1017	1050	1117	...	1152	1217	1250
Kitzbühel .... d.	|	...	...	...	...	...	0620	0646	...	0712	0725	...	0803	0825	0901	0930	...	1003	1025	1101	1125	...	1203	1225	1301
St Johann in Tirol .... d.	|	...	...	...	...	...	0629	0655	...	0720	0732	...	0812	0832	0910	0938	...	1012	1032	1110	1132	...	1212	1232	1310
Hochfilzen .... d.	|	...	...	...	...	...	0646	0713	...	0741	0747	...	0830	0847	0928	|	...	1030	1047	1128	1147	...	1230	1247	1328
Saalfelden .... d.	|	...	...	0458	0546	0705	0705	0730	0735	0758	0805	...	...	0905	...	1006	...	...	1105	...	1205	...	...	1305	...
Zell am See .... d.	|	...	...	0508	0556	0715	0715	...	0748	0809	0815	...	...	0915	...	1017	...	...	1115	...	1215	...	...	1315	...
Schwarzach - St Veit.......... a.	0317	...	...	0541	0633	0747	0747	...	0823	...	0847	...	...	0947	...	1046	...	...	1147	...	1247	...	...	1347	...
Schwarzach - St Veit...**970** ‡ d.	0324	0320	...	0542	0635	0749	0749	...	0824	...	...	0850	...	0949	...	1056	1050	...	1149	...	...	1250	...	1349	...
St Johann im Pongau ..**970** ‡ d.	|	|	...	0548	0642	0755	0755	...	0829	...	...	0856	...	0955	...	1102	1056	...	1155	...	...	1256	...	1355	...
Bischofshofen.....**970 975** ‡ d.	0336	|	...	0558	0652	0804	0804	...	0840	...	...	0905	...	1004	...	1110	1105	...	1204	...	...	1305	...	1404	...
Golling-Abtenau ....**970** ‡ d.	...	|	...	0620	0716	0825	0825	...	0904	...	...	0925	...	1025	...	...	1125	...	1225	...	...	1325	...	1425	...
Salzburg Hbf. **951 970 975** ‡ a.	...	0409	...	0645	0744	0851	0851	...	0940	...	...	0948	...	1051	...	...	1148	...	1251	...	...	1348	...	1451	...
Wien Hbf **950** .... a.	...	0755	...	...	...	...	...	...	...	...	...	1305	...	...	...	...	...	...	...	...	...	...	...	...	...

	EC	*RJ*			*IC*		*RJ*		*RJ*				*RJ*	*IC*					*IC*						
	163	**793**			**947**		**797**		**1261**				**110**	**1281**					**591**						
				Ⓐ**d**	Ⓒ	Ⓐ			⑥		Ⓐ			⑥**P**		Ⓐ**d**	Ⓐ				Ⓐ	Ⓐ	Ⓒ		
	Z✕	✕⊖	2	2	🍷	2	✕⊖	2	✕	2	2	2	✕⊖		2	2	2	2	🍷⊖	2	2	2	2	2	2
Innsbruck Hbf .... **951** d.	1221	...	...	...	...	...	...	...	...	...	...	...	...	...	...	...	...	...	...	...	...	...	...	...	...
Jenbach .... **951** d.	1244	...	...	...	...	...	...	...	...	...	...	...	...	...	...	...	...	...	...	...	...	...	...	...	...
Wörgl Hbf .... **951** d.	1300	...	1322	1352	1452	1452	...	1522	...	1552	1620	1652	...	1657	1722	1752	1820	1852	...	1922	1952	2052	2052	2238	0037
Kirchberg in Tirol .... d.	1321	...	1352	1417	1514	1517	...	1552	...	1617	1650	1717	...	1730	1752	1817	1850	1917	...	1952	2017	2117	2122	2308	0105
Kitzbühel .... d.	1330	...	1403	1425	1522	1525	...	1603	...	1625	1701	1725	...	1741	1803	1825	1901	1925	...	2003	2025	2125	2133	2319	0113
St Johann in Tirol .... d.	1338	...	1412	1432	1530	1532	...	1612	...	1632	1710	1732	...	1750	1812	1832	1910	1932	...	2012	2032	2132	2142	2328	0122
Hochfilzen .... d.	|	...	1431	1447	|	1547	...	1630	...	1647	1728	1747	...	1811	1830	1847	1928	1947	...	2031	2046	2147	2200	2346	0138
Saalfelden .... d.	1406	...	1448e	1505	1600	1605	...	...	...	1705	...	1805	...	1828	...	1905	...	2005	...	2048b	...	2205	2217	0003	0155
Zell am See .... d.	1417	...	...	1515	1610	1615	...	...	1705	1715	...	1815	...	1839	...	1915	...	2015	...	...	...	2217	...	...	...
Schwarzach - St Veit.......... a.	1446	...	...	1547	1639	1647	...	...	1735	1747	...	1847	...	1910	...	1947	...	2047	...	...	...	2250	...	...	...
Schwarzach - St Veit...**970** ‡ d.	1456	1450	...	1549	1641	...	1650	...	1737	1749	...	...	1850	...	...	1949	...	...	2050	...	...	...	...	...	...
St Johann im Pongau ..**970** ‡ d.	1502	1456	...	1555	1647	...	1656	...	1744	1755	...	...	1856	...	...	1955	...	...	2056	...	...	...	...	...	...
Bischofshofen.....**970 975** ‡ d.	1510	1505	...	1604	1656	...	1705	...	1753	1804	...	...	1905	...	...	2004	...	...	2105	...	...	...	...	...	...
Golling-Abtenau ....**970** ‡ d.	...	1525	...	1625	1718	...	1725	...	1817	1825	...	...	1925	...	...	2025	...	...	2125	...	...	...	...	...	...
Salzburg Hbf. **951 970 975** ‡ a.	...	1548	...	1651	|	...	1748	...	1844	1851	...	...	1948	...	...	2051	...	...	2148	...	...	...	...	...	...
Wien Hbf **950** .... a.	...	1905	...	...	2037	...	...	...	...	...	...	...	...	...	...	...	...	...	...	...	...	...	...	...	...

A – *ÖBB nightjet.* ZÜRICHSEE – 🛏 1, 2 cl., ▬ 2 cl. and [2] Graz - Feldkirch - Buchs 🏛 - Zürich and v.v. Conveys from / to Schwarzach 🛏 1, 2 cl.*, ▬ 2 cl.* and [2] Beograd - Zagreb - Ljubljana - Villach - Zürich and v.v.
G – From / to Graz (Table **975**).
M – ⑦ Jan. 8 - Mar. 26 (also Dec. 26); ⑦ June 25 - Sept. 10. [12] Schwarzach - München - Hamburg - Flensburg.
N – ⑥ Jan. 7 - Mar. 25; ⑥ July 1 - Sept. 9. [12] Zell am See - München.
P – ⑥ Jan. 7 - Mar. 25 (also Dec. 25); ⑥ June 24 - Sept. 9. [12] München - Schwarzach.
Q – ⑥ Jan. 7 - Mar. 25. [12] München - Zell am See.
Z – TRANSALPIN – [12] ✕ Graz - Selzthal - Bischofshofen - Innsbruck - Buchs 🏛 - Zürich and v.v.

b – Not ⑥.
c – Ⓒ only.
d – Runs daily Salzburg - Saalfelden and v.v.
e – Ⓐ only.
j – Runs Bischofshofen - Schwarzach on the mornings of Ⓒ only.

* – 🛏 1, 2 cl., ▬ 2 cl. from / to Zagreb.
⊖ – See Table **970** for further details.
§ – Runs as *RJ* **717** Apr. 14 - July 16.
‡ – See panel below main table for other local stopping trains.

Freilassing .... **890** d.	0607		2207	2307	0007
Salzburg Hbf...... **890** d.	0621	and	2221	2321	0021
Golling-Abtenau ....d.	0659	hourly	2259	2359	0059
Bischofshofen..........d.	0724	until	2324	0024	0124
St Johann im Pongau d.	0734		2334	0034j	0134
Schwarzach - St Veit.a.	0739		2339	0039j	0139

Schwarzach - St Veit.d.	0524	0554	0624		2224
St Johann im Pongau d.	0529	0559	0629	and	2229
Bischofshofen..........d.	0540	0610	0640	hourly	2240
Golling-Abtenau ....d.	0604	0634	0704	until	2304
Salzburg Hbf...... **890** a.	0640	0710	0740		2340
Freilassing .... **890** a.	0657	0726	0754		2354

ATTNANG-PUCHHEIM - STAINACH-IRDNING 961

2nd class only

km		⚒		Ⓐ									ⒸA											
	Wien Hbf 950 d.	...	...	...	...	...	...	...	...	...	...	...	1015	...	...	...	...	...	...	...	...	...	...	...
0	**Attnang-Puchheim** d.	...	...	0459	...	0603	0715	0811	0911	1011	1111	1211	1211	1311	1411	1511	1611	1711	1811	1911	2005	2109	...	...
12	**Gmunden** d.	...	...	0515	...	0621	0732	0826	0932	1026	1132	1226	1226	1332	1426	1532	1626	1732	1826	1932	2022	2128	...	...
17	Altmünster am Traunsee d.	...	...	0522	...	0626	0738	0832	0938	1032	1138	1232	1232	1338	1432	1538	1632	1738	1832	1938	2028	2134	...	...
22	Traunkirchen d.	...	...	0528	...	0633	0744	0838	0944	1038	1144	1238	1238	1344	1438	1544	1638	1744	1838	1944	2033	2140	...	...
27	Ebensee Landungsplatz d.	...	...	0534	...	0640	0752	0844	0952	1044	1152	1244	1244	1352	1444	1552	1644	1752	1844	1952	2040	2147	...	...
28	Ebensee d.	...	...	0537	...	0643	0758	0847	0958	1047	1158	1247	1247	1358	1447	1558	1647	1758	1847	1958	2042	2150	...	...
44	**Bad Ischl** d.	...	...	0556	...	0705	0820	0903	1020	1103	1220	1303	1303	1420	1503	1620	1703	1820	1903	2020	2102	2211	...	...
54	Bad Goisern d.	...	...	...	...	0719	0833	0913	1033	1113	1233	1313	1313	1433	1513	1633	1713	1833	1913	2033	2115	...	...	...
64	Hallstatt ⊡ d.	...	...	...	...	0731	0848	0925	1048	1125	1248	1325	1325	1448	1525	1648	1725	1848	|	|	|	...	...	...
67	Obertraun-Dachsteinhöhlen d.	...	...	...	...	0735	0851	0928	1051	1128	1251	1328	1328	1451	1528	1651	1728	1851	1928	2051	2131	...	...	...
78	**Bad Aussee** d.	0503	0632	...	...	0749	...	0942	...	1142	...	1342	1342	...	1542	...	1742	...	1942	2104	2143	...	...	...
93	Bad Mitterndorf d.	0521	0650	...	...	0804	...	0959	...	1159	...	1359	1359	...	1559	...	1759	...	1959	...	...	...	...	...
108	**Stainach-Irdning** a.	0538	0707	...	...	0818	...	1015	...	1215	...	1415	1415	...	1615	...	1815	...	2015	...	...	...	...	...

			Ⓐ	⚒	⚒											ⒸB	Ⓒ	Ⓐ				Ⓒ	Ⓐ	
Stainach-Irdning d.	...	...	...	...	0611	...	0713	...	0940	...	1140	...	1340	...	1540	1540	...	...	1740	...	...	1940	1940	2047
Bad Mitterndorf d.	...	...	...	...	0629	...	0730	...	0959	...	1159	...	1359	...	1559	1559	...	...	1759	...	...	1959	1959	2104
Bad Aussee d.	...	0456	...	0604	0650	0650	0811r	...	1016	...	1216	...	1416	...	1616	1616	...	...	1816	...	...	2016	2016	2121
Obertraun-Dachsteinhöhlen d.	...	0508	...	0616	0702	0702	0824	0904	1028	1104	1228	1304	1428	1504	1628	1628	1704	1704	1828	1905	...	2028	...	...
Hallstatt ⊡ d.	...	|	...	|	0706	0706	0828	0907	1032	1107	1232	1307	1432	1507	1632	1632	1707	1707	1832	|	...	|	...	...
Bad Goisern d.	...	0523	...	0631	0720	0720	0842	0922	1043	1122	1243	1322	1443	1522	1643	1643	1722	1722	1843	1922	...	2042	...	...
Bad Ischl d.	0433	0536	0601	0644	0733	0733	0853	0935	1053	1135	1253	1335	1453	1535	1653	1653	1735	1740	1853	1935	...	2052	...	...
Ebensee d.	0453	0559	0622	0707	0758	0758	0911	0958	1111	1158	1311	1358	1511	1558	1711	1711	1758	1758	1911	1958	...	2108	...	...
Ebensee Landungsplatz d.	0456	0601	0624	0710	0800	0800	0913	1001	1113	1201	1313	1401	1513	1601	1713	1713	1801	1801	1913	2001	...	2110	...	...
Traunkirchen d.	0503	0609	0633	0718	0808	0808	0919	1009	1119	1209	1319	1409	1519	1609	1719	1719	1809	1809	1919	2009	...	2116	...	...
Altmünster am Traunsee d.	0509	0614	0639	0724	0814	0814	0925	1016	1125	1216	1325	1416	1525	1616	1725	1725	1816	1816	1925	2016	...	2122	...	...
Gmunden d.	0516	0621	0645	0732	0826	0826	0931	1026	1131	1226	1331	1426	1531	1626	1731	1731	1826	1826	1931	2023	...	2128	...	...
Attnang-Puchheim a.	0531	0638	0703	0748	0842	0842	0947	1044	1147	1244	1347	1444	1547	1644	1747	1747	1844	1844	1947	2041	...	2145	...	...
Wien Hbf 950 a.	...	...	...	...	...	...	...	...	...	...	...	...	...	...	...	1946	...	...	...	...	...	...	...	...

A – (2) Wien (**528**) - Attnang-Puchheim - Stainach-Irdning.
B – (2) Stainach-Irdning - Attnang-Puchheim (**725**) - Wien.

d – Runs daily May - October.
r – Arrives 0748.

⊡ – services operate Hallstatt Bahnhof - Hallstatt Markt. Journey: 8 minutes.
Operator: Hallstättersee-Schifffahrt Hemetsberger KG ✆ +43 (0)6134 8228.
From Hallstatt Bahnhof at 0707⚒, 0735⚒**d**, 0830, 0900, 0930, 1035, 1100, 1130, 1235, 1300, 1330, 1435, 1500, 1530, 1635, 1700, 1730 and 1850.
From Hallstatt Markt at 0650⚒, 0715⚒, 0810⚒**d**, 0845, 0915, 1015, 1045, 1215, 1245, 1315, 1415, 1445, 1515, 1615, 1645, 1715 and 1815.

LINZ - PASSAU and SIMBACH 962

km										ICE 228					ICE 28	5914					ICE 26				
		Ⓐ 2	⚒ 2	G2	2	B2	Ⓐ 2	Ⓒ 2	Ⓒ 2	✕	2	2	2	Ⓐ 2	✕	⊖2	2	2	2	⚒ 2	D✕	2	2	⚒ 2	⚒ 2
	Wien Hbf 950 d.	...	...	...	...	...	...	...	...	0650	...	...	...	...	0850	0655f	...	...	...	...	1050	...	...	...	...
0	**Linz** Hbf 950 d.	...	0452	0543	0600	0700	...	0736	...	0817	0852	...	0952	...	1017	1038	1052	...	1152	...	1217	1252	...	1352	...
25	**Wels** Hbf 950 d.	0445	0516	0612	0620	0731	...	0754	...	0833	0909	...	1009	...	1033	1054	1109	...	1209	...	1233	1309	...	1409	...
54	Neumarkt-Kallham d.	0509	0543	0642	0646	0757	0811	0823	0832	|	0936	0940	1033	1040	|	1116	1140	1140	1233	1240	|	1336	1340	1433	1440
	Ried im Innkreis d.	0529	|	|	0710	|	0831	|	0855	|	|	1001	|	1101	|	|	1201	|	|	1301	|	|	1401	|	1501
	Braunau am Inn a.	0603	|	|	0740	|	0907	|	0940	|	|	1040	|	1140	|	|	1240	|	|	1340	|	|	1440	|	1540
	Simbach (Inn) 🚌 893 a.	*0644*	|	|	0744	|	*0945*	|	0945	|	|	1045	|	1145	|	|	1245	|	|	1345	|	|	1445	|	1545
92	Schärding d.	...	0615	0714	...	0827	...	0853	...	|	1009	...	1059	...	|	1141	...	1213	1259	...	|	1409	...	1459	...
106	**Passau** Hbf a.	...	0628	0727	...	0840	...	0906	...	0918	1021	...	1111	...	1118	1153	...	1225	1311	...	1318	1421	...	1511	...
	Nürnberg Hbf 920 a.	...	...	...	...	...	...	...	...	1126	...	...	...	...	1326	...	...	...	...	...	1526	...	...	...	...
	Frankfurt (Main) Hbf 920 ▲ a.	...	...	...	...	...	...	...	...	1336	...	...	...	...	1536	...	...	...	...	...	1736	...	...	...	...

	ICE 90					ICE 22								ICE 20						RJ 748			EN 490	RJ 840	
	H✕	2	2	2	⚒ 2	D✕	Ⓐ 2	Ⓐ 2	2	2	Ⓐ 2	Ⓐ 2	2	✕	2	Ⓐ 2	2	2	2	✕	2		⊡♣	✕	2
Wien Hbf 950 d.	1250	...	...	...	...	1450	...	...	...	...	...	...	...	1650	...	...	...	...	...	1955	...	...	2039	2055	...
Linz Hbf 950 d.	1417	1452	...	1552	...	1617	1625	1636	1652	...	1725	1752	1752	1817	1852	...	1952	...	2052	2132	...	...	2215	2232	...
Wels Hbf 950 d.	1433	1509	...	1609	...	1633	1642	1653	1709	...	1742	1809	1814k	1833	1909	...	2009	...	2109	2143	2148	...	2232	2243	2248
Neumarkt-Kallham d.	|	1540	1540	1633	1640	|	1704	1720	1736	1740	1809	1833	1840	|	1936	1940	2036	2040	2136	|	2216	...	|	|	2315
Ried im Innkreis d.	|	1601	|	|	1701	|	|	1737	|	1801	|	|	1901	|	|	2001	|	2105	|	|	2237	...	|	|	|
Braunau am Inn a.	|	1640	|	|	1740	|	|	1809	|	1840	|	|	1940	|	|	2040	|	2141	|	|	2311	...	|	|	|
Simbach (Inn) 🚌 893 a.	|	1645	|	|	1745	|	|	...	|	1845c	|	|	1945	|	|	2045	|	2145	|	...	...	...	|	|	|
Schärding d.	|	...	1613	1659	...	|	1730	...	1809	...	1842	1859	...	|	2009	...	2110	...	2209	...	...	...	|	|	2347
Passau Hbf a.	1518	...	1625	1711	...	1718	...	...	1821	...	1858	1913	...	1918	2021	...	2123	...	2221	...	...	...	2320	...	...
Nürnberg Hbf 920 a.	1726	...	...	...	...	1926	...	...	...	...	...	...	...	2126	...	...	...	...	...	...	...	...	0127	...	...
Frankfurt (Main) Hbf 920 ▲ a.	...	...	...	...	...	2136	...	...	...	...	...	...	...	2340	...	...	...	...	...	...	...	...	...	...	...

km						EN 491															ICE 21				
		⚒ 2	Ⓐ 2	2		⊡♣	⚒ 2	† 2	2	⚒ 2	Ⓐ 2	Ⓐ 2	2	⚒ 2	Ⓐ 2	2	2	Ⓒ 2	2	2	✕	Ⓐ 2	2	2	2
	Frankfurt (Main) Hbf 920 ▲ d.	...	...	...	...	...	...	...	...	...	...	...	...	...	...	...	...	...	...	...	0621	...	...	...	...
	Nürnberg Hbf 920 d.	...	...	...	...	0307	...	...	...	...	...	...	...	...	...	...	...	...	...	...	0830	...	...	...	...
	Passau Hbf d.	...	0410	0419c	...	0524	...	...	0538	0605	...	0624	...	0649	...	...	0806	...	0935	...	1040	...	1044	...	1138
	Schärding d.	0359	0423	0432	...	|	...	...	0551	0618	...	0637	...	0702	...	...	0819	...	0948	...	|	...	1056	...	1151
0	**Simbach** (Inn) 🚌 893 d.	|	|	|	...	|	...	...	|	|	...	|	...	|	0717	...	|	0817	|	0919	|	1019	|	1119	|
2	**Braunau** am Inn d.	|	|	|	...	|	0513	0525	|	|	0610	|	0628	|	0723	0751	|	0821	|	0923	|	1023	|	1123	|
39	Ried im Innkreis d.	|	|	|	...	|	0552	0601	|	|	0643	|	0710	|	0755	0831	|	0855	|	1001	|	1101	|	1201	|
61	Neumarkt-Kallham d.	0430	0451	0504	...	|	0613	0619	0623	0644	0702	0706	0730	0736	0812	0850	0854	0912	1019	1024	|	1119	1125	1219	1224
90	**Wels** Hbf 950 d.	0457	0515	0531	...	0619	0636	...	0651	0712	...	0727	0758z	0807	0835	...	0923	0935	...	1051	1129	...	1151	...	1251
115	**Linz** Hbf 950 a.	0520	0532	0555	...	0633	0652e	...	0708	0741	...	0745	...	0824	0855	...	0940	0955	...	1108	1143	...	1208	...	1308
	Wien Hbf 950 a.	...	...	...	...	0819	...	...	...	...	...	...	...	...	...	...	...	...	...	...	1309	...	...	...	...

	ICE 23					ICE 91					ICE 27				5927	ICE 29			RJ 749		RJ 841	ICE 229			RJ 843
	D✕	⚒ 2	2	2	2	H✕	⚒ 2	⚒ 2	2	2	D✕	⚒ 2	2	2	⊖2	✕	2	2	✕	2	✕	✕	Ⓐ 2	2	
Frankfurt (Main) Hbf 920 ▲ d.	0819v	...	...	...	...	...	...	...	...	...	1221	...	...	...	...	1421	...	...	...	...	...	1621	...	...	...
Nürnberg Hbf 920 d.	1030	...	...	...	...	1230	...	...	...	...	1431	...	...	...	...	1630	...	...	...	...	...	1830	...	...	...
Passau Hbf d.	1240	...	1244	1335	...	1440	...	1444	...	1538	1640	...	1644	...	1747	1840	...	1851	...	...	...	2040	...	2053	...
Schärding d.	|	...	1256	1348	...	|	...	1456	...	1551	|	...	1656	...	1800	|	...	1905	...	...	...	|	...	2105	...
Simbach (Inn) 🚌 893 d.	|	1219e	|	|	1319	|	1419	|	1519	|	|	1619	|	1719	|	|	1819	|	|	1919	|	|	2017	|	...
Braunau am Inn d.	|	1223	|	|	1323	|	1423	|	1523	|	|	1623	|	1723	|	|	1823	|	|	1923	|	|	2023	|	...
Ried im Innkreis d.	|	1301	|	|	1401	|	1501	|	1601	|	|	1701	|	1801	|	|	1901	|	|	2001	|	|	2101	|	...
Neumarkt-Kallham d.	|	1319	1325	1419	1424	|	1519	1525	1619	1624	|	1719	1725	1824	1835	|	1924	1937	|	2024	|	|	2119	2137	...
Wels Hbf 950 d.	1329	...	1351	...	1451	1529	...	1551	...	1651	1729	...	1751	1851	1905	1929	1951	2006	2016	2051	2116	2129	...	2204	2216
Linz Hbf 950 a.	1343	...	1408	...	1508	1543	...	1608	...	1708	1743	...	1808	1908	1922	1943	2008	2023c	2028	...	2128	2143	...	...	2228
Wien Hbf 950 a.	1509	...	...	...	...	1709	...	...	...	...	1909	...	...	...	2233f	2109	...	...	2205	...	2305	2309	...	...	...

B – From Amstetten (d. 0613) and St Valentin (d. 0636).
D – To / from Dortmund (Table **800**).
G – From Garsten (Table **976**).
H – To / from Hamburg (Table **900**).

c – Ⓒ only.
e – Ⓐ only.
f – Wien **Franz-Josefs-Bahnhof**.
k – 1817 on Ⓐ.
v – 0821 on ⑦.
z – † only.

⊖ – May 1 - Oct. 26. (2) Wien Franz-Josefs-Bf - Tulln - St Pölten - Passau and v.v.
⊡ – *ÖBB nightjet*. 🛏 1, 2 cl., ▬ 2 cl. and (2) Wien - Nürnberg - Hamburg and v.v.; 🛏 1, 2 cl., ▬ 2 cl. and (2) (**40490**/**40421**) Wien - Frankfurt - Köln - Düsseldorf and v.v.
♣ – Ⓡ for journeys to Germany.
▲ – Frankfurt timings are subject to alteration on ⑥⑦ Feb. 11 - Apr. 2 (also Apr. 14 – 17).

963   SALZBURG and ST WOLFGANG - STROBL - BAD ISCHL   Routes 150, 546

km	Route 150	※	†	Ⓐ	※		k	Ⓜ	※	Ⓒ	Ⓒ	Ⓒ	Ⓐ		Ⓐ		Ⓐ	Ⓐ	Ⓐ	Ⓐ	Ⓐ	†	※
0	Salzburg Hbf △ ....d.	0555	...	0625	0645	0815	0915	0915	1115	1115	1215	1220	1320r	1415	1420	1520r	1615	1625	1715	1815	1820	1915	2015	2015	2215
32	St Gilgen (Busbahnhof)d.	0645	0650	0730	0735	0910	1010	1110	1210	1210	1310	1315	1410	1510	1510	1610	1710	1710	1810	1910	1910	2005	2058	2105	2258
45	Strobl (Busbahnhof) .....d.	0703	0706	0748	0751	0928	1028	1128	1228	1235	1328	1333	1428	1528	1528	1628	1728	1728	1828	1928	1928	2021	2113	2121	2313
57	Bad Ischl Bahnhof .....a.	0722	0723	0807	0808	0947	1047	1147	1247	1254	1347	1352	1447	1547	1547	1647	1747	1747	1847	1947	1947	2038	2129	2138	2329

	Route 150	※	※		Ⓐ	※		†		※		IC		Ⓒ		Ⓒ	※				※		Ⓐ		⑥	※
	Bad Ischl Bahnhof ......d.	0504	0541	...	0611	0646	0746	0824	0924	1024	1124	1224	1224	1324	1336	1424	1524	1624	1724	1724	1824	1924	2024			
	Strobl (Busbahnhof) ....d.	0520	0600	0615	0630	0707	0807	0845	0945	1045	1145	1245	1245	1345	1357	1445	1545	1645	1745	1745	1845	1945	2040	...		
	St Gilgen (Busbahnhof)d.	0535	0615	0630	0645	0728	0828	0906	1006	1106	1206	1306	1316	1406	1416	1506	1606	1706	1806	1806	1906	2006	2054	2106	2206
	Salzburg Hbf △ ....a.	0619	0655	0715	0730	0819	0919	0953	1057	1157	1257	1357	1407	1457	1507	1557	1657	1757	1853	1857	1953	2053	...	2150	2250

km	Route 546	Ⓐ	Ⓐ	Ⓐ	Ⓒ		†	Ⓐ		Ⓒ		Ⓒ	Ⓒ		Ⓐ		Ⓐ	Ⓐ		Ⓐ	Ⓐ			
0	St Wolfgang ⊡ ‡ ... ♥ d.	0500	0600	0648	0735	0735	0740	0753	0900	0913	1013	1013	1100	1213	1318	1413	1513	1613	1713	1713	1813	1813	1828	1913	2003
7	Strobl (Busbahnhof) ♥ d.	0512	0612	0703	0746	0747		0804		0926		1028		1228	1333	1428	1528	1628	1726	1728		1828	1841	1926	2016
19	Bad Ischl Bahnhof .....a.	0531	0639	0729	...	0806	0811		0931		1044	1050	1131	1250	1359	1450	1554	1650		1754	1844	1850		...	...

	Route 546	Ⓐ		Ⓐ		Ⓐ	Ⓒ		Ⓐ			Ⓐ					Ⓐ			Ⓐ		
	Bad Ischl Bahnhof .....d.	0605	0642		0823	0913		0913	1023		1113	1223		1330	1423		1513	1623		1713	1843	1913	
	Strobl (Busbahnhof) ....d.	0630	0706	0806		0930	0945	1045	1045	1135	1245	1245	1355	1445	1535	1645	1645	1735	1845	1845	1930	2040
	St Wolfgang ⊡ ‡ ....a.	0642	0718	0817	0850	0940	0942	0947	1057	1057	1147	1257	1257	1407	1457	1457	1547	1657	1657	1747	1857	1857	1940	1942	2052

k – ⑥ (also June 6, Nov. 2; runs on ※ Dec. 24 - Jan. 7, Feb. 11–18, Apr. 8–18 and July 8 - Sept. 9).
m – Not Dec. 27 - Jan. 5, Feb. 13–17, Apr. 10–18, June 6, July 10 - Sept. 8, Nov. 2.
r – 5 minutes **earlier** on ⑥.

△ – All services also call at Mirabellplatz.
⊡ – St Wolfgang Schafbergbahnhof. All services also call at St Wolfgang Markt.
♥ – Additional services St Wolfgang - Strobl: 1028 Ⓐ, 1113 Ⓒ, 1313 Ⓒ and 1513 Ⓒ.
‡ – The **Schafbergbahn** narrow-gauge steam rack railway operates St Wolfgang - Schafbergspitze (6 km). Services operate subject to demand and weather conditions **Apr. 29 - Oct. 26,** 2017. 2nd class only. Special fares payable. Journey time: 35 minutes each way. ✆ +43 (0) 6138 2232 0.

964   STROBL - ST GILGEN (WOLFGANGSEE)   March 25 - April 23 *

	A	C	A		A	C	A	C	A		A	C	
Strobl Schiffstation ⊡ ....d.	...	1045	1100	...	1230	1300	1400	1515	1530	...	1700	1720	...
St Wolfgang Schafbergbahnhof d.	1009												
St Wolfgang Markt ....d.	1017	1100	1130	...	1300	1315	1430	1530	1600	...	1725	1730	...
St Wolfgang Schafbergbahnhof ....d.		1110	1138		1308	1325	1438	1540	1608		1733	1740	
St Gilgen Schiffstation ● ......a.	1050	1145	1215	...	1345	1400	1515	1615	1645	...			

	C	A		A	C	A	A	C	A		A	C	A	
St Gilgen Schiffstation ● .....d.	...	...	...	1100	1155	1230	1400	1410	...	...	1530	1620	1700	...
St Wolfgang Schafbergbahnhof ....d.	1015	1027	...	1137	1230	1307	1437	1445	...		1607	1650		
St Wolfgang Markt ....d.	1025	1035	...	1150	1240	1320	1450	1455	...	...	1620	1700	1737	
St Wolfgang Schafbergbahnhof ....a.													1745	
Strobl Schiffstation ⊡ ....a.	1040	1050	...	1215	1255	1345	1515	1510	...	...	1645	1715	...	...

A – Apr. 13–17 only.
C – ⑥⑦ (not Apr. 15, 16).

* – Subject to lake conditions.
⊡ – Approximately 400 metres from Strobl Busbahnhof.
● – Approximately 500 metres from St Gilgen Busbahnhof.

969   TAUERN TUNNEL CAR-CARRYING TRAINS

BÖCKSTEIN - MALLNITZ-OBERVELLACH   11 km.   Transit time: 11 minutes.   Passengers without cars are also conveyed.   ✆ 05-1717.   E-mail: autoschleuse.tauernbahn@pv.oebb.a
From Böckstein at 0620, 0720 and hourly until 2320.   **From Mallnitz-Obervellach** at 0550, 0650 and hourly until 2250.

970   SALZBURG - VILLACH - KLAGENFURT

km		EN 499 R ♦	EN 237 R ♦	EN 40465 ※ R 2		※ 2		IC 590 �MΥ	RJ 898 L✕	EC 111 ✕	RJ 596 ✕	EC 113 ✕♦	EC 115 ⊗♦	RJ 698 Ⓐ ✕	EC 117 ⊗	RJ 717 S ✕	EN 295 R ♦
	Wien Hbf 950 ....d.	...	2127	...	...	...	...	...	...	...	0855	...	...	1455	...	...	...
	München Hbf 890 ...d.	2335r	...	...	...	2	...	...	0818	...	1217	1417	...	...	1817	...	2010z
0	Salzburg Hbf ... 960 975 d.	0134	0134	...	...	...	...	0612	0812	1012	1212	1412	1612	1812	2012	2012	2111	2202
29	Golling-Abtenau ......960 d.	...	...	...	...	...	...	0633	0833	1033	1233	1433	1633	1833	2033	2033	2136	
53	Bischofshofen ... 960 975 d.	...	...	...	...	...	...	0654	0854	1054	1254	1454	1654	1854	2054	2054	2158	
61	St Johann im Pongau ...960 d.	...	...	...	...	...	...	0703	0903	1103	1303	1503	1703	1903	2103	2103	2206	
67	Schwarzach-St Veit .....960 d.	0226	0226	...	0420	...	...	0711	0911	1111	1311	1511	1711	1911	2111	2111	2214	2254
86	Bad Hofgastein ....d.	...	...	...	0437	...	...	0729	0929	1129	1329	1529	1729	1929	2129	2129	2230	
97	Bad Gastein ....d.	...	...	...	0501	...	...	0742	0942	1142	1342	1542	1742	1942	2142	2142	2241	
113	Mallnitz-Obervellach ....d.	...	...	...	0516	...	0647	0756	0956	1156	1356	1556	1756	1956	2156	2156	...	
146	Spittal-Millstättersee ... 971 d.	0328	0328	...	0542	...	0717	0820	1020	1220	1420	1620	1820	2020	2220	2220		
182	Villach Hbf ....971 a.	0351	0351	...	0605	...	0753	0843	1043	1243	1443	1643	1843	2043	2243	2243		0019
182	Villach Hbf ....971 d.	...	...	0450		0620	...	0755	0847	1047	1247	1447	1649	1847	2047	2247	2247	
198	Velden am Wörthersee ...971 d.	...	...	0505		0634	...	0806	0858	1058	1258	1458	1700	1858	2058	2258	2258	
207	Pörtschach am Wörthersee 971 d.	...	...	0513		0642.	...	...	0904	1104	1304	1504	1707	1904	2104	2304	2304	
220	Klagenfurt Hbf ....971 a.	...	...	0528		0656	...	0822	0913	1113	1316	1513	1718	1916	2116	2316	2316	

		EN 236 R ♦	EN 498 R ♦	EN 294 R ♦		RJ 691 ✕ F 2	EC 114 ✕	EC 112 ♦✕♦	RJ 793 ✕	RJ 797 ✕		Ⓐ 2		RJ 110 ✕	IC 591 Υ		EN 414 R ♦
	Klagenfurt Hbf ....971 d.	...	...	...	...	0645	0842	1027	1245	1445	1532	...	1642	1845	...	2232	...
	Pörtschach am Wörthersee . 971 d.	...	...	...	...	0655	0855	1040	1255	1455	1547	...	1655	1855	...	2247	...
	Velden am Wörthersee ....971 d.	...	...	...	...	0702	0902	1047	1302	1502	1554	...	1702	1902	...	2254	...
	Villach Hbf ....971 d.	...	...	...	...	0713	0913	1058	1313	1513	1609	...	1713	1913	2309		...
	Villach Hbf ....971 d.	0146	0146	0400	...	0529	0716	0916	1116	1316	1516	1610	...	1716	1916	...	2316	
	Spittal-Millstättersee ....971 d.	0209	0209		0604	0740	0940	1140	1340	1540	1634	1644	1740	1940		2341	
	Mallnitz-Obervellach .....d.	...	...		0633	0804	1004	1204	1404	1604	...	1714	1804	2004		0010	
	Bad Gastein ....d.	...	...		0625	0817	1017	1217	1417	1617	...		1817	2017		0027	
	Bad Hofgastein ....d.	...	...		0636	0830	1030	1430	1430	1630	...		1830	2030		0041	
	Schwarzach-St Veit ....960 d.	0320	0320	0520	0655	0850	1050	1250	1450	1650	...		1850	2050		0057	
	St Johann im Pongau ...960 d.	...	...		0700	0855	1055	1255	1455	1655	...		1855	2055			
	Bischofshofen ... 960 975 d.	...	...		0709	0903	1103	1303	1503	1703	...		1903	2103			
	Golling-Abtenau ......960 d.	...	...			0924	1124	1324	1524	1724	...		1924	2124			
	Salzburg Hbf ... 960 975 a.	0409	0409	0615	0748	0948	1148	1348	1548	1748	...		1948	2148			
	München Hbf 890 ....a.	...	0610	0819v			1341	1541					2142t				
	Wien Hbf 950 ....a.	0755				1305			1905	2105							

♦ – NOTES (LISTED BY TRAIN NUMBER)
112 – ⊑ and ✕ Klagenfurt - München - Stuttgart - Frankfurt; ⊑ Zagreb (212) - Villach (112) - Frankfurt.
113 – ⊑ and ✕ Frankfurt - Stuttgart - München - Klagenfurt; ⊑ Frankfurt - Villach (213) - Zagreb.
114 – WÖRTHERSEE – ⊑ and ⊗ Klagenfurt - München - Stuttgart - Köln - Dortmund.
115 – WÖRTHERSEE – ⊑ and ⊗ Münster - Köln - Stuttgart - München - Klagenfurt.
117 – Not Apr. 14 - July 16. ⊑ and ⊗ (Frankfurt Ⓑ / Karlsruhe Ⓒ -) Stuttgart - München - Salzburg - Klagenfurt. Train number 1217 on ⑥.
236/7 – ÖBB nightjet. ⊱ 1, 2 cl., ◢ 2 cl. and ⊑ Venezia - Tarvisio ⬛ - Villach - Salzburg - Wien and v.v.
294/5 – ÖBB nightjet. ⊱ 1, 2 cl., ◢ 2 cl. and ⊑ Roma - Firenze - Bologna - München and v.v.; ⊱ 1, 2 cl., ◢ 2 cl. and ⊑ (40235/40295) Milano - Verona - München and v.v.
414 – ⊑ Beograd - Zagreb - Ljubljana - Villach - Schwarzach (464); ⊱ 1, 2 cl. and ◢ 2 cl. ⊑ Ljubljana - Villach - Schwarzach (464) - Innsbruck - Feldkirch - Zürich.
498/9 – LISINSKI – ⊱ 1, 2 cl., ◢ 2 cl. and ⊑ Zagreb - Dobova - Ljubljana - Jesenice ⬛ - München and v.v. ⊱ 1, 2 cl., ◢ 2 cl. and ⊑ (ÖBB nightjet 40236/40463) Venezia - München and v.v.

40465 – ⊑ Zürich (465) - Feldkirch - Innsbruck - Schwarzach (415) Villach - Ljubljana - Zagreb - Beograd; ⊱ 1, 2 cl. and ◢ 2 cl. Zürich (465) - Feldkirch - Innsbruck - Schwarzach (415) - Villach - Ljubljana - Zagreb.

F – To Freilassing (a. 0800).
L – From Linz (Table 950).
R – Ⓡ for international journeys.
S – Apr. 14 - July 16.

r – 2154 on ⑥⑦ Apr. 15 - July 16 (not May 20, 21).
t – 2 minutes later Apr. 14 - July 16.
v – 0827 from Apr. 14.
z – 1917 from Apr. 14.

LIENZ - VILLACH - KLAGENFURT - FRIESACH (- WIEN) 971

	EN 234 ★ 2	⚒ 2	*RJ* 530 ✕	U 2	2	2	2	*D* 734 Ⓐ 2	*RJ* 532 ✕	2	2	⚒ 2	*IC* 590 ◐ 🍷	*RJ* 534 ✕	2	⚒ 2	*RJ* 898 ◐ ✕	2	*D* 736 ⑥ 2	*RJ* 536 ✕	2	Ⓐ 2	⚒ 2	*RJ* 111 ◐ ✕	*RJ* 538 ✕
Lienz d.	...	...	...	...	...	...	0524	0548	...	...	0629	...	...	...	0719	0824e	...	0924	0953	...	...	...	1024e	...	...
Spittal-Millstättersee a.	...	...	...	...	...	...	0627	0632	...	...	0727	...	...	...	0822	0922e	...	1022	1042	...	...	...	1122e	...	...
Spittal-Millstättersee 970 d.	...	...	...	0448r	0530e	...	0630	0637	...	0642e	0729	0732	0820	...	0832	0932	1020	1032	1046	...	...	...	1132	1220	...
Villach Hbf 970 a.	...	...	...	0520r	0558e	...	0656	0701	...	0715e	0753	0804	0843	...	0904p	1004	1043	1104	1109	...	←	...	1204	1243	...
Villach Hbf 970 d.	0418	0450	0526	0529	0604	0620	0659e	...	0714	0720	0755	0820	0847	0914	0920	1020	1047	1120	...	1114	1120	1150	1220	1247	1314
Velden am Wörthersee 970 d.	|	0505	|	0543	|	0634	0711e	...	0725	0734	0806	0834	0858	|	0934	1034	1058	→	...	1125	1134	1204	1234	1258	|
Pörtschach am W'see ⊡ 970 d.	|	0513	|	0551	|	0642	|	...	|	0742	|	0842	0904	0929	0942	1042	1104	...	...	|	1142	1212	1242	1304	1329
Krumpendorf d.	|	0519	|	0557	|	0648	|	...	|	0748	|	0848	|	|	0948	1048	|	...	...	|	1148	1218	1248	1310	|
Klagenfurt Hbf 970 a.	0439	0528	0547	0605	0625	0656	0728e	...	0737	0756	0822	0856	0913	0937	0956	1056	1113	...	...	1137	1156	1226	1256	1316	1337
Klagenfurt Hbf 980 d.	0440	...	0549	0607	0627	0704	...	...	0739	0804	0823	0904	...	0939	1004	1104	...	...	...	1139	1204	1228	1304	...	1339
St Veit an der Glan 980 d.	|	...	0602	0627	0640	0724	...	...	0753	0824	0838	0924	...	0953	1024	1124	...	...	...	1153	1224	1247	1324	...	1353
Friesach 980 a.	|	...	|	0659	0703	0756	...	...	|	0856	...	0956	...	1015	1056	1156	...	...	...	|	1256	...	1356	...	1415
Wien Hbf 980 a.	0846	...	0935	...	...	...	...	...	1135	...	...	...	...	1335	...	...	...	...	...	1535	...	...	...	...	1735

	2	Ⓐ 2	⚒ 2	*RJ* 596 ◐ ✕	*RJ* 630 ✕	2	Ⓐ 2	⚒ 2	*EC* 113 ◐ ✕	2	*RJ* 632 ✕	2	Ⓐ 2	*D* 732 ⑦w 2	⚒ 2	*EC* 115 ◐ ⊗	*EC* 30 V ✕	2	⚒ 2	⚒ 2	*RJ* 698 ◐ ✕	◇ 2	⚒ 2	*EC*§ 117 1217 ◐ ⊗	2
Lienz d.	1124	...	1224e	...	...	1324	...	1424e	...	1524	1553	...	...	...	1624e	...	...	1724	1824e	...	...	1924	2024e	...	...
Spittal-Millstättersee a.	1222	...	1322e	...	...	1422	...	1522e	...	1622	1642	...	...	...	1722e	...	...	1822	1922e	...	...	2022	2122e	...	...
Spittal-Millstättersee 970 d.	1232	...	1332	1420	...	1432	...	1532	1620	1632	1646	...	...	...	1732	1820	...	1832	1932	...	2020	2032	2132	2220	...
Villach Hbf 970 a.	1304p	...	1404	1443	...	1504p	...	1604	1643	1704	1709	←	...	...	1804	1843	...	1904p	2004	...	2043	2104	2204	2243	...
Villach Hbf 970 d.	1320	1350	1420	1447	1514	1520	1550	1620	1649	1720	1714	1720	1750	1814	1820	1847	1914	1920	...	2020	2047	2120	2220	2247	2350
Velden am Wörthersee 970 d.	1334	1404	1434	1458	1525	1534	1604	1634	1700	→	|	1734	1804	1825	1834	1858	1925	1934	...	2034	2058	2134	2234	2258	0004
Pörtschach am W'see ⊡ 970 d.	1342	1412	1442	1504	|	1542	1612	1642	1707	...	1729	1742	1812	1831	1842	1904	|	1942	...	2042	2104	2142	2242	2304	0012
Krumpendorf d.	1348	1418	1448	|	|	1548	1618	1648	1712	...	|	1748	1818	|	1848	1910	|	1948	...	2048	2110	2148	2248	2310	0018
Klagenfurt Hbf 970 a.	1356	1426	1456	1513	1537	1556	1626	1656	1718	...	1737	1756	1826	1839	1856	1916	1937	1956	...	2056	2116	2156	2256	2316	0026
Klagenfurt Hbf 980 d.	1404	1428	1504	...	1539	1604	1628	1704	...	...	1739	1804	1828	1841	1904	...	1939	2004	...	2104	...	2204	2304	...	0028
St Veit an der Glan 980 d.	1424	1447	1524	...	1553	1624	1647	1724	...	...	1753	1824	1847	1854	1924	...	1953	2024	...	2124	...	2224	2324	...	0047
Friesach 980 a.	1456	...	1556	...	|	1656	...	1756	...	...	1815	1856	...	1918	1956	...	|	2056	...	2156	...	2256	2356	...	...
Wien Hbf 980 a.	...	...	...	...	1935	...	...	...	...	...	2135	...	...	2235	...	...	2335	...	...	...	...	...	...	...	...

km		⚒ 2	⚒ 2	2	⚒ 2	*RJ* 691 ◐ ✕	⚒ 2	⚒⊖ U 2	◇ 2	*EC* 114 ◐ ⊗	⚒ 2	2	*EC* 31 V ✕	*EC* 112 ◐ ✕	⚒ 2	2	*RJ* 533 ✕	2	Ⓐ 2	*RJ* 793 ◐ ✕	⚒ 2	Ⓐ 2	2	*RJ* 535 ✕	*RJ* 797 ◐ ✕
	Wien Hbf 980 d.	...	...	...	...	...	...	...	...	...	...	...	0625	...	...	...	0825	...	...	...	...	...	...	1025	...
0	Friesach 980 d.	...	...	0508	0545	...	0608	0643	0708	...	0808	0908	|	...	1008	1108	1144	...	...	...	1208	...	1308	|	...
33	St Veit an der Glan 980 d.	...	0512	0542	0616	...	0642	0718	0742	...	0842	0942	1008	...	1042	1142	1208	...	1212	...	1242	1312	1342	1408	...
53	Klagenfurt Hbf 980 a.	...	0530	0600	0631	...	0700	0738	0800	...	0900	1000	1020	...	1100	1200	1220	...	1230	...	1300	1330	1400	1420	...
53	Klagenfurt Hbf 970 d.	...	0532	0602	0633	0645	0702	0744	0802	0842	0902	1002	1022	1027	1102	1202	1222	...	1232	1245	1302	1332	1402	1422	1445
60	Krumpendorf d.	...	0541	0611	0643	|	0711	0752	0811	0849	0911	1011	|	1034	1111	1211	|	...	1241	|	1311	1341	1411	|	|
66	Pörtschach am W ⊡ 970 d.	...	0547	0617	0648	0655	0717	0757	0817	0855	0917	1017	|	1040	1117	1217	1232	...	1247	1255	1317	1347	1417	|	1455
75	Velden am Wörthersee 970 d.	...	0554	0624	0654	0702	0724	0804	0824	0902	0924	1024	1036	1047	1124	1224	|	...	1254	1302	1324	1354	1424	1436	1502
91	Villach Hbf 970 a.	...	0609	0639	0710	0713	0739	0820	0839	0913	0939	1039	1046p	1058	1139	1239	1246	←	1309	1313	1339	1409	1439	1446p	1513
91	Villach Hbf 970 d.	0529	0617e	0654	...	0716	0754	...	0854	0916	0954	1054	...	1116	1154	1254	1250	1254	...	1316	1354	...	1454	...	1516
127	Spittal-Millstättersee 970 a.	0602	0650e	0726	...	0738	0826	...	0926	0938	1026	1126	...	1138	1226	→	1314	1326	...	1338	1426	...	1526	...	1538
127	Spittal-Millstättersee d.	0632	...	0737	...	...	0837e	...	0937	...	1037e	1137	...	...	1237e	...	1316	1337	...	...	1437e	...	1537	...	...
195	Lienz a.	0732	...	0837	...	...	0937e	...	1037	...	1137e	1237	...	...	1337e	...	1406	1437	...	...	1537e	...	1637	...	...

	⚒ 2	Ⓐ 2	2	*RJ* 537 ✕	*D* 735 Ⓑb 2	2	Ⓐ 2	*RJ* 110 ◐ ✕	⚒ 2	Ⓐ 2	2	*RJ* 539 ✕	Ⓐ 2	*IC* 591 ◐ 🍷	⚒ 2	Ⓐ 2	2	*RJ* 631 ✕	⚒ 2	2	*RJ* 633 ✕	Ⓑ 2	2	*EN* 233 ★ 2	2
Wien Hbf 980 d.	...	...	...	1225	...	...	...	...	...	...	...	1425	...	...	...	...	...	1625	...	...	1825	...	...	1923	...
Friesach 980 d.	1408	...	1508	1544	...	...	...	...	1608	...	1708	|	...	...	1808	...	1908	1944	2008	2108	|	...	...	2301	...
St Veit an der Glan 980 d.	1442	1512	1542	1608	...	...	1612	...	1642	1712	1742	1808	1812	...	1842	1912	1942	2008	2042	2142	2200	...	...	|	...
Klagenfurt Hbf 980 a.	1500	1530	1600	1620	...	...	1630	...	1700	1730	1800	1820	1830	...	1900	1930	2000	2020	2100	2200	2212	...	...	2335	...
Klagenfurt Hbf 970 d.	1502	1532	1602	1622	...	...	1632	1642	1702	1732	1802	1822	1832	1845	1902	1932	2002	2022	2102	...	2214	...	2232	2337	2341
Krumpendorf d.	1511	1541	1611	|	...	...	1641	1649	1711	1741	1811	|	1841	|	1911	1941	2011	|	2111	...	|	...	2241	|	2350
Pörtschach am W'see ⊡ 970 d.	1517	1547	1617	1632	...	...	1647	1655	1717	1747	1817	|	1847	1855	1917	1947	2017	2032	2117	...	|	...	2247	|	2357
Velden am Wörthersee 970 d.	1524	1554	1624	|	...	...	1654	1702	1724	1754	1824	1836	1854	1902	1924	1954	2024	|	2124	...	|	...	2254	|	0004
Villach Hbf 970 a.	1539	1609	1639	1646	...	←	1709	1713	1739	1809	1839	1846p	1909	1913	1939	2009	2039	2046p	2139	...	2236	...	2309	2400	0019
Villach Hbf 970 d.	1554	1610	1654	...	1650	1654	1710	1716	1754	1810	1854	...	...	1916	1954	...	2054	...	2154	...	...	2254	2316	...	...
Spittal-Millstättersee 970 a.	1626	1634	→	...	1714	1726	1734	1738	1826	1834	1926	...	...	1938	2026	...	2126	...	2226	...	...	2326	2339	...	...
Spittal-Millstättersee d.	...	1637	...	...	1716	1737	...	...	1837e	...	1937	...	...	...	2037e	...	2137	...	...	...	...	...	...	...	...
Lienz a.	...	1737	...	...	1806	1837	...	...	1937e	...	2037	...	...	...	2136e	...	2235	...	...	...	...	...	...	...	...

U – To / from Unzmarkt (Table **980**).
V – 🚆12 Venezia - Tarvisio 🚌 - Villach - Wien and v.v.

b – Not Dec. 25, Apr. 16, 30, June 4.
e – Ⓐ only.
p – Connects with train in previous column.

r – ⚒ only.
w – Also Dec. 26, Apr. 17, May 1, June 5; not Dec. 25, Apr. 16, 30, June 4.

§ – Runs as *RJ* **717** Apr. 14 - July 16.
◇ – Change trains at Spittal-Millstättersee on Ⓐ.

⊖ – Change trains at Klagenfurt on Ⓐ to July 7 / from Sept. 11.
★ – See Table **980** for through cars to / from Roma and Milano.
◐ – See Table **970** for further details.
⊡ – Pörtschach am Wörthersee.

LINZ - SELZTHAL 974

2nd class only

km		⚒						*IC* 503 🍷					Ⓐ			Ⓐ		*IC* 601 🍷		Ⓐ						
0	Linz Hbf d.	0506	0536	0636	0712	0736	0836	0914	1058	1136	1258	1336	1404	1458	1536	1558	1636	1714	1736	1800	1858	1936	2036	2136	2236	2336
28	Rohr - Bad Hall d.	0539	0609	0709	0736	0809	0909	0935	1121	1209	1321	1409	1429	1521	1609	1622	1709	1735	1809	1825	1921	2009	2109	2209	2309	0009
32	Kremsmünster d.	0545	0615	0715	|	0815	0915	|	1125	1215	1325	1415	1436	1525	1615	1627	1715	|	1815	1829	1925	2015	2115	2215	2315	0015
51	Kirchdorf a. d. Krems d.	0604	0633	0734	0750	0834	0933	0949	1140	1233	1340	1434	1453	1540	1633	1644	1733	1750	1833	1843	1939	2033	2134	2233	2333	0033
68	Hinterstoder ★ d.	0625	...	0755	0807	0856	...	|	1201	...	1401	1456c	1514	1601	...	1705	...	|	...	1904	2001	...	2156	...	...	...
82	Windischgarsten d.	0639	...	...	0821	0910	...	1020	1215	...	1415	1510c	1528	1615	...	1719	...	1820	...	1918	2015	...	2211	...	...	...
87	Spital am Pyhrn d.	0646	...	...	0827	0916	...	1026	1221	...	1421	1516c	1534	1621	...	1725	...	1826	...	1924	2021	...	2218	...	...	...
104	Selzthal a.	0702	...	...	0843	...	...	1040	1239	...	1439	...	...	1639	...	1743	...	1840	...	...	2039	...	2234	...	...	...
	Liezen 975 a.	...	...	...	0851e	...	...	|	1251e	...	1451e	...	...	1648e	...	...	...	|	...	...	...	...	...	...	...	...
	Graz Hbf 975 a.	...	...	...	...	...	...	1214	...	...	...	...	...	...	...	...	...	2014	...	...	...	...	...	...	...	...

		Ⓐ		⚒		⚒	Ⓐ	Ⓒ			*IC* 502 🍷								Ⓐ		*IC* 600 🍷					
Graz Hbf 975 d.	...	...	...	...	...	...	...	...	...	...	0745	...	...	...	...	...	...	...	...	...	1545	...	...	...	...	...
Liezen 975 d.	...	...	...	...	...	...	...	...	...	...	|	...	...	...	...	1305e	...	1505e	...	...	|	...	...	...	...	...
Selzthal d.	...	0428	...	...	...	0547	0615	0615	0721	...	0919	...	...	1121	...	1321	...	1521	...	...	1719	...	...	1921	...	...
Spital am Pyhrn d.	...	0445	...	...	...	0604	0632	0632	0738	...	0934	...	1044	1140	...	1340	...	1540	...	1643	1734	...	...	1940	2043e	...
Windischgarsten d.	...	0451	...	...	...	0610	0640	0649f	0744	...	0940	...	1050	1146	...	1346	...	1546	...	1649	1740	...	...	1947	2049e	...
Hinterstoder ★ d.	...	0504	...	...	...	0625	0654	0702	0758	...	|	...	1104	1200	...	1400	...	1600	...	1704	|	...	...	2000	2103e	...
Kirchdorf a. d. Krems d.	0425	0525	0525	0555	0625	0646	0717	0725	0821	0925	1011	1025	1125	1221	1325	1421	1525	1621	1650	1725	1811	1825	1925	2021	2125	2225
Kremsmünster d.	0445	0545	0545	0615	0645	0703	0731	0746	0836	0945	|	1045	1145	1236	1345	1436	1545	1636	1714	1745	|	1845	1945	2036	2145	2246
Rohr - Bad Hall d.	0449	0549	0549	0619	0649	0708	0737	0750	0840	0949	1025	1049	1149	1240	1349	1440	1549	1640	1718	1749	1825	1849	1949	2040	2149	2250
Linz Hbf a.	0524	0624	0624	0654	0724	0735	0803	0824	0903	1024	1047	1124	1224	1303	1424	1503	1624	1703	1754	1824	1847	1924	2024	2103	2224	2324

c – Kirchdorf - Spital am Pyhrn on Ⓒ only.
e – Ⓐ only.
f – Arrives 0637.

★ – 🚌 services operate Hinterstoder rail station - Hinterstoder town centre and v.v. Journey time: 18 minutes. Operated by Riedler Reisen & Touristik GmbH. **Subject to confirmation**.
From Hinterstoder rail station at 0655 ⑥, 0810, 0900, 1203, 1403, 1515 Ⓐ, 1603 and 1715.
From Hinterstoder Gemeindehaus at 0600 Ⓐ, 0630 ⚒, 0735 Ⓐ, 0739 Ⓒ, 1138, 1338, 1538 and 1638.

AUSTRIA

975 SALZBURG - BISCHOFSHOFEN - SELZTHAL - GRAZ

km		⚒ 2	*EN* 465 A	⚒ 2	Ⓐ 2	Ⓐ 2	Ⓐ 2	2	*IC* 719 ⊗	Ⓐ 2	2	*IC* 513 🍷	*IC* 503 🍷	2	*RJ* 111 ✕	*IC* 515 🍷	Ⓐ 2L	2	*EC* 217 ◇ S⊗	Ⓐ 2L	Ⓑ 2	*EC* 113 ✕	*EC* 163 Z✕	Ⓐ 2
0	**Salzburg** Hbf ... **960 970** d.	...	...	...	...	...	...	...	0615	...	...	0815	...	...	1012	...	...	...	1215	...	...	1412	...	...
	Innsbruck Hbf **960** ... d.	...	0056	...	...	...	...	...	|	...	...	|	...	...	|	0821	...	...	|	...	...	|	1221	...
53	**Bischofshofen** ... **960 970** a.	...	0336	...	...	...	...	...	0702	...	...	0902	...	...	1052	1110	...	...	1302	...	...	1452	1510	...
53	**Bischofshofen** ... d.	...	0338	...	...	...	...	...	0713	...	0741r	0913	...	...	...	1113	...	...	1313	...	...	...	1513	...
77	Radstadt ... d.	...	|	...	...	...	...	0610	0736	...	0809	0936	...	...	...	1136	...	...	1336	...	...	...	1536	...
94	Schladming ... d.	...	0416	0500	...	...	...	0629	0752	...	0831	0952	...	1031	...	1152	...	1231	1352	...	1431	...	1552	...
133	**Stainach-Irdning** ... d.	0415	0447	0541	...	...	...	0710	0821	...	0912	1021	...	1112	...	1221	...	1312	1421	...	1512	...	1621	...
145	Liezen ... d.	0427	|	0553	...	...	...	0726	0832	0857	0926	1032	...	1126	...	1232	1305	1326	1432	1505	1526	...	1632	1704
	Linz Hbf **974** ... d.	|	|	|	...	...	...	|	|	|	|	|	0914	|	...	|	|	|	|	|	|	...	|	|
152	**Selzthal** ... a.	0433	0504	0559	...	...	...	0733	0839	0904	0933	1039	1040	1133	...	1239	1312	1333	1439	1512	1533	...	1639	1711
152	**Selzthal** ... d.	0440	0513	0606	...	0716	...	0739	0846	...	0939	1048	1048	1139	...	1248	...	1339	1446	...	1539	...	1648	...
158	Stadt Rottenmann ... d.	0447	|	0613	...	0722	...	0745	0853	...	0945	|	|	1145	...	|	...	1345	1453	...	1545	...	|	...
169	Trieben ... d.	0455	|	0621	...	0729	...	0753	|	...	0953	|	|	1153	...	|	...	1353	|	...	1553	...	|	...
215	St Michael ... a.	0530	0550	0655	...	0802	...	0828	0921	...	1028	1121	1121	1228	...	1321	...	1428	1521	...	1628	...	1721	...
215	St Michael ... **980** d.	0531	0551	0701	0706	0803	...	*0833*	0922	...	*1033*	1122	1122	*1233*	...	1322	...	*1433*	1522	...	*1633*	...	1722	...
225	Leoben Hbf ... **980** d.	0540	0601	0709	0715	0811	0818	*0841*	0930	...	*1041*	1130	1130	*1241*	...	1330	...	*1441*	1530	...	*1641*	...	1730	...
	Bruck a. d. Mur ... **980** a.	|	0612	|	0728	0824	|	*0853*	|	...	*1053*	|	|	*1253*	...	|	...	*1453*	|	...	*1653*	...	|	...
293	**Graz** Hbf ... **980** a.	0633	0700	0801	...	...	0903	...	1014	...	...	1214	1214	...	...	1414	...	...	1614	...	...	...	1814	...

	2	*IC* 611 🍷	*IC* 601 🍷	2	Ⓐ 2	*EC* 219 ◇ F⊗	*EC* 117 1217 §⊗	2	Ⓑ 2
Salzburg Hbf ... **960 970** d.	...	1615	...	...	*1641*	1815	2012	...	...
Innsbruck Hbf **960** ... d.	...	|	...	...	|	|	|	...	...
Bischofshofen ... **960 970** a.	...	1702	...	...	*1733*	1902	2052	...	...
Bischofshofen ... d.	...	1713	...	...	1741	1913	...	2100	...
Radstadt ... d.	...	1736	...	...	1810	1936	...	2130	...
Schladming ... d.	1631	1752	...	1831	...	1952	...	2149	2155
Stainach-Irdning ... d.	1712	1821	...	1912	...	2021	...	...	2234
Liezen ... d.	1726	1832	...	1926	...	2032	...	...	...
Linz Hbf **974** ... d.	|	|	1714	|	...	|	...	...	...
Selzthal ... a.	1733	1839	1840	1933	...	2039	...	...	...
Selzthal ... d.	1739	1848	1848	1939	...	2046	...	...	...
Stadt Rottenmann ... d.	1745	|	|	1945	...	2053	...	...	...
Trieben ... d.	1753	|	|	1953	...	|	...	...	...
St Michael ... a.	1828	1921	1921	2028	...	2121	...	...	...
St Michael ... **980** d.	*1833*	1922	1922	*2033*	...	2122	...	...	...
Leoben Hbf ... **980** d.	*1841*	1930	1930	*2041*	...	2130	...	...	...
Bruck a. d. Mur ... **980** a.	*1853*	|	|	*2053*	...	|	...	...	...
Graz Hbf ... **980** a.	...	2014	2014	...	...	2214	...	...	...

	⚒ 2	⚒ 2	2	Ⓐ 2	⚒ 2	*EC* 218 F⊗	2	Ⓐ 2L	*IC* 502 🍷	*IC* 512 🍷
Graz Hbf ... **980** d.	...	...	...	...	...	0545	...	...	0745	0745
Bruck a. d. Mur ... **980** d.	...	...	...	*0536*	0613	|	*0706*	...	|	|
Leoben Hbf ... **980** d.	...	...	...	*0549*	0625	0631	*0721*	...	0831	0831
St Michael ... **980** a.	...	...	...	*0556*	...	0637	*0728*	...	0837	0837
St Michael ... d.	...	...	...	0600	...	0638	0731	...	0838	0838
Trieben ... d.	...	...	...	0636	...	|	0805	...	|	|
Stadt Rottenmann ... d.	...	...	...	0644	...	0708	0812	...	|	|
Selzthal ... a.	...	...	...	0650	...	0713	0818	...	0911	0911
Selzthal ... d.	...	0544	...	...	...	0719	0823	0844	0919	0919
Linz Hbf **974** ... a.	...	|	...	...	...	|	|	|	1047	|
Liezen ... d.	...	0552	...	...	...	0727	0832	0851	...	0927
Stainach-Irdning ... d.	...	0604	...	...	...	0737	0845	...	...	0937
Schladming ... d.	0506	0648	0648	...	...	0810	0928	...	...	1010
Radstadt ... d.	0525	0706	0706	...	...	0826	...	...	...	1026
Bischofshofen ... a.	0554	0735	0735	...	...	0848	...	...	...	1048
Bischofshofen ... **960 970** d.	*0610*	*0740*	*0740*	...	...	0857	...	...	...	1057
Innsbruck Hbf **960** ... a.	|	|	|	...	...	|	...	...	...	|
Salzburg Hbf ... **960 970** a.	*0710*	*0840*	*0840*	...	...	0944	...	...	...	1144

	2	*EC* 164 Z✕	*EC* 112 ✕	Ⓑ 2	Ⓐ 2L	*EC* 216 S⊗	2	Ⓐ 2L	*IC* 518 🍷	*RJ* 797 ✕	2	Ⓐ 2L	⚒ 2	*IC* 600 🍷	*IC* 610 🍷	Ⓐ 2	Ⓑ 2	⚒ 2	⚒ 2	*IC* 718 ⊗	Ⓑ 2	⑥ 2		*EN* 464 A
Graz Hbf ... **980** d.	...	0945	...	...	...	1145	...	...	1345	...	...	...	1501	1545	1545	...	...	1701	...	1745	...	...	...	2224
Bruck a. d. Mur ... **980** d.	*0906*	|	...	*1106*	...	|	*1306*	...	|	...	*1506*	...	|	|	|	...	*1706*	|	...	|	*1906*	*1906*	...	2317
Leoben Hbf ... **980** d.	*0921*	1031	...	*1121*	...	1231	*1321*	...	1431	...	*1521*	...	1557	1631	1631	...	*1721*	1755	1801	1831	*1921*	*1921*	...	2331
St Michael ... **980** a.	*0928*	1037	...	*1128*	...	1237	*1328*	...	1437	...	*1528*	...	1605	1637	1637	...	*1728*	...	1809	1837	*1928*	*1928*	...	2338
St Michael ... d.	0931	1038	...	1131	...	1238	1331	...	1438	...	1531	...	1608	1638	1638	...	1731	...	1810	1838	1931	1931	...	2340
Trieben ... d.	1005	|	...	1205	...	|	1405	...	|	...	1605	...	1644	|	|	...	1805	...	1846	|	2005	2005	...	|
Stadt Rottenmann ... d.	1012	|	...	1212	...	1308	1412	...	|	...	1612	...	1652	|	|	...	1812	...	1854	1908	2012	2012	...	|
Selzthal ... a.	1018	1111	...	1218	...	1313	1418	...	1511	...	1618	...	1658	1711	1711	...	1818	...	1900	1913	2018	2018	...	0017
Selzthal ... d.	1023	1119	...	1223	1244	1319	1423	1444	1519	...	1623	1641	...	1719	1719	...	1823	...	...	1919	2023	2023	...	0029
Linz Hbf **974** ... a.	|	|	...	|	|	|	|	|	|	...	|	|	...	1847	|	...	|	...	...	|	|	|	...	|
Liezen ... d.	1032	1127	...	1232	1251	1327	1432	1451	1527	...	1632	1648	...	...	1727	...	1832	...	...	1927	2032	2032	...	|
Stainach-Irdning ... d.	1045	1137	...	1245	...	1337	1445	...	1537	...	1645	...	...	...	1737	...	1845	...	...	1937	2045	2045	...	0046
Schladming ... d.	1128	1210	...	1328	...	1410	1528	...	1610	...	1728	...	...	...	1810	...	1929	...	...	2010	2126	2127	...	0118
Radstadt ... d.	...	1226	...	...	...	1426	...	...	1626	...	...	...	...	...	1826	1920	1952	...	...	2026	...	2147	...	|
Bischofshofen ... a.	...	1248	...	...	...	1448	...	...	1648	...	...	...	...	...	1848	1950	...	...	...	2048	...	...	...	0156
Bischofshofen ... **960 970** d.	...	1250	1305	...	...	1457	...	...	1650	1705	...	...	...	...	1857	*2004*	...	...	...	2057	...	...	...	0158
Innsbruck Hbf **960** ... a.	...	1540	|	...	...	|	...	...	1939	|	...	...	...	...	|	|	...	...	...	|	...	...	...	0449
Salzburg Hbf ... **960 970** a.	...	...	1348	...	...	1544	...	...	...	1748	...	...	...	...	1944	*2051*	...	...	...	2144	...	...	...	...

A – *ÖBB nightjet*. ZÜRICHSEE – 🛏 1, 2 cl., ▬ 2 cl. and [2] Graz - Innsbruck - Buchs ▦ - Zürich and v.v.
F – [12] and ⊗ Graz - München - Stuttgart - Frankfurt and v.v. See note ◇.
L – To / from Linz (Table **974**).
S – [12] and ⊗ Graz - München - Stuttgart - Saarbrücken and v.v. See note ◇.
Z – TRANSALPIN – [12] and ✕ Zürich - Buchs ▦ - Innsbruck - Graz and v.v.

r – ⚒ only.
◇ – Apr. 14 - July 16 runs with a different train number and does not run to / from Germany (**216** runs as **616**; **217** runs as **617**; **218** runs as **618**; **219** runs as **619**).
§ – Runs as *RJ* **717** Apr. 14 - July 16.

976 LINZ - STEYR - KLEINREIFLING - WEISSENBACH

2nd class only

km		⚒	Ⓐ		Ⓐ	Ⓒ		Ⓒ	Ⓐ			Ⓒ	Ⓐ			Ⓒ	Ⓐ		Ⓐ		Ⓒ	Ⓐ		Ⓐ		Ⓒ
0	**Linz** Hbf ... **950 992** d.	0430	0514	0614	0649	0649	0752	0752	*0830*	0852	0952	0952	*1030*	1052	1152	1152	1222	1252	1252	1352	1352	1422	1452	*1530*	1552	1552
17	Enns ... **992** d.	0448	0532	0632	0707	0707	0810	0810	|	0910	1010	1010	|	1110	1210	1210	1240	1310	1310	1410	1410	1440	1510	|	1610	1610
25	St Valentin ... **950** d.	0509	0540	0649	0721	0721	0821	0821	0851	0921	1021	1021	1051	1121	1221	1221	1251	1321	1321	1421	1421	1451	1521	1551	1621	1621
45	**Steyr** ... d.	0532	0605	0714	0754t	0754t	0846	0846	0912	0946	1046	1046	1112	1146	1246	1246	1312	1346	1346	1446	1446	1512	1546	1612	1646	1646
47	Garsten ... d.	0536	0608	0717	0758	0758	0849	0850	0916	0949	1049	1050	1116	1149	1249	1250	1316	1349	1350	1449	1450	1516	1549	1616	1649	1650
67	Losenstein ... d.	0601	...	...	0822	0822	...	0917	0937	...	...	1117	1137	...	...	1317	1337	...	1423	...	1517	1537	...	1640	...	1717
89	Kastenreith ... **977** a.	0628	...	...	0848	0852	...	0941	1004	...	...	1141	1204	...	...	1341	1404	...	1447	...	1541	1603	...	1704	...	1741
92	**Kleinreifling** ... **977** a.	0633	...	...	0852	0856	...	0946	1008	...	...	1146	1208	...	...	1346	1408	...	1451	...	1546	1607	...	1708	...	1746
106	Weißenbach ⊡ .. **977** a.	0648e	...	...	0907	*0916*	...	...	...	...	...	*1216*	...	...	...	*1416*	...	...	...	...	...	1622	...	1723	...	*1816*

	Ⓐ		Ⓐ		Ⓒ	Ⓐ					
Linz Hbf ... **950 992** d.	1622	1652	*1730*	1752	1752	1822	*1852*	1952	*2052*	2152	2252
Enns ... **992** d.	1640	1710	|	1810	1810	1840	*1910*	2010	*2110*	2210	2310
St Valentin ... **950** d.	1651	1721	1751	1821	1821	1851	1921	2021	2121	2221	2321
Steyr ... d.	1712	1746	1812	1846	1846	1912	1946	2045	2146	2246	2346
Garsten ... d.	1716	1749	1816	1849	1850	1916	1949	2048	2149	2249	2349
Losenstein ... d.	1737	...	1841	...	1917	1937	...	2111	...	...	...
Kastenreith ... **977** a.	1803	...	1905	...	1941	2002	...	2135	...	...	...
Kleinreifling ... **977** a.	1807	...	1910	...	1946	2006	...	2139	...	...	...
Weißenbach ⊡ ... **977** a.	1822	...	1924	...	...	...	...	...	...	...	...

	P	Ⓐ	⚒		Ⓐ			Ⓐ	Ⓐ	Ⓒ	
Weißenbach ⊡ . **977** d.	...	...	...	...	...	0603e	...	0706	...	...	...
Kleinreifling ... **977** d.	...	0437	0513	...	...	0618	...	0721	0754	0812	...
Kastenreith ... **977** d.	...	0441	0517	...	...	0622	...	0724	0758	0816	...
Losenstein ... d.	...	0505	0540	...	...	0647	...	...	0822	0843	...
Garsten ... d.	0442	0527	0601	0609	0637	0709	0809	...	0843	0909	0909
Steyr ... d.	0446	0532	0606	0614	0642	0714	0814	...	0847	0914	0914
St Valentin ... **950** a.	0508	0555	0622	0637	0705	0737	0837	...	0907	0937	0937
Enns ... **992** a.	0520	0602	0628	0647	0719	0749	0849	...	|	0949	0949
Linz Hbf ... **950 992** a.	0538	0618	0641	0704	0738	0808	0908	...	*0930*	1008	1008

		Ⓐ	Ⓒ			Ⓐ	Ⓒ			Ⓐ	Ⓒ			Ⓐ	Ⓒ		Ⓐ	Ⓐ		Ⓐ	Ⓒ					
Weißenbach ⊡ ... **977** d.	...	0940	...	...	...	...	...	...	...	1338	*1341*	...	...	...	*1541*	...	...	1641	...	1738	*1747*	...	...	1939	...	...
Kleinreifling ... **977** d.	...	0954	1015	...	...	1154	1215	...	...	1354	1415	...	...	1554	1615	...	...	1708	...	1753	1815	...	...	1953	2021	...
Kastenreith ... **977** d.	...	0958	1019	...	...	1158	1219	...	...	1358	1419	...	...	1558	1619	...	...	1712	...	1757	1819	...	...	...	2025	...
Losenstein ... d.	...	1022	1044	...	...	1222	1244	...	...	1422	1444	...	...	1621	1644	...	...	1744	...	1821	1844	...	...	...	2050	...
Garsten ... d.	1009	1043	1109	1109	1209	1243	1309	1309	1409	1443	1509	1509	1609	1643	1709	1709	1743	1809	1809	1843	1909	1909	2009	...	2113	2209
Steyr ... d.	1014	1047	1114	1114	1214	1247	1314	1314	1414	1447	1514	1514	1614	1647	1714	1714	1747	1814	1814	1847	1914	1914	2014	...	2116	2214
St Valentin ... **950** a.	1037	1107	1137	1137	1237	1307	1337	1337	1437	1507	1537	1537	1637	1707	1737	1737	1807	1837	1837	1907	1937	1937	2037	...	2139	2237
Enns ... **992** a.	1049	|	1149	1149	1249	|	1349	1349	1449	|	1549	1549	1649	|	1749	1749	|	1849	1849	|	1949	1949	2049	...	2149	2249
Linz Hbf ... **950 992** a.	1108	*1130*	1208	1208	1308	*1330*	1408	1408	1508	*1530*	1608	1608	1708	*1730*	1808	1808	*1830*	1908	1908	*1930*	2008	2008	2108	...	2208	2308

P – To Passau (Table **962**).
e – Ⓐ only.
k – ⑥ only.
t – Arrives 0745.
⊡ – Weißenbach-St Gallen.

AMSTETTEN - KLEINREIFLING - SELZTHAL — 977

2nd class only

km		⑥	Ⓐ	⚒W	†◇	Ⓒ	Ⓒ	Ⓐ	Ⓐ	Ⓒ	Ⓐ	Ⓐ	Ⓒ	Ⓐ	Ⓐ	Ⓒ	Ⓐ	Ⓐ	Ⓒ	Ⓐ	†	Ⓐ	Ⓒ	Ⓐ	Ⓑt	
0	**Amstetten** d.	0515	0515	0621	0705	0805	0905	0905	1005	1105	1105	1205	1305	1305	1405	1505	1505	1605	1705	1705	1805	1805	1905	1905	2005	2105
23	Waidhofen a. d. Ybbs. d.	0541	0550	0703j	0731	0831	0931	0931	1030	1131	1131	1231	1331	1331	1431	1531	1531	1631	1731	1731	1831	1831	1931	1933	2030	2132
41	Weyer d.	0604	0608	0729	0749	0850	0949	0949	...	1149	1149	1249	1349	1349	1449	1549	1553	1649	1749	1749	1849	1849	1949	2008f	...	...
44	Kastenreith **976** d.	0608	0612	0733	0753	0856	0953	0952	...	1153	1152	1253	1353	1352	1453	1553	1556	1653	1753	1752	1853	1853	1953	2012	...	...
47	**Kleinreifling** **976** a.	0611	0615	0737	0757	0859	0957	*1008*	...	1157	*1208*	1257	1357	*1408*	1457	1557	*1607*	1657	1757	*1807*	1857	1857	1957	2015	...	...
61	Weißenbach ⊡ **976** a.	...	*0648*	...	...	0916	...	...	...	*1216*	...	*1316*	*1416*	...	...	...	*1622*	*1723*	*1816*k	*1822*	1912	*1924*	...	...	...	...
119	**Selzthal** a.	...	...	...	...	1019	...	...	...	...	...	...	...	...	...	...	...	...	...	...	...	...	...	...	...	...

	⚒		ⒶP	Ⓒ		Ⓐ	Ⓐ		⚒	Ⓐ	Ⓒ	Ⓐ	Ⓐ	Ⓒ	Ⓐ	Ⓐ	Ⓒ	Ⓐ	Ⓐ	Ⓒ	Ⓐ	Ⓐ	Ⓒ	†	Ⓐ	Ⓒ
Selzthal d.	...	...	...	...	...	...	...	...	...	...	...	...	...	...	...	...	...	...	...	...	...	...	1644	...	...	...
Weißenbach ⊡ **976** d.	...	...	...	...	...	*0603*	0706	...	...	*0940*	...	...	...	...	...	*1338*	*1341*	...	...	*1541*	*1641*	*1738*	1747	...	*1939*	*1939*
Kleinreifling **976** d.	...	...	0519	0556	...	0622	0721	0802	...	*0954*	1002	...	*1154*	1202	1302	*1354*	1402	1502	*1554*	1602	1658	*1753*	1802	1902	1956	2002
Kastenreith **976** d.	...	...	0523	0600	...	0630	0725	0806	...	1006	1006	...	1206	1206	1306	1406	1406	1506	1606	1606	1706	1806	1806	1906	2004	2006
Weyer d.	...	...	0527	0608	...	0634	0728	0810	...	1010	1010	...	1210	1210	1310	1410	1410	1510	1610	1610	1710	1810	1810	1910	2010	2010
Waidhofen a. d. Ybbs. d.	0430	0518	0547	0629	0629	0653	...	0830	0930	1030	1030	1130	1230	1230	1330	1430	1430	1530	1630	1630	1730	1830	1830	1930	2031	2031
Amstetten a.	0455	0546	0614	0655	0655	0719	...	0857r	0955	1055	1055	1155	1255	1255	1355	1455	1455	1555	1655	1655	1755	1855	1855	1955	2055	2055

W – From Wien (Table **950**).
P – To St Pölten (Table **950**).
f – Arrives 1952.
j – Arrives 0652.
k – ⑥ only.
r – 0855 on †.
t – Not Dec. 25, Jan. 5, Apr. 16, 30, May 24, June 4, 14, Aug. 14, Oct. 25, 31, Dec. 7.
◇ – Runs daily Amstetten - Waidhofen.
⊡ – Weißenbach-St Gallen.

WIEN and WIENER NEUSTADT - SOPRON - DEUTSCHKREUTZ — 978

2nd class only

WIEN - EBENFURTH - SOPRON - DEUTSCHKREUTZ *Operated by GySEV Győr-Sopron-Ebenfurti Vasút (in German Raab-Oedenburg-Ebenfurter Eisenbahn – ROeEE)*

km		Ⓐ	Ⓐ		Ⓐ		Ⓐ		Ⓐ		Ⓐ		Ⓐ		Ⓐ				Ⓑw
	Bratislava-P ⊖ **997** d.	...	...	0615	0715	0815	0915	1015	1115	1215	1315	1415	1515	1615z	...	1815z	1915e	...	...
0	**Wien** Hbf d.	0520	0619	0719	0819	0919	1019	1119	1219	1319	1419	1519	1619	1719	1819	1919	2019	...	...
4	**Wien** Meidling d.	0525	0625	0725	0825	0925	1025	1125	1225	1325	1425	1525	1625	1725	1825	1925	2025	...	...
42	Ebenfurth d.	0600	0701	0801	0902	1002	1102	1202	1302	1402	1502	1602	1702	1802	1902	2002	2102	...	2243
74	**Sopron** 🏛 a.	0637	0738	0837	0937	1037	1137	1237	1337	1437	1537	1637	1737	1837	1937	2037	2137	...	2318
83	**Deutschkreutz** a.	0657	0754	0847	0947	1047	1147	1247	1347	1447	1547	1647	1747	1847	1947	2047	2147	...	2331

	Ⓐ	Ⓐ	Ⓐ		Ⓐ		Ⓐ	Ⓐ		Ⓐ		Ⓐ		Ⓐ		Ⓐ		Ⓐ	
Deutschkreutz d.	0413	0513	0535	0613	0635	0712	0735	0813	0913	1013	1113	1213	1313	1413	1513	1613	1713	1813	1913
Sopron 🏛 d.	0423	0523	0545	0623	0646	0722	0746	0823	0923	1023	1123	1223	1323	1423	1523	1623	1723	1823	1923
Ebenfurth ▷ d.	0504	0604	0626	0704	0726	0804	0826	0904	1004	1104	1204	1304	1404	1504	1604	1704	1804	1904	2004
Wien Meidling a.	0535	0635	0700	0735	0800	0835	0900	0935	1035	1135	1235	1335	1435	1535	1635	1735	1835	1935	2035
Wien Hbf a.	0542	0642	0707	0742	*0811*	0842	0907	0942	1042	1142	1242	1342	1442	1542	1642	1742	1842	1942	2041
Bratislava-P ⊖ **997** a.	0644	0744	...	0844e	...	0944	...	1044	1144	1244	1344z	1444	1544	...	1744z	1844	1944	...	2144

e – Ⓐ only.
h – Continues to Wien Hbf (arrives 7 minutes later).
w – From Wiener Neustadt Hbf (d. 2233).
z – Ⓒ only.
⊖ – Bratislava-Petržalka. Trains do not run from / to Bratislava July 3 - Sept. 3.
▷ – Ebenfurth departures may be 2 minutes earlier July 3 - Sept. 3.
⊠ – **Additional journeys** from Wiener Neustadt to Sopron at 1301 Ⓐ, 1337 Ⓒ, 1401 Ⓐ, 1501 Ⓐ, 1537 Ⓒ, 1601 Ⓐ, 1701 Ⓐ, 1801 Ⓐ, 1901 Ⓐ.

WIENER NEUSTADT - SOPRON - DEUTSCHKREUTZ ⊠ *Operated by ÖBB*

km		Ⓐ						Ⓐ			Ⓐ	Ⓐ		Ⓐ	Ⓐ	Ⓒ	Ⓐ	Ⓒ	Ⓐ	Ⓒ	Ⓐ		Ⓐ		Ⓑ	
	Wien Meidling **980/1** d.	...	...	...	...	...	...	...	...	...	...	...	...	...	1600	...	1700	...	1800	...	...	...	...	...	...	...
0	**Wiener Neustadt** Hbf d.	0503	0603	0703	0739	0837	0937	1037	1137	1237	1331	1431	1437	1531	1631	1637	1731	1737	1831	1837	1931	1937	2037	2137	2233	2237
16	Mattersburg d.	0527	0626	0726	0803	0902	1002	1102	1202	1302	1344	1444	1502	1544	1644	1702	1744	1802	1844	1902	1944	2002	2102	2202	|	2302
33	**Sopron** 🏛 a.	0542	0641	0741	0818	0917	1017	1117	1217	1317	1400	1500	1517	1600	1700	1717	1800	1817	1900	1917	2000	2017	2117	2217	2318	2317
42	**Deutschkreutz** a.	...	...	...	...	...	...	...	...	...	1410	1510	...	1610	1710	...	1810	...	1910	...	2010	...	...	2227e	2331	...

	Ⓐ	Ⓐ	Ⓐ		Ⓐ	⑥	Ⓑ	Ⓐ				Ⓐ										Ⓐ			Ⓐ	
Deutschkreutz d.	...	...	0459	...	0559	0635	...	0659	...	...	...	...	...	...	...	...	...	...	...	...	...	...	...	...	2234	...
Sopron 🏛 d.	0418	0447	0509	0547	0609	0645	0647	0709	0747	0844	0944	1044	1144	1244	1344	1444	1544	1644	1744	1844	1944	2044	2144	...	2244	2244
Mattersburg d.	0434	0503	0527	0603	0627	0702	0703	0727	0803	0902	1002	1102	1202	1302	1402	1502	1602	1702	1802	1902	2002	2102	2202	...	2302	2302
Wiener Neustadt Hbf a.	0453	0525	0539	0625	0639	0725	0725	0739	0825	0925	1025	1125	1225	1325	1425	1525	1625	1725	1825	1925	2025	2125	2225	...	2325	2325
Wien Meidling **980/1** a.	...	...	0615h	...	0715h	...	...	0815	...	...	...	...	...	...	...	...	...	...	...	...	...	...	...	...	...	...

WIEN and GRAZ - KLAGENFURT (- VILLACH) — 980

km		⚒ 2	⚒ 2	⚒ 2	RJ 72 ✕	2	2	🚌 851 ☆	RJ 551 ✕	RJ 554 ✕	EC 31 V✕	🚌 853 ☆	RJ 553 H✕	2	EC 151 E✕	RJ 558 ✕	RJ 533 L✕	RJ 557 ✕	2	🚌 855 ☆	RJ 559 H✕	EC 158 ✕	RJ 535 ✕	RJ 71 P✕	2
0	**Wien** Hbf **981** d.	...	...	...	...	...	...	...	0558	...	0625	...	0658	...	0758	...	0825	0858	...	...	0958	...	1025	1058	...
4	**Wien** Meidling **981** d.	...	...	...	...	...	...	...	0605	...	0632	...	0705	...	0805	...	0832	0905	...	...	1005	...	1032	1105	...
49	**Wiener Neustadt** Hbf **981** a.	...	...	...	...	...	...	...	0628	...	0655	...	0728	...	0828	...	0855	0928	...	...	1028	...	1055	1128	...
49	**Wiener Neustadt** Hbf **981** d.	...	...	...	...	...	...	...	0632	...	0657	...	0732	...	0832	...	0857	0932	...	...	1032	...	1057	1132	...
104	Semmering **981** d.	...	...	...	...	...	...	...	|	...	|	...	|	...	0915	...	|	1015	...	...	1115	...	|	|	...
118	Mürzzuschlag **981** d.	...	0521	...	...	0621r	0621h	...	0730	...	|	...	0830	...	0930	...	|	1030	...	...	1130	...	|	1230	...
	Graz Hbf **975** d.	...	|	...	0626	|	|	0630	|	0726	|	0800	|	*0826*	|	0926	|	|	*1026*	1030	|	1126	|	|	*1226*
158	**Bruck** an der Mur a.	...	0602	...	0701	0702r	0702h	|	0756	0801	0813	|	0856	*0901*	0956	1001	1013	1056	*1101*	|	1156	1201	1213	1256	*1301*
158	**Bruck** an der Mur **975** ‡ d.	0436	0608	0613	...	0706	0708	|	0758	...	0815	|	0858	0906	0958	...	1015	1058	1106	|	1158	...	1215	1258	1306
212	**Graz** Hbf ‡ a.	|	0655	|	...	|	0755	|	0833	...	|	|	0933	|	1033	...	|	1133	|	|	1233	...	|	1333	|
174	Leoben Hbf **975** d.	0450	▬	0626	...	0721	...	|	...	...	0827	|	...	0921	...	...	1027	...	1121	|	...	...	1227	...	1321
◧	St Michael **975** a.	0458	...	|	...	0728	...	|	...	...	|	|	...	0928	...	...	|	...	1128	|	...	...	|	...	1328
◧	St Michael d.	0507	...	|	...	0734	...	|	...	...	|	|	...	0934	...	...	|	...	1134	|	...	...	|	...	1334
205	Knittelfeld d.	0527	...	0648	...	0752	...	|	...	...	0847	|	...	0952	...	...	1047	...	1152	|	...	...	1247	...	1352
213	Zeltweg d.	0534	⚒	0654	...	0758	...	|	...	...	|	|	...	0958	...	...	|	...	1158	|	...	...	|	...	1358
220	Judenburg d.	0542	2	0702	...	0806	...	|	...	...	0859	|	...	1006	...	...	1059	...	1206	|	...	...	1259	...	1406
239	Unzmarkt d.	0558	0608	0718	...	0822	...	|	...	...	0913	|	...	1022	...	...	1113	...	1222	|	...	...	1313	...	1422
276	Friesach **971** a.	...	0642	...	...	0855	...	|	...	...	|	|	...	1055	...	...	1143	...	1255	|	...	...	|	...	1455
309	St Veit an der Glan **971** a.	...	0716	...	...	...	...	|	...	...	1006	|	...	...	...	...	1206	...	...	|	...	...	1406	...	...
329	**Klagenfurt** Hbf **971** a.	...	0738	...	...	...	...	0830	...	...	1020	1000	...	...	...	...	1220	...	...	1230	...	...	1420	...	...
	Villach Hbf **970 971** a.	...	0820t	...	...	...	...	...	...	...	1046	...	...	...	...	...	1246	...	...	...	...	...	1446	...	...

	🚌 857 ☆	RJ 653 H✕	RJ 656 ✕	RJ 537 ✕	RJ 73 P✕	2	🚌 859 ☆	RJ 657 H✕	RJ 750 ✕	RJ 539 ✕	RJ 75 P✕	2	🚌 951 ☆	⚒ 2	EC 159 F✕	RJ 754 ✕	RJ 631 ✕	RJ 77 P✕	2	🚌 953 ☆	Ⓐ 2	D 459 Ⓐ 2	RJ 755 1255 H✕	2	RJ 633 ✕
Wien Hbf **981** d.	...	1158	...	1225	1258	...	...	1358	...	1425	1458	...	...	...	1558	...	1625	1658	...	...	...	1725	1758	...	1825
Wien Meidling **981** d.	...	1205	...	1232	1305	...	...	1405	...	1432	1505	...	...	...	1605	...	1632	1705	...	...	...	1732	1805	...	1832
Wiener Neustadt Hbf **981** a.	...	1228	...	1255	1328	...	...	1428	...	1455	1530	...	...	...	1630	...	1655	1730	...	...	...	1755	1830	...	1855
Wiener Neustadt Hbf **981** d.	...	1232	...	1257	1332	...	...	1432	...	1457	1532	...	...	...	1632	...	1657	1732	...	...	...	1757	1832	...	1857
Semmering **981** d.	...	1315	...	|	|	...	...	|	...	|	1615	...	...	...	|	...	|	1815	...	...	...	1849	1915	...	|
Mürzzuschlag **981** d.	...	1330	...	|	1430	...	...	1530	...	|	1630	...	...	...	1730	...	|	1830	...	...	...	1902	1930	...	|
Graz Hbf **975** d.	1230	|	1326	|	|	*1426*	1430	|	1526	|	|	*1626*	1630	1701	|	1726	|	|	*1826*	1845	1901	...	|	*1926*	|
Bruck an der Mur a.	|	1356	1401	1413	1456	*1501*	|	1556	1601	1613	1656	*1701*	|	|	1756	1801	1813	1856	*1901*	|	|	...	1956	*2001*	2013
Bruck an der Mur **975** ‡ d.	|	1358	...	1415	1458	1506	|	1558	...	1615	1658	1706	|	|	1758	...	1815	1858	1906	|	|	...	1958	2006	2015
Graz Hbf ‡ a.	|	1433	...	|	1533	|	|	1633	...	|	1733	|	|	|	1833	...	|	1933	|	|	|	...	2033	|	|
Leoben Hbf **975** d.	|	...	...	1427	...	1521	|	...	...	1627	...	1721	|	1758	...	...	1827	...	1921	|	1956	...	...	2021	2027
St Michael **975** a.	|	...	...	|	...	1528	|	...	...	|	...	1728	|	|	...	...	|	...	1928	|	2003	...	...	2028	|
St Michael d.	|	...	...	|	...	1534	|	...	...	|	...	1734	|	|	...	...	|	...	1934	|	2009	...	...	2034	|
Knittelfeld d.	|	...	...	1447	...	1552	|	...	...	1647	...	1752	|	1821	...	...	1847	...	1952	|	2027	...	...	→	2047
Zeltweg d.	|	...	...	|	...	1558	|	...	...	|	...	1758	|	1827	...	...	|	...	1958	|	2034	...	...	...	|
Judenburg d.	|	...	...	1459	...	1606	|	...	...	1659	...	1806	|	1835	...	...	1859	...	2006	|	2042	...	...	...	|
Unzmarkt d.	|	...	...	1513	...	1622	|	...	...	1713	...	1822	|	1851	...	...	1913	...	2021	|	2057	...	...	...	|
Friesach **971** a.	|	...	...	1543	...	1655	|	...	...	|	...	1855	|	...	...	...	1943	...	...	|	...	...	...	...	|
St Veit an der Glan **971** a.	|	...	...	1606	...	...	|	...	...	1806	...	...	|	...	...	...	2006	...	...	|	...	...	...	...	2158
Klagenfurt Hbf **971** a.	1430	...	...	1620	...	...	1630	...	...	1820	...	...	1830	...	...	...	2020	...	...	2045	...	...	...	...	2212
Villach Hbf **970 971** a.	...	...	...	1646	...	...	...	...	...	1846	...	...	...	...	...	...	2046	...	...	...	...	...	...	...	2236

FOR NOTES SEE NEXT PAGE →

12 *For explanation of standard symbols see page 4* 461

980 WIEN and GRAZ - KLAGENFURT (- VILLACH)

	2	RJ 79 P✗	2	EN 233 AR	RJ 759 H✗	2	EN 1237 D R	RJ 371 P✗	REX 1975 2
Wien Hbf ... 981 d.	...	1858	...	1923	1958	...	2023	2058	2259
Wien Meidling ... 981 d.	...	1905	...	1931	2005	...	2031	2105	2305
Wiener Neustadt Hbf ... 981 a.	...	1928	...	1956	2028	...	2056	2128	2330
Wiener Neustadt Hbf ... 981 d.	...	1932	...	1958	2032	...	2058	2132	2332
Semmering ... 981 d.	...	|	...	|	|	...	|	|	0029
Mürzzuschlag ... 981 d.	...	2030	...	|	2130	...	|	2230	0043
Graz Hbf ... 975 d.	...	|	*2026*	|	|	*2105*r	|	|	...
Bruck an der Mur ... a.	...	2056	*2101*	2125	2156	*2151*r	2220	2256	...
Bruck an der Mur ... 975 ‡ d.	...	2058	2106	2127	2158	2206	2222	2258	...
Graz Hbf ... ‡ a.	...	2133	|	|	2233	|	|	2333	...
Leoben Hbf ... 975 d.	...	...	2121	2142	...	2219	2236	...	...
St Michael ... 975 a.	←	...	2128	|	...	|	|	...	...
St Michael ... d.	2034	...	2134	|	...	|	|	...	...
Knittelfeld ... d.	2052	...	2152	2205	...	2241	|	...	...
Zeltweg ... d.	2058	...	2158	|	...	2248	|	...	...
Judenburg ... d.	2106	...	2206	|	...	2255	|	...	...
Unzmarkt ... d.	2121	...	2221	|	...	2311	|	...	...
Friesach ... 971 a.	...	...	...	2300	...	...	|	...	...
St Veit an der Glan ... 971 a.	...	...	...	|	...	...	|	...	...
Klagenfurt Hbf ... 971 a.	...	...	...	2335	...	...	0019	...	...
Villach Hbf 970 971 ... a.	...	...	...	2400	...	...	0043	...	...

	REX 1956 Ⓒ 2	D 458 Ⓐ 2	⚒ 2	⚒ 2	RJ 550 G✗	EN 1234 B R	EN 234 AR	⚒ 2	⚒ 2	RJ 72 P✗	Ⓐ 2
Villach Hbf 970 971 ... d.	...	...	...	...	...	0344	0418	...	...	...	...
Klagenfurt Hbf ... 971 d.	...	...	...	...	...	0409	0440	...	...	...	...
St Veit an der Glan ... 971 d.	...	...	...	...	...	|	|	...	...	...	*0501*
Friesach ... 971 d.	...	...	...	...	...	|	|	...	...	...	*0527*
Unzmarkt ... d.	...	...	0437	...	...	|	|	0527	0548	...	0608
Judenburg ... d.	...	...	0453	...	...	|	|	0543	0604	...	0624
Zeltweg ... d.	...	...	0501	...	...	|	|	0552	0612	...	0632
Knittelfeld ... d.	...	...	0507	...	...	|	|	0558	0618	...	0638
St Michael ... a.	...	...	0526	...	...	|	|	|	|	...	0657
St Michael ... 975 d.	...	...	0535	0531	...	|	|	|	|	...	0706
Leoben Hbf ... 975 d.	...	...	0543	0540	...	0608	0627	0623	0642	...	0715
Graz Hbf ... ‡ d.	...	...	|	|	0528	|	|	|	|	0626	|
Bruck an der Mur ... 975 ‡ a.	...	...	0557	|	0603	0621	0639	|	0654	0701	0728
Bruck an der Mur ... d.	...	...	...	|	0605	0624	0641	|	*0708*	0703	...
Graz Hbf ... 975 a.	...	...	...	0633	|	|	|	0714	*0755*	|	...
Mürzzuschlag ... 981 d.	0521	0524	...	...	0634	|	|	...	...	0732	...
Semmering ... 981 d.	0537	0538	...	...	|	|	|	...	...	0746	...
Wiener Neustadt Hbf ... 981 a.	0626	0626	...	...	0728	0751	0801	...	...	0828	...
Wiener Neustadt Hbf ... 981 d.	0630	0630	...	...	0730	0754	0803	...	...	0832	...
Wien Meidling ... 981 a.	0655	0655	...	...	0755	0905y	0839	...	...	0855	...
Wien Hbf ... 981 a.	0702	0702	...	...	0802	0913y	0846	...	...	0902	...

	⚒ 2	2	RJ 530 ✗	RJ 551 ✗	2	2	RJ 74 P✗	🚌 852 ☆	RJ 532 ✗	EC 151 ✗	RJ 558 G✗	🚌 854 ☆	2	RJ 76 P✗	RJ 534 ✗	RJ 559 ✗	EC 158 F✗	🚌 856 ☆	2	RJ 78 P✗	RJ 536 ✗	RJ 653 ✗	RJ 656 G✗	2	RJ 370 P✗
Villach Hbf 970 971 ... d.	...	...	0526	...	0529	...	...	...	0714	...	...	...	...	...	0914	...	...	...	...	...	1114	...	...	...	...
Klagenfurt Hbf ... 971 d.	...	...	0549	...	0607	...	...	0720	0739	...	...	0920	...	...	0939	...	...	1120	...	...	1139	...	...	...	...
St Veit an der Glan ... 971 d.	...	...	0602	...	0627	...	...	|	0753	...	...	|	...	...	0953	...	...	|	...	...	1153	...	...	...	...
Friesach ... 971 d.	...	...	|	...	0700	...	...	|	|	...	...	|	0903	...	1016	...	...	|	1103	...	|	...	...	1303	...
Unzmarkt ... d.	...	0637	|	...	0733	0737	...	|	0847	...	...	|	0937	...	1047	...	...	|	1137	...	1247	...	...	1337	...
Judenburg ... d.	...	0653	|	...	▬	0753	...	|	0901	...	...	|	0953	...	1101	...	...	|	1153	...	1301	...	...	1353	...
Zeltweg ... d.	...	0701	|	...	...	0801	...	|	|	...	...	|	1001	...	|	...	...	|	1201	...	|	...	...	1401	...
Knittelfeld ... d.	...	0707	|	...	*RJ*	0807	...	|	0914	...	...	|	1007	...	1114	...	...	|	1207	...	1314	...	...	1407	...
St Michael ... a.	...	|	|	...	**554**	0826	...	|	|	...	...	|	1026	...	|	...	...	|	1226	...	|	...	...	1426	...
St Michael ... 975 d.	0701	|	|	...		0833	...	|	|	...	...	|	1033	...	|	...	...	|	1233	...	|	...	...	1433	...
Leoben Hbf ... 975 d.	0709	0728	0734	...	G✗	0841	...	|	0934	...	...	|	1041	...	1134	...	...	|	1241	...	1334	...	...	1441	...
Graz Hbf ... ‡ d.	|	|	|	...	0726	|	0826	|	|	...	0926	|	|	1026	|	...	1126	|	|	1226	|	...	1326	|	1426
Bruck an der Mur ... 975 ‡ a.	|	0739	0744	...	0801	0853	0901	|	0944	...	1001	|	1053	1101	1144	...	1201	|	1253	1301	1344	...	1401	1453	1501
Bruck an der Mur ... d.	|	...	0746	0758	0803	*0858*	0903	|	0946	0958	1003	|	*1058*	1103	1146	1158	1203	|	*1258*	1303	1346	1358	1403	*1458*	1503
Graz Hbf ... 975 a.	0801	...	|	0833	|	*0933*	|	0920	|	1033	|	1120	*1133*	|	|	1233	|	1320	*1333*	|	|	1433	|	*1533*	|
Mürzzuschlag ... 981 d.	...	...	|	...	0832	...	0932	...	|	...	1032	...	...	1132	|	...	1232	...	...	1332	|	...	1432	...	1532
Semmering ... 981 d.	...	...	|	...	0846	...	0946	...	|	...	|	...	...	1146	|	...	|	...	...	1346	|	...	|	...	1546
Wiener Neustadt Hbf ... 981 a.	...	...	0903	...	0928	...	1028	...	1103	...	1128	...	...	1228	1303	...	1328	...	...	1428	1503	...	1528	...	1628
Wiener Neustadt Hbf ... 981 d.	...	...	0905	...	0932	...	1032	...	1105	...	1132	...	...	1232	1305	...	1332	...	...	1432	1505	...	1532	...	1632
Wien Meidling ... 981 a.	...	...	0928	...	0955	...	1055	...	1128	...	1155	...	...	1255	1328	...	1355	...	...	1455	1528	...	1555	...	1655
Wien Hbf ... 981 a.	...	...	0935	...	1002	...	1102	...	1135	...	1202	...	...	1302	1335	...	1402	...	...	1502	1535	...	1602	...	1702

	🚌 858 ☆	RJ 538 ✗	RJ 657 ✗	RJ 750 G✗	2	RJ 372 P✗	🚌 950 ☆	RJ 630 ✗	EC 159 ✗	RJ 754 G✗	2	RJ 756 ✗	🚌 952 ☆	RJ 632 L✗	D 15030 ⑦z 2	RJ 755 1255 ✗	EC 150 E✗	2	D 732 ⑦z 2	2	RJ 758 ✗	🚌 954 ☆	EC 30 V✗	RJ 759 ✗	⑤–⑦ 2
Villach Hbf 970 971 ... d.	...	1314	...	...	...	...	...	1514	...	...	...	...	...	1714	...	...	...	...	1814	...	...	...	1914	...	...
Klagenfurt Hbf ... 971 d.	1345	1339	...	...	...	...	1545	1539	...	...	...	...	1745	1739	...	...	...	...	1841	...	...	1945	1939	...	...
St Veit an der Glan ... 971 d.	|	1353	...	...	...	...	|	1553	...	...	...	...	|	1753	...	...	...	...	1854	...	...	|	1953	...	...
Friesach ... 971 d.	|	1416	...	...	1503	...	|	|	...	...	1703	...	|	1816	...	...	...	1903	1919	...	...	|	|	...	...
Unzmarkt ... d.	|	1447	...	...	1537	...	|	1647	...	...	1737	...	|	1847	1856	...	...	1937	|	...	...	|	2047	...	2137
Judenburg ... d.	|	1501	...	...	1553	...	|	1701	...	...	1753	...	|	1901	1910	...	...	1953	2002	...	...	|	2101	...	2153
Zeltweg ... d.	|	|	...	...	1601	...	|	|	...	...	1801	...	|	|	1918	...	...	2001	|	...	...	|	|	...	2201
Knittelfeld ... d.	|	1514	...	...	1607	...	|	1714	...	...	1807	...	|	1914	1924	...	...	2007	2014	...	...	|	2114	...	2207
St Michael ... a.	|	|	...	...	1626	...	|	|	...	...	1826	...	|	|	|	...	...	2026	|	←	...	|	|	...	2226
St Michael ... 975 d.	|	|	...	...	1633	...	|	|	...	...	1833	...	|	|	|	...	...	2033	|	2033	...	|	|	...	2233
Leoben Hbf ... 975 d.	|	1534	...	...	1641	...	|	1734	...	...	1841	...	|	1934	1945	...	...	→	2034	2041	...	|	2134	...	2241
Graz Hbf ... ‡ d.	|	|	...	1526	|	1626	|	|	...	1726	|	1826	|	|	|	...	1926	...	|	|	2026	|	|	...	|
Bruck an der Mur ... 975 ‡ a.	|	1544	...	1601	1653	1701	|	1744	...	1801	1853	1901	|	1944	|	...	2001	...	2044	2053	2101	|	2144	...	2253
Bruck an der Mur ... d.	|	1546	1558	1603	*1658*	1703	|	1746	1758	1803	*1858*	1903	|	1946	|	1958	2003	...	2046	*2058*	2103	|	2146	2158	*2258*
Graz Hbf ... 975 a.	1545	|	1633	|	*1733*	|	1745	|	1833	|	*1933*	|	1945	|	2030	2033	|	...	|	*2133*	|	2145	|	2233	*2333*
Mürzzuschlag ... 981 d.	...	|	...	1632	...	1732	...	|	...	1832	...	1932	...	|	...	...	2032	...	|	...	2132	...	|	...	...
Semmering ... 981 d.	...	|	...	1646	...	1746	...	|	...	1846	...	|	...	|	...	...	|	...	|	...	|	...	|	...	...
Wiener Neustadt Hbf ... 981 a.	...	1703	...	1728	...	1828	...	1903	...	1928	...	2028	...	2103	...	...	2128	...	2203	...	2228	...	2303	...	...
Wiener Neustadt Hbf ... 981 d.	...	1705	...	1732	...	1832	...	1905	...	1932	...	2032	...	2105	...	...	2132	...	2205	...	2232	...	2305	...	...
Wien Meidling ... 981 a.	...	1728	...	1755	...	1855	...	1928	...	1955	...	2055	...	2128	...	...	2155	...	2228	...	2255	...	2328	...	...
Wien Hbf ... 981 a.	...	1735	...	1802	...	1902	...	1935	...	2002	...	2102	...	2135	...	...	2202	...	2235	...	2302	...	2335	...	...

Local stopping trains **BRUCK AN DER MUR - GRAZ - SPIELFELD-STRASS** (for international services Graz - Spielfeld Straß - Maribor - Ljubljana / Zagreb see Table **1315**).

km				Ⓐ				◇									◇			⚒			⚒	⚒	
	Bruck a. d. Mur ... d.	0457	0608	0650	*0708*	*0808*	*0908*	0958	*1008*	*1108*	*1208*	*1308*	*1408*	*1508*	*1608*	*1708*	1758	*1808*	*1908*	*2008*	*2108*	2208	2208	2308	...
	Graz Hbf ... a.	0544	0655	0729	*0755*	*0855*	*0955*	1033	*1055*	*1155*	*1255*	*1355*	*1455*	*1555*	*1655*	*1755*	1833	*1855*	*1955*	*2055*	*2155*	2255	2255	2355	...
0	**Graz** Hbf ... 1315 d.	0558	0708	0738	0808	0908	1008	1038	1108	1208	1308	1408	1508	1608	1708	1808	1838	1908	2008	2108	2208	...	2308	...	0008
9	Flughafen Graz ✈ ... d.	0610	0720	0750	0820	0920	1020	|	1120	1220	1320	1420	1520	1620	1720	1820	|	1920	2020	2120	2220	...	2320	...	0020
35	Leibnitz ... d.	0636	0750	0820	0850	0950	1047	1059	1150	1250	1350	1450	1550	1650	1749	1847	1859	1950	2047	2147	2247	...	2347	...	0047
47	**Spielfeld-Straß** ... 1315 a.	0648	0800	0830	0900	1000	1100	1108	1200	1300	1400	1500	1600	1700	1759	1900	1908	2000	2057	2157	2257	...	2357	...	0057

	Ⓐ				Ⓐ						◇									◇		⚒		⚒	
Spielfeld-Straß ... 1315 d.	0357	0431	0504	...	0549	0609	0709	0809	0909	1009	1048	1109	1209	1309	1409	1509	1609	1709	1809	1848	1909	2009	2109	2209	...
Leibnitz ... d.	0408	0442	0515	...	0600	0620	0720	0820	0920	1020	1058	1120	1220	1320	1420	1520	1620	1720	1820	1858	1920	2020	2120	2220	...
Flughafen Graz ✈ ... d.	0436	0510	0542	...	0628	0649	0748	0848	0948	1048	|	1148	1248	1348	1448	1548	1648	1748	1848	|	1948	2048	2148	2248	...
Graz Hbf ... 1315 a.	0447	0521	0554	...	0639	0701	0759	0859	0959	1059	1120	1159	1259	1359	1459	1559	1659	1759	1859	1920	1959	2059	2159	2259	...
Graz Hbf ... d.	0449	...	0559e	0611	0642	*0708*	*0805*	*0905*	*1005*	*1105*	1126	*1205*	*1305*	*1405*	*1505*	*1605*	*1705*	*1805*	*1905*	1926	*2005*	*2105*	*2205*	2305	0005
Bruck a. d. Mur ... a.	0535	...	0641e	0657	0728	*0754*	*0851*	*0951*	*1051*	*1151*	1201	*1251*	*1351*	*1451*	*1551*	*1651*	*1751*	*1851*	*1951*	2001	*2051*	*2151*	*2251*	2351	0051

A – *ÖBB nightjet.* 1, 2 cl., 2 cl. and (2) Milano - Wien and v.v.; 1, 2 cl., 2 cl. and (2) (**40294/40233**) Roma - Bologna - Venezia - Wien and v.v.
B – *ÖBB nightjet.* Fom Villach on ⑤⑦ Apr. 7 - Oct. 29 (also Apr. 18, May 2, June 6, Aug. 16). Previous night from Livorno. 1, 2 cl., 2 cl. and (2) Livorno - Pisa - Firenze - Bologna - Wien.
D – *ÖBB nightjet.* ③⑤ Apr. 5 - Oct. 27 (also Apr. 16, 30, June 4, Aug. 14). 1, 2 cl., 2 cl. and (2) Wien - Bologna - Firenze - Pisa - Livorno.
E – EMONA – (12) and ✗ Ljubljana - Maribor - Spielfeld-Straß 🚌 - Graz - Wien and v.v.
F – CROATIA – (12) and ✗ Zagreb - Maribor - Spielfeld-Straß 🚌 - Graz - Wien and v.v.
G – To Flughafen Wien ✈ (arrives 25 minutes after Wien Hbf).
H – From Flughafen Wien ✈ (departs 25 minutes before Wien Hbf).
L – To / from Lienz (Table **971**).
P – (12) and ✗ Graz - Wien - Břeclav 🚌 - Praha and v.v.
R – Ⓡ for journeys from / to Italy.
V – (12) and ✗ Wien - Villach - Tarvisio 🚌 - Udine - Venezia and v.v.

e – Ⓐ only.
h – † only.
r – ⚒ only.
t – Change trains at Klagenfurt on Ⓐ to July 7 / from Sept. 11.
y – On ⑦ arrives Wien Meidling 0826, Wien Hbf 0832.
z – Also Dec. 26, Apr. 17, May 1, June 5; not Dec. 25, Apr. 16, 30, June 4.

◇ – *EC* train (see main panel, also Table **1315**).
‡ – For other local journeys see panel below main table.
▬ – Leoben - St Michael is *10 km*. St Michael - Knittelfeld is *22 km*.
☆ – **ÖBB** *Intercitybus*. Rail tickets valid. 1st and 2nd class. 🍸 in 1st class. Number of seats limited so reservation is recommended.

Local trains WIEN - WIENER NEUSTADT - MÜRZZUSCHLAG 981

WIEN - WIENER NEUSTADT ⊡

km		⚒P						P
0	**Wien** Praterstern d.	0418	0518	0548		2218	2248	2348
2	**Wien** Mitte-Landstraße d.	0422	0522	0552	and at	2222	2252	2352
5	**Wien** Hbf d.	0429	0529	0559	the same	2229	2259	2359
9	**Wien** Meidling ● d.	0437	0537	0607	minutes	2237	2307	0007
21	Mödling d.	0449	0549	0619	past each	2249	2319	0019
32	Baden d.	0457	0557	0627	hour until	2257	2327	0027
54	**Wiener Neustadt** Hbf a.	0521	0621	0649		2321	2349	0049

	P	P	P	P	P						P
Wiener Neustadt Hbf d.	0533	0603	0633	0703	0733	0811	0838		2111	2138	2238
Baden d.	0553	0623	0653	0723	0753	0832	0902	and at	2132	2202	2302
Mödling d.	0600	0630	0700	0730	0800	0839	0909	the same	2139	2209	2309
Wien Meidling ● a.	0612	0642	0712	0742	0812	0853	0923	minutes	2153	2223	2323
Wien Hbf a.	0620	0650	0720	0750	0820	0859	0929	past each	2159	2229	2329
Wien Mitte-Landstraße a.	0628	0658	0728	0758	0828	0907	0937	hour until	2207	2237	2337
Wien Praterstern a.	0632	0702	0732	0802	0832	0911	0941		2211	2241	2341

WIENER NEUSTADT - PAYERBACH-REICHENAU - MÜRZZUSCHLAG ⊡

km		⚒P							Q	P		⚒	†	⚒		Ⓒ	Ⓐ	Ⓒ	Ⓐ	Ⓒ	Ⓐ	Ⓒ	ⒶY	Ⓐ	Ⓒ
0	**Wiener Neustadt** Hbf d.	0535	0635	0735	and	2035	2135	2235	2332	0102		...	...	...	...	...	...	...	...	...	...	...	1757	...	...
14	Neunkirchen NÖ d.	0546	0646	0746	hourly	2046	2146	2246	2343	0113	A	...	...	...	...	...	...	...	...	...	...	...	|	...	...
27	Gloggnitz d.	0559	0659	0759	until	2059	2159	2259	2355	0126	L	...	...	...	...	...	...	...	...	...	...	...	1813	...	...
34	Payerbach-Reichenau d.	0608	0708	0808		2108	2208	2308	0005	0135	S	0710	0811	0838	1011	1211	1238	1411	1538	1611	1738	1811	1823	1938	2011
55	Semmering a.	...	...	...		...	...	...	0029	...	O	0734	0840	0907	1040	1240	1307	1440	1607	1640	1807	1840	1848	2007	2040
69	**Mürzzuschlag** a.	...	...	...		...	...	...	0043	...		...	0856	...	1056z	1256	1323	1456	...	1656	...	1856	1902	2023	2056

	ⒶD	ⒶP	ⒶG	ⒸP	⚒P	ⒸR	ⒶW	H	P				P		⚒		Ⓒ	Ⓐ	Ⓒ	Ⓐ	Ⓒ	Ⓐ	Ⓒ	Ⓐ	Ⓒ
Mürzzuschlag d.	0345	...	...	...	...	0521	0524	...	*0603*	...		...	...		...	0907t	1107	...	1307	1337	1507	...	1700	...	1900
Semmering d.	0400	...	...	...	...	0537	0538	...	*0618*	...		...	...	A	0752	0922	1122	1152	1322	1352	1522	1652	1715	1852	1915
Payerbach-Reichenau d.	0427	0452	0527	0527	0552	0604	0604	0627	0655	0755	and	1955	2158	L	0822	0952	1152	1222	1352	1422	1552	1722	1752	1922	1952
Gloggnitz d.	0436	0501	0536	0536	0601	0612	0612	0636	0704	0804	hourly	2004	2217	S	...	...	...	...	...	...	...	...	...	...	...
Neunkirchen NÖ d.	0447	0512	0547	0547	0612	|	|	0647	0715	0815	until	2015	2228	O	...	...	...	...	...	...	...	...	...	...	...
Wiener Neustadt Hbf a.	0458	0522	0558	0558	0622	0626	0626	0658	0725	0825		2025	2238		...	...	...	...	...	...	...	...	...	...	...

D – To Wien Meidling (a. 0529) and Wien Hbf (a. 0536).
G – To Wien Meidling (a. 0629) and Wien Hbf (a. 0638).
H – On Ⓐ to Wien Meidling (a. 0729). On Ⓒ note **P** applies.
P – (2) Wien Praterstern - Wiener Neustadt - Payerbach-Reichenau and v.v.
Q – *REX* **1975**. From Wien (Table **980**).

R – *REX* **1956**. To Wien (Table **980**).
W – *D* **458**. To Wien (Table **980**).
Y – *D* **459**. From Wien (Table **980**).
t – † only.

z – Ⓒ only.
⊡ – Only selected services are shown Wien - Wiener Neustadt - Payerbach-Reichenau and v.v. Additional trains run at peak times. See Table **980** for long-distance services.

WIEN - BŘECLAV 982

Austrian Holiday dates apply

km		2	*RJ* 70 ✕	*EC* 104 ✕♠	2	*RJ* 72 ✕	2	2 Ⓐ	*RJ* 74 ✕	2	*RJ* 76 ✕	*EC* 102 ✕♠	2	*RJ* 78 ✕	2 Ⓐ	2	*RJ* 370 ✕	2 Ⓐ	*D* 100 B	2	*RJ* 372 ✕	2	2	2	*EN* 40406 2★
	Graz Hbf 980 d.	...	...	...	...	0626	...	...	0826	...	1026	...	...	1226	...	...	1426	...	...	...	1626	...	...	...	...
	Wiener Neustadt Hbf **980/1** d.	0516e	...	...	0716e	0832	0911	1011	1032	1111	1232	...	1311	1432	1438	1511	1632	1638	...	1711	1832	1911	2011	2138	...
0	**Wien** Meidling **980/1** d.	0557	...	...	0800	0857	0954	1054	1057	1154	1257	...	1354	1457	1524	1554	1657	1724	...	1754	1857	1954	2054	2224	...
4	**Wien** Hbf **980/1** d.	0603	0710	0810	0806	0910	1000	1100	1110	1200	1310	1410	1400	1510	1530	1600	1710	1730	1810	1800	1910	2000	2100	2230	2250
7	**Wien** Mitte-Landstraße. **981** d.	0611	|	|	0814	|	1008	1108	|	1208	|	|	1408	|	1538	1608	|	1738	|	1808	|	2008	2108	2238	|
9	**Wien** Praterstern **981** d.	0615	|	|	0818	|	1012	1112	|	1212	|	|	1412	|	1542	1612	|	1742	|	1812	|	2012	2112	2242	|
14	**Wien** Floridsdorf d.	0623	|	|	0826	|	1020	1120	|	1220	|	|	1420	|	1550	1620	|	1750	|	1820	|	2020	2120	2250	|
40	Gänserndorf d.	0645	|	|	0848	|	1042	1142	|	1242	|	|	1442	|	1612	1642	|	1812	|	1842	|	2042	2142	2323	|
74	Hohenau 🏛 a.	0717	|	|	0920	|	1114	1214	|	1314	|	|	1514	|	1644	1714	|	1842	|	1914	|	2114	2214	2355	|
92	**Břeclav** 🏛 a.	...	0804	0904	0935	1004	1129	...	1204	...	1404	1504	1529c	1604	1658	1729c	1804	1857	1904	1929c	2004	...	...	...	2349
	Praha hlavní **1150** a.	...	1106	...	...	1306	...	...	1506	...	1706	...	...	1906	...	...	2106	...	...	...	2313	...	...	...	0345

	EN 40477 2★	2 Ⓐ	2	*D* 101 B	2	*RJ* 71 ✕	2	*RJ* 73 ✕	2	*EC* 103 ♠✕	2 Ⓐ	*RJ* 75 ✕	2	2 Ⓐ	*RJ* 77 ✕	2	2 Ⓐ	*RJ* 79 ✕	2	*EC* 105 ♠✕	2 Ⓐ	*RJ* 371 ✕	2	*RJ* 373 ✕	2
Praha hlavní **1150** d.	2358	...	...	...	...	0650	...	0852	...	...	...	1052	...	...	1252	...	...	1452	...	...	...	1652	...	1852	...
Břeclav 🏛 d.	0549	0557	0627k	0855	...	0955	1027	1155	1227	1255	...	1355	...	...	1555	1627c	1727	1755	1827c	1855	1927	1955	2027c	2155	...
Hohenau 🏛 d.	|	0612	0642	|	0842	|	1042	|	1242	|	1342	|	1442	1542	|	1642	1742	|	1842	|	1942	|	2042	|	2242
Gänserndorf d.	|	0645	0715	|	0915	|	1115	|	1315	|	1415	|	1515	1615	|	1715	1815	|	1915	|	2015	|	2115	|	2315
Wien Floridsdorf a.	|	0708	0738	|	0938	|	1138	|	1338	|	1438	|	1538	1638	|	1738	1838	|	1938	|	2038	|	2138	|	2338
Wien Praterstern **981** a.	|	0717	0747	|	0947	|	1147	|	1347	|	1447	|	1547	1647	|	1747	1847	|	1947	|	2047	|	2147	|	2347
Wien Mitte-Landstraße . **981** a.	|	0721	0751	|	0951	|	1151	|	1351	|	1451	|	1551	1651	|	1751	1851	|	1951	|	2051	|	2151	|	2351
Wien Hbf **980/1** a.	0655	0728	0758	0949	0958	1049	1158	1249	1358	1349	1458	1449	1558	1658	1649	1758	1858	1849	1958	1949	2058	2049	2158	2249	2358
Wien Meidling **980/1** a.	...	0734	0804	...	1004	1103	1204	1303	1404	...	1504	1503	1604	1704	1703	1804	1904	1903	2004	...	2104	2103	2204	...	0004
Wiener Neustadt Hbf **980/1** a.	...	0821	0849	...	1049	1128	1249	1328	1449	...	1549	1530	1649	1749	1730	1849	1949	1928	2049	...	2149	2128	2249	...	0049
Graz Hbf **980** a.	...	...	...	...	...	1333	...	1533	...	...	...	1733	...	...	1933	...	...	2133	...	...	...	2333	...	...	...

B – To / from Bohumín (Table **1155**).
c – Ⓒ only.
e – Ⓐ only.
k – ⑥ only.
♠ – International service to / from Poland (see Table **99**).
★ – See Tables **60** and **99** for details of through cars.

WIEN - RETZ - ZNOJMO 983

2nd class only; Austrian holiday dates apply

km		⚒	⚒		⚒d	⑥		Ⓐ		Ⓐ		Ⓐ		Ⓐ	Ⓐ	Ⓐ		Ⓐ	Ⓐ	Ⓐ		Ⓐ			
0	**Wien** Meidling d.	...	0545	0645	0745	0745	0845	0945	1045	1145	1245	1345	1445	1515	1545	1615	1645	1715	1745	1815	1845	1945	2045	2151	2315
4	**Wien** Hbf d.	...	0551	0651	0751	0751	0851	0951	1051	1151	1251	1351	1451	1521	1551	1621	1651	1721	1751	1821	1851	1951	2051	2157	2321
7	**Wien** Mitte-Landstraße d.	...	0559	0659	0759	0759	0859	0959	1059	1159	1259	1359	1459	1529	1559	1629	1659	1729	1759	1829	1859	1959	2059	2205	2329
9	**Wien** Praterstern d.	...	0603	0703	0803	0803	0903	1003	1103	1203	1303	1403	1503	1533	1603	1633	1703	1733	1803	1833	1903	2003	2103	2209	2333
14	**Wien** Floridsdorf d.	...	0611	0711	0811	0811	0911	1011	1111	1211	1311	1411	1511	1541	1611	1641	1711	1741	1811	1841	1911	2011	2111	2217	2341
34	Stockerau d.	...	0628	0728	0828	0828	0928	1028	1128	1228	1328	1428	1528	1601	1628	1701	1728	1801	1828	1901	1928	2028	2128	2243	2358
60	Hollabrunn d.	...	0645	0745	0845	0845	0945	1045	1145	1245	1345	1445	1545	1623	1645	1723	1745	1823	1845	1923	1945	2045	2154	...	0024
90	**Retz** 🏛 d.	0617	0712	0815	0912	0915	1012	1112	1215	1312	1415	1512	1615	1652	1712	1752	1815	1852	1912	1952	2012	2112	2220	...	0050
96	Šatov 🏛 a.	0625	...	0823	...	0923	...	...	1223	...	1423	...	1623	...	...	...	1823n	...	...	...	...	...	...	...	...
107	**Znojmo** a.	0634	...	0834	...	0934	...	...	1234	...	1434	...	1634	...	...	...	1834n	...	...	...	...	...	...	...	...

	Ⓐ	Ⓐ	Ⓐ	⑥	Ⓒ	Ⓒ	Ⓐ	Ⓐ	⚒	Ⓐ		⚒		⑥	⚒		Ⓐ		Ⓐ		Ⓐ		Ⓐ		
Znojmo d.	...	...	...	...	...	...	...	...	...	...	0653r	...	0855	0955	...	...	...	1255	...	1455	...	1655	...	1855n	...
Šatov 🏛 d.	...	...	...	...	...	...	...	...	...	...	0704r	...	0906	1006	...	...	...	1306	...	1506	...	1706	...	1906n	...
Retz 🏛 d.	0359	0434	0510	0510	...	0514t	0530	0552	0617	0636	0715	0817	0917	1017	1017	1117	1217	1317	1417	1517	1617	1717	1817	1917	2017
Hollabrunn d.	0427	0502	0539	0539	...	0543	0558	0620	0645	0706	0745	0845	0945	1045	1045	1145	1245	1345	1445	1545	1645	1745	1845	1945	2045
Stockerau d.	0444	0527	0556	0556	...	0615	0625	0640	0702	0728	0802	0902	1002	1102	1102	1202	1302	1402	1502	1602	1702	1802	1902	2002	2102
Wien Floridsdorf a.	0459	0547	0617	0617	0630	0641	0647	0659	0717	0747	0817	0917	1017	1117	1117	1217	1317	1417	1517	1617	1717	1817	1917	2017	2117
Wien Praterstern a.	0511	0556	0626	...	0638	0650	0656	0708	0726	0756	0826	0926	1026	1126	1126	1226	1326	1426	1526	1626	1726	1826	1926	2026	2126
Wien Mitte-Landstraße a.	0515	0600	0630	...	0642	0654	0700	0712	0730	0800	0830	0930	1030	1130	1130	1230	1330	1430	1530	1630	1730	1830	1930	2030	2130
Wien Hbf a.	0522	0607	0637	...	0649	0701	0707	0719	0737	0807	0837	0937	1037	1137	1137	1237	1337	1437	1537	1637	1737	1837	1937	2037	2137
Wien Meidling a.	0528	0613	0643	...	0655	0707	0713	0725	0743	0813	0843	0943	1043	1143	1143	1243	1343	1443	1543	1643	1743	1843	1943	2043	2143

WIEN - STOCKERAU - ABSDORF-HIPPERSDORF

km											
	Wien Meidling d.	0533	0751	0951	1151	1351	1521	...	1751	1851	1951
	Wien Hbf d.	0539	0757	0957	1157	1357	1527	...	1757	1857	1957
	Wien Mitte-Landstraße d.	0547	0805	1005	1205	1405	1535	...	1805	1905	2005
	Wien Praterstern d.	0551	0809	1009	1209	1409	1539	...	1809	1909	2009
	Wien Floridsdorf d.	0559	0817	1017	1217	1417	1547	...	1817	1917	2017
0	Stockerau ✣ d.	0631j	0845	1045	1245	1445	1613	1631	1845	1945	2045
17	**Absdorf-Hippersdorf** ✣ a.	0646	0900	1100	1300	1500	...	1646	1900	2000e	2100

									Ⓐ
Absdorf-Hippersdorf ✣ d.	0626	*0811*	0928	1128	1328	1528	*1811*	1928	2028
Stockerau ✣ d.	0645	0845	0945	1145	1345	1545	1845	1945	2045
Wien Floridsdorf a.	0711	0911	1011	1211	1411	1611	1911	2011	2111
Wien Praterstern a.	0720	0920	1020	1220	1420	1620	1920	2020	2120
Wien Mitte-Landstraße a.	0724	0924	1024	1224	1424	1624	1924	2024	2124
Wien Hbf a.	0731	0931	1031	1231	1431	1631	1931	2031	2131
Wien Meidling a.	0737	0937	1037	1237	1437	1637	1937	2037	2137

d – Runs daily May 1 - Oct. 28.
e – Ⓐ only.
j – Arrives 0622.
n – Not Dec. 24, 25, 31.
r – ⚒ only.
t – † only.
✣ – **Additional journeys** Stockerau - Absdorf-Hippersdorf and v.v.
From Stockerau at 0435Ⓐ, 0501Ⓐ, 0531Ⓐ, 0731Ⓐ, 1345Ⓐ, 1545Ⓐ and 1731Ⓐ.
From Absdorf-Hippersdorf at 0458Ⓐ, 0528Ⓑ, 0711Ⓐ, 1428Ⓐ, 1628Ⓐ, 1711Ⓐ and 1911Ⓐ.

984 WIENER NEUSTADT - PUCHBERG am Schneeberg - HOCHSCHNEEBERG
2nd class only

WIENER NEUSTADT - **PUCHBERG** am Schneeberg *28 km*. Journey time: ± 45 minutes.
From Wiener Neustadt at 0043 **t**, 0611 Ⓐ, 0737, 0837 **A**, 0937, 1037 **E**, 1137, 1237 **E**, 1337, 1437 **E**, 1537, 1637, 1737, 1837 Ⓑ, 1937, 2037 Ⓑ and 2137.
From Puchberg at 0454 Ⓐ, 0524 Ⓐ, 0554 ⚒, 0624 Ⓐ, 0638 Ⓒ, 0647 Ⓐ, 0738, 0838, 0938 **C**, 1038, 1138 **E**, 1238, 1338 **E**, 1438, 1538 **E**, 1638, 1738, 1838, 1938 Ⓑ and 2038 ⑤⑥ **t**.

PUCHBERG am Schneeberg - **HOCHSCHNEEBERG** *Schneebergbahn* (narrow-gauge rack railway). *9 km*. Journey time: ± 40 minutes.
Services run **Apr. 30 - Oct. 26, 2017** subject to demand and weather conditions. **Operator**: NÖ Schneebergbahn GmbH, Bahnhofplatz 1, A-2734 Puchberg. ✆ +43 (0) 2636 3661 20.
From Puchberg at 0900, 1030, 1200, 1400, 1530. **From Hochschneeberg** at 0945, 1115, 1315, 1445, 1615. Additional trains operate during July and August, also at other times when there is sufficient demand. A steam service operates on ⑦ July 2 - Sept. 3 (also Aug. 15): Departs Puchberg 1120, departs Hochschneeberg 1517 (journey time ± 80 minutes – special fares apply).

A – Ⓐ (daily Apr. 24 - Nov. 3).
C – Ⓒ Apr. 29 - Nov. 1.
E – ⚒ (daily Apr. 24 - Nov. 4).
t – Also Dec. 25, Jan. 5, Apr. 16, 30, May 24, June 4, 14, Aug. 14, Oct. 25, 31, Dec. 7.

985 FLUGHAFEN WIEN ✈ Schwechat
CAT ★; S-Bahn (2nd class only)

km		Ⓐ			★		★		★			★		★		★						
0	**Wien** Praterstern ..... d.	0415	0445	0515	...	0545	...	0615	...	0645	and at the same	...	2215	...	2245	...	...	2345	...	...	...	...
2	**Wien** Mitte-Landstraße ..... d.	0419	0449	0519	0536	0549	0606	0619	0636	0649	minutes past	2206	2219	2236	2249	2306	...	2349	...	...	...	...
21	**Flughafen Wien** ✈ ..... a.	0442	0512	0542	0552	0612	0622	0642	0652	0712	each hour until	2222	2242	2252	2312	2322	...	0012	...	...	...	...

		Ⓐ			★		★		★		★		★		★			★		★		★
Flughafen Wien ✈ ..... d.	0018	0448	0518	0548	0609	0618	0639	0645	0709	0718	0739	0745	0809	0818	0839	0848	and at the same	2239	2248	2309	2318	2339
Wien Mitte-Landstraße ..... a.	0043	0513	0543	0613	0625	0643	0655	0710	0725	0743	0755	0810	0825	0843	0855	0913	minutes past	2255	2313	2325	2343	2355
Wien Praterstern ..... a.	0047	0517	0547	0617	...	0647	...	0714	...	0747	...	0814	...	0847	...	0917	each hour until	...	2317	...	2347	...

★ – *City Airport Train (CAT)*. Non-stop service with special fares.

RJ trains **Wien Hbf** - **Flughafen Wien** ✈ and v.v. Journey time: 15 – 18 minutes. Most trains run from / to Salzburg, Linz and St Pölten (see Table **950**) or Graz (Table **980**).
From Wien Hbf at 0542, 0612, 0642 and at 12 and 42 minutes past each hour until 2112, 2142 and 2212. Variations: Wien Hbf d. 0939 (not 0942), 1539 (not 1542) and 1839 (not 1842).
From Flughafen Wien ✈ at 0633, 0703, 0733 and at 03 and 33 minutes past each hour until until 2203, 2233 and 2303.

🚌 *Vienna Airport Lines*: Wien Westbahnhof (Europaplatz) – Flughafen Wien ✈ and v.v. Journey time: 45 minutes Westbahnhof - Flughafen / 35 minutes Flughafen - Westbahnhof.
🚌 From **Wien Westbahnhof**: 0515, 0545 and every 30 minutes until 2315, 2345. 🚌 From **Flughafen Wien** ✈: 0005, 0605, 0635 and every 30 minutes until 2305, 2335.

🚌 ÖBB-Postbus / Slovak Lines: **Bratislava**, AS Mlynské nivy (bus station) – **Flughafen Wien** ✈ and v.v. Journey time: 60 minutes.
Reservation recommended ✆ +43 (0) 810 222333-6 or +421 2 55422734. Please note that a much reduced service operates on Dec. 24, 25, 26, 31, Jan. 1.
🚌 From **Bratislava** AS Mlynské nivy at 0400, 0500 and hourly until 1500; then 1530 ①–⑤, 1555, 1700, 1755, 1900, 2000 and 2205.
🚌 From **Flughafen Wien** ✈ at 0630, 0730, 0800 ①–⑤, 0830, 0930 and hourly until 2230 and 0000.

986 GRAZ - SZENTGOTTHÁRD - SZOMBATHELY
ÖBB, GySEV •; 2nd class only

km		A ✓	W		W				Ⓒ W	Ⓐ		Ⓐ ◇		Ⓐ		Ⓐ	P	Ⓐ ⊡		⚒		Ⓐ		⚒		
0	**Graz** Hbf ..... d.	0608	0708	0808	0908	1008	1108	1208	1308	1308	1408	1438	1508	1538	1608	1638	1708	1738	1808	1838	1908	1938	2008	2108	2213	0008
29	Gleisdorf ..... d.	0650	0750	0850	0950	1050	1150	1250	1350	1350	1450	1513	1550	1613	1650	1713	1750	1813	1850	1913	1950	2013	2050	2150	2253	0047
53	Feldbach ..... d.	0715	0814	0914	1014	1114	1214	1314	1414	1414	1514	1529	1614	1629	1714	1729	1814	1829	1914	1929	2014	2029	2114	2217	2316	0111
62	Fehring ..... d.	0726	0824	0925	1024	1125	1233t	1325	1424	1430	1525	1542	1624	1638	1725	1738	1824	1842	1925	1941	2024	2040	2125	2227	2326	0121
82	**Szentgotthárd** 🏛 ..... a.	0747	...	0947	...	1147	1255	1347	...	1451	1547c	1603	...	*1702*	1747c	*1803*	...	1903	1947c	2002e	...	2101	2146	...	...	...

		Ⓐ	Ⓐ		Ⓐ	Ⓐ	⑥	†	Ⓐ	⚒	Ⓐ H			P		W								N	Ⓐ	B ✓
Szentgotthárd 🏛 ..... d.	...	...	*0445*	0516k	*0532*	...	...	0616	*0619*	0640k	...	...	0816	...	1016	...	1210	1303	1408	*1509*e	1616	1716e	1813	...	...	2147
Fehring ..... d.	0409	0440	0511	0540	0557	0615	0615	0640	0644	0703	0730	0740	0840	0940	1040	1140	1240t	1327	1430	1540	1640	1740	1840	1940	2040	2207
Feldbach ..... d.	0420	0450	0522	0550	0606	0627	0627	0650	0654	0715	0742	0750	0850	0950	1050	1150	1250	1350z	1450z	1550	1650	1750	1850	1950	2050	2217
Gleisdorf ..... d.	0443	0513	0540	0613	0626	0650	0655	0713	0713	0738	0802	0813	0913	1013	1113	1213	1313	1413	1513	1613	1713	1813	1913	2013	2113	2232
Graz Hbf ..... a.	0519	0553	0615	0652	0703	0724	0734	0753	0748	0816	0837	0853	0953	1053	1153	1253	1353	1453	1553	1653	1753	1853	1953	2053	2153	2300

SZENTGOTTHÁRD - SZOMBATHELY •

km		S	Ⓐ ⊖				A ✓	S		S			Ⓐ S			S	S		S		n S		S	Ⓐ		n
0	**Szentgotthárd** 🏛 ..... d.	0406	0506	0606	0636	0706	0822	0836	...	1006	...	1206	1236	1306	1406	1436	1536	1636	1706	1806	1836	...	2006	2106	...	2236
28	Körmend ..... d.	0430	0530	0630	0700	0730	0841	0900	...	1030	...	1230	1300	1330	1430	1500	1600	1700	1730	1830	1900	...	2030	2132	...	2300
64	**Szombathely** ..... a.	0453	0553	0653	0723	0753	0900	0923	...	1053	...	1253	1323	1353	1453	1523	1623	1723	1753	1853	1923	...	2053	2153	...	2323

		S	S		S							Ⓐ		Ⓐ	S	S	S	S	n	Ⓐ ⊖		n	B ✓	n		n
Szombathely ..... d.	0436	0506	0606	0636	0706	...	0906	...	1106	...	1236	1306	1336	1406	1436	1536	1636	1736	1836	1906	...	2036	2058	2136	...	2236
Körmend ..... d.	0500	0530	0630	0700	0730	...	0930	...	1130	...	1300	1330	1400	1430	1500	1600	1700	1800	1900	1930	...	2100	2118	2200	...	2300
Szentgotthárd 🏛 ..... a.	0524	0554	0654	0724	0754	...	0954	...	1154	...	1324	1354	1424	1459	1524	1624	1724	1824	1924	1954	...	2124	2135	2224	...	2324

A – [12] Graz (**317**) - Szentgotthárd (*IC* **317**) - Budapest.
B – [12] Budapest (*IC* **318**) - Szentgotthárd (**318**) - Graz.
H – From Hartberg (Table **995**).
N – From Wiener Neustadt on Ⓒ (Table **995**).
P – To / from Wiener Neustadt on Ⓐ (Table **995**).
S – From / to Sopron (Table **1233**).
W – To / from Wiener Neustadt (Table **995**).
c – Ⓒ only.
e – Ⓐ only.
k – ⑥ only.
n – Not Dec. 24, 31.
t – Arrives 8 – 9 minutes earlier.
z – Arrives 11 – 13 minutes earlier.
◇ – On ⑤ change trains at Fehring (Fehring d. *1546*, Szentgotthárd a. *1607*).
⊡ – Change trains at Fehring on ①–④.
⊖ – *IC* train to / from Budapest (Table **1250**). 🅁 and supplement payable.
✓ – 🅁 and supplement payable in Hungary.
• – Szentgotthárd - Szombathely operated by Győr-Sopron-Ebenfurti Vasút.

990 WIEN - GMÜND - ČESKÉ VELENICE
2nd class only

km				⚒		⚒					⑤ f			Ⓐ	Ⓐ		Ⓐ		B		A			Ⓐ
0	**Wien** Franz-Josefs-Bf.. **991/3** d.	0628	...	0730	0828	0930	1028	1130	1228	1330	1358	1428	1528	1557	1617	1628	1655	1728	1755	1828	1855	1928	2028	2057
1	Wien Spittelau ..... ● **991/3** d.	0631	...	0733	0831	0933	1031	1133	1231	1333	1401	1431	1531	1600	1620	1631	1658	1731	1758	1831	1858	1931	2031	2100
3	Wien Heiligenstadt .. △ **991/3** d.	0634	...	0736	0834	0936	1034	1136	1234	1336	1404	1434	1534	1603	1623	1634	1702	1734	1802	1834	1902	1934	2034	2103
33	Tulln a. d. Donau ..... **991/3** d.	0656	...	0759	0856	0959	1056	1159	1256	1359	|	1456	1556	1626	|	1656	1727	1756	1827	1856	1927	1956	2056	2126
44	Absdorf-Hippersdorf ..... **991** d.	0705	...	0808	0905	1008	1105	1208	1305	1408	|	1505	1605	1634	|	1705	|	1805	1837	1905	|	2005	2105	2135
79	Eggenburg ..... d.	0734	...	0838	0934	1038	1134	1238	1333	1438	1454	1534	1638	1705	1715	1734	1803	1838	1905	1933	2003	2038	2134	2205
89	Sigmundsherberg ..... d.	0742	...	0846	0942	1046	1142	1246	1341	1446	1502	1542	1646	1713	1723	1742	1814	1846	1913	1941	2013	2046	2142	2213
121	Göpfritz an der Wild ..... d.	0806	...	...	1006	...	1206	...	1406	...	1523	1606	...	...	1747	1806	1839	...	1935	2006	2037	...	2206	...
138	Schwarzenau im Waldviertel . d.	0820	...	...	1020	...	1220	...	1419	...	1535	1620	...	...	1801	1820	1851	...	1951	2019	2051	...	2220	...
162	**Gmünd** NÖ ..... a.	0841	...	...	1041	...	1241	...	1440	...	1553	1641	...	...	1822	1841	1914	...	2013	2040	2112	...	2241	...
162	**Gmünd** NÖ 🏛 ..... d.	0844	...	...	1044	...	1244	...	1444	...	...	1646	...	...	...	1844	...	...	...	2044	...	...	...	...
164	**České Velenice** 🏛 ..... **1133** a.	0848	...	...	1048	...	1248	...	1448	...	...	1650	...	...	...	1848	...	...	...	2048	...	...	...	...

	Ⓐ	⚒	⚒	Ⓑ	Ⓐ	Ⓐ		Ⓐ		Ⓐ			⚒						Ⓐ	Ⓒ		†		⑦ w
České Velenice 🏛 ..... **1133** d.	...	...	...	...	...	...	...	...	0602	0707	...	0907	...	1107	...	1307	...	1507	...	...	1705	...	1907	...
Gmünd NÖ 🏛 ..... a.	...	...	...	...	...	...	...	...	0606	0711	...	0911	...	1111	...	1311	...	1511	...	...	1709	...	1911	...
Gmünd NÖ ..... d.	...	0350	...	...	...	0453	0508	...	0612	0714	...	0914	...	1114	...	1314	...	1514	...	...	1712	...	1914	2051
Schwarzenau im Waldviertel .. d.	...	0412	...	...	...	0517	0531	...	0633	0735	...	0935	...	1135	...	1335	...	1535	...	...	1733	...	1935	|
Göpfritz an der Wild ..... d.	...	0425	...	...	...	0532	0545	...	0646	0749	...	0949	...	1149	...	1349	...	1549	...	...	1749	...	1949	2122
Sigmundsherberg ..... d.	0409	0449	0455	0509	0539	0557	0610	0639	0710	0814	0909	1014	1109	1214	1309	1414	1509	1614	1656	1709	1814	1909	2014	2143
Eggenburg ..... d.	0418	0458	0503	0518	0548	0606	0618	0648	0718	0822	0918	1022	1118	1222	1318	1422	1518	1622	1718	1718	1822	1918	2022	2151
Absdorf-Hippersdorf ..... **991** d.	0448	|	0533	0548	0617	|	0648	0717	0748	0852	0948	1052	1148	1252	1348	1456	1548	1652	1748	1748	1852	1948	2052	|
Tulln a. d. Donau ..... **991/3** d.	0457	|	0543	0559	0627	|	0658	0726	0757	0901	0959	1101	1159	1301	1359	1504	1557	1701	1800	1757	1901	1957	2101	|
Wien Heiligenstadt ... △ **991/3** a.	0521	0549	0605	0621	0649	0658	0721	0750	0818	0923	1021	1123	1221	1323	1421	1526	1619	1723	1822	1819	1923	2019	2123	2246
Wien Spittelau ..... ● **991/3** a.	0524	0552	0609	0624	0652	0702	0725	0753	0822	0926	1024	1126	1224	1326	1424	1530	1623	1726	1825	1823	1926	2023	2126	2249
Wien Franz-Josefs-Bf .. **991/3** a.	0527	0555	0612	0627	0655	0705	0728	0756	0825	0929	1027	1129	1227	1329	1427	1533	1626	1729	1828	1826	1929	2026	2129	2252

A – ①–④ (not Dec. 26, Jan. 5, Apr. 17, May 1, 24, 25, June 5, 14, 15, Aug. 14, 15, Oct. 25, 26, 31, Nov. 1, Dec. 7).
B – ①–④ (not Dec. 26, Apr. 17, May 1, 25, June 5, 15, Aug. 15, Oct. 26, Nov. 1).
f – Not Jan. 6, Dec. 8.
w – Also Dec. 26, Apr. 17, May 1, June 5; not Dec. 25, Apr. 16, 30, June 4.
△ – S-Bahn trains run every 10 – 15 minutes from / to Wien Hütteldorf (journey: 21 – 23 minutes).
● – Direct U-Bahn links: Line **U4** – Wien Mitte - Spittelau.
Line **U6** – Wien Meidling - Westbahnhof - Spittelau - Floridsdorf.

2nd class only — WIEN - KREMS an der Donau - EMMERSDORF — 991

km		Ⓐ						Ⓐ	Ⓐ	Ⓒ	Ⓐ		Ⓐ		Ⓐ		Ⓐ					
0	**Wien** Franz-Josefs-Bf 990/3 d.	0504	0604	0704		1404	1504	1532	1601	1604	1632	1704	1732	1804	1832	1904	1932	2004	2104	2204	2307	0008
1	Wien Spittelau ● 990/3 d.	0507	0607	0707	and	1407	1507	1535	1604	1607	1635	1707	1735	1807	1835	1907	1935	2007	2107	2207	2310	0011
3	Wien Heiligenstadt △ 990/3 d.	0510	0610	0710	hourly	1410	1510	1538	1607	1610	1638	1710	1738	1810	1838	1910	1938	2010	2110	2210	2313	0014
33	Tulln a. d. Donau 990/3 d.	0533	0633	0733		1433	1533	1602	1633	1633	1701	1733	1801	1833	1901	1933	2001	2033	2133	2233	2336	0051
44	Absdorf-Hippersdorf 990 d.	0542	0642	0742	until	1442	1542	1611	1642	1642	1711	1742	1811	1842	1911	1942	2011	2042	2142	2242	2345	...
76	**Krems** a. d. Donau a.	0614	0716	0814		1514	1614	1636	1714	1714	1736	1814	1836	1914	1936	2014	2036	2114	2214	2314	0017	...

	Ⓐ	⚒	Ⓐ		Ⓐ	Ⓐ		Ⓐ				Ⓐ	Ⓒ									
Krems a. d. Donau d.	0429	0451	0529	0551	0616	0629	0651	0729	0751		1251	1343	1351	1451	1551	1651	1751	1851	1951	2051	2151	...
Absdorf-Hippersdorf 990 d.	0454	0523	0554	0623	0642	0654	0723	0754	0823	and	1323	1423	1423	1523	1623	1723	1823	1923	2023	2123	2223	...
Tulln a. d. Donau 990/3 d.	0504	0532	0604	0632	0651	0704	0732	0804	0832	hourly	1332	1432	1432	1532	1632	1732	1832	1932	2032	2132	2232	...
Wien Heiligenstadt △ 990/3 a.	0525	0553	0625	0653	0718	0725	0753	0825	0853		1353	1453	1453	1553	1653	1753	1853	1953	2053	2153	2253	...
Wien Spittelau ● 990/3 a.	0528	0557	0628	0657	0721	0728	0757	0828	0857	until	1357	1457	1457	1557	1657	1757	1857	1957	2057	2157	2257	...
Wien Franz-Josefs-Bf 990/3 a.	0531	0600	0631	0700	0724	0731	0800	0831	0900		1400	1500	1500	1600	1700	1800	1900	2000	2100	2200	2300	...

KREMS - EMMERSDORF ⊠

km		R		R		R			
0	**Krems** an der Donau d.	1020	...	1320	...	1620	...	...	...
18	**Spitz** an der Donau d.	1054	...	1354	...	1654	...	...	...
34	**Emmersdorf** an der Donau a.	1120	...	1420	...	1720	...	...	...

	R		R		R			
Emmersdorf an der Donau d.	1145	...	1445	...	1745	...	...	...
Spitz an der Donau d.	1212	...	1512	...	1812	...	...	...
Krems an der Donau a.	1245	...	1545	...	1845	...	...	...

R – Ⓒ Apr. 15 - Oct. 26 (daily July 1 - Oct. 1). Special fares apply.

● – Direct U-bahn links: Line **U4** – Wien Mitte - Spittelau. Line **U6** – Wien Meidling - Westbahnhof - Spittelau - Floridsdorf.
△ – S-Bahn trains run every 10 – 15 minutes from / to Wien Hütteldorf (journey: 21 – 23 minutes).
⊠ – Operated by NÖVOG. ✆ +43 (0) 2742 360 990-99. A connecting 🚌 service operates Emmersdorf - Melk and v.v. Journey time: 10 minutes. From Emmersdorf at 1135 and 1735. From Melk at 1120 and 1720.

2nd class only — LINZ and ST VALENTIN - GREIN - SARMINGSTEIN — 992

km		Ⓐ	Ⓐ	⚒						Ⓐ		⚒		Ⓐ	⚒	Ⓐ	Ⓐ		Ⓐ	Ⓐ		Ⓐ	Ⓒ	Ⓐ	
0	**Linz** Hbf 976 d.	*0430*	0524	*0630*	*0649*	...	0834	...	1034	*1130*	*1230*	*1330*	1434	*1452*	*1530*	1530	1606	1634	1706	*1730*	*1752*	1834	*1930*	1934	*2030*
17	Enns 976 d.	*0448*	0538	|	*0707*	...	0848	...	1048	|	|	|	1448	*1510*	|	|	1620	1648	1720	|	*1810*	1848	|	1948	|
	St Valentin d.	0502	|	0649	0719	...	|	...	|	1150	1250	1350	|	1521	1550	1550	|	|	|	1750	1821	|	1950	|	2050
34	Perg d.	0526	0609	0713	0744	...	0914	...	1114	1214	1314	1414	1514	1545	1614	1614	1644	1714	1745	1814	1845	1914	2014	2014	2113
55	Grein-Bad Kreuzen d.	0601	0644	0744	0816	...	0945	...	1145	1245	1345	1445	1545	1613	1644	1645	1714	1745	1816	1845	1915	1945	2043	2043	2142
57	Grein Stadt d.	0604	0648	0747	0819	...	0948	...	1148	1248	1348	1448	1548	...	...	1648	...	1748	1819	1847	1918	1948	2046	2046	...
62	St Nikola-Struden a.	0610	0655	0753	0825	...	0954	...	1154	1254	1354	1454	1554	...	...	1654	...	1754	1825	...	1924	1954	2052	2052	...
65	Sarmingstein a.	0615	...	...	...	...	...	...	...	...	...	...	...	...	...	...	...	...	1830	...	...	1959	2057	2057	...

km		Ⓐ	Ⓐ		Ⓐ	⚒		Ⓐ			Ⓐ	Ⓐ	Ⓒ	⚒		Ⓐ	Ⓐ	Ⓒ	Ⓐ	Ⓐ	Ⓐ	Ⓒ	Ⓐ	Ⓑ	
0	Sarmingstein d.	...	0511	0525	...	...	0627	...	...	...	...	...	...	...	...	...	...	...	...	...	...	...	1858	...	...
3	St Nikola-Struden d.	...	0516	0530	...	...	0632	0703	0803	1003	...	1203	1203	1303	1403	1503	1603	1603	...	1703	1803	1803	1903	...	1933
8	Grein Stadt d.	0401	0523	0537	...	...	0639	0710	0810	1010	1110	1210	1210	1310	1410	1510	1610	1610	...	1710	1810	1810	1910	1910	1940
10	Grein-Bad Kreuzen d.	0405	0526	0540	0601	0612	0644	0714	0815	1015	1115	1215	1215	1315	1415	1515	1615	1615	1644	1715	1815	1815	1915	1915	1945
31	Perg d.	0432	0554	0610	0630	0641	0713	0744	0844	1044	1144	1244	1244	1344	1444	1544	1644	1644	1714	1744	1844	1844	1944	1944	2014
49	**St Valentin** a.	0454	|	0632	|	0706	|	0807	|	|	1207	|	1307	1407	|	|	|	1707	1738	1807	|	1907	2007	2007	2036
	Enns 976 a.	*0520*	0613	*0647*	0652	|	0736	|	0907	1107	|	1307	|	|	1507	1607	1707	|	*1749*	|	1907	|	|	|	*2049*
	Linz Hbf 976 a.	*0538*	0628	*0704*	0709	*0730*	0752	*0830*	0922	1122	*1230*	1322	*1330*	*1430*	1522	1622	1722	*1730*	*1808*	*1830*	1922	*1930*	*2030*	*2030*	*2108*

2nd class only — ST PÖLTEN - KREMS and TULLN — 993

ST PÖLTEN - KREMS

km		⚒	Ⓐ		Ⓐ					Ⓐ					Ⓐ		Ⓐ		Ⓐ			Ⓐ		T
0	**St Pölten** Hbf d.	0505	0539	0605	0639	0705	0805	0905	1005	1105	1205	1305	1405	1505	1539	1605	1639	1705	1739	1805	1905	2005	2105	2205
10	Herzogenburg d.	0514	0548	0614	0648	0714	0814	0914	1014	1114	1214	1314	1414	1514	1548	1614	1648	1714	1748	1814	1914	2014	2114	2214
30	**Krems** a. d. Donau a.	0541	0626	0641	0726	0741	0841	0941	1041	1141	1241	1341	1441	1541	1612	1641	1712	1741	1812	1841	1941	2041	2141	2241

	⚒	⚒		Ⓐ	⚒	Ⓐ			Ⓐ				Ⓒ	Ⓐ						Ⓐ			T
Krems a. d. Donau d.	0519	0546	0617	0646	0718	0746	0819	0919	1019	1119	1219	1319	1419	1421	1519	1619	1719	1819	1919	2019	2119	...	2219
Herzogenburg d.	0547	0613	0646	0715	0746	0813	0847	0947	1047	1147	1246	1347	1447	1446	1547	1646	1747	1846	1947	2047	2147	...	2247
St Pölten Hbf a.	0555	0622	0655	0724	0755	0822	0855	0955	1055	1155	1255	1355	1455	1455	1555	1655	1755	1855	1955	2055	2155	...	2255

ST PÖLTEN - TULLN - WIEN

km		⚒		⑥	Ⓐ			Ⓐ		Ⓐ		Ⓐ		Ⓐ		Ⓐ		Ⓐ		Ⓐ	P			
0	**St Pölten** Hbf 950 d.	0401	...	0512	0545	0612	0715	0812	0912	...	1112	1212	1312	1412	1512	1612	1712	1812	1912	2012	2118	...	...	...
10	Herzogenburg d.	0415	...	0532	0603	0632	0732	0835	0931	...	1132	1232	1332	1432	1532	1632	1732	1832	1932	2032	2127	...	...	...
40	Tullnerfeld 950 a.	0449	...	0612	0638	0712	0809	0912	1012	...	1212	1312	1412	1512	1612	1712	1812	1912	2012	2112	|	...	...	...
40	Tullnerfeld d.	0450	...	0624	0654	0724	0824	0924	1024	1124	1224	1324	1424	1524	1624	1724	1824	1924	2024	2124	|	...	...	...
46	**Tulln** Stadt d.	0456	...	0630	0700	0730	0830	0930	1030	1130	1230	1330	1430	1530	1630	1730	1830	1930	2030	2130	2200	...	2235	2335
47	**Tulln** a. d. Donau 990/1 a.	0459	...	0632	0702	0732	0832	0932	1032	1132	1232	1332	1432	1532	1632	1732	1832	1932	2032	2132	|	...	2237	2337
77	Wien Heiligenstadt 990/1 a.	0545	...	0715	0745	0815	0915	1015	1115	1215	1315	1415	1515	1615	1715	1815	1915	2015	2115	2215	2226	...	2315	0015
79	Wien Spittelau 990/1 a.	0548	...	0718	0748	0818	0918	1018	1118	1218	1318	1418	1518	1618	1718	1818	1918	2018	2118	2218	2229	...	2318	0018
80	**Wien** Franz-Josefs-Bf 990/1 a.	0551	...	0721	0751	0821	0921	1021	1121	1221	1321	1421	1521	1621	1721	1821	1921	2021	2121	2221	2233	...	2321	0021

	Ⓐ		⚒		⚒		P	Ⓐ		Ⓐ		Ⓐ		Ⓐ		Ⓐ		Ⓐ		Ⓐ			
Wien Franz-Josefs-Bf 990/1 d.	...	...	0508	0538	0608	0638	0655	0738	0838	0938	1038	1138	1238	1338	1438	1538	1638	1738	1838	1938	2038	2138	2238
Wien Spittelau 990/1 d.	...	...	0511	0541	0611	0641	|	0741	0841	0941	1041	1141	1241	1341	1441	1541	1641	1741	1841	1941	2041	2141	2241
Wien Heiligenstadt 990/1 d.	...	...	0514	0544	0614	0644	0703	0744	0844	0944	1044	1144	1244	1344	1444	1544	1644	1744	1844	1944	2044	2144	2244
Tulln a. d. Donau 990/1 d.	0442	...	0559	0627	0658	0727	|	0827	0927	1027	1127	1227	1327	1427	1527	1627	1727	1827	1927	2027	2127	2223	2323
Tulln Stadt d.	0444	...	0601	0629	0700	0729	0745	0829	0929	1029	1129	1229	1329	1429	1529	1629	1729	1829	1929	2029	2129	2225	2325
Tullnerfeld a.	0449	...	0606	0634	0705	0734	0750	0834	0934	1034	1134	1234	1334	1434	1534	1634	1734	1834	1934	2034	2134	...	...
Tullnerfeld 950 d.	0450	...	0619	0647	0718	0747	0810	0847	0947	...	1147	1247	1347	1447	1547	1647	1747	1847	1947	2047	...	...	...
Herzogenburg d.	0525	...	0658	0730	0753	0830	0841	0930	1030	...	1230	1330	1430	1530	1630	1732	1830	1930	2030	2130	...	...	...
St Pölten Hbf 950 a.	0538	...	0714	0744	0805	0844	0850	0944	1044	...	1248	1348	1444	1548	1648	1748	1844	1944	2044	2144	...	...	...

P – May 1 - Oct. 26. 🚃2 Wien Franz-Josefs-Bf - St Pölten - Linz - Passau and v.v.

T – ④⑤⑥ (not Jan. 6, May 25, June 15, Oct. 26, Dec. 8).

Narrow gauge 2nd class only — ST PÖLTEN - MARIAZELL — 994

km				★	C	S 🅁					
0	**St Pölten** Hbf d.	0635	0737	0837	0907	0907	1037	1237	1437	1637	1837
12	Ober Grafendorf d.	0654	0754	0854	0925	0925	1054	1254	1454	1654	1854
31	Kirchberg a. d. Pielach d.	0723	0823	0923	1000	1006	1123	1323	1523	1723	1923
43	Frankenfels ⊗ d.	0741	0841	0941	1021	1031	1141	1341	1541	1741	1941
48	Laubenbachmühle d.	0751	0851	0951	1041	1051	1151	1351	1551	1751	1949
67	Gösing ⊗ d.	0820	0920‡	1020	1115	1140	1220	1420	1620	1820	...
80	Mitterbach ⊗ d.	0845	0945‡	1045	1140	1215	1245	1445	1645	1845	...
84	**Mariazell** a.	0852	0952‡	1052	1147	1222	1252	1452	1652	1852	...

						C	S 🅁	★		
Mariazell d.	...	0907	1107	1307	1507	1527	1522	1607‡	1707	1907
Mitterbach ⊗ d.	...	0913	1113	1313	1513	1533	1529	1613‡	1713	1913
Gösing ⊗ d.	...	0938	1138	1338	1538	1600	1600	1638‡	1738	1938
Laubenbachmühle d.	0655	1010	1210	1410	1610	1633	1650	1710	1810	2010
Frankenfels ⊗ d.	0702	1017	1217	1417	1617	1642	1659	1717	1817	2017
Kirchberg a. d. Pielach d.	0726	1036	1236	1436	1636	1702	1722	1736	1836	2036
Ober Grafendorf d.	0754	1104	1304	1504	1704	1735	1754	1804	1904	2104
St Pölten Hbf a.	0812	1122	1322	1522	1722	1802	1817	1822	1922	2122

C – Runs on Dec. 17, 2016, ⑥ May 6 - Oct. 21, 2017 (also Nov. 25, Dec. 2, 9, 2017). ÖTSCHERBÄR – Traditional loco-hauled electric train. Conveys 🚃12 and ✕.
S – Runs on May 14, June 11, July 9, Aug. 13, Sept. 10, Oct. 8 and Dec. 8 only. Steam train with special fares. Conveys 🚃12 and ✕.

★ – Runs daily. On Dec. 11, 17, 18, 2016, Ⓒ May 1 - Oct. 26 and Ⓒ from Nov. 25, 2017 also conveys first class panorama cars with special fares (🅁).
‡ – Dec. 11 – 18, 2016, May 1 - Oct. 26, 2017 and from Nov. 25, 2017.

⊗ – Trains call on request only.

Operator: NÖVOG. ✆ +43 (0) 2742 360 990 99. www.noevog.at/mariazellerbahn

995 (WIEN -) WIENER NEUSTADT - FEHRING

2nd class only

km		⚒	Ⓐ			Ⓐ			⑤†	Ⓐ		Ⓐ	Ⓐ		Ⓑ	Ⓑ	
0	**Wien** Meidling 980/1 d.	...	...	...	...	...	...	...	1435k	...	...	1735	...	...	...	...	...
44	**Wiener Neustadt** Hbf 980/1 d.	...	0639	0903	1103	...	1303	1503	1503	1633	1703	1801	1833	1903	2003	2103	2139
99	Friedberg d.	...	0802	1002	1202	...	1402	1602	1602	1734	1802	1857	1931	2002	2100	2200	2247
126	Hartberg d.	0621	0835	1035	1234	1326	1435	1634	1635	1812	1835	1929	...	2035	2132e	2232	...
157	Fürstenfeld d.	0653	0910	1110	...	1359	1510	...	1710	...	1910	...	...	2110	...	...	...
177	**Fehring** a.	0723	0937	1137	...	1426	1537	...	1737	...	1937	...	...	2137	...	...	...
	Graz Hbf **986** a.	0837e	1053	1253	...	...	...	...	...	...	2053z	...	...	...	...	...	...

	Ⓐ	Ⓐ	Ⓐ	⚒	Ⓐ	Ⓑ	Ⓐ				Ⓐ			⑤†			†k
Graz Hbf **986** d.	...	...	...	...	...	...	...	...	0708	0908	...	...	1308z	...	...	1708e	...
Fehring d.	...	...	...	...	0501	...	...	0622	0827	1027	1227	...	1427	1627	...	1827	1827
Fürstenfeld d.	...	...	...	...	0530	...	...	0653	0855	1055	1255	...	1455	1655	...	1855	1855
Hartberg d.	...	...	0435	0533	0602	...	...	0724	0927	1127	1327	1327	1527	1727	1727	1929	1929
Friedberg d.	0347	0428	0509	0607	0636	0636	0700	0758	1002	1202	1402	1402	1602	1802	1802	2002	2002
Wiener Neustadt Hbf 980/1 a.	0453	0529	0611	0711	0735	0735	0757	0851	1057	1257	1457	1457	1657	1857	1857	2057	2057
Wien Meidling 980/1 a.	...	0559	0644	0744e	...	...	...	...	...	...	...	...	...	...	...	...	2131
Wien Hbf 980/1 a.	...	0606	0651	...	...	...	...	...	...	...	...	...	...	...	...	...	2138

e – Ⓐ only.
k – † (not Dec. 25, Jan. 6, Apr. 16, 30, June 4, Dec. 8).
z – Ⓒ only.

996 WIEN - BRATISLAVA via Marchegg

2nd class only; Austrian holiday dates apply

km						Ⓐ				
0	**Wien** Hbf d.	0516	0616		1816	1916	2016	2133	2216	...
4	**Wien** Simmering ⊖ d.	0522	0622	and	1822	1922	2022	2139	2222	...
47	Marchegg 🏛 d.	0602	0702	hourly	1902	2002	2102	2230	2302	...
53	Devínska Nová Ves 🏛 d.	0610	0710	until	1910	2010	2110	...	2310	...
66	**Bratislava** hlavná a.	0623	0723		1923	2023	2123	...	2323	...

		Ⓐ					
Bratislava hlavná d.	0537	0605	0637		1837	2037	2237
Devínska Nová Ves 🏛 d.	0551	0619	0651	and	1851	2051	2251
Marchegg 🏛 d.	0601	0629	0701	hourly	1901	2101	2301
Wien Simmering ⊖ a.	0637	0714	0737	until	1937	2137	2337
Wien Hbf a.	0643	0721	0743		1943	2143	2343

⊖ – For U-Bahn connections (line U3) from / to Wien Mitte and Wien Westbahnhof.

997 WIEN - BRATISLAVA via Bruck an der Leitha

2nd class only; Austrian holiday dates apply

km					Ⓐ		Ⓐ		Ⓐ		Ⓐ		Ⓐ		Ⓐ		Ⓐ		Ⓐ						
0	**Wien** Hbf d.	0050	...	0445	0545	0645	0745	0845	0945	1045	1145	1245	1345	1445	1545	1645	1745	1845	1945	2045	...	2250	...	...	...
41	Bruck an der Leitha d.	0129	...	0513	0613	0713	0813	0913	1013	1113	1213	1313	1413	1513	1613	1713	1813	1913	2013	2113	...	2329	...	...	...
69	Kittsee 🏛 a.	0154	...	0538	0638	0738	0838	0938	1038	1138	1238	1338	1438	1538	1638	1738	1838	1938	2038	2138	...	2354	...	...	...
74	**Bratislava** - Petržalka 🏛 ☆ a.	0200	...	0544	0644	0744	0844	0944	1044	1144	1244	1344	1444	1544	1644	1744	1844	1944	2044	2144	...	2400	...	...	...

		Ⓐ	Ⓐ		Ⓐ	Ⓐ		Ⓐ		Ⓐ		Ⓐ		Ⓐ		Ⓐ		Ⓐ		Ⓐ				
Bratislava - Petržalka 🏛 ☆ d.	0427	0515	0546	0615	0646	0715	0815	0915	1015	1115	1215	1315	1415	1515	1615	1715	1815	1915	2015	2115	...	2245	...	...
Kittsee 🏛 d.	0433	0521	0552	0621	0652	0721	0821	0921	1021	1121	1221	1321	1421	1521	1621	1721	1821	1921	2021	2121	...	2251	...	...
Bruck an der Leitha d.	0458	0547	0617	0647	0717	0747	0846	0946	1046	1146	1246	1346	1446	1546	1646	1746	1846	1946	2046	2146	...	2316	...	...
Wien Hbf a.	0539	0616	0646	0716	0746	0815	0914	1014	1114	1214	1314	1414	1514	1614	1714	1815	1914	2014	2114	2214	...	2355	...	...

☆ – Bus 93 links Petržalka station with Bratislava hlavná every 5–10 minutes (journey time ±12 minutes).

☛ Many services run as through trains from / to Deutschkreutz (Table **978**).

998 UNZMARKT - TAMSWEG

2nd class only; Narrow gauge

km		Ⓐ	H		⑤C 🚂	④B 🚂	Ⓒ 🚌	Ⓐ	②A 🚂		Ⓒ	Ⓐ	Ⓒ 🚌	Ⓐ	Ⓐ 🚌			🚌
0	**Unzmarkt** d.	0719	0719	0922	...	...	1118	1122	...	1322	*1518**	1522	1718	1722	...	1922	...	2125
27	Murau-Stolzalpe d.	0759	0800	1000	1015	1015	1200	1200	1250	1400	1600	1600	1800	1758	1805	2000	...	2200
34	St Lorenzen d.	...	0813	1013	1035	1035	1212	1213	1310	1413	1613	1613	1812	...	1816s	2013	...	2208s
44	Stadl an der Mur d.	...	0827	1027	1055	1105	1225	1227	1343	1427	1627	1627	1825	...	1827s	2027	...	2219s
65	**Tamsweg** a.	...	0857	1057	...	1153	1252	1257	1431	1457	1657	1657	1852	...	1850	2057	...	2240

	Ⓐ	Ⓐ	Ⓒ		Ⓐ	Ⓒ 🚌	⑤C 🚂		Ⓒ 🚌	Ⓐ	④B 🚂	Ⓒ	Ⓐ	②A 🚂		Ⓐ 🚌	🚌	Ⓒ 🚌
Tamsweg d.	...	0655	0703	...	0903	0910	...	1103	1310	1303	1335	1503	1503	1615	1703	1820	...	1910
Stadl an der Mur d.	...	0724	0731	...	0931	0930	1110	1131	1330	1331	1425	1531	1531	1710	1731	1840	...	1930
St Lorenzen d.	...	0738	0745	...	0945	0945	1130	1145	1345	1345	1446	1545	1545	1732	1745	1853	...	1945
Murau-Stolzalpe d.	0635	0802	0802	...	1002	1000	1145	1202	1400	1402	1500	1559	1602	1745	1804	1905	2000	2000
Unzmarkt a.	0713	0840	0840	...	1040	1040	...	1240	1440	1440	...	*1640**	1640	...	1842	...	2035	2035

A – June 27 - Sept. 5.
B – June 22 - Sept. 21.
C – July 21 - Aug. 25.
H – Dec. 27–30, Jan. 2–5, Apr. 10–14, 18, June 6, Ⓐ July 10 - Sept. 8.

s – Stops to set down only.

* – By 🚌.
🚂 – Steam train. Special fares payable.

Operator: Steiermärkische Landesbahnen.

999 Danube shipping: BUDAPEST - BRATISLAVA - WIEN - LINZ - PASSAU

Hydrofoil services. 🍸	W	E	B	Q	W	P	W	Y	T
	R♠	R♠	R◇	⊙	R♠	⊙	R♠	⊙	R♠
Wien Reichsbrücke ▲ d.	...	...	0900	0945	...	1600	...	1730	...
Wien Schwedenplatz ▲ d.	0830	0900	|	|	1230	|	1630	|	1800
Bratislava d.	0945	1015	|	1115	1345	1730	1745	1900	1915
Budapest § a.	...	...	1430	...	...	...	...	...	...

Hydrofoil services. 🍸	Z	W	A	W	E	R	S	W	T
	⊙	R♠	R◇	R♠	R♠	⊙	⊙	R♠	R♠
Budapest § d.	...	...	0900	...	...	...	...	...	...
Bratislava d.	0900	1030	|	1430	1600	1600	1730	1830	2100
Wien Schwedenplatz a.	|	1200	|	1600	1730	|	|	2000	2230
Wien Reichsbrücke ▲ a.	1045	...	1530	...	...	1745	1915	...	...

All sailings convey ✕	J	C	C	⑦N	K	⑦D	K	K	K
	⊡	⊡	◐	⊖	◐	◐R	⊡	◐	◐
Wien Reichsbrücke ▲ d.	...	...	...	...	...	0830	...	...	...
Tulln d.	...	...	...	0900n	...	1120	...	...	...
Krems an der Donau d.	0900	1010	1015	1150	1310	1400	1540	1545	...
Dürnstein d.	0930	1040	1050	1220	1340	1430	1610	1620	...
Spitz an der Donau d.	...	1140	1145	1315	1445r	...	1700	1720	1730
Melk a.	...	1300	1320	1450	1605	...	*1730**	...	1850
Grein d.	...	...	...	1820	...	...	...	...	...
Linz Lentos a.	...	...	...	2220	...	...	...	...	...

All sailings convey ✕	J	K	C	C	⑥N	⑦D	K	K	K
	⊡	◐	⊡	◐	⊖	◐R	⊡	◐	◐
Linz Lentos d.	...	...	...	...	0900	...	...	...	...
Grein d.	...	...	...	...	1200	...	...	...	...
Melk d.	...	1100	1345	1350	1440	...	...	1625	...
Spitz an der Donau d.	...	1200t	1435	1440	1520	...	1705	1710	1725
Dürnstein d.	0930	1230	1505	1510	1600	1640	1730	...	1750
Krems an der Donau d.	0950	1250	1530	1530	1620	1700	1755	...	1810
Tulln d.	...	...	...	...	1820q	1900	...	...	...
Wien Reichsbrücke ▲ a.	...	...	...	...	2030q	2100	...	...	...

All sailings convey ✕	⊖H	⊖N		⊖M
Linz Lentos d.	...	...	...	1420
Schlögen d.	...	1425	...	1800
Obernzell d.	...	1615	...	1935
Passau Liegestelle 11 🏛 d.	1515	1715	...	2050
Deggendorf a.	2030	...	...	...

All sailings convey ✕	⊖L		⊖N	⊖G
Deggendorf d.	...	...	...	1000
Passau Liegestelle 11 🏛 d.	0900	...	1200	1400
Obernzell d.	0945	...	1245	...
Schlögen a.	1110	...	1410	...
Linz Lentos a.	1410	...	...	...

A – ②④⑥ May 10 - Sept. 29.
B – ③⑤⑦ May 11 - Sept. 30.
C – Apr. 15 - Oct. 29.
D – ⑦ May 21 - Sept. 24 (not June 25, July 23).
E – Mar. 31 - Oct. 29.
G – ④⑥ May 14 - Sept. 8 (not June 18, Aug. 13, 27).
H – ④ May 19 - Sept. 8 (not June 16, July 7).
J – July 1 - Aug. 31.
K – Apr. 29 - Oct. 1.
L – ②–⑦ Apr. 29 - Oct. 2 (also Oct. 8, 15, 22).

M – ②③④⑥⑦ Apr. 30 - Oct. 2 (also Oct. 8, 15, 22; not May 26, June 15, 16, Aug. 11).
N – Apr. 30 - Oct. 3.
P – ⑤–⑦ Sept. 16 - Oct. 23.
Q – ③–⑦ Apr. 20 - June 19; daily June 22 - Aug. 28; ③–⑦ Aug. 31 - Sept. 25; ⑤–⑦ Sept. 30 - Oct. 23.
R – ③–⑦ Sept. 14–25; ⑤–⑦ Sept. 30 - Oct. 23.
S – ③–⑦ Apr. 20 - June 19; daily June 22 - Aug. 28; ③–⑦ Aug. 31 - Sept. 11.
T – ⑤⑥ May 5 - Sept. 2.
W – ⑤–⑦ Mar. 31 - Apr. 23 (also Apr. 17); daily Apr. 28 - Oct. 1; ⑤–⑦ Oct. 6–29 (also Oct. 26).
Y – ③–⑦ Apr. 20 - June 26; daily June 29 - Sept. 4 (also Sept. 9, 10, 11).
Z – ③–⑦ Apr. 20 - June 26; daily June 29 - Sept. 4; ⑤–⑦ Sept. 9 - Oct. 23.

n – Not June 19, Sept. 4.
q – Not June 18, Sept. 3.
r – Arrives 1435.
t – Arrives 1140.

* – By 🚌 from Spitz.
§ – Nemzetközi Hajóállomás (International shipping terminal).

▲ – DDSG operates Wien sightseeing cruises Schwedenplatz - Reichsbrücke and v.v. Daily Apr. 1 - Oct. 31.
From Schwedenplatz (duration 1 h 55 m via Schleuse Freudenau) at 1030, 1400 (also 1130, 1500 Apr. 15 - Oct. 1).
From Reichsbrücke (duration 1 h 20 m via Schleuse Nussdorf) at 1230, 1600 (also 1330, 1700 Apr. 15 - Oct. 1).
Also shorter *City Cruise* available daily throughout the year from Schwedenplatz at 1100, 1230, 1430 and 1600 (duration 1 h 15 m).

Operators:
⊡ – Brandner Schiffahrt GmbH, Ufer 15, A-3313 Wallsee. ✆ +43 (0) 7433 25 90 21. www.brandner.at
◐ – DDSG Blue Danube Schiffahrt GmbH, Handelskai 265, A-1020 Wien. ✆ +43 (0)1 588 80. www.ddsg-blue-danube.at
⊖ – Wurm und Köck, Höllgasse 26, D-94032 Passau. **2016 service**. ✆ +49 (0) 851 92 92 92. www.donauschiffahrt.de
⊙ – SPaP - LOD – Slovenská Plavba a Prístavy - Lodná Osobná Doprava a.s., Fajnorovo nábrežie 2, 811 02 Bratislava. Reservation recommended. Check-in 15 minutes before departure. **2016 service**. Bratislava: ✆ +421 2 529 32 226. www.lod.sk
◇ – MAHART PassNave, H-1056 Budapest, Belgrád rakpart. Check-in 60 minutes before departure. **2016 service**. Budapest: ✆ +36 1 484 4013. www.mahartpassnave.hu
♠ – *Twin City Liner*. DDSG Blue Danube GmbH, Handelskai 265, A-1020 Wien. Check-in 30 minutes before departure. ✆ +43 (0)1 904 88 80. Internet booking: www.twincityliner.com

Operators: Express services are operated by PKP Intercity www.intercity.pl. Most local trains are operated by Przewozy Regionalne (PR) www.przewozyregionalne.pl. Certain local services are operated by regional companies owned by local government: e.g. Koleje Dolnośląskie, Koleje Mazowieckie, Koleje Śląskie and Koleje Wielkopolskie.

Services: PKP InterCity : Note reservation is compulsory (Ⓡ) on all services operated by PKP InterCity (*EC, EIC, EIP, EN, IC, MP, TLK*) :

EC, EIC and *EIP* trains are fast premium-rate trains on long-distance routes (*EC* or *EuroCity* trains run on international routes) - first and second class seats, higher rate of fares apply and a supplement is payable for pass holders. *EC, EIC* and *EIP* trains normally convey ✕ or 🍴 for at least part of the route.

IC and *TLK* trains are lower-cost long distance trains with first and second class seats (also sleepers and couchettes on nights routes as shown in the tables). *TLK* is short for *Twoje Linie Kolejowe* (Your Railway Lines). Certain trains convey 🍴 but it is not possible to identify these in the tables.

MP is the classification (within Poland) for other international trains; *TLK* fares apply within Poland. Note that Russian/Ukrainian sleeping car services cannot be used for journeys in or between Poland and Germany unless seating cars are also conveyed. *EN* trains are *EuroNight* services with 'global' fares which include the sleeping accommodation. Descriptions of sleeping (🛏) and couchette (🛌) cars appear on page 8.

Przewozy Regionalne and other local operators :

IR (InterRegio) and *RE (Regional Express)* trains are semi-fast trains operated by Przewozy Regionalne on longer distance routes, with second class seats. Fares are cheaper than *TLK* services but slightly higher than local *Regio* trains.

All other trains are local *R (Regio)* trains, second class only, calling at all or most stations en route. No train category is shown in our tables for these trains. They are operated by Przewozy Regionalne unless otherwise shown in the table heading or by a footnote. Fares on *Regio* trains are the cheapest available.

Timings: Valid until **March 11, 2017** except where shown otherwise. However, alterations are possible at any time (particularly on and around public holidays) and readers are advised to check locally before travelling. Engineering work can often affect schedules; major changes are shown in the tables where possible but other changes may occur at short notice. A number of long-distance trains running only in high summer (particularly to coastal resorts) are not shown owing to lack of space. Note that train numbers often change en route by one or two digits. In station names, Gł. is short for Główny or Główna, meaning main station.

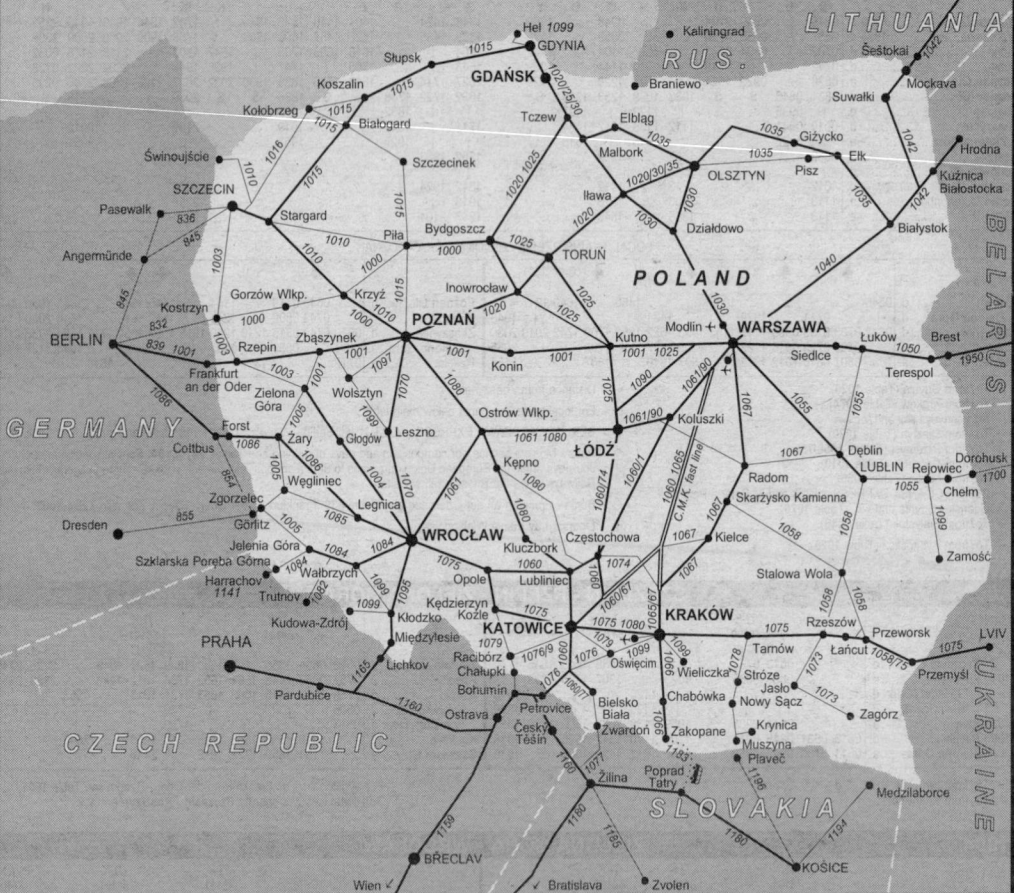

KOSTRZYN - KRZYŻ - POZNAŃ and BYDGOSZCZ — 1000

km			TLK 85108 n Gd	TLK 81106 Sd				a		TLK 85152 Eh	x		TLK 81100 W				x		TLK 88170 Ⓡ x
0	Kostrzyn d.	...	...	0533	...	...	0649	0859	...	a	...	1059	...	1356	...	1507	1559	...	1756	2103	...
43	Gorzów Wlkp. d.	...	...	0614	0551	...	0729	0939	...	...	...	1138	...	1439	1457	1546	1638	...	1838	2145	2312
103	Krzyż ....1010 d.	0454	...	0708	0656r	...	0821	0832	1041j	1038	...	1230	1335	1530	1544	1640	1739	1746	1930	2019	2237	2358
186	Poznań ....1010 a.	...	...	0829	...	...	...	1148	...	...	...	...	...	...	1839	...	...	...	...	...
163	Piła Gł. d.	0544	0549	...	0739	0900	...	0922	...	1127	1152	1219	...	1425	...	1645t	1745	...	1836	1952	...	2108	...
248	Bydgoszcz a.	...	0717	...	...	1019	...	...	...	1323	1336	...	1618	...	1754	1913	...	2120	...	...

	TLK 80171 d x			x	TLK 18101 n W		a	x	TLK 58153 Eg a			TLK 58109 Gb		TLK 18107 Sb
Bydgoszcz d.	...	...	...	...	...	1016	...	1146	...	1429	...	1548	...	1738	...	1918	1940
Piła Gł. d.	...	...	0729	...	0905	0909	...	1141	...	1334	1439	...	1538	1543	1712	1717	...	1946	1903	...	2010	2029	2105
Poznań ....1010 d.	...	...	...	...	...	0850	...	1221	...	...	...	...	...	1856	...	...
Krzyż ....1010 d.	0442	0513	0623	0823	0835	...	1001	1005	1226	1324	1425	1502	1531	1613	...	1636	...	1808	1816	2125	...	2007	2102	...
Gorzów Wlkp. d.	0532	0608	0722	...	0931	...	1100	1316	1418	...	1557	...	1710	...	1912	2218	...	2101	...
Kostrzyn a.	...	0647	0800	...	1011	...	1138	...	1456	1636	...	1748	...	1950	...	2139	...

E – To/from Kołobrzeg (Table 1015).
G – To/from Gdynia.
S – To/from Szczecin (Table 1010).
W – To/from Warszawa (Table 1001 / 1025).

a – ①–⑤ (not Dec. 26, Jan. 6).
b – ⑧ (not Dec. 25).
d – ①–⑥ (not Dec. 26).
g – ⑥ (also Dec. 23, 30, Jan. 5; not Dec. 24, 31, Jan. 7).

h – ⑦ (also Dec. 26; not Dec. 25).
j – Arrive 1033.
n – Not Dec. 25, 26, Jan. 1, 6.

r – Arrive 0642.
t – Arrive 1628.
x – Not Dec. 25.

1001 — BERLIN - POZNAŃ - WARSZAWA

km		TLK 81170 81171	TLK 71100 71101	TLK 71150 71151	EIC 7104 7105	TLK 83106 83107	EIC 7100 7101	EIC 8102 8103	EC 41 8154/5	TLK 73100 71002	EIC 8104/5	TLK 75104 71123	MP 453	EC 81122 71004	TLK 75106 75000	EC 45	TLK 70108	EC 55	TLK 82100 82101	EIC 8100 8101	TLK 75102	EC 47 71006
		①–⑥	⑦			①–⑥		①–⑥		⊠												
		N			K			☕	P		G			Y	O		☕		X	U	b	
0	Berlin Hbf ⊖ d.	N	...	...	K	...	☕ 0637	P	...	G	...	0713	0937	...	1237	...	1437	...	X	U	b 1637	
5	Berlin Ostbahnhof ⊖ d.						0650						0950		1250		1450				1650	
87	Frankfurt an der Oder ⚇ ⊖ d.						0745					0855	1045		1345		1545				1745	
98	Kunowice ⚇ ⊖ d.																					
110	Rzepin ▷ d.						0808					1016	1108		1408		1608				1808	
●58	Zielona Góra ▷ d.		0253			0552			0846				1255		1542			1737				
185	Zbąszynek ▷ d.		0336			0635	0846		0928			1146	1337	1446		1624	1646			1819	1846	
191	Zbąszyń ▷ d.		0342						0934				1343			1630				1825		
266	Poznań Gł. ▷ a.	S	0428			S 0717	S 0923		S	1024	1130	1223	S 1432	1523		1718	1723	S	S	1913	1923	
266	Poznań Gł. d.	0248	0448	0448	0624	0711	0720	0825	0926	0936	1024		1135	1226	1333		1526		1736	1834		1926
366	Konin d.	0355	0557	0557		0824	0809		1014	1049			1314	1438		1614		1842			2014	
445	Kutno 1025 d.	0458	0645	0645	0906	0852		1055	1141	1154		1355	1524		1656		1930	2003			2055	
572	Warszawa Cent 1025 d.	0630	0800	0800	0900		1100	1101	1200	1320	1308	1425	1500	1641		1800		2040	2110		2156	
577	Warszawa Wsch 1025 a.	0641	0831	0831	0916		1036	1112	1216	1401	1319	1436	1511	1706		1811		2056	2126		2211	

		EC 46 17000	TLK 57103	TLK 1800 1801	EIC 28100 28101	TLK 54 57001	EIC 77109	EC 44 17002	EIC 57107	TLK 18102/3 18122/3	EC 42 17004	MP 452	EC 57105	TLK 37100 37101	TLK 1804/5 1854/5	EIC 1700 1701	TLK 1802 1803	EIC 38106 38107	EC 40 17006	EIC 1704 1705	EC 17150 17151	EIC 17100 17101	TLK 18170 18171
																⑧		⑧					
		☕	b	U	X		☕	O	Y		☕		G	P			K	☕	⑧				N
Warszawa Wsch 1025 d.		0546		0649	0704		0948		1109		1348	1424		1404	1446	1539	1649		1742	1844	1949	1949	2252
Warszawa Cent 1025 d.		0557		0659	0720		0959		1125		1359		1425	1457	1600	1700		1758	1900	2000	2000	2305	
Kutno 1025 d.		0702		0804	0833		1104		1242		1504		1616	1603	1705		1847	1903		2118	2118	0032	
Konin d.		0742			0919		1144		1329		1543		1705	1747		1926	1943		2202	2202	0128		
Poznań Gł. a.		0826		0929	1021		1228		1429		1627	1714	1816	1728	1833	1930	2032	2027	2128	2306	2306	0235	
Poznań Gł. ▷ d.		0831	0845		S	1033	1039	1233	1338	S	1632	1722	1738		S	1836	S	2030		2318	S		
Zbąszyń ▷ d.			0935			1129		1427				1832											
Zbąszynek ▷ d.		0910	0941		1112	1135	1312	1434			1711		1840		1919			2109		0012			
Zielona Góra ▷ d.			1022			1215	1515				1927		1958						0053				
Rzepin ▷ d.		0952			1152	1352					1752	1903						2148					
Kunowice ⚇ ⊖ d.																							
Frankfurt an der Oder ⚇ ⊖ a.		1012			1212	1412					1812	1924						2208					
Berlin Ostbahnhof ⊖ a.		1118			1306	1518					1918							2258					
Berlin Hbf ⊖ a.		1143			1315	1543					1943	2104						2321					

LOCAL TRAINS RZEPIN / ZIELONA GORA - POZNAŃ

	♣					♣	① (–⑤ ⑥⑦)			♣
Rzepin d.	0540			1038		1450		1640	1917	
Zielona Góra d.			0711	1029		1431				1948
Zbąszynek d.	0642	0703 0753	0908	1117 1152	1403	1522 1552	1703 1742	2019	2030	
Zbąszyń d.	0708	0759	0913 1122	1408	1527	1708	2035			
Poznań Gł. a.	0807 0846	1012 1212	1507 1619	1807	2151					

		♣		♣	♣	①(–⑤)		
Poznań Gł. d.		0645 0719	1144	1445 1544		1645 1950 2047		
Zbąszyń d.		0743 0809	1244	1547 1646		1744 2050 2145		
Zbąszynek d.	0610 0749 0815	1210 1250	1515 1553 1652 1716	1744 2050 2145				
Zielona Góra a.	0858	1337		1844 2137				
Rzepin a.	0712	1312	1617	1818				

G – To / from Gdynia (Table 1020).
K – To / from Kraków (Table 1074).
N – Also conveys 🛏 and / or 🍴.
O – To / from Olsztyn (Table 1020).
P – To / from Przemyśl (Tables 1058/75).
S – To / from Szczecin (Table 1010).
U – To / from Lublin (Table 1055).
X – BERLIN GDANSK EXPRESS – 🚲 and 🍴 Berlin - Poznań - Gdansk - Gdynia and v.v. (Table 1020).
Y – To / from Białystok (Table 1040).
b – To / from Bydgoszcz (Table 1020).

● – Distance from Zbąszynek.
▷ – For local trains see panel below main table.
☕ – BERLIN WARSZAWA EXPRESS – 🚲 🍴 🛏, Berlin - Warszawa and v.v. Special fares apply. See Table 56.
⊠ – Paris - Moskva service; for composition and days of running see Tables 24/56/94. Special conditions apply. Journeys within the European Union (e.g. Paris to Berlin) are possible, but only bookable through agents of Russian Railways or via the Russian rail website.
⊖ – Berlin - Frankfurt an der Oder: see also Table 839. Frankfurt an der Oder - Rzepin: see also Table 1003.
♣ – Operated by Koleje Wielkopolskie.

1003 — SZCZECIN - RZEPIN - ZIELONA GÓRA

km		TLK 86100 Cd	TLK 84100 T						
0	Szczecin Gł. d.	0613 0706	0845		1135 1245 1545				
104	Kostrzyn d.	0807 0836	1023		1307 1425 1733				
	Frankfurt / Oder. d.			1120		1818			
	Kunowice d.			1131		1829			
136	Rzepin a.	0844 0905	1059 1139	1338 1500	1810 1837				
136	Rzepin d.	0513 0631 0845 0911	1100 1140	1342 1506	1838				
207	Zielona Góra a.	0611 0730 0949 0959	1158 1241	1430 1605	1939				

		TLK 48101 T					TLK 68101 ⑧C		⑦–④	⑤⑥
Zielona Góra d.		0656 0834	1355 1406	1550 1629	1823 1849			2225	2240	
Rzepin a.		0757 0933	1443 1504	1652 1730	1912 1948			2323	2338	
Rzepin d.		0758 0934	1445 1505	1653 1731	1913		1953			
Kunowice d.		0806			1739					
Frankfurt / Oder. a.		0817			1750					
Kostrzyn d.		1016	1533 1555	1745	1958		2043			
Szczecin Gł. a.		1154	1650 1723	1918	2110					

C – To/from Wrocław.   d – ①–⑥ only.
T – To/from Katowice.

For additional trains Frankfurt an der Oder - Rzepin see Table 1001.
Additional services operate Szczecin - Kostrzyn and v.v.

1004 — ZIELONA GÓRA - WROCŁAW

km		IC 76104 P	TLK 86100 d	TLK 84100 T							
0	Zielona Góra d.	0529 0555 0647 0844	1008 1029	1439 1556	1801 1955						
23	Nowa Sól d.	0547 0612 0706 0902	1025 1048	1455 1614	1820 2013						
54	Głogów d.	0621 0640 0738 0934	1057 1122	1532 1647	1852 2045						
154	Wrocław Gł. a.	0802 0810 0920 1116	1231 1305	1702 1828	2032 2225						
	Kraków 1075 a.										

		①–⑤	⑥⑦		TLK 48101 T		TLK 68101 ⑧		⑤⑥	IC 67105 P
Kraków 1075 d.										
Wrocław Gł. d.		0537	0651	0903	1125 1252	1455	1546 1700	1938		2022
Głogów d.		0733	0840	1101	1305 1444	1645	1715 1851	2141		2159
Nowa Sól d.		0807	0915	1136	1337 1518	1720	1803 1927	2216		2229
Zielona Góra a.		0827	0934	1157	1352 1537	1740	1819 1947	2235		2244

P – To/from Przemyśl (Table 1075).   T – To/from Katowice.

1005 — ZIELONA GÓRA - WEGLINIEC - JELENIA GÓRA

km		⊖	⊖	⊖	⊖	①–⑤	⑥⑦	⊖	⊖
0	Zielona Góra d.		0741			1849		2151	
54	Żary 1086 d.		0841			1644 1949		2256	
67	Żagań 1086 d.					2001		2308	
94	Węgliniec 1085 d.	0524	0943	1539		1744	▬ 2242		
118	Zgorzelec Miasto d.	0545	1006	1602		1805	⊖ 2303		
	Görlitz 1085 d.	0746	1346	1546 1746	1808	1928			
120	Zgorzelec 1085 d.	0749	1020 1351	1549 1749	1934				
144	Lubań Śląski d.	0616 0821	1056 1421	1605 1620	1820	2004 2334			
196	Jelenia Góra a.	0716 0920	1156 1522	1720 1920	2111				

		⊖	⊖	⊖	①–⑤ ⑥⑦	⑦	⊖	⊖
Jelenia Góra d.			0550 0753 0954	1317 1454	1553 1753	1946		
Lubań Śląski d.		0441 0526 0657 0900	1101 1423	1622 1700	1900 2047			
Zgorzelec 1085 d.		0727 0932	1132 1508	1712 1732	2118			
Görlitz 1085 d.		0731 0936	1136	1736	2122			
Zgorzelec Miasto d.		0512 0603 ①–⑤	1511 1715	1930				
Węgliniec 1085 d.		0534 0625 ①–⑤	1546 1742	1952				
Żagań 1086 d.		0508	0825					
Żary 1086 d.		0520	0843	1640 1835				
Zielona Góra a.		0619	0942	1744 1934				

⊖ – Operated by Koleje Dolnośląskie.
▬ Local 🚌 service 'P' links Görlitz Bahnhof with Zgorzelec Miasto station every 30 mins (journey 22 mins).

Reservation is compulsory for travel by all EC, EIC, EIP, EN, IC, MP and TLK trains

SZCZECIN - POZNAŃ — 1010

Świnoujście / Szczecin - Stargard and v.v. is subject to alteration from March 1

km		IC 83106	TLK 84106	EIC 8102		TLK 83102 8104	EIC 8105	TLK 8154	IC 84104	IC 8303 8302		IC 81122	TLK 8314		IC 83104	IC 8405 8404	TLK 82100		EIC 8100	IC 81120	TLK 8754		IC 83174	TLK 83196	TLK 81171 81170
		①–⑥			①–⑥		⑦				①–⑤							⑧	⑤⑦		n			
						P		Y	P			U				L		*			NP	NZ	N
0	Świnoujście ....d.					0622			0816	0824		1022			1321d						1935	1909	2043
0	**Szczecin Gł. 1015** d.	0450	0544	0556	0600	0658	0753	0753	0849	0952	1010	1149	1210	1254	1350	1443	1517	1559	1654	1749	1808	1935	1909	2216
15	Szczecin Dąbie **1015** d.	0504	0558	0610	0615	0712	0807	0807	0903	1006	1024	1055	1203	1224	1308	1404	1457	1533	1613	1708	1804	1822	1923	2250
40	Stargard ....**1015** d.	0521	0617	0629	0636	0730	0827	0827	0921	1024	1045	1114	1222	1246	1326	1425	1517	1557	1633	1726	1822	1843	2009	1942	2309
130	Krzyż ....**1000** d.	0614	0737	0721	0756	0828	0920	0920	1014	1122	1157	1216	1319	1357	1421	1524	1619	1712	1723	1819	1924	2004	2039	2033
213	**Poznań Gł. ....1000** a.	0708	0840	0815	0910	0924	1014	1014	1108	1302	1302	1313	1417	1505	1514	1630	1717	1832	1817	1914	2022	2112	2209	2137	0138
	Wrocław Gł. **1070** .....a.		1047‡						1439			1649				1855‡						0023		
	Warszawa Cent. **1001** a.			1101		1301‡	1301‡				1641					2040		2110					0630	
	Katowice **1075 1080** ....a.		1321						1710					2109								0328		
	Kraków Gł **1075 1080** ...a.	1249			1447				1817		2041		2052									0550	0359	

km		TLK 18171	TLK 38197	IC 38175		IC 18121	EIC 1801	TLK 28101		IC 4805 4804		IC 3815 18123	TLK 1803	IC 48105			EIC 1805	EIC 1855	TLK 38103	EIC 1803	TLK 48107	IC 38107	TLK 7855
					①–⑥		①–⑥							⑧	⑥								⑤⑦
		N	NZ	NP		L		U				P	Y	P									
	Kraków Gł. **1075 1080** .....d.		2308‡	2204						0831			1010				1327			1452			
	Katowice **1075 1080** ....d.			0020				0728				1028					1504						
	Warszawa Cent. **1001** ....d.	2305				0659		0720			1125			1457	1457		1700						
	Wrocław Gł. **1070** ....d.		2335	0415‡						1057		1157		1343						1740			
	Poznań Gł. .....**1000** d.	0315	0540	0642	0648	0834	0940	0954	1037		1212	1345	1423	1441	1608	1644	1650	1741	1741	1850	1943	1958	2052	2145
	Krzyż ....**1000** d.	0432	0648	0741	0801	0930	1034	1110	1136		1313	1453	1522	1540	1707	1741	1813		1836	1836	1947	2040	2111	2149	2247
	Stargard ....**1015** d.	0530	0746	0839	0917	1025	1125	1223	1234		1411	1607	1622	1640	1803	1833	1920		1930	1930	2042	2131	2206	2241	2344
	Szczecin Dąbie ....**1015** d.	0548	0803	0857	0941	1044	1142	1247	1252		1429	1630	1644	1657	1820	1850	1942		1947	1947	2101	2151	2223	2258	0002
	Szczecin Gł. ....**1015** a.	0602	0818	0912	0955	1056	1156	1301	1306		1442	1644	1659	1711	1834	1903	1958		2000	2002	2114	2206	2237	2312	0016
	Świnoujście ....a.	0749			1143			1457			1618	1855b			2013			2153		2131				

km					a	a		d		b					a	a		d		b	
0	Świnoujście ....d.	0439	0558	0821	1022		1321	1535	1728		1957	**Szczecin Gł.** ....d.	0404	0530	0735	1000		1315	1523	1708		2008
101	Szczecin Dąbie ....a.	0606	0724	0949	1148		1446	1703	1853		2133	Szczecin Dąbie ....d.	0417	0544	0750	1015		1329	1537	1722		2023
116	**Szczecin Gł.** ....a.	0621	0739	1004	1204		1500	1718	1910		2148	**Świnoujście** ....a.	0543	0711	0916	1143		1457	1705	1855		2153

km			81106 d§						⑧					d					⑦	①–⑥		18107 b§
0	**Szczecin Gł.** ....d.		0549		0726	1124		1506		1945	**Piła Główna** ....d.		0734		1320	1553		1908	1908		2046
12	Szczecin Dąbie ....d.		0604		0742	1139		1524		2004	Wałcz ....d.	0347	0806		1357	1622		1936	1936		2113
37	Stargard ....d.	0455	0623		0801	1201		1552		2026	Kalisz Pomorski ....d.	0430	0848		1439	1705		2016	2016		2152
102	Kalisz Pomorski ....d.	0604	0725		0911	1310		1708		2153	Stargard ....d.	0549	1001		1550	1821		2120	2123		2254
146	Wałcz ....d.	0648	0812		0955	1355		1752		2237	Szczecin Dąbie ....a.	0611	1026		1614	1841		2138			2312
176	**Piła Główna** ....a.	0717	0840		1024	1425		1820			**Szczecin Gł.** ....a.	0626	1047		1629	1857		2155			2327

L – To/from Łódź (Table **1025**).
N – Also conveys 🛏 and/or 🍴.
P – To/from Przemyśl (Tables **1058/75**).
U – To/from Lublin (Table **1055**).
Y – To/from Białystok (Table **1040**).
Z – To/from Zakopane (Table **1066**).

a – ①–⑤ only.
b – ⑧ only.
d – ①–⑥ only.
m – Dec. 23, 25, 26, 29, 30, Jan. 1, 6 - 8, Jan. 14 - Feb. 26.
n – Dec. 22, 23, 25, 28 - 30, Jan. 5 - 7, Jan. 13 - Feb. 25.

§ – TLK service.
‡ – Time varies – see main table.

SZCZECIN - KOSZALIN - GDYNIA - GDAŃSK — 1015

km		EIP 8300 ①–⑥	TLK 83100	TLK 85100		TLK 81104	IC 4809 4808	TLK 80103		TLK 85106	TLK 48103		TLK 58153	TLK 85104		TLK 83170 ⑧	IC 3805 3804 ①–⑥
				O		Y	T			O	T		b			KN	P
0	**Szczecin Gł.** § d.		0718	0740		1109		1304	1420		1527			1717	1735		2102
15	Szczecin Dąbie .... § d.		0732	0755		1123		1318	1434		1541			1731	1750		2119
40	Stargard .... § d.		0750	0818		1143		1340	1453		1609			1751	1822		2144
*231	**Poznań Gł.** .... d.				0629	0823	0947			1238	1329		1432			1634	1819
*135	Piła Gł. .... d.				0835	1031	1131			1435	1512	1541	1638			1847	2006
*64	Szczecinek .... d.				0939	1157	1234			1541	1617	1641	1802			1959	2059
151	Białogard .... a.		0903	0950	1045	1254	1259	1326		1518	1609	1640	1708	1736	1745	1900	1903	1949			2056	2151	2312
151	Białogard .... d.		0905	0951	1050	1310	1301	1338	1350	1530	1610	1642	1709	1750	1746	1909	1906	1951			2058	2206	2313
187	Kołobrzeg .... a.				1124			1427		1716	1737		1815	1944			2047
**43	Kołobrzeg .... d.	0610	0719														
175	**Koszalin** .... d.	0645	0807	0921	1010		1340	1318	1407		1549	1625		1809			1922	2017	2140	2116	2223	2329
242	Słupsk .... d.	0724	0857	1003	1057		1402	1502		1642	1707		1857			2005	2117	2225			2301
294	Lębork .... d.	0754	0928	1039		1433		1739			2046	2259				
353	**Gdynia Gł.** .... a.	0831	1012	1122		1516		1822			2128	2349				
353	**Gdynia Gł.** .... ▷ a.	0834	1043	1137		1536		1845			2138	0011				
362	Sopot .... ▷ a.	0843	1052	1145		1545		1858			2147	0020				
374	**Gdańsk** **1025/30** .... a.	0858	1106	1201		1600		1908			2203	0035				
	Warszawa C. **1025/30** .... a.	1150	1439										0425			

km		IC 8305 ①–⑥ 8304	TLK 38171	TLK 58105		TLK 85152	TLK 84102	TLK 58107 ⑦		IC 8409 ①–⑥ 8408	TLK 88102		TLK 18105		TLK 58101		TLK 38101	EIP 3801 ⑧
		P	KN			b	K	O		T			Y		O		K	K
	Warszawa C. **1025/30** .... d.		0002					0904		1200			1555		1651		1321	1620
	Gdańsk Gł. .... ▷ d.		0350	0555				0904		1200			1555	1651			1321	1620
	Sopot .... d.		0405	0609				0918		1215			1609	1706			1917
	Gdynia Gł. .... ▷ d.		0414	0618				0927		1224			1618	1715			1926
	Gdynia Gł. .... d.		0427	0631				0938		1242			1629	1742			1929
	Lębork .... d.		0525	0722				1019		1327			1718	1829			2006
	Słupsk .... d.	0522	0532	0626	0806			1100		1225	1326		1402	1417		1801	1825	1859		2036	2044
	Koszalin .... d.	0454	0608	0629	0740	0848		1141		1216	1317	1410		1443	1520	1657	1850	1929	1952		2115	2141
	Koszalin .... a.			0830													2031	2149
	Kołobrzeg .... a.					0849	0929	1020			1353	1450						
	Kołobrzeg .... d.	0509	0622	0650		0902	0922	0958	1048	1156	1239		1335	1427	1422	1533	1458	1550	1718	1904	1948		2200
	Białogard .... a.	0510	0645	0652		0905	0924	1003	1049	1156	1243		1345	1447		1535	1459	1551	1719	1905	1958	
	Szczecinek .... d.	0625	0737			1034	1103	1141		1400			1540		1639		1830	
	Piła Gł. .... d.	0737	0830			1138	1208	1247		1505			1643		1744		1946	
	Poznań Gł. .... a.	0939	1008			1328	1436	1731		1825			1935		2144			
	Stargard .... § d.			0817		1018			1315		1517			1619	1748		2019	2137
	Szczecin Dąbie .... § d.			0841		1039			1338		1541			1649	1812		2037	2203
	Szczecin Gł. .... § a.			0855		1053			1352		1556			1702	1828		2052	2218

K – To/from Kraków (Tables **1065/67**).
N – Also conveys 🛏 and/or 🍴.
O – To/from Olsztyn (Table **1035**).
P – To/from Przemyśl (Table **1075**).
T – To/from Katowice (Table **1075**).
Y – To/from Białystok (Table **1035**).

b – To/from Bydgoszcz (Table **1000**).

* – Distance from Białogard.
** – Distance from Koszalin.
§ – See also Table **1010**.
▷ – Frequent local trains runs between Gdynia and Gdansk.

1016 SZCZECIN - KOŁOBRZEG

km		①–⑥	⑥⑦			①–⑤				①–⑥	⑤⑦
0	Szczecin Gł. d.	0630	0829	1049	...	1227	1459	1658	...	1938	2150
35	Goleniów ✈ d.	0704	0903	1122	...	1301	1535	1731	...	2012	2223
106	Kołobrzeg a.	0903	1032	1300	...	1501	1715	1917	...	2206	2348

	①–⑤	①	②–⑥							
Kołobrzeg d.	0354	0435	0446	...	0632	0943	1331	1537	1722	...
Goleniów ✈ d.	0523	0616	0616	...	0827	1114	1530	1725	1914	...
Szczecin Gł. a.	0558	0648	0648	...	0901	1148	1603	1758	1949	...

1020 GDYNIA - GDAŃSK - BYDGOSZCZ - POZNAŃ

km		TLK 56112 56113 ①–⑥ m	①–⑤	TLK 57102 57103 F		TLK 5606 5607	TLK 57100 57101 ①–⑥	EC 54 57000 X	①–⑤	TLK 56104 56105		TLK 57106 57107 F		TLK 54108 54109 T		IC 5600 5601		TLK 16112 16152 Y	TLK 57104 57105 F		IC 5604 5605	Ⓑ	TLK 57108 57109	IC 5700 5701	TLK 56170 56171 NJ
0	Gdynia Gł. ▷ d.	...	...	...	...	0603	...	0709	...	0751	...	...	...	0934	...	1211	...	...	1334	...	1604	...	...	1807	2244
9	Sopot ▷ d.	...	...	...	...	0612	...	0717	...	0800	...	...	...	0943	...	1219	...	...	1343	...	1613	...	...	1815	2253
21	Gdańsk Gł. ▷ d.	...	...	...	...	0630	...	0733	...	0818	...	...	...	1001	...	1236	...	...	1405	...	1633	...	...	1836	2310
53	Tczew ▷ d.	...	...	...	...	0648	...	0750	...	0839	...	...	...	1022	...	1254	...	...	1426	...	1652	...	...	1854	2331
181	Bydgoszcz Gł. ▷ a.	...	...	...	...	0759	...	0855	...	0958	...	...	...	1140	...	1405	...	...	1543	...	1804	...	...	2005	0050
181	Bydgoszcz Gł. d.	0544	0553	0700	...	0802	...	0858	...	1001	1046	...	...	1143	...	1408	1442	...	1545	...	1807	...	...	2008	0053
•198	Olsztyn Gł. d.	|	|	|	...	|	0609	|	...	|	|	0925	...	|	...	|	|	1316	|	...	|	...	1739	|	|
•129	Iława d.	|	|	|	...	|	0703	|	...	|	|	1017	...	|	...	|	|	1410	|	...	|	...	1832	|	|
•35	Toruń Gł. d.	|	|	|	0700	|	0832	|	0939	|	|	1138	...	|	1307	|	|	1542	|	1703	|	1855	2000	|	|
227	Inowrocław d.	0615	0636	0731	0738	0831	0857	0926	1013	1031	1130	1202	...	1213	1342	1437	1529	1606	1615	1739	1836	1934	2025	2037	0125
283	Gniezno d.	0654	0725	0809	0827	0907	0935	0957	1114	1108	1219	1239	...	1258	1430	1511	1620	1649	1659	1831	1910	2025	2103	2114	0205
334	Poznań Gł. a.	0737	0831	0841	0935	0940	1008	1027	1203	1142	1309	1316	...	1338	1527	1542	1720	1724	1735	1924	1942	2116	2136	2146	|
	Wrocław 1070 a.	0944	...	...	...	1144	...	...	...	1413‡	...	...	...	1601y	...	1757‡	...	1948	...	...	2155	...	...	...	0618

	TLK 65171 65170 NJ	①–⑥	IC 7500 7501	TLK 75108 75109	IC 6505 6504		TLK 75104 75105 F	TLK 61113 61153 Y	①–⑤	IC 6501 6500		TLK 75106 75107 F	TLK 45108 45109 Tj	TLK 75110 75111 g	TLK 45108 45109 Tk		TLK 65105 65104	EC 55 75000 X		TLK 75100 75101 Ⓑ		TLK 6507 6506	TLK 75102 75103 F		TLK 65113 65112 Ⓑ m
Wrocław 1070 d.	2312	...	...	...	0615	...	...	0800	...	1033	...	...	1240	...	1240	...	1327‡	...	...	...	...	1630	...	...	1822
Poznań Gł. d.	0243	0545	0631	0651	0833	0950	1028	1041	1146	1249	1346	1437	1511	1511	1511	1552	1636	1726	...	1745	1750	1852	1930	1945	2047
Gniezno d.	0317	0639	0658	0722	0905	1047	1103	1116	1237	1316	1437	1510	1546	1546	1552	1648	1708	1755	...	1820	1840	1919	2004	2036	2121
Inowrocław d.	0357	0726	0734	0759	0938	1134	1145	1155	1326	1353	1528	1551	1625	1625	1632	1737	1744	1825	...	1857	1935	1955	2041	2124	2159
Toruń Gł. d.	|	0759	|	0821	|	1206	|	1222	|	|	1601	1615	|	|	|	|	|	|	...	1926	|	|	|	2157	|
Iława d.	|	...	|	0944	|	...	|	1348	|	|	...	1735	|	|	|	|	|	|	...	2044	|	|	|	...	|
Olsztyn Gł. a.	|	...	|	1034	|	...	|	1438	|	|	...	1825	|	|	|	|	|	|	...	2134	|	|	|	...	|
Bydgoszcz Gł. a.	0425	...	0800	...	1005	...	1213	...	1408	1420	...	...	1652	1653	1700	1811	1812	1850	...	...	2015	2022	2109	...	2230
Bydgoszcz Gł. ▷ d.	0435	...	0803	...	1009	...	1216	...	...	1427	...	...	1656	1656	1704	...	1818	1853	...	...	...	2025	...	...	...
Tczew ▷ d.	0558	...	0913	...	1120	...	1333	...	...	1539	...	...	1814	1814	1822	...	1936	1958	...	...	...	2136	...	...	...
Gdańsk Gł. ▷ a.	0618	...	0933	...	1137	...	1415	...	...	1557	...	...	1834	1834	1842	...	2002	2014	...	...	...	2204	...	...	...
Sopot ▷ a.	0636	...	0950	...	1155	...	1432	...	...	1616	...	...	1853	1853	1901	...	2020	2031	...	...	...	2222	...	...	...
Gdynia Gł. ▷ a.	0644	...	0958	...	1203	...	1440	...	...	1624	...	...	1901	1901	1909	...	2028	2039	...	...	...	2230	...	...	...

F – To/from Zielona Góra (Table **1001**).
J – To/from Jelenia Góra/Szklarska Poreba Górna (Table **1084**).
N – Also conveys 🛏 and/or 🛌.
T – To/from Katowice (Table **1075**).
X – ⟨12⟩ and ✕ Gdynia - Poznań - Berlin and v.v. (Table **1001**).
Y – To/from Białystok (Table **1035**).

g – Dec. 11-31.
j – Jan. 1-30.
k – Jan. 31 - Mar. 11.
m – From Jan. 17.
y – From Jan. 1.

‡ – Time varies – see main table.
• – Distance from Inowrocław.
▷ – See also Table **1025**. Frequent local services run between Gdynia and Gdansk (see Table **1035**).

1025 GDYNIA - GDAŃSK - BYDGOSZCZ - WARSZAWA/ŁODŹ

km		TLK 51114 51115 ①–⑥	IC 51120 51121	TLK 53112 53152 R	TLK 54100 54101	IC 83106 83107	TLK 51118 51119 ①–⑥	TLK 51116 51117		TLK 81106 81107 ①–⑥ S	TLK 51128 51129 ⑦	IC 53106 53107	IC 84104 84105 S	IC 51112 51113	TLK 52102 52103 U	IC 54102 54103	IC 83104 83105 S	IC 51110 51111		TLK 81100 81101 H	IC 81120 81121 Ⓑ S	IC 51104 51105	TLK 54170 54171 BN
0	Gdynia Gł. ▷ d.	...	...	...	0433	...	...	...	...	...	...	0848	...	...	1142	1304	...	...	...	...	...	1711	2132
9	Sopot ▷ d.	...	...	...	0442	...	...	...	...	...	...	0857	...	...	1151	1312	...	...	...	...	...	1719	2141
21	Gdańsk Gł. ▷ d.	...	...	...	0500	...	...	...	...	...	...	0914	...	...	1209	1330	...	...	...	...	...	1736	2159
53	Tczew ▷ d.	...	...	...	0522	...	...	...	...	...	...	0932	...	...	1230	1348	...	...	...	...	...	1757	2220
181	Bydgoszcz Gł. ▷ a.	...	...	...	0640	...	...	...	...	...	...	1040	...	...	1348	1456	...	...	...	...	...	1907	2338
181	Bydgoszcz Gł. d.	0323	0438	0546	0655	...	0737	0812	...	1024	1024	1100	...	1224	1404	1504	...	1603	...	1811	...	1915	2343
	Inowrocław d.	|	|	|	|	...	0807	|	...	|	|	|	...	|	|	1533	...	|	...	|	...	1944	0015
232	Toruń Gł. d.	0406	0521	0629	0738	...	|	0855	...	1107	1107	1143	...	1307	1447	|	...	1646	...	1854	...	|	|
287	Włocławek d.	0451	0606	0720	0823	...	|	0936	...	1153	1153	1227	...	1351	1529	|	...	1730	...	1940	...	|	|
	Poznan Gł. d.	|	|	|	|	0711	|	|	...	|	|	|	1118	|	|	|	1530	|	...	|	1934	|	|
	Konin d.	|	|	|	|	0824	|	|	...	|	|	|	1215	|	|	|	1627	|	...	|	2037	|	|
342	Kutno d.	0528	0654	0809	0903	0907	0935	1012	...	1230	1230	1303	1304	1428	1607	1704	1713	1817	...	2015	2122	2126	|
469	Warszawa Centralna a.	0700	0805	0930	|	|	1057	1152	...	1350	1350	|	|	1539	1736	|	|	1930	...	2136	|	2236	|
474	Warszawa Wschodnia a.	0711	0816	0956	|	|	1108	1212	...	1414	1414	|	|	1610	1756	|	|	1941	...	2147	|	2247	|
410	Łódź Kaliska a.	...	...	...	1011	|	...	...	...	...	...	|	1411	...	...	1811	|	...	...	...	2230	...	|
	Katowice 1060 a.	...	...	...	1305	|	...	...	...	...	...	|	|	...	...	2115	|	...	...	...	...	...	0551
	Kraków 1062/65 a.	...	...	...	...	1249	...	...	...	...	...	1701	1658	...	...	...	2128	...	...	...	...	...	...

	TLK 45171 BN	IC 18120 18121 ①–⑥ S	IC 15105	TLK 18100 18101 H	IC 15110 15111	IC 38104 38105 S	IC 45102 45103		TLK 25103 U	IC 15112 15113	IC 35106 35107	IC 48104 48105 S	TLK 15114 15115 Ⓑ	TLK 15128 15129 ⑥	TLK 18106 18107 Ⓑ S		TLK 15116 15117	IC 38106 38107	TLK 15118 15119 Ⓑ	TLK 45100 45101		TLK 35113 35153 R	IC 15120 15121
Kraków 1062/65 d.	...	...	...	...	...	0652	...	...	...	...	1052	...	...	...	...	...	...	1452	...	...	...	...	...
Katowice 1060 d.	2316	...	...	...	...	|	0700	...	...	...	|	1028	...	...	...	...	...	|	...	1438	...	...	...
Łódź Kaliska d.	|	0533	...	...	...	|	0952	...	...	...	|	1324	...	...	...	...	...	|	...	1751	...	...	...
Warszawa Wschodnia d.	|	|	0514	0619	0819	|	|	...	1009	1219	|	|	1409	1514	1514	...	1620	|	1714	|	...	1804	2019
Warszawa Centralna d.	|	|	0525	0630	0830	|	|	...	1030	1230	|	|	1420	1530	1530	...	1631	|	1730	|	...	1830	2030
Kutno d.	|	0644	0655	0752	0939	1046	1101	...	1157	1340	1451	1454	1541	1655	1655	...	1753	1847	1856	1900	...	1956	2142
Konin d.	|	0726	|	|	|	1129	|	...	|	|	|	1534	|	|	|	...	|	1926	|	|	...	|	|
Poznan Gł. a.	|	0830	|	|	|	1235	|	...	|	|	|	1633	|	|	|	...	|	2042	|	|	...	|	|
Włocławek d.	|	...	|	0828	1015	...	1146	...	1234	1416	1526	...	1622	1736	1736	...	1829	...	|	1937	...	2033	2218
Toruń Gł. d.	|	...	|	0913	1101	...	1231	...	1327	1500	1609	...	1714	1830	1830	...	1924	...	|	2021	...	2125	2301
Inowrocław d.	0505	...	0812	|	|	...	|	...	|	|	|	...	|	|	|	...	|	...	2021	|	...	|	|
Bydgoszcz Gł. a.	0533	...	0851	1004	1141	...	1321	...	1413	1543	1648	...	1754	1913	1913	...	2004	...	2054	2104	...	2206	2344
Bydgoszcz Gł. ▷ d.	0544	...	0854	...	...	...	1331	...	1433	...	1700	...	...	...	...	...	...	...	...	2125	...	...	...
Tczew ▷ d.	0701	...	1007	...	...	...	1442	...	1554	...	1810	...	...	...	...	...	...	...	...	2244	...	...	...
Gdańsk Gł. ▷ a.	0722	...	1026	...	...	...	1459	...	1613	...	1846	...	...	...	...	...	...	...	...	2304	...	...	...
Sopot ▷ a.	0740	...	1043	...	...	...	1518	...	1631	...	1906	...	...	...	...	...	...	...	...	2322	...	...	...
Gdynia Gł. ▷ a.	0749	...	1052	...	...	...	1526	...	1640	...	1914	...	...	...	...	...	...	...	...	2331	...	...	...

B – To/from Bielsko Biała (Table **1060**).
H – To/from Gorzów Wlkp (Table **1000**).
N – Also conveys 🛏 and/or 🛌.

R – To/from Rzeszów (Tables **1055/8**).
S – To/from Szczecin (Table **1010**).
U – To/from Lublin (Table **1055**).

▷ – See also Table **1020**. Frequent local services run between Gdynia and Gdansk.

GDYNIA - GDAŃSK - (OLSZTYN -) WARSZAWA — 1030

	IC 53104 53105 ①-⑥ K	TLK 51102	EIP 5400 5401 B	EIP 5302 5303 K	TLK 54104 54105 B	EIP 5402 5403 T	EIP 8300 8301 B	IC 53102 53103 K	EC 54000 105 K	X	EIP 5304 5305 K	TLK 83100 83101	EIP 5306 5307 K	IC 53100 53101 §	EIP 5404 5405 T	EIP 5308 5309 K	EIP 5406 5407 B	EIP 5310 5311 K	IC 51108 51109	IC 5102	EIP 5100 51101	IC 51100	TLK 53170 53171 NZ	TLK 83170 83171 KN
Kołobrzeg 1015 ...d.							0610d				0719													2047
0 Gdynia Gł. ▶d.		0428	0534	0627		0727	0834		0923		1027	1043	1227		1327	1421	1526	1627		1720	1827		1922	2011
9 Sopot ▶d.		0436	0543	0636		0735	0843		0931		1036	1052	1236		1336	1436	1535	1636		1729	1836		1931	0020
21 Gdańsk Gł. ▶d.		0453	0601	0654		0753	0901		0948		1054	1109	1254		1354	1454	1553	1654		1746	1854		1949	0038
53 Tczew ▶d.		0514		0711		0810			1006		1111	1131	1311		1411	1511		1711		1803	1911		2008	0059
72 Malbork ▶d.		0526		0723		0822			1018		1123	1145	1323		1423	1523	1620	1723		1816	1923		2021	0113
Olsztyn ▶d.	0518				0734			0941						1336					1739			1925		
141 Iława Gł. ▶d.		0611		0757		0856			1053		1157	1225	1357		1557	1654	1757				1957	2016	2102	0158
201 Działdowo ...d.	0626	0647				0840		1049	1125		1259		1444		1726		1846				2047	2141		0235
251 Ciechanów ...d.	0651	0711				0911		1114			1327		1509	1547				1912	1943		2112	2211		0308
305 Modlin ✛...d.	0718	0739				0946		1140			1357		1537					1937			2139	2240		
345 Warszawa Wsch. ...a.	0747	0803	0832	0932	1017	1032	1132	1208	1233		1332	1427	1532	1603	1632	1732	1832	1932	2004	2032	2132	2206	2308	0411
350 Warszawa Cent. ...a.	0755	0825	0855	0945	1025	1050	1150	1215	1255		1350	1439	1550	1610	1650	1750	1850	1950	2011	2045	2145	2225	2320	0425

	IC 15100 15101 NZ	EIP 1501	TLK 35170 35171 K	EIP 1503	IC 15108 15109 T	EIP 3510 3511 K	EIP 4506 4507 K	IC 3508 3509 K	EIP 4504 4505 K	EIP 35100 35101	IC 3506 3507	EIP 38100 38101	IC 3504 3505	EC 104 45000 X	IC 35102 35103 K	EIP 3800 3801 T	TLK 4502 4503 B	EIP 45104 45105 K	EIP 3502 3503 B	EIP 4500 4501 K	IC 35104 45101	TLK 15103	TLK 38170 38171 KN
Warszawa Centralna ...d.	0555	0620	0625	0720	0755	0820	0920	1020	1120	1154	1220	1321	1420	1520	1555	1620	1720	1735	1820	1920	1955	2005	0002
Warszawa Wschodnia ...d.	0603	0628	0637	0727	0808	0828	0928	1028	1128	1204	1228	1329	1428	1528	1602	1628	1728	1743	1828	1928	2005	2015	0017
Modlin ✛...d.	0630		0706		0836					1231		1359			1635			1814			2033	2040	
Ciechanów ...d.	0657		0734	0816	0903			1214		1259		1431			1700			1852			2103	2108	0117
Działdowo ...d.	0722		0804		0929		1034			1323		1501		1636	1725			1926			2103	2134	0150
Iława Gł. ▶d.	0755	0803	0837		1003	1106	1203			1403	1535	1603		1708			1903		2003			2206	0228
Olsztyn ...a.	0845				1032					1428				1830			2032		2232				
Malbork ...d.		0837	0916	0943		1037	1140	1237	1337		1437	1614	1637	1742			1937		2037			2246	0311
Tczew ...d.		0850	0930	0956		1050		1250	1350		1444	1628	1650	1755			1950		2050			2259	0327
Gdańsk Gł. ▶a.		0906	0947	1013		1106	1207	1306	1407		1506	1648	1706	1811	1859	2006		2106	2159			2319	0347
Sopot ▶a.		0924	1005	1032		1124	1225	1324	1425		1524	1706	1724	1828	1917	2024		2124	2217			2337	0405
Gdynia Gł. ▶a.		0933	1014	1042		1133	1234	1333	1434		1533	1715	1733	1836	1926	2033		2133	2226			2345	0414
Kołobrzeg 1015 ...a.											2031			2149b									0830

B – To/from Bielsko Biała (Table 1060).
K – To/from Kraków (Tables 1065/7).
N – Also conveys ◄ and/or ►.
T – To/from Katowice (Table 1060).
X – SOBIESKI - ◻ and X Gdynia - Warszawa - Katowice - Wien and v.v.
Z – To/from Zakopane (Table 1066).
b – Ⓡ only.
d – ①-⑥ only.
§ – Train number varies on some days / dates: 3508/9 runs as 3500/1; 3800/1 runs as 3518/9; 5308/9 runs as 5300/1; 8300/1 runs as 5318/9.
▶ – For additional trains Gdynia - Gdansk - Iława (- Olsztyn) see Table 1035. Frequent local trains (every 10 - 30 minutes) run between Gdynia and Gdańsk operated by SKM.
• – Olsztyn - Działdowo: 84 km.

GDYNIA - GDAŃSK - EŁBLAG - OLSZTYN - BIAŁYSTOK — 1035

km		TLK 51106 51107	TLK 85100 85101	TLK 61112 61152 C	TLK 81104 81105	TLK 85106 85107 ①-⑥
	Szczecin Gł. 1015 ..d.			0718	1109	1420
0	Gdynia Gł. ▶d.	0543	0742	0844 1137	1348 1536 1654 1752	1845 2052
9	Sopot ▶d.	0552	0751	0852 1145	1357 1545 1703 1801	1854 2101
21	Gdańsk Gł. ▶d.	0605	0808	0905 1204	1411 1606 1717 1815	1911 2115
53	Tczew ▶d.	0637	0828	0927 1225	1446 1627 1751 1849	1932 2150
72	Malbork ▶d.	0656	0842	0948 1242	1506 1646 1811 1909	1948 2210
101	Elbląg ...d.	0719	1001	1007 1301	1531 1708 1837 1935	2007 2235
	Iława Gł. ▶a.					
*200	Olsztyn ...a.	1022	1422		1847	2134
200	Olsztyn ...d.	1040	1458		1903	
319	Giżycko ...a.	1216	1647		2038	
366	Ełk ...a.	1253	1726		2116	
366	Ełk ...d.	1305	1728		2118	
470	Białystok ...a.	1419	1845		2232	

		TLK 58106 58107	TLK 18104 18105	TLK 16113 16153	TLK 58100 58101 C	TLK 15106 15107 Ⓡ
	Białystok ...d.		0550	0921		1331
	Ełk ...a.		0706	1040		1456
	Ełk ...d.		0707	1042		1508
	Giżycko ...a.		0746	1121		1554
	Olsztyn ...a.		0916	1256		1723
	Olsztyn ...d.	0641	0931	1330		1738
	Iława Gł. ▶a.					
	Iława Gł. ▶d.					
	Elbląg ...d.	0536 0805	1059 1323	1459 1545	1645 1858	1946
	Malbork ...d.	0604 0826	1119 1348	1519 1621	1712 1918	2013
	Tczew ...d.	0624 0841	1133 1407	1533 1641	1745 1932	2042
	Gdańsk Gł. ▶d.	0649 0900	1153 1440	1552 1715	1819 1951	2115
	Sopot ▶d.	0704 0918	1215 1454	1609 1732	1834 2009	2130
	Gdynia Gł. ▶a.	0714 0927	1224 1503	1618 1742	1844 2018	2141
	Szczecin Gł. 1015 ..a.	1352	1655	2052		

LOCAL SERVICES OLSZTYN - EŁK - BIAŁYSTOK

km		①-⑥	①									
0	Olsztyn ...d.	0359	0821	0850		1401	1443	1615	1730	2042		
45	Szczytno ...d.		0901			1529		1818				
102	Pisz ...d.			1018		1645		1934				
	Giżycko ...d.	0619		1043		1553		1816		2235		
157	Ełk ...d.	0548 0702	1157	1134 1417	1620 1638		1900 2113	2319				
261	Białystok ...a.	0729		1555 1755								

								⑤	⑥	
	Białystok ...d.			1019		1428				1824
	Ełk ...d.	0330 0535	0725	1200 1151	1218	1609	1650	1921	2007	
	Giżycko ...d.	0618 0809			1309		1742	2005		
	Pisz ...d.	0509		1339		1701				
	Szczytno ...d.	0626		1456		1817				
	Olsztyn ...a.	0706 0810	1000	1536 1500		1857	1935	2203		

C – To/from Wrocław (Table 1020).
▶ – For additional trains Gdynia - Gdansk - Iława (- Warszawa) see Table 1030. Frequent local trains run between Gdynia and Gdańsk operated by SKM (every 10 - 30 minutes).
• – 210 km via Iława.

WARSZAWA - BIAŁYSTOK — 1040

km		IC 10107 ①-⑥	TLK 31113	IC 10101	TLK 61109 V	IC 10109	TLK 10109 C	IC 10109 B	TLK 81123 Sg	IC 15127	IC 61103 J
0	Warszawa Cent ...d.	0640	0800	1005	1158	1400	1510	1600	1700	1825	2000
5	Warszawa Wsch ...d.	0651	0808	1013	1207	1408	1518	1608	1708	1833	2009
95	Malkinia ...d.	0754	0914	1116	1310	1511	1622	1711	1814	1936	2113
184	Białystok ...a.	0852	1014	1214	1408	1609	1719	1809	1913	2034	2211

		IC 16102 ⑥ J	IC 51156 ①-⑤ S	IC 51126 ①-⑥ S	TLK 10114 ⑦	TLK 18102 Ⓡ B	TLK 18122	IC 14104	IC 10118	IC 16108	IC 10110	TLK 13112	IC 10116 X
	Białystok ...d.	0525	0654	0654	0743	0904	0904	0947	1143	1411	1610	1800	2012
	Malkinia ...d.	0623	0752	0752	0841	1003	1003	1045	1242	1510	1709	1900	2111
	Warszawa Wsch ...d.	0723	0853	0853	0942	1107	1107	1146	1342	1610	1808	2007	2217
	Warszawa Cent ...a.	0730	0900	0900	0950	1115	1115	1153	1350	1618	1815	2015	2225

B – To/from Bielsko Biała (Table 1060).
C – To/from Wrocław (Table 1061).
N – To/from Jelenia Góra (Table 1084).
S – To/from Szczecin (Table 1010).
V – HAŃCZA ◻ Kraków - Warszawa - Białystok - Suwałki. Conveys Dec. 11-24: ◻ Kraków - Warszawa - Białystok (10015) - Hrodna (Tables 1042/65).
X – HAŃCZA ◻ Suwałki - Białystok - Warszawa - Kraków. Conveys Dec. 11-24: ◻ Hrodna (10016) - Białystok - Warszawa - Kraków (Tables 1042/65).
g – Conveys Ⓡ Dec. 11-23, Mar. 1-10: ◻ Białystok - Warszawa (10153) - Suwałki.

1042   (WARSZAWA) - BIAŁYSTOK - VILNIUS and HRODNA   PKP, BCh, LG

km			TLK 143	TLK 31113	10015		149	TLK 10153		
			⑥⑦	V	V		⑤-⑦	⑧g	⑧	
0	Warszawa Cent. 1040 .... d.			0800	0800j			1700t		
5	Warszawa Wsch. 1040 ... d.			0808	0808j			1708t		
184	Białystok .... d.		0625	0714	1030	1044	1222	1443	1515	1834	1838	1937	2009
225	Sokółka .... d.		0703	0805	1108		1259	1522	1616	1915	2032	2055
324	Suwałki .... a.		0925	1217			1658	1742		2141	2223
	Mockava 🚃 ◐ ....§ a.		...	...			...	...		...	...
377	Šeštokai ....§ a.		...	...			...	...		...	...
471	Kaunas ....1811 § a.		1313				2130			
575	Vilnius ....1811 § a.		...				...			
241	Kuźnica Białostocka 🚃 ...... a.		0719		1134	1315		1933		
241	Kuźnica Białostocka 🚃 ...... d.				1234					
268	Hrodna 🚃 ....‡ a.				1512					

			TLK 18102		142	y	TLK 10016	13112	y	146
			①-⑥	①-⑥	①-⑤		p	①-⑥	X	X	①-⑥	⑥⑦
	Hrodna 🚃 ....‡ d.							1631		
	Kuźnica Białostocka 🚃 ...... a.							1509		
	Kuźnica Białostocka 🚃 ...... d.		0520				1342	1625		1944	
	Vilnius ....1811 § d.									
	Kaunas ....1811 § d.					0900			1717
	Šeštokai ....§ d.						...	...		...
	Mockava 🚃 ◐ ....§ d.						...	...		...
	Suwałki .... d.		0510	0646	0757	1051		1537	1907
	Sokółka .... d.		0536	0645	0758	0925	1223	1358		1651	2000	2016
	Białystok .... a.		0614	0732	0834	1013	1301	1435	1711	1733	2037	2053
	Warszawa Wsch. 1040 a.		...	1107					2007j	2007	...
	Warszawa Cent. 1040 ... a.		...	1115					2015j	2015	...

V – HAŃCZA – 🛏 Kraków - Warszawa - Białystok - Suwałki. Conveys Dec. 11-24: 🛏 Kraków (31011) - Warszawa - Białystok (10015) - Hrodna (Tables 1040/65).
X – HAŃCZA – 🛏 Suwałki - Białystok - Warszawa - Kraków. Conveys Dec. 11-24: 🛏 Hrodna (10016) - Białystok - Warszawa (13010) - Kraków (Tables 1040/65).
g – Conveys ⑧ Dec. 11-23, Mar. 1-10: 🛏 Warszawa (81123) - Białystok (10153) - Suwałki.

j – Dec. 11-24.
p – ①⑥⑦ only.
t – Dec. 11-23, Mar. 1-10.
y – From Jan. 2.

§ – Lithuanian time (Polish time +1 hour).
‡ – Belarus time (Polish time +1 hour in summer; +2 hours in winter).
◐ – 🚃 = Trakiszki (Poland) / Mockava (Lithuania); ticketing point is Mockava.

1050   WARSZAWA - TERESPOL - BREST

km		EN 441	TLK 11103	IC 31107	MP 453	TLK 11105		TLK 11107	MP 11011	
		14	①-⑥	⊠	⑧				10	
		☐ M		K					☐ M	
0	Warszawa Centralna .... d.	0033	0700		1010		1430	1612		1810	1940
5	Warszawa Wschodnia ...... d.	0033	0707		1026		1525	1619		1819	2021
93	Siedlce .... a.		0801		1115			1715		1916	2116
93	Siedlce .... d.		0803		1117			1716		1918	2117
121	Łuków .... d.		0821		1132			1733		1935	2136
173	Biała Podlaska .... d.		0853		1200			1807		2007	2211
210	Terespol 🚃 .... a.	0213	0922	1125	1226	1512	1707	1838	1955	2036	2237
217	Brest Tsentralny 🚃 ....‡ a.	0538		1346		1733	2033		2216		0156

		MP 9	TLK 11116	TLK 11114	MP 452		IC 13106		TLK 11112	EN 13	
		11016			⑧					440	
		☐ M			K		K			☐ M	
	Brest Tsentralny 🚃 ....‡ d.	0620	0804			1303	1515		1924		0032
	Terespol 🚃 .... d.	0518	0623	0723	1038	1206	1333	1623	1742	1918	2357
	Biała Podlaska .... a.	0545		0753	1109		1652		1949	
	Łuków .... a.	0621		0824	1143		1719		2022	
	Siedlce .... a.	0639		0841	1159		1733		2038	
	Siedlce .... d.	0640		0841	1200		1735		2040	
	Warszawa Wschodnia ...... a.	0737		0937	1253	1354		1823		2134	0138
	Warszawa Centralna .... a.	0740		0945	1300	1430		1830		2145	0156

K – To / from Kraków (Table 1065).
M – To / from Minsk / Moskva (Table 94).

‡ – Belarus time (Polish time +1 hour in summer; +2 hours in winter).
☐ – For composition and days of running see Tables 56 / 94.
⊠ – Paris - Moskva service; for composition and days of running see Tables 24 / 56 / 94. Special conditions apply. Journeys within the European Union (e.g. Paris to Berlin) are possible, but only bookable through agents of Russian Railways or via the Russian rail website.

1055   WARSZAWA - LUBLIN - CHEŁM - DOROHUSK

km		TLK 13108 13109	TLK 32105 42103	IC 42102	IC 12103	TLK 42101	TLK 53113 53153	IC 12105	TLK 62103	TLK 73100 73101	TLK 62106 62107	MP 68	TLK 12101	TLK 62103	TLK 32101 52103	IC 42150 42151	IC 42106 42107	TLK 82100 82101
		①-⑤	①-⑥	⑦	①-⑥									⑧		⑥⑦	①-⑤	⑧
		R	K			Q		C	M		C	X	C	V	K			S
0	Warszawa Cent ......d.	0550	0750	0750	0950	1150			1355	1550	1650	1750			1950	1950	2050
5	Warszawa Wsch...d.	0558	0758	0758	0958	1158			1403	1558	1658	1758			1958	1958	2058
•62	Łuków ....d.	0622					1301			1620			1910				
104	Dęblin ....d.	0719	0728	0928	0928	1119	1318	1358		1519	1717	1720	1823		1919	2007	2119	2119	2226
125	Puławy Miasto .....d.	0744	0841	0943	0943	1055	1135	1333		1509	1535	1735	1839	1911	1935	2004	2133	2133	2241
175	Lublin ....a.	0818	0915	1015	1015	1127	1209	1405		1543	1610	1807	1913	1944	2008	2036	2205	2205	2314
175	Lublin ....d.						1225	1455		1555			1920			2131		2250	
228	Rejowiec ....d.						1321	1551		1651			2003			2227		2346	
249	Chełm ....a.						1338	1608		1708			2019			2244		0003	
270	Dorohusk .... 🚃 a.												2103					

		TLK 28100 28101	IC 24106 24154		TLK 23100	MP 67	TLK 25102 25103		TLK 26100		IC 26106 26107	TLK 37100 37101		TLK 26102	TLK 26102	IC 21104		TLK 35112 35152	TLK 24100 24103		IC 24102	TLK 21102		IC 23104		TLK 31108
							①-⑥		⑥⑦				①-⑤		y	z			⑧			⑥			⑧		⑧
		S	B		K	X	G		C		C	M		C	C			Q			K			R
Dorohusk .... 🚃 a.					0502																			
Chełm ....d.			0448		0546			0743					1258			1532			1828		
Rejowiec ....d.			0506		0604			0801					1315			1549			1845		
Lublin ....a.			0600		0646			0855					1410			1644			1940		
Lublin ....d.	0500	0548		0643	0657	0755		0820		0950	1158		1223	1306	1350		1540	1625		1750	1750		1846		1955
Puławy Miasto ......d.	0534	0621		0717	0731	0831		0854		1024	1232		1258	1341	1424		1615	1649		1823	1823		1920		2030
Dęblin ....d.	0548	0636	0639		0748	0847	0909		1039	1248	1350		1439		1550	1638		1837	1837	1853			2047
Łuków ....a.		0747					1007			1448			1648				1951				
Warszawa Wsch...a.	0703	0753		0903	1003			1153	1403			1554			1803		1953	1953			2201
Warszawa Cent ...a.	0710	0800		0910	1015			1200	1410						1810		2000	2000			2210

B – To / from Bielsko Biała (Table 1060).
C – To / from Wrocław (Table 1067).
G – To / from Gdynia (Table 1025).
K – To / from Kraków (Table 1067).
M – 🛏 Przemyśl / Rzeszów - Warszawa - Poznań and v.v. (Tables 1010/58).
Q – 🛏 Piła / Bydgoszcz - Warszawa - Lublin - Rzeszów and v.v. (Tables 1000/25/58).
R – To / from Rzeszów (Table 1058).

S – To / from Szczecin (Table 1010).
V – 🛏 Przemyśl / Rzeszów / Lublin - Warszawa - Bydgoszcz and v.v. (Tables 1025/58).
X – KYIV EKSPRES / KIEV EXPRESS – 🛏 1, 2 cl. Warszawa - Kyiv and v.v. (Table 1730). International journeys only.

y – Until Jan. 16.
z – From Jan. 17.
• – Distance from Dęblin.

1058   LUBLIN - RZESZÓW - PRZEMYŚL

km		TLK 13109	TLK 53113 53153		TLK 73101	TLK 23103		TLK 32102	TLK 37100	TLK 35112 35152	TLK 31108
			①-⑥			⑧		①-⑥			⑧
				Q		M				M	Q
	Warszawa Cent. 1055 .. d.		0550		0950		1355		Przemyśl ......1075 d.	0333		0639	0739	1018		1451		1531	...
	Warszawa Wsch. 1055 .. d.		0558		0958		1403		Jarosław ....1075 d.	0404		0727	0810	1101		1534		1613	...
0	Lublin .... d.	0545	0840	1229	1300	1635	1728	2030	Przeworsk ....1075 d.	0415		0741	0821	1114		1547		1627	...
103	Skarżysko Kamienna 1067 d.								Rzeszów ....1075 a.	0440		0822	0846	1150		1624		1709	...
103	Stalowa Wola Rozwadów a.	0745		1344	1500		1922		Rzeszów ....1075 d.	0454	0557		0908		1220	1259		1654		1931
132	Tanobrzeg ....a.	0812	1021		1528		1807	1948	2215	Tanobrzeg .... d.	0544	0727		0958		1411		1744		1842
204	Rzeszów ....a.	0933	1112	1529	1652		1905	2100	2305	Stalowa Wola Rozwadów .. d.		0803			1357	1450			1926
	Rzeszów ....1075 d.								Skarżysko Kamienna 1067 d.									
178	Przeworsk ....1075 d.	0938	1150	1555		1757	1920		2319	Lublin .... a.	0727	0942		1130		1519	1630		1925		2107
193	Jarosław ....1075 d.	1016	1218	1240	1644		1856	1957	2355	Warszawa Wsch. 1055 ... a.		1403		1803		2201	
228	Przemyśl ....1075 a.	1115	1327	1731		1938	2030		0028	Warszawa Cent. 1055 .... a.		1410		1810		2210	

M – 🛏 Przemyśl / Rzeszów - Warszawa - Poznań and v.v. (Tables 1010/55).
Q – 🛏 Piła / Bydgoszcz - Warszawa - Lublin - Rzeszów and v.v. (Tables 1000/25/55).

WARSZAWA/ŁÓDŹ - KATOWICE and BIELSKO BIAŁA — 1060

km		TLK 54171 116	EC 14004 14113	TLK 14112 103	EC 14000	IC 24154 24155	EC 24106 24107	TLK 5400 5401	IC 131	EC 14002	TLK 54101	TLK 54104 54105	EC 5402 5403	TLK 14104	EC 54000	IC 14006 105	TLK 84105 112	EC 14110 14111	EIP 1400 1401		EIP 14100 14101	TLK 5404 5405	EC 14008 110	EIP 5406 5407	IC 54103 24103	IC 24102	MP 14010 407
				§		⑥⑦	①-⑤						⑧		⑧	⑧					⑧		⑧		⑧		
		GN	Z	P		U	G	V	G	O	G	Y	S	M	s	A				B	G	Q	G	G	U	C
0	Warszawa Wschodnia d.		0539	0604	0644	0754	0754	0834	0924	...	1019	1034	1147	1234	1339	...	1436	1544	...	1634	1738	1834	...	1954	2109
5	Warszawa Centralna d.		0550	0615	0655	0815	0815	0855	0955	...	1045	1050	1225	1255	1355	...	1447	1555	...	1614	1650	1754	1850	...	2010	2120
	Łódź Kaliska d.									1014					1414							1814				
	Koluszki d.			0720		0915	0915			1154			1324			1559				1728				2117		
	Piotrków Trybunalski d.	0344		0743		0940	0940		1105	1218			1347			1506	1624			1752			1906	2140		
	Częstochowa d.	0445		0840		1032	1032		1157	1311			1440			1602	1719			1846			1959	2234		
259	Zawiercie d.	0516	0750	0913	0847	1104	1104		1150	1229	1344		1512	1448	1553	1634	1751	1745		1919		1952		2039		2316
294	Sosnowiec Gł. d.	0542	0814	0941	0911	1130	1130	1104	1214	1256	1411	1302	1539	1512	1617	1701	1818	1807		1946	1902	2014	2054	2106		2340
302	Katowice a.	0551	0823	0950	0920	1139	1139	1113	1222	1305	1420	1311	1548	1521	1626	1710	1827	1816		1955	1911	2023	2103	2115		2349

km		MP 406 41010	IC 42102 42103	TLK 41100 41101	EIC 4100 4101	IC 4506 4507	EIP 45102	IC 111 41111	TLK 41110 4505	EC 4504	IC 48104	s	EC 113 41006	TLK 41104 45000	EC 104 45104	IC 45104 45105	TLK 45100	EC 4502 4503	IC 130	EC 42106 41004	TLK 42150 42151	EIP 4500 4501	IC 41112 41113	EIP 102 41000	TLK 117 41002	EC	TLK 45170
		①-⑥	①-⑥				①-⑥						①-⑥					⑧		①-⑤	⑥⑦		§			
		C	U	B			G	Q	A	G	s		M	Y	S	O	G	V	U		G	1646	G	P	Z	GN
	Katowice d.	0431		0540	0608	0655	0700	0737	0810	0851	1028		1133	1224	1233	1347	1438	1448	1533	1600	1646	1759	1834	1937	2316
	Sosnowiec Gł. d.	0440		0549	0617	0704	0709	0746	0821	0900	1037		1142	1233	1242	1356	1447	1500	1542	1609	1655	1808	1843	1946	2326
0	Zawiercie d.	0505		0618	0641		0737	0809	0852		1105		1207	1301	1307	1425	1517		1607	1637	1637		1836	1908	2011	2352
43	Częstochowa d.		0510	0657			0808		0925		1137			1334		1501	1558			1710	1710		1911			0049
129	Piotrków Trybunalski d.		0604	0751			0900		1017		1229			1426		1553	1651			1802	1802		2004			0143
168	Koluszki d.		0628	0818					1041					1450		1617				1827	1827		2028			
	Łódź Kaliska a.						0950				1321					1749										0218z
273	Warszawa Centralna a.	0705	0726	0924	0830	0910		1005	1148	1110			1405	1550	1505	1725			1710	1805	1925	1925	1905	2125	2101	2209
278	Warszawa Wschodnia a.	0716	0756	0936	0846	0926		1031	1208	1126			1418	1606	1526	1741			1726	1836	1956	1956	1926	2136	2112	2226

km		TLK 54171 116	TLK 14002 103	EC 14000	IC 48103	TLK 14151	IC 14113		EC 5401	IC 24107 24155	EC 14004 131	TLK 14105		EC 54000 105	IC 14105	EC 14006 112	EIP 1401		TLK 14111	TLK 14111	TLK 14101		EC 14008 110	TLK 5407		MP 14010 407
						⑥⑦	①-⑤									⑧			v	w	⑧					
		GN	Z						G	U	V	O		S		M			A	A			Q	G		C
0	Katowice 1075 d.	0600	0828	0923	0927	0955	0955		1117	1146	1230	1430		1526	1553	1631	1819		1832	1839	2015		2027	2106		0005
45	Tychy d.	0617		0937		1010	1011		1133	1202	1243	1448		1540	1609		1833				2033			2120		0021
	Rybnik 1075 d.		0909													1711			1856	1903			2108			
	Gliwice 1075 d.				0949				1049																	
	Bielsko Biała ▷ a.	0650				1049		1207	1234		1521			1648	1907				2106			2154			

km		MP 406 41010	TLK 41100	EIP 4100		EC 111 41008	TLK 41110	EIP 4504		EC 113 41006	EC 41104	EC 104 45000	TLK 45104		EC 130 41004	TLK 42106	TLK 42150	EIP 4500		IC 41112 41152	EC 102 41000	TLK 84102		EC 117 41002	TLK 45170
		①-⑥	①-⑥			①-⑥											①-⑤	⑥⑦							
		C		Q	A	G			M	Y	S	O		V	U	U	G			P		Z	GN	
0	Bielsko Biała ▷ d.		0436	0515		0800			1131		1254			1458		1556	1707						2206	
	Gliwice 1075 d.				0741															1823				
	Rybnik ▷ a.				0643				1048												1851			
39	Tychy d.	0357	0515	0548		0834			1204	1216	1230	1329		1517	1531	1531	1629		1740	1816			2239	
55	Katowice 1075 a.	0414	0531	0602		0728	0807	0848		1129	1220	1230	1344		1530	1546	1546	1643		1756	1830	1847		1933	2257

- To/from Racibórz (Table **1076**).
- To/from Bielsko Biała.
- CHOPIN – Warszawa - Budapest/Praha/Wien and v.v. For days of running and composition see Table **99**.
- To/from Gdynia (Tables **1025/30**).
- PORTA MORAVICA – [restaurant] and X Warszawa - Praha and v.v.
- Also conveys [bike] and/or [couchette].
- To/from Olsztyn (Table **1030**).
- POLONIA – [restaurant] and X Warszawa - Wien and v.v.
- COMENIUS – [restaurant] and X Warszawa - Ostrava and v.v.
- SOBIESKI – [restaurant] and X Gdynia - Warszawa - Wien and v.v.
- To/from Lublin (Table **1055**).
- VARSOVIA – [restaurant] and X Warszawa - Budapest and v.v.
- To/from Białystok (Table **1040**).
- PRAHA – [sleeping] and X Warszawa - Praha and v.v.

s – To/from Szczecin.
v – Until Dec. 31.
w – From Jan. 1.
z – Łódź Widzew.

§ – Train number varies on some days/dates: 14112/3 runs as 14150/1; 41112/3 runs as 41152/3.
▷ – For local trains Katowice - Bielsko Biała and Rybnik – see Tables **1077/79**.

WARSZAWA - ŁÓDŹ - WROCŁAW — 1061

km		IC 16101 16100	EIP 1600 1601	EIC 1620 1650	IC 16102 16103	EIP 1602 1603	IC 16104 16105	IC 26106 26107	EIC 1622	IC 16108 16109	EIP 1604 1605	EIP 1614 1615	IC 16110 16111	EIC 1608 1609	IC 17102 17103
		①-⑥							⑧		⑧			⑧	⑧
		J			JY			U		Y		J			
0	Warszawa Wsch d.	0454	0554	...	0714	0724	...	0954	...	1119	1154	...	1442	...	1612	...	1616	1616	...	1749	...	1854	1904
4	Warszawa Cent d.	0505	0610	...	0735	0745	...	1005	...	1135	1205	...	1453	...	1635	...	1627	1627	...	1805	...	1905	1914
	Piotrków Trybunalski d.				0855					1257										1931			
●	Częstochowa d.				0948					1352										2028			
130	Łódź Widzew ▷ d.	0617				0854				1316					1745							2027	
257	Kalisz ▷ d.	0757				1032				1455					1922							2209	
281	Ostrów Wlkp ▷ d.	0816				1051				1515					1940							2227	
	Opole Gł d.		0900		1048			1254	1452		1749		1918	1918			2130	2155	
	Brzeg d.								1517										
482*	Wrocław Gł ▷ a.	0938	0943	...	1140	1214	...	1337	...	1549	1640	...	1834	...	2114	...	2000	2000	...	2221	...	2240	

		EIP 6108 6109	IC 71102 71103	EIC 6122 6123	EIP 6104 6105	EC 6114 6115	IC 61109 61108	IC 61110 61111	EIP 6100 6101	IC 62107 62106	EIP 6102 6103	IC 61102 61103	EIC 6120 6150	IC 61100 61101	IC 61104 61105
		①-⑥	①-⑥		①-⑥	①-⑥	⑦						⑧		
		J			Y				U		JY		J		
	Wrocław Gł ▷ d.	0503	...	0611	0709	0709	...	0651	...	0835	...	1017	1054	...	1416	...	1522	...	1630	...	1850	...	1906	
	Brzeg d.							0907												1936	
	Opole Gł d.	0548	...	0658	0753	0753	...	0936	...	1101	...	1501	...	1720	...	2003	
	Ostrów Wlkp ▷ d.		0538					0818				1216			1647			2022	...	
	Kalisz ▷ d.		0538					0835				1234			1705			2039	...	
	Łódź Widzew ▷ d.		0742					1014				1412			1843			2219	...	
	Częstochowa a.							1041							1833			2123	
	Piotrków Trybunalski a.							1132							1922			2216	
	Warszawa Cent a.	0841	0855	...	0956	1047	1047	...	1126	...	1255	1355	1525	...	1753	1950	...	2048	2330	...	2340	
	Warszawa Wsch a.	0901	0906	...	1011	1058	1058	...	1204	...	1410	1556	...	1810	2006	...	2101	2342	...	2356	

- To/from Jelenia Góra/Szklarska Poręba Górna (Table **1084**).
- To/from Lublin (Table **1055**).
- To/from Białystok (Table **1040**).
▷ – For local trains see Table **1080**.
* – 406 km via CMK.
● – Częstochowa - Opole Gł: 91 km.

POLAND

1065 — WARSZAWA - KRAKÓW

km	For trains via Kielce see Table 1067	TLK 13100 13101	EIP 1300 1301 ①-⑥	EIP 1304 1305 ⑦	IC 53104	IC 13104	EIC 1322 1352	EIP 5302 5303	IC 13102 13103	EIC 1320 1321 ①-⑥	EIP 8300 8301	EIC 5318 5303	EIP 5102 53103	IC 1302 1303	EIC 5304 5305	EIP 83100 83101	EIC 5306 5307	EIP 53100 53101	EIC 1324 1325 ⑧		EIP 5308 5309 ⑧	EIP 5300 5301	IC 13106 13107 ⑧	EIC 1326 1327 ⑥	EIP 5310 5311	TLK 1311 1311
		§																	L				L			
0	Warszawa Wschodnia ...... d.	0524	0639	0734	0749	0749	0849	0934	1024	1044	1134	1134	1209	1239	1334	1428	1534	1604	1644	...	1734	1734	1824	1839	1934	2009
5	Warszawa Centralna ...... d.	0535	0650	0750	0820	0820	0900	0945	1055	1050	1150	1150	1220	1250	1350	1439	1550	1622	1655	...	1750	1750	1835	1855	1950	2022
297	Kraków Gł. ...... a.	0818	0905	1005	1225	1225	1123	1200	1400	1317	1405	1405	1624	1505	1607	1718	1806	2036	1921	...	2004	2004	2154	2118	2209	2301

		TLK 31112 31113	EIP 3510 3511	EIC 3124 3125 ①-⑥	IC 31106 31107 ⑦	IC 53106 53101 ①-⑥	EIP 3508 3509	IC 3500 3501	EIP 3126 3127	EIP 3506 3507	TLK 38100 38101	EIC 35102 35103	IC 3502 3505			EIP 3800 3801	EIP 3518 3519 ⑧	EIC 3120 3103 ⑥	IC 31102 31103	IC 35105 35105	EIP 3502 3503	EIC 3104 3105	IC 3122 3152	EIP 31100 31101	TLK 310 310
		V			L																		§		
Kraków Gł. ...... d.		0500	0553	0638	0559	0720	0753	0753	0842	0953	1024	1132	1153	...	1353	1353	1438	1510	1522	1522	1553	1653	1753	1843	1924	1959
Warszawa Centralna ...... a.		0740	0810	0905	0919	1140	1010	1010	1105	1210	1312	1535	1410	...	1610	1610	1701	1840	1940	1940	1810	1910	2010	2106	2205	2217
Warszawa Wschodnia ...... a.		0806	0826	0931	1016	1200	1026	1026	1116	1226	1327	1601	1426	...	1626	1626	1716	1856	2001	2001	1826	1931	2026	2117	2216	223

L – Conveys 🛏 Warszawa - Kraków (6300/3607) - Przemyśl - Lviv and v.v. See Table 1075.
V – HANCZA – 🛏 Kraków - Warszawa - Białystok - Suwałki and v.v.
　　　Conveys Dec. 11 - 24: 🛏 Kraków - Warszawa - Białystok (10015/16) - Hrodna and v.v. (Tables 1040/42).

§ – Train number varies on some days / dates:
　　13100/1 runs as 13150/1;
　　31100/1 runs as 31150/1.

1066 — KRAKÓW - ZAKOPANE

Southbound dates apply from Kraków

km		TLK 53171	TLK 13191	TLK 53171	TLK 83197	TLK 43191		TLK 33101	EIC 1353	EIC 1353				TLK 31190	EIC 3152	TLK 30100	EIC 3154	TLK 34190	TLK 38196		TLK 35170	TLK 3517
		Na		Nb	Nx	Ny		v	h	w					s		g	Nu	Nz		Nd	Nc
	Warszawa Cent. 1065 ... d.	2320	2230	2320					0805	0900		Zakopane ...... d.		0931	1522	1532	1714	1915	1933	...	2140	2244
0	Kraków Gł. ...... d.	0313	0325	0405	0410	0643			1037	1132		Nowy Targ ...... d.		0954	1541	1559	1733	1938	1956	...	2203	2307
5	Kraków Płaszów ...... d.	0357	0414	0437	0432	0714		0902	1112	1155		Chabówka ...... a.		1032	1607	1625	1805	2004	2022	...	2231	2341
68	Sucha Beskidzka ...... d.	0521	0543	0601	0601	0841		1021	1248	1313		Chabówka ...... d.		1046	1621	1639	1819	2018	2042	...	2243	2347
103	Chabówka ...... a.	0558	0629	0647	0647	0918		1103	1323	1348		Sucha Beskidzka ...... d.		1154	1710	1731	1908	2109	2134	...	2335	0039
103	Chabówka ...... d.	0612	0649	0701	0701	0943		1117	1337	1402		Kraków Płaszów ...... a.		1321	1813	1924	2017	2214	2242	...	0040	0150
126	Nowy Targ ...... d.	0638	0716	0728	0728	1009		1144	1404	1429		Kraków Gł. ...... a.		1355	1834	1841	2038	2234	2304	...	0127	0232
147	Zakopane ...... a.	0701	0740	0751	0751	1032		1206	1422	1447		Warszawa Cent. 1065 ... a.		1655	2106		2322			...	0620	0620

N – Also conveys 🛏 and / or 🍴.
a – Not Dec. 13 - 15, 25, Jan. 1, Feb. 4, Mar. 10.
b – Dec. 13 - 15, Feb. 4, Mar. 10.
c – Not Dec. 12 - 14, Feb. 3, Mar. 9.
d – Dec. 12 - 14, Feb. 3, Mar. 9.
g – ⑥⑦ Jan. 7 - Feb. 26 (also Dec. 25 - 30, Jan. 1).

h – ⑥⑦ Jan. 7 - Feb. 26 (also Dec. 24, 26 - 31).
j – Feb. 11 - 26 (also Dec. 23, 26, 29).
s – Dec. 17, 18, 23, 25, 26, 29, 30, Jan. 1, 6 - 8, Jan. 14 - Feb. 26, Mar. 4, 5, 11.
t – Dec. 11, 17, 18, 23, 24, 25 - 30, Jan. 1, Jan. 6 - Feb. 26, Mar. 4, 5, 11 (not Jan. 9 - 13).
u – Dec. 25, 26, Jan. 1, 6, 8, Jan. 14 - Feb. 26.

v – Dec. 17, 18, 23, 24, 26, 29 - 31, Jan. 6 - 8, Jan. 14 - Feb. 26, Mar. 4, 5, 11.
w – ①-⑥ Dec. 23 - 31; daily Jan. 6 - Feb. 26 (also Dec. 12, 17, 18, Mar. 4, 5, 11; not Jan. 9 - 13).
x – Dec. 23, 24, 26, 29 - 31, Jan. 6 - 8, Jan. 14 - Feb. 26.
y – Dec. 24, 26, 31, Jan. 6, 8, Jan. 14 - Feb. 26.
z – Dec. 23, 25, 26, 29, 30, Jan. 1, 6 - 8, Jan. 14 - Feb. 26.

1067 — WARSZAWA and LUBLIN - KIELCE - KATOWICE and KRAKÓW

km	For fast trains to Kraków see Table 1065	TLK 83170 83171	TLK 23101 ①-⑥		IC 53104 53105 ①-⑥	IC 13104 13105 ⑦	TLK 26101		IC 53102 53103	IC 26103		TLK 26103		IC 53100 53101		TLK 24101 ⑧		TLK 23105	TLK 12108 12109 ⑧		TLK 1319
		Q			O		C		O	Cy		Cz		O							NZa
0	Warszawa Centralna ...... d.	0425	...		0749	0749			1220					1622				1918			2230
4	Warszawa Wschodnia ...... d.	0414j	...		0820j	0820j			1209j					1604j				1909j			2237
•	Dęblin ...... d.																				2357
107*	Lublin ...... d.		0643				0820		1223		1306			1625	1846					
148	Radom ...... d.	0708	0806				0945		1348		1429			1746		2010	2135		0042
192	Skarżysko Kamienna 1058 ...... d.	0735	0835				1013		1415		1455			1812		2038	2202		0112
	Kielce ...... d.	0812	0913		1055	1055	1105		1455	1507		1550	1858	1903		2117	2237		0149
	Zawiercie ...... d.						1223			1623		1706		2019				
	Sosnowiec Gł. ...... d.						1250			1650		1723		2045				
	Katowice ...... a.						1259			1659		1741		2054				
324	Kraków Gł. ...... a.	0945	1041		1225	1225			1624					2036			2247		0318

km		TLK 21108 21109 ①-⑥		TLK 32104	TLK 42100 ①-⑥		IC 35100 35101	IC 35102 35103		TLK 62102		IC 35104 35105 ⑧	IC 31104 31105 ⑧		TLK 62100		TLK 32100 ⑧		TLK 38170 38171
							O	O				C			C				
0	Kraków Gł. ...... d.			0519			0720	1132				1522	1522			1641		1913	
0	Katowice ...... d.				0645			1102				1505			1505				
9	Sosnowiec Gł. ...... d.				0654			1111				1515			1515				
44	Zawiercie ...... d.				0732			1139				1545			1545				
161	Kielce ...... d.	0524		0652	0903		0909	1306		1319		1703	1703		1721		1815		2050
	Skarżysko Kamienna 1058 ...... d.	0600		0728	0940			1356				1758			1851		2128
	Radom ...... d.	0629		0754	1007			1423				1824			1917		2155
	Lublin ...... a.			0914	1127			1543				1944	2036				
	Dęblin ...... d.																	
	Warszawa Wschodnia ...... a.	0856j					1200j	1601j				2001j	2001j				0008j	
	Warszawa Centralna ...... a.	0836					1140	1535				1940	1940				2357	

C – To / from Wrocław (Table 1075).
N – Also conveys 🛏 and / or 🍴.
O – To / from Olsztyn (Table 1030).

Q – 🛏 1, 2 cl., 🍴 2 cl. and 🛏 Kolobrzeg - Gdynia - Gdańsk - Kraków and v.v. (Table 1015).
Z – To / from Zakopane (Table 1066).

a – ⑤⑥ Feb. 10 - 25 (also Dec. 22, 25, 28).
j – Via Warszawa Centralna.
y – Until Jan. 16.
z – From Jan. 17.

• – Lublin - Radom : 121 km.
* – 161 km via Dęblin.

1070 — POZNAŃ - WROCŁAW

km		IC 7300	TLK 56113 56112 ①-⑥	TLK 84106	TLK 84106		TLK 5607 5606	IC 8304	TLK 56105 56104	TLK 56105 56104		IC 8302	IC 8302	IC 54109 54108		IC 8314	TLK 5601 5600	TLK 5601 5600		IC 8404	TLK 16113 16153	TLK 8408		IC 5605 5604	IC 8317
			bt	Vq	Vp		B	P	Gq	Gp		Vw	Vx	Tq		S	Gq	Gp		V	Y	T		G	
0	Poznań Gł ...... d.	0552	0741	0843	0843	...	0938	1027	1156	1156	...	1236	1245	1355	...	1445	1547	1554	...	1649	1745	1841	...	1946	2227
69	Leszno ...... d.	0655	0839	0944	1002	...	1040	1124	1258	1306	...	1336	1336	1453	...	1542	1646	1655	...	1746	1841	1936	...	2042	2322
165	Wrocław Gł ...... a.	0758	0944	1047	1106	...	1144	1234	1405	1413	...	1439	1439	1601	...	1649	1749	1757	...	1855	1948	2044	...	2155	002

		IC 38175	IC 6505 6504	TLK 4809	TLK 61113 61153	TLK 61113 61153		IC 4805	IC 6500		IC 3815	TLK 45109 45108	IC 3803	IC 3803	IC 65105 65104		IC 3805	IC 3805	TLK 6507 6506		TLK 48107	TLK 65113 65112 ⑧		IC 3701
		Q	G	T	Yx	Yw		V	G		S	Tq	Sq	Sp	Gq		Pq	Pp	G		V	bt		
Wrocław Gł ...... d.		0415	0615	0717	0800	0800	...	0950	1033	...	1157	1240	1343	1343	1408	...	1545	1545	1630	...	1740	1822	...	2010
Leszno ...... d.		0521	0722	0824	0911	0911	...	1057	1139	...	1304	1352	1449	1449	1529	...	1654	1654	1741	...	1846	1933	...	2117
Poznań Gł ...... a.		0635	0826	0931	1009	1028	...	1200	1243	...	1407	1455	1552	1604	1632	...	1756	1805	1845	...	2001	2042	...	2229

G – To / from Gdynia (Tables 1015/20).
P – To / from Przemyśl (Table 1075).
Q – 🛏 1, 2 cl., 🍴 2 cl. and 🛏 Szczecin - Poznań - Wrocław - Przemyśl and v.v. (Tables 1010/75).
S – To / from Szczecin (Table 1010).

T – To / from Katowice (Table 1075).
V – 🛏 Katowice - Wrocław - Poznań - Szczecin and v.v. (Tables 1010/75).
Y – To / from Białystok (Table 1035).

b – To / from Bydgoszcz.
p – Until Dec. 31.
q – From Jan. 1.

t – From Jan. 1.
w – Until Feb. 6.
x – From Feb. 7.

RZESZÓW - JASŁO - ZAGÓRZ — 1073

km		TLK 33177				TLK 53153			
			⑦	⑦	①-⑥		⑤	⑦	
		g				h			
0	Rzeszów Gł .... d.	...	...	1433	1520	...	1539	...	1600 1950
9	Boguchwała .... d.	...	...	1446	1533	...	1550	...	1613 2003
52	Przybówka .... d.	...	...	1539	1625	...	...	1706	2056
71	Jasło .... d.	0653	0721	1559	1644	...	1708	...	1732 2114
94	Krosno .... d.	0721	0752	...	...	1737	...	1803	...
133	Sanok .... d.	0821	0849	...	...	1839	...	1900	...
139	Nowy Zagórz .... a.	...	0856	...	...	1907	...		
140	Zagórz .... a.	0832	0859	...	...	1850	...	1910	

		TLK 35152			TLK 30178		
		①-⑤		⑦		⑤	
			g		h		
	Zagórz .... d.	...	...	0905	...	1605	...	2030 2058
	Nowy Zagórz .... d.	...	...	...	...	1607	...	...
	Sanok .... d.	...	...	0916	...	1615	...	2042 2107
	Krosno .... d.	...	...	1018	...	1711	...	2141 2159
	Jasło .... d.	0456	0551	1100	...	1755	...	2209 2226
	Przybówka .... d.	0514	0609	...	...	1813	...	...
	Boguchwała .... d.	0607	0701	1158	...	1906	...	...
	Rzeszów Gł .... a.	0620	0715	1208	...	1919	...	...

■ – Dec. 17, 18, 23, 26, 29-31, Jan. 6, 8, Jan. 14 - Feb. 26, Mar. 4, 5, 11 (not Feb. 4).
h – Dec. 17, 18, 23, 26, 29, 30, Jan. 1, 6, 8, Jan. 14 - Feb. 26, Mar. 4, 5, 11.

ŁÓDŹ - KRAKÓW — 1074

km		IC 13111	IC 83106 83107	IC 53106 53107	IC 83104 83105	IC 83104 83105
		①-⑥	S	G	Sy	Sz
0	Łódź Kaliska .... 1060 d.	...	...	...	...	...
15	Łódź Widzew .... d.	0605	1024	1434	1824	1839
67	Piotrków Trybunalski . 1060 d.	0643				
153	Częstochowa .... 1060 d.	0741				
299*	Kraków Gł. .... a.	0919	1249	1701	2052	2128

		IC 38104 38105	IC 38106 35107	IC 38106 38107	IC 31110
		S	D	S	⑧
	Kraków Gł. .... d.	0652	1052	1452	1829
	Częstochowa .... 1060 d.	...	...	...	2010
	Piotrków Trybunalski . 1060 d.	...	...	...	2103
	Łódź Widzew .... d.	0924	1320	1729	2139
	Łódź Kaliska .... 1060 a.	...	...	...	...

■ – To/from Poznan. (Table 1025).
■ – To/from Gdynia. (Table 1025).
■ – To/from Szczecin (Table 1010).
y – Dec. 11-16, Dec. 19 - Feb. 28.
z – Dec. 17, 18, Mar. 1-11.
* – 274 km via CMK.

WROCŁAW - KATOWICE - KRAKÓW - PRZEMYŚL — 1075

For other trains Poznań - Katowice/Kraków see Tables 1080 (via Ostrów Wlkp) and 1025 (via Łódź)

km		IC 83174 83175	IC 6300 6301	TLK 73170	IC 6302 6303	IC 64104	IC 7300 7301	IC 62102	IC 6304 6305	TLK 84106	IC 62100	IC 8304 8305	TLK 73101	IC 62100	IC 8302 8303	TLK 54108	EIP 5309	IC 8314 8315	TLK 84100 64101	TLK 23103	TLK 6306 6307	IC 8404	IC 8408
		①-⑥		N			U	J	S	U	k	D	U		j	⑧		S	S	⑧		L S	k
		SN		N			U	J	S	U	k	D	U		j	⑧		S	S	⑧		L S	k
0	Wrocław Gł .... 1061 d.	0029	0418	0452	0616	0748	0828	0840	1053	1058	1233	1240	...	1252	1446	...	1607	1714	1719	1745	1842	1900	2044
42	Brzeg .... 1061 d.	0101	0447	0530	0645	0823	0902	0912	1123	1132	1313	1310	...	1321	1517	...	1641	1744	1750	1817	1914	1931	2114
82	Opole Gł. .... 1061 d.	0129	0510	0557	0714	0849	0927	0938	1147	1206	1339	1333	...	1347	1548	...	1707	1810	1816	1850	1938	1954	2136
162	Gliwice .... 1060 d.	0243	...	0709	...	0940	...	1027	...	1256	1428	...	1436	...	...	1758	...	1905	...	...	...	2045	2229
190	Katowice .... 1060 a.	0328	...	0734	...	1005	...	1051	...	1321	1452	...	1500	...	...	1824	...	1930	...	...	...	2109	2251
190	Katowice .... d.	0332	...	0739	...	...																	
	Częstochowa Stradom .... d.			0808	...	1032	...	1242	...	...	1430	...	...	1643	...	1907	...	...	2032	...			
268	Kraków Gł. .... a.	0550	...	0945	0937	...	1212	...	1415	...	...	1559	...	...	1817	...	2041	...	2200	...			
268	Kraków Gł. .... 1078 d.	0600	...	...	0944	...	1235	...	1418	...	...	1606	...	...	1836	...	2007	2046	...	2214	...		
273	Kraków Płaszów .... 1078 d.	0607	0800	...	0955	...	1242	...	1425	...	...	1613	...	...	1843	...	2014	2053	...	2221	...		
346	Tarnów .... 1078 d.	0703	0844	...	1046	...	1346	...	1513	...	...	1701	...	...	1934	...	2053	2140	...	2307	...		
379	Dębica .... d.	0730	0911	...	1123	...	1419	...	1541	...	...	1727	...	...	2002	...	2119	2207	...	2336	...		
426	Rzeszów .... 1058 d.	0814	0954	...	1206	...	1507	...	1624	...	...	1810	1920	...	2059	...	2154	2252	2319	...	0019		
463	Przeworsk .... 1058 d.	0841	1021	...	1233	...	1537	...	1651	...	...	1837	1946	...	2126	...	2319	2344	...	0046			
478	Jarosław .... 1058 d.	0853	1033	...	1246	...	1550	...	1704	...	...	1849	1957	...	2138	...	2331	2355	...	0059			
513	Przemyśl .... 1058 a.	0925	1119	...	1318	...	1634	...	1735	...	...	1921	2030	...	2210	...	0004	0028	...	0130			

		TLK 4809	IC 4805	IC 3606 3607	TLK 46100 46101	TLK 32102	IC 48101	IC 3814 3815	EIP 3508	TLK 3802	TLK 37100	TLK 26101	IC 3804 3805	IC 48107	TLK 3604 3605	TLK 3700 3701	TLK 26103	IC 26103	IC 46105 46120	IC 46120	IC 3602 3603	IC 46105	IC 37171	IC 3600 3601	IC 38175 38174
				①-⑥-①-⑥													y	z			y	⑦	z	⑧	
		k	S	M		U	S	S		S	D	U	k	S	J	U	U						N	SN
	Przemyśl .... 1058 d.	...	0222	0333	...	0431	...	0627	0739	...	0849	1116	...	1226	...	1429	...						1636	1826
	Jarosław .... 1058 d.	...	0254	0404	...	0503	...	0659	0810	...	0922	1149	...	1259	...	1502	...						1708	1858
	Przeworsk .... 1058 d.	...	0306	0415	...	0516	...	0711	0821	...	0934	1201	...	1312	...	1514	...						1720	1910
	Rzeszów .... 1058 d.	...	0334	0440	...	0545	0600	0759	0846	...	1002	1229	...	1343	...	1542	...						1748	1938
	Dębica .... d.	...	0416	...	...	0627	0636	0841	...	...	1044	1311	...	1429	...	1630	...						1832	2023
	Tarnów .... 1078 d.	...	0444	...	...	0656	0702	0904	...	...	1112	1339	...	1459	...	1700	...						1900	2055
	Kraków Płaszów .... 1078 d.	...	0531	...	...	0749	0744	0958	...	...	1159	1427	...	1550	...	1747	...						1950	2146
	Kraków Gł. .... 1078 a.	...	0538	...	...	0756	0750	1005	...	...	1206	1433	...	1557	...	1754	...						1957	2153
	Kraków Gł. .... d.	...	0611	...	...	0831	...	1010	...	...	1211	1445	...	1612	1800	1855							2025	2204
	Częstochowa Stradom .. d.	...	0744	...	...	1003	...	1138	...	...	1346	1616	...	1750	1929	...						2057	2156	
	Katowice .... a.																					2057	0009	
	Katowice .... 1060 d.	0505	0728	...	...	0857	...	1012	...	1319	1504	1702	1744	1812	...	1955	2102						0020	
	Gliwice .... 1060 d.	0528	0751	...	...	0919	...	1037	...	1343	1528	1725	1806	1835	...	2018	2125						0123	
	Opole Gł. .... 1061 d.	0620	0843	0850	0934	...	1011	1102	1129	1243	1434	1442	1621	1711	1816	1901	1938	1946	2035	2111	2244	2254	0243
	Brzeg .... 1061 d.	0642	0905	0911	0959	...	1035	1123	1153	1305	1459	1504	1646	1733	1841	1920	1925	2003	2012	2057	2136	2309	2316	0309
	Wrocław Gł. .... 1061 a.	0711	0934	0939	1028	...	1106	1152	1234	1333	1529	1533	1718	1801	1910	1950	1955	2034	2048	2126	2207	2339	2344	0340

A – Runs on uneven dates in Jan.; even dates in Dec., Feb., Mar.
B – Runs on even dates in Jan.; uneven dates in Dec., Feb., Mar.
D – To/from Poznan (Table 1001).
J – To/from Jelenia Góra (Table 1084).
L – LVIV EXPRESS / MATEJKO – 🛏 2 cl. Wrocław - Kraków - Przemyśl (35/51) - Lviv. Conveys 🛏 Warszawa (1326/7) - Kraków - Lviv.
M – LVIV EXPRESS / MATEJKO – 🛏 2 cl. Lviv (36/52) - Przemyśl - Kraków - Wrocław. Conveys 🛏 Lviv - Kraków (3124/5) - Warsaw.
N – Also conveys 🛏 and/or 🛏.
S – To/from Szczecin/Świnoujście (Tables 1010/70).
J – To/from Lublin (Table 1067).

h – From Jan. 1.
k – To/from Słupsk (Table 1015).
y – Until Jan. 16.
z – From Jan. 17.

‡ – Ukrainian (East European) time.

PRZEMYŚL - LVIV

km		33015 51 BL				52 33016 AM
	Kraków Gł. (see above) .... d.	2214	...	Lviv .... d.	2315
0	Przemyśl .... d.	0356	...	Mostiska II ‡ d.	0101
13	Medyka .... d.	...		Medyka .... d.	...
20	Mostiska II ‡ d.	0600		Przemyśl .... a.	0036
98	Lviv ‡ a.	0715	...	Kraków Gł. (see above) .. a.	0538

1076 KATOWICE and KRAKÓW - BOHUMÍN - OSTRAVA

km		EC	EC	EC	EC	EC	EC	MP	MP	MP	MP
		116	103	131	105	112	110	402	402	407	407
		✕⁄	✕⁄	✕⁄	✕⁄	✕⁄	✕⁄	444	407	444	
							Ⓑ	🅁			
		Y		V	S	M	N	W	K	P	C
	Warszawa Cent. **1060** ... d.	0550	0655	0955	1255	1355	1754	...	...	2120	2120
0	**Katowice** ... d.	0828	0923	1230	1526	1631	2027	...	...	0010	0010
•116	**Kraków** Gł. ... ▷ d.	|	|	|	|	|	|	2202	2202	|	|
•51	Oświecim ... ▷ d.	|	|	|	|	|	|	2342	2342	|	|
74	Zebrzydowice 🛃 ... d.	|	1023	1323	1623	|	|	0054	0054	0103	0103
45	Rybnik ... ▷ d.	0908	|	|	|	1712	2109	|	|	|	|
82	Racibórz ... ▷ d.	|	|	|	|	|	|	|	|	|	|
102	Chałupki ... ▷ d.	0941	|	|	|	1743	2145	|	|	|	|
∆94	Bohumín 🛃 ... a.	0947	1040	1340	1640	1749	|	0112	0112	0121	0121
94	Bohumín 🛃 ... **1160** d.	1008	1050	1350	1650	1808	|	0212	0220	0212	0220
102	**Ostrava** hlavní ... **1160** a.	1016	1058	1358	1658	1816	2155	0220	0228	0220	0228
	Praha hlavní **1160** ... a.	1339	|	|	|	2139	...	0633	|	0633	|
	Wien Hbf **1150** ... a.	...	1349	|	1949	...	...	...	0655	...	0655
	Budapest Keleti ... a.	...	...	1935	...	...	...	...	...	...	...

	MP	MP	MP	MP	EC	EC	EC	EC	EC	EC
	406	406	445	445	111	113	104	130	102	117
		403	406	403	✕⁄	✕⁄	✕⁄	✕⁄	✕⁄	✕⁄
				🅁	①–⑥					
	C	K	P	W	N	M	S	V		Y
Budapest Keleti ... d.	...	...	...	...	...	...	...	0822	...	...
Wien Hbf **1150** ... d.	2250	2250	...	...	...	...	0810	|	1410	...
Praha hlavní **1160** ... d.	|	|	2200	2200	...	0622	|	|	|	1422
Ostrava hlavní ... **1160** d.	0156	0156	0217	0217	0556	0944	1101	1401	1701	1744
Bohumín 🛃 ... **1160** a.	0203	0203	0226	0226	|	0952	1108	1408	1708	1752
Bohumín 🛃 ... d.	0300	0404	0300	0404	|	1007	1120	1420	1720	1809
Chałupki ... ▷ d.	|	|	|	|	0611	1016	|	|	|	1817
Racibórz ... ▷ d.	|	|	|	|	|	|	|	|	|	|
Rybnik ... ▷ d.	|	|	|	|	0643	1048	|	|	|	1851
Zebrzydowice 🛃 ... d.	0319	0424	0319	0424	|	|	1138	1439	1738	|
Oświecim ... ▷ a.	|	0534	|	0534	|	|	|	|	|	|
Kraków Gł. ... ▷ a.	|	0708	|	0708	|	|	|	|	|	|
Katowice ... a.	0411	...	0411	...	0728	1129	1230	1530	1830	1933
Warszawa Cent. **1060** a.	0705	...	0705	...	1005	1405	1505	1805	2101	2210

C – CHOPIN – 🛏 1, 2 cl., ▬ 2 cl. and (2) Warszawa - Wien and v.v.; 🛏 1, 2 cl., ▬ 2 cl. and (2) Warszawa - Bratislava - Budapest and v.v.
K – 🛏 1, 2 cl. Kraków - Wien and v.v.; 🛏 1, 2 cl. and ▬ 2 cl. Kraków - Bratislava - Budapest and v.v.
M – PORTA MORAVICA – (12) and ✕ Warszawa - Praha and v.v.
N – COMENIUS – (12) and ✕ Warszawa - Ostrava and v.v.
P – 🛏 1, 2 cl. and (2) Warszawa - Praha and v.v. Also conveys ▬ 2 cl. on dates in Table **99**.
S – SOBIESKI – (12) and ✕ Gdynia - Warszawa - Wien and v.v.
V – VARSOVIA – (12) and ✕ Warszawa - Budapest and v.v.
W – SILESIA – 🛏 1, 2 cl., ▬ 2 cl. and (2) Kraków - Praha and v.v.
Y – PRAHA – (12) and ✕ Warszawa - Praha and v.v.
⁄ – Supplement payable.
▷ – For local trains see Tables **1079/99**.
• – Distance from Zebrzydowice
∆ – *106 km* via Chałupki.

1077 KATOWICE - BIELSKO BIAŁA - ZWARDOŃ - ŽILINA

Koleje Śląskie, 2nd class

km				a	c										b
0	**Katowice** ... **1060** d.	0536	0701	0739	0819	0940	1138	1339	1441	1540	1641	1739	1937	2127	2256
17	Tychy ... d.	0555	0718	0757	0837	0958	1205	1357	1500	1558	1659	1758	1956	2145	2317
44	Czechowice Dziedzice .. d.	0625	0738	0827	0906	1028	1236	1427	1528	1627	1729	1827	2027	2214	2345
55	**Bielsko Biała** ... **1060** d.	0651	0752	0847	0924	1045	1258	1450	1545	1644	1755	1850	2046	2231	0003
76	Zywiec ... a.	0727	0842	0917	1000	1115	1328	1523	1625	1714	1825	1922	2117	2301	0032
113	**Zwardoń** ... a.	0834	0948	1017	1100	1225	1435	1624	1723	1816	1933a	2031	2218	0001	...

				a							c	a			
Zwardoń ... d.	0347	0442	0546	0623	0739	0916	...	1130	1341	1448	1627	1627	1821	1936	...
Zywiec ... d.	0447	0543	0647	0733	0841	1035	...	1235	1447	1557	1751	1748	1921	2039	...
Bielsko Biała ... **1060** d.	0521	0619	0722	0813	0915	1110	...	1318	1523	1642	1825	1823	1956	2114	2224
Czechowice Dziedzice ... d.	0537	0636	0739	0830	0932	1127	...	1335	1539	1700	1836	1840	2012	2131	2241
Tychy ... d.	0606	0705	0808	0859	1003	1156	...	1404	1608	1731	1857	1909	2041	2200	2311
Katowice ... **1060** a.	0625	0722	0826	0917	1022	1214	...	1422	1626	1750	1913	1927	2059	2218	2330

		a	⑦		a	a	d	b
Czech. Dziedzice .. d.	0609	0847	0935	...	1308	1434	1634	1930
Zebrzydowice ... d.	0658	0934	1022	...	1356	1521	1723	2025
Cieszyn ★ ... a.	0730	1007	1054	...	1428	1553	1755	2058

	d	b	⑥		a	b	a	d
Cieszyn ★ ... d.	0546	0802	1039	...	1300	1438	1611	1845
Zebrzydowice ... d.	0628	0844	1121	...	1342	1520	1653	1927
Czech. Dziedzice .. a.	0706	0922	1200	...	1420	1559	1732	2005

a – Ⓐ only.
b – Ⓑ only.
c – Ⓒ only.
d – ⚒ only.

★ – Cieszyn station (Poland) is situated ± 1500 metres from Český Těšín station (Czech Republic).

ZWARDÓN - ŽILINA

km					a	
0	**Zwardoń** 🛃 ... d.	0642	...	1541	1642	1952
22	Čadca ... **1160** a.	0726	...	1626	1732	2026
52	**Žilina** ... **1160** a.	0813	...	1713	1813	2113

			a		
Žilina ... **1160** d.	0448	1348	1448	...	1757
Čadca 🛃 ... **1160** d.	0537	1437	1537	...	1837
Zwardoń 🛃 ... a.	0617	1510	1610	...	1910

1078 KRAKÓW - NOWY SĄCZ - KRYNICA

km		TLK			□	TLK		□	□	□	□
		30171	①–⑤			13151					
		y				h				x	
0	**Kraków** Gł. ... **1075** d.	...	...	0414	0544	0832	...	...	1514	1644	2018
5	Kraków Płaszów ... **1075** d.	0335	...	0420	0550	0854	...	...	1520	1650	2024
78	Tarnów ... **1075** a.	0418	...	0529	0640	0942	...	...	1627	1737	2131
78	Tarnów ... d.	0419	0431	0530	0642	0944	1327	...	1628	1738	2132
136	Stróze ... d.	0540	0550	0651	0745	1047	1438	...	1746	1837	2248
167	**Nowy Sącz** ... d.	0617	0630	0730	0822	1126	1516	1525	1825	1913	2326
217	Muszyna ... d.	0732	...	...	0924	1241	...	1643	...	2019	...
228	**Krynica** ... a.	0749	...	...	0939	1300	...	1700	...	2036	...

	□		□			TLK		□	□	TLK
						31150				3317
	x	①–⑤				j	Ⓑ		w	z
Krynica ... d.	...	...	0953	...	...	1410	...	1828	...	211
Muszyna ... d.	...	...	1018	...	...	1441	...	1851	...	214
Nowy Sącz ... d.	0403	0655	1124	1129	1525	1545	1746	1948	2020	225
Stróze ... d.	0442	0734	...	1208	1604	1623	1825	2022	2059	234
Tarnów ... a.	0600	0852	...	1319	1718	1746	1943	2120	2211	004
Tarnów ... **1075** d.	0601	...	...	...	...	1748	2000	2121	2212	004
Kraków Płaszów ... **1075** a.	0650	...	...	...	...	1836	2118	2231	2321	012
Kraków Gł. ... **1075** a.	0657	...	...	...	...	1908	2127	2238	2327	...

h – Dec. 17, 18, 23, 24, 26, 29 - 31, Jan. 6, 8, Jan. 14 - Feb. 26, Mar. 4, 5, 11.
j – Dec. 17, 18, 23, 25, 26, 29, 30, Jan. 1, 6, 8, Jan. 14 - Feb. 26, Mar. 4, 5, 11.
w – From Jan. 1.
x – From Dec. 31.
y – Dec. 11, 17, 18, 23, 26, 29 - 31, Jan. 6, 8, Jan. 14 - Feb. 26, Mar. 4, 5, 11 (not Feb. 4).
z – Dec. 11, 17, 18, 23, 26, 29, 30, Jan. 1, 6, 8, Jan. 14 - Feb. 26, Mar. 4, 5, 11 (not Feb. 3).
□ – Operator: Koleje Małopolskie

1079 LOCAL SERVICES IN SILESIA

2nd class

KATOWICE - OSWIECIM

Operator: Koleje Śląskie

km		①					a		a			
0	Katowice ... d.	0457	0635	0835	...	1240	1440	1540	1647	...	1840	...
33	Oswiecim ... d.	0552	0726	0925	...	1330	1530	1630	1738	...	1931	...

	a							a			⑤
Oswiecim ... d.	0534	0632	0844	...	1240	1441	...	1542	...	1730	205
Katowice ... a.	0627	0725	0936	...	1332	1533	...	1635	...	1823	215

KATOWICE - RYBNIK - RACIBÓRZ

Operator: Koleje Śląskie

km									a			
0	Katowice ... d.	0416	...	0527	0834	1129	1332	1520	1636	...	1929	2138
45	Rybnik ... d.	0514	0523	0629	0928	1224	1427	1621	1738	...	2024	2233
81	Racibórz ... a.	...	0612	0721	1016	1312	1515	1709	1827	...	2114	2322

						c					
Racibórz ... d.	0441	0538	0739	1037	1250	1433	1538	1748	1934	2150	...
Rybnik ... d.	0536	0631	0831	1135	1342	1531	1639	1840	2027	2240	224
Katowice ... a.	0631	0734	0939	1238	1444	1634	1744	1940	2123	...	234

RACIBÓRZ - CHAŁUPKI

Operator: Koleje Śląskie

km		a							a			
0	Racibórz ... d.	0530	0750	...	1337	...	1519	...	1627	...	1950	...
22	Chałupki △ ... a.	0604	0825	...	1412	...	1553	...	1702	...	2024	...

	a							a			
Chałupki △ ... d.	0436	...	0636	...	0900	...	1435	1603	...	1906	...
Racibórz ... a.	0507	...	0707	...	0932	...	1506	1635	...	1937	...

(WROCŁAW -) OPOLE - KEDZIERZYN-KOŹLE - RACIBÓRZ

Operator: Przewozy Regionalne

km		a						a				
	Wrocław Gł ... d.	...	...	0753	0931	1145	...	1336	1434	1659	...	1847
0	Opole Gł. ... d.	...	...	0909	1055	1300	...	1505	1605	1805	...	2024
42	Kedzierzyn-Koźle ... d.	0601	0701	1001	1146	1352	1401	1556	1701	1856	1901	2116
74	Racibórz ... a.	0645	0745	1046	...	...	1445	...	1746	...	1945	2201

										j	
Racibórz ... d.	0512	...	0715	1015	...	...	1518	...	1719	1946	...
Kedzierzyn-Koźle ... a.	0551	0556	0758	1059	...	1357	1557	1602	1807	2033	203
Opole Gł. ... a.	...	0700	0910	1210	...	1521	...	1725	1923	...	213
Wrocław Gł ... a.	...	0806	1023	1329	...	1624	...	1849	2044	...	225

a – Ⓐ only.
c – Ⓒ only.
j – From Jan. 1.

△ – Chałupki station is situated ± 1600 metres from Stary Bohumín, where a 🚌 service runs approximately every 30 minutes from the main square (náměsti Svobody) to Bohumín (journey 15 mins) and Ostrava (journey 45 mins).

POZNAŃ - OSTRÓW - KATOWICE - KRAKÓW — 1080

For other trains Poznań - Katowice - Kraków (via Wrocław) see Table **1075**; for Poznań - Kraków via Łódź see Table **1025**

km					TLK 83102			TLK 84102			TLK 73104					TLK 37105 ①–⑥			TLK 48103			TLK 38103			
		⊗	⊗	⊗		⊗		⊗	⑧	⑥⑦	⊗						⊗	⊗		⊗		⊗	⊗	⊗	⊗
					S			**E**											**E**			**S**			
0	Poznań Gł............d.	...	...	0932	...	...	1440	...	...	1728		Kraków Gł............d.	0444	...	...	0540	0810	0927	...	1342	...	1538	1826	2047
67	Jarocin ....d.	...	...	1029	...	...	1528	...	...	1822		Katowice ....d.	...	0540	0810	0927	...	1342	...	1538	1826	2047		
114	Ostrów Wlkp.........d.	...	...	1103	...	...	1602	...	...	1855		Bytom ....d.	...	0605	0834		...	1406	...	1602	1850	2111		
160	Kępno ....d.	...	...	1134	...	...	1633	...	...	1925		Gliwice ....d.	...	...	0951	...		...	...					
201	Kluczbork ....d.	...	...	1200	...	...	1659	...	...	1954		Lubliniec ....d.	0654	0709	0939	1035	...	1511	1528	1707	1956	2214		
252	Lubliniec ....d.	0703	0912	1211	1235	...	1525	1735	1748	1931	2028	Kluczbork ....d.	0729	...	1110	...	...	1605	...	...			
	Gliwice ....d.						1823					Kępno ....d.	0759	...	1136	...	...	1631	...	...			
302	Bytom ....d.	0759	1007	1304		1620		1843	2026			Ostrów Wlkp.........d.	0836	...	1209	...	...	1709	...	...			
20	**Katowice** ....d.	0822	1030	1328		1643	1847	1908	2049			Jarocin ....d.	0909	...	1243	...	...	1745	...	...			
398	**Kraków** Gł. ....a.	...	...	1447		...	...	...	...	2234		Poznań Gł............a.	0957	...	1326	...	...	1835	...	...			

2nd class — LOCAL TRAINS POZNAŃ / WROCŁAW - OSTRÓW WLKP - ŁÓDŹ

			Ⓐ																			
Poznań Gł. ....d.	...	0546	0850	...	1052	1248	1450	...	1852	...	2048	**Łódź** Kaliska ... **1061**	0520	...	0725	...	1020	1219	1425	...	1627	1820	...
Jarocin ....d.	...	0646	0949	...	1153	1349	1550	...	1953	...	2149	Kalisz **1061**	0707	...	0908	...	1159	1405	1608	...	1806	1957	...
Wrocław Gł. **1061** d.	...	...	...	0805	...	...	1615	...	1935	...	...	Ostrów Wlkp.........**1061**	0733	0746	0940	1040	1238	1440	1632	1642	1845	2020	2036
Ostrów Wlkp.... **1061** d.	0505	0740	1026	1033	1241	1440	1656	1830	2030	2132	2231	**Wrocław** Gł. **1061** a.	0928	...		...	...	1831	...	...			
Kalisz .... **1061** d.	0529	0802	...	1057	1303	1503	1718	1854	...	...	...	Jarocin ....d.	...	0824	1017	1118	1315	1520	...	1719	1923	...	2118
Łódź Kaliska ... **1061** a.	0710	0943	...	1244	1443	1643	1857	2040	...	...	...	Poznań Gł............a.	...	0920	1112	1212	1410	1617	...	1818	2019	...	2224

- To / from Kołobrzeg (Table **1015**).
- To / from Szczecin / Świnoujście (Table **1010**).

⊗ – Operator: Koleje Śląskie.
* – 331 km via Gliwice.

JELENIA GÓRA - TRUTNOV — 1082

Valid Summer 2016 (no winter service)

km			**S**	**S**	**S**				**S**	**S**	**S**
0	Jelenia Góra.................d.	...	...	1158	1628		Trutnov hlavní ....d.	...	0929	...	1425	1909
27	Sędzisław ....d.	...	0809	1234	1703		Královec 🚲...........d.	...	1000	...	1501	1943
43	Lubawka 🚲 ....d.	...	0833	1259	1728		Lubawka 🚲 ....d.	...	1010	...	1511	1945
48	Královec 🚲...........d.	...	0842	1308	1737		Sędzisław ....d.	...	1039	...	1540	2008
65	**Trutnov** hlavní ....a.	...	0911	1337	1806		**Jelenia Góra** ....a.	...	1111	...	1610	...

- ⑥⑦ Apr. 23 - Aug. 28 (also May 3, 26, 27, Aug. 15).

Operated by Koleje Dolnośląskie (in Czech Republic by GW Train Regio).

SZKLARSKA PORĘBA GÓRNA - JELENIA GÓRA - WAŁBRZYCH - WROCŁAW — 1084

km		EIP 6104 ①–⑥	IC 6304 P		IC 61102 M		EIC 6150 Dm	IC 61100 Dn z	TLK 65170 N				TLK 56171 N	⊖	IC 16101 D	EIC 1651 y	IC 16103 M		IC 3605 P	EIP 1605 ⑧	
0	Jelenia Góra .... d.	0528	0834	0937	1142	1305	1351	1409	1440	1630	1928	2032	Warszawa C. △ d.	...	...	0505	0735	0745	...	...	1627	...
27	Sędzisław ....d.		0859	1003	1209	1331	1419	1437		1656	1955	2101	**Wrocław** Gł. ....d.	0703	0710	0922	0950	1143	1240	1457	1713	1828	2003	2104
47	Wałbrzych Gł.........d.		0920	1025	1229	1351	1440	1459	1519	1715	2016	2122	Jaworzyna Śląska ...d.	0741	0757	1004	1025	1218	1320	1539	1800	1903		2152
78	Jaworzyna Śląska ..d.		0954	1059	1302	1424	1515	1532	1551	1751	2051	2200	Wałbrzych Gł.........d.	0822	0833	1041	1103	1252	1356	1618	1836	1941		2228
127	**Wrocław** Gł. ....a.	0706	1028	1140	1345	1459	1556	1614	1625	1826	2135	2235	Sędzisław ....d.	0842	0854	1102	1123		1416	1639	1858	2001		2249
	Warszawa C. △ ..a.	1047	...	...	1950	...	...	2048	2330	...			**Jelenia Góra** .... a.	0911	0921	1132	1149	1332	1443	1706	1924	2026	2147	2316

km			N	⊖	D	⊖		⊖	⊖	⊖	⊖				⊖	⊖	Dm	Dn	⊖	⊖	N
0	Jelenia Góra ....d.	...	0722	0952	0925	1135	...	1311	1527	1726	1926		Szklarska Poręba Górna ....d.	0624	0826	1044	1255	1316	1436	1635	1835	1909
32	Szklarska Poręba Górna ....a.	...	0810	1039	1013	1223	...	1406	1616	1814	2015		Jelenia Góra ....a.	0713	0915	1133	1348	1404	1525	1724	1924	2002

- To / from Poznań (Table **1070**).
- 🚃 Białystok - Warszawa - Jelenia Góra and v.v. (Table **1040**).
- Also conveys 🛏 and / or 🍴.
- To / from Przemyśl (Table **1075**).

m – Dec. 11-21, Feb. 3-9.
n – Dec. 22 - Feb. 2, Feb. 10 - Mar. 11.
y – Dec. 11, 17, 18, 23, 24, 26 - 31, Jan. 6-8, Jan. 14 - Feb. 26, Mar. 4, 5, 11.
z – Dec. 11, 17, 18, 23, 24, 26 - 30, Jan. 1, 6 - 8, Jan. 14 - Feb. 26, Mar. 4, 5, 11.

⊖ – Operated by Koleje Dolnośląskie.
△ – **1060** via Katowice; **1070** via Poznań; **1090** via Łódź.

GÖRLITZ - WROCŁAW — 1085

Operator : Koleje Dolnośląskie

km																		**F**			
	Dresden 855 ...... d.	...	...	0608	...	...	1208	...	1808	...	...	**Wrocław** Gł. **1086** d.	0452	0616	0945	...	1213	1339	1540	...	1646	1815	1945
0	Görlitz 🚲 ...... d.	...	...	0739	...	1107	1335	...	1939	...	2207	Legnica .... **1086** d.	0545	0709	1040	...	1307	1436	1635	...	1742	1908	2044
1	Zgorzelec 🚲.. **1005** d.	...	...	0744	0909	...	1112	1340	...	1944	...	2212	Bolesławiec ...... d.	0619	0748	1116	...	1346	1511	1710	...	1817	1947	2119
3	Zgorzelec Miasto .. d.	...	...	0747	0912	...	1115	1343	...	1947	...	2215	Węgliniec ...... **1005** d.	0637	0809	1133	1146	1406	1528	1728	1744	1834	2009	2136
28	Węgliniec ...... **1005** d.	0516	0641	0810	0935	0946	1138	1407	1546	2011	2146	2236	Zgorzelec Miasto .. d.	...	0829	...	1209	1404	1602	...	1805	...	2029	...
53	Bolesławiec ...... d.	0534	0659	0830	...	1004	...	1427	1604	2031	2204	...	Zgorzelec 🚲.. **1005** d.	...	0833	...	1213	1433	1605	...	1808	...	2033	...
99	Legnica .... **1086** d.	0608	0734	0910	...	1041	...	1508	1639	2110	2239	...	Görlitz 🚲 ...... a.	...	0837	...	1217	1437	...	...	...	...	2037	...
164	**Wrocław** Gł. .. **1086** a.	0701	0827	1003	...	1135	...	1600	1733	2202	2332	...	Dresden 855 ...... a.	...	1000	...	1600	...	...	...	...	...	2200	...

⤧ – From Zielona Góra (Table **1005**).

COTTBUS - FORST - WROCŁAW — 1086

km			⊖	⊖	①–⑤	⑥⑦	①–⑤		①–⑤	①–⑤	⑥⑦	⑤				①–⑤			⊖	⊖		⊖	⊖	⑤		⊖	⊖
	Berlin Licht ....d.	...	...	...	...	...	...	...							**Wrocław** Gł. **1085** d.	...	...	0815	...	1305	...	...	1715	1850			
0	**Cottbus** ...... 854 d.	...	0607	...	...	1607	...	...							Legnica ...... **1085** d.	...	0618	0907	...	1406	...	1552	1813	1953			
22	Forst 🚲 ...... 854 d.	...	0625	...	...	1626	...	...							Żagań ...... **1005** d.	0539	0728	1023	...	1521	1541	1701	1922	2103			
22	Forst...........d.	...	0635	...	...	1638	...	...							Żary ...... **1005** d.	0551	0740	1035	...	1534	1553	1713	1934	2115			
36	Tuplice ....d.	...	0650	...	...	1653	...	...							Tuplice ....d.	0612	...	...	...	1614	...	...	...	...			
57	Żary ....**1005** d.	0529	0711	0830	1307	1330	1556	1714	1817	1911	2055		Forst ....d.	0628	...	...	...	1629	...	...	...	...			
70	Żagań ...... **1005** d.	0546	0723	0846	1320	1343	1609	1726	1830	1924	2108		Forst 🚲 ...... 854 d.	0633	...	...	...	1633	...	...	...	...			
144	Legnica ...... **1085** d.	0703	...	0956	1430	1459	1724	...	2041	2041	2217		**Cottbus** ...... 854 a.	0651	...	...	...	1651	...	...	...	...			
210	**Wrocław** Gł. **1085** a.	...	...	1046	...	1817	...	2044	2140	...	...		Berlin Licht ....a.	...	...	...	...	...	...	...	...	...			

⊖ – Operated by Koleje Dolnośląskie.

Reservation is compulsory for travel by all EC, EIC, EIP, EN, IC, MP and TLK trains

1090 WARSZAWA - ŁÓDŹ

km		IC 16100 16101 ①–⑥ J	IR 10120 10121 ①–⑥	TLK 19112 19113	IC 16102 16103 ①–⑤	IC 10854 51127	TLK 19104 51126 ①–⑤ J	IR 10122 10123	♣	IC 26106 26107 ⑧	TLK 19102 19103 ⑥⑦	♣	IC 10124 10125 ⑥⑦	IR 10118 10119 ①–⑤	IC 19106 19107 ⑥⑦	♣	IR 10126 10127 ①–⑤	TLK 19114 19115 ①–⑤	IC 16108 16109 ⑪	TLK 19132 19133 ①–⑤	IC 1910 1911	IC 19110 19111 ⑦	TLK 19116 19117 ①–⑤	IR 10128 10129 ⑥	♣ ①	IC 1911 1911
0	Warszawa Wschodnia d.	0454	0504	0624	0724	0854	1004	1054	1124	1154	1309	1324	1324	1344	1504	1509	1509	1524	1612	1625	1654	1654	1704	1719	1724	172
4	Warszawa Centralna d.	0505	0515	0635	0705	0905	1015	1105	1145	1205	1320	1345	1345	1415	1515	1520	1520	1544	1635	1645	1705	1705	1715	1735	1735	174
70	Skierniewice d.	0545	0558	0715	0822	0951	1055	1150	1220	1245	1359	1420	1429	1455	1555	1555	1555	1602	1631		1732		1745	1805	1818	1813	185
109	Koluszki d.	0605	0622	0734	0842	1014	1115	1213	1239	1304	1419	1439	1452	1515	1614	1614	1614	1624	1656	1733	1805		1805	1830	1843	1832	185
137	Łódź Chojny d.	0627			0904					1327								1755								
144	Łódź Kaliska ■ a.		0634	0745	...	1028	1126	1226	1249		1430	1449	1505	1526	1625	1624	1637	1710		1820	1812	1816	1844	1855	1842	190

		IC 10110 10111		IC 19108 17103 ⑦	IC 17102 17103 ⑥	IR 10130 10131 ①–⑤	IC 51108 51109 ⑥⑦		IC 10110 10111	IC 19100 19101
	Warszawa Wschodnia d.	1809	1819	1904	1904	1914	2005	2124	2214	2324	...
	Warszawa Centralna d.	1820	1845	1914	1914	1922	2035	2135	2235	2335	...
	Skierniewice d.	1900	1923	1956	2005	2115	2210	2313	0016		
	Koluszki d.	1922	1942	2015	2015	2028	2135	2229	2333	0036	...
	Łódź Chojny a.			2037							
	Łódź Kaliska a.	1935	1953	2027	...	2040	2148	2245	2346	0048	...

		IC 10107 10106 ①–⑤	TLK 91101 91100 ①–⑤	TLK 91117 91116 ①–⑤	IC 15109 15108 ①–⑤	IR 9111 9110 ①–⑤	IC 91133 91132 ①–⑤	TLK 10133 10132 ①–⑤	IR 71103 71102 ①–⑤	IC 91109 91108 ⑥	IC 1010 1010 ⑦
	Łódź Kaliska ■ d.	0513	0521	0553	0635	0648	0655	0705		0742	083
	Łódź Chojny d.								0730		
	Koluszki d.	0525	0536	0608	0647		0709	0718	0754	0754	085
	Skierniewice d.		0605	0635	0712		0735	0741	0814	0814	090
	Warszawa Centralna a.	0625	0650	0722	0755	0820	0824	0855	0855	0955	095
	Warszawa Wschodnia a.	0646	0701	0736	0801	0811	0836	0841	0906	0906	101

		IR 10135 10134 ①–⑤	♣ ⑥⑦	IC 91111 91110 ①–⑥	IC 61109 61108	♣ ⑥⑦	IC 91107 91106 ①–⑤		IC 10109 10108 ①–⑤	IC 10137 10136 ⑥⑦		IC 62107 62106 ①–⑤	IR 10139 10138 ⑥⑦	♣ ①–⑤	IC 91103 91102 ⑧	IC 15127 15126		IR 10141 10140 ①–⑤	♣ ⑥⑦	IC 91105 91104 ①–⑤	IC 61103 61102 ⑧	IR 10143 10142		IC 91113 91112 ⑧	IC 61101 61100 ⑧
	Łódź Kaliska ■ d.	0901	0922	0938		1119	1138		1228	1311	1323		1507	1512	1538	1629		1711	1720	1738		1916		2038	
	Łódź Chojny d.				1003						1401						1831				1916			2208	
	Koluszki d.	0915	0933	0951	1026	1131	1150		1240	1324	1335		1424	1525	1524	1550	1642		1725	1732	1750	1855	1930		2050	2232
	Skierniewice d.	0938	0952	1011	1045	1150	1209		1259	1347	1354		1443	1548	1542	1609	1705		1748	1750	1810	1914	1955		2110	2251
	Warszawa Centralna a.	1020	1030	1051	1126	1225	1250		1340	1430	1430		1525	1630	1620	1648	1748		1830	1825	1850	1950	2036		2150	2330
	Warszawa Wschodnia a.	1041	1041	1102	1204	1236	1301		1406	1441	1441		1556	1641	1631	1701	1831		1841	1841	1901	2006	2046		2201	2341

J – To / from Jelenia Góra / Szklarska Poręba Górna (Tables **1061/84**).

■ – Time shown is for Łódź **Widzew** (not Kaliska). During the currency of this timetable most services stop at Łódź **Widzew** and terminate / originate at Łódź **Fabryczna**.

♣ – Operator: Łódzka Kolej Aglomeracyjna (ŁKA)

1095 WROCŁAW - KŁODZKO

Certain trains continue beyond Kłodzko – see Table **1165**

km		⊖ a	⊖ a c			d						⑧				
0	Wrocław Gł. d.	0526	0608	0628	...	0831	1048	...	1308	1358	...	1450	1554	1654	...	1849	1943	2054	2254
72	Kamieniec Ząbkowicki d.	0637	0717	0738	·	0940	1203	...	1412	1505	...	1556	1703	1801	...	1951	2051	2208	0001
94	Kłodzko Gł. 1165 a.	0707	0742	0807	...	1009	1231	...	1437	1533	...	1628	1731	1829	...	2015	2119	2237	0030

		⊖ a c	a		d		⊖					⊖ a c	c			
Kłodzko Gł. 1165 d.	0343	0426	0426	0540	0610	...	0637	0738	0845	...	1051	1256	...	1447	1447	...	1610	1640	...	1900	...	2043
Kamieniec Ząbkowicki d.	0409	0455	0455	0607	0637	...	0706	0807	0912	...	1115	1324	...	1514	1514	...	1633	1708	...	1927	...	2111
Wrocław Gł. a.	0513	0600	0600	0714	0742	...	0820	0911	1019	...	1217	1429	...	1629	1629	...	1739	1817	...	2031	...	2219

a – ①–⑤ only.   c – ⑥⑦ only.   d – ①–⑥ only.   ⊖ – Operated by Koleje Dolnośląskie.

1099 OTHER LOCAL SERVICES

Subject to alteration on and around holidays   2nd class onl

GDYNIA - HEL   *77 km, journey 1 hr 50 mins - 2 hrs*

Gdynia Główna depart : 0508, 1035, 1423, 1534, 1654, 2009, 2121.
Hel depart : 0453, 0553, 0647, 1359, 1609, 1705, 1823.

KŁODZKO - KUDOWA-ZDRÓJ   *44 km, journey 1 hr 10 mins*

Kłodzko Główne depart : 0710 a, 0742 c, 0906, 1158, 1438, 1603, 1745, 2022.
Kudowa-Zdrój depart : 0617 a, 0717 c, 0943, 1140, 1320 a, 1454 c, 1622, 1722, 1911.
Operator : Koleje Dolnośląskie.

KRAKÓW - LOTNISKO (for Kraków John Paul II Airport ✈)

Kraków Główny depart : 0437, 0607, 0707, 0737, 0806, 0907, 0937, 1007, 1107, 1137, 1207, 1307, 1337, 1407, 1507, 1533, 1607, 1705, 1735, 1807, 1907, 1935, 2007, 2103, 2137, 2207, 2307, 2337.
Kraków Lotnisko depart : 0548, 0648, 0748, 0818, 0845, 0948, 1018, 1048, 1148, 1218, 1245, 1348, 1418, 1448, 1548, 1615, 1645, 1745, 1815, 1848, 1948, 2018, 2044, 2148, 2218, 2248.

12 km, journey 18 mins.

KRAKÓW - OŚWIĘCIM (for Auschwitz-Birkenau Memorial and Museum)

VIA TRZEBINIA   *65 km   Journey 1 hr 45 mins - 1 hr 50 mins*
Kraków Główny depart : 0536 a, 0635, 0808, 1032, 1145, 1340, 1446, 1515 a, 1547, 1708, 1740, 1950, 2140.
Oświęcim depart : 0330, 0400, 0426 a, 0501, 0603, 0704, 0851, 1102 a, 1231, 1340, 1429, 1537, 1741, 1918.

KRAKÓW - WADOWICE   *62 km, journey 1 hr 45 mins*

Kraków Płaszów depart : 5 – 8 trains daily; times vary.
Wadowice depart : 5 – 8 trains daily; times vary.
Wadowice is the birthplace of Pope John Paul II.

KRAKÓW - WIELICZKA (for Salt Mine)   *15 km, journey 25 – 30 mins*

Kraków Główny depart : 0010⑥⑦, 0110⑥⑦, 0210⑥⑦, 0310⑥⑦, 0510⑥⑦, 0610, 0710, 0810, 0840, 0910, 1010, 1040, 1110, 1210, 1240, 1310, 1410, 1440, 1510, 1610, 1640, 1710, 1810, 1840, 1910, 2010, 2040, 2110, 2210, 2240, 2310.
Wieliczka Rynek depart : 0040⑥⑦, 0140⑥⑦, 0240⑥⑦, 0410, 0538, 0640, 0710, 0740, 0840, 0910, 0940, 1040, 1110, 1140, 1240, 1310, 1340, 1440, 1510, 1540, 1640, 1710, 1740, 1840, 1910, 1940, 2040, 2110, 2140, 2240, 2310.

LESZNO - WOLSZTYN - ZBĄSZYNEK   Operator : *Koleje Wielkopolskie*

		d	d			a				
Leszno d.	0527	0756	...	1026	...	1345	1434	...	1627	182
Wolsztyn d.	0628	0903	...	1127	...	1446	1535	...	1728	193
Zbąszyń d.	0654	...	...	1154	...	...	1602	...	...	...
Zbąszynek a.	0701	...	...	1200	...	...	1608	...	...	...

		d	d			a				
Zbąszynek d.	...	0708	...	...	1210	...	...	1618	...	...
Zbąszyń d.	...	0714	...	...	1216	...	...	1624	...	...
Wolsztyn d.	0630	0741	0924	...	1243	1458	...	1651	...	194
Leszno a.	0730	0841	1024	...	1343	1605	...	1758	...	204

POZNAN - WOLSZTYN   *81 km, journey 1 hr 25 mins - 2 hrs*

Poznan Główny depart : 0621, 0735 a, 0948, 1201 a, 1342, 1450 a, 1559, 1709 a, 1857, 2004.
Wolsztyn depart : 0447 a, 0553, 0810, 0944 a, 1148, 1340 a, 1539, 1653 a, 1744, 1945.
Operator : Koleje Wielkopolskie.

REJOWIEC - ZAMOŚĆ   *63 km, journey 1 hr 10 mins*

Rejowiec depart : 0956, 1425, 1754, 2114 b.
Zamość depart : 0525 d, 0717, 1254, 1603.

WAŁBRZYCH - KŁODZKO   *51 km, journey 1 hr 25 mins*

Wałbrzych Główny depart : 0618 a, 0740, 1045, 1234, 1435, 1630, 1904.
Kłodzko Główne depart : 0450 a, 0553, 0749 a, 0848 c, 1100, 1252, 1452, 1739.
Operator : Koleje Dolnośląskie.

WARSZAWA - WARSZAWA MODLIN AIRPORT ✈   *40 km, journey 36 min*

Warszawa Centralna depart : 0325, 0415, 0515, 0615, 0715 and hourly until 2315.
Modlin ✈ depart : 0022, 0423, 0522, 0622, 0722 and hourly until 2322.
Minor time variations are possible
A 🚌 connects the rail station with the terminal. Additional slower trains run Modlin ✈ to Warszawa Gdańska, with metro connection to city centre.
Operator : Koleje Mazowieckie.

a – ①–⑤ only.   b – ⑧ only.   c – ⑥⑦ only.   d – ①–⑥ only.

   Reservation is compulsory for travel by all EC, EIC, EIP, EN, IC, MP and TLK trains

CZECH REPUBLIC

ervices: Operator: České Dráhy (ČD), www.cd.cz. Railway infrastructure and timetables are the responsibility of Správa železniční dopravní cesty (SŽDC), www.szdc.cz.
All daytime trains convey first and second classes of travel unless otherwise shown by '2' at the top of the column or by a note (which may be in the table heading).

mings: Valid **December 11, 2016 - December 9, 2017**. Certain trains are cancelled during the Christmas / New Year period, particularly the evening of Dec. 24, 31 and the morning of Dec. 25, 26, Jan. 1; passengers travelling during this period are advised to confirm train times before travel.

eservations: It is possible to reserve seats on most Express trains.

upplements: SuperCity (*SC*) tilting trains have a compulsory reservation fee of 250 CZK. *Business* class on Railjet (*RJ*) trains requires a first class ticket and a supplement of 250 CZK.

tation names: hlavní = main; západ = west; východ = east; horní = upper; dolní = lower; střed = centre; starý = old; město = town; předměstí = suburban; nádraží = station.

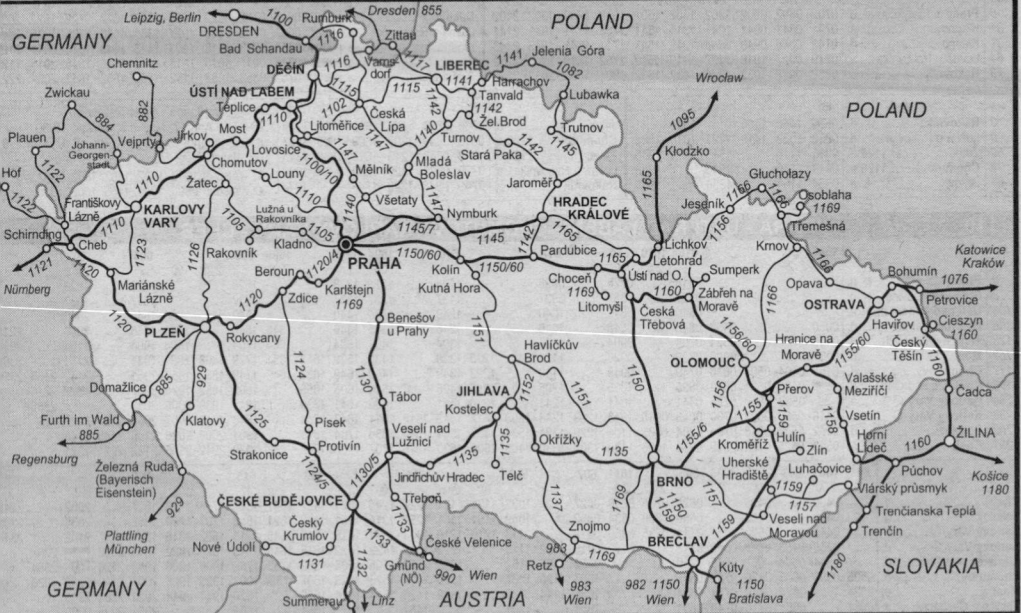

PRAHA - ÚSTÍ NAD LABEM - DĚČÍN - DRESDEN 1100

km	Praha - Ústí : see also **1110**	EN 476 M	616 C	EC 178 B	692 H	EC 176 H	690	EC 174 H	688	EC 378 K	686	EC 172 J	684	682 Ⓐ	EC 170 B	680	678 Ⓐ	EC 258	EC 258 N	676 Ⓐ	EC 674	672		670
0	Praha hlavní ....▷d.	0406	0518	0628		0828		1028		1228		1428			1628			1828	1828					2321
	Praha Masarykovo ....d.				0653		0853		1053		1253		1453	1553		1653	1753			1853	1953	2053	2141	
3	Praha Holešovice ......▷d.	0415	0527	0637		0837		1037		1237		1437			1637			1837	1837					2330
27	Kralupy nad Vltavou ....d.		0549		0718		0918		1118		1318		1518	1618		1718	1818			1918	2018	2118	2216	2351
84	Roudnice nad Labem ....d.		0610		0742		0942		1142		1342		1542	1642		1742	1842			1942	2042	2142	2251	0015
	Lovosice ....d.		0624		0758		0958		1158		1358		1558	1658		1758	1858			1958	2058	2158	2307	0031
106	Ústí nad Labem hlavní ...▷a.	0520	0640	0740	0814	0940	1014	1140	1214	1340	1414	1540	1614	1714	1740	1814	1914	1940	1940	2014	2114	2214	2327	0047
106	Ústí nad Labem hlavní ...▷d.	0522	0658	0741	0816	0941	1016	1141	1216	1341	1416	1541	1616	1727	1741	1816	1916	1941	1941	2016	2119	2216	2328	0049
129	Děčín ....▷a.	0537	0724	0755	0831	0955	1031	1155	1231	1355	1431	1555	1631	1743	1755	1831	1931	1955	1955	2031	2135	2231	2347	0105
129	Děčín ....▷d.	0542		0800		1000		1200		1400		1600			1800			2000						
151	Bad Schandau ▦ ....857 d.			0816		1017		1217		1417		1617			1817			2017						
191	Dresden Hbf ....857 a.	0627		0843		1043		1243		1443		1643			1843			2045						

					EC 259 P	EC 259	677	EC 679 Ⓐ	681	EC 171 B	683	EC 173 J	1655 2Ⓐ	685	EC 379 K	687	EC 175 B	689	EC 691 H	691	EC 179 H		617 C	EN 477 M	2
		671	673 Ⓐ	675	677	259 P	259		679 Ⓐ	681	171 B	683	173 J	1655	685	379 K	687	175 B	689	691 H	691	179 H		617 C	477 M	2
Dresden Hbf ....857 d.						0708				0908		1108			1308		1508		1708		1908			2108	
Bad Schandau ▦ ⊖ ....**857** d.						0738				0938		1138			1338		1538		1738		1938			2153	
Děčín ⊖ ....a.						0753				0953		1153			1353		1553		1753		1953			2153	
Děčín ⊖ ....▷d.	0424	0524	0624	0724	0756	0756	0816	0924	0956	1124	1156		1324	1356	1524	1556	1724	1756	1924	1956	2042		2156	2228
ŭsti nad Labem hlavní ...▷a.	0439	0539	0639	0739	0811	0811	0832	0939	1011	1139	1211		1339	1411	1539	1611	1739	1811	1939	2011	2108		2211	2257
Ústí nad Labem hlavní ...▷d.	0441	0541	0641	0741	0815	0815	0841	0941	1041	1141	1241		1341	1415	1541	1615	1741	1815	1941	2015		2115	2215	2300
ovosice ....d.	0458	0558	0658	0758			0858	0958		1158		1257	1358		1558		1758		1958			2133		2323
Roudnice nad Labem ....d.	0513	0613	0713	0813			0913	1013		1213		1311	1413		1613		1813		2013			2145		2337
Kralupy nad Vltavou ....d.	0538	0638	0738	0838			0938	1038		1238			1438		1638		1838		2038			2209		
Praha Holešovice ....a.					0917	0917			1117		1317		1517		1717		1917	2059	2117			2228	2317	
Praha Masarykovo ....a.							1002	1102		1302			1502		1702		1902							
raha hlavní................▷a.	0602	0702	0802	0902			0927	0927		1127		1327		1527		1727		1927	2109	2127			2238	2327

ADDITIONAL LOCAL TRAINS DĚČÍN - DRESDEN AND V.V.

			W			S		b						S			W		b
itomerice mesto ....d.	...	...	...	...	...	1613			**Dresden Hbf** ◇ **857** d.	0559	0750	0759	0959	1159	1359	1600	1559	1759	1959	2259
Jsti n. L. hlavní ....d.	...	...	0918	...	...	1650			**Bad Schandau** .. **857** a.	0643	0825	0843	1043	1243	1443	1628	1643	1843	2043	2343
Děčín ....**1116** d.	0641	0841	0936	1041	1241	1441	1641	1710	1841	2041	2241	**Bad Schandau 1116** d.	0648	0826	0848	1048	1248	1448	1629	1648	1848	2048	2350
Bad Schandau .. 1116 a.	0710	0910	0951	1110	1315	1510	1710	1728	1910	2110	2310	**Děčín** .. **1116** a.	0716	0844	0916	1116	1316	1516	1645	1716	1916	2116	0013
Bad Schandau .. 857 d.	0715	0915	0952	1115	1315	1515	1715	1730	1915	2115	2315	**Ústí n. L. hlavní** ....a.		0904					1703				
Dresden Hbf ◇ .. **857** a.	0758	0958	1021	1158	1358	1558	1758	1807	1958	2158	2358	**Litomerice mesto** ......a.		0940									

B — 🍴 Praha - Dresden - Berlin and v.v.
C — 🍴 Praha - Ústí nad Labem - Karlovy Vary - Cheb and v.v.
H — 🍴 ✕ Praha - Dresden - Berlin - Hamburg and v.v. (Table 60).
J — HUNGARIA - 🍴 ✕ Budapest - Bratislava - Brno - Praha - Dresden - Berlin - Hamburg and v.v.
K — 🍴 ✕ Praha - Dresden - Berlin - Hamburg - Kiel and v.v. (Table 60).
M — METROPOL - 🛏 1,2 cl., 🛏 2 cl., 🛏 (🚊) Budapest - Bratislava - Brno - Praha - Dresden - Berlin and v.v.; 🛏 1,2 cl., 🛏 2 cl., 🚊 (🚊) Wien - Brno - Praha - Dresden - Berlin and v.v. (Table 60).
N — KOPERNIKUS, ⑥ (not Dec. 25, Apr. 16) - 🍴 ✕ Praha - Dresden - Leipzig.
N — KOPERNIKUS, ①–⑤ (not Dec. 26, Apr. 17) - 🍴 ✕ Leipzig - Dresden - Praha.
S — ⑥⑦ Apr. 1- Oct. 29, also Apr. 14-17, May 1, 25, June 5, Oct. 3, 31.
W — Dec. 11, 17, 18 (2016); Dec. 2, 3, 9 (2017) only.
b — Not Dec. 24, 31, Mar. 20 - June 17.

► - Ústi nad Labem - Děčín : see also Table **1115** and foot of Table **1110**.
▷ - For other non-stop trains Praha - Ústí nad Labem and v.v. see Table **1110**.
◇ - Local trains continue to / from Meissen.
⊖ - Routeing point for international tickets: Schöna.
🗆 - Ⓡ for international journeys.

FOR OTHER TRAIN NAMES SEE TABLE 60.

*For additional non-stop trains Praha - Ústí nad Labem see Table **1110**.*

1102 LOVOSICE - LITOMĚŘICE - ČESKÁ LIPA

2nd class

km										
0	**Lovosice 1100** d.	0601	0801	1001	1201	1401	1601	1801	2001	2214
8	Litoměřice horní d.	0616	0816	1016	1216	1416	1616	1816	2016	2227
50	**Česká Lípa** a.	0723	0923	1123	1323	1523	1723	1923	2123	...

		Ⓐ									
Česká Lípa d.	...	0443	0633	0833	1033	1233	1433	1633	1833	2033	...
Litoměřice horní d.	0018	0559	0740	0940	1140	1340	1540	1740	1940	2141	225
Lovosice 1100 a.	0029	0614	0752	0952	1152	1352	1552	1752	1952	2153	230

Also: Lovosice - Litoměřice horní: 0054, 0500, 0638Ⓐ, 0736, 0836, 0936, 1036, 1136, 1236, 1336, 1436, 1501Ⓐ, 1536, 1636, 1701Ⓐ, 1736, 1836, 1901Ⓐ, 1936, 2036, 2138, 2238Ⓐ, 232
Litoměřice horní - Lovosice: 0502, 0531Ⓐ, 0640Ⓐ, 0659Ⓐ, 0759, 0840Ⓐ, 0903, 0959, 1103, 1159, 1303, 1359, 1439Ⓐ, 1459, 1559, 1639Ⓐ, 1659, 1759, 1839Ⓐ, 1859, 1959, 2114, 221

1105 PRAHA - RAKOVNIK - CHOMUTOV - JIRKOV

km											
			2◧		2◧			2Ⓐ			P
0	**Praha** Masarykovo d.	0702	0802	0902	1002	1302	1502	1618	1702	1902	2102
31	Kladno a.	0741	0841	0941	1041	1341	1541	1708	1741	1941	2141
31	Kladno d.	0743	*0846*	0943	*1046*	1343	1543	1711	1743	1943	2143
64	Lužná u Rakovnika a.	0819	*0927*	1019	*1127*	1419	1619	1752	1819	2019	2219
73	**Rakovník** a.	0832	*0948*	1032	*1140*	1432	1632	1804	1832	2032	2232

	⚒n	2			2◐				⑦e	2
Rakovník d.	0516	0618	0722	0922	*1006*	1322	1522	1722	1922	*203*
Lužná u Rakovnika d.	0527	0632	0735	0935	*1021*	1335	1535	1735	1935	*204*
Kladno a.	0604	0711	0813	1013	*1103*	1413	1613	1813	2013	*212*
Kladno d.	0608	0715	0815	1015	1115	1415	1615	1815	2015	212
Praha Masarykovo a.	0650	0752	0852	1052	1152	1452	1652	1852	2052	222

km	*2nd class*						
		Ⓒ					
0	**Rakovník** d.	*0806*	*1006*	1406	...	1806	...
9	Lužná u Rakovnika d.	0823	1023	1418	1423	1818	1823
50	Žatec **1126** d.	0915	1115	...	1513	...	1915
75	**Chomutov** **1126** a.	0943	1140	...	1540	...	1943
81	Jirkov a.	0954	1154	...	1554	...	1954

	Ⓐ	Ⓒ				⑦e
Jirkov d.	0606	0759	1159	1559	1759	1759
Chomutov **1126** d.	0616	0809	1209	1609	1809	1809
Žatec **1126** d.	0643	0843	1243	1643	1838	1843
Lužná u Rakovnika a.	0729	0929	1329	1729	...	1929
Rakovník a.	0749	*0948*	*1348*	*1748*	...	*1944*

P – Ⓑ to Kladno; ⑦**e** to Rakovnik.
e – Also Apr. 17, May 1, 8; not Apr. 16, 30, May 7
n – ①–⑥ (not Dec. 24, 26, Apr. 15, 17, May 1, 8, July 6, Nov. 18).
◧ – Also at 1202, 1402, 1602, 1802, 2002.
◐ – Also at *0806*, *1206*, *1406*, *1606*, *1806*.

1110 PRAHA - ÚSTI NAD LABEM - CHOMUTOV - KARLOVY VARY - CHEB

km		1686				616	1670	614		612			610		1694	608		1696	606			604		602		
		2	2	Ⓐ			2S	K	Ⓐm		m	Ⓐ			Ⓐ			2Ⓐ		2Ⓒ	Ⓐ		2			
0	**Praha** hlavní ▶ d.	...	...	...	...	0518	...	0728	...	0928	...	...	1128	...	*1228*	1328	...	...	1528	...	...	1728	...	1928	...	...
3	**Praha** Holešovice ▶ d.	...	...	...	...	0527	...	0737	...	0937	...	...	1137	...	*1237*	1337	...	...	1537	...	...	1737	...	1937	...	...
106	**Ústí nad Labem** hl ▶ a.	...	...	...	...	0640	...	0840	...	1040	...	...	1240	...	*1340*	1440	...	...	1640	...	...	1840	...	2040	...	...
106	**Ústí nad Labem** hl d.	0050	...	...	0458	0646	...	0846	...	1046	...	...	1246	...	1345	1446	...	1546	1646	...	*1746*	1846	...	2046	...	2218
123	Teplice v Čechách d.	0110	...	...	0521	0704	...	0904	...	1104	...	...	1304	...	1404	1504	...	1604	1704	...	*1804*	1904	...	2104	...	2238
152	**Most** d.	0137	...	...	0600	0729	...	0929	...	1129	...	*1213*	1329	...	1431	1529	1613	1631	1729	1808	*1831*	1931	...	2131	...	2308
177	**Chomutov** d.	0155	0404	0508	0625	0749	...	0949	...	1149	...	*1233*	1349	...	1449	1549	1633	1649	1749	1833	1853	1951	...	2149	2153	2326
196	Klášterec nad Ohři d.	▬	0438	0531	0643	0805	...	1005	...	1205	...	*1252*	1405	...	1520	1605	1655	...	1805	1852	1921	2007	...	▬	2215	...
236	**Karlovy Vary** ⊙ a.	...	0523	0619	0726	0841	...	1041	...	1241	...	*1336*	1441	...	1606	1641	1739	...	1841	1939	2005	2043	...	2	2258	...
236	**Karlovy Vary** ⊙ d.	0418	*0530*	0622	0730	0843	0915	1043	1203	1243	1308	1412	1443	1518	1611	1643	1744	...	1843	1940	2007	2045	2122	2222	...	...
262	Sokolov d.	0442	*0554*	0648	0754	0904	0933	1104	1229	1304	1334	1437	1504	1544	1636	1704	1811	...	1904	2008	2035	2106	2148	2248	...	...
291	**Cheb** a.	0513	*0625*	0722	0825	0930	1005	1130	1300	1330	1405	1509	1530	1615	1707	1730	1842	...	1930	2042	2106	2132	2221	2321	...	...

	601	1691	603		1695	605		1671	607		609			611			613		615			617				
	Ⓐ	2Ⓐ		2	Ⓐ		2Ⓒ	2S				Ⓒ	Ⓐn		Ⓐ	Ⓒ			K	Ⓒ	Ⓐ			2	2	2
Cheb d.	...	0400	...	0425	...	0625	0735	0800	0827	...	1027	1121	1121	1227	*1245*	1321	1427	1547	1627	*1706*	1723	1827	...	2002	...	2248
Sokolov d.	...	0425	...	0456	...	0650	0809	0834	0852	...	1052	1151	1151	1252	*1316*	1351	1452	1621	1652	*1737*	1754	1852	...	2035	...	2321
Karlovy Vary ⊙ a.	...	0448	...	0520	...	0711	0835	0850	0913	...	1113	1216	1216	1313	*1341*	1416	1513	1645	1713	*1802*	1818	1913	...	2102	...	2346
Karlovy Vary ⊙ d.	...	0456	*0456*	▬	0558	0713	...	...	0915	1022	1115	...	1222	1315	1422	1422	1515	1648	1715	1822	1822	1915	2022	▬	2257	...
Klášterec nad Ohři d.	...	0544	*0544*	Ⓐ	0643	0750	...	...	0952	1106	1152	...	1306	1352	1506	1506	1552	1733	1752	1906	1906	1952	2126	Ⓐ	2354	...
Chomutov d.	0505	0558	0605	0626	0702	0805	...	...	1007	1125	1207	...	1325	1407	1525	1525	1607	1750r	1807	1925	1925	2007	2143	*2253*	0023	...
Most d.	0524	...	0624	0649	0721	0824	...	...	1026	1144	1226	...	1349	1426	1544	1544	1626	...	1826	1944	1944	2026	2202	2315		...
Teplice v Čechách d.	0551	...	0651	0716	0749	0851	...	...	1051	...	1251	...	...	1451	...	...	1651	...	1851	...	...	2051	2235	0000	...	...
Ústí nad Labem hl a.	0609	...	0709	0734	0808	0909	...	...	1109	...	1309	...	...	1509	...	...	1709	...	1909	...	...	2109	2257	0023	...	...
Ústí nad Labem hl ▶ d.	0615	...	0715	...	*0815*	0915	...	...	1115	...	1315	...	...	1515	...	...	1715	...	1915	...	...	2115	...	...	...	...
Praha Holešovice ▶ a.	0717	...	0817	...	*0917*	1017	...	...	1217	...	1417	...	...	1617	...	...	1817	...	2017	...	...	2228	...	...	...	...
Praha hlavní ▶ a.	0727s	...	0827	...	*0927*	1027	...	...	1227	...	1427	...	...	1627	...	...	1827	...	2027	...	...	2238	...	...	...	...

km	*via Louny (2 cl.)*	Ⓒ§	Ⓐ§
0	**Praha** Masarykovo d.	0718	1622
47	Slaný d.	0821	1726
90	Louny d.	0911	1820
115	**Most** a.	0940	...

via Louny (2 cl.)	Ⓐ§	Ⓒ§
Most d.	...	1647
Louny d.	0529	1713
Slaný d.	0627	1800
Praha Masarykovo a.	0732	1858

Local trains (2 cl.)				⊡
Děčín ▶ d.	0530	and	1930	2042
Ústí n. L. hlavní ▶ d.	0558	hourly	1958	2118
Teplice v Čechách d.	0621	⊡	2021	2138
Most a.	0654	until	2054	2207

Local trains (2 cl.)				
Most d.	0502	and	2002	2102
Teplice v Čechách d.	0535	hourly	2035	2135
Ústí n. L. hlavní ▶ d.	0558	⊖	2058	2157
Děčín ▶ a.	0624	until	2124	...

K – Also conveys 🛏 1, 2 cl. Cheb - Karlovy Vary - Praha (**445/4**) - Žilina - Košice and v.v. (not Dec. 25, Jan. 1).
S – Ⓒ July 1 - Sept. 3.
m – To Mariánské Lázní (arrive 1348 and 1445).
n – From Mariánské Lázní (depart 1040).
r – Ⓐ only (on Ⓒ terminates at Klášterec nad Ohři).
s – Praha **Masarykovo**.
▶ – For other non-stop trains see Table **1100**.
⊙ – Known locally as Karlovy Vary horní (upper).
⊖ – Also Ústí - Děčín at 0457, 0528, 1432Ⓐ, 1632Ⓐ, 2227.
⊡ – Also Děčín - Ústí at 0016, 0600Ⓐ, 0658Ⓐ, 2124, 2228.
§ – For other journeys Praha - Louny change at Kralupy n. Vlt.

1115 ÚSTÍ NAD LABEM - DĚČÍN - ČESKÁ LIPA - LIBEREC

km		1997	1999	1161	1163	1165	1167	1169	1171	1173	1175
		2Ⓐ									Ⓑh
0	**Ústí nad Labem** hl. § d.	...	...	0727	0927	1127	1327	1527	1727	1927	2119
23	**Děčín** § d.	0427	0526	0745	0945	1145	1345	1545	1745	1945	2136
54	Česká Lipa d.	0511	0608	0828	1028	1228	1428	1628	1828	2022	2211
113	**Liberec** a.	0623	0729	0943	1143	1343	1543	1743	1943	2131	...

	1174	1172	1170	1168	1166	1164	1162	1160		
	⚒n								2	2
Liberec d.	...	0628	0828	1028	1228	1428	1628	1828	2040	...
Česká Lipa d.	0608	0738	0938	1138	1338	1538	1738	1938	2207	2225
Děčín § d.	0648	0816	1016	1216	1416	1616	1816	2016	...	2310
Ústí nad Labem hl. § a.	0704	0832	1032	1232	1432	1632	1832	2032	...	...

h – Not Dec. 25, Apr. 14, 16, 30, May 7, July 5, Nov. 17.
n – ①–⑥ (not Dec. 24, 26, Apr. 15, 17, May 1, 8, July 6, Nov. 18).
§ – See also Table **1100** and foot of Table **1110**.

1116 DĚČÍN - RYBNIŠTĚ - RUMBURK / DĚČÍN - SEBNITZ - RUMBURK

km											
								Ⓐ			
0	**Děčín** d.	0643	0835	1035	1235	1435	1635	1735	1835	2035	2235
25	Česká Kamenice d.	|	0906	1106	1306	1506	1706	1806	1906	2106	2306
50	Rybniště a.	0823	0938	1138	1338	1538	1738	1837	1938	2135	2333
61	**Rumburk** a.	0837	0952	1152	1352	1552	1752	1852	1952	2149	2347

			ⒸS							G
Rumburk d.	0604	0800	0839	1000	1200	1400	1601	1800	2000	2100
Rybniště d.	0617	0813	0852	1013	1213	1413	1614	1813	2013	2113
Česká Kamenice d.	0647	0847	0923	1047	1247	1447	1647	1847	2047	2144
Děčín a.	0720	0920	0946	1120	1320	1520	1720	1920	2120	2214

km											
							Ⓐ				
0	**Děčín** ▷ d.	...	0641	0841	1041	1241	...	1441	1641	1841	2041
22	Bad Schandau ▦ ▷ d.	...	0718	0918	1118	1318	...	1518	1718	1918	2118
37	Sebnitz d.	0629	0741	0941	1141	1341	...	1541	1741	1941	2141
38	Dolní Poustevna ▦ d.	0633	0745	0945	1145	1345	1505	1545	1745	1945	2145
65	**Rumburk** a.	0724	0835	1026	1226	1427	1546	1625	1826	2026	2225

						Ⓐ				
Rumburk d.	0533	0728	0920	1120	1320	1400	1520	1720	1920	2039
Dolní Poustevna ▦ d.	0614	0812	1012	1212	1412	1440	1612	1812	2012	2120
Sebnitz d.	0618	0818	1018	1218	1418	...	1618	1818	2018	2123
Bad Schandau ▦ ▷ a.	0639	0839	1039	1239	1439	...	1639	1839	2039	...
Děčín ▷ a.	0716	0916	1116	1316	1516	...	1716	1916	2116	...

G – ⑤⑥ (also Dec. 25, Apr. 13 - 16, 30, May 7, July 4, 5, Sept. 27, Nov. 16; not Dec. 24. 31).
S – Apr. 1 - Oct. 29.
▷ – See also Table **1100**.

1117 RYBNIŠTĚ - VARNSDORF - ZITTAU - LIBEREC

2nd class

Service January 8 - August 12. *For service December 11 - January 7 see page 494*

km																									
					d										Ⓒ			Ⓐ							
	[illegible]ište d.	...	0627	...	...	...	0940	...	1127	1227	...	1340	...	...	...	1540	...	...	*1740*	...	1839	...	...	2027	...
	[illegible]dorf ▦ d.	0557	0650	0730	...	*0851*	0957	1029	1152	1244	1256	1357	...	1451	...	1557	1651	...	1805	...	1856	...	*2005*	2044	2130
	[illegible] ▦ d.	0616	0714	0749	0844	0920	...	1049	1213	...	1317	1417	1447	1516	1547	1617	1716	1746	1823	1847	1915	1921	2044	...	2150
	[illegible] a.	0655	0755	0824	0915	0955	...	1127	1253	...	1355	1455	1524	1555	1624	1655	1755	1824	...	1920	...	1955	2115	...	2229

						d								Ⓒ					Ⓐ		d				
[illegible] d.	0500	0602	0702	0802	...	0838	...	1002	1038	...	...	1231	1402	1433	1502	1602	1633	...	1732	1802	1838	...	2005	2251	...
[illegible] d.	0537	0644	0740	0836	0845	0910	0943	1040	1129	...	...	1308	1446	1510	1545	1646	1708	...	1809	1844	1912	1930	2046	2327	...
[illegible] d.	0555	0703	0758	...	0904	...	1001	1104	1147	1149	1304	1326	1504	...	1607	1704	1726	1801	...	1906	...	1948	2104	2345	...
[illegible] a.	0613	...	...	...	0922	...	...	1122	...	1207	1322	...	1522	...	...	1722	...	1819	...	...	...	2006	...	...	...

[illegible] Table **855**).

Operator: **Die Länderbahn** *Trilex*.

479

PRAHA - PLZEŇ - MARIÁNSKÉ LÁZNĚ - CHEB 1120

km		768	EC 356	1980	766	778	1982	764	EC 354	762	SC• 512	776	760	Ex 352	1988	758	774	1990	756	SC• 506	Ex 350	754	772	752	770	750
		🍸	🍸	2	🍸	🍸	2		🍸	🍸	🅁🍸	🍸	🍸	🍸	2	🍸	🍸	2	🍸	🅁🍸	🍸	🍸	🍸	🍸	🍸	🍸
		⚒n	M	a		z	E	⊡	M		b	z		M			k	Ⓑh			M		k	Ⓑh		Ⓑh
	Ostrava hl. **1160** d.	...	...	...	...	...	...	...	...	...	0721	...	...	...	...	...	...	...	...	1321	...	...	...	...	...	...
0	**Praha** hlavní **1124** d.	...	0512	...	0612	0712	...	0812	0912	1012	1037	1112	1212	1312	...	1412	1512	...	1612	1637	1712	1812	1912	2012	2112	2322
4	Praha Smíchov **1124** d.	...	0520	...	0620	0720	...	0820	0920	1020	1045	1120	1220	1320	...	1420	1520	...	1620	1645	1720	1820	1920	2020	2120	2330
43	Beroun **1124** d.	...	0550	...	0650	0750	...	0850	0950	1050	|	1150	1250	1350	...	1450	1550	...	1650	|	1750	1850	1950	2050	2150	2359
52	Zdice **1124** d.	...	|	...	0658	|	...	0858	|	1058	|	|	1258	|	...	1458	|	...	1658	|	|	1858	|	2058	|	0007
90	Rokycany d.	...	0627	...	0727	0827	...	0927	1027	1127	|	1227	1327	1427	...	1527	1627	...	1727	|	1827	1927	2027	2127	2227	0033
113	**Plzeň** hlavní a.	...	0649	...	0749	0849	...	0949	1049	1149	1201	1249	1349	1449	...	1549	1649	...	1749	1801	1849	1949	2049	2149	2249	0054
113	**Plzeň** hlavní d.	0604	...	0702	0804	...	0900	1004	...	1151e	1203	...	1404	...	1501	1604	...	1700	▬	1803	...	2004	...	▬	▬	▬
146	Stříbro d.	0629	...	0732	0829	...	0930	1029	...	1214e	1227	...	1429	...	1531	1629	...	1728	...	1827	...	2029	...	...	...	...
177	Planá u Marián. Lázni d.	0653	...	0800	0853	...	1001	1053	...	1237e	1246	...	1453	...	1602	1653	...	1757	Ⓑh	1846	...	2053	...	Ⓐ	Ⓐ	Ⓐ
189	Mariánské Lázně d.	0704	...	0813	0908	...	1011	1108	...	1246e	1255	...	1504	...	1630*	1708	...	1807	1840	1855	...	2104	...	0455	0552	0648
219	**Cheb** **1122** a.	0724	...	0842a	0928	...	...	1128	...	...	1314	...	1523	...	1701	1728	...	...	1910	1914	...	2126	...	0523	0621	0720
226	Františkovy Lázně **1122** a.	...	...	...	...	...	...	...	...	...	1323	...	...	...	...	...	...	...	...	...	...	...	...	...	...	...

	771	753	1981	773	SC• 505	755	1983	Ex 351	757	775	759	Ex 353	761	1987	777	SC• 515	763	763	1989	EC 355	765	1991	779	767	EC 357	
	🍸	🍸	2	🍸	🅁🍸	🍸	2	🍸	🍸	🍸	🍸	🍸	🍸		🍸	🅁🍸	🍸		2	🍸	🍸	2	🍸	🍸	🍸	☆
	★	⚒n	⚒n	k				M‡		z		M		Ⓐ	z	b		⑦e		M		E	z	⊡	M	
Františkovy Lázně **1122** d.	...	...	...	...	...	...	...	...	...	...	...	...	...	...	...	1435	...	...	...	...	...	...	...	...	...	...
Cheb **1122** d.	...	0432	0504	...	0642	...	...	...	0834	...	1034	...	1234	*1317*	...	1444	...	...	1519	...	1634	...	...	1834	...	2003
Mariánské Lázně d.	...	0455	0548	...	0703	...	0749	...	0855	...	1055	...	1255	*1349*	...	1503	...	1506	1550	...	1655	1746	...	1855	...	2034
Planá u Marián. Lázni d.	...	0505	0559	...	0711	...	0801	...	0905	...	1105	...	1305	1402	...	1511	...	1516	1602	...	1705	1757	...	1905	...	...
Stříbro d.	...	0529	0630	...	0732	...	0830	...	0929	...	1130	...	1329	1429	...	1531	...	1539	1630	...	1729	1827	...	1929	...	...
Plzeň hlavní a.	...	0554	0658	...	0756	...	0859	...	0954	...	1155	...	1354	1457	...	1555	...	1603	1659	...	1754	1856	...	1954	...	...
Plzeň hlavní d.	0506	0606	...	0706	0758	0806	...	0906	1006	1106	1206	1306	1406	...	1506	1557	1606	1606	...	1706	1806	...	1906	2006	2107	...
Rokycany d.	0525	0625	...	0725	|	0825	...	0925	1025	1125	1225	1325	1425	...	1525	|	1625	1625	...	1725	1825	...	1925	2025	2125	...
Zdice **1124** d.	0551	0651	...	|	|	0851	...	|	1051	|	1251	|	1451	...	|	|	1651	1651	...	|	1851	...	|	2051	|	...
Beroun **1124** d.	0601	0701	...	0801	|	0901	...	1001	1101	1201	1301	1401	1501	...	1601	|	1701	1701	...	1801	1901	...	2001	2101	2201	...
Praha Smíchov **1124** a.	0633	0733	...	0833	0907	0933	...	1033	1133	1233	1333	1433	1533	...	1633	1706	1733	1733	...	1833	1933	...	2033	2133	2233	...
Praha hlavní **1124** a.	0641	0741	...	0841	0916	0941	...	1041	1141	1241	1341	1441	1541	...	1641	1716	1741	1741	...	1841	1941	...	2041	2141	2241	...
Ostrava hl. **1160** a.	...	...	...	...	1238	...	...	...	...	...	...	...	...	...	...	2038	...	...	...	...	...	...	...	...	...	...

E – Ⓒ May 1 - Sept. 30 (daily July 1 - Aug. 31).
M – 🚌12 Praha - Regensburg - München and v.v. (Table **76**, **885**). In Germany operated by Die Länderbahn *Alex*.
a – Daily to Mariánské Lázně, Ⓐ to Cheb.
b – From/to Bohumín (Table **1160**).
e – ⑦ (also Apr. 17, May 1, 8; not Dec. 25, Apr. 16, 30, May 7).
h – Not Dec. 25, Apr. 14, 16, 30, May 7, July 5, Nov. 17.
k – To/from Klatovy (Table **929**).
n – ①-⑥ (not Dec. 24, 26, Apr. 15, 17, May 1, 8, July 6, Nov. 18).
z – To/from Klatovy and Železná Ruda (Table **929**).
• – *SUPERCITY PENDOLINO* tilting train, 🅁, 🍸, reservation fee CZK 250 (Plzeň - Cheb - F. Lázně 🅁 in 1st class only).
⊡ – Conveys 🛏 1, 2 cl. Cheb - Plzeň - Praha (**443/2**) - Žilina - Košice - Humenné and v.v.
☆ – Additional journey: 2248 Ⓐ.
★ – Additional journey: 0406 ⚒n.
‡ – Starts from Schwandorf on ⑦ (Table **885**).
* – Arrive 1611.

TRAIN NAMES trains **350** - **357**: see Table **76**.

CHEB - MARKTREDWITZ 1121

*27 km**													
Cheb d.	0629	0829	0938	1027	1227	1338	1427	1538	1627	1738	1827	1938	2027
Schirnding 🛃 d.	0642	0842	|	1040	1240	|	1440	|	1640	|	1840	|	2040
Marktredwitz a.	0654	0854	0958	1052	1252	1358	1452	1558	1652	1758	1852	2004	2052
Nürnberg § a.	*0819*	*1020*	1122	*1220*	*1420*	1522	*1620*	1722	*1820*	1922	*2022*	2122	*2222*

Nürnberg § d.	*0535*	0637	*0738*	*0938*	1037	*1138*	1237	*1338*	1437	*1538*	1637	*1738*	*2055*
Marktredwitz d.	0712	0802	0908	1108	1202	1308	1402	1508	1602	1708	1802	1911	2218
Schirnding 🛃 d.	0724	|	0920	1120	|	1320	|	1520	|	1720	|	1923	2230
Cheb a.	0737	0822	0933	1133	1222	1333	1422	1533	1622	1733	1822	1936	2243

* – Cheb - Schirnding = 13 km, Cheb - Marktredwitz = 27 km. Local trains Cheb - Marktredwitz are operated by Die Länderbahn *Oberpfalzbahn* (2nd class).
§ – See Table **880**.

CHEB - FRANTIŠKOVY LÁZNĚ - HOF / PLAUEN 1122

Operator: Die Länderbahn. 2nd class

km		◇	◇	⊖	◇	⊖	◇	◇	⊖	◇	⊖	◇
0	**Cheb** ▶ d.	0738	0937	1005	1137	1205	1337	1537	1605	1737	1805	1937
7	Františkovy Lázně ▶ d.	0745	0945	1012	1145	1212	1345	1545	1612	1745	1812	1945
30	Aš 🛃 d.	0808	1008	|	1208	|	1408	1608	|	1808	|	2008
62	**Hof** a.	0843	1048	|	1243	|	1443	1643	|	1848	|	2043
24	Bad Brambach 🛃 a.	...	...	1036	...	1236	...	...	1636	...	1836	...
73	**Plauen** a.	...	...	1127	...	1327	...	...	1727	...	1927	...

	◇	⊖	◇	⊖	◇	◇	⊖	◇	⊖	◇	◇
Plauen d.	...	0830	...	1030	...	...	1430	...	1630	...	...
Bad Brambach 🛃 d.	...	0921	...	1121	...	...	1521	...	1721	...	...
Hof d.	0709	|	0907	|	1107	1307	|	1507	|	1707	1907
Aš d.	0747	|	0947	|	1147	1347	|	1547	|	1747	1947
Františkovy Lázně ▶ d.	0812	0945	1012	1145	1212	1412	1545	1612	1745	1812	2012
Cheb ▶ a.	0819	0952	1019	1152	1219	1419	1552	1619	1752	1819	2019

⊖ – Trains continue beyond Plauen to/from Zwickau.
◇ – Marktredwitz (Table **1121**) - Cheb - Hof and v.v.
▶ – For *SC* trains see Table **1120**. Additional trains: From Cheb 0458Ⓐ, 0518⑥, 0600Ⓐ, 0637, 1420Ⓐ, 2250. From Františkovy Lázně 0507Ⓐ, 0527⑥⑦, 0609Ⓐ, 0614⑥, 0617Ⓐ, 0714Ⓐ, 2119.

KARLOVY VARY - MARIÁNSKÉ LÁZNĚ 1123

Operator: GW TrainRegio. 2nd class

km										
0	**Karlovy Vary** dolní (lower) d.	...	0617	0901	1055	1258	1502	1707	1927	2127
33	Bečov nad Teplou d.	0448	0649	0934	1127	1331	1535	1739	1959	2159
53	**Mariánské Lázně** a.	0539	0740	1024	1217	1421	1625	1830	2050	2250

Mariánské Lázně d.	0556	0824	1034	1221	1425	1630	1906	2106	2255
Bečov nad Teplou d.	0650	0915	1128	1312	1516	1721	2000	2200	2346
Karlovy Vary dolní (lower) a.	0722	0949	1200	1346	1550	1755	2032	2232	...

PRAHA - BEROUN - PŘÍBRAM - PISEK - ČESKÉ BUDĚJOVICE 1124

2nd class

km		1254	1252	1250		1248	1246	1244	1242	1240
		Ⓐ	①d		◧	Ⓒ	Ⓐ	⑤f		
0	**Praha** hlavní **1120** d.	...	0542	0742	*0812*	0942	1142	1342	1542	1742
4	Praha Smíchov **1120** d.	...	0550	0750	*0820*	0950	1150	1350	1550	1750
43	Beroun **1120** d.	...	0619	0819	0857	1019	1219	1419	1619	1819
52	Zdice **1120** d.	...	0627	0827	0907	1027	1227	1427	1627	1827
82	Příbram d.	...	0656	0856	0949	1056	1256	1456	1656	1856
100	Březnice d.	...	0714	0914	1015	1114	1314	1514	1715	1914
142	Pisek d.	0555	0756	0955	1108	1155	1355	1555	1755	1955
155	Protivín **1125** d.	0611	0811	1011	1123	1211	1411	1611	1811	2011
192	**České Budějovice** **1125** a.	0643	0843	1043	...	1243	1443	1643	1843	2043r

	1241	1243		1245	1247	1249	1251	1253	
			◐	⑤f			⑦e		
České Budějovice **1125** d.	0509z	0709	...	1109	1309	1509	1709	1909	...
Protivín **1125** d.	0540	0740	1034	1140	1340	1540	1740	1940	2213
Pisek d.	0555	0755	1049	1155	1355	1555	1755	1953	2229
Březnice d.	0636	0836	1143	1236	1436	1636	1836	...	2315
Příbram d.	0656	0856	1208	1256	1456	1656	1856	...	...
Zdice **1120** d.	0725	0925	1244	1325	1525	1725	1925	...	...
Beroun **1120** a.	0733	0933	1254	1333	1533	1733	1933	...	...
Praha Smíchov **1120** a.	0803	1003	*1333*	1403	1603	1803	2003	...	...
Praha hlavní **1120** a.	0811	1011	*1341*	1411	1611	1811	2011	...	...

d – Also Apr. 18, May 2, 9; not Dec. 26, Apr. 17, May 1, 8.
e – Also Apr. 17, May 1, 8; not Dec. 25, Apr. 16, 30, May 7.
f – Also Dec. 22, Apr. 12, 13, July 4, Sept. 27, Nov. 16; not Dec. 30, Apr. 14, July 7, Sept. 29, Nov. 17.
r – ⑤-⑦ (also Dec. 22, 26, Apr. 12, 13, 17, May 1, 8, July 4 - 6, Sept. 27, 28, Nov. 16; not Dec. 24, 31).
z – ① (also Dec. 23, 27, Apr. 13, 18, May 2, 9, July 7, Sept. 29; not Dec. 26, Apr. 17, May 1, 8).
◧ – Also at 1012, 1212Ⓐ, 1412Ⓑ, 1612 (change at Beroun).
◐ – Also at 0834, 1234, 1434Ⓐ, 1634Ⓑ, 1834 (change Beroun).

For direct trains Praha - České Budějovice see Table **1130**

PLZEŇ - ČESKÉ BUDĚJOVICE 1125

km		653	661	663	665	667	669	655	657	659
		⚒n						h		Ⓑr
0	**Plzeň** hlavní d.	...	0602	0802	1002	1202	1402	1602	1802	2002
34	Nepomuk d.	...	0631	0831	1031	1231	1431	1631	1831	2031
59	Horaždovice předměstí d.	...	0652	0852	1052	1252	1452	1652	1852	2052
76	Strakonice d.	0457	0707	0907	1107	1307	1507	1707	1907	2108
99	Protivín **1124** d.	0517	0726	0926	1126	1326	1526	1726	1926	2127
136	**České Budějovice** **1124** a.	0551	0755	0955	1155	1355	1555	1755	1955	2155
	Jihlava **1135** a.	0833	1033	1233z	1433	1633	1833	2031r	...	...
	Brno **1135** a.	1036	1236	1436z	1636	1836	2036	...	...	...

	658	656	654	668	666	664	662	660	
			h					Ⓑr	Ⓑr
Brno **1135** d.	...	...	...	0720	0920z	1120	1320	1520	...
Jihlava **1135** d.	...	0525a	0725	0925	1125z	1325	1525	1725	...
České Budějovice **1124** d.	0604	0804	1004	1204	1404	1604	1804	2004	2243
Protivín **1124** d.	0632	0832	1032	1232	1432	1632	1832	2032	2327
Strakonice d.	0653	0853	1053	1253	1453	1653	1853	2053	2350
Horaždovice předměstí d.	0709	0909	1109	1309	1509	1709	1909	2109	...
Nepomuk d.	0729	0929	1129	1329	1529	1729	1929	2129	...
Plzeň hlavní a.	0757	0957	1157	1357	1557	1757	1957	2157	...

a – Ⓐ (also Dec. 31, July 8, Sept. 30).
h – To/from Havlíčkův Brod on dates in Table **1152**.
n – ①-⑥ (not Dec. 24, 26, Apr. 15, 17, May 1, 8, July 6, Nov. 18).
r – Ⓑ (not Dec. 25, Apr. 14, 16, 30, May 7, July 5, Nov. 17).
z – ⑤⑥⑦ (daily May 26 - Sept. 10), also Dec. 26, Apr. 17, May 1, 8, Sept. 27, 28, Nov. 16.

CZECH REPUBLIC

1126 PLZEŇ - CHOMUTOV - MOST

km		1798	1080	1082	1188	1084	1086	1182	1088	
		2Ⓐ						Ⓑh	⑦e	
0	**Plzeň** hlavní ... d.	...	0605	1005	1205	1405	1605	1805	2005	...
59	Blatno u Jesenice ... d.	0454	0709	1109	1309	1509	1709	1909	2109	...
107	Žatec ... **1105** d.	0550	0802	1202	1402	1602	1802	2002	2202	...
130	Chomutov ... **1110** d.	0616	0823	1223	1428	1623	1823	2028	2223	...
155	**Most** ... **1110** a.	...	0842	1242	1449	1642	1842	2049	2242	...

	1181	1081	1083		1085	1189	1087	1799	1089
	⚒n							2Ⓐ	⑦e
Most ... **1110** d.	0505	0710	0910	...	1310	1505	1710	*1859*	1910
Chomutov ... **1110** d.	0528	0730	0930	...	1330	1528	1730	1928	1930
Žatec ... **1105** d.	0553	0752	0952	...	1352	1553	1752	1954	1952
Blatno u Jesenice ... d.	0645	0845	1045	...	1445	1645	1845	2049	2045
Plzeň hlavní ... a.	0754	0954	1154	...	1554	1754	1954	...	2154

FOR NOTES SEE TABLE **1130**

1130 PRAHA - TÁBOR - ČESKÉ BUDĚJOVICE

km		*Ex* 1541	⊡ 703	705	*Ex* 531	707	*AEx* 1059	709	*Ex* 1543	711	713	715	*Ex* 1545	717	*Ex* 533	719	*Ex* 535	721	*Ex* 537	723	*Ex* 1547	725	*Ex* 539	727	729	731
		🍸	⚒n		K🍸	⚒n	A♣		🍸	🍸	Ⓐ		🍸		Ⓐ🍸		Ⓐ🍸		🍸		P🍸		⑦e			
	Praha Holešovice ... d.	...	...	0712n	0742n	0812	...	0912	0942	1112	1212	1312	1342	1412	1442	1512	...	1612	1642	1712	1742	1812	...	1912r	...	2142
0	**Praha** hlavní ... d.	0602	0632	0732	0802	0832	0902	0932	1002	1132	1232	1332	1402	1432	1502	1532	1602	1632	1702	1732	1802	1832	1902	1932	2032	2202
49	Benešov u Prahy ... d.	|	0712	0812	|	0912	|	1012	|	1212	1312	1412	|	1512	|	1612	|	1712	|	1812	|	1912	|	2012	2112	2242
103	**Tábor** ... d.	0715	0758	0858	0915	0958	1022	1058	1115	1258	1358	1458	1515	1558	1615	1658	1715	1758	1815	1858	1915	1958	2015	2058	2158	2328
130	Veselí nad Lužnicí ▷ a.	|	0820	0920	|	1020	|	1120	|	1320	1420	1520	|	1620	|	1720	|	1820	|	1920	|	2020	|	2120	2220	2350
169	**České Budějovice** ▷ a.	0800	0852	0952	1002	1057	1110	1152	1200	1352	1457	1552	1600	...	1702	1752	1802	1857e	1902	1952	2000	2057	2102	2152	2252	0022
	Linz Hbf **1132** ... a.	1007	...	...	...	...	...	...	1407	...	...	...	1807	...	...	...	...	...	...	...	2207	...	...	...	...	...

	730	728	*Ex* 538	726	*Ex* 536	724	*Ex* 534	722	*Ex* 1540	720	718	716	714	*Ex* 1542	712	*Ex* 532	710	708	*Ex* 530	706	*Ex* 1544	704	*AEx* 1058	702	700	*Ex* 1546
	⚒n	⚒n	Ⓐ🍸		🍸		Ⓐ🍸		P🍸	⚒n		🍸	Ⓐ	🍸		K🍸			⑦e		🍸		A♣	🍸	🍸	🍸
Linz Hbf **1132** ... d.	...	...	...	...	...	...	...	...	0635	...	...	...	...	1152	...	...	...	...	...	...	1552	...	...	...	...	1835
České Budějovice ▷ d.	0453	...	0553	0605	0653	...	0753	0805	0853	0901	1005	1205	1301	1353	1405	1453	1501	1605	1653	1701n	1753	1805	1854	1901	2005	2053
Veselí nad Lužnicí ▷ d.	|	0537	|	0637	|	0737	|	0837	|	0937	1037	1237	1337	|	1437	|	1537	1637	|	1737	|	1837	|	1937	2037	2126
Tábor ... d.	0544	0601	0644	0701	0744	0801	0844	0901	0944	1001	1101	1301	1401	1444	1501	1544	1601	1701	1744	1801	1844	1901	1944	2001	2101	2145
Benešov u Prahy ... d.	|	0648	|	0748	|	0848	|	0948	|	1048	1148	1348	1448	|	1548	|	1648	1748	|	1848	|	1948	|	2048	2148	2219
Praha hlavní ... a.	0700	0727	0757	0827	0857	0927	0957	1027	1057	1127	1227	1427	1527	1557	1627	1657	1727	1827	1857	1927	1957	2027	2102	2127	2227	2257
Praha Holešovice ... a.	0719	0746	0819	0846	0919	0946	1019	1046	1119	1146	1246	1446	...	1619	1646	1719	1746	1846r	...	...	...	2046	...	2146x	...	...

A – Ⓒ (daily June 3 - Oct. 1).
K – [12] Praha - Český Krumlov and v.v. (Table **1131**).
P – [12] Praha - Linz and v.v.; 🛏 1,2 cl., [2] (Ⓡ) Praha - Linz - Zürich and v.v.
e – ⑦ (also Apr. 17, May 1, 8; not Dec. 25, Apr. 16, 30, May 7).
h – Ⓑ (not Dec. 25, Apr. 14, 16, 30, May 7, July 5, Nov. 17).
n – ①–⑥ (not Dec. 24, 26, Apr. 15, 17, May 1, 8, July 6, Nov. 18).
r – ①–⑥ (also Apr. 16, 30, May 7; not Apr. 17, May 1, 8).
x – ⑥ (also Apr. 14 - 16, 30, May 7, July 5, Nov. 17).
⊡ – Additional train runs one hour earlier (0532 ⚒ **n**).
▷ – See also Table **1135**.
♣ – Operated by ARRIVA. 2nd class, 🍸. Separate fare tariff. To / from Český Krumlov and Horní Planá (Table **1131**).

1131 ČESKÉ BUDĚJOVICE - ČESKÝ KRUMLOV - NOVÉ ÚDOLÍ

2nd class (except *Ex*)

km		T		*Ex*531		1059 A♣	R		B			Ⓐ‡
	Praha hl. **1130** ... d.	...	...	0802	...	0902	...	...	...	...	...	...
0	**České Budějovice** d.	0607	0809	1013	1023	1118	1211	1422	1515	1611	1822	2010
31	Český Krumlov ... d.	0656	0900	1050	1108	1202	1302	1506	1604	1656	1908	2055
68	Horní Planá ... a.	0802	1000	...	1200	1254	1400	1600	...	1800	1959	...
96	**Nové Údolí** ... a.	...	1042	...	1242c	...	1442	1642	...	1842r	...	...

	P	N		R	*Ex*532			1058 A♣		V
Nové Údolí ... d.	...	...	0919z	1119	...	1319c	1519	...	1719	...
Horní Planá ... d.	0717	0803	1002	1209	...	1401	1601	1704	1801	...
Český Krumlov ... d.	0811	0859	1052	1301	1402	1451	1657	1759	1852	2101
České Budějovice a.	0856	0943	1137	1345	1440	1535	1741	1842	1936	2147
Praha hl. **1130** ... a.	...	...	...	...	1657	...	...	2102	...	...

A – Ⓒ (daily June 3 - Oct. 1).
B – Ⓐ (not Dec. 23 - Jan. 2, Feb. 3, Apr. 13, July 3 - Sept. 1, Oct. 26, 27).
N – Ⓒ (daily Dec. 23 - Jan. 2, July 1 - Sept. 3).
P – Ⓐ (not Dec. 23 - Jan. 2, July 3 - Sept. 1).
R – Ⓐ (daily Apr. 10 - Nov. 3).
T – Ⓐ (daily Jan. 2 - Mar. 31, Apr. 10 - Oct. 6).
V – Ⓐ (daily Apr. 10 - Oct. 6).
c – Apr. 14 - Oct. 1 (also Apr. 1, 2, 8, 9; Ⓒ from Oct. 7).
r – Apr. 14 - Oct. 1 (also Ⓒ Oct. 7 - 29).
z – Ⓒ (daily Apr. 14 - Oct. 1).
♣ – Operated by ARRIVA. 2nd class, 🍸 Separate fare tariff.
‡ – Additional journey runs at 2245.

1132 ČESKÉ BUDĚJOVICE - LINZ

km		3801	*Ex* 1541	3803	*Ex* 1543	3805	*Ex* 1545	3807	*Ex* 1547	
		2	🍸	2	🍸	2	🍸	2	P	2
	Praha hlavní **1130** ... d.	...	0602	...	1002	...	1402	...	1802	...
0	**České Budějovice** ... d.	0600	0804	1003	1206	1400	1606	1800	2004	2020
50	Rybnik ... a.	0653	0851	1052	1251	1452	1651	1851	2051	2124
72	Lipno nad Vltavou ... ⊡ a.	*0745*	*0945*	*1145*	*1345*	*1545*	*1745*	*1945*	|	...
64	Summerau 🏛 ... d.	0713	0909	1113	1309	1513	1709	1913	2109	...
73	Freistadt ... d.	0721	0918	1121	1318	1521	1718	1921	2118	...
126	**Linz** Hbf ... a.	0824	1007	1224	1407	1624	1807	2024	2207	...

	Ex 1540	3800	3802	*Ex* 1542	3804	*Ex* 1544	3806	*Ex* 1546	
	P	2	2	🍸	2	🍸	2	🍸	2Ⓐ
Linz Hbf ... d.	0635	0752	0935	1152	1335	1552	1735	1835	...
Freistadt ... d.	0742	0842	1039	1242	1439	1644	1839	1942	...
Summerau 🏛 ... d.	0753	0852	1051	1252	1451	1653	1851	1952	2112
Lipno nad Vltavou ... ⊡ d.	|	*0814*	*1014*	*1214*	*1414*	*1614*	*1814*	*1906*a	*2046*
Rybnik ... d.	0806	0908	1108	1306	1508	1706	1907	2005	2129
České Budějovice ... a.	0851	0958	1200	1351	1600	1751	1959	2050	2227
Praha hlavní **1130** ... a.	1057	...	...	1557	...	1957	...	2257	...

P – [12] Praha - Linz and v.v.; 🛏 1,2 cl., [2] (Ⓡ) Praha - Linz - Zürich and v.v.
a – Ⓐ only.
⊡ – Change trains at Rybnik.

TRAIN NAMES: **1540/1** F. A. GERSTNER, **1542/3** ANTON BRUCKNER, **1544/5** MATTHIAS SCHÖNERER, **1546/7** VÁŠA PŘÍHODA.

1133 ČESKÉ BUDĚJOVICE and VESELÍ NAD LUŽNICÍ - ČESKÉ VELENICE

For connections České Velenice - Wien see Table **990**. For connections Praha - Veselí nad Lužnicí see Table **1130**.

km		2Ⓐ	2Ⓐ			N		R	Ⓑh		Ⓑh	
0	České Budějovice . d.	0511	0632	0809	1009	1209	1409	1509	1609	1809	2009	2246
50	České Velenice 🏛 a.	0559	0726	0857	1057	1257	1457	1602	1657	1857	2057	2333

	Ⓐ	2	2Ⓐ		Ⓐ		Ⓑh		F	
České Velenice 🏛 . d.	0400	0500	0626	0903	1103	1303	1503	1703	1903	2103
České Budějovice .. a.	0449	0555	0715	0952	1152	1352	1552	1752	1952	2152

km	*2nd class*		Ⓐ	Ⓒ			E				Ⓒ	Ⓐ
0	Veselí nad Lužnicí d.	0452	0624	0725	0937	1137	1337	1537	1737	1937	2155	2230
21	Třeboň ... d.	0517	0647	0748	0959	1159	1359	1559	1759	1959	2216	2252
55	České Velenice 🏛 a.	0555	0725	0824	1036	1236	1436	1636	1836	2036	2253	2325

	Ⓐ		Ⓒ		E					
České Velenice 🏛 . d.	0419	0607	0734	0921	1121	1321	1521	1721	1921	2216
Třeboň ... d.	0457	0647	0812	1000	1200	1400	1600	1800	2000	2251
Veselí nad Lužnicí . a.	0519	0710	0833	1021	1221	1421	1621	1821	2021	2310

E – Ⓐ (daily Apr. 10 - Oct. 6).
F – Ⓑ **h** (daily June 25 - Sept. 1).
N – Ⓐ (also ⑥ July 1 - Aug. 26), also July 5.
R – Ⓐ (not Dec. 23 - Jan. 2, Feb. 3, Apr. 13, July 3 - Sept. 1, Oct. 26, 27).
h – Not Dec. 25, Apr. 14, 16, 30, May 7, July 5, Nov. 17.

1135 ČESKÉ BUDĚJOVICE - JIHLAVA - BRNO

km		1869	651	653	661	663	665	667	669	2	655
		2Ⓐ	⚒n			H					Ⓑh
	Plzeň **1125** ... d.	...	...	...	0602	0802	1002	1202	1402	...	1602
0	**České Budějovice** ... d.	...	0413z	0613	0813	1013	1213	1413	1613	...	1813
39	Veselí nad Lužnicí ... ▷ d.	...	0445z	0645	0845	1045	1245	1445	1645	...	1845
65	Jindřichův Hradec ... ▷ d.	...	0516z	0716	0916	1116	1316	1516	1716	...	1916
117	Kostelec u Jihlavy ... d.	...	0615z	0815	1015	1215	1415	1615	1815	...	2013
132	**Jihlava** ... a.	...	0633z	0833	1033	1233	1433	1633	1833	...	2031
132	**Jihlava** ... d.	0530	0640	0840	1040	1240	1440	1640	1840	1930	▽
161	Okříšky ... d.	0603	0707	0907	1107	1307	1507	1707	1907	2018	...
173	Trebíč ... d.	0620	0724	0924	1124	1324	1524	1724	1924	2046	...
236	**Brno** hlavní ... a.	0737	0836	1036	1236	1436	1636	1836	2036	2211	...

	656	654	668	666	664	662	660	652	650
	Ⓐt			H					Ⓑh
Brno hlavní ... d.	...	...	0720	0920	1120	1320	1520	1720	1920
Trebič ... d.	...	...	0833	1033	1233	1433	1633	1833	2036
Okříšky ... d.	...	...	0847	1047	1247	1447	1647	1847	2051
Jihlava ... a.	...	▽	0918	1118	1318	1518	1718	1918	2117
Jihlava ... d.	0525	0725	0925	1125	1325	1525	1725	1934s	...
Kostelec u Jihlavy ... d.	0543	0743	0943	1143	1343	1543	1743	1953s	...
Jindřichův Hradec ... ▷ d.	0643	0843	1043	1243	1443	1643	1843	2056s	...
Veselí nad Lužnicí ... ▷ d.	0715	0915	1115	1315	1515	1715	1915	2126s	...
České Budějovice ... a.	0746	0946	1146	1346	1546	1746	1946	2158s	...
Plzeň **1125** ... a.	0957	1157	1357	1557	1757	1957	2157h	...	...

H – ⑤⑥⑦ (daily May 26 - Sept. 10), also Dec. 26, Apr. 13, 17, Sept. 27, 28, Nov. 16.
J – ⚒ (daily Feb. 13 - Dec. 9).
e – Also Apr. 17, May 1, 8; not Dec. 25, Apr. 16, 30, May 7.
f – Also Apr. 13, July 4, Sept. 27, Nov. 16; not Apr. 14, Nov. 17).
h – Ⓑ (not Dec. 25, Apr. 14, 16, 30, May 7, July 5, Nov. 17).
n – ①–⑥ (not Dec. 24, 26, Apr. 15, 17, May 1, 8, July 6, Nov. 18).
s – ⑤⑦ (also Apr. 13, 17, May 1, 8, July 4, Sept. 27, Nov. 16; not Dec. 24 - 30, Apr. 14, 16, 30, May 7, July 7, Sept. 29, Nov. 17).
t – Also Dec. 31, July 8, Sept. 30.
z – ① (also Apr. 18, May 2, 9; not Dec. 26, Apr. 17, May 1, 8).
▷ – Additional trains: from Veselí nad Lužnicí 0740, 0935, 1135Ⓐ, 1335, 1559Ⓑ **h**, 1735, 1935Ⓐ, 2130, 2225, 2320; from Jindřichův Hradec 0555Ⓐ, 0642Ⓒ, 0730, 0947, 1147, 1347Ⓐ, 1547Ⓑ **h**, 1747, 1947, 2142, 2236Ⓐ. Journey 31 - 36 minutes.
▽ – To / from Havličkův Brod on dates in Table **1152**.
⊡ – To Jihlava, arrive 2105.

KOSTELEC U JIHLAVY - TELČ 36 mins, *23* km:
From Kostelec: 0457Ⓐ, 0637Ⓐ, 0820, 1018, 1111Ⓐ, 1316, 1421Ⓐ, 1512Ⓒ, 1522Ⓐ, 1710, 1818⑦**e**, 1907⚒, 2019⑦**e**, 2128Ⓐ.
From Telč: 0404⚒**n**, 0516Ⓐ, 0719Ⓑ**h**, 0803Ⓐ, 0901Ⓒ, 0935Ⓐ, 1204, 1327Ⓐ, 1404Ⓒ, 1441Ⓐ, 1604, 1655⑦**e**, 1823⚒, 1910⑦**e**, 2028Ⓐ.

OKŘÍŠKY - ZNOJMO 1137

km		Ⓐ	Ⓐ	J				Ⓑh			⑤f
0	Okříšky d.	0443	0610	0710	0917	1117	1317	1517	1717	1920	1920
32	Moravské Budějovice a.	0518	0645	0744	0952	1152	1352	1552	1752	2000	2000
70	Znojmo a.	0631	0730	0848	1047	1247	1447	1647	1847	...	2047

	Ⓐ	J				Ⓐ			⊡
Znojmo d.	0529	0659n	0902	1102	1302	...	1502	1702	1859
Moravské Budějovice d.	0623	0803	1003	1203	1346	1427	1603	1803	1941
Okříšky a.	0703	0839	1039	1239	...	1503	1639	1839	2016

FOR NOTES SEE TABLE **1135**

PRAHA - MLADÁ BOLESLAV - TURNOV - (LIBEREC) 1140

2nd class

km			1148 T	1146 T		1144 T	1142 T	1944 Ⓐ	1140	1940	
0	**Praha** hlavní d.	0548	0725	0925	1148	1325	1525	1625	1725	1925	2106
34	Neratovice d.	0632	0800	1000	1232	1400	1600	1703	1800	2000	2149
40	Všetaty d.	0641	0807	1007	1240	1407	1607	1712	1807	2007	2157
72	**Mladá Boleslav** a.	0718	0833	1033	1321	1433	1633	1747	1833	2033	2232
72	**Mladá Boleslav** d.	...	0834	1034	*1344*	1434	1634	*1749*	1834	2034	2241
88	Mnichovo Hradiště d.	...	0859	1059	*1408*	1459	1659	*1811*	1859	2058	2259
102	**Turnov** a.	...	0912	1112	*1428*	1512	1712	*1831*	1912	2116	2315
	Turnov 1142 d.	...	*0921*	*1121*	*1440**	*1521*	*1721*	*1840**	*1921*	*2121*	*2319*
	Liberec 1142 a.	...	*0956*	*1156*	*1524**	*1556*	*1756*	*1924**	*1956*	*2156*	*2356*

	1941 Ⓐ	1141	1143 T		1145	1147 T	1149 T	1151 T		Ⓒ
Liberec 1142 d.	*0400*	*0602*	*0802*	*0830**	*1202*	*1402*	*1602*	*1802*	...	*2030*
Turnov 1142 a.	*0437*	*0639*	*0839*	*0915**	*1239*	*1439*	*1639*	*1839*	...	*2114*
Turnov d.	0441	0644	0844	*0927*	1244	1444	1644	1844	*1927*	2122
Mnichovo Hradiště d.	0459	0658	0858	*0945*	1258	1458	1658	1858	*1945*	2140
Mladá Boleslav a.	0519	0715	0915	*1010*	1315	1515	1715	1915	*2010*	2200
Mladá Boleslav d.	0521	0724	0924	1037	1324	1524	1724	1924	2037	2207
Všetaty d.	0550	0751	0951	1121	1351	1551	1751	1951	2121	2247
Neratovice d.	0558	0800	1000	1130	1400	1600	1800	2000	2130	2257
Praha hlavní a.	0635	0837	1037	1212	1437	1638	1838	2037	2212	2336

T – To/from Tanvald on dates in Table **1142**. * – Change at Turnov.

LIBEREC - TANVALD - HARRACHOV - SZKLARSKA POŖEBA 1141

2nd class

km		S	R		R	S		S		E
0	**Liberec** ▶ d.	0635	0735	0835	0935	1035	1235	1435	1635	1835
12	Jablonec nad Nisou ▶ d.	0656	0756	0856	0956	1056	1256	1456	1656	1856
27	**Tanvald** ▶ a.	0725	0825	0925	1025	1125	1325	1525	1725	1925
27	**Tanvald** d.	0730	0830	0933	1027	1130	1330	1530	1730	1930
39	Harrachov d.	0757	0857	0957	1057	1157	1357	1557	1757	1957
55	**Szklarska Poŗeba** ‡ a.	0821	0921	1021	1121	1221	1421	1621	1821	2021

	S	R		R	S		S		E
Szklarska Poŗeba ‡ d.	0829	0929	1029	1129	1229	1429	1629	1829	2029
Harrachov d.	0857	0957	1057	1157	1257	1457	1657	1900	2057
Tanvald a.	0923	1023	1123	1223	1323	1523	1723	1925	2123
Tanvald ▲ d.	0929	1029	1129	1229	1329	1529	1729	1929	2129
Jablonec nad Nisou ▲ d.	0957	1057	1157	1257	1357	1557	1757	1957	2157
Liberec ▲ a.	1018	1118	1218	1318	1418	1618	1818	2018	2218

E – June 24 - Sept. 3.
R – ⑥⑦ Dec. 31 - Jan. 22 (also Dec. 26 - 30); daily Jan. 28 - Mar. 19; ⑥⑦ Apr. 29 - June 18 (also May 1, 3, 8, June 15); daily June 24 - Sept. 3; ⑥⑦ Sept. 9 - Oct. 29 (also Sept. 28).
S – Daily Dec. 26 - Mar. 19; ⑥⑦ Mar. 25 - June 18 (also Apr. 14, 17, May 1, 3, 8, June 15); daily June 24 - Sept. 3; ⑥⑦ Sept. 9 - Oct. 29 (also Sept. 28).
‡ – Szklarska Poŗeba Górna. 🏛 Czech Republic / Poland = Jakuszyce.

▶ – **Liberec - Tanvald**: 0035, hourly 0535 - 2235 (on Ⓐ also 0437 and hourly 0505 - 0705, 1305 - 1805).
▲ – **Tanvald - Liberec**: hourly 0429 - 2229 (on Ⓐ also hourly 0459 - 0759, 1259 - 1659).

Additional trains **Liberec - Harrachov** and v.v.:
From Liberec: 0635, 0735, 0935, 1135, 1335, 1435, 1535**S**, 1735.
From Harrachov: 0757Ⓒ, 0857, 0957, 1157**S**, 1257, 1357, 1557, 1657, 1757**S**, 1957**E**.

LIBEREC - HRADEC KRÁLOVÉ - PARDUBICE 1142

2nd class

km		1261	1263	1265		1275	1277
0	**Liberec** d.	0400	0602	0802		1802	2002
38	Turnov d.	0438	0642	0842		1842	2042
52	Železný Brod ★ d.	0455	0659	0859	and	1859	2059
76	Stará Paka d.	0525	0727	0927	every	1927	2127
107	Dvůr Králové n. L. d.	0600	0800	1000	two	2000	2201
122	Jaroměř d.	0617	0818	1018	hours	2020	2221
139	**Hradec Králové** a.	0631	0832	1032	until	2034	2237
139	**Hradec Králové** ▶ d.	0634	0839	1036		2037	2239
161	**Pardubice** ▶ a.	0652	0857	1054		2055	2302

	1276		1262	1260
Pardubice ▶ d.	0502		1903	2107
Hradec Králové ▶ a.	0521		1922	2125
Hradec Králové d.	0525	and	1926	2127
Jaroměř d.	0542	every	1942	2144
Dvůr Králové n. L. d.	0558	two	1956	2158
Stará Paka d.	0631	hours	2031	2232
Železný Brod ★ d.	0700	until	2100	2301
Turnov d.	0721		2121	2319
Liberec a.	0756		2156	2356

	△		d		Ⓑh	Ⓑh
Praha hl 1140 d.	...	0725	0925	1325	1525	*1725*
Turnov d.	...	0919	1119	1519	1719	1926
Železný Brod d.	0701	0936	1136	1536	1736	1946
Tanvald a.	0727	1003	1210	1603	1803	2010

	▽	⑥u	Ⓐ	Ⓒ	d	
Tanvald d.	0627	0751	1340	1349	1550	1751
Železný Brod a.	0653	0817	1407	1415	1617	1817
Turnov a.	...	0835	1431	1435	1635	1835
Praha hl 1140 a.	...	1037	*1638*	1638	1838	2037

d – Change at Turnov on Ⓐ.
h – Not Dec. 25, Apr. 14, 16, 30, May 7, July 5, Nov. 17.
s – Ⓐ (daily Apr. 29 - Sept. 24).
u – ⑥ (also ①-⑤ July 3 - Sept. 1), also Dec. 23, 27 - 30, Apr. 14, Sept. 28, Nov. 17; not Apr. 15, July 6, Nov. 18.
△ – Also 0901, 1101Ⓒ, 1301, 1414Ⓐ, 1501, 1701, 1901, 2101, 2301**s**.
▽ – Also 0427⚒, 0527Ⓐ, 0827, 1027, 1227, 1427, 1627, 1827, 2027, 2227**s**.

★ – For Pardubice - Tanvald and v.v. change at Železný Brod (see right hand panel).
▶ – Additional trains **Hradec Kralové - Pardubice** and v.v. (journey 20 - 30 minutes):
From Hradec Kralové: 0038, 0428, 0505Ⓐ, 0532Ⓐ, 0545, 0603, 0703, 0730, 0804, 0903, 0935Ⓐ, 1004, 1104, 1136, 1204, 1304, 1336, 1404, 1504, 1537, 1604, 1704, 1735, 1804, 1904, 1936Ⓒ, 2004, 2104, 2204.
From Pardubice: 0111, 0432Ⓐ, 0533, 0605Ⓐ, 0628Ⓐ, 0634Ⓒ, 0719Ⓐ, 0736, 0805, 0836, 0932, 1033, 1132, 1205, 1233, 1332, 1406, 1434, 1534, 1605, 1634, 1732, 1805, 1833, 1933, 2001Ⓒ, 2033, 2134, 2241.

PRAHA - HRADEC KRÁLOVÉ - TRUTNOV 1145

km		1780	941 Ⓐ	1782 ⑥t	921	943	1784 2	923	945	1786 2Ⓐ	925	1788 2	927	947 Ⓐu	1790 2	929	935 L	1792 2	931	949	951	1796	953	955	957
0	**Praha** hlavní d.	...	0507	...	0607	0707	...	0807	0907	...	1007	...	1207	1307	...	1407	1507	...	1607	1707	1807	...	1907	2007	2207
35	Lysá nad Labem ▷ d.	...	0540	...	0640	0740	...	0840	0940	...	1040	...	1240	1340	...	1440	1540	...	1640	1740	1840	...	1940	2040	2240
50	Nymburk ▷ d.	...	0555	...	0655	0755	...	0855	0955	...	1055	...	1255	1355	...	1455	1555	...	1655	1755	1855	...	1955	2055	2255
57	Poděbrady ▷ d.	...	0601	...	0701	0801	...	0901	1001	...	1101	...	1301	1401	...	1501	1601	...	1701	1801	1901	...	2001	2101	2301
116	**Hradec Králové** a.	...	0651	...	0751	0851	...	0951	1051	...	1151	...	1351	1451	...	1551	1651	...	1751	1851	1951	...	2051	2151	2348
116	**Hradec Králové** d.	0601	...	0702	0804	...	0902	1004	...	1102	1204	1302	1404	...	1501	1604	...	1702	1804	...	...	2001	...	...	...
137	Jaroměř d.	0617	...	0718	0819	...	0917	1019	...	1117	1219	1317	1419	...	1517	1619	...	1717	1819	...	...	2020	...	...	...
189	**Trutnov** hlavní a.	0720	...	0820	0920	...	1017	1120	...	1218	1320	1417	1520	...	1621	1720	...	1817	1920	...	...	2118	...	...	...

	952 Ⓐ	950	1785	934 L	932	1787 2	948	930	1789 2Ⓐ	928	1791 2	946 Ⓐu	926	1793 2	944	924	1795 2	942	922	1795 2Ⓒ	940	920	2	2	2⊡
Trutnov hlavní d.	...	...	0542	...	0643	0743	...	0843	0942	1043	1141	...	1243	1341	...	1443	1541	...	1643	1742	...	1843	...	...	2041
Jaroměř d.	...	0540r	0641	...	0742	0843	...	0942	1043	1142	1243	...	1342	1443	...	1542	1643	...	1742	1843	...	1942	...	...	2142
Hradec Králové a.	...	0555r	0657	...	0755	0856	...	0955	1056	1155	1256	...	1355	1458	...	1555	1657	...	1755	1856	...	1955	...	...	2200
Hradec Králové d.	0508	0608	...	0708	0808	...	0908	1008	...	1208	...	1308	1408	...	1508	1608	...	1708	1808	...	1908	2008	...	...	...
Poděbrady ▷ d.	0554	0654	...	0754	0854	...	0954	1054	...	1254	...	1354	1454	...	1554	1654	...	1754	1854	...	1954	2054	2153	...	...
Nymburk ▷ d.	0602	0702	...	0802	0902	...	1002	1102	...	1302	...	1402	1502	...	1602	1702	...	1802	1902	...	2002	2102	2206	2312	...
Lysá nad Labem ▷ d.	0616	0716	...	0816	0916	...	1016	1116	...	1316	...	1416	1516	...	1616	1716	...	1816	1916	...	2016	2116	2225	2331	...
Praha hlavní a.	0648	0748	...	0848	0948	...	1048	1148	...	1348	...	1448	1548	...	1648	1748	...	1848	1948	...	2048	2148	2303	0008	...

L – To/from Letohrad (Table **1165**).
r – ①-⑥ (not Dec. 24, 26, Apr. 15, 17, May 1, 8, July 6, Nov. 18).
t – Also Apr. 14, July 5, Sept. 28, Nov. 17; not Apr. 15, Nov. 18.
u – Not Dec. 27 - 30.
▷ – See also Table **1147**.
⊡ – Change at Starkoč.

DĚČÍN - ÚSTÍ NAD LABEM - MĚLNÍK - KOLÍN and RUMBURK - KOLÍN 1147

km		781 ⚒n	783		793	795 Ⓑh
0	**Ústí n. L západ** d.	0439	0639		1639	1839
2	**Ústí n. L Střekov** d.	0444	0644		1644	1844
27	Litoměřice město d.	0503	0703	and	1703	1903
63	**Mělník** d.	0532	0732	every	1732	1932
73	Všetaty d.	0541	0741	two	1741	1941
85	Stará Boleslav d.	0551	0751	hours	1751	1951
96	Lysá nad Labem ▷ d.	0559	0759	until	1759	1959
111	Nymburk ▷ d.	0614	0814		1814	2014
118	Poděbrady ▷ d.	0621	0821		1821	2021
134	**Kolín** d.	0638	0838		1838	2038

	794 ⚒n	792		782	780 Ⓑh
Kolín d.	0715	0915		1915	2115
Poděbrady ▷ d.	0731	0931		1931	2131
Nymburk ▷ d.	0739	0939	and	1939	2139
Lysá nad Labem ▷ d.	0752	0952	every	1952	2152
Stará Boleslav d.	0800	1000	two	2000	2200
Všetaty d.	0812	1012	hours	2012	2212
Mělník d.	0822	1022	until	2022	2222
Litoměřice město d.	0853	1053		2053	2253
Ústí n. L Střekov a.	0910	1110		2110	2310
Ústí n. L západ a.	0915	1115		2115	2315

km	⊖						
0	**Děčín** hlavní d.	0601	0801	1201	1401	1601	1801
28	**Ústí n. L Střekov** a.	0639	0839	1239	1439	1639	1839

⊖						
Ústí n. L Střekov d.	0655	0913	1313	1513	1713	1913
Děčín hlavní a.	0734	0955	1355	1555	1755	1955

RUMBURK - ČESKA LIPÁ - KOLÍN

						E
Rumburk d.	0507**a**	0716	1113	1316	1516	1716
Česka Lipá d.	0623	0823	1223	1423	1623	1823
Mladá Boleslav d.	0722	0922	1322	1522	1722	1922
Nymburk ▷ d.	0748	0948	1348	1548	1748	1948
Poděbrady ▷ d.	0756	0956	1356	1556	1756	1956
Kolín a.	0811	1011	1411	1611	1811	2011

						E
Kolín d.	0744	0944	1344	1544	1744	1944
Poděbrady ▷ d.	0759	0959	1359	1559	1759	1959
Nymburk ▷ d.	0808	1008	1408	1608	1808	2008
Mladá Boleslav a.	0835	1035	1435	1635	1835	2035
Česka Lipá a.	0935	1135	1535	1735	1935	2135
Rumburk a.	1036	1237	1639	1837	2037	...

E – ⑤⑥⑦ (daily May 26 - Sept. 17), also Dec. 26, Apr. 13, 17, Sept. 27, 28, Nov. 16; not Dec. 24, 25, 31.
a – Ⓐ only.
h – Not Dec. 25, Apr. 14, 16, 30, May 7, July 5, Nov. 17.
n – ①-⑥ (not Dec. 24, 26, Apr. 15, 17, May 1, 8, July 6, Nov. 18).
▷ – See also Table **1145**.
⊖ – 2nd class only. For Dečín - Ústí nad Labem hlavni see Table **1100**.

1150 PRAHA - PARDUBICE - BRNO - BŘECLAV - WIEN / BRATISLAVA

km	FAST TRAINS	EC 271	Ex 571	EC 273	RJ 71	EC 275	RJ 73	EC 277	RJ 75	EC 279	RJ 77	EC 131	EC 173	RJ 79	EC 281	Ex 573	RJ 371	EC 283	Ex 577	RJ 373	RJ 579	Ex 581	EN 477	477 407	Ex 525
		✕	🍷	✕	✕	✕	✕	✕	✕	✕	✕	✕	✕	✕	✕	🍷	✕	✕	🍷	✕	✕	✕	§	§	
			Ⓐu		G		G	S	G		G	V	H	G		Ⓐu	G	≋	⑦e				M	W	
0	**Praha** hlavní ..... **1160** d.	...	0449	0549	0650	0752	0852	0952	1052	1152	1252	...	1352	1452	1552	1619	1652	1752	1819	1852	1947	2100	2358	2358	0001
62	Kolín ..... **1160** d.	...	0525	0625	|	0827	|	1027	|	1227	|	...	1427	|	1627	|	|	1827	|	|	2025	2137	|	|	0039
104	**Pardubice** ..... **1160** d.	...	0547	0647	0747	0849	0947	1049	1147	1249	1347	...	1449	1547	1649	1718	1747	1849	1918	1947	2047	2201	0108	0108	0104
164	Česká Třebová .. **1160** d.	...	0621	0721	0821	|	1021	|	1221	|	1421	...	|	1621	|	|	1821	|	|	2021	2121	2241	|	|	...
255	**Brno** hlavní ..... a.	...	0720	0820	0920	1020	1120	1220	1320	1420	1520	...	1620	1720	1820	1851	1920	2020	2051	2120	2220	2344	0245	0245	...
255	**Brno** hlavní ..... **1159** d.	0622	...	0823	0923	1023	1123	1223	1323	1423	1523	...	1623	1723	1823	...	1923	2028	...	2123	...	...	0315	0315	...
314	**Břeclav** ..... **1159** a.	0652	...	0852	0952	1052	1152	1252	1352	1452	1552	...	1652	1752	1852	...	1952	2057	...	2152	...	...	0347	0347	...
314	**Břeclav** ..... d.	0659	...	0859	0955	1059	1155	1259	1355	1459	1555	1559	1659	1755	1859	...	1955	2059	...	2155	...	...	0440	0549	...
	Wien Hbf **982** ..... a.	|	...	*0949**	1049	|	1249	*1349**	1449	|	1649	|	|	1849	*1949**	...	2049	|	...	2249	...	...	|	0655	...
332	Kúty 🏛 ..... d.	0713	...	0913	...	1113	...	1313	...	1513	...	1613	1713	...	1913	...	...	2113	...	...	...	...	0455	...	...
396	**Bratislava** hlavná ..... a.	0750	...	0950	...	1150	...	1350	...	1550	...	1650	1750	...	1950	...	...	2150	...	...	...	...	0536	...	...
	Budapest K. **1175** ..... a.	1035	...	1235	...	1435	...	1635	...	1835	...	1935	2035	...	2235	...	...	...	...	...	...	...	0837	...	...

FAST TRAINS	Ex 524	RJ 580	Ex 578	IC 574	EC 282	Ex 572	RJ 70	EC 280	RJ 72	EC 172	EC 130	RJ 74	EC 278	RJ 76	Ex 570	EC 276	RJ 78	EC 274	RJ 370	EC 272	RJ 372	EC 270	406 476	EN 476	476 524
	Ⓐ		✕	✕	✕	🍷	✕	✕	✕	✕	✕	✕	✕	✕	🍷	✕	✕	✕	✕	✕	✕	✕	§	§	§
					≋	Ⓐu			G	H	V	G		G	⑦e	S	G		G		G		W	M	P
Budapest K. **1175** ..... d.	...	...	...	...	...	...	...	0525	...	0725	0822	...	0925	...	...	1125	...	1325	...	1525	...	1725	...	2005	2005
Bratislava hlavná ..... d.	...	...	...	...	0610	...	...	0810	...	1010	1110	...	1210	...	...	1410	...	1610	...	1810	...	2010	...	2301	2301
Kúty 🏛 ..... d.	...	...	...	...	0649	...	...	0849	...	1049	1149	...	1249	...	...	1449	...	1649	...	1849	...	2049	...	2343	2343
Wien Hbf **982** ..... d.	...	...	...	...	|	...	0710	*0810**	0910	|	|	1110	|	1310	...	*1410**	1510	|	1710	*1810**	1910	|	2250	|	|
Břeclav ..... a.	...	...	...	...	0701	...	0804	0901	1004	1101	1201	1204	1301	1404	...	1501	1604	1701	1804	1901	2004	2101	2349	2355	2355
Břeclav ..... **1159** d.	...	...	...	0607	0706	...	0807	0907	1007	1107	...	1207	1307	1407	...	1507	1607	1707	1807	1907	2007	2107	0024	0024	0024
Brno hlavní ..... **1159** a.	...	...	...	0636	0734	...	0836	0936	1036	1136	...	1236	1336	1436	...	1536	1636	1736	1836	1936	2036	2136	0054	0054	0054
Brno hlavní ..... d.	...	0431	0538	0638	0738	0809	0838	0938	1038	1138	...	1238	1338	1438	1509	1538	1638	1738	1838	1938	2038	...	0111	0111	0111
Česká Třebová ... **1160** d.	...	0538	0637	0738	|	|	0938	|	1138	|	...	1338	|	1538	|	|	1738	|	1938	2038	2144	...	|	|	|
Pardubice ..... **1160** d.	0533	0612	0710	0812	0910	0946	1012	1110	1212	1310	...	1412	1510	1612	1646	1710	1812	1910	2012	2112	2218	...	0252	0252	0533
Kolín ..... **1160** d.	0559	|	0730	|	0930	|	|	1130	|	1330	...	|	1530	|	|	1730	|	1930	|	2132	2238	...	|	|	0559
Praha hlavní ..... **1160** a.	0639	0706	0806	0906	1006	1042	1106	1206	1306	1406	...	1506	1606	1706	1742	1806	1906	2006	2106	2209	2313	...	0345	0345	0639r

SEMI-FAST TRAINS *For fast trains Praha - Olomouc see Table 1160*

km		883	861	885	863	865	889	867	891	869	893	871	895	873	897	875	Ex581	877
		◇	T	◇			◇		◇		⊡		▽		⊙			
0	**Praha** hlavní ..... d.	...	0555	0653	0755	0955	1055	1155	1255	1355	1455	1555	1655	1755	1855	2001	2100	2200
62	Kolín ..... d.	⊖	0635	0733	0835	1035	1135	1235	1335	1435	1535	1635	1735	1835	1935	2042	2137	2240
104	**Pardubice** ..... d.	0605	0705	0805	0905	1105	1205	1305	1405	1505	1605	1705	1805	1905	2005	2105	2201	2304
139	Choceň ..... d.	0625	0725	0825	0925	1125	1225	1325	1425	1525	1625	1725	1825	1925	2025	2125	2217	...
154	Ústí nad Orlicí ..... d.	0638	0738	0838	0938	1138	1238	1338	1438	1538	1638	1738	1838	1938	2038	2138	2229	...
164	**Česká Třebová** ..... d.	0649	0749	0849	0949	1149	1249	1349	1449	1549	1649	1749	1849	1949	2049	2148	2241	...
	Brno hl. (below) ... a.	|	0902	|	1102	1302	|	1502	|	1702	|	1904	|	2102	|	...	2344	...
250	**Olomouc** ..... a.	0729	...	0929	...	...	1329	...	1529	...	1729	...	1929	...	2129	...	...	...

	876	898	874	894	872	892	870	868	888	866	886	864	884	862	882	860	860	Ex120
		Ⓐd	Ⓐ	⊙		▽			◇		◇		◇		◇	Ⓑh	⑦e	z
Olomouc ..... d.	...	...	...	0631	...	0831	...	...	1231	...	1431	...	1631	...	1831	...	...	2009
Brno hl (below) ..... d.	...	...	0500	|	0656	|	0857	1057	|	1257	|	1455	|	1655	|	1857	1857	|
Česká Třebová ..... d.	...	0514	0614	0714	0814	0914	1014	1214	1314	1414	1514	1614	1714	1814	1914	2014	2014	2105
Ústí nad Orlicí ..... d.	...	0523	0623	0723	0823	0923	1023	1223	1323	1423	1523	1623	1723	1823	1923	2023	2023	2115
Choceň ..... d.	...	0536	0636	0736	0836	0936	1036	1236	1336	1436	1536	1636	1736	1836	1936	2036	2036	2128
Pardubice ..... d.	0458	0558	0658	0758	0858	0958	1058	1258	1358	1458	1558	1658	1758	1858	1958	2053	2056	2146
Kolín ..... d.	0523	0623	0723	0823	0923	1023	1123	1323	1423	1523	1623	1723	1823	1923	2023	...	2121	2210
Praha hlavní ..... a.	0603	0703	0803	0903	1003	1103	1203	1403	1503	1603	1703	1803	1903	2003	2103	...	2159	2248

REGIOJET ♥	1035	1031	1033
Praha hl. ..... d.	0719	1519	1719
Kolín ..... d.	0755	|	|
Pardubice ..... d.	0818	1613	1813
Ústí nad Orlicí ..... d.	|	1642	1842
Česká Třebová ... d.	|	1653	1853
Brno hlavní ..... d.	0953	1753	1953
Břeclav ..... a.	1022	1822	2025
Kúty 🏛 ..... a.	1034	1834	s
Bratislava hl. ..... a.	1112	1912	...

REGIOJET ♥	1030	1032	1038
Bratislava hl. ..... d.	...	0545	1526
Kúty 🏛 ..... d.	s	0623	1618
Břeclav ..... d.	0533	0635	1633
Brno hlavní ..... d.	0609	0709	1709
Česká Třebová ... d.	0710	0810	|
Ústí nad Orlicí ..... d.	0719	0819	|
Pardubice ..... d.	0751	0848	1846
Kolín ..... d.	|	|	1906
Praha hl. ..... a.	0847	0942	1942

km		1973	1975	861	863	865	867	1977	869	871	873	Ex581
		⚒n	2Ⓐ	T				2Ⓐ				
	Praha hlavní ▷ .. d.	...	...	0555	0755	0955	1155	...	1355	1555	1755	2100
0	**Česká Třebová** ..... d.	0541	0643	0749	0949	1149	1349	1448	1549	1754	1949	2241
17	Svitavy ..... d.	0559	0700	0801	1001	1201	1401	1505	1601	1805	2001	2251
44	Letovice ..... d.	0628	0729	0821	1020	1220	1420	1532	1620	1826	2020	2309
69	Blansko ..... d.	0650	0752	0841	1042	1242	1442	1552	1642	1844	2042	2324
91	**Brno** hlavní ..... a.	0714	0814	0902	1102	1302	1502	1612	1702	1904	2102	2344

	580	874	872	870	868	866	864	862	860	372
	•	Ⓐ								•
Brno hlavní ..... d.	0431	0500	0656	0857	1057	1257	1455	1655	1857	2038
Blansko ..... d.	0452	0520	0718	0918	1118	1318	1518	1718	1918	2059
Letovice ..... d.	0509	0538	0738	0939	1139	1339	1539	1739	1939	2116
Svitavy ..... d.	0527	0601	0803	1001	1201	1401	1601	1803	2001	2133
Česká Třebová ..... a.	0537	0611	0813	1011	1211	1411	1611	1813	2011	2143
Praha hlavní ▷ .. a.	0706	0803	1003	1203	1403	1603	1803	2003	2159e	2313

G – [12] ✕ Praha - Brno - Wien - Graz and v.v. (Table **60**).
H – HUNGARIA – [12] ✕ Hamburg - Berlin - Dresden - Praha - Bratislava - Budapest and v.v. Conveys on ②⑤ June 16 - Sept. 1 🛏 1, 2 cl. Praha - Budapest - Beograd - Bar, returning from Bar on ④⑦ June 18 - Sept. 3.
M – METROPOL – 🛏 1, 2 cl., ▬ 2 cl., [2] Berlin - Dresden - Praha - Bratislava - Budapest and v.v. For other cars Břeclav - Budapest and v.v. see Tables **95**/**99**.
P – 🛏 1, 2 cl., ▬ 2 cl., [2] Budapest (**476**) - Bratislava - Pardubice (**524**Ⓐ / **898**Ⓒ) - Praha. On Ⓒ Pardubice d. 0558 (train **898**), Kolín d. 0623, Praha hlavní a. 0703.
S – SLOVAN – [12] ✕ Praha - Budapest and v.v. On ②⑤ June 20 - Sept. 1 conveys 🛏 1, 2 cl. Praha - Budapest (**1204/5**) - Zagreb - Split, returning ③⑥ June 21 - Sept. 2.
T – From Praha on ① **g**; from Pardubice on ①–⑥ **n**; runs daily Česká Třebová - Brno.
V – VARSOVIA – [12] ✕ Warszawa - Katowice - Ostrava - Břeclav - Budapest and v.v.
W – 🛏 1, 2 cl., ▬ 2 cl., [2] Berlin - Dresden - Praha - Břeclav (**407/6**) - Wien Hbf and v.v.
d – Daily from Pardubice.

e – ⑦ (also Apr. 17, May 1, 8; not Dec. 25, Apr. 16, 30, May 7).
g – Also Apr. 18, May 2, 9; not Dec. 26, Apr. 17, May 1, 8.
h – Not Dec. 25, Apr. 14, 16, 30, May 7, July 5, Nov. 17.
n – ①–⑥ (not Dec. 24, 26, Apr. 15, 17, May 1, 8, July 6, Nov. 18).
r – 0703 on Ⓒ.
s – To / from Staré Město u Uherské Hradiště (a. 2114 / d. 0444).
u – Ⓐ (not Dec. 27 - 30, July 7, Sept. 29).
z – From Žilina (Table **1160**).
♥ – Operated by REGIOJET. Separate fare tariff applies.
≋ – Conveys 🛏 1, 2 cl. Brno (**283/2**) - Bratislava (**801/0**) - Košice - Prešov and v.v. on dates in Table **1190**.
⊡ – To / from Staré Město u Uherské Hradiště (Table **1159**).
▽ – To / from Veseli nad Moravou (Table **1159**).
◇ – To / from Luhačovice (Table **1159**).

⊖ – From Hradec Králové (d. 0545).
⊙ – To / from Zlín (Table **1159**).
§ – Reservation compulsory for international journeys.
▷ – See table above.
• – Railjet train (*RJ*).
* – Change at Břeclav.

OTHER TRAIN NAMES: SEE TABLE **60**.

1151 PRAHA - HAVLIČKŮV BROD - BRNO

See also Table **1150**

km		975	977	979	981	983	985	987	961	989	991	963
		⚒n					Ⓐ		Ⓑh		G	
0	**Praha** hlavní ..... ▷ d.	0604	0804	1004	1204	1404	1504	1604	1704	1804	1904	2004
62	Kolín ..... ▷ d.	0646	0846	1046	1246	1446	1546	1646	1746	1846	1946	2046
73	Kutná Hora ..... d.	0656	0856	1056	1256	1456	1556	1656	1756	1856	1956	2056
82	Čáslav ..... d.	0704	0904	1104	1304	1504	1604	1704	1804	1904	2004	2104
136	**Havlíčkův Brod** ..... d.	0802	1002	1202	1402	1602	1702	1802	1902	2002	2104	2200
	Jihlava **1152** ..... a.	|	|	|	|	|	|	|	1923	|	|	...
169	Žďár nad Sázavou .. d.	0829	1029	1229	1429	1629	1729	1829	...	2029	2129	...
257	**Brno** hlavní ..... a.	0941	1141	1341	1541	1741	1841	1941	...	2143	2238	...

	962	960	990	988	986	984	982	980	978	976	972
	⚒n		E						Ⓑh		
Brno hlavní ..... d.	...	...	0520	0620	0820	1020	1220	1420	1520	1620	1820
Žďár nad Sázavou . d.	...	...	0634	0734	0934	1134	1334	1534	1634	1734	1934
Jihlava **1152** ..... d.	...	0537n	|	|	|	|	|	|	|	|	|
Havlíčkův Brod ..... d.	0500	0600	0700	0800	1000	1200	1400	1600	1700	1800	2000
Čáslav ..... d.	0549	0649	0749	0849	1049	1249	1449	1649	1749	1849	2049
Kutná Hora ..... d.	0600	0700	0800	0900	1100	1300	1500	1700	1800	1900	2100
Kolín ..... ▷ d.	0612	0712	0812	0912	1112	1312	1512	1712	1812	1912	2112
Praha hlavní ..... ▷ a.	0651	0751	0851	0951	1151	1351	1551	1751	1851	1951	2151

E – ① **v** from Brno, Ⓐ from Žďár nad Sázavou, ⚒ **n** from Havlíčkův Brod.
G – Ⓑ **h** to Havlíčkův Brod, ⑤ **z** to Brno.
h – Not Dec. 25, Apr. 14, 16, 30, May 7, July 5, Nov. 17.

n – ①–⑥ (not Dec. 24, 26, Apr. 15, 17, May 1, 8, July 6, Nov. 18).
v – Also Apr. 18, May 2, 9, July 7, Sept. 29; not Apr. 17, May 1, 8.
z – Also Apr. 13, July 4, Sept. 27, Nov. 16; not Apr. 14, Nov. 17.
▷ – See also Tables **1150** / **60**.

ADDITIONAL JOURNEYS:
0502Ⓐ, 0602, 0802 Havlíčkův Brod - Brno.
1720Ⓐ Brno - Havlíčkův Brod.
2204 Praha - Čáslav (to Havlíčkův Brod night of ⑤⑥).

1152 HAVLÍČKŮV BROD - JIHLAVA

2nd class

27 km																	
		Ⓐ		R§				Ⓐ		Ⓐ		Ⓐ		P	Ⓐz		
Havlíčkův Brod ... d.	0448	0603	0647	0701	0805	1005	1205	1313	1405	1513	1605	1712	1805	1902	2005	2105	2208
Jihlava ..... a.	0516	0632	0717	0723	0833	1033	1234	1343	1435	1542	1635	1742	1834	1923	2033	2134	2237

		P		Ⓐ				Ⓐ		Ⓐ		Ⓐ		Ⓐz		S§	
Jihlava ..... d.	0519	0537	0605	0655	0727	0922	1122	1237	1322	1436	1521	1614	1721	1813	1924	2034	2135
Havlíčkův Brod ... a.	0548	0558	0643	0735	0751	0950	1150	1305	1351	1504	1550	1642	1750	1841	1952	2056	2204

P – To / from Praha. For days of running see Table **1151**.
R – ①⑥ (also Apr. 14, 18, May 2, 9, July 5, Sept. 28, Nov. 17; not Dec. 26 - 31, Apr. 15, 17, May 1, 8, July 8, Sept. 30, Nov. 18
S – ⑤⑦ (also Apr. 13, 17, May 1, 8, July 4 - 6, Sept. 27, Nov. 16; not Dec. 25, 30, Apr. 14, 16, 30, May 7, Sept. 29, Nov. 17).
z – Not Dec. 27 - 30. § – To / from Plzeň (Table **1135**).

BRNO - PŘEROV - OSTRAVA - BOHUMÍN 1155

km		EN 406	821	823	Ex 590	825	EC 104	827	829	EC 130	831	833	835	EC 102	837	839	841	843	Ex* 100	845	847	849	
		C	✕n	✕n		🍷	S	🍷	🍷	V	🍷	🍷	🍷	P	🍷	🍷	🍷	Ⓑh	M	🍷	⑦e	🍷	
0	**Brno** hlavní 1156 d.	...	0502	0602	...	0702	...	0902	1102	...	1202	1302	1402	...	1502	1602	1702	1802	...	1902	2002	2102	...
45	Vyškov na Moravě 1156 d.	...	0540	0640	...	0740	...	0940	1140	...	1240	1340	1440	...	1540	1640	1740	1840	...	1940	2040	2140	...
71	Kojetín d.	...	0606	0706	...	0806	...	1006	1206	...	1306	1406	1506	...	1606	1706	1806	1906	...	2006	2106	2206	...
	Wien Hbf **982** d.	2250	|	|	...	|	0810	|	|	...	|	|	|	1410	|	|	|	|	1810	|	|	|	...
	Břeclav **1159** d.	0013	|	|	0711	|	0911	|	|	1211	|	|	|	1511	|	|	|	|	1911	|	|	|	...
88	**Přerov** 1160 d.	0105	0623	0723	0809	0823	1009	1023	1223	1309	1323	1423	1523	1609	1623	1723	1823	1923	2009	2023	2123	2223	...
117	Hranice na Moravě 1160 d.	|	0641	0741	0826	0841	1026	1041	1241	1326	1341	1441	1541	1626	1641	1741	1841	1941	2026	2041	2141	2241	...
167	Ostrava Svinov 1160 a.	0145	0714	0814	0851	0914	1051	1114	1314	1351	1414	1514	1614	1651	1714	1814	1914	2014	2051	2114	2214	2314	...
172	**Ostrava** hlavní 1160 a.	0154	0722	0822	0859	0922	1059	1122	1322	1359	1422	1522	1622	1659	1722	1822	1922	2022	2059	2122	2222	2322	...
180	Bohumín 1160 a.	0203	0732	0832	0908	0932	1108	1132	1332	1408	1432	1532	1632	1708	1732	1832	1932	2032	2108	2132	2232	2332	...

	EN 407	848	846	844	Ex* 101	842	840		838	EC 103	836	834	EC 131	832	830	828	EC 105	826	824	Ex 591	822	820	
	C	✕n	✕n	🍷	M	🍷	🍷		🍷	P	🍷	🍷	V	🍷	🍷	🍷	S	Ⓑh	🍷		⑦e	🍷	
ohumín 1160 d.	0220	0429	0529	0629	0650	0729	0829	...	1029	1050	1229	1329	1350	1429	1529	1629	1650	1729	1829	1850	1929	2029	...
strava hlavní 1160 d.	0231	0439	0539	0639	0700	0739	0839	...	1039	1100	1239	1339	1400	1439	1539	1639	1700	1739	1839	1900	1939	2039	...
)strava Svinov 1160 d.	0240	0447	0547	0647	0708	0747	0847	...	1047	1108	1247	1347	1408	1447	1547	1647	1708	1747	1847	1908	1947	2047	...
ranice na Moravě 1160 d.	|	0519	0619	0719	0733	0819	0919	...	1119	1133	1319	1419	1433	1519	1619	1719	1733	1819	1919	1933	2019	2119	...
řerov 1160 d.	0322	0538	0638	0738	0751	0838	0937	...	1137	1151	1338	1438	1451	1538	1638	1738	1751	1838	1938	1951	2038	2138	...
Břeclav **1159** a.	0414	|	|	|	0850	|	|	...	|	1250	|	|	1550	|	|	|	1850	|	|	2050	|	|	...
Wien Hbf **982** a.	0655	|	|	|	0949	|	|	...	|	1349	|	|	...	|	|	|	1949	|	|	...	|	|	...
ojetín d.	...	0553	0653	0753	...	0853	0953	...	1153	...	1353	1453	...	1553	1653	1753	...	1853	1953	...	2053	2153	...
yškov na Moravě 1156 d.	...	0617	0717	0817	...	0917	1017	...	1217	...	1417	1517	...	1617	1717	1817	...	1917	2017	...	2117	2217	...
rno hlavní 1156 d.	...	0659	0757	0857	...	0957	1057	...	1257	...	1459	1559	...	1659	1759	1859	...	1957	2053	...	2156	2253	...

- – CHOPIN – 🛏 1, 2 cl., 🛌 2 cl., (2) Wien - Bohumín - Katowice - Warszawa and v.v.; 🛏 1, 2 cl. Wien - Bohumín (**403/2**) - Kraków and v.v. (also 🛌 2 cl. on dates in Table **99**); 🛏 1, 2 cl., 🛌 2 cl., (2) Budapest (**476/7**) - Bratislava - Břeclav (**406/7**) - Warszawa and v.v.; 🛏 1, 2 cl., 🛌 2 cl. Budapest (**476/7**) - Bratislava - Břeclav (**406/7**) - Bohumín (**403/2**) - Kraków and v.v.; 🛏 1, 2 cl. Wien - Bohumín (**445/4**) - Košice and v.v.
- – MORAVIA – (12) Wien - Břeclav - Bohumín and v.v. Conveys on dates in Table **95** 🛏 1, 2 cl. Wien - Bohumín (**405/4**) - Minsk - Moskva / St Peterburg and v.v.
- – POLONIA – (12) ✕ Wien - Břeclav - Ostrava - Katowice - Warszawa and v.v.
- – SOBIESKI – (12) ✕ Wien - Břeclav - Ostrava - Katowice - Warszawa - Gdansk - Gdynia and v.v.
- V – VARSOVIA – (12) ✕ Budapest - Bratislava - Břeclav - Ostrava - Katowice - Warszawa and v.v.
- e – Also Apr. 17, May 1, 8; not Dec. 25, Apr. 16, 30, May 7.
- h – Not Dec. 25, Apr. 14, 16, 30, May 7, July 5, Nov. 17.
- n – ①-⑥ (not Dec. 24, 26, Apr. 15, 17, May 1, 8, July 6, Nov. 18).
- * – Classified *D* in Austria.

BRNO - OLOMOUC - ŠUMPERK and JESENÍK 1156

km		901	903	905	907	909	909	911	913	915	917
		Ⓐb	Ⓒ			Ⓐ	Ⓒ				E
0	**Brno** hlavní ▷ d.	0523	0628	0718	0918	1118	1118	1318	1518	1718	1918
45	Vyškov na Moravě ▷ d.	0559	0703	0759	0959	1159	1159	1359	1559	1759	1959
61	Nezamyslice d.	0620	0720	0820	1020	1220	1220	1420	1620	1820	2020
80	Prostějov d.	0635	0735	0835	1035	1235	1235	1435	1635	1835	2035
100	**Olomouc** a.	0652	0752	0852	1052	1252	1252	1452	1652	1852	2052
100	**Olomouc** ▽ d.	0656	0754	0856	1056	1256	▬	1456	1656	1856	2056
146	Zábřeh na Moravě ▽ a.	0722	0822	0922	1122	1322	Ⓒ	1522	1722	1924	2124
146	Zábřeh na Moravě d.	0731	0834	0931	1131	1331	1331	1531	1731	1926	2126
159	**Šumperk** a.	0740r	0840r	0939r	1139r	1339r	|	1539r	1739r	1942	2141
171	Hanušovice a.	0759	0901	0959	1159	1359	1359	1559	1759	*2000*x	...
203	Lipová Lázně a.	0859	0959	1059	1259	1459	1459	1659	1859	*2052*x	...
207	**Jeseník** a.	0911	1007	1111	1311	1511	1511	1711	1911	*2102*x	...

	1638	914	912	910	908	1708	906	904	902	900
	Ⓐ	F			Ⓐ	Ⓒ				Ⓒ
Jeseník d.	...	...	0654	0854	1054	1054	1254	1454	1654	*1845*z
Lipová Lázně d.	...	...	0703	0903	1103	1103	1303	1503	1703	*1855*z
Hanušovice d.	...	...	0800	1000	1200	1200	1400	1600	1800	*1953*z
Šumperk d.	0449	0610	0808s	1008s	1208s	|	1408s	1608s	1808s	2013
Zábřeh na Moravě a.	0510	0630	0824	1024	1224	1224	1424	1624	1824	2031
Zábřeh na Moravě ▽ d.	0512	0632	0832	1032	1232	▬	1432	1632	1832	2032
Olomouc ▽ a.	0548	0701	0858	1058	1258	Ⓒ	1458	1658	1858	2058
Olomouc d.	0558	0706	0906	1106	1306	1306	1506	1706	1906	2106
Prostějov d.	0616	0723	0923	1123	1323	1323	1523	1723	1923	2123
Nezamyslice d.	0637	0739	0939	1139	1339	1339	1539	1739	1939	2139
Vyškov na Moravě ▷ d.	0700	0800	1000	1200	1400	1400	1600	1800	2000	2200
Brno hlavní ▷ a.	0745	0842	1042	1242	1443	1443	1643	1842	2038	2236

- – Daily Brno - Olomouc, Ⓑ **h** to Šumperk.
- – ①-⑥ **n** from Šumperk, daily Olomouc - Brno.
- – Runs daily Olomouc - Jeseník (no Šumperk portion on Ⓒ).
- – Not Dec. 25, Apr. 14, 16, 30, May 7, July 5, Nov. 17.
- n – Not Dec. 24, 26, Apr. 15, 17, May 1, 8, July 6, Nov. 18.
- r – Šumperk portion detatches at Zabreh (dep. xx25).
- s – Šumperk portion attaches at Zabreh (arr. xx21).
- x – Change at Bludov (a. 1935 / d. 1939).
- z – Change at Bludov (a. 2016 / d. 2021).
- ▷ – See also Table **1155**.
- ▽ – See also Table **1160**.

Different train numbers apply between Zabreh and Jeseník.

2nd class BRNO - UHERSKÉ HRADIŠTĚ - LUHAČOVICE / TRENČIANSKA TEPLÁ 1157

km										
0	**Brno** hlavní d.	0735	0928	1128	1328	1528	1730	1928	2128	2225
67	Kyjov d.	0837	1032	1232	1432	1632	1832	2032	2232	2340
90	Veselí nad Moravou d.	0907	1102	1302	1502	1702	1902	2102	2258	...
108	Uherské Hradiště ▷ a.	0925	1120	1320	1520	1720	*1925*r	*2127*r	...	...
113	**Staré Město u Uh. H** ▷ a.	0933z	*1128*	*1328*	*1528*	*1728*	*1939*r	*2133*r	...	...

Staré Město u Uh. H ▷ d.	...	...	*0832*	*1032*	1233	*1432*	*1632*	1835	2030	...
Uherské Hradiště ▷ d.	...	0635	0840	1040	1240	1440	1640	1842	2037	...
Veselí nad Moravou d.	0601	0701	0901	1101	1301	1501	1701	1901	2054	2101
Kyjov d.	0628	0728	0928	1128	1328	1528	1728	1928	...	2128
Brno hlavní a.	0733	0834	1033	1233	1433	1633	1833	2033	...	2233

km				G♣			Y♣			
	Praha hlavní **1160** d.	...	...	0819	...	...	1419	...	...	...
	Brno hl. (above) ▷ d.	...	...	|	...	...	|	...	1730	1928
0	**Staré Město u Uh. H** ▷ d.	*0935*	1135	1150	1335	1535	1750	1805	*1905*r	|
5	Uherské Hradiště ▷ a.	*0941*	1141	1156	1341	1541	1756	1811	*1911*r	|
5	Uherské Hradiště ▷ d.	0943	1144	1205	1344	1544	1757	1830	*1914*r	*2114*r
7	Kunovice d.	0947	1147	|	1347	1550	|	1835	1920	2123
22	Uherský Brod ▷ d.	1009	1209	1225	1416	1616	1815	1902	1942	2142
26	Újezdec u Luhačovic a.	1013	1213	|	1420	1620	|	1906	1946	2146
36	**Luhačovice** ▷ a.	*1031*	*1231*	|	*1436*	*1636*	|	*1924*s	*2016*x	*2202*
35	Bojkovice město d.	1030	1230	1243	1446	1646	1843	1925	2004	2204
63	Bylnice d.	...	...	1313	1519a	1650a	1913	...	2037	2237
68	Vlárský průsmyk 🏛 a.	...	...	|	1527a	...	|	...	...	...
90	Trenčianska Teplá **1180** a.	...	...	1332	...	...	1932	...	...	...
98	**Trenčín** **1180** a.	...	...	1340	...	...	1940	...	...	...
	Nitra **1177** a.	...	...	1514v	...	...	2115	...	...	...

	Ⓒ		Z♣				G♣			Ⓒ
Nitra **1177** d.	...	...	0646	...	...	...	1254n	...	...	...
Trenčín **1180** d.	...	...	0810	...	...	...	1418	...	...	...
Trenčianska Teplá **1180** d.	...	...	0817	...	...	...	1425	...	...	*1737*t
Vlárský průsmyk 🏛 d.	...	*0743*	|	...	...	...	|	...	...	1756t
Bylnice d.	...	0754	0838	...	...	...	1447	...	...	1804
Bojkovice město d.	0702	0828	0906	0920	1120	1320	1520	1532	1738	1838
Luhačovice ▷ d.	*0703*	|	|	*0924*	*1124*	*1318*	|	*1534*	*1738*	*1838*s
Újezdec u Luhačovic d.	0720	0856	|	0940	1140	1340	|	1550	1755	1855
Uherský Brod ▷ d.	0725	0901	0934	0951	1151	1351	1537	1555	1800	1900
Kunovice a.	0742	0918	|	1010	1210	1410	|	1614	1817	1917
Uherské Hradiště ▷ a.	0745	0922	0949	1013	1213	1413	1551	1617	1820	*1925*r
Uherské Hradiště ▷ d.	0746	0927u	0950	1020	1217	1420	1552	1620	1821	*1933*r
Staré Město u Uh. H ▷ a.	0751	0933u	0956	1026	1223	1426	1558	1626	1827	*1939*r
Brno hl. (above) ▷ a.	...	...	|	...	...	...	|	...	...	...
Praha hlavní **1160** a.	...	...	1329	...	...	...	1932	...	...	...

- – ⑦ Dec. 18 - Apr. 2; ⑤⑥⑦ from Apr. 7 (daily June 12 - Oct. 1), also Dec. 26, Apr. 13, 17, May 1, 8, Nov. 16; not Dec. 25, Apr. 15, 16, 30, May 7, Nov. 18.
- – ⑤ to Mar. 31; daily from Apr. 1.
- – ⑥ to Apr. 1; daily from Apr. 2.
- – Ⓐ only.
- n – ⑥⑦ from Apr. 8 (also Apr. 14, 17, May 1, 8, July 5, 6, Sept. 28, Nov. 17; not Apr. 15, 16, 30, May 7, Sept. 30, Nov. 18).
- r – Change at Kunovice.
- s – Ⓑ (not Dec. 25, Apr. 14, 16, 30, May 7, July 5, Nov. 17).
- t – ⑦ (also Apr. 17, May 1, 8; not Dec. 25, Apr. 16, 30, May 7, July 2 - Aug. 27).
- u – Change at Uherské Hradiště on Ⓐ.
- v – ⑥ from Apr. 8 (also Apr. 14, July 5, 6; not Apr. 15).
- x – ⑥ (also Apr. 14 - 16, 30, May 7, July 5, Nov. 17).
- z – Change at Uherské Hradiště on Ⓒ.
- ♣ – Operated by ARRIVA. 2nd class, 🍷. Separate fares.
- ▷ – See also Table **1159**.

(PRAHA) - OLOMOUC - VSETÍN - HORNÍ LIDEČ - ŽILINA 1158

For faster trains Praha - Olomouc - Žilina via Ostrava (including through trains Praha - Žilina - Košice) see Table **1160**

km			121*	123*	125*	127*	221*	129*	521*	523*
		2	✕	✕	✕	✕	✕	✕	✕	✕
	Praha hlavní **1160** d.	...	0522	0722	0922	1122	1322	1522	1722	1922
0	**Olomouc** d.	...	0751	0951	1151	1351	1551	1751	1951	2151
51	Hranice na Moravě d.	0635	0823	1023	1223	1423	1623	1823	2029	2223
77	Valašské Meziříčí d.	0707	0849	1049	1249	1449	1649	1849	2054	2249
96	**Vsetín** d.	0726	0907	1107	1307	1507	1707	1907	2110	2305
114	Horní Lideč 🏛 d.	...	0925	1125	1325	1525	1725	1925	...	...
142	**Púchov** a.	...	0948	1148	1348	1548	1748	1948	...	...
	Poprad Tatry **1180** a.	...	*1235*r	*1435*r	*1635*r	*1835*r	*2035*r	*2231*s	...	...
	Košice **1180** a.	...	*1352*r	*1552*r	*1752*r	*1952*r	*2152*r	*2349*s	...	...
142	**Púchov** d.	...	1001	1201	1401	1601	1801	2001	...	...
153	Považská Bystrica d.	...	1016	1216	1416	1616	1816	2016	...	...
187	**Žilina** a.	...	1048	1248	1448	1648	1848	2048	...	...

	522*	520*	220*	128*	126*	124*	122*	120*	
	✕	✕	✕	✕	✕	✕	✕	✕	2
Žilina d.	...	...	0712	0912	1112	1312	1512	1712	...
Považská Bystrica d.	...	...	0745	0945	1145	1345	1545	1745	...
Púchov a.	...	...	0759	0959	1159	1359	1559	1759	...
Košice **1180** d.	...	...	*0408*s	*0608*r	*0808*r	*1008*r	*1208*r	*1408*r	...
Poprad Tatry **1180** d.	...	...	*0525*s	*0725*r	*0925*r	*1125*r	*1325*r	*1525*r	...
Púchov d.	...	...	0812	1012	1212	1412	1612	1812	...
Horní Lideč 🏛 d.	...	...	0837	1037	1237	1437	1637	1837	...
Vsetín d.	0455	0652	0855	1055	1255	1455	1655	1855	1952
Valašské Meziříčí d.	0512	0709	0912	1112	1312	1512	1712	1912	2012
Hranice na Moravě d.	0535	0735	0935	1135	1335	1535	1735	1935	2044
Olomouc 1160 a.	0607	0807	1007	1207	1407	1607	1807	2007	...
Praha hlavní **1160** a.	0839	1039	1239	1439	1639	1839	2039	2248	...

- – Change at Púchov.
- s – For days of running see Table **1180**. Change at Púchov.
- * – Classified *Ex*.

1159 OLOMOUC - UHERSKÉ HRADIŠTĚ - BŘECLAV - BRNO

For direct services Olomouc - Brno see Table **1156**. For night train **406/7** Warszawa - Wien see Tables **99** and **1155** (also calls at Otrokovice: **406** at 0048, **407** at 0338)

km					*Ex*				*LE*♠	*EC*				*EC*					*EC*	*RJ*♥		*LE*♠		*Ex*		
		881	**814**	**883**	**101**	**812**	**885**	**810**	**1355**	**103**	**887**	**808**	**889**	**131**	**806**	**891**	**804**	**893**	**105**	**1015**	**802**	**1365**	**895**	**591**	**800**	**897**
		Ⓐ		⊡	**M**				🅁 🍷	**P**§				**V**§					**S**§	🍷		🅁 🍷		**b**	Ⓑ**h**	
	Praha hl. **1150/60** .. d.	...	...	...	...	...	0653	...	0913	...	...	...	1055	...	...	1255	...	1455	...	1644	...	1713	1655	...	...	1855
0	**Olomouc** ▽ d.	0559	0710	0731	...	0910	0931	1110	1126	...	1159	1310	1331	...	1510	1531	1710	1731	...	1902	1910	1926	1931	...	2110	2131
	Ostrava hl. **1155** .... d.	|	|	|	0700	|	|	|	|	1100	|	|	|	1400	|	|	|	|	1700	|	|	|	|	1900	|	|
22	Přerov ▽ d.	0614	0724	0746	0751	0924	0948	1124	1140	1151	1215	1324	1348	1451	1524	1548	1724	1746	1751	1917	1924	1940	1945	1951	2124	2147
37	Hulín d.	0625	0735	0756	|	0935	0958	1135	1150	|	1225	1335	1358	|	1535	1558	1735	1756	|	1929	1935	1950	1956	|	2135	2157
50	Otrokovice d.	0635	0744	0805	0808	0944	1008	1144	1158	1208	1235	1344	1408	1508	1544	1608	1744	1805	1808	1939	1944	1958	2005	2008	2144	2215
61	**Zlín** střed ▷ a.	|	|	|	|	|	|	|	|	|	|	|	|	|	|	|	|	|	|	|	|	|	|	|	|	2228
68	Staré Město U.H. ⊖ .. a.	0646	0753	0815	0818	0953	1018	1153	1208	1218	1246	1353	1418	1518	1553	1618	1753	1815	1818	1950	1953	2008	2015	2018	2153	▬
68	Staré Město U.H. ⊖ .. d.	0656	0754	0832	0819	0954	1032	1154	...	1219	1300	1354	1432	1519	1554	1632	1754	*1835*	1819	...	1954	...	2030	2019	2154	...
73	Uherské Hradiště ... a.	0702	|	0838	|	|	1038	|	...	|	1306	|	1438	|	|	1638	|	*1841*	|	...	|	...	2036	|	|	...
90	Uherský Brod a.	0722	|	0900	|	|	1059	|	...	|	1330	|	1459	|	|	1659	|	...	|	...	|	...	v	|	|	**816**
104	**Luhačovice** a.	0744	|	0923	|	|	1123	|	...	|	1354	|	1523	|	|	1723	|	...	|	...	|	...	...	|	|	⚒**n**
102	Hodonin d.	▬	0818	...	0837	1018	...	1218	...	1237	...	1418	...	1537	1618	...	1818	...	1837	...	2018	...	...	2037	2213	0618
122	**Břeclav** a.	⚒**n**	0830	...	0850	1030	...	1230	...	1250	...	1430	...	1550	1630	...	1830	...	1850	...	2030	...	...	2050	2225	0632
122	**Břeclav** **1150** d.	0740	0840	...	*0907*	1040	...	1240	...	*1307*	...	1440	...	*1607*	1640	...	1840	...	*1907*	...	2040	...	...	*2107*	...	0640
181	**Brno** hlavní **1150** a.	0824	0924	...	*0936*	1124	...	1324	...	*1336*	...	1524	...	*1636*	1724	...	1924	...	*1936*	...	2124	...	...	*2136*	...	0724

				RJ♥	*LE*♠	*Ex*				*EC*				*EC*	*LE*♠			*EC*						*Ex*		
	896	**894**	**801**	**1002**	**1354**	**590**	**892**	**803**	**890**	**104**	**805**	**888**	**807**	**130**	**1362**	**886**	**809**	**102**	**884**	**811**	**882**	**813**	**880**	**100**	**815**	**817**
			⚒**n**	🍷	🅁 🍷	**b**			Ⓐ	**S**§				**V**§	🅁 🍷			**P**§						**M**		Ⓑ**h**
Brno hlavní **1150** d.	...	...	...	...	...	*0622*	...	0636	...	*0823*	0836	...	1036	*1123*	...	...	1236	*1423*	...	1436	...	1636	...	*1823*	1836	2036
Břeclav **1150** a.	...	...	...	...	...	*0652*	...	0719	...	*0852*	0919	...	1119	*1152*	...	...	1319	*1452*	...	1519	...	1719	...	*1852*	1919	2119
Břeclav d.	...	...	0531	...	...	0711	...	0728	...	0911	0928	...	1128	1211	...	...	1328	1511	...	1528	...	1728	...	1911	1928	2128
Hodonin d.	...	...	0543	...	...	0724	...	0743	...	0924	0943	...	1143	1224	...	...	1343	1524	...	1543	...	1743	...	1924	1943	2141
Luhačovice d.	...	...	|	...	...	|	...	|	0813	|	|	1038	|	|	...	1238	|	|	1438	|	1638	|	1820	|	|	...
Uherský Brod d.	...	...	|	...	...	|	v	|	0832	|	|	1101	|	|	...	1301	|	|	1501	|	1701	|	1839	|	|	...
Uherské Hradiště d.	...	...	|	...	...	|	0722	|	0852	|	|	1122	|	|	...	1322	|	|	1522	|	1722	|	1856	|	|	...
Staré Město U.H. ⊖ .. a.	...	...	0601	...	...	0741	0728	0801	0858	0941	1001	1128	1201	1241	...	1328	1401	1541	1528	1601	1728	1801	1902	1941	2001	...
Staré Město U.H. ⊖ .. d.	0423	...	0604	0608	0627	0742	0745	0804	0911	0942	1004	1141	1204	1242	1327	1341	1404	1542	1545	1604	1741	1804	1915	1942	2004	...
Zlín střed ▷ d.	|	0528	|	|	|	|	|	|	|	|	|	|	|	|	|	|	|	|	|	|	|	|	|	|	|	...
Otrokovice d.	0434	0552	0615	0619	0637	0753	0756	0815	0923	0953	1015	1153	1215	1253	1337	1353	1415	1553	1556	1615	1753	1815	1927	1953	2015	...
Hulín d.	0442	0602	0624	0628	0645	|	0805	0824	0933	|	1024	1202	1224	|	1345	1402	1424	|	1605	1624	1802	1824	1937	|	2024	...
Přerov ▽ a.	0452	0612	0633	0639	0659	0808	0815	0833	0943	1008	1033	1211	1233	1308	1359	1411	1433	1608	1614	1633	1811	1833	1947	2008	2033	...
Ostrava hl. **1155** ..... a.	|	|	|	|	|	0859	|	|	|	1059	|	|	|	1359	|	|	|	1659	|	|	|	|	|	2059	|	...
Olomouc ▽ a.	0507	0629	0647	0652	0711	...	0829	0847	0958	...	1047	1229	1247	...	1411	1429	1447	...	1629	1647	1829	1847	2002	...	2047	...
Praha hl. **1150/60** ... a.	0739	0903	...	0912	0919	...	1103	...	...	...	...	1503	...	...	1619	1703	...	...	1903	...	2103	...	...	...	...	...

M – MORAVIA – 🚃12 Bohumín - Ostrava - Břeclav - Wien and v.v. Conveys on dates in Table **95** 🛏 1, 2 cl. Moskva / St Peterburg - Bohumín - Břeclav - Wien and v.v.
P – POLONIA – 🚃12 🍴 Warszawa - Katowice - Ostrava - Břeclav - Wien and v.v. (Table **99**).
S – SOBIESKI – 🚃12 🍴 Gdynia - Gdansk - Warszawa - Katowice - Ostrava - Břeclav - Wien and v.v. (Table **99**).
V – VARSOVIA – 🚃12 Warszawa - Katowice - Ostrava - Břeclav - Bratislava - Budapest and v.v. (Table **99**).
b – From / to Bohumín (Table **1155**).
h – Not Dec. 25, Apr. 14, 16, 30, May 7, July 5, Nov. 17.
n – ①-⑥ (not Dec. 24, 26, Apr. 15, 17, May 1, 8, July 6, Nov. 18).
v – To / from Veseli nad Moravou (a. 2054 / d. 0708).

♥ – Operated by REGIOJET. Separate fare tariff applies.
♠ – Operated by LEO Express. Separate fare tariff applies.
⊖ – Full name: Staré Město u Uherské Hradiště.
⊡ – From Hradec Králové via Pardubice (Table **1160**).
▽ – See also Table **1160**.
▷ – Local trains Otrokovice - Zlín: 1-2 per hour (or trolleybus every 10 minutes).
§ – 🅁 for international journeys to / from Poland.

ADDITIONAL TRAINS Přerov - Otrokovice - Staré Mesto u U.H. ♠ 🅁 🍷 journey 27 mins From Přerov 0459, 0559, 2059. From Staré Mesto u U.H. 0428, 0527, 2027.

For ARRIVA Praha - Přerov - Staré Mesto u U.H. - Trenčin trains see Table **1157**.

1160 PRAHA - OLOMOUC - OSTRAVA - ŽILINA - (KOŠICE)

FAST TRAINS. For semi-fast trains Praha - Česká Třebová - Olomouc see Table **1150**. For additional trains Přerov - Ostrava - Bohumín see Table **1155**.

km			*Ex*		*Ex*		*RJ*♥	*EC*	*SC*●	*LE*♠	*Ex*	*RJ*♥	*LE*♠	*Ex*	*AEx*	*LE*♠	*Ex*	*SC*●	*RJ*♥	*Ex*	*LE*♠	*Ex*	*SC*●	
		341	**541**	**641**	**121**	**343**	**1001**	**113**	**241**	**1351**	**123**	**1003**	**1353**	**141**	**1041**	**1355**	**125**	**505**	**1005**	**115**	**1357**	**127**	**507**	**345**
				2	🍷		🍷	🍴	🅁 🍷	🅁 🍷	🍷	🍷	🅁 🍷	🍷	♣	🅁 🍷	🍷	🅁 🍷	🍷	🍷	🅁 🍷	🍴	🅁 🍷	
			①**g**	**J**			⚒	♦	♦	**U**					**G**			⊕		♦				
0	**Praha** hlavní **1150** d.	...	0422	...	0522	...	0544	0622	0707	0713	0722	0744	0813	0822	0819	0913	0922	0937	0944	1022	1113	1122	1137	...
62	Kolín **1150** d.	...	0459	...	0559	...	|	0659	0741	0750	0759	|	0850	0859	0903	0950	0959	|	|	1059	1150	1159	|	...
104	**Pardubice** **1150** d.	...	0521	...	0621	...	0639	0721	0802	0809	0821	0839	0909	0921	0928	1009	1021	1030	1039	1121	1209	1221	1230	...
164	Česká Třebová **1150** d.	...	0556	...	0656	...	0714	0756	0835	|	0856	|	|	0956	|	|	1056	|	1114	1156	|	1256	|	...
206	Zábřeh na Moravé d.	...	0618	...	0718	...	0736	0818	|	0901	0918	0936	1001	1018	|	1101	1120	|	1136	1218	1301	1320	|	...
252	**Olomouc** d.	...	0641	0641	0751	...	0801	0841	0916	0926	0951	1001	1026	1041	1058	1126	1151	1142	1201	1241	1326	1351	1342	...
	Přerov **1159** **1155** d.	...	|	|	|	...	|	|	|	0942	|	|	1042	|	1114	1138	|	|	|	|	1342	|	|	...
303	Hranice na Moravě **1155** d.	...	0712	0712	0823	...	0830	0909	|	0959	1023	1030	1059	1109	♡	⊡	1223	|	1230	1309	1359	1423	|	...
353	Ostrava Svinov **1155** d.	0643	0746	0746	|	0843	0857	0936	1004	1028	|	1057	1128	1136	...	...	|	1230	1257	1336	1428	|	1430	1443
381	Opava východ a.	|	|	|	|	|	|	|	|	|	|	|	|	|	...	...	|	|	|	|	|	|	|	|
358	**Ostrava** hlavní **1155** d.	0650	0754	0754	|	0850	0905	0944	1013	1034	|	1105	1134	1144	...	...	|	1238	1305	1344	1436	|	1438	1450
366	Bohumín **1155** d.	0658	0802	0802	|	0859	|	0952	|	1043	|	|	1143	1157	...	...	|	...	|	1352	1445	|	...	1458
381	Karviná hlavní d.	0714	...	...	⇊	0914	|	...	|	...	⇊	|	...	1213	...	...	⇊	...	|	...	1502	⇊	...	1514
376	Havířov d.	|	...	...	|	|	0924	...	|	...	|	1125	...	|	...	...	|	...	1324	...	...	|	...	|
397	**Český Těšín** d.	0734	...	...	|	0934	...	...	1048	...	|	1145	...	1234	...	...	|	...	...	...	...	|	...	1534
405	Trinec centrum d.	0742	...	...	|	0942	...	...	|	...	|	1152	...	1242	...	...	|	...	...	...	...	|	...	1542
417	Návsi d.	0750	...	...	|	0950	...	...	|	...	|	|	...	1250	...	...	|	...	...	...	...	|	...	1550
435	Čadca 🏛 d.	0808	...	...	|	1008	...	...	1112	...	|	1215	...	1308	...	...	|	...	...	...	...	|	...	1608
∆ *466*	**Žilina** a.	0833	...	...	1048	1033	...	...	1134	...	1248	1237	...	1335	...	...	1448	...	...	...	...	1648	...	1633
	Poprad Tatry **1180** a.	△	...	...	*1235*r	...	...	...	1315	...	*1435*r	1422	...	...	...	...	*1635*r	...	...	...	...	*1835*r	...	△
	Košice **1180** a.	...	...	...	*1352*r	...	...	...	1423	...	*1552*r	1544	...	...	...	...	*1752*r	...	...	...	...	*1952*r	...	...

	RJ♥	*Ex*	*IC*	*EC*	*Ex*	*SC*●		*RJ*♥	*LE*♠	*EC*	*AEx*	*RJ*♥	*LE*♠	*Ex*	*SC*●	*RJ*♥	*LE*♠	*Ex*	*IC*	*RJ*♥	*LE*♠	*Ex*	*SC*●	
	1007	**143**	**543**	**243**	**221**	**509**	**347**	**1009**	**1359**	**117**	**1043**	**1011**	**1361**	**129**	**511**	**1013**	**1363**	**145**	**513**	**1015**	**1365**	**521**	**515**	
	🍷	🍷	🅁 🍷	🅁 🍷	🍴	🅁 🍷		🍷	🅁 🍷	🍴	♣	🍷	🅁 🍷	🍴	🅁 🍷	🍷	🅁 🍷	🍴	🅁 🍷	🍷	🅁 🍷	🍴	🅁 🍷	
			⑤**f**	⑤**f**					**P**	♦	**G**					**m**		**R**	Ⓑ**h**			**V**	⊗	
Praha hlavní **1150** d.	1144	1222	1319	1319	1322	1337	...	1344	1413	1422	1419	1444	1513	1522	1537	1544	1613	1622	1637	1644	1713	1722	1737	...
Kolín **1150** d.	|	1259	|	|	1359	|	...	|	1450	1459	1503	|	1550	1559	|	|	1650	1659	|	|	1750	1759	|	...
Pardubice **1150** d.	1239	1321	1416u	1416u	1421	1430	...	1439	1509	1521	1530	1539	1609	1621	1630	1639	1709	1721	1730	1739	1809	1821	1830	...
Česká Třebová **1150** d.	1314	1356	|	|	1456	|	...	1514	|	1556	|	1614	|	1656	|	1714	|	1756	|	1814	|	1856	|	...
Zábřeh na Moravé d.	1336	1418	|	|	1520	|	...	1536	1601	1618	|	1636	1701	1720	|	1736	1801	1818	|	1836	1901	1920	|	...
Olomouc d.	1401	1441	1534	1534	1551	1542	...	1601	1626	1641	1658	1702	1726	1751	1742	1801	1826	1841	1844	1902	1926	1951	1942	...
Přerov **1159** **1155** d.	|	|	|	|	|	|	...	|	1642	|	1713	|	1742	|	|	|	1842	|	|	1915	1938	|	|	...
Hranice na Moravě **1155** d.	1430	1509	|	|	1623	|	...	1630	1659	1709	♡	1730	1759	1823	|	1830	1859	1909	|	⊡	⊡	2022	|	...
Ostrava Svinov **1155** d.	1457	1536	1630	1637	|	1630	1643	1657	1728	1736	...	1757	1828	|	1830	1857	1928	1936	1940	...	...	...	2030	...
Opava východ a.	|	|	1650	|	|	|	|	|	|	|	...	|	|	|	|	|	|	|	1959	...	...	...	|	...
Ostrava hlavní **1155** d.	1505	1544	...	1644	|	1638	1650	1705	1736	1744	...	1805	1834	|	1838	1905	1934	1944	...	...	...	...	2038	...
Bohumín **1155** d.	|	1557	...	|	|	...	1658	|	1745	1752	...	|	1843	|	1848	|	1943	1957	...	...	...	...	2048	...
Karviná hlavní d.	|	1613	...	|	⇊	...	1714	|	1803	...	...	|	...	⇊	...	|	...	2013	...	...	...	...	...	...
Havířov d.	1524	|	...	|	|	...	|	1724	|	...	...	1825	...	|	...	1925	...	|	...	...	...	...	...	...
Český Těšín d.	...	1634	...	1718	|	...	1734	...	1823	...	...	1845	...	|	...	1945	...	2034	...	...	...	...	...	...
Trinec centrum d.	...	1642	...	|	|	...	1742	...	1830	...	...	1852	...	|	...	1952	...	2042	...	...	...	...	...	...
Návsi d.	...	1650	...	1730	|	...	1750	...	|	...	...	|	...	|	...	2004	...	2050	...	...	...	...	...	...
Čadca 🏛 d.	...	1708	...	1748	|	...	1808	...	1855	...	...	1915	...	|	...	...	...	2108	...	...	...	...	...	...
Žilina a.	...	1735	...	1810	1848	...	1833	...	1917	...	...	1937	...	2048	...	...	...	2135	...	...	...	...	...	...
Poprad Tatry **1180** a.	...	...	...	1958	*2035*r	...	▽	...	2057	...	...	▽	...	...	...	...	...	...	...	...	...	...	...	...
Košice **1180** a.	...	...	...	2110	*2152*r	...	...	...	2238	...	...	...	...	...	...	...	...	...	...	...	...	...	...	...

PRAHA - OLOMOUC - OSTRAVA - ŽILINA - (KOŠICE) 1160

	RJ♥ 1017	Ex 545	Ex 523	SC• 517	RJ♥ 1019	LE♠ 1367	Ex 547	RJ♥ 1021	EN 445	EN 443
	🍷	🍷	✕	[R] 🍷	🍷	[R] 🍷	🍷	🍷	⊖	⊖
		S♦	V			D P	N	♦	♦	♦K
Praha hlavní .... 1150 d.	1744	1822	1922	1937	1944	2013	2122	2144	2200	2309
Kolín .... 1150 d.	|	1859	1959	|	|	2050	2200	|	2251	2359
Pardubice .... 1150 d.	1839	1921	2021	2030	2039	2109	2221	2239	2316	0023
Česká Třebová .... 1150 d.	1914	1956	2056	|	2114	|	2258	|	|	0102
Zábřeh na Moravé .... d.	1936	2018	2120	|	2136	2201	2320	2337	|	0127
Olomouc .... d.	2001	2041	2151	2142	2201	2226	2343	0001	0041	0155
Přerov **1159** .... 1155 d.	|	|	|	|	|	2242	|	|	0126z	|
Hranice na Moravě .... 1155 d.	2030	2109	2222	|	2230	2259	0012	0031	|	|
Ostrava Svinov .... 1155 d.	2057	2142	...	2230	2257	2328	0038	0100	|	0252
Opava východ .... a.	|	|	...	|	|	|	|	|	|	|
Ostrava hlavní .... 1155 d.	2105	2151	...	2238	2305	2336	0046	0108	0216	0302
Bohumín .... 1155 d.	|	2202	...	2248	|	2344	0054	|	0245	0336
Karviná hlavní .... d.	|	2216	...	...	|	2358	...	|	|	0352
Havířov .... d.	2125	|	...	...	2325	|	...	0129	|	|
Český Těšín .... d.	2145	2236	...	...	2345	0018	...	0150	|	0413
Třinec centrum .... d.	2152	2243	...	...	2352	0026	...	0158	|	0420t
Návsi .... d.	2204	2255	...	...	0004	|	...	|	|	|
Čadca 🏛 .... d.	...	...	...	...	...	0049	...	0225	|	0446
Žilina .... a.	...	...	...	...	...	0110	...	0250	0414	0514
Poprad Tatry **1180** .... a.	...	...	...	...	...	0251	...	0451	0622	0703
Košice **1180** .... a.	...	...	...	...	...	0432	...	0614	0741	0839

	EN 444	RJ♥ 1020	EN 442	Ex 546	LE♠ 1350	RJ♥ 1000	LE♠ 1352	SC• 516	
	⊖	🍷	⊖	[R] 🍷	[R] 🍷	🍷	[R] 🍷	[R] 🍷	
	♦	♦	♦L	Ⓐ	P	⚒			
Košice **1180** .... d.	2024	2122	2208	...	2306	...	...	...	...
Poprad Tatry **1180** .... d.	2159	2241	2325	...	0048	...	...	...	...
Žilina .... d.	0012	0042	0134	...	0230	...	...	...	...
Čadca 🏛 .... d.	|	0110	0201	...	0252	...	...	...	...
Návsi .... d.	|	|	|	...	|	0347	...	...	...
Třinec centrum .... d.	|	0133	0223t	...	0313	0358	...	...	...
Český Těšín .... d.	|	0142	0231	...	0321	0406	...	...	...
Havířov .... d.	|	0207	|	...	|	0430	...	...	...
Karviná hlavní .... d.	|	|	0251	...	0340	|	...	...	...
Bohumín .... 1155 d.	0212z	|	0329	0343	0355	|	0455	0512	...
Ostrava hlavní .... 1155 d.	0223	0227	0338	0353	0403	0449	0503	0521	...
Opava východ .... d.	|	|	|	|	|	|	|	|	...
Ostrava Svinov .... 1155 d.	|	0236	0347	0401	0411	0501	0511	0529	...
Hranice na Moravě .... 1155 d.	|	|	|	0432	0439	0527	0539	|	...
Přerov **1159** .... 1155 d.	0341z	|	|	|	0459	|	0559	|	...
Olomouc .... d.	0358	0330	0443	0505	0513	0556	0613	0618	...
Zábřeh na Moravé .... d.	|	0354	0508	|	0535	0619	0635	|	...
Česká Třebová .... 1150 d.	0447	|	0534	|	|	0642	|	|	...
Pardubice .... 1150 d.	0525	0455	0615	0621	0626	0717	0726	0729	...
Kolín .... 1150 d.	0550	|	|	|	0645	|	0745	|	...
Praha hlavní .... 1150 a.	0633	0558	0722	0712	0719	0812	0819	0822	...

	Ex 522	RJ♥ 1002	IC 514	LE♠ 1354	Ex 544	RJ♥ 1004	SC• 512	Ex 520	RJ♥ 1006	EC* 144	RJ♥ 1008	346	SC• 510	Ex 220	AEx 1040	LE♠ 1356	EC 116	RJ♥ 1010	LE♠ 1358	Ex 128	LE♠ 1360	Ex 142	RJ♥ 1012	LE♠ 1362
	✕	🍷	[R] 🍷	[R] 🍷	🍷	🍷	[R] 🍷	✕	🍷	✕	🍷		[R] 🍷	✕	♣	[R] 🍷	✕	🍷	[R] 🍷	✕	[R] 🍷	🍷	🍷	[R] 🍷
	V		⚒n		T♦		⊗	V	k						G	E P	♦		U					
Košice **1180** .... d.	...	...	...	...	...	...	...	...	...	...	...	...	...	...	...	0501	...	...	...	*0608*r	...	...	0800	...
Poprad Tatry **1180** .... d.	...	...	...	...	...	...	...	...	...	...	▽	▽	...	...	...	0648	...	...	...	*0725*r	...	...	0915	...
Žilina .... d.	...	...	...	...	...	...	...	...	...	0625n	0708	0727	...	0712	...	0830	...	...	...	0912	...	1025	1108	...
Čadca 🏛 .... d.	...	...	...	...	...	...	...	...	...	0654n	0735	0754	...	|	...	0852	...	...	...	|	...	1054	1135	...
Návsi .... d.	...	...	...	...	0458	0547	...	...	0647	0709	0750	0809	...	|	...	|	...	0947x	...	|	...	1109	1150	...
Třinec centrum .... d.	...	...	...	...	0505	0558	...	...	0658	0717	0758	0817	...	|	...	0913	...	0958x	...	|	...	1117	1158	...
Český Těšín .... d.	...	...	...	...	0515	0606	...	...	0706	0726	0806	0826	...	|	...	0921	...	1006x	...	|	...	1126	1206	...
Havířov .... d.	...	...	...	...	|	0630	...	...	0730	|	0830	|	...	|	...	|	...	1030	...	|	...	|	1230	...
Karviná hlavní .... d.	...	...	...	...	0535	|	...	...	|	0746	|	0846	...	≋	...	0940	...	|	...	≋	...	1146	|	...
Bohumín .... 1155 d.	...	...	...	...	0558	|	0712	...	|	0808	|	0902	0912	|	...	0955	1008	|	1055	|	1155	1208	|	...
Ostrava hlavní .... 1155 d.	...	...	...	...	0607	0649	0721	...	0749	0818	0849	0911	0921	|	...	1003	1018	1049	1104	|	1203	1218	1249	...
Opava východ .... d.	...	...	0602	...	|	|	|	...	|	|	|	|	|	|	...	|	|	|	|	|	|	|	|	...
Ostrava Svinov .... 1155 d.	...	...	0625	...	0615	0701	0729	...	0758	0827	0901	0917	0929	|	...	1011	1027	1101	1111	|	1211	1227	1301	...
Hranice na Moravě .... 1155 d.	0535	⊡	|	⊡	0652	0727	|	0735	0824	0852	0927	...	|	0935	♡	1039	1052	1127	1139	1135	1239	1252	1327	⊡
Přerov **1159** .... 1155 d.	|	0639	|	0659	|	|	|	|	|	|	|	...	|	|	1029	1059	|	|	1159	|	1259	|	|	1359
Olomouc .... d.	0609	0654	0718	0713	0721	0756	0818	0809	0854	0921	0956	...	1018	1009	1045	1113	1121	1156	1213	1209	1313	1321	1356	1413
Zábřeh na Moravé .... d.	0643	0718	|	0735	0743	0819	|	0843	0918	0943	1019	...	|	1043	|	1135	1143	1219	1235	1243	1335	1343	1419	1435
Česká Třebová .... 1150 d.	0705	0741	|	|	0805	0842	|	0905	0942	1005	1042	...	|	1105	|	|	1205	1242	|	1305	|	1405	1442	|
Pardubice .... 1150 d.	0738	0817	0829	0826	0838	0917	0929	0938	1017	1038	1117	...	1129	1138	1217	1226	1238	1317	1326	1338	1426	1438	1517	1526
Kolín .... 1150 d.	0800	|	|	0845	0900	|	|	1000	|	1100	|	...	|	1200	1249	1245	1300	|	1345	1400	1445	1500	|	1545
Praha hlavní .... 1150 a.	0839	0912	0922	0919	0939	1012	1022	1039	1112	1139	1212	...	1222	1239	1329	1319	1339	1412	1419	1439	1519	1539	1612	1619

	344	SC• 506	Ex 126	Ex 114	RJ♥ 1014	SC• 504	Ex 124	AEx 1042	LE♠ 1364	EC 242	IC 542	Ex 140	RJ♥ 1016	342	SC• 502	Ex 122	EC 112	RJ♥ 1018	SC• 240	Ex 120	LE♠ 1366	Ex 540	640	340
		[R] 🍷	✕	🍷	🍷	[R] 🍷	✕	♣	[R] 🍷	[R] 🍷	[R] 🍷	🍷	🍷		[R] 🍷	✕	🍷	🍷	[R] 🍷	🍷	[R] 🍷	🍷	2	
		⊕		♦				G		⑦e	⑦e						♦		♦			⑦e	Ⓐ	
Košice **1180** .... d.	...	...	*0808*r	...	...	...	*1008*r	...	...	1122	...	...	...	...	...	*1208*r	...	...	1503	*1408*r	...	...	...	...
Poprad Tatry **1180** .... d.	△	...	*0925*r	...	...	...	*1125*r	...	...	1238	...	...	...	△	...	*1325*r	...	...	1612	*1525*r	...	...	...	△
Žilina .... d.	1127	...	1112	...	...	...	1312	...	...	1420	...	1425	...	1527	...	1512	...	...	1753	1712	...	...	...	1927
Čadca 🏛 .... d.	1154	...	|	...	...	...	|	...	...	1444	...	1454	...	1554	...	|	...	...	1817	|	...	...	...	1954
Návsi .... d.	1209	...	|	...	...	...	|	...	...	1459	...	1509	...	1609	...	|	...	...	|	|	...	...	...	2009
Třinec centrum .... d.	1217	...	|	...	...	...	|	...	...	|	...	1517	...	1617	...	|	...	...	|	|	...	...	...	2017
Český Těšín .... d.	1226	...	|	...	...	...	|	...	...	1514	...	1526	...	1626	...	|	...	...	1841	|	...	...	...	2026
Havířov .... d.	|	...	|	...	1430	...	|	...	...	|	...	|	1630	|	...	|	...	1830	|	|	...	...	...	|
Karviná hlavní .... d.	1247	...	≋	...	|	...	≋	...	1538	|	...	1546	|	1646	...	≋	...	|	|	≋	...	...	...	2046
Bohumín .... 1155 d.	1302	...	|	1408	|	...	|	...	1555	|	...	1608	|	1702	...	|	1808	|	|	|	1955	2002	2002	2102
Ostrava hlavní .... 1155 d.	1311	1321	|	1418	1449	1521	|	...	1603	1553	...	1618	1649	1711	1721	|	1818	1849	1921	|	2003	2012	2012	2111
Opava východ .... d.	|	|	|	|	|	|	|	...	|	|	1553	|	|	|	|	|	|	|	|	|	|	|	|	|
Ostrava Svinov .... 1155 d.	1317	1329	|	1427	1501	1529	|	...	1611	1624v	1624	1627	1701	1717	1729	|	1827	1901	1929	|	2011	2021	2021	2117
Hranice na Moravě .... 1155 d.	...	|	1335	1452	1527	|	1535	♡	1639	|	|	1652	1727	...	|	1735	1852	1927	|	1935	2039	2052	2052	...
Přerov **1159** .... 1155 d.	...	|	|	|	|	|	|	1629	1659	|	|	|	|	...	|	|	|	|	|	|	2059	|	|	...
Olomouc .... d.	...	1418	1409	1521	1556	1618	1609	1645	1713	1716	1716	1721	1756	...	1818	1809	1921	1956	2018	2009	2113	2121	2119	...
Zábřeh na Moravé .... d.	...	|	1443	1543	1619	|	1643	|	1735	|	|	1743	1819	...	|	1843	1943	2019	|	2043	2135	2143	...	...
Česká Třebová .... 1150 d.	...	|	1505	1605	1642	|	1705	|	|	|	|	1805	1842	...	|	1905	2005	2041	2058	2105	|	2205	...	...
Pardubice .... 1150 d.	...	1529	1538	1638	1717	1729	1738	1819	1826	1829	1829	1838	1917	...	1929	1938	2038	2117	2131	2146	2226	2243	...	...
Kolín .... 1150 d.	...	|	1600	1700	|	|	1800	1851	1845	|	|	1900	|	...	|	2000	2100	|	2151	2210	2245	2305	...	...
Praha hlavní .... 1150 a.	...	1622	1639	1739	1812	1822	1839	1932	1919	1922	1922	1939	2012	...	2022	2039	2139	2212	2224	2248	2319	2344	...	...

♦ – **NOTES** (LISTED BY TRAIN NUMBER)

112/3 – PORTA MORAVICA – [12] 🍷 Praha - Ostrava - Bohumín - Katowice - Warszawa and v.v.

114 – CRACOVIA – [12] 🍷 (Kraków Apr. 14 - Oct. 1 -) Bohumín - Ostrava - Praha.

115 – CRACOVIA – [12] 🍷 Praha - Ostrava - Bohumín (- Kraków Apr. 13 - Sept. 30).

116/7 – PRAHA – [12] ✕ Praha - Ostrava - Bohumín - Katowice - Warszawa and v.v.

240/1 – PENDOLINO KOŠIČAN.

442/3 – BOHEMIA – 🛏 1, 2 cl., ▬ 2 cl., [2] Praha - Bohumín - Košice - Humenné and v.v.; 🛏 1, 2 cl. Cheb (**767/4**) - Plzeň - Praha (**443/2**) - Žilina - Košice - Humenné and v.v.; 🛏 1, 2 cl. Praha - Košice - Čierna nad Tisou - Čop - Lviv - Kyïv and v.v. (Table **96**); 🍷 Praha - Ostrava and v.v.

444/5 – SLOVAKIA – 🛏 1, 2 cl., ▬ 2 cl., [2] Praha - Bohumín - Košice and v.v.; 🛏 1, 2 cl., [2] Praha - Bohumín (**406/7**) - Katowice - Warszawa and v.v. (also ▬ 2 cl. on dates in Table **99**); 🛏 1, 2 cl. Cheb (**615/4**) - Karlovy Vary - Praha (**445/4**) - Košicé and v.v. Conveys on dates in Table **1185** 🛏 1, 2 cl. Praha - Žilina - Banská Bystrica - Zvolen and Banská Bystrica - Praha. Not Dec. 24, 31.

544/5 – Conveys on ⑥ from Praha (returning on ⑤ from Moskva, ④ from St Peterburg) 🛏 1, 2 cl. Praha - Bohumín (**405/4**) - Katowice - Minsk - Moskva and v.v.; 🛏 1, 2 cl. Praha - Bohumín (**405/4**) - Orsha - St Peterburg and v.v. (Table **95**).

1020/1 – 🛏 (1,2,3 berth), ▬ (6 berth), [12] Praha - Košice and v.v.

D – Daily to Karviná; ③–⑦ to Prešov and Košice.
E – ①④⑤⑥⑦ from Košice and Prešov; daily from Karviná.
G – For days of running see Table **1157**.
K – Conveys 🛏 1, 2 cl., [2] Praha (**443**) - Bohumín (**403**) - Kraków (also ▬ 2 cl. Dec. 15 - 23, 25 - 30, Jan. 1 - 8, Apr. 5 - Nov. 5).
L – Conveys 🛏 1, 2 cl., [2] Kraków (**402**) - Bohumín (**442**) - Praha (also ▬ 2 cl. Dec. 16 - 23, 25 - 30, Jan. 1 - 9, Apr. 6 - Nov. 6 from Kraków).
N – ①②③④⑦ (not Dec. 25, Apr. 13, 16, 30, May 7, July 4, 5, Sept. 27, Nov. 16).
P – [12] Praha - Prešov - Košice and v.v. (Table **1180**).
R – Daily to Návsi; ⑧ **h** to Žilina.
S – Daily to Bohumin; ⑧ **h** to Návsi.

T – ①–⑥ **n** from Návsi, daily from Bohumín.
U – Daily except ②.
V – To / from Vsetín (Table **1158**).
W – Daily to Karviná; ③–⑦ to Prešov and Košice.
e – Also Apr. 17, May 1, 8; not Dec. 25, Apr. 16, 30, May 7.
f – Also Apr. 13, July 4, Sept. 27, Nov. 16; not Dec. 30, Apr. 14, July 7, Sept. 29, Nov. 17.
g – Also Apr. 18, May 2, 9; not Dec. 26, Apr. 17, May 1, 8.
h – Not Dec. 25, Apr. 14, 16, 30, May 7, July 5, Nov. 17.
k – Not Dec. 25 - Jan. 1, Apr. 17, May 1, 8, July 6.
m – Not Dec. 24 - 31, Apr. 16, 30, May 7, July 5.
n – ①–⑥ (not Dec. 24, 26, Apr. 15, 17, May 1, 8, July 6, Nov. 18).
r – Change at Púchov (Tables **1158** / **1180**).
t – Trinec (not Trinec centrum).
u – Calls to pick up only.
v – Arrive 1559; attached to *IC* **542** from Ostrava Svinov.
x – ⑦ (also Dec. 24, 26, Apr. 14, 17, May 1, 8, July 5, 6, Sept. 28, Nov. 17).
z – **445** arrives Přerov 0056. **444** arrives Bohumín 0141, Přerov 0309.

♥ – Operated by REGIOJET. Separate fare tariff applies.
♠ – Operated by LEO Express. Separate fare tariff.
♣ – Operated by ARRIVA. 2nd class, 🍷. Separate fares.
≋ – Via Vsetín and Horní Lideč (Table **1158**).
• – *SUPERCITY PENDOLINO* train, [R] (fee CZK 250).
⊡ – To / from Staré Město u Uherské Hradiště (Table **1159**).
⊕ – From / to Cheb via Plzeň (Table **1120**).
⊗ – From / to Františkovy Lázně via Plzeň (Table **1120**).
♡ – To / from Nitra via Trenčin (Table **1157**).
△ – To / from Banská Bystrica (Table **1185**).

▽ – To / from Zvolen via Banská Bystrica (Table **1185**).
⊖ – [R] for international journeys.
Δ – *439 km* via Vsetin.
* – Classified *Ex* in Slovakia.

Český Těšín - Havířov - Ostrava:
From Český Těšín every two hours 0610Ⓐ - 1810Ⓐ, from Ostrava hlavní every two hours 0654Ⓐ - 1854Ⓐ, journey 45 - 47 mins. Local trains run hourly Český Těšín - Havířov - Ostrava Svinov (journey 50 mins).

Český Těšín - Cieszyn (Poland):
From Český Těšín 0521 then every two hours 0820 - 2220; from Cieszyn 0532 then every two hours 0831 - 2231. Journey 5 minutes. Trains continue beyond Český Těšín to / from Frýdek-Mistek.

12 *Subject to alteration on Dec. 24, 25, 31, Jan. 1.* 487

1165 ÚSTI NAD ORLICI - LETOHRAD - LICHKOV - KLODZKO

Most trains 2nd class

km			Ⓒ	Ⓐ								
	Praha hlavní ... **1150** d.	...	...	*0653*	*0755*	*1055*	*1255*	...	*1455*	*1655*	...	*1755*
	Pardubice .... **1150** d.	*0605*	0731	*0805*	*0905*	*1205*	*1405*	...	*1605*	*1805*	...	*1905*
	Ústi nad Orlici. **1150** a.	*0637*	0823	*0837*	*0937*	*1237*	*1437*	...	*1637*	*1837*	...	*1937*
0	**Ústi nad Orlici** .... d.	0649	0825	0846	0946	1246	1446	...	1648	1848	...	1941
14	Letohrad .... a.	0711	0845	0906	1007	1306	1507	...	1707	1908	...	2002
14	Letohrad .... d.	0714	0849	0908	1008	1307	1508	...	1708	1909	...	...
35	Lichkov .... a.	0742	0916	0936	1036	1333	1537	...	1735	1934	...	...
35	Lichkov .... ◇ d.	0745	...	...	...	*1348*	...	1542	...	...	1940	...
44	Międzylesie 🏛 .... ◇ a.	0753	...	...	...	*1356*	...	1550	...	...	1948	...
80	**Klodzko** Gl. .... ◇ a.	*0844*	...	...	...	*1439*	...	1639	...	...	2042	...
	Wroclaw **1095** .... ◇ a.	*1019*	...	...	...	...	...	1817	...	...	2219	...

	Ⓐ								
Wroclaw **1095** ..... ◇ d.	...	*0628*	...	...	1048	...	...	...	*1654*
Klodzko Gl. .... ◇ d.	...	*0808*	...	...	1232	...	*1446*	...	*1830*
Międzylesie 🏛 .... ◇ d.	...	0906	...	...	1314	...	*1529*	...	*1920*
Lichkov .... ◇ a.	...	0915	...	...	1322	...	*1538*	...	*1929*
Lichkov .... d.	0803	0918	1217	1301	...	1504	1603	1704	1935
Letohrad .... a.	0830	0945	1243	1330	...	1530	1630	1730	2000
Letohrad .... d.	0846	0946	1246	1346	...	1546	1648	1746	2004
Ústi nad Orlici .... a.	0909	1009	1309	1409	...	1609	1712	1809	2017
Ústi nad Orlici **1150** d.	*0923*	*1023*	*1323*	*1423*	...	*1623*	*1723*	*1823*	*2023*
Pardubice .... **1150** a.	*0953*	*1053*	*1353*	*1453*	...	*1653*	*1753*	*1853*	*2053*
Praha hlavní ... **1150** a.	*1103*	*1203*	*1503*	*1603*	...	*1803*	*1903*	*2003*	*2159*

km		Ⓐ	Ⓒ						**935**		
	Praha hlavní **1145** ..... d.	...	...	...	...	...	...	...	1507	...	...
0	**Hradec Králové** .... d.	0705	0705	0905	1105	...	1305	1505	1705	1905	...
21	Týniště nad Orlicí .... d.	0733	0733	0931	1131	...	1331	1531	1731	1931	...
36	Doudleby nad Orlici .... d.	0752	0753	0951	1151	...	1351	1551	1751	1951	...
62	**Letohrad** .... a.	...	0829	1027	1231	...	1431	1631	1831	2028	...

	934	Ⓐ	Ⓒ							**d**
Letohrad .... d.	0533	...	0729	0833	1133	1333	1533	1733	2009	...
Doudleby nad Orlici ...... d.	0610	0810	0810	0910	1210	1410	1610	1810	2057	2106
Týniště nad Orlicí .... d.	0630	0831	0831	0931	1230	1431	1631	1831	...	2132
Hradec Králové .... a.	0653	0853	0853	0953	1253	1453	1653	1853	...	2157
Praha hlavní **1145** ..... a.	0848	...	...	...	...	...	...	...	...	...

d – Change at Častolovice (a. 2115 / d. 2118).
e – Also Apr. 17, May 1, 8; not Dec. 25, Apr. 16, 30, May 7.
h – Not Dec. 25, Apr. 14, 16, 30, May 7, July 5, Nov. 17.
t – Ⓑ**h** to Pardubice (⊡); ⑦**e** to Praha.
⊡ – On other dates stay on train to Pardubice, a. 2120.
◇ – Timings in Poland subject to alteration from Mar. 12.

1166 OLOMOUC - KRNOV - OPAVA - OSTRAVA

2nd class

km										Ⓐ	Ⓐ	Ⓐ
0	**Olomouc** .... d.	...	0705**r**	*0901*	1105	1305	1505	1705	1905	...	...	...
64	Bruntál .... d.	...	0828**r**	*1028*	1228	1428	1628	1828	2028	...	...	...
87	Krnov .... a.	...	0852**r**	*1052*	1252	1452	1652	1852	2052	...	...	...
87	Krnov .... d.	0706	0906	1106	1306	1506	1706	1906	*2101*	...	...	...
116	**Opava** východ... ▷ d.	0737	0937	1137	1337	1537	1737	1937	*2138*	0615	every	1815
144	Ostrava Svinov.. ▷ a.	0757	0957	1157	1357	1557	1757	2001	...	0639	**two**	1839
149	**Ostrava** hlavní ...... a.	0807	...	1207	1407	1607	...	...	...	0653	hours	1853

									Ⓐ	Ⓐ	Ⓐ
Ostrava hlavní ...... d.	...	...	0948	...	1348	1548	1748	...	0656	every	1856
Ostrava Svinov .. ▷ d.	0601	0801	1001	1201	1401	1601	1801	...	0713	**two**	1913
Opava východ ... ▷ d.	0628	0828	1028	1228	1428	1628	1828	2023	0736	hours	1936
Krnov .... a.	0656	0856	1056	1256	1456	1656	1856	2100	...	...	...
Krnov .... d.	0705	0905	*1105*	1305	1505	1705	...	*2112*	...	...	...
Bruntál .... d.	0734	0934	*1131*	1334	1534	1734	...	*2138*	...	...	...
Olomouc .... a.	0853	1053	*1255*	1453	1653	1853	...	*2304*	...	...	...

km								
0	Jesenik .... d.	0530	0930	...	1325	...	1725	...
22	Glucholazy (Poland) .d.	0611	1011	...	1406	...	1806	...
43	Tremešná ve Slezsku .d.	0640	1040	1240	1440	1643	1840	2040
60	Krnov .... a.	0658	1058	1259	1458	1702	1858	2059

Krnov .... d.	0704	0908	1104	1308	1504	1708	1904
Tremešná ve Slezsku d.	0725	0928	1125	1328	1523	1728	1925
Glucholazy (Poland). d.	0800	...	1200	...	1600	...	2000
Jesenik .... a.	0837	...	1237	...	1637	...	2037

r – ①–⑥ (not Dec. 24, 26, Apr. 15, 17, May 1, 8, July 6, Nov. 18).
▷ – Local trains run approx hourly (journey 35 minutes).

1169 OTHER LOCAL SERVICES

2nd class. May vary on holidays.

BRNO - ZNOJMO *89 km* Journey 2 hours Change at Miroslav and Hrušovany

From Brno: 0649⑥**t**, 0849Ⓒ, 1254Ⓒ, 1454 **R**, 1654Ⓒ.
From Znojmo: 0903Ⓒ, 1303Ⓒ, 1503 **R**, 1703Ⓒ.

CHOCEŇ - LITOMYŠL *24 km* Journey 55 minutes

From Choceň: 0504Ⓐ, 0627, 0839, 1039, 1239Ⓒ, 1429Ⓐ, 1539Ⓒ, 1639Ⓐ, 1839Ⓒ.
From Litomyšl: 0440Ⓐ, 0603Ⓐ, 0720Ⓐ, 0734Ⓒ, 0942, 1232, 1532, 1732, 1934Ⓒ.
Change at Vysoké Myto město on certain journeys.

JINDŘICHŮV HRADEC - NOVÁ BYSTŘICE *33 km* Narrow gauge, 80 mins

Ⓒ (daily Apr. 14 - Sept. 30): from Jindřichův Hradec 0925, 1725 (also 0725, 1125, 1325, 1525 July 1 - Sept. 3). Round trip approx 3 hours. Operator: JHMD www.jhmd.cz
Steam train: daily July 1 - Sept. 2: from Jindřichův Hradec 1044, returning 1515.
⑥ May 6 - June 24, ⑥ Sept. 9 - 30: from Jindřichův Hradec 1044, returning 1422.

KOJETIN / HULIN - KROMĚŘÍŽ *8 km* Journey 8 minutes

Kojetin - Kroměříž: approx hourly. *9 km*, journey 12 minutes.
Hulin - Kroměříž: 1 - 2 trains per hour connecting with trains in Table **1159**.

PRAHA - KARLŠTEJN *33 km* Journey 42 minutes

From Praha hlavní: hourly 0417 - 2317 (every 30 minutes 1217 - 1917). From Karlštejn: hour 0453 - 2253 (every 30 mins 1253 - 1953). Most trains continue to / from Beroun (8 mins).

TŘEMEŠNÁ VE SLEZSKU - OSOBLAHA *20 km* Narrow gauge, 45 minutes

From Třemešná: 0450Ⓐ **n**, 0650Ⓐ **n**, 0730⑥ **u**, 1045 **s**, 1130, 1525, 1930.
From Osoblaha: 0350 Ⓐ **n**, 0550 ⚒, 0950, 1350, 1510 **s**, 1750.

ZNOJMO - BŘECLAV *69 km* Journey 90 minutes

From Znojmo: 0658, 0903, 1103, every 2 hours 1255 - 1655 (hourly 1155-1755 on Ⓐ), 190
From Břeclav: approx every 2 hours 0731 - 1931 (also 1233Ⓐ, 1433Ⓐ, 1633Ⓐ, 2136Ⓐ).

R – Ⓒ Apr. 14 - Oct. 1.
n – Not Dec. 23 - 30, July 3 - Sept. 1.
s – ⑥ June 3 - Sept. 16, ⑦ July 2 - Aug. 27 (also May 8, July 5, 6, Nov. 11). Steam journey; special fares.
t – Also Apr. 14, July 5, Sept. 28, Nov. 17; not Apr. 15, Nov. 1
u – Also Ⓐ July 3 - Sept. 1.

SLOVAKIA

Operator: National railway operator is Železničná spoločnosť Slovensko (ŽSSK), www.slovakrail.sk, which runs on the network of Železníce Slovenskej Republiky (ŽSR), www.zsr.sk

Services: All trains convey first and second class seating, **except** where shown otherwise in footnotes or by '2' in the train column, or where the footnote shows sleeping and/or couchet cars only. Descriptions of sleeping (🛏) and couchette (🛏) cars appear on page 8.

Timings: Valid **December 11, 2016 - December 9, 2017.** Holiday cancellation dates of mainline trains are shown in the tables, but certain local trains may also be cancelled during th period Dec. 24 - Jan. 1 and these cancellations may not be shown in the tables.

Supplements: A higher level of fares applies to travel by *EC* and *IC* trains. It is possible to reserve seats on most Express trains.

1170 BRATISLAVA - LEVICE - ZVOLEN - BANSKÁ BYSTRICA

km		**831**	**833**	**835**	**837**	**839**	**851**	**841**	**843**	**845**	**847**	**801**
							Ⓐ		Ⓐ			Ⓑ
							2**z**		**z**			**P**
0	**Bratislava** hlavná ▷ d.	0601	0801	1001	1201	1401	1431	1601	1657	1801	2001	2349
49	Galanta .... ▷ d.	0637	0837	1037	1237	1437	1513	1637	1731	1837	2037	0027
60	Šal'a .... ▷ d.	0647	0847	1047	1247	1447	1522	1647	1740	1847	2047	0037
89	Šurany .... d.	0709	0909	1109	1309	1509	1546	1709	1804	1909	2109	0101
132	Levice .... d.	0749	0949	1149	1349	1549	...	1749	1850	1949	2149	0148
187	Žiar nad Hronom ..... d.	0839	1039	1239	1439	1639	...	1839	1939	2039	2239	0238
209	**Zvolen** osob. .... a.	0857	1057	1257	1457	1657	...	1857	1957	2057	2257	0257
209	**Zvolen** osob. .... d.	0901	1101	1301	1501	1701	...	1901	2001	2101	2301	...
230	**Banská Bystrica** ..... a.	0925	1125	1325	1525	1725	...	1925	2025	2125	2325	...

	830	*Ex* **530**	**832**	**834**	**836**	**838**	**840**	**17840**	**842**	**844**	**80(**
		Ⓐ						⑦			Ⓑ
	△	✕**z**						**e**			**P**
Banská Bystrica ..... d.	0435	0535	0635	0835	1035	1235	1435	1511	1635	1835	...
Zvolen osob. .... a.	0459	0553	0659	0859	1059	1259	1459	1540	1659	1859	...
Zvolen osob. .... d.	0503	0555	0703	0903	1103	1303	1503	1553	1703	1903	021
Žiar nad Hronom ...... d.	0521	0613	0721	0921	1121	1321	1521	1614	1721	1921	023
Levice .... d.	0613	0659	0813	1013	1213	1413	1613	1710	1813	2013	033
Šurany .... d.	0651	0740	0851	1051	1251	1451	1651	1756	1851	2051	041
Šal'a .... ▷ d.	0714	|	0914	1114	1314	1514	1714	1817	1914	2114	043
Galanta .... ▷ d.	0725	|	0925	1125	1325	1525	1725	1826	1925	2125	044
Bratislava hlavná ▷ a.	0759	0836	0959	1159	1359	1559	1759	1901	1959	2159	052

LOCAL TRAINS ZVOLEN - BANSKÁ BYSTRICA

	J		▶		Ⓐ	Ⓐ**z**		Ⓐ**z**							Ⓐ**z**	§	Ⓐ**z**		⊡			Ⓐ**z**			
Zvolen .... d.	0427	0439	0502	0522	0557	0639	0700	0733	0801	1001	1110	1201	1310	1401	1430	1510	1539	1601	1710	1814	1910	2019	2116	2221	...
Banská Bystrica .... a.	0501	0512	0529	0555	0629	0711	0731	0803	0831	1031	1141	1231	1340	1431	1511	1541	1611	1631	1741	1848	1941	2051	2149	2252	...

			Ⓐ**z**	Ⓐ**z**		Ⓐ**z**							Ⓐ**z**			Ⓐ**z**					▶	J			
Banská Bystrica .... d.	0447	0542	0606	0646	0718	0749	0818	0929	...	1129	1218	1327	1346	1418	1528	1546	1618	1728	1818	1929	2029	2126	2135	2228	...
Zvolen .... a.	0521	0614	0635	0718	0751	0821	0850	0959	...	1159	1250	1359	1418	1450	1559	1619	1650	1759	1850	1959	2053	2150	2207	2259	...

J – Operated by RegioJet. 12 🍸 Praha - Zvolen and v.v. (Table **1185**).
P – POL'ANA – For days of running see Table **1190**. 🛏 1, 2 cl. 2 Bratislava - Zvolen - Košice - Prešov and v.v.; 🛏 1, 2 cl. Brno (**283/2**) - Bratislava (**801/0**) - Košice - Prešov and v.v. Conveys 🛏 1, 2 cl. Bratislava - Košice - Lviv - Kyïv and v.v. on dates in Table **96**.
e – Also Apr. 17, May 1, 8, Nov. 1; not Dec. 25, Jan. 1, Apr. 16, 30, May 7.
z – Not Dec. 24 - Jan. 8.
▶ – 12 Ostrava - Zvolen - Žilina and v.v. (train **347/346**, Table **1185**).
△ – Additional train on Ⓐ**z**: Šurany d. 0603, Šal'a d. 0632, Galanta d. 0641, Bratislava a. 0716 (train **850**).
▷ – For additional trains see Table **1175**.
⊡ – 11 minutes later on ⑦**e** (daily July 2 - Aug. 27).
§ – 10 minutes later on ⑦**e**.

1171 BRATISLAVA - KOMÁRNO

Operator: RegioJet. 2nd clas

km		Ⓒ	Ⓐ					Ⓐ		Ⓐ		
0	**Bratislava** hlavná .... d.	0605	0705	0805	1005	1205	1405	1513	1605**r**	1705	1805	2005
42	Dunajská Streda ...... d.	0711	0821	0911	1111	1311	1511	1606	1711	1808	1914	2111
94	**Komárno** .... a.	0813	0922	1013	1213	1413	1613	1703	1813	1906	2015	2213

	Ⓐ					Ⓐ	Ⓒ	Ⓐ	Ⓒ	Ⓐ	
Komárno .... d.	0643	0743	0943	1143	1343	1433	1543	1635	1743	1838	194
Dunajská Streda ...... d.	0750	0850	1050	1250	1450	1550	1650	1750	1850	1949	205
Bratislava hlavná .... a.	0841	0952	1152	1352	1552	1652	1752	1852	1952	2051	215

r – Depart 1613 on Ⓐ.

Subject to alteration Dec. 24 - Jan. 8.

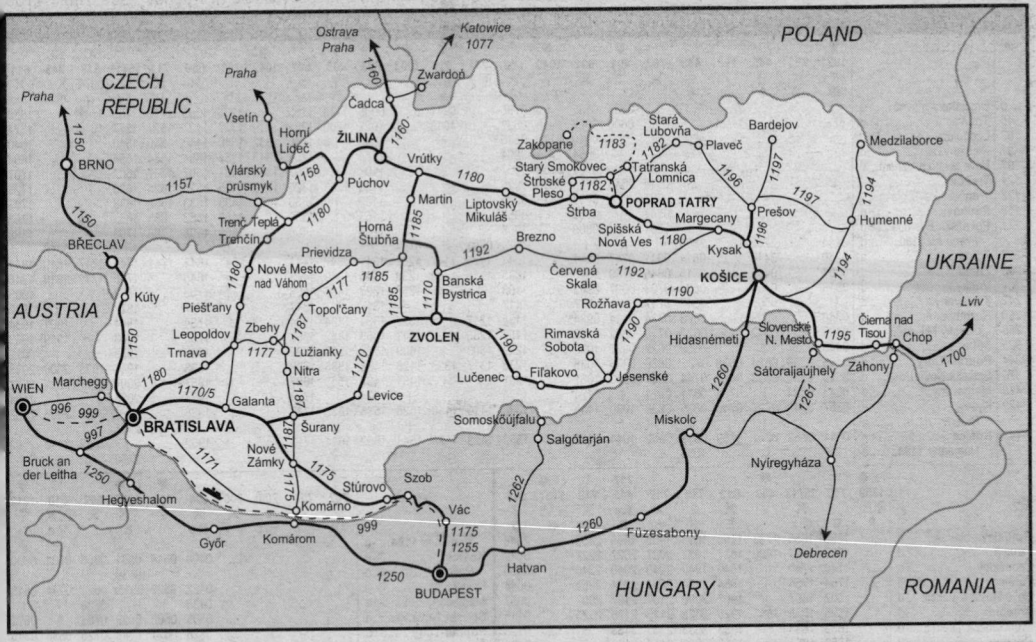

BRATISLAVA - ŠTÚROVO - BUDAPEST — 1175

km		EN 477	EC 271 ✕	EC 273 ✕	EC 275 ✕	EC 277 ✕	EC 279 ✕	EC 131 ✕	EC 173 ✕	EC 281 ✕
		MP				S		V	H	
	Praha hlavní **1150**......d.	2358	...	0549	0752	0952	1152	...	1352	1552
	Brno hlavní **1150**......d.	0315	0622	0823	1023	1223	1423	...	1623	1823
	Bratislava hlavná **1150**.d.	0440	0659	0859	1059	1259	1459	1559	1659	1859
0	**Bratislava hlavná**......d.	0548	0753	0953	1153	1353	1553	1653	1753	1953
91	Nové Zámky......d.	0644	0846	1046	1246	1446	1646	1746	1846	2046
135	Štúrovo 🚂......d.	0713	0914	1114	1314	1514	1714	1814	1914	2114
150	Szob 🚂......d.		0925	1025	1325	1525	1725	1825	1925	2125
180	Nagymaros-Visegrád..▷ d.		0935	1135	1335	1535	1735	1835	1935	2135
197	Vác......d.		0750	0950	1150	1350	1550	1750	1850	2150
214	**Budapest Keleti**....▷ a.	0837	1035	1235	1435	1635	1835	1935	2035	2235

		EC 280 ✕	EC 172 ✕	EC 130 ✕	EC 278 ✕	EC 276 ✕	EC 274 ✕	EC 272 ✕	EC 270 ✕	EN 476	476 524
						S				MP	
Budapest Keleti......▷ d.		0525	0725	0822	0925	1125	1325	1525	1725	2005	2005
Vác......▷ d.		0610	0810	0910	1010	1210	1410	1610	1810	2048	2048
Nagymaros-Visegrád..▷ d.		0624	0824	0924	1024	1224	1424	1624	1824		
Szob 🚂......▷ d.		0636	0836	0936	1036	1236	1436	1636	1838		
Štúrovo 🚂......d.		0649	0849	0949	1049	1249	1449	1649	1850	2124	2124
Nové Zámky......d.		0716	0916	1016	1116	1316	1516	1716	1916	2152	2152
Bratislava hlavná......a.		0807	1007	1107	1207	1407	1607	1807	2007	2246	2246
Břeclav **1150**......a.		0901	1101	1201	1301	1501	1701	1901	2101	2355	2355
Brno hlavní **1150**......a.		0936	1136	...	1336	1536	1736	1936	2136	0054	0054
Praha hlavní **1150**......a.		1206	1406	...	1606	1806	2006	2209	...	0345	0639r

2nd class — LOCAL TRAINS BRATISLAVA - NOVÉ ZAMKY

	Ⓐz			Ⓐ			Ⓐz					Ⓐ	
Bratislava hl....§ d.	0707	0907	1107	1207	1307	1501	1507	1707	1831	1907	2107	2307
Galanta......§ d.	0757	0957	1157	1257	1357	1537	1557	1757	1913	1957	2157	2357
Šaľa......§ d.	0807	1007	1207	1307	1407	1547	1607	1807	1922	2007	2207	0007
Nové Zámky......a.	0836	1036	1236	1336	1436	1607	1636	1836	1940	2036	2236	0036

		Ⓐ	Ⓐz					Ⓐ			Ⓐz	
Nové Zámky ... d.		0518	0618	0722	0922	1122	1322	1522	1622	1722	1822	1922
Šaľa......§ d.		0539	0639	0752	0952	1152	1352	1552	1652	1753	1852	1952
Galanta......§ d.		0549	0649	0809	1004	1204	1404	1604	1704	1804	1904	2004
Bratislava hl....§ a.		0630	0730	0857	1052	1252	1452	1652	1752	1852	1952	2052

H — HUNGARIA – 🚃 ✕ Hamburg - Berlin - Dresden - Praha - Budapest and v.v. Conveys ②⑤ June 16 -
  Sept. 1 🛏 1,2 cl. Praha - Budapest (**341/0**) - Beograd - Bar, returning from Bar ④⑦ June 18 - Sept. 3.
M — METROPOL – 🛏 1,2 cl., 🍽 2 cl., 🚃 Berlin - Dresden - Praha - Bratislava - Budapest and v.v.;
  🛏 1,2 cl., 🍽 2 cl., 🚃 Warszawa (**407/6**) - Břeclav (**477/6**) - Budapest and v.v.; 🛏 1,2 cl.,
  🛏 1,2 cl., 🚃 Kraków (**402/3**) - Bohumín (**407/6**) - Břeclav (**477/6**) - Budapest and v.v.
P — 🛏 1,2 cl., 🍽 2 cl. Praha - Bratislava - Budapest and v.v.
S — SLOVAN – 🛏 ✕ Praha - Bratislava - Budapest and v.v. On ②⑤ June 20 - Sept. 1 conveys
  🛏 1,2 cl. Praha - Budapest (**1204/5**) - Zagreb - Split, returning from Split ③⑥ June 21 - Sept. 2.
V — VARSOVIA – 🚃 ✕ Warszawa - Katowice - Ostrava - Břeclav - Bratislava - Budapest and v.v.
r — Arrive 0703 on ⓒ (conveyed in train **898** Pardubice - Praha).
— Not Dec. 24 - Jan. 8.

▷ — For local trains Szob - Budapest Nyugati see Table **1255**.
△ — Also at: 0444, 1407Ⓐz, 1607Ⓐz, 1807Ⓐ.
▽ — Also at: 0326, 0430, 0454Ⓐz, 0530, 0554Ⓐz, 1422Ⓐz.
§ — See also Table **1170**.

OTHER TRAIN NAMES: **270/1** PETROV, **272/3** CSÁRDÁS,
274/5 JAROSLAV HAŠEK, **278/9** DANUBIUS, **280/1** JÁN JESENIUS.

Nové Zámky - Komárno (29 km, journey 30 minutes):
From Nové Zámky every 2 hours 0452 - 2052 (also 0552Ⓐz, 0735Ⓐz,
1352Ⓐz, 1552Ⓐz, 1752Ⓐz). From Komárno every 2 hours 0442 - 2042
(also 0542Ⓐz, 0737Ⓐz, 1342Ⓐz, 1542Ⓐz, 1742Ⓐz).

2nd class — BRATISLAVA - NITRA and PRIEVIDZA — 1177

km		1721		1723				1725				1727			1043		
							♣					⑥h ⑦e Ⓐz	♣	①–⑥ ⑦			
0	**Bratislava hl.** .... **1180** d.	0555	0639	...	0755	0955	1039	...	1155	...	1355	1439	...	1555	1655	...	1755	1839	...	1955	1955	2100
46	Trnava **1180** ....d.	0627	0716	...	0827	1027	1116	...	1227	...	1427	1516	...	1627	1727	...	1827	1916	...	2027	2027	2202
63	Leopoldov **1180** ....d.	0638	0728	...	0838	1038	1128	...	1238	...	1438	1528	...	1638	1738	...	1838	1928	...	2038	2038	2204
63	Leopoldov ....d.	0642	0743	...	0842	1042	1143	...	1242	1431	1442	1543	...	1642	1748	...	1842	1943	...	2035	2042	2125
87	Zbehy ....d.	0713	0807	0819	0909	1113	1207	1219	1313	1419	...	1513	1607	1619	1713	1822	1822	1913	2007	2011	2019	...	2113	2152
91	Lužianky ....d.	0719	...	0825	0915	1120	...	1225	1320	1425	...	1520	...	1625	1720	1828	1828	1920	...	2017	2025	...	2120	2159
98	**Nitra** ....d.	0730	...	0841	0926	1139	...	1249	1336	1448	1514	1539	...	1649	1738	1849	1849	1939	...	2028	2049	2115	2131	2210
114	Topoľčany ....▷ a.	...	0832	...	...	...	1232	...	...	...	...	1632	...	...	2032	...	...	...
131	Partizánske ....▷ a.	...	0900	...	...	...	1300	...	...	...	...	1700	...	...	2100	...	...	...
158	**Prievidza** ....▷ a.	...	0934	...	...	...	1334	...	...	...	...	1734	...	...	2134	...	...	...

		1720	1040		1722			1042	1724			1726		17728	
		✕b ✕b	✕b	♣	Ⓐ			♣		Ⓐ				⑥h ⑦e	⑦e
Prievidza......▽ d.			0442			0833			1233			1633		1840	
Partizánske......▽ d.			0515			0915			1315			1715		1914	
Topoľčany......▽ d.			0539		◊	0939	◊	◊	1339	◊		1739	◊	1939	
Nitra ......d.		0423 0537	0630 0646	0747	0942	...	1026 1144 1226 1254 1342		1426 1515 1544 1626 1742		1826 1944	...	2026
Lužianky ......d.		0439 0549		0641	0754	0952	...	1041 1154 1241	...	1352	1441 1534 1554 1641 1752	...	1837 1954	...	2041
Zbehy ......d.		0446 0555	0605 0648	0809	0959	1005 1048 1201 1248	1359	1448 1542 1600 1648 1759	1805 1848 2010	2049	
Leopoldov ......a.		0513	0627 0715 0724 0835		1027 1115		1315 1327	1427 1515 1615		1715	1827 1915		2035 2115
Leopoldov ...... **1180** d.			0642 0720		0856	1042 1120	1320		1442 1520 1620		1720	1842 1920		2040 2120
Trnava ...... **1180** d.			0657 0734		0912	1057 1134	1334		1534 1634		1734	1857 1934		2056 2134
Bratislava hl. ...... **1180** a.			0733 0805		0959	1133 1205	1405		1533 1605 1705		1805	1933 2005		2135 2205

b — ①–⑥ (not Dec. 26 - Jan. 7, Apr. 15, 17, May 1, 8,
  Sept. 2, 16, Nov. 18).
e — Also Apr. 17, May 1, 8, Nov. 1; not Dec. 25, Jan.
  1, Apr. 16, 30, May 7.
h — Not Dec. 24 - Jan. 6, Apr. 14, 16, 30, May 7, Sept.
  1, 15, Nov. 17.

z — Not Dec. 24 - Jan. 8.

⬟ — Operated by ARRIVA. For days of running see Table **1157**.
▷ — Local trains Topoľčany - Prievidza (journey 60 - 80 mins) §:
  0356Ⓐ, 0451, 0550Ⓐ, 0649, 0917, 1115, 1307, 1404Ⓐz,
  1527, 1718, 1839 (not ⑦e) 1942⑦Ⓐ 2223Ⓐ.

◊ — To/from Nové Zámky (Table **1187**).
▽ — Local trains Prievidza - Topoľčany (journey 60 - 80 mins)
  0414Ⓐ, 0520, 0623, 0717Ⓐ, 0928, 1115, 1328, 1425Ⓐ,
  1525, 1728 (not ⑦e), 1810⑦e, 1840 (not ⑦e), 2231Ⓐ.
§ — Certain journeys run from/to Nitra (see Table **1187**).

1180 BRATISLAVA - ŽILINA - POPRAD TATRY - KOŠICE

km																									
		♥		*EN*				♥		♣		*SC*•	*IC*	♥		♥		♣					*IC*	*EC*	
		1021	**763**	**445**	**765**	**443**	**767**	**401**	**601**	**1040**	**603**	**241**	**511**	**1003**	**605**	**405**	**607**	**1042**	**709**	**609**	**711**	**15711**	**513**	**243**	**611**
		🍷	✖	⊖	2	⊖	✖	🍷	✖	🍷	✖	🅁✖	🅁✖	🍷	✖	🍷	✖	🍷		✖	✖	✖	🅁✖	✖⊖	✖
		≋	Ⓐ	♦	Ⓐ	♦				T△			v					U△	2Ⓐ		H	⑤f	w	⑤n	
0	**Bratislava** hlavná ... ▷ d.	...	...	...	...	...	...	0533	0555	...	0755	...	0947	...	0955	1133	1155	...	1255	1355	1455	1455	1547	...	1555
46	Trnava ▷ d.	...	...	...	...	...	...	0600	0627	...	0827	...	1013	...	1027	1200	1227	...	1327	1427	1527	1527	1613	...	1627
63	Leopoldov ▷ d.	...	...	...	...	...	...	|	0640	0729	0840	...	|	...	1040	|	1240	1332	1340	1440	1540	1540	|	...	1640
81	Piešťany d.	...	...	...	...	...	...	|	0654	0741	0854	...	|	...	1054	|	1254	1345	1354	1454	1554	1554	|	...	1654
99	Nové Mesto n. Váhom ... d.	...	...	...	...	...	...	|	0707	0752	0907	...	|	...	1107	|	1307	1356	1407	1507	1607	1607	|	...	1707
124	**Trenčín** d.	...	...	...	...	...	0514	0643	0725	0810	0925	...	|	...	1125	1243	1325	1418	1425	1525	1625	1625	|	...	1725
132	Trenčianska Teplá d.	...	...	...	...	...	0522	|	0733	0816	0933	...	|	...	1133	|	1333	1424	1433	1533	1633	1633	|	...	1733
159	**Púchov** ▷ d.	...	...	...	...	...	0547	|	0753	...	0953	...	|	...	1153	|	1353	...	1453	1553	1653	1653	|	...	1753
171	Považská Bystrica .. ▷ d.	...	...	...	...	...	0601	|	0808	...	1008	...	|	...	1208	|	1408	...	1508	1608	1708	1708	|	...	1808
	Praha hl. **1160** d.	2144	...	2200	...	2309	|	|	|	...	|	0707	|	0744	|	|	|	...	|	|	|	|	|	1319	|
203	**Žilina** ▷ a.	0250	...	0414	...	0514	0641	0747	0841	...	1041	1134	1147	1237	1241	1347	1441	...	1541	1641	1741	1741	1747	1810	1841
203	**Žilina** ▷ d.	0301	...	0435	...	0516	0645	0749	0845	...	1045	1136	1149	1239	1245	1349	1445	...	...	1645	...	1755	1749	1819	1845
224	Vrútky ▷ d.	0319	...	0453	...	0534	0703	0807	0903	...	1103	|	|	1256	1303	1407	1503	...	...	1703	...	1813	|	|	1903
242	Kraľovany d.	|	...	0507	...	0547	0717	|	0917	...	1117	|	|	|	1317	|	1517	...	...	1717	...	1827	|	|	1917
260	Ružomberok d.	0348	...	0523	...	0603	0734	0834	0934	...	1134	1217	|	1323	1334	1434	1534	...	...	1734	...	1844	|	1901	1934
286	Liptovský Mikuláš d.	0409	...	0542	...	0622	0753	0852	0953	...	1153	1235	|	1341	1353	1452	1553	...	...	1753	...	1903	|	1919	1953
325	Štrba d.	0438	...	|	...	0650	0822	0920	1022	...	1222	1303	|	1409	1422	1520	1622	...	...	1822	...	1933	|	|	2022
344	**Poprad-Tatry** d.	0456	0538	0624	0638	0725*	0838	0935	1038	...	1238	1317	1323	1428	1438	1535	1638	...	...	1838	...	1948	1923	2000	2038
370	Spišská Nová Ves d.	0516	0557	0643	0657	0744	0857	0953	1057	...	1257	|	|	1451	1457	1553	1657	...	...	1857	...	2007	|	2019	2057
410	Margecany d.	0543	0624	|	0724	0811	0924	|	1124	...	1324	|	|	|	1524	|	1724	...	...	1924	...	2035	|	|	2124
429	Kysak ▷ a.	0557	0640	0727	0740	0825	0938	1030	1138	...	1338	1410	1416	1528	1538	1630	1738	...	...	1938	...	|	2016	2056	2138
	Prešov a.	|	|	|	|	|	|	|	|	...	|	|	|	|	|	|	|	...	...	|	...	2105	|	|	|
445	**Košice** ▷ a.	0614	0652	0741	0752	0839	0952	1044	1152	...	1352	1423	1429	1544	1552	1644	1752	...	...	1952	...	|	2029	2110	2152
	Humenné **1194** a.	...	...	...	...	1033	...	...	...	...	...	...	...	...	...	...	...	...	...	...	...	2230	...	...	...

	LE♠			♥				717		*LE*♠	
	1359	**713**	**15713**	**409**	**613**	**715**	**717**	**445**	**719**	**1367**	**615**
	🍷🅁		✖	🍷	✖	2	✖	🛏	✖	🍷🅁	2
	P	G	⑤k		E	F		R	Ⓑh	N	♦
Bratislava hlavná ▷ d.	...	1655	1655	1733	1755	1855	1955	1955	2155	...	2345
Trnava ▷ d.	...	1727	1727	1800	1827	1927	2027	2027	2227	...	0017
Leopoldov ▷ d.	...	1740	1740	|	1840	1940	2040	2040	2240	...	0030
Piešťany d.	...	1754	1754	|	1854	1954	2054	2054	2254	...	0044
Nové Mesto n. Váhom d.	...	1807	1807	|	1907	2006	2107	2107	2307	...	0057
Trenčín d.	...	1825	1825	1843	1925	2025	2125	2125	2323	...	0115
Trenčianska Teplá d.	...	1833	1833	|	1933	2033	2133	2133	...	...	0123
Púchov ▷ d.	...	1853	1853	|	1953	2053	2153	2153	...	...	0143
Považská Bystrica ▷ d.	...	1908	1908	|	2008	2108	2208	2208	...	...	0158
Praha hl. **1160** d.	1413	|	|	|	|	|	|	|	...	2013	|
Žilina ▷ a.	1917	1941	1941	1947	2041	2141	2241	2241	...	0110	0231
Žilina ▷ d.	1919	...	1956	1949	2045	...	...	0435	...	0112	0243
Vrútky ▷ d.	1935	...	2014	2007	2103	...	...	0453	...	0129	0301
Kraľovany d.	|	...	2028	|	2117	...	...	0507	...	|	0315
Ružomberok d.	2001	...	2044	2034	2134	...	...	0523	...	0155	0332
Liptovský Mikuláš d.	2018	...	2103	2052	2153	...	...	0542	...	0212	0351
Štrba d.	2045	...	2131	2120	2222	...	...	|	...	0238	|
Poprad-Tatry d.	2058	...	2146	2135	2238	...	...	0624	...	0252	0432
Spišská Nová Ves d.	2116	...	2204	2153	2257	...	...	0643	...	0309	0451
Margecany d.	|	...	2230	|	2324	...	...	|	...	|	0518
Kysak ▷ a.	2225r	...	2244	2230	2338	...	...	0727	...	0419r	0532
Prešov a.	2206	...	|	|	|	...	...	|	...	0359	|
Košice ▷ a.	2238	...	2257	2244	2352	...	...	0741	...	0432	0546
Humenné **1194** a.	...	...	...	...	...	...	...	...	...	...	0750

						♥	*LE*♠		*IC*	♥
	702	**704**	**706**	**600**	**600**	**400**	**1356**	**602**	**510**	**1012**
	🍷	✖	2	✖	✖	🍷	🍷🅁	✖	🅁✖	🍷
	Ⓐz		Ⓐt		⚒b		N		⚒d	
Humenné **1194** d.	...	...	...	...	...	...	...	...	...	...
Košice ▷ d.	...	...	...	...	0408	0516	0501	0608	0731	0800
Prešov d.	...	...	...	...	|	|	0538	|	|	|
Kysak ▷ d.	...	...	...	...	0422	0529	0513r	0622	0744	0813
Margecany d.	...	...	...	...	0438	|	|	0638	|	|
Spišska Nová Ves d.	...	...	...	...	0505	0608	0629	0705	|	0852
Poprad-Tatry d.	...	...	...	...	0525	0627	0648	0725	0836	0915
Štrba d.	...	...	...	...	0541	0642	0701	0742	|	0930
Liptovský Mikuláš d.	...	...	...	...	0611	0709	0729	0810	|	0959
Ružomberok d.	...	...	...	...	0628	0727	0746	0828	|	1018
Kraľovany d.	...	...	...	...	0645	|	|	0845	|	|
Vrútky ▷ d.	...	...	...	...	0659	0753	0812	0859	|	1044
Žilina ▷ a.	...	...	...	...	0715	0810	0828	0915	1010	1100
Žilina ▷ d.	0419	0519	0619	0719	0719	0812	0830	0919	1012	1108
Praha hl. **1160** a.	|	|	|	|	|	|	1319	|	|	1612
Považská Bystrica ▷ d.	0454	0554	0654	0754	0754	|	...	0954	|	...
Púchov ▷ d.	0509	0609	0709	0809	0809	|	...	1009	|	...
Trenčianska Teplá d.	0527	0627	0727	0827	0827	|	...	1027	|	...
Trenčín d.	0535	0635	0735	0835	0835	0918	...	1035	|	...
Nové Mesto n. Váh. d.	0554	0654	0754	0854	0854	|	...	1054	|	...
Piešťany d.	0607	0707	0807	0907	0907	|	...	1107	|	...
Leopoldov ▷ d.	0620	0720	0820	0920	0920	|	...	1120	|	...
Trnava ▷ d.	0634	0734	0834	0934	0934	1001	...	1134	1150	...
Bratislava hlavná ▷ a.	0705	0805	0905	1005	1005	1027	...	1205	1213	...

		IC	♣		♥		*EC*					*SC*•	♣		*IC*			♥		*EN*	♥		442	*LE*♠	
	604	**514**	**1041**	**606**	**404**	**714**	**242**	**608**	**17716**	**610**	**17610**	**240**	**1043**	**760**	**512**	**17612**	**612**	**408**	**762**	**444**	**1020**	**442**	**704**	**1350**	**614**
	✖	🅁✖	🍷	✖	🍷		✖⊖	✖	2	✖	✖	🅁✖	🍷	2	🅁✖	✖	✖	✖	✖	⊖	🍷	⊖	🛏	🍷🅁	
		⑦e	V△			Ⓑh	⑦s		⑦c		⑦g		W△	Ⓐz	w	⑦u			Y	♦	≋	♦	S	P	♦‡
Humenné **1194** d.	...	...	...	...	...	...	...	...	...	...	...	...	...	...	...	1406	...	...	...	...	...	1946	...	...	2154
Košice ▷ d.	0808	0931	...	1008	1116	...	1122	1208	...	1408	1432	1503	...	1508	1531	|	1608	1716	1808	2024	2122	2208	2208	2306	2345
Prešov d.	|	|	...	|	|	...	|	|	...	|	|	|	...	|	|	1536	|	|	|	|	|	|	|	2338	|
Kysak ▷ d.	0822	0944	...	1022	1129	...	1135	1222	...	1422	1447	1516	...	1522	1544	|	1622	1729	1822	2041	2136	2222	2222	2318r	2359
Margecany d.	0838	|	...	1038	|	...	|	1238	...	1438	1503	|	...	1538	|	1605	1638	|	1838	|	2151	2238	2238	|	0015
Spišska Nová Ves d.	0905	|	...	1105	1208	...	1215	1305	...	1505	1530	|	...	1605	|	1634	1705	1808	1905	2120	2219	2305	2305	0029	0042
Poprad-Tatry d.	0925	1036	...	1125	1227	...	1238	1325	...	1525	1551	1612	...	1623	1636	1654	1725	1827	1925	2159	2241	2325	2325	0048	0102
Štrba d.	0942	|	...	1140	1242	...	|	1342	...	1542	1608	1626	...	...	|	1709	1740	1842	1942	|	2257	2342	2342	0101	|
Liptovský Mikuláš d.	1010	|	...	1208	1309	...	1319	1410	...	1610	1637	1652	...	...	|	1737	1808	1909	2010	2242	2326	0010	0010	0129	0144
Ružomberok d.	1028	|	...	1226	1327	...	1337	1428	...	1628	1655	1710	...	...	|	1757	1826	1927	2028	2301	2345	0028	0028	0146	0203
Kraľovany d.	1045	|	...	1243	|	...	|	1445	...	1645	1712	|	...	...	|	1814	1843	|	2045	2318	|	0045	0045	|	0219
Vrútky ▷ d.	1059	|	...	1257	1353	...	|	1459	...	1659	1726	|	...	...	|	1828	1857	1953	2059	2334	0016	0059	0059	0212	0233
Žilina ▷ a.	1115	1210	...	1313	1410	...	1418	1515	...	1715	1742	1751	...	...	1810	1844	1913	2010	2115	2350	0032	0115	0115	0228	0249
Žilina ▷ d.	1119	1212	...	1319	1412	1419	1420	1519	1615	1719	1748	1753	...	...	1812	1848	1919	2012	2119	0012	0042	0134	0519	0230	0307
Praha hl. **1160** a.	|	|	...	|	|	|	1922	|	|	|	|	2224	...	...	|	|	|	|	|	0633	0558	0722	|	0719	|
Považská Bystrica ▷ d.	1154	|	...	1354	|	1454	...	1554	1652	1754	1822	...	...	...	|	|	1954	|	2156	...	...	...	0554	...	0342
Púchov ▷ d.	1209	|	...	1409	|	1509	...	1609	1707	1809	1836	...	...	...	|	|	2009	|	2210	...	...	...	0609	...	0401
Trenčianska Teplá d.	1227	|	1334	1427	|	1527	...	1627	1733	1827	1853	...	1934	...	|	|	2027	|	2234	...	...	...	0627	...	0419
Trenčín d.	1235	|	1343	1435	1519	1535	...	1635	1741	1835	1901	...	1943	...	|	1959	2035	2118	2241	...	...	...	0635	...	0427
Nové Mesto n. Váhom d.	1254	|	1401	1454	|	1554	...	1654	1803	1854	1933	...	2001	...	|	|	2054	|	2301	...	...	...	0654	...	0446
Piešťany d.	1307	|	1414	1507	|	1607	...	1707	1816	1907	1947	...	2014	...	|	|	2107	|	2313	...	...	...	0707	...	0459
Leopoldov ▷ d.	1320	|	1424	1520	|	1620	...	1720	1829	1920	2000	...	2024	...	|	|	2120	|	2326	...	...	...	0720	...	0512
Trnava ▷ d.	1334	1350	...	1534	1601	1634	...	1734	1844	1934	2015	...	...	...	1950	2047	2134	2201	2339	...	...	...	0734	...	0527
Bratislava hlavná ▷ a.	1405	1413	...	1605	1627	1705	...	1805	1918	2005	2045	...	...	...	2013	2119	2205	2227	0013	...	...	...	0805	...	0611

♦ – **NOTES** (LISTED BY TRAIN NUMBERS)

442/3 – BOHEMIA – 🛏 1, 2 cl., ▬ 2 cl., [2] Praha - Žilina - Košice - Humenné and v.v.; 🛏 1, 2 cl. Cheb (**767/4**) - Plzeň - Praha (**443/2**) - Žilina - Košice - Humenné and v.v.; 🛏 1, 2 cl. Praha - Košice - Čierna nad Tisou - Čop - Lviv - Kyïv and v.v. (Table **96**).

444/5 – SLOVAKIA – 🛏 1, 2 cl., ▬ 2 cl., [2] Praha - Bohumín - Žilina - Košice and v.v.; 🛏 1, 2 cl. Cheb (**615/4**) - Karlovy Vary - Praha (**445/4**) - Košice and v.v.; 🛏 1, 2 cl. Wien (**406/7**) - Bohumín (**445/4**) - Košice and v.v. Not Dec. 24, 31.

614/5 – ZEMPLÍN – 🛏 1, 2 cl., ▬ 2 cl., [2] Bratislava - Humenné and v.v. Not Dec. 24, 31.

E – Terminates at Žilina (train **16613**) on ⑥, also Dec. 25, Jan. 6, Apr. 14, 16, 30, May 7, Sept. 1, 15, Nov. 17.

F – Ⓐ to Trenčin, ⑤ to Žilina (also Apr. 13, July 4, Aug. 28, 31, Sept. 14, Oct. 31, Nov. 16; not Dec. 30, Jan. 6, Apr. 14, Sept. 1, 15, Nov. 17). Also runs Bratislava - Žilina (train **17715**) on ⑦**g**.

G – ①②③④⑦ (also ⑤ July 7 - Aug. 25); not Dec. 23 - Jan. 7, Apr. 13, 16, 30, May 7, Aug. 31, Sept. 14, Oct. 31, Nov. 16.

H – ①–④ (not Dec. 23 - Jan. 8, Apr. 13, 17, May 1, 8, July 5, Aug. 29, 31, Sept. 14, Oct. 31, Nov. 1, 16).

N – ①④⑤⑥⑦ (not Dec. 25, Jan. 1).

P – [12] Praha (**1359/50**) - Prešov (**1361/48**) - Košice and v.v.

R – 🛏 1, 2 cl. Bratislava (**717**) - Žilina (**445**) - Košice. Not Dec. 24, 31.

S – 🛏 1, 2 cl. Košice (**442**) - Žilina (**704**) - Bratislava. Not Dec. 24, 31.

T – ⑥ to Apr. 1; daily from Apr. 2.

U – ⑥⑦ from Apr. 8 (also Apr. 14, 17, May 1, 8, July 5, 6, Sept. 28, Nov. 17; not Apr. 15, 16, 30, May 7, Sept. 30, Nov. 18).

V – For days of running see Table **1157**.

W – ⑤ to Mar. 31; daily from Apr. 1.

Y – Daily to Trenčin; ⑦**u** to Bratislava.

b – ①–⑥ (not Dec. 26, Jan. 7, Apr. 15, 17, May 1, 8, Sept. 2, 16, Nov. 18).

c – Also Apr. 17, May 1, 8, July 5, Aug. 29, Nov. 1; not Jan. 1, Apr. 16, 30, May 7.

d – ①–⑥ (not Dec. 26, Apr. 15, 17, May 1, 8).

e – Also May 1, 8; not Dec. 25, Jan. 1, Apr. 16.

f – Also Apr. 13, Aug. 31, Sept. 14, Oct. 31, Nov. 16; not Dec. 30, Jan. 6, Apr. 14, Sept. 1, 15, Nov. 17.

g – Also Apr. 17, May 1, 8, Nov. 1; not Jan. 1, Apr. 16, 30, May 7, July 9 - Aug. 27.

h – Not Jan. 6, Apr. 14, 16, 30, May 7, Sept. 1, 15, Nov. 17.

k – Also Apr. 13, Aug. 31, Sept. 14, Oct. 31, Nov. 16; not Dec. 30, Jan. 6, Apr. 14, July 7 - Aug. 25, Sept. 1, 15, Nov. 17.

n – Also Apr. 13, July 4, Sept. 27, Nov. 16; not Dec. 30, Apr. 14, July 7, Sept. 29, Nov. 17.

r – Calls after Prešov (before Prešov towards Praha).

s – Also Apr. 17, May 1, 8; not Dec. 25, Apr. 16, 30, May 7.

t – Also ⚒**b** from Trenčin.

u – Also Apr. 17, May 1, 8, Nov. 1; not Dec. 25, Jan. 1, Apr. 16, 30, May 7.

v – Not Dec. 25, 26, Jan. 1, Apr. 15 - 17.

w – Not Dec. 24, 25, 31, Apr. 14 - 16.

z – Not Dec. 24 - Jan. 8.

△ – [2] Nitra - Praha and v.v. (Table **1157**).

▷ – For other trains see Table **1177** Bratislava - Leopoldov, **1160** Puchov - Žilina, **1185** Žilina - Vrútky, **1196** Kysak - Košice.

⊖ – 🅁 for international journeys.

• – *SUPERCITY PENDOLINO*, 🅁, supplement payable.

♥ – Operated by REGIOJET. Separate fares.

♠ – Operated by LEO Express. Separate fares.

♣ – Operated by ARRIVA. 🍷. Separate fares.

≋ – 🛏 (1,2,3 berth), ▬ (6 berth), [12].

‡ – Train number **17614** on ⑤⑥ (Bratislava arrive 0605).

* – Arrive 0703.

LOCAL LINES IN POPRAD TATRY AREA — 1182

2nd class

km																									
														Ⓐz			⑦e	Ⓐz	Ⓐz			Ⓐz			
0	**Poprad Tatry** d.	0402	...	0546	...	0646	...	0846	...	1046	...	1246	...	1346	1446	...	...	1546	...	1646	...	1746	1846	...	2200
8	Studený Potok a.	0414	0423	0558	0602	0658	0702	0858	0904	1058	1104	1258	1304	1358	1458	1504	...	1558	1604	1658	1704	1758	1858	1904	2212
17	**Tatranská Lomnica** a.	|	0434	|	0613	|	0713	|	0915	|	1115	|	1315	|	|	1515	...	|	1615	|	1715	|	|	1915	|
14	Kežmarok a.	0448	...	0618	...	0712	...	0914	...	1114	...	1314	...	1412	1514	...	...	1612	...	1714	...	1812	1914	...	2224
44	**Stará Lubovňa** a.	0533	...	0703a	...	...	...	0957	...	1157z	...	1357	...	...	1600	...	1705	...	...	1757	...	...	1957r	...	2307
60	Plaveč a.	...	...	...	...	...	...	...	...	...	...	...	...	...	1619f	...	1724	...	...	...	...	...	...	...	...

												Ⓐz			Ⓐz	⑦e				Ⓐz	⑤f				
Plaveč d.	...	...	...	...	...	...	...	...	...	...	...	...	...	...	...	...	...	...	...	...	1635	...	1740e	...	...
Stará Lubovňa d.	...	...	0458	...	0558a	...	0803	...	1003	...	1203z	...	...	1403	...	1453	...	...	1603	...	1653	...	1803	...	2203r
Kežmarok d.	...	0446	0550	...	0650	...	0850	...	1050	...	1250	1350	...	1450	...	1550	1550	...	1650	1750	...	...	1850	...	2254
Tatranská Lomnica d.	0439	|	|	0643	|	0843	|	1043	|	1243	|	|	1443	|	1543	|	|	1643	|	|	...	1843	|	2158	|
Studený Potok d.	0452	0457	0601	0656	0701	0856	0901	1056	1101	1256	1301	1401	1456	1501	1556	1601	1601	1656	1701	1801	...	1856	1901	2214	2305
Poprad Tatry a.	...	0510	0614	...	0714	...	0914	...	1114	...	1314	1414	...	1514	...	1614	1614	...	1714	1814	...	...	1914	2227	2318

Poprad Tatry - Starý Smokovec (24 mins, *13* km, narrow gauge): 0504, 0604, 0629Ⓐ, 0729 **k**, 0829, 0929, 1004 **N**, 1029, 1129 **N**, 1229, 1329, 1429, 1504, 1529, 1629, 1729, 1829, 1929, 2029 **S**, 2129, 2240. Most continue to Štrbské Pleso (see below).

Starý Smokovec - Štrbské Pleso (41 mins, *16* km, narrow gauge): 0531, 0631, 0701Ⓐ, 0801 **d**, 0901, 1001, 1031 **N**, 1101, 1201 **N**, 1301, 1401, 1501, 1531, 1601, 1701, 1801, 1901, 2001, 2101 **S**, 2201, 2308. Most start from Poprad Tatry (see above).

Starý Smokovec - Tatranská Lomnica (14 mins, *6* km, narrow gauge): 0416, 0556, 0656, 0802 **k**, 0902, 1002, 1102, 1202 **N**, 1302 and hourly to 2202 (1902 is **d**).

Štrbské Pleso - Štrba (18 mins, *5* km, rack): 0520, 0620, 0720, 0814, 0914, 1014, 1114, 1214, 1254, 1344, 1444, 1544, 1644, 1744, 1844, 1944, 2244.

Starý Smokovec - Poprad Tatry (23 mins, *13* km, narrow gauge): 0437, 0555, 0655, 0735Ⓐ, 0755, 0855, 0955, 1055, 1155 **N**, 1255, 1355, 1455, 1555, 1635 **N**, 1655, 1755, 1855 **k**, 1955, 2055, 2155, 2306. Most start from Štrbské Pleso (see below).

Štrbské Pleso - Starý Smokovec (39 mins, *16* km, narrow gauge): 0513, 0613, 0643Ⓐ, 0715, 0813, 0913, 1013, 1113 **N**, 1213, 1313, 1413, 1513, 1543 **N**, 1613, 1713, 1813 **d**, 1913, 2013, 2113, 2213. Most continue to Poprad Tatry (see above).

Tatranská Lomnica - Starý Smokovec (14 mins, *6* km, narrow gauge): 0514, 0614, 0716 **b**, 0834, 0934, 1034, 1134 **N**, 1234, 1334, 1434, 1534, 1634, 1734, 1824 **k**, 1934, 2034, 2134, 2234.

Štrba - Štrbské Pleso (15 mins, *5* km, rack): 0456, 0556, 0659, 0746, 0836, 0946, 1036, 1146, 1236, 1326, 1426, 1516, 1626, 1716, 1826, 1926, 2026.

N – Dec. 11 - Apr. 18, May 15 - Sept. 24.
S – May 15 - Sept. 24.
a – Ⓐ only.
b – 0734 on Ⓒ (daily Dec. 24 - Jan. 8, July 1 - Sept. 3).
d – Štrbské Pleso - Starý Smokovec - Tatranská Lomnica and v.v.
e – ⑦ (also Apr. 18, May 1, 8, Nov. 1; not Dec. 25, Jan. 1, Mar. 5, Apr. 16, 30, May 7, July 2 - Aug. 27, Oct. 29).
f – ⑤ (also Dec. 22, Feb. 2, Apr. 12, Sept. 14, Nov. 16; not Dec. 23 - Jan. 6, Feb. 3, Mar. 10, Apr. 14, July 7 - Sept. 1, Sept. 15, Nov. 17).
k – Tatranská Lomnica - Starý Smokovec - Poprad Tatry and v.v.
r – Ⓑ (not holidays).
z – Ⓐ (not Dec. 24 - Jan. 8).

POPRAD TATRY - ZAKOPANE — 1183

STRAMA 🚌 No winter service

	S	S	S	S	V	V
Poprad Tatry (Bus Stn stand 4) d.	0850	1150	1650	1750	1150	1650
Starý Smokovec (Bus Station) d.	0910	1210	1710	1810	1210	1710
Tatranská Lomnica (Bus Stn) d.	0924	1224	1724	1824	1224	1724
Zakopane (Bus Station) a.	1033	1333	1833	1933	1333	1833
Zakopane (ul Balzera Nosal) a.	...	1339	1839	1939	1339	1839

	S	S	S	S	V	V
Zakopane (ul Balzera Nosal) d.	0600	0900	...	1600	0900	1500
Zakopane (Bus Stn stand 3) d.	0615	0915	1115	1615	0915	1515
Tatranská Lomnica (Bus Stn) d.	0727	1027	1227	1727	1027	1627
Starý Smokovec (Bus Station) d.	0737	1037	1237	1737	1037	1637
Poprad Tatry (Bus Station) a.	0753	1053	1253	1753	1053	1653

S – June 17 - Sept. 30, 2016.
V – Oct. 1 - 16, 2016.
Rail tickets not valid.
🏛 = Lysa Polana. Bus stations at Poprad Tatry and Zakopane are adjacent to railway station.

ŽILINA - VRÚTKY - MARTIN - BANSKÁ BYSTRICA and ZVOLEN — 1185

2nd class ♣

km																										
		941	941		943		945		341		949		951				953			345			347		1011	
		s	P		Ⓐu	Ⓐu									Ⓐ	Ⓐz			Ⓐz			⚒		R	♥	n
	Praha hl. **1160** d.	...	2200	...	...	...	...	...	...	...	...	...	...	...	...	...	...	...	...	...	...	...	...	...	1444	...
	Ostrava Svinov **1160** d.	...	|	...	...	...	...	...	0643	...	...	...	...	...	...	...	...	...	...	1443	...	...	1643	...	1757	...
0	**Žilina** 1180 d.	0454	0454	...	0554	*0627*	0654	...	0854	...	1054	...	1254	...	*1334*	*1428*	1454	...	*1555*	1654	...	*1727*	1854	...	1939	...
21	Vrútky 1180 a.	0511	0511	...	0611	*0647*	0711	...	0911	...	1111	...	1311	...	*1353*	*1447*	1511	...	*1615*	1711	...	*1746*	1911	...	1955	...
21	Vrútky d.	0513	0513	0520	0620	0650	0713	0720	0913	0920	1113	1120	1313	1320	1420	1450	1513	1520	1620	1713	1720	1820	1913	1920	1957	2120
28	**Martin** d.	0520	0520	0528	0627	0658	0720	0728	0920	0928	1120	1128	1320	1328	1428	1458	1520	1528	1628	1720	1728	1828	1920	1928	2019	2128
51	Turčianske Teplice d.	0538	0538	0558	0645	0728	0738	0758	0938	0958	1138	1158	1338	1358	1458	1528	1538	1558	1658	1738	1758	1858	1938	1958	2037	2158
97	**Banská Bystrica** a.	0626	0626	|	0729	|	0826	|	1026	|	1226	|	1426	|	|	|	1626	|	|	1826	|	|	2026	|	2121	|
60	Horná Štubňa d.	...	|	0610	...	0738	...	0808	...	1008	...	1210	...	1417	1508	1538	...	1610	1708	...	1808	1908	|	2015	|	2208
80	Kremnica d.	...	|	0636	...	...	...	...	...	...	...	1236	...	◇	...	...	...	1636	...	...	...	...	|	2041	|	...
106	Hronská Dúbrava d.	...	|	0709	...	...	...	...	...	...	...	1309	...	...	...	...	...	1709	...	...	...	...	|	2114	|	...
117	**Zvolen osob.** a.	...	0821r	0718	...	...	...	...	...	...	...	1318	...	...	...	...	...	1718	...	...	...	...	2053	2123	2150	...

				1008	346			942		344		946			342		950		952			340	956	956		
		Ⓐ	Ⓒ	♥		Ⓐz		k					Ⓐ			Ⓐ	Ⓐu			Ⓐz				Q		
Zvolen osob. d.	...	0425	...	0427	0502	...	0619	...	...	...	...	...	...	...	...	...	...	1425	...	1525	...	...	...	...	1904	...
Hronská Dúbrava d.	...	0435	...	|	|	...	0629	...	...	...	...	...	...	...	...	...	...	1435	...	1535	...	...	...	...	1914	...
Kremnica d.	...	0515	...	|	|	...	0708	...	◇	...	...	...	...	...	...	...	...	1509	...	1609	...	...	...	...	1948	...
Horná Štubňa d.	0452	0547	0547	|	|	0652	0752	...	0952	...	1152	...	1252	1352	...	1452	...	1552	...	1652	1752	...	...	...	2020	...
Banská Bystrica d.	|	|	|	0516	0534	|	|	0734	|	0934	|	1134	|	|	1334	|	1434	|	1534	|	|	1734	1934	1934	|	...
Turčianske Teplice d.	0502	0557	0557	0606	0621	0702	0802	0821	1002	1021	1202	1221	1302	1402	1421	1502	1521	1602	1621	1702	1802	1821	2021	2021	2030	...
Martin d.	0532	0632	0632	0637	0640	0732	0832	0840	1032	1040	1232	1240	1332	1432	1440	1532	1540	1632	1640	1732	1832	1840	2040	2040	2100	...
Vrútky a.	0540	0640	0640	0644	0647	0740	0840	0847	1040	1047	1240	1247	1340	1440	1447	1540	1547	1640	1647	1740	1840	1847	2047	2047	2108	...
Vrútky 1180 d.	*0546*a	...	...	0645	0649	*0746*	...	0849	...	1049	...	1249	...	...	1449	...	1549	...	1649	*1805*	...	1849	2049	2049	*2113*	...
Žilina 1180 a.	*0605*a	...	...	0701	0706	*0805*	...	0906	...	1106	...	1306	...	...	1506	...	1606	...	1706	*1825*	...	1906	2106	2106	*2132*	...
Ostrava Svinov **1160** a.	...	...	...	0857	0917	...	...	...	...	1317	...	...	...	...	1717	...	...	...	...	...	...	2117	...	|	...	...
Praha hl. **1160** a.	...	...	...	1212	...	...	...	...	...	...	...	...	...	...	...	...	...	...	...	...	...	...	...	0633	...	...

km											
							◇				
0	Horná Štubňa d.	0417	0617	0817	1017	1217	1417	1617	1817	2017	...
18	Handlová d.	0440	0640	0840	1040	1240	1440	1640	1840	2040	...
37	Prievidza a.	0511	0711	0911	1111	1311	1511	1711	1911	2111	...

			◇							
Prievidza d.	0438	0641	0841	1041	1241	1441	1641	1841	2141	...
Handlová d.	0521	0717	0917	1117	1317	1517	1717	1917	2221	...
Horná Štubňa a.	0544	0741	0941	1141	1341	1541	1741	1941	2244	...

P – ④⑤⑥ (also Apr. 13 - 16, 30, May 7, July 4, 5, Sept. 27; not Dec. 25, Jan. 5). 🛏 1, 2 cl. Praha (**445**) - Žilina (**941**) - Banská Bystrica (**7311** or **7313**) - Zvolen.
Q – ⑤⑥⑦ (also Dec. 26, Apr. 17, May 1, 8, July 5, 6, Sept. 28; not Dec. 24, 25, 31, Jan. 6). 🛏 1, 2 cl. Banská Bystrica - Žilina (**444**) - Praha.
R – ⑤⑦ (daily to Horná Štubňa).
a – Ⓐ only.
k – Not Dec. 25, 26, Jan. 6.
n – Runs one hour later on ⚒.
r – 0850 on ⑥⑦.
s – Not Dec. 25, 26, Jan. 6.
u – Not Dec. 24 - Jan. 8, July 1 - Sept. 3.
z – Not Dec. 24 - Jan. 8.
◇ – 🚌 Vrutky - Horná Štubňa - Prievidza and v.v.
♥ – Operated by RegioJet, 🍸.
♣ – Trains showing a train number also have 1st class.

NOVÉ ZAMKY - NITRA - TOPOL'ČANY — 1187

2nd class

km																									
												Ⓐ			Ⓐ					Ⓐ	Ⓒ				
0	**Nové Zamky** d.	...	0427	0520	0629	0726	0920	1120	1250	1320	1413	1423	1450	1520	1620	1650	1720	1820	1853	1920	1920	2052	...	2242	...
10	Šurany a.	...	0440	0532	0640	0736	0932	1132	1305	1334	1424	1436	1505	1531	1634	1705	1734	1834	1905	1934	1934	2103	...	2253	...
10	Šurany d.	...	0443	0537	0641	0741	0935	1135	...	1335	...	1437	...	1535	1635	...	1735	1835	...	1935	1935	2114	...	2254	...
36	**Nitra** a.	...	0516	0616	0719	0813	1007	1207	...	1407	...	1512	...	1607	1716	...	1807	1916	...	2007	2007	2147	...	2331	...
36	**Nitra** d.	0423	0547	0638	0744	0817	1017	1217	...	1417	...	1515	...	1617	1742	...	1817	...	...	2017	...	...	2240	...	...
40	Lužianky d.	0436	0601	0648	0754	0828	1028	1228	...	1428	...	1529	...	1628	1752	...	1830	...	...	2028	...	...	2253	...	...
69	**Topoľčany** a.	0512	0647	0730	◇	0904	1104	1304	...	1504	...	1613	...	1704	...	...	1904	...	...	2105	...	...	2329	...	...
	Prievidza **1177** a.	...	0806	...	...	1036	1216	1417	...	1625	...	...	...	1835	...	...	...	...	...	...	...	...	...	...	...

			Ⓐ						Ⓐ			Ⓐ			Ⓐ	Ⓐ						Ⓒ	Ⓐ		
Prievidza **1177** d.	...	0414a	0520	...	0623	0717a	0928	...	...	1115	...	...	1328	...	1425	...	1525	...	...	...	1728r	...	...	...	...
Topoľčany d.	0425	0521	0626	◇	0737	0844	1044	◇	...	1244	◇	...	1444	◇	1526	...	1644	◇	...	◇	1844	...	...	2044	...
Lužianky d.	0515	0600	0704	0720	0831	0925	1129	1129	1239	1328	1328	1438	1529	1529	1601	1639	1728	1728	...	1839	1929	...	...	2131	...
Nitra a.	0525	0610	0715	0730	0841	0935	1139	1139	1249	1338	1338	1448	1539	1539	1612	1649	1738	1738	...	1849	1939	...	...	2143	...
Nitra d.	0528	0631	—	0750	—	0945	...	1145	1253	...	1345	1450	1545	1545	—	1653	...	1745	...	1853	...	2034	2058	...	2243
Šurany a.	0558	0701	Ⓐ	0828	...	1023	...	1223	1323	...	1423	1528	1623	1623	...	1723	...	1823	...	1923	...	2104	2134	...	2315
Šurany d.	0604	0711	0746	0828	0855	1024	...	1224	1324	...	1426	1533	1624	1624	1655	1724	...	1824	1855	1924	...	2111	2134	...	2316
Nové Zamky a.	0615	0721	0757	0840	0907	1036	...	1236	1336	...	1440	1545	1636	1636	1707	1736	...	1836	1909	1936	...	2123	2146	...	2328

a – Ⓐ only.
r – ⑦ (also Apr. 17, May 1, 8, Nov. 1; not Dec. 25, Jan. 1, Apr. 16, 30, May 7).
◇ – To/from Leopoldov (Table **1177**).

1190 ZVOLEN - LUČENEC - KOŠICE

2nd class (also 1st in 930 - 937)

km		931			933		935	17935		937		801
		R				n		⑦e				ⒷP
	Bratislava hl. 1170 d.	...	...	...	...	...	...	...	...	...	...	2349
0	**Zvolen** osob. d.	0713	0723	0923	1113	1323	1513	1713	1723	1913	2223	0316
54	Lučenec d.	0801	0835	1035	1201	1435	1601	1801	1835	2001	2335	0407
69	Fil'akovo d.	0814	0853	1053	1214	1453	1614	1814	1853	2014	2353	0421
98	Jesenské d.	0841	...	...	1241	...	1641	1841	...	2041	...	0449
162	Rožňava d.	0939	...	...	1339	...	1737	1939	...	2139	...	0546
202	Moldava nad Bodvou d.	1012	...	...	1412	...	1810	2012	...	2212	...	0621
233	**Košice** a.	1037	...	...	1437	...	1837	2037	...	2237	...	0648
	Prešov 1196 a.	...	...	...	...	...	...	...	...	...	...	0739

		930		932		934		936			800
											ⒷP
Prešov 1196 d.	...	...	...	...	...	...	...	...	...	...	2127
Košice d.	...	0523	...	0923	...	1323	...	1523	...	...	2220
Moldava nad Bodvou d.	...	0550	...	0948	...	1348	...	1548	...	...	2247
Rožňava d.	...	0623	...	1020	...	1420	...	1619	...	...	2325
Jesenské d.	...	0720	...	1120	...	1520	...	1720	...	...	0018
Fil'akovo d.	0700	0746	0910	1146	1310	1546	1710	1746	2016	...	0046
Lučenec d.	0729	0801	0929	1201	1329	1601	1729	1801	2033	2235	0059
Zvolen osob a.	0840	0849	1040	1249	1440	1649	1840	1849	...	2346	0155
Bratislava hl. 1170 a.	...	...	...	...	...	...	...	...	...	...	0525

km												
0	Fil'akovo d.	0600	...	...	0855	1055	...	1455	...	1655	1855	...
29	Jesenské d.	0644	0725	0844	0944	1144	1244	1544	1644	1744	1940	2044
40	Rimavská Sobota a.	0658	0739	0858	0958	1158	1258	1558	1658	1758	1954	2058

				Ⓐz							
Rimavská Sobota d.	0600	0700	0817	1017	1101	1217	1417	1501	1617	1701	1917
Jesenské a.	0614	0714	0831	1031	1115	1231	1431	1515	1631	1715	1931
Fil'akovo a.	0649	...	0908	1108	...	1308	1508	...	1708	...	2008

P – POL'ANA – Ⓑ (not Dec. 25, Jan. 6, Apr. 14, 16, 30, May 7, Sept. 1, 15, Nov. 17). 🛏 1, 2 cl., (2) Bratislava - Prešov and v.v.; 🛏 1, 2 cl. Brno (**283/2**) - Bratislava (**801/0**) - Košice - Prešov and v.v. Conveys on dates in Table **96** 🛏 1, 2 cl. Bratislava - Košice - Chop - Lviv - Kyïv and v.v.

R – ①–⑥ (daily July 2 - Aug. 27), also Dec. 25, Jan. 1, Apr. 16, 30, May 7; not Apr. 17, May 1, 8, Nov. 1.

e – Also Apr. 17, May 1, 8, Nov. 1; not Dec. 25, Jan. 1, Apr. 16, 30, May 7, July 2 - Aug. 27.

n – Change at Lučenec on Ⓒ.

z – Not Dec. 24 - Jan. 8.

1192 BANSKÁ BYSTRICA - BREZNO - MARGECANY - (KOŠICE)

2nd class

km		1781	1785				1783				
		Ⓐ	Ⓒ						Ⓐz		
0	**Banská Bystrica** ▷ d.	0536	0739	0836	1036	1236	1330	1436	...	1635	1746
43	Brezno ▷ d.	0626	0834	0935	1136	1336	1419	1541	1606	1739	1849
86	Červená Skala d.	0721	0938	▬	▬	▬	1514	...	1723	...	▬
106	Dobšinká L'adová Jas. d.	0744	1000	...	...	...	1536	...	▬	...	1935
114	Dedinky d.	0754	1010	...	...	...	1546	...	...	...	1945
139	Nálepkovo d.	0831	1036	1039r	1239	1424	1621	...	1837	...	2017
171	Gelnica d.	0905	1108	1141	1341	1521	1654	...	1930	...	2109
179	**Margecany** a.	0914	1117	1152	1352	1532	1703	...	1941	...	2120
	Margecany 1185 d.	*0924*	*1124*	...	...	...	*1724*	...	...	...	...
	Košice 1185 a.	*0952*	*1152*	...	...	...	*1752*	...	...	...	...

		1780					1782			
	Ⓐ		Ⓒ							
Košice 1185 d.	...	*0608*	...	...	...	...	*1408*	...	...	...
Margecany 1185 a.	...	*0636*	...	...	...	...	*1436*	...	...	...
Margecany d.	...	0646	0808	1008	1208	1408	1446	1608	1808	2008
Gelnica d.	...	0656	0820	1020	1220	1427	1456	1620	1820	2019
Nálepkovo d.	...	0729	0903	1115	1305	1509	1529	1716	1903	2103
Dedinky d.	...	0806	▬	▬	▬	▬	1603	1753	▬	2137
Dobšinká L'adová Jas. d.	...	0816	...	...	...	...	1614	1803	...	2147
Červená Skala d.	...	0837	...	...	...	Ⓑ	1637	...	...	...
Brezno ▽ d.	0820	0940	1020	1220	1421	1514	1740	...	2022	...
Banská Bystrica ▽ a.	0924	1030	1124	1324	1524	1613	1830	...	2121	...

r – 1046 on Ⓒ.

z – Not Dec. 24 - Jan. 8.

▷ – Also at 0618, 1544Ⓐz, 1854, 1946Ⓐz, 2031, 2230.

▽ – Also at 0557, 0726, 0804Ⓒ, 1626⚒, 1821, 2215.

1194 KOŠICE - HUMENNÉ - MEDZILABORCE

2nd class

km		615	443	1901	1903	1905	1907	1909	1911	1913	1915
		H	B		Ⓐ		Ⓐz				△
	Bratislava hl 1180 d.	2345	...	...	...	...	...	...	...	...	...
0	**Košice** d.	0608	0901	1101	1301	1501	1537	1701	1901	2101	2252
68	Trebišov d.	0657	0947	1150	1350	1550	1630	1750	1950	2150	2341
88	Michalovce d.	0723	1011	1211	1411	1611	1651	1811	2011	2218	0002
112	**Humenné** a.	0750	1033	1233	1433	1633	1713	1833	2033	2240	0024

	1900	1902	1904	1906	1908	1910	1912	1914	442	614
	Ⓐ			Ⓐ		P			B	H
Humenné d.	0333	0528	0728	0928	1128	1328	1528	1728	1946	2154
Michalovce d.	0356	0551	0751	0951	1151	1351	1551	1751	2012	2216
Trebišov d.	0418	0613	0813	1013	1213	1413	1613	1813	2041	2238
Košice a.	0504	0659	0859	1059	1259	1459	1659	1859	2128	2325
Bratislava hl 1180 a.	...	...	...	...	...	...	...	...	...	0611

km					Ⓐ	Ⓐ		Ⓐ			Ⓐ
0	Humenné d.	0637	0837	1037	1237	1329	1437	1529	1637	1837	2037
41	Medzilaborce a.	0746	0946	1146	1346	1423	1546	1623	1746	1946	2146
43	Medzilaborce mesto a.	0756a	0956	1156	1356	...	1556	...	1756	1956	...

		Ⓐ				P				
Medzilaborce mesto d.	0418	...	0618	0818a	1018	1223	1417	1617	1818	2018
Medzilaborce d.	0427	0504	0628	0828	1028	1227	1428	1628	1828	2028
Humenné a.	0524	0558	0724	0924	1124	1324	1524	1724	1924	2124

B – BOHEMIA – 🛏 1, 2 cl., 🛌 2 cl., (2) Praha - Košice - Humenné and v.v.

H – ZEMPLÍN – 🛏 1, 2 cl., 🛌 2 cl., (2) Bratislava - Košice - Humenné and v.v. Not Dec. 24, 31.

P – Runs 5 minutes earlier on ⑦ (also Apr. 17, May 1, 8, Nov. 1; not Dec. 25, Jan. 1, Apr. 16, 30, May 7).

a – Ⓐ only.

z – Not Dec. 24 - Jan. 8.

△ – Runs 9 minutes later on certain dates (mostly ⑤).

1195 KOŠICE - ČIERNA NAD TISOU - CHOP

2nd class

km					8807				1965			
				⚒	K			Ⓐ		Ⓐ		△
0	**Košice** d.	0506	0706	0806	1006	1206	1416	1516	1631	1716	1906	2036
62	Slovenské N. Mesto d.	0614	0814	0914	1114	1314	1520	1622	1723	1821	2014	2142
95	**Čierna nad Tisou** a.	0651	0851	0951	1151	1351	1559	1659	1802	1859	2051	2219

		1964								8820	
	▽			Ⓐ			E	Ⓐ		K	
Čierna nad Tisou d.	0505	0556	0705	0805	1005	1205	1405	1505	1605	1805	2005
Slovenské N. Mesto d.	0543	0638	0743	0843	1043	1243	1443	1545	1643	1843	2044
Košice a.	0654	0728	0854	0954	1154	1354	1554	1654	1754	1954	2154

km			K
0	Čierna nad Tisou 🛃 d.	0700	1215
10	Chop 🛃 ⊕ a.	0840	1410

		K
Chop 🛃 ⊕ d.	0943	1735
Čierna nad Tisou 🛃 a.	0947	1740

K – Conveys 🛏 1, 2 cl. Praha (**443/2**) - Košice - Čierna nad Tisou - Chop - Lviv - Kyïv and v.v. (Table **96**). Conveys on dates in Table **96** 🛏 1, 2 cl. Bratislava (**801/0**) - Košice - Čierna nad Tisou - Chop - Lviv - Kyïv and v.v.

⊕ – East European time (one hour ahead).

△ – Additional journey: 2257.

▽ – Also at 0305, 0405.

E – Approx 30 min earlier on ⑦ (also Dec. 26, Apr. 17, 18, May 1, 8, Nov. 1; not Apr. 16).

1196 KOŠICE - PREŠOV - PLAVEČ

2nd class

km			1354			801																				1348
			♠🅁			P			⑥	Ⓑ	Ⓐ	⑦	①–⑥	Ⓐ				Ⓐ			†	⚒	b		n	♠🅁
0	**Košice** 1180 d.	0358	0501	0536	0636	0710	0736	0836	*0927*	0936	1036	*1127*	1136	1236	1336	1436	1536	1636	1736	1836	*1927*	1936	...	*2127*	2213	2306
16	Kysak 1180 d.	0433	0513	0553	0653	0725	0753	0853	0953	0953	1053	1153	1153	1253	1353	1453	1553	1653	1753	1853	1953	1953	2025	2203	2230	2318
33	**Prešov** a.	0455	0528	0615	0715	0741	0815	0915	1015	1015	1115	1215	1215	1315	1415	1515	1615	1715	1815	1915	2015	2015	2040	2229	2252	2333
33	**Prešov** d.	0519	...	0636a	0726a	...	0819	...	1019	1019	...	1219	1219	1319	1419	1519r	1619	1719	1819	1919	2019	2019	...	...	2254	...
65	Lipany a.	0556	...	0713a	0803a	...	0856	...	1056	1056	...	1256	1256	1356	1456	1556r	1656	1756	1856	1956	2056	2056	...	...	2331	...
88	**Plaveč** a.	...	...	...	...	...	...	...	...	...	...	...	...	...	...	1629x	...	...	...	...	...	...	...	...	...	...

		1369																				800		1361	
	⚒	♠🅁			Ⓐ		⑦		⑦e				Ⓐ	Ⓑ	⑥			Ⓐ	⑥	⑦			R		♠🅁	⑦
Plaveč d.	...	...	...	...	...	...	...	...	...	...	...	...	...	...	...	...	...	...	...	...	1730x	...	...	...	...	...
Lipany d.	...	...	0420	0503	0557	0646	...	0903	...	1103	1203a	1303	...	1403	...	1503	1603a	1703	...	1703	1803	...	...	2029	...	...
Prešov a.	...	...	0457	0540	0634	0724	...	0940	...	1140	1240a	1340	...	1440	...	1540	1640a	1740	...	1740	1840	...	...	2107	...	...
Prešov d.	0341	0404	0458	0542	0642	0742	0918	0942	1111	1142	1242	1342	1418	1442	1442	1542	1642	1742	1742	1742	1842	1953	2127	2136	2211	2333
Kysak 1180 a.	0404	0419	0524	0606	0706	0806	0933	1006	1133	1206	1306	1406	1440	1506	1506	1606	1706	1806	1806	1806	1906	2018	2142	2202	2225	2348
Košice 1180 a.	*0441*	0432	0541	0624	0724	0824	...	1024	...	1224	1324	1432	1457	1524	1524	1624	1724	1824	*1832*	*1832*	1924	...	2158	2221	2238	...

P – ①–⑥ (not Dec. 26, Jan. 7, Apr. 15, 17, May 1, 8, Sept. 2, 16, Nov. 18). From Bratislava previous day. 🛏 1, 2 cl., (2) Bratislava - Prešov (Table **1190**).

R – Ⓑ (not Dec. 25, Jan. 6, Apr. 14, 16, 30, May 7, Sept. 1, 15, Nov. 17). 🛏 1, 2 cl., (2) Prešov - Bratislava.

a – Ⓐ only.

b – Not Dec. 24, 25, 31, Apr. 14 - 16.

e – Also Apr. 17, May 1, 8; not Dec. 25, Apr. 16, 30, May 7.

n – Runs 18 mins later on ⑤ (also Apr. 13, Aug. 31, Sept. 14, Oct. 31; not Dec. 30, Jan. 6, Apr. 14, Sept. 1, 15).

r – Ⓑ only.

x – ⑤⑦ (also Feb. 2, Apr. 12, 18, May 1, 8, Sept. 14, Nov. 1, 16; not Dec. 23 - Jan. 6, Feb. 3, Mar. 5, 10, Apr. 14 16, 30, May 7, July 2 - Sept. 1, Sept. 15, Oct. 29, Nov. 17).

♠ – Operated by LEO Express, 🅁, 🍸. (12) Praha - Prešov - Kysak - Košice and v.v. (Table **1180**).

1197 PREŠOV - BARDEJOV and HUMENNÉ

2nd class

km		§	Ⓐ	Ⓒ		Ⓐz					§	
0	Prešov d.	0416	0603	0626	0824	1024	1224	1424	1624	1824	2044	...
45	Bardejov a.	0532	0710	0733	0931	1131	1331	1531	1731	1931	2155	...

		Ⓐ	Ⓒ		Ⓐz		⚒			§	u
Bardejov d.	0430	0608	0631	0829	1029	1229	1429	1629	1829	1958	2216
Prešov a.	0535	0713	0736	0934	1134	1334	1534	1734	1934	2110	2326

km						Ⓐz	Ⓐ					⑤b
0	Prešov d.	0416	0610	0844	1044	1244	1344	1444r	1644	1844	2044	2122
70	Humenné a.	0602	0803	1020	1220	1420	1520	1620	1820	2020	2216	2230

		Ⓐ		△				⑦b			
Humenné d.	0350	0440	0540	0728	0940	1140	1335	1406	1540	1740	1934
Prešov a.	0527	0633	0723	0908	1108	1308	1508	1519	1708	1908	2110

b – (12) Bratislava - Prešov - Humenné and v.v. For days of running see Table **1180**.

r – 1434 on ⑦ (also Apr. 17, May 1, 8, Nov. 1; not Dec. 25, Jan. 1, Apr. 16, 30, May 7).

u – Runs 17 - 21 minutes later on certain dates (mostly ⑤).

z – Not Dec. 24 - Jan. 8.

△ – Change at Strážske (a. 0737 / d. 0750).

§ – Change at Kapušany pri Prešove.

HUNGARY

Operator:	MÁV-START (www.mav-start.hu) running on the network of MÁV (www.mav.hu). Certain services in the west are operated by Györ - Sopron - Ebenfurthi Vasút (GySEV).
Services:	All trains convey first and second class seating, **except** where shown otherwise in footnotes or by '2' in the train column, or where the footnote shows sleeping- and / or couchette cars only. Descriptions of sleeping- (🛏) and couchette (🛌) cars appear on page 8. Certain international services, as indicated in the tables, cannot be used for internal journeys in Hungary, whilst others generally convey dedicated carriages for internal journeys, which may be made without reservation.
Timings:	Valid from **December 11, 2016**. Summer services June 17 - August 27 for the Lake Balaton area will be shown in summer editions. Engineering work alterations may affect travel - it is not always possible to show short-term changes in our tables. Many trains are cancelled on the evening of Dec. 24, 31 and on the morning of Dec. 25 and Jan. 1.
Reservations:	Most InterCity (*IC*) and Express (*Ex*) trains have **compulsory** reservation, as shown by ℝ in the tables. *IC* trains also require a supplement; the amount depends on distance of the journey. Passengers having passes which include the supplement (e.g. Eurail) have to pay the reservation fee only. Higher supplements and reservation fees apply at peak times (Friday and Sunday afternoons), and if purchased on day of travel. For **domestic** journeys on **international** *EC*/*IC*/*RJ*/*EN* trains, a supplement is required (and seat reservation is compulsory where shown as ℝ in tables). For **international** journeys on these trains the supplement does not apply but seat reservation is possible (and is **compulsory** where shown in the tables). If a seat reservation or supplement is not paid in advance, an additional supplement of 500 HUF must be paid on the train.

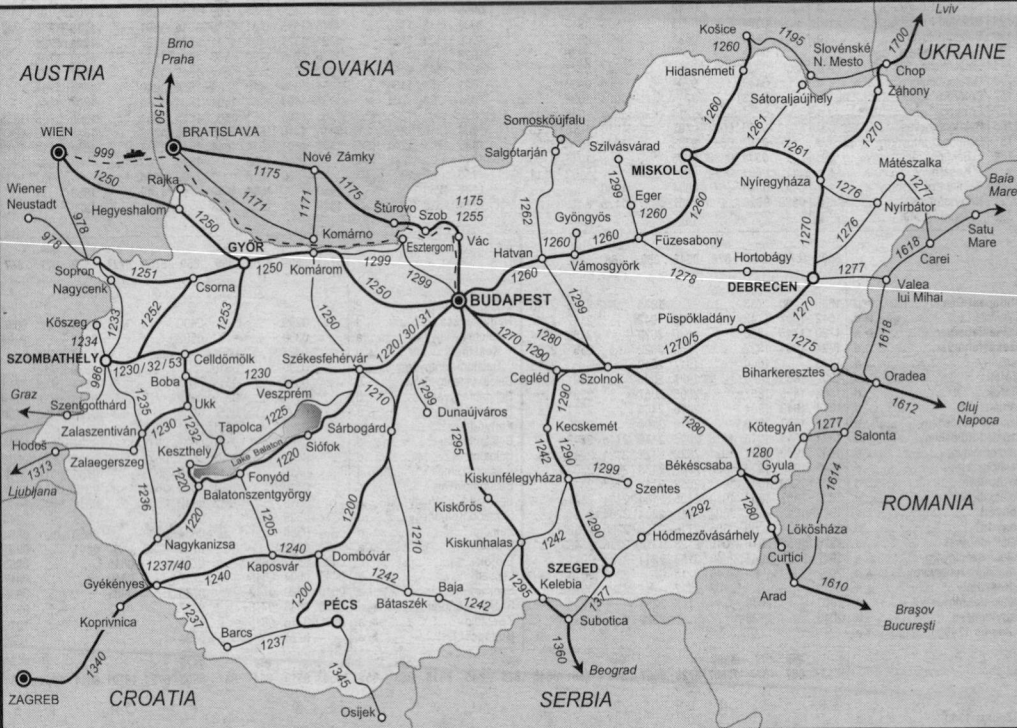

BUDAPEST - DOMBÓVÁR - PÉCS · 1200

km		IC 800 IC 200 ⊘	IC 800		IC 802 ℝ	IC 812 ℝ	IC 804 ℝ		IC 814 ℝ R	IC 204 ℝ	IC 806 ℝ	IC 816 ℝ	IC 828 2 ℝ		IC 808 ℝ	IC 818 ℝ
		JK		2 ◇				2 ◇					n			
0	Budapest Keleti ... d.	0545	0545	...	0745	0945	1145	...	1345	1445	1545	1645	1645	...	1745	1945
	Budapest Déli ... d.							1255						1655		
13	Kelenföld ... d.	0559	0559	0702	0759	0959	1159	1302	1359	1459	1559	1659	1659	1702	1759	1959
93	Sárbogárd ... d.	0659	0659	0826	0859	1059	1259	1426	1459	...	1659	...	1826	1859	1909	2059
173	Dombóvár ... a.	0749	0749	0942	0949	1149	1349	1542	1549	1655	1749	1855	1855	1942	1949	2149
173	Dombóvár ... d.		0753	1005	0953	1153	1353	1603	1553	...	1753	1859	...	2005	1953	2153
218	Szentlörinc ... d.		0826	1046	1026	1226	1426	1646	1646	...	1826	1939	...	2046	2026	2226
237	Pécs ... a.		0840	1102	1040	1240	1440	1702	1640	...	1840	1953	...	2102	2040	2240

		IC 809 ℝ	IC 819 ℝ	IC 829 2 ℝ n	IC 807 ℝ		IC 817 ℝ		IC 805 ℝ	IC 815 ℝ	IC205 ℝ K	IC 803 ℝ	IC 801 ℝ	IC201 ℝ JR	IC 811 ℝ	
						2 ◇		2 ◇							2	2
Pécs ... d.		0514	0602	...	0714	0646	0914	0847	1114	1310	...	1514	1714	...	1910	1845	2047
Szentlörinc ... d.		0528	0616	...	0728	0707	0928	0907	1128	1324	...	1528	1728	...	1924	1903	2107
Dombóvár ... a.		0601	0647	...	0801	0750	1001	0950	1201	1354	...	1601	1801	...	1954	1948	2151
Dombóvár ... d.		0605	0658	0805	0810	1005	1010	1205	1405	1405	1605	1805	2005	2005	2010
Sárbogárd ... d.		0659	...	0859	0927	1059	1127	1259	1459	1459	1659	1859	2059	2059	2127
Budapest Déli ... a.						1104		1304							2304	
Budapest Keleti ... a.		0814	0914	0914	1014		1214		1414	1614	1614	1814	2014	2014	2214	2214

J – Dec. 11 - June 16. (Runs via Fonyód June 17 - Aug. 27, Table 1220).
K – KVARNER – 🛏 and ✕ Budapest - Zagreb - Rijeka and v.v.
R – RIPPL-RÓNAI – 🛏 and ✕ Budapest - Zagreb and v.v.
n – To/from Gyékényes (Table 1240). For other cars see Table 1240.

● – Budapest Déli - Kelenföld : 4 km.
⊖ – ℝ for domestic journeys within Hungary.
◇ – Local trains run in similar pattern every 2 hours.

FONYÓD - PÉCS · 1205

km	2nd class	8807 K		8873 K	8803 P
	Tapolca **1232** ... d.	0830	...	1718	1718
	Keszthely **1220** ... d.	0903	...	1757	1757
0	Fonyód ... ▶ a.	1007	1510	1858	1858
53	Kaposvár ... a.	1135	1646	2018	2018
82	Dombóvár alsó ... a.	...	...	...	2049
92	Szentlörinc ... a.	...	...	...	2125
148	Pécs ... a.	...	...	...	2139

	8872 K	8802 P		8806 c
Pécs ... d.	...	0719	...	...
Szentlörinc ... d.	...	0733	...	...
Dombóvár alsó ... d.	...	0814	...	...
Kaposvár ... ▶ d.	0857	0857	1308	1505	1652
Fonyód ... a.	1008	1008	1448	1645	1832
Keszthely **1220** ... a.	1111	1111	...	...	1936
Tapolca **1232** ... a.	1148	1148	...	...	2006

K – Ⓐ (not Apr. 29 - Sept. 17).
P – Ⓒ (daily Apr. 29 - Sept. 17).
c – From/to Celldömölk or Szombathely (Table 1232).
▶ – **Also:** Fonyód - Kaposvár : 0318🅇, 0524, 0728, 1140, 1310Ⓐ, 1703, 2118. Kaposvár - Fonyód : 0311, 0529, 0724, 1007Ⓐ, 1855, 2244🅇.

Dec. 11 - June 16: by 🚂 Fonyód - Kaposvár and v.v. in timings shown. See also Table 1220.

BUDAPEST - SÁRBOGÁRD - SZEKSZÁRD - BAJA · 1210

2nd class (except *Ex* trains)

km		IR 8300	IR 8302 ✕	IR 8304		IR 8306	Ex 1836 F	IR 18308 ⑥‡	IR 18398 ⑦	Ex 838 ✕	IR 8308	IR 8318
0	Budapest Keleti ▷ d.						1515			1715		
4	Kelenföld ... d.						1529			1729		
84	Sárbogárd ▷ d.	0702	0902	1102	...	1502	1702	1705	...	1902	2102	
149	Szekszárd ... d.	0757	0957	1157	1422	1557	1722	1757	1916	1957	2205	
168	Bátaszék ... a.	0818	1018	1218	1441	1618	1741	1818	1839	1932	2018	2249
184	Baja **1242** ... a.	0838	1038	1239	1503	1639r	1800	1837	1901	1951	2037	2311

		Ex 839 ℝ	IR 8307	IR 8305 ✕	IR 18395 ⑦	IR 18398 ⑥‡	IR 8305 Ⓐ	IR 8313	IR 1833 N	IR 8303	IR 8301	
Baja **1242** ... d.		0557	0701	0913	1312	1450	1515	1514	1601	1712v	1912	
Bátaszék **1242** ... d.		0616	0723	0934	1334	1509	1534	1534	1620	1734v	1934	
Szekszárd ... d.		0636	0759	0959	1357	1535	1559	1620	1637	1759	1959	
Sárbogárd ▷ a.		...	0854	1054	1454	1645	1733	...	...	1854	2054	
Kelenföld ▷ a.		0828							1828			
Budapest Keleti ▷ a.		0844							1844			

F – ⑤ (not Dec. 23, 30, June 16 - Aug. 25).
N – ⑦ (not Dec. 25, Jan. 1, June 18 - Aug. 27).
r – 1654 on dates in note N.

v – On ⑤F Baja d. 1659, Bátaszék d. 1718.
▷ – For connections see Table **1200**.
‡ – Also public holidays.

Sárbogárd - Székesfehérvár 39 km. Journey 54 mins.
From Sárbogárd 0903, 1703Ⓒ, 1741Ⓐ.
From Székesfehérvár 1000, 1600Ⓒ, 1950Ⓐ.

Supplements are payable for domestic journeys on EC, EN and IC trains

1220 BUDAPEST - SIÓFOK - FONYÓD - KESZTHELY / NAGYKANIZSA

2nd class

Service December 11 - June 16. Shaded timings are by 🚌

km		8540	8530	🚌 8612	8510	8710	850	🚌 860	8872 8802	8722	18502	852	🚌 862	🚌 8624	854	🚌 864	8514	844	🚌 874	8524	8724	856	🚌 866	8806 18806
		Ⓐ	d						P	Y	Z			Ⓐ						J	Ⓐ			Q
0	**Budapest** Déli ▶ d.	...	...	...	0405	*0505*	0735	...	...	...	0805	0935	...	...	1135	...	...	1335	...	...	...	1535	...	...
4	Kelenföld ⊡ ▶ d.	...	...	...	0412	*0512*	0742	...	...	*0742*	0812	0942	...	...	1142	...	*1142*	1342	...	*1342*	*1442*	1542	...	...
67	**Székesfehérvár** ▶ a.	...	...	...	0509	*0609*	0820	...	...	*0840*	0851	1020	...	...	1220	...	*1240*	1420	...	*1440*	*1540*	1620	...	...
67	**Székesfehérvár** d.	...	...	...	0511	0617	0822	...	...	0850	0852	1022	...	...	1222	...	1250	1422	...	1450	1556	1622	...	...
95	Lepsény d.	...	...	...	0536	0644	0840	...	...	0917	0917	1040	...	...	1240	...	1317	1440	...	1517	1621	1640	...	...
115	**Siófok** a.	...	...	...	0559	0704	0855	...	...	0937	0937	1055	...	...	1255	...	1337	1455	...	1537	1645	1655	...	...
115	**Siófok** d.	...	0340	...	0601	...	0857	...	...	...	0941	1057	...	...	1257	...	1340	1457	...	1540	...	1657	...	...
124	Zamárdi d.	...	0353	...	0614	...	0904	...	...	...	0952	1104	...	...	1304	...	1351	1504	...	1551	...	1704	...	...
128	Szántód-Kőröshegy a.	...	0357	...	0618	...	0908	...	...	...	0955	1108	...	...	1308	...	1354	1508	...	1554	...	1708	...	...
128	Szántód-Kőröshegy d.	...	0404	...	0625	...	0915	0915	...	...	1002	1115	1115	...	1315	1315	1401	1515	1515	1601	...	1715	1715	...
130	Balatonföldvár d.	...	0410	...	0631	...	0921	0921	...	...	1008	1121	1121	...	1321	1321	1407	1521	1521	1607	...	1721	1721	...
139	Balatonszemes d.	...	0425	...	0646	...	0936	0936	...	...	1023	1136	1136	...	1336	1336	1422	1536	1536	1622	...	1736	1736	...
146	Balatonlelle d.	...	0436	...	0657	...	0947	0947	...	...	1034	1147	1147	...	1347	1347	1433	1547	1547	1633	...	1747	1747	...
149	Balatonboglár d.	...	0443	...	0704	...	0954	0954	...	...	1041	1154	1154	...	1354	1354	1440	1554	1554	1640	...	1754	1754	...
157	**Fonyód** a.	...	0453	...	0714	...	1004	1004	...	...	1051	1204	1204	...	1404	1404	1450	1604	1604	1650	...	1804	1804	...
157	**Fonyód** d.	...	0454	0613	0715	...	1005	1005	1011	...	1052	1205	1205	1300	1405	1405	1451	1605	1605	1651	...	1805	1805	1835
165	Balatonfenyves d.	...	0506	0625	0727	...	1016	1016	1023	...	1104	1216	1216	1312	1416	1416	1503	1616	1616	1703	...	1816	1816	1847
181	Balatonszentgyörgy a.	...	0537	0656	0758	...	1044	1044	1054	...	1135	1244	1244	1343	1444	1444	1534	1644	1644	1734	...	1844	1844	1918
181	Balatonszentgyörgy ▲ d.	...	*0549*	0658	*0805*	...	|	1046	1100	...	*1143*	|	1246	1345	|	1446	*1606*	|	1646	*1743*	...	|	1846	1925
	Keszthely ▲ a.	...	*0601*	0714	*0817*	...	|	1102	1111	...	*1155*	|	1302	1401	|	1502	*1618*	|	1702	*1755*	...	|	1902	1936
181	Balatonszentgyörgy d.	0447	0543	...	0804	...	1050	...	...	...	1141	1250	...	...	1450	...	1540	1650	...	1740	...	1850	...	...
221	**Nagykanizsa** a.	0529	0626	...	0857	...	1128	...	...	...	1224	1328	...	...	1528	...	1623	1728	...	1822	...	1928	...	...
352	*Zagreb* **1340** a.	...	...	...	...	...	...	...	...	...	...	...	...	...	...	...	...	...	...	...	...	...	...	...

	8506	18706	846	🚌 876	8518	858	🚌 868	1868	
		⑤R						F	
Budapest Déli ▶ d.	1635	1700	1735	...	...	1935	...	2105	*2140*
Kelenföld ⊡ ▶ d.	1642	1707	1742	...	*1742*	1942	...	2112	*2147*
Székesfehérvár ▶ a.	1720	1748	1820	...	*1840*	2020	...	2150	*2244*
Székesfehérvár d.	1721	1801	1822	...	1850	2022	...	2151	2250
Lepsény d.	1743	|	1840	...	1917	2040	...	|	2315
Siófok a.	1802	1833	1855	...	1937	2055	...	2221	2334
Siófok d.	1803	1835	1857	...	2005	2057	...	2224	...
Zamárdi d.	1814	1843	1904	...	2016	2104	...	2231	...
Szántód-Kőröshegy a.	1817	1847	1909	...	2019	2108	...	2235	...
Szántód-Kőröshegy d.	1824	1854	1915	1915	2026	2115	2115	2242	...
Balatonföldvár d.	1830	1900	1921	1921	2032	2121	2121	2248	...
Balatonszemes d.	1845	1915	1936	1936	2047	2136	2136	2303	...
Balatonlelle d.	1856	1926	1947	1947	2058	2147	2147	2314	...
Balatonboglár d.	1903	1933	1954	1954	2105	2154	2154	2321	...
Fonyód a.	1913	1943	2004	2004	2115	2204	2204	2331	...
Fonyód d.	1914	1944	2005	2005	2116	2205	2205	2332	...
Balatonfenyves d.	1926	1955	2016	2016	2128	2216	2216	2343	...
Balatonszentgyörgy a.	1957	2023	2044	2044	2159	2244	2244	0011	...
Balatonszentgyörgy ▲ d.	*2007*	...	|	2046	*2215*	|	2246	0013	...
Keszthely ▲ a.	*2019*	...	|	2102	*2227*	|	2302	0029	...
Balatonszentgyörgy d.	2003	...	2050	...	...	2250	...	...	...
Nagykanizsa a.	2046	...	2128	...	...	2329	...	...	...
Zagreb **1340** a.	...	...	...	...	...	...	...	...	...

	8749	8509	8769	🚌 869	859	8759	8727	8529	🚌 877	847
			Ⓐ			Ⓐ				
Zagreb **1340** d.	...	...	...	...	...	...	...	...	...	...
Nagykanizsa d.	...	0259	...	...	0430	...	...	0554	...	0630
Balatonszentgyörgy a.	...	0339	...	...	0508	...	...	0637	...	0708
Keszthely ▲ d.	...	*0327*	...	0454	|	...	...	*0627*	0654	|
Balatonszentgyörgy ▲ a.	...	*0339*	...	0510	|	...	...	*0639*	0710	|
Balatonszentgyörgy d.	...	0344	...	0513	0513	...	...	0644	0713	0713
Balatonfenyves d.	...	0413	...	0539	0539	...	...	0713	0739	0739
Fonyód a.	...	0425	...	0550	0550	...	...	0725	0750	0750
Fonyód d.	...	0427	...	0551	0551	0605	...	0727	0751	0751
Balatonboglár d.	...	0437	...	0601	0601	0615	...	0737	0801	0801
Balatonlelle d.	...	0444	...	0608	0608	0622	...	0744	0808	0808
Balatonszemes d.	...	0455	...	0619	0619	0633	...	0755	0819	0819
Balatonföldvár d.	...	0510	...	0634	0634	0648	...	0810	0834	0834
Szántód-Kőröshegy a.	...	0518	...	0642	0642	0656	...	0818	0842	0842
Szántód-Kőröshegy d.	...	0525	...	...	0649	0703	...	0825	...	0849
Zamárdi d.	...	0530	...	...	0654	0708	...	0830	...	0854
Siófok a.	...	0542	...	...	0701	0720	...	0841	...	0901
Siófok d.	0425	0543	0625	...	0703	...	0815	...	...	0903
Lepsény d.	0445	0604	0645	...	0717	...	0840	...	...	0917
Székesfehérvár a.	0510	0629	0712	...	0735	...	0905	...	...	0935
Székesfehérvár ▶ d.	*0518*	0635	*0718*	...	0737	...	*0918*	...	...	0937
Kelenföld ⊡ ▶ a.	*0615*	0716	*0815*	...	0816	...	*1015*	...	...	1016
Budapest Déli ▶ a.	...	0724	...	...	0824	...	...	...	...	1024

	18537	🚌 867	857	8807 18807	8725	9657	🚌 865	855	9645	🚌 875	845	8615	🚌 863	853	18503	8513	🚌 861	851	8873 8803	8721	18701	8511	1861	8531
	©R			Q											Z	Ⓐ			P		⑦R		F	b
Zagreb **1340** d.	...	...	...	...	...	...	...	...	...	...	...	...	...	...	...	...	...	...	...	...	...	...	...	...
Nagykanizsa d.	0818	...	0830	...	...	...	...	1026	...	...	1226	...	...	1426	1511	1511	...	1626	...	...	...	1912	...	2130
Balatonszentgyörgy a.	0903	...	0908	...	...	...	...	1108	...	...	1308	...	...	1508	1603	1603	...	1708	...	...	...	1958	...	2211
Keszthely ▲ d.	...	0850	|	0903	...	0957	1054	|	1157	1254	|	1357	1454	|	*1550*	*1550*	1654	|	1757	...	...	*1940*	2048	*2157*
Balatonszentgyörgy ▲ a.	...	0906	|	0914	...	1009	1110	|	1209	1310	|	1413	1510	|	*1602*	*1602*	1710	|	1809	...	...	*1952*	2104	*2209*
Balatonszentgyörgy d.	...	0909	0913	0919	...	...	1113	1113	...	1313	1313	1416	1513	1513	1608	1608	1713	1713	1814	...	1816	2003	2107	2216
Balatonfenyves d.	...	0938	0939	0948	...	...	1139	1139	...	1339	1339	1445	1539	1539	1637	1637	1739	1739	1843	...	1845	2032	2133	2245
Fonyód a.	...	0950	0950	1000	...	...	1150	1150	...	1350	1350	1457	1550	1550	1649	1649	1750	1750	1855	...	1857	2044	2144	2257
Fonyód d.	...	0951	0951	...	...	...	1151	1151	...	1351	1351	1459	1551	1551	1652	1652	1751	1751	...	...	1859	2046	2145	2259
Balatonboglár d.	...	1001	1001	...	...	...	1201	1201	...	1401	1401	1509	1601	1601	1702	1702	1801	1801	...	...	1909	2056	2155	2309
Balatonlelle d.	...	1008	1008	...	...	...	1208	1208	...	1408	1408	1516	1608	1608	1709	1709	1808	1808	...	...	1916	2103	2202	2316
Balatonszemes d.	...	1019	1019	...	...	...	1219	1219	...	1419	1419	1527	1619	1619	1720	1720	1819	1819	...	...	1927	2114	2213	2327
Balatonföldvár d.	...	1034	1034	...	...	...	1234	1234	...	1434	1434	1542	1634	1634	1735	1735	1834	1834	...	...	1942	2129	2228	2342
Szántód-Kőröshegy a.	...	1042	1042	...	...	...	1242	1242	...	1442	1442	1550	1642	1642	1743	1743	1842	1842	...	...	1950	2137	2236	2350
Szántód-Kőröshegy d.	...	...	1049	...	...	...	...	1249	...	...	1449	1557	...	1649	1750	1750	...	1849	...	...	1957	2144	2245	2357
Zamárdi d.	...	...	1054	...	...	...	...	1254	...	...	1454	1602	...	1654	1755	1755	...	1854	...	...	2002	2149	2250	0002
Siófok a.	...	...	1101	...	...	...	...	1301	...	...	1501	1614	...	1701	1806	1806	...	1901	...	...	2014	2202	2257	0015
Siófok d.	...	...	1103	...	1215	...	...	1303	...	...	1503	1615	...	1703	1807	...	...	1903	...	2015	2015	2205	2259	...
Lepsény d.	...	...	1117	...	1240	...	...	1317	...	...	1517	1640	...	1717	1840	...	...	1917	...	2040	2040	2227	|	...
Székesfehérvár a.	...	...	1135	...	1305	...	...	1335	...	...	1535	1705	...	1735	1905	...	...	1935	...	2105	2105	2247	2333	...
Székesfehérvár ▶ d.	...	...	1137	...	*1318*	...	...	1337	...	...	1537	*1718*	...	1737	1906	...	...	1937	...	...	2107	2248	2334	...
Kelenföld ⊡ ▶ a.	...	...	1216	...	*1415*	...	...	1416	...	...	1616	*1815*	...	1816	1946	...	...	2016	...	...	2146	2345	0011	...
Budapest Déli ▶ a.	...	...	1224	...	...	...	...	1424	...	...	1624	...	...	1824	1954	...	...	2024	...	...	2154	2354	0019	...

F – ⑤⑥⑦ Apr. 28 - June 16 (also May 1, June 5).
J – ⑧ (daily Apr. 29 - June 16).
P – Kaposvár - Fonyód - Keszthely - Tapolca and v.v. (Table **1205**). From/to Pécs on © and daily Apr. 29 - Sept. 17.
Q – (2) Kaposvár - Fonyód - Keszthely - Tapolca - Celldömölk (- Szombathely Apr. 29 - Aug. 27) and v.v., Table **1205**.
R – Apr. 28 - June 16.

Y – Not dates in note **Z**.
Z – ⑥⑦ Apr. 1-23 (also Apr. 17); daily Apr. 29 - Aug. 27.
b – Not Dec. 20-31 Fonyód - Siófok.
d – Not Dec. 21 - Jan. 1 Siófok - Fonyód.
⊡ – Connection with metro line 4 (see city plan page 29).
▶ – See also Tables **1225** and **1230**.

▲ – *Italic* times: change at Balatonszentgyörgy
• – Keleti - Kelenföld: *13 km*.

Dec. 11 - June 16: shaded journeys are by replacement 🚌 in the timings shown due to track reconstruction.

1117 RYBNIŠTĚ - VARNSDORF - ZITTAU - LIBEREC

Die Länderbahn *Trilex* 2nd class

Service December 11 - January 7 only. TEMPORARILY RELOCATED FROM PAGE 480.

km					d									d			d				d				
0	**Rybniště** d.	...	0627	...	...	...	0940	...	...	1127	1227	...	1340	...	...	1540	...	...	1740	...	...	1839	...	2027	...
11	Varnsdorf 🏛 d.	0557	0650	0730	...	0851	0957	1029	...	1152	1244	1256	1357	...	1451	1557	...	1651	1757	1805	...	1856	2011	2044	2130
29	**Zittau** 🏛 d.	0616	0714	0749	0844	0916	...	1048	1051	1213	...	1317	1417	1444	1516	1616	1644	1716	...	1823	1847	1916	2044	...	2150
56	**Liberec** a.	0655	0755	0824	0915	0955	...	...	1127	1253	...	1355	1455	1524	1555	...	1716	1755	...	...	1920	1955	2115	...	2229

					d		Ⓐz		d					d			d				d				
Liberec d.	0500	0602	0702	0802	0838	...	0854	1002	1038	...	...	1231	1402	1433	1502	1602	1633	...	...	1802	1838	...	2005	2251	...
Zittau 🏛 d.	0537	0644	0740	0845	0910	0943	0943	1040	1114	1130	...	1308	1446	1510	1545	1646	1709	1712	...	1844	1912	1930	2046	2327	...
Varnsdorf 🏛 d.	0555	0703	0758	0904	...	1001	1001	1104	...	1149	1304	1326	1504	...	1607	1704	...	1730	1801	1906	...	1948	2104	2345	...
Rybniště a.	0613	...	...	0922	...	...	...	1122	...	1207	1322	...	1522	...	...	1722	...	...	1819	...	...	2006	...	...	...

d – From/to Dresden (Table **855**).
z – Not Dec. 27-30.

2nd class BUDAPEST - SZÉKESFEHÉRVÁR - BALATONFÜRED - TAPOLCA 1225

Service December 11 - June 16

km		9740	9710	8510	9720	900	9712	972	246	9722	1974	904	9714	974	9004	9724	9006	9716	976	906	9726	1978	908	9718	9738
		Ⓐ									D			H								⑤F			
0	**Budapest** Déli ▶ d.	...	...	0405	...	0630	...	0800	0830	0825z	1000	1030	...	1200	1230	...	1430	...	1600	1630	...	1800	1830	...	*2140*
4	Kelenföld ▶ d.	...	...	0412	...	0637	...	0807	0837	0832z	1007	1037	...	1207	1237	...	1437	...	1607	1637	...	1807	1837	...	*2147*
67	**Székesfehérvár** ▶ a.	...	...	0509	...	0715	...	0845	0915	0912z	1045	1115	...	1245	1315	...	1515	...	1645	1715	...	1845	1915	...	*2244*
67	**Székesfehérvár** d.	...	0429r	...	0530	...	0722	0855	...	0924	1055	...	1124	1255	...	1324	▬	1524	1655	...	1724	1855	...	1924	2250
105	Balatonkenese d.	...	0512r	...	0615	...	0810	0929	...	1010	1129	...	1210	1329	...	1410	...	1610	1729	...	1810	1929	...	2010	2335
117	Balalatonalmádi d.	...	0526r	...	0629	...	0827	0943	...	1027	1143	...	1227	1343	...	1427	...	1627	1743	...	1827	1943	...	2027	2348
123	Alsóörs d.	...	0533r	...	0636	...	0834	0949	...	1034	1149	...	1234	1349	...	1434	C	1634	1749	...	1834	1949	...	2034	2355
132	**Balatonfüred** d.	0400	0546	...	0654	...	0848	1000	...	1048	1200	...	1248	1400	...	1448	1543	1648	1800	...	1848	2000	...	2048	0006
157	Révfülöp d.	0437	0627	...	0730	...	0930	1027	...	1130	1227	...	1330	1427	...	1530	1625	1730	1827	...	1930	2027	...	2125	...
168	Badacsonytomaj d.	0455	0642	...	0745	...	0945	1038	...	1145	1238	...	1345	1438	...	1545	1640	1745	1838	...	1945	2038	...	2140	...
170	Badacsony d.	0458	0645	...	0748	...	0948	1041	...	1148	1241	...	1348	1441	...	1548	1643	1748	1841	...	1948	2041	...	2143	...
184	**Tapolca** a.	0516	0703	...	0810	...	1010	1057	...	1210	1255	...	1410	1457	...	1610	1659	1810	1857	...	2005	2055	...	2200	...

	9739	9719	9069	9729	979	9729	909	9717	907	9727	19745	9715	9005	975	9725	247	1973	9713	903	971	9723	901	1971	9711	9711
			Ⓐ								C			H			⑦N						D	Ⓑ	⑥
apolca d.	...	0435	...	0530	0558	...	...	0750	...	0950	1059	1150	...	1301	1350	...	1503	1550	...	1701	1750	...	1903	2015	2015
adacsony d.	...	0452	...	0547	0613	...	...	0807	...	1007	1113	1207	...	1316	1407	...	1516	1607	...	1716	1807	...	1916	2032	2032
adacsonytomaj d.	...	0455	...	0550	0616	...	...	0810	...	1010	1116	1210	...	1319	1410	...	1519	1610	...	1719	1810	...	1919	2038	2038
évfülöp d.	...	0510	...	0605	0627	...	...	0827	...	1027	1130	1227	...	1330	1427	...	1530	1627	...	1730	1827	...	1930	2052	2052
alatonfüred d.	0345	0544	...	0641	0655	←	...	0908	...	1108	1212	1308	...	1359	1508	...	1559	1708	...	1759	1908	...	1959	2129	2125
lsóörs d.	0356	0555	...	→	0703	0708	...	0919	...	1119	▬	1319	...	1407	1519	...	1607	1719	...	1807	1919	...	2007	2139	▬
alalatonalmádi d.	0403	0602	...	...	0709	0727	...	0927	...	1127	...	1327	...	1413	1527	...	1613	1727	...	1813	1927	...	2013	2147	...
alatonkenese d.	0416	0615	...	...	0723	0743	...	0943	...	1143	...	1343	...	1427	1543	...	1627	1743	...	1827	1943	...	2027	2200	...
zékesfehérvár a.	0505	0700	...	...	0800	0834	...	1034	...	1234	...	1434	...	1502	1634	...	1702	1834	...	1902	2034	...	2102	2244	...
zékesfehérvár ▶ d.	*0518*	...	0704	...	0812	...	0842	...	1042	...	1242	...	1442	1512	...	1642	1712	1845z	1842	1912	...	2042	2112	...	2248
elenföld ▶ a.	*0615*	...	0746	...	0851	...	0921	...	1121	...	1321	...	1521	1551	...	1721	1751	1925z	1921	1951	...	2121	2151	...	2345
udapest Déli ▶ a.	...	...	0754	...	0859	...	0929	...	1129	...	1329	...	1529	1559	...	1729	1759	1944z	1929	1959	...	2129	2159	...	2354

– Ⓒ Apr. 29 - June 16.
– Ⓒ Apr. 15 - June 16.
– ⑤ (not Dec. 23, 30, June 16 - Aug. 25).
H – Mar. 25 - Oct. 29.
N – ⑦ (not Dec. 25, Jan. 1, June 18 - Aug. 27).
r – ⚒ only.
z – ⑥⑦ Mar. 25 - Apr. 16; daily Apr. 17 - Sept. 22; ⑥⑦ Sept. 23 - Oct. 29.
▶ – See also Tables **1220** and **1230**.

2nd class BUDAPEST - SZÉKESFEHÉRVÁR - ZALAEGERSZEG and SZOMBATHELY 1230

For faster trains Budapest - Szombathely (via Györ) see Table **1252**. The section of line between Szombathely and Porpác (17 km) is operated by GySEV.

km		9510	900	900 9590	246	246 902	962	904	904 9594	9064	9004	9004 9504	964	9006	9006 9596	9526	966	906	906 956	*IC* 958	9518	908	968	9008	9008 1246
					C															🅁					R
0	**Budapest** Déli ▶ d.	...	0630	0630	0830	0830	0930	1030	1030	1130	1230	1230	1330	1430	1430	...	1530	1630	1630	1730	...	1830	1930	2030	2030
4	Kelenföld ▶ d.	...	0637	0637	0837	0837	0937	1037	1037	1137	1237	1237	1337	1437	1437	...	1537	1637	1637	1737	...	1837	1937	2037	2037
67	**Székesfehérvár** ▶ d.	...	0716	0716	0916	0916	1016	1116	1116	1216	1316	1316	1416	1516	1516	...	1616	1716	1716	1816	...	1916	2016	2116	2116
90	Várpalota d.	...	0736	0736	0936	0936	1033	1136	1136	1233	1336	1336	1433	1536	1536	...	1633	1736	1736	|	...	1936	2033	2135	2135
112	Veszprém d.	...	0802	0802	1002	1002	1055	1202	1202	1255	1402	1402	1455	1602	1602	...	1655	1802	1802	1854	...	2002	2055	2157	2157
148	Ajka d.	...	0833	0833	1033	1033	▬	1233	1233	▬	1433	1433	▬	1633	1633	...	...	1833	1833	1925	...	2035	▬	2231	2231
	Celldömölk d.	0606	|	|	|	|	1206	|	|	1401	|	|	1606	|	|	1801	...	|	|	|	2006	|	2206	|	|
181	Boba a.	0614	0900	0900	1100	1100	1214	1300	1300	1409	1500	1500	1614	1700	1700	1809	...	1900	1900	|	2014	2108	2214	2302	2302
181	Boba d.	0615	0905	0909	1109	1105	1215	1305	1309	1410	1505	1509	1615	1705	1709	1810	...	1905	1909	|	2015	2109	2215	2306	2314
199	Ukk d.	0635	|	0929	1124	|	1235	|	1329	1435	|	1524	1635	|	1724	1835	...	|	1924	2001	2035	|	2235	|	|
230	Zalaszentiván a.	0705	|	0959	1145	|	1305	|	1359	1505	|	1545	1705	|	1759	1905	...	|	1945	2023	2105	|	2305	|	|
239	**Zalaegerszeg** a.	0714	|	1012	1155	|	1314	|	1412	1514	|	1555	1714	|	1812	1914	...	|	1955	2032	2114	|	2314	|	2355
191	Celldömölk ▷ d.	...	0914	...	...	1114	...	1314	...	...	1514	...	...	1714	...	...	...	1914	...	...	...	2120	...	2315	...
236	**Szombathely** ▷ a.	...	0947	...	...	1147	...	1347	...	...	1547	...	...	1747	...	...	...	1947	...	...	...	2159	...	...	...

	9009	*IC* 959	1247 959	909	9517	907	957 907	905	9597 905	9005	9505 9005	9525	247	9003 247	9513	903	953 903	9523	*IC* 1951	961	901	9591 901	9511	9021	9521
		🅁	R										C						🅁N						
zombathely ▷ d.	...	...	...	0605	...	0805	...	1005	...	1205	...	...	...	1403	...	1605	...	...	...	...	1805	...	...	2004	...
elldömölk ▷ d.	0440	...	...	0644	...	0843	...	1043	...	1243	...	...	...	1444	...	1643	...	...	...	...	1843	...	...	2048	...
Zalaegerszeg d.	|	0527	0527	|	0646	|	0804	|	0945	|	1204	1246	1345	|	1446	|	1604	1646	1716	...	|	1745	1846	|	2046
Zalaszentiván d.	|	0535	0535	|	0654	|	0812	|	1002	|	1212	1254	1402	|	1454	|	1612	1654	|	...	|	1802	1854	|	2054
Ukk d.	|	0601	0601	|	0723	|	0835	|	1032	|	1235	1328	1432	|	1523	|	1635	1728	|	...	|	1832	1923	|	2123
oba a.	0448	|	|	0652	0740	0851	0851	1051	1051	1251	1251	1345	1451	1452	1540	1651	1651	1745	|	...	1851	1851	1940	2057	2140
oba d.	0449	|	|	0654	0741	0901	0901	1101	1101	1301	1301	1346	1501	1501	1541	1701	1701	1746	|	...	1901	1901	1941	2058	2141
Celldömölk a.	|	|	|	|	0752	|	|	|	|	|	|	1357	|	|	1552	|	|	1757	|	...	|	|	1952	|	2152
jka d.	0524	0635	0635	0723	▬	0926	0926	1126	1126	1326	1326	▬	1526	1526	▬	1726	1726	...	1818	...	1926	1926	...	2142	...
eszprém d.	0602	0705	0705	0802	0902	1002	1002	1202	1202	1402	1402	1502	1602	1602	1702	1802	1802	...	1855	1902	2002	2002	...	2223	...
árpalota d.	0624	|	|	0821	0924	1021	1021	1221	1221	1421	1421	1524	1621	1621	1724	1821	1821	...	|	1924	2021	2021	...	...	...
zékesfehérvár ▶ d.	0642	0742	0742	0842	0942	1042	1042	1242	1242	1442	1442	1542	1642	1642	1742	1842	1842	...	1932	1942	2042	2042	...	...	...
elenföld ▶ a.	0722	0822	0822	0922	1022	1122	1122	1322	1322	1522	1522	1622	1722	1722	1822	1922	1922	...	2012	2022	2122	2122	...	...	...
udapest Déli ▶ a.	0729	0829	0829	0929	1029	1129	1129	1329	1329	1529	1529	1629	1729	1729	1829	1929	1929	...	2019	2029	2129	2129	...	...	...

– CITTADELLA – [12] ✕ Budapest - Zalaegerszeg - Hodoš - Ljubljana and v.v.; [2] Budapest - Ljubljana - Koper and v.v.
– ⑦ (not Dec. 25, Jan. 1, June 18 - Aug. 27).
R – ISTRIA – from Budapest June 23 - Aug. 25, from Rijeka / Koper June 24 - Aug. 26. 🛏 1, 2 cl., ━ 2 cl., [2] Budapest - Ljubljana - Rijeka and v.v.; ━ 2 cl. Budapest - Koper and v.v. (also [2] on ⑤, returning ⑦).
▶ – See also Tables **1220** and **1225**.
▷ – See also Tables **1232** and **1253**.

2nd class SZOMBATHELY - CELLDÖMÖLK - UKK - TAPOLCA - KESZTHELY 1232

Service December 11 - June 16

km		9639	9619		9637	9629	8807		9617	19807	9645	9625		9615	9613	9603		9623	8803	9611		9621		
							k			E									n					
0	**Szombathely** 1230 d.	...	...	...	...	...	0643r	...	...	0925	...	...	...	...	...	...	...	...	...	...	...	...	...	...
45	Celldömölk 1230 d.	...	*0453*	...	...	*0606*	0730	...	...	1000	...	...	...	...	*1401*	1501	...	*1606*	...	*1801*	...	*2006*	...	...
55	Boba 1230 d.	...	*0502*	...	...	*0615*	0741	...	*0909*	|	...	...	...	*1309*	*1410*	1514	...	*1615*	...	*1810*	...	*2015*	...	...
73	**Ukk** 1230 d.	...	0522	...	...	0636	0800	...	0936	|	...	...	...	1336	1436	1538	...	1636	...	1831	...	2036	...	...
81	Sümeg d.	...	0533	...	...	0647	0810	...	0947	1030	...	...	...	1347	1447	1549	...	1647	...	1842	...	2048	...	...
101	**Tapolca** a.	...	0555	...	...	0709	0828	...	1009	1047	...	...	...	1409	1509	1610	...	1709	...	1904	...	2109	...	...
101	**Tapolca** d.	0418	0556	...	0645	...	0830	...	1015	1048	...	1218	...	1418	1518	1613	...	...	1718	1905	...	2110	...	...
126	**Keszthely** a.	0449	0626	...	0716	...	0859	...	1046	1113	...	1249	...	1449	1549	1645	...	...	1749	1934	...	2141	...	...
126	*Keszthely* **1220** d.	...	0627	...	...	...	0903	...	...	...	1157	...	...	...	1550	...	...	...	1757	1940	...	2157	...	...
136	*B'tonszentgyörgy* **1220** a.	...	0639	...	...	...	0914	...	...	...	1209	...	...	...	1602	...	...	...	1809	1952	...	2209	...	...

	9610	9630	9630	9620	9632	9652	9612	9597	8802	9604	9654	9624	9616	953	9626	9636	19804	9636	9646	8806	9618	9618	9658	9658
		Ⓐ	Ⓒ						n								E			k				
B'tonszentgyörgy **1220** d.	...	...	...	0549	...	0805	...	...	1100	...	1143	...	...	...	...	*1606*	...	...	1743	1925	2007	*2046z*	2215	*2246z*
Keszthely **1220** a.	...	...	...	0601	...	0817	...	...	1111	...	1155	...	...	...	...	*1618*	...	...	1755	1936	2019	*2102z*	2227	*2302z*
eszthely d.	...	0523	...	0605	0655	...	0905	...	1117	...	...	1406	1506	...	...	1627	1647	1706	1803	1937	...	2119	...	2306
apolca a.	...	0553	...	0639	0727	...	0936	...	1148	...	...	1439	1539	...	...	1658	1712	1739	1834	2006	...	2153	...	2337
apolca d.	0440	0600	0600	0640	...	...	0940	...	...	1200	...	1440	1540	...	1640	...	1713	...	1835	2007	...	...	...	...
ümeg d.	0500	0621	0621	0708	...	...	1008	...	...	1221	...	1508	1608	...	1708	...	1731	...	1908	2025	...	...	...	...
kk 1230 a.	0512	0633	0633	0720	...	...	1020	1032	...	1233	...	1520	1620	1635	1720	...	|	...	1920	2033	...	...	...	...
oba 1230 a.	*0540*	0652	0652	*0740*	...	...	...	1051	...	1259	...	*1540*	...	1651	*1745*	...	|	...	*1940*	2051	...	...	...	...
elldömölk 1230 a.	*0552*	0704	0704	*0752*	...	...	...	...	...	1319	...	*1552*	...	...	*1757*	...	1801	...	*1952*	2104	...	...	...	...
zombathely 1230 a.	...	...	...	...	...	...	...	...	...	...	...	...	...	...	...	...	1854	...	...	2141r	...	...	...	...

– Ⓒ Apr. 29 - Oct. 23.
– To / from Kaposvár (Table **1205**).
n – To / from Kaposvár (train **8872/3**) or Pécs (train **8802/3**), Table **1205**.
r – Apr. 29 - Aug. 27 (train **18807/6**).
z – By 🚌.
▷ – See also Table **1230**.

1233 SOPRON - SZOMBATHELY
GySEV. 2nd class

km																	
		◇	◇	◇		P		◇		◇	Ⓐ◇	◇	◇		Ⓐ		
0	**Sopron** d.	0408	0455	0549	0644	0810	0934	1108	1208	1343	1443	1543	1643	1756	1907	2011	2230
38	Bük d.	0440	0528	0630	0717	0837	1007	1140	1240	1415	1515	1615	1715	1828	1945	2044	2306
62	**Szombathely** a.	0500	0548	0653	0737	0852	1026	1200	1300	1433	1533	1633	1733	1851	2005	2103	2325

		◇			◇	◇				Ⓐ◇	◇		◇	Q	Ⓐ◇	◇	
Szombathely d.	0422	0508	0632	0715	0926	1100	1238	1331	1435	1535	1635	1711	1826	1910	1942	2110	2225
Bük d.	0441	0527	0651	0734	0944	1118	1257	1353	1453	1553	1653	1731	1845	1925	2002	2128	2244
Sopron a.	0517	0600	0727	0807	1017	1152	1330	1428	1528	1628	1728	1812	1917	1950	2034	2200	2316

P – To Pécs (Table **1237**). Q – From Pécs (Table **1237**). ◇ – To/from Szentgotthárd (Table **986**).

1234 KÖSZEG

18 km, journey time 20 - 25 minutes
Operated by GySEV. 2nd class

From **Szombathely**: 0506, 0606, 0706Ⓐ, 0806, 0906, 1006Ⓐ, 1106, 1206Ⓐ, 1306Ⓒ, 1335Ⓐ, 1430Ⓐ, 1506Ⓒ, 1522Ⓐ, 1606Ⓒ, 1614Ⓐ, 1706, 1806Ⓐ, 1906, 2106, 2236.

From **Köszeg**: 0432, 0532, 0632, 0732Ⓐ, 0832, 0932Ⓐ, 1032, 1132Ⓐ, 1232, 1401Ⓐ, 1432Ⓒ, 1456Ⓐ, 1532Ⓒ, 1548Ⓐ, 1632Ⓒ, 1640Ⓐ, 1732Ⓐ, 1832, 2032, 2208.

1235 SZOMBATHELY - ZALASZENTIVÁN - ZALAEGERSZEG
MÁV-START / GySEV. 2nd class

km																									
		△						△				△		Ⓐ					Ⓐ	△					
	Sopron **1233** d.	...	...	...	...	...	...	0810	...	...	...	...	...	...	...	...	...	...	...	...	...	...	...	...	...
0	**Szombathely** d.	0509	...	0612	...	0709	...	0909	...	1109	...	1309	...	1402	...	1432	1602	...	1638	1709	...	1805	1909	2230	...
24	Vasvár d.	0530	...	0638	...	0735	...	0930	...	1135	...	1330	...	1428	...	1457	1628	...	1704	1730	...	1833	1934	2255	...
49	Zalaszentiván a.	0551	...	0701	...	0758	...	0951	...	1158	...	1351	...	1451	...	1520	1651	...	1727	1751	...	1855	1957	2318	...
49	Zalaszentiván ▶ d.	...	0557	...	0706	...	0812	...	1004	...	1212	...	1404	...	1506	1524	...	1706	...	...	1804	1900	2004	2324	...
58	**Zalaegerszeg** ▶ a.	...	0606	...	0714	...	0821	...	1012	...	1221	...	1412	...	1514	1532	...	1714	...	...	1812	1908	2013	2333	...

								△				△		Ⓐ	Ⓐ	Ⓒ				△			△		
Zalaegerszeg ▶ d.	0348	0446	...	0547	0740	...	0945	...	1135	...	1345	...	1446	...	1536	1536	1646	...	1745	...	1935	2135	...	2243	...
Zalaszentiván ▶ a.	0357	0453	...	0556	0749	...	0954	...	1144	...	1354	...	1453	...	1544	1544	1653	...	1754	...	1944	2144	...	2251	...
Zalaszentiván d.	0402	...	0455	0602	...	0802	...	1003	...	1202	...	1403	...	1502	1602	1602	...	1655	...	1803	2002	...	2203	...	...
Vasvár d.	0426	...	0519	0626	...	0826	...	1025	...	1226	...	1427	...	1529	1627	1627	...	1721	...	1830	2026	...	2225	...	...
Szombathely a.	0451	...	0545	0653	...	0851	...	1045	...	1251	...	1451	...	1554	1700	1652	...	1746	...	1850	2051	...	2250	...	...
Sopron **1233** a.	...	...	...	0807	...	...	...	...	...	...	...	...	...	...	...	...	...	...	...	1950	...	...	...	...	...

△ – To/from Pécs (Tables **1236/7**). ▶ – See also Tables **1230** and **1236**.

1236 ZALAEGERSZEG - ZALASZENTIVÁN - NAGYKANIZSA
2nd class

km											
					△						
	Szombathely **1235** d.	...	0509	...	0909	...	1309	...	...	1709	...
0	**Zalaegerszeg** ▶ d.	0547	|	0945	|	1345	|	1652	1745	|	...
9	Zalaszentiván ▶ a.	0556	0551	0954	0951	1354	1351	1700	1754	1751	...
9	Zalaszentiván d.	...	0558	...	1000	...	1400	1712	...	1800	...
61	**Nagykanizsa** a.	...	0648	...	1048	...	1448	1818	...	1848	...
	Pécs **1237** a.	...	0936	...	1342	...	1736	...	...	2146	...

						▽			
Pécs **1237** d.	...	0615	...	1015	...	1415	...	1815	...
Nagykanizsa d.	0608	0910	...	1310	...	1710	...	2110	...
Zalaszentiván a.	0708	0958	...	1358	...	1758	...	2200	...
Zalaszentiván ▶ d.	0713	1003	1004	1403	1404	1803	1804	2203	2203
Zalaegerszeg ▶ a.	0722	|	1012	|	1412	|	1812	|	2212
Szombathely **1235** a.	...	1045	...	1451	...	1850	...	2250	...

△ – From Sopron (depart 0810, Table **1233**). ▽ – To Sopron (arrive 1950, Table **1233**). ▶ – See also Tables **1232** and **1235**.

1237 NAGYKANIZSA - PÉCS
2nd class

km		8910	8900	8954	8902	8914	8904	18958	8906	
				Ⓐ	△			⑦		
	Szombathely **1235** d.	...	0509	...	0909	...	1309	...	1709	...
0	**Nagykanizsa** **1240** d.	0353	0651	...	1051	...	1451	...	1851	...
29	Gyékényes **1240** d.	0435	0720	...	1120	1255	1520	...	1920	...
84	Barcs d.	0611	0826	1012	1226	1412	1626	1812	2026	...
114	Szigetvár d.	0658	0857	1056	1257	1455	1657	1855	2110	...
129	Szentlőrinc d.	0734	0913	1115	1325	1529	1713	1925	2129	...
148	**Pécs** a.	0754	0936	1138	1342	1549	1736	1945	2146	...

	8907	8905	8955	8903	8953	8913	8901	8961	⊡
				▽					Ⓑ
Pécs d.	0615	1015	1212	1415	1453	1612	1815	2012	2225
Szentlőrinc d.	0638	1038	1237	1438	1518	1637	1838	2050	2250
Szigetvár d.	0654	1054	1258	1454	1536	1658	1854	2109	2309
Barcs d.	0725	1125	1337	1525	1615	1738	1925	2148	2348
Gyékényes **1240** a.	0838	1238	...	1638	...	1843	2038	...	...
Nagykanizsa **1240** a.	0907	1307	...	1707	...	1935	2107	...	...
Szombathely **1235** a.	1045	1451	...	1845	...	...	2250	...	...

△ – From Sopron (depart 0810, Table **1233**). ▽ – To Sopron (arrive 1950, Table **1233**). ⊡ – Runs earlier on ⑦ June 18 - Aug. 27 (Pécs 2218, Barcs 2348).

1240 (BUDAPEST) - DOMBÓVAR - KAPOSVÁR - NAGYKANIZSA
2nd class

For Budapest - Nagykanizsa (via Siófok and Fonyód) see Table **1220**

km		8250	8212	*IC* 200	*IC* 1200	8202	8222	8214	8905	8254	8216	8256	8903	8226	8236	*IC* 204	8913	8206	*IC* 828	8561	1204	8218	8208	8208	
				K⊖	K⊖											R			Ⓡ		Ⓡ				
				T	S	S	T				Ⓐb			Ⓐ		⊖					A		Ⓑ	⑥	
	Budapest Keleti **1200** d.	...	...	0545	0600	...	...	...	...	...	...	...	...	...	...	1445	...	...	1645	...	1815	...	...	...	...
0	**Dombóvár** d.	0422r	0625	0803	|	0807	...	1007	...	1207	...	1407	...	...	1607	1700	...	1807	1909	...	|	2005	2207	2207	...
31	**Kaposvár** a.	0457r	0704	0829	❦	0833	...	1042	...	1242	...	1442	...	...	1642	1726	...	1833	1935	...	❦	2043	2233	2233	...
31	**Kaposvár** d.	0500	0707	0831	|	0907	0907	1107	...	1257	1407	1507	...	1557	1705	1731	...	1907	1937	...	|	2110	2241	...	...
71	Somogyszob d.	0610	0800	0912	|	1000	1000	1200	...	1351	1459	1600	...	1649	1757	1821	...	2000	2018	...	|	2211	2330	...	...
101	Gyékényes a.	0640	0830	0945	0942	1030	1030	1236	...	1430	1529	1630	...	1719	1827	1848	...	2030	2045	...	2218	2241	2400	...	...
101	Gyékényes **1237** d.	0720	*0839*	1011	1011	...	...	...	1239	1431	...	1658	1639	...	...	1916	1859	*2039*	...	2047	2255	...	...	...	...
130	**Nagykanizsa** **1237** a.	0750	*0907*	|	|	...	...	...	1307	1506	...	1732	1707	...	...	|	1935	*2107*	...	2123	|	...	...	...	...
	Zagreb **1340** a.	...	...	1139	1139	...	...	...	...	...	...	...	...	...	...	2059	...	...	...	...	0022	...	...	...	...

	8219	8219	8229	8910	*IC* 829	1205	8259	8207	8217	8215	8564	*IC* 205	18225	8225	8253	8904	8253	8263	*IC* 201	*IC* 1201	8201	8568	8251	18251	
					Ⓡ	Ⓡ						K							R⊖	R⊖					
	⚒	†	Ⓐ			A						⊖	S	T					T	S		Ⓑ	Ⓑ	⑥	
Zagreb **1340** d.	...	...	...	...	...	0232	...	...	...	...	...	1003	...	...	...	...	...	...	1536	1640	...	...	...	...	...
Nagykanizsa **1237** d.	...	...	...	0417	...	|	0458	0635	...	*1051*	1105	|	...	...	1428	1451	...	1635	|	|	*1851*	1918	2109	2109	...
Gyékényes **1237** a.	...	...	...	0451	...	0418	0528	0706	...	*1119*	1138	1135	...	...	1512	1519	←	1719	1709	1809	*1919*	1954	2139	2139	...
Gyékényes d.	0339	...	0422	...	0512	0529	0530	0722	0920	1129	...	1211	1320	1329	→	...	1530	1726	1745	1835	1929	...	2140	2140	...
Somogyszob d.	0410	...	0453	...	0540	|	0606	0800	1000	1200	...	1239	1400	1400	...	...	1600	1757	1821	|	2018	...	2211	2211	...
Kaposvár a.	0458	...	0541	...	0620	|	0700	0852	1048	1248	...	1319	1448	1448	...	...	1648	1845	1901	|	2106	...	2303	2259	...
Kaposvár d.	0514	0514	...	...	0622	❦	0714	0923	1114	...	...	1322	1514	1514	...	...	1705	1903	1912	❦	2124	...	2304	...	...
Dombóvár a.	0549	0549	...	...	0648	|	0749	0949	1149	...	...	1348	1549	1549	...	...	1743	1942	1946	|	2150	...	2339	...	...
Budapest Keleti **1200** a.	...	...	...	...	0914	0936	...	...	...	...	...	1614	...	...	...	...	...	...	2214	2230	...	...	...	...	...

A – ADRIA – from Budapest ②⑤⑦ June 18 - Sept. 1, returning from Split ①③⑥ June 19 - Sept. 2 (next day from Zagreb). 🛏 1, 2 cl., 🛏 2 cl., (2) Budapest - Zagreb - Split and v.v. On ②⑤ June 20 - Sept. 1 conveys 🛏 1, 2 cl. Praha (**277/6**) - Budapest (**1204/5**) - Zagreb - Split, returning from Split ③⑥ June 21 - Sept. 2.

K – KVARNER – (12) 🍸 Budapest - Zagreb - Rijeka and v.v.
R – RIPPL-RÓNAI – (12) ✕ Budapest - Zagreb and v.v.
S – June 17 - Aug. 27.
T – Not June 17 - Aug. 27.
b – Not Dec. 22 - Jan. 2, June 16 - Sept. 1.

r – ⚒ only.
❦ – Via Fonyód, Nagykanizsa (Table **1220**).
⊖ – Ⓡ for domestic journeys within Hungary.

1242 DOMBÓVAR - BAJA - KISKUNFÉLEGYHÁZA - KECSKEMÉT
2nd class (*Ex* also 1st)

km											
							⑤F	G		Ⓡ	
0	**Dombóvár** d.	...	0606	...	1406	...	1606	1606	1811	...	...
60	Bátaszék **1210** d.	0520	0723	...	1513	...	1717	1732	1920	1933	...
80	**Baja** **1210** a.	0540	0744	...	1538	...	1738	1753	...	1951	...

	⚒	Ⓐ	Ⓡ							
Baja **1210** d.	0425	...	0557	...	...	1407	...	1555x	...	1812
Bátaszék **1210** d.	0444	0448	0615	0633	...	1429	...	1633	...	1838
Dombóvár a.	...	0554	...	0740	...	1540	...	1740	...	1945

km											
			Ⓐ						Ⓐr		
0	**Baja** d.	0413	0517	0609	0809	1009	1209	1409	1511	1609	1809
76	Kiskunhalas a.	0520	0630	0720	0920	1120	1320	1520	1630	1720	1920
76	Kiskunhalas d.	0532	0639	0732	0932	1132	1332	1532	...	1732	1932
122	Kiskunfélegyháza **1290** d.	0615	0719	0815	1015	1215	1415	1615	...	1815	2014
147	**Kecskemét** **1290** a.	0636	...	0836	1036	1236	1436	1636	...	1836	...

	Ⓐ						Ⓐ			
Kecskemét **1290** d.	...	0510	0722	0922	1122	1322	...	1522	1722	1922
Kiskunfélegyháza **1290** d.	...	0545	0745	0945	1145	1345	1438	1545	1745	1945
Kiskunhalas a.	...	0625	0825	1025	1225	1425	1518	1625	1825	2025
Kiskunhalas d.	0528	0637	0837	1037	1237	1437	1528r	1637	1837	2037
Baja a.	0638	0742	0942	1142	1342	1542	1638r	1742	1942	2142

F – ⑤ (not Dec. 23, 30, June 16 - Aug. 25). G – Not dates in note F. r – Not June 17 - Aug. 27. x – 1611 on ⑦ (not Dec. 25, Jan. 1, June 18 - Aug. 27).

BUDAPEST - GYŐR - WIEN 1250

km				IC	RJ	IC	RJ	IC	EC	IC	RJ	IC	IC	RJ	IC	IC	RJ	IC		IC	RJ		IC	EC	
		9430	346	910	162	930	60	912	140	932	62	922	942	64	914	934	66	924	9204	936	68	9304	916	344	9306
		2	§	R	✕⊖	R	✕⊖	R	✕R	R	✕⊖	R	R	✕⊖	R	R	✕⊖	R	2	R	✕⊖	2	R	✕§	2
			D		Z		M		H		M			M			M f				M	Ⓐ		A	Ⓐ
0	**Budapest** Keleti d.	...	0540	0610	0640	0710	0740	0810	0840	0910	0940	1010	1110	1140	1210	1310	1340	1410	1440	1510	1540	1553	1610	1640	1653
7	Ferencváros d.	...	0549	|	|	|	|	|	|	|	|	|	|	|	|	|	|	|	1449	|	|	1601	|	|	1701
13	Kelenföld ☆ d.	...	0555	0625	0655	0725	0755	0825	0855	0925	0955	1025	1125	1155	1225	1325	1355	1425	1455	1525	1555	1608	1625	1655	1708
75	Tatabánya d.	...	0626	0656	0726	0756	0826	0856	0926	0956	1026	1056	1156	1226	1256	1356	1426	1456	1533	1556	1626	1650	1656	1726	1750
83	Tata d.	...	|	0704	|	0804	|	0904	|	1004	|	1104	1204	|	1304	1404	|	1504	1542	1604	|	1659	1704	|	1759
103	Komárom d.	...	|	0717	|	0817	|	0917	|	1017	|	1117	1217	|	1317	1417	|	1517	1556	1617	|	1719	1717	|	1819
140	**Győr** a.	...	0700	0735	0800	0835	0900	0935	1000	1035	1100	1135	1235	1300	1335	1435	1500	1535	1625	1635	1700	1743	1735	1800	1843
140	**Győr** d.	0448	0702	△	0802	▽	0902	△	1002	▽	1102	△	▽	1302	△	▽	1502	△	u	▽	1702	...	△	1802	...
176	Mosonmagyaróvár d.	0514	0720	...	0820	...	0920	...	1020	...	1120	...	...	1320	...	...	1520	...	...	...	1720	...	...	1820	...
187	Hegyeshalom ▦ d.	0526	0732	...	0832	...	0932	...	1032	...	1132	...	...	1332	...	...	1532	...	...	...	1732	...	...	1832	...
256	**Wien** Hbf a.	0624	0821	...	0918	...	1021	...	1121	...	1221	...	...	1421	...	...	1618	...	...	...	1821	...	...	1921	...

	IC	RJ		IC	EC	IC	Ex	IC	EN	
	946	42	9308	318	148	938	1948	948	462	
	R	✕⊖	2	R	🍷R	R	2R	R	R	2
		S	Ⓐ	G			⑦		K	⊡
Budapest Keleti d.	1710	1740	1753	1810	1840	1910	1940	2010	2040	2120d
Ferencváros d.	|	|	1801	|	|	|	1949	|	|	|
Kelenföld ☆ d.	1725	1755	1808	1825	1855	1925	1956	2025	2055	2128
Tatabánya d.	1756	1826	1850	1856	1926	1956	2034	2056	2126	2215
Tata d.	1804	|	1859	1904	|	2004	2042	2104	|	2226
Komárom d.	1817	|	1919	1917	|	2017	2055	2117	|	2249
Győr a.	1835	1900	1943	1935	2000	2035	2120	2135	2200	2316
Győr d.	▽	1902	...	△	2002	▽	...	...	2202	...
Mosonmagyaróvár d.	...	1920	...	...	2020	...	...	...	2220	...
Hegyeshalom ▦ d.	...	1932	...	...	2032	...	...	...	2232	...
Wien Hbf a.	...	2021	...	...	2121	...	...	...	2321	...

		IC			IC		EN	IC	RJ	IC
	9409	949	7701	9407	919	9209	463	917	41	937
	2	R	2	2	R	2	⊖	R	✕⊖	R
	Ⓐ		c	Ⓐ			K			
Wien Hbf d.	...	...	0445	...	...	...	0639	...	0739	...
Hegyeshalom ▦ d.	0506	...	0545	0606	...	...	0728	...	0828	...
Mosonmagyaróvár d.	0514	...	...	0614	...	...	0736	...	0836	...
Győr a.	0540	...	...	0640	△▽	u	0753	△	0853	▽
Győr d.	0547	0621	...	0643	0721	0726	0756	0821	0856	0921
Komárom d.	0609	0639	...	0709	0739	0751	|	0839	|	0939
Tata d.	0623	0652	...	0723	0752	0807	|	0852	|	0952
Tatabánya d.	0631	0700	...	0731	0800	0816	0830	0900	0930	1000
Kelenföld ☆ a.	0707	0732	...	0807	0832	0901	0907	0932	1002	1032
Ferencváros a.	0714	|	...	0814	|	0910	|	|	|	|
Budapest Keleti a.	0722	0749	...	0822	0849	0919	0924	0949	1019	1049

	EC	IC	RJ	IC	IC	RJ	IC	IC	RJ	IC	EC	IC	RJ	IC	Ex	EC	IC	RJ	IC	RJ	IC				
	345	317	49	947	927	61	945	915	63	933	145	925	65	943	1943	147	913	67	931	165	911	347			
	✕§	R	✕⊖	R	R	✕⊖	R	R	✕⊖	R	🍷R	R	✕⊖	R	2R	✕R	R	✕⊖	R	✕⊖	R	§	2	2b	2
	A	G	v			M			M f				M		⑦	H		M		Z		D			
Wien Hbf d.	0839	...	0942	...	...	1139	...	...	1339	...	1439	...	1542	...	...	1639	...	1739	...	1842	...	1939	...	2045	...
Hegyeshalom ▦ d.	0928	...	1028	...	...	1228	...	...	1428	...	1528	...	1628	...	...	1728	...	1828	...	1928	...	2028	...	2146	...
Mosonmagyaróvár d.	0936	...	1036	...	...	1236	...	...	1436	...	1536	...	1636	...	...	1736	...	1836	...	1936	...	2036	...	2154	...
Győr a.	0953	△	1053	▽	△	1253	▽	△	1453	▽	1553	△	1653	▽	...	1753	△	1853	▽	1953	△	2053	...	2220	...
Győr d.	0956	1021	1056	1121	1221	1256	1321	1421	1456	1521	1556	1621	1656	1721	1735	1756	1821	1856	1921	1956	2021	2056	2139	...	2239
Komárom d.	|	1039	|	1139	1239	|	1339	1439	|	1539	|	1639	|	1739	1800	|	1839	|	1939	|	2039	|	2204	...	2304
Tata d.	|	1052	|	1152	1252	|	1352	1452	|	1552	|	1652	|	1752	1815	|	1852	|	1952	|	2052	|	2222	...	2322
Tatabánya d.	1030	1100	1130	1200	1300	1330	1400	1500	1530	1600	1630	1700	1730	1800	1824	1830	1900	1930	2000	2030	2100	2130	2233	...	2332
Kelenföld ☆ a.	1102	1132	1202	1232	1332	1402	1432	1532	1602	1632	1702	1732	1802	1832	1857	1902	1932	2002	2032	2102	2132	2202	2320	...	...
Ferencváros a.	|	|	|	|	|	|	|	|	|	|	|	|	|	|	1905	|	|	|	|	|	|	2211	|	...	...
Budapest Keleti a.	1119	1149	1219	1249	1349	1419	1449	1549	1619	1649	1719	1749	1819	1849	1914	1919	1949	2019	2049	2119	2149	2220	2329d	...	...

A – AVALA – [12] ✕ Beograd - Budapest - Wien and v.v.
D – DACIA – 🛏 1, 2 cl., 🛏 2 cl., [12] Wien - Budapest - Bucureşti and v.v.
G – RÁBA – [12] Budapest - Szombathely - Graz and v.v.
H – HORTOBÁGY – [12] ✕ Nyíregyháza - Debrecen - Budapest - Wien and v.v.
K – KÁLMÁN IMRE / WIENER WALZER – 🛏 1, 2 cl., 🛏 2 cl., [2] Budapest - Wien - München and v.v.; 🛏 1, 2 cl., 🛏 2 cl., [2] Budapest - Wien - Salzburg (**466/7**) - Zürich and v.v.
M – [12] and ✕ Budapest - Wien - Salzburg - München and v.v. (Table **65**).
S – [12] and ✕ Budapest - Wien - Salzburg and v.v. (Table **65**).
Z – [12] ✕ Budapest - Wien - Salzburg - Innsbruck - Zürich and v.v. (Table **86**).
b – Change at Bruck an der Leitha (a. 2112 / d. 2118).
c – Change at Bruck an der Leitha (a. 0512 / d. 0520).
d – Budapest **Déli**.
f – Extended to / from Frankfurt on dates in Tables **912** / **930**.
u – To / from Szombathely via Celldömölk (Table **1253**).
v – From Innsbruck and Salzburg on dates in Table **86**.
⊖ – Reservation compulsory for domestic journeys within Hungary.

△ – To / from Szombathely (Table **1252**).
▽ – To / from Sopron (Table **1251**).
⊡ – Additional trains run Budapest Déli - Komárom at 2220, 2320.
☆ – See also Tables **1200**, **1220**, **1225**, **1230**. Kelenföld is also served by metro line 4 from Budapest Keleti.
§ – Reservation compulsory for international journeys.
RJ – *Railjet* service, first and economy (2nd) class. *Business class* also available to first class ticket holders (supplement payable).

Győr - Hegyeshalom - Bruck an der Leitha *79 km* Journey 1h 15m - 1h 22m
From Győr 0448, 0748, 0948, 1148, 1348, 1548, 1748, 1948.
From Bruck an der Leitha 0748, 0948, 1048, 1248, 1448, 1748, 1848, 2118.

Komárom - Székesfehérvár *82 km* Journey 1h 25m
From Komárom 0845, 1610; from Székesfehérvár 1035, 1835.

GYŐR - SOPRON 1251

Operator: GySEV

km							IC		IC		IC			IC			IC			IC			IC		
		9910	9920	9912	9922	9932	930	9942	932	9914	942	9924	9934	934	9916	9926	936	9936	9946	946	9918	9948	938	9928	9938
			Ⓐ			Ⓐ	R		R		R		Ⓐ	R			R			R		⑦e	R		
	Budapest Kel. **1250** d.	...	...	...	...	...	0710	...	0910	...	1110	...	...	1310	...	...	1510	...	...	1710	...	...	1910	...	...
0	**Győr** d.	0408	0519	0603	0649	0751	0838	0851	1038	1051	1238	1251	1351	1438	1451	1551	1638	1651	1751	1838	1851	1951	2038	2051	2251
31	Csorna d.	0435	0546	0631	0723	0821	0859	0921	1059	1121	1259	1323	1421	1459	1520	1621	1659	1720	1821	1859	1920	2020	2059	2117	2317
85	**Sopron** a.	0523	0647	0723	0813	0908	0938	1006	1138	1205	1338	1414	1513	1538	1613	1713	1738	1814	1913	1938	2013	2106	2138	2201	0001

				IC				IC		IC		IC		IC				IC			IC				
	9919	9929	9939	939	9917	9927		937	9937	947	9915	945	9925	933		9913	9923	943	9933	9943	931	9911	9921	9931	
				R	Ⓐ			R		R		R		R		Ⓐ		R	Ⓐ		R				
Sopron d.	0350	0446	0548	0608	0617	0745	...	0821	0944	1021	1144	1221	1345	1421	...	1446	1545	1621	1646	1746	1821	1846	1944	2229	...
Csorna d.	0435	0530	0639	0659	0706	0834	...	0859	1034	1059	1233	1259	1434	1459	...	1535	1634	1659	1735	1834	1859	1935	2034	2317	...
Győr a.	0501	0601	0708	0719	0733	0906	...	0919	1106	1119	1307	1319	1506	1519	...	1606	1706	1719	1806	1906	1919	2006	2106	2343	...
Budapest Kel. **1250** a.	...	...	...	0849	...	...	...	1049	...	1249	...	1449	...	1649	...	...	...	1849	...	...	2049	...	...	...	...

e – Not Dec. 25, Jan. 1, June 18 - Aug. 27.

GYŐR - CSORNA - SZOMBATHELY 1252

For alternative services Budapest - Szombathely via Székesfehérvár see Table **1230**

km		IC	IC	IC	IC	IC	IC	IC	IC	
		910	912	922	914	924	916	318	938	
		R	R	R	R	R	R	R	R	2
	Budapest Keleti **1250** d.	0610	0810	1010	1210	1410	1610	1810	1910	...
0	**Győr** d.	0738	0938	1138	1338	1538	1738	1938	2038	...
31	Csorna d.	0759	0959	1159	1359	1559	1759	1959	2058	2107
103	**Szombathely** a.	0849	1049	1249	1449	1649	1849	2049	...	2218
	Graz **986** a.	...	...	...	...	...	...	2300	...	...

	IC	IC	IC	IC	IC	IC	IC	IC	
	919	917	317	927	915	925	913	911	
	R	R	R	R	R	R	R	R	2
Graz **986** d.	...	...	0608	...	...	...	...	...	...
Szombathely d.	0600	0710	0910	1110	1310	1510	1710	1910	2230
Csorna d.	0659	0759	0959	1159	1359	1559	1759	1959	2340
Győr a.	0719	0819	1019	1219	1419	1619	1819	2019	...
Budapest Keleti **1250** a.	0849	0949	1149	1349	1549	1749	1949	2149	...

GYŐR - CELLDÖMÖLK - SZOMBATHELY 1253

km								b				
0	**Győr** d.	0741	0840	0933	1040	1237	1456	1640	1750	1840	1948	2040
47	Pápa d.	0848	0927	1032	1127	1333	1600	1727	1848	1927	2046	2127
72	Celldömölk a.	0919	0953	1103	1153	1404	1634	1753	1919	1953	2117	2153
72	Celldömölk d.	...	1006	...	1206	...	...	1806	...	2006	...	2206
117	**Szombathely** a.	...	1044	...	1244	...	...	1844	...	2044	...	2242

	b										
Szombathely d.	0519	0704	...	...	1304	...	1504	...	1704	...	...
Celldömölk a.	0551	0748	...	...	1351	...	1551	...	1751	...	...
Celldömölk d.	0606	0806	0926	1126	1406	1449	1606	1649	1806	1926	2126
Pápa d.	0631	0831	1000	1200	1431	1523	1631	1735	1831	2000	2200
Győr a.	0716	0916	1054	1254	1516	1619	1716	1831	1916	2056	2301

b – From / to Budapest Keleti (Table **1250**, note **u**).

Additional trains: Győr - Celldömölk 0506, 0636, 1350Ⓐ, 1602; Celldömölk - Győr 0440, 0650, 1249Ⓐ.

1255 BUDAPEST - VÁC - SZOB

Local trains, 2nd class

km										
0	**Budapest** Nyugati ..... d.	0048	0441	0541	0707	then	2107	2148	2248	2348
34	Vác .... d.	0134	0534	0630	0734	hourly	2134	2234	2334	0034
51	Nagymaros-Visegrád ¶ d.	0149	0549	0645	0749	until	2149	2249	2349	0049
64	**Szob** .... a.	0205	0605	0700	0805		2205	2305	0005	0105

Szob .... d.	0456	0556	0656	then	1856	2001	2101	2201	2301
Nagymaros-Visegrád ¶ .d.	0511	0611	0711	hourly	1911	2016	2116	2216	2316
Vác .... d.	0528	0628	0728	until	1928	2034	2134	2234	2334
Budapest Nyugati ...... a.	0554	0654	0754		1954	2117	2217	2317	0017

¶ – A ferry operates across the river to Visegrád.

For *EC* trains see Table **1175**.

1260 BUDAPEST - MISKOLC - KOŠICE

Most Budapest Keleti - Nyíregyháza *IC* trains continue to / from Debrecen and Budapest Nyugati. For trains Budapest - Debrecen - Nyiregyháza see Table **1270**

km		5520	5030	5040	5500	520	*IC** 182 [R]	542	*IC* 560 [R]	522	*IC* 502 [R]	552	*IC* 562 [R]	*IC* 512 [R]	544	*IC* 564 [R]	524	*IC* 504 [R]	554	*IC* 566 [R]	526 ⑤⑦	*IC* 514 [R]	546	*IC* 568 [R]	528
0	**Budapest** Keleti .... d.	...	...	...	0500	0600	0630	0700	0730	0800	0830	0900	0930	1030	1100	1130	1200	1230	1300	1330	1400	1430	1500	1530	1600
67	Hatvan .... d.	0405	...	0505	0555	0653	|	0753	|	0853	|	0953	|	|	1153	|	1253	|	1353	|	1453	|	1553	|	1652
87	Vámosgyörk ⊡ .... d.	0421	...	0521	0608	0706	|	0805	|	0906	|	1005	|	|	1205	|	1306	|	1405	|	1506	|	1605	|	1705
126	Füzesabony .... a.	0457	...	0556	0640	0729	0750	0828	0850	0929	0950	1028	1050	1150	1228	1250	1329	1350	1428	1450	1529	1550	1628	1650	1728
126	Füzesabony .... d.	0504	0503	*0603*	0650	0733	0751	0831	0851	0933	0951	1031	1051	1151	1231	1251	1333	1351	1431	1451	1533	1551	1632	1651	1733
143	**Eger** ⊙ .... a.	0523	|	|	0710	|	|	0850	|	|	|	1050	|	|	1250	|	|	|	1450	|	|	|	1650	|	|
139	Mezőkövesd .... d.	...	0514	*0614*	...	0744	|	...	|	0944	|	...	|	|	...	|	1344	|	...	|	1544	|	...	|	1744
183	**Miskolc** .... a.	...	0552	*0652*	...	0822	0827	...	0927	1022	1027	...	1127	1227	...	1327	1422	1427	...	1527	1622	1627	...	1727	1822
183	**Miskolc** .... d.	...	...	...	...	0835	0830	...	0930	1035	...	...	1130	...	...	1330	1435	...	...	1530	1635	...	...	1730	1835
	Nyíregyháza **1261** ... a.	...	...	...	...	▽	|	...	1029	▽	...	...	1229	...	...	1429	▽	...	...	1629	▽	...	...	1829	▽
244	Hidasnémeti ▦ .... § d.	...	...	...	...	...	0937	...	...	...	...	...	...	...	...	...	...	...	...	...	...	...	...	...	...
270	**Košice** .... a.	...	...	...	...	...	0959	...	...	...	...	...	...	...	...	...	...	...	...	...	...	...	...	...	...

	IC 506 [R]	556	*IC* 586 [R]	5208	*IC** 186 [R]	5508	*IC* 508 [R]	5008	5018	
Budapest Keleti .... d.	1630	1700	1730	1800	1830	1900	1930	2100	2235	...
Hatvan .... d.	|	1753	|	1853	|	1954	|	2158	2353	...
Vámosgyörk ⊡ .... d.	|	1805	|	1906	|	2009	|	2212	0007	...
Füzesabony .... a.	1750	1828	1850	1929	1950	2043	2050	2242	0041	...
Füzesabony .... d.	1751	1831	1851	1933	1951	2052	2051	2250	...	...
Eger ⊙ .... a.	|	1850	|	|	|	2109	|	• |	...	...
Mezőkövesd .... d.	|	...	|	1944	|	...	|	2301	...	...
Miskolc .... a.	1827	...	1927	2022	2027	...	2127	2340	...	...
Miskolc .... d.	...	...	1929	2035	2030	...	...	...	...	...
Nyíregyháza **1261** .... a.	...	...	2101	▽	|	...	...	...	...	...
Hidasnémeti ▦ .... § d.	...	...	...	...	2137	...	...	...	...	...
Košice .... a.	...	...	...	...	2159	...	...	...	...	...

	5009 2	5509 2	529 2	*IC* 519 [R]	547 2	*IC** 187 [R]	527 2	*IC* 682 [R]	557 2	*IC* 517 [R]
Košice .... d.	...	...	...	...	...	0602	...	...	...	...
Hidasnémeti ▦ .... § d.	...	...	...	...	...	0633	...	...	...	...
Nyíregyháza **1261** .... d.	...	...	▽	0526	...	|	▽	0726	...	...
Miskolc .... a.	...	...	0522	0627	...	0727	0722	0827	...	...
Miskolc .... d.	0328	...	0534	0629	...	0729	0734	0829	...	0929
Mezőkövesd .... d.	0406	...	0612	|	...	|	0812	|	...	|
Eger ⊙ .... d.	|	0438	|	|	0704	|	|	|	0904	|
Füzesabony .... a.	0417	0455	0624	0704	0723	0804	0824	0904	0923	1004
Füzesabony .... d.	0419	0500	0626	0705	0728	0805	0826	0905	0928	1005
Vámosgyörk ⊡ .... d.	0454	0536	0652	|	0752	|	0852	|	0952	|
Hatvan .... d.	0511	0554	0706	|	0806	|	0906	|	1006	|
Budapest Keleti .... a.	0620	0715	0800	0830	0900	0930	1000	1030	1100	1130

	525 2	*IC* 650 [R]	545 2	*IC* 515 [R]	*IC* 652 [R]	555 2	*IC* 505 [R]	5205 2	*IC* 654 [R]	543 2	*IC* 513 [R]	523 ⑤⑦	*IC* 656 [R]	553 2	*IC* 503 [R] N	*IC* 1521 [R] G	521 2 E	15201 2 G	*IC* 658 [R]	541 2	*IC** 181 [R]	5203 2	5203 2 ⑦	511 2	5021 2
Košice .... d.	...	...	...	...	...	...	...	...	...	...	...	...	...	...	...	...	...	...	...	...	1802	...	...	...	...
Hidasnémeti ▦ .... § d.	...	...	...	...	...	...	...	...	...	...	...	...	...	...	...	...	...	...	...	...	1833	...	...	...	...
Nyíregyháza **1261** .... d.	▽	0926	...	...	1126	...	...	▽	1326	...	...	▽	1526	...	...	▽	▽	...	1726	...	|	▽	▽	1926	...
Miskolc .... a.	0922	1027	...	...	1227	...	...	1322	1427	...	...	1522	1627	...	...	1716	1722	...	1827	...	1927	1922	1922	2027	...
Miskolc .... d.	0934	1029	...	1129	1229	...	1329	1334	1429	...	1529	1534	1629	...	1729	1729	1734	1734	1829	...	1929	1934	1934	2034	2300
Mezőkövesd .... d.	1012	|	...	|	|	...	|	1412	|	...	|	1612	|	...	|	|	1812	1812	|	...	|	2012	2012	2112	2338
Eger ⊙ .... d.	|	|	1104	|	|	1304	|	|	|	1504	|	|	|	1704	|	|	|	|	|	1904	|	|	|	|	|
Füzesabony .... a.	1024	1104	1123	1204	1304	1323	1404	1424	1504	1523	1604	1624	1704	1723	1804	1804	1824	1824	1904	1920	2004	2024	2024	2124	2350
Füzesabony .... d.	1026	1105	1128	1205	1305	1328	1405	1426	1505	1528	1605	1626	1705	1728	1805	1805	1826	1826	1905	1926	2005	...	2026	2126	...
Vámosgyörk ⊡ .... d.	1052	|	1152	|	|	1352	|	1452	|	1552	|	1652	|	1752	|	|	1852	1852	|	1955	|	...	2052	2152	...
Hatvan .... d.	1106	|	1206	|	|	1406	|	1506	|	1606	|	1706	|	1806	|	|	1906	1906	|	2009	|	...	2106	2205	...
Budapest Keleti .... a.	1200	1230	1300	1330	1430	1500	1530	1600	1630	1700	1730	1800	1830	1900	1930	1930	2000	2000	2030	2105	2130	...	2200	2300z	...

E – Not dates in note **G**.
G – ⑦ (not Dec. 25, Jan. 1, June 18 - Aug. 27).
z – ⑦ only.
▽ – To / from Sátoraljaújhely (Table **1261**).
§ – Local trains run Miskolc - Hidasnémeti 14 times daily (no local trains Hidasnémeti - Košice).
• – Classified *EC* in Slovakia.

⊙ – Local trains **Füzesabony - Eger** and v.v. (journey 17 mins):
From Füzesabony: 0422, 0604, 0708Ⓐ, 0808Ⓐ, 0908, 1008Ⓐ, 1108, 1208Ⓐ, 1308, 1408Ⓐ, 1508, 1608Ⓐ, 1708, 1808Ⓐ, 2008Ⓐ, 2208Ⓐ, 2255.
From Eger: 0322, 0531Ⓐ, 0631, 0731Ⓐ, 0831, 0931Ⓐ, 1031, 1131Ⓐ, 1231, 1331Ⓐ, 1431, 1531Ⓐ, 1631, 1731Ⓐ, 1831, 1931Ⓐ, 2031, 2131Ⓐ, 2231.

⊡ – Connecting trains **Vámosgyörk - Gyöngyös** and v.v. (journey 16 mins):
From Vámosgyörk: 0522, 0610, 0708, 0908, 1108, 1308, 1408Ⓐ, 1508, 1608, 1708, 1908.
From Gyöngyös: 0546, 0633, 0732, 0932, 1132, 1332, 1432Ⓐ, 1532, 1632, 1732, 1932.

TRAIN NAMES: **181/2** RÁKÓCZI, **186/7** HERNÁD / HORNÁD

1261 MISKOLC - SÁTORALJAÚJHELY and NYÍREGYHÁZA

Most Budapest Keleti - Nyíregyháza - Debrecen *IC* trains continue to / from Budapest Nyugati. For trains Budapest - Debrecen - Nyiregyháza see Table **1270**

km		*IC* 580 [R]	5140 2 ⊡	510 2	520 2	*IC* 560 [R]	522 2	*IC* 562 [R]	5122 2	5234 2	*IC* 564 [R]	5114 2	524 2	*IC* 566 [R]	5124 2	5236 2 ④–⑦	*IC* 568 [R]	5116 2	528 2	*IC* 586 [R]	1528 [R] F	5118 2	5208 2	5128 2	5158 2 Ⓑ
	Budapest Kel. **1260**..d.	...	...	...	0600*	0730	0800*	0930	...	...	1130	...	1200*	1330	...	1400r	1530	...	1600*	1730	1730	...	1800*	...	...
0	**Miskolc** .... d.	0626	0635	0730	0835	0930	1035	1130	1135	1235	1330	1335	1435	1530	1535	1635	1730	1735	1835	1929	1929	1935	2035	2135	2310
38	Szerencs .... a.	0650	0712	0754	0912	0954	1112	1154	1212	1312	1354	1412	1512	1554	1612	1712	1754	1812	1912	1954	1954	2012	2112	2212	2347
38	Szerencs .... d.	0651	0716	0755	0914	0955	1114	1155	1216	1314	1355	1416	1514	1555	1616	1714	1755	1816	1914	1955	2014	2016	2114	2216	2348
74	Sárospatak .... a.	|	*0802*	|	1002	|	1202	|	*1302*	1402	|	*1502*	1602	|	*1702*	1802	|	*1902*	2002	|	2102	*2102*	2202	*2306*	|
84	**Sátoraljaújhely** .... a.	|	*0812*	|	1012	|	1212	|	*1312*	1412	|	*1512*	1612	|	*1712*	1812	|	*1912*	2012	|	2112	*2112*	2212	*2316*	|
56	Tokaj .... a.	0704	0734	0808	...	1008	...	1208	1234	*1334*	1408	1434	*1534*	1608	1634	*1734*	1808	1834	*1934*	2008	...	2034	*2134*	2234	0006
88	**Nyíregyháza** .... a.	0725	0815	0829	...	1029	...	1229	1315	*1415*	1429	1515	*1615*	1629	1715	*1815*	1829	1915	*2015*	2029	...	2115	*2215*	2315	0040
	Debrecen **1270** .... a.	0801	...	...	...	1101	...	1301	...	...	1501	...	...	1701	...	...	1901	...	...	2101	...	...	...	...	...

	529 2	*IC* 519 [R]	5139 2	527 2	5169 2	*IC* 682 [R]	525 2	5117 2	*IC* 650 [R]	5237 2	*IC* 652 [R]	5205 2	5115 2⊙	*IC* 654 [R]	5235 ④–⑦	*IC* 656 [R]	*IC* 1521 [R] G	521 E	5113 2	*IC* 658 [R]	5203 2	5123 2	511 2	5221 2	5231 2
Debrecen **1270** .... d.	...	...	...	...	...	0654	... •	...	0854	...	1054	...	...	1254	...	1454	...	...	...	1654	...	...	...	...	...
Nyíregyháza .... d.	*0343*	0526	0539	...	0639	0726	...	0839	0926	...	1126	...	1239	1326	...	1526	...	...	1639	1726	...	1839	1926	*1939*	*2039*
Tokaj .... d.	*0418*	0548	0620	...	0720	0748	...	0920	0948	...	1148	...	1320	1348	...	1548	...	...	1720	1748	...	1920	1948	*2021*	*2120*
Sátoraljaújhely .... d.	0353	|	|	0548	*0648*	|	0748	|	|	0948	|	1148	*1248*	|	1348	|	1548	1548	*1648*	|	1748	*1848*	|	1948	2048
Sárospatak .... d.	0404	|	|	0604	*0704*	|	0804	|	|	1004	|	1204	*1304*	|	1404	|	1604	1604	*1704*	|	1804	*1904*	|	2004	2104
Szerencs .... a.	0443	0601	0639	0643	0739	0801	0843	0939	1001	1043	1201	1243	1339	1401	1443	1601	1643	1643	1739	1801	1843	1939	2001	2043	2143
Szerencs .... d.	0445	0602	0640	0645	0745	0802	0845	0945	1002	1045	1202	1245	1345	1402	1445	1602	1644	1645	1745	1802	1845	1945	2002	2045	*2220*
Miskolc .... a.	0522	0627	0713	0722	0822	0827	0922	1022	1027	1122	1227	1322	1422	1427	1522	1627	1716	1722	1822	1827	1922	2022	2027	2122	2257
Budapest Kel. **1260**... a.	0800	0830	...	1000*	...	1030	1200*	...	1230	...	1430	1600*	...	1630	1800r	1830	1930	2000*	...	2030	2200*	...	2300z	...	...

E – Not dates in note **G**.
F – ⑤ (not Dec. 23, 30, June 16 - Aug. 25).
G – ⑦ (not Dec. 25, Jan. 1, June 18 - Aug. 27).
r – ⑤⑦ only (train **526 / 523**) *.
z – ⑦ only.
⊡ – Similar journeys run at 0435, 0535, 0735.
⊙ – Similar journeys run at 1039, 1439.
* – Faster connection is available by changing at Miskolc (see Table **1260**).
Italic times indicate a change at Szerencs

1262 HATVAN - SALGÓTARJÁN - SOMOSKÖÚJFALU

2nd class

km										n	
0	Hatvan .... d.	0410	0610	0810	1013	1213	1410	1610	1813	2013	2213
59	Salgótarján .... a.	0540	0740	0940	1140	1340	1540	1740	1940	2140	2340
65	Somosköújfalu ▦ .... a.	0551	0751	0951	1151	1351	1551	1751	1951	2151	2351

						⑦b				
Somosköújfalu ▦ ...... d.	0617	0817	1017	1217	1417	1600	1617	1817	2017	2217
Salgótarján .... d.	0629	0829	1029	1229	1429	1612	1629	1829	2029	2229
Hatvan .... a.	0750	0950	1150	1350	1550	1727	1750	1950	2150	2350

b – ⑦ (not Dec. 25, Jan. 1, June 18 - Aug. 27). To Budapest Keleti, arrive 1840.
n – On ⑦ (not Dec. 25, Jan. 1, June 18 - Aug. 27) starts from Budapest Keleti, depart 1905.

Additional trains: Hatvan to Somosköújfalu: 0510Ⓐ, 0710Ⓐ, 1310Ⓐ, 1510Ⓐ, 1910Ⓐ.
Somosköújfalu to Hatvan: 0317, 0417, 0517Ⓐ, 0717Ⓐ, 1317Ⓐ, 1517Ⓐ.

BUDAPEST - DEBRECEN - NYÍREGYHÁZA - ZÁHONY - CHOP 1270

For trains to / from Romania see Table **1275**.

km		IC 682	IC 650	IC 34	IC 652	IC 612	IC 654	IC 614	IC 656	IC 624	IC 658	IC 626	IC 628	IC 616	IC 616	IC 608	IC 618	EC 147				6260	6202		6208	
		R	R	R	R	R	R	R	R	R	R	R	R	R	R	R	R	⊖		2	2	2	2		2	2
				L											⑤			H								d
0	**Budapest** Nyugati ◧ d.	...	0623	0723	0823	0923	1023	1123	1223	1323	1423	1523	1623	1723	1723	1823	1923	1940k	S	...	...	0503	0628	E	1828	2028
11	Kőbánya Kispest ◧ d.	...	0637	0737	0837	0937	1037	1137	1237	1337	1437	1537	1637	1737	1737	1837	1937	|	L	...	...	0518	0642	V	1842	2042
18	Ferihegy ✈ ◧ d.	...	0643	0743	0843	0943	1043	1143	1243	1343	1443	1543	1643	1743	1743	1843	1943	|	O	...	...	0527	0648	E	1848	2048
73	Cegléd ◧ d.	...	0718	0818	0918	1018	1118	1218	1318	1418	1518	1618	1718	1818	1818	1918	2018	|	W	...	...	0624	0724	R	1924	2130
100	**Szolnok** ◧ d.	...	0738	0838	0938	1038	1138	1238	1338	1438	1538	1638	1738	1838	1838	1938	2038	2105		...	0550	0650	0750	Y	1950	2156
177	Püspökladány d.	...	0821	0921	1021	1121	1221	1321	1421	1521	1621	1721	1821	1921	1921	2021	2121	2204	T	0455	0655	0755	0855		2055	2259
201	Hajdúszoboszló d.	...	0837	0937	1037	1137	1237	1337	1437	1537	1637	1737	1837	1937	1937	2037	2137	2220	R	0514	0714	0814	0914	2	2114	2318
221	**Debrecen** a.	...	0852	0952	1052	1152	1252	1352	1452	1552	1652	1752	1852	1952	1952	2052	2152	2235	A	0529	0729	0829	0929		2129	2333
221	**Debrecen** d.	0654	0854	0954	1054	1154	1254	1354	1454	1554	1654	1757	1854	1954	1954	2054	2154	2237	I	0534	0741	0834	0934	H	2134	...
270	**Nyíregyháza** a.	0724	0924	1024	1124	1224	1324	1424	1524	1624	1724	1827	1924	2024	2024	2124	2224	2307	N	0616	0823	0916	1016	O	2216	...
270	**Nyíregyháza** d.	◇	◇	1031	◇	...	◇	...	◇	1631	◇	1831	1931	...	2031	...	...	...	S	0648	0848	0948	1048	U	2248	...
313	Kisvárda d.	...	...	1102	...	...	...	...	...	1702	...	1902	2002	...	2102	...	...	...		0732	0932	1032	1132	R	2332	...
335	Záhony ▶ a.	...	...	1121	...	...	...	...	...	1721	...	1921	2021	...	2121	...	...	...		0757	0957	1057	1157	S	2357	...
341	**Chop** ⊙ ▶ a.	...	...	1340	...	...	...	...	...	...	...	...	...	...	...	...	...	...		...	...	...	...		...	...

	EC 140	IC 619	IC 629	IC 580	IC 627	IC 617	IC 560	IC 605	IC 562	IC 615	IC 564	IC 33	IC 566	IC 1623	IC 613	IC 568	IC 586			6109	6207	6297		6293		
	⊖	R	R	R	R	R	R	R	R	R	R	R	R	R	R	R	R		2	2	2	2		2	2	2
	H											L		⑦	①–⑥											h
Chop ⊙ ▶ d.	...	...	...	...	...	...	...	...	...	...	...	1420	...	...	...	...	...	S	...	...	...	...		...	...	...
Záhony ▶ d.	...	...	0528	...	0735	...	...	...	...	...	...	1440	...	1623	...	...	...	L	0358	...	0553	0803	E	1603	1703	1803
Kisvárda d.	...	...	0547	...	0754	...	...	...	...	...	...	1459	...	1642	...	...	...	O	0423	...	0618	0828	V	1628	1728	1828
Nyíregyháza a.	...	...	0618	◇	0825	...	◇	...	◇	...	◇	1530	◇	1714	...	◇	◇	W	0507	...	0702	0912	E	1712	1812	1912
Nyíregyháza d.	0451	0531	0622	0731	0831	0931	1031	1131	1231	1331	1431	1531	1631	1731	1731	1831	2031		—	0544	0744	0944	R	1744	1844	1944
Debrecen a.	0521	0601	0653	0801	0901	1001	1101	1201	1301	1401	1501	1601	1701	1801	1801	1901	2101	T	2	0626	0826	1026	Y	1826	1926	2026
Debrecen d.	0523	0603	0703	0803	0903	1003	1103	1203	1303	1403	1503	1603	1703	1803	1803	1903	...	R	0414	0631	0831	1031		1831	1931	—
Hajdúszoboszló d.	0539	0619	0719	0819	0919	1019	1119	1219	1319	1419	1519	1619	1719	1819	1819	1919	...	A	0430	0647	0847	1047	2	1847	1947	...
Püspökladány d.	0557	0637	0737	0837	0937	1037	1137	1237	1337	1437	1537	1637	1737	1837	1837	1937	...	I	0455	0708	0908	1108		1908	2008	2
Szolnok ◧ d.	0657	0722	0822	0922	1022	1122	1222	1322	1422	1522	1622	1722	1822	1922	1922	2022	...	N	0605	0815	1015	1215	H	2015	2115	2225
Cegléd ◧ d.	|	0743	0843	0943	1043	1143	1243	1343	1443	1543	1643	1743	1843	1943	1943	2043	...	S	0628	0838	1038	1238	O	2038	2148	2250
Ferihegy ✈ ◧ d.	|	0815	0915	1015	1115	1215	1315	1415	1515	1615	1715	1815	1915	2015	2015	2115	...		0715	0910	1110	1310	U	2110	2240	2348
Kőbánya Kispest ◧ a.	|	0820	0920	1020	1120	1220	1320	1420	1520	1620	1720	1820	1920	2020	2020	2120	...		0720	0915	1115	1315	R	2115	2248	2358
Budapest Nyugati ◧ a.	0820k	0837	0937	1037	1137	1237	1337	1437	1537	1637	1737	1837	1937	2037	2037	2137	...		0737	0932	1132	1332	S	2132	2305	0014

H – HORTOBÁGY – 12 ✕ Wien - Budapest - Nyíregyháza and v.v.
L – LATORCA – 12 Budapest - Záhony and v.v.; 2 Záhony - Chop and v.v.; 🛏 1, 2 cl. Budapest - Chop - Kyïv and v.v.; 🛏 1, 2 cl. Budapest - Chop - Lviv and v.v.
d – An additional journey runs 2 hours later.
h – Additional journeys run at 1929, 2003.
k – Budapest **Keleti**.
⊙ – Ukrainian (East European) time, one hour ahead of Hungarian time.
⊖ – Compulsory reservation for domestic journeys within Hungary.

◧ – Also **1290** Budapest - Cegléd; **1280** Budapest - Szolnok. Ferihegy ✈ is served by 5 - 6 trains per hour.
◇ – To / from Miskolc, Table **1261** (most trains continue beyond Miskolc to / from Budapest Keleti).

▶ – Full service Záhony - Chop, 2nd class (minimum 15 minutes connection time at Záhony required):

				L								L			
Záhony .. d.	0342	0634	0835	1223	1422	1802	2015	Chop ⊙ d.	0530	0822	1025	1420	1615	1957	2220
Chop . ⊙ a.	0500	0752	0953	1340	1540	1920	2133	Záhony .. a.	0448	0740	0943	1337	1533	1915	2138

BUDAPEST - BIHARKERESZTES - ORADEA 1275

km				IC*				IC*	IC*	
			369	367	6204	365		363	407	
		2		H R	2	2	2	A R	C R	2
0	**Budapest Keleti** 1270 d.	...	...	0645	1028n	...	...	1340	1740	...
100	Szolnok 1270 d.	0526	...	0816	1150	...	...	1503	1903	...
177	Püspökladány 1270 d.	0628	0633	0927	1252	1309	1409	1609	2009	2125
228	Biharkeresztes a.	...	0737	1034	...	1417	1517	1717	2113	2229
228	Biharkeresztes d.	...	0802	1121	...	1437	...	1757	2153	...
241	Episcopia Bihor ⊙ a.	...	0917	1243	...	1552	...	1912	2308	...
241	Episcopia Bihor ⊙ d.	...	0932	1303	...	1607	...	1937	2323	...
247	**Oradea** ⊙ a.	...	0941	1311	...	1615	...	1945	2331	...
	Cluj Napoca **1612** ⊙ a.	...	▽	1550	...	...	...	2228	0211	...

	IC*	IC*					IC	IC*	
	406	362	364	6205		368	33	366	
	C R	A R	2	2	2	2	R	H R	2
Cluj Napoca **1612** ⊙ d.	0225	0644	...	...	...	▽	...	1444	...
Oradea ⊙ d.	0502	0922	1130	...	...	1441	...	1731	...
Episcopia Bihor ⊙ a.	0510	0930	1138	...	...	1449	...	1739	...
Episcopia Bihor ⊙ d.	0533	0949	1153	...	...	1504	...	1759	...
Biharkeresztes a.	0448	0904	1108	...	...	1419	...	1714	...
Biharkeresztes d.	0528	0944	1144	...	1344	1444	...	1744	1944
Püspökladány 1270 a.	0632	1052	1252	1308	1452	1552	1637	1852	2052
Szolnok 1270 a.	0752	1156	...	1410	...	...	1720	1957	...
Budapest Keleti 1270 a.	0920	1320	...	1532n	...	...	1837n	2120	...

A – ADY ENDRE – 12 🍷 Budapest - Oradea - Cluj Napoca and v.v.
C – CORONA – 🛏 1, 2 cl., 🛏 2 cl., 12 🍷 Budapest - Cluj Napoca - Deda - Brasov and v.v.
H – HARGITA – 12 🍷 Budapest - Oradea - Cluj Napoca - Deda - Braşov and v.v.; 2 Budapest - Cluj Napoca - Târgu Mures and v.v.
n – Budapest **Nyugati**.
⊙ – Romanian (East European) time, one hour ahead of Hungary.
▽ – To / from Salonta (Table **1614**).
* – Classified *IR* in Romania.

2nd class DEBRECEN and NYÍREGYHÁZA - MÁTÉSZALKA 1276

km									△		Ⓑ	
0	**Debrecen** d.	0455	0712	0912	1112	1312	1512	1708	1807	1912	2118	2246
58	Nyírbátor d.	0624	0838	1038	1238	1438	1638	1838	1920	2035	2243	0009
78	**Mátészalka** a.	0647	0901	1101	1301	1501	1701	1901	1938	2058	2306	0032

			▽								
Mátészalka d.	0358	0446	0520	0703	0903	1103	1303	1503	1703	1914	2108
Nyírbátor d.	0421	0509	0541	0726	0926	1126	1326	1526	1727	1941	2131
Debrecen a.	0546	0631	0649	0848	1048	1248	1448	1648	1853	2112	2253

km		⚒				⚒	⑦					
0	**Nyíregyháza** d.	0538	...	0837	...	1435	1435	...	1635	...	...	...
38	Nyírbátor d.	0702	...	0954	...	1558	1558	...	1754	...	...	...
58	**Mátészalka** a.	0727	...	1016	...	1620	1636	...	1816	...	...	...

		▽									
Mátészalka d.	...	0520	...	...	0734	...	1534	...	1725	...	...
Nyírbátor d.	...	0540	0559	...	0758	...	1557	...	1755	...	...
Nyíregyháza a.	...	...	0715	...	0922	...	1722	...	1911	...	...

△ – 2 R Budapest Nyugati (*IC* **626** d. 1523) - Debrecen (*IC* **638**) - Mátészalka.
▽ – 2 R Mátészalka (*IC* **639**) - Debrecen (*IC* **629**) - Budapest Nyugati (a. 0937).

2nd class DEBRECEN - ORADEA and BAIA MARE and other cross-border services 1277

km		6812	6822	6826
				b
0	**Debrecen** d.	0712	0912	1512
30	Nyirábrány a.	0751	0951	1551
39	Valea lui Mihai ⊙ a.	0921	1121	1726
39	Valea lui Mihai ⊙ d.	0945	1141	1756
105	**Oradea** ⊙ a.	1109	|	|
70	Carei 1618 ⊙ a.	...	1216	1832
106	Satu Mare 1618 ⊙ a.	...	1300	1925
165	**Baia Mare** 1616 ⊙ a.	...	...	2203

	6827	6823	6811
	d		
Baia Mare 1616 ⊙ d.	0414	...	...
Satu Mare 1618 ⊙ d.	0621	1500	...
Carei 1618 ⊙ d.	0710	1544	...
Oradea ⊙ d.	|	|	1638
Valea lui Mihai ⊙ a.	0749	1617	1820
Valea lui Mihai ⊙ d.	0839	1639	1839
Nyirábrány d.	0809	1609	1809
Debrecen a.	0848	1648	1848

km				
0	**Békéscsaba** 1280 d.	0638	1550	...
16	Gyula 1280 d.	0659	1609	...
36	Kötegyán a.	0727	1645	...
50	**Salonta** ⊙ a.	0900	1805	...

Salonta ⊙ d.	0940	1830	...
Kötegyán d.	0915	1815	...
Gyula 1280 d.	0950	1854	...
Békéscsaba 1280 a.	1010	1910	...

km				
0	**Mátészalka** d.	0535	1410	...
18	Tiborszállás a.	0605	1440	...
18	Tiborszállás d.	0620	1455	...
33	**Carei** ⊙ a.	0746	1621	...

Carei ⊙ d.	0927	1738	...
Tiborszállás a.	0853	1704	...
Tiborszállás d.	0908	1719	...
Mátészalka a.	0952	1803	...

b – To Jibou (arrive 2357).
d – From Jibou (depart 0301).
⊙ – Romanian (East European) time, one hour ahead of Hungary.

2nd class DEBRECEN - FÜZESABONY 1278

km										Ⓑ	
0	**Debrecen** d.	0450	0645	0845	1045	1245	1445	1645	1850	2000	2245
42	Hortobágy d.	0536	0736	0936	1136	1336	1536	1736	1936	2050	2331
73	Tiszafüred d.	0612	0812	1012	1212	1412	1612	1812	2012	2125	0006
103	**Füzesabony** a.	0647	0847	1047	1247	1447	1647	1847	2047	...	...

			Ⓐ							
Füzesabony d.	0459	0659	...	0859	1059	1259	1459	1659	1859	2158
Tiszafüred d.	0535	0735	0827	0935	1135	1335	1535	1735	1935	2233
Hortobágy d.	0616	0816	0901	1016	1216	1416	1616	1816	2016	...
Debrecen a.	0700	0900	0950	1100	1300	1500	1700	1904	2100	...

1280 BUDAPEST - BÉKÉSCSABA - LÖKÖSHÁZA - ARAD (- BUCURESTI)

km				7400	IC* 73	7402	IC* 75	7404	IC 752	1471 1481	7504	754	7506	IC* 79	1696	7406	IC 756	748	IC* 473		17408	347	
		2	2	2	△	2	△	2	Ⓡ	2	2	2	2	△	Ⓡ	2	Ⓡ	2	△	2	2		
					T		R			N				K	Y				B	b	⑤	D	
0	**Budapest** Keleti ... **1270** d.	...	...	0610	0710	0810	0910	1010	1110	1110	1210	1310	1410	1510	...	1610	1710	1810	1910	...	2010	2250	...
100	Szolnok ... **1270** d.	0445**a**	0545	0734	0834	0934	1034	1134	1234	1234	1334	1434	1534	1634	...	1734	1834	1934	2034	...	2134	0016	...
141	Mezőtúr ... d.	0529	0629	0759	0859	0959	1059	1159	1259	1259	1359	1459	1559	1659	...	1759	1859	1959	2059	...	2159	|	...
159	Gyoma ... d.	0547	0647	0814	0912	1012	1112	1212	1312	1312	1414	1512	1612	1712	...	1812	1912	2012	2112	...	2212	|	...
196	**Békéscsaba** ... a.	0617	0717	0840	0940	1040	1140	1240	1340	1340	1440	1540	1640	1740	...	1840	1940	2040	2140	...	2236	0110	...
196	**Békéscsaba** ... d.	0635	...	...	0943	...	1143	...	1343	1343	1443	1543	1643	1743	...	...	1943	...	2143	2235	*2243*	0115	...
225	Lökösháza ... a.	0713	...	...	1010	...	1210	...	1410	1410	1513	1613	1713	1813	...	...	2010	...	2210	2302	*2310*	0140	...
225	Lökösháza 🛃 ... d.	...	...	...	1050	...	1250	...	...	1440	...	...	...	1853	...	...	...	...	2251	...	...	0225	...
236	Curtici 🛃 ... ⊙ d.	...	...	...	1230	...	1425	...	...	1620	...	...	...	2028	...	...	...	...	0025	...	...	0405	...
253	**Arad** ... ⊙ a.	...	...	...	1244	...	1439	...	...	1634	...	...	...	2042	...	...	...	...	0039	...	...	0419	...
	Timisoara **1614** ... ⊙ a.	...	...	...	1333	...	|	...	...	...	...	...	...	2133	2230	...	...	...	|	...	...	|	...
	Brasov **1600** ... ⊙ a.	...	...	...	|	...	2310	...	...	...	...	...	...	...	|	...	...	...	0932	...	...	1316	...
	Bucuresti Nord **1600** ... ⊙ a.	...	...	...	2238	...	...	...	...	...	...	...	...	...	0822	...	...	...	1210	...	...	1600	...

	346	7509	IC* 472	IC 759	7507	1695	IC* 78	7407	757	7405	IC 755	7403	1470 1480	IC* 74		IC* 72	IC 753	7501	751		7441	7451	
		2	△	Ⓡ	2	Ⓡ	△	2	2	2	Ⓡ	2	2	△		△	Ⓡ	2	2	2	2	2	
	D		B			Y	K						N	R		T							
Bucuresti Nord **1600** ... ⊙ d.	1400	...	1745	...	...	2125	...	...	...	...	...	...	...	...	...	0545	...	...	...	...	...	...	...
Brasov **1600** ... ⊙ d.	1637	...	2019	...	...	|	...	...	...	...	...	...	...	0545	...	|	...	...	...	...	...	...	...
Timisoara **1614** ... ⊙ d.	|	...	|	...	...	0646	0730	...	...	...	...	...	...	|	...	1438	...	...	...	...	...	...	...
Arad ... ⊙ d.	0116	...	0518	...	...	...	0820	...	...	...	...	...	1234	1415	...	1531	...	...	...	...	...	...	...
Curtici 🛃 ... ⊙ d.	0200	...	0559	...	...	...	0859	...	...	...	...	...	1320	1459	...	1614	...	...	...	...	...	...	...
Lökösháza 🛃 ... a.	0110	...	0509	...	...	...	0809	...	...	...	...	...	1230	1409	...	1524	...	...	...	...	...	...	...
Lökösháza ... d.	0150	0450	0549	0649	0749	...	0849	...	1049	...	1249	...	1310	1449	...	1549	1649	1749	1849	...	...	...	...
Békéscsaba ... a.	0215	0517	0616	0716	0816	...	0916	...	1116	...	1316	...	1335	1516	...	1616	1716	1816	1916	...	...	...	...
Békéscsaba ... d.	0220	0532	0619	0719	0819	...	0919	1019	1119	1219	1319	1419	1419	1519	...	1619	1719	1819	1919	...	2040	2240	...
Gyoma ... d.	|	0601	0648	0746	0848	...	0948	1048	1148	1248	1346	1448	1448	1548	...	1648	1748	1848	1948	...	2111	2311	...
Mezőtúr ... d.	|	0616	0701	0801	0901	...	1001	1101	1201	1301	1401	1501	1501	1601	...	1701	1801	1901	2001	...	2126	2326	...
Szolnok ... **1270** d.	0318	0649	0727	0827	0927	...	1027	1127	1227	1327	1427	1527	1527	1627	...	1727	1827	1927	2027	2219	...	...	...
Budapest Keleti ... **1270** a.	0450	0815	0850	0950	1050	...	1150	1250	1350	1450	1550	1650	1650	1750	...	1850	1950	2050	2150	0015	...	...	...

B – ISTER – 🛏 1,2 cl., ▬ 2 cl., (12) 🍷 Budapest - Sighisoara - Brasov - Bucuresti and v.v.
D – DACIA – 🛏 1,2 cl., ▬ 2 cl., (12) Wien - Budapest - Sibiu - Brasov - Bucuresti and v.v.
K – KÖRÖS / CRIS – (12) Budapest - Lökösháza and v.v.; (12) Budapest - Arad - Timisoara - Bucuresti and v.v. (conveyed in train **Y** Timisoara - Bucuresti and v.v.).
N – NESEBAR - ALBENA – ②⑤ June 16 - Sept. 1 from Budapest; ③⑥ June 17 - Sept. 2 from Burgas and Varna (next day from Arad). ▬ 2 cl., (2) Budapest - Craiova - Ruse - Burgas and v.v.; (2) Budapest - Ruse - Varna and v.v.
R – TRANSSYLVANIA – (12) Budapest - Arad - Simeria - Sibiu - Brasov and v.v.
T – TRAIANUS – (12) Budapest - Timisoara - Craiova - Bucuresti and v.v.
Y – 🛏 1,2 cl., ▬ 2 cl. and (12) Timisoara - Bucuresti and v.v.
a – Ⓐ only.

b – Not ⑤.
s – Not Dec. 25, Jan. 1, June 18 - Aug. 27. To / from Szeged (Table **1292**).
⊙ – Romanian (East European) time, one hour ahead of Hungary.
△ – Reservation compulsory for international journeys (Ⓡ in Romania).
* – Classified *IR* in Romania.

Note: *IC* trains on this line have designated carriages for the use of passengers without seat reservations.

BÉKÉSCSABA - GYULA

16 km 2nd class. Journey 17 - 20 mins

From **Békéscsaba**: 0523, 0638, 0725, 0950, 1150, 1250, 1350, 1427 Ⓐ, 1450, 1550, 1617⑦**s**, 1650, 1750, 1950, 2050, 2230**b**, 2241⑤.

From **Gyula**: 0459, 0548, 0617Ⓐ, 0659, 0750, 0854, 0950, 1054, 1250, 1450, 1550, 1650, 1728⑦**s**, 1750, 1854, 1950, 2107.

1290 BUDAPEST - KECSKEMÉT - SZEGED

km		7020	IC 700	IC 702	IC 712		IC 708	IC 718	IC 728	
		2	Ⓡ	Ⓡ	Ⓡ		Ⓡ	Ⓡ	Ⓡ	
									⑤⑦	
0	**Budapest** Nyugati ... ▷ d.	0400	0553	0653	0753		1853	1953	2053	...
11	Kőbánya Kispest ... ▷ d.	0415	0607	0707	0807	and	1907	2007	2107	...
18	Ferihegy ✈ ... ▷ d.	0424	0613	0713	0813	hourly	1913	2013	2113	...
73	Cegléd ... ▷ d.	0531	0648	0748	0848	until	1948	2048	2148	...
106	**Kecskemét** ... d.	0605	0711	0811	0911		2011	2111	2211	...
131	Kiskunfélegyháza ... d.	0630	0730	0830	0930		2030	2130	2228	...
191	**Szeged** ... a.	0715	0815	0915	1015		2115	2215	2317	...

	7029	7009	IC 709	IC 707	IC 717		IC 701	IC 711	IC 721
	2	2	Ⓡ	Ⓡ	Ⓡ		Ⓡ	Ⓡ	Ⓡ
									⑤⑦
Szeged ... d.	...	0436	0547	0645	0745		1845	1945	2045
Kiskunfélegyháza ... d.	...	0523	0631	0731	0831	and	1931	2031	2131
Kecskemét ... d.	0431	0539	0648	0748	0848	hourly	1948	2048	2147
Cegléd ... ▷ d.	0508	0608	0713	0813	0913	until	2013	2113	2214
Ferihegy ✈ ... ▷ a.	0554	0654	0744	0844	0944		2044	2144	2248
Kőbánya Kispest ... ▷ a.	0600	0700	0750	0850	0950		2050	2150	2254
Budapest Nyugati ... ▷ a.	0617	0717	0807	0907	1007		2107	2207	2310

▷ – For additional trains see Table **1270**.

Note : *IC* trains on this line have designated carriages for the use of passengers without seat reservations.

1292 SZEGED - BÉKÉSCSABA

2nd class

km				d	d		Ⓐ				
0	**Szeged** ... d.	0521	0621	0721	0921	1121	1221	1321	and	1921	2021
31	Hódmezővásárhely ... d.	0601	0705	0801	1001	1201	1305	1401	hourly	2001	2105
62	Orosháza ... d.	0631	0731	0831	1031	1231	1331	1431	until	2031	2133
97	**Békéscsaba** ... a.	0712	0810	0910	1110	1310	1410	1510		2110	...

				h	h	Ⓐ			
Békéscsaba ... d.	0547	0647	0747	0947	1147	1247	1345	and	1947
Orosháza ... d.	0632	0732	0832	1032	1232	1332	1432	hourly	2032
Hódmezővásárhely ... d.	0702	0802	0902	1102	1302	1402	1502	until	2102
Szeged ... a.	0740	0840	0940	1140	1340	1440	1540		2140

d – Additional journeys run at 0821Ⓒ, 1021Ⓒ.
h – Additional journeys run at 0847Ⓒ, 1047Ⓒ.

1295 BUDAPEST - KISKUNHALAS - KELEBIA - (BEOGRAD)

km		7920	7912	343	EC 345	7916	7926	7918	7928	341
		2	2	D	L	2	2	2	2	B
0	**Budapest Keleti** ... d.	...	0605	0805	1205	1405	1605	1805	1932**r**	2225
7	Ferencváros ... d.	...	0614	0814	1214	1414	1614	1814	1941	2234
61	Kunszentmiklós-Tass ... d.	0510	0709	0909	1309	1509	1709	1909	2050	2320
107	Kiskőrös ... d.	0601	0801	1001	1401	1601	1801	2001	2138	0006
134	Kiskunhalas ... a.	0632	0832	1032	1432	1632	1832	2032	2208	0035
163	**Kelebia** 🛃 ... a.	0711	0911	1111	1511	1711	1911	2111	...	0106
	Subotica **1360** ... a.	...	...	1155	1555	...	...	...	...	0154
	Beograd **1360** ... a.	...	...	1622	2015	...	...	...	...	0613

	340	7929	7927	7937	EC 344	7923	342	7911	
	B	2	2	2	L	2	D	2	
Beograd **1360** ... d.	2150	...	...	...	0736	...	1135	...	...
Subotica **1360** ... d.	0216	...	...	...	1202	...	1602	...	...
Kelebia 🛃 ... d.	0300	0448	0646	0846	1246	1446	1646	1846	...
Kiskunhalas ... d.	0329	0525	0725	0925	1325	1525	1725	1925	...
Kiskőrös ... d.	0358	0600	0800	1000	1400	1600	1800	2000	...
Kunszentmiklós-Tass ... d.	0442	0649	0850	1050	1450	1650	1850	2050	...
Ferencváros ... a.	0537	0749	0945	1145	1545	1745	1945	2145	...
Budapest Keleti ... a.	0546	0758	0954	1154	1554	1754	1954	2154	...

B – BEOGRAD – ▬ 2 cl., (12) Budapest - Beograd and v.v. Conveys on ②⑤ June 16 - Sept. 1 🛏 1,2 cl. Praha (**173/2**) - Budapest - Beograd - Bar, returning from Bar on ④⑦ June 18 - Sept. 3.
D – IVO ANDRIĆ – (12) Budapest - Beograd and v.v.
L – AVALA – (12) ✕ Wien - Györ - Budapest - Beograd and v.v. Conveys on ②⑤ June 16 - Sept. 1 🛏 1,2 cl., ▬ 2 cl., (2) Budapest - Subotica - Podgorica - Bar, returning from Bar on ③⑥ June 17 - Sept. 2 (next day from Subotica).
r – Kőbánya Kispest.

1299 OTHER LOCAL SERVICES

2nd class

BUDAPEST - DUNAÚJVÁROS *80* km, journey 85 - 90 minutes
From **Budapest** Déli: 0555, 0655, 0855, 1055, 1255, 1355, 1455, 1555, 1655, 1855, 2055.
From **Dunaújváros**: 0631, 0731, 0831, 1035, 1231, 1435, 1535, 1635, 1731, 1835, 2031.

BUDAPEST - ESZTERGOM *53 km*, journey 84 - 88 minutes
From **Budapest** Nyugati: 0420, 0550, 0614, 0720 and hourly until 2320. Additional faster journeys on Ⓐ (journey 68 minutes) run hourly 0800Ⓐ - 2000Ⓐ.
From **Esztergom**: 0340, 0416, 0445, 0545Ⓐ, 0559, 0640, 0715, 0811 and hourly until 2211. Additional journeys on Ⓐ (journey 70 mins) run hourly 0747Ⓐ - 1247Ⓐ, 1348Ⓐ - 1848Ⓐ.
Ⓒ Mar. 25 - Nov. 5: 1020, 1120, 1320 call at **Vasútmúzeum**, returning 1429, 1529, 1629.

BUDAPEST - SZENTENDRE *21 km*, journey time 41 minutes
HÉV suburban trains from Budapest Batthyány tér, every 20 - 30 minutes.

ESZTERGOM - KOMÁROM *53 km*, journey time 1h 30m – 1h 45m
From **Esztergom**: 0658, 1423. From **Komárom**: 0513, 1210.

EGER - SZILVÁSVÁRAD *34 km*, journey time 65 minutes
From **Eger**: 0638 **G**, 0900, 1257, 1638 **G**.
From **Szilvásvárad**: 0748 **G**, 1112, 1512, 1750 **G**.
Via Szilvásvárad-Szalajkavölgy (for the forest railway), 5 minutes before Szilvásvárad.

HATVAN - SZOLNOK *68 km*, journey 71 - 73 minutes
From **Hatvan**: every two hours 0613 - 2213 (on Ⓐ also 0513, 0713, hourly 1413 - 2213).
From **Szolnok**: every two hours 0431 - 2031, also 2131 (on Ⓐ also 0731, hourly 1431 - 2131).

KISKUNFÉLEGYHÁZA - CSONGRÁD - SZENTES *39 km*, journey time 53 minutes
From **Kiskunfélegyháza**: 0534Ⓐ, 0734, 0934, 1334, 1534, 1734, 1934, 2134.
From **Szentes**: 0428Ⓐ, 0634, 0834, 1234, 1434, 1634, 1834 (calls Csongrád 18 mins later).

G – Apr. 1 - Oct. 23.

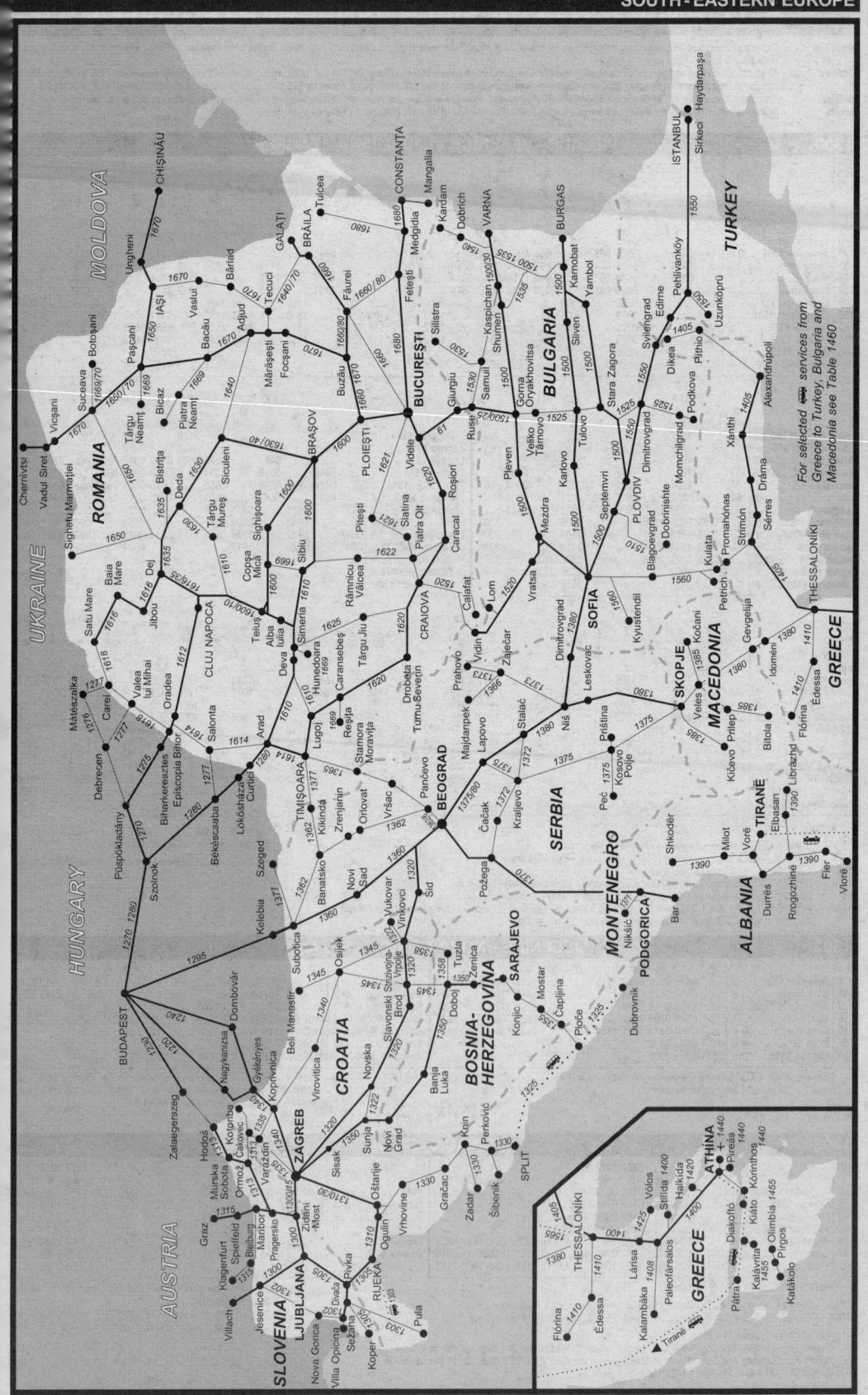

SLOVENIA, CROATIA and BOSNIA-HERZEGOVINA

Operators: Slovenske Železnice (SŽ): www.slo-zeleznice.si; Hrvatske Željeznice (HŽ): www.hzpp.hr; Željeznice Federacije Bosne i Hercegovine (ŽFBH): www.zfbh.ba; and Željeznice Republike Srpske (ŽRS): www.zrs-rs.com.

Services: All trains convey first and second class seating, **except** where shown otherwise in footnotes or by '2' in the train column, or where the footnote shows sleeping and / or couchette cars only. Descriptions of sleeping (🛏) and couchette (🛌) cars appear on page 8. In Slovenia, travel by *ICS* train requires reservation and payment of a special fare.

Timings: Valid from **December 11, 2016** except where indicated otherwise. Readers should note, however, that services in the Bosnian Federation are subject to alteration.

Tickets: A supplement is payable for travel by internal express trains. Reservation of seats is possible on most express trains.

1300   VILLACH - JESENICE - LJUBLJANA - ZAGREB   SŽ, HŽ, ÖBB

km				499				415										211	631				
			2	2	2	2	2	2	2	2	2	2	2	2	2	2	2	2	2	2	2	2
			Ⓐ			Ⓐ		Ⓐ	Ⓐ	Ⓒ	Ⓐ		Ⓐ		Ⓐ	Ⓐ	Ⓐ		Ⓐ	Ⓐ		Ⓑ
	München Hbf 890 ..d.		2335																			
	Salzburg Hbf 970 ..d.		0140																			
0	Villach Hbf...........d.		0415				0625									1253					
38	Jesenice 1302 .. 🚲 .d.	0430	0505	0532		0608	0626	0715	0732		0754		0946		1120		1235	1340		1418	
51	Lesce-Bled ....d.	0444	0517	0547		0623	0641	0731	0746		0813		1003		1134		1249	1351		1435	
74	Kranj ....d.	0508	0539	0611		0648	0709	0753	0814		0838		1031		1158		1321	1411		1500	
102	Ljubljana ....a.	0539	0559	0645		0723	0745	0813	0844		0908		1101		1228		1352	1431		1531	
102	Ljubljana 1315 ....d.	0450a		0550	0620		0650		0825	0850		0955	1050		1150		1250	1350		1445	1448	1535	1545	1648
166	Zidani Most 1315 ..d.	0604		0658	0713		0801		0917		1003		1100	1157		1300		1401	1455		1541	1602	1635	1700	1802
182	Sevnica 1315 ......d.	0623		0717	0729		0820		0933		1022		1118	1215		1319		1420	1513		1557	1621	1651	1719	1821
215	Dobova 1315 .. 🚲 .d.	0653		0748	0805		0851		1012		1052		1147	1244		1350		1449	1542		1639	1652	1721	1749	1852
245	Zagreb 1315 ....a.			0836					1043								1710				
	Beograd 1320 ......a.								1737													

		EC 213				315	411							630			410	632	314				EC 212
		2	2	2	2	2	2	2				2	2	2	2	2	2	2	2	2	2	2
		Ⓐ	♦			N	♦	♦	Ⓐ				Ⓐ	Ⓒ N			Ⓐ			Ⓐ		♦
	München Hbf 890 .. d.		1217								Beograd 1320 ....d.				2120	2120						0655
	Salzburg Hbf 970 .. d.		1412								Zagreb 1315 ......d.			0437		0437						0655
	Villach Hbf..........d.		1653			1853					Dobova 1315 .. 🚲 d.			0453		0505	0508	0530	0540	0600		0708	0744
	Jesenice 1302 .. 🚲 .d.	1531	1740		1807	1925	1945		2034		Sevnica 1315 ....d.		0410		0526		0535		0558	0605	0630		0739	0808
	Lesce-Bled ....d.	1545	1751		1821	1942	2001		2048		Zidani Most 1315 ..d.		0428		0546		0555		0615	0621	0658		0800	0824
	Kranj ....d.	1624	1812		1847	2007	2021		2114		Ljubljana 1315 ..a.		0531		0642		0659		0710	0717	0800		0906	0915
	Ljubljana ....a.	1653	1832		1920	2038	2041		2147		Ljubljana ....d.	0433		0611		0655			0727		0824		0923
	Ljubljana 1315 ....d.		1755	1835	1855		2105			2205	Kranj ....d.	0508		0648		0725			0753		0858		0943
	Zidani Most 1315 ..d.		1905	1928	2001		2202			2308	Lesce-Bled ....d.	0547		0712		0756			0813		0922		1003
	Sevnica 1315 ......d.		1923	1944	2019		2118			2355	Jesenice 1302 .. 🚲 .a.	0601		0725		0812			0824	0935			1014
	Dobova 1315 .. 🚲 .d.		1952	2021	2048		2305	2305		2355	Villach Hbf........a.					0908							1058
	Zagreb 1315 ....a.		2052				2336	2336			Salzburg Hbf 970 .. a.												1348
	Beograd 1320 ......a.						0555	0555			München Hbf 890 .. a.												1541

					210											414			498
		2	2	2	2	2	2	2	2	2	2	2	2	2	2	2	2	2	2
			Ⓐ		Ⓐ		♦		Ⓐ	Ⓐ					Ⓑ	♦	Ⓑ	♦	♦
	Beograd 1320 ......d.															1055			
	Zagreb 1315 ....d.						1237									1837			2120
	Dobova 1315 .. 🚲 .d.	0911	1011		1106		1211		1311	1338		1408		1510		1613		1706	1808		1910	1926	2010	2206
	Sevnica 1315 ......d.	0943	1041		1136		1241		1341	1402		1440		1540		1643		1738	1839		1942	1950	2040	2232
	Zidani Most 1315 ..d.	1003	1100		1200		1300		1400	1418		1500		1600		1701		1800	1902		2009	2006	2106	2248
	Ljubljana 1315 ....a.	1109	1202		1305		1402		1502	1510		1606		1701		1803		1906	2007		2115	2057	2203	2339
	Ljubljana ....d.	1000		1250		1332		1445		1527	1532	1549		1622		1718	1754		1846		2042		2110	2355
	Kranj ....d.	1031		1321		1411		1518		1552	1604	1624		1656		1750	1827		1919		2114		2131	0016
	Lesce-Bled ....d.	1055		1351		1435		1545		1613	1628	1649		1720		1821	1851		1942		2138		2151	0036
	Jesenice 1302 .. 🚲 .d.	1108		1404		1448		1559		1624	1641	1703		1733		1834	1904		1955		2151		2202	0047
	Villach Hbf..........a.								1709											2243		0131
	Salzburg Hbf 970 ... a.																					0404
	München Hbf 890 ... a.																					0611

♦ – NOTES (LISTED BY TRAIN NUMBER)

210/1 – SAVA – 🛌 Vinkovci - Zagreb - Ljubljana - Villach and v.v.
212/3 – MIMARA – 🛌 Zagreb - Villach (**112/3**) - München - Frankfurt and v.v.
314/5 – 🛌 Villach - Ljubljana - Dobova and v.v.
410 – Dec. 23 - Jan. 15, June 25 - Sept. 11: 🛌 Beograd - Dobova (**314**) - Ljubljana.
411 – Dec. 22 - Jan. 14, June 24 - Sept. 10: 🛌 Ljubljana (**315**) - Dobova - Beograd.
414/5 – ALPINE PEARLS – 🛏 1, 2 cl., 🛌 2 cl. and 🛌 Zagreb - Ljubljana - Villach - Schwarzach-St Veit (**464/5**) - Zürich and v.v.; 🛌 Beograd - Zagreb - Ljubljana - Villach and v.v.

498/9 – LISINSKI – 🛏 1, 2 cl., 🛌 2 cl. and 🛌 Zagreb - Salzburg (**462/3**) - München and v.v.
N – Conveys on Ⓒ: 🛌 Ljubljana - Jesenice - Nova Gorica and v.v.
a – Ⓐ only.

1302   JESENICE - NOVA GORICA - SEŽANA   2nd class only   SŽ

km		Ⓐ		Ⓐ	N		Z			k				Ⓐ			w	Ⓐ		Ⓒ N		Ⓑ y	h
0	Jesenice 1300 ....d.		0415	0605	0822	1115		1432	1651		1918	Sežana 1305 ....d.			0626q	1023a		1430		1635		2050	2140
10	Bled Jezero ....d.		0431	0621	0838	1131		1448	1706		1934	Nova Gorica.... ♣ a.			0719q	1116a		1522		1728		2143	2232
28	Bohinjska Bistrica ...d.		0451	0648	0858	1151		1508	1726		1954	Nova Gorica.... ♣ d.	0330	0528	0735	1120	1447		1555	1720		1946	
56	Most na Soči ....d.		0526	0724	0934	1227		1553	1802		2030	Most na Soči.....d.	0407	0607	0814	1159	1526		1634	1804		2032	
89	Nova Gorica ...... ♣ a.		0604	0813	1011	1304		1632	1840		2107	Bohinjska Bistrica ..d.	0453	0646	0900	1245	1604		1727	1840		2111	
89	Nova Gorica ...... ♣ d.	0455	0608q	0912		1411	1530		1847			Bled Jezero......d.	0513	0707	0921	1306	1624		1747	1900		2130	
130	Sežana 1305 ....d.	0551	0707q	1008		1512	1626		1943			Jesenice 1300 ...a.	0529	0722	0937	1322	1640		1803	1916		2146	

N – Conveys on Ⓒ: 🛌 Ljubljana - Jesenice - Nova Gorica and v.v.
Z – Runs 33 – 38 minutes later on some dates.
a – Ⓐ only.
h – June 24 - Aug. 27.
k – Ⓑ (daily June 24 - Aug. 27).
q – Ⓐ (daily Aug. 28 - Aug. 31).
w – Not Ⓒ June 26 - Aug. 31.
y – Not June 24 - Aug. 27.
♣ – Line 1 🚌 service operates between Nova Gorica (bus stop 100 metres from station on Italian side) and Gorizia Centrale (Italy) stations. Total journey time ± 20 minutes.

1303   DIVAČA - PULA   2nd class only   HŽ, SŽ

km				1274	1272				z	Ⓐ						w	z			1273	1275
			Ⓐ		w													Ⓐ	v	♦	♦
	Ljubljana 1305 .....d.				0612	0612						Pula ....d.	0500	0650	0913		1320		1435	1530	1720	1756	1756	1940
0	Divača 1305 ....d.				0745	0745	0955			z		Lupoglav ..... ▲ a.	0636	0827	1048		1507		1615	1718	1902	1926	1926	2115
12	Hrpelje-Kozina ......d.				0800	0800	1009					Buzet 🚲 ....d.	0658	0846	1107		1530		1649	1750	1921r	2000	2000	2140
30	Rakitovec 🚲 ....d.				0835	0835	1032					Rakitovec 🚲 ......d.			1129		1713				2021	2021	
36	Buzet 🚲 ....d.		0515z	0705	0902	0902		1117	1300		1710	1955r	Hrpelje-Kozina ....d.			1153		1737				2050	2050	
43	Lupoglav..... ▲ d.	0437	0536	0726	0921	0921		1138	1321	1518	1731	2016	Divača 1305 ......d.			1205		1749				2102	2102	
117	Pula ....a.	0617	0724	0904	1045	1045		1311	1508	1656	1907	2153	Ljubljana 1305 ...a.										2238	2238	

♦ – NOTES (LISTED BY TRAIN NUMBER)

1272/3 – June 24 - Aug. 27: 🛌 Maribor (**1604/5**) - Hrpelje-Kozina - Pula and v.v.
1274/5 – Ⓐ Apr. 22 - June 18; daily Aug. 28 - Sept. 24: 🛌 Ljubljana - Pula and v.v.

▲ – 🚌 service Lupoglav - Rijeka and v.v.: Journey 40 minutes. Subject to alteration.
From Lupoglav: 0639✕, 1110, 1618, 2120.
From Rijeka: 0555✕, 1025, 1425Ⓐ, 1535Ⓒ, 1930.

r – Apr. 22 - May 1, June 24 - Sept. 24.
v – Ⓐ until Apr. 21; daily Apr. 22 - May 1; Ⓐ May 2 - June 23; daily June 24 - Sept. 24; Ⓐ from Sept. 25.
w – ✕ until Apr. 22; daily Apr. 23 - May 1; ✕ May 2 - June 24; daily June 25 - Sept. 24; ✕ from Sept. 26.
z – Ⓐ (not Dec. 27 - Jan. 11, Apr. 13 - 21, June 16 - Sept. 1).

1305 LJUBLJANA - RIJEKA, KOPER, SEŽANA and VILLA OPICINA

SŽ, HŽ   2nd class only except where shown

km		1274	1605		481		IC 503								483		IC 509				A
		Ⓐ	Ⓒ			♦			Ⓐ	Ⓐ					♦	Ⓑ	Ⓐ	♦		Ⓐ	
	Maribor 1315 .... d.	...	...	...	0335	...	...	0655	...	...	...	...	...	...	...	...	...	...	...	...	...
0	Ljubljana .... d.	0434	...	0550	0612	0612	...	0635	0810	...	0943	...	1044	1210	1317	...	1435	1510	1545	1610	1657	1745	1855	1950	...	2102
67	Postojna............... d.	0535	...	0653	0710	0710	...	0732	0912	...	1041	...	1146	1315	1419	...	1537	1611	1649	1708	1802	1846	1958	2052	...	2206
80	Pivka ▲................ d.	0548	...	0706	0722	0722	...	0745	0926	...	1054	...	1159	1329	1433	...	1549	1623	1702	1720	1816	1857	2011	2106	...	2220
	Ilirska Bistrica ▲ d.	...	...	...	...	...	0814	...	...	...	...	...	...	...	...	...	1650	...	...	...	...	...	...	...	...	...
	Šapjane .... d.	...	...	...	...	...	0843	...	...	...	...	...	...	...	...	...	1718	...	...	...	...	...	...	...	...	...
	Rijeka 1310 .... a.	...	...	...	...	...	0925	...	...	...	...	...	...	...	...	...	1800	...	...	...	...	...	...	...	...	...
104	Divača 1303 .... a.	0607	...	0726	0742	0742	...	...	0945	...	1115	...	1219	1350	1453	...	1611	...	1723	1742	1837	1917	2032	2126	...	2241
104	Divača .... d.	0612	...	0727	0745	0757	...	...	0946	1120	1117	...	1220	1351	1454	1538	1612	...	1724	1743	1838	1919	2033	2127	2127	2242
116	Hrpelje-Kozina ⊡ d.	...	...	...	0800	0805	0809	...	...	...	1129	...	...	...	...	...	...	...	1737	...	...	1931	...	...	...	...
153	Koper .... ⊡ a.	...	...	...	0840	0845	...	...	...	...	1204	...	...	...	...	...	...	...	1812	...	...	2004	...	...	...	...
113	Sežana ▥............ a.	0621	...	0736	...	...	...	...	0955	...	...	1130	1229	1401	1504	1548	1622	...	1751	1848	...	...	2043	2136	2136	2252
113	Sežana ▥............ d.	0622	0622	...	...	...	...	...	0956	...	...	1230	...	...	...	...	1628	...	...	...	...	...	2054	2137	2137	...
120	Villa Opicina 601 a.	0632	0632	...	...	...	...	...	1006	...	...	1240	...	...	...	...	1638	...	...	...	...	...	2054	2147	2147	...

km		IC 508			482			502				IC 653			1275	1604	480		B
		Ⓐ	Ⓐ	Ⓐ	♦	Ⓐ		Ⓐ	Ⓐ		Ⓐ		Ⓐ	Ⓑ	C	♦	♦	♦		B
	Villa Opicina 601 d.	...	...	...	0700	...	1030	...	1327	...	...	1740	...	...	...	...	...	2119	2158
	Sežana ▥............. a.	...	...	...	0710	...	1040	...	1337	...	...	1750	...	...	...	...	...	2129	2208
	Sežana ▥............. d.	...	0430	0508	0558	0711	0925	1041	1338	1433	1516	...	1650	1751	1820	1952	...	...	...	...
	Koper .... ⊡ d.	...	...	...	0525	...	...	1003	...	...	...	1445	...	...	...	1915	...	2015	...	...
	Hrpelje-Kozina ⊡ d.	...	...	...	0557	...	...	1036	...	...	...	1518	...	...	...	1952	2050	2050	...	...
	Divača 1303 .... a.	...	0439	0518	0608	0609	0720	0934	1052	1048	1347	1443	1526	1529	1659	1800	1828	2002	2005	2102	2102
	Divača .... d.	...	0440	0519	...	0611	0721	0935	...	1100	1348	1444	...	1531	1700	1801	1829	...	2006	2107	2107
0	Rijeka 1310 .... d.	...	...	...	...	...	...	...	1155	...	...	...	...	...	...	...	...	...	2050	...
28	Šapjane .... d.	...	...	...	...	...	...	...	1253	...	...	...	...	...	...	...	...	...	2148	...
40	Ilirska Bistrica ▲ d.	...	...	...	0632	...	...	...	1323	...	...	...	...	...	...	...	...	...	2217	...
56	Pivka ▲................ d.	...	0410	0502	0542	...	0637	0650	0742	0956	...	1121	1339	1409	1506	...	1552	1723	1822	1849	...	2037	2129	2129	2233
	Postojna................ d.	...	0423	0516	0556	...	0650	0703	0755	1009	...	1135	1353	1422	1519	...	1604	1737	1835	1901	...	2051	2141	2141	2246
	Ljubljana............... a.	...	0525	0618	0702	...	0747	0805	0857	1110	...	1235	1448	1526	1625	...	1704	1838	1936	2000	...	2153	2238	2238	2339
	Maribor 1315 .... a.	...	...	...	...	...	...	...	...	...	...	...	...	...	...	...	1947	...	...	...	...	...	...	...	...

NOTES (LISTED BY TRAIN NUMBER)

480/1 – OPATIJA – 🛏 Rijeka - Ljubljana and v.v. Conveys 🛏 1, 2 cl., ━ 2 cl. and 🛏 Rijeka - Ljubljana (1604/5) - Maribor (1246/7) - Budapest.

482/3 – LJUBLJANA – 🛏 Rijeka - Ljubljana and v.v.

508/9 – 🛏 Ljubljana - Koper and v.v. Conveys June 17 - Aug. 27 (from Budapest); June 18 - Aug. 27 (from Koper): 🛏 and ✗ Budapest (246/7) - Ljubljana - Koper and v.v.

1274/5 – Ⓒ Apr. 22 - June 18; daily Aug. 28 - Sept. 24: 🛏 Pula - Ljubljana and v.v.

1604 – ISTRA – June 24 - Aug. 27: 🛏 Koper - Ljubljana - Maribor. Conveys ━ 2 cl. and 🛏 Koper - Ljubljana (1247) - Hodoš - Budapest; 🛏 1, 2 cl., ━ 2 cl. and 🛏 Rijeka (480) - Ljubljana - Budapest.

1605 – ISTRA – June 24 - Aug. 27: 🛏 Maribor - Ljubljana - Koper. Conveys ━ 2 cl. and 🛏 Budapest (1246) - Hodoš - Ljubljana - Koper; 🛏 1, 2 cl., ━ 2 cl. and 🛏 Budapest - Maribor - Ljubljana (481) - Rijeka.

A – Ⓒ Apr. 22 - Sept. 24.
B – Ⓐ (also Ⓒ Apr. 22 - Sept. 24).
C – Ⓑ (daily June 24 - Aug. 27).

☐ – 🚌 service **Koper - Trieste and v.v.**: Journey 45 minutes.
From **Koper**: 0600✗, 0642Ⓐ, 0700Ⓐ, 0730✗, 1030✗, 1200Ⓐ, 1400✗, 1730✗.
From **Trieste**: 0700✗, 0900Ⓐ, 1115Ⓐ, 1230✗, 1300✗, 1400Ⓐ, 1530✗, 1900✗.
Service subject to alteration. No service on ⑦, Slovenian and Italian holidays.
Operator: Veolia Transport Slovenija.
An irregular 🚌 service also operates Trieste - Hrpelje-Kozina and v.v.

1310 RIJEKA - ZAGREB

HŽ   2nd class only except where shown

km		205				701								200			702	
		✗		✗		Ⓐ					Osijek 1340 ... d.		Ⓐ	♦		Ⓐ		Ⓐ
0	Rijeka 1305 ..... d.	...	0535	0727	...	1323	1543	1730	...	1938		...	...	1204	...	...
61	Delnice .... d.	...	0644	0840	...	1440	1701	1835	...	2056	Zagreb 1330/40 d.	...	0636	0812	1200	1316	...	1439	1545	1705	1714	2140
90	Moravice .... d.	...	0608	0717	0915	...	1515	1736	1911	1950	2131	Karlovac 1330 .. d.	...	0726	0907	1241	1410	...	1536	1640	1746	1808	2235
120	Ogulin 1330 ..... d.	0413	0640	0747	0945	1027	1212	...	1613	1808	1939	2021	2201	Ostarije 1330 ... d.	...	0825	1007	...	1513	...	1637	1745	1833	1908	2335
126	Oštarije 1330 ... d.	0420	0647	...	...	1035	1219	...	1620	...	1946	2029	...	Ogulin 1330 ..... d.	0420	0605	0831	1014	1341	1519	1555	1643	1753	1841	1914	2342
176	Karlovac 1330 ... d.	0522	0754	0850	...	1136	1327	...	1728	...	2035	2128	...	Moravice .... d.	0451	0637	...	1045	1410	...	1626	...	1823	1910	...
229	Zagreb 1330/40 a.	0615	0850	0931	...	1233	1423	...	1825	...	2115	2218	...	Delnice .... d.	0525	0716	...	1119	1439	...	1700	...	1940	...
	Osijek 1340 ..... a.	...	1445	...	...	...	...	...	...	...	...	...	...	Rijeka 1305 ..... a.	0640	0834	...	1233	1541	...	1818	...	2043

NOTES (LISTED BY TRAIN NUMBER)

200 – KVARNER – 🛏 and ⓘ Budapest - Zagreb - Rijeka.
205 – KVARNER – 🛏 and ⓘ Rijeka - Zagreb - Budapest; 🛏 Rijeka - Koprivnica (703) - Osijek.

1313 MARIBOR - ČAKOVEC, MURSKA SOBOTA and ZALAEGERSZEG

SŽ, MÁV   2nd class only except where shown

km		1247						640	247										1642	518	520			642	
			Ⓐ	Ⓐ	Ⓐ	Ⓐ		Ⓐ			Ⓐ	✗	g	Ⓐ	Ⓐ				j	Ⓐ	y		Ⓐ	♦	Ⓐ
	Ljubljana 1315 ... d.	0015							0908										1519						
0	Maribor 1315 ..... d.		...	...	...	...	0705	...	1100	1253	1253	1350	...	1432	...	1527	...	...	1837	...	2205
19	Pragersko 1315 .. d.	0225	...	0616	...	0736	0949	1114	1130	1322	1322	...	1503	...	...	1603	1725	1725	...	1905	1940	2235
37	Ptuj.................... d.	0238	...	0640	0749	...	0802	1001	1126	1152	1345	1345	1435	...	1526	...	1611	...	1627	1738	1738	...	1926	1952	2257
59	Ormož.................. d.	...	0447	0534	0703	0813	0815	0826	1016	1141	1215	1410	1410	1457	...	1551	1555	1635	1643	1650	1753	1753	1758	...	1951	2007	2320
	Središče ▥..... a.	...	0458	...	...	0828	...	...	...	...	...	...	1508	...	...	1606	...	1654	...	...	1811	...	...
	Čakovec 1335 ... a.	...	...	...	...	0841	...	...	...	...	...	...	...	...	...	...	...	...	1824	...	...
98	Murska Sobota .... d.	0319	0330	...	0618	...	0857	...	0910	1048	1213	...	1452	1452	...	1537	1635	...	1720	...	1734	1828	1828	...	2051	...
127	Hodoš .... d.	0338	0356	...	...	...	...	...	1230	...	...	...	1603	...	...	...	1856	1856	...	2116	...
127	Hodoš ▥.............. d.	0353	...	0620	...	...	...	1252	...	...	...	...	1610	...	...	1930	...	...
174	Zalaegerszeg .... a.	0431	...	0710	...	...	...	1330	...	...	...	...	1706	...	...	2020	...	...
	Budapest D 1230 .. a.	0829						1729													

km		1246	521	519		643		513						246						1641			1643		
			y	Ⓐ		p		Ⓐ			Ⓐ				Ⓐ	✗	g	Ⓐ			g			g		Ⓐ
	Budapest D 1230 .. d.	2030											0830										
	Zalaegerszeg .... d.	0010	...	...	0520	...	...	...	1212	...	...	...	...	1450	...	1645	1825	...
	Hodoš .... d.	0048	...	...	0611	...	...	...	1250	...	...	...	...	1540	...	1735	1916	...
	Hodoš ▥.............. d.	0103	0430	0430	...	...	...	...	1305	...	...	...	...	1615	1617	...	...	1919
	Murska Sobota .... d.	0121	0458	0458	...	0623	...	0710	...	0935	...	1222	...	1325	1509	1509	...	1644	1643	...	1825	1855	1945
	Čakovec 1335 ..... d.					0945													1832		
12	Središče ▥..... d.		0434		0537		1000					1529			1614		1710		1847	
22	Ormož.................. d.	...	0446	0529	0529	0624	0702	0703	0735	1010	1016	1223	1304	1357	1540	1550	1550	1625	1701	1722	1727	...	1857	1901	1937	...
	Ptuj.................... d.	0205	0510	0543	0543	0613	0641	...	0725	0744	1037	1246	1327	1412	...	1611	1611	...	1723	...	1752	...	1921	2006	...
	Pragersko 1315 .. d.	0356t	0541	0554	0607	0645	0651	0757	0800	1106	1316	1401	1424	...	1640	1640	...	1746	...	1823	...	1939	2039	...
	Maribor 1315 ..... a.	0231	0604	...	0708	...	0819	...	1128	1339	1424	...	1700	1700	...	...	...	...	2102	...
	Ljubljana 1315 ... a.	0605	...	0805	...	...	...	...	1630	...	...	...	2023	...	...	2136	...

NOTES (LISTED BY TRAIN NUMBER)

246/7 – CITADELLA – 🛏 Budapest - Ljubljana and v.v. Conveys June 17 - Aug. 27 (from Budapest, June 18 - Aug. 27 (from Koper): 🛏 and ✗ Budapest - Ljubljana (508/9) - Koper and v.v.

518/9 – PTUJ – Ⓐ (not June 24 - Aug. 27): 🛏 Ljubljana - Hodoš and v.v.

642 – MURA – 🛏 Pragersko - Hodoš.

1246 – ISTRA – June 23 - Aug. 25: ━ 2 cl. and 🛏 Budapest - Hodoš - Maribor (1605) - Koper; 🛏 1, 2 cl., ━ 2 cl. and 🛏 Budapest - Ljubljana (481) - Rijeka.

1247 – ISTRA – June 24 - Aug. 27: ━ 2 cl. and 🛏 Koper - Ljubljana - Hodoš - Budapest; 🛏 1, 2 cl., ━ 2 cl. and 🛏 Rijeka (480) - Ljubljana - Budapest.

g – ⑦ Dec. 11 - June 18, Sept. 3 - Dec. 3 (also Feb. 8, Apr. 17, May 2; not Dec. 25, Apr. 16, 30, Oct. 29).
j – ⑤ Dec. 16 - June 16, Sept. 8 - Dec. 8 (also Feb. 7, Apr. 26, not Dec. 30, Apr. 28, Nov. 3).
p – Dec. 11 - June 10.
t – Via Maribor.
y – Ⓐ June 24 - Aug. 27.

SLOVENIA and CROATIA

1315 LJUBLJANA and ZAGREB - MARIBOR - GRAZ

SŽ, HŽ, ÖBB

km		1247			512		IC 514	EC 158	247		IC 522		IC 506			IC 524		IC 518	EC 150		IC 526	IC 502	IC 528		1604	604
			2	2		2		✕		2		2		2	2		2	2	✕					2	2	2
		♦	h	Ⓐ			p	♦	♦		p		Ⓐ	⚒	Ⓐ	p		♦	♦		p	♦	p		♦	w
	Koper **1305** d.	...	...	...	...	...	...	...	...	...	...	...	...	...	...	...	...	...	...	...	...	...	...	...	2015	...
0	**Ljubljana 1300** d.	0015	0045	...	0545	...	...	...	0908	1050	...	1250	1345	1350	...	...	...	1519	1600	...	...	1725	...	2050	2250	2250
*	**Zagreb 1300** d.	|	|	...	|	...	...	0725	|	|	...	|	|	|	...	...	...	|	|	...	...	|	...	|	|	|
	Dobova **1300** ⊞ d.	|	|	...	|	...	...	0813	|	|	...	|	|	|	...	...	...	|	|	...	...	|	...	|	|	|
	Sevnica **1300** d.	|	|	...	|	...	...	0840	|	|	...	|	|	|	...	...	...	|	|	...	...	|	...	|	|	|
64	Zidani Most **1300** d.	0108	0143	...	0637	0700	0847	|	1004	1200	1357	1402	1443	1500	...	1600	1604	1611	1657	...	1800	1825	2057	2154	2351	2355
89	Celje d.	0133	0208	...	0702	0725	0908	0919	1030	1225	1419	1427	1510	1525	...	1621	1629	1639	1723	...	1825	1851	2120	2219	0017	0021
137	Pragersko **1313** d.	0212	0248	...	0742	0810	0944	1000	1109	1311	1455	1511	1551	1611	...	1657	1715	1722	1800	...	1901	1932	2155	2304	0059	0103
156	**Maribor 1313** ▲ a.	...	0301	...	0756	0828	0956	1014	...	1328	1507	1529	1607	1629	...	1709	1733	...	1816	...	...	1947	2208	2322	0113	0117
156	**Maribor** d.	...	...	0502	...	0833	...	1019	...	1333	...	...	...	...	1635	...	1735	...	1819	...	...	...	...	...	...	...
172	Spielfeld-Straß ⊞ a.	...	...	0525	...	0852	...	1036	...	1352	...	...	...	...	1658	...	1755	...	1836	...	...	...	...	...	...	...
172	Spielfeld-Straß **980** ⊞ d.	...	...	...	...	...	...	1048	...	...	...	...	...	...	...	...	...	...	1848	...	...	...	...	...	...	...
219	**Graz** Hbf **980** a.	...	...	...	...	...	...	1120	...	...	...	...	...	...	...	...	...	...	1920	...	...	...	...	...	...	...
	Wien Hbf **980** a.	...	...	...	...	...	...	1402	...	...	...	...	...	...	...	...	...	...	2202	...	...	...	...	...	...	...

		605	1605		IC 511	IC 519		IC 503		IC 517	EC 151		246		IC 525	1611			IC 527	1615	1641		1643	IC 523	EC 159	1613
	2	2		2		2	2		2		✕	2		2		2	2	2		2	2	2	2		✕	2
	h	w	♦		p	♦	Ⓐ	♦		p	♦	Ⓐ	♦		p	g	Ⓐ	Ⓐ	p	g	♦		♦	p	♦	g
Wien Hbf **980** d.	...	...	...	...	...	...	...	...	...	...	0758	...	...	...	...	...	...	...	...	...	...	...	...	...	1558	...
Graz Hbf **980** d.	...	...	...	...	...	...	...	...	...	...	1038	...	...	...	...	...	...	...	...	...	...	...	...	...	1838	...
Spielfeld-Straß **980** ⊞ a.	...	...	...	...	...	...	...	...	...	...	1108	...	...	...	...	...	...	...	...	...	...	...	...	...	1908	...
Spielfeld-Straß ⊞ d.	...	...	...	...	...	...	0545	...	0903	...	1120	...	...	1405	...	...	...	1710	...	...	...	1802	...	...	1920	...
Maribor a.	...	...	...	...	...	...	0608	...	0923	...	1137	...	...	1423	...	...	...	1731	...	...	...	1818	...	...	1937	...
Maribor 1313 ▲ d.	0115	0335	0335	0425	0543	...	...	0655	0927a	1045	1150	1320	...	1427	1518	1620	1620	...	1740	1800	...	1825a	...	1945	1955	2005
Pragersko **1313** d.	0133	0351	0351	0444	0557	0607	...	0715	0946a	1059	1206	1339	1429	1446	1532	1639	1639	...	1754	1817	1823	1844a	1939	2000	2011	2022
Celje d.	0214	0435	0435	0529	0634	0649	...	0757	1031a	1135	1245	1424	1507	1531	1609	1724	1724	...	1831	1858	1905	1928a	2018	2038	2050	2104
Zidani Most **1300** d.	0238	0502	0502	0553	0654	0713	...	0821	1100a	1155	1310	1500	1531	1555	1629	1750	1800	...	1851	1924	1929	1951a	2041	2101	|	2131
Sevnica **1300** d.	|	|	|	...	...	|	...	|	|	...	|	|	|	...	...	|	|	...	...	|	|	...	|	...	2130	|
Dobova **1300** ⊞ d.	|	|	|	...	...	|	...	|	|	...	|	|	|	...	...	|	|	...	...	|	|	...	|	...	2211	|
Zagreb 1300 a.	|	|	|	...	...	|	...	|	|	...	|	|	|	...	...	|	|	...	...	|	|	...	|	...	2242	|
Ljubljana 1300 a.	0334	0601	0601	...	...	0805	...	0925	1202a	...	1406	1606	1630	...	...	1841	1906	...	...	2017	2023	...	2136	...	...	2222
Koper **1305** a.	...	...	0840	...	...	...	...	...	...	...	...	...	...	...	...	...	...	...	...	...	...	...	...	...	...	...

ADDITIONAL SERVICES MARIBOR - ZIDANI MOST and v.v.: 2nd class only

		Ⓐ	Ⓐ	Ⓐ		Ⓐ		Ⓐ		Ⓐ		Ⓐ		Ⓑ
Maribor ▲ d.	0520	0620	0720	0820	1020	1120	...	1220	1522	1620	1720	1920	2020	2115
Pragersko d.	0539	0640	0739	0839	1039	1139	...	1239	1541	1639	1739	1939	2039	2134
Celje d.	0624	0726	0825	0924	1124	1225	...	1324	1626	1724	1824	2024	2124	2219
Zidani Most d.	0648	0750	0849	0948	1148	1249	...	1348	1650	1748	1848	2048	2148	2243

		Ⓐ	Ⓐ	Ⓐ	Ⓐ	Ⓐ	Ⓐ		Ⓐ			Ⓐ
Zidani Most d.	0500	0600	0800	0922	1008	1104	1305	1705	1803	1900	2008	2101
Celje d.	0525	0625	0825	0947	1035	1129	1330	1730	1828	1925	2035	2126
Pragersko d.	0610	0711	0910	1032	1119	1214	1414	1817	1914	2010	2121	2211
Maribor ▲ a.	0628	0729	0928	1050	1139	1232	1431	1835	1932	2028	2139	2229

♦ – **NOTES** (LISTED BY TRAIN NUMBER)

150/1 – EMONA – [12] and ✕ Ljubljana - Wien and v.v.
158/9 – CROATIA – [12] and ✕ Zagreb - Wien and v.v.
246/7 – CITADELLA – [12] Budapest - Ljubljana and v.v. Conveys June 17 - Aug. 27 (from Budapest, June 18 - Aug. 27 (from Koper): [2] and ✕ Budapest - Ljubljana (**508/9**) - Koper and v.v.
502/3 – POHORJE – [12] Ljubljana - Maribor and v.v.
518/9 – PTUJ – Ⓐ (not June 24 - Aug. 27): [2] Ljubljana - Hodoš and v.v.
1247 – ISTRA – June 24 - Aug. 27: ▬ 2 cl. and [2] Koper (**1604**) - Ljubljana - Hodoš - Budapest; 🛏 1, 2 cl., ▬ 2 cl. and [2] Rijeka (**480**) - Ljubljana - Hodoš - Budapest.
1604 – ISTRA – June 24 - Aug. 27: [2] Koper - Ljubljana - Maribor. Conveys ▬ 2 cl. and [2] Koper - Ljubljana (**1247**) - Hodoš - Budapest; 🛏 1, 2 cl., ▬ 2 cl. and [2] Rijeka (**480**) - Ljubljana - Hodoš - Budapest.
1605 – ISTRA – June 24 - Aug. 27: [2] Maribor - Ljubljana - Koper. Conveys ▬ 2 cl. and [2] Budapest (**1246**) - Hodoš - Maribor - Koper; 🛏 1, 2 cl., ▬ 2 cl. and [2] Budapest - Maribor - Ljubljana (**481**) - Rijeka.
1641 – ⑦ Dec. 11 - June 18, Sept. 3 - Dec. 3 (also Feb. 8, Apr. 17, May 2; not Dec. 25, Apr. 16, 30, Oct. 29): [2] Hodoš - Ljubljana.
1643 – ⑦ Dec. 11 - June 18, Sept. 3 - Dec. 3 (also Feb. 8, Apr. 17, May 2; not Dec. 25, Apr. 16, 30, Oct. 29): [2] Murska Sobota - Ljubljana.

a – Ⓐ only.
g – ⑦ Dec. 11 - June 18, Sept. 3 - Dec. 3 (also Feb. 8, Apr. 17, May 2; not Dec. 25, Apr. 16, 30, Oct. 29).
h – Dec. 18 - Jan. 1, June 11 - Sept. 24.
p – Dec. 11 - June 10.
w – Not June 24 - Aug. 27.

▲ – For Maribor - Bleiburg (- Klagenfurt) services see panel below.

* – Zagreb - Celje: *104 km*.

MARIBOR - BLEIBURG (- KLAGENFURT) and v.v.:

km		Ⓐ	Ⓐ		Ⓐ	Ⓐ
0	Maribor d.	0520	1445	*Klagenfurt* d.	*0806*	*1636*
87	Bleiburg ⊞ a.	0736	1705	Bleiburg ⊞ d.	0854	1726
126	*Klagenfurt* a.	*0837*	*1750*	Maribor a.	1101	1933

Other services are available Bleiburg - Klagenfurt and v.v.

1320 ZAGREB - VINKOVCI - BEOGRAD

SŽ, HŽ, ŽS

km		741		415	743	745	211		747	411
			2					2		
				♦	⚒		♦	⚒		♦
	Ljubljana **1300** d.	...	...	0825	...	...	1445	...	...	2105
0	**Zagreb** d.	0614	0744	1107	1307	1520	1742	1907	2138	2352
105	Novska d.	0809	1009	1258	1507	1717	1934	2125	2332	0143
191	Slavonski Brod d.	0909	1129	1359	1612	1816	2033	2244	0040	0240
224	Strizivojna-Vrpolje **1345** d.	0927	1159	1417	1631	1834	2051	2314	0103	0258
	Osijek **1345** a.	|	|	|	|	|	|	|	|	|
256	**Vinkovci** d.	0943	1223	1447	1648	1850	2107	2339	0128	0318
288	Šid ⊞ a.	...	...	1515	...	...	...	...	...	0345
407	**Beograd** a.	...	...	1737	...	...	...	...	...	0555

	740	742	744	210	746	414	748		410
								2	
			⚒	♦		♦		Ⓐ	♦
Beograd d.	...	...	...	...	...	1055	...	...	2120
Šid ⊞ d.	...	...	...	...	...	1353	...	...	0025
Vinkovci d.	0256	0555	0735	0900	1204	1442	1715	1947	0105
Osijek **1345** d.	|	|	|	|	|	|	|	|	|
Strizivojna-Vrpolje **1345** d.	0319	0612	0752	0916	1221	1500	1739	2012	0121
Slavonski Brod d.	0341	0629	0810	0935	1239	1519	1804	2041	0140
Novska d.	0449	0731	0906	1031	1335	1622	1911	2158	0236
Zagreb a.	0644	0928	1055	1224	1525	1813	2109	0010	0425
Ljubljana **1300** a.	...	...	...	1510	...	2057	...	...	0717

♦ – **NOTES** (LISTED BY TRAIN NUMBER)

210/1 – SAVA – [12] Vinkovci - Zagreb - Ljubljana - Villach and v.v.
410 – Dec. 23 - Jan. 15, June 25 - Sept. 11: [12] Beograd - Dobova (**314**) - Ljubljana.
411 – Dec. 22 - Jan. 14, June 24 - Sept. 10: [12] Ljubljana (**315**) - Dobova - Beograd.
414/5 – ALPINE PEARLS – 🛏 1, 2 cl., ▬ 2 cl. and [2] Zagreb - Ljubljana - Villach Schwarzach-St Veit (**464/5**) - Zürich and v.v.; [2] Beograd - Zagreb - Ljubljana Villach and v.v.

1322 Subject to alteration LOCAL SERVICES in Croatia

2nd class only HŽ

ZAGREB - SISAK CAPRAG and v.v.: Journey 60–75 minutes. All services call at Sisak (6 minutes from Sisak Caprag).
From Zagreb: 0544Ⓐ, 0633, 0751Ⓐ, 1101, 1159Ⓐ, 1353, 1454Ⓐ, 1547, 1649Ⓐ, 1746Ⓐ, 1854, 1958, 2051Ⓐ, 2251.
From Sisak Caprag: 0416⚒, 0520, 0613, 0702Ⓐ, 0812Ⓐ, 1037⚒, 1214, 1414Ⓐ, 1513, 1608Ⓐ, 1655, 1807Ⓐ, 2000, 2112.

SISAK CAPRAG - SUNJA and v.v.: Journey 25 minutes.
From Sisak Caprag: 0350⚒, 0704Ⓐ, 0744, 1215, 1456, 1656, 1853Ⓐ, 1959, 2350.
From Sunja: 0454⚒, 0547, 0636Ⓐ, 1148, 1253Ⓐ, 1629, 1930, 2046, 2140Ⓐ.

SUNJA - NOVSKA and v.v.: Journey 70 minutes.
From Sunja: 0810, 1241, 2035Ⓑ.
From Novska: 0436, 0525Ⓐ, 1037, 1758Ⓑ.

VINKOVCI - VUKOVAR and v.v.: Journey 40 minutes.
From Vinkovci: 0400Ⓐ, 1000Ⓐ, 1520, 1933Ⓐ.
From Vukovar: 0452Ⓐ, 1111Ⓐ, 1633, 2022Ⓐ.

1325 🚌 SPLIT - PLOČE - DUBROVNIK

🚌 SPLIT - DUBROVNIK: Up to 18 departures per day. Journey 4 hrs - 5 hrs 10 mins.
🚌 SPLIT - PLOČE: Up to 22 departures per day. Journey 2 hrs - 2 hrs 50 mins.
🚌 PLOČE - DUBROVNIK: Up to 17 departures per day. Journey 2 hrs - 2 hrs 20 mins.

Note: various operators run on these routes; tickets are not interchangeable.
Split and Ploče bus stations are situated adjacent to the railway stations.
Buses pass through Bosnia between Ploče and Dubrovnik (passports required).

HŽ 2nd class only except where shown ZAGREB - ZADAR, ŠIBENIK and SPLIT 1330

Knin - Zadar and v.v. 🚌 service is subject to alteration

km	km							ICN 521								ICN 523							821	1204	
			⚒	Ⓐ		Ⓐq	🚌 Ⓐ	Ⓡ 🍷	Ⓐ	🚌 Ⓒ	Ⓐ			🚌		Ⓡ 🍷	Ⓐ	Ⓐ	p				♦	♦	🚌 h
0		**Zagreb 1310** d.	...	...	...	...	...	0735	...	...	...	...	...	...	...	1521	...	...	...	...	...	...	2305	0035	...
53		Karlovac **1310** d.	...	...	...	...	...	0813	...	...	...	...	...	...	...	1556	...	...	...	...	...	...	2344	|	...
103		Oštarije **1310** d.	...	...	...	...	...	|	...	...	...	...	...	...	...	|	...	...	...	...	...	...	|	|	...
109		**Ogulin 1310** d.	...	...	...	...	...	|	...	...	...	...	...	...	...	|	...	...	...	...	...	...	0049	0218	...
225		Gospić d.	...	...	...	...	...	1030	...	...	...	...	...	...	...	1815	...	...	...	...	...	...	0256	|	...
269		Gračac d.	...	...	...	...	...	1103	...	...	...	...	...	...	...	1847	...	...	...	...	...	...	0333	|	...
333		Knin a.	...	...	...	...	...	1154	...	...	...	...	...	...	...	1938	...	...	...	...	...	...	0438	0603	...
333	0	Knin d.	...	0756	...	...	1110	1205	...	1200	...	1507	...	1715	...	1939	1950	...	...	0418	...	...	0439	0604	0505
	95	**Zadar** ⊡ a.	...	|	...	...	1328	|	...	1418	...	|	...	1933	...	|	|	...	...	|	...	...	|	|	0724
387	—	Perković a.	...	0901	...	...	...	1251	...	...	...	1616	...	...	...	2037	2057	...	...	0523	...	←	0539	0659	...
387	0	Perković d.	0705	0906	0913	1221	...	1252	1257	...	1508	1630	1645	...	...	2038	2102	2104	2250	→	0534	0542	0550	0700	...
	22	**Šibenik** ⊡ a.	0738	0938	|	|	...	|	1331	...	1540	1703	|	...	...	|	2135	|	2318	...	|	0615	|	|	...
435		**Split** ⊡ a.	...	...	1007	1315	...	1337	...	...	...	...	1739	...	...	2123	...	2205	...	...	0628	...	0648	0757	...

							ICN 520						ICN 522					1205						820	
	Ⓐv	Ⓐw	⚒	🚌 h			Ⓡ 🍷		Ⓐ	Ⓐq		Ⓐ	Ⓡ 🍷	🚌		Ⓐ		♦		Ⓐ		🚌	p	♦	
Split ⊡ d.	...	...	...	...	0800	...	0822	...	...	1035	...	...	1421	...	1530	...	...	1817	...	1953	...	...	...	2144	...
Šibenik ⊡ d.	0500	0500	0624	...	|	0832	|	...	1108	|	...	1425	|	...	|	1555	...	|	...	|	2028	...	2215	|	...
Perković a.	0531	0531	0656	...	0855	0904	0908	←	1156	1130	...	1457	1507	...	1625	1628	...	1917	...	2054	2100	...	2244	2246	...
Perković d.	0541	0541	...	...	...	→	0909	0922	...	...	...	...	1508	...	...	1631	...	1918	...	...	2102	...	...	2247	...
Zadar ⊡ d.	|	|	...	0735	...	...	|	|	...	...	...	...	|	1440	...	|	...	|	...	...	|	2030	...	|	...
Knin a.	0650	0700	...	0956	...	...	1000	1034	...	...	...	...	1559	1701	...	1743	...	2045	...	...	2214	2251	...	2355	...
Knin d.	...	...	...	...	...	...	1001	...	...	...	...	...	1600	...	...	...	...	2046	...	...	...	...	...	2356	...
Gračac d.	...	...	...	...	...	...	1106	...	...	...	...	...	1654	...	...	...	...	|	...	...	...	...	...	0113	...
Gospić d.	...	...	...	...	...	...	1139	...	...	...	...	...	1727	...	...	...	...	|	...	...	...	...	...	0151	...
Ogulin 1310 d.	...	...	...	...	...	...	|	...	...	...	...	...	|	...	...	...	...	0041j	...	...	...	...	...	0408	...
Oštarije **1310** d.	...	...	...	...	...	...	|	...	...	...	...	...	|	...	...	...	...	|	...	...	...	...	...	|	...
Karlovac **1310** d.	...	...	...	...	...	...	1354	...	...	...	...	...	1958	...	...	...	...	|	...	...	...	...	...	0506	...
Zagreb 1310 a.	...	...	...	...	...	...	1430	...	...	...	...	...	2037	...	...	...	...	0213	...	...	...	...	...	0547	...

♦ – **NOTES** (LISTED BY TRAIN NUMBER)

820 – ②④⑦ (daily Apr. 29 - Oct. 29): 🛏 1, 2 cl., ▬ 2 cl. and (2) Split - Zagreb.
821 – ①③⑤ (daily Apr. 28 - Oct. 28): 🛏 1, 2 cl., ▬ 2 cl. and (2) Zagreb - Split.
1204 – ADRIA – ②⑤⑦ June 18 - Sept. 1 (from Budapest, one day later from Zagreb): 🛏 1, 2 cl., ▬ 2 cl. and (2) Budapest - Gyékényes - Zagreb - Split. Conveys on ②⑤: 🛏 1, 2 cl. Praha - Budapest - Split.
1205 – ADRIA – ①③⑥ June 19 - Sept. 2: 🛏 1, 2 cl., ▬ 2 cl. and (2) Split - Zagreb - Gyékényes - Budapest. Conveys on ③⑥: 🛏 1, 2 cl. Split - Budapest - Praha.

h – ⚒ (daily May 1 - Oct. 30).
j – Arrive 0028.
p – ②④⑦ (daily Apr. 29 - Oct. 29).
q – Not June 16 - Sept. 1.
v – Not June 19 - Sept. 1.
w – June 19 - Sept. 1.
⊡ – Frequent 🚌 services operate Zadar - Šibenik - Split and v.v.; some continue to Ploče and Dubrovnik (see Table **1325**). Bus station locations: Zadar, Split and Ploče are adjacent to rail station, Šibenik approximately 10 minutes walk.

HŽ, MÁV 2nd class only except where shown ZAGREB - VARAŽDIN - NAGYKANIZSA 1335

There is currently no service Kotoriba - Murakeresztúr and v.v.

km														992		790		770										
		⚒			Ⓐ			⚒		⚒	⚒	Ⓐ	Ⓐ			Ⓐ		♦			Ⓐ	ⒶV	⚒	V				
0	**Zagreb** d.	...	...	...	0541	0730	...	0859	...	1117	...	...	1308	1424	...	1520	1524	1536	...	...	1647	...	1818	...	1920	...	2124	2226
38	Zabok d.	...	...	...	0655	0835	...	1002	...	1222	...	...	1414	1525	...	1609	1628	k	...	...	1748	...	1924	...	2026	...	2227	2325
104	**Varaždin** ▲ d.	0523	0653	...	0835	1016	...	1140	1305	1355	1414	1522	1556	1653	1657	1744	1810	1737	...	1921	1936	2020	2101	2119	2159	2218	0000	0055
115	Čakovec **1313** d.	0535	0710	...	0845	1027	...	▬	1322	...	1425	1539	...	▬	1708	1755	...	...	...	1941	▬	2032	...	2131	...	2229	0010	...
145	Kotoriba 🏛 d.	0612	0742	...	...	1059	...	...	1355	...	1500	1614	...	...	1745	1823	...	...	...	2016	...	2105	...	2208a	...	2306	...	...
151	Murakeresztúr 🏛 d.	...	...	0854	...	...	...	1255	...	...	...	...	...	1655	...	...	...	...	...	...	2055	...	...	...	...	...	...	...
165	**Nagykanizsa** a.	...	...	0907	...	...	...	1307	...	...	...	...	...	1707	...	...	...	...	...	...	2107	...	...	...	...	...	...	...

				991	771																995						
		⚒	⚒	⚒	♦		⚒			⚒		Ⓐ	Ⓐ	Ⓐ	⚒	⚒			Q				Ⓐ		Ⓐ		
Nagykanizsa d.	...	...	...	...	...	...	...	...	0651	...	...	1051	...	...	...	...	...	...	1451	...	...	...	...	...	1851	...	...
Murakeresztúr 🏛 d.	...	...	...	...	...	...	...	...	0703	...	...	1103	...	...	...	...	...	...	1503	...	...	...	...	...	1903	...	...
Kotoriba 🏛 d.	...	...	...	0422	...	...	...	0634	...	0803	...	...	1109	...	1156	1246	...	1503d	...	1605	...	...	1832	1923	...	2120	2219
Čakovec **1313** d.	...	...	...	0458	...	...	...	0709	...	0848	...	...	1143	...	1234	1320	...	1538d	...	1639	...	...	1908	2007	...	2154	2252
Varaždin ▲ d.	0246	0336	0425	0508	0524	0533	0644	0719	...	0858	1041	...	1153	1213	1244	1330	1415	1600	...	1649	...	1754	1920	2017	...	2204	2302
Zabok d.	0423	0510	0625	...	0654	k	0836	...	...	...	1221	...	...	1352	...	...	1632	1749	...	...	...	1923	2105	...	...	...	...
Zagreb a.	0521	0610	0729	...	0748	0726	0935	...	...	...	1321	...	...	1450	...	...	1732	1846	...	...	...	2021	2203	...	...	...	...

▲ – **VARAŽDIN - KOPRIVNICA and v.v.** 2nd class only except where shown:

km			771								
		⚒	♦		⚒	⚒		⚒	Q		Ⓐ
0	Varaždin d.	0430	0533	0652	1020	1303	1426	1607	1707	1923	2215
42	Koprivnica a.	0515	0609	0736	1105	1348	1510	1652	1752	2007	2259

								770			
	Ⓐ			⚒	⚒	Ⓐ		♦	⑦	ⒶV	V
Koprivnica d.	0432	0545	0842	1125	1303	1443	1541	1702	1800	1920	2022
Varaždin a.	0518	0638	0927	1210	1352	1535	1634	1737	1845	2009	2106

♦ – **NOTES** (LISTED BY TRAIN NUMBER)

770/1 – Ⓐ: (2) Zagreb - Koprivnica - Varaždin and v.v.

Q – ⑦: (2) Kotoriba - Varaždin - Koprivnica.
V – (2) Koprivnica - Varaždin - Kotoriba and v.v.

a – Ⓐ only.
d – ⚒ only.
k – Via Koprivnica.

HŽ, MÁV ZAGREB - KOPRIVNICA - NAGYKANIZSA and OSIJEK 1340

km			1205	783	703	205	981	770	201	581	1201	971	
		2	♦		♦	♦	2	♦	♦		♦	2	2
	Rijeka **1310** d.	...	...	...	0535	0535	...	...	...	...	...	...	...
0	**Zagreb** d.	...	0232	0652	1003	1003	1249	1536	1536	1640	1640	1845	2031
57	Križevci d.	...	0319	0741	1052	1052	1348	1626	1629	1728	1728	1940	2102
88	Koprivnica **1335** d.	...	0404	0814	1120	1121	1436	1644	1655	1801	1755	2014	2158
103	Gyékényes 🏛 d.	...	0529	|	|	1211	|	...	1745	|	1835	...	...
132	**Nagykanizsa** a.	...	0554	|	|	|	|	...	|	|	1905	...	...
	Budapest Keleti **1240** a.	...	0936	|	|	1614	|	...	2214	|	2230	...	...
153	Virovitica d.	0349	...	0929	1230	...	1601	...	...	1918	...	...	...
225	Našice d.	0509	...	1045	1354	...	1738	...	...	2030	...	...	...
275	**Osijek 1345** a.	0622	...	1136	1445	...	1838	...	...	2121	...	...	...

	980	771	580	200	1200	702		204	782	1204	
	2	♦		♦	♦		2	♦	♦	♦	2
Osijek 1345 d.	0106a	...	0527	...	...	1204	...	...	1620	...	1957
Našice d.	0159a	...	0618	...	...	1255	...	...	1712	...	2107
Virovitica d.	0321a	...	0734	...	...	1416	...	...	1830	...	2227
Budapest Kel **1240** d.	|	...	|	0545	0600	|	...	1445	|	1815	...
Nagykanizsa d.	|	...	|	|	0917	|	...	|	|	2154	...
Gyékényes 🏛 d.	|	...	|	1011	1011	|	...	1916	|	2253	...
Koprivnica **1335** d.	0444	0619	0848	1030	1030	1531	1723	1949	1949	2313	...
Križevci d.	0525	0640	0911	1053	1053	1551	1756	2011	2011	2335	...
Zagreb a.	0627	0726	0954	1139	1139	1636	1853	2059	2059	0022	...
Rijeka **1310** a.	...	...	...	1541	1541	2043	...	...	...	...	...

♦ – **NOTES** (LISTED BY TRAIN NUMBER)

200 – KVARNER – Dec. 11 - June 16, Aug. 28 - Dec. 9: (12) and 🍷 Budapest - Zagreb - Rijeka.
201 – RIPPL-RÓNAI – Dec. 11 - June 16, Aug. 28 - Dec. 9: (12) and ✕ Zagreb - Budapest.
204 – RIPPL-RÓNAI – (12) and ✕ Budapest - Gyékényes - Zagreb; (12) Osijek (**782**) - Koprivnica - Zagreb.
205 – KVARNER – (12) and 🍷 Rijeka - Zagreb - Budapest; (12) Rijeka - Koprivnica (**703**) - Osijek.
703 – (12) Koprivnica - Osijek.
770/1 – Ⓐ: (2) Zagreb - Koprivnica - Varaždin and v.v.
782 – (12) Osijek - Koprivnica (**204**) - Zagreb.
1200 – KVARNER – June 17 - Aug. 27: (12) and 🍷 Budapest - Zagreb - Rijeka.
1201 – RIPPL-RÓNAI – June 17 - Aug. 27: (12) and ✕ Zagreb - Budapest.
1204 – ADRIA – ②⑤⑦ June 18 - Sept. 1: 🛏 1, 2 cl., ▬ 2 cl. and (2) Budapest - Gyékényes - Zagreb - Split. Conveys on ②⑤: 🛏 1, 2 cl. Praha (**277**) - Budapest - Split.
1205 – ADRIA – ①③⑥ June 19 - Sept. 2 (from Split, one day later from Zagreb): 🛏 1, 2 cl., ▬ 2 cl. and (2) Split - Zagreb - Gyékényes - Budapest. Conveys on ③⑥: 🛏 1, 2 cl. Split - Budapest (**276**) - Praha.

1345 PÉCS - OSIJEK - DOBOJ

2nd class only except where shown   HŽ, MÁV, ŽRS

There is currently no service Slavonski Šamac - Šamac - Doboj and v.v. Strizivojna-Vrpolje - Slavonski Šamac and v.v. 🚌 bus service is subject to alteration

km		Ⓐ	✗	Ⓐ		✗	Ⓐ	✗	✗	Ⓐ		✗	Ⓐ		🚌	✗				Ⓑ	Ⓐ	Ⓑ	Ⓐ
	Budapest Déli 1200 .....d.	...	...	...	...	...	...	...	...	...	...	...	...	...	...	...	...	...	...	...	...	...	...
0	Pécs..................d.	...	...	0512	...	...	...	...	...	...	...	...	...	1710	...	...	...	...	...	...	...	...	...
36	Villány................d.	...	...	0558	...	...	...	...	...	...	...	...	...	1755	...	...	...	...	...	...	...	...	...
43	Magyarbóly ● ▦ d.	...	...	0605	...	...	...	...	...	...	...	...	...	1802	...	...	...	...	...	...	...	...	...
54	Beli Manastir ● ▦ d.	...	0542	0701	...	0820	...	1051	1219	...	1410	...	1615	...	1846	...	...	2006	2300				
82	Osijek 1340 ....a.	...	0610	0729	...	0848	...	1119	1247	...	1438	...	1643	...	1914	...	...	2034	2328				
82	Osijek 1340 ....d.	0439	...	0745	0816	...	1050	1103	...	1347	1353	...	1623	1815	...	...	1954	2027	2230				
	Vinkovci.............d.	...	...	0827	...	1132		...	...	1435	...	1705	1857	...	...	2109	2312						
130	Strizivojna-Vrpolje 1320...d.	0507	0532	...	...	0910	...	1155	...	1440	...	1650	...	...	2046	...	...	...	...				
150	Slavonski Šamac ▦ d.	0530	...	...	...	...	...	...	...	...	1713	...	...	...	...	...	...	...	...				
154	Šamac............d.	...	...	...	...	...	...	...	...	...	...	...	...	...	...	...	...	...	...				
226	Doboj 1350 ....a.	...	...	...	...	...	...	...	...	...	...	...	...	...	...	...	...	...	...				

km		Ⓐ	✗		Ⓐ	Ⓐ	✗	✗	✗		Ⓐ	✗		Ⓐ				🚌		Ⓐ	Ⓑ	🚌	Ⓑ	Ⓐ
	Doboj 1350 ....d.	...	...	...	...	...	...	...	...	...	...	...	...	...	...	...	...	...	...	...	...	...	...	...
	Šamac............d.	...	...	...	...	...	...	...	...	...	...	...	...	...	...	...	...	...	...	...	...	...	...	...
	Slavonski Šamac ▦ d.	...	...	...	0537	...	...	...	...	...	...	...	...	...	...	...	...	1717	...	...	...	...	...	...
	Strizivojna-Vrpolje 1320...d.	...	...	0540	0600	0622	...	...	1008	...	1202	...	...	1650	...	...	...	1740	2111	...	...	...	...	...
0	Vinkovci.............d.	0536		0640	...	...	0834	...	1201		...	1522		1723	...	...	1905	2114		...	...	...	...	
35	Osijek 1340 ....a.	0618	...	0632	...	0715	0722	...	0916	...	1100	...	1243	1255	...	1604	1742	1805	...	...	1947	2156	2203	...
	Osijek 1340 ....d.	0502	0624	...	0740	...	1010	1141	...	1325	1530	...	...	1808	1926	...	...	...	...	2222				
	Beli Manastir ● ▦ d.	0530	0652	...	0808	...	1038	1209	...	1353	1558	...	...	1836	1954	...	...	...	...	2250				
	Magyarbóly ● ▦ d.	...	0736	...	...	...	...	...	...	...	...	...	...	1939	...	...	...	...	...	...				
	Villány................a.	...	0743	...	...	...	...	...	...	...	...	...	...	1946	...	...	...	...	...	...				
	Pécs..................a.	...	0842	...	...	...	...	...	...	...	...	...	...	2042	...	...	...	...	...	...				
	Budapest Déli 1200 ...a.	...	...	...	...	...	...	...	...	...	...	...	...	...	...	...	...	...	...	...				

● – Magyarbóly - Beli Manastir and v.v. is currently suspended.

1350 ZAGREB - DOBOJ - SARAJEVO

2nd class only except where shown   HŽ, ŽFBH, ŽRS

km			715									397					
0	Zagreb 1322 ....d.	...	...	...	...	...	...	...	...	...	0910	...	...	...	...	
72	Sunja 1322 ....d.	...	...	...	...	...	...	...	...	...	1025	...	...	...	...	
92	Volinja ....▦ d.	...	...	...	...	...	...	...	...	...	1112	...	...	...	...	
98	Dobrljin ....▦ d.	...	...	...	...	...	...	0631	...	...	1145	...	...	...	1832	
112	Novi Grad ....d.	...	...	...	...	0440	...	0702	...	...	1201	...	...	...	1905	
214	Banja Luka ....d.	...	0528	...	0442	...	0631	0732	...	0859	1339	...	1532	...	1931	2106
324	Doboj 1345 ....a.	...	0707	...	0637	...	...	0939	...	...	1524	...	1738	...	2138	
324	Doboj 1345 ....d.	...	0707	...	...	...	...	...	...	...	1524	...	...	...	...	
347	Maglaj ....d.	...	0735	0515	...	...	...	0930	...	...	1555	...	1708	...	...	
370	Zavidovici ....d.	...	0804	0543	...	...	...	0958	...	...	1621	...	1736	...	...	
419	Zenica ....d.	0457	0857	0643	0748	...	1058	1114	1527	...	1714	...	1836	1917	...	
447	Kakanj ....d.	0531	0926	...	0830	...	...	1153	1601	...	1743	1745	...	1951	...	
465	Visoko ....d.	0553	0943	...	0852	...	...	1215	1630	...	1744	1813	...	2013	...	
472	Podlugovi ....d.	0602		...	0901	...	...	1224	1638	...	1800	1822	...	2022	...	
496	Sarajevo 1355 ....a.	0639	1027	...	0938	...	...	1301	...	...	1838	1859	...	2059	...	

			396									714					
	Sarajevo 1355 ....d.	...	...	0439	...	0717	...	1012	...	1101	...	...	1540	1539	...	1924
	Podlugovi ....d.	...	...	0517	...	0755	...	1139	...	1139	...	...	1618		1732	2002
	Visoko ....d.	...	...	0526	...	0804	1051	1148	...	1148	...	...	1627	1618	1746	2015
	Kakanj ....d.	...	...	0559	...	0826	1108	1216	...	1216	...	...	1648	1635	1808	2037
	Zenica ....d.	...	...	0632	0723	0859	...	1138	1249	...	1531	...	1705	1841	1923	2110
	Zavidovici ....d.	...	...	0824	...	...	...	1229	...	...	1632	...	1802	2024	...	
	Maglaj ....d.	...	...	0851	...	...	...	1255	...	...	1659	...	1828	2051	...	
	Doboj 1345 ....a.	...	...	...	...	...	...	1335	...	...	...	...	1903	...	...	
	Doboj 1345 ....d.	...	0424	...	0725	...	...	1335	...	1525	...	...	1903	1932	...	
	Banja Luka ....d.	...	0624	0725	0922	...	...	1511	1525	1728	...	...	1925	2026	2142	
	Novi Grad ....d.	0600	0921	...	...	...	...	1645	1730	...	...	...	2122	...	...	
	Dobrljin ....▦ d.	0618	...	...	...	...	...	1721	1848	...	...	...	...	...	...	
	Volinja ....▦ d.	...	...	...	...	...	...	1802	...	...	...	...	...	...	...	
	Sunja 1322 ....d.	...	...	...	...	...	...	1830	...	...	...	...	...	...	...	
	Zagreb 1322 ....a.	...	...	...	...	...	...	1944	...	...	...	...	...	...	...	

1355 SARAJEVO - PLOČE

Most services 2nd class only   HŽ, ŽFBH

Sarajevo - Čapljina is currently closed. There is no rail service Čapljina - Metković and v.v. (see note below).

km		🚌	🚌	723	🚌	⊗	🚌	721						720	🚌	🚌	🚌	722
		✗	✗		Ⓐ	⊗	✗		⊗	⊗				⊗	🚌		✗	⊗
	Zagreb 1350 ....d.	...	...	0715	...	...	1530	...	1857	1921		Ploče...................d.	...	0550	1245	1420	...	
0	Sarajevo 1350 ....d.	...	...	0855	...	...	1709	...	2024	2105		Metković................d.	...	0625	1320	1455	...	
67	Konjic ....d.	...	...	0959	...	...	...	...	2128	...		Čapljina ....▦ d.	0637	...	...	...	...	1843
129	Mostar ....d.	...	...	1016	...	...	...	...	2145	...		Žitomislići ....d.	0654	...	...	...	...	1900
149	Žitomislići ....d.	...	...	1032	...	...	...	...	2201	...		Mostar ....d.	0712	...	...	...	...	1918
163	Čapljina ....▦ d.	0510	0630	...	1325	...	1705	...	...	...		Konjic ....d.	0503	0815	...	...	1716	2027
173	Metković...............d.	0545	0705	...	1400	...	1740	...	...	...		Sarajevo 1350 ......a.	0642	0948	...	...	1855	2153
194	Ploče ....a.											Zagreb 1350 ....a.	...	...	...	...	...	...

⊗ – Service temporarily suspended owing to engineering work.

Alternative 🚌 services are available Sarajevo - Mostar - Metković - Dubrovnik and v.v.
Connections are possible at Metković to / from Ploče.

1358 LOCAL SERVICES in Bosnia

2nd class only   HŽ, ŽFBH, ŽRS

VINKOVCI - TUZLA and v.v. :

There is currently no service Gunja - Brčko - Tuzla and v.v.

km		Ⓐ					Ⓐ				Ⓐ				Ⓐ
0	Vinkovci............d.	0328	...	0950	...	1500	...	1935		Tuzla.................d.	...	...	...	...	...
49	Gunja ....d.	0426	...	1049	...	1600	...	2034		Brčko...............▦ d.	...	...	...	...	...
53	Brčko ....▦ d.	...	...	...	...	...	...	...		Gunja ....d.	0433	...	1056	1609	...	2042
127	Tuzla.................a.	...	...	...	...	...	...	...		Vinkovci............a.	0531	...	1155	1708	...	2141

TUZLA - DOBOJ and v.v. :

km			Ⓐ								Ⓐ				
0	Tuzla.................d.	0452	1020	...	1709	...	...		Doboj.................d.	0438	0728	...	1310	1528	1928
32	Petrovo Novo ......d.	0536	1104	1408	1753	2028	...		Petrovo Novo ......d.	0526	0821	...	1402	1621	2021
60	Doboj.................a.	0628	1156	1500	1841	2116	...		Tuzla.................a.	...	0904	...	1704	2104	

SERBIA, MONTENEGRO and FYRO MACEDONIA *MAP PAGE 501*

Operators:	Železnice Srbije (ŽS): www.zeleznicesrbije.com; Železnice Crne Gore (ŽCG): www.zcg-prevoz.me; Makedonski Železnici (MŽ): www.mztransportad.com.mk; Trainkos (KŽ/HK): www.trainkos.com.
Services:	All trains convey first- and second-class seating, except where shown otherwise in footnotes, by a '2' in the train column, or where the footnote shows that the train conveys sleeping- (🛏) and / or couchette (🛌) cars only. Descriptions of sleeping- and couchette cars are given on page 8.
Timings:	Valid from **December 11, 2016** except where indicated otherwise. Readers should note, however, that only partial information was available at press date and consequently all domestic services are subject to alteration. *Services may be amended or cancelled at short notice and passengers are strongly advised to check locally before travelling.*
Tickets:	A supplement is payable for travel by internal express trains. Reservation of seats is possible on most express trains.
Visas:	Most nationals do not require a visa to enter Serbia and Montenegro, but must obtain an entry stamp in their passport, sight of which will be required by officials on leaving the country. These must be obtained at a border crossing recognised by the authorities - this excludes Kosovo's external borders with Montenegro, Former Yugoslav Republic Of Macedonia (FYROM) and Albania. Note also that Serbia should not be entered from Kosovo unless initial travel into Kosovo was via Serbia. Visas are not required for entry into FYROM for most nationals.
Currency:	Visitors must declare large amounts of foreign currency upon arrival; currently € 2000 in Montenegro, and € 10000 in Serbia and FYROM. It is reported, however, that FYROM may now be operating on a threshold of € 2000. A certificate issued by the customs officer must be presented on departure, otherwise any funds held may be confiscated.
Security:	Following the declaration of independence by Kosovo (which has not been recognised by Serbia) caution should be exercised when travelling in southern Serbia and northern Kosovo. Caution is also advised in the northern and western border regions of the Former Yugoslav Republic Of Macedonia.

ŽS — (BUDAPEST -) KELEBIA - SUBOTICA - BEOGRAD — 1360

km		341	741	743	841	IC 541	745		747	749	843		641	IC 343	751		753		845	EC 345	755	757	1137	
		✪				R 2	2					2		✪		2		2		✎			2	2
		B												C						V		P		
	Budapest Keleti **1295**...... d.	2225	...	...	...	...	...		...	...	...		0805		...		...		...	1205		...	...	...
0	Kelebia .... a.	0106											1111							1511				
10	Subotica **1362** ...... 🚌 a.	0154											1155							1555				
10	Subotica .... d.	0206	...	0345	...	0545	0713		...	1011	...		1226		1320		...		1531	1630		1837	1907	...
108	Novi Sad **1362** ...... a.	0445	...	0628	...	0803	0951		...	1252	...		1454		1551		...		1808	1849		2108	2142	
108	Novi Sad .... d.	0447	0540	0617	...	0711	0807	0910	...	1008	1105		1321	1445	1457	1524		1700	1756		1851	1928	2030	2131	2245
181	Novi Beograd .... d.	0601	0706	0752	...	0851	0921	1037	...	1129	1239		1456	1608	1610	1651		1821	1936		2003	2053	2207	2250	0013
186	Beograd .... a.	0613	0717	0803	...	0902	0932	1049c	...	1140	1250c		1507	1619	1622	1702		1832	1947		2015	2104	2218	2256c	0025

		740	1136		840	742	EC 344		744	746	842		IC 342		640	748		750		752	IC 540	754	844		340	756
		2			2	2	2						✪			2		2		2	R 2			2	✪	
			P				V						C								B					
	Beograd .... d.	...	0340	0502c	0458	...	0557	0736		0835	1005	...	1044	1135	...	1232c	1318		1428c	1530	1635	1705	1835		2020	2150	2305
	Novi Beograd......... d.	...	0352	0508	0509	...	0608	0749		0846	1016	...	1055	1148		1238	1330		1444	1542	1646	1716	1846		2031	2203	2316
	Novi Sad **1362** ...... a.	...	0520	0635	0639	...	0733	0900		...	1007	1139		1220	1259		1352	1504		1607	1719	1815	1828	2010		2201	2314	0039
	Novi Sad .... d.	0355	...	0658	...	0708	...	0904	0958		...	1204		1301		...	1546		...		1838		2028		2318		
	Subotica **1362** ...... a.	0625	...	0937	...	0945	...	1123	1223		...	1434		1520		...	1819		...		2102		2310		0139		
	Subotica .... 🚌 a.	...	...	...	...	...	...	1202						1602											0216		
	Kelebia .... 🚌 a.	...	...	...	...	...	...	1216						1616											0230		
	Budapest Keleti **1295** ...... a.	...	...	...	...	...	...	1554						1954											0546		

– **BEOGRAD** – 🛏 1, 2 cl., 🛌 2 cl. and 🍴 Budapest - Beograd and v.v. Conveys ②⑤ June 16 - Sept. 1 (from Praha); ④⑦ June 18 - Sept. 3 (from Bar): 🛏 1, 2 cl. and 🛌 2 cl. Praha (**172/3**) - Beograd (**430/1**) - Bar and v.v.
– **IVO ANDRIĆ** – 🍴 Beograd - Budapest and v.v.
– **PANONIJA** – June 2 - Sept. 3 (from Subotica); June 3 - Sept. 4 (from Bar): 🛏 1, 2 cl., 🛌 2 cl. and 🍴 Subotica - Bar and v.v. Conveys ②⑤ June 16 - Sept. 1 (from Budapest); ③⑥ June 17 - Sept. 2 (from Bar): 🛏 1, 2 cl., 🛌 2 cl. and 🍴 Budapest (**344/5**) - Subotica - Bar and v.v.
– **AVALA** – 🍴 and ✕ Wien - Budapest - Beograd and v.v. Conveys ②⑤ June 16 - Sept. 1 (from Budapest); ③⑥ June 17 - Sept. 2 (from Bar): 🛏 1, 2 cl., 🛌 2 cl. and 🍴 Budapest - Subotica (**1136/7**) - Bar and v.v.

c – Beograd **Centar**.
🌐 – Train with 'global' price.
✪ – Supplement payable for travel in Serbia.
✎ – Supplement payable for travel in Hungary and Serbia.

ŽS — 2nd class only — SUBOTICA and KIKINDA - ZRENJANIN - PANČEVO - BEOGRAD — 1362

km															
	Subotica **1360** .... ⊖ d.	...	...	0730	...	...		Beograd Dunav **1365**.... d.	...	...	1040	...	1725	...	
	Senta .... ⊖ d.	...	...	0853	...	...		Pančevački most **1365/6** .. d.	...	...	1044	...	1729	...	
	Banatsko Miloševo ..... ⊖ d.	...	...	0943	...	...		Pančevo glavna **1365/6** .. d.	...	...	1108	...	1753	...	2250
0	**Kikinda 1377** .... ⊖ d.	...	0435	1000	1131	...	1635	Orlovat stajalište.......... d.	0623	...	1224	...	1911	...	0008
19	Banatsko Miloševo ..... ⊖ d.	...	0453	...	1149	...	1653	**Zrenjanin** .... d.	0717	0915	1318	1420	2005	2015	0102
71	**Zrenjanin** .... d.	0400	0641	0740	1337	1415	1841	2020	Banatsko Miloševo ..... a.	...	1103	...	1608	...	2203	...
96	Orlovat stajalište .... d.	0455	...	0835	...	1510	...	2115	**Kikinda 1377** .... ⊖ a.	...	1010	1121	...	1626	...	2221
145	**Pančevo glavna 1365/6** ... d.	...	...	0951	...	1626	...	2232	Banatsko Miloševo ..... ⊖ d.	1035						
160	Pančevački most **1365/6** ... d.	...	...	1018	...	1654	...		Senta .... ⊖ d.	1125						
161	Beograd Dunav **1365** .... a.	...	...	1021	...	1657	...		Subotica **1360** .... ⊖ a.	1240						

🚌 – For alternative 🚌 services Subotica - Kikinda and v.v. see www.polazak.com.

ŽS, CFR — BEOGRAD - VRŠAC - TIMISOARA — 1365

km		2		2	2		2			2		2	2		2
0	**Beograd Dunav 1362**.... d.	0725	...	1150	1615	...	2020	**Timisoara Nord**............ § d.	...	0749	...	...	1638	...
1	Pančevački most **1362/6**.. d.	0729	...	1154	1619	...	2024	Stamora Moravita.......... § a.	...	0900	...	...	1753	...
16	Pančevo glavna **1362/6**.. d.	0753	...	1218	1643	...	2048	Stamora Moravita 🚉 .... § d.	...	0930	...	...	1823	...
83	Vršac 🚉 .... a.	0903	...	1328	1753	...	2200	Vršac 🚉 .... a.	...	0852	...	...	1745	...
83	Vršac 🚉 .... d.	...	1018	...	...	1835	...	Vršac 🚉 .... d.	0520	...	0940	1410	...	1825
103	Stamora Moravita 🚉 ... § a.	...	1140	...	...	1957	...	Pančevo glavna **1362/6**..... d.	0634	...	1052	1522	...	1937
103	Stamora Moravita .... § d.	...	1217	...	...	2026	...	Pančevački most **1362/6**.... d.	0702	...	1120	1550	...	2005
159	**Timisoara Nord** .... § a.	...	1322	...	...	2130	...	**Beograd Dunav 1362**..... d.	0705	...	1123	1553	...	2008

§ – Romanian (East European) time.

ŽS — 2nd class only — NOVI BEOGRAD - PANČEVO — 1366

Novi Beograd.................. d.	0617	and	2117	...	2147	2232	...	Pančevački most **1362/5**..d.	0604	and	1504	1602	and	2002	2104	2149	2219	2304
Beograd centar.............. d.	0623	hourly	2123	...	2153	2238	...	Beograd centar.............. d.	0614	hourly	1514	1613	hourly	2013	2114	2159	2229	2314
Pančevački most **1362/5**.. d.	0632	until	2132	...	2202	2247	...	Novi Beograd................. a.	0619	until	1519	1618	until	2018	2119	2204	2234	2319

Pančevački most **1362/5**.. d.	0500	0640	0820	0955	1145	1320	1500	1810	1945	2150	Pančevo glavna **1362/5**..... d.	0601	0739	0916	1104	1240	1421	1725	1906	2106	2301
Pančevo glavna **1362/5**.. a.	0518	0658	0838	1014	1203	1338	1518	1828	2003	2208	Pančevački most **1362/5**..... a.	0622	0800	0937	1138	1301	1442	1746	1927	2127	2322

SERBIA and MONTENEGRO

1370 — BEOGRAD - PODGORICA - BAR — ŽCG, ŽS

km										431		713		IC 581 R K ⊗	IC 513 R		433				1137	
		2	2	2	2	2	2	2	2	2 T	2	2	2			2	2 L	2	2	2	2	2 P
0	Beograd.............d.	...	0250		0704	...		0910	...	1030	1245	1454	1655	1655	...	1905	2110	...	...	2259c
93	Valjevo...............d.	...	0507		0924	...		1103	...	1243	1434	1709	1844	1844	...	2122	2303	...	...	0046
159	Požega 1372.......d.	...	0648		1059	...		1229	...	1432	1559	1854	2007	2022	...	2303	0029	...	...	0222
185	Užice.................d.	...	0727		1135	...		1255	...	1508	1632	1934		2042	...	2333	0055	...	0236	0248
292	Prijepolje teretna.....d.	...	0959		1403	...		1603	...	1747		2203		2249	...		0428	...	0513	0650
328	Vrbnica ▥..........a.	...				...		1649	...						...			...		
338	Bijelo Polje ▥.......d.	...	0903			...		1806	1833						...	0552		0630		0815
468	Podgorica 1371....d.	1030	1130		1250	...	1520	1650	1801	2015	2115			0535	...	0805	0750	0855		1036
524	Bar...................a.	1128	1234		1348	...	1618	1756	1858	2110	2213			0629	...	0902	0848			1157

		IC 580 R K ⊗	IC 512 R						430		714					1136			432		
		2	2	2	2	2	2	2	2 T	2	2	2	2	2	2	2 P	2	2	2 L	2	2
Bar....................d.				0515	0640	...		0710	0913	1140	...	1405		1440	1635		1650	...	1825	1900	1930	...
Podgorica 1371......d.				0625	0739	...		0810	1017	1238	...	1503		1550	1736		1753	...	1929	2005	2035	...
Bijelo Polje ▥.......d.				0843		...		1045			...			1814			2035	...		2240		...
Vrbnica ▥..........d.						...		1123			...							...				...
Prijepolje teretna.......d.			0305	0330	0740	...	1115		1215		...			1530			1949	2204	...	0004		...
Užice.................d.	0235		0521	0612	1026	...	1403		1532		1757			1813			2245	0127	...	0224		0235
Požega 1372.........d.	0305	0437	0542	0649	1100	...	1431		1554		1821			1855				0149	...	0246		0305
Valjevo...............d.	0442	0605	0711	0841	1244	...	1612		1721		1955			2049				0316	...	0412		0442
Beograd..............a.	0644	0751	0852	1055	1449	...	1840		1913		2155			2201				0429c	...	0602		0644

K – ⊒ Beograd - Požega - Kraljevo and v.v.
L – LOVĆEN – ⊒ 1,2 cl., ◢ 2 cl. and ⊒ Beograd - Bar and v.v.
P – PANONIJA – June 2 - Sept. 3 (from Subotica); June 3 - Sept. 4 (from Bar): ⊒ 1,2 cl., ◢ 2 cl. and ⊒
   Subotica - Bar and v.v. Conveys ②⑤ June 16 - Sept. 1 (from Budapest); ③⑥ June 17 - Sept. 2 (from Bar):
   ⊒ 1,2 cl., ◢ 2 cl. and ⊒ Budapest (344/5) - Subotica - Bar and v.v.
T – TARA – ⊒ and ✕ Beograd - Bar and v.v. Also conveys cars from / to Moskva / Minsk / Praha. See Table
   1360 for composition and dates.

c – Beograd Centar.
⊗ – Service currently suspended.

1371 — PODGORICA - NIKŠIĆ — ŽCG

km																						
0	Podgorica 1370.......d.	0630	0740	0930	1105	1245	1400	1510	1614	1900	2040	Nikšić................d.	0620	0805	0910	1055	1235	1425	1535	1650	1740	2030
25	Danilovgrad..........d.	0701	0807	0957	1136	1316	1427	1537	1645	1927	2111	Danilovgrad...........d.	0700	0850	0958	1135	1315	1510	1620	1730	1820	2110
61	Nikšić...............a.	0740	0846	1036	1215	1355	1506	1616	1728	2005	2150	Podgorica 1370......a.	0726	0926	1024	1202	1341	1541	1646	1756	1846	2137

1372 — POŽEGA - KRALJEVO - STALAĆ — 2nd class only — ŽS

tariff km								581 K ⊗							580 K ⊗						
0	Požega 1370.........d.			0830		1250		1650	2025	Stalać 1380..........d.					0915			1945
45	Čačak................d.		0525	0905		1325	1725	2052	Kraljevo 1375.......d.	0342	0410	0630		1050	1138	1440	1830	2208
83	Kraljevo 1375.......a.	0434	0603	0942	1402	1425	1802	2116	Čačak................d.	0410	0445	0705		1129		1519	1909
155	Stalać 1380..........a.	0657				1648			Požega 1370.........a.	0435		0737		1204		1554	1944

K – ⊒ Beograd - Požega - Kraljevo and v.v.
⊗ – Service currently suspended.

1373 — MAJDANPEK and PRAHOVO - ZAJEČAR - NIŠ — 2nd class only except where shown — ŽS

tariff km																			
0	Majdanpek...........d.	0345			0855		1705			Niš 1380.............d.	0225		1053		1540		
★	Prahovo pristanište...d.		0425	0845		1750			Knjaževac...........d.	0434		1259		1751		
97	Zaječar..............d.	0558	0611	0625	1031	1109	1150	1919	1936	1956	Zaječar..............d.	0540	0620	0635	1402	1430	1530	1857	2225	2240
144	Knjaževac...........d.		0729			1304		2102	Prahovo pristanište...a.		0820		1716		002?
221	Niš 1380.............a.		0936		1509		2307	Majdanpek...........a.		0831		1641		0036

★ – Prahovo - Zaječar : 81 km.

1375 — LAPOVO and PRIŠTINA - KOSOVO POLJE - SKOPJE — 2nd class only — ŽS, KŽ

km							760 ⊠		⊠	⊠	892 ⊠ h
	Beograd 1380........d.						Skopje 1380/5........d.				1610
0	Lapovo 1380.........d.		0338	1110		1853	Deneral Janković / Hani I Elezit ▥.d.	...	0548		1050		1745
28	Kragujevac..........d.		0432	1204		1947	Uroševac / Ferizaj....d.	...	0632		1135		1829
82	Kraljevo 1372.......d.	0240	0623	0640	1355	1455	2138	Peć / Pejë............d.		0532		1210	
163	Raška...............d.	0418	0821		1636	Kosovo Polje / Fushë Kosovë ♣.d.	...	0714	0721		1219	1359	1910
180	Lešak / Leshak.......d.		0853		1708	Priština / Prishtinë....d.		0732		1410		1920
210	Zvečan / Zveçan.....♣.d.		1002		1817	Mitrovica / Mitrovicë....♣.d.					

		891 ⊠ h		⊠	761 ⊠		
214	Mitrovica / Mitrovicë....♣.d.					Zvečan / Zveçan......d.			1028		1843	...
	Priština / Prishtinë....d.	0710	0750		1630		Lešak / Leshak.......d.			1135		1950	...
247	Kosovo Polje / Fushë Kosovë.d.	0722	0801	1605	1641	1848	Raška...............d.	0435		1210		2025	...
*	Peć / Pejë............a.		0950		1826		Kraljevo 1372.......d.	0611	0644	1346	1449	2201	2225
276	Uroševac / Ferizaj....d.	0802		1649		1935	Kragujevac..........d.		0836		1641		0017
304	Deneral Janković / Hani I Elezit.... ▥.d.	0900		1730		2016	Lapovo 1380.........d.		0929		1734		0112
331	Skopje 1380/5........a.	0951					Beograd 1380........a.					

h – A change of train may be necessary at Deneral Janković / Hani I Elezit
   (connection between trains is guaranteed).
⊠ – Service operated by KŽ (see country heading).
♣ – Currently no service Zvečan - Mitrovica - Kosovo Polje and v.v.
* – Kosovo Polje - Peć : 82 km.

1377 — MINOR BORDER CROSSINGS — 2nd class only — ŽS, MÁV, CFF

SUBOTICA - SZEGED and v.v. :	Service suspended
km			
0	Subotica...d.	Szeged.....d.
24	Horgoš ▥..d.	Röszke ▥.d.
31	Röszke ▥a.	Horgoš..▥d.
43	Szeged ....d.	Subotica....a.

KIKINDA - JIMBOLIA - TIMISOARA and v.v. :									
km										
0	Kikinda 1362...d.	...		...		...		Timisoara .... § d.	0704	0812	1340	1624	1936	232?
19	Jimbolia... ▥.§ d.	0515	0608	0840	1240	1440	1740	Jimbolia... ▥.§ d.	0755	0927	1431	1714	2027	001?
58	Timisoara .... § a.	0608	0701	0933	1333	1532	1833	Kikinda 1362.. a.	...		...		...	

§ – East European time, one hour ahead of Central European time.

ŽS, MŽ, BDŽ | **BEOGRAD - NIŠ - SOFIA, SKOPJE and THESSALONÍKI** | **1380**

Services subject to disruption owing to engineering work between Niš and Preševo; Beograd - Skopje / Thessaloníki services are suspended

km		2	2	2	2	2	2	2	2✗	**791** 2	2	0714	**491** B	2	←	2	2x	2	2	**795** 2	2	2	**335** H⊗	2
0	Beograd 1375 ....d.	...	...	...	...	0335	...	0610	...	0714	...	0925	←	...	1110	...	...	1515	...	1527	...	1835	1920
110	Lapovo 1375 ....d.	...	...	0350	...	0610	...	0819	...	0952	...	1121	1003	...	1342	1551	...	1714	...	1806	...	2039	2153
135	Jagodina ....d.	...	...	0418	...	0638	...	0844	...	→	...	1151	1031	...	1410	1619	...	1739	...	1834	...	2109	...
155	Paraćin ....d.	...	...	0433	...	0653	...	0900	...	...	...	1205	1046	...	1424	1634	...	1755	...	1849	...	2125	...
176	Stalać 1372 ....d.	...	...	0458	...	0717	...	0923	...	...	...	1234	1111	...	...	1659	...	1818	...	1914	...	2154	...
244	Niš 1373 ....a.	...	...	0631	...	0855	...	1032	...	...	...	1342	1249	...	...	1831	...	1927	...	2045	...	2302	...
244	Niš ....d.	...	0335	...	...	0711	...	...	...	...	...	1415	...	1526	1550	...	...	1932	...	...	...	2317	...
	Dimitrovgrad ......▦ d.	...		...	...		...	...	...	...	...	1718	...		...	...	...		...	...	...		...
	Dragoman ....▦ § d.	...		...	...		...	...	...	...	...	1925	...		...	...	...		...	...	...		...
	Sofia ....§ a.	...		...	...		...	...	...	...	...	2010	...		...	...	...		...	...	...		...
288	Leskovac...................d.	...	0437	...	...	0824	...	...	...	...	...	...	1630	1655	...	...	...	...	2032	...	...	0002	...
392	Preševo ....d.	...	0712x	...	...	...	...	...	...	...	...	2	...	1925	...	2	...	...	2257x	...	...	0301	...
401	Tabanovci..............▦ d.	0516	...	0747	...	...	...	...	...	...	...	1750	...	...	2016	...	...	...	...	...	...	0340	...
462	Skopje ....a.	0610	...	0841	...	...	...	...	...	...	...	1844	...	...	2110	...	...	...	...	...	...	0420	...
462	Skopje 1375/85 ....d.	0620	...	0900	...	...	1320	...	1655	...	...	...	...	...	...	2233	...	...	...	...	...	0445	...
511	Veles 1385 ....d.	0722	...	0951	...	...	1411	...	1746	...	...	...	...	...	...	2328	...	...	...	...	...	0526	...
638	Gevgelija ....d.	0908	...	...	...	...	...	...	1938	...	...	...	...	...	...	...	...	...	...	...	...	0651	...
638	Gevgelija ....▦ d.	...	...	...	...	...	...	...	...	...	...	...	...	...	...	...	...	...	...	...	...	0723t	...
641	Idoméni ....▦ a.	...	...	...	...	...	...	...	...	...	...	...	...	...	...	...	...	...	...	...	...	0828t	...
641	Idoméni ....d.	...	...	...	...	...	...	...	...	...	...	...	...	...	...	...	...	...	...	...	...	0900t	...
717	Thessaloníki 1400.....§ a.	...	...	...	...	...	...	...	...	...	...	...	...	...	...	...	...	...	...	...	...	1005t	...

km		2	2	2	2	**790** 2	2	2✗	2	2	2	**490** B	2	2	2	2	2	2✗	2	2x	2	2	**334** H⊗	2
	Thessaloníki 1400.....§ d.	...	...	...	...	...	...	...	...	...	...	...	...	...	...	...	...	...	...	...	...	...	1830t	...
	Idoméni ....a.	...	...	...	...	...	...	...	...	...	...	...	...	...	...	...	...	...	...	...	...	...	1937t	...
	Idoméni ....▦ d.	...	...	...	...	...	...	...	...	...	...	...	...	...	...	...	...	...	...	...	...	...	2011t	...
	Gevgelija ....▦ a.	...	...	...	...	...	...	...	...	...	...	...	...	...	...	...	...	...	...	...	...	...	1916t	...
	Gevgelija ....d.	...	...	...	...	...	...	0443	...	...	...	...	...	...	...	...	...	...	...	...	1655	...	1948	...
	Veles 1385 ....d.	...	...	...	0503	...	0610	0635	...	...	...	...	1148	...	1423	...	...	...	...	...	1840	...	2113	...
	Skopje 1375/85 ....a.	...	...	...	0558	...	0705	0733	...	...	...	...	1239	...	1520	...	...	...	...	1931	...	...	2154	...
	Skopje ....d.	...	...	...	0630	...	...	...	...	...	...	...	...	...	...	...	1634	...	1900	...	...	...	2219	...
	Tabanovci ....▦ a.	...	...	...	0724	...	...	...	...	...	...	...	...	...	...	...	1729	...	1955	...	...	...	2329	...
	Preševo ....▦ d.	...	...	0250x	...	...	...	...	0815x	...	...	...	...	...	...	...	...	2005	...	...	...	...	0016	...
	Leskovac.....................d.	...	...	0520	...	...	...	...	1048	...	1250	...	...	...	1715	...	...	2233	...	...	...	...	0235	...
0	Sofia ....§ d.	...	...		...	...	...	...	...	...	...	0940	...	...		...	...		...	...	...	...		...
42	Dragoman ....▦ § d.	...	...		...	...	...	...	...	...	...	1027	...	...		...	...		...	...	...	...		...
63	Dimitrovgrad ....▦ d.	...	...		...	...	...	...	...	...	...	1100	...	...		...	...		...	...	...	...		...
161	Niš 1373 ....a.	...	...	0623	...	...	...	2	...	1152	...	1400	1338	2	1819	...	...	2339	...	...	...	...	0319	...
	Niš ....d.	...	0310	...	0632	...	0730	1105	...	...	...	1408	...	1545	1924	...	...	...	...	...	...	...	0329	...
	Stalać 1372 ....d.	...	0450	0657	0745	...	0901	1239	...	...	...	1517	...	1727	2059	...	...	...	...	...	...	...	0438	...
	Paraćin ....d.	...	0513	0726	0805	...	0924	1301	...	...	1444	1537	...	1749	2121	...	...	...	...	...	...	...	0458	...
	Jagodina ....d.	...	0528	0741	0821	...	0939	1323	...	...	1459	1709	...	1812	2147	...	...	...	...	...	...	...	0514	...
	Lapovo 1375 ....d.	0346	0606	...	0845	...	1016	1351	...	...	1532	1613	...	1850	2214	...	...	...	...	...	...	...	0545	...
	Beograd 1375 ....a.	0613	0838	...	1118	...	1242	...	...	...	1752	1814	...	2126	...	...	...	...	...	...	...	...	0746	...

B – BALKAN – 🛏 Beograd - Sofia and v.v.
H – HELLAS – 🛏 2 cl. and 🛏 Beograd - Skopje - Thessaloníki and v.v.
– By 🚌.
x – Service temporarily suspended.

⊗ – Service suspended owing to engineering work (expected to resume late-May).
§ – East European time.

MŽ 2nd class only | **BRANCH LINES in FYRO Macedonia** | **1385**

SKOPJE - KOČANI and BITOLA and v.v. :

km		R §					
0	Skopje 1380 .....d.	0135	0642	1430	1640	1710	2010
49	Veles 1380 ....d.	0217	0748	1524	1734	1752	2113
★	Kočani ....a.			1926			
134	Prilep ....d.	0355	0934	1710	...	1921	2310
178	Bitola ....a.	0430	1016	1752	...	1956	2352

	R §			R §		
Bitola ....d.	0310	0520	...	1250	1830	2100
Prilep ....d.	0350	0556	...	1334	1928	2136
Kočani ....d.			0500	...		
Veles 1380 ....d.	0540	0726	0657	1522	2117	2307
Skopje 1380 ..a.	0635	0807	0750	1614	2205	2348

SKOPJE - KIČEVO and v.v. :

km						
0	Skopje....d.	...	1650	...	Kičevo ... d.	...	0533	...
86	Tetovo ..d.	...	1753	...	Tetovo ... d.	...	0633	...
163	Kičevo ..a.	...	1854	...	Skopje ... a.	...	0735	...

§ – Also conveys 🛏.
⊗ – Service reported as temporarily suspended.
★ – Veles - Kočani : 110 km.

ALBANIA
SEE MAP PAGE 501

Operator: Hekurudha Shqiptarë (HSH).
Services: Trains convey one class of accommodation only. Tickets are not sold in advance, only for the next available departure.
Timings: Timings have been compiled from the latest information received, but readers should be aware that timetable amendments usually come into effect at short notice, and are advised to check information locally before travelling.
Security: Most visits to Albania are reported to be trouble free, but travellers are advised to avoid the north-east of the country.

HSH One class only | **ALBANIAN RAILWAYS** | **1390**

All services currently suspended
Kashar - central Tiranë and v.v. is operated by 🚌 (approximately 7.5 km)

km	km				km	km		
	0	Shkodër ....d.				Vlorë.................d.		
	82	Vorë...................d.				Fier....................d.		
	98	Tiranë ..... 🚌 d.	ALL			Lushnjë..............d.	ALL	
0	—	Kashar ..... 🚌 d.				Librazhd.......d.		
9		Vorë...................a.	SERVICES			Elbasan.........d.	SERVICES	
31		Durrës ....a.				Rrogozhinë.......d.		
—	0	Durrës...............d.	SUSPENDED			Durrës.............a.	SUSPENDED	
0	36	Rrogozhinë.........d.				Durrës.............d.		
	77	Elbasan..............a.				Vorë.................d.		
	98	Librazhd ....a.				Kashar ..... 🚌 a.		
17		Lushnjë...............a.				Tiranë ..... 🚌 a.		
49		Fier ....a.				Vorë.................a.		
83		Vlorë ....a.				Shkodër ....a.		

GREECE

SEE MAP PAGE 501

Operator: TRAINOSE S.A., ΤΡΑΙΝΟΣΕ Α.Ε.: www.trainose.gr.

Services: All trains convey first and second class seating except where shown otherwise in footnotes or by '2' in the train column, or where the footnote shows sleeping and/or couchett cars only. Descriptions of sleeping (🛏) and couchette (🛏) cars appear on page 8. Services that convey catering may vary from day to day.

Timings: Timings have been compiled from the latest information received. Readers should be aware that timetable amendments may come into effect at short notice, and are advised t check information locally before travelling.

Tickets: Reservation of seats is possible (and recommended) on most express trains. IC trains carry a supplement which varies depending upon distance travelled. Break of journey i only permitted when tickets are so endorsed before travel with the station quoted.

1400 — ATHÍNA - LÁRISA - THESSALONÍKI

km			590		IC50		884		2590	IC52		3520		IC56		IC58		IC60		1510		600
		2	2	2	✗✓	2	☕	2	2	✗✓	2	⑤⑦	2	✗✓	2	☕✓	2	✗✓	2		2
0	Athína Lárisa **1420**......d.	...	...	...	0718	...	0827	...	...	1018	...	1118	1418	...	...	1616	...	1818	...	1917	...	2355
7	SKA (Acharnon) **1420/40**..d.	...	...	...	0728	...	0836	...	...	1028	...	1127	1427	...	...	1625	...	1827	...	1926	...	
61	Inói **1420**.......d.	...	...	...	0808	...	0916	...	...	1108	...	1206	1508	...	...	1706	...	1908	...	2005	...	0047
89	Thíva...........d.	...	...	...	0824	...	0931	...	...	1124	...	1222	1524	...	...	1721	...	1924	...	2021	...	0105
129	Levadiá...........d.	...	...	...	0843	...	0953	...	...	1143	...	1247	1543	...	...	1741	...	1943	...	2046	...	0128
154	Tithoréa...........d.	...	...	...		...	1006	...	...		...	1308		...	...		...	1955	...	2107	...	0142
169	Amfíklia...........d.	...	...	...		...	1019	...	...		...	1320		...	...	1804	...	2006	...	2119	...	
210	Lianokládi...........d.	0515	0645	...	0815	0941	1015	1102	1115	...	1241	1315	1402	1515	1641	1650	1810	1839	1958	2041	2110	2202	2215	0230
	Lamia ....d.	0525	0655	...	0825		1024		1125	...		1325		1525		1659	1820		2007		2119	...	2225	
	Stilida ....d.	0548	0718	...	0848				1148	...		1348		1548			1843					...	2248	
291	Paleofársalos **1408**...........d.	...	0917	...	1100		1222		1232	1400	...			1805	...	...	1958	...	2200	...	...	...	0353
	Kalambáka **1408**...........a.	...	0819p	...			1318				...				...	...		...		...	...	...	
333	**Lárisa 1425** ▲ d.	...	0941	...	1120		1252		1252	1420	...			1824	...	...	2017	...	2219	...	...	...	0418
417	Katerini ....▲ d.	...	1031	...	1157		1338		1457		...			1902	...	...	2055	...	2257	...	...	...	0507
465	Plati **1410** ....▲ d.	...	1057	...	1218		1402		1518		...			1923	...	...	2117	...	2318	...	...	...	0534
502	**Thessaloniki 1410** ....▲ a.	...	1124	...	1241		1428		1541		...			1946	...	...	2139	...	2341	...	...	...	0601

km			1511		IC51		IC53		IC55			3521		IC59		591		885		IC61		601
		2	2	2	☕✓	2	✗✓	2	✗✓	2	2	⑤⑦	2	✗✓	2	☕	2	✗✓	2	2
	Thessaloníki 1410 ▲ d.	...	...	...	0513	...	0704	...	1004	...	...	...	1504	1617	...	...	...	1804	...	...	2300
	Plati **1410** ....▲ d.	...	...	...	0536	...	0728	...	1028	...	...	...	1528	1645	...	...	...	1828	...	...	2328
	Katerini ....▲ d.	...	...	...	0556	...	0749	...	1049	...	...	...	1549	1712	...	...	...	1849	...	...	2355
	Lárisa 1425 ....▲ d.	...	...	...	0633	...	0826	...	1126	...	...	...	1626	1801	...	...	...	1926	...	...	0043
	Kalambáka **1408** ....d.	...	...	...		...		...		...	...	...		1925p	...	1722	...	...	...	...	
	Paleofársalos **1408** ....d.	...	...	...	0652	...	0845	...	1145	...	...	...	1645	1824	...	1830	...	1945	...	...	0107
0	Stilida ....d.	0607	...	0723		0857		1157		1357	1557	...			1857				...	...	2254	
17	Lamia ....d.	0630	...	0746		0922	1045	1220		1420	1620	...	1741		1920		2021	...	...	2145	2317	
23	Lianokládi ....d.	0639	0649	0755	0810	0929	1006	1054	1229	1306	1429	...	1629	1642	1750	1803	...	1929	1945	2030	2105	2154	2326	0231
	Amfíklia ....d.	...	0729	...	0844							...		1722	1840		...	2025					
	Tithoréa ....d.	...	0740	...	0854		1050		1350			...		1733	1850		...	2036				0317
	Levadiá ....d.	...	0800	...	0904		1101		1401			...		1753	1901		...	2048		2201		0331
	Thíva ....d.	...	0825	...	0921		1121		1421			...		1818	1921		...	2110		2221		0354
	Inói **1420** ....d.	...	0841	...	0936		1137		1437			...		1837	1937		...	2125		2236		0411
	SKA (Acharnon) **1420/40**..d.	...	0919	...	1015		1216		1516			...		1912	2016		...	2204		2315		
	Athína Lárisa **1420**...........a.	...	0928	...	1023		1224		1524			...		1922	2024		...	2212		2324		0501

▲ – Local service Thessaloníki - Litóhoro - Lárisa and v.v. :

Thessaloníki ....d.	0537	0640	0800	...	1258	1425	1714	1837	2147	Lárisa...........d.	0600	0723	0830	1043	...	1450	1645	1900	2109
Plati...........d.	0604	0707	0827	...	1325	1452	1741	1904	2214	Litóhoro...........⚠ d.	0637	0800	0907	1120	...	1527	1722	1937	2146
Katerini...........d.	0628	0731	0851	...	1349	1516	1805	1928	2238	Katerini...........d.	0646	0809	0916	1129	...	1536	1731	1946	2155
Litóhoro...........⚠ d.	0638	0741	0901	...	1359	1526	1815	1938	2248	Plati...........d.	0711	0834	0941	1154	...	1601	1756	2011	2220
Lárisa...........a.	0712	0815	0935	...	1433	1600	1849	2012	2322	Thessaloniki...........a.	0736	0859	1006	1214	...	1626	1821	2036	2245

FOR NOTES SEE TABLE 1405

1405 — THESSALONÍKI - ALEXANDRÚPOLI - DÍKEA

OSE, BDZh

There are currently no cross-border services from/to Turkey

km		1682	600	1684	IC 90				IC 91	1683	601	1685
		2		2	✓				✓	2		2
0	Thessaloníki...........d.	...	0655	...	1601	...	Díkea...........d.	0411	1208	...	1905
42	Kilkis...........d.	...	0735	...	1637	...	Néa Orestiáda...........d.	0442	1239	...	1936
97	Rodópoli...........d.	...	...	...	...	...	*Istanbul Sirkeci* **1550**...........d.			...	
130	Strimón...........d.	...	...	...	...	...	Píthio...........d.	0455	1257	...	1954
162	Sérres...........d.	...	0930	...	1806	...	**Alexandrúpoli**...........d.	0619	1426	...	2124
232	Dráma...........d.	...	1021	...	1853	...	Komotiní...........d.	0751	...	1519	...
327	Xánthi...........d.	...	1222	...	2054	...	Xánthi...........d.	0821	...	1618	...
374	Komotiní...........d.	...	1255	...	2124	...	Dráma...........d.	1020	...	1652	...
443	**Alexandrúpoli**...........a.	...	1354	...	2220	...	Sérres...........d.	1108	...	1854	...
443	**Alexandrúpoli**...........d.	0745	...	1441	2252	...	Strimón...........d.		...	1944	...
556	Píthio...........d.	0915	...	1611	0018	...	Rodópoli...........d.		...		...
*	*istanbul Sirkeci* **1550**...........d.		...			...	Kilkis...........d.	1237	...	2145	...
574	Néa Orestiáda...........d.	0933	...	1629	0031	...	**Thessaloníki**...........a.	1312	...	2222	...
611	Díkea...........a.	1004	...	1700	0101	...					

p – Via Paleofársalos.

✗ – ® with supplement payable. *Icity* train.
⚠ – Station for Mount Ólimbos.
* – Píthio - istanbul : 268 km.

1408 — LÁRISA - PALEOFÁRSALOS - KALAMBÁKA

km		880	882	884	886	888			881	883	885	887	889
		♦		☕	♦					♦	☕		♦
	Thessaloníki **1400**...........d.	...	...	...	...	1617	...	Kalambáka **1400**...........☐ d.	0542	0819	1732	1930	2148
	Athína **1400**...........d.	...	...	...	0827	...	...	Tríkala...........d.	0558	0835	1742	1946	2204
	Lárisa **1400**...........d.	0411	...	...	1801	...	Karditsa...........d.	0617	0854	1809	2005	2222
0	Paleofársalos **1400**...........d.	0438	0658	1222	1831	2029	...	Paleofársalos **1400**...........d.	0636	0913	1828	2024	2242
31	Karditsa...........d.	0458	0718	1242	1851	2049	...	**Lárisa 1400**...........a.	...	0940	...	...	2310
60	Tríkala...........d.	0517	0737	1303	1910	2108	...	Athína **1400**...........a.	...	...	2212	...	
82	**Kalambáka 1400**...........☐ a.	0532	0752	1318	1925	2123	...	Thessaloníki **1400**...........a.	...	1124	...	...	

♦ – **NOTES (LISTED BY TRAIN NUMBER)**

880 – 🛏 Lárisa (561) - Paleofársalos - Kalambáka.
883 – 🛏 Kalambáka - Paleofársalos (590) - Thessaloníki.
886 – 🛏 Thessaloníki (591) - Paleofársalos - Kalambáka.
889 – 🛏 Kalambáka - Paleofársalos (562) - Lárisa.

✗ – ® with supplement payable. *Icity* train.

☐ – An infrequent bus service operates Kalambáka - Igumenitsa and v.v. (approximately 250 km).

THESSALONÍKI - ÉDESSA - FLÓRINA — 1410

km		IC81	IC83		IC85					IC82	IC84	IC86	
0	Thessaloníki 1400/05......d.	0714	1223	1547	1930	2132	...	Flórina ....d.	...	0615	0959	1612	...
38	Platí 1400.........................d.	0741	1250	1616	1957	2203	...	Amíndeo ....d.	...	0644	1027	1639	...
69	Véria ....d.	0803	1311	1645	2018	2232	...	Édessa ....d.	0450	0727	1111	1723	2056
97	Skidra ....d.	0822	1330	1708	2037	2255	...	Skidra ....d.	0504	0742	1126	1738	2110
112	Édessa ....a.	0837	1345	1722	2052	2309	...	Véria ....d.	0528	0802	1145	1757	2133
162	Amíndeo ....d.	0921	1429	...	2136	...	...	Platí 1400 ....d.	0556	0822	1205	1818	2202
196	Flórina ....a.	0947	1455	...	2202	...	...	Thessaloníki 1400/05..a.	0624	0848	1231	1845	2230

PIREÁS - ATHÍNA - HALKÍDA — 1420

km			Ⓐ						Ⓐ					
0	Pireás...............................d.	...	0525	0625	0825	1025	1225	1425	1525	1625	1825	2025	2225	...
10	Athína Lárisa 1400.........d.	0427	0544	0644	0844	1044	1244	1444	1544	1644	1844	2044	2244	...
17	SKA (Acharnon) 1400/40..d.	0439	0556	0656	0856	1056	1256	1456	1556	1656	1856	2056	2256	...
	Afidnai.............................d.	0458	0621	0721	0921	1121	1321	1521	1621	1721	1921	2121	2321	...
71	Inói 1400 ....d.	0500	0525	0650	0750	0950	1150	1350	1550	1650	1750	1950	2150	2350
94	Halkída ....a.	0520	...	0712	0812	1012	1212	1412	1612	1712	1812	2012	2212	0012

			Ⓐ						Ⓐ					
Halkída...............................d.	...	0627	0727	0827	1027	1227	1427	1627	1727	1827	2027	2227	0020
Inói 1400 ....d.	0529	0651	0751	0851	1051	1251	1451	1651	1751	1851	2051	2251	0040
Afidnai...............................d.	0557	0722	0822	0922	1122	1322	1522	1722	1822	1922	2122	2322	...
SKA (Acharnon) 1400/40..d.	0617	0742	0842	0942	1142	1342	1542	1742	1842	1942	2142	2342	...
Athína Lárisa 1400.........a.	0628	0753	0853	0953	1153	1353	1553	1753	1853	1953	2153	2353	...
Pireás...............................a.	0651	0814	...	0914	1014	1214	1414	1614	1814	...	1914	2014	2214	0014

- change of train is necessary at Afidnai.

LÁRISA - VÓLOS — 1425

km			🚌		🚌								
0	Lárisa 1425.......d.	0437	0637	0837	0950	1130	1230	1430	1510	1630	1830	2018	2230
61	Vólos................a.	0525	0725	0925	1035	1218	1330	1518	1610	1718	1918	2106	2318

			🚌										
Vólos ....d.	0530	0730	0830	1025	1120	1225	1340	1525	1725	1925	2125	2335
Lárisa 1425. a.	0618	0818	0930	1113	1220	1313	1440	1613	1813	2013	2213	0023

ATHÍNA AIRPORT ✈ and ATHÍNA - KÓRINTHOS - KIÁTO — 1440

2nd class. *Subject to confirmation*

km	km															
0		Athína Airport ✈ ....▲ d.	0526	...	0544	0611	and	2111	2126	...	2144	Kiáto 1450.................d.	...	0525	and	...	2125	...
25		Neratziótissa.................▲ d.	0549	...	0607	0634	at the	2134	2149	...	2207	Kórinthos....................d.	...	0539	at the	...	2139	...
	0	Athína Lárisa ....d.	...	0550		same	...	...	2150	...	Ano Liosia ....d.	0602	0628	0647	same	2147	2202	2228	...
31	7	SKA (Acharnon) 1400/20.d.	0555	0600	0613	0640	minutes	2140	2155	2200	2213	SKA (Acharnon) 1400/20..d.	0605	0632	0641	0650	minutes	2150	2205	2232	2241
34		Ano Liosia ....d.	0558	...	0617	0643	past each	2143	2158	...	2217	Athína Lárisa ....a.	...	...	0650	past each	...	...	...	2250
W04		Kórinthos.......................d.	...	...	0706	hour	...	...	2306	...	Neratziótissa ....▲ a.	0612	0638	...	0657	hour	2157	2212	2238	...
W25		Kiáto 1450 ....a.	...	...	0719	until	...	...	2319	...	Athína Airport ✈..........▲ a.	0635	0701	...	0720	until	2220	2235	2301	...

▲ – Frequent Metro services operate as follows:
  Line 1 (green): Pireás - Monastiraki - Omónia - Attiki - Neratziótissa - Kifissia.
  Line 2 (red): Aghios Dimitrios - Syntagma - Omónia - Athína Lárisa (for Athína mainline station) -
  Attiki - Aghios Antonios.
  Line 3 (blue): Egaleo - Monastiraki - Syntagma - Athína Airport ✈.
  Operators: ISAP Line 1; Attiko Metro Lines 2 and 3.

Additional trains operate on Ⓐ Athína Airport - Neratziótissa and v.v.

KIÁTO - PÁTRA 🚌 services (including Pireás, Athína and Athína Airport connections) — 1450

Subject to confirmation

Pireás............................d.	0530	...	0730	...	1030	...	1330	...	1530	...	1730	...
Athína Lárisa ....d.	0550	...	0750	...	1150	...	1350	...	1550	...	1750	...
Athína Airport ✈....d.		0544		0744		1144		1344		1544		1744
Neratziótissa................d.		0607		0807		1207		1407		1607		1807
SKA (Acharnon)..........d.	0600	0613	0800	0813	1200	1213	1400	1413	1600	1613	1800	1813
Kórinthos......................d.	0706		0906		1306		1506		1706		1906	
Kiáto.............................a.	0719		0919		1319		1519		1719		1919	

change to bus

		🚌		🚌				🚌	🚌	🚌	
Kiáto 1440 ....d.		0730		0930		1330		1530		1730	1830	1930
Xilókastro.....................d.										1850		
Diakoftó 1455 ....d.					1415				1930		
Pátra.............................a.	...	0900	...	1100	...	1510	...	1700	...	1900	2030	2100

		🚌			🚌			🚌		🚌	
Pátra ....d.	0730		0830	0945	1130	...	1415		1630	...	1830	...
Diakoftó 1455 ....d.				1045			1500				
Xilókastro.....................d.				1135							
Kiáto 1440 ....a.	0915		1015	1210	1315	...	1615		1815	...	2015	...

change to train

Kiáto ....d.	0925		1025		1325	...	1625		1825		2025	
Kórinthos......................d.	0939		1039		1339	...	1639		1839		2039	
SKA (Acharnon)...........d.	1032	1041	1132	1141	1432	1541	1732	1741	1932	1941	2132	2141
Neratziótissa................d.	1038		1138		1438		1738		1938		2138	
Athína Airport ✈....a.	1101		1201		1501		1801		2001		2201	
Athína Lárisa ....a.		1050		1150		1550		1750		1950		2150
Pireás...........................a.		1108		1208		1608		1808		2008		2208

PELOPÓNNISOS narrow-gauge branches — 1455

Diakoftó – Kalávrita
2nd class only, rack railway

km				Ⓒ		Ⓒ	
0	Diakoftó 1450 ....d.		0845	1115	1233	1432	1550
23	Kalávrita ....a.		0952	1222	1343	1542	1700

			Ⓒ		Ⓒ	
Kalávrita ....d.		0957	1227	1430	1550	1650
Diakoftó 1450. a.		1104	1337	1540	1700	1757

Ⓒ – Service currently suspended.

Katákolo – Pírgos – Olimbía
2nd class only

km					⊗	⊗		⊗	⊗	⊗
0	Katákolo......d.	...	0840	...	1030	1211	...	1405	1550	1730
12	Pírgos..........a.	0700	0904	...	1050	1233	1235	...	1425	1610	1752
33	Olimbía ....a.	0728	0932	...	1112	...	1303	...	1447	1632	...

			⊗			⊗	⊗		⊗	⊗	⊗
Olimbía..............d.	0733	...	0937	1120	...	1308	...	1500	1637	...
Pírgos................d.	0804	1000	1005	1144	...	1336	1338	1524	1701	...
Katákolo ....a.	0826	1018	...	1202	...	1400	1542	1719	...

INTERNATIONAL BUS SERVICES — 1460

A number of operators run long-distance 🚌 services to and from Greece, and selected services are listed below. Details should be checked with the relevant operator before travel. Rail tickets and passes are not valid. Further details about travelling to Greece by bus can be found on www.europebyrail.eu

ATHÍNA - ISTANBUL: Depart Athina 1700. Depart Istanbul 1800. Journey 16 hours. Operator: Metro www.metroturizm.com.tr

THESSALONIKI - ISTANBUL: Depart Thessaloniki 2100. Depart Istanbul 2100. Journey 10 hours. Operator: Simeonidis Tours www.simeonidistours.gr
Depart Thessaloniki 1000, 2200, 2330. Depart Istanbul 1000, 1800, 2200. Journey 10 - 11 hours. Operator: Metro www.metroturizm.com.tr

THESSALONIKI - SKOPJE: Depart Thessaloniki 0830, 1730. Depart Skopje 0600, 1700. Journey 3½ - 4 hours. Operator: Simeonidis Tours www.simeonidistours.gr

THESSALONIKI - SOFIA: Coach services are operated by Union Ivkoni (www.union-ivkoni.com) as follows :
Pireás (0730) → Athína (0830) → Thessaloniki (1530) → Sofia (2030) → Varna (0500).
Varna (2345) → Sofia (0800) → Thessaloniki (1300) → Athína (2000) → Pireás (2100).
Kórinthos → Pireás → Athína (1900) → Thessaloniki (0130) → Sofia (0645) → Plovdiv → Burgas.
Burgas → Plovdiv → Sofia (2000) → Thessaloniki (0100) → Athína (0800) → Pireás → Kórinthos.

BULGARIA and TURKEY IN EUROPE

SEE MAP PAGE 501

Operators: Bâlgarski Dârzhavni Zheleznitsi (BDZh) www.bdz.bg
Türkiye Cumhuryeti Devlet Demiryolları (TCDD) www.tcdd.gov.tr

Services: Trains convey first- and second-class seating, except where shown otherwise in footnotes or by '2' in the train column, or where the footnote shows sleeping and/or couchette cars only. Descriptions of sleeping (🛏) and couchette (▬) cars appear on page 8. Seat reservation is possible on most long-distance trains (compulsory on express trains).

Timings: BDŽ schedules valid **from December 11**, 2017. **Timetable amendments are possible at short notice so it is advisable to confirm timings locally before travelling.** Please refer to Tables **61**, **98** and **99** for international through cars to/from Burgas and Varna (summer only). TCDD schedules are the latest available.
For services in Asian Turkey see pages 514–516.

1500 SOFIA - RUSE, BURGAS and VARNA

km	km						8631	8611	3621	2601	460/2	2611			8601	2613	8613	3623	4612	3601	8641	2641	9647	8637	3637	8627	2627
										⚡[R]	[R]								⚡[R]	⚡[R]		⚡[R]					
			2	2	2	2					A		2	2						⑤⊠			L	Z	ZD	Z	Z
0	0	**Sofia** .... **1520** d.	...	...	...	...	...	0635	0640	0700	0900	1000	...	...	1050	1300	1315	1315	1600	1640	1715	1800	2120	...	2230	2240	2250
	103	Septemvri .... d.	...	...	...	...	...	0820	|	|	|	|	...	...	1246	|	1510	|	|	|	1910	|	|	...	|	0038	|
	119	Pazardzhik .... d.	...	...	...	...	...	0832	|	|	|	|	...	...	1258	|	1521	|	|	|	1921	|	|	...	|	0052	|
	156	**Plovdiv** .... a.	...	...	...	...	...	0858	|	|	|	|	...	...	1325	|	1546	|	|	|	1947	|	|	...	|	0120	|
	156	**Plovdiv** .... d.	...	...	...	...	0705	0903	|	|	|	|	...	...	1330	|	1550	|	|	|	1950	|	|	2330	|	0128	|
	262	Stara Zagora .... d.	...	...	...	...	0914	1053	|	|	|	|	...	...	1521	|	1742	|	|	|	2145	|	|	0125	|	0326	|
	340	Yambol .... d.	...	0605	...	...	1002	1141	|	|	|	|	...	...	1610	|	1834	|	|	|	...	|	|	0216	|	0419	|
		Karlovo .... **1525** d.	...	|	0540	...	|	|	0927	|	|	|	...	*1120*	|	|	|	1600	|	1856	...	|	|	|	0108	|	|
		Kazanlak ..... **1525** d.	...	|	0715j	...	|	|	1028	|	|	|	...	1335	|	|	|	1701	|	1955	...	|	|	|	0207	|	|
		Tulovo .... **1525** d.	...	|	0732	...	|	|	1043	|	|	|	...	1352	|	|	|	1717	|	2010	...	|	|	|	0222	|	|
		Sliven .... d.	0450	|	0917	0932	|	|	1159	|	|	|	1420	1533	|	|	|	1836	|	2116	...	|	|	|	0335	|	|
		Zimnitsa .... d.	0514	0620	▬	0956	1014	|	1216	|	|	|	1444	1555	1622	|	1847	1857	|	2133	...	|	|	|	|	|	|
	389	Karnobat ..... **1535** d.	0543	0650	...	1054t	1039	1213	1241	|	|	|	1513	...	1647	|	1912	1923	|	2155	...	|	|	0252	0423	0457	|
	450	**Burgas** .... **1535** a.	0700	0810	**2655**	1210	|	1300	1328	|	|	|	1632	...	|	|	2000	2010	|	2242	...	|	|	|	|	0547	|
88		Mezdra .... **1520** d.	▬	▬		...	|	...	...	0827	1029	1135	▬	...	|	1429	...	...	1725	▬	...	1934	2308	|	|	...	002
194		Pleven .... d.	...	...	0705	...	|	...	...	0942	1148	1259	...	...	|	1548	...	...	1843	...	...	2052	0028	|	|	...	0139
239		Levski .... d.	...	...	0737	...	|	...	...	1014	1217	1331	...	...	|	1620	...	...	1915	**4640**	...	2124	0057	|	|	...	0212
294		Gorna Oryakhovitsa . a.	...	...	0821	...	|	...	...	1055	1255	1415	...	...	|	1701	...	...	1956	**p**	...	2205	0138	|	|	...	0255
294		Gorna Oryakhovitsa . d.	...	...	0825	...	|	...	...	1105	1310	1425	...	...	|	1711	...	...	2000	2006	...	...	0143	|	|	...	0305
405		**Ruse** 🏛 .... a.	2	2	|	...	|	...	...	|	1505	|	2	...	|	|	...	...	2155	|	...	...	0338	|	|	...	|
435		Shumen .... **1530/5** d.	0520	0717	1017	...	|	...	...	1253	...	1620	1700	...	|	1901	...	...	...	2204	...	...	...	|	|	...	0503
459		Kaspichan .... **1530/5** d.	0548	0745	1036	...	|	...	...	|	...	1639	1728	...	|	1920	...	...	...	2223	...	...	...	|	|	...	0524
518		Povelyanovo **1530/5** d.	0658	0854	1131	...	1250	...		1402	...	1731	1836	...	1853	2011	...	...	...	|	...	...	...	0501	0647	...	0622
543	546	**Varna** .... **1530/5** a.	0729	0925	1156	...	1314	...		1425	...	1755	1907	...	1917	2035	...	...	...	2340	...	...	...	0526	0711	...	0650

km		2640	8640	3602	4641	4611		2602	3622	8602		2612	4613	2614		3624	8612	461/3	8632	2654			8626	2626	9646	3636	863
		⚡[R]		⚡[R]		⚡[R]		⚡[R]										[R]									
				⑥⊠	p		2				2				2⊠			A			2	2	Z	Z	N	ZD	Z
	Varna .... **1530/5** d.	...	...	...	0432	...	0600	0730	...	0850	...	1035	...	1325	1415	...	...	...	1530	1645	1700	1935	...	2210	...	2220	231
	Povelyanovo. **1530/5** d.	...	...	...	0457	...	0632	0752	...	0916	...	1100	...	1350	1447	...	...	...	1555	|	1732	2009	...	2243	...	2304f	234
	Kaspichan ..... **1530/5** d.	...	...	...	0553	...	0743	0846	...	|	...	1158	...	1446	1558	...	...	...	|	1805	1842	2120	...	2339	...	|	|
	Shumen .... **1530/5** d.	...	...	...	0612	...	0810	0906	...	|	...	1218	...	1506	1624	...	...	...	|	1824	1907	2147	...	2359	...	|	|
	Ruse 🏛 .... d.	...	...	...	|	0623	▬	|	...	|	...	|	1315	|	▬	...	...	1630	|	|	▬	▬	...	|	2343	|	|
	Gorna Oryakhovitsa .. a.	...	...	...	0813	0819	...	1056	...	|	...	1414	1523	1658	...	...	...	1828	|	2019	...	...	...	0155	0138	|	|
	Gorna Oryakhovitsa .. d.	0500	...	...	▬	0831	...	1105	...	|	...	1425	1535	1708	...	...	...	1833	|	2027	...	...	...	0215	0215	|	|
	Levski .... d.	0542	...	...	...	0915	...	1147	...	|	...	1508	1620	1750	...	...	...	1911	|	2111	...	...	...	0300	0300	|	|
	Pleven .... d.	0613	...	...	...	0948	**8610**	1218	...	|	...	1540	1652	1821	...	...	...	1939	|	2143	...	...	...	0333	0333	|	|
	Mezdra .... **1520** d.	0730	...	...	2⊠	1104		1332	...	|	...	1659	1821	1942	2	...	...	2055	|	...	2	2	...	0458	0458	|	|
0	**Burgas** .... **1535** d.	|	...	0540	0530	|	0705	|	0910	|	1150	|	|	|	1410	1455	1525	|	|	...	1710	1955	2220	|	|	|	|
61	Karnobat ...... **1535** d.	|	...	0627	0645	|	0756	|	0959	1125	1310	|	|	|	1526	1544	1614	|	1757	...	1825	2112	2312	|	|	0124	015
95	Zimnitsa .... d.	|	...	0648	0714	|	0820	|	1023	|	1341	|	|	|	1603	1608	|	|	1821	...	1856	2143	|	|	|	|	021
119	Sliven .... d.	|	...	0704	0738	|	|	|	1040	|	1401	|	|	|	|	1625	|	|	|	...	1916	|	|	|	|	0207	|
195	Tulovo .... **1525** d.	|	...	0809	0904	|	|	|	1150	|	...	|	|	|	|	1734	|	|	|	...	...	|	|	|	|	0323	|
210	Kazanlak ...... **1525** d.	|	...	0824	0921	|	|	|	1206	|	...	|	|	|	|	1749	|	|	|	...	...	|	|	|	|	0338	|
269	Karlovo .... **1525** d.	|	...	0925	1040	|	|	|	1305	|	...	|	|	|	|	1857	|	|	|	...	...	|	|	|	|	0436	|
	Yambol .... d.	|	...	|	...	|	0833	|	|	1205	...	|	|	|	1624	|	1645	|	1833	...	...	2157	2349	|	|	|	023
	Stara Zagora .... d.	|	0610	|	...	|	0925	|	|	1255	...	|	|	|	...	|	1736	|	1934	...	...	...	0046	|	|	|	033
	Plovdiv .... a.	|	0756	|	...	|	1108	|	|	1435	...	|	|	|	...	|	1912	|	2117	...	...	...	0235	|	|	|	052
	Plovdiv .... d.	|	0800	|	...	|	1113	|	|	1440	...	|	|	|	...	|	1917	|	...	...	...	...	0245	|	|	|	*060*
	Pazardzhik .... d.	|	0828	|	...	|	1141	|	|	1508	...	|	|	|	...	|	1940	|	...	...	...	...	0312	|	|	|	*062*
	Septemvri .... d.	|	0839	|	...	|	1152	|	|	1520	...	|	|	|	...	|	1951	|	...	...	...	...	0323	|	|	|	*063*
418	**Sofia** .... **1520** a.	0855	1045	1145	...	1230	1357	1455	1540	1727	...	1828	2000	2110	...	2124	2143	2225	...	...	...	...	0530	0630	0630	0723	*084*

Other trains **SOFIA - PLOVDIV**

	⊠	1621		1625		1627	493
	Ⓐ2	s	2	s	2		T
Sofia .... d.	0535	0830	1430	1510	1815	1915	2040
Septemvri .... d.	0745	1027	1636	1706	2032	2110	2226
Pazardzhik .... d.	0800	1039	1652	1718	2051	2121	2236
Plovdiv .... a.	0833	1105	1725	1745	2130	2146	2300

	1620	492		⊠	1624		1626
		V	2	Ⓐ2		2	s
Plovdiv .... d.	0600	0645	0715	1000	1310	1635	1805
Pazardzhik .. d.	0628	0709	0751	1035	1336	1716	1831
Septemvri .... d.	0639	0719	0806	1050	1347	1734	1842
Sofia .... a.	0845	0910	1023	1303	1548	1957	2040

Other local trains **GORNA ORYAKHOVITSA - RUSE**

	2	2	2	2	2
Gorna Oryakhovitsa .... d.	0425	0725	1115	1450	171
Ruse .... a.	0649	1000	1341	1720	193
	2	2	2		2
Ruse .... d.	0757	1126	1415	...	184
Gorna Oryakhovitsa .... a.	1018	1403	1652	...	211

A – To/from Bucureşti on dates in Table **61**.
D – Conveys 🛏 1, 2 cl. and (2) Sofia - Povelyanovo - Dobrich and v.v. See Table **1540**.
L – 🛏 1, 2 cl. and (2) Sofia - Ruse - Silistra (Table **1530**).
N – 🛏 1, 2 cl. and (2) Silistra - Ruse - Gorna (**2626**) - Sofia.
T – BALKAN EXPRESS – (2) Sofia - Svilengrad; ▬ 2 cl. Sofia - Çerkezköy (Table **1550**).
V – BALKAN EXPRESS – (2) Svilengrad - Sofia, ▬ 2 cl. Çerkezköy - Sofia (Table **1550**).
Z – Conveys 🛏 1, 2 cl. and (12).

f – Arrives 2246.
j – Arrives 0656.
p – From/to Plovdiv via Tulovo (Table **1525**).
s – To/from Svilengrad (Table **1550**).
t – Arrives 1024.
⊠ – Days of running are subject to confirmation.
⚡ – Express train. Higher fare payable.

1510 SEPTEMVRI - DOBRINISHTE

Narrow gauge; 2nd class only

km										
0	**Septemvri** .... d.	0205	...	0832	...	1310	...	1550	...	...
39	Velingrad .... d.	0352	...	1004	...	1450	...	1733	...	...
119	Bansko .... d.	0708	...	1308	...	1758	...	2036	...	...
125	**Dobrinishte** .... a.	0720	...	1320	...	1810	...	2048	...	...

Dobrinishte .... d.	...	...	0520	...	1010	...	1350	...	1845	...
Bansko .... d.	...	...	0535	...	1028	...	1407	...	1903	...
Velingrad .... d.	0450	...	0839	...	1329	...	1659	...	2214	...
Septemvri .... a.	0620	...	1013	...	1455	...	1824	...	2340	...

1520 SOFIA - VIDIN - CRAIOVA

km				⊠	7620		7622			7624		7630
		2	2	Ⓐ2		2		2	2		2	
0	**Sofia** ..... **1500** d.	...	...	...	0725	...	1200	...	...	1700	...	1900
88	Mezdra .. **1500** d.	0550	...	0654	|	...	1340	...	1605	1849	...	2058
106	Vratsa .... d.	0609	...	0714	0907	...	1356	...	1624	1907	...	2114
182	Brusartsi ..... ⊖ d.	0734	0740	0856	1021	1026	1515	1520	1750	2028	2038	2233
204	Lom .... ⊖ a.	|	0808	0924	|	1054	|	1547	|	|	2105	2300
269	**Vidin** ★ .... a.	0920	...	...	1153	...	1645	...	1942	2202	...	...

	2660	7631		7621	⊠				7623				762
			2		Ⓐ2	2	2	2		2	2	2	
Vidin ★ ...... d.	...	...	...	0555	...	...	1020	...	1225	...	1440	...	173
Lom ..... ⊖ d.	...	0545	0655	|	0825	1110	|	1315	|	1600	|	1838	|
Brusartsi .. ⊖ d.	...	0614	0722	0735	0858	1136	1209	1343	1356	1625	1630	1902	190
Vratsa .... d.	0525	0743	...	0853	1029	...	1347	...	1515	...	1755	...	202
Mezdra **1500** a.	0539	0758	...	|	1047	...	1405	...	|	...	1813	...	|
Sofia .. **1500** a.	0730	0947	...	1030	...	...	...	...	1655	...	...	...	220

km		①–⑥			
	Vidin 🏛 ...... d.	...	...	...	1235
0	**Calafat** .... d.	0335	0625	1252	|
107	**Craiova** .... a.	0630	0920	1557	1557

km					Ⓑ
0	**Craiova** .... d.	0810	0810	1700	1950
	Calafat .... a.	|	1135	2000	2250
119	**Vidin** 🏛 ..... a.	1125	...	...	...

⊖ – Other services Brusartsi - Lom and v.v.: **From Brusartsi** at 0613, 1213, 1400, 1640, 1800 and 1917. **From Lom** at 0940, 1440, 1720 and 1958.
⊠ – Days of running are subject to confirmation.

RUSE - STARA ZAGORA - DIMITROVGRAD - MOMCHILGRAD - PODKOVA 1525

km				4641					465	
		2	Ⓐ2	V	2C	2	2	2	ⓇB	2
0	**Ruse** 1500 d.	...	...	0623	...	0757	1126	...	1630	...
111	**Gorna Oryakhovitsa** 1500 d.	0515	...	0835	...	1120	1430	...	1925	2047
125	Veliko Târnovo d.	0533	...	0852	...	1141	1451	...	1948	2107
	Karlovo 1500 d.	|	0725	|	...	|	|	1802	|	...
	Kazanlak 1500 d.	|	0846	|	...	|	|	1927	|	...
226	Tulovo 1500 d.	0814t	0916f	1056	...	1405	1737r	2015r	|	...
253	Stara Zagora 1500 d.	0857	0956	1138	1355	1445	1817	2055	2220	...
	Plovdiv 1500 a.	...	...	1329	|	...	...	...	|	...
310	**Dimitrovgrad** a.	...	...	...	1519	...	...	...	2335	...

			464					4640	
	2	2	ⓇB	2	2	2	2	V	2
Dimitrovgrad d.	...	...	0730	...	1040	...	...	...	...
Plovdiv 1500 d.	...	...	|	...	|	...	...	1440	...
Stara Zagora 1500 d.	...	0705	0910t	0958	1202	1315	1505	1632	...
Tulovo 1500 d.	...	0745	0956	1053f	...	1404	1603f	1708	...
Kazanlak 1500 a.	...	|	|	|	...	|	1619	|	...
Karlovo 1500 a.	...	|	|	|	...	|	1740	|	...
Veliko Târnovo d.	0700	1015	1202	1316	...	1621	...	1928	2112
Gorna Oryakhovitsa 1500 a.	0720	1035	1218	1335	...	1641	...	1945	2132
Ruse 1500 a.	1000	1341	1505	1720	...	1937	...	2155	...

km		2	2	2C
0	**Dimitrovgrad** d.	0505	...	1537
23	Haskovo d.	0536	...	1608
87	Kârdzhali d.	0723	1320	1749
101	**Momchilgrad** a.	0743	1340	1810
119	**Podkova** a.	0806	1404	1836

	2	2	2	P2
Podkova d.	0620	0815	1410	...
Momchilgrad d.	0645	0840	1433	1720
Kârdzhali d.	0724t	0859	...	1752
Haskovo d.	0907	...	...	1936
Dimitrovgrad a.	0933	...	...	2003

B – (2) Gorna - Dimitrovgrad and v.v. On dates in Table **61** conveys (2) Bucureşti - Dimitrovgrad and v.v., 🛏 1, 2 cl. and ▬ 2 cl. Bucureşti - Çerkezköy and v.v.
C – (2) Stara Zagora - Dimitrovgrad - Podkova.
P – To Plovdiv (Table **1550**).
V – From/to Varna (Table **1500**).
f – Arrives 14 – 17 minutes earlier.
r – Arrives 30 – 32 minutes earlier.
t – Arrives 20 – 24 minutes earlier.

RUSE - SILISTRA and VARNA 1530

km		9647		9621			2655		9623		
		H	g2		2	2		Ⓐ2		2	2
0	**Ruse** d.	0341	...	0600	0736	...	...	1418	1730	1741	...
5	Ruse Razpr d.	0354	...	0614	0746	...	...	1427	1739	1832	...
71	Razgrad d.	0503	...	0723	0906	...	...	1546	1846	1958	...
93	Samuil d.	0554f	0550	0744	0928	0935	...	1607	1907	2019	2036
	Silistra a.	0823	|	|	|	1210	...	...	|	...	2307
142	Kaspichan 1500 a.	...	0654	0834	1028	...	1036	...	2003	...	...
	Shumen 1500 a.	...	0732	|	1119	...	|	...	|	...	...
201	Povelyanovo 1500 a.	...	...	0929	...	...	1130	...	2100	...	...
226	**Varna** 1500 a.	...	...	0954	...	...	1156	...	2125	...	...

km			4641			9620				9622	9646
		2		2	2			2	2		D
	Varna 1500 d.	...	0432	...	...	0915	...	...	...	1815	...
	Povelyanovo 1500 d.	...	0457	...	...	0941	...	...	...	1843	...
	Shumen 1500 d.	...	|	...	0547	|	...	...	1555	|	...
	Kaspichan 1500 d.	...	0552	...	0632	1040	...	...	1655	1942	...
0	**Silistra** d.	...	...	0440	|	|	...	1455	|	|	1920
113	Samuil d.	0540	...	0713	0745	1131	...	1732	1758	2033	2201
	Razgrad d.	0601	...	...	0807	1151	...	...	1819	2053	2221
	Ruse Razpr a.	0725	...	...	0930	1259	...	...	1952	2203	2327
	Ruse a.	0734	...	...	0940	1308	...	...	2005	2216	2340

H – 🛏 1, 2 cl. and (2) Sofia - Ruse - Silistra.
D – 🛏 1, 2 cl. and (2) Silistra - Gorna Oryakhovitsa (**2626**) - Sofia.
f – Arrives 0522.
g – To Gorna Oryakhovitsa (a. 1005).

VARNA and SHUMEN - BURGAS 1535

km			8602	8611				8632			
		2			2	2	2		2	2	2
	Varna 1500 d.	0625	0850	...	1105	...	1350	1530	...	1825	...
	Povelyanovo 1500 d.	0657	0916	...	1138	...	1422	1555	...	1859	...
	Kaspichan 1500 d.	|	|	...	|	...	|	|	...	|	1842
0	Shumen 1500 d.	|	|	...	|	1405	|	|	...	|	1915
50	Komunari d.	0749	0958	...	1231	1505	1515	1636	...	1958	2015
133	Karnobat 1500 d.	0946r	1124	1213	...	...	1720j	1756	1812	2147	...
194	**Burgas** 1500 a.	1059	...	1300	...	...	1836	...	1923	...	...

					3622	8631			8612	8601	
	2	2		2			2	2			2
Burgas 1500 d.	...	...	...	0730	0910	...	...	...	1525	...	1615
Karnobat 1500 d.	0320	...	...	0902r	0958	1039	...	...	1613	1647	1744r
Komunari d.	0512	0610	...	1055	...	1207	1243	1518	...	|	1931
Shumen 1500 a.	|	0712	...	|	...	|	1345	|	...	|	|
Kaspichan 1500 a.	|	0744	...	|	...	|	...	|	...	|	|
Povelyanovo 1500 d.	0608	...	...	1151	...	1250	...	1618	...	1853	2025
Varna 1500 a.	0639	...	...	1223	...	1314	...	1650	...	1917	2055

j – Arrives 1702.
r – Arrives 12 – 13 minutes earlier.

VARNA - DOBRICH - KARDAM 1540

km		2	D	2	2	2	2	2
0	**Varna** 1500 d.	0600	...	...	1340	...	1715	1850
	Sofia 1500 d.	|	2230	...	|	...	|	|
25	Povelyanovo 1500 d.	0631	0705	...	1413	...	1747	1923
93	**Dobrich** a.	...	0830	0840	1530	1550	1902	2047
131	Kardam a.	...	...	0945	...	1655	...	...

	2	2	2	2	2	E
Kardam d.	...	...	1100	...	1935	...
Dobrich d.	0605	0915	1204	1215	2039	2115
Povelyanovo 1500 a.	0730	1041	...	1332	...	2237
Sofia 1500 a.	|	|	...	|	...	0723
Varna 1500 a.	0803	1115	...	1406	...	...

D – 🛏 1, 2 cl. and (2) Sofia (**3637**) - Povelyanovo (**2637**) - Dobrich.
E – 🛏 1, 2 cl. and (2) Dobrich (**2636**) - Povelyanovo (**3636**) - Sofia.

(SOFIA -) PLOVDIV - SVILENGRAD - İSTANBUL 1550

BDŽ; TCDD

km	*Bulgarian train number*			1621				1625			493	
	Turkish train number										81031	81721
		2	2		2	2	2		2	2	ⓇA	
0	*Sofia* 1500 d.	...	...	0830	...	...	...	1510	...	...	2040	...
156	**Plovdiv** ⊡ d.	0610	0910	1120	1210	1420	1610	1750	1923	2020	2310	...
202	Parvomaj ⊡ d.	0650	0956	1159	1251	1504	1652	1828	2003	2107	2338	...
234	Dimitrovgrad ⊡ a.	0719	1021	1219	1316	1529	1723	1848	2028	2136	2355	...
234	Dimitrovgrad d.	0721	1025	1220	...	1534	...	1900	...	...	0012	...
299	Svilengrad a.	0815	1121	1310	...	1632	...	1951	...	...	0102	...
299	Svilengrad 🏛 d.	...	...	...	...	...	...	...	...	...	0147	...
318	**Kapıkule** 🏛 a.	...	...	...	...	...	...	...	...	...	0205	...
318	**Kapıkule** d.	...	...	...	...	...	...	...	...	...	0256	0710
338	Edirne d.	...	...	...	...	...	...	...	...	...	0320	0730
	Uzunköprü d.	...	...	...	...	...	...	...	...	...	|	|
385	Pehlivanköy d.	...	...	...	...	...	...	...	...	...	|	0806
406	Alpullu d.	...	...	...	...	...	...	...	...	...	0427	0826
506	Çerkezköy a.	...	...	...	...	...	...	...	...	...	0544	0956
593	Halkalı ¶ a.	...	...	...	...	...	...	...	...	...	0706*	1138
621	**İstanbul** Sirkeci ¶ a.	...	...	...	...	...	...	...	...	...	0750*	...

km	*Turkish train number*	81724	81032								
	Bulgarian train number		492						1626		
			ⓇA		2	2	2	2		2	M2
0	**İstanbul** Sirkeci ¶ d.	...	2200*	...	...	...	...	...	...	...	...
28	Halkalı ¶ d.	1800	2238*	...	...	...	...	...	...	...	...
115	Çerkezköy d.	1944	0002	...	...	...	...	...	...	...	...
215	Alpullu d.	2114	0124	...	...	...	...	...	...	...	...
237	Pehlivanköy d.	2133	|	...	...	...	...	...	...	...	...
258	Uzunköprü a.	|	|	...	...	...	...	...	...	...	...
	Edirne d.	2209	0230	...	...	...	...	...	...	...	...
	Kapıkule a.	2227	0250	...	...	...	...	...	...	...	...
	Kapıkule 🏛 d.	▬	0345	...	...	...	...	...	...	...	...
	Svilengrad 🏛 a.	...	0405	...	...	...	...	...	...	...	...
	Svilengrad d.	...	0450	0525	0840	...	1125	...	1610	1720	...
	Dimitrovgrad a.	2	0540	0630	0933	...	1218	...	1701	1814	...
	Dimitrovgrad ⊡ d.	0440	0550	0632	0938	1130	1230	1555	1703	1827	2006
	Parvomaj ⊡ d.	0506	0610	0704	1009	1200	1305	1628	1724	1858	2040
	Plovdiv ⊡ a.	0549	0640	0748	1048	1248	1345	1708	1801	1938	2130
	Sofia 1500 a.	...	0910	...	...	...	...	...	2040	...	...

A – BALKAN EXPRESS – ▬ 2 cl. Sofia - Çerkezköy and v.v.; (2) Sofia - Svilengrad and v.v. See Table **61** for through cars from / to Bucureşti.
M – From Momchilgrad (Table **1525**).
* – By 🚌 from / to Çerkezköy. During certain periods the bus connection may operate from / to Kapıkule (in similar timings), or train may run through to Halkalı.
¶ – For İstanbul suburban services via the Marmaray tunnel see Table **1570**.
⊡ – Additional trains Plovdiv - Dimitrovgrad and v.v.: **From Plovdiv** at 0710, 0810 and 1710 Ⓐ. **From Dimitrovgrad** at 0840, 1330 and 1735.

SOFIA - KYUSTENDIL, PETRICH, KULATA and THESSALONÍKI 1560

Most trains 2nd class only

km									361 Ⓡ				
0	**Sofia** d.	...	0520	0740	0845	1000	1200	1300	1500	...	1700	1840	2000
33	Pernik d.	...	0613	0832	0928	1051	1248	1400	1540	...	1748	1945	2051
48	Radomir d.	...	0642	0854	0950	1117	1313	1426	1600	1605	1809	2011	2113
102	**Kyustendil** a.	...	|	|	1117	|	|	1555	|	1745	|	2142	|
91	Dupnitsa d.	0630	0756	0934	▬	1207	1352	▬	1640	▬	1852	▬	2154
123	**Blagoevgrad** a.	0718	0837	1004	...	1247	1419	...	1708	...	1926	...	2222
123	**Blagoevgrad** d.	0719	▬	1015	...	...	1424	...	1709	...	1927	...	...
186	Sandanski d.	0831	...	1134	...	...	1532	...	1803	...	2029	...	...
197	General Todorov. a.	0843	...	1146	...	...	1544	...	1813	...	2040	...	...
197	General Todorov. d.	0844	0855	1158	1156	...	1554	1555	1814	1820	2045	2050	...
207	**Petrich** a.	|	0908	1211	|	...	1607	|	|	1833	2100	|	...
210	Kulata 🏛 a.	0858	...	...	1210	...	...	1609	1825	...	...	2105	...
211	Promahónas 🏛 a.	...	...	...	...	...	...	...	1921‡	...	...	...	...
354	**Thessaloníki** a.	...	...	...	...	...	...	...	2222‡	...	...	...	...

						360 Ⓡ					
Thessaloníki d.	...	...	...	...	...	0655‡	...	...	...	...	...
Promahónas 🏛 d.	...	...	...	...	...	0950‡	...	...	...	...	...
Kulata 🏛 d.	0500	...	0645	...	...	1050	1405	...	1638	...	1915
Petrich d.	|	0505	|	0645	1042	|	|	1408	|	1645	1907t
General Todorov a.	0514	0517	0659	0658	1055	1100	1419	1422	1652	1659	1928
General Todorov d.	▬	0522	▬	0710	▬	1101	▬	1433	▬	1709	1929
Sandanski d.	...	0534	...	0723	...	1111	...	1446	...	1722	1942
Blagoevgrad a.	...	0635	...	0841	...	1204	...	1600	...	1835	2100
Blagoevgrad d.	0525	0636	...	0851	0935	1205	1422	1605	...	1840	2101
Dupnitsa d.	0601	0705	...	0930	1022	1234	1458	1641	...	1919	2138
Kyustendil d.	|	|	0700	...	|	|	|	|	1755	|	...
Radomir d.	0642	0743	0831	...	1118	1313	1552	1719	1927	2000	...
Pernik d.	0700	0800	0858	...	1140	1328	1620	1737	1944	2020	...
Sofia a.	0750	0856	0948	...	1235	1407	1710	1831	2033	2111	...

☛ Additional journeys Radomir - Kyustendil and v.v.: **From Radomir** at 0707, 1130 and 1813. **From Kyustendil** at 0445, 0930, 1130, 1410 and 1605. Journey: 87 – 100 minutes.

▬ – Change trains at General Todorov.
‡ – Greek timings are subject to confirmation.

TURKEY IN ASIA

Operator: Türkiye Cumhuriyeti Devlet Demiryolları (TCDD).

Services: YHT (high-speed) trains convey first and second class seating. Long distance trains convey a single class of seating known locally as 'Pullman' (shown as ⊡ in footnotes) and may also convey sleeping and/or couchette cars. Local trains convey 2nd class seating, shown as '2' in the train column. Descriptions of sleeping (🛏) and couchette (🛌) cars appear on page 8. Reservation of seats (free of charge) is required for YHT and express trains.

Timings: Schedules are the latest available. Timetable amendments are possible at short notice so please confirm timings locally before travelling.

1570 — İSTANBUL - ESKİŞEHİR - KONYA and ANKARA — TCDD

km		YHT 91052	YHT 91202		91054	YHT 91002	91204	91302	11604	91004	91206	91056	91006	91208	11606	91008	91210	91012	91212	91010	11612	91304	91060	91214	91012	11616
	İstanbul (Pendik) d.				0630		0730	0800	0855				1135		1020	1345				1730	1650	1815			1920	2030
	İzmit d.				0720		0820	0850	0945				1225		1110					1820	1740	1905			2010	2120
	Arifiye d.				0741		0841	0917					1246		1137					1841	1807	1926				2147
	Adapazarı a.								0940						1230						1830					2210
	Bilecik d.						0824		0927						1539					1927	2012					
	Bozüyük d.						0851		0951											1951	2036					
0	Eskişehir d.	0630				0840	0913		1013	1131		1325	1412			1621		1820		2013		2058	2110		2156	
355	Konya a.								1156														2241				
	Konya d.		0630				0915			1130			1410			1620		1900					2115			
156	Polatlı YHT d.	0719	0735			0929	1001	1020			1414	1500	1515			1723	1909	2005	2101			2159	2220			
220	Sincan d.	0739	0755			0949	1021	1040			1236	1250	1434	1520	1535		1727	1742	1929	2025	2122		2219	2240	2303	
245	Ankara a.	0806	0822			1016	1048	1107			1303	1317	1501	1547	1602		1754	1809	1956	2052	2149		2246	2307	2330	

km		YHT 11601	11603	91001	91051	91301	91201	91003	91203	91053	91205	11609	91005	91207	91007	91055	91209	91009	91303	91057	91211	91011	91059	11611	91213
0	Ankara d.			0600	0630		0645	0840	0855	1105	1140		1200	1350	1405	1600	1635	1700		1800	1840	1900	2050		2140
25	Sincan d.			0628	0658		0713	0908	0923	1133	1208		1228	1418	1433	1628	1703	1723		1828	1908	1928	2118		2208
89	Polatlı YHT d.			0647	0718		0733		0943	1153			1247	1438		1648	1723	1747		1848	1928		2138		2228
309	Konya a.						0840		1050	1332			1545			1830				2035			2335		
245	Konya d.				0700													1745							
245	Eskişehir d.			0740	0806	0844		1017	1241		1340		1542	1736		1840	1930	1936		2037	2226				
	Bozüyük d.			0758		0902										1857	1947								
	Bilecik d.			0819		0924										1919	2009								
	Adapazarı d.	0545	0720								1320									1835					
	Arifiye d.	0605	0731	0903		1009					1345	1457				2003	2053			1900					
	İzmit d.	0636	0802	0926		1032	1156			1416	1520		1721			2026	2116			2216		1931			
506	İstanbul (Pendik) a.	0725	0851	1016		1121	1245			1505	1608		1810			2115	2205			2305		2020			

🚌 CONNECTIONS

km 0										
Eskişehir d.	0815	0900	1035	1355	1555	1750	1855	1950	2055	...
Bursa a.	1030	1110	1250	1610	1810	2005	2110	2205	2310	...

Bursa d.	0401	0645	0901	1055	1140	1350	1550	1745	1831	1925
Eskişehir a.	0616	0900	1116	1310	1355	1604	1805	2000	2046	1931

km 0						
Konya d.	0850	0915	1130	1440	1730	2305
Alanya a.	1330				2215	0420
Antalya a.		1415	1615	1920		0420

Antalya d.		1000	1230	1430	
Alanya d.	0730	1000			1600
Konya a.	1205	1445	1500	1750	2040	2040

A – ADA EKSPRES TRENİ – ⊡ İstanbul (Pendik) - Arifiye and v.v.

* – The Marmaray tunnel (13.6km from near Kazlıçeşme station to near Ayrılıkçeşmesi station) includes the world's deepest immersed tube tunnel at 60.46 metres below sea level (1.4km in length, between Sirkeci and Üsküdar).

"MARMARAY*" SUBURBAN SERVICES

Kazlıçeşme d.	0600	and at	2400		Ayrılıkçeşmesi d.	0600	and at	2400
Yenikapı d.	0605	least	0005		Üsküdar d.	0605	least	0005
Sirkeci d.	0609	every 10	0009		Sirkeci d.	0609	every 10	0009
Üsküdar d.	0613	minutes	0013		Yenikapı d.	0613	minutes	0013
Ayrılıkçeşmesi a.	0618	until	0018		Kazlıçeşme a.	0618	until	0018

TCDD ESKIŞEHIR, BANDIRMA and AFYON - IZMIR 1571

km		71136 A	21316	32526	21130 B	31622	32420	32528	31002 C	31004 D	72616
	Ankara **1570** d.	...	...	...	...	...	...	...	...	...	...
0	**Eskişehir** ♧ d.	...	...	...	2245	...	...	...	...	...	...
78	Kütahya ♧ d.	...	...	...	0020	...	...	...	...	...	1625
128	Tavşanllı d.	...	...	...	|	...	...	...	...	...	1731
‡	**Bandirma** Şehir d.	...	...	...	|	...	0700	...	...	...	|
‡	**Bandirma** Gar d.	...	...	...	|	...	0703	...	...	...	|
331	Ballıkesir d.	...	0400**b**	...	|	...	0847	...	...	...	2203
413	Soma d.	...	0533**a**	...	|	...	...	...	1530	1830	▬
454	Akhisar d.	...	0616	...	|	...	...	...	1616	1913	**31620**
◇	**Afyon** Ali Çetinkaya d.	0001	|	...	0214	...	...	...	|	|	
◇	Usak d.	0231	|	...	0502	0615	...	...	|	|	1620
◇	Alaşehir d.	0449	|	0520	0725	0847	...	1500	|	|	1900
506	Manisa d.	0625	0708	0723	0902	1050	...	1700	1713	2008	2107
572	**Izmir** Alsancak a.	0748	0830	0859	1029	1222	...	...	1839	2127	2236

	31001 C	31619	32525	31003 D	32421	31621	32527	31315	31129 B	31135 A
Izmir Alsancak d.	0650	0730	1100	1400	...	1525	...	1755	1930	2110
Manisa d.	0818	0907	1229	1525	...	1701	1840	1931	2101	2236
Alaşehir d.	|	1110	1428	|	...	1901	2038	|	2238	0010
Usak d.	|	1347	...	|	...	2139	...	|	0120	0229
Afyon Ali Çetinkaya a.	|	...	...	|	...	...	...	|	0410	0500
Akhisar d.	0914	...	...	1615	...	...	...	2026	|	▬
Soma d.	0958	...	...	1656	...	...	...	2110**c**	|	**72615**
Ballıkesir d.	...	...	...	...	1800	...	...	2241**b**	|	0600
Bandirma Gar a.	...	...	...	...	1945	...	...	...	|	|
Bandirma Şehir a.	...	...	...	...	1947	...	...	...	|	|
Tavşanllı d.	...	...	...	...	...	...	...	...	|	1035
Kütahya ♧ d.	...	...	...	...	...	...	...	...	0612	1137
Eskişehir ♧ a.	...	...	...	...	...	...	...	...	0740	...
Ankara **1570** a.	...	...	...	...	...	...	...	...	...	...

⛴ İstanbul - Bandirma

İstanbul Deniz Otobüsleri *

km											
0	**İstanbul** Yenikapi d.	0700	...	...	...	...	...	1830	...	...	...
	Bandirma Şehir a.	0910	...	...	...	...	...	2040	...	...	...

	①-⑤	⑥								
Bandirma Şehir d.	0730	0930	...	...	...	...	1830	...	...	...
İstanbul Yenikapi a.	0940	1140	...	...	...	...	2040	...	...	...

A – KONYA MAVI TRENI – 🛌, 🛏, 🚃(1) and ✕ Konya - Izmir Basmane and v.v.
B – IZMIR MAVI TRENI – 🛌, 🚃(1) and ✕ Izmir - Eskişehir and v.v.
C – 6 EYLÜL EKSPRESI – 🚃(1) Bandirma - Soma - Izmir and v.v. ♠
D – 17 EYLÜL EKSPRESI – 🚃(1) Bandirma - Soma - Izmir and v.v. ♠
a – From Savaştepe, depart 0503.
b – Non confirmed connection by bus.
c – To Savaştepe, arrive 2138.

♧ – For local services see Table **1581**.
♠ – All services currently only operate to/from Soma.
‡ – Bandirma Sehir - Bandirma Gar: *1 km*. Bandirma Sehir - Ballıkesir *101 km*.
◇ – Afyon - Manisa: *355 km*. Usak - Manisa: *220 km*. Alaşehir - Manisa: *122 km*.
* – İstanbul Deniz Otobüsleri ✆ +90 (212) 455 6900. www.ido.com.tr

TCDD 2nd class IZMIR - TIRE, ÖDEMIŞ, SÖKE and DENIZLI 1572

km		32333	32321	32251	32253	32323	32393	32415	32255	32325	32395	32263	32417	32397	32327	32257	32413	32259	32329	32335	32261	32419	32351	32331	32333 ⑤–⑦
0	**Izmir** Basmane ⊡ d.	...	0620	0745	0900	0920	...	1000	1125	1220	...	1340	1400	...	1510	1535	1550	1645	1710	...	1825	1905	1925	2025	2200
18	Adnan Menderes ⊡ d.	...	0641	0805	0926	0947	...	1025	1149	1246	...	1407	1424	...	1535	1557	1612	1710	1733	...	1848	1930	1949	2048	2225
49	Torballı d.	...	0710	0838	0954	1016	...	1055	1220	1317	...	1433	1457	...	1605	1624	1646	1739	1807	...	1914	2002	2023	2118	2255
86	Çatal d.	0600	0759	|	|	1103	...	1138	|	1356	...	|	1541	...	1657	|	1731	|	1853	1855	|	2045	|	2200	2321
96	**Tire** a.	0610	|	|	|	|	...	1151	|	|	...	|	1554	...	|	|	1744	|	|	1906	|	2581	|	|	|
111	**Ödemiş** Gar a.	▬	0828	|	|	1129	...	...	|	1421	...	|	...	...	1730	|	...	|	1920	...	|	...	|	2227	2355
112	**Ödemiş** Şehir a.	**32391**	0831	|	|	1132	...	...	|	1424	...	|	...	...	1733	|	...	|	1923	...	|	...	|	2230	2358
77	Selçuk d.		...	0908	1024	...	...	...	1247	...	...	1500	...	...	...	1653	...	1807	...	...	1943	...	2054	...	...
	Söke d.	0620	...	|	|	...	1110	...	|	...	1445	|	...	1615	...	|	...	|	...	...	|	...	2153	...	...
100	Ortaklar d.	0645	...	0942	1058	...	1135	...	1321	...	1510	1534	...	1641	...	1728	...	1841	...	...	2020	...	2130↑	...	...
130	Aydin d.	0728	...	1017	1132	...	1210	...	1354	...	1544	1609	...	1718	...	1801	...	1917	...	...	2054	...	...	...	...
175	Nazilli d.	0830	...	1109	1226	...	1306	...	1448	...	...	1658	...	1825	...	1854	...	2009	...	...	2145	...	...	...	...
251	Goncali **1587** d.	0945	...	1218	1335	...	...	...	1557	...	...	...	...	1944	...	2002	...	2118	...	...	2254	...	...	...	...
260	**Denizli** **1587** a.	0957	...	1230	1347	...	...	...	1609	...	...	...	...	1956	...	2014	...	2130	...	...	2306	...	...	...	...

km		32334	32322	32412	32352	32252	32324	32414	32254	32326	32392	32256	32394	32328	32396	32330	32258	32418	32260	32398	32332	32264	⑤–⑦	32334 ⑤–⑦	32262
0	**Denizli** **1587** d.	...	...	...	...	0420	...	...	0545	...	0655	0825	1030	...	...	...	1245	...	1435	...	...	...	...	...	1730
9	Goncali **1587** d.	...	...	...	...	0433	...	...	0557	...	0708	0838	1043	...	...	...	1258	...	1449	...	...	...	...	...	1743
85	Nazilli d.	...	...	...	...	0543	...	...	0706	...	0829	0954	1200	...	1325	...	1408	...	1602	...	...	1734	...	...	1853
130	Aydin d.	...	...	...	...	0633	...	...	0800	...	0928	1045	1302	...	1422	...	1459	...	1655	1805	...	1829	...	...	1946
160	Ortaklar d.	...	...	...	0620	0707	...	...	0834	...	1004	1118	1344	...	1511	...	1533	...	1729	1842	...	1904	...	...	2021
183	**Söke** a.	...	...	...	0555↑	|	...	...	|	...	1027	|	1407	...	1534	...	|	...	|	1905	...	|	...	...	|
183	Selçuk d.	...	...	...	0654	0740	...	...	0909	...	...	1151	▬	...	...	...	1606	...	1808	▬	...	1942	...	...	2055
	Ödemiş Şehir d.	...	0520	...	|	|	0700	...	|	0845	...	|	**32416**	1205	...	1450	|	...	|	**32336**	1750	|	...	1955	|
	Ödemiş Gar d.	...	0524	...	|	|	0705	...	|	0849	...	|	...	1210	...	1455	|	...	|	...	1754	|	...	2000	|
	Tire d.	0535	|	0615	|	|	|	0752	|	|	...	|	1203	|	...	|	|	1640	|	1810	|	|	1955	|	|
	Çatal d.	0545	0556	0629	|	|	0731	0807	|	0915	...	|	1217	1235	...	1519	|	1700	|	1820	1826	|	2005	2024	|
211	Torballı d.	...	0644	0711	0724	0807	0817	0852	0937	1001	...	1218	1259	1317	...	1605	1635	1754	1833	...	1915	2010	...	2104	2122
242	Adnan Menderes ⊡ a.	...	0714	0738	0754	0835	0846	0922	1005	1029	...	1245	1329	1344	...	1634	1704	1823	1859	...	1945	2036	...	2133	2148
260	**Izmir** Basmane ⊡ a.	...	0738	0800	0818	0856	0911	0947	1030	1053	...	1308	1353	1410	...	1659	1729	1848	1918	...	2009	2100	...	2157	2212

⊡ – Frequent local trains operate 0600 - 2300.

TCDD ANKARA - KARS, KURTALAN, TATVAN and TEHRAN 1575

km		42102	42104	21512	11532	11542	42822	52546	21410	21124	51516
				③	②⑦	△					②
		2	2	A ❈	B	C	2	2	D	E ❈	F ❈
0	**Ankara** **1582** d.	...	...	1025	*1119**	*1119**	...	...	*1758**	1900	...
70	Irmak **1582** d.	...	...	1200	1249	|	...	...	1929	2022	...
92	Kirikkale **1582** d.	...	...	|	1316	1316	...	...	1953	2046	...
365	Boğazköprü **1582** d.	...	...	1654	1805	1805	...	...	0020	0104	...
381	Kayseri d.	...	...	1730	1836	1836	...	...	0048	0136	...
603	**Sivas** a.	...	...	2055	2221	2221	...	...	0406	0500	...
603	**Sivas** d.	0900	1940	2136	2231	2231	...	...	0412	0512	...
715	Çetinkaya d.	1023	2108	|	0021	0021	...	...	0549	0702	...
779	Divrïgi d.	1139	2224	|	|	|	0502	...	0709	|	...
935	Erzincan d.	▬	...	|	|	|	0828	...	1007	|	...
1150	Erzurum d.	...	...	|	|	|	▬	...	1357	|	...
1235	Horasan d.	...	...	|	|	|	...	...	1519	|	...
1307	Sarkamis d.	...	...	|	|	|	...	...	1703	|	...
1366	**Kars** a.	...	...	|	|	|	...	...	1801	|	...
854	Malatya d.	**52538**	...	0302	0302	0302	...	...	...	0925	...
949	Yolçatı d.	2	...	|	0525	0513	...	...	...	...	...
1107	Diyarbakir d.	0730	...	|	|	0904	**52862**	1758	...	...	...
1198	Batman d.	0950	...	|	|	1046	②⑤⑦	2017	...	...	...
1267	**Kurtalan** a.	...	...	|	|	1201	2 **a**	...	...	...	...
973	Elâzig d.	...	...	0631	0620	...	0705	...	...	...	...
1201	Mus d.	...	...	1223	1149	...	1408	...	...	...	...
1295	**Tatvan** Gar a.	...	...	1440	1331	...	1650	...	...	...	...
1300	**Tatvan** Iskele ♡ a.	...	...	1453	...	...	...	...	...	...	...
0	**Van** Iskele ♡ d.	...	...	2130	...	...	...	...	...	...	...
3	**Van** Gar d.	...	...	2154	...	...	...	...	...	...	2000
114	Kapiköy 🏛 d.	...	...	0130	...	...	...	...	...	...	2315
120	Razi d.	...	...	0235	...	...	...	...	...	...	0110
342	Tabriz a.	...	...	0635	...	...	...	...	...	...	0625
342	Tabriz d.	...	...	0823	...	...	...	...	...	...	...
1078	**Tehran** a.	...	...	2020	...	...	...	...	...	...	...

	42103	51123	52545	41409	51511	52861	51515	51541	51531	52537
					③	①③⑥	①	▽	②④	
	2	E ❈	2	D	A ❈	2 a	F ❈	C	B	2
Tehran d.	...	...	...	...	2125	...	...	...	...	...
Tabriz a.	...	...	...	...	0926	...	...	...	...	...
Tabriz d.	...	...	...	...	1056	...	2230	...	...	...
Razi d.	...	...	...	...	1540	...	0400	...	...	...
Kapiköy 🏛 d.	...	...	...	...	1740	...	0415	...	...	...
Van Gar a.	...	...	...	...	1933	...	0606	...	...	...
Van Iskele ♡ a.	...	...	...	...	1956	...	...	...	...	...
Tatvan Iskele ♡ d.	...	...	...	...	0457	...	...	...	...	...
Tatvan Gar d.	...	...	...	...	0715	0715	...	...	0800	...
Mus d.	...	...	...	...	0944	0946	...	...	0938	...
Elâzig d.	...	...	...	...	1545	1621	...	...	1506	...
Kurtalan d.	...	...	...	...	|	...	...	0930	|	...
Batman d.	...	...	0504	...	|	...	...	1050	|	1500
Diyarbakir d.	...	...	0721	...	|	...	...	1224	|	1715
Yolçatı d.	...	...	▬	...	|	...	...	1540	1540	▬
Malatya d.	...	1530	...	...	1820	...	...	1753	1753	...
Kars d.	...	|	...	0810	|	...	...	|	|	...
Sarkamis d.	...	|	...	0916	|	...	...	|	|	...
Horasan d.	...	|	**42821**	1048	|	...	...	|	|	...
Erzurum d.	...	|	2	1226	|	...	...	|	|	**42101**
Erzincan d.	...	|	1400	1616	|	...	...	|	|	2
Divrïgi d.	1630	|	1723	1912	|	...	...	|	|	0557
Çetinkaya d.	1746	1757	...	2029	|	...	...	2043	2043	0715
Sivas a.	1905	1937	...	2202	2238	...	...	2218	2218	0835
Sivas d.	...	1947	...	2207	2255	...	...	2233	2233	...
Kayseri d.	...	2318	...	0126	0241	...	...	0222	0222	...
Boğazköprü **1582** d.	...	2346	...	0153	|	...	...	0245	0245	...
Kirikkale **1582** d.	...	0415	...	0616	|	...	...	0736	0736	...
Irmak **1582** a.	...	0438	...	0638	|	...	...	0801	0801	...
Ankara **1582** a.	...	0610	...	*0805**	0922	...	...	*0936**	*0936**	...

A – TRANSASYA EKSPRESI – 🛏 and ✕ Ankara(**21512/51511**) - Tatvan and v.v.;
🛏 and ✕ Van (**21512/51511**) - Razi (**59/60**) - Tehran and v.v.
B – VAN GÖLÜ EKSPRESI – 🛌 🛏 and 🚃(2) Ankara - Tatvan and v.v.
C – GÜNEY KURTALAN EKSPRESI – 🛌 🛏 and 🚃(2) Ankara - Kurtalan and v.v.
D – DOĞU EKSPRESI – 🛌 🛏 🚃(12) Ankara - Kars and v.v.
E – 4 EYLÜL MAVI – 🚃(12) 🛏 and ✕ Ankara - Malatya and v.v.
F – 🚃(2) and 🍸 Tabriz(**494/495**) - Kapiköy(**51515/51516**) - Van and v.v.

a – Subject to confirmation.
△ – ①③④⑤⑥.
▽ – ①③⑤⑥⑦.
* – 🚌 connection to/from Ankara.
❈ – Service currently suspended.
♡ – By ⛴ Tatvan - Van and v.v. Passengers must leave the train at Tatvan and rejoin it at Van. Note that different sets of coaching stock are used either side of the ferry.

TURKEY in Asia

1576 ANKARA - ZONGULDAK `TCDD`

km		22302					22301	
0	Ankara.............d.		...	...	Zonguldak........♡ d.	1330	...
70	Irmak...............d.		...	...	Karabük...........d.	1704	...
172	Çankırı.............d.		...	...	Çankırı............d.		...
364	Karabük............d.	0830	...	...	Irmak..............d.		...
486	Zonguldak......♡ a.	1203	...	...	Ankara.............a.		...

Note : Services Çankırı - Zonguldak and v.v. are suspended for engineering work with no
re-opening date given. Please check with operator before travelling.

♡ – Local service Zonguldak - Filyos - Gokçebey and v.v. (journey 1 hr 50 minutes,
Zonguldak – Filyos 50 minutes). From Zonguldak at 0640, 0945, 1550, 1730, 1835.
From Gokçebey at 0535, 0630, 1225, 1400, 1830.

1577 SIVAS - AMASYA - SAMSUN `TCDD`

Services are suspended for engineering works until December 2017

km								
0	Sivas..............d.	...	...	...	Samsun...........d.	...	...	...
111	Yenice.............d.	...	...	...	Havza.............d.	...	...	...
181	Turhal.............d.	...	...	...	Suluova............d.	...	...	...
245	Amasya............d.	...	...	...	Amasya............d.	...	...	...
272	Suluova............d.	...	...	...	Turhal.............d.	...	...	...
292	Havza.............d.	...	...	...	Yenice.............d.	...	...	...
378	Samsun............a.	...	...	...	Sivas..............a.	...	...	...

1581 ESKİŞEHİR - KONYA - ADANA `TCDD`

For YHT (high-speed) services between Eskişehir and Konya, see Table 1570.

km		31135 F	72442 2 ☙	72444 2 ☙	72202 H	71306 2	72204 G	71322 2	72406 H	72206 2	21130 C
0	Eskişehir......1571 d.				0850		1415	1540	1810	1950	2245
79	Kütahya.......1571 d.				1009		1536	1715	1939	2108	0020
163	Afyon Ali Çetinkaya..d.	0500						1906	2126		0214
261	Akşehir..............d.	0627	0630	1220							
435	Konya............♡ d.	0858	0902	1452							
537	Karaman.........♡ d.				1530						
	Ereğli...............d.				1640						
672	Ulukışla.......1582 d.				1724						
781	Yenice.........1582 d.				1922						
804	Adana.........1582 d.				1945						

km		31129 C	72201 2	72405 2	72203 H	72441 2 ☙	61305 2	72205 H	71321 2	72443 2 ☙	71136 F
	Adana.........1582 d.					0745		...			...
	Yenice.........1582 d.					0815		...			...
	Ulukışla.......1582 d.					1017		...			...
	Ereğli...............d.					1105		...			...
	Karaman.........♡ d.					1215		...			...
	Konya...........♡ d.					0920			1730	2000
	Akşehir..............d.					1150			2000	2235
	Afyon Ali Çetinkaya..d.	0410		0707				2011		0001
	Kütahya.......1571 d.	0612	0707	0855	1146			1805	2211	
	Eskişehir......1571 a.	0740	0823	1030	1300			1921	2340	

km		🚌	🚌	🚌	🚌	🚌	🚌
0	Konya............♡ d.	0850	1130	1230	1445	1700	2030
102	Karaman..........♡ a.	1020	1300	1400	1615	1830	2200

		🚌	🚌	🚌	🚌	🚌	🚌
	Karaman..........♡ d.	0750	1030	1300	1530	1610	1900
	Konya............♡ a.	0920	1200	1430	1700	1740	2030

C – IZMIR MAVI TRENI – 🛏, 🍴 and ✕ Izmir - Eskişehir and v.v.
F – KONYA MAVI TRENI – 🛏, 🍴, 🍴 and ✕ Konya - Izmir Basmane and v.v.
G – TOROS EKSPRESİ – 🍴 Adana - Karaman and v.v.
H – PAMUKKALE EKSPRESİ – 🍴 and ✕ Eskişehir - Denizli and v.v.

♡ – Rail services Konya - Karaman and v.v. are suspended until Dec. 31.
☙ – Service suspended.

1582 ANKARA - ADANA `TCDD`

km		11512 A ③☙	11532 B △	22576 2	21410 D	21124 2	21302 G	21206 J	71306
0	Ankara............1575 d.	1025	1119*	1737	1758*	1900			...
70	Irmak.............1575 d.	1200	1249	1910	1928	2022			...
92	Kırıkkale.........1575 d.		1316	1933	1953	2046			...
365	Boğazköprü......1575 d.	1654	1805		0023	0104			...
381	Kayseri...........1575 d.	1713	1824		0043	0124	0510	1535	...
479	Niğde...............d.					0721	1746		...
542	Ulukışla.........1581 d.					0836	1901	1724	...
651	Yenice..........1581 d.					1032	1212	1922	...
674	Adana...........1581 d.					1054	1234	1945	...

km		61205	51123	61301	22571 E ☙	41409 2	51511 ⑥☙	51531 B ▽	61305 J
	Adana...........1581 d.	1645		1730					0745
	Yenice..........1581 d.	1710		1757					0815
	Ulukışla.........1581 d.	1936		2004					1017
	Niğde...............d.	2041		2115					
	Kayseri...........1575 d.	2233	2318	2321		0126	0241	0222	
	Boğazköprü......1575 d.		2346			0153		0245	
	Kırıkkale.........1575 d.		0415			0600	0616	0736	
	Irmak............1575 d.		0437			0624	0648	0801	
	Ankara...........1575 a.		0610			0802	0805*	0922	0936*

A – TRANSASYA EKSPRESİ – 🍴 and ✕ Ankara (11512/51511) - Tatvan and v.v.;
🍴 and ✕ Van (11512/51511) - Razi (59/60) - Tehrän and v.v.
B – VAN GÖLÜ EKSPRESİ – 🛏 and 🍴 Ankara - Tatvan and v.v.
C – GÜNEY EKSPRESİ – 🛏 and 🍴 Ankara - Kurtalan and v.v.
D – DOĞU EKSPRESİ – 🛏 and 🍴 Ankara - Kars and v.v.
E – 4 EYLÜL MAVI – 🍴 🛏 and ✕ Ankara - Malatya and v.v.

G – ERCIYES EKSPRESİ – 🍴 Kayseri - Adana and v.v.
J – TOROS EKSPRESİ – 🍴 Adana - Konya and v.v.
* – 🚌 connection to/from Ankara.
△ – Runs as 21542 on ①②③④⑤⑥ (see note C).
▽ – Runs as 51541 on ①②④⑥⑦ (see note C).
☙ – Service suspended.

1583 ADANA - ELAZIG `TCDD`

km		61502 L		
0	Adana..............d.	0740	...
79	Toprakkale.........d.	0858	...
142	Fevzipaşa..........d.	1042	...
211	Narlı...............d.	1205	...
336	Doğanşehir.........d.	1459	...
392	Malatya............d.	1638	...
487	Yolçatı.............d.	1844	...
511	Elazig..............a.	1904	...

		51501 L	
Elazig..............d.	0735	...
Yolçatı.............d.	0801	...
Malatya............d.	1016	...
Doğanşehir.........d.	1131	...
Narlı...............d.	1418	...
Fevzipaşa..........d.	1559	...
Toprakkale.........d.	1716	...
Adana..............a.	1823	...

L – FIRAT EKSPRESİ – 🍴 Elazig - Adana and v.v.

1584 GAZIANTEP - ALEPPO & NUSAYBIN `TCDD`

km								
0	Gaziantep..........d.	...	...	Nusaybin...........d.	...	...
	Nizip...............d.	...	...	Şenyurt............d.	...	...
88	Karkamış...........d.	...	...	Aleppo.............d.	...	...
143	Çöbanbey........🚃 d.	...	...	Çöbanbey........🚃 d.	...	...
218	Aleppo.............a.	...	...	Karkamış...........d.	...	...
356	Şenyurt............d.	...	...	Nizipden...........d.	...	...
381	Nusaybin...........a.	...	...	Gaziantep..........a.	...	...

SERVICE SUSPENDED.

1585 MERSIN - ADANA `TCDD`

km																		J	K									
0	Mersin.........d.	0600	0637	0707	0800	0900	0930	1030	1100	1200	1330	1420	1500	1610	1630	1705	1720	1730	1810	1840	1910	2005	2050	2133	2234
26	Tarsus.........d.	0618	0707	0736	0823	0918	0953	1048	1129	1218	1348	1449	1518	1628	1659	1723	1749	1819	1839	1858	1939	2023	2113	2159	2314
43	Yenice.........d.	0629	0722	0751	0836	0929	1006	1059	1143	1229	1359	1502	1529	1639	1712	1734	1804	1834	1852	1909	1955	2035	2126	2213	2314
67	Adana.........a.	0645	0746	0815	0856	0945	1026	1115	1206	1245	1415	1526	1545	1655	1734	1750	1829	1857	1916	1925	2018	2051	2146	2236	2336

									K	J																	
Adana.........d.	0600	0630	0646	0738	0820	0901	0932	1003	1100	1115	1200	1220	1330	1420	1510	1600	1630	1710	1750	1830	1910	2015	2115	2215	2315
Yenice.........d.	0617	0656	0713	0755	0844	0918	0957	1030	1117	1140	1217	1242	1347	1445	1527	1618	1656	1728	1817	1847	1936	2032	2137	2239	2340
Tarsus.........d.	0628	0709	0727	0806	0858	0929	1011	1044	1128	1153	1228	1255	1358	1458	1538	1629	1709	1739	1832	1858	1950	2043	2150	2253	2353
Mersin.........a.	0645	0736	0754	0824	0929	0946	1040	1113	1145	1218	1245	1306	1415	1525	1555	1646	1734	1758	1900	1915	2017	2100	2211	2319	0015

J – 🍴 Islahiye - Adana - Mersin and v.v.
K – 🍴 Iskenderun - Adana - Mersin and v.v.

1587 AFYON - BURDUR, ISPARTA & DENIZLI `TCDD`

km		71322 H	🚌	🚌			71321 H
	Eskişehir ◇. d.	1540			Denizli....1572 d.		1540
0	Afyon AC ♡...d.	1906	...	...	Goncalı....1572 d.		1552e
114	Karakuyu......d.	2108	...	...	Isparta........d.	0830	
129	Dinar..........d.	2127	1640	1640	Burdur........d.		0830
	Burdur........a.		1740		Dinar..........d.	0930	0930	1749
	Isparta........a.			1740	Karakuyu......d.		1808
254	Goncalı........d.	2327	...	...	Afyon AC ◇...a.		2011
263	Denizli.........a.	2339	...	...	Eskişehir ◇..a.		2340

H – PAMUKKALE EKSPRESİ – 🍴 and ✕ Eskişehir - Denizli and v.v.
e – Goncalı Muselles.
◇ – See Table 1581.
♡ – Afyon Ali Çetinkaya.

1590 ADANA - ALEPPO - DIMASHQ `CFS, TCDD`

All trains in Syria are believed to have been withdrawn.

km		2J	2K			2K	2J
0	Adana.................d.	1835	1900	Dimashq Kadem....d.		...	...
79	Toprakkale............d.	1942	2008	Hims II.............d.		...	...
138	Iskenderun...........d.		2115	Hamah.............d.		...	...
142	Fevzipaşa............d.	2057		Aleppo.............d.		...	...
	Islahiye..............d.	2109		Meydan Ekbez 🚃 d.		...	...
174	Meydan Ekbez 🚃 a.			Islahiye...........a.		0723
274	Aleppo.............a.			Fevzipaşa..........a.		0738
418	Hamäh...............d.			Iskenderun.........d.	0715	...
479	Hims II..............d.			Toprakkale........d.	0822	0857
623	Dimashq Kadem.....a.			Adana..............a.	0929	1001

J – 🍴 Islahiye - Adana - Mersin and v.v.
K – 🍴 Iskenderun - Adana - Mersin and v.v.

Route 32: The Semmering railway

CITIES: ★★★ CULTURE: ★★ HISTORY: ★★ SCENERY: ★★★
COUNTRIES COVERED: AUSTRIA (AT), ITALY (IT)
JOURNEY TIME: 7 HRS | DISTANCE: 620 KM

This is a tremendous journey over one of **Europe's first mountain rail routes** and links two very fine cities: Vienna and Venice. The railway between the two was fostered by imperial ambition, with the Austrian authorities keen to see a rail link between the capital and the country's only major port at Trieste. (For more on Trieste as an important Adriatic outpost of Austrian life and culture see p211). But the notion of building a main-line railway over the rugged Alpine terrain south-west of Vienna was daunting. In 1844 **Carlo Ghega** stepped up to the challenge. Ghega was born in Venice of Albanian parents; as a young engineer he has worked on several early railway projects in Moravia.

The **Semmering Railway** opened in 1854. In 1998, it was inscribed on UNESCO's World Heritage List. The citation commends the route as "one of the greatest feats of civil engineering during the pioneering phase of railway building. Set against a spectacular mountain landscape, the railway line remains in use today thanks to the quality of its tunnels, viaducts, and other works, and has led to the e̶ along its tracks."

A number of other **Alpine**
36) follow routes whic
is different: it was de
heavy passenger train
book for capturing t
comfortable long-dist

Fifty years ago, t
Moscow to Rome ser
over the Semmering,
25). Today, the Semr
from Vienna to Graz
of Styria and Carinth
cities in Italy. And it'

ITINERARY HINTS

This is a journey you'll de
which leaves Vienna ever
train in each direction bet
windows – perfect for sig

There's talk of a **se**
likely that Railjets will be
daytime train leaves Vien

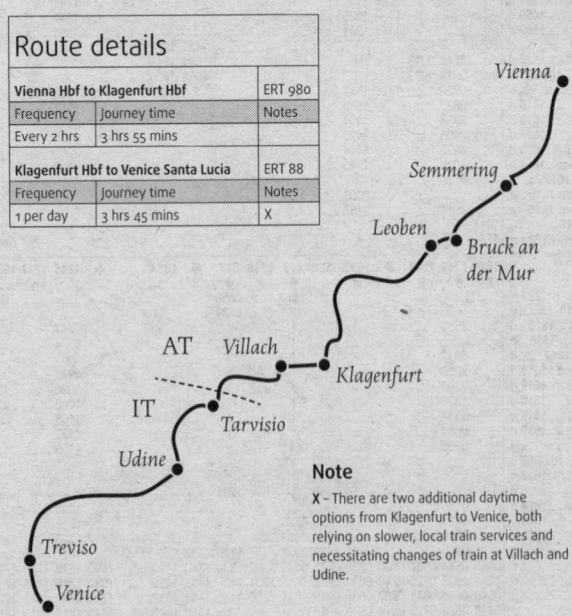

270 | ALPINE ADVENTURES

Route details

Vienna Hbf to Klagenfurt Hbf		ERT 980
Frequency	Journey time	Notes
Every 2 hrs	3 hrs 55 mins	

Klagenfurt Hbf to Venice Santa Lucia		ERT 88
Frequency	Journey time	Notes
1 per day	3 hrs 45 mins	X

Vienna
Semmering
Leoben
Bruck an
der Mur
AT Villach
IT Klagenfurt
Tarvisio
Udine
Treviso
Venice

Note

X – There are two additional daytime options from Klagenfurt to Venice, both relying on slower, local train services and necessitating changes of train at Villach and Udine.

ROMANIA

SEE MAP PAGE 501

Operator: Societatea Naţională de Transport Feroviar de Călători (CFR Călători): www.cfrcalatori.ro. Additionally, Regiotrans, Trans-Feroviar and Softrans operate some services and these are identified in the relevant tables where applicable.

Services: Trains convey 1st- and 2nd-class seating accommodation unless otherwise indicated. Sleeping- (🛏) and couchette (▬) cars are described on page 8. Russian-type sleeping-cars, as used in trains to and from destinations in Belarus, Moldova, Russia and Ukraine, are described on page 530; these cars are not accessible to passengers making journeys wholly within Romania or between Romania and Bulgaria.

Timings: Valid **December 11, 2016 - June 10, 2017** unless stated otherwise. Local services (those shown without a train number) are subject to alteration.

Tickets: Reservation is obligatory for travel by all CFR Călători services for which a train number is shown in the tables, and passengers boarding without a prior reservation are surcharged. Supplements are payable for travel by **Intercity** (*IC*) and most other fast trains. Trains shown without numbers are slow stopping-services calling at all, or most, stations.

♦ – **NOTES for all tables in Romania section** (LISTED BY TRAIN NUMBER)

- **72/3** – TRAIANUS – [12] and ✕ Bucureşti - Arad - Budapest and v.v.
- **74/5** – TRANSILVANIA – [12] Braşov - Budapest and v.v.
- **78/9** – CRIŞ – [12] Budapest - Arad - Timişoara and v.v.; [2] Budapest - Timişoara (**1695/6**) - Bucureşti and v.v.
- **346/7** – DACIA – 🛏 1, 2 cl., ▬ 2 cl., [12] and ✕ Bucureşti - Budapest - Wien and v.v.
- **362/3** – ADY ENDRE – [12] Budapest - Oradea / Cluj Napoca and v.v.
- **366/7** – HARGHITA – [12] and ✕ Braşov - Cluj Napoca - Budapest and v.v.; [2] Târgu Mureş (**4536/7**) - Cluj Napoca - Budapest and v.v.
- **380/1** – [12] Bucureşti - Suceava and v.v.; [2] Bucureşti - Suceava - Vadul Siret and v.v. Conveys 🛏 1, 2 cl. Bucureşti - Suceava - Vadul Siret - Chernivtsi - Kyïv and v.v. on ⑦ from Bucureşti, ⑤ from Kyïv (see Table **1700**).
- **401/2** – PRIETENIA – 🛏 1, 2 cl. and [2] Bucureşti - Ungheni (**106/5**) - Chişinău and v.v.
- **406/7** – CORONA – 🛏 1, 2 cl., ▬ 2 cl. and [12] Budapest - Cluj Napoca - Braşov and v.v.
- **472/3** – ISTER – 🛏 1, 2 cl., ▬ 2 cl., [12] and ✕ Bucureşti - Budapest and v.v.
- **1540/1** – [12] Braşov - Siculeni - Iaşi and v.v.
- **1621/2** – [12] Bucureşti - Sibiu - Timişoara and v.v.
- **1638/9** – 🛏, ▬ and [2] Cluj Napoca - Dej (**1641/2**) - Bucureşti and v.v.
- **1641** – 🛏, ▬ and [12] Bucureşti - Baia Mare; 🛏 and [2] Bucureşti - Sărăţel (**1648**) - Bistriţa; 🛏, ▬ and [2] Bucureşti - Dej (**1639**) - Cluj Napoca; [2] Bucureşti - Baia Mare (**4090**) - Satu Mare; [2] Bucureşti - Deda (**4541**) - Târgu Mureş.
- **1642** – 🛏, ▬ and [12] Baia Mare - Bucureşti; 🛏 and [2] Bistriţa (**1649**) - Sărăţel - Bucureşti; 🛏, ▬ and [2] Cluj Napoca (**1638**) - Dej - Bucureşti; [2] Satu Mare (**4091**) - Baia Mare - Bucureşti.
- **1643** – 🛏, ▬ and [2] Bucureşti - Beclean pe Someş; 🛏, ▬ and [2] Bucureşti - Beclean pe Someş (**4133**) - Sighetu Marmaţiei.
- **1644** – 🛏, ▬ and [2] Beclean pe Someş - Bucureşti; 🛏, ▬ and [2] Sighetu Marmaţiei (**4136**) - Beclean pe Someş - Bucureşti; [2] Târgu Mureş (**4550**) - Deda - Bucureşti.
- **1645** – [12] Bucureşti - Târgu Mureş; [12] Bucureşti - (**1539**) - Cluj Napoca.
- **1646** – [12] Târgu Mureş - Bucureşti.
- **1648/9** – 🛏 and [2] Bucureşti (**1641/2**) - Sărăţel - Bistriţa and v.v.
- **1651** – [12] Bucureşti - Suceava; [2] Bucureşti - Bacău (**5481**) - Bicaz.
- **1652** – [12] Suceava - Bucureşti; [2] Piatra Neamţ (**1858**) - Bacău - Bucureşti.
- **1653/4** – 🛏, ▬ and [12] Bucureşti - Suceava - Vatra Dornei Băi and v.v.
- **1659** – [12] Bucureşti - Suceava; [2] Bucureşti - Bacău (**1859**) - Piatra Neamţ.
- **1695/6** – 🛏, ▬ and [12] Bucureşti - Timişoara and v.v.; [2] Bucureşti - Timişoara (**78/9**) - Budapest and v.v.; [2] Bucureşti - Caransebeş (**9161/70**) - Reşiţa Sud and v.v.
- **1736/7** – [12] Râmnicu Vâlcea - Sibiu - Cluj Napoca and v.v.
- **1741** – 🛏, ▬, [12] and 🍷 Bucureşti - Cluj Napoca - Oradea - Satu Mare.
- **1742** – 🛏, ▬, [12] and 🍷 Satu Mare - Oradea - Cluj Napoca - Bucureşti.
- **1743/4** – [12] Timişoara - Arad - Oradea - Baia Mare and v.v.
- **1754** – 🛏, ▬ and [12] Suceava - Bucureşti; [2] Bicaz (**5482**) - Bacău - Bucureşti.
- **1765** – ▬ and [12] Iaşi - Cluj Napoca - Timişoara; [2] Sighetu Marmaţiei (**4136**) - Timişoara.
- **1766** – ▬ and [12] Timişoara - Cluj Napoca - Iaşi.
- **1821/2** – 🛏, ▬ and [12] Arad - Craiova - Bucureşti - Constanţa and v.v.
- **1824** – [12] Deva - Târgu Jiu - Craiova - Bucureşti.
- **1829** – [12] Bucureşti (**1835**) - Simeria - Deva.
- **1831/2** – [12] Galaţi - Iaşi - Cluj Napoca and v.v.
- **1833/4** – [12] Iaşi - Cluj Napoca - Oradea - Timişoara and v.v.
- **1835** – [12] Bucureşti - Târgu Jiu - Cluj Napoca; [12] Bucureşti - Simeria (**1829**) - Deva.
- **1836** – [12] Cluj Napoca - Târgu Jiu - Bucureşti.
- **1837/8** – 🛏, ▬ and [12] Iaşi - Cluj Napoca - Timişoara and v.v.
- **1843** – [12] Timişoara - Beclean pe Someş; [2] Timişoara - Beclean pe Someş (**4135**) - Sighetu Marmaţiei.
- **1856/7** – [2] Suceava Nord - Mărăşeşti (**1861/2**) - Constanţa and v.v.
- **1861/2** – [12] Iaşi - Constanţa and v.v.; [2] Suceava Nord - Mărăşeşti (**1856/7**) - Constanţa and v.v.
- **4090/1** – [2] Bucureşti (**1641/2**) - Baia Mare - Satu Mare and v.v.
- **4133** – 🛏, ▬ and [2] Bucureşti (**1643**) - Beclean pe Someş - Sighetu Marmaţiei.
- **4135** – [2] Timişoara (**1843**) - Beclean pe Someş - Sighetu Marmaţiei.
- **4136** – 🛏, ▬ and [2] Sighetu Marmaţiei - Beclean pe Someş (**1644**) - Bucureşti; [2] Sighetu Marmaţiei (**1765**) - Timişoara.
- **4541/50** – [2] Bucureşti (**1641/4**) - Deda - Târgu Mureş and v.v.
- **9161/70** – [2] Bucureşti (**1695/6**) - Caransebeş - Reşiţa Sud and v.v.

★ – Train runs in summer only (2016 times shown). 2017 schedules to be confirmed.

♣ – Operated by Regiotrans. § – Operated by Transferoviar Grup SA.
□ – Operated by Softrans S.R.L. • – Subject to cancellation for scheduled maintenance.

1600 BUCUREŞTI - BRAŞOV - SIBIU and CLUJ NAPOCA

km		74 ♦	1737 ♦	2•	♣⑥ 2T	1745	1631	1636	1732 g	♣ 2	1621 ♦	2	♣ 2	1645 ♦	1539	1937 ★	346 ♦	1527	1633 w	♣ 2	472 ♦	1643 ♦		1741 ♦	1945 ★	1931 ★	1641 ♦	♣ 2
	Constanţa **1680** d.	...	...	...	...	...	...	0530	...	...	...	...	...	...	...	1030	...	...	...	...	...	...	...	...	1715	1745	...	...
0	**Bucureşti** Nord d.	...	...	...	...	0600	0700	0822	...	0850	1000	...	1145	1215	...	1315	1400	1510	1645	1723	1745	1800	...	1845	1940b	2045	2055	2107
59	Ploieşti Vest d.	...	...	...	...	0643	0742	0904	0929	0957	1048	...	1236	1258	...	1358	1440	1553	1735	1829	1825	1846	...	1930	2028	2132	2137	2204
92	Câmpina d.	...	...	...	...	0708	0807	0927	0955	1036	1113	...	1311	1322	...	|	|	1620	1759	1903	|	1911	...	1955	2055	2157	2204	2238
121	Sinaia d.	...	...	...	...	0739	0833	0953	1020	1117	1140	...	1359	1348	...	1445	1526	1646	1826	1954	1909	1940	...	2021	2122	2225	2228	2319
140	Predeal d.	...	...	...	...	0805	0900	1022	1047	1144	1208	...	1428	1417	...	1509	1548	1714	1853	2022	1933	2006	...	2050	2148	2252	2254	2346
166	**Braşov** a.	...	...	...	...	0842	0937	1100	1124	1223	1245	...	1507	1457	...	1545	1625	1752	1930	2102	2010	2042	...	2127	2226	2329	2331	0025
166	**Braşov** d.	0545	...	0612	0730	0851	...	...	...	...	1300	1430	...	...	1505	...	1637	1804	...	...	2019	...	...	2137	2238	2343	2343	...
294	Sighişoara **1669** d.	|	...	|	1006	1134	...	...	...	...	|	|	...	...	1741	...	|	|	...	...	2252	...	...	0023	|	0216	|	...
332	Mediaş **1669** d.	|	...	|	1120	1225	...	...	...	...	|	|	...	...	1831	...	|	|	...	...	2343	...	...	0123	|	0312	|	...
343	Copşa Mică **1669** d.	|	...	|	1141	1241	...	...	...	...	|	|	...	...	1851	...	|	|	...	...	|	...	...	0137	|	0328	|	...
	Făgăraş d.	0656	...	0805	|	|	...	...	...	...	1421	1628	...	...	|	...	1750	1942	...	...	|	...	...	|	|	|	|	...
	Podu Olt **1622** d.	|	0546	0943	|	|	...	...	...	...	1521	1745	...	...	|	...	|	2100	...	...	|	...	...	|	|	|	|	...
	Sibiu **1622/69** a.	0821	0618	1022	|	|	...	...	...	...	1555	1830	...	...	|	...	1915	2140	...	...	|	...	...	|	|	|	|	...
373	Blaj d.	|	0759	...	1238	1321	...	...	...	...	...	...	...	...	1928	...	|	...	...	...	0034	...	...	0216	◐	0411	◐	...
394	Teiuş **1610** d.	|	0826	...	...	1350	...	...	...	...	...	...	...	...	1957	...	|	...	...	...	|	...	...	0251	|	0442	|	...
407	Aiud **1610** d.	|	0838	...	...	1404	...	...	...	...	...	...	...	...	2011	...	|	...	...	...	|	...	...	0307	|	0454	|	...
427	Războieni **1610** d.	|	0905	...	...	1426	...	...	...	...	...	...	...	...	2035	...	|	...	...	...	|	...	...	0331	|	0513	|	...
444	Câmpia Turzii **1610** d.	|	0922	...	...	1444	...	...	...	...	...	...	...	...	2052	...	|	...	...	...	|	...	...	0347	|	0529	|	...
496	**Cluj Napoca** **1610** a.	|	1020	...	...	1540	...	...	...	...	...	...	...	...	2149	...	|	...	...	...	|	...	...	0443	|	0624	|	...
	Oradea **1612** a.	|	...	...	...	|	...	...	...	...	...	...	...	...	...	...	|	...	...	...	|	...	...	0750	|	0930	|	...
	Baia Mare **1616** a.	|	...	...	...	2008	...	...	...	...	...	...	...	...	...	...	|	...	...	...	|	...	...	|	|	...	0930	...
	Satu Mare **1616** a.	|	...	...	...	2157	...	...	...	...	...	...	...	...	...	...	|	...	...	...	|	...	...	1006	1014	...	1122	...
	Arad **1610** a.	1411	...	...	...	...	...	...	...	...	...	...	...	...	...	...	0106	...	...	...	0515	...	...	...	...	...	...	...
	Budapest K **1280** a.	1750	...	...	...	...	...	...	...	...	...	...	...	...	...	...	0450	...	...	...	0850	...	...	...	...	...	...	...

km		1630	1742 ♦x	1644 ♦	♣ 2	1632 w	1526	473 ♦	1936 ★	347 ♦	♣ 2	1634		♣ 2	1746	1731 g	1635	①–⑤ 2	1622 ♦	1646 ♦	⑥⑦ 2	1538	♣⑦ 2T	1736 ♦	75 ♦	1944 ★	1642 ♦	1932 ★
	Budapest K **1280** d.	...	...	...	...	...	...	1910	...	2250	...	...	...	...	...	...	...	...	...	...	...	...	...	...	0910	...	...	...
	Arad **1610** d.	...	...	...	...	...	...	0041	...	0434	...	...	...	...	...	...	...	...	...	...	...	...	...	...	1444	...	...	...
	Satu Mare **1616** d.	...	1650	...	...	...	...	|	...	|	...	...	...	...	0347	...	...	...	...	...	...	...	...	...	|	1330	1610	...
	Baia Mare **1616** d.	...	|	...	...	...	...	|	...	|	...	...	...	...	0524	...	...	...	...	...	...	...	...	...	|	|	1820	...
	Oradea **1612** d.	...	1912	...	...	...	...	|	...	|	...	...	...	...	|	...	...	...	...	...	...	...	...	...	|	|	|	1839
	Cluj Napoca **1610** d.	...	2209	...	...	...	...	|	...	|	...	...	...	...	0930	...	...	...	...	...	...	1330	...	1600	|	|	|	2140
	Câmpia Turzii **1610** d.	...	2306	...	...	...	...	|	...	|	...	...	...	...	1026	...	...	...	...	...	...	1426	...	1654	|	|	|	2234
	Războieni **1610** d.	...	2326	...	...	...	...	|	...	|	...	...	...	...	1046	...	...	...	...	...	...	1446	...	1717	|	|	|	2253
	Aiud **1610** d.	...	2347	...	...	...	...	|	...	|	...	...	...	...	1108	...	...	...	...	...	...	1506	...	1737	|	|	|	2312
	Teiuş **1610** d.	...	0004	...	...	...	...	|	...	|	...	...	...	...	1127	...	...	...	...	...	...	1525	...	1753	|	|	|	2331
	Blaj d.	...	0035	...	...	...	...	0516	...	|	...	...	...	...	1156	...	...	...	...	...	...	1553	1612	1817	|	◐	◐	0003
0	**Sibiu** **1622/69** d.	...	|	...	...	...	0500	|	...	1032	...	...	1154	...	|	...	...	1440	1513	...	1540	|	|	2007	2026	|	|	|
22	Podu Olt **1622** d.	...	|	...	...	...	0534	|	...	|	...	...	1232	...	|	...	...	1530	1547	...	1615	|	|	2041	|	|	|	|
84	Făgăraş d.	...	|	...	...	...	0658	|	...	1201	...	...	1415	...	|	...	...	1702	1649	...	1829	|	|	...	2159	|	|	|
	Copşa Mică **1669** d.	...	0110	...	...	...	|	|	...	|	...	...	|	...	1240	...	...	|	|	...	|	1631	1709	...	|	|	|	0045
	Mediaş **1669** d.	...	0124	...	...	...	|	0606	...	|	...	...	|	...	1256	...	...	|	|	...	|	1647	1730	...	|	|	|	0104
	Sighişoara **1669** d.	...	0218	...	...	...	|	0659	...	|	...	...	|	...	1348	...	...	|	|	...	|	1739	1843	...	|	|	|	0203
149	**Braşov** a.	...	0500	...	...	...	0830	0932	...	1316	...	...	1551	...	1627	...	...	1838	1818	...	2002	2009	2110	...	2310	0100	0319	0437
	Braşov d.	0445	0514	0537	0700	0735	0845	0941	1200	1330	1340	1415	...	1600	1640	1740	1720	...	1830	1900	...	2018	...	...	...	0115	0331	0450
	Predeal d.	0521	0602	0620	0740	0812	0922	1018	1234	1407	1418	1450	...	1639	1716	1816	1756	...	1906	1935	...	2054	...	...	...	0200	0413	0530
	Sinaia d.	0546	0630	0648	0807	0838	0949	1041	1255	1430	1444	1517	...	1706	1740	1842	1824	...	1934	2001	...	2121	...	...	...	0228	0435	0558
	Câmpina d.	0618	0659	0722	0846	0910	1018	|	|	|	1522	1549	...	1748	1815	1910	1852	...	2004	2029	...	2148	...	...	...	0256	0503	0627
	Ploieşti Vest d.	0647	0726	0749	0926	0935	1043	1131	1344	1520	1600	1617	...	1824	1842	1934	1917	...	2031	2054	...	2214	...	...	...	0323	0531	0653
	Bucureşti Nord a.	0730	0810	0833	1029	1021	1125	1210	1425	1600	1649	1703	...	1922	1925	...	1959	...	2117	2136	...	2254	...	...	...	0418b	0613	0735
	Constanţa **1680** a.	...	...	...	...	...	...	...	1740	...	...	...	...	...	...	...	2248	...	...	...	...	...	...	...	...	0654	...	1104

T – From / to Timişoara (Table **1610**).
b – Bucureşti **Băneasa**.
g – From / to Galaţi via Ploieşti Sud (Table **1660**).
w – Not June 10 - Sept. 10.
x – Not June 9 - Sept. 9.
◐ – Via Miercurea Ciuc (Table **1630**).
For notes ♦, ★, ♣, §, □ and • see heading.

CLUJ NAPOCA and SIBIU - DEVA - ARAD and TIMIŞOARA 1610

km		1765		1811	1821	1837				1836	74						1621			1736	1819	346						472
		♦	2		♦k	♦	2	2	2	♦	♦	2	2	♣ 2⑥	2	2	♦	2	2	♦		♦	2		2	2	2	♦
0	**Cluj Napoca** 1600 d.	0040	...	...	...	0444	0530	...	...	0702	...	...	...	...	...	1207	...	...	1445	1600	...	...	...	...	...	1945	...	...
52	Câmpia Turzii 1600 d.	0135	...	...	...	0539	0640	...	...	0759	...	...	...	...	...	1317	...	...	1600	1654	...	...	...	...	...	2055	...	...
	Târgu Mureş d.	|	...	...	...	|	|	...	0303	|	...	0710	...	...	...	|	...	1438	|	|	1620	...	1735	...	1920	|	2220	...
	Luduş d.	|	...	...	...	|	|	...	0417	|	...	0816	...	...	...	|	...	1545	|	|	1713	...	1846	...	2036	|	2330	...
69	Războieni 1600 d.	0154	...	...	...	0559	0703	...	0448	0819	...	0843	...	...	...	1340	...	1610	1624	1717	1741	...	1912	...	2105	2118	2358	...
90	Aiud 1600 d.	0215	...	...	...	0621	0728	...	0516	0840	...	...	...	...	...	1407	...	...	...	1737	1803	...	1935	...	...	2149	...	...
103	Teiuş 1600 d.	0232	...	...	...	0637	0745	...	0534	0856	...	...	...	...	...	1421	...	...	...	1753	1819	...	1949	...	...	2204	...	...
	Bucureşti Nord 1600 d.	|	...	...	2345	|	|	...	|	|	...	...	...	...	...	...	1000	...	...	|	|	1400	...	...	...	...	...	1745
	Braşov 1600 d.	|	...	...	|	|	|	...	|	|	0545	...	...	0730	...	...	1300	...	...	|	|	1637	...	...	...	...	...	2019
83∆	**Sibiu** d.	|	...	0330	|	|	|	...	0948	|	0824	...	...	|	...	...	1603	...	...	2000	|	1920	...	...	...	...	...	|
9∆	Sebeş Alba d.	|	...	0510	▽	|	|	...	...	|	0956	...	...	|	...	...	1738	...	...	...	|	|	...	...	...	...	...	|
122	**Alba Iulia** d.	0301	...	|	|	0709	0828	...	...	0929	|	...	...	1342	...	...	|	...	...	...	1852	|	...	...	...	...	...	0125
132	Vinţu de Jos d.	0313	...	0521	|	0722	0846	...	...	0944	1008	...	...	1400	...	...	1750	...	...	...	1905	2107	...	...	...	...	...	|
176	Simeria 1625 d.	0424	0620	0626	0744	0838	1007	1014	...	1052	1121	...	1240	1518	1543	...	1911	...	...	...	2015	2225	...	...	...	...	...	0240
185	Deva 1625 d.	0438	0632	0639	0758	0851	1019	1027	...	...	1136	...	1254	1528	1557	...	1925	...	...	...	2029	2239	...	...	...	...	...	0254
208	Ilia d.	0511	0715	0712	0830	0921	...	1100	...	...	1208	...	1328	1552	1631	...	1956	...	...	...	2102	|	...	...	...	...	...	|
298	Radna d.	0638	0913	|	0956	|	...	1245	...	...	1336	...	1518	1700	1816	...	2123	...	...	...	|	|	...	...	...	...	...	|
333	**Arad** a.	0712	0955	|	1030	|	...	1325	...	...	1411	...	1559	1730	1856	...	2156	...	...	...	|	0106	...	...	...	...	...	0515
	Budapest Keleti 1280 a.	|	...	|	...	|	...	...	...	...	1750	...	...	|	...	...	|	...	...	...	|	0450	...	...	...	...	...	0850
291	Lugoj 1620 a.	|	...	0845	...	1113	...	...	...	...	...	...	...	|	...	...	|	...	...	...	2244	...	...	...	...	...	...	...
355	**Timişoara** Nord 1620 a.	0835	...	0952	...	1219	...	...	...	...	...	...	...	1845	...	...	2310	...	...	...	2350	...	...	...	...	...	...	...

			1737		347			1820		1622					75	1766			1812		1838	1822			1835	1843	473	
		2	♦	2Ⓐ	♦	2•	2		2	♦		♣ 2⑦	2	2	♦	♦	2	2		2	♦	♦j	2	2	♦	♦	♦	
	Timişoara Nord 1620 d.	...	...	...	...	...	...	0733	...	0745	...	0954	...	...	...	1350	1351	...	1601	...	1800	...	...	...	...	2140	...	...
	Lugoj 1620 d.	...	...	...	...	...	...	0847	...	|	...	|	...	...	...	|	|	...	1709	...	1906	...	...	...	...	|	...	...
	Budapest Keleti 1280 d.	...	...	...	2250	...	...	|	...	|	...	|	...	...	0910	|	|	...	|	...	|	...	...	...	...	|	1910	...
	Arad d.	...	...	...	0434	...	0748	|	...	0907	...	1104	...	...	1444	1512	1521	...	|	1638	|	1930	1814	1956	...	2228n	0041	...
	Radna d.	...	...	...	|	...	0829	|	...	0941	...	1136	...	...	1517	1549	1602	...	|	1719	|	2005	1900	2037	...	2309	|	...
	Ilia d.	...	...	...	|	...	1015	1024	...	1104	...	1249	...	...	1639	1713	1755	...	1840	1914	2037	2127	2128	2252	...	0031	|	...
	Deva 1625 d.	...	...	...	0656	...	1049	1054	...	1135	...	1313	1415	...	1713	1746	1833	...	1909	1947	2105	2157	2204	2326	...	0102	0259	...
	Simeria 1625 d.	...	...	...	0721	...	1102	1111	...	1200	...	1326	1429	...	1741	1812	1846	...	1925	2000	2129	2210	2217	2339	0034	0116	0320	...
	Vinţu de Jos d.	...	...	...	0833	...	...	1214	...	1313	...	1441	1545	...	1838	1921	...	...	2035	...	2227	|	...	...	0137	0222	|	...
	Alba Iulia d.	...	...	...	|	...	...	1228	...	|	...	1458	1602	...	|	1935	...	...	|	...	2240	|	...	...	0151	0236	0426	...
	Sebeş Alba d.	...	...	...	|	...	...	|	...	1325	...	|	|	...	1849	|	...	...	2050	...	|	▽	...	...	|	|	|	...
	Sibiu a.	...	0618	...	1023	...	...	|	...	1505	...	|	|	1553	2026	|	...	...	2233	...	|	|	...	...	|	|	|	...
	Braşov 1600 a.	...	|	...	1316	...	...	|	...	1818	...	2110	|	|	2310	|	...	...	...	...	|	|	...	...	|	|	0932	...
	Bucureşti Nord 1600 a.	...	|	...	1600	...	...	|	...	2117	...	...	|	|	...	|	...	...	...	...	|	0600	...	...	|	|	1210	...
	Teiuş 1600 d.	0630	0826	1050	...	...	...	1304	1423	...	...	...	1640	1914	...	2009	...	1950	...	...	2310	...	...	...	0224	0323	...	...
	Aiud 1600 d.	0642	0838	1101	...,	...	...	1320	1434	...	...	...	1651	1925	...	2022	...	2002	...	...	2323	...	...	...	0236	0335	...	...
	Războieni 1600 d.	0707	0905	1129	...	1146	...	1344	1500	...	1638	...	1714	2005	...	2045	...	2029	...	...	2347	...	...	...	0257	0356	...	...
	Luduş d.	0735	|	|	...	1214	...	1410	|	...	1708	...	|	2035	...	|	...	|	...	...	|	...	...	...	|	|	...	...
	Târgu Mureş a.	0847	|	|	...	1328	...	1454	|	...	1815	...	|	2139	...	|	...	|	...	...	|	...	...	...	|	|	...	...
	Câmpia Turzii 1600 d.	...	0922	1150	...	...	...	...	1519	...	...	...	1733	...	...	2103	...	2048	...	...	0003	...	...	...	0314	0412	...	...
	Cluj Napoca 1600 a.	...	1020	1309	...	...	...	...	1633	...	...	...	1849	...	...	2158	...	2158	...	...	0057	...	...	...	0414	0505	...	...

– Not Apr. 27-30, June 9 - Sept. 9.
k – Not Apr. 28 - May 1, June 10 - Sept. 10.
n – Aradu **Nou**.
▽ – Via Craiova and Târgu Jiu (Table **1625**).
∆ – Distance from Vinţu de Jos.
For notes ♦, ♣, §, □ and • see page 518.

CLUJ NAPOCA - ORADEA 1612

km		406	1741	1531	1931	362			1533	366	1833		1535
		♦	♦	ⒷT	★	♦	§	⚒§		♦	♦	§	
	Bucureşti N 1600 d.	...	1845	...	2045	...	...	...	...	...	...	...	...
	Braşov 1600/35 d.	1850	2137	...	2343	...	...	...	...	0703	...	...	...
0	**Cluj Napoca** d.	0225	0457	0545	0640	0644	0731	0912	1336	1444	1549	1621	2023
50	Huedin d.	0317	0552	0637	0737	0737	0832	1010	1436	1540	1647	1718	2115
153	**Oradea** a.	0457	0750	0825	0930	0920	1045	1228	1624	1729	1844	1943	2315
	Budapest K 1275 a.	0920	...	...	...	1320	...	...	...	2120	...	...	...

		1532	1834	367		1534	1742	1932	363	1536	407
	⚒§		♦	♦	§	Ⓑ	♦	★	♦	T	♦
Budapest K 1275 d.	...	...	...	0645	...	...	...	...	1340	...	1740
Oradea d.	0500	0600	0955	1313	1521	1712	1912	1839	1949	2019	2330
Huedin d.	0706	0752	1146	1458	1745	1853	2101	2031	2136	2213	0120
Cluj Napoca a.	0802	0842	1237	1550	1842	1948	2154	2124	2228	2302	0211
Braşov 1600/35 a.	...	...	...	2338	...	...	0500	0437	...	...	0942
Bucureşti N 1600 a.	...	...	...	...	...	...	0810	0735	...	...	...

– From/to Timişoara (Table **1614**).
For notes ♦, ★, ♣, §, □ and • see page 518.
Additional services **Cluj Napoca - Oradea and v.v.**:
From Cluj Napoca: 0213, 0740, 1640Ⓑ. From Oradea: 0247, 0730, 1530Ⓑ.

ORADEA - ARAD - TIMIŞOARA 1614

km		1744			1531	369	73			79	1833	
		m	2	2⚒	Ⓑ	P2	♦	2	2	♦	♦	2
	Cluj Napoca 1612 d.	...	...	...	0545	...	...	...	...	...	1549	...
0	**Oradea** d.	0435	0505	0740	0829	0956	...	...	1600	...	1848	1954
39	Salonta d.	0517	0553	0835	0915	1038	...	...	1648	...	1935	2103
21	**Arad** a.	0639	0738	1020	1038	...	...	...	1849	...	2100	2253
21	**Arad** 1669 d.	0646	0751	...	1041	...	1246	1625	1902	2044	2116	2330j
78	**Timişoara** Nord 1669 a.	0743	0921	...	1131	...	1333	1747	2017	2133	2216	0049j

		1834	78	368		72	1743	1536			
	2	♦	♦	P2	2	♦	m		2	2	
Timişoara N. 1669 d.	0518	0633	0730	...	1303	1438	1550	1715	1735	2019	...
Arad 1669 a.	0644	0733	0818	...	1411	1528	1645	1807	1851	2137	...
Arad d.	0656	0748	...	...	1425	...	1655	1812	1906	...	...
Salonta d.	0834	0914	...	1342	1607	...	1819	1934	2102	...	...
Oradea a.	0927	0953	...	1426	1702	...	1906	2016	2149	...	...
Cluj Napoca 1612 a.	...	1237	...	...	...	...	...	2302	...	...	...

– From/to Püspökladány (Table **1275**).
– (12) Timişoara - Arad - Budapest and v.v. (Table **1280**).
j – Not nights of ⑤/⑥ and ⑥/⑦.
m – From/to Baia Mare (Table **1618**).
For Cluj - Timişoara via Teiuş see Table **1610**.
For notes ♦, ♣, §, □ and • see page 518.

CLUJ NAPOCA - BAIA MARE - SATU MARE 1616

km			1741	1945	1641 4090				1546	1745	1544	1744
		D2	♦	★	♦	2	2	2			Ⓐ	♦
	Bucureşti N 1600 d.	...	1845	1940b	2055	...	...	...	...	0600	...	...
	Braşov 1600 d.	...	2137	2238	2343	...	...	...	...	0851	...	...
0	**Cluj Napoca** d.	...	0457	▽	▽	0535	...	1410	1410	1555	1820	...
59	Dej Călători d.	...	|	0546	0645	0720	...	1528	1528	1722	1941	...
35	Jibou d.	0301	△	0726	0825	0857	...	1708	1714	1844	2121	...
93	**Baia Mare** a.	0400	|	0835	0930	...	...	1818	|	2008	2223	...
93	**Baia Mare** 1669 d.	0414	|	0850	0948	...	1545	...	|	2022	...	0100
52	**Satu Mare** 1669 a.	0605	1006	1014	1122	...	1724	...	1945	2157	...	0220

	1746			1545		1944	1543	4091 1642	1742		1743
		2Ⓐ	2		2	★	⑦	♦	♦x	D2	♦
Satu Mare 1669 d.	0347	0512	...	0733	0743	1330	...	1610	1650	1953	2119
Baia Mare 1669 a.	0510	0707	...	|	0934	1452	...	1802	|	2203	2241
Baia Mare d.	0524	...	0845	|	...	1507	1702	1820	|	2247	...
Jibou d.	0639	...	1019	1019	...	1618	1824	1933	△	2358	...
Dej Călători d.	0811	...	1149	1149	...	1745	2001	2110	|	...	...
Cluj Napoca a.	0918	...	1253	1253	...	▽	2109	▽	2154	...	...
Braşov 1600 a.	1627	...	...	...	...	0100	...	0319	0500	...	...
Bucureşti N 1600 a.	1925	...	...	...	...	0418b	...	0613	0810	...	...

– From/to Debrecen (Table **1277**).
b – Bucureşti **Băneasa**.
x – Not June 9 - Sept. 9.
△ – Via Oradea (Tables **1612**/**1618**).
▽ – Via Miercurea Ciuc (Table **1630**).
For notes ♦, ★, ♣, §, □ and • see page 518.

ORADEA - CAREI - SATU MARE 1618

km		①–⑥	1741			1546				1743	
		2	♦	2	D2		2	D	D2	♦	2
0	**Oradea** d.	0310	0802	0750	...	...	1536	...	1635	1914	1937
66	Valea lui Mihai d.	0441	0910	0919	1138	...	1719	1757	1837	2019	2127
97	Carei d.	0518	0936	...	1214	1916	1756	1840	...	2043	2200
33	**Satu Mare** a.	0602	1006	...	1256	1945	1838	1925	...	2112	2239
	Baia Mare 1616 a.	...	...	...	...	...	...	2203	...	2241	...

	1744	⚒		1545					1742	
	♦	2	D2		2	D2	D2	2	♦x	2
Baia Mare 1616 d.	0100	...	0414	...	...	...	...	...	...	...
Satu Mare d.	0225	0327	0620	0733	0740	...	1500	1543	1650	2000
Carei d.	0257	0359	0708	0803	0837	...	1543	1625	1725	2045
Valea lui Mihai d.	0322	0432	0837	...	0928	0943	1637	1731	1752	2123
Oradea a.	0426	0555	...	...	...	1118	...	1855	1900	2247

– From/to Debrecen (Table **1277**).
x – Not June 9 - Sept. 9.
For notes ♦, ♣, §, □ and • see page 518.

1620 BUCUREŞTI - CRAIOVA - TIMISOARA

km		1821	1698		1991	1999		72	1591		1823		1521	1691	1599	1697	1595		1825	1693	1835	1593	1597		1695	1695 9161
		♦k	2Ⓐ	2	★	★		♦		2	2T	2		2		⚒		2⚒	T		♦	w	2		♦p	♦
0	**Bucureşti** Nord d.	2345	...	...	0010b	0010b	...	0545	0630	0748	0845	...	0930	1045	1215	...	1350	...	1445	1545	1625	1741	1945	...	2125	2125
51	Videle d.	0036	...	...	0105	0105	...	0638	0723	0900	0945	...	1020	1136	1316	...	1446	...	1536	1636	1715	1836	2035	...	2218	2218
100	Roşiori Nord d.	0120	...	...	0148	0148	...	0718	0807	1002	1037	...	1105	1220	1419	...	1530	...	1620	1720	1800	1920	2122	...	2305	2305
155	Caracal d.	0210	...	...	0237	0237	...	0804	0852	1106	1132	...	1153	1308	1515	...	1616	...	1710	1806	1848	2008	2210	...	2352	2352
209	**Craiova** a.	0250	...	...	0318	0318	...	0845	0932	1210	1218	...	...	1348	1601	...	1655	...	1750	1847	1928	2048	2250	...	0035	0035
209	**Craiova** **1625** d.	0300	...	...	0330	0330	...	0855	0935	▬	1222	1232	...	1355	...	...	▬	...	1755	1855	1935	...	...	...	0045	0045
245	Filiaşi **1625** d.	0328	...	...	|	|	...	0924	1003	...	1251	1320	...	1424	...	...	2⑦	...	1823	1924	2002	...	...	...	0114	0114
323	Drobeta Turnu Severin d.	...	...	...	0530	0530	...	1050	1129	...	...	1516	...	1557	...	1750	1750	1819	...	2050	...	...	...	...	0244	0244
347	Orşova d.	...	...	...	0600	0600	...	1118	...	...	...	1543	...	1624	...	1817	1817	1847	...	2119	...	...	...	...	0315	0315
364	Băile Herculane d.	...	...	...	0624	0624	...	1142	...	2	...	...	...	1651	...	1843	1843	1914	...	2144	...	...	...	...	0340	0340
435	Caransebeş d.	...	0638	0740	0802	0815	...	1302	...	1314	...	...	...	1811	...	2055	2023	2139	...	2305	...	...	...	...	0510	0542
	Reşiţa Sud **1669** a.	...	0515r	|	|	0910	...	|	...	|	...	...	...	|	...	|	|	|	...	|	...	...	...	...	|	0702
474	Lugoj **1610** d.	...	0708	0838	0834	...	...	1330	...	1400	...	...	...	1839	...	2122	2050	2226	...	2335	...	...	...	...	0540	...
533	**Timişoara** Nord **1610** a.	...	0805	0953	0940	...	...	1428	...	1530	...	...	...	1937	...	2228	2157	2344	...	0033	...	...	...	...	0646	...

		1826	1692	1824	1596		1522	1590	1836			1694	73				1699			1998	1992	1822	1592	1594	1696	9170 1696
	2	T		♦	2		R		♦	2	2		♦	2	2		2Ⓐ	2	2	★	★	♦j	2	w	♦q	♦
Timişoara Nord **1610** d.	...	...	0530	...	...	...	...	...	...	...	1251	1300	1355	...	1425	...	1622	1627	1918	...	1902	...	...	...	2230	...
Lugoj **1610** d.	...	...	0630	...	...	...	...	...	...	...	1416	1421	1501	...	1542	...	1723	1758	2050	...	2009	...	...	...	2334	...
Reşiţa Sud **1669** d.	...	...	|	...	...	...	...	...	...	...	|	|	|	...	|	...	1911r	|	|	1921	|	...	...	...	|	2230
Caransebeş d.	...	...	0658	...	...	...	...	...	...	...	1458	1450	1528	←	1626	...	1812	1843	2134	2053	2053	...	...	...	0020	0020
Băile Herculane d.	...	...	0820	...	...	...	...	...	...	...	1704	1620	1650	1704	...	...	...	...	...	2229	2229	...	...	...	0144	0144
Orşova d.	...	...	0843	...	...	...	...	...	...	1602	→	1650	1713	1732	...	...	...	...	...	2253	2253	...	...	...	0209	0209
Drobeta Turnu Severin d.	0420	...	0910	...	...	...	...	1426	...	1642	...	1715	1740	1759	...	...	...	...	...	2332	2332	...	...	...	0245	0245
Filiaşi **1625** d.	0617	0644	1041	1154	...	...	...	1552	1625	1847	...	...	1903	...	...	...	...	...	...	|	|	0221	...	...	0420	0420
Craiova **1625** a.	0706	0711	1107	1220	...	...	...	1618	1655	1945	...	...	1930	...	...	...	...	...	...	0133	0133	0247	...	...	0449	0449
Craiova d.	...	0715	1115	1228	1410	...	...	1624	1710	...	...	...	1940	...	...	...	...	...	...	0145	0145	0256	0305	0430	0500	0500
Caracal d.	...	0754	1152	1310	1450	...	1632	1705	1805	...	...	...	2018	...	...	...	...	...	...	0223	0223	0335	0351	0508	0545	0545
Roşiori Nord d.	...	0845	1240	1400	1538	...	1721	1750	1900	...	...	...	2102	...	...	...	...	...	...	0310	0310	0423	0450	0600	0635	0635
Videle d.	...	0934	1330	1449	1627	...	1816	1840	1956	...	...	...	2150	...	...	...	...	...	...	0357	0357	0512	0547	0653	0725	0725
Bucureşti Nord a.	...	1028	1418	1544	1724	...	1905	1940	2047	...	...	...	2238	...	...	...	...	...	...	0456b	0456b	0600	0648	0744	0822	0822

R – From / to Râmnicu Vâlcea (Table **1622**).
T – From / to Târgu Jiu (Table **1625**).
b – Bucureşti **Băneasa**.
j – Not Apr. 27 - 30, June 9 - Sept. 9.
k – Not Apr. 28 - May 1, June 10 - Sept. 10.
p – Apr. 28 - May 1.
q – Apr. 27 - 30.
r – Via Caransebeş.
w – Not June 10 - Sept. 10.

For notes ♦, ★, ♣, §, □ and • see page 518.

1621 BUCUREŞTI - PITESTI - CRAIOVA

km		1891	1781	1783	1893	1785	1895	1787	1897	1789	1791	1793	1922 ★
0	**Bucureşti** Nord d.	0607	0730	0930	1330	1430	1530	1630	1730	1830	1930	2030	2312
108	Piteşti d.	0815	0928	1132	1538	1630	1735	1833	1938	2025	2125	2225	0140
189	Slatina d.	0939	...	...	1650	...	1858	...	2052	...	...	...	0255
206	Piatra Olt **1622** d.	1001	...	...	1715	...	1920	...	2114	...	...	...	0314
250	**Craiova** **1622** a.	1049	...	...	1832	...	2010	...	2202	...	...	...	...

	1780	1782	1890	1892	1784	1786	1788	1894	1790	1792	1896	1921 ★
Craiova **1622** d.	...	...	0425	0725	...	...	...	1225	...	...	1625	...
Piatra Olt **1622** d.	...	...	0514	0814	...	...	...	1316	...	...	1714	2245
Slatina d.	...	...	0535	0835	...	...	...	1337	...	...	1735	2308
Piteşti d.	0500	0600	0700	1000	1100	1300	1400	1500	1600	1700	1900	0055
Bucureşti Nord a.	0640	0740	0840	1140	1234	1440	1540	1634	1740	1850	2034	0228

For notes ♦, ★, ♣, §, □ and • see page 518.

1622 SIBIU - RÂMNICU VÂLCEA - CRAIOVA

km		1722		1720			1522			1725	1921	1736
			2⚒		2⚒			2⚒	2		★	♦
0	**Sibiu** **1600** d.	0240	0328	0642	0740	...	...	...	1610	1650	1842	2007
	Braşov **1600** d.	|	|	|	|	...	...	...	|	|	|	|
22	Podu Olt **1600** d.	|	0400	0717	0820	...	...	1310	1647	1727	|	2042
83	Călimănesti d.	0444	0539	0849	1008	...	1423	1453	1849	1916	2043	2212
99	**Râmnicu Vâlcea** d.	0510	0605	0910	1035	...	1442	1520	1945	1935	2102	2230
186	Piatra Olt **1621** d.	0633	0809	1034	...	...	1558	1732	2204	2046	2245	...
*	Caracal a.	0707	...	|	...	...	1630	...	|	|	|	...
	Bucureşti N **1620** a.	...	...	|	...	...	1905	...	|	|	0228	...
230	**Craiova** **1621** a.	...	...	1128	...	...	...	...	2312	2133	...	...

		1737	1922			1724	1521		1721	1723	
	2⚒	♦	★	2⚒	2			2Ⓑ			
Craiova **1621** d.	...	...	...	...	0510	0750	...	...	1450	...	...
Bucureşti N **1620** d.	...	...	2312	...	|	|	0930	...	|	...	...
Caracal d.	...	...	|	...	|	|	1155	...	|	1810	...
Piatra Olt **1621** d.	...	...	0332	0352	0632	0910	1239	...	1557	1853	2044
Râmnicu Vâlcea d.	0250	0405	0450	0630	0910	1022	1345	1608	1710	2022	2259
Călimănesti d.	0315	0421	0515	0654	0935	1040	1408	1634	1728	2039	...
Podu Olt **1600** a.	0527	0545	0656	0855	1117	1203	...	1821	|	2202	...
Braşov **1600** a.	|	|	|	...	|	|	...	|	|	|	...
Sibiu **1600** a.	0605	0616	0725	...	1152	1235	...	1857	1923	2235	...

* – *32 km* from Piatra Olt.

For notes ♦, ★, ♣, §, □ and • see page 518.

1625 CRAIOVA - TÂRGU JIU - DEVA

Local trains 2nd class only

km			1821			1995	1823		1825	1835	1829	
		2	♦k	2	2	★		2		♦	♦	2
	Bucureşti N **1620** d.	...	2345	...	...	0010b	0845	...	1445	1625	1625	...
0	**Craiova** **1620** d.	...	0300	0305	...	0342	1222	1612	1755	1935	1935	...
36	Filiaşi **1620** d.	...	0330	0407	...	0411	1252	1712	1825	2003	2003	...
107	**Târgu Jiu** d.	...	0441	0552	...	0540	1418	1855	1950	2118	2118	2302
157	Petroşani a.	...	0551	0730	...	0655	▬	2028	...	2227	2227	0025
157	Petroşani d.	0320	0555	...	0735	0657	1850	...	...	2230	2230	0026
237	Simeria **1610** d.	0552	0744	...	1014	0850	2117	...	...	0034	0040	0212
246	**Deva** **1610** a.	0604	0756	...	1027	0902	2127	...	...	|	0052	...
	Cluj Napoca **1610** a.	...	|	...	|	...	...	...	...	0414	...	...
	Arad **1610** a.	...	1030	...	1325	...	...	...	...	...	...	...

	1826			1824	1836					1996	1822
		2	2	♦	♦	2	2	2Ⓐ	2	★	♦j
Arad **1610** d.	...	...	...	...	...	...	...	...	...	...	1930
Cluj Napoca **1610** d.	...	...	...	...	0702	...	...	...	...	...	|
Deva **1610** d.	...	...	...	0715	|	...	1550	...	...	2003	2157
Simeria **1610** d.	...	...	*0445*	0733	1118	...	1605	...	1906	2023	2215
Petroşani a.	...	...	*0715*	0928	1315	...	1830	...	2124	2210	2357
Petroşani d.	...	0440	0805	0932	1325	1430a	...	1905	2150	2212	0001
Târgu Jiu d.	0520	0628	0951	1045	1505	1616	...	2044	2320	2335	0113
Filiaşi **1620** a.	0644	0808	1129	1154	1625	1755	...	2226	...	0053	0221
Craiova **1620** a.	0711	0920	1218	1220	1655	1845	...	2315	...	0123	0247
Bucureşti N **1620** a.	1028	...	...	1544	2047	...	...	...	...	0456b	0600

a – Ⓐ only.
b – Bucureşti **Băneasa**.
e – ⑤⑥† only.
j – Not Apr. 27 - 30, June 9 - Sept. 9.
k – Not Apr. 28 - May 1, June 10 - Sept. 10.

For notes ♦, ★, ♣, §, □ and • see page 518.

1630 BRAŞOV - MIERCUREA CIUC - DEDA - TÂRGU MURES

km			366		1540	1645		406	1643	1945	1641	4541
		2	♦	2	♦	♦	2	♦	♦	★	♦	♦
	Bucureşti N **1600** d.	...	...	...	...	1215	...	...	1800	1940b	2055	2055
0	**Braşov** **1640** d.	0355	0703	...	1413	1509	1617	1850	2053	2238	2343	2343
32	Sfântu Gheorghe **1640** d.	0459	0733	...	1447	1540	1657	1920	2123	2309	0013	0013
95	**Miercurea Ciuc** **1640** d.	0742	0847	1540	1601	1645	1923	2023	2238	0024	0118	0118
	Galaţi **1640** d.	|	|	|	|	|	|	|	|	|	|	|
103	Siculeni **1640** d.	0755	0858	1554	1610	1659	1931	2032	2249	0038	0132	0132
150	Gheorghieni d.	0909	0946	1710	...	1749	2045	2129	2338	0138	0224	0224
184	Topliţa d.	...	1023	1753	...	1827	2126	2205	0023	0222	0309	0309
228	**Deda** a.	...	1120	1910	...	1927	...	2303	0122	0322	0409	0418
228	**Deda** d.	...	...	1923	...	1943	...	...	...	0401t	...	0433
250	Reghin d.	...	...	2004	...	2007	...	...	...	0432t	...	0502
282	**Târgu Mureş** a.	...	...	2057	...	2040	...	...	...	0507t	...	0545

	407		1541		1646		367	1944	1642	4550	1644
	♦	2	♦	2		2	♦	★	♦	♦	♦
Târgu Mureş d.	...	...	...	1055	1307	1423	...	1830j	...	2250	...
Reghin d.	...	...	...	1144	1349	1509	...	1915j	...	2338	...
Deda a.	...	...	...	1225	1412	1542	...	1941j	...	0011	...
Deda d.	0544	...	...	1239	1425	1555	1928	2022	2305	0054	0054
Topliţa d.	0640	0419	...	1350	1524	1705	2029	2128	0004	0202	0202
Gheorghieni d.	0718	0504	...	1437	1602	1802	2108	2213	0041	0242	0242
Siculeni **1640** d.	0806	0625	1128	1553	1701	1913	2157	2314	0134	0337	0337
Galaţi **1640** a.	|	|	|	|	|	|	|	|	|	|	|
Miercurea Ciuc **1640** d.	0816	0706	1138	1617	1712	1936	2208	2325	0145	0348	0348
Sfântu Gheorghe **1640** d.	0914	0828	1253	1750	1817	2105	2310	0031	0250	0453	0453
Braşov **1640** a.	0642	0908	1323	1827	1846	2151	2338	0100	0319	0522	0522
Bucureşti N **1600** a.	...	...	...	...	2136	...	...	0418b	0613	0833	0833

b – Bucureşti **Băneasa**.
j – Train number **1948**.
t – Train number **1949**.

For notes ♦, ★, ♣, §, □ and • see page 518.

DEDA and BISTRIŢA - DEJ - CLUJ NAPOCA 1635

km			1945	1641	1639	366				1649	406	1643
		2	★	♦	♦	♦	2	2	2	♦	♦	♦
	Bucureşti Nord **1600** d.	...	1940b	2055	2055	...	...	...	...	...	...	1800
	Braşov **1630** d.	...	2238	2343	2343	0703	...	...	...	...	1850	2053
0	**Deda** d.	...	0335	0421	0421	1127	...	...	...	...	2308	0125
10	**Bistriţa** Nord d.	0345	|	|	|	|	0730	1533	1920	2257	|	|
47	Sărăţel d.	0407	0433	0521	0521	1220	0747	1551	1936	2309	0003	0214
72	Beclean pe Someş **1650** d.	0441	0504	0546	0546	1246	0821	1633	2019	...	0029	0238
97	Dej Călători **1616/50** d.	0524	0546	0619	0632	1320	0903	1716	2102	...	0104	...
	Baia Mare **1616** a.	|	0835	0930	|	|	|	|	...	...	|	...
56	**Cluj Napoca** **1616/50** a.	0649	...	...	0735	1425	1030	1843	...	...	0210	...
	Budapest Keleti **1275** a.	...	...	...	...	2120	...	...	...	...	0920	...

	1648			367	1944		1638	1642		1644	407
	♦	2	2	♦	★		♦	♦	2	♦	♦
Budapest Keleti **1275** d.	...	...	...	0645	...	...	...	...	...	...	1740
Cluj Napoca **1616/50** d.	...	...	1127	1610	...		1925	...	1935	...	2333
Baia Mare **1616** d.	...	...	|	|	1507	...	|	1820	|	...	|
Dej Călători **1616/50** d.	...	0502	1306	1729	1758	...	2110	2110	2124	...	0340
Beclean pe Someş **1650** d.	...	0544	1342	1805	1843	...	2146	2146	2202	2240	0415
Sărăţel d.	0530	0623	1415	1830	1910	...	2212	2212	2235	2330	0442
Bistriţa Nord a.	0544	0642	1432	|	|	...	|	|	2253	|	|
Deda a.	...	...	...	1923	2000	...	2301	2301	...	0032	0540
Braşov **1630** a.	...	...	...	2338	0100	...	0319	0319	...	0522	0942
Bucureşti Nord **1600** a.	...	...	...	...	0418b	...	0613	0613	...	0833	...

– Bucureşti **Băneasa**.

Δ – Distance from Sărăţel.

For notes ♦, ★, ♣, §, □ and • see page 518.

BRAŞOV - MIERCUREA CIUC - ADJUD - GALAŢI 1640

km									1540		
		2	2	2	2	2	2•	2		2	2
0	**Braşov** **1630** d.	...	0355	...	0606	...	1224	...	1413	...	...
32	Sfântu Gheorghe **1630** d.	...	0459	...	0650	...	1311	...	1447	...	...
95	**Miercurea Ciuc** **1630** a.	...	0631	...	0817	...	1440	...	1557	...	...
95	**Miercurea Ciuc** **1630** d.	...	▬	0712	▬	1152	1446	...	1601	1615	1945
	Târgu Mureş **1630** d.	...	2	|	...	|	|	...	|	|	|
03	Siculeni **1630** d.	...	0420	0725	...	1205	1454	...	1615	1626	2003
44	Ghimeş d.	...	0532	0828	2	1313	▬	...	1713	1733	2114
79	Comăneşti d.	0425	0620	0917	1000	1408	...	...	1754	1825	2205
16	Oneşti d.	0525	0740	▬	1101	1507	...	1540	1839	1938	2323
54	**Adjud** **1670** d.	0630	0839	...	1202	...	...	1636	1955	2031	0017
79	Mărăşeşti **1670** a.	0704	0913	2	1239	...	2	1714	|	2107	0053
79	Mărăşeşti d.	...	...	1105	...	...	1608	...	|	...	...
	Iaşi **1670** a.	...	...	|	...	...	|	...	2248	...	...
98	Tecuci **1670** d.	...	...	1131	...	...	1633	...	...	...	...
83	**Galaţi** **1670** a.	...	...	1344	...	...	1836	...	...	...	...

			1541							
	2	2		2	2	2	2	2	2	2
Galaţi **1670** d.	...	...	...	...	0740	...	...	1540	...	1945
Tecuci **1670** d.	...	...	...	...	0946	...	...	1745	...	2150
Iaşi **1670** d.	...	...	0505	...	|	...	...	|	...	|
Mărăşeşti a.	...	...	|	...	1011	...	...	1810	...	2217
Mărăşeşti **1670** d.	...	0420	|	0840	▬	...	1420	...	1852	...
Adjud **1670** d.	...	0515	0823	0918	...	1259	1510	...	1932	...
Oneşti d.	...	0605	0903	1012	...	1347	1558	...	2026	...
Comăneşti d.	0410	0704	0948	1116	...	1458	1659	...	2124	...
Ghimeş d.	0501	0754	1029	...	2	1547	1751	...	...	...
Siculeni **1630** a.	0618	0915	1128	...	1332	...	1906	...	...	...
Târgu Mureş **1630** a.	|	|	|	...	|	...	|	...	...	...
Miercurea Ciuc **1630** a.	0627	0924	1136	...	1340	...	1915	...	...	...
Miercurea Ciuc **1630** d.	...	...	1138	...	1343	...	...	...	...	...
Sfântu Gheorghe **1630** d.	...	...	1253	...	1511	...	...	...	...	...
Braşov **1630** a.	...	...	1323	...	1557	...	...	...	...	...

For notes ♦, ♣, §, □ and • see page 518.

IAŞI - SUCEAVA - DEJ - CLUJ NAPOCA 1650

km			1653	1833	1947	1831		4136	1765	1837
		2⚒	♦		★		2	♦	♦	♦
0	**Iaşi** d.	...	...	0610	...	1058	...	...	1510	1925
76	Paşcani **1670** d.	...	0327	0719	...	1207	...	...	1619	2034
22	Vereşti **1670** d.	...	0408	0758	...	1246	...	...	1658	2113
37	**Suceava** **1670** a.	...	0421	0811	...	1259	...	...	1711	2126
37	**Suceava** d.	...	0438	0826	...	1314	...	...	1726	2141
87	Gura Humorului Oraş d.	...	0536	0914	...	1402	...	...	1814	2229
219	Câmpulung Moldovenesc d.	...	0618	0956	...	1449	...	...	1857	2311
257	Vatra Dornei Băi d.	...	0725	1101	...	1552	...	...	2002	0015
351	Năsăud d.	...	...	1303	...	1755	...	...	2203	0217
18	**Sighetu Marmaţiei** d.	0100	...	|	1419	|	1550	1735	|	|
61	Vişeu de Jos d.	0317	...	|	1610	|	1754	1944	|	|
357	Salva d.	0512	...	1311	1741	1803	1938	2123	2211	0225
379	Beclean pe Someş **1635** d.	0543	...	1336	1811	1828	2013	2200	2236	0250
402	Dej Călători **1635** d.	0625	...	1412	...	1907	2051	...	2311	0326
460	**Cluj Napoca** **1635** a.	0748	...	1519	...	2014	2204	...	0019	0432
	Oradea **1612** a.	...	...	1844	...	...	...	...	|	|
	Timişoara N **1610/14** a.	...	...	2216	...	...	...	...	0835	1219

	4133	1838	1946	1843	4135	1832	1834		1654	1766
	♦	♦	★	♦	♦	♦		2⚒	♦	♦
Timişoara N **1610/14** d.	...	1800	...	2140	...	...	0633	...	...	1350
Oradea **1612** d.	...	|	...	|	...	...	0955	...	...	|
Cluj Napoca **1635** d.	...	0109	...	0519	...	0914	1252	1435	...	2215
Dej Călători **1635** d.	...	0223	...	0636	...	1030	1409	1615	...	2334
Beclean pe Someş **1635** d.	0303	0258	0515	0710	0718	1106	1444	1650	...	0009
Salva d.	0338	0321	0548	...	0802	1129	1508	1739	...	0032
Vişeu de Jos d.	0510	|	0716	...	0957	|	|	1927	...	|
Sighetu Marmaţiei a.	0711	|	0906	...	1200	|	|	2122	...	|
Năsăud d.	...	0330	...	...	...	1138	1519	...	...	0040
Vatra Dornei Băi d.	...	0529	...	...	...	1343	1732	...	2115	0241
Câmpulung Moldovenesc d.	...	0642	...	...	...	1448	1838	...	2223	0346
Gura Humorului Oraş d.	...	0725	...	...	...	1531	1922	...	2314	0430
Suceava a.	...	0811	...	...	...	1614	2007	...	0001	0515
Suceava **1670** d.	...	0823	...	...	...	1624	2022	...	0021	0527
Vereşti **1670** d.	...	0838	...	...	...	1638	2036	...	0034	0540
Paşcani **1670** d.	...	0921	...	...	...	1719	2118	...	0113	0623
Iaşi a.	...	1031	...	...	...	1827	2228	...	...	0733

Δ – Distance from Salva.

For notes ♦, ★, ♣, §, □ and • see page 518.

BUCUREŞTI - GALAŢI 1660

km		1961	1573			§			1971		1731
		★		2	2Ⓑ		2		★	2Ⓑ	V
0	**Bucureşti** Nord **1670** d.	...	0830	...	...	1520	1540	...	...	...	...
	Ploieşti Sud **1670** d.	...	0918	...	...	|	|	...	...	...	1943
**	Buzău **1670** d.	...	1032	1341	1520	|	|	...	...	1852	2055
71	Urziceni d.	...	|	|	|	1634	1726	...	...	|	|
Δ	Feteşti d.	...	|	|	|	|	|	...	1740	|	|
138	Făurei d.	0114	1111	1447	1625	1746	1847	...	|	2014	2135
198	Brăila d.	0202	1200	1612	1719	1836	1946	...	1959	2116	2223
229	**Galaţi** a.	...	1240	1633	1800	1917	2030	...	2038	2203	2302

	1962	1732		§	1970			1576		
	★	V	2	•	★	2			2	2
Galaţi d.	...	0552	0608	0650	0730	1110	...	1430	1530	1950
Brăila d.	0316	0632	0652	0735	0812	1158	...	1511	1620	2038
Făurei d.	0406	0722	0752	0823	|	1259	...	1600	1724	2138
Feteşti a.	...	|	|	|	1013	|	...	|	|	|
Urziceni d.	...	|	0912	0938	...	|	...	|	|	|
Buzău **1670** d.	...	0810	|	|	...	1359	...	1641	1827	2235
Ploieşti Sud **1670** d.	...	0921	|	|	...	...	...	1756	...	...
Bucureşti Nord **1670** a.	...	...	1037	1052	...	...	...	1841	...	...

– From/to Braşov (Table **1600**).

** – Buzău - Făurei: *40 km*.

Δ – Feteşti - Făurei: *89 km*.

For notes ♦, ★, ♣, §, □ and • see page 518.

LOCAL SERVICES 1669

.ocal trains, 2nd class only

BACĂU - PIATRA NEAMŢ - BICAZ:

km								
							B	B
0	**Bacău** d.	0414	0525	0715	1430	1635	1902	2206
60	Piatra Neamţ d.	0543	0657	0857	1608	1817	2033	2318
86	**Bicaz** a.	0627	...	...	...	1901b	2118	...
				B			Ⓑ	B
	icaz d.	...	0700	...	...	...	1949b	2200
	iatra Neamţ d.	0455	0738	0915	1622	1731	2036	2238
	acău a.	0642	0907	1028	1751	1900	2205	0003

BISTRIŢA - DEDA:

km							
			Ⓐ				
0	Bistriţa Nord d.	0345	0446	0730	1220	1543	1938
10	Sărăţel d.	0401	0501	0746	1236	1615	2012
57	Deda a.	...	...	...	...	1721	2114
	eda d.	0457	...	...	...	1658	
	ărăţel d.	0617	0901	...	1415	1831	2235
	strita Nord a.	0633	0917	...	1432	1846	2253

or long-distance trains see Table **1635**.

OTES for all routes

- – Conveys [2-berth] from/to Bucureşti (see Table **1670**).
- – Ⓑ only.
- – ①②③④⑦ only.

or notes ♦, ♣, §, □ and • see page 518.

SIGHIŞOARA - SIBIU:

km								
		⚒						•
0	**Sighişoara** d.	...	...	0620	...	1500	...	...
39	Mediaş d.	0429	0540	0742	1213	1612	...	2035
50	Copşa Mică d.	0450	0610	0804	1247	1656	...	2110
95	**Sibiu** a.	0557	0720	0913	1355	1805	...	2217
				•	•		•	Ⓑ
	Sibiu d.	0730	...	1204	1543	...	1935	2323
	Copşa Mică d.	0841	...	1322	1657	...	2055	0034
	Mediaş d.	0900	...	1341	1715	...	2134	0052
	Sighişoara a.	...	...	1450	...	...	2248	...

TÂRGU MUREŞ - RÂZBOIENI:

km								
				•				
0	**Târgu Mureş** d.	0303	0710	1154	1438	1735	1920	2220
40	Luduş d.	0417	0816	1255	1545	1846	2036	2330
59	**Războieni** a.	0446	0843	1322	1610	1911	2105	2358
					•			
	Războieni d.	0345	0520	0707	1146	...	1638	2005
	Luduş d.	0416	0546	0735	1214	...	1708	2035
	Târgu Mureş a.	0525	0651	0847	1328	...	1815	2139

For long-distance trains see Table **1610**.

ARAD - TIMISOARA *57 km*, ± 75 minutes

From Arad: 0440, 0554, 0751, 1340, 1625, 1751, 1902y.
From Timişoara: 0418Ⓐ, 0518, 1303, 1351, 1627, 1735, 2019, 2354.
For long-distance trains see Table **1614**.

BAIA MARE - SATU MARE *59 km*, ± 110 minutes

From Baia Mare: 0414, 0740, 0945•, 1221⚒•, 1545, 1928Ⓑ.
From Satu Mare: 0512Ⓐ, 0743, 1122⚒•, 1610, 1953.
For long-distance trains see Table **1616**.

PAŞCANI - TÂRGU NEAMT *31 km*, ± 45 minutes

From Paşcani: 0440, 0700, 1000•, 1425•, 1634, 1918.
From Târgu Neamt: 0555, 0802, 1102•, 1527•, 1736, 2020.

REŞIŢA - CARANSEBEŞ *43 km*, ± 80 minutes

From Reşiţa Sud: 0550, 0848, 1320, 1510, 1755, 2230.
From Caransebeş: 0345, 0551, 0730, 1333, 1631, 1932.
For long-distance trains see Table **1620**.

SIMERIA - HUNEDOARA *16 km*, ± 30 minutes

From Simeria: 0450, 1335, 1720.
From Hunedoara: 0545, 1430, 1820.

VEREŞTI - BOTOŞANI *44 km*, ± 65 minutes

From Vereşti: 0528, 0636, 0813, 1335•, 1748, 1850.
From Botoşani: 0508, 0804, 1122, 1511, 1917, 2100.
For long-distance trains see Table **1670**.

1670   BUCUREŞTI - BUZĂU - BACĂU - IAŞI and SUCEAVA

km		1961	1857	1861	1953	1831	1661	380	1655	♣	§	1753	1663	§	1651	1657	♣	1540	1665	1659	§	402	1559	§	1653	1667	175
☆		★	◆k	◆p	★	◆	◆	◆		J2•		◆	◆		◆	◆		B2•	V	◆		⊠◆	◆	⑦	◆	☉	☉
0	Bucureşti Nord ...1660 d.						0550	0615	0715			1015	1100	1205	1208	1350	1500			1610	1700	1737	1915	2005	2115	2135	2225	233
59	Ploieşti Sud ...1660 d.						0634	0702	0801	0936	1111	1146	1250	1309	1434	1546	1613			1656	1746	1837	2006	2051	2205	2220	2342	001
128	Buzău ...1660/80 d.		0144	0144	0309		0748	0817	0914	1046	1221	1300	1403	1434	1549	1659	1728			1811	1855	1950	2128	2201	2315	2332	0055	012
161	Râmnicu Sărat ....d.		0216	0216	0343		0819	0849	0946	1118		1331	1434		1621	1730	1801			1842	1926		2201			0004	0127	015
199	Focşani ....d.		0256	0256	0423		0859	0930	1026	1157		1411	1514		1701	1810	1841			1921	2006		2243			0044	0207	023
219	Mărăşeşti ...1640 d.		0330	0332	0449			0953	1049	1225		1433			1723	1833	1913			2029			2310			0108		030
244	Adjud ...1640 d.		0357		0518			1022	1117			1501			1751	1901		1955		2057			2340			0136		032
303	Bacău ....d.		0436		0559			1115	1156			1548	1866	1842	1940		2041			2148			0027			0225		041
346	Roman ....d.		0507		0631			1146				1619	2	1914			2113			2220			0104			0257		044
	Galaţi ...1640 d.				0600								1642															
238	Tecuci ...1640 d.	0400		0357n		0746	0954					1608	1827				2016									0303		
288	Bârlad ....d.	0445		0444		0838	1042		1330			1703	1924		2029		2110									0350		
340	Vaslui ....d.	0530		0531		0921	1126		1412			1737	2011		2117		2155									0436		
408	Iaşi ....a.	0638		0641		1030	1236	2	1520			1857	2120		2232	2248	2304					0247	2			0545		
408	Iaşi ....RO d.					1312																0309	0451					
431	Ungheni 1720 MD a.					1505																0502	0655					
538	Chişinău 1720 ....a.																					0906						
387	Paşcani ...1650 d.	0537		0702		1216			1649			1944			2250					0327				051
432	Vereşti ...1650 d.	0616		0738	1384	1256			1727			2022			2335					0408				060
476	Botoşani 1669 ....a.				2				1850x													0750
448	Suceava ...1650 a.	0629		0750	1055	1309			1749			2036			2352					0421				061
450	Suceava Nord ...▲ RO a.	0636		0801	1101	1331						2043												
499	Vadul Siret ....UA a.				1255	1540																		
539	Chernivtsi ....UA a.					1910r																		

km		1654	1558	§	1658	1650	1541	1662	1652	§	1863	1752	§	1656	1664	§	381	1666	1832	1385	1952	1962	1856	1862	1754	401	166
		◆	◆			🍴	V	◆		2	⑦			K2•	◆		2	◆	◆	2	★	★	◆j	◆q		⊠◆	◆
	Chernivtsi ....UA d.													0925t													
	Vadul Siret ....UA d.													1340					1635								
	Suceava Nord ...▲ RO d.													1545						1841	2025		2235				
	Suceava ...1650 d.	0021			0500		0852			1230				1603	1624					1847	2032		2242		2205		
	Botoşani 1669 ....d.									1119x															2056x
	Vereşti ...1650 d.	0034					0906			1259				1617	1638					2048		2256		2233		
	Paşcani ...1650 d.	0117			0554		0947			1341				1658	1719					2128		2338		2315		
	Chişinău 1720 ....d.																								1645	
	Ungheni 1720 MD d.														1700										2045	
	Iaşi ....RO a.													1827	1829										2220	
	Iaşi ....d.				0505	0600			0746			1425	1531	1630	1839						2235		2235		2239	231
	Vaslui ....d.					0715			0900			1540	1649	1746	1949						2348		2349			003
	Bârlad ....d.					0806			0950			1630	1732	1835	2037						0033		0039			012
	Tecuci ...1640 d.					0907			1045			1714n	1814n	1933	2127						0117		0128n			022
	Galaţi ...1640 d.								1226						2310											
	Roman ....d.	0148			0623	0641		1018			1411				1720					2155	0009		2346	0024		
	Bacău ....d.	0232			0440	0655	0723	1104			1451	1624			1805					2228	0041	0031	0103		
	Adjud ...1640 d.	0315			0523	0741	0804	1148			1535	1707			1848					2312	0125	0115	0151		
	Mărăşeşti ...1640 d.	0344			0553	0810		1217			1603	1753	1753	1850	1916					2341	0152	0209	0144	0219	035
	Focşani ....d.	0410			0619	0836		0954	1242		1629	1819	1819	1917	1942	2019				0009		0234	0210	0245	031
	Râmnicu Sărat ....d.	0448			0657	0915		1032	1320		1707			1848	2012	2057				0050		0313	0249	0323	035
	Buzău ....1660/80 d.	0520	0640	0715	0729	0955		1104	1353	1455		1740	1900	1929	1929	2028	2052	2129		0123		0344	0321	0402	042
	Ploieşti Sud ....1660 d.	0635	0755	0827	0841	1110		1217	1504	1605		1853	2013	2041	2041	2140	2204	2241				0434	0512	053
	Bucureşti Nord ...1660 a.	0720	0847	0917	0925	1154		1303	1550	1704		1938	2100	2125	2125	2247	2323					0520	0605	062

B – 🚃 Braşov - Ploieşti Vest (d. 1606) - Iaşi.
J – ①⑥⑦: 🚃 Braşov - Ploieşti Vest (d. 0930) - Iaşi.
K – ⑤⑥⑦: 🚃 Iaşi - Ploieşti Vest (a. 2148) - Braşov.
V – From/to Braşov (Table 1640).

j – Not June 9 - Sept. 9.
k – Not June 11 - Sept. 11.
n – Tecuci Nord.
p – Not Apr. 28 - May 1, June 10 - Sept. 10.
q – Not Apr. 27-30, June 9 - Sept. 9.
r – 🚃 Vadul Siret - Chernivtsi - Kyïv. On ⑦ also conveys 🛏 1, 2 cl. Bucureşti - Suceava - Vadul Siret - Kyïv.
t – 🚃 Kyïv - Chernivtsi - Vadul Siret. On ⑥ (⑤ from Kyïv) also conveys 🛏 1, 2 cl. Kyïv - Chernivtsi - Vadul Siret - Suceava - Bucureşti.
x – Portion attached to/detached from main train at Vereşti.

☉ – Also conveys 🛏 1, 2 cl.
⊠ – For international journeys only.
▲ – 🚃 is Vicşani (RO).
☆ – Tecuci - Galaţi *85km*; Iaşi - Roman *114km*.
MD Moldova. RO Romania. UA Ukraine.
For notes ◆, ★, ♣, §, □ and • see page 518.

1680   BUCUREŞTI - CONSTANŢA - MANGALIA   Winter service

km		1862	1822	1581	1583	1585	1587	1589	163
		2 ◆j	2 ◆j	2 w	2 w	2 2	2 2 🍴	2 p	R
0	Bucureşti Nord ....d.		0620	0730	0932	1400	1600 1700		2020
	Buzău ....d.	0404		0645					1620
	Făurei ....d.	0444		0753					1725
146	Feteşti ....d.	0608	0743	1051	0928	1520	1820	1901	2140
190	Medgidia ....d.	0654	0829 0910	1137	1031	1605 1619	1905	2002	2225
334	Tulcea Oraş ....a.		1239			1945			
225	Constanţa ....a.	0721	0852	0935	1200 1114	1628	1805 1928	2045	2248
225	Constanţa ....d.	0620 0740		1000	1420	1640	1840	2000	
239	Eforie Sud ....d.	0654 0814		1031	1451	1711	1914	2034	
268	Mangalia ....a.	0740 0911		1117	1539	1759	2000	2120	

km		1636	1580	1582	1584	1586	1588	1821	1861
		R	2 2	q 2	w	2 2	2 🍴	2 ◆k	◆k
	Mangalia ....d.	0525	0637	0805	1125	1430	1606	1857	
	Eforie Sud ....d.	0613	0732	0855	1213	1529	1653	1953	
	Constanţa ....a.	0648	0807	0927	1245	1601	1735	2028	
0	Constanţa ....d.	0530 0748	0830	1300 1400	1629 1700	1900	2050 2200
35	Medgidia ....d.	0554 0832	0848 0854	1424	1713 1724	1942	2114 2226
79	Feteşti ....d.	0640 0933	0940	1510	1821 1810		2200 2312
168	Făurei ....d.	1125			2008		0045
208	Buzău ....d.	1215		2114			0124
	Bucureşti Nord ....a.	0800	1057	1505 1627	1927	2105	2323

R – From/to Braşov.

j – Not Apr. 27-30, June 9 - Sept. 9.
k – Not Apr. 28 - May 1, June 10 - Sept. 10.
p – Not Apr. 28 - May 1.
q – Not Apr. 29 - May 2.
w – Not June 10 - Sept. 10.

For notes ◆, ♣, §, □ and • see page 518.

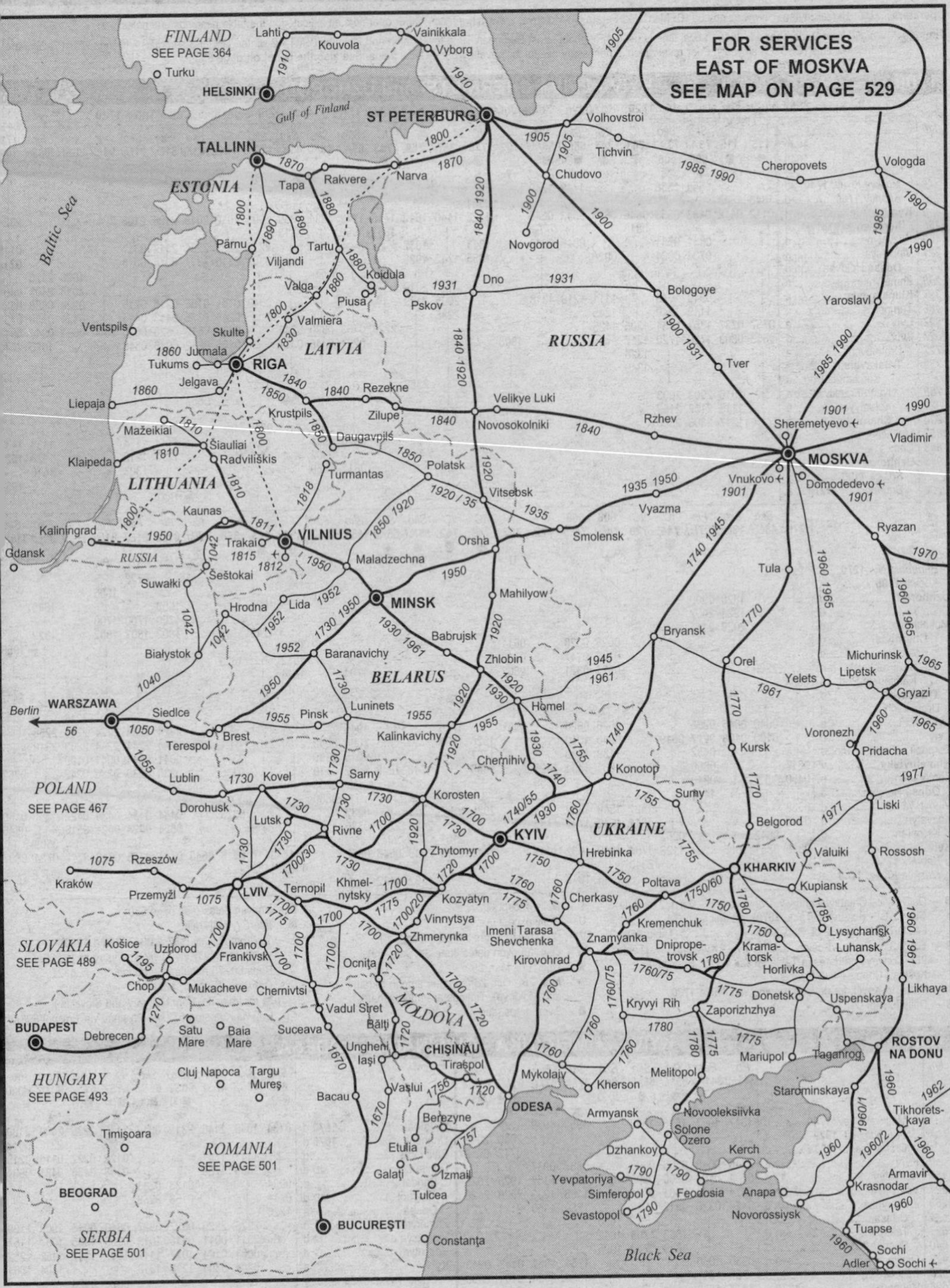

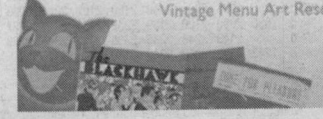

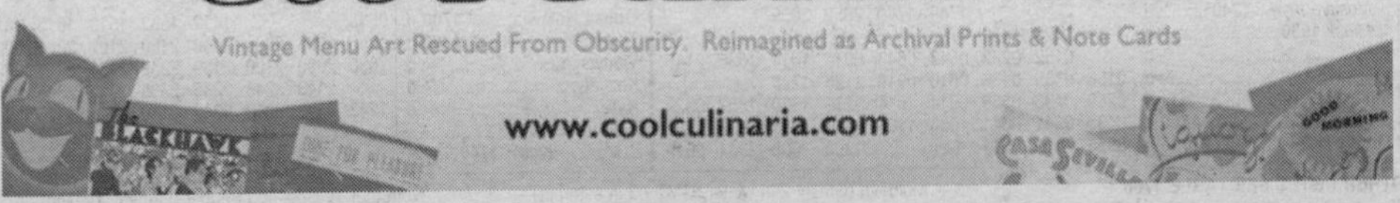

UKRAINE and MOLDOVA

SEE MAP PAGE 52

Operators: UZ: Ukrzaliznytsya, www.uz.gov.ua **CFM**: Calea Ferată din Moldova, www.railway.md Other operators as indicated in the table headings and notes.

Timings: Valid from **December 11, 2016**. Local time is used throughout: East European Time for Ukraine and Moldova (GMT+2 winter, GMT+3 summer) – timings within Russia are Moskva time (GMT+3 all year). Prior reservation is necessary except for travel by purely local trains. **See also the panel on page 530.**

1700 KYÏV - LVIV - CHERNIVTSI and UZHOROD

UZ, CF

Kyïv - Zhmerynka: see also Table **1720**. Kozyatyn - Zhmerynka - Lviv: see also Table **1775**. Odesa - Zhmerynka: see also Table **1720**.

km		113 ●	115 ■	Sko 73AJ 608 ★	Sko 73AJ 608 ☆	IC 741 ≋	IC 747 ≋	Sko 55MJ ■(3) ★	Sko 55MJ ■(3) ☆	702 T	IC 719 ≋ S	357	769	IC 743 ≋	Sko 99KJ	Sko 13KJ	Sko 43KJ	Sko 117LJ B	Fir 49KJ	Sko 143KJ	Sko 81DJ L	Sko 81DJ	Fir 91KJ	Fir 26SH	Fir 108SH	771 108 P
	Moskva Kiyev. **1740** d.	...	...	1558	1558	...	...	1749	1749	...	...	...	...	...	...	...	...	...	...	...	...	...	...	...	...	...
	Kharkiv **1750** d.	1848	1848	|	|	...	...	|	|	...	0551	...	...	...	...	...	...	...	...	...	...	...	...	...	...	...
0	**Kyïv** d.	0112	0112	0433	0533	0645	0655	0543	0643	...	1128	1440	1642	1718	1742	1834	1850	2005	2012	2019	2108	2108	2241	...	...	232
156	Korosten d.	|	|	|	|	0818	|	|	|	...	|	|	|	1851	1950	|	2113	|	|	|	|	|	|	...	...	|
159	Kozyatyn d.	|	|	0631	0731	|	|	0849	0949	...	1313	|	1832	|	|	|	|	2210	2221	2236	2317	2317	|	...	...	011
221	Vinnytsya d.	|	|	0734	0834	|	0928	|	|	...	1355	1742	1923	|	|	|	|	2303	2315	2331	0015	0015	|	...	...	021
	Odesa Holovna d.	|	|	|	|	|	|	|	|	...	...	|	|	|	|	⊙	|	|	|	|	|	|	|	1826	2126	|
268	Zhmerynka d.	|	|	|	|	|	|	|	|	...	...	|	2019	|	|	|	|	|	|	|	|	|	|	0053	0403	040
367	**Khmelnytsky** d.	|	|	0949	1049	|	1111	1218	1318	...	...	2005	2139	|	|	|	|	0049	0101	0156	0215	0215	|	0226	0538	053
486	Ternopil d.	|	|	1149	1249	|	1245	...	...	...	...	2235	|	|	|	|	|	|	0245	0355	0413	0413	|	0424	0738	073
*627	**Lviv** a.	0737	0737	1351	1451	1205	1425	...	...	...	...	|	|	2223	0153	0320	0247	|	0432	0610	0620	0620	0600	0633	0944	094
*627	**Lviv** d.	0803	0803	1720	1720	1217	...	...	...	1908	...	|	|	...	0221	0346	0311	|	0455	0632	0646	0646	...	...	1010	101
727	Drohobych a.	|	|	|	|	1328	...	...	...	|	...	|	|	...	|	|	|	|	0730	|	|	|	...	...	|	|
739	**Truskavets** a.	|	|	|	|	1349	...	...	...	|	...	|	|	...	|	|	|	|	0759	|	|	|	...	...	|	|
	Kamianets-Pod. a.	|	|	|	|	...	...	...	...	|	...	|	2358	...	|	|	|	0327	...	|	|	|	...	...	|	|
768	Ivano-Frankivsk a.	|	1016	2003	2003	...	...	...	...	2055	...	|	...	...	|	|	0544	|	...	0857	|	|	...	...	|	|
823	Kolomyya a.	|	1115	2152	2152	...	...	...	...	2142	...	0537	...	...	|	|	...	|	...	...	|	|	...	...	|	|
894	**Chernivtsi** a.	|	1217	2306	2306	...	...	...	...	2244	...	⊡	...	...	|	|	...	0710	...	...	|	|	...	...	|	|
852	Mukacheve d.	1208	...	...	...	...	...	...	...	...	...	...	...	...	0646	0811	...	...	...	...	1114	1114	...	...	1433	143
893	Chop § a.	|	...	...	...	...	...	...	...	...	...	...	...	...	|	0902	...	...	...	...	1212	1212	...	...	1523	152
915	**Uzhhorod** a.	1333	...	...	...	...	...	...	...	...	...	...	...	...	0812	0950	...	...	...	...	|	1303	...	...	1616	|
	Košice **1195** a.	...	...	...	...	...	...	...	...	...	...	...	...	...	...	...	...	...	...	...	|	...	...	...	...	195
	Budapest Ny. **1270** a.	...	...	...	...	...	...	...	...	...	...	...	...	...	...	...	...	...	...	...	1837	...	...	...	...	...

	770	Sko 43CJ	Sko 13LJ	Fir 107LJ	IC 744 ≋	IC 720 ≋ S	608 74LJ ★	608 74LJ ☆	772	702 U	IC 748 ≋	IC 742 ≋	Sko 55KJ ● ★	Sko 55KJ ● ☆	Sko 143LJ	Fir 26LJ ▽	116 ●	113 ■	358	Fir 92LJ	Fir 81LJ	Fir 81LJ L	Fir 81LJ P	Fir 50LJ	Sko 99LJ	Sko 118S B
Budapest Ny. **1270** d.	...	...	...	...	...	...	...	...	...	...	...	...	...	...	...	...	...	...	...	...	...	0723	...	...	...	...
Košice **1195** d.	...	...	...	...	...	...	...	...	...	...	...	...	...	...	...	...	...	...	...	...	...	|	1006	...	...	...
Uzhhorod d.	...	...	1828	1900	...	...	...	...	...	...	...	...	...	...	...	...	...	1625	...	...	1550	|	|	...	1649	...
Chop § d.	...	...	1924	2002	...	...	...	...	...	...	...	...	...	...	...	...	...	|	...	...	1700	1700	1700	...	|	...
Mukacheve d.	...	...	2029	2112	...	...	...	...	...	...	...	...	...	...	...	...	...	1748	...	...	1802	1802	1802	...	1822	...
Chernivtsi d.	...	...	|	|	...	...	0028	0028	...	0611	...	...	...	...	...	...	1707	|	⊡	...	|	|	|	...	|	1955
Kolomyya d.	...	...	|	|	...	...	0147	0147	...	0712	...	...	...	...	...	...	1812	|	1629	...	|	|	|	...	|	|
Ivano-Frankivsk d.	...	2200	|	|	...	...	0321	0321	...	0802	...	...	...	...	1701	...	1914	|	|	...	|	|	|	...	|	|
Kamianets-Pod. d.	0054	|	|	|	...	...	|	|	...	|	...	...	...	...	|	...	|	|	|	...	|	|	|	...	|	2329
Truskavets d.	|	|	|	|	...	...	|	|	...	|	...	1543	...	...	|	...	|	|	|	...	|	|	|	1949	|	|
Drohobych d.	|	|	|	|	...	...	|	|	...	|	...	1604	...	...	|	...	|	|	|	...	|	|	|	2016	|	|
Lviv a.	|	0040	0045	0205	...	...	0626	0626	...	0951	...	1715	...	...	1945	...	2121	2134	|	...	2224	2224	2224	2246	2258	|
Lviv d.	|	0100	0108	0227	0619	...	0940	1040	...	...	1526	1728	...	...	2005	2040	2154	2154	|	2255	2244	2244	2244	2308	2318	|
Ternopil d.	|	|	|	0432	|	...	1139	1239	...	...	1707	|	...	...	2215	2300	|	|	2344	|	0041	0041	0041	0100	|	|
Khmelnytsky d.	0317	|	|	0650	|	...	1351	1451	1425	...	1845	|	1748	1848	0032	0110	|	|	0136	|	0230	0230	0230	0242	|	0252
Zhmerynka d.	0456	|	|	0840	|	...	|	|	1559	...	|	|	|	|	|	0258	|	|	|	|	|	|	|	|	|	|
Odesa Holovna a.	|	|	⊙	1440	|	...	|	|	|	...	|	|	|	|	|	0850	|	|	|	|	|	|	|	|	|	|
Vinnytsya d.	0538	|	|	...	|	1527	1549	1649	1643	...	2025	|	|	|	0233	...	|	|	0323	|	0434	0434	0434	0427	|	0450
Kozyatyn d.	0630	|	|	...	|	1611	1642	1742	1735	...	|	|	2148	2248	0326	...	|	|	|	|	0524	0524	0524	0516	|	0546
Korosten d.	|	0642	|	...	0953	|	|	|	|	...	|	2101	|	|	|	...	|	|	|	|	|	|	|	|	0509	|
Kyïv a.	0835	0851	1005	...	1123	1754	1852	1952	1939	...	2245	2233	2348	0048	0552	...	0417	0417	0618	0646	0743	0743	0743	0717	0724	0807
Kharkiv **1750** a.	...	...	...	...	...	2340	|	|	...	...	...	...	|	|	...	...	1132	1132	...	...	...	...	...	...	...	...
Moskva Kiyev. **1740** a.	...	...	...	...	...	...	1043	1043	...	...	...	...	1432	1432	...	...	...	...	...	...	...	...	...	...	...	...

B – Daily Kyïv - Chernivtsi and v.v. Conveys on ⑤ 🛏 1, 2 cl. Kyïv - Chernivtsi - Bucuresti (Table **1670**), returning on ⑦.
L – LATORCA – 🛏 1, 2 cl. Budapest - Kyïv and v.v. (Table **96**).
P – 🛏 1, 2 cl. Praha - Košice - Chop - Lviv - Kyïv and v.v. (Table **96**). Conveys on dates in Table **96** 🛏 1, 2 cl. Bratislava - Košice - Chop - Lviv - Kyïv and v.v.
R – From / to Kovel; for days of running see Table **1730**.
S – Daily except ②.

T – Daily except ③.
U – Daily except ④.
V – ②⑤ (even dates June 2 - Sept. 26).
W – ③⑥ (uneven dates June 3 - Sept. 29).
★ – Dec. 11 - Mar. 25.
☆ – Mar. 26 - Oct. 28 (summer time in Ukraine and Moldova). Timings are approximate.
● – Even dates (see page 530).

■ – Uneven dates (see page 530).
≋ – *InterCity* fast train.
⊡ – To / from Rakhiv (**357** a. 0943 / **358** d. 1230).
⊙ – Via Berdychiv (Kyïv - Lviv via this route is *566 km*).
▽ – Runs 60 - 75 minutes later June 15 - Aug. 27.
⊖ – Odessa - Tiraspol: *120 km*.
§ – 🛃 for trains to / from Hungary and Slovakia.
* – Lviv via Korosten *572 km*, Chişinău via Tiraspol *698 km*

1720 KYÏV - ZHMERYNKA - CHIŞINĂU and ODESA

UZ, CFM

km		Pas 341FJ ★	Pas 341FJ ☆	Sko 65MJ ● ★	Sko 65MJ ● ☆	Sko 642 ⑥⑦	Sko 47MZ ★	Sko 47MZ ☆	Sko 61MZ ■(3) ★	Sko 61MZ ■(3) ☆
	Moskva Kiyev. **1740** d.	1047	1047	1618	1618	...	1959	1959	...	...
	St P'burg Vit. **1920** d.	|	|	|	|	...	|	|	2040	2040
	Orsha Tsent. **1920** d.	|	|	|	|	...	|	|	0712	0712
0	**Kyïv** ▷ d.	2348	0048	0508	0608	...	0837	0937	|	|
157	Kozyatyn ▷ d.	0204	0104	0700	0800	...	1052	1152	1925	2025
221	Vinnytsya ▷ d.	0314	0214	0801	0901	...	1153	1253	2020	2120
268	Zhmerynka UA d.	0426	0326	0912	1012	...	1259	1359	2121	2221
⊖	**Odesa** d.	|	|	|	|	1600	|	|	|	|
627	Tiraspol MD d.	|	|	1603	1703	1842	|	|	|	|
640	Bender 2 d.	|	|	1649	1749	1925	|	|	|	|
422	Ocniţa MD d.	0950	1050	|	|	|	1751	1851	0143	0243
520	Bălţi Oraş d.	1237	1337	|	|	|	1954	2054	0400	0500
598	Ungheni **1670** a.	1443	1543	|	|	|	|	|	|	|
*705	**Chişinău** **1670** a.	1749	1849	1832	1932	2106	2344	0044	0745	0845

	Sko 642 ⑥⑦	Sko 47SZ ★	Sko 47SZ ☆	Sko 66SZ ■(3) ★	Sko 66SZ ■(3) ☆	Sko 61SZ ■(1) ★	Sko 61SZ ■(1) ☆	Pas 341MZ ★	Pas 341M ☆
Chişinău **1670** d.	0734	1048	1148	2312	0012	2136	2236	2009	2109
Ungheni **1670** d.	|	|	|	|	|	|	|	2318	0018
Bălţi Oraş d.	|	1441	1541	|	|	0122	0222	0110	0210
Ocniţa MD d.	|	1659	1759	|	|	0338	0438	0431	0531
Bender 2 d.	0924	|	|	0133	0233	|	|	|	|
Tiraspol MD d.	0944	|	|	0158	0258	|	|	|	|
Odesa a.	1225	|	|	|	|	|	|	|	|
Zhmerynka UA d.	...	2225	2325	0827	0927	0846	0946	1009	1109
Vinnytsya ▷ d.	...	2311	0011	0918	1018	0935	1035	1057	1157
Kozyatyn ▷ d.	...	0004	0104	1012	1112	1047	1147	1152	1252
Kyïv ▷ a.	...	0204	0304	1218	1318	|	|	1404	1504
Orsha Tsent. **1920** a.	...	|	|	|	|	0028	0028	|	|
St P'burg Vit. **1920** a.	...	|	|	|	|	1144	1144	|	|
Moskva Kiyev. **1740** a.	...	1651	1651	0508	0508	...	...	0524	0524

km		84 R	Sko 93 V ★	Sko 93 V ☆	Sko 89KJ ■(3) ★	Sko 89KJ ■(3) ☆	Fir 23MJ ★	Fir 23MJ ☆	IC 763 ≋	Fir 105KJ
	Moskva Kiyev. **1740** d.	...	...	...	1749	1749	2059	2059	...	...
	Minsk **1930** d.	...	1420	1420	|	|	|	|	...	...
0	**Kyïv** ▷ d.	...	0132	0232	0543	0643	0914	1014	1636	2115
159	Kozyatyn ▷ d.	0156	0336	0436	0816	0916	1126	1226	|	|
221	Vinnytsya ▷ d.	0259	0436	0536	0914	1014	1230	1330	1852	0027
268	Zhmerynka **1700** d.	0406	0541	0641	1003	1103	1336	1436	1927	|
387	**Odesa** Holovna **1700** a.	0956	1111	1211	...	...	1905	2005	2334	0619

	IC 764 ≋	Sko 90KJ ● ★	Sko 90KJ ● ☆	Sko 94 W ★	Sko 94 W ☆	Fir 24SH ★	Fir 24SH ☆	84 R	Fir 106SH
Odesa Holovna **1700** d.	0543	...	...	1432	1532	1513	1613	1816	2225
Zhmerynka **1700** d.	0955	1906	2006	2050	2150	2102	2202	0033	|
Vinnytsya ▷ d.	1030	2000	2100	2139	2239	2151	2251	0127	0358
Kozyatyn ▷ d.	|	2148	2248	2235	2335	2245	2345	0223	|
Kyïv ▷ a.	1243	2348	0048	0040	0140	0046	0146	...	0710
Minsk **1930** a.	...	|	|	1344	1344	|	|	...	...
Moskva Kiyev. **1740** a.	...	1432	1432	...	...	1514	1514	...	...

FOR OTHER NOTES SEE TABLE 1700
▷ – See also Table **1700**.

MD – Moldova (GMT+2 in winter, GMT+3 in summer).
UA – Ukraine (GMT+2 in winter, GMT+3 in summer).

Note that Tiraspol and Bender (formerly Tighina) are located in the unrecognised *de facto* autonomous region of Transnistria

UZ, PKP — KYÏV - RIVNE - KOVEL and DOROHUSK — 1730

km		804	84	77	77	806	141	67	97	371	371
		①–⑥	R	M	M	Ⓑ		K		■(1)	■(1)
				★	☆					★	☆
	Moskva Kiyev. **1740** d.	...	...	1558	1558	...	...	...	...	...	...
0	**Kyïv** d.	...	...	0448	0548	...	1544	1724	2122	...	...
156	Korosten d.	...	...	0654	0754	...	1825	|	2322	...	...
658	**Minsk** d.	...	...	|	|	...	|	|	|	1947	1947
517	Baranavichy Pol. d.	...	...	|	|	...	|	|	|	2234	2234
401	Luninets BY d.	...	...	|	|	...	|	|	|	0035	0035
311	Sarny ‡UA d.	...	▽	|	|	...	2142	|	|	0312	0412
383	**Rivne** d.	0646	0648	1114	1214	1315	|	|	0352	0453	0553
461	Lutsk d.	|	0830	1253	1353	|	|	|	0534	|	|
545	**Kovel** d.	|	1018	1445	1545	|	0018	|	0735	|	|
744	**Lviv** a.	0936	...	...	...	1606	0440	|	...	0820	0920
604	Yahodyn UA d.	...	...	...	...	...	...	|	...	...	...
613	**Dorohusk** PL a.	...	...	...	...	...	...	0346	...	...	...
	Lublin **1055** a.	...	...	...	...	...	...	0646	...	...	...
	Warszawa C. **1055** a.	...	...	...	...	...	...	0910	...	...	...

	804	78	78	806	84	372	372	98	68	142
	①–⑥	M	M	Ⓑ	S	●	●		K	
		★	☆			★	☆			
Warszawa C. **1055** d.	...	...	...	...	...	...	...	...	1650	...
Lublin **1055** d.	...	...	...	...	...	...	...	...	1920	...
Dorohusk PL d.	...	...	...	...	...	...	...	...	2203	...
Yahodyn UA d.	...	...	...	...	...	...	...	...	0116	...
Lviv d.	0950	...	...	1630	...	1816	1916	...	|	2146
Kovel d.	|	0946	1046	|	1755	|	|	2016	|	0210
Lutsk d.	|	1206	1306	|	2012	|	|	2226	|	|
Rivne d.	1228	1323	1423	1916	2136	2152	2252	2348	|	|
Sarny ‡UA d.	...	|	|	...	▽	2325	0025	|	|	0440
Luninets BY d.	...	|	|	...	...	0427	0427	|	|	|
Baranavichy Pol. d.	...	|	|	...	...	0708	0708	|	|	|
Minsk a.	...	|	|	...	...	0924	0924	|	|	|
Korosten d.	...	1702	1802	...	...	...	...	0353	|	0810
Kyïv a.	...	1908	2008	...	...	...	...	0558	0922	1028
Moskva Kiyev. **1740** a.	...	1043	1043	...	...	...	...	...	...	...

– KYÏV EKSPRES / KIEV EXPRESS – 1, 2 cl. Kyïv - Warszawa and v.v.
– Moskva (**73/4**) - Kyïv (**77/8**) - Kovel and v.v.
– From Odesa ● (daily June 3 - Oct. 1).
S – ■(1) (daily June 2 - Sept. 30).
★ – Dec. 11 - Mar. 25.
☆ – Mar. 26 - Oct. 28 (summer time in Ukraine). Timings are approximate.
▽ – To / from Odesa (Table **1720**).
● – Even dates (see page 530).
■ – Uneven dates (see page 530).
‡ – : Horyn (BY) / Udrytsk (UA).
* – Distance from Lviv.
BY – Belarus (GMT + 3 all year).
PL – Poland (Central European Time).
UA – Ukraine (East European Time).

RZhD, UZ — MOSKVA - BRYANSK - KONOTOP - KYÏV — 1740

km		*Pas* 341*FJ*	*Pas* 341*FJ*	*Sko* 103*MJ*	*Sko* 61*KH*	*Sko* 61*KH*	*Sko* 73*AJ*	*Sko* 73*AJ*	*Sko* 65*MJ*	*Sko* 65*MJ*
					●	●	L	L	●	●
		★	☆		★	☆	★	☆	★	☆
0	**Moskva** Kiyevskaya d.	1047	1047	1330	1533	1533	1558	1558	1618	1618
387	Bryansk Orlovski d.	1724	1724	1745	|	|	2207	2207	2230	2230
504	Suzemka RU d.	|	|	...	2348	2348	|	|	0045	0045
519	Zernove UA d.	|	|	...	2347	0047	|	|	|	|
651	Konotop d.	2035	2135	...	0133	0233	0130	0230	0227	0327
829	Chernihiv a.	|	|	...	△	△	|	|	|	|
872	**Kyïv** a.	2328	0028	...	...	...	0413	0513	0453	0553
	Odesa Holovna **1720** a.	|	|	...	...	...	|	|	|	|
	Chişinău **1720** a.	1749	1849	...	...	...	|	|	1832	1932
	Lviv **1700** a.	...	...	...	...	...	1351	1451	...	...
	Chernivtsi **1700** a.	...	...	...	...	...	2306	2306	...	...

		Sko 55*MJ*	*Sko* 55*MJ*	*Sko* 105*MJ*	*Fir* 5*JA*	*Fir* 5*JA*	*Fir* 5*JA*	*Fir* 5*JA*	*Sko* 47*MZ*	*Sko* 47*MZ*	*Fir* 23*MJ*	*Fir* 23*MJ*	*Fir* 99*CH*
		■(3)	■(3)										
		★	☆		★	★	☆	☆	★	☆	★	☆	
Moskva Kiyevskaya d.	...	1749	1749	1920	1935	1935	1935	1935	1959	1959	2059	2059	2355
Bryansk Orlovski d.	...	2327x	2327x	2335	|	|	|	|	0214	0214	0235x	0235x	0656
Suzemka RU d.	...	0142	0142	...	|	|	|	|	|	|	0440	0440	...
Zernove UA d.	...	|	|	...	|	|	|	|	|	|	|	|	...
Konotop d.	...	|	|	...	|	|	|	|	0528	0628	|	|	...
Chernihiv a.	...	|	|	...	|	0733	|	0833	|	|	|	|	...
Kyïv a.	...	0533	0633	...	0631	...	0731	...	0817	0917	0840	0940	...
Odesa Holovna **1720** a.	...	▽	▽	...	...	...	...	...	|	|	1905	2005	...
Chişinău **1720** a.	...	...	...	...	...	...	...	...	2344	0044	...	...	...
Lviv **1700** a.	...	...	...	...	...	...	...	...	...	...	...	...	...
Chernivtsi **1700** a.	...	...	...	...	...	...	...	...	...	...	...	...	...

	Sko 55*KJ*	*Sko* 55*KJ*	*Fir* 24*SH*	*Fir* 24*SH*	*Sko* 47*SZ*	*Sko* 47*SZ*	*Sko* 104*MJ*	*Sko* 106*MJ*	*Sko* 66*SZ*	*Sko* 66*SZ*	*Pas* 341*MZ*	*Pas* 341*MZ*	*Fir* 100*CH*
	●	●‡							■(3)	■(3)			
	★	☆	★	☆	★	☆			★	☆	★	☆	
Chernivtsi **1700** d.	...	...	...	...	...	...	...	...	...	...	...	...	...
Lviv **1700** d.	...	...	...	...	...	...	...	...	...	...	...	...	...
Chişinău **1720** d.	...	...	...	...	1048	1148	...	...	2312	0012	2009	2109	...
Odesa Holovna **1720** d.	▽	▽	1513	1613	|	|	...	...	|	|	|	|	...
Kyïv d.	2358	0058	0103	0203	0219	0319	...	...	1238	1338	1424	1524	...
Chernihiv d.	|	|	|	|	|	|	...	...	|	|	|	|	...
Konotop d.	|	|	|	|	0513	0613	...	...	1552	1652	1725	1825	...
Zernove UA d.	|	|	|	|	|	|	...	...	|	|	|	|	...
Suzemka RU d.	0659	0659	0757	0757	0945	0945	...	...	2041	2041	2201	2201	...
Bryansk Orlovski d.	|	|	0949	0949	1127	1127	1330	1900	2305	2305	2332	2332	2350
Moskva Kiyevskaya a.	1432	1432	1514	1514	1651	1651	1745	2315	0508	0508	0524	0524	0644

		Fir 6*OJ*	*Fir* 6*OJ*	*Fir* 6*OJ*	*Fir* 6*OJ*		*Sko* 74*LJ*	*Sko* 74*LJ*	*Sko* 61*SH*	*Sko* 61*SH*
			⊙		⊙		L	L	■(1)	■(1)
		★	★	☆	☆		★	☆	★	☆
Chernivtsi **1700** d.	...	...	...	...	...	...	0028	0028	...	...
Lviv **1700** d.	...	...	...	...	...	...	0940	1040	...	...
Chişinău **1720** d.	...	...	...	...	...	...	|	|	...	...
Odesa Holovna **1720** d.	...	...	...	...	...	...	|	|	...	...
Kyïv d.	...	1933	...	2033	...	...	1952	2052	...	...
Chernihiv d.	...	|	1903	|	2003	...	|	|	△	△
Konotop d.	...	|	|	|	|	...	2249	2349	2321	0021
Zernove UA d.	...	|	|	|	|	...	|	|	0200	0300
Suzemka RU d.	...	|	|	|	|	...	0332	0332	|	|
Bryansk Orlovski d.	...	|	|	|	|	...	0451x	0451x	|	|
Moskva Kiyevskaya a.	...	0948	0948	0948	0948	...	1043	1043	1112	1112

L – Also conveys Moskva - Kyïv - Kovel and v.v. (Table **1730**).
x – Bryansk **Lgovski**.
△ – To / from Mykolaiv and Kherson (Table **1760**).
▽ – To / from Khmelnytsky (Table **1700**) and Zhmerynka (Table **1720**).
★ – Dec. 11 - Mar. 25.
☆ – Mar. 26 - Oct. 28. Timings are approximate.
● – Even dates (see page 530).
■ – Uneven dates (see page 530).
⊙ – Train number **658***KJ* Chernihiv - Konotop.
‡ – Next day from Kyïv.
RU – Russia (Moskva Time GMT + 3).
UA – Ukraine (GMT + 2 in winter, GMT + 3 in summer).

UZ — KYÏV - POLTAVA - KHARKIV — 1750

km		113 116	*IC* 712	*IC* 722	*IC* 724	*IC* 726	*IC* 720		126	124	64
		u	⚡	⚡	⚡	⚡	E⚡				
	Lviv **1700** d.	2154	...	...	...	...	v	...	...	...	...
0	**Kyïv** d.	0437	0622	0646	1333	1801	1809	...	2028	2118	2222
150	Hrebinka d.	|	|	|	|	|	1940	...	2238	|	0024
335	**Poltava** Kyïvska d.	0831	0926	0951	1636	2106	2200	...	0212	▽	0342
493	**Kharkiv** a.	1132	|	1123	1811	2240	2340	...	|	0651	0627
635	Slovyansk a.	...	1213	...	...	...	...	...	0716	1058	...
649	Kramatorsk a.	...	1224	...	...	...	...	...	0738	1140	...
679	Kostiantynivka a.	...	1246	...	...	...	...	...	0812	1217	...
744	**Donetsk** ◇ a.	...	...	...	...	...	...	...	...	...	...

	IC 719	*IC* 725	*IC* 723	*IC* 712	*IC* 721	113 115		63	124	126
	E⚡	⚡	⚡	⚡	⚡	u				
Donetsk ◇ d.	...	...	...	...	...	...	...	...	...	...
Kostiantynivka d.	...	...	...	1629	...	...	...	...	1838	2111
Kramatorsk d.	...	...	...	1653	...	...	...	...	1915	2142
Slovyansk d.	...	...	...	1704	...	...	...	...	2001	2202
Kharkiv d.	0551	0722	1315	|	1838	1848	...	2207	0016	|
Poltava Kyïvska d.	0742	0900	1453	1951	2016	2106	...	0104	▽	0324
Hrebinka d.	0943	|	|	|	|	|	...	0413	|	0651
Kyïv a.	1113	1202	1754	2258	2319	0052	...	0623	0927	0856
Lviv **1700** a.	v	...	...	...	...	0737	...	...	...	...

E – Daily except ②.
u – From / to destinations in Table **1700**.
v – From / to Vinnytsya (Table **1700**).
⚡ – *InterCity* fast train.
▽ – Via Sumy (Table **1755**).
◇ – Service suspended.

UZ — KYÏV - SUMY - KHARKIV — 1755

km		776	798	143	143	100	100	780	124	134	
				●	●	■(1)	K				
			M	★	☆	★	☆				
	St Peterburg **1930** d.	...	...	1531	1531	...	...	...	...	...	...
	Minsk **1930** d.	...	...	|	|	0744	0744	...	...	...	...
	Homel **1930** d.	...	...	0759	0759	1249	1249	...	...	...	...
0	**Kyïv** d.	0022	...	|	|	|	|	1709	2118	2320	...
221	Konotop d.	0312	...	1345	1445	1754	1854	1932	0016	0219	...
350	Sumy d.	0536	1617	1648	1748	2050	2150	2127	0308	0541	...
552	**Kharkiv** a.	0825	1940	2020	2120	0015	0115	...	0651	0929	...
	Lysychansk **1785** a.	...	...	...	...	⊡	⊡	...	△	1520	...

	124	779	100	100	143	143	797	775	134	
			■(3)	L	■(1)	■(1)				
			★	☆	★	☆	M			
Lysychansk **1785** d.	△	...	⊡	⊡	...	...	...	...	1636	...
Kharkiv d.	0016	...	0523	0623	0616	0716	1002	2116	2224	...
Sumy d.	0400	0535	0907	1007	0957	1057	1325	0023	0225	...
Konotop d.	0633	0735	1149	1249	1241	1341	...	0243	0509	...
Kyïv a.	0927	0952	|	|	|	|	...	0526	0823	...
Homel **1930** a.	...	...	1832	1832	2014	2014	...	...	...	...
Minsk **1930** a.	...	...	2345	2345	|	|	...	...	...	...
St Peterburg **1930** a.	...	...	...	...	1220	1220	...	...	...	...

K – ■(1) (daily June 1 - Sept. 21).
L – ■(3) (daily June 3 - Sept. 23).
M – Conveys Sumy - Kharkiv - Moskva (Table **1770**) and v.v.
★ – Dec. 11 - Mar. 25.
☆ – Mar. 26 - Oct. 28 (summer time in Ukraine). Timings are approximate.
● – Even dates (see page 530).
■ – Uneven dates (see page 530).
△ – To / from Kostiantynivka (Table **1750**).
⊡ – To / from Zaporizhzhya (Table **1780**) extended to Novooleksiivka in summer.

CFM — CHIŞINĂU - BASARABEASCA — 1756

km	*Subject to alteration*	821	6820*
		⑥⑦	④–⑦
0	**Chişinău** **1720** d.	0643	1855
	Ungheni **1720** a.	0855	|
	Iasi Socola a.	1056	|
195	Basarabeasca a.	...	2334
331	Etulia ◇ a.	...	...

Subject to alteration	6819*	822
	⑤–①	⑥⑦
Etulia ◇ d.	...	...
Basarabeasca d.	0202	...
Iasi Socola d.	|	1708
Ungheni **1720** d.	|	1917
Chişinău **1720** a.	0625	2113

* – only.
◇ – Service suspended.

UZ — ODESA - BEREZYNE and IZMAÏL — 1757

km		686*PC*	686*OJ*
		P	P
0	**Odesa** Holovna d.	1620	1620
85	Bilhorod-Dnistrovsky d.	1847	1847
175	Artsyz d.	2040	2057
210	Berezyne a.	|	2252
282	**Izmaïl** a.	2254	...

	686*SH*	686*KJ*
	P	P
Izmaïl d.	...	2359
Berezyne d.	2312	|
Artsyz d.	0239	0239
Bilhorod-Dnistrovsky d.	0435	0435
Odesa Holovna a.	0639	0639

P – ⑤⑦ (also ③⑥ May 31 - Aug. 30).

1760 KYÏV and KHARKIV - MYKOLAIV - KHERSON UZ

km		766	61KH	61KH	91	318	793	63	59	102	121
			● ★	● ☆		●		E			
	Moskva Kiyev. **1740** d.	...	1533	1533	...	...	...	...	...	...	...
	Konotop d.	...	0138	0238	...	...	...	...	...	...	...
	Cherkasy d.	...	0712	0812	...	...	...	...	...	...	...
0	**Kyïv** d.	0746	|	|	...	...	...	...	...	2048	2139
216	Im. T. Shevchenka d.	|	0812	0912	...	...	...	...	...	0034	0151
*353	**Kharkiv** d.	|	|	|	0941	...	1530	...	1747	|	|
*213	Poltava Pivdenna d.	|	|	|	1211	...	1743	...	2106	|	|
*94	Kremenchuk d.	|	|	|	1417	...	2008	...	2320	|	|
*224	**Dnipropetrovsk** d.	|	|	|	...	...	|	1910	|	|	|
308	Znamyanka d.	|	1005	1105	...	...	2150	2350	0123	|	|
362	Kirovohrad d.	|	|	|	...	...	...	0043	0226	|	|
720	**Odesa** Holovna d.	|	|	|	...	1441	...	0628	0759	|	|
448	Kryvyi Rih d.	|	|	|	...	|	...	...	...	0455	|
651	**Mykolaiv** a.	1407	1349	1449	...	1952	...	...	...	|	0656
706	Kherson a.	1454	1540	1640	...	2112	...	...	...	0855	...
1062	Zaporizhzhya I a.	...	...	...	...	0540	...	...	...	...	...
	Simferopol ◇ a.	...	...	...	...	...	...	...	...	...	...

	61SH	61SH	60	765	122	102	794	64	318	92
	■(1) ★	■(1) ☆						F	■(1)	
Simferopol ◇ d.	...	...	...	...	...	...	...	...	...	...
Zaporizhzhya I d.	...	...	...	...	...	...	...	...	1950	...
Kherson d.	0810	0910	...	1557	...	1848	...	...	0419	...
Mykolaiv d.	1012	1112	...	1642	1941	|	...	...	0534	...
Kryvyi Rih d.	|	|	...	|	|	2306	...	...	|	...
Odesa Holovna d.	|	|	1844	|	|	|	...	2157	1046	...
Kirovohrad d.	|	|	0029	|	|	|	...	0329	...	...
Znamyanka d.	1451	1551	0136	|	|	|	0227	0436	...	...
Dnipropetrovsk d.	|	|	|	|	|	|	|	0850	...	...
Kremenchuk d.	|	|	0346	|	|	|	0428	...	...	145
Poltava Pivdenna d.	|	|	0557	|	|	|	0619	...	...	171
Kharkiv d.	|	|	0919	|	|	|	0817	...	...	195
Im. T. Shevchenka d.	1644	1744	...	|	0127	0346	...	...	...	...
Kyïv a.	|	|	...	2307	0546	0710	...	...	...	...
Cherkasy d.	1724	1824	...	...	...	...	...	...	...	...
Konotop a.	2316	0016	...	...	...	...	...	...	...	...
Moskva Kiyev. **1740** a.	1112	1112	...	...	...	...	...	...	...	...

E – Uneven dates (daily May 24 - Sept. 29).
F – Even dates (daily May 25 - Sept. 30).
◇ – Service suspended.
★ – Dec. 11 - Mar. 25.
☆ – Mar. 26 - Oct. 28 (summer time in Ukraine). Timings are approximate.
● – Even dates (see page 530).
■ – Uneven dates (see page 530).
* – Distance from Znamyanka.

1770 MOSKVA - OREL - KHARKIV RZhD, UZ

km		717	723	719	73JA	73JA	715	735	19	19	105
			≋		d ★	d ☆		≋	s ★	s ☆	
0	**Moskva** Kurskaya d.	0650	0830	1200	1450	1450	1600	1755	2145	2145	2330
194	Tula I d.	0846	1028	1356	1815	1815	1756	1953	0015	0015	0204
383	Orel d.	1030	1217	1540	2125	2125	1940	2146	0232	0232	0524
537	Kursk d.	1157	...	1707	2343	2343	2107	2327	0421	0421	0750
697	Belgorod § RU d.	1343	...	1859	0253	0253	2248	...	0727	0727	...
781	**Kharkiv** § UA a.	...	...	...	0311	0411	...	...	0751	0851	...
	Kryvyi Rih **1780** a.	...	...	...	1330	1430	...	...	...	...	...

	722	716	720	726	718	106	20	20	74	74
	≋			≋			s ★	s ☆	d ★	d ☆
Kryvyi Rih **1780** d.	...	...	...	...	...	...	...	...	1052	115
Kharkiv § UA d.	...	...	...	...	...	...	2116r	2216r	2244	234
Belgorod § RU d.	...	0724	1227	...	1639	...	0035	0035	0204	020
Kursk d.	0621	0909	1424	...	1829	2110	0257	0257	0424	042
Orel d.	0806	1042	1557	1911	2002	0013	0454	0454	0621	062
Tula I d.	1000	1231	1746	2105	2146	0326	0705	0705	0852	085
Moskva Kurskaya a.	1200	1430	1945	2305	2345	0630	0952	0952	1130	113

d – Conveys portion to / from Dnipropetrovsk (Table **1780**).
r – Passengers must board by 2045 ★ 2145 ☆.
s – Conveys portion to / from Sumy (Table **1755**).
★ – Dec. 11 - Mar. 25.
☆ – Mar. 26 - Oct. 28. Timings are approximate.
≋ – *Lastochka* (Swallow) fast day train.
§ – 🏛 : Krasny Khutor (RU) / Kozacha Lopan (UA).
RU – Russia (Moskva Time GMT + 3).
UA – Ukraine (GMT + 2 winter, GMT + 3 summer).

1775 LVIV and KYÏV - DNIPROPETROVSK - MARIUPOL and MELITOPOL UZ

km		IC 732	70	IC 736	84	IC 734	12	86	76	80	52	42
		≋		L≋		≋		J			E	△
0	**Lviv** ▷ d.	...	0116	...	...	...	...	1047	...	...	...	1536
141	Ternopil ▷ d.	...	0332	...	...	...	...	1258	...	...	...	1745
260	Khmelnytsky ▷ d.	...	0601	...	...	...	...	1457	...	...	...	1946
359	Zhmerynka ▷ d.	...	0758	...	...	...	...	1643	...	...	...	2136
406	Vinnytsya ▷ d.	...	0857	...	...	...	...	1734	...	...	...	2225
468	Kozyatyn ▷ d.	...	0957	...	...	...	...	1840	...	...	...	2336
*216	**Kyïv** d.	0715	|	1449	1637	1735	1945	|	2125	2300	2344	|
772	Im. T. Shevchenka d.	0922	1436	1656	2007	1942	2219	2341	0054	0143	0219	0356
864	Znamyanka d.	1022	1559	1757	2124	2043	2332	0102	0220	0257	0330	0521
909	Oleksandria d.	1052	1640	1827	2204	2112	|	0145	0259	0342	0407	0602
1046	**Kryvyi Rih** a.	|	|	|	|	|	|	|	0605	|	|	|
1052	Dniprodzerzhynsk d.	1225	1901	1959	0027	2244	0223	0418	...	0610	0620	0843
1088	**Dnipropetrovsk** d.	1301	1954	2035	0121	2323	0315	0517	...	0647	0710	0920
1291	Krasnoarmiisk a.	|	|	|	|	0143	|	|	...	...	|	...
1357	Donetsk ◇ a.	|	|	|	|	...	|	|	...	...	|	...
1214	Zaporizhzhya I d.	1422	2200	2157	0328	...	0507	0722	...	...	0900	...
1589	Mariupol a.	...	0630	...	1115	...	|	|	...	...	...	...
1326	**Melitopol** a.	...	...	...	...	...	0650	0910	...	...	...	...
1417	Novooleksiivka a.	...	...	...	...	...	0825	1108	...	...	...	...
1570	Simferopol ◇ a.	...	...	...	...	...	...	...	...	...	...	...

	IC 733	41	IC 732	86	76	79	70	52	IC 736	12	84
	≋	▽	≋	K				F	L≋		
Simferopol ◇ d.	...	...	...	...	...	...	...	...	...	...	...
Novooleksiivka d.	...	...	...	1207	...	...	...	...	...	1955	...
Melitopol d.	...	...	...	1358	...	...	...	...	...	2135	...
Mariupol d.	...	...	...	|	...	...	1250	...	...	|	182
Zaporizhzhya I d.	...	...	1537	1551	...	...	2033	2157	2258	2322	020
Donetsk ◇ d.	...	...	|	|	...	...	|	|	|	|	|
Krasnoarmiisk d.	0441	...	|	|	...	...	|	|	|	|	|
Dnipropetrovsk d.	0710	1430	1709	1800	...	2225	2241	2357	0029	0131	041
Dniprodzerzhynsk d.	0738	1506	1737	1842	...	2302	2315	0030	0057	0207	045
Kryvyi Rih d.	|	|	|	|	2101	|	|	|	|	|	|
Oleksandria d.	0912	1739	1911	2137	0014	0137	0149	0245	0231	|	073
Znamyanka d.	0940	1824	1939	2224	0106	0221	0235	0327	0259	0512	081
Im. T. Shevchenka d.	1042	2003	2041	0026	0221	0339	0432	0441	0401	0628	094
Kyïv a.	1250	|	2249	|	0518	0658	|	0717	0610	0940	131
Kozyatyn ▷ d.	...	0033	...	0438	...	...	0902	...	...	...	...
Vinnytsya ▷ d.	...	0133	...	0540	...	...	1006	...	...	...	...
Zhmerynka ▷ d.	...	0243	...	0645	...	...	1116	...	...	...	...
Khmelnytsky ▷ d.	...	0420	...	0826	...	...	1259	...	...	...	...
Ternopil ▷ d.	...	0626	...	1023	...	...	1503	...	...	...	...
Lviv ▷ a.	...	0833	...	1238	...	...	1723	...	...	...	...

E – Even dates Jan., Apr., May, Aug., Nov.; uneven dates Dec., Feb., Mar., June, July, Sept., Oct.
F – Uneven dates Jan., Apr., May, Aug., Nov.; even dates Dec., Feb., Mar., June, July, Sept., Oct.
J – Uneven dates ■(1) (daily June 16 - Sept. 14).
K – Even dates (daily June 17 - Sept. 15).
L – ①③④⑤⑦.
■ – Uneven dates (see page 530).
≋ – *InterCity* fast train.
△ – From Truskavets (d. 1256).
▽ – To Truskavets (a. 1111).
▷ – See also Table **1700**.
◇ – Service suspended.
* – Distance from Im. T. Shevchenka.

1780 KHARKIV - DNIPROPETROVSK, KRYVYI RIH and MELITOPOL UZ

km		100	100	73JA	73JA 106	73JA	73JA 106	120	795 84	81
		■(1) ★	K ☆	★	★	☆	☆			
	Moskva Kurs. **1770** d.	...	...	1450	1450	1450	1450	...	...	...
	Minsk **1930** d.	0744	0744	|	|	|	|	...	...	...
0	**Kharkiv** d.	0037	0037	0401	0401	0501	0501	...	1805	2325
303	**Dnipropetrovsk** a.	|	|	|	0947	|	1047	...	2208	|
327	Zaporizhzhya I d.	0450	0450	0935	...	1035	...	1220	0313	0405
512	Kryvyi Rih a.	...	|	1330	...	1430	...	1654	|	|
702	Mariupol a.	...	|	...	...	...	...	...	1115	|
439	**Melitopol** a.	...	0637s	...	...	...	...	...	...	0550
530	Novooleksiivka a.	...	0805s	...	...	...	...	...	...	0715
683	Simferopol ◇ a.	...	...	...	...	...	...	...	...	...

	84 796	106 74	74	106 74	74	120	100	100	82
		★	★	☆	☆		■(3) ★	L ☆	
Simferopol ◇ d.	...	...	...	...	...	...	...	...	...
Novooleksiivka d.	...	...	...	...	...	...	...	2115s	2148
Melitopol d.	...	...	...	...	...	...	...	2256s	233
Mariupol d.	1827	...	...	...	...	...	...	|	|
Kryvyi Rih d.	|	...	1052	...	1152	1147	...	|	|
Zaporizhzhya I d.	0205	...	1602	...	1702	1620	0031	0031	0112
Dnipropetrovsk d.	0633	1548	|	1648	|	...	|	|	|
Kharkiv a.	1047	2145	2145	2245	2245	...	0459	0459	0553
Minsk **1930** a.	...	|	|	|	|	...	2345	2345	...
Moskva Kurs. **1770** a.	...	1130	1130	1130	1130	...	...	...	...

K – ■(1) (daily June 1 - Sept. 21).
L – From Zaporizhzhya ■(3) (daily June 3 - Sept. 23).
s – June 2 - Sept. 22.
★ – Dec. 11 - Mar. 25.
☆ – Mar. 26 - Oct. 28 (summer time in Ukraine). Timings are approximate.
■ – Uneven dates (see page 530).
◇ – Service suspended.

1785 KHARKIV - LYSYCHANSK UZ

km			134 K		609		409				
0	**Kharkiv** d.	...	0959	...	1445	...	2200	...	...	...	...
129	Kupiansk-Vuslov d.	...	1237	...	1744	...	0308	...	...	...	...
254	Lysychansk a.	...	1520	...	2026	...	0554	...	...	...	...
382	**Luhansk** ◇ a.	...	...	...	...	...	...	...	...	...	...
280	Horlivka ◇ a.	...	...	...	...	...	...	...	...	...	...
333	**Donetsk** ◇ a.	...	...	...	...	...	...	...	...	...	...

			410		134 K		610			
Donetsk ◇ d.	...	...	...	...	...	...	...	...	...	...
Horlivka ◇ d.	...	...	...	...	...	...	...	...	...	...
Luhansk ◇ d.	...	...	...	...	...	...	...	...	...	...
Lysychansk d.	...	...	0633	...	1636	...	2138	...	...	...
Kupiansk-Vuslov d.	...	...	0935	...	1938	...	0040	...	...	...
Kharkiv a.	...	...	1204	...	2156	...	0533	...	...	...

K – Kyïv (Table **1755**) - Kharkiv - Lysychansk and v.v.
◇ – Service suspended.

CRIMEAN PENINSULA

Although recognised by most countries as part of Ukraine, the region is *de facto* controlled by Russia. There are currently no rail services between Ukraine and Crimea; access to the region is from mainland Russia by way of the ferry across the Kerch Strait. A road and rail bridge is under construction across the strait. For local services see Table **1790**.

526 BCh – Belarusian Railways RZhD – Russian Railways UZ – Ukrainian Railways

CRIMEAN PENINSULA — 1790

Crimean Railway. GMT+3

km														
0	Solone Ozero ....d.	..	0525	...	...	0930	...	1400	...	...	1835
20	Dzhankoy ....d.	...	0600	...	0700	1005	1140	1450	...	1710	1908
11	Simferopol ....a.	...	0820	...	...	1225	1400	1710	...	1930	2105
11	Simferopol ....▷d.	0515	...	0850	...	...	1445	...	1755	...	...
90	Yevpatoriya ....▷a.	...	...	...	1005	...	...	...	...	...	...
89	Sevastopol ....a.	0730	...	1100	...	...	1700	...	2010	...	...

km												
0	Armyansk ....d.	...	...	...	0715	...	...	...	1450
78	Dzhankoy ....d.	0135	...	0620	...	0930	1435	...	1720
79	Vladyslavivka.............d.	0438	0613	0906	0920	1145	1138	1656	1705	1908	...
96	Feodosia ....d.	...	0703	...	1002	...	1220	...	1745	1945	...
70	Kerch.........................a.	0705	...	1130	...	1345	...	1930	...	...

Sevastopol ....d.	...	0510	0810	...	1120	...	...	1720	...	...
Yevpatoriya ....▷d.	...	...	...	...		...	...	1715	...
Simferopol ....▷a.	...	0725	1020	...	1330	...	1930	...	...
Simferopol ....d.	0535	0845	...	1050	1350	1530	1830	...	...	2040
Dzhankoy ....d.	0810	1100	...	1310	1605	1747	2050	...	2020	2255
Solone Ozero..............a.	0840	...	...	1340	...	1815	2120	...	...

Kerch..........................d.	...	...	0830	...	1350	1625	...	...	2045
Feodosia ....d.	...	0805	1025	...	1505	...	1815	2015	
Vladyslavivka ....d.	...	0846	1109	1135	1550	1614	1833	1905	2115	0020
Dzhankoy ....d.	0950	...	...	1355	...	1840	...	2130	...	0255
Armyansk....................a.	1145	...	...	...	...	...	...	...	...

– From Simferopol 0520, 0830, 1435, 1800. From Yevpatoriya 0515, 0820, 1230, 1755. Journey 2 hrs to 2 hrs 10 mins.   *Subject to alteration.*

LITHUANIA, LATVIA and ESTONIA   *SEE MAP PAGE 523*

Operators: Lithuania: **LG** (Lietuvos Geležinkeliai), www.litrail.lt   Latvia: **LDz** (Latvijas Dzelzceļš), www.ldz.lv   Estonia: **Elron** www.edel.ee

Services: Trains convey first- and second-class seating unless indicated otherwise. International trains to and from Belarus, Russia and Ukraine are composed of Russian-style sleeping-cars (for details of train types and classes of travel see the panel on page **530**).

Timings: Valid from **December 11, 2016**. Timings are expressed in local time at the station concerned (time comparison chart: page 2). Timings of local trains in Estonia are often subject to short-term changes and passengers are advised to check times before travel.

Reservations: Reservation is compulsory for travel by international services to / from Russia.

RIGA - TALLINN, ST PETERBURG, VILNIUS and KALININGRAD — 1800

RIGA - TALLINN ☐
Journey time: 4 hours 25 mins.
From Riga: 0305, 0700, 0900, 1000, 1115, 1230, 1445, 1600, 1700, 1830, 2035.
From Tallinn: 0600, 0700, 0830, 1000, 1115, 1245, 1445, 1600, 1700, 1830, 2230.

RIGA - ST PETERBURG ☐
Journey time: approx 11 hours.
From Riga: 0855, 1845, 2245, 2355.
From St Peterburg Coach Station: 1115, 1945, 2100, 2335.
From Baltiski station 35-40 mins later.

RIGA - VILNIUS ☐
Journey time: 4h 10m - 4h 30m
From Riga: 0250, 0700, 0900, 1035, 1230, 1445, 1530, 1620, 1700, 1815, 2250.
From Vilnius: 0630, 0700, 0800, 1000, 1115, 1230, 1415, 1610, 1830, 2300.

RIGA - KALININGRAD ☐
Journey time: 7 hours 40 mins.
From Riga: 2330.
From Kaliningrad: 2230◊.

☐ – Operator: Lux Express (www.luxexpress.eu).
☐ – Operator: Ecolines (ecolines.net).

◊ – One hour earlier when Latvia is on summer time (Mar. 26 - Oct. 28).

Riga and Vilnius coach stations are adjacent to the railway stations. Tallinn coach station is 3 km from the railway station (by tram).

VILNIUS - ŠIAULIAI - KLAIPEDA — 1810

LG 2nd class §

km		781	17	23	36	783	19		18	780	24	782	38	20
					⑥		Ⓐ			⑥		⑤⑦		Ⓐ
					m					m				
0	Vilnius......... 1811 d.	...	0650	0720	0950	...	1415	...	1645	1710	1745	Klaipeda...............d.	0640	0815	...	1030	...	1445	1605	...	1800	...	Ⓐ
67	Kaišiadorys ... 1811 d.	...	0732	0805	...	...	1500	...	...	1755	1827	Šiauliai.................d.	0831	1045	1156	1218	1325	1725	1734	1757	1830	1943	2020
**	Kaunas..................d.	...	...	...	...	...	...	1530	...	...	...	Radviliškis ....d.	0848	1127	1231	...	1345	1745	1806	1814	1852	...	2040
192	Radviliškis ....d.	0550	0851	0933	...	1340	1628	1635	1723	...	1923	1949	Kaunas ....a.	...	...	...	...	...	...	...	...	2049	...	...
212	Šiauliai ....d.	0617	0913	0952	1201	1411	1647	1709	1744	1855	1941	2011	Kaišiadorys ... 1811 d.	1008	...	...	1515	1916	...	1934	...	...	2210	
376	Klaipeda ....a.	0900	1102	...	1338	...	2001	...	2029	...	2157	Vilnius ... 1811 a.	1052	...	...	1426	1601	2003	...	2017	...	2151	2256

km				m							m			
0	Šiauliai ....d.	...	0920	1413	...	1800	...	2055	...	Mažeikiai ....d.	...	0705	...	1045	...	1550	...	1930	...
78	Mažeikiai ....a.	...	1034	1526	...	1915	...	2210	...	Šiauliai ....a.	...	0818	...	1156	...	1703	...	2043	...

– Radviliškis - Mažeikiai and v.v.   § – Trains where no train number is shown are 3rd class.   ** – 138 km Kaunas - Radviliškis.

VILNIUS - KAUNAS — 1811

LG 1,2 class

km		Ⓐ																				Ⓑ	
0	Vilnius .... 1810 d.	0440	0445	0620	0730	0850	0935	1025	1115	1140	1225	1405	1445	1550	1630	1650	1730	1755	1850	1945	2100	...
67	Kaišiadorys .... 1810 d.	0523	0546	0710	0820	0948	1016	1111	1202	1236	1306	1453	1542	1633	1711	1749	1814	1847	1950	2035	2154	...
104	Kaunas ....a.	0550	0621	0737	0849	1024	1040	1137	1231	1311	1330	1520	1617	1657	1735	1825	1839	1918	2026	2102	2231	...

km		⊀		Ⓐ																	
	Kaunas..........................d.	0502	0530	0623	0705	0810	0915	1100	1208	1350	1440	1540	1632	1705	1721	1755	1845	1920	1950	2010	2149
	Kaišiadorys .... 1810 d.	0529	0602	0652	0736	0837	0943	1132	1234	1419	1505	1611	1657	1730	1753	1821	1910	1950	2015	2045	2216
	Vilnius .... 1810 a.	0631	0709	0738	0837	0924	1041	1239	1320	1519	1549	1714	1738	1816	1900	1910	1910	1954	2054	2102	2136	2305

VILNIUS - VILNIUS AIRPORT — 1812

LG 3rd class

km											Ⓐ							
0	Vilnius......................d.	0545	0800	0845	0935	...	1100	1145	1248	1330	1406	1450	...	1605	1657	1745	1920	2025	2200
4	Vilnius Airport ☐ ....a.	0552	0807	0852	0942	...	1107	1152	1255	1337	1413	1457	...	1612	1704	1752	1927	2032	2207

Vilnius Airport ☐ ....d.	0557	0812	0857	0947	...	1112	1157	1300	1342	1418	1505	...	1617	1712	1757	1932	2037	2216
Vilnius..........................a.	0605	0820	0905	0955	...	1120	1205	1308	1350	1426	1513	...	1625	1720	1805	1940	2045	2224

☐ – Oro uostas in Lithuanian.

VILNIUS - TRAKAI — 1815

LG 3rd class

km			Ⓐ										Ⓐ							
0	Vilnius........................d.	0428	0518	0610	0740	1230	1330	1610	1815	2046	Trakai.......................d.	0520	0603	0705	0830	1315	1420	1705	1945	2132
27	Trakai.........................a.	0510	0600	0655	0825	1310	1410	1655	1905	2130	Vilnius......................a.	0605	0647	0751	0916	1400	1506	1752	2030	2219

VILNIUS - TURMANTAS — 1818

LG 3rd class

km			Ⓐ									Ⓐ						
0	Vilnius........................d.	0534	0812	1144	1510	1645	1753	1925	2111	Turmantas ....d.	...	0434	0526	0834	1206	1610	1753	...
101	Ignalina......................d.	0718	1000	1332	1653	1808	1917	2113	2242	Ignalina......................d.	0424	0511	0602	0917	1249	1653	1836	2030
147	Turmantas ....a.	0801	1043	1415	1736	...	1955	...	2319	Vilnius......................a.	0605	0630	0723	1101	1433	1834	2017	2153

RIGA - VALMIERA - VALGA — 1830

LDz

km							Ⓑ								Ⓐ	Ⓒ
0	Riga..........................d.	0621	0754	1038	1230	1400	1542	1728	1810	1837	1938	2130	Valga ... 🚎EE d.	...	0517	...	...	1438	...	1639
53	Sigulda.......................d.	0743	0907	1148	1343	1513	1655	1841	1900	1951	2051	2243	Lugaži ... 🚎LV d.	...	0524	...	...	1445	...	1646
93	Cesis..........................d.	0825	...	1230	...	...	1932	2033	...	Valmiera ....d.	0457	0606	...	0947	...	1530	...	1731
121	Valmiera.....................d.	0856	...	1302	...	...	1958	2104	...	Cesis.........................d.	0531	0632	...	1021	...	1602	...	1802
164	Lugaži ... 🚎LV a.	...	1347	...	...	2044	...	Sigulda.......................d.	0613	0704	0802	0922	1103	1405	1535	1644	1710	1844	2133
168	Valga ... 🚎EE a.	...	1353	...	...	2049	...	Riga..........................a.	0725	0751	0916	1036	1215	1519	1649	1737	1824	1948	2247

🚎E – Estonia.   LV – Latvia.   🚎 For trains Valga - Tallinn see Table **1880**.

1840 RIGA - REZEKNE - ST PETERBURG and MOSKVA

LDz, RZhD

km		808	Pas 662AJ 664AJ M	702 ©	Fir 2RJ L ★	Fir 38RJ B ★	816	Fir 2RJ L ☆	Fir 38RJ B ☆
0	**Riga** 1850 d.	0947	...	1138	1650	1650	1700	1730	1730
51	Lielvarde 1850 d.	1037	...	|	|	|	1750	|	|
129	Krustpils ⊡ 1850 d.	1150	...	1320	1838	1838	1858	1920	1920
224	**Rezekne II** d.	1323	...	1428	2002	2002	2032	2055	2055
279	Zilupe LV d.	1426	...	...	2140	2140	2135	2240	2240
306	Sebezh RU d.	...	...	...	2358	2358	...	2358	2358
417	Novosokolniki d.	...	...	...	0224	0334	...	0224	0334
593	Dno d.	...	...	...	|	0606	...	|	0606
838	**St Peterburg** Vitebski a.	...	...	...	|	0930	...	|	0930
446	**Velikiye Luki** d.	...	2115	...	0258	...	...	0258	...
687	Rzhev d.	...	0227	...	0602	...	...	0602	...
922	**Moskva** Rizhskaya a.	...	0658	...	1017	...	...	1017	...

	815	Fir 1RJ L ★	Fir 37RJ B ★	Fir 1RJ L ☆	Fir 37RJ B ☆	Pas 661AJ 663RJ N	701 ©	807
Moskva Rizhskaya d.	...	1705	...	1705	...	1956	...	...
Rzhev d.	...	2110	...	2110	...	0035	...	...
Velikiye Luki d.	...	0035	...	0035	...	0605	...	...
St Peterburg Vitebski d.	...	|	1720	|	1720	...	...	...
Dno d.	...	|	2101	|	2101	...	...	...
Novosokolniki d.	...	0135	0135	0135	0135	...	...	...
Sebezh RU d.	...	0410	0410	0410	0410	...	...	...
Zilupe LV d.	0334	0422	0422	0522	0522	...	...	1526
Rezekne II d.	0439	0522	0522	0622	0622	...	1505	1632
Krustpils ⊡ 1850 d.	0611	0637	0637	0733	0733	...	1613	1820
Lielvarde 1850 d.	0725	|	|	|	|	...	|	1937
Riga 1850 a.	0820	0828	0828	0924	0924	...	1758	2027

B – BALTIJA – 🛏 1, 2 cl. [R]
L – LATVIJAS EKSPRESIS – 🛏 1, 2 cl. [R]
M – ②③④⑤⑦.
N – ①③④⑤⑦.
★ – Dec. 11 - Mar. 25.
☆ – Mar. 26 - Oct. 28 (summer time in Latvia). Approx times.
⊡ – Station for Jekabpils.
LV – Latvia (GMT+2 winter, GMT+3 summer).
RU – Russia (Moskva Time GMT+3).

1850 RIGA - DAUGAVPILS - MINSK

LDz, BCh

km		802	©		810 ⑤–⑦		704	818	Sko 88BJ ●(4) ★	Sko 88BJ ●(4) ☆	
0	**Riga** ▷ d.	0740	0830	0947	1258	1525	1612	1738	1920	2020	2110
51	Lielvarde ▷ d.	0829	0930	1037	1348	1620	|	1826	|	|	2215
129	Krustpils ⊡ ▷ d.	0947	1052	1150	1500	1741	1754	1941	2100	2200	2333
218	**Daugavpils** LV d.	1107	...	...	1630	...	1858	2101	2224	2324	...
379	Polatsk § BY d.	...	...	...	...	...	...	...	0330	0330	...
578	Maladzechna d.	...	...	...	...	...	...	...	0639	0639	...
655	**Minsk** a.	...	...	...	...	...	...	...	0750	0750	...

		703	Sko 87BJ ■(3) ★	Sko 87BJ ■(3) ☆	817	©	801 ⑤–⑦			809
Minsk d.	...	...	2226	2226	...	...	...	...	...	...
Maladzechna d.	...	...	0002	0002	...	...	...	...	...	...
Polatsk § BY d.	...	...	0310	0310	...	...	...	...	...	...
Daugavpils LV d.	...	0615	0607	0707	0716	...	1255	...	...	1735
Krustpils ⊡ ▷ d.	0454	0721	0710	0810	0843	1150	1421	...	...	1906
Lielvarde ▷ d.	0617	|	|	|	1001	1312	1539	1647	1739	2022
Riga ▷ a.	0729	0907	0900	1000	1052	1411	1630	1751	1842	2113

⊡ – Station for Jekabpils.
★ – Dec. 11 - Mar. 25.
☆ – Mar. 26 - Oct. 28 (summer time in Latvia). Approx times.
● – Even dates (see page 530).
■ – Uneven dates (see page 530).
▷ – See also Table **1840**. Local trains run Riga - Lielvarde.
§ – : Indra (LV) / Bihosava (BY).
LV – Latvia (GMT+2 winter, +3 summer).
BY – Belarus (GMT+3).

1860 RIGA - LIEPAJA, TUKUMS and SAULKRASTI

LDz

km		⑤		⑦
0	**Riga** ▷ d.	1825	**Liepaja** d.	1730
43	Jelgava ▷ d.	1911	Saldus d.	1850
125	Saldus d.	2027	Jelgava ▷ d.	2005
223	**Liepaja** a.	2146	**Riga** ▷ a.	2043

RIGA - JURMALA ◧ - TUKUMS *65 km* Journey 1h 25m

From **Riga**: 0548, 0737, 0920, 1300, 1417, 1556, 1706, 1856, 2140, 2240, 2336. From **Tukums** II: 0451, 0548, 0622, 0813, 0925, 1117, 1451, 1633, 1745, 1933, 2100.

Riga - Jurmala (Sloka) ◧ 1 - 2 trains per hour. journey ± 50 mins.

RIGA - SAULKRASTI *48 km* Journey 1 hour

From **Riga**: 0615, 0720, 0814, 1018, 1220, 1440, 1556Ⓐ, 1632, 1743, 1830, 1929, 2033, 2225. From **Saulkrasti**: 0507, 0641, 0747, 0832, 0948, 1150, 1350, 1622, 1708Ⓐ, 1804, 1919, 2212.

Certain trains continue to/from Skulte, *56 km* ± 70 minutes.

▷ – Riga - Jelgava: 1 - 2 trains per hour.
◧ – Jurmala's 33 km coastline has several stations; principal stations are Majori (*22 km*) and Sloka (*32 km*). There is no station called Jurmala.

1870 TALLINN - ST PETERBURG - MOSKVA

Elron, GoRail, RZhD

km		220		34KH A§ ★	34KH A ☆		222	224	226	
0	**Tallinn** 1880 d.	0852	...	1610	1710	...	1527	1853	2126	...
77	Tapa 1880 d.	0952	...	1701	1801	...	1627	1953	2226	...
104	Rakvere d.	1010	...	|	|	...	1646	2012	2244	...
165	Jõhvi d.	1101	...	1758	1858	...	1734	2104	...	...
209	Narva EE d.	1135	...	1913	2013	...	1807	2138	...	...
380	**St Peterburg** Glavni RU a.	...	...	2354	2354	...	...	...	...	...
633	Bologoye 1900 a.	...	...	0445	0445	...	...	...	...	...
797	Tver 1900 a.	...	...	0718	0718	...	...	...	...	...
964	**Moskva** Oktyabrskaya 1900 a.	...	...	0940	0940	...	...	...	...	...

	221	223		34AJ A ★	34AJ A ☆		225	227	
Moskva Oktyabrskaya 1900 d.	...	...	...	2215	2215	...	...	...	...
Tver 1900 d.	...	...	...	0031	0031	...	...	...	...
Bologoye 1900 d.	...	...	...	|	|	...	...	...	...
St Peterburg Glavni RU d.	...	...	...	0625	0625	...	...	...	...
Narva EE d.	...	0705	...	1005	1105	...	1303	1932	...
Jõhvi d.	...	0740	...	1040	1140	...	1337	2006	...
Rakvere d.	0615	0829	...	|	|	...	1426	2054	...
Tapa 1880 d.	0635	0849	...	1142	1242	...	1446	2114	...
Tallinn 1880 a.	0733	0947	...	1235	1335	...	1544	2212	...

Lux Express (www.luxexpress.eu) 🚌 TALLINN - ST PETERBURG Reservation compulsory

🚌	Ⓑ				©				
Tallinn coach station ◇ d.	0600	0700	0800	1015	1135	1430	1545	2300	2359
St Peterburg coach station ¶ a.	1325*	1525*	1550*	1915*	1925*	2220*	2310*	0700*	0850*

🚌					Ⓑ		©		
St Peterburg coach station ¶ d.	0645	0815	1030	1315	1700	1810	2200	2230	2315
Tallinn coach station ◇ a.	1300r	1415r	1810r	1955r	2320r	0015r	0500r	0545r	0540r

A – 🛏 1, 2 cl. [R]. Operated by Go Rail.
★ – Dec. 11 - Mar. 25.
☆ – Mar. 26 - Oct. 28 (approximate times).
r – One hour later Mar. 26 - Oct. 28.
¶ – Also calls at Baltiski station.
§ – Dep. 1530 Dec. 23 - Jan. 9, Feb. 23 - 26.
◇ – 3 km by tram from railway station.
* – One hour earlier Mar. 26 - Oct. 28.
EE – Estonia (GMT+2 winter, GMT+3 summer).
RU – Russia (Moskva Time GMT+3).

1880 TALLINN - TARTU - VALGA

Elron

km		210	10 ◇	12 ◇	14 ◇	212	16 ◇	214	18 ◇	216
0	**Tallinn** 1870 d.	0611	0805	1006	1315	1413	1513	1651	1742	2021
77	Tapa 1870 d.	0711	0855	1056	1405	1513	1603	1751	1832	2122
142	Jõgeva d.	0800	0940	1135	1445	1604	1645	1846	1917	2208
190	**Tartu** a.	0834	1007	1203	1513	1641	1713	1922	1946	2242
190	**Tartu** d.	...	1010	...	1517	...	1716	...	...	...
215	Elva d.	...	1037	...	1544	...	1746	...	...	...
273	**Valga** a.	...	1122	...	1629	...	1831	...	...	...
	Riga 1830 a.	...	...	...	*1948c*	...	...	...	...	...

	211	11 ◇	13 ◇	15 ◇	213	17 ◇	215	19 ◇	217
Riga 1830 d.	...	...	...	...	...	*1038*	...	...	...
Valga d.	...	0615a	0724c	...	...	1405	...	1701	...
Elva d.	...	0659a	0808c	...	...	1449	...	1745	...
Tartu a.	...	0726a	0835c	...	...	1516	...	1813	...
Tartu d.	0624	0729	0838	1206	1408	1520	1722	1816	1958
Jõgeva d.	0702	0759	0906	1235	1444	1549	1757	1846	2033
Tapa 1870 d.	0749	0839	0947	1315	1538	1630	1848	1931	2123
Tallinn 1870 a.	0847	0928	1036	1404	1636	1719	1946	2020	2221

km			
0	Tartu d.	1012	1718
43	Põlva d.	1054	1800
72	Orava d.	1119	1825
85	Koidula a.	1129	1835
92	Piusa a.	1155s	...

	Ⓐ	©	
Piusa d.	...	...	1533s
Koidula d.	0601	0710	1550
Orava d.	0611	0720	1600
Põlva d.	0635	0744	1624
Tartu a.	0719	0828	1708

a – Ⓐ only.
c – © only.
s – Apr. 29 - Oct. 1 (approx time).
◇ – Classified *Ekspress* between Tallinn and Tartu (higher fares apply). Different train numbers apply between Tartu and Valga but trains normally run through.
☛ Fast 🚌 services operate between Tallinn and Tartu approx 18 times daily (journey: 2½ hrs); operator Lux Express (www.luxexpress.eu). Tallinn coach station is located 3 km south of Tallinn railway station (by tram).

1890 TALLINN - VILJANDI and PÄRNU

Elron

km												
0	**Tallinn** d.	0744	0744	0951	1136	1417	1614	1726	1802	1830	1930	2202
54	Rapla d.	0843	0843	1058	1242	1523	1720	1825	1901	1940	2040	2309
72	Lelle d.	0859	0900	1114	...	1539	1736	1841	1920	1956	2056	2325
98	Türi a.	0923	|	1135	...	1601	1757	1903	|	2017	2118	2346
151	**Viljandi** a.	1004	|	...	...	1642	...	1944	|	...	2159	...
136	**Pärnu** a.	...	1002	...	...	...	...	...	2022	...	...	...

				©	Ⓐ						
Pärnu d.	...	...	0723	...	...	...	...	...	...	1816	...
Viljandi d.	...	0628	|	0838	0847	...	1320	...	1737	|	...
Türi d.	0551	0710	|	0921	0921	1256	1402	...	1819	|	2033
Lelle d.	0613	0732	0826	0943	0943	1318	1424	...	1842	1921	2056
Rapla d.	0629	0746	0842	0957	0957	1334	1440	1721	1900	1940	2112
Tallinn a.	0737	0843	0938	1053	1053	1443	1547	1828	1956	2036	2217

☛ Pärnu railway station is situated approx 4 km from the centre. 🚌 services operate between Tallinn coach station and Pärnu 7 times daily (journey 1h 50m); operator Lux Express (www.luxexpress.eu). Tallinn coach station is located 3 km south of Tallinn railway station (by tram).

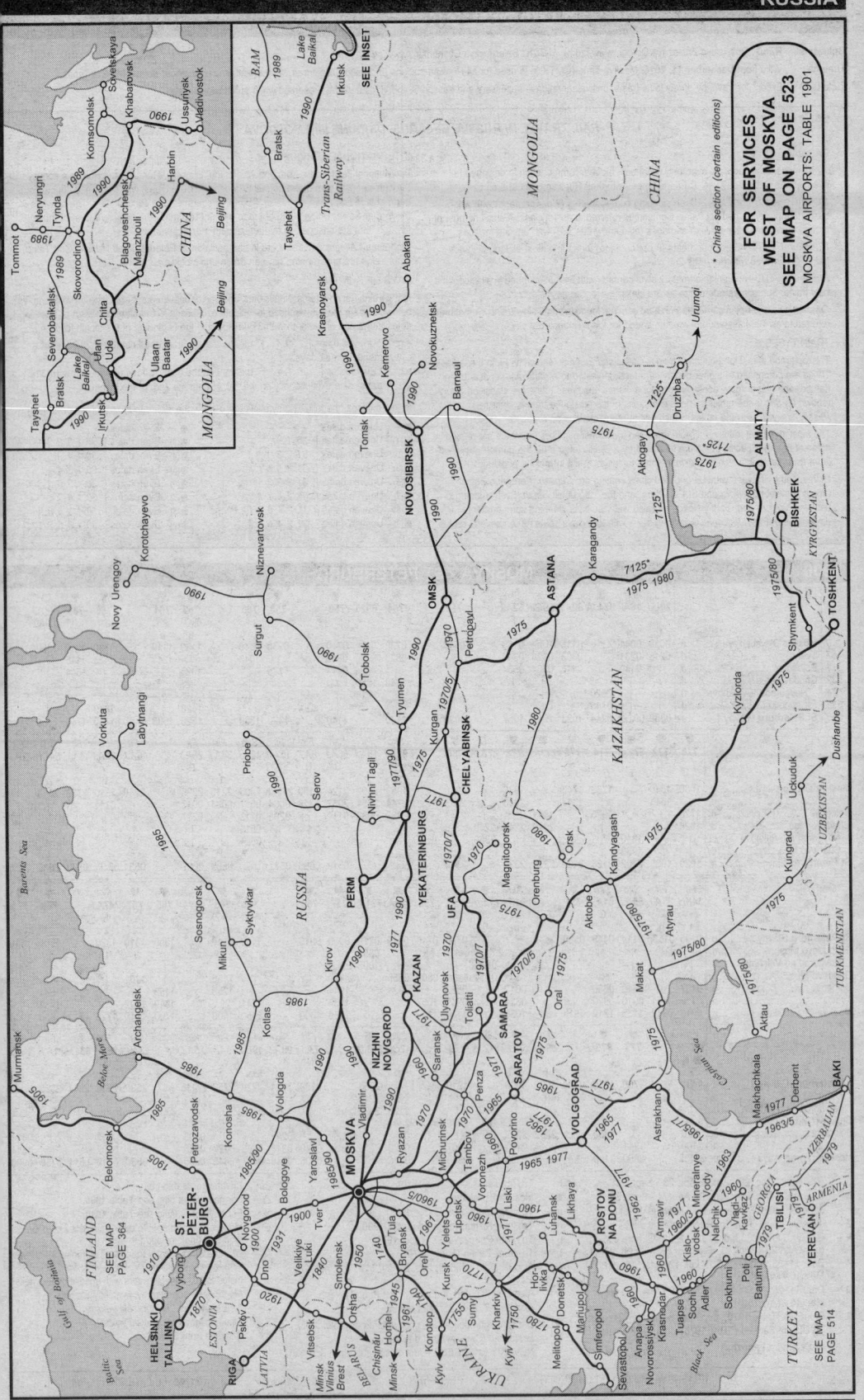

RUSSIA and BELARUS

Operators : RZhD : Rossiskiye Zheleznye Dorogi, www.rzd.ru BCh : Belaruskaya Chyhunka, www.rw.by

Timings :   Valid from **December 11, 2016.** Moskva Time (GMT +3) is used for all Russian stations (including Kaliningrad, where local time is one hour behind Moskva Time).

Tickets :   Except for travel by purely local trains, prior reservation is necessary and passports and visas must be presented when purchasing tickets.

RAIL TRAVEL IN RUSSIA, BELARUS, UKRAINE and MOLDOVA

CARRIAGE TYPES

As trains generally operate over long distances, most accommodation is designed for overnight as well as day use. Carriage types (with their Russian names) are:

Spálny vagón SV or CB – 2-berth sleeping compartments (9 per carriage) with wash basin, found only in the best trains. Sometimes referred to as 1st class. A small number of named trains also have *de luxe* carriages (also known as *VIP*) with ensuite facilities.

Kupéiny K – 4-berth compartments (9 per carriage) found in almost all long-distance trains. Sometimes referred to as 2nd class.

Platskártny ПЛ – open-plan dormitory-style carriage with 54 bunks, found in all except the best trains. Sometimes referred to as 3rd class.

Óbshchi О – open-plan carriages with hard seating, found in some slow trains. Sometimes referred to as 4th class and not recommended for long-distance travel.

TRAIN TYPES

The top grade of fast long-distance train is classified *Firménny* (shown as *Fir* in the tables). These are composed of higher-quality carriages dedicated to a particular service (often named) and higher fares apply. Normal long-distance express trains are classified *Skóry* (shown as *Sko* in the tables). The lowest class of long-distance train is classified *Passazhírsky* (*Pas* in the tables) which call at many stations en-route.

The most important trains on a route are given the lowest numbers (numbers are reused in different areas). Specific trains are identified by a cyrillic letter after the number, or a two-letter transliteration which is shown in some tables to assist in making bookings.

High-speed train types with 1st and 2nd class seating are *Sapsan* (Peregrine Falcon) running between Moskva and St Peterburg, and the Talgo-built *Strizh* (Swift) running between Moskva and Nizhny Novgorod (also with 1st class sleeping compartments for daytime use). Fast *Lastochka* (Swallow) trains with 2nd class seats run on several routes.

INTERNATIONAL SERVICES

International services to, from and via Poland, Slovakia, Hungary and Romania convey through sleeping cars of the normal European (`RIC`) types, with single and double compartments in first class, and 3- or 4-berth compartments in second class. The railways of the former Soviet Union being of broad gauge (1520mm), the bogies (trucks) of these through cars are changed at the frontier with these countries.

High-speed *Allegro* day trains are in use between St Peterburg and Helsinki, and Talgo hotel trains are now running beween Berlin and Moskva.

DAYS OF RUNNING

Many trains run on alternate days only, on even or uneven numbered dates. The examples below illustrate the system used to indicate exceptions to the pattern of even or uneven dates at the end of a month with 31 days and at the beginning of the month following:

e.g.   "Uneven dates [... 29, 1 ...]" means that the train does not run on the 31st of a month with 31 days.

e.g.   "Even dates [... 30, 1, 4 ...]" means that the train, **following a month with 31 days,** runs exceptionally on the 1st, but not the 2nd, of the month.

In these cases, the following symbols are used in the tables to indicate days of running:

■ – Uneven dates.	● – Even dates.
■(1) – Uneven dates [.. 29, 1 ..]	●(3) – Even dates [.. 30, 1, 3, 8 ..]
■(2) – Uneven dates [.. 31, 2, 3 ..]	●(4) – Even dates [.. 30, 1, 4 ..]
■(3) – Uneven dates [.. 31, 3 ..]	●(5) – Even dates [.. 30, 1, 3, 4 ..]
■(5) – Uneven dates [.. 31, 2, 5 ..]	●(6) – Even dates [.. 30, 1, 3, 6 ..]
■(7) – Uneven dates [.. 31, 2, 4, 7 ..]	●(7) – Even dates [.. 30, 1, 6 ..]
■(8) – Uneven dates [.. 31, 2, 4, 6, 8, 10, 11 ..]	●(8) – Even dates [.. 30, 1, 3, 5, 8 ..]
■(9) – Uneven dates [.. 31, 2, 4, 6, 9 ..]	●(9) – Even dates [.. 30, 1, 3, 5, 7, 10 ..]

1900   MOSKVA - ST PETERBURG   RZhD

km		☐ 20UJ	Fir 16AJ	⚡ 874JA	Sko 30AJ	Fir 59GJ	Sko 62AJ F		♥ 752		♥ 754	6925	♥ 756		♥ 758	♥ 760		♥ 762 ⑥⑦ u	♥ 764 ⑥⑦ u		♥ 766	♥ 768	☐ 748AJ ①–⑥ w
0	Moskva Oktyabrskaya § .... d.	0020	0041	...	0115	0135k	0153		0540		0730		0740		0930	0940		1130	1140		1330	1340	1350
167	Tver .... d.	0215	0231	...	0303	0328	0344				0833		0845		1043			1243		1433	1445	
331	Bologoye .... d.		0440		0448	0504	0534						0944		1125			1325			1544	
532	Chudovo Mos. .... d.										1040	1050										
*74	Novgorod na Volkhove ...... d.			0620							1214											
532	Chudovo Mos. .... d.			0746																		
650	St Peterburg Glavny ‡ .... a.	0859	0912c	0944	1023	1011	1057		0920		1130		1140		1320	1330		1520	1530		1730	1740	1755

		♥ 770	♥ 772	⚡ 872JA	♥ 774	♥ 776	⚡ 722AJ	♥ 778	⚡ 873JA	♥ 780		Sko 92AJ △ m	Fir 18AJ p	Sko 56AJ D	Fir 9AJ N	Fir 107JI S	Sko 42AJ ☆	Fir 34AJ	Fir 26AJ P		Fir 6AJ ☆ ⊙	Fir 32AJ ▽ h	♥ 4AJ ☆	☒ 54CH ☒	Fir 2AJ ☆
	Moskva Oktyabrskaya § .... d.	1530	1540	...	1730	1740	...	1930	...	1940		1953	2102	2124	2150	2156k	2205	2215	2228		2250	2310	2330	2340	2355
	Tver .... d.		1643	...		1843		2033		2045		2144	2254	2332	2356	0004	0011	0031	0047		...	0111			
	Bologoye .... d.	1725	...	1925		1841		...		2144		2332	0038	0117		0205	0213	0227							
	Chudovo Mos. .... d.	1828				2049	2240	2249								0515									
	Novgorod na Volkhove ...... d.			1810				2359								0624									
	Chudovo Mos. .... d.			1932																					
	St Peterburg Glavny ‡ .... a.	1920	1930	2102	2120	2130	2211	2300		2340		...	0519	0606	0532		0539	0627			0634	0546c	0830	0836	0756

		Fir 34KH t	Fir 31AJ ▽	Sko 55AJ E	Sko 61AJ G	♥ 751		Sko 91AJ △ m	⚡ 874JA	♥ 753	♥ 755	⚡ 721AJ	721AJ	♥ 757	♥ 759		♥ 761 ⑥⑦ u	♥ 763 ⑥⑦ u		♥ 765	♥ 767	♥ 747AJ Ⓑ z		♥ 769	♥ 771
	St Peterburg Glavny ‡ .... d.	0105	0153c	0114	0145	0530		...	...	0700	0710	0719	0719	0900	0910		1100	1110		1300	1310	1320		1500	1510
	Chudovo Mos. .... d.												0857												
	Novgorod na Volkhove ...... d.								0620				1008												
	Chudovo Mos. .... d.							0734		0800	0855														
	Bologoye .... d.	0457		0648	0630			0612		0852		1034		1044			1259			1452		1644			
	Tver .... d.	0719	0651	0910	0920			0821		0949	1007			1139			1341			1549	1602	1739			
	Moskva Oktyabrskaya § .... a.	0940	0919	1138	1210	0910		1036		1100	1110			1250	1300		1450	1500		1700	1710	1725		1850	1900

		Fir 107ZH ■(3) T	♥ 773	♥ 775		Fir 59AJ n	♥ 777	⚡ 872JA	♥ 779		Sko 42CH ☆	⚡ 873JA		Fir 7AJ N	Sko 29AJ	☐ 19UJ ☆ ☒	Fir 5AJ △	Fir 15AJ		Fir 3AJ ☆ ⊙	Fir 25AJ ☒ Q	☐ 53CH	Fir 1AJ ☆	Fir 77AJ p
	St Peterburg Glavny ‡ .... d.	1431	...	1700	1710		1803	1900		1910		...	2055		2150	2211	2229	2250	2241c		2330	2336	2344	2355	...
	Chudovo Mos. .... d.											2249													
	Novgorod na Volkhove ...... d.							1810				2120	2359												
	Chudovo Mos. .... d.							1922	2000			2247													
	Bologoye .... d.	1910			1859		2232	2052		0132			0201				0303								0411
	Tver .... d.	2100		1941			0014	2149		2207		0340	0348	0355	0427	0426				0502				0644
	Moskva Oktyabrskaya § .... a.	2348k		2050	2100		0209k	2300		2310		0515		0606	0549	0557	0645	0650			0830	0719	0814	0756	0900

D – ⑤⑦ (daily Dec. 26 - Jan. 8, Apr. 23 - Sept. 24).	h – To/from Helsinki (Table **1910**).
E – ①⑥ (daily Dec. 26 - Jan. 10, Apr. 24 - Sept. 25).	k – Moskva **Kurskaya**.
F – June 24 - Aug. 27 (also certain dates in June).	m – To/from Murmansk (Table **1905**).
G – June 26 - Aug. 31 (also certain dates in June).	n – To/from Nizhni Novgorod (Table **1990**).
N – ①⑤⑥⑦ to Dec. 30; daily Jan. 1- 13, ⑧ from Jan. 15 (daily Apr. 23 - Sept. 8), also Feb. 25; not Feb. 23, 24.	p – To/from Petrozavodsk (Table **1905**).
P – Dec. 11- 26, ①②③④⑤⑥⑦ Jan. 12 - Mar. 14; daily Mar. 16 - May 26.	S – From Ufa (Table **1970**), depart ■(1). Journey 2 nights.
Q – Dec. 11- 25, ①②③④⑤⑥⑦ Jan. 10 - Mar. 14; daily Mar. 16 - May 26.	T – To Ufa via Samara (Table **1970**). Journey 2 nights.
S – From Ufa (Table **1970**), depart ■(1). Journey 2 nights.	
c – St Peterburg **Ladozhski**.	

☐ – Privately operated train.	
△ – For days of running see Table **1905**.	
▽ – For days of running see Table **1910**.	
⊙ – Modern low-cost double deck train, 🍴 2 cl. only, food and drink included in fare.	
☒ – *Grand Express* luxury train: 🛏 1 cl. (ensuite), shower sofa, air conditioning, TV, DVD, wi-fi, 🛏 1,2 cl., ✕.	
☆ – Includes Lux Sleeping cars with ensuite shower/toilet.	
◐ – *Megapolis* - operated by Tverskoy Express.	
‡ – Also known as *Leningradski vokzal*.	
‡ – Also known as *Moskovski vokzal*.	
* – Distance from Chudovo.	
🟦 – *Sapsan* high-speed train, special fares payable. ✕ 🅡	
⚡ – *Lastochka* (Swallow) fast day train.	
♡ – NEVSKIY EKSPRESS – first class seats only.	

Named trains :	1 / 2 KRASNAYA STRELA (RED ARROW)	3/4 EKSPRESS	25/26 SMENA	31/32 LEV TOLSTOI

MOSKVA AIRPORTS ✈ 1901

MOSKVA DOMODEDOVO AIRPORT ✈
Aeroexpress rail service Moskva Paveletskaya - Moskva Domodedovo ✈. *35 km* Journey time 40 - 47 minutes.
From **Moskva Paveletskaya**: 0600, 0630, 0700 and every 30 minutes (not 1230) until 2330, 0000, 0030.
From **Domodedovo ✈**: 0600, 0630, 0700 and every 30 minutes (not 1230) until 2330, 0000.

MOSKVA SHEREMETYEVO AIRPORT ✈
Aeroexpress rail service Moskva Belorusskaya - Moskva Sheremetyevo ✈. *35 km* Journey time 35 minutes.
From **Moskva Belorusskaya**: 0530, 0600, 0630 and every 30 minutes (not 1300) until 2330, 0000, 0030.
From **Sheremetyevo ✈**: 0500, 0600, 0630 and every 30 minutes (not 1200) until 2330, 0000, 0030.

MOSKVA VNUKOVO AIRPORT ✈
Aeroexpress rail service Moskva Kiyevskaya - Moskva Vnukovo ✈. *28 km* Journey time 34 - 42 minutes.
From **Moskva Kiyevskaya**: 0600 and every 60 minutes (also 1030, 1530, 1730, 1930; not 1200) until 2300, 0000.
From **Vnukovo ✈**: 0600 and every 60 minutes (also 0937, 1630, 1830) until 2300, 0000.

(MOSKVA) - ST PETERBURG - PETROZAVODSK - MURMANSK 1905

RZhD

km		Fir 18AJ	Sko 92AJ E	804CH	Fir 16AJ	806CH	Sko 22CH	Sko 12AJ Ⓑ	
	Moskva Oktyabrskaya **1900** . d.	2102	1953	...	0041	...	...	...	...
0	**St Peterburg** Ladozhski .... d.	|	|	0632	0950	1800	1948	2320	...
*114	Volkhovstroi I .... d.	0425v	0402v	0819	1157	|	2151	0122	...
394	**Petrozavodsk** .... d.	0855	0947	1152	1715	2255	0249	0700	...
773	Belomorsk .... d.	...	1908	...	2358	...	1003	...	...
1161	Kandalaksha .... d.	...	0315	...	0653	...	1705	...	...
1438	**Murmansk** .... a.	...	0910	...	1155	...	2215	...	...

	Sko 21CH	803CH	Fir 15AJ	805CH	Fir 17AJ	Sko 91AJ F	Sko 11AJ Ⓑ	
Murmansk .... d.	0940	...	1920	...	...	2045	...	...
Kandalaksha .... d.	1514	...	0109	...	...	0236	...	...
Belomorsk .... d.	2155	...	0758	...	...	1009	...	...
Petrozavodsk .... d.	0442	0636	1517	1800	1955	2027	2240	...
Volkhovstroi I .... d.	1002	1012	2011	|	0031v	0123v	0427	...
St Peterburg Ladozhski .... a.	1150	1200	2216	2255	|	|	0624	...
Moskva Oktyabrskaya **1900** . a.	...	...	0650	...	0900	1036	...	...

E – ②③④⑤⑦ (daily Mar. 21 - Apr. 2, Apr. 25 - Sept. 1).
F – ②④⑤⑥⑦ (daily Mar. 23 - Apr. 4, Apr. 27 - Sept. 1).
v – Volkhovstroi II.
* – Moskva - Vokhovstroi : *641 km.*

MOSKVA - ST PETERBURG - HELSINKI 1910

RZhD, VR

km		WINTER 781 AE30 A ★	Fir 32AJ BL ★	783 AE34 A ★	785 AE36 A ★	787 AE38 A ★	SUMMER 781 AE30 A ☆	Fir 32AJ BL ☆	783 AE34 A ☆	785 AE36 A ☆	787 AE38 A ☆
	Moskva Okt. § .... d.	...	2310	...	...	...	...	2310	...	...	...
	Tver .... d.	...	0111	...	...	...	...	0111	...	...	...
**	**St Peterburg** Lad. ‡ ..... d.	...	0601	...	...	...	...	0601	...	...	...
0	**St Peterburg** Fin. ‡ ..... d.	0640	|	1130	1530	2030	0640	|	1030	1530	2030
129	Vyborg .... a.	0734	0754	1224	1624	2124	0734	0754	1124	1624	2124
129	Vyborg .... 🛃 RU d.	0744	0834	1234	1634	2134	0744	0834	1134	1634	2134
159	Vainikkala .... 🛃 FIN a.	0707	0814	1157	1557	2057	0807	0814	1157	1657	2157
159	Vainikkala .... d.	0714	0914	1204	1604	2104	0814	0914	1204	1704	2204
250	**Kouvola** .... 797 a.	0753	1009	1243	1643	2143	0853	1009	1243	1743	2243
312	Lahti .... 797 a.	0819	1048	1309	1709	2209	0919	1048	1309	1809	2309
400	Tikkurila .... 797 a.	0853	1143	1343	1743	2243	0953	1143	1343	1843	2343
413	Pasila .... 797 a.	|	1219	|	|	|	|	1219	|	|	|
416	**Helsinki** .... 797 a.	0907	1227	1357	1757	2257	1007	1227	1357	1857	2357

	WINTER AE33 782 A ★	AE35 784 A ★	AE37 786 A ★	Fir 31AJ BL ★	AE39 788 A ★	SUMMER AE33 782 A ☆	AE35 784 A ☆	AE37 786 A ☆	Fir 31AJ BL ☆	AE39 788 A ☆
Helsinki .... 797 d.	0620	1000	1500	1747	1900	0620	1100	1600	1747	2000
Pasila .... 797 d.	|	|	|	1753	|	|	|	|	1753	|
Tikkurila .... 797 d.	0633	1013	1513	1803	1913	0633	1113	1613	1803	2013
Lahti .... 797 d.	0707	1047	1547	1854	1947	0707	1147	1647	1854	2047
Kouvola .... 797 d.	0733	1113	1613	1942	2013	0733	1213	1713	1942	2113
Vainikkala .... a.	0813	1153	1653	2037	2053	0813	1253	1753	2037	2153
Vainikkala .... 🛃 FIN d.	0820	1200	1700	2122	2100	0820	1300	1800	2122	2200
Vyborg .... 🛃 RU a.	0942	1322	1822	2303	2222	0842	1322	1822	2303	2222
Vyborg .... d.	0947	1327	1827	2343	2227	0847	1327	1827	2343	2227
St Peterburg Fin. ‡ .... a.	1047	1427	1927	|	2327	0947	1427	1927	|	2327
St Peterburg Lad. ‡ .... a.	...	...	...	0118	...	...	...	...	0118	...
Tver .... a.	...	...	...	0650	...	...	...	...	0650	...
Moskva Okt. § .... a.	...	...	...	0919	...	...	...	...	0919	...

A – *Allegro* (R) ✕ Ⓡ St Peterburg - Helsinki and v.v.
B – Ⓑ (also Dec. 24, Jan. 7, Feb. 25, Apr. 29, May 6; daily May 28 - Sept. 1).
L – LEV TOLSTOI – 🛏 1 cl. (ensuite), 🛏 1, 2 cl., ✕.
★ – Dec. 11 - Mar. 25.
☆ – Mar. 26 - Oct. 28 (summer time in Finland). Approximate times.
§ – Moskva Oktyabrskaya, also known as Leningradski.
‡ – Lad. = Ladozhski; Fin. = Finlyandski.
** – *143 km* St Peterburg Ladozhski - Vyborg.
FIN – Finland (GMT + 2 in winter, GMT + 3 in summer).
RU – Russia (Moskva Time GMT + 3).

ST PETERBURG - HOMEL and KOZYATYN 1920

RZhD, BCh, UZ

km		Sko 49BJ A	Fir 53AJ ● ⊡	Sko 79CH K	Fir 55BJ ◇	Sko 83AJ	Fir 51BJ	Sko 61MZ ■(3) ★	Sko 61MZ ■(3) ☆	Sko 57BJ D 🚃
0	**St Peterburg** Vitebski .... d.	1403	1531	1610	...	1720	1823	2040	2040	2146
245	Dno .... d.	1733	1911	1949	...	2101	2203	0010	0010	0141
421	Novosokolniki .... RU d.	2039	2206	2249	...	0008	0050	0316	0316	0519
568	Vitsebsk .... § BY d.	2318	0040	0116	...	0249	0314	0529	0529	0755
670	Polatsk .... d.	|	|	0307	...	|	|	|	|	|
868	Maladzechnia .... a.	|	|	0546	...	|	|	|	|	|
	Moskva Bel. **1950** .... d.	|	|	▽	2100	|	|	|	|	|
652	**Orsha** Tsentralnaya .... a.	0037	0154	...	0343	0417	0426	0650	0650	0907
652	**Orsha** Tsentralnaya .... d.	0100	0216	...	0410	0439	0448	0712	0712	0929
	Minsk **1950** .... a.	0338	|	...	|	|	0715	|	|	1212
	Hrodna **1952** .... a.	|	|	...	|	|	|	|	|	1938
	Brest Tsent. **1950** .... a.	0818	|	...	|	|	1359x	|	|	...
726	Mahilyow I .... d.	...	0340	...	0600	0651	...	0840	0840	...
853	Zhlobin .... **1930** d.	...	0602	...	0819	0900	...	1100	1100	...
	Homel .... **1930** a.	...	0736	...	0938	1036	...	|	|	...
	Kyïv **1930** .... a.	...	1257r	...	...	...	...	|	|	...
954	Kalinkavichy .... BY d.	...	...	...	...	...	...	1242	1242	...
1109	Korosten .... ‡ UA d.	...	...	...	...	...	...	1546	1646	...
1191	Zhytomyr .... d.	...	...	...	...	...	...	1724	1824	...
1267	**Kozyatyn** .... a.	...	...	...	...	...	...	1903	2003	...
	Chişinău **1720** .... a.	...	...	...	...	...	...	0745	0845	...

	Fir 52BJ 🚃	Sko 50BJ B	Sko 83BJ	Sko 80CH K	Fir 55MZ ◇	Sko 61SZ ■(1) ★	Sko 61SZ ■(1) ☆	Sko 54KJ ■(1) ⊡	Sko 58BJ E
Chişinău **1720** .... d.	...	...	...	...	...	2136	2236	...	...
Kozyatyn .... d.	...	...	...	...	...	1047	1147	...	...
Zhytomyr .... d.	...	...	...	...	...	1216	1316	...	...
Korosten .... UA d.	...	...	...	...	...	1404	1504	...	...
Kalinkavichy .... ‡ BY d.	...	...	...	...	...	1906	1906	...	...
Kyïv **1930** .... d.	...	...	...	...	...	|	|	1245s	...
Homel .... **1930** d.	...	...	1716	...	1819	|	|	2039	...
Zhlobin .... **1930** d.	...	...	1831	...	2000	2104	2104	2159	...
Mahilyow I .... d.	...	...	2140	...	2220	2306	2306	0039	...
Brest Tsent. **1950** .... d.	1157z	1405	|	...	|	|	|	|	...
Hrodna **1952** .... d.	|	|	|	...	|	|	|	|	1733
Minsk **1950** .... d.	1800	1842	|	...	|	|	|	|	0058
Orsha Tsentralnaya .... a.	2032	2132	2245	...	2337	0028	0028	0149	0328
Orsha Tsentralnaya .... d.	2055	2156	2307	...	2359	0050	0050	0211	0351
Moskva Bel. **1950** .... a.	|	|	|	▽	0657	|	|	|	|
Maladzechnia .... d.	|	|	|	2036	...	|	|	|	|
Polatsk .... d.	|	|	|	2356	...	|	|	|	|
Vitsebsk .... BY d.	2215	2326	0036	0155	...	0221	0221	0338	0517
Novosokolniki .... § RU d.	0114	0252	0334	0444	...	0527	0527	0633	0822
Dno .... d.	0345	0533	0606	0733	...	0813	0813	0900	1119
St Peterburg Vitebski .... a.	0723	0916	0930	1109	...	1144	1144	1220	1525

A – Dec. 23 - Jan. 10, Mar. 24 - Apr. 4, Apr. 28 - May 11, June 2 - Sept. 1.
B – Dec. 22 - Jan. 9, Mar. 23 - Apr. 3, Apr. 27 - May 10, June 1 - Aug. 31.
D – ④⑦ (also ②⑤ May 30 - Sept. 1). Train **57***MJ* certain dates.
E – ③⑥ (also ①④ May 29 - Aug. 31).
K – For days of running see Table **1950**.
r – Arrive approx one hour later Mar. 26 - Oct. 28.
s – Depart approx one hour later Mar. 26 - Oct. 28.
x – Not dates in note **A**. Train **681***BJ*.
z – Not dates in note **B**. Train **652***BJ*.
★ – Dec. 11 - Mar. 25.
☆ – Mar. 26 - Oct. 28 (summer time in Ukraine). Approx. times.
🚃 – Conveys on ④ from St Peterburg and ⑥ from Praha / Wien 🛏 1, 2 cl. St Peterburg - Orsha (**21***JA* / **22***AJ*) - Brest - Warszawa - Praha / Wien and v.v. (Table **95**). See Table **1950** for Orsha - Brest times.
▽ – To / from Vilnius and Kaliningrad (Table **1950**).
⊡ – For St Peterburg - Kharkiv portion see Tables **1930** / **1755**.
◇ – For Moskva - Homel via Bryansk see Table **1945**.
● – Even dates (see page 530).
■ – Uneven dates (see page 530).
BY – Belarus (GMT + 3)
RU – Russia (Moskva Time GMT + 3).
UA – Ukraine (GMT + 2 winter, GMT + 3 summer).
§ – 🛃 : Yezyaryshcha (BY) / Zaverezhye (RU).
‡ – 🛃 : Slovechno (BY) / Berezhest (UA).

MINSK - HOMEL - KYÏV 1930

BCh, UZ

km		WINTER Sko 100FJ ■(1) ★	Sko 94BJ E ★	Fir 86BJ ★	Fir 53AJ ● ★	Sko 143 ● ★	SUMMER Sko 100FJ K ☆	Sko 94BJ E ☆	Fir 86BJ ☆	Fir 53AJ ● ☆	Sko 143 ● ☆
	St P'burg Vit. **1920** . d.	...	...	...	1531	1531	...	...	...	1531	1531
0	**Minsk** .... d.	0744	1420	2240	|	|	0744	1420	2240	|	|
214	Zhlobin .... **1920** d.	1106	1736	0128	0602	0602	1106	1736	0128	0602	0602
304	**Homel** .... **1920** a.	1226	1851	0245	0736	0736	1226	1851	0245	0736	0736
304	**Homel** .... BY d.	1249	1926	0309	0759	0759	1249	1926	0309	0759	0759
415	Chernihiv .... § UA d.	|	2226	|	1009	1009	|	2326	|	1109	1109
624	**Kyïv** .... a.	|	0112	0752	1257	|	|	0212	0852	1357	|
	Kharkiv **1755** .... a.	0015	|	...	...	2020	0115	|	...	...	2120
	Odesa **1720** .... a.	▽	1111	...	...	...	▽	1211	...	...	...

	WINTER Sko 100PC ■(3) ★	Fir 54KJ ■(1) ★	Sko 143PC ■(1) ★	Fir 86KJ ★	Sko 94SH F ★	SUMMER Sko 100PC L ☆	Fir 54KJ ■(1) ☆	Sko 143PC ■(1) ☆	Fir 86KJ ☆	Sko 94SH F ☆
Odesa **1720** .... d.	▽	...	...	...	1432	▽	...	...	...	1532
Kharkiv **1755** .... d.	0523	...	0616	...	|	0623	...	0716	...	|
Kyïv .... d.	|	1245	|	2119	0110	|	1345	|	2219	0210
Chernihiv .... § UA d.	|	1637	1637	|	0412	|	1737	1737	|	0512
Homel .... BY a.	1832	2014	2014	0416	0843	1832	2014	2014	0416	0843
Homel .... **1920** d.	1914	2039	2039	0440	0906	1914	2039	2039	0440	0906
Zhlobin .... **1920** d.	2039	2159	2159	0546	1018	2039	2159	2159	0546	1018
Minsk .... a.	2345	|	|	0838	1344	2345	|	|	0838	1344
St P'burg Vit. **1920** . a.	...	1220	1220	...	...	...	1220	1220	...	...

E – ②⑤ (even dates June 2 - Sept. 26).
F – ③⑥ (uneven dates June 3 - Sept. 29).
K – ■(1) (daily June 1 - Sept. 21).
L – ■(3) (daily June 3 - Sept. 23).
★ – Dec. 11 - Mar. 25.
☆ – Mar. 26 - Oct. 28 (summer time in Ukraine). Approx. times.
● – Even dates (see page 530).
■ – Uneven dates (see page 530).
▽ – To / from Zaporizhzhya or Novooleksiivka (Table **1780**).
§ – 🛃 : Teryukha (BY) / Hornostayivka (UA).
BY – Belarus (GMT + 3).
UA – Ukraine (GMT + 2 winter, GMT + 3 summer).

RUSSIA and BELARUS

1931 MOSKVA - PSKOV

km		Fir 10AJ		Fir 10CH
0	Moskva Okt. ▷ d.	2023	Pskov .... d.	1930
167	Tver ▷ d.	2236	Dno .... d.	2112
331	Bologoye ▷ d.	0053	Bologoye ▷ d.	0221
588	Dno ▷ d.	0627	Tver ▷ d.	0408
687	Pskov .... a.	0805	Moskva Okt. ▷ a.	0614

▷ – See also Table 1900.

1935 MOSKVA - POLATSK

km		Fir 39SZ		Fir 39BJ
0	Moskva Bel....d.	2029	Polatsk .... BY d.	1830
243	Vyazma ....d.	2359	Vitsebsk.. ‡ RU d.	2045
419	Smolensk ....d.	0232	Smolensk ....d.	2337
560	Vitsebsk.. ‡ RU d.	0535	Vyazma ....d.	0219
662	Polatsk .... BY a.	0710	Moskva Bel. ..... a.	0519

‡ – 🚍 : Rudnya (RU) / Zavolsha (BY)
BY Belarus (GMT + 3).
RU Russia (GMT + 3).

1945 MOSKVA - HOMEL

km		Sko 75BJ		Sko 76BJ
0	Moskva Bel.......d.	1532	Homel .... d.	2019
485	Bryansk Orlov....d.	0005	Dobrush.. BY d.	2049
713	Zlynka .... RU d.	0408	Zlynka .... RU d.	0005
739	Dobrush... BY d.	0433	Bryansk Orlov. .... d.	0300
764	Homel .... a.	0500	Moskva Bel. ..... a.	1140

▽ – Conveys portion to/from Brest (Table 1955).
BY RU See Table 1935. For train via Orsha see Table 1920.

1950 — MOSKVA - MINSK - VILNIUS, KALININGRAD and BREST   RZhD, BCh, LG

Block 1

km	Station	805BJ/803BJ (Pas)	57BJ (Pas)	607BJ (Sko) E	57MJ (Fir)	21JA (Sko)④ H	21JA (Fir) V	701BJ (Sko)	731MJ (Fir)	807BJ (Sko)	25BJ (Sko)⑤⑦	711BJ (Fir)	17BJ (Sko)★ N	17BJ (Sko) N	13MJ (Fir) B	13MJ (Fir) B	9JA (Sko)★ P	9JA (Sko) P	27BJ (Fir)★	29CH (Fir)	735MJ (Fir)	49BJ (Sko)	95BJ (Sko) Y
0	Moskva Belorusskaya d.					0533	0633	0710			0946	1018	1118	1205k	1305k		1409	1509	1515	1720	1820		2000
243	Vyazma d.					0820	0920	0932			1301	1336	1436	1700	1800		1825	2030	2059				2318
419	Smolensk RU d.					1009	1109	1116			1515	1538	1638	1616	1716		1852	1952	2026	2239	2245		0201
538	St Peterburg Vitebski ◐ a.			2146	2146																	1403	
538	Orsha Tsentralnaya BY a.			0907	0907	1121	1221				1658	1649	1749	1732	1832		2002	2102	2143	0003	0037		0318
538	Orsha Tsentralnaya d.			0929		1138	1238	651BJ			1712	1705	1805	1747	1847		2017	2117	2200	0017	0100		0332
750	Minsk a.			1212		1359	1459			1950		1923	2023	1955	2055		2227	2327	0038	0237	0338		0638
750	Minsk d.	0800	1258	1226	1330	1414	1514	1646	1730	1952	2010	1938	2038	2009	2109		2301	0001	0108	0300	0353		
827	Maladzechna BY d.	0900	1155							2054									0410				
943	Vilnius LT a.	0930r	1242r							2122r									0623r				
943	Vilnius LT d.																		0658r				
1285	Kaliningrad Ka a.																		1348				
892	Baranavichy Tsentralnye d.		1413p	1525		1603	1703	1916									0039	0139	0308			0543	0921p
1094	Brest Tsentralny a.			1801		1756	1856	2001	2148		2348	2324	0024	2324	0024		0228	0328	0540			0818	1210
	Warszawa Wsch. 1050 a.					2230	2230					0349	0349	0138	0138		0737	0737					

Block 2

Station	79CH (Sko) K	55BJ (Fir) T	23JI (Sko) T	3BJ (Sko)	51BJ (Fir)	1BJ (Sko)	147CH (Fir) Z	131BJ (Sko) F	33ZH (Fir)
Moskva Belorusskaya d.		2100	2115	2215	2203	2140	2232	2322	2354
Vyazma d.		0025		0008	0054	0125	0159	0249	0353
Smolensk RU d.		0225	0155	0255		0319	0354	0447	0630
St Peterburg Vitebski ◐ d.	1610				1823				
Orsha Tsentralnaya BY a.		0343	0305	0405	0355	0426	0439	0512	0606
Orsha Tsentralnaya d.	□ 0410	0320	0420	0409	0448	0456	0535	0622	
Minsk a.	△ 0545	0645	0622	0715	0725	0808	0903		
Minsk d.	0559	0659	0659	0647	0929v		0834	0929	
Maladzechna BY d.	0600					0942			
Vilnius LT a.	0820r				1152r				
Vilnius LT d.	0837r				1209r				
Kaliningrad Ka a.	1548				1914				
Baranavichy Tsentralnye d.		0756	0856	0838	1125v			1125	
Brest Tsentralny a.		0950	1050	1041	1359v			1359	
Warszawa Wsch. 1050 a.		1354	1354						

Block 3

Station	702BJ (Pas)	804TJ (Pas)	608BJ (Sko)	734MJ (Sko)	18BJ (Sko)★ M	18BJ (Sko) M	22AJ (Sko)★ W	22AJ (Sko) W	52BJ (Fir)☆ J
Warszawa Wsch. 1050 d.					0328	0328	0328	0328	
Brest Tsentralny d.	0620		0628		1001	1101	1001	1101	
Baranavichy Tsentralnye d.			0908		1202	1302	1202	1302	
Kaliningrad Ka d.									
Vilnius LT a.									
Vilnius LT d.	0615r								
Maladzechna BY d.	0847								
Minsk a.	0935	0945	1056		1346	1446	1346	1446	
Minsk d.					1401	1501	1401	1501	
Orsha Tsentralnaya d.					1617	1717	1617	1717	
Orsha Tsentralnaya BY a.					1634	1734	1634	1734	2055
St Peterburg Vitebski ◐ d.									0723
Smolensk RU d.					1835	1753	1853	1753	1853
Vyazma d.					2021	1956	2056	1956	2056
Moskva Belorusskaya a.					2250	2225	2325	2225	2325

Block 4

Station	52BJ (Fir)	50BJ (Sko)	808TJ (Fir)	26BJ (Sko)	712BJ (Fir)⑤⑦	34ZH (Fir)	80CH (Sko) L	55MZ (Fir)	8BJ (Sko) ♡	806TJ (Fir)
Warszawa Wsch. 1050 d.										
Brest Tsentralny d.	1157x	1405			1550		1740		1750	
Baranavichy Tsentralnye d.	1449x	1641					1944		2024	
Kaliningrad Ka d.					1028				1347	
Vilnius LT a.					1530r				1835r	
Vilnius LT d.					1547r				1910r	
Maladzechna BY d.					2036				2042	
Minsk a.	1638x	1827	1845	1930			2125	2140		
Minsk d.	1800	1842		1902			2140	2208		
Orsha Tsentralnaya d.	2032	2132		2142			2337	2357		
Orsha Tsentralnaya BY a.	2055	2156		2156			2359	0011		
St Peterburg Vitebski ◐ d.	0723	0916			1109					
Smolensk RU d.				2324		2354		0138		
Vyazma d.				0204		0250		0406		
Moskva Belorusskaya a.				0510		0628		0657		

Block 5

Station	2BJ (Fir)	28BJ (Sko)	30CH (Sko)	58BJ (Sko)	24JI (Fir)	668BJ (Pas)★	732MJ (Sko)⑦	148CH (Sko) G	96BJ (Sko)	10ZH (Fir) P	14MJ (Sko)★ B	14MJ (Sko) B
Brest Tsentralny d.			1525	1525					2021	2021	0033	0033
Baranavichy Tsentralnye d.		2243	2243	2230				2324	0318	0418	0446	0546
Kaliningrad Ka d.	2248p	2347	0530p			0047	0247p	0516	0616			
Vilnius LT a.	1729						2230r					
Vilnius LT d.	2247r											
Maladzechna BY d.	0305											
Minsk a.	0411	0446	0702	0802	0812	0912						
Minsk d.	0434	0505	0732	0832	0826	0926						
Orsha Tsentralnaya d.	0709	0736	1000	1100	1043	1143						
Orsha Tsentralnaya BY a.	0726	0750	1015	1115	1058	1158						
St Peterburg Vitebski ◐ d.	1525											
Smolensk RU d.	0935	1159	1231	1335	1435							
Vyazma d.	1150	1530	1440	1134	1234	1312						
Moskva Belorusskaya a.	1330	1709	1625k	1725k								

Notes

B – ⑥⑦ from Moskva; ①⑦ from Berlin. 🛏 1cl (lux), 🛏 1,2 cl., 🍴 Moskva - Warszawa - Berlin and v.v. (Table 56). Strizh (Swift) Talgo train.
E – St Peterburg - Minsk - Hrodna and v.v. For days of running see Table 1920.
F – Dec. 28 - Jan. 10, Feb. 22, 26; four times per week May 27 - Aug. 31.
G – Dec. 27 - Jan. 9, Feb. 21, 25; four times per week May 26 - Aug. 30.
H – Conveys on ④ from St Peterburg 🛏, 1,2 cl. St Peterburg - Orsha - Warszawa - Praha/Wien, on ⑥ (Table 95). Conveyed in train V from Orsha.
J – Conveys on ⑥ from Praha/Wien 🛏, 1,2 cl. Praha/Wien - Warszawa - Orsha - St Peterburg, on ⑤ (Table 95). Conveyed in train W to Orsha.
K – ③⑤⑦ (also ① May 29 - Sept. 1). Days of running vary Dec. 27 - Jan. 11.
L – ②④⑥ (also ⑦ May 28 - Sept. 3). Days of running vary Dec. 26 - Jan. 10.
M – ⑥ from Nice, arrive Moskva ①. 🛏 1cl (lux), 🛏 1,2 cl. Nice - Milano - Katowice - Warszawa (Table 25); 🍴 Brest - Moskva.
N – ④ from Moskva, arrive Nice ⑥. 🛏 1cl (lux), 🛏 1,2 cl. Moskva - Warszawa - Katowice - Milano - Nice (Table 25); 🍴 Moskva - Brest.
P – POLONEZ – 🛏 1,2 cl., 🍴 Moskva - Warszawa and v.v. (Table 95); 🍴 Moskva - Brest and v.v.; 🛏 1,2 cl. Moskva - Warszawa - Kraków and v.v.
T – TRANSEUROPEAN EXPRESS – ③ from Moskva, arrive Paris ⑤. 🛏 1,2 cl. Moskva (23JI) - Brest (452) - Berlin - Paris (Table 24); 🍴 Moskva - Brest.
U – TRANSEUROPEAN EXPRESS – ⑤ from Paris, arrive Moskva ⑦. 🛏 1,2 cl. Paris (453) - Berlin - Brest (24JI) - Moskva (Table 24); 🍴 Brest - Moskva.
V – VLTAVA – ⑤ from Moskva, arrive Praha/Wien ⑦. 🛏 1,2 cl. Moskva - Warszawa - Katowice - Praha/Wien and v.v. (Table 95); 🍴 Moskva - Brest.
W – VLTAVA – ⑥ from Praha/Wien, arrive Moskva ⑦. 🛏 1,2 cl. Praha/Wien - Katowice - Warszawa - Moskva (Table 95); 🍴 Brest - Moskva.

Y – Dec. 23 - Jan. 10, Mar. 24 - Apr. 4, Apr. 28 - May 11, June 2 - Sept. 1.
Z – Dec. 22 - Jan. 9, Mar. 23 - Apr. 3, Apr. 27 - May 10, June 1 - Aug. 31.
k – Moskva Kurskaya.
p – Baranavichy Polesskiye.
r – One hour later Mar. 26 - Oct. 28 (summer time in Lithuania).
v – Not when train Y runs. Train 681BJ.
z – Not when train Z runs. Train 652BJ.
★ – Dec. 11 - Mar. 25.
☆ – Mar. 26 - Oct. 28 (summer time in Lithuania / Poland). Timings are approximate.
△ – To/from Homel (Table 1920).
⬡ – Via Vitsebsk (Table 1920).
♤ – Not 31st of month. Train 7MJ on uneven dates.
♡ – Not 31st of month. Train 4BJ on uneven dates.
▼ – Fast day train.
◐ – See Table 1920.
■ – Even dates (see page 530).
■ – Uneven dates (see page 530).
■(1) – Uneven dates [.. 29, 1..]

BY – Belarus (GMT + 3).
Ka – Kaliningrad region of Russia (train times are Moskva time GMT + 3, local time is GMT + 2).
LT – Lithuania (GMT + 2 in winter, GMT + 3 in summer).
RU – Russia (Moskva Time GMT + 3).

BORDER CROSSINGS
Between Smolensk and Orsha: Krasnoye (RU) / Osinovka (BY).
Between Maladzechna and Vilnius: Hudahai (BY) / Kena (LT).
Between Vilnius and Kaliningrad: Kybartai (LT) / Nesterov (Ka).

OTHER NAMED TRAINS
1/2 BELORUSSIYA/BELARUS
3/4 MINSK
7/8 SLAVYANSKI EKSPRESS
29/30 YANTAR

1952 MINSK - HRODNA   BCh

km		673BJ S	57BJ	627BJ/629BJ			630BJ/674BJ	58BJ	628BJ
0	Minsk d.	0701	1226	1535 1705	Hrodna d.		0625 1512	1733	2356
77	Maladzechna d.	0805		1816	Baranavichy Pol. d.			2248	0520
205	Lida d.	0956		2027	Lida d.		0818	1706	
141	Baranavichy Pol. d.		1451	1800	Maladzechna d.		1029	1900	
*337	Hrodna a.	1145	1938	2305 2220	Minsk a.		1132 2002	0039	0723

S – From/to St Peterburg. For days of running see Table 1920.   * – 361 km via Baranavichy.

1955 HOMEL - BREST   BCh

km		675FJ	603BJ			676FJ	604BJ
	Moskva Bel. ....d.	1532r		Brest Tsentralny . d.		1020	1934
0	Homel ....d.	0537	2011	Luninets ....d.		1430	0019
128	Kalinkavichy ....d.	0808	2241	Kalinkavichy ....d.		1733	0328
305	Luninets ....d.	1118	0154	Homel ....a.		1934	0533
533	Brest Tsentralny .. a.	1511	0600	Moskva Bel. ....a.		1140r	

r – Train 75/76 (Table 1945).

MOSKVA - VORONEZH - ROSTOV NA DONU - SOCHI - ADLER 1960

km		43SJ Fir	87GJ Fir	126EI Sko	49AJ Sko	35AJ Fir	302BJ Pas	70GJ Fir	4SJ Fir	12MJ Fir	104VJ Fir	115AJ Sko	102MJ Fir	30SJ Fir	46VJ Fir	20SJ Fir	139NJ Sko	306MJ Pas	34SJ Sko	202MJ Sko	25JA Fir	77CH Sko	29MJ Fir	156MJ Sko
		■(5)				◇			☆	☆	◇		☆	☆	◇	☆					☆			
			E	N	L	Q	n					J	C				U	S		G		◧		A
	St Peterburg Glavny .... d.	1406	...	...	1330	2027	...	...	...	...	...	2036r	...	...	...	...	...	...	...	...	...	...	...	...
	Bologoye .... d.	1825	...	...	1724	0003	...	...	...	...	...	0020	...	...	...	...	...	...	...	...	...	...	...	...
	Tver .... d.	2052	g	...	1903	0141	...	...	...	...	...	0212	...	...	...	...	...	...	...	...	...	...	...	...
0	**Moskva** Kazanskaya .... d.	|	|	0025	2150k	|	...	0814	0822	1042	1052	0431k	1408	1418	1650	1842	...	1950	2150	2316	...	...	...	2328
0	**Moskva** Paveletskaya .... d.	|	|	|	|	|	...	|	|	|	|	|	|	|	|	|	...	|	|	|	2114	2104	2142	|
198	Ryazan II .... d.	0247	0427	0351	|	0629	...	1035	1049	1302	1312	|	1653	1703	1911	2143	...	2257	0111	0203	|	|	|	0237
408	Michurinsk Uralski .... d.	0645	0733	0818	|	|	...	|	|	|	|	♡	|	|	|	|	...	|	0420	|	|	0518	|	0635
412	Michurinsk Voronezhski .... d.	|	|	|	|	0917	⊡	1247	1303	1523	1540	|	1916	1933	2121	0014	...	0141	|	0444	0453	|	|	|
426	Yelets .... d.	|	|	|	0615	|	0801	|	|	|	|	1213	|	|	|	|	...	|	|	|	|	|	0545	|
504	Lipetsk .... d.	|	|	|	0739	|	0913	|	|	|	|	1354	|	|	|	|	...	|	|	|	|	|	0700	|
469	Gryazi Voronezhski .... d.	0750	0838	0919	|	1016	|	1329	|	1605	|	|	|	|	2203	0058	...	0227	0520	0529	0544	0623	...	0738
588	**Voronezh** I .... d.	|	|	|	|	1240	1215	1449	|	|	|	|	|	|	2323	|	...	0522	|	0800	0758	|	...	|
591	**Voronezh** Pridacha .... d.	1018	1040	1121	1108	|	|	...	1518	1740	1755	1725	2133	2146	...	0245	d	|	0750	|	...	0844	...	1006
667	Liski .... d.	1133	1205	1233	1223	1427	1435	...	1634	1852	1906	1834	2246	2258	...	0347	0449	0710	0918	0947	...	0955	...	1116
786	Rossosh .... d.	1447	1423	1435	1508	1623	1645	...	1820	2025	2041	2049	0018	0033	...	0529	0713	0933	1140	1149	...	1328	...	1304
1062	Likhaya .... d.	1951	|	1900	1938	2030	2126	...	|	|	|	0138	|	|	...	0923	1155	1413	1638	1620	...	1824	...	1741
1226	**Rostov na Donu** .... a.	2303	2223	2244	2253	2312	0042	...	2352	0157	0207	0459	0546	0558	...	1155	1450	1730	1942	1915	...	2203	...	2051
1226	**Rostov na Donu** .... d.	2320	2241	2301	2311	2328	0100	...	0009	0212	0222	0517	0610	0620	...	...	1528	1814	2013	1941	...	2225	...	2111
1405	Tikhoretskaya .... d.	|	|	|	0210	|	|	...	0231	|	|	|	|	|	...	...	1820	|	2304	2215	...	0102	...	|
1332	Starominskaya Tim. .... d.	0104	0005	0050	|	|	0231	...	|	|	|	0642	|	|	...	...	|	1939	|	|	...	u	...	2244
1510	**Krasnodar** I .... d.	0402	0305	|	|	0325	0517	...	|	|	0538	1010	|	0942	...	...	|	2232	|	|	...	...	...	|
1645	Novorossiysk .... a.	0725	|	0625	|	|	|	...	|	|	|	|	|	1255	...	...	|	|	|	|	...	...	...	|
1636	Anapa .... a.	...	|	...	|	|	|	...	|	0945	|	|	|	...	...	...	|	|	|	|	...	...	...	0500
1533	Armavir Rostovski .... d.	...	|	...	0447	|	|	...	0422	...	|	|	|	...	...	...	2121t	|	0134	0111t	...	...	...	...
1721	Mineralnye Vody .... d.	...	|	...	0830	|	|	...	0658	...	|	|	|	...	...	...	|	|	0516	|	...	...	...	...
1747	Pyatigorsk .... d.	...	|	...	0916	|	|	...	0736	...	|	|	|	...	...	...	|	|	v	|	...	...	...	...
1785	**Kislovodsk** .... a.	...	|	...	1011	|	|	...	0828	...	|	|	|	...	...	...	|	|	...	|	...	...	...	...
1658	Tuapse .... d.	...	0657	...	...	0710	1013	...	...	...	0820	1602	1146	...	...	...	0240	0212	...	0609	...	...	...	...
1738	**Sochi** .... a.	...	0911	...	...	0930	1230	...	...	...	1008	1803	1334	...	...	...	0436	0408	...	0848	...	...	...	...
1761	**Adler** .... a.	...	0959	...	...	1011	1315	...	...	...	1047	1844	1405	...	...	...	0521	0453	...	0929	...	...	...	...
1800	Gagra ◐ .... a.	...	...	...	...	...	...	...	...	...	...	...	...	...	...	...	...	0815	...	...	...	...	...	...
1873	**Sukhumi** ◐ .... a.	...	...	...	...	...	...	...	...	...	...	...	...	...	...	...	...	1024	...	...	...	...	...	...

	49CH Sko	104ZH Fir	30JI Fir	44SJ Fir	88SJ Fir	36AJ Fir	302SJ Pas	102SJ Fir	3SJ Fir	69VJ Fir	77SJ Sko	140NJ Sko	306SJ Pas	33SJ Sko	202SJ Sko	29VJ Fir	25VJ Fir	19SJ Fir	155SJ Sko	11EI Fir	45VJ Fir	126SJ Sko	116SJ Sko	
		◇	☆	■(3)		◇	■(3)	☆	☆								☆	☆		☆	◇			
	M				F	R		D			◧	V	T		H				B			P	K	
Sukhumi ◐ .... d.	...	...	...	...	...	...	...	...	...	...	...	...	1403	...	...	...	...	...	...	...	...	...	...	...
Gagra ◐ .... d.	...	...	...	...	...	...	...	...	...	...	...	...	1618	...	...	...	...	...	...	...	...	...	...	...
Adler .... d.	...	1834	...	...	1529	1726	1659	2037	...	...	...	1351	1934	...	2054	...	...	...	...	...	...	...	1102	...
Sochi .... d.	...	1914	...	...	1609	1808	1740	2113	...	...	...	1430	2013	...	2139	...	...	...	...	...	...	...	1144	...
Tuapse .... d.	...	2105	...	...	1820	2040	1956	2303	...	...	...	1635	2225	...	2345	...	...	...	...	...	...	...	1403	...
Kislovodsk .... d.	1336	|	...	...	|	|	|	|	1958	...	...	|	|	...	|	...	...	...	...	...	...	...	|	...
Pyatigorsk .... d.	1433	|	...	...	|	|	|	|	2054	...	...	|	|	w	|	...	...	...	...	...	...	...	|	...
Mineralnye Vody .... d.	1542	|	...	...	|	|	|	|	2143	...	...	|	|	2231	|	...	...	...	...	...	...	...	|	...
Armavir Rostovski .... d.	1831	|	...	...	|	|	|	|	0002	...	...	2241t	|	0109	0542t	...	...	...	...	...	...	...	|	...
Anapa .... d.	|	|	...	...	|	|	|	|	|	...	...	|	|	|	|	...	...	...	0910	1345	...	...	|	...
Novorossiysk .... d.	|	|	2052	1655	|	|	|	|	|	...	...	|	|	|	|	...	...	...	|	|	...	1335	|	...
Krasnodar I .... d.	|	2324	2334	2002	2302	2355	2311	|	|	...	...	|	0130	|	|	...	...	...	|	|	...	|	1718	...
Starominskaya Tim. .... d.	|	|	|	2345	0231	|	0243	|	|	...	u	|	0436	|	|	...	...	...	1532	|	...	1916	2116	...
Tikhoretskaya .... d.	2038	|	|	|	|	|	|	|	0203	...	0149	0130	|	0310	0755	...	...	...	|	|	...	|	|	...
Rostov na Donu .... a.	2325	0242	0252	0112	0348	0338	0408	0428	0436	...	0501	0446	0603	0636	1026	...	...	...	1652	2043	...	2115	2249	...
Rostov na Donu .... d.	2345	0257	0307	0131	0407	0357	0426	0443	0453	...	0525	0507	0627	0703	1053	...	...	1433	1710	2103	...	2133	2307	...
Likhaya .... d.	0255	|	|	0444	|	0710	0815	|	|	...	0845	0828	1043	1114	1359	...	...	1720	2037	|	...	0058	0225	...
Rossosh .... d.	0725	0822	0838	0945	1120	1108	1331	1008	1024	...	1311	1340	1522	1609	1740	...	...	2105	0038	0241	...	0523	0650	...
Liski .... d.	0920	1011	1022	1128	1308	1242	1527	1155	1205	...	1518	1549	1655	1805	1912	...	...	2235	0230	0423	...	0711	0833	...
Voronezh Pridacha .... d.	1142	1115	1128	1237	1424	|	|	1303	1318	...	1625	b	|	1926	|	...	...	2340	|	0528	...	0822	1018	...
Voronezh I .... d.	|	|	|	|	|	1451	1802	|	|	1617	|	...	1937	|	2115	...	2130	|	0435	|	0725	|	|	...
Gryazi Voronezhski .... d.	|	|	|	1557	1633	1644	|	|	|	1737	1828	...	2125	2140	2300	...	2320	0123	0710	0657	0845	1103	|	...
Lipetsk .... d.	1512	|	|	|	|	|	2113	|	|	|	|	...	|	|	|	2035	|	|	|	|	|	|	1438	...
Yelets .... d.	1704	|	|	|	|	|	2310	|	|	|	|	...	|	|	|	2227	|	|	|	|	|	|	1630	...
Michurinsk Voronezhski .... d.	|	1330	1348	|	|	1747	⊡	1524	1544	1818	|	...	2230	|	2356	|	0039	0214	0817	0757	0926	|	|	...
Michurinsk Uralski .... d.	|	|	|	1755	1824	|	...	|	|	|	2009	...	|	0004	|	|	|	|	|	|	|	1259	♡	...
Ryazan II .... d.	|	1555	1605	2151	2141	2052	...	1752	1802	2034	|	...	0134	0317	0245	|	|	0451	1122	1028	1140	1643	|	...
Moskva Paveletskaya .... a.	|	|	|	|	|	|	...	|	|	|	0500	...	|	|	|	0615	0750	|	|	|	|	|	|	...
Moskva Kazanskaya .... a.	0202k	1823	1833	|	|	|	...	2015	2055	2253	...	...	0452	0628	0555	...	...	0735	1435	1338	1358	1937	2336k	...
Tver .... d.	0415	...	...	0336	h	0223	...	...	...	...	...	...	...	...	...	...	...	...	...	...	...	...	0207	...
Bologoye .... d.	0601	...	...	0512	...	0409	...	...	...	...	...	...	...	...	...	...	...	...	...	...	...	...	0355	...
St Peterburg Glavny .... a.	1155	...	...	1017	...	0745	...	...	...	...	...	...	...	...	...	...	...	...	...	...	...	...	0952r	...

A – May 24 - Sept. 17.
B – May 26 - Sept. 19.
C – Dec. 24 - Jan. 14; even dates ●(4) from Jan. 16 (daily from Apr. 28).
D – Dec. 22 - Jan. 12; even dates from Jan. 14 (daily from Apr. 26).
E – Uneven dates ■(3) (daily May 25 - Oct. 11).
F – Uneven dates ■(5) (daily May 27 - Oct. 13).
G – Uneven dates ■(3) May 23 - Sept. 25.
H – Uneven dates ■(5) May 27 - Sept. 29.
J – Uneven dates ■(5) (daily Apr. 23 - May 13, June 2 - Oct. 3).
K – Uneven dates ■(3) (daily Apr. 21 - May 11, June 1 - Sept. 30).
L – ②④⑤⑦ (daily Dec. 22 - Jan. 8, Apr. 23 - Sept. 24).
M – ②④⑥⑦ (daily Dec. 24 - Jan. 10, Apr. 25 - Sept. 25).
N – Uneven dates ■(3) (daily Dec. 27 - Jan. 13, Apr. 29 - May 13).
P – Uneven dates ■(1) (daily Dec. 25 - Jan. 11, Apr. 27 - May 11).
Q – Even dates (daily Apr. 28 - Nov. 6).
R – Even dates ●(4) (daily May 1 - Nov. 8).
S – Every four days Dec. 13 - 29, Jan. 2 - 30, Feb. 3 - 27, Mar. 3 - 31, Apr. 4 - 20; daily Apr. 24 - Sept. 30. Journey 2 nights.
T – Every four days Dec. 15 - 27, Jan. 4 - 28, Feb. 1 - 25, Mar. 1 - 29, Apr. 2 - 22; daily Apr. 26 - Oct. 2. Journey 2 nights.

U – From Novosibirsk on even dates (daily June 20 - Aug. 30).
V – Even dates ●(6) (daily June 24 - Sept. 3).
Y – From Rostov every 4 days Apr. 22 - 30, May 4 - 28, June 1 - 29, July 3 - 31, Aug. 4 - 28, Sept. 1 - 29, Oct. 3 - 15; from Baki 2 days later.

b – To Novosibirsk (Table **1990**). Via Penza (d. 0314 3rd day), Saransk (d. 0613 3rd day). Arrive Novosibirsk 5th day.
d – From Novosibirsk (Table **1990**). Via Saransk (1433 3rd day), Penza (1810 3rd day). Departs Liski on 4th day, arrive Adler on 5th day.
g – From Nizhni Novgorod (d. 1907) via Vladimir (d. 2253).
h – To Nizhni Novgorod (a. 0718) via Vladimir (a. 0352).
k – Moskva **Kurskaya**.
n – ■(1) from Minsk, next day from Yelets (Table **1961**).
r – St Peterburg **Ladozhski**.
t – Armavir **Tuapsinkii**.
u – To / from Stavropol (arrive 0600; depart 2116).
v – To Vladikavkaz (arrive 0953) and Nalchik ⚲ (a. 0750).
w – From Vladikavkaz (d. 1746) and Nalchik ⚲ (d. 1810, train **689**SJ).

◐ – Abkhazia Autonomous Region (⊞ = Veseloe / Tsandryphsh).
☆ – Includes Lux sleeping car with ensuite shower/toilet.

⊡ – From / to Minsk (Table **1961**).
◧ – Runs 2 - 3 times per week.
◇ – Train consists of double-deck sleeping cars.
⚲ – Nalchik portion runs in separate train **62**CH / **61**SJ June - Sept.
♡ – Via Tula (**J** 0720, **K** 2112).

● – Even dates. See page 530.
●(4) – Even dates [.. *30, 1, 4* ..]
●(6) – Even dates [.. *30, 1, 3, 6* ..]

■ – Uneven dates. See page 530.
■(1) – Uneven dates [.. *29, 1* ..]
■(3) – Uneven dates [.. *31, 3* ..]
■(5) – Uneven dates [.. *31, 2, 5* ..]

AZ – Azerbaijan (GMT + 4). ⊞ = Yalama.
BY – Belarus (GMT + 3).
RU – Russia (Moskva time GMT + 3).

MINSK - ADLER 1961

km		302BJ Pas ■(1)		302SJ Pas ■(3)
0	**Minsk** ..... 1930 d.	1221	**Adler** .... d.	1659
306	Homel .... BY d.	1740	Sochi .... d.	1740
577	Bryansk O... RU d.	0100	**Rostov na D.** .. d.	0426
908	Yelets .... d.	0801	Yelets .... d.	2310
1787	**Rostov na D.** ... d.	0100	Bryansk O. .. RU d.	0715
2298	Sochi .... a.	1230	Homel .... BY a.	1217
2321	**Adler** .... a.	1315	**Minsk** ..... 1930 a.	1740

■ – Uneven dates, see page 530. For further stations between Yelets and Adler see Table **1960**.

SARATOV - ADLER 1962

km		14ZH Sko △		14SJ Sko ▽
0	**Saratov** I .... d.	0947	**Adler** .... d.	1820
429	Volgograd I .... d.	1654	Sochi .... d.	1900
964	Tikhoretskaya .. d.	0234	Tuapse .... d.	2121
1100	**Krasnodar** I .... d.	0526	**Krasnodar** I .... d.	0045
1248	Tuapse .... d.	0941	Tikhoretskaya .. d.	0326
1328	Sochi .... a.	1145	Volgograd I .... d.	1414
1351	**Adler** .... a.	1226	**Saratov** I .... a.	2047

△ – Uneven dates ■(3) (daily May 25 - Oct. 1).
▽ – Even dates ●(4) (daily May 26 - Oct. 2).

ROSTOV - BAKI 1963

km		392SJ Pas Y		391SZ Pas Y
0	**Rostov na D.** .. d.	1807	**Baki** .... AZ d.	2300
307	Armavir Rost. ... d.	2328	Derbent .... d.	0725
495	Mineralnye Vody d.	0222	Makhachkala .... d.	1017
773	Gudermes .... d.	0952	Gudermes .... d.	1520
896	Makhachkala ... d.	1355	Mineralnye Vody d.	0015
1025	Derbent .... d.	1625	Armavir Rost. ... d.	0254
1286	**Baki** .... AZ a.	0215	**Rostov na D.** ... a.	0810

FOR NOTES SEE TABLE **1960**.

RUSSIA

1965 MOSKVA - SARATOV, VOLGOGRAD and BAKI

km		79AJ Sko B	1IJ Fir	9GJ Fir ☆	17MJ Fir	15JI Sko	55CH Sko ⑥t	86VJ Sko	7CJ Sko ●(4)	31CH Fir	5GJ Fir
	St Peterburg Glavny . d.	2035	...	...	...	...	...	...	...	...	...
	Tver d.	0151	...	...	...	...	...	...	...	...	...
0	**Moskva** Paveletskaya d.	0410r	1405	1813	2000	2009	2240r	2112k	2133	2200	2359
198	Ryazan II d.	|	|	|	|	|	△	0040	|	|	|
408	Michurinsk Uralski d.	|	2013v	0118	0331	0400v	|	0402	0547	0612	0908
426	Yelets d.	1336	|	|	|	|	0635	|	|	|	|
504	Lipetsk d.	1501	|	|	|	|	0807	|	|	|	|
541	Gryazi Voronezhski d.	1625	2140	|	|	0523	0930	|	|	|	|
481	Tambov I d.	|	|	0229	0444	|	|	0524	0658	0730	1026
861	**Saratov** I a.	|	|	0850	1141	|	|	1203	1322	...	1733
778	Povorino d.	2230	0200	...	...	1010	1350	|	a	...	|
1145	**Volgograd** I a.	0458	0819	...	...	1655	2056	|	...	...	|
1595	Astrakhan I a.	...	...	...	...	...	0506	2337	...	...	0543
⊡	Makhachkala a.	...	...	...	...	...	1520	1235	...	...	...
2212	Derbent a.	...	...	...	...	...	1822	...	...	...	...
2473	**Baki** AZ a.	...	...	...	...	...	0410	...	...	...	...

	9ZH Fir ☆	1ZH Fir	17ZH Fir	7RJ Sko E	15ZH Sko	5ZH Fir	79ZH Sko C	55SZ Sko ④t	85SJ Sko	31VJ Fir
Baki AZ d.	...	...	...	...	...	...	...	0135	...	...
Derbent d.	...	...	...	...	...	...	...	0825	...	...
Makhachkala d.	...	...	...	...	...	...	...	1105	1445	...
Astrakhan I d.	...	...	...	...	...	1030	...	2055	0145	...
Volgograd I d.	...	1523	...	...	1713	|	0107	0506	|	...
Povorino d.	...	2205	...	a	2359	|	0830	1240	|	...
Saratov I d.	1630	|	1903	1936	|	2249	|	|	1341	...
Tambov I d.	2253	|	0153	0216	|	0530	|	|	2032	2119
Gryazi Voronezhski d.	|	0222	|	|	0436	|	1445	1755	|	|
Lipetsk d.	|	|	|	|	|	|	1544	1841	|	|
Yelets d.	|	|	|	|	|	|	1800	2023	|	|
Michurinsk Uralski d.	0032	0313v	0336	0355	0540v	0710	|	|	2242	2306
Ryazan II d.	|	|	|	|	|	|	|	▽	0220	|
Moskva Paveletskaya a.	0720	0930	1029	1038	1400	1437	0256r	0322r	0530k	0624
Tver a.	...	...	...	...	...	...	0525	...	...	...
St Peterburg Glavny a.	...	...	...	...	...	...	1223	...	...	...

B – Even dates (daily May 24 - Sept. 3).
C – Uneven dates ■(3) (daily May 25 - Sept. 5).
E – ■(1) from Almaty, from Saratov 3rd day.
a – To / from Almaty (Table 1975).
k – Moskva **Kazanskaya**.
r – Moska **Kurskaya**.
t – Journey 3 nights.
v – Michurinsk **Voronezhski**.
● – Even dates. See page 530.
■ – Uneven dates. See page 530.
△ – Via Tula I (d. 0149).
▽ – Via Tula I (d. 0058).
⊡ – *1537 km (2083 km via Volgograd).*
☆ – Includes Lux 🛏 with ensuite shower/toilet.
AZ – Azerbaijan (GMT + 4).

1970 MOSKVA - SAMARA - UFA - CHELYABINSK

km		116JI Sko	66JI Sko	32UJ Fir F	50MJ Sko	10JI Fir	14EJ Fir	6FJ Sko T	18SZ Sko B	84CJ Fir A	107ZH Fir S
0	**Moskva** Kaz. d.	1226	1708	1716	1808	2008	2122	2240	2240	2248	0014k
197	Ryazan I d.	1533	2024	2034	2101	2259	0037	0146	0146	0209	0457
601	Ruzayevka ⊡ d.	2217	0155	0210	0238	0347	0544	0805	0805	0903	1150
712	Inza d.	0025	0339	0355	0410	|	0716	1005	1005	|	◇
908	Syzran I d.	|	0623	0637	0648	0738	0939	|	|	1351	1924
1044	**Samara** a.	|	t	0856	0847	0911	1120	1522	1522	1552	2156
1044	**Samara** d.	♡	...	0954	...	...	1156	1602	1602	1637	2237
1216	Buzuluk' d.	|	...	1328	...	...	|	1917	1917	|	|
1462	Orenburg a.	|	...	1735	...	...	|	2303	2303	|	|
1567	**Ufa** a.	1703	...	...	...	...	1920	...	...	0101	0700
1933	Magnitogorsk a.	...	...	...	...	...	0537e	...	...	|	...
2048	**Chelyabinsk** a.	...	...	...	...	...	0420	...	...	1015	...

	49JI Sko	13UJ Fir	9JI Fir	31UJ Fir G	66EI Sko	17SZ Sko B	5FJ Sko T	107JI Fir S	83CJ Sko A	115JI Sko
Chelyabinsk d.	...	2100	...	...	...	...	...	...	0252	...
Magnitogorsk d.	...	1945e	...	...	...	...	...	...	|	...
Ufa d.	...	0653	...	...	...	...	...	1255	1245	2354
Orenburg d.	...	|	...	0948	...	1056	1056	|	|	|
Buzuluk' d.	...	|	...	1410	...	1507	1507	|	|	|
Samara a.	...	1500	...	1718	...	1812	1812	2125	2135	♡
Samara d.	1433	1554	1850	1808	t	1904	1904	2210	2220	|
Syzran I d.	1637	1801	2033	2041	2053	|	|	0041	0108	|
Inza d.	1929	2034	|	2320	2336	0027	0027	◇	|	1711
Ruzayevka ⊡ d.	2112	2214	0031	0111	0124	0215	0215	0838	0540	1919
Ryazan I d.	0239	0309	0501	0653	0643	0810	0810	1459	1213	0152
Moskva Kaz. a.	0545	0620	0753	1029	1024	1115	1115	2133k	1520	0512

MOSKVA - PENZA, SARANSK, ULYANOVSK

km		22JI Fir	132UJ Sko	52JI Fir	42JI Fir
0	**Moskva** Kaz d.	1908	1510	2040	2132
197	Ryazan I d.	2238	1833r	0001r	0049
313	Ryazhsk I d.	|	2032	0143	|
710	**Penza** I a.	|	0437	0800	|
601	Ruzayevka ⊡ d.	0421	n	...	0632
627	**Saransk** I a.	|	...	...	0705
712	Inza d.	0630	...	...	...
873	**Ulyanovsk** a.	0909	...	...	...

	41JI Fir	131UJ Sko	51JI Fir	21JI Fir
Ulyanovsk d.	...	...	...	1950
Inza d.	...	...	...	2306
Saransk d.	2043	...	...	|
Ruzayevka ⊡ d.	2127	o	...	0049
Penza I d.	|	1927	2056	|
Ryazhsk I d.	|	0408	0317	|
Ryazan I d.	0259	0556r	0508r	0550
Moskva Kaz a.	0603	0938	0823	0930

PENZA - SAMARA - CHELYABINSK - OMSK

km		124VJ Sko ●v	110JI Fir	12UJ Sko △
0	**Penza** I d.	0601	0713	...
253	Syzran I d.	0928	1004	...
389	**Samara** d.	1243	1138	...
912	Ufa d.	2231	...	...
1393	**Chelyabinsk** d.	0822	...	1905
1651	Kurgan d.	1219	...	2250
1918	Petropavl § d.	1649	...	0327
2191	**Omsk** a.	2101	...	0810

	123NJ Sko ■w	11UJ Sko ▽	109JI Fir
Omsk d.	1948	0054	...
Petropavl § d.	0056	0546	...
Kurgan d.	0511	1009	...
Chelyabinsk d.	0929	1346	...
Ufa d.	1933	...	...
Samara d.	0448	...	1754
Syzran I a.	0724	...	1934
Penza I a.	1129	...	2226

A – To / from Astana (for days of running see Table **1975**).
B – To / from Bishkek (for days of running see Table **1975**).
F – Even dates (daily Dec. 22 - Jan. 14, May 26 - Sept. 4).
G – Uneven dates (daily Dec. 21 - Jan. 13, May 25 - Sept. 3).
S – St P'burg - Moskva - Ufa ■(3); Ufa - Moskva - St P'burg ■(1).
T – To / from Toshkent (for days of running see Table **1975**).
e – Portion detached / attached at Ufa (**675EI** / **676UJ**). From Moskva and Magnitogorsk on unven dates in Jan., Apr., May, Aug., Nov., even dates in Dec., Feb., Mar., June, July, Sept. Oct.
k – Moskva **Kurskaya**.
n – To Samara (a. 1208), Orenburg (a. 2038), Orsk (a. 0307).
o – From Orsk (d. 2040), Orenburg (d. 0314), Samara (d. 1140).
r – Ryazan II.
t – To / from Toliatti (a. 1010 / d. 1730).
v – Runs ● (daily Apr. 24 - Oct. 2). From Belgorod (0910), Voronezh I (1748), Tambov (2315). To Novosibirsk (0549).
w – Runs ■ (daily Apr. 27 - Oct. 5). From Novosibirsk (1052). To Tambov (a. 1820), Voronezh I (a. 0028), Belgorod (a. 1010).
△ – From Chelyabinsk ■(1). To Chita (Table **1990**).
▽ – From Chita ■(5) (Table **1990**). Omsk 4th day.
⊡ – Also known as Saransk Gorod or Saransk II.
♡ – Via Ulyanovsk (**116** a. 0322, **115** d. 1313).
◇ – Via Penza I (d. 1530 to Ufa; 0502 from Ufa).
§ – Petropavl (Kazakhstan). Moskva time.
● – Even dates. See page 530.
■ – Uneven dates. See page 530.

1975 TRAINS TO KAZAKHSTAN AND BEYOND

km	TOSHKENT	6FJ Sko E	18SZ Sko G	381EI Pas M
0	*Moskva Kaz* ‡ d.	2240	2240	...
1044	**Samara** d.	1602	1602	...
	Ufa d.	...	...	1110
1462	Orenburg d.	2348	2348	2013
1734	Aktobe KA d.	1106	1106	0833
1828	Kandyagash KA d.	1242	1242	1016
2767	Kyzlorda KA d.	0450	0450	0400
3315	**Toshkent** UZ a.	1650	|	1827
3240	Shymkent KA a.	...	1346	...
3720	**Bishkek** II KY a.	...	2300	...

	5FJ Sko F	17SZ Sko H	381MZ Pas N
Bishkek II KY d.	...	0906	...
Shymkent KA d.	...	0034	...
Toshkent UZ d.	1850	|	0145
Kyzlorda KA d.	0944	0944	1744
Kandyagash KA d.	0225	0225	1221
Aktobe KA d.	0405	0405	1406
Orenburg d.	1056	1056	2136
Ufa a.	|	|	0630
Samara a.	1812	1812	...
Moskva Kaz ‡ a.	1115	1115	...

km	ALMATY	7CJ Sko ●(4)	34TJ Sko	310KH Pas
0	*Moskva Pav* § d.	2133	...	...
856	**Saratov** I d.	1400	...	...
1291	Oral / Uralsk KA d.	0413	...	...
1750	**Aktobe** KA d.	1458	2335	0050
1844	Kandyagash KA d.	1653	0118	0313
2940	**Aktau** ⊙ KA a.	|	|	0630*
2783	Kyzlorda KA d.	0858	1826	...
3256	Shymkent KA d.	1721	0344	...
4008	**Almaty** I KA a.	0652	1719	...
4017	**Almaty** II KA a.	0719	...	...

	309KH Pas	7RJ Sko ■(1)	33CJ Sko
Almaty II KA d.	...	0633	...
Almaty I KA d.	...	0700	2314
Shymkent KA d.	...	2106	1238
Kyzlorda KA d.	...	0648	2218
Aktau ⊙ KA d.	1407	|	|
Kandyagash KA d.	1704*	2241	1451
Aktobe KA d.	1846	0039	1615
Oral / Uralsk KA d.	...	1115	...
Saratov I a.	...	1856	...
Moskva Pav § a.	...	1038	...

km	ASTANA	90UJ Sko ■(3)	84CJ Sko ●(4)	304CJ Pas ③	306SZ Pas ④d	316FJ Pas ①
0	*Moskva Kaz* **1970** d.	1850	2248	...	...	...
1044	**Samara** d.	|	1637	...	...	...
2048	Chelyabinsk d.	▽	1056	...	...	...
	Yekaterinburg d.	2155*	|	1730	1730	1730
2306	Kurgan d.	0431	1427	0011	0011	0011
2573	Petropavl ⊡ KA d.	0918	2005	0628	0628	0628
3064	**Astana** KA a.	...	0804	1850	1850	1850
3064	**Astana** KA d.	...	0844	1930	1930	1930
3305	Karagandy KA d.	...	1253	0034	0034	0034
4407	**Almaty** II KA a.	...	...	2013	|	|
4356	Bishkek II KY a.	...	...	...	1847	|
4522	Shymkent KA a.	...	...	...	...	2216
4755	**Toshkent** UZ a.	...	...	...	...	0547

	89UJ Sko ■(1)	83CJ Sko ●	315FJ Pas ⑥	305SZ Pas ②e	303CJ Pas ①
Toshkent UZ d.	...	...	0355	...	...
Shymkent KA d.	...	...	1308	...	...
Bishkek II KY d.	...	...	|	1048	...
Almaty II KA d.	...	...	|	|	1512
Karagandy KA d.	...	0656	1303	1303*	1303
Astana KA a.	...	1054	1721	1721	1721
Astana KA d.	...	1124	1800	1800	1800
Petropavl ⊡ KA d.	1313	1745	0248	0248	0248
Kurgan d.	1904	2241	0844	0844	0844
Yekaterinburg a.	0047	|	1515	1515	1515
Chelyabinsk d.	▽	0252			
Samara a.	|	2135			
Moskva Kaz **1970** a.	0457*	1520			

km	DUSHANBE *Arrive 5th day*	320EI 330CH Pas P
0	**Moskva** Kaz. d.	1216
198	Ryazan II d.	1530
409	Michurinsk Vor . d.	1834
1073	**Volgograd** d.	1210
1802	Atyrau KA d.	0824
1932	Makat KA d.	1121
2639	Kungrad UZ d.	0243
3190	Uckuduk II UZ d.	1234
3467	Navoi UZ d.	1733
3712	Karshi UZ d.	2113
4044	Termez UZ d.	...
4269	**Dushanbe** I . TA a.	1648

Arrive Moskva on 5th day	319ZJ 329ZJ Pas Q
Dushanbe I . TA d.	0310
Termez UZ d.	...
Karshi UZ d.	2210
Navoi UZ d.	0151
Uckuduk II UZ d.	0628
Kungrad UZ d.	1519
Makat KA d.	0828
Atyrau KA d.	1120
Volgograd d.	0252
Michurinsk Vor d.	1658
Ryazan II d.	2019
Moskva Kaz. a.	0001

km	VIA AKTOGAY	369NJ J	301NJ ●(7)
0	**Novosibirsk** d.	1434	1434
228	Barnaul d.	2041	2041
1121	Aktogay KA d.	2048*	2048*
1678	**Almaty** I KA a.	0817	0817
1687	**Almaty** II KA a.	|	0909
2424	Shymkent KA d.	2345	...
2657	**Toshkent** UZ a.	0714	...

	302CJ ♥	369FJ J
Toshkent UZ d.	...	1615
Shymkent KA d.	...	0226
Almaty II KA d.	1633	|
Almaty I KA d.	1725	1725
Aktogay KA d.	0510	0510
Barnaul d.	2336	2336
Novosibirsk a.	0459	0459

E – ⑦ (also ② from Feb. 28). Arrive T'kent 4th day.
F – ④ (also ⑥ from Mar. 4). Arrive Moskva 4th day.
G – ④⑥. Arrive Bishkek on 4th day.
H – ①③. Arrive Moskva on 4th day.
J – Runs approximately every 4 days.
M – ⑥ (also ②④ from Mar. 7).
N – ④ (also ②⑦ from Mar. 5).
P – ①③⑥ (also ⑤ Mar. 10 - June 2).
Q – ②④⑥ (also ① Mar. 6 - May 29).
d – Also ⑥ May 6 - Sept. 30.
e – Also ④ May 4 - Sept. 28.
⊙ – Mangyshlak station (12 km from Aktau).
⊡ – Petropavl (KA) times are in Moskva time.
▽ – Via Kazan (Table **1990**).
* – More than 24 hrs after previous time shown.
● – Even dates. See page 530.
■ – Uneven dates. See page 530.
♥ – Even dates [.. *30*, *4* ..] (see page 530).
§ – See Table **1965**.
‡ – See Table **1970**.
KA – Kazakhstan (GMT + 6). Oral, Aktau, Aktobe are GMT + 5.
KY – Kyrgyzstan (GMT + 6).
TA – Tajikistan (+ 5).
UZ – Uzbekistan (+ 5).

TYUMEN - MAKHACHKALA · YEKATERINBURG - KISLOVODSK · KHARKIV - BAKI — 1977

km		373EJ Pas ●		373SJ Pas ■(5)
0	**Tyumen** d.	1832	**Makhachkala** d.	1635
326	**Yekaterinburg** a.	0010	Astrakhan I d.	0250
326	**Yekaterinburg** d.	0050	**Saratov** I a.	1502
578	Chelyabinsk d.	0810	**Saratov** I d.	1557
1059	Ufa d.	1820	**Samara** d.	0130
1582	**Samara** d.	0324	Ufa d.	1056
2019	**Saratov** I a.	1212	Chelyabinsk d.	2045
2019	**Saratov** I d.	1300	**Yekaterinburg** a.	0303
2695	Astrakhan I d.	0136	**Yekaterinburg** d.	0351
3183	**Makhachkala** a.	1122	**Tyumen** a.	0921

km		45EJ Fir ●		45SJ Fir ■(5)
0	**Yekaterinburg** d.	2330	**Kislovodsk** d.	2157
515	Sarapul d.	0931	Pyatigorsk d.	2254
875	**Kazan** d.	1658	Mineral. Vody d.	0004
1121	Ulyanovsk d.	2350	Armavir Ros. d.	0242
1576	**Saratov** I d.	0930	Volgograd I a.	1555
2005	Volgograd I d.	1750	**Saratov** I d.	2346
2665	Armavir Ros. d.	0810	Ulyanovsk d.	0915
2853	Mineral. Vody a.	1050	**Kazan** d.	1457
2879	Pyatigorsk a.	1244	Sarapul d.	2045
2917	**Kislovodsk** a.	1355	**Yekaterinburg** a.	0411

km		449OJ Pas D‡		449SZ Pas E‡
0	**Kharkiv** UA d.	2335	**Baki** AZ d.	0340
129	Kupiansk UA a.	0214	Derbent d.	0825
368	Liski d.	0906	Makhachkala d.	1105
593	Povorino d.	1350	Astrakhan I a.	2010
960	Volgograd d.	2137	Astrakhan I d.	2055
1410	Astrakhan I a.	0506	Volgograd d.	0506
1410	Astrakhan I d.	0551	Povorino d.	1300
1898	Makhachkala d.	1555	Liski d.	1740
2027	Derbent d.	1827	Kupiansk UA a.	2220
2272	**Baki** AZ a.	0410	**Kharkiv** UA a.	0114

D – ①④ Apr. 24 - Oct. 16.
E – ②⑥ Apr. 22 - Oct. 14.
● – Even dates (see page 530).
■ – Uneven dates (see page 530).
‡ – A winter service operates every four days via Rostov na Donu (train **369**OJ).
AZ – Azerbaijan (GMT+4).
UA – Ukraine (GMT+2 winter, GMT+3 summer).

GEORGIA — 1979

GMT+4 *Subject to alteration*

km		870	872	682	802	698	18	684	678	874	804	602	860 A
0	**Tbilisi** d.	0800	0820	...	0910	...	1015	...	1530	1750	1820	2145	0035
221	Kutaisi a.	|	|	0940	|	1245	1515	1730	2057	|	|	|	|
317	Zugdidi a.	1330	|	|	|	1605	...	|	...	|	|	0605	|
312	Poti a.	...	1316	|	|	...	...	|	...	2245	|	...	|
348	**Batumi** a.	...	...	1333	1409	...	...	2125	...	...	2319	...	0615

	677	803	873	697	683	17	801	871	869	681	601	859 A
Batumi d.	...	0735	...	...	0825	...	1705	...	...	1845	...	0135
Poti d.	...	|	0815	...	|	...	|	1740	...	|	...	|
Zugdidi d.	...	|	|	0755	|	...	|	|	1750	|	2215	|
Kutaisi d.	0500	|	|	1110	1210	1215	|	|	|	2223	|	|
Tbilisi a.	1045	1230	1340	...	...	1740	2200	2239	2320	...	0630	0705

km		37 🛏		38 🛏
0	Tbilisi d.	1730	Baki AZ d.	2030
551	Baki AZ a.	0745	Tbilisi a.	1045

km	🛏	372 W	202 S	🛏	201 S	371 Y
	Batumi d.	...	1535	Yerevan AR d.	1530	2130
0	Tbilisi d.	2020	2216	Tbilisi a.	0012	0750
374	Yerevan AR a.	0655	0725	Batumi a.	0710	...

A – Every second day.
S – Every second day mid June - late Sept.
W – ■(3) late Sept to mid June.
Y – ● late Sept. to mid June.
● ■ See page 530.
AR – Armenia (GMT+4).
AZ – Azerbaijan (GMT+4).

KAZAKHSTAN and UZBEKISTAN — 1980

KA	4CJ	2TJ	10TJ	87KH ■(1)	80KH ●
Astana d.	1145	1853	2210	2235	2335
Aktobe a.	|	|	|	1529	|
Karagandy d.	1625	2124	0217	...	0206
Almaty I a.	0825	|	1700	...	|
Almaty II a.	0852	0747	...	...	|
Shymkent a.	...	...	...	...	1520

KA	1TJ	80TJ ■(3)	3KH	88KH ●	9TJ
Shymkent d.	...	1633	...	...	...
Almaty II d.	1931	|	1334	...	...
Almaty I d.	|	|	1400	...	2052
Karagandy d.	0623	0637	0528	...	1231
Aktobe d.	|	|	|	2055	|
Astana a.	0846	0900	0930	1352	1552

KA	37 ■(5)	19 ●
Astana d.	1625	1840
Kandyagash d.	1745*	1044
Atyrau a.	|	1705
Aktau ⊙ a.	1435	...

KA	37 ■(3)	19 ■(3)
Aktau ⊙ d.	1655	...
Atyrau d.	|	2000
Kandyagash d.	1333	0237
Astana a.	1225	1907

UZ	760‡	762‡	10FJ	56/58	662 ⑦–④
Toshkent d.	0700	0800	0854	2020	2205
Samarkand d.	0908	1013	1228	0013	0225
Bukhara I a.	▽	1147	1442	...	0559

UZ	55/57	9FJ	761‡	759‡	661 ①–⑤
Bukhara I d.	...	0801	1521	▽	2236
Samarkand d.	0305	1034	1700	1800	0233
Toshkent a.	0708	1352	1910	2010	0634

⊙ – Mangyshlak station (12 km from Aktau).
▽ – To/from Karshi (a. 1020/d. 1648).
‡ – AFROSIYOB – high-speed Talgo train.
* – More than 24 hours after previous time.
● – Even dates (see page 530).
■ – Uneven dates (see page 530).
KA – Kazakhstan (GMT +6). Aktau is GMT+5.
UZ – Uzbekistan (GMT +5).

MOSKVA - ARCHANGELSK, LABYTNANGI and VORKUTA — 1985

km		16MJ Sko	34JA Fir F	90GJ Sko ●	78JA Sko H	98JA Sko J	10JA Sko D	22JA Fir B	118MJ Fir ■	42VJ Fir	653MJ Pas
0	**Moskva** Yarolslavsk d.	1005	1305	...	...	...	...	1950	2020	2150	...
282	Yaroslavl d.	1438	1726	...	...	...	...	0006	0032	0156	...
	St Peterburg Lad. ▷ d.	|	|	...	1020	1020	1454	|	|	|	...
496	Vologda I ▷ d.	1845	2133	...	|	|	|	0357	0434	0547	...
707	Konosha I d.	2200	0100	...	0123	0123	0508	0705	0813	0919	...
1134	**Archangelsk** a.	0600	|	...	|	|	1345	|	1821	|	...
825	Velsk d.	...	0306	n	0350	0350	...	0916	...	1135	...
1084	**Kotlas** Yuzhny d.	...	0738z	0910	0957	0957	...	1318	...	1631	...
1325	Mikun d.	...	1215	1331	1427	1536	...	1818	...	2038	...
1412	**Syktyvkar** a.	...	1355	|	1750x	1750x	...	|	...	|	...
1571	Sosnogorsk d.	...	...	1855	1948	...	...	2250	...	0134	...
2406	Labytnangi a.	...	...	|	|	...	...	1644	...	|	1045
2277	**Vorkuta** a.	...	...	0820	0950	...	...	...	...	1435	2104

	117JA Fir ■(2)	34MJ Fir F	41MJ Fir	89GJ Sko ●(4)	77JA Sko K	97VJ Sko L	15JA Sko	9SJ Sko E‡	21NJ Fir C	653JA 655JA y
Vorkuta d.	...	...	1635	1905	2030	...	...	...	...	0910
Labytnangi d.	...	...	|	|	|	...	...	...	0750	2211
Sosnogorsk d.	...	...	0551	0855	0930	...	...	...	0057	...
Syktyvkar d.	...	0745	|	|	0840x	0840x	...	...	|	...
Mikun d.	...	1004	1125	1332	1424	1424	...	...	0531	...
Kotlas Yuzhny d.	...	1419z	1552	1813	1922	1922	...	...	1000	...
Velsk d.	...	1847	2103	u	0110	0110	...	...	1458	...
Archangelsk d.	0725	|	|	...	|	|	2010	2043	|	...
Konosha I d.	1807	2142	2315	...	0333	0333	0427	0554	1720	...
Vologda I ▷ d.	2154	0049	0208	...	|	|	0812	|	2021	...
St Peterburg Lad ▷ a.	|	|	|	...	1845	1845	|	2055	|	...
Yaroslavl d.	0221	0522	0611	...	...	...	1221	...	0055	...
Moskva Yarolslavsk a.	0623	0912	0958	...	...	...	1643	...	0446	...

B – ②⑤ (runs 2-3 times per week June - Sept.).
C – ①⑤ (runs 2-3 times per week June - Sept.).
D – ①④⑤ (daily Dec. 26 - Jan. 9, June 22 - Aug. 31).
E – ②⑤⑥ (daily Dec. 27 - Jan. 10; June 23 - Sept. 1).
F – Approx every 3 days (June - Aug also runs as *Sko* **224**CH, **228**JA).
H – Approx every 3 days; uneven dates ■(5) Apr. 25 - Aug. 31.
J – Approx every 3 days; even dates ●(6) Apr. 28 - Aug. 30.
K – Approx every 3 days; uneven dates ■(3) Apr. 25 - Aug. 31.
L – Approx every 3 days; uneven dates ■(3) Apr. 23 - Aug. 31.

n – From Niz. Novgorod (1610), Kirov (2352).
u – To Kirov (0218), Niz. Novgorod (0915).
x – Syktyvkar portion: **305**JA and **304**JA.
y – Arrive 2018 on even dates.
z – Kotlas **Uzlovoy**.
▷ – See also Table **1990**.
● – Even dates. See page 530.
■ – Uneven dates. See page 530.
‡ – Train **289**MJ on certain dates.

km		♡		♧
0	**Murmansk** § d.	0830	**Archangelsk** d.	1518
277	Kandalaksha § d.	1407	Belomorsk § d.	0325
665	Belomorsk § d.	2142	Kandalaksha § d.	1128
1151	**Archangelsk** a.	0950	**Murmansk** § a.	1730

♡ – ①⑥ (● May/Aug; ■ June/July/Sept. 1-13). **373**JA/**371**JA.
♧ – ④⑥ (● May/Aug; ■ June/July/Sept. 1-11). **371**CH/**374**JA.
§ – See also Table **1905**.

NOVOSIBIRSK - SEVEROBAIKALSK - TYNDA - NERYUNGRI - TOMMOT — 1989

km	*Baikal-Amur Magistrale (BAM)*	87IJ 348Y ●	348Y Pas ●	71IJ Sko ■(1)	76EI Sko ■(7) n	92IJ Sko D n	324JI Pas	78EI Sko ■ v	
	Moskva Yar. **1990** d.	...	...	...	1310r	1620	...	...	...
0	**Novosibirsk** **1990** d.	...	...	...	1455	1649	...	1746	...
762	Krasnoyarsk **1990** d.	...	1700	...	0325	0527	...	0635	...
	Ulan Ude **1990** d.	...	|	1103	|	|	...	|	...
	Irkutsk **1990** d.	1428	|	1848	|	|	...	|	...
1180	**Tayshet** a.	0202	0205	0602	1016	1227	...	1316	...
1180	**Tayshet** d.	0320	0340	0637	1056	1257	...	1335	...
1473	Bratsk d.	1320	1320	1320	1654	1925	...	|	...
2243	**Severobaikalsk** d.	0459	0459	0459	0734	0905	...	▽	...
3972	Skovorodino d.	...	...	...	|	...	...	2046x	...
3528	**Tynda** a.	...	...	...	1008*	...	...	0154	...
∆	**Tynda** d.	...	...	...	1152	...	...	0311	...
3757	Neryungri d.	...	...	...	1717	...	0156	0842	...
4125	Tommot a.	...	...	...	...	...	0945	...	...
4493	Nizhny Bestyakh ⊕ a.	...	...	...	...	...	...	...	...

Local time (Moskva time +)		323JI Pas	75EI Sko ■(1) u	91IJ Sko E s	77EI Sko ■(3)		71Y Sko ■(3)	347Y 87Y ●(4)	347Y Pas ●(4)
+6	Nizhny Bestyakh ⊕ d.	...	...	...	...	...	...	...	...
+6	Tommot d.	1306	...	...	...	...	...	...	...
+6	Neryungri d.	2117	2302	...	0305	...	...	...	...
+6	**Tynda** a.	...	0427	...	0813	...	...	...	...
+6	**Tynda** d.	...	0647	...	0943	...	...	...	...
+6	Skovorodino d.	...	|	...	1445	...	...	...	...
+5	**Severobaikalsk** d.	...	1030*	1151	▽	...	1720	1720	1720
+5	Bratsk d.	...	0011	0202	|	...	0749	0811	0811
+5	**Tayshet** a.	...	0557	0824	2002z	...	1336	1829	1854
+5	**Tayshet** d.	...	0654	0854	2007z	...	1414	1944	2014
+5	**Irkutsk** **1990** a.	...	|	|	|	...	0119	0710	|
+5	Ulan Ude **1990** a.	...	|	|	|	...	0903	...	|
+4	Krasnoyarsk **1990** a.	...	1331	1548	0338	...	...	...	0525
+4	**Novosibirsk** **1990** a.	...	0218	0448	1550	...	...	...	...
0	*Moskva Yar.* **1990** a.	...	0442r	0552	...	...	...	...	...

D – Even dates ●(6) (daily June 6 - Sept. 4).
E – Even dates (daily June 2 - Aug. 31).
n – Novosibirsk on 3rd day, Severobaikalsk on 5th day.
r – Moskva Kazanskaya.
s – Novosibirsk 3rd day, Moskva 5th day.
u – Novosibirsk 5th day, Moskva 7th day.
v – Uneven dates [.. *31*, *1*, *3*, *7*..] (see page 530).
x – 4th day. z – 3rd day.
▽ – Via Irkutsk (Table **1990**).
● – Even dates. See page 530.
■ – Uneven dates. See page 530.
∆ – *4182* via Skovorodino.
⊕ – Under construction. In summer a ferry (15 km from station) runs to Yakutsk.
* – Following day (more than 24 hours after previous time shown).

		364EI	667ZH		667EI	363EI
0	**Tynda** d.	1216	...	**Khabarovsk** d.	1410	...
951	Novy Urgal d.	1131	...	Komsomolsk d.	2327	1153
1469	Komsomolsk d.	0040	1413	Novy Urgal d.	...	0237
1857	**Khabarovsk** a.	...	2341	**Tynda** a.	...	0153

1990 MOSKVA - YEKATERINBURG - NOVOSIBIRSK - IRKUTSK - VLADIVOSTOK

km	*Trans-Siberian Railway*	140*NJ* Sko Q	36*EI* Fir	44*EI* Sko ■(9)	100*EI* Sko ●(9) ◇	59*AJ* Fir d	64*BJ* Sko D	702*NJ* ♠ ①③ ④–⑥	704*NJ* ♠ ④ ⑤⑦	728*GJ* ≋	706*NJ* ♠ ④–⑥	76*EI* Sko ■(7)	82*IJ* Sko ●(6)	56 *Y* Fir ●(6)	118*EJ* Sko ■(5)	708*NJ* ♠ ①⑤ ⑥⑦	12*UJ* Sko ■(1)	78*EI* Sko ■(6)	84*MJ* Fir ♡	50*EJ* Fir ♤	70*CH* Sko	710*NJ* ♠	730*GJ* ≋	41*GJ* Fir
0	**Moskva** Yaroslavskaya ▷ d.	...	0010	0035	0035	...	...	...	...	...	...	...	...	...	...	...	...	...	1335	1335	1350	...	...	...
	Moskva Kazanskaya d.	...	|	|	|	0221k	0335r	0635k	0715k	0930k	1100k	1310	1310	1318	1318	1400k	...	...	|	|	|	1540k	1635k	...
282	Yaroslavl ▷ d.	...	|	0427	0427	|	|	|	|	|	|	|	|	|	|	|	...	...	|	|	1817	|	|	...
210	Vladimir d.	...	0320	|	|	0457	0653	0816	0856	1116	1241	|	|	|	|	1541	...	...	1650	1650	|	1721	1821	...
461	**Nizhni Novgorod** d.	...	0624	|	|	0753	1120	1010	1105	1336	1443	|	|	|	|	1743	...	...	2010	2010	|	1923	2041	2125
	St Peterburg Ladozhski d.	...	...	|	|	...	|	...	▬	...	...	|	|	|	|	...	...	...	|	|	|	...	...	|
	Vologda I d.	...	...	|	|	...	|	...	...	...	...	|	|	|	|	...	...	...	|	|	|	...	...	|
917	**Kirov** d.	...	...	1837	1837	...	1847	...	...	...	...	|	|	|	|	...	...	...	0220	0220	0609	...	...	|
1397	Perm II d.	...	...	0350	0350	...	0400	...	...	...	...	|	|	|	|	...	...	...	1110	1110	1406	...	...	|
	Murom I d.	a	...	|	|	...	|	...	...	...	...	1750	1750	1801	1801	...	...	...	y	|	|	...	...	|
	Kazan d.	1545	...	|	|	...	|	...	...	...	...	0203	0203	0213	0213	...	...	...	...	w	|	...	...	0617
	Sarapul d.	2200	...	|	|	...	|	...	...	...	...	0759	0759	0809	0809	...	...	...	...	|	|	...	...	...
1778	**Yekaterinburg** a.	0559	...	0918	0918	...	0930	...	...	...	...	1612	1612	1602	1602	...	...	...	...	2212	1941	...	...	...
1778	**Yekaterinburg** d.	0629	...	0952	0952	...	1000	...	...	...	...	1641	1641	1633	1633	...	...	...	...	...	2016	...	...	...
2104	Tyumen d.	1243	...	1512	1512	...	1523	...	...	...	...	2217	2217	2227	2227	...	c	...	...	...	0323	...	...	...
2676	**Omsk** a.	2016	...	2301	2301	...	2327	...	...	...	...	0538	0538	0614	0614	...	0810	...	...	...	1158	...	...	...
2676	**Omsk** d.	2101	...	2317	2317	...	2343	...	...	...	...	0600	0600	0632	0632	...	0826	...	...	...	1215	...	...	...
3303	**Novosibirsk** a.	0534	...	0732	0732	...	0818	...	...	...	...	1403	1403	1424	1424	...	1656	...	...	...	2010	...	...	...
3303	**Novosibirsk** d.	...	...	0832	0832	...	...	...	...	...	...	1455	1455	1445	1529	...	1746	1746	...	...	2102	...	...	...
3532	Tayga d.	...	...	1150	1150	...	...	...	...	...	...	1836	1836	1823	o	...	2127	2127	...	...	0103	...	...	...
4065	**Krasnoyarsk** d.	...	...	2106	2106	...	...	...	...	...	...	0325	0325	0347	...	...	0635	0635	...	...	1045	...	...	...
4483	Tayshet d.	...	...	0406	0406	...	...	...	...	...	...	1056	1019	...	...	...	1335	1335	...	...	1750	...	...	...
5152	**Irkutsk** a.	...	...	1547	1547	...	...	...	...	...	...	u	2152	...	...	...	0109	0109	...	...	0631	...	...	...
5152	**Irkutsk** d.	...	...	1617	1617	...	...	...	...	...	...	...	2232	...	...	...	0146	0146	...	...	0706	...	...	...
5608	Ulan Ude d.	...	...	0019	0019	...	...	...	6*EI*	...	...	...	0629	...	...	...	1001	1001	...	...	1555	...	...	...
6165	Chita II d.	...	...	1215	1215	...	...	...	Fir	...	...	...	...	...	...	...	2151	2227	...	...	0302	...	...	...
7274	Skovorodino d.	...	...	1127	1127	...	...	...	...	...	...	...	...	...	...	...	...	2046	...	...	...	...	...	...
8492	**Khabarovsk** d.	...	...	0920	1020	...	...	...	1410	...	...	...	...	...	...	...	...	u	...	...	...	...	...	...
9147	Ussuriysk d.	...	...	...	2139	...	...	...	2335	...	...	...	...	...	...	...	...	...	...	...	...	...	...	...
9258	**Vladivostok** a.	...	...	...	2340	...	...	...	0130	...	...	...	...	...	...	...	...	...	...	...	...	...	...	...

local time ★		92*IJ* Sko E	60*UJ* Fir ♡	16*EJ* Fir ♤	8 *EJ* Fir ♡	12 *JA* Fir ♤	712*NJ* ♠	90*UJ* Sko ■(3)	96*NJ* Sko ▽	2 *JI* Fir ☆	714*NJ* ♠ ⑧	32*GJ* Fir	110*EI* Sko	30*NJ* Fir ■(3)	38*NJ* Fir ●(2)	68 *Y* Sko	2 *MJ* Fir ■(1) R	8*NJ* Sko ●(4)	4*ZJ* Sko ② B	6 Sko ③④ A	20*SZ* Sko ⑥ P	14*AJ* Fir ●(4)	74*EJ* Sko ■(3)	72*EJ* Fir
	Moskva Yaroslavskaya ▷ d.	1620	...	...	1650	1650	...	...	...	...	...	2005	2235	2250	2250	2305	2345	...	2355	2355	2355	...	...	...
	Moskva Kazanskaya d.	|	1638	1638	|	|	1835k	1850	1920	1940	2020k	|	|	|	|	|	|	...	|	|	|	...	...	...
	Yaroslavl ▷ d.	|	|	|	|	|	|	|	|	|	|	|	|	|	|	0320	|	...	|	|	|	...	...	...
	Vladimir d.	1948	|	|	2025	2025	2016	|	|	|	2201	2322	0152	0202	0202	|	0252	...	0302	0302	0302	...	...	...
	Nizhni Novgorod d.	2315	|	|	2325	2325	2218	|	|	|	2355	0219	0458	0508	0508	|	0550	...	0600	0600	0600	...	...	...
	St Peterburg Ladozhski d.	|	|	|	|	|	...	|	|	|	...	|	|	|	|	|	|	...	|	|	|	1530	1530	1709
	Vologda I d.	|	|	|	|	|	...	|	|	|	...	|	|	|	|	|	|	...	|	|	|	0239	0239	0505
	Kirov d.	0539	|	|	0559	0559	...	|	|	|	...	0833	1148	1202	1202	1444	1222	...	1232	1232	1232	1251	1251	1504
+2	Perm II d.	1343	|	|	1333	1353	...	|	|	|	...	...	2031	2001	2001	2223	2011	...	2021	2021	2021	2040	2040	2300
	Murom I d.	|	2110	2110	...	|	...	0007	0020	0034	...	...	|	|	|	|	|	...	|	|	|	|	|	|
	Kazan d.	|	0538	0538	...	|	...	0748	0805	0748	...	...	|	|	|	|	|	...	|	|	|	|	|	|
	Sarapul d.	|	1050	1050	...	|	...	1333	1344	...	...	...	|	|	|	|	|	...	|	|	|	|	|	|
+2	**Yekaterinburg** a.	1913	1804	1804	...	1923	...	2125	2233	...	...	...	0149	0117	0117	0339	0125	...	0137	0137	0137	0206	0206	0434
+2	**Yekaterinburg** d.	1950	1856	...	...	1958	...	2155	2304	...	...	...	0217	0146	0146	0424	0154	...	0205	0205	0205	0234	0234	...
+2	Tyumen d.	0040	0224	...	...	0234	...	p	0441	...	...	...	0833	0752	0752	1014	0622	...	0632	0632	0632	0813	0728	...
+3	**Omsk** a.	0746	n	...	...	t	...	...	1223	...	...	...	s	1544	1544	1825	1320	...	1349	1349	1349	1606	...	...
+3	**Omsk** d.	0811	...	...	...	...	...	...	1253	...	...	...	...	1600	1600	1841	1339	...	1407	1407	1407	1641	...	...
+4	**Novosibirsk** a.	1611	...	...	...	...	...	...	b	...	...	...	...	2350	2350	0200	2100	...	2115	2115	2115	0054	...	...
+4	**Novosibirsk** d.	1649	...	...	...	...	...	...	...	...	...	...	...	0040	0040	0250	2121	2121	2136	2136	2136	0147	...	...
+4	Tayga d.	2011	...	...	...	...	...	...	...	...	...	...	...	m	0427	0633	0034	0034	0043	0043	0043	o	...	...
+4	**Krasnoyarsk** d.	0527	...	...	...	...	...	...	...	...	...	...	...	...	z	q	0910	0910	0920	0920	0920	...	...	...
+5	Tayshet d.	1257	...	...	...	...	...	...	...	...	...	...	...	...	...	...	1545	1545	|	|	|	...	...	...
+5	**Irkutsk** a.	x	...	...	...	...	...	...	...	...	...	...	...	...	...	...	0218	0218	0227	0227	0227	...	...	...
+5	**Irkutsk** d.	...	...	...	...	...	...	...	...	...	...	...	...	...	...	...	0247	0247	0312	0312	0312	...	...	...
+5	Ulan Ude d.	...	...	...	...	...	...	...	...	...	...	...	...	...	...	...	0944	0944	1047	1047	1128	...	...	...
+6	Chita II d.	...	...	...	...	...	...	...	...	...	...	...	...	...	...	...	1920	1920	...	...	2257	...	...	...
+6	Skovorodino d.	...	...	...	...	...	...	...	...	...	...	...	...	...	...	...	1614	1614	...	...	...	...	...	...
+7	**Khabarovsk** d.	...	...	...	...	...	...	...	...	...	...	...	...	...	...	...	1234	1234	...	...	...	...	...	...
+7	Ussuriysk d.	...	...	...	...	...	...	...	...	...	...	...	...	...	...	...	2206	2206	...	...	...	...	...	...
+7	**Vladivostok** a.	...	...	...	...	...	...	...	...	...	...	...	...	...	...	...	2355	2355	...	...	...	...	...	...

ROSSIYA SUMMARY

km	*Moskva time*	2 *MJ* Fir ■(1) R	
0	**Moskva** Yar. d.	2345	*1st day*
461	Nizhni Novgorod d.	0550	*2nd day*
917	Kirov d.	1222	*2nd day*
1778	Yekaterinburg d.	0154	*3rd day*
2676	Omsk d.	1339	*3rd day*
3303	Novosibirsk d.	2121	*3rd day*
4065	Krasnoyarsk d.	0910	*4th day*
5152	Irkutsk d.	0247	*5th day*
5608	Ulan Ude d.	0944	*5th day*
8492	Khabarovsk d.	1234	*7th day*
9258	**Vladivostok** a.	2355	*7th day*

MOSKVA - BEIJING via Ulaan Baatar

km	*Trans-Mongolian Railway*	362 *Y* Pas ♤ e	4 *ZJ* Sko ②	6 *ZJ* Sko § ③ J	6 *MZ* Sko ④ K	24 Exp ④ ◧
0	*Moskva Yar.* △ d.	...	2355 ②	2355 ③	2355 ④	...
3303	*Novosibirsk* △ d.	...	2136 ④	2136 ⑤	2136 ⑥	...
5152	**Irkutsk** d.	1600	0312 ⑥	0312 ⑦	0312 ①	...
5608	Ulan Ude d.	0115	1047 ⑥	1047 ⑦	1047 ①	...
5863	Naushki 🛃 d.	1220	1656 ⑥	1656 ⑦	1656 ①	...
5886	Suche Bator 🛃 MO d.	*2055	*0014 ⑦	*0014 ①	*0014 ②	...
6265	**Ulaan Baatar** MO a.	*0545	*0650 ⑦	*0650 ①	*0650 ②	...
6265	**Ulaan Baatar** MO d.	...	*0730 ⑦	...	...	*0730 ④
6770	Dzamin Uud 🛃 MO d.	...	*2035 ⑦	...	...	*2035 ④
6780	Erlan 🛃 CH a.	...	2100 ⑦	...	...	2100 ④
7622	**Beijing** CH a.	...	1140 ①	...	...	1140 ⑤

MOSKVA - BEIJING via Harbin

km	*Trans-Manchurian Train name: Vostok*	20*SZ* Sko ⑥	602*CH* 684*CH* ④⑥
0	*Moskva Yar.* △ d.	2355 ⑥	...
1778	*Yekaterinburg* △ d.	0205 ①	...
3303	*Novosibirsk* △ d.	2136 ①	...
5152	**Irkutsk** d.	0312 ③	...
6165	Chita II d.	2257 ③	1330
6625	Zabaikalsk 🛃 d.	1305 ④	0535
6637	Manzhouli 🛃 CH d.	2359 ④	1100
7572	Harbin CH d.	1317 ⑤	...
7814	Changchun CH d.	1600 ⑤	...
8119	Shenyang CH d.	1934 ⑤	...
8961	**Beijing** CH a.	0549 ⑥	...

A – To Ulaanbaatar (see panel below main table). Runs on **J** and **K**.
B – To Ulaanbaatar and Beijing (see panel below main table).
D – ② from Brest (d. 1142 **104***BJ*), ②⑤⑦ from Minsk (d. 1622), Smolensk (d. 1919), Moskva next day.
E – Even dates ●(6) (daily June 6 - Sept. 4).
J – Dec. 14, 28, Jan. 11, 25, Feb. 8, 22, Mar. 8, 22, Apr. 5, 19, May 3, 17; ③ from May 31.
K – Dec. 22, Jan. 5, 19, Feb. 2, 16, Mar. 2, 16, 30, Apr. 13, 27, May 11; ④ from May 25.
P – VOSTOK. To Beijing via Harbin (see panel below main table).
Q – From Adler on even dates ●(6) (daily June 24 - Sept. 3). Depart Yekaterinburg on 4th day.
R – ROSSIYA (see also summary below main table). Also conveys 🛏 Moskva - Tumangan (North Korea) on 1st, 5th, 17th, 21st of month.
a – From Adler, Sochi, Rostov (Table **1960**).
b – To Barnaul (a. 0455). On ●(6) to Barnaul (a. 0316), Biisk (0745).
c – From Chelyabinsk ■(1) (Table **1970**), next day from Omsk.
d – From St Peterburg (Table **1900**).
e – Naushki a. 0751, Suche Bator a. 1758. **364***Y* / **264***IJ* from Naushki.
k – Moskva **Kurskaya**.
m – To Kemerovo (a. 0516).
n – To Tobolsk (a. 0615), Surgut (a. 1523) and Niznevartovsk (a. 2046).
o – To Novokuznetsk (train **14** a. 0838; train **118** a. 0044).
p – To Petropavl (Table **1975**).
q – To Abakan (a. 0140).
r – Moskva **Belorusskaya**.
s – To Tobolsk (a. 1205), Surgut (a. 2022), Korotchayevo (a. 1044), Novy Urengoy (a. 1250).
t – To Tobolsk (a. 0636), Surgut (a. 1703), Korotchayevo (a. 0600), Novy Urengoy (a. 0800).
u – To Neryungri (Table **1989**).
w – Via Nivhni Tagil (a. 1932).
x – To Severobaikalsk (Table **1989**).
y – To Serov (a. 2318), Priobe (a. 1240).
z – To Tomsk I (a. 0558), Tomsk II (a. 0629).
♠ – *Strizh* (Swift) high-speed Talgo train.
≋ – *Lastochka* (Swallow) fast day train.
★ – Shows the number of hours that local time is ahead of Moskva time (all timings within Russia are shown in Moskva time).
◧ – Also ⑤ in summer. Days of running are subject to alteration.
♡ – Even dates Jan., Apr., May, Aug., Nov.; uneven dates Dec., Feb., Mar., June, July, Sept., Oct.
♤ – Uneven dates Jan., Apr., May, Aug., Nov.; even dates Dec., Feb., Mar., June, July, Sept., Oct.
△ – For timings Moskva - Irkutsk see main table.
▽ – Train **96***NJ* on uneven dates ■(5), **136***MJ* on even dates ●(6).
▷ – Fast day trains run from Moskva Yaroslavskaya to Yaroslavl at 0735, 1445, 1905 (journey 3h 20m).
◇ – Journey 7 days (7 nights) Moskva - Vladivostok. Conveys 🛏 Moskva -Ussuriysk - Pyongyang (North Korea) on 12th, 26th of month.
☆ – Premium class train; includes Lux sleeping cars with shower/toilet.
§ – Operated by Mongolian Railways.
* – One hour later Mar. 25 - Sept. 29.
● – Even dates (see page 530).
●(2) – Even dates [.. *30, 1, 2* ..]
●(4) – Even dates [.. *30, 1, 4* ..]
●(6) – Even dates [.. *30, 1, 3, 6* ..]
●(9) – Even dates [.. *30, 1, 3, 5, 7, 10* ..]
■ – Uneven dates (see page 530).
■(1) – Uneven dates [.. *29, 1* ..]
■(3) – Uneven dates [.. *31, 3* ..]
■(5) – Uneven dates [.. *31, 2, 5* ..]
■(6) – Uneven dates [.. *31, 1, 3, 7* ..]
■(7) – Uneven dates [.. *31, 2, 4, 7* ..]
■(9) – Uneven dates [.. *31, 2, 4, 6, 9* ..]
CH – China (GMT + 8).
MO – Mongolia (GMT + 8 in winter, GMT + 9 Mar. 25 - Sept. 29).

VLADIVOSTOK - IRKUTSK - NOVOSIBIRSK - YEKATERINBURG - MOSKVA 1990

Trans-Siberian Railway	67 Y	77EI	11UJ	701NJ	3ZJ	5	41EI	703NJ	1MJ	7NJ	727GJ	37NJ	29NJ	705NJ	139NJ	19CH	707NJ	709NJ	729GJ	69JA	71EJ	63BJ	103NJ	73EJ
	Sko	Sko	Sko	♠	Sko	Sko	Fir	♠	Fir	Sko	❦	Fir	Fir	♠	Sko	Sko	♠	♠	❦	Sko	Fir	Sko	Sko	Sko
		■(3)	■(5)	①–⑥	⑤‡	③⑥‡			●(8)	■(9)		■(0)	●(2)	①④		①‡	④	④				②④	⑥	■(1)
					B	A			R					⑤–⑦	Q	P	⑤⑦	⑤⑦				C	D	
adivostok d.	...	...	...	...	...	...	...	...	1210	1210	...	...	...	...	...	...	...	...	...	...	...	...	...	...
ssuriysk d.	...	...	...	...	...	...	...	...	1425	1425	...	...	...	...	...	...	...	...	...	...	...	...	...	...
habarovsk d.	...	u	...	...	...	...	...	...	0125	0125	...	...	...	...	...	...	...	...	...	...	...	...	...	...
kovorodino d.	...	1445	...	...	...	...	...	...	2121	2121	...	...	...	...	...	...	...	...	...	...	...	...	...	...
hita II d.	...	1320	1320	...	...	...	...	...	1842	1842	...	...	...	...	...	1843	...	...	...	1604	...	...	...	...
an Ude d.	...	2359	2359	...	0208	0208	...	...	0411	0411	...	...	...	...	...	0538	...	...	...	0318	...	...	...	...
kutsk a.	...	0757	0757	...	1017	1017	...	...	1046	1046	...	...	...	...	...	1341	...	...	...	1137	...	...	...	...
kutsk d.	...	0825	0825	...	1105	1105	...	...	1115	1115	...	...	...	...	...	1411	...	...	...	1218	...	...	...	...
yshet d.	...	2007	2007	...	|	|	...	...	2135	2135	...	...	...	...	...	|	...	...	...	2355	...	...	...	...
rasnoyarsk d.	q	0338	0338	...	0419	0419	...	...	0429	0429	...	z	...	...	...	0720	...	...	...	0738	...	...	...	...
yga d.	0853	1219	1219	...	1230	1230	...	...	1254	1254	...	1025	m	...	...	|	...	...	...	1735	...	...	...	...
ovosibirsk a.	1216	1550	1550	...	1539	1539	...	...	1604	1604	...	1403	1403	...	...	1839	...	...	...	2050	...	...	...	...
ovosibirsk d.	1306	...	1646	...	1601	1601	...	...	1625	...	...	1459	1459	...	1805	1858	...	...	...	2144	...	0015	0015	...
msk a.	2112	...	0038	...	2329	2329	...	...	2339	...	...	2300	2300	...	0249	0303	...	...	...	0558	...	0756	0756	...
msk d.	2128	...	0054	...	2345	2345	...	...	2355	...	...	2316	2316	...	0319	0328	...	...	...	0616	...	0812	0812	...
umen d.	0456	...	c	...	0649	0649	...	...	0659	...	...	0619	0619	...	1046	1045	...	...	...	1442	...	1557	1557	1547
katerinburg a.	1037	...	...	...	1130	1130	...	...	1139	...	...	1147	1147	...	1547	1445	...	...	...	2005	...	2114	2114	2105
katerinburg d.	1134	...	...	...	1200	1200	...	...	1209	...	...	1218	1218	...	1618	1517	...	...	...	2114	2103	2144	2144	2134
Sarapul d.	|	...	...	...	|	|	...	...	|	...	...	|	|	...	0004	|	...	...	...	|	|	|	|	|
Kazan d.	|	...	...	...	|	|	2207	...	|	...	...	|	|	...	0534	|	...	...	...	|	|	|	|	|
Murom I d.	|	...	...	...	|	|	|	...	|	...	...	|	|	...	a	|	...	...	...	|	|	|	|	|
rm II d.	1726	...	...	...	1736	1736	|	...	1746	...	...	1830	1830	...	...	2118	...	...	...	0259	0249	0330	0330	0340
rov d.	0105	...	...	...	0115	0115	|	...	0125	...	...	0333	0333	...	...	0508	...	...	...	1113	1103	1134	1134	1200
Vologda I d.	|	...	...	...	|	|	|	...	|	...	...	|	|	...	...	|	...	...	...	|	2116	|	|	2233
St Peterburg Ladozhski a.	|	...	...	...	|	|	|	...	|	...	...	|	|	...	...	|	...	...	...	|	0838	|	|	1000
zhni Novgorod d.	|	...	...	0643	0702	0702	0655	0739	0712	...	0940	0950	0950	1050	...	1115	1343	1553	1755	|	...	1815	1815	...
adimir d.	|	...	...	0840	1057	1057	...	0945	1107	...	1200	1305	1305	1256	...	1448	1549	1759	2015	|	...	2223	2223	...
Yaroslavl ▷ d.	1306	...	...	|	|	|	...	|	|	...	|	|	|	|	...	|	|	|	|	0004	...	|	|	...
oskva Kazanskaya a.	|	...	...	1020k	|	|	...	1126k	|	...	1345k	|	|	1440k	...	|	1730k	1940k	2200k	|	...	0115r	0115r	...
oskva Yaroslavskaya ▷ a.	1658	...	...	...	1358	1358	...	...	1413	...	...	1558	1558	...	...	1758	...	...	...	0411	...	...	...	...

	13NJ	711NJ	713NJ	59GJ	75EI	81IJ	89UJ	95NJ	55 Y	117NJ	7EJ	11EJ	91IJ	35GJ	5EI	1GJ	43EI	99EI	59EJ	15EJ	31GJ	109MJ	49EJ	84EJ
	Fir	♠	♠	Fir	Sko	Sko	Sko	Sko	Fir	Sko	Fir	Fir	Sko	Fir	Fir	Fir	Sko	Sko	Fir	Fir	Fir	Sko	Fir	Fir
	■(1)	①⑤			■(1)	●(2)	■(1)		■(3)	●(2)	♤	♡	E				●(2)	●(2)	♤	♤			♡	♡
		⑥⑦		d				▽								☆		◇						
adivostok d.	...	...	...	...	...	...	...	...	...	...	...	...	...	...	1400	...	...	1802	...	...	...	...	...	...
ssuriysk d.	...	...	...	...	...	...	...	...	...	...	...	...	...	...	1559	...	...	2013	...	...	...	...	...	...
habarovsk d.	...	...	...	...	...	...	...	...	...	...	...	...	...	...	0115	...	0727	0727	...	...	...	...	...	...
kovorodino d.	...	...	...	...	...	...	...	...	...	...	...	...	...	...	...	...	0500	0500	...	...	...	...	...	...
hita II d.	...	...	...	...	...	...	...	...	...	...	...	...	...	...	...	...	0340	0340	...	...	...	...	...	...
an Ude d.	...	...	...	...	...	1054	...	...	...	...	...	...	...	...	...	...	1422	1422	...	...	...	...	...	...
kutsk a.	...	...	...	...	...	1813	...	...	...	...	...	...	...	...	...	...	2202	2202	...	...	...	...	...	...
kutsk d.	...	...	...	...	u	1858	...	...	...	...	...	...	x	...	...	...	2237	2237	...	...	...	...	...	...
yshet d.	...	...	...	...	0654	0654	...	...	...	...	...	...	0854	...	...	...	1001	1001	...	...	...	...	...	...
asnoyarsk d.	...	...	...	...	1420	1420	...	...	1450	...	...	...	1624	...	...	...	1714	1714	...	...	...	...	...	...
yga d.	o	...	...	...	2244	2244	...	...	2326	o	...	...	0137	...	...	...	0156	0156	...	...	...	...	...	...
ovosibirsk a.	2307	...	...	...	0218	0218	...	...	0238	0215	...	...	0448	...	...	...	0505	0505	...	...	...	...	...	...
ovosibirsk d.	2352	...	...	...	0325	0325	...	b	0305	0305	...	...	0539	...	...	...	0557	0557	...	...	...	...	...	...
msk a.	0723	...	...	...	1142	1142	...	1020	1130	1130	...	...	1417	...	...	...	1444	1444	...	...	...	...	...	...
msk d.	0800	...	...	...	1212	1212	...	1108	1200	1200	...	t	1442	...	...	...	1503	1503	n	...	...	s	...	...
umen d.	1547	...	...	...	1945	1945	p	1925	1935	1935	...	2114	2252	...	...	...	2302	2302	0112	...	...	2312	...	...
katerinburg a.	2105	...	...	...	0038	0038	0047	0059	0110	0110	...	0252	0319	...	...	...	0328	0328	0738	...	...	0440	...	...
katerinburg d.	2134	...	...	...	0108	0108	0120	0204	0212	0212	...	0339	0349	...	...	...	0403	0403	0812	0812	...	0517	0220	...
Sarapul d.	|	...	...	...	0950	0950	1007	1026	1016	1016	...	|	|	...	...	...	|	|	1603	1603	...	|	|	...
Kazan d.	|	...	...	...	1555	1555	1613	1642	1630	1630	...	|	|	...	...	1945	|	|	2157	2157	...	|	w	...
Murom I d.	|	...	...	...	0015	0015	0027	0104	0052	0052	...	|	|	...	...	0255	|	|	0456	0456	...	|	|	y
rm II d.	0340	...	...	...	|	|	|	|	|	|	0935	0935	0945	...	...	|	0955	0955	|	|	...	1240	1250	1250
rov d.	1200	...	...	...	|	|	|	|	|	|	1710	1710	1725	...	...	|	1735	1735	|	|	2030	2114	2124	2124
Vologda I d.	2233	...	...	...	|	|	|	|	|	|	|	|	|	...	...	|	|	|	|	|	|	|	|	|
St Peterburg Ladozhski a.	1000	...	...	...	|	|	|	|	|	|	|	|	|	...	...	|	|	|	|	|	|	|	|	|
zhni Novgorod d.	...	1858	2011	1919	|	|	|	|	|	|	2310	2310	2320	2335	...	|	|	|	|	|	0307	0323	0333	0333
adimir d.	...	2055	2217	2305	|	|	|	|	|	|	0206	0206	0300	0323	...	|	|	|	|	|	0620	0700	0710	0710
Yaroslavl ▷ d.	...	|	|	|	|	|	|	|	|	|	|	|	|	|	...	|	0719	0719	|	|	|	|	|	|
oskva Kazanskaya a.	...	2235k	2358k	0123k	0442	0442	0457	0545	0538	0538	|	|	|	|	...	0710	|	|	0923	0923	|	|	|	|
oskva Yaroslavskaya ▷ a.	...	...	...	...	...	...	...	...	...	...	0522	0522	0552	0629	...	...	1113	1113	...	...	0943	1030	1038	1038

ROSSIYA SUMMARY

km	*Moskva time*	1MJ Fir ●(8) R	
0	**Vladivostok** d.	1210	1st day
766	Khabarovsk d.	0125	2nd day
3650	Ulan Ude d.	0411	4th day
4106	Irkutsk d.	1115	4th day
5193	Krasnoyarsk d.	0429	5th day
5955	Novosibirsk d.	1625	5th day
6582	Omsk d.	2355	5th day
7480	Yekaterinburg d.	1209	6th day
8341	Kirov d.	0125	7th day
8797	Nizhni Novgorod d.	0712	7th day
9258	**Moskva** Yar. a.	1413	7th day

BEIJING - MOSKVA via Ulaan Baatar

km	*Trans-Mongolian Railway*	5VJ Sko ②J	3ZJ Sko ③	5SZ Sko § ⑤K	23 Exp ⑥◧	263IJ Pas ♡e
0	**Beijing** CH d.	...	1122 ③	...	1122 ⑥	...
842	Erlan 🏛 CH d.	...	0059 ④	...	0059 ⑦	...
852	Dzamin Uud 🏛 MO d.	...	*0240 ④	...	*0240 ⑦	...
1356	**Ulaan Baatar** MO a.	...	*1435 ④	...	*1435 ⑦	...
1356	**Ulaan Baatar** MO d.	*1522 ②	*1522 ④	*1522 ⑤	...	2040
1735	Suche Bator 🏛 MO d.	*2310 ②	*2310 ④	*2310 ⑤	...	*1008
1758	Naushki 🏛 d.	2110 ②	2110 ④	2110 ⑤	...	0951
2013	Ulan Ude d.	0208 ③	0208 ⑤	0208 ⑥	...	1721
2469	**Irkutsk** a.	1017 ③	1017 ⑤	1017 ⑥	...	0220
4319	*Novosibirsk* △ a.	1539 ④	1539 ⑥	1539 ⑦	...	...
7622	*Moskva Yar.* △ a.	1358 ⑥	1358 ①	1358 ②	...	...

BEIJING - MOSKVA via Harbin

km	*Trans-Manchurian Train name: Vostok*	19CH Sko ⑥	653CH 683CH ⑤⑦
0	**Beijing** CH d.	2300 ⑥	...
841	Shenyang CH d.	0855 ⑦	...
1141	Changchun CH d.	1229 ⑦	...
1388	Harbin CH d.	1544 ⑦	...
2323	Manzhouli 🏛 CH d.	0701 ①	1400
2335	Zabaikalsk 🏛 d.	0812 ①	1346
2795	Chita II d.	1843 ①	0158
3808	**Irkutsk** a.	1341 ②	...
5658	*Novosibirsk* △ a.	1839 ③	...
7183	*Yekaterinburg* △ a.	1445 ④	...
8961	*Moskva Yar.* △ a.	1758 ⑤	...

– From Ulaanbaatar (see below main table). Runs on **J** and **K**.
– From Beijing and Ulaanbaatar (see panel below main table).
– To Smolensk a. 0640 ④⑥ and Minsk a. 1123 ④⑥.
– To Smolensk a. 0640 ①, Minsk a. 1123 ①, Brest a. 1621 ①.
– From Severobaikalsk on even dates (daily June 2 - Aug. 31).
– Dec. 13, 27, Jan. 10, 24, Feb. 7, 21, Mar. 7, 21, Apr. 4, 18, May 1, 16; ② from May 30.
– Dec. 23, Jan. 6, 20, Feb. 3, 17, Mar. 3, 17, 31, Apr. 14, 28, May 12, ⑤ from May 26.
– VOSTOK. From Beijing via Harbin (see below main table).
– Even dates (daily June 20 - Aug. 30). Arrive Adler on 5th day.
– ROSSIYA (see also summary below main table). Also conveys 🛏 Tumangan (North Korea) - Ussuriysk - Moskva four times per month.
– To Rostov, Sochi, Adler (Table **1960**).
– From Barnaul (d. 1903 on even dates, 2111 on uneven dates).
– To Chelyabinsk (Table **1970**).
– To St Peterburg (Table **1900**).
– Arrives Suche Bator 0436, Naushki 0600. Train number **363**IJ from Suche Bator, **361**IJ from Naushki.
– Moskva **Kurskaya**.
– From Kemerovo (d. 0903).
– From Niznevartovsk (d. 0458), Surgut (d. 1013), Tobolsk (1946).
– From Novokuznetsk (train **13** d. 1628; train **117** d. 1736).

p – From Petropavl (Table **1975**).
q – From Abakan (d. 1440).
r – Moskva **Belorusskaya**.
s – From Novy Urengoy (d. 1450), Korotchayevo (d. 1650), Surgut (d. 0833 2nd day), Tobolsk (d. 1755 2nd day).
t – From Novy Urengoy (d. 1000), Korotchayevo (d. 1226), Surgut (d. 0308 2nd day), Tobolsk (d. 1630 2nd day).
u – From Neryungri (Table **1989**). Train **75** departs Tayshet on 4th day.
w – Via Nivhni Tagil (depart 0456).
x – From Severobaikalsk (Table **1989**), next day from Tayshet.
y – From Priobe (d. 1420), Serov (d. 0145). From Perm 2nd day.
z – From Tomsk II (d. 0746), Tomsk I (d. 0820).

♠ – *Strizh* (Swift) high-speed Talgo train.
❦ – *Lastochka* (Swallow) fast day train.
◧ – Also ② in summer. Days of running are subject to alteration.
♡ – Even dates Jan., Apr., May, Aug., Nov.; uneven dates Dec., Feb., Mar., June, July, Sept., Oct.
♤ – Uneven dates Jan., Apr., May, Aug., Nov.; even dates Dec., Feb., Mar., June, July, Sept., Oct.
▷ – Fast day trains run from Yaroslavl to Moskva Yaroslavskaya at 0700, 1352, 1934 (journey 3 hours 20 mins).
△ – For timings Irkutsk - Moskva see main table.
▽ – Train **95**NJ on even dates ●(2), **136**NJ on uneven dates ■(3).

◇ – Journey 8 days (7 nights) Vladivostok - Moskva. Also conveys 🛏 Pyongyang (North Korea) - Ussuriysk - Moskva twice monthly.
‡ – For day of running from point of origin see panel below main table.
§ – Operated by Mongolian Railways.
☆ – Premium class train; includes Lux sleeping cars with shower/toilet.
* – One hour later Mar. 25 - Sept. 29.

● – Even dates (see page 530).
●(2) – Even dates [.. *30, 2* ..]
●(8) – Even dates [.. *30, 1, 3, 5, 8* ..]

■ – Uneven dates (see page 530).
■(0) – Uneven dates [.. *31, 1* ..]
■(1) – Uneven dates [.. *29, 1* ..]
■(3) – Uneven dates [.. *31, 3* ..]
■(5) – Uneven dates [.. *31, 2, 5* ..]
■(9) – Uneven dates [.. *31, 2, 4, 6, 9* ..]

CH – China (GMT + 8).
MO – Mongolia (GMT + 8 in winter, GMT + 9 Mar. 25 - Sept. 29).

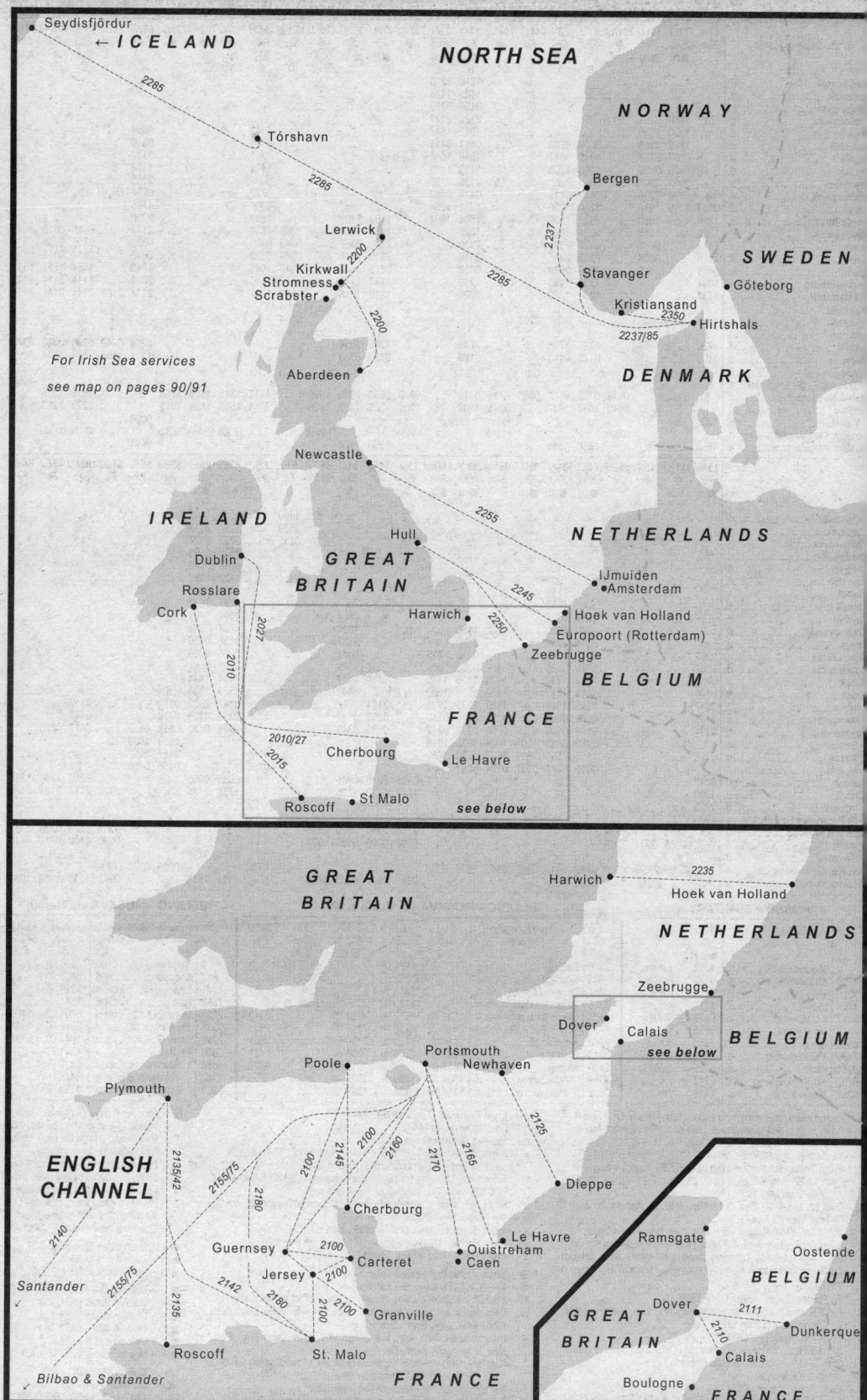

Seydisfjördur
← I C E L A N D
2285

Tórshavn
2265

NORTH SEA

N O R W A Y

Bergen
2237
Stavanger

S W E D E N

Göteborg

Lerwick
2200
Kirkwall
Stromness
Scrabster
2200

Kristiansand
2350
2237/85
Hirtshals

For Irish Sea services
see map on pages 90/91

Aberdeen

D E N M A R K

Newcastle
2255

I R E L A N D

Hull

Dublin

G R E A T
B R I T A I N

Rosslare
Cork
2027
2010

N E T H E R L A N D S

IJmuiden
Amsterdam

Harwich
2245
2250
Hoek van Holland
Europoort (Rotterdam)
Zeebrugge

B E L G I U M

F R A N C E

2010/27
Cherbourg
Le Havre
2015
Roscoff
St Malo
see below

G R E A T
B R I T A I N

Harwich
2235
Hoek van Holland

N E T H E R L A N D S

Zeebrugge

Dover
Calais
see below

B E L G I U M

Plymouth

Poole
Portsmouth
Newhaven

2125

ENGLISH
CHANNEL

2135/42
2155/75
2180
2100
2145
2100
2160
2170
2165

Dieppe

2140

Cherbourg

Le Havre

Santander
2155/75
2135

Guernsey
2100
Carteret
Ouistreham
Caen

Jersey
2142
2180
2100
2100
2100
Granville

Ramsgate
Oostende

B E L G I U M

Roscoff

St. Malo

Bilbao & Santander

F R A N C E

Dover
2111
2110
Calais
Dunkerque
Boulogne

G R E A T
B R I T A I N

F R A N C E

538

11

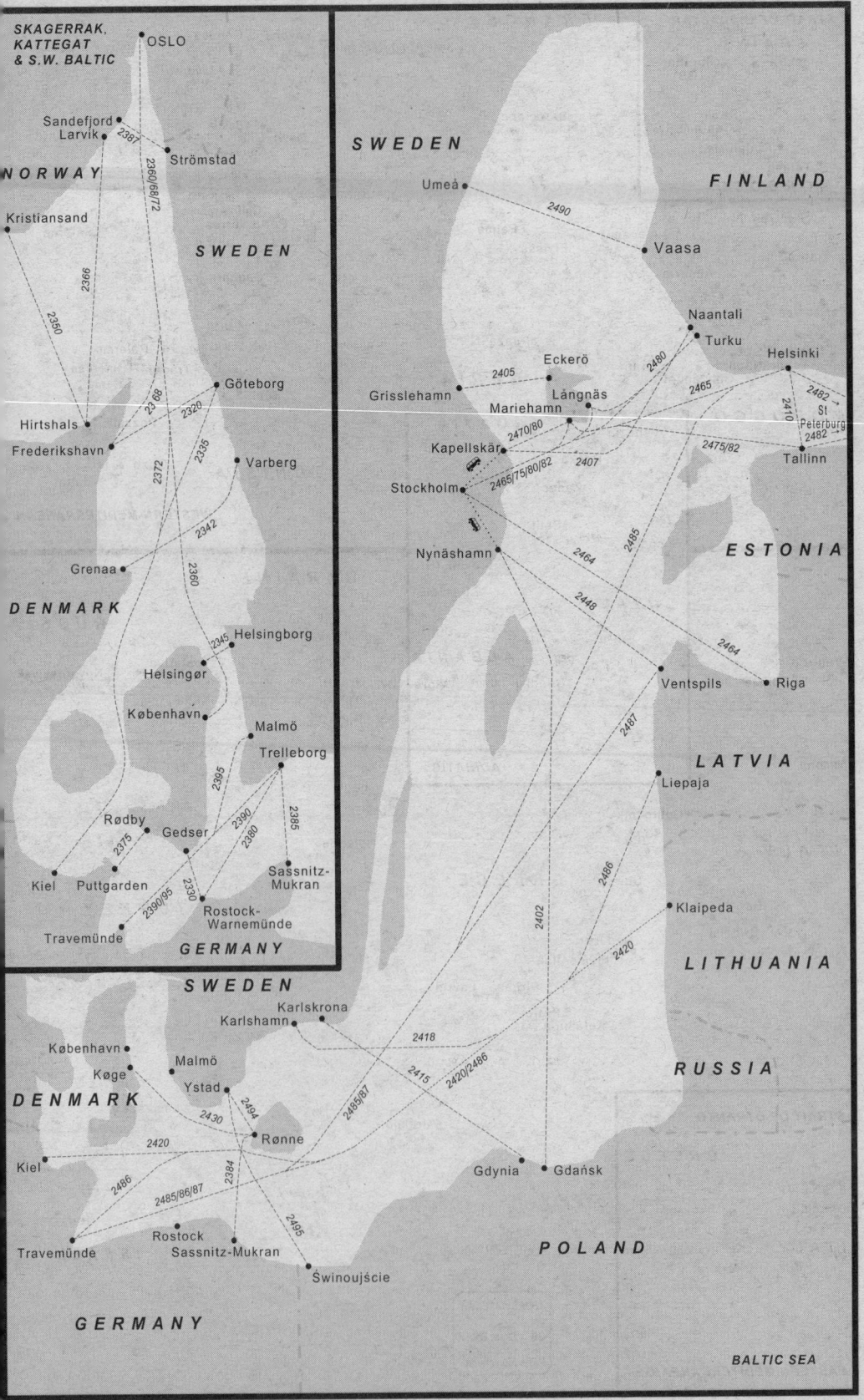

SKAGERRAK, KATTEGAT & S.W. BALTIC

OSLO

Sandefjord
Larvik
2387

NORWAY
Strömstad

Kristiansand

2360/68/72

SWEDEN

2366

2350

Göteborg

23 68
2320

Hirtshals
2335
Frederikshavn
2372
Varberg

2342

Grenaa
2360

DENMARK

2345 Helsingborg

Helsingør

København
Malmö

2395 Trelleborg

Rødby
2390
2375 Gedser 2380 2385
Kiel Puttgarden
2390/95 2330
Travemünde Rostock-Warnemünde
Sassnitz-Mukran

GERMANY

SWEDEN

Umeå
2490
Vaasa

FINLAND

Naantali
Turku
Eckerö
2405 2480 Helsinki
Grisslehamn Långnäs 2465 2482
Mariehamn 2410 St Peterburg
2470/80 2482
Kapellskär 2475/82 Tallinn
2407
Stockholm 2465/75/80/82

ESTONIA

Nynäshamn 2485
2464
2448
2464

Ventspils Riga

2487

LATVIA

Liepaja

2486

Klaipeda

2402 2420

LITHUANIA

SWEDEN

Karlskrona
Karlshamn
København
2418
Køge
Malmö
Ystad 2415 2420/2486
DENMARK
2430 2494 2485/87
Kiel 2420 Rønne
2384
2486 RUSSIA
2485/86/87
Rostock Gdynia Gdańsk
Travemünde Sassnitz-Mukran 2495

Świnoujście

POLAND

GERMANY

BALTIC SEA

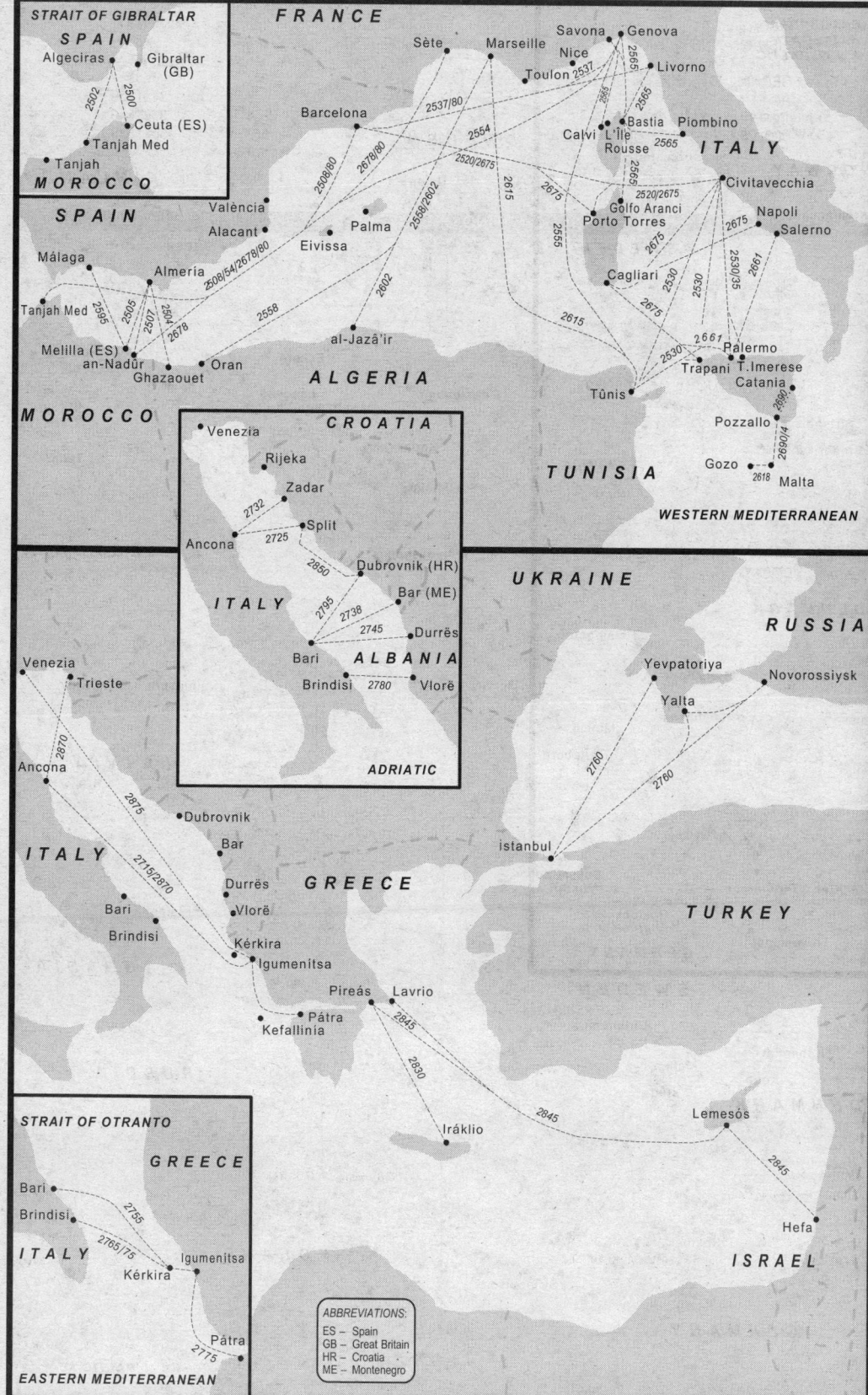

STRAIT OF GIBRALTAR

SPAIN

Algeciras · Gibraltar (GB)

2502 · 2500

Ceuta (ES)

Tanjah Med

Tanjah

MOROCCO

FRANCE

Sète · Marseille

Savona · Genova

Nice

Toulon 2537

Livorno

2537/80

Barcelona 2554

2678/80 2520/2675

2508/80 2558/2602

2565 2565

Calvi L'Île
Rousse

Bastia · Piombino

ITALY

Civitavecchia

2615 2675

2520/2675 2675 Napoli

Golfo Aranci
Porto Torres 2555

Salerno

Cagliari 2530 2530/35 2661

2675 2530 2530 2675

Tûnis

2661 Palermo

Trapani T.Imerese

Catania

València

Alacant

Palma

Eivissa

SPAIN

Málaga

Almeria

Tanjah Med 2605 2505 2507 2504

Melilla (ES)

an-Nadûr 2678

Ghazaouet

Oran

al-Jazá'ir

ALGERIA

2602

2558 2615

Pozzallo

Gozo 2618 Malta

TUNISIA

WESTERN MEDITERRANEAN

CROATIA

Venezia

Rijeka

Zadar

2732

Ancona Split 2725

2850

Dubrovnik (HR)

2795 2738 Bar (ME)

2745 Durrës

Bari **ALBANIA**

Brindisi 2780 Vlorë

ITALY

ADRIATIC

UKRAINE

RUSSIA

Yevpatoriya Novorossiysk

Yalta

2760 2760

Venezia

Trieste

2870

Ancona

2875

Dubrovnik

2715/2870

Bar

Durrës

Vlorë

Bari

Brindisi

Kérkira

Igumenitsa

GREECE

istanbul

TURKEY

Pireás Lavrio

2845

Pátra

Kefallinía

2830

Iráklio

2845

Lemesós

2845

Hefa

ISRAEL

STRAIT OF OTRANTO

GREECE

Bari

Brindisi

2755

2765/75

Igumenitsa

Kérkira

ITALY

Pátra

2775

EASTERN MEDITERRANEAN

ABBREVIATIONS:
ES – Spain
GB – Great Britain
HR – Croatia
ME – Montenegro

SHIPPING OPERATORS

AG EMS   www.ag-ems.de
Postfach 11 54, 26691 Emden-Außenhafen: ✆ +49 (0)1805 180 182,
fax +49 21 89 07 405.

ALILAURO   www.alilauro.it
Stazione Marittima, Piazzale Angioino, 80133 Napoli: ✆ +39 081 497 2222,
fax +39 081 497 2228. Reservations: ✆ +39 (0)81 497 2238.

ALSFÆRGENS   www.faergen.dk
Færgen, Dampskibskajen 3, 3700 Rønne: ✆ +45 70 23 15 15.

ANEK LINES   www.anek.gr
22 Akti Kondili Str., 18545 Pireás: ✆ +30 210 4197 420, +30 210 4197 430.
U.K. agent: Viamare Ltd., Suite 3, 447 Kenton Road, Harrow, HA3 0XY:
✆ 020 8206 3420, fax 020 8206 1332.

BALEÀRIA (EUROLÍNIES MARÍTIMES)   www.balearia.com
Estació Marítima s/n, 03700 Dénia: ✆ +34 96 642 86 00; call centre: ✆ +34 96 642 87 00.

BLUE LINE   www.blueline-ferries.com
29/11 Vincenti Buildings - Strait Street, Valletta, VLT 1432, Malta
✆ +356 2122 3299
Croatia agent: ✆ +385 21 352 533, fax +385 21 352 482.
Italy agent: ✆ +39 071 20 40 41, fax +39 071 20 26 18.

BLUE STAR FERRIES   www.bluestarferries.com
123 - 125 Syngrou Avenue & 3 Torva Street, 117 45 Athína: ✆ +30 210 891 9800,
fax +30 210 891 9829.

BLUFERRIES   www.bluferries.it
✆ +39 090 6786 406, fax +39 090 6406 508.

BORNHOLMERFÆRGEN   www.faergen.dk
Færgen, Dampskibskajen 3, 3700 Rønne: ✆ +45 70 23 15 15.

BRITTANY FERRIES: www.brittany-ferries.co.uk
Millbay, Plymouth, PL1 3EW: ✆ 0871 244 1401.
Reservations: U.K. ✆ 0871 244 0744; France ✆ +33 825 828 828;
Spain ✆ +34 942 36 06 11.

BUMERANG SHIPPING COMPANY TOURISM TRAVEL & TRADE S.A.
Rihtim Cad. Veli Alemdar Han Kat. 6, 80030 Karaköy - Istanbul: ✆ +90 (0)212 251 7373,
fax +90 (0)212 251 1472.

CAREMAR   www.caremar.it
See Tirrenia for details.

COLOR LINE   www.colorline.com
Postboks 1422 Vika, N-0115 Oslo: ✆ + 47 22 94 44 00, fax +47 22 83 04 30.
Reservations: Norway ✆ +47 22 94 42 00; Denmark ✆ +45 99 56 19 77;
Germany ✆ +49 431 7300 300; Sweden ✆ +46 526 62 000.

COMARIT   www.comarit.com
Avenue Mohamed VI, Tanjah: ✆ +212 539 32 00 32, fax +212 539 32 59 00.

COMPAGNIE TUNISIENNE DE NAVIGATION   www.ctn.com.tn
5 Avenue Dag Hammarskjoeld, 1001 Tünis: ✆ +216 (71) 341 777, fax +216 (71) 345 736.
Reservations: ✆ +33 825 88 80 88.
U.K. agent: Southern Ferries (see Trasmediterranea).

CONDOR FERRIES   www.condorferries.co.uk
New Harbour Road South, Hamworthy, Poole, BH15 4AJ.
Reservations: ✆ 0845 609 1024.
Information: U.K. ✆ 01202 207 216; Jersey ✆ 01534 872 240; Guernsey 12023 (local
calls only); St Malo ✆ (0)825 165 463; Cherbourg ✆ +33 2 33 88 44 88.

CORSICA FERRIES   www.corsica-ferries.fr
5 bis Rue Chanoine Leschi, 20296 Bastia: ✆ +33 4 95 32 95 95, fax +33 4 95 32 14 71.

DESTINATION GOTLAND   www.destinationgotland.se
Korsgatan 2, Box 1234, 621 23 Visby: ✆ +46 (0)498 20 18 00, fax +46 (0)498 20 18 90.
Reservations: ✆ +46 (0)771 22 33 00, fax +46 (0)498 20 13 90.

DFDS SEAWAYS   www.dfdsseaways.co.uk
International Port, Parkeston, Harwich CO12 4SR.
International Passenger Terminal, Royal Quays, North Shields, Newcastle, NE29 6EE.
Reservations: U.K. ✆ 0871 522 9955; Denmark ✆ +45 33 42 30 00, +45 7917 7917;
Netherlands ✆ +31 255 54 66 66; Norway ✆ +47 21 62 10 00;
Ostuferhafen 15, 24149 Kiel: ✆ +49 (0)431 20976 420, fax +49 (0)431 20976 102;
Klaipeda: ✆ +370 46 395 051.

ECKERÖ LINE   www.eckeroline.fi
Mannerheimintie 10, 00100 Helsinki: ✆ +358 6000 4300, fax +358 9 2288 5547.
Passanger Harbour, Sadama 29, 10111 Tallinn: ✆ +372 664 6000,
fax +372 631 8690.

ECKERÖ LINJEN   www.eckerolinjen.fi
P.O. Box 158, Torggatan 2, AX-22101 Mariehamn, Åland: ✆ +358 (0)18 28 000,
fax +358 (0)18 28 380.
SE-760 45 Grisslehamn: ✆ +46 (0)175 258 00, fax +46 (0)175 330 54.
Berghamn, AX-22270 Eckerö, Åland: ✆ +358 (0)18 28 300, fax +358 (0)18 38 230.

E N T M V   www.algerieferries.com
27, Boulevard des Dames, 13002 Marseille: ✆ +33 (0)4 91 90 64 70,
fax +33 (0)4 91 91 59 58. Reservations: ✆ +213 (021) 42 46 50.

EUROPEAN SEAWAYS   www.europeanseaways.com
Machis Analatou 111, Neos Kosmos 117 44 Athína: ✆ +30 210 9561630,
fax +30 210 9537263.
Customer support: ✆ +30 210 9561630.

FANØFÆRGEN   www.faergen.dk
Færgen, Dampskibskajen 3, 3700 Rønne: ✆ +45 70 23 15 15.

FINNLINES   www.finnlines.com
Porkkalankatu 20A, FI-00180 Helsinki: ✆ +358 (0)10 343 4500, (0)10 343 4600.

FJORD LINE   www.fjordline.com
Skoltegrunnskaien, N-5003, 5003 Bergen: ✆ +47 51 46 40 99, fax +47 55 31 88 00.
Reservations: ✆ +47 51 46 40 99.

FRED. OLSEN S.A.   www.fredolsen.es
Polígono Industrial de Añaza s/n, 38109 Santa Cruz de Tenerife: ✆ +34 922 628 200,
fax +34 922 628 232. Reservation: ✆ +34 902 100 107.

F R S   www.frs.es
Estación Marítima. P.O. / Apto de correos 13, E-11380 Tarifa - Cádiz: ✆ +34 956 68 18 30,
fax +34 956 62 71 80.

FRS HELGOLINE   www.helgoline.de
Norderhofenden 19 - 20, D 24937 Flensburg: ✆ +49 (0)461 864 0, fax +49 (0)461 864 70.

GOZO CHANNEL   www.gozochannel.com
Mgarr Harbour, Mgarr Gozo: ✆ +356 2210 9000, fax +356 2155 6743.

GRANDI NAVI VELOCI   www.gnv.it
Via Fieschi 17, 16121 Genova: ✆ +39 010 5509 465, fax +39 010 5509 301.
Contact centre: ✆ +39 010 2094 591.
U.K. agent: Viamare (see Anek Lines).

GRIMALDI LINES   www.grimaldi-lines.com
Via Marchese Campodisola 13, 80133 Napoli: ✆ +39 081 496 444, fax +39 081 551 7716.
U.K. agent: Viamare (see Anek Lines).

HURTIGRUTEN (NORWEGIAN COASTAL VOYAGE)   www.hurtigruten.no
Fredrik Langes gate 14, Postboks 6144, 9008 Tromsø: ✆ +47 970 57 030.
Reservations: ✆ +47 810 30 000.
U.K. reservations: ✆ 0203 603 6213.

INTERNATIONAL MARITIME TRANSPORT CORPORATION (I M T C)   www.imtc.co.ma
50 Avenue Paster, 20 300 Casablanca: ✆ +212 (22) 437 620, fax +212 (22) 543 548.
Spain agent: Vapores Suardiaz Andalucia S.A. (VS), Avda. Del Puerto 1 - 6, SP-11006
Cádiz: ✆ +34 956 282 111, fax +34 956 282 846.

IRISH FERRIES   www.irishferries.com
P.O. Box 19, Alexandra Road, Dublin 1: ✆ +353 (0)1 855 2222, fax +353 (0)1 855 2272.
Corn Exchange Building, Ground Floor, Brunswick Street, Liverpool L2 7TP:
✆ 08717 300 400, fax 0151 236 0562.
France reservations: ✆ +33 1 70 72 03 26, fax +33 1 70 72 03 27.

ISLE OF MAN STEAM PACKET CO.   www.steam-packet.com
Sea Terminal, Douglas, Isle of Man IM1 2RF.
Reservations: ✆ 661 661; U.K. ✆ 08722 992 992; Ireland ✆ +44 8722 992 992.

ISLES OF SCILLY STEAMSHIP CO.   www.islesofscilly-travel.co.uk
Travel Centre, Quay Street, Penzance, TR18 4BZ: ✆ 0845 710 5555, fax 01736 334 228.
Overseas reservations: ✆ +44 (0)1736 334 228.

JADROLINIJA   www.jadrolinija.hr
Riva 16, 51000 Rijeka: ✆ +385 (51) 666 111, fax +385 (51) 213 116.
U.K. agent: Viamare (see Anek Lines).

KAPETAN LUKA   www.krilo.hr
M.B. Kapetan Luka TP, Poljička cesta - Krilo 4, 21314 Krilo Jesenice.
✆ +385 (021) 645 476, fax +385 (021) 872 877.

L D LINES   www.ldlines.co.uk
Continental Ferry Port, Wharf Road, Portsmouth, PO2 8QW: ✆ 0844 576 8836,
fax 01235 84 56 08.
Terminal de la Citadelle, BP 90746, F-76060 Le Havre: ✆ 0825 304 304.
Outside U.K. and France: ✆ +33 (0)2 32 14 52 09.

LINDA LINE OY   www.lindaline.fi
Makasiiniterminaali, 00140 Helsinki: ✆ +358 (0)9 668 9700, fax +358 (0)9 668 97070.
Ädala 4a, 10614 Tallinn: ✆ +372 6 999 340, fax +372 6 999 340.
Tallinn port: ✆ +372 6 999 333, fax +372 6 999 330.
Reservations: ✆ +358 (0)600 0668970.

L N P   www.lnp.hr
Linijska Nacionalna Plovidba d.d., Boktuljin put b.b., 21000 Split: ✆ +385 (0)21 338 310,
fax +385 (0)21 352 447.

MANCHE ÎLES EXPRESS   www.manche-iles-express.com
Albert Quay, St Helier, Jersey: ✆ 01534 880 756, fax 01534 880 314.
Terminal Building, New Jetty, White Rock, St Peter Port, Guernsey: ✆ 01481 701 316,
fax 01481 701 319.

MARITIMA FERRIES   www.maritima-ferries.eu
✆ +33 (0)825 88 80 88.
Information: Bordeaux ✆ 05 56 44 46 07; Le Havre ✆ 02 35 21 53 50;
Marseille ✆ 04 91 56 33 90; Toulon ✆ 04 94 16 66 62.
U.K. agent: Southern Ferries (see Trasmediterranea).

continued on next page

continued from previous page

MEDMAR www.medmargroup.it
Terminal Porta di Massa, Napoli: ✆ +39 (0)81 333 44 11, fax +39 (0)81 333 44 36.

MINOAN LINES www.minoan.gr
17, 25th August Street, 712 02 Heraklion: ✆ +30 2810 399800, fax +30 2810 330308.
  Reservations: ✆ +30 210 414 5700.
  U.K. agent: Viamare (see Anek Lines).

MOBY LINES www.moby.it
Via Ninci 1, 57037 Portoferraio: ✆ +390 (565) 91 41 33, fax +390 (565) 91 76 52.
  Outside Italy: ✆ +49 (0)611 14020, fax +49 (0)611 140 2244.
  U.K. agent: Viamare (see Anek Lines).

MOLS-LINIEN www.mols-linien.dk
Færgehavnen, 8400 Ebeltoft: ✆ +45 89 52 52 00, fax +45 89 52 52 90.
  Reservations: ✆ +45 70 10 14 18.

MONTENEGRO LINES www.montenegrolines.net
Barska Plovidba, Obala 13 jula bb, 85000 Bar: ✆ +382 30 312 366, fax +382 30 311 652.
  Reservations: ✆ +382 30 303 469.

NAVIERA ARMAS www.naviera-armas.com
Juan Rejón 32 - 5 y 6, 35008 Las Palmas de Gran Canaria, España. ✆ +34 (928) 22 72 82,
  fax +34 (928) 46 99 91.
  Call centre: ✆ +34 902 456 500.

NAVIGAZIONE LIBERA del GOLFO www.navlib.it
Molo Beverello, 80133 Napoli: ✆ +39 081 552 07 63, fax +39 081 552 55 89.

NORDIC FERRY SERVICES www.nordic-ferry.com
Damoskibskajen 3, DK-3700 Rønne: ✆ +45 70 23 15 15.

NORDLANDSEKSPRESSEN www.torghatten-nord.no
Postboks 2380, 9271 Tromsø: ✆/fax +47 906 20 700.

NORFOLK LINE www.norfolkline.com
Kranenburgweg 180, 2583 ER The Hague: ✆ +31 70 35 27 400, fax +31 70 35 27 435.
  Reservations: Dover - Dunkerque ✆ 0871 574 7235.
  Irish Sea: ✆ 0871 200 0621, 01 800 806 118.

NORTHLINK FERRIES www.northlinkferries.co.uk
Ferry Road, Stromness, KW16 3BH, Orkney: ✆ 01856 88 55 00, fax 01856 85 17 95.
  Reservations: ✆ 0845 6000 449.

P & O FERRIES www.poferries.com
Channel House, Channel View Road, Dover, CT17 9TJ: ✆ 08716 645 645; outside U.K.:
  ✆ +44 1304 863 000.
  Belgium ✆ +32 070 70 77 71; France ✆ +33 0825 12 01 56;
  Germany ✆ +49 0180 500 9437; Netherlands ✆ +31 020 200 8333;
  Spain ✆ +34 902 02 04 61; other countries ✆ +352 34 20 80 82 94.

P & O IRISH SEA www.poirishsea.com
Arran House, 100 Port Ranald Drive, Troon, KA10 6HH.
  Larne Harbour, Larne BT40 1AW.
  Reservations: U.K. ✆ 0871 66 44 77; Dublin ✆ 01 407 34 34.

POLFERRIES www.polferries.pl
Polish Baltic Shipping Co., ul. Portowa 41, 78 100 Kolobrzeg: ✆ +48 94 35 52 102,
  fax +48 94 35 52 208.
  Reservations: ✆ +48 94 35 52 119, +48 94 35 52 233.

REEDEREI CASSEN EILS www.cassen-eils.de
Bei der Alten Liebe 12, 27472 Cuxhaven: ✆ +49 (0)4721 35082, fax +49 (0)4721 31161.

REGINA LINE www.reginaline.dk
Contact: office@reginaline.dk

ST PETER LINE www.stpeterline.com
1, ul. Karavannaya, St Peterburg: ✆ +7 (812) 702 07 77.

SALAMIS CRUISE LINES www.salamiscruiselines.com
1, G. Katsounotos Str., P.O. Box 50531, 3607 Limassol: ✆ +357 2586 0000,
  fax +357 2537 4437.

SAMSØFÆRGEN www.faergen.dk
Færgen, Dampskibskajen 3, 3700 Rønne: ✆ +45 70 23 15 15.

SARDINIA FERRIES www.corsica-ferries.fr
5 bis Rue Chanoine Leschi, 20296 Bastia: ✆ +33 4 95 32 95 95, fax +33 4 95 32 14 71.

SCANDLINES GmbH www.scandlines.de
Hochhaus am Fährhafen, 18119 Rostock: ✆ +49 (0)381 5435-0,
  fax +49 (0)381 5435-678.
  Reservations: Germany ✆ +49 (0)1805 11 66 88; Denmark ✆ +45 33 15 15 15,
  fax +45 3529 02 01; Latvia ✆ +371 6362 07 83, fax +371 6362 06 90;
  Lithuania ✆/fax +370 46 310561.

SIREMAR
See Tirrenia for details.

SMYRIL LINE www.smyrilline.com
Yviri Vid Strond 1, Postboks 370, FO-110 Tórshavn: ✆ +298 34 59 00, fax +298 34 59 50.
  Reservations: Iceland ✆ +354 570 8600, fax +354 552 9450;
  Denmark ✆ +45 96 55 03 60, fax +45 96 55 03 61.
  U.K. agent: The Travel Gateway, 2 Morrow Court, Appleford Road, Sutton Courtenay,
  OX14 4FH: ✆ 0844 576 5503, fax 01235 845108.

SNAV www.snav.
Stazione Marittima, Molo Angioino, 80133 Napoli: ✆ +39 081 428 55 55,
  fax +39 081 428 52 59.
  U.K. agent: Viamare (see Anek Lines).

STENA LINE www.stenaline.com
Stena House, Station Approach, Holyhead, LL65 1DQ: ✆ 08447 70 70 70.
  Reservations: Denmark ✆ +45 96 200 200; Germany ✆ +49 1805 91 66 66;
  Ireland ✆ +353 (0)1204 7777; Netherlands ✆ +31 174 31 58 11;
  Northern Ireland ✆ +44 8447 70 70 70; Norway ✆ +47 23 17 91 30;
  Poland ✆ +48 58 660 92 00; Sweden ✆ +46 31 704 00 00.

SUPERFAST FERRIES www.superfast.com
123 - 125 Syngrou Av. & 3 Torva Str., 117 45, Athina: ✆ +30 210 891 9000,
  fax +30 210 891 9029.
  Reservations: ✆ +30 210 891 9800; Germany ✆ +49 451 88 00 61 66,
  fax +49 451 88 00 61 29.
  U.K. agents: The Travel Gateway (see Smyril Line); Viamare (see Anek Lines).

TALLINK SILJA www.tallinksilja.com
Keilaranta 9, 02151 Espoo: ✆ +358 9 180 41, fax +358 9 180 4402.
  Södra Hamnvägen 50A, 10253 Stockholm: ✆ +46 8 666 3330.
  Reservations: ✆ +358 600 174 552; rest of Europe ✆ +49 451 58 99 222,
  fax +49 451 58 99 203; outside Europe ✆ +358 600 15700.

TIRRENIA www.tirrenia.
Rione Sirignano 2, Casella Postale 438, 80121 Napoli: ✆ +39 091 749 31 11,
  fax +39 091 749 33 66. Call centre: ✆ +39 02 2630 2803.
  U.K. agent: The Travel Gateway (see Smyril Line).

TOREMAR www.toremar.i
Via Calafati 6, 57123 Livorno. Call centre: ✆ +39 02 2630 2803.
  U.K. agent: S.M.S. Travel & Tourism, 40 /42 Kenway Road, London, SW5 0RA:
  ✆ 020 7244 8422, fax 020 7244 9829.

TORGHATTEN NORD AS www.torghatten-nord.no
P.O. Box 2380, 9271 Tromsø: ✆ +47 906 20 700, fax +47 907 20 700.

TRANSMANCHE FERRIES www.transmancheferries.com
Ferry Port, Railway Approach, Newhaven, BN9 0DF.
  7 Quai Gaston Lalitte, 76200 Dieppe.
  Reservations: ✆ 0844 576 8836, fax 01235 84 56 08; outside U.K. and France
  ✆ +33 (0)2 32 14 52 09.

TRASMEDITERRANEA www.trasmediterranea.es
Avda. de Europa 10, Parque Empresarial La Moraleja, C.P. 28108 Alcobendas, Madrid:
  ✆ +34 (0)91 423 85 00, fax +34 (0)91 423 85 55.
  Reservations: ✆ +34(0) 902 45 46 45.
  U.K. agent: Southern Ferries, 22 Sussex Street, London SW1V 4RW:
  ✆ 0844 815 7785, fax 0844 815 7795.

TT-LINE www.ttline.com
Zum Hafenplatz 1, 23570 Lübeck-Travemünde: ✆ +49 (0)4502 801-81.
  Rostock: ✆ +49 (0)381 67079-0; Trelleborg ✆ +46 (0)410 56-200.

UNITY LINE www.unityline.p
Plac Rodja 8, 70-419, Szczecin: ✆ +48 (0)91 35 95 795, fax +48 (0)91 35 95 885.
  Reservations: ✆ +48 (0)91 35 95 600.
  Färjeterminalen, 271 39 Ystad: ✆ +46 (0)411 55 69 00, fax +46 (0)411 55 69 53.

USTICA LINES www.usticalines.i
Via Serraino Vulpitta 5, 91100 Trapani: ✆ +39 0923 873 813, fax +39 0923 593 200.

VENTOURIS FERRIES www.ventouris.
17 Gr. Lampraki Str., 185 33 Pireás: ✆ +30 210 482 8001-4, fax +30 210 483 2909.
  UK agent: Viamare (see Anek Lines).

VIKING LINE www.vikingline.fi
Lönnrotinkatu 2, FIN-00100 Helsinki: ✆ +358 (0)9 12 351, fax +358 (0)9 647 075.
  U.K. agent: Emagine U.K. Ltd, Leigh, WN7 1AZ: ✆ 01942 262 662, fax 01942 606 500.

VIRTU FERRIES LTD www.virtuferries.com
Sea Passenger Terminal, Pinto Road, Valletta, FRN 1910, Malta: ✆ +356 2206 9022,
  fax +356 21 235 435.

WASALINE www.wasaline.com
Vaasanlaivat, Laivanvarustajankatu 3, FIN- 65170 Vaasa.
  Reservations: ✆ +358 (0)207 716 810.

TIME COMPARISON

COMPARAISON DES HEURES   COMPARAZIONE DELLE ORE   ZEITVERGLEICH   COMPARACIÓN DE LAS HORAS

West European Time	*WINTER: GMT* *SUMMER: GMT +1*	Algeria Morocco Canaries Tunisia Faeroe Islands	East European Time	*WINTER: GMT +2* *SUMMER: GMT +3*	Cyprus
Central European Time	*WINTER: GMT +1* *SUMMER: GMT +2*	Israel			

Daylight Saving Time ('Summer Time') applies between 0100 GMT on March 27 and 0100 GMT on October 30, 2016 *(GMT = Greenwich Mean Time = UTC)*

Time comparison for countries with their own section in the ERT is shown on page 2

BELFAST - CAIRNRYAN 2002

Stena Line　by ship　　　2016 service
Sailings from Stranraer and Belfast.　(No service Dec. 25)

Belfast		Cairnryan			Cairnryan		Belfast		
0330§	→	0550	②③④⑤⑥		0400§	→	0620	②③④⑤⑥	
0730	→	0950			0500	→	0720	⑦	
1130	→	1350			0730	→	0950	①②③④⑤⑥	
1530	→	1750			1130	→	1350		
1930	→	2150			1530	→	1750		
2300§	→	0120	⑥⑦		1930	→	2150		
2330§	→	0150	①②③④⑤		2300§	→	0120	⑥⑦	
					2330§	→	0150	①②③④⑤	

§ – No foot passengers conveyed.

Subject to alteration during Easter and Xmas / New Year periods

CAIRNRYAN - LARNE 2005

⚓ & O Irish Sea　by ship　Journey 2 hours　2016 service

Until July 2 and August 22 - December 23
Depart Cairnryan and Larne: 0400①②③④⑤⑥, 0730, 1030①②③④⑤⑥, 1300⑦, 1330①②③④⑤⑥, 1630, 2000, 2300⑦, 2359①②③④⑤.

July 3 - August 21
Depart Cairnryan and Larne: 0400①②③④⑤⑥, 0730, 1030, 1330, 1630, 2000, 2300⑦, 2359①②③④⑤.

Subject to alteration during Easter and Xmas / New Year periods,
and ship's maintenance (Apr. 30 - May 1, May 28, 29).

CHERBOURG - ROSSLARE 2010

Irish Ferries　　　Service to May 31, 2017

Cherbourg		Rosslare	
1700	→	1100	Dec. 30.
1800	→	1130	May 8, 10, 16, 22, 24, 30.
2000	→	1400	② Sept. 27 - Dec. 13, Mar. 7 - May 2.
2130	→	1430	⑥ Sept. 24 - Dec. 10, Mar. 4 - Apr. 29 (also May 4).
2130	→	1500	④ Sept. 22 - Dec. 15, Mar. 2 - Apr. 27.

Rosslare		Cherbourg	
1530	→	1100	May 7, 9, 15, 21, 23, 29.
1800	→	1400	⑦ Sept. 25 - Dec. 11, Mar. 5 - Apr. 30.
2130	→	1630	⑤ Sept. 23 - Dec. 9, Mar. 3 - Apr. 28.
2130	→	1700	③ Sept. 21 - Dec. 14, Mar. 1 - May 3.

Stena Line　by ship　　　2016 service

Cherbourg		Rosslare		Rosslare		Cherbourg	
1545⑦	→	0815①		1630①	→	1030⑦	
2030⑤	→	1230⑥		2030④	→	1630⑤	
2030③	→	1530④		2130②	→	1615③	

Subject to alteration during Easter and Xmas / New Year periods

CORK - ROSCOFF 2015

Brittany Ferries　　　Service to May 31, 2017
Sailings from Cork (Ringaskiddy) and Roscoff.　(No winter service)

Cork		Roscoff	
1600⑥	→	0700⑦	Oct. 1 - Nov. 5, Apr. 1 - May 27.

Roscoff		Cork	
2030⑤	→	0930⑥	Sept. 30 - Nov. 4. Mar. 31 - May 19 (not May 12).
2130⑤	→	1000⑥	May 12, 26.

Times may vary owing to tidal conditions.

DOUGLAS - BELFAST 2020

Isle Of Man Steam Packet Co.　by SeaCat　2016 service
Sailings from Belfast Albert Quay.　(No winter service)

Douglas		Belfast			Belfast		Douglas	
0700	→	0945	See note **A**.		0100	→	0545	See note **D**.
1500	→	1745	Mar. 25.		0200	→	0630	June 14.
1930	→	0015	See note **C**.		0300	→	0545	June 12.
2000	→	0030	June 13.		1045	→	1330	See note **B**.
2345	→	0230	June 11.		1115	→	1400	Aug. 24.
					1145	→	1430	Aug. 28.
					1845	→	1930	Mar. 25.

A – Mar. 30, Apr. 3, 10, 20, 27, May 4, 8, 11, 22, 25, June 19, 22, 26, 29, July 3, 6, 10, 13, 15, 17, 20, 24, 27, 31, Aug. 3, 10, 17, 24, 28, 30, Sept. 4, 7, 14.
B – Mar. 30, Apr. 3, 10, 20, 27, May 4, 8, 11, 22, 25, June 19, 22, 26, 29, July 3, 6, 10, 13, 15, 17, 20, 24, 27, 31, Aug. 3, 10, 17, 30, Sept. 4, 7, 14.
C – May 14, Aug. 6, 13, 20, Sept. 10, 17, 24.
D – May 15, Aug. 7, 14, 21, Sept. 11, 18, 25.

A special service operates during the TT Race period (May 28 - June 10)

DOUGLAS - DUBLIN 2025

Isle Of Man Steam Packet Co.　by SeaCat　2016 service
Sailings from Dublin North Wall.　(No regular winter service)

Douglas		Dublin			Dublin		Douglas	
0700	→	0955	See note **E**.		0100	→	0545	See note **H**.
0745	→	1040	June 7.		1045	→	1340	See note **F**.
1930	→	0015	See note **G**.		1130	→	1425	May 29.
					1145	→	1440	June 7.

E – Mar. 23, 27, May 29, June 15, 21, 28, July 4, 12, 19, 26, Aug. 2, 9, 16, 21, 31.
F – Mar. 23, 27, June 15, 21, 28, July 4, 12, 19, 26, Aug. 2, 9, 16, 21, 31.
G – July 9, 16, 23, Dec. 17, 26.
H – July 17, 24, Dec. 18, 27.

A special service operates during the TT Race period (May 28 - June 10)

DUBLIN - CHERBOURG 2027

Irish Ferries　　　Service to May 31, 2017
Conveys passengers with vehicles only

Dublin		Cherbourg	
1530⑥	→	1130⑦	Oct. 1 - May 27 (also Dec. 29; not Dec. 24, 31).

Cherbourg		Dublin	
1700⑦	→	1130①	Oct. 2 - May 28 (not Dec. 25, Jan. 1).

FISHGUARD - ROSSLARE 2030

Stena Line　by ship　　　2016 service
　　　　　　　　　　　　(No service Dec. 25, 26)

Fishguard		Rosslare		Rosslare		Fishguard	
0230	→	0600		0900	→	1230	
1430	→	1800		2115	→	0030	

HEYSHAM - DOUGLAS 2035

Isle Of Man Steam Packet Co.　2016 service
Sailings from Heysham Port and Douglas.　(No service Dec. 25)

Heysham		Douglas	
0100	→	0545	Nov. 11.
0130	→	0500	Apr. 12, May 4.
0130	→	0545	Nov. 12, Dec. 12.
0145	→	0515	Nov. 13.
0145	→	0545	July 1.
0215	→	0545	Daily Feb. 1 - Apr. 11, May 5 - July 9; ①②③④⑤⑥ July 11 - Dec. 31 (also Aug. 28, Sept. 4, Oct. 9, 16, 30, Nov. 6, 27, Dec. 4; not Feb. 28, Mar. 27, May 15, 22, June 14, 26, 30, July 1, Aug. 26, Nov. 11, 12, Dec. 12, 19, 26 - 28).
0315	→	0645	June 30, Aug. 26.
1115	→	1315	June 14.
1200	→	1400	Apr. 12-19, 21-26, 28-30, May 1-3, Oct. 2.
1330	→	1700	May 4.
1345	→	1715	Sept. 23, Nov. 11.
1415	→	1745	①②③④⑤ Feb. 1 - Mar. 11; daily Mar. 14 - Apr. 11, May 5 - Nov. 10; ①②③④⑤⑥ Nov. 14 - Dec. 30 (not June 30, Aug. 25, Sept. 23, Oct. 2).
1500	→	1830	Aug. 25.
1530	→	1900	June 30.

Douglas		Heysham	
0730	→	0930	June 11, 12, 14.
0800	→	1000	Apr. 12-19, 21-26, 28-30, May 1-3.
0800	→	1130	May 4, 25-27, Sept. 23, Nov. 11.
0815	→	1145	Aug. 26.
0845	→	1045	Oct. 2.
0845	→	1215	①②③④⑤ Feb. 1 - Mar. 11; daily Mar. 14 - Apr. 11, May 5 - Nov. 10; ①②③④⑤⑥ Nov. 14 - Dec. 30 (not June 28, July 27, Aug. 26, Sept. 23, Oct. 2).
0915	→	1300	July 27.
0930	→	1300	June 28.
1700	→	2130	June 13.
1900	→	2230	June 14.
1945	→	2315	①②③④⑤⑥⑦ Feb. 1 - Apr. 11, May 4 - Dec. 30 (not June 13, 27, 30, July 26, Aug. 24, 25, Sept. 22, 23, Dec. 18, 26, 27).
2000	→	2330	Feb. 6, 13, 20, Mar. 5, 12, 19, Apr. 2, 9, May 7, 28, 31, June 4, 10, 11, 18, July 2, Aug. 27, Sept. 3, Oct. 8, 15, 29, Nov. 5, 12, 26, Dec. 3.
2030	→	2359	June 12, Aug. 24, Sept. 22.
2045	→	0015	June 30.
2100	→	0030	July 26.
2130	→	0100	Aug. 25.

A special service operates during the TT Race period (May 28 - June 10)

HOLYHEAD - DUBLIN 2040

Irish Ferries　by ship　　　2016 service
Sailings from Holyhead and Dublin Ferryport.　(No service Dec. 25, 26)

Holyhead		Dublin			Dublin		Holyhead		
0240	→	0555	Not Dec. 27.		0155§	→	0525	②③④⑤⑥	
0800§	→	1130	②③④⑤⑥		0805	→	1130		
1410	→	1725			1415§	→	1745	②③④⑤	
2000§	→	2315	②③④⑤		2055	→	0020	Not Dec. 24.	

§ – No foot passengers conveyed.

Sailing times may vary owing to tidal conditions.
🚌 Dublin Ferryport - Dublin Busaras (Central Bus Station).

Irish Ferries　by fast ferry　Journey 2 hours　2016 service
Sailings from Holyhead and Dublin Ferryport.　(No service Dec. 25, 26)
Depart Holyhead: 1150, 1715 (not Dec. 24).
Depart Dublin: 0845, 1430 (not Dec. 24).
🚌 Dublin Ferryport - Dublin Busaras (Central Bus Station).

Stena Line　by ship　　　2016 service
Sailings from Holyhead and Dublin Ferryport.　(No service Dec. 25, 26)

Holyhead		Dublin		Dublin		Holyhead	
0230	→	0545		0215	→	0530	
0855	→	1210		0820	→	1150	
1350	→	1705		1510	→	1825	
2030	→	2345		2040	→	2355	

Subject to alteration during Easter and Xmas / New Year periods

BIRKENHEAD (LIVERPOOL) - BELFAST 2050

Stena Line　　　2016 service
　　　　　　　　　　　　(No service Dec. 24-26, 31)

Sailings from Birkenhead Twelve Quays Terminal and Belfast Victoria Terminal.

Birkenhead		Belfast			Belfast		Birkenhead		
1030	→	1830	②③④⑤⑥⑦		1030	→	1830	②③④⑤⑥⑦	
2200	→	0600	①⑦		2200	→	0600	①⑦	
2230	→	0630	②③④⑤⑥		2230	→	0630	②③④⑤⑥	

2052   LIVERPOOL - DUBLIN

P & O Irish Sea   Service to January 2, 2017

Conveys passengers with vehicles only

Liverpool		Dublin		Dublin		Liverpool	
0300	→	1030	①②③④⑤⑥	0900	→	1700	②③④⑤⑥
0930	→	1730	②③④⑤⑥	1500	→	2330	①②③④⑤
2100	→	0500		1600	→	2359	⑦
				2130	→	0530	

Subject to alteration during holiday periods

2053   LIVERPOOL - DOUGLAS

Isle Of Man Steam Packet Co.   2016 service
(No winter service)

Sailings from Liverpool Landing Stage and Douglas.

Liverpool		Douglas	
1115	→	1400	Mar. 18, 19, 21, 24, 26, 28, 29, 31, Apr. 1, 2, 4 - 9, 11, May 5 - 7, 9, 12 - 14, 16, 19 - 21, 23, 24, 26 - 28; ①④⑤⑥ June 13 - Sept. 17 (also July 5, Aug. 7, 14, Sept. 6, 19; not July 4, 15, Sept. 8, 15).
1845	→	2130	June 12.
1915	→	2200	Mar. 17 - Oct. 17; ①④⑤⑥⑦ Oct. 20 - Nov. 6 (not Mar. 25, Apr. 9, Sept. 4).
1945	→	2230	Apr. 9.
2000	→	2245	June 13 - 15.
2030	→	2315	Sept. 4.

Douglas		Liverpool	
0730	→	1015	Mar. 18, 19, 21, 24, 26, 28, 29, 31, Apr. 1, 2, 4 - 9, 11, May 5 - 7, 9, 12 - 14, 16, 19 - 21, 23, 24, 26 - 28; ①④⑤⑥ June 13 - Sept. 17 (also Aug. 7, 14, Sept. 6; not June 30, July 15, Sept. 8, 15, 19).
1000	→	1245	⑥ Sept. 24 - Nov. 5.
1500	→	1745	Daily Mar. 17 - Sept. 23; ①②③④⑤⑦ Sept. 25 - Oct. 14; ①④⑤⑦ Oct. 16 - Nov. 6 (not Mar. 25, Sept. 4).
1600	→	1845	June 13 - 15.
1630	→	1915	Sept. 4.
2345	→	0230	June 12.

Sailing times may vary.

Subject to alteration May 28 - June 11, Aug. 21 - Sept. 3

2055   PEMBROKE - ROSSLARE

Irish Ferries   2016 servic
(No service Dec. 25, 26

Pembroke		Rosslare		Rosslare		Pembroke
0245	→	0645		0845	→	1245
1445	→	1845		2045	→	0045

Sailing times may vary owing to tidal conditions

2065   ROSSLARE - ROSCOFF

Irish Ferries   2017 servic
(No winter service

Rosslare		Roscoff		Roscoff		Rosslare	
1600	→	1030	See note **R**.	1830	→	1100	See note **S**.
1730	→	1100	May 5 only.				

R – May 11, 13, 17, 19, 25, 27, 31, June 2, 8, 10, 14, 16, 22, 24, 28, 30, July 6, 12, 14, 20, 26, Aug. 3, 11, 17, 25, 31, Sept. 6, 8, 14.

S – May 6, 12, 14, 18, 20, 26, 28 June 1, 3, 9, 11, 15, 17, 23, 25, 29, July 1, 7, 13, 15, 21, 27, Aug. 4, 12, 18, 26, Sept. 1, 7, 9, 15.

ENGLISH CHANNEL & BAY OF BISCAY

2100   CHANNEL ISLAND SERVICES

Condor Ferries   *Departure times vary owing to tidal conditions*

POOLE - GUERNSEY by fast ferry   Service to May 31, 2017

From Poole: Dec. 2, 9, 10, 12, 16, 17, 19, 21 - 23, 27 - 30, Jan. 2 - 4, 6, 13, 20, 27, Feb. 3, 6, 10, 13, 17, 18, 20, 24 - 27, Mar. 3, 4, 6, 10, 11, 13, 17, 18, 20, 24, 27, 31, Apr. 1, 3, 7, 8, 10, 12 - 17, 19, 21 - 24, 26, 28 - 30, May 1 - 3, 5 - 10, 12 - 15, 17 - 22, 24 - 31.
From Guernsey: Dec. 5, 9, 10, 12, 16, 17, 19, 21 - 23, 27 - 30, Jan. 2 - 4, 9, 16, 23, 30, Feb. 4, 6, 10, 13, 17, 18, 20, 24 - 27, Mar. 3, 4, 6 - 8, 11, 13, 17, 18, 20, 24, 27, 31, Apr. 1, 3, 7, 8, 10, 12 - 17, 19, 21 - 24, 26, 28 - 30, May 1 - 3, 5 - 10, 12 - 14, 17 - 22, 24 - 31.

POOLE - JERSEY by fast ferry   Service to May 31, 2017

From Poole: Dec. 2, 9, 10, 12, 16, 17, 19, 21 - 23, 27 - 30, Jan. 2 - 4, 6, 13, 20, 27, Feb. 3, 6, 10, 13, 17, 18, 20, 24 - 27, Mar. 3, 4, 6, 10, 11, 13, 17, 18, 20, 24, 27, 31, Apr. 1, 3, 7, 8, 10, 12 - 17, 19, 21 - 24, 29 - 30, May 1 - 3, 5 - 10, 12 - 15, 17 - 22, 24 - 31.
From Jersey: Dec. 5, 9, 10, 12, 16, 17, 19, 21 - 23, 27 - 30, Jan. 2 - 4, 9, 16, 23, 30, Feb. 4, 6, 10, 13, 17, 18, 20, 24 - 27, Mar. 3, 4, 6, 10, 11, 13, 17, 18, 20, 24, 27, 31, Apr. 1, 3, 7, 8, 10, 12 - 17, 19 - 24, 26, 28 - 30, May 1 - 3, 5 - 10, 12 - 15, 17 - 22, 24 - 31.

PORTSMOUTH - GUERNSEY by ship   2017 service

Sailings from Portsmouth Continental Ferry Port and St Peter Port.

Portsmouth		St Peter Port	
0900	→	**A**	①②③④⑤⑥ Jan. 2 - May 31; daily June 1 - Sept. 12; ①②③④⑤⑥ Oct. 12 - 31.

St Peter Port		Portsmouth	
D	→	0630	①②③④⑤⑥ Jan. 2 - May 31; daily June 1 - Sept. 13; ①②③④⑤⑥ Oct. 20 - 31 (also Apr. 2; not Apr. 1, Sept. 3).

A – Most arrivals 1600, but variations possible between 1555 and 2300.
D – Most departures 1720, but variations possible between 1720 and 2359.

PORTSMOUTH - JERSEY by ship   2017 service

Sailings from Portsmouth Continental Ferry Port and St Helier.

Portsmouth		St Helier	
0900	→	**B**	①②③④⑤⑥ Jan. 2 - May 31; daily June 1 - Sept. 12; ①②③④⑤⑥ Oct. 20 - 31.

St Helier		Portsmouth	
C	→	0630	①②③④⑤⑥ Jan. 2 - May 31; daily June 1 - Sept. 13; ①②③④⑤⑥ Oct. 20 - 31 (not Sept. 3).

B – Most arrivals 1920, but variations possible between 1705 and 2050.
C – Most departures 2120, but variations possible between 1835 and 2220.

ST MALO - GUERNSEY by fast ferry   Service to May 31, 2017

From St Malo: Dec. 5, 10, 19, 29, 30, Jan. 2 - 4, 9, 16, 23, 30, Feb. 4, 13, 17, 26, 27, Mar. 3, 4, 13, 17, 18, 27, 30, 31, Apr. 1, 2, 4, 6, 11 - 20, 23, 25 - 30, May 1 - 5, 7, 10, 11, 13, 14, 16 - 18, 21, 23, 24, 26 - 30.
From Guernsey: Dec. 2, 9, 10, 12, 16, 17, 19, 21, 22, 23, 27 - 30, Jan. 2, 3, 6, 13, 20, 27, Feb. 3, 6, 10, 17, 18, 24, 27, Mar. 3, 6, 10, 11, 13, 17, 20, 24, 27, 30, Apr. 2 - 4, 6 - 8, 10 - 14, 16, 18 - 27, 30, May 2 - 7, 9 - 30.

ST MALO - JERSEY by fast ferry   Service to May 31, 2017

From St Malo and Jersey: Dec. 2 - 5, 9 - 12, 15 - 19, 21 - 23, 27 - 30, Jan. 2 - 4, 6 - 9, 13 - 16, 20 - 23, 27 - 30, Feb. 3 - 6, 10 - 13, 17 - 20, 23 - 27, Mar. 2 - 6, 9 - 13, 16 - 20, 23 - 27, 30, 31, Apr. 1 - 4, 6 - 30, May 1 - 31.

GUERNSEY - JERSEY by fast ferry   Service to May 31, 2017

From Guernsey: Dec. 1, 2, 4 - 10, 12, 14 - 23, 27 - 30, Jan. 2 - 6, 12 - 14, 16 - 21, 23, 26 - 28, 30, 31, Feb. 1 - 4, 6, 10, 11, 13 - 18, 20 - 22, 24 - 28, Mar. 1 - 4, 6, 7, 10, 11, 13 - 18, 20 - 24, 27 - 31, Apr. 1 - 8, 10 - 30, May 1 - 31.
From Jersey: Dec. 3, 5, 9 - 13, 16, 17, 19, 21 - 23, 27 - 30, Jan. 2 - 4, 7, 9 - 11, 16, 23 - 25, 30, Feb. 4, 6 - 10, 13, 17, 18, 20, 23 - 27, Mar. 3, 4, 6, 8 - 11, 13, 17, 18, 20, 24, 25, 27, 30, 31, Apr. 1 - 4, 6 - 8, 10 - 30, May 1 - 31.

OTHER SERVICES:

Manche îles Express operate catamaran services in summer from Jersey to Carteret, Granville, Sark and Guernsey, and from Guernsey to Alderney and Diélette.

2110   DOVER - CALAIS

DFDS Seaways   by ship   2016 service

Sailings from Dover Eastern Docks and Calais Maritime.   Journey 90 minutes

Conveys passengers with vehicles only.

Depart Dover: 0045, 0240①②③④⑤⑥, 0410①②③④⑤⑥, 0550①②③④⑤⑥, 0740, 0910, 1040①②③④⑤⑥, 1215, 1345, 1515, 1650, 1820, 1955, 2135①②③④⑤⑦, 2305①②③④⑤⑦.

Depart Calais: 0105①②③④⑤⑥, 0230①②③④⑤⑥, 0415①②③④⑤⑥, 0610, 0740, 0920①②③④⑤⑥, 1055, 1225, 1355, 1530, 1700, 1830, 2010①②③④⑤⑦, 2140①②③④⑤⑦, 2315.

P & O Ferries   Journey 90 minutes   Service to January 15, 2017
(No service Dec. 25)

Sailings from Dover Eastern Docks and Calais Maritime.
On night services, conveys passengers with vehicles only (foot passengers may travel 0825 - 1915 from Dover, 0645 - 2145 from Calais). Timings subject to variation.

March 13 - December 17
Depart Dover: 0050, 0220, 0320, 0420, 0640, 0735, 0825, 0925, 1015, 1110, 1205, 1255, 1355, 1445, 1540, 1640, 1725, 1835, 1915, 2015, 2120, 2205, 2315.
Depart Calais: 0030, 0120, 0240, 0435, 0545, 0645, 0745, 0840, 0950, 1045, 1135, 1235, 1325, 1420, 1520, 1605, 1715, 1755, 1850, 1945, 2035, 2145, 2335.

December 18 - 24
Depart Dover: 0045, 0225①②③④⑤⑥, 0340, 0450①②③④⑤⑥, 0630, 0740, 0845, 0955, 1100, 1210, 1315, 1425, 1530 **X**, 1645 **X**, 1745 **X**, 1905 **X**, 2005 **X**, 2125①②③④⑤⑦ **X**, 2225 **X**, 2345 **X**.
Depart Calais: 0035①②③④⑤⑥, 0140, 0310①②③④⑤⑥, 0425, 0550①②③④⑤⑥, 0705, 0815, 0940, 1050, 1155, 1305, 1410, 1525, 1625, 1745, 1840 **X**, 2000 **X**, 2055 **X**, 2215 **X**, 2325 **X**.

December 26 - January 15
Depart Dover: 0045 **Y**, 0225 **Z**, 0340 **Y**, 0450 **Z**, 0630 **Y**, 0740, 0845 **Z**, 0955, 1100 **Z**, 1210, 1315 **Z**, 1425, 1530 **Z**, 1645, 1745 **Z**, 1905, 2005 **Z**, 2125①②③④⑤⑦, 2225 **Z**, 2345.
Depart Calais: 0035①②③④⑤⑥ **Z**, 0140 **Y**, 0310①②③④⑤⑥ **Z**, 0425 **Y**, 0550①②③④⑤⑥ **Z**, 0705 **Y**, 0815 **Z**, 0940 **Y**, 1050, 1155 **Z**, 1305, 1410 **Z**, 1525, 1625 **Z**, 1745, 1840 **Z**, 2000, 2055 **Z**, 2215, 2325 **Z**.

X – Not Dec. 24.
Y – Not Dec. 26, 27.
Z – Not Dec. 26.

🚌 connections:
Calais Port - Calais Ville station 1100 – 1745; Calais Ville station - Calais Port 1030 – 1800.

DOVER - DUNKERQUE — 2111

DFDS Seaways by ship — 2016 service

Sailings from Dover Eastern Docks and Dunkerque. Journey 2 hours
Conveys passengers with vehicles only

Depart Dover: 0200②③④⑤⑥⑦, 0400①②③④⑤⑥, 0600①②③④⑤⑥, 0800,
1000①②③④⑤⑥, 1200, 1400, 1600, 1800, 2000①②③④⑤⑦, 2200,
2359①②③④⑤⑦.

Depart Dunkerque: 0200①②③④⑤⑥, 0400①②③④⑤⑥, 0600, 0800①②③④⑤⑥,
1000, 1200, 1400, 1600, 1800①②③④⑤⑦, 2000, 2200①②③④⑤⑦,
2359①②③④⑤⑦.

NEWHAVEN - DIEPPE — 2125

DFDS Seaways — 2016 service
Sailings from Newhaven and Dieppe. — (No service Dec. 25)

Newhaven		Dieppe		Dieppe		Newhaven
1000	→	1500		0530	→	0830
2300	→	0400		1800	→	2100

Newhaven ferry terminal is adjacent to Newhaven Town rail station.
For rail services see Table **101**.

Departure times may vary owing to tidal conditions.

PENZANCE - ST. MARY'S — 2130

Isles Of Scilly Steamship Co. — 2016 service

Sailings from Penzance Lighthouse Pier (South Pier) and St Mary's. — (No winter service)
From Penzance and St Mary's: sailings on: ①③⑤⑥ Mar. 14-19; ①②③④⑤⑥ Mar. 21 -
June 25; daily June 27 - Sept. 17; ①②③④⑤⑥ Sept. 19 - Oct. 8; ①③⑤⑥ Oct. 10 -
Nov. 5 (also Nov. 6).

Departure times vary owing to tidal conditions
(most sailings Penzance depart 0915, St Mary's depart 1630).

PLYMOUTH - ROSCOFF — 2135

Brittany Ferries Departure times vary — Service to May 31, 2017

Sailings from Plymouth Millbay and Roscoff.
From Plymouth: daily Oct. 1 - Nov. 6; ②③⑤⑦ Nov. 8-18; daily Dec. 1, 3, 4, 6, 7, 9, 11, 13,
14, 16, 18, 20-23, 27-29, Jan. 2, Feb. 6; ②④⑤⑦ Feb. 10 - Mar. 26; daily Mar. 28 -
May 31.
From Roscoff: daily Oct. 1 - Nov. 7; ①③④⑥ Nov. 9-19; daily Dec. 1, 3-5, 7, 8, 10, 12,
14, 15, 17, 19, 21-23, 27-29, Jan. 2, Feb. 7; ①③⑤⑥ Feb. 11 - Mar. 27; daily Mar. 29 -
May 31 (not Apr. 7, 28, May 5, 12).

PLYMOUTH - SANTANDER — 2140

Brittany Ferries — Service to May 31, 2017
Sailings from Plymouth Millbay and Santander. — (No regular winter service)

Plymouth		Santander	
1545	→	1215	⑦ Oct. 2 - Nov. 6, Apr. 2 - May 28.
1600	→	1300	② Nov. 8 - Dec. 20 (also Dec. 4).
2030	→	1730	Oct. 7, Nov. 25, Feb. 3.
Santander		**Plymouth**	
1800	→	1300	① Nov. 7 - Dec. 19 (also Nov. 30).
2115	→	1615	③ Oct. 5 - Nov. 2, Mar. 29 - May 31.

PLYMOUTH - ST MALO — 2142

Brittany Ferries — Service to May 31, 2017
— (No summer service)

Sailings from Plymouth Millbay and St Malo Terminal Ferry du Naye.

Plymouth		St Malo	
2045	→	0815	Feb. 8.
2200	→	0730	Dec. 2.
St Malo		**Plymouth**	
1230	→	2010	Dec. 3, Feb. 6.

POOLE - CHERBOURG — 2145

Brittany Ferries — Service to May 31, 2017

Poole		Cherbourg		Cherbourg		Poole	
0830	→	1345	See note **R**.	1300	→	1615	Jan. 2 only.
				1830	→	2145	See note **P**.
				2215	→	0700	See note **Q**.

P – ①④⑤⑥⑦ Sept. 15 - May 29 (not Nov. 17-21, 28, Dec. 23-25, 31, Jan. 1, 2).
Q – ②③ Oct. 4 - May 31 (also Nov. 20, 21, 28).
R – Not Nov. 18-20, Dec. 24-26, Jan. 1, 2.
🚌 Cherbourg Port - Cherbourg station (operated by Zéphir).

PORTSMOUTH - BILBAO — 2155

Brittany Ferries — Service to May 31, 2017
Conveys passengers with vehicles only

Portsmouth		Bilbao	
0845	→	1415§	② Oct. 4 - Nov. 1, Dec. 6 - Jan. 3; ⑥ Feb. 18 - Mar. 25; ② Mar. 28 - May 30; not Dec. 20).
1030	→	1130§	Dec. 22 only.
1145③	→	1245④	Oct. 5 - Feb. 8, Mar. 29 - May 31 (not Dec. 21, 28).
2230⑦	→	0745②	Oct. 2 - Feb. 5, Apr. 2 - May 28 (not Dec. 25, Jan. 1).
2345	→	0800§	Dec. 19 only.
Bilbao		**Portsmouth**	
1030②	→	0900③	Oct. 4 - Feb. 7, Apr. 4 - May 30 (also Dec. 29; not Dec. 27, Jan. 3).
1300	→	1630§	Dec. 21 only.
1530④	→	1415⑤	Oct. 13 - Feb. 9, Mar. 30 - May 25 (not Nov. 24, Dec. 22, 29, Feb. 2).
1715	→	2045§	③ Oct. 5 - Nov. 2, Dec. 7 - Jan. 4; ⑦ Feb. 19 - Mar. 26; ③ Mar. 29 - May 31 (not Dec. 21).
1900	→	1915§	Dec. 26 only.

§ – One day later.

PORTSMOUTH - CHERBOURG — 2160

Brittany Ferries by fast ferry — 2016 service
Sailings from Portsmouth Continental Ferry Port and Cherbourg. **(No regular winter service)**

Portsmouth		Cherbourg	
0715	→	1115	July 3 only.
0730	→	1130	⑤⑥⑦ May 27 - Sept. 4 (not July 3).
0815	→	1500	Jan. 11, Feb. 4, Apr. 25, May 17.
0900	→	1300	Daily Apr. 27 - May 26; ①②③④ May 30 - Sept. 6.
1200	→	1730	Jan. 4 only.
1515	→	1915	⑤⑥⑦ May 27 - Sept. 4 (not July 3).
Cherbourg		**Portsmouth**	
1230	→	1430	⑤⑥⑦ May 27 - Sept. 4 (not July 3).
1630	→	2100	Jan. 11.
1630	→	2115	Feb. 4, Apr. 25, May 17.
1700	→	1900	Daily Apr. 27 - May 26; ①②③④ May 30 - Sept. 5.
2015	→	2215	⑤⑥⑦ May 27 - Sept. 4 (not July 3).
2045	→	2245	July 3 only.

🚌 Cherbourg Port - Cherbourg station (operated by Zéphir).

PORTSMOUTH - LE HAVRE — 2165

Brittany Ferries by ship — Service to May 31, 2017
Sailings from Portsmouth Continental Ferry Port and Le Havre Terminal de la Citadelle.

Portsmouth		Le Havre	
1045	→	1715	⑤ Dec. 9 - Feb. 10; ② Feb. 14 - Mar. 21 (not Dec. 23, 30).
2145	→	0800	Dec. 22, 23 only.
2315	→	0830	daily Oct. 1 - Nov. 6 (not Oct. 18).
2315	→	0900	Oct. 18 only.
2330	→	0810	Mar. 30 only.
2330	→	0830	daily Nov. 7 - May 31 (not Dec. 8, 15, 22-25, 31, Jan. 1, 5, Mar. 29, 30, Apr. 27, 28, May 27, 28).
2330	→	0840	Apr. 27 only.
2330	→	0850	Mar. 29, May 28 only.
2330	→	0900	May 27 only.
2330	→	0920	Apr. 28 only.
Le Havre		**Portsmouth**	
1200	→	1645	⑤ Jan. 13 - Feb. 10; ② Feb. 14 - Mar. 21 (also Jan. 2).
1700	→	2130	daily Nov. 7 - Dec. 7, Dec. 10-14, 17-21, 26-28, Jan. 3, 4; ①②③④⑥⑦ Jan. 7 - Feb. 12; ①③④⑤⑥⑦ Feb. 13 - Mar. 27; ①②③⑥⑦ Mar. 28 - May 31.
1715	→	2145	①②③⑥⑦ Oct. 1 - Nov. 6.
2200	→	0600	⑤ Oct. 7 - Nov. 4, Dec. 9 - Feb. 10; ② Feb. 14 - Mar. 21; ⑤ Mar. 31 - May 26 (also Dec. 26, Jan. 2; not Dec. 23, 30).
2200	→	0715	④ Oct. 6 - Nov. 3, Dec. 8 - 29, Mar. 30 - May 18.
2200	→	0800	May 25 only.
2200	→	0845	Jan. 5 only.

A shuttle 🚌 service operates between the terminal and railway station

PORTSMOUTH - OUISTREHAM (CAEN) — 2170

Brittany Ferries by ship — Service to May 31, 2017
— (No service Dec. 25, Jan. 1)

Sailings from Portsmouth Continental Ferry Port and Ouistreham.

Portsmouth		Ouistreham	
0815	→	1500	Daily (not Dec. 26, Feb. 10).
1445	→	2130	①②④⑤⑥⑦ Oct. 1 - Nov. 6; ①②③④⑥⑦ Nov. 7 - Feb. 28; ①②④⑤⑥⑦ Mar. 2 - May 30 (not Nov. 16, Dec. 24, 31, Jan. 3, Apr. 7).
2200	→	0645	③ Oct. 5 - Nov. 2; ⑤ Nov. 11 - Feb. 24; ③ Mar. 1 - May 31 (not Dec. 23).
2245	→	0645	①④⑤⑥⑦ Oct. 1 - Nov. 7; daily Nov. 8, 9, 12-14, 16; ①②③⑥⑦ Nov. 19 - Feb. 22; ①④⑤⑥⑦ Feb. 25 - May 29 (also Dec. 22, 23; not Dec. 24, 31, Feb. 28, Mar. 1).
2245	→	0730	② Oct. 4 - Nov. 1; ④ Nov. 10 - Feb. 23; ② Feb. 28 - May 30 (not Dec. 20).
Ouistreham		**Portsmouth**	
0830	→	1315	①②④⑤⑥⑦ Oct. 1 - Nov. 6; ①②③④⑥⑦ Nov. 7 - Feb. 26; ①②④⑤⑥⑦ Feb. 27 - May 30 (also Dec. 23; not Nov. 16, Dec. 24, 31, Mar. 27, Apr. 3).
1400	→	1915	③ Oct. 5 - Nov. 2; ⑤ Nov. 11 - Feb. 24; ③ Mar. 1 - May 31 (not Dec. 23).
1630	→	2115	①②④⑤⑥⑦ Oct. 1 - Nov. 6; ①②③④⑥⑦ Nov. 7 - Feb. 26; ①②④⑤⑥⑦ Feb. 27 - May 30 (not Dec. 24, 31).
2300	→	0645	Daily (not Nov. 16, Dec. 24, 31).

🚌 Ouistreham - Caen station (journey 45 minutes) to connect with most sailings.

2175 — PORTSMOUTH - SANTANDER

Brittany Ferries Journey time approx. 24 hours **Service to May 31, 2017**
Sailings from Portsmouth Continental Ferry Port and Santander.

Portsmouth		Santander	
0845	→	1415	⑥ Oct. 1 - Nov. 5; ②⑥ Jan. 7 - Feb. 11; ③ Feb. 15 - Mar. 22; ⑥ Apr. 1 - May 27 (also Dec. 10, 17).
1100	→	1200	Nov. 13, 20 only.
1100	→	1300	Nov. 27, Dec. 11, 18 only.
1100	→	1215	②⑤ Feb. 14 - Mar. 24.
1145	→	1215	Dec. 30 only.
1700	→	1730	⑤ Oct. 14 - Feb. 10, Mar. 31 - May 26 (not Nov. 25, Dec. 23, 30, Feb. 3).
1715	→	1815	② Oct. 4 - Nov. 1, Mar. 28 - May 30.
2345	→	0800	Nov. 7 only.

Santander		Portsmouth	
1030	→	0900	Mar. 28 only.
1515	→	1415	① Oct. 3 - 31, Apr. 3 - May 29.
1530	→	1800	Jan. 2 only.
1715	→	2045	⑦ Oct. 2 - Nov. 6, Dec. 4 - 18; ③⑦ Jan. 8 - Feb. 12; ④ Feb. 16 - Mar. 23; ⑦ Apr. 2 - May 28.
1730	→	1700	③⑥ Feb. 15 - Mar. 25.
1800	→	1700	③ Nov. 9 - Dec. 21 (not Nov. 30).
2030	→	1945	⑥ Oct. 1 - Feb, 4, Apr. 1 - May 27 (not Dec. 24, 31).

2180 — PORTSMOUTH - ST MALO

Brittany Ferries **Service to May 31, 2017**
Sailings from Portsmouth Continental Ferry Port and St. Malo Terminal Ferry du Naye.

From Portsmouth: daily July 6 - Sept. 5; ①③④⑤⑥⑦ Sept. 7 - Dec. 21; ①③⑤⑦ Jan. 1 - Feb. 5; ①③⑤⑥⑦ Mar. 1 - 31; ①③④⑤⑥⑦ Apr. 1 - May 31 (also Dec. 27, 28, 30, Feb. 10, 12, 15, 17 - 20, 22, 24 - 27; not Dec. 3, Apr. 6).

From St. Malo: daily July 7 - Sept. 6; ①②④⑤⑥⑦ Sept. 8 - Dec. 23; ①②④⑥ Jan. 2 - Feb. 4; ①②④⑥⑦ Mar. 2 - 30; ①②④⑤⑥⑦ Apr. 1 - May 30 (also Dec. 26 - 29, Feb. 9, 11, 13, 14, 16, 19 - 21, 23, 25 - 28; not Dec. 4, Apr. 7).

Departure times vary: most sailings Portsmouth d. 2015 (St. Malo a. 0815); St. Malo d. 1030 (Portsmouth a. 1820).

2200 — ABERDEEN - KIRKWALL - LERWICK

NorthLink Ferries **2017 service**

Aberdeen		Kirkwall		Kirkwall		Lerwick	
January 2 - March 28 and November 1 - December 30							
1700④⑥⑦	→	2300④⑥⑦	→	2345⑤⑥⑦	→	0730⑤⑦①	
1900①②③⑤	→	→		→		0730②③④⑥	
March 29 - October 31							
1700②④⑥⑦	→	2300②④⑥⑦	→	2345②④⑥⑦	→	0730③⑤⑦①	
1900①③⑤	→	→		→		0730②④⑥	

Lerwick		Kirkwall		Kirkwall		Aberdeen	
January 2 - March 27 and November 1 - December 30							
1730③⑤	→	2300③⑤	→	2345③⑤	→	0700④⑥	
1900①②④⑥⑦	→	→		→		0700②③⑤⑦①	
March 28 - October 31							
1730①③⑤	→	2300①③⑤	→	2345①③⑤	→	0700②④⑥	
1900②④⑥⑦	→	→		→		0700③⑤⑦①	

Subject to alteration during ship maintenance
A 🚌 transfer service is available Kirkwall - Stromness and v.v.
in conjunction with evening sailings.

2235 — HARWICH - HOEK VAN HOLLAND

Stena Line by ship **2016 service**
  (No service Dec. 25, 26)
Sailings from Harwich International Port and Hoek van Holland.

Harwich		Hoek			Hoek		Harwich	
0900	→	1715	①②③④⑤⑥		1345	→	1945	⑥⑦
1000	→	1800	⑦		1415	→	1945	①②③④⑤
2300	→	0800			2200	→	0630	

See Table 15a for connecting rail services London - Harwich and v.v. and
Hoek van Holland - Amsterdam and v.v.

2237 — HIRTSHALS - STAVANGER - BERGEN

Fjord Line **Service to May 31, 2017**
  (No service Jan. 1)

Hirtshals		Stavanger		Bergen		Stavanger		Hirtshals	
September 1 - December 31									
2000 W	→	0630 X	→	1230 X / 1330 Y	→	2000 Y	→	0800 Z	
January 2 - May 31 ♦									
2000	→	0630	→	1230 / 1330	→	2000	→	0800	

W – Not Dec. 24, 25. X – Not Dec. 25, 26.
Y – Not Dec. 30, 31. Z – Not Dec. 31, Jan. 1.

♦ – Variations:
No departure from Hirtshals Jan. 3, 5, 7, 9, 12, 14, 16, 18;
no departure from Bergen and Stavanger Jan. 4, 6, 8, 10, 13, 15, 17, 19;
no departures between Stavanger and Bergen Jan. 5, Apr. 20.
Subject to alteration during Xmas / New Year period

2239 — LOFOTEN ISLANDS (map page 341)

Torghatten Nord by fast ferry **Service to January 31, 2017**
BODØ - SVOLVÆR (subject to alteration)

Bodø		Svolvær			Svolvær		Bodø	
1715	→	2050	①②③④⑥		0630	→	1000	①②③④⑤⑥
1800	→	2135	⑤		1600	→	1930	⑦
2030	→	2330	⑦					

Torghatten Nord by ship **Service to January 31, 2017**
BODØ - MOSKENES

Bodø		Moskenes			Moskenes		Bodø	
February 1 June 9 and August 29 - January 31								
0015	→	0330	②④⑤		0700	→	1015	①②③④⑤⑥
0215	→	0630	③		1200	→	1900	⑦
1300	→	1630	⑦		1700	→	2359	⑦
1530	→	1845	③		1900	→	2345	③
1630	→	1945	①②④⑤⑥		2030	→	2345	①②④
2100	→	0015	⑦					
June 10 - August 28								
0045	→	0415			0600	→	0915	
0430	→	0800	①②③④⑤⑥		1030	→	1430	
0600	→	1000			1400	→	1715	
1015	→	1330			1930	→	2330	
1530	→	1900			2115	→	0030	
1745	→	2100			2359	→	0330	①②③④⑤⑦

2240 — NORWEGIAN COASTAL SERVICES (map page 341)

Hurtigruten **2017 service**
BERGEN - TRONDHEIM - TROMSØ - KIRKENES (subject to alteration)

	NORTHBOUND						SOUTHBOUND			
	WINTER		SUMMER					ALL YEAR		
	arrive	depart	arrive	depart	day			arrive	depart	day
Bergen ♣	...	2230	...	2000	A	Kirkenes		...	1230	A
Florø	0430	0445	0200	0215	B	Vadsø		...	...	
Måløy	0715	0730	0415	0430	B	Vardø		1545	1645	A
Torvik	1030	1045	0715	0730	B	Båtsfjord		1945	2015	A
Ålesund	1200	1500	0845	0930	B	Berlevåg		2200◇	2215◇	A
Geiranger ▲			1325 g	1330 g	B	Mehamn		0045	0100	B
Ålesund	1200	1500	1815¶	1900	B	Kjøllefjord		0245	0300	B
Molde	1800	1830	2145	2200	B	Honningsvåg		0530	0545	B
Kristiansund	2215	2300	0145	0200	B / C	Havøysund		0745	0800	B
Trondheim	0600	1200	0600	1200	C	Hammerfest		1045	1245 §	B
Rørvik	2045	2115	2045	2115	C	Øksfjord		1530 §	1545 §	B
Brønnøysund	0045	0100	0045	0100	D	Skjervøy		1915△	1945△	B
Sandnessjøen	0345	0415	0345	0415	D	Tromsø		2345	0130	B / C
Nesna	0525	0530	0525	0530	D	Finnsnes		0415	0445	C
Ørnes	0915	0930	0915	0930	D	Harstad		0745	0830	C
Bodø	1230	1500	1230	1500	D	Risøyhamn		1045	1100	C
Stamsund	1900	1930	1900	1930	D	Sortland		1230	1300	C
Svolvær	2100	2200	2100	2200	D	Stokmarknes		1415	1515	C
Stokmarknes	0100	0115	0100	0115	E	Svolvær		1830	2030	C
Sortland	0245	0300	0245	0300	E	Stamsund		2200	2230	C
Risøyhamn	0415	0430	0415	0430	E	Bodø		0230	0415	D
Harstad	0645	0800	0645	0745	E	Ørnes		0700	0715	D
Finnsnes	1115	1145	1100	1130	E	Nesna		1100	1115	D
Tromsø	1430	1830	1415	1830	E	Sandnessjøen		1230	1300	D
Skjervøy	2230	2245	2230	2245	E	Brønnøysund		1545	1700	D
Øksfjord	0200	0215	0200	0215	F	Rørvik		2030	2130	D
Hammerfest	0515	0600	0515	0600	F	Trondheim		0630	1000	E
Havøysund	0845	0915	0845	0915	F	Kristiansund		1630	1700	E
Honningsvåg	1145	1445	1115	1445	F	Molde		2100	2130	E
Kjøllefjord	1700	1715	1700	1715	F	Ålesund		0030	0100	F
Mehamn	1915	1930	1915	1930	F	Geiranger ▲				
Berlevåg	2145 ‡	2200 ‡	2200	2215	F	Ålesund		0030	0100	F
Båtsfjord	2345	0015	2345	0015	F / G	Torvik		0215	0230	F
Vardø	0315	0330	0315	0330	G	Måløy		0515	0545	F
Vadsø	0645	0715	0645	0715	G	Florø		0745	0815	F
Kirkenes	0900	...	0900	...	G	Bergen ♣		1430		F

A – 1st day .... G – 7th day.

g – June 2 - Sept. 1.

◇ – 15 minutes earlier Apr. 1 - Sept. 1.
‡ – 15 minutes later Apr. 1 - June 1.
△ – 15 minutes earlier Apr. 1 - June 1.
¶ – 60 minutes earlier Sept. 2 - Nov. 1.
§ – 60 minutes earlier June 2 - Sept. 1.

♣ – Sailings from Bergen Frilenesset.

▲ – Embarkation and disembarkation take place by tender - passengers are required to be at the quay 30 minutes before departure.

2242 — HELGOLAND (Germany) services

2017 services

From:		Operator:
BREMERHAVEN	May 20 - Sept. 24, 2017	Reederei Cassen Eils
BÜSUM	Apr. 8 - Oct. 22, 2017	Reederei Cassen Eils
CUXHAVEN	Mar. 19 - Oct. 30, 2016	FRS Helgoline
	All year service	Reederei Cassen Eils
HAMBURG	Mar. 19 - Oct. 30, 2016	FRS Helgoline

HULL - ROTTERDAM 2245

P & O Ferries
2016 service
(No service Dec. 24, 25, 30, 31)

Sailings from Hull King George Dock and Rotterdam Europoort.

Hull	Rotterdam		Rotterdam	Hull	
2030	→	0815	①②③④⑤	2030	→	0800	⑥⑦
2030	→	0900	⑥⑦	2100	→	0800	①②③④⑤

Subject to alteration during Xmas/New Year period

🚍 connections (reservation recommended):
Hull railway station (depart 1715) - King George Dock and v.v.
Rotterdam Centraal Station (depart 1700) - Europoort and v.v.
Amsterdam Centraal Station (depart 1700) - Europoort and v.v.

HULL - ZEEBRUGGE 2250

P & O Ferries
2016 service

Sailings from Hull King George Dock and Zeebrugge Leopold II Dam.

Hull	Zeebrugge		Zeebrugge	Hull	
1830	→	0845	①②③④⑤	1900	→	0830	①②③④⑤
1830	→	0930	⑥⑦	1900	→	0900	⑥⑦

Subject to alteration during Xmas/New Year period

🚍 connections (reservation recommended):
Hull railway station (depart 1715) - King George Dock and v.v.
Brugge Station (depart 1730) - Zeebrugge and v.v.

NEWCASTLE - IJMUIDEN (AMSTERDAM) 2255

DFDS Seaways
2016 service
(No service Dec. 24, 25)

Sailings from Newcastle International Ferry Terminal, Royal Quays and IJmuiden Felison Terminal.

Newcastle	IJmuiden		IJmuiden	Newcastle	
1700	→	0930 §	1730	→	0900 §

§ – Arrive 30 minutes later on ⑦.

🚍 connections:
Newcastle rail station - International Ferry Terminal (North Shields) and v.v.
depart Newcastle station 2½ and 1¼ hours before sailing; depart Ferry Terminal following arrival of ship).
Victoria Hotel Amsterdam (near Centraal station) - IJmuiden and v.v.
(depart hotel every 10 minutes 1530 - 1630; depart Ferry Terminal following arrival of ship).

SCRABSTER - STROMNESS 2280

NorthLink Ferries
2017 service
(No service Dec. 25, 26)

Scrabster	Stromness	
0845	→	1015	①②③④⑤ Jan. 3 - May 12; ①②③④⑤⑥ May 15 - Sept. 2 (also Aug. 13, Sept. 4, 9, 15, 16, 18, 23, 30, Oct. 14, 21, 28).
1200	→	1330	⑥⑦ Jan. 7 - May 19; ⑦ May 21 - Oct. 1; ⑥⑦ Oct. 7 - Dec. 31 (not Apr. 1, 15, Aug. 13, Oct. 14, 21, 28).
1315	→	1445	①②③④⑤⑥ May 20 - Sept. 4 (also Apr. 1, 15, Aug. 13, Sept. 9, 15, 16, 18, 23, 30, Oct. 14, 21, 28).
1900	→	2030	Daily Jan. 3 - Dec. 31 (not Dec. 25, 26).

Stromness	Scrabster	
0630	→	0800	①②③④⑤ Jan. 3 - May 12; ①②③④⑤⑥ May 15 - Sept. 2 (also Aug. 13, Sept. 4, 9, 15, 16, 18, 23, 30, Oct. 14, 21, 28).
0900	→	1030	⑥⑦ Jan. 7 - May 19; ⑦ May 21 - Oct. 1; ⑥⑦ Oct. 7 - Dec. 31 (not Apr. 1, 15, Aug. 13, Oct. 14, 21, 28).
1100	→	1230	①②③④⑤⑥ May 20 - Sept. 4 (also Apr. 1, 15, Aug. 13, Sept. 9, 15, 16, 18, 23, 30, Oct. 14, 21, 28).
1645	→	1815	Daily Jan. 3 - Dec. 31 (not Dec. 25, 26).

Subject to alteration during Xmas/New Year period

ICELAND and the FAEROE ISLANDS 2285

Smyril Line
2017 service

	arrive	depart
January 1 - June 9 and August 26 - December 31 ▲		
Hirtshals	1000⑥	1500⑥
Tórshavn	0500①	1400①w
Seydisfjördur	0900②w	2000③w
Tórshavn	1500④w	2100④
June 10 - August 25 ▲		
Hirtshals	1230⑥	1530⑥
Tórshavn	2230⑦	2330⑦
Hirtshals	0930②	1130②
Tórshavn	1730③	1800③
Seydisfjördur	0830④	1030④
Tórshavn	0300⑤	0330⑤

w – Jan. - Mar. and Oct. - Dec. Tórshavn - Seydisfjördur and v.v.: times may be advanced, delayed or cancelled at short notice owing to adverse weather conditions. Contact operator for more details.

▲ – Variations:
Jan. 4 Hirtshals d. 0800; June 10 Hirtshals a. 1000; Aug. 26 Hirtshals a. 1230, d. 1630.

In poor weather conditions sailings may dock at Klaksvík or Kollafjördur (for Tórshavn), and Frederikshavn or Hanstholm (for Hirtshals).

SKAGERRAK, KATTEGAT & SOUTH WEST BALTIC

BØJDEN - FYNSHAV 2304

AlsFærgen Journey 50 minutes
2016 service

August 8 - 31
Depart Bøjden: 0700①②③④⑤⑥, 0900, 1000, 1100, 1200, 1300, 1400, 1500, 1600, 1700, 1900, 2100①④⑤⑥⑦.
Depart Fynshav: 0600①②③④⑤⑥, 0800, 1000, 1100, 1200, 1300, 1400, 1500, 1600, 1700, 1800, 2000①④⑤⑥⑦.

September 1 - 30
Depart Bøjden: 0700①②③④⑤⑥, 0900, 1100, 1300, 1500, 1700, 1900, 2100④⑤⑥⑦.
Depart Fynshav: 0600①②③④⑤⑥, 0800, 1000, 1200, 1400, 1600, 1800, 2000④⑤⑥⑦.

October 1 - December 17
Depart Bøjden: 0700①②③④⑤⑥, 0900, 1100, 1300, 1500, 1700, 1900, 2100⑥⑦ (also Oct. 14, 21, Dec. 16).
Depart Fynshav: 0600①②③④⑤⑥, 0800, 1000, 1200, 1400, 1600, 1800, 2000⑥⑦ (also Oct. 14, 21, Dec. 16).

December 18 - 24
Depart Bøjden: 0700①②③④⑤⑥, 0900, 1100, 1300, 1500, 1700①②③④⑤⑦, 1900①②③④⑤⑦, 2100①②③④⑤⑦.
Depart Fynshav: 0600①②③④⑤⑥, 0800, 1000, 1200, 1400, 1600, 1800①②③④⑤⑦, 2000①②③④⑤⑦.

December 25 - 31
Depart Bøjden: 0700②③④⑤⑥⑦, 0900, 1100, 1300, 1500, 1700①②③④⑤⑦, 1900①②③④⑤⑦, 2100①.
Depart Fynshav: 0600②③④⑤⑥⑦, 0800, 1000, 1200, 1400, 1600, 1800①②③④⑤⑦, 2000①.

Subject to alteration on and around holidays

EBELTOFT - SJÆLLANDS ODDE 2310

Mols-Linien by catamaran
2016 service
Journey 65 minutes

Ebeltoft - Sjællands Odde and v.v.: 6 - 13 sailings daily in summer; 2 - 9 in winter.
Subject to alteration during holiday periods

ESBJERG - FANØ 2312

FanøFærgen Journey 12 minutes
2016 service

Up to 3 departures hourly: 0530 - 0015 from Esbjerg, 0510 - 0030 from Fanø.
Subject to alteration on and around holidays

FREDERIKSHAVN - GÖTEBORG 2320

Stena Line Journey 2½ - 3½ hours
2016 service
(No service Dec. 25)

Sailings from Frederikshavn Trafikhavn and Göteborg.

From Frederikshavn and Göteborg: June 1 - 27: 3 - 4 sailings daily; June 28 - Aug. 14: 5 - 6 sailings daily; Aug. 15 - Dec. 31: 3 - 4 sailings daily. Departure times vary.

Subject to alteration on and around holidays

GEDSER - ROSTOCK 2330

Scandlines Journey 2 hours
2016 service

Sailings from Rostock International Port and Gedser.

Until May 1
Depart Gedser: 0130①②③④⑥, 0330⑤, 0340①, 0700, 0900, 1115, 1330, 1530, 1745, 2000, 2215.
Depart Rostock: 0030⑤, 0130①, 0430①⑥, 0600, 0900, 1115, 1330, 1530, 1745, 2000, 2215.

May 2 - December 18
Depart Gedser: 0230 A, 0330①, 0700, 0900, 1100, 1300, 1500, 1700, 1900, 2100, 2345 H.
Depart Rostock: 0130①, 0400 J, 0600, 0900, 1100, 1300, 1500, 1700, 1900, 2100, 2345 H.

G – ②③④⑤⑥ (also ⑦ June 26 - Aug. 14).
H – ①②③④⑤ (also ⑥ June 25 - Aug. 13).
J – ①②③④⑤⑥ (also ⑦ June 26 - Aug. 14).

Subject to alteration on and around holidays

🚍 services connect with most sailings:
Nykøbing (Falster) railway station - Gedser Færge and v.v. (route 740, journey time 40 minutes); Rostock Fähre - Rostock Hbf Süd (route 40, journey time 40 minutes).

GÖTEBORG - KIEL 2335

Stena Line
2016 service
(No service Dec. 24, 25)

Sailings from Kiel Schwedenkai and Göteborg.

Göteborg	Kiel		Kiel	Göteborg	
1845	→	0915	1845	→	0915

Subject to alteration during Easter and Xmas/New Year periods

2342 GRENAA - VARBERG

Stena Line Journey 4 - 5½ hours   2016 service

Grenaa		Varberg		Varberg		Grenaa	
			May 7 - June 26				
0100	→	0615	①②③④⑤⑥	0700	→	1125	②③④⑤
1420	→	1845		0850	→	1315	①⑥⑦
				1945	→	0005	①②③④⑤⑦
			June 27 - August 14				
0100	→	0615	June 27 only.	0805	→	1245	
1315	→	1740	Not June 27.	1835	→	2255	
2350	→	0415					
			August 15 - December 22				
0100	→	0615	See note G.	0700	→	1125	②③④⑤
1420	→	1845	①②③④⑤⑦	0850	→	1315	①
				1945	→	0005	①②③④⑤⑦

G – ①②③④⑤ (not Aug. 15).

Grenaa port is located approximately 3 km from railway station (currently closed for conversion as part of the Aarhus Light Rail scheme).

2345 HELSINGØR - HELSINGBORG

Scandlines Journey 20 minutes   2016 service

From Helsingør and Helsingborg: sailings every 15 minutes (every 30 minutes at night).

Subject to alteration on and around holidays

2350 HIRTSHALS - KRISTIANSAND

Color Line   by ship   2016 service
                    (No service Dec. 24)

Hirtshals		Kristiansand		Kristiansand		Hirtshals	
			February 1 - March 28 and April 7 - December 23				
1215	→	1530	See note M.	0800	→	1115	See note M.
2045	→	2400		1630	→	1945	
			March 29 - April 6				
2130	→	0045	Not Apr. 6.	0800	→	1115	Not Mar 29.

M – Not Apr. 18, May 2, 23, June 6, 20, Aug. 15, 29, Sept. 12, 26, Oct. 10, 24, Nov. 7, 21, Dec. 5, 19.

Fjord Line   by catamaran   2017 service
                    (No winter service)

Hirtshals		Kristiansand		Kristiansand		Hirtshals	
			April 7 - June 15 and August 21 - September 4				
1145	→	1400	See note P.	0830	→	1045	
1800	→	2015		1500	→	1715	See note P.
			June 16 - August 20				
1000	→	1215		0645	→	0900	
1700	→	1915		1330	→	1545	
2330	→	0145	See note Q.	2015	→	2230	See note Q.

P – Not Apr. 13, 18 - 20, 25, 26, May 2 - 4, 9, 10, 16, 17, 23, 30, June 13, 14, Aug. 22, 23, 29, 30.

Q – Not June 20, 21, 27, 28, July 4, 5, 11, 12, 18, 19, Aug. 1, 2, 8, 9, 15, 16.

2355 KALUNDBORG - SAMSØ

SamsøFærgen   Service to January 2, 2017
Journey 75 – 90 minutes

July 26 - August 14
Depart Kalundborg: 0845, 1215⑥⑦, 1545, 1915.
Depart Ballen (Samsø): 0700, 1030⑥⑦, 1400, 1730.

August 15 - 28
Depart Kalundborg: 0845, 1215⑥⑦, 1545①②③④⑤⑦ (also June 25), 1915.
Depart Ballen (Samsø): 0700, 1030⑥⑦, 1400①②③④⑤⑦ (also June 25), 1730.

August 29 - October 30
Depart Kalundborg: 0845, 1215⑥⑦B, 1545⑤⑦, 1745①②③④, 1915⑤⑥⑦.
Depart Ballen (Samsø): 0700, 1030⑥⑦B, 1400⑤⑦, 1600①②③④, 1730⑤⑥⑦.

October 31 - December 19
Depart Kalundborg: 0845, 1545⑤⑦, 1745①②③④⑥, 1915⑤⑦.
Depart Ballen (Samsø): 0700, 1400⑤⑦, 1600①②③④⑥, 1730⑤⑦.

December 20 - 26
Depart Kalundborg: 0845①②③④⑤⑥, 1215①⑥⑦, 1545⑤⑦, 1745②③④, 1915①⑤.
Depart Ballen (Samsø): 0700①②③④⑤⑥, 1030①⑥⑦, 1400⑤⑦, 1600②③④, 1730①⑤.

December 27 - January 2
Depart Kalundborg: 0845①②③④⑤⑥, 1215⑥, 1545⑤⑦, 1745①②③④, 1915⑤⑦.
Depart Ballen (Samsø): 0700①②③④⑤⑥, 1030⑥, 1400⑤⑦, 1600①②③④, 1730⑤⑦.

B – Not Oct. 2, 9, 16, 30.

Subject to alteration during holiday periods

2360 KØBENHAVN - OSLO

DFDS Seaways   2016 service
Sailings from København Dampfærgevej and Oslo Vippetangen (Utstikker 2).

København		Oslo		Oslo		København	
1630	→	0945	Not Dec. 24.	1630	→	0945	Not Dec. 24.

🚌 connections:
Movia route 20E operates DFDS terminal - Østerport (Folke Bernadottes Allé) - København (Det Kongelige Teater, Kongens Nytorv) and v.v.
Departs at regular intervals 1000 - 1040 ①–⑥, 1000 - 1025 ⑦ from DFDS terminal; 1345 - 1545 ①–⑥, 1415 - 1545 ⑦ from København. Free to DFDS passengers.

2366 LARVIK - HIRTSHALS

Color Line   2016 service
                    (No service Dec. 24)

Larvik		Hirtshals		Hirtshals		Larvik	
			August 15 - December 23				
0800	→	1145	②③④⑤⑥⑦	1245	→	1630	②③④⑤⑥⑦
1730	→	2115		2215	→	0200	
			December 25 - 31				
0800	→	1145	Dec. 26 - 31.	1245	→	1630	Dec. 26 - 31.
1730	→	2115	Dec. 25, 26.	2215	→	0200	Dec. 25, 26.

2368 OSLO - FREDERIKSHAVN

Stena Line   2016 service
Sailings from Oslo Vippetangen and Frederikshavn.   (No service Dec. 24, 25)

Oslo		Frederikshavn		Frederikshavn		Oslo	
1930§	→	0730	See note F.	0915‡	→	1845	See note G.
				1830	→	0730	See note H.

F – ②③④⑤⑥⑦ until June 26; daily June 27 - Aug. 21; ②③④⑤⑥⑦ Aug. 22 - Dec. 31 (also Oct. 3).

G – ③④⑤⑥⑦ until June 26; daily June 27 - Aug. 31; ③④⑤⑥⑦ Aug. 22 - Dec. 31 (also Oct. 3, 4; not June 4, 5).

H – ① until June 20 and from Aug. 22 (also June 4; not Oct. 3).

§ – Depart 1830 on Dec. 31.   ‡ – Depart 0830 on Dec. 31.

Subject to alteration on and around holidays

2372 OSLO - KIEL

Color Line   2016 service
                    (No service Dec. 24, 31)

Sailings from Oslo Color Line Terminalen, Hjortnes and Kiel Oslo-Kai.

Oslo		Kiel		Kiel		Oslo	
1400	→	1000		1400	→	1000	

🚌 Oslo Color Line Terminal - Oslo Sentral rail station.
Kiel Oslo-Kai - Hamburg ZOB (Central Bus Station).

2375 PUTTGARDEN - RØDBY

Scandlines Journey 45 minutes   2016 service

Departures every 30 minutes (at 15 and 45 minutes past each hour). Sailing times between 2215 and 0415 may vary.

Subject to alteration on and around holidays

2380 ROSTOCK - TRELLEBORG

Stena Line Journey 6 - 7½ hours   2016 service
Sailings from Rostock Überseehafen and Trelleborg.   (No service Dec. 24, 25, 31)
From Rostock and Trelleborg: June 1 - 19: 5 sailings daily; June 20 - Sept. 4: 5 - 6 sailings daily; Sept. 5 - Dec. 22: 2 - 3 sailings daily; Dec. 23 - 30: 1 sailing per day. Journey times vary.

Subject to alteration on and around holidays

TT Line Journey 5½ - 6½ hours   2016 service
Sailings from Rostock Überseehafen and Trelleborg.
Up to 6 sailings per day.

Subject to alteration during holiday periods

2384 SASSNITZ-MUKRAN - RØNNE

BornholmerFærgen   2017 service
                    (No winter service)

Sassnitz		Rønne		Rønne		Sassnitz	
			April 1 - 20				
1150	→	1510	See note N.	0800	→	1120	See note N.
			April 21 - June 12				
1150	→	1510	See note P.	0800	→	1120	See note P.
1400	→	1800	See note Q.	0900	→	1245	See note Q.
			June 13 - 21				
1150	→	1510	①④⑥	0730	→	1100	⑦
1200	→	1530	⑦	0800	→	1120	①④⑥
1400	→	1800	⑥	0900	→	1245	⑥
			June 22 - September 3				
1150	→	1510	See note R.	0800	→	1120	See note R.
1400	→	1800	⑥⑦ (also Aug. 4, 11).	0900	→	1245	⑥⑦ (also Aug. 4, 11
			September 4 - October 8				
1150	→	1510	See note S.	0800	→	1120	See note S.
1400	→	1800	See note T.	0900	→	1245	See note T.
			October 9 - November 4				
1150	→	1510	See note V.	0800	→	1120	See note V.
1400	→	1800	⑥ (not Nov. 4).	0900	→	1245	⑥ (not Nov. 4).

N – ④⑥ (also Apr. 9, 17; not Apr. 6).
P – ④ (also Apr. 23, May 7, 14, June 5).
Q – ⑥⑦ (also May 25; not Apr. 23, May 7, 14).
R – Not June 25, 26, July 2, 9, Sept. 3.
S – ④⑥⑦ (not Sept. 10, 16, 17, 23).
T – ⑥ (also Sept. 10, 17; not Sept. 30, Oct. 7).
V – ④⑦ (also Nov. 4; not Oct. 29, Oct. 2).

For international shipping maps – see pages 538 - 540

SASSNITZ-MUKRAN - TRELLEBORG 2385

Stena Line Journey 4 hours Service to December 31, 2016
Sailings from Fährhafen Sassnitz-Mukran and Trelleborg. (No service Dec. 24)

May 9 - June 12 and August 29 - December 15
From Sassnitz: 1345②, 1530①⑦, 1700③④⑤⑥.
From Trelleborg: 0800①②③⑤⑥, 0945⑦, 1130④.

June 13 - August 28 and December 16 - 19
From Sassnitz: 1300, 2300.
From Trelleborg: 0745, 1800.

December 20 - 31
From Sassnitz: 1300 (Dec. 23), 1345 (Dec. 20, 27), 1530 (Dec. 25, 26),
 1715 (Dec. 21, 22, 28 - 30).
From Trelleborg: 0745 (Dec. 23), 0800 (Dec. 20, 21, 26 - 28, 30), 0945 (Dec. 31),
 1130 (Dec. 22, 29), 1800 (Dec. 23).

Subject to alteration on and around holidays

STRÖMSTAD - SANDEFJORD 2387

Color Line Journey 2½ hours 2016 service
Sailings from Strømstad and Sandefjord: frequent daily departures.

Fjord Line Journey 2½ hours Service to December 31, 2017
 (No service Dec. 24 - Jan. 26)

Strømstad	Sandefjord		Sandefjord	Strømstad	
1200	→	1430	0830	→	1100	Not Dec. 23.
1830	→	2100	Not Dec. 23.	1520	→	1750	Not Dec. 23.

TRAVEMÜNDE - TRELLEBORG 2390

TT Line 2016 service
Sailings from Travemünde Skandinavienkai and Trelleborg.
Up to 8 sailings per day.

Subject to alteration during holiday periods

🚍 connection available Trelleborg - Malmö railway station and v.v. for certain sailings.

TRAVEMÜNDE - MALMÖ 2395

Finnlines 2016 service (until further notice)

Travemünde		Malmö		Malmö		Travemünde	
0100	→	1015	⑦	1000	→	1900	③④⑤⑥
0230	→	1115	②③④⑤	1330	→	2315	⑥
0300	→	1145	①⑥	1600	→	0045	①②③④⑤
1000	→	1900	②③④⑤	1600	→	0100	⑦
1100	→	2000	⑥	2200	→	0700	①②③④⑤⑦
2200	→	0700	Daily.	2300	→	0830	⑥

Subject to alteration during Xmas / New Year period

GDAŃSK - NYNÄSHAMN 2402

Polferries Service to January 31, 2017

Gdańsk		Nynäshamn		Nynäshamn		Gdańsk	
1800	→	1200	See note A.	1800	→	1200	See note B.

A – Feb. 16, 18, 20, 23, 25, 27, Mar. 1, 3, 5, 8, 10, 12, 15, 17, 19, 22, 24, 29, 31, Apr. 2, 5, 7,
 9, 12, 14, 16, 19, 21, 23, 26, 28, 30, May 3, 5, 7, 10, 12, 14, 17, 19, 21, 24, 26, 28, 31,
 June 2, 4, 7, 9, 11, 14, 16, 18, 21, 23, 25, 27, 29, July 1, 3, 5, 7, 9, 11, 13, 15, 17, 19,
 21, 23, 25, 27, 29, 31, Aug. 2, 4, 6, 8, 10, 12, 14, 16, 18, 20, 22, 24, 26, 28, 30, Sept. 1, 3,
 6, 8, 10, 13, 15, 17, 20, 22, 24, 27, 29, Oct. 1, 4, 6, 8, 11, 13, 15, 18, 20, 22, 25, 27, 29,
 Nov. 1, 3, 5, 8, 10, 12, 15, 17, 19, 22, 24, 26, 29, Dec. 1, 3, 6, 8, 10, 13, 15, 17, 19, 21, 27,
 Jan. 2, 4, 6, 8, 10, 12, 14, 17, 19, 21, 24, 26, 28, 31.
B – Feb. 1, 17, 19, 22, 24, 26, 29, Mar. 2, 4, 7, 9, 11, 14, 16, 18, 21, 23, 25, 30, Apr. 1, 4, 6,
 8, 11, 13, 15, 18, 20, 22, 25, 27, 29, May 2, 4, 6, 9, 11, 13, 16, 18, 20, 23, 25, 27, 30,
 June 1, 3, 6, 8, 10, 13, 15, 17, 20, 22, 24, 27, 29, July 2, 4, 6, 8, 10, 12, 14, 16, 18, 20,
 22, 24, 26, 28, 30, Aug. 1, 3, 5, 7, 9, 11, 13, 15, 17, 19, 21, 23, 25, 27, 29, 31, Sept. 2, 5,
 7, 9, 12, 14, 16, 19, 21, 23, 26, 28, 30, Oct. 3, 5, 7, 10, 12, 14, 17, 19, 21, 24, 26, 28, 31,
 Nov. 2, 4, 7, 9, 11, 13, 16, 18, 21, 23, 25, 28, Dec. 2, 5, 7, 9, 12, 14, 16, 18, 20, 22, 29,
 Jan. 3, 5, 7, 9, 11, 13, 16, 18, 20, 23, 25, 27, 30.

Suburban rail service operates every 30 minutes (60 minutes on Ⓒ) Nynäshamn -
Stockholm and v.v.: Nynäshamn depart xx19Ⓐ, xx49; Stockholm depart xx04, xx34Ⓐ.

GRISSLEHAMN - ECKERÖ 2405

Eckerö Linjen Service to June 15, 2017
 (No service Dec. 24, 25)

Grisslehamn		Eckerö		Eckerö		Grisslehamn	
1000	→	1300		0830	→	0915	①⑤⑥⑦
1500	→	1800		1330	→	1430	
2000	→	2245	④⑤⑥⑦	1830	→	1930	

NAANTALI - KAPELLSKÄR 2407

Finnlines 2016 service
Conveys passengers with vehicles only (No service Dec. 24, 25)

Naantali		Kapellskär		Kapellskär		Naantali	
0930	→	1700	May 23 - Sept. 30.	0100	→	1040	See note K.
1100	→	1815	From Oct. 1.	0915	→	1900	
1615	→	2315	See note L.	2145	→	0715	
2245	→	0615					

K – ②③④⑤⑥ May 24 - Aug. 31.
L – ①②③④⑤ May 23 - Sept. 4.

Subject to alteration on and around holidays

HELSINKI - TALLINN 2410

Eckerö Line by ship 2016 service
 (No service Dec. 24, 25)
Sailings from Helsinki Länsiterminaali and Tallinn A-terminal.

Helsinki		Tallinn		Tallinn		Helsinki	
0830	→	1100		0145	→	0645	③④ from Feb. 17.
1530	→	1745		1200	→	1430	
2215	→	0045	②③ from Feb. 16.	1845	→	2115	

Connection: Tram route 9 Helsinki railway sation - Länsiterminaali

Linda Line Oy by hydrofoil 2016 service
Linda Line Express Journey 1 hour 40 minutes
Sailings from Helsinki Makasiiniterminaali and Tallinn Linnahalli.

August 15 - October 16
Depart Helsinki: 0800①②③④⑤⑥, 1000, 1200①②③⑥⑦, 1600, 1800, 2000④⑤⑦.
Depart Tallinn: 0800①②③④⑤⑥, 1000, 1200①②③⑥⑦, 1600, 1800, 2000④⑤⑦.

October 17 - December 22
Depart Helsinki: 0800①, 1000①②③④⑤⑥, 1200⑦, 1400④⑤, 1600⑤⑥⑦, 1800,
 2000⑦.
Depart Tallinn: 0800①②③④⑤, 1000⑤⑥⑦, 1200④, 1400⑤, 1600, 1800⑤⑥⑦, 2000⑦.

Tallink Silja by ship 2016 service
Sailings from Helsinki Länsiterminaali and Tallinn D-terminal.
Journey 2 hours (§ – 3½ hours, ‡ – 4 hours, ¶ – 4½ hours)

June 1 - December 18
Depart Helsinki: 0730, 1030, 1330, 1630, 1830§, 1930①②③④⑤⑦, 2030⑥,
 2230①②③④⑤⑦.
Depart Tallinn: 0730, 1030, 1230§, 1330, 1630, 1930①②③④⑤⑦, 2030⑥,
 2230①②③④⑤⑦.

December 19 - 31
Depart Helsinki: 0730①②③④⑤, 1030, 1330①②③④⑤, 1400⑥⑦, 1630①②③④⑤,
 1730⑥⑦, 1830§, 1930①②③④⑤, 2230①②③④⑤.
Depart Tallinn: 0730①②③④⑤, 1030, 1230§, 1330①②③④⑤, 1400⑥⑦,
 1630①②③④⑤, 1730⑥⑦, 1930①②③④⑤, 2230①②③④⑤.

Subject to alteration during Xmas / New Year period
Connection: Tram route 9 Helsinki railway sation - Länsiterminaali

Viking Line by ship Journey 2½ hours 2016 service
Sailings from Helsinki Katajanokka terminal and Tallinn A-terminal. (No service Dec. 24, 25)

Until June 17 and from August 15
Depart Helsinki: 1130, 2000⑦, 2130①②③④⑤⑥.
Depart Tallinn: 0800, 1630⑦, 1800①②③④⑤⑥.

June 18 - August 14
Depart Helsinki: 1030⑦, 1130, 2000⑦, 2130①②③④⑤⑥.
Depart Tallinn: 0800, 1400⑦, 1630⑦, 1800①②③④⑤⑥.

KARLSKRONA - GDYNIA 2415

Stena Line 2016 service (No service Dec. 24, 25)

Karlskrona		Gdynia		Gdynia		Karlskrona	
0830	→	1900	①	0800	→	1830	⑤
0900	→	1930	②③⑥⑦	0900	→	1930	②③④⑥⑦
1000	→	2030	④	1800	→	0530	③⑦
1800	→	0700	②④	1900	→	0630	①
1900	→	0800	⑤	1930	→	0730	⑤
1930	→	0745	①	2100	→	0900	②③⑥⑦
2030	→	0830	⑥	2130	→	0930	④
2100	→	0900	②③④⑦	2200	→	1000	①
2159	→	0930					

Subject to alteration on and around holidays

2418 KARLSHAMN - KLAIPEDA

DFDS Seaways   2016 service

Sailings from Karlshamn Ferry Terminal and Klaipeda International Ferry Port.

Karlshamn		Klaipeda	Klaipeda		Karlsham
1900	→	0900	1900	→	0900

2420 KIEL - KLAIPEDA

DFDS Seaways   2016 service

Sailings from Kiel Ostuferhafen and Klaipeda International Ferry Port.

Kiel		Klaipeda	Klaipeda		Kiel
Until April 3					
1400①	→	1230②	1500①	→	1230②
1600②	→	1400③	1730②	→	1400③
1800③	→	1630④	1900③	→	1600④
2000④	→	1800⑤	2100④	→	1800⑤
2200⑤	→	2000⑥	2300⑤	→	1900⑥
2300⑥	→	2200⑦	0100⑦	→	2200⑦
From April 4					
2000	→	1630	2100	→	1600

Departure times may vary owing to tidal conditions.
Subject to alteration during Xmas/New Year period

2430 KØGE - RØNNE

BornholmerFærgen   2016 service

Køge	Rønne		Rønne	Køge
0030	→ 0600		1700	→ 2230

2445 NYNÄSHAMN - VISBY

Destination Gotland   2016 service

Nynäshamn	Visby		Visby	Nynäshamn	
October 3 - 20					
1125	→ 1455	①	0730	→ 1045	①
1200	→ 1530	⑦	0805	→ 1120	⑦
1215	→ 1530	②③④⑤	0830	→ 1145	②③④⑤⑥
1220	→ 1535	⑥	1600	→ 1915	⑥⑦
2005	→ 2320	⑥⑦	1630	→ 1950	①②③④⑤
2100	→ 0020	①②③④⑤			
October 21 - November 6					
1125	→ 1455	Not Oct. 23.	0730	→ 1045	Not Oct. 23.
1200	→ 1515	Oct. 23 only.	0805	→ 1120	Oct. 23 only.
1250	→ 1605	⑦ (not Oct. 23).	0855	→ 1210	⑦ (not Oct. 23).
2005	→ 2320	⑤⑥ (not Oct. 27-29).	1600	→ 1915	See note S.
2100	→ 0020	See note Q.	1630	→ 1950	See note Q.
2105	→ 0020	See note R.	1645	→ 2000	See note T.
November 7 - December 31					
1125	→ 1455	See note V.	0730	→ 1045	See note Z.
1200	→ 1515	See note W.	0805	→ 1120	See note W.
2005	→ 2320	See note X.	1600	→ 1915	⑤⑦ (also Dec. 26).
2100	→ 0020	See note Y.	1630	→ 1950	See note Y.

Q – ①②③④ (not Oct. 27,28).
R – ⑦ (also Oct. 27,28; not Oct. 29).
S – ⑤⑥ (also Oct. 23; not Oct. 27-29).
T – ⑦ (also Oct. 27,28; not Oct. 23).
V – ①②③④⑤ (also Dec. 10,31; not Dec. 26).
W – ⑦ (also Dec. 26; not Dec. 25).
X – ⑤⑥⑦ (also Dec. 26; not Dec. 10,24,25,31).
Y – ①②③④ (not Dec. 26).
Z – ①②③④⑤⑥ (not Dec. 24-26).

Additional services operate at peak times;
subject to alteration during Easter and Xmas/New Year periods

Suburban rail service operates every 30 minutes (60 minutes on ⓒ) Nynäshamn - Stockholm and v.v.: Nynäshamn depart xx19Ⓐ, xx49; Stockholm depart xx04, xx34Ⓐ.

2448 NYNÄSHAMN - VENTSPILS

Stena Line   2016 service
                                                    (No service Dec. 24, 25)

Nynäshamn	Ventspils	Ventspils	Nynäshamn
0800⑦	→ 1900⑦	0001②	→ 1000②
0900①③	→ 2000①③	1000③	→ 1900③
1900②④	→ 0700③⑤	1800⑥	→ 0600⑦
2200③⑤	→ 1000④⑥	2100④	→ 0900⑤
		2200⑦	→ 0800①
		2300③⑦	→ 0900④①

Subject to alteration on and around holidays

Suburban rail service operates every 30 minutes (60 minutes on ⓒ) Nynäshamn - Stockholm and v.v.: Nynäshamn depart xx19Ⓐ, xx49; Stockholm depart xx04, xx34Ⓐ.

2450 OSKARSHAMN - VISBY

Destination Gotland   2016 service

Oskarshamn	Visby			Visby	Oskarshamn	
October 3 - 20						
0400	→ 0650	① (not Oct. 3).		0010	→ 0300	① (not Oct. 3).
0500	→ 0750	②③④⑤		0110	→ 0400	②③④⑤
1100	→ 1400	⑥		0715	→ 1015	⑥
1730	→ 2025	⑤		1400	→ 1655	⑤
2010	→ 2305	⑦		1620	→ 1915	⑦
2110	→ 0005	②④		1705	→ 2000	②④
October 21 - November 6						
1100	→ 1400	② (also Oct. 29).		0715	→ 1015	②⑥
2010	→ 2305	See note W.		1620	→ 1915	⑤ (not Oct. 28).
2110	→ 0005	See note V.		1640	→ 1935	Oct. 23 only.
				1700	→ 1955	②
				1705	→ 2000	See note X.
November 7 - December 31						
2010	→ 2305	⑤⑦ (also Dec. 26).		1620	→ 1915	⑤⑥ (also Dec. 26).
2110	→ 0005	See note Y.		1700	→ 2000	See note Y.

V – ①②③④⑦ (also Oct. 28; not Oct. 23).
W – ⑤⑥ (also Oct. 23; not Oct. 28,29).
X – ①③④⑦ (also Oct. 28; not Oct. 23).
Y – ①②③④ (not Dec. 26).

Additional services operate at peak times;
subject to alteration during Easter and Xmas/New Year periods

2464 STOCKHOLM - RIGA

Tallink Silja   2016 service

Sailings from Stockholm Frihamnsterminalen and Riga passenger port.

Stockholm	Riga	
1700	→ 1100	Even dates Feb., Apr., May, Aug., Nov., Dec.; uneven dates Jan., Mar., June, July, Sept., Oct.

Riga	Stockholm	
1730	→ 1030	Even dates Jan., Mar., June, July, Sept., Oct.; uneven dates Feb., Apr., May, Aug., Nov., Dec.

2465 STOCKHOLM - MARIEHAMN - HELSINKI

Tallink Silja   Service to May 21, 2017
                                                    (No service Dec. 24)

Sailings from Stockholm Värtahamnen and Helsinki Olympiaterminaali.

Stockholm	Mariehamn	Helsinki	Helsinki	Mariehamn	Stockholm
March 31 - November 8 and March 30 - May 21					
1645	→ 2355	→ 0955	1700	→ 0405	→ 0930
November 9 - March 29					
1645	→ 2355	→ 1030	1700	→ 0405	→ 0945

🚌 Stockholm Värtahamnen - Ropsten metro station (for Stockholm Centralen).

Viking Line   2016 service
                                                    (No service Dec. 24, 25)

Sailings from Stockholm Stadsgården and Helsinki Katajanokka.

Stockholm	Mariehamn	Helsinki	Helsinki	Mariehamn	Stockholm
Until June 16 and August 16 - December 31					
1630	→ 2345	→ 1010	1730	→ 0430	→ 1000
June 17 - August 15					
1600	→ 2255	→ 0915	1800	→ 0430	→ 0950

Connections:
🚌 Stockholm Cityterminalen (near Central station) - Slussen metro station - Viking Line terminal. Tram no. 4T runs daily from Helsinki city centre to the Viking Line Terminal.

2470 (STOCKHOLM -) KAPELLSKÄR - MARIEHAMN

Viking Line   2016 service
Sailings from Kapellskär and Mariehamn.   (No service Dec. 24, 25, Jan. 7 - 28)

Stockholm	Kapellskär	Mariehamn		Mariehamn	Kapellskär	Stockholm	
(by 🚌)						*(by 🚌)*	
January 29 - April 1 and October 2 - December 31							
1000♦	→ 1200	→ 1530	①②③④	0730	→ 0900	→ 1035♦	①②③④⑤⑥
1230♦	→ 1445	→ 1800	⑤⑥⑦	1245	→ 1400	→ 1540♦	⑦
1700♦	→ 1900	→ 2230	①②③④	1600	→ 1730	→ 1915♦	①②③④
1800♦	→ 2000	→ 2320	⑤⑥⑦	1830	→ 1945	→ 2115♦	⑤⑥⑦
April 2 - 28							
0700♦	→ 0900	→ 1215	⑥	0730	→ 0845	→ 1025♦	⑥
1000♦	→ 1200	→ 1530	①②③④	0900	→ 0900	→ 1035♦	①②③④⑤
1230♦	→ 1445	→ 1800	⑤⑥⑦	1245	→ 1400	→ 1540♦	⑥⑦
1700♦	→ 1900	→ 2230	①②③④	1600	→ 1730	→ 1915♦	①②③④
1800♦	→ 2000	→ 2320	⑤⑥⑦	1830	→ 1945	→ 2115♦	⑤⑥⑦
April 29 - June 12 and August 19 - October 1							
0700♦	→ 0900	→ 1215	⑤⑥	0730	→ 0845	→ 1025♦	⑤⑥
1000♦	→ 1200	→ 1530	①②③④	0900	→ 0900	→ 1035♦	①②③④
1230♦	→ 1445	→ 1800	⑤⑥⑦	1245	→ 1400	→ 1540♦	⑤⑥⑦
1700♦	→ 1900	→ 2230	①②③④	1600	→ 1730	→ 1915♦	①②③④
1800♦	→ 2000	→ 2320	⑤⑥⑦	1830	→ 1945	→ 2115♦	⑤⑥⑦
June 13 - August 18							
0700♦	→ 0900	→ 1215		0730	→ 0845	→ 1025♦	
1230♦	→ 1445	→ 1800		1245	→ 1400	→ 1540♦	
1800♦	→ 2000	→ 2320		1830	→ 1945	→ 2125♦	

♦ – Connecting 🚌 service from/to Stockholm Cityterminalen (near Central station).

STOCKHOLM - TALLINN via Mariehamn — 2475

Tallink Silja Service to March 29, 2017
Sailings from Stockholm Värtahamnen and Tallinn D-terminal.

Stockholm	Mariehamn	Tallinn	Tallinn	Mariehamn	Stockholm
1730 →	0100 →	1045	1800 →	0500 →	1015

STOCKHOLM - TURKU via Mariehamn / Långnäs — 2480

Tallink Silja Service to December 31, 2017
Sailings from Stockholm Värtahamnen and Turku.

Stockholm	Mariehamn	Långnäs§	Turku
0710 →	1345 →	→	1915
1930 →	→	0255 →	0700
Turku	Långnäs§	Mariehamn	Stockholm
0815 →	→	1345	1815
2015 →	0045 →	→	0610

§ – Långnäs is 28km from Mariehamn.
Nearest metro station to Stockholm Värtahamnen is Gärdet (for Stockholm Centralen).

Subject to alteration during Xmas / New Year period

Viking Line 2016 service
Sailings from Stockholm Stadsgården and Turku Linnansatama. (No service Dec. 24, 25)

Stockholm	Mariehamn	Långnäs§	Turku
0745 →	1425 →	→	1950
2000 →	→	0320 →	0735
Turku	Långnäs§	Mariehamn	Stockholm
0845 →	→	1425 →	1855
2055 →	0110 →	→	0630

§ – Långnäs is 28km from Mariehamn.

🚌 connections: Stockholm Cityterminalen (near Central station) - Slussen metro station - Viking Line terminal; Turku city centre - harbour (bus no. 1).

ST PETERBURG - HELSINKI - STOCKHOLM - TALLINN — 2482

St Peter Line 2016 service

St Peterburg	Helsinki	Stockholm	Tallinn	St Peterburg
♣ 1900 A →	0800 B / 1600 B →	0800 C / 1800 C →	1130 D / 1900 D →	0930 E

♣ – Sailings from St Peterburg: contact operator for sailing dates and exact times as all timings may vary.

A – 1st day; B – 2nd day; C – 3rd day; D – 4th day; E – 5th day.

Subject to alteration during Easter and Xmas / New Year periods

TRAVEMÜNDE - HELSINKI — 2485

Finnlines 2016 service
Sailings from Travemünde Skandinavienkai and Helsinki Vuosaaren satama.

Travemünde	Helsinki	Helsinki	Travemünde
0300 ②–⑤ →	0900 ③–⑥	1700 ①–⑥ →	2130 ②–⑦
0300⑦ →	0900①		
0330⑥ →	0930⑦		

Subject to alteration on and around German and Finnish holidays

TRAVEMÜNDE - LIEPAJA — 2486

Stena Line 2016 service

Travemünde	Liepaja	Liepaja	Travemünde
2100③⑦ →	0030⑤②	0400② →	0730③
		1600⑥ →	1800⑦

Subject to alteration on and around holidays

TRAVEMÜNDE - VENTSPILS — 2487

Stena Line 2016 service

Travemünde	Ventspils	Ventspils	Travemünde
1730⑥ →	1930⑦	1000⑤ →	1330⑥

Subject to alteration on and around holidays

VAASA - UMEÅ (HOLMSUND) — 2490

Wasaline 2016 service
(No service Dec. 24, 25)

Vaasa	Umeå		Umeå	Vaasa	
February 1 - June 10 and August 15 - December 22					
0800 →	1130	⑦	0800 →	1330	③
0900 →	1230	④⑤⑥	0900 →	1430	①②
1430 →	1800	③	1300 →	1830	⑦
2000 →	2330	①②⑦	1800 →	2330	④⑤⑥
			1900 →	0030	③
June 11 - August 14					
0800 →	1100	⑥	0800 →	1330	③
0830 →	1200	⑦	0900 →	1430	①②
0900 →	1230	④⑤	1145 →	1645	⑥
1430 →	1800	③	1330 →	1900	⑦
1730 →	2030	⑥	1800 →	2330	④⑤
2000 →	2330	①②	1900 →	0030	③
2030 →	2400	⑦	2100 →	0200	⑥

YSTAD - RØNNE — 2494

BornholmerFærgen by fast ferry 2017 service
3 - 8 sailings daily (less frequent in winter), departure times vary, journey 80 minutes.
See Table **727** for rail connections Ystad - København and v.v.

(KØBENHAVN -) YSTAD - ŚWINOUJŚCIE — 2495

Polferries 2016 service

København	Ystad	Świnoujście		
▲ →	1400 →	2000	Daily (not Dec. 10, 24 - 26, 31, Jan. 1).
▲ →	2130 →	0530	①②③④⑤ Mar. 25 - June 17; ①②③④⑤⑦ June 18 - Aug. 26; ①②③④⑤ Aug. 27 - Dec. 9; daily Dec. 12 - 23 (not May 2 - 6).
Świnoujście	**Ystad**	**København**		
1230 →	1900 →	▲	②③④⑤ Mar. 25 - June 17; ①②③④⑤⑦ June 18 - Aug. 26; ②③④⑤ Aug. 27 - Dec. 9; daily Dec. 10 - 23 (not May 3 - 6, Dec. 10).
1500 →	2200 →	▲	⑦ Mar. 25 - June 17, Aug. 27 - Dec. 9 (not May 1).
2230 →	0615 →	▲	Daily (not Dec. 23 - 26, 30, 31).

▲ – 🚆 operates København railway station - Polferries Terminal and v.v. Times vary - contact operator.

Unity Line 2016 service
(No service Dec. 24, 25, 31)

Ystad	Świnoujście		Świnoujście	Ystad
1330 →	2000		1300 →	2015
2230 →	0645		2230 →	0630

A connecting 🚆 service operates Świnoujście terminal - Szczecin Hotel Radisson SAS and v.v.: Świnoujście depart 0730, Szczecin arrive 0900. Return journey Szczecin depart 1000, Świnoujście arrive 1130.

WESTERN MEDITERRANEAN

ALGECIRAS - CEUTA — 2500

Baleària (Eurolínies Marítimes) 2016 service
Journey 1¼ - 1½ hours
Depart Algeciras: 0600, 0800, 0930, 1230, 1400, 1600, 1800, 1900, 2000, 2200, 2330.
Depart Ceuta: 0600, 0730, 1030, 1115, 1415, 1600, 1715, 2000, 2015, 2330.

Trasmediterranea by fast ferry 2016 service
Subject to alteration at Easter and Christmas. Journey 55 minutes
Depart Algeciras and Ceuta: 3 – 5 sailings daily, departure times vary.

ALGECIRAS - TANJAH (TANGIERS) MED — 2502

Trasmediterranea Journey 1½ hours 2016 service
From Algeciras and Tanjah Med: 4 – 6 sailings daily, departure times vary.
Tanjah (Tangiers) Med port is located approximately 45km east of Tanjah.
A connecting 🚌 operates between Tanjah Med and Tanjah.

ALMERÍA - GHAZAOUET — 2504

Trasmediterranea Service to November 30, 2016

Almería	Ghazaouet	
2359 →	0800	②⑤ Feb. 2 - June 28; ③⑤⑥ July 1-22; daily July 25, 27, 28, 30, Aug. 2, 3, 10, 11, 15, 17, 18, 20, 24, 26, 29, 31, Sept. 2, 5, 6, 9, 13, 16, 21, 23, 28, 30, Oct. 5, 7, 12, 14, 19, 21, 26, 28; ② Nov. 1 - 29.
Ghazaouet	**Almería**	
1400 →	2200	③⑥ Feb. 3 - June 29; ④⑥⑦ July 2 - 23; daily July 26, 28, 29, 31, Aug. 3, 4, 11, 12, 16, 18, 19, 21, 25, 27, 30, Sept. 1, 3, 6, 7, 10, 14, 17, 22, 24, 29, Oct. 1, 6, 8, 13, 15, 20, 22, 27, 29.
2100 →	0600	③ Nov. 2 - 30.

ALMERÍA - MELILLA — 2505

Trasmediterranea Journey 6 - 8 hours 2016 service
Depart Almería: 1700①, 2359②③④⑤⑥⑦.
Depart Melilla: 0930①, 1400⑤, 1500②③④⑥⑦.

Times may vary (particularly in August and September).
Additional sailings by fast ferry in summer (journey 3 hours).
Subject to alteration during Easter and Xmas / New Year periods

ALMERÍA - AN-NADÛR (NADOR) — 2507

Trasmediterranea Journey 5 - 8 hours 2016 service
From Almería and an-Nadûr: Feb. - June: daily sailings; July - Aug.: up to 3 sailings daily; Oct. - Dec.: daily sailings.

2508 BARCELONA - TANJAH (TANGIERS) MED

Grandi Navi Veloci   Journey 27 - 32 hours   **2016 service**
Departure times vary.
From Barcelona: June 3, 7, 10, 12, 14, 15, 17, 19, 21, 23, 24, 26, 28, July 1, 3, 5, 8, 9, 10, 12, 15, 17, 19, 22, 24, 25, 26, 29, 31, Aug. 2, 5, 7, 9, 10, 12, 14, 16, 18, 19, 21, 26, 28, Sept. 2, 4, 9, 11, 16, 18, 23, 25, 30, Oct. 2, 7, 11, 13, 16, 21, 22, 25, 30, 31, Nov. 4, 8, 9, 13, 18, 22, 27, Dec. 2, 6, 11, 15, 16, 20, 24, 25, 30.
From Tanjah Med: June 4, 8, 13, 15, 20, 22, 27, 29, July 4, 6, 11, 13, 18, 20, 25, 27, Aug. 1, 3, 8, 10, 11, 13, 15, 17, 19, 20, 22, 24, 27, 29, 31, Sept. 3, 4, 5, 7, 10, 12, 14, 17, 19, 20, 21, 24, 26, 28, Oct. 3, 5, 6, 12, 17, 22, 26, 31, Nov. 5, 9, 14, 19, 23, 28, Dec. 3, 7, 12, 17, 21, 26, 31.

Tanjah (Tangiers) Med port is located approximately 45 km east of Tanjah.
A connecting ⛌ operates between Tanjah Med and Tanjah.

2510 BALEARIC ISLANDS   (map page 320)

Baleària (Eurolínies Marítimes)

BARCELONA - CIUTADELLA (MENORCA)   **Service to January 22, 2017**

Barcelona		Ciutadella		Ciutadella		Barcelona	
2230	→	0800	①②③④⑤⑦	1000	→	1930	①②③④⑤

BARCELONA - EIVISSA (IBIZA)   **Service to January 22, 2017**

Barcelona		Eivissa		Eivissa		Barcelona	
2130	→	0600	See note S.	1000	→	1845	②③④⑤ until Oct. 2.
2130	→	0600	⑥⑦ July 2 - Sept. 25.	1000	→	1845	① July 2 - Sept. 25.
2215	→	0630	See note R.	1030	→	1845	See note T.
				1130	→	1945	⑥⑦ July 2 - Sept. 25.
				2230	→	0700	See note Q.

Q –   ⑦ May 21 - July 1, Sept. 26 - Oct. 2.   R –   ①②③④⑤⑦ Oct. 3 - Jan. 22.
S –   ①②③④⑤ until Oct. 2.   T –   ①②③④⑤⑥ Oct. 3 - Jan. 22.

BARCELONA - PALMA   **Service to January 22, 2017**

Barcelona		Palma		Palma		Barcelona	
			August 14 - October 2				
2230	→	0500	①②③④⑤⑦	1130	→	2030	⑦ Sept. 5 - 25.
2300	→	0630	⑥ until Sept. 4.	1400	→	2030	①②③④
2359	→	0900	⑥ Sept. 5 - 25.	1400	→	2030	⑤⑥⑦ until Sept. 4.
				1400	→	2030	⑤⑥ from Sept. 5.
			October 3 - January 22				
2300	→	0630	①②③④⑤	1230	→	1945	①②③④⑤
2300	→	0700	⑦	1230	→	2015	⑥

DÉNIA - EIVISSA (IBIZA) - PALMA   **Service to January 22, 2017**

Dénia		Eivissa		Palma
1730	→	2100 / 2145	→	0115

Palma		Eivissa		Dénia
0800	→	1130 / 1230	→	1600

OTHER SERVICES:
Dénia - Sant Antoni and v.v.:   1 – 2 sailings daily, journey ± 3½ hours.
Formentera - Eivissa and v.v.:   frequent daily services (0700 - 2130), journey 30 - 60 minutes.
València - Palma and v.v.:   6 sailings per week (daily in summer), journey ± 7½ hours (some services via Eivissa).

Trasmediterranea   **2016 services**
Departure times may vary. All routes subject to alteration on and around holidays.

BARCELONA - EIVISSA (IBIZA)   **by ship**   Journey 8 - 14 hours
Depart Barcelona: Apr. 18 - June 17: sailings on ①②③④⑤; June 20 - Sept. 10: sailings on ①②③④⑤⑥; Sept. 12 - Dec. 31: sailings on ①②③④⑤.
Depart Eivissa: Apr. 18 - June 12: sailings on ②③④⑤⑦; June 14 - Sept. 11: sailings on ②③④⑤⑥⑦; Sept. 13 - Dec. 31: sailings on ②③④⑤⑦.
Most sailings overnight; additional sailings available.

BARCELONA - MAÓ (MAHÓN)   **by ship**   Journey 8 - 9 hours
Depart Barcelona: Feb. 1 - Apr. 17: sailings on ①③⑤; Apr. 18 - June 10: sailings on ①②③④⑤; June 13 - Sept. 10: daily sailings; Sept. 12 - Dec. 31: sailings on ①②③④⑤.
Depart Maó: Feb. 1 - Apr. 17: sailings on ②④⑥; Apr. 18 - June 11: sailings on ②③④⑤⑥; June 14 - Sept. 11: daily sailings; Sept. 13 - Dec. 31: sailings on ②③④⑤⑥.
Most sailings overnight; additional sailings available.

BARCELONA - PALMA   **by ship**   Journey 6½ - 8½ hours, departure times vary
Depart Barcelona: Feb. 1 - Apr. 17: sailings on ①②③④⑤⑦; Apr. 18 - June 12: 2230⑦, 2300①②③④⑤; June 13 - Sept. 16: 2300; Sept. 18 - Oct. 31: 2230⑦, 2300①②③④⑤; Nov. 1 - Dec. 31: 2300①②③④⑤⑦.
Depart Palma: Feb. 1 - Apr. 17: daily sailings; Apr. 18 - Dec. 31: daily sailings.

PALMA - MAÓ (MAHÓN)   **by ship**   Journey 5½ hours
Depart Palma: Feb. 1 - Dec. 18: 0800⑦.
Depart Maó: Feb. 1 - Dec. 18: 1715⑦.

VALÈNCIA - MAÓ (MAHÓN) via Palma   **by ship**   Journey 14 - 15 hours
Depart València: Feb. 1 - Dec. 17: 2300⑥.
Depart Maó: Feb. 1 - Dec. 18: 1715⑦.

VALÈNCIA - PALMA   **by ship**   Journey 8 hours
Depart València: Feb. 1 - Dec. 30: 2300①②③④⑤⑥ (not Dec. 24).
Depart Palma: Feb. 1 - Dec. 31: 1130②③④⑤⑥, 2345⑦ (not Dec. 25).

2512 CANARY ISLANDS

Fred. Olsen   Inter-Island services   **2016 services**
Playa Blanca (Lanzarote) - Corralejo (Fuerteventura), journey 15 minutes;
Morro del Jable (Fuerteventura) - Las Palmas de Gran Canaria (Gran Canaria), journey 100 minutes;
Agaete (Gran Canaria) - Santa Cruz de Tenerife (Tenerife), journey 60 minutes;
Los Cristianos (Tenerife) - San Sebastián de la Gomera (La Gomera), journey 35 minutes;
Santa Cruz de La Palma (La Palma) - Los Cristianos (Tenerife).

Naviera Armas   **2016 services**
Huelva - Arrecife (Lanzarote) - Las Palmas (Gran Canaria) - Santa Cruz (Tenerife): 1 sailing per week.

Inter-Island services
Corralejo (Fuerteventura) - Playa Blanca (Lanzarote)	5 – 6 sailings daily.
Las Palmas (Gran Canaria) - Arrecife (Lanzarote)	5 sailings per week
Las Palmas (Gran Canaria) - Morro Jable (Fuerteventura)	1 sailing daily.
Las Palmas (Gran Canaria) - Puerto del Rosario (Fuerteventura)	3 sailings per week
Las Palmas (Gran Canaria) - Santa Cruz (Tenerife)	2 – 3 sailings daily.
Los Cristianos (Tenerife) - San Sebastián (La Gomera)	1 – 3 sailings daily.
Los Cristianos (Tenerife) - Valverde (El Hierro)	3 sailings per week
Santa Cruz (Tenerife) - Arrecife (Lanzarote)	4 sailings per week

Sailing frequencies may change

Trasmediterranea   **2016 service**
CÁDIZ - GRAN CANARIA - TENERIFE - PALMA - LANZAROTE - CÁDIZ

	arrive	depart
Cádiz	1230①	1700②
Lanzarote (Arrecife)	2300③	2359③
Gran Canaria (Las Palmas)	0800④	1300④
Tenerife (Santa Cruz)	1700④	2330④
Palma (Santa Cruz)	0800⑤	1600⑤
Tenerife (Santa Cruz)	2130⑤	2330⑤
Gran Canaria (Las Palmas)	0800⑥	1400⑥
Lanzarote (Arrecife)	2330⑥	0100⑦

2520 CIVITAVECCHIA - BARCELONA

Grimaldi Lines   **2016 service**

Civitavecchia		Barcelona			Barcelona		Civitavecchia	
2215	→	1815	①②③④⑤⑥		2215	→	1845	①②③④⑤⑥

2530 CIVITAVECCHIA - SICILY - TÛNIS

Grandi Navi Veloci   **2016 service**

Civitavecchia		Palermo		Tûnis		Palermo		Civitavecchia
			July 1 - September 15					
1800⑤	→	0700⑥ / 1100⑥	→	2100⑥ / 2300⑥	→	0900⑦ / 1900⑦	→	1000①
2100①③	→	1000②④				2100②④	→	1200③⑤
			September 16 - October 31					
1800⑤‡	→	0700⑥ / 1100⑥	→	2100⑥ / 2300⑥	→	0900⑦ / 1900⑦	→	1000①
			November 1 - December 24					
2000⑤	→	0900⑥ / 1100⑥	→	2100⑥ / 2300⑥	→	0900⑦ / 1800⑦	→	0900①

‡ –   Depart 2000 Oct. 21, 28.

Grimaldi Lines   **2016 service**

Civitavecchia		Trapani		Tûnis		Trapani		Civitavecchia
1730③	→		→	1400④ / 1700②	→		→	1430③

2535 CIVITAVECCHIA - TERMINI IMERESE

Grandi Navi Veloci   **2016 service**
                     (No summer service)

Civitavecchia		Termini Imerese		
2030①③	→	1130②④	Mar. 2 - June 15, Sept. 19 - Dec. 21.

Termini Imerese		Civitavecchia		
0200③	→	1700③	Mar. 2 - June 15, Sept. 21 - Dec. 21.
2200④	→	1300⑤	Mar. 3 - June 16, Sept. 22 - Dec. 22.

2537 GENOVA - BARCELONA

Grandi Navi Veloci   **2016 service**

Genova		Barcelona			Barcelona		Genova	
1300	→	0700	See note K.		1300	→	0730	See note N.
1800	→	1100	See note L.		2300	→	1730	See note P.
2000	→	1300	See note M.					

K –   Mar. 10, 24, Apr. 7, 21, May 5, 19; ④ June 2 - Oct. 20; Nov. 3, 17, Dec. 1, 15, 29.
L –   Mar. 5, 19, Apr. 2, 16, 30, May 14, 28; ⑥ June 11 - Oct. 29; Nov. 12, 26, Dec. 10, 24.
M –   Mar. 14, 28, Apr. 11, 25, May 9, 23, June 6, Oct. 24, Nov. 7, 21, Dec. 5, 19.
N –   Mar. 4, 9, 18, 23, 27, Apr. 1, 6, 15, 20, 29, May 4, 13, 18, 27, June 1; ③⑤ June 10 - Oct. 28; Nov. 2, 11, 16, 25, 30, Dec. 9, 14, 23, 28.
P –   Mar. 13, 27 Apr. 10, 24, May 8, 22, June 5, Oct. 23, Nov. 6, 20, Dec. 4, 18.

2547 GENOVA - PALERMO

Grandi Navi Veloci   Journey 21 hours   **2016 service**
From Genova: 2100 P, 2300 Q.   From Palermo: 2100 P, 2300 T, 2359 V.

P –   Daily June 13 - Sept. 10 (not June 19, Aug. 15).
Q –   ①②③④⑤ Mar. 1 - June 11, Sept. 12 - Dec. 29 (not Dec. 24).
T –   ①②③④⑤ Mar. 1 - June 10; ①②③④⑤⑥ Sept. 12 - 30; ①②③④⑤ Oct. 3 - Dec. 29.
V –   ⑥ Mar. 5 - June 11, Oct. 1 - Dec. 17.

GENOVA - TANJAH (TANGIERS) MED — 2554

Grandi Navi Veloci
2016 service

Genova		Tanjah Med			Tanjah Med		Genova	
1300	→	1130	See note **A**.		1600	→	0030	See note **D**.
1800	→	1630	See note **B**.		2300	→	0730	See note **E**.
2000	→	1830	See note **C**.					

A – ④ June 2 - Oct. 20; Nov. 3, 17, Dec. 1, 15, 29.
B – ⑥ June 11 - Oct. 29; Nov. 12, 26, Dec. 10, 24.
C – Oct. 24, Nov. 7, 21, Dec. 5, 19.
D – Oct. 22, Nov. 5, 19, Dec. 3, 17, 31.
E – ①③ June 8 - Oct. 31; Nov. 9, 14, 23, 28, Dec. 7, 12, 21, 26 (not Oct. 12).

Tanjah (Tangiers) Med port is located approximately 45 km east of Tanjah.
A connecting 🚌 operates between Tanjah Med and Tanjah.

All sailings via Barcelona (see Table **2508**)

GENOVA - TÙNIS — 2555

Grandi Navi Veloci Departure times vary. Journey 24 hours
2016 service

From Genova: ③⑥ Mar. 2 - June 11; ①③⑥ June 13 - Aug. 10; ②⑤⑦ Aug. 14 - Sept. 11; ③⑥ Sept. 14 - Dec. 28 (also Dec. 19).
From Tùnis: ④⑦ Mar. 3 - June 12; ②④⑦ June 14 - Aug. 11; ①③⑥ Aug. 15 - Sept. 12; ④⑦ Sept. 15 - Dec. 29 (also Dec. 19).

MARSEILLE - ORAN — 2558

ENTMV Journey 24 - 25 hours
2016 service

From Marseille: Feb. 10, 24, Mar. 9, 23, Apr. 13, 27, May 10, 20, 31, June 7, 19, 26, July 4, 9, 14, 19, 24, Aug. 1, 5, 12, 18, 25, Sept. 1, 8, 16, 23, 29.
From Oran: Feb. 7, 21, Mar. 5, 20, Apr. 9, 24, May 8, 18, 29, June 9, 21, 28, July 2, 9, 14, 18, 23, 28, Aug. 3, 12, 19, 26, 30, Sept. 6, 9, 17, 24, 30.

Departure times vary.

Other services operate from Marseille to Annâbah and Sakîkdah.

GULF OF NAPOLI — 2560
(including Gulf of Salerno and Ponziane Islands)

Alilauro
2016 services

Napoli Beverello - Forio: up to 5 sailings daily (summer only). Sailings via Ischia in winter.
Napoli Beverello or Mergellina - Ischia: up to 15 sailings daily.
Napoli Beverello - Sorrento: 5 sailings daily.
Salerno - Capri: daily sailing.
Sorrento - Capri: up to 8 sailings daily (summer only).
Additional infrequent services to Capri operate (summer only) from Ischia, Castellammare di Stàbia, Positano and Amalfi.
Sailing frequencies may change

Caremar
2016 services

Napoli - Capri: 3 sailings daily by catamaran, 3 sailings by ship (4 / 3 in summer).
Napoli - Ischia: 5 sailings daily by catamaran, 7 sailings by ship (6 / 8 in summer).
Napoli - Procida: 7 sailings daily by catamaran, 6 sailings by ship (8 / 7 in summer).
Pozzuoli - Procida: 1 sailing by catamaran, 5 sailings by ship (1 / 4 in summer).
Procida - Ischia: 5 sailings daily by catamaran, 7 - 10 sailings by ship.
Sorrento - Capri: 4 sailings daily by catamaran.

Medmar
2016 services

Napoli - Ischia: 3 - 5 sailings daily.
Ischia - Pozzuoli: up to 8 sailings daily.
Additional infrequent services operate between Pozzuoli, Procida and Ischia.

Navigazione Libera del Golfo by Linea Jet
2016 services

Napoli (Molo Beverello) - Capri: up to 10 sailings daily (more in summer). Journey 40 minutes.
Sorrento - Capri: 6 sailings daily (more in summer). Journey 25 minutes.
Additional services operate (summer only) between Castellammare di Stàbia and Capri.

SNAV Journey 40 minutes
2016 services

Napoli (Beverello) - Capri: 0700, 0805, 0930, 1135, 1240, 1440, 1630, 1915.
Capri - Napoli (Beverello): 0650, 0805, 0910, 1035, 1240, 1340, 1630, 1810.

Sorrento - Capri: 0715①②③④⑤⑥, 0830, 0950, 1145, 1330, 1550, 1705.
Capri - Sorrento: 0800①②③④⑤⑥, 0855, 1120, 1300, 1515, 1635, 1740.

CORSICA — 2565

Sailings from mainland FRANCE (map page 171)

MARSEILLE - AJACCIO Service to November 5, 2016

Maritima Ferries Journey 9 - 12 hours

From Marseille:
Uneven dates: Feb., Apr., May, Aug., Nov.; even dates: Mar., June, July, Sept., Oct.
From Ajaccio:
Uneven dates: Mar., June, July, Sept., Oct.; even dates: Feb., Apr., May, Aug., Nov.
Sailings depart 1900 from Marseille and Ajaccio. Additional departures available in summer.

MARSEILLE - BASTIA Service to November 5, 2016

Maritima Ferries Journey 10 - 13 hours

From Marseille:
Uneven dates: Mar., June, July, Sept., Oct.; even dates: Feb., Apr., May, Aug., Nov.
From Bastia:
Uneven dates: Feb., Apr., May, Aug., Nov.; even dates: Mar., June, July, Sept., Oct.
Sailings depart 1900 from Marseille, 1830 (1900⑥) from Bastia. Additional departures available in summer.

MARSEILLE - L'ÎLE ROUSSE Service to November 5, 2016

Maritima Ferries Departure times vary Journey 8 - 11½ hours

From Marseille: ①⑤ Feb. 1 - 19; ①③⑤ Feb. 22 - Mar. 4; ①⑤ Mar. 7 - Apr. 8; ①③⑤ Apr. 11 - Nov. 4 (also Mar. 30; not Mar. 28).
From L'île Rousse: ②⑥ Feb. 2 - 20; ②④⑥ Feb. 23 - Mar. 5; ②⑥ Mar. 8 - Apr. 9; ②④⑥ Apr. 12 - Nov. 5 (also Mar. 31; not Mar. 29).

CORSICA continued — 2565

MARSEILLE - PORTO VECCHIO Service to November 5, 2016

Maritima Ferries Departure times vary Journey 14 hours

From Marseille: ③⑤ Feb. 3 - 12; ①③⑤ Feb. 15 - Mar. 4; ③ Mar. 9 - 23; ①③⑤ Apr. 6 - Nov. 4 (also Mar. 28).
From Porto Vecchio: ④⑥ Feb. 4 - 13; ②④⑥ Feb. 16 - Mar. 5; ④ Mar. 10 - 24; ②④⑥ Apr. 7 - Nov. 5 (also Mar. 29).

MARSEILLE - PROPRIANO 2016 service

Maritima Ferries Departure times vary Journey 9½ - 12½ hours

From Marseille and Propriano: occasional sailings.

NICE - AJACCIO 2016 service

Corsica Ferries Journey 4½ - 9 hours

From Nice and Ajaccio: Apr. - June: 5 – 11 sailings per month; July – Aug.: 14 – 19 sailings per month; Sept.: 7 sailings per month.
Most sailings by day, departure times vary.

NICE - BASTIA 2016 service

Corsica Ferries Journey 5 - 6 hours

From Nice and Bastia: 3 – 5 sailings per week (daily July / Aug.).
Most sailings by day, departure times vary.

Moby Lines

Nice		Bastia	
1100	→	1830	Aug. 16 - Sept. 25.
2230	→	0730	Daily June 1 - Aug. 14; ③⑤ Sept. 28 - Oct. 28; ⑤ Nov. 4 - Dec. 16.

Bastia		Nice	
1100	→	1830	June 2 - Aug. 14.
2230	→	0730	Daily Aug. 15 - Sept. 25; ④⑥ Sept. 29 - Oct. 29; ⑥ Nov. 5 - Dec. 17.

NICE - CALVI 2016 service

Corsica Ferries Journey 4 - 5½ hours

From Nice and Calvi: late-May - early-Sept.: 5 – 7 sailings per week.
Most sailings by day, departure times vary.

NICE - L'ÎLE ROUSSE 2016 service

Corsica Ferries Journey 5 - 5½ hours

From Nice and L'île Rousse: May - June: occasional sailings; July - Aug.: 2 - 3 sailings per week; Sept.: occasional sailings.
Most sailings by day, departure times vary.

TOULON - AJACCIO 2016 service

Corsica Ferries Journey 6 - 10 hours

From Toulon and Ajaccio: Apr. - Sept.: 1 – 2 sailings daily (including daily night sailing). Departure times vary.

TOULON - BASTIA 2016 service

Corsica Ferries Journey 9 - 10 hours

From Toulon and Bastia: Apr. - Sept.: 1 – 2 sailings daily.
Most sailings by night. Departure times vary.

TOULON - L'ÎLE ROUSSE 2016 service

Corsica Ferries Journey 6 - 7 hours

From Toulon and L'île Rousse: Apr. - May: 1 - 2 sailings per week; June: 2 - 3 sailings per week; July - Aug.: 3 – 6 sailings per week; Sept.: 1 – 3 sailings per week.
All sailings by day, departure times vary.

Other sailings available from Nice and Toulon to Porto Vecchio, and Toulon to Calvi.

Sailings from ITALY

GENOVA - BASTIA 2016 service

Moby Lines

Genova		Bastia			Bastia		Genova	
2200	→	0800	May 12 - Sept. 29.		1100	→	1730	May 13 - Sept. 30.

LIVORNO - BASTIA 2016 service

Corsica Ferries Journey 4 hours (night sailings 7½ hours)

From Livorno and Bastia: Apr. - June: 1 – 2 sailings daily; July - Sept: up to 3 sailings daily.
Most sailings by day, departure times vary.

Moby Lines

Livorno		Bastia	
0800	→	1205	May 26 - Sept. 30.
1400	→	1805	June 18 - Sept. 11.
2100	→	0600	④⑤⑥⑦ July 14 - Sept. 4 (not July 21 - 24).

Bastia		Livorno	
0800	→	1205	June 19 - Sept. 11.
1400	→	1805	May 26 - Sept. 30.
2100	→	0600	④⑤⑥⑦ July 14 - Sept. 4 (also Sept. 11; not July 21 - 24).

PIOMBINO - BASTIA 2016 service

Corsica Ferries Journey 2½ hours. Departure times vary.

From Piombino: ③④ June 29 - Sept. 1.
From Bastia: ④⑤ June 30 - Sept. 2.

SAVONA - BASTIA 2016 service

Corsica Ferries Journey 6 - 10 hours. Departure times vary.

From Savona and Bastia: Apr. - May: 2 – 4 sailings per week; June: 1 – 2 sailings daily; July - Aug.: 2 – 3 sailings daily; Sept.: up to 3 sailings daily.

Other sailings available from Livorno and Savona to L'île Rousse.

2566 CORSICA - SARDINIA (map page 287)

BONIFACIO - SANTA TERESA DI GALLURA
2016 service

Moby Lines Journey 50 minutes **Mar. 24 - Sept. 30 only**
From Bonifacio: 0830, 1200, 1700, 2000.
From Santa Teresa di Gallura: 0700, 1000, 1500, 1830.

Saremar Journey 1 hour
From Bonifacio and Santa Teresa di Gallura: up to 3 sailings per day.

PORTO VECCHIO - GOLFO ARANCI
2016 service

Corsica Ferries / Sardinia Ferries
From Porto Vecchio and Golfo Aranci: June - Sept.: up to 3 sailings per week.

2570 ITALIAN ISLAND SERVICES (map page 287)
(Egadi, Eolie, Pantelleria, Pelagie and Ustica Islands)

Alilauro **May 28 - September 11, 2016**
Napoli Mergellina - Stromboli - Panarea - Salina - Vulcano - Lipari and v.v.:
2 – 3 sailings per week (daily July 1 - Sept. 5).
Sailing frequencies may change

Siremar **2016 services**
NAPOLI - MILAZZO via Stromboli, Ginostra, Panarea, Lipari and Vulcano.

Napoli	Milazzo		Milazzo	Napoli	
2000②⑤→	1215③⑥		1350①④→	0800②⑤	Not Apr. 1 - Oct. 31.
			1430①④→	0800②⑤	Apr. 1 - Oct. 31.

OTHER SERVICES:
Inter-island sailings operate, also from mainland Sicily to the islands. Services operate to differing frequencies (additional sailings in summer).

EOLIE ISLANDS:
Alicudi to Filicudi, Lipari, Milazzo, Rinella, Salina and Vulcano.
Filicudi to Alicudi, Lipari, Milazzo, Rinella, Salina and Vulcano.
Ginostra to Lipari, Milazzo, and Panarea.
Lipari to Alicudi, Filicudi, Ginostra, Milazzo, Panarea, Rinella, Salina, Stromboli and Vulcano.
Milazzo to Alicudi, Filicudi, Ginostra, Lipari, Panarea, Rinella, Salina, Stromboli and Vulcano.
Panarea to Filicudi, Ginostra, Lipari, Milazzo, Rinella, Salina, Stromboli and Vulcano.
Rinella to Alicudi, Filicudi, Lipari, Milazzo, Panarea, Salina, Stromboli and Vulcano.
Salina to Alicudi, Filicudi, Lipari, Milazzo, Panarea, Rinella, Stromboli and Vulcano.
Stromboli to Alicudi, Filicudi, Lipari, Milazzo, Panarea, Rinella, Salina and Vulcano.
Vulcano to Alicudi, Filicudi, Lipari, Milazzo, Panarea, Rinella, Salina and Stromboli.

EGADI ISLANDS:
Favignana to Levanzo, Marettimo and Trapani.
Levanzo to Favignana, Marettimo, and Trapani.
Marettimo to Favignana, Levanzo and Trapani.
Trapani to Favignana, Levanzo and Marettimo.

PANTELLERIA ISLAND:
Trapani - Pantelleria and v.v.

PELAGIE ISLANDS:
Porto Empedocle (Agrigento) - Linosa - Lampedusa and v.v.

USTICA ISLAND:
Palermo - Ustica and v.v.

Ustica Lines (Liberty Lines) by hydrofoil **2016 services**
EGADI & EOLIAN ISLANDS and USTICA
The Sicilian ports of Messina, Milazzo, Palermo and Trapani are linked by island-hopping services serving Alicudi, Favignana, Filicudi, Levanzo, Lipari, Marettimo, Panarea, Rinella, Salina, Stromboli, Ustica and Vulcano.
Services operate to differing frequencies (additional sailings in summer).

MILAZZO - VULCANO by hydrofoil Journey 50 minutes
Late Summer service
Depart Milazzo: 0630, 0700, 0800, 0830, 0940, 1045, 1230, 1300, 1400, 1430①②③⑤⑥, 1510, 1630, 1745, 1845, 1930.
Depart Vulcano: 0715, 0755, 0850, 0915, 1035, 1215, 1245①②③⑤⑥, 1320, 1405, 1420, 1620, 1725, 1755, 1820, 1940①②③⑤⑥, 1945④⑦, 2005.
Winter service
Depart Milazzo: 0600, 0700, 0730, 0830, 0930, 1215, 1320, 1500, 1600, 1700, 1815①②③④⑤⑦, 1910.
Depart Vulcano: 0715, 0815, 0845, 0945, 1155, 1225, 1315, 1355, 1445, 1620, 1735, 1750①②③④⑤⑦, 1815, 1945⑤⑦.

MILAZZO - PALERMO by hydrofoil
Journey 2½ hours

Milazzo		Palermo		Milazzo
0630	→	1145/1350	→	1910

2580 LIVORNO - BARCELONA - TANJAH (TANGIERS) MED

Grimaldi Lines **2016 service**

Livorno		Barcelona		Tanjah Med		Barcelona		Livorno
2330⑥	→	2000/2359⑦	→	1030/1700②	→	2000/2359③	→	2030④

Tanjah (Tangiers) Med port is located approximately 45km east of Tanjah.
A connecting 🚌 operates between Tanjah Med and Tanjah.

2595 MÁLAGA - MELILLA

Trasmediterranea Journey 6 - 8 hours **2016 service**
From Málaga: 0030②, 1430②③④⑤⑥, 2300⑦.
From Melilla: 0030②③④⑤⑥⑦, 1400①.

Departure times may vary at peak times
Subject to alteration during Easter & Xmas / New Year periods
Also daily sailings by fast ferry in summer (journey 4 hours).

2602 MARSEILLE - AL-JAZÂ'IR (ALGIERS)

ENTMV **Service to January 31, 2017**

Marseille		al-Jazâ'ir	
1200	→	0800	Aug. 6, 8, 13, 15, 18, 20, 24, 27, 29, 31, Sept. 3, 5, 19, 22, 24, 28, Oct. 20.
1200	→	0900	Oct. 1, 8, 15, 29, Nov. 5, 12, 26, Dec. 10, 24, 29, Jan. 7, 21, 28.
1400	→	0900	Sept. 10.
1500	→	1000	Aug. 1, 3, Sept. 8, 17.
1600	→	1200	Oct. 22, Nov. 19, Dec. 3, 17, Jan. 2, 14.

al-Jazâ'ir		Marseille	
1200	→	0800	Aug. 7, 11, 14, 16, 19, 23, 26, 28, 30, Sept. 2, 4, 6, 23, Jan. 1.
1200	→	0900	Sept. 20, 26, 29.
1200	→	1000	Sept. 16, Oct. 3, 10, 17, 21, 24, Nov. 1, 7, 14, 21, 28, Dec. 5, 12, 19, 26, Jan. 9, 16, 23, 30.
1400	→	1000	Sept. 9.
1500	→	1100	Aug. 2, 4.
1600	→	1200	Jan. 3.

Other services operate from Marseille to Annâbah and Sakîkdah.

2615 MARSEILLE - TÚNIS

Compagnie Tunisienne de Navigation **2016 service**
Departure times vary. Journey 20 - 24 hours

Until June 9
From Marseille: 1200④. From Túnis: 1200②.
June 10 - October 1 (departure times vary)
From Marseille: June 12, 16, 18, 21, 23, 25, 28, 30, July 2, 5, 7, 9, 12, 14, 16, 18, 21, 23, 26, 28, 30, Aug. 2, 4, 6, 8, 10, 13, 15, 17, 19, 21, 24, 26, 28, 30, Sept. 2, 4, 7, 9, 11, 13, 16, 18, 22, 25, 29.
From Túnis: June 11, 14, 17, 20, 22, 24, 27, 29, July 1, 4, 6, 8, 11, 13, 15, 17, 20, 22, 25, 27, 29, Aug. 1, 3, 5, 7, 9, 12, 14, 16, 18, 20, 21, 23, 25, 27, 29, Sept. 1, 3, 6, 8, 10, 12, 15, 17, 20, 24, 27, Oct. 1.
October 2 - December 22
From Marseille: 1200④. From Túnis: 1200②.
Additional sailings Dec. 11 (d. 1500), Dec. 17, 24 (d. 1600), Dec. 28 (d. 1500).

2618 MGARR (Gozo) - CIRKEWWA (Malta)

Gozo Channel Co. Journey 25 minutes **2016 service**
June 13 - November 6
From Mgarr: 0045, 0200, 0330, 0500, 0600, 0630, 0700, 0730, 0815, 0900, 0945, 1030, 1115, 1200, 1245, 1330, 1415, 1500, 1545, 1630, 1715, 1800, 1845, 1930, 2015, 2100, 2145, 2230, 2315.
From Cirkewwa: 0120, 0230, 0400, 0545, 0630, 0700, 0730, 0815, 0900, 0945, 1030, 1115, 1200, 1245, 1330, 1415, 1500, 1545, 1630, 1715, 1800, 1845, 1930, 2015, 2100, 2145, 2230, 2315, 2400.

2625 NAPOLI - PALERMO

Grandi Navi Veloci **2016 service**

Napoli		Palermo			Palermo		Napoli	
0900	→	1930	See note N.		0900	→	1930	See note N.
2000	→	0630	See note P.		2000	→	0630	See note P.
2100	→	0730	See note N.		2100	→	0730	See note N.

N – July 23, 29-31, Aug. 4 - 6, 8, 11, 13 - 15, 19 - 21, 26 - 28.
P – Daily Mar. 1 - July 28; Aug. 1 - 3, 7, 9, 10, 12, 16 - 18, 22 - 25; daily Aug. 29 - Nov. 5; ①②③④⑤⑥ Nov. 7 - Dec. 17; ①②③④⑤ Dec. 19 - 30 (also Dec. 18; not Mar. 6, July 23).

Tirrenia **2016 service**

Napoli		Palermo		Palermo		Napoli
2015	→	0630		2015	→	0630

2630 NAPOLI - TRAPANI

Ustica Lines (Liberty Lines) by hydrofoil **July 2 - September 3, 2016**
(No winter service)

⑥: Napoli 1500 → Ustica 1905/1925 → Favignana 2125/2135 → Trapani 2200.
⑥: Trapani 0615 → Favignana 0635/0640 → Ustica 0840/0900 → Napoli 1315.

2661 SALERNO - PALERMO - TÚNIS

Grimaldi Lines **2016 service**

Salerno		Palermo		Túnis		Palermo		Salerno
1200①	→	2300①/0100②	→	1430②/1730④	→	0730⑤/1000⑤	→	2000⑤
2330⑤	→	1000⑥/1200⑥	→	2300⑥/0001⑦	→	1530⑦/1900⑦	→	0700①

SARDINIA	2675

Sailings from FRANCE

NICE - GOLFO ARANCI 2016 service

Sardinia Ferries Journey 16 hours

From Nice and Golfo Aranci: up to 3 sailings per week.

Most sailings by night, departure times vary.

Sailings from mainland ITALY (map page 287)

CIVITAVECCHIA - ARBATAX 2016 service

Tirrenia

Civitavecchia		Arbatax	
1900	→	0500	③⑤ May 18 - July 22; ①③ July 25 - Aug. 24; ③⑤ Aug. 31 - Oct. 14; ③⑤ Dec. 21-30.
1930	→	0430	③⑤ Oct. 19 - Dec. 16.
Arbatax		Civitavecchia	
2359	→	1030	③⑦ May 18 - July 24; ②④ July 26 - Aug. 25; ③⑦ Aug. 31 - Oct. 12; ②⑥ Oct. 15 - Dec. 17; ③⑦ Dec. 21-28.

CIVITAVECCHIA - CAGLIARI 2016 service

Tirrenia

Civitavecchia		Cagliari	
1900	→	1030	③⑤ May 25 - July 22; ①③ July 25 - Aug. 24; ③⑤ Aug. 31 - Oct. 14; ③⑤ Dec. 21-28.
1930	→	1000	③⑤ Oct. 19 - Dec. 16.
2000	→	0845	①②④⑥⑦ May 17 - July 24; ②④⑤⑥ July 26 - Aug. 27; ①②④⑤⑦ Aug. 29 - Oct. 13; ① Oct. 17 - Dec. 26 (also Aug. 14, Dec. 20, 22, 24, 25, 27, 29, 31; not Aug. 6).
2330	→	1215	⑦ July 31 - Aug. 28 (also Aug. 6; not Aug. 14).
Cagliari		Civitavecchia	
1900	→	1030	③⑦ May 18 - July 24; ②④ July 26 - Aug. 25; ③⑦ Aug. 31 - Oct. 12; ②⑥ Oct. 15 - Dec. 17 (also Dec. 21, 25, 28).
2000	→	0845	①②④⑤⑥ May 16 - July 23; ①③⑤⑥⑦ July 25 - Aug. 28; ①②④⑤⑥ Aug. 29 - Oct. 14; ④ Oct. 20 - Dec. 15 (also Dec. 19, 20, 22-24, 26, 27, 29-31).

CIVITAVECCHIA - OLBIA 2016 service

Moby Lines Journey 5-5½ hours (night sailings 8 hours). Departure times vary.

From Civitavecchia and Olbia: Jan. - Mar.: 1 sailing daily; Apr.: 1-2 sailings daily; May: 1 sailing daily; June - July: up to 3 sailings daily; Aug.: 2-4 sailings daily; Sept.: up to 3 sailings daily; Oct. - Dec.: 1 sailing daily.

Tirrenia Journey 5 hours (night sailings 8 hours)

From Civitavecchia and Olbia: night sailing every day (d. 2230). Additional day sailings in summer.

CIVITAVECCHIA - PORTO TORRES 2016 service

Grandi Lines

Civitavecchia		P. Torres	
2215	→	0530	②⑥ Feb. 1 - Mar. 22; ②⑤⑥ Mar. 29 - Apr. 30; ①④⑤⑥ May 2 - June 4; ①②④⑤⑥ June 6 - Sept. 17; ②⑥ Sept. 19 - Dec. 27.
P. Torres		Civitavecchia	
1130	→	1845	③⑦ Feb. 1 - Mar. 20; ③⑥⑦ Mar. 30 - Apr. 24; ②③⑥⑦ Apr. 26 - June 5; ②③⑤ June 7 - Sept. 18; ③⑦ Sept. 20 - Dec. 28.
1230	→	1915	⑥⑦ June 11 - Sept. 18.

GENOVA - ARBATAX 2016 service
No winter service

Tirrenia

Genova		Arbatax	
2130	→	1300	①⑥ July 18 - Aug. 13; ①⑤ Aug. 15 - Sept. 2.
Arbatax		Genova	
1400	→	0730	②⑦ July 19 - Aug. 14; ②⑥ Aug. 16 - Sept. 3.

GENOVA - OLBIA 2016 service

Moby Lines Journey 9-12 hours. Departure times vary.

From Genova and Olbia: Jan. - mid-May: 3 sailings per week; mid-May - end-May: 1 sailing daily; June - July: 2-3 sailings daily; Aug: 2-4 sailings daily; Sept.: 2-3 sailings daily; Oct.: 1 sailing daily; Nov. - Dec.: 3 sailings per week.

Tirrenia 2016 service

Genova		Olbia	
0900	→	2000	③④⑦ Aug. 17 - Sept. 4.
2030	→	0845	①③⑤ May 23 - July 15, Sept. 5 - 23; Sept. 25, 27, 29, Oct. 2; uneven dates Oct. 3 - 29; ①③⑤ Oct. 31 - Dec. 30.
2130	→	0945	①③④⑤⑥ July 18 - Aug. 13; ①⑤ Aug. 15 - Sept. 2.
Olbia		Genova	
0900	→	2000	④⑤⑥ July 21 - Aug. 13.
2030	→	0845	②④⑥ May 24 - July 16, Sept. 6 - 24; Sept. 26, 28, 30; even dates Oct. 2 - 30; ②④⑥ Nov. 1 - Dec. 31.
2130	→	0945	②⑦ July 19 - Aug. 14; ②④⑥⑦ Sept. 4.

GENOVA - PORTO TORRES 2016 service

Grandi Navi Veloci Journey 10-12 hours

From Genova: depart 2030: ①③⑤ Mar. 23 - May 27; even dates June 2 - July 30; uneven dates Aug. 1 - 31; even dates Sept. 2 - 16 (also May 29, 31, Sept. 19, 21, 23).
From Porto Torres: depart 2030: ②④⑥ Mar. 24 - May 28; uneven dates June 1 - July 31; even dates Aug. 2 - 30; uneven dates Sept. 1 - 17 (also May 30, Sept. 20, 22, 24).

Tirrenia

Genova		Porto Torres		Porto Torres		Genova
2030	→	0830		2030	→	0830

LIVORNO - GOLFO ARANCI 2016 service

Sardinia Ferries Journey 6½-10 hours. Departure times vary.

From Livorno and Golfo Aranci: Apr. - May: daily sailings; June: 1-2 sailings daily; July - Sept.: 2-3 sailings daily.

SARDINIA continued	2675

LIVORNO - OLBIA 2016 service

Moby Lines Journey 6½ hours (night sailings 8 hours).

From Livorno and Olbia: Jan. - May: 1 sailing daily (by night); June - mid-Sept.: day and night sailings; mid-Sept. - Dec.: 1 sailing daily (by night).

Departure times vary (most night sailings d.2100, day sailings d.0800).

NAPOLI - CAGLIARI 2016 service

Tirrenia

Napoli		Cagliari	
1800	→	0730	② July 19 - Aug. 30.
1900	→	0830	②④ until July 14; ⑤ July 22 - Sept. 2; ②④ Sept. 6 - Dec. 29.
Cagliari		Napoli	
1900	→	0830	①③ until July 13; ①④ July 18 - Sept. 1; ①③ Sept. 5 - Dec. 28.

PIOMBINO - OLBIA 2016 service

Moby Lines

Piombino		Olbia		Olbia		Piombino	
1430	→	1930	See note Q.	0815	→	1330	See note Q.

Q – June 1, 4, 5, 11, 12, 16 - 19, 25 - 27, July 2 - 4, 7 - 11, 15 - 18, 22 - 25; ①③④⑥⑦ July 27 - Sept. 11; Sept. 17, 18.

Sailings from SICILY (map page 287)

PALERMO - CAGLIARI 2016 service

Tirrenia

Palermo		Cagliari	
1930	→	0730	⑥ until July 16; ⑦ July 24 - Sept. 4; ⑥ Sept. 10 - Dec. 31.
2359	→	1200	③ July 20 - Aug. 31.
Cagliari		Palermo	
1030	→	2230	③ July 20 - Aug. 31.
1930	→	0730	⑤ until July 15; ⑥ July 23 - Sept. 3; ⑤ Sept. 9 - Dec. 30.

Sailings from SPAIN

BARCELONA - PORTO TORRES 2016 service

Grimaldi Lines

Barcelona		Porto Torres		Porto Torres		Barcelona
2215①②④⑤⑥	→	1030②③⑤⑥⑦		0630②③⑤⑥⑦	→	1815②③⑤⑥⑦

SÈTE - AN-NADÛR (NADOR)	2678

Grandi Navi Veloci Journey 28 - 30 hours 2016 service
Departure times vary.

From Sète: Mar. 9, 17, 26, Apr. 3, 12, 20, 29, May 7, 16, 25, June 2, 10; ③ June 15 - Sept. 28; Oct. 8, 17, 26, Nov. 4, 13, 22, Dec. 1, 10, 19, 31.
From an-Nadûr: Mar. 2, 11, 19, 28, Apr. 5, 14, 22, May 1, 9, 18, 27, June 4, 12, 20; ⑤ June 24 - Sept. 30; Oct. 2, 10, 19, 28, Nov. 6, 15, 24, Dec. 3, 12, 21.

SÈTE - TANJAH (TANGIERS) MED	2680

Grandi Navi Veloci Journey ±36 hours 2016 service
Departure times vary.

From Sète: Mar. 5, 9, 13, 17, 22, 26, 30, Apr. 3, 8, 12, 16, 20, 25, 29, May 3, 7, 12, 16, 20, 29, June 6, 13, 14, 19, 20, 26, 27, July 3, 4, 10, 11, 17, 18, 24, 25, 31, Aug. 1, 7, 8, 14, 15, 21, 22, 28, 29, Sept. 4, 5, 11, 12, 18, 19, 25, 26, Oct. 3, 4, 8, 10, 12, 17, 21, 26, 30, Nov. 4, 8, 13, 17, 22, 26, Dec. 1, 5, 10, 14, 19, 23.
From Tanjah Med: Mar. 3, 7, 11, 15, 20, 24, 28, Apr. 1, 6, 10, 14, 18, 23, 27, May 1, 5, 10, 14, 18, 22, 31, June 8, 11, 16, 18, 21, 25, 28, July 2, 5, 9, 12, 16, 19, 23, 26, 30, Aug. 2, 6, 9, 13, 16, 20, 22, 27, 29, Sept. 3, 5, 10, 12, 17, 19, 24, 26, Oct. 1, 2, 6, 8, 10, 14, 15, 19, 23, 28, Nov. 1, 6, 10, 15, 19, 24, 28, Dec. 3, 7, 12, 16, 21, 25.

Tanjah (Tangiers) Med port is located approximately 45km east of Tanjah.
A connecting 🚌 operates between Tanjah Med and Tanjah.

VALLETTA - CATANIA	2690

Virtu Ferries by catamaran Journey 4 hours 2016 service
(No service Dec. 25)

From Valletta and Catania: Apr. - May: 4 sailings per week; June - Sept.: 5-6 sailings per week (daily mid-July - mid-Aug.); Oct. - Dec.: 3 sailings per week.
Departure times vary.

All sailings by catamaran Valletta - Pozzallo and v.v., then by 🚌 to/from Catania (see also Table 2694).

Subject to alteration during Xmas/New Year period

VALLETTA - POZZALLO	2694

Virtu Ferries by catamaran Journey 1½ hours 2016 service
(No service Dec. 25)

From Valletta and Pozzallo: Apr. - Dec.: sailings on ①②③⑤⑥⑦ (daily mid-July - mid-Aug.). 1-2 sailings per day, departure times vary.

Subject to alteration during Xmas/New Year period

2695 STRETTO DI MESSINA

MESSINA - REGGIO DI CALABRIA 2016 service

Ustica Lines by hydrofoil Journey 30 minutes *Times may vary*

From Messina:
①–⑤: 0600, 0700, 0730, 0830, 0930, 1025, 1130, 1305, 1340, 1430, 1505, 1600, 1630, 1740, 1905, 2015.
⑥⑦: 0800, 0930, 1100, 1340, 1530, 1700.

From Reggio di Calabria:
①–⑤: 0645, 0745, 0810, 0910, 0940, 1105, 1210, 1345, 1420, 1510, 1545, 1640, 1710, 1820, 1945, 2055.
⑥⑦: 0840, 1010, 1140, 1420, 1610, 1740.

MESSINA - VILLA SAN GIOVANNI 2016 service

Bluferries by hydrofoil Journey 20 minutes

From Messina:
①–⑤: 0615, 0740, 0925, 1120, 1255, 1420, 1650, 1810, 1915.
⑥⑦: 0615, 0925, 1120, 1420, 1810, 1915.

From Villa San Giovanni:
①–⑤: 0710, 0810, 1000, 1210, 1335, 1510, 1735, 1845, 2020.
⑥⑦: 0810, 1000, 1210, 1510, 1845, 2020.

2699 OTHER SERVICES

Corsica Ferries by fast ferry 2016 service
(No winter service)

From Piombino and Portoferraio (Elba): June - Sept.: up to 7 sailings daily; journey time 30 minutes.

Moby Lines 2016 service
(No service Dec. 25)

Piombino - Portoferraio (Elba): up to 15 sailings daily in high-summer, less frequent at other times; journey time 1 hour.

Toremar 2016 services

Services operate from Piombino to Cavo, Pianosa, Portoferraio and Rio Marina; from Livorno to Capraia and Gorgona; from Porto Santo Stefano to Isola del Giglio.

ADRIATIC / EASTERN MEDITERRANEAN / BLACK SEA

2715 ANCONA - PÁTRA via Kérkira and Igumenítsa

Anek Lines / Superfast Ferries 2016 service

January 1 - June 30 and September 11 - December 31

Ancona		Igumenítsa		Pátra
1330③④⑤	→	0800④⑤⑥	→	1430④⑤⑥
1630⑥⑦	→	0900⑦①	→	1430⑦①
1900②	→	1430③	→	2100③

Pátra		Igumenítsa		Ancona
1730⑤⑥	→	2300⑤⑥	→	1330⑥⑦
1730①②③④	→	2359①②③④	→	1630②③④⑤

July 1 - September 10

Ancona		Kérkira		Igumenítsa		Pátra
1330	→			0600	→	1130
1630⑥	→			0900⑦	→	1430⑦
1630②④	→	0800③⑤	→	0930③⑤	→	1500③⑤

Pátra		Igumenítsa		Kérkira		Ancona
1430	→	2000	→		→	1030
1730⑤	→	2300⑤	→		→	1330⑥
1730①③	→	2300①③	→	0030②④	→	1400②④

🚌 connection Pátra - Pireás - Athína and v.v. operates most days in summer.
For international journeys only

Minoan Lines 2016 service

January 1 - July 31 and August 30 - December 31

Ancona		Igumenítsa		Pátra		Pátra		Igumenítsa		Ancona
1730①	→	1030②	→	1630②		1900①	→	0102②	→	1530②
1400③	→	0700④	→	1300④		1900②	→	0103③	→	1530③
1400④	→	0700⑤	→	1300⑤		1700④	→	2300④	→	1330⑤
1630⑤	→	0930⑥	→	1530⑥		1700⑤	→	2300⑤	→	1330⑥
1630⑥	→	0930⑦	→	1530⑦		1800⑥	→	2359⑥	→	1430⑦
1730⑦	→	1030①	→	1630①		1800⑦	→	2359⑦	→	1430①

August 1 - 29
From Ancona: daily departures (not Aug. 9, 16); sailings on Aug. 23, 24 do not serve Igumenítsa.
From Pátra: daily departures (not Aug. 10, 17); sailings on Aug. 3, 4 do not serve Igumenítsa.

2725 ANCONA - SPLIT

Blue Line / SNAV March 21 - November 5, 2016
(No winter service)

Ancona		Split	
2015	→	0700	①③⑤ Mar. 21 - Apr. 15; ①②③④⑤⑥ Apr. 18 - June 25; daily June 27 - Sept. 17; ①②③④⑤⑥ Sept. 19 - Oct. 22; ①③⑤ Oct. 24 - Nov. 4 (not July 17).

Split		Ancona	
2015	→	0700	②④⑦ Mar. 22 - Apr. 14; ①②③④⑤⑦ Apr. 17 - June 24; daily June 26 - Sept. 16; ①②③④⑤⑦ Sept. 18 - Oct. 21; ②④⑦ Oct. 23 - Nov. 5 (not July 16).

Jadrolinija 2016 service
(No service Dec. 25, 26)

Ancona		Split		Split		Ancona	
January 3 - March 21 and November 3 - December 30							
1945	→	0700	①⑤	2000	→	0700	④⑦
March 22 - July 23 and August 29 - November 2							
1945	→	0700	①③⑤	2000	→	0700	②④⑦
July 24 - August 28							
1100	→	1900	⑦ Aug. 21 - 28.	1430	→	2230	⑥ Aug. 6 - 13.
1945	→	0600	⑤	2000	→	0700	②④
1945	→	0700	①③	2030	→	0945	⑦
2359	→	1030	⑥ Aug. 6 - 13.	2200	→	0940	⑥ Aug. 20 - 27.

2732 ANCONA - ZADAR

Jadrolinija 2016 service
(No winter service)

Ancona		Zadar		Zadar		Ancona
June 3 - July 5 and September 9 - 27▲						
2200②⑥	→	0700③⑦		2200①⑤	→	0700②⑥
July 6 - 14 and August 31 - September 8						
2200②④⑥	→	0700③⑤⑦		2200①③⑤	→	0700②④⑥
July 15 - 28 and August 24 - 30						
2200②④⑤⑥	→	0700③⑤⑥⑦		1130⑤⑥	→	1800⑤⑥
				2200①③	→	0700②④
July 29 - August 23						
1230⑦	→	1830⑦		0800⑥	→	1400⑥
1600⑥	→	2200⑥		1130②③④⑤	→	1800②③④⑤
2200⑤	→	0530⑥		2200⑦	→	0700①
2200①②③④	→	0600②③④⑤		2345⑤	→	0700⑦

▲ – June 17, Sept. 9: Zadar depart 1130, Ancona arrive 1800.

2738 BARI - BAR

Montenegro Lines 2016 service

Bari		Bar	
1200	→	0900	Aug. 19 - 23, 26 - 28.
2200	→	0900	Aug. 1, 3 - 6, 8, 10 - 13, 15, 17, 24, 29, 31; ①③⑤ Sept. 2 - 30; ②⑤ Oct. 4 - Dec. 2 (also Oct. 31; not Nov. 1).

Bar		Bari	
1200	→	0900	Aug. 4 - 6, 11 - 13.
2200	→	0900	Aug. 2, 7, 9, 14, 16, 18 - 23, 25 - 28, 30; ②④⑦ Sept. 1 - 29; ④⑦ Oct. 2 - Dec. 1.

2745 BARI - DURRÉS

Ventouris Ferries Service to June 30, 2017

Bari		Durrës	
1200	→	2100	Dec. 17, 18, Jan. 6, 7.
2200	→	0800	Daily.

Durrës		Bari	
1200	→	2100	Dec. 17, 18, Jan. 6, 7.
2200	→	0800	Daily.

BARI - PÁTRA via Kérkira and Igumenítsa · 2755

Anek Lines / Superfast Ferries · 2016 service

Bari	Kérkira	Igumenítsa	Pátra
January 1 - May 1 and October 1 - December 31			
1330⑦	→	→	2300⑦ →	0700①
1930①–⑥	→	→	0530②–⑦ →	1300②–⑦
May 2 - June 26 and September 12 - 30			
1330⑦	→	→	2300⑦ →	0700①
1930①②③⑤⑥	→	→	0530②③④⑥⑦ →	1300②③④⑥⑦
1930④	→	0430⑤	0600⑤ →	1300⑤
June 27 - July 24 and August 29 - September 11			
1330⑦	→	→	2300⑦ →	0700①
1930①②③→	→	0530②③④	1300②③④	
1930④⑤⑧	→	0430⑤⑥⑦	0600⑤⑥⑦ →	1300⑤⑧⑦
July 25 - August 28			
1300⑤⑥	→	2200⑤⑥	2330⑤⑥ ...	...
1330⑦	→	→	2300⑦ →	0700①
1930①②③⑥	→	→	0530②③④⑦ →	1300②③④⑦
1930④	→	0430⑤	0600⑤ →	1300⑤

Pátra	Igumenítsa	Kérkira	Bari
January 1 - May 1 and October 1 - December 31			
1800	0030	→	→	0930
May 2 - June 26 and September 12 - 30			
1800①②④⑤⑥⑦	0030②③⑤⑥⑦①	→	→	0930②③⑤⑥⑦①
1800③	0030④	→	0200④ →	1000④
June 27 - July 24 and August 29 - September 11			
1800①②④⑤	0030②③⑤⑥	→	→	0930②③⑤⑥
1800③⑥⑦	0030④⑦①	→	0200④⑦① →	1000④⑦①
July 25 - August 28			
1800①②④⑤⑦	0030②③⑤⑥①	→	→	0930②③⑤⑥①
1800③	0030④	→	0200④ →	1000④
...	0200⑥⑦	→	0330⑥⑦ →	1030⑥⑦

Subject to alteration during ship maintenance periods
🚢 connection Pátra - Pireás - Athína and v.v.
Tickets available on-board ship and from 30 Amalias av., Sindagma, Athína.

BLACK SEA services · 2760

Bumerang Shipping Company Tourism Travel & Trade S.A.

İSTANBUL - YALTA - NOVOROSSIYSK	Irregular sailings, journey 30 hours
İSTANBUL - YEVPATORIYA	Journey 24 hours

BRINDISI - IGUMENÍTSA · 2765

Grimaldi Lines · 2016 service

Brindisi	Igumenítsa		Igumenítsa	Brindisi
1400①③⑥	→	2300①③⑥	0100①③⑤⑥	→	0830①③⑤⑥
1630②⑤⑦	→	0130③⑥①	0300①③⑥	→	1100①③⑥
2100①③④⑥	→	0530②④⑤⑦	2359①③⑥	→	0830②④⑦

BRINDISI - PÁTRA · 2775

Grimaldi Lines · 2016 service

Brindisi	Pátra		Pátra	Brindisi
2100①③④⑥	→	1400②④⑤⑦	1700②④⑤⑦	→	0830③⑤⑥①

BRINDISI - VLORË · 2780

European Seaways · 2016 service

Brindisi	Vlorë		Vlorë	Brindisi
May 20 - July 15 and from September 9				
2330①②③④⑤⑥	→	0700②③④⑤⑥①	1430①②③④⑤⑥	→	1930①②③④⑤⑥
July 16 - September 8				
2330	→	0700	1430	→	1930

DUBROVNIK - BARI · 2795

Jadrolinija · 2016 service (No winter service)

Dubrovnik	Bari		Bari	Dubrovnik
March 23 - May 19 and October 3 - 27				
2200①③	→	0800②④	2200②④	→	0800③⑤
May 20 - June 26 and September 12 - October 2				
2200①③⑤	→	0800②④⑥	2200④⑥	→	0800③⑤⑦
June 27 - July 18 and August 30 - September 11				
1200⑦	→	1930⑦	2200②④⑥⑦	→	0800③⑤⑦①
2200①③⑤	→	0800②④⑥			
July 19 - August 1				
1200⑤⑥⑦	→	1930⑤⑥⑦	2200②④⑤⑥⑦①	→	0800③⑤⑥⑦①
2200①③	→	0800②④			
August 2 - 16				
1200③④⑤⑥⑦	→	1930③④⑤⑥⑦	2200②③④⑤⑥⑦	→	0800③④⑤⑥⑦①
2200①	→	0800②			
August 17 - 29				
2200①③④⑤⑥⑦	→	0800②④⑤⑥⑦①	1200①④⑤⑥⑦	→	1930①④⑤⑥⑦
			2200②	→	0800③

GREEK ISLANDS · 2800

Summary table of regular 🚢 services to the Greek Islands.

Each route is operated by various shipping companies to differing schedules. Additional inter-island routes are operated at less regular intervals.

Pireás to Égina, Póros, Ídra, Spétses, Kithira, Andikíthira.
Pireás to Sérifos, Sífnos, Milos, Folégandros.
Pireás to Páros, Íos, Thíra (Santoríni), Iráklio.
Pireás to Náxos, Amorgós, Astipálea.
Pireás to Pátmos, Léros, Kálimnos, Kos, Nísiros, Tílos, Sími, Ródos, Kárpathos, Kásos.
Pireás to Ikaría, Sámos, Híos, Lésvos.
Pireás and **Rafína** to Síros, Dílos, Míkonos, Tínos, Ándros.
Pátra to Zákinthos (Zante), Kefallinía, Itháki, Kérkira (Corfu), Igumenítsa.
Vólos, Ágios Konstantínos and **Kimi** to Skíathos, Skópelos, Alónissos, Skíros.
Kavála to Thásos, Samothráki, Límnos.

PIREÁS - IRÁKLIO · 2830

Minoan Lines · 2016 service

Pireás	Iráklio		Iráklio	Pireás	
2100	→	0600	Not July 1 - Aug. 31.	2130 → 0600	Not July 1 - Aug. 31.
2200	→	0630	July 1 - Aug. 31.	2200 → 0630	July 1 - Aug. 31.

Additional sailings on July 2, 9, 16, 23, 24, 29-31, Aug. 5- 7, 12, 13, 19-21, 26-28, Sept. 3 at 1100 from Pireás and Iráklio.

Anek Lines / Blue Star Ferries · 2016 service

Pireás	Iráklio		Iráklio	Pireás
2100	→	0600	2100 →	0600

PIREÁS / LAVRIO - LEMESÓS (LIMASSOL) - HEFA · 2845

Grimaldi Lines · 2016 service
Pireás - Lemesós - Hefa: 1 sailing per week – contact operator for details.

Salamis Cruise Lines · 2016 service
Lavrio - Lemesós - Hefa: occasional service – contact operator for details.

SPLIT - DUBROVNIK · 2850

Kapetan Luka · 2016 service (No winter service)

Split	Hvar	Korčula	Dubrovnik	
0740 →	0855 →	1010 →	1200	①②⑤⑥ May 2-31; daily June 1 - Oct. 9; ⑤⑥⑦ Oct. 10-30.

Dubrovnik	Korčula	Hvar	Split	
1600 →	1800 →	1915 →	2020	Daily Sept. 1 - Oct. 9; ⑤⑥⑦ Oct. 10-30.
1630 →	1830 →	1945 →	2050	①②⑤⑥ May 2-31; daily June 1 - Aug. 31.

TRIESTE - PÁTRA via Igumenítsa · 2870

Minoan Lines · 2016 service

Trieste	Ravenna	Ancona	Igumenítsa	Pátra
0430③④ →	→	1400③④ →	0700④⑤ →	1300④⑤
Pátra	**Igumenítsa**	**Ancona**	**Ravenna**	**Trieste**
1900①② →	0100②③ →	1530②③ →	→	2330②③

Variations: no departure from Trieste on Aug. 3, 4, 24, 25; from Pátra on Aug. 1, 2, 22, 23.
For full service Ancona - Igumenítsa - Pátra and v.v. see Table **2715**.

VENEZIA - PÁTRA via Igumenítsa · 2875

Anek Lines / Superfast Ferries · 2016 service

Venezia	Igumenítsa	Pátra	Igumenítsa	Venezia
January 1 - June 30 and September 12 - December 31				
1200⑥ →	1430⑦ →	2100⑦ / 2359⑦ →	0630① →	0700②
1200⑦ →	1430① →	2100① / 2359① →	0630⑥ →	0700⑦
July 1 - September 11				
1200③ →	1430④ →	2100④ / 2359④ →	0630⑤ →	0700⑥
1200⑥ →	1430⑦ →	2100⑦ / 2359⑦ →	0630① →	0700②

For international journeys only

OTHER SERVICES · 2899

Jadrolinija · 2016 services
Many local services operate to the Islands along the Croatian coast.

L N P · 2016 services
All-year services operate Split - Rogač and Šibenik - Kaprije - Žirje.

Salamis Cruise Lines · 2016 services
Cruises around Greece and the Greek Islands (2- 9 days, June - Sept.).

Venezia Lines · 2016 services
Services operate Apr. 30 - Oct. 2 from Venezia to Poreč, Pula, Rovinj and Umag.

FINLAND

Some branch lines, which have reportedly been under threat of closure, have seen an improved level of service from the timetable change. This includes the Joensuu to Pieksämäki route which has a second daily service added in each direction (Table **793**). An additional journey has also been added between Tampere and Haapamäki (Table **795**) meaning there are now two daily journeys available in each direction.

GERMANY

Engineering work at various locations around Germany will once again cause disruption to journeys during certain periods. The Frankfurt – Erfurt – Leipzig / Berlin route (Table **850**) will be particularly badly affected during the first half of 2017 with various track improvement projects taking place. Unfortunately we are unable to show all timing variations, but a special version of the table, covering the period from March 11 to May 22 when the most significant alterations occur, will be found on page 561. Other work taking place in the Frankfurt, Halle and Leipzig areas will complicate schedules further at certain times and so readers intending to use services in Table **850**, particularly from February 11 to May 22, are strongly advised to check timings before travelling.

The route from Berlin to Stralsund (Table **845**) is another with significant changes, this time from February 9 through to the December 2017 timetable change. All trains are diverted between Berlin and Bernau resulting in extended journey times. Most regional services between Berlin and Stralsund run from / to Berlin Lichtenberg whilst those between Berlin and Lutherstadt Wittenberg / Falkenberg continue to serve Berlin Hbf (meaning no direct connection between the two routes). A special version of Table **845** will be found on page 560 with full details of amended timings from February 9 for both long-distance and regional services.

To help readers plan their journeys in Germany, we have included a summary of the most significant alterations affecting long distance journeys on page 367. Please note that this list is not exhaustive and other alterations may occur, particularly at weekends and during holiday periods.

There have been some changes to the Rhein-Ruhr *Regional Express* network (Table **802**) with some routes now benefitting from an increased frequency. *RE6*, which previously ran from Düsseldorf to Bielefeld and Minden, is now extended to run on an hourly basis from Köln/Bonn Flughafen via Köln Hbf and Neuss. *RE11* no longer runs Mönchengladbach – Duisburg – Hamm, but is diverted to provide an extra service each hour on the Düsseldorf – Duisburg – Hamm section (which now has three fast regional connections per hour in each direction). Certain *RE11* services are extended to run through to Kassel via Paderborn (Table **805**). The Mönchengladbach to Duisburg section, previously part of *RE11*, is now part of an extended route *RE42* running Mönchengladbach – Duisburg – Recklinghausen – Münster. Finally, *RE5* from Koblenz now only runs as far as Wesel, no longer serving Emmerich. However, a new route *RE19*, operated by Abellio Rail NRW, provides an hourly service Düsseldorf – Duisburg – Emmerich; this service is expected to be extended to run across the border to and from Arnhem from April 6.

Private operator *Locomore* is scheduled to start running its daily return service between Stuttgart and Berlin from December 14. Timings have been included in Tables **902** and **912**. Tickets may be purchased from the operator's website and are also available on board the train.

AUSTRIA

Railjet services between Wien and Bregenz / Zürich have been modified to produce a regular hourly service over the Arlberg mountain section between Innsbruck and Feldkirch (Table **951**). This has been achieved by running most Wien to Bregenz and Wien to Zürich services separately (rather than combined between Wien and Feldkirch). Stopping patterns between Innsbruck and Feldkirch alternate every two hours; all trains call at Landeck and Bludenz with, for most of the day, alternate trains calling at Ötztal and St Anton or Imst-Pitztal and Langen. The only downside to this calling pattern is only a limited service is available for short journeys between St Anton and Langen.

All services between Wien and Salzburg operated by Austrian Railways are now formed of *Railjet* rolling stock (Table **950**).

Six *Railjet* services in each direction between Graz and Wien are extended to serve Wien Flughafen (Table **980**). This does mean that certain services between Salzburg and Wien no longer serve the airport.

POLAND

Polish Railways' schedules have been updated and are now valid until March 11. As is usual, there are many variations even within this short time period and it is always advisable to confirm times locally when travelling in Poland.

CZECH REPUBLIC

Czech Railways has introduced a through train between Praha and Český Krumlov (Table **1131**) via České Budějovice, whilst *Arriva* also has a journey on the route at weekends, increasing to daily in summer. Praha to Linz (Table **1132**) now has four journeys each way, with journey times improved to just over four hours.

Regiojet has a new Praha – Brno – Bratislava service (Table **1150**), with two trains each way. A third train runs between Praha and Brno, continuing to Staré Město u Uherské Hradiště. *Arriva* has increased its cross-border Praha to Trenčín service and extended it to Nitra (Table **1157**); initially running two days per week, there will be a daily service from April.

The Praha – Ostrava – Žilina service has been recast once again (Table **1160**) and there are new trains from Ostrava Svinov to Banská Bystrica, some extending to Zvolen (Table **1185**).

SLOVAKIA

Slovak Railways has reintroduced *Intercity* trains to the Bratislava – Košice route (Table **1180**) with two journeys each way. The Praha to Banská Bystrica sleeper service (Table **1185**) is reduced to three days per week.

A new Brno – Košice – Prešov sleeping car has been introduced, conveyed in train **283/2** between Brno and Bratislava, then in train **801/800** to and from Prešov. A further new sleeping car runs between Wien and Košice conveyed in trains **406/445**, returning in **444/407**.

HUNGARY

Bus substitution in the Fonyód area will take place until June 16, as shown in Table **1220**. Budapest to Zagreb trains will therefore run via Dombóvár during this period (Table **1240**). Tables **1260**, **1261** and **1265** have been recast to improve our coverage of the services from Budapest to Miskolc and beyond.

SLOVENIA, CROATIA and BOSNIA-HERZEGOVINA

Schedules have been updated where possible, but it should be noted that no information was available at press date for the Bosnian Federation, although major changes are not expected.

Refurbishment to Slovenian Railways' fleet of tilting trains is currently taking place resulting in *ICS* category services being replaced by *IC* trains until June 10.

SERBIA and FYRo MACEDONIA

Engineering work between Niš and Preševo is expected to be completed in late May which should see the resumption of international trains from Beograd to Skopje and Thessaloníki (Table **1380**).

ALBANIA

The somewhat perilous state of Albanian Railways continues and services have been suspended once again, apparently owing to lack of finance. The situation will be reviewed by Government in January (Table **1390**).

BULGARIA

Services on the recently upgraded route between Plovdiv and Svilengrad have been adjusted with more through journeys now available (Table **1550**). These include two eastbound through journeys from Sofia to Svilengrad and one in the opposite direction.

ROMANIA

Tables have been updated and all principal services - those shown with a train number - have been checked. However, services run by private operators *Regiotrans*, *Softrans* and *Transferoviar*, and all local services are subject to alteration.

CONTINUED ON PAGE 559

What's new this month (continued from page 558)

UKRAINE

Amongst the changes is a new early-morning *Intercity* train from Kharkiv to Vinnytsya via Kyïv, returning in the evening, running daily except Tuesdays (Tables **1750** and **1700**). A further new *Intercity* departs Kyïv at 1449 for Zaporizhzhya (Table **1775**) on five days per week, returning overnight.

In Table **1700**, train **113** Kharkiv – Mukacheve is extended to Uzhorod whilst **115** from Kharkiv continues to Chernivtsi instead of Ivano-Frankivsk.

RUSSIA

The principal train on the Trans-Siberian route, the *Rossiya* (Table **1990**), has been retimed to leave Moskva late evening instead of early afternoon: from December 11 train **2** *MJ* leaves Moskva Yaroslavskaya at 2345, whilst train **1** *MJ*, its westbound equivalent, leaves Vladivostok at 1210 (1910 local time). The train continues to run on alternate days, taking seven days to complete the journey.

BEYOND EUROPE

In this expanded Winter edition of the European Rail Timetable, we are showing all eight of our Beyond Europe sections. A list of the areas covered and their locations within the timetable will be found on page 577. Please note that only limited updates have been made to most sections since they last appeared in the regular monthly editions.

In the section covering Israel we have created a new table, numbered **4513**, which shows timings for the newly opened Haifa to Bet She'an line. This service follows the route of the old Jezreel Valley Railway which ceased operations in 1948.

845 LUTHERSTADT WITTENBERG - BERLIN - STRALSUND

RE services except where shown

SERVICE FROM FEBRUARY 9 (see page 396 for service to February 8)

Block 1

Train identification: IC 2217 (Ⓐ, N); ICE 1731 (⑥ b, L✗); ICE 1524 (⑥ h, C✗); ICE 1712 (O✗, S)

km		Ⓒ	✗			Ⓐ		Ⓐ	S	L✗		C✗		O✗	S
	Berlin Hbf .....d.	…	…	…	…	…	…	0924	…	…	1138	…	1338	…
	Berlin Gesundbrunnen …d.	…	…	…	…	…	…	0931	…	…	…	…	1344	…
	Berlin Lichtenberg …d.	0018	0018	0428	0533	0633	0733 0800 0833	0933 1033 1133	1233 1333	1433 1447
	Bernau (b. Berlin) …d.	0038	0038	0448	0553	0653	0753 0822 0853	0953 1053 1153	1253 1353	1453 1509
	Eberswalde Hbf …d.	0058	0100	0509	0609	0709	0809 0838 0909	1009 1109 1209 1228	1309 1409 1428	1509 1527
0	Angermünde …a.	…	0119	0528	0628	0728	0828 0853 0928	1028 1128 1228	1328 1428 1443	1528 1543
23	Angermünde …d.	…	0120	0533	0634c 0634	0731	0834 0933	1034 1133 1235	1333 1434 1445	1533
	Schwedt (Oder) …a.	…	0142		0656c 0656		0856	1056 1258	1456	
	Prenzlau …d.	…	…	0601		0759	1001	1201 1401	1508	1601
	Pasewalk …d.	…	0419	0620		0817	1019	1219 1419	1526	1619
	Anklam …d.	…	0451	0652		0849	1051	1251 1344 1451	1552	1651
	Züssow 846 d.	…	0505	0706		0903 1140	1105	1305 1356 1505	1605	1705
	Greifswald 846 d.	…	0520 0701	0721		0918 1153	1120	1320 1409 1520	1620	1720
	Stralsund Hbf 846 a.	…	0541 0722	0744		0939 1213	1141	1342 1435 1541	1641	1741

Block 2

Train identification: IC 2424 (O); IC 2428 (S, ①–④, m); IC 1924 (⑦ R); IC 1970 (⑤ f, O); IC 1924 (⑦ P); (⑤ n, S); ♠; (⑤⑥, k); Ⓑ; (⑦, w)

	Ⓐ	O	S m	⑦R	⑤f O	⑦P	⑤n S		♠	⑤⑥ k	Ⓑ	⑦ w
Berlin Hbf …d.	…	1521	…	1723	1810 1817	1928	…	…	…	…	…	…
Berlin Gesundbrunnen …d.	…	1529	…	1729								
Berlin Lichtenberg …d.	1533	1633 1716	1733	1834	1933 2033 2102 2133	2233 2233 2233						
Bernau (b. Berlin) …d.	1553	1653 1737	1753	1854	2008 1953 2053 2153	2253 2253 2253						
Eberswalde Hbf …d.	1609 1619	1709 1752	1809	1904 1904	1910 2028 2009 2137 2214	2314 2314 2314						
Angermünde …a.	1628 1634	1728 1807	1837 1828	1920 1920	1929 2043 2028 2128 2153	2233 2335 2335 2335						
Angermünde …d.	1634 1636	1733	1840 1834	1922 1922	1933 2045 2036 2133	2234 2337 2345 2345 2345						
Schwedt (Oder) …d.	1656			1856	2058	2256 2359						
Prenzlau …d.	1700 1801	1903	1945 1945 2001 2108	2201	0013 0013 0013						
Pasewalk …d.	1717 1819	1919	2001 2001 2019 2137	2219	0029 0029 0029						
Anklam …d.	1743 1851	1944	2027 2027 2051 2203	2251	0102						
Züssow 846 d.	1755 1905	1956	2039 2039 2105 2216	2305	0115						
Greifswald 846 d.	1808 1920	2010	2053 2053 2120 2234	2320	0130						
Stralsund Hbf 846 a.	1835 1941	2030	2114 2113 2141 2248	2341	0151						

Block 3

Train identification: IC 2429 (①–④, m); IC 2425 (S, O); ICE 1513 (C✗)

km		Ⓐ		①g	Ⓐ	✗		Ⓐ		m		S O		C✗	
0	Stralsund Hbf 846 d.	…	0406	0416		0616 0708	0816	0911	1016 1111	1216
31	Greifswald 846 d.	…	0425	0438		0638 0729	0838	0931	1038 1134	1238
49	Züssow 846 d.	…	0430	0454		0654 0749	0854	0951	1054 1149	1254
66	Anklam …d.	…	0449	0506		0706 0800	0906	1005	1106 1200	1306
109	Pasewalk …d.	…	0519	0544j 0544		0744j 0837	0944j	1039	1144j 1239	1344j
133	Prenzlau …d.	…	0537 0537	0601 0601		0801 0852	1001	1054	1201 1255	1401
	Schwedt (Oder) …d.	…	0506		0701 0704c	0906		1106	1306	
170	Angermünde …a.	…	0528 0603 0603 0628 0628	0723 0726c	0828 0913 0920 1028	1115 1128 1228 1316 1328 1428						
170	Angermünde …d.	0410	0531 0605 0605 0631 0631 0707	0733	0831 0915 0931 1031	1107 1117 1131 1231 1318 1331 1431						
196	Eberswalde Hbf …d.	0431 0431	0552 0625 0625 0652 0724 0754	0852 0932 0952 1052	1124 1134 1152 1252 1335 1352 1452							
218	Bernau (b. Berlin) …d.	0451 0451	0606 0641 0641 0706 0706 0741 0808	0906 0947 1006 1106 1140	1206 1306 1406 1506							
	Berlin Lichtenberg …a.	0509 0509	0624 0724 0724 0800 0826	0924 1024 1124 1200	1224 1324 1424 1524							
239	Berlin Gesundbrunnen …a.	…	0710 0710		1025	1222	1419						
243	Berlin Hbf …a.	…	0716 0716		1034								

Block 4

Train identification: IC 2325 (⑤ f, J✗); ICE 1715 (⑦ d, J✗); ICE 1536 (⑥ b, H✗); IC 1932 (⑤ n, ⑦ R, S A); IC 1932 (⑦ P, A); IC 2216 (Ⓐ, N); S; (①–⑥, t); (⑤⑥, k); (⑦, w)

	⑤f J✗	⑦d J✗	⑥b H✗		⑤n⑦R S A		⑦P A	N S			t	k	w
Stralsund Hbf 846 d.	1310 1312	1347* 1419	1608 1619 1648	1813 1825	2016	2216 2216 2237						
Greifswald 846 d.	1331 1336	1407 1441	1628 1641 1709	1833 1847	2038	2238 2238 2259						
Züssow 846 d.	1349 1349	1420 1457	1642 1657 1721	1903	2054	2254 2254 2315						
Anklam …d.	1401 1409	1509	1655 1709 1733	1915	2106	2306 2306 2327						
Pasewalk …d.	1431 1439	1544	1734v 1744 1759	1947	2144j	2336 2344 2357						
Prenzlau …d.	1450 1455	1601	1750 1801 1815	2004	2201	0002						
Schwedt (Oder) …d.	1506	1706	1906	2106 2306								
Angermünde …a.	1512 1516 1528	1628 1728	1812 1828 1837 1928	2031 2033 2046	2131 2231 2331	0028						
Angermünde …d.	1514 1518 1531	1631 1731	1808 1816 1831 1839 1931	2033 2046	2131 2231 2331	0031						
Eberswalde Hbf …d.	1532 1535 1552	1652 1752	1825 1831 1852 1857 1952	2054 2104 2152	2152 2252 2352	0052						
Bernau (b. Berlin) …d.	1547	1606	1706 1806 1841 1852 1906 2006	2108 2119 2206 2311	0006	0112						
Berlin Lichtenberg …a.		1624	1724 1824 1900 1924 2024	2126 2142 2224 2329	0024	0130						
Berlin Gesundbrunnen …a.			1626●	1928 1938								
Berlin Hbf …a.	1621 1622	1635*										

LUTHERSTADT WITTENBERG / FALKENBERG - BERLIN

km		Ⓒ																			
0	Lutherstadt Wittenberg 851 d.	0024	0613	0812	1012	1212	1412	1612	1813	2013	2225									
	Falkenberg (Elster) …d.		0449	0643	0843	1043	1243	1443	1643	1843	2043									
32	Jüterbog …d.	0053	0433 0533 0641 0733 0837r	0936 1037r	1136 1237r	1336 1437r	1536 1637r	1736 1837r	1936 2037r	2136 2252									
45	Luckenwalde …d.	0100	0441 0545 0649 0740 0846r	0944 1046r	1144 1246r	1344 1446r	1544 1646r	1744 1846r	1944 2046r	2144 2300									
91	Berlin Südkreuz 851 d.	0148	0520 0618 0719 0819 0921	1018 1121	1218 1321	1418 1521	1618 1721	1818 1921	2018 2121	2218 2346									
97	Berlin Hbf 851 a.	0154	0529 0628 0729 0831 0930	1028 1130	1227 1330	1427 1530	1627 1730	1827 1930	2027 2130	2227 2355									

km		Ⓒ																			
0	Berlin Hbf 851 d.	0044	0532 0631 0731 0831 0931	1030 1131	1231 1331	1431 1531z	1631 1731	1831 1931	2031 2137	2236									
6	Berlin Südkreuz 851 d.	0053	0540 0640 0740 0840 0940	1040 1140	1240 1340	1440 1540z	1640 1740	1840 1940	2040 2146	2246									
52	Luckenwalde …d.	0133	0614 0711r 0814 0911r	1014 1111r	1214 1311r	1414 1511r	1614z 1711r	1814 1911r	2014 2111	2328									
65	Jüterbog …d.	0141	0625 0719r 0825 0919r	1025 1119r	1225 1319r	1425 1519r	1625 1719r	1825 1919r	2025 2119	2336									
114	Falkenberg (Elster) …d.		0707	0907	1107	1307	1507	1907	2107	2310										
	Lutherstadt Wittenberg 851 a.	0157c	0748	0948	1148	1348	1548y	1748	1946	2142	0003									

Footnotes

A – 🚃 and 🍴 Stralsund - Berlin - Hannover - Bremen - Oldenburg.
C – 🚃 and ✗ Ostseebad Binz - Berlin - Leipzig - München und v.v.
H – 🚃 and ✗ Stralsund - Berlin - Erfurt / Frankfurt.
J – 🚃 and ✗ Stralsund - Berlin - Stralsund - Berlin - Leipzig - München.
L – 🚃 and ✗ Erfurt - Berlin - Stralsund (- Ostseebad Binz from Apr. 22).
N – Ⓐ (not May 26). 🚃 and 🍴 Greifswald - Hamburg - Köln - Stuttgart and v.v.
O – To / from Ostseebad Binz (Table 844).
P – ⑦ from May 14 (also June 5; not June 4).
R – ⑦ to May 7 (also Apr. 17, May 1; not Apr. 16, 30).
S – To / from Szczecin (Table 949).
b – Also Apr. 14, May 25; not Apr. 15, May 27.
c – Ⓒ only.

d – Also Apr. 15, 17, May 1, June 5.
f – Also Apr. 13, May 24; not Apr. 14, May 26.
g – Also Apr. 18, May 2, June 6; not Apr. 17, May 1, June 5.
h – Also Apr. 14, 16, 30, June 4.
j – Arrives 8 minutes earlier.
k – Also Apr. 13, 17, 30, May 24, June 4.
m – Not Apr. 13, 17, May 1, 24, 25, June 5.
n – Also Apr. 13; not Apr. 14.
r – 3–4 minutes later on certain dates.
t – Also Apr. 16, 30, June 4; not Apr. 17, May 1, June 5.
v – Arrives 1720.
w – Also Apr. 17, May 1, June 5; not Apr. 16, 30, June 4.
y – 1557 on ⑤⑦ Mar. 12 - Apr. 16 (also Apr. 13, 17).

z – 3–4 minutes later on ⑤⑦ (also May 24).
♠ – ①②③④⑦ (not Apr. 13, 16, 30, May 24, June 4).
* – From Mar. 11.
* – Departs Stralsund 1344 from May 25. Arrives Berlin 1630 until Mar. 4.
* – From / to Halle on Ⓒ (Tables 848).

BERLIN and LEIPZIG - ERFURT - KASSEL and FRANKFURT 850

Other regional services: Table **845** Berlin - Lutherstadt Wittenberg. Table **848** Lutherstadt Wittenberg - Halle. Table **849** Leipzig / Halle - Erfurt - Eisenach - Bebra.

SERVICE MARCH 11 - MAY 22 (see pages 398 and 399 for service to March 10)

SEE NOTE ⊠	*IC* **1950**	*IC* **1950**	*ICE* **1646**	*ICE* **1656**	*ICE* **1644**	*ICE* **1654**	*ICE* **1636**	*ICE* **1642**	*ICE* **1652**	*ICE* **1634**	*ICE* **1640**	*ICE* **1650**	*ICE* **1632**	*ICE* **1548**	*ICE* **1558**	*ICE* **1630**	*ICE* **1546**	*ICE* **1556**	*ICE* **1538**	*ICE* **1544**	*IC* **1962**	*ICE* **1594**	*ICE* **1554**	*ICE* **1536**	*ICE* **1542**
	①	Ⓐ	Ⓐ	①–⑥	①–⑥		Ⓐ														⑤⑦		Ⓑq		
			⊙	e	e																d		S	T	
			✕	✕	✕	✕	✕	✕	✕	✕	✕	✕	✕	✕	✕	✕	✕	✕	✕	✕	U	🍸◧	✕	✕	✕
Berlin Hbf .... **851 902** d.	0029	...	...	...	...	...	0659	...	...	0900	...	...	1100	...	...	1300	...	...	1500	...	1450	...	...	1700	...
Berlin Südkreuz .... **851** d.	0036	...	...	...	...	...	0707	...	...	0907	...	...	1107	...	...	1307	...	...	1507	...	1458	...	...	1707	...
Lutherstadt Wittenberg .. **851** d.	0113	...	...	...	...	...	|	...	...	|	...	...	|	...	...	|	...	...	|	...	1600	...	...	|	...
Bitterfeld .... **851** d.	0129	...	...	...	...	...	|	...	...	|	...	...	|	...	...	|	...	...	|	...	|	...	...	|	...
Halle (Saale) Hbf .... **851** d.	0154	...	...	...	...	...	0814	...	...	1014	...	...	1214	...	...	1414	...	...	1614	...	1636	...	...	1814	...
Dresden Hbf **842** .... d.	|	...	...	...	...	0613e	|	...	0813	|	...	1013	|	...	1213	|	...	1420	|	...	|	1613h	1620	|	...
Leipzig Hbf .... **851** d.	0238	...	0422	0529	0613	0729	|	0808	0929	|	1008	1129	|	1208	1329	|	1408	1529	|	1608	|	1729	1729	|	1808
Naumburg (Saale) Hbf ... d.	|	...	|	|	|	|	|	|	|	|	|	|	|	|	|	|	|	|	|	|	|	|	|	|	|
Weimar .... d.	0336	...	|	|	|	|	|	|	|	|	|	|	|	|	|	|	|	|	|	|	|	|	|	|	|
Erfurt Hbf .... d.	0353	...	0509	0613	0659	0813	0848	0901	1013	1047	1101	1213	1247	1301	1413	1447	1501	1613	1647	1701	|	1813	1813	1847	1901
Gotha .... d.	0408	...	0526	0630	0720	0831	...	|	1031	...	|	1231	...	|	1431	...	|	1631	...	|	|	1831	1831	...	|
Eisenach .... d.	0426	...	0546	|	0740	|	...	0936	|	...	1136	|	...	1336	|	...	1536	|	...	1736	|	|	|	...	1936
Bebra .... **901** d.	0500	0500	|	|	|	|	...	|	|	...	|	|	...	|	|	...	|	|	...	|	|	|	|	...	|
Kassel Wilhelmshöhe **901** a.	|	|	|	|	|	|	...	|	|	...	|	|	...	|	|	...	|	|	...	|	1929	|	|	...	|
Bad Hersfeld .... **901** d.	0511	0511	0619	|	0819	|	...	1019	|	...	1219	|	...	1419	|	...	1619	|	...	1819	...	|	|	...	2019
Fulda .... **900/1/2** d.	0541	0541	0645	0744	0845	0944	...	1045	1144	...	1245	1344	...	1445	1544	...	1645	1744	...	1845	...	1944	1944	...	2045
Hanau Hbf .... **900/1/2** d.	0624	0624	|	|	|	|	...	|	|	...	|	|	...	|	|	...	|	|	...	|	...	|	|	...	2125
Frankfurt (Main) Süd .... a.	|	|	0737	|	0937	|	...	1137	|	...	1337	|	...	1537	|	...	1737	|	...	|	...	|	|	...	2138
Frankfurt (Main) Hbf **900/1/2** a.	0642	0642	|	0837	|	1037	...	|	1237	...	|	1437	...	|	1637	...	|	1837	...	1940	...	2036	2036	...	|
Frankfurt Flughafen ✈ § .. a.	...	...	0751	0855	0949	1055	...	1149	1255	...	1349	1455	...	1549	1655	...	1749	1855	...	...	...	2057	...	...	2149
Wiesbaden Hbf **911** .... a.	...	...	...	0933	...	1133	...	...	1333	...	...	1533	...	...	1733	...	...	1933	...	...	...	2133	...	...	...

SEE NOTE ⊠	*ICE* **1552**	*ICE* **1572**	*ICE* **1534**	*IC* **1938**	*ICE* **1717**	*ICE* **1550**		*EN* **471**	
		⑦w	⑤f	⑦w		⑦w		Ⓡ	
	K	K						A	
	✕	✕	✕		H✕	✕			
Wiesbaden Hbf **911** .... d.	...	...	1903	1903	1927	...	...	2204	...
Frankfurt Flughafen ✈ § .. d.	...	...	1911	1911	1934	...	...	2214	...
Frankfurt (Main) Hbf **900/1/2** d.	...	...	|	|	2009	...	...	|	...
Frankfurt (Main) Süd .... d.	...	...	|	|	2026	...	...	|	...
Hanau Hbf .... **900/1/2** d.	...	...	2017	2022	|	...	...	2344	...
Fulda .... **900/1/2** d.	1813	...	|	...	|	2013	...	|	...
Bad Hersfeld .... **901** d.	1929	1929	|	...	2051	2129	...	|	...
Kassel Wilhelmshöhe **901** d.	|	|	|	...	|	|	...	|	...
Bebra .... **901** d.	|	|	|	...	|	|	...	|	...
Eisenach .... d.	2013	2013	2050	...	2139	2213	...	|	...
Gotha .... d.	2031	2031	...	...	2154	2231	...	|	...
Erfurt Hbf .... d.	|	|	...	...	2213	|	...	|	...
Weimar .... a.	|	|	...	...	...	|	...	|	...
Naumburg (Saale) Hbf ... a.	|	|	...	...	...	|	...	|	...
Leipzig Hbf .... **851** a.	|	|	...	...	...	|	...	|	...
Dresden Hbf **842** .... a.	2158	2158	...	...	...	2344	...	0300	...
Halle (Saale) Hbf .... **851** d.	2239	2239	...	...	...	|	...	|	...
Bitterfeld .... **851** d.	|	|	...	...	...	|	...	0359	...
Lutherstadt Wittenberg .. **851** d.	2254	2254	...	...	...	0037	...	...	...
Berlin Südkreuz .... **851** a.	...	...	...	...	...	...	...	...	...
Berlin Hbf .... **851 902** a.	...	...	...	...	...	...	...	...	...

SEE NOTE ⊠	*EN* **470**	*ICE* **1531**	*ICE* **1716**	*ICE* **1731**	*ICE* **1553**	*ICE* **1626**	*ICE* **1543**	*ICE* **1533**	*IC* **1937**	*ICE* **1555**
	Ⓡ	Ⓐ	Ⓐ	⑥	①–⑥	⑦	①–⑥	Ⓐ	⑥	
	B	J		p	e	b	e		y	
		🍸	✕	T✕	✕	H✕	✕	✕		✕
Wiesbaden Hbf **911** .... d.	...	...	...	...	...	...	...	...	...	...
Frankfurt Flughafen ✈ § .... d.	...	...	...	...	...	...	...	...	...	...
Frankfurt (Main) Hbf ...... **900/1/2** d.	...	...	...	...	0437g	...	0617	...	...	0718
Frankfurt (Main) Süd .... d.	0054	...	...	...	|	...	|	...	...	|
Hanau Hbf .... **900/1/2** d.	|	...	...	...	|	...	0633	...	...	|
Fulda .... **900/1/2** d.	0147	...	...	...	0532g	...	0714	...	...	0814
Bad Hersfeld .... **901** d.	|	...	...	...	0559g	...	0740	...	...	|
Kassel Wilhelmshöhe ...... **901** d.	|	...	...	...	|	...	|	...	...	|
Bebra .... **901** d.	|	...	...	...	|	...	|	...	...	|
Eisenach .... d.	|	...	0545	...	0647	0744	0812	...	...	0918
Gotha .... d.	|	...	0604	...	0706	0805	|	...	...	0938
Erfurt Hbf .... d.	|	...	0627	0712	0727	0827	0847	0912	...	0958
Weimar .... a.	|	...	|	|	|	|	|	|	...	|
Naumburg (Saale) Hbf .... a.	|	...	|	|	|	|	|	|	...	|
Leipzig Hbf .... **851** a.	|	...	0709	|	0810	0910	0933	|	...	1042
Dresden Hbf **842** .... a.	|	...	|	|	0935	|	...	|	...	1155
Halle (Saale) Hbf .... **851** d.	0459	0646	|	0748	...	|	...	0948	0948	...
Bitterfeld .... **851** d.	|	|	|	|	...	|	...	|	|	...
Lutherstadt Wittenberg .... **851** d.	|	|	0748	|	...	0948	...	|	|	...
Berlin Südkreuz .... **851** a.	|	0754	0822	0854	...	1022	...	1054	1054	...
Berlin Hbf .... **851 902** a.	0633	0801	0829	0901	...	1030	...	1101	1102	...

SEE NOTE ⊠	*ICE* **1545**	*ICE* **1535**	*ICE* **1557**	*ICE* **1597**	*ICE* **1547**	*ICE* **1537**	*ICE* **1559**	*ICE* **1549**	*ICE* **1539**	*ICE* **1651**	*IC* **1969**	*ICE* **1641**	*ICE* **1631**	*ICE* **1653**	*ICE* **1643**	*IC* **2398**	*ICE* **1633**	*ICE* **1655**	*IC* **2157**	*ICE* **1645**	*ICE* **1657**	*ICE* **1647**	*ICE* **1659**	*ICE* **1659**	*ICE* **1659**
			①–⑥								⑤⑦					①–④	Ⓑq		Ⓑ	Ⓑq			Ⓑ	⑤⑦	⑦
			e								c					m			Q				q	v	w
	✕	✕	S✕	🍸◐	✕	✕	✕	✕	✕	✕	U	✕	✕	✕	✕		✕	✕		✕	✕	✕	✕	✕	✕
Wiesbaden Hbf **911** .... d.	...	...	...	0824z	...	...	1024	...	...	1224	...	...	...	1424	...	...	...	1624	...	...	1824	...	2024	2024	2024
Frankfurt Flughafen ✈ § .. d.	0811	...	...	0901	1011	...	1101	1211	...	1301	...	1411	...	1501	1610	...	...	1701	...	1811	1901	...	2101	2101	2101
Frankfurt (Main) Hbf **900/1/2** d.	|	...	0919	0919	|	...	1119	|	...	1319	...	|	...	1520	|	1617	...	1720	...	|	1919	2022	2119	2119	2119
Frankfurt (Main) Süd .... d.	0822	...	|	|	1022	...	|	1222	...	|	...	1422	...	|	1622	|	...	|	...	1822	|	|	|	|	|
Hanau Hbf .... **900/1/2** d.	|	...	|	|	|	...	|	|	...	|	...	|	...	|	|	1641	...	|	...	|	|	2038	|	|	|
Fulda .... **900/1/2** d.	0914	...	1014	1014	1114	...	1214	1314	...	1414	...	1514	...	1614	1714	1723	...	1814	...	1914	2014	2118	2214	2214	2214
Bad Hersfeld .... **901** d.	0940	...	|	|	1140	...	|	1340	...	|	...	1540	...	|	1740	1753	...	|	...	1940	|	2144	2239	2239	2239
Kassel Wilhelmshöhe **901** d.	|	...	|	|	|	...	|	|	...	|	1425	|	...	|	|	|	...	|	1909	|	|	|	|	|	|
Bebra .... **901** d.	|	...	|	|	|	...	|	|	...	|	|	|	...	|	|	1803	...	|	|	|	|	|	|	|	|
Eisenach .... d.	1012	...	1118	1118	1212	...	1318	1412	...	1518	|	1612	...	1718	1812	...	...	1918	|	2012	2117	|	2318	2318	2318
Gotha .... d.	|	...	1138	1138	|	...	1338	|	...	1538	|	|	...	1738	|	...	...	1938	|	2031	2133	|	2337	2337	2337
Erfurt Hbf .... d.	1048	1112	1158	1158	1248	1312	1358	1448	1512	1558	|	1648	1712	1757	1858t	...	1912	1958	|	2058t	2158	2258	2351	2353	2353
Weimar .... a.	|	|	|	|	|	|	|	|	|	|	|	|	|	|	|	...	|	|	|	|	|	|	...	|	|
Naumburg (Saale) Hbf ... a.	|	|	|	|	|	|	|	|	|	|	|	|	|	|	|	...	|	|	|	|	|	|	...	|	|
Leipzig Hbf .... **851** a.	1132	|	1242	1242	1332	|	1442	1532	|	1642	|	1732	|	1842	1947	...	|	2042	|	2142x	2242‡	2342	...	0037	0037
Dresden Hbf **842** .... a.	...	|	1355	1355j	...	|	1555	...	|	1755	|	...	|	1955	...	...	|	2155	|	...	0004n	...	...	...	0151
Halle (Saale) Hbf .... **851** d.	...	1148	...	...	...	1348	...	...	1548	...	1716	...	1748	...	...	...	1948	...	2206	...	...	...	...	...	...
Bitterfeld .... **851** d.	...	|	...	...	...	|	...	...	|	...	|	...	|	...	...	...	|	...	...	...	...	...	...	...	...
Lutherstadt Wittenberg .. **851** d.	...	|	...	...	...	|	...	...	|	...	1756	...	|	...	...	...	|	...	...	...	...	...	...	...	...
Berlin Südkreuz .... **851** a.	...	1254	...	...	...	1454	...	...	1654	...	1837	...	1854	...	...	...	2054	...	...	...	...	...	...	...	...
Berlin Hbf .... **851 902** a.	...	1301	...	...	...	1501	...	...	1701	...	1845	...	1901	...	...	...	2102	...	...	...	...	...	...	...	...

A – *ÖBB nightjet.* 🛏 1, 2 cl., 🛏 2 cl. and (2) Hamburg Hbf (d. 1956) - Berlin - Basel - Zürich. From Apr. 18 departs Berlin Hbf 2212, Südkreuz 2219, Halle 2337.
B – *ÖBB nightjet.* 🛏 1, 2 cl., 🛏 2 cl. and (2) Zürich - Basel - Berlin - Hamburg Hbf (a. 0849). From Apr. 18 arrives Berlin Hbf 0608, Hamburg Hbf 0831.
H – From / to Hamburg (Table **840**).
J – Not Mar. 16, 23, 30, Apr. 6, 13. From Jena (Table **851**). Until Apr. 12 arrives Berlin Südkreuz 0829, Berlin Hbf 0837.
K – To / from Stuttgart on dates in Table **912**.
Q – Ⓑ to May 5 (not Apr. 14, 16, 19, 26, 30). (12) Köln - Hamm - Kassel - Halle.
S – To / from Saarbrücken (Table **919**).
T – From / to Ostseebad Binz and Stralsund on dates in Tables **844** and **845**.
U – To / from Düsseldorf (Tables **800**/**805**).

b – Also Apr. 15, 17, May 1.
c – ⑤⑦ to May 5 (also Apr. 13, 17, May 1; not Apr. 14, 16, 30).
d – ⑤⑦ to Apr. 28 (also Apr. 13, 17, May 1; not Apr. 14, 16).
e – ①–⑥ (not Apr. 15, 17, May 1).
f – Also Apr. 13, May 24; not Apr. 14, May 26.
g – ① (also Apr. 18, May 2; not Apr. 17, May 1).
h – ⑥ (also Apr. 14, 16, 30).
j – ⑦ (also Apr. 15, 17, May 1).

m – Not Apr. 13, 17, May 1, 15, 24, 25.
n – Leipzig - Dresden on Ⓑ (not Mar. 13, 14, Apr. 14, 16, 30, May 15, 16, 22).
p – Also Apr. 14, May 25; not Apr. 15, May 27.
q – Not Apr. 14, 16, 30.
t – Arrives 12 minutes earlier.
v – Also Apr. 13, 17, May 1, 24; not Apr. 14, 16, 30, May 26.
w – Also Apr. 17, May 1; not Apr. 16, 30.
x – Not ①② Mar. 20 - May 9. Arrives 2159 on Mar. 13, 14, May 15, 16, 22.
y – Also Apr. 16, 30; not Apr. 15, 29.
z – Ⓒ only.

‡ – 2258 on Mar. 13, 14, May 15, 16, 22.
◧ – Conveys ✕ on ⑥ **h**.
◐ – Conveys ✕ on ⑦ **j**.
⊙ – Also calls at Leipzig/Halle Flughafen (d. 0435).
⊠ – **WARNING!** Berlin timings may vary by up to 25 minutes until Apr. 17 (earlier departures / later arrivals possible). Timings at Frankfurt Flughafen, Frankfurt (Main) Hbf and Hanau are subject to alteration on ⑥⑦ Feb. 11 - Apr. 2 (also Apr. 14 – 17). See also engineering work panel on page 367.

Scenic Rail Routes of Europe

The following is a list of some of the most scenic rail routes of Europe, timings for most of which can be found within the timetable (the relevant table number has been specified in bold). Routes marked * are some of the editorial team's favourite journeys. Please note that this list does not include specialised mountain and tourist railways.

Types of scenery : C-Coastline, F-Forest, G-Gorge, L-Lake, M-Mountain, R-River.

ALBANIA

Elbasan - Pogradec	ML G		R		1390

AUSTRIA

Bruck an der Mur - Villach	M		R		980
Gmunden - Stainach Irdning*	ML				961
Innsbruck - Brennero	M				595
Innsbruck - Garmisch*	M				895
Innsbruck - Schwarzach-St Veit	M G				960
Krems - Emmersdorf			R		991
Landeck - Bludenz*	M				951
St Pölten - Mariazell*	M				994
Salzburg - Villach*	M G				970
Selzthal - Kleinreifling - Steyr	M G		R		976/977
Wiener Neustadt - Graz	M				980

BELGIUM and LUXEMBOURG

Liège - Luxembourg*			R		444
Liège - Marloie			R		447
Namur - Dinant			R		440

BULGARIA

Septemvri - Dobriniste	M				1510
Sofia - Burgas	M				1500
Tulovo - Gorna Oryakhovitsa	M				1525

CROATIA and BOSNIA

Rijeka - Ogulin	M				1310
Ogulin - Split	M				1330
Sarajevo - Ploče	M G		R		1355

CZECH REPUBLIC

Karlovy Vary - Mariánské Lázně		R F			1123
Karlovy Vary - Chomutov		R			1110
Praha - Děčín		R			1100

DENMARK

Struer - Thisted	C				716

FINLAND

Kouvola - Joensuu	L		F		797

FRANCE

Aurillac - Neussargues	M G				331
Bastia - Ajaccio	M				369
Bourg-en-Bresse - Bellegarde	M				341
Chambéry - Bourg St Maurice	M				366
Chambéry - Modane	ML				367
Chamonix - Martigny*	M G				572
Clermont Ferrand - Béziers	M G				332
Clermont Ferrand - Nîmes*	M G		R		333
Gap - Briançon	ML				362
Genève - Aix les Bains	M		R		364
Grenoble - Veynes - Marseille	M				632
Marseille - Ventimiglia		C			360/361
Mouchard - Montbéliard			R		378
Nice - Digne	M				359
Nice - Cuneo*	M				581
Perpignan - Latour de Carol*	M G				354
Portbou - Perpignan		C			355
Sarlat - Bergerac			R		318
Toulouse - Latour de Carol	M				312
Valence - Veynes	M				362

GERMANY

Arnstadt - Meiningen	M				870
Dresden - Děčín		G R			1100
Freiburg - Donaueschingen		G	F		938
Garmisch - Reutte - Kempten	M				888
Heidelberg - Neckarelz			R		923/924
Koblenz - Mainz*		G R			911/914
München - Lindau	M				935
Murnau - Oberammergau	ML				897
Naumburg - Saalfeld			R		849/851
Niebüll - Westerland		C			821
Nürnberg - Pegnitz		G R			880

GERMANY - continued

Offenburg - Konstanz	M		F		916
Pforzheim - Nagold / Wildbad			F		941
Plattling - Bayerisch Eisenstein			F		929
Rosenheim - Berchtesgaden	ML				890/891
Rosenheim - Wörgl	M				951
Siegburg/Bonn - Siegen			R		807
Stuttgart - Singen			F		940
Titisee - Seebrugg	L				938
Trier - Koblenz - Giessen			R		906/915
Ulm - Göppingen	M				930
Ulm - Tuttlingen			R		938

GREAT BRITAIN and IRELAND

Alnmouth - Dunbar		C			180
Barrow in Furness - Maryport		C			159
Coleraine - Londonderry		C			231
Dun Laoghaire - Wicklow		C			237
Edinburgh - Aberdeen		C			224
Exeter - Newton Abbot		C			115/116
Glasgow - Oban / Mallaig*	ML				218
Inverness - Kyle of Lochalsh*	M	C			226
Lancaster - Carlisle - Carstairs	M	G	R		151
Liskeard - Looe			R		118
Llanelli - Craven Arms	M				146
Machynlleth - Pwllheli	M	C			148
Perth - Inverness	M				221
Plymouth - Gunnislake			R		118
St Erth - St Ives		C			118
Sheffield - Chinley	M				193/206
Shrewsbury - Aberystwyth	M		R		147
Skipton - Settle - Carlisle	M				173

GREECE

Korinthos - Patras		C			1450
Diakoptó - Kalávrita	M	G			1455

HUNGARY

Budapest - Szob			R		1255
Eger - Szilvásvárad	M				1299
Székesfehérvár - Balatonszentgyörgy	L				1220
Székesfehérvár - Tapolca	L				1225

ITALY

Bologna - Pistoia	M				609
Bolzano - Merano	M				597
Brennero - Verona*	M				595
Brig - Arona	ML				590
Domodossola - Locarno*	M G				551
Firenze - Viareggio	M				614
Fortezza - San Candido	M				596
Genova - Pisa		C			610
Genova - Ventimiglia		C			580
Lecco - Tirano	ML				593
Messina - Palermo		C			641
Napoli - Sorrento		C			639
Roma - Pescara		C			624
Salerno - Reggio Calabria		C			640
Taranto - Reggio Calabria		C			635
Torino - Aosta	M				586
Ventimiglia - Cuneo*	M G				581

NORWAY

Bergen - Oslo*	ML				780/781
Bodø - Trondheim	ML				787
Dombås - Åndalsnes	M				785
Drammen - Larvik		C			783
Myrdal - Flåm*	M	C			781
Oslo - Kongsvinger			R		750
Oslo / Røros - Trondheim	ML				784/785
Stavanger - Kristiansand	M				775

POLAND

Jelenia Góra - Walbrzych	M				1084
Kraków - Zakopane	M				1066
Olsztyn - Elk	L				1035
Olsztyn - Morag	L				1035
Tarnów - Krynica	M				1078

PORTUGAL

Covilhã - Entroncamento	M		R		69*
Pampilhosa - Guarda	M				692
Porto - Coimbra		C R			690
Porto - Pocinho*			R		69*
Porto - Valença	M	C			69(

ROMANIA

Brasov - Ploesti	M				1600
Caransebes - Craiova	M G		R		1620
Fetesti - Constanta			R		1680
Oradea - Cluj Napoca			R		1612

SERBIA and MONTENEGRO

Priboj - Bar	ML				1370

SLOVAKIA

Banská Bystrica - Brezno - Košice	M				1192
Žilina - Poprad Tatry	M				1180

SLOVENIA

Jesenice - Sežana	M G		R		1302
Maribor - Zidani Most	M				1315
Maribor - Bleiburg	M G		R		1315
Villa Opicina - Ljubljana - Zagreb		G	R		1305

SPAIN

Algeciras - Ronda	M		R		673
Barcelona - Latour de Carol	M				656
Bilbao - San Sebastián	M				686
Bilbao - Santander	M				687
Ferrol - Gijón*		C			687
Granada - Almería	M				673
Huesca - Canfranc	M G		R		670
León - Monforte de Lemos	M				682
León - Oviedo	M				685
Lleida - La Pobla de Segur	ML				655
Málaga - Bobadilla		G			673
Santander - Oviedo	M	C			687
Zaragoza - València	M				670

SWEDEN

Bollnäs - Änge - Sundsvall	ML				761
Borlänge - Mora	ML		F		758
Borlänge - Ludvika - Frövi	ML		F		755
Narvik - Kiruna	M		F		765
Östersund - Storlien	L		F		761

SWITZERLAND

Andermatt - Göschenen		G			576
Basel - Delémont - Moutier	M		R		505
Chur - Arosa	M G				541
Chur - Brig - Zermatt*	M				575/576
Chur - St Moritz*	M G				540
Davos - Filisur	M G				545a
Davos - Landquart	M				545
Interlaken Ost - Jungfraujoch*	M				564
Interlaken Ost - Luzern	ML				560
Interlaken West - Spiez	L				560
Lausanne - Brig	ML		R		570
Lausanne - Neuchâtel - Biel	ML				505
Montreux - Zweisimmen - Lenk	ML G				566
Rorschach - Kreuzlingen	L				532
St Moritz - Scuol Tarasp	M				546
St Moritz - Tirano*	M				547
Spiez - Zweisimmen		G			563
Thun - Kandersteg - Brig*	ML				562
Zürich / Luzern - Chiasso	ML				550
Zürich - Chur	ML				520

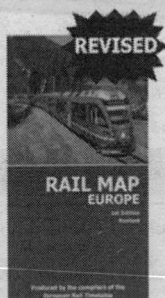 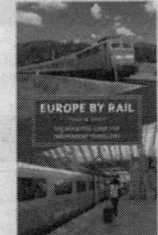
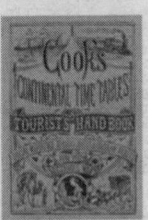 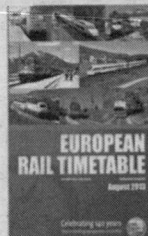
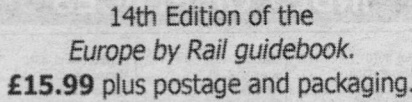
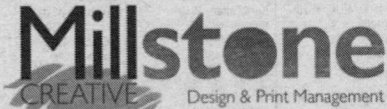

BEYOND EUROPE
Africa and the Middle East

INDEX OF PLACES

A

Aba, 4270
Abeokuta, 4270
Abidjan, 4260
Abu Hamed, 4200
Abqaiq, 4620
Accra, 4250
Ad Dammam, 4620
Ad Dwanyah, 4610
Agboville, 4260
Agege, 4270
Aïn M'Lila, 4030
Ain Seeba, 4000, 4005
Aïn Touta, 4030
Akko, 4500, 4510
Al Basrah, 4610
Aleppo, 4600
Alexandria, 4100, 4110, 4120, 4130
Alger, 4020, 4040
Al Hasakah, 4600
Al Hillah, 4610
Al Hufuf, 4620
Ali Sabieh, 4215
Al Ladhiqyah, 4600
Al Mawsil, 4610
Al Qâmishli, 4600
Ambila-Lemaitso, 4340
Amritsar, 4650
Andasibe, 4340
Annaba, 4040
An Nasiriyah, 4610
Anyama, 4260
Ar Raqqah, 4600
Ar Riyad, 4620
Asilah, 4000
Asmara, 4210
Asoprochona, 4250
Aswân, 4150
Asyût, 4150
Atari, 4650
Atbara, 4200
Azzaba, 4040

B

Babanusa, 4200
Bafoulabé, 4240
Baghdâd, 4610
Ba'iji, 4610
Balaka, 4360
Bamako, 4240
Bandar e Abbas, 4630
Banfora, 4260
Bannockburn, 4380
Barika, 4030
Batna, 4030
Bauchi, 4270
Beaufort West, 4400
Béchar, 4010
Be'er Sheva, 4510
Beira, 4370
Beit Bridge, 4380
Béja, 4050
Béjaïa, 4040
Belabo, 4280
Bellville, 4400
Benguerir, 4000
Ben Gurion Airport, 4500, 4510
Benha, 4110
Beni Mansour, 4040
Beni Nsar, 4000
Béni Suef, 4150
Berber, 4200
Bet She'an, 4513
Bet Shemesh, 4515
Bibala, 4350
Bilila, 4360
Binyamina, 4500, 4510
Bir Bou Rekba, 4080
Biskra, 4030

Bismaron, 4600
Bizerte, 4060
Blida, 4020
Blantyre, 4360
Bloemfontein, 4400
Bobo Dioulasso, 4260
Boké, 4230
Booué, 4290
Bordj Bou Arreridj, 4040
Borj Cédria, 4080
Bouaké, 4260
Bouchegouf, 4040
Bouira, 4040
Brazzaville, 4300
Bulawayo, 4380
Buni, 4270
Burgersdorp, 4400
Bûr Sa'îd, 4130
Bûr Sûdan, 4200

C

Caála, 4350
Cairo, 4100, 4110, 4120, 4130, 4140, 4150.
Cambuio, 4350
Cape Town, 4400
Casablanca, 4000, 4005
Catete, 4350
Chegutu, 4380
Chicualacuala, 4370, 4380
Chiredzi, 4380
Chisamba, 4330
Chlef, 4020
Chókwe, 4370
Choma, 4330
Conakry, 4230
Constantine, 4030, 4040
Cradock, 4400
Cuamba, 4370

D

Dagash, 4200
Dahmani, 4070
Dalbandin, 4640
Damanhûr, 4110
Dango, 4350
Dar es Salaam, 4330
Dayr az Zawr, 4600
De Aar, 4400
Dete, 4380
Dewelé, 4215
Dilolo, 4320
Dimbokro, 4260
Diré Daoua, 4215
Djamâa, 4030
Djibouti, 4215
Djulfa, 4630
Dodoma, 4330
Dolisie, 4300
Dondo (Cuanza), 4350
Dondo (Lubango), 4350
Dondo (M'bique), 4370
Douala, 4280
Dreá, 4040
Dumyat, 4120
Durban, 4400

E

East London, 4400
Ed. Dâmer, 4200
Ede, 4270
Edéa, 4280
El Affroun, 4020
El Alamein, 4100
El Daien, 4200
El Giza, 4150
El Harrouch, 4040
El Jadida, 4000
El Jem, 4080

El Kef, 4070
El Menya, 4150
El Milia, 4040
El Obeid, 4200
El Suweis, 4140
Enugu, 4270
Er Rahad, 4200
Eséka, 4280
Esfahan, 4630

F

Ferkessédougou, 4260
Fès, 4000
Fianarantsoa, 4340
Franceville, 4290
Francistown, 4345, 4380

G

Gaafour, 4070
Gabès, 4080
Gaborone, 4345
Gafsa, 4080
Gebeit, 4200
Germiston, 4400
Ghardimaou, 4050
Ghazaouet, 4010
Ghinda, 4210
Ghraïba, 4080
Gombe, 4270
Grünau, 4390
Guercif, 4000
Gwayi, 4380
Gweru, 4380

H

Haifa, 4500, 4510, 4513
Haiya, 4200
Hammamet, 4080
Halte Kilomètre 36, 4230
Hamah, 4600
Harare, 4380
Hertsliyya, 4515
Hims, 4600
Huambo, 4350
Hwange, 4380

I

Iapala, 4370
Ibadan, 4270
Ifakara, 4330
Ilebo, 4320
Ilorin, 4270
Inhaminga, 4370
Inhamitanga, 4370
Itigi, 4330

J

Jacobabad, 4650
Jebba, 4270
Jendouba, 4050
Jerissa, 4070
Jerusalem, 4515
Jijel, 4040
Jisr ash Shughur, 4600
Johannesburg, 4400

K

Kaapmuiden, 4400
Kabalo, 4320
Kabwe, 4330
Kadoma, 4380
Kaduna, 4270
Kafanchan, 4270
Kafue, 4330
Kalaâ Kasbah, 4070
Kalaâ Séghira, 4080
Kalemie, 4320
Kaliua, 4330

Kalkrand, 4390
Kalomo, 4330
Kamina, 4320
Kamsar, 4230
Kananga, 4320
Kano, 4270
Kapiri Mposhi, 4330
Karasburg, 4390
Karibib, 4390
Kasama, 4330
Katchiungo, 4350
Kati, 4240
Katiola, 4260
Kayes, 4024 .
Keetmanshoop, 4390
Kenitra, 4000, 4005
Khanewal, 4650
Khartoum, 4200
Khémis Miliana, 4020
Khorramshahr, 4630
Kigoma, 4330
Kilosa, 4330
Kimberley, 4400
Kindu, 4320
Kinshasa, 4320
Kiryat Gat, 4510
Kisaki, 4330
Kisangani, 4320
Kisumu, 4310
Kita, 4240
Kitwe, 4330
Klerksdorp, 4400
Komatipoort, 4400
Kôsti, 4200
Koudougou, 4260
Kranzberg, 4390
Kroonstad, 4400
Kuhi Taftan, 4640
Kumasi, 4250
Kumba, 4280
Kwekwe, 4380

L

Ladysmith, 4400
Lafia, 4270
Lahore, 4650
Lastourville, 4290
Le Sers, 4070
Libreville, see Owendo
Limbe, 4360
Livingstone, 4330
Liwonde, 4360
Lobatse, 4345
Lobita, 4350
Lod, 4510, 4515
Lohariandava, 4340
Loutété, 4300
Luanda, 4350
Luau, 4350
Lubango, 4350
Lubumbashi, 4320
Luena, 4350
Lundi, 4380
Lusaka, 4330
Luxor, 4150

M

Macheke, 4380
Maghnia, 4010
Mahalapye, 4345
Mahdia, 4080, 4090
Maiduguri, 4270
Makambako, 4330
Makhanga, 4360
Makhado, 4400
Makindu, 4310
Makurdi, 4270
Malange, 4350
Malema, 4370
Manakara, 4340

Manampatrana, 4340
Manyoni, 4330
Maotiza, 4370
Maputo, 4370
Mariental, 4390
Marondera, 4380
Marrakech, 4000
Marromeu, 4370
Mashhad, 4630
Masvingo, 4380
Matadi, 4320
Matala, 4350
Mateur, 4060
Mazabuka, 4330
Mbanga, 4280
Mbeya, 4330
Mbitom, 4280
Mechraa Bel Ksiri, 4000
Mechrouha, 4040
Meknes Amir, 4000
Menongue, 4350
Mersa Matruh, 4100
Metlaoui, 4080
Middelburg, 4400
Mindouli, 4300
Minna, 4270
Mirjawa, 4640
Mitande, 4370
Mitsiwa, 4210
Mlimbe, 4330
Mkushi Boma, 4330
Moambe, 4370
Moanda, 4290
Modi'in, 4510
Mohammadia, 4020
Moknine, 4090
Mokopane, 4400
Mombasa, 4310
Monastir, 4080, 4090
Monculo, 4210
Monze, 4330
Moramanga, 4340
Morogoro, 4330
Mostaganem, 4020
Mpanda, 4330
Mpika, 4330
M'Sila, 4030, 4040
Mtito Andei, 4310
Mulobezi, 4330
Muanza, 4370
Musina, 4400
Mutare, 4380
Mutuali, 4370
Mwanza, 4330
Mwene Ditu, 4320

N

Nador, 4000
Naâma, 4010
Nabeul, 4080
Nahariyya, 4500, 4510
Nairobi, 4310
Nakonde, 4330
Nakuru, 4310
Namibe, 4350
Nampula, 4370
Nanga Eboko, 4280
Nayuchi, 4360, 4370
N'dalatando, 4350
Ndjole, 4290
Ndola, 4330
Nefasit, 4210
Nelspruit, 4400
Newcastle, 4400
N'gaoundéré, 4280
Ngezi, 4380
Ngoumou, 4280
Ngwezi, 4330
Nhamalabue, 4370
Niangoloko, 4260
Nkaya, 4360
Nkayi, 4300

Nok Kundi, 4640
Norton, 4380
Nouadhibou, 4220
Nsawam, 4250
Nushki, 4640
Nyálá, 4200
Nyazura, 4380

O

Okahandja, 4390
Omaruru, 4390
Omuthiya, 4390
Ondangwa, 4390
Oran, 4010, 4020
Oshikango, 4390
Oshivelo, 4390
Oshogbo, 4270
Otjiwarongo, 4390
Otumlo, 4210
Oturkpo, 4270
Ouagadougou, 4260
Ouangolodougou, 4260
Oued Kébérit, 4040
Oujda, 4000
Oum el Bouaghi, 4030
Owendo, 4290

P

Pemba, 4330
Pietermaritzburg, 4400
Pointe Noire, 4300
Polokwane, 4400
Pont Du Fahs, 4070
Port Elizabeth, 4400
Port Harcourt, 4270
Pretoria, 4400

Q

Qena, 4150
Qiryat, 4500, 4510
Qom, 4630
Queenstown, 4400
Quetta, 4640, 4650

R

Rabat, 4000, 4005
Ramdane Djamel, 4040
Ranomena, 4340
Rehoboth, 4390
Relizane, 4020
Ressano Garcia, 4370
Rohri, 4650
Rusápe, 4380
Rutenga, 4380
Ruvu, 4330

S

Safi, 4000
Sahasinaka, 4340
Sakania, 4320
Salé, 4005
Samarra, 4610
Sangaredi, 4230
Sarakhs, 4630
Sennâr, 4200
Serenje, 4330
Setif, 4040
Settat, 4000
Sfax, 4080
Shangani, 4380
Shendî, 4200
Shiraz, 4630
Sibi, 4650
Sidi Bel Abbès, 4010
Sidi El Hémissi, 4040
Sidi Kacem, 4000
Sidi Yahia, 4030
Simbaya, 4230
Sinkat, 4200

Skikda, 4040
Sohâg, 4150
Somabhula, 4380
Souk Ahras, 4040
Sousse, 4080, 4090
Spezand, 4640
Standerton, 4400
Swakopmund, 4390

T

Tabora, 4330
Tabriz, 4630
Tafiré, 4260
Takoradi, 4250
Tampolo, 4340
Tanger, 4000
Tanta, 4110
Taourirt, 4000
Tartus, 4600
Tataouine, 4080
Taza, 4000
Tebessa, 4030, 4040
Tebourba, 4050
Tehran, 4630
Tel Aviv, 4500, 4510, 4515
Tendelti, 4200
Tenke, 4320
Thénia, 4040
Thomson, 4380
Tikrit, 4610
Tlemcen, 4010
Toamasina, 4340
Tolongoina, 4340
Touggourt, 4030
Tozeur, 4080
Triangle, 4380
Tses, 4390
Tsumeb, 4390
Tunduma, 4330
Tunis, 4050, 4060, 4070, 4080

U

Ubundu, 4320
Umm Qasr, 4610
Umuahia Ibeku, 4270
Usakos, 4390
Uvinza, 4330

V

Vereeniging, 4400
Viana, 4350
Victoria Falls, 4380
Voi, 4310

W

Wali Khan, 4640
Walvisbaai, 4390
Wadi Halfa, 4200
Wagah, 4650
Windhoek, 4390
Witbank, 4400
Worcester, 4400

Y

Yaoundé, 4280

Z

Zâhedân, 4630, 4640
Zaria, 4270
Zenza, 4350
Zouérate, 4220
Zungeru, 4270

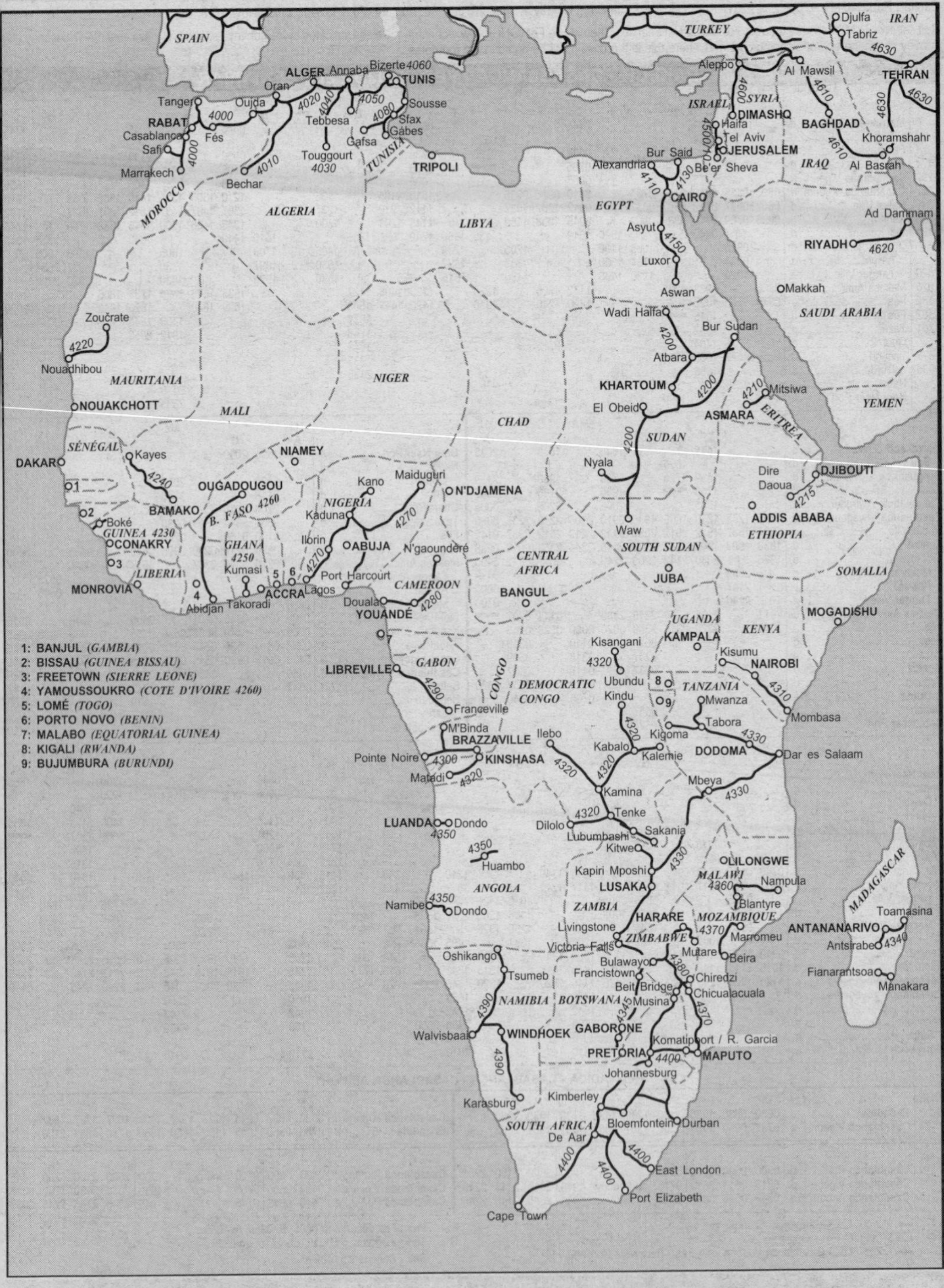

Map of Africa and the Middle East showing railway routes.

SPAIN

Tanger, Oujda, RABAT, Casablanca, Fés, Safi, Marrakech, Bechar — *MOROCCO* — 4000, 4010

Oran, ALGER, Annaba, Bizerte 4060, TUNIS, Sousse, Sfax, Gabès, Gafsa, Tebbesa, Touggourt 4030, 4020, 4040, 4050, 4080 — *TUNISIA*

TRIPOLI — *LIBYA*

ALGERIA, Zoucrate 4220, Nouadhibou, NOUAKCHOTT — *MAURITANIA*

NIGER, *MALI*, *CHAD*

DAKAR, *SÉNÉGAL*, Kayes 4240, BAMAKO, OUAGADOUGOU 4260, *B. FASO*, NIAMEY

GUINEA 4230, Boké, CONAKRY, *LIBERIA*, MONROVIA, Kumasi, *GHANA*, Abidjan, Takoradi, ACCRA, Kano, Kaduna, Ilorin, ABUJA, *NIGERIA*, Lagos, Port Harcourt, N'gaoundéré, Douala, YOUANDÉ, *CAMEROON*, 4270, 4280

N'DJAMENA, Maiduguri, *CENTRAL AFRICA*, BANGUI, Waw 4200, *SOUTH SUDAN*, JUBA

EGYPT, CAIRO, Alexandria, Asyut 4150, Luxor, Aswan, Wadi Halfa, Bur Said, Be'er Sheva, 4110, 4130

TURKEY, Aleppo, Al Mawsil 4610, *SYRIA*, DIMASHQ, Haifa, Tel Aviv, JERUSALEM, *ISRAEL*, Djulfa, Tabriz 4630, *IRAN*, TEHRAN, 4630, BAGHDAD, Khoramshahr, *IRAQ*, Al Basrah

Ad Dammam, RIYADH 4620, Makkah, *SAUDI ARABIA*, *YEMEN*

Bur Sudan 4200, Atbara, KHARTOUM, El Obeid, Nyala, *SUDAN*, 4200, 4210, Mitsiwa, ASMARA, *ERITREA*, DJIBOUTI 4215, Dire Daoua, ADDIS ABABA, *ETHIOPIA*, *SOMALIA*, MOGADISHU

DEMOCRATIC CONGO, Kisangani 4320, Ubundu, Kindu, Kabalo 4320, Kamina, Tenke, Dilolo, Lubumbashi, Sakania, Kitwe 4320

UGANDA, KAMPALA, Kisumu, NAIROBI 4310, Mombasa, *KENYA*, *TANZANIA*, Mwanza, Tabora, DODOMA, Dar es Salaam 4330, Kigoma, Kalemie, Mbeya

LIBREVILLE, *GABON*, Franceville, M'Binda, BRAZZAVILLE 4290, Pointe Noire 4300, Matadi, KINSHASA 4320, Ilebo, *CONGO*

LUANDA, Dondo 4350, Huambo, Namibe, Dondo, *ANGOLA*, Oshikango, Tsumeb 4390, Walvisbaai, WINDHOEK, *NAMIBIA*

Kapiri Mposhi, LUSAKA 4360, *ZAMBIA*, Livingstone, Victoria Falls, HARARE, *ZIMBABWE* 4370, Bulawayo, Francistown, *BOTSWANA*, GABORONE

LILONGWE, *MALAWI*, Blantyre, Nampula, Beira, Marromeu, *MOZAMBIQUE*, Mutare, Chiredzi, Chicualacuala, Beit Bridge, Musina, 4380, 4370

ANTANANARIVO, Toamasina, Antsirabe 4340, Fianarantsoa, Manakara, *MADAGASCAR*

PRETORIA 4400, Johannesburg, Kimberley, Karasburg, De Aar, Bloemfontein, Durban, East London, Port Elizabeth, Cape Town 4400, Komatipoort / R. Garcia, MAPUTO, *SOUTH AFRICA*

Legend:
1: BANJUL (*GAMBIA*)
2: BISSAU (*GUINEA BISSAU*)
3: FREETOWN (*SIERRA LEONE*)
4: YAMOUSSOUKRO (*COTE D'IVOIRE 4260*)
5: LOMÉ (*TOGO*)
6: PORTO NOVO (*BENIN*)
7: MALABO (*EQUATORIAL GUINEA*)
8: KIGALI (*RWANDA*)
9: BUJUMBURA (*BURUNDI*)

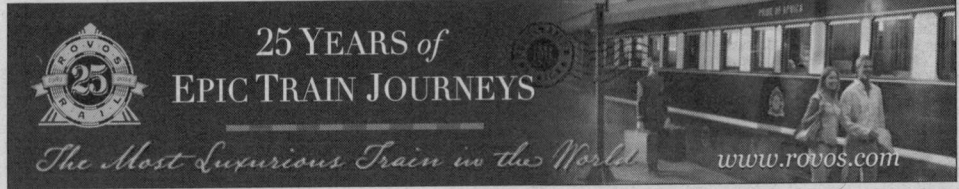

MOROCCO

Capital: **Rabat** (GMT + 0).   2017 Public Holidays: Jan. 1, 11, May 1, June 26, July 30, Aug. 14, 20, 21, Sept. 2, 22, Nov. 6, 18, Dec. 11.

Rail services in Morocco are operated by Office National des Chemins de Fer (ONCF. www.oncf.ma). Unless indicated trains convey 1st and 2nd class seating. Trains may also convey couchette and/or sleeping cars and where this is the case it will be noted in the footnotes.

4000   MARRAKECH - CASABLANCA - FÈS - OUJDA and BENI NSAR   ONCF

km						F		F		B		B						F
0	Marrakech Guéliz … d	…	…	…	…	0445	…	0645	…	0845	…	1045	…	…	…	…	…	1245
*	Safi … d						0525		0725									
74	Benguerir … d					0539		0739		0939		1139						1339
174	Settat … d					0705		0905		1105		1305						1505
257	Casablanca V'geurs … a					0805		1005		1205		1405						1605
257	Casablanca V'geurs … d	0505	0535	0610	0750 0735	0810	0905 0935	1010 1105	1135	1210 1305	1335	1410 1505	1535	1610				
346	Rabat Ville … d	0607	0637	0712	0807 0837	0912	1007 1037	1112 1210	1237	1307 1407	1437	1512 1607	1637	1712				
386	Kenitra … d	0638	0709	0745	0838 0909 fa	0945 1038 1109 fb	1145 1241	1309	1345 1438 1509	1545	1638 1709 fc	1745						
471	Sidi Kacem … d			0840		1000 1040	1135 1150 1240	1335	1610 1440		1640		1825 1840						
	Mechraa Bel Ksiri … d		0805		1005 1100		1205 1233		1405 1700		1605		1805 1905						
	Asilah … a		0934		1134 1300		1333 1437		1530 1837		1730		1927 2037						
620	Tanger Ville … a		1020		1230 1405		1430 1515		1630 1925		1830		2020 2130						
526	Meknes Amir … d	0806		0933 1006		1132 1206	1229	1333 1408 1427		1533 1606	▬ 1733 1806		1933					
582	Fès … a	0840		1020 1040		1220 1240	1310	1420 1443 1503		1620 1640	1820 1840		2020					
582	Fès … d			1045				1535		1700	1845							
701	Taza … d			1302				1748		1910 2050								
	Guercif … d			1404				1843		2015								
818	Taourirt … d			1500 1550				1933		2125								
935	Oujda … a			1655				2135										
	Nador … a			1735						2310								
	Beni Nsar Port … a			1800						2335								

		⚒		C		MA ▬		MT ▬ A					TM A	C	▬		⚒	
Marrakech Guéliz … d			1445		1645		1845		2045	Beni Nsar Port … d				2010				
Safi … d			1525							Nador … d				2033				
Benguerir … d			1539 1725		1739		1939		2139	Oujda … d		1935	2055					
Settat … d			1705		1905		2105		2305	Taourirt … d		2118	2245					
Casablanca Voyageurs … a			1805		2005		2205		0005	Guercif … d		2203 2246	2330					
Casablanca Voyageurs … d	1705	1735	1810 1905	1935	2010 2105	2210 2235	0030			Taza … d		2301 2344	0030					
Rabat Ville … d	1807	1837	1912 2012	2037	2112 2212	2312 2337	0140			Fès … a		0100 0150	0240					
Kenitra … d	1838	1909	1945 2047	2111	2145 2244	2353 0018	0228			Fès … d		0130 0210 0230 0305 0440	0535	0640				
Sidi Kacem … d	1925		2040 2142	2200	2240	0047 0112	0400			Meknes Amir … d		0210 0246 0307	0517	0606	0717			
Mechraa Bel Ksiri … d		2005					0438			Tanger Ville … d	2155				0525			
Asilah … a		2147					0600			Asilah … d	2244				0605			
Tanger Ville … a		2240					0700			Mechraa Bel Ksiri … d	0000				0725			
Meknes Amir … d	2011		2133 2234	2215	2333	0144 0225	▬			Sidi Kacem … d	0100 0308 0335 0404	0605 0649	0805					
Fès … a	2045		2220 2315	2350	0020 0050	0225 0245				Kenitra … d	0202 0420 0440 0502 0530 0705	0738 0835 0905						
Fès … d			0020		0110	0310				Rabat Ville … d	0300 0510 0530 0545 0615 0745	0815 0915 0945						
Taza … d			0237		0318	0509				Casablanca Voyageurs … a	0430 0615 0630 0645 0715 0845	0920 1020 1050						
Guercif … d			0337		0419	0607				Casablanca Voyageurs … d	0450	0650 0850	1050					
Taourirt … d					0510	0650 0820				Settat … d	0542	0742 0942	1142					
Oujda … d			0557		0705	0840	1003			Benguerir … d	0708	0908 1110 1200	1402					
Nador … d							1003			Safi … a			1402					
Beni Nsar Port … a			0625				1025			Marrakech Guéliz … a	0810	1010 1210	1410					

		⚒			G		B		G		B				G		
Beni Nsar Port … d									0840				1200		1655		
Nador … d									0906				1220		1715		
Oujda … d								0805		1115		1240 1400 1423		1855			
Taourirt … d								1005		1201		1507					
Guercif … d				0615				1046		1300		1606					
Taza … d				0822				1145		1510		1815					
Fès … a								1350									
Fès … d		0740	0811	0840 0940		1040 1140		1240	1340	1415 1440	1540	1640 1740	1840	2040			
Meknes Amir … d		0811		0917 1011		1117 1211		1317	1411	1457 1517	1611	1717 1811	1917	2118			
Tanger Ville … d			0725		0815 0925		1030 1125		1250	1320		1525	1725	1840			
Asilah … d			0805		0859 1008		1106 1206		1335	1406		1605	1806	1930			
Mechraa Bel Ksiri … d			0925		1045 1125		1256 1325		1501	1525		1725	1925	2111			
Sidi Kacem … d			1005		1122		1205 1331		1405 1536	1548 1605		1805	2005	2206			
Kenitra … d		0940 1035	1105 1140 ga	1235 1305 1340		1435 1505	gb 1540 1635		1705	1740 1835 1905 1940	2035 2105 gc	2305					
Rabat Ville … d		1015 1115	1145 1215	1315 1345 1415		1515 1545	1615 1715		1745	1815 1915 1945 2015 2115 2145	2355						
Casablanca Voyageurs … a		1120 1220	1245 1320	1420 1445 1520		1620 1645	▬ 1720 1820		1845	1920 2020 2045 2120 2220 2245	0115						
Casablanca Voyageurs … d			1250		1450		1650		1850	2050							
Settat … d			1342		1542		1742		1942	2142							
Benguerir … d			1508		1708		1908 2000		2108	2308							
Safi … d							2202										
Marrakech Guéliz … a			1610		1810		2010		2210	0010							

EL JADIDA - CASABLANCA - CASABLANCA AIRPORT

km		①–⑥								7			Casablanca V'geurs d	0627 0827 0915 1027 1227 1427 1627 1727 1932 …
0	El Jadida … d	0630	0830	1030	1130	1230	1430	1730	1830	1930			El Jadida … a	0750 0950 1045 1150 1350 1550 1750 1853 2100 …
123	Casablanca V'geurs … a	0747	0950	1151	1256	1351	1551	1851	1951	2055				

km												Casablanca Airport … d	0400 0600 0700 and hourly 1900 2000 2100 2200 2345
0	Casablanca Port … d	0300	0500	0600	0700		1900	2000 2100 2200				Casablanca V'geurs … a	0430 0630 0730 until 1930 2030 2130 2230 0017
	Casablanca V'geurs … d	0313	0513	0613	0713 and hourly	1913	2013 2113 2213					Casablanca Port … a	0445 0645 0745 1945 2045 2145 2245 0035
	Casablanca Airport … a	0345	0545	0645	0745 until	1945	2045 2145 2245						

A – ⚑ 1, 2 cl., 🛏 Marrakech - Tanger and v.v.
B – 🛏 Tanger - Fès - Oujda and v.v.
C – ⚑ 1, 2 cl., 🛏 Casablanca Voyageurs. - Fès - Beni Nsar Port and v.v.
* – Safi - Benguerir : 142 km.

F – From Fez departs: **fa** 0805, **fb** 0955, **fc** 1655.
G – To Fez arrives: **ga** 1310, **gb** 1715, **gc** 2330.

4005   CASABLANCA - RABAT - KENITRA   ONCF

km		↓	⚒	A	⚒	⚒		C																			C
93	Casablanca Port … d	0620	0650	0720	0750	0850	0950	1020	1050	1120	1150	1220	1320	1350	1420	1450	1520	1550	1620	1650	1720	1750	1820	1850	1920	1950
	Ain Seeba … d	0629	0659	0729	0759	0859	0959	1029	1059	1129	1159	1229	1329	1359	1429	1459	1529	1559	1629	1659	1729	1759	1829	1859	1929	1959
0	Rabat Ville … d	0732	0802	0832	0855	0952	1052	1132	1155	1222	1252	1322	1422	1452	1552	1622	1652	1732	1752	1852	1932	1952	2032			
7	Salé Ville … d	0740	0800	0840	0903	1000	1100	1140	1203	1124	1300	1340	1430	1500	1540	1630	1700	1740	1840	1940	1940	2040	2100			
40	Kenitra … a	0803	0823		0926	1023	1124	1227		1323	1403	1452	1523	1603	1652	1723	1803	1823	1903	1923	2003	2103	2123			

		⚒	⚒	A	⚒	⚒		B																			
Kenitra … d		0550	0605	0620	0650	0720	0755	0824		0920	1020			1224		1320	1355	1450	1520	1555		1650	1720	1755	1824	1850	1920
Salé Ville … d		0617	0632	0647	0717	0746	0820	0849	0919	0947	1047	1117	1216	1249	1317	1347	1420	1517	1547	1620	1646	1717	1747	1820	1849	1917	1947
Rabat Ville … d		0630	0645	0700	0730	0800	0830	0900	0930	1000	1100	1130	1230	1300	1330	1400	1430	1530	1600	1630	1700	1730	1800	1830	1900	1930	2000
Ain Seeba … d		0729	0738	0809	0839	0853	0929	0950	1029	1050	1150	1220	1320	1350	1420	1450	1530	1620	1650	1720	1750	1829	1850	1929	1950	2029	2050
Casablanca Port … a		0740	0750	0803	0840	0903	0940	1040	1040	1140	1230	1340	1340	1440	1500	1540	1630	1700	1740	1830	1900	1940	2000	2040			

A – Additional trips: 0820, 0920, 1250.   B – Additional trips: 1016, 1445.   C – Additional trips: 2020, 2120, 2150.   D – Additional trips: 1120, 2024, 2120.

ALGERIA

Capital: **Alger** (GMT +1).   2017 Public Holidays: Jan. 1, May 1, June 26, 27, July 5, Sept. 2, 3, 22, 30, Nov. 1, Dec. 11.

Rail services are operated Société Nationale des Transports Ferroviaires (SNTF. www.sntf.dz). Unless otherwise noted, trains convey first and second class seated accommodation. Long distance overnight trains may convey sleeping cars and/or couchettes and where this is the case it will be shown in the footnotes. Timings are the most recent available and are subject to alteration at any time.

ORAN - GHAZAOUET and BÉCHAR — 4010

SNTF   2nd class unless indicated

km		2✕	2	2	2	✕A			2	✕A	2	2	2	2	2
0	Oran ....d.	0730	1250	...	1600	1700	2030	Béchar ....d.	2000	...	...	...	...	...	...
76	Sidi bel Abbès ....d.	0835	1355	...	1711	1822	2134	Naâma ....d.	0009	...	...	...	...	...	...
163	Tlemcen ....d.	0956	1512	1700	1832	1942	...	Ghazaouet ....d.			0430	...	...	...	...
219	Maghnia ....d.	1105	1622	1823	1942	...	...	Maghnia ....d.			0445	0618	0850	...	1405
284	Ghazaouet ....a.	...	...	2010	...	...	...	Tlemcen ....d.			0550	0740	0955	...	1510	2000
350	Naâma ....a.	...	...	...	...	...	0130	Sidi bel Abbès ....d.	0323	0540	0706	...	1120	1629	2119
676	Béchar ....a.	...	...	...	...	...	0546	Oran ....a.	0500	0658	0809	...	1222	1726	...

A — 🛏, 🍴 and ✕ Oran - Béchar and v.v.

ORAN - ALGER — 4020

SNTF

km		2	✕	2B		✕	✕	2	✕	2✕	2			2	2C	2✕	✕	2	✕	✕	2
0	Oran ....d.	...	0625	...	0800	1230	1500	...	1615	1630	1715	Alger Agha☆ d.	...	0625	...	0800	1230	1500	1655	1800
77	Mohammadia ...d.	...	0716	0730	...	1320	...	...	1700	1728	1813	Blida ....☆ d.	...	0700	...	0829	1305	1529	1732	1854
	Mostaganem .a.	...	...	0820	...							El Affroun...☆ d.	...	0713	...		1318	...	...	1910
126	Relizane ....d.	...	0750	...	0903	1354	1607	...	1731	1802	1847	Khémis Miliana d.	...	0545	0756	...	1401	...	1800	...
213	Chlef ....d.	0530	0846	...		1448	1653	1730	1829	1856	...	Chlef ....d.	...	0650	0709	0854	...	1004	1503	1704	1932
303	Khémis Miliana .d.	...	0625	0954	...	1554	...	1844	...	...	...	Relizane ....d.	0525	0745	...	1001	...	1051	1604	1751	...
354	El Affroun .....☆ d.	0620		1038	...	1645						Mostaganem ..d.	...	0540	...		1030	...			
372	Blida ....☆ d.	0634	0721	1051	...	1129	1658	1829				Mohammadia ..d.	0600	0630	0823	...	1034	1120	1642	...	
421	Alger Agha .....☆ a.	0725	0757	1129	...	1200	1737	1900				Oran ....a.	0717	...	0911	...	1130	1200	1739	1900	...

☆ – Additional local trains available.   B – Additional trips: 1215, 1740.   C – Additional trip: 1630.

TEBESSA, TOUGGOURT and M'SILA — 4030

SNTF   2nd class only

km			A						A	
0	Constantine ....d.	...	0515	0545	...	M'Sila ....d.	...	1644	...
49	Aïn M'Lila ....d.	...	0601		...	Barika ....d.	...	1807	...
115	Oum el Bouaghi ....d.	...	0658		...	Touggourt ....d.	...	0100	...
212	Sidi Yahia ....d.	...	0837		...	Djamāa ....d.	...	0158	...
258	Tebessa ....a.	...	0916		...	Biskra ....d.	...	0512	1500
118	Batna ....d.	0430		0724	...	Aïn Touta ....d.	...		1631
151	Aïn Touta ....d.				...	Batna ....d.	...	1909	1656
238	Biskra ....d.		0921	2000	...	Tebessa ....d.	...		1510
403	Djamāa ....d.			2310	...	Sidi Yahia ....d.	...		1548
455	Touggourt ....a.		0016		...	Oum el Bouaghi ....d.	...		1726
202	Barika ....d.	0530			...	Aïn M'Lila ....d.	...		1821
299	M'Sila ....a.	0649			...	Constantine ....a.	...	1838	1908

ALGER - CONSTANTINE - TEBESSA — 4040

SNTF   2nd class unless indicated

km		✕B		A			✕C		✕C		A		✕B	
0	Alger ....☆ d.	0725	...	1230	1530	1620	2130	Tebessa ....d.	...	0430	...	...
54	Thénia ....☆ d.	0811	...	...	1705	1736	2214	Oued Kéberit ....d.	...	0541	...	...
123	Bouira ....d.	0940	...	1412	1713	1824	1906	2326	Dreâ ....d.	...	0618	...	...
171	Beni Mansour ....d.	1026	1040	1451	...	...	0011	Sidi El Hémissi ....d.	...	...	...	0719	1602
259	Béjaïa ....a.	...	1229	...	...	...	...	Souk Ahras ....d.	...	0656	...	0828	1714
237	Bordj Bou Arreridj .d.	0615	1143	1553	1850	1610	0115	Mechrouha ....d.	...	0722	...	...
289	M'Sila ....d.	0703		1642	...	...	...	Bouchegouf ....d.	...	0810	...	...
308	Setif ....d.		1230	...	1932	1650	0204	Annaba ....d.	...	0932	...	...
464	Constantine ....a.		1430	...	...	1854	0430	Annaba ....d.	2130	...	...	...
464	Constantine ....d.			1455	...	...	0435	Azzaba ....d.	2226	...	...	...
521	El Harrouch ....d.			1541	...	...	...	Skikda ....d.				
582	El Milia ....d.			1658	...	...	...	Ramdane Djamal ......d.	2251			
620	Jijel ....d.			1739	...	...	...	Jijel ....d.			0645	
532	Ramdane Djamel ...d.				...	...	0545	El Milia ....d.			0725	
550	Skikda ....d.				...	...	...	El Harrouch ....d.			0843	
557	Azzaba ....d.				...	...	0610	Constantine ....a.	2359		0941	
631	Annaba ....a.				...	...	0713	Constantine ....d.	0004		0640	0741
631	Annaba ....d.			1640	...	...	...	Setif ....d.	0227	0540	0845	1007
686	Bouchegouf ....d.			1752	...	...	...	M'Sila ....a.				1700
721	Mechrouha ....d.			1848	...	...	...	Bordj Bou Arreridj ....d.	0317	0620	0740	0929	1050	1748
738	Souk Ahras ....d.	0600	1335	1910	...	...	...	Béjaïa ....d.	...	0800	...	1650	
787	Sidi El Hémissi ....d.	0709	1444		...	...	...	Beni Mansour ....d.	0429	...	0844	0959	1037	1850
762	Dreâ ....d.			1957	...	...	...	Bouira ....d.	0519	0535	0757	0933	1015	1121	1720
794	Oued Kéberit ....d.			2036	...	...	...	Thénia ....☆ d.	0636	0700		1133	1230	1838
862	Tebessa ....a.			2149	...	...	...	Alger ....☆ a.	0729	0753	0942	1115	1315	...

A — 🚌 Alger - Batna and v.v.   B — 🚌 and ✕ Alger - Constantine and v.v.   C — 🛏🚌 and ✕ Alger - Annaba and v.v.   ☆ – Additional local trains available.

TUNISIA

Capital: **Tunis** (GMT +1).   2017 Public Holidays: Jan. 1, 14, Mar. 20 Apr. 9, May 1, July 5, 25, Sept. 13, Oct. 3, 15, Dec. 12.

Rail services are operated Société Nationale des Chemins de Fer Tunisiens (SNCFT. www.sncft.com.tn). Unless otherwise noted, trains convey first and second class seated accommodation. Long distance overnight trains may convey sleeping cars and/or couchettes and where this is the case it will be shown in the footnotes. Timings are the most recent available and are subject to alteration at any time.

SNCFT offers the **Carte Bleue** pass. The pass allows unlimited travel on all scheduled SNCFT services (except the Lézard Rouge tourist train) for a period of 7, 15, or 21 days, and are available for each of the three classes of accommodation. Supplements are payable in advance for using certain services. For more information, please visit the website of the European agent www.fahrplancenter.com   Prices (in Euros): Grand Confort Class 7 days 31.00, 15 days 62.00, 21 days 93.00. First Class 7 days 28.00, 15 days 56.00, 21 days, 84.00. Second Class 7 days 20.00, 15 days 40.00, 21 days 60.00.

GHARDIMAOU - TUNIS — 4050

SNCFT

km		①–⑥	①–⑥						⑥	①–⑤	①–⑤
0	Ghardimaou ....d.	...	...	0500	1030	1215	1455	Tunis Ville ....d.	...	0600	1005	1300	1435	1625	1715	...	1800
34	Jendouba ....d.	...	...	0528	1058	1238	1517	Tebourba ....d.	...	0646	1044	1346	1517	1716	1758	...	1842
92	Béja ....d.	...	0520	0620	1144	1324	1606	Béja ....d.	...	0755	1150	1459	1631	1833	...	...	1951
177	Tebourba ....d.	0600	0738	1301	1433	1715	Jendouba ....d.	...	0843	1237	1550	...	1927	...	...
211	Tunis Ville ....a.	0641	0726	0830	1342	1515	1757	Ghardimaou ....a.	...	0904	1258	1616	...	1953	...	...

BIZERTE - TUNIS — 4060

SNCFT

km		①–⑥			①–⑤				①–⑥		①–⑤	
0	Bizerte ....d.	0520	0740	1515	1810	...	Tunis Ville ....d.	0525	1215	1525	1820	...
34	Mateur ....d.	0554	0813	1549	1842	...	Mateur ....d.	0642	1322	1637	1931	...
98	Tunis Ville ....a.	0708	0919	1704	1953	...	Bizerte ....a.	0714	1354	1708	2002	...

BEYOND EUROPE - AFRICA and THE MIDDLE EAST

4070 KALAÂ KASBAH - TUNIS

SNCFT

km		⊡			⊡	1	⊡			
0	**Tunis** Ville ... d.	0555	0930	...	1330	1530	1805	...	...	...
63	Pont du Fahs ... d.	0714	|	...	1447	|	1920	...	...	...
120	Gaafour ... d.	0803	1058	...	1539	1703	2009	...	...	...
166	Le Sers ... d.	0900	1143	...	1637	1748	2105	...	...	...
191	Dahmani ... d.	0929	1205	...	1706	|	2132	...	...	...
214	Jerissa ... a.	|	1240	...	|	|	...	...	...	...
235	**Kalaâ Kasbah** ... a.	1031	...	...	1808a	|	...	...	...	...
202	**El Kef** ... a.	...	...	...	...	1824	...	...	...	...

	⊡	1	⊡						
El Kef ... d.	...	0515	...	...	...	...	...	...	...
Kalaâ Kasbah ... d.	...	|	0530a	...	...	1330	...	...	...
Jerissa ... d.	...	|	|	...	1330	|	...	...	...
Dahmani ... d.	0355	|	0633	...	1405	1434	...	...	...
Le Sers ... d.	0423	0552	0702	...	1438	1503	...	...	...
Gaafour ... d.	0519	0638	0802	...	1524	1604	...	...	...
Pont du Fahs ... d.	0610	0713	0822	...	1601	1702	...	...	...
Tunis Ville ... a.	0732	0804	1010	...	1654	1819	...	...	...

a – Runs Nov. 26 - Dec. 4, Dec. 7–22, Jan. 7–22, Feb. 25 - Mar. 5, Apr. 8–16 only. ⊡ – Supplement payable.

4080 TUNIS - SOUSSE - SFAX - TOZEUR

SNCFT

km				⊡		⊡	⊡				⊡	1		⚒⊡	1			⊡		⊡	⊡	⊡	🚌	
0	**Tunis** Ville ... d.	...	0600	0630	...	0845	0930	...	...	1235	1305	1420	...	1535	1620	1715	1745	1800	...	1830	2045	2215	...	...
23	Borj Cédria ... ◇ d.	0605	|	|	...	|	|	...	...	|	|	|	1455	|	|	|	1805	|	...	1855	|	|	...	...
59	Bir Bou Rekba ... ◇ d.	0641	0650	0721	...	0938	1023	...	...	1328	1356	1502	1527	1637	|	1757	1848	1855	...	1922	2143	2307	...	...
64	Hammamet ... ◇ d.	0647	|	|	...	|	|	...	...	|	|	|	1533	|	|	|	1854	|	...	|	|	|	...	...
76	**Nabeul** ... ◇ a.	0706	|	|	...	|	|	...	...	|	|	|	1552	|	|	|	1913	|	...	|	|	|	...	...
142	Kalaâ Séghira ... d.	...	0739	0818	0830	|	|	...	...	|	1455	|	...	1741	1802	1845	...	1955	...	2028	|	|	...	...
149	**Sousse** ... d.	...	0746	|	0838	1100	1137	...	...	1443	|	1557	...	1749	|	|	...	2015	...	2035	2250	0020	...	...
174	Monastir ... d.	...	...	|	...	1140	|	...	...	1523	|	...	...	...	|	1938	...	|	...	...	|	|	...	...
217	**Mahdia** ... a.	...	...	|	...	...	|	...	...	...	|	...	...	...	|	2022	...	|	...	...	|	|	...	...
215	El Jem ... d.	...	...	0908	...	...	1234	...	...	...	1548	...	...	...	|	...	...	2112	...	...	2347	0117	...	...
278	**Sfax** ... d.	...	...	1000	...	...	1327	...	...	...	1643	...	...	...	1935	...	...	2201	...	...	0040	0215	...	...
340	Ghraïba ... d.	...	...	1052	...	...	1418	...	...	...	1735	...	...	...	|	...	...	...	...	...	0134	|	...	...
422	**Gabès** ... a.	...	...	1204	...	...	|	...	...	...	1843	...	...	...	2125	...	...	...	...	...	|	0413	0420	...
	Tataouine ... a.	...	...	...	...	...	|	...	...	...	...	...	...	...	...	...	...	...	...	...	|	...	0700	...
482	Gafsa ... d.	...	...	...	...	...	1634	...	...	...	...	...	...	...	...	...	...	...	...	...	0347	...	...	...
521	Metlaoui ... d.	...	...	...	...	...	1711	...	...	...	...	...	...	...	...	...	...	...	...	...	0424	...	...	...
574	**Tozeur** ... a.	...	...	...	...	...	1759	...	...	...	...	...	...	...	...	...	...	...	...	...	0512	...	...	...

		⊡	🚌	⊡	⚒1	⊡	⚒⊡			⊡	1	1	⊡			⊡	1	1			⊡			
Tozeur ... d.	...	2030	...	...	...	...	...	...	...	...	...	...	0630	...	...	...	...	...	...	...	...	...	...	...
Metlaoui ... d.	...	2121	...	...	...	...	...	...	...	...	...	...	0721	...	...	...	...	...	...	...	...	...	...	...
Gafsa ... d.	...	2200	-...	...	...	...	...	...	...	...	...	...	0800	...	...	...	...	...	...	...	...	...	...	...
Tataouine ... d.	...	|	2100	...	...	...	...	...	...	...	...	...	|	...	...	...	...	...	...	...	...	...	...	...
Gàbes ... d.	...	|	2355	0005	...	...	...	...	...	...	0500	...	|	...	...	1115	...	1400	...	...	...	...	...	...
Ghraïba ... d.	...	0011	...	|	...	...	...	...	...	...	|	...	1011	...	...	1229	...	1513	...	...	...	...	...	...
Sfax ... d.	...	0115	...	0210	...	...	...	...	...	0530	0653	...	1110	...	...	1332	...	1610	...	...	...	...	...	...
El Jem ... d.	...	0209	...	0258	...	...	...	...	...	0620	|	...	1158	...	...	1422	...	1653	...	...	...	...	...	...
Mahdia ... d.	...	|	...	|	...	...	...	...	0535	|	|	...	|	...	...	|	...	|	...	...	...	...	...	...
Monastir ... d.	...	|	...	|	...	...	...	...	0630	|	|	...	|	1250	...	|	...	|	...	...	1715	...	...	...
Sousse ... d.	...	0315	...	0405	...	0450	0550	...	|	0727	|	0950	1312	1340	...	|	1640	|	...	...	1810	...	...	...
Kalaâ Seghira ... d.	...	|	...	|	...	0503	0559	...	0700	|	0820	|	|	|	...	1511	|	1738	...	...	|	...	...	...
Nabeul ... ◇ d.	...	|	...	|	0500	|	|	...	|	|	|	|	|	|	...	|	|	|	...	...	|	...	1925	...
Hammamet ... ◇ d.	...	|	...	|	0517	|	|	...	|	|	|	|	|	|	...	|	|	|	...	...	|	...	1944	...
Bir Bou Rekba ... ◇ d.	...	0418	...	0508	0523	0609	0659	...	0746	0832	|	1042	1418	1446	...	1607	1735	1832	...	...	1915	...	1951	...
Borj Cédria ... ◇ d.	...	|	...	|	0556	0641	0730	...	0814	0902	|	|	1451	|	...	|	|	|	...	...	|	...	2022	...
Tunis Ville ... a.	...	0513	...	0601	...	0707	0757	...	0835	0926	1003	1129	1516	1541	...	1703	1823	1922	...	...	2009	...	...	...

⊡ – Supplement payable. ◇ – Additional services available with connections from/to Tunis.

4090 SOUSSE - MONASTIR AIRPORT - MAHDIA

SNCFT

km		503		505	507 ⚒	509		513		517	519	521	523	525		527	529	531	533	535	537		539	
0	**Sousse** Bab El Jedid ... d.	0540	...	0710	0740	0830	...	1000	...	1115	1145	1225	1315	1355	...	1445	1545	1620	1705	1755	1840	...	1950	...
3	**Sousse** Sud ... d.	0546	...	0716	0746	0836	...	1006	...	1121	1151	1231	1321	1401	...	1451	1551	1626	1711	1801	1846	...	1956	...
15	Monastir Airport ✈ ... d.	0600	...	0730	0800	0850	...	1020	...	1135	1205	1248	1335	1416	...	1505	1605	1640	1725	1815	1900	...	2010	...
24	Monastir ... d.	0620	...	0750	0815	0905	...	1035	...	1155	1225	1310	1355	1435	...	1525	1625	1700	1750	1840	1920	...	2030	...
47	Moknine ... d.	0651	...	0821	...	...	...	1106	...	1225	1302	1341	1430	1510	...	1556	1656	1731	1826	1916	1950	...	2101	...
73	**Mahdia** ... a.	0735	...	0850	...	...	...	1150	...	...	1335	1420	...	1545	...	1645	1745	1810	1905	2000	2025	...	2135	...

		506 ⚒	508	510		512	516	518	520	522	526	528	530		532	534		538	540		542	544	546	
Mahdia ... d.	...	0500	0530	0615	...	0640	0745	...	0910	0945	1115	...	1225	...	1350	1430	...	...	1615	...	1715	1835	1930	...
Moknine ... d.	...	0530	0600	0650	...	0720	0815	...	0940	1020	1150	1235	1305	...	1422	1500	...	1620	1648	...	1756	1907	2014	...
Monastir ... d.	...	0610	0645	0740	...	0810	0900	0940	1020	1055	1230	1315	1400	...	1500	1540	...	1705	1740	...	1845	1950	2055	...
Monastir Airport ✈ ... d.	...	0620	0655	0750	...	0820	0910	0950	1030	1105	1240	1325	1410	...	1512	1550	...	1715	1750	...	1855	2000	2105	...
Sousse Sud ... d.	...	0639	0714	0809	...	0839	0929	1009	1045	1120	1259	1340	1425	...	1530	1605	...	1734	1809	...	1910	2015	2120	...
Sousse Bab El Jedid ... a.	...	0645	0720	0815	...	0845	0935	1015	1050	1125	1305	1345	1430	...	1535	1610	...	1740	1815	...	1915	2020	2125	...

a – Runs Sept. 14, 2015 - May 14, 2016 only.

EGYPT

Capital: **Cairo** (GMT +2). 2017 Public Holidays: Jan. 7, 25, Apr. 16, 17, 25, May 1, June 26 - 28, 30, July 23, Sept. 2 - 5, Oct. 6, Dec. 1.

Rail services are operated Egyptian National Railways (ENR. www.enr.gov.eg). Unless otherwise noted, trains convey first and second class seated accommodation. Long distance overnight trains may convey sleeping cars and/or couchettes and where this is the case it will be shown in the footnotes. Timings are the most recent available and are subject to alteration at any time.

4100 MERSA MATRUH - CAIRO and ALEXANDRIA

Egyptian National Railways

km		2	A	2	B					
0	**Mersa Matruh** ... d.	0705	1335	1545	2200	...	...	...	...	...
84	El Alamein ... d.	1024	1620	1830	|	...	...	...	...	...
311	**Alexandria** ... a.	1330	|	2115	|	...	...	...	...	...
509	**Cairo** Main ... a.	...	2135	...	0540	...	...	...	...	...

	2	A	2	B					
Cairo Main ... d.	...	0640	...	2330	...	...	...	...	...
Alexandria ... d.	0640	|	1330	|	...	...	...	...	...
El Alamein ... d.	0924	1145	1717	|	...	...	...	...	...
Mersa Matruh ... a.	1205	1415	2020	0635	...	...	...	...	...

A – June – Sept. only. B – 🛏 (1, 2 class). July - Sept. From Mersa on ②④⑦, from Cairo on ①③⑥. see www.wataniasleepingtrains.com

4110 CAIRO - ALEXANDRIA

Egyptian National Railways

km		903	965	905	901	909	911	89		913	907	949	917	919	2001	915	923	925	921	927	961	931	935	
0	**Cairo** Main ... d.	0600	0735	0800	0815	0900	1000	1100	...	1200	1250	1315	1400	1420	1500	1515	1600	1715	1800	1900	1950	2015	2230	...
45	Benha ... d.	0636	0812	|	0851	|	1036	|	...	1236	1326	1357	|	1458	|	1551	1636	1751	|	|	2040	2050	|	...
86	Tanta ... d.	0720	0845	|	0923	|	1108	1205	...	1308	1358	1440	|	1542	|	1623	1720	1832	1903	|	...	2132	2335	...
147	Damanhūr ... d.	0815	...	|	1007	|	1153	|	...	1352	1443	...	|	1647	|	1708	1813	1918	|	|		2223	|	...
208	**Alexandria** ... a.	0915	...	1030	1100	1130	1250	1340	...	1445	1540	...	1630	1745	1720	1805	1920	2015	2030	2130	...	2320	0105	...

	936	948	1904	902	906	952	904	900	910	912	914	916	918	966	922		88	994	928	926	2008	930	934	1908
Alexandria ... d.	...	...	...	0600	0700	...	0800	0815	1000	1200	1300	1400	1500	...	1530	...	1645	...	1800	1900	2000	2010	2200	2130
Damanhūr ... d.	...	...	...	0700	|	...	|	0920	1100	|	1400	|	|	...	1635	...	|	...	|	|	|	2110	|	2232
Tanta ... d.	0600	0655	0715	0756	|		|	1008	1145	1330	1500	|	|	1635	1725	...	1825	1900	1930	|	2129	2200	2330	|
Benha ... d.	0642	0739	0757	0840	|	0910	|	1042	1222	|	1542	|	|	1722	1757	...	|	1942	|	|	|	2232	|	|
Cairo Main ... a.	0715	0820	0830	0915	0940	0955	1040	1115	1255	1430	1615	1630	1730	1755	1830	...	1925	2015	2030	2130	2230	2305	0030	0020

ALEXANDRIA and CAIRO - DUMYAT — 4120

Egyptian National Railways 2nd class only

km									
240	Alexandria .... d.			1815	...	...	...	...	...
205	Cairo Main .... d.	0515	0725		1935	...	...	...	...
0	Dumyat .... a.	1015	1125	2230	2355	...	...	...	...

Dumyat .... d.	0640	0715	1315	1630	...	...	...	...
Cairo Main .... a.	1005		1800	2020	...	...	...	...
Alexandria .... a.		1210	...	...	...	...	...	...

☛ All services are subject to confirmation.

ALEXANDRIA and CAIRO - BÛR SA'ÎD — 4130

Egyptian National Railways 2nd class only

km			12	12					
334	Alexandria .... d.		0430		1530	...	...	...	...
236	Cairo Main .... d.	0615		1345	1440		1945	...	...
0	Bûr Sa'îd .... a.	1015	1110	1800	1905	2210	2350	...	...

					12			12	
Bûr Sa'îd .... d.	0530	0725	0930	1300	1730	1825	1815	...
Cairo Main .... a.	0945		1335	1710	2135		0050	...
Alexandria .... a.		1330	...	...	...	0035	...	...

☛ All services are subject to confirmation.

CAIRO - EL SUWEIS — 4140

Egyptian National Railways 2nd class only

km									
0	Cairo Ain Shams .... d.	0630	0510n	0920	1310	1615	1845	2145	
127	El Suweis .... a.	0840	0950	1135	1520	1830	2100	2400	

El Suweis .... d.	0600	1010	1310	1525	1550	1900	2125	...
Cairo Ain Shams ..... a.	0815	1215	1525	2005n	1805	2110	2335	...

☛ All services are subject to confirmation.   n –   Cairo Main.

CAIRO - ASWÂN — 4150

Egyptian National Railways

km		1902	934	980	982	986	988	88	86 B	996	2008
0	Cairo Main .... ◇ d.	0005	0100	0800	1200	1300	1900	2000	2015	2200	2305
13	El Giza .... ◇ d.	0030	0130	0825	1225	1325	1925	2025	2045	2230	2330
124	Béni Suef .... ◇ d.		0250	0940	1350	1443	2045	2147		2348	
247	El Menya .... ◇ d.		0425	1110	1510	1630	2220	2330			
375	Asyût .... ◇ d.	0455	0620	1300	1715	1830	0010	0125		0310	0410
467	Sohâg .... ◇ d.	0630	0740	1430	1850	2000	0125	0250		0435	0530
609	Qena .... ◇ d.	0845	1000	1710	2120	2235	0340	0525		0655	0745
671	Luxor .... ◇ d.	0950	1055	1825	2235	...	0445	0640	0303	0800	0850
879	Aswân .... a.	1305		2200	0205	...	0800	1015	1002	1120	1200

		981	983	935	2007	1903	87 B	997	89	989	987
	Aswân .... d.	0530	0700		1500	1615	1900	1945	2000	2200	...
	Luxor .... d.	0915	1035	1200	1820	1945	2230	2320	2345	0130	...
	Qena .... ◇ d.	1025	1145	1305	1920	2045		0020	0050	0230	0600
	Sohâg .... ◇ d.	1310	1430	1530	2145	2300		0245	0340	0450	0850
	Asyût .... ◇ d.	1440	1610	1705	2305	0030		0405	0515	0615	1025
	El Menya .... ◇ d.	1630	1810	1845	0055			0600	0710	0805	1225
	Béni Suef .... ◇ d.	1805	1942	2025				0740	0855	0940	1410
	El Giza .... ◇ d.	1930	2110		0525	0804	0900		1100	1525
	Cairo Main ...... ◇ a.	1950	2130	2205	0410	0545	0830	0920	1040	1120	1545

B – 🛏 (1, 2 class). www.wataniasleepingtrains.com   ◇ – Additional services available.

OTHER AFRICAN STATES

For details of capital cities and public holiday dates please see individual tables.

Unless otherwise noted, trains convey first and second class seated accommodation. Some operators also offer third class seating. This will not normally be mentioned in the tables, and where it is the only class available will be noted as second class. Long distance overnight trains may convey sleeping cars and/or couchettes. As a general rule, first class sleepers have two berths per cabin, whilst second class has four. The standard of accommodation varies widely with no two countries beng the same. Timings are the latest available and are valid until further notice, but may change at any time so we suggest you confirm them locally before travelling. In Muslim countries a different timetable may be operated during the festival of Ramadan.

SUDAN and SOUTH SUDAN — 4200

Sudan Railways Corporation

Sudan: **Khartoum** (GMT +3). 2017 Public Holidays: Jan. 1, 8, Apr. 16, June 26, 300, Sept. 2, 22, Dec. 1.
South Sudan: **Juba** (GMT +3). 2017 Public Holidays: Jan. 1, 9, Mar. 27, May 1, 16, Jul. 9, 30, Sept. 2, Dec. 25, 28, 31.

km		222 ②	101 ④A	212 E	551 B	202 ④C	D01 ④D		
926	Wadi Halfa .... d.	1800b		...	...	0200d	...		
576	Abu Hamed .... d.	0600c		...	...	0800e	...		
551	Dagash .... d.			...	...	1030e	...		
351	Berber .... d.			...	...	2300e	...		
810	Bûr Sûdan .... d.		1530d	...	...		...		
	Sinkat .... d.		2000d	...	...		...		
720	Gebeit .... d.		2240d	...	...		...		
620	Haiya Junction .... d.		0445e	...	...		...		
310	Atbara .... a.		1255e	...	...	2345e	...		
310	Atbara .... d.			2130	...	0200f	...		
295	Ed Dâmer .... d.			2300	...	0300g	...		
170	Shendî .... d.			0300	...	0930g	...		
0	Khartoum Bahri .... a.			0730	...	1700g	...		
0	Khartoum Bahri .... d.				...	2000d	...		
270	Sennâr Junction .... d.				...	0600e	...		
383	Kôsti .... d.				...	1030e	...		
470	Tendelti .... d.				⊖	1500e	...		
605	Er Rahad .... d.				⊖	2100e	...		
629	El Obeid .... a.				⊖	2230e	...		
983	Babanusa .... d.				⊖		...		
	El Daien .... d.				⊖		...		
1318	Nyâlâ .... a.				⊖		...		

km		552 B	221 ④	201 ①C	502 ①D	102 ①A	211 E
	Nyâlâ .... d.	⊖					
	El Daien .... d.	⊖					
	Babanusa .... d.	⊖					
	El Obeid .... d.	⊖			0700a		
	Er Rahad .... d.	⊖			0830a		
	Tendelti .... d.				1445a		
	Kôsti .... d.				1930a		
	Sennâr Junction .... d.				0000b		
	Khartoum Bahri .... a.				1030b		
	Khartoum Bahri .... d.			0800a			2130
	Shendî .... d.			1545a			0200
	Ed Dâmer .... d.			2200a			0600
	Atbara .... a.			2300a			0730
	Atbara .... d.			0100b		2000a	
	Haiya Junction .... d.					0415b	
	Gebeit .... d.					1015b	
	Sinkat .... d.					1120b	
	Bûr Sûdan .... d.					1545b	
	Berber .... d.			0345b			
	Dagash .... d.			1530b			
	Abu Hamed .... d.			1730d	1745b		
	Wadi Halfa .... a.			0545e	2230b		

A – 🛏 From Bûr Sûdan 1st and 3rd ④ of each month, from Atbara on following ①. Service temporarily withdrawn March 2014
B – 🛏 1 cl., 🛏. From El Rahad/ Nyâlâ every two weeks day and time not fixed.
C – 🛏 1 cl., 🛏. From Khartoum on 1st and 3rd ① of each month, from Wadi Halfa on following ④. Service temporarily withdrawn March 2014
D – 🛏 1 cl., 🛏 2 cl., 🛏 and 🍴. From Khartoum on 2nd ④ of each month, from El Obeid on following ①. Service temporarily withdrawn March 2014. Not operated by SRC.
E – 🛏 1 cl., 🛏.

a –	①.	e –	⑤.
b –	②.	f –	⑥.
c –	③.	g –	⑦.
d –	④.		

⊖ – No timings available.

ERITREA — 4210

Chemins de Fer d'Eritrea

km		①–⑥ 2	⑦ A	B			①–⑥ 2	⑦ A	B
0	Mitsiwa .... d.	⊖	A	...	Asmara ...... d.		...	A	0800
0	Otumlo .... d.	⊖	A	...	Nefasit ...... d.		...	A	0915
8	Moncullo ..... d.		A	...	Ghinda ...... d.		...	A	
70	Ghinda .... d.		A	...	Moncullo .... d.		...	A	
92	Nefasit .... d.		A	1000	Otumlo ...... d.		⊖	A	
118	Asmara .... a.		A	1200	Mitsiwa ...... d.		⊖	A	

Capital: **Asmara** (GMT +3).
2017 Public Holidays: Jan. 1, Mar. 8, Apr. 14, 16, May 1, 24, June 26, Sept. 1, 2, 27, Dec. 1, 25.

A – No regular service. Charter service available.
B – Minimum 10 passengers required.

ETHIOPIA — 4215

Chemins de Fer Djibouti Ethiopien

km		②⑤			③⑥	
0	Diré Daoua .... d.	0400	...	Djibouti .... d.	0600	...
210	Dewelé .... 🚊 a.	1400	...	Ali Sabieh .... 🚊 d.	1000	...
228	Ali Sabieh ..... 🚊 d.	1700	...	Dewelé .... 🚊 a.	1300	...
318	Djibouti .... a.	2200	...	Diré Daoua ...... d.	2200	...

Capital: **Addis Abeba** (GMT +3).   2017 Public Holidays: Jan. 7, 19, Mar. 2, Apr. 14, 16, May 1, 5, 28, June 26, Sept. 2, 11, 27, Dec. 1.

A new standard-gauge line between Djibouti and Addis Abeba is under construction and nearly complete. It will be operated by ETHIOPIA RAILWAYS CORP. Services may start in late 2016, then activities of the old metre-gauge railway will cease.

MAURITANIA — 4220

SNIM   2nd class only

km							
0	Nouadhibou .... d.	1450	...	Zouèrate .... d.	1215	...
652	Zouèrate .... a.	0540	...	Nouadhibou .... a.	0618	...

Capital: **Nouakchott** (GMT +0).
2017 Public Holidays: Jan. 1, May 1, 25, June 26, Sept. 2, 14, 15, Oct. 3, Nov. 28 Dec. 1.
SNIM – Société Nationale Industrielle et Minière.

BEYOND EUROPE - AFRICA and THE MIDDLE EAST

4230 — GUINEA

2nd class only   Chemins de Fer Guinea, Chemins de Fer de Boké

km		①–⑤	①–⑤	①–⑤			①–⑤	①–⑤	①–⑤	①–⑤
0	Conakry Portovoya..d.	...	0847	1725	Halte Km 36 ....d.		0645			1916
	Simbaya ....d.	0600	0940	1829	Simbaya ....d.		0730	1630	1950
36	Halte Km 36 ....a.	0640	...	1906	Conakry P'voya...a.		0837	1710		

km		B					B
0	Kamsar ....d.	0930	...	...	Sangaredi ....d.		1415
55	Boké ....d.	1130	...	...	Boké ....d.		1630
136	Sangaredi ....a.	1345	...	...	Kamsar ....a.		1830

Capital: **Conakry** (GMT +0).
2017 Public Holidays : Apr. 17, May 1, 25, Jun. 21, 26, Aug. 15, Sept. 2, Oct. 2, Dec. 1, 25.
B – ①④⑤⑦.

4240 — MALI

2nd class only   Transrail

km		B				A
0	Kayes ....d.	0715	...	Bamako ....d.		0715
160	Bafoulabé ....d.	1130	...	Kati ....d.		0815
308	Kita ....d.	1805	...	Kita ....d.		1300
468	Kati ....d.	2250	...	Bafoulabé ....d.		1935
493	Bamako ....a.	2345	...	Kayes ....a.		2350

Capital: **Bamako** (GMT +0).
2017 Public Holidays : Mar. 26, Apr. 17, May 25, Jun. 5, 26, Sept. 2, 22, Dec. 1, 25.
A – ①②④⑥.
B – ②③⑤⑦.

4250 — GHANA

Ghana Railway Corporation

km		A			A
0	Takoradi ....d.	2030	...	Kumasi ....d.	2030
276	Kumasi ....a.	0930a	...	Takoradi ....a.	0930a

km		①–⑥	①–⑥	①–⑥			①–⑥	①–⑥	①–⑥
0	Accra ....d.	0500	1215	1700	Tema ....d.		0630		1830
	Asoprochona ....a.	0558	1313	1759	Asoprochona ....a.		0655	1415	1855
	Tema ....a.	0625		1825	Accra ....a.		0755	1515	1955

km		2B	2B	2B			2B	2B	2B
0	Accra ....d.	0740	1000	1400	Nsawam ....d.		0600	1140	1220
40	Nsawam ....a.	0920	1140	1540	Accra ....a.		0740	1320	1400

Capital: **Accra** (GMT +0).
2017 Public Holidays : Jan. 1, 2, Mar. 6, Apr. 14, 17, May 1, 25, Jun. 26, Sep. 2, 21, Dec. 1, 25, 26.
A – Service operates every second day, also may be suspended.   a – Approximate timings.
B – ①–⑥. Additional trains from Accra at 1900, from Nsawam at 1730.

4260 — BURKINA FASO - CÔTE D'IVOIRE

Sitarail

km		②④⑥	⑥			①③⑤	④
		2	A			2	A
0	Ouagadougou ....d.		⊖	Abidjan Treichville ....d.		0900	0700
93	Koudougou ....d.		⊖	Abidjan Plateau ......d.		0920	⊖
349	Bobo Dioulasso ......d.		1400	Anyama ....d.		1015	0755
446	Banfora ....d.		1715	Agboville ....d.		1240	0918
495	Niangoloko ......🚉..d.		2030	Dimbokro ....d.		1615	1140
539	Ouangolodougou .....d.		2200	Bouaké ....d.		⊖	1515
576	Ferkessédougou ......d.		2310	Katiola ....d.		⊖	1730
658	Tafiré ....d.		0125	Tafiré ....d.		⊖	2020
769	Katiola ....d.		0430	Ferkessédougou ......d.		⊖	2235
820	Bouaké ....d.		0645	Ouangolodougou .....d.		⊖	2345
958	Dimbokro ....d.	0900	0955	Niangoloko ......🚉.d.		⊖	0215
1064	Agboville ....d.	1255	1219	Banfora ....d.		⊖	0345
1115	Anyama ....d.	1515	1344	Bobo Dioulasso ......d.		⊖	0700
1141	Abidjan Plateau .....a.	1610	...	Koudougou ....d.		⊖	
1143	Abidjan Treichville ..a.	1625	1430	Ouagadougou ....a.		⊖	

Capitals: **Ouagadougou** (Burkina Faso, GMT +0), **Yamoussoukro** (Côte d'Ivoire, GMT +0).
2017 Public Holidays :
Burkina Faso : Jan. 1, Apr. 17, May 1, 25, Jun. 26, Aug. 15, Sept. 2, Nov. 1, Dec. 1, 25.
Côte d'Ivoire : Jan. 1, Apr. 17, May 1, 26, Jun. 5, 21, 26, Aug. 7, 15, Sept. 2, Nov. 1, 15, Dec. 1, 25.
A – 🛏 and 🍴 Abidjan - Ouagadougou and v.v. Journey time 43 - 48 hours.
⊖ – No timings available.

4270 — NIGERIA

Nigerian Railways Corporation

Capital: **Abuja** (GMT +1). 2017 Public Holidays : Jan. 1, Apr. 14, 17, May 1, 29, Jun. 26, 27, Sept. 2, 3, Oct. 1, Dec. 1, 25, 26.

km		⑤A	⑤B	②⑤⑧		km		①A	⑤B	③⑥⑦
0	Lagos Terminal ....d.	1200	...	0900	Kano ....d.		0900	⊖	⊖
14	Agege ....d.	⊖		⊖	Zaria ....d.		⊖	⊖	⊖
91	Abeokuta ....d.	⊖		⊖	Kaduna Junction d.		⊖	⊖	⊖
193	Ibadan ....d.	⊖		⊖	Minna ....d.		⊖	⊖	⊖
280	Ede ....d.	⊖		⊖	Zungeru ....d.		⊖	⊖	⊖
295	Oshogbo ....d.	⊖		⊖	Jebba ....d.		⊖	⊖	⊖
391	Ilorin ....d.	⊖	1834		Ilorin ....d.		⊖	⊖	0900
488	Jebba ....d.	⊖		⊖	Oshogbo ....d.		⊖	⊖	⊖
685	Zungeru ....d.	⊖		⊖	Ede ....d.		⊖	⊖	⊖
744	Minna ....d.	⊖		⊖	Ibadan ....d.		⊖	⊖	⊖
902	Kaduna Junction ...d.	⊖		⊖	Abeokuta ....d.		⊖	⊖	⊖
986	Zaria ....d.	⊖		⊖	Agege ....d.		⊖	⊖	⊖
1126	Kano ....a.	1701a		⊖	Lagos Terminal .....a.		1424a	⊖	2059

km		C	⑤B				C	⑤B
0	Port Harcourt New ...d.	⊖	⊖	Maiduguri ....d.		⊖	⊖
63	Aba ....d.	⊖	⊖	Buni ....d.		⊖	⊖
113	Umuahia Ibeku ......d.	⊖	⊖	Gombe ....d.		⊖	⊖
243	Enugu ....d.	⊖	⊖	Bauchi ....d.		⊖	⊖
375	Oturkpo ....d.	⊖	⊖	Kaduna Junction ...d.		⊖	⊖
463	Makurdi ....d.	⊖	⊖	Kafanchan ....d.		⊖	⊖
565	Lafia ....d.	⊖	⊖	Lafia ....d.		⊖	⊖
737	Kafanchan ....d.	⊖	⊖	Makurdi ....d.		⊖	⊖
916	Kaduna Junction ....d.	⊖	⊖	Oturkpo ....d.		⊖	⊖
1333	Bauchi ....d.	⊖	⊖	Enugu ....d.		⊖	⊖
1499	Gombe ....d.	⊖	⊖	Umuahia Ibeku ......d.		⊖	⊖
1658	Buni ....d.	⊖	⊖	Aba ....d.		⊖	⊖
1801	Maiduguri ....a.	⊖	⊖	P Harcourt New .....a.		⊖	⊖

A – Conveys 🛏 (1 cl.), �GPS and 🍴.
B – Port Harcourt - Kaduna - Kano and v.v.
C – Port Harcourt - Kaduna - Maiduguri and v.v. Once per week in each direction. Subject to confirmation.
⊖ – No timings available.
a – Next day.

4280 — CAMEROON

Camrail

Capital: **Youandé** (GMT +1). 2017 Public Holidays : Jan. 1, Feb. 11, Apr. 14, May 20, 25, Jun. 26, Aug. 15, Sept. 2, Dec. 11, 25.

km		151	181	103	191	153	113
		A		①③⑤	B	A	②④⑥
0	Douala Bessengué ..d.	0600	0730	0900	...	1445	...
72	Edéa ....d.		0910	1210	...	...	...
152	Eséka ....d.		1050	1510	...	...	...
220	Ngoumou ....d.		1230	1720	...	...	...
263	Yaoundé ....d.	0945	1315	1820	1910	1830	...
477	Nanga Eboko ....d.		...	2300	...	...	...
582	Belabo ....d.		...	0230	...	0830	...
686	Mbitom ....d.		...	0450	...	1115	...
910	N'gaoundéré ....a.		...	1000	...	1800	...

		184	112	104	192	152	154
			①③⑤②⑥	B	A	A	A
	N'gaoundéré ....d.		0800		1915		...
	Mbitom ....d.		1140		0000		...
	Belabo ....d.		1730		0230		...
	Nanga Eboko ....d.				0600		...
	Yaoundé ....d.		0800	0915	0840	1025	1920
	Ngoumou ....d.		0855	1030			...
	Eséka ....d.		1045	1250			...
	Edéa ....d.		1225	1600			...
	Douala Bessengué ....a.		1350	1910		1410	2305

km		173	175	177			172	174	176
0	Douala Bonaberi ....d.		...	...	Kumba ....d.		0750	1130	1530
	Mbanga ....d.		0920	1300	1730	Mbanga ....d.		0900	1240	1640
	Kumba ....d.		1030	1410	1840	Douala Bonaberi ....a.		...	...	...

A – Conveys �GPS and 🍴.   B – Conveys 🛏 2 cl. (2 & 4 berth) 🍴.   🍴 – Note: All intermediate and arrival times are approximate.

4290 — GABON

Chemins de Fer Trans Gabonnais

Capital: **Libreville** (GMT +1). 2017 Public Holidays : Jan.1, Apr. 16, 17, May 1, Jun. 5, 26, Aug. 15, 16, 17, Sept. 2, Nov. 1, Dec. 25.

km		A		B				A		B
		①③⑤		②④⑦				②④⑦		①③⑤
0	Owendo (Libreville) .d.	1850	...	1850	...	Franceville ....d.		1950	...	1900
183	Ndjole ....d.	2303	...	2313	...	Moanda ....d.		2030	...	1940
340	Booué ....d.	0151	...	0225	...	Lastourville ....d.		2235	...	2151
485	Lastourville ....d.	0402	...	0441	...	Booué ....d.		0044	...	0005
625	Moanda ....d.	0609	...	0654	...	Ndjole ....d.		0332	...	0319
670	Franceville ....a.	0651	...	0736	...	Owendo (Libreville) ..a.		0745	...	0742

A – Trans-Ogooué Conveys VIP, �GPS, 🍴.   B – L'Equateur Conveys �GPS, 🍴.   Note: Services may be less frequent than shown.

CONGO — 4300

Chemins de Fer Congo Océan

km			①③⑤	①	①③⑥	⑥				②④⑦	①	②	①③⑥
			A	B						A	B		
0	Brazzaville	d.	0700	1310	1430	...	Pointe Noire	d.	0700	0925	1330	...
137	Mindouli	d.	1000	1715	1730	...	Dolisie	d.	1130	1800	2015	...
190	Loutété	d.	1130		1850	...	Nkayi	d.	1335	...	2300	0750
261	Nkayi	d.	1255	2100	2050	...	Loutété	d.	1520	...	2245	0930
342	Dolisie	d.	1530	0045		0400	Mindouli	d.	1650	...	0030	1100
509	Pointe Noire	a.	1915	0919		1200	Brazzaville	a.	1950	...	0500	1350

Capital : **Brazzaville** (GMT +1).
2017 Public Holidays : Jan. 1, Apr. 16, 17, May 1, 25, June 5, 10, Aug. 15, Nov. 1, Dec. 25.
A – GAZELLE – 🛏 and ✕.
B – OCEAN – 🛏 and ✕.

KENYA — 4310

Kenya Railways

km			②④⑦	①③⑤				②④⑦	①③⑤
			A	⊠				⊠	A
0	Mombasa	d.	1900	...	Kisumu	d.	1830	...
164	Voi	d.	2320	...	Nakuru	d.	0255	...
263	Mtito Andei	d.	0150	...	Nairobi	a.	0900	...
337	Makindu	d.	0350	...	Nairobi	d.	...	1900
530	Nairobi	a.	1100	...	Makindu	d.	...	2315
0	Nairobi	d.	...	1830	Mtito Andei	d.	...	0111
183	Nakuru	d.	...	0105	Voi	d.	...	0400
400	Kisumu	a.	...	0920	Mombasa	a.	...	1100

Capital : **Nairobi** (GMT +3).
2017 Public Holidays : Jan. 1, 2, Apr. 14, 17, May, 1, June 1, 27, Sept. 2, Oct. 20, Dec. 12, 25, 26.
A – JAMBO KENYA DELUXE – 🛏 and ✕.
⊠ – Currently suspended.

DEMOCRATIC CONGO — 4320

Société Nationale des Chemins de Fer du Congo

Capital : **Kinshasa** (GMT +1). 2017 Public Holidays : Jan. 1, 4, 16, 17, Apr. 29, 30, May 1, 17, June 30, Aug. 1, Dec. 25.

km			2A	C	B	2D	②④	2				2D	C	B	2A	②③	2
255	Sakania	d.	...	...	...	...	2000	...	Ilebo	d.	...	...	1600	...	...	...
0	Lubumbashi	d.	0300	0700	0700	1300	0822	...	Kananga	d.	...	...	0500	...	...	...
237	Tenke	d.	1500	2000	2000	0200	...	...	Mwene Ditu	d.	...	1600	0700	...	...	...
757	Dilolo	d.	...	...	2200		...	...	Kalemie	d.	...	...	...	...	...	...
600	Kamina	d.	1300	1600	2000		...	...	Kindu	d.	...	...	...	⊖	...	...
1047	Kabalo	d.	2000				...	...	Kabalo	d.	...	...	0600	⊖	...	...
1583	Kindu	d.					⊖	...	Kamina	d.	...	1100	1100	1400	...	...
1320	Kalemie	d.					⊖	...	Dilolo	d.	1500				...	...
913	Mwene Ditu	d.	...	1000	2000		...	...	Tenke	d.	1400	1200	1400	1600	...	...
1156	Kananga	d.	...	...	2200		...	...	Lubumbashi	a.	0300	1900	2100	2300	0800	...
1578	Ilebo	a.	...	...	0900		...	...	Sakania	a.	...	...	2000		...	...

km			⑥2						⑦2						2③						2④	
0	Kinshasa Est	d.	0730	...	Matadi	d.	0715	0	Kisangani	d.	0700	Ubundu	d.	1700
366	Matadi	a.	1500	...	Kinshasa Est	a.	1445	125	Ubundu	a.	1700	Kisangani	a.	0700

🚩 All timings are approximate.
A – From Lubumbashi 2nd and 4th ⑥ of each month. From Kabalo 1st and 3rd ④.
B – From Lubumbashi 1st ⑥ of each month. From Ilebo on following ①.
C – From Lubumbashi 1st and 3rd ① of each month. From Mwene on following ④.
D – From Lubumbashi 1st and 3rd ④. From Dilolo on following ⑦.
⊖ – No information available.

TANZANIA and ZAMBIA — 4330

Tanzania Railways, TAZARA, Zambian Railways

Capitals : **Dodoma** (Tanzania, GMT +3), **Lusaka** (Zambia, GMT +2).
2017 Public Holidays : Tanzania : Jan. 1, 12, Apr. 7, 14, 17 26, May 1, June 1, July 7, Aug. 8, Sept. 2, Oct. 14, Dec. 1, 9, 25, 26.
2017 Public Holidays : Zambia : Jan. 1, Mar. 8, 12, Apr. 14, 17, May 1, 25, July 3, 4, Aug. 3, Oct. 24, Dec. 25.

km		②⑤⑦	①③⑤	①③⑤	④		Tanzania Railways		⑥	②④⑦	②④⑦	
		A	B	B						B	B	
0	2100	...	...	0800	↓	Dar es Salaam	◧ d.	↑	1730	...	1330
78	2332	...	1005	↓	Ruvu	d.		1525	...	1115
203	0400	...	1330	↓	Morogoro	d.		1215	...	0744
290	0636	...		↓	Kilosa	d.			...	0508
465	1230	...	2000	↓	Dodoma	d.		0535	...	0000
578	1657	...		↓	Manyoni	d.			...	1850
637	1804	...		↓	Itigi	d.			...	1758
840	2340	...	0530	↓	Tabora	d.		1920	...	1130
840	0125	1700	1900	0630	↓	Tabora	d.	1820	0300	0330	0907
975	0456	2330			↓	Kaliua	d.		2313		0521
1051		0500			↓	Mpanda	d.		1500		↑
			0500			Mwanza	d.			1700	↑
1144	0925			1700	↑	Uvinza	d.			...	0047
1256	1310			1700	↑	Kigoma	a.	↓	0800	...	2100

km		TAZARA		②	⑤				⑤	②
				C	D				D	C
0	Dar es Salaam	◧ d.	1550	1350	New Kapiri Mposhi	◧ d.	1400	1600
226	Kisaki	d.	2013	1910	Mkushi Boma	d.	⊖	...
360	Ifakara	d.	2258	2230	Serenje	d.	1817	1947
496	Mlimba	d.	0152	0144	Mpika	d.	2329	0010
652	Makambako	d.	0746	0803	Kasama	d.	0309	0329
849	Mbeya	d.	1323	1440	Nakonde	🚉 a.	0915	0839
969	Tunduma	d.	1717	1853				
970	Nakonde	🚉 a.	1622	1758	Nakonde	🚉 d.	0925	0905
						Tunduma	d.	1045	1029
970	Nakonde	🚉 d.	1647	1813	Mbeya	d.	1500	1428
1226	Kasama	d.	2227	0031	Makambako	d.	2129	2030
1412	Mpika	d.	0148	0445	Mlimba	d.	0351	0208
1652	Serenje	d.	0556	0931	Ifakara	d.	0628	0512
1761	Mkushi Boma	d.	⊖	...	Kisaki	d.	1035	0757
1852	New Kapiri Mposhi	◧ a.	0926	1337	Dar es Salaam	◧ a.	1546	1210

km	Zambia Railways		①	③	⑤			⑦	①	⑤	
			2	E	2				2	E	2
					⊠				⊠		
0	Kitwe	d.	1600	1600	...	Livingstone	d.	1800	2000	2000
66	Ndola	d.	1855	1855	...	Kalomo	d.	2131	0100	0100
199	Kapiri Mposhi	◧ d.	2357	2357	...	Choma	d.	2311	0345	0345
262	Kabwe	d.	0255	0255	...	Pemba	d.	0054	0609	0609
331	Chisamba	d.	0500	0500	...	Monze	d.	0153	0749	0749
384	Lusaka	a.	0656	0656	...	Mazabuka	d.	0333	1015	1015
384	Lusaka	d.	0736	0736	1800	Kafue	d.	0515	1244	1244
432	Kafue	d.	0946	0946	1942	Lusaka	a.	0627	1424	1424
481	Mazabuka	d.	1155	1155	2104	Lusaka	d.	...	1524	1524
540	Monze	d.	1417	1417	2244	Chisamba	d.	...	1656	1656
577	Pemba	d.	1558	1558	0021	Kabwe	d.	...	1946	1946
643	Choma	d.	1834	1834	0145	Kapiri Mposhi	◧ d.	...	2216	2216
713	Kalomo	d.	2108	2108	0301	Ndola	d.	...	0336	0336
851	Livingstone	a.	0200	0200	0627	Kitwe	a.	...	0600	0600

km	Zambia Railways		③⑤					②⑤	
			2					2	
0	Mulobezi	d.	1200	...	Livingstone	d.	1400
85	Ngwezi	d.	2030	...	Ngwezi	d.	1905
163	Livingstone	a.	0200	...	Mulobezi	a.	0200

A – 🛏 1, 2 cl., 🚐 and ✕ Dar es Salaam - Kigoma and v.v. Subject to confirmation.
B – Subject to confirmation.
C – 🛏 2 cl., 🛏 1, 2 cl., 🚐 and ✕. Kilimanjaro/Mukuba Express Train.
D – 🛏 1cl. 🛏 1 cl, 🚐 and ✕. Kilimanjaro/Mukuba Ordinary Train.
E – 🛏, 3 and 6 berth 🛏 and ✕. Zambezi Train.
◧ – Stations are approximately 8 km from each other.
◨ – Stations are approximately 2 km from each other.
⊖ – No information available.
⊠ – Possibly suspended.

MADAGASCAR — 4340

Chemins de Fer Fianarantsoa-Côte Est / Madarail

Capital : **Antananarivo** (GMT +3). 2017 Public Holidays : Jan. 1, Mar. 29, May 1, 25, June 5, 26, Aug. 15, Nov. 1, Dec, 11, 25.

km	Madarail		⑤	②				①	④		km	CFFCE		②⑥				③⑦
			2	2				2	2									
0	Toamasina	d.	...	0820	Moramanga	d.	0700	1500	0	Fianarantsoa	d.	0700	...	Manakara	d.	0645
43	Tampolo	d.	...	0951	Andasibe	◇ d.	0830	1600	39	Ranomena	d.	0855	...	Sahasinaka	d.	0900
86	Ambila-Lemaitso	d.	0800	1125	Lohariandava	d.	1050	1820	62	Tolongoina	d.	1015	...	Manampatrana	d.	1130
162	Lohariandava	d.	1150	1515	Ambila-Lemaitso	d.	1340	2200	79	Manampatrana	d.	1110	...	Tolongoina	d.	1225
223	Andasibe	◇ d.	1515	1725	Tampolo	d.	1520		118	Sahasinaka	d.	1330	...	Ranomena	d.	1355
249	Moramanga	a.	1740	1855	Toamasina	a.	1650		163	Manakara	a.	1600	...	Fianarantsoa	a.	1600

◇ – Special tour trains using Michelin railcars run Andasibe - Antananarivo and v.v, For dates contact operator.

BOTSWANA — 4345

Botswana Railways

km			502					501	
0	Francistown	4380 d.	2100	...	Lobatse	d.	1910
235	Mahalapye	d.	0216	...	Gaborone	d.	2125
435	Gaborone	d.	0605	...	Mahalapye	d.	0056
507	Lobatse	a.	0731	...	Francistown	4380 a.	0611

Capital : **Gaborone** (GMT +2).
2017 Public Holidays : Jan. 1, Apr. 14, 17, May 1, 25, July 1, 20, Sept. 30, Dec, 25.
501/502 – 🛏, 🚐 and ✕.

BEYOND EUROPE - AFRICA and THE MIDDLE EAST

4350 ANGOLA

INCFA

km		①–⑤	①–⑤	③	⑥	①–⑤	②	⑥	⑥	①–⑤
0	**Luanda** Textang ⊗ d.	0500a	...	...	...	0721	0744	0750	1525	1640
23	Viana ⊗ d.	0528	0700	0700	0745	0803	0930	0834	1610	1732
65	Catete d.	...	0740	0747	0834	0909	|	0927	1704	1827
135	Zenza d.	...	0839	0859	0948	...	1127	...	...	...
190	**Dondo** (Cuanza) a.	...	|	|	1048	...	1220	...	...	...
241	N'dalatando d.	...	1200	1227	...	...	...	...	...	...
424	**Malange** a.	...	1625	1652	...	...	...	...	...	...

	①–⑤	⑥	②	⑥	②⑦	①–⑤	④	⑥	①–⑤
Malange d.	...	...	...	...	0730	...	0730	...	...
N'dalatando d.	...	...	...	...	1215	...	1215	...	...
Dondo (Cuanza) d.	...	...	1320	1340	|	...	|	...	...
Zenza d.	...	...	1418	1450	1516	...	1538	...	...
Catete d.	1000	1020	|	1600	1615	...	1647	1730	1850
Viana ⊗ d.	1052	1110	1620	1649	1655	1708	1730	1822	1945
Luanda Textang ⊗ a.	1137	114	1701	...	...	1750	...	1855a	2021a

km		①–⑤	①–⑤	③
0	**Lobita** ◧ d.	...	...	0530
33	Benguela ◧ a.	...	...	|
395	**Caála** d.	0630	...	|
408	Dango d.	0730	...	|
423	Huambo d.	0755	1000	1714
453	Cambuio d.	...	1100	▬
478	**Katchiungo** a.	...	1155	③
1016	Luena d.	...	...	0600
1332	Luau a.	...	...	1235

	①–⑤	①–⑤	④
Luau d.	...	...	0600
Luena d.	...	...	1240
Katchiungo d.	1300	...	▬
Cambuio d.	1355	...	⑤
Huambo d.	1455	1600	0600
Dango d.	...	1622	|
Caála a.	...	1730	|
Benguela ◧ d.	...	...	|
Lobita ◧ a.	...	...	1648

km		✥		①④
0	**Namibe** d.	...	...	0500
162	Bibala d.	...	...	0845
246	Lubango d.	0600	...	1010
424	Matala d.	1040	...	1320
509	**Dondo** (Lubango) a.	1240	...	|
756	Menongue a.	...	...	1900

	②⑤		✥
Menongue d.	0500	...	...
Dondo (Lubango) a.	|	...	1715
Matala d.	1045	...	1910
Lubango d.	1400	...	2340
Bibala d.	1530	...	...
Namibe a.	1920	...	...

Capital: **Luanda** (GMT +1). 2017 Public Holidays: Jan. 1, Feb. 4, 28, Mar. 8, Apr. 4, 14, May 1, Sept. 17, Nov. 2, 11, Dec. 25.

⊗ – Additional local trains available. ✥ – Service suspended. **a** – Luanda Muceques.

◧ – Services dep. Lobita and Benguela at 0600, 1700 journey time 65 min.

4360 MALAWI

2nd class only Central East African Railway

km		⑥	④	⑤	③
22	Bilila d.	...	0730	...	1625
0	**Balaka** d.	...	0940	0600	1735
16	Nkaya d.	...	1030	0840	...
42	Liwonde d.	...	1115	|	...
114	**Nayuchi** a.	...	1427	|	...
104	Blantyre d.	...	...	1640	...
112	Limbe d.	0900	...	1737	...
233	**Makhanga** a.	1715	...	...	...

	④	③	⑦	④
Makhanga d.	...	...	0700	...
Limbe d.	...	0700	1645	...
Blantyre d.	...	0745	...	...
Nayuchi d.	...	|	...	1500
Liwonde d.	...	|	...	1800
Nkaya d.	...	1315	...	1900
Balaka d.	0600	1453	...	1940
Bilila a.	0710	1605	...	...

Capital: **Lilongwe** (GMT +2).

2017 Public Holidays: Jan. 1, 15, Mar. 3, Apr. 14, 17, May 1, 14, June 14, 26, July 6, Dec. 25.

4370 MOÇAMBIQUE

2nd class only CD do Norte / CF Moçambique

Capital: **Maputo** (GMT +2). 2017 Public Holidays: Jan. 1, Feb. 3, Apr. 7, 14, May 1, June 25, Sep. 7, 25, Oct. 4, Dec. 25.

km		②④⑥	A	
0	**Nampula** d.	0600	...	...
173	Iapala d.	1051	...	...
252	Malema d.	1342	...	...
302	Mutuáli d.	1533	...	...
356	Cuamba d.	1704	⊖	...
464	Mitande d.	...	⊖	...
541	**Nayuci** a.	...	⊖	...

	③⑤⑦	A	
Nayuci d.	...	⊖	...
Mitande d.	...	⊖	...
Cuamba d.	0600	⊖	...
Mutuáli d.	0735	...	...
Malema d.	0933	...	...
Iapala d.	1220	...	...
Nampula a.	1708	...	...

km		⑥⑦	⑥	③
0	**Maputo** d.	0730	0955	1300
208	Chókwe d.	1216	1910	1950
534	**Chicualacuala** a.	...	0349	0342

	④	⑦	⑥⑦
Chicualacuala d.	1300	1015	...
Chókwe d.	2323	2020	1420
Maputo a.	0549	0810	1909

km		③⑥	②	
0	**Beira** d.	0600	1100	...
28	Dondo d.	0731	1224	...
120	Muanza d.	1021	1509	...
187	Inhaminga d.	1208	1656	...
214	Inhamitanga d.	1259	1742	...
302	Marromeu a.	1600	|	...
320	**Nhamalabue** a.	...	2125	...
577	Maotize a.	...	0526	...

	④⑦		③
Moatize d.	...	...	1600
Nhamalabue d.	...	...	0011
Marromeu d.	0800	...	|
Inhamitanga d.	1108	...	0426
Inhaminga d.	1159	...	0517
Muanza d.	1346	...	0705
Dondo d.	1639	...	0935
Beira a.	1800	...	1050

km		①–⑤	⑥⑦	⑦–⑤
0	**Maputo** d.	0745	0800	1815
53	Moambe d.	0927	0952	2032
88	**Ressano Garcia** a.	1020	1045	2124

	①–⑥	①–⑤	⑥⑦
Ressano Garcia d.	0346	1205	1225
Moambe d.	0506	1317	1346
Maputo a.	0645	1511	1540

A – Once a week. Day of operation varies.

⊖ – No information available.

4380 ZIMBABWE

National Railways of Zimbabwe

Capital: **Harare** (GMT +2). 2017 Public Holidays: Jan. 1, Apr. 14, 17, 18, May 1, 25, Aug. 8, 14, Dec. 22, 25, 26.

km		①④⑥ A		
0	**Mutare** d.	2100	...	...
77	Nyazura d.	2307	...	...
99	Rusape d.	0010	...	...
166	Macheke d.	0239	...	...
201	Marondera d.	0345	...	...
273	**Harare** a.	0605	...	...

	③⑤⑦ A		
Harare d.	2130	...	...
Marondera d.	2345	...	...
Macheke d.	0100	...	...
Rusape d.	0320	...	...
Nyazura d.	0409	...	...
Mutare a.	0600	...	...

km		B		
0	**Bulawayo** d.	1930	...	...
126	Gwayi d.	2310	...	...
266	Dete d.	0200	...	...
339	Hwange d.	0347	...	...
351	Thomson Junction d.	0455	...	...
472	**Victoria Falls** a.	0800	...	...

	B		
Victoria Falls d.	1900	...	...
Thomson Jct d.	2230	...	...
Hwange d.	2303	...	...
Dete d.	0110	...	...
Gwayi d.	0340	...	...
Bulawayo a.	0805	...	...

km		②⑤⑦ A	①③⑤	
0	**Harare** d.	2000	...	...
44	Norton d.	2120	...	...
127	Chegutu d.	2227	...	...
160	Kadoma d.	2320	...	...
237	Kwekwe d.	0054	...	...
**	Masvingo d.	|	2000	...
302	Gweru d.	0242	0345	...
336	Somabhula d.	|	...	...
369	Shangani d.	|	...	...
486	**Bulawayo** a.	0700	...	...

	①④⑥ A	①③⑤	
Bulawayo d.	2000	...	...
Shangani d.	|	...	...
Somabhula d.	|	...	...
Gweru d.	0030	0245	...
Masvingo a.	|	0955	...
Kwekwe d.	0227	...	...
Kadoma d.	0412	...	...
Chegutu d.	0502	...	...
Norton d.	0620	...	...
Harare a.	0730	...	...

km		③ A	⑦ A	
0	**Bulawayo** d.	1215	1730	...
113	Shangani d.	1513	2045	...
150	Somabhula d.	1607	2140	...
229	Bannockburn d.	1755	2335	...
309	Ngezi d.	1941	0135	...
401	Rutenga d.	2300	0455	...
433	Lundi d.	|	0636	...
500	**Chicualacuala** a.	0251a	|	...
499	Triangle d.	...	0720	...
523	**Chiredzi** a.	...	0758	...

	④ A	① A	
Chiredzi d.	...	1530	...
Triangle d.	...	1620	...
Chicualacuala d.	1520a	|	...
Lundi d.	|	1701	...
Rutenga d.	2000	2000	...
Ngezi d.	2255	2255	...
Bannockburn d.	0135	0135	...
Somabhula d.	0450	0450	...
Shangani d.	0552	0556	...
Bulawayo a.	0910	0910	...

km	⊠	④⑦ 2		
0	**Bulawayo** d.	1800	...	...
	Beit Bridge a.	0540	...	...

⊠	①⑤ 2		
Beit Bridge d.	2100	...	...
Bulawayo a.	0845	...	...

km	⊠	①⑤ 2	
0	**Bulawayo** ‡ d.	0900	...
196	**Francistown** ‡ **4345** a.	1425	...

⊠	②⑥ 2	
Francistown ‡ **4345** d.	1230	...
Bulawayo ‡ a.	1715	...

A – 1, 2 cl. and 2 R.
B – 1 cl., 2 cl. and 2.

a – Sango Halt.

⊖ – No information available.
** – Masvingo - Gweru *199 km*.

‡ – is Plumtree.
⊠ Service suspended

4390 NAMIBIA

Starline

Capital: **Windhoek** (GMT +1). 2017 Public Holidays: Jan. 1, Mar. 21, Apr. 14, 17, May 1, 4, 14, 25, Aug. 26, Dec. 10, 25, 26.

km	①–⑤ 12	⑥ A			⑤ A	①–⑤ 12
412	1900	...	↓	d.**Walvisbaai** a. ↑	...	0715
373	2045	1500		d.Swakopmund d.	1000	0530
222	0045	|	↓	d.Usakos d. ↑	|	0150
419	|	|		d. **Otjiwarongo** d.	|	|
282	|	|	↓	d. Omaruru d. ↑	|	|
210	0135	|		d.Kranzberg d.	|	0130
191	0220	|	↓	d.Karibib d. ↑	|	0040
70	0510	|		d.Okahandja d.	|	2205
0	0700	1030	↓	a.**Windhoek** d. ↑	1200a	1915

km	Ⓑ b	③⑥			④⑦	Ⓑ c
0	1940	...	↓	d.**Windhoek** a. ↑	...	0700
97	2210	...		d.Rehobeth d.	...	0425
192	2400	...	↓	d.Kalkrand d. ↑	...	0230
274	0220	...		d.Mariental d.	...	0020
423	0510	...	↓	d.Tses d. ↑	...	2040
505	0700	...		a.**Keetmanshoop** d.	...	1850
505	...	0850	↓	d.**Keetmanshoop** a. ↑	1630	...
681	...	1310		d.Grünau d.	1225	...
732	...	1430	↓	a.**Karasburg** d. ↑	1120	...

km	①–⑥	⑦			①–⑥	⑦
0	0850	1120	↓	d.**Oshikango** ♣ a. ↑	1640	1805
60	1010	1235		a.**Ondangwa** ♠ d.	1520	1650
	1120	1320	↓	d.**Ondangwa** ♠ a. ↑	1420	1647
	1317	1515	↓	d.Omuthiya ♥ d. ↑	1212	1505
	1443	1631		d.Oshivelo d.	1056	1326
306	1640	1840	↓	a.**Tsumeb** d. ↑	0850	1120

♣ – Rev. Theofelus Hamutumbangela.
♠ – Nehale Lya Mpingana. ♥ – Sam Nujoma.

A – DESERT EXPRESS – , 1 and ✕. Special service including meals and excursions.

a – departs 1300 in the summer.
b – Also conveys 2 cl. on ①③⑤. **c** – Also conveys 2 cl. on ②④⑦.

SOUTH AFRICA 4400

Gautrain / Shosholoza Meyl

Capital: **Pretoria** (GMT +2). 2017 Public Holidays: Jan. 1, 2, Mar. 21, Apr. 14, 17, 27, May 1, June 16, Aug. 9, Sep. 24, 25, Dec. 16, 25, 26.

km			③⑤⑦	③⑤⑦	②	⑤	④	③⑤⑦		
		G	A	B	C	2	2	E	D	...	...
0	**Johannesburg** d.	1230	1230	1315	1730	...	...	1030	1840	...	...
14	Germiston d.	1302	│	1350	│	...	...	│	1918	...	...
172	Standerton d.	│	│	│	│	...	...	│	│	...	...
315	Newcastle d.	│	│	│	│	...	...	│	0027	...	...
438	Ladysmith d.	│	│	│	│	...	...	│	0245	...	...
617	Pietermaritzburg d.	│	│	│	│	...	...	│	0630	...	...
722	**Durban** a.	│	│	│	│	...	...	│	0915	...	...
75	Vereeniging d.	1420	│	1455	1920	...	...	│	...	...	...
210	Kroonstad d.	1652	│	1725	2150	...	...	│	...	...	...
407	**Bloemfontein** a.	1935	│	2020	0032	...	...	│	...	...	...
407	**Bloemfontein** d.	...	│	2030	0055	...	...	│	...	...	...
664	Burgersdorp d.	...	│	│	0634	...	...	│	...	...	...
809	Queenstown d.	...	│	│	0912	1445	1445	│	...	...	...
1023	**East London** a.	...	│	│	1325	1000↑	│	│	...	...	...
835	Cradock d.	...	│	0445	...	│	│	│	...	...	...
1112	**Port Elizabeth** a.	...	│	0915	...	│	│	│	...	...	...
186	Klerksdorp d.	...	1625	...	...	│	│	│	...	...	...
495	Kimberley d.	...	2120	...	...	│	│	1907	...	...	...
908	De Aar d.	...	0135	...	...	0100	0100	2305	...	...	...
988	Beaufort West d.	...	0600	...	...	0500	0500	0340	...	...	...
1355	Worcester d.	...	1205	...	...	1055	1055	│	...	...	...
1511	Bellville d.	...	1500	...	...	1345	1345	│	...	...	...
1530	**Cape Town** a.	...	1530	...	...	1410	1410	1240	...	...	...

			③⑤⑦	③⑤⑦		②	③⑤⑦		⑦	④
			D	C	G	E	B	A	2	2
Cape Town d.	...	...	...	...	...	0905	...	1000	1025	1025
Belleville d.	...	...	...	...	...	│	...	1035	1105	1105
Worcester d.	...	...	...	...	...	│	...	1330	1355	1355
Beaufort West d.	...	...	...	...	...	1845	...	1950	2005	2005
De Aar d.	...	...	...	...	...	2235	...	2345	0010	0010
Kimberley d.	...	...	...	...	...	0300	...	0346	│	│
Klerksdorp d.	...	...	...	...	...	│	...	0826	│	│
Port Elizabeth d.	...	...	...	...	...	│	1500	│	│	│
Cradock d.	...	...	...	...	...	│	1932	│	│	│
East London d.	...	...	...	0900	...	│	│	│	1425↓	│
Queenstown d.	...	...	...	1326	...	│	│	│	1012	1005
Burgersdorp d.	...	...	...	1828	...	│	│	│	...	...
Bloemfontein a.	...	...	...	2136	...	│	0426	│	...	...
Bloemfontein d.	...	...	...	2156	2325	│	0446	│	...	...
Kroonstad d.	...	...	...	0110	0216	│	0752	│	...	...
Vereeniging d.	...	...	...	0325	0500	│	1010	│	...	...
Durban d.	...	...	1915	│	│	│	│	│	...	...
Pietermaritzburg d.	...	...	2153	│	│	│	│	│	...	...
Ladysmith d.	...	...	0145	│	│	│	│	│	...	...
Newcastle d.	...	...	0407	│	│	│	│	│	...	...
Standerton d.	...	...	│	│	│	│	│	│	...	...
Germiston d.	...	...	0917	│	0610	│	1112	│	...	...
Johannesburg a.	...	...	0935	0500	0625	1103	1135	1220	...	...

km		③⑤ H		
0	**Johannesburg** d.	1800	...	...
14	Germiston d.	1827	...	...
70	Pretoria d.	1930	...	...
183	Witbank d.	2205	...	...
218	Middelburg d.	2302	...	...
422	Nelspruit d.	0402	...	...
461	Kaapmuiden d.	0505	...	...
530	**Komatipoort** ▼ a.	0638	...	...
292	Mokopane d.	...	...	...
357	Polokwane d.	...	...	...
504	Makhado d.	...	...	...
633	**Musina** ▶ a.	...	...	...

	④⑦ H		
Musina ▶ d.	...	...	...
Makhado d.	...	...	...
Polokwane d.	...	...	...
Mokopane d.	...	...	...
Komatipoort ▼ d.	1800	...	...
Kaapmuiden d.	1926	...	...
Nelspruit d.	2025	...	...
Middelburg d.	0134	...	...
Witbank d.	0215	...	...
Pretoria d.	0500	...	...
Germiston d.	0557	...	...
Johannesburg a.	0616	...	...

Johannesburg - Pretoria and v.v. 56 km. Journey 36 mins. Operator: Gautrain.

From **Johannesburg** Park: Train call at Sandton* 8 mins later.

Ⓐ: 0530, 0550, 0610, 0620, 0630, 0640, 0650, 0700, 0710, 0720, 0730, 0740, 0750, 0800, 0810, 0820, 0830, 0840, 0900, 0920, 0938, 0958, 1018, and every 20mins until 1438, 1538, then every 10 mins until 1828, 1848, 1910, 1930, 1950, 2010, 2030.

Ⓒ: 0530, 0600 and every 30 mins. until 2030.

From **Pretoria**: Trains call at Sandton* 27 mins later.

Ⓐ: 0533, 0553, 0608, 0613, 0623, 0633, 0643, 0653, 0703, 0713, 0723, 0733, 0743, 0753, 0803, 0813, 0823, 0833, 0843, 0853, 0911 and every 20 mins until 1531, 1541, 1551, 1611, then every 10 mins until 1831, 1843, 1903, 1923, 1943, 2003, 2023, 2037.

Ⓒ: 0533, 0603 and every 30 mins until 2003, 2037.

* – Frequent services run throughout the day to/from Sandon and OR Tambo Airport.

A – TRANS KAROO – [sleeper], [T2] [car] and ✕ Johannesburg - Cape Town and v.v. From Johannesburg ②③⑤⑦ (No [2] on ②). From Cape Town ③⑤⑥⑦ (No [2] on ⑥).
B – ALGOA – [sleeper], [T2] and ✕ Johannesburg - Port Elizabeth and v.v.
C – AMATOLA – [sleeper], [T2] and ✕ Johannesburg - East London and v.v.
D – TRANS NATAL – [sleeper], [T2] [car] and ✕ Durban - Johannesburg and v.v. - PREMIER CLASSE – [sleeper] (1 cl.) [1] and ✕ Johannesburg - Durban and v.v.
E – PREMIER CLASSE – [sleeper] (1 cl.) [1] and ✕ Johannesburg - Cape Town and v.v. Note: Intermediate stops are operational only.
G – [2] From Johannesburg on last ⑤ of each month, from Bloemfontein on following ⑦.
H – KOMATI – [T2] and 🍸 Johannesburg - Komatipoort and v.v.
NOTE: These are the published schedules in some cases the actual timings could vary.
▶ – Musina - Beit Bridge (Zimbabwe): *12 km.* ▼ – Komatipoort - Ressano Garcia (Mozambique): *5 km.*
Train Classes: [1] Premier Class coaches consist of one or two berth deluxe compartments that convert to sleeper accommodation at night and can accomodate up to 14 passengers.
[T] Tourist Class coaches consist of two or four berth compartments that convert to sleeper accommodation at night and can accomodate up to 28 passengers.
[2] Economy Class consitsts of sitting accommodation only and hold up to 72 passengers.

ISRAEL

Capital: **Jerusalem** (GMT +2, add 1 hour in summer). 2017 Public Holidays: Mar. 12, 13, Apr. 6, 11, 17, May 2, 24, 31, Sept. 21, 22, 30, Oct. 5, 12.

Rail services are operated Israel Railways (www.rail.co.il). All services convey a single class of seated accommodation. Timings are the most recent available and are subject to alteration at any time, particularly around religious holidays. Tickets and reservations may be purchased up to 7 days in advance of travel at stations or through the website.

NAHARIYYA - TEL AVIV - BEN GURION AIRPORT - MODI'IN 4500

Israel Railways

km		⑦–⑤	⑦–⑤	⑦–⑤	⑦–⑤	⑦–⑤	⑦–④	⑦–④	⑤	⑦–④	⑦–④	⑤		⑦–④	⑦–④	⑤	⑦–④	⑤b	⑦–④	⑤	⑦–④	⑤a	⑦–④	⑦–④
0	**Nahariyya** d.	0013	0113	0213	0313	0357	...	0452	0451	0515	0554	0551		1215	1254	1251	1315	1327	1354	1351	...	1451	1454	1515
	Akko d.	0021	0121	0221	0321	0405	...	0459	0458	0522	0601	0558		1222	1301	1158	1322	1334	1401	1358	...	1458	1501	1522
20	Qiryat Motzkin d.	0032	0132	0232	0332	0415	...	0509	0508	0532	0611	0608	and at	1232	1311	1308	1332	1344	1411	1408	...	1808	1511	1532
38	Haifa Hof HaKarmel d.	0052	0152	0252	0352	0435	0503	0536	0539	0603	0636	0639	the same	1303	1336	1339	1403	1413	1436	1439	1503	1539	1536	1603
71	Binyamina d.	0112	0212	0312	0412	0455	0526	0556	0602	0626	0656	0702	minutes	1326	1356	1402	1426	1432	1456	1502	1526	1302	1556	1626
123	**Tel Aviv** Savidor Center a.	0154	0254	0354	0454	0538	0558	0628	0634	0658	0728	0734	past each	1358	1428	1434	1458	1503	1528	1534	1558	1634	1628	1658
123	**Tel Aviv** Savidor Center d.	0156	0256	0356	0456	0540	0601	0631	0637	0701	0731	0737	hour until	1401	1431	1437	1501	1506	1531	1537	1601	1637	1631	1701
137	Ben Gurion Airport a.	0210	0310	0410	0510	0558	0619	0649	0655	0719	0749	0755		1419	1449	1455	1533	1523	1549	1555a	1619	1655	1649	1719
158	**Modi'in** Center a.	...	...	...	...	...	0643	0713	0719	0743	0813	0819		1443	1513	1519	1543	1546	1613	1619a	1643	1719	1713	1743

	⑤a	⑦–④	⑦–④	⑦–④	⑦–④		⑦–④	⑦–④	⑦–④	⑦–④	⑥		⑥b	⑥b		⑥b	⑥a	⑥b	⑥a	⑥b	⑥a	⑥ab	
Nahariyya d.	1525	...	1554	1615	1654		2015	2054	2148	2313		...	1855	1951	...	2051	2055	2129	2151	2151	2229	2313	...
Akko d.	1532	...	1601	1622	1701	and at	2022	2101	2155	2321		...	1902	1958	...	2058	2102	2136	2158	2158	2236	2321	...
Qiryat Motzkin d.	1542	...	1611	1632	1711	the same	2032	2111	2205	2332		...	1912	2008	...	2108	2112	2146	2208	2208	2246	2332	...
Haifa Hof HaKarmel d.	1610	...	1636	1703	1736	minutes	2103	2136	2236	2352		...	1939	2039	...	2139	2139	2213	2239	2239	2313	2352	...
Binyamina d.	1632	...	1656	1726	1756	past each	2126	2156	2256	0012		...	2002	2102	...	2202	2202	2232	2302	2302	2332	0012	...
Tel Aviv Savidor Center a.	1703	...	1728	1758	1828	hour until	2158	2228	2347	0054		...	2034	2134	...	2254	2234	2322	2334	2354	0025	0054	...
Tel Aviv Savidor Center d.	1703	1713	1731	1801	1831		2201	2231	2350	0056		...	2037	2137	...	2257	2237	2325	2337	2357	0028	0056	...
Ben Gurion Airport a.	1723	1731	1749	1819	1849		2219	2349	0008	0110		...	2055	2155	...	2315	2255	2342	2355	0015	0045	0110	...
Modi'in Center a.	1746	1755	1813	1843	1913		2243	2313	0032	...		...	2119	2219	...	2339	2319	...	0019	0039	...	...	...

	⑦–⑤	⑦–⑤	⑦–⑤	⑦–⑤	⑦–⑤	⑤	⑦–④	⑦–④		⑤	⑦–④	⑦–④	⑤	⑦–④	⑦–④	⑤		⑦–④	⑦–④		⑦–④	⑦–④
Modi'in Center d.	...	...	...	...		0511	0518	0548		1211	1218	1248	1311	1318	1348	1411	...	1418	1448		1818	1848
Ben Gurion Airport d.	0053	0153	0253	0353	0453	0528	0535	0605		1228	1235	1305	1328	1335	1405	1428	...	1435	1505	and at	1835	1905
Tel Aviv Savidor Center a.	0106	0206	0306	0406	0506	0549	0556	0626	and at	1249	1256	1326	1349	1356	1426	1449	...	1456	1526	the same	1856	1926
Tel Aviv Savidor Center d.	0108	0208	0308	0408	0508	0552	0559	0629	the same	1252	1259	1329	1352	1359	1429	1452	...	1459	1529	minutes	1859	1929
Binyamina d.	0145	0245	0345	0445	0545	0623	0630	0700	minutes	1323	1330	1400	1423	1430	1500	1523	...	1530	1600	past each	1930	2000
Haifa Hof HaKarme d.	0205	0305	0405	0505	0610	0647	0649	0724	past each	1347	1349	1424	1447	1449	1524	1542	...	1549	1624	hour until	1949	2024
Qiryat Motzkin d.	0226	0326	0426	0528	0641	0718	0715	0755	hour until	1418	1415	1455	1518	1515	1555	1618a	...	1615	1655		2015	2055
Akko d.	0236	0336	0436	0838	0652	0727	0724	0804		1427	1424	1504	1527a	1524	1604	1627a	...	1624	1704		2024	2104
Nahariyya a.	0246	0346	0446	0548	0702	0736	0733	0813		1436	1433	1513	1536a	1533	1613	1636a	...	1633	1713		2033	2113

	⑦–④	⑦–④	⑦–④	⑦–④	⑦–④	⑦–④	⑦–④		⑥		⑥b	⑥b	⑥ab	⑥a	⑥b	⑥ab								
Modi'in Center d.	1918	1948	2018	2048	2118	2218	2318	...		...	1911	2011	2111	2211	2208	2308	...	...	...	...	...	...	...	...
Ben Gurion Airport d.	1935	2005	2035	2105	2135	2235	2335	...		...	1928	2028	2128	2228	2225	2325	...	...	...	...	...	...	...	...
Tel Aviv Savidor Center d.	1956	2026	2056	2126	2156	2256	2356	...		...	1949	2049	2149	2249	2246	2346	...	...	...	...	...	...	...	...
Tel Aviv Savidor Center d.	1959	2029	2059	2129	2159	2259	2359	...		...	1952	2052	2152	2252	2249	2349	...	...	...	...	...	...	...	...
Binyamina d.	2030	2100	2130	2200	2230	2330	0047	...		...	2023	2123	2223	2323	2337	0037	...	...	...	...	...	...	...	...
Haifa Hof HaKarme a.	2049	2124	2149	2224	2249	2349	0105	...		...	2047	2147	2247	2347	0001	0101	...	...	...	...	...	...	...	...
Qiryat Motzkin d.	2115	...	2219	...	2317	0017	0132	...		...	2118	2218	2318	0018	0032	0132	...	...	...	...	...	...	...	...
Akko a.	2124	...	2228	...	2326	0026	0141	...		...	2127	2228	2328	0027	0041	0141	...	...	...	...	...	...	...	...
Nahariyya a.	2133	...	2237	...	2335	0035	0150	...		...	2136	2236	2336	0036	0050	0150	...	...	...	...	...	...	...	...

a – Mar. 24, 2017 - June 30, 2017 only. b – Nov. 5, 2016 - Mar. 23, 2017 only.

4510 NAHARIYYA - TEL AVIV - BE'ER SHEVA

Israel Railways

km		⑦–④	⑦–④	⑤ B	⑤	⑦–④	①–④	⑦	⑤ B	⑤	⑦–④	①–④	⑦	⑤ B	⑤	⑦–④	①–④	⑦	⑤ B	⑤	⑦–④	⑦–④	⑤ B	
0	**Nahariyya** d.	...	...	...	0527	0527	...	...	...	0627	0627	...	...	...	0727	0727	...	...	...	0827	0827	...	...	...
	Akko d.	...	...	...	0534	0534	...	...	...	0634	0634	...	...	...	0734	0734	...	...	...	0834	0834	...	...	...
20	Qiryat Motzkin d.	...	...	...	0544	0544	...	...	...	0644	0644	...	...	...	0744	0744	...	...	...	0844	0844	...	...	...
38	Haifa Hof HaKarmel d.	...	...	...	0613	0616	0645	0645	...	0713	0716	0745	0745	...	0813	0816	0846	0846	...	0913	0916	0946	...	...
71	Binyamina d.	...	...	...	0632	|	|	|	...	0732	|	|	|	...	0832	|	|	|	...	0932	|	|	...	...
123	**Tel Aviv** Savidor Ctr a.	...	...	...	0703	0704	0734	0734	...	0803	0804	0834	0834	...	0903	0904	0934	0934	...	1003	1004	1034	...	...
123	**Tel Aviv** Savidor Ctr d.	0607	0637	0644	0706	0707	0737	0737	0744	0806	0807	0837	0837	0844	0906	0907	0937	0937	0944	1006	1007	1037	1044	...
143	Lod d.	0627	0656	0713	0726	0727	|	0758	0813	0826	0827	|	0858	0913	0926	0927	|	0958	1013	1026	1027	|	1113	...
186	Kiryat Gat d.	0654	0718	0738	0751	0754	0818	0822	0838	0851	0854	0918	0922	0938	0951	0954	1018	1022	1038	1051	1054	1118	1138	...
230	**Be'er Sheva** Center a.	0729	0750	0814	0827	0829	0850	0855	0914	0927	0929	0950	0955	1014	1027	1029	1050	1055	1114	1127	1129	1150	1214	...

	⑤	⑦–④	⑤ B	⑤	⑦–④	⑤ B	⑤	⑦–④	⑤ B	⑤	⑦–④	⑤ aB	⑤ a	⑦–④	⑤ aB	⑤ a	⑦–④	⑦–④	⑦–④	⑦–④	⑦–④	⑦–④	⑦–④
Nahariyya d.	0927	0927	...	1027	...	...	1127	...	...	1227	...	...	1327	...	...	1427	1427	...	1527	...	1627	...	1727
Akko d.	0934	0934	...	1034	...	...	1134	...	...	1234	...	...	1334	...	...	1434	1434	...	1534	...	1634	...	1734
Qiryat Motzkin d.	0944	0944	...	1044	...	...	1144	...	...	1244	...	...	1344	...	...	1444	1444	...	1544	...	1644	...	1744
Haifa Hof HaKarmel d.	1013	1016	...	1113	...	...	1213	...	...	1313	...	...	1413	...	...	1513	1516	1546	1616	1646	1716	1746	1816
Binyamina d.	1032	|	...	1132	...	...	1232	...	...	1332	...	...	1432	...	...	1532	|	|	|	|	|	|	|
Tel Aviv Savidor Centre a.	1103	1104	...	1203	...	...	1303	...	...	1403	...	...	1503	...	...	1603	1604	1634	1704	1734	1804	1834	1904
Tel Aviv Savidor Centre d.	1106	1107	1144	1206	1207	1244	1306	1307	1344	1406	1407	1444	1506	1507	1544	1606	1607	1637	1707	1737	1807	1837	1907
Lod d.	1126	1127	1213	1226	1227	1313	1326	1327	1413	1426	1427	1513	1526	1527	1613	1626	1627	|	1727	|	1827	|	1927
Kiryat Gat d.	1151	1154	1238	1251	1254	1338	1351	1354	1438	1451	1454	1538	1551	1554	1638	1651	1654	1718	1754	1818	1854	1918	1954
Be'er Sheva Center a.	1227	1229	1314	1327	1329	1414	1427	1429	1514	1527	1529	1614	1627	1629	1714	1727	1729	1750	1829	1850	1929	1950	2029

	⑦–④	⑦–④	⑦–④	⑦–④	⑦–④		⑥			⑥ b	⑥ b	⑥ b	⑥ b	⑥ b	⑥ a		⑥ a	⑥ b	⑥ a	⑥ a			
Nahariyya d.	...	1827	1927	...	...	...		...	...	...	...	...	1843	1929	...	...	...	2029	2043	2129	...	...	...
Akko d.	...	1834	1934	...	...	...		...	...	...	...	...	1850	1936	...	...	...	2036	2050	2136	...	...	...
Qiryat Motzkin d.	...	1844	1944	...	...	...		...	...	...	...	1847	1900	1946	...	...	2047	2046	2100	2146	...	...	...
Haifa Hof HaKarmel d.	1846	1916	2016	...	...	...		...	...	...	1858	1913	1931	2013	...	...	2113	2113	2131	2213	...	...	...
Binyamina d.	|	|	|	...	...	...		...	...	...	1921	1932	1951	2032	...	...	2132	2132	2151	2232	...	...	...
Tel Aviv Savidor Centre a.	1934	2004	2104	...	...	...		...	...	...	1959	2004	2029	2104	...	...	2204	2222	2229	2304	...	...	...
Tel Aviv Savidor Centre d.	1937	2007	2107	2207	2307	...		...	...	1907	...	2007	2031	2107	2107	...	2207	2225	2231	2307	...	...	...
Lod d.	|	2027	2127	2227	2327	...		...	...	1927	...	2027	2052	2127	2127	...	2227	2245	2252	2327	...	...	...
Kiryat Gat d.	2018	2054	2154	2254	2354	...		...	...	1952	...	2052	2120	2152	2152	...	2252	2310	2320	2352	...	...	...
Be'er Sheva Center a.	2050	2129	2229	2329	0029	...		...	...	2028	...	2128	2156	2228	2228	...	2328	2346	2356	0028	...	...	...

	⑦–④	⑤	⑦–④	⑤	⑤ B	⑦–④	⑦–④	⑤	⑤ B	⑦–④	⑦–④	⑤	⑤ B	⑦–④	⑦–④	⑤	⑤ B	⑦–④	⑤	⑤ B	⑦–④	⑤	⑤ B
Be'er Sheva Center d.	0459	0501	0559	0601	0628	0638	0659	0701	0728	0738	0759	0801	0828	0838	0859	0901	0928	0959	1001	1028	1059	1101	1128
Kiryat Gat d.	0532	0535	0632	0635	0702	0708	0732	0735	0801	0808	0832	0835	0902	0908	0932	0935	1002	1032	1035	1102	1132	1135	1212
Lod d.	0559	0559	0659	0659	0726	|	0759	0759	0826	|	0859	0859	0926	|	0959	0959	1026	1059	1059	1126	1159	1159	1226
Tel Aviv Savidor Centre a.	0620	0620	0720	0720	0755	0750	0820	0820	0855	0850	0920	0920	0955	0950	1020	1020	1055	1120	1120	1155	1220	1220	1255
Tel Aviv Savidor Centre d.	0623	0623	0723	0723	...	0753	0823	0823	...	0853	0923	0923	...	0952	...	1023	...	...	1123	...	...	1223	...
Binyamina d.	|	0653	|	0753	...	|	|	0853	...	|	|	0953	...	|	...	1053	...	...	1153	...	...	1253	...
Haifa Hof HaKarmel d.	0708	0712	0808	0812	...	0838	0908	0912	...	0938	1008	1012	...	1038	...	1112	...	...	1212	...	...	1312	...
Qiryat Motzkin d.	0741	0742	0841	0842	...	...	0941	0942	...	...	1041	1042	...	...	...	1143	...	...	1242	...	...	1342	...
Akko d.	0751	0751	0851	0851	...	...	0951	0951	...	...	1051	1051	...	...	...	1151	...	...	1251	...	...	1351	...
Nahariyya a.	0800	0800	0900	0900	...	...	1000	1000	...	...	1100	1100	...	...	...	1200	...	...	1300	...	...	1400	...

	⑦–④	⑤	⑤ B	⑦–④	⑤	⑤ B	⑦–④	⑤ a		⑤ aB	⑦–④	⑦–④	⑤ a	⑤ aB	⑦–④	⑦–④	⑦–④	⑦–④	⑦–④	⑦–④	⑦–④	⑦–④	
Be'er Sheva Center d.	1159	1201	1228	1259	1301	1328	1359	1401	...	1428	1438	1459	1501	1528	1538	1559	1638	1659	1738	1759	1838	1859	...
Kiryat Gat d.	1232	1235	1302	1332	1335	1402	1432	1435	...	1502	1508	1532	1535	1602	1608	1632	1708	1732	1808	1832	1908	1932	...
Lod d.	1352	1259	1326	1359	1359	1426	1459	1459	...	1526	|	1559	1559	1626	|	1659	|	1759	|	1859	|	1959	...
Tel Aviv Savidor Centre a.	1320	1320	1355	1420	1420	1455	1520	1520	...	1555	1550	1620	1620	1655	1650	1720	1750	1820	1850	1920	1950	2020	...
Tel Aviv Savidor Centre d.	...	1323	...	1423	1423	...	1523	1523	...	...	1553	1623	1623	...	1653	1723	1753	1823	1853	1923	1953	2023	...
Binyamina d.	...	1353	...	|	1453	...	|	1553	...	...	|	|	1653	...	|	|	|	|	|	|	|	|	...
Haifa Hof HaKarmel d.	...	1412	...	1508	1512	...	1608	1612	...	...	1640	1708	1712	...	1740	1808	1840	1908	1938	2008	2038	2108	...
Qiryat Motzkin d.	...	1442	...	1541	1542a	...	1641	1642	...	...	...	1741	...	...	...	1841	...	1941	...	2041	...	2141	...
Akko d.	...	1451	...	1551	1551a	...	1651	1651	...	...	...	1751	...	...	...	1842	...	1951	...	2051	...	2151	...
Nahariyya a.	...	1500	...	1600	1600a	...	1700	1700	...	...	...	1800	...	...	...	1900	...	2000	...	2100	...	2200	...

	⑦–④	⑦–④	⑦–④	⑦–④	⑥		⑥ b	⑥ b	⑥ b	⑥ b	⑥ b	⑥ a	⑥ b	⑥ a	⑥ a	⑥ a							
Be'er Sheva Center d.	1959	2059	2159	2259		...	1840	1901	1920	2001	2020	2040	2101	2101	2201	2220	...	...	...	...	...	...	...
Kiryat Gat d.	2032	2132	2232	2332		...	1914	1935	|	2035	|	2114	2135	2135	2235	|	...	...	...	...	...	...	...
Lod d.	2059	2159	2259	2359		...	1943	1959	|	2059	|	2143	2159	2159	2259	|	...	...	...	...	...	...	...
Tel Aviv Savidor Centre a.	2120	2220	2320	0020		...	2005	2020	2107	2120	2207	2205	2220	2220	2320	0007	...	...	...	...	...	...	...
Tel Aviv Savidor Centre d.	...	...	...	...		...	...	2023	...	2123	...	...	2223	2223	2323	...	...	...	...	...	...	...	...
Binyamina d.	...	...	...	...		...	...	2253	...	2210	...	...	2310	2253	0010	...	...	...	...	...	...	...	...
Haifa Hof HaKarmel d.	...	...	...	...		...	...	2112	...	2228	...	...	2328	2312	0028	...	...	...	...	...	...	...	...
Qiryat Motzkin d.	...	...	...	...		...	...	2141	...	...	...	...	...	2341	...	...	...	...	...	...	...	...	...
Akko d.	...	...	...	...		...	...	2150	...	...	...	...	...	2350	...	...	...	...	...	...	...	...	...
Nahariyya a.	...	...	...	...		...	...	2159	...	...	...	...	...	2359	...	...	...	...	...	...	...	...	...

4513 BET SHE'AN - HAIFA Hof HaKarmel

Israel Railways

km		⑦–④		⑦–④	⑤		⑦–④	⑤	⑦–④	⑤ a	⑦–④	⑤ a	⑦–④		⑦–④		⑥	b	b	a	a
	Bet She'an d.	0532	...	0632	0635	and hourly until	1432	1435	1532	1535	1632	1635	1732	and hourly until	2132	...		1908	2008	2108	2208
	Haifa Hof HaKarmel a.	0629	...	0729	0732		1529	1532	1629	1632	1729	1732	1829		2229	...		2005	2105	2205	2305

	⑦–④	⑤	⑦–④	⑤		⑦–④	⑤	⑦–④	⑥ a	⑦–④	⑥ a	⑦–④		⑦–④		⑥	b	b	a	a	
Haifa Hof HaKarmel d.	0603	0621	0703	0721	and hourly until	1403	1421	1503	1521	1603	1621	1703	and hourly until	2103	...		1954	2054	2154	2254	...
Bet She'an a.	0701	0721	0801	0821		1501	1521	1601	1621	1701	1721	1801		2201	...		2054	2154	2254	2354	...

4515 HERTSLIYYA - TEL AVIV - JERUSALEM

Israel Railways

km		⑦–④	⑤	⑦–④	⑤	⑦–④	⑤	⑦–④	⑤	⑦–④	⑤	⑦–④	⑤	⑦–④	⑤	⑦–④	⑤	⑦–④	⑤ a	⑦–④	⑤ a	⑦–④	⑦–④	⑦–④	⑦–④
	Hertsliyya d.	...	0602	0629	0702	0729	0802	0829	0902	0929	1002	1029	1102	1129	1202	1229	1302	1329	1402	1429	1502	1529	1629	1729	1829
0	**Tel Aviv** Savidor C d.	0544	0614	0644	0714	0744	0814	0844	0914	0944	1014	1044	1114	1144	1214	1244	1314	1344	1414	1444	1514	1544	1644	1744	1844
20	Lod d.	0604	0634	0704	0734	0804	0834	0904	0934	1004	1034	1104	1134	1204	1234	1304	1334	1404	1434	1504	1534	1604	1704	1804	1904
51	Bet Shemesh d.	0629	0659	0729	0759	0829	0839	0929	0959	1029	1059	1129	1159	1229	1259	1329	1359	1429	1459	1529	1559	1629	1729	1829	1929
82	**Jerusalem** Malha a.	0709	...	0810	0840	0910	0940	1010	1040	...	1140	1210	1239	...	1339	1409	1439a	...	1539	1609	...	1709	1809	1909	2009

		⑦–④	⑥ b	⑦–④	⑦–④	⑥ a	⑦–④		
Hertsliyya d.	...	1929	...	2029	2129	...	2229	...	...
Tel Aviv Savidor C d.	...	1944	2014	2044	2144	2214	2244	...	...
Lod d.	...	2004	2034	2104	2204	2234	2304	...	...
Bet Shemesh d.	...	2029	2059	2129	2229	2259	2329	...	...
Jerusalem Malha a.	...	2109	2139	...	...	2339	...	...	...

	⑦–④	⑤	⑦–④	⑤	⑦–④	⑦–④	⑤	⑦–④	⑤
Jerusalem Malha d.	...	...	0617	...	...	0717	0747	0817	0847
Bet Shemesh d.	0559	0629	0659	0729	0730	0759	0829	0859	0929
Lod d.	0623	0653	0723	0853	0753	0823	0853	0923	0953
Tel Aviv Savidor C a.	0644	0714	0744	0814	0814	0844	0914	0944	1014
Hertsliyya a.	0658	0727	0758	0827	...	0858	0927	0958	1027

	⑦–④	⑤	⑦–④	⑤	⑦–④	⑤	⑦–④	⑤	⑦–④	⑤	⑦–④	⑤ a	⑦–④	⑤ a	⑦–④	⑦–④	⑦–④	⑦–④	⑥ b	⑦–④		⑦–④	⑥ a	
Jerusalem Malha d.	0917	0947	...	1046	1117	1146	...	1246	1316	1346a	...	1446	1516	...	1616	1716	1816	1916	1945	2017	...	2117	2145	...
Bet Shemesh d.	0959	1029	1100	1129	1159	1229	1300	1329	1359	1429	1500	1529	1559	1629	1659	1759	1859	1959	2023	2059	...	2159	2223	...
Lod d.	1023	1053	1123	1153	1223	1253	1323	1353	1423	1453	1523	1553	1623	1653	1723	1823	1923	2023	2047	2123	...	2223	2247	...
Tel Aviv Savidor C a.	1044	1114	1144	1214	1244	1314	1344	1414	1444	1514	1544	1614	1644	1714	1744	1844	1944	2044	2109	2144	...	2244	2309	...
Hertsliyya a.	1058	1127	1158	1227	1258	1327	1358	1427	1458	1527a	1558	1627	1658	...	1758	1858	1958	2058	...	2158	...	...	...	...

B – Also calls at Ben Gurion Airport 18 mins before/after Tel Aviv. a – Mar. 24, 2017 - June 30, 2017 only. b – Nov. 5, 2016 - Mar. 23, 2017 only.

LUXURY and CRUISE TRAINS

THE BLUE TRAIN :
A luxury cruise train running regularly between Pretoria and Cape Town with excursions along the way. Also occasional trips from Pretoria to Durban. ✆ +27 12 334 8459. Fax +27 12 334 8464. www.bluetrain.co.za.

ROVOS RAIL :
Luxury cruise train running regularly between: Pretoria and Cape Town, Pretoria and Victoria Falls and Pretoria and Durban. Also occasonial trips to Swakopmund and Dar es Salaam. Most tours feature haulage by the company's preserved steam locomotives. ✆ +27 12 315 8242. Fax +27 12 323 0843. www.rovos.com.

SHONGOLOLO EXPRESS :
Various 16 day train journeys throughout Southern Africa with excursions along the way. Tours start from Johannesburg or Cape Town and destinations include Dar es Salaam, Victoria Falls and Swakopmund. ✆ +27 11 486 4357. Fax +27 11 486 4057. www.shongololo.com.

SYRIA 4600

Chemins de fer Syriens   Services suspended due to hostilities

Capital : **Dimashq** (GMT +2, add 1 hour in summer). 2017 Public Holidays :

km				
0	**Al Qamishli** d.	...	...	...
81	Al Hasakah d.	...	...	...
210	Dayr az Zawr d.	...	...	...
346	Ar Raqqah d.	...	...	...
550	**Aleppo** (Halab) a.	...	...	...
550	**Aleppo** (Halab) d.	...	...	...
694	Hamah d.	...	...	...
755	Hims 2 d.	...	...	...
899	**Dimashq** Kadem a.	...	...	...

Dimashq Kadem d.	...	...	...
Hims 2 d.	...	...	...
Hamah d.	...	...	...
Aleppo (Halab) a.	...	...	...
Aleppo (Halab) d.	...	...	...
Ar Raqqah d.	...	...	...
Dayr az Zawr d.	...	...	...
Al Hasakah d.	...	...	...
Al Qamishli a.	...	...	...

km				
0	**Aleppo** (Halab) d.	...	...	...
68	Bismaron d.	...	...	...
95	Jisr ash Shughur d.	...	...	...
199	**Al Ladhiqyah** a.	...	...	...
199	**Al Ladhiqyah** d.	...	...	...
280	Tartus d.	...	...	...
382	Hims 2 d.	...	...	...
526	**Dimashq** Kadem a.	...	...	...

Dimashq Kadem d.	...	...	...
Hims 2 d.	...	...	...
Tartus d.	...	...	...
Al Ladhiqyah a.	...	...	...
Al Ladhiqyah d.	...	...	...
Jisr ash Shughur d.	...	...	...
Bismaron d.	...	...	...
Aleppo (Halab) a.	...	...	...

IRAQ 4610

Iraq Railways

km			21
		2C	B
609	Umm Qasr d.	1130	...
541	**Al Basrah** Ma'qil d.	1400	1800
370	An Nasiriyah (for Ur) d.	▬	|
182	Ad Dawanyah d.	...	|
107	Al Hillah (for Babylon) d.	**11**	|
0	**Baghdad** West a.	**A**	0615
0	**Baghdad** West d.	1920	...
117	Samarra d.	2310	...
171	Tikrit d.	|	...
211	Ba'iji d.	|	...
406	**Al Mawsil** a.	0755	...

	20	12
	B	A
Al Mawsil d.	...	1900
Ba'iji d.	...	|
Tikrit d.	...	|
Samarra d.	...	0400
Baghdad West a.	...	0800
Baghdad West d.	1700	▬
Al Hillah (for Babylon) d.	|	...
Ad Dawanyah d.	|	...
An Nasiriyah (for Ur) d.	|	**2C**
Al Basrah Ma'qil a.	0520	0800
Umm Qasr a.	...	1025

Capital : **Baghdad** (GMT +3).

2017 Public Holidays : Jan. 1, 6, May 1, June 26 - 28, July 14, Sept. 2 - 5, 22, Oct. 1, 3, Dec. 1, 25

Rail services in Iraq are operated by Iraq Railways. Trains convey second class seating and also sleeping cars where indicated. Information regarding rail services is still very hard to obtain and the schedules shown should be treated as subject to confirmation.

A – 🛏 2 cl. Runs when required.
B – 🛏 2 cl.
C – Runs once per week. Days of operation unknown.

SAUDI ARABIA 4620

Saudi Railways Organization

Capital : **Riyadh** (GMT +3).   2017 Public Holidays : June 26, 29, July 2, Sep. 2, 4, 5, 23.

Rail services are operated by the Saudi Railways Organization (www.saudirailways.org). There are two types of trains: Modern (shown as **M** in the tables) and Regular (shown as **R**). **M** trains convey first (called Premium and includes refreshments in the waiting rooms) and second class (Standard) seating. **R** trains convey first (called Al-Rihab), second (called Al-Taleaa) and ordinary class (called Al Qafela) seating. Reservations are available from 6 months until 1 hour before departure time

km		M	R	M	M		M	M	M	M	R
			⑦–④								⑥–③
0	**Ad Dammam** d.	0345	0522	0837	0947	...	1332	1519	1716	1935	2049
74	Abqaiq d.	0426	0603	0918	|	...	|	1603	1757	|	2138
139	Al Hufuf d.	0512	0652	1011	|	...	|	1700	1853	2108	2219
449	**Ar Riyad** a.	0755	...	1247	1342	...	1727	1939	2136	2345	...

	R	M	M	M	R	M	M	M	M	
	⑦–④				⑦–④					
Ar Riyad d.	...	0930	0929	1120	...	1300	1518	1738	2045	...
Al Hufuf d.	0525	1113	|	1401	1604	|	1758	2014	2325	...
Abqaiq d.	0604	1152	|	1446	1643	|	1837	2053	|	...
Ad Dammam a.	0655	1240	1324	1540	1734	1655	1928	2148	0055	...

IRAN 4630

Raja Trains

Capital : **Tehran** (GMT +3.5, add 1 hour in summer).
2017 Public Holidays : Feb. 11, Mar. 2, Apr. 10, 24, May 12, June 26, 27, July 20, Sept. 1, 9, 30, Oct. 1, Nov. 10, 19, Dec. 6.
Rail services are operated by Raja Trains, an associate of Islamic Republic of Iran Railways (www.raja.ir). Except where noted as convey 2nd class only, all trains convey sleeping cars which convert to seating for daytime travel (for services to/from Turkey see Table **1575**).

km							●	●				●								●				
0	**Tehran** d.	...	...	0605	0640	0730	0800	1105	1120	1210	1605	1635	1705	1735	1820	1920	1940	2020	2040	2054	2120	2130	2145	2210
926	**Mashhad** a.	...	...	1345	1415	1505	1735	1805	2300	0010	0145	0325	0250	0315	0400	0525	0540	0615	0640	0645	0840	0715	0905	0745

							●		●			●			●				●					
Mashhad d.	...	...	...	0535	0600	0615	0700	0735	1210	1400	1500	1550	1700	1720	1730	1820	1905	1955	2012	2015	2115	2135	2225	2330
Tehran a.	...	...	...	1310	1330	1355	1650	1915	2005	0135	1005	0120	0255	0615	0430	0420	0500	0610	0615	0640	0640	0920	1010	1125

km				
0	**Tehran** d.	1605	...	1745
736	**Tabriz** a.	0430	...	0640

Tabriz d.	1735	...	1855
Tehran a.	0645	...	0750

km		A		
0	**Tabriz** d.	0820	...	...
146	**Djulfa** a.	1110	...	...

	A		
Djulfa d.	1730	...	...
Tabriz a.	2040	...	...

km				●
0	**Tehran** d.	1325	1445	1800
1329	**Bandar e Abbas** a.	0805	0945	1240

			●
Bandar e Abbas d.	1345	1435	1700
Tehran a.	0900	0855	1220

km			●	
0	**Tehran** d.	1555	1940	2215
494	**Eşfahan** d.	|	|	0545
	Shiraz a.	0715	0930	

			●
Shiraz d.	...	1820	1900
Eşfahan d.	2350	|	|
Tehran a.	0720	0955	0935

km			
0	**Tehran** d.	1530	1820
924	**Khorramshahr** a.	0945	1300

Khorramshahr d.	1240	1520
Tehran a.	0645	1015

km			
0	**Tehran** d.	1155	...
	Zahedan a.	1100	...

Zahedan d.	1530	...
Tehran a.	1325	...

km			
0	**Mashhad** d.	1000	2045
165	**Sarakhs** a.	1240	2325

Sarakhs d.	0530	1440
Mashhad a.	0825	1745

km			
0	**Mashhad** d.	1445	1610
	Eşfahan a.	0855	0930

Eşfahan d.	1515	1540
Mashhad a.	0840	093

km			
0	**Mashhad** d.	0010	1532
	Qom a.	1440	0420

Qom d.	1150	2045
Mashhad a.	0035	1125

A – ②④⑤⑦.
● – Every other day.   ▲ – Odd dated days.

ZAHEDAN - QUETTA 4640

km		404
		A
0	**Zahedan** d.	1000
84	Mirjawa 🏛 a.	1220
84	Mirjawa 🏛 d.	1300
100	Kuhi Taftan a.	1550
100	Kuhi Taftan d.	1700
222	Nok Kundi d.	2157
389	Dalbandin d.	0540
578	Nushki d.	1257
689	Wali Khan d.	1740
712	Spezand d.	1930
737	**Quetta** a.	2025

	403
	B
Quetta d.	0800
Spezand d.	0920
Wali Khan d.	1016
Nushki d.	1510
Dalbandin d.	2240
Nok Kundi d.	0557
Kuhi Taftan a.	1100
Kuhi Taftan d.	1230
Mirjawa 🏛 a.	1505
Mirjawa 🏛 d.	1515
Zahedan a.	1740

NOTE : Pakistan Railways and Raja Trains give different schedules for this train. This table shows the Pakistan Railways version. The Raja version is : Quetta d. 0830 - Zahedan a. 1335 / Zahedan d. 0800 - Quetta a. 1515.
A – ⑫ departs on 3rd and 17th of the month.
B – ⑫ departs on 1st and 15th of the month.

QUETTA - AMRITSAR 4650

km		23	402	14002
		A	①④	①④
0	**Quetta** d.	1015	...	...
131	Sibi d.	1520	...	...
296	Jacobabad d.	1820	...	...
385	Rohri d.	2045	...	...
840	Khanewal d.	0720	...	...
1127	**Lahore** Junction a.	0955	...	...
1127	**Lahore** Junction d.	...	0800	...
	Wagah a.	...	0835	...
	Wagah d.	...	1130	...
1147	Atari 🏛 a.	...	1150	...
1147	Atari 🏛 d.	...	...	2000
1173	**Amritsar** a.	...	...	2037

	14001	401	24
	①④	①④	A
Amritsar d.	0650	...	...
Atari 🏛 a.	0715	...	...
Atari 🏛 d.	...	1100	...
Wagah a.	...	1410	...
Wagah d.	...	1610	...
Lahore Junction a.	...	1645	...
Lahore Junction d.	...	...	1700
Khanewal d.	...	...	2250
Rohri d.	...	...	0630
Jacobabad d.	...	...	0840
Sibi d.	...	...	1155
Quetta a.	...	...	1700

A – AKBAR EXPRESS operated by Pakistan Railways.
NOTE : Timings are subject to confirmation and connections are not guaranteed.

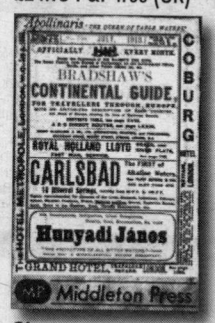
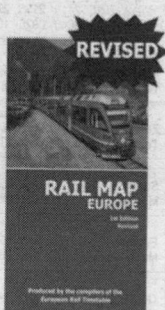
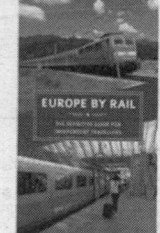
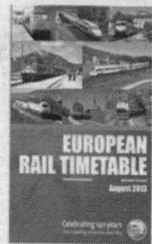

As an added extra for readers of this seasonal Winter edition we are including the remaining BEYOND EUROPE sections, in addition to the pages for **Africa and the Middle East** which appear in the preceding pages.

The tables covering **India**, **South East Asia**, **Australia and New Zealand**, **China**, **Japan**, **North America**, **South America** and **South Korea** previously appeared in our regular editions from July to November 2016. Limited updates have been made to these tables for this seasonal edition.

	Tables	Pages
Africa & the Middle East	From **4000**	564 – 575
India	From **5000**	578 – 589
S. E. Asia, Australia, New Zealand	From **6000**	590 – 601
China	From **7000**	602 – 615
Japan	From **8000**	616 – 627
North America	From **9000**	628 – 641
South America	From **9900**	642 – 644
South Korea	From **9970**	646 – 647

BEYOND EUROPE
India

Introduction

The Beyond Europe section covers principal rail services in a different area of the world each month. There are six areas, each appearing as follows:

Winter (December) and Summer (June): all the latest Beyond Europe pages will be included.

January and July (digital only): India.

February and August: India; South East Asia, Australia and New Zealand; North America.

March and September (digital only): China.

April and October: China; Japan; South America; South Korea.

May and November (digital only): North America.

The months have been chosen so that we can bring you up-to-date information for those countries which make seasonal changes.

Contents

INDEX OF PLACES

by table number

INDIA

Capital : **New Delhi** (GMT +5.5).   2017 Public Holidays : Jan. 26, Feb, 24, Apr. 9, 14, May 10, Aug. 15, Sept. 2, 30, Oct. 1, 2, 19, Nov. 4, Dec. 2, 25.

Rail services in India are operated by Indian Railways. Most trains convey a selection of first and second class accommodation from the several available. Trains which convey second class only are noted in either the column head or footnotes. Note that Rajdhani and Shatabdi trains convey first class accommodation only. The exact carriage types available on each train varies. A brief summary of train types and accommodation follows :

Rajdhani (shown as *RDi* in column heads). Air-conditioned first class night trains. Special fares payable. Conveys First Class 2 or 4-berth sleepers (code 1A); two-tier (code 2A) or three-tier (code 3A) first class open plan berths. **Shatabdi** (shown as *SDi* in column heads). Air-conditioned first class daytime trains. Special fares payable. Conveys Chair Class seats (code CC); Executive Chair Class. **Duronto** (shown in column heads as *Duro*). Some non-stop trains, some very limited stop trains. Conveys first class sleeping accommodation (codes 1A, 2A, 3A as above); second class non air-conditioned 6-berth (code SL). **Express** (shown in column heads as *Exp*). Most services convey first class air conditioned two-tier (code 2A) or three-tier (code 3A) open plan berths; second class 'Sleeper Class' non air-conditioned six-berth (code SL); non air-conditioned second class seats (code 2S). **Yuva** (shown in column heads as *Yuva*). Low-cost air-conditioned train. Seating accommodation only. During the day, all sleepers and berths convert to seated accommodation. The codes shown are those used by Indian Railways.

Timings are valid until further notice. Short notice changes are possible, especially around religious festivals and during monsoon seasons. Tickets can be purchased from stations or through authorised agents. Reservations are required for travel on all trains shown in this section.

For multiple journies the best value ticket is the Indrail Pass. This is only available to foreign nationals and non-resident Indians. It is personal and non-transferable. Holders should always have their passports ready for inspection. Holders of Indrail Passes are exempted from all reservation fees, sleeping car charges and can travel as they like, from any point in any train in the class it is issued for, within the period of validity. Reservations are essential, particularly on overnight journeys and are allocated on a first come first served basis and can be made up to 360 days in advance. There is a maximum luggage allowance of 70Kgs. The exact amount depends upon the type of pass or class of travel. Prices for AC CLASS Adult pass : ½ day US$57, 1 day US$95, 2 days US$160, 4 days US$220, 7 days US$270, 15 days US$370, 21 days US$396, 30 days US$495, 60 days US$800, 90 days US$1060. A Child pass is available at half price.

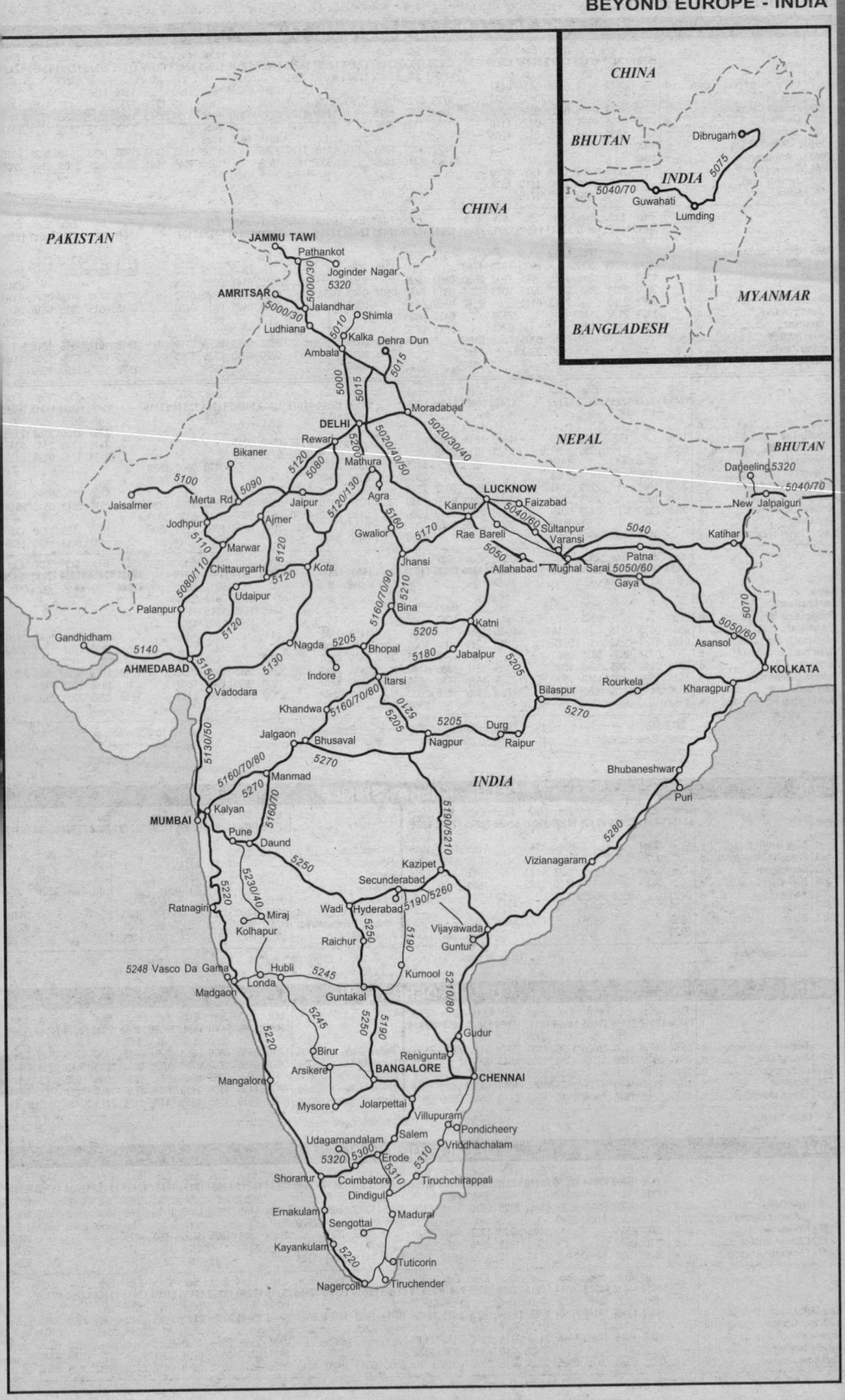

CHINA

BHUTAN

Dibrugarh
5075
5040/70 INDIA
Guwahati
Lumding

BANGLADESH MYANMAR

PAKISTAN

CHINA

JAMMU TAWI
Pathankot
Joginder Nagar
5320
5000/30
AMRITSAR
Jalandhar Shimla
Ludhiana Kalka Dehra Dun
5010
Ambala
5000
5015

Moradabad

DELHI
Rewari
Bikaner 5120 5080 Mathura 5020/40/60 5020/30/40 NEPAL BHUTAN
5100 5090 Darjeeling 5320
Jaisalmer Merta Rd. Jaipur Agra LUCKNOW Faizabad New Jalpaiguri 5040/70
Jodhpur Ajmer Kanpur Sultanpur 5040 Katihar
Marwar 5120/130 Rae Bareli Varansi
Chittaurgarh 5120 Kota 5160 5170 Patna 5050/60
5080/110 Gwalior Allahabad Mughal Sarai
Palanpur Udaipur Jhansi 5050 Gaya 5070
5160/70/90 Bina 5050/60
Nagda 5210 Katni Asansol
Gandhidham 5140 5205 Bhopal Jabalpur KOLKATA
AHMEDABAD 5130 Indore 5180 5205 Bilaspur Rourkela Kharagpur
Vadodara Itarsi Durg 5270
Khandwa 5160/70/80 Nagpur Raipur
5130/50 Jalgaon 5205 5205
5160/70/80 Bhusaval BHUBANESHWAR
Manmad 5270 INDIA Puri
5270
MUMBAI Kalyan 5190/5210 5280
Pune Daund Vizianagaram
5250 Kazipet
Secunderabad
5230/40 Miraj Wadi Hyderabad 5190/5260
Ratnagiri Kolhapur Raichur 5190 Vijayawada
5220 5250 Guntur
5248 Vasco Da Gama Hubli 5245 Kurnool 5210/80
Madgaon Londa Guntakal
5220 5245 5250 5190 Gudur
Birur
Arsikere BANGALORE Renigunta CHENNAI
Mangalore Mysore Jolarpettai
Udagamandalam Villupuram
5320 5300 Salem Pondicheery
Shoranur Coimbatore 5310 Vriddhachalam
Ernakulam Dindigul Tiruchchirappali
Sengottai Madurai
Kayankulam 5220
Nagercoil Tiruchender Tuticorin

5000 DELHI - AMRITSAR and JAMMU TAWI

Indian Railways

km		Exp	Exp	Exp	Exp	Exp	Exp		SDi	SDi	Exp	SDi	Exp	Exp	Exp	Exp	Exp	Exp	Exp	Exp	Exp	Exp	Exp	Exp
		15707	12471	12473	12475	12477	12919		12029	12031	12497	12037	14037	18215	11057	12549	12925	12483	12379	12715	19325	12203	12459	12421
			A	⑦	④	③			ex ④	④		12043	ex④	④		③		⑤	⑥		③⑥	①②⑤		④
7	**Delhi** Hazrat Nizamuddin d.	...	0414	0414	0414	0414	0437	...	...	...	...	...	...	...	0349	0930f	1005	1100	...	1148	1130	...	...	...
0	**New Delhi** d.	0325j	0450	0450	0450	0450	0520	...	0720	0720	0640	0700	0800j	0800	0430	|	1105	1150	1225j	1230	|	1410	1340	1330
199	Ambala Cantonment d.	0700	0805	0805	0805	0805	0905	...	0957	0957	1015	|	1125	1125	0940	1310	1455	1505	1525	1550	1640	1655	1720	|
304	Ludhiana d.	0930	0955	0955	0955	0955	1115	...	1133	1133	1207	1225	1313	1313	1345	1520	1652	1707	1717	1755	1835	1835	1923	1937
356	Jalandhar Cantonment d.	|	1050	1045	1045	1045	1205	...	|	|	|	...	|	|	1445	1615	1739	|	|	|	|	|	|	|
361	Jalandhar City d.	1040	|	|	|	|	|	...	1227	1227	1303	...	1410	1410	1505	|	1758	1815	1815	1900	1930	1940	2025	2040
440	**Amritsar** a.	1245	|	|	|	|	|	...	1345	1345	1420	...	1535	1535	1630	|	1920	1945	1945	2020	2105	2105	2145	2205
468	Chakki Bank ♥ d.	...	1235	1230	1230	1230	1400	...	...	...	...	...	p	1850k	...	1800	...	...	...	...	...	...	...	...
568	**Jammu Tawi** a.	...	1440	1440	1440	1440	1610	...	...	...	...	...	...	2110	...	2110	...	...	...	...	...	...	...	...
646	**Katra** a.	...	1710	1710	1710	1710	...	...	...	...	...	...	...	...	...	...	...	...	...	...	...	...	...	...

		Exp	Exp	Exp	Exp	Exp	SDi	Exp	Exp	Exp	RDi	Exp	Duro		Exp	Exp	Exp	Exp		Exp	Exp	Exp	Exp	Exp
		14649	14673	18507	22941	14645	12013	22461	12903	18237	12425	12445	12265		22401	12413	14033	11077		11449	16031	16317	16687	18101
		①③⑥	B	③⑥⑦	②								②⑤⑦		①③⑥					②	①④⑤	⑦	③	
Delhi Hazrat Nizamuddin d.	...	...	...	1417	1420f	...	...	...	1915	2030	...	...	2215a	...	2215a	...	...	2028	...	2235	2235	2110	2110	...
New Delhi d.	...	1320j	1320j	1500	|	1550j	1630	1730	|	|	2040	2050	|	...	|	2230j	2010j	2120	...	0010	0010	0010	0010	2200j
Ambala Cantonment d.	...	1755	1755	1845	1845	2145	1907	2030	0100	0225	|	2358	|	...	0110	0142	0025	0145	...	|	|	|	|	0245
Ludhiana d.	...	2010	2010	2027	2027	0010	2043	2215	0313	0450	0107	0147	0258	...	0258	0332	0220	0352	...	0710	0710	0710	0710	0516
Jalandhar Cantonment d.	...	2103	2103	|	2123	0110	|	2312	0359	0547	|	0238	|	...	0350	0425	0312	0450	...	0815	0815	0815	0815	0618
Jalandhar City d.	...	2120	2120	2155	|	|	2136	|	0420	0605	|	|	|	...	|	|	0350	|	...	|	|	|	|	0635
Amritsar a.	...	2330	2325	2355	|	|	2245	|	0545	0810	|	|	|	...	|	|	|	|	...	|	|	|	|	0750
Chakki Bank ♥ d.	...	...	...	...	2310	0305	...	0105	...	...	0340	0430	|	...	0533	0615	0630k	0710	...	1018	1018	1018	1018	|
Jammu Tawi a.	...	...	...	...	0120	0525	...	0310	...	...	0545	0635	0720	...	0720	0810	0925	1005	...	1300	1300	1300	1300	1410
Katra a.	...	...	...	...	...	...	...	0510	...	...	...	0840	...	...	...	...	1150	...	...	1520	1520	1520	1520	...

	Exp	Exp	Duro	Exp	Exp		RDi	Exp	Exp	Exp		Exp	Exp	Exp	Exp	Exp	Exp	SDi	Exp		Exp	Exp	Exp	Exp
	12414	18238	12266	22402	18102		12426	14034	12446	12904		18508	19326	11078	22462	14646	12204	12014	12716		11450	16032	16318	16688
			①③⑥	②④⑦								③⑥⑦	③⑥				③⑥⑦				③	②⑤⑥	①	④
Katra d.	...	...	...	...	...	...	...	1420	1910	...	...	...	...	...	2255	...	...	...	...	...	2155	2155	2155	2155
Jammu Tawi d.	1810	...	1920	1920	1420	...	1940	1615	2100	...	...	...	...	2145	0040	2040	...	...	...	...	2345	2345	2345	2345
Chakki Bank ♥ d.	2005	...	|	2053	|	...	2123	1915	2250	...	...	...	...	2350	0220	2310	...	...	...	...	0138	0138	0138	0138
Amritsar d.	|	1610	|	|	1935	...	|	|	|	2125	...	2345	2315	|	|	|	0420	0500	0535	...	|	|	|	|
Jalandhar City d.	|	1735	|	|	2058	...	|	2205	|	2238	...	0100	0040	|	|	|	0535	0606	0645	...	|	|	|	|
Jalandhar Cantonment d.	2200	1746	|	2232	2108	...	|	2215	0032	2248	...	|	|	0150	0430	0115	|	|	|	...	0350	0350	0350	0350
Ludhiana d.	2305	1925	2325	2325	2220	...	0005	2345	0125	2358	...	0220	0150	0315	0550	0235	0630	0702	0755	...	0515	0515	0515	0515
Ambala Cantonment d.	0100	2220	|	0120	0040	...	|	0150	0340	0200	...	0420	0410	0550	0800	0500	0820	0838	1000	...	|	|	|	|
New Delhi a.	0355j	|	|	|	0430j	...	0500	0545j	0650	|	...	0750	|	0955	1045	1055j	1055	1115	1300	...	1330	1330	1330	1330
Delhi Hazrat Nizamuddin a.	...	0410	0420a	0420a	...	...	...	...	...	0705	...	0830	0945	...	...	...	...	...	...	...	1433	1433	1433	1433

	Exp	Exp	Exp	Exp	Exp		Exp	Exp	Exp	Exp		Exp	Exp		Exp	Exp	Exp	Exp		SDi	Exp	SDi	SDi	Exp
	12484	12460	15708	12550	12926		14038	12380	12920	11058		14650	14674		12472	12474	12476	12478		12038	12498	12030	12032	12422
	⑦			④			ex⑤	⑦				①③⑥	B		C	④	①	⑦		12044		ex ④	④	①
Katra d.	...	...	...	...	...	...	...	...	...	...	...	...	...	...	0910	0910	0910	0910	...	...	...	...	...	...
Jammu Tawi d.	...	...	...	0500	...	...	...	...	0900	...	...	...	...	...	1115	1115	1115	1115	...	...	...	...	...	...
Chakki Bank ♥ d.	...	...	...	0645	...	...	pp	...	1045	...	...	...	...	...	1305	1305	1305	1305	...	...	...	...	...	...
Amritsar d.	0555	0615	0715	|	0810	...	0930	1055	|	0830	...	1155	1155	...	|	|	|	|	...	...	1510	1650	1650	1430
Jalandhar City d.	0710	0727	0840	|	0920	...	1045	1210	|	1005	...	1315	1315	...	|	|	|	|	...	...	1620	1757	1757	1542
Jalandhar Cantonment d.	|	0737	0850	0835	0930	...	|	|	1243	1015	...	1325	1325	...	1450	1450	1450	1450	...	...	|	|	|	|
Ludhiana d.	0815	0840	1005	0945	1035	...	1155	1310	1350	1145	...	1435	1435	...	1550	1550	1550	1550	...	1640	1723	1855	1855	1700
Ambala Cantonment d.	1015	1055	1200	1150	1305	...	1355	1520	1540	1550	...	1710	1710	...	1800	1800	1800	1800	...	|	1918	2032	2032	|
New Delhi a.	1320	1415	1505j	1500f	1625	...	1725j	1820j	1855	2020	...	2040j	2040j	...	2130	2130	2130	2130	...	2210	2250	2305	2305	2315
Delhi Hazrat Nizamuddin a.	1353	...	...	...	...	...	...	...	...	2103	...	...	...	...	...	...	...	...	...	...	...	...	...	...

A – ①②⑤⑥. B – ②④⑤⑦. C – ②③⑤⑥. a – Delhi Sarai Rohilla. f – Delhi Safdarjang. j – Delhi Junction. k – Pathankot Junction. ♥ – Pathankot Cantonment. p – To Pathankot Junction arr.1830. pp – From Pathankot Junction dep.0700.

5010 DELHI - KALKA - SHIMLA

Indian Railways

km		Exp	Exp	Exp	Exp	Exp	SDi	Exp	Exp	SDi	SDi
		52457	12311	52451	52453	14095	12011	52455	22925	12005	12045
											①–⑥
0	**New Delhi** d.	...	2125j	...	...	0535a	0740	...	1105	1715	1915
199	Ambala Cantonment d.	...	0220	...	...	0950	1030	...	1515	1958	2200
268	Chandigarh d.	...	0350	...	...	1033	1113	...	1612	2048	2245
305	**Kalka** a.	...	0430	...	...	1110	1145	...	1645	2120	...
305	**Kalka** ¶ d.	0400	...	0530	0600	...	...	1210	...	...	...
347	Barog ¶ d.	0625	...	|	0815	...	...	1425	...	...	...
351	Solan ¶ d.	0639	...	|	0829	...	...	1439	...	...	...
401	**Shimla** ¶ a.	0920	...	1015	1105	...	...	1720	...	...	...

	SDi	SDi	Exp	Exp	Exp	SDi	Exp	Exp	Exp	Exp
	12006	12046	22926	52456	14096	12012	52458	52542	52454	12312
		①–⑥								
Shimla ¶ d.	...	...	...	1035	...	...	1425	1740	1815	...
Solan ¶ d.	...	...	...	1314	...	...	1725	|	2050	...
Barog ¶ d.	...	...	...	1340	...	...	1750	|	2110	...
Kalka ¶ a.	...	...	...	1610	...	...	2010	2225	2320	...
Kalka d.	0615	...	1020	...	1650	1745	...	...	...	2355
Chandigarh d.	0653	1200	1120	...	1730	1823	...	...	...	0110
Ambala Cantonment d.	0738	1242	1305	...	1830	1905	...	...	...	0220
New Delhi a.	1025	1525	1625	...	2240a	2155	...	...	...	0630j

a – Delhi Sarai Rohilla. j – Delhi Junction. ¶ – Narrow gauge railway.

5015 DELHI - DEHRA DUN

Indian Railways

km		Exp	SDi	Exp	Exp	Exp	Exp	SDi	Exp	Exp	Exp
		19019	12017	22659	19565	14309	14317	12055	12687	14041	12205
				⑦	⑥	④⑤	①⑦		②⑤		
0	**Delhi** H. Nizamuddin d.	0550	0645n	1100	1100n	1130	1130	1520n	2110	2210j	2350n
76	Meerut City d.	0845	0805	1230	1230	1255	1255	1642	2251	|	0110
190	Saharanpur d.	1245	1010	|	|	1535	1535	|	0205	|	|
271	Haridwar d.	1525	1127	1600	1715	1655	1655	1937	0320	0625	0355
323	**Dehra Dun** a.	1735	1240	1810	1940	1940	1940	2110	0500	0820	0540

	SDi	Exp	Exp	Exp	Exp	Exp	Exp	SDi	Exp	Exp
	12056	22660	14310	14318	19566	12688	19020	12018	14042	12206
		①	②③	⑤⑥	⑦	①⑤				
Dehra Dun d.	0510	0550	0550	0550	0550	0645	1030	1700	2120	2330
Haridwar d.	0625	0750	0750	0750	0750	0850	1245	1815	2315	0052
Saharanpur d.	|	|	0955	0955	|	1050	1605	1950	|	|
Meerut City d.	0927	1136	1136	1136	1136	1230	1910	2117	|	0337
Delhi H. Nizamuddin a.	1115n	1310	1310	1310	1310n	1405	2115	2245n	0740j	0520n

j – Delhi Junction. n – New Delhi.

5020 DELHI - LUCKNOW

Indian Railways

km		Exp	Exp	SDi	Exp	Exp	RDi	RDi	Exp	Exp	Exp	Exp	Exp	Exp	Exp	Exp	Exp	Exp	Exp	Exp	Exp	SDi	Exp	Exp
		12328	19403	12004	12876	15910	12236	12436	12204	14258	12420	12392	12584	12566	12558	14312	19601	12372	19407	12524	22412	12034	15708	15280
		12370	③		②⑤⑦		②	④⑦	③⑥⑦				⑤⑦			①③⑤	⑥	④	⑤	③⑦	⑦	①–⑥		①⑤
0	**New Delhi** d.	...	0035j	0610	0625	0745j	0925	0925	1110	1135	1225	1310	1405v	1415	1450v	1455	1505j	1505j	1505j	1505	1550	1550	1520j	1655j
	Kanpur Central d.	...	|	1125	1240	|	|	|	|	|	1955	|	|	2020	|	|	|	|	|	|	2055	2050	2300	|
167	Moradabad d.	0300	0355	|	|	1125	1222	1222	1400	1520	|	1605	1715	|	1745	1845	1825	1830	1830	1825	|	...	|	2030
258	Bareilly Junction d.	0430	0530	|	|	1305	1345	1345	1521	1652	|	1733	1843	|	|	2040	|	1955	1955	|	|	...	|	2215
493	**Lucknow** Junction a.	0820	0930	1240	1405	1745	1725	1725	1840	2135	2125	2115	2255	2145	2240	...	2335	2335	2335	2335	2210	...	0025	0200

		Exp	Exp	Exp	Exp	Exp	Exp	Exp	Exp	Exp	Exp	Exp	Exp	Exp	Exp	Exp	Exp	Exp	Exp	Exp	Exp	Exp	Exp	
		14018	14016	14008	14014	14004	22408	14206	22418	22420	12226	12554	14208	12556	15716	19269	12212	14650	14674	13414	13484	12230	12430	
		③	⑤⑦	②④	①⑥	④⑦	①③⑤		①③⑤	②④⑥					①②④	⑤⑥	③	①③⑥	A	①③⑥	A			
New Delhi d.	...	1615j	1615j	1615j	1615j	1755	1815v	1830j	1835	1845v	1915j	1950	1950j	2025	2040j	2040j	2055v	2110j	2110j	2140j	2140j	2205	2325	...
Kanpur Central d.	...	|	|	|	|	|	|	|	|	|	0140	0225	|	0315	|	|	|	|	|	0545	0545	|	|	...
Moradabad d.	...	1945	1945	1945	1945	2115	2115	2210	2140	2140	|	|	2305	|	2358	2358	2358	0030	0030	|	|	0120	0225	...
Bareilly Junction d.	...	|	|	|	|	2240	2240	2352	2338	2338	|	|	0037	|	0127	0127	0127	0207	0207	|	|	0255	0345	...
Lucknow Junction a.	...	0325	0325	0325	0325	0225	0225	0350	0310	0310	0300	0345	0420	0445	0515	0515	0515	0610	0610	0720	0720	0645	0730	...

A – ②④⑤⑦. j – Delhi Junction. v – Delhi Anand Vihar Terminal.

For return service see next page ▷ ▷ ▷

LUCKNOW - DELHI 5020

Indian Railways

km		Exp 14205	Exp 22407 ①③⑤	Exp 12371 ②	SDi 12033 ①–⑥	Exp 22411 ④	Exp 14311 ④⑤⑦	Exp 14649 ①③⑥	Exp 14673 A	Exp 12523 ③⑦	Exp 19602 ②	Exp 15279 ①⑤	Exp 22411 ④	Exp 12211 ⑥	Exp 19270 ①②	Exp 15715 ①③⑥	Exp 12583 ⑤⑦	Exp 12203 ①②⑤	Exp 12419	Exp 14003 ③⑦	Exp 15909	RDi 12235 ⑥	RDi 12435 ③⑦	Exp 12203 ①②⑤
0	**Lucknow** Junction d.	0055	0130	0130	...	0420	...	0115	0115	0330	0330	0330	0520	0430	0430	0455	0500	0610	0600	0550	0535	0610	0610	0610
	Bareilly Junction d.	0425	0502	0502	...	|	0605	0500	0500	|	|	0712	|	0805	0805	0825	0825	0933	|	0958	0920	0933	0933	0933
	Moradabad d.	0620	0700	0705	...	|	0800	0835	0835	0905	0905	0905	|	0950	0950	1005	1010	1107	|	1140	1125	1107	1107	1107
72	Kanpur Central d.	|	|	|	0600	0620	|	|	|	|	|	|	0620	|	|	|	|	|	0740	|	|	|	|	|
511	**New Delhi** a.	0950j	1010v	1020j	1120	1140	1130	1230j	1230j	1210	1210	1210j	1140	1235v	1240j	1310j	1300v	1355	1455	1440	1505j	1355	1355	1355

	Exp 12875 ①③⑥	SDi 12003	Exp 15707	Exp 14017 ⑤	Exp 14007 ④⑥	Exp 14015 ①③	Exp 14013 ②⑦	Exp 13413 ②⑤⑦	Exp 13483 B	Exp 12391	Exp 14257	Exp 19408 ⑥	Exp 19404 ③	Exp 12565		Exp 14207	Exp 12555	Exp 12229	Exp 12553	Exp 12225	Exp 12429	Exp 12557	Exp 22417 ③⑤⑦	Exp 22419 ②④⑥
ucknow Junction d.	1345	1535	1825	1850	1850	1850	1850	1930	1930	2030	2045	2130	2130	2120	...	2140	2150	2215	2225	2315	2330	2345	2358	2358
areilly Junction d.	|	|	|	|	|	|	|	|	|	0010	0045	0105	0105	|	...	0127	|	0155	|	|	0245	|	0322	0322
oradabad d.	|	|	|	0120	0120	0120	0120	|	|	0155	0230	0310	0250	|	...	0325	|	0345	|	|	0425	0450	0500	0500
Kanpur Central d.	1528	1655	2000	|	|	|	|	2115	2115	|	|	|	|	2258	...	|	2328	|	0005	0050	|	|	|	|
ew Delhi a.	2145	2215	0250j	0450j	0450j	0450j	0450j	0440j	0440j	0510	0610	0620j	0620j	0535	...	0645j	0550	0715	0640	0705j	0725	0750v	0825	0810v

– ②④⑤⑦. B – ①③④⑥. j – Delhi Junction. v – Delhi Anand Vihar Terminal.

JAMMU TAWI and AMRITSAR - LUCKNOW 5030

Indian Railways

km		Exp 15708	Exp 18104 ③⑤	Exp 14650 ①③⑥	Exp 14674 A		Exp 12238	Exp 15934 ⑤	Exp 13050	Exp 13006		Exp 12356 ③⑦		Exp 12588 ⑥	Exp 15652 ③	Exp 15654 ⑤	Exp 15098 ②	Exp 12332 ①④⑦	Exp 13152	Exp 12204 ③⑥⑦		Exp 12318 ②⑤	Exp 12358 ①④	
0	**Jammu Tawi** d.	...	...	...	...	...	1400	...	...	...	...	2010	...	2245	2245	2245	2245	2245	1855	...	...	...	...	...
100	Chakki Bank ♥ d.	...	...	...	...	...	1545	...	...	...	...	2150	...	0030	0030	0030	0030	0030	2210	...	...	...	...	...
**	**Amritsar** d.	0715	1235	1155	1155	...	|	1550	1810	1845	...	|	...	|	|	|	|	|	|	0420	...	0555	0555	...
**	Jalandhar City d.	0840	1350	1315	1315	...	|	1700	1930	1957	...	|	...	|	|	|	|	|	|	0535	...	0710	0710	...
213	Jalandhar Cantonment d.	0850	|	1325	1325	...	1735	|	1940	2007	...	2335	...	0220	0220	0220	0220	0220	0015	|	...	|	|	...
265	Ludhiana d.	1005	1505	1435	1435	...	1835	1800	2050	2115	...	0035	...	0330	0330	0330	0330	0330	0205	0630	...	0815	0815	...
378	Ambala Cantonment d.	1200	1655	1710	1710	...	2100	2030	2310	2330	...	0235	...	0525	0525	0525	0525	0525	0430	0820	...	1015	1015	...
460	Saharanpur d.	|	1830	|	|	...	2225	2200	0055	0115	...	0405	...	0700	0700	0700	0700	0700	0620	|	...	1145	1145	...
652	Moradabad d.	|	2132	0030	0030	...	0135	0105	0420	0445	...	0705	...	1010	1010	1010	1010	1010	1045	1402	...	1450	1455	...
743	Bareilly Junction d.	|	2257	0207	0207	...	|	0240	|	0620	...	0833	...	1142	1142	1142	1142	1142	1230	1521	...	1620	|	...
978	**Lucknow** Junction a.	0025	0240	0610	0610	...	0710	0800	1145	1025	...	1225	...	1520	1520	1520	1520	1520	1705	1840	...	2005	2005	...

		Exp 12317 ①④	Exp 12357 ③⑦	Exp 12203 ①②⑤	Exp 15933 ④		Exp 14649 ①③⑥	Exp 14673 A	Exp 13151	Exp 18103 ②④		Exp 13005	Exp 13049	Exp 12355 ②⑥	Exp 12237		Exp 15707		Exp 12331 ③⑥⑦	Exp 15097 ⑤	Exp 15651 ②	Exp 15563 ④	Exp 12587 ①	
ucknow Junction d.	...	0225	0255	0610	0610	...	0115	0115	1040	1525	...	1545	1610	1735	1815	...	1825	...	1950	1950	1950	1950	1950	...
areilly Junction d.	...	0620	|	0933	0933	...	0500	0500	1515	1917	...	1935	|	2053	|	...	|	...	2330	2330	2330	2330	2330	...
oradabad d.	...	0815	0815	1107	1110	...	0835	0835	1725	2105	...	2125	2255	2235	2315	...	|	...	0110	0110	0110	0110	0110	...
aharanpur d.	...	1130	1130	|	1450	...	|	|	2130	0030	...	0125	0305	0145	0230	...	|	...	0425	0425	0425	0425	0425	...
mbala Cantonment d.	...	1300	1300	1655	1615	...	1755	1755	2310	0210	...	0315	0445	0325	0420	...	0700	...	0548	0548	0548	0548	0548	...
udhiana d.	...	1452	1452	1835	1815	...	2010	2010	0202	0405	...	0556	0723	0543	0640	...	0930	...	0742	0742	0742	0742	0742	...
alandhar Cantonment d.	...	|	|	|	|	...	2103	2103	0305	|	...	0649	0825	0638	0735	...	|	...	0845	0845	0845	0845	0845	...
Jalandhar City d.	...	1548	1548	1940	1940	...	2120	2120	|	0510	...	0707	0845	|	|	...	1040	...	|	|	|	|	|	...
Amritsar a.	...	1720	1720	2105	2105	...	2330	2325	|	0630	...	0855	1020	|	|	...	1245	...	|	|	|	|	|	...
hakki Bank ♥ d.	...	...	...	...	...	...	...	...	0505	...	...	...	...	0830	0920	...	...	...	1043	1043	1043	1043	1043	...
ammu Tawi a.	...	...	...	...	...	...	...	...	0835	...	...	...	...	1030	1125	...	...	...	1235	1235	1235	1235	1235	...

– ②④⑤⑦. ♥ – Pathankot Cantonment. ** – Amritsar - Jalandhar Cantonment: *84 km*. Jalandhar City - Jalandhar Cantonment: *5 km*.

DELHI - GUWAHATI 5040

Indian Railways

km	km		Exp 12506	Exp 15934 ⑥	Exp 15910	RDi 12436 ④⑦	RDi 12236 ②	Exp 12204 ③⑥⑦	RDi 12424	Exp 15708	Exp 12502 ③④⑦	Exp 12370 E
0	0	**New Delhi** d.	0645v	...	0745j	0925	0925	1110	1355	1520j	2345	...
	167	Moradabad d.	|	...	1125	1222	1222	1400	|	|	|	0300
	258	Bareilly Junction d.	|	...	1305	1345	1345	1521	|	|	|	0430
	493	Lucknow Junction d.	|	0810	1810	1735	1735	1850	|	0050	|	0830
	981	Chhapra d.	|	2045	0405	0155	0155	0325	|	1005	|	|
440		Kanpur Central d.	1300	|	|	|	|	|	1839	2300↑	0620	|
634		Allahabad d.	1552	|	|	|	|	|	2042	|	0900	|
787		Mughal Sarai d.	1825	|	|	|	|	|	2255	|	|	1425
999		Patna Junction d.	2220	|	|	|	|	|	0210	|	|	1750
109	1128	Barauni d.	0105	0020	0905	0505	|	0750	0445	1525	|	...
288	1308	Katihar d.	0500	0410	1350	0845	0845	...	0750	2010	2050	...
471	1491	New Jalpaiguri d.	0840	0805	1805	1205	1205	...	1105	...	0020	...
723	1742	New Bongaigaon d.	1350	1245	2330	1610	1610	...	1512	...	0510	...
879	1899	**Guwahati** a.	1650	1545	0300	1900	1900	...	1730	...	0845	...

	RDi 12235 ⑤	RDi 12435 ②⑥	Exp 12203 ①④⑦	Exp 12501 ②③⑥	Exp 12369 F	RDi 12423	Exp 12505	Exp 15933 ②	Exp 15909	Exp 15707
Guwahati d.	0540	0540	...	0615	...	0700	0945	1945	2200	...
New Bongaigaon d.	0807	0807	...	0905	...	0920	1245	2330	0115	...
New Jalpaiguri d.	1215	1215	...	1345	...	1315	1725	0420	0620	...
Katihar d.	1525	1525	...	1705	...	1625	2110	0900	1045	2345
Barauni d.	|	1855	1715	|	...	1920	0015	1320	1425	0320
Patna Junction d.	|	|	|	|	2110	2150	0305	|	|	|
Mughal Sarai d.	|	|	|	|	0047	0107	0720	|	|	|
Allahabad d.	|	|	|	0425	|	0256	0945	|	|	|
Kanpur Central d.	|	|	|	0650	|	0508	1255	|	|	2000↓
Chhapra d.	2155	2155	2120	|	|	|	|	1710	1940	0845
Lucknow Junction d.	0610	0610	0610	|	0730	|	|	0600	0535	1825
Bareilly Junction d.	0933	0933	0933	|	1110	|	|	...	0920	|
Moradabad d.	1107	1107	1107	|	1240	|	|	...	1125	|
New Delhi a.	1355	1355	1355	1300	...	1015	1920v	...	1505j	0250j

– ①②③⑤⑥.
– ①③④⑥⑦.
j – Delhi Junction.
v – Delhi Anand Vihar Terminal.

DELHI - PATNA - KOLKATA 5050

Indian Railways

km		Exp 12506	Exp 12324 ④⑦	Duro 12274 ②⑥	Exp 12312	Exp 12488	Exp 15484		Exp 12332 ①②⑤	Exp 13258	RDi 12424	Exp 12368	Exp 13132	SDi 12034 ①–⑥	RDi 12302 ⑥–④	RDi 12314	RDi 12306 ⑤		SDi 12024 ①–⑥	Exp 12570 ②⑥	Exp 22406 ①③⑤	Exp 12316 ①	Exp 12318 ③⑥	Exp 12326 ⑦
0	**New Delhi** d.	0645v	0705v	1255	0700j	0730v	0635j	...	...	1330v	1355	1440v	1530v	1550	1655	1625	1655	...	...	1655v	1655v	...	...	...
440	Kanpur Central d.	1300	1340	1750	1430	1355	1520	...	...	|	1839	|	0340	2050	2143	2125	2143	...	...	2217	2217	2005	...	...
634	Allahabad Junction d.	1552	1645	|	1730	1655	1805	...	...	|	2042	|	0755	...	2346	|	2346	...	...	0019	0019	2245	...	...
787	Muhgal Sarai d.	1825	1940	|	2025	2005	2115	...	2215	|	2255	|	1215	...	0155	0138	0155	...	...	0232	0232	0255	0238	0238
998	**Patna** Junction d.	2155	|	|	|	2325	0035	...	0150	0705f	0200	0645	1720	...	|	|	0455	...	0545	0555	0555	0615	0615	0615
992	Gaya d.	...	2225	|	2325	...		...	|	...	...	...	|	...	0404	0353	|	...	|	...	...	|	|	|
189	Dhanbad d.	...	0200	0252	0325	...	...	...	|	...	...	...	|	...	0645	0628	|	...	|	...	...	|	|	|
247	Asansol d.	...	0300	|	0436	...	...	...	0820	...	...	...	0247	...	|	0719	|	...	1047	...	...	1203	1203	1203
447	**Kolkata** Howrah a.	...	0600	0610	0755	...	...	...	1130	...	...	...	0730	...	0955	1015e	1240	...	1325	...	...	1510e	1515e	1515k

	Exp 13152	Exp 12372 ④	Exp 12304 A	Exp 12382 ①②⑤	RDI 12310	Exp 12394	Exp 12330 ③	Exp 12380 ⑦	Yuva 12250 ⑦	Duro 12260 C	Exp 11106 ⑥	Exp 12402	Duro 12276 ③⑤⑦		Exp 14056	Exp 12350 ②	Exp 12370 E	Exp 12328 ④⑦	Exp 12360 ③⑤⑦	Duro 22214 ②④⑥	Exp 12352	Exp 13006	Exp 12334
ew Delhi d.	...	1505j	1615	1615	1715	1725	1905j	1905j	1950v	1940	...	2000	2240	...	2340j	2345	...	...	...	...	...	...	...
anpur Central d.	...	|	2345	2345	2203	|	0120	0120	0034	0032	0130	0235	|	...	0600	0620	...	...	...	...	...	...	...
llahabad Junction d.	...	|	0215	0250	0009	|	|	|	0236	|	0400	0513	0610	...	0840	0900	...	...	...	...	...	...	1540a
luhgal Sarai d.	0300	0635	0450	0635	0215	|	|	|	0438	|	0715	0755	...	...	1145	|	1425	1425	...	...	...	1815	1910
atna Junction d.	|	|	0805	|	0540	0655	|	|	|	|	1055	1130	...	...	1445	1500	1800	1800	2005	2040	2110b	2155	2325
Gaya d,	0639	0915	|	0918	...	...	|	0935	|	|	|	...	...	...	...	...	|	|	|	|	|	|	|
Dhanbad d.	1035	1218	|	1228	...	...	1245	1245	0905	0905	|	...	...	...	...	...	|	|	|	|	|	|	|
sansol d.	1150	1322	1341	1341	...	...	1357	1357	1001	|	1710	...	...	...	...	...	0006	0006	0207	|	0333	0404	0424
olkata Howrah a.	1555k	1630	1655	1655	...	...	1725e	1725e	1240	1235e	2145k	...	...	...	...	...	0315	0315	0515k	0540h	0635	0720	0730

– ③④⑥⑦. D – ①③④⑦. a – Allahabad City. f – Danapur. v – Delhi Anand Vihar Terminal.
– ①②⑤⑥. E – ①②③⑤⑥. b – Patna Saheb. h – Kolkata Shalimar.
– ①②④⑤. F – ①③④⑥⑦. c – Kolkata Chitpur. j – Delhi Junction.
e – Kolkata Sealdah. k – Kolkata.

For return service see next page ▷ ▷ ▷

5050 KOLKATA - PATNA - DELHI
Indian Railways

km			Duro	Duro	Exp	Exp	Exp	Exp	Exp	Exp	Exp	RDi	Exp	Exp	Exp	Exp	Exp	Exp	Exp	Exp	SDI	RDI	Exp	RD
			12273	12275	14055	11105	12317	12325	12303	12381	12371	12309	12367	13257	12393	12569	22405	12327	12315	12369	12023	12305	12301	1242
			①⑤	②④⑥		⑦	③⑦	④	B	③④⑦	①					①⑤	②④⑥	②⑤	④	F	①–⑥	⑦	①–⑥	
0	**Kolkata** Howrah d.	...	1245	...	...	0730k	0740e	0740k	0805	0815	0815	...	...	...	...	...	...	1300	1310e	1300	1405	1405	1655	...
200	Asansol d.	...	|	...	...	1140	1040	1040	1040	1053	1053	...	...	...	...	...	...	1534	1605	1534	1642	|	|	...
	Dhanbad d.	...	1558	...	...	|	|	|	|	1205	1205	...	...	...	...	...	...	|	|	|	|	|	2001	...
	Gaya d.	...	|	...	...	|	|	|	|	1455	1455	...	...	...	...	...	...	|	|	|	|	|	2238	...
532	**Patna** Junction d.	...	|	...	1315	1820	1615	1615	1615	|	|	1925	1705	1600f	1800	1915	1915	2110	2200	2110	2215	2125	|	215
744	Mughal Sarai d.	...	|	...	1657	2309	1932	1932	1947	1802	1817	2235	|	|	|	2300	2300	0037	0205	0037	...	0055	0057	010
896	Allahabad Junction d.	...	|	2240	1925	0115	...	...	2155	2155	|	0028	|	|	|	0055	0055	...	0425	...	...	0246	0243	025
1091	Kanpur Central d.	...	0055	|	2210	0345	...	...	0030	0013	|	0235	|	|	|	0300	0300	...	0645	...	...	0453	0453	050
1530	**New Delhi** a.	...	0620	0620	0605j	...	...	...	0735	0735	1020j	0740	0800v	1040v	0750	0820v	0820v	...	...	...	...	1000	1000	101

			RDi	Yuva	Duro	SDi	Exp		Exp	Exp	Exp	Exp	Exp	Exp	Exp	Exp	Exp	Exp	Exp		Exp	Duro	Exp
			12313	12249	12259	12033	12401		12329	12379	12349	12323	15483	12505	13005	12311	12333	12359	12487		12351	22213	1233
				⑥	D	①–⑥			②	⑤	①	②⑤						②④⑥				①③⑤	②⑤
Kolkata Howrah d.	...	...	1650e	1840	1830e	...	...	...	1310e	1310e	...	1850	...	...	1910	1940	2000	2005	...	...	2035	2205h	235
Asansol d.	...	...	1920	2052	|	...	...	...	1605	1605	...	2118	...	...	2154	2222	2238	2251	...	...	2322	|	023
Dhanbad d.	...	...	2025	2156	2156	...	...	...	1715	1715	...	2250	...	...	|	2336	|	|	...	...	|	|	|
Gaya d.	...	...	2255	|	|	...	...	...	|	2017	...	0210	...	...	|	0300	|	|	...	...	|	|	|
Patna Junction d.	...	...	|	|	|	...	1810	...	|	|	2235	|	0150	0305	0420	|	0435	0530	0520	...	0543b	0640	101
Mughal Sarai d.	...	...	0117	0232	|	...	2217	...	|	|	|	0520	0545	0720	0807	0638	0842	...	0937	...	...	...	134
Allahabad Junction d.	...	...	|	0420	|	...	0045	...	|	|	0425	0740	0855	0945	...	0935	1200a	...	1155	...	...	...	...
Kanpur Central d.	...	...	0518	0628	0625	0600	0325	...	0400	0400	0650	1020	1225	1255	...	1245	...	...	1440	...	...	...	...
New Delhi a.	...	...	1025	1120	1130	1120	1150	...	1205j	1205j	1300	1700	2240j	1920v	...	2045j	...	...	2100v	...	...	...	...

For footnotes and return service see previous page.

5060 LUCKNOW - MUGHAL SARAI - PATNA - KOLKATA
Indian Railways

km		Exp	Exp	Exp	Exp	Exp	Exp	Exp	Exp	Exp	Exp	Exp	Exp	Exp	Exp		Exp	Exp		Exp	Exp	Exp	Exp	Exp
		12354	22408	18104	22418	12238	12328	12370	13010	13006	12356	12876	12332	12358	12318		12326	13050		13152	12392	14258	12372	194
		⑦	②④⑦	④⑥	①③⑤		④⑦	A			①④	②⑤⑦	①②⑤	①④	②⑤		⑥						④	⑤
493	Haridwar d.	...	...	...	...	...	2355p	2355	2230q	...	...	...	...	...	...	...	...	...	...	...	...	...	...	...
0	**Lucknow** Junction d.	0125	0235	0305	0320	0720	0830	0830	0845	1050	1235	1430	1530	2015	2015	...	2015	1210	...	1720	2130	2150	2345	234
77	Rae Bareli d.	0425	0406	|	|	|	|	|		1216	1402	1553	|	|	|	...	|	|	...	|	|	2330	0105	|
127	Faizabad d.	|	|	0503	|	|	|	|	1105	|	|	|	|	|	|	...	|	|	...	2052	|	|	|	|
140	Sultanpur d.	|	|	|	0540	0940	1039	1039		|	|	|	1805	|	2223	...	|	1448	...	|	2340	|	|	051
283	Varanasi Junction d.	0720	0805	1005	0825	1240	1305	1305	1610	1655	1855	2010	2105	0110	0115	...	0115	1915	...	0130	0240	0445	0520	054
300	**Mughal Sarai** d.	0835	...	1135	...	...	1425	1425	1730	1815	1950	2120	2215	0220	0238	...	0238	2040	...	0300	0345	...	0635	...
512	**Patna** Junction d.	|	...	|	...	...	1800	1800	|	2155	2235	|	0150	|	0615	...	0615	0230	...	|	0715	...	|	...
***	Gaya d.	1130	...	1428	...	...	|	|		|	...	0025	|	0445	|	...	|	|	...	0639	...	...	0915	...
***	Dhanbad d.	1445	...	...	...	...	|	|	0125	|	...	...	|	0730	|	...	|	|	...	1035	...	...	1218	...
843	Asansol d.	1550	...	...	...	...	0006	0006	0230	0404	...	...	0820	0825	1203	...	1203	1105	...	1150	...	...	1322	...
1055	**Kolkata** Howrah a.	1855	...	...	...	...	0315	0315	0655	0720	...	...	1130	1120k	1510k	...	1515k	1545	...	1555k	...	...	1630	...

	Exp	Exp	Exp	Exp	Exp	Exp		Exp	Exp	Exp	Exp	Exp	Exp	Exp	Exp	Exp	Exp	Exp	Exp	Exp	Exp	Exp		
	22417	12353	12371	22407	12317	12325		12357	12327	12369	13151	12875	18103	13005	13049	13009	12355	12237	14257	12331	12391	19408		
	②④⑥	⑤	①	②④⑦	③⑦	④		②⑥	②⑤	B		①③⑥	②④				②⑥			②⑤⑥		⑥		
Kolkata Howrah d.	...	0815	0815	...	0740k	0740k	...	1220k	1300	1300	1145k	...	...	1910	1350	2030	...	...	...	2355	...	...	...	...
Asansol d.	...	1053	1053	...	1040	1040	...	1457	1534	1534	1520	...	...	2154	1811	0016	...	...	...	0236	...	...	...	...
Dhanbad d.	...	1205	1205	...	|	|	...	1602	|	|	1657	...	...	|	|	0130	...	...	...	|	...	...	...	...
Gaya d.	...	1455	1455	...	|	|	...	1843	|	|	2115	0315	0408	|	|	0500	...	...	...	|	...	...	...	...
Patna Junction d.	...	|	|	...	1615	1615	...	|	2110	2110	|	|	|	0420	0215	|	0730	...	...	1015	1050	...	...	...
Mughal Sarai d.	...	1817	1817	...	1947	1947	...	2122	0047	0047	0152	0647	0722	0827	0737	0937	1047	...	...	1402	1427	...	...	...
Varanasi Junction d.	1835	1930	1930	1930	2040	2040	...	2205	0155	0155	0250	0738	0815	0927	0840	1030	1140	1250	1400	1447	1512	1535	...	...
Sultanpur d.	2118	|	|	|	2250	|	...	|	0400	0400	|	|	|	|	1205	|	|	1450	|	1650	1710	1745	...	...
Faizabad d.	|	|	|	|	|	|	...	|	|	|	0620	|	1145	|	|	1449	|	|	|	|	|	|	...	...
Rae Barali d.	|	2328	2328	2328	|	|	...	|	|	|	|	1113	|	1315	|	|	1519	|	1820	|	|	|	...	...
Lucknow Junction a.	2350	0120	0120	0120	0210	0210	...	0245	0715	0715	1030	1315	1500	1520	1545	1820	1720	1805	2035	1940	2020	2110	...	...
Haridwar a.	...	...	...	...	...	...	...	...	1535l	1605	...	...	...	...	...	0435n	...	...	...	...	...	...	...	...

A – ①②③⑤⑥. e – Kolkata Sealdah. l – To Dehra Dun arr. 1810. n – To Dehra Dun arr. 0725. p – From Dehra Dun dep. 2210. q – From Dehra Dun dep. 203

B – ①③④⑥⑦. k – Kolkata. *** – Mughal Sarai - Dhanbad: *402 km*. Gaya - Dhandab: *199 km* Dhanbad - Asansol: *58 km*.

5070 KOLKATA - NEW JALPAIGURI - GUWAHATI
Indian Railways

km		Exp	Exp	SDi	Exp	Exp	Exp	Exp	Exp	Exp	Exp
		15657	12509	12041	12507	15901	12345	15959	12525	12517	22511
			A	①–⑥	④	③			③	④⑦	④
0	**Kolkata** Howrah d.	0635e	1115	1415	1415	1425	1550	1735	2140k	2140k	2155
213	Rampurhat d.	1050	1428	|	1743	1743	1859	|	|	|	0210
335	Malda Town d.	1355	1730	1910	2015	2015	2145	0210	0410	0410	0520
480	Kishanganj d.	1617	1932	2104	2205	2205	2337	0425	0602	0602	|
567	**New Jalpaiguri** d.	1830	2145	2225	0010	0010	0200	0635	0805	0805	0920
819	New Bongaigaon d.	0040	0225	...	0435	0645	0627	1150	1237	1237	1540
975	**Guwahati** a.	0415	0600	...	0815	1025	0935	1535	1540	1540	1825c

	Exp	Exp	Exp	Exp	Exp	SDi	Exp	Exp	Exp	Exp
	15902	12508	12510	15960	12346	12042	22512	12526	12518	156
	⑥	⑤	B			①–⑥	⑥	②	③⑥	
Guwahati d.	0520	0620	0620	0745	1230	...	1800c	2100	2100	224
New Bongaigaon d.	0840	0940	0940	1145	1522	...	2120	2355	2355	022
New Jalpaiguri d.	1425	1425	1425	1655	1925	0530	0320	0355	0355	075
Kishanganj d.	1530	1530	1530	1810	2032	0635	|	0458	0458	090
Malda Town d.	1845	1845	1845	2210	2340	0850	0750	0825	0825	124
Rampurhat d.	2110	2110	2110	|	0158	|	1030	|	|	151
Kolkata Howrah a.	0045	0045	0045	0545	0510	1335	1410	1500k	1500k	192

A – ①②⑤⑥⑦. Runs as **12513** on ① and as **12515** on ②. c – Kamakhya Junction. k – Kolkata.

B – ①②③④⑦. Runs as **12514** on ④ and as **12516** on ③. e – Kolkata Sealdah.

5075 GUWAHATI - DIBRUGARH
Indian Railways

km		Exp	Exp	Exp	Exp	Exp	Exp	RDi	RDi	RDi	Exp	Exp
		15910	15929	15901	14056	15934	15959	12424	12236	12436	15905	15904
			⑦	④		⑦			③	①⑤	⑦	②⑤
0	**Guwahati** d.	0320	0510	1045	1500	1600	1550	1755	1925	1925	1925	2005
87	Chaparmukh d.	0530	0715	|	1640	1727	1800	|	|	|	|	|
184	Lumding d.	0715	0925	1510	1930	1945	2015	2112	2242	2242	2245	2325
250	Dimapur d.	0900	1045	1657	2050	2106	2140	2230	0015	0015	0015	0050
323	Furkating d.	1057	1232	|	2257	2322	2355	|	|	|	0152	0242
358	Mariani d.	1140	1320	1920	2355	0020	0120	0100	0240	0240	0240	0335
513	New Tinsukia d.	1510	1635	|	0310	0410	0435	0345	|	0515	0525	0610
561	**Dibrugarh** a.	1625	1800	2230	0425	0525	0600	0455	0530	0615	0715	0735

	Exp	Exp	Exp	Exp	RDi	RDi	RDi	Exp	Exp	Exp	Exp
	15933	15903	15909	15902	12435	12235	12423	15960	15906	14055	159
	②	①⑤		⑤	①⑤	④			⑥		⑦
Dibrugarh d.	0700	0700	0920	1830	1920	1925	2035	1825	2245	2310	233
New Tinsukia d.	0805	0805	1040	|	2025	|	2140	1940	2350	0020	004
Mariani d.	1100	1100	1356	2135	2235	2225	0012	2310	0235	0340	041
Furkating d.	1242	1242	1452	2230	|	|	|	0010	0335	0447	052
Dimapur d.	1405	1400	1613	2342	0045	0045	0205	0145	0515	0621	065
Lumding d.	1535	1535	1745	0135	0217	0217	0327	0325	0710	0800	084
Chaparmukh d.	1720	|	1913	|	|	|	|	0530	|	1020	111
Guwahati a.	1920	1920	2140	0455	0515	0515	0635	0730	1130	1235	144

5080 DELHI - JAIPUR - AHMEDABAD
Indian Railway

km		Exp	Exp	SDi	Exp	Exp	Exp	Exp	Exp	Exp	RDi	Exp
		19708	12414	12015	19408	19264	12215	14311	19270	12916	12958	19032
					⑦	①④	A	④⑤⑦	①②			
0	**Delhi** Junction d.	...	0425	0605n	0640	0820a	0920a	1145	1255	1520	1955n	2230
83	Rewari d.	...	0615	0747	0832	1005	1050	1352	1458	1707	|	0035
157	Alwar d.	...	0716	0842	0927	1110	1145	1452	1557	1806	|	0139
308	**Jaipur** d.	0845	1010	1040	1145	1325	1420	1730	1850	2035	0025	0425
444	Ajmer d.	1115	1220	1245	1410	1600	1640	2015	2140	2250	0229	0650
581	Marwar Junction d.	1315	...	...	1630	1855	|	2226	2359	|	|	0910
749	Abu Road d.	1650	...	...	1913	2205	2120	0125	0245	0350	0605	1200
801	Palanpur d.	1825	...	...	2037	2317	2217	0247	0412	0502	0707	1318
866	Mahesana d.	1951	...	...	2150	0014	|	0416	|	0602	0805	1430
934	**Ahmedabad** a.	2205	...	...	2355	0210	0110	0615	0715	0740	0940	1655

	Exp	RDi	Exp	Exp	Exp	Exp	Exp	Exp	Exp	SDI	Ex
	19031	12957	12915	12216	14312	19407	19263	19269	12413	12016	197
				B	②④⑦	④	③⑦	⑤⑥			
Ahmedabad d.	1005	1740	1830	1940	2020	2100	0050	0050	...	...	052
Mahesana d.	1202	1850	1951	|	2200	2219	0240	|	...	...	065
Palanpur d.	1357	2004	2109	2250	2342	0004	0412	0412	...	...	090
Abu Road d.	1450	2050	2210	2345	0045	0118	0542	0542	...	...	101
Marwar Junction d.	1740	|	|	|	0327	0413	0830	0830	...	...	134
Ajmer d.	2050	0055	0230	0500	0610	0630	1105	1105	1405	1545	163
Jaipur d.	2315	0250	0440	0720	0845	0910	1320	1320	1625	1750	185
Alwar d.	0141	|	0643	0919	1110	1134	1543	1543	1842	1938	...
Rewari d.	0320	|	0825	1050	1235	1255	1802	1802	2017	2102	...
Delhi Junction a.	0505	0730n	1010	1215a	1435	1445	1935a	2000	2200	2240n	...

A – ①②④⑥. B – ②③⑤⑦. a – Delhi Sarai Rohilla. n – New Delhi.

Indian Railways — DELHI - JODHPUR — 5090

km	Exp 15014	Exp 14659	Exp 12461	Exp 12463 ③⑤⑦		Station		Exp 15013	Exp 12464 ②④⑥	Exp 12462	Exp 14660
0	0440	1735	2115	2225a	↓	d.Delhi Junction .... a.	↑	2010	0535a	0645	1115
83	0645	1945	2322	|	↓	d.Rewari .... d.		1855	|	0455	0915
157	0755	2055	0017	0052		d.Alwar .... d.	↑	1703	0233	0310	0717
308	1110	2345	0245	0315		d.Jaipur .... d.		1435	0025	0100	0500
471	|	0241	0514	0550	↓	d.Degana .... d.	↑	|	2120	2208	0127
516	|	0322	0600	0635		d.Merta Road .... d.		|	2035	2132	0043
620	1735	0450	0705	0825	↓	a.Jodhpur .... d.	↑	0630	1900	2000	2315

Indian Railways — JODHPUR - JAISALMER — 5100

km	Exp 14659	Exp 22931 ⑥	Exp 15014	Exp 14810		Station		Exp 15013	Exp 14809	Exp 14660	Exp 22932 ⑥
0	0520	0735	1750	2345	↓	d.Jodhpur .... a.	↑	0615	1330	2240	2345
65	0634	0835	1903	0058	↓	d.Osian .... d.		0429	1101	2112	2236
137	0744	0940	2007	0207		d.Phalodi .... d.	↑	0327	0942	2001	2138
184	0823	1019	2049	0313		d.Ramdevra .... d.		0223	0857	1913	2052
194	0907	|	|	0400	↓	d.Pokaran .... d.	↑	|	0838	1855	|
198	0915	|	2111	0408		d.Ashapura .... d.		0210	0811	1823	|
301	1130	1250	2315	0600	↓	a.Jaisalmer .... d.	↑	0045	0645	1700	1920

Indian Railways — JODHPUR - AHMEDABAD — 5110

km	Exp 16311 ③	Exp 19028 ②	Exp 16507 ④⑥	Exp 16533 ③	Exp 19224	Exp 14707	Exp 12489 ②⑥	Exp 12479	Exp 19066 ⑥	Exp 22473 ①	Exp 17038 D⑤⑦	Exp 22932 ⑥	Station
277	2140	...	...	...	0045	0930	1340	...	...	1450	1540	...	d. Bikaner Junction a.
0	0300	0330	0540b	0540b	0610	1430	1815	1845	1930b	1920	2115	2355	d.Jodhpur .... a.
31	0332	0402	0606	|	0641	1502	1847	1916	|	1956	2147	0027	d.Luni .... d.
103	0520	0553	0740	0740	0805	1657	2204c	2032	2138	2138	2315	0202	d.Marwar Junction .. d.
268	0750	0825	1030	1030	1055	1933	|	2345	0040	0040	0213	0450	d.Abu Road .... d.
321	0907	0952	1153	|	1217	2135	0140	0100	|	0155	0327	0557	d.Palanpur .... d.
386	1028	1114	1309	|	1335	2245	|	0155	0305	0308	0435	0702	d.Mahesana .... d.
459	1230	1310	1430	1430	1500	0035	0410	0320	0435	0435	0625	0910	a.Ahmedabad .... d.

Station	Exp 14708	Exp 17037 ④⑤	Exp 16125 ①	Exp 16312 ①	Exp 16508 ③⑤	Exp 16534 ②	Exp 19065 ⑥	Exp 19223	Exp 19027 ⑥	Exp 12480	Exp 12490 ③⑦	Exp 22931 C②⑤
Bikaner Junction a.	1535	1700	...	2150	...	...	...	0135	...	...	1310	...
Jodhpur a.	0945	1050	1050	1630	1645b	1645b	1710b	2000	0430	0635	0745	0725
Luni d.	0909	1011	1014	1554	1554	|	|	1916	0358	0546	0709	0651
Marwar Junction d.	0805	0910	0910	1450	1450	1450	1520	1812	0255	0442	0426c	0550
Abu Road d.	0443	0608	0608	1155	1155	1155	1237	1530	2345	0132	|	0250
Palanpur d.	0328	0503	0503	1056	1056	|	|	1428	2250	0033	0155	0155
Mahesana d.	0154	0308	0240	0912	0912	|	1007	1245	2123	2245	|	2346
Ahmedabad d.	0010	0110	0050	0735	0705	0705	0805	1120	1955	2135	2230	2230

– Bhagat Ki Koth. c – Marwar Bhinmal. C – Runs as **22474** on ② to Bikaner arr. 1235. D – Also runs from Jodhpur as **16126** on ①.

Indian Railways — DELHI and JAIPUR - UDAIPUR - AHMEDABAD — 5120

km	Station	Exp 12992	Exp 12315 ⑤	Exp 19602 ②	Exp 15715 ①③⑥	Exp 12986	Exp 19665	Exp 12963 A	Exp 12981	52927	Exp 19943
0	Delhi Sarai Rohilla .... d.	...	...	1230j	1335j	1735	...	1900h	1940	...	...
83	Rewari .... d.	...	...	1522	1522	|	...	|	2107	...	...
**	Jaipur .... d.	1400	1745	1910	1910	2205	2300	|	|	...	...
73	Ajmer .... d.	1610	2030	2140	2130	...	0125	|	0210	...	...
59	Chittaurgarh .... d.	1925	0020	0145	...	...	0425	0505	0533	...	...
73	Udaipur City .... d.	2130	0300	0405	...	...	0645	0720	0750	0810	1745
83	Himmatnagar .... d.	...	...	...	...	...	...	...	...	1810	0155
71	Ahmedabad .... a.	...	...	...	...	...	...	...	...	2125	0425

Station	Exp 12316 ①	Exp 19601 ⑥	Exp 15716 ①②④	Exp 12991	Exp 19944	Exp 12982	Exp 12964 B	52928	Exp 19666	Exp 12985
Ahmedabad .... d.	...	...	...	...	2300	...	...	0710	...	...
Himmatnagar .... d.	...	...	...	...	0150	...	...	1030	...	...
Udaipur City .... d.	0020	0020	...	0600	0920	1715	1815	1900	2220	...
Chittaurgarh .... d.	0235	0235	...	0820	...	1930	2050	...	0035	...
Ajmer .... d.	0630	0630	1105	1130	...	2245	|	...	0340	...
Jaipur .... a.	0845	0900	1320	1330	...	|	|	...	0545	0600
Rewari .... d.	...	1255	1802	...	...	0345	|	...	...	|
Delhi Sarai Rohilla ... a.	...	1445j	2000j	...	...	0510	0635h	...	...	1030

– Via Mathura (d. 2110), Sawai Madhopur (d. 2358) and Kota (d. 0125).
– Via Kota (d. 2340), Sawai Madhopur (d. 0055) and Mathura (d. 0430).
h – Delhi Hazrat Nizamuddin.
j – Delhi Junction.
** – Jaipur - Ajmer: *136 km*.

Indian Railways — DELHI and JAIPUR - MUMBAI and AHMEDABAD — 5130

km	Station	Exp 12904	Exp 19708	Exp 12956	Exp 12215 D	Duro 12264 ①④	Exp 12918 ②④⑥	Exp 12910 ③⑤⑦	RDi 12952	Yuva 12248 ⑥	RDi 12954	Duro 12240 ②④	Exp 12980 ①③⑤	Exp 22926	Duro 22210 ②⑥	Exp 12908 ①④	Exp 12472 A	Exp 12478 ⑦E	Exp 19024	Exp 19020
0	Delhi H Nizamuddin ... d.	0735	...	...	0920h	1055	1355	1535	1625n	1535	1650	...	...	1645n	2330n	2135	2150n	2150n	1325n	2155
24	Mathura .... d.	1000	...	...	|	|	1605	1712	|	1712	1840	...	...	1915	|	|	0010	0010	1705	0135
	Jaipur .... d.	|	0845	1400	1420	|	|	|	|	|	|	1910	2025	|	|	|	|	|	|	|
340	Sawai Madhopur .... d.	1300	|	1610	|	|	|	|	|	|	2038	2105	2245	2205	|	|	0229	0229	2110	0525
48	Kota Junction .... d.	1425	△	1730	△	1540	1955	2010	2105	2010	2150	|	0010	2345	0425	0310	0355	0355	2320	0750
73	Nagda .... d.	1757	|	2105	|	|	|	|	|	|	0024	|	0308	0320	|	|	0727	0727	0445	1315
14	Ratlam .... d.	1910	|	2150	|	1845	2350	2325	0005	2325	0055	0155	0350	0410	0740	|	0820	0820	0600	1425
76	Vadodara .... d.	2330	0030	0144	0313	2236	0430	0307	0324	0307	0423	0600	0805	0821	1121	1107	1215	1230	1053	2005
75	Ahmedabad .... a.	|	|	|	|	P	0645	|	|	|	|	|	|	|	|	|	|	1415	|	|
04	Surat .... d.	0120	0222	0335	0451	...	...	0450	0503	0520	0602	|	1013	1025	|	|	1410	...	1335	2238
40	Borivali .... d.	0428	0548	0642	0730	...	...	0730	0731	|	0854	|	1329	1355	|	1554	1723	...	1850	0332
60	Mumbai Bandra .... a.	0520c	0635	0740c	0810	...	...	0810	0815c	0920	0945c	1140c	1420	1445	1615c	1635	1805	...	2010c	0420

km	Station	Exp 19019	Exp 19023	Exp 12471 B	Exp 12477 ②F	Exp 22925	Exp 12216 C	Duro 12263 ②⑤	Exp 12979 ②④⑥	RDi 12951	Exp 12907 ③⑦	Exp 12909 ②④⑥	Yuva 12247 ⑤	Exp 12917 ①③⑤	RDi 12953	Exp 12955	Exp 19707	Exp 12903	Duro 12239 ②⑦	Duro 22209 ①⑤
0	Mumbai Bandra .... d.	0005	0725c	0755	...	1135	1245	...	1545	1700c	1635	1635	1635	...	1740c	1850c	2100	2130c	2315c	2315c
19	Borivali .... d.	0040	0810	0831	...	1214	1315	...	1627	1734	1713	1709	|	...	1821	1930	2145	2209	|	|
252	Surat .... d.	0445	1337	1147	...	1547	1600	...	2035	1958	|	2005	2010	...	2055	2245	0102	0115	|	|
	Ahmedabad .... d.	|	|	|	1125	|	|	P	|	|	|	|	|	1720	|	|	|	|	|	|
381	Vadodara .... d.	0655	1607	1345	1343	1740	1738	1849	2242	2128	2305	2146	2146	1935	2231	0039	0254	0305	0405	0405
542	Ratlam .... d.	1240	2055	1805	1805	2200	|	2223	0255	0040	|	0110	0110	2340	0220	0440	|	0720	0740	0740
584	Nagda .... d.	1425	2205	1905	1905	2325	△	|	0355	|	|	|	|	|	0312	0538	△	0815	|	|
909	Kota Junction .... d.	1935	0135	2140	2140	0215	|	0110	0635	0325	0635	0345	0345	0300	0520	0855	|	1105	|	1035
017	Sawai Madhopur .... d.	2130	0320	2257	2257	0350	|	|	0845	|	|	|	|	|	0628	1040	|	1230	1225	|
48	Jaipur .... a.	|	|	|	|	|	0705	|	1045	|	|	|	|	|	|	1240	1855	|	1435	|
	Mathura .... d.	0225	0935	0205	0205	0750	|	|	...	|	|	0727	0727	0802	0902	...	...	1620	...	|
	Delhi H Nizamuddin ... a.	0520	1245n	0412	0412	1040n	1215h	0655	...	0835n	1345	0940	0940	1040	1055	...	...	1845	...	1630n

A – ②③⑤⑥.
B – ①④⑤⑦.
C – ②③⑤⑦.
D – ①②④⑥.
E – Runs as **12476** on ①. Also as **12474** on ④
F – Runs as **12475** on ③. Also as **12473** on ⑥
P – To/from Pune see Table **5160**

c – Mumbai Central.
h – Delhi Sarai Rohilla.
n – New Delhi.

△ – Via Ahmedabad (Table **5080**).

Indian Railways — GANDHIDHAM - AHMEDABAD — 5140

km	Station	Exp 16335 ⑤	Exp 22952 ④	Exp 16505 ②	Exp 11091 ③	Exp 14312 ②④⑦	Exp 15667 ⑥	Exp 22904 ①④⑥	Exp 19132	Exp 12993 ⑤	Exp 19116
0	Gandhidham .... d.	0700	0650	0900	1005	1410	1315	1625	2115	2245	2340
53	Samakhiali .... d.	0800	0747	0956	1105	1510	1420	1718	2215	2345	0041
94	Maliya Miyana .... d.	0838	0827	|	|	1547	1507	|	2252	|	0119
170	Dhrangadhra .... d.	0930	|	1136	1306	1658	|	|	0004	0127	0235
236	Viramgam .... d.	1117	1245	1307	1423	1825	1942	|	0115	|	0345
301	Ahmedabad .... a.	1240	1355	1430	1530	1945	2105	2150	0235	0410	0505

Station	Exp 19131	Exp 14311 ①⑤⑥	Exp 16336 ④	Exp 16506 ①	Exp 12994 ③	Exp 11092 ②	Exp 22093 ①④⑥	Exp 22951 ⑤	Exp 15668 ⑤	Exp 19115
Ahmedabad .... d.	0200	0645	0735	0705	0745	0805	0645	0815	1920	2359
Viramgam .... d.	0304	0800	0841	0822	|	0918	|	0924	2029	0107
Dhrangadhra .... d.	0404	0900	0952	0927	0952	1015	|	|	|	0208
Maliya Miyana .... d.	0515	1022	1056	|	|	|	|	1355	0119	0335
Samakhiali .... d.	0607	1114	1146	1140	1146	1216	1025	1432	0207	0430
Gandhidham .... a.	0715	1215	1300	1300	1300	1320	1125	1530	0320	0530

Indian Railways — AHMEDABAD - MUMBAI — 5150

km	Station	Exp 12972	Exp 12215 A	Exp 22452 ①④	Exp 14707	Exp 19132	Exp 12479	Exp 12489 A B	Exp 12934	Exp 12990 ①④⑥	Exp 19066 ⑦	Exp 22473 ②	Exp 12932 ①–⑥	Exp 19116	Exp 22954	Exp 22932 ⑦	Exp 19216	SDi 12010 ①–⑥	Exp 19028 ②	Exp 22952 ④	Exp 19018	Exp 22928	Duro 12268	Exp 12902	Exp 22904 ①④⑥	Exp 19708	Exp 22946
0	Ahmedabad ... d.	2359	0130	0130	0100	0300	0345	0430	0455	0455	0455	0455	0600	0525	0700	0930	0710	1440	1400	1415	2030	2110	2345	2200	2210	2230	2300
64	Anand ... d.	0105	|	0225	0205	0408	0453	0539	0557	0610	|	0610	0658	0634	0813	1035	0839	1534	1515	|	2146	2221	|	2315	|	2339	0002
00	Vadodara ... d.	0152	0313	0317	0252	0455	0540	0626	0644	0700	0700	0700	0745	0721	0902	1130	0947	1616	1603	1625	2245	2308	|	0013	2339	0028	0053
229	Surat ... d.	0350	0451	0520	0442	0705	0735	0820	0840	0855	0855	0855	0927	1000	1115	1350	1230	1758	1835	1835	0055	0108	|	0205	0130	0222	0238
462	Borivali ... d.	0800	0730	0834	0844	1038	1050	1125	1151	1202	1202	1202	1218	1322	1502	1650	1807	2037	2145	2142	0450	0508	|	0526	0413	0543	0607
480	Mumbai Bandra a.	0810	0810	0920	0940	1125	1135	1200d	1235c	1240d	1245	1245	1300c	1405	1555c	1735	1915c	2120c	2225	2225	0540	0550	0600c	0625c	0455	0635	0710c

Station	Exp 12959 ③⑥	SDi 12009 ①–⑥	Exp 22953	Exp 19215	Exp 19027 ⑥	Exp 22451 ①④	Exp 12216 A	Exp 12480	Exp 12933	Exp 12931 ①–⑥	Exp 12490 ③⑦	Exp 12989 ①④⑥	Exp 22931 C②⑤	Exp 19115	Exp 14708	Exp 19131	Exp 19017	Exp 22927	Exp 19707	Exp 12971	Exp 22945	Duro 12267	Exp 12901	Exp 19065 ⑤	Exp 22951 ④	Exp 22903 ③⑤⑦
umbai Bandra .... d.	0005d	0625c	0545c	0820c	1205	1205	1245	1330	1340c	1420c	1435d	1435d	1435	1450	1505	1710	1735	1940	2055	2130	2135c	2325c	2200c	2325	2355	2355
rivali .... d.	0036	0659	0627	0902	1243	1243	1315	1403	1417	1457	1509	1509	1509	1519	1551	1747	1820	2019	2132	2206	2221	|	2253	0005	0027	0027
rat .... d.	0420	0931	1028	1415	1600	1600	1600	1727	1740	1800	1827	1827	1827	1906	1925	2139	2202	0027	0052	0120	0135	|	0215	0355	0420	0318
adodara .... d.	0610	1107	1237	1705	1748	1748	1738	1915	1928	1940	2018	2018	2018	2135	2151	2340	0006	0226	0244	0307	0326	|	0423	0545	0610	0448
nand .... d.	0642	1136	1312	1750	1819	1819	|	1948	2000	2011	2053	2053	2053	2211	2222	0016	0042	0257	0315	0339	0359	|	0456	|	|	|
nmedabad .... a.	0755	1245	1440	1945	1930	1930	1920	2115	2125	2140	2210	2210	2210	2340	2350	0140	0210	0420	0430	0455	0535	0550	0635	0745	0755	0625

– ②③⑤⑦. B – Runs as **12960** on ②⑤. C – Runs as **22474** on ②. c – Mumbai Central. d – Mumbai Dadar.

5160 DELHI - PUNE and MUMBAI

Indian Railway

km		Exp	Exp	Duro	Exp	Exp	Exp	Exp	Exp	Exp	Exp
		12172	**12138**	**12264**	**12148**	**12782**	**12630**	**11078**	**12780**	**22110**	**11058**
		③⑥		①④	④	①	**A**			③	
0	**Delhi** H Nizamuddin ..d.	0010	0515**n**	1055	0555	0555	0845	1015**n**	1500	1545	2105
134	Mathura Junction ....d.	|	0740	|	0801	0801	|	1240	1645	|	2343
188	Agra Cantonment.......d.	0300	0835	|	0852	0855	|	1335	1733	1751	0048
306	Gwalior ....d.	|	1036	|	1104	1104	|	1536	1945	1911	0300
403	Jhansi.......................d.	0610	1235	|	1245	1245	1505	1730	2122	2027	0500
556	Bina..........................d.	|	1450	|	1505	1505	|	2010	|	|	0900
694	Bhopal.......................d.	1035	1655	|	1710	1710	1925	2220	0115	2345	1115
786	Itarsi ....d.	|	1840	▽	1855	1855	|	0020	0250	|	1325
969	Khandwa ....d.	|	2145	|	2200	2200	|	0325	0535	|	1645
1093	Bhusaval ....d.	1645	2335	|	2355	2355	|	0515	0730	0530	1855
1277	Manmad ....d.	|	0155	|	0215	0215	|	0750	0950	|	2150
1513	Daund ....d.	|	|	|	0755	0755	|	1310	1500	|	|
1589	**Pune** ....a.	|	|	0710	0915	0915	1105	1510	1620	|	|
1484	Kalyan ....d.	2255	0625	...	...	...	...	...	...	1050	0245
1521	**Mumbai** LTT ....a.	2345	0735**h**	...	...	...	...	...	...	1145	0405**h**

	Exp	Exp	Exp	Duro	Exp	Exp	Exp	Exp	Exp	Ex
	11057	**12779**	**12171**	**12263**	**22109**	**12629**	**12147**	**12781**	**11077**	**121**
			①④	②⑤	②	**B**	②	⑥		
Mumbai LTT.............d.	2330**h**	...	0755	...	1430	...	...	...	...	194
Kalyan ....d.	0033	...	0830	...	1507	...	...	...	...	204
Pune ....d.	|	0410	|	1110	|	0900	1610	1610	1720	|
Daund ....d.	|	0550	|	|	|	|	1745	1745	1850	|
Manmad ....d.	0405	1020	|	|	|	|	2155	2155	2325	002
Bhusaval....................d.	0645	1255	1410	|	2020	|	0025	0025	0200	025
Khandwa.....................d.	0930	1500	|	|	|	|	0220	0220	0430	050
Itarsi.........................d.	1250	1735	|	▽	|	|	0445	0445	0715	074
Bhopal ....d.	1505	1940	2035	|	0210	0045	0630	0630	0910	094
Bina...........................d.	1745	|	|	|	|	|	0825	0825	1120	120
Jhansi........................d.	2040	2358	0038	|	0531	0605	1038	1038	1347	143
Gwalior ....d.	2218	0115	|	|	0632	|	1157	1157	1520	160
Agra Cantonment.....d.	0016	0305	0405	|	0757	|	1405	1405	1712	175
Mathura Junction .....d.	0117	0402	|	|	|	|	1500	1500	1805	184
Delhi H Nizamuddin.a.	0347	0620	0655	0655	1025	1300	1710	1710	2026	205

A – ②③⑤⑥ Runs as **22686** on ②⑥.
B – ③④⑤⑦ Runs as **22685** on ④⑦.
d – Mumbai Dadar.
h – Mumbai CST.
n – New Delhi.
▽ – Via Kota and Vadodara, see Table **5130**.

5170 LUCKNOW - PUNE and MUMBAI

Indian Railway

km		Exp	Exp	Exp	Exp	Exp	Exp	Exp	Exp	Exp	Exp
		11016	**12541**	**12144**	**12174**	**12104**	**15101**	**12597**	**12533**	**15029**	**12108**
				②	②④	⑦	③	②		④	②④⑦
0	**Lucknow** Junction.....d.	0040	0355	0235	0550	0630	0630	1335	1945	2240	2245
72	Kanpur Central ....d.	0225	0535	0425	0800	0800	0800	1515	2132	0040	0020
292	Jhansi........................d.	0715	0942	1020	1200	1200	1155	1905	0142	0437	0345
445	Bina...........................d.	0950	|	1250	|	1410	|	|	|	0710	|
583	Bhopal........................d.	1200	1345	1445	1635	1635	1630	2320	0605	0935	0820
674	Itarsi ....d.	1355	1525	|	|	1820	1820	0100	0745	1205	|
858	Khandwa ....d.	1720	1810	1850	|	2105	2105	|	1030	1450	|
981	Bhusaval ....d.	1920	1955	2035	2255	2255	2255	0530	1220	1700	1450
1166	Manmad ....d.	2220	|	2245	|	0115	0110	|	1419	1940	|
1402	Daund ....d.	|	|	|	|	0620	|	|	|	|	|
1477	**Pune** ....a.	|	|	|	|	0805	|	|	|	0405	|
1372	Kalyan ....d.	0315	|	|	0455	...	|	1100	1845	...	2135
1409	**Mumbai** LTT ....a.	0420	0400	0410	0600	...	0615**h**	1215**h**	2005**h**	...	2235

	Exp	Exp	Exp	Exp	Exp	Exp	Exp	Exp	Exp	Exp
	12534	**12542**	**15030**	**12598**	**15102**	**12173**	**12107**	**12103**	**12143**	**110**
			⑥	③	⑤	②⑦	①③⑥	⑤	⑦	
Mumbai LTT.............d.	0820**h**	1110	...	1420	1535**h**	1625	1625	...	1640	224
Kalyan ....d.	0913	|	...	1510	1633	1710	1710	...	|	232
Pune ....d.	|	|	1045	|	|	|	|	1615	|	|
Daund ....d.	|	|	|	|	|	|	|	1745	|	|
Manmad ....d.	1245	|	1725	|	2015	|	|	2155	2145	031
Bhusaval....................d.	1510	1750	2020	2055	2230	2240	2240	0025	0025	055
Khandwa.....................d.	1715	2105	2345	|	0235	|	|	0220	0235	090
Itarsi ....d.	1930	2335	0225	0135	0515	|	|	0505	|	115
Bhopal ....d.	2105	0115	0430	0330	0720	0505	0505	0655	0720	135
Bina...........................d.	|	|	0645	|	|	|	|	0900	0940	163
Jhansi........................d.	0210	0527	0855	0735	1225	0925	0925	1112	1225	192
Kanpur Central.........d.	0700	0955	1445	1140	1715	1335	1350	1545	1545	002
Lucknow Junction ...a.	0840	1125	1615	1310	1905	1455	1510	1710	1715	014

h – Mumbai CST.

5180 MUGHAL SARAI, VARANASI and ALLAHABAD - MUMBAI

Indian Railway

km		Exp	Exp	Exp	Exp	Exp	Exp	Exp	Exp	Exp	Exp	Exp	Duro	Exp	Exp	Exp	Exp	Exp	Exp	Exp	Exp	Exp	Exp	Exp
		11062	**22104**	**15267**	**12545**	**12361**	**19050**	**12321**	**13201**	**18609**	**12168**	**11094**	**12294**	**12142**	**11060**	**11056**	**15018**	**12335**	**15646**	**15648**	**11070**	**11068**	**12166**	**1107**
		A	③	⑦	⑤	①	④			④			②⑥		①④⑥	**E**		②⑤⑦	①④	③	①③**Z**	④⑦	②⑤⑥	**X**
	Mughal Sarai.....................d.	...	...	...	0532	0532	0307	0837	0422	0700	...	...	...	1450	...	...	...	1755	1755	1755	...	...	...	...
	Varanasi.......................d.	2320	...	0345	|	|	|	|	|	0800	1025	1120	...	|	...	...	1115	|	|	|	...	...	2020	155
0	**Allahabad** Junction ....d.	0315	0703	0745	|	|	|	|	|	1220	|	|	1930	|	1710	1710	1630	|	|	|	1615	2108	2330	194
103	Manikpur ....d.	0510	0900	|	|	|	|	1335	1050	|	1430	1710	|	|	|	|	1832	|	|	|	1800	2300	|	213
178	Satna.................................d.	0625	1025	1100	1100	1100	0805	1500	1220	1550	1610	1830	2220	2020	2040	2040	2000	2310	2310	2310	|	0025	|	225
278	Katni..................................d.	0825	1135	1220	1220	1220	0920	1620	1350	1705	1725	1950	|	|	|	|	2115	0030	0030	0030	|	0140	0225	002
369	Jabalpur ....d.	0950	1305	1400	1400	1400	1110	1755	1520	1930	1855	2120	|	2310	2320	2320	2340	0200	0200	0200	|	0315	0500	|
614	Itarsi ....d.	1405	1720	|	1810	1810	|	2225	2045	2345	2320	0130	|	|	0350	0350	0430	0720	0720	0720	0800	0800	0905	093
791	Khandwa ....d.	1700	|	2045	2045	2045	|	0105	0035	0235	0310	0415	|	|	|	|	0820	1005	1005	1005	1130	1130	|	125
915	Bhusaval ....d.	1900	|	2230	2230	2230	1930	0300	0235	0420	0455	0615	0905	0740	0810	0810	1020	1155	1155	1155	1335	1335	1345	144
1099	Manmad ....d.	2115	|	|	0050	0050	|	0535	0455	0640	|	0820	|	0955	|	|	1245	1405	1405	1405	1600	1600	1600	174
1306	Kalyan ....d.	0235	0400	0455	0455	0455	|	1015	1023	1100	1125	1255	|	1415	1450	1450	1709	1854	1854	1854	2025	2025	2025	215
1349	**Mumbai** LTT ....a.	0340	0500	0600	0600	0615**h**	0735**b**	1125**h**	1130	1205	1225	1415**h**	1450	1515	1555	1555	1805	2000	2000	2000	2130	2130	2130	225

		Exp	Exp	Exp	Exp	Exp	Exp	Exp	Exp	Exp	Exp	Exp	Exp	Exp	Exp	Exp	Duro	Exp	Exp	Exp	Exp	Exp	Exp	Exp
		12167	**11093**	**11067**	**12165**	**15017**	**11069**	**12336**	**15645**	**15647**	**11055**	**12362**	**12546**	**11061**	**11065**	**22103**	**12293**	**11071**	**19049**	**15268**	**18610**	**12322**	**12141**	**132**
				③⑥	①④⑤		②⑦**Y**	②④⑦	③⑥	⑤	**B**	③	**C**①④	**F**	②④⑦	①	①⑤	**W**	①	②	⑥			
Mumbai LTT ....d.	...	0035	0010**h**	0520	0520	0635	0520	0805	0805	0805	1055	1105**h**	1120	1215	1215	1430	1725	1240	1545**b**	1550	1550	2130**h**	2325	221
Kalyan ....d.	...	0123	0115	0608	0608	0722	0608	0840	0840	0840	1138	1200	1200	1300	1300	1507	|	1325	|	1633	1633	2235	0021	230
Manmad ....d.	...	|	0455	0940	0940	1105	0940	1215	1215	1215	|	1550	1550	1630	1630	|	|	1650	|	|	2015	0213	0400	030
Bhusaval...................................d.	...	0730	0720	1200	1200	1335	1200	1440	1440	1440	1740	1815	1815	1905	1905	|	2305	1920	0420	2230	2230	0435	0620	052
Khandwa ....d.	...	1015	1000	1420	|	1635	1420	1730	1730	1730	|	2040	2040	2130	2130	|	|	2150	|	0235	0235	0655	|	080
Itarsi ....d.	...	1315	1250	1710	1710	2120	1700	2010	2010	2010	2230	2315	2315	0025	0025	0130	|	0030	|	|	0520	0940	|	114
Jabalpur ....d.	...	1640	1620	2050	2050	0105	|	2330	2330	2330	0155	0235	0235	0350	0350	0440	|	|	1245	0850	0850	1320	1425	160
Katni...d.	...	1755	1735	2210	2210	0225	|	0045	0045	0045	|	0350	0350	0515	0515	0555	|	1010	1408	1030	1030	1435	|	173
Satna...d.	...	1945	1930	0010	0010	0400	|	0215	0215	0215	0500	0520	0520	0655	0655	0735	0850	1150	1530	1200	1200	1620	1725	191
Manikpur...................................d.	...	2212	2155	0145	|	0555	0650	|	|	|	|	|	|	0855	0855	0937	|	1330	|	|	|	1812	|	211
Allahabad Junction ....a.	...	|	|	0350	0350	0810	0850	|	|	|	0940	|	|	1040	1040	1140	1235	1530	|	1550	1558	|	|	|
Varanasi.............................a.	...	0345	0440	...	0705	1240	...	|	|	|	...	|	|	1355	1355	...	...	1925	|	1945	1945	|	|	|
Mughal Sarai ....a.	...	...	...	...	...	...	...	0855	0855	0855	...	1215	1215	...	...	...	...	...	2210	...	2040	2352	0040	035

A – Runs as **11066** on ②④⑥.
B – Runs as **11059** on ②④⑥.
C – Runs as **15548** on ④.
E – ②③⑤⑦. F – ①③⑤⑥.
W – Via Bhopal (d. 0235) and Bina (d. 0535).
X – Via Bina (d. 0535) and Bhopal (d. 0740).
Y – Via Bhopal (d. 1845), Bina (d. 2140) and Jhansi (d. 0030).
Z – Via Jhansi (d. 0030), Bina (d. 0245) and Bhopal (d. 0455).
b – Mumbai Bandra.
d – Mumbai Dadar.
h – Mumbai CST.

5190 DELHI - SECUNDERABAD - TIRUPATI and BANGALORE

Indian Railway

km		Exp	Exp	Exp	Duro	RDi	Exp	RDi	RDi	Duro	Exp
		12650	**12708**	**12648**	**12286**	**12438**	**12724**	**22692**	**22694**	**12214**	**12722**
		A	③⑤⑦	③	①⑤	⑦		**C**	③④⑦	①	
0	**Delhi** H Nizamuddin ..d.	0640	0715	0835	1545	1555	1725**n**	2045	2045	2300**h**	2300
134	Mathura Junction ....d.	|	|	1023	|	|	1925	|	|	|	0100
188	Agra Cantonment.......d.	|	|	1115	|	|	2013	|	|	|	0200
306	Gwalior ....d.	|	|	1305	|	|	2210	|	|	|	0348
403	Jhansi.......................d.	1215	1355	1445	2027	2043	2347	0120	0120	|	0530
556	Bina..........................d.	|	|	1705	|	|	|	|	|	|	0800
694	Bhopal.......................d.	1615	1750	1905	|	0005	0330	0440	0440	|	1015
786	Itarsi ....d.	|	|	2100	|	|	|	|	|	|	1220
1083	Nagpur ....d.	2220	0015	0150	0520	0535	0950	1010	1010	|	1745
1528	Kazipet ....d.	|	0650	0932	|	1127	1647	1607	1607	|	0140
1660	**Secunderabad**..........a.	|	|	|	1400	1400	1915	1835	1835	2115	0405
***	**Secunderabad**..........d.	|	|	|	...	...	1920**c**	1850	1850	2130	0410**c**
1666	Kacheguda ....d.	0715	1000	1230	...	...	...	|	|	|	▬
1772	Mahabubnagar.............d.	|	1124	1400	...	...	...	|	|	|	*Duro*
1902	Kurnool Town ....d.	1107	1338	1610	...	...	...	|	|	|	**12245**
1951	Raichur ....d.	|	|	|	...	...	...	2310	|	|	①③④
1956	Dhone ....d.	|	1515	1745	...	...	...	|	|	|	⑥⑦
2292	Renigunta.................d.	|	2102	|	...	...	...	|	|	|	1030
2302	**Tirupati** ....a.	|	2135	|	...	...	...	|	|	|	|
	Guntakal...........d.	|	...	|	...	...	...	|	|	0302	|
2101	Dharmavaram..............d.	1520	...	2055	...	...	...	0330	|	|	|
2336*	**Bangalore** City..........a.	1910**y**	...	0030**y**	...	...	...	0640	0640	0755**y**	1600**y**

	RDI	RDi	Duro	Exp	Exp	RDi	Duro	Exp	Exp	Dur
	22691	**22693**	**12213**	**12723**	**12649**	**12437**	**12285**	**12647**	**12707**	**122**
	D	②⑤⑥	⑥		**B**	③	④⑦	⑦	①③⑤	ex③
Bangalore City........d.	2000	2000	2340**y**	...	2200**y**	...	...	2340**y**	...	1115
Dharmavaram ....d.	2322	|	|	...	0045	...	...	0245	...	|
Guntakal........d.	|	|	0350	...	|	...	...	|	...	|
Tirupati................d.	|	|	|	...	|	...	...	|	0540	|
Renigunta.............d.	|	|	|	...	|	...	...	|	0605	165
Dhone.......................d.	|	|	|	...	|	...	...	0545	1210	...
Raichur ....d,	0245	|	|	...	|	...	...	|	|	▬
Kurnool Town............d.	|	|	|	...	0427	...	...	0635	1304	*Exp*
Mahabubnagar.........d.	|	|	|	...	|	...	...	0835	1506	**127**
Kacheguda ....d.	|	|	|	...	0830	...	...	1040	1715	
Secunderabad ....a.	0735	0735	0855	0645**e**	|	...	...	|	|	2255
Secunderabad ....d.	0750	0750	0910	0650	|	1245	1310	|	|	230
Kazipet ....d.	0930	0930	|	0842	|	1447	|	1320	1950	013
Nagpur.......................d.	1530	1530	|	1550	1715	2045	1815	2110	0210	091
Itarsi ....d.	|	|	|	|	|	|	|	0145	|	145
Bhopal ....d.	2130	2130	|	2200	2305	0210	|	0330	0815	165
Bina...........................d.	|	|	|	|	|	|	|	0525	|	190
Jhansi........................d.	0056	0056	|	0220	0300	0531	0550	0745	1210	213
Gwalior ....d.	|	|	|	0332	|	|	|	0925	|	225
Agra Cantonment.....d.	|	|	|	0523	|	|	|	1124	|	005
Mathura Junction .....d.	|	|	|	0608	|	|	|	1215	|	013
Delhi H Nizamuddin.a.	0555	0555	0700**h**	0838	0915	1025	1035	1415	1800	040

A – ①②④⑥⑦.
B – ①③⑤⑥⑦.
C – ①②⑤⑥.
D – ①③④⑦.
c – To Hyderabad Decan.
e – From Hyderabad Decan.
h – Delhi Sarai Rohilla.
n – New Delhi.
y – Bangalore Yesvantpur Junction.
* – *2415 Kms* via Raichur.
*** – Secunderabad - Kacheguda : *7 km*.

DELHI - AGRA 5200

Indian Railways

km		Exp 12172 ③⑥	SDi 12002	Exp 18238	Exp 12138	Exp 12148 ④	Exp 12644 ⑤	Exp 12646 ②	Exp 12782 ①	Exp 12804 ③⑦	Exp 12280	Exp 12642 ①⑥	SDi 12050 ex ⑤	Exp 12808 A	Exp 18508 ①④⑦	Exp 13008	Exp 12618	Exp 11078	Exp 12626	Exp 18478	Exp 14624	Exp 19326 ④	Exp 12716	Exp 14310 ②③
7	**New Delhi** d.	...	0600	...	0515	...	...	...	...	...	...	...	...	...	0810	0700	...	1015	1125	...	1220h	...	1320	...
0	**Delhi** Hazrat Nizamuddin d.	0010	|	0440	|	0555	0555	0555	0555	0555	0705	0715	0810	0835	0845	|	0915	|	|	1210	|	1005	|	1340
134	Mathura Junction d.	|	0724	0700	0740	0801	0801	0801	0801	0801	0858	|	|	1023	1036	1010	1111	1240	1321	1420	1520	1155	1530	1550
188	**Agra** Cantonment a.	0255	0757	0812	0830	0850	0850	0850	0850	0850	0947	1010	0950	1110	1125	1145	1205	1330	1405	1515	1605	1250	1620	1640

	Exp 14318 ⑤⑥	Exp 12191	Exp 12780	Exp 11450 ④	Exp 16032 ③⑥⑦	Exp 16318 ②	Exp 12688 ①⑤	Exp 16688 ⑤	Exp 12550 ④	RDi 12434 ③⑤	Exp 12612 ①	Exp 12190	Exp 12724	Exp 12616	Exp 14212	Exp 12920	Exp 12448	Exp 12156	Exp 12628	Exp 11058	Exp 12622	Exp 12722	Exp 12422 ①	Exp 12486 ②⑤⑥
New Delhi d.	...	1405	...	1415	1415	1415	...	1415	1510f	...	...	...	1725	1840	1735	1915	...	...	2115	2050	2230	...	2345	2345
Delhi Hazrat Nizamuddin d.	1340	1421	1500	1435	1435	1435	1435	1445	|	1555	1555	1605	|	|	1757	|	2010	2055	|	2105	|	2300	|	|
Mathura Junction d.	1550	1613	1645	1708	1708	|	|	|	|	|	|	1815	1925	2047	2031	2140	2212	|	2303	2343	|	0100	|	0151
Agra Cantonment a.	1640	1657	1730	1812	1812	1812	1812	1840	1840	1800	1800	1910	2010	2135	2205	2225	2305	2320	2347	0040	0100	0155	0225	0240

	Exp 11057	Exp 12721	Exp 12919	Exp 22181	Exp 12447	Exp 12615	Exp 14623	Exp 12779	Exp 12621	Exp 12171 ②⑤	Exp 12155	Exp 12723	Exp 12549 ③	Exp 14211	Exp 12627	Exp 14309 ④⑤	Exp 14317 ①⑦	Exp 19325 ③	Exp 12192	Exp 12611 ⑦	RDi 12433 ①⑥	Exp 12189	Exp 12715	Exp 12485 ①②⑤
Agra Cantonment d.	0016	0050	0125	0209	0225	0250	0155	0305	0353	0405	0450	0523	0536	0600	0645	0708	0623	0623	0735	0757	0757	0818	0840	0915
Mathura Junction d.	0117	0139	0216	0255	0311	0350	0242	0402	|	|	|	0609	|	0702	0737	0810	0810	0810	0830	|	|	0920	0930	1010
Delhi Hazrat Nizamuddin a.	0347	0405	0435	0515	0525	0600	|	0620	0642	0655	0800	0838	|	0947	0955	1110	1110	1110	1118	1025	1025	1140	1146	|
New Delhi a.	0415	...	0500	...	...	0625	0615h	...	0705	...	...	0905	0920f	1020	1030	...	...	...	1150	...	...	...	1210	1300

	Exp 12421 ④	Exp 12617	Exp 12625	Exp 18477	Exp 12647 ②	Exp 18507 ③⑥⑦	Exp 12807 B	Exp 12781 ⑦	Exp 12643 ④	Exp 12803 ②⑥	Exp 12147 ③	Exp 12645 ①	Exp 12641 ⑤⑦	Exp 13007	Exp 18237	Exp 11077	Exp 16787 ③⑦	Exp 12687 ⑤	SDi 12049 ex ⑤	Exp 12137	Exp 16031 ①④⑤	Exp 11449 ②	Exp 12279	SDi 12001	Exp 22403 ④
Agra Cantonment d.	0915	1018	1025	1058	1124	1129	1344	1405	1405	1405	1405	1405	1515	1525	1635	1712	1730	1730	1750	1755	1833	1833	1855	2115	2350
Mathura Junction d.	|	1108	1115	1157	1215	1215	1435	1500	1500	1500	1500	1500	|	1640	1733	1805	|	|	|	1845	2000	2000	1946	2150	0037
Delhi Hazrat Nizamuddin a.	|	1315	1321	1440	1415	1415	1645	1710	1710	1710	1710	1710	1800	1913	2005	2022	2040	2040	1930	2051	2215	2215	2205	|	|
New Delhi a.	1300	...	1345	...	...	1440	...	...	...	...	...	...	...	1940	...	2045	2140	...	...	2115	2300	2300	...	2330	0320

A – ①②④⑤⑥. Also runs as **12648** on ③.
B – ①③④⑤⑦.

f – Delhi Safdarjang.
h – Delhi Sarai Rohilla.

DELHI - BILASPUR 5205

Indian Railways

km	km		SDi 12002	Exp 18508 ①④⑦	Exp 18478	Exp 18238	Exp 12410 A	Exp 12550 ④	Exp 12824 ②⑤⑦	RDi 12442 ②⑥	Exp 12920
0	0	**Delhi** Hazrat Nizamuddin d.	0600	0845	1210	0440	1520	1510f	1725	1545n	1915n.
135	135	Mathura Junction d.	0724	1036	1420	0700	1730	|	|	|	2140
189	189	Agra Cantonment d.	0802	1130	1523	0820	1830	1845	|	|	2230
307	307	Gwalior d.	0933	1323	1736	1050	2030	|	|	1923	0035
404	404	Jhansi d.	1051	1505	1925	1320	2200	2240	2330	2043	0235
557	557	Bina d.	|	|	|	1640	0015	|	|	|	0515
	632	Saugor d.	|	1847	2330	|	|	0210	0240	|	|
	819	Katni Murwara d.	|	2205	0410	|	|	0540	0610	|	|
	985	Anupper d.	|	0110	0745	|	|	0835	0900	|	|
695		Bhopal d.	1400	|	|	1845	0215	|	|	0005	0740
		Indore Junction a.		|	|	|	|	|	|	|	1250
788		Itarsi d.	...	|	|	2115	0400	|	|	|	...
1085		Nagpur d.	...	|	|	0355	0940	|	|	0545	...
1215		Gondia d.	...	|	|	0556	1128	|	|	0723	...
1349		Durg d.	...	|	|	0855	1330	1420↓	1510↓	0930	...
1387		Raipur Junction d.	...	|	|	0955	1415	1320↓	1415↓	1015	...
1498	1136	**Bilaspur** a.	...	0430	1055	1220	1645	1115	1155	1200	...

	Exp 12409 B	Exp 12823 ①④⑥	Exp 12549 ②	RDi 12441 ①④	Exp 18477	Exp 18507 ②⑤⑥	Exp 18237	SDi 12001	Exp 12919
Bilaspur d.	0555	1450	1450	1400	1545	1905	1415	...	...
Raipur Junction d.	0745	1240↑	1240↑	1540	|	|	1620	...	...
Durg d.	0845	1200↑	1200↑	1635	|	|	1715	...	...
Gondia d.	1039	|	|	1824	|	|	1923	...	...
Nagpur d.	1300	|	|	2045	|	|	2205	...	...
Itarsi d.	1750	|	|	|	|	|	0425	...	...
Indore Junction d.	|	|	|	|	|	|	|		1225
Bhopal d.	1950	|	|	0210	|	|	0635	1515	1735
Anupper d.	|	1725	1725	|	1840	2140	|	|	|
Katni Murwara d.	|	2045	2045	|	2310	0135	|	|	|
Saugor d.	|	2320	2320	|	0200	0420	|	|	|
Bina d.	2205	|	|	|	|	|	0920	|	1940
Jhansi d.	0050	0240	0240	0531	0640	0810	1220	1840	2157
Gwalior d.	0230	|	|	|	0805	0925	1400	1945	2325
Agra Cantonment d.	0418	|	0536	|	1058	1129	1635	2115	0125
Mathura Junction d.	0510	|	|	|	1157	1215	1733	2150	0216
Delhi Hazrat Nizamuddin a.	0720	0905	0929f	1055n	1440	1415	2005	2330	0435

A – ①②③④⑥.
B – ①③④⑤⑥.

f – Delhi Safdarjang.
n – New Delhi.

DELHI - NAGPUR - TIRUPATI and CHENNAI 5210

Indian Railways

km		Exp 12650 C	Exp 12804 ③⑦	Exp 12644 ⑤	Exp 12646 ②	Exp 12642 ①⑥	Exp 12652 ②④	Exp 12708 ③⑤⑦	Exp 18238	Exp 12626	RDi 12442 ②⑥	Duro 12270 ②⑥	RDi 12438 ⑦	RDi 12434 ③⑤	Exp 12612 ①	Exp 12688 ①⑤	Exp 16318 ②	Exp 16688 ⑤	Exp 12724	RDi 22692 A	RDi 22694 ③④⑦	Exp 16032 ③⑥⑦	Exp 12616	Exp 12622	Exp 12722	Exp 22404 ⑦
0	**Delhi** H Nizamuddin d.	0640	0555	0555	0555	0715	0715	0715	0440	1125n	1545n	1545	1555	1555	1555	1435	1435	1443	1725n	2045	2045	1435	1840n	2230n	2300	2345n
135	Mathura Junction d.	|	0801	0801	0801	|	|	|	0700	1321	|	|	|	|	|	|	|	|	1925	|	|	1708	2047	|	0100	0138
189	Agra Cantonment d.	|	0855	0855	0852	1015	|	|	0820	1410	|	|	|	1802	1802	1817	1817	1845	2013	|	|	1817	2140	0103	0200	0230
307	Gwalior d.	|	1104	1104	1104	|	|	|	1050	1610	|	|	|	1925	1925	2015	2015	2055	2210	|	|	2015	2331	0235	0348	|
404	Jhansi d.	1215	1245	1245	1245	1355	1355	1355	1320	1752	2043	2032	2043	2043	2043	2145	2145	2240	2347	0120	0120	2145	0107	0412	0530	0555
557	Bina d.	|	1505	1505	1505	|	|	|	1630	1955	|	|	|	|	|	|	|	|	|	|	|	0110	0320	|	0800	|
695	Bhopal d.	1615	1710	1710	1710	1750	1750	1750	1845	2145	0005	|	0005	0005	0005	0150	0150	0305	0330	0440	0440	0305	0525	0800	1015	1105
788	Itarsi d.	|	1900	1900	1900	1935	|	|	2115	2355	|	|	|	|	|	|	0335	0530	|	|	|	0530	0725	0945	1220	1305
1085	**Nagpur** d.	2210	2325	2325	2325	0015	0015	0015	0330	0410	0530	0520	0525	0535	0535	0840	0840	1045	0950	1000	1000	1045	1230	1430	1745	1845
1298	Balharshah d.	...	0305	0305	0305	0340	|	|	—	0750	...	0815	...	|	0820	1210	1210	1440	1320	—	...	1440	1605	1740	2145	2250
1543	Warangal d.	...	0632	0632	0632	|	|	S	Exp	1107	...	|	...	1126	|	1533	1533	1843	...	Exp	...	1843	1935	2050	...	0302
1752	Vijayawada d.	...	1105	1040	1040	1050	1050	|	**16115**	1500	...	1430	...	1430	1430	1920	1920	2345	...	**12867**	...	0100	2325	0025	...	0730
2046	Gudur d.	...	...	1512	1512	1505	|	|	...	1920	...	|	...	|	1825	|	2343	0430	...	②	...	0740	0400	|	...	1200
2122	Renigunta a.	...	...	1620	1620	|	|	2100	...	2040	...	|	...	|	|	|	0055	0540	...		...	|	|	|	...	|
2132	**Tirupati** a.	...	...	1650	1650	|	|	2135	...	2052	...	|	...	|	|	|	0120	0605	...	0122	...	|	|	|	...	|
2184	**Chennai** Central a.	...	...	...	...	1805e	1805e	...	1810e	...	...	2010	...	2015	2015	0215	...	...	...	|	...	1020	0620	0710	...	1425e
2384	Pondicherry a.	...	...	...	...	...	...	...	2230	...	...	...	...	...	...	...	...	...	...	0850	...	...	...	...	...	1845

	Exp 22403 ③	Exp 12868 ③	RDi 22691 B	RDi 22693 ③⑥⑦	Exp 12615	Exp 12621	Exp 12723	Exp 12649 D	RDi 12437 ③	RDi 12433 ⑤⑦	Exp 12611 ⑥	Duro 12269 ①⑤	RDi 12441 ①④	Exp 12625	Exp 12643 ③	Exp 12645 ⑦	Exp 12803 ①⑤	Exp 12641 ④⑥	Exp 12651 ②⑦	Exp 12707 ①③⑤	Exp 18237	Exp 16687 ②	Exp 16317 ⑥	Exp 16116	Exp 12687 ①④	Exp 16031 ③④⑦
Pondicherry d.	0905	1230	...	...	...	...	...	...	...	...	...	...	...	...	...	...	...	...	...	...	...	...	...	0535	...	...
Chennai Central d.	1300e	|	...	...	1915	2200	...	...	...	0610	0610	0640	...	...	...	...	...	0905e	0905e	...	...	...	...	0930e	0945	0515
Tirupati d.	|	1945	...	...	|	|	...	...	...	|	|	|	...	0357	0735	0735	...	|	|	0540	...	0935	0935	...	|	|
Renigunta d.	|	...	...	...	|	|	...	...	...	|	|	|	...	0420	0800	0800	...	|	|	0605	...	1000	1000	...	|	|
Gudur d.	1552	—	...	...	2132	|	...	...	...	|	0801	|	...	0557	0935	0935	...	|	|	|	...	1140	1140	...	|	0817
Vijayawada d.	2020	Exp	...	...	0205	0420	...	...	...	1200	1200	1240	...	1015	1435	1435	1435	1610	1610	|	...	1625	1625	...	1700	1450
Warangal d.	2355	**12721**	...	...	0500	0705	...	...	...	1440	|	|	...	1305	1735	1735	1735	|	|	S	...	1945	1945	...	2035	1800
Balharshah d.	0420		...	...	0855	1110	...	...	...	|	1800	1815	...	1710	2125	2125	2125	2315	|	|	...	2340	2340	...	0040	2250
Nagpur d.	0745	0915	1530	1530	1225	1420	1550	1715	2045	2045	2045	2105	2045	2015	0030	0030	0030	0210	0210	0210	2205	0255	0255	...	0350	0245
Itarsi d.	1300	1455	|	|	1720	1843	|	|	|	|	|	|	|	0110	0445	0445	0445	0630	|	|	0425	0730	0730	...	|	0810
Bhopal d.	1455	1650	2130	2130	1930	2020	2200	2305	0210	0210	0210	|	0200	0300	0630	0630	0630	0815	0815	0815	0635	0920	0920	...	0950	1000
Bina d.	|	1905	|	|	2130	|	|	|	|	|	|	|	|	0455	0825	0825	0825	|	|	|	0920	|	|	...	|	1235
Jhansi d.	1930	2130	0056	0056	2340	0028	0220	0300	0531	0531	0531	0550	0531	0707	1038	1036	1036	1210	1210	1210	1220	1412	1412	...	1412	1455
Gwalior d.	|	2252	|	|	0055	0140	0333	|	|	0632	0632	|	0630	0825	1157	1157	1157	|	|	|	1400	1535	1535	...	1535	1620
Agra Cantonment d.	2350	0050	|	|	0250	0353	0523	|	|	0757	0757	|	|	1025	1405	1405	1405	1515	|	|	1635	1730	1730	...	1730	1833
Mathura Junction d.	0037	0139	|	|	0350	|	0608	|	|	|	|	|	|	1115	1500	1500	1500	|	|	|	1733	|	|	...	|	2000
Delhi H Nizamuddin a.	0320n	0405	0555	0555	0600	0642	0838	0915	1025	1025	1025	1035	1055n	1321	1710	1710	1710	1800	1800	1800	2005	2040	2040	...	2040	2215

A – ①②⑤⑥.
B – ①②④⑤.
C – ①②④⑥⑦.
D – ①②④⑥⑦.

S – Via Kacheguda (Table **5190**).

e – Chennai Egmore.
n – New Delhi.

5220 DELHI, AHMEDABAD and MUMBAI - GOA - MANGALORE - TRIVANDRUM

Indian Railways

km		22150	12133	16333	16335	16311	16348	10111	16603	16630	12432	12450	12051	10103	12218	12484	22660	16649	16345	19578	16605	12284	12619	12201	1222
		Exp	Exp	Exp	Exp	Exp	Exp	Exp	Exp	Exp	RDi	Exp	SDi	Exp	Exp	Exp	Exp	Exp	Exp	Exp	Exp	Duro	Exp	Exp	Dur
		③⑦ A		④	⑤	③					②③⑦	①⑥			③⑤	⑦	①			⑥⑦		⑥		①⑤	②⑥
0	**Delhi** Hazrat Nizamuddin d.	...	...	...	...	...	...	...	...	...	1055	0725	...	...	1340	1355	1355	...	...	...	...	2135	...	...	...
458	Kota Junction d.	...	...	...	...	...	...	...	...	...	1540	1320	...	...	1950	1955	1950	...	...	...	...	0310	...	...	...
****	**Ahmedabad** d.	...	...	1300	1300	1300	...	...	...	...	|	|	...	...	|	|	|	...	...	0327	...	|	...	...	...
986	Vadodara Junction d.	...	...	1505	1458	1458	...	...	...	...	2238	2146	...	...	0417	0417	0417	...	...	0517	...	1115	...	...	...
***	**Mumbai** CST d.	...	2200	|	|	|	...	2305	...	...	|	|	0525d	0710	|	|	|	...	1140t	|	...	|	1520t	1655t	205
1397	Panvel d.	2125	2315	2205	2205	2205	...	0030	...	...	0430	0510	0638	0830	1215	1215	1215	...	1255	1315	...	1800	1625	1810	|
1678	Ratnagiri d.	0200	0345	0255	0255	0255	...	0530	...	...	0915	0945	1045	1315	1750	1750	1750	...	1900	1945	...	2305	2135	2305	020
1917	**Madgaon** d.	0555	0715	0740	0740	0740	...	1045	...	...	1242	1445	1405	1845	2110	2110	2110	...	2310	2345	...	0225	0135	0225	055
2166	Udupi d.	0940	1111	1156	1156	1156	...	...	...	...	1620	...	...	...	0040	0112	0112	...	0302	0402	...	|	0540	0622	|
2234	**Mangalore** Junction d.	1120	1240	1350	1350	1350	1420c	...	1745c	1815c	1800	...	...	...	0225	0310	0310	0500c	0435	0605	0720c	0810	0730c	0810	102
2365	Cannanore d.	1320	...	1605	1605	1555	1700	...	2015	2110	1955	...	...	...	0420	0510	0510	0715	0645	0815	0935	|	...	1015	|
2455	Calicut d.	1445	...	1745	1745	1735	1845	...	2200	2305	2120	...	...	...	0550	0620	0620	0900	0825	0950	1125	1135	...	1140	135
2541	Shoranur d.	1620	...	1950	1950	1950	2105	...	0001	0120	2245	...	...	...	0805	0820	0820	1120	1035	1145	1400	|	...	1320	|
2574	Trichur d.	1704	...	2038	2038	2038	2150	...	0045	0203	2330	...	...	...	0840	0905	0905	1200	1125	1223	1447	|	...	1415	|
2645	**Ernakulam** Town d.	1850j	...	2200	2200	2200	2335	...	0225j	0330	0055j	...	...	...	1015j	1110j	1040	1345	1305j	1400j	1625j	1520j	...	1520	174
2762	Kayankulam d.	...	...	|	0005	0005	0215	...	0432	0555	|	...	...	...	1232	1302	|	1610	1512	1602	1827	...	...	1755	...
2789	Quilon d.	...	...	0110	0110	0110	0305	...	0535	0705	0315	...	...	...	1310	1350	1350	1715	1615	1710	1930	...	...	1840	...
2866	**Trivandrum** Central a.	...	...	0250	0240	0250k	0445	...	0715	0905	0455	...	...	...	1445k	1515k	1515k	1830	1755	1815	2100	...	...	2025k	...
2937	Nagercoil a.	...	...	...	0415	...	...	...	...	...	...	...	...	...	...	...	...	2050	...	2008	2315	...	...	...	...

		12224	10104	12431	12449	16312	16336	16334	12283	16604	16629	16347	12052	10112	22149	12134	12620	16606	16650	12202	22659	12217	12483	19577	1634
		Duro	Exp	RDi	Exp	Exp	Exp	Exp	Duro	Exp	Exp	Exp	SDi	Exp	Exp	Exp	Exp	Exp	Exp	Exp	Exp	Exp	Exp	Exp	Exp
		③⑦		②④⑤	②③	⑥	②	①	②						②⑤ B					④⑦	⑤	⑥	③	①②	
Nagercoil d.	...	...	...	...	...	...	1400	...	...	...	...	...	...	...	...	...	...	0200	0420	...	...	...	...	0920	...
Trivandrum Central d.	...	...	...	1915	...	1535k	1535	1535	...	1925	1845	2040	...	...	...	...	...	0340	0620	0845k	0845k	0920k	0920k	1055	0950
Quilon d.	...	...	...	2012	...	1630	1630	1630	...	2030	2000	2150	...	...	...	...	...	0445	0723	0940	0940	1015	1015	1155	1055
Kayankulam d.	...	...	...	|	...	1710	1710	|	...	2112	2048	2242	...	...	...	...	...	0526	0810	1015	|	1100	1100	1230	1135
Ernakulam Town d.	...	2330j	...	2235j	...	2005	2005	2005	2330j	2340j	2350	0125	...	...	0515j	...	...	0745j	1100	1250	1250	1250j	1250j	1435j	1405
Trichur d.	...	|	...	2350	...	2120	2120	2120	|	0053	0135	0255	...	...	0610	...	...	0920	1230	1357	1357	1357	1357	1545	1520
Shoranur d.	...	|	...	0050	...	2230	2230	2230	|	0200	0305	0405	...	...	0720	...	...	1035	1400	1505	1505	1505	1505	1700	1650
Calicut d.	...	0100	...	0205	...	0020	0020	0020	0255	0340	0505	0605	...	...	0855	...	...	1230	1555	1635	1635	1635	1635	1830	1905
Cannanore d.	...	|	...	0325	...	0155	0155	0155	|	0525	0655	0755	...	...	1020	...	...	1415	1740	1805	1805	1805	1805	2000	2045
Mangalore Junction d.	...	0425	...	0530	...	0445	0445	0445	0635	0805c	1015c	1055c	...	...	1225	1355	1435c	1715c	2040c	2025	2025	2025	2025	2215	2325
Udupi d.	...	|	...	0650	...	0622	0622	0622	|	...	...	...	...	...	1350	1459	1558	...	...	2146	2146	2146	2146	2340	0052
Madgaon d.	...	0855	0915	1110	1225	1130	1130	1130	1205	...	...	...	1430	1800	1720	1850	2040	...	...	0130	0130	0130	0130	0400	0505
Ratnagiri d.	...	1245	1410	1330	1715	1615	1615	1615	1655	...	...	...	1750	2305	2045	2220	0030	...	...	0505	|	|	|	0810	0915
Panvel d.	...	|	1930	1810	2300	2125	2125	2125	2220	...	...	...	2150	0410	0230	0250	0515	...	...	1020	1100	1100	1100	1340	1515
Mumbai CST a.	...	1815t	2140	|	|	|	|	|	|	...	...	...	2305d	0550	...	0425	0635t	...	...	1155t	|	|	|	|	1640
Vadodara Junction d.	...	...	...	0023	0720	0522	0522	0522	0522	...	...	...	...	...	...	...	...	...	...	...	1820	1820	1820	2115	...
Ahmedabad a.	...	...	...	|	|	0715	0715	0715	|	...	...	...	...	...	...	...	...	...	...	...	|	|	|	2300	...
Kota Junction d.	...	...	...	0650	1500	...	...	...	1300	...	...	...	...	...	...	...	...	...	...	...	0300	0300	0300	...	...
Delhi Hazrat Nizamuddin a.	...	...	...	1240	2240	...	...	...	1940	...	...	...	...	...	...	...	...	...	...	...	1040	1040	1040	...	...

A – From Pune (d. 1845 ③⑦). B – To Pune (a. 1030 ③⑥).
c – Mangalore Central. d – Mumbai Dadar.
j – Ernakulam Junction. k – Trivandrum Kochuveli.
t – Mumbai Lokmaniya Tilak Terminus. z – Journey time 42 - 44 hours.
*** – Mumbai CST - Panvel: *68 km*. **** – Ahmedabad - Vadodara: *100 km*.

5230 MUMBAI - PUNE - KOLHAPUR

Indian Railways

km		11049	22105	12148	12127	11007	11301	11029	16331	17031	11041	11009	11019	16381	11046	12125	12123	11023	17411	22107	12701	12115	11027	11040
		Exp	Exp	Exp	Exp	Exp	Exp	Exp	Exp	Exp	Exp	Exp	Exp	Exp	Exp	Exp	Exp	Exp	Exp	Exp	Exp	Exp	Exp	Exp
		①		⑤					A						③									
0	**Mumbai** CST d.	...	0540	...	0640	0700	0805	0840	1210	1245	1400	1430	1510	1545	...	1625	1710	1750	2023	2100	2150	2245	2345	...
54	Kalyan d.	0450	0635	...	|	0755	0900	0935	1308	1340	1500	1530	1608	1640	...	|	|	1850	2123	2153	2240	2345	0040	...
192	**Pune** a.	0750	0908	0930	0957	1105	1140	1240	1545	1630	1800	1840	1900	1915	1930	1950	2025	2155	0010	0030	0120	0210	0325	0450
471	Miraj d.	1400	...	1505	...	...	...	1910	...	...	...	...	...	...	0215	...	...	0443	0555	...	...	...	...	1120
518	**Kolhapur** a.	1525	...	1620	...	...	...	2025	...	...	...	...	...	...	0335	...	...	0605	0725	...	...	...	...	1245

		16382	12702	12116	17412	22108	11010	12124	12126	11024	11045	17032	11042	11008	11302	11030	12147	16332	12128	22106	11050	11039	11028	11020
		Exp	Exp	Exp	Exp	Exp	Exp	Exp	Exp	Exp	Exp	Exp	Exp	Exp	Exp	Exp	Exp	Exp	Exp	Exp	Exp	Exp	Exp	Exp
											④						②	B			⑥			
Kolhapur d.	...	...	...	...	2030	...	...	...	...	2250	2345	...	...	...	...	0755	0905	...	...	...	1250	1530	...	...
Miraj d.	...	...	...	...	2138	...	...	...	...	0005	0045	...	...	...	...	0910	1020	...	...	...	1345	1640	...	...
Pune d.	...	0050	0115	0310	0335	0415	0605	0715	0750	0700	0725	0910	0935	1530	1555	1545	1555	1640	1755	1835	1950	2305	2340	2350
Kalyan d.	...	0325	0343	0540	0610	0645	0847	|	|	1035	...	1150	1220	1823	1835	1850	...	1930	|	2052	2217	...	0230	0240
Mumbai CST a.	...	0440	0455	0650	0725	0805	0953	1025	1115	1150	...	1305	1335	1935	1950	2005	...	2050	2105	2200	...	...	0345	0355

A – Runs as **16339** on ③④⑤⑦ and as **16351** on ②⑥. B – Runs as **16340** on ②③④⑥ and as **16352** on ①⑤.

5240 MUMBAI - KALYAN - PUNE - HUBLI

Indian Railways

km		16531	16533	16209	16507	16505	11005	11035	11021	12782	12630	12780
		Exp	Exp	Exp	Exp	Exp	Exp	Exp	Exp	Exp	Exp	Exp
		②	④	①⑥	⑤⑦	③	①⑤⑦	④	②③⑥	②	A	
0	**Mumbai** Dadar d.	...	...	...	...	...	2130	2130	2130	...	...	...
54	Kalyan d.	0105	0105	0105	0105	0105	2213	2213	2213	...	...	...
192	**Pune** d.	0420	0420	0420	0420	0420	0110	0110	0110	0930	1120	1635
338	Satara d.	0713	0713	0713	0713	0713	0400	0400	0400	1208	|	1920
472	Miraj d.	1035	1035	1035	1035	1035	0655	0655	0655	1500	1645	2230
610	Belgaum d.	1330	1330	1330	1330	1330	0905	0905	0905	1710	1850	0050
661	Londa d.	1417	1417	1417	1417	1417	1000	1000	1000	|	|	0205
731	Dharwad d.	1555	1555	|	1625	|	1127	1127	1127	1920	2114	...
751	**Hubli** a.	1645	1645	1700	1700	1700	1230	1230	1230	2020	2215	...

	12781	16532	16534	16210	16506	16508	11006	11036	11022	12779	12629
	Exp	Exp	Exp	Exp	Exp	Exp	Exp	Exp	Exp	Exp	Exp
	⑥	⑥	①	③⑤	⑦	②④	①③④	⑦	②⑤⑥		B
Hubli d.	0440	0635	0635	0635	0635	0635	1515	1515	1515	...	2150
Dharwad d.	0505	0700	0700	0700	0700	0700	1540	1540	1540	...	2218
Londa d.	|	0825	0825	0825	0825	0825	1710	1710	1710	1845	|
Belgaum d.	0720	0940	0940	0940	0940	0940	1805	1805	1805	1950	0032
Miraj d.	1020	1245	1245	1245	1245	1245	2050	2050	2050	2230	0320
Satara d.	1238	1503	1503	1503	1503	1503	2308	2308	2308	0040	|
Pune d.	1555	1850	1850	1850	1850	1850	0220	0220	0220	0355	0845
Kalyan a.	...	2127	2127	2127	2127	2124	0447	0447	0447	...	...
Mumbai Dadar a.	...	...	...	...	...	...	0545	0545	0545	...	...

A – ③④⑥⑦. Runs as **22686** on ③⑦. B – ②③④⑥. Runs as **22685** on ③⑥.

5245 HUBLI - BANGALORE - MYSORE

Indian Railways

km		17310	12726	12777	11005	11021	11035	12080	17315	16507	16505	16209	16531	16533	14806	12782	17312	17314	16591	17302	12630	16590	16536	
		Exp	Exp	Exp	Exp	Exp	Exp	SDi	Exp	Exp	Exp	Exp	Exp	Exp	Exp	Exp	Exp	Exp	Exp	Exp	Exp	Exp	Exp	
		②⑦		③	①②⑥	③④⑦	⑤		①	⑤⑦	③	①⑥	②	④	⑥	②	④	⑥			A			
0	**Hubli** d.	0220	0600	0645	1240	1240	1240	1400	1440	1710	1710	1710	1655	1655	1820	2025	2025	2025	1820	2115	2220	2245	2300	...
129	Harihar d.	0445	0800	0850	1445	1445	1445	1555	|	1935	1935	1935	|	|	|	2235	2235	2235	|	2335	|	0045	0105	...
258	Birur d.	0640	1010	1050	1705	1705	1705	1750	1930	2130	2130	2130	|	|	|	0040	0040	0040	|	0145	|	0250	0320	...
303	Arsikere d.	0740	1100	1200	1810	1810	1810	1840	2020	2255	2255	2255	G	G	0007	0135	0135	0135	G	0305	|	0350	0425	...
393	Tumkur d.	0940	1230	1327	1930	1930	|	2000	2140	0110	0110	0110	|	|	|	|	0325	0325	|	|	0445	0530	0625	...
469	**Bangalore** City a.	1125y	1405	1510y	2130y	2130y	|	2125	2310y	0315	0315	0315	0445	0445	0315y	|	0500y	0500y	0610	|	0620y	0700	0805	...
614	**Mysore** a.	...	...	...	...	...	2140	...	...	...	...	0600	...	...	...	0455	...	...	0915	0700	...	...	1105	...

			12778	12079	11006	11022	11036	14805	12629	12725	17309	16535	12781	16589	16532	16534	17311	17313	16508	16210	16506	17301	16592	
			Exp	SDi	Exp	Exp	Exp	Exp	Exp	Exp	Exp	Exp	Exp	Exp	Exp	Exp	Exp	Exp	Exp	Exp	Exp	Exp	Exp	
			⑤		①③④	②⑤⑥	⑦	①	B		②⑦		⑤		⑤	⑦	⑤	⑦	①③	②④	⑥			
Mysore d.	...	...	...	...	...	...	0605	...	...	...	...	1600	2010	...	...	...	...	...	...	1815	...	2230	1840	...
Bangalore City d.	...	...	0440y	0600	0630y	0630y	|	1030y	1345y	1300	1430y	1900	|	2115	1700	1700	2155y	2155y	2150	2150	2150	|	2200	...
Tumkur d.	...	...	0535	0705	0732	0732	|	1120	1450	1405	1535	2020	|	2227	|	|	2305	2305	2305	2305	2305	|	|	...
Arsikere d.	...	...	0720	0835	0915	0915	0915	1315	|	1545	1700	2205	2320	0010	G	G	0050	0050	0050	0050	0050	0145	G	...
Birur d.	...	...	0810	0915	1005	1005	1005	|	|	1632	1750	2250	0005	0100	|	|	0135	0135	0135	0135	0135	0225	|	...
Harihar d.	...	...	1010	1105	1205	1205	1225	|	|	1845	|	0110	0210	0310	|	|	0330	0330	0330	0330	0330	0450	|	...
Hubli a.	...	...	1240	1325	1505	1505	1505	1930	2140	2110	2345	0350	0430	0535	0625	0625	0635	0625	0630	0630	0625	0735	1040	...

A – ③④⑥⑦. Runs as **22686** on ③⑦. B – ②③④⑥. Runs as **22685** on ③⑥. G – Via Guntakal. y – Bangalore Yesvantpur Junction.

VASCO DA GAMA - MADGAON - HUBLI — 5248

Indian Railways

km		Exp 18048 A	56962	Exp 17315 ①	56964	Exp 17312 ④	Exp 12779	56966	Exp 12741 ③	Exp 17310 ①⑥	
0	**Vasco Da Gama** d.	0710	0735	0900	1310	1430	1510	1730	1800	2045	...
28	**Madgaon** d.	0750	0815	0935	1347	1520	1550	1815	1845	2125	...
62	Kulem d.	0830	0905	1025	1500	1610	1635	1910	...	2210	...
146	Londa d.	1005	...	1205	...	1750	1855	...	...	2340	...
236	**Hubli** a.	1220	...	1430	...	2015	...	...	...	0210	...

	Exp 17309 ②⑦	Exp 17316 ③	Exp 12780	56961	Exp 12742 ①	Exp 17311 ⑥	56963	Exp 18047 B	56965	
Hubli d.	2350	2350	...	...	...	0645	...	0900	...	...
Londa d.	0145	0145	0215	...	...	0835	...	1040	...	...
Kulem d.	0415	0415	0440	0630	...	1105	1220	1300	1715	...
Madgaon d.	0520	0520	0545	0730	0900	1200	1315	1400	1810	...
Vasco Da Gama a.	0600	0600	0630	0820	0950	1300	1405	1505	1900	...

– ②④⑤⑥. B – ①③④⑥.

MUMBAI - PUNE - SECUNDERABAD, BANGALORE and CHENNAI — 5250

Indian Railways

km		Exp 11301	Exp 11017 ⑥	Exp 16331 ①	Exp 16339 A	Exp 16351 ②⑥	Exp 17222 ④⑦	Exp 17031	Exp 11073 ①	Exp 11041	Exp 11019	Exp 16381	Exp 19568 ⑤	Exp 16613 ⑦	Exp 17203 ⑥	Exp 17017 ①③④	Exp 19202 ②	Exp 12163	Exp 12701	Exp 11013	Duro 12219 ③⑥	Exp 11043 ⑤	Exp 11027	SDi 12025 ③–①
0	**Mumbai** CST d.	0805	1205t	1210	1210	1210	1225t	1245	1320t	1400	1510	1545	...	...	...	...	...	2030d	2150	2235t	2305t	0015t	2345	...
54	Kalyan d.	0900	1255	1308	1308	1308	|	1340	1408	1500	1608	1640	1945	1945	1945	1945	1945	2110	2240	2318	|	0100	0040	...
192	**Pune** d.	1145	1535	1550	1550	1550	1535	1635	1645	1810	1905	1925	2230	2230	2230	2230	2230	0010	0125	0155	0215	0358	0335	0550
263	Daund d.	1310	|	1705	1705	1705	|	1815	|	1930	2040	2055	|	2355	2355	2355	2355	|	|	|	|	0530	0510	|
456	Solapur d.	1615	1945	2025	2025	2025	1945	2225	2120	2325	0025	0055	0300	0300	0300	0300	0300	0405	0535	0635	|	0845	0940	0913
568	Gulbarga d.	1844	2155	2230	2230	2230	2155	0030	2310	0110	0233	0300	0453	0453	0453	0453	0453	0610	0720	0848	|	1055	1148	1042
605	Wadi d.	1945	2240	2320	2320	2320	2240	0135	0025	0225	0350	0420	0600	0600	0600	0600	0600	0710	0840	1000	|	1205	1255	1130
717	Vikarabad d.	|	|	|	|	|	|	0359	|	|	|	|	|	|	0820	|	|	|	1032	|	|	|	|	1245
800	**Secunderbad** a.	|	|	|	|	|	0150	0555h	|	|	0745	|	|	|	1030	1030	1030	|	1210h	|	1105	|	|	1420
713	Raichur d.	2135	0010	0050	0050	0050	...	...	0155	0400	...	0610	0720	0720	...	...	...	0835	...	1130	...	1330	1435	...
783	Adoni d.	2250	|	0230	0230	0230	...	...	0310	0510	...	0725	0840	0840	...	...	...	0950	...	1250	...	1450	1640	...
834	Guntakal d.	0010	0210	0400	0400	0400	...	...	0405	0630	...	0840	0950	0950	...	...	...	1110	...	1400	...	1630	1800	...
863	Gooty d.	0055	0240	0435	0435	0435	...	...	0445	0655	...	0910	|	1030	...	...	...	1135	...	1430	...	1702	1830	...
913	Anantapur d.	0240	|	0540	0540	|	...	...	|	|	...	|	1155	1155	...	...	...	|	...	1535	...	|	|	...
942	Dharmavaram d.	0415	|	0655	0655	|	...	...	|	|	...	|	1305	1305	...	...	...	|	...	1655	...	|	|	...
1041	Hindupur d.	0545	|	0820	0820	|	...	...	|	|	...	|	1420	1420	...	...	...	|	...	1820	...	|	|	...
1177	**Bangalore** City a.	0850	|	1028k	1028k	|	...	...	|	|	...	|	1620k	1620k	...	...	...	|	...	2150	...	|	|	...
1017	Cuddapah d.	...	0500	...	...	0720	...	...	0720	1005	...	1145	...	...	...	...	...	1400	...	...	...	1925	2135	...
1142	Renigunta d.	...	0815	...	...	1050	...	...	1015	1300	...	1435	...	...	...	...	...	1650	...	...	...	2230	0100	...
1152	**Tirupati** a.	...	|	...	...	...	...	...	|	|	...	1510	...	...	...	...	...	|	...	...	...	|	|	...
1214	Arakkonam d.	...	0920	...	...	...	...	...	1135	1430	...	...	...	...	...	...	...	1755	...	...	...	2340	0225	...
1283	**Chennai** Central a.	...	1100e	...	...	...	...	...	1310	1630	...	...	...	...	...	...	...	1945e	...	...	...	...	0425	...

		Exp 11018 ①	Exp 11028	Exp 11020	SDi 12026 ③–①	Exp 16382	Exp 12702	Exp 19201 ③	Exp 17018 ①②⑥	Exp 17204 ④	Exp 16614 ⑤	Exp 11044 ⑦	Exp 12164	Exp 19567 ①	Exp 17221 ③⑥	Duro 12220 ②⑤	Exp 17032	Exp 11042	Exp 11014	Exp 11074 ②	Exp 11302	Exp 16332 ⑥	Exp 16340 B	Exp 16352 ④⑦
Chennai Central d.	...	2215e	2250	...	...	...	...	...	...	...	...	...	0650e	...	...	...	...	1155	...	1515	...	...	...	...
Arakkonam d.	...	2343	0005	...	...	...	...	...	...	...	...	0430	|	...	...	...	...	1300	...	1620	...	...	...	...
Tirupati d.	...	|	|	...	...	0320	...	...	...	...	...	|	|	...	...	...	...	|	...	|	...	...	...	...
Renigunta d.	...	0135	0205	...	...	0350	...	...	...	...	...	0720	0925	...	...	...	...	1430	...	1810	...	...	...	2200
Cuddapah d.	...	0335	0425	...	...	0600	...	...	...	...	...	0930	1125	...	...	...	...	1640	...	2017	...	...	...	0015
Bangalore City d.	...	|	|	...	...	|	...	...	...	...	0720k	|	|	1115k	...	...	...	|	1600	|	2045	2130k	2130k	|
Hindupur d.	...	|	|	...	...	|	...	...	...	...	0930	|	|	1305	...	...	...	|	1810	|	2235	2330	2330	|
Dharmavaram d.	...	|	|	...	...	|	...	...	...	...	1145	|	|	1435	...	...	...	|	2020	|	0025	0125	0125	|
Anantapur d.	...	|	|	...	...	|	...	...	...	...	1220	|	|	1500	...	...	...	|	2055	|	0110	0215	0215	|
Gooty d.	...	0615	0800	...	...	0900	...	...	...	...	1320	1215	1355	|	...	...	...	1930	2210	2232	0250	0345	0345	0345
Guntakal d.	...	0735	0850	...	...	1015	...	...	...	...	1420	1315	1500	1715	...	...	...	2025	2245	2305	0320	0420	0420	0420
Adoni d.	...	|	0935	...	...	1120	...	...	...	...	1500	1400	1540	1802	...	...	...	2105	2325	2355	0410	0500	0500	0500
Raichur d.	...	0930	1105	...	...	1250	...	...	...	...	1610	1505	1650	1915	...	...	...	2220	0030	0105	0540	0630	0630	0630
Secunderabad d.	...	|	|	1145	1445	|	1445h	1500	1500	1500	|	|	|	|	2025	2305	2040h	|	|	|	|	|	|	|
Vikarabad d.	...	|	|	|	1541	|	1602	|	|	1619	|	|	|	|	|	|	2205	|	|	|	|	|	|	|
Wadi d.	...	1220	1500	1610	1722	1740	1805	1845	1845	1845	1845	1845	1910	2145	0035	|	0050	0145	0305	0405	0800	0905	0905	0905
Gulbarga d.	...	1255	1545	1645	1756	1813	1845	1925	1925	1925	1925	1925	1950	2230	0111	|	0130	0225	0343	0440	0845	0943	0943	0943
Solapur d.	...	1500	1820	1855	1940	2015	2100	2125	2125	2125	2125	2125	2200	0015	0310	|	0350	0440	0600	0650	1120	1150	1150	1150
Daund d.	...	|	2155	2230	|	2320	|	0030	0030	0030	0030	0030	|	|	|	|	0735	0805	0930	|	1425	1510	1510	1510
Pune d.	...	1955	2340	2350	2310	0050	0115	0205	0205	0205	0205	0205	0235	0505	0755	0757	0910	0935	1045	1200	1555	1640	1640	1640
Kalyan d.	...	2230	0230	0240	...	0325	0343	0437	0437	0437	0437	0440	0500	0747	|	|	1150	1220	1315	1505	1835	1930	1930	1930
Mumbai CST a.	...	2345t	0345	0355	...	0440	0455	...	...	...	...	0545	0600d	...	1105t	1105t	1305	1335	1430t	1620	1950	2050	2050	2050

A – ③④⑤⑦. B – ①②③⑤. d – Mumbai Dadar. e – Chennai Egmore. h – Hyderabad Decan. k – Bangalore Krishnarajapuram. t – Mumbai Lokmaniya Tilak Terminus.

HYDERABAD - SECUNDERABAD - TIRUPATI and CHENNAI — 5260

Indian Railways

km		Exp 17406	Exp 18646	Exp 17230	Exp 12839	Exp 12704	Exp 12604	Exp 12734	Exp 12764 A	Exp 12760	Exp 12710
	Hyderabad Decan d.	...	0950	1125	...	...	1650	...	...	1830	...
0	**Secunderabad** d.	0605	1020	1155	...	1555	1715	1805	1830	1855	2255
281	Guntur d.	|	|	1720	...	2030	2225	2310	|	|	|
132	Kazipet d.	0820	1240	|	...	|	|	|	2020	2055	0050
351	Vijayawada d.	1315	1630	|	2040	2125	|	|	0040	0110	0435
382*	Tenali d.	1400	...	1810	2115	...	2312	0002	0108	0138	0502
643	Gudur d.	1930	...	2225	0125	...	0320	0415	0510	0540	0920
726	Renigunta d.	2045	...	2355	|	...	|	0532	0632	|	...
736	**Tirupati** a.	2125	...	0010	|	...	|	0605	0700	|	...
793	**Chennai** Central a.	...	...	...	0345	...	0555	...	...	0815	...

	Exp 12603	Exp 12763 B	Exp 12733	Exp 12759	Exp 12709	Exp 12703	Exp 12840	Exp 17229	Exp 18645	Exp 17405
Chennai Central d.	1645	...	...	1810	...	...	2345	...	...	...
Tirupati d.	|	1700	1825	|	...	...	|	0035	...	0525
Renigunta d.	|	1717	1842	|	...	...	|	0100	...	0545
Gudur d.	1918	1857	2017	2045	2210	...	0152	0247	...	0742
Tenali d.	2317	2208	0010	0015	0137	...	0516	0644	...	1150
Vijayawada d.	|	2335	|	0120	0250	0335	0625	|	1135	1330
Kazipet d.	|	0250	|	0442	0605	|	...	|	1445	1720
Guntur d.	0015	|	0105	|	|	0430	...	0735	|	|
Secunderabad a.	0515	0550	0625	0715	0835	0935	...	1310	1800	2040
Hyderabad Decan a.	0545	...	...	0800	...	...	...	1340	1830	...

A – ①②④⑤⑦ B – ①②③⑤⑥. * – *311 km* via Guntur.

MUMBAI and PUNE - KOLKATA — 5270

Indian Railways

km		Exp 12859	Exp 12869 ⑦	Duro 12261 C	Duro 12221 ①⑥	Exp 22511 ③	Duro 12289	Exp 12101 A	Exp 12129	Exp 12809	Exp 18029
0	**Mumbai** CST d.	0600	1105	1715	...	1130t	2015	2035t	...	2035	2200t
53	Kalyan d.	0655	1200	|	...	1210	|	2118	...	2134	2250
*	**Pune** d.	|	|	|	1515	|	|	|	1825	|	|
260	Manmad d.	|	|	|	|	1620	|	|	0035	0115	0245
420	Jalgaon d.	1200	|	|	2033	|	|	|	0240	0310	0440
441	Bhusaval d.	1250	1815	2305	2255	1845	0205	0300	0330	0350	0515
584	Akola d.	1445	2010	|	|	2040	|	0450	0525	0610	0745
663	Badnera d.	1615	2205	|	|	|	|	0645	0700	0745	0945
759	Wardha d.	1722	|	|	|	|	|	|	0840	0918	1120
837	Nagpur d.	1905	0145	0415	0415	0145	0720	1000	1020	1125	1330
967	Gondia d.	2048	0323	|	|	0323	...	1138	1208	1316	1555
1101	Durg d.	2250	0525	|	|	|	...	1343	1410	1530	1835
1139	Raipur Junction d.	2335	0610	|	|	0610	...	1430	1455	1615	1935
1250	Bilaspur d.	0130	0810	1005	1005	0820	...	1625	1650	1815	2225
1454	Jharsuguda d.	0427	1107	|	|	1152	...	|	1947	2140	0200
1554	Raurkela d.	0550	1237	|	|	1325	...	2056	2117	2311	0335
1718	Tatanagar d.	0830	1500	1600	1605	1635	...	2327	2345	0140	0700
1853	Kharagpur d.	1025	1655	|	|	1930	...	0130	0147	0340	0930
1969	**Kolkata** Howrah a.	1230	1930	1940	1940	2130	...	0335	0350	0550	1225h

	Duro 12262 D	Duro 12222 ④⑥	Exp 12860	Exp 22512 ⑦	Exp 12870 ⑤	Exp 18030	Exp 12810	Exp 12130	Exp 12102 B	Duro 12290
Kolkata Howrah d.	0820	0820	1350	1435	1435	1500h	2015	2150	2250	...
Kharagpur d.	|	|	1535	1625	1620	1750	2200	2335	0035	...
Tatanagar d.	1145	1145	1732	1815	1815	2005	2352	0132	0230	...
Raurkela d.	|	|	2003	2050	2050	2310	0224	0405	0457	...
Jharsuguda d.	|	|	2143	2220	2220	0055	0400	0552	|	...
Bilaspur d.	1745	1745	0045	0125	0125	0445	0725	0915	0940	...
Raipur Junction d.	|	|	0225	0310	0310	0645	0910	1055	1130	...
Durg d.	|	|	0325	|	0410	0755	1005	1145	1225	...
Gondia d.	|	|	0515	0600	0600	1015	1200	1339	1415	...
Nagpur d.	2325	2325	0730	0830	0830	1340	1420	1550	1630	2040
Wardha d.	|	|	0835	|	|	1505	1533	1646	|	|
Badnera d.	|	|	1015	|	1125	1700	1743	1825	1910	|
Akola d.	|	|	1115	1224	1224	1805	1845	1925	2005	|
Bhusaval d.	0347	0347	1320	1425	1425	2045	2115	2130	2200	0125
Jalgaon d.	|	|	1340	|	|	2110	2140	2155	|	|
Manmad d.	|	0558	|	1630	|	2315	2340	2355	|	|
Pune a.	|	1145	|	|	|	|	|	0650	|	|
Kalyan d.	|	...	2005	2205	2205	0350	0410	...	0440	|
Mumbai CST a.	1030	...	2120	2315	2315	0450t	0520	...	0545t	0755

A – ①②⑤⑥. B – ①③④⑦. C – ②③④⑦. D – ①②③⑤. h – Kolkata Shalimar. t – Mumbai Lokmaniya Tilak Terminus. * – *314 km* from Manmad.

5280 KOLKATA - PURI, SECUNDERABAD, TIRUPATI and CHENNAI

Indian Railways

km		Exp	Exp	Exp	Duro	Exp	Exp	Duro	Exp	Exp	Exp	SDi	SDi	Exp	Exp	Duro	Exp	Exp	Exp	Exp	Exp	Exp	Exp	Exp	Exp	Exp
		12514	12510	12821	22203	12703	11020	12245	18645	22825	22849	12073	12277	12841	12663	22201	18409	12863	12881	12837	22642	12660	15228	15644	12867	1283
		⑤	A		②④⑦	K		ex①④	K	②	③	①–⑥	④–②		C	①③⑤			F		②⑦	③	①	⑤	⑦	
0	**Kolkata** Howrah d.	0105	0105	0600	...	0725	...	1100	1145	1210h	1210h	1325	1425	1450	1610	2000d	1900	2035	2055	2235	2300h	2300h	2315	2315	2330	234
116	Kharagpur d.	0300	0300	0745	...	0910	...	|	1352	1405	1405	1515	1615	1635	1800	2220	2055	2230	2250	0025	0145	0145	0145	0115	0115	013
232	Balasore d.	0427	0427	0930	...	1037	...	|	1550	1540	1540	1644	1743	1805	1927	|	2305	2357	0027	0155	0325	0325	0325	|	0242	030
409	Cuttack d.	0705	0705	1210	...	1310	...	|	1900	1815	1815	1920	1953	2045	|	|	0159	0235	0320	0435	0600	0600	0600	0515	|	053
437	Bhubaneswar d.	0755	0755	1250	...	1355	1525	1700	1950	1900	1900	2010	2040	2130	2250	|	0250	0320	0400	0520	0640	0640	0640	0600	0600	061
456	Khurda Road d.	0840	0840	1325	...	1445	1555	|	2040	1945	1945	...	|	2210	2330	|	0325	0405	0440	0555	0730	0730	0730	0640	0650	071
500	**Puri** a.	|	|	1425	...	|	|	|	|	|	|	...	2200	|	|	0400	0435	|	0550	0710	|	|	|	0740	|	|
819	Vizianagram d.	1400	1400	...	...	2005	2115	2205	0240	0120	0120	...	...	|	0435	...	...	0915	...	...	1300	1300	1300	...	1137	124
879	Visakhapatanam d.	1550	1550	...	1945	2130	2245	|	0415	0245	0245	...	...	0440	0555	...	...	1100	...	...	1430	1430	1430	...	1255	141
1081	Rajahmundry d.	1852	1855	...	|	0031	0150	|	0812	0554	0554	...	...	0733	0852	...	...	1357	...	...	1750	1750	1750	...	|	173
1259	Vijayawada d.	2155	2155	...	0044	0335	0520	0435	1135	0850	0850	...	...	1035	1155	...	...	1700	...	...	2055	2055	2055	...	1905	204
1574	**Secunderabad** a.	0420	|	...	0610	0935	1135	|	1800	|	1500	...	...	|	|	...	...	|	...	...	|	|	|	...	|	|
1637	Renigunta d.	...	|	...	...	...	...	1025	...	|	...	...	...	|	|	...	...	2305	...	...	|	0310	|	...	0105	|
1647	**Tirupati** a.	...	|	...	...	...	...	...	...	|	...	...	...	|	|	...	...	2320	...	...	|	0325	|	...	0120	|
1691	**Chennai** Central a.	...	0430	...	...	...	...	...	...	1700	...	...	...	1720	1950e	...	...	...	...	...	0355	...	0355	...	...	034

	Exp	Duro	Exp	Exp	Exp	Exp	Exp	Exp	Exp	Exp	Exp	Exp	Exp	SDi	SDi	Exp	Exp	Exp	Duro	Exp	Exp	Duro	Exp	Exp	Exp
	12664	22202	12840	12838	12864	12882	15643	18410	22850	12509	12513	11019	12842	12074	12278	12659	12507	15227	12246	18646	12704	22204	12822	22826	1286
	D	②④⑥				G	⑥		⑤	B	⑦			①–⑥	④–②	①	③	E	ex③⑥	K	K	①③⑥		④	③
Chennai Central d.	2230e	...	2345	...	...	...	...	...	...	0630	...	...	0845	...	...	...	1000	1000	...	...	...	...	...	1625	...
Tirupati d.	|	...	|	...	0235	...	...	...	...	|	...	...	|	...	...	0935	|	|	...	...	...	...	...	|	1950
Renigunta d.	|	...	|	...	0300	...	...	...	...	|	...	...	|	...	...	1000	|	|	1655	...	...	...	...	|	2015
Secunderabad d.	|	...	|	...	|	...	...	...	0530	|	0730	0800	|	...	...	|	|	|	|	1020	1555	2015	...	|	|
Vijayawada d.	0540	...	0640	...	0940	...	...	...	1125	1320	1320	1420	1525	...	...	1620	1700	1700	2235	1650	2140	0125	...	2345	0255
Rajahmundry d.	0753	...	0914	...	1205	...	...	...	1338	1529	1527	1641	1737	...	...	1845	1912	1912	|	1927	0003	|	...	0203	|
Visakhapatanam d.	1205	...	1325	...	1615	...	...	...	1750	1935	1935	2120	2210	...	...	2310	2310	2310	|	2355	0350	0635	...	0635	0850
Vizianagram d.	1304	...	1430	...	1715	...	...	...	1855	2038	2038	2220	|	...	...	0010	0010	0010	0445	0112	0455	...	...	0745	0950
Puri d.	|	1945	|	2000	|	2215	2215	2230	|	|	|	|	|	...	0545	|	|	|	|	|	|	...	1140	|	|
Khurda Road d.	1825	|	2010	2120	2230	2315	2315	2330	0045	0210	0210	0355	0415	...	|	0540	0540	0540	|	0645	1020	...	1235	1340	1500
Bhubaneswar d.	1850	|	2040	2147	2255	2340	2340	2355	0110	0235	0235	0425	0445	0600	0705	0615	0615	0615	1015	0710	1045	...	1300	1405	1525
Cuttack d.	|	|	2120	2230	2330	0025	0025	0045	0150	0315	0315	...	0525	0632	0730	0650	0650	0650	|	0745	1120	...	1335	1445	|
Balasore d.	2248	|	0014	0105	0217	0250	|	0337	0437	0622	0622	...	0806	0904	1001	0943	0943	0943	|	1143	1352	...	1621	1732	1844
Kharagpur d.	0100	0117	0152	0240	0355	0445	0445	0600	0620	0830	0830	...	0948	1050	1145	1135	1135	1135	|	1347	1530	...	1808	1930	2033
Kolkata Howrah a.	0320	0400d	0410	0450	0610	0705	0705	0810	0905h	1055	1055	...	1150	1240	1340	1350h	1355	1355	1610	1615	1745	...	2015	2130h	2240

A – ①②③④⑥. Runs as **12516** on ④. **12508** on ⑥

B – ①④⑤⑥. Runs as **12515** on ①.

C – ①④⑦. Runs as **12665** on ①.

D – ②⑤⑥. Runs as **12666** on ⑥.

E – ④⑤⑦. Runs as **22641** on ⑤⑦ but arrives Kolkata Shalimar at 1350.

F – ①②④⑤. Runs as **12887** on ①, **12895** on ⑤. Also as **22835** on ③ but departs from Kolkata Shalimar.

G – ①③④⑦. Runs as **12896** on ④, **12888** on ⑦. Also as **22836** on ② but arrives Kolkata Shalimar at 0720.

K – See Table **5260**.

d – Kolkata Sealdah.

e – Chennai Egmore.

h – Kolkata Shalimar.

5290 CHENNAI - BANGALORE - MYSORE

Indian Railways

km		Exp	Exp	SDi	Exp	Exp	Exp	Exp	Exp	Exp	Exp	Exp	Exp	Exp	SDi	Exp	Exp	Exp	Exp	Exp		Exp	Exp	Exp
		15228	12510	12007	22625	12639	12614	12552	12609	12296	17311	17313	12577	12607	12027	16209	16021	12657	12691	22682		12292	16591	1653
		③	②③④	④–②				⑤			⑤	⑦	④		③–①	②⑦			⑤	④		⑥		
0	**Chennai** Central d.	0415	0455	0600	0725	0750	...	1140	1335	1355	1345	1345	1445	1535	1730	...	2100	2315	2330	2330	...	2330	...	...
68	Arakkonam d.	0525	0600	|	0830	0855	...	|	1440	1505	1450	1450	1540	1640	|	...	2205	0015	0030	0030	...	0028	...	...
130	Katpadi d.	0625	0655	0740	0920	0955	...	1345	1545	1600	1555	1555	1630	1745	1905	...	2325	0110	0125	0120	...	|	...	...
214	Jolarpettai d.	0740	0820	|	1035	1107	...	1515	1708	1730	1745	1745	1755	1855	|	...	0042	0225	0245	0240	...	0245	...	...
350	Krishnarajapuram d.	1000	1040	|	1220	1250	...	|	1915	1935	2010	2010	|	2045	|	...	0240	|	0445	0445	...	0445	...	...
361	**Bangalore** City a.	1150y	1150z	1050	1310	1400	1500	1830y	2005	2020	2135y	2135y	2040	2135	2230	0330	0345	0510	0525	0525	...	0600y	0630	0815
506	**Mysore** a.	...	...	1300	...	...	1730	...	...	...	...	...	2330	...	...	0600	0650	...	...	0820	...	...	0915	1105

		SDi	Exp	Exp	Exp	Exp	Exp	Exp	Exp	Exp	Exp	Exp	SDi	Exp	Exp	Exp	Exp	Exp	Exp	Exp	Exp	Exp	Exp	
		12028	17312	17314	12608	12610	12251	12295	12578	12613	22626	12640	12008	16535	16210	16592	12658	12291	12692	22681	12509	16022	15227	
		③–①	⑤	⑦			⑥		⑥				④–②		②④			⑤	⑦	③	③④⑤		③	
Mysore d.	...	...	...	...	...	...	...	...	0720	1115	...	...	1415	1600	1815	1900	...	...	...	2010	...	2030	...	...
Bangalore City d.	...	0600	0530y	0530y	0630	0800	0830y	0900	1010	1345	1430	1500	1625	1850	2130	2150	2240	2245y	2300	2300	2330z	2345	2355y	...
Krishnarajapuram d.	...	|	0610	0610	0653	0823	|	0923	|	...	1453	1523	|	...	...	...	|	2323	2323	2323	2353	0010	0035	...
Jolarpettai d.	...	|	0825	0825	0845	1030	1115	1130	1230	...	1645	1715	|	...	...	...	0100	0132	0132	0132	0210	0255	0425	...
Katpadi d.	...	0900	0930	0930	0950	1150	1235	1240	1340	...	1800	1830	1925	...	...	...	0210	|	0245	0245	0320	0410	0710	...
Arakkonam d.	...	|	1025	1025	1045	1300	|	1335	1430	...	1855	1925	|	...	...	...	0300	0340	0340	0340	0410	0510	0805	...
Chennai Central a.	...	1100	1155	1155	1215	1430	1535	1515	1555	...	2030	2105	2125	...	...	...	0440	0515	0515	0515	0605	0700	0930	..

5300 CHENNAI and BANGALORE - TRIVANDRUM

Indian Railways

km		Exp	Exp	SDi	Exp	Exp	Exp	Exp	Exp	Exp	Exp	Exp	Exp	Exp	Exp	Exp	Exp	Exp	Exp	Exp	Exp	Exp	Exp	Exp	Exp
		22642	12516	12243	22619	16331	22207	15906	12697	12777	12695	16315	16381	12644	12646	12623	12257	16526	12626	22645	12511	22647	17230	16318	12660
		②④	⑤⑦A	③–①	③	②	②⑤	②	⑦	③				⑥	③		②④⑦			②	①⑤⑥	④⑦		④	⑤
0	**Chennai** Central d.	0415	0445	0715	...	...	1630	...	1515	...	1525	...	...	...	...	1945	...	...	...	2350	2350	2350	...	...	...
	Tirupati d.	|	|	|	...	...	|	...	|	...	|	...	1515	1655	1655	|	...	...	2054	|	|	|	0015	0122	0327
130	Katpadi d.	0625	0655	|	1135	...	|	1610	1705	...	1720	...	1800	1922	1922	2130	...	...	2320	0150	0150	0150	0235	0350	0542
214	Jolarpettai d.	0730	0830	|	|	...	|	1755	1820	...	1840	...	1930	|	2035	|	...	...	0035	0310	0310	0310	0400	0505	0655
	Bangalore City d.	|	|	|	|	...	|	|	|	1520y	|	1700	|	|	|	|	2100y	2000	|	|	|	|	|	|	|
	Krishanrajapuram d.	|	|	|	|	1030	|	|	|	|	|	1725	|	|	|	|	|	2024	|	|	|	|	|	|	|
	Bangarapet d.	|	|	|	|	1205	|	|	|	1640	|	1810	|	|	|	|	|	2125	|	|	|	|	|	|	|
335	Salem Junction d.	0905	0955	1125	1420	1540	2035	1940	1950	1930	2015	2115	2105	2210	2210	0010	0120	0030	0215	0445	0445	0445	0535	0640	0830
394	Erode Junction d.	1020	1120	1225	1540	1700	|	2040	2050	2030	2125	2230	2210	2320	2320	0110	0220	0130	0320	0610	0610	0610	0705	0815	0950
494	Coimbatore Junction d.	1200	1325	1415	1720	1850	2308	2235	|	|	2310	0015	2350	0120	0120	0250	0415	0315	0510	0745	0745	0745	0845	1000	1130
548	Palghat Junction d.	1310	1440	...	1830	2010	0015	2355	2330	2330	0030	0135	0115	0235	0235	0405	0535	0435	0625	0900	0900	0900	0950	1110	1240
626	Trichur d.	1430	1607	...	1948	2130	0123	0110	0040	0040	0145	0253	0240	0400	0400	0518	0655	0555	0740	1050	1050	1050	1148	1238	1353
697	Ernakulam Town d.	1605j	1735	...	2125j	2305j	0245j	0230	0205	0205	0300	0430j	0450	0545j	0600j	0655	0825	0735	0945j	1217	1217	1230	1315	1405	1525
814	Kayankulam d.	1820	1950	...	2322	0050	|	|	|	|	0510	0632	0735	0830	...	0905	1037	1005	1217	1445	1445	1445	1550	1622	1750
842	Quilon d.	1920	2045	...	0015	0150	0515	0525	0505	0505	0610	0725	0845	0920	...	1000	1125	1105	1305	1550	1550	1550	1650	1725	1845
919	**Trivandrum** Central a.	2045	2235	...	0120	0320	0645	0705	0635	0630k	0735	0900k	1005	1100	...	1145	1300k	1244	1435	1715	1715	1715	1820	1845	2000
	Nagercoil a.	...	...	...	0243	...	...	0922	...	...	...	...	1152	...	...	...	...	1430	...	...	...	...	...	2047	2150

km		Exp	Exp	Exp	SDi	Exp	Exp	Exp	Exp	Exp	Exp	Exp	Exp	Exp	Exp	Exp	Exp	Exp	Exp	Exp	Exp	Exp	Exp	Exp	Exp
		15905	22620	16332	12244	22646	22648	17229	16382	12625	12778	12515	16525	12645	12643	12624	16316	16317	12659	22641	12258	12507	12696	22208	12698
		④	⑦	⑥	③–①	B	①④				④	⑦		⑥	②		②④⑥	⑤	⑦	④⑥	①③⑤	②		③⑦	⑥
72	Nagercoil d.	2320	0225	...	...	...	...	...	0715	...	...	...	1050	...	...	...	...	1435	1440	...	...	...	...	...	...
0	**Trivandrum** Central d.	0045	0425	0425	...	0610	0610	0715	0855	1115	1250k	1240	1245	...	1415	1450	1645k	1600	1600	1700	1700k	1700	1715	2130	2020
77	Quilon d.	0145	0525	0525	...	0710	0710	0820	1005	1215	1340	1340	1405	...	1500	1550	1740	1705	1705	1758	1758	1758	1815	2225	2115
105	Kayankulam d.	|	0602	0602	...	0745	0745	0900	1044	1257	|	1410	1450	...	1547	1630	1816	1736	1736	1836	1836	1836	1853	|	|
222	Ernakulam Town d.	0530	0815j	0815j	...	1015j	1020	1155	1325	1545j	1655	1705	1805	1900j	1850j	1930	2030j	2040	2040	2055j	2110	2110	2135	0040j	0020
293	Trichur d.	0640	0940	0940	...	1145	1145	1303	1455	1703	1800	1805	1908	2003	2003	2045	2155	2205	2205	2220	2220	2220	2303	0205	0133
371	Palghat Junction d.	0815	1215	1215	...	1405	1405	1520	1650	1845	1945	2005	2120	2145	2145	2225	2330	2355	2355	2355	0015	2355	0045	0315	0330
425	Coimbatore Junction d.	0935	1335	1335	1520	1525	1525	1635	1805	2000	|	2130	2255	2320	2320	2350	0100	0125	0125	0125	0140	0125	0210	0443	|
525	Erode Junction d.	1110	1520	1520	1645	1715	1715	1830	2000	2200	2250	2315	0040	0055	0055	0120	0245	0330	0315	0305	0315	0305	0350	|	0600
584	Salem Junction d.	1210	1615	1615	1746	1810	1810	1930	2100	2300	2345	0010	0140	0155	0155	0220	0340	0430	0415	0400	0415	0400	0450	0720	0655
	Bangarapet d.	|	|	1950	|	|	|	|	|	|	0235	|	0510	|	|	|	0635	|	|	|	|	|	|	|	|
	Krishnarajapuram d.	|	|	2120	|	|	|	|	|	|	|	|	0620	|	|	|	0735	|	|	|	|	|	|	|	|
853	**Bangalore** City a.	|	|	...	|	|	|	|	|	|	0430y	|	0720	|	|	|	0835	|	|	|	0930y	|	|	|	|
705	Jolarpettai d.	1355	|	...	|	1950	1950	2120	2320	0045	...	0155	...	0345	|	|	...	0610	0605	0550	...	0550	0635	|	0850
789	Katpadi d.	1503	1903	...	|	2055	2055	2240	0050	0202	...	0320	...	0530	0530	0500	...	0725	0725	0710	...	0710	0745	|	1000
912	**Tirupati** a.	...	...	...	|	|	|	0030	0315	0355	...	|	...	0730	0730	|	...	0933	0933	|	...	|	|	|	|
919	**Chennai** Central a.	...	...	...	2215	2305	2305	...	...	...	...	0605	...	...	...	0730	...	...	...	0930	...	0930	1000	1150	1225

Notes for Tables **5290** and **5300**

A – ⑤⑦. Runs as **12516** on ⑤ and as **12508** on ⑦.

B – ②③⑥⑦. Runs as **12512** on ②③⑦ and as **22646** on ⑥.

j – Ernakulam Junction.

k – Trivandrum Kochuveli.

y – Bangalore Yesvantpur Junction.

z – Bangalore Cantonment.

ndian Railways — CHENNAI - SENGOTTAI, TUTICORIN, TIRUCHENDER and NAGERCOIL — 5310

km		Exp 12688 ③⑦	56768 2	Exp 16127	56735 2	Exp 12635	Exp 12633	Exp 16612	Exp 16105	Exp 12667 ④	Exp 12642 ②⑦	Exp 12652 ③⑤	56761 2	Exp 12693	Exp 16723	Exp 12631	Exp 12661	Exp 12637	Exp 12665 ②	56763 2	Duro 22205 ①③	56731 2	56767 2	Exp 16236	Exp 22623 ⑤⑦	56733 2
0	**Chennai** Egmore ... d.	0240	...	0740	...	1320	1730	...	1605	1850	1830	1830	...	1915	1935	2010	2055	2120	2020	...	2230**c**	...	...	...	2245	...
56	Chengalpattu ... d.	|	...	0840	...	1420	1830	...	1705	1945	1930	1930	...	2015	2035	2110	2155	2220	2120	...	|	...	...	...	2340	...
59	Villupuram ... d.	**A**	...	1035	...	1550	2015	...	1905	2115	2120	2120	...	2205	2225	2240	2330	2345	2255	...	**C**	...	...	...	0120	...
214	Vriddhachalam Jct ... d.	|	...	1112	...	1630	2057	...	|	2207	2207	2207	...	2247	2312	2322	0012	0027	2337	...	|	...	...	...	|	...
340	Tiruchchirappalli Jct ... d.	|	...	1315	...	1835	2255	...	1953	0035	0035	0035	...	0055	0200	0210	0240	0305	0320	...	|	...	...	...	0600	...
433	Dindigul ... d.	1115	...	1445	...	2005	0035	0100	0200	0215	0215	0215	...	0235	0347	0330	0410	0435	0440	...	|	...	...	0615	0730	...
95*	Madurai Junction ... d.	1245	...	1615	1715	2125	0155	0205	0300	0325	0325	0345	...	0345	0500	0435	0530	0615	0635	...	0710	0715	...	0725	0850	1125
538	Virudunagar ... d.	▬	...	1655	1800	▬	0240	0250	0342	0412	0412	...	...	0430	0540	0515	0617	▬	0717	...	...	0802	...	0807	...	1220
562	Tenkasi ... d.	**56765**	...	|	1957	**56741**	|	|	|	|	|	...	...	|	|	|	0817	**56742**	|	...	...	1010	...	|	...	1430
570	**Sengottai** ... a.	2	...	|	2050	2	|	|	|	|	|	...	...	|	|	|	0905	2	|	...	...	1045	...	|	...	1500
623	Vanchi Maniyachchi ... d.	...	1720	1840	...	1905	|	0510	0510	|	0530	...	...	0601	0700	|	...	0820	0846	...	...	...	1000	1000	...	...
656	**Tuticorin** ... a.	...	1845	|	...	|	|	0610	|	|	|	...	...	0710	|	|	...	0925	|	...	...	...	|	1115	...	...
652	Tirunelveli Junction ... d.	1840	...	1935	...	2040	0455	...	0620	0630	0630	...	0720	...	0825	0800	...	...	0940	0935	...	...	1115	...	...	...
714	**Tiruchender** ... a.	2040	...	|	...	...	|	...	0825	|	|	...	0910	...	|	...	...	...	|	1105	...	...	1310	...	...	...
726	**Nagercoil** Junction ... a.	...	...	2130	...	...	0615	...	...	0805	0811	...	...	...	1000	...	...	...	1055	...	...	...	...	...	...	...

	56734 2	56736 2	56768 2	Exp 16235	56741 2	56764 2	Exp 12668 ⑤	Exp 12662	Exp 12634	Exp 12632	Duro 22206 ②④	56766	Exp 12694	Exp 16724	Exp 12641 ③⑤	Exp 12651 ②⑦	Exp 12687 ③⑦	Exp 16106	Exp 16611	Exp 12636	56732 2	Exp 16128	56742 2	56767 2	56762 2	Exp 12666 ⑥
Nagercoil Junction ... d.	...	...	...	...	...	...	1705	...	1740	...	...	...	...	1755	1940	...	...	...	...	...	...	0525	...	...	...	0815
Tiruchender ... d.	...	...	1435	...	...	1630	|	...	|	...	...	1755	...	|	|	...	...	1850	...	...	...	|	...	...	0705	|
Tirunelveli Junction ... d.	...	...	1620	...	...	1810	1820	...	1905	1925	...	1940	...	1950	2115	...	...	2040	...	...	...	0745	0720	...	0855	0940
Tuticorin ... d.	...	...	|	1635	1750	...	|	...	|	|	...	▬	1950	|	|	...	...	|	2130	...	...	|	|	0845	...	|
Vanchi Maniyachchi ... d.	...	...	1719	1713	1850	...	|	...	|	|	...	*Exp*	2023	2035	2141	...	...	2105	2230	...	...	0835	0818	0950	...	1015
Sengottai ... d.	1200	1550	...	|	▬	...	|	1830	|	|	...	**22624**	|	|	|	...	...	|	|	...	0700	|	...	...	...	|
Tenkasi ... d.	1215	1604	...	|	*Exp*	...	|	1845	|	|	...	④⑥	|	|	|	...	...	|	|	...	0713	|	...	...	...	|
Virudunagar ... d.	1430	1807	...	1835	**12638**	...	2017	2042	2105	2120	...		2145	2200	2307	...	...	2222	0005	...	0925	1000	...	...	...	1135
Madurai Junction ... d.	1545	1935	...	1950	2035	...	2115	2130	2150	2210	2245	2115	2250	2305	0015	0015	2335	2345	0105	0700	1045	1115	...	...	...	1250
Dindigul ... d.	...	...	...	2115	2140	...	2212	2235	2252	2315	|	2212	2350	0010	0112	0112	0035	0117	0220	0755	...	1218	...	...	...	1350
Tiruchchirappalli Jct ... d.	...	...	...	...	2310	...	2355	0020	0035	0105	|	2350	0130	0200	0300	0300	|	0330	...	0900	...	1410	...	...	...	1600
Vriddhachalam Jct ... d.	...	...	...	...	0104	...	0155	0215	0235	0245	**D**	|	0320	0350	0450	0450	**B**	|	...	1045	...	1620	...	...	...	1755
Villupuram ... d.	...	...	...	...	0220	...	0302	0325	0335	0355	|	0410	0425	0510	0550	0550	|	0825	...	1142	...	1720	...	...	...	1855
Chengalpattu ... d.	...	...	...	...	0355	...	0435	0455	0515	0540	|	0600	0610	0710	0730	0730	|	1010	...	1320	...	1910	...	...	...	2040
Chennai Egmore ... a.	...	...	...	...	0535	...	0605	0640	0650	0710	0720**c**	0720	0745	0840	0850	0850	0920**c**	1125	...	1440	...	2115	...	...	...	2210

– Via Katpadi (d. 0440), Salem (d. 0730) and Erode (d. 0850).
– Via Erode (d.0305), Salem (d. 0400) and Katpadi (d. 0705).
C – Via Salem d. 0305.
D – Via Salem d. 0230.
c – Chennai Central.
* – *596 km* via Salem.

ndian Railways — HILL and MOUNTAIN RAILWAYS — 5320

DARJEELING HIMALAYAN RAILWAY

km	¶	52541 ①③⑤	52587	52546	52548 🚂	52574	52575	52571 🚂 ②④⑦	52547 🚂		52559 🚂
0	**New Jalpaiguri** Jct ... d.	0830	...	...	...	...	...	...	...	...	...
8	Siliguri Junction ... d.	0900	...	...	...	...	...	...	...	...	1030
18	Sukna ... d.	0932	...	...	...	...	...	...	...	...	1120
26	Rangtong ... d.	1005	...	...	...	...	...	...	...	...	1150
32	Chunbhati ... d.	|	...	...	...	...	...	...	...	...	...
38	Tindharia ... d.	1112	...	...	...	...	...	...	...	...	...
50	Mahanadi ... d.	1214	...	...	...	...	...	...	...	...	...
57	Kurseong ... d.	1255	0700	...	...	...	...	1400	...	...	...
65	Tung ... d.	1326	0734	...	...	...	...	1445	...	...	...
73	Sonada ... d.	1405	0815	...	...	...	...	1550	...	...	...
82	Ghum ... d.	1455	0900	0920	1200	1220	1450	1655	1725	...	...
88	**Darjeeling** ... a.	1535	0935	1000	1240	1300	1530	1745	1805	...	...

¶	52546	52570 🚂 ②④⑥		52540 ②④⑥	52548 🚂	52574	52575		52588	52547 🚂
Darjeeling ... d.	0800	0910	...	1015	1040	1100	1330	...	1600	1605
Ghum ... d.	0850	1015	...	1050	1130	1150	1420	...	1635	1655
Sonada ... d.	...	1105	...	1131	...	...	...	...	1717	...
Tung ... d.	...	1205	...	1210	...	...	...	...	1758	...
Kurseong ... d.	...	1245	...	1250	...	...	...	...	1830	...
Mahanadi ... d.	...	...	...	1321	...	...	...	...	▬	...
Tindharia ... d.	...	...	...	1423	...	...	...	...	**52559**	...
Chunbhati ... d.	...	...	...	|	...	...	...	...	🚂	...
Rangtong ... d.	...	...	...	1534	...	...	...	...	1220	...
Sukna ... d.	...	...	...	1606	...	...	...	...	1255	...
Siliguri Junction ... d.	...	...	...	1645	...	...	...	...	1335	...
New Jalpaiguri Jct ... a.	...	...	...	1715	...	...	...	...	...	...

KANGRA VALLEY RAILWAY

km		52464 2	52466 2	18102	52472 2	14034	52468 2	52474 2	14036 ②④⑥	52470 2
0	**Joginder Nagar** ... d.	...	...	...	0720	...	...	1220	...	...
23	Baijnath Paprola ... d.	0400	0720	...	1050	...	1410	1555	...	1735
37	Palampur Himachal ... d.	0438	0800	...	1130	...	1451	1641	...	1813
66	Kangra Mandir ... d.	0550	0946	...	1246	...	1605	1756	...	1946
164	**Pathankot Junction** ... a.	1050	1420	...	1730	...	2025	2235	...	2355
164	Pathankot Junction ... ‡ d.	...	...	1645	...	1905	...	...	2320	...
653	Delhi Junction ... ‡ a.	...	...	0430	...	0545	...	...	1025	...

	52471 2	52463 2	14033	56465 2	14035 ①③⑤	52473 2	18101	52467 2	52469 2
Delhi Junction ... ‡ d.	...	...	2010	...	2245	...	2200	...	...
Pathankot Junction ... ‡ d.	...	...	0610	...	0820	...	1100	...	...
Pathankot Junction ... d.	0215	0400	...	0645	...	1000	...	1320	1550
Kangra Mandir ... d.	0647	0843	...	1110	...	1503	...	1858	2032
Palampur Himachal ... d.	0806	1001	...	1310	...	1634	...	2014	2139
Baijnath Paprola ... d.	0950	1045	...	1400	...	1805	...	2055	2230
Joginder Nagar ... a.	1125	...	...	...	...	1945	...	...	...

MATHERAN HILL RAILWAY

km		96003 2	52111	52101	11007	52103	11029	95107 2	92105	95119 2	52109
90	Mumbai CST ... ♥ d.	0424	...	...	0700	...	0840	0908	...	1454	...
0	Neral ... ♥ a.	0625	...	...	0825	...	1004	1040	...	1626	...
0	**Neral** ... ♣ d.	...	0640	0750	...	0910	...	...	1040	...	1705
21	**Matheran** ... ♣ a.	...	0840	0950	...	1120	...	...	1235	...	1900

	52102	11024	52104	95122 2	52106	95128 2	52108	95130	52110	95134
Matheran ... ♣ d.	0720	...	0955	...	1250	...	1515	...	1630	...
Neral ... ♣ a.	0855	...	1140	...	1425	...	1655	...	1810	...
Neral ... ♥ d.	...	1000	...	1217	...	1543	...	1627	...	1858
Mumbai CST ... ♥ a.	...	1150	...	1354	...	1721	...	1803	...	2045

NILGIRI MOUNTAIN RAILWAY

km		56141	12671	56136		56143		56138		
0	Chennai Central ... ‡ d.	...	2115	...	...	...	...	...	...	...
530	Mettupalaiyam ... ‡ a.	...	0615	...	...	...	...	...	...	...
0	**Mettupalaiyam** ... d.	...	...	0710	...	...	...	...	...	...
28	Coonor ... d.	0745	...	1040	...	1235	...	1630	...	...
46	**Udagamandalam** (Ooty) ... a.	0905	...	1200	...	1350	...	1745	...	...

	56139	56142	56137	12672	56140				
Udagamandalam (Ooty) ... d.	0915	1215	1400	...	1800	...	...	...	...
Coonor ... d.	1025	1320	1515	...	1910	...	...	...	...
Mettupalaiyam ... a.	...	...	1735	...	...	...	...	...	...
Mettupalaiyam ... ‡ d.	...	...	...	1945	...	...	...	...	...
Chennai Central ... ‡ a.	...	...	...	0505	...	...	...	...	...

– By main-line train (*Exp*).
– Services normally suspended during Monsoon season.
– By main-line train. Frequent additional trains (2 cl. only) are available. Journey 1½ – 2 hours.
¶ – For up-to-date information see www.dhrs.org

ndian/Pakistan Rlys — LAHORE - DELHI — 5400

km		402 ①④	Exp 14002 ①④
0	**Lahore** Jct ... d.	0800	...
	Wagah ... a.	0835	...
	Wagah ... d.	1130	...
20	Atari 🛃 ... a.	1150	...
20	Atari 🛃 ... d.	...	2000
46	**Delhi** Junction ... a.	...	0320

	Exp 14001 ③⑥	401 ①④
Delhi Junction ... d.	2305	...
Atari 🛃 ... a.	0715	...
Atari 🛃 ... d.	...	1100
Wagah ... a.	...	1410
Wagah ... d.	...	1610
Lahore Jct ... a.	...	1645

OTE: Timings are subject to confirmation and connections are not guaranteed.

Bangladesh/Indian Rlys — KOLKATA - DHAKA — 5450

km		Exp 13108 ①⑥	Exp 13109 ②
0	**Kolkata** Chitpur ... d.	0710	0710
122	Gede ... a.	0925	0925
122	Gede ... d.	1055	1055
	Darsana 🛃 ... a.	1105	1105
540	**Dhaka** Cantonment ... a.	1735	1735

	Exp 13107 ⑤⑦	Exp 13110 ③
Dhaka Cantonment ... d.	0740	0740
Darsana 🛃 ... d.	1420	1350
Gede ... a.	1430	1400
Gede ... d.	1600	1600
Kolkata Chitpur ... a.	1810	1810

NOTE: Timings are subject to confirmation.

BEYOND EUROPE
South East Asia, Australia and New Zealand

Introduction

The Beyond Europe section covers principal rail services in a different area of the world each month. There are six areas, each appearing as follows:

Winter (December) and Summer (June): all the latest Beyond Europe pages will be included.

January and July (digital only): India.

February and August: India; South East Asia, Australia and New Zealand; North America.

March and September (digital only): China.

April and October: China; Japan; South America; South Korea.

May and November (digital only): North America.

The months have been chosen so that we can bring you up-to-date information for those countries which make seasonal changes.

Contents

INDEX OF PLACES

by table number

A
Adelaide, 6390, 6395, 6400
Albury, 6355, 6365
Alexandra, 6510
Alice Springs, 6320, 6400
Almaden, 6310
Alor Setar, 6000
Alpha, 6330
Aranyaprathet, 6050
Ararat, 6385, 6395
Arau, 6000
Armadale, 6410
Armidale, 6345
Arthur's Pass, 6505
Ashburton, 6510
Atherton, 6325
Auckland, 6500
Aungban, 6160
Ayr, 6330
Ayutthaya, 6060, 6065

B
Bacchus Marsh, 6385
Bagan, 6165
Bago, 6165, 6170
Bahau, 6010
Bairnsdale, 6375
Ballan, 6385
Ballarat, 6385
Bandung, 6205, 6220
Bangkok, 6000, 6020, 6050, 6055, 6060, 6065, 6070, 6075
Bang Pa In, 6060
Bang Saphan Yai, 6055
Banjar, 6220
Ban Plu Ta Luang, 6050
Banyuwangi Baru, 6215
Barcaldine, 6330
Barkly Homestead, 6320
Barrow Creek, 6320
Bathurst, 6340
Beaufort, 6015
Beijing, 6100
Benalla, 6355, 6365
Bendigo, 6380
Blackbull, 6305
Blayney, 6340
Blenheim, 6505
Blitar, 6215, 6220
Bojonegoro, 6210
Bowen, 6330
Broadmeadow, 6345
Brisbane, 6330, 6335, 6345
Broken Hill, 6340, 6390
Brunner, 6505
Brunswick, 6410
Bua Yai, 6065
Bukit Mertajam, 6000
Bunbury, 6410
Bundaberg, 6330
Buri Ram, 6065
Butterworth, 6000,

C
Cairns, 6300, 6310, 6325, 6330
Camooweal, 6320
Canberra, 6355
Cardwell, 6330
Casino, 6345
Castlemaine, 6380
Cepu, 6210
Chachoengsao, 6050

Changsha, 6100
Charleville, 6335
Charters Towers, 6315, 6320
Chiang Mai, 6060
Christchurch, 6505, 6510
Chumphon, 6055
Cirebon, 6210, 6215
Cloncurry, 6315, 6320
Coffs Harbour, 6345
Colac, 6370
Condoblin, 6340
Cook, 6390
Cooladdi, 6335
Coonamia, 6400
Cooroy, 6330
Cootamundra, 6355
Cromwell, 6510
Croydon, 6305, 6325
Crystal Brook, 6400
Culcairn, 6355
Cunnamulla, 6335

D
Dabong, 6010
Dalby, 6335
Da Nang, 6115
Dandenong, 6375
Darwin, 6400
Dawei Port, 6170
Den Chai, 6060
Điêu Trị, 6115
Dimboola, 6395
Dong Dang, 6100
Đông Hới, 6115
Dubbo, 6340
Duchess, 6315
Dunedin, 6510

E
Echuca, 6380
Einasleigh, 6310
Emerald, 6330
Esperance, 6415

F
Fairlie, 6510
Forsayth, 6310
Fox Glacier, 6510
Franz Josef, 6510
Freshwater, 6300

G
Geelong, 6370, 6395
Gemas, 6000, 6001, 6010
Georgetown, 6325
Geraldine, 6510
Gladstone, 6330
Gokteik, 6155
Gordonvale, 6330
Gosford, 6345, 6350
Goulburn, 6355
Grafton City, 6345
Greymouth, 6505, 6510
Griffith, 6355
Gua Masang, 6010
Guilin, 6100
Gunnedah, 6345
Gympie, 6330

H
Haast, 6510
Hai Phòng, 6110
Hamilton (Aus.), 6350
Hamilton (NZ), 6500
Hà Nội, 6100, 6105, 6110, 6115
Hai Duong, 6110
Harden, 6355
Harvey, 6410
Hat Yai, 6000, 6055
Heho, 6160
Herberton, 6325
Ho Chi Minh, see Sai Gòn
Hokitika, 6510
Home Hill, 6330
Hornsby, 6345
Horsham, 6395
Hsipaw, 6155
Hua Hin, 6055
Hua Takhe, 6050
Huế, 6115
Hughenden, 6315, 6320

I
Ingham, 6330
Innisfail, 6330
Ipoh, 6000
Ipswich, 6335
Ivanhoe, 6340

J
Jakarta, 6205, 6210, 6215
Jerantut, 6010
Jericho, 6330
Johor Baru, 6001
Jombang, 6215, 6220
Julia Creek, 6315, 6320
Junee, 6355

K
Kabin Buri, 6050
Kaeng Khoi, 6065
Kalaw, 6160
Kaikoura, 6505
Kalgoorlie, 6390, 6405, 6415
Kampar, 6000
Kampot, 6090
Kanchanaburi, 6020, 6070
Kantang, 6055
Karumba, 6325
Katherine, 6400
Katoomba, 6340
Kawlin, 6150
Kediri, 6210, 6215
Kellerberrin, 6405
Kempsey, 6345
Kemubu, 6010
Kerang, 6380
Kertosono, 6210, 6220
Khon Kaen, 6065
Khun Tan, 6060
Kluang, 6001
Kota Kinabalu, see Tanjong Aru
Krai, 6010
Kroya, 6215, 6220
Kuala Kangsar, 6000, 6020
Kuala Lipis, 6010
Kuala Lumpur, 6000, 6020
Kulai, 6001
Kuranda, 6300, 6310, 6325

Kutoarjo, 6215, 6220
Kyaikto, 6170
Kyaukme, 6155
Kyneton, 6380

L
Lamphun, 6060
Lào Cai, 6105
Lashio, 6155
Levin, 6500
Lithgow, 6340
Long Reach, 6330
Lop Buri, 6060
Lubuk Linggau, 6200

M
Madiun, 6210, 6215, 6220
Mackay, 633
Macksville, 6345
Maitland, 6345
Makkasan, 6050
Malang, 6210, 6215, 6220
Mandalay, 6150, 6155, 6160, 6165
Mareeba, 6310, 6325
Maria, 6400
Maryborough QLD, 6330
Maryborough VIC, 6385
Mawlamyine, 6170
Medan, 6200
Melbourne, 6355, 6360, 6365, 6370, 6375, 6380, 6385, 6395
Melton, 6385
Menindee, 6340
Mentakab, 6010
Merak, 6215
Merredin, 6405
Midland, 6405
Miles, 6335
Milton, 6510
Mitchell, 6335
Moana, 6505
Moe, 6375
Moree, 6345
Morwell, 6375
Morven, 6335
Moss Vale, 6355
Mount Cook, 6510
Mount Garnet, 6325
Mount Isa, 6315, 6320
Mount Suprise, 6310, 6325
Mount Victoria, 6343
Murray Bridge, 6395
Murchison, 6360
Muswellbrook, 6345
Myitkyina, 6150

N
Nakhon Lampang, 6060
Nakhon Pathom, 6055, 6070
Nakhon Ratchasima, 6065
Nakhon Sawan, 6060
Nakhon Si Thammarat, 6055
Nambour, 6330
Nambucca Heads, 6345
Nam Dinh, 6115
Nam Tok, 6070
Nanning, 6100
Narrabri, 6345
Narrandera, 6355
National Park, 6500

Naypyitaw, 6165
Newcastle, 6350
Newcastle Waters, 6400
Nha Trang, 6115
Nhill, 6395
Ninh Binh, 6115
Nong Khai, 6065
Nong Pla Duk, 6070
Normanton, 6305, 6325
Norseman, 6415
Northam, 6405

O
Oamaru, 6510
Ohakune, 6500
Orange, 6340
Otira, 6505
Otorohanga, 6500

P
Padang, 6200
Padang Besar, 6000
Pak Chong, 6065
Palembang, 6200
Palmerston North, 6500
Paloh, 6001
Panjang, 6200
Papakura, 6500
Papar, 6015
Paraparaumu, 6500
Pariaman, 6200
Paringa, 6510
Parkes, 6340
Pasir Mas, 6010
Pattani, 6055
Pattaya, 6050
Pekalongan, 6210
Pematangsiantar, 6200
Penrith, 6340
Perth, 6390, 6405, 6410
Phattalung, 6055
Phitsanulok, 6060
Phnom Penh, 6090
Phô Lu, 6105
Phun Phin, 6055
Phú Thái, 6110
Picton, 6505
Pingxiang, 6100
Pinjarra, 6410
Port Augusta, 6400
Port Pirie, 6400
Prachin Buri, 6050
Prosperine, 6330
Purwokerto, 6215
Pyay, 6165, 6175
Pyin Oo Lwin, 6155

Q
Quang Ngai, 6115
Queanbeyan, 6355
Queenstown, 6510
Quilpie, 6335

R
Rangiora, 6505
Rantau Prapat, 6200
Rachaburi, 6055
Ravenshoe, 6325
Rawlinna, 6390
Richmond, 6315, 6320
River Kwae Bridge, 6070
Rochester, 6380
Rockhampton, 6330

Roma, 6335
Roxburgh, 6510

St / Ste / S.
St Lawrence, 6330

S
Sagaing, 6150
Saï Gòn, 6115
Sale, 6375
Saraburi, 6065
Sarina, 6330
Savarnabhumi International Aiport, 6075 (also see Hua Takhe).
Scone, 6345
Segamat, 6001
Semarang, 6210
Seremban, 6000
Seymour, 6360, 6365
Shepparton, 6360
Shwebo, 6150
Shwenyaung, 6160
Sikanoukville, 6090
Sila At, 6060
Singapore, see Woodlands
Si Racha, 6050
Si Sa Ket, 6065
Snowtown, 6400
Solo, 6215, 6220
Southern Cross, 6405
Springfield, 6505
Sunbury, 6380
Sungai Kolok, 6055
Surabaja, 6210, 6215, 6220
Surat Thani, 6055
Surin, 6065
Swan Hill, 6380
Sydney, 6340, 6345, 6350, 6355, 6390

T
Taiping, 6000, 6001
Takeo, 6090
Tampin, 6000
Tamworth, 6345
Tanah Merah, 6010
Tanjong Aru, 6015
Tanjong Balai, 6200
Tanjong Malim, 6000
Tanjungkarang Telukbetang, see Panjang.
Tapah Road, 6000
Tapan Hln, 6060
Taree, 6345
Tasikmalaya, 6220
Taungoo, 6165
Tegal, 6210
Tennant Creek, 6320, 6400
Tenom, 6015
Tha Na Laeng, 6065
Thanh Hóa, 6115
Thazi, 6160, 6165
The Rock, 6355
Thung Song, 6055
Timaru, 6510
Toowoomba, 6335
Townsville, 6315, 6320, 6330
Trang, 6055
Traralgon, 6375
Tully, 6330
Tumpat, 6010

U
Ubon Ratchathani, 6065
Udon Thani, 6065
Undara, 6325
Uttaradit, 6060

V
Vinh, 6115

W
Wagga Wagga, 6355
Waipara, 6505
Wakaf Bharu, 6010
Wanaka, 6510
Wangaratta, 6355, 6365
Wang Po, 6020
Waroona, 6410
Warragul, 6375
Warrnambool, 6370
Wauchope, 6345
Wellington, 6500, 6505
Werris Creek, 6345
Wickham, 6350
Wodonga, 6365
Woodend, 6380
Woodlands, 6001, 6020
Wuhan, 6100
Wyandra, 6335

Y
Yala, 6055
Yaksauk, 6160
Yangon, 6165, 6170, 6175
Yass, 6355
Ye, 6170
Yên Bái, 6105
Yogyakarta, 6215, 6220

Z
Zhengzhou, 6100

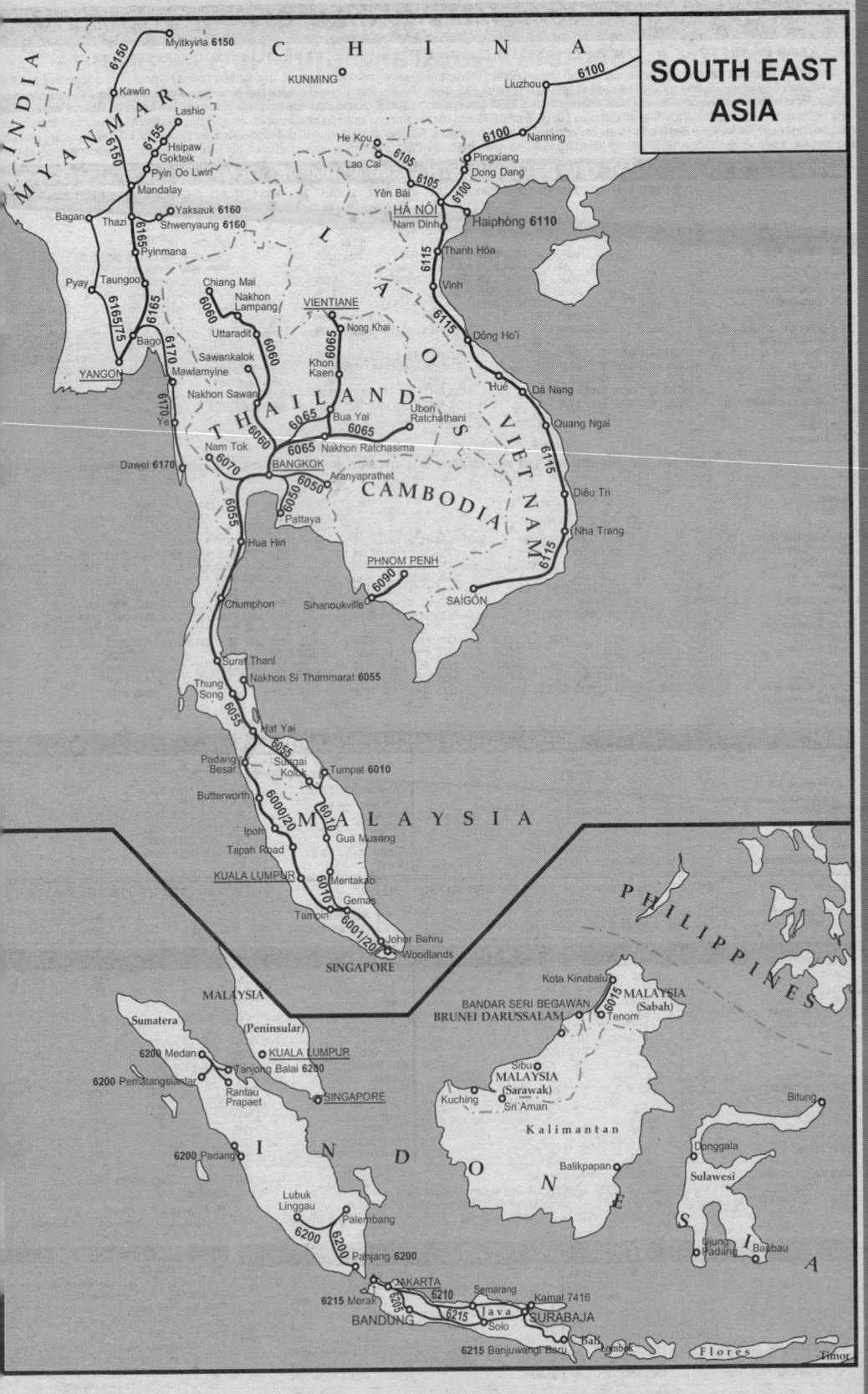

SOUTH EAST ASIA

BEYOND EUROPE - SOUTH EAST ASIA, AUSTRALIA and NEW ZEALAND

MALAYSIA

Capital: **Kuala Lumpur** (GMT +8). 2017 Public Holidays: Feb. 8, 9, May 1, 21, June 4, July 6, 7, 8, Aug. 31, Sept. 12, 13, 16, Oct. 2, 29, Dec. 12, 25.

Rail services in Malaysia are operated by Keretapi Tanah Melayu Berhad (Malayan Railways, www.ktmb.com.my), a government owned agency. Trains numbered **9XXX** a *Electric Train Service – ETS* and convey one class of seating only either ETS Silver, Gold or Platinum and a buffet car, all are air-conditioned. Trains **29XX** are classed Commuter service and use air-conditioned EMUs. Overnight trains **26/27** convey air-conditioned second class and thirdclass seating (known locally as Superior and Econom and air-conditioned couchettes which have 40 curtained bunks. Train **35/36** also convey air conditioned couchettes which have 40 curtained bunks. All non *ETS* trains conv second class only. The Malaysia Rail Pass offers unlimited travel on Intercity services. Reservations are required and supplements are payable for the use of sleeping car bert on overnight trains. Prices: 5 days US$35.00, 10 days US$55.00, 15 days US$70.00. Child fares approximately half price. For full information go to www.ktmintercity.com.m

6000 HAT YAI - BUTTERWORTH - KUALA LUMPUR - GEMAS

Keretapi Tanah Melayu Berha

km		9301	9231	9303	9235	2941	9201	2945	2949	9203	947	9213	9247	35	2957	2961	9233	9237	949	2967	9209	9215	2977	9221	9249	9217	29
		R	R	R	R	2	R	2	2	R	2	R	R	R	2	2	R	R	2	2	R	R	2	R	R	R	2
						A							⑤–⑦	♦											⑤–⑦		
	Bangkok **6055** d.	...	...	...	...	...	...	...	...	...	...	...	...	1445t	...	...	...	...	...	...	...	...	...	...	...	...	...
0	**Hat Yai** Junction d.	...	...	...	...	...	...	...	...	...	0730t	...	...	0700t	...	...	...	...	1305t	...	...	...	...	...	...	...	...
45	Padang Besar 🏛 d.	...	...	...	...	0525	...	0625	0725	0745	0925	0930	...	0855	1025	1225	...	...	1500	1525	1615	1715	1825	2000	...	...	222
76	Arau d.	...	...	...	...	0544	...	0644	0744	0801	...	0946	...	...	1044	1244	...	...	▬	1544	1631	1733	1844	2016	...	...	224
114	Alor Setar d.	...	...	...	...	0608	...	0708	0808	0819	...	1004	...	...	1108	1308	...	...		1608	1648	1755	1908	2034	...	...	230
205	Bukit Mertajam d.	...	...	...	...	0705	...	0805	0905	|	...	|	...	...	1205	1405	...	...	...	1705	1735	1849	2005	|	...	...	000
216	**Butterworth** d.	...	0500	...	0630	0716	0745	0816	0916	|	...	|	1155	...	1216	1416	1455	1600	...	1716	1758	1908	2016	|	2200	2250	00
227	Bukit Mertajam d.	...	0509	...	0639	▬	0755	...	...	|	▬	|	1204	▬	▬	...	1504	1609	...	...	1807	1918	...	|	2209	2259	...
312	Taiping d.	...	0550	...	0724	**9305**	0841	...	...	0945	**9401**	1129	1245	**9307**	**9309**	...	1549	1654	**9311**	...	1852	2005	...	2202	2254	2340	...
344	Kuala Kangsar d.	...	|	...	|	R	0857	...	...	1002	R	|	|	R	R	...	1606	1711	R	...	1909	2026	...	2219	2311	2357	...
398	**Ipoh** d.	0500	0633	0730	0810	0900	0930	...	...	1032	1100	1214	1328	1300	1600	...	1635	1740	1800	...	1939	2056	...	2249	2340	0030	...
434	Kampar d.	0521	|	0751	0829	0921	0951	...	...	|	1121	|	|	1321	1621	...	1654	1759	1821	...	1958	2115	...	2310	2359	...	...
450	Tapah Road d.	0533	|	0803	0839	0933	1001	...	...	|	1133	|	|	1333	1633	...	1704	1809	1833	...	2008	2124	...	2320	0009	...	...
517	Tanjong Malim d.	0616	|	0846	0913	1016	1037	...	...	1135	1217	|	|	1416	1716	...	1738	1843	1916	...	2044	2158	...	2358	0043	...	...
604	**Kuala Lumpur** Sentral d.	0725	0835	0955	1022	1125	1159	...	...	1254	1335	1435	1453	1525	1825	...	1857	1952	2025	...	2200	2310	...	0122	0152	...	...
677	Seremban d.	...	...	...	...	...	1313	...	...	1415	...	1600	...	...	...	...	...	...	...	...	...	...	...	0238	...	...	...
726	Tampin d.	...	...	...	...	...	1347	...	...	1446	...	...	...	...	...	...	...	...	...	...	...	...	...	0313	...	...	...
779	**Gemas** d.	...	...	...	...	...	1415	...	...	1525	...	...	...	...	...	...	...	...	...	...	...	...	...	0340	...	...	...

	9500	2948	948	2956	9220	9246	9302	2960	9232	9208	9236	9214	9402	36	2968	9304	9248	9306	9202	9216	9204	9308	9234	9238	9404	931
	R	2	2	2	R	R	R	2	R	R	R	R	R	R	2	R	R	R	R	R	R	R	R	R	R	R
		B				⑤–⑦								♦			⑤–⑦									
Gemas d.	...	...	...	...	0430	...	...	...	...	...	...	...	...	...	...	...	...	...	1500	...	1600	...	...	...	...	...
Tampin d.	...	...	...	...	0500	...	...	...	...	...	...	...	...	...	...	...	...	...	1526	...	1628	...	...	...	...	...
Seremban d.	...	...	...	...	0534	...	...	...	...	...	...	...	...	...	...	...	...	...	1600	1630	1701	...	...	...	...	...
Kuala Lumpur Sentral d.	...	...	...	...	0656	0750	0830	...	0900	0930	1038	1100	1230	...	...	1445	1600	1610	1721	1750	1822	1900	2000	2030	2100	234
Tanjong Malim d.	...	...	...	...	0758	|	0939	...	|	1033	1141	|	1344	...	...	1554	1703	1719	1833	1859	1924	2009	2103	2133	2214	004
Tapah Road d.	...	...	...	...	0836	|	1020	...	|	1112	1220	|	1428	...	...	1635	1742	1800	1909	1940	|	2050	2142	2212	2258	013
Kampar d.	...	...	...	...	0845	|	1029	...	|	1122	1230	|	1440	...	...	1644	1752	1809	1919	1949	|	2059	2152	2222	2310	013
Ipoh d.	0530	...	...	...	0908	0951	1055	...	1101	1144	1251	1306	1505	...	...	1710	1813	1835	1941	2011	2029	2125	2213	2243	2335	020
Kuala Kangsar d.	0559	...	...	...	0934	|	...	...	|	1213	1320	|	▬	...	...	▬	1842	▬	2010	2040	2055	▬	2242	2312	...	...
Taiping d.	0620	...	...	...	0953	1034	...	...	1144	1230	1337	1350	**2964**	...	...	**2976**	1859	**2984**	2028	2057	2114	**2988**	2259	2329	...	...
Bukit Mertajam d.	0707	...	...	...	|	1117	...	...	1227	1315	1422	|	2	...	...	2	1944	2	2116	2142	|	2	2344	0014	...	...
Butterworth d.	0728	0735	...	1025	|	1125	...	1225	1252	1338	1430	|	1425	...	1625	1825	1952	2025	2130	2200	|	2225	2352	0022	...	...
Bukit Mertajam d.	0737	0756	...	1036	|	...	...	1236	...	1348	▬	|	1436	...	1636	1836	...	2036	...	...	|	2236	...	...	...	...
Alor Setar d.	0830	0843	...	1133	1122	...	...	1333	...	1435	**950**	1518	1533	...	1733	1933	...	2133	...	...	2243	2333	...	...	...	...
Arau d.	0853	0907	...	1157	1141	...	...	1357	...	1454	2	1537	1557	...	1757	1957	...	2157	...	...	2302	2357	...	...	...	...
Padang Besar 🏛 d.	0910	0926	0955	1216	1210	...	...	1416	...	1515	1540	1555	1616	1840	1816	2016	...	2216	...	...	2340	0016	...	...	...	...
Hat Yai Junction a.	...	...	0950t	...	...	...	...	...	...	...	1535t	...	...	1845t	...	...	...	...	...	...	...	...	...	...	...	...
Bangkok **6055** a.	...	...	...	...	...	...	...	...	...	...	...	...	...	1030t	...	...	...	...	...	...	...	...	...	...	...	...

6001 GEMAS - JOHOR BAHRU - SINGAPORE

Keretapi Tanah Melayu Berhad

km		ES43	ES41	ES45	27					
		2	2	2	R ♦					
53	Tampin d.	...	1455	...	...	...	...	...	...	...
0	**Gemas** d.	1450	1540	0410	0830	...	...	...	...	...
26	Segamat d.	1520	1613	0440	0903	...	...	...	...	...
85	Paloh d.	1629	1725	0548	|	...	...	...	...	...
112	Kluang d.	1701	1757	0622	1046	...	...	...	...	...
163	Kulai d.	1758	1858	0724	1158	...	...	...	...	...
195	**Johor Bahru** Sentral a.	1840	2000	0820	1300	...	...	...	...	...

	ES40	ES42	26	ES44					
	2	2	R ♦	2					
Johor Bahru Sentral d.	0845	1010	1900	2340	...	...	...	...	...
Kulai d.	0930	1053	1953	0025	...	...	...	...	...
Kluang d.	1106	1209	2101	0122	...	...	...	...	...
Paloh d.	1142	1237	|	0150	...	...	...	...	...
Segamat d.	1303	1355	2257	0300	...	...	...	...	...
Gemas d.	1338	1435	2356	0340	...	...	...	...	...
Tampin d.	1428	...	...	...	...	...	...	...	...

km	◄	ST63	ST65	ST67	ST69	ST71	ST73	ST77	ST81	ST83	ST87	ST91	ST93
0	**Johor Bahru** Sentral d.	0530	0600	0630	0700	0830	0900	1230	1530	1700	1900	2100	2215
4	**Woodlands** ◇ a.	0535	0605	0635	0705	0835	0905	1235	1535	1705	1905	2105	2220

◄	ST70	ST74	ST78	ST82	ST84	ST86	ST88	ST90	ST92	ST9
Woodlands ◇ d.	0800	1000	1330	1630	1800	1845	2000	2045	2200	231
Johor Bahru Sentral d.	0805	1005	1335	1635	1805	1850	2005	2050	2205	232

6010 TUMPAT - GEMAS

Keretapi Tanah Melayu Berhad

km			51	53	55	57	59			27
			3	3	3	3	3			R ♦
0	**Tumpat** d.	...	0420	...	1000	1400	...	...	...	1930
14	Wakaf Bharu d.	...	0439	...	1018	1419	...	...	...	1948
25	Pasir Mas d.	...	0457	...	1035	1436	...	...	...	2004
53	Tanah Merah d.	...	0529	...	1107	1512	...	...	...	2031
85	Krai d.	...	0608	...	1205	1610	...	...	...	2110
135	Dabong d.	...	0740	...	1347	1820	...	...	...	2234
	Kemubu d.	...	0754	...	...	1834	...	...	...	|
206	**Gua Masang** d.	...	0959	1005	...	2030	2036	...	...	2300
300	Kuala Lipis d.	...	...	1236	...	...	2307	...	...	0246
353	Jerantut d.	...	...	...	...	...	...	...	...	0412
406	Mentakab d.	...	...	...	...	...	...	...	...	0512
492	Bahau d.	...	...	...	...	...	...	...	...	0718
528	**Gemas** a.	...	...	...	...	...	...	...	...	0830

	26		50	52		56		58	60
	R ♦		3	3		3		3	3
Gemas d.	2356	...	...	...	...	...	...	...	...
Bahau d.	0102	...	...	...	...	...	...	...	...
Mentakab d.	0313	...	...	...	...	...	...	...	...
Jerantut d.	0420	...	...	...	...	...	...	...	...
Kuala Lipis d.	0534	...	0300	...	...	...	...	1345	...
Gua Masang d.	0750	...	0516	0522	...	...	...	1550	1552
Kemubu d.	|	...	...	0719	...	...	...	...	1744
Dabong d.	0946	...	...	0745	...	1430	...	...	1805
Krai d.	1112	...	...	0914	...	1554	...	...	1933
Tanah Merah d.	1151	...	...	0954	...	1632	...	...	2035
Pasir Mas d.	1218	...	...	1040	...	1706	...	...	2107
Wakaf Bharu d.	1234	...	...	1057	...	1723	...	...	2124
Tumpat a.	1300	...	...	1130	...	1735	...	...	2155

Notes for Tables **6000**, **6001**, **6010**. ♦ – Notes, listed by train number.

26/27 – EKSPRES RAKYAT TIMURAN – 🛏 2 cl., (23) Johor Bahru - Gua Musang -Tumpat and v.v.
35/36 – INTERNATIONAL EXPRESS – See Table **6055**. For connections to/from Butterworth use *ETS* services.
A – Additional trips: 0725, 1425, 1625, 1725, 1925, 2025. **B** – Additional services: 0525, 0625, 0825, 0925, 1725, 1925.
2XXX – Komuter Electric Train Service (2).

9XXX – Electric Train Service (2) 🍷.
t – Thai time.
◇ – Border point with Singapore.
◄ – Connections with intercity trains are not guaranteed

6015 TENOM - TANJONG ARU

JKNS

km		201	401	505	502	508	504	504A
			①-⑥	⑦		⑦	①-⑥ ☛	①-⑥
0	**Tenom** d.	...	...	...	0730	1230	1300	...
	Halogilat d.	...	0600	0810	0854	1353	1444	1740
49	Beaufort a.	...	0658	0911	0951	1455	1545	1839
49	Beaufort d.	0500	...	...	1101	1630	1700	...
101	Papar d.	0611	...	...	1216	1750	1828	...
134	**Tanjong Aru** ◐ a.	0657	...	...	1310	1845	1910	...

	301	303	101A	101	106A	102A	103	104	104
	①-⑥	⑦			⑦	①-⑥	☛	⑦	①-⑥
Tanjong Aru ◐ d.	...	...	...	0745	...	...	1340	1706	1736
Papar d.	...	...	...	0829	...	...	1428	1750	1823
Beaufort a.	...	...	...	0940	...	...	1542	1900	1934
Beaufort d.	0500	0700	0750	...	1330	1330	1630a	...	...
Halogilat d.	0556	0758	0853	...	1444	1444	1730a	...	...
Tenom a.	...	...	1013	...	1555	1555	...	...	...

a – ①–⑥ only. ◐ – Kota Kinabalu. ☛ – This service is often cancelled.

Operator: Jabatan Keretapi Negeri Sabah (Sabah State Railways).

6020 BANGKOK - WOODLANDS

EOE

The EASTERN AND ORIENTAL EXPRESS is a Luxury cruise train operating between Bangkok an Woodlands ◇. 2017 departure dates:
From **Bangkok** depart 1750, journey 3 nights on Jan. 3, 26, Feb. 5, 14, 23, Mar. 5, 14, 24, Apr. 26, Sept. 19, 28, Oct. 10, 22, Nov.1, 10.
From **Woodlands** depart 1500, journey 2 nights o Jan. 19, Feb. 1, 10, 19 Mar. 1, 10, 19, Apr. 2, 22, Sept. 14, 24, Oct. 15, 27, Nov. 6, 18.
Operator: Eastern and Oriental Express
✆ UK 0845 077 2222.

◇ – Border point with Singapore.

THAILAND

Capital: **Bangkok** (GMT +7).   2017 Public Holidays: Jan. 1, 2, Apr. 6, 13, 14, 15, 17, May 1, 5, 10, July 8, Aug. 11, 12, Oct. 23, Dec. 5, 10, 11.

Rail services are operated by State Railway of Thailand (www.railway.co.th). Trains may convey any combination of first, second or third class seating as shown in either columns or footnotes. Overnight trains may also convey sleeping cars or couchettes. Sleeping cars have lockable two berth compartments which convert into seats during the day. Couchettes are arranged 'open plan' along the coach and during the day the bottom bunks are used as seats. Dining cars are operated on all important trains. The Thailand Rail Pass offers twenty days unlimted travel in seated accommodation. Two passes are available. Pass A costs 1550 Baht and does not include supplements for express trains or sleeping cars. Pass B costs 3000 Baht and includes all supplements.

BANGKOK - BAN PLU TA LUANG and ARANYAPRATHET — 6050

State Railway of Thailand

km	3rd class only		275	283	281	367	389	279	277	391	371
										A	
0	**Bangkok** Hua Lampong	d.	0555	0655	0800	1010	1210	1305	1525	1635	1740
5	Makkasan	d.	0620	0716	0816	1030	1228	1317	1545	1654	1802
31	Hua Takhe ‡	d.	0703	0814	0857	1109	1304	1348	1618	1730	1842
61	Chachoengsao Junction	d.	0740	0859	0932	1145	1330	1421	1644	1755	1924
131	Si Racha Junction	d.	|	1013a	|	...	...	|	|	...	|
155	Pattaya	d.	|	1035a	|	...	...	|	|	...	|
184	**Ban Plu Ta Luang**	a.	|	1120a	|	...	...	|	|	...	|
122	Prachin Buri	d.	0858	...	1046	...	...	1522	1741	...	2032
161	Kabin Buri	d.	0948	...	1135	...	...	1612	1820	...	...
255	**Aranyaprathet**	a.	1135	...	...	...	...	1735	...	...	...

3rd class only		372	278	280	368	390	282	284	276	386
						B				①–⑤
Aranyaprathet	d.	...	...	0640	...	...	...	...	1355	...
Kabin Buri	d.	...	0630	0823	...	...	1325	...	1539	...
Prachin Buri	d.	0500	0719	0921	...	...	1416	...	1630	...
Ban Plu Ta Luang	d.	|	|	|	...	...	|	1335a	|	...
Pattaya	d.	|	|	|	...	...	|	1421a	|	...
Si Racha Junction	d.	|	|	|	...	...	|	1452a	|	...
Chachoengsao Junction	d.	0619	0831	1022	1235	1405	1534	1620	1800	2005
Hua Takhe ‡	d.	0701	0911	1107	1316	1435	1609	1711	1855	2038
Makkasan	d.	0751	0958	1148	1354	1512	1655	1807	1940	2116
Bangkok Hua Lampong	a.	0815	1015	1205	1410	1525	1715	1825	1955	2130

A – Also at 1700 Ⓐ, 1825.
B – Also at 0545 Ⓐ, 0705.

a – ①–⑤ only.
‡ – For Suvarnabhumi International Airport.

BANGKOK - HAT YAI - SUNGAI KOLOK — 6055

State Railway of Thailand

km			453	175	43	261	171	35	37	463	169	451	83	173	447	167	85	39	41	455	445	457
			3	23	2 🍸	3	C	A	B	3	C	3	B	C	3	C	B	2 🍸	2 🍸	3	3	3
0	**Bangkok** Hua Lampong	d.	...	...	0805	0920	1300	1445	1510	...	1535	...	1705	1735	...	1830	1930	2250	2250	...	...	...
64	Nakhon Pathom	d.	...	...	0922	1048	1437	1611	1638	...	1715	...	1833	1912	...	1958	2059	0009	0009	...	...	...
117	Rachaburi	d.	...	...	1004	1145	1526	1701	1730	...	1820	...	1924	2007	...	2050	2150	0052	0052	...	...	...
229	Hua Hin	d.	...	...	1129	1335	1717	1845	1913	...	2010	...	2110	2154	...	2234	2336	0224	0224	...	...	...
377	Bang Saphan Yai	d.	...	...	1321	...	1946	2107	2143	...	2249	...	2341	0048	...	0111	0232	0433	0433	...	...	...
485	Chumphon	d.	...	...	1441	...	2121	2245	2324	...	0052	...	0127	0258	...	0328	0423	0559	0559	...	0630	...
651	Surat Thani ♥	d.	...	...	1645	...	0027	0126	0203	...	0348	...	0427	0603	0613	0628	0716	0805	0815	...	0946	...
773	Thung Song Junction	d.	...	...	...	...	0239	0322	0400	...	0556	...	0635	0832	0907	0855	0932	...	0954	...	1219	1415
832	**Nakhon Si Thammarat**	a.	...	...	...	...	|	|	|	...	|	0600	|	0955	|	|	1055	...	|	0958	|	|
845	Trang	a.	...	...	...	...	|	|	|	...	|	|	0805	...	|	1036	...	...	|	|	|	|
866	**Kantang**	a.	...	...	...	...	|	|	|	...	|	|	...	...	|	1120	...	...	|	|	|	1655
862	Phatthalung	d.	...	...	...	...	0422	0506	0548	0602	0738	0822	...	...	1123	...	...	...	1112	1224	1420	...
943	Hat Yai Junction	d.	...	0630	...	...	0645	0700	0735	0755	0930	1018	...	...	1312	...	...	...	1250	1433	1650	...
1009	Pattani	d.	...	0739	...	...	0810	...	0858	0919	1050	1145	...	...	1448	...	...	...	1404	1616	...	...
1055	Yala	d.	0630	0806	...	...	0848	...	0929	0958	1120	1227	...	...	1545	...	...	...	1430	1710	...	...
1159	**Sungai Kolok**	a.	0840	1000	...	...	1045	...	1120	1210	...	1450	...	...	1800	...	...	...	...	...	...	...

		458	262	40	446	174	456	168	448	86	452	170	42	44	84	172	464	38	176	36	454
		3	3	2 🍸	2	C	3	C	3	B	3	C	2 🍸	2 🍸	B	C	3	B	2	A	2
Sungai Kolok	d.	...	...	...	...	...	...	...	0630	...	0855	...	...	...	...	1130	1225	1420	1455	...	1525
Yala	d.	...	...	...	...	...	0635	...	0828	...	1122	1235	1455	...	...	1326	1432	1609	1637	...	1740
Pattani	d.	...	...	...	...	...	0716	...	0920	...	1206	1306	1519	...	...	1405	1528	1640	1704	...	...
Hat Yai Junction	d.	...	...	...	0640	...	0918	...	1058	...	1350	1445	1623	...	...	1539	1705	1810	1815	1845	...
Phatthalung	d.	0600	...	...	0853	...	1118	...	1300	...	1534	1623	1736	...	...	1713	1850	1947	...	2019	...
Kantang	d.	|	...	...	|	...	|	1240	|	...	|	|	|	...	...	|	...	|	...	|	...
Trang	d.	|	...	...	|	...	|	1329	|	...	|	|	|	...	1725	|	...	|	...	|	...
Nakhon Si Thammarat	d.	0830	...	...	|	1300	1355	|	|	1500	1805	|	|	...	|	|	...	|	...	|	...
Thung Song Junction	d.	...	...	...	1058	1424	...	1517	1531	1620	...	1813	1903	...	1912	1927	...	2138	...	2207	...
Surat Thani ♥	d.	...	...	1040	1325	1647	...	1738	1755	1837	...	2014	2041	2041	2104	2126	...	2328	...	2357	...
Chumphon	d.	...	...	1246	1630	1936	...	2031	...	2122	...	2323	2249	2249	2359	0044	...	0206	...	0234	...
Bang Saphan Yai	d.	...	...	1407	...	2128	...	2216	...	2308	...	0112	0019	0019	0148	0219	...	0336	...	0404	...
Hua Hin	d.	...	1410	1601	...	0045	...	0116	...	0147	...	0428	0222	0222	0415	0456	...	0605	...	0629	...
Rachaburi	d.	...	1600	1741	...	0244	...	0306	...	0404	...	0625	0350	0350	0608	0649	...	0749	...	0813	...
Nakhon Pathom	d.	...	1716	1826	...	0340	...	0405	...	0500	...	0726	0438	0438	0704	0744	...	0842	...	0903	...
Bangkok Hua Lampong	a.	...	1900	1945	...	0510	...	0535	...	0630	...	0900	0555	0555	0835	0915	...	1010	...	1030	...

A – INTERNATIONAL EXPRESS – 🛏 1, 2 cl. and ✕ Bangkok (**35/36**) - Hat Yai and v.v.; 🛏 2 cl. Hat Yai (**35/36**) - Padang Besar and v.v. **Note**: Trains **35/36** are to be replaced by Trains **31/32**, timings shoud not alter but **31/32** will convey new Chinese sleepers between Bangkok and Hat Yai.

B – 🛏 1, 2 cl., [23].
C – 🛏 2 cl., [23].
♥ – Station is at Phun Phin, 13 km away.

BANGKOK - CHIANG MAI — 6060

State Railway of Thailand

km			403	407	401	409	111	7	201	3	209	211	109	207	9	13	107	105	51
			3	3	3	3	23 ✕	2 🍸	23	2 🍸	3	23	B ✕	3	A ✕	A ✕	B ✕	23 🍸	B ✕
0	**Bangkok** Hualampong	d.	...	...	...	...	0700	0830	0925	1050	1120	1255	1345	1405	1810	1935	2010	2100	2200
58	Bang Pa In	d.	...	...	...	...	0825	|	1114	|	1251	1419	|	1543	|	|	|	2211	|
71	Ayutthaya	d.	...	...	...	0600	0838	0948	1128	1216	1305	1432	1519	1558	1945	2107	2144	2223	2236
133	Lop Buri	d.	...	...	0600	0715	0944	1029	1241	1300	1423	1538	1623	1727	2042	2200	2239	2316	0031
246	Nakhon Sawan	d.	...	0500	0811	...	1124	1140	1511	1407	...	1753	1827	1935	2217	2331	0006	0050	0224
319	Taphan Hin	d.	...	0617	0936	...	1242	1226	1640	1457	...	1915	1937	...	|	|	0130	0210	0337
389	Phitsanulok	d.	0555	0729	1055	...	1345	1322	1755	1604	...	...	2037	...	0018	0149	0238	0309	0440
485	Uttaradit	d.	0737	0907	...	...	1524	1427	...	1912	...	...	2223	...	|	0308	0405	0436	0606
488	Sila At	d.	0740	0917	...	...	1529	1433	...	1915	...	...	2237	...	0154	0321	0418	0440	0620
534	Den Chai	d.	...	1013	...	...	1630	1524	...	...	...	...	2342	...	0251	0419	0515	...	0720
642	Nakhon Lampang	d.	...	1236	...	...	...	1733	...	...	...	...	0204	...	0501	0633	...	...	1001
683	Khun Tan	d.	...	1330	...	...	...	1823	...	...	...	...	0258	...	0606	0737	...	...	1105
729	Lamphun	d.	...	1415	...	...	...	1915	...	...	...	...	0344	...	0651	0821	...	...	1150
751	**Chiang Mai**	a.	...	1435	...	...	...	1930	...	...	...	...	0405	...	0715	0840	...	...	1210

		208	212	202	106	112	210	102	8	402	408	410	4	108	52	14	10
		3	3	23	23 🍸	23 ✕	3	B ✕	2 🍸	3	3	3	2 🍸	B ✕	B ✕	A ✕	A ✕
Chiang Mai	d.	...	...	...	...	...	...	0630	0850	...	0930	...	...	...	1530	1700	1800
Lamphun	d.	...	...	...	...	...	...	0652	0905	...	1000	...	...	...	1548	1720	1820
Khun Tan	d.	...	...	...	...	...	...	0736	0947	...	1103	...	...	...	1650	1824	1921
Nakhon Lampang	d.	...	...	...	...	...	...	0837	1041	...	1202	...	...	...	1804	1927	2017
Den Chai	d.	...	...	...	...	0730	...	1046	1239	...	1419	...	...	1905	2026	2141	2236
Sila At	d.	...	...	...	0730	0827	...	1147	1326	...	1533	1630	1950	2012	2130	2236	2333
Uttaradit	d.	...	...	...	0735	0833	...	1153	1332	...	1538	1633	2000	2019	2137	2242	|
Phitsanulok	d.	...	...	0605	0855	1003	...	1318	1444	1345	1724	1810	2140	2209	2301	0001	0050
Taphan Hin	d.	...	0530	0718	0952	1112	...	1428	1532	1458	1842	...	2239	2320	0007	|	|
Nakhon Sawan	d.	0500	0701	0835	1048	1242	...	1556	1622	1630	1955	...	0006	0048	0114	0159	0241
Lop Buri	d.	0706	0918	1056	1220	1438	1732	1806	1728	1845	...	...	0130	0228	0245	0324	0405
Ayutthaya	d.	0826	1027	1248	1311	1559	1848	1916	1806	...	...	...	0227	0321	0339	0424	0459
Bang Pa In	d.	0840	1039	1229	1323	1616	1903	|	|	...	...	...	|	|	|	|	|
Bangkok Hualampong	a.	1020	1210	1405	1440	1800	2035	2110	1925	...	...	...	0400	0510	0525	0615	0650

A – Conveys 🛏 1, 2 cl.

B – Conveys 🛏 2 cl., [23].

6065 BANGKOK - NONG KHAI and UBON RATCHATHANI

State Railway of Thailand

km		425	421	415	431	21	419	135	75	71	427	417	233	145	77	139	25	69	913	23	67	133	917	73	141
		3	3	3	3	2 🍸	3	23	23 🍸	23 🍸	3	3	3	23 ✕	23 🍸	B	D	A	23	C	A	B	23	23 🍸	23 ✕
0	**Bangkok** Hua Lampong d.	...	...	...	...	0545	...	0640	0820	1005	...	...	1140	1520	1835	1855	2000	2000	...	2030	2030	2045	...	2150	2225
71	Ayutthaya d.	...	...	...	...	0659	...	0826	0942	1125	...	...	1307	1657	2002	2026	2141	2141	...	2153	2151	2218	...	2309	2354
113	Saraburi d.	...	...	...	...	0734	...	0910	1018	1204	...	...	1353	1801	2040	2110	2223	2223	...	|	2232	2302	...	2345	0036
125	Kaeng Khoi Junction d.	...	...	...	0500	0745	...	0923	1030	1216	...	...	1406	1815	2051	2124	2235	2235	...	|	2246	2315	...	2355	0053
180	Pak Chong d.	...	...	...	0618	0856	...	1056	|	1327	...	...	1524	1949	2158	2249	|	|	...	0010	0017	|	...	0105	0226
264	Nakhon Ratchasima d.	...	0610	0620	0829	1011	1115	1224	|	1443	1420	1600	1705	2125	2333	0023	|	|	...	0146	0153	|	...	0231	0352
346	Bua Yai Junction d.	...	|	0758	1009	|	|	|	1414	|	|	1742	|	|	0048	|	0250	0250	...	|	|	0357	...	|	|
450	Khon Kaen d.	...	|	0935	1155	|	|	|	1527	|	|	1917	|	|	0206	|	0419	0419	...	|	|	0535	...	|	|
569	Udon Thani d.	...	|	1133	...	|	|	|	1710	|	|	2140	|	|	0336	|	0558	0558	...	|	|	0740	...	|	|
621	**Nong Khai** a.	...	|	1200	...	|	|	|	1745	|	|	...	|	|	0415	|	0645	0645	0730	|	|	0835	1445	|	|
627	**Tha Na Laeng** (Laos) a.	...	|	...	...	|	|	|	...	|	|	...	|	|	...	|	...	...	0745	|	|	...	1500	|	|
376	Buri Ram d.	...	0810	...	...	1137	1317	1422	...	1617	1635	...	1916	2341	...	0226	...	...	...	0334	0344	...	...	0428	0605
420	Surin d.	0538	0910	...	...	1211	1403	1510	...	1711	1723	...	2000	0032	...	0317	...	...	...	0414	0432	...	...	0516	0701
515	Si Sa Ket d.	0718	1107	...	...	1320	1550	1703	...	1840	1906	...	...	0221	...	0509	...	...	...	0539	0620	...	...	...	0900
575	**Ubon Ratchathani** a.	0830	1215	...	...	1400	1645	1800	...	...	2015	...	...	0335	...	0615	...	...	...	0635	0725	...	...	...	1020

	234	424	72	416	76	428	136	146	432	426	22	914	418	142	74	918	78	68	24	420	134	70	26	140
	3	3	23 🍸	3	23 🍸	3	23 ✕	23 ✕	3	3	2 🍸	23	3	23 ✕	23 ✕	23	23 ✕	A	C	3	B	A	D	B ✕
Ubon Ratchathani d.	...	...	...	...	...	0620	0700	0845	...	1235	1450	...	...	1650	...	...	...	1830	1900	1845	...	...	...	1930
Si Sa Ket d.	...	...	...	...	...	0716	0804	0951	...	1344	1531	...	...	1757	1905	...	...	1930	1956	1948	...	...	...	2028
Surin d.	0520	0703	0749	...	...	0905	0939	1130	...	1528	1641	...	...	1931	2025	...	...	2059	2123	2120	...	...	...	2202
Buri Ram d.	0606	0752	0835	...	...	0953	1027	1226	...	1615	1715	...	...	2028	2110	...	...	2143	2204	...	...	...	...	2250
Tha Na Laeng (Laos) d.	|	|	|	...	...	|	|	|	...	|	|	1000	...	|	|	1730	...	|	|	...	...	...	...	|
Nong Khai d.	|	|	|	...	0700	|	|	|	...	|	|	1015	1255	|	|	1745	1815	|	|	...	1830	1910	1910	|
Udon Thani d.	|	|	|	0555	0738	|	|	|	...	|	|	...	1340	|	|	...	1852	|	|	...	1919	1959	1959	|
Khon Kaen d.	|	|	|	0757	0912	|	|	|	1355	|	|	...	1536	|	|	...	2019	|	|	...	2106	2138	2138	|
Bua Yai Junction d.	|	|	|	0938	1045	|	|	|	1546	|	|	...	1714	|	|	...	2136	|	|	...	2246	2317	2317	|
Nakhon Ratchasima d.	0822	0950	1018	1125	|	1145	1233	1454	1740	1825	1847	...	1900	2234	2254	...	2304	2337	2359	...	|	|	|	0051
Pak Chong d.	1009	...	1127	...	|	...	1400	1635	1914	...	1948	...	...	0003	0026	...	0042	0127	0131	...	|	|	|	0228
Kaeng Khoi Junction d.	1136	...	1228	...	1444	...	1530	1750	2030	...	2053	...	...	0132	0158	...	0222	0246	|	...	0237	0308	0308	0352
Saraburi d.	1151	...	1241	...	1455	...	1545	1805	...	...	2106	...	...	0148	0210	...	0235	0304	|	...	0252	0321	0321	0413
Ayutthaya d.	1240	...	1317	...	1535	...	1637	1905	...	...	2142	...	...	0237	0254	...	0315	0355	0342	...	0348	0404	0404	0525
Bangkok Hua Lampong a.	1415	...	1455	...	1710	...	1840	2100	...	...	2255	...	...	0425	0435	...	0500	0550	0515	...	0545	0600	0600	0730

A – Conveys 🛏 1, 2 cl., [23] ✕. B – Conveys 🛏 2 cl., [23] ✕. C – Conveys 🛏 1, 2 cl., ✕. D – Conveys 🛏 1, 2 cl., ✕. Awaiting exact timings.

6070 BANGKOK - NAM TOK

State Railway of Thailand

km	485	909	257	259		3rd class only		260	258	910	486
		ⓒ A								A	
0	...	0630h	0750	1335	↓	**Bangkok** Thon Buri d.		1025	1740	1925h	...
64	...	0820	0902	1503		Nakhon Pathom d.	↑	0921	1631	1809	...
82	0435	0836	0922	1522	↓	Nong Pla Duk Jct d.		0835	1602	1755	1850
133	0607	0927	1035	1626		Kanchanaburi d.	↑	0719	1448	1653	1741
210	0820	...	1235	1830	↓	**Nam Tok** a.	↑	0520	1255	1425	1530

A – Tourist train to River Khwae Bridge (a. 0935) and allied war cemetery at Kanchanaburi. Conveys [23]. Ⓡ. Special fare payable. 740 Baht.
h – Bangkok Hua Lampong.

6075 SUVARNABHUMI INTERNATIONAL AIRPORT

Bangkok Makksan - Suvarnabhumi International Airport (jouney 15 minutes non-stop): **Service suspended**.

Suvarnabhumi International Airport - Bangkok Makksan (jouney 15 minutes non-stop): **Service suspended**.

Bangkok Makksan - Suvarnabhumi International Airport (jouney 22 minutes): 0606 and at least 4 journeys a hour until 2351, 0006.

Suvarnabhumi International Airport - Bangkok Makksan (jouney 22 minutes): 0556, 0608 and at least 4 journeys a hour unti 2347, 0002.

6090 CAMBODIA

Royal Railway

km		⑥ a	⑦	⑤		⑥	⑦ a	⑦
0	**Phnom Penh** d.	0700	0700	1500	**Sihanoukville** d.	0700	0700	1600
75	Takeo d.	0830	0830	1630	Kampot d.	0840	0840	1740
166	Kampot d.	1140	1140	1940	Takeo d.	1150	1150	2050
263	**Sihanoukville** a.	1400	1400	2200	**Phnom Penh** a.	1400	1400	2300

Capital: **Phnom Penh** (GMT +7).
2017 Public Holidays: Jan. 1, 7, Mar. 8, Apr. 13 May 1, 14 - 16, June 1, Sept. 24, Oct. 15, 29, Nov. 4 - 6, 9, Dec. 10.
a – Air-conditioned service.

VIÊT NAM

Capital: **Há Nôi** (GMT +7). 2017 Public Holidays: Jan. 1, 2, 26 - 31, Feb. 1, Apr. 6, 7, 30, May 1, 2, Sept. 2, 4.

Rail services are operated by Duóng Sát Viêt Nam (Viêt Nam Railways, www.vr.com.vn). Unless stated trains convey first and second class accommodation. First class has four berth compartments, whilst second class has six. Dining facilities (meals brought to your seats) are provided on some trains.

6100 HÁ NOI - BEIJING

Duóng Sát Viêt Nam

km				MR1	T8702	Z6	Z286			DD5
				BC	BC	C				
0	**Há Nôi** Gia Lam d.	...	...	2140	...	...	...	...	...	0730
162	Dong Dang a.	...	...	0155	...	...	...	...	...	1140
162	Dong Dang 🏛 d.	...	...	0250	...	...	...	...	...	...
207	Pingxiang 🏛 a.	...	...	0431	...	...	...	...	...	...
207	Pingxiang d.	...	...	...	0615	...	...	...	...	...
430	Nanning a.	...	...	...	1007	...	...	...	...	...
430	Nanning d.	...	...	...	...	1055	1745	...	...	...
861	Guilin d.	...	...	...	...	1422	2125a	...	...	...
1409	Changsha d.	...	...	...	...	1942	0255	...	...	...
1771	Wuhan Wuchang d.	...	...	...	...	2311	0622	...	...	...
2307	Zhengzhou d.	...	...	...	...	0352	1108	...	...	...
2996	**Beijing** xi a.	...	...	...	...	0948	1730	...	...	...

	Z5	T8701	MR2	Z285				DD6	
	D	BD	BD						
Beijing xi d.	1609	...	...	2110	...	...	...	...	...
Zhengzhou d.	2212	...	...	0310	...	...	...	...	...
Wuhan Wuchang d.	0252	...	...	0753	...	...	...	...	...
Changsha d.	0615	...	...	1122	...	...	...	...	...
Guilin d.	1140	...	...	1635a	...	...	...	...	...
Nanning a.	1546	...	...	2040	...	...	...	...	...
Nanning d.	...	1805	...	...	...	...	...	...	...
Pingxiang a.	...	2210	...	...	...	...	...	...	...
Pingxiang 🏛 d.	...	...	2241	...	...	...	...	...	...
Dong Dang 🏛 a.	...	...	2322	...	...	...	...	...	...
Dong Dang d.	...	...	0022	...	...	...	...	1530	...
Há Nôi Gia Lam a.	...	...	0520	...	...	...	...	1946	...

B – Conveys 🛏 1 cl. Nanning (**T8701/2**) - Pingxiang (**MR2/1**) - Há Nôi and v.v.
C – Runs daily. On ②⑤ (from Há Nôi) conveys 🛏 1 cl. Há Nôi – Beijing (2 nights).
D – Runs daily. On ④⑦ (from Beijing) conveys 🛏 1 cl. Beijing - Há Nôi (2 nights).
a – Guilin bei.

6105 HÁ NOI - LÂO CAÍ

Duóng Sát Viêt Nam

km		LC3	YB1	SP1	SP3	SP7				
				AB	A					
0	**Há Nôi** d.	0610	1315	2140	2200	2230	...	...	...	...
6	**Há Nôi** Gia Lâm d.	0628	1342	2158	2218	2248	...	...	...	...
155	Yên Bái d.	1150	1810	0140	0223	0300	...	...	...	...
262	Phõ Lu d.	1441	...	0435	0520	0600	...	...	...	...
296	**Lâo Caí** a.	1546	...	0535	0620	0700	...	...	...	...

	LC4			SP8	SP2	SP4	YB2		
				B	AB	A			
Lâo Caí d.	1005	...	...	1940	2035	2110	...	...	...
Phõ Lu d.	1108	...	...	2036	2134	2209	...	...	...
Yên Bái d.	1453	...	...	2338	0036	0128	0735	...	...
Há Nôi Gia Lâm a.	1914	...	...	0405	0430	0507	1203	...	...
Há Nôi a.	1932	...	...	0420	0445	0522	1235	...	...

A – 🛏 1, 2 cl., [12] Há Nôi - Lâo Caí and v.v.
B – Conveys private sleeping cars operated by Livitrans: www.livitrans.com

6110 HÁ NOI - HAI PHÒNG

Duóng Sát Viêt Nam

km		HP1	LP3	LP5		LP7				
				2						
0	**Há Nôi** Long Bien d.	0600h	0928	1520	...	1838	...	...	...	...
6	**Há Nôi** Gia Lâm d.	0616	0948	1530	...	1854	...	...	...	...
57	Hai Duong d.	0720	1055	1652	...	1958	...	...	...	...
76	Phú Thái d.	0748	1123	1721	...	2026	...	...	...	...
102	**Hai Phòng** a.	0825	1200	1800	...	2105	...	...	...	...

	LP2	LP6	LP8	HD2	HP2				
		2							
Hai Phòng d.	0610	0905	1500	...	1845	...	...	...	...
Phú Thái d.	0646	0941	1537	...	1922	...	...	...	...
Hai Duong d.	0718	1008	1650	1628	1955	...	...	...	...
Gia Lâm d.	0832	1119	1726	1747	2101	...	...	...	...
Há Nôi Long Bien a.	0840	1126	1734	1757	2115h	...	...	...	...

h – Há Nôi.

HÁ NÔI - SAI GÔN — 6115

Duöng Sát Viêt Nam

km		SE5 A	SPT1	TN1	SNT1		SE1 A	SE19 A	SE3 A	SE7 A♣			SE8 A♣	SPT2	SE6 A	TN2 B		SE2 A	SNT2 A	SE4 A	SE20 A
					B																
0	Hà Nôi ....d.	0900	...	1310	...	...	1930	2010	2200	0600	Sai Gôn (Ho Chi Minh)....d.	0600	0640	0900	1310	...	1930	2030	2200	...
87	Nam Dinh ....d.	1046	...	1510	...	...	2114	2149	2340	0747	Binh Thuan ....d.	0930	1010	1236	1704	...	2255	0033	0115	...
116	Ninh Binh ....d.	1121	...	1548	...	...	2149	2225	0013	0822	Phan Thiet ....a.		1026			...				...
175	Thanh Hóa ....d.	1237	...	1711	...	...	2258	2339	0116	0933	Nha Trang ....d.	1326	...	1629	2119	...	0321	0530	0500	...
319	Vinh ....d.	1511	...	1950	...	...	0141	0225	0332	1208	Diêu Tri ....d.	1729	...	2117	0150	...	0713	...	0846	...
522	Dông Hó'i ....d.	1940	...	0039	...	...	0550	0639	0740	1636	Quang Ngai ....d.	2018	...	0011	0521	...	1007	...	1127	...
688	Huê ....d.	2250	...	0347	...	...	0856	0950	1035	1955	Dà Nang ....d.	2259	...	0302	0835	...	1246	1413	1840	...
791	Dà Nang ....d.	0143	...	0715	...	...	1141	1220	1315	2247	Huê ....d.	0136	...	0539	1214	...	1531	1647	2133	...
928	Quang Ngai ....d.	0421	...	1005	...	...	1434	...	1535	0121	Dông Hó'i ....d.	0450	...	0916	1535	...	1845	1952	0049	...
095	Diêu Tri ....d.	0725	...	1338	...	...	1741	...	1836	0423	Vinh ....d.	0926	...	1327	2033	...	2251	2353	0553	...
315	Nha Trang ....d.	1123	...	1755	1910	...	2122	...	2212	0835	Thanh Hóa ....d.	1154	...	1611	2336	...	0119	...	0217	0823
	Phan Thiet ....d.	...	1310			...		...			Ninh Binh ....d.	1314	...	1727	0106	...	0230	...	0321	0956
551	Binh Thuan ....d.	1543	1327	2207	2333	...	0118	...	0214	1239	Nam Dinh ....d.	1350	...	1803	0143	...	0305	...	0653	1049
726	Sai Gôn (Ho Chi Minh) ......a.	1911	1717	0230	0324	...	0439	...	0520	1608	Hà Nôi ....a.	1533	...	1958	0330	...	0450	...	0530	1233

A – Conveys ⊨ 1, 2 cl., ⊑ and ✕.   B – Conveys ⊨ 2 cl., ⊑ .   ♣ – Runs only at peak periods.

MYANMAR

Capital: **Yangon** (GMT +6½).   2017 Public Holidays: Jan. 4, Feb. 12, Mar. 2, 12, 27, Apr. 13 - 17, May 1, July 19, Dec. 25.

Rail service in Myanmar is provided by Myanmar Railways Corporation (MRC). Unless noted all trains convey first and second class seating (known locally as upper and ordinary). All seating is allocated on purchase of tickets. Sleeping cars are operated on overnight trains and bedding is supplied. Sleepers have 6 compartments comprising 4 x 4-berth and 2 x 2-berth.

MYITKYINA - MANDALAY — 6150

Myanmar Railways

km		38	56	42	34	58				37	33 B	55	57	41
0	Myitkyina ....d.	0430	0745	0910	1350	1510	...	Mandalay ....d.	0430	1300	1410	1620	1945
299	Kawlin ....d.	1441	1925	0100	0006	0351	...	Sagaing ....d.	0510		1504	1714	2041
	Shwebo ....d.	1842	0019	0713	0400	0828	...	Shwebo ....d.	0713	1533	1724	1934	0020
529	Sagaing ....d.		0300	1020		1104	...	Kawlin ....d.	1103	1933	2208	0057	0608
539	Mandalay ....a.	2200	0411	1120	0720	1220	...	Myitkyina ....a.	2200	0630	1045	1330	2105

B – ⊨ and ⊑ Myitkyina - Mandalay and v.v.

LASHIO - MANDALAY — 6155

Myanmar Railways

km		132				131
0	Lashio ....d.	0500	Mandalay ....d.	0400
74	Hsipaw ....d.	0940	Pyin Oo Lwin ....a.	0752
	Kyaukme ....d.	1125	Pyin Oo Lwin ....d.	0822
	Gokteik ....d.	1325	Gokteik ....d.	1108
213	Pyin Oo Lwin ....a.	1605	Kyaukme ....d.	1339
213	Pyin Oo Lwin ....d.	1740	Hsipaw ....d.	1515
280	Mandalay ....a.	2240	Lashio ....a.	1935

THAZI - YAKSAUK — 6160

Myanmar Railways

km		141 z	143 ◫			142 z	144 ◫
0	Thazi ....d.	0700	0500	Yaksauk ....d.	...	0600
197	Kalaw ....d.	1330	1140	Shwenyaung ....a.	...	0910
	Aungban ....⊖		1230	Shwenyaung ....d.	0800	0940
	Heho ....d.	1540	1345	Heho ....d.	0920	1110
247	Shwenyaung ....a.	1700	1400	Aungban ....⊖		1235
	Shwenyaung ....d.		1520	Kalaw ....d.	1145	1325
	Yaksauk ....a.		1930	Thazi ....a.	1900	2045

z – From / to Naypyitaw (Table 6165).   ⊖ – Information unavailable at press date.
◫ – This service is reported as suspended.

MANDALAY - BAGAN - YANGON — 6165

Myanmar Railways

km		8 A	6 A	4 A	120 B	62	10/142	32	12	118			11 A	31 A	9/141 B	5 A	61 A	3 A	7 A	119	117
0	Mandalay ....d.		1500	1700	2100	z			0600	0720	Yangon ....d.	0600	0800	1100	1500	1600	1700	2030	...	...
129	Thazi ....d.		1749	1949		2200		0854			Bago ....d.	0748	0943	1313	1644		1848	2213	...	...
	Naypyitaw ....a.		2000	2036	2251		0209	0800	1154		Taungoo ....d.	1231	1410	1937	2059		2325	0223	...	...
***	Bagan ....a.					0450				1845	Bagan ....a.				0931				...	...
***	Bagan ....d.						1700				Bagan ....d.								0700	0400
335	Taungoo ....d.		2235	2318	0127		0536	1059	1451		Naypyitaw ....d.	1522	1700	2255	2332		0157	0500	...	...
548	Bago ....d.		0258	0316	0549		1211	1523	1859		Thazi ....d.	1815		0330	0211		0458		...	...
622	Yangon ....a.		0435	0500	0745		1030	1440	1700	2100	Mandalay ....a.	2100	z	0500	0745				1430	1555

A – ⊨ and ⊑ Yangon - Mandalay and v.v.   y – From Shwenyaung (Table 6160).   *** – Yangon - Bagan : 644 km. Mandalay - Bagan : 179 km.
B – ⊨ and ⊑ Runs via Pyay line.   z – To Shwenyaung (Table 6160).

YANGON - MAWLAMYINE - DAWEI — 6170

Myanmar Railways

km		89	175	35			90	36	176
0	Yangon ....d.	0715	1825	1900	Dawei Port ....d.	...	0540	...
78	Bago ....d.	0904	2019	2250	Ye ....d.	...	1438	...
	Kyaikto ....d.	1157	2320	0130	Mawlamyine ....a.	...	2025	...
281	Mawlamyine ....a.	1650	0400	0600	Mawlamyine ....d.	0800	1930	2055
281	Mawlamyine ....d.		0430		Kyaikto ....d.	1233	2355	0130
	Ye ....d.		1025		Bago ....d.	1524	0245	0413
	Dawei Port ....a.		1900		Yangon ....a.	1730	0420	0620

YANGON - PYAY — 6175

MRC

km		63	75	71
0	Yangon ....d.	0700	1100	1300
257	Pyay ....a.	1800	2215	2130
		76	64	72
	Pyay ....d.	0200	0615	2330
	Yangoon ....a.	1340	1730	0750

⊖ – Information unavailable at press date.   * – Trains 63, 64, 75, 76 use Rangoon Kyemyindine station.

INDONESIA

Capital: **Jakarta** (GMT +7).   2017 Public Holidays: Jan. 1, 28, Mar. 28, Apr. 14, 24, May 1, 11, 25, Jun. 26, 27, Aug. 17, Sept. 2, 22, Dec. 1, 25.

Rail services in Indonesia are operated by PT Kereta Api (Indonesian Railways, www.kereta-api.co.id). Trains may convey any of three classes of seated accommodation which are known locally as Eksekutif, Bisnis and Ekonomi, shown in the tables as 1, 2 and 3.

SUMATRA — 6200

PT Kereta Api

Medan - Pematangsiantar: *127 km*   Journey 4 hours
Medan depart: 1327⊙.
Pematangsiantar depart: 0725⊙.

Medan - Rantau Prapat: *266 km*   Journey 5½ - 6 hours
Medan depart: 0840, 1037, 1537, 2235.
Rantau Prapat depart: 0840, 1530, 1730, 2310.

Medan - Tanjung Balai: *173 km*   Journey 4½ hours
Medan depart: 0735⊙, 1232⊙, 1755⊙.
Tanjung Balai depart: 0855⊙, 1435⊙, 1940⊙.

Padang - Pariaman: Journey 2 hours.
Padang depart: 0600⊙, 0910⊙, 1400⊙, 1640⊙.
Pariaman depart: 0545⊙, 0850⊙, 1415⊙, 1620⊙.

Palembang - Lubuk Linggau: *305 km*   Journey 7 - 8½ hours
Palembang Kertapati depart: 2000.
Lubuk Linggau depart: 2000.

Palembang - Panjang: ♠ *401 km*   Journey 8 - 8½ hours
Palembang Kertapati depart: 0830⊙, 2100.
Panjang depart: 0830⊙, 2100.

⊙ – Conveys 3rd class only.   ♠ – Panjang is also known as Tanjungkarang Telukbetang.

BEYOND EUROPE - SOUTH EAST ASIA, AUSTRALIA and NEW ZEALAND

6205 JAKARTA - BANDUNG

PT Kereta Api

km		20		22	24	32	34	26	28	30
		12		12	12	⑥⑦	12	12	12	12
0	**Jakarta** Gambir d.	0500	...	0830	1015	1145	1245	1530	1815	2000
12	**Jakarta** Jatinegara d.	|	...	|	|	|	|	|	|	|
173	**Bandung** a.	0834	...	1159	1335	1457	1547	1828	2127	2312

	19	21	31	33		23	25	27	29
	12	12	⑥⑦	12		12	12	12	12
Bandung d.	0500	0630	0735	0835	...	1150	1430	1615	1925
Jakarta Jatinegara a.	0754	0929	1045	1136	...	1447	1736	1920	2223
Jakarta Gambir a.	0804	0940	1056	1148	...	1457	1747	1931	2234

6210 JAKARTA - SEMARANG - SURABAJA

PT Kereta Api

km		202	62	14	160	16	2	93	64	66	152	68	178	78	56	12		18	176	70	48	158	97	4	75
		3	12	1	3	1	1	12	12	12	3	12	3	12	1	1		1	3	12	1	3	12	1	12
	Bandung d.	...	...	...	...	...	...	0955	...	...	...	...	...	...	...	...	...	...	...	...	...	...	1945	...	2125
	Jakarta Kota d.	...	...	...	...	...	...	|	...	...	...	...	...	...	...	...	...	...	...	...	...	...	|	...	|
	Jakarta Gambir d.	...	2145	0700	...	1000	0930	|	0905	1100	...	1210	...	...	1500	1615	...	1715	...	1945	1915	...	|	2130	|
	Jakarta Pasar Senen d.	2300	|	|	0715	|	|	|	|	|	1200	|	1400	1545	|	|	...	|	1600	|	|	1945	|	|	|
0	**Jakarta** Jatinegara d.	|	|	|	|	|	|	|	|	|	|	|	|	|	|	|	...	|	|	|	|	|	|	|	|
212	Cirebon d.	0212p	0058	0952	1013p	1246	1212	1405	1225	1410	1501	1521	1715p	1847	1752	1907	...	1958	1930p	2302	2212	2247p	2350	0016	0144
288	Tegal d.	0327	...	1052	1122	...	|	...	1347	1532	1610	...	1822	2019	1900	2008	...	...	2033	0024	2315	2356	...	|	0254
348	Pekalongan d.	0427	...	1143	1221	...	1350	...	...	...	1707	...	1918	2121	2003	2100	...	...	...	...	2357	0053	...	|	0348
443	**Semarang** Tawang d.	0552n	...	1300	1343	...	1506	...	...	...	1845n	...	2105	2300	2147	2215	...	...	...	...	0135	0216	...	0304	0535
644	Madiun d.	...	...	...	...	...	|	...	...	...	|	...	|	|	0120	...	...	...	...	...	|	...	...	|	|
737	Kediri d.	...	...	...	...	...	|	...	...	...	|	...	|	|	|	...	...	...	...	...	|	...	...	|	|
573	Cepu d.	...	...	...	...	...	|	...	...	...	|	...	2318	0109	♣	...	...	...	...	...	0329	...	...	|	0745
610	Bojonegoro d.	...	...	...	...	...	|	...	...	...	2134	...	2355	0146	|	...	...	...	...	...	0406	...	...	|	0822
713	**Surabaja** Pasar Turi a.	...	...	...	...	...	1830	...	...	...	2258	...	0130	0320	0346b	...	...	...	...	...	0535	...	...	0630	0957
881	**Malang** a.	...	...	...	...	...	...	...	...	...	0117	...	...	...	...	...	...	...	...	...	...	...	...	...	...

	91	61	15	171		63	11	65	157	17	1	95	67	69	13	201	151	77	159	55	73	47	3	177
	13	12	1	3		12	1	12	3	1	1	13	12	12	1	3	3	12	3	1	12	1	1	3
Malang d.	...	...	...	...	...	...	...	...	...	...	...	...	...	...	...	...	1145	...	...	...	...	...	...	...
Surabaja Pasar Turi d.	...	...	...	...	...	...	...	...	...	...	0800	...	...	...	...	...	1415	1530	...	1600b	1615	1750	2000	2100
Bojonegoro d.	...	...	...	...	...	...	...	...	...	...	|	...	...	...	...	...	1544	1710	...	|	1753	1922	|	2233
Cepu d.	...	...	...	...	...	...	...	...	...	...	|	...	...	...	...	...	1622	1747	...	♥	1830	1956	|	2309
Kediri d.	...	...	...	...	...	...	...	...	...	...	|	...	...	...	...	...	|	|	...	|	|	|	|	|
Madiun d.	...	...	...	...	...	...	...	...	...	...	|	...	...	...	...	...	|	|	...	1845	|	|	|	|
Semarang Tawang d.	...	...	...	0250	...	...	0600	...	0800	...	1130	...	...	...	1600	1400n	1841n	2005	2100	2230	2043	2205	2331	0142
Pekalongan d.	...	...	...	0419	...	...	0718	...	0928	...	1243	...	...	...	1718	1525	2005	2133	2228	2350	2212	2329	|	|
Tegal d.	...	...	...	0514	...	0530	0810	...	1030	...	|	...	1445	1605	1810	1625	2110	2238	2330	0050	2304	0023	|	0410
Cirebon d.	0500	0520	0620	0630p	...	0715	0913	0820	1140p	1400	1422	1500	1604	1800	1913	1738p	2218	2357	0033p	0157	0021	0128	0219	0519p
Jakarta Jatinegara a.	|	0825	0904	0936	...	1012	1148	1119	1427	1636	1649	|	1907	2058	2155	2029	0107	0249	0321	0435	|	0405	0447	0814
Jakarta Pasar Senen a.	|	|	|	0948	...	|	|	|	1436	|	|	|	|	|	|	2038	0116	0258	0330	|	|	|	|	0823
Jakarta Gambir a.	|	0838	0916	...	...	1023	1159	1131	...	1648	1700	|	1918	2110	2206	...	...	...	...	0446	|	0416	0457	...
Jakarta Kota a.	|	...	...	...	...	...	...	...	...	...	...	|	...	...	...	...	...	...	...	...	|	...	...	...
Bandung a.	0908	...	...	...	...	...	...	...	...	...	...	1908	...	...	...	...	...	...	...	...	0426	...	...	...

b – Surabaya Gubeng. n – Semerang Poncol. p – Cirebon Prujakan. ♣ – Via Jombang (d. 0245). ♥ – Via Jombang (d. 1704).

6215 JAKARTA - YOGYAKARTA - SURABAJA

PT Kereta Api

km		192	210	136	164	10	140	52	86	89	174	166	176	44	42	142	8	54	138	162	134	58	87	84	144
		3	3	2	3	1	12	1	12	12	3	3	3	1	1	12	1	1	2	3	2	12	12	12	2
	Jakarta Kota d.	...	...	...	...	...	...	...	...	...	...	♠	...	...	...	...	...	...	...	...	...	...	...	...	...
	Jakarta Gambir d.	...	...	...	...	0800	...	0850	...	...	...	...	...	1645	1745	...	2015	2045	...	...	...	2215	...	...	...
	Jakarta Pasar Senen d.	0530	...	0615	0645	|	0815	|	...	...	1030	1300	1600	|	|	1800	|	|	1900	2145	2200	|	...	...	...
0	**Jakarta** Jatinegara d.	|	...	|	|	|	|	|	...	...	|	|	|	|	|	|	|	|	|	|	|	|	...	...	...
212	Cirebon d.	0851p	...	0927	0950p	1053	1118	1150	...	...	1345p	1630	1930p	1938	2033	2108	2308	2344	2159	0050p	0107	0124	...	...	...
343	Purwokerto d.	1058	...	1142	1207	1258	1333	1400	...	...	1615	1836	|	2140	2237	2325	0115	0155	0026	0257	0320	0335	...	...	...
370	Kroya d.	1148	...	1222	1235	1332	1405	|	...	...	|	|	◄	|	|	2356	|	|	|	0332	|	0403	...	...	...
445	Kutoarjo d.	1318	...	1340	1357	1444	1526	1540	...	...	1819	2054	|	|	0053	0134	0254	0329	|	0448	0502	...	...	...	...
508	**Yogyakarta** d.	...	...	1440	1505l	1542	...	1632	1630	...	|	2206l	|	0105	0200	...	0352	0420	0316	0555l	0605	...	...	0645	...
568	Solo Balapan d.	...	...	...	...	1635	...	...	1725	...	|	|	0218j	0200	0300	...	0445	...	...	...	0658	...	...	0744	...
663	Madiun d.	...	...	...	...	...	...	...	1912	...	2255	0050	0450	0325	0433	...	...	...	...	...	...	...	...	0907	1330
756	Kediri d.	...	...	...	...	...	...	...	|	...	|	0235	0636	|	0615	...	...	...	...	...	...	...	...	|	|
826	Blitar d.	...	...	...	...	...	...	...	|	...	|	...	...	|	0735	...	...	...	...	...	...	...	...	|	|
900	**Malang** a.	...	1555	...	...	...	...	...	|	...	|	...	...	0810	0920	...	...	...	...	...	...	...	...	|	|
750	Jombang d.	...	|	...	...	...	...	...	2048	...	0022	...	...	0446↑	...	...	...	...	...	...	...	...	...	1037	1526
831	**Surabaja** Gubeng a.	...	|	...	...	...	...	...	2151	2200	0125	...	...	0620↑	...	...	...	...	...	...	...	...	0900	1140	1655
	Jember d.	...	2040	...	...	...	...	...	...	0155	...	...	...	...	...	...	...	...	...	...	...	...	1300	...	...
1140	**Banyuwangi Baru** a.	...	2330	...	...	...	...	...	...	0430	...	...	...	...	...	...	...	...	...	...	...	...	1530	...	...

		139	135	51	208	7	161	90	143	83	165	57	191	173	175	141	137	163	133	53	41	9	88	43	85
		12	2	1	3	1	3	12	2	12	3	12	3	3	3	12	2	3	2	1	1	1	12	1	12
Banyuwangi Baru d.	...	...	...	...	0500	...	...	2200	...	...	♦	...	...	...	...	...	...	...	...	...	...	...	0900	...	...
Jember d.	...	...	...	...	0750	...	...	0037	...	...	...	...	...	...	...	...	...	...	...	...	...	...	1135	...	...
Surabaja Gubeng d.	...	...	...	...	|	...	...	0426	0935	0730	...	...	...	1200	...	...	...	...	...	...	...	...	1526	1700	1725
Jombang d.	...	...	...	...	|	...	...	...	1053	0849	...	...	...	1306	...	...	...	...	...	...	...	...	...	1804	1832
Malang d.	...	...	...	...	1256	...	...	...	|	|	...	...	...	|	...	...	...	...	...	...	1330	...	...	1425↑	|
Blitar d.	...	...	...	...	...	...	...	...	|	|	...	...	...	|	...	...	...	...	...	...	1515	...	...	|	|
Kediri d.	...	...	...	...	...	...	...	...	1237	|	0745	...	...	|	1300	...	...	...	...	...	1627	...	...	|	|
Madiun d.	...	...	...	...	...	...	...	...	...	1028	1000	...	...	1432	1515	...	...	...	...	...	1807	...	...	1938	2016
Solo Balapan d.	...	...	...	...	...	0800	...	...	...	1200	|	...	...	|	1657j	...	...	...	1730	...	0930	2000	...	2058	2142
Yogyakarta d.	...	...	0700	0800	...	0857	0900l	...	...	1255	1243l	...	...	|	|	...	1745	1800l	1835	2000	2035	2057	...	2200	2232
Kutoarjo d.	...	0700	0804	0857	...	0953	1010	...	...	...	1354	...	1700	1817	►	1900	|	1910	1941	2056	2132	2153	...	|	...
Kroya d.	...	0823	|	|	...	|	1128	...	...	...	|	1530	1845	|	|	2034	|	2049	2103	|	|	|	...	|	...
Purwokerto d.	...	0900	0952	1040	...	1130	1212	...	...	...	1625	1610	1928	2030	|	2110	2050	2136	2151	2245	2310	2333	...	0030	...
Cirebon d.	...	1125	1200	1245	...	1334	1430p	...	...	...	1849	1820	2142p	2240p	2310p	2334	2300	2343p	2356	0050	0115	0140	...	0235	...
Jakarta Jatinegara a.	...	1409	1457	1521	...	1611	1713	...	...	...	2144	2112	0032	0139	0205	0222	0153	0232	0303	0331	0352	0417	...	0518	...
Jakarta Pasar Senen a.	...	1418	1506	|	...	|	1722	...	...	...	2153	|	0041	0148	0214	0231	0202	0241	0312	|	|	|	...	|	...
Jakarta Gambir a.	...	...	...	1533	...	1622	...	...	...	...	...	2123	...	...	...	...	...	...	...	0342	0403	0428	...	0529	...
Jakarta Kota a.	...	...	...	...	...	...	...	...	...	...	...	...	...	...	...	...	...	...	...	...	...	...	...	...	...

j – Solo Jebres. l – Yogyakarta Lempuyangan. p – Cirebon Prujakan. ♠ – From Merak dep. 0815. ♦ – To Merak arr. 0207. ► – Via Semarang Tawang (d. 1925) and Tegal (d. 2155). ◄ – Via Tegal (d. 2042) and Semarang Twang (d. 2327).

6220 BANDUNG - SURABAYA

PT Kereta Api

km		180	80	6	132	100	82	50	102	104
			12	1	2	123	12	1	13	13
0	**Bandung** d.	...	0720	0830	1545	1650	1855	1930	...	...
124	Tasikmalaya d.	0825	1016	1119	1853	2002	2153	2224	...	...
156	Banjar d.	0930	1115	1215	1955	2058	2255	2325	...	...
249	Kroya d.	|	|	1356	2127	2239	0035	0122	...	...
324	Kutoarjo d.	1308	1414	1505	2340	0033	0200	0234	...	...
387	**Yogyakarta** d.	1425l	1520	1602	0048	0135	0304	0332	0730	2045
447	Solo Balapan d.	|	1615	1652	0141	0250	0400	0424	0834	2152
542	Madiun d.	1737	...	1810	0305	0408	...	0545	1035	2320
635	Kediri d.	|	...	|	|	0552	...	|	1238	0108
705	Blitar d.	|	...	|	|	0707	...	|	1351	0223
779	**Malang** a.	|	...	|	|	0901	...	|	1537	0400
629	Jombang d.	2032	...	1925	0427	...	...	0706	...	...
710	**Surabaya** Gubeng a.	2136	...	2019	0531	...	...	0812	...	...

	79	5	81	49	99	131	103	179	101
	12	1	12	1	123	2	13	3	13
Surabaya Gubeng d.	...	0700	...	1630	...	1900	...	0815	...
Jombang d.	...	0756	...	1735	...	2041	...	0920	...
Malang d.	...	|	...	|	1600	|	2015	|	0825
Blitar d.	...	|	...	|	1746	|	2155	|	1007
Kediri d.	...	|	...	|	1856	|	2308	|	1118
Madiun d.	...	0910	...	1915	2055	2146	0115	1112	1310
Solo Balapan d.	0700	1029	1900	2034	2235	2325	0303	|	1445
Yogyakarta d.	0808	1125	2008	2128	2332	0030	0357	1400l	1540
Kutoarjo d.	0910	1225	2109	2223	0031	0141	...	1509	...
Kroya d.	|	1345	2230	0002	0252	0334	...	|	...
Banjar d.	1212	1525	0030	0140	0425	0500	...	1845	...
Tasikmalaya d.	1308	1621	0126	0236	0526	0620	...	2004	...
Bandung a.	1600	1906	0418	0521	0825	0959	...	...	...

596 ITE

AUSTRALIA

Capital: **Canberra** (GMT + 10).   2017 Public Holidays: Jan. 1, 2, 26, Apr. 14, 17, 25, June 8(not WA), Dec. 25, 26.

Interstate trains are operated by Great Southern Rail (GSR) (www.gsr.com.au). Intrastate services are operated by Government owned agencies NSW Train Link (New South Wales, www.nswtrainlink.info), Queensland Rail (QR) (Queensland, www.qr.com.au), V/Line (Victoria, www.vline.com.au) and Transwa (Western Australia, www.transwa.wa.gov.au). Unless indicated all trains convey first and second class seated accommodation. On GSR and some overnight trains the first class accommodation is usually a private compartment which converts to sleeping berths for night time travel. The exact offering varies by operator and by train. Most longer distance trains also convey a refreshment facility. Due to the low frequency of trains reservations are recommended, even if they are not always compulsory. GSR offer the Rail Explorer Pass which gives either 2 or 3 months unlimited travel in a Red Daynighter Seat on their services. Prices : 2 months AU$545, 3 months AU$655. NSW Train Link offer the Discovery Pass which gives either 14 day, 1 month, 3 months or 6 months unlimited travel on their rail and coach network and are available for travel in either economy or premium. Prices range from AU$ 232 for a 14 day economy pass to AU$ 550 for a 6 month premium pass. QR have the Explorer Pass which offers either 1 month (AU$ 299) or 2 months (AU$ 389) unlimited travel on their services. They also offer the Costal Pass for unlimited travel in one direction between Brisbane and Cairns or vice versa. Prices 1 month AU$ 209, 2 months AU$ 289. Reservations are required for all journeys and supplements may also be payable. See www.railaustralia.com.au or www.acprail.com

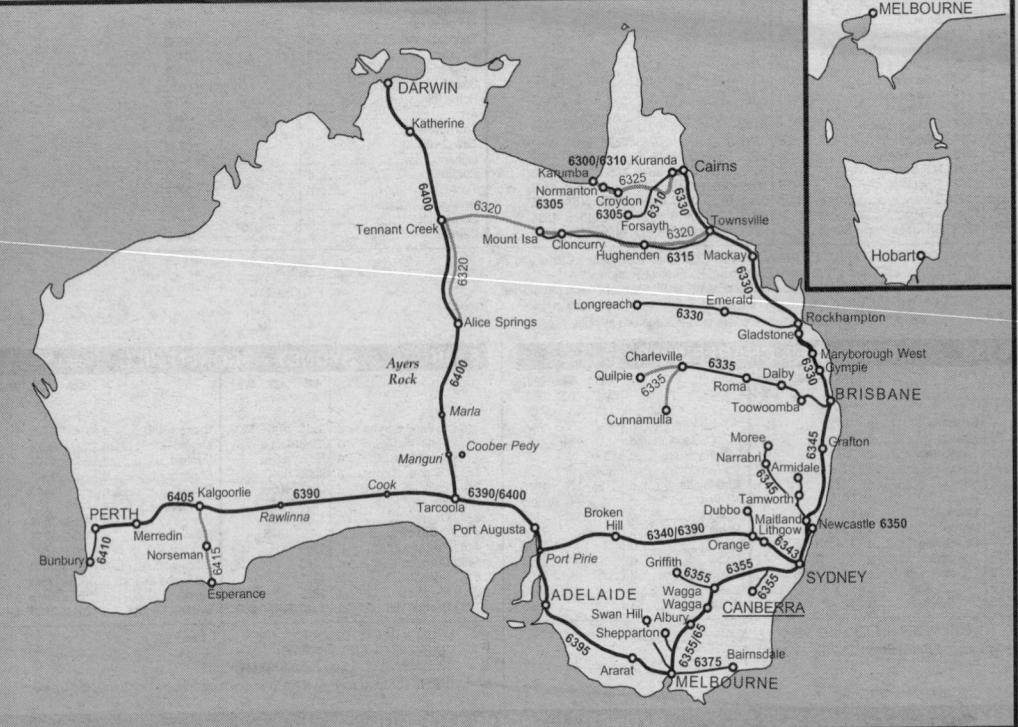

CAIRNS - KURANDA — Queensland Rail — 6300

km		3K30 2 ab	3K32 2 a			3C61 2 ab	3C65 2 a
0	Cairns .... d.	0830	0930	Kuranda .... d.	1400	1530
	Freshwater ...... d.	0850	0950	Freshwater .... d.	1532	1702
33	Kuranda .... a.	1025	1125	Cairns .... a.	1555	1725

a – Not Apr. 20, 21, June 8, 9, 15, 16, Oct. 12, 13, Nov. 13, 14, 20, 21, Dec. 4, 5, 25.
b – Not March 24, 25, 26.

CAIRNS - FORSAYTH — CKST — 6310

km		4 ③ B	4 ④ B			5 ⑤ B	6 ⑥ B
0	Cairns .... d.	0630	...	Forsayth .... d.	0830	...
33	Kuranda .... d.	0810	...	Einasleigh .... d.	1215	...
74	Mareeba .... d.	0930	...	Mount Suprise .... a.	1415	...
194	Almaden .... a.	1315	...	Mount Suprise .... d.	...	0815
194	Almaden .... d.	...	0800	Almaden .... a.	...	1145
302	Mount Suprise ... a.	...	1130	Almaden .... d.	...	1215
302	Mount Suprise ... d.	...	1215	Mareeba .... a.	...	1650
357	Einasleigh .... d.	...	1445	Kuranda .... a.	...	1650
423	Forsayth .... a.	...	1730	Cairns .... a.	...	1830

B – SAVANNAHLANDER – 🚃 – Mar. 1 - Dec. 13.
Operator: Cairns Kuranda Steam Ltd ✆ +61 7 4053 6848.

TOWNSVILLE - TENNANT CREEK — Greyhound — 6320

km		489 🚌 D			849 🚌 E
0	Townsville .... d.	1900	Alice Springs .... d.	0900	...
135	Charters Towers .... d.	2040	Barrow Creek .... d.	1235	...
378	Hughenden .... d.	0010	Tennant Creek ...... d.	1545	...
490	Richmond .... d.	0135	Barkly Homestead ... d.	1815	...
634	Julia Creek .... d.	0315	Camooweal .... d.	2130	...
768	Cloncurry .... d.	0440	Mount Isa .... a.	0010	...
886	Mount Isa .... a.	0630	Mount Isa .... d.	0010	...
886	Mount Isa .... d.	0705	Cloncurry .... d.	0135	...
1074	Camooweal .... d.	0915	Julia Creek .... d.	0310	...
1353	Barkly Homestead .. d.	1205	Richmond .... d.	0440	...
1547	Tennant Creek ...... a.	1415	Hughenden .... d.	0640	...
1771	Barrow Creek .... d.	1650	Charters Towers ..... d.	0935	...
2072	Alice Springs .... a.	2030	Townsville .... a.	1120	...

D – ③⑦.   E – ②⑤.   Operator : Greyhound Australia ✆ 07 3258 1600.

NORMANTON - CROYDON — Queensland Rail — 6305

km		③ A			④ A
0	Normanton .... d.	0830	Croydon .... d.	0830	...
90	Blackbull .... a.	1115	Blackbull .... a.	1015	...
152	Croydon .... a.	1330	Normanton .... a.	1330	...

A – GULFLANDER – 🚃 . Services usually suspended mid Dec. - mid Feb.

TOWNSVILLE - MOUNT ISA — Queensland Rail — 6315

km		3M34 ③⑥ C			3231 ④⑦ C
0	Townsville .... d.	1240	Mount Isa .... d.	1330	...
138	Charters Towers ... d.	1540	Duchess .... d.	1515	...
388	Hughenden .... d.	2020	Cloncurry .... d.	1745	...
502	Richmond .... d.	2245	Julia Creek .... d.	2100	...
648	Julia Creek .... d.	0210	Richmond .... d.	0005	...
780	Cloncurry .... d.	0520	Hughenden .... d.	0240	...
890	Duchess .... d.	0745	Charters Towers ... d.	0705	...
977	Mount Isa .... a.	0935	Townsville .... a.	1010	...

C – INLANDER – 🚌 and 🍴 Townsville - Mount Isa and v.v. Ⓡ.

CAIRNS - KARUMBA — Trans North Bus — 6325

km		🚌 ①③⑤			🚌 ②④⑥
0	Cairns Central ...... d.	0630	Karumba .... d.	0630	...
33	Kuranda .... d.	0705	Normanton .... d.	0725	...
75	Mareeba .... d.	0740	Croydon .... d.	0925	...
109	Atherton .... d.	0820	Georgetown .... d.	1055	...
140	Herberton .... d.	0835	Mount Suprise ..... d.	1240	...
160	Ravenshoe .... d.	0945	Undara .... d.	1305	...
211	Mount Garnet ...... d.	1015	Mount Garnet ...... d.	1355	...
287	Undara .... d.	1105	Ravenshoe .... d.	1450	...
321	Mount Suprise ..... d.	1130	Herberton .... d.	1520	...
422	Georgetown .... d.	1325	Atherton .... d.	1540	...
579	Croydon .... d.	1505	Mareeba .... d.	1615	...
744	Normanton .... d.	1645	Kuranda .... d.	1640	...
820	Karumba .... a.	1730	Cairns Central ..... a.	1730	...

Operator: Trans North Bus and Coach ✆ 07 4095 8644.

6330 CAIRNS, TOWNSVILLE and LONGREACH - BRISBANE

Queensland Rail

km	km			V9Q4	Q904	Q904	A960	Q902	Q902	Q902	
				◄	②⑤	①④⑥	①④	①④⑥	②③⑤	⑦	
				A	B	B*	C	B	B*	B*	
0		**Cairns**	d.	0900	...	...	...	...	...	...	...
23		Gordonvale	d.	0926	...	...	...	...	...	...	...
87		Innisfail	d.	1043	...	...	...	...	...	...	...
135		Tully	d.	1150	...	...	...	...	...	...	...
178		Cardwell	d.	1242	...	...	...	...	...	...	...
232		Ingham	d.	1331	...	...	...	...	...	...	...
340		**Townsville**	a.	1509	...	...	...	...	...	...	...
340		**Townsville**	d.	1524	...	...	...	...	...	...	...
421		Ayr	d.	1627	...	...	...	...	...	...	...
432		Home Hill	d.	1644	...	...	...	...	...	...	...
531		Bowen	d.	1750	...	...	...	...	...	...	...
596		Proserpine	d.	1841	...	...	...	...	...	...	...
717		Mackay	d.	2026	...	...	...	...	...	...	...
754		Sarina	d.	2057	...	...	...	...	...	...	...
869		St Lawrence	d.	2220	...	...	...	...	...	...	...
	0	**Longreach**	d.	|	...	...	1000	...	...	...	...
	108	Barcaldine	d.	|	...	...	1227	...	...	...	...
	194	Jericho	d.	|	...	...	1403	...	...	...	...
	249	Alpha	d.	|	...	...	1518	...	...	...	...
	422	Emerald	d.	|	...	...	1933	...	...	...	...
1042	687	Rockhampton	d.	0110	...	...	0037	0710	0730	0730	...
1152	797	Gladstone	d.	0225	...	...	0255	0826	0901	0901	...
1330	975	Bundaberg	d.	0403	0515	0515	0526	1005	1122	1122	...
1414	1059	Maryborough West	d.	0457	0601	0623	0635	1058	1236	1236	...
1507	1152	Gympie North	d.	0609	0701	0748	0811	1205	1409	1409	...
1550	1195	Cooroy	d.	0642	0737	0837	0856	1240	1457	1505	...
1575	1220	Nambour	d.	0705	0757	0916	0925	1302	1526	1534	...
1681	1326	**Brisbane** Roma Street	a.	0920	0955	1140	1155	1450	1755	1755	...

		Q301	Q301	AW57	VCQ5		Q303	Q303	AW57	
		②⑤⑦	①④⑥	⑥	►		△	①④	②	
		B	B*	C	A		B*	B	C	
Brisbane Roma Street	d.	1100	1100	1355	1545	...	1625	1655	1810	...
Nambour	d.	1235	1316	1619	1731	...	1842	1838	2023	...
Cooroy	d.	1258	1342	1649	1754	...	1908	1858	2049	...
Gympie North	d.	1337	1443	1745	1828	...	1954	1929	2145	...
Maryborough West	d.	1440	1606	1905	1928	...	2117	2028	2305	...
Bundaberg	d.	1531	1719	2036	2019	...	2330	2125	0013	...
Gladstone	d.	1712	1943	2309	2207	...	...	...	0246	...
Rockhampton	d.	1845	2125	0103	2341	...	...	...	0440	...
Emerald	d.	...	...	0602	|	...	...	...	0940	...
Alpha	d.	...	...	1012	|	...	...	...	1350	...
Jericho	d.	...	...	1121	|	...	...	...	1459	...
Barcaldine	d.	...	...	1316	|	...	...	...	1655	...
Longreach	a.	...	...	1540	|	...	...	...	1920	...
St Lawrence	d.	...	...	...	0200	...	...	...	...	...
Sarina	d.	...	...	...	0330	...	...	...	...	...
Mackay	d.	...	...	...	0424	...	...	...	...	...
Prosperine	d.	...	...	...	0602	...	...	...	...	...
Bowen	d.	...	...	...	0639	...	...	...	...	...
Home Hill	d.	...	...	...	0748	...	...	...	...	...
Ayr	d.	...	...	...	0802	...	...	...	...	...
Townsville	a.	...	...	...	0908	...	...	...	...	...
Townsville	d.	...	...	...	0923	...	...	...	...	...
Ingham	d.	...	...	...	1056	...	...	...	...	...
Cardwell	d.	...	...	...	1152	...	...	...	...	...
Tully	d.	...	...	...	1259	...	...	...	...	...
Innisfail	d.	...	...	...	1348	...	...	...	...	...
Gordonvale	d.	...	...	...	1521	...	...	...	...	...
Cairns	a.	...	...	...	1605	...	...	...	...	...

A – SPIRIT OF QUEENSLAND TILT TRAIN – R, (2) and 🍸 Brisbane - Cairns and v.v.
B – TILT TRAIN – (12) and 🍸 Brisbane - Bundaberg, Rockhampton and v.v.
B* – (2) and 🍸 Traditional diesel replacement service whilst Tilt trains are being refurbished.
C – SPIRIT OF THE OUTBACK – 1cl ✕, (2) and 🍸 Brisbane - Longreach and v.v.
R – RailBed – This is a seat by day and converts to a lie-flat bed at night.

△ – ②③⑤⑦.
► – ①②③⑤⑥.
◄ – ①③④⑤⑦.

6335 BRISBANE - CHARLEVILLE

Queensland Rail

km			3S86	🚌	🚌
			②④	③⑤	③⑤
			D		
0	**Brisbane** ‡	d.	1915	...	...
38	Ipswich	d.	2013	...	...
161	Toowoomba	d.	2325	...	...
244	Dalby	d.	0117	...	...
371	Miles	d.	0325	...	...
512	Roma	d.	0615	...	...
597	Mitchell	d.	0805	...	...
687	Morven	d.	0955	...	...
777	**Charleville**	a.	1145	1155	1155
875	Wyandra	a.	...	1315	|
972	Cunnamulla	a.	...	1425	|
876	Cooladdi	a.	...	...	1305
998	Quilpie	a.	...	...	1430

		🚌	🚌	3907
		③⑤	③⑤	③⑤
				D
Quilpie	d.	...	1500	...
Cooladdi	d.	...	1640	...
Cunnamulla	d.	1500	|	...
Wyandra	d.	1625	|	...
Charleville	d.	1735	1740	1815
Morven	d.	...	...	1955
Mitchell	d.	...	...	2145
Roma	d.	...	...	2335
Miles	d.	...	...	0210
Dalby	d.	...	...	0447
Toowoomba	d.	...	...	0700
Ipswich	d.	...	...	1012
Brisbane ‡	a.	...	...	1125

D – WESTLANDER – (2) and 🍸. 🅁.
‡ – Brisbane **Roma Street**.

6340 SYDNEY - BROKEN HILL

NSW Train Link

km			445	427	WE1
			①		③
			E	F	G
0	**Sydney** Central	d.	0618	0718	1503
	Penrith	d.	0704u	0806u	|
	Katoomba	d.	0759u	0859u	|
155	Lithgow	d.	0839u	0940	|
240	Bathurst	d.	0947	1052	|
290	Blayney	d.	1035	1138	|
323	Orange	d.	1059	1202	|
462	**Dubbo**	a.	|	1345	|
446	Parkes	d.	1248	|	|
546	Condobolin	d.	1400	|	|
816	Ivanhoe	d.	1631	|	|
1017	Menindee	d.	1822	|	|
1125	**Broken Hill**	a.	1910	*2245**	0600

		428	446	WE2
			②	②
		F	E	G
Broken Hill	d.	*0345**	0745	1855
Menindee	d.	|	0924	|
Ivanhoe	d.	|	1107	|
Condobolin	d.	|	1341	|
Parkes	d.	|	1443	|
Dubbo	d.	1415	|	|
Orange	d.	1554	1644	|
Blayney	d.	1621	1716	|
Bathurst	d.	1707	1801	|
Lithgow	d.	1823	1913s	|
Katoomba	d.	1905s	1954s	|
Penrith	d.	1956s	2045s	|
Sydney Central	a.	2044	2130	1107

E – BROKEN HILL OUTBACK EXPLORER – (2) and 🍸.
F – DUBBO XPT – (12) and 🍸.
G – INDIAN PACIFIC – See Table **6390/6400**.
s – Calls to set down only. u – Calls to pick up only. * – Connection by 🚌.

6343 SYDNEY - LITHGOW - BATHURST

Sydney Trains, NSW Train Link

km			505	507	A	509	529	525	527	503	501	533	4501
			①–⑤	①–⑤		①–⑤	⑥⑦	①–⑤	⑦	⑦	①–⑤	①–⑤	
0	**Sydney** Central	d.	0420	0818	1018	1218	1218	1418	1418	1618	1621	1721	1752
55	Penrith u	d.	0508	0906	1106	1305	1309	1505	1509	1709	1708	1808	1839
110	Katoomba	d.	0619	1016	1217	1416	1419	1616	1619	1819	1812	1912	1940
127	Mount Victoria	d.	0642	1037	1237	1437	1440	1637	1640	1840	1833	1933	2001
155	**Lithgow**	a.	0710	1110	1305	1505	1510	1705	1710	1910	1911	2011	2025
240	**Bathurst**	a.	*0815**	*1225**	...	*1625**	*1625**	*1820**	*1820**	*2015**	*2015**	2121	2135

		4502	504	502	506	4506	508	510	534	536	538	548
		①–⑤	①–⑤	①–⑤	①–⑤	⑥	①–⑤	Ⓒ	①–⑤	⑦	①–⑤	⑦
		C		B								
Bathurst	d.	0549	*0535**	...	*1005**	*1005**	*1205**	*1205**	*1410**	*1420**	*1820**	*1750**
Lithgow	d.	0657	0724	0925	1125	1137	1325	1337	1525	1537	1934	1937
Mount Victoria	d.	0724	0754	0954	1154	1205	1354	1405	1554	1605	2002	2005
Katoomba	d.	0740	0814	1013	1213	1225	1413	1425	1613	1625	2021	2025
Penrith s	d.	0838	0925	1123	1324	1335	1524	1535	1724	1735	2132	2135
Sydney Central	a.	0927	1014	1214	1414	1431	1614	1631	1814	1831	2222	2231

A – Additional services: ① – ⑤ 0018, 0621, 1752, 1836, 2018, 2218; ⑥⑦ 0018, 0348, 0548, 0818, 1418, 1618, 1818, 2018, 2218.
B – Additional services: ① – ⑤ 0300, 0415, 0508, 0538, 0608, 1733, 2134; ⑥⑦ 0338, 0438, 0637, 0737, 0937, 1137, 1537, 1737, 1937, 2208.
C – Additional service: ⑥⑦ 0725. **s** – Calls to set down only. **u** – Calls to pick up only. * – Connection by 🚌.

6345 BRISBANE, ARMIDALE and MOREE - SYDNEY

NSW Train Link

km	km			036	244	224	032	034	
				H	J	K	L	M	
0		**Brisbane** Roma Street	d.	...	...	...	0555	*1500**	...
182		Casino	d.	...	...	...	0820	1930	...
291		Grafton City	d.	0515	...	...	0953	2058	...
379		Coffs Harbour	d.	0626	...	...	1105	2210	...
		Nambucca Heads	d.	0708	...	...	1147	2251r	...
		Macksville	d.	0721	...	...	1200	2305r	...
483		Kempsey	d.	0805	...	...	1243	2347	...
532		Wauchope	d.	0844	...	...	1322	0024	...
608		Taree	d.	0952	...	...	1441	0131	...
	0	**Armidale**	d.	|	...	0840	|	|	...
	124	Tamworth	d.	|	...	1027	|	|	...
	◐	**Moree**	d.	|	0805	|	|	|	...
	◐	Narrabri	d.	|	0910	|	|	|	...
	◐	Gunnedah	d.	|	1014	|	|	|	...
	168	Werris Creek	d.	|	1107	1107	|	|	...
	264	Scone	d.	|	1228	1228	|	|	...
	290	Muswellbrook	d.	|	1248	1248	|	|	...
794	387	Maitland	d.	1253	1355	1355	1732	0410	...
824	416	Broadmeadow	d.	1319	1419	1419	1754	0433	...
897	499	Gosford	d.	1419s	1521s	1521s	1855s	0538s	...
953	545	Hornsby	d.	1459s	1603s	1603s	1936s	0622s	...
987	579	**Sydney** Central	a.	1539	1638	1638	2012	0659	...

		033	243	223	035	031	
		M	J	K	H	L	
Sydney Central	d.	0711	0929	0929	1141	1441	...
Hornsby	d.	0750u	1005u	1005u	1220u	1520u	...
Gosford	d.	0832u	1044u	1044u	1300u	1601u	...
Broadmeadow	d.	0936	1145	1145	1405	1704	...
Maitland	d.	1000	1210	1210	1429	1727	...
Muswellbrook	d.	|	1316	1316	|	|	...
Scone	d.	|	1337	1337	|	|	...
Werris Creek	d.	|	1457	1457	|	|	...
Gunnedah	d.	|	1545	|	|	|	...
Narrabri	a.	|	1652	|	|	|	...
Moree	a.	|	1800	|	|	|	...
Tamworth	a.	|	...	1537	|	|	...
Armidale	a.	|	...	1735	|	|	...
Taree	d.	1241	...	...	1725	2008	...
Wauchope	d.	1348	...	...	1831	2113	...
Kempsey	d.	1426	...	...	1910	2152	...
Macksville	d.	1507	...	...	1955	2234	...
Nambucca Heads	a.	1519	...	...	2009	*2305**	...
Coffs Harbour	d.	1558	...	...	2050	2335	...
Grafton City	d.	1712	...	...	2215	0049	...
Casino	a.	1841	...	...	...	0219	...
Brisbane Roma Street	a.	*2234**	...	...	...	0453	...

H – GRAFTON XPT – (12). 🅁.
J – MOREE EXPLORER – (12) and 🍸. 🅁.
K – ARMIDALE XPLORER – (12) and 🍸. 🅁.
L – BRISBANE XPT – (12) Brisbane - Sydney; 1 cl., (2) Sydney - Brisbane. 🅁.
M – CASINO XPT – 1 cl., (2) Casino - Sydney; (12) Sydney - Casino. 🅁.

r – Calls on request.
s – Calls to set down only.
u – Calls to pick up only.
* – Connection by 🚌.
◐ – Moree - Narrabri: *97 km.* Moree - Gunnedah: *190 km.* Moree - Werris Creek: *255 km.*

NEWCASTLE - SYDNEY 6350

Sydney Trains

km		Ⓐ	Ⓐ	Ⓐ	Ⓐ	Ⓐ	Ⓐ	Ⓐ	Ⓐ	Ⓐ	Ⓐ	Ⓐ		Ⓐ	Ⓐ	Ⓐ	Ⓐ	Ⓐ	Ⓐ	Ⓐ	Ⓐ	Ⓐ	Ⓐ
0	**Newcastle** d.	0210*	0405*	0420*	0503*	0530*	0603*	0623*	0701*	0712*	0801*	0812*	and at the same minutes past each hour until	1301*	1312*	1359*	1413*	1453*	1512*	1601*	1612*	1701*	1803*
	Wickham d.	0216*	0411*	0426*	0509*	0536*	0609*	0629*	0707*	0718*	0806*	0818*		1307*	1318*	1405*	1419*	1459*	1518*	1607*	1618*	1707*	1809*
	Hamilton d.	0231	0425	0440	0525	0552	0625	0645	0725	0736	0825	0836		1325	1336	1423	1437	1517	1536	1625	1636	1725	1825
88	Gosford d.	0357	0536	0606	0635	0705	0735	0806	0835	0900	0936	1000		1436	1500	1533	1601	1638	1700	1736	1800	1836	1936
168	**Sydney** Central a.	0527	0656	0726	0756	0826	0855	0926	0955	1025	1056	1126		1556	1626	1659	1729	1759	1826	1856	1926	1956	2056

	Ⓐ	Ⓐ	Ⓐ	Ⓐ	Ⓐ	Ⓒ	Ⓒ	Ⓒ	Ⓒ	Ⓒ	Ⓒ	Ⓒ	Ⓒ	Ⓒ	Ⓒ	Ⓒ	Ⓒ	Ⓒ	Ⓒ	Ⓒ	Ⓒ	Ⓒ	Ⓒ	Ⓒ
ewcastle d.	1814*	1903*	1914*	2014*	2113*	0228*	0419*	0508*	0617*	0706*	0816*	0906*	1016*	1106*	1216*	1306*	1416*	1506*	1616*	1705*	1818*	1851*	1952*	2122*
ickham d.	1820*	1907*	1920*	2020*	2119*	0234*	0425*	0514*	0623*	0714*	0822*	0914*	1022*	1112*	1222*	1312*	1422*	1512*	1622*	1711*	1824*	1857*	1958*	2128*
amilton d.	1836	1925	1936	2036	2135	0248	0439	0530	0639	0730	0840	0930	1040	1130	1240	1330	1430	1530	1640	1729	1840	1913	2014	2144
osford d.	2000	2036	2101	2200	2302	0414	0551	0651	0751	0851	0951	1051	1151	1251	1351	1451	1551	1651	1751	1851	1951	2039	2140	2304
ydney Central a.	2126	2156	2226	2325	0029	0541	0710	0810	0910	1010	1110	1210	1310	1410	1510	1610	1710	1810	1910	2010	2110	2210	2310	0045

	Ⓐ	Ⓐ	Ⓐ	Ⓐ	Ⓐ	Ⓐ	Ⓐ	Ⓐ	Ⓐ	Ⓐ		Ⓐ	Ⓐ	Ⓐ	Ⓐ	Ⓐ	Ⓐ	Ⓐ	Ⓐ	Ⓐ	Ⓐ	Ⓐ	Ⓐ
ydney Central d.	0145	0345	0445	0515	0545	0615	0645	0715	0745	0815	and at the same minutes past each hour until	1315	1345	1415	1515	1545	1615	1645	1715	1745	1815	1915	2015
osford d.	0311	0512	0612	0635	0712	0735	0812	0841	0912	0935		1435	1513	1536	1635	1705	1735	1805	1833	1905	1935	2035	2135
amilton a.	0441	0637	0737	0746	0837	0858	0937	0956	1038	1047		1558	1641	1704	1746	1819	1848	1920	1943	2020	2046	2158	2258
ickham d.	0424*	0648*	0748*	0757*	0848*	0909*	0948*	1007*	1049*	1058*		1609*	1652*	1715*	1757*	1830*	1859*	1931*	1954*	2031*	2057*	2209*	2309*
ewcastle a.	0456*	0654*	0754*	0803*	0854*	0915*	0954*	1013*	1055*	1104*		1615*	1658*	1721*	1803*	1836*	1905*	1937*	2000*	2037*	2103*	2215*	2315*

	Ⓐ	Ⓐ	Ⓐ	Ⓐ	⑥	Ⓒ	Ⓒ	Ⓒ	Ⓒ	Ⓒ	Ⓒ	Ⓒ	Ⓒ	Ⓒ	Ⓒ	Ⓒ	Ⓒ	Ⓒ	Ⓒ	Ⓒ	Ⓒ	Ⓒ	Ⓒ	Ⓒ
ydney Central d.	2115	2145	2245	2345	0145	0445	0545	0715	0815	0915	1015	1115	1215	1315	1415	1515	1615	1715	1815	1915	2015	2145	2245	2345
osford d.	2235	2313	0015	0115	0311	0615	0717	0841	0936	1036	1136	1236	1336	1436	1536	1636	1736	1836	1936	2036	2142	2315	0015	0115
amilton a.	2359	0042	0143	0244	0441	0740	0843	0953	1058	1148	1258	1348	1458	1548	1658	1748	1858	1948	2058	2154	2308	0042	0142	0242
ickham d.	0008*	0051*	0152*	0253*	0450*	0751*	0854*	1004*	1109*	1159*	1309*	1359*	1509*	1559*	1709*	1759*	1909*	1959*	2109*	2205*	2319*	0051*	0151*	0251*
ewcastle a.	0014*	0057*	0158*	0259*	0456*	0757*	0900*	1010*	1115*	1205*	1315*	1405*	1515*	1605*	1715*	1805*	1915*	2005*	2115*	2211*	2325*	0057*	0157*	0257*

* – By 🚌.

Operator: Sydney Trains ✆ 02 4907 7500.

SYDNEY - CANBERRA, GRIFFITH and MELBOURNE 6355

NSW Train Link/Vline

km		631 ⑥⑦A	641 ⑥B	631 ⒶA	Vline 🚌	Vline	NSW 🚌	623 C		633 A	635 A	621 D
0	**Sydney** Central d.	0657	0657	0704	...	...	...	0732	...	1208	1812	2032
143	Moss Vale d.	0839	0839	0854	...	...	...	0921	...	1354	2004	2218
222	Goulburn d.	0929	0929	0944	...	...	...	1012	...	1444	2054	2309
318	Queanbeyan d.	1051	|	1106	...	...	...	|	...	1606	2216	|
326	**Canberra** a.	1107	|	1122	0810v	...	0937v	|	...	1622	2230	|
320	Yass Junction d.	...	1053	...	0855	...	1045	1120	...	...	...	0017r
383	Harden d.	...	1144r	...	|	...	1153	1211r	...	...	...	0107r
427	Cootamundra d.	...	1217	...	|	...	1222	1246	...	...	...	0142
483	Junee d.	...	1258	...	|	...	...	1327	...	...	...	0220
580	Narrandera d.	...	1414	...	g	...	...	|	...	...	...	|
658	**Griffith** a.	...	1520	...	|	...	...	|	...	...	...	|
518	Wagga Wagga a.	...	...	...	|	...	...	1354	...	...	...	0247
547	The Rock d.	...	...	...	|	...	...	1414r	...	...	...	0305r
594	Culcairn d.	...	...	...	|	...	...	1441r	...	...	...	0332r
643	**Albury** 6365 a.	...	...	...	1225	1245	...	1511	...	...	...	0403
727	Wangaratta 6365 d.	...	...	...	...	1341	...	1553	...	...	...	0445
765	Benalla 6365 d.	...	...	...	...	1408	...	1617	...	...	...	0509
961	**Melbourne** S Cross a.	...	...	...	...	1635	...	1830	...	...	...	0725

	632 A	642 ⑦B	634 ⑥⑦A	634 ⒶA	624 C	NSW 🚌	636 ⑥⑦A	636 ⒶA	Vline	Vline 🚌	622 D
Melbourne S Cross d.	...	...	...	...	0830	...	...	...	1205	...	1950
Benalla 6365 d.	...	...	...	...	1041	...	...	...	1425	...	2154
Wangaratta 6365 d.	...	...	...	...	1106	...	...	...	1450	...	2220
Albury 6365 d.	...	...	...	...	1149	...	...	...	1600	1610	2305
Culcairn d.	...	...	...	...	1221r	...	...	...	...	|	2334r
The Rock d.	...	...	...	...	1249r	...	...	...	...	|	0002r
Wagga Wagga d.	...	...	...	...	1307	...	...	...	...	|	0022
Griffith d.	...	0720	...	...	|	...	...	...	...	|	|
Narrandera d.	...	0821	...	...	|	...	...	...	...	g	|
Junee d.	...	0941	...	...	1351	...	...	...	...	|	0048
Cootamundra d.	...	1032	...	...	1438	1450	...	...	...	|	0135
Harden d.	...	1108r	...	...	1514r	1521	...	...	...	|	0241r
Yass Junction d.	...	1159	...	...	1605	1620	...	...	...	|	0305r
Canberra d.	0650	|	1140	1153	|	1722v	1720	1725	...	2025v	|
Queanbeyan d.	0659	|	1149	1202	|	...	1729	1734	...	...	|
Goulburn d.	0820	1313	1310	1323	1715	...	1851	1856	...	...	0413
Moss Vale d.	0913	1413	1413	1415	1804	...	1944	1950	...	...	0502
Sydney Central a.	1056	1556	1556	1559	1953	...	2125	2137	...	...	0653

A – CANBERRA XPLORER – [12] and 🍷.
B – GRIFFITH XPLORER – [12] and 🍷.
C – MELBOURNE XPT – [12] and 🍷.
D – MELBOURNE XPT – 🛏 1 cl., [12] and ✕.
b – 1432 on ⑥⑦.
r – Calls on request.
g – Via Gundagai.
v – Canberra Civic Centre.

MELBOURNE - SHEPPARTON 6360

V/Line

km		①-⑤	⑥	⑦	①-⑤	①-⑤	①-⑤	⑦	①-⑤	①-⑤ x	⑥⑦
0	**Melbourne** S Cross d.	0701	0912	0930	0932	1252	1432	1512	1631	1822	1832
99	Seymour ☛ a.	0833	1027	1052	1053	1410	1554	1632	1808	1945	1951
99	Seymour d.	0845*	1032	1057	1058	1415	1605*	1640*	1815*	1950	1956
147	Murchison East d.	|	1107	1132	1133	1450	1650*	|	|	2025	2031
	Murchison d.	|	|	|	|	|	1653*	1728*	1903*	|	|
182	**Shepparton** a.	0955*	1141	1206	1207	1523	1723*	1800*	1935*	2059	2105

	①-⑤ F	⑥⑦ E	①-⑤	①-⑤	①-⑤	⑦	⑥	①-⑤	⑦	⑤ x
Shepparton d.	0631	0704	0850*	1040*	1250	1342*	1605	1606	1705	1800*
Murchison d.	|	|	0920*	1107*	|	1407*	|	|	|	1832*
Murchison East d.	0659	0732	|	|	1317	|	1633	1633	1733	|
Seymour d.	0734	0807	1015*	1155*	1352	1457*	1708	1708	1808	1920*
Seymour ☛ d.	0736	0809	1034	1214	1354	1512	1710	1710	1810	1955
Melbourne S Cross a.	0910	0928	1154	1335	1515	1635	1829	1835	1929	2122

E – 10 - 12 minutes later on ⑦.
F – Additional service ①-⑤ dep. Shepparton 0515 arr. Melbourne S Cross 0759.
x – Schedule will alter from Jan. 29.
* – By 🚌.

MELBOURNE - ALBURY 6365

V/Line

km			C		①-⑤		D				
0	**Melbourne** S Cross d.	0705	0830	1205	1432	1802	1950	...	...	...	...
99	Seymour ☛ a.	0824	|	1319	1554	1930	|	...	...	...	...
99	Seymour d.	0826	0948u	1321	1605*	1932	2059u	...	...	...	...
196	Benalla d.	0930	1041	1425	1720*	2036	2154	...	...	...	...
234	Wangaratta d.	0955	1106	1450	1755*	2101	2220	...	...	...	...
301	Wodonga d.	1043	|	1538	1840*	2149	|	...	...	...	...
318	**Albury** a.	1055	1149	1550	1850*	2200	2305	...	...	...	...

	D		①-⑤		C					
Albury d.	0403	0635	0900*	1245	1511	1720	...	...	...	...
Wodonga d.	|	0645	0910*	1255	|	1730	...	...	...	...
Wangaratta d.	0445	0731	1000*	1341	1553	1816	...	...	...	...
Benalla d.	0509	0758	1035*	1408	1617	1843	...	...	...	...
Seymour a.	|	0900	1200*	1510	|	1945	...	...	...	...
Seymour ☛ d.	0605s	0902	1214	1512	1711s	1947	...	...	...	...
Melbourne S Cross a.	0725	1030	1335	1635	1830	2140	...	...	...	...

C – MELBOURNE XPT – [12] and 🍷 Sydney Central - Melbourne Southern Cross and v.v.
D – MELBOURNE XPT – 🛏 1 cl., [12] and ✕ Sydney Central - Melbourne Southern Cross and v.v.
s – Calls to set down only. u – Calls to pick up only. * – By 🚌.
☛ Additional trains are available Melbourne - Seymour and v.v.

MELBOURNE - WARRNAMBOOL 6370

V/Line

km		⑥	①-⑤	⑦	⑥	①-⑤	⑦	①-⑤	⑥⑦	①-⑤	
0	**Melbourne** S Cross d.	0700	0720	0900	1300	1321	1610	1622	1900	1912	...
73	Geelong ☛ a.	0810	0828	1008	1408	1426	1708	1732	2008	2020	...
73	Geelong d.	0813	0833	1013	1413	1431	1720*	1745*	2013	2025	...
133	Colac d.	0915	0936	1115	1515	1534	1825*	1912*	2115	2128	...
267	**Warrnambool** a.	1030	1052	1230	1630	1650	2000*	...	2230	2249	...

	⑥	①-⑤	⑦		⑥	①-⑤	⑦		⑥⑦	①-⑤
Warrnambool d.	0550	0600	0725	...	1130	1208	1210*	...	1730	1750
Colac d.	0708	0719	0843	...	1248	1326	1405*	...	1848	1908
Geelong a.	0810	0825	0945	...	1350	1428	1520*	...	1950	2010
Geelong ☛ d.	0812	0828	0947	...	1352	1430	1552	...	1952	2012
Melbourne S Cross a.	0917	0931	1052	...	1457	1535	1654	...	2057	2117

☛ Additional trains are available Melbourne - Geelong and v.v. **Note: Schedules will alter from Jan. 29.** * – By 🚌.

MELBOURNE - TRARALGON - BAIRNSDALE 6375

V/Line

km		①-⑤ [R]	⑥ [R]	⑦ [R]	⑦ [R] C	⑥ [R]	①-⑤ [R]	⑥⑦	①-⑤	⑥⑦ [R]	①-⑤ [R]
0	**Melbourne** S Cross d.	0720	0725	0804	1025	1156	1320	1336	1520	1816	1834
32	Dandenong d.	0805u	0800u	0840u	1100u	1239u	1403u	1419u	1603u	1859u	1916u
101	Warragul d.	0859	0859	0929	1152	1333	1457	1513	1657	1951	2007
131	Moe d.	0918	0918	0948	1213	1352	1516	1531	1715	2010	2026
145	Morwell d.	0932	0932	1001	1223	1404	1528	1541	1728	2023	2039
159	**Traralgon** ☛ a.	0942	0942	1011	1235	1414	1538	1553	1740	2033	2049
207	Sale d.	1019	1020	1049	1400*	1451	1615	1700*	1835*	2111	2126
276	**Bairnsdale** a.	1113	1113	1142	1500*	1541	1709	...	...	2204	2218

	①-⑤ [R]	⑥ [R]	①-⑤ B	⑦ [R]	⑥ [R]	①-⑤ [R]	⑦ [R] A	⑥	⑥⑦ [R]	①-⑤ [R] x
Bairnsdale d.	0610	0630	...	0750	1222	1245	1255*	...	1637	1820
Sale d.	0659	0720	0755*	0840	1312	1335	1415	1520*	1727	1910
Traralgon ☛ d.	0736	0755	0920	0916	1348	1413	1454	1629	1803	1947
Morwell d.	0747	0806	0929	0927	1359	1424	1503	1638	1814	1958
Moe d.	0759	0817	0939	0938	1413	1436	1512	1647	1825	2009
Warragul d.	0818	0836	0958	0957	1432	1457	1533	1708	1844	2032
Dandenong d.	0909s	0928s	1049s	1046s	1524s	1549s	1626s	1804s	1934s	2138s
Melbourne S Cross a.	0957	1006	1137	1130	1610	1635	1710	1850	2019	2222

A – Additional trips ①-⑤ 0435, 1515.
B – Additional trip ①-⑤ 0920.
C – Additional trips ①-⑤ 0813, 1658.
s – Calls to set down only.
u – Calls to pick up only.
x – Schedule will alter from Jan. 29.
* – By 🚌.
☛ Frequent additional trains are available Melbourne - Traralgon and v.v.

6380 MELBOURNE - BENDIGO - SWAN HILL and ECHUCA *V/Line*

km		①–⑤	①–⑤	⑥⑦	⑥⑦	①–⑤	⑥⑦	①–⑤	⑥⑦	①–⑤	①③⑤	②④	①–⑤	⑥⑦	①–⑤	⑥⑦	①–⑥	⑤	①–⑤	⑦	⑥	①–⑤	①–⑤	⑥⑦	⑤	⑥
			[R] 🍷	[R] 🍷	[R]						🚌	🚌	[R]	[R]	[R] 🍷	[R] 🍷		🚌								
0	**Melbourne** S Cross d.	0617	0742	0836	0939	1015	1039	1215	1219	1315	...	...	1515	1719	1824	1836	1923	...	2023	2025	2050	2123	2223	2220	2350	235
38	Sunbury d.	0652	|	|	1011	1048	1109	1248	1251	1351	...	...	1553	1749	|	|	1952	...	2053	2054	2119	2153	2253	2249	0022	001
78	Woodend d.	0720	0847	0939	1039	1109	1130	1309	1319	1419	...	...	1621	1817	1932	1942	2020	...	2121	2122	2147	2222	2321	2317	0050	004
92	Kyneton d.	0728	0857	0949	1046	1117	1137	1317	1326	1426	...	...	1628	1824	1942	1952	2027	...	2128	2129	2154	2228	2328	2324	0057	005
125	Castlemaine d.	0747	0926	1011	1109	1134	1155	1334	1345	1445	...	...	1647	1844	2006	2014	2044	...	2147	2148	2213	2245	2347	2343	0116	011
162	**Bendigo** ☛ a.	0816	0956	1040	1131	1204	1219	1400	1409	1506	1530	1530	1710	1907	2034	2038	2109b	2120	2208	2213	2238	2306	0012	0008	0140	013
289	Kerang a.	|	1128	1212	|	1356*	1406*	|	|	...	|	1750	|	|	2208	2212	...	2330	...	...	...	...	...	...	...	...
345	**Swan Hill** a.	|	1210	1254	|	1439*	1448*	|	|	...	1840	1835	|	|	2251	2255	...	0014	...	...	...	...	...	...	...	...
222	Rochester a.	0940*	...	...	1234	...	...	1510*	1515*	...	...	...	1813	2010	...	...	...	...	...	...	...	...	...	...	...	...
248	**Echuca** a.	1003*	...	...	1259	...	...	1533*	1538*	...	...	...	1838	2035	..	...	...	...	...	...	...	...	...	...	...	...

	⑥	①–⑤	⑦	⑥	①–⑤	①–⑤	⑥⑦	①–⑤	⑥	⑦	①③⑤	②④	①–⑤	⑥	①–⑤	⑦	①–⑤	①–⑤	⑦	⑥	⑥⑦	⑥	⑦	①–⑤	①–⑤	⑥⑦
				[R]	[R]	[R] 🍷	[R] 🍷			[R]	🚌	🚌			[R]			[R] 🍷		[R] 🍷	[R]		[R] 🍷			
Echuca d.	...	...	...	0703	0716	...	...	0855*	0855*	0903	...	...	...	...	...	1250*	1240*	...	...	...	1608	...	...	...	...	...
Rochester d.	...	...	...	0726	0739	...	...	0920*	0920*	0926	...	...	...	...	...	1315*	1320*	...	...	...	1631	...	...	...	...	...
Swan Hill d.	...	...	...	|	|	0710	0710	|	|	|	0900	0900	...	1000*	1050*	|	|	1243	1305*	1330	|	...	1623	1525a	...	...
Kerang d.	...	...	...	|	|	0750	0751	|	|	|	|	0950	...	1046*	1136*	|	|	1323	1351*	1410	|	...	1703	1605a	...	...
Bendigo ☛ d.	0730	0745	0800	0829	0845	0922	0923	1030	1030	1030	1215	1215	1230	1232	1336	1424	1438	1456	1537	1544	1735	1840	1836	1847	2038	204
Castlemaine d.	0751	0806	0821	0850	0908	0948	0947	1051	1053	1053	...	...	1251	1253	1357	1446	1501	1527	1558	1608	1756	1906	1903	1910	2101	210
Kyneton d.	0811	0825	0841	0910	0930	1013	1012	1111	1113	1113	...	...	1311	1313	1416	1505	1521	1551	1617	1631	1816	1929	1931	1934	2121	212
Woodend d.	0819	0833	0849	0918	0939	1024	1023	1120	1121	1121	...	...	1320	1321	1425	1513	1530	1601	1625	1641	1824	1937	1941	1942	2129	213
Sunbury d.	0850	0858	0919	0950	1011	|	|	1152	1153	1153	...	...	1352	1353	1450	1545	1602	|	1651	|	1856	2002	|	2014	2201	220
Melbourne S Cross a.	0922	0927	0950	1022	1042	1133	1129	1222	1224	1224	...	...	1422	1424	1521	1618	1632	1704	1722	1743	1927	2032	2041	2043	2230	223

☛ Additional trains are available Melbourne - Bendigo and v.v. a – Connection by 🚌 on ⑤ only. b – 2115 on ⑥. * – By 🚌.

6385 MELBOURNE - MARYBOROUGH and ARARAT *V/Line*

km		⑥	⑦	①–⑤	②⑥	①–⑤	⑥	⑥	①–⑤	⑥	①–④	①②④	⑦	⑦	①–⑤	①–⑤	⑤	①–⑤	⑥⑦	①–⑤	⑦	①–⑤	⑥⑦	E	①–⑤
		[R]	[R]	[R]	A			🚌	[R]			🚌					🚌		[R]	[R]				🚌	
0	**Melbourne** S Cross d.	0815	0815	0817	0805	0917	0915	...	1217	1215	1317	...	1335	1515	1633	1633	...	1751	1815	1826	1915	2025	2055	2125	2225
41	Melton d.	0849	0851	0849	|	0949	0949	...	1249	1249	1349	...	1411	1549	|	|	...	|	1849	1854	1949	2055	2129	|	2255
53	Bacchus Marsh d.	0902	0902	0904	|	1004	1002	...	1304	1302	1404	...	1422	1602	|	|	...	1823	1902	1902	2002	2107	2138	|	2307
82	Ballan d.	0919	0919	0921	|	1021	1019	...	1321	1319	1421	...	1439	1619	1722	1722	...	1840	1919	1919	2019	2124	2155	|	2324
122	**Ballarat** ☛ a.	0941	0942	0944	|	1044	1041	1055	1344	1344	1444	1500	1502	1644	1738	1738	1810	1857	1937	1935	2037	2143	2211	2255	2343
180	**Maryborough** a.	|	|	|	|	|	...	1201	|	|	|	1607	|	|	1839	|	1917	|	*2039*	|	|	...	...	2358	...
210	**Ararat** a.	1043	1040	1044	1139	1216*	...	...	1444	1517*	1616*	...	1642*	1820*	...	1909*	...	2021*	2035	2034	2205*	...	...	...	...

		①–⑥	①–⑤	⑥	⑥	⑥	①–⑤	①–⑤	①–⑤	⑦	⑥⑦	D	①–⑤	⑥	⑥	①–⑤	⑦	①–⑤	⑥⑦	①⑤	⑥⑦	①–⑤	⑦	①–⑤	⑥⑦
		🚌				[R]		[R]			[R]	🚌						[R]		A	[R]	[R]			
Ararat d.	...	...	...	...	...	0716	...	0718	...	...	0816a	...	0817*	0825*	0922*	1031*	1131*	1228	1535*	1531	1609	1649	1745*	1730*	...
Maryborough d.	...	0400	...	...	0710	|	0712	|	...	0810	|	0829	|	|	|	|	|	|	|	|	|	|	|	|	...
Ballarat ☛ d.	...	0510	0519	0619	0803	0819	0805	0821	0921	0903	0919	0938	1021	1019	1139	1221	1319	1321	1714	|	1714	1802	1914	1912	2121
Ballan d.	...	|	0536	0635	...	0835	...	0837	0937	...	0935	...	1037	1035	1155	1237	1335	1337	1735	|	1735	1825	1935	1935	2138
Bacchus Marsh d.	0500	|	0553	0652	...	0852	...	0854	0954	...	0952	...	1054	1052	1212	1254	1352	1354	1752	|	1752	1845	1952	1952	2158
Melton d.	0508	|	0601	0701	...	0901	...	0903	1003	...	1001	...	1103	1101	1221	1303	1401	1403	1801	|	1801	1854	2001	2003	2207
Melbourne S Cross a.	0542	0640	0631	0739	...	0939	...	0940	1040	...	1040	...	1140	1139	1259	1340	1439	1440	1839	1850	1839	1927	2039	2038	2243

☛ Additional trains are available Melbourne - Ballarat and v.v. A – See Table **6395**. D – ①②④⑤⑥. E – ①②③④⑤⑦. a – ⑦ only. * – By 🚌.
Note: Schedules will alter after Jan 29.

6390 SYDNEY - PERTH *Great Southern Rail*

km		WE1 [R] ③A			WE2 [R] ⑦A	
0	**Sydney** Central d.	1503	③	East **Perth** d.	1000	⑦
1125	Broken Hill a.	0600	④	Kalgoorlie a.	2050	:
1125	Broken Hill d.	0820	:	Kalgoorlie d.	0001	①
1688	**Adelaide** Parklands a.	1515	:	**Adelaide** Parklands a.	0720	②
1688	**Adelaide** Parklands d.	2140	:	**Adelaide** Parklands d.	1015	:
	Rawlinna a.	1755	⑤	Broken Hill a.	1725	:
	Rawlinna d.	2035	:	Broken Hill d.	1930	:
4343	East **Perth** a.	1457	⑥	**Sydney** Central a.	1107	③

Note: Train **WE2** has a additional off train excursion at Cook (arr. 1445, dep. 1545). From April 2017 both services will have off train excursions at Nullabor and Cook. For footnotes see Table **6400**.

6395 MELBOURNE - ADELAIDE *Great Southern Rail*

km		8701 [R] B ②⑥			8702 [R] B ①⑤	
0	**Melbourne** S Cross d.	0805	...	**Adelaide** Parklands d.	0745	...
74	Geelong North Shore d.	0942	...	Murray Bridge d.	0949	...
265	Ararat d.	1140	...	Nhill d.	1305	...
381	Horsham d.	1255	...	Dimboola d.	1334	...
416	Dimboola d.	1318	...	Horsham d.	1358	...
454	Nhill d.	1343	...	Ararat d.	1531	...
734	Murray Bridge d.	1605	...	Geelong North Shore d.	1738	...
828	**Adelaide** Parklands a.	1753	...	**Melbourne** S Cross a.	1850	...

B – THE OVERLAND – (12) and 🍷 Melbourne - Adelaide and v.v.

6400 DARWIN - ADELAIDE *Great Southern Rail*

km		8506 [R] ③C			8505 [R] ⑦C	
0	**Darwin** △ d.	1000	③	**Adelaide** Parklands d.	1215	⑦
310	Katherine a.	1340	:	Snowtown d.	1446	:
310	Katherine d.	1820	:	Crystal Brook d.	1520	:
	Newcastle Waters d.	2220	:	Coonamia ◇ d.	1536	:
947	Tennant Creek a.	0253	④	Port Augusta a.	1645	:
947	Tennant Creek d.	0427	:	Port Augusta d.	1700	:
1414	**Alice Springs** a.	0910	:	**Alice Springs** a.	1345	①
1414	**Alice Springs** d.	1245	:	**Alice Springs** d.	1800	:
2661	Port Augusta a.	0648	⑤	Tennant Creek a.	2300	:
2661	Port Augusta d.	0730	:	Tennant Creek d.	0105	②
2751	Coonamia ◇ d.	0825	:	Newcastle Waters d.	0445	:
2775	Crystal Brook d.	0845	:	Katherine a.	0900	:
2827	Snowtown d.	0925	:	Katherine d.	1300	:
2973	**Adelaide** Parklands a.	1130	⑤	**Darwin** △ a.	1730	②

A – INDIAN PACIFIC – 🛏 1 cl., (12) and ✕ Sydney - Adelaide - Perth and v.v. From Sydney on ③. From Perth on ⑦. **Note:** From April 2017 **WE1** will arrive at Perth at 150 and **WE2** will depart Perth at 0900 and arrive Sydney at 1130,

C – THE GHAN – 🛏 1 cl., (2), ✕ (in 1st class) and 🍷 Darwin - Adelaide and v.v. Fron Adelaide on ⑦ service will also stop at Maria and Katherine for an off train excursion From Darwin on ③ service will also stop at Katherine and Manguri for an off train excursion. The Ghan will not operate between Dec. 18, 2016 and Jan. 18, 2017. also Dec. 17, 2017 and Jan. 17, 2018.

Note: From April 2017 **8506** will arrive Adelaide at 1300. There will be a special timetable for the Darwin - Adelaide Ghan between May and Oct. 2017. Service departs Darwin on ③ a 1000 arriving Adelaide on ⑥ at 1045 and has an extended stop at Coober Pedy on ⑤

△ – Darwin station is in the suburb of Berrimah. 🚌 connections to and from Darwin city centre are provided by the operator. ◇ – For Port Pirie.

6405 KALGOORLIE - PERTH *All trains 2 cl. and [R] TransWA*

km		AVM2 ①–⑤	AVM8 ⑥	AVM4 d	KPA ①–⑤	KPL ⑥	MEP2 ③	AVM6 d	KPA4 ⑦	KPL2 ①	KPL4 ⑤
0	**Kalgoorlie** d.	...	...	...	0705	0705	...	...	1405	1500	1500
250	Southern Cross d.	...	...	...	0912	0917	...	...	1612	1707	1715
371	Merredin d.	...	...	...	1023	1028	1310	...	1723	1818	1829
427	Kellerberrin d.	...	...	...	1102c	1107	1341	...	1802	1857	1908
531	Northam d.	0630	0830	1000	1209	1212	1454	1600	1907	2002	2013
641	Midland d.	0750	0950	1120	1323	1323	1610	1720	2020	2115	2125
653	East **Perth** a.	...	...	...	1345	1345	1630	...	2040	2135	2145

	PKA a	PKL ③	MAV1 d	MEP2 ③	MAV3 d	PKA1 ⑦	PKL1 ①	MAW7 ⑥	PKL3 ⑤	MAV5 ①–⑤
East **Perth** d.	0710	0710	...	0855	...	1410	1515	...	1515	...
Midland d.	0727	0727	0815	0912	1400	1427	1533	1535	1532	1750
Northam d.	0850	0850	0935	1027	1520	1547	1645	1655	1655	1910
Kellerberrin d.	0956	|	...	1138	...	1653	1750	...	1800	...
Merredin d.	1027	1027	...	1210	...	1728	1821	...	1831	...
Southern Cross d.	1144	1144	...	...	...	1845	1938	...	1948	...
Kalgoorlie a.	1400	1400	...	...	...	2100	2150	...	2205	...

a – ①②④⑤⑥ only. c – ①②④⑤ only. d – ①②④⑤ only. NOTE: Trains will only call at intermediate stations if bookings are made in advance.

6410 PERTH - BUNBURY *TransWA*

km		103 2 [R]	105 2 [R]		102 2 [R]	108 2 [R]
0	**Perth** City d.	0930	1755	**Bunbury** d.	0600	1445
30	Armadale d.	0956	1825	Brunswick Junction d.	0617	1502
85	Pinjarra d.	1042	1911	Harvey d.	0632	1517
111	Waroona d.	1100	1929	Waroona d.	0656	1538
136	Harvey d.	1121	1950	Pinjarra d.	0712	1555
157	Brunswick Junction d.	1136	2005	Armadale d.	0755	1639
183	**Bunbury** a.	1155	2025	**Perth** City a.	0830	1715

NOTE: Trains will only call at intermediate stations if bookings are made in advance.

6415 KALGOORLIE - ESPERANCE *TransWA*

km		671 🚌 ①③	651 🚌 ⑤			700 🚌 ⑦	690 🚌 ③⑤	
0	**Kalgoorlie** d.	1430	1430	...	**Esperance** d.	0800	0835	...
208	Norseman d.	1715	1730	...	Norseman d.	1045	1120	...
409	**Esperance** a.	1930	1945	...	**Kalgoorlie** a.	1315	1335	...

NEW ZEALAND

Capital : **Wellington** (GMT + 12, add one hour in Summer). 2017 public holidays : Jan. 1, 2, 3, Feb. 6, Apr. 14, 17, 25, June 5, Oct. 23, Dec. 25, 26.

Long distance rail services are operated by Tranz Scenic (www.tranzscenic.co.nz). Only one class of accommodation is offered, which is referred to in the tables as second class. All services operated by TranzScenic require compulsory reservation. There are two types of Scenic Rail Passes; the Fixed Pass offers unlimited travel on the TranzScenic network (not the Capital Connection) and also allows one journey on the Interislander ferry service. Adult prices : 7 days NZ$599, 14 days NZ$699, 21 days NZ$799. The Freedom Pass offers flexible travel from 3 to 10 days. Adult prices : 3 days NZ$ 417 to 10 days NZ$ 1290. For full information go to www.kiwirailscenic.co.nz.

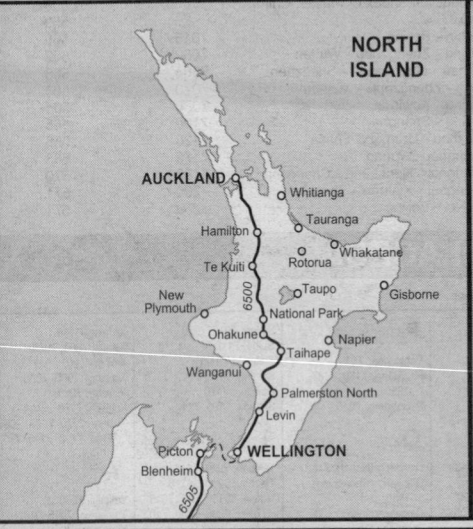

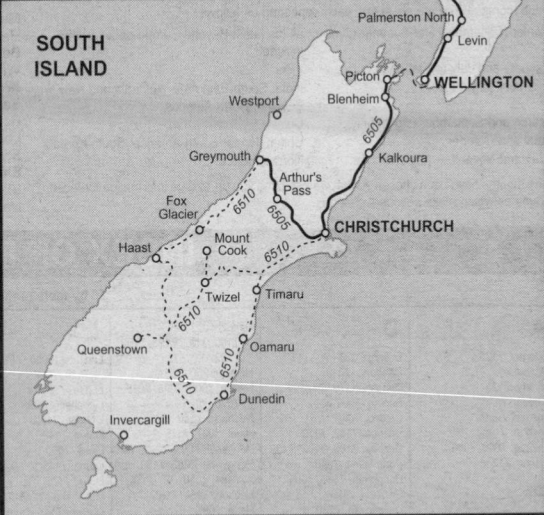

KiwiRail Scenic AUCKLAND - WELLINGTON 6500

km		1203 Ⓡ ①–⑤ B	0201 Ⓡ ①④⑥ A			0200 Ⓡ ②⑤⑦ A	1205 Ⓡ ①–⑤ B
0	**Auckland** Strand .... d.	...	0745	**Wellington** .... ☐ d.	0755	1715
34	Papakura .... d.	...	0840	Paraparaumu .... d.	0845	1803
139	Hamilton .... d.	...	1015	Levin .... d.	...	1842
183	Otorohanga .... d.	...	1054	**Palmerston North** .... d.	1000	1920
314	National Park .... d.	...	1315	Ohakune .... d.	1245	...
364	Ohakune .... d.	...	1345	National Park .... d.	1315	...
544	**Palmerston North** .... d.	0615	1620	Otorohanga .... d.	1545	...
590	Levin .... d.	0653		Hamilton .... d.	1630	...
632	Paraparaumu .... d.	0732	1730	Papakura .... d.	1755	...
681	**Wellington** .... ☐ a.	0820	1825	**Auckland** Strand .... a.	1850	...

Note: Trains are permitted to depart from intermediate stations earlier than advertised provided that all pre-booked passengers are on board.

A – NORTHERN EXPLORER – 🚌 and ♀. Not Dec. 25, 28. 29.
B – CAPITAL CONNECTION – 🚌 and ♀. Not public holidays or Dec. 25 – Jan 4.
s – Calls to set down only.
u – Calls to pick up only.

KiwiRail Scenic PICTON - CHRISTCHURCH 6505

km		803 Ⓡ D	0701 Ⓡ C			0700 Ⓡ C	0804 Ⓡ D
0	**Picton** .... ☐ d.	...	1315	**Greymouth** .... d.	...	1345
28	Blenheim .... d.	...	1353	Brunner .... d.	...	1405
157	Kaikoura .... d.	...	1550	Moana .... d.	...	1442
285	Waipara .... d.	...	1740	Otira .... d.	...	1533
318	Rangiora .... d.	...	1809	Arthur's Pass .... d.	...	1557
348	**Christchurch** .... a.	...	1833	Springfield .... d.	...	1712
348	**Christchurch** .... d.	0815	...	**Christchurch** .... a.	...	1805
417	Springfield .... d.	0915	...	**Christchurch** .... d.	0700	...
484	Arthur's Pass .... d.	1042	...	Rangiora .... d.	0732	...
498	Otira .... d.	1103	...	Waipara .... d.	0758	...
	Moana .... d.	1147	...	Kaikoura .... d.	0959	...
565	Brunner .... d.	1221	...	Blenheim .... d.	1153	...
579	**Greymouth** .... a.	1245	...	**Picton** .... ☐ a.	1220	...

Note: Trains are permitted to depart from intermediate stations earlier than advertised provided that all pre-booked passengers are on board.

C – COASTAL PACIFIC – 🚌 and ♀. **Due to the recent earthquake this service is suspended and will not operate until at least September 2017.**
D – THE TRANZALPINE – 🚌 and ♀. Not Dec. 25.

☐ – Wellington - Picton 🚢 service ('Interislander'). Journey 3½ hours. Operator: Interislander ✆ +64 4 498 3302.

Dec. 26 - Jan. 8.
Wellington – Picton.
0830, 1100, 1445, 1830, 0030 ②–⑥.
Picton – Wellington.
0545 ②–⑥, 1045, 1330, 1600, 1845 2330.

Jan. 9 - Feb. 5.
Wellington – Picton.
0330 ②–⑥, 0900, 1445, 1700 ①–⑥, 2000 ⑦–⑤, 2030 ⑥.
Picton – Wellington.
0905 ②–⑥, 1045 ②–⑥, 1115 ①, 1415, 1845, 2215 ①–⑥.

Feb. 6 - Mar. 31.
Wellington – Picton.
0330 ②–⑥, 0900, 1445, 1700, 2000 ②, 2030 ①–⑤.
Picton – Wellington.
0905 ②–⑥, 1045 ②–⑦, 1115 ①, 1415, 1845, 2215 ①–⑥.

April 1 - May 31.
Wellington – Picton.
0330 ②–⑥a, 0900, 1445, 1700 ②–⑥a, 2000 ⑦–⑤.
Picton – Wellington.
0905 ②–⑥a, 1045 ②–⑦, 1415, 1845, 2215 ①–⑥a.
a – NOT April 18 – May 14.

🚌 SELECTED SOUTH ISLAND BUS SERVICES 6510

km		Operator	AS	IC	IC	AS	NM	IC	AS	IC ⑤⑦			Operator	IC	AS	NM	IC	IC	AS	AS	IC ⑤⑦
0	**Christchurch** .... d.		0730	0730	0745	0800	0830	1400	1500	1715	...	**Queenstown** .... d.			0805	0745			1500	
82	Ashburton .... d.		0845	0850	0915	0920	0950	1525	1630	1850	...	Cromwell .... d.			0910	0920			1555	
160	Timaru .... d.				1030	1025		1700	1800	2030	...	Twizel .... d.			1110	1130			1805	
240	Oamaru .... d.				1205	1200		1815	1910	2135	...	**Mount Cook** .... a.				1230				
366	**Dunedin** .... a.				1340	1350		1950	2045	2305	...	**Mount Cook** .... d.				1345				
144	Geraldine .... d.		0925	1000			1045				...	Fairlie .... d.			1315	1550			1920	
191	Fairlie .... d.		1000	1025			1125				...	Geraldine .... d.			1410	1655			2000	
341	**Mount Cook** .... a.			1300							...	**Dunedin** .... d.		0745	0800		1250	1430		1715
341	**Mount Cook** .... d.			1425							...	Oamaru .... d.		0930	1000		1500	1635		1855
281	Twizel .... d.		1120	1515			1330				...	Timaru .... d.		1120	1110		1700	1840		2030
435	Cromwell .... d.		1340	1715			1530				...	Ashburton .... d.		1225	1210	1455	1735	1730	1845	2040	2135
496	**Queenstown** .... a.		1430	1830			1630				...	**Christchurch** .... a.		1345	1350	1630	1910	1855	2000	2145	2250

km		Operator	IC	AS	AS	AS	IC			Operator	IC	AS	AS	IC	AS
0	Greymouth .... d.		...	...	...	...	1330		Dunedin .... d.		...	1000	1355	1530
41	Hokitika .... d.		...	...	...	...	1455		Milton .... d.		...	1040	1445	1620
189	Franz Josef .... d.		...	...	0800	1705	...		Roxburgh .... d.		...	1220	1605	1740
213	**Fox Glacier** .... d.		...	...	0845	1740	...		Alexandra .... d.		...	1250	1640	1805
	Paringa .... d.		...	...	1005	...	...		Cromwell .... d.		...	1340	1705	1830
331	Haast .... d.		...	...	1120	...	...		**Queenstown** .... a.		0810	1430	1815	1935
476	Wanaka .... d.		...	...	1435	...	...		Wanaka .... d.		0945			
593	**Queenstown** .... d.		0745	0915	1500	1615	...		Haast .... d.		1250			
654	Cromwell .... d.		0850	1015	1555	...	...		Paringa .... d.		1435			
685	Alexandra .... d.		0920	1050	1630	...	...		**Fox Glacier** .... d.		0830	1525		
727	Roxburgh .... d.		0955	1120	1715	...	...		Franz Josef .... d.		0915	1610		
817	Milton .... d.		1130	1240	1830	...	...		Hokitika .... d.		1230			
873	**Dunedin** .... a.		1235	1345	1930	...	...		Greymouth .... a.		1315			

AS –	Atomic Travel. ✆ 03 349 0697.	IC –	Intercity Coachlines. ✆ 09 583 5780.	NM –	Newmans. ✆ 09 583 5780.

BEYOND EUROPE
China

Contents

INDEX OF PLACES

by table number

China

Capital: Beijing (GMT + 8). 2017 Public Holidays: Jan. 1, 27 - 29, Apr. 2, 4, 5, May 1, 28 - 30, Oct. 1, 2, 3, 4.

Rail services in the People's Republic are generally operated by Chinese Railways. High-speed services are operated by China Rail High Speed. All times shown are Beijing time unless otherwise stated. Schedules in this section are as per the latest information available and are liable to change at any time.

Trains are numbered using a combination of letters and numbers, with the letter indicating the type of train. The fastest trains carry prefixes C and G. These use the new high-speed railways and run at speeds up to 300 km/h on routes such as Wuhan to Guangzhou and Beijing to Tianjin. Other high-speed trains running at speeds of up to 200 km/h are prefixed with the letter D and Z. These trains use both dedicated high-speed railways and normal lines. Ordinary long distance trains are prefixed T or K. T trains make fewer stops and thus are considerably quicker than K trains. Most K trains in this section are only shown to highlight additional connections between major points and may not be shown in their entirety. Also shown are a few trains without prefix letters. These are essentially similar to K trains but are slower still and are only shown in this section where there are no higher category trains.

In total seven classes of accommodation are available, but not all will be available on every train. Seated accommodation can be either Hard, Soft, Second or First class. Hard seats are generally padded plastic seats. This is the cheapest class available and is often very busy. Soft seats are cloth covered and generally can be reclined. Second class seats have five seats per row and are similar to economy class seating on an aeroplane. First class has four seats per row. Sleeping accommodation is available in either Hard, Soft or Deluxe Soft classes. Hard sleepers consist of cabins of six berths (upper, middle and lower), with three beds attached to the wall on either side. The cabin is open and has no door. Soft sleepers have four berths and a sliding door. Deluxe Soft cabins have two berths and an en-suite bathroom. Generally K, T and Z trains convey Soft and Hard sleepers, and Hard Seats whilst C, D and G trains convey First and Second class seats. Exact train compositions are **not** shown in the tables.

All travel should be reserved in advance either at stations or through an agent. At many stations you may find it possible to only book for trains calling there, however in major cities such as Beijing, Shanghai and Guangzhou you may be able to purchase all tickets. Some major stations may have English speakers available at ticket desks. Reservations for Z and D usually open 10 - 21 days in advance. Other classes of train are only usually available 7 - 10 days before departure. In peak seasons such as Spring Festival holidays reservations may only open 5 days before departure. Identity documents, such as passports for most foreigners or ID cards for Chinese citizens, are required to buy tickets for and to board C, D and G trains.

More comprehensive train schedules are available (in Chinese!) from Chinese Railways official website: and www.tielu.org. Other unofficial websites such as www.cnvol.com and www.chinatravelguide.com offer timetable search facilities in English.

A printed English language timetable is available from Duncan Peattie (CTT) 29 Watford Field Road, Watford UK, WD18 0BG or see www.chinatt.org.

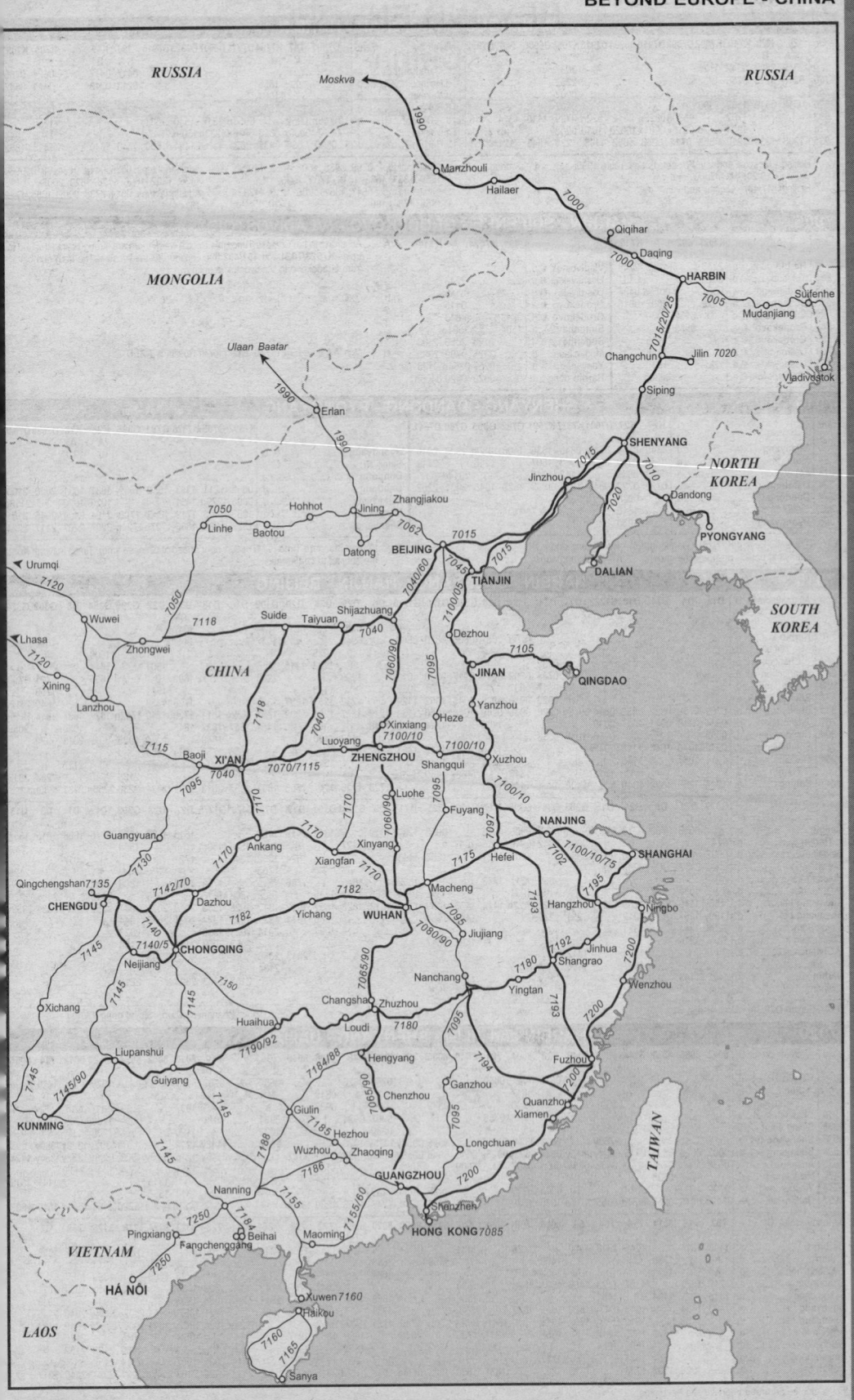

7000 MANZHOULI and QIQHAR - HARBIN

Chinese Railways, China Rail High Speed

km	20 ⑤A	K20 B	K7193	K7092	D7902	D7910	D6904	D7918 W	K7058	D6906	T48 C	D7992	Read Down	Read Up	D7991 U	T47 C	K7194	D7911 X	D6907	D7923	D6915	19 ⑦A	K19 B		K7057	K709
0	2359	2359	0542	1725	...	...	...	...	2037	...	...	...	↓ d.**Manzhouli**	a. ↑	...	...	...	...	...	...	...	0417	0417	...	0624	0755
186	0215	0215	0758	1952	...	...	...	...	2253	...	...	...	d.Hailaer	d.	...	...	1855	...	...	...	...	0213	0213	...	0411	0547
268	|	|	0921	2102	...	...	...	...	0002	...	...	...	↓ d.Yakeshi	d. ↑	...	...	1504	...	...	...	...	|	|	...	0234	0412
396	0519	0519	1132	2300	...	...	...	...	0207	...	...	...	d.Boketu	d.	...	...	1259	...	...	...	...	2251	2251	...	0039	|
693	|	|	1702	|	0530n	0822n	0912	1022n	0729	1415	1814	2116	↓ d. Qiqihar	a. ↑	0700n	0952	|	0953n	1317	1540	1831	|	|	...	1956	|
776	|	|	1907	0425	0615x	0901x	1002d	1103d	0932	|	1918x	2154x	d.Daqing	d.	0617d	0830x	0626	0916x	1233d	1509x	1747d	|	|	...	1709	2044
935	1238	1238	2210	0653	0712	0958	1052	1148	1225	1543	2121	2251	↓ a.**Harbin**	d. ↑	0520	0636	0435	0829	1136	1404	1656	1540	1540	...	1413	1852

A – Beijing - Moscow and v.v. For details see Table **1990**.
B – Beijing(**K19/20**) - Manzhouli and v.v.
C – Beijing(**T47/48**) - Qiqihar and v.v.
d – dong.
n – nan.
x – xi.
U – Additional trips: 0709, 0938, 1008, 1033, 1208, 1258, 1333, 1533, 1612, 1702, 1935.
V– Additional trips: 0547, 1052, 1205, 1216, 1433, 1459, 1754, 1900.
W – Additional trips: 0536, 0648, 0734, 0810, 0936 1136, 1302, 1600, 1738, 1820, 2007.
X – Additional trips: 0614, 0738, 0902, 1055, 1712 1904.

7005 HARBIN - SUIFENHE - GRODEKOVO - (VLADIVOSTOK)

Chinese Railways

km		K7023	402 2	A ③⑥	K7193		401 2	K7024	A ①④	K7194
0	**Harbin** dong ... d.	2236	...	1835	2248	**Vladivostok** ◐ d.	...	...	1400	...
161	Yimianpo ... d.	0026	...	|	0131	Ussruiysk ... ◐ a.	...	...	2246	...
355	Mudanjiang ... a.	0331	...	0059a	0437	Ussruiysk ... ◐ d.	...	...	0200c	...
648	**Suifenhe** ... a.	0522	...	0602	0616	**Grodekovo** ◐ a.	...	...	0415	...
648	**Suifenhe** ▦ ... d.	...	0930	0930	...	**Grodekovo** ◐ d.	0843	...	0843	...
669	**Grodekovo** .. ◐ a.	...	0559	0553	...	**Suifenhe** ▦ ... a.	1504	...	1504c	...
669	**Grodekovo** .. ◐ a.	...	...	1115	...	**Suifenhe** ... d.	...	2123	2055	2100
766	Ussruiysk ... ◐ a.	...	...	1328	...	Mudanjiang ... d.	...	2325	0709	2300
766	Ussruiysk ... ◐ d.	...	...	1537	...	Yamianpo ... d.	...	0257	0354d	0128
878	**Vladivostok** ◐ a.	...	...	0030b	...	**Harbin** dong ... a.	...	0520	0620	0405h

A – Accordng to the Chinese Timetable twice a week there are through cars attached to trains **K7023/7024** and **401/402** that continue to Vladivostok. The train number from Grodekovo to Vladivostok is unknown.
a – ④⑦.
b – ①⑤.
c – ②⑤.
d – ③⑥.
h – Harbin.
◐ – Moscow time (GMT +3). Operator in Russia is **RZhD**.

7010 SHENYANG - DANDONG - PYONGYANG

China Rail High Speed, Chinese Railways

km		K27 A	K27 A	D7601	K7377	K7591	G782	G395	G786	D7641		K7592	G785	K7378	G781	G396	K28 A	K28 A	D7638	D7640
0	**Shenyang** ... d.	0340	0340	0532	0848	1356	1406	1430n	1808	2046	**Pyongyang** ... ⊗ d.	...	...	...	...	...	...	1010	...	...
84	Muxi ... d.	0448	0448	0605	0956	1507	|	1456	|	2119	Sinuiji ▦ ... ⊗ d.	...	...	...	...	...	...	|	...	...
217	Fengcheng ... d.	0633	0633	|	1142	1748	|	|	2014d	|	**Dandong** ... a.	...	...	...	...	...	...	1623	...	...
224	**Dandong** ... a.	0722	0722	0648	1231	1859	1528	1545	2031	2202	**Dandong** ... d.	0652	1211	1353	1552	1609	1831	1831	2000	2100
224	**Dandong** ... d.	...	0935	...	...	...	...	...	...	...	Fengcheng ... d.	0806	1229d	1451	|	|	1920	1920	|	2118d
282	Sinuiji ▦ ... ⊗ d.	...	1346	...	...	...	...	...	...	...	Muxi ... d.	1053	1302	1719	1643	1700	2104	2104	2045	2151
506	**Pyongyang** ... ⊗ a.	...	1930	...	...	...	...	...	...	...	**Shenyang** ... a.	1322	1335	1836	1727b	1724n	2207	2207	2117	2224

A – ①③④⑥. Beijing(**K27/28**) - Dandong(**6/5**) - Pyongyang and v.v.
b – Shenyang bei. **d** – Fengcheng dong. **n** – Shenyang nan.
⊗ – Korean Standard Time (GMT +9, 1 hour ahead of Chinese time). Times in North Korea are subject to confirmation.

7015 HARBIN - SHENYANG - TIANJIN - BEIJING

China Rail High Speed

km	All trains prefix 'D'	D12	D4	D14	D10	G1222	D2	D24	G394	D28	G1206	G1203	G1276	D6	D26	D74	D20	D102	D16	D18	D30 D	D22	G396	G384	D8	G382	G374
	Qiqihar ... d.	...	...	...	...	...	...	...	...	...	...	...	...	...	0753	...	...	...	...	...	1247	...	...	...	...	...	...
0	**Harbin** xi ... d.	...	...	...	...	...	...	...	0708	0657	0805	0820	0859	...	0946	...	...	1037	...	...	1441	...	...	...	...	1622	1651
	Jilin ... d.	...	...	...	...	...	...	...	|	|	|	|	|	...	|	1025	...	|	...	...	|	1517	...	1600	...	|	|
* *	Changchun .. d.	...	...	...	...	...	...	0732	|	|	|	|	|	...	|	1108	1115	|	...	...	|	1601	...	1644	...	|	|
240	Changchun xi .. d.	...	...	...	...	...	...	0744	0809	0817	0917	0933	1010	...	1109	|	|	1203	...	...	1600	|	...	1656	...	1721	1756
358	Siping dong ... d.	...	...	...	...	...	...	0817	0837	|	0951	1001	1039	...	|	1148	|	|	...	...	|	1641	...	|	...	1750	|
538	**Shenyang** bei. a.	...	...	...	...	...	...	0923	0930	0939	1045	1052	1129	...	1232	1251	1307	1334	...	...	1726	1738	...	1822	...	1840	1912y
538	**Shenyang** bei. d.	0709	0750	0822	0852	0814	0919y	0926	0938	0949	1048	1056	1132	1217	1237	1256	1309	1337	1432y	1511	1729	1740	1742n	1827	1837	1844	1915y
761	Jinzhou nan ... d.	0834	0918	0947	1017	0939	|	|	|	1118	|	1214	1249	1348	|	|	|	1454	1557	1632	1846	|	|	|	1956	|	2059
804	Huludao bei ... d.	0852	|	|	|	0956	1050	1058	|	|	|	|	1307	|	1412	1430	|	|	|	1649	|	|	1925	|	2013	2022	|
926	Shanhaiguan ... d.	0940	1020	1046	1118	1041	|	|	|	1218	|	1318	1351	|	|	|	|	|	1658	1733	1944	1955	|	|	|	|	|
964	Beidaihe ... d.	1014	1051	|	1145	|	|	|	|	1249	|	1344	|	|	|	1515	|	1623	1728	|	|	2027	|	|	2127	|	|
	Tianjin ... a.	|	|	|	|	1212	|	|	1348	|	1453x	1450	1529x	|	|	|	|	|	|	|	|	|	2138	2210	|	2238	2317
1241	**Beijing** ... a.	1217	1259	1328	1349	...	1408	1414	1444	1451	...	...	...	1723	1728	1747	1753	1831	1937	2013	2222	2231	2230	2256n	2331	2333n	...

	G373	D29 D	D5	D21	D15	G383	G381	G395	D17	G1205	D25	D11	D9	G1221	D101	D19	D73	G1201	G1275	D27	D23	G393	D7	D1	D3	D13
Beijing ... d.	...	0658	0703	0713	0731	0730n	0753n	0905	0915	...	0958	1237	1319	...	1349	1418	1428	...	...	1515	1533	1505	1745	1808	1815	1851
Tianjin ... d.	0747	|	|	|	|	0820	0842	0949	|	1047	|	|	|	1427	|	|	|	1529	1535	|	|	1554	|	|	|	|
Beidaihe ... d.	0902	|	|	0920	0938	0954	|	1101	1121	|	1208	1443	|	|	|	1624	1630	1645	|	1721	|	|	|	2017	|	|
Shanhaiguan ... d.	|	|	|	0959	|	|	|	|	|	|	1241	|	|	|	|	|	1703	|	|	|	|	|	|	|	|	|
Huludao bei ... d.	|	|	|	|	1101	|	1050	1217	1233	|	|	1602	|	1645	|	1736	|	|	1759	1842	|	1808	2102	|	2137	2129
Jinzhou nan ... d.	|	1030	1037	|	|	|	1108	1234	|	|	1342	1620	1653	1702	1735	|	1800	1808	1816	|	1908	|	2119	|	2157	2229
Shenyang bei ... a.	1156y	1146	1153	1209	1237y	1248	1228	1412n	1414	1436	1459	1740	1813	1823	1852	1912	1919	1926	1933	2018	2031	1941	2253	2321y	2331	2359y
Shenyang bei ... d.	1159y	1151	...	1212	...	1251	1230	...	...	1440	1501	...	...	...	1856	1914	1921	1931	1937	2021	2036	1944	...	...	...	...
Siping dong ... d.	1256	1244	...	1321	...	|	|	...	...	|	|	...	...	...	1954	|	2014	2023	2030	|	|	2037	...	...	...	...
Changchun xi ... d.	1325	1316	...	|	...	|	1346	...	...	1603	1647	...	...	...	2027	|	|	2052	2059	2154	|	2106	...	...	...	...
Changchun ... a.	|	|	...	1404	...	1412	|	...	...	|	|	...	...	...	|	2043	2050	|	|	|	2209	|	...	...	...	...
Jilin ... a.	|	|	...	1447	...	1455	|	...	...	|	|	...	...	...	|	...	2134	|	|	|	...	|	...	...	...	...
Harbin xi ... a.	1422	1443	...	...	...	...	1459	...	...	1703	1809	...	...	...	2139	...	...	2153	2203	2300	...	2212	...	...	...	...
Qiqihar ... a.	...	1630	...	...	...	...	...	...	...	...	2028	...	...	...	...	...	...	...	...	...	...	...	...	...	...	...

D – Beijing(**D29/30**) - Qiqihar and v.v.
n – nan. x – Tianjin xi. y – Shenyang.
* * – Changhcun *0 km* - Siping dong *130 km*.

7020 HARBIN and JILIN - SHENYANG - DALIAN

China Rail High Speed

km	All trains prefix 'G'	8042	8068	8070	8044	8002	8046	702	8004	704	8048	8006	706	708	48	8008	8050	754		710	8010	8052	8054	712	8012	714	8056
0	**Harbin** xi ... d.	...	...	...	...	...	...	0616	...	0650	...	...	0729	0756	0828	...	...	0850	...	0907	...	...	...	1028	...	1128	...
* *	**Jilin** ... d.	...	...	...	...	...	...	|	0617	|	...	...	|	|	|	0849	...	|	...	|	...	...	...	|	...	|	...
* *	Changchun .. d.	...	...	...	...	0621	...	|	0700	|	...	0819	|	|	|	0932	...	|	...	|	1037	...	...	|	1207	|	...
240	Changchun xi .. d.	...	...	...	...	|	...	|	|	0756	...	|	0840	0902	0924	|	...	0954	...	1017	|	...	...	1138	1219	1232	...
358	Siping dong ... d.	...	...	...	...	0657	...	|	|	|	...	|	|	0930	|	1008	...	1022	...	|	1120	...	...	1206	|	|	...
538	**Shenyang** bei. a.	...	...	...	...	0758y	...	0834	0824y	0920y	...	0945	0953y	1025y	1028	1058	...	1112	...	1143y	1212	...	...	1302y	1329y	1350y	...
538	**Shenyang** bei. d.	0602	0625	0635	0715	0801y	0815y	0838	0828y	0923y	0919	0948	0956y	1039y	1030	1101	1122	...	...	1146y	1215	1228y	1303	1306y	1332y	1354y	1424
638	Anshan xi ... d.	0638	|	0724	|	0833	0855	0921	0907	|	1009	|	1033	|	|	1137	|	...	...	1225	1251	|	1354	1345	1411	|	|
677	Haicheng xi ... d.	|	|	0738	|	|	|	|	|	1009	|	|	|	|	|	1151	|	...	...	1239	|	1315	|	|	|	1441	1513
715	Yinkou dong ... d.	0700	|	|	0814	|	|	0943	0929	|	|	1039	1055	1133	|	|	|	...	...	1254	1314	1330	|	|	|	|	|
921	**Dalian** bei ... a.	0812d	0816	0853	0934d	0955	1017d	1036	1029	1116	1136	1143	1210	1247	1203	1259	1353d	...	...	1347	1424d	1450d	1522d	1453	1531d	1549	1633

All trains prefix 'G'	782	716	8014	718	764	50	8016	758	8058	720	8018	8060	8020	8062	722	724	786	8064	726	8022	8024	728	8126	730	732	
Harbin xi ... d.	1143	1211	...	1246	1318	1400	...	1425	...	1431	...	...	...	...	1543	1608	1642	...	1700	...	...	1747	...	1828	1908	...
Jilin ... d.	|	|	1238	|	|	|	1409	|	...	|	1458	...	1538	...	|	|	|	...	|	...	1726	|	1814	|	|	...
Changchun ... d.	|	|	1321	|	|	|	1452	|	...	|	1541	...	1621	...	|	|	|	...	|	1723	1808	|	1859	|	|	...
Changchun xi ... d.	1247	1322	|	1357	1423	1456	1504	1523	...	1530	|	...	|	...	1647	1709	1742	...	1809	1734	|	1846	1911	1934	2011	...
Siping dong ... d.	1315	|	1404	|	1451	|	|	|	...	1558	|	...	1658	...	|	1737	1811	...	1838	1803	|	|	1940	|	2039	...
Shenyang bei ... a.	1403	1434	1451y	1516	1547y	1600	1615	1642	...	1653y	1713y	...	1750	...	1810y	1828	1905	...	1921	1857y	1941	2002y	2034y	2046	2130	...
Shenyang bei ... d.	...	1438	1456y	1519	1553y	1602	1618	...	1642y	1656y	1716y	1740	1755	1806y	1814y	1832	...	1924y	1926	1902y	1944	2006y	2037y	2049	2133	...
Anshan xi ... d.	...	|	1528	1555	1642	|	1655	...	1714	1735	|	1816	|	1838	1853	1917	...	|	|	1934	|	2045	|	2125	|	...
Haicheng xi ... d.	...	|	|	1609	1654	|	|	...	|	|	1802	|	|	1852	|	1931	...	|	|	|	|	2059	2123	2139	|	...
Yinkou dong ... d.	...	|	1551	1624	...	|	1717	...	|	|	|	|	1847	|	1915	|	...	2011	2025	1957	|	2114	2139	|	|	...
Dalian bei ... a.	...	1628	1702	1724	...	1735	1822	...	1836	1850	1903	1936d	1947	2012d	2015	2032	...	2111	2124	2103	2147d	2221	2231	2240	2317	...

For footnotes and return service see next page.

DALIAN - SHENYANG - JILIN and HARBIN — 7020

China Rail High Speed

ll trains prefix 'G'	751	701	8041	8001	703	8043	8003	705	8005	47	8045	707	8007	709	755	8047	8049	8009	711	8011	713	785	8051	8013	715
alian bei d.	...	0603	0610	0615	0646	0702	0717	0731	0835	0830	0830d	0911	0915d	0943	...	0952d	1038d	1019	1105	1121	1136	...	1154d	1201d	1223
'inkou dong d.	...	|	0705	|	0748	|	0812	|	|	|	0938	1013	1038	|	...	1114	|	|	|	|	1237	...	|	1310	|
laicheng xi d.	...	0706	|	|	|	0812	0827	|	|	|	0953	|	|	|	...	|	|	|	1208	|	|	...	|	|	|
nshan xi d.	...	|	0727	0753	|	|	0841	0855	|	|	1007	1035	|	|	...	1136	1202	1143	|	|	|	...	1318	|	|
henyang bei a.	...	0750y	0757y	0823y	0840y	0900	0918y	0925y	1019	1003	1048	1105y	1127y	1130y	...	1206y	1236	1213y	1252y	1308y	1326	...	1352	1359	1404
henyang bei d.	0620	0753y	...	0826y	0844y	...	0921y	0928y	1022	1005	...	1108y	1130y	1133y	1143	...	...	1217y	1256y	1311y	1329	1338	...	1402	1423
iping dong d.	0705	|	...	0923	|	...	1011	|	|	|	...	1205	1216	|	|	...	...	1307	|	1408	|	1442	...	1455	|
hangchun xi d.	0734	0912	...	|	1003	...	1040	1047	|	1111	...	1233	|	1252	1304	...	...	1335	1421	|	1450	1510	...	|	1538
Changchun a.	|	|	...	0954	|	...	1051	|	1140	|	...	|	1248	|	|	...	...	1345	|	1441	|	|	...	1530	|
Jilin a.	|	|	...	...	|	...	1135	|	...	|	...	|	1330	|	|	...	...	1427	|	1521	|	|	...	1610	|
larbin xi a.	0830	1008	...	...	1106	...	...	1156	...	1205	...	1339	...	1348	1400	...	...	...	1523	...	1546	1619	...	...	1641

ll trains prefix 'G'	717	8015	8053	49	719	781	8017	8055	721	8057	723	8019	725	8059	8021	727	729	8023	8061		731	8063	8067		8069
)alian bei d.	1239	1335	1352d	1400	1416	...	1442d	1508d	1532	1541d	1610	1605d	1650	1651d	1740d	1746	1822	1840	1902	...	1912	1954d	2015	...	2115
'inkou dong d.	|	|	1459	|	1519	...	|	1631	|	|	|	|	1745	|	|	|	1924	1942	|	...	|	|	2124	...	|
laicheng xi d.	1403	|	|	|	|	...	1606	|	|	1702	1713	|	|	|	|	|	|	|	2012	...	|	|	|	...	|
nshan xi d.	1417	1452	1521	|	1541	...	|	|	1703	|	1727	1742	|	1815	|	1903	1946	2004	|	...	2036	|	2146	...	|
ihenyang bei a.	1447y	1540	1558y	1533	1611y	...	1701	1720	1733y	1745y	1804y	1820	1831y	1852y	1948y	1940y	2027	2045	2053	...	2106y	2158	2216y	...	2252
ihenyang bei d.	1450y	1542	...	1535	1614y	1730	1704	...	1736y	...	1807y	1824	1834y	...	1953y	1947y	2030	2048	...	...	2109y	...	...	...	...
iping dong d.	|	1628	...	|	|	|	1757	...	|	...	1901	1922	1931	...	2101	2043	2116	2142	...	...	|	...	...	...	...
hangchun xi d.	1609	|	...	1641	1733	1851	|	...	1901	...	1929	|	1959	...	|	2112	2144	|	...	...	|	...	...	...	...
Changchun a.	|	1705	...	|	|	|	1835	...	|	...	|	1954	|	...	2134	|	|	2215	...	...	2232	...	...	...	...
Jilin a.	|	...	...	|	|	|	1918	...	|	...	|	2038	|	...	...	|	|	...	...	...	|	...	...	...	...
larbin xi a.	1712	...	...	1735	1842	1954	...	...	2010	...	2025	...	2102	...	...	2222	2240	...	...	...	2331	...	...	...	...

d – Dalian. y – Shenyang. * * – Changhcun *0 km* - Jilin *111 km.* - Siping dong *130 km.*

HARBIN - TIANJIN and BEIJING — 7025

Chinese Railways

km	Z188	K20	T244	Z62	K28	Z16	Z18	Z238	T122	Z118	T48	T184	Z158	↓ ↑	T47	K27	Z117	Z237	Z15	Z61	T121	Z187	K19	T243	Z157	T183	Z15
	◆	◆			◆			◆	◆		◆				◆	◆		◆			◆	◆	◆				
0	...	1317	1057x	...	...	2120	2128	2136	...	...	2208	0659	1043	d.Harbin a.	0612	...	...	0732	0726	...	...	...	1512	1546x	1655	1824x	0726
242	...	1557	1342	2200	...	|	|	|	2128	2341	|	1029	1248	d.Changchun d.	|	...	0517	|	|	0637	0656	...	1237	1343	1458	1544	|
546	...	1926y	1703	|	...	|	|	0159	0012	0213	0257	1335y	1512	a.Shenyang bei d.	0124	...	0252	0233	|	|	0351	...	0859y	1040	1227	1234	|
546	1735	1934y	1711	|	2224y	|	|	0205	0019	0219	0303	1345y	1518	d.Shenyang bei a.	0116	0318y	0245	0227	|	|	0327	0530	0847y	1032	1219	1227	|
934	2338	0022	|	|	0304	|	|	|	0410	|	|	1813	|	d.Shanhaiguan d.	|	2242	|	|	|	|	2303	2327	0413	|	|	0753	|
972	|	|	|	|	|	|	|	|	|	|	|	1908	|	d.Beidaihe d.	2124	|	|	|	|	|	|	|	|	|	|	|	|
1235	0303	0352	0234	|	0649	|	|	0750	0800	|	|	2139	|	a. Tianjin d.	|	1909	|	2040	|	|	1935	2013	0041	0357	|	0409	|
1249	...	0546	...	0608	0838	0724	0730	...	...	0836	0914	...	2108	a.Beijing d.	1857	1727	2109	...	2121	2210	...	...	2300	...	0558	...	2121

BEIJING - BADALING — 7035

Chinese Railways

km	S201	S203	S205	S207	S209	S211	S213	S215	S217	S219	S221	S227	↓ ↑	S208	S210	S212	S214	S216	S218	S220	S222	S224	S226	S228	S232
0	0612	0758	0834	0902	1057	1242	1314	1335	1524	1711	1741	2128	d.Beijing ▽ d.	09417	1212	1240	1312	1500	1643	1725	1739	1854	2111	2143	2303
82	0731	0920	0947	1015	1213	1401	1425	1450	1643	1830	1857	2244	a.Badaling △ a.	0823	1051	1119	1150	1340	1508	1552	1621	1733	1934	2006	2133

BEIJING - TAIYUAN - XI'AN — 7040

China Rail High Speed

km		D2501 A	D2505	D2531	G601	D2001	G91	D2533	G603	D2515	G605	G607	G609	D2519	G611	D2521	D2003	G613	D2525 E	G615	D2529 D	D2005	G617	G619	G621	G623	G625
0	Beijing xi d.	...	...	...	0721	0752	0840	...	1010	...	1028	1114	1133	...	1239	...	1318	1410	...	1506	...	1529	1657	1802	1807	1905	2005
281	Shijiazhuang d.	...	...	...	0853	0934	0950	...	1142	...	1200	1243	1256	...	1411	...	1520	1533	...	1633	...	1725	1819	1924	1939	2021	2115
384	Yangquan bei d.	...	...	...	0936	1017	|	...	1225	...	1243	|	1339	...	1454	...	1603	1615	...	1718	...	1808	|	2007	2023	2104	2157
513	Taiyuan nan a.	...	...	...	1022	1103	1112	...	1311	...	1329	1405	1425	...	1540	...	1649	1701	...	1804	...	1854	1941	2053	2110	2150	2243
513	Taiyuan nan d.	0700	0825	0925	...	1113	...	1212	...	1334	1347	...	...	1510	...	1611	1700	...	1750	...	1913	1902	...	...	...	...	...
746	Linfen xi d.	0829	0940	1108	...	1307	...	|	...	1517	1537	...	...	1639	...	1747	1838	...	|	...	|	2053	...	...	...	...	...
869	Yuncheng bei d.	0921	1018	|	...	1353	...	1433	...	|	1620	...	...	1717	...	1825	1932	...	2011	...	|	...	...	...	...	...	...
1092	Xi'an bei a.	1047	1125	1312	...	...	...	1553	...	1715	...	...	...	1837	...	1945	...	...	2131	...	2240	...	...	...	...	...	...

	G602 B	G604	G606	G92	D2002	G610	D2004	G612	D2502	D2506 C	D2508	D2510 F	G614	G616	G618	G620	G622	D2006	D2520	G624	G626	D2532	D2526	D2528	D2534	D2530
Xi'an bei d.	...	...	...	...	...	...	...	...	0810	0938	0945	1000	...	...	...	...	...	...	1410	...	...	1612	1751	1832	1850	1905
Yuncheng bei d.	...	...	...	...	...	...	0806	...	|	1044	|	|	...	1152	...	...	...	1425	|	...	...	1740	1919	|	|	2025
Linfen xi d.	...	...	...	...	0739	...	0909	...	1030	1129	|	1206	...	1238	...	...	...	1512	|	...	...	1832	|	|	|	2110
Taiyuan nan a.	...	...	...	...	0916	...	1101	...	1152	1258	1313	1328	...	1420	...	...	...	1657	1737	...	...	2008	2131	2006	2224	2246
Taiyuan nan d.	0648	0700	0805	0825	0926	1100	1108	1143	...	...	...	...	1346	1429	1458	1525	1650	1707	...	1800	1850	...	...	...	...	...
Yangquan bei d.	|	|	0853	|	1017	|	1158	1231	...	...	...	...	1435	1518	1547	1614	1738	1758	...	1849	1940	...	...	...	...	...
Shijiazhuang d.	0817	0827	0935	0950	1102	1226	1252	1314	...	...	...	...	1518	1605	1634	1658	1821	1844	...	1931	2032	...	...	...	...	...
Beijing xi a.	0935	0956	1054	1100	1255	1344	1503	1434	...	...	...	...	1637	1728	1745	1816	1943	2039	...	2050	2151	...	...	...	...	...

km	All trains prefix 'D'	6801	6877	6803	6805	6807	6809	6811	2531	6813	G671	6815	2533	6869	6817	6819	5091	G673	6821	6823					
0	Xi'an beii d.	0730	0800	0830	0930	1030	1130	1230	1320	1400	1440	1500	1600	1640	1700	1800	1900	2045	2145	2200	...	...	...	...	...
167	Baoji nan d.	0835	0853	0935	1035	1135	1235	1335	1425	1505	1539	1605	1705	1745	1805	1905	2005	2144	2250	2305	...	...	...	...	...

All trains prefix 'D'	G672	6822	6802	5082	6804	6806	6824	6808	6810	5096	2532	6812	G674	6814	2534	6816	6870	6818	6820					
Baoji nan d.	0800	0830	0900	0935	1000	1100	1130	1200	1300	1400	1500	1530	1600	1630	1730	1830	1815	1930	2030	...	...	...	...	...
Xi'an bei d.	0905	0935	1005	1040	1105	1205	1235	1259	1405	1459	1605	1635	1705	1735	1835	1935	1920	2035	2135	...	...	...	...	...

A – Additional trips: 1245, 1318. B – Additional trip 0843. C – Additional trips: 1107, 1210, 1250, 1725.
D – Additional trips: 1015, 1033, 1718, 1830. E – Additional trips: 0800, 1434. F – Additional trips: 0905, 1340, 1458.

BEIJING - TIANJIN — 7045

China Rail High Speed

High-speed '**C**' trains (numbers **C20xx**, **C21xx** and **C22xx**). *120 km.* Journey 33 - 41 minutes.

Beijing nan depart: 0601, 0614, 0627, 0632, 0643, 0651, 0702, 0713, 0731, 0746, 0808, 0819, 0827, 0839, 0852, 0903, 0908, 0917, 0925, 0937, 0945, 1000, 1008, 1016, 1027, 1040, 1048, 1054. 1110, 1112, 1118, 1130, 1142, 1154, 1206, 1223, 1232, 1250, 1300, 1313, 1318, 1340, 1352, 1402, 1418, 1440, 1449, 1500, 1512, 1532, 1545, 1550, 1602, 1608, 1619, 1632, 1641, 1649, 1709, 1723, 1731, 1745, 1752, 1806, 1825, 1835, 1840, 1852, 1906, 1926, 1942, 2002, 2008, 2015, 20026, 2034, 2056, 2107, 2126, 2150, 2218, 2243, 2305.

Tianjin depart: 0618, 0630, 0638, 0652, 0700, 0715, 0728, 0744, 0802, 0811, 0823, 0838, 0851, 0907, 0912, 0923, 0937, 0951, 0957, 1002, 1014, 1029, 1039, 1047, 1105, 1114, 1135, 1140, 1155, 1207, 1213, 1219, 1225, 1236, 1247, 1302, 1315, 1338, 1350, 1406, 1429, 1441, 1447, 1505, 1517, 1525, 1531, 1539, 1609, 1623, 1633, 1645, 1706, 1718, 1723, 1735, 1741, 1747, 1801, 1810, 1815, 1823, 1841, 1859, 1917, 1930, 1938, 1955, 2009, 2018, 2019, 2031, 2046, 2054, 2103, 2111, 2127, 2139, 2153, 2203, 2209, 2233, 2252.

HOHHOT - LANZHOU — 7050

Chinese Railways

km	K888	2635	K41		Z179	↓ ↑	Z180	K887	2636		K42
	◆		◆		◆		◆	◆			◆
0	0835	1545h	0921	...	2250	d.Hohhot dong a.	0131	0643	0621	...	0940
165	1047	1821	1149	...	0046	d.Baotou d.	2343	0446	0413	...	0729
383	1327	2052	1407	...	0309	d.Linhe d.	2119	0225	0117	...	0501
676	1846	0058	1818	...	0708	d.Yinchuan d.	1734	2240	1959	...	0122
838	2213	0335	2129	...	0942	d.Zhongwei d.	1511	1922	1741	...	2152
1095	|	|	0055	...	1318	a. Wuwei d.	1019	|	|	...	1812
1562	|	|	0711	...	1753	a. Jiayuguan d.	0534	|	|	...	1236
970	0037	0541	...	...	...	d.Jingtai d.	...	1702	1442	...	...
1057	0241	0710	...	...	...	d.Beiyin xi d.	...	1526	1315	...	...
1144	0423	0906	...	...	...	a.Lanzhou d.	...	1309	1121	...	...

◆ – **NOTES** for Tables **7025 - 7050** (by train number):

K19/20 – Beijing(**K19/20**) - Manzhouli and v.v.
K27/28 – ①③④⑥. Beijing(**K27/28**) - Dandong(**6/5**) - Pyongyang and v.v.
K42/41 – Jiayuggan(**K42/41**) - Beijing.
T47/48 – Qiqihar(**T48/47**) - Beijing.
T121/122 – Changchun(**T122/21**) - Tianjin(**T123/24**) - Guangzhou and v.v.
Z179/180 – Beijing(**Z178/180**) - Urümqi and v.v.
Z187/188 – Shenyang bei(**Z188/87**) - Tianjin(**Z185/86**) - Shenzhen and v.v.
Z237/238 – Harbin(**Z238/37**) - Tianjin(**Z235/36**) - Guangzhou and v.v.
K887/88 – Beijing(**K887/88**) - Lanzhou and v.v.

b – Beijing bei. **h** – Hohhot. **t** – Taiyuan.
x – xi. **y** – Shenyang. △ – For Great Wall of China.
▽ – Services now depart from Huangtudian station and departure / arrival times may alter slightly.

BEYOND EUROPE - CHINA

7060 BEIJING - ZHENGZHOU - WUHAN (- GUANGZHOU)

China Rail High Speed

km	All trains prefix 'G'	93	551	D2201	D295	541	423	507		501	529	817	71	531	307	83	421	98	73	511	309	79	821	831	65
0	**Beijing** xi d.	...	...	...	...	...	...	0653	...	0710	0726	...	0740	...	0830	0900	0907	...	...	0927	0932	1000	...	...	1033
281	Shijiazhuang d.	...	...	...	...	...	0800	0816	...	0847	0857	...	0909	0915	0955	1010	1022	...	...	1050	1055	1109	...	...	1202
403	Xingtai dong d.	...	...	...	...	...	|	|	...	0925	0934	...	0939	0949	|	|	|	...	...	1120	1135	|	...	...	1236
456	Handan dong d.	...	...	...	...	...	0847	0858	...	|	|	...	0957	|	1046	|	1103	...	...	1145	1153	|	...	...	|
516	Anyang dong d.	...	...	...	...	...	|	0917	...	|	1004	...	|	1022	1105	|	1123	...	...	1204	1212	|	...	...	1306
626	Xinxiang dong d.	...	...	...	...	...	0934	|	...	|	|	...	|	1049	|	|	1150	...	...	1232	|	|	...	...	|
	Xi'an bei **7070** d.	...	...	...	...	...	|	|	...	|	|	0803	|	|	|	|	|	0953	...	|	|	|	1054	1128	|
693	**Zhengzhou** dong a.	...	...	...	...	...	0956	1007	...	1029	1046	1022	1058	1111	1154	1131	1212	1147**z**	...	1253	1302	1230	1312**z**	1342**z**	1348
693	**Zhengzhou** dong d.	0756	...	0804**z**	0824**z**	0825	1000	1010	...	1034	1052	1045	1106	1114	1158	1134	1218	1150**z**	1212	1256	1308	1233	1315**z**	1346**z**	1352
848	Luohe xi d.	|	0800	0907	0923	0902	1037	|	...	|	1129	|	|	|	|	|	1305	|	1254	1329	|	|	1412	|	|
1030	Xinyang dong d.	|	0854	1000	1016	0949	1124	1128	...	1150	|	1203	|	1246	|	|	1352	|	1339	1409	|	|	1452	|	1508
1229	**Wuhan** a.	0955	0944	1056**h**	1122**h**	1033	1208	1224**h**	...	1234	1253	1248	1305	1331	1349**h**	1324	1436	1348	1423	1455	1517**h**	1417	1535	1605	1552
	Changsha nan **7065** a.	1118	1127	...	...	1204	1348	...	...	1410	1449	1417	1427	1505	...	1443	1609	1511	1554	...	...	1538	1706	1737	1727
	Guangzhou nan **7065** a.	1350	1423	...	...	1456	...	...	...	...	...	1657	1714	1752	...	...	...	1739	1837	...	...	1803	1950	2025	2016
	Shenzhen bei **7065** a.	...	1458	...	...	...	...	...	...	...	...	1736	1753	1830	...	...	...	...	1909	...	...	...	2030	...	...

All trains prefix 'G'	545	429	553	75	835	825	839	555	67	69	89	547	519	503	858	642	587	521	505	573	585	523	525	563
Beijing xi d.	...	1153	...	...	...	...	...	1251	1213	1305	1330	...	1405	1438	...	...	1455	1523	1540	1618	1623	1630	1714	1731
Shijiazhuang d.	...	1316	...	...	...	...	...	1406	1342	1428	1439	...	1527	1600	...	...	1642	1652	1703	1742	1758	1753	1836	1853
Xingtai dong d.	...	1346	...	...	...	...	...	|	1419	|	|	...	|	1630	...	...	|	|	1733	|	1828	1723	1906	|
Handan dong d.	...	|	...	...	...	...	...	|	1447	1516	|	...	|	|	...	...	1723	|	1751	|	1848	|	|	1941
Anyang dong d.	...	1417	...	...	...	...	...	|	|	1535	|	...	1627	1700	...	...	|	1753	|	|	1907	1853	1936	2000
Xinxiang dong d.	...	1445	...	...	...	...	...	|	1527	|	|	...	1655	|	...	...	|	1821	|	1905	1953	1921	2011	2028
Xi'an bei **7070** d.	...	|	...	...	1229	1235	1305	|	|	|	|	...	|	|	...	1520	|	|	|	|	|	|	|	|
Zhengzhou dong a.	...	1506	...	...	1442**z**	1501**z**	1533**z**	1534	1548	1617	1600	...	1716	1742	...	1740	1825	1842	1853	1926	1956	1943	2032	2049
Zhengzhou dong d.	1407	...	...	1430	1447**z**	1504**z**	1536**z**	1537	1551	1620	...	1643	1720	1745	1726**z**	1755	1829	1845	1856	1929	1959	1946	2035	...
Luohe xi d.	1445	...	...	1517	|	1552	|	|	1633	|	...	1727	|	1820	|	|	1911	1938	|	|	2043	2023	2118	...
Xinyang dong d.	|	...	1530	1604	1613	|	|	1645	1713	|	...	|	1844	|	1903	1910	1951	2034	2025	2044	2123	2103	2205	...
Wuhan a.	1613	...	1624	1650	1657	1717	1742	1734**h**	1759	1812	...	1858	1928	1937	1949	1954	2035	2139**h**	2056	2128	2207	2149	2255**h**	...
Changsha nan **7065** a.	1745	...	1756	1811	1829	1850	1920	...	1929	1933	...	2026	...	2123	...	2122	...	...	2232	...	...	...	...	...
Guangzhou nan **7065** a.	2032	...	2043	210	2117	2138	2208	...	2218	2223	...	2310	...	...	...	...	...	...	...	...	...	...	...	...
Shenzhen bei **7065** a.	...	...	...	2141	...	2219	...	...	...	...	...	...	...	...	...	...	...	...	...	...	...	...	...	...

All trains prefix 'G'	527	565	509	567	569	D901 A	D903 A	D909 A	D927 A	D923 A
Beijing xi d.	1812	1829	1900	1916	2000	2010	2015	2020	2025	2035
Shijiazhuang d.	1942	1951	2009	2038	2109	2135	2140	2145	2156	2206
Xingtai dong d.	|	|	|	2108	|	|	|	2217	|	|
Handan dong d.	2023	2045	|	2126	|	|	2225	|	|	|
Anyang dong d.	2043	2105	|	|	|	2236	|	|	|	|
Xinxiang dong d.	2117	|	|	|	2218	|	|	|	|	|
Xi'an bei **7070** d.	|	|	|	|	|	|	|	|	|	|
Zhengzhou dong a.	2140	2147	2131	2227	2240	|	2327	2332	2337	2347
Zhengzhou dong d.	2143	...	2134	...	...	|	2332	2337	2342	2352
Luohe xi d.	|	...	|	...	...	|	|	|	|	|
Xinyang dong d.	2259	...	|	...	...	|	|	|	|	|
Wuhan a.	2342	...	2324**h**	...	...	|	|	|	|	|
Changsha nan **7065** a.	...	...	...	...	...	|	|	|	|	|
Guangzhou nan **7065** a.	...	...	...	...	...	0628	0633	0638	0648	0643
Shenzhen bei **7065** a.	...	...	...	...	...	0706	0711	0716	0725	...

All trains prefix 'G'	520	90	508	564	510	588	502	512	856	640
Shenzhen bei **7065** d.	...	...	...	...	...	...	...	...	...	...
Guangzhou nan **7065** d.	...	...	...	...	...	...	...	...	...	...
Changsha nan **7065** d.	...	...	...	...	...	...	0743	...	...	0852
Wuhan d.	0700**h**	...	0708**h**	...	0816	0825	0911	0923**h**	0922	1027
Xinyang dong d.	|	...	0759	...	0901	0917	|	1014	1019	|
Luohe xi d.	|	...	0847	...	0950	1004	|	|	1107	|
Zhengzhou dong a.	0851	...	0930	...	1033	1045	1102	1127	1201**z**	1200
Zhengzhou dong d.	0854	0900	0933	0940	1036	1050	1105	1132	1205**z**	1212
Xi'an bei **7070** a.	|	|	|	|	|	|	|	|	1437	1450
Xinxiang dong d.	|	|	|	1002	1059	1112	1131	|	...	...
Anyang dong d.	|	|	|	1030	|	1140	|	1220	...	...
Handan dong d.	|	|	1035	1051	1139	|	|	|	...	...
Xingtai dong d.	|	|	|	|	|	1215	1228	1252	...	...
Shijiazhuang d.	1018	1024	1117	1137	1220	1247	1259	1324	...	...
Beijing xi a.	1126	1131	1229	1302	1339	1423	1418	1447	...	...

All trains prefix 'G'	84	586	641	572	514	566	94	556	832	96	516	552	66	72	430	74	568	542	818	532	822	310	524	68
Shenzhen bei **7065** d.	...	...	...	...	...	...	...	...	...	...	...	...	...	0753	...	0842	...	...	0935	0940	1000	...	...	...
Guangzhou nan **7065** d.	...	...	...	...	...	...	0740	...	0711	0855	...	0933	1000	0827	...	0922	...	0944	1016	1023	1040	...	...	1115
Changsha nan **7065** d.	0900	...	0853	...	...	...	1020	...	0956	1120	...	1232	1220	1114	...	1211	...	1238	1303	1308	1325	...	...	1401
Wuhan d.	1020	0917	1026	1013	1035	...	1143	1035**h**	1133	1241	1330	1402	1341	1246	...	1347	...	1414	1435	1440	1456	1509**h**	1530	1535
Xinyang dong d.	|	1004	|	1103	1120	...	1233	1139	|	|	|	1452	|	|	...	1432	...	1459	1520	1526	1541	|	1615	1620
Luohe xi d.	|	1056	|	1150	1207	...	|	1240	|	|	|	...	|	1421	...	1519	...	1539	1600	1609	|	|	|	1707
Zhengzhou dong a.	1205	1142	1224**z**	1233	1241	...	1347	1327	1344**z**	1438**z**	1516	...	1526	1456	...	1602	...	1619	1649**z**	1648	1714**z**	1712	1731	1743
Zhengzhou dong d.	1208	1151	1229	1236	1249	1259	...	1332	1355**z**	1441**z**	1519	...	1529	1459	1545	...	1610	...	1653**z**	1654	1718**z**	1715	1734	1746
Xi'an bei **7070** a.	|	|	1456	|	|	|	...	|	1610	1635	|	...	|	|	|	...	|	...	1915	|	1933	|	|	|
Xinxiang dong d.	|	1213	...	1259	|	1322	...	|	...	...	|	...	|	|	1607	...	|	...	...	|	...	|	|	1808
Anyang dong d.	|	1254	...	|	1339	1358	...	1423	...	...	|	...	|	1543	1635	...	1700	...	...	|	...	1758	1824	1843
Handan dong d.	|	1313	...	1345	1358	|	...	1442	...	...	|	...	|	|	|	...	1719	...	...	1756	...	|	|	|
Xingtai dong d.	|	|	...	|	|	1429	...	|	...	...	|	...	|	1630	1705	...	|	...	...	|	...	1828	|	|
Shijiazhuang d.	1332	1402	...	1426	1449	1500	...	1524	...	...	1642	...	1653	1703	1736	...	1809	...	...	1845	...	1859	1919	1944
Beijing xi a.	1440	1521	...	1553	1609	1632	...	1643	...	...	1750	...	1800	1821	1856	...	1933	...	...	...	...	2020	2044	2056

All trains prefix 'G'	836	422	308	504	570	80	424	506	D2202	840	70	530	826	528	D296	544	546	76	548	D924 A	D902 A	D904 A	D910 A	D928 A
Shenzhen bei **7065** d.	...	...	...	...	...	1131	...	...	...	...	...	...	1250	...	...	...	...	1540	...	...	1940	1945	1950	1955
Guangzhou nan **7065** d.	1130	...	...	...	...	1211	...	...	...	1230	1250	...	1330	...	...	1356	1414	1624	1629	2010	2015	2020	2025	2030
Changsha nan **7065** d.	1417	1412	...	1430	...	1456	1501	1506	...	1517	1538	1553	1616	...	...	1647	1712	1914	1923	2303	|	2313	2318	2323
Wuhan d.	1546	1556	1615**h**	1611	...	1633	1639	1644	1649**h**	1653	1707	1724	1748	1757	1811**h**	1832	1849	2041	2056	|	|	|	|	|
Xinyang dong d.	1632	1644	|	|	...	1718	1724	1716	1816	1739	1752	1810	1833	1843	1924	1917	1934	2126	2142	|	|	|	|	|
Luohe xi d.	1718	|	|	1736	...	|	1804	1809	1908	|	|	1857	1913	|	2018	2005	|	2223	2230	|	|	|	|	|
Zhengzhou dong a.	1809**z**	1801	1824	1811	...	1832	1842	1851	1956**z**	1914**z**	1906	1932	1957	2002	2114**z**	2043	2109	2301	2313	|	|	|	|	|
Zhengzhou dong d.	1813**z**	1806	1830	1814	1825	1835	1847	1854	...	1918**z**	1911	1935	2012	2008	...	...	...	...	...	|	|	|	|	|
Xi'an bei **7070** a.	2029	|	|	|	|	|	|	|	...	2139	|	|	2224	|	...	...	...	...	...	|	|	|	|	|
Xinxiang dong d.	...	|	|	|	|	1855	1911	1918	...	...	|	|	...	|	...	...	...	...	...	|	|	|	|	|
Anyang dong d.	...	1849	1920	1857	1915	1925	1952	|	...	...	1957	2027	...	|	...	...	...	...	...	|	|	|	|	|
Handan dong d.	...	|	|	1917	|	1944	|	2001	...	...	2017	|	...	2111	...	...	...	...	...	|	|	|	|	0459
Xingtai dong d.	...	1919	1950	|	1945	|	2024	|	...	...	|	|	...	|	...	...	...	...	...	|	|	|	0507	|
Shijiazhuang d.	...	1950	2021	2000	2016	2027	2052	2044	...	...	2100	2130	...	2152	...	...	...	...	...	0520	0525	0530	0540	0545
Beijing xi a.	...	2109	2141	2126	2136	2146	...	2206	...	...	2227	2250	...	2312	...	...	...	...	...	0621	0656	0701	0713	0718

A – Conveys 1cl, Runs ①⑤⑥⑦ only.

h – Wuhan Hankou.
z – Zhengzhou.

7062 BEIJING - HOHHOT

Chinese Railways

km	K217	K58	K617	Z315	Z179	K263	K573	K597	K41	K89	Z317	K888			Z180	K887	Z316	K42	K618	Z318	K218	K598	K57	K264	K90	K574
					♦				♦			♦	↓	↑	♦	♦		♦								
0	0033**x**	0255	1024**x**	1533**x**	1515	2013	2035**x**	2126**x**	2140	2216**x**	2249	2341	d.**Beijing**	a.	0939	1358	1426**x**	1942	1935**x**	2150	0405**x**	0454**x**	0427	0710	0726**x**	0858**x**
190	0405	0623	1419	1856	1839	2339	0007	0051	0147	0136	0214	0329	d.Zhangjiakou nan	d.	0619	1043	1112	1617	1554	1825	2359	0136	0105	0331	0414	0538
368	0656	|	|	|	|	|	0301	0346	0450	|	|	|	d. Datong	d.	|	|	|	1340	|	|	2053	2304	|	|	|	0307
374	0843	0832	1715	2046	2104	0329	0446	0531	0730	0504	|	0647	d.Jining nan	d.	0359	0841	0922	1145	1326	|	1854	2110	2221	0050	0038	0031
524*	1006	1016	1838	2154	2227	0514	0609	0652	0853	0703	0511**h**	0810	a.**Hohhot** dong	d.	0215	0717	0814	1006	1158	1518**h**	1638	1940	2052	2318	2308	2301
697	1247	1236	...	...	0038	0730	0845	0908	1140	...	0701	1039	a.Baotou	d.	2343	...	...	0729	...	1338	1453	1728	1819	2055	...	2012

♦ – **NOTES** by train number
K41/42 – Jiayuggan(**K41/42**)- Beijing.
Z179/180 – Beijing(**Z179/180**) - Urümqi and v.v.
K887/88 – Beijing(**K887/88**) - Lanzhou and v.v.

h – Hohhot.
x – Beijing xi.

* – 645km via Datong.

China Rail High Speed — (BEIJING -) XIA'N - WUHAN - GUANGZHOU - SHENZHEN — 7065

km	All trains prefix 'G'	6011	6101	1103	1001	1105	1107	77	1111	1007	93	551	541	85	1011	1034	501	73	71	531	83	1015	98	79	820	1017
1229	*Beijing xi* **7060** d.	...	...	...	...	...	...	...	...	...	...	...	...	...	...	...	0710	...	0740	...	0900	...	...	1000	...	...
1050	**Xi'an** bei d.	...	...	...	...	...	...	...	...	...	...	...	...	...	...	...	|	...	|	...	|	...	0958	|	0942	...
929	Huashan bei d.	...	...	...	...	...	...	...	...	...	...	...	...	...	...	...	|	...	|	...	|	...	|	|	|	...
793	Sanmenxia nan d.	...	...	...	...	...	...	...	...	...	...	...	...	...	...	...	|	...	|	...	|	...	|	|	1050	...
670	Luoyang Longmen d.	...	...	...	...	...	...	...	...	...	...	...	...	...	...	...	|	...	|	...	|	...	|	|	1123	...
536	Zhengzhou dong **7060** d.	...	...	...	...	...	...	...	...	...	0756	...	0825	...	...	...	1034	1041	1106	1116	1134	...	1150z	1233	1201z	...
0	**Wuhan** ♥ d.	...	...	0700	0725	0737	0831	0900	0910	0930	0958	0951	1039	...	1053	1140	1238	1251	1308	1336	1324	1344	1351	1420	1427	1439
209	Yueyang dong d.	...	...	0751	|	0828	0936	|	1008	1028	|	1054	|	...	|	1238	|	1343	|	|	|	1447	|	|	1818	1530
347	**Changsha** nan ♥ d.	0700	0706	0828	0854	0912	1014	1021	1045	1105	1119	1130	1207	1228	1222	1316	1410	1420	1430	1505	1443	1523	1515	1541	1601	1607
387	Zhuzhou xi d.	|	|	0845	|	|	1035	|	1055	1122	|	1148	|	|	|	|	...	|	|	|	...	|	|	|	|	|
496	Hengyang dong d.	|	0745	0921	|	0951	1104	|	|	1151	1159	1217	1246	|	|	1355	...	|	1509	|	...	1603	|	|	1640	1646
628	Chenzhou xi d.	0807	0820	|	1008	1026	1139	|	1159	1231	|	1251	1321	|	1340	1430	...	1527	|	1612	...	1646	|	|	|	|
758	Shaoguan d.	0840	0853	|	|	|	|	|	|	|	|	|	1359	|	1411	1503	...	1600	1617	1648	...	1720	|	|	|	1754
968	**Guangzhou** nan ♥ a.	0951	0957	1126	1131	1156	1309	1243	1329	1401	1349	1423	1456	1451	1517	1600	...	1657	1714	1752	...	1816	1739	1803	1837	1851
1070	**Shenzhen** bei a.	1032	...	...	1212	...	...	1317	...	1441	...	1458	...	...	1549	1643	...	1736	1753	1830	...	1857	...	1835	1909	1924

All trains prefix 'G'	824	1019		65	834	545	553	75	1021	838	828	1151	839	6027	67	1133	69	1135	1305	547	1139	1141	6121	503	505
Beijing xi **7060** d.	...	...	...	1033	...	...	...	...	...	...	...	...	...	...	1213	...	1305	...	...	...	...	...	...	1438	1540
Xi'an bei d.	1100	...	...	|	1123	...	...	...	...	1230	1235	...	1312	...	|	...	|	...	...	...	...	...	...	|	|
Huashan bei d.	1132	...	...	|	|	...	...	...	...	1303	1321	...	|	...	|	...	|	...	...	...	...	...	...	|	|
Sanmenxia nan d.	|	...	...	|	|	...	...	...	...	|	1352	...	1425	...	|	...	|	...	...	...	...	...	...	|	|
Luoyang Longmen d.	1235	...	...	|	1304	...	...	...	...	1406	1425	...	1258	...	|	...	|	...	...	...	...	...	...	|	|
Zhengzhou dong **7060** d.	1315z	...	...	1352	1346z	1407	...	1430	...	1447z	1504z	...	1536z	...	1551	...	1620	...	...	1643	...	...	...	1745	1856
Wuhan ♥ d.	1538	1543	...	1555	1609	1620	1628	1653	1658	1704	1722	1736	1748	...	1803	1757	1815	1808	...	1901	1923	1946	...	1941	2059
Yueyang dong d.	1629	|	...	1653	|	|	1722	|	1800	1755	|	1834	|	...	1855	1905	|	1911	...	1952	2014	|	...	2032	2158
Changsha nan ♥ d.	1706	1712	...	1731	1741	1748	1759	1816	1837	1832	1854	1912	1924	1929	1934	1948	1939	1958	2020	2031	2100	2116	2105	2107	2232
Zhuzhou xi d.	|	|	...	|	|	|	|	1833	1854	1849	|	1929	|	|	|	|	1954	|	|	|	|	|	2122	...	...
Hengyang dong d.	1745	|	...	|	1820	1827	|	1902	|	|	1933	|	|	2008	|	2030	2025	2045	2100	2110	|	2156	|	...	...
Chenzhou xi d.	1820	|	...	1846	1855	1902	|	|	|	1947	2008	2026	|	2043	2048	2105	|	|	|	2145	2214	2231	2219	...	...
Shaoguan d.	1853	1859	...	|	|	|	1946	2003	|	|	|	2057	2104	|	|	|	2126	2148	|	|	|	|	2252	...	...
Guangzhou nan ♥ a.	1950	1956	...	2016	2025	2032	2043	2100	2122	2117	2138	2156	2208	2213	2218	2235	2223	2245	2255	2308	2344	2354	2349	...	...
Shenzhen bei a.	2030	2036	...	...	...	...	...	2141	2202	...	2219	...	...	2255	...	...	...	...	...	...	...	...	...	...	...

All trains prefix 'G'	502	6102	84	833	1002	94	1104	86	72	1106	97	1004	1108	74	552	542	66	1006	819	532	823	1114	1008	68	504
Shenzhen bei d.	...	...	...	...	0700	...	...	...	0753	...	...	0826	...	0847	...	...	...	0930	0935	0940	1000	...	1016	...	...
Guangzhou nan ♥ d.	...	0706	...	0711	0734	0740	0746	0800	0827	0834	0855	0907	0917	0922	0933	0944	1000	1011	1016	1023	1040	1102	1057	1115	...
Shaogun d.	...	0759	...	|	|	|	0839	|	0921	|	|	|	1010	|	1033	1039	|	1104	|	|	|	1202	1150	1208	...
Chenzhou xi d.	...	|	...	0838	0853	0859	|	|	0955	1001	|	1026	|	1049	1106	1116	|	|	1144	1150	1207	|	1223	|	...
Hengyang dong d.	...	0907	...	0913	0928	0934	0945	|	1030	1039	|	1102	1119	|	|	|	|	|	|	1225	1242	1303	|	|	...
Zhuzhou xi d.	...	|	...	|	|	|	|	|	|	1108	|	|	|	|	1206	1213	|	1235	|	|	|	|	1322	1338	...
Changsha nan ♥ d.	0743	0949	0900	0956	1013	1020	1030	1021	1114	1132	1120	1148	1205	1211	1232	1238	1220	1257	1303	1308	1325	1350	1345	1401	1430
Yueyang dong d.	0818	...	|	1032	|	|	|	...	|	|	|	|	|	1252	1307	|	|	|	|	1344	1400	1425	1420	1437	|
Wuhan ♥ a.	0908	...	1017	1129	1138	1148	1158	...	1246	1301	1238	1321	1331	1343	1357	1411	1338	1416	1429	1434	1452	1522	1512	1528	1606
Zhengzhou dong **7060** d.	1102	...	1205	1355z	...	1347	...	...	1456	...	1418z	...	...	1602	...	1619	1526	...	1653z	1648	1703z	...	...	1743	1811
Luoyang Longmen d.	|	...	|	1436	...	...	...	...	|	...	|	...	...	...	...	...	|	...	1732	...	1748	...	...	|	|
Sanmenxia nan d.	|	...	|	1508	...	...	...	...	|	...	|	...	...	...	...	...	|	...	1805	...	1827	...	...	|	|
Huashan bei d.	|	...	|	1538	...	...	...	...	|	...	|	...	...	...	...	...	|	...	1835	...	|	...	...	|	|
Xi'an bei a.	|	...	|	1610	...	...	...	...	|	...	1635	...	...	...	...	...	|	...	1906	...	1929	...	...	|	|
Beijing xi **7060** a.	1418	...	1440	...	...	...	...	...	1821	...	...	...	...	...	...	...	1800	...	...	...	...	...	...	2056	2126

All trains prefix 'G'	837	80	506	841	70	1032	827	544	546	78	554	1128	1130	1306	1018	1016	548	76	1132	1020	1134	1136	1138	1022	6122
Shenzhen bei d.	...	1131	...	...	...	1239	1250	...	...	1400	1328	...	...	...	1504	1510	...	1540	...	1625	...	...	...	1710	...
Guangzhou nan ♥ d.	1130	1211	...	1230	1250	1319	1330	1356	1414	1434	1409	1513	1526	1539	1544	1550	1629	1624	1647	1705	1730	1740	1746	1751	2100
Shaogun d.	|	1311	...	1323	1343	1412	1423	1449	1507	|	|	|	1631	|	1637	1643	1729	|	|	|	1823	1833	1839	|	2153
Chenzhou xi d.	1249	|	...	|	1416	1445	1456	1522	1540	|	1529	1632	1704	|	1710	1716	|	1753	1814	1831	1856	1906	1912	1917	2226
Hengyang dong d.	1324	|	...	|	|	1527	1532	1557	1620	|	1604	1707	1739	1726	1745	1751	|	1828	1849	1906	1931	1941	1947	|	2301
Zhuzhou xi d.	1354	|	...	1454	|	|	|	1626	1649	|	1633	1740	|	|	|	1820	|	|	|	|	|	|	2016	|	|
Changsha nan ♥ d.	1417	1456	1506	1517	1538	1610	1616	1647	1712	1700	1654	1804	1825	1807	1831	1842	1923	1914	1933	1950	2016	2027	2039	2045	2343
Yueyang dong d.	1452	|	1541	1553	1613	1645	|	1723	1747	|	1741	1846	1900	...	1913	|	1959	|	|	2026	2052	2109	2114	2127	...
Wuhan ♥ a.	1546	1633	1638	1643	1704	1749	1743	1825	1837	1820	1854	1944	1957	...	2003	2015	2049	2041	2106	2123	2149	2207	2212	2175	...
Zhengzhou dong **7060** a.	1813z	1832	1851	1918z	1906	...	2041z	2043	2109	...	...	...	...	...	...	...	2313	2301	...	...	...	...	...	...	...
Luoyang Longmen d.	1852	|	|	2004	|	...	2121	...	...	...	...	...	...	...	...	...	...	...	...	...	...	...	...	...	...
Sanmenxia nan d.	|	|	|	|	|	...	|	...	...	...	...	...	...	...	...	...	...	...	...	...	...	...	...	...	...
Huashan bei d.	1848	|	|	|	|	...	|	...	...	...	...	...	...	...	...	...	...	...	...	...	...	...	...	...	...
Xi'an bei a.	2029	|	|	2137	|	...	2239	...	...	...	...	...	...	...	...	...	...	...	...	...	...	...	...	...	...
Beijing xi **7060** a.	...	2146	2206	...	2227	...	...	...	...	...	...	...	...	...	...	...	...	...	...	...	...	...	...	...	...

z – Zhengzhou.

♥ – Additional services operate Wuhan/Changsha – Guangzhou and v.v.

China Rail High Speed — BEIJING - ZHENGZHOU - XI'AN — 7066

km	651	653	671	655	659	87	673	661	663	665	669	25	All trains prefix 'G'	652	26	672	656	662	660	658	88	664	666	674	670
0	0658	0757	0815	0943	1207	1400	1443	1448	1545	1600	1731	1855	d.**Beijing** xi a.	1326	1350	1511	1533	1641	1711	1826	1755	2025	2131	2300	2329
281	0821	0920	0945	1120	1329	|	1605	1618	1708	1730	1853	2004	d.Shijiazhuang d.	1155	1241	1345	1414	1511	1540	1708	1648	1906	2011	2141	2215
403	0851	0957	|	1152	1359	|	1635	1649	1738	1800	|	|	d.Xingtai dong d.	|	|	1315	1343	|	|	|	|	1835	|	|	|
456	0914	1015	1026	1211	|	|	1653	|	1758	|	1941	|	d.Handan dong d.	|	|	1257	|	1429	1458	1625	|	|	1922	2100	2127
516	0933	|	|	|	1429	|	1712	|	|	1830	2000	|	d.Anyang dong d.	|	|	|	|	1410	1434	1606	|	1803	1903	|	2103
626	|	1055	|	|	|	|	1740	1754	1845	1858	|	|	d.Xinxiang dong d.	|	|	1202	|	1335	1359	|	|	1735	|	2012	|
693	1028	1122	1149	1324	1526	1631	1812	1820	1911	1928	2054	2131	d.**Zhengzhou** dong d.	1010	1112	1140	1229	1313	1336	1509	1524	1708	1820	1950	2020
836	1109	|	1230	1405	|	|	1855	1901	1959	2016	2135	|	d.Luoyang Longmen d.	|	|	|	1145	1230	1247	1419	|	1621	1734	1905	1931
959	1141	1242	1302	1437	1641	|	|	1933	|	2048	|	|	d.Sanmenxia nan d.	0857	|	1023	|	1157	|	|	|	1547	1701	1830	|
1095	1211	1312	1332	|	|	|	2010	2017	2054	|	|	|	d.Huashan bei d.	|	|	0953	|	1127	1144	|	|	1509	|	1800	1835
1216	1250	1343	1418	1530	1742	1823	2041	2048	2125	2150	2253	2323	a.**Xi'an** Bei d.	0752	0915	0921	1007	1055	1112	1242	1320	1433	1558	1720	1803

China Rail High Speed — XI'AN - ZHENGZHOU - XUZHOU — 7070

km	Prefix 'G' unless noted	1914	1982	1900	1844	2002	1896	362	1918	2006	1922	2008	1856	1884	1836	1930	1876	1934	1938	1942	2012	1832	2014	D308 ♦	2016
0	**Xi'an** Bei d.	0623	0645	0735	0742	0820	0836	0845	0929	1026	1020	1151	1253	1333	1345	1402	1427	1453	1512	1529	1650	1708	2028	1950	2108
121	Huashan bei d.	0643	0718	0807	0831	0901	0924	|	|	1059	1052	1233	|	|	1417	|	1459	1529	|	|	|	|	2110	2036	2140
257	Sanmenxia nan d.	0734	0748	0837	0908	0939	1008	|	|	|	1122	|	|	1436	1447	1505	1529	|	|	|	1753	1803	2147	2110	|
380	Luoyang Longmen d.	0808	|	0910	0942	1019	1041	|	|	1202	1155	1342	1431	1509	1520	1538	1602	1628	1633	1719	1841	1836	2228	2149	2244
523	**Zhengzhou** dong d.	0850	0906	0953	1034	1108	1123	1043	1147	1245z	1237	1426	1515	1551	1606	1620	1629	1720	1715	1808	1916z	1921	2327z	2241	2325
713	Shangqui d.	0951	1015	1052	1143	1205	1229	|	1246	...	1344	1516	1614	1651	1713	1721	1805	1812	|	1914	...	2019	...	|	...
883	**Xuzhou** dong a.	1040	1110x	1144	1228	...	1321	1213	1338	...	1435	...	1706	1745	1820	1815	1901	1911	1845	2008	...	2118	...	0030	...

Prefix 'G' unless noted	D307 ♦	2015	2001	2003	1981	1879	1831	1913	1887	1875	1917	361	2007	1983	1883	1921	1835	1895	1925	2009	1929	2013	1937	1941
Xuzhou dong. d.	...	...	...	...	0640	0837	0846	0914	0940	1020	1032	1115	...	1130	1148	1221	1304	1404	1445	...	1607	...	1909	1942
Shangqui d.	...	...	...	...	0748	0938	0946	1007	1036	1113	1125	|	...	1228	|	|	1350	1459	1539	1616	1700	...	|	2030
Zhengzhou dong d.	0642z	0742	0814	0840	0904	1039	1047	1109	1137	1216	1221	1249	1306z	1329	1340	1416	1444	1601	1646	1716	1807	1940	2059	2136
Luoyang Longmen d.	0729	|	0853	0927	0952	1121	1135	|	1218	1257	1304	|	1345	1410	1422	1458	|	1649	1727	1800	1848	2021	|	|
Sanmenxia nan d.	0807	0906	0925	1007	1025	1154	|	1222	|	1334	|	|	1417	|	1455	1530	1550	1721	|	|	|	|	2213	|
Huashan bei d.	0842	0936	0955	1039	1102	1224	1231	1254	1322	1418	|	|	1447	1512	1526	1622	|	1800	|	1903	1948	2123	|	|
Xi'an Bei a.	0930	1018	1035	1122	1143	1256	1309	1335	1353	1449	1423	1442	1518	1544	1606	1956	1645	1839	1901	1942	2031	2202	2306	2336

D305/306 – Shanghai(**D306/305**) - Zhengzhou(**D307/308**) - Xi'an bei.

7085 BEIJING, SHANGHAI and GUANGZHOU - SHENZHEN and HONG KONG

GUANGZHOU DONG - SHENZHEN via Dongguan

China Rail High Speed

High-speed '**C**' trains (numbers **C70xx** and **C71xx**). *139 km.* Journey 70 minutes. Trains call at **Dongguan** 34–37 minutes after Guangzhou and 28–32 minutes after Shenzhen.

Guangzhou dong depart: 0616, 0630, 0640, 0648, 0656, 0704, 0712, 0720, 0728, 0748, 0800, 0820, 0830, 0840, 0850, 0900, 0923, 0932, 0942, 0950, 0958, 1006, 1014, 1022, 1036, 1052, 1105, 1113, 1122, 1140, 1155, 1206, 1228, 1238, 1246, 1254, 1302, 1310, 1318, 1326, 1348, 1358, 1407, 1415, 1435, 1445, 1457, 1508, 1520, 1534, 1544, 1552, 1600, 1610, 1620, 1630, 1640, 1658, 1706, 1715, 1725, 1735, 1747, 1808, 1816, 1832, 1840, 1848, 1900, 1913, 1923, 1934, 1942, 1950, 2010, 2022, 2030, 2040, 2050, 2058, 2106, 2114, 2130, 2146, 2205, 2222, 2237, 2245.

Shenzhen depart: 0620, 0635, 0651, 0702, 0712, 0726, 0740, 0754, 0804, 0812, 0820, 0828, 0836, 0844, 0852, 0913, 0928, 0947, 0956, 1006, 1016, 1027, 1048, 1100, 1108, 1116, 1124, 1132, 1140, 1148, 1200, 1217, 1230, 1239, 1248, 1307, 1320, 1335, 1352, 1402, 1410, 1420, 1436, 1444, 1452, 1512, 1522, 1531, 1539, 1600, 1610, 1621, 1632, 1644, 1700, 1708, 1716, 1724, 1735, 1745, 1755, 1805, 1824, 1832, 1840, 1850, 1900, 1910, 1932, 1940, 1956, 2005, 2015, 2025, 2037, 2058, 2106, 2114, 2134, 2147, 2155, 2204, 2214, 2222, 2230, 2238.

GUANGZHOU NAN - SHENZHEN BEI

China Rail High Speed

High-speed '**G**' trains (numbers **G62xx G97XX**)*102 km.* Journey 29 - 44 minutes.

Guangzhou nan depart: 0702, 0717, 0722, 0731, 0820, 0825, 0847, 0908, 0917, 0931, 1018, 1025, 1037, 1044, 1050, 1055, 1100, 1110, 1125, 1145, 1154, 1252, 1312, 1320, 1445, 1457, 1517, 1535, 1555, 1620, 1722, 1748, 1814, 1848, 1937, 2013, 2020, 2042, 2207, 2230.

Shenzhen bei depart: 0725, 0758, 0808, 0839, 0945, 0950, 0955, 1008, 1027, 1033, 1134, 1210, 1215, 1221, 1341, 1349, 1420, 1425, 1522, 1600, 1652, 1718, 1747, 1759, 1813, 1826, 1844, 1903, 1917, 1923, 1931, 2012, 2040, 2059, 2115, 2125, 2136, 2148, 2226.

Certain trains continue from/to Changsha, Wuhan, Xi'an and Beijing. See Tables **7060**, **7065** and **7070**.

GUANGZHOU - KOWLOON

MTR Corporation

km		Z801	Z807	Z813	Z823	Z817	Z809	Z825	Z815	Z803	Z819	Z827	Z811
0	**Guangzhou** dong .... d.	0819	0904	0955	1037	1203	1404	1538	1614	1733	1820	2030	2132
82	Dongguan (Changping)..... d.	0903	0948	1039	1121	|	1448	1622	1658	1817	1904	2114	|
174	**Kowloon** Hung Hom .... a.	1017	1102	1153	1233	1356	1602	1734	1812	1931	2018	2226	2325

		Z812	Z824	Z820	Z804	Z808	Z814	Z826	Z818	Z810	Z828	Z816	Z802
Kowloon Hung Hom .... d.	...	0725	0815	0924	1052	1132	1223	1311	1432	1635	1800	1844	2001
Dongguan (Changping)...... d.	...	0839	0927	1038	1204	|	|	1420	1546	1749	1912	1958	2115
Guangzhou dong .... a.	...	0924	1012	1123	1251	1326	1417	1508	1631	1834	1957	2043	2200

BEIJING & SHANGHAI - KOWLOON

Chinese Railways

	Z97 A	Z99 B
Beijing xi .... d.	1240	...
Shanghai............. d.	|	1745
Kowloon Hung Hom . a.	1301	1301

	Z100 A	Z98 B
Kowloon Hung Hom d.	1515	1515
Shanghai........... a.	1037	|
Beijing xi............. a.	...	1530

Note: Trains make no intermediate passenger stops.

A – Odd dates in (2017); Jan., Apr., May, Aug., Nov., Dec: Even dates in (2017) Feb., Mar., June, July, Sept., Oct.

B – Odd dates in (2017) Feb., Mar., June, July, Sept., Oct.: Even dates in (2017) Jan., Apr., May, Aug., Nov., Dec.

7090 BEIJING and TIANJIN - WUHAN - NANCHANG and GUANGZHOU

Chinese Railways

km		T126 ♦	T95	Z35	Z235 ♦	Z189	T123 ♦	T145	Z97	Z89	Z161 ♦	T167	Z13	T9 ♦	Z5 ♦	T253	Z77 ♦	Z1	Z151 ♦	Z201 ♦	T179	Z121	Z167 ♦	Z285 ♦	Z263 ♦	Z137 ♦
0	**Beijing** xi.................. d.	...	...	1149	...	...	...	1238**b**	1240	...	1234	1462	...	1505	1609	...	1615	1800	1557	1754	...	...	...	2110	...	...
	Tianjin .... d.	...	...	|	0758	...	0811	|	|	...	|	|	1308	|	|	1150	|	|	|	|	...	...	...	|	...	...
281	Shijiazhuang .... d.	...	...	|	1150	...	1236	1547	|	1500	1508	1712	1820	1746	1838	1742	1844	2030	1822	2024	...	...	...	2340	...	...
689	Zhengzhou................ d.	...	...	1742	1558	1643	1702	2010	1831	1859	1847	2136	2206	2229	2212	2246	2218	2359	**A**	2353	...	...	0150	0310	0335	0449
1225	**Wuhan** Wuchang...... a.	...	...	2218	2047	2150	2255	0139	2305	2328	2327	0306	0240	...	0246	0350	0252	0433	...	0427	...	...	0653	0747	0812	0935
1225	**Wuhan** Wuchang...... d.	1544	1735	2224	2053	2217	2323	0147	2311	2346	2333	0326	0246	...	0252	0406	0258	0439	...	0433	0631	0356	0705	0753	0827	0950
1587	Changsha .... a.	|	2115	0140	0010	0130	0249	0520	0226	0259	0255	|	0603	...	0609	0734	0615	0802	...	0755	0952	1022	1032	1116	1155	1309
1587	Changsha .... d.	|	2121	0146	0016	0136	0255	0537	0231	0305	...	|	0609	...	...	0740	...	...	...	0807	1000	1028	1038	...	1201	1315
1639	Zhuzhou.................. d.	|	|	|	0055	|	0333	0623	|	|	...	|	|	...	...	0819	...	...	...	|	1039	|	1117	...	|	1355
2006	**Nanchang**............ a.	1920	|	|	|	|	|	1027	|	|	...	0720	|	...	...	|	...	...	...	|	|	|	|	...	|	|
2297	**Guangzhou**............ a.	...	0431**f**	0910	0822**d**	0914	1048	...	1001**d**	1023	...	...	1343**d**	...	...	1535	...	...	...	1542	1725	1800	1837	...	1950	2103

km		Z138 ♦	Z202 ♦	Z162 ♦	T146	Z264 ♦	T10 ♦	T168	Z6 ♦	Z78 ♦	Z90	Z2	T128 ♦	Z190	Z36	Z14	Z98	T124 ♦	Z286 ♦	Z236 ♦	T254	T96	Z152 ♦	T180	Z122	Z168 ♦
0	**Guangzhou**............. d.	0830	0850	...	...	1144	...	...	...	...	1355	...	...	1545	1645	1712**d**	1806	1741	...	1950**d**	1930	1920**g**	...	2120	2210	2318
	Nanchang............. d.	|	|	...	1220	|	...	1850	...	...	|	...	21315	|	|	|	|	|	...	|	|	|	...	|	|	|
655	Zhuzhou.................. d.	1526	|	...	1634	|	...	|	...	...	|	...	|	|	|	|	|	0043	...	0311	|	|	...	0402	|	0624
707	Changsha .... a.	1604	1624	...	1711	1856	...	|	...	...	2113	...	|	2259	2352	0042	0119	0120	...	0348	0312	0238	...	0449	0525	0701
707	Changsha .... d.	1610	1630	1636	1726	1918	...	|	1942	2148	2123	1750	|	2305	2358	0048	0125	0126	0255	0400	0320	0244	...	0445	0651	0707
1069	**Wuhan** Wuchang...... a.	1938	1957	2003	2125	2243	...	2344	2302	0108	0045	2117	0056	0227	0320	0415	0448	0511	0615	0726	0647	0629	...	0808	0902	1044
1069	**Wuhan** Wuchang...... d.	1956	2003	2015	2131	2302	...	0004	2311	0126	0103	2123	...	0250	0326	0421	0454	0522	0622	0742	0702	...	...	...	...	1051
1605	Zhenghzou................ d.	0112	0046	0058	0308	0335	0432	0532	0352	0609	0541	0203	...	0812	0804	0917	0934	1131	1108	1250	1221	...	**B**	...	...	1624
2017	Shijiazhuang .... d.	...	0410	0422	0749	...	0833	0949	0716	0935	0912	0528	...	...	|	1241	|	1542	1433	1657	1658	...	1152	...	...	...
2436	**Tianjin** .... a.	...	|	|	|	...	|	|	|	|	...	|	...	...	|	1557	|	1925	|	2032	2208	...	|	...	...	...
2297	**Beijing** xi................. a.	...	0640	0652	1052**b**	...	1113	1305	0948	1210	...	0758	...	...	1343	...	1513	...	1703	...	...	...	1426	...	...	...

♦ – NOTES (by train number):

Z5/6 – Beijing(**Z5/6**) - Nanning and v.v. **T9/10** –Beijing(**T9/10**) - Chongqing bei and v.v.
Z77/78 – Beijing xi (**Z77/78**) - Guiyang and v.v.
T123/124 – Changchun (**T122/121**) - Tianjin (**T123/124**) - Guangzhou and v.v.
Z151/152 – Beijing xi (**Z151/152**) - Xining xi and v.v.
T127/28 – Chengdu (**T126/25**) - Wuhan Wuchang (**T127/28**) - Dongguan dong and v.v.
Z137/38 – Urumqi (**Z136/35**) - Zhengzhou (**Z137/38**) - Guangzhou and v.v.
Z168/70 – Guangzhou dong (**Z168/67**) - Jinan (**Z169/70**) - Qingdao and v.v.
Z161/62 – Beijing (**Z161/62**) - Kunming and v.v. **Z201/02** –Beijing(**Z201/02**) - Sanya and v.v.
Z235/236 – Harbin (**Z238/237**) - Tianjin (**Z235/36**) - Guangzhou and v.v.
Z263/264 – Lhasa (**Z266/265**) - Zhengzhou (**Z263/64**) - Guangzhou and v.v.
Z285/286 – Beijing (**Z285/286**) - Nanning and v.v.
A – Via Xi'an (Table **7115**. a. 0323). **B** – Via Xi'an (Table **7115**. d. 0226).
b – Beijing. **d** – Guangzhou dong. **f** – To Shenzhen a. 0613. **g** – From Shenzhen d. 1730.

7095 BEIJING - NANCHANG - SHENZHEN

Chinese Railways

km		Z167 ♦	Z133	Z65	Z107	Z67	K105	Z185 ♦	K1619	T127 ♦
0	**Beijing** xi.......................... d.	...	1924	1949	1955	2001	2321	...	...	...
* *	**Tianjin**........................... d.	...	|	|	|	|	|	0314	2220	...
147	Renqiu................................ d.	...	|	|	|	|	0103	|	|	...
274	Hengshui .... d.	...	2130	|	2210	|	0230	0618	|	...
426	Liaocheng........................... d.	...	2252	|	2332	|	0419	0742	|	...
582	Heze.................................... d.	...	|	|	0043	|	0553	0853	0506	...
687	Shangqiu nan .... d.	...	|	|	|	|	0711	1000	0625	...
* * *	**Jinan** .... d.	1755	|	|	|	|	|	|	|	...
* * *	Xuzhou............................. d.	2202	|	|	|	|	|	|	|	...
855	Fuyang .... d.	|	|	|	0304	|	0932	1154	0905	...
1091	Macheng.............................. d.	|	|	|	|	|	1208	1408	1249	...
1314	Jiujiang .... d.	|	0616	0644	|	0655	1432	1615	1545	...
1449	**Nanchang** .... a.	|	0720**x**	0747	0753**x**	0822	1548	1719**x**	1703	...
1449	**Nanchang** .... d.	|	0737**x**	...	0801**x**	...	1605	1733**x**	1711	1946
1675	Ji'an.................................... d.	|	0952	...	1008	...	1835	1941	2026	2155
1861	Ganzhou............................. d.	|	...	...	1217	...	2045	2155	2253	0006
2102	Longchuan.......................... d.	|	...	...	|	...	0010	0033	0216	0247
2248	Huizhou.............................. d.	|	...	...	1632	...	0224	0235	0408	0436
2310	Dongguan dong .... d.	|	...	...	|	...	0348	0342	0459	0520
2396	**Guangzhou** dong............. a.	1837	...	...	|	...	|	|	|	...
2372	**Shenzhen** .... a.	...	...	...	1751	...	0448	0506	0625**d**	...

	Z68	Z66	Z134	T128 ♦	K1620	Z108	K106	Z168 ♦	Z186 ♦
Shenzhen .... d.	...	...	...	...	0920**d**	1500	1054	...	1957
Guangzhou dong .... d.	...	...	...	...	|	|	|	2318	|
Dongguan dong.................. d.	...	...	...	1140	|	|	|	|	2046
Huizhou.............................. d.	...	...	...	1227	1056	1632	1235	|	2132
Longchuan .... d.	...	...	...	1432	1313	|	1434	|	2327
Ganzhou .... d.	...	...	...	1724	1641	2051	1803	|	0225
Ji'an .... d.	...	...	1751	1920	1907	2253	2025	|	0421
Nanchang........................ a.	...	...	1951**x**	2124	2208	0104	2319	|	0623**x**
Nanchang........................ d.	1941	1935	2007**x**	...	2233	0122	2333	|	0636**x**
Jiujiang.............................. d.	2050	2044	2114	...	2359	|	0057	|	0744
Macheng .... d.	|	|	|	...	0236	|	|	|	0950
Fuyang............................... d.	|	|	|	...	0530	0616	0628	|	1210
Xuzhou .... d.	|	|	|	...	|	|	|	2044	|
Jinan.............................. a.	|	|	|	...	|	|	|	0114	|
Shangqiu nan .... d.	|	|	|	...	0739	|	0841	...	1345
Heze .... d.	|	|	|	...	|	0831	|	...	1445
Liaocheng.......................... d.	|	|	|	...	1042	0941	1127	...	1557
Hengshui............................ d.	|	|	0546	...	1243	|	1320	...	1721
Renqiu .... d.	|	|	|	...	|	|	1439	...	|
Tianjin........................... a.	|	|	|	...	1606	|	|	...	2005
Beijing xi .... a.	0746	0738	0803	...	...	1315	1618	...	...

♦ – NOTES (by train number):

T127/28 – Chengdu(**T126/25**) - Wuhan Wuchang(**T127/28**) - Dongguan dong and v.v.
Z168/67 – Guangzhou dong(**Z168/57**) - Jinan(**Z169/70**) - Qingdao and v.v.
Z185/86 – Shenyang bei(**Z188/87**) - Tianjin(**Z185/86**) - Shenzhen and v.v.
d – Shenzhen dong. **x** – Nanchang xi.
* * – Tianjin *0 km* - Renqiu *142 km.* * * * – Jinan *0 km* - Xuzhou *319 km* - Fuyang *542 km.*

7097 BEIJING - BENGBU - HEFEI

China Rail High Speed

All trains prefix '**G**'

km	1673 C	345 C	433	261	355 C	241 C	323 C	7405	325 C	29	267	271	↓
0	...	...	...	0715	0840	...	1010	...	1205	1335	1738	1854	d.**Beijing** nan
406	...	0657	0851	0903	1031	1025**j**	1159	...	1354	1515	1922	2039	d.Jinan xi
692	0658	0823	1018	|	1200	1211	1317	...	1459	|	2034	2151	d.Xuzhou dong
848	0743	0909	1104	1050	1250	|	1356	1400	|	|	2113	2230	d.**Bengbu** nan
911	|	0927	1123	1108	|	1331	|	1419	1558	|	2131	|	d.Huainan dong
980	0840**n**	1006**n**	1149	1142	1340**n**	1417**n**	1452**n**	1505**n**	1638**n**	1734**n**	2210	2319**n**	a.**Hefei**

↑	246	262	266	268	30	322 C	242 C	324 C	356 C	1434	272	348 C
Beijing nan......... a.	...	1147	1353	1814	1739	1826	...	2013	2219	...	2236	...
Jinan xi .... d.	0947**j**	1008	1200	1622	1602	1638	1731**j**	1833	2026	2031	2057	2232
Xuzhou dong....... d.	0826	0850	1044	1444	|	1518	1544	1704	1857	1915	|	2101
Bengbu nan........ d.	0748	0805	0957	1404	|	|	1503	1614	1817	1830	|	2016
Huainan dong...... d.	0728	0746	0936	1342	|	|	1444	|	1752	|	|	|
Hefei.................. d.	0648	0706**n**	0908	1302**n**	1340**n**	1345**n**	1404	1515**n**	1705**n**	1750	1818**n**	1917**n**

C – To/from Table **7193**. **j** – Jinan. **n** – Hefei nan.

China Rail High Speed

BEIJING, ZHENGZHOU and NANJING - SHANGHAI and HANGZHOU 7100

km		G7505	G7349	D2281 A	G7177	D3135	G7589 a	G7291	D5431 A	G297	G101	G103	G105	G11	G221 Q	G107	G109	G111	G1	G113	G211	G41	G115	G117	G13	D291
0	**Beijing** nan d.	...	...	...	...	...	...	...	...	...	0644	0705	0735	0800	...	0805	0815	0835	0900	0853	0931T	0916	0922	0940	1000	...
314	Dezhou dong d.	...	...	...	...	...	...	...	...	...	0813	│	│	│	...	0921	0931	│	│	1020	1025	1034	1044	1055	│	...
406	Jinan xi d.	...	...	...	...	...	...	...	...	0720	0840	0846	0924	0934	0936j	0949	1008	1017	│	1048	1052	1102	1110	1123	1134	...
	Zhengzhou d.	...	...	...	...	...	...	...	...	│	│	│	│	│	│	│	│	│	│	│	│	│	│	│	│	0855
	Shangqiu d.	...	...	...	...	...	...	...	...	│	│	│	│	│	│	│	│	│	│	│	│	│	│	│	│	1034
692	Xuzhou dong d.	...	...	...	...	...	0708	0755	0721	0845	1000	1006	1029	│	1108	1100	1119	│	│	1153	│	│	1222	│	│	1236
848	Bengbu nan d.	...	...	...	...	...	0753	0840	0815	0924	│	1045	│	│	│	│	│	│	│	│	│	1247	│	│	│	1341
1023	**Nanjing** nan d.	0713	0730	0745f	0750	0810f	0847	0939	0922	1008	1117	1128	1151	1155	1224	1216	1246	1304	1241	1310	1314	1331	1339	1410	1348	1431
1088	Zhenjiang nan d.	0734	0751	0821	│	0835	0909	│	0944	1029	1138	│	│	│	1245	│	│	│	│	│	1335	│	│	│	│	│
1153	Changzhou bei d.	0753	0810	0853	0830	0910	0928	1013	1005	1049	│	│	1228	│	│	│	1320	1338	│	│	│	│	│	│	│	│
1210	Wuxi dong d.	0812	0829	0910	0849	0927	0947	1032	1025	│	│	1214	│	│	1316	│	│	│	│	│	1406	1417	1432	│	│	│
1237	Suzhou bei d.	0825	0842	0929	0902	0945	0959	1044	1038	1113	1215	│	1252	│	│	1315	1344	│	│	1407	│	│	│	1508	│	│
1318	**Shanghai** Hongqiao a.	0855	0907	1015	0932	1037	1030	1111h	1104	1136	1238	1242	1315	1310	1344	1338	1407	1425	1348	1430	1434	1446	1507	1531	1455	1549
1477	Hangzhou dong a.	0954	1005	1131	...	1205	1141	...	1234	...	...	...	...	...	...	...	...	...	...	...	...	1544	...	...	...	...

	G229 Q	G213	G121	G15	G123	G125	G127	G129	G133	G7293	G135	G139	G3	G43	G141	G143	G215	D281	G17	G225 Q	G145	G1202	G19	G147	D285
Beijing nan d.	...	1044T	1028	1100	1105	1110	1135	1210	1240	...	1255	1340	1400	1405	1410	1431	1438T	...	1500	...	1436	1452T	1600	1541	...
Dezhou dong d.	...	1144	1157	│	1227	1232	1258	1332	1404	...	│	1502	│	1519	1525	│	1531	...	│	...	│	│	│	1720	...
Jinan xi d.	1207j	1210	1224	1234	1253	1258	1324	1358	1430	...	1445	1532	│	1545	1551	1612	1600	...	1634	1630j	1622	1644	1741	1746	...
Zhengzhou d.	│	│	│	│	│	│	│	│	│	...	│	│	│	│	│	│	│	1420	│	│	│	│	│	│	1510
Shangqiu d.	│	│	│	│	│	│	│	│	│	...	│	│	│	│	│	│	│	1555	│	│	│	│	│	│	1640
Xuzhou dong d.	1336	1322	1343	│	│	│	1438	1504	1543	1551	1558	1644	│	1657	1702	1724	1714	1746	│	1806	1743	1806	1847	│	1902
Bengbu nan d.	│	│	│	│	│	1444	│	│	│	1633	│	1723	│	│	1752	│	│	1830	│	│	│	1853	│	│	│
Nanjing nan d.	1453	1439	1459	1448	1521	1529	1601	1628	1707	1724	1728	1826	1741	1816	1841	1858	1831	2013	1848	1924	1908	1938	2004	2020	2035
Zhenjiang nan d.	│	│	│	│	│	│	│	1649	1730	│	│	│	│	│	│	1919	│	│	│	│	1929	2000	│	2041	2108
Changzhou bei d.	1527	│	1534	│	1555	1610	│	│	1749	1758	│	│	│	1850	1921	│	│	2059	│	1958	1948	2020	│	│	2137
Wuxi dong d.	│	1532	1553	│	│	│	1648	1721	1808	│	1824	│	│	│	│	1950	1919	2123	│	│	2007	2040	│	│	2220
Suzhou bei d.	1550	1544	1605	│	1619	1634	│	│	│	1822	│	1921	│	1915	1950	2003	1938	2136	│	2022	2020	2056	│	2126	2232
Shanghai Hongqiao a.	1612	1607	1628	1555	1650	1659	1916	1749	1837	1850h	1857	1952	1848	1938	2013	2026	2002	2213	1956	2045	2043	2127	2115	2150	2258
Hangzhou dong a.	...	...	...	...	...	...	...	...	...	...	...	...	...	2047	...	...	...	...	...	...	...	...	...	...	...

	G149	G151	G21	G153	G157	G233 Q	G201	G203	D321	D305 ♦
Beijing nan d.	1625	1635	1700	1715	1743	...	1755	1900	2123	...
Dezhou dong d.	1749	1758	│	│	1900	...	│	│	│	...
Jinan xi d.	1819	1824	1841	1858	1926	1909j	1943	2041	│	...
Zhengzhou d.	│	│	│	│	│	│	│	│	│	2241
Shangqiu d.	│	│	│	│	│	│	│	│	│	│
Xuzhou dong d.	1933	1947	2000	2011	2045	2027	2105	2153	│	0033d
Bengbu nan d.	│	│	│	2049	│	│	2142	2232	│	│
Nanjing nan d.	2054	2113	2118	2134	2202	2151	...	2310	0644f	0330f
Zhenjiang nan d.	2116	│	2139	│	│	│	...	...	│	│
Changzhou bei d.	│	2147	│	│	2236	│	...	...	│	│
Wuxi dong d.	2148	│	│	│	2255	2238	...	...	│	│
Suzhou bei d.	│	2211	2216	2227	│	2250	...	...	0822g	0534g
Shanghai Hongqiao a.	2224	2235	2239	2252	2323	2313	...	...	0913h	0635h
Hangzhou dong a.	...	...	...	...	...	...	...	...	...	...

	G202	G204	D282	G102	G222 Q	G104	G106	G108	D286	G110
Hangzhou dong d.	...	...	...	...	...	...	...	...	...	...
Shanghai Hongqiao d.	...	...	0625	0639	0705	0653	0710	0720	0734	0730
Suzhou bei d.	...	...	│	0704	│	│	0735	│	0807	0756
Wuxi dong d.	...	...	0658	│	0734	0728	│	0757	│	│
Changzhou bei d.	...	...	0723	0728	│	│	│	│	│	0820
Zhenjiang nan d.	...	...	│	│	0805	│	0812	│	0908	0841
Nanjing nan d.	...	0732	0800	0803	0826	0814	0833	0851	0930	0903
Bengbu nan d.	0735	0829	│	│	│	│	│	0937	│	│
Xuzhou dong d.	0821	0909	1030	│	0944	0939	0950	1018	1151	1037
Shangqiu d.	│	│	1159	│	│	│	│	│	1257	│
Zhengzhou a.	│	│	1336	│	│	│	│	│	1429	│
Jinan xi d.	0940	1028	...	1039	1053j	1044	1103	1132	...	1149
Dezhou dong d.	│	│	...	│	...	│	│	1158	...	│
Beijing nan a.	1133	1213	...	1218	...	1223	1242	1311	...	1333

	G12	G2	G112	G114	G212	G230 Q	G116	G1204	G14	G118	G42	G122	G7292	G16	G124	G128	G130	G412	G134	G136	G138	G140	G4	G226 Q	G214
Hangzhou dong d.	...	...	...	...	...	...	...	...	...	...	0925	...	...	...	...	...	...	...	...	...	...	...	...	...	...
Shanghai Hongqiao d.	0800	0900	0805	0816	0853	0908	0934	0939	1000	0954	1028	1046	1155h	1100	1105	1115	1126	1223	1302	1317	1330	1341	1400	1405	1454
Suzhou bei d.	│	│	0830	│	│	0933	│	1004	│	1023	│	1112	1225	│	│	1140	1151	│	│	│	1354	1405	│	1430	1522
Wuxi dong d.	│	│	│	0855	0931	│	1006	1016	│	1035	1058	│	│	│	1135	│	1203	│	1339	│	│	1417	│	1442	│
Changzhou bei d.	0842	│	│	│	│	0957	1025	1039	│	│	│	1140	1249	│	│	│	1222	│	│	1405	1418	│	│	│	│
Zhenjiang nan d.	│	│	│	0927	1004	1017	│	1100	│	│	1130	│	1308	│	│	1217	│	│	│	1425	│	1453	│	│	│
Nanjing nan d.	0916	1009	0921	0949	1026	1038	1101	1122	1109	1128	1151	1216	1330	1209	1221	1238	1256	1349	1427	1446	1452	1514	1509	1528	1624
Bengbu nan d.	│	│	│	1040	│	1122	1151	│	│	│	│	│	│	│	1305	│	│	│	1511	│	│	│	│	│	│
Xuzhou dong d.	1032	│	1056	1122	1148	1203	1230	1246	│	1254	1311	1334	1524	│	1345	1407	1420	1513	1557	1602	│	│	│	1652	1750
Shangqiu d.	│	│	│	│	│	│	│	│	│	│	│	│	...	│	│	│	│	│	│	│	│	│	│	│	│
Zhengzhou a.	│	│	│	│	│	│	│	│	│	│	│	│	...	│	│	│	│	│	│	│	│	│	│	│	│
Jinan xi d.	1144	│	1209	1233	1302	1318j	1343	1403	1321	1412	1427	1452	...	1423	1502	1524	1544	1643	1702	1720	1735	1745	│	1823j	1905
Dezhou dong d.	│	│	│	│	│	...	1409	│	│	│	│	1519	...	│	1528	1550	1610	1709	1728	│	│	1811	│	...	│
Beijing nan a.	1316	1348	1408	1412	1418T	...	1523	1526T	1458	1544	1606	1633	...	1555	1655	1713	1723	1840	1852	1908	1923	1931	1848	...	2022T

	G142	G18	G146	G148	G20	G150	G152	D292	G234 Q	G216	G22	G154	G44	G158	G7294	G206	G298	D3136	G7391	D5432 A	D3126	D322	G7590 b	D2282 A	D306 ♦
Hangzhou dong d.	...	...	...	...	...	...	...	...	...	...	...	...	1615	...	...	...	...	1638	...	1706	2009	...	1747	1730	...
Shanghai Hongqiao d.	1421	1500	1505	1532	1600	1605	1619	1610	1632	1638	1700	1714	1724	1734	1744	...	1758	1802	1805	1831	2123	1953h	1904	1847	2224h
Suzhou bei d.	│	│	1530	1557	│	1630	│	1637	│	1703	│	1739	1755	│	1816	...	1830	1849g	│	1903	2153g	│	1936	1944	2314g
Wuxi dong d.	1458	│	1542	│	1630	│	│	1659	│	│	1730	│	│	│	1828	...	1842	1906	│	1915	2212	│	1948	2001	│
Changzhou bei d.	│	│	│	1620	│	│	│	│	│	1727	│	│	│	1823	1847	...	1901	1933	│	1941	2228	2114	2007	2018	│
Zhenjiang nan d.	│	│	1614	│	│	│	│	│	1726	│	│	1816	1834	│	│	...	│	2005	│	2002	│	│	│	2053	│
Nanjing nan d.	1544	1609	1637	1657	1716	1727	1735	1752	1747	1801	1816	1837	1856	1906	1924	2000	1943	2028f	2119	2024	2312f	2225f	2042	2116	0149f
Bengbu nan d.	1628	│	│	│	│	│	│	1857	│	│	│	│	│	1950	2019	│	2040	...	...	2126	...	│	2134	...	│
Xuzhou dong d.	1710	│	1756	1821	│	1843	1853	1952	1903	1926	1934	│	2011	│	2103	2115	2133	...	...	2215	...	│	2218	...	0448d
Shangqiu d.	│	│	│	│	│	│	│	2121	│	│	│	│	│	│	...	│	│	...	...	...	...	│	...	...	│
Zhengzhou a.	│	│	│	│	│	│	│	2255	│	│	│	│	│	│	...	│	│	...	...	...	...	│	...	...	0637
Jinan xi d.	1838	1823	1911	1933	1938	2001	2006	...	2019j	2038	2052	2108	2118	2140	...	2221	2250	...	...	...	...	│	...	...	...
Dezhou dong d.	...	│	│	│	│	2027	2032	...	...	│	│	│	│	│	...	│	...	...	...	...	...	│	...	...	...
Beijing nan a.	2018	1955	2050	2112	2117	2147	2152	...	...	2156T	2224	2240	2301	2318	...	2352	...	...	...	...	...	0745	...	...	...

China Rail High Speed

BEIJING and NANJING - HANGZHOU and NINGBO 7102

km	All trains prefix 'G'	1671 C	1503 B	7615	7609	7607	61 B	63 A	51	1481 B	57	31	55 A	7639	7611	1483 B	1222	167 A	D658	59	35	7605	53	45 B	D2224	37	39
0	**Beijing** nan d.	...	...	...	...	...	...	...	0700T	...	0720	0830	0810	...	...	...	1212T	1250	...	1345	1505	...	1535T	1515	...	1605	1647
314	Dezhou dong d.	...	...	...	...	...	...	...	0800	...	0847	│	0926	...	...	...	1316	1414	...	1512	│	...	│	1649	...	1738	│
406	Jinan xi d.	...	...	...	...	...	0708	0726j	0826	...	0913	1004	0957	...	...	...	1343	1441	...	1538	1653	...	1656	1715	...	1804	1835
692	Xuzhou dong d.	...	...	...	...	...	0834	0857	0939	...	1024	│	1114	...	...	...	1455	1548	...	1650	1811	...	1814	1827	...	1909	1955
1023	**Nanjing** nan d.	0654	0832	0081	0938	0953	1002	1033	1056	1128	1149	1222	1238	1338	1357	1518	1616	1711	1805	1819	1928	1848	1933	1943	2026	2039	2116
1152	Yixing d.	0736	0914	0934	1027	1035	1045	1109	1141	1217	1225	│	│	1434	1439	1600	1659	│	1923	1855	│	1937	2020	2027	2112	2122	│
1208	Huzhou d.	0801	0932	0959	1045	1109	1103	│	1200	1248	│	1310	1333	1452	1504	1625	1718	1814	1947	1914	2030	2002	│	2046	2149	2141	2218
1279	**Hangzhou** dong a.	0829	0955	1021	1113	1131	1125	1154	1221	1309	1304	1331	1354	1513	1525	1646	1739	1835	2029	1935	2052	2023	2059	2114	2221	2202	2239
1439	Ningbo a.	...	...	1134	...	...	...	1248	1328	...	1410	...	1455	...	1621	...	1838	1940	2149	2040	...	...	...	...	...	...	...

	34	D2223	D656	32	1221	58	36	54	46 B	7640	1492 B	168 A	7604	7606	56 A	1482 B	7612	52	40	60	1484 B	7636	62 B	64 A	1504 B
Ningbo d.	...	...	0630	...	0736	0747	...	...	...	...	...	1033	...	...	1155	...	1300	1351	...	1438	...	1732	...	1705	...
Hangzhou dong d.	0711	0733	0750	0830	0836	0852	0905	0927	0952	0958	1103	1138	1209	1220	1249	1328	1413	1447	1518	1544	1621	1837	1737	1806	2044
Huzhou d.	0734	0806	0831	0853	0900	│	0935	0958	1015	1028	1126	1213	1232	1250	1312	│	1436	1510	1541	│	1651	1900	1807	│	2107
Yixing d.	0753	0836	0910	│	0919	│	│	1017	1041	1047	1152	1232	1258	1309	│	│	1502	1536	1607	│	1711	1926	1834	│	2139
Nanjing nan d.	0845	0952	1006	0942	1002	1019	1031	1055	1117	1119	1238	1323	1337	1348	1421	1458	1548	1619	1643	1703	1753	2012	1919	1938	2218
Xuzhou dong d.	1013	...	...	│	1133	1141	1153	1222	1234	...	...	1500	...	...	1539	...	...	1741	1800	1830	...	...	2056	2122	...
Jinan xi d.	1126	...	...	1156	1252	1257	1308	1334	1348	...	...	1616	...	...	1657	...	...	1849	1917	1950	...	...	2214	2246	...
Dezhou dong d.	1152	...	...	│	1318	1323	1335	│	1414	...	...	1642	...	...	│	...	...	1916	│	│	...	...	...	...	...
Beijing nan a.	1305	...	...	1328	1408T	1439	1449	1451T	1533	...	...	1803	...	...	1843	...	...	2006T	2056	2129	...	...	...	...	...

A – To/from Table **7200**. **B** – To/from Table **7192**. **C** – To/from Table **7193**. **Q** – To/from Qingdao (**T7105**). **T** – Time at Tianjin xi not Beijing. **a** – To Ningbo a. 1239. **b** – From Ningbo d.1645.
c – Changzhou. **d** – Xuzhou. **f** – Nanjing. **g** – Suzhou. **h** – Shanghai. **j** – Jinan. **k** – Hangzhou. **D305/306** – Shanghai(**D306/305**) - Zhengzhou(**D307/308**) - Xi'an bei and v.v.

7105 BEIJING - JINAN - QINGDAO

Chinese Railways, China Rail High Speed

km	All unmarked trains prefix 'D'	Z169 A	6001	6003		G175	6005	G177	G247	G221 S	G179	G171	G181	6007	G231 S	G183	G185	G187	6009	G189	6011	G173	G1207	G191	G193
0	**Beijing** nan d.	...	...	...	...	0621	...	0725	...	...	0935	...	1045	...	...	1153	1220	1245	...	1318	...	...	...	1420	1446
122	**Tianjin** nan d.	...	...	...	...	0658	...	0803	...	...	|	1051x	1121	...	...	|	|	1313	...	|	...	1352x	1505x	|	1534
314	Dezhou dong d.	...	...	...	...	0750	...	0852	...	...	1050	1151	1213	...	...	1316	|	1409	...	|	...	|	|	1540	|
426	**Jinan** d.	0140	0600	0710	...	0849	0959	0939	0949	1055	1135	1241	1259	1316	1322	1401	1422	1458	1452	1525	1531	1547	1647	1630	1706
536	Zibo d.	0248	0644	0753	...	0933	1046	1022	1034	1139	1218	1332	1343	1400	1406	1448	1511	1542	1535	1608	1615	1631	1730	1713	1749
636	Weifang d.	0349	0722	0830	...	1011	1124	1059	1112	1221	1255	1418	1426	1438	1444	1527	1555	1619	1612	1645	1653	1715	1812	1751	1832
819	**Qingdao** a.	0528	0835	0948	...	1131	1248	1212	1226	1334	1408	1532	1539	1535	1602	1651	1708	1738	1739	1803	1812	1828	1909b	1909	1945

	6013	G243	G195	G227 S	G197	6015	G199	6017	G235 S
Beijing nan d.	...	...	1610	...	1642	...	1725	...	...
Tianjin nan d.	...	...	|	...	1718	...	|	...	...
Dezhou dong d.	...	...	1733	...	1804	...	1848	...	...
Jinan d.	1712	1743	1819	1825	1849	1906	1934	1951	2021
Zibo d.	1759	1826	1906	1954	1933	1955	2018	2035	2104
Weifang d.	1837	1903	1944	1954	2017	2038	2101	2113	2147
Qingdao a.	1951	2022	2058	2112	2130	2151	2219	2238	2300

	6002	G1208	G176	6004	G224 S	G178	G180		G182
Qingdao d.	0551	0616b	0622	0643	0655	0702	0710	...	0820
Weifang d.	0701	0720	0732	0759	0804	0816	0826	...	0934
Zibo d.	0745	0758	0812	0839	0846	0859	0910	...	1011
Jinan d.	0832	0852	0901	0929	0934	0953	0959	...	1101
Dezhou dong d.	...	0943	0948	...	...	|	1047	...	|
Tianjin nan a.	...	1033x	1034	...	...	|	|	...	|
Beijing nan a.	...	...	1114	...	...	1151	1201	...	1258

	G244	G172	G232 S	6006	G184	6008	G186	G188	G190	6010	G192	Z170 A	G248	6012	G228 S	G194	G196	6014	G174	G236 S	G198	G200	6016	6018
Qingdao d.	0813	0902	0917	0910	0929	1009	1022	1127	1214	1221	1232	1310	1324	1337	1354	1430	1600	1601	1610	1623	1711	1835	1845	1947
Weifang d.	0927	1017	1032	1024	1045	1121	1138	1242	1323	1331	1341	1522	1444	1451	1503	1540	1715	1658	1726	1737	1826	1949	2001	2104
Zibo d.	1017	1055	1115	1102	1128	1202	1221	1321	1401	1425	1419	1609	1522	1528	1540	1623	1752	1735	1804	1814	1913	2027	2047	2148
Jinan d.	1110	1145	1203	1150	1218	1250	1311	1414	1452	1513	1513	1734	1610	1616	1630	1712	1842	1841	1856	1909	2002	2125	2201	2242
Dezhou dong d.	...	|	...	...	|	...	|	1507	1538	...	|	...	...	...	...	|	|	...	1948	...	|	2218	...	...
Tianjin nan a.	...	1321x	...	...	|	...	1434	|	1631	...	|	...	...	...	...	1836	2006	...	2039x	...	|	2304	...	...
Beijing nan a.	...	...	...	...	1418	...	1514	1622	1705	...	1717	...	...	...	...	1917	2040	...	...	...	2202	2338	...	...

A – Guangzhou dong(**Z168/57**) - Jinan(**Z169/70**) - Qingdao and v.v. S – To/from Shanghai Hongqiao (Table **7100**). b – Qingdao bei. x – Tianjin xi.

7110 SHANGHAI - NANJING - ZHENGZHOU

Chinese Railways

km		K290 ♦	T112 ♦	Z167 ♦	T116 ♦	Z252 ♦	K152	Z40 ♦	Z164 ♦		K282 ♦
0	**Shanghai** d.	0850	A	...	1532	1552	1631	1940	2010	...	2046
84	Suzhou d.	1000	1316	...	1635	1643	1735	2028	2058	...	2204
126	Wuxi d.	1032	1352	...	1703	1709	1816	2114	2123	...	2235
165	Changzhou d.	1103	1421	...	1730	1736	1847	2138	|	...	2305
237	Zhenjiang d.	|	1505	...	|	|	|	|	|	...	|
301	**Nanjing** d.	1250	1555	...	1903	1909	2044	2259	2305	...	0100
485	Bengbu d.	151	1737	...	2048	2054	0012	0034	0040	...	0322
649	Xuzhou d.	1733	1926	2202	2224	2230	|	0209	0220	...	0514
795	Shangqiu d.	1923	|	|	2357	2349	0500	|	|	...	0653
998	**Zhengzhou** a.	2139	2248	0130	0203	0142	0727	0453	0507	...	0909

	Z254 ♦	Z163 ♦	Z39 ♦	T115 ♦	T111 ♦	Z168 ♦	K289 ♦	K151	K284 ♦	
Zhengzhou d.	0347	0258	0305	0313	0612	1643	1746	1813	1920	...
Shangqiu d.	0525	|	|	0503	|	|	2006	2050	2155	...
Xuzhou d.	0656	0558	0604	0640	0925	2044	2157	|	2342	...
Bengbu d.	0832	0722	0728	0846	1101	...	2347	0046	0130	...
Nanjing d.	1010	0900	0906	1033	1246	...	0152	0250	0334	...
Zhenjiang d.	|	|	|	|	1331	...	|	0339	|	...
Changzhou d.	|	|	1011	|	1414	...	0322	0427	0459	...
Wuxi d.	1139	1030	1036	1206	1443	...	0353	0457	0530	...
Suzhou d.	1205	1101	1107	1235	1517	...	0429	0528	|	...
Shanghai a.	1255	1151	1157	1330	B	...	0534	0643	0657	...

For footnotes see Table **7120**.

7115 ZHENGZHOU - XI'AN - LANZHOU

Chinese Railways

km	Z135 ♦	T117 ♦	Z252 ♦	Z265 ♦	Z165 ♦	Z41 ♦		T197 ♦	T193 ♦	T113 ♦	Z151 ♦	Z323 ♦	Z223 ♦	Read Down		Read Up	Z254 ♦	Z136 ♦	T118 ♦	Z324 ♦	Z224 ♦	Z166 ♦	Z266 ♦	Z42 ♦	T114 ♦	T194 ♦	T198 ♦	Z152 ♦	
0	0128	0210	0150	0352	0514	0500	...	2118	2250	2301	...	...	...	↓	d. **Zhengzhou** a.	↑	0340	0439	0242	...	...	0250	0313	0257	0604	0554	0640	...	...
124	0254	0337	|	|	|	0624	...	2303	0020	0034	...	...	...		d. Luoyang d.		|	0319	|	...	...	|	|	|	0441	0433	0517	0700	...
512	0726	0812	0757	0941	1114	1100	...	0341	0455	0501	0323	...	...	↓	a. **Xi'an** d.	↑	2135	2241	2015	...	...	2044	2115	2050	0005	2353	0040	0226	...
512	0738	0821	...	1000	1124	1110	...	0349	0505	0513	0333	...	...		d. **Xi'an** a.		...	2233	2003	...	...	2034	2107	2040	2344	2334	0025	0213	...
685	0918	1020	...	|	|	1249	...	0535	0654	0702	0517	0330	0330	↓	d. Baoji d.	↑	...	2056	1824	0109	0109	|	|	1910	2200	2153	2248	|	...
840	1100	1202	...	|	|	1435	...	0712	0831	0839	0653	|	|	↓	d. Tianshui d.	↑	...	1818	1542	|	|	|	|	1628	1920	1911	2004	2215	...
1188	1511	1558	...	1647	1817	1824	...	1114	1219	1235	1057	0858	0858	↓	a. **Lanzhou** d.	↑	...	1357	1115	1836	1836	1226	1305	1218	1440	1457	1540	1744	...

For footnotes see Table **7120**.

7118 BEIJING - LANZHOU

Chinese Railways

km		Z69 ♦	T175 ♦	T41	Z55		T7 ♦	Z21 ♦		
0	**Beijing** xi d.	1000	1312	1422	1500	...	1640	2010	...	...
291	Shijiazhuang bei d.	1307	1626	1732	1759	...	2003	2255	...	...
395	Yangquan bei d.	1404	|	|	1915	...	2116	|	...	...
516	**Taiyuan** d.	1510n	1836	2000	2025n	...	2215	0044	...	...
701	Lvliang d.	1640	2047	2210	|	...	2358	|	...	...
790	Suide d.	1736	2143	2338	|	...	|	|	...	...
1283	**Xi'an** a.	|	|	0507	|	...	0621	|	...	...
1267	Zhongwei d.	2253	0242	...	0301	...	...	0725	...	...
1524	**Wuwei** a.	0216	|	...	|	...	...	|	...	...
1573	**Lanzhou** a.	...	0744	...	0800	...	...	1226	...	...

	Z22 ♦	T42	T176 ♦	T8 ♦		Z56	Z70 ♦		
Lanzhou d.	1617	...	150/	...	...	2040	...	...	...
Wuwei d.	|	...	|	...	...	|	0505	...	...
Zhongwei d.	2131	...	2038	...	...	0217	0837	...	...
Xi'an d.	|	1936	|	2247	...	|	|	...	...
Suide d.	|	0141	0200	|	...	|	1253	...	...
Lvliang d.	|	0238	0259	|	...	|	1351	...	...
Taiyuan d.	0351	0427	0448	0727	...	0847n	1533n	...	...
Yangquan bei d.	|	|	0542	0832	...	|	1641	...	...
Shijiazhuang bei d.	0548	0631	0643	0941	...	1107	1744	...	...
Beijing xi a.	0820	0922	0929	1231	...	1336	2020	...	...

7120 LANZHOU - ÜRÜMQI and LHASA

Chinese Railways, China Rail High Speed

km		D2701	D2703	D2711 C	Z151 ♦	Z179 ♦	T197 ♦	T193 ♦	Z135 ♦	T295	Z41 ♦	Z69 ♦
	Zhongwei d.	...	...	...	...	0942	...	...	...	...	...	2253
0	**Lanzhou** d.	0812x	0830x	1050x	1112	|	1130	1234	1527	1638	1839	|
188	Xining d.	0921	0956	1201	1348	|	|	|	1717	|	2025	0222
303	Wuwei d.	|	|	|	...	1318	1438	1544	|	1954	|	
770	Jiayuguan d.	1243n	1310n	1527n	...	1801	1930	2039	2137	0057	0030	0654
1067	Liuyuan d.	1434n	1454n	1719n	...	2054	2233	2339	0048	0402	0318	1004
1339	Hami d.	1619	1635	1856	...	0020	0139	0245	0401	0718	|	1310
1749	Turpan d.	1838b	1854b	2115b	...	0454	0549	0640	0742	1112	0905b	1651
1892	**Ürümqi** nan a.	1937	1953	2214	...	0631	0718	0809	0908	1241	1022	1835

	Z70 ♦	T296	T194 ♦	Z180 ♦	Z42 ♦	T198 ♦	Z136 ♦	Z152 ♦	D2704	D2706	D2712 D
Ürümqi nan d.	1302	1430	1732	1808	1920	1908	1917	...	0921	0946	1059
Turpan d.	1434	1605	1920	1941	2126b	2104	2056	...	1022b	1047b	1200b
Hami d.	1820	2003	2357	2338	|	0109	0051	...	1249	1312	1424
Liuyuan d.	2128	2308	0345	0245	0315	0430	0406	...	1431n	1452n	1602n
Jiayuguan d.	0032	0216	0652	0534	0609	0736	0719	...	1626n	1640n	1759n
Wuwei d.	0505	0716	1138	1019	|	1217	|	...	|	|	|
Xining d.	|	|	|	|	1007	|	|	1500	1958	2009	2129
Lanzhou a.	|	1022	1440	|	1203	1521	1342	1729	2114x	2122x	2234x
Zhongwei a.	0822	...	...	1454	...	...	...	...	...	...	...

km		D2741	D2747	D2745	D2749	D2743	Z21 ♦	T175 ♦	Z323 ♦	Z223 ♦	Z265 ♦	Z165 ♦
0	**Zhongwei** d.	...	...	...	...	...	0725	0242	...	...	...	...
306	**Lanzhou** d.	0740x	0755	1345x	1710	1745x	1241	0802	0913	0913	1702	1832
534	Xining d.	0849	0914	1454	1828	1900	1530	1031	1214	1214	1939	2135
	Jiayuguan nan a.	1153	1202	1822	2124	2214	|	...	|	|	|	|
1352	Golmud d.	...	...	...	...	...	2250	...	1954	1954	0245	0444
2172	Naqu d.	...	...	...	...	...	0841	...	0558	0558	1201	1452
2449	**Lhasa** a.	...	...	...	...	...	1355	...	0955	0955	1625	1950

	Z324 ♦	Z224 ♦	Z166 ♦	Z266 ♦	Z22 ♦	T176 ♦	D2750	D2744	D2748	D2742	D2746
Lhasa d.	1830	1830	1105	1300	1530	...	...	...	...	...	...
Naqu d.	2155	2155	1456	1625	1900	...	...	...	...	...	...
Golmud d.	0830	0830	0200	0306	0600	...	...	...	...	...	...
Jiayuguan nan a.	|	|	|	|	|	...	0717	0825	1240	1255	1845
Xining d.	1549	1549	0926	1030	1333	1215	1023	1157	1530	1607	2156
Lanzhou a.	1821	1821	1211	1249	1557	1452	1136x	1304x	1649	1720x	2301x
Zhongwei a.	...	...	...	...	2121	2025	...	...	...	...	...

♦ – **NOTES** for Tables **7110**, **7115 7118** and **7120** (by train number):

T7/8 – Beijing xi(**T7/8**) - Chengdu and v.v.
Z21/22 – Beijing xi(**Z21/22**) - Lhasa and v.v.
Z39/41 – Urumqi(**Z42/41**) - Zhengzhou(**Z39/40**) - Shanghai and v.v.
Z69/70 – Beijing xi(**Z69/70**) - Urumqi and v.v.
T111/114 – Lanzhou(**T114/13**) - Zhengzhou(**T111/12**) - Hangzhou and v.v.
T115/118 – Lanzhou(**T118/17**) - Zhengzhou(**T115/16**) - Shanghai and v.v.
Z135/36 – Urumqi(**Z136/35**) - Zhengzhou(**Z137/38**) - Guangzhou and v.v.
Z252/54 – Xian(**Z254/252**) - Zhengzhou - Shanghai and v.v.
Z151/152 – Beijing xi(**Z151/152**) - Xining and v.v.
Z163/166 – Lhasa(**Z166/165**) - Zhengzhou(**Z163/164**) - Shanghai and v.v.
Z168/70 – Guangzhou dong(**Z168/67**) - Jinan(**Z169/70**) - Qingdao and v.v.
T175/176 – Beijing xi(**T175/176**) - Xining xi and v.v. **Z179/180** –Beijing(**Z179/80**) - Urumqi and v.v.
T193/194 – Zhengzhou(**T193/194**) - Urumqi and v.v. **T197/198** –Zhengzhou(**T197/198**) - Urumqi and v.v.
Z223/224 – Lhasa(**T224/223**) - Chongqing and v.v. See note **E**.
Z323/24 – Chengdu(**Z322/21**) - Lanzhou(**Z323/24**) - Lhasa and v.v. see note **E**.
Z265/266 – Lhasa(**Z266/265**) - Zhengzhou(**Z263/64**) - Guangzhou and v.v.
K282/284 – Shanghai(**K282/284**) - Zhengzhou(**K283/281**) – Chengdu and v.v.
K289/290 – Shanghai(**K290/289**) - Zhengzhou(**K291/292**) – Chengdu and v.v.
A – From Hangzhou dep. 1020. B – To Hangzhou arr. 1851.
C – Additional trip: 0938. D – Additional trip: 1027. E – Runs alternate days only.
b – bei. n – nan. x – xi.

ÜRÜMQI - ALMATY - ASTANA 7125

km		5801	13 CJ ①⑥n	13/53 ①
0	**Ürümqi** d.	2358	2314	2314
144	Shihezi d.	0258	|	|
241	Kuitun d.	0456	|	|
477	Alashankou a.	0950	0800	0800
477	Alashankou 🏛 d.	...	1100	1100
493	Druzhba 🏛 a.	...	0930	0930
493	Druzhba d.	...	1240	1240
654	Beskol' d.	...	1617	1617
797	**Aktogay** a.	...	1814	1814
797	**Aktogay** d.	...	1844	1906
1051	Ush Tobe d.	...	2315	|
1283	Kapchagay d.	...	0351	|
1354	**Almaty** I a.	...	0500	|
1363	**Almaty** II a.	...	0547	|
1657	Karagandy a.	...	...	0832
1898	**Astana** a.	...	...	12456

	5802	54/14 ⑥	14 TJ ②⑦u
Astana d.	...	1620	...
Karagandy d.	...	2132	...
Almaty II d.	...	|	0016
Almaty I d.	...	|	0103
Kapchagay d.	...	|	0213
Ush Tobe d.	...	|	0650
Aktogay a.	...	1030	1102
Aktogay d.	...	1131	1131
Beskol' d.	...	1343	1343
Druzhba a.	...	1635	1635
Druzhba 🏛 d.	...	1950	1950
Alashankou 🏛 a.	...	2210	2210
Alashankou d.	2308	2350	2350
Kuitun d.	0511	|	|
Shihezi d.	0716	|	|
Ürümqi a.	1043	1019	1019

n – Numbered 13 *KH* on ⑥
u – Numbered 14 *CJ* on ②

For connections to Moscow see Table **1975**. Operators: Chinese Railways and Kazakstan Temir Zholy.

Chinese Railways — XI'AN - CHENGDU 7130

km		K291 C	K245	T7 A	K5	Z324 B	Z224 E	K879	K869	K165 D
	Zhengzhou d.	2146	2335	...	...	...	...	...	1336	...
0	**Xi'an** d.	0449	0701	0641	1320	...	...	1945	2119	2210
173	Baoji d.	0720	0934	0842	1546	0138	0138	2213	2329	0034
523	Guangyuan d.	1626	1810	1545	0037	1002	1002	0646	0819	0917
727	Mianyang d.	1954	2133	1908	0359	|	...	1016	1144	|
842	**Chengdu** a.	2135	2316	2036	0529	1436	...	1144	1337	1426

		T8 A	K880	K166 D	K870	K292 C	Z223 E	Z323 B	K6	K246
Chengdu d.	...	0900	1255	1326	1438	1747	...	1448	2105	2120
Mianyang d.	...	1039	1435	1506	1638	1925	...	|	2245	2304
Guangyuan nan d.	...	1421	1820	1844	2108	2301	1944	1944	0222	0244
Baoji d.	...	2048	0340	0430	0629	0719	0305	0305	1017	1046
Xi'an a.	...	2227	0550	0628	0840	0917	...	...	1220	1243
Zhengzhou a.	...	...	...	...	1636	1730	...	...	...	1934

A – Bejing xi(**T7/8**) - Chengdu and v.v.
B – Chengdu(**X323/21**) - Lanzhou(**Z323/24**) - Lhasa and v.v. Runs alternate days only.
C – Shanghai(**K290/289**) - Zhengzhou(**K291/292**) – Chengdu and v.v.
D – Xi'an(**K165/66**) - Kunming and v.v.
E – Lhasa(**Z224/23**) - Chongqing. Runs alternate days only.

CHENGDU - QINGCHENGSHAN 7135

All unmarked trains prefix 'C'

km	6101	6103	6105	6107	6109	6111	6113	6115	6117	6121	6123		6102	6104	6106	6108	6110	6112	6114	6116	6120	6122	6124
0	0648	0854p	0922p	1035p	1301p	1619	1620	1808p	1916	2107p	2125p	↓ d. **Chengdu** a. ↑	0823p	1027p	1059p	1228p	1413p	1738p	1850	1911p	2055p	2239	2258
57	0725	0826	0955	1110	1328	1650	1716	1827	1957	|	2157	↓ d. Dujiangyan d. ↑	0802	1003	1029	1149	|	1703	1753	1840	2031	2210	2229
65	0733	0934	1003	1118	1336	...	1724	...	2005	2140	2205	↓ a. **Qingchengshan** d. ↑	0750	0952	1018	1139	1349	...	1742	...	2020	2153	2218

p – Xipu.

China Rail High Speed — CHENGDU - CHONGQING 7140

km	All unmarked trains prefix 'D'	G308	2244	2202	638	G8553 B	2224	354	2208	G8501	2256	2264	2238	G314	2374	G8681	2260	G8511	368	G8517	G8519	634	G8523	G8525
0	**Chengdu** dong d.	0718	0645	0700	0712	0748	0736	0801	0820	0823	0826	0905	0911	0917	0929	1005n	1020	1057	1055	1213	1250	1333	1335	1406
146	Suining d.	|	0744	0805	|	|	0845	|	0920	|	0935	|	|	|	1029	|	|	|	|	|	|	1437	|	|
198	Tongnan d.	0846	0815	|	0839	|	|	0925	|	|	1008	|	1032	1041	1102	|	1136	|	1212	|	|	1508	|	|
247	Hechuan d.	0915	0841	0857	0906	|	|	0952	|	|	1034	|	1059	1108	1128	|	1203	|	1239	|	|	|	|	|
313	**Chongqing** bei **7182** a.	0940	0906	0922	0931	0937	0951	1017	1030	1010	1059	1112	1124	1133	1153	1136	1228	1237	1304	1401	1430	1552	1515	1539

All trains prefix 'D'	G8527	G8529	G8533	5102	G8545	G8547	G8549	G8551	G8683
Chengdu dong d.	1424	1459	1549	1749	1814	1919	1935	2100	2143n
Suining d.	|	|	|	1849	|	|	|	|	|
Tongnan d.	|	|	|	1922	|	|	|	|	|
Hechuan d.	|	|	|	1949	|	|	|	|	|
Chongqing bei **7182** a.	1605	1625	1729	2014	2001	2059	2115	2233	2321

All trains prefix 'D'	G8682	5105	G8504 A	G8506	G8508	G8510	G8512	G8514	G8516
Chongqing bei **7182** d.	0734	0751	0820	0845	0908	1000	1030	1123	1142
Hechuan d.	|	0818	|	|	|	|	|	|	|
Tongnan d.	|	0844	|	|	|	|	|	|	|
Suining d.	|	0915	|	|	|	|	|	|	|
Chengdu dong a.	0923n	1012	0954	1026	1047	1127	1212	1304	1328

All trains prefix 'D'	G8520	G8522	633	G8528	367	G8532	2373	2259	G8542	2201	G312	G8544	2255	2237	637	2207	G8550	2223	G8552	2243	G307	2263	G8556
Chongqing bei **7182** d.	1240	1308	1359	1420	1507	1529	1649	1718	1734	1731	1743	1823	1842	1859	1911	1926	1951	1954	2020	2007	2031	2057	2205
Hechuan d.	|	|	1427	|	1535	|	1716	|	|	1758	1810	|	1909	|	1938	1953	|	2021	|	2035	2058	2124	|
Tongnan d.	|	|	1454	|	1603	|	1742	1805	|	1824	|	|	|	1946	2005	2019	|	2048	|	2101	|	2151	|
Suining d.	|	|	1526	|	|	|	1813	1836	|	|	|	|	|	|	|	2051	|	|	|	|	|	|	|
Chengdu dong a.	1421	1456	1627h	1602	1727	1703	1917	1932	1915	1940	1955	2009	2054	2101	2128	2156	2125	2203	2210	2217	2236	2308	2339

A – Additional trips: 1213, 1344, 1404, 1451, 1551, 1609, 1636, 1711, 1849, 1930, 2119.
B – Additional trips: 0916, 0933, 1033, 1130, 1145, 1308, 1522, 1605, 1640, 1706, 1723, 1753.

h – Chengde. n – Chengdu nan.
Note: All trains numbered **G8XXX** go via Neijiang.

China Rail High Speed — CHENGDU - DAZHOU 7142

km	All trains prefix 'D'	5182	5184	5186	5162	5188	5164	5192	5174	5156 A	5194
0	**Chengdu** dong d.	0813h	0930h	1017	1219h	1429	1602	1648	1703	1846	2038
146	Suining d.	|	|	1116	|	|	|	|	1804	1945	2137
213	Nanchong d.	|	1106	1153	1351	|	1730	1818	1840	2019	2213
372	**Dazhou** a.	1104	1224	1311	...	1703	...	1948	...	...	2325

All trains prefix 'D'	5181	5179	5185	5161 C	5189	5163 B	6195	5191	5193	5195
Dazhou d.	0659	...	1119	...	1332	...	...	1718	1912	2015
Nanchong d.	0834	1024	1247	1407	1459	1753	1642	1847	2040	213/
Suining d.	|	1058	|	|	1531	1826	|	1921	2113	2212
Chengdu dong a.	0957	1159h	1411	1532	1628	1923	1859h	2018	2214	2313h

h – Chengdu. A – Additional trips: 0750, 1141, 1953. B – Additional trips: 1149, 2204. C – Additional trips: 1516, 2058.

Chinese Railways — CHENGDU - NANNING and KUNMING 7145

km		K853	K829 B	K1139	K1273	K485	K1223	K144	T8897	K482 B
0	**Chengdu** dong d.	0854h	1011h	1030h	1052h	1400	1457h	1455	1907	...
217	Neijiang d.	1301	1416	1444	1159	|	1851	|	|	...
337	Yibin d.	1525	1648	1713	1825	|	2107	|	|	...
744	Liupanshui d.	0054	0108	0146	0225	|	0535	|	|	...
502	Chongqing d.	|	|	|	|	1929	|	2035	|	...
810	Zunyi d.	|	|	|	|	0231	|	0338	0426	...
965*	Guiyang d.	|	0519	|	0536	0542	1014	0718	0732	...
1424	Jinchengjiang d.	|	1227	|	...	...	1542	1203	—	...
1585	Liuqiao a.	|	1454	|	...	...	1842	1438	**K364**	...
1720	Litang d.	|	1644	|	...	...	...	|	**B**	...
1840	**Nanning** a.	|	...	|	...	...	...	1817	2215	1010
1014	Qujing d.	0445	...	0700	...	...	...	...	|	|
1171	**Kunming** a.	0651	...	0838	...	...	...	...	1141	2257

	K854	K1224	K830 B	K486	K1140	K363 B	K1274	K143	K481 B
Kunming d.	0826	...	...	...	0952	0800	...	...	1715
Qujing d.	1038	...	...	...	1133	|	...	...	|
Nanning d.	|	...	...	...	|	2020	...	0925	0520
Litang d.	|	...	...	...	|	—	...	1059	...
Liuqiao d.	|	0217	0610	...	|	**T8898**	...	1300	...
Jinchengjiang d.	|	0450	0850	...	|		...	1513	...
Guiyang d.	|	1110	1343	1440	|	1942	1654	2046	...
Zunyi d.	|	|	|	1902	|	2240	|	2359	...
Chongqing d.	|	|	|	0226	|	|	|	0741	...
Liupanshui d.	1438	1538	1741	|	1707	|	2135	|	...
Yibin d.	2301	2336	0030	|	0058	|	0824	|	...
Neijiang d.	0131	0205	0258	|	0340	|	1153	|	...
Chengdu dong a.	0526h	0546h	0640h	0710	0829h	0728	1738h	1256	...

km		K113	K165 D	K145	K1501	K117	T8869			
0	**Chengdu** d.	1300	1457	1430	1655	1728	1755	...	...	...
557	Xichang d.	2311	0054	0017	0148	0210	0455	...	...	...
749	Panzhihua d.	0215	0422	0402	0548	0453	0756	...	...	...
1100	**Kunming** a.	0731	1016	0923	1038	...	...	...	...	...

	K114		T8870		K146	K1502	K166 D	K118	
Kunming d.	0848	...	...	...	1815	1905	1932	...	...
Panzhihua d.	1403	...	1649	...	2313	2346	0035	1153	...
Xichang d.	1645	...	1936	...	0417	0254	0343	1440	...
Chengdu a.	0405	...	0926	...	1324	1222	1251	2332	...

B – To/from Guangzhou (Table **7155**). D – Xi'an(**K165/66**) - Kunming and v.v. b – Chongqing bei. h – Chengdu. * – *993 km* via Yibin.

Chinese Railways — CHONGQING - ZHUZHOU - GUANGZHOU 7150

km			K72 F	K204	K334	K578	K194	K686	K778	
0	**Chongqing** bei d.	...	0800	1225	1320	1350	1419	1520	1550	...
100	Fuling d.	...	0916	1339	1434	1511	1530	1639	1710	...
280	Qianjiang (Chongqing) d.	...	1139	1648	1732	1805	|	1906	2006	...
602	Huaihua d.	...	1550	2058	2252	2220	2311	2331	0026	...
917	Loudi d.	...	1953	|	0311	0216	|	0331	|	...
1042	**Zhuzhou** a.	...	2200	0248	0525	0426	0512	0518	0608	...
1323	Chenzhou d.	...	...	0615	...	...	0907	0851	0929	...
1697	**Guangzhou** a.	...	...	1045	...	...	1342	1257	1400	...

	K777	K71 F	K577	K333	K193		K685	K203	
Guangzhou d.	1603	...	...	...	1449	...	1621	1951	...
Chenzhou d.	2013	...	...	...	1915	...	2029	2351	...
Zhuzhou d.	0004	0352	1538	1202	2346	...	2358	0305	...
Loudi d.	|	0528	1726	1412	0122	...	0131	|	...
Huaihua d.	0553	1012	2207	1858	0625	...	0537	0916	...
Qianjiang (Chongqing) d.	1028	1519	0235	0323	1209	...	0946	1352	...
Fuling d.	1313	1756	0453	0600	1435	...	1228	1638	...
Chongqing bei a.	1434	1966	0602	0721	1558	...	1345	1805	...

F – Shanghai nan (**K71/2**) - Chongqing and v.v.

7155 NANNING - GUANGZHOU *Chinese Railways*

km		K829 A	K363 B	K481 B
0	**Nanning** d.	...	2035	0540
**	**Liuqiao** d.	1454	|	|
120	Litang d.	1659	|	|
263	Yuli d.	1901	2359	0927
438	Maoming dong d.	2300	0255	1259
700	Zhaoqing d.	0248	0558	1637
787	Fuoshan d.	0407	0742	1852
809	**Guangzhou** a.	0512	0839	1957

	K364 B	K830 A	K482 B
Guangzhou d.	0942	1642	2115
Fuoshan d.	1012	1712	2152
Zhaoqing d.	1148	1848	2313
Maoming dong d.	1541	2244	|
Yuli d.	1829	0214	0606
Litang d.	|	|	|
Liuqiao a.	|	0557	|
Nanning a.	2153	...	0954

A – To / from Chendgu (Table **7145**).
B – To / from Kunming (Table **7145**).
** – Liuqiao - Litang: *135 km.*

7160 GUANGZHOU - SANYA *Chinese Railways*

km		K511 C	Z201 B	K1167
0	**Guangzhou** d.	1730	1602	1908
22	Fuoshan d.	1758	1633	1939
109	Zhaoqing d.	1950	1741	2132
361	Maoming dong d.	2331	2031	0042
488	Zhanjiang xi d.	0111	2155	|
601	Xunwen d.	|	0026	0426
794	Haikou a.	0620	0454	0757
1157	**Sanya** a.	...	0850	...

	K512 C	K1168	Z202 B
Sanya d.	...	...	1716
Haikou d.	2320	2008	2135
Xunwen d.	0314	|	|
Zhanjiang xi d.	0433	0040	0220
Maoming dong d.	0545	0201	0347
Zhaoqing d.	0850	0510	0640
Fuoshan d.	1017	0712	0805
Guangzhou a.	1045	0749	0830

B – Beijing(**Z201/02**) - Sanya and v.v.
C – Shanghai(**K511/12**) - Haikou and v.v.

7165 HAIKOU - SANYA *China Rail High Speed*

High-speed '**D**' trains (numbers **D73xx**). *289 km 284km from Haikou dong.* Journey 2 - 2¼ hours. * – To/from Haikou.

Haikou dong depart : 0700, 0724, 0800, 0840*, 0843, 0900, 0915, 0935, 1000*, 1025, 1038, 1050, 1120, 1200 1228, 1300, 1330, 1355, 1430*, 1440, 1450, 1508, 1510, 1550, 1600, 1610, 1645*, 1710, 1735*, 1755, 1812, 1830, 1900, 1930, 2029, 2045, 2045*, 2100, 2120*, 2120, 2205.

Sanya depart : 0700*, 0700, 0715, 0730, 0740, 0750*, 0815, 0820, 0930*, 1015, 1050, 1115, 1137, 1205, 1225, 1245, 1250, 1305, 1330, 1410, 1430*, 1435, 1500, 1515*, 1545, 1625, 1650, 1720, 1755*, 1820*, 1830, 1900, 2000, 2020, 2050, 2105*, 2125, 2200.

7170 ZHENGZHOU and WUHAN - CHENGDU and CHONGQING *Chinese Railways*

km		K389	K257	K1269	K507	K205	K351	Z122	K283 D	Z224 A	K385	K805	K909	T247	K819	K15	K817	T125 C	K1063	K117		K357		T9 B	K1257
	Zhengzhou d.	...	0358	...	0612	0638	...	...	0930	...	1313	...	1355	...	1610	1617	1725	...	2000	2055	...	...	...	2255	...
0	**Wuhan** Wuchang d.	0602	|	2107	|	|	0829	0946h	|	...	|	1134	|	1920	|	|	|	0120	|	|	...	2341	...	|	1109
165	Suizhou d.	0759	|	|	|	|	|	|	|	...	|	1423	|	2111	|	|	|	|	|	|	...	|	...	|	|
334	Xiangyang d.	0942y	1114	|	1317	1340	1326y	1225y	|	...	|	1642y	2245	2310	|	2309	|	0440	0256	0424	...	|	...	0517	|
500	Shiyan d.	1232	1310	|	1528	1544	1600	|	1922	...	|	1855	0051	0116	|	0130	|	0646	0517	0625	...	|	...	0709	|
*	**Xi'an** d.	|	|	|	|	|	|	|	|	...	2102n	|	|	|	|	|	|	|	|	|	...	|	...	|	|
702	Ankang d.	1525	1555	|	1803	1815	1831	1614	2154	...	0044	2222	0322	0341	0218	0352	0358	0901	0753	0850	...	|	...	0926	|
978	Dazhou d.	|	|	0827	2151	|	2233	1950	|	X	0420	0245	0707	0716	0620	0734	0742	1246	1156	1226	...	1232	...	1317	0320
1137	Nanchong d.	|	|	|	|	|	0050	|	|	1203	0605	|	|	0858	|	|	0951	1449	|	1421	...	|	...	|	0522
1204	Suining d.	|	|	|	|	|	0301	2150	|	|	0652	|	|	0944	|	|	1042	1601	|	1504	...	|	...	|	0616
1375	**Chengdu** a.	0442	0558	|	|	0830	0451	2309	1119	|	0852	|	|	1120d	|	|	1234	1750	|	1702	...	|	...	|	0746d
1233	**Chongqing** bei a.	...	...	1133	0219a	...	...	...	...	1341		0535	0948	...	0917	1018	...	...	1452	...	...	1527	...	1619	...

			K508	K806	K910	T10 B	K1258	K16	T248	K390	K386	K1270	Z223 A	K818	K820	K258	Z124	K1064	K206		K281 D	T126 C	K358	K352	K118
Chongqing bei d.	...	...	0804a	0807	1054	1038	...	1223	...	...	...	1808	1542	...	2140	...	...	2300	...	...	...	...	2320	...	...
Chengdu d.	...	...	|	|	|	|	0948d	|	1244	0830	1252	|	|	1930	|	1353	1720	|	1623	...	1820	2235	|	2351	2359
Suining d.	...	...	|	|	|	|	|	|	1425	|	1511	|	|	2136	|	|	|	|	|	...	|	0034	|	0129	0150
Nanchong d.	...	...	|	|	|	|	1254	|	1529	|	1607	|	1725	2224	|	|	|	|	|	...	|	0128	|	0222	0245
Dazhou d.	...	...	1221	1124	1357	1335	1441	1510	1739	|	1803	2106	X	0021	0033	|	2037	0157	|	...	|	0330	0208	0441	0456
Ankang d.	...	...	1547	1505	1713	1640	|	1822	2046	2238	2130	|	...	0336	0341	0330	2334	0511	0601	...	0612	0644	|	0801	0807
Xi'an a.	...	...	|	|	|	|	|	|	|	|	0002n	|	...	|	|	|	|	|	|	...	|	|	|	|	|
Shiyan d.	...	...	1842	1750	2011	1925	|	2056	2330	0115	|	|	...	|	|	|	|	0757	0904	...	0854	0938	|	|	|
Xiangyang d.	...	...	2130	2027y	2300	2154	|	2339	0154	0331y	|	|	...	|	|	0855	0351y	1041	1156	...	1138	|	|	1338y	1352
Suizhou d.	...	...	|	2201	|	|	|	|	0319	|	|	|	...	|	|	|	|	|	|	...	|	1306	|	|	|
Wuhan Wuchang a.	...	...	|	0108	|	|	0419	|	0507	0809	|	0846	...	|	|	|	0627h	|	|	...	|	1528	1703	1916	|
Zhengzhou a.	...	...	0539	...	0745	0410	...	0628	...	...	0825	...	...	1304	1330	1550	...	1822	1842	...	1858	...	...	...	2108

A – Lhasa(**Z224/23**) - Chongqing. Runs alternate days only. B – Beijing(**T9/10**) - Chongqing.
C – Chengdu(**T126/25**) - Wuhan Wuchang(**T127/28**) - Dongguan dong and v.v.
D – Shanghai(**K282/284**) - Zhengzhou(**K283/281**) – Chengdu and v.v.
X – Via Table **7130**.
a – Chongqing. d – Chengdu dong.
h – Wuhan Hankou. n – Xi'an nan.
y – Xiangfan dong.
* – Xian *0 km* - Dazhou *535 km*.

7175 SHANGHAI - NANJING - WUHAN *China Rail High Speed*

km	All trains prefix 'D'	3077	637	3003	2207	3073	G599	3057	2213	3065	G577	2216	G677	3022	3091	3061	3069	3081	3027	3094	3007	3011	3033	3015	3043	3087	3047
0	**Shanghai** ♣ d.	...	0609	0630	0638	0650	0715	0715	0730	0820	0834	0839	0840	0915	1015	0942	1018	...	1330	1427	1353	1452	1507	1607	1647	1652	1753
84	Suzhou d.	...	0643	0710	0718	0736	0740b	0752	0810	0857	0859b	0919	0905b	0946	1055b	1018	1054	...	1406	|	1434	1532	1543	1643	1739	1730b	1832
126	Wuxi d.	...	0702	0734	0749	0755	|	0809	0829	0920	0911d	0938	0917d	1004	1112d	1100	1111	...	1423	1514d	1451	1549	1600	1700	1806	|	1850
165	Changzhou d.	...	0721	0753	0808	0814	0806b	0832	0848	0937	0930b	|	0940b	1022	|	1119	1128	...	1440	1549b	1509	1606	1617	1717	|	1800b	1907
237	Zhenjiang d.	...	0750	0836	0842	0849	0834n	0859	0923	1004	|	1036	|	1054	|	1152	1200	...	1508	|	1536	1633	1653	1749	1843	1826n	|
311	**Nanjing** nan d.	0738	0835	0910	0916	0922	0905	0932	0957	1037	1005	1110	1015	1126	1211	1228	1232	1510	1539	1629	1608	1703	1724	1821	1915	1853	1959
468	Hefei nan d.	0846	0945	1012	1017	1031	1007	1042	1103	1156	1115	1217	1121	1241	1319	1330	1341	1616	1641	1737	1710	1805	1826	1923	2021	1955	2114
555	Liuan d.	0916	1015	1042	1047	1101	1037	1112	1133	1226	1146	1247	1151	1311	1349	1400	1411	1646	1711	|	1740	1835	1856	1953	2051	2025	2145
827	**Wuhan** Hankou a.	1103	1204	1224h	1234	1246	1217	1300	1323	1407	1325h	1424	1336h	1522g	1529	1602	1625	1831	1858	2001	1918	2022	2048	2144	2232	2211	2324
1119	*Yichang dong* **7182** a.	1302	1420	...	1436	1457	...	...	1537	...	...	1634	...	...	...	...	...	2041	...	...	2123	...	...	...	...	...	...

All trains prefix 'D'	3028	3016	3093	3012	3034	3008	3044	3082	3088	3048	3004	3058	G678	2214	3066	G600	G578	2218	3092	3074	3024	3062	638	3070	3078	2208
Yichang dong **7182** d.	...	...	...	...	...	0640	...	0830	...	...	...	...	...	1139	...	...	...	1300	...	1333	...	...	1414	...	1517	1456
Wuhan Hankou d.	0720	0735	0805	0820	0838	0907	0947	1050	1019	1121g	1251h	1334	1335h	1353	1435	1501	1511h	1517	1556	1547	1546g	1630	1632	1700	1731	1721
Liuan d.	0914	0926	0955	1013	1039	1102	1142	1250	1203	1342	1500	1530	|	1554	1641	1635	1647	1720	1753	1739	1758	1819	1835	1904	1933	1924
Hefei nan d.	0950	1001	1031	1048	1114	1140	1218	1330	1242	1417	1531	1608	1547	1636	1717	1707	1723	1755	1829	1815	1833	1856	1912	1943	2008	1957
Nanjing nan d.	1057	1113	1137	1159	1215	1246	1328	1431	1340	1538	1629	1724	1645	1755	1820	1805	1834	1856	1931	1914	1946	2009	2027	2051	2102	2101
Zhenjiang d.	|	1145	1200n	|	1247	1325	1358	...	1407n	|	1701	1753	1712n	1829	1850	|	|	1929	1953n	1946	2021	|	|	2129	...	2136
Changzhou d.	1154	1217	1221b	1315	1328	1357	1434	...	1433b	1628	1730	1825	|	1858	1927	|	1909b	2010	2017b	2015	2059	|	|	2156	...	2205
Wuxi d.	1213	1234	1301d	1332	1344	1414	1513	...	1505d	1645	1750	1842	1750d	1917	2003	1852d	1932d	2029	2051d	2034	2116	2123	2141	2213	...	2224
Suzhou d.	1232	1252	1313b	1351	1407	1432	1531	...	1537b	1702	1809	1900	1802b	1936	2022	1909b	1945b	2048	2104b	2053	2133	2142	2200	2231	...	2243
Shanghai Hongqiao a.	1307	1325	1353	1426	1447	1506	1605	...	1619	1730	1857	1934	1826	2015	2058	1944	2008	2130	2139	2134	2208	2220	2238	2259	...	2315

♣ – **Shanghai** Hongqiao. b – Changzhou/Shuzhou bei. d – Wuxi dong. g – Wuhan Wuchang. h – Wuhan. n – Zhenjiang nan.

7180 SHANGHAI - NANCHANG and ZHUZHOU - GUANGZHOU *Chinese Railways*

km		K1185	T169	K71 F.	T81 A	T77 B	Z99	K79 D	K527	K739 E	K511 C
0	**Shanghai** nan d.	0848	1050	1434	1606	1127	1745a	1834	1914	1936	1920
80	Jiaxing d.	0952	1135	1532	1652	1212	|	1933	2003	2038	2009
188	Hangzhou dong d.	1107	1246	1646	1804	1319	|	2053	2119	2200	2147
312	Yiwu d.	1224	1352	1809	1919	1418	|	2210	2306	2321	2312
360	Jinhua d.	1311	1436	1857	2003	1511	2059	2303	2353	0025	2359
446	Quzhou d.	|	|	|	|	|	|	|	|	|	|
557	Shangrao d.	1605	1644	2126	2209	1717	|	0138	0312	|	0306
673	Yingtan d.	1751	1803	2248	2322	1830	|	0345	0436	0500	0428
817	**Nanchang** a.	1952	|	|	|	|	|	|	|	|	|
1128	Wuchang a.	...	|	|	|	|	|	|	|	|	|
1044	Pingxiang d.	...	|	|	|	|	|	0739	0908	0933	|
1125	**Zhuzhou** a.	...	|	0337	0400	2246	0255	0836	1018	1048	|
1125	**Zhuzhou** d.	...	|	...	0416	2306	0313	0848	1036	1105	|
1259	Hengyang d.	...	|	...	0537	0045	|	...	1205	...	|
1406	Chenzhou d.	...	|	...	...	...	|	...	1351	...	|
1559	Shaoguan dong d.	...	0247	...	...	...	|	...	1536	...	1445
1780	**Guangzhou** a.	...	0530	...	...	...	1008d	...	1812	...	1710

	K528	K1186	K80 D	K512 C	T170	K740 E	Z100	T82 A	K72 F	T78 B
Guangzhou d.	0748	...	...	1103	1455	...	1812d	...	...	...
Shaogun dong d.	1013	...	...	1332	1717	...	|	...	...	...
Chenzhou d.	1155	...	...	1538	|	...	|	...	...	...
Hengyang d.	1352	...	...	1730	|	...	|	0038	...	2107
Zhuzhou a.	1516	...	1530	1857	|	2307	0051	0202	...	2229
Zhuzhou d.	1533	...	1546	1915	|	2330	0111	0220	2222	2254
Pingxiang d.	1629	...	1642	|	|	|	|	0312	|	|
Wuchang d.	|	...	|	|	|	|	|	|	|	|
Nanchang d.	|	1828	|	|	|	|	|	|	|	|
Yingtan d.	2054	2127	2114	0002	0115	0517	|	0636	0328	0306
Shangrao d.	2205	2308	2226	0130	|	0649	|	|	|	0412
Quzhou d.	|	|	|	|	|	|	|	|	|	|
Jinhua d.	0025	0209	0046	0408	0526	0932	0706	0940	0710	610
Yiwu d.	0102	0253	|	0446	0603	1026	|	1012	0755	0642
Hangzhou nan d.	0226	0429	0252	0629	0726	1159	|	1135	0952	0758
Jiaxing d.	|	0537	0400	0733	0835	1301	|	1232	1054	0905
Shanghai nan a.	0414	0706	0516	0855	0941	1433	1022a	1327	1215	1019

A – Shanghai nan(**T81/82**) - Nanning and v.v.
B – Shanghai nan(**T77/78**) - Guilin and v.v.
C – Shanghai(**K511/12**) - Haikou and v.v.
D – Shanghai nan(**K79/80**) - Kunming and v.v.
E – Shanghai nan(**K739/40**) - Kunming and v.v.
F – Shanghai nan (**K71/2**) - Chongqing and v.v.
a – Shanghai.
d – Guangzhou dong.

WUHAN - YICHANG - CHONGQING 7182

China Rail High Speed

km	All unmarked trains prefix 'D'	633	2251	2277	366	2259	2201	3077	2255	2237	637	2207	3073	2213	2223	2242	G307	657	2216	G309	2226	2271	2232	3257	3081	3007
	Shanghai **7175** d.	...	...	...	...	...	...	...	...	...	0609	0638	0650	0730	...	...	...	...	0839	...	...	...	...	...	...	1353
	Nanjing nan **7175** d.	...	...	...	...	...	...	0738	0830	...	0830	0916	0922	0957	0952	...	...	1020	1110	...	...	...	...	...	1510	|
	Nanchang **7194** d.	...	...	...	...	...	...	|	|	0840	|	|	|	|	|	1029x	...	|	|	...	1230x	...	1054x	1513	|	|
0	**Wuhan** Hankou d.	0705	0755	0838	0805	1043	1100	1109	1151	1208	1214	1241	1255	1333	1316	1323	1355	1400	1432	1528	1547	1522	1535	1816	1834	1924
83	Tianmen nan d.	|	|	0915	0847	1119	|	|	|	|	1256	|	1331	|	1353	1405	1431	1440	|	|	1629	1605	1617	|	|	2000
114	Xiantao xi d.	0751	0841	|	|	|	|	1155	|	1254	|	|	|	1428	|	|	1447	|	1525	|	|	|	1633	|	1927	|
134	Qianjiang (Hubei) d.	|	|	0937	0909	1141	1152	|	1249	|	|	1333	1354	|	1415	1427	|	1504	|	1620	|	1628	|	1908	|	2022
204	Jingzhou d.	0825	0916	1005	0937	1209	1220	1229	1317	1328	1340	1401	1422	1504	1443	1455	1522	1532	1600	1649	1716	1658	1707	1936	2002	2050
292	**Yichang** dong d.	0910	1006	1042	1021	1247	1300	1302	1358	1412	1428	1444	1457	1537	1523	1534	1601	1611	1640	1727	1809	1736	1744	2009	2041	2123
567	Lichuan d.	1149	1245	1317	1257	1521	1534	...	1634	1651	1700	1719	...	1818	1751	1809	1835	1846	1915	|	2042	2024	2016	...	...	...
845	**Chongqing** bei **7140** a.	1346	1443	1521	1458	1710	1723	...	1829	1852	1901	1914	...	2013	1946	1958	2024	2035	2120	2146	2245	2219	2213	...	...	...

All unmarked trains prefix 'D'	3008	3082	3258	2214	658	2234	G310	2272	2218	2228	3074	G308	2202	2244	638	2224	2208	3078	2238	2256	2260	365	2278	2252	634
Chongqing bei **7140** d.	...	...	...	0715	0727	0739	0817	0829	0839	0902	...	0946	0931	0921	0939	1001	1039	...	1133	1105	1234	1314	1323	1532	1604
Lichuan d.	...	...	...	0910	|	|	|	1024	1034	|	...	1136	1126	1110	1146	1156	|	...	|	|	|	|	|	1727	|
Yichang dong d.	0640	0830	0900	1139	1145	1206	1243	1253	1300	1322	1333	1405	1359	1347	1414	1423	1456	1517	1553	1519	1659	1740	1800	1955	2038
Jingzhou d.	0720	0911	0940	1214	1226	1247	1317	1328	1340	1357	1407	1440	1434	1429	1450	1506	1537	1551	1628	1609	1735	1816	1835	2037	2111
Qianjiang (Hubei) d.	0748	|	1008	1242	|	1315	1346	1357	1408	1424	1435	|	1507	|	1517	|	|	1619	1656	|	|	1844	|	2105	|
Xiantao xi d.	0800	|	1020	|	1300	1327	|	|	|	|	|	|	1530	|	|	1540	1612	|	|	1643	1809	|	1910	|	|
Tianmen nan d.	0816	0959	|	1304	1316	|	1409	1419	1429	|	|	1524	1545	1514	|	|	|	1641	1718	1659	1825	|	|	|	|
Wuhan Hankou a.	0859	1042	1111	1347	1359	1420	1453	1500	1507	1520	1534	1603	1640	1552	1621	1634	1705	1718	1802	1736	1904	1935	1955	2156	2226
Nanchang **7194** a.	|	|	1443	|	|	1804	...	...	|	1843x	|	...	...	|	|	|	|	|	2159	|	...	...	...	...	...
Nanjing nan **7175** a.	1241	1431	...	1751	1756	...	...	...	1851	...	1910	...	...	1932	2023	2018	2057	2102	...	2113	...	...	...	...	...
Shanghai Hongqiao **7175** a.	1506	...	...	2015	...	...	...	...	2130	...	2134	...	...	...	2238	...	2315	...	...	...	...	...	...	...	...

km	All unmarked trains prefix 'D'	5921	5931	5927	5923	5817	5712	5906	5819	5936	5996	5853	5993	5702	5857	5716		5877	5863	5722	5801	G555	G1032	5867	5803	5726
0	**Wuhan** Hankou d.	0601	0612	0619	0635	0655	0730c	0736	0800	0815	0852	0944	0950	1020c	1238	1233c	...	1456	1609	1620c	1710	1739	1823	1850	2000	2059c
83	Tianmen nan d.	|	|	|	|	|	0818	|	0836	|	|	1021	|	1108	|	|	...	1533	1651	|	|	1816	1900	1932	|	|
114	Xiantao xi d.	|	|	|	|	|	|	|	|	|	0939	1037	|	1123	|	1337	...	|	|	|	|	|	|	|	|	|
134	Qianjiang (Hubei) d.	|	|	|	|	0747	0840	0829	0858	0916	|	|	1043	|	|	|	...	1555	1713	1730	1803	1838	1921	|	|	|
204	Jingzhou d.	0715	0727	0736	0747	0815	0907	0858	0928	0946	1014	1113	1111	1158	1355	1413	...	1623	1741	1757	1832	1906	1949	2016	2115	2225
292	**Yichang** dong a.	0754	0800	0808	0822	0848	0940	0930	1001	1020	1048	1147	1150	1231	1428	1448	...	1656	1816	1838	1905	1945	2023	2055	2148	2259

All unmarked trains prefix 'D'	5854	5711	5896	G556	G1034	5858	5701	5878		5864		5868	5820	5998	5994	5725		5826	5721	5802		5932	5924	5928	5922
Yichang dong d.	0617	0730	0800	0820	0840	0919	1000	1024	...	1225	...	1523	1608	1629	1704	1810	...	1833	1843	1930	...	2017	2030	2043	2130
Jingzhou d.	0657	0810	0834	0900	0922	0954	1034	1104	...	1307	...	1605	1648	1709	1740	1844	...	1909	1923	2007	...	2057	2106	2112	2204
Qianjiang (Hubei) d.	0725	0838	|	0928	|	1022	|	|	...	1335	...	|	1716	1737	1809	1912	...	1936	1951	2035	...	|	|	2145	|
Xiantao xi d.	0737	0850	|	|	|	|	|	|	...	1347	...	|	1728	1749	1821	|	...	|	|	|	...	|	|	|	|
Tianmen nan d.	0754	0907	0918	0950	1010	1044	1118	1148	...	|	...	1652	1744	1805	1837	|	...	1958	2013	2059	...	|	|	2208	|
Wuhan Hankou a.	0837	1002c	0959	1027	1051	1119	1206c	1223	...	1444	...	1727	1822	1843	1913	2017c	...	2036	2059c	2136	...	2210	2220	2246	2317

c – Wuchang. h – Wuhan. x – Nanchang xi.

CHANGSHA - GUILIN - NANNING - BEIHAI and FANGCHENGGANG 7184

China Rail High Speed

km	D8232	431	D8236	423 A	1505 E	1503 E	529 A	1501 E	D8240	421 A	433 D		All unmarked trains prefix 'G'		434 D	422 A	424 A	1502 E	530 A	D8231	1504 E	1506 E	D8235	432	D8242
362	...	0706	...	1216	...	...	1301	...	...	1444	1449	↓	d.Wuhan a.	↑	1457	1548	1633	...	1720	...	...	...	...	2333	...
0	...	0841	...	1351	1406	1440	1452	1530	...	1617	1632	↓	d.**Changsha** nan a.	↑	1316	1402	1458	1523	1547	...	1603	1702	...	2155	...
177	...	0927	...	1437	1453	1522	1532	1609	...	1704	1714	↓	d.Hengyang dong d.	↑	1235	1313	1414	1435	1505	...	1514	1609	...	2113	...
*	0810	|	1356	|	|	|	|	|	1758	|	|		d. Hezhou d.		|	|	|	|	|	1334	|	|	1727	|	2232
519	0958	1228	1505b	1721	1727	1819	1831	1906	1938	1950	2000	↓	d.**Guilin** d.	↑	0956	1035	1123	1144	1207	1217b	1228	1325	1546	1826	2051
675	1109	1333	1626	1827	1833	1932	1950	2024	2040	2056	2109	↓	d.Liuqiao d.	↑	0850	0925	1004	1031	1048	1055	1112	1216	1429	1703	1946
887	1231	1455	1754	2002n	1949	2054	2113n	2140	2201	2224	2231	↓	a.**Nanning** dong d.	↑	0730	0800	0835n	0905	0913n	0930	0940	1057	1258	1535	1815

km	8201	8293	8203	3561	3563	8295	G1505	8205 X	8267	6244	3565 V		All trains prefix 'D'		8204 Z	3652 W	G1506	8262	8264	8266	8294	3568	8214	8296	8252
0	0720	0817	1026	0950	1101	1310	1727	1352	1455	1525b	1629b	↓	d.**Guilin** a.	↑	1005	1037b	1318	1312	1428	1607	1710	1936	2212	2241	
156	0825	0934	1131	1118	1216	1427	1833	1504	1610	1643	1754	↓	d.Liuqiao d.	↑	0903	0910	1216	1210	1320	1506	1605	1818	2110	2122	2319
368	0953	1102	1247	1241	1332	1555	1949	1620	1733	1805	1922	↓	a.**Nanning** dong d.	↑	0744	0750	1057	1042n	1157	1347	1434	1651	1945	1951	2157n
368	...	1125	...	1306	1355	1616	2010	...	1753	1825	...	↓	d.**Nanning** dong a.	↑	...	...	...	1020n	1152	1343	1431	1647	...	1946	2153n
496	...	|	...	1353	1440	|	2058	...	1840	1913	...	↓	d.Qinzhou dong d.	↑	...	...	...	0927	1028	1219	|	1523	...	|	2029
587	...	|	...	1440	1529	|	2139	...	1927	1954	...	↓	a.Beihai d.	↑	...	...	...	0838	0945	1130	|	1440	...	|	1946
539	...	1228	...	...	...	1718	...	...	...	...	...	↓	a.Fangchenggang bei d.	↑	...	...	...	...	...	...	1250	...	...	1805	...

A – To/from Table **7060**. **D** – To/from Table **7097**. **E** – To/from Table **7192**. **V** – Additional trip: 1912.
W – Additional trips: 1015. **X** – additional trips: 1630, 1813, 2010, 2055. **Z** – Additional trips: 1025, 1715, 1844.
b – Guilin bei. **n** – Nanning. * *185* km from Guilin.

GUIYANG - GUILIN - GUANGZHOU 7185

China Rail High Speed

km	3591 A	211	2803 B	2815	2821	2879	3565	G2917	2829	2831	2841	2843		All trains prefix 'D'		3592	2804 E	3562 D	2806	G2918	2877	2820	212	2832	2836	2838	2844
0	0637	0800	0808	1013	1204	1327	1345	1425	1536	1542	1735	1803	↓	d.**Guiyang** bei a.	↑	1150	1302	1325	1417	1404	1705	1730	1812	2048	2144	2209	2321
408	0905x	|	1034	12504	1430	1600	1621x	|	1803	1810	2015	2044	↓	d.**Guilin** xi d.	↑	0925x	1018	1041x	1136	|	1421	1439	|	1804	1853	1953	2056
593	...	|	1146	1404	1541	1710	...	|	1919	1927	2139	2154	↓	d.Hezhou d.	↑	...	0915	...	1027	|	1309	1336	|	1655	1744	1826	1953
778	...	|	|	|	1628	|	...	|	2017	2030	2236	2253	↓	d.Zhaoqing dong d.	↑	...	|	...	0931	|	1210	1237	|	|	1642	1730	1849
854	...	1211	1325	1542	1719	1854n	...	1858	2054	2106	2312	2329	↓	a.**Guangzhou** nan d.	↑	...	0730	...	0848	0930	1128n	1200	1400	1516	1605	1647	1812

A – Additional trips: 1623, 1828. **B** – Additional trips: 0846, 0859, 0915, 0938, 1044, 1123, 1214, 1448, 1512, 1640, 1655. **D** – Additional trip: 1305, 2117.
E – Additional trips: 0900, 0925, 0943, 1036, 1049, 1235, 1436, 1504, 1532, 1647, 1711, 1752. **n** – Guangzhou. **x** –Guilin bei.

BEIHAI - NANNING - GUANGZHOU 7186

China Rail High Speed

km	All unmarked trains prefix 'D'	3601	3605 A	3607	G2911	3611	201	3615	3708	3684	G2913	3704	3716	3623	3625	3627	203	3637	3641	3724	3628	3643	G2915	3645	3692	3647
	Fangchenggang bei d.	...	...	...	...	...	...	...	...	0900	...	...	...	...	...	...	...	...	...	...	...	...	...	...	1740	...
0	**Beihai** ▶ d.	...	...	...	...	...	...	...	0806	|	...	1015	1038	...	...	...	...	...	...	1452	1512	...	...	...	|	...
91	Qinzhou dong d.	...	...	...	...	...	...	...	0849	|	...	1058	1127	...	...	...	...	...	...	1541	1601	...	...	...	|	...
197	**Nanning** dong ▶ d.	0700	0731	0740	0750	0808	0830	0900	0955	1025	1138	1205	1235	1300	1322n	1355	1500	1600	1630	1649	1709	1719	1800	1820	1907	1915
337	Guigang d.	|	0823	|	0842	0900	|	0952	1047	1123	1230	1257	1327	1352	1421	1447	|	1652	1722	1741	1801	1811	1854	1918	1959	2013
514	Wuzhou nan d.	0907	0942	0957	0949	1021	|	1105	1206	1242	1337	1404	1452	1520	1538	1600	|	1812	1841	1848	1914	1924	2005	2031	2118	2128
684	Zhaoqing dong d.	|	1058	1106	1052	1132	|	1208	1321	|	|	1513	1555	|	|	|	|	1921	1951	1957	2023	|	|	|	2228	2243
760	**Guangzhou** nan a.	1059	1135	1143	1128	1217	1149	1246	1358	1428	1518	1551	1638	1707	1725	1740	1819	1958	2029	2035	2100	2112	2145	2219	2306	2320
862	Shenzhen bei a.	...	...	...	1200	...	...	...	...	...	11554	...	...	...	...	...	...	...	...	...	...	...	2229	...	...	...

All unmarked trains prefix 'D'	3602	G2912	2372 B	3706	2362	2364	3604	3710	202	3608	3616	3682	3620	3622	3714	G2914	3624	204	3718	3722	3686	3726	G2916	3632	3640	3650
Shenzhen bei d.	...	0705	...	...	...	...	...	...	...	...	...	...	...	...	...	1220	...	...	...	...	...	...	1620	...	...	...
Guangzhou nan d.	0745	0737	0753	0836	0806	0818	0824	0906	1005	0950	1125	1153	1206	1214	1312	1300	1352	1430	1451	1525	1616	1555	1652	1738	1840	1943
Zhaoqing dong a.	0823	|	|	0914	0844	0856	0907	|	|	1028	1203	|	1245	1258	|	1338	|	|	|	1603	1654	1639	1730	1816	1918	2021
Wuzhou nan a.	0934	0922	0945	1029	0955	1009	1019	1055	|	1150	1315	1343	1350	1410	1507	1443	1541	|	1642	1714	1805	1746	1835	1927	2029	2133
Guigang d.	1039	1027	1056	1148	1106	1127	1136	1207	|	1307	1438	1454	1507	1527	1624	1548	1652	|	1747	1832	1916	1909	1940	2032	2140	2251
Nanning dong ▶ a.	1129	1117	1146	1238	1202	1218	1232	1258	1324	1403	1528	1544	1557	1623	1714	1638	1742	1749	1837	1922	2012	1959	2030	2122	2230	2341
Qinzhou dong d.	...	...	...	1347	...	...	...	1406	...	...	...	|	...	...	1822	...	...	...	1948	2032	|	2108	...	...	...	...
Beihai ▶ a.	...	...	...	1429	...	...	...	1447	...	...	...	|	...	...	190	...	...	...	2029	2119	|	2155	...	...	...	...
Fangchenggang bei a.	...	...	...	...	...	...	...	...	...	...	...	1708	...	...	...	...	...	...	...	...	2137	...	...	...	...	...

A – Additional trips. 0910, 0922, 0940**x**, 1005, 1110, 1150, 1215, 1225, 1247, 1340, 1510, 1520, 1735. **n** – Nanning. **x** – To/from Guangzhou.
B – Additional trips. 0842, 0845, 1043, 1055, 1405**x**, 1443, 1622, 1658, 1730, 1800, 1818, 1923. ▶ – Additional trains are available Nanning dong – Beihai and v.v.

BEYOND EUROPE - CHINA

7188 CHANGSHA/ZHUZHOU - NANNING Chinese Railways

km	T81 A	T77 B	Z5 C	Z285 D		T82 A	Z6 C	Z286 D	T78 B
0	...	...	...	...	d.**Nanchang** ... d.	...	...	...	...
231	...	...	...	...	d.Pingxiang ... a.	0307	...	...	...
* *	...	...	0615	1122	d. **Changsha** ... d.	|	1936	0249	...
312	0400	2246	|	|	a.**Zhuzhou** ... d.	0220	|	|	2254
312	0416	2306	|	|	d.**Zhuzhou** ... a.	0202	|	|	2229
437	|	|	|	|	d.Loudi ... d.	|	|	|	|
446	0555	0045	0815	1322	d. Hengyang ... d.	0038	1740	0053	2107
808	|	0530**b**	1140	1635**b**	d.Guilin ... d.	|	1422	2131**b**	1644
989	|	...	1324	1842	d.Liuqiao ... d.	|	1253	1952	...
1124	1650	...	|	|	d.Litang ... d.	1244	|	|	...
1244	1827	...	1546	2040	a.**Nanning** ... a.	1110	1055	1745	...

A – Shanghai nan(**T81/82**) - Nanning and v.v. B – Shanghai nan(**T77/78**) - Guilin and v.v.
C – Beijing(**Z5/6**) - Nanning and v.v. D – Beijing(**Z285/6**) - Nanning and v.v.
* * – Changsha *0 km* - Zhuzhou *52 km*. **b** – Guilin bei.

7190 CHANGSHA/ZHUZHOU - KUNMING Chinese Railways

km	Z161 G	Z77 F	K79 H	K739 E		K80 H	Z162 G	Z78 F	K740 E
* *	0301	0621	...	...	d.**Changsha** ... a.	...	1630	2140	...
0	|	|	0848	1105	d. **Zhuzhou** ... a.	1530	|	|	2307
145	0505	0821	1031	1249	d.Loudi ... d.	1342	1424	1940	2031
440	0916	1228	1505	1712	d.Huaihua ... d.	0933	1021	1542	1602
709	1259	1609	1855	2107	d.Kaili ... d.	0534	0632	1149	1122
917	1525	1835	2123	2335	a.**Guiyang** ... d.	0306	0408	0925	0844
917	1537	...	2141	2356	d.**Guiyang** ... a.	0247	0356	...	0819
948	|	...	2259	|	d.Anshun ... d.	0133	|	...	0705
1146	1854	...	0140	0330	d.Liupanshui ... d.	2336	0058	...	0456
1378	2117	...	0434	0632	d.Qujing ... d.	2050	2231	...	0118
1525	2234	...	0608	0818	a.**Kunming** ... a.	1908	2105	...	2335

E – Shanghai nan(**K739/40**) - Kunming and v.v. F – Beijing xi(**Z77/78**) - Guiyang and v.v.
G – Beijing(**Z161/62**) - Kunming and v.v. H – Shanghai nan(**K79/80**) - Kunming and v.v.
* * – Changsha *0 km* - Loudi *177 km*.

7192 SHANGHAI - HANGZHOU - NANCHANG - CHANGSHA – GUIYANG China Rail High Speed

km	All trains prefix 'G'	1321	1383	1371	1341	85 C	1505 B	1323	1343	1503 AB	1325	1347	1501 B	61 A	1349	1327	1481 A	1387	1373	1355	1357	1305 C	1483 A	1361	1365	45 A	
0	**Shanghai** ♥ ... d.	0625	0645	0723	0733	0800	...	0822	0900	...	0930	0950	1003	...	1049	1139	...	1220	1240	1348	1501	1525	...	1643	1740	...	...
84	Jiaxing nan ... d.	|	0715	0754	0810	|	...	0854	|	...	|	1020	1032	...	1118	|	...	1249	|	|	1530	|	...	1719	1810	...	...
159	**Hangzhou** ♣ .. d.	0721	0749	0828	0838	0848	0919	0930	0949	0958	1033	1053	1103	1134	1152	1244	1312	1325	1342	1452	1557	1615	1652	1746	1842	2128	...
268	Yiwu ... d.	0755	0830	0902	|	|	0953	|	|	1040	1107	1134	|	|	1226	1325	|	1359	1423	1526	|	|	1727	1820	|	2210	...
320	Jinhua ... d.	0813	|	0920	0937	|	1012	1022	1035	1058	|	|	1155	1221	1244	|	1358	|	|	1544	|	1700	|	1838	1927	2228	...
398	Quzhou ... d.	|	|	0946	|	|	1036	1045	|	1121	|	|	|	1244	|	|	1422	|	|	|	|	|	1808	1901	|	2248	...
500	Shangrao ... d.	0909	0935	|	1027	|	1107	1124	|	1151	1219	|	1247	1313	|	1429	|	1502	1519	1629	|	1749	1837	1930	2019	...	...
604	Yingtan bei ... d.	0937	1012	1046	|	|	1135	1152	1142	1219	|	|	|	1341	1353	1457	1520	1530	1548	1958	1742	|	1905	1959	|	...	...
744	**Nanchang** xi... a.	1016	1111	1121	1135	1100	1210	1227	1217	1254	1316	1341	1343	1417	1440	1532	1602	1613	1623	1740	1817	1845	1947	2034	2111	...	...
1086	**Changsha** nan a.	1151	...	1253	1311	1225	1402	1408	1343	1432	1454	1517	1525	...	1615	1711	1749	...	1808	1924	1942	2013	2141	2213	2254	...	...
1211	Loudi nan ... d.	1246	...	1343	...	...	...	1458	...	...	1544	...	...	...	...	1802	|	...	1900	...	...	...	...	...	...	...	...
1418	Huaihua nan ... a.	1343	...	1440	...	...	...	1558	...	...	1641	...	...	...	...	1858	1935	...	1957	...	...	...	...	...	...	...	...
1586	**Guiyang** bei ... a.	1537	...	...	...	...	...	1750	...	...	1829	...	...	...	...	2055	2128	...	...	...	...	...	...	...	...	...	...

All trains prefix 'G'	46 A	1492 A	1382	1384	1342	1346	1482 A	1348	1350	86 C	1352	1374	1354	1322	62 A	1484 A	1686	1356	1324	1358	1502 B	1328	1504 AB	1506 B	1330	1306 C
Guiyang bei ... d.	...	...	...	...	...	...	......	...	...	...	...	...	...	0909	...	0804	0936	...	1008	...	...	1159	...	...	1401	...
Huaihua nan ... d.	...	...	...	...	...	...	...	...	...	...	...	0923	...	1102	...	0953	1123	...	1155	...	...	1352	...	...	1555	...
Loudi nan ... d.	...	...	...	...	...	...	...	...	...	...	...	1023	...	1203	...	1053	1223	...	1255	...	...	1453	...	...	1648	...
Changsha nan ... d.	...	...	...	...	0700	0800	0840	0900	0927	1024	1040	1108	1142	1245	...	1132	1318	1340	1348	1500	1527	1532	1608	1708	1727	1812
Nanchang xi ... d.	...	0810	0732	0804	0846	0943	1035	1026	1113	1147	1216	1244	1318	1428	1437	1324	1520	1533	1527	1622	1707	1712	1748	1843	1917	1943
Yingtan bei ... d.	...	0846	0815	0858	|	1024	|	1102	1150	|	1253	1321	|	1507	1520	1400	1557	|	1615	1701	1743	|	1824	1921	1954	|
Shangrao ... d.	...	0914	0843	0939	|	|	1140	|	|	|	1322	1350	1417	1535	1548	1428	1634	|	1643	|	1811	1835	1852	1952	2022	|
Quzhou ... d.	0825	|	0913	|	1006	1110	|	|	|	|	|	1420	|	1605	1618	1458	...	|	|	|	|	1912	|	2022	|	2103
Jinhua ... d.	0848	1000	0936	1032	|	|	1226	1208	1304	|	1415	1443	1511	|	1641	1522	...	1724	1743	1808	1904	1942	1948	2052	2117	2126
Yiwu ... d.	0906	1018	|	1050	|	1144	1244	|	|	|	1433	1501	1529	1639	1659	1540	...	1743	|	|	1922	2000	2008	2110	2136	2144
Hangzhou dong ... d.	0946	1059	1030	1125	1114	1220	1325	1255	1350	1402	1515	1536	1603	1715	1733	1613	...	1821	1832	1856	2010	2048	2039	2143	2210	2220
Jiaxing nan ... d.	...	...	1055	1151	1147	|	...	|	|	|	|	|	1635	|	...	...	...	1854	1859	|	2037	2120	...	...	|	|
Shanghai Hongqiao . a.	...	...	1129	1218	1214	1319	...	1340	1454	1450	1607	1638	1703	1822	...	...	...	1921	1926	1942	2115	2148	...	...	2302	2305

A – To/from Table **7102**. B – To/from Table **7184**. C – To/from Table **7065**. ♥ – Shanghai Hongqiao. ♣ – Hangzhou dong.

7193 BEIJING - HEFEI - SHANGHAI - HANGZHOU - FUZHOU - XIAMEN China Rail High Speed

km	All trains prefix 'G'	1651	1611	1671	1631	1621	1653	1673	1655	1601	345 A	1657	1633	1659	355 A	1686	241 A	1635	323 A	301	1637	325 A	303	1639	7371	7381	7383
	Beijing nan ... d.	...	...	...	...	...		...	...	...	...	...	...	...	0840	...	...	...	1010	1040	...	1205	1230	...	...	...	...
	Xuzhou dong . d.	...	...	...	...	...		0658	...	...	0823	...	...	...	1200	...	1253	...	1317	1350	...	1459	1538	...	...	...	...
	Hefei nan ... d.	...	0733	...	...	0758	...	0846	...	0923	1010	...	...	...	1347	...	1438	...	1506	1531	...	1644	1720	...	1454	...	...
0	**Shanghai** ♥ ... d.	0658	|	...	0754	|	0816	|	0925	|	|	1018	1228	1258	|	...	|	1435	|	|	1519	|	|	1724	1814	1917	2033
84	Jiaxing nan ... d.	|	|	...	0826	|	|	|	0955	|	|	1048		1335	|	...	|	1506	|	|	1558	|	|	1800	|	1956	2102
159	**Hangzhou** ♣ .. d.	0805	|	0832	0853	|	0905	|	1028	|	|	1120	1330	1400	|	...	|	1538	|	|	1625	|	|	1828	1930	2029	2152
304	Yiwu ... d.	0846	|	0907	|	|	|	|	|	|	|	1155		1434	|	...	|	1612	|	|	1659	|	|	|	2015	2110	2233
352	Jinhua ... d.	0904	|	0930	0945	|	0957	|	1114	|	|	|	1422	|	|	...	|		|	|	1717	|	|	|	2034	2128	2251
438	Quzhou ... d.	|	|	1006	|	|	|	|		|	|	|	|	|	|	...	|	1646	|	|	|	|	|	|	2055	2150	2313
549	Shangrao ... d.	0958	1009	1042	1033	1049	1116	1121	1206	1218	1246	1305	1512	1547	1626	1639	1715	1722	1748	1814	1827	1913	1956	2018	...	...	...
768	Nanping bei ... d.	1108	1113	1152	1138	1159	1219	1231	1316	|	|	1408	1632	1650	|	1750	1819	1832	1851	1922	|	|	2110	2128	...	...	...
889	**Fuzhou** ... d.	1147	1159	1246	1222	1234	1258	1317	1407	1413	1429	1502	1715	1750	1816	1843	1900	1908	1937	1958	2020	2100	2146	2211	...	...	...
1063	Quanzhou ... d.	1305	1316	1403	...	...	1414	1430	1518	1524	...	|	...	1910	1940	2002	2026	...	|	...	...	2217	...	...	...	...	...
1134	**Xiamen** bei ... a.	1331	1343	1429	...	...	1440	1501	1544	1550	...	1645	...	1943	2007	2034	2058	...	2127	...	...	2244	...	...	...	...	...

All trains prefix 'G'	7382	7372	302	1632	1634	322 A	242 A	1652	1672	324 A	1688	7380	304	1636	1638	356 A	1624	1602	348 A	1654	1656	1676	1612	1640	1658	1660
Xiamen bei ... d.	...	...	...	...	...	0720	0747	0757	...	0849	0929	...	...	...	...	1059	...	1254	...	1336	1409	1454	1503	...	1615	1706
Quanzhou ... d.	...	...	...	...	...	|	0820	0830	...	0922	0957	...	...	...	...	1127	...	1321	...	1403	1436	1526	1531	...	1648	1733
Fuzhou ... d.	...	...	0703	0800	0855	0914	0933	0959	1030	1054	1122	...	1215	1225	1245	1252	1300	1435	1450	1529	1555	1644	1651	1752	1807	1846
Nanping bei ... d.	...	...	0739	0836	|	|	1010	1043	1113	|	1206	...	1251	1302	1321	|	1343	1512	|	1612	1632	1721	1743	|		1930
Shangrao ... d.	...	...	0841	0952	1049	1058	1113	1155	1227	1237	1314	...	1402	1408	1441	1432	1500	1615	1637	1728	1748	1838	1849	1943	1956	2042
Quzhou ... d.	0624	0647	|	1025	|	|	|	|	|	|	...	1343	|	|	1513	|	|	|	|	1809	1827	|	|	2015	2032	
Jinhua ... d.	0654	0717	|	|	|	|	|	1241	1320	|	...	1420	|	1506	|	|	|	|	|	1839	1850	|	|	2039	2102	2132
Yiwu ... d.	0712	0735	|	1106	1203	|	|	1310	1338	|	...	1442	|	|	1548	|	|	|	|	|	1908	|	|	2057	2121	2150
Hangzhou dong ... d.	0753	0817	|	1142	1244	|	|	1345	1412	|	...	1523	|	1555	1627	|	|	|	|	1935	1945	|	|	2140	2157	2234
Jiaxing nan ... d.	|	0849	|	1209	|	|	|	1410	...	|	...	...	|	1620	|	|	|	|	|	|	|	|	|	|	|	|
Shanghai Hongqiao . a.	0859	0924	|	1237	1336	|	|	1438	...	|	...	...	|	1655	1723	|	|	|	|	2029	2047	|	|	2233	2243	2319
Hefei nan ... a.	...	1234	1124	...	...	1335	1357	...	...	1509	...	...	1638	...	...	1657	1734	1841	1917	...	...	2111	2122	...	...	...
Xuzhou dong ... d.	...	...	1303	...	...	1518	1541	...	...	1704	...	...	1837	...	...	1857	...	...	2057	...	...	2310	...	...	...	...
Beijing nan ... a.	...	...	1618	...	...	1826	...	...	...	2013	...	...	2141	...	...	2219	...	...	...	...	...	...	...	...	...	...

A – Via Table **7097**. ♥ – Shanghai Hongqiao. ♣ – Hangzhou dong.

7194 WUHAN - NANCHANG - FUZHOU and XIAMEN China Rail High Speed

km	All trains prefix 'D'	6501	6521	6503	6523	6525	6527	6505	3262	3241	3276	6529	6507	3223	3258	6509	295	3272	6531	6533	2234	3245	2228	6511	2244	3227	2238
0	**Wuhan** Hankou d.	...	...	...	...	...	...	...	0810	0825	0830	...	...	1110**c**	1116	...	1145	1232	...	...	1452	1525	1526	...	1609	1749**c**	1815
118	Huangshi ... d.	...	...	...	...	...	...	...	0929	0941	|	...	...	1205	1233	...	|	1354	...	...	1603	1622	1637	...	|	1843	1941
368	**Nanchang** xi... d.	0648**x**	0725**x**	0751**x**	0855	0909	0953	1026**x**	1133	1141	1203	1250**x**	1345**x**	1407	1443	1450	1510	1601	1720**x**	1758	1808	1850	1849	1915	1938	2042	2159**x**
732	Sanming bei ... d.	0915	1005	1025	1119	1139	1215	1301	1349	...	1420	1531	1600	...	...	1711	1732	1824	1956	2015	2034	...	2111	2149	2154	...	...
927	**Fuzhou** ... a.	1030	|	1148	|	|	|	1415	1504	...	|	|	1709	...	...	1826	1847	|	|	|	|	...	2233	2258	2303	...	...
1068	**Xiamen** bei ... a.	...	1220	...	1321	1357	1418	...	...	...	1628	1745	...	...	...	...	...	2047	2233**z**	2229	2237	...	...	...	...	...	...

All trains prefix 'D'	3222	2237	2242	2232	3247	6502	2226	6522	3274	6524	3226	296	3257	6504	6506	6508	6526	3278	3242	3261	6528	6510	6530	6512	6532	6534
Xiamen bei ... d.	...	...	...	0715	...	...	...	0850	0918	0910	...	...	...	...	...	...	1421	1445	...	...	1548	...	1653	...	1814**z**	1853
Fuzhou ... d.	...	...	0650	|	...	0827	0839	|	|	|	...	1054	...	1314	1407	1440	|	|	...	1535	|	1724	|	1910	|	|
Sanming bei ... d.	...	...	0807	0932	...	0946	0956	1108	1138	1124	...	1211	...	1431	1524	1558	1627	1709	...	1652	1827	1842	1858	2021	2054	2111
Nanchang xi ... d.	0802	0840**x**	1029	1159	1209**x**	1218**x**	1230	1327**x**	1403	1340	1428**x**	1436	1513	1655**x**	1739	1819	1859**x**	1940	1910	1919	2042	2111**x**	2113	2245	2318**x**	2314
Huangshi ... d.	|	1054	|	1359	1411	...	1422	...	|	...	1625	1640	|	...	...	...	...	2132	2059	|	...	...	...	...	...	...
Wuhan Hankou ... a.	1040**c**	1202	1314	1525	1518	...	1539	...	1706	...	1719**c**	1756	1813	...	...	...	...	2301	2210	2227	...	...	...	...	...	...

c – Wuchang. **x** – Nanchang. **z** – Xiamen.

China Rail High Speed — SHANGHAI - HANGZHOU - FUZHOU - XIAMEN - SHENZHEN and LONGYAN — 7200

km	All trains prefix D	3111	3145	3131	2287	3125	2285	3107	2281 B	3135	2283	2293
	Nanjing nan ......d.	...	...	...	...	0625n	...	...	0745	0810	...	...
0	**Shanghai** ♥.....d.	...	0640	0737	0747	0849	0905	0940	1028	1042	1124	...
84	Jiaxing nan.......d.	...	0710	0813	0842	0934	0946	1027	1105	1133	1155	...
159	**Hangzhou** ♣ ...d.	0733	0743	0843	0909	1014	10204	1125	1135	1206	1229	...
314	Ningbo..............d.	0850	0909	0952	1017	1125	1131	1225	1236	1325	1339	...
466	Taizhou ....d.	0951	1010	|	|	1226	1232	1327	1343	1426	1434	...
589	Wenzhou nan ...d.	1043	1102	1152	1210	1318	1330	1425	1442	1519	1532	1549
883	**Fuzhou** nan .....d.	1254	1316	1356	1414	1529	1535	1621	1639	1729	1746	1757
1038	Quanzhou..........d.	1358	1420	1458	1513	1628	1634	1726	1745	|	1839	|
1109	**Xiamen** bei.......d.	1428	1453	1528	1543	1657	1703	1756	1815	1913	1908	1920
1151	Zhangzhou ....d.	1449	|	1549	1605	|	1725	1817	|	1935	1930	1942
	Longyan.......a.	|	1558	1640	|	|	|	|	|	2019	|	|
1318	Chaoshan ....d.	1601	...	...	1704	1824	1830	1923	1941	...	2040	2052
1567	Huizhou nan .....d.	1744	...	...	1846	2006	2012	2111	2129	...	|	2234
1623	**Shenzhen** bei...a.	1816	...	...	1919	2039	2045	2144	2209	...	2256	2308

All trains prefix D	3136	2282 B	2294	3108	3132	2284	3126	3146	2286	2288	3112
Shenzhen bei d.	...	0700	0755	0811	...	0847	0913	...	0955	1040	1117
Huizhou nan ..d.	...	0735	0830	0840	...	|	0942	...	1024	1109	1146
Chaoshan ......d,	...	0921	1016	1031	...	1107	1132	...	1215	1306	1343
Longyan....d.	0821	|	|	|	1057	|	|	1254	|	|	|
Zhangzhou.....d.	0912	|	|	|	1148	1220	1247	|	1328	|	1451
Xiamen bei ....d.	0934	1046	1147	1158	1211	1243	1312	1357	1351	1439	1516
Quanzhou ......d.	|	1113	|	1226	1245	|	1339	1425	1419	1513	1545
Fuzhou nan...d.	1119	1215	1316	1335	1352	1427	1442	1532	1547	1618	1647
Wenzhou nan.d.	1325	1427	1527	1542	1559	1624	1649	1738	1748	1832	1900
Taizhou..........d.	1422	|	...	1633	1655	1720	1739	1828	|	|	|
Ningbo ....d.	1532	1622	...	1741	1758	1832	1847	1934	1954	2022	2050
Hangzhou ♣.d.	1632	1730	...	1904	1926	1942	2002	2050	2110	2140	2201
Jiaxing nan ....d.	1713	|	...	1938	|	2008	|	2131	2142	|	...
Shanghai ♥..a.	1742	1843	...	2007	2030	2038	2120	2200	2212	2235	...
Nanjing nan ...a.	2028k	2116k	...	...	...	...	2312k	...	...	...	...

km	All unmarked trains prefix 'D'	6201 R	3231	G7541 P	G7501	379	G7543	377	G7505	3201	3213	3205	G63 A	5431 B	3215	3207	G7511	3209	G55 A	3217	3101	381	G7545	3103	G7521	G167 A
	Nanjing nan .... d.	...	...	...	...	...	...	...	0713	...	0752	...	1033	0922	...	...	...	...	1238	...	...	...	...	...	...	1711
0	**Shanghai** Hongqiao.. d.	...	...	0614	0650	0702	0707	...	0900	0820	|	0935	|	1119	...	1148	1153	1215	|	...	1509	1445	1552	1557	1647	|
84	Jiaxing nan .... d.	...	...	|	0728	0743	0738	...	0929	0901	|	1009	|	1150	...	1228	|	1245	|	...	|	1535	|	|	1723	|
159	**Hangzhou** dong........ d.	...	0716	0708	0800	0815	0810	0824	0959	0931	0941	1041	1156	1239	...	1302	1256	1319	1408	1558	1630	1620	1655	1700	1755	1841
314	Ningbo .... d.	...	0834	0817	0856	0922	0914	0947	1100	1047	1103	1200	1252	1353	1414	1426	1359	1440	1459	1729	1751	1740	1807	1813	1907	1952
466	Taizhou...................... d.	...	0929	0918	0957	1023	1015	1048	...	|	1204	1301	1353	1454	|	1527	1500	|	1554	1830	1852	|	1902	1914	2008	2053
589	Wenzhou nan.............. d.	...	1027	1015	1047	1121	1103	1140	...	1234	1256	1359	1445	1602	1613	1620	1557	1634	1647	1922	1944	1933	1959	2007	2058	2144
883	**Fuzhou** nan.............. d.	0639	1236	...	...	1324	...	1349	...	1450	1502	1601	...	...	1822	1839	...	1845	1859f	2137	2150f	2138	...	2211	...	...
1038	Quanzhou.................. d.	0744	1335	...	...	1425	...	1453	...	1549	1614	|	...	...	1935	1946	...	1951	...	|	...	...	...	...	...	...
1109	**Xiamen** bei .... a.	0828	1402	...	...	1451	...	1519	...	1615	1640	1721	...	...	2001	2012	...	2017	...	2311	...	...	...	...	...	...

All unmarked trains prefix 'D'	G7504 T	G7506	G168 A	G7540	3102	G56 A	382	3104	G7542	6202 Q	G7546	3216	G7516	3218	3208	3296	5432 B	3210	G64 A	3206	3202	3146	378	380	3232
Xiamen bei........................ d.	...	...	...	...	...	...	...	...	...	0829	...	0816	...	0844	0953	1015		...	...	1300	1323	1357	1426	1535	1557
Quanzhou.......................... d.	...	...	...	...	...	...	...	...	...	0902	...	0849	...	0917	|	1042	..	1040	...	1327	1350	1425	1459	1602	1630
Fuzhou nan....................... d.	...	...	...	...	0740f	0755f	0737	0830	...	1030f	...	0956	...	1024	1130	1144	...	1107	...	1436	1501	1532	1606	1705	1743
Wenzhou nan .... d.	0631	0729	0836	0906	0958	1007	0943	1038	1052	...	1121	1200	1216	1225	1337	1356	1402	1208	1510	1637	1708	1738	1819	1911	1944
Taizhou .... d.	0721	0825	0926	1002	1043	1057	1034	|	1142	...	1217	1250	1306	1321	1427	1446	1452	1415	1600	|	|	1828	|	2002	2040
Ningbo................................ d.	0825	0930	1033	1106	1148	1155	1133	1234	1255	...	1315	1352	1417	1427	1538	1548	1558	1505	1705	1837	1905	1938	2013	2107	2140
Hangzhou dong .... d.	0920	1036	1138	1202	1300	1249	1238	1340	1409	...	1419	...	1519	1533	1647	1700	1706	1604	1806	1954	2020	2050	2130	2218	2237
Jiaxing nan .... d.	0945	1108	|	1234	|	|	1304	1425	1441	...	1452	...	1551	...	1723	|	|	1751	|	2019	2108	2131	2157	...	...
Shanghai Hongqiao .... a.	1020	1135	|	1308	1414	|	1355	1524	1516	...	1520	...	1629	...	1806	|	1813	1838	|	2052	2147	2200	2227	...	...
Nanjing nan .... a.	...	...	1320	...	...	1419	...	...	...	...	...	...	...	...	...	1846	2022	...	1933	...	...	...	...	...	...

km	All trains prefix 'D'	681	6571	2327	6403	2311	2295	6405	2297	2301	6407	2323	6409	2325	6451	2331	6381	G1601	6575	2307	685	2309	6415	671	6417	6419
	Fuzhou .... d.	...	0658	...	0712	...	...	0819	...	...	0923	...	0943	1023	...	1225	...	1413	1425	...	...	...	1633	...	1829	2005
0	**Fuzhou** nan.............. d.	...	|	0720	0730	0757	0813	0835	...	0919	0941	0936	|	|	1004	1243	1342	|	|	1456	...	1548	1651	1816	1850	2024
155	Quanzhou .... d.	0728	0821	|	0849	0856	0914	0942	1000	1024	1040	1046	|	1140	1112	1344	1447	1524	1542	1555	....	1047	1757	1930	1956	2129
226	**Xiamen** bei .... d.	0804	|	0908	0919	0932	0949	1016	1044	1055	1108	1115	1129	1217	1203	1419	|	1557	1616	1624	1712	1717	1827	2000	2025	2203
268	Zhangzhou................ d.	|	|	0933	|	0953	1010	1037	1105	|	1129	|	1150	|	|	|	1536	1618	1639	1645	1744	1738	1854	2021	2046	2224
382	**Longyan** .... a.	|	0947	|	1032	|	|	1121	|	|	1219	|	1234	|	1302	|	1626	|	1729	|	|	|	1938	|	2142	2308
435	Chaoshan .... d.	0931	...	1038	...	1100	1122	...	1205	1214	...	1242	...	1337	...	1547	...	1729	...	1757	1849	1854	...	2127	...	...
682	Huizhou nan............... d.	1119	...	1226	...	|	1304	...	1347	1356	...	1424	...	|	...	|	...	1905	...	|	2032	2043	...	|	...	...
740	**Shenzhen** bei .... a.	1152	...	1259	...	1319	1343	...	1427	1434	...	1503	...	1559	...	1759	...	1937	...	2012	2110	2116	...	2338	...	...

All trains prefix 'D'	6382	6576	2308	G1602	6434	682	2310	3146	6436	6438	6440	684	2324	6442	2304	6444	6572	2296	2328	2306	672	2326	2312	6448	686
Shenzhen bei.................... d.	...	...	0832	0852	...	0924	0945	...	...	...	...	1215	1354	...	1455	...	...	1538	1525	1607	1614	1619	1643	...	1800
Huizhou nan .... d.	...	...	|	0927	...	0953	|	...	...	...	...	|	1429	...	1524	...	...	|	1554	1636	1643	1648	|	...	1830
Chaoshan............................ d.	...	...	1053	1117	...	1137	1206	...	...	...	...	1429	1615	...	1703	...	...	1756	1742	1828	1836	1847	1906	...	2022
Longyan........................... d.	0716	1027	|	|	1145	|	|	1254	1300	1344	1510	|	|	1703	|	1740	1804	|	|	|	|	|	|	1959	|
Zhangzhou .... d.	0801	1112	1200	1230	1237	1242	|	|	1352	1435	1604	1537	1734	1754	|	1832	1851	1953	1856	1938	|	1958	2018	2044	|
Xiamen bei......................... d.	0824	1136	1237	1254	1305	1315x	1340	1357	1414	1510	1630	1607x	1809	1815	1836	1853	1915	1923	1922	2000	2009	2030	2042	2114	2209
Quanzhou............................ d.	0857	1203	1304	1321	1334	...	1407	1425	1454	1539	1658	...	|	1843	|	1927	1942	1954	1948	2027	2036	|	2110	2141	2240
Fuzhou nan......................... a.	1000	1300	1402	|	|	...	1512	1527	|	1638	1801	...	1935	2002	2016	2024	2039	...	2047	2131	2138	2156	2208	2250	...
Fuzhou .... a.	...	1319	...	1430	1437	...	...	...	1609	1656	1819	...	...	2021	...	2043	2100	...	...	...	...	...	...	2310	...

China Rail High Speed — SHANGHAI - HANGZHOU - NINGBO — 7202

km	All trains prefix 'G'	7331 U	7301	7357	7351	7303	7305	7307	7309	7311	7557	7315
0	**Shanghai** ♥.....d.	0620	0635	0836	1008	1134	1330	1430	1632	1729	1932	2130
84	Jiaxing nan ....d.	|	0704	0908	1038	1210	|	1501	1708	1805	2001	2159
169	**Hangzhou**.........d.	0712d	0740	0944	1107	1249	1436	1537	1744	1841	2032d	2228

All trains 'G'	7556	7558	7302 V	7330	7304	7306	7308	7360	7310	7336	7312
Hangzhou .....d.	0659d	0714d	0758	0858d	1130	1306	1451	1537	1553	1653d	1800
Jiaxing nan ....d.	0732	0746	0836	|	1212	|	|	1615	1625	1718	1833
Shanghai ♥..d.	0807	0827	0910	1007	1239	1404	1550	1650	1659	1754	1901

km	All trains prefix 'G'	7503 W	7505	7507	7509	7511	7595	7515	7517	7519	7525	7527
0	**Shanghai** ♥.....d.	0805	0905	1013	1100	1153	1305	1400	1456	1547	1800	2021
84	Jiaxing nan ....d.	0834	0934	1043	1128	|	1341	1429	1525	1613	1830	2052
159	**Hangzhou** dong.d.	0859	0959	1109	1204	1302	1418	1501	1551	1652	1903	2124
314	**Ningbo**.............a.	0952	1059	1209	1257	1356	1511	1554	1644	1752	2003	2231

	7502 X	7504	7572	7506	7510	7512	7514	7518	7520	7522	7524
Ningbo.........d.	0711	0825	0857	0929	1124	1228	1321	1527	1619	1727	1820
Hangzhou dong d.	0822	0920	1000	1038	1226	1330	1424	1632	1725	1826	1920
Jiaxing nan ....d.	0854	0946	1032	1110	1258	1355	|	1704	1757	1904	1952
Shanghai ♥..a.	0928	1012	1108	1138	1325	1433	1530	1732	1832	1931	2020

Notes for Tables **7200** and **7202**.

A – To/from Beijing Table **7102**. **B** – To/from Table **7100**.
P – Additional trip: 1800.
Q – Additional trips: 0651**x**, 0923, 1005, 1003**x**, 1053, 1204, 1227, 1318, 1329, 1524, 1529, 1534**x**, 1629**x**, 1718**x**, 1723, 1808**x**, 1945, 2019, 2024, 2049, 2102, 2108.
R – Additional trips: 0640**f**, 0700, 0741, 0824, 0848**n**, 0856, 0912**n**, 0913, 0950, 1027, 1119, 1211**n**, 1305, 1406, 1419**n**, 1509, 1611, 1529**n**, 1720, 1810, 1852**n**.
T – Additional trips: 1837, 1928. **U** – Additional trips: 1230, 1823. **V** – Additional trips: 1900, 1959. **W** – Additional trips: 0832, 1030, 1440. **X** – Additional trips: 0732, 1023, 1700, 1737.
d – Hangzhou dong. **f** – Fuzhou. **h** – Hangzhou. **k** – Nanjing. **n** – Fuzhou nan. **x** – Xiamen. ♥ – Shanghai Hongqiao. ♣ – Hangzhou dong.

Chihese Railways, Duóng Sát Viêt Nam — HÁ NOI - BEIJING — 7250

km				MR1 BC	T8702 BC	Z6 C	Z286			DD5
0	**Há Nôi** Gia Lam ....d.	...	...	2140	...	...	...	...	...	0730
162	Dong Dang ....a.	...	...	0155	...	...	...	...	...	1140
162	Dong Dang 🛃.....................d.	...	...	0250	...	...	...	...	...	...
207	Pingxiang 🛃 ....a.	...	...	0431	...	...	...	...	...	...
207	Pingxiang..........................d.	...	...	...	0615	...	...	...	...	...
430	Nanning.............................a.	...	...	...	1007	...	...	...	...	...
430	Nanning.............................d.	...	...	...	...	1055	1745	...	...	...
861	Guilin...............................d.	...	...	...	...	1422	2125a	...	...	...
1409	Changsha ....d.	...	...	...	...	1942	0255	...	...	...
1771	Wuhan Wuchang ....d.	...	...	...	...	2311	0622	...	...	...
2307	Zhengzhou.........................d.	...	...	...	...	0352	1108	...	...	...
2996	**Beijing** xi..........................a.	...	...	...	...	0948	1730	...	...	...

	Z5 D	T8701 BD	MR2 BD	Z285					DD6	
Beijing xi .... d.	1609	...	...	2110	...	...	...	...	...	...
Zhengzhou .... d.	2212	...	...	0310	...	...	...	...	...	...
Wuhan Wuchang .... d.	0252	...	...	0753	...	...	...	...	...	...
Changsha.................................. d.	0615	...	...	1122	...	...	...	...	...	...
Guilin.. d.	1140	...	...	1635a	...	...	...	...	...	...
Nanning..................................... a.	1546	...	...	2040	...	...	...	...	...	...
Nanning..................................... d.	...	1805	...	...	...	...	...	...	...	...
Pingxiang.................................. a.	...	2210	...	...	...	...	...	...	...	...
Pingxiang 🛃............................. d.	...	...	2241	...	...	...	...	...	...	...
Dong Dang 🛃 .... a.	...	...	2322	...	...	...	...	...	...	...
Dong Dang.................................. d.	...	...	0022	...	...	...	...	...	1530	...
Há Nôi Gia Lam .... a.	...	...	0520	...	...	...	...	...	1946	...

B – Conveys 🛏 1 cl. Nanning (**T8701/2**) - Pingxiang (**MR2/1**) - Há Nôi and v.v.
C – Runs daily. On ②⑤ (from Há Nôi) conveys 🛏 1 cl. Há Nôi – Beijing (2 nights).
D – Runs daily. On ④⑦ (from Beijing) conveys 🛏 1 cl. Beijing - Há Nôi (2 nights).
a – Guilin bei.

BEYOND EUROPE
Japan

Introduction

The Beyond Europe section covers principal rail services in a different area of the world each month. There are six areas, each appearing as follows:

Winter (December) and Summer (June): all the latest Beyond Europe pages will be included.

January and July (digital only): India.

February and August: India; South East Asia, Australia and New Zealand; North America.

March and September (digital only): China.

April and October: China; Japan; South America; South Korea.

May and November (digital only): North America.

The months have been chosen so that we can bring you up-to-date information for those countries which make seasonal changes.

Contents

INDEX OF PLACES

by table number

JAPAN

Capital:	Tokyo (GMT + 9). 2017 Public Holidays: Jan. 1, 2, 9, Feb. 11, Mar, 20, Apr. 29, May 3 - 5, July 17, Aug. 11, Sep. 18, 23, Oct. 9, Nov. 3, 23, Dec. 23
Operators:	Most rail services in Japan are operated by the six private regional railway companies which are marketed as a whole as Japan Railways (JR); there are also a number of private railways, some quite large, which are not shown in this section. The six regional operators are JR Central (jr-central.co.jp), JR East (www.jreast.co.jp), JR Hokkaido (www.jrhokkaido.co.jp), JR Kyushu (www.jrkyushu.co.jp), JR Shikoku (www.jr-shikoku.co.jp) and JR West (www.westjr.co.jp).
Services:	Except where noted, all trains convey first and second class seated accommodation (known locally as "Green" and "Standard" respectively). Seat reservation is obligatory in first class and a supplement must be paid. No trains convey restaurant cars, but nearly all main-line services have some kind of refreshment service available, often in the form of box-meals or in vending machines. The few remaining overnight trains have one or two berths in first class and 2 or 4 berths in second. Trains are very punctual and delays are rare.
Timings:	The latest available timings are shown. The availability of english language timetable information varies by operator. An english language booklet of timetables for high-speed and principal long distance trains is available on application from the Japan National Tourism Organization in London (℘ 020 7398 5678 or www.seejapan.co.uk), however it does not list all stations. Much more detailed information can be obtained using the Hyperdia Timetable and Route Search website, which is also available in english (www.hyperdia.com/en).
Tickets:	Tickets can be purchased from windows or machines at stations. A basic one-class fare structure applies according to the distance travelled. Rural lines have a slightly higher fare. Supplements are payable for travel on high-speed and express services, for the use of first class, and in some cases where a JR group train uses the line of a private operator.
Passes:	The Japanese Railways Group offers the Japan Rail Pass (www.japanrailpass.net). To qualify for a pass you must enter the country under the status of "temporary visitor" and your passport must be endorsed with this stamp. When you purchase your pass, which cannot be done in Japan, you will receive an Exchange Order which must be exchanged, within 3 months, for an actual pass. This is done at any of 43 JR stations most of which do not open until 1000. The JR Pass is not valid on Nozomi and Mizuho trains and a supplement is payable for any sleeping berths, but it is valid for all other JR Group Railways, some JR buses and the JR ferry from Miyajima to Miyajimaguchi. You can travel in a higher class by paying the relevant supplements. The pass is valid from the date it is first used. Ages for the child pass are from 6 to 11.
	Prices: Adult first (Green) class 7 Day ¥38800/14 Day ¥ 62950/21 Day ¥84870, Adult second (Ordinary) class 7 Day ¥29110/14 Day ¥46390/21 Day ¥59350. Child first (Green) class 7 Day ¥19440/14 Day ¥31470/21 Day ¥40930, Child second (Ordinary) class 7 Day ¥14550/14 Day ¥23190/21 Day ¥29670. A variety of more region specific passes are also available.

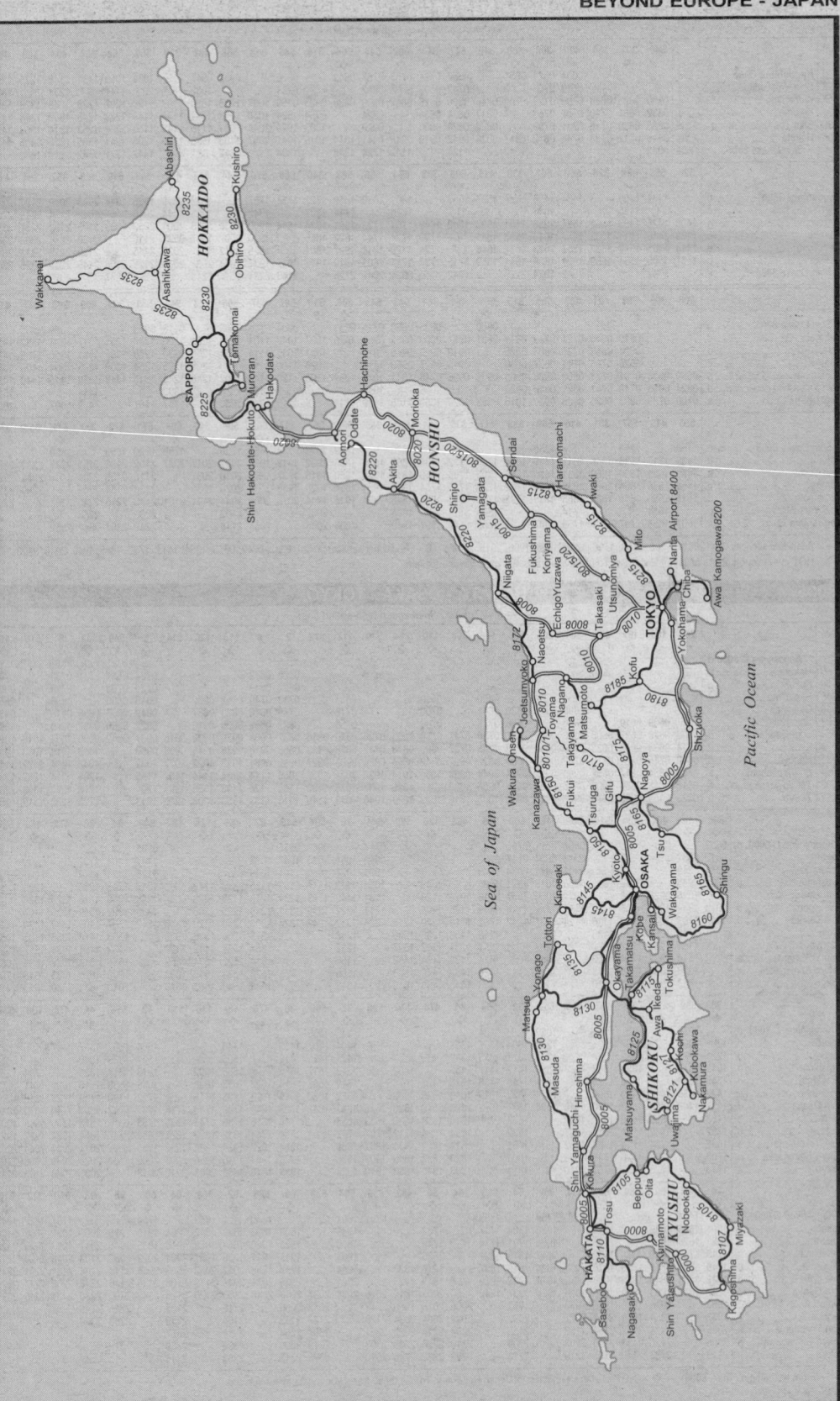

8000 KAGOSHIMA - HAKATA

JR Kyushu

Kyushu Shinkansen high-speed line

km		540	302 A	304	400	308	600 ❖	310	542	314	602 ❖	544	604 ❖	316	546	318	548	402	320	550	552	554	404	556	40
0	**Kagoshima** Chuo d.	...	...	...	0604	0621	0651	...	0657	0724	0753	0757	0849	...	0856	...	0935	0947	...	1034	1059	1134	1146	1235	125
126	Shin Yatsushiro d.	...	...	...	0649	0706	|	...	0742	0809	|	0842	|	...	0941	...	|	1032	...	|	1144	|	1231	|	133
158	Kumamoto d.	0600	0623	0639	0706	0723	0742	0746	0800	0826	0842	0900	0938	0923	0959	1007	1028	1050	1107	1128	1202	1228	1248	1328	135
224	Kurume d.	0632	0654	0710	0727	0755	|	0817	0824	0858	|	0924	|	0954	1024	1039	1048	1111	1138	1149	1223	1248	1309	1348	141
230	Shin Tosu d.	0635	0659	0715	0731	0759	|	0822	0828	0906	|	0929	|	1003	1029	1044	1053	1115	1143	1153	1228	1253	1314	1353	142
256	**Hakata** a.	0649	0712	0728	0744	0812	0817	0836	0842	0919	0915	0941	1011	1018	1041	1057	1105	1128	1155	1206	1241	1305	1326	1405	143
	Shin Osaka **8005** a.	0942	...	...	...	...	1042	...	1124	...	1142	1224	1242	...	1324	...	1342	...	...	1442	1524	1542	...	1642	...

	326	558	408	328	560	562	330	410	606 ❖	332	564	566	568	340	608 ❖	570	344	572	412	348	610 ❖	458	352	354	414
Kagoshima Chuo d.	...	1334	1350	...	1434	1454	...	1527	1553	...	1601	1630	1659	1722	1754	1757	...	1822	1859	1925	1944	2003	2049	2134	221
Shin Yatsushiro d.	...	|	1435	...	|	1546	...	|	|	...	1646	|	1744	1807	|	1842	...	1908	1944	2010	|	2048	2134	2219	225
Kumamoto d.	1408	1428	1453	1501	1527	1558	1601	1620	1642	1649	1704	1723	1801	1824	1844	1900	1936	1926	2001	2039	2033	2105	2152	2237	231
Kurume d.	1439	1448	1514	1533	1547	1619	1633	1641	|	1720	1724	1744	1822	1856	|	1920	2007	1947	2022	2110	|	2126	2224	2308	233
Shin Tosu d.	1444	1453	1518	1537	1552	1623	1637	1646	|	1724	1729	1748	1827	1901	|	1925	2012	1951	2027	2115	|	2130	2228	2313	234
Hakata a.	1457	1505	1531	1550	1604	1636	1651	1659	1715	1737	1741	1801	1840	1913	1917	1937	2024	2004	2039	2128	2106	2145	2243	2325	235
Shin Osaka **8005** a.	...	1742	...	...	1842	1924	...	...	1942	...	2034	2048	2125	...	2142	2221	...	2249	...	...	2337	...	...	...	...

	303	305	307	401	403	405	313	601 ❖	451	541	543	545	603 ❖	319 B	547	407	605 ❖	323	549	551	325	409	553	327	41
Shin Osaka **8005** d.	...	...	...	...	...	...	...	0600	...	0625	0650	0715	0753	...	0804	...	0859	...	0918	0959	...	...	1059	...	...
Hakata d.	...	...	0610	0645	0721	0749	0811	0831	0857	0909	0932	0958	1020	1007	1042	1101	1128	1151	1206	1236	1251	1317	1336	1352	141
Shin Tosu d.	...	...	0624	0658	0737	0803	0826	|	0910	0922	0946	1012	|	1021	1055	1114	|	1205	1220	1250	1305	1331	1350	1405	143
Kurume d.	...	...	0628	0703	0741	0807	0830	|	0915	0927	0950	1016	|	1026	1100	1119	|	1209	1225	1254	1309	1335	1354	1409	143
Kumamoto d.	0606	0638	0701	0723	0803	0828	0908	0905	0936	0948	1011	1037	1054	1103	1120	1140	1202	1240	1245	1315	1345	1356	1415	1440	145
Shin Yatsushiro d.	0624	0655	0719	0741	0821	0846	0926	|	|	1006	|	1055	|	...	|	1158	|	...	1303	|	...	1414	|	...	151
Kagoshima Chuo a.	0709	0739	0803	0825	0905	0930	1010	0953	1029	1050	1105	1139	1144	...	1213	1242	1250	...	1347	1407	...	1459	1507	...	155

	555	413	557	331	415	559	333	417	335	561	563	339	565	567	343	607 ❖	569	347	609 ❖	571	573	353	611 ❖	355	377
Shin Osaka **8005** d.	1159	...	1259	...	...	1359	...	...	...	1459	1520	...	1559	1620	...	1659	1720	...	1759	1820	1859	...	1959	...	...
Hakata d.	1436	1517	1536	1546	1617	1636	1644	1708	1722	1736	1802	1816	1836	1902	1919	1932	2002	2017	2027	2102	2136	2151	2227	2232	230
Shin Tosu d.	1450	1531	1550	1559	1631	1650	1658	1722	1735	1750	1818	1829	1850	1916	1933	|	2016	2031	|	2116	2150	2204	|	2245	232
Kurume d.	1454	1535	1554	1604	1635	1654	1702	1726	1740	1754	1822	1834	1854	1920	1938	|	2020	2035	|	2120	2154	2209	|	2250	232
Kumamoto d.	1515	1556	1615	1634	1656	1715	1733	1748	1811	1815	1848	1904	1915	1944	2015	2006	2044	2111	2101	2143	2215	2240	2301	2320	235
Shin Yatsushiro d.	|	1614	|	...	1714	|	...	1805	...	|	1905	...	|	2002	...	|	2102	...	|	2200	|	2258	|	...	...
Kagoshima Chuo a.	1607	1658	1707	...	1759	1807	...	1850	...	1907	1949	...	2008	2046	...	2054	2146	...	2150	2245	2307	2342	2352	...	...

A – Additional services 0711, 0810, 1208, 1308, 1708, 1735, 1806, 1906, 2015, 2119. B – Additional services: 0700, 0732, 0842, 0916, 1054, 1448, 1752, 1845, 1946, 2045, 2122.

❖ – NOT available to holders of Japan Rail Pass. To use these trains you must pay the full fare.

8005 HAKATA - OSAKA - TOKYO

JR Central, JR West

Sanyo and *Tokaido Shinkansen* high-speed lines

km		200 ❖	100 ❖	102 ❖	504	104 ❖	506	106 ❖	108 ❖	508	110 ❖	214 ❖	510	112 ❖	512	2 ❖	4 ❖	118 ❖	120 ❖	514	6 ❖	540 k	122 ❖	8 ❖	516	10 ❖
	Kagoshima C **8000** d.	...	...	...	...	...	...	...	...	...	...	...	...	...	...	...	...	...	...	...	...	...	...	...	...	...
0	**Hakata** d.	...	...	...	...	...	...	...	...	...	...	...	...	...	...	0605	0632	...	...	...	0704	0651	...	0732	...	074
56	Kokura d.	...	...	...	...	...	...	...	...	...	...	...	...	...	...	0622	0649	...	...	...	0721	0708	...	0749	...	080
248	Hiroshima d.	...	...	...	...	...	...	...	0600	...	0619	...	...	0637	...	0713	0740	0752	0800	...	0813	0806	...	0835	...	085
393	Okayama d.	...	...	...	...	0600	...	0620	0641	...	0700	...	...	0718	...	0749	0816	0833	0837	...	0849	0853	0858	0916	...	093
521	Shin Kobe d.	...	0609	0619	...	0636	...	0656	0716	...	0736	...	...	0756	...	0822	0849	0906	0916	...	0922	0930	0936	0949	...	100
554	Shin **Osaka** d.	0600	0623	0633	0608	0650	0627	0710	0730	0717	0750	0803	0726	0810	0816	0837	0903	0920	0930	0916	0937	0942	0950	1003	1016	102
593	Kyoto d.	0614	0638	0648	0623	0706	0642	0726	0745	0732	0805	0818	0742	0826	0833	0853	0918	0936	0945	0933	0953	...	1005	1018	1033	103
727	Nagoya d.	0649	0715	0724	0718	0742	0734	0803	0822	0827	0842	0854	0834	0903	0927	0932	0954	1012	1022	1027	1032	...	1042	1054	1127	111
1044	Shin Yokohama a.	0806	0834	0844	0852	0904	0922	0924	0944	0952	1004	1014	1022	1024	1052	1055	1114	1134	1144	1152	1155	...	1204	1214	1252	123
1063	**Tokyo** Shinagawa a.	0817	0846	0856	0903	0916	0933	0936	0956	1003	1016	1026	1033	1036	1103	1106	1126	1146	1156	1203	1206	...	1216	1226	1303	124
1069	**Tokyo** a.	0823	0853	0903	0910	0923	0940	0943	1003	1010	1023	1033	1040	1043	1110	1113	1133	1153	1203	1210	1213	...	1223	1233	1310	125

	600 ❖	14 ❖	464	124 ❖	518	542	16 ❖	602 ❖	18 ❖	466	126 ❖	520	544	20 ❖	604 ❖	546	22 ❖	468	128 ❖	522	548	24 ❖	26 ❖	470	130 ❖	524
Kagoshima C **8000**. d.	0652	...	...	...	...	0657	...	0753	...	...	...	...	0757	...	0849	0856	...	...	...	...	0935	...	...	...	...	...
Hakata d.	0817	0832	...	...	...	0843	0904	0917	0932	...	...	...	0943	1004	1013	1043	1032	...	...	...	1107	1104	1132	...	...	...
Kokura d.	0834	0849	...	...	...	0901	0921	0934	0949	...	...	...	1001	1021	1030	1101	1049	...	...	...	1125	1121	1149	...	...	...
Hiroshima d.	0921	0935	...	0949	...	0953	1013	1021	1035	...	1049	...	1053	1113	1117	1153	1135	...	1149	...	1217	1213	1235	...	1252	...
Okayama d.	0957	1016	0928	1028	...	1034	1050	1057	1116	1023	1128	...	1134	1149	1153	1234	1216	1123	1228	...	1258	1249	1316	1223	1328	...
Shin Kobe d.	1029	1049	1025	1106	...	1111	1122	1129	1149	1125	1206	...	1211	1222	1230	1311	1249	1225	1306	...	1330	1322	1349	1325	1406	...
Shin **Osaka** d.	1042	1103	1040	1120	1116	1124	1137	1142	1203	1140	1220	1216	1224	1237	1242	1324	1303	1240	1320	1316	1342	1337	1403	1340	1420	1416
Kyoto d.	...	1118	1056	1136	1133	...	1153	...	1218	1156	1236	1233	...	1253	...	...	1318	1256	1335	1333	...	1353	1418	1356	1435	1433
Nagoya d.	...	1154	1134	1212	1227	...	1232	...	1254	1234	1312	1327	...	1332	...	...	1354	1334	1412	1427	...	1432	1454	1434	1512	1527
Shin Yokohama a.	...	1314	1322	1334	1352	...	1355	...	1414	1422	1434	1452	...	1455	...	...	1514	1522	1534	1552	...	1555	1614	1622	1634	1652
Tokyo Shinagawa a.	...	1326	1333	1346	1403	...	1406	...	1426	1433	1446	1503	...	1506	...	...	1526	1533	1546	1603	...	1606	1626	1633	1646	1703
Tokyo a.	...	1333	1340	1353	1410	...	1413	...	1433	1440	1453	1510	...	1513	...	...	1533	1540	1553	1610	...	1613	1633	1640	1653	1710

	28 ❖	550	232 ❖	30 ❖	132 ❖	526	552	32 ❖	554	34 ❖	474	134 ❖	528	36 ❖	556	38 ❖	476	40 ❖	136 ❖	530	42 ❖	558	44 ❖	478	138 ❖	532
Kagoshima C **8000**. d.	...	1034	...	...	...	...	1059	...	1134	...	...	...	...	...	1235	...	...	...	...	...	...	1334	...	...	...	...
Hakata d.	1204	1208	...	1232	...	...	1243	1304	1307	1332	...	...	...	1404	1407	1432	...	1448	...	...	1504	1507	1532	...	...	...
Kokura d.	1221	1225	...	1249	...	...	1301	1321	1325	1349	...	...	...	1421	1425	1449	...	1505	...	...	1521	1525	1549	...	...	...
Hiroshima d.	1313	1317	...	1335	1352	...	1356	1413	1417	1435	...	1452	...	1513	1517	1535	...	1556	1602	...	1613	1617	1635	...	1704	...
Okayama d.	1349	1358	...	1416	1428	...	1434	1449	1458	1516	1423	1528	...	1549	1558	1616	1523	1632	1638	...	1649	1658	1716	1622	1741	...
Shin Kobe d.	1422	1430	...	1449	1506	...	1511	1522	1530	1549	1525	1606	...	1622	1630	1649	1625	1705	1716	...	1722	1730	1749	1725	1816	...
Shin **Osaka** d.	1437	1442	1450	1503	1520	1516	1524	1537	1542	1603	1540	1620	1616	1637	1642	1703	1640	1720	1730	1716	1737	1742	1803	1740	1830	1816
Kyoto d.	1453	...	1505	1518	1536	1533	...	1553	...	1618	1556	1636	1633	1653	...	1718	1656	1736	1745	1733	1753	...	1818	1756	1845	1833
Nagoya d.	1532	...	1542	1554	1612	1627	...	1632	...	1654	1634	1712	1727	1732	...	1754	1734	1812	1822	1827	1832	...	1854	1834	1922	1927
Shin Yokohama a.	1655	...	1704	1714	1734	1752	...	1755	...	1814	1822	1834	1852	1855	...	1914	1922	1934	1944	1952	1955	...	2014	2022	2044	2052
Tokyo Shinagawa a.	1706	...	1716	1726	1746	1803	...	1806	...	1826	1833	1846	1903	1906	...	1926	1933	1946	1956	2003	2006	...	2026	2033	2056	2103
Tokyo a.	1713	...	1723	1733	1753	1810	...	1813	...	1833	1840	1853	1910	1913	...	1933	1940	1953	2003	2010	2013	...	2033	2040	2103	2110

	48 ❖	560	50 ❖	480	52 ❖	534	562	54 ❖	606 ❖	254 ❖	56 ❖	482	536	564	538	60 ❖	566	62 ❖	568	64 ❖	608 ❖	96 ❖	98 ❖	570	572	610 ❖
Kagoshima C **8000**. d.	...	1434	...	...	...	...	1454	...	1553	...	...	...	...	1601	...	...	1630	...	1659	...	1754	...	...	1757	1822	1944
Hakata d.	1604	1606	1632	...	1648	...	1638	1704	1717	...	1732	...	...	1743	...	1806	1803	1832	1842	1858	1919	1928	2000	1939	2006	2108
Kokura d.	1621	1625	1649	...	1705	...	1655	1721	1734	...	1749	...	...	1800	...	1825	1820	1849	1859	1915	1935	1945	2017	1957	2023	2126
Hiroshima d.	1713	1717	1735	...	1752	...	1747	1813	1821	...	1835	...	...	1903	...	1917	1911	1935	1951	2001	2022	2037	2103	2048	2120	2213
Okayama d.	1749	1758	1816	1723	1828	...	1834	1849	1857	...	1916	1823	...	1944	...	1953	1958	2012	2032	2036	2058	2114	2144	2131	2201	2249
Shin Kobe d.	1822	1830	1849	1825	1906	...	1911	1922	1929	...	1949	1925	...	2021	...	2025	2034	2049	2113	2108	2130	2146	2216	2208	2237	2325
Shin **Osaka** d.	1837	1842	1903	1840	1920	1916	1924	1937	1942	1950	2003	1940	2026	2034	2037	2040	2048	2103	2125	2123	2142	2200	2230	2221	2249	2337
Kyoto d.	1853	...	1918	1856	1936	1933	...	1953	...	2005	2018	1956	2042	...	2053	2056	...	2118	...	2137	...	2215	2246	...	...	...
Nagoya d.	1932	...	1954	1934	2012	2027	...	2032	...	2042	2054	2034	2125	...	2129	2132	...	2154	...	2212	...	2250	2320	...	...	...
Shin Yokohama a.	2055	...	2114	2122	2134	2152	...	2155	...	2204	2214	2222	2251	...	2307	2254	...	2314	...	2327	...	...	...	...	...	...
Tokyo Shinagawa a.	2106	...	2126	2133	2146	2203	...	2206	...	2216	2226	2233	2303	...	2319	2306	...	2325	...	2338	...	...	...	...	...	...
Tokyo a.	2113	...	2133	2140	2153	2210	...	2213	...	2223	2233	2240	2310	...	2326	2313	...	2332	...	2345	...	...	...	...	...	...

k – From Kumamoto (Table **8000**). ❖ – NOT available to holders of Japan Rail Pass. To use these trains you must pay the full fare.

For return service see next page ▷ ▷ ▷

HAKATA - OSAKA - TOKYO 8005

JR Central, JR West

Sanyo and *Tokaido Shinkansen* high-speed lines

	601	541	543	95	545	603	97	547	99	1	3	605	501	5	549	7	461	9	551	11	503	13	463	15	553	17
	❖			❖		❖	❖		❖	❖	❖	❖		❖		❖		❖		❖		❖		❖		❖
okyo d.	...	...	...	...	...	...	...	...	...	0600	0616	...	0626	0630	...	0650	0703	0710	...	0730	0733	0750	0803	0810	...	0830
okyo Shinagawa d.	...	...	...	...	...	...	...	...	0600	0607	0623	...	0634	0637	...	0657	0710	0717	...	0737	0740	0757	0810	0817	...	0837
hin Yokohama d.	...	...	...	...	...	...	...	...	0611	0618	0634	...	0646	0649	...	0709	0722	0729	...	0749	0752	0809	0822	0829	...	0849
agoya d.	...	...	...	0620	...	...	0706	...	0729	0735	0754	...	0821	0812	...	0835	0911	0851	...	0914	0919	0933	1011	0951	...	1014
yoto d.	...	...	...	0656	...	...	0743	...	0803	0809	0830	...	0916	0849	...	0913	0949	0927	...	0952	1013	1010	1049	1027	...	1052
hin **Osaka** d.	0600	0625	0650	0712	0715	0753	0759	0804	0818	0824	0845	0859	0930	0905	0918	0929	1005	0942	0959	1009	1026	1025	1105	1042	1059	1109
hin Kobe d.	0613	0638	0703	0725	0729	0806	0812	0817	0832	0838	0859	0913	...	0919	0932	0942	1019	0956	1012	1023	...	1039	1119	1056	1112	1123
kayama d.	0651	0716	0741	0757	0807	0839	0844	0855	0904	0910	0931	0946	...	0951	1011	1020	1123	1028	1046	1056	...	1111	1220	1128	1146	1156
iroshima d.	0727	0757	0822	0838	0848	0915	0920	0936	0940	0951	1007	1023	...	1032	1052	1056	...	1109	1127	1132	...	1147	...	1209	1227	1232
okura d.	0813	0851	0913	0925	0940	1002	1012	1023	1032	1037	1059	1110	...	1119	1147	1143	...	1156	1218	1223	...	1239	...	1256	1318	1323
akata a.	0829	0907	0930	0941	0956	1018	1028	1040	1048	1053	1115	1126	...	1135	1204	1159	...	1211	1234	1240	...	1255	...	1311	1334	1339
Kagoshima C **8000** a.	0953	1050	1105	...	1139	1144	...	1213	...	...	...	1250	...	...	1347	...	...	...	1407	...	...	...	...	...	1507	...

	505	103	465	19	555	21	507	105	467	23	557	25	509	225	469	27	559	29	511	109	471	31	561	33	563	513
		❖		❖		❖		❖		❖		❖		❖		❖		❖		❖		❖		❖		
okyo d.	0833	0850	0903	0910	...	0930	0933	0950	1003	1010	...	1030	1033	1100	1103	1110	...	1130	1133	1150	1203	1210	...	1230	...	1233
okyo Shinagawa d.	0840	0857	0910	0917	...	0937	0940	0957	1010	1017	...	1037	1040	1107	1110	1117	...	1137	1140	1157	1210	1217	...	1237	...	1240
hin Yokohama d.	0852	0909	0922	0929	...	0949	0952	1009	1022	1029	...	1049	1052	1119	1122	1129	...	1149	1152	1209	1222	1229	...	1249	...	1252
agoya d.	1019	1033	1111	1051	...	1114	1119	1133	1211	1151	...	1214	1219	1242	1311	1251	...	1314	1319	1333	1411	1351	...	1414	...	1419
yoto d.	1113	1110	1148	1127	...	1152	1213	1210	1248	1227	...	1252	1313	1319	1349	1327	...	1352	1413	1410	1449	1427	...	1452	...	1513
hin **Osaka** d.	1126	1125	1205	1142	1159	1209	1226	1225	1305	1242	1259	1309	1326	1333	1405	1342	1359	1409	1426	1425	1505	1442	1459	1509	1520	1526
hin Kobe d.	...	1139	1219	1156	1212	1223	...	1239	1319	1256	1312	1323	...	...	1419	1356	1412	1423	...	1439	1519	1456	1512	1523	1534	...
kayama d.	...	1216	1320	1228	1246	1256	...	1316	1420	1328	1346	1356	...	...	1520	1428	1446	1456	...	1516	1620	1528	1546	1556	1612	...
iroshima d.	...	1252	...	1309	1327	1332	...	1352	...	1409	1427	1432	...		...	1509	1526	1532	...	1553	...	1609	1627	1632	1653	...
okura d.	...	...	...	1356	1418	1423	...	...	...	1456	1518	1523	...	...	...	1556	1618	1623	...	...	...	1656	1718	1723	1744	...
akata a.	...	...	...	1411	1434	1439	...	...	...	1511	1534	1539	...	...	...	1611	1634	1639	...	...	...	1711	1734	1739	1800	...
Kagoshima C **8000** a.	...	...	...	...	1607	...	...	...	...	...	1707	...	...	...	...	...	1807	...	...	...	...	...	1907	...	1949	...

	111	473	35	565	37	567	515	113	475	39	607	41	569	517	115	477	43	609	45	519	571	117	479	47	573	49
	❖		❖		❖			❖		❖	❖	❖			❖		❖	❖	❖			❖		❖		❖
okyo d.	1250	1303	1310	...	1330	...	1333	1350	1403	1410	...	1430	...	1433	1450	1503	1510	...	1530	1533	...	1550	1603	1610	...	1630
okyo Shinagawa d.	1257	1310	1317	...	1337	...	1340	1357	1410	1417	...	1437	...	1440	1457	1510	1517	...	1537	1540	...	1557	1610	1617	...	1637
hin Yokohama d.	1309	1322	1329	...	1349	...	1352	1409	1422	1429	...	1449	...	1452	1509	1522	1529	...	1549	1552	...	1609	1622	1629	...	1649
lagoya d.	1433	1511	1451	...	1514	...	1519	1533	1611	1551	...	1614	...	1619	1633	1711	1651	...	1714	1719	...	1733	1811	1751	...	1814
yoto d.	1510	1548	1527	...	1552	...	1613	1610	1648	1627	...	1652	...	1713	1710	1749	1727	...	1752	1813	...	1810	1849	1827	...	1852
hin **Osaka** d.	1525	1605	1542	1559	1609	1620	1626	1625	1705	1642	1659	1709	1720	1726	1725	1805	1742	1759	1809	1826	1820	1825	1905	1842	1859	1909
hin Kobe d.	1539	1619	1556	1612	1623	1634	...	1639	1719	1656	1712	1723	1734	...	1739	1819	1756	1813	1823	...	1834	1839	1919	1856	1912	1923
kayama d.	1616	1720	1628	1646	1656	1712	...	1716	1820	1728	1750	1756	1812	...	1816	1920	1828	1846	1856	...	1912	1916	2020	1928	1946	1956
iroshima d.	1656	...	1709	1726	1732	1753	...	1756	...	1809	1826	1832	1853	...	1856	...	1904	1922	1932	...	1953	1956	...	2004	2027	2032
okura d.	...	...	1756	1818	1823	1844	...	...	...	1856	1913	1923	1944	...	...	...	1956	2009	2023	...	2044	...	...	2056	2118	2123
akata a.	...	...	1811	1834	1839	1900	...	...	...	1911	1930	1939	2000	...	...	...	2011	2025	2039	...	2100	...	...	2111	2134	2139
Kagoshima C **8000** a.	...	...	...	2008	...	2046	...	...	...	...	2054	...	2146	...	...	...	...	2150	...	...	2245	...	...	...	2307	...

	521	51	481	53	611	55	523	119	765	121	57	123	527	59	529	125	127	531	129	257	533	131	133	135	263	265
		❖		❖	❖	❖		❖		❖	❖	❖		❖		❖	❖		❖	❖		❖	❖	❖	❖	❖
okyo d.	1633	1650	1703	1710	...	1730	1733	1750	...	1800	1810	1830	1833	1850	1903	1910	1930	1933	1950	2000	2003	2010	2030	2050	2110	2123
okyo Shinagawa d.	1640	1657	1710	1717	...	1737	1740	1757	...	1807	1817	1837	1840	1857	1910	1917	1937	1940	1957	2007	2010	2017	2037	2057	2117	2130
hin Yokohama d.	1652	1709	1722	1729	...	1749	1752	1809	...	1819	1829	1849	1852	1909	1922	1929	1949	1952	2009	2019	2022	2029	2049	2109	2129	2142
lagoya d.	1819	1833	1911	1851	...	1914	1919	1933	...	1942	1951	2014	2019	2033	2111	2051	2114	2119	2133	2142	2210	2151	2212	2233	2250	2258
yoto d.	1913	1910	1949	1927	...	1952	2013	2010	...	2019	2027	2052	2113	2110	2203	2127	2152	2213	2210	2219	2302	2227	2250	2309	2326	2332
hin **Osaka** d.	1926	1925	2005	1942	1959	2009	2026	2026	2052	2035	2042	2109	2126	2126	2216	2142	2209	2226	2226	2233	2316	2242	2306	2325	2339	2345
hin Kobe d.	...	1939	2019	1956	2013	2023	...	2039	2105	2048	2056	2122	...	2139	...	2156	2222	...	2239	...	...	2256	2320	2339	...	...
kayama d.	...	2016	2111	2028	2046	2056	...	2116	2152	2124	2129	2200	...	2213	...	2232	2259	...	2313	...	...	2332	2357	...	...	...
iroshima d.	...	2052	...	2109	2122	2132	...	2156	...	...	2205	2240	...	2250	...	2312	...	...	2354	...	...	...	...	...	...	...
okura d.	...	2140	...	2156	2209	2223	...	...	...	...	2256	...	...	2341	...	...	...	...	...	...	...	...	...	...	...	...
akata a.	...	2155	...	2211	2225	2239	...	...	...	...	2311	...	...	2356	...	...	...	...	...	...	...	...	...	...	...	...
Kagoshima C **8000** a.	...	...	...	...	2352	...	...	...	...	...	...	...	...	...	...	...	...	...	...	...	...	...	...	...	...	...

❖ – NOT available to holders of Japan Rail Pass. To use these trains you must pay the full fare.

TOKYO - ECHIGO YUZAWA - NIIGATA 8008

JR East JR West

Joetsu Shinkansen high-speed line

km		481	301	401	303	305	403	307	309	311	313	315	317	319	321	323	325	327	329	331	333	405	335	337
0	**Tokyo** **8010/15/20** d.	...	0608	0636	0700	0748	0804	0824	0852	0912	0928	1016	1040	1140	1240	1340	1440	1516	1540	1616	1640	1708	1716	1740
4	**Tokyo** Ueno **8010/15/20** d.	...	0614	0642	0706	0754	0810	0830	0858	|	0934	1022	1046	1146	1246	1346	1446	1522	1546	1622	1646	1714	1722	1746
31	Omiya **8010/15/20** d.	...	0634	0702	0726	0814	0830	0850	0918	0935	0954	1042	1105	1206	1306	1406	1506	1542	1606	1642	1706	1734	1742	1806
109	Takasaki d.	...	0659	0737	0811	0839	0906	0919	0950	|	1027	1105	1134	1231	1331	1431	1531	|	1631	1713	1731	1806	1816	1834
183	**Echigo Yuzawa** d.	0700	0724	0806	0836	0909	0935	0945	1025	|	1053	1136	1200	1301	1401	1501	1601	|	1701	|	1801	1835	1842	1904
245	Nagaoka d.	0726	0750	...	0846	0935	...	1008	1052	|	1114	1201	1221	1326	1427	1526	1626	1645	1726	1754	1828	...	1903	1931
269	Tsubame Sanjo d.	0737	0800	...	0859	0946	...	1018	1102	|	1124	1211	1231	1336	1437	1536	1636	|	1736	1804	1839	...	1913	1941
301	**Niigata** a.	0750	0813	...	...	0959	...	1031	1115	1049	1136	1223	1243	1348	1450	1548	1648	1704	1747	1816	1852	...	1925	1954

	407	339	409	411	341	413	343	415	345	347	349	473	351	417	475								
Tokyo **8010/15/20** d.	1752	1812	1816	1832	1852	1912	1936	1952	2004	2024	2052	2112	2140	2228	2300	...	...	...	...	...	...	...	...
Tokyo Ueno **8010/15/20** d.	1758	1818	1822	1838	1858	1918	1942	1958	2010	2030	2058	2118	2146	2234	2306	...	...	...	...	...	...	...	...
Omiya **8010/15/20** d.	1818	1838	1842	1858	1918	1938	2002	2018	2030	2050	2118	2138	2206	2254	2326	...	...	...	...	...	...	...	...
Takasaki d.	1850	1902	1916	1931	1950	2011	2031	2057	|	2123	2153	2210	2239	2326	2358	...	...	...	...	...	...	...	...
Echigo Yuzawa d.	1920	1929	1945	2000	2016	2040	2058	2126	|	2153	2223	...	2309	2355	...	...	...	...	...	...	...	...	...
Nagaoka d.	...	1950	...	...	2042	...	2119	...	2134	2219	2244	...	2333	...	...	...	...	...	...	...	...	...	...
Tsubame Sanjo d.	...	2000	...	...	2052	...	2129	...	2144	2230	2254	...	2343	...	...	...	...	...	...	...	...	...	...
Niigata a.	...	2012	...	...	2105	...	2141	...	2156	2243	2306	...	2356	...	...	...	...	...	...	...	...	...	...

	470	400	472	300	402	302	304	404	306	308	310	312	406	314	408	316	410	318		320	322	324	326
Niigata d.	...	...	...	0605	...	0631	0656	...	0719	0751	0825	0904	...	0920	...	1015	...	1119	...	1218	1319	1413	1419
Tsubame Sanjo d.	...	...	...	0617	...	0644	0709	...	0731	0804	0837	|	...	0932	...	1028	...	1131	...	1231	1331	|	1431
Nagaoka d.	...	...	...	0628	...	0655	0720	...	0742	0815	0848	|	...	0943	...	1039	...	1142	...	1242	1342	1432	1442
Echigo Yuzawa d.	...	0607	...	|	0708	0722	|	0748	0808	0842	0909	|	0928	1009	1030	1105	1130	1208	...	1308	1408	|	1508
Takasaki d.	0617	0637	0653	0713	0738	0748	0802	0817	0838	0912	0934	|	1003	1034	1102	1135	1202	1238	...	1338	1438	|	1538
Omiya **8010/15/20** d.	0651	0710	0727	0747	0815	0823	0835	0851	0915	0939	1003	1020	1035	1103	1135	1203	1235	1303	...	1403	1503	1535	1603
Tokyo Ueno **8010/15/20** d.	0711	0731	0747	0807	0835	0843	0855	0911	0935	0959	1023	|	1055	1123	1155	1223	1255	1323	...	1423	1523	1555	1623
Tokyo **8010/15/20** a.	0716	0736	0752	0812	0840	0848	0900	0916	0940	1004	1028	1043	1100	1128	1200	1228	1300	1328	...	1428	1528	1600	1628

	328	330	332	334	336	338	340	342	412	344	346	414	348	416	350								
Niigata d.	1504	1513	1609	1623	1649	1723	1744	1812	...	1856	1916	...	2018	...	2134	...	...	...	...	...	...	...	...
Tsubame Sanjo d.	1516	1525	1622	1635	1701	1735	1756	1824	...	1908	1929	...	2031	...	2147	...	...	...	...	...	...	...	...
Nagaoka d.	1527	1536	1633	1646	1712	1746	1807	1835	...	1919	1940	...	2042	...	2158	...	...	...	...	...	...	...	...
Echigo Yuzawa d.	1548	1602	|	1712	1733	1812	1828	1901	1913	1940	2006	2036	2109	2140	2224	...	...	...	...	...	...	...	...
Takasaki d.	|	1631	|	1742	1803	1842	1858	|	1942	2010	2035	2107	2138	2210	2250	...	...	...	...	...	...	...	...
Omiya **8010/15/20** d.	1635	1703	1725	1815	1835	1915	1927	1947	2015	2035	2103	2143	2203	2243	2315	...	...	...	...	...	...	...	...
Tokyo Ueno **8010/15/20** d.	1655	1723	1755	1835	1855	1935	1947	2007	2035	2055	2123	2203	2223	2303	2335	...	...	...	...	...	...	...	...
Tokyo **8010/15/20** a.	1700	1728	1800	1840	1900	1940	1952	2012	2040	2100	2128	2208	2228	2308	2340	...	...	...	...	...	...	...	...

8010 TOKYO - NAGANO - TOYAMA - KANAZAWA

JR East JR West

Hokuriku Shinkansen high-speed line

km		591	501 R	551	601	503 R	603	553	521	505 R	555	507 R	557	605 A	509 R	559	607	561	609	563	611	565	613	567
0	**Tokyo** 8008/15/20 d.	...	0616	0628	0652	0720	0724	0752	0812	0836	0844	0920	0932	0944	1024	1032	1104	1124	1204	1224	1304	1324	1404	142
4	**Tokyo** Ueno 8008/15/20 d.	...	0622	0634	0658	0726	0730	0758	0818	0842	0850	0926	0938	0950	|	1038	1110	1130	1210	1230	1310	1330	1410	143
31	Omiya 8008/15/20 d.	...	0642	0654	0718	0746	0750	0818	0838	0902	0909	0946	0958	1010	1048	1058	1130	1150	1230	1250	1330	1350	1430	145
109	Takasaki d.	...	|	0719	0749	|	0823	0843	|	|	0934	|	|	1042	|	1123	1202	1216	1302	1316	1402	1416	1502	151
151	Karuizawa d.	...	|	0735	0810	|	0844	0900	|	|	0950	|	1035	1103	|	1140	1218	|	1323	|	1418	|	1523	|
194	Ueda d.	...	|	0754	0828	|	0902	0918	|	|	1009	|	1054	1121	|	1155	1237	|	1341	|	1437	|	1541	|
226	**Nagano** d.	0611	0740	0808	0840	0845	0914	0932	0941	1002	1021	1047	1107	1133	1146	1209	1248	1254	1353	1358	1448	1454	1553	155
285	Joetsumyoko d.	0635	|	0931	...	|	...	0958	|	|	1048	|	1130	...	|	1235	...	1312	...	1421	...	1512	...	162
392	**Toyama** d.	0716	0827	0912	...	0932	...	1039	1028	1049	1129	1135	1212	...	1233	1317	...	1353	...	1502	...	1553	...	170
412	Shin Takaoka d.	0725	|	0921	...	|	...	1048	|	|	1138	|	1221	...	|	1326	...	1402	...	1511	...	1602	...	171
454	**Kanazawa** a.	0738	0846	0935	...	0951	...	1102	1047	1108	1152	1154	1235	...	1252	1339	...	1416	...	1525	...	1616	...	172

		615	569	617	511 R	571	619	513 R	621	573	515 R	623	575	517 R	625	539	577	627	519 R	629	631		
Tokyo 8008/15/020 d.	...	1504	1524	1552	1624	1632	1652	1724	1732	1804	1824	1840	1904	1924	1932	1956	2012	2036	2104	2132	2208	...	...
Tokyo Ueno 8008/15/20 d.	...	1510	1530	1558	1630	1638	1658	1730	1738	1810	1830	1846	1910	1930	1938	2002	2018	2042	2110	2138	2214	...	...
Omiya 8008/15/20 d.	...	1530	1550	1618	1650	1658	1718	1750	1758	1830	1850	1906	1930	1950	1958	2022	2038	2102	2130	2158	2234	...	...
Takasaki d.	...	1602	1616	1650	|	1723	1750	|	1827	|	|	1934	1956	|	2023	|	2104	2127	|	2227	2302	...	...
Karuizawa d.	...	1618	1632	1711	|	1739	1806	|	1848	1911	|	1955	2013	|	2044	|	2121	2149	|	2248	2323	...	...
Ueda d.	...	1637	|	1730	|	1758	1825	|	1906	1931	|	2014	2032	|	2103	|	2140	2206	|	2307	2342	...	...
Nagano d.	...	1649	1657	1742	1748	1812	1837	1851	1918	1955	1951	2026	2055	2051	2114	2121	2154	2218	2228	2319	2353	...	...
Joetsumyoko d.	...	...	1716	...	|	1835	...	|	...	2018	|	...	2118	|	...	|	2217	...	|	...	...	...	...
Toyama d.	...	...	1757	...	1835	1916	...	1938	...	2059	2038	...	2159	2138	...	2208	2258	...	2316	...	...	...	...
Shin Takaoka d.	...	...	1806	...	|	1925	...	|	...	2108	|	...	2208	|	...	2216	2307	...	|	...	...	...	...
Kanazawa a.	...	...	1820	...	1854	1938	...	1958	...	2122	2058	...	2222	2158	...	2230	2321	...	2335	...	...	...	...

	600	602	604 B	500 R	606	608	552	502 R	536	610	504 R	554	612	506 R	556	508 R	558	560	614	616	562	618	564
Kanazawa d.	...	...	...	0600	...	...	0612	0700	0708	...	0748	0723	...	0848	0823	0946	0921	1056	...	...	1156	...	1256
Shin Takaoka d.	...	...	...	|	...	...	0628	|	0722	...	|	0737	...	|	0837	|	0939	1110	...	...	1210	...	1310
Toyama d.	...	...	...	0619	...	...	0637	0719	0732	...	0807	0747	...	0907	0847	1005	0945	1119	...	...	1219	...	1319
Joetsumyoko d.	...	...	...	|	...	...	0717	|	|	...	|	0827	...	|	0927	|	1028	1159	...	...	1259	...	1359
Nagano d.	0602	0618	0642	0707	0711	0722	0742	0807	0820	0824	0855	0900	0926	0955	1000	1053	1100	1224	1126	1227	1320	1323	1424
Ueda d.	0614	|	0654	|	0723	0734	0754	|	|	0836	|	0912	0939	|	1012	|	1112	|	1138	1239	|	1336	|
Karuizawa d.	0634	0642	0714	|	0742	0754	0814	|	|	0856	|	0932	0959	|	1032	|	1132	|	1158	1259	|	1355	|
Takasaki d.	0650	0702	0734	|	0758	0814	0830	|	|	0916	|	0948	1019	|	|	|	1148	1301	1218	1315	1401	1415	1501
Omiya 8008/15/20 d.	0715	0735	0759	0807	0827	0843	0855	0907	0919	0947	0955	1015	1047	1055	1115	1155	1215	1327	1247	1347	1427	1447	1527
Tokyo Ueno 8008/15/20 d.	0735	0755	0819	0827	0847	0903	0915	0927	0939	1007	1015	1035	1107	1115	1135	1215	1235	1347	1307	1407	1447	1507	1547
Tokyo 8008/15/20 a.	0740	0800	0824	0832	0852	0908	0920	0932	0944	1012	1020	1040	1112	1120	1140	1220	1240	1352	1312	1412	1452	1512	1552

	620	566	622	568	624	530	626	570	510 R	572	512 R	574	514 R	576	516 R		630	578	518 R	590			
Kanazawa d.	...	1356	...	1450	...	1552	...	1609	1647	1650	1751	1809	1851	1902	1947	...	...	2017	2100	2135	...	...	...
Shin Takaoka d.	...	1410	...	1504	...	|	...	1623	|	1704	|	1823	|	1916	|	...	...	2031	|	2149	...	...	...
Toyama d.	...	1419	...	1513	...	1612	...	1632	1706	1713	1811	1832	1911	1925	2006	...	...	2041	2120	2158	...	...	...
Joetsumyoko d.	...	1459	...	1553	...	|	...	1713	|	1757	|	1913	|	2009	|	...	...	2121	|	2238	...	...	...
Nagano d.	1427	1520	1523	1618	1623	1700	1709	1734	1755	1822	1859	1938	1959	2034	2055	...	2115	2146	2208	2302	...	...	...
Ueda d.	1439	|	1536	1630	1636	|	1721	1746	|	1834	|	1950	|	2046	|	...	2127	2158	|	...	...	...	...
Karuizawa d.	1459	|	1555	1646	1655	|	1740	1806	|	1854	|	2009	|	2105	|	...	2147	2218	|	...	...	...	...
Takasaki d.	1515	1601	1615	1715	1715	|	1800	1822	|	1910	|	2026	|	2121	|	...	2207	2234	|	...	...	...	...
Omiya 8008/15/20 d.	1547	1627	1647	1727	1747	1803	1827	1847	1855	1935	1959	2051	2057	2147	2155	...	2235	2259	2307	...	...	...	...
Tokyo Ueno 8008/15/20 d.	1607	1647	1707	1747	1807	1823	1847	1907	1915	1955	2019	2111	|	2207	2215	...	2255	2319	2327	...	...	...	...
Tokyo 8008/15/20 a.	1612	1652	1712	1752	1812	1828	1852	1912	1920	2000	2024	2116	2119	2212	2220	...	2300	2324	2332	...	...	...	...

8011 TOYAMA - KANAZAWA

JR East JR West

Tsurugi Shinkansen high-speed lines

km		701	703	705	707	709	711	713	715	717	719		721	723	725	727	729	731	733	735			
0	**Toyama** d.	0612	0642	0725	0751	0831	1022	1112	1253	1417	1517	...	1542	1617	1711	1811	1959	2016	2127	2333	...	...	...
19	Shin Takaoka d.	0621	0651	0734	0800	0840	1031	1121	1302	1426	1526	...	1551	1626	1720	1820	2008	2025	2136	2342	...	...	...
59	**Kanazawa** a.	0635	0705	0748	0813	0853	1045	1135	1317	1439	1540	...	1604	1639	1734	1833	2022	2038	2150	2356	...	...	...

		700	702	704	706	708	710	712	714	716	718	720	722	724	726	728	730	732	734			
Kanazawa d.	...	0647	0758	0949	1034	1128	1228	1328	1428	1509	1709	1738	1838	1923	2025	2106	2219	2306	2337	...	...	...
Shin Takaoka d.	...	0701	0812	1003	1048	1142	1242	1342	1442	1523	1723	1752	1852	1937	2039	2120	2233	2320	2351	...	...	...
Toyama d.	...	0710	0821	1012	1057	1151	1251	1351	1451	1532	1732	1801	1901	1946	2048	2129	2242	2329	2359	...	...	...

8015 TOKYO - SHINJO and MORIOKA

JR East

Yamagata and *Tohoku Shinkansen* high-speed line

km		41	121	201	203	123	123	125	205 B	127	127	43	129	129	131	131	45	133	133	47	135	135	49	137	137	51
0	**Tokyo** 8010/20 d.	0604	0612	0620	0640	0712	0712	0732	0744	0808	0808	0848	0856	0856	0924	0924	0940	1000	1000	1036	1100	1100	1136	1200	1200	1236
4	**Tokyo** Ueno 8010/20 d.	0610	0618	0626	0646	0718	0718	0738	0750	0814	0814	0854	0902	0902	|	|	0946	1006	1006	1042	1106	1106	1142	1206	1206	1242
31	Omiya 8010/20 d.	0630	0638	0646	0706	0738	0738	0758	0810	0834	0834	0914	0922	0922	0948	0948	1006	1026	1026	1102	1126	1126	1202	1226	1226	1302
109	Utsunomiya d.	0654	0702	0719	0737	0806	0806	0824	0844	0905	0905	0939	0946	0946	|	|	1031	1050	1050	1131	1150	1150	1229	1250	1250	1331
214	Koriyama d.	0725	0731	0757	0822	0834	0834	0856	0926	0933	0933	1007	1017	1017	|	|	1059	1119	1119	1200	1219	1219	1257	1319	1319	1402
255	Fukushima d.	0740	0747	0815	0841	0850	0853	0915	0940	0949	0950	1025	1033	1034	1048	1051	1114	1135	1138	1217	1235	1238	1317	1335	1338	1417
295	Yonezawa d.	|	0820	|	|	0926	|	|	|	1025	|	|	1105	|	1121	|	|	1210	|	|	1307	|	|	1409	|	|
342	Yamagata d.	|	0859	|	|	1008	|	|	|	1104	|	|	1137	|	1152	|	|	1246	|	|	1344	|	|	1444	|	|
369	Murayama d.	|	0927	|	|	1031	|	|	|	...	|	|	...	|	1212	|	|	1308	|	|	...	|	|	1507	|	|
404	**Shinjo** a.	|	0955	|	|	1054	|	|	|	...	|	|	...	|	1235	|	|	1331	|	|	...	|	|	1530	|	|
325	Sendai (Honshu) d.	0802	...	0841	0902	...	0919	0938	1006	...	1011	1049	...	1100	...	1114	1136	...	1204	1239	...	1304	1339	...	1404	1439
497	**Morioka** a.	0919	...	...	...	...	...	...	...	...	...	1207	...	...	...	...	1254	...	...	1354	...	...	1454	...	...	1554

	139	139	53	141	141	55	143	143	57	145	145	147	149	149	151	153	153 A	157	157	219	59	159	159	221	223
Tokyo 8010 8020 d.	1300	1300	1336	1400	1400	1436	1500	1500	1536	1600	1600	1636	1700	1700	1728	1800	1800	1916	1916	1928	2020	2044	2044	2056	2144
Tokyo Ueno 8010 8020 d.	1306	1306	1342	1406	1406	1442	1506	1506	1542	1606	1606	1642	1706	1706	1734	1806	1806	1922	1922	1934	2026	2050	2050	2102	2150
Omiya 8010 8020 d.	1326	1326	1402	1426	1426	1502	1526	1526	1602	1626	1626	1702	1726	1726	1754	1826	1826	1942	1942	1954	2046	2110	2110	2122	2210
Utsunomiya d.	1350	1350	1431	1450	1450	1531	1550	1550	1631	1650	1650	1731	1750	1750	1818	1850	1850	2008	2008	2026	2110	2134	2134	2150	2235
Koriyama d.	1419	1419	1502	1519	1519	1602	1619	1619	1702	1719	1719	1800	1819	1819	1855	1919	1919	2038	2038	2103	2138	2203	2203	2228	2308
Fukushima d.	1435	1438	1517	1535	1538	1617	1635	1638	1717	1735	1738	1818	1836	1838	1910	1936	1937	2056	2057	2117	2156	2219	2220	2243	2322
Yonezawa d.	1512	|	|	1611	|	|	1707	|	|	1808	|	|	1909	|	|	2012	|	2128	|	|	|	2251	|	|	|
Yamagata d.	1550	|	|	1650	|	|	1746	|	|	1844	|	|	1945	|	|	2047	|	2159	|	|	|	2326	|	|	|
Murayama d.	...	|	|	1714	|	|	...	|	|	1906	|	|	...	|	|	...	|	2221	|	|	|	...	|	|	|
Shinjo a.	...	|	|	1740	|	|	...	|	|	1929	|	|	...	|	|	...	|	2245	|	|	|	...	|	|	|
Sendai (Honshu) d.	...	1504	1539	...	1604	1639	...	1704	1739	...	1804	1842	...	1904	1930	...	1958	...	2123	2143	2220	...	2246	2303	2347
Morioka a.	...	...	1654	...	...	1754	...	...	1854	...	...	...	...	...	...	...	...	...	...	...	2331	...	...	...	...

A – Additional trip: 1828. **B** – Additional trips: 1012, 1212, 1412, 1612, 1736, 1836.

For return service see next page ▷ ▷ ▷

TOKYO - SHINJO and MORIOKA — 8015

JR East

Yamagata and *Tohoku Shinkansen* high-speed line

	202	204	206 C	120	120	122	122	124	126	128	128	210	130	132	132	134	136	136	42	138	138	212	44	140	140	46
Morioka d.	...	...	...	...	...	...	0631	...	...	...	...	...	...	...	...	...	...	...	1007	...	...	...	1107	...	...	1207
Sendai (Honshu) d.	0606	0624	0650	...	0712	...	0743	0805	0824	...	0844	0900	0924	...	0941	1024	...	1041	1124	...	1144	1200	1224	...	1244	1324
Shinjo d.	|	|	|	0540	|	...	|	|	|	0716	|	|	|	...	|	|	0916	|	|	...	|	|	|	1117	|	|
Murayama d.	|	|	|	0603	|	...	|	|	|	0740	|	|	|	...	|	|	0940	|	|	...	|	|	|	1140	|	|
Yamagata d.	|	|	|	0625	|	0708	|	|	|	0802	|	|	|	0903	|	|	1002	|	|	1057	|	|	|	1208	|	|
Yonezawa d.	|	|	|	0703	|	0738	|	|	|	0840	|	|	|	0937	|	|	1037	|	|	1136	|	|	|	1238	|	|
Fukushima d.	0633	0646	0716	0739	0739	0814	0814	0835	0846	0916	0916	0922	0951	1013	1013	1049	1116	1116	1150	1216	1216	1223	1250	1316	1316	1350
Koriyama d.	0647	0704	0730	0753	0753	|	|	0849	0902	0930	0930	0936	1006	1027	1027	1104	1130	1130	1205	1230	1230	1239	1305	1330	1330	1405
Utsunomiya d.	0723	0742	0810	0822	0822	|	|	0918	0934	0958	0958	1020	1038	1058	1058	1134	1158	1158	1234	1258	1258	1320	1334	1358	1358	1434
Omiya **8010/20** d.	0751	0811	0839	0847	0847	0913	0913	0943	0959	1023	1023	1051	1103	1123	1123	1159	1223	1223	1259	1323	1323	1351	1359	1423	1423	1459
Tokyo Ueno **8010/20** d.	0811	0831	0859	0907	0907	|	|	1003	1019	1043	1043	1111	1123	1143	1143	1219	1243	1243	1319	1343	1343	1411	1419	1443	1443	1519
Tokyo **8010/20** a.	0816	0836	0904	0912	0912	0935	0935	1008	1024	1048	1048	1116	1128	1148	1148	1224	1248	1248	1324	1348	1348	1416	1424	1448	1448	1524

	142	142	214	48	144	144	50	146	146	52	148	148	150	150	152	154	154	156	156	54	56	158	158	58	160	60
Morioka d.	...	...	...	1307	...	...	1407	...	...	1507	...	...	...	...	...	...	...	...	...	1754	1840	...	...	1940	...	2029
Sendai (Honshu) d.	...	1344	1400	1424	...	1444	1524	...	1544	1624	...	1634	...	1644	1725	...	1744	...	1844	1910	2000	...	2017	2054	...	2147
Shinjo d.	...	|	|	|	1318	|	|	...	|	|	...	|	1517	|	|	...	|	1711	|	|	|	1843	|	|	1957	|
Murayama d.	...	|	|	|	1342	|	|	...	|	|	...	|	1542	|	|	...	|	1737	|	|	|	1906	|	|	2021	|
Yamagata d.	1304	|	|	|	1404	|	|	1504	|	|	1546	|	1607	|	|	1705	|	1803	|	|	|	1931	|	|	2043	|
Yonezawa d.	1340	|	|	|	1438	|	|	1540	|	|	1623	|	1638	|	|	1741	|	1838	|	|	|	2012	|	|	2117	|
Fukushima d.	1416	1416	1423	1450	1516	1516	1550	1616	1616	1650	1701	1701	1716	1716	1750	1816	1816	1916	1916	1933	2023	2049	2049	2124	2155	2209
Koriyama d.	1430	1430	1439	1505	1530	1530	1605	1630	1630	1705	1715	1715	1730	1730	1805	1830	1830	1930	1930	1947	2042	2104	2104	2138	2209	2224
Utsunomiya d.	1458	1458	1520	1534	1558	1558	1631	1658	1658	1734	1746	1716	1758	1758	1836	1859	1859	1959	1959	2022	2110	2134	2134	2206	2238	2253
Omiya **8010/20** d.	1523	1523	1551	1559	1623	1623	1659	1723	1723	1759	1811	1811	1823	1823	1903	1923	1923	2023	2023	2047	2135	2159	2159	2231	2303	2319
Tokyo Ueno **8010/20** d.	1543	1543	1611	1619	1643	1643	1719	1743	1743	1819	1831	1831	1843	1843	1923	1943	1943	2043	2043	2107	2155	2219	2219	2251	2323	2339
Tokyo **8010/20** a.	1548	1548	1616	1624	1648	1648	1724	1748	1748	1824	1836	1836	1848	1848	1928	1948	1948	2048	2048	2112	2200	2224	2224	2256	2328	2344

C – Additional trips: 0734, 1600, 1808, 1920, 2037. For return service see previous page ▷ ▷ ▷

TOKYO - AKITA and AOMORI - HAKODATE — 8020

JR East

Akita, Tohoku and Hokkaido Shinkansen high-speed lines

km			91 [R]		93 [R]	95 [R]	95 [R]	1 [R]	1 [R]	111 [R]	3 [R]	3 [R]	101 [R]	5 [R]	7 [R]	7 [R]	9 [R]	9 [R]	11 [R]	13 [R]	13 [R]	15 [R]	17 [R]	17 [R]
0	**Tokyo** 8010 8015 d.	...	...	...	...	...	...	0632	0632	0716	0736	0736	0756	0820	0840	0840	0908	0908	0936	1020	1020	1044	1120	1120
4	**Tokyo** Ueno 8010 8015 d.	...	...	...	...	...	...	0638	0638	0722	0742	0742	0802	|	0846	0846	0914	0914	|	1026	1026	1050	1126	1126
31	Omiya 8010 8015 d.	...	...	...	...	...	...	0658	0658	0742	0802	0802	0822	0844	0906	0906	0933	0933	1000	1046	1046	1110	1146	1146
325	Sendai (Honshu) d.	...	...	...	...	0640	0640	0806	0806	0858	0912	0912	0936	0952	1016	1016	1042	1042	1108	1154	1154	1217	1254	1254
497	Morioka d.	...	...	...	0654	0758	0800	0849	0848	1011	0954	0956	1049	1032	1057	1059	1123	1125	1148	1235	1237	1301	1335	1337
537	Tazawako d.	...	...	...	|	0831	|	|	0921	...	1025	|	...	|	1128	|	1158	|	|	1311	|	...	1407	|
555	Kakunodate d.	...	...	...	|	0845	|	|	0935	...	1039	|	...	|	1142	|	1217	|	|	1325	|	...	1421	|
572	Omagari d.	...	...	...	|	0859	|	|	0947	...	1051	|	...	|	1154	|	1229	|	|	1337	|	...	1433	|
624	**Akita** a.	...	...	...	|	0932	|	|	1024	...	1124	|	...	|	1230	|	1301	|	|	1408	|	...	1504	|
593	Hachinohe d.	...	...	...	0727	...	0836	0922	...	...	...	1032	...	|	...	1127	...	1202	|	...	1305	...	...	1414
675	Shin **Aomori** a.	...	0632	...	0755	...	0904	0950	...	...	...	1100	...	1119	...	1151	...	1229	1235	...	1329	...	...	1443
824	Shin **Hakodate Hokuto** ♥ a.	0654	0738	0814	0903	...	1007	1058	...	...	...	...	...	1222	...	...	...	...	1338	...	1437	...	...	...
842	*Hakodate* ♥ a.	0713	*0809*	0833	*0934*	...	*1046*	*1125*	...	...	...	...	...	*1249*	...	...	...	...	*1406*	...	*1502*	...	...	...

	19 [R]	19 [R]		21 [R]	21 [R]	23 [R]	23 [R]	25 [R]	25 [R]	27 [R]	27 [R]	113 [R]	29 [R]	29 [R]	115 [R]	31 [R]	31 [R]	103 [R]	33 [R]	33 [R]	105 [R]	35 [R]	35 [R]	37 [R]
Tokyo 8010 8015 d.	1220	1220	...	1320	1320	1420	1420	1520	1520	1620	1620	1656	1720	1720	1756	1820	1820	1856	1920	1920	1940	2016	2016	2136
Tokyo Ueno 8010 8015 d.	1226	1226	...	1326	1326	1426	1426	1526	1526	1626	1626	1702	1726	1726	1802	1826	1826	1902	1926	1926	1946	|	|	|
Omiya 8010 8015 d.	1246	1246	...	1346	1346	1446	1446	1546	1546	1646	1646	1722	1746	1746	1822	1846	1846	1922	1946	1946	2006	2040	2040	2200
Sendai (Honshu) d.	1354	1354	...	1454	1454	1554	1554	1654	1654	1754	1754	1839	1854	1854	1939	1954	1954	2030	2055	2055	2115	2148	2148	2307
Morioka d.	1435	1437	...	1535	1537	1635	1637	1735	1737	1835	1837	1954	1935	1937	2054	2035	2037	2143	2136	2138	2223	2230	2231	...
Tazawako d.	1511	|	...	1607	|	1712	|	1809	|	1913	|	...	2008	|	...	2112	|	...	2207	|	...	|	|	...
Kakunodate d.	1525	|	...	1621	|	1728	|	1823	|	1928	|	...	2022	|	...	2125	|	...	2220	|	...	|	|	...
Omagari d.	1537	|	...	1633	|	1741	|	1835	|	1942	|	...	2034	|	...	2138	|	...	2232	|	...	2323	|	...
Akita a.	1608	|	...	1708	|	1812	|	1906	|	2013	|	...	2105	|	...	2208	|	...	2303	|	...	2353	|	...
Hachinohe d.	...	1505	...	...	1614	...	1705	...	1814	...	1909	...	...	2013	...	...	2109	...	...	2206	...	...	2308	...
Shin **Aomori** a.	...	1529	...	...	1643	...	1729	...	1843	...	1937	...	...	2040	...	...	2137	...	...	2230	...	...	2336	...
Shin **Hakodate Hokuto** ♥ a.	...	1634	1730	...	1751	...	1832	...	1950	...	...	...	...	2148	...	...	...	...	...	2333	...	...	...	...
Hakodate ♥ a.	...	*1705*	1749	...	*1820*	...	*1859*	...	*2015*	...	...	...	...	*2229*	...	...	...	...	...	*0005*	...	...	...	...

	2 [R]	102 [R]	4 [R]	112 [R]	6 [R]		8 [R]	104 [R]	10 [R]	10 [R]	114 [R]	12 [R]	12 [R]		14 [R]	14 [R]	16 [R]	16 [R]	18 [R]	18 [R]	20 [R]	20 [R]	22 [R]	22 [R]
Hakodate ♥ d.	...	...	...	...	...	...	...	...	...	*0601*	...	...	*0657*	0746	...	...	...	*0848*	...	*0956*	...	...	...	*1153*
Shin **Hakodate Hokuto** ♥ d.	...	...	...	...	...	...	...	...	...	0635	...	...	0734	0808	...	...	...	0931	...	1049	...	...	...	1244
Shin **Aomori** d.	...	...	0617	...	...	...	0649	...	...	0743	...	...	0837	...	...	0952	...	1039	...	1152	...	1239	...	1352
Hachinohe d.	...	...	0641	...	...	...	0717	...	...	0811	...	...	0905	...	...	1016	...	1107	...	1216	...	1307	...	1416
Akita d.	...	...	|	...	0608	...	|	...	0715	|	...	0810	|	...	0912	|	1006	|	1106	|	1213	|	1306	|
Omagari d.	...	...	|	...	0640	...	|	...	0747	|	...	0842	|	...	0949	|	1038	|	1140	|	1246	|	1339	|
Kakunodate d.	...	...	|	...	|	...	|	...	0757	|	...	0855	|	...	0959	|	1054	|	1156	|	1257	|	1350	|
Tazawako d.	...	...	|	...	|	...	|	...	0811	|	...	0908	|	...	1013	|	1108	|	1210	|	1311	|	1408	|
Morioka d.	...	0610	0711	0716	0736	...	0800	0810	0850	0850	0857	0950	0950	...	1050	1050	1150	1150	1250	1250	1350	1350	1450	1450
Sendai (Honshu) d.	0636	0721	0752	0833	0816	...	0855	0921	0930	0930	1013	1030	1030	...	1130	1130	1230	1230	1330	1330	1430	1430	1530	1530
Omiya 8010 8015 a.	0743	0830	0859	0950	0925	...	1006	1030	1038	1038	1130	1138	1138	...	1238	1238	1338	1338	1438	1438	1538	1538	1638	1638
Tokyo Ueno 8010 8015 a.	|	0851	|	1011	|	...	1026	1050	1058	1058	1150	1158	1158	...	1258	1258	1358	1358	1458	1458	1558	1558	1658	1658
Tokyo 8010 8015 a.	0807	0856	0923	1016	0947	...	1032	1056	1104	1104	1156	1204	1204	...	1304	1304	1404	1404	1504	1504	1604	1604	1704	1704

		24 [R]	24 [R]	106 [R]	26 [R]	26 [R]	108 [R]	28 [R]	28 [R]	30 [R]	30 [R]	32 [R]	32 [R]	34 [R]		36 [R]	36 [R]	38 [R]	38 [R]	96 [R]	96 [R]	98 [R]	100 [R]	
Hakodate ♥ 8225 d.	...	...	*1302*	...	...	*1414*		...	...	...	*1545*	...	...	*1651*	1727	...	...	...	*1801*	...	*1906*	*2000*	*2116*	2213
Shin **Hakodate Hokuto** ♥ d.	...	...	1335	...	...	1444		...	...	...	1617	...	...	1721	1749	...	...	...	1836	...	1937	2039	2159	2235
Shin **Aomori** d.	...	...	1438	...	...	1552	...	...	1638	...	1722	...	1744	1824	...	...	1838	...	1944	...	2040	2147	2305	...
Hachinohe d.	...	...	1506	...	...	1616	...	...	1706	...	|	...	1812	|	...	...	1906	...	2012	...	2108	2215	...	...
Akita d.	...	1413	|	...	1506	|	...	1612	|	1634	|	1710	|	|	...	1817	|	1911	|	2015	|	|	...	...
Omagari d.	...	1447	|	...	1539	|	...	1647	|	1708	|	1743	|	|	...	1849	|	1944	|	2048	|	|	...	...
Kakunodate d.	...	1458	|	...	1551	|	...	1658	|	1718	|	1754	|	|	...	1859	|	1954	|	2058	|	|	...	...
Tazawako d.	...	1512	|	...	1608	|	...	1712	|	1734	|	1810	|	|	...	1913	|	2010	|	2112	|	|	...	...
Morioka d.	...	1550	1550	1607	1650	1650	1707	1750	1750	1815	1815	1850	1850	1913	...	1950	1950	2050	2050	2151	2151	2247	...	...
Sendai (Honshu) d.	...	1630	1630	1721	1730	1730	1821	1830	1830	1857	1857	1930	1930	1953	...	2030	2030	2130	2130	2301	2301	...	...	...
Omiya 8010 8015 a.	...	1738	1738	1830	1838	1838	1930	1938	1938	2006	2006	2038	2038	2100	...	2138	2138	2238	2238	...	...	...	...	...
Tokyo Ueno 8010 8015 a.	...	1758	1758	1850	1858	1858	1950	1958	1958	2025	2026	2058	2058	|	...	2158	2158	2258	2258	...	...	...	...	...
Tokyo 8010 8015 a.	...	1804	1804	1856	1904	1904	1956	2004	2004	2032	2032	2104	2104	2123	...	2204	2204	2304	2304	...	...	...	...	...

♥ – Services to/from Hakodate change at Shin Hakodate Hokuto. NOT [R].

Some trains run on a different schedule on ©.

8105 HAKATA - MIYAZAKI

JR Kyushu

km																										
0	**Hakata** d.	...	...	...	...	...	...	...	0622	...	0700	0731	0802	0823	0902	...	0921	0957	...	1019	1057	...	1119	1157	...	121
67	Kokura d.	...	...	...	...	...	...	0639	0715	...	0800	0833	0857	0917	0948	...	1009	1040	...	1109	1139	...	1209	1239	...	130
186	Beppu d.	...	...	...	...	...	0739	0804	0833	...	0922	0951	1014	1034	1057	...	1128	1150	...	1225	1249	...	1327	1349	...	142
198	Oita d.	...	...	...	...	0700	0750	0815	0844	0909	0932	1006	1024	1044	1106	1111	1138	1200	1207	1235	1258	1304	1336	1359	1406	143
322	Nobeoka d.	0515	0645	0712	0806	0911	...	1028	...	1104	...	1208	...	...	...	1309	...	...	1408	...	...	1512	...	...	1613	...
405	**Miyazaki** a.	0624	0800	0832	0916	1019	...	1136	...	1210	...	1309	...	...	...	1413	...	...	1516	...	...	1624	...	...	1723	...
412	**Miyazaki** Airport a.	0634	0814	0842	0930	1029	...	1147	...	1220	...	1317	...	...	...	1422	...	...	1524	...	...	1632	...	...	1732	...

Hakata d.	1257	...	1319	1357	...	1419	1457	...	1519	1557	...	1619	1657	...	1719	1757	...	1819	1857	1920	1959	2020	2103	2205	225
Kokura d.	1339	...	1409	1439	...	1509	1541	...	1609	1641	...	1709	1741	...	1808	1841	...	1911	1941	2012	2047	2115	2153	2304	235
Beppu d.	1449	...	1525	1550	...	1627	1650	...	1726	1752	...	1827	1852	...	1925	1953	...	2035	2052	2136	2205	2238	2314	0027	011
Oita d.	1459	1504	1535	1600	1605	1636	1700	1706	1736	1802	1805	1837	1906	...	1935	2002	2018	2045	2102	2149	2216	2248	2325	0036	012
Nobeoka d.	...	1730	...	...	1814	...	...	1910	...	...	2017	...	...	2127	...	...	2227	...	...	...	...	...	...	...	...
Miyazaki a.	...	1837	...	...	1925	...	...	2016	...	...	2122	...	...	2236	...	...	2330	...	...	...	...	...	...	...	...
Miyazaki Airport a.	...	1846	...	...	1937	...	...	...	...	...	...	...	...	...	...	...	...	...	...	...	...	...	...	...	...

Miyazaki Airport d.	...	...	...	...	...	...	...	...	...	...	...	...	...	...	...	...	...	...	0925	...	...	1020	...	...	1126	...
Miyazaki d.	...	...	...	...	...	...	...	...	0558	...	...	0700	...	...	0806	...	...	...	0936	...	...	1030	...	...	1136	...
Nobeoka d.	...	...	...	...	...	...	...	...	0706	...	...	0806	...	...	0911	...	...	...	1036	...	...	1141	...	...	1242	...
Oita d.	0445	0521	0558	0640	0713	0746	0810	0842	0908	0910	0939	1006	1011	1045	1108	1111	1145	1210	1238	1245	1311	1340	1345	1411	1440	144
Beppu d.	0453	0530	0606	0648	0722	0755	0818	0851	...	0919	0947	...	1020	1053	...	1120	1153	1218	...	1253	1320	...	1353	1420	...	145
Kokura d.	0613	0650	0731	0810	0844	0919	0939	1005	...	1041	1105	...	1141	1205	...	1241	1305	1341	...	1405	1441	...	1505	1539	...	160
Hakata a.	0716a	0749a	0830b	0855a	0940a	1003	1022c	1047e	...	1128	1148	...	1228	1247	...	1328	1346	1428	...	1446	1528	...	1547	1628	...	164

Miyazaki Airport d.	...	1215	...	...	1321	...	...	1422	...	...	1525	...	1626	...	...	1719	1753	...	1825	1930	2023	...	...	2119	...	...
Miyazaki d.	...	1229	...	...	1331	...	...	1433	...	...	1535	...	1639	...	...	1731	1803	...	1841	1943	2040	...	...	2130	2235	234
Nobeoka d.	...	1338	...	...	1437	...	...	1539	...	...	1641	...	1745	...	...	1840	1918	...	1949	2053	2143	...	...	2235	2346	004
Oita d.	1511	1540	1545	1610	1640	1645	1710	1740	1745	1811	1842	1911	1939	1941	2012	2055	...	2143	2148	...	...	2255	...	...	...	...
Beppu d.	1520	...	1553	1618	...	1653	1718	...	1753	1820	1851	1919	...	1950	2020	2104	...	2151	...	...	...	2304	...	...	...	...
Kokura d.	1639	...	1705	1739	...	1805	1840	...	1905	1943	2009	2041	...	2112	2139	2229	...	2311	...	...	...	...	...	...	...	...
Hakata a.	1728	...	1748	1830	...	1848	1930	...	1947	2030	2057	2128	...	2201	2227	2323	...	2359	...	...	...	...	...	...	...	...

a – Arrival time 2–3 minutes earlier on Ⓒ. b – Arrival time 0819 on Ⓒ. c – Arrival time 1023 on Ⓒ. e – Arrival time 1050 on Ⓒ.

8107 MIYAZAKI - KAGOSHIMA

JR Kyushu

km											
0	**Miyazaki** d.	0557	0716	0815	0919	1015	1225	1416	1621	1736	1855
79	Kirishima-Jingu d.	0717	0836	0938	1038	1137	1342	1537	1739	1855	2022
95	Hayato d.	0733	0852	0954	1057	1154	1359	1553	1756	1912	2041
123	**Kagoshima** d.	0803	0922	1021	1123	1222	1424	1619	1827	1937	2110
126	**Kagoshima** Chuo a.	0807	0926	1025	1127	1226	1428	1623	1831	1941	2114

Kagoshima Chuo d.	0559	0737	0849	0959	1150	1419	1618	1716	1828	2021
Kagoshima d.	0603	0741	0854	1004	1154	1424	1623	1721	1833	2027
Hayato d.	0634	0819	0921	1032	1220	1448	1649	1748	1904	2054
Kirishima-Jingu d.	0652	0836	0938	1050	1238	1504	1706	1805	1921	2111
Miyazaki a.	0823	1002	1057	1209	1402	1620	1826	1934	2038	2230

8110 HAKATA - SASEBO and NAGASAKI

JR Kyushu

km																									
						Ⓐ	Ⓒ																		
0	**Hakata** d.	0558	0633	0717	0729	0753	0754	0814	0834	0856	0915	0931	0955	1015	1032	1055	1115	1132	1155	1232	1255	1332	1355	1432	...
29	Tosu d.	0619	0655	0740	0758	0816	0816	0838	0857	0916	0938	0956	1016	1038	1058	1115	1138	1158	1215	1258	1315	1358	1415	1458	...
	Shin Tosu d.	0623	0659	0744	0801	0820	0820	0843	0901	0920	0942	1000	1020	1042	1102	1121	1142	1202	1219	1302	1320	1402	1419	1502	...
54	Saga d.	0636	0712	0801	0815	0833	0833	0857	0915	0933	0956	1016	1033	1056	1117	1134	1156	1216	1233	1316	1333	1416	1433	1516	...
117	**Sasebo** a.	|	|	|	0925	|	|	...	1024	|	|	1125	|	|	1227	|	|	1324	|	1425	|	1524	|	1625	...
154	**Nagasaki** a.	0801	0835	0926	...	0950	0950	...	...	1049	1123	...	1149	1222	...	1250	1322	...	1349	...	1450	...	1550	...	...

Hakata d.	...	1455	1515	1532	1555	1615	1632	...	1655	1715	1732	1755	1815	1833	1900	1915	1933	2000	2033	2100	2133	2211	2233	2256	2335	...
Tosu d.	...	1515	1538	1558	1615	1638	1658	...	1716	1739	1758	1815	1837	1858	1920	1942	1957	2021	2058	2120	2158	2230	2256	2317	2358	...
Shin Tosu d.	...	1519	1542	1602	1619	1642	1702	...	1720	1743	1802	1820	1842	1902	1924	1946	2001	2025	2103	2124	2202	2234	2300	2321	0002	...
Saga d.	...	1533	1556	1616	1633	1656	1716	...	1733	1756	1816	1833	1857	1916	1938	2002	2016	2038	2117	2138	2217	2247	2313	2335	0016	...
Sasebo a.	...	|	|	1724	|	|	1826	...	|	|	1925	|	|	2023	|	...	2128	|	2229	|	2321	|	...	0038	...	...
Nagasaki a.	...	1650	1724	...	1755	1823	...	...	1853	1926	...	1953	2026	...	2056	...	...	2158	...	2257	...	2359	...	...	...	...

		Ⓒ	Ⓐ	Ⓒ	Ⓐ	Ⓒ	Ⓐ	Ⓒ	Ⓐ			Ⓒ	Ⓐ	Ⓒ	Ⓐ	Ⓒ										
Nagasaki d.	...	...	...	0558	0600	...	...	0625	0625	...	0728	...	...	...	...	...	0829	...	0846	0920	...	0946	1020	...	1046	112
Sasebo d.	...	...	...	|	|	0621	0621	|	|	0708	|	...	0806	0806	...	...	|	0847	|	|	0944	|	|	1043	|	|
Saga d.	0626	0705	0705	0718	0718	0731	0731	0756	0756	0819	0845	0859	0912	0912	0926	0926	0945	0953	1013	1034	1053	1113	1135	1153	1213	1235
Shin Tosu d.	0640	0717	0717	0730	0730	0745	0745	0809	0809	0834	0858	0914	0925	0925	0940	0940	0958	1006	1026	1047	1107	1126	1148	1207	1226	1248
Tosu d.	0645	0722	0722	0735	0735	0749	0749	0813	0813	0839	0902	0918	0932	0932	0944	0944	1002	1012	1031	1052	1112	1130	1152	1212	1230	1252
Hakata a.	0707	0743	0747	0756	0759	0809	0815	0830	0835	0905	0920	0938	0953	0954	1005	1006	1021	1034	1053	1112	1134	1152	1213	1234	1253	1313

Nagasaki d.	...	1220	...	1320	...	1420	...	1446	1520	...	1546	1620	...	1647	1720	...	1751	1820	...	1854	1919	...	2023	...	2131	...
Sasebo d.	1143	|	1243	|	1342	|	1443	|	|	1541	|	|	1642	|	|	1743	|	|	1845	|	|	1952	|	2100	|	...
Saga d.	1252	1334	1353	1434	1453	1535	1552	1612	1635	1653	1713	1736	1753	1814	1836	1853	1914	1936	1954	2018	2039	2057	2142	2210	2246	2321
Shin Tosu d.	1306	1347	1407	1447	1507	1547	1607	1626	1647	1707	1426	1749	1807	1827	1848	1907	1927	1949	2007	2031	2051	2107	2156	2223	2258	2334
Tosu d.	1312	1351	1412	1452	1512	1552	1613	1630	1652	1712	1730	1753	1812	1831	1852	1912	1931	1953	2013	2035	2055	2113	2200	2227	2302	2338
Hakata a.	1334	1412	1434	1513	1534	1613	1636	1651	1713	1734	1753	1814	1835	1852	1914	1935	1951	2013	2038	2055	2115	2135	2222	2250	2321	2359

8115 TAKAMATSU - TOKUSHIMA

JR Shikoku

km																								
									a											a				
0	**Takamatsu** d.	...	0705	0823	0910	1011	...	1107	1206	1312	...	1412	1512	1612	...	1715	1813	...	1917	2005	2120	...	2223	2320
10	Yashima d.	...	0714	0833	0920	1022	...	1117	|	1323	...	1423	1522	1622	...	1725	1822	...	1927	2016	2131	...	2234	2329
64	Ikenotani d.	...	0804	0924	1009	1115	...	1205	|	1407	...	|	1612	|	...	1814	|	...	2017	2106	2225	...	|	0020
75	**Tokushima** a.	...	0814	0936	1018	1125	...	1213	1304	1415	...	1520	1620	1716	...	1823	1924	...	2027	2115	2234	...	2334	0030

				b											b							
Tokushima d.	0543	0701	...	0823	0922	...	1028	1131	1224	...	1325	1426	...	1528	1646	1728	...	1830	1932	2034	...	2202	...
Ikenotani d.	0554	0712	...	0834	0932	...	|	1140	1233	...	|	1436	...	1537	|	1737	...	1838	|	|	...	2211	...
Yashima d.	0644	0804	...	0920	1022	...	|	|	1322	...	1423	1522	...	1622	|	1822	...	1926	2028	2130	...	2308	...
Takamatsu a.	0654	0813	...	0931	1032	...	1137	1234	1331	...	1433	1532	...	1632	1744	1832	...	1937	2038	2140	...	2318	...

a – From Okayama (dep. 1 hour earlier). b – To Okayama (arr. 1 hour later).

8118 TOKUSHIMA - AWA IKEDA

JR Shikoku

km													
		LEX	*LEX*	**A**	*LEX*		*LEX*		*LEX*			*LEX*	
0	**Tokushima** d.	0648	0903	0950	1201	1317	1501	1532	1757	1800	1927	2017	2106
74	**Awa Ikeda** a.	0810	1014	1151	1315	1515	1616	1730	1916	2005	2117	2134	2253

	LEX	**B**	*LEX*		*LEX*		*LEX*		*LEX*	*LEX*		
Awa Ikeda d.	0648	0652	0834	0943	1125	1237	1333	1539	1637	1950	2007	2149
Tokushima a.	0803	0855	0947	1128	1236	1422	1445	1720	1746	2104	2157	2335

A – Additional trips: 0540, 0609, 0721, 1145, 1446, 1905. B – Additional trips: 0622, 0753, 1032, 1429, 1654, 1809. 1841Ⓐ.

UWAJIMA - KUBOKAWA — 8121

JR Shikoku

km																		
0	Uwajima........‡d.	...	0604	0939	1136	1535	1730	1830	...	...	Kubokawa........d.	...	0622	0940	1324	1517	1658	1843	...	...
82	Kubokawa........a.	...	0809	1145	1347	1750	1937	2040	...	...	Uwajima........‡a.	...	0828	1215	1534	1721	1915	2044	...	...

– Japan Rail Pass holders must pay a supplement to travel between these stations.

OKAYAMA and TAKAMATSU - MATSYUAMA and UWAJIMA — 8125

JR Shikoku

km																						
72	Okayama........d.	...	...	...	...	...	...	0723	...	0832	...	0845	...	0925	...	1035	...	1135	...	1235	...
0	Takamatsu........d.	...	0517	...	0600	...	0737	...	0845	...	0940	...	1047	...	1150	...	1250
46	Utazu........d.	...	...	0629	0711	...	0756	0802 0802	...	0913 0913	...	1006 1006	...	1116 1113	...	1214 1214	...	1314 1314
164	Imabari........d.	...	...	0629 0711	...	0756	0930 0930	...	1041 1041	...	1135 1135	...	1241 1241	...	1339 1339	...	1443 1443
214	Matsuyama........a.	0548 0648	0710 0758	0808 0836	0903	1005 1005	1014	1115 1115	1125	1210 1210	1227	1315 1315	1324	1413 1413	1428	1517 1517
311	Uwajima........a.	0713 0813	...	0930	1024	...	1131	...	1244	...	1350	...	1446	...	1551	...

kayama........d.	...	1335	...	1435	...	1535	...	1635	...	1735	1750	1835	...	1935	...	2039	2059 2220	2200
Takamatsu........d.	...	1350	...	1450	...	1550	...	1650	...	1750	...	1858	...	1952	...	2114 2117 2239	2235
tazu........d.	1414 1414	...	1515 1515	...	1615 1615	...	1715 1715	...	1814 1814	1912 1917	...	2009 2012	...	2114 2117 2239	2235
nabari........d.	1541 1541	...	1645 1645	...	1745 1745	...	1847 1847	...	1947 1947	2052 2052	...	2156 2156	...	2255 2255 0019	0019
Matsuyama........a.	1527 1616 1616	1632 1724 1724	1730 1827 1827	1842 1924 1924	1935 2028 2028	2132 2132	2148 2236 2236	2246 2331 2331	0055 0055
wajima........a.	1650	...	1749	...	1857	...	2009	...	2057 2204	...	2306	...	0005	...	0055

wajima........d.	...	...	...	0533	...	0635 0635	0738	...	0840	...	0949	...	1042	...	1155
Matsuyama........d.	0505 0505	0613 0613	0658	0720 0720	0810 0810	0903 0915 0915	1007	1021 1021	1118 1123 1123	1213 1220 1220	1317
nabari........d.	0437 0541 0541	0650 0650	0756 0756	0847 0847	0957 0957	1059 1059	1202 1202	1259 1259
tazu........d.	0606 0715 0714	0753 0827 0826	0926 0925	1020 1021	1133 1132	1234 1233	1335 1334	1435 1434
Takamatsu........d.	...	0737 0811	...	0844	...	0944 1038	...	1133 1154	...	1254	...	1355	...	1455
kayama........a.	0643 0751	...	0900	...	0959	...	1058	1210	...	1310	...	1410	...	1511	...

wajima........d.	...	1256	...	1358	...	1456	...	1603	...	1708	...	1809	...	1907	...	2018	2116	2304
Matsuyama........d.	1326 1326	1413	1423 1423	1528 1526	1618 1628 1628	1726 1737 1737	1834 1841 1841	1927 1932 2030 2036	2135 2140 2238	2304
nabari........d.	1405 1405	1501 1501	1606 1606	1704 1704	1813 1813	1919 1919	2009 2111	2215	2343
tazu........d.	1535 1534	1635 1636	1735 1736	1835 1836	1938 1939	2052 2051	2109 2155	2258 0004
Takamatsu........a.	1555	1655	1754	1854	1956	...	2109	2155	2258 0004
kayama........a.	1611	...	1711	...	1811	...	1911	...	2011	2129	...	...	...

OKAYAMA and TAKAMATSU - KOCHI - NAKAMURA — 8127

JR Shikoku

km																					
0	Okayama........d.	...	...	0708	...	0851	1005	1105	...	1205	1305	1405	1505	1605	...	1705	...	1805	1905	...	2005	...	2139
97	Takamatsu........d.	0604	0720	...	0825	...	...	1826	...	2027
97	Awa Ikeda........d.	0706 0829	0829	0924	1020 1122	1234	1332 1425	1523 1630 1734	1834	1935 1935 2029	2138 2138 2257
179	Kochi........a.	0817 0939	0939	0953	1037 1130	1229 1341	1349 1442	1543 1639 1741 1848	1855 1945 1953 2050 2050	2146 2153 2250 2250 0004
251	Kubokawa........d.	0927	...	1057	...	1249	...	1454	...	1651 1806	...	2010	2104	...	2300	...
294	Nakamura........a.	1004	...	1132	...	1324	...	1531	...	1727 1846	...	2049	2139	...	2336	...

km																					
	Nakamura........d.	...	...	0608	0700	...	0924	...	1111	...	1324	...	1510	...	1647	...	1745	1934	...
	Kubokawa........d.	...	...	0648	0741	...	1004	...	1157	...	1402	...	1551	...	1728	...	1824	2012	...
0	Kochi........d.	0451 0600	0700 0700	0801 0904	0913 1013	1113 1213	1302 1313 1413	1504 1513 1613 1713 1834	1837 1934 2115	2120
82	Awa Ikeda........d.	0600 0709	0813 0813	0907	...	1020 1122 1223 1322	1424 1523	1620 1719 1823 1823	1946 2040 2040	2228
158	Takamatsu........a.	0702	0921	...	...	...	1925	...	2142	...	2325
	Okayama........a.	...	0838	...	0938 1033	...	1140 1240 1340 1441	...	1541 1641	...	1741 1847 1941	...	2111	2157	...

TOTTORI and OKAYAMA - IZUMOSHI - YAMAGUCHI — 8130

JR West

km																									
	Tottori........d.	...	0704	...	0824	...	0944	...	1140	...	1338	...	1508	...	1742	...	1843	...	...	2049	...
	Kurayoshi........d.	...	0733	...	0858	...	1012	...	1209	...	1409	...	1539	...	1811	...	1914	...	...	2122	...
0	Okayama........d.	...	...	0705	...	0804	...	0904 1004	...	1104 1204	...	1304 1404	...	1504 1604	...	1704	...	1804 1904	...	2005 2140
80	Niimi........d.	...	...	0810	...	0908	...	1011 1107	...	1207 1312	...	1413 1508	...	1610 1707	...	1807	...	1907 2008	...	2111 2243
159	Yonago........d.	0551 0808	0917 0930	1016	1047 1118	1219 1241	1318 1418	1441 1520	1620 1613 1723	1823 1846	1921 1948	2027 2123 2156	2219 2351
188	Matsue........d.	0614 0836	0942	...	1040 1111	1141 1242	1303 1340	1443 1504	1544 1644 1637 1746	1847 1912	1946	...	2050 2146	2242 0013
220	Izumoshi........d.	0639 0906	1010	...	1104 1136	1209 1307	1326 1408	1509 1527	1609 1716 1707 1813	1919 1941 2017	...	2115 2210	2307 0037
	Hamada........d.	0758 1014	...	...	1250	...	1438	...	1641	...	1824	...	2050	...	...
	Masuda........d.	0840 1051	...	...	1325	...	1514 1616	...	1718	...	1903	...	2122	...	...
	Tsuwano........d.	0911 1205	...	...	1355	...	1656	...	1749	...	...	...
	Yamaguchi........a.	1000 1316	...	...	1443	...	1816	...	1837	...	...	...
	Shin Yamaguchi........a.	1014 1356	...	...	1457	...	1841	...	1851	...	...	...

km																									
0	Shin Yamaguchi........d.	...	...	...	...	...	...	0852	...	0912	...	...	1253	...	1329	...	...	1712	...
13	Yamaguchi........d.	...	...	...	0907	...	0946	...	1307	...	1358	...	1727	...
63	Tsuwano........d.	...	...	...	0958	...	1110	...	1355	...	1519	...	1815	...
94	Masuda........d.	...	0552	...	0702	...	1031	...	1150 1217	...	1430	...	1600 1607	...	1851
135	Hamada........d.	...	0624	...	0738	...	1103	...	1250	...	1503	...	1640	...	1924
224	Izumoshi........d.	0443 0531	...	0627 0720	0736 0831	0854 0934 1032	1134 1210	1300 1359 1433 1530	1614 1630 1717 1748 1827 2035
256	Matsue........d.	0508 0556	...	0658 0751	0800 0857	0924 1001 1057	1201 1235	1301 1400 1424 1459 1600	1645 1659 1743 1815 1907 2104
285	Yonago........d.	0533 0622 0700	0724 0819	0825 0922 0950 1026 1125	1217 1226 1303	1325 1428 1450 1527 1628	1711 1726 1815 1841 1923 2127 2040
	Niimi........d.	0640 0729	...	0834 0934	...	1036	...	1136 1235	1337	1438 1537	1637 1737	1837 1925	2033
338	Okayama........a.	0741 0834	...	0938 1035	1138	1238 1338	1438	1539 1638	1738 1838	1938 2024	2136
	Kurayoshi........d.	...	0733	...	0858	...	1027	...	1258	...	1521	...	1743	...	1914
378	Tottori........a.	...	0804	...	0927	...	1058	...	1327	...	1552	...	1816	...	1942

KYOTO - KURAYOSHI

JR West

km		1	3	5	7		9	11	13			2	4	6	8	10
0	Kyoto........d.	0706	0850	1052	1252	...	1452	1656	1935	Kurayoshi........d.	0608	0812	1014	1218	1434
39	Shin Osaka........d.	0730	0916	1116	1316	...	1516	1719	2000	Tottori........d.	0639	0853	1046	1254	
43	Osaka........d.	0737	0924	1124	1324	...	1524	1726	2006	Chizu........‡d.	0708	0921	1115	
131	Himeji........d.	0836	1022	1220	1420	...	1620	1822	2108	Kamigori........‡d.	0751	1003	120	
166	Kamigori........‡d.	0902	1048	1243	1444	...	1644	1845	2131	Himeji........d.	0814	1025	
222	Chizu........‡d.	0944	1130	1323	1524	...	1725	1931	2214	Osaka........d.	0924	11	
254	Tottori........d.	1014	1159	1353	1556	...	1753	2001	2242	Shin Osaka........d.	0925		
294	Kurayoshi........a.	1044	1229	1422	1623	...	2032		Kyoto........a.			

OKAYAMA - TOTTORI

JR West

km														
0	Okayama........d.	...	0647	0914	1105	1343	1724	1946	...	Tottori		
54	Kamigori........‡d.	...	0725	0950	1142	1419	1803	2022	...	Chizu		
110	Chizu........‡d.	...	0811	1036	1226	1501	1845	2104	...	Kam		
142	Tottori........a.	...	0838	1104	1253	1533	1917	2311	...			

‡ – Japan Rail Pass holders must pay a supplement to travel between these stations.

8145 — KYOTO and OSAKA - KINOSAKI
JR West

km																					
0	Kyoto ....d.	0732	0836	0925	1025	1125	...	1225	1325	...	1425	1525	...	1625	1728	...	1828	1928	...	2037	...	2137	...
76	Ayabe ....d.	0839	0945	1032	1135	1231	...	1340	1431	...	1535	1631	...	1735	1841	...	1945	2045	...	2149	...	2243	...
89	Fukuchiyama ....d.	0849	0953	1041	1144	1245	...	1349	1444	...	1544	1640	...	1743	1854	...	1954	2054	...	2158	...	2252	...
148	Toyooka	0943	...	...	...	1340	...	...	1541	...	...	...	...	1950									
158	Kinosaki Onsen ......a.	0952	...	...	...	1349	...	...	1549														

Kinosaki Onsen ......d.							1039		1232				1612							
Toyooka ....d.					0742		1049		1242				1622							
Fukuchiyama ....d.	0602	0657		0743	0838	0947	1044	1145	1244	1346	1444	1543	1644	1728	1825		1929			
Ayabe ....d.	0612	0712		0753	0855	0958	1059	1156	1300	1356	1459	1556	1659	1740	1842		1942			
Kyoto ....a.	0719	0821		0903	1007		1107	1207		1307	1407		1507	1607		1707	1808		1849	1953		2048

km																			
0	Shin Osaka ....d.	0806		0904	1005		1105		1205	1305		1405		1505	1705		1801		1906	2006	...	2107	...	220-
4	Osaka ....d.	0812		0910	1012		1111		1211	1311		1411		1511	1711		1811		1912	2012	...	2110	...	221(
118	Fukuchiyama ....d.	0955			1046	1146		1243		1350	1442		1546		1647	1853		2002		2055	2155	...	2255	...	235-
178	Toyooka	1049			1143	1242				1445		1641		1747		2056						
188	Kinosaki Onsen ......a.	1058			1152	1250				1454		1650		1756								

Kinosaki Onsen ......d.							0933		1133		1330		1435		1530		1702	1818		
Toyooka ....d.							0943		1143		1339		1445		1540		1712	1828		
Fukuchiyama ....d.	0550	0652		0745		0840		0949	1046		1246		1442		1545	1646	1722	1817	1927	2025
Osaka ....a.	0733	0839		0926		1019	1123		1223		1423		1621		1720	1820	1855	1949	2101	220-
Shin Osaka ....a.	0739	0846		0932		1025	1129		1229		1429		1628		1726	1828	1901	1955	2106	220(

8150 — KANAZAWA - NAGOYA and OSAKA
IR, JR West

km																										
0	Osaka ....d.				0630	0700		0740		0758	0810	0840	0857		0912	0942		1012	1042		1112	1142		1212
4	Shin Osaka ....d.				0634	0705		0744		0803	0814	0844	0901		0917	0946		1016	1046		1116	1146		1216
43	Kyoto ....d.				0858	0729		0810		0831	0841	0909	0925		0942	1010		1040	1110		1140	1210		1240
	Nagoya ......8175 d.								0750		1058	0850		0948								1148	
	Gifu ....8170 d.							0810	0955		1037	0911		1012								1212	
	Maibara ....d.						0809	0859	0921		1005	0956		1056		1156						1256	
137	Tsuruga ....d.				0758	0822	0840	0902	0927		0938		1026	1035		1126	1134		1226	1234		1326	1334
191	Fukui ....d.	0600	0650	0720	0744	0830	0855	0915	0937	1002		1012	1031		1101	1110	1133	1201	1208	1232	1301	1308	1335	1401	1408
268	Kanazawa .....8155 d.	0648	0737	0809	0833	0913	0938	1003	1024	1049		1102	1113		1148	1156	1217	1248	1256	1317	1348	1356	1420	1448	1456
334	Nanao ....d.				0948										1217			1401	1401					1552	1552
339	Wakura Onsen ....a.				0954										1222			1407	1407					1557	1557

km																					
0	Osaka ....d.		1312		1412		1512			1612	1642		1712	1742		1812	1842		1927		2007	...	2054	...
	Shin Osaka ....d.		1316		1416		1516			1616	1646		1716	1746		1816	1846		1931		2012	...	2058	...
	Kyoto ....d.		1340		1440		1540			1640	1709		1740	1809		1840	1909		1954		2037	...	2121	...
30	Nagoya ......8175 d.			1348					1548					1748					1948			
	Gifu ....8170 d.			1410					1611					1811					2012			
80	Maibara ....d.	1356		1456		1556			1656		1756		1856			1956		2056			
126	Tsuruga ....d.	1426	1434	1526	1534	1626	1634		1724	1733		1826	1834	1926	1933	2006	2026	2126	2133		2218	2226	2248
180	Fukui ....d.	1501	1508	1601	1607	1701	1708		1759	1807	1830	1900	1908	1930	2001	2007	2038	2101	2124	2201	2208		2247	2301	2317
257	Kanazawa .....8155 d.	1548	1556	1648	1654	1750	1756		1847	1853	1913	1950	1957	2015	2050	2056	2122	2148	2209	2250	2256		2329	2348	0039
323	Nanao ....d.												2105				1932					2351
328	Wakura Onsen ....a.												2111				1938					2357

Wakura Onsen ....d.									0701			0841	0841			1014	1014			
Nanao ....d.									0707			0848	0848			1020	1020			
Kanazawa .....8155 d.	0500	0535	0548	0607	0648		0645	0715	0748	0805		0815	0848	0903		0948	0953	1048	1056	1124	1148	1155	1248	1253
Fukui ....d.	0548	0621	0639	0658	0739		0729	0803	0838	0848		0905	0936	0946		1036	1042	1136	1143	1209	1236	1244	1336	1342
Tsuruga ....d.	0622	0653	0712	0736	0812		0801	0837	0912			0939	1010			1110	1116	1209	1216		1310	1316	1410	1416
Maibara ....d.	0656		0752		0844				0950				1044			1150		1244			1350		1444	
Gifu ....8170 d.			0829						1026							1227					1427			
Nagoya ......8175 d.			0851						1048							1248					1448			
Kyoto ....a.		0751		0837			0855	0934		1011		1037		1109		1209		1309	1337		1409		1509	
Shin Osaka ....a.		0815		0901			0919	0958		1035		1101		1132		1232		1332	1401		1432		1532	
Osaka ....a.		0819		0906			0925	1003		1039		1106		1137		1237		1337	1406		1437		1537	

Wakura Onsen ....d.		1300	1300						1520	1520			1730	1730						
Nanao ....d.		1306	1306						1527	1527			1737	1737						
Kanazawa .....8155 d.	1348	1356	1417			1548	1600	1613		1648	1655		1748	1754	1842	1853	1947	2006	2047	2108	2135	2206	2321
Fukui ....d.	1436	1443				1636	1644	1706		1736	1744		1837	1842	1928	1942	2035	2056	2132	2155	2224	2253	2531
Tsuruga ....d.	1510							1741		1810	1815		1910	1915	2001	2015	2109	2129	2203				0008
Maibara ....d.									1802	1850		1825	1944			2055		2201				
Gifu ....8170 d.									1725	1925		1743				2129						
Nagoya ......8175 d.									1703	1946						2150						
Kyoto ....a.						1809	1838	1850		1908	1922		2009	2054		2202		2300				
Shin Osaka ....a.						1833	1903	1914		1933	1946		2032	2117		2225		2323				
Osaka ....a.						1839	1909	1918		1939	1951		2037	2122		2230		2327				

... KA - SHINGU
JR West

	13	15	17		19	21	23		25	27	29		31
							1747						
	1315	1415	1515		1615	1715	1815		1915	2015	2115		2146
	1332	1432	1532		1632	1736	1836		1936	2036	2136		2206
	1417	1518	1618		1717	1822	1936		2025	2125	2224		2253
	1538	1646	1747		1845	1946	2055		2156	2253			
	1831		1843			2036			2259				
	1916					2109			2335				
	1932					2134			2352				

	16	18	20		22	24		26	28	30	32	34
		1028			1243			1418	1541		1755	
		1045			1258			1435	1557		1810	
		1120			1330			1512	1630		1843	
	1227	1317			1433	1518		1621	1728	1819	1945	
	1350	1450			1553	1649		1748	1818	1850	1949	2106
	1435	1535			1635	1734		1834	1904	1934	2034	2149
	1450	1550			1650	1750		1851	1920	1950	2050	2206
						1834				2019		

NAGOYA - SHINGU 8165

JR Central

km		1	3	5	7						
0	**Nagoya** d.	0805	1001	1258	1947	...	...	...	...	...	...
37	Yokkaichi ‡ d.	0837	1037	1337	2019	...	...	...	...	...	...
48	Suzuka ‡ d.	0845	1046	1345	2027	...	...	...	...	...	...
66	Tsu ‡ d.	0901	1101	1400	2042	...	...	...	...	...	...
86	Matsusaka d.	0916	1116	1416	2057	...	...	...	...	...	...
93	Taki d.	0924	1129	1424	2104	...	...	...	...	...	...
206	Kumano Shi d.	1114	1318	1605	2253	...	...	...	...	...	...
228	**Shingu** a.	1134	1337	1624	2314	...	...	...	...	...	...
244	**Kii Katsuura** a.	1156	1356	1642	...	...	...	...	...	...	...

	2	4	6	8						
Kii Katsuura d.	...	0855	1224	1711	...	...	...	...	...	...
Shingu d.	0620	0913	1244	1730	...	...	...	...	...	...
Kumano Shi d.	0640	0933	1305	1750	...	...	...	...	...	...
Taki d.	0819	1118	1449	1931	...	...	...	...	...	...
Matsusaka d.	0826	1126	1456	1938	...	...	...	...	...	...
Tsu ‡ d.	0841	1142	1512	1954	...	...	...	...	...	...
Suzuka ‡ d.	0854	1154	1525	2006	...	...	...	...	...	...
Yokkaichi ‡ d.	0904	1204	1534	2015	...	...	...	...	...	...
Nagoya a.	0941	1241	1610	2049	...	...	...	...	...	...

‡ – Japan Rail Pass holders must pay a supplement to travel between these stations.

NAGOYA - TOYAMA 8170

JR Central, JR West

km											
0	**Nagoya** d.	0745	0843	0939	1048	1143	1248	1448	1543	1743	1943
30	Gifu 8150 d.	0805	0903	1010	1108	1206	1308	1508	1606	1805	2006
58	Mino Ota d.	0826	0923	1032	1129	1226	1328	1529	1629	1829	2030
119	Gero d.	0919	1014	1129	1227	1325	1423	1626	1733	1933	2130
167	Takayama d.	1002	1100	1219	1315	1409	1510	1716	1807	2019	2215
182	Hida Furukawa d.	...	1113	1233	1329	...	1524	1731	...	...	...
256	**Toyama** a.	...	1229	...	1445	...	1636	1852	...	...	...

Toyama d.	...	...	0800	0952	...	...	1302	...	...	1713
Hida Furukawa d.	...	...	0918	1106	...	1306	1418	...	...	1826
Takayama d.	0646	0800	0938	1132	1233	1331	1438	1535	1632	1846
Gero d.	0732	0845	1026	1211	1318	1418	1524	1621	1715	1928
Mino Ota d.	0827	0948	1119	1315	1420	1519	1619	1715	1817	2020
Gifu 8150 d.	0852	1012	1141	1341	1441	1541	1641	1741	1841	2043
Nagoya a.	0913	1033	1202	1402	1502	1602	1702	1802	1903	2102

NIIGATA - NAOETSU - JOETSUMYOKO 8172

JR East

km		LEX	LEX	LEX			LEX		LEX	Ⓡ	
0	**Niigata** d.	0737	1021	1304	1522	1702	1624	1758	2002	2100	...
63	Nagaoka d.	0828	1117	1355	1626	1804	1715	1901	2054	2203	...
136	Naoetsu d.	0925	1212	1449	1739	1910	1809	2004	2149	2303	...
146	**Joetsumyoko** ‡ a.	0939	1225	1504	1754	1927	1822	...	2202	...	...

	Ⓡ	LEX			LEX	LEX	LEX		LEX	
Joetsumyoko ‡ d.	...	0725	...	0900	1033	1307	1726	1828	2128	...
Naoetsu d.	0615	0741	0831	0921	1047	1322	1740	1840	2142	...
Nagaoka d.	0722	0834	0935	1027	1140	1415	1834	1952	2233	...
Niigata a.	0831	0925	1033	1127	1230	1507	1925	2053	2325	...

‡ – Japan Rail Pass holders must pay a supplement to travel to/from this station.

NAGOYA - NAGANO 8175

JR Central

km																								
0	**Nagoya** 8150 d.	0700	0800	...	0900	1000	...	1100	1200	...	1300	1400	...	1500	1600	...	1740	1840	...	1940	...	...	...	...
80	Nakatsugawa d.	0750	0850	...	0950	1050	...	1150	1250	...	1350	1450	...	1550	1650	...	1830	1930	...	2032	...	...	...	...
133	Kiso Fukushima d.	0829	0925	...	1025	1126	...	1226	1325	...	1425	1525	...	1626	1726	...	1907	2007	...	2110	...	...	...	...
175	Shiojiri d.	0859	0956	...	1055	1155	...	1255	1354	...	1454	1554	...	1655	1755	...	1936	2035	...	2138	...	...	...	...
188	Matsumoto d.	0909	1007	...	1105	1205	...	1305	1404	...	1504	1604	...	1705	1806	...	1946	2046	...	2149	...	...	...	...
251	**Nagano** a.	1001	1058	...	1157	1254	...	1353	1456	...	1555	1655	...	1753	1858	...	2039	2134	...	2239	...	...	...	...

Nagano d.	...	0609	0745	...	0900	1000	...	1100	1201	...	1300	1404	...	1500	1600	...	1700	1811	...	1940	...	...	...	...
Matsumoto d.	...	0704	0836	...	0951	1050	...	1153	1253	...	1352	1453	...	1553	1653	...	1751	1907	...	2031	...	...	...	...
Shiojiri d.	...	0714	0846	...	1003	1103	...	1203	1303	...	1403	1503	...	1603	1703	...	1803	1919	...	2041	...	...	...	...
Kiso Fukushima d.	...	0743	0913	...	1030	1130	...	1230	1330	...	1430	1530	...	1630	1730	...	1830	1948	...	2108	...	...	...	...
Nakatsugawa d.	...	0822	0950	...	1106	1206	...	1306	1406	...	1506	1608	...	1710	1810	...	1910	2026	...	2144	...	...	...	...
Nagoya 8150 a.	...	0917	1045	...	1201	1301	...	1401	1501	...	1601	1701	...	1805	1905	...	2005	2121	...	2234	...	...	...	...

SHIZUOKA - KOFU 8180

JR Central

km											
0	**Shizuoka** d.	0817	0941	1140	1340	1540	1740	1940	...	...	...
34	Fuji d.	0844	1014	1211	1411	1611	1811	2011	...	...	...
131	**Kofu** a.	1028	1208	1402	1602	1802	1959	2204	...	...	...

Kofu d.	0622	0844	1043	1237	1435	1636	1836	...	...	...
Fuji d.	0811	1037	1234	1429	1629	1828	2032	...	...	...
Shizuoka a.	0837	1102	1301	1456	1656	1855	2059	...	...	...

TOKYO - KOFU - MATSUMOTO 8185

JR East

km			B																						
0	**Tokyo** Shinjuku d.	0700	0730	0800	0830	0900	1000	1100	1200	1300	1400	1500	...	1600	...	1700	1730	1800	...	1900	...	2000	2100	...	...
37	Hachioji d.	0729	0803	0833	0908	0939	1034	1130	1231	1331	1430	1531	...	1631	...	1734	1808	1837	...	1935	...	2034	2133	...	...
124	Kofu d.	0829	0908	0929	1016	1039	1129	1232	1329	1431	1524	1632	...	1728	...	1834	1915	1936	...	2036	...	2131	2240	...	...
185	Chino d.	0908	0952	1007	1059	1124	1204	1314	1407	1515	1600	1716	...	1804	...	1916	1958	2012	...	2121	...	2208	2324	...	...
192	Kami Suwa d.	0915	0957	1012	1104	1130	1209	1319	1412	1521	1605	1722	...	1809	...	1922	2004	2017	...	2126	...	2214	2329	...	...
212	Shiojiri d.	0931	1015	1029	1119	1146	|	1336	1426	1537	|	1738	...	1825	...	1940	2021	2033	...	2143	...	2229	2346	...	...
225	**Matsumoto** a.	0939	1023	1038	1128	1156	1231	1346	1435	1546	1626	1748	...	1834	...	1950	2031	2042	...	2152	...	2238	2355	...	...

																A							
Matsumoto d.	...	0608	0651	0800	0851	...	0914	0954	1108	1200	...	1302	1347	...	1449	1519	1547	1658	...	1718	1835	1921	2000	...
Shiojiri d.	...	0617	0659	0809	0900	...	0924	1003	|	1208	...	1311	1356	...	1458	1527	1555	1707	...	1727	1843	1930	2008	...
Kami Suwa d.	...	0634	0713	0825	0915	...	0941	1021	1130	1225	...	1328	1413	...	1512	1544	1615	1722	...	1744	1859	1946	2025	...
Chino d.	...	0639	0719	0831	0921	...	0946	1026	1135	1230	...	1333	1419	...	1518	1550	1620	1728	...	1750	1905	1951	2031	...
Kofu d.	...	0724	0756	0910	1003	...	1031	1106	1211	1312	...	1409	1503	...	1555	1632	1702	1805	...	1833	1942	2030	2109	...
Hachioji d.	...	0831	0851	1005	1104	...	1133	1204	1305	1410	...	1504	1601	...	1650	1732	1801	1902	...	1934	2036	2135	2206	...
Tokyo Shinjuku a.	...	0914	0926	1040	1136	...	1204	1233	1333	1441	...	1533	1634	...	1726	1807	1836	1935	...	2009	2106	2207	2236	...

km		C										
0	**Tokyo** Shinjuku d.	1030	1130	1230	1330	1430	1530	1630	1830	1930	2200	2300
37	Hachioji d.	1103	1202	1302	1402	1502	1602	1704	1906	2008	2234	2336
124	Kofu d.	1208	1310	1408	1509	1608	1709	1809	2012	2113	2341	0040

	D										
Kofu d.	0708	0812	0929	1129	1229	1329	1425	1527	1610	1727	1856
Hachioji d.	0821	0919	1033	1233	1333	1433	1531	1630	1714	1832	2003
Tokyo Shinjuku a.	0904	0956	1104	1305	1405	1504	1603	1707	1751	1909	2037

Note: Some trains run on a slightly different schedule on ©. **A** – From Minami Otari dep. 1422. **B** – To Minami Otari arr. 1142. **C** – Additional trip 0930. **D** – Additional trip 2002.

TOKYO - IZUKYU SHIMODA and SHUZENJI 8195

JR East

km				Ⓡ		©B	©D	Ⓡ			Ⓡ
0	**Tokyo** d.	0900	0900	0925j	1000	1030	1030	1100	1200	1200	1300
29	Yokohama d.	0924	0924	0959	1024	1054	1054	1124	1224	1224	1324
84	Odawara d.	1002	1002	|	1102	1132	1132	|	1301	1301	|
105	Atami d.	1023	1025	1056	1122	1154	1156	1219	1323	1325	1419
122	Ito ‡ d.	1047	|	1118	1146	1216	|	1237	1346	|	1442
168	**Izukyu Shimoda** ‡ a.	1146	|	1215	1236	1324	|	1329	1448	|	1541
121	Mishima ‡ d.	...	1040	...	...	...	1211	...	...	1340	...
141	**Shuzenji** ‡ a.	...	1108	...	...	...	1239	...	...	1406	...

	©	Ⓡ				Ⓡ		C	Ⓡ	© A
Shuzenji ‡ d.	...	...	...	1235	...	...	...	1539	...	
Mishima ‡ d.	...	...	...	1305	...	...	...	1606	...	...
Izukyu Shimoda ‡ d.	...	1006	1208	|	1302	1413	1504	|	1605	1649
Ito ‡ d.	1004	1105	1305	|	1406	1510	1602	|	1700	1805
Atami d.	1032	1128	1332	1332	1429	1533	1629	1629	1726	1830
Odawara d.	1050	1146	1349	1349	1449	|	1646	1646	|	1848
Yokohama d.	1129	1222	1426	1426	1526	1627	1723	1723	1824	1934
Tokyo a.	1154	1241	1449	1449	1549	1649	1746	1746	1859j	1958

A – Additional trips on © at 1135Ⓡ, 1342.
B – Additional trip on © at 1330.
C – Additional trip on © at 1418.
D – Additional trip on ⑥ at 1330.
j – Tokyo **Shinjuku**.
‡ – Japan Rail Pass holders must pay a supplement to travel between these stations.

TOKYO - AWA KAMOGAWA 8200

JR East

km												
0	**Tokyo** d.	0715	0900	1000	1100	1300	1500	1700	1800	1900	2100	2200
43	Soga d.	0753	0935	1033	1134	1334	1534	1733	1834	1935	2134	2232
62	Oami d.	0805	0947	1046	1146	1346	1546	1745	1848	1949	2148	2246
74	Mobara d.	0813	0955	1054	1154	1353	1553	1753	1856	1957	2158	2254
82	Kazusa Ichinomiya d.	0820	1002	1105	1202	1401	1601	1800	1908	2008	2206	2301
110	Katsuura a.	0846	1030	1130	1227	1426	1625	1832	...	2033	2230	2326
133	**Awa Kamogawa** a.	...	1054	1155	1252	1453	...	...	...	...	...	...

Awa Kamogawa d.	...	0738	0838	...	1137	1407	1534	1638	...	...	...
Katsuura d.	0726	0808	0905	1009	1206	1436	1559	1704	1811	...	2007
Kazusa Ichinomiya d.	0753	0833	0930	1034	1234	1502	1631	1738	1836	1929	2039
Mobara d.	0759	0839	0937	1041	1241	1508	1638	1744	1842	1936	2045
Oami d.	0810	0847	0945	1049	1249	1516	1646	1752	1850	1948	2053
Soga d.	0824	0902	1002	1102	1302	1531	1700	1805	1903	2001	2106
Tokyo a.	0859	0934	1036	1135	1335	1603	1734	1840	1936	2034	2139

BEYOND EUROPE - JAPAN

8205 TOKYO - MANZA KAZAWAGUCHI and MAEBASHI

JR East

km		Ⓒ			[R]	[R]	Ⓐ[R]	Ⓒ	Ⓐ	Ⓐ[R]	Ⓐ[R]
0	**Tokyo** Ueno d.	0900	1000	1212	1900	2000	2100	2129j	2129j	2200	2250
27	Omiya d.	0926	1026	1237	1925	2025	2124	2201	2201	2227	2316
62	Kumagaya d.	0952	1052	1302	1951	2053	2151	2228	2228	2254	2342
102	**Takasaki** d.	1021	1123	1335	2022	2126	2221	2301	2301	2326	0012
164	**Naganohara Kusatsuguchi** a.	1126	1231	1441	|	|	|	|	|	|	...
112	**Maebashi** a.	...	...	...	*2046*	2136	*2247*	2313	2313	2337	...

	Ⓐ[R]	Ⓐ[R]	Ⓒ		Ⓒ		Ⓒ		Ⓐ	Ⓐ
Maebashi d.	0726	*0748*k	*0748*k	0835	0908	...	...	...	1734k	*2047*
Naganohara Kusatsuguchi d.	|	|	|	|	|	1102	1356	1543	|	|
Takasaki d.	0739	0810	0810	0848	0922	1206	1503	1646	1741	2104
Kumagaya d.	0810	0842	0842	0920	0953	1238	1530	1716	1810	2146
Omiya d.	0841	0912	0912	0951	1022	1306	1600	1744	1837	2225
Tokyo Ueno a.	0911j	0939	0939	1014	1054j	1331	1624	1809	1900	2257

j – Tokyo **Shinjuku**. **k** – Shim-Maebashi.

8210 TOKYO - NIKKO

JR East

km		[R]	[R]	[R]	[R]						
0	**Tokyo** Shinjuku d.	0730	1031	1301	1732	...	...	...	...	...	...
27	Omiya d.	0802	1102	1332	1802	...	...	...	...	...	...
135	Tobu **Nikko** ‡ d.	0929	|	|	|	...	...	...	...	...	...
140	**Kinugawa** Onsen ‡ a.	...	1238	1512	1940	...	...	...	...	...	...

	[R]	[R]	[R]	[R]						
Kinugawa Onsen ‡ d.	0813	1038	1505	...	...	...	...	...	...	...
Tobu **Nikko** ‡ d.	|	|	|	1639	...	...	...	...	...	...
Omiya d.	0949	1217	1646	1804	...	...	...	...	...	...
Tokyo Shinjuku a.	1018	1248	1719	1836	...	...	...	...	...	...

‡ – Japan Rail Pass holders must pay a supplement to travel to / from this station.

8215 TOKYO - SENDAI

JR East

km	All trains [R]																							
	Tokyo Shinagawa d.	0644	...	...	...	...	...	...	0944	...	1014	1044	1114	...	1144	1214	1244	1314	...	1344	1414	1444	...	151
0	**Tokyo** Ueno d.	0700	0730	0800	...	0830	0900	0930	1000	...	1030	1100	1130	...	1200	1230	1300	1330	...	1400	1430	1500	...	153
67	Tsuchiura d.	0742	0818	0850	...	0916	|	1016	|	...	1115	|	1215	...	|	1313	|	1413	...	|	1513	|	...	161
118	Mito d.	0811	0850	0919	...	0950	1016	1048	1106	...	1148	1207	1248	...	1307	1345	1407	1445	...	1507	1546	1607	...	164
124	Katsuta d.	0817	0855	0925	...	0955	1021	1053	1111	...	1153	1212	1252	...	1312	1350	1412	1450	...	1512	1551	1612	...	165
150	Hitachi d.	0834	0915	0941	...	...	1040	...	1126	...	...	1232	...	...	1327	...	1430	1511	...	1527	...	1630	...	...
212	Iwaki △ a.	0918	...	1023	...	...	1124	...	1207	...	...	1315	...	...	1409	...	1514	...	...	1609	...	1714	...	...
290	Haranomachi △ d.	...	...	...	...	...	...	...	...	...	...	...	...	...	...	...	...	...	...	...	...	...	...	...
361	**Sendai** (Honshu) △ a.	...	...	...	...	...	...	...	...	...	...	...	...	...	...	...	...	...	...	...	...	...	...	...

All trains [R]																								
Tokyo Shinagawa d.	...	1544	1614	1644	...	...	1744	...	...	1844	...	...	...	1944	...	...	2044	...	...	...	2144	...	...	224
Tokyo Ueno d.	...	1600	1630	1700	1730	...	1800	1815	1830	1900	...	1915	1930	2000	2015	2030	2100	2115	2130	...	2200	2215	2230	2300
Tsuchiura d.	...	|	1711	|	1816	...	1839	1905	1915	1939	...	2008	2015	2040	2107	2117	2142	2208	2216	...	2239	2310	2321	235
Mito d.	...	1706	1744	1808	1848	...	1909	...	1947	2009	...	...	2051	2110	2142	2150	2211	...	2250	...	2312	2342	2355	002
Katsuta d.	...	1712	1749	1813	1853	...	1914	...	1952	2014	...	...	2056	2118	2147	2156	2217	...	2256	...	2317	2347	2359	002
Hitachi d.	...	1730	...	1831	...	...	1932	...	2012	2032	...	...	...	2135	...	2214	2235	...	2316	...	...	...	...	...
Iwaki △ a.	...	1811	...	1915	...	...	2015	...	...	2116	...	...	...	2217	...	2256	2319	...	...	...	...	...	...	...
Haranomachi △ d.	...	...	...	...	...	...	...	...	...	...	...	...	...	...	...	...	...	...	...	...	...	...	...	...
Sendai (Honshu) △ a.	...	...	...	...	...	...	...	...	...	...	...	...	...	...	...	...	...	...	...	...	...	...	...	...

All trains [R]				Ⓐ									Ⓒ											
Sendai (Honshu) △ d.	...	...	...	...	...	...	...	...	...	...	...	...	...	...	...	...	...	...	...	...	...	...	...	...
Haranomachi △ d.	...	...	...	...	...	...	...	...	...	...	...	...	...	...	...	...	...	...	...	...	...	...	...	...
Iwaki △ d.	...	...	...	...	...	...	...	0613	...	...	0703	0739	...	0818	...	0920	...	1017	...	...	1120	...	...	121
Hitachi d.	...	...	...	...	0542	...	...	0701	0719	...	0745	0822	...	0901	...	1002	1027	1102	...	...	1202	...	...	130
Katsuta d.	...	...	0539	0553	0602	0620	0700	0720	0739	...	0804	0841	0904	0921	0947	1021	1047	1121	...	1147	1221	1247	...	132
Mito d.	...	...	0545	0559	0608	0626	0706	0726	0745	...	0810	0848	0911	0927	0953	1027	1053	1127	...	1153	1227	1253	...	132
Tsuchiura d.	...	0606	0620	0631	0640	0700	0739	0758	0819	...	0839	0920	0942	|	1025	|	1125	|	...	1225	|	1325	...	|
Tokyo Ueno a.	...	0705	0723	0734	0746	0804	0843	0858	0910	...	0935	1006	1023	1037	1108	1137	1208	1237	...	1308	1337	1408	...	143
Tokyo Shinagawa a.	...	...	...	...	...	...	...	0913	...	...	0952	1021	...	1051	1122	1151	1222	1251	...	1322	1351	1422	...	145

All trains [R]																								
Sendai (Honshu) △ d.	...	...	...	...	...	...	...	...	...	...	...	...	...	...	...	...	...	...	...	...	...	...	...	...
Haranomachi △ d.	...	...	...	...	...	...	...	...	...	...	...	...	...	...	...	...	...	...	...	...	...	...	...	...
Iwaki △ d.	...	...	1323	...	...	1418	...	1518	...	...	...	1618	...	1721	...	...	...	1816	...	1918	...	...	2016	...
Hitachi d.	...	...	1405	...	...	1502	...	1602	...	1626	...	1702	...	1803	...	...	...	1900	...	2000	...	...	2100	...
Katsuta d.	...	1347	1421	1447	...	1521	1547	1621	...	1647	...	1721	1747	1821	...	1847	...	1921	1947	2021	...	2047	2121	214
Mito d.	...	1353	1427	1453	...	1527	1553	1627	...	1653	...	1727	1753	1827	...	1853	...	1927	1953	2027	...	2053	2127	215
Tsuchiura d.	...	1425	|	1525	...	|	1625	|	...	1725	...	|	1824	|	...	1924	...	|	2024	|	...	2124	2156	222
Tokyo Ueno a.	...	1509	1537	1609	...	1639	1706	1738	...	1807	...	1839	1907	1938	...	2006	...	2037	2106	2139	...	2205	2238	230
Tokyo Shinagawa a.	...	1522	1551	1623	...	1653	...	1752	...	...	...	1852	...	1952	...	...	...	2052	...	2154	...	...	2253	...

△ – Limited Express services Iwaki - Sendai and v.v. are suspended due to earthquake damage. Some local services may be available.

8220 NIIGATA - AOMORI

JR East

km				LEX	LEX	LEX	LEX	LEX	LEX	LEX	LEX	LEX
0	**Niigata** d.	...	...	...	0827	...	1058	1233	1501	...	1717	2120
168	Sakata d.	0535	0634	...	1039	...	1305	1441	1731	...	1931	2329
273	Akita d.	0725	0828	0834	1204	1241	...	1604	1841	1932	...	...
377	Odate d.	...	...	1004	...	1414	...	...	...	2103	...	...
421	Hirosaki d.	...	...	1042	...	1452	...	...	...	2142	...	...
455	Shin Aomori d.	...	...	1111	...	1523	...	...	...	2211	...	...
459	**Aomori** d.	...	...	1117	...	1529	...	...	...	2216	...	...

	LEX	LEX	LEX	LEX	LEX	LEX	LEX	LEX	LEX	LEX	
Aomori d.	...	...	...	...	0908	...	...	1242	...	1601	...
Shin Aomori d.	...	...	...	...	0912	...	...	1248	...	1607	...
Hirosaki d.	...	...	...	...	0939	...	...	1321	...	1634	...
Odate d.	...	...	...	...	1016	...	...	1400	...	1711	...
Akita d.	...	...	...	0915	1143	1258	...	1527	1635	1841	204
Sakata d.	0528	0646	0901	1047	...	1426	1557	...	1804	...	223
Niigata a.	0731	0851	1104	1257	...	1632	1801	...	2007	...	...

8225 HAKODATE and MURORAN - SAPPORO

JR Hokkaido

km				1		3		5	7	9		11	13			15			17	19	21	23	
0	**Hakodate** d.	...	...	0610	...	0728	...	0854	1005	1048	...	1216	1351	...	...	1456	...	...	1635	1751	1849	1955	...
18	Shin **Hakodate Hokuto** 8020 d.	...	...	0628	...	0748	...	0913	1024	1109	...	1234	1411	...	...	1515	...	...	1655	1811	1909	2014	...
112	Oshamambe d.	...	...	0734	...	0901	...	1021	1132	1220	...	1343	1522	...	...	1625	...	...	1808	1923	2016	2122	...
154	Toya d.	...	...	0758	...	0928	...	1047	1156	1246	...	1409	1548	...	...	1649	...	...	1833	1950	2042	2147	...
	Muroran d.	0527	0656	|	...	|	...	|	|	|	1348	|	|	1626	...	|	...	1812	|	|	|	|	...
190	Higashi-Muroran d.	0541	0710	0825	0923	0956	...	1115	1223	1315	1400	1437	1615	1638	...	1717	...	1824	1905	2019	2110	2214	...
207	Noboribetsu d.	0556	0724	0837	0937	1009	...	1128	1235	1328	1415	1450	1628	1653	...	1730	...	1839	1918	2032	2122	2227	...
248	Tomakomai d.	0622	0749	0900	1002	1035	...	1153	1259	1353	1441	1514	1652	1719	...	1755	...	1904	1943	2057	2146	2251	...
275	Minami Chitose d.	0641	0807	0916	1022	1052	...	1211	1316	1410	1459	1530	1708	1737	...	1811	...	1923	2000	2114	2203	2307	...
319	**Sapporo** a.	0714	0838	0948	1101	1127	...	1241	1348	1441	1534	1604	1741	1811	...	1841	...	1955	2034	2148	2233	2340	

km		2	4		6	8	10		12			14	16	18		20	22			24			
0	**Sapporo** d.	0600	0652	0730	0839	0930	1044	1124	1215	...	1355	1332	1444	1539	1602	1632	1810	1854	...	2000	2200	...	...
44	Minami Chitose d.	0628	0702	0759	0911	1000	1115	1158	1245	...	1427	1401	1515	1611	1632	1705	1841	1927	...	2028	2234	...	...
71	Tomakomai d.	0644	0739	0818	0929	1018	1132	1219	1302	...	1445	1419	1533	1627	1651	1725	1858	1945	...	2044	2253	...	...
112	Noboribetsu d.	|	0804	0845	0955	1043	1156	1245	1327	...	1509	1443	1557	1654	1721	1750	1923	2011	...	2108	2309	...	...
129	Higashi-Muroran d.	0718	0817	0859	1008	1057	1210	1300	1340	...	1524	1456	1610	1708	1737	1803	1936	2026	...	2120	2334	...	...
136	**Muroran** a.	|	|	...	|	|	|	1311	|	...	1536	|	|	|	1748	|	|	2037	...	|	2346	...	...
	Toya d.	|	0844	...	1036	1124	1235	...	1408	...	...	1525	1636	1734	...	1831	2004	...	...	2146	...	...	...
	Oshamambe d.	0806	0944	...	1104	1152	1302	...	1436	...	...	1549	1701	1802	...	1857	2031	...	...	2211	...	...	...
	Shin **Hakodate Hokuto** 8020 a.	0911	1023	...	1218	1307	1410	...	1551	...	...	1654	1809	1908	...	2004	2139	...	...	2316	...	...	...
	Hakodate a.	0927	1038	...	1234	1324	1425	...	1608	...	...	1709	1825	1924	...	2020	2155	...	...	2331	...	...	...

SAPPORO - KUSHIRO — 8230

JR Hokkaido

km				A			A	A				
0	Sapporo ....d.	0700	0754	0854	1024	1153	1416	1608	1724	1832	1940	2104
44	Minami Chitose .....d.	0730	0826	0926	1056	1226	1448	1641	1756	1905	2011	2132
143	Tomamu ....d.	0833	0934	1040	1212	1338	1602	1758	1918	2020	2126	2246
220	Obihiro ....d.	0926	1145	1140	1310	1553	1837	1900	2018	2121	2220	2341
349	Kushiro ....a.	1100	1322	1320		1734	2015		2159		2355	

				A			A		A		
Kushiro ....d.		0626		0823		1124	1339		1450		1900
Obihiro ....d.	0645	0802	0847	1020	1101	1257	1240	1520	1645	1922	2034
Tomamu ....d.	0740	0903	0955	1212	1212	1400	1432	1612	1836	2020	2126
Minami Chitose .....d.	0900	1014	1108	1324	1324	1507	1544	1722	1944	2143	2228
Sapporo ....a.	0933	1045	1140	1356	1356	1541	1619	1756	2015	2215	2258

NOTE: Because of typhoon damage most services are suspended unill at least the end of December 2016.
Services marked A are operating but with a bus connection between Tomamu and Obihiro and v.v.

SAPPORO - WAKKANAI and ABASHIRI — 8235

JR Hokkaido

km									
0	Sapporo ....d.	0721	0748	0941	1230	1508	1730	1748	...	...
	Takikawa ....d.	0820	0842	1039	1331	1603	1829	1839	...	...
137	Asahikawa ....d.	0900	0917	1118	1411	1642	1908	1917	...	...
396	Wakkanai ....a.		1253		1822			2258	...	...
185	Kamikawa ....d.	0940		1201		1728	1953	...	...	...
375	Abashiri ....a.	1240		1506		2037	2301	...	...	...

Abashiri ....d.	0620		0923	1326			1718	...	...
Kamikawa ....d.	0924		1229	1629			2021	...	...
Wakkanai ....d.		0700			1344	1700		...	...
Asahikawa ....d.	1011	1041	1311	1713	1734	2045	2105	...	...
Takikawa ....d.	1047	1114	1347	1749	1810	2118	2140	...	...
Sapporo ....a.	1146	1206	1446	1847	1914	2209	2240	...	...

SHIN CHITOSE AIRPORT - SAPPORO - ASAHIKAWA — 8240

JR Hokkaido

km																											
0	Shin Chitose Airport.d.	...	...	...	...	...	...	...	...	...	...	...	...	...	...	...	...	...	...	...	...	...	...	...	...	...
3	Minami Chitose ......d.	...	...	...	...	...	...	...	...	...	...	...	...	...	...	...	...	...	...	...	...	...	...	...	...	...
47	Sapporo ....d.	0635	0800	0825	0900	0930	...	1000	1100	1200	1300	1400	1430	1500	1600	1630	1700	1800	1830	1900	1930	2000	2100	2200	2305
	Takikawa ....d.	0727	0852	0917	0952	1022	...	1052	1152	1252	1352	1452	1522	1552	1652	1722	1752	1852	1922	1952	2022	2052	2152	2252	2357
184	Asahikawa ....a.	0800	0925	0950	1025	1055	...	1125	1225	1325	1425	1525	1555	1625	1725	1754	1825	1925	1955	2025	2055	2125	2225	2325	0030

Asahikawa ....d.	...	0518	0600	0645	0718	0755	0830	0900	...	1000	1100	1200	1300	1400	1430	1500	1530	1600	1630	1700	1800	1830	1900	2000	2200
Takikawa ....d.	...	0550	0632	0717	0750	0827	0902	0932	...	1032	1132	1232	1332	1432	1502	1532	1602	1632	1702	1732	1832	1902	1932	2032	2232
Sapporo ....a.	...	0643	0733	0826	0834	0920	0955	1025	...	1125	1225	1325	1425	1525	1555	1625	1655	1725	1755	1825	1925	1955	2025	2125	2325
Minami Chitose ......a.	...	...	...	...	...	...	...	...	...	...	...	...	...	...	...	...	...	...	...	...	...	...	...	...	...
Shin Chitose Airport..a.	...	...	...	...	...	...	...	...	...	...	...	...	...	...	...	...	...	...	...	...	...	...	...	...	...

SUMMARY OF OVERNIGHT TRAINS — 8300

km	km			A [H]	B [R]					B [R]	A [R]
0		Takamatsu ....d.	...		2126	...	Tokyo ....d.	...	...	2200	2200
44		Kojima ....d.	...		2201	...	Yokohama ....a.	...	...	2224	2224
	0	Izumoshi ....d.	...	1851			Shiuoka ....a.	...	...	0020	0020
	33	Matsue ....d.	...	1927			Osaka ....a.	...	...		
	62	Yonago ....d.	...	1956			Okayama ....a.	...	...	0627	0627
	140	Niimi ....d.	...	2120			Okayama ....d.	...	...	0631	0634
72	221	Okayama ....a.	...	2230	2222		Niimi ....a.	...	...		0744
		Okayama ....d.	...	2234	2234		Yonago ....a.	...	...		0905
248	397	Osaka ....a.	...	0034	0034		Matsue ....a.	...	...		0931
624	773	Shizuoka ....a.	...	0440	0440		Izumoshi ....a.	...	...		0958
776	925	Yokohama ....a.	...	0645	0645		Kojima ....a.	...	...	0653	
805	954	Tokyo ....a.	...	0708	0708		Takamatsu ....a.	...	...	0727	

A – SUNRISE IZUMO 🛏 1,2 cl. 🚃 Izumoshi - Tokyo and v.v. • B – SUNRISE SETO 🛏 1,2 cl. 🚃 Takamatsu - Tokyo and v.v.

Note: As well as De-lux, single and twin berth compartments both trains have *Nobinobi* – open-plan sleeping areas categorised as seats.

AIRPORT RAIL LINKS — 8400

CHUBU CENTRAL JAPAN INTERNATIONAL AIRPORT

SKY' Limited Express [R] service Meitetsu Nagoya - Central Japan International Airport and v.v. *44 km.* Journey 30 minutes. (Frequent additional slower trains are available, not [R]). Operator : Meitetsu.

From Meitetsu Nagoya at 0600Ⓐ, 0602Ⓒ, 0628Ⓐ, 0630Ⓒ, 0648Ⓐ, 0653Ⓒ, 0720, 0750Ⓒ, 0751Ⓐ, 0820Ⓒ, 0823Ⓐ, 0850, 0920, 0950, 1020, 1050, 1120, 1150, 1220, 1250, 1320, 1350, 1420, 1450, 1520, 1550, 1620, 1650, 1719Ⓐ, 1720Ⓒ, 1749Ⓐ, 1750Ⓒ, 1819Ⓐ, 1820Ⓒ, 1849Ⓐ, 1850Ⓒ, 1919Ⓐ, 1920Ⓒ, 1949Ⓐ, 1950Ⓒ, 2019Ⓐ, 2020Ⓒ, 2049Ⓐ, 2050Ⓒ, 2119Ⓐ, 2120Ⓒ.
From Central Japan International Airport at 0703Ⓐ, 0713Ⓒ, 0726Ⓐ, 0729Ⓒ, 0759Ⓒ, 0800Ⓐ, 0829Ⓒ, 0834Ⓐ, 0907, 0937, 1007, 1037, 1107, 1137, 1207, 1237, 1307, 1337, 1407, 1437, 1507, 1537, 1607, 1637, 1706Ⓐ, 1707Ⓒ, 1736Ⓐ, 1737Ⓒ, 1806Ⓐ, 1807Ⓒ, 1836Ⓐ, 1837Ⓒ, 1906Ⓐ, 1907Ⓒ, 1936Ⓐ, 1937Ⓒ, 2007, 2037, 2107, 2137, 2207.

KANSAI AIRPORT

HARUKA' Limited Express service Kyoto - Shin Osaka ■ - Kansai Airport and v.v. *100 km.* Journey 80 - 90 minutes. Operator : JR West.
From Kyoto at 0545, 0621, 0644, 0714, 0745, 0817, 0848, 0930, 1000, 1030, 1100, 1130, 1200, 1230, 1300, 1330, 1400, 1430, 1500, 1530, 1600, 1630, 1700, 1730, 1800, 1830, 1900, 1930, 2000, 2030.
From Kansai Airport at 0630, 0727, 0755, 0845, 0916, 0946, 1016, 1046, 1114, 1144 and ½ hourly until 1614, 1644, 1716, 1746, 1816, 1846, 1916, 1946, 2016, 2046, 2125, 2216.
■ – Trains call at Shin Osaka 28 - 33 minutes after Kyoto and 45 - 50 minutes after Kansai Airport.

TOKYO HANEDA AIRPORT

Limited Express service Tokyo Shinagawa - Haneda Airport International Terminal △ and v.v. *14 km.* Journey 20 minutes. Operator : Keikyu Railway.
From Tokyo Shinagawa at 0552 and every 10 - 15 minutes until 2300.
From Haneda Airport International Terminal at 0530 and every 10 - 15 minutes until 2330.
△ – Most trains continue to/from Haneda Aiport Domestic Terminal, journey 3 minutes.
MONORAIL service Tokyo Hamamatsucho – Haneda Airport International Terminal☐ and v.v. (JR pass valid) *14 km.* Journey 13 minutes(Haneda Express), 15 minutes, (rapid) 24 minutes (stopping). Operator : Tokyo Monorail Co Ltd.
From Tokyo Hamamatsucho at 0458 and every 3 - 10 minutes until 0001.
From Haneda Airport International Terminal at 0517 and every 3 - 10 minutes until 0010.
☐ – All trains continue to/from Haneda Aiport Domestic Terminal 1, journey 3 - 5 minutes and Aiport Domestic Terminal 2, journey 5 - 7 minutes.

TOKYO NARITA AIRPORT

"NARITA EXPRESS' Limited Express [R] service Tokyo - Narita Airport Terminal 1 ▽ and v.v. *79 km.* Journey 55 minutes. Operator : JR East.
From Tokyo at 0618, 0700, 0715, 0731, 0800, 0830, 0900, 1003, 1033, 1103, 1134, 1203, 1233, 1303, 1333, 1403, 1433, 1503, 1533, 1603, 1633, 1703, 1733, 1803, 1833, 1903, 2003.
From Narita T1 at 0744, 0813, 0850, 0915, 0945, 1015, 1045, 1114, 1145, 1220, 1245, 1314, 1345, 1418, 1444, 1514, 1544, 1619, 1644, 1716, 1744, 1815, 1848, 1912, 1946, 2044, 2144.
▽ – Trains also call at Narita Aiport Terminal two, 2/3 minutes before/after Terminal one. Additional slower trains(not [R]) are available about hourly each direction.

'SKYLINER' Limited Express [R] service Tokyo Ueno Keisei - Narita Airport Terminal one ▷ and v.v. *69 km.* Journey 45 minutes. Operator : Keisei Electric Railway.
From Tokyo Ueno Keisei at 0558, 0620, 0640, 0700, 0720, 0740, 0800, 0825Ⓐ, 0826Ⓒ, 0850, 0920, 1000, 1040, 1100, 1140, 1220, 1300, 1340, 1400, 1440, 1500, 1520, 1540, 1600, 1620, 1640, 1700, 1740, 1820.
From Nanta Airport Terminal 1 at 0726Ⓐ, 0757Ⓒ, 0820Ⓐ, 0821Ⓒ, 0911Ⓐ, 0912Ⓒ, 0958, 1038, 1118, 1158, 1258, 1338, 1358, 1418, 1438, 1458, 1518, 1538, 1558, 1618, 1638, 1658, 1718Ⓒ, 1719Ⓐ, 1738Ⓒ, 1740Ⓐ, 1810Ⓐ, 1818Ⓒ, 1848Ⓐ, 1858Ⓒ, 1927Ⓐ, 1938Ⓒ, 2008Ⓒ, 2011Ⓐ, 2038Ⓒ, 2043Ⓐ, 2109, 2149Ⓐ, 2230.
▷ – Trains also call at Nanta Airport Terminal two, 3/5 minutes before/after Terminal one. Additional slower trains are available.

SAPPORO SHIN CHITOSE AIRPORT

Local and Rapid service Sapporo - Shin Chitose Airport and v.v. *47 km.* Journey 48minutes (local *) 38 minutes (rapid). All services call at Minami-Chitose 3/4 minutes before/after Shin Chitose Airport. Operator : JR Hokkaido.
From Sapporo at 0602*, 0616, 0631, 0643, 0703, 0716, 0733, 0748, 0805, 0820, 0835, 0850, 0905, 0920, 0935, 0950, 1005, 1020, 1035, 1050 and at the same minutes past the hour until 1805, 1820, 1835, 1850, 1905, 1920, 1935, 1950, 2005*, 2015*, 2025, 2045, 2055*, 2110*, 2138*, 2151.
From Shin Chitose Airport at 0656*, 0704*, 0723*, 0734*, 0748*, 0815, 0830, 0845, 0900, 0915, 0930, 0945, 1000, 1015, 1030, 1045 and at the same minutes past the hour until 2000, 2015, 2030, 2045, 2104, 2116, 2130, 2150, 2205, 2215, 2235, 2253.

BEYOND EUROPE
North America

Introduction

The Beyond Europe section covers principal rail services in a different area of the world each month. There are six areas, each appearing as follows:

Winter (December) and Summer (June): all the latest Beyond Europe pages will be included.

January and July (digital only): India.

February and August: India; South East Asia, Australia and New Zealand; North America.

March and September (digital only): China.

April and October: China; Japan; South America; South Korea.

May and November (digital only): North America.

The months have been chosen so that we can bring you up-to-date information for those countries which make seasonal changes.

Contents

INDEX OF PLACES

A

Agassiz, 9050
Agawa Canyon, 9040
Albany (NY), 9210, 9235
Albany (OR), 9315
Albuquerque, 9295
Aldershot, 9020
Alexandria, 9015
Alliance, 9235
Alpine, 9310
Alton, 9260
Altoona, 9225
Amherst (Canada), 9000
Anaheim, 9320, 9362, 9364
Anchorage, 9105
Ann Arbor, 9275
Anniston, 9245
Ardmore, 9300
Arkadelphia, 9300
Atlanta, 9245
Austin, 9300

B

Bakersfield, 9330
Baltimore, 9215, 9240
Banff, 9065
Barstow, 9295
Battle Creek, 9275
Beaumont, 9310
Belleville, 9015
Bellingham, 9315
Bellows Falls, 9220
Bennett, 9100
Benson, 9310
Benton Harbor, 9275
Biggar, 9050
Birmingham, 9245
Biscotasing, 9035
Bloomington, 9260
Bonaventure, 9000
Boston, 9200, 9215, 9235
Brampton, 9030
Brantford, 9020
Brattleboro, 9220
Brockville, 9015
Brunswick, 9200
Buffalo, 9210, 9235
Burbank, 9354, 9356
Burlington (Canada), 9020
Burlington (IA), 9290
Burlington (VT), 9220
BWI Airport, 9215

C

Calgary, 9065, 9090
Campbellton, 9000
Canora, 9055
Capreol, 9050
Carcross, 9100
Carlinville, 9260
Carbondale, 9255
Carlsbad Village, 9366
Centralia (IL), 9255
Centralia (WA), 9305, 9315
Chambord, 9005
Champaign, 9255
Chapleau, 9035
Charleston (SC), 9240
Charleston (WV), 9250
Charlotte, 9245
Charlottesville, 9215, 9250
Charny, 9000, 9010
Chatham, 9020
Chatsworth, 9354
Chemult, 9305
Chicago, 9235, 9250, 9255, 9260, 9265, 9270, 9275, 9285, 9290, 9295, 9300
Chico, 9305
Churchill, 9055
Cincinnati, 9250
Claremont, 9220
Cleveland, 9235

Clifton Forge, 9250
Clova, 9005
Cobalt, 9025
Cochrane, 9025
Columbia, 9240
Columbus, 9285
Coquitlam, 9070
Cormorant, 9055
Cornwall, 9015
Couber, 9015
Covina, 9358
Cranberry Portage, 9045
Crawfordsville, 9250
Croton Harmon, 9210
Culpeper, 9250
Cumberland, 9235

D

Dallas, 9300
Dauphin, 9055
Dearborn, 9275
Del Rio, 9310
Denali, 9105
Denver, 9290
Detroit , 9275
Devils Lake, 9285
Dodge City, 9295
Dorval, 9015
Dover, 9200
Drummondville, 9010
Dunsmuir, 9305
Durand, 9275
Durham, 9200

E

East Lansing, 9275
Edmonton, 9050, 9090
Edson, 9050
Effingham, 9255
Elizabethtown, 9230
Elkhart, 9235
Elko, 9290
El Monte, 9358
El Paso, 9310
Emeryville, 9290, 9305, 9325, 9330
Encinitas, 9366
Endeavour, 9055
Engleheart, 9025
Erie, 9235
Escondido, 9368
Essex, 9285
Eton, 9040
Eugene, 9305, 9315
Everett, 9285, 9315
Exeter, 9200

F

Fairbanks, 9105
Fargo, 9285
Fayetteville, 9240
Flagstaff, 9295
Flint, 9275
Florence, 9240
Foleyet, 9050
Fort Fraser, 9060
Fort Lauderdale, 9240
Fort Madison, 9295
Fort Worth, 9300
Franz, 9035, 9040
Fraser, 9100
Fraserdale, 9025
Fredericksburg, 9215
Freemont, 9352
Freeport, 9200
Fresno, 9330
Fullerton, 9360, 9364

G

Gainesville (GA), 9245
Gainesville (TX), 9300
Galesburg, 9265, 9290, 9295

Gallup, 9295
Gaspé, 9000
Georgetown, 9030
Gillam, 9055
Girdwood, 9105
Glasgow, 9285
Glenwood Springs, 9290
Granby, 9290
Grand Canyon, 9295
Grand Forks, 9285
Grand Junction, 9290
Grand Rapids, 9275
Grandview, 9105
Gravenhurst, 9025
Great America, 9352
Green River, 9290
Greensboro, 9245
Greensburg, 9225
Greenville, 9245
Greenwood, 9255
Guelph, 9030

H

Halifax, 9000
Hammond, 9255
Hanford, 9330
Harper's Ferry, 9235
Harrisburg, 9225, 9230
Hartford, 9215
Hastings, 9290
Hattiesburg, 9245
Haverhill, 9200
Havre, 9285
Hawk Junction, 9040
Hearst, 9040
Herchmer, 9055
Hervey, 9005
High Point, 9245
Homepayne, 9050
Houston, 9310
Hudson, 9210
Hudson Bay, 9055
Huntingdon, 9225
Huntington, 9250
Huntsville, 9025
Hurricane, 9105

I

Indianapolis, 9250
Industry, 9360
Irvine, 9362, 9364

J

Jackson (MI), 9275
Jackson (MS), 9255
Jacksonville, 9240, 9310
Jasper, 9050, 9060, 9065
Jefferson City, 9260
Johnstown, 9225
Joliet, 9260
Jonquière, 9005

K

Kalamazoo, 9275
Kamloops, 9050, 9065
Kankakee, 9255
Kansas City, 9260, 9295
Kelso, 9305, 9315
Kingman, 9295
Kingston, 9015
Kirkwood, 9260
Kissimmee, 9240
Kitchener, 9030
Kitimat, see Terrace
Klamath Falls, 9305

L

Lac Édouard, 9005
La Crosse, 9285
Lafayette (IN), 9250
Lafayette (LA), 9310
La Junta, 9295

Lake Charles, 9310
Lake Louise, 9065
Lamar, 9295
Lamy, 9295
Lancaster, 9230, 9356
Las Vegas (NM), 9295
Las Vegas (NV), 9280
Latrobe, 9225
La Tuque, 9005
Lee's Summit, 9260
Lewistown, 9225
Lincoln (IL), 9260
Lincoln (NB), 9290
Little Rock, 9300
Livermore, 9352
Lodi, 9330
London, 9020, 9030
Longlac, 9050
Longview, 9300
Lordsburg, 9310
Los Angeles, 9280, 9295, 9300, 9305, 9310, 9320, 9330, 9354, 9356, 9358, 9360, 9364
Lynchburg, 9215

M

Madera, 9330
Malta, 9285
Matapedia, 9000
Matapédia, 9000
McBride, 9060
McComb, 9255
McCook, 9290
Melville, 9050
Memphis, 9255, 9280
Menlo Park, 9350
Merced, 9330
Meridian, 9245
Miami, 9240
Michigan City, 9275
Millbrae, 9350
Milwaukee, 9270, 9285
Minneapolis, 9285
Minot, 9285
Miramichi, 9000
Mission City, 9070
Mobile, 9310
Modesto, 9330
Moncton, 9000
Mont Joli, 9000
Montpelier, 9220
Montréal, 9005, 9010, 9015, 9210
Moorpark, 9354
Moose River, 9025
Moosonee, 9025
Mosher, 9040
Mountain View 9350
Mount Vernon, 9315

N

Nashville, 9280
Needles, 9295
Nelson River, see Gillam
Newark (NJ), 9215, 9230, 9240
Newbern, 9255
New Hazelton, 9060
New Haven, 9215
New Iberia, 9310
New Liskeard, 9025
New London, 9215
New Orleans, 9245, 9255, 9310
Newport News, 9215
Newton, 9295

New York, 9210, 9215, 9230, 9240
Niagara Falls (Canada), 9020
Niagara Falls (USA), 9210
Niles, 9275
Norfolk, 9215
North Bay, 9025
Northampton (USA), 9220

O

Oakland, 9305, 9325, 9330
Oakville, 9020
Oba, 9040, 9050
Oceanside, 9320, 9362, 9364, 9366, 9368
Oklahoma City, 9300
Old Orchard Beach, 9200
Olympia, 9305, 9315
Omaha, 9290
Orlando, 9240, 9310
Orange, 9362, 9364
Oshawa, 9015
Ottawa, 9015
Ottumwa, 9290
Oxnard, 9320, 9354

P

Palm Springs, 9310
Palo Alta 9350
Paoli, 9230
Parent, 9005
Parry Sound, 9050
Pasco, 9285
Paso Robles, 9305
Percé, 9000
Perris, 9360
Petersburg, 9240, 9245
Philadelphia, 9215, 9230, 9240
Phoenix, 9295
Pittsburgh, 9225, 9235
Pitsfield, 9235
Plattsburgh, 9210
Pleasanton, 9352
Pomona, 9310, 9358, 9360
Pontiac (IL), 9260, 9300
Pontiac (MI), 9275
Poplar Bluff, 9300
Portage, 9105
Portage la Prairie, 9050, 9055
Port Huron, 9275
Portland (ME), 9200
Portland (OR), 9285, 9305, 9315
Poughkeepsie, 9210
Prince George, 9060
Prince Rupert, 9060
Princeton, 9265
Providence, 9215
Provo, 9290
Pukatawagan, 9045

Q

Québec City, 9010
Quesnel, 9065
Quincy, 9265

R

Raleigh, 9240, 9245
Randolph, 9220
Raton, 9295
Redding, 9305
Red Lake Road, 9050
Redwood City, 9350
Reno, 9290
Rhinecliff Kingston, 9210
Richmond (VA), 9215, 9240, 9245
Rimouski, 9000
Rivière à Pierre, 9005
Rivière du Loup, 9005

Rivers, 9050
Riverside, 9360, 9362
Rochester, 9210, 9235
Rocky Mount, 9240, 9245
Rutland, 9210

SAN, ST.

San Antonio, 9300, 9310
San Bernardino, 9295, 9358, 9362
San Clemente, 9362, 9364
San Diego, 9320, 9366
San Francisco, 9290, 9305, 9325, 9330, 9350
San Jose, 9305, 9325, 9350, 9352
San Juan Capistrano, 9320, 9362, 9364
San Luis Obispo, 9305, 9320
San Marcos, 9300, 9368
Santa Ana, 9362, 9364
Santa Barbara, 9305, 9320
Santa Clara, 9350, 9352, 9356
Santa Maria, 9320
St. Albans, 9220
St. Catharines, 9020
St. Cloud, 9285
Ste. Foy, 9010
St. Hyacinthe, 9010
St. Lambert, 9010
St. Louis, 9260, 9300
St. Paul, 9285

S

Saco, 9200
Sacramento, 9290, 9305, 9325, 9330
Salem, 9305, 9315
Salinas, 9305
Salisbury, 9245
Salt Lake City, 9290
Sandpoint, 9285
Sandusky, 9235
Saratoga Springs, 9210
Sarnia, 9030
Saskatoon, 9050
Sault Ste. Marie, 9040
Savannah, 9240
Schenectady, 9210
Seattle, 9285, 9305, 9315
Sebring, 9240
Sedalia, 9260
Senneterre, 9005
Seward, 9105
Shawinigan, 9005
Shelby, 9285
Sioux Lookout, 9050
Skagway 9100
Smithers, 9060
Smiths Falls, 9015
Solana Beach, 9320, 9366
Sorrento Valley, 9366
South Bend, 9235
South Portsmouth, 9250
Spartanburg, 9245
Spencer, 9105
Spokane, 9285
Springfield (IL), 9260, 9300
Springfield (MA), 9215, 9220, 9235
Stamford, 9215
Stockton, 9330, 9352
Stratford, 9030
Sturtevant, 9270
Sudbury, 9035, 9050
Sunnyvale, 9350
Swastika, 9025
Syracuse, 9210, 9235

T

Tacoma, 9305, 9315

Talkeetna, 9105
Tallahassee, 9310
Tampa, 9240
Taylor, 9300
Temple, 9300
Terrace, 9060
Texarkana, 9300
The Pas, 9045, 9055
Thicket Potage, 9055
Thompson, 9055
Toledo, 9235
Tomah, 9285
Topeka, 9295
Toronto, 9015, 9020, 9025, 9030, 9050
Tracy, 9352
Trinidad, 9295
Truckee, 9290
Truro, 9000
Tucson, 9310
Tukwila, 9315
Tuscaloosa, 9245
Tyrone, 9225

U

Utica, 9210

V

Valemount, 9050
Vancouver (Canada), 9050, 9065, 9070, 9285, 9315
Vancouver (USA) 9285, 9305, 9315
Van Nuys, 9354
Via Princessa, 9356
Victorville, 9295
Virginia Beach, 9215
Vista, 9368

W

Wabowden, 9055
Wainwright, 9050
Walnut Ridge, 9300
Washago, 9025, 9050
Washington DC, 9215, 9235, 9240, 9245, 9250
Wasilla, 9105
Waterbury, 9220
Waterloo, 9235
Wells, 9200
Wenatchee, 9285
West Corona, 9360, 9362
West Palm Beach, 9240
Westport, 9210
Weymont, 9005
Whistler, 9065
Whitefish, 9285
Whitehorse, 9100
White Pass, 9100
White River, 9035
White River Junction, 9250
White Sulphur Springs, 9250
Whittier, 9105
Williams, 9295
Windsor (Ont Canada), 9020
Windsor (VT USA) 9220
Winnemucca, 9290
Winnipeg, 9050, 9055
Winslow, 9295
Winter Haven, 9240
Winter Park (CO), 9290
Winter Park (FL), 9240
Wisconsin Dells, 9285
Woodstock, 9020
Worcester, 9235

Y

Yazoo City, 9255
Yonkers, 9210
Yuma, 9310

ITE

CANADA

Capital: **Ottawa** (GMT -5).   2017 Public Holidays: Jan. 1, 2, Apr. 14, July 1, 3, Sep. 4, Oct. 9, Nov. 11, Dec. 25.

The principal operator in Canada is Via Rail (Via Rail ✆ 1 888 842 7245. www.viarail.ca). Timings shown are the most recently available and are subject to alteration at any time, but especially around public holidays. Details of other operators can be found in relevant tables. Unless otherwise noted all trains carry first and second class seated accomodation. In Canada first class is called 'Via1' and second class is called 'Economy'. Most very long distance trains convey sleeping cars, and where this is the case it is detailed in the footnotes. Almost all sleeping car accommodation in North America has two berths per compartment, some of which are en-suite, although the exact product offering varies by operator and route. Most trains also convey some form of catering, but again the actual service offered varies considerably. Tickets are available from staffed stations, websites and through authorised ticketing agents. A reservation is neccessary for travel on very long distance Via Rail trains, but generally not for corridor services such as Montréal - Ottawa/Toronto and Toronto - Windsor/London/Sarnia.

Via Rail offers the CANRAIL PASS which is a convenient and flexible pass that allows you to choose between 7, 10 or unlimited one-way trips to a destination of your choice. You have the choice of travelling between Quebec and Ontario for 21 consecutive days with our Corridor pass, or across Canada for 60 consecutive days with our System Pass. The BASE PASS for Economy or Escape fare tickets costs: - Corridor, $299 for 7 one-way tickets, $399 for 10 one-way tickets. System, $699 for 7 one-way tickets, $899 for 10 one-way tickets. Note: these have limited seat availability. EXTRA PASS for Economy or Escape fare tickets and Economy Plus fare seats booked the day before departure costs :- Corridor, $369 for 7 one-way tickets, $499 for 10 one-way tickets. System, $769 for 7 one-way tickets, $999 for 10 one-way tickets. The unlimited Corridor pass costs $699 for unlimited travel over 21 consecutive days and the unlimited System pass costs $1299 for unlimited travel over 60 consecutive days. There are reductions for 60 +, students and youths. For conditions see www.viarail.ca.

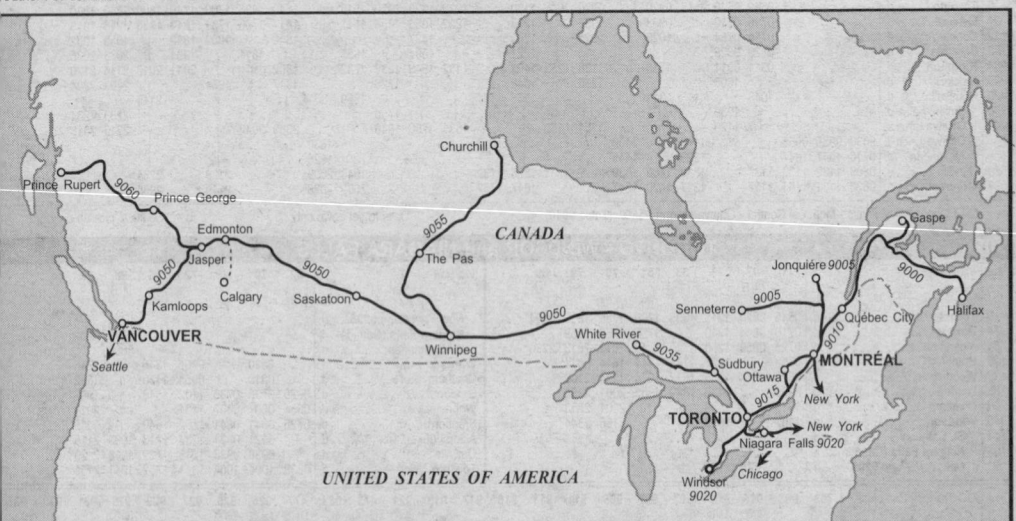

GASPÉ and HALIFAX — Via Rail — 9000

km			15 Ⓡ ③⑤⑦ A	17 Ⓡ ③⑤⑦ Z	B			16 Ⓡ ③⑤⑦ Z	14 Ⓡ ③⑤⑦ B	A
1099	Halifax	d.	1300	...		Montréal Central 9010	d.	1900	1900	
996	Truro	d.	1431	...		Sainte Foy 9010	d.	2249	2249	
872	Amherst	d.	1608	...		Rivière du Loup	d.	0113	0113	
795	Moncton	d.	1717	...		Rimouski	d.	0301	0301	
795	Moncton	d.	1732	...		Mont Joli	d.	0339	0339	
666	Miramichi	d.	1937	...		Matapédia	d.	0610	0610	
494	Campbellton	d.	2318	...		Bonaventure	d.	0909		
800	Gaspé	d.		1520		Percé	d.	1158		
737	Percé	d.		1639		Gaspé	a.	1317		
618	Bonaventure	d.		1930		Campbellton	d.	...	0748	
475	Matapédia	d.	2252	2252		Miramichi	d.	...	1123	
325	Mont Joli	d.	0126	0126		Moncton	a.	...	1323	
296	Rimouski	d.	0201	0201		Moncton	d.	...	1338	
192	Rivière du Loup	d.	0353	0352		Amherst	d.	...	1442	
0	Sainte Foy 9010	a.	0613	0613		Truro	d.	...	1622	
	Montréal Central 9010	a.	1003	1003		Halifax	d.	...	1751	

A – OCEAN – 🛏 Montréal - Halifax and v.v.
B – 🛏 Montréal - Gaspé and v.v.
Z – During infrastructure work currently in progress, trains 16 and 17 are not operating and train services between Matapédia and Gaspé are suspended. As an alternative you can travel on trains 14 and 15 between Montréal and Matapédia.

JONQUIÈRE and SENNETERRE — Via Rail — 9005

km			604 Ⓡ 2 ②④	606 Ⓡ 2 ⑦	600 Ⓡ 2 ②④	602 Ⓡ 2 ⑦
717	Senneterre	d.	0545	0845	...	...
561	Clova	d.	0750	1050	...	...
495	Parent	d.	0850	1150	...	...
	Weymont	d.	1001	1301	...	...
297	La Tuque	d.	1153	1453	...	...
510	Jonquière	d.	...	...	0810	1110
444	Chambord	d.	...	...	0911	1211
341	Lac Édouard	d.	...	...	1105	1405
251	Rivière à Pierre	d.	...	...	1240	1540
217	Hervey	a.	1325	1625	1350	1650
217	Hervey	d.	1400	1700	1400	1700
170	Shawinigan	d.	1448	1748	1448	1748
0	Montréal Central	a.	1715	2015	1715	2015

			601 Ⓡ 2 ①③	605 Ⓡ 2 ⑤	603 Ⓡ 2 ①③	607 Ⓡ 2 ⑤
	Montréal Central	d.	0815	0910	0815	0910
	Shawinigan	d.	1043	1138	1043	1138
	Hervey	a.	1130	1225	1130	1225
	Hervey	d.	1140	1235	1200	1255
	Rivière à Pierre	d.	1234	1329	...	...
	Lac Édouard	d.	1408	1503	...	...
	Chambord	d.	1605	1700	...	...
	Jonquière	a.	1710	1805	...	...
	La Tuque	d.	...	...	1318	1413
	Weymont	d.	...	...	1504	1559
	Parent	d.	...	...	1625	1720
	Clova	d.	...	...	1721	1816
	Senneterre	a.	...	...	1940	2035

QUÉBEC CITY - MONTRÉAL — Via Rail — 9010

km			15 2 ①④⑥ A*	17 2 ①④⑥ ZB*	33 C	35 C	37 ①–⑤ C	25 ⑥ C	637 ⑦ C	39 ①–⑤ C	29 C
0	Québec City Palais	▽ d.	...	...	0527	0805	1300	1300	1300	1500	1745
21	Ste. Foy	▽ d.	0628	0628	0553	0830	1326	1326	1326	1526	1811
23	Charny	▽ d.	...	...	0838						
72	Drummondville	d.	0836	0836	0711	1014	1507	1507	1507	1652	1949
219	St. Hyacinthe	d.	0915	0915	...	1043					2020
265	St. Lambert	d.	0950	0950	0814	1111	1601	1601	1601	1757	2047
272	Montréal Central	▽ a.	1003	1003	0825	1122	1612	1612	1612	1808	2058

			20 ①–⑤	622 ⑤⑦ C	22 ①–⑤	24 C	26 ①–⑥⑦ C	28 C ①–⑥⑦		16 2 ③⑤⑦ ZB*	14 2 ①④⑥ A*
	Montréal Central	▽ d.	0605	0853	0843	1245	1610	1815	...	1900	1900
	St. Lambert	▽ d.	0618	0905	0905	1308	1632	1838	...	1925	1925
	St. Hyacinthe	d.	0645	0930				1905	...	1958	1958
	Drummondville	d.	0714	0958	0958	1401	1740	1942	...	2047	2047
	Charny	▽ d.	...	...	1555				...		
	Ste. Foy	▽ d.	0911	1143	1143	1603	1919	2111	...	2204a	2234a
	Québec City Palais	▽ a.	0934	1206	1206	1626	1941	2133	...		

A – OCEAN – 🛏 Montréal Central - Halifax and v.v. (Table 9000).
B – 🛏 Montréal Central - Gaspé and v.v. (Table 9000).
C – 🛏 Québec City Palais - Montréal Central - Ottawa Union and v.v. (Table 9015).
Z – During infrastructure work currently in progress, trains 16 and 17 are not operating and train services between Matapédia and Gaspé are suspended.

a – Arrival time.
s – Calls to set down only.
* – A shuttle operates between Sainte-Foy and Québec City Palais Ⓡ required.
▽ – Local traffic not carried Montréal Central - St Lambert and v.v., or Québec City Palais - Charny and v.v.
u – Request stop. Calls to pick up only.

9015 MONTRÉAL - OTTAWA - TORONTO

Via Rail

km		41	641	43	51	61	643	33	633	63	45	65	47	35	645	55	635	67	647	69	59	37	637	669		39	639
								A						A								A	A			A	
		①–⑤	⑥	①–⑤	①–⑤	①–⑥	⑥⑦	①–⑤	⑥⑦							⑦–⑤	⑦–⑤		⑦–⑤			①–⑤	⑦			①–⑤	⑥
0	**Montréal** Central d.	...	...	...	0610	0635	...	0900	0900	0855	...	1055	...	1137	...	...	1500	1545	...	1640	...	1650	1650	1840	...	1850	1900
19	Dorval d.	...	...	...	0634	0703	...	0932	0925	0920	...	1119	...	1210	...	...	1525	1608	...	1704	...	1724	1824	1904	...	1924	1924
100	Alexandria d.	...	...	...	0718	|	...	1016	1012	|	...	|	...	1259	...	...	|	|	...	|	...	1807	1807	|	...	2011	2011
187	**Ottawa** Union a.	...	...	...	0810	|	...	1106	1105	|	...	|	...	1345	...	...	1655	|	...	|	...	1856	1856	|	...	2055	2055
187	**Ottawa** Union d.	0530	0640	0720	0825	|	0910	...	...	|	1030	|	1230	1345	1430	1530	...	|	1700	|	1817	...	...	|	...		
253	Smiths Falls d.	0622	0726	|	0913	|	0959	...	...	|	|	|	|	...	|	|	...	|	|	|	1916	...	...	|	...	**651**	**655**
	Cornwall d.	|	|	|	|	0755	|	...	...	1013	|	1211	|	...	|	|	...	1659	|	|	|	...	...	1955	...	2	2
298	Brockville d.	0651	0755	|	0942	|	1033	...	...	|	|	1257	1357	...	|	1654	...	|	|	1834	1951	...	...	|	...	①–⑤	⑥
378	**Kingston** d.	0734	0838	0914	1026	0924	1116	...	...	1143	1233	1341	1446	...	1635	1738	...	1826	1856	1917	2035	...	...	2120	...	0532	0645
451	Belleville d.	0816	0919	|	|	1002	1200	...	...	|	|	1422	1529	...	1716	1818	...	|	|	|	2117	...	...	|	...	0614	0725
520	Cobourg d.	0851	0951	|	1137	|	1234	...	...	|	|	1459	|	...	|	1852	...	|	|	|	2157	...	...	|	...	0659	0806
581	Oshawa d.	0927	1029	|	|	1111	1314	...	...	1355	|	1532	1638	...	1823	1925	...	2010	2044	2101	2232	...	...	2304	...	0739	0842
633	**Toronto** Union a.	1002	1102	1125	1242	1141	1347	...	...	1407	1448	1603	1715	...	1905	1957	...	2039	2116	2130	2307	...	...	2333	...	0825	0914

km		22	32	632	60	50	34	62	26	52	40	64	28	42	644	44	66	38	46	646	68	650	668	48	648		
		A							A				A														
		①–⑤	①–⑤	⑥⑦	①–⑥	①–⑥			①–⑥				⑦–⑤	①–⑤					⑦–⑤	⑦–⑤	⑦–⑤	①–⑤		①–⑥	⑦		
0	**Toronto** Union d.	...	...	...	0640	0640	...	0920	...	0920	1045	1130	...	1220	1320	1420	1515	...	1540	1635	1700	1740	1800	1840	1840	...	...
51	Oshawa d.	...	...	...	0719	0719	...	0953	...	0953	|	1208	...	1252	1353	1454	1547	...	1617	1706	1731	1814	1833	1916	1915	...	...
113	Cobourg d.	...	...	...	0754	0754	...	1025	...	1025	|	1243	...	|	1427	|	|	...	1650	|	1802	1849	|	1953	1952	...	...
182	Belleville d.	...	...	...	0829	0829	...	|	...	|	|	1321	...	|	1504	|	1653	...	|	1811	|	1931	|	2036	2035	...	...
254	**Kingston** d.	...	...	...	0911	0911	...	1138	...	1138	1252	1402	...	1432	1543	1636	1732	...	1802	|	|	2011	2016	2116	2120	...	...
335	Brockville d.	...	...	...	|	1008	...	|	...	1235	|	1448	...	|	|	1720	|	...	1847	|	1954	...	|	2203	2204	...	...
428	Cornwall d.	...	...	...	1048	|	...	1311	...	|	|	1535	...	|	|	|	1859	...	|	|	|	...	2143	|	|	...	...
380	Smiths Falls d.	...	...	...	|	1039	...	|	...	|	|	|	...	|	|	1750	|	...	|	|	|	...	|	2233	2234	...	...
446	**Ottawa** Union a.	...	...	...	|	1129	...	|	...	1351	1455	|	...	1631	1750	1846	|	...	2009	2042	|	...	|	2316	2318	...	...
	Ottawa Union d.	0630	0955	0955	|	...	1140	|	1400	...	...	|	1610	...	...	...	|	1830	...	...	|	...	|	...	...	...	...
	Alexandria d.	0716	1047	1047	|	...	1229	|	1445	...	...	|	|	...	...	...	|	1925	...	...	|	...	|	...	...	...	...
520	Dorval d.	0809	1132	1132	1137	...	1318	1400	1529	...	...	1626	1739	...	...	...	1948	2009	...	...	2129	...	2234	...	...	...	...
539	**Montréal** Central a.	0828	1151	1151	1157	...	1337	1420	1547	...	...	1647	1757	...	...	...	2009	2028	...	...	2149	...	2255	...	...	...	...

A – 12 Québec City Palais - Montréal Central - Ottawa Union and v.v. (Table **9010**). s – Calls to set down only. u – Calls to pick up only.

9020 TORONTO - WINDSOR and NIAGARA FALLS

GO Transit, Via Rail

km	Via Rail	71	97	73	83	81	75	79	69	
			R B							
					①–⑤	⑥	⑦–⑤			
0	**Toronto** Union d.	0645	0820	1215	1635	1730	1730	1935	2204	...
34	Oakville d.	0710	0844	1240	|	1756	1756	1959	2227	...
56	Aldershot d.	0725	0859	1258	1713	1812	1812	2013	2239	...
96	Brantford d.	0753	|	1327	1743	1844	1844	2041	...	...
139	Woodstock d.	0825	|	1355	1812	1914	1914	2109	...	...
185	London d.	0905	|	1430	1849	1955	2001	2150	...	...
290	Chatham d.	1013	|	1539	...	...	2104	2253	...	...
360	**Windsor** a.	1102	|	1630	...	...	2156	2344	...	...
114	St. Catharines d.	...	0954	...	...	...	...	...	...	...
133	**Niagara Falls** (Canada) a.	...	1016	...	...	...	...	...	...	...
	*New York Penn **9205*** a.	...	2145	...	...	...	...	...	...	...

Via Rail	82	70	80	72	76	98	78		
						R B			
	①–⑤	①–⑥	⑦						
*New York Penn **9205*** d.	...	...	...	...	...	0715	...	...	...
Niagara Falls (Canada) d.	...	...	...	...	...	1745	...	...	...
St. Catharines d.	...	...	...	...	...	1808	...	...	...
Windsor d.	...	0530	...	0905	1345	|	1745	...	...
Chatham d.	...	0618	...	0951	1430	|	1832	...	...
London d.	0625	0730	0730	1102	1543	|	1942	...	...
Woodstock d.	0654	0807	0807	1131	|	|	2014	...	...
Brantford d.	0725	0841	0841	1202	1640	|	2045	...	...
Aldershot d.	|	0921	0921	1234	1713	1903	2115	...	...
Oakville d.	|	0938	0938	1248	1727	1918	2129	...	...
Toronto Union a.	0835	1004	1004	1311	1752	1941	2151	...	...

km	GO Transit - 2nd class.	703	903	905	905	907	907	909	911	913	915	917	919	921	473	923	477	925	925	927	929	929	931	933	935
		①–⑤		⑥⑦	①–⑤	⑥⑦	①–⑤							⑥⑦	①–⑤	⑥⑦	①–⑤	①–⑤	⑥⑦		①–⑤	⑥⑦			
0	**Toronto** Union ☛ d.	0613	0643	0743	0748	0843	0848	0943	1043	1143	1243	1343	1443	1543	1600	1643	1700	1740	1743	1843	1943	1943	2043	2143	2243
34	Oakville d.	0651	0724	0824	0829	0924	0929	1024	1124	1224	1324	1424	1524	1624	1631	1724	1731	1821	1824	1924	2024	2024	2124	2224	2324
51	Burlington ☛ a.	0710	0744	0844	0849	0944	0949	1044	1144	1244	1344	1444	1544	1644	1651	1744	1751	1841	1844	1944	2044	2044	2144	2244	2344
114	St. Catharines a.	*0820**	*0854**	*0959**	*0959**	*1059**	*1059**	*1159**	*1254**	*1354**	*1459**	*1559**	*1659**	*1759**	*1816**	*1859**	*1911**	*1956**	*1959**	*2059**	*2154**	*2154**	*2254**	*2354**	*0054**
133	**Niagara Falls** (Canada) a.	*0845**	*0924**	*1024**	*1024**	*1124**	*1124**	*1224**	*1324**	*1424**	*1524**	*1624**	*1724**	*1824**	*1841**	*1924**	*1936**	*2021**	*2024**	*2124**	*2219**	*2224**	*2324**	*0019**	*0119**

GO Transit - 2nd class only.	900	470	704	496	908	710	910	912	914	916	918	920	922	922	924	726	926	928	730	930	932	934	936	938
		①–⑤	①–⑤	①–⑤	⑥⑦	①–⑤	⑥⑦						⑥⑦	①–⑤	⑥⑦	①–⑤	⑥⑦		⑤					
Niagara Falls (Canada) d.	...	*0454**	*0524**	*0554**	*0627**	*0652**	*0722**	*0827**	*0922**	*1017**	*1117**	*1217**	*1317**	*1314**	*1417**	*1441**	*1517**	*1617**	...	*1717**	*1817**	*1917**	*2022**	*2127**
St. Catharines d.	...	*0514**	*0544**	*0619**	*0652**	*0717**	*0747**	*0852**	*0947**	*1042**	*1142**	*1242**	*1342**	*1339**	*1442**	*1506**	*1542**	*1642**	*1742**	*1742**	*1842**	*1942**	*2047**	*2152**
Burlington ☛ d.	0539	0629	0658	0738	0807	0842	0907	1007	1107	1207	1307	1407	1507	1504	1607	1631	1707	1807	1842	1907	2007	2107	2207	2307
Oakville d.	0557	0647	0717	0757	0834	0901	0926	1026	1126	1226	1326	1426	1526	1523	1626	1650	1726	1826	1901	1926	2026	2126	2226	2326
Toronto Union ☛ a.	0640	0720	0750	0830	0910	0946	1010	1116	1211	1311	1411	1511	1610	1608	1710	1735	1810	1911	1946	2011	2111	2211	2311	0011

B – THE MAPLE LEAF – 12 and 🍷 Toronto (**97/98**) - Niagara Falls (**64/63**) - New York and v.v. (Table **9210**). * – Connection by 🚌 (Route 12).
☛ – Additional trains are available Toronto – Burlington and v.v.

9025 TORONTO - COCHRANE

Ontario Northland

km		421	🚌
		①–⑤	
		C	
0	**Toronto** Bay Street d.	...	0915
143	Washago d.	...	1145
164	Gravenhurst d.	...	1205
219	Huntsville d.	...	1315
351	**North Bay** a.	...	1450
351	**North Bay** d.	...	1615*
513	Cobalt d.	...	1755
529	New Liskeard d.	...	1825
571	Engleheart d.	...	1920
643	Swastika d.	...	2010r
677	Matheson d.	...	2115*
754	**Cochrane** a.	...	2230
754	**Cochrane** d.	0900	...
	Fraserdale d.	1045r	...
	Moose River d.	1235r	...
1053	**Moosonee** a.	1350	...

	🚌	422
		①–⑤
		C
Moosonee d.	...	1700
Moose River d.	...	1807r
Fraserdale d.	...	1957r
Cochrane a.	...	2145
Cochrane d.	0815	...
Matheson d.	0935*	...
Swastika d.	1025r	...
Engleheart d.	1115	...
New Liskeard d.	1205	...
Cobalt d.	1230	...
North Bay a.	1420	...
North Bay d.	1600*	...
Huntsville d.	1740	...
Gravenhurst d.	1835	...
Washago d.	1910	...
Toronto Union a.	2145	...

C – POLAR BEAR EXPRESS – 2 and 🍷 Cochrane - Moosonee and v.v. R, also ⑦ in summer. r – Calls on request. * – Change buses.

9030 TORONTO - SARNIA

2nd class Via Rail

km		85	87
0	**Toronto** Union d.	1055	1740
34	Brampton d.	1129	1814
47	Georgetown d.	1140	1826
79	Guelph d.	1206	1851
101	Kitchener d.	1232	1918
143	Stratford d.	1309	1955
195	London d.	1417	2114
290	**Sarnia** a.	...	2220

	84	88
Sarnia d.	0610	...
London d.	0732	1951
Stratford d.	0840	2105
Kitchener d.	0918	2142
Guelph d.	0944	2212
Georgetown d.	1010	2237
Brampton d.	1020	2247
Toronto Union a.	1053	2317

9035 WHITE RIVER - SUDBURY

Via Rail

km		186	
		2	
		③⑤⑦	
0	**White River** d.	0700	...
79	Franz d.	0820	...
209	Chapleau d.	1045	...
341	Biscotasing d.	1245	...
484	**Sudbury** § a.	1550	...

	185	
	2	
	②④⑥	
Sudbury § d.	0900	...
Biscotasing d.	1130	...
Chapleau d.	1415	...
Franz d.	1630	...
White River a.	1745	...

§ – Sudbury is 10 km from Sudbury Junction (Table **9050**).

9040 HEARST - SAULT STE MARIE

km		632	632
		2D	2D
		②⑤⑦	②⑤⑦
0	**Hearst** d.	0800	0830
82	Oba d.	0915	0945
126	Mosher d.	0955	1030
162	Franz d.	1045	1115
211	Hawk Junction d.	1150	1225
282	Eton d.	1310	1340
292	Agawa Canyon d.	1325	1355
475	**Sault Ste. Marie** a.	1740	1810

	631	631
	2D	2D
	①④⑥	①④⑥
Sault Ste. Marie d.	0900	0920
Agawa Canyon d.	1305	1325
Eton d.	1320	1340
Hawk Junction d.	1500	1520
Franz d.	1545	1605
Mosher d.	1630	1650
Oba d.	1710	1730
Hearst a.	1840	1900

D – Service suspended until further notice.

9045 THE PAS - PUKATAWAGAN

Keewatin Railway

km		291	
		F	
		①④	
0	**The Pas 9055** d.	1115	...
88	Cranberry Portage d.	1355	...
251	**Pukatawagan** a.	1845	...

	290	
	F	
	②⑤	
Pukatawagan d.	1000	...
Cranberry Portage d.	1515	...
The Pas 9055 a.	1730	...

F – Operated by Keewatin Railway Company. To book ✆ 204 623 5255.

TORONTO - VANCOUVER 9050

Via Rail

km		1 R A			2 R A
0	Toronto Union....d.	2200 ② ⑥	Vancouver Pacific...a.		2030 ② ⑤
143	Washago....d.	0040 ③ ⑦	Agassiz....d.		2233
241	Parry Sound....d.	0242	Kamloops North....d.		0600 ③ ⑥
422	Sudbury Junction..§ d.	0513	Kamloops North....a.		0635
444	Capreol....a.	0538	Valemount....d.		1250
444	Capreol....d.	0608	Jasper....a.		1600
683	Foleyet....d.	1059	Jasper....d.		1730
859	Oba....d.	1351	Edson....d.		2020
921	Homepayne....d.	1520	Edmonton....a.		2300
1084	Longlac....d.	1749	Edmonton....d.		2359
1537	Sioux Lookout....d.	0009 ④ ①	Wainwright....d.		0315 ④ ⑦
1652	Red Lake Road....d.	0209	Biggar....d.		0645
1943	Winnipeg....a.	0800	Saskatoon....a.		0800
1943	Winnipeg....d.	1145	Saskatoon....d.		0825
2032	Portage la Prairie....d.	1309	Melville....d.		1120
2173	Rivers....d.	1458	Rivers....d.		1645
2394	Melville....d.	1727	Portage la Prairie....d.		1930
2702	Saskatoon....a.	2207	Winnipeg....a.		2045
2702	Saskatoon....d.	2232	Winnipeg....d.		2230
2792	Biggar....d.	2359	Red Lake Road....d.		0251 ⑤ ①
3017	Wainwright....d.	0300 ⑤ ②	Sioux Lookout....d.		0542
3221	Edmonton....a.	0622	Longlac....d.		1303
3221	Edmonton....d.	0737	Homepayne....d.		1610
3430	Edson....d.	1013	Oba....d.		1710
3600	Jasper....a.	1300	Foleyet....d.		1958
3600	Jasper....d.	1430	Capreol....a.		0018 ⑥ ②
3721	Valemount....d.	1607	Capreol....d.		0048
4052	Kamloops North....a.	2309	Sudbury Junction..§ d.		0117
4052	Kamloops North....d.	2344	Parry Sound....d.		0433
4360	Agassiz....d.		Washago....d.		0649
4466	Vancouver Pacific....a.	0942 ⑥ ②	Toronto Union....a.		0930 ⑥ ②

A – THE CANADIAN – ➡ 1 cl., 🛏 and ✕ Toronto - Vancouver and v.v. From Toronto on ②⑥ (also ④ May 4 - Oct. 12). From Vancouver on ②⑤ (also ⑦ April 30 - Oct. 8).
- Request stop.
§ – Sudbury Junction is 10 km from Sudbury (Table **9035**).

ROCKY MOUNTAINEER TOURS 9065

RMR

	D	E	G	H		H	E	D	G
Seattle....d.				1510	Calgary....d.		...		...
Vancouver ‡....a.				2045	Banff....d.		0740		...
Vancouver ‡....d.	0730	0730			Lake Louise....d.		0900		...
N. Vancouver....d.			0740		Jasper....d.		0810		0655
Whistler....♥ a.			1130		Kamloops....♥ a.		1700	1815	
Whistler....♥ d.			0710		Kamloops....♥ d.		0735	0735	
Quesnel....♥ a.			1930		Quesnel....♥ a.				1930
Quesnel....♥ d.			0710		Quesnel....♥ d.				0710
Kamloops....♥ a.			1730	1730	Whistler....♥ a.				1930
Kamloops....♥ d.	0625	0745			Whistler....♥ d.				1510
Jasper....a.		1800	2030		N. Vancouver....a.				1900
Lake Louise....a.	1830				Vancouver ‡....a.		0810		
Banff....a.	1930				Vancouver ‡....d.				
Calgary....a.					Seattle....a.		1315		

D – FIRST PASSAGE TO THE WEST – For 2017 dates contact operator. ◀
E – JOURNEY THROUGH THE CLOUDS – For 2017 dates contact operator. ◀
G – RAINFOREST TO GOLD RUSH – For 2017 dates contact operator. ★
H – COASTAL PASSAGE – For 2017 dates contact operator. ★
◀ – Services operate on selected dates from late April to early October.
★ – Services operate on selected dates from mid May to early October.
‡ – Vancouver Cottrell Street.
♥ – Compulsory overnight stop, arrival times are flexible.
Operator : Rocky Mountaineer Railtours (www.rockymountaineer.com)

WINNIPEG - CHURCHILL 9055

Via Rail

km		693 R B				692 R B
0	Winnipeg....d.	1205 ②⑦	Churchill....d.		1930	②④⑥
88	Portage la Prairie....d.	1315r	Herchmer....d.		0003	③⑤⑦
283	Dauphin....d.	1706r	Giliam (Nelson River)....d.		0530	
484	Canora a....d.	1946	Thompson....a.		1130	
549	Endeavour a....d.	2054r	Thompson....d.		1400	
635	Hudson Bay a....d.	2232r	Thicket Potage....d.		1622	
777	The Pas 9045....a.	0145 ③①	Wabowden....d.		1811	
777	The Pas 9045....d.	0230 ③①⑤	Cormorant....d.		2147	
843	Cormorant....d.	0412	The Pas 9045....a.		2330	③⑤⑦
996	Wabowden....d.	0748	The Pas 9045....d.		0315	⑥①
1073	Thicket Potage....d.	0937	Hudson Bay a....d.		0427r	
1149	Thompson....a.	1200	Endeavour a....d.		0555r	
1149	Thompson....d.	1700	Canora a....d.		0718	
1401	Giliam (Nelson River)....d.	2330	Dauphin....d.		1206	
1540	Herchmer....d.	0426 ④②⑥	Portage la Prairie....d.		1537r	
1697	Churchill....a.	0900 ④②⑥	Winnipeg....a.		1645	⑥①

B – 🛏 1 cl., 🛏 and ✕ Churchill - Winnipeg and v.v. Note: only runs on days shown.
a – Sasakatchewan, always standard time.
r – Request stop.

PRINCE RUPERT - JASPER 9060

Via Rail

km		5 R ③⑤⑦			6 R ③⑤⑦
0	Jasper....d.	1245 ③⑤⑦	Prince Rupert....d.		0800 ③⑤⑦
174	McBride....d.	1444	Terrace (Kitimat)....d.		1025
409	Prince George....a.	1908	New Hazelton....d.		1230r
409	Prince George....d.	0800 ④⑥①	Smithers....d.		1424
560	Fort Fraser....d.	1032r	Fort Fraser....d.		1757r
795	Smithers....d.	1420	Prince George....a.		2029
869	New Hazelton....d.	1537r	Prince George....d.		0945 ④⑥①
1007	Terrace (Kitimat)....d.	1805	McBride....d.		1348
1160	Prince Rupert....a.	2025	Jasper....a.		1830

Compulsory overnight stop in **Prince George**. Passengers must arrange their own accommodation.
r – Request stop.

VANCOUVER - MISSION CITY 9070

West Coast

km		①-⑤	①-⑤		①-⑤	①-⑤	①-⑤
0	Vancouver Waterfront....d.	1550	1620		1650	1730	1820
26	Coquitlam....d.	1619	1649		1719	1759	1849
68	Mission City....a.	1705	1735		1805	1845	1935

		①-⑤	①-⑤		①-⑤	①-⑤	①-⑤
Mission City....d.		...	0525	0555		0625	0655	0725
Coquitlam....d.		...	0610	0640		0710	0740	0810
Vancouver Waterfront....a.		...	0640	0710		0740	0810	0840

Operator : West Coast Express ✆ 604 488 8906.

🚌 CALGARY - EDMONTON 🚌 9090

Greyhound

km		5200 ex⑦	5204 ①⑤⑥	5206	5208	5210 a	5214	5216 ⑤⑦	5218 ex②	5222	5224 ⑤⑦
0	Calgary....d.	0030	0700	0800	1130	1300	1600	1700	1800	1900	1945
303	Edmonton....a.	0655	1040	1150	1530	1730	1940	2100	2200	2240	2345

		5201 ①⑤⑥	5205	5207	5211 ex⑥	5209	5215 ex②③	5217 ex⑥	5219 ⑤⑦	5223 ex②	5225 ⑤⑦
Edmonton....d.		0100	0700	0800	1300	1400	1600	1700	1800	1900	2000
Calgary....a.		0635	1100	1159	1730	1940	2100	2100	2300	2300	2340

a – ①④⑤⑦.

UNITED STATES OF AMERICA

Capital : **Washington DC** (GMT -5, add one hour in summer). 2017 Public Holidays : Jan. 1, 2, 16, Feb. 20, May 29, July 4, Sep. 4, Oct. 9, Nov. 11, 23, Dec. 25.

The principal operator in the USA is Amtrak (✆ 1 800 872 7245. www.amtrak.com). Details of other operators can be found in relevant tables. Unless otherwise noted all trains carry first and second class seated accomodation known as 'Business' and 'Coach' class respectively. Acela Express trains running between Boston, New York and Washington convey business class and an enhanced seated accommodation, confusingly called 'First Class'. Most very long distance trains convey sleeping cars, and where this is the case it is detailed in the footnotes. Almost all sleeping car accommodation in North America has two berths per compartment, some of which are en-suite, although the exact product offering varies by operator and route. Most trains also convey some form of catering, but again the actual service offered varies considerably. Timings shown are the latest available and are subject to alteration around public holidays and it is recommended that you confirm all timings locally as short notice changes are possible. Tickets are available from staffed stations, websites and through authorised ticketing agents. Amtrak requires reservations on practically all of its services, and also requires that you have identity documents available for inspection.

Amtrak offers the 'USA Rail Pass' It is available to both US citizens and foreign nationals and has the option of three validity periods: 15 day/8 segments of travel, 30 day/12 segments of travel and 45 day/18 segments of travel. The pass is valid in coach class on the entire Amtrak system. Be warned though: this program is now revenue/capacity managed and may not be available on all trains all the time. The pass is not valid on the Autotrain, Acela Express trains, Thruway buses numbered 7000 – 7999 and the Canadian portion of trains operated jointly by Amtrak and VIA Rail Canada. The pass alone is not valid for travel; tickets and, where neccessary, reservations must be obtained for each segment of travel. Upgrades to higher levels of accommodation may be possible subject to capacity and the payment of relevant supplements. Travel is limited to no more than four one-way journeys over any given route segment. A segment is any time you get on and then get off a train or bus, regardless of the length of that journey. A 7 day California Rail Pass is also available. For full details on both passes see the Amtrak website (www.amtrak.com).

SKAGWAY - WHITEHORSE 9100

White Pass and Yukon Railroad

km		-1 A	Ba	Bb	🚌			Ba	Bb	2 C
0	Skagway Shops....d.	0730	0740	1210	1400	Whitehorse....d.	0730	...	...	...
22	White Pass ►....🚌 d.		...	...	...	Carcross....a.	0845	...	...	...
41	Fraser....a.	0900	0925	1415	1445	Carcross....d.	0845	...	...	1300
41	Fraser....d.	0900	...	...	1500	Bennett....a.		...	...	1430
65	Bennett....a.	1015				Bennett....d.		...	...	1515
65	Bennett....d.	1100				Fraser....a.	1000	...	...	1600
108	Carcross....a.	1230			1600	Fraser....d.	1000	1020	1445	1600
108	Carcross....d.				1600	White Pass ►....🚌 d.		...	...	...
177	Whitehorse....a.				1730	Skagway Shops....a.	1100	1205	1630	1745

A – May 23 – Sept. 9. From Skagway ②③④⑤.
B – May 28 – Sept. 28. Not May 5, 6, 7, 8, 15. Sept. 15, 17, 18, 22, 24, 28. **a** – Not Sept. 22, 27. **b** – Not May 2, 4, 11, 12, 13, 18. June 4, Sept. 23, 28.
C – May 23 – Sept. 9. From Carcross ②③④ Also from Carcross ⑥ departing 1200.

🚌 – For services crossing the US / Canadian border passengers must provide proof of citizenship. All services ℝ. All times shown are Alaska time.
► – Between May 2 and Sept. 28 a White Pass Summit round trip excursion operates. Departs Skagway daily 0815 c and 1245 e. Additional trips 1630 on ②③ between May 30 and Aug. 30.
c – Not May 5, 6, 7, 8, 15, June 4, Sept. 10, 15, 17, 18, 22, 24, 25.
e – Not May 5, 6, 7, 8, 15, June 4, 18, July 2, 16, Aug. 13, 27, Sept. 10, 15, 17, 18, 22, 24, 25.
Operator : White Pass & Yukon Railroad ✆ Skagway 907 983 2217. www.wpyr.com

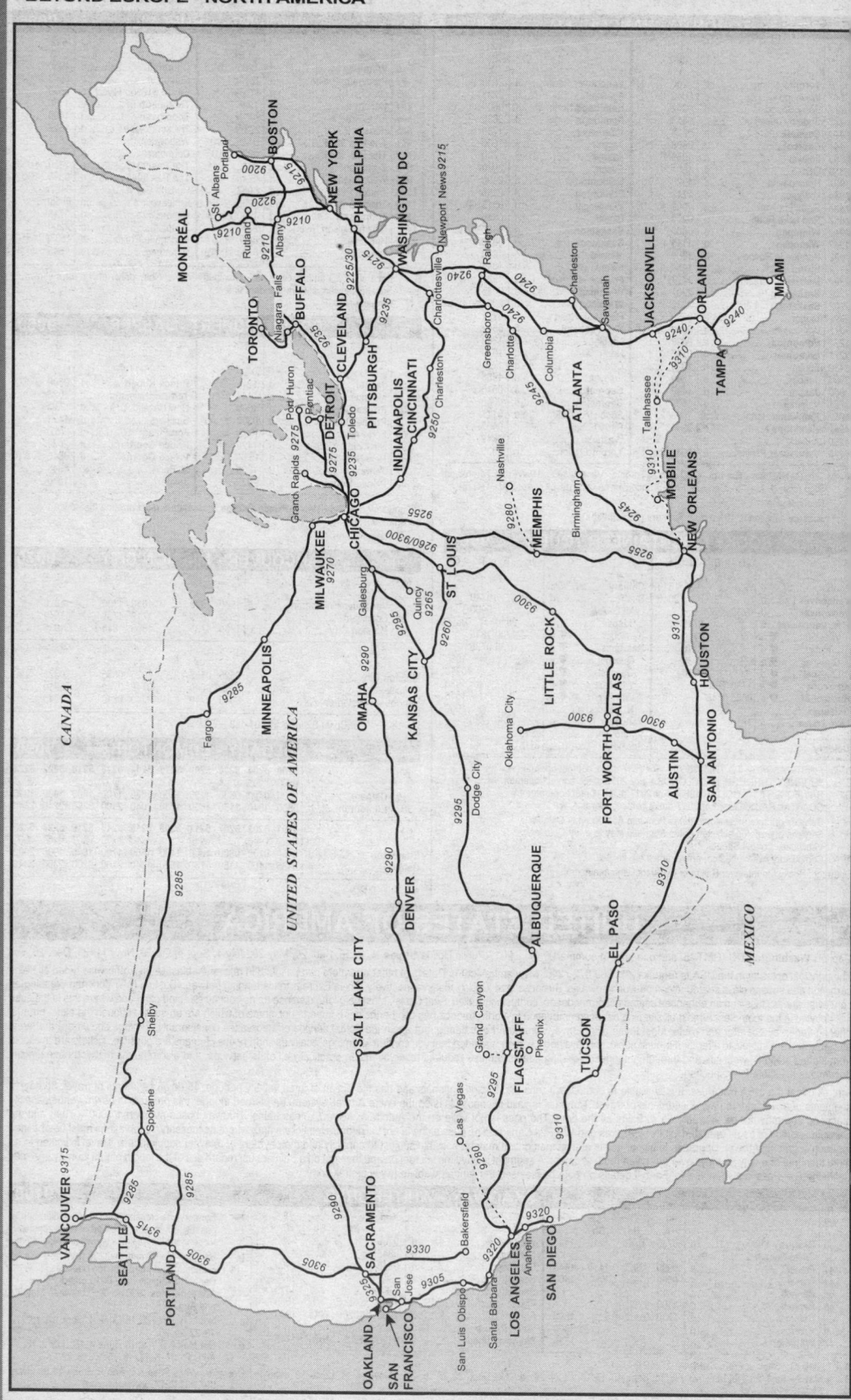

ALASKA 9105

Alaska Railroad

km			E	F	Ab ④	C ⑦	Be ④-①	D					Aa ⑥	Bd ④	C	D ④-①	F	E
0	Fairbanks	d.			0815	...	0830	...	Seward	d.			...	...	...	...	...	1800
195	Denali	d.			1230	...	1230	...	Grandview	a.			...	...	...	1530	...	...
305	Hurricane	d.			1445	1445	1630	...	Spencer	a.			...	...	...	1630		...
392	Talkeetna	d.			1655	1650	1650	1915	Spencer	d.			...	...	...	1640		...
498	Wasilla	d.			1815	1825	1825	...	Portage	a.			...	...	...	1715		...
572	Anchorage	a.			2000	2000	2000	...	Whittier	d.			...	...	...	1845		...
572	Anchorage	d.	0645	0945				...	Portage	d.			...	...	...	1920		...
636	Girdwood	d.	0800	1100				...	Girdwood	d.			...	...	...	1940	2055	...
652	Portage	a.		1130				...	Anchorage	a.			...	...	...	2115	2215	...
20a	Whittier	d.		1245				...	Anchorage	d.			0815	0830	0830			...
652	Portage	d.		1325				...	Wasilla	d.			0935	0950	0950			...
666	Spencer	a.		1345				...	Talkeetna	d.			1120	1125	1125	1300		...
666	Spencer	d.		1355				...	Hurricane	d.			...	1340	1340	1530		...
683	Grandview	d.		1520				...	Denali	d.			1600	1555				...
750	Seward	a.	1105					...	Fairbanks	a.			2000	2000				...

- DENALI STAR – 🚃 and ✗ (Aa May 17 - Sept. 16. Ab May 18 - Sept. 17).
- AURORA 🚃 and ✗ Sept. 24, 2016 - May 14, 2017. d – Also Dec. 27, Jan. 3, Feb. 21, 28, Mar. 7, 9, 14, 16, 21, 28. e – Also Dec. 26, Jan. 4, Feb. 22, Mar. 1, 8, 10, 15, 17, 22, 29.
- HURRICANE TURN (WINTER) 🚃 1st ④ of every month Oct. 6, 2016 - May 25, 2017.
- HURRICANE TURN – (SUMMER) 🚃 May 11 - Sept. 18.

- E – COASTAL CLASSIC – 🚃 and ✗ May 13 - Sept. 17.
- F – GLACIER DISCOVERY – 🚃 and ✗ May 27 - Sept. 18.
- a – Kms from Portage.

Operator : Alaska Railroad ✆ Anchorage 907 265 2620. Fax 907 265 2323.

BRUNSWICK - PORTLAND - BOSTON 9200

Amtrak

km			680 ①-⑤	690 ⑥⑦	682 ①-⑤	692 ⑥⑦	684 ①-⑤	694 ⑥⑦	686 ①-⑤	696 ⑥⑦	688 ①-⑤	698 ⑥⑦
0	Brunswick	d.	...	...	0705	0725	...	...	...	...	1825	1825
14	Freeport	d.	...	...	0720	0740	...	...	...	...	1840	1840
47	Portland	d.	0520	0600	0800	0820	1240	1305	1435	1505	1920	1920
66	Old Orchard Beach ◀◀	d.	0535	0613	0813	0835	1255	1320	1450	...	1933	1935
72	Saco	d.	0542	0622	0822	0842	1300	1327	1457	1527	1942	1942
98	Wells	d.	0559	0639	0839	0859	1317	1345	1514	1544	1959	1959
124	Dover	d.	0617	0657	0857	0917	1335	1402	1532	1602	2017	2017
133	Durham	d.	0625	0704	0905	0925	1343	1510	1540	1610	2025	2025
151	Exeter	d.	0639	0717	0918	0938	1356	1423	1553	1623	2038	2038
178	Haverhill	d.	0700	0737	0939	0959	1419	1444	1614	1644	2104	2058
232	Boston North	a.	0750	0825	1030	1050	1510	1535	1705	1735	2200	2150

			681 ①-⑤	691 ⑥⑦	683 ①-⑤	693 ⑥⑦	685 ①-⑤	695 ⑥⑦	687 ①-⑤	697 ⑥⑦	689 ①-⑤	699 ⑥⑦
Boston North	d.		...	0905	0925	1125	1155	1700	1700	1805	2000	2325	2325
Haverhill	d.		...	0953	1013	1212	1243	1748	1748	1852	2048	0013r	0013r
Exeter	d.		...	1014	1034	1232	1304	1809	1809	1912	2114	0034r	0034r
Durham	d.		...	1027	1047	1245	1317	1822	1822	1925	2127	0047r	0047r
Dover	d.		...	1035	1055	1252	1324	1830	1830	1932	2134	0055r	0055r
Wells	d.		...	1053	1113	1310	1341	1848	1848	1950	2151	0113r	0113r
Saco	d.		...	1110	1130	1328	1358	1905	1905	2006	2208	0127r	0127r
Old Orchard Beach ◀◀	d.		...	1115	1137	1335	1403	1910	1910	2013	2213	0132r	0132r
Portland	a.		...	1135	1125	1355	1420	1925	1920	2035	2320	0150	0150
Freeport	a.		...	1215	1230	...	...	2005	2005	...	...	...	...
Brunswick	a.		...	1230	1245	...	...	2020	2020	...	...	...	...

- Calls on request.   ◀◀ – Seasonal stop. Station open mid-June to mid-October only.

NEW YORK - ALBANY - RUTLAND, MONTRÉAL and NIAGARA FALLS 9210

Amtrak

km			63 F	69 2H	281 J	233	283 J	235 ⑤-⑥	291 ⑥-④	255 ⑤	49 G	237 ①-⑤	253 ⑤	239 ①-④	293 K	241	243	259 ⑤	245 ①-⑤	261 ⑥⑦
0	New York Penn. ▼	d.	0715	0815	1020	1120	1320	1420	1515	1515	1540	1640	1715	1747	1747	1915	2055	2115	2245	2335
24	Yonkers ▼	d.	0744	0844	...	1144	1344	1444	1539	1539	...	...	1739	...	...	1939	2119	2139	...	...
54	Croton Harmon ▼	d.	0803	0903	1101	1203	1403	1503	1558	1558	1626u	...	1758	1832	1832	1958	2138	2158	2326	0016
118	Poughkeepsie ▼	d.	0845	0945	1143	1245	1445	1545	1640	1640	1710u	...	1840	1922	1922	2040	2220	2240	0008	0058
142	Rhinecliff Kingston	d.	0900	1000	1158	1300	1500	1600	1655	1655	...	1813	1855e	1937e	1937e	2055e	2236e	2255e	0023e	0113e
184	Hudson	d.	0920	1020	1218	1320	1520	1620	1715	1715	...	1833	1915	1957e	1957e	2115e	2256e	2315e	0043e	0134e
229	Albany Rensselaer	a.	0950	1050	1245	1350	1545	1650	1745	1745	1820u	1900	1945	2020	2020	2145	2325	2345	0115	0205
229	Albany Rensselaer	d.	1000	1110	1300	...	1600	...	1800	...	1905u	...	...	...	2030	...	...	...	...	...
258	Schenectady	d.	1024	1134	1323	...	1623	...	1824	...	1932	...	...	...	2054	...	...	...	...	...
288	Saratoga Springs	d.	...	1202	...	...	...	...	1850	...	...	...	...	...	2123	...	...	...	...	...
391	Rutland	a.	...	...	...	...	...	...	2048	...	...	...	...	...	2318	...	...	...	...	...
436	Westport	d.	...	1404	...	...	...	...	...	...	...	...	...	...	...	...	...	...	...	...
500	Plattsburgh	d.	...	1517	...	...	...	...	...	...	...	...	...	...	...	...	...	...	...	...
617	Montréal Central	a.	...	1911	...	...	...	...	...	...	...	...	...	...	...	...	...	...	...	...
382	Utica	d.	1141	...	1440	...	1740	...	...	...	2048	...	...	...	...	...	...	...	...	...
459	Syracuse	d.	1243	...	1544	...	1844	...	...	...	2149	...	...	...	...	...	...	...	...	...
597	Rochester	d.	1358	...	1708	...	2006	...	...	...	2309	...	...	...	...	...	...	...	...	...
706	Buffalo Exchange St.	a.	1514	...	1833e	...	2133e	...	...	...	2355d	...	...	...	...	...	...	...	...	...
745	Niagara Falls USA	a.	1621	...	1945	...	2245	...	...	...	...	...	...	...	...	...	...	...	...	...
	Toronto Union 9020	a.	1942	...	...	...	...	...	...	...	...	...	...	...	...	...	...	...	...	...

			230 ①-⑤	232 ①-⑤	250 ⑥⑦	234 ①-⑤	252 ⑥	260 ⑥⑦	236 ①-⑤	280 J	254 ⑦	290 ①-⑤	238 ⑦	284	292 ⑥	256 ⑦	242 ①-⑤	48 G	244	68 2H	64 F	296 ⑦ K	288 ⑦ J
Toronto Union 9020	d.		...	...	...	...	...	...	...	...	...	...	...	...	...	...	...	...	...	0820	...	...	...
Niagara Falls USA	d.		...	...	...	...	...	...	...	0330	...	0625	...	...	...	...	...	...	...	1230	...	1440
Buffalo Exchange St	d.		...	...	...	...	...	...	...	0405	...	0700	...	...	...	...	...	0851d	...	1305	...	1515
Rochester	d.		...	...	...	...	...	...	...	0516	...	0844	...	...	...	...	...	0950	...	1413	...	1626
Syracuse	d.		...	...	...	...	...	...	...	0636	...	0931	...	...	...	...	...	1118	...	1528	...	1746
Utica	d.		...	...	...	...	...	...	...	0731	...	1029	...	...	...	...	...	1215	...	1629	...	1841
Montréal Central	d.		...	...	...	...	...	...	...	...	...	...	...	...	...	...	...	...	1020	...	...	...
Plattsburgh	d.		...	...	...	...	...	...	...	...	...	...	...	...	...	...	...	...	1325	...	...	...
Westport	d.		...	...	...	...	...	...	...	...	...	...	...	...	...	...	...	...	1429	...	...	...
Rutland	d.		...	...	...	...	...	...	...	...	0800	...	...	1100	...	...	...	...	...	1705	...	...
Saratoga Springs	d.		...	...	...	...	...	...	...	...	0937	...	...	1246	...	...	...	...	...	1847	...	...
Schenectady	a.		...	...	...	...	...	...	...	0923	1017	1218	...	1328	1358	...	1727	1827	1923	2033
Albany Rensselaer	a.		...	...	...	...	...	...	...	0950	1050	1250	...	1355	1455	...	1755	1855	1955	2100
Albany Rensselaer	d.		0505	0555	0610	0655	0710	0810	0820	1005	1005	1110	1205	1305	1410	1410	1510	1545	1605	1815	1915	2015	2115
Hudson	d.		0530	0619	0635	0720	0735	0835	0845	1030	1030	1135	1231	1330	1435	1435	1536	1630	1840	1940	2040	2140
Rhinecliff Kingston	d.		0550	0640	0657	0743	0757	0857	0907	1051	1051	1156	1253	1350	1455	1455	1558	1633s	1652	1901	2001	2101	2200
Poughkeepsie ▼	d.		0710	...	0810	0910	0920	1111	1110	1210	1310	1410	1510	1510	1615	1651s	1710	1915	2015	2115	2217
Croton Harmon ▼	d.		0643	0731	0750	0850	0950	1959	1150	1150	1250	1350	1450	1550	1550	1655	1731s	1750	1956	2055	2155	2257
Yonkers ▼	d.		...	0811	0911	1011	1021	1311	1411	1511	1611	1611	1716	1823	1845	2017	2116	2216	...
New York Penn. ▼	a.		0730	0815	0845	0920	0945	1040	1050	1245	1245	1345	1345	1550	1645	1645	1748	1823	1845	2050	2150	2250	2345

9215 BOSTON - NEW YORK - WASHINGTON - NEWPORT NEWS

Most trains 🍸 Amtrak

km		65	67	151	111	Acela 2103	89	89	131	51	Acela 2107	183	79	79	Acela 2109	Acela 2203	153	185	Acela 2151	Acela 2205	155	141	Acela 2153	Acela 2207
		⑤⑥	⑦–④	①–⑤	①–⑤	①–⑤	⑥⑦ ♦	①–⑤ ♦	⑥	③⑤⑦ ♦	①–⑤	①–⑤	⑥⑦ ♦	①–⑤ ♦	①–⑤	⑥	⑥⑦	①–⑤	①–⑤	⑦	⑥⑦	①–⑤	①–⑤	⑥
0	**Boston** South d.	2130	2130	...	...	...	...	...	...	...	...	...	...	...	...	...	...	...	0505	...	...	...	0605	...
69	Providence d.	2222	2222	...	...	...	...	...	...	...	...	...	...	...	...	...	...	...	0540	...	...	...	0643	...
169	New London d.	2331	2331	...	...	...	...	...	...	...	...	...	...	...	...	...	...	...	0624	...	...	...	|	...
	Springfield MA d.	|	|	...	...	...	...	...	...	...	...	...	...	...	...	...	...	...	|	...	...	0555	|	...
	Hartford d.	|	|	...	...	...	...	...	...	...	...	...	...	...	...	...	...	...	|	...	...	0635	|	...
251	New Haven d.	0050	0050	...	...	...	...	...	...	...	...	...	...	...	...	...	...	...	0706	...	...	0737	0814	...
301	Stamford d.	0136	0136	...	...	...	...	...	...	...	...	...	...	...	...	...	...	...	0752	...	...	0827	0900	...
373	**New York** Penn a.	0230	0230	...	...	...	...	...	...	...	...	...	...	...	...	...	...	...	0844	...	...	0921	0945	...
373	**New York** Penn d.	0300	0325	0440	0530	0600	0602	0602	0645	0645	0700	0705	0717	0725	0800	0800	0805	0810	0900	0900	0905	0935	1000	1000
389	Newark NJ d.	0320	0345	0457u	0546u	0615u	0619u	0619u	0702	0705u	0715u	0722	0739u	0744u	0815u	0814	0822u	0827	0915	0914u	0922	0952	1015	1014
519	**Philadelphia** 30th St. d.	0432	0500	0607	0657	0718	0732u	0740u	0815	0815u	0816	0832	0854	0854	0916	0916	0935	0939	1013	1016	1032	1112	1112	1116
670	Baltimore Penn d.	0543	0610	0732	0800	0821	0842u	0850u	0930	0930u	0919	0938	1004	1004	1019	1019	1044	1046	1113	1119	1145	1220	1216	1219
687	BWI Airport d.	0556	0625	0745	0815	|	0855u	0903	0944	|	|	0952	|	|	|	1032	1057	1059	1129	1132	1201	1233	1229	1232
735	**Washington** Union a.	0630	0700	0820	0850	0855	0930u	0930u	1020	1100u	0953	1028	1045	1045	1053	1053	1135	1136	1155	1153	1235	1306	1255	1253
735	**Washington** Union d.	0700	0730	...	...	...	1000u	1000u	...	1100u	...	...	1110	1110	...	...	...	...	...	...	...	...	...	...
822	Fredricksburg d.	0805	0836	...	...	...	|	|	...	|	...	...	1221	1221	...	...	...	...	...	...	...	...	...	...
911	Richmond d.	0908	0944	...	...	...	1211	1211	...	|	...	...	1324	1324	...	...	...	...	...	...	...	...	...	...
1042	**Newport News** a.	1115	1145	...	...	...	...	...	...	|	...	...	...	...	...	...	...	...	...	...	...	...	...	...
1092	Norfolk a.	*1215**	*1250**	...	...	...	...	...	...	|	...	...	...	...	...	...	...	...	...	...	...	...	...	...
	Virgina Beach a.	*1255**	*1330**	...	...	...	...	...	...	|	...	...	...	...	...	...	...	...	...	...	...	...	...	...
915	Charlottesville d.	...	...	...	...	...	...	...	...	1352	...	...	...	...	...	...	...	...	...	...	...	...	...	...
1012	**Lynchburg** a.	...	...	...	...	...	...	...	...	...	...	...	...	...	...	...	...	...	...	...	...	...	...	...

	143	🚌 3495	95	Acela 2155	Acela 2211	91	405	195	Acela 2295	125	Acela 2117	Acela 2251	Acela 2213	157	147	145	171	99	Acela 2159	133	Acela 2121	🚌 3493	93	83
	⑥⑦	①–⑤	①–⑤	①–⑤	⑦	♦	⑥⑦ 2	⑥⑦	⑥	①–⑤	①–⑤	⑥	⑦	⑦	⑥	⑦	①–⑤	⑥⑦	①–⑤	⑤	①–⑤	①–⑤	①–④	⑤
Boston South d.	...	...	0610	0715	...	...	...	0640	0735	...	...	0805	...	...	...	...	0815	0840	0910	...	...	...	0930	0930
Providence d.	...	...	0650	0750	...	...	...	0720	0813	...	...	0840	...	...	...	...	0855	0919	0946	...	...	...	1011	1011
New London d.	...	...	0745	|	...	...	...	0817	|	...	...	|	...	...	...	...	0948	1019	|	...	...	...	1112	1112
Springfield MA d.	0630	0640	|	|	...	...	0730	|	|	...	...	|	...	0800	0835	...	|	|	|	...	...	1000	|	|
Hartford d.	0708	0715	|	|	...	...	0805	|	|	...	...	|	...	0837	0909	...	|	|	|	...	...	1033	|	|
New Haven d.	0809	0835	0843	|	...	...	0855	0909	0943	...	...	1013	...	0939	1018	...	1040	1109	1113	...	...	1150	1209	1209
Stamford d.	0858	...	0930	0959	...	...	...	0958	|	...	...	1058	...	1028	1111	...	1129	1158	1158	...	...	...	1258	1258
New York Penn a.	0950	...	1021	1045	...	...	...	1050	1115	...	...	1145	...	1125	1213	...	1220	1253	1245	...	...	...	1348	1348
New York Penn d.	1005	...	1035	1100	1100	1102	...	1105	...	1135	1200	1200	1200	1205	1250	1255	1235	1317	1300	1309	1400	...	1402	1402
Newark NJ d.	1022	...	1053	1115	1114u	1122u	...	1123	...	1152	1215u	1214	1214u	1222	1307	1312	1252	1335	1315	1325u	1415u	...	1419	1419
Philadelphia 30th Street d.	1135	...	1202	1216	1216	1235u	...	1234	...	1303	1316	1316	1316	1333	1418	1417	1414	1448	1413	1430	1513	...	1527	1532
Baltimore Penn d.	1247	...	1320	1320	1319	1355u	...	1340	...	1420	1419	1419	1419	1443	1525	1525	1527	1553	1516	1541	1616	...	1633	1638
BWI Airport d.	1300	...	1333	|	1332	|	...	1353	...	1434	|	1432	1432	1456	1538	1535	1544	1606	1529	1556	1629	...	1646	1651
Washington Union a.	1336	...	1403	1355	1353	1505u	...	1425	...	1506	1453	1455	1453	1530	1610	1612	1620	1635	1555	1630	1653	...	1715	1720
Washington Union d.	...	...	1430	...	...	1505u	...	1450	...	1555	...	...	...	1600	1635	1650	1650	1700	...	...	...	...	1750	1750
Fredricksburg d.	...	...	1540	...	...	|	...	1601	...	1712	...	...	...	1710	|	|	|	1808	...	...	...	...	1901	1901
Richmond d.	...	...	1648	...	...	1707	...	1704	...	1824	...	...	...	1822	|	|	|	1911	...	...	...	...	2006	2016
Newport News a.	...	...	1852	...	...	...	...	...	...	|	...	...	...	|	|	|	|	2106	...	...	...	...	...	2215
Norfolk a.	...	...	*1950**	...	...	...	...	...	...	2038	...	...	...	2036	|	|	|	*2155**	...	...	...	...	...	*2255*
Virgina Beach a.	...	...	*2030**	...	...	...	...	...	...	...	...	...	...	...	|	|	|	*2225**	...1	...	...	...	...	*2325*
Charlottesville d.	...	...	...	...	...	...	...	...	...	...	...	...	...	...	1901	1916	1923	...	...	...	...	...	...	...
Lynchburg a.	...	...	...	...	...	...	...	...	...	...	...	...	...	...	2014	2029	2036	...	...	...	...	...	...	...

	401	161	19	Acela 2253	Acela 2163	85	87	71	97	173	Acela 2165	Acela 2221	127	463	163	129	Acela 2167	Acela 2255	159	193	Acela 2119	Acela 2225	135	137
	⑥⑦ 2	⑥⑦	♦	⑥⑦	①–⑤	①–⑤	⑦	⑥	♦	①–⑤	①–⑤	⑦	①–⑤	⑥⑦ 2	⑥⑦	①–⑤	①–⑤	⑦	⑥⑦	①–⑤	①–⑤	⑦	⑥⑦	①–⑤
Boston South d.	...	0940	...	1100	1105	...	...	...	...	1115	1210	...	...	...	1140	...	1305	1310	...	...	...	...	1340	1340
Providence d.	...	1020	...	1145	1143	...	...	...	...	1156	1246	...	...	...	1220	...	1341	1344	...	...	...	...	1419	1421
New London d.	...	1115	...	|	|	...	...	...	...	1248	|	...	...	...	1318	...	|	|	...	...	...	...	1513	1514
Springfield MA d.	1040	|	...	|	|	...	...	...	...	|	|	...	...	1240	|	...	|	|	...	...	...	...	|	|
Hartford d.	1114	|	...	|	|	...	...	...	...	|	|	...	...	1316	|	...	|	|	...	...	...	...	|	|
New Haven d.	1200	1209	...	1313	1313	...	...	...	...	1340	1413	...	...	1405	1409	...	1513	1513	...	...	...	...	1609	1609
Stamford d.	...	1258	...	1358	1358	...	...	...	...	1429	1458	...	...	...	1458	...	1558	1558	...	...	...	...	1658	1658
New York Penn a.	...	1352	...	1445	1445	...	...	...	...	1520	1545	...	...	...	1550	...	1645	1645	...	...	...	...	1750	1800
New York Penn d.	...	1405	1415	1500	1500	1505	1504	1504	1515	1535	1600	1600	1605	...	1605	1642	1700	1700	1705	1739	1800	1800	1805	1825
Newark NJ d.	...	1422	1437u	1514	1515	1522	1521	1521	1538u	1553	1615	1614u	1622	...	1622	1658	1715	1714	1722	1756	1815u	1814u	1822	1842
Philadelphia 30th Street d.	...	1535	1555u	1616	1613	1630	1635	1635	1658u	1657	1713	1716	1735	...	1737	1814	1813	1816	1835	1914	1913	1916	1935	1957
Baltimore Penn d.	...	1647	1712u	1719	1716	1742	1748	1748	1817u	1802	1814	1819	1842	...	1849	1924	1915	1919	1946	2025	2016	2019	2049	2100
BWI Airport d.	...	1700	|	1732	1729	1756	1800	1800	|	1815	1827	1832	1855	...	1903	1937	1929	1932	1959	2038	2029	2032	2102	2113
Washington Union a.	...	1736	1830u	1755	1755	1825	1835	1835	1925u	1851	1855	1853	1930	...	1941	2010	1955	1955	2035	2113	2053	2053	2140	2150
Washington Union d.	...	...	1830u	...	...	1905	1900	1900	1925u	...	...	...	...	...	...	...	...	...	...	...	...	...	...	...
Fredricksburg d.	...	...	|	...	...	2017	2012	2010	|	...	...	...	...	...	...	...	...	...	...	...	...	...	...	...
Richmond d.	...	...	|	...	...	2116	2113	2122	2134	...	...	...	...	...	...	...	...	...	...	...	...	...	...	...
Newport News a.	...	...	|	...	...	...	...	|	...	...	...	...	...	...	...	...	...	...	...	...	...	...	...	...
Norfolk a.	...	...	|	...	...	...	...	2336	...	...	...	...	...	...	...	...	...	...	...	...	...	...	...	...
Virgina Beach a.	...	...	|	...	...	...	...	...	...	...	...	...	...	...	...	...	...	...	...	...	...	...	...	...
Charlottesville d.	...	...	2052	...	...	...	...	...	...	...	...	...	...	...	...	...	...	...	...	...	...	...	...	...
Lynchburg a.	...	...	2200	...	...	...	...	...	...	...	...	...	...	...	...	...	...	...	...	...	...	...	...	...

	55	Acela 2171	Acela 2257	57	465	165	475	175	Acela 2259	Acela 2173	467	167	Acela 2297	123	Acela 2175	187	177	139	497	169	🚌 3479	179
	①–⑤ ♦	①–⑤	⑦	⑥⑦ ♦	⑦ 2	⑥⑦	①–⑤ 2	①–⑤	⑦	①–⑤	⑥ 2	⑥	⑦	⑦	①–⑤	①–⑤	①–⑤	⑦	⑦ 2	⑥⑦	①–⑤	①–⑤
Boston South d.	...	1510	1505	...	...	1510	...	1520	1605	1615	...	1635	1710	...	1720	...	1735	1740	...	1840	...	1845
Providence d.	...	1545	1543	...	...	1550	...	1601	1640	1650	...	1714	1748	...	1755	...	1814	1820	...	1920	...	1925
New London d.	...	|	|	...	...	1649	...	1657	|	|	...	1813	|	...	|	...	1915	1915	...	2016	...	2017
Springfield MA d.	1450	|	|	1450	1610	|	1605	|	|	|	1727	|	|	...	|	...	|	|	1940	|	1855	|
Hartford d.	1532	|	|	1526	1647	|	1642	|	|	|	1806	|	|	...	|	...	|	|	2015	|	1931	|
New Haven d.	1639	1713	1713	1639	1731	1739	1735	1745	1813	1826	1900	1909	1913	...	1920	...	2013	2009	2100	2109	2050	2110
Stamford d.	1728	1759	1758	1728	...	1828	...	1833	1858	1911	...	1958	1958	...	2005	...	2103	2058	...	2158	...	2159
New York Penn a.	1825	1845	1845	1825	...	1927	...	1926	1945	1958	...	2050	2045	...	2050	...	2151	2150	...	2250	...	2250
New York Penn d.	1845	1900	1900	1901	...	2001	...	1940	2000	2013	...	2105	...	2105	2105	2110	2205	2205	...	2305	...	...
Newark NJ d.	1903	1915	1914	1918	...	2018	...	1958	2014	2028	...	2122	...	2122u	2120	2127	2222	2222	...	2322	...	...
Philadelphia 30th Street d.	2014	2013	2016	2028	...	2132	...	2114	2116	2128	...	2235	...	2233	2218	2237	2332	2335	...	0032	...	...
Baltimore Penn d.	2121	2114	2119	2136	...	2241	...	2228	2219	2230	...	2344	...	2342	2321	2343	0042	0044	...	0142	...	...
BWI Airport d.	|	2128	2132	2149	...	2255	...	2242	2232	2240	...	2357	...	2355	|	2356	0055	0057	...	0155	...	...
Washington Union a.	2201	2155	2155	2225	...	2334	...	2312	2255	2305	...	0035	...	0035	2355	0031	0132	0135	...	0232	...	...
Washington Union d.	...	...	...	...	...	...	...	...	...	...	...	...	...	...	...	...	...	...	...	...	...	...
Fredricksburg d.	...	...	...	...	...	...	...	...	...	...	...	...	...	...	...	...	...	...	...	...	...	...
Richmond d.	...	...	...	...	...	...	...	...	...	...	...	...	...	...	...	...	...	...	...	...	...	...
Newport News a.	...	...	...	...	...	...	...	...	...	...	...	...	...	...	...	...	...	...	...	...	...	...
Norfolk a.	...	...	...	...	...	...	...	...	...	...	...	...	...	...	...	...	...	...	...	...	...	...
Virgina Beach a.	...	...	...	...	...	...	...	...	...	...	...	...	...	...	...	...	...	...	...	...	...	...
Charlottesville d.	...	...	...	...	...	...	...	...	...	...	...	...	...	...	...	...	...	...	...	...	...	...
Lynchburg a.	...	...	...	...	...	...	...	...	...	...	...	...	...	...	...	...	...	...	...	...	...	...

♦ – NOTES, LISTED BY TRAIN NUMBER:

19/20 – CRESCENT – 🛏 1, 2 cl., (2) and ✕ New York - Washington - New Orleans and v.v.
50/51 – CARDINAL – 🛏 1, 2 cl., (2) and 🍸 Chicago - Washington - New York and v.v.
54/55 – VERMONTER – (12) and 🍸 Washington - New York - New Haven - St Albans and v.v.
56/57 – VERMONTER – (12) and 🍸 Washington - New York - New Haven - St Albans and v.v.
79/80 – CAROLINIAN – (12) and 🍸 New York - Washington - Charlotte and v.v.
89/90 – PALMETTO – (12) and 🍸 New York - Washington - Savannah and v.v.

Amtrak Most trains 🍸

NEWPORT NEWS - WASHINGTON - NEW YORK - BOSTON 9215

km		66	Acela 2190 ①-⑤	190 ①-⑤	🚌 3490 ①-⑤	150 ⑥⑦	450 ⑥⑦ 2		110 ①-⑤	Acela 2150 ①-⑤	Acela 2290 ⑥	170 ①-⑤	🚌 3470 ①-⑤		160 ⑥⑦	460 ⑥⑦	180 ①-⑤	Acela 2100 ①-⑤	162 ⑥⑦	130 ①-⑤	Acela 2154 ①-⑤	98 ♦	172 ①-⑤	54 ⑥⑦ ♦
	Lynchburg d.	...	...	...	...	...	...	...	...	...	...	...	...	...	...	...	...	...	...	...	...	...	...	...
	Charlottesville d.	...	...	...	...	...	...	...	...	...	...	...	...	...	...	...	...	...	...	...	...	...	...	...
	Virginia Beach d.	*1430**	...	...	...	...	...	...	...	...	...	...	...	...	...	...	...	...	...	...	...	...	...	...
	Norfolk d.	*1515**	...	...	...	...	...	...	...	...	...	...	...	...	...	...	...	...	...	...	...	...	...	...
	Newport News d.	1720	...	...	...	...	...	...	...	...	...	...	...	...	...	...	...	...	...	...	...	...	...	...
	Richmond d.	1900	...	...	...	...	...	...	...	...	...	...	...	...	...	...	...	...	...	...	...	0432	...	...
	Fredericksburg d.	1957	...	...	...	...	...	...	...	...	...	...	...	...	...	...	...	...	...	...	...	|	...	...
	Washington Union a.	2120	...	...	...	...	...	...	...	...	...	...	...	...	...	...	...	...	...	...	...	0707s	...	...
	Washington Union d.	2210	...	0315	...	0315	...	...	0400	0500	...	0442	...	...	0525	...	0530	0600	0620	0630	0700	0707s	0725	0730
	BWI Airport d.	2238	...	0340	...	0340	...	...	0425	|	...	0520	...	...	0553	...	0557	0621	0648	0657	0721	|	0753	0757
	Baltimore Penn d.	2254	...	0355	...	0355	...	...	0441	0530	...	0535	...	...	0608	...	0613	0634	0703	0714	0734	0812s	0809	0812
	Philadelphia 30th Street d.	0010	...	0515	...	0515	...	...	0550	0632	...	0646	...	...	0719	...	0727	0736	0820	0830	0836	0930s	0920	0920
	Newark NJ d.	0122	...	0622	...	0622	...	...	0702	0728	...	0757	...	...	0827	...	0825s	0833s	0926	0942	0930	1040s	1026	1027
	New York Penn a.	0140	...	0641	...	0642	...	...	0724	0745	...	0816	...	...	0846	...	0849	0856	0946	1003	0946	1100	1046	1047
	New York Penn d.	0241	0615	0655	...	0701	...	...	...	0800	0803	0830	...	...	0901	...	...	...	1000	...	1003	...	1100	1130
	Stamford d.	0330	0701	0747	...	0748	...	...	...	0847	0848	0919	...	...	0948	...	...	...	1048	...	1048	...	1148	1218
0	New Haven d.	0440	0753	0837	0840	0840	0842	...	...	0936	0937	1013	1030	...	1044	1046	...	...	1144	...	1137	...	1244	1323
60	Hartford d.	|	|	|	0929	|	0923	...	...	|	|	|	1114	...	|	1128	...	...	|	...	|	...	|	1411
101	**Springfield** MA a.	|	|	|	1010	|	1003	...	...	|	|	|	1155	...	|	1205	...	...	|	...	|	...	|	1458
	New London d.	0534	0831e	0926	...	0929	...	...	...	|	|	1100	...	...	1129	...	...	...	1234	...	|	...	1332	...
	Providence d.	0656	0913	1020	...	1028	...	...	...	1053	1102	1155	...	...	1228	...	...	...	1334	...	1256	...	1426	...
	Boston South a.	0758	0958	1105	...	1120	...	...	...	1140	1150	1245	...	...	1318	...	...	...	1423	...	1345	...	1515	...

	Acela 2104 ①-⑤	56 ①-⑤ ♦	152 ⑥⑦		86 ①-⑤	Acela 2158 ①-⑤	Acela 2250 ⑥⑦	184 ①-⑤	164 ⑥⑦	464 ⑥⑦	20 ♦	Acela 2160 ①-⑤	Acela 2208 ⑦	174 ①-⑤	82 ⑥	154 ⑦	Acela 2110 ①-⑤	Acela 2252 ⑦	84 ①-⑤	88 ⑥⑦	488 ⑥⑦		Acela 2164 ①-⑤	Acela 2212 ⑥⑦
Lynchburg d.	...	...	...	...	...	...	...	...	...	...	0556	...	...	...	...	...	...	...	...	...	...	...	...	...
Charlottesville d.	...	...	...	...	...	...	...	...	...	...	0709	...	...	...	...	...	...	...	...	...	...	...	...	...
irginia Beach d.	...	...	...	...	...	...	...	...	...	...	|	...	...	...	...	...	...	...	...	...	...	...	...	...
orfolk d.	...	...	...	...	...	...	...	...	...	...	|	...	...	...	...	...	...	...	0610	0615	...	...	...	...
ewport News d.	...	...	...	...	...	...	...	...	...	...	|	...	...	...	...	...	...	...	|	|	...	...	...	...
ichmond d.	...	...	...	...	0600	...	...	...	0635	...	|	...	...	0700	0735	...	...	...	0818	0825	...	...	...	...
redericksburg d.	...	...	...	...	0656	...	...	...	0733	...	|	...	...	0800	0832	...	...	...	0919	0925	...	...	...	...
/ashington Union a.	...	...	...	...	0815	...	...	...	0900	...	0953s	...	...	0933	0944	...	...	...	1039	1056	...	...	...	...
/ashington Union d.	0800	0810	0810	...	0840	0900	0900	0920	0925	...	0953s	1000	1000	1010	1020	1020	1100	1100	1110	1125	...	...	1200	1200
WI Airport d.	0821	0835	0838	...	0908	0921	0921	0948	0953	...	|	1021	1021	1037	1048	1047	1121	1121	1138	1153	...	...	|	1221
altimore Penn d.	0834	0852	0854	...	0923	0934	0934	1004	1008	...	1055s	1034	1031	1053	1104	1104	1134	1134	1154	1208	...	...	1230	1234
hiladelphia 30th Street d.	0936	1101	1012	...	1040	1036	1039	1115	1120	...	1208s	1136	1139	1205	1218	1218	1236	1239	1305	1319	...	...	1332	1339
ewark NJ d.	1031s	1103	1125s	...	1147	1130	1136	1222	1229	...	1325s	1230	1236s	1315	1328	1328	1331s	1336	1411	1428	...	...	1430	1436s
ew York Penn a.	1051	1121	1147	...	1205	1148	1153	1242	1247	...	1346	1248	1258	1335	1346	1348	1353	1353	1430	1446	...	...	1446	1458
ew York Penn d.	...	1133	...	...	1230	1203	1203	...	1300	...	...	1303	...	1400	1400	...	...	1403	...	1500	...	...	1500	...
tamford d.	...	1218	...	...	1318	1248	1247	...	1348	...	...	1348	...	1448	1448	...	...	1448	...	1548	...	...	1545	...
ew Haven d.	...	1325	...	...	1410	1337	1335	...	1444	1450	...	1437	...	1544	1544	...	...	1537	...	1644	1650	...	|	...
Hartford d.	...	1413	...	...	|	|	|	...	|	1541	...	|	...	|	|	...	...	|	...	|	1736	...	|	...
Springfield MA a.	...	1500	...	...	|	|	|	...	|	1616	...	|	...	|	|	...	...	|	...	|	1815	...	|	...
ew London d.	...	...	...	...	1455	|	|	...	1532	...	...	|	...	1635	1634	...	...	|	...	1353	...	...	|	...
rovidence d.	...	...	...	...	1547	1454	1457	...	1633	...	...	1556	...	1733	1729	...	...	1657	...	1827	...	...	1751	...
oston South a.	...	...	...	...	1635	1545	1519	...	1723	...	...	1645	...	1830	1820	...	...	1749	...	1920	...	...	1845	...

	176 ①-⑤	476 ①-⑤	140 ⑥⑦	Acela 2166 ①-⑤	Acela 2254 ⑦	186 ①-⑤	194 ⑦	96 ⑥	Acela 2168 ①-⑤	Acela 2260 ⑥	94 ①-⑤	494 ①-⑤	156 ⑥⑦	Acela 2170 ①-⑤	Acela 2256 ⑦	148 ①-⑤	92 ♦	168 ⑥	132 ⑦	432 ⑦	134 ④⑤	Acela 2172 ①-⑤	Acela 2220 ⑥	Acela 2258 ⑦
Lynchburg d.	0738	...	...	...	...	...	...	...	...	...	...	...	0959	...	...	...	...	...	...	...	...	...	...	...
Charlottesville d.	0852	...	...	...	...	...	...	...	...	...	...	...	1113	...	...	...	...	...	...	...	...	...	...	...
'irginia Beach d.	|	...	...	...	...	...	*0610**	*0610**	...	...	*0700**	...	|	...	...	...	...	...	...	...	...	...	...	...
orfolk d.	|	...	...	...	...	...	*0650**	*0650**	...	...	*0740**	...	|	...	...	...	...	...	...	...	...	...	...	...
ewport News d.	|	...	...	...	...	...	0830	0830	...	...	0900	...	|	...	...	...	...	...	...	...	...	...	...	...
ichmond d.	|	...	...	...	...	...	1019	1019	...	...	1051	...	|	...	...	...	1216	...	...	...	...	...	...	...
redericksburg d.	|	...	...	...	...	...	1117	1117	...	...	1150	...	|	...	...	...	|	...	...	...	...	...	...	...
/ashington Union a.	1120	...	...	...	...	...	1235	1235	...	...	1325	...	1335	...	...	...	1438s	...	...	...	...	...	...	...
/ashington Union d.	1205	...	1225	1300	1300	1305	1305	1325	1400	1400	1405	...	1420	1500	1500	1505	1438s	1525	1525	...	1530	1600	1600	1600
WI Airport d.	1232	...	1252	|	1321	1332	1332	1352	|	1421	1433	...	1447	1521	1521	1532	|	1552	1552	...	1554	|	1621	1621
altimore Penn d.	1247	...	1308	1330	1334	1347	1351	1411	1430	1434	1449	...	1504	1534	1534	1548	1547s	1608	1608	...	1609	1630	1634	1634
hiladelphia 30th Street d.	1358	...	1418	1432	1439	1501	1505	1523	1532	1539	1559	...	1619	1636	1639	1700	1705s	1718	1718	...	1734	1732	1739	1739
ewark NJ d.	1502	...	1528	1530	1536	1612	1615	1632	1630	1636	1705	...	1727	1730	1736	1810	1823s	1828	1828	...	1837s	1830	1837s	1837
ew York Penn a.	1520	...	1548	1546	1553	1632	1635	1650	1646	1653	1722	...	1746	1746	1753	1831	1850	1846	1848	...	1858	1846	1857	1853
ew York Penn d.	1530	...	1630	1600	1603	...	1700	1725	1700	1703	1742	...	...	1800	1803	1845	...	1900	1930	...	...	1900	...	1903
tamford d.	1618	...	1718	|	1648	...	1748	1812	1748	1748	1831	...	...	1847	1848	1935	...	1948	2018	...	...	1945	...	1948
lew Haven d.	1734	1720	1826	1733	1737	...	1840	1901	1837	1837	1932b	1930	...	1936	1937	2044	...	2044	2114	2120	...	2034	...	2037
Hartford d.	|	1810	1919	|	|	...	|	|	|	|	|	2016	...	|	|	2131	...	|	|	2210	...	|	...	|
Springfield MA a.	|	1850	2000	|	|	...	|	|	|	|	|	2055	...	|	|	2220	...	|	|	2250	...	|	...	|
ew London d.	1824	...	...	|	|	...	1932	1951	|	|	2024	...	...	|	|	...	...	2135	2207	...	...	2111e	...	|
'rovidence d.	1919	...	...	1854	1856	...	2028	2047	1956	1929	2119	...	...	2054	2050	...	...	2235	2302	...	...	2154	...	2154
oston South a.	2012	...	...	1940	1946	...	2120	2138	2045	2050	2210	...	...	2145	2148	...	...	2330	2358	...	...	2245	...	2250

		178 ①-⑤	126 ⑦	146 ⑥		80 ♦	Acela 2122 ①-⑤	Acela 2222 ⑦	136 ⑤	196 ①-④	192 ⑥		166 ⑦	Acela 2124 ①-⑤	138 ①-⑤	50 ③⑤⑦ ♦	158 ⑥⑦	Acela 2126 ①-⑤	188 ①-⑤	182 ⑥⑦	90 ♦	Acela 2128 ①-⑤	Acela 2228 ⑦	
Lynchburg d.	...	...	...	...	...	...	...	...	...	...	...	...	...	...	...	...	...	...	...	...	...	...	...	...
Charlottesville d.	...	...	...	...	...	...	...	...	...	...	...	...	...	...	...	1519	...	...	...	...	...	...	...	...
irginia Beach d.	...	...	...	...	...	...	...	...	...	...	...	...	...	...	...	|	...	...	...	...	...	...	...	...
orfolk d.	...	...	...	...	...	...	...	...	...	...	...	...	...	...	...	|	...	...	...	...	...	...	...	...
lewport News d.	...	...	...	...	...	...	...	...	...	...	...	...	...	...	...	|	...	...	...	...	...	...	...	...
ichmond d.	...	...	...	...	...	1412	...	...	...	...	...	...	...	...	...	|	...	...	...	...	1714	...	...	...
redericksburg d.	...	...	...	...	...	1506	...	...	...	...	...	...	...	...	...	|	...	...	...	...	|	...	...	...
/ashington Union a.	...	...	...	...	...	1629s	...	...	...	...	...	...	...	...	...	1819s	...	...	...	...	1942s	...	...	...
/ashington Union d.	...	1602	1625	1625	...	1629s	1700	1700	1705	1705	1720	...	1720	1800	1805	1819s	1820	1900	1910	1920	2030s	200	2000	...
WI Airport d.	...	1629	1651	1652	...	|	|	1721	1732	1732	1747	...	1747	|	1833	|	1847	|	1937	1947	2057	|	2021	...
altimore Penn d.	...	1645	1707	1708	...	1747s	1730	1734	1748	1748	1804	...	1804	1830	1850	1916s	1904	1930	1954	2004	2115s	2030	2034	...
hiladelphia 30th Street d.	...	1758	1818	1819	...	1900s	1832	1839	1902	1902	1919	...	1919	1932	2001	2026s	2015	2035	2110	2120	2228s	2135	2139	...
ewark NJ d.	...	1903	1923s	1925	...	2013s	1930s	1936s	2022	2020s	2027	...	2027	2029s	2112	2138s	2123s	2134s	2214s	2226	2336s	2232s	2236s	...
lew York Penn a.	...	1925	1947	19465	...	2035	1952	1958	2043	2042	2047	...	2046	2051	2133	2158	2147	2154	2236	2251	2356	2252	2257	...
lew York Penn d.	...	1950	...	2000	...	...	...	...	2057	...	...	...	2100	...	...	...	...	...	...	...	...	...	...	...
itamford d.	...	2045	...	2048	...	...	...	...	2149	...	...	...	2148	...	...	...	...	...	...	...	...	...	...	...
lew Haven d.	...	2142	...	2154	...	...	...	...	2259	...	...	...	2241	...	...	...	...	...	...	...	...	...	...	...
Hartford d.	...	|	...	2250e	...	...	...	...	2347	...	...	...	|	...	...	...	...	...	...	...	...	...	...	...
Springfield MA a.	...	|	...	2320	...	...	...	...	0030	...	...	...	|	...	...	...	...	...	...	...	...	...	...	...
lew London d.	...	2232	...	...	...	...	...	...	...	...	...	...	2331	...	...	...	...	...	...	...	...	...	...	...
'rovidence d.	...	2329	...	...	...	...	...	...	...	...	...	...	0020	...	...	...	...	...	...	...	...	...	...	...
3oston South a.	...	0020	...	...	...	...	...	...	...	...	...	...	0113	...	...	...	...	...	...	...	...	...	...	...

1/92 – SILVER STAR – 🛏 1, 2 cl., 💺 and ✕ New York - Washington - Tampa - Miami and v.v.
7/98 – SILVER METEOR – 🛏 1, 2 cl., 💺 and ✕ New York - Washington - Orlando - Miami and v.v.

a – Arrives 1712.
b – Arrives 1921.
e – May leave earlier than time shown.

s – Calls to set down only.
u – Calls to pick up only.
* – Connection by 🚌.

BEYOND EUROPE - NORTH AMERICA

9220 ST ALBANS - SPRINGFIELD — Amtrak

km		55	57
		①–⑤	⑥⑦
		A	A
0	**St. Albans** d.	0925	0925
38	Burlington Essex Jct. d.	0954	0954
70	Waterbury d.	1019	1019
90	Montpelier d.	1032	1032
133	Randolph d.	1105	1105
189	White River Jct. d.	1142	1142
205	Windsor VT d.	1159	1159
225	Claremont d.	1209	1209
252	Bellows Falls d.	1230	1230
291	Brattleboro d.	1301	1301
360	Northampton d.	1401	1401
397	**Springfield** MA a.	1435	1435
609	*New York Penn* **9215** a.	1825	1825
974	*Washington U* **9215** a.	2159	2225

	54	56
	⑥⑦	①–⑤
	A	A
Washington U **9215** d.	0730	0810
New York P **9215** d.	1130	1133
Springfield MA d.	1515	1515
Northampton d.	1557	1557
Brattleboro d.	1656	1656
Bellows Falls d.	1726	1726
Claremont d.	1745	1745
Windsor VT d.	1754	1754
White River Jct. d.	1815	1815
Randolph d.	1852	1852
Montpelier d.	1927	1927
Waterbury d.	1939	1939
Burlington Essex Jct. d.	2008	2008
St. Albans a.	2040	2040

A – VERMONTER – (12) and 🍸 Washington - New York - New Haven - St Albans and v.v.

9225 HARRISBURG - PITTSBURGH — Amtrak

km		43	
		B	
	New York Penn **9230** d.	1052	...
	Philadelphia **9230** d.	1242	...
0	**Harrisburg** d.	1436	...
95	Lewistown d.	1546	...
154	Huntingdon d.	1622	...
186	Tyrone d.	1648r	...
213	Altoona d.	1706	...
275	Johnstown d.	1800	...
334	Latrobe d.	1841r	...
346	Greensburg d.	1852	...
401	**Pittsburgh 9235** a.	2005	...

	42	
	B	
Pittsburgh 9235 d.	0730	...
Greensburg d.	0811	...
Latrobe d.	0821r	...
Johnstown d.	0904	...
Altoona d.	1001	...
Tyrone d.	1017r	...
Huntingdon d.	1044	...
Lewistown d.	1121	...
Harrisburg a.	1255	...
Philadelphia **9230** a.	1455	...
New York Penn **9230** a.	1650	...

B – PENNSYLVANIAN – (12) and 🍸 Pittsburgh - Harrisburg - New York and v.v.
r – Calls on request.

9230 NEW YORK - PHILADELPHIA - HARRISBURG — Amtrak

KEYSTONE SERVICE

km		601s	605	607s	611	661	641s	663	643s	43s	645s	615	609	665	647	649s	667	651	653s	669	655s	671		619s	
		Ⓐ	Ⓐ	Ⓐ	⑥	Ⓒ	Ⓐ	Ⓒ	Ⓐ	B	Ⓐ	⑦	Ⓐ	Ⓒ	Ⓐ	Ⓐ	Ⓒ	Ⓐ	Ⓐ	Ⓒ	Ⓐ	Ⓒ		Ⓐ	
0	**New York** Penn **9215** d.	*0325*	*0440*	*0530*	*0300*	0700	0717	0909	0930	1052	1205	*1205*	1254	1305	1411	1444	1513	1603	1710	1717	1835	1953	...	*2110*	...
16	Newark NJ **9215** d.	*0345*	0457u	0546u	*0320*	0717u	0734u	0927u	0946u	1109u	1222u	*1222*	1310u	1323u	1428	1459	1532u	1620u	1727u	1734u	1852u	2009u	...	*2127*	...
146	**Philadelphia** 30th St a.	*0452*	*0602*	*0653*	*0427*	0820	0846	1035	1050	1215	1325	*1330*	1417	1426	1533	1612	1638	1723	1830	1836	2000	2015	...	*2234*	...
146	**Philadelphia** 30th St d.	0520	0625	0725	0725	0835	0900	1055	1100	1242	1335	1355	1445	1445	1545	1645	1655	1735	1842	1855	2015	2145	...	2259	...
178	Paoli d.	0546	0651	0751	0750	0900	0923	1120	1123	1312	1359	1420	1510	1510	1610	1711	1721	1802	1907	1921	2040	2210	...	2324f	...
255	Lancaster d.	0632	0735	0830	0834	0945	1007	1203	1207	1352	1443	1504	1555	1555	1650	1758	1805	1847	1953	2007	2125	2255	...	0009f	...
300	Elizabethtown d.	0651	0752	0845	0850	1001	1024	1220	1224	1406	1500	1521	1611	1611	1704	1814	1821	1903	2009	2026	2141	2311	...	0025f	...
315	**Harrisburg** a.	0715	0818	0905	0915	1025	1050	1245	1250	1426	1525	1540	1635	1635	1730	1840	1845	1930	2035	2050	2205	2330	...	0050	...

	640s	642	600s	660	644s	662	646	664	648s	666	650s	42s	670	652s	654s	672	656	618s	658s	674	610	612	620	622s
	Ⓐ	Ⓐ	Ⓐ	Ⓒ	Ⓐ	⑥	Ⓐ	Ⓒ	Ⓐ	Ⓒ	Ⓐ	B	Ⓒ	Ⓐ	Ⓐ	Ⓒ	Ⓐ	①–④	⑤	⑦	⑥	⑦	Ⓐ	Ⓐ
Harrisburg d.	0500	0555	0645	0720	0755	0820	0900	0930	1000	1120	1200	1305	1400	1520	1630	1705	1735	1840	1840	1905	1905	2020	2030	2115
Elizabethtown d.	0517	0612	0702	0737	0812	0837	0917	0947	1016	1137	1217	1323	1417	1537	1647	1722	1752	1857	1857	1922	1922	2037	2047	2132
Lancaster d.	0535	0630	0721	0755	0832	0855	0933	1005	1032	1155	1235	1340	1434	1554	1705	1740	1810	1912	1912	1940	1940	2055	2102	2147
Paoli d.	0619	0723	0809	0841	0910	0941	1018	1049	1110	1241	1316	1424	1522	1637	1750	1825	1855	1955	1955	2025	2025	2140	2144	2229
Philadelphia 30th St a.	0645	0750	0835	0905	0935	1005	1040	1110	1135	1305	1345	1455	1550	1705	1825	1850	1923	2020	2020	2050	2050	2210	2210	2255
Philadelphia 30th St d.	0700	0805	0850	0823	0945	1030	1055	1125	1145	1330	1405	1525	1610	1718	1850	1910	1940	*2110*	2036	2110	*2120*	*0010*	...	*0010*
Newark NJ a.	0812f	0906f	0955s	1031	1047f	1142f	1157f	1231f	1245s	1440f	1508f	1630s	1713f	1833f	1954f	2014f	2045f	*2214*s	2142f	2214f	*2226*s	*0122*s	...	*0122*
New York Penn a.	0830	0926	1015	1049	1105	1159	1215	1249	1303	1457	1526	1650	1732	1853	2012	2034	2103	2236	2200	2234	*2251*	*0140*	...	*0140*

B – PENNSYLVANIAN – see Table **9225**.
f – May leave before time shown.
s – Calls to set down only.
u – Calls to pick up only.

NOTE: On weekdays during periods of severe weather trains MAY operate on a special schedule when only trains marked **XXXs** will operate.

9235 BOSTON - CHICAGO — Amtrak

km		29	449	49
		E	C	D
0	**Boston** South d.	...	1250	...
70	Worcester d.	...	1403	...
157	Springfield MA d.	...	1523	...
242	Pittsfield d.	...	1639	...
	New York **9205** d.	...	|	1540
320	**Albany** R'laer d.	...	1800	1905
349	Schenectady d.	...	...	1932
558	Syracuse d.	...	...	2149
686	Rochester d.	...	...	2309
784	Buffalo Depew d.	...	...	2359
931	Erie d.	...	...	0148
◇	**Washington** U d.	1605	...	|
◇	Harper's Ferry d.	1716	...	|
◇	Martinsburg d.	1745	...	|
◇	Cumberland d.	1924	...	|
◇	Pittsburgh **9225** d.	2359	...	|
◇	Alliance d.	0139	...	|
1083	**Cleveland** d.	0259	...	0345
1179	Sandusky d.	0402	...	0455
1254	Toledo d.	0522	...	0615
1379	Waterloo d.	0636	...	0733
1467	Elkhart d.	0729	...	0825
1494	South Bend d.	0751	...	0849
1629	**Chicago** Union a.	0845	...	0945

	30	48	448
	E	D	C
Chicago Union d.	1840	2130	...
South Bend d.	2109	2359	...
Elkhart d.	2129	0022	...
Waterloo d.	2023	0115	...
Toledo d.	2349	0320	...
Sandusky d.	0040	0412	...
Cleveland d.	0154	0550	...
Alliance d.	0305	|	...
Pittsburgh **9225** d.	0520	|	...
Cumberland d.	0932	|	...
Martinsburg d.	1101	|	...
Harper's Ferry d.	1131	|	...
Washington U a.	1305	|	...
Erie d.	...	0720	...
Buffalo Depew d.	...	0851	...
Rochester d.	...	0950	...
Syracuse d.	...	1118	...
Schenectady d.	...	1358	...
Albany R'laer a.	...	1455	1505
New York **9205** a.	...	1823	|
Pittsfield d.	...	...	1609
Springfield MA d.	...	...	1733
Worcester d.	...	...	1844s
Boston South a.	...	...	2001

9240 WASHINGTON - MIAMI — Amtrak

km		89	91	97
		F	G	H
0	**New York** Penn d.	0602	1102	1515
146	Philadelphia 30th St d.	0732v	1235u	1658u
297	Baltimore Penn d.	0842v	1355u	1817u
362	**Washington** Union d.	1000	1505u	1925u
536	Richmond d.	1219	1717	2144
581	Petersburg d.	1254	1751	2218
738	Rocky Mount d.	1429	1921	2350
852	**Raleigh** d.	|	2101	|
882	Fayetteville d.	1605	|	0122
1015	Florence d.	1744	|	0313
1167	Charleston SC d.	1919	|	0451
1176	Columbia d.	|	0138	|
1328	Savannah d.	2104	0418	0640
1565	**Jacksonville** a.	...	0639	0909
1565	**Jacksonville** d.	...	0659	0934
1792	Winter Park d.	...	0943	1226
1800	Orlando d.	...	1020	1304
1829	Kissimmee d.	...	1044	1326
1959	**Tampa** d.	...	1237	|
	Winter Haven d.	...	1335	1413
1955	Sebring d.	...	1416	1454
2120	West Palm Beach a.	...	1617s	1647s
2189	Fort Lauderdale a.	...	1717s	1743s
2224	**Miami** Amtrak a.	...	1758	1839

	98	92	90
	H	G	F
Miami Amtrak d.	0810	1150	...
Fort Lauderdale d.	0850u	1230u	...
West Palm Beach d.	0947u	1327u	...
Sebring d.	1123	1502	...
Winter Haven d.	1207	1548	...
Tampa d.	|	1727	...
Kissimmee d.	1256	1848	...
Orlando d.	1335	1932	...
Winter Park d.	1352	1949	...
Jacksonville a.	1647	2225	...
Jacksonville d.	1707	2303	...
Savannah d.	1931	0122	0820
Columbia d.	|	0401	|
Charleston SC d.	2117	|	1000
Florence d.	2312	|	1139
Fayetteville d.	0037	|	1305
Raleigh d.	|	0845	|
Rocky Mount d.	0209	1003	1452
Petersburg d.	0333	1128	1620
Richmond d.	0432	1216	1714
Washington Union a.	0707s	1438s	1942s
Baltimore Penn a.	0812s	1547s	2115
Philadelphia 30th St a.	0930s	1705s	2224s
New York Penn a.	1100	1850	2356

Notes for Table **9235** and **9240**.

C – 🛏 1, 2 cl., (2) and 🍸 Boston(**449/448**) - Albany(**48/49**) - Chicago and v.v.
D – LAKE SHORE LIMITED – 🛏 1, 2 cl., (2) and ✕ New York(**49/48**) - Albany(**49/48**) - Chicago and v.v.; conveys 🛏 1, 2 cl., (2) and 🍸 Boston(**449/448**) - Albany(**48/49**) - Chicago and v.v.
E – CAPITOL LIMITED – 🛏 1, 2 cl., (2) and ✕ Washington - Chicago and v.v.
F – PALMETTO – (12) and 🍸 New York - Washington - Savannah and v.v.
G – SILVER STAR – 🛏 1, 2 cl., (2) and ✕ New York - Washington - Tampa - Miami and v.v.
H – SILVER METEOR – 🛏 1, 2 cl., (2) and ✕ New York - Washington - Orlando - Miami and v.v.

s – Calls to set down only.
u – Calls to pick up only.
v – Calls to pick up only and on ①–⑤ runs 8–9 mins later than shown.

◇ – Washington - Cleveland distances: Washington *0 km*, Harper's Ferry *88 km*, Martinsburg *118 km*, Cumberland *234 km*, Pittsburgh *478 km*, Alliance *613 km*, Cleveland *702 km*.

9245 WASHINGTON - CHARLOTTE - NEW ORLEANS — Amtrak

km		73		75	79	19				
		2		2	A	B				
	New York Penn **9215** d.	...	...	...	0725a	1415	...	...	...	...
0	**Washington** Union d.	...	...	...	1110	1830	...	...	...	...
174	Richmond d.	...	...	...	1334	|	...	...	...	...
219	Petersburg d.	...	...	...	1408	|	...	...	...	...
376	Rocky Mount d.	...	...	...	1536	|	...	...	...	...
490	**Raleigh** d.	0645	...	1145	1716	|	...	...	...	...
619	Greensboro d.	0821	...	1321	1858	0022	...	...	...	...
645	High Point d.	0838	...	1338	1919	0039	...	...	...	...
699	Salisbury d.	0914	...	1414	1955	0117	...	...	...	...
766	**Charlotte** a.	1004	...	1504	2044	0245	...	...	...	...
890	Spartanburg d.	...	...	...	...	0414	...	...	...	...
940	Greenville d.	...	...	...	...	0501	...	...	...	...
1102	Gainesville d.	...	...	...	...	0658	...	...	...	...
1179	**Atlanta** d.	...	...	...	...	0838	...	...	...	...
1344	Anniston d.	...	...	...	...	1000	...	...	...	...
1447	Birmingham d.	...	...	...	...	1208	...	...	...	...
1536	Tuscaloosa d.	...	...	...	...	1307	...	...	...	...
1692	Meridian d.	...	...	...	...	1504	...	...	...	...
1829	Hattiesburg d.	...	...	...	...	1638	...	...	...	...
2018	**New Orleans** a.	...	...	...	...	1932	...	...	...	...

	20	80	74	76					
	B	A	2	2					
New Orleans d.	0700	...	...	...	...	...	...	...	...
Hattiesburg d.	0930	...	...	...	...	...	...	...	...
Meridian d.	1107	...	...	...	...	...	...	...	...
Tuscaloosa d.	1244	...	...	...	...	...	...	...	...
Birmingham d.	1424	...	...	...	...	...	...	...	...
Anniston d.	1559	...	...	...	...	...	...	...	...
Atlanta d.	2004	...	...	...	...	...	...	...	...
Gainesville d.	2059	...	...	...	...	...	...	...	...
Greenville d.	2258	...	...	...	...	...	...	...	...
Spartanburg d.	2339	...	...	...	...	...	...	...	...
Charlotte d.	0146	0700	1200	1715	...	...	...	...	...
Salisbury d.	0232	0743	1244	1759	...	...	...	...	...
High Point d.	0316	0817	1320	1835	...	...	...	...	...
Greensboro d.	0344	0839	1342	1857	...	...	...	...	...
Raleigh d.	|	1025	1521	2036	...	...	...	...	...
Rocky Mount d.	|	1152	...	...	...	...	...	...	...
Petersburg d.	|	1317	...	...	...	...	...	...	...
Richmond d.	|	1412	...	...	...	...	...	...	...
Washington Union a.	0953	1629	...	...	...	...	...	...	...
New York Penn **9215** a.	1346	2035	...	...	...	...	...	...	...

A – CAROLINIAN – (12) and 🍸 New York - Washington - Charlotte and v.v. **a** – 0717 ⑥⑦.
B – CRESCENT – 🛏 1, 2 cl., (2) and ✕ New York - Washington - New Orleans and v.v.

636 ITE

WASHINGTON - CHICAGO 9250

Amtrak

km		51	851
		③⑤⑦	
		A	B
	New York P **9215** ...... d.	0645	...
0	**Washington** Union .... d.	1100	...
109	Culpeper .... d.	1225	...
181	Charlottesville .... d.	1352	...
338	Clifton Forge .... d.	1613	...
393	White Sulpher Springs .. d.	1705	...
528	Charleston WV .... d.	2029	...
606	Huntington .... d.	2151	...
678	South Portsmouth .... d.	2257	...
872	Cincinnati .... d.	0141	...
069	**Indianapolis** .... a.	0515	...
069	**Indianapolis** .... d.	0600	0600
144	Crawfordsville .... d.	0658	0658
187	Lafayette .... d.	0736	0736
383	**Chicago** Union .... a.	1005	1005

	50	851
	②④⑥	
	A	B
Chicago Union .... d.	1745	1745
Lafayette .... d.	2157	2157
Crawfordsville .... d.	2231	2231
Indianapolis .... a.	2350	2350
Indianapolis .... d.	2359	...
Cincinnati .... d.	0327	...
South Portsmouth .... d.	0545	...
Huntington .... d.	0716	...
Charleston WV .... d.	0821	...
White Sulpher Spings .... d.	1139	...
Clifton Forge .... d.	1244	...
Charlottesville .... d.	1519	...
Culpepper .... d.	1635	...
Washington Union .... a.	1819	...
New York P **9215** ...... a.	2158	...

– CARDINAL – 1,2 cl., (2) and Chicago - New York and v.v.
– HOOSIER STATE – (2) Chicago - Indianapolis and v.v. Runs on days Trains **50/51** do not operate.

CHICAGO - NEW ORLEANS 9255

Amtrak

km		391	393	59
		D	E	C
0	**Chicago** Union ..... d.	0815	1605	2005
92	Kankakee .... d.	0922	1712	2123r
208	Champaign ‡ .... d.	1025	1815	2234
323	Effingham .... d.	1129	1919	2337r
408	Centralia .... d.	1216	2006	0025r
498	Carbondale .... d.	1345	2135	0126
725	Newbern .... d.	...	...	0356r
850	Memphis .... d.	...	...	0650
1051	Greenwood .... d.	...	...	0900
1136	Yazoo City .... d.	...	...	0951r
1207	Jackson .... d.	...	...	1120
1334	McComb .... d.	...	...	1240r
1419	Hammond .... d.	...	...	1328
1503	**New Orleans** .... a.	...	...	1532

	58	390	392
	C	D	E
New Orleans .... d.	1345	...	...
Hammond .... d.	1445	...	...
McComb .... d.	1532r	...	...
Jackson .... d.	1744	...	...
Yazoo City .... d.	1842r	...	...
Greenwood .... d.	1937	...	...
Memphis .... d.	2240	...	...
Newbern .... d.	0022r	...	...
Carbondale .... d.	0316	0730	1615
Centralia .... d.	0410r	0823	1708
Effingham .... d.	0457r	0907	1752
Champaign ‡ .... d.	0610	1014	1859
Kankakee .... d.	0713r	1115	2000
Chicago Union ..... a.	0900	1300	2145

C – CITY OF NEW ORLEANS – 1,2 cl., (2) and Chicago - New Orleans and v.v.
D – SALUKI – (12) and Chicago - Carbondale and v.v.
E – ILLINI – (12) and Chicago - Carbondale and v.v.
r – Request stop.
‡ – Champaign Urbana.

CHICAGO - ST. LOUIS - KANSAS CITY 9260

Amtrak

km		311	301	303	313	21	3	305	307	
		F	G	G	F	H	J	G	G	
0	**Chicago** Union .... d.	...	0700	0925	...	1345	1500	1715	1900	...
60	Joliet Union .... d.	...	0757	1015	...	1440u	|	1805	1950	...
148	Pontiac .... d.	...	|	1106	...	1527	|	1856	2041	...
204	Bloomington .... d.	...	0914	1139	...	1604	|	1929	2114	...
252	Lincoln .... d.	...	|	1210	...	1637	|	2002	2147	...
298	Springfield IL .... d.	...	1015	1250	...	1714	|	2039	2224	...
360	Carlinville .... d.	...	|	1328	...	1749r	|	2119	2304	...
414	Alton .... d.	...	1122	1359	...	1822	|	2150	2335	...
457	**St. Louis** .... d.	0915	1220	1500	1600	1921	|	2245	0030	...
480	Kirkwood .... d.	0944	...	...	1629	...	|	...	...	...
658	Jefferson City .... d.	1136	...	...	1822	...	|	...	...	...
760	Sedalia .... d.	1246	...	...	1939	...	|	...	...	...
866	Lee's Summit .... d.	1404	...	...	2050	...	|	...	...	...
912	**Kansas City** .... a.	1455	...	...	2140	...	2211	...	...	...

	300	302	22	4	314	304	306	316	
	G	G	H	J	F	G	G	F	
Kansas City .... d.	...	...	...	0743	0815	...	...	1600	...
Lee's Summit .... d.	...	...	...	|	0851	...	...	1636	...
Sedalia .... d.	...	...	...	|	1004	...	...	1749	...
Jefferson City .... d.	...	...	...	|	1118	...	...	1903	...
Kirkwood .... d.	...	...	...	|	1313	...	...	2058	...
St. Louis .... d.	0435	0640	0755	|	1355	1500	1730	2140	...
Alton .... d.	0520	0725	0843	|	...	1545	1815	...	...
Carlinville .... d.	0550	0755	0915r	|	...	1614	1845	...	...
Springfield IL .... d.	0632	0837	0955	|	...	1656	1932	...	...
Lincoln .... d.	0700	0905	1025	|	...	1724	2000	...	...
Bloomington .... d.	0731	0946	1108	|	...	1756	2036	...	...
Pontiac .... d.	0759	1014	1139	|	...	1823	2104	...	...
Joliet Union .... d.	0859	1119	1256s	|	...	1926	2202	...	...
Chicgo Union .... a.	1000	1220	1352	1515	...	2040	2310	...	...

– RIVER RUNNER – (12) and St Louis - Kansas City and v.v.
– LINCOLN SERVICE – (12) and Chicago - St. Louis and v.v.
H – TEXAS EAGLE. See Table **9300**.
J – SOUTHWEST CHIEF. See Table **9295**.
r – Request stop.
s – Calls to set down only.
u – Calls to pick up only.

CHICAGO - QUINCY 9265

Amtrak

km		381	5	3	383					
		A	C	D	B					
0	**Chicago** Union .... d.	0735	1400	1500	1755	...	...	...	...	...
166	Princeton .... d.	0921	1544	1646	1941	...	...	...	...	...
259	Galesburg .... d.	1018	1638	1738	2038	...	...	...	...	...
413	**Quincy** .... a.	1158	...	...	2218	...	...	...	...	...

	380	4	382						
	B	D	A						
Quincy .... d.	0612	...	1730	...	...	...	...	...	...
Galesburg .... d.	0738	1208	1856	...	...	...	...	...	...
Princeton .... d.	0831	1258	1949	...	...	...	...	...	...
Chicago Union .... a.	1035	1515	2153	...	...	...	...	...	...

– CARL SANDBURG – (12) and Chicago Union - Quincy and v.v.
– ILLINOIS ZEPHYR – (12) and Chicago Union - Quincy and v.v.
C – CALIFONIA ZEPHYR – See Table **9290**.
D – SOUTHWEST CHIEF – See Table **9295**.

CHICAGO - MILWAUKEE 9270

Amtrak 2nd class

km		329	331	333	335	337	339	341	8307	343
		①–⑤							🚌	⑥
0	**Chicago** Union .... d.	0610	0825	1020	1305	1515	1708	2005	2115	2310
100	Sturtevant .... d.	0710	0925	1120	1405	1615	1814	2105	|	0010
125	**Milwaukee** Airport .... a.	0724	0939	1134	1419	1629	1828	2119	|	0024
138	**Milwaukee** .... a.	0739	0954	1149	1434	1644	1845	2134	2330	0039

	8337	330	332	334	336	338	340	342	344
	🚌	①–⑤							⑥
Milwaukee .... d.	0600	0615	0805	1100	1300	1500	1745	1935	2340
Milwaukee Airport .... d.	|	0626	0815	1110	1310	1510	1755	1945	2350
Sturtevant .... d.	|	0643	0828	1123	1323	1523	1808	1958	2303
Chicago Union .... a.	0735	0757	0934	1229	1429	1629	1914	2104	0009

CHICAGO - GRAND RAPIDS, PORT HURON, DETROIT and PONTIAC 9275

Amtrak

km		8465	350	8150	352	8365	364	354	370	8354	8356
		🚌		🚌		🚌				🚌	🚌
			K		K	P	L	K	M		
0	**Chicago** Union ..... CT d.	...	0720	...	1250	...	1600	1800	1830	...	2235
140	Benton Harbour . ET d.	...	|	...	|	...	|	|	2115	...	|
282	**Grand Rapids** .. ET a.	0803	|	...	|	1630	|	|	2339	...	|
34	Michigan City .... CT d.	|	|	...	1358	|	|	1901	...	...	|
141	Niles .... ET d.	|	1007	...	1533	|	1833	2035	...	...	|
221	Kalamazoo .... a.	0900	1052	...	1608	1735	1912	2110	...	2200d	0245
258	Battle Creek .... a.	...	1124	1201d	1640	...	1945	2147	...	|	|
335	East Lansing .... d.	...	|	1330	|	...	2054	|	...	0025	|
382	Durand .... d.	...	|	|	|	...	2131	|	...	|	|
409	Flint .... d.	...	|	1535	|	...	2202	|	...	0125	|
513	**Port Huron** .... a.	...	|	...	|	...	2338	|	...	...	|
331	Jackson .... d.	...	1218	...	1733	...	...	2237	...	...	|
390	Ann Arbor .... d.	...	1305	...	1816	...	...	2320	...	...	|
439	Dearborn .... d.	...	1333e	...	1844e	...	...	2348e	...	...	0520
450	**Detroit** .... d.	...	1401e	...	1911e	...	...	0015e	...	...	0555
494	**Pontiac** .... a.	...	1500	...	2011	...	...	0117	...	...	f

	371	351	365	8351	8353	8364	353	8555	355	8651
				🚌	🚌	🚌		🚌		🚌
	M	K	L				K		K	
Pontiac .... d.	...	0545	...	...	...	...	1035	...	1740	g
Detroit .... d.	...	0628	...	...	...	...	1120	...	1823	|
Dearborn .... d.	...	0650	...	...	...	...	1142	...	1844	|
Ann Arbor .... d.	...	0724	...	...	...	...	1215	...	1919	|
Jackson .... d.	...	0806	...	...	...	...	1256	...	1959	|
Port Huron .... d.	...	|	0620	...	...	...	|	...	|	|
Flint .... d.	...	|	0732	...	0845	...	|	1600	|	|
Durand .... d.	...	|	0804	...	|	...	|	|	|	|
East Lansing .... d.	...	|	0845	...	0950	...	|	1750	|	|
Battle Creek .... d.	...	0901	0952	...	1115	...	1353	|	2054	|
Kalamazoo .... d.	...	0934	1025	1030	...	1415	1424	2020	2125	|
Niles .... ET d.	...	|	1103	|	...	|	1457	...	2202	|
Michigan City ..... CT d.	...	|	|	|	...	|	|	...	2133	|
Grand Rapids ET d.	0600	|	|	1122	...	1625	|	...	|	|
Benton Harbour ET d.	0816	|	|	...	...	...	|	...	|	|
Chicago Union .. CT a.	0911	1046	1145	...	...	...	1557	...	2256	0605

– WOLVERINE – (12) and Chicago - Pontiac and v.v.
– BLUE WATER – (12) and Chicago - Port Huron and v.v.
– PERE MARQUETTE – (2) Chicago - Grand Rapids and v.v.
P – Additional trip 1923.
d – Departure time.
e – Can leave before time shown.
f – To Toronto arr. 1305.
g – From Toronto dep. 1830.
CT – Central Time.
ET – Eastern Time.

SELECTED BUS ROUTES 9280

Greyhound

km	*Greyhound 🚌 service*	1529	1535	1539	1537	1511				
0	**Nashville** .... d.	0315	0645	1125	1700	2235	...	...	...	...
337	**Memphis** .... a.	0700	1045	1525	2055	0220	...	...	...	...

Greyhound 🚌 service	1502	1510	1514	1508	1504				
Memphis .... d.	0510	0920	1340	2030	2300	...	...	...	...
Nashville .... a.	0905	1315	1740	0015	0255	...	...	...	...

km	*Greyhound 🚌 service*	6001	1683	6021	6023	6005	6009	6029	6013	6017	6025
										⑦	
0	**Las Vegas** NV .... d.	0135	0345	0700	0800	0915	1201	1545	1715	1930	0001
501	**Los Angeles** .... a.	0825	0900	1440	1325	1600	1715	2245	2230	0105	0500

Greyhound 🚌 service	6034	6002	1682	6006	6012	6010	6014	6044	1302	6048
								⑤		
Los Angeles .... d.	0030	0615	0815	1000	1215	1415	1500	1815	1830	2300
Las Vegas NV .... a.	0530	1410	1325	1655	1730	2140	2020	2330	0020	0430

9285 CHICAGO - SEATTLE

Amtrak

km			7 A	27 B	[bus] 8948			[bus] 8909	28 B	8 A
0	**Chicago** Union	d.	1415	...	...	**Vancouver BC**	d.	1130	...	...
137	Milwaukee	d.	1552u	...	...	**Portland**	d.	|	1645	...
241	Columbus	d.	1702	...	...	Vancouver WA	d.	|	1707	...
314	Wisconsin Dells	d.	1749	...	...	Pasco	d.	|	2057	...
386	Tomah	d.	1827	...	...	**Seattle** King St.	d.	1530	|	1640
452	La Crosse	d.	1911	...	...	Everett	d.	...	|	1739
673	**Minneapolis / St Paul**	a.	2201	...	...	Wenatchee	d.	...	|	2042
673	**Minneapolis / St Paul**	d.	2228	...	...	**Spokane**	a.	...	0013	0040
773	St. Cloud	d.	0024	...	...	**Spokane**	d.	...	...	0125
1058	Fargo	d.	0324	...	...	Sandpoint	d.	...	...	0230
1194	Grand Forks	d.	0441	...	...	Whitefish	d.	...	...	0741
1332	Devils Lake	d.	0602	...	...	Essex	d.	...	...	0850r
1522	Minot	d.	0906	...	...	Shelby	d.	...	...	1133
1958	Glasgow	d.	1226	...	...	Havre	d.	...	...	1322
2072	Malta	d.	1325	...	...	Malta	d.	...	...	1442
2212	Havre	d.	1504	...	...	Glasgow	d.	...	...	1537
2381	Shelby	d.	1722	...	...	Minot	d.	...	...	2147
2537	Essex	d.	1941r	...	...	Devils Lake	d.	...	...	2337
2624	Whitefish	d.	2116	...	...	Grand Forks	d.	...	...	0102
2924	Sandpoint	d.	1349	...	...	Fargo	d.	...	...	0218
3030	**Spokane**	a.	0140	...	...	St. Cloud	d.	...	...	0519
3030	**Spokane**	d.	0215	0245	...	**Minneapolis / St Paul**	a.	...	...	0743
3306	Wenatchee	d.	0535	|	...	**Minneapolis / St Paul**	d.	...	...	0800
3501	Everett	d.	0838	|	...	La Crosse	d.	...	...	1047
3554	**Seattle** King St.	a.	1025	|	1045	Tomah	d.	...	...	1126
3265	Pasco	d.	...	0535	|	Wisconsin Dells	d.	...	...	1208
3621	Vancouver WA	d.	...	0918	|	Columbus	d.	...	...	1257
3638	**Portland**	a.	...	1010	|	Milwaukee	d.	...	...	1407s
	Vancouver BC	a	...	...	1415	**Chicago** Union	a.	...	...	1555

A – EMPIRE BUILDER – [sleeper] 1,2 cl., [2nd class] and [bar] Chicago - Spokane - Seattle and v.v.
B – EMPIRE BUILDER – [sleeper] 1,2 cl., [2nd class] Chicago - Spokane - Portland and v.v.
s – Calls to set down only. u – Calls to pick up only.

9290 CHICAGO - SAN FRANCISCO

Amtrak

km			5 C	[bus]			[bus]	6 C
0	**Chicago** Union	d.	1400	...	**San Francisco** ‡	d.	0750	...
261	Galesburg	d.	1638	...	**Emeryville**	d.	0825	091
330	Burlington	d.	1725	...	Martinez	d.	...	095
450	Ottumwa	d.	1853	...	Sacramento	d.	...	110
806	**Omaha**	a.	2255	...	Truckee	d.	...	143
806	**Omaha**	d.	2305	...	Reno	d.	...	160
892	Lincoln	d.	0014	...	Winnemucca	d.	...	190
1049	Hastings	d.	0147	...	Elko	d.	...	213
1261	McCook	d.	0343	...	**Salt Lake City**	a.	...	030
1668	**Denver** Union	a.	0715	...	**Salt Lake City**	d.	...	033
1668	**Denver** Union	d.	0805	...	Provo	d.	...	043
1770	Winter Park	d.	1007	...	Green River	d.	...	075
1791	Granby	d.	1037	...	Grand Junction	d.	...	102
1966	Glenwood Springs	d.	1353	...	Glenwood Springs	d.	...	121
2109	Grand Junction	d.	1610	...	Granby	d.	...	151
2279	Green River	d.	1758	...	Winter Park	d.	...	155
2516	Provo	d.	2126	...	**Denver** Union	a.	...	183
2587	**Salt Lake City**	a.	2305	...	**Denver** Union	d.	...	191
2587	**Salt Lake City**	d.	2330	...	McCook	d.	...	234
3010	Elko	d.	0303	...	Hastings	d.	...	014
3232	Winnemucca	d.	0540	...	Lincoln	d.	...	032
3514	Reno	d.	0836	...	**Omaha**	a.	...	045
3569	Truckee	d.	0937	...	**Omaha**	d.	...	051
3785	Sacramento	d.	1413s	...	Ottumwa	d.	...	090
3879	Martinez	d.	1526s	...	Burlington	d.	...	103
3922	**Emeryville**	a.	1610	1625	Galesburg	d.	...	1141
3936	**San Francisco** ‡	a.	...	1700	**Chicago** Union	a.	...	145

C – CALIFORNIA ZEPHYR – [sleeper] 1,2 cl., [2nd class] and [bar] Chicago - Emeryville and v.v.
s – Calls to set down only.
‡ – San Francisco Transbay Temporary Terminal.

9295 CHICAGO - LOS ANGELES

Amtrak

km			3 D				4 D	
0	**Chicago** Union	d.	1500	...	**Los Angeles** Union	d.	1810	...
261	Galesburg	d.	1738	...	San Bernardino	d.	1954	...
329	Fort Madison	d.	1842	...	Victorville	d.	2105	...
677	**Kansas City**	a.	2211	...	Barstow	d.	2151	...
677	**Kansas City**	d.	2245	...	Needles	d.	0018	...
783	Topeka	d.	0029	...	Kingman *	d.	0128*	...
1001	Newton	d.	0245	...	Williams Junction *	d.	0345*	...
1247	Dodge City	d.	0525	...	**Flagstaff * a**	d.	0437*	...
1488	Lamar	d.	0659	...	Winslow *	d.	0535*	...
1572	La Junta	d.	0830	...	Gallup	d.	0821	...
1704	Trinidad	d.	0950	...	**Abuquerque**	a.	1142	...
1741	Raton	d.	1056	...	**Abuquerque**	d.	1210	...
1918	Las Vegas NM	d.	1238	...	Lamy	d.	1317	...
2022	Lamy	d.	1424	...	Las Vegas NM	d.	1503	...
2132	**Abuquerque**	a.	1555	...	Raton	d.	1650	...
2132	**Abuquerque**	d.	1645	...	Trinidad	d.	1749	...
2391	Gallup	d.	1908	...	La Junta	d.	1941	...
2595	Winslow *	d.	1950*	...	Lamar	d.	2240	...
2690	**Flagstaff * a**	d.	2057*	...	Dodge City	d.	0027	...
2768	Williams Junction *	d.	2133*	...	Newton	d.	0259	...
2967	Kingman *	d.	2346*	...	Topeka	d.	0518	...
3067	Needles	d.	0049	...	**Kansas City**	a.	0724	...
3337	Barstow	d.	0339	...	**Kansas City**	d.	0743	...
3398	Victorville	d.	0418	...	Fort Madison	d.	1109	...
3472	San Bernardino	d.	0532	...	Galesburg	d.	1208	...
3588	**Los Angeles** Union	a.	0815	...	**Chicago** Union	a.	1515	...

D – SOUTHWEST CHIEF – [sleeper] 1,2 cl., [2nd class] and [bar] Chicago - Los Angeles and v.v.
a – Thruway buses operate to/from the Grand Canyon and Pheonix.
* – Do not observe DST, schedule times will be one hour later from November 1, 2016.

9300 CHICAGO - SAN ANTONIO

Amtrak

km			821 2 E	21 F			22 F	822 2 E
0	**Chicago** Union	d.	...	1345	**Los Angeles** Union	d.	2200b	...
148	Pontiac	d.	...	1527	**San Antonio**	a.	0450b	...
298	Springfield IL	d.	...	1714	**San Antonio**	d.	0700	...
457	**St. Louis**	a.	...	1921	San Marcos	d.	0832	...
457	**St. Louis**	d.	...	1955	Austin	d.	0931	...
717	Poplar Bluff	d.	...	2342	Taylor	d.	1022	...
813	Walnut Ridge	d.	...	0037	Temple	d.	1125	...
1007	Little Rock	d.	...	0310	**Fort Worth**	a.	1358	...
1127	Arkadelphia	d.	...	0420	**Fort Worth**	d.	1420	1725
1240	Texarkana	d.	...	0558	Gainesville	d.	|	1830
1384	Longview	d.	...	0828	Ardmore	d.	|	191
1588	**Dallas**	a.	...	1130	**Oklahoma City**	a.	|	2127
1588	**Dallas**	d.	...	1150	**Dallas**	a.	1520	...
336c	**Oklahoma City**	d.	0825	|	**Dallas**	d.	1540	...
172c	Ardmore	d.	1024	|	Longview	d.	1815	...
109c	Gainesville	d.	1110	|	Texarkana	d.	2043	...
1638	**Fort Worth**	a.	1227	1325	Arkadelphia	d.	2202	...
1638	**Fort Worth**	d.	...	1410	Little Rock	d.	2339	...
1844	Temple	d.	...	1643	Walnut Ridge	d.	0141	...
1906	Taylor	d.	...	1736	Poplar Bluff	d.	0244	...
1962	Austin	d.	...	1830	**St. Louis**	a.	0719	...
2011	San Marcos	d.	...	1912	**St. Louis**	d.	0755	...
2060	**San Antonio**	a.	...	2155	Springfield IL	d.	0955	...
2060	**San Antonio**	d.	...	0245a	Pontiac	d.	1139	...
4389	**Los Angeles** Union	a.	...	0535a	**Chicago** Union	a.	1352	...

E – HEARTLAND FLYER – [2nd class] [bar].
F – TEXAS EAGLE – [sleeper] 1,2 cl., [2nd class] and [restaurant] [bar] Chicago (**21/22**) - San Antonio (**421/422**) - Los Angeles and v.v.
a – San Antonio - Los Angeles ②④⑦ only. Arrives Los Angeles ①③⑤. See Table **9310**.
b – Los Angeles - San Antonio ③⑤⑦ only. Arrives San Antonio ①④⑥. See Table **9310**.
c – km from Fort Worth.

9305 SEATTLE - LOS ANGELES

Amtrak

km			[bus]	11 G	[bus] 5011			[bus] 5014	14 G	[bus] 6014
	Vancouver BC	d.	0530	...	...	**Los Angeles** ◐	d.	...	1010	...
0	**Seattle** King St.	d.	0900	0935	...	Santa Barbara	d.	...	1240	...
64	Tacoma	d.	▬	1021	...	San Luis Obispo	d.	...	1535	...
114	Olympia	d.	...	1111	...	Paso Robles	d.	...	1637	...
151	Centralia	d.	...	1135	...	Salinas	d.	...	1828	...
219	Kelso Longview	d.	...	1219	...	San Jose	d.	...	2023	...
282	Vancouver WA	d.	...	1258	...	**Oakland**	a.	...	2124	...
298	**Portland**	a.	...	1350	...	**Oakland**	d.	...	2139	2135
298	**Portland**	d.	...	1425	...	**San Francisco** ‡	d.	2110	|	2205
382	Salem	d.	...	1537	...	Emeryville	a.	2145	2154	▬
496	Eugene	d.	...	1710	...	Emeryville	d.	...	2204	...
691	Chemult	d.	...	2008	...	Martinez	d.	...	2246	...
808	Klamath Falls	d.	...	2200	...	**Sacramento**	d.	...	2359	...
976	Dunsmuir	d.	...	0035	...	Chico	d.	...	0147	...
1067	Redding	d.	...	0221	...	Redding	d.	...	0306	...
1186	Chico	d.	...	0350	...	Dunsmuir	d.	...	0456	...
1320	**Sacramento**	d.	...	0635	...	Klamath Falls	d.	...	0817	...
1397	Martinez	d.	...	0734	...	Chemult	d.	...	0932	...
1441	Emeryville	a.	[bus]	0810	...	Eugene	d.	...	1236	...
1441	Emeryville	d.	**6011**	0820	0825	Salem	d.	...	1355	...
	San Francisco ‡	a.	0745	|	0855	**Portland**	a.	...	1532	...
1449	**Oakland**	a.	0825	0835	...	**Portland**	d.	...	1602	...
1449	**Oakland**	d.	...	0850	...	Vancouver WA	d.	...	1621	...
1573	San Jose	d.	...	1007	...	Kelso Longview	d.	...	1654	...
1624	Salinas	d.	...	1148	...	Centralia	d.	...	1739	...
1780	Paso Robles	d.	...	1338	...	Olympia	d.	...	1804	...
1835	San Luis Obispo	d.	...	1520	...	Tacoma	d.	...	1853	[bus]
2025	Santa Barbara	d.	...	1802	...	**Seattle** King St.	a.	...	2012	2100
2190	**Los Angeles** ◐	a.	...	2100	...	Vancouver BC	a.	...	...	0015

G – COAST STARLIGHT – [sleeper] 1,2 cl., [2nd class] and [bar] Seattle - Los Angeles and v.v.
‡ – San Francisco Transbay Temporary Terminal.
◐ – Los Angeles Union.
NOTE: Due to extensive trackwork schedules are subject to change.

9310 NEW ORLEANS - LOS ANGELES

Amtrak

km			1257 [bus] J	1 ①③⑥ H			2 ③⑤⑦ H	1562 [bus] J
0	Orlando	d.	1855	...	**Los Angeles** Union	d.	2200	...
235	**Jacksonville**	d.	*2145*	...	Pomona	d.	2241	...
509	Tallahassee	d.	0115	...	Palm Springs	d.	0036	...
998	Mobile	d.	*0535*	...	Yuma *	d.	0247	...
1230	**New Orleans**	a.	*0755*	...	Maricopa *	d.	0540	...
1230	**New Orleans**	d.	...	0900	Tucson *	d.	0815	...
1434	New Iberia	d.	...	1156r	Benson *	d.	0915r	...
1462	Lafayette	d.	...	1224	Lordsburg	d.	1215r	...
1581	Lake Charles	d.	...	1355	**El Paso**	a.	1510	...
1678	Beaumont	d.	...	1548	**El Paso**	d.	1535	...
1810	Houston	d.	...	1855	Alpine	d.	2045	...
2146	**San Antonio**	a.	...	0005	Del Rio	d.	0102	...
2146	**San Antonio**	d.	...	0245	**San Antonio**	a.	0450	...
2418	Del Rio	d.	...	0549	**San Antonio**	d.	0625	...
2765	Alpine	d.	...	1038	Houston	d.	1210	...
3114	**El Paso**	a.	...	1322	Beaumont	d.	1405	...
3114	**El Paso**	d.	...	1347	Lake Charles	d.	1529	...
3350	Lordsburg	d.	...	1613r	Lafayette	d.	1715	...
3539	Benson*	d.	...	1718r	New Iberia	d.	1741r	...
3619	Tucson*	d.	...	1935	**New Orleans**	a.	2140	...
3757	Maricopa*	d.	...	2102	**New Orleans**	d.	...	1030
4021	Yuma*	d.	...	2349	Mobile	a.	...	1350
4253	Palm Springs	d.	...	0202	Tallahassee	a.	...	*2325*
4371	Pomona	d.	...	0404s	**Jacksonville**	a.	...	*0200*
4422	**Los Angeles** Union	a.	...	0535	Orlando	a.	...	0420

H – SUNSET LIMITED – [sleeper] 1,2 cl., [2nd class] and [restaurant] [bar]; Conveys TEXAS EAGLE (**421/2**) San Antonio - Los Angeles and v.v.
J – Operated by Greyhound USA. Change at Mobile.
r – Calls on request.
s – Calls to set down only.
* – Do not observe DST, schedule times will be one hour later from November 6, 2016.

VANCOUVER - SEATTLE - PORTLAND - EUGENE 9315

Amtrak Most trains 🍸

km		503 ①-⑤ A	🚌 D	505 ⑥⑦ A	501 A	11 B	513 A	507 A	🚌	509 A	🚌	517 A
0	**Vancouver** (Canada) d.	...	...	...	...	*0530**	0630	*0900**	...	*1130**	1600	1735
93	Bellingham d.	...	...	...	...	|	0832	|	1510	|	|	1937
135	Mount Vernon d.	...	...	...	...	|	0902	|	1545	|	|	2007
198	Everett d.	...	...	...	...	|	0952	|	1630	|	|	2059
251	**Seattle** King Street a.	...	...	...	...	*0900**	1055	*1245**	1730	*1530**	1945	2200
251	**Seattle** King Street d.	...	...	...	0725	0935	1115	1410	—	1805	—	...
269	Tukwila ✈ d.	...	...	...	0739	|	1129	1424	...	1819	...	...
315	Tacoma d.	...	...	...	0808	1021	1158	1453	...	1848	...	...
365	Olympia d.	...	...	...	0845	1111	1235	1530	...	1925	...	...
402	Centralia d.	...	...	...	0906	1135	1256	1551	...	1945	...	...
470	Kelso Longview d.	...	...	...	0947	1219	1337	1632	...	2027	...	...
533	Vancouver WA d.	...	...	...	1025	1258	1415	1710	...	2105	...	...
549	**Portland** a.	...	...	...	1105	1350	1505	1750	🚌	2145	🚌	...
549	**Portland** d.	0600	0700	0935	*1125**	1425	*1525**	1805	1900	...	2155	...
633	Salem d.	0707	0820	1140	*1225**	1537	*1645*c	1911	2005t	...	2320t	...
678	Albany d.	0736	0855	1110	*1300**	1610	*1720*c	1940	2040t	...	2359t	...
747	**Eugene** a.	0835	0945	1210	*1350**	1703	*1810*c	2040	2130	...	0050	...

	510 A	🚌	500 ①-⑤ A	502 ⑥⑦ A	🚌	504/6 A	516 A	14 B	🚌 C	508 A
Eugene d.	...	...	0530	*0530**	0720	0900a	*1140**	1236	1315	1600
Albany d.	...	...	0611	*0620**	0810	0943a	*1235**	1322	1405	1643
Salem d.	...	...	0641	*0655**	0850	1012a	*1305**	1355	1440	1712
Portland a.	...	...	0805	*0805**	1010	1135a	*1415**	1532	1545	1835
Portland d.	...	...	0820	0820	—	1200	1450	1602	...	1850
Vancouver WA d.	...	...	0835	0835	...	1215	1505	1621	...	1905
Kelso Longview d.	...	...	0910	0910	...	1250	1540	1654	...	1940
Centralia d.	...	...	0951	0951	...	1331	1621	1739	...	2021
Olympia d.	...	...	1012	1012	...	1352	1642	1804	...	2042
Tacoma d.	...	...	1054	1054	...	1434	1724	1853	...	2124
Tukwila ✈ d.	...	...	1122	1122		1502	1752	|	...	2152
Seattle King Street a.	...	...	1200	1200	🚌	1550	1830	2012	...	2230
Seattle King Street d.	0745	1045	*1225**	...	1345	*1645*b	1850	*2100**	...	...
Everett d.	0836	|	*1310**	...	|	|	1942	|	...	...
Mount Vernon d.	0926	|	*1355**	...	|	|	2027	|	...	...
Bellingham d.	0957	|	*1425**	...	|	|	2100	|	...	...
Vancouver (Canada) a.	1145	1415	...	...	1715	*2015*b	2250	*0015**	...	....

– CASCADES – ⑫ and 🍸.
– COAST STARLIGHT – Table **9305**.
– Additional trips: 1445, 1730.
– Additional trip: 1040.

a – By 🚌 on ①–⑤ timings Eugene 0825, Albany 0920, Salem 1000 arrive Portland 1130.
b – Connection by 🚌 ⑥⑦ only.
c – Connection by 🚌 on ⑥⑦ runs 10 mins. earlier.

t – Paid ticket required to board.
✈ – Sea Tac Airport.
* – Connection by 🚌.

SAN LUIS OBISPO - LOS ANGELES - SAN DIEGO 9320

Amtrak Most trains 🍸

PACIFIC SURFLINER

km			5818 🚌	562	564	1566 ©	566 Ⓐ			🚌	768		572	774	580	🚌	582	🚌	784	790 ①–⑤	1790 ©	592	🚌	796
0	**San Luis Obispo** d.	...	...	...	...	...	...	...	...	0350	....	...	...	0655	...	...	...	1030	...	1335	1400	...	1540	...
40	Santa Maria d.	...	...	...	...	...	...	...	...	0440	....	...	...	0731a	...	...	...	1120u	...	1411a	1436a	...	1635	...
190	Santa Barbara d.	...	...	...	...	...	...	...	...	0630	0649	...	...	0927	...	1255	...	1345	1404	1612	1640	...	1840	1859
248	Oxnard d.	...	...	...	...	...	...	...	...	...	0743	...	...	1018	...	1350	...	...	1457	1707	1735	...	...	1951
355	**Los Angeles** Union a.	...	...	...	...	...	...	...	...	...	0935	...	...	1215	...	1535	...	...	1650	1910	1920	...	...	2145
355	**Los Angeles** Union d.	...	0230	0608	0725	0819	0841	...	...	...	0955	...	1120	1233	1458	...	1608	...	1710	1931	1940	2025	...	2210
406	Anaheim d.	...	|	0648	0804	0858	0920	...	...	...	1034	...	1159	1312	1537	...	1647	...	1751	2010	2019	2049	...	2249
448	San Juan Capistrano d.	...	0355s	0726	0842	0931	0954	...	...	...	1109	...	1239	1349	1614	...	1724	...	1827	2047	2054	2324	...	2324
495	Oceanside d.	...	0430s	0805	0916	1019	1038	...	...	...	1147	...	1313	1424	1652	...	1801	...	1903	2120	2127	2357	...	2357
522	Solana Beach d.	...	0450s	0821	0934	1038	1056	...	...	...	1208	...	1331	1443	1713	...	1820	...	1929	2147	2155	1226	...	0026
560	**San Diego** a.	...	0515	0858	1016	1118	1135	...	...	...	1249	...	1411	1525	1750	...	1902	...	2009	2230	2239	0106	...	0106

		761 Ⓐ	1761 ©	763	🚌	565	1567 ©	567 Ⓐ	769	🚌	573	777	579	583			785	🚌	591	🚌			595	5811 🚌
an Diego d.	...	0400	0440	0606	...	0657	0805	0823	0918	...	1041	1157	1336	1447	...	...	1558	...	1850	...	...	...	2059	2145
olana Beach d.	...	0437	0517	0644	...	0737	0843	0903	0958	...	1122	1232	1411	1538	...	...	1636	...	1928	...	...	...	2139	2215
ceanside d.	...	0453	0537	0703	...	0755	0911	0929	1015	...	1150	1247	1429	1545	...	...	1653	...	1944	...	...	...	2203	2245
an Juan Capistrano d.	...	0528	0609	0736	...	0827	0945	1007	1047	...	1222	1319	1501	1622	...	...	1734	...	2017	...	...	...	2235	2320
naheim d.	...	0606	0648	0814	...	0903	1021	1042	1122	...	1257	1353	1536	1701	...	...	1810	...	2052	...	...	...	2310	|
os Angeles Union a.	...	0703	0730	0857	...	0946	1104	1125	1205	...	1340	1440	1621	1745	...	...	1855	...	2135	...	...	...	2352	0100
os Angeles Union d.	...	0735	0750	0920	...	...	...	...	1230	...	...	1505	...	...	...	...	1915	...	...	2150	...	...	...	...
xnard d.	...	0921	0921	1053	...	...	...	...	1405	...	...	1638	...	...	...	...	2046	...	...	2345	...	...	...	...
anta Barbara d.	...	1022	1022	1155	1205	...	...	...	1505	1510	...	1743	...	...	...	...	2150	2155	...	0035	...	...	...	...
anta Maria d.	...	1216a	1216a	...	1330	...	...	...	...	1635	...	1937a	...	...	...	...	...	2325	...	...	...	...	...	...
an Luis Obispo a.	...	1300	1300	...	1425	...	...	...	...	1715	...	2035	...	...	...	...	...	0015	...	...	...	...	...	...

– Guadalupe - Santa Maria.

s – Calls to set down only.

SAN JOSE and SAN FRANCISCO - SACRAMENTO 9325

Amtrak 2nd class Most trains 🍸

CAPITOL CORRIDOR

km		520 ①–⑤	522 ①–⑤	524 ①–⑤	720 ⑥⑦	724 ⑥⑦	528 ①–⑤	728 ⑥⑦	530 ①–⑤	532 ①–⑤	732 ⑥⑦	534 ①–⑤	734 ⑥⑦	536 ①–⑤	736 ⑥⑦	538 ①–⑤	540 ①–⑤	738 ⑥⑦	542 ①–⑤	544 ①–⑤	742 ⑥⑦	546 ①–⑤	744 ⑥⑦	548 ①–⑤	550 ①–⑤	748 ⑥⑦
0	**San Jose** d.	...	...	0640	...	0810	0905	1010	...	1220	1305	...	...	...	A	1510	...	1610	1620	...	1710	1750	1845	1915	...	2110
75	Oakland JLS ¶ d.	0525	0625	0745	0815	0915	1015	1115	1215	1325	1410	1450	1500	1530	1610	1620	1650	1720	1730	1810	1820	1855	1950	2020	2210	2215
	San Francisco ‡ d.	*0505*e	*0600*e	*0715*e	*0750*e	*0845*e	*0945*e	*1045*e	*1145*e	*1255*e	*1340*e	*1420*e	*1430*e	*1500*e	*1540*e	*1550*e	*1620*e	*1645*e	*1655*e	*1735*e	*1745*e	*1815*e	*1910*e	*1955*e	*2140*e	*2145*e
83	Emeryville d.	0535	0635	0755	0825	0925	1025	1125	1225	1335	1420	1500	1510	1540	1620	1630	1700	1730	1745	1820	1830	1905	2000	2030	2220	2225
128	Martinez d.	0614	0714	0834	0804	1004	1104	1204	1304	1414	1459	1539	1549	1619	1659	1709	1739	1809	1824	1859	1909	1944	2039	2109	2259	2304
219	**Sacramento** a.	0723	0823	0948	1013	1118	1218	1318	1413	1528	1613	1648	1658	1722	1808	1823	1848	1921	1938	2008	2012	2058	2153	2228	0008	0018

	521 ①–⑤	523 ①–⑤	723 ⑥⑦	525 ①–⑤	527 ①–⑤	529 ①–⑤	727 ⑥⑦	531 ①–⑤	729 ⑥⑦	535 ①–⑤	733 ⑥⑦	537 ①–⑤	737 ⑥⑦	541 ①–⑤	741 ⑥⑦	543 ①–⑤	743 ⑥⑦	545 ①–⑤	745 ⑥⑦	747 ⑥⑦	547 ①–⑤	549 ①–⑤	749 ⑥⑦	551 ①–⑤	751 ⑥⑦	553 ①–⑤
acramento d.	0430	0530	0610	0620	0700	0740	0810	0855	0915	1010	1030	1210	1210	1410	1410	1535	1555	1640	1700	1740	1740	1855	1935	2110	2230	2230
lartinez d.	0529	0629	0709	0719	0759	0839	0909	0954	1014	1109	1129	1309	1309	1509	1509	1634	1654	1739	1759	1839	1839	1954	2034	2209	2329	2329
meryville d.	0610	0710	0750	0800	0840	0920	0950	1035	1055	1150	1210	1350	1350	1550	1550	1715	1735	1820	1840	1920	1920	2035	2113	2250	0010	0010
San Francisco ‡ a.	*0640*e	*0750*e	*0820*e	*0835*e	*0915*e	*0950*e	*1020*e	*1105*e	*1125*e	*1220*e	*1240*e	*1420*e	*1420*e	*1620*e	*1620*e	*1745*e	*1805*e	*1850*e	*1910*e	*1950*e	*1950*e	*2100*e	*2140*e	*2315*e	*0035*e	*0035*e
akland JLS ¶ a.	0621	0721	0801	0811	0851	0938	1001	1051	1106	1206	1226	1401	1401	1608	1601	1726	1746	1838	1858	1931	1931	2051	2133	2308	0028	0028
an Jose a.	0738	0838	0918	0928	1013	...	1118	...	1223	...	...	1518	1518	...	1718	1848	1908	...	...	2048	2058	*2355*b	*2355*b	...	...	...

– Also Train **746** on ⑥⑦ departs Oakland 2030.
– Connection by 🚌, change at **Emeryville**.
– Connection by 🚌 San Francisco - Emeryville and v.v.

‡ – San Francisco Transbay Temporary Terminal.
¶ – Oakland Jack London Square.

OAKLAND and SAN FRANCISCO - BAKERSFIELD 9330

Amtrak 2nd class Most trains 🍸

SAN JOAQUIN

km		🚌 ◧	702	710	712	714	716	🚌 ◧	704	718	
0	**Oakland** JLS ¶ d.	0515	...	0735	0955	1235	1430	1440	...	1755	...
	San Francisco ‡ d.	0435	...	*0705*e	*0925*e	*1205*e	*1400*e	1400	...	*1655*e	...
8	Emeryville d.	0500	...	0745	1005	1245	1440	1425	...	1805	...
53	Martinez d.	|	...	0824	1044	1324	1519	|	...	1904	...
90	**Sacramento** d.	|	0635	|	|	|	|	|	1710	|	...
148	Lodi d.	|	0713	|	|	|	|	|	1748	|	...
167	Stockton San Joaquin d.	0700d	0731d	0925	1137	1423	1621	1720d	1806d	1939	...
215	Modesto d.	...	0804	0953	1207	1451	1649	...	1839	2012	...
271	Merced d.	...	0846	1037	1251	1535	1735	...	1919	2055	...
329	Madera d.	...	0914	1105	1325	1608	1803	...	1947	2128	...
364	Fresno d.	...	0948	1144	1401	1643	1834	...	2016	2203	...
412	Hanford d.	...	1022	1219	1436	1718	1911	...	2052	2237	...
542	**Bakersfield** a.	...	1200	1349	1604	1849	2046	...	2225	2358	...
704	Los Angeles a.	...	*1425**	*1615**	*1830**	*2115**	*2310**	...	*0045**	*0220**	...

	711	701	713		715	717	719	703	🚌 ◧	
Los Angeles d.	*0115**	*0255**	*0455**	...	*0750**	*1030**	*1250**	*1510**	...	...
Bakersfield d.	0425	0600	0800	...	1025	1325	1545	1825	...	...
Hanford d.	0543	0717	0921	...	1147	1447	1705	1946	...	...
Fresno d.	0618	0753	1004	...	1227	1526	1747	2027	...	...
Madera d.	0643	0821	1029	...	1252	1551	1814	2052	...	...
Merced d.	0718	0858	1108	...	1331	1625	1847	2125	...	...
Modesto d.	0753	0936	1143	...	1406	1700	1925	2201	...	...
Stockton S.Joaquin d.	0833	1009d	1218	...	1447	1743	2006	2234d	2245d	...
Lodi d.	|	1024	|	...	|	|	|	2249	|	...
Sacramento a.	|	1120	|	...	|	|	|	2340	|	...
Martinez d.	0929	...	1313	...	1544	1834	2059	...	|	...
Emeryville d.	1019s	...	1358s	...	1628s	1919s	2146s	...	0020	...
San Francisco ‡ a.	*1040*e	...	*1430*e	...	*1700*e	*1950*e	*2215*e	...	0040	...
Oakland JLS ¶ a.	1026	...	1410	...	1640	1933	2158	...	0005	...

– Stockton **Downtown**. Also known as ACE station.
– Connection by 🚌 San Francisco - Emeryville and v.v.
– Calls to set down only.

* – Connection by 🚌.
◧ – Calling order is San Francisco - Emeryville - Oakland - Stockton and v.v.

‡ – San Francisco Transbay Temporary Terminal.
¶ – Oakland Jack London Square.

CALIFORNIA

This section is intended to give a brief overview of rail services in California that are not operated by Amtrak. All services in this section are operated using modern air-conditione rolling stock and convey a single class of accommodation, known locally as coach class, equivelant to european 2nd class. Timings are the latests available and may change a any time. Tickets must be purchased seperately for each network and are generally not valid on parallel Amtrak services.

9350 SAN FRANCISCO - SAN JOSE

Caltrain

km			ex①	Ⓐ	Ⓐ	Ⓐ	Ⓐ	Ⓐ	Ⓐ	Ⓐ	Ⓐ	Ⓐ	Ⓐ	Ⓐ	Ⓐ	Ⓐ	Ⓐ	Ⓐ	Ⓐ	Ⓐ		Ⓐ	Ⓐ	Ⓐ	Ⓐ
0	**San Francisco** △ d.	Ⓐ	0001	0455	0525	0606	0624	0644	0656	0712	0719	0724	0744	0756	0812	0819	0824	0844	0856	0900	and	1500	1537	1610	1619
22	Millbrae d.		0025	0519	0549	0624	0649	0702	0717	0732	|	0749	0802	0817	0832	|	0849	0902	0917	0922	at the	1525	1556	1626	|
44	Redwood City d.		0051	0545	0615	0645	0715	0722	0732	|	|	0815	0822	0832	|	|	0915	0922	0932	0948	same	1551	1620	|	|
47	Menlo Park d.		0056	0550	0620	0650	|	0728	0738	|	0806	|	0828	0838	|	0906	|	0928	0938	0953	minutes	1556	1626	|	|
55	Palo Alto d.		0059	0553	0623	0653	0722	0732	0741	0754	0809	0822	0832	0841	0854	0909	0922	0932	0941	0958	past each	1601	1630	1647	1702
58	Mountain View d.		0110	0605	0635	0703	|	0744	0749	0801	0817	|	0844	0849	0901	0917	|	0944	0949	1010	hour	1613	1643	1654	1712
	Sunnyvale d.		0116	0610	0640	|	|	0749	|	|	|	|	0849	|	|	|	|	0949	|	1015	until	1618	1648	|	1717
71	Santa Clara d.		0125	0619	0649	|	0736	0802	|	|	|	0836	0902	|	|	|	0936	1002	|	1025		1628	1657	|	|
75	**San Jose** Diridon a.		0134	0628	0658	0720	0745	0811	0803	0816	0834	0845	0910	0903	0916	0934	0945	1010	1003	1034		1638	1704	1709	1728

	Ⓐ	Ⓐ	Ⓐ	Ⓐ	Ⓐ	Ⓐ	Ⓐ	Ⓐ	Ⓐ	Ⓐ	Ⓐ	Ⓐ	Ⓐ	Ⓐ	Ⓐ	Ⓐ	Ⓐ		Ⓒ		Ⓒ	⑥		Ⓒ	Ⓒ
San Francisco △ d.	1633	1628	1655	1712	1720	1733	1728	1755	1812	1820	1833	1828	1855	1933	2040	2140	2240	Ⓒ	0815	and	2115	2215		1159	185
Millbrae d.	1650	1657	1714	1730	|	1750	1757	1814	1830	|	1850	1857	1914	1957	2105	2205	2305		0839	at the	2139	2239		1215	191
Redwood City d.	1708	1724	1730	|	|	1808	1824	1830	|	|	1908	1924	1930	2023	2131	2231	2331		0909	same	2209	2309	A	1235	193
Menlo Park d.	|	1730	1736	|	|	|	1830	1836	|	|	|	1930	1936	2028	2136	2236	2336		0916	minutes	2216	2316	L	|	|
Palo Alto d.	1716	|	1740	1752	1804	1816	|	1840	1852	1904	1916	|	1940	2031	2140	2240	2340		0919	past each	2219	2319	S	1241	194
Mountain View d.	|	1738	1752	1759	1814	|	1838	1852	1859	1914	|	1938	1952	2043	2152	2252	2352		0931	hour	2231	2331	O	1249	194
Sunnyvale d.	1726	1743	1757	|	1820	1826	1843	1857	|	1920	1926	1943	1957	2048	2157	2257	2357		0936	until	2236	2336		1954	195
Santa Clara d.	|	1752	1810	|	|	|	1852	1910	|	|	|	1952	2010	2057	2206	2306	0006		0945		2245	2345		|	|
San Jose Diridon a.	1736	1800	1820	1814	1830	1835	1900	1920	1914	1930	1935	2000	2018	2106	2213	2313	0013		0953		2253	2353		2005	200

		Ⓐ	Ⓐ	Ⓐ	Ⓐ	Ⓐ	Ⓐ	Ⓐ	Ⓐ	Ⓐ	Ⓐ	Ⓐ	Ⓐ	Ⓐ	Ⓐ	Ⓐ	Ⓐ		Ⓐ	Ⓐ	Ⓐ	Ⓐ	Ⓐ	Ⓐ	Ⓐ
San Jose Diridon d.	Ⓐ	0430	0505	0545	0557	0603	0645	0650	0657	0703	0718	0745	0750	0757	0803	0822	0915	and	1415	1440	1505	1545	1608	1622	163
Santa Clara d.		0436	0511	|	0604	|	|	|	0704	|	0724	|	|	0806	|	0828	0921	at the	1421	1446	1512	1551	1614	|	|
Sunnyvale d.		0445	0520	|	0621	0616	|	0702	0721	0716	0734	|	0802	0823	0816	0836	0931	same	1431	1455	1522	1600	|	|	|
Mountain View d.		0450	0525	0600	0626	|	0700	0707	0726	|	0740	0800	0807	0829	|	0842	0937	minutes	1437	1459	1527	1605	|	1635	164
Palo Alto d.		0502	0537	0608	0639	0626	0708	0719	0739	0726	|	0808	0819	0842	0827	|	0949	past each	1449	1511	1540	1618	1629	1644	165
Menlo Park d.		0505	0540	|	0642	|	|	|	0742	|	0748	|	|	0845	|	0851	0942	hour	1452	1514	1543	1621	|	1648	165
Redwood City d.		0510	0545	|	0648	0633	|	|	0748	0733	0754	|	|	0851	0835	0857	0958	until	1458	1519	1548	1627	1637	1654	|
Millbrae d.		0535	0610	0629	0703	0650	0729	|	0803	0750	0821	0829	|	0908	0852	0924	1023	⊠	1523	1543	1613	1646	1704	1709	|
San Francisco △ a.		0603	0638	0647	0722	0707	0747	0803	0822	0807	0851	0847	0903	0927	0909	0950	1050		1550	1604	1640	1706	1732	1727	174

	①–⑤	Ⓐ	Ⓐ	Ⓐ	Ⓐ	Ⓐ	Ⓐ	Ⓐ	Ⓐ	Ⓐ	Ⓐ	Ⓐ	Ⓐ	Ⓐ	Ⓐ	Ⓐ		⑥	Ⓒ		Ⓒ	⑥		Ⓒ	Ⓒ
San Jose Diridon d.	1640	1645	1708	1722	1731	1740	1745	1808	1822	1831	1845	1850	1930	2030	2130	2230	Ⓒ	0700	0800	and	2100	2230		1035	173
Santa Clara d.	1646	|	1714	|	|	1746	|	1814	|	|	|	1856	1936	2036	2136	2236		0705	0805	at the	2105	2235		|	|
Sunnyvale d.	1700	|	|	|	|	1800	|	|	|	|	|	1905	1946	2046	2146	2246		0714	0814	same	2114	2244	A	1045	174
Mountain View d.	1705	1700	|	1735	1748	1805	1800	|	1835	1848	1901	1910	1951	2051	2151	2251		0719	0819	minutes	2119	2249	L	1050	175
Palo Alto d.	1720	1708	1729	1744	1756	1820	1808	1829	1844	1856	1911	1922	2004	2104	2204	2304		0731	0831	past each	2131	2301	S	1058	175
Menlo Park d.	1723	|	|	1748	1759	1923	|	|	1848	1859	1914	1925	2007	2107	2207	2307		0734	0834	hour	2134	2304	O	|	|
Redwood City d.	1729	|	1737	1754	|	1829	|	1837	1854	|	1920	1930	2012	2112	2212	2312		0741	0841	until	2141	2311		1104	180
Millbrae d.	1748	1729	1804	1809	|	1848	1829	1904	1909	|	1943	1955	2038	2138	2238	2338		0810	0910		2210	2340		1123	182
San Francisco △ a.	1806	1749	1833	1827	1843	1906	1849	1932	1927	1943	2002	2023	2104	2204	2304	0004		0838	0938		2238	0008		1141	184

⊠ – On Ⓐ, the 11xx, 12xx and 13xx trains depart 1110, 1210 and 1310 and run 5 minutes earlier throughout.

△ – San Francisco 4th and King Street.

9352 SAN JOSE - STOCKTON

Altamont Corridor Expres

km		①–⑤	①–⑤	①–⑤	①–⑤								①–⑤	①–⑤	①–⑤	①–⑤						
0	**San Jose** Diridon d.	1535	1635	1735	1838	...	...	...	...	...	...	**Stockton** Downtown d.	0420	0535	0640	0705	...	...	...	...	...	...
	Santa Clara d.	1540	1640	1740	1843	...	...	...	...	...	...	Tracy d.	0451	0606	0711	0736	...	...	...	...	...	...
	Great America d.	1549	1649	1749	1852	...	...	...	...	...	...	Livermore d.	0525	0640	0745	0810	...	...	...	...	...	...
	Fremont d.	1605	1705	1805	1908	...	...	...	...	...	...	Pleasanton d.	0533	0648	0753	0818	...	...	...	...	...	...
	Pleasanton d.	1628	1728	1828	1931	...	...	...	...	...	...	Fremont d.	0555	0710	0815	0840	...	...	...	...	...	...
	Livermore d.	1637	1737	1837	1940	...	...	...	...	...	...	Great America d.	0613	0728	0833	0858	...	...	...	...	...	...
	Tracy d.	1711	1811a	1911a	2014a	...	...	...	...	...	...	Santa Clara d.	0620a	0735a	0840a	0905a	...	...	...	...	...	...
125	**Stockton** Downtown a.	1747	1847	1947	2050	...	...	...	...	...	...	**San Jose** Diridon a.	0632	0747	0852	0917	...	...	...	...	...	...

a – Trains may leave early after all passengers have exited.

9354 OXNARD - LOS ANGELES

Metrolin

km		①–⑤	①–⑤	①–⑤	①–⑤	①–⑤		①–⑤	①–⑤	①–⑤ A	⑥⑦ B	①–⑤	①–⑤		B	①–⑤	①–⑤	①–⑤	B		①–⑤	①–⑤	①–⑤ B	⑥⑦ B	①–⑤	B
0	**Oxnard** d.	...	...	0535	0612	0652	...	...	...	0743	0743	...	...	...	1018	...	...	...	1457	...	...	...	1707	1735	...	195
32	Moorpark d.	0502	...	0557	0634	0714	...	...	...	0808	0808	0828	...	...	|	1419	...	...	1520	...	...	1709	1736	1804	...	|
62	Chatsworth d.	0526	...	0622	0658	0738	...	...	0828	0840	0840	0854	1100	...	1114	1446	...	...	1552	...	1639	1736	1812	1833	...	205
77	Van Nuys d.	0540	...	0635	0712	0752	...	...	0843	0856	0856	0909	1114	...	1128	1500	...	...	1614	...	1653	1754	1831	1845	...	210
86	Burbank Airport ✈ d.	0547	0614	0643	0726	0759	...	0839	0850	0904	0904	0917	1122	...	1135	1507	1541	1556	1622	...	1700	1801	1839	1853	2031	211
92	Downtown Burbank d.	0555	0619	0648	0733	0804	...	0845	0855	0909	|	0922	1127	...	|	1513	1546	1601	|	...	1705	1806	|	|	2036	|
107	**Los Angeles** Union a.	0615	0638	0713	0751	0833	...	0904	0917	0935	0935	0941	1149	...	1215	1536	1605	1621	1650	...	1726	1827	1910	1920	2055	214

	①–⑤	①–⑤	①–⑤	①–⑤ A	⑥⑦ B	①–⑤		①–⑤	①–⑤	B	①–⑤	B		①–⑤	①–⑤	B	①–⑤	①–⑤		①–⑤	①–⑤	①–⑤	①–⑤	B	①–
Los Angeles Union d.	0538	0651	0716	0735	0750	0800	...	0823	0855	0920	0952	1230	...	1243	1448	1505	1514	1537	...	1628	1710	1752	1846	1915	194
Downtown Burbank d.	0554	0709	0734	|	|	0818	...	0841	0914	|	1010	|	...	1301	1506	|	1532	1555	...	1646	1728	1811	1906	|	200
Burbank Airport ✈ d.	0603	0715	0740	0800	0812	0825	...	0848	0921	0942	1016	1252	...	1307	1513	1527	1538	1600	...	1652	1734	1815	1912	1937	201
Van Nuys d.	...	0725	0748	0810	0821	...	...	...	...	0952	1024	1302	...	1316	...	1537	1546	1608	...	1659	1741	1823	1919	1947	...
Chatsworth d.	...	0739	0811	0832	0833	...	...	...	...	1004	1041	1314	...	1331	...	1549	1603	1624	...	1713	1803	1847	1933	1959	...
Moorpark d.	...	0806	...	0857	0857	...	...	...	...	|	...	1339	...	1400	...	|	...	1656	...	1741	1826	1914	1958	|	...
Oxnard a.	...	...	...	0921	0921	...	...	...	...	1053	...	1405	...	...	...	1638	...	...	...	1803	1848	...	2019	2046	...

9356 LANCASTER - LOS ANGELES

Metrolin

km		①–⑤	①–⑤	①–⑤	①–⑤		①–⑤	⑥⑦	①–⑤	①–⑥		⑥⑦	①–⑤	①–⑤	⑥⑦		①–⑤	⑥⑦	①–⑤	①–⑤		①–⑤	⑥⑦	①–⑤	⑥⑦	①–
0	**Lancaster** d.	0347	0449	0519	...	...	0603	0625	0651	...	...	0855	0903	...	1110	...	1135	1240	...	1342	...	...	1425	...	1815	181
	Via Princessa d.	0443	0545	0615	...	...	0659	0719	0751	0907	...	0953	0958	1129	1204	...	1236	1332	1348	1438	...	1523	1519	...	1912	192
82	Santa Clarita d.	0449	0551	0621	0649	...	0705	0725	0758	0913	...	1000	1005	1135	1210	...	1242	1338	1354	1444	...	1530	1525	1714	1918	193
106	Downtown Burbank d.	0525	0627	0704	0725	...	0745	0800	0836	0951	...	1035	1046	1212	1248	...	1323	1413	1436	1528	...	1620	1559	1751	1953	201
121	**Los Angeles** Union a.	0553	0655	0725	0744	...	0809	0825	0857	1013	...	1100	1108	1234	1315	...	1347	1440	1447	1551	...	1641	1630	1814	2020	203

	①–⑤	①–⑤	①–⑤	⑥⑦		①–⑤	①–⑤	⑥⑦	①–⑤		①–⑤	⑥⑦	①–⑤	⑥⑦		①–⑤	①–⑤	⑥⑦	①–⑤		①–⑤	①–⑤	①–⑤	⑥⑦	①–
Los Angeles Union d.	0624	0729	0829	0845	...	0945	1111	1140	1205	...	1355	1415	1528	1550	...	1553	1650	1725	1732	...	1758	1838	1936	2055	212
Downtown Burbank d.	0643	0748	0849	0902	...	1004	1130	1157	1224	...	1414	1432	1549	1607	...	1612	1709	1742	1748	...	1817	1857	1955	2112	214
Santa Clarita d.	0729	0836	0930	0938	...	1048	1213	1233	1304	...	1457	1508	1630	1643	...	1655	1752	1818	1824	...	1856	1946	2038	2148	222
Via Princessa d.	0736	0845	0937	0944	...	1056	1220	1239	1316	...	1504	1513	1637	1649	...	...	1759	1824	...	...	1903	1953	2045	2154	223
Lancaster a.	0844	...	1050	1055	...	...	1323	1350	...	...	...	1620	1741	1755	...	...	1901	1925	...	...	2010	2054	2148	2300	233

A – Operated by Amtrak. Metrolink tickets valid on this service. B – Operated by Amtrak. Metrolink tickets not valid on this service.

LOS ANGELES - SAN BERNARDINO 9358

Metrolink

km		⑥	①–⑤	①–⑤	⑥⑦	①–⑤	⑦	⑥	①–⑤	⑥⑦	①–⑤	⑥⑦	①–⑤	①–⑤	⑥⑦	①–⑤	①–⑤	⑥⑦	①–⑤	①–⑤	⑥	①–⑤	①–⑤	⑥⑦	①–⑤	⑥
			A																							
0	**Los Angeles Union** ... d.	0615	0725	0906	0900	1019	1010	1035	1106	1210	1242	1345	1356	1503	1600	1556	1656	1735	1739	1825	1910	1930	2042	2100	2149	2330
25	El Monte ... d.	0635	0759	0935	0920	1042	1031	1057	1136	1232	1311	1407	1420	1526	1621	1620	1722	1757	1804	1848	1932	1952	2105	2121	2211	2350
30	Covina ... d.	0651	0822	0953	0938	1100	1050	1115	1153	1250	1329	1425	1437	1544	1638	1637	1740	1815	1823	1906	1950	2010	2122	2139	2229	0005
70	Pomona North ... d.	0702	0835	1006	0950	1113	1059	1127	1206	1302	1342	1436	1450	1557	1649	1650	1753	1827	1836	1919	2001	2023	2135	2150	2242	0016
95	**San Bernardino** ... a.	0754	0931	1053	1045	1200	1152	1222	1255	1400	1429	1530	1538	1650	1745	1743	1841	1922	1923	2014	2054	2110	2222	2240	2329	0105

	①–⑤	①–⑤	①–⑤	⑥⑦	①–⑤	⑥	①–⑤	⑥⑦	①–⑤	⑥⑦	①–⑤	⑦	①–⑤	⑥	①–⑤	⑥⑦	①–⑤	⑥⑦	①–⑤	⑥	①–⑤	①–⑤	⑥⑦	①–⑤	⑥
	B																								
San Bernardino ... d.	0602	0624	0700	0700	0801	0825	0849	0950	1000	1130	1135	1230	1229	1305	1336	1407	1513	1535	1601	1655	1718	1816	1830	1950	2115
Pomona North ... d.	0648	0710	0746	0741	0847	0906	0938	1034	1047	1213	1223	1308	1317	1349	1423	1449	1601	1618	1649	1739	1813	1918	1914	1037	2200
Covina ... d.	0659	0722	0757	0751	0858	0916	0949	1044	1058	1223	1234	1317	1329	1359	1435	1459	1612	1628	1700	1749	1824	1930	1924	2048	2210
El Monte ... d.	0716	0738	0814	0807	0915	0935	1006	1101	1115	1243	1251	1332	1345	1419	1451	1514	1632	1647	1723	1809	1848	1952	1944	2106	2230
Los Angeles Union ... a.	0738	0802	0836	0835	0939	1005	1030	1130	1139	1315	1315	1400	1408	1450	1514	1540	1700	1715	1753	1840	1910	2014	2015	2129	2255

A – Also from Los Angeles Union on ①–⑤ at 0546, 1534, 1625, 1716, 1806. B – Also from San Bernardino on ①–⑤ at 0350, 0423, 0441, 0514, 0540.

LOS ANGELES - RIVERSIDE 9360

Metrolink

km		①–⑤	①–⑤	①–⑤	①–⑤	①–⑤	①–⑤				
0	**Los Angeles Union** ... d.	1320	1615	1700	1730	1800	1835	...	...	...	...
	Industry ... d.	1355	1650	1735	1805	1835	1910	...	...	...	...
70	Downtown Pomona ... d.	1404	1659	1744	1814	1844	1919	...	...	...	...
101	**Riverside** Downtown ... a.	1448	1742	1827	1858	1925	2002	...	...	...	...

	①–⑤	①–⑤	①–⑤	①–⑤	①–⑤	①–⑤				
Riverside Downtown d.	0447	0542	0615	0650	0810	1507	...	...	...	...
Downtown Pomona . d.	0520	0615	0648	0723	0843	1540	...	...	...	...
Industry ... d.	0529	0624	0657	0732	0852	1549	...	...	...	...
Los Angeles Union . a.	0610	0707	0735	0815	0935	1635	...	...	...	...

km		①–⑤	①–⑤	①–⑤	①–⑤	⑥⑦	①–⑤	①–⑤	①–⑤	①–⑤	⑥⑦
0	**Los Angeles Union** ... d.	0545	...	...	...	1515	1535	1620	1730	1850	1912
	Fullerton ... d.	0619	...	...	...	1549	1609	1654	1804	1924	1946
	West Corona ... d.	0643	...	...	...	1613	1635	1718	1828	1948	2010
99	**Riverside** Downtown ... a.	0715	0810	1200	1453	1652	1703	1745	1855	2025	2052
	Perris Downtown ... a.	...	0846	1236	1529	...	1739	1821	1931	...	...

	①–⑤	①–⑤	①–⑤	①–⑤	⑥⑦	⑥⑦	①–⑤	①–⑤	①–⑤	
Perris Downtown ... d.	0447	0516	0552	0655	...	...	1040	1355	...	...
Riverside Downtown d.	0527	0556	0632	0735	0750	0900	1120	1435	1807	...
West Corona ... d.	0551	0618	0656	...	0814	0924	...	...	1831	...
Fullerton ... d.	0616	0643	0721	...	0839	0949	...	...	1854	...
Los Angeles Union . a.	0705	0732	0810	...	0930	1040	...	...	1945	...

RIVERSIDE - OCEANSIDE 9362

Metrolink

km		①–⑤	①–⑤	①–⑤	①–⑤	⑥⑦	①–⑤	⑥⑦	①–⑤	①–⑤	①–⑤
0	**San Bernardino** ... d.	0436	0520	0557	...	0705	...	0900	...	1222	...
	Riverside Downtown ... d.	0455	0539	0616	0659	0725	0728	0920	1018	1240	1501
25	West Corona ... d.	0518	0604	0639	0722	0849	0752	0944	1041	1304	1526
	Anaheim Canyon ... d.	0541	0625	0658	0742	0811	0812	1007	1059	1325	1545
	Orange ... d.	0548	0633	0707	0753	0822	0822	1017	1106	1334	1554
78	Santa Ana ... d.	0553	0638	0712	0758	0827	0828	1023	1111	1340	1600
94	Irvine ... d.	0607	0655	0726	0813	0842	0842	1039	1127	1354	1615
113	San Juan Capistrano ... d.	0626	...	...	...	0903	...	1100	...	1409	...
126	San Clemente ... d.	0636	...	...	...	0913	...	1110	...	1418	...
160	**Oceanside** ... a.	0703	...	...	...	0955	...	1150	...	1453	...

	①–⑤	①–⑤	①–⑤	①–⑤	⑥⑦	①–⑤	①–⑤	⑥⑦	①–⑤	①–⑤
Oceanside ... d.	0739	...	...	...	1451	...	...	1628	1625	...
San Clemente ... d.	0802	...	...	...	1514	...	...	1650	1646	...
San Juan C'strano ... d.	0811	...	...	...	1529	...	...	1700	1657	...
Irvine ... d.	0827	0923	1250	1537	1548	1606	1655	1718	1728	1845
Santa Ana ... d.	0839	0935	1303	1550	1601	1619	1707	1730	1741	1857
Orange ... d.	0844	0940	1308	1557	1607	1624	1712	1735	1746	1902
Anaheim Canyon ... d.	0851	0946	1314	1603	1616	1631	1719	1742	1753	1909
West Corona ... d.	0909	1004	1334	1622	1638	1652	1738	1804	1811	1930
Riverside D'town ... a.	0944	1029	1410	1657	1708	1717	1806	1833	1837	2005
San Bernardino ... a.	...	1058	...	...	1738	1741	1830	1913	1905	...

LOS ANGELES - OCEANSIDE 9364

Metrolink

km		①–⑤	①–⑤	⑥⑦		①–⑤	⑥⑦	①–⑤		⑥⑦	①–⑤	①–⑤		①–⑤	①–⑤	①–⑤	⑥⑦	①–⑤	①–⑤		①–⑤	①–⑤		①–⑤	
0	**Los Angeles Union** ... d.	0650	0758	0840	...	...	1050	...	...	1400	1411	1519	...	1547	...	1630	1640	1650	1746	...	1840	*1850*	...	...	...
42	Fullerton ... d.	0725	0833	0915	...	1000	1125	1340	...	1435	1446	1556	...	1625	1655	1710	1715	1725	1823	...	1916	1935	...	2210	...
51	Anaheim ... d.	0732	0840	0922	...	1007	1132	1347	...	1442	1454	1603	...	1633	1702	1717	1722	1733	1831	...	1923	1943	...	2218	...
	Orange ... d.	0738	0845	0927	...	1012	1137	1352	...	1447	1459	1608	...	1638	1707	1722	1727	1739	1837	...	1928	1947	...	2223	...
58	Santa Ana ... d.	0744	0850	0932	...	1017	1142	1357	...	1452	1505	1613	...	1643	1712	1727	1732	1745	1842	...	1933	1952	...	2227	...
74	Irvine ... d.	0800	0904	0946	...	1031	1156	1411	...	1506	1521	1627	...	1702	1726	1741	1746	1801	1856	...	1947	2005	...	2241	...
93	San Juan Capistrano .. d.	...	0920	1001	...	...	1213	...	...	1521	...	1646	...	...	...	1757	1801	...	1912	...	2004	...	...	2258	...
106	San Clemente ... d.	...	0930	1012	...	...	1225	...	...	1534	...	1659	...	...	...	1806	1815	...	1922	...	2017	...	...	2307	...
140	**Oceanside** ... a.	...	1001	1052	...	...	1300	...	...	1615	...	1728	...	...	...	1837	1855	...	1954	...	2046	...	...	2335	...

	①–⑤	①–⑤	①–⑤		①–⑤	①–⑤	①–⑤		①–⑤	①–⑤	⑥⑦		①–⑤	①–⑤	⑥⑦		⑥⑦	①–⑤	①–⑤		①–⑤	①–⑤	⑥⑦		①–⑤
Oceanside ... d.	...	0438	0516	...	0542	...	0634	...	...	...	0815	...	...	...	1124	...	1324	1459	1526	...	...	...	1736	...	
San Clemente ... d.	...	0501	0538	...	0604	...	0656	...	...	...	0838	...	...	...	1150	...	1346	1521	1548	...	...	...	1758	...	
San Juan Capistrano ... d.	...	0511	0547	...	0613	...	0705	...	...	...	0850	...	...	...	1200	...	1400	1531	1557	...	...	...	1811	...	
Irvine ... d.	0415	0527	0603	...	0629	0710	0722	...	0813	0854	0908	...	0908	1140	1219	...	1417	1550	1615	...	1717	1805	1829	...	2100
Santa Ana ... d.	0427	0539	0616	...	0643	0722	0734	...	0825	0906	0920	...	0920	1152	1231	...	1429	1604	1629	...	1729	1817	1841	...	2112
Orange ... d.	0432	0547	0621	...	0649	0727	0739	...	0830	0911	0925	...	0925	1157	1236	...	1434	1609	1634	...	1734	1822	1846	...	2117
Anaheim ... d.	0436	0552	0626	...	0655	0732	0744	...	0835	0916	0930	...	0929	1201	1241	...	1439	1614	1639	...	1739	1827	1851	...	2122
Fullerton ... d.	0443	0559	0635	...	0702	0741	0751	...	0842	0925	0937	...	0941	1215	1248	...	1446	1624	1646	...	1746	1840	1858	...	2135
Los Angeles Union ... a.	0525	0640	0720	...	0745	0819	0840	...	0926	1004	1030	...	...	...	1337	...	1539	...	1726	...	1827	*1945*	1956	...	...

OCEANSIDE - SAN DIEGO 9366

Coaster

km		①–⑤	①–⑤	①–⑤	①–⑤	①–⑤	⑥⑦		①–⑤	①–⑤	⑥⑦		⑥⑦	①–⑤	①–⑤		①–⑤	⑥⑦	①–⑤			①–⑤	⑥⑦		
																					C	C	C	C	C
0	**Oceanside** ... d.	0507	0600	0630	0713	0742	0823	...	0937	1108	1109	...	1356	1442	1532	...	1712	1721	1741	...	1903	2120	2127	2219	2357
	Carlsbad Village ... d.	0511	0604	0635	0717	0746	0828	...	0942	1113	1113	...	1401	1447	1536	...	1717	1726	1746	...	1908	2125	2132	|	0003
	Encinitas ... d.	0522	0614	0646	0728	0757	0839	...	0954	1125	1124	...	1412	1500	1549	...	1728	1737	1756	...	1923	2140	2148	|	0019
27	Solana Beach ... d.	0527	0619	0655	0736	0802	0845	...	1000	1133	1131	...	1420	1505	1554	...	1735	1744	1801	...	1929	2147	2155	2236	0026
	Sorrento Valley ... d.	0537	0628	0708	0746	0814	0854	...	1011	1142	1140	...	1429	1514	1603	...	1744	1753	1811	...	1939	2157	2206	|	0036
	San Diego Old Town . a.	0559	0654	0731	0810	0837	0916	...	1033	1207	1206	...	1450	1536	1628	...	1808	1814	1837	...	2001s	2219s	2227s	2312	0058s
68	**San Diego** SF Depot . a.	0608	0701	0738	0817	0845	0924	...	1040	1214	1214	...	1458	1544	1635	...	1816	1823	1845	...	2009	2230	2239	2324	0106

	Ⓐ	Ⓒ	①–⑤	①–⑤	⑥⑦	①–⑤	⑥⑦	①–⑤				⑥⑦	①–⑤	①–⑤	⑥⑦	①–⑤	①–⑤	①–⑤		①–⑤	①–⑤	⑥⑦	①–⑤		
	C	C			C	C				C															C
San Diego SF Depot ... d.	0400	0440	0624	0741	0805	0823	0939	0940	...	1041	...	1229	1251	1405	1517	1538	1623	1655	...	1740	1826	1911	1915	...	2059
San Diego Old Town ... d.	0407	0447	0630	0747	0812	0830u	0945	0946	...	1048u	...	1236	1257	1411	1524	1544	1629	1701	...	1746	1832	1918	1921	...	2106u
Sorrento Valley ... d.	|	|	0652	0809	0834	0854	1008	1009	...	1111	...	1300	1319	1433	1545	1606	1651	1724	...	1808	1854	1943	1943	...	2128
Solana Beach ... d.	0437	0517	0702	0822	0843	0903	1017	1020	...	1122	...	1309	1330	1443	1554	1617	1700	1734	...	1820	1904	1953	1953	...	2139
Encinitas ... d.	|	|	0709	0829	0850	0909	1022	1026	...	1130	...	1314	1336	1449	1600	1623	1708	1740	...	1826	1910	1958	1959	...	2145
Carlsbad Village ... d.	|	|	0722	0841	0904	0923	1040	1038	...	1142	...	1329	1347	1501	1612	1635	1721	1752	...	1838	1922	2010	2011	...	2157
Oceanside ... a.	0453	0537	0727	0846	0911	0929	1045	1043	...	1150	...	1335	1354	1507	1620	1641	1728	1758	...	1845	1930	2016	2018	...	2203

C – Operated by Amtrak. Coaster tickets generally valid on this service. s – Calls to set down only. u – Calls to pick up only.

OCEANSIDE - ESCONDIDO 9368

Sprinter

km		D	D	D	D		D	D	D	D
0	**Oceanside** ... d.	0533	0633	0733	0833	and at	1733	1833	1933	2033
	Vista Transit Center ... d.	0556	0656	0756	0856	the same	1756	1856	1956	2056
	San Marcos Civic Ctr. . d.	0613	0713	0813	0913	minutes past each	1813	1913	2013	2113
34	**Escondido** ... a.	0626	0726	0826	0926	hour until	1826	1926	2026	2126

	D	D	D	D		D	D	D	D
Escondido ... d.	0533	0633	0733	0833	and at	1733	1833	1933	2033
S. Marcos Civic Ctr . d.	0544	0644	0744	0844	the same	1744	1844	1944	2044
Vista Transit Center . d.	0557	0657	0757	0857	minutes past each	1757	1857	1957	2057
Oceanside ... a.	0626	0726	0826	0926	hour until	1826	1926	2026	2126

D – Additional services: from **Oceanside** at 0403 ①–⑤ and hourly until 1003 ①–⑤, 1103 and hourly until 1803, 1903 ①–⑤, 2003 ①–⑤; from **Escondido** at 0403 ①–⑤ and hourly until 0903 ①–⑤, 1003 and hourly until 1703, 1803 ①–⑤, 1903 ①–⑤, 2003 ①–⑤. Additional later evening services are available on ⑤⑥.

BEYOND EUROPE - SOUTH AMERICA

9900 MEXICO — Ferromex

km		▶ A	①④⑥ B
0	**Chihuahua** d.	0600	0600
132	Cuauhtémoc d.	0825	0825
295	Creel d.	1120	1147
355	Divisadero d.	1304	1341
358	Posada Barrancas d.	1311	1352
370	San Rafael d.	1337	1416
400	Bahuichivo d.	1428	1512
440	Témoris d.	1525	1612
570	El Fuerte d.	1823	1919
655	**Los Mochis** a.	2022	2128

	⊕ A	②⑤⑦ B
Los Mochis d.	0600	0600
El Fuerte d.	0816	0819
Témoris d.	1120	1124
Bahuichivo d.	1220	1224
San Rafael d.	1325	1328
Posada Barrancas d.	1343	1346
Divisadero d.	1422	1414
Creel d.	1544	1539
Cuauhtémoc d.	1837	1907
Chihuahua a.	2054	2134

km		⑥ C	
0	**Guadalajara** d.	1045	...
	Amatitán a.	1145	...

	⑥ C	
Amatitán d.	1700	...
Guadalajara a.	1800	...

A – EL CHEPE – (1) and ✕. B – EL TARAHUMARA – (2) and 🍸.
C – TEQUILA EXPRESS – (1) Currently trip by 🚌 as train is being refurbished.
▶ – ②③⑤⑦. ⊕ – ①③④⑥.

9905 HONDURAS — FC de Honduras

km		①–⑤	①–⑤	①–⑤	①–⑤	①–⑤	①–⑤	①–⑤	①–⑤	①–⑤
0	**S Pedro Sula** Est d.	0730	0830	0930	1030	1130	1230	1330	1430	1530
3	**S Pedro Sula** Central a.	0750	0850	0950	1050	1150	1250	1350	1450	1550

		①–⑤	①–⑤	①–⑤	①–⑤	①–⑤	①–⑤	①–⑤	①–⑤	①–⑤
S Pedro Sula Central d.	...	0800	0900	1000	1100	1200	1300	1400	1500	1600
S Pedro Sula Est a.	...	0820	0920	1020	1120	1220	1320	1420	1520	1620

All services subject to confirmation.

9910 PANAMA — Panama Canal Rly

km		①–⑤	
0	**Ciudad Panama** d.	0715	...
77	**Colon** a.	0815	...

	①–⑤	
Colon d.	1715	...
Ciudad Panama a.	1815	...

9915 COSTA RICA — INCOFER

km		①–⑤	①–⑤	①–⑤	①–⑤	①–⑤	①–⑤	①–⑤	①–⑤	①–⑤	①–⑤	①–⑤	①–⑤	
0	**San José** Pacifico d.	0500	0612	0617	0635	0728	0805	1612	1611	1707	1738	1737	1842	...
8	Pavas Metropolis III d.	0535	|	0648	|	|	|	|	1651	|	|	1816	|	...
10	**S Antonio de Belén** a.	...	0640	...	0710	0803	0841	1643	...	1742	1814	...	1919	...

	①–⑤	①–⑤	①–⑤	①–⑤	①–⑤	①–⑤	①–⑤	①–⑤	①–⑤	①–⑤	①–⑤	①–⑤	①–⑤	①–⑤
S Antonio de Belén d.	...	0557	0642	...	0715	0815	0845	1621	1645	...	1800	...	1830	1920
Pavas Metropolis III d.	0537	|	|	0649	|	|	|	|	|	1655	|	1818	|	|
San José Pacifico a.	0615	0631	0715	0726	0755	0840	0917	1655	1720	1737	1830	1900	1905	2000

km		①–⑤	①–⑤	①–⑤	①–⑤	①–⑤
0	**Freses de Curidabat** d.	0651	0801	1705	1811	1925
4	Universidad Costa Rica d.	0700	0808	1714	1819	1934
15	**San José** Pacifico a.	0728	0832	1739	1841	1953

		①–⑤	①–⑤	①–⑤	①–⑤	①–⑤
San José Pacifico d.	...	0617	0728	1628	1739	1900
Universidad Costa Rica d.	...	0641	0750	1654	1800	1919
Freses de Curidabat a.	...	0650	0759	1701	1807	1925

km		①–⑤	①–⑤	①–⑤	①–⑤	①–⑤	①–⑤	①–⑤	①–⑤	①–⑤	①–⑤	△
0	**San José** Atlantico d.	0530	0600	0630	0700	0730	0800	1530	1600	1630	1700	1730
10	**Heredia** a.	0600	0630	0700	0730	0800	0830	1600	1630	1700	1730	1800

	①–⑤	①–⑤	①–⑤	①–⑤	①–⑤	①–⑤	①–⑤	①–⑤	①–⑤	①–⑤	▽
Heredia d.	0600	0630	0700	0730	0800	0830	1600	1630	1700	1730	1800
San José Atlantico a.	0630	0700	0730	0800	0830	0900	1630	1700	1730	1800	1830

△ – ①–⑤. Also at 1800①–⑤, 1830①–⑤, 1900①–⑤, 1930①–⑤.
▽ – ①–⑤. Also at 1830①–⑤, 1900①–⑤, 1930①–⑤, 2000①–⑤.

9920 CUBA — Unión de los Ferrocarriles Cubanos

km					9	11	15	13	7		73
			2	2		1	2		2		
		◧	◧	◧	◧	◧	◧	◧	◧	◧	◧
0	**Habana** La Coubre d.	...	0740	0840	...	1813	1853	1925	2121	...	0715a
90	Matanzas d.	...	|	|	...	|	2210	2104	2354	...	|
	Varadero d.	...	|	|	...	|	|	|	|	0815	|
286	Santa Clara d.	...	1200	1325	1425	2319	2329	0042	0540	|	|
	Cienfuegos d.	...	|	|	|	|	|	|	|	1325	1335
	Trinidad d.	0800	|	|	|	|	|	|	|	1500	1745
	Sancti Spiritus d.	0925	1320	|	1550	|	|	|	0833	...	▬
436	Ciego de Avila d.	1045	1525	|	1710	|	0300	0400	...	...	...
538	Camagüey d.	1240	1720	1735	2126	0407	0450	0524	...	...	...
714	Bayamo d.	|	|	|	|	|	|	1017	...	...	...
770	**Manzanillo** a.	|	|	|	|	|	|	1150	...	...	...
652	Las Tunas d.	1440	2000	|	0110	|	|	...	...	...	...
729	Cacocúm d.	|	|	|	|	|	1017	...	...	...	...
806	Combinado d.	|	|	|	|	|	|	...	...	...	...
	Holguim d.	1555	|	2035	0235	|	|	...	...	...	◧
	Baracoa d.	|	|	...	|	|	|	...	...	...	1330
884	**Guantanamo** a.	|	|	...	|	|	1238	...	...	...	1640
854	**Santiago de Cuba** a.	1925	2340	...	0605	1005	...	...	...	...	1820

			14	16	8		12		10	
	2	2	2		2	◧		2		
	◧	◧	◧	◧	◧		◧	◧	◧	◧
Santiago de Cuba d.	0735	...	...	...	...	1930	2345	2315	0720	...
Guantanamo d.	0930	...	...	0850	...	|	|	|	|	...
Baracoa a.	1235	...	...	|	...	|	|	|	|	...
Holguim d.	▬	0840	...	|	...	2035	|	|	1105	...
Combinado d.	...	|	...	|	...	|	|	|	|	...
Cacocúm d.	...	|	...	1300	...	|	0300	|	|	...
Las Tunas d.	...	0955	...	|	...	0020	|	0335	1305	...
Manzanillo d.	...	|	§	|	...	|	|	|	|	...
Bayamo d.	...	|	2211	|	...	|	|	|	|	...
Camagüey d.	...	1150	0346	1655	...	0220	0600	0515	1552	...
Ciego de Avila d.	**74**	1425	§	1916	...	0415	0830	0700	1725	...
Sancti Spiritus d.	◧	1545	|	|	2045	0535	|	0825	1910	...
Trinidad a.	0530	|	|	|	|	0655	|	|	|	1500
Cienfuegos d.	0700		|	|	|	...	|	|	|	1640
Santa Clara d.	|	1705	0852	2147	0015	...	1115	1005	2243	|
Valadero a.	|	|	|	|	|	...	|	|	...	2145
Matanzas d.	|	|	§	0100	0526	...	1400	|	...	...
Habana La Coubre a.	1730a	2050	1350	0233	0755	...	1532	1541	...	...

a – Havana Tulipan. ◧ – Services run about every second, third or forth day and **ALL are subject to confirmation, please check locally**. § – Timings unknown.

9925 VENEZUELA

km			①–⑤	①–⑤	①–⑤		①–⑥	①–⑥	①–⑥	①–⑥	①–⑥	①–⑥		①–⑥	①–⑥	①–⑥	①–⑤	①–⑤	①–⑤		①–⑤	①–⑤	①–⑤
0	**Caracas** d.		0500	0520	0540	and every	0900	1000	1100	1200	1300	1400	...	1500	1600	1700	1720	1740	1800	and every	2020	2040	2100
24	Charallave Norte d.		0517	0537	0557	20 minutes	0917	1017	1117	1217	1317	1417	...	1517	1617	1717	1737	1757	1817	20 minutes	2037	2057	2117
32	Charallave Sur d.		0522	0542	0602	until	0922	1022	1122	1222	1322	1422	...	1522	1622	1722	1742	1802	1822	until	2042	2002	2122
41	**Cúa** a.		0531	0551	0611		0931	1031	1131	1231	1331	1431	...	1531	1631	1731	1751	1811	1831		2051	2011	2131
	Cúa d.	...	0500	0520	0540	and every	0900	1000	1100	1200	1300	1400	...	1500	1600	1700	1720	1740	1800	and every	2020	2040	2100
	Charallave Sur d.	...	0509	0529	0549	20 minutes	0909	1009	1109	1209	1309	1409	...	1509	1609	1709	1729	1749	1809	20 minutes	2029	2049	2109
	Charallave Norte d.	...	0514	0534	0554	until	0914	1014	1114	1214	1314	1414	...	1514	1614	1714	1734	1754	1814	until	2034	2054	2114
	Caracas a.	...	0531	0551	0611		0931	1031	1131	1231	1331	1431	...	1531	1631	1731	1751	1811	1831		2054	2011	2131

9930 COLOMBIA

BARRANCABERMEJA — Coopsercol Ltda

km										
0	**Puerto Parra** d.	...	...	0510	...	...	...	...	...	1655
65	Barrancabermeja d.	0600	...	0725	...	1130	...	1430	1700	1910
95	**García Cardena** a.	0700	...	...	...	1230	...	1530	1800	...

García Cardena d.	...	0700	...	...	...	1230	...	1530	...	1800
Barrancabermeja d.	0500	0800	...	1300	...	1330	...	1630	...	1900
Puerto Parra a.	0715	...	...	1515	...	...	...	...	...	...

All services subject to confirmation, please check locally.

BOGOTÁ - ZAPAQUIRÁ — Turistren

km		⑥⑦	
0	**Bogotá Sabana** d.	0815	...
15	Usaquen d.	0915	...
34	La Caro d.	1015	...
40	Cajicá d.	|	...
53	**Zapaquirá** a.	1105	...

	⑥⑦	⑥⑦
Zapaquirá d.	1235	...
Cajicá d.	1305	1515
La Caro d.	...	1540
Usaquen d.	...	1650
Bogotá Sabana a.	...	1730

9935 ECUADOR — FC del Ecuador

km	All trains [R]		②	
0	**Quito** d.	...	0800	...
45	Machachi d.	...	1010	...
62	Cotopaxi d.	...	1100	...
80	Lasso d.	...	...	...
110	**Latacunga** a.	...	...	...

All trains [R]			③
Latacunga d.	...	...	...
Lasso d.	...	...	...
Cotopaxi d.	...	...	1500
Machachi d.	...	...	1550
Quito a.	...	...	1756

km	All trains [R]	31 ⑤–⑦		
0	**Otavalo** a.	0800	...	...
30	**Ibarra** d.	1120	...	...
61	**Salinas** a.	1310	...	...

All trains [R]		32 ⑤–⑦	
Salinas d.	...	1510	...
Ibarra a.	...	1700	...
Otavalo d.	...	1750	...

km	All trains [R]	A ②–⑦	②–⑤	②–⑦
0	**Riobamba** d.	...	0630	...
41	Colta d.	...	0730	...
98	Alausi d.	0800	1040	1100
111	Sibambe d.	0900	...	1200
154	**Bucay** a.	...	...	...
			④–⑦	
87	**Bucay** d.	...	1440	...
21	Yaguachi d.	...	1645	...
0	**Duran** a.	...	1800	...

All trains [R]	④–⑦		
Duran d.	0800	...	...
Yaguachi d.	0910	...	...
Bucay a.	1135	...	...
	②–⑦	B ②–⑦	②–⑤
Bucay d.	...	...	...
Sibambe d.	1000	1300	...
Alausi d.	1030	1330	1245
Colta d.	...	...	1645
Riobamba a.	...	...	1745

A – Additional trip 1600. B – Additional trip 1600.

PERU 9940

POROY - MACHU PICCHU
Inca Rail / Perurail

km		71 B	81 B	41 I1	301 A	61 I2	83 B	601 B	31 A	501 A	33 B	203 C	11 A	43 I1E		73 B	303 A	603 A	45 I1	75 B	51 B
0	Poroy △.........d.						0555	...	0640	...	0735	0825	0905	...		...	...	...	...	...	...
48	Ollantaytambo...d.	0505	0610	0640	0705	0720	0745	0800	...	0853	...	1032	...	1115		1255	1327	1537	1636	1904	2100
86	Machu Picchu ..a.	0635	0740	0801	0827	0848	0915	0925	0954	1029	1052	1211	1224	1245		1425	1450	1702	1809	2045	2245

		50 B	72 B	42 I1		302 A	204 A	44 I1	74 B	32 A	304 A	64 I2	504 A	34 B	604 C	12 A	606 B	84 A	46 I1		76 B
	Machu Picchu ....d.	0535	0853	0830		1056	1337	1430	1455	1520	1548	1610	1622	1643	1723	1750	1810	1820	1900		2150
	Ollantaytambo..............d.	0744	1052	1010		1232	1504	1556	1631		1729	1750	1810			1951	2005	2032			2335
	Poroy △..............a.									1905	U	1938			2023	2052	2116				...

A – VISTADOME – 🚃 and ☕.
B – EXPEDITION – 🚃 and ☕.
C – HIRAM BINGHAM – 🚃 and ✕.
D – 2016 Mar. 24, Apr. 15, May 27, June 26, July 28, Aug. 27, Sept. 16, Oct. 7, 29.
E – 2016 Mar. 27, Apr. 17, May 29, June 29, July 31, Aug.30, Sept.18, Oct. 9, Nov. 1. Inca Rail. www.incarail.com
U – To/ From Urubamba d. 0650, a.1843.
△ – Poroy is 13 km from Cusco, connection by bus.

CUSCO - PUNO
ANDEAN EXPLORER. 385 km. Journey 10 hours.
From Cusco at 0800 ①③⑥ (also ⑤ Apr. - Oct.).
From Puno at 0800 ①③⑥ (also ⑤ Apr. - Oct.).
Trains convey 🚃 and ✕. Operator: Perurail.
NOTE: From May 2017 this service will extend to/ from Arequipa.

LIMA - HUANCAYO
TREN DE LA SIERRA. 332 km. Journey 12 hours.
From Lima at 0700 on dates in note D but may vary.
From Huancayo at 0700 on dates in note E but may vary.
Trains convey 🚃 and ✕. Operator: FC Central Andino.

TACNA - ARICA
62 km. Journey 1½ hours. 2nd class.
From Tacna. 0600, 1630
From Arica. 0800, 1830
Operator: FC Tacna Arica.

HUANCAYO - HUANCAVELICA
127 km. Journey 5¼ hours.
From Huancayo. ①③⑤ 0630.
From Huancavelica. ②④⑥ 0630
Operator: FC HH.

BOLIVIA 9945

Ferroviária Andina / Ferroviária Oriental

PUERTO QUIJARRO - SANTA CRUZ DA LA SIERRA
FO

km		13 ②④⑦①③⑤	7			14 ①③⑤②④⑥	8
0	Puerto Quijarro ....d.	1300	1800	SC da la Sierra.... d.	1320	1800
125	Rivero Torrez ......d.	1540	2010	Pozo del Tigre .... d.	1626	...
240	Roboré ....d.	1914	2248	San José Chiquitos d.	1945	2308
374	San José Chiquitos d.	2323	0152	Roboré ....d.	2357	0212
	Pozo del Tigre ....d.	0229	...	Rivero Torrez .... d.	0312	0448
640	SC da la Sierra....a.	0540	0700	Puerto Quijarro .. a.	0602	0700

SANTA CRUZ DE LA SIERRA - YACUIBA
FO

km		2 ④			1 ⑤
0	SC de la Sierra.... a.	1530	Yacuíba..........d.	1700
115	Cabezas ....d.	1945	Villa Montes.. d.	1948
239	Charaguá ....d.	2322	Boyuibe .... d.	2235
360	Boyuibe ....d.	0229	Charaguá ...... d.	0135
434	Villa Montes....d.	0513	Cabezas .... d.	0535
533	Yacuíba ....a.	0805	SC de la Sierra .. a.	0955

OURO - VILLAZÓN
FA

km		2 ②⑤	16 ③⑥	68 ①④			1 ③⑥	15 ①④	67 ①④
0	Oruro................d.	1430	1900		Villazón............d.	1530	1530	
313	Uyuni...............d.	2140	0250	0330	Tupiza ....d.	1825	1905	...
391	Avaroa ....d.			0930	Atocha ....d.	2145	2300	...
404	Atocha ....d.	2355	0520		Avaroa ....d.			1810
501	Tupiza ....d.	0310	0905		Uyuni ....d.	0005	0145	1810
602	Villazón ....a.	0605	1205		Oruro ....a.	0710	0910	...

OTHER SERVICES IN BOLIVIA
FA

km ②④⑥			③⑤⑦	km ①④			②⑤
0	0800	d.Cochabamba....	1645	0	0800	d.Viacha............ d.	1410
216	1645	a.Aiquile............ a.	0800	208	1420	a.Charaña.......... a.	0800

km ②④⑥			①③⑤	km A			A
0	0800	d.Potosí............ d.	1400	0	0800	d.El Alto........... d.	1820
171	1400	a.Sucre El Tejar .... a.	0800	77	1320	a.Guaqui .... a.	1600

A – 2nd Sunday of every month.

BRAZIL 9950

Estrada de Ferro do Carajás / Estrada de Ferro Vitória a Minas

SÃO LUIS - PARAUAPEBAS
EFC

km		⑥ 12		⑦ 12
0	...	0800	d.São Luís .... a.	↑ 2200
126	1016	d.Arari .... d.	↓ 1941
145	1040	d.Vitória do Mearim ... d.	↓ 1913
213	1156	d.Santa Inês ...... d.	↓ 1804
264	1255	d.Alto Alegre ..... d.	↓ 1659
281	1319	d.Mineirinho...... d.	↓ 1634
299	1340	d.Auzilândia...... d.	↓ 1613
315	1402	d.Altamira.......... d.	↓ 1551
334	1430	d.Presa de Porco .. d.	↓ 1525
384	1526	d.Nova Vida ...... d.	↓ 1429
513	1741	d.Acailandia...... d.	↓ 1219
650	1957	d.São Pedro ...... d.	↓ 0956
738	2131	d.Marabá............ d.	↓ 0829
785	2222	d.Itainopolis...... d.	↓ 0731
861	2350	a.Parauapebas ... d.	↓ 0600

BELO HORIZONTE - VITÓRIA
EFVM

km		2		2
0	0730	d.Belo Horizonte ... a.	↑ 2010
71	0903	d.Dois Irmãos .... d.	↓ 1830
97	1002	d.Rio Piracicaba .... d.	↓ 1732
149	1048	d.Drumond.......... d.	↓ 1639
173	1116	d.Antonio Dias ...... d.	↓ 1605
	1152	d.Mario Carvalho ... d.	↓ 1532
286	1315	d.Periquito .... d.	↓ 1405
339	1420	d.G Valadares .... d.	↓ 1314
415	1547	d.Conselheiro Pena .. d.	↓ 1125
484	1704	d.Aimorés.......... d.	↓ 1026
532	1804	d.Colatina.......... d.	↓ 0927
588	1859	d.Piraqueaçú ...... d.	↓ 0829
612	1926	d.Fundão............ d.	↓ 0802
657	2012	d.Flexal............ d.	↓ 0715
664	2030	a.Vitória .... d.	↓ 0700

DRUMOND - ITABIRA
EFVM

km		2		2
0	1645	d.Drumond.............. d.	1026
35	1741	a.Itabira................ d.	↑ 0930

PORTO SANTANA - SERRA DO NÁVIO
EFVM

km ②④⑦	Temporarily suspended.	①③⑥
	2	2
0	1000	d.Porto Santana ...... a.	↑ 1205
	1320	d.Porto Grande ...... d.	↑ 0847
130	1403	d.Dona Maria ...... d.	↑ 0807
150	1445	d.Cupixi............ d.	↑ 0725
162	1505	d.Munquba .... d.	↑ 0705
179	1540	d.Pedra Branca do Amapari.. d.	↑ 0630
194	1610	a.Serra do Návio ... d.	↑ 0600

URUGUAY 9955

Ferrocarriles del Estado

km		①–⑤	①–⑤	⑥	⑥ ①–⑤	①–⑤	①–⑤	⑥	①–⑤ ⑥	⑥	①–⑤ ⑥ ①–⑤
0	Montevideo Nueva Terminal ....d.	...	0655	...	1015 1035 1320 1330	...	1500	...	1545 1550 1730 1750	...	1810 1845 2010
8	Sayago ....d.	...	0709	...	1029 1048 1333 1344	...	1514	...	1600 1604 1744 1804	...	1824 1900 2024
19	Las Piedras ....d.	...	0730	...	1050 1111 1356 1405	...	1535	...	1627 1629 1807 1825	...	1847 1922 2045
26	Progreso ....d.	...	0743	...	1103 1124 1409	...	1548	...	1641 1643 1824 1838	...	1901 1936 2058
42	Canalones ....d.								1707 1844		1924 1959
63	25 de Augusto ....d.								1737 1914		1954 2029

		①–⑤	①–⑤	⑥	①–⑤①–⑤ ⑥	①–⑤	⑥	①–⑤ ⑥ ①–⑤	⑥	①–⑤ ①–⑤
25 de Augusto ....d.		0435	...	0530 0530	...	0635				
Canalones ....d.		0504	...	0600 0559	...	0705				
Progreso ....d.		0529	...	0623 0623 0715 0728 0755	...	1120 1135	...	1555 1555 1700 1850		
Las Piedras ....d.		0544	...	0638 0638 0731 0743 0807	...	1132 1147	1415	1607 1609 1714 1901		
Sayago ....d.		0607	...	0701 0702 0754 0806 0829	...	1154 1209	1436	1628 1631 1738 1926		
Montevideo N Terminal ....a.		0622	...	0716 0717 0809 0821 0843	...	1208 1223	1450	1642 1645 1753 1940		

ARGENTINA 9960

Ferrobaires — BUENOS AIRES - MAR DEL PLATA — 9960A

km	Service suspended	6701 ①–⑤	6701 ⑥⑦	305 ①③⑤	307 ⑥	315 ①③⑤	319 ⑥	6073 Ⓐ
0	Buenos Aires ‡.....d.	0355	0824	1345	1510	1640	1640	1648
114	Chascomús ....d.	0551	1018	...	1830	1830	1830	1847
204	Dolores ....d.			1658	1832	2002	2002	...
271	Maipú ....d.					2107		...
346	Pinamar ....a.						2258	...
399	Mar del Plata ....a.			2018	2147	2323		...

	Service suspended	6702 ①–⑤	308 ⑦	6704	306 ⑦	320 ⑦	316 ②④⑦
Mar del Plata ....d.			1155		1420		1630
Pinamar ....d.						1630	
Maipú ....d.							1846
Dolores ....d.			1536		1736	1911	1957
Chascomús ....d.		1104		1919		2040	2136
Buenos Aires ‡.........a.		1305	1837	2044	2103	2230	2330

‡ – Buenos Aires Plaza Constitución.

SOFSE — BUENOS AIRES - BAHÍA BLANCA / TANDIL — 9960C

km		133 ②⑤ ②⑤ ⑤			134 ②⑤ ⑦
0	1848	1952	↓ d.Buenos Aires ‡.... a. ↑	0849	0754
64	2011	2020	↓ d.Cañuelas............ d. ↑	0715	...
107	...	2121	2204	↓ d.Monte .... d. ↑	0614	0535
179	...	2329	↓ d.Las Flores .... d. ↑		0410
269	...	↓ d. Rauch .... d. ↑		
330	...	a. Tandil .... d. ↑		
374	...	d. Vela .... d. ↑		
289	...	0124	↓ d.Azul .... d. ↑		0215
332	...	0235	↓ d.Olavarria .... d. ↑		0110
420	...	↓ d. Laprida .... d. ↑		
490	...	d. Pringles .... d. ↑		
488	...	0513	↓ d.Coronel Suárez .... d. ↑		2226
538	...	0606	↓ d.Pigüé .... d. ↑		2133
	0707	↓ d.Tornquist.......... d. ↑		2032
680*	...	0828	↓ a.Bahía Blanca Sud .. d. ↑		1915

* – 640 km via Pringles.
‡ – Buenos Aires Plaza Constitución.

9960 ARGENTINA

9960D BUENOS AIRES - LINCOLN / REALICÓ / PEHUAJO — Ferrobaires / SOFSE

km	Service suspended	1331 ①-⑤	115 ①②⑥	115 ③	115 ④	153 ⑤	101 ⑥	103 ⑥	111 ⑤	
0	**Buenos Aires** Once d.	1730	1835	1835	1835	1953	...	...	2105	...
98	Mercedes DFS d.	2003	2103	2103	2103	2220	...	...	2332	...
158	Chivilcoy Sud d.	...	2231	2231	2231	2349	...	...	0101	...
209	Bragado d.	...	0013	0013	2349	0125	0133	...	0240	...
261	9 de Julio d.	...	0111	0111	...	0214	|	...	0338	...
310	Carlos Casares a.	...	0155	0155	...	0250	|	...	0422	...
363	**Pehuajo** a.	...	...	...	...	0402	|	...	...	...
523	Catriló a.	...	...	...	...	1000	|	0943	...	...
606	Santa Rosa a.	...	...	...	...	|	|	1225	...	...
263	Los Toldos d.	...	...	...	...	|	0348	...	...	...
313	**Lincoln** d.	...	...	...	...	|	0536	...	...	...
336	General Pinto d.	...	...	...	...	|	0641	...	...	...
390	Ameghino d.	...	...	...	...	|	0841	...	...	...
446	General Villegas d.	...	...	...	...	|	1003	...	...	...
559	**Realicó** a.	...	...	...	...	|	1303	...	...	...
644	General Pico a.	...	...	...	...	1150	1534	...	...	...

Service suspended	102 ⑦	104 ⑦	154 ⑦	1332 ①-⑤	1112 ①②③	112 ⑤	116 ④	1112 ⑥	
General Pico d.	1116	...	1521	...	...	...	...	...	...
Realicó d.	1351	...	|	...	...	...	...	...	...
General Villegas d.	1648	...	|	...	...	...	...	...	...
Ameghino d.	1810	...	|	...	...	...	...	...	...
General Pinto d.	2010	...	|	...	...	...	...	...	...
Lincoln d.	2115	...	|	...	...	...	...	...	...
Los Toldos d.	2303	...	|	...	...	...	...	...	...
Santa Rosa d.	|	1429	|	...	...	...	...	...	...
Catriló a.	|	1720	1725	...	...	...	...	...	...
Pehuajo d.	|	...	2232	...	...	...	...	...	...
Carlos Casares d.	|	...	0007	...	0502	0502	...	0713	...
9 de Julio d.	|	...	0056	...	0546	0546	...	0757	...
Bragado d.	0130	...	0200	...	0701	0701	0701	0912	...
Chivilcoy Sud d.	...	...	0314	...	0821	0821	0821	1032	...
Mercedes DFS d.	...	...	0443	0610	0949	0949	0949	1200	...
Buenos Aires Once a.	...	...	0709	0849	1210	1210	1210	1421	...

9960E BUENOS AIRES - GENERAL ALVEAR — Ferrobaires

km	377 ⑦	375 ⑤	383 ⑦	381 ⑤				376 ⑥	378 ①	384 ①	382 ⑥
0	...	...	...	...	↓	d.**B. Aires** P Constitución a.	↑	...	...	...	...
17	1730	1825	1830	2002		d.Temperley a.		0807	0808	1015	1344
98	1920	2014	2020	2140	↓	d.Empalme Lobos d.	↑	0620	0621	0937	1159
136	2053	2247	2153	2312		d.Roque Pérez d.		0446	0447	0703	1025
185	2230	2324	2330	0050	↓	a.Saladillo d.	↑	0308	0309	0525	0847
233	...	...	0143	0303		a.**General Alvear** d.		...	...	0313	0635
205	...	...	...	...	↓	a. **25 de Mayo** d.	↑	...	...	...	...

9960F BASAVILBASO - CONCORDIA — SOFSE

km	Service suspended	613 ①-⑤		Service suspended	614 ①-⑤	
0	**Basavilbaso** d.	0700	...	**Concordia** d.	...	...
56	Villaguay Este d.	0828	...	Villaguay Este d.	...	...
61	Villaguay Central d.	...	...	Villaguay Central d.	...	...
56	Villaguay Este d.	...	...	Villaguay Este d.	1643	...
171	**Concordia** a.	...	...	**Basavilbaso** a.	1812	...

9960G BUENOS AIRES - TUCUMÁN — SOFSE

km		265 ①	277	265 ⑤		266 ③	266 ⑥	278
0	**B. Aires** Retiro d.	0930	1725	1500	**Tucumán** d.	0920	1520	...
294	Rosario Sur d.	|	2352	|	La Banda d.	1318	1918	...
314	Rosario Norte d.	1653	0030	0225	Colonia Dora d.	1633	2233	...
523	Rafaela d.	2131	...	0703	Pinto d.	1814	0014	...
684	Ceres d.	0100	...	1032	Ceres d.	2033	0233	...
791	Pinto d.	0307	...	1239	Rafaela d.	2354	0554	...
858	Colonia Dora d.	0455	...	1427	Rosario Norte d.	0440	1040	0125
1020	La Banda d.	0810	...	1742	Rosario Sur d.	|	|	0200
1170	**Tucumán** a.	1158	...	2130	**B. Aires** Retiro a.	1150	1750	0830

9960H BUENOS AIRES - CÓRDOBA — SOFSE

km		215 ①②	215 ⑥	269 ①⑤		268 ④⑦		216 ①⑤⑦
0	**B. Aires** Retiro d.	*	**	1900	**Córdoba** Mitre d.	1335	...	1800
314	Rosario Norte d.	...	...	0225	Villa Maria d.	1720		2151
384	Cañada de Gómez d.	...	...	0444	C de Gómez d.	2136		
566	Villa Maria d.	0500	0700	0905	Rosario Norte d.	2335		
708	**Córdoba** Mitre a.	0851	1051	1240	**B. Aires** Retiro a.	0650		

* – Not on holiday ①. ** – Runs on holiday ①.

9960J VILLA BALLESTER - ZÁRATE — SOFSE

km		2051	2503	2505		2500	2502	2504
0	**Villa Ballester** d.	0210	0931	1830	**Zárate** d.	0510	1202	2147
52	Escobar d.	0318	1043	1934	Escobar d.	0600	1255	2248
92	**Zárate** a.	0408	1133	2024	**Villa Ballester** a.	0704	1403	2349

9960K SÁENZ PEÑA - CHOROTOS — SOFSE

km		102			101	
0	**Sáenz Peña** d.	1700	...	**Chorotis** d.	0326	...
119	General Pinedo d.	2046	...	General Pinedo d.	0524	...
187	**Chorotis** a.	2244	...	**Sáenz Peña** a.	0912	...

9960L VIEDMA - BARILOCHE — TP

km		361 ①⑤		363 ⑤			362 ①⑤	364 ⑦
0	**Viedma** ◨ d.	...	...	1800	**Bariloche** d.	...	1700	1700
189	San Antonio Oeste d.	...	...	2220	Ing Jacobacci d.	...	2145	2204
625	Ing Jacobacci d.	0530	...	0730	S Antonio Oeste d.	...	...	0744
819	**Bariloche** a.	1010	...	1227	**Viedma** ◨ a.	...	...	1134

◨ – 🚌 connections available to / from B. Blanca and Buenos Aires (operator El Pinguino).

9960M PARANÁ - CONCEPCIÓN DEL URUGUAY — SOFSE

km	Service suspended	①③⑤	2302 ⑤	Service suspended	①③⑤	2303 ⑦
0	**Paraná** d.	...	1300	**C del Uruguay** d.	1230	1300
46	Crespo d.	...	1415	Basavilbaso d.	1400	1430
120	Nogoyá d.	...	1600	Nogoyá d.	...	1710
216	Basavilbaso d.	0600	1830	Crespo d.	...	1900
280	**C del Uruguay** a.	0735	2010	**Paraná** a.	...	2010

9960N BUENOS AIRES - ALBERDI - RUFINO — Ferrobaires

km		565 ⑤	513 ①-④	1513 ⑤		566 ⑦	514 ②-⑤	1514 ①
0	**B. Aires** Retiro d.	1715	1800	1800	**Rufino** d.	2224	...	...
111	Mercedes d.	|	2030	2031	**Alberdi** d.	0002	...	0145
209	Chacabuco d.	2049	2216	2217	Junin d.	0147	0450	0450
255	Junin a.	2145	2304	2304	Chacabuco d.	0237	0545	0545
336	**Alberdi** a.	2320	...	0205	Mercedes d.	|	0749	0749
421	**Rufino** a.	0054	...	...	**B. Aires** Retiro a.	0605	1024	1024

9960P SALTA - SOCOMPA — Tren a las Nubes

km		809 ✕a			810 ✕a	
0	**Salta** d.	0700b	🚌	**Socompa** d.	...	...
53	Alfarcito d.	1035	🚌	Viaducto La Polvorilla d.	1330	...
	San Antonio de los Cobres d.	1200	...	San Antonio de los Cobres a.	1400	...
218	Viaducto La Polvorilla a.	1300	...	Tastil d.	1800	🚌
570	**Socompa** a.	...	...	**Salta** a.	2000	🚌

a – Operates ②④⑥ untill Nov. 26: then Dec 1, 3, 9, 10, 17, 22, 29: ④ ⑥ Jan 2017.
b – Passengers should arrive at 0615.

9960Q SALTA - GÜEMES — SOFSE

km		2802 ①-⑥	2804 ①-⑤		2801 ①-⑥	2803 ①-⑤
0	**Salta** d.	1230	1930	**Güemes** d.	0630	1500
46	**Güemes** a.	1407	2107	**Salta** a.	0807	1637

9960R RESISTENCIA - LOS AMORES — SOFSE

km		①-⑤	⑥⑦		①-⑤	⑥⑦	
	Resistencia d.	1255	...	**Los Amores** d.	0053	0053	...
0	Cacui d.	1346	1346	La Sabana d.	0210	0210	...
120	La Sabana d.	1812	1812	Cacui a.	0635	0635	...
147	**Los Amores** a.	1928	1928	**Villa Ballester** a.	0717	...	...

9960S EL TREN DEL FIN DEL MUNDO

km	a	b	c					a	b	c	
0	0930	1000	1200	1500	↓	d.**Fin Del Mundo** a.	↑	1140	1155	1410	1710
8	1030	1050	1300	1600		a.**Parque Nacional** d.		1040	1115	1310	1610

a – Sept. 1 - Apr. 30. b – May 1 - Aug. 31. c – Departs 30 mins later during b.

9965 CHILE

Empresa de los Ferrocarriles del Estado

SANTIAGO - CHILLÁN — EFE

km	22001 ①-⑤	22003 ⑥⑦	22017 ⑦	22011 ⑤				22206 ⑦ C	22202 ⑤⑥	22002 ①-④	22020 ①
0	0745	0815	1930	2000	↓	d.**Santiago** Alameda a.	↑	1845	1945	2140	0618
	0809	0839	1954	2024	↓	d.San Bernardo d.	↑	1822	1922	2117	|
85	0903	0933	2048	2118		d.Rancagua d.		1728	1828	2023	0502
138	0942	1012	2127	2157	↓	d.San Fernando d.	↑	1649	1749	1944	|
191	1011	1041	2156	2226		d.Curicó d.		1620	1720	1915	|
	1024	1054	2209	2239	↓	d.Molina d.	↑	1607	1707	1902	|
258	1059	1129	2244	2314		d.**Talca** d.		1532	1632	1827	0309
278	1117	1147	2302	2332	↓	d.San Javier d.	↑	1514	1614	1809	|
308	1136	1206	2321	2351		d.Linares d.		1455	1555	1750	|
348	1201	1231	2346	0016	↓	d.Parral d.	↑	1430	1530	1725	|
382	1223	1253	0008	0038		d.San Carlos d.		1408	1508	1703	|
400	1240	1310	0025	0055	↓	a.**Chillán** d.	↑	1350	1450	1645	0130

VICTORIA - TEMUCO

km		22931 ①-⑤	22933	22935		22932 ①-⑤	22934	22936
0	**Victoria** d.	0630	1140	1820	**Temuco** d.	0930	1645	2000
44	Lautaro d.	0718	1228	1908	Lautaro d.	1010	1725	2040
73	**Temuco** a.	0757	1307	1947	**Victoria** a.	1057	1812	2127

TALCA - CONSTITUCIÓN

km		20701		20703		20702		20704
0	**Talca** d.	0730	...	1645	**Constitución** d.	0715	...	1630
	Gonzalez Bastias d.	0907	...	1822	Gonzalez Bastias d.	0907	...	1822
89	**Constitución** a.	1054	...	2009	**Talca** a.	1039	...	1954

SANTIAGO - SAN FERNANDO — Ferrobaires

km		501 ⑥⑦	507 ⑦	509 ⑦	511 ⑦	517 ⑦-④	521 ⑤	523 ⑥			
0	**Santiago** Alameda d.	0845	1030	1130	1230	2000	2030	2100	...	...	...
	San Bernardo d.	0909	1054	1154	1254	2024	2054	2124	...	...	...
85	Rancagua a.	1014	1159	1259	1359	2129	2159	2229	...	...	...
138	**San Fernando** a.	...	...	...	...	...	...	...	...	...	...

		502 Ⓐ	510 ⑥⑦		514 ⑦	518 ⑦	520 ⑦	526 ⑦		528 ⑥
San Fernando d.	...	...	...	...	...	...	...	...	...	...
Rancagua d.	...	0600	0630	...	1520	1600	1640	1740	...	1915
San Bernardo d.	...	0706	0736	...	1626	1706	1746	1846	...	2021
Santiago Alameda a.	...	0729	0759	...	1649	1729	1809	1909	...	2044

C – Additional trips ⑦ 1710, ⑤⑦1800.

Route 32: The Semmering railway

CITIES: ★★★ CULTURE: ★★ HISTORY: ★★ SCENERY: ★★★
COUNTRIES COVERED: AUSTRIA (AT), ITALY (IT)
JOURNEY TIME: 7 HRS | DISTANCE: 620 KM

This is a tremendous journey over one of **Europe's first mountain rail routes** and links two very fine cities: Vienna and Venice. The railway between the two was fostered by imperial ambition, with the Austrian authorities keen to see a rail link between the capital and the country's only major port at Trieste. (For more on Trieste as an important Adriatic outpost of Austrian life and culture see p211). But the notion of building a main-line railway over the rugged Alpine terrain south-west of Vienna was daunting. In 1844 **Carlo Ghega** stepped up to the challenge. Ghega was born in Venice of Albanian parents; as a young engineer he has worked on several early railway projects in Moravia.

The **Semmering Railway** opened in 1854. In 1998, it was inscribed on UNESCO's World Heritage List. The citation commends the route as "one of the greatest feats of civil engineering during the pioneering phase of railway building. Set against a spectacular mountain landscape, the railway line remains in use today thanks to the quality of its tunnels, viaducts, and other works, and has led to the e̶ along its tracks."

A number of other **Alpine** 36) follow routes whi is different: it was de heavy passenger trai book for capturing t comfortable long-dis

Fifty years ago, Moscow to Rome ser over the Semmering, 25). Today, the Semi from Vienna to Graz of Styria and Carinth cities in Italy. And it's

ITINERARY HINTS

This is a journey you'll de which leaves Vienna ever train in each direction be windows – perfect for sig

There's talk of a **se** likely that Railjets will be daytime train leaves Vien

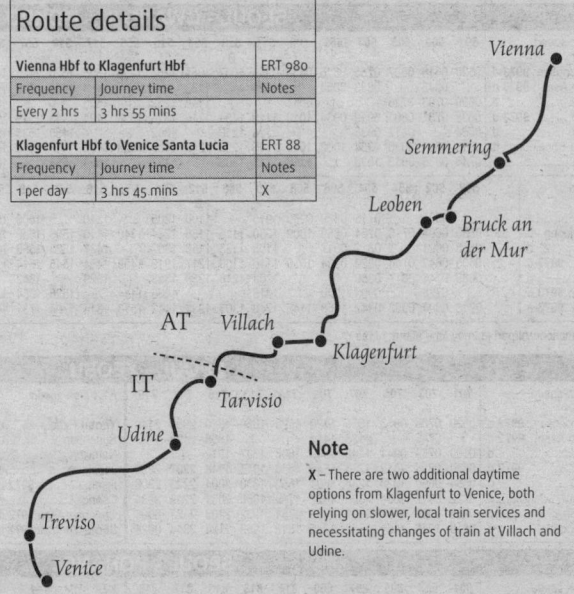

Europe by Rail
The Definitive Guide for Independent Travellers
Now available at www.europeanrailtimetable.eu

270 | ALPINE ADVENTURES

Route details

Vienna Hbf to Klagenfurt Hbf		ERT 980
Frequency	Journey time	Notes
Every 2 hrs	3 hrs 55 mins	

Klagenfurt Hbf to Venice Santa Lucia		ERT 88
Frequency	Journey time	Notes
1 per day	3 hrs 45 mins	X

Note
X – There are two additional daytime options from Klagenfurt to Venice, both relying on slower, local train services and necessitating changes of train at Villach and Udine.

South Korea

Rail services in South Korea are operated by Korea National Railways under the brand names 'Korail' and 'AREX'. All services convey at least Economy class seating (shown in the tables as '2nd class') with many trains (and all KTX high-speed services) also conveying 1st class accommodation. Timings shown are the latest available.

9970 SEOUL - BUSAN

Korail

km	KTX high-speed	101	103 A	107	109	111	113	115	117 B	351	119	121	123	301	125 B	353	127	129	131	133	135	303	137 B	139	141	143
0	**Seoul** Main .... 9971 d.	0515	0530	0625	0640	0700	0730	0745	0800	0822	0830	0900	0930	0955	1000	1020	1030	1050	1100	1200	1230	1240	1300	1310	1330	1350
96	Cheonan Asan .. 9971 d.	|	0609	0704	0720	0740	|	|	0839	|	0905	|	1009	1030	|	|	1105	|	1139	1235	|	1314	|	|	1405	|
160	Daejeon .... 9971 d.	0615	0635	0730	0751	0811	0836	0846	0911	1004	0931	1000	1035	1057	1102	1157	1132	1151	1206	1301	1336	1341	1405	1417	1432	1450
293	Dongdaegu .... 9971 d.	0659	0719	0820	0841	0856	0920	0936	0955	1054	1021	1044	1119	1141	1146	1241	1216	1235	1250	1351	1420	1425	1458	1509	1517	1540
348	Miryang .... 9971 d.	|	|	|	|	|	|	|	|	|	|	|	|	1213	|	|	|	|	|	|	|	1456	|	|	|	|
372	Ulsan .... d.	0730	0751	|	|	0923	|	1007	1022	|	1047	1114	1146	|	1213	1307	|	1301	|	1417	|	|	1530	1536	|	1606
409*	**Busan** .... a.	0752	0813	0909	0925	0945	1004	1029	1044	1143	1110	1137	1208	1252	1235	1330	1305	1324	1339	1440	1509	1535	1553	1559	1607	1629

KTX high-speed	145	147	149	151	305	153	155	355	157	307	159 B	161	163	309	165	167	357	169 B	171	173	311	175	177 B	179	181	183
Seoul Main .... 9971 d.	1415	1430	1455	1530	1540	1555	1630	1640	1700	1720	1725	1800	1830	1840	1850	1900	1905	1930	2000	2030	2040	2100	2130	2200	2230	2300
Cheonan Asan ... 9971 d.	|	1505	|	1604	|	|	1705	|	|	1755	1805	|	1905	|	1929	|	|	|	2035	|	2115	2140	|	2239	2309	|
Daejeon .... 9971 d.	1516	1536	1551	1631	1640	1655	1731	1817	1806	1822	1831	1905	1931	1942	1956	2008	2054	2030	2107	2131	2141	2206	2235	2304	2335	0000
Dongdaegu .... 9971 d.	1600	1620	1642	1715	1731	1739	1821	1901	1850	1911	1921	1955	2015	2026	2040	2058	2140	2114	2157	2215	2231	2250	2319	2348	0019	0044
Miryang .... 9971 d.	|	|	|	|	1802	|	|	|	|	1944	|	|	|	2101	|	|	|	|	|	|	2302	|	|	|	|	|
Ulsan .... d.	|	1646	1710	|	|	1805	1852	|	1916	|	|	2021	2106	|	|	|	2211	2146	2223	2241	|	2321	|	0019	0045	0110
Busan .... a.	1649	1709	1732	1759	1841	1828	1914	1950	1939	2023	2010	2044	2108	2141	2129	2141	2233	2208	2246	2304	2341	2344	0008	0042	0108	0133

KTX high-speed	102 B	104	106 ①–⑤	108	302	110	112	114	116 B	304	118	120	122	124	126	128	352	130	132	134 B	306	136	138	354	140	142
Busan .... d.	0500	0515	0530	0600	0610	0630	0655	0730	0755	0820	0830	0900	0920	0930	0950	1000	1015	1030	1100	1200	1210	1220	1225	1240	1300	1320
Ulsan .... d.	0522	0537	|	0622	|	|	0717	|	0817	|	|	0922	|	0952	|	1022	|	1052	1123	1223	|	|	1247	1601	1322	1342
Miryang .... 9971 d.	|	|	|	|	0649	|	|	|	|	0858	|	|	|	|	|	|	|	|	|	|	1249	|	|	|	|	|
Dongdaegu .... 9971 d.	0550	0610	0620	0650	0726	0720	0745	0820	0850	0933	0920	0950	1010	1020	1040	1050	1105	1125	1151	1251	1324	1310	1320	1330	1350	1410
Daejeon .... 9971 d.	0642	0656	0707	0742	0818	0806	0831	0906	0942	1019	1006	1042	1056	1106	1132	1136	1151	1217	1243	1337	1416	1356	1407	1422	1437	1456
Cheonan Asan ... 9971 d.	0705	|	|	0805	0841	|	0854	|	1005	|	1035	1105	|	|	|	1200	|	|	1307	1400	1439	|	|	|	|	|
Seoul Main.* ...... 9971 a.	0745	0755	0812	0845	0917	0910	0934	1005	1045	1122	1112	1141	1154	1158	1231	1236	1334	1317	1342	1440	1514	1455	1506	1601	1530	1556

KTX high-speed	144	146 B	148	150	308	152	154	156	158 B	160	162	164	356	166	310	168	170	172	174	358	176	178	312	180	182	184
Busan .... d.	1400	1410	1430	1440	1445	1510	1540	1600	1630	1640	1700	1725	1750	1800	1820	1825	1900	1925	2000	2020	2030	2050	2055	2125	2200	2220
Ulsan .... d.	1422	|	1452	|	|	1532	|	1623	|	1702	1723	|	1812	1822	|	1847	1922	1948	2022	2042	|	2113	|	2147	2222	2242
Miryang .... 9971 d.	|	|	|	|	1523	|	|	|	|	|	|	|	|	|	1900	|	|	|	|	|	|	|	2135	|	|	|
Dongdaegu .... 9971 d.	1450	1500	1520	1530	1557	1605	1630	1651	1720	1730	1756	1811	1845	1855	1938	1920	1950	2021	2050	2110	2120	2141	2209	2220	2255	2310
Daejeon .... 9971 d.	1542	1546	1606	1623	1643	1652	1722	1743	1806	1816	1842	1903	1931	1947	2024	2006	2042	2107	2142	2156	2206	2233	2255	2312	2341	2356
Cheonan Asan ... 9971 d.	1605	|	|	|	|	|	1745	|	|	1840	|	1927	|	|	2053	2029	2105	|	2205	|	2235	|	2324	|	0010	0019
Seoul Main .... 9971 a.	1640	1649	1710	1720	1742	1747	1820	1837	1910	1916	1946	2007	2115	2046	2133	2109	2145	2212	2241	2340	2315	2337	0004	0010	0051	0059

A – Additional trip: ①–⑤ 0600. B – To/from Incheon Airport journey time about 1 hour. * – *424km* via Ulsan.

9971 SEOUL - MASAN - JINJU

Korail

km	KTX high-speed	401	403	405	407	409	411 B	413	415	417	419
0	**Seoul** Main .... 9970 d.	0515	0545	0840	0910	1040	1345	1610	1705	1910	2210
96	Cheonan Asan ... 9970 d.	|	0624	|	|	|	|	|	|	1950	|
160	Daejeon .... 9970 d.	0615	0656	0947	1011	1140	1442	1716	1811	2017	2310
293	Dongdaegu .... 9970 d.	0702	0743	1034	1101	1230	1526	1802	1855	2109	0002
348	Miryang .... 9970 d.	|	0819	1107	1131	1303	1558	|	1927	|	0034
387	Changwon Jungang .... d.	0801	0845	1132	|	1329	1624	1902	1953	2207	|
397	Changwon .... d.	0809	|	|	1206	1338	|	|	2003	2215	0105
401	**Masan** .... a.	0814	0855	1143	1211	1343	1634	1912	2008	2220	0110
450	Jinju .... a.	...	0922	...	1236	1409	1701	...	...	2247	...

KTX high-speed	402	404 B	406	408	410	412	414	416	418	420
Jinju .... d.	...	0615	...	0958	...	1305	1500	1733	...	...
Masan .... d.	0513	0641	0915	1024	1230	1331	1526	1800	1950	2116
Changwon .... d.	0519	0647	|	1030	1236	|	1532	|	1956	|
Changwon Jungang . d.	0527	|	0928	1039	|	1342	|	1811	|	2128
Miryang .... 9970 d.	0555	0719	|	1103	1304	|	1604	|	2028	2153
Dongdaegu ...... 9970 d.	0629	0759	1033	1138	1343	1436	1638	1905	2103	2233
Daejeon .... 9970 d.	0715	0851	1119	1225	1429	1522	1730	1951	2150	2319
Cheonan Asan 9970 d.	|	0915	|	|	|	|	|	2014	|	2342
Seoul Main ..... 9970 a.	0820	0955	1223	1325	1526	1620	1834	2054	2249	0022

B – To/from Incheon Airport journey time about 1 hour.

9972 SEOUL - GWANGJU - MOKPO

Korail

km	KTX high-speed	501	503	505	507	551	509	511	513 B	553	515	555	517	519	557	521	559	523	525 B	561	527		563	529	565	531
0	**Seoul** Yongsan. 9973 d.	0520	0610	0637	0755	0815	0853	0950	1037	1055	1205	1250	1305	1320	1405	1420	1510	1550	1650	1733	1857	...	1920	2010	2115	2215
93	Cheonan Asan .. 9973 d.	|	0648	|	0833	0854	|	1024	|	1133	|	|	|	1358	|	1454	|	|	|	1811	|	...	|	2048	|	2254
121	Osong .... d.	0609	0703	0726	|	|	0941	|	|	1148	1252	|	1353	|	|	1509	|	|	1737	|	1945	...	2008	2103	|	2309
240	Iksan .... 9973 d.	0638	0731	0801	0919	0934	1010	1110	1154	1216	1326	1356	1421	1443	1519	1543	1623	1656	1812	1856	2020	...	2042	2132	2233	2337
287	Jeongeup .... d.	0654	|	0817	0935	|	|	1126	1210	|	1342	|	|	1459	1535	1559	1640	|	1828	1913	2036	...	2058	2148	|	2353
337	**Gwangju** Songjeong .. d.	0713	0801	0836	0954	1008	1039	1145	1228	1243	1400	1423	1450	1517	1552	1617	1657	1736	1846	1931	2054	...	2115	2206	2300	0011
405	**Mokpo** .... a.	0746	0838	0913	1030	...	1116	1218	1305	...	1437	...	1523	1554	...	1654	...	1802	1923	...	2131	...	...	2243	...	0048

KTX high-speed		552	502	554	504	506	508	510	556	512 B	514	558	516	560	518	520	562	522	564	524		526 B	528	566	530	532
Mokpo .... d.	...	...	0525	...	0715	0820	0930	1015	...	1100	1205	...	1340	...	1500	1600	...	1705	...	1805	...	1850	2000	...	2105	2210
Gwangju Songjeong .. d.	...	0530	0603	0715	0754	0859	1009	1050	1115	1138	1244	1340	1419	1505	1539	1639	1655	1744	1815	1844	...	1926	2039	2125	2140	2248
Jeongeup .... d.	...	0548	0621	|	0812	0917	|	1108	1133	1156	1302	|	1437	1523	1558	1657	1713	|	1834	1902	...	1944	2057	|	2188	2306
Iksan .... 9973 d.	...	0605	0642	0744	0829	0934	1038	1130	1150	1217	1319	1409	1454	1545	1614	1715	1729	1812	1850	1919	...	2000	2114	2154	2215	2323
Osong .... d.	...	0632	0716	0817	0856	|	|	1203	1218	1250	1353	|	1529	|	1642	|	1803	|	1924	1953	...	2027	2149	|	|	2351
Cheonan Asan ... 9973 d.	...	|	0728	|	0909	1020	|	1215	|	|	1405	1444	|	1626	1654	1750	|	1847	1936	|	...	2039	|	|	2250	0003
Seoul Yongsan .. 9973 a.	...	0716	0804	0902	0947	1058	1145	1248	1303	1334	1442	1518	1614	1704	1731	1825	1847	1924	2010	2038	...	2117	2233	2258	2327	0040

B – To/from Incheon Airport journey time about 1 hour.

9973 SEOUL - YEOSU

Korail

km	KTX high-speed	701	703	705	707	709	711	713	715	717	719
0	**Seoul** Yongsan .. 9972 d.	0520	0705	0853	1055	1420	1520	1650	1820	2050	2140
93	Cheonan Asan ... 9972 d.	|	0745	|	1133	1454	|	|	1858	2128	|
	Osong .... d.	0609	0759	0941	1148	1509	1608	1737	1912	|	|
240	Iksan .... 9972 d.	0640	0834	1012	1218	1545	1636	1814	1948	2207	2252
266	Jeonju .... d.	0656	0850	1028	1234	1601	1653	1830	2004	2223	2308
326	Namwon .... d.	0722	0917	1054	1300	1627	1719	1856	2031	2249	2334
394	Suncheon .... d.	0755	0949	1132	1331	1706	1751	1932	2103	2323	0005
434	**Yeosu** Expo .... a.	0816	1011	1154	1352	1725	1812	1953	2124	2344	0024

KTX high-speed	702	704	706	708	710	712	714	716	718	720
Yeosu Expo .... d.	0500	0740	0945	1030	1250	1400	1610	1755	1915	2105
Suncheon .... d.	0521	0802	1004	1052	1312	1422	1632	1816	1937	2127
Namwon .... d.	0554	0836	1038	1126	1343	1455	1706	1853	2007	2157
Jeonju .... d.	0620	0903	1106	1153	1410	1522	1733	1920	2034	2224
Iksan .... 9972 d.	0642	0919	1130	1217	1426	1545	1750	1937	2050	2240
Osong .... d.	0716	|	1203	1250	1454	|	|	2011	|	2308
Cheonan Asan 9972 d.	0728	|	1215	|	1507	1626	1825	|	|	|
Seoul Yongsan 9972 a.	0804	1027	1248	1334	1544	1704	1903	2057	2158	2353

9974 SEOUL - POHANG

Korail

km	KTX high-speed	801	803	805	807	809 B	811	813	815	817	819
0	**Seoul** Main .... 9971 d.	0545	650	0840	0945	1300	1435	1610	1655	1910	2210
96	Cheonan Asan ... 9971 d.	0624	0730	|	|	|	1514	|	|	1950	|
160	Daejeon .... 9971 d.	0656	0801	0947	1046	1405	1542	1716	1755	2017	2310
293	Dongdaegu .... 9971 d.	0740	0851	1032	1130	1455	1626	1800	1839	2107	0000
	Pohang .... a.	0815	0926	1107	1204	1530	1701	1835	1914	2142	0035

KTX high-speed	802	804 B	806	808	810	812	814	816	818	820
Pohang .... d.	0525	0715	0950	1046	1300	1408	1700	1850	2000	2150
Dongdaegu ...... 9971 d.	0610	0759	1033	1120	1343	1445	1737	1927	2035	2233
Daejeon .... 9971 d.	0656	0851	1119	1207	1429	1531	1829	2019	2121	2319
Cheonan Asan 9971 d.	|	0915	|	|	|	|	1852	|	2143	2342
Seoul Main ..... 9971 a.	0755	0955	1223	1312	1526	1624	1932	2125	2221	0022

B – To/from Incheon Airport journey time about 1 hour.

SEOUL - CHUNCHEON 9975

2nd class Korail

Seoul Yongsan - **Namchuncheon** and v.v. *93 km*. Journey 69 – 78 minutes.

From **Seoul** Yongsan. Most trains call at **Gapyeong** 56 – 64 minutes later: On ①–⑤ at 0600, 0800, 0830, 0900, 1000, 1200, 1400, 1600, 1700, 1830, 2000, 2035, 2200, 2244; on ⑥⑦ at 0600, 0700, 0800, 0830, 0900, 0930, 1000, 1100, 1130, 1200, 1300, 1400, 1430, 1500, 1630, 1730, 1800, 1830, 1930, 2030, 2100, 2200.

From **Namchuncheon**. Most trains call at **Gapyeong** 15 – 19 minutes later: On ①–⑤ at 0611, 0643, 0711, 0813, 1013, 1213, 1413, 1513, 1613, 1813, 1913, 2013, 2213; on ⑥⑦ at 0613, 0713, 0829, 1003, 1031, 1129, 1229, 1303, 1329, 1503, 1603, 1629, 1655, 1803, 1900, 1929, 2003, 2103, 2213.

SEOUL - ANDONG and DAEGU - BUSAN 9976

Korail

km		1771	1773			1601				1621	1783		1785	1605	1787			1681		1791		1795	1609	1623
		2	2							2	2		2		2			2A		2		2		2
0	**Seoul** Cheongnyangni .. **9977** d.	...	...	...	...	0640	...	...	...	0825	...	...	...	1305	...	...	...	...	...	...	...	...	1907	2113
105	Wonju **9977** d.	...	...	...	...	0746	...	...	...	0934	...	...	...	1413	...	...	...	...	...	...	...	...	2029	2219
155	Jecheon **9977** d.	...	...	...	...	0829	...	...	...	1016	...	...	...	1453	...	...	...	...	...	...	...	...	2110	2300
219	Yeongju **9978** d.	...	...	...	...	0932	...	...	...	1117	...	...	...	1552	...	...	...	...	...	...	...	...	2209	0000
256	**Andong** **9978** d.	...	...	...	...	1000	...	...	...	1147	...	...	...	1621	...	...	...	1736	...	...	...	...	2239	0032
	Dongdaegu **9978** d.	0700	0730	...	...	...	...	...	...	|	1400	...	1600	...	1700	...	...	|	...	1905	...	2120	...	|
383	Gyeongju d.	0813	0842	...	...	...	...	...	...	1408	1510	...	1709	...	1809	...	...	1933	...	2023	...	2236	...	0229
422	Taehwagang (Ulsan) d.	0853	0918	...	...	...	...	...	...	1453	1551	...	1748	...	1848	...	...	2008	...	2106	...	2312	...	0306
	Haeundu d.	0951	1006	...	...	...	...	...	...	1553	1647	...	1845	...	1934	...	...	2102	...	2206	...	0004	...	0353
497	**Busan** Bujeon a.	1010	1022	...	...	...	...	...	...	1612	1707	...	1901	...	1952	...	...	2122	...	2226	...	0022	...	0409

		1602	1772	1774	1622		1682	1604		1778	1780								1610	1796	1792	1794		1624
			2	2	2		2A			2	2									2	2	2		2
Busan Bujeon d.	...	...	0547	0603	0720	...	0912	...	...	0925	1152	...	...	...	...	...	...	...	...	1645	1736	1957	...	2245
Haeundu d.	...	...	0602	0621	0738	...	0930	...	...	0942	1210	...	...	...	...	...	...	...	...	1701	1754	2016	...	2301
Taehwagang (Ulsan) d.	...	...	0646	0717	0832	...	1024	...	...	1040	1305	...	...	...	...	...	...	...	...	1749	1849	2108	...	2350
Gyeongju d.	...	...	0721	0757	0916	...	1106	...	...	1119	1342	...	...	...	...	...	...	...	...	1826	1932	2149	...	0026
Dongdaegu **9978** a.	...	...	0841	0911	|	...	|	...	...	1228	1454	...	...	...	...	...	...	...	...	1942	2055	2255	...	|
Andong **9978** d.	...	0715	...	...	1119	...	1258	1325	...	...	...	...	...	...	...	...	...	...	1920	...	...	...	...	0220
Yeongju **9978** d.	...	0750	...	...	1159	...	...	1402	...	...	...	...	...	...	...	...	...	...	1957	...	...	...	...	0253
Jecheon **9977** d.	...	0843	...	...	1253	...	...	1455	...	...	...	...	...	...	...	...	...	...	2053	...	...	...	...	0350
Wonju **9977** d.	...	0934	...	...	1342	...	...	1534	...	...	...	...	...	...	...	...	...	...	2135	...	...	...	...	0429
Seoul Cheongnyangni .. **9977** a.	...	1043	...	...	1452	...	...	1642	...	...	...	...	...	...	...	...	...	...	2241	...	...	...	...	0538

A – To/from Donghae (Table **9978**).

SEOUL - DONGHAE 9977

Korail

km		1631	1633		1637			1641		
0	**Seoul** Cheongnyangni . **9976** d.	0705	0910	...	1413	...	...	2325	...	...
105	Wonju **9976** d.	0828	1017	...	1515	...	...	0032	...	...
155	Jecheon **9976** d.	0921	1106	...	1558	...	...	0112	...	...
	Yemi d.	1016	1201	...	1649	...	...	0202	...	...
	Mindungsan d.	1037	1221	...	1710	...	...	0222	...	...
	Taebaek d.	1109	1251	...	1744	...	...	0254	...	...
	Dogye d.	1139	1321	...	1813	...	...	0322	...	...
	Donghae a.	1220	1358	...	1855	...	...	0400	...	...
	Jeongdongjin a.	1248	1427	...	1924	...	...	0428	...	...

			1634		1638	1640	1642		
Jeongdongjin d.	...	...	0715	...	1040	1500	1640	...	...
Donghae d.	...	...	0743	...	1109	1528	1710	...	...
Dogye d.	...	...	0824	...	1151	1611	1753	...	...
Taebaek d.	...	...	0852	...	1219	1639	1824	...	...
Mindungsan d.	...	...	0926	...	1251	1711	1856	...	...
Yemi d.	...	...	0949	...	1311	1732	1921	...	...
Jecheon **9976** d.	...	...	1049	...	1403	1829	2017	...	...
Wonju **9976** d.	...	...	1129	...	1447	1918	2104	...	...
Seoul C'yangni **9976** a.	...	...	1243	...	1554	2029	2216	...	...

DAEGU - DONGHAE 9978

Korail 2nd class

km		1672	1682	1674						
			A							
0	**Dongdaegu** **9976** d.	0615	...	1630	...	...	...	...	...	...
127	Andong **9976** d.	0802	1259	1820	...	...	...	...	...	...
164	Yeongju **9976** d.	0839	1331	1859	...	...	...	...	...	...
	Cheoram d.	1022	1516	2044	...	...	...	...	...	...
	Dogye d.	1052	1547	2114	...	...	...	...	...	...
	Donghae a.	1132	1628	2151	...	...	...	...	...	...
	Jeongdongjin a.	1200	1702	2220	...	...	...	...	...	...

	1671	1681	1691						
		A							
Jeongdongjin d.	0630	1335	1405	...	...	...	...	...	...
Donghae d.	0658	1402	1435	...	...	...	...	...	...
Dogye d.	0738	1444	1514	...	...	...	...	...	...
Cheoram d.	0804	1514	1540	...	...	...	...	...	...
Yeongju **9976** d.	0954	1702	1726	...	...	...	...	...	...
Andong **9976** d.	1025	1734	|	...	...	...	...	...	...
Dongdaegu **9976** a.	1239	...	2033	...	...	...	...	...	...

A – To/from Busan Bujeon (Table **9976**).

DAEGU - POHANG 9979

Korail 2nd class

km			1753	1755						
0	**Dongdaegu** d.	...	0900	1500	...	...	...	...	...	...
	Yeongcheon d.	...	0935	1535	...	...	...	...	...	...
103	**Pohang** a.	...	1052	1653	...	...	...	...	...	...

	1752		1756	1758					
Pohang d.	0620	...	1425	1915	...	...	...	...	...
Yeongcheon d.	0735	...	1553	2035	...	...	...	...	...
Dongdaegu a.	0808	...	1629	2107	...	...	...	...	...

DAEGU - MASAN 9980

Korail 2nd class

km		1901	1903	1271		1909	1911	1913		1031
	Seoul d.	...	...	0853						1914
0	**Dongdaegu** d.	0640	0920	1253	...	1630	1700	1840	...	2257
57	Miryang d.	0722	1007	1335	...	1714	1746	1931	...	2329
	Changwon Jungang d.	0755	1039	1409	...	1748	1825	2009	...	0000
	Changwon d.	0803	1048	1418	...	1756	1835	2018	...	0009
105	**Masan** a.	0808	1053	1423	...	1801	1840	2023	...	0014

	1902	1904	1032			1910	1272	1914	1916
Masan d.	0540	0835	0924	...	...	1600	1745	1843	2057
Changwon d.	0546	0841	0930	...	...	1606	1751	1849	2103
Changwon Jungang d.	0556	0850	0939	...	...	1616	1802	1858	2113
Miryang d.	0633	0920	1005	...	...	1651	1833	1929	2144
Dongdaegu a.	0729	1006	1037	...	...	1745	1915	2016	2238
Seoul a.	...	...	1416	...	...	...	2023	...	...

MOKPO - BUSAN 9981

Korail 2nd class

km		1944	1972	1952	1954	1441				
0	**Mokpo** d.	...	...	...	0935	...	...	...	...	...
	Gwangju Songjeong d.	...	0640	...	1035	...	...	...	...	...
85	Seogwangju d.	...	0649	...	1044	1351	...	...	...	...
	Boseong d.	...	0804	...	1152	1500	...	...	...	...
206	**Suncheon** d.	0628	0905	0920	1250	1556	...	...	...	...
284	Jinju d.	0727	...	1020	1350	...	...	...	...	...
350	Masan d.	0815	...	1105	1437	...	...	...	...	...
354	Changwon d.	0821	...	1111	1443	...	...	...	...	...
	Changwon Jungang d.	0830	...	1121	1452	...	...	...	...	...
385	Samnangjin d.	0857	...	1149	1519	...	...	...	...	...
433	**Busan** Bujeon a.	0940	...	1236	1603	...	...	...	...	...

		1442	1951		1953	1973	1943		
Busan Bujeon d.	...	...	0620	...	1325	...	1854	...	...
Samnangjin d.	...	...	0709	...	1410	...	1947	...	...
Changwon Jungang d.	...	...	0737	...	1427	...	2018	...	...
Changwon d.	...	...	0746	...	1446	...	2027	...	...
Masan d.	...	...	0753	...	1453	...	2034	...	...
Jinju d.	...	...	0840	...	1539	...	2118	...	...
Suncheon d.	...	0725	0938	...	1635	1735	2214	...	...
Boseong d.	...	0826	1038	...	...	1831	...	...	...
Seogwangju d.	...	0935	1149	...	...	1941	...	...	...
Gwangju Songjeong a.	...	...	1158	...	...	1953	...	...	...
Mokpo a.	...	...	1254	...	...	...	...	...	...

INCHEON AIRPORT ✈ - SEOUL 9984

AREX

Incheon Airport ✈ - Seoul Main and v.v. *61 km*. 2nd class only. Journey 45 minutes.

From **Incheon Airport** ✈ at 0520, 0600, 0630, 0720, 0802, 0835, 0920, 0954, 1032, 1056, 1130, 1156, 1230, 1301, 1332, 1400, 1434, 1500, 1526, 1607, 1641, 1715, 1759, 1847, 1915, 1954, 2016, 2100, 2145. Frequent additional slower services (calling at Gimpo Airport ✈) run 5 – 6 times per hour 0523 – 2342 (journey 55 – 60 minutes Incheon - Seoul).

From **Seoul** Main at 0600, 0626, 0700, 0734, 0816, 0900, 0938, 1027, 1106, 1135, 1158, 1228, 1257, 1337, 1405, 1428, 1511, 1530, 1602, 1635, 1720, 1745, 1820, 1901, 1943, 2026, 2050, 2121, 2200. Frequent additional slower services (calling at Gimpo Airport ✈) run 5 – 6 times per hour 0520 – 2338 (journey 55 – 60 minutes Seoul - Incheon).

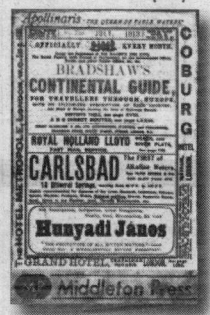
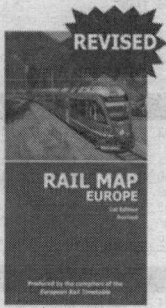
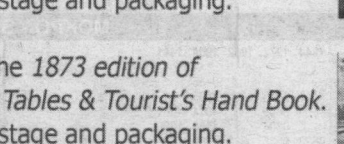
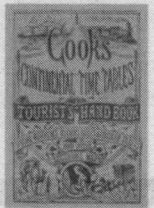
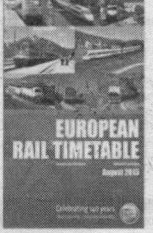